D0762175

Almanac

& Culture

Associations

Broadcasting

Business & Finance

Education

Government: Federal & Provincial

Government: Municipal

Government: Judicial

Health

Law Firms

Libraries

Publishing

Religion

Sports

Transportation

Utilities

Entry Name Index

CANADIAN ALMANAC & DIRECTORY

RÉPERTOIRE ET ALMANACH CANADIEN

2012

Additional Publications

For more detailed information or to place an order, see the back of the book.

ASSOCIATIONS CANADA 2011

Le Répertoire des Associations du Canada 2011
1984 pages, 8 1/2 x 11, Hardcover
32nd edition, February 2011
ISBN 978-1-59237-764-0
ISSN 1186-9798

Nearly 20,000 entries profile Canadian and international organizations active in Canada. Over 2,000 subject classifications index activities, professions and interests served by associations. Includes listings of NGOs, institutes, coalitions, social agencies, federations, foundations, trade unions, fraternal orders, political parties. Fully indexed by subject, geographic location, electronic addresses, executive name, acronym, mailing list availability, conferences and publications.

CANADIAN PARLIAMENTARY GUIDE 2011

1180 pages, 6 x 9, Hardcover
ISBN 978-1-59237-765-7
ISSN 0315-6168

Published annually since before Confederation, this indispensable guide to government in Canada provides information on Federal and Provincial governments, with biographical sketches of government members, descriptions of government institutions, and historical text and charts. With significant bilingual sections, the Guide covers elections from Confederation to the present, including the most recent provincial elections.

CANADIAN ENVIRONMENTAL RESOURCE GUIDE 2011-2012

1566 pages, 8 1/2 x 11, Softcover
16th edition, July 2011
ISBN 978-1-59237-768-8
ISSN 1187-1202

Canada's most complete and ONLY national listing of environmental Associations and Organizations, Governmental Regulators and Purchasing Groups, Product and Service Companies, Special Libraries, and more! All indexed and categorized for quick and easy reference. Also included are companies registered by ISO 9001, 9002, 9003 and 14001.

FINANCIAL SERVICES CANADA 2011-2012

1540 pages, 8 1/2 x 11, Softcover
14th edition, May 2011
ISBN 978-1-59237-766-4

This directory of Canadian financial institutions and organizations includes banks and depository institutions, non-depository institutions, investment management firms, financial planners, insurance companies, accountants, major law firms, government and regulatory agencies, and associations. Fully indexed.

LIBRARIES CANADA 2011-2012

916 pages, 8 1/2 x 11, Hardcover
26th edition, August 2011
ISBN 978-1-59237-767-1
ISSN 1191-1603

Offers comprehensive information on Canadian libraries, resource centres, business information centres, professional associations, regional library systems, archives, library schools, government libraries, and library technical programs.

CANADIAN ALMANAC & DIRECTORY

RÉPERTOIRE ET ALMANACH CANADIEN

2012

GREY HOUSE PUBLISHING CANADA

165th YEAR

Grey House Publishing Canada
PUBLISHER: Leslie Mackenzie
GENERAL MANAGER: Bryon Moore
MANAGING EDITOR: Tannys Williams
ASSOCIATE EDITORS: Elena Anton, Janet Hawtin, Maral Moradipour, Stuart Paterson, Heather Saunders
OPERATIONS & MARKETING COORDINATOR: Caitlin Beatty

Grey House Publishing
EDITORIAL DIRECTOR: Laura Mars
MARKETING DIRECTOR: Jessica Moody
COMPOSITION: David Garoogian

CONTRIBUTORS: Maj. (Ret.) Richard K. Malott, C.D., M.Sc., B.A., F.R.P.S.C., F.R.P.S.L., A.H.F. (British & Commonwealth Honours), Duy Cuong Nguyen (Astronomical Calculations)

Grey House Publishing Canada
555 Richmond Street West, Suite 301
Toronto, ON M5V 3B1
866-433-4739
FAX 416-644-1904
www.greyhouse.ca
e-mail: info@greyhouse.ca

Printed and bound in Canada by Webcom Inc.

Cataloguing in Publication Data

Library and Archives Canada has catalogued this publication as follows:
Canadian almanac & directory.
Annual.
v. 101- ; 1948-
Continues: Canadian almanac and legal and court directory, ISSN 0316-227X.
ISSN: 0068-8193
ISBN: 978-1-59237-769-5 (165th edition)

1. Almanacs, Canadian. 2. Canada - Directories. I. Title: Canadian almanac & directory.
AY414.C2 101- 1948- 971'.0025 C75-032392-2

PRIME MINISTER • PREMIER MINISTRE

Foreword from the Prime Minister

On behalf of the Government of Canada, I am delighted to extend my warmest greetings to the readers of the ***Canadian Almanac & Directory 2012 Edition****.*

From national statistics to information about business, recreation and Canadiana, these pages contain an array of facts as vast as our great country.

I commend Grey House Publishing Canada for compiling this impressive tome of current information about our nation's institutions, organizations and prominent citizens. I am certain that it will serve as a valuable resource for Canadians across the country.

I invite you to discover what has made the ***Canadian Almanac & Directory*** *the most comprehensive national sourcebook since 1847.*

Avant-propos par le Premier ministre

Au nom du gouvernement du Canada, je suis heureux d'offrir mes plus cordiales salutations aux lecteurs de l'édition 2012 du ***Répertoire et almanach canadien.***

Des statistiques nationales aux affaires, en passant par les loisirs et autres sujets intéressants, l'information dont regorgent ces pages est aussi vaste que notre grand pays.

Je félicite Grey House Publishing Canada d'avoir compilé cet impressionnant recueil d'information à jour au sujet d'institutions, d'organisations et d'éminents citoyens du Canada. Je suis persuadé qu'il sera pour les Canadiens de toutes les régions une précieuse ressource.

Je vous invite à découvrir pourquoi, depuis 1847, le ***Répertoire et almanach canadien*** *reste le guide national le plus complet.*

Sincerely / Sincères salutations,

The Rt. Hon. Stephen Harper, P.C., M.P. / Prime Minister of Canada
Le très hon. Stephen Harper, C. P., député / Premier ministre du Canada

Introduction

First published 165 years ago as *Canadian Mercantile Almanac for 1847,* the *Canadian Almanac & Directory* is now published by Grey House Publishing Canada. The 2012 edition of this significant work includes over 44,000 entries covering hundreds of topics, making this the number one reference for collected facts and figures about Canada.

The *Almanac* continues to be widely used by business professionals, government officials, information specialists, researchers, publishers, and anyone needing current, accessible information on all topics relevant to those who live and work in Canada. This latest edition provides the most comprehensive picture of Canada, from physical attributes to economic and business summaries to leisure and recreation. It combines textual material, charts, color photographs and directory listings. This 2012 edition includes hundreds more listings and thousands more details than its predecessor. The comprehensiveness and currency of data is unparalleled.

Each of the 17 sections in this year's *Almanac* includes a detailed Table of Contents, outlining hundreds of subcategories. A *Topical Table of Contents* on the following pages and a comprehensive *Entry Name Index* at the end of the work make navigation of the massive amount of material easier than ever before.

Section 1: Almanac comprises 10 major categories, including History, Geography, Science, Awards & Regulations, Economics, Vital Statistics and more. Readers will find articles, color maps and photographs, charts and tables for a fact-filled snapshot of Canada. This resource section, invaluable for residents, politicians, and the business community, includes a detailed Table of Contents for easy access.

DIRECTORY SECTIONS

Section 2: Arts & Culture includes nine categories: Aquaria, Art Galleries, Botanical Gardens, Museums, National Parks, Observatories, Performing Arts, Science Centres and Zoos. Categories are arranged by province and city. All listings include address, phone, fax, website, email, key executives and a brief description.

Section 3: Associations lists thousands of associations and organizations arranged in 113 topics from Accounting to Writers. Each listing includes valuable descriptions and current contact information. An Association Name Index precedes the listings.

Section 4: Broadcasting begins with Canada's Major Broadcasting Companies, then lists, by Province, all Radio and Television Stations, as well as Cable Companies and Specialty Broadcasters.

Section 5: Business & Finance combines Accounting, Banking, Insurance, and Canada's Major Companies and Stock Exchanges. It includes a separate section for Major Accounting Firms with company descriptions.

Section 6: Education is arranged by Province, and includes Government Agencies, Districts, Specialized and Independent Schools, University and Technical facilities, many with valuable descriptions.

Section 7: Federal Government begins with a Quick Reference Guide to help you find your way around government agencies. The Guide is followed by Federal and Provincial listings, plus information on The Royal Family and Foreign Diplomatic Representation.

Section 8: Municipal Government details all County and Municipal Districts and segregated Major Municipalities. All profiles include date of incorporation, square miles, and population figures. Also included are District Maps for all Provinces.

Section 9: Judicial Government provides thorough coverage for Courts in Canada, including Federal and Provincial. Listings are categorized by type of Court and City within each Province, and include presiding judges.

Section 10: Hospitals and Health Care Facilities is an overview of available facilities by Province. Government agencies, hospitals, community health centres, retirement care and mental health facilities, are all arranged alphabetically by city for easy access.

Originairement publié sous le nom « Canadian Mercantile Almanac for 1847 » il y a plus de 165 ans, le *Répertoire et Almanach Canadien* est maintenant publié par Grey House Publishing Canada. L'édition 2012 comprend plus de 44 000 entrées couvrant des centaines de sujets, faisant de ce répertoire l'*Almanach* le plus complet jamais publié sur les faits et données concernant le Canada.

Le *Répertoire et Almanach Canadien* continu d'être largement consulté par les éditeurs, les gens d'affaires, les bureaux gouvernementaux, les spécialistes de l'information, les chercheurs et par tous ceux qui ont besoin d'une information à jour et facilement accessible sur tous les sujets imaginables concernant le travail et la vie au Canada. La présente édition brosse le tableau le mieux documenté qui soit du Canada en un seul volume, comprenant ses attributs physiques et économiques en passant par les activités commerciales, les divertissements et les loisirs qu'on y pratique. Il constitue un amalgame exceptionnel de textes, de chartes, de photographies couleur et de listes de répertoire. Cette édition comprend un plus grand nombre de données, de profils détaillés et des quantités de mises à jour.

En plus d'offrir un contenu plus riche en information, l'*Almanach* est restructuré de manière à faciliter la recherche. Des tables des matières détaillées pour chacune des 17 sections, une *Table des matières par sujets,* et un *Index par nom* détaillé, rendent la consultation de ces données imposantes plus aisée et accessible que jamais.

La section 1 : Almanach s'étend maintenant sur 10 catégories, dont Histoire, Géographie, Science, Prix et citations, Économies et Mensurations. Il contient plus d'articles, de cartes et de photographies couleur, de chartes et de tableaux qui offrent un portrait juste et à jour des faits et données importants sur le Canada. Elle constitue une source unique de renseignements pour tous les citoyens, les politiciens et les communautés d'affaires. Les tables des matières détaillées de chacune des catégories rendent maintenant la consultation plus facile.

RÉPERTOIRES

La section 2 : Arts et Culture comprend neuf matières principales, des galeries d'art aux parcs zoologiques. Les renseignements y sont regroupés par province et par ville. Chaque entrée comprend des données d'identification, dont l'adresse, numéros de téléphone et télécopieur, site Internet, courriel, cadres, ainsi qu'une brève description.

La section 3 : Associations répertorie des milliers d'associations et d'organismes regroupés sous 113 catégories. Chaque entrée comprend des données d'identification, dont celles de contacts. Un index par nom au début des catégories facilite la recherche.

La section 4 : Radiodiffusion et télédiffusion présente une liste des principales sociétés de radiodiffusion et télédiffusion au pays suivie des listes, par province, des stations de radio et de télévision ainsi que des entreprises de distribution par câble et des émetteurs spécialisés.

La section 5 : Affaires et finance comprend de l'information sur les cabinets comptables, les banques, les compagnies d'assurances, les plus grandes sociétés canadiennes et les bourses. Comprend aussi une liste des principaux cabinets de comptables et une description des sociétés répertoriées.

La section 6 : Éducation est divisée par province et donne des renseignements sur les agences gouvernementales, les commissions scolaires, les écoles privées et spécialisées, les institutions universitaires, collégiales et techniques. Vous y trouverez également plusieurs autres renseignements d'intérêts en matière d'éducation.

La section 7 : Gouvernement fédéral commence par un Guide de références rapide qui vous aidera à trouver votre chemin parmi la multitude d'agences gouvernementales répertoriées, suivi de leurs listes au niveau du pays et des provinces. Cette section comprend également les plus récents résultats d'élection de l'année 2008. Vous y trouverez de plus de l'information sur la Famille royale et les délégations diplomatiques à l'étranger.

La section 8 : Gouvernement municipal fournit de l'information sur les comtés, les municipalités régionales de comté et les principales villes canadiennes. Chaque profil a été revu pour y incorporer la date

Section 11: Law Firms includes a separate section of Major Law Firms with descriptions and Senior Partners. Following the Majors are law firms arranged by Province.

Section 12: Libraries begins with Canada's main Library/Archive and Government Departments for Libraries. Provincial listings follow, with Regional Systems listed first, then Public Libraries and Archives.

Section 13: Publishing includes Publishers—Book, Magazine, Newspapers—and Newspapers by Province. Magazine listings are arranged in six major categories, preceded by a Magazine Name Index for easy searching. Details include frequency and circulation figures.

Section 14: Religion starts off with broad information on religious groups, then lists Associations, arranged alphabetically by 18 denominations, from Anglican to United Church of Christ.

Section 15: Sports provides Associations for 88 single sports, plus detailed League and Team listings for Baseball, Basketball, Football, Hockey, Lacrosse and Soccer. You'll also find the major sports venues in Canada, both stadiums and racetracks.

Section 16: Transportation offers comprehensive listings for major transportation modes, plus industry Associations, Government Agencies and Port Authorities.

Section 17: Utilities includes Associations, Government Agencies and Provincial Utility Companies.

In addition, this edition of the *Canadian Almanac & Directory* includes a **Topical Table of Contents** in the front of the book, and a comprehensive **Entry Index** in the back of the book. These documents, used together with the three indexes in the body of the work, and the tables of contents for each individual section, make easy work of finding exactly what you are looking for.

The *Canadian Almanac & Directory 2012* is also available as part of **Grey House Publishing Canada's Canada Information Resource Center (CIRC)** on the web (www.greyhouse.ca) where subscribers have full access to this rich database right at their computer. Trial subscriptions are available to the CIRC database by calling 866-433-4739.

We acknowledge the valuable contributions of those individuals and organizations that have responded to our information gathering process. Their help and responses to our phone calls, faxes and questionnaires are greatly appreciated.

Every effort has been made to assure the accuracy of the information included in this edition of the *Canadian Almanac & Directory*. Do not hesitate to contact the editorial offices in Toronto with comments, or if revisions are necessary.

d'incorporation, la superficie et la population approximative. Vous trouverez aussi des cartes de comtés de chaque province.

La section 9 : Gouvernement - Juridique dresse la liste de tous les tribunaux judiciaires au Canada, tant fédéraux que provinciaux. Les renseignements y sont regroupés par genre de tribunal et par ville, au niveau de chaque province. On y trouve également le nom des juges actuellement en fonction.

La section 10 : Hôpitaux et soins de santé donne une vue d'ensemble des établissements de santé par province. Pour simplifier la consultation, les agences gouvernementales, les hôpitaux, les centres de santé communautaire, les centres de santé mentale et les établissements de soins de longues durées pour personnes âgées sont regroupés par ville, en ordre alphabétique.

La section 11 : Bureaux d'avocats inclue une sous-section détaillant les principaux cabinets d'avocats au Canada et donnant une brève description de ceux-ci et de leurs principaux associés. Vient ensuite, la liste des bureaux d'avocats regroupés par province.

La section 12 : Bibliothèque présente en premier lieu les principales bibliothèques au Canada et les bibliothèques gouvernementales et d'archives. On y trouve ensuite des renseignements sur les bibliothèques, par province, où sont décrits les systèmes régionaux, suivis des principales bibliothèques publiques et d'archives.

La section 13 : Édition fournit de l'information, détaillé par province, sur les éditeurs des livres, magazines et journaux, ainsi que les quotidiens et autres journaux. La nomenclature des magazines est présentée en six catégories précédées d'un index par nom pour faciliter la recherche. Plusieurs données ont été ajoutées dont celles concernant la fréquence de publication et le tirage.

La section 14 : Religion fournit une vaste quantité d'informations sur les groupements religieux, suivie de celles sur les dix-huit principales confessions, d'Anglicane à United Church of Christ.

La section 15 : Sports fournit des principales informations sur 88 associations de sports individuels et des données sur les ligues et équipes de baseball, basketball, football, hockey, lacrosse et soccer. Vous y trouverez aussi des renseignements sur les majeures installations sportives du Canada comprenant les stades et les pistes de course.

La section 16 : Transport donne une liste détaillée des principaux modes de transport et organismes œuvrant dans le domaine au pays, ainsi qu'une liste des associations de l'industrie, des agences gouvernementales et des autorités portuaires.

La section 17 : Services publics regroupe sous un même chapitre les associations, les agences gouvernementales et les entreprises œuvrant dans les services publics de chaque province.

De plus, la présente édition du *Répertoire et Almanach Canadien* profite d'une **Table des matières par sujets** au début du volume, et un **Index par nom** à la fin du volume, avec référence au numéro de la page où se trouve l'information. Ces index, qui s'ajoute aux trois autres index contenus dans le répertoire, ont été incorporés pour faciliter davantage votre consultation.

Le *Répertoire et Almanach Canadien 2012* fait partie des vaste données électroniques du **Canada Information Resource Centre (CIRC) de Grey House Publishing Canada** (www.greyhouse.ca) auquel les abonnés peuvent avoir accès de leur ordinateur personnel. Vous pouvez obtenir un abonnement d'essai aux données du CIRC en composant le 866 433-4739.

Nous tenons à souligner la précieuse contribution des personnes et des organismes qui ont collaboré tout au long de l'année à notre procédé de cueillette d'information; votre aide, vos réponses à notre questionnaire dans les délais impartis, vos appels téléphoniques et vos envois par télécopieur sont grandement appréciés.

Nous avons mis tous les efforts pour nous assurer de l'exactitude de l'information contenue dans cette édition du *Répertoire et Almanach Canadien*. N'hésitez pas à communiquer avec le bureau de la rédaction pour faire part de vos commentaires ou si des modifications s'avèrent nécessaires.

Table of Contents

Table des matières

Topical Table of Contents

Table des Matières par Sujets

SECTION 1

ALMANAC

History

History of Canada

Over the past 400 years, Canada has evolved from a sparsely populated trading post to the eighth-richest sovereign power in the world. It stands alone as the only country to separate from its colonial power through peaceful means.

The political boundary of what is now known as Canada recorded thousands of years of history before European colonization, but was one of the last places on Earth to host human habitation. While modern *Homo sapiens* emerged from the eastern region of Africa 200,000 years ago, most scientists agree that it took another 175,000 years for humans to find their way across the ice bridge that once joined Alaska and Eastern Siberia. The land that now constitutes Canada has seen the longest period of human habitation in the New World: from the original migration 25,000 years ago came all the indigenous cultures of North and South America including the Arctic Inuit, Blackfoot, Cree, Algonquin, Dene, and Iroquois League of Five Nations. Estimates put the number of native peoples in the United States and Canada before European contact at about two million.

Columbus may have been given credit for the "discovery" of America in 1492, but proof exists that Vikings voyaged to Greenland and further west as early as 982 A.D. Archeological evidence points to Norse settlements in Newfoundland at L'Anse aux Meadows dating back to approximately 1000 A.D., making Canada the actual site of the European discovery of North America. The Vikings, however, were not concerned with permanent colonization, only Canadian natural resources. By the time Christopher Columbus arrived, the Norse settlements had been abandoned.

With Christopher Columbus came the European fervour of colonizing the New World. Seeking a way to circumvent the long land trade routes to Asian goods by crossing the Atlantic to what he thought was India, Columbus inadvertently began the Age of Discovery. European powers established colonies, seeking spice, gold, slaves, and new crops, as well as the promotion of Christianity among the native peoples. The earlier colonies, mostly Spanish and Portuguese, were concentrated in South America, Central America, and the Caribbean. England and France, however, turned their attention north. John Cabot, an Italian-born English explorer, is credited as being the first European explorer after the Vikings to set foot in North America. Although this exploration occurred only five years after Columbus's discoveries, it was not until 1605 that permanent settlements were established. Many explorers, including Henry Hudson, still attempted to find the Northwest Passage, a reputed waterway through the New World to Asia. The reasons for this 100-year gap have more to do with European affairs than those of the New World.

Two events slowed the colonization of North America: religious unrest and war in Europe. In 1517, Martin Luther distributed his list of 95 grievances against the Catholic Church by means of a new invention, the printing press. Thus began the Protestant Reformation. This schism was to have far-reaching consequences across all of European history, but in the short term, it created rancorous religious strife. Most of Europe turned inward to deal with unrest and religious crisis. Escalating political conflicts enveloped most of Western Europe for decades, drawing resources away from colonization efforts. The French Wars of Religion, the Italian Wars, and popular uprisings combined with new religious uprisings to turn the attention of Europe away from the New World for more than a century.

France looked to North America as the best possible source of wealth and power and as a relief from war debt. When French explorer Jacques Cartier sailed up the St. Lawrence River in 1534, he claimed the territory for France, and gave it the name it still bears today: Canada. Once fur traders arrived in Eastern Canada in the 1500s, France monopolized the fur trade. While the French made an effort to establish friendly trading relations with the native population, the Iroquois in particular proved openly hostile. Conflicts with local tribes soon convinced the crown that if traders were to make a profit in Canada, a permanent military and civilian presence was essential. King Henry IV sent his royal "hydrographer," Samuel de Champlain to map the region.

In 1605, after exploring the coast of North America as far south as Cape Cod, Champlain established the first permanent French settlement at Port Royal, and in 1608 he founded Quebec City. New France, as it was then called, grew slowly, mainly due to disinterest from the mainland and war with the Iroquois. The settlers survived attacks from native peoples through their alliance with the Algonquin, Montagnais, and Huron peoples. These alliances not only secured their survival, but greatly increased France's control of the fur trade. Europeans had little experience in the thick wilderness of the area, an expertise that the native peoples supplied.

Once again religious tensions in Europe interfered with Canada's settlement and growth. By the mid-seventeenth century, while England's American and Caribbean colonies grew self-sufficient, New France remained underpopulated. The struggling colony drained France's resources. The French crown decided to take action by creating land incentives for emigrants to New France. Only one caveat stood in the way: all settlers must be Roman Catholic, or convert to Roman Catholicism before leaving Europe. This change of policy, undertaken at the urging of the fanatical Catholic Cardinal Richelieu, closest advisor to King Louis XIII, created friction. Previously, French Protestants, especially the persecuted sect known as Huguenots, had fled to New France to escape religious persecution. Cardinal Richelieu's new edict would have a lasting impact on the religious and political makeup of modern Canada.

In the late seventeenth century, English and French colonies in the New World began to take a stronger foothold. Both nations finally saw a large-scale financial return on their investments, but a war in Europe again infringed on Canada's nascent growth. New France, already in the middle of brutal intertribal warfare with the Algonquins, conflicted with the Iroquois confederacy opposing them. With the War of the Grand Alliance in 1688, which pitted France against almost all of continental Europe, the Iroquois began to receive English weapons as part of government policy. This escalation by the English heightened the already bloody warfare. English armies and their Iroquois allies captured Port Royal, but were turned back from Quebec City, due mainly to a decimation of forces by disease. The war eventually petered out, and a peace was signed in 1697. The Iroquois, however, continued the fight without British help, and eventually suffered a series of major defeats, forcing them to sue for peace four years later.

New France, and thereby Canada, seemed securely in the mother country's domain following the end of the War of the Grand Alliance. However, France's control of the region was not to last. Queen Anne's War, which began only a year after the French peace with the Iroquois, lead England to claim Nova Scotia and Newfoundland, as well as the rights to the land surrounding Hudson Bay. Fighting broke out again three decades later in 1744, in a battle known as King George's War, but neither side was able to enlarge their colonial positions.

By 1754 the long-standing animosity between the English and French seeped into the New World, culminating in the Seven Years War, known in the Americas as the French and Indian War. The causes of the conflict were threefold. The lucrative fur trade, rich fishing grounds, ample lumber, and mineral deposits all promised great wealth to whoever controlled Canada. Secondly, the fiercely anti-Catholic British felt that the Protestant French were heretics, a feeling that was reciprocated by the French. Thirdly, possession of colonies overseas could be used as diplomatic bargaining chips should the war in Europe go badly.

The Seven Years War was the first worldwide war, fought on five continents: North America, South America, Africa, Europe and Asia. More than a million died, and the war resulted in a complete change in the power structure of the New World. Britain gained all of France's colonial possessions in North America, and Canada became a British colony. However, 150 years of French colonization didn't disappear overnight. Even today, French-English relations in Canada can be contentious.

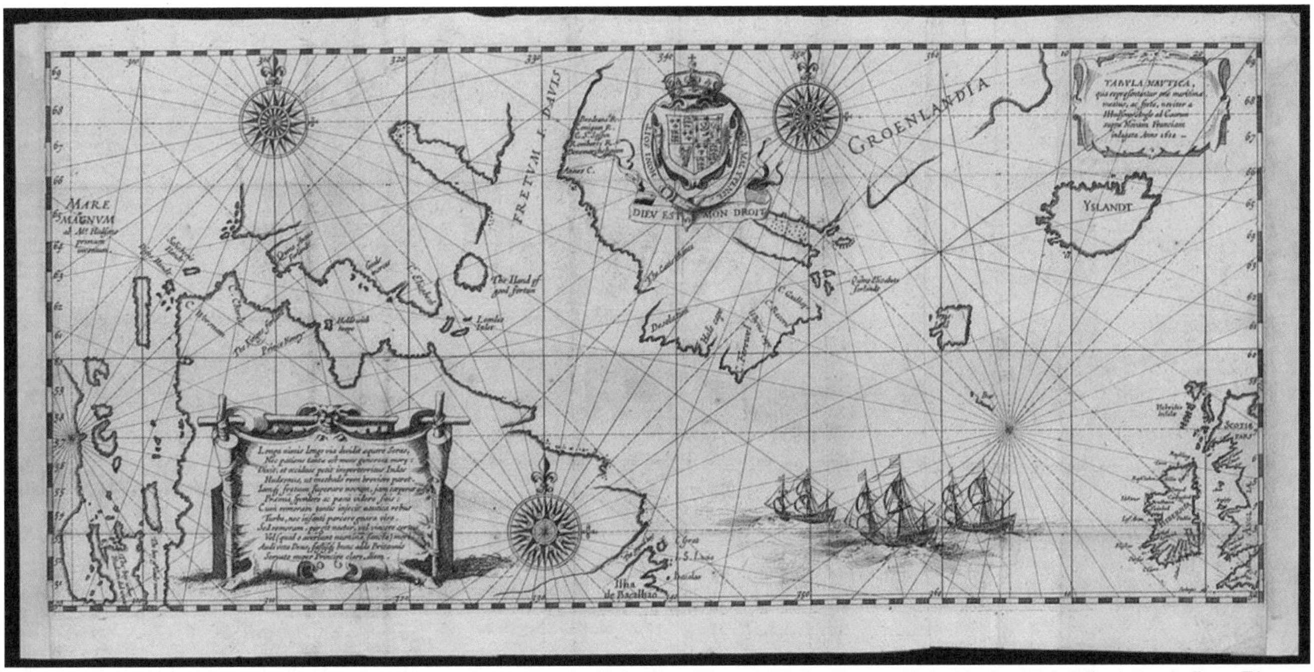

Henry Hudson arrived in Arctic waters in 1610 determined to find the Northwest Passage. He explored Hudson Bay and the mouth of the Bay. His crew mutinied and abandoned him in 1611 and returned to Europe. This map by Dutch cartographer Gerritsz is based on Hudson's discoveries.

Champlain's Map 1632

The British, upon taking control of Canada in 1764, left intact the religious and economic systems already in place, to the relief of the Catholic French colonists. The Quebec Act of 1774 allowed a separate system of French law to continue in Quebec. The British now controlled the entire eastern half of North America, from the eastern seaboard to the Mississippi River. However, George III's mistreatment of the American colonies would soon cause a shift in the balance of power in the New World.

As a base for the British forces, a refuge for fleeing Americans loyal to the British crown, and a source of militia for both the British and American armies, Canada played a large role in the American Revolution. The American army originally attempted to convince Canada to join their revolution but Canadians had just finished rebuilding after the Seven Years War and most did not want no take part in another feud. On June 27, 1775, American troops attacked Quebec and Montreal was taken without a fight. The attack on Quebec City was eventually defeated and in 1776, the American troops evacuated Montreal.

When America gained independence from Britain in 1783, citizens loyal to the British Empire were exiled. Over 35,000 of these loyalists flooded into Nova Scotia. This massive influx prompted the British government to divide Nova Scotia, creating the new colony of New Brunswick. Soon, the loyalists in Quebec were also making demands for their own colony, while the French Canadians were equally determined to have their own elected assembly. In 1791, Quebec was divided into Upper Canada and Lower Canada in order to meet the distinct needs of the English loyalists and the French Canadians.

Tensions between Britain and America remained high in the proceeding decades, and once again a conflict erupted that ensnared Canada. The United States declared war on Britain in 1812 over the arming and supplying of hostile Native American tribes and the forced conscription of American sailors into the British Navy. Canada became one of the primary battlegrounds in this conflict, with the United States planning to seize Canada and use it as leverage against the British. America expected support from the people of Canada, who they assumed were unhappy under English colonial rule. However, many Canadians at that time were children of British loyalists who fled America and saw the United States as invaders and occupiers.

The American army suffered a loss early in the war when they were soundly defeated by General Isaac Brock and his force of Indian allies and local military men at the Battle of Queenston Heights. But the American army did go on to occupy and loot many cities, including York (now Toronto) and Newark (now Niagara-on-the-Lake), eventually controlling much of present day Ontario and Quebec. Ultimately, the American army was driven back, and although the war ended with no real victor, the fact that an attempted American takeover had been thwarted gave Canadians confidence and stimulated national pride.

While Canadians rejected the idea of American invaders on their soil, the political example of the United States resonated throughout the country. Rebellions broke out against the British in 1837. Canadians, angry over the unfair distribution of wealth derived from Canada's natural resources, balked against not being represented in the British government. Based on the opinion of the British that friction between the French and English people was causing conflict in Canada, all of the Canadian colonies were merged together into the United Province of Canada in 1840. In 1849 the United States and the British Empire agreed that the 49th north parallel would be the boundary between the two nations, and the British extended Canada to the western seaboard, encompassing British Columbia.

Canadian independence had been debated in Britain and in Canada almost since the American Revolution. Some advocated violent revolution and total Canadian independence. Others wanted a slower, more gradual autonomy. On July 1st, 1867, the British parliament passed the British North America Act, which established The Dominion of Canada as a separate and self-governing colony. While it was not completely severed from England, especially in matters of foreign policy, domestically, Canada was allowed free reign.

During the next decades, Canada continued to expand westward. With the purchase of two huge northern territories, The North-Western Territory and Rupert's Land, from the Hudson Bay Company, the country more than doubled its size. The sections of Canada west of Ontario housed a large population of French-speaking, Catholic Métis, the children of indigenous people and white settlers. After the sale of Rupert's Land, many settlers from Ontario flooded into the region hoping to claim land. The Métis became worried that this influx of mostly English Protestant settlers would threaten their rights to language, religion and land. The Métis leader Louis Riel organized the Red River Resistance in 1869 in order to ensure that these rights were guaranteed. The revolt led to the creation of Manitoba, a province with strong laws protecting the Métis, French-speaking people and Catholics. By 1905, the founding provinces of Upper and Lower Canada, New Brunswick, and Nova Scotia were soon joined by British Columbia, Saskatchewan, Prince Edward Island, and Alberta.

The construction of a transcontinental railroad, completed in 1885, spurred Canada's expansion. While the railroad enabled additional settlers to move west into the new provinces, it also pushed the Native people aside. Again rebellion flared, resulting in more bloodshed. The sentiment that the Canadian government didn't heed the concerns of French-speaking Catholic citizens caused a political crisis resulting in the resignation of prime minister Mackenzie Bowell in 1896, when the government tried to ban French as an official language of Manitoba, contrary to the laws of the province.

Both Canada and the United States shared a period of western expansion in the late nineteenth century, based on the prominence of the railroad, the promise of free land and the discovery of mineral deposits. These factors, joined with a large influx of European immigrants, led to Canada becoming the fastest-growing economy in the world between 1896 and 1911. During that time, the Canadian government created the Yukon Territory, a land mass about the size of Germany, Austria and Switzerland combined, then populated by only 8,500 people.

On the verge of the twentieth century, Canada faced the first serious conflict with its colonial power. When Britain entered the Boer War in 1899, most English-speaking Canadians supported bringing South Africa into the fold of the British Empire. French Canadians, however, had little interest in British imperialism, seeing themselves as a separate concern, only nominally part of the Empire. As a compromise, volunteers were allowed to serve in the Boer War, but the Canadian Army stayed uninvolved. The view of French Canada as a separate entity, exacerbated by rebellion and anti-French laws of the past decades, would continue to play out in Canadian politics in years to come.

Arctic regions 1953

Although many French Canadians wanted out from under the British Empire's yoke, the country was still obligated to fall in line with British foreign policy. With the assassination of Archduke Ferdinand on June 28, 1914, Canada was swept into the chaotic system of alliances that created World War I. When Britain declared war on the central powers on August 4th, Canadian troops were called into action. Like most of the allied powers, internal disputes were put aside and support for the war remained high, even among French Canadians. After suffering more than 200,000 dead and wounded casualties out of a population of seven million, support for the war began to wane. By the time the government attempted to introduce conscription in 1917, many Canadians, especially in French Canada, were fiercely anti-war. Despite the popular sentiment, World War I greatly increased the sense of Canadian nationalism and identity, fed by the country's significant role in the largest war mankind had ever known. Massive Canadian casualties in what many Canadians saw as a "British" war also created additional animosity towards the Empire.

World War I radically changed Canada's political landscape. Soldiers returned home from the horrors of the conflict with altered political ideologies. Socialism, communism, trade unionism and other left-wing progressive movements gained traction in the years immediately after the war, as the influx of soldiers returning home caused high unemployment and wage cuts. The Winnipeg General Strike of 1919, the largest of a wave of strikes that swept the country, was violently crushed by police, killing one man and wounding 30. When women's suffrage was enacted nationwide in 1918, the ruling Conservative Party collapsed, partly because of their actions during the strike. The Liberal Party, upon assuming control of the government, enacted many of the original strike committee's demands, including the right to form unions without government permission. Progressive and socialist parties formed in subsequent years, including the Progressive Party of Canada and the Cooperative Commonwealth Federation.

In 1931, the British Parliament passed the Statute of Westminster, establishing all the colonies and dominions of the British Empire, including Canada, Australia, New Zealand, and Ireland as separate legislative entities. This act allowed these countries to write their own constitutions and removed the power of the British Government to legislate in these areas, effectively making them independent, while still being contained in a worldwide British Commonwealth.

When the American Stock Market crashed on Black Tuesday in 1929 kicking off the Great Depression, the Canadian economy soon felt the effects. By 1933, the Canadian gross national product had dropped 40 percent. Manufacturing and farming suffered the most, with the price of wheat, Canada's main export, cut in half. At its worst point in 1933, 30 percent of Canadians were out of work. Newfoundland, deciding that Canadian government policy was the cause of the economic difficulty, voted to leave the Canadian federation and rejoin the British Empire.

When both the Liberal and Conservative parties were unable to produce any solutions to the crisis, many Canadians began to turn to third parties, such as the socialist Cooperative Commonwealth Federation and the Social Credit Party of Canada. After the Conservative government of R.B. Bennett put unemployed men into work camps to offset the great cost of supporting a huge welfare system, the Workers' Unity League put together a massive protest called the "On to Ottawa Trek" in order to call for improved conditions and benefits. Bennett's attempt to repress the Trek resulted in the Regina Riot, and contributed to his defeat in the 1935 election. The new Liberal government did away with the camps and instituted social programs to help lessen the effects of the Depression, but Canada was still severely affected. Almost one-fifth of the population was surviving on government payouts and social support systems. Even after a resurgent boom in Canada's economy, brought on by World War II, these systems remained in place, and continued to evolve.

World War II officially began on September 1, 1939. Canada did not immediately enter the war upon the British declaration as it had in World War I. With its growing independence from England, Canada decided to declare war on its own nine days later. While the Japanese and Nazi onslaught was still in full effect, Canadian supplies and war material were instrumental in keeping Britain from succumbing to German invasion. Once the Allies were in a position to counterattack, Canadian troops were deployed all over the world, and served valiantly in some of the major battles, including the invasion of Sicily and Italy in 1943, the allied landing at Normandy in 1944, the liberation of the Netherlands, and the drive across France and Germany to end the war. However, Canada endured its own share of loss. A predominantly Canadian raid, at Dieppe, France, resulted in more than 3,000 dead, wounded or captured and German U-boats, which prowled Canadian waters, sank many supply ships. In the end, Canada suffered a total of 42,000 casualties.

When the Japanese bombed Pearl Harbor on December 7, 1941, the 22,000 Japanese Canadians then living in British Columbia took the brunt of the resulting pain and anger. The anti-Asian sentiment in the province was further fueled when thousands of Canadians were killed or captured in the Japanese invasion of Hong Kong. In 1942, all people of Japanese descent were sent to internment camps, and after the war, all Japanese

Canadians were deported from British Columbia. It was not until 1949 that they became free to live anywhere in Canada. Japanese Canadians were finally compensated in 1988 for the wrongs that they had suffered during the war.

At the close of World War II, Canada and the United States alone benefited from never having seen fighting on their home soil. Each country was, therefore, in a unique economic position. Due to a revitalized manufacturing sector, the discovery of oil in Alberta, and as the main trading partner to the economic superpower on their southern border, the Canadian economy exploded. This newfound wealth was put into a radical new program of social support. Based upon the centralized welfare state of the late 1930s and early 1940s, as well as many of the policies of the socialist Cooperative Commonwealth Federation, Canadians enjoyed hospital insurance, old-age pensions, veterans' pensions, and family allowance. These progressive social policies convinced Newfoundland to rejoin Canada in a 1949 referendum.

Canada cemented its position in the Cold War with its founding membership in NATO in 1949. The country's fortunes were firmly rooted with the United States. Canada participated in the Korean War, and Canadian troops were stationed in West Germany, on the border of the communist Eastern Bloc. Canada's voting record in the United Nations was not always aligned with the United States, but there is no question that Canada was an American ally pitted against the Soviet Union.

Canada's treatment of its Native peoples has a sad history. As far back as the late 1800s, when the buffalo were hunted almost to extinction and the expansion of the railroad brought more settlers to native territories, First Nations people were treated as second-class citizens. Starvation, assimilation and a crushed rebellion largely put an end to the native resistance movement, but it gained strength again after World War II. Decolonialization and a newfound spirit of democracy was being put forth by the Western powers in their opposition to Soviet tyranny, yet most First Nations people could not vote as late as 1950. In order to vote, First Nations people had to gain suffrage by renouncing their status as "Indians." It was not until 1960 (1969 in Quebec) that all First Nations people were allowed to vote freely.

As Canada entered the 1960s, the government faced growing radicalism and organization among its populace. Quebec nationalism had been growing ever since the British took Canada from the French in 1764. French Canadians saw themselves as a separate nation, and frequently found themselves disagreeing with the policies of the Canadian government. The more radical French Canadian factions felt they were being oppressed, and that their language and culture were under attack. Inspired by revolutions around the world, nationalist and left-wing terrorism began to rise, Canada was not unaffected. The Front de Libération du Québec (FLQ), committed more than 200 bombings, and killed five people in pursuit of an independent Quebec. While violence was rejected by a majority of the population, a genuine desire for independence fueled Québécois protests. When Pierre Elliott Trudeau was elected prime minister in 1968, he declared martial law in Quebec, arresting most members of the FLQ.

While the crisis in Quebec worsened throughout the 1970s, the United States became involved in one of the most controversial conflicts in modern history: the war in Indochina. The Vietnam War resulted in over 1,500,000 dead, and radicalized an entire generation. Canada was no exception. Young people throughout the country protested against what they saw as American imperialism. The Canadian government refused to participate in the war, and granted citizenship to as many as 125,000 American draft dodgers over the course of the conflict. This led to serious friction between the governments of Canada and the US. To this day Vietnam and Canada have a close relationship, and hundreds of thousands of Vietnamese have immigrated to Canada's west coast. The period of the Vietnam War also saw the rise of the New Democratic Party (NDP), the successor to the socialist Cooperative Commonwealth Federation. Since its beginning in 1962, the NDP has altered the balance of Canadian politics, regularly receiving between 10 and 20 percent of the national vote, and often having the ability to form a majority coalition by grouping itself with the winning party. In the 2011 federal election, the NDP had its best result, winning 30 percent of the vote and the role of official opposition for the first time. It has fought for the continuation of Canada's welfare state, a humanitarian foreign policy, and native rights.

Young people across Canada became increasingly involved in politics as a result of the Vietnam War, and this new political awareness allowed the question of Quebec sovereignty to be addressed. The Parti Québécois was formed in 1968 and elected to govern Quebec in 1976, making French the official language of the province in 1977. Finally, the party made good on its biggest promise and introduced a referendum to decide Quebec's fate. The actual referendum simply said that Quebec would "negotiate a new agreement with the rest of Canada, based on the equality of nations; this agreement would enable Quebec to acquire the exclusive power to make its laws, levy its taxes and establish relations abroad - in other words, sovereignty." The fact that the referendum did not advocate full independence, in combination with a full-out public relations assault from the federal government, doomed the referendum.

While Canada became a sovereign entity in 1867, and had its independence increased in 1931, it was not technically a separate nation. Canada could not make amendments to its own constitution and the power of Canada to act directly against the wishes of the British government was in question. In 1982, Trudeau finally sealed Canada's status as its own unique nation by signing the Canada Act and the Charter of Rights and Freedoms. Although still a member of the British Commonwealth, Canada was now free from control by the British parliament.

With Canada's complete independence from Britain, the question of trade with the United States became central to the Canadian economy. The Canada-United States Free Trade Agreement drafted in 1988 set the model for the subsequent North American Free Trade Agreement and Central American Free Trade Agreement. The criticism of the agreement, as well as later free trade agreements, was that by eliminating trade barriers, Canadian consumers and labour unions would be at the mercy of more powerful US corporations. The agreement was a decisive issue in the 1988 elections, with the Liberal Party and NDP in opposition, and the ruling Progressive Conservatives attempting to pass it. A 57 percent majority voted against the Progressive Conservatives, but because they received the most votes for one single party, they were rewarded with the most seats in parliament, and passed the free trade agreement.

The Parti Québécois, after failing in its referendum of 1980, had formed a national party, the Bloc Québécois, and doggedly pursued its agenda of an independent Quebec. A second referendum, called in 1995, created an even bigger debate than the referendum of 1980, with massive media campaigns on both sides of the issue. When the vote finally came up, it failed by a slim 54,000 votes, but the issue illustrated a true divide in Quebec. Considering that 86,000 ballots were thrown out as invalid, the question of Quebec independence failed by a razor-thin margin, and the probability of it arising again in the future is still possible.

In 1990, in a small town called Oka, west of Montreal, a First Nations revolt led to the intervention of the Canadian Army and three deaths. While this was far from the first violent conflict between First Nations people and the Canadian government, it has marked a new era of militant native resistance. With more than one million people of Aboriginal descent living in Canada, many native organizations have called for more indigenous control over resources in their lands, resulting in violent conflicts between First Nations people and corporations attempting to mine, fish, or harvest lumber. One effect of these protests was the creation of a new territory, Nunavut, in the far north of Canada in 1999. While the population is less than 30,000, more than 85 percent of its inhabitants claim Inuit status, and the territory has adopted many laws securing their rights and claims to land and resources.

Today, Canada continues to deal with its internal relations with French speaking Canadians and First Nations people. As a unified country, it also faces other issues such as participation in peacekeeping missions, drug decriminalization, immigration, global warming, and control over Arctic seaways.

Histoire du Canada

Au cours des 400 dernières années, le Canada est passé de simple poste de traite peu peuplé au huitième état souverain le plus riche au monde. Il s'agit de plus du seul pays à s'être séparé pacifiquement de sa puissance coloniale.

Malgré que le grand territoire composant aujourd'hui le Canada avait déjà une histoire vieille de plusieurs millénaires au début de la colonisation européenne, il a néanmoins été un des derniers endroits au monde à accueillir des populations humaines. Alors que l'*Homo Sapiens* moderne aurait émergé dans l'est de l'Afrique il y a 200 000 ans, la majorité des scientifiques conviennent qu'il aura fallu 175 000 années de plus pour que les hommes traversent le pont de glace reliant jadis l'Alaska et l'est de la Sibérie. Sur ce nouveau continent, c'est l'espace que délimitent les frontières canadiennes actuelles qui est habité depuis le plus longtemps; la migration originale qui a eu lieu il y a 25 000 ans est la source des cultures indigènes d'Amérique du Nord et du Sud, incluant les Inuits de l'Arctique, les Pieds-Noirs, les Cris, les Algonquins, les Dénés et la Ligue iroquoise des Cinq-Nations. On estime à environ deux millions le nombre d'Autochtones vivant aux États-Unis et au Canada avant l'arrivée des Européens dans le Nouveau Monde.

Christophe Colomb est peut-être celui à qui l'on attribue la « découverte » de l'Amérique en 1492, mais l'on sait aujourd'hui avec certitudes que les Vikings ont atteint et dépassé le Groenland en 982 apr. J.-C. Des traces archéologiques qui dateraient d'environ 1000 ans indiquent la présence à cette époque de peuples norois à L'Anse aux Meadows, à Terre-Neuve, ce qui ferait du Canada le véritable lieu de découverte de l'Amérique du Nord par les Européens. Les Vikings ne visaient pas toutefois à établir une colonisation permanente, mais étaient plutôt intéressés aux ressources naturelles du Canada. Quand Christophe Colomb foula le sol américain pour la première fois, les installations qui y avaient été construites par les peuples norois étaient abandonnées depuis longtemps déjà.

Le voyage de Christophe Colomb déclencha en Europe une course à la colonisation du Nouveau Monde. En traversant l'Atlantique vers ce qu'il croyait être l'Inde pour trouver une voie alternative aux longues routes de commerce terrestres menant à l'Asie et à ses produits, Christophe Colomb donna sans le vouloir le coup d'envoi à l'Ère des grandes découvertes. Les puissances européennes établirent des colonies à la recherche d'épices, d'or, d'esclaves et de nouvelles cultures, ainsi que pour convertir les peuples autochtones au christianisme. Les premières colonies, principalement espagnoles et portugaises, étaient concentrées en Amérique du Sud, en Amérique Centrale et dans les Caraïbes. L'Angleterre et la France ont plutôt tourné leurs efforts vers le Nord. Jean Cabot, un explorateur anglais d'origine italienne, est considéré comme le premier explorateur européen à avoir mis le pied en Amérique du Nord après les Vikings. Bien que cette exploration eut lieu seulement cinq années après les découvertes de Christophe Colomb, il faudra attendre jusqu'en 1605 pour que des installations permanentes soient établies. À cette époque, beaucoup d'explorateurs, dont Henry Hudson, tentaient encore de trouver le passage du Nord-Ouest, la fameuse voie navigable qui devait relier le Nouveau Monde à l'Asie. Si plus de cent ans se sont écoulés avant ces premières installations permanentes, c'est davantage en raison d'événements se déroulant en Europe que de facteurs attribuables au Nouveau Monde.

Deux événements sont venus ralentir la colonisation de l'Amérique du Nord : l'agitation religieuse et la guerre en Europe. En 1517, Martin Luther diffusa sa liste de 95 griefs contre l'Église catholique en utilisant une invention toute nouvelle, la presse à imprimer. Ainsi débuta la réforme protestante. Ce schisme détournera de façon importante le cours de l'Histoire en Europe, mais à court terme, il suscita surtout un conflit religieux tumultueux. Presque toute l'Europe connut un repli sur soi pour faire face à cette agitation ainsi qu'à cette crise religieuse. Des conflits politiques croissants secouèrent la majeure partie de l'Europe de l'Ouest durant des décennies, accaparant les ressources qui auraient dû être attribuées aux efforts de colonisation. Les guerres de religion en France, les guerres en Italie et les révoltes populaires combinées aux soulèvements religieux ont détourné l'attention de l'Europe du Nouveau Monde pendant plus d'un siècle.

La France voyait l'Amérique du Nord comme la meilleure source de richesse et de puissance possible et souhaitait, en exploitant ces contrées, arriver à alléger ses dettes de guerre. Quand l'explorateur français Jacques Cartier navigua sur le fleuve Saint-Laurent en 1534, il revendiqua le territoire au nom de la France et lui donna le nom qu'il porte encore aujourd'hui : le Canada. Après que les commerçants de fourrure se furent implantés dans l'Est du Canada, la France monopolisa le commerce de la fourrure. Bien que les Français tentèrent d'établir des relations commerciales amicales avec les peuples autochtones, certains d'entre eux, dont les Iroquois, se révélèrent particulièrement hostiles. Les conflits avec les tribus locales ont rapidement fait de convaincre la Couronne que pour assurer la rentabilité du commerce au Canada, une présence militaire et civile permanente était essentielle. Le roi Henri IV dépêcha donc sur place son « hydrographe » Samuel de Champlain pour cartographier la région.

En 1605, après avoir exploré la côte de l'Amérique du Nord jusqu'à Cape Cod, Champlain établira un premier peuplement français à Port-Royal et fondera ensuite la ville de Québec en 1608. La Nouvelle-France, comme on l'appelait à l'époque, se développa lentement, principalement en raison du manque d'intérêt de la mère patrie et de la guerre avec les Iroquois. Les colons survécurent aux attaques des Autochtones grâce à leurs alliances avec les Algonquins, les Montagnais et les Hurons. En plus de garantir la survie des colons, ces alliances permirent à la France d'affermir son contrôle du commerce des fourrures. Les Européens n'avaient aucune notion du milieu sauvage de la région, connaissances que les Autochtones leur procureront.

Une fois de plus, des tensions religieuses en Europe vinrent interférer avec le développement des établissements au Canada. Vers le milieu du dix-septième siècle, alors que les colonies anglaises en Amérique et dans les Caraïbes devenaient autosuffisantes, la Nouvelle-France demeurait sous-peuplée. Cette colonie éprouvait des difficultés et épuisait les ressources de la France. La monarchie française décida de prendre les choses en mains en offrant des primes à ceux qui décideraient d'émigrer en Nouvelle-France. Une seule condition s'imposait : tous les colons en partance devaient être catholiques ou se convertir au catholicisme avant de quitter l'Europe. Ce changement de politique, imposé à la demande du fervent cardinal Richelieu, le conseiller le plus proche du roi Louis XIII, créera de nombreuses frictions. Auparavant, les protestants français, particulièrement la secte persécutée connue sous le nom de Huguenots, s'exilaient souvent en Nouvelle-France pour fuir les persécutions religieuses. Ce nouveau décret du cardinal Richelieu aura un effet durable sur la composition politique et religieuse du Canada moderne.

Vers la fin du dix-septième siècle, les assises des colonies anglaises et françaises du Nouveau Monde commençaient enfin à gagner en solidité. Les deux nations avaient remporté leur mise et leurs colonies dégageaient un bon profit, mais une guerre en Europe devait venir gêner une fois de plus la croissance balbutiante du Canada. La Nouvelle-France, déjà au cœur d'une brutale guerre intertribale avec les Algonquins, entra en conflit avec la confédération iroquoise qui s'opposait à elle. Avec la guerre de Neuf Ans, qui débuta en 1688 et vit la France entrer en conflit avec presque tout le reste de l'Europe, les Iroquois commencèrent à recevoir des armes de la part des Anglais, en accord aux politiques de leur gouvernement. Cette escalade de violence des Anglais envenima cette guerre déjà sanglante. L'armée anglaise et ses alliés iroquois capturèrent Port-Royal, mais furent repoussés de Québec, principalement en raison des maladies qui décimaient les forces. La guerre finit par s'essouffler sur le Continent, et un traité de paix fut signé en 1697. Les Iroquois continueront cependant à se battre sans les Britanniques, mais subiront finalement d'importantes défaites qui les forceront à établir la paix quatre ans plus tard.

La Nouvelle-France (et le Canada par le fait même) semblait bien acquise à la mère patrie à la suite de la conclusion de la guerre de Neuf Ans. Toutefois, le contrôle de la région par la France ne durera pas longtemps. La guerre de Succession d'Espagne, qui commencera un an seulement après la signature du traité de paix entre la France et les Iroquois, permettra à l'Angleterre de prendre possession de la Nouvelle-Écosse et de Terre-Neuve, ainsi que des droits sur la région entourant la baie d'Hudson. Un nouveau conflit, nommé la guerre du roi George, débutera trois décennies plus tard, soit en 1744, mais aucun des deux belligérants ne réussira à élargir alors ses positions coloniales.

En 1754, l'animosité de longue date entre les Anglais et les Français gagnera le Nouveau Monde, avec comme point culminant la guerre de Sept Ans, appelée aussi en Amérique guerre franco-indienne. Trois causes principales étaient à la base de ce conflit. D'abord, le lucratif commerce de la fourrure, l'abondance des poissons, la richesse des forêts et les gisements de minerais étaient tous des sources de fortune pour quiconque contrôlerait le Canada. Ensuite, les Anglais, anticatholiques invétérés, croyaient que les Français étaient des hérétiques, un sentiment qui était d'ailleurs réciproque! Enfin, le contrôle des colonies outre-mer pourrait servir comme monnaie d'échange diplomatique si la guerre en Europe devait se détériorer.

La guerre de Sept Ans fut la première guerre à l'échelle mondiale et qui fit rage sur cinq continents : l'Amérique du Nord, l'Amérique du Sud, l'Afrique, l'Europe et l'Asie. Plus d'un million de personnes perdront la vie et la conclusion de cette guerre changera totalement le partage du pouvoir dans le Nouveau Monde. La Grande-Bretagne obtiendra le contrôle de toutes les colonies françaises en Amérique du Nord, faisant ainsi du Canada une colonie britannique. Toutefois, 150 années de colonisation française ne pouvaient disparaître du jour au lendemain. Encore aujourd'hui, les relations entre Anglais et Français au Canada connaissent leurs tensions et contrariétés.

Les Britanniques, suite à leur prise de contrôle du Canada en 1764, ne touchèrent pas aux systèmes religieux et économiques en place, au grand soulagement des colons catholiques français. L'Acte de Québec de 1774 permit qu'un système indépendant de lois françaises continue au Québec. Les Britanniques contrôlaient maintenant complètement la portion est de l'Amérique du Nord, depuis la rive est du fleuve Mississippi jusqu'à la côte Atlantique. Le mauvais traitement réservé aux colonies américaines par George III viendrait cependant bientôt modifier de nouveau l'équilibre du pouvoir dans le Nouveau Monde.

À titre de base pour les forces britanniques, de refuge pour les Américains loyaux à la monarchie britannique qui étaient en fuite et de source de milice pour les armées britanniques et américaines, le Canada joua un rôle important dans la guerre de l'Indépendance américaine. L'armée américaine tenta à l'origine de convaincre le Canada de prendre part à sa révolution, mais les Canadiens se relevaient à peine de la guerre de Sept Ans, et la majorité d'entre eux ne voulaient pas d'un autre conflit. Le 27 juin 1775, les troupes américaines attaquèrent Québec. Montréal fut pris sans résistance, mais l'attaque sur la ville de Québec se solda par une défaite, et en 1776, les troupes américaines évacuèrent Montréal.

Lorsque l'Amérique gagna son indépendance de la Grande-Bretagne en 1783, les citoyens loyaux à l'Empire britannique durent s'exiler. Plus de 35 000 d'entre eux se rendirent en Nouvelle-Écosse. Cet important mouvement de masse força le gouvernement britannique à diviser la Nouvelle-Écosse, créant ainsi la nouvelle colonie du Nouveau-Brunswick. Peu de temps après, les loyalistes établis au Québec commencèrent à présenter des demandes pour obtenir leur propre colonie, alors que les Canadiens français étaient aussi déterminés à avoir leur propre assemblée d'élus. En 1791, le Québec fut divisé en deux parties, le Haut-Canada et le Bas-Canada, afin de répondre aux exigences des loyalistes anglais et des Canadiens français.

Au cours des décennies qui suivirent, les tensions entre la Grande-Bretagne et l'Amérique demeurèrent vives, et encore une fois, un conflit déchira le Canada. Les États-Unis déclarèrent la guerre à la Grande-Bretagne en 1812 en raison de l'approvisionnement en armes des tribus amérindiennes hostiles et du service militaire obligatoire des marins américains à la marine britannique. Le Canada fut un des champs de bataille principaux de ce conflit puisque les États-Unis avaient planifié s'emparer du Canada et l'utiliser comme monnaie d'échange pour négocier avec les Britanniques. Les Américains s'attendaient à gagner le soutien des Canadiens qu'ils croyaient malheureux sous le contrôle colonial des Anglais. Toutefois, beaucoup de Canadiens, descendants de loyalistes britanniques qui avaient fui l'Amérique, percevaient les États-Unis comme des envahisseurs et des occupants.

L'armée américaine subit une défaite tôt dans le conflit lorsqu'elle fut battue par le général Isaac Brock et ses forces d'alliés indiens et de militaires locaux lors de la bataille de Queenston Heights. L'armée américaine en arriva quand même occuper et à piller un grand nombre de villes, incluant York (aujourd'hui Toronto) et Newark (aujourd'hui Niagra-on-the-Lake), jusqu'à contrôler à un certain moment presque tout le territoire correspondant à l'Ontario et au Québec d'aujourd'hui, mais en fin de compte, l'armée américaine fut repoussée, et bien que la guerre finit sans réel vainqueur, le fait qu'une prise de contrôle américaine fut empêchée donna aux Canadiens un regain de confiance et devint source de fierté nationale.

Même si les Canadiens rejetaient l'idée d'un envahisseur américain sur leur sol, l'exemple politique des États-Unis laissait sa marque à travers le pays. Des rébellions éclatèrent contre les Britanniques en 1837. Les Canadiens, insatisfaits de la distribution inéquitable des richesses tirées des ressources naturelles du Canada, s'insurgeaient de ne pas être représentés au sein du gouvernement britannique. Puisque les Britanniques considéraient que les frictions entre les Français et les Anglais étaient la source des conflits qu'ils vivaient avec le Canada, toutes les colonies canadiennes furent réunies en 1840 sous le nom de la Province du Canada, aussi appelée le Canada-Uni. En 1849, les États-Unis et l'Empire britannique se mirent d'accord pour que le 49e parallèle nord serve de frontière entre les deux nations, et les Britanniques étendirent le Canada jusqu'au au littoral ouest, annexant ainsi la Colombie-Britannique.

C'est pratiquement depuis la guerre d'Indépendance américaine que l'indépendance du Canada fait l'objet de débats en Grande-Bretagne comme au Canada. Certains prônaient une révolution violente et une indépendance canadienne totale. D'autres désiraient suivre un processus vers l'autonomie plus lent et graduel. Le 1er juillet 1867, le Parlement britannique édicta l'Acte de l'Amérique du Nord britannique, qui établit le Dominion du Canada comme une colonie distincte et dotée d'un gouvernement autonome. Sans être complètement détaché de l'Angleterre, particulièrement en ce qui a trait à la politique étrangère, sur le plan de la politique intérieure, le Canada gagnait pleine liberté et souveraineté.

Au cours des décennies suivantes, le Canada continua son expansion vers l'Ouest. Grâce à l'achat de deux énormes territoires au nord, les Territoires du Nord-Ouest et la Terre de Rupert, acquis de la Compagnie de la Baie d'Hudson, le pays doubla pratiquement sa superficie. Beaucoup de francophones et de Métis catholiques, les enfants d'Autochtones et de pionniers, vivaient à l'ouest de l'Ontario. Après la vente de la Terre de Rupert, plusieurs colons ontariens affluèrent dans cette région en espérant réclamer ces terres. Les Métis se mirent à craindre que cette arrivée massive de protestants anglais mette en péril leurs droits linguistiques, religieux et territoriaux. Le chef Métis Louis Riel organisa la Rébellion de la rivière Rouge en 1869 dans le but de garantir la protection de ces droits. Cette révolte mena à la création du Manitoba, une province qui mit en place des lois rigoureuses protégeant les Métis, les francophones et les catholiques. En 1905, la Colombie-Britannique, la Saskatchewan, l'Île-du-Prince-Édouard et l'Alberta furent coup sur coup jointes aux provinces fondatrices du Haut et du Bas-Canada, au Nouveau-Brunswick et à la Nouvelle-Écosse.

La construction d'un chemin de fer transcontinental, complété en 1885, stimula l'expansion du Canada. Ce chemin de fer incita de nouveaux colons à déménager dans l'Ouest pour s'établir dans les nouvelles provinces, mais ces nouveaux arrivants voulurent chasser les Autochtones de leurs terres, ce qui, une fois de plus, fit éclater des rébellions qui finirent en bains de sang. Le sentiment que le gouvernement canadien n'écoutait pas les préoccupations des catholiques francophones engendra une crise politique qui entraîna la démission du premier ministre Mackenzie Bowell en 1896 lorsque le gouvernement tenta de retirer au français son statut de langue officielle au Manitoba, ce qui allait à l'encontre des lois de la province.

Le Canada et les États-Unis connurent une période d'expansion vers l'ouest à la fin du dix-neuvième siècle grâce au développement du chemin de fer, à l'attrait qu'exerçaient ses contrées vierges et à la découverte de gisements de minerais. Ces facteurs, additionnés de l'arrivée massive d'immigrants en provenance d'Europe, permirent au Canada d'être le pays présentant la croissance économique la plus forte entre 1896 et 1911. Durant cette période, le gouvernement canadien créa le Yukon, un territoire dont la superficie se compare à celle de l'Allemagne, l'Autriche et la Suisse combinées, et dont la population se chiffrait à seulement 8 500 habitants à ce moment.

À l'aube du vingtième siècle, le Canada connut son premier conflit d'importance avec sa puissance coloniale. Lorsque la Grande-Bretagne entra dans la Guerre des Boers en 1889, la majorité des Anglo-canadiens appuyaient l'annexion de l'Afrique du Sud à l'Empire britannique. Les Canadiens français, toutefois, ne s'intéressaient pas vraiment à l'impérialisme britannique, car ils se considéraient comme un cas à part et considéraient qu'ils faisaient partie de l'Empire britannique uniquement pour la forme. En guise de compromis, tous ceux se portant volontaires purent servir dans la Guerre des Boers, mais l'Armée canadienne comme telle ne s'impliqua pas dans ce conflit. Cette vision du Canada français comme une entité à part, vision exacerbée par les rébellions et par les lois anti-françaises des décennies précédentes, continuera de se manifester dans la politique du Canada des années à venir.

Bien qu'un grand nombre de Canadiens français désirait se départir du joug de l'Empire britannique, le pays devait tout de même se plier à la politique étrangère britannique. Avec l'assassinat de l'Archiduc Ferdinand le 28 juin 1914, le Canada fut pris dans le chaotique système d'alliances que suscita la Première Guerre mondiale. Lorsque la Grande-Bretagne déclara la guerre aux puissances centrales le 4 août, les troupes canadiennes furent appelées en renfort. Comme pour la majorité des puissances alliées, les disputes internes furent temporairement mises de côté, et l'appui à la guerre demeura massif, même chez les Canadiens français. Après plus de 200 000 morts et blessés de guerre, sur une population de 7 millions d'habitants, l'effort de guerre commença à s'essouffler. Au moment où le gouvernement tenta d'introduire le service obligatoire en 1917, beaucoup de Canadiens, et principalement des Canadiens français, s'opposèrent farouchement à la guerre. Malgré l'opinion populaire, la Première Guerre mondiale contribua à alimenter le sentiment de nationalisme et d'identité canadienne, surtout grâce au rôle important que joua le Canada dans la guerre la plus importante de l'histoire de l'humanité. Les très nombreuses victimes canadiennes occasionnées par ce conflit que plusieurs considéraient comme une guerre « britannique » vint aussi augmenter le ressentiment accumulé envers l'Empire.

La Première Guerre mondiale changea radicalement le visage politique du Canada. Après les horreurs vécues pendant ce conflit, les soldats rentrèrent chez eux avec de nouvelles idéologies politiques. Le socialisme, le communisme, le syndicalisme et d'autres courants progressistes de gauche gagnèrent en popularité dans les années suivant la guerre, tandis que le retour massif des soldats faisait augmenter le taux de chômage et diminuer les salaires. La grève générale de Winnipeg de 1919, la plus importante d'une série de grèves qui paralysèrent le pays, fut brutalement mise fin par la police, au prix d'un mort et de 30 blessés. Lorsque le Canada accorda le droit de vote aux femmes en 1918, le Parti conservateur en place s'effondra, en partie en raison de ses actions durant la grève. Le Parti libéral, en prenant le contrôle du gouvernement, acquiesça à une bonne partie des demandes originales du comité de grève, incluant le droit de former des syndicats sans la permission du gouvernement. Des partis progressistes et socialistes se formèrent les années suivantes, incluant le Parti progressiste du Canada et la Fédération du Commonwealth coopératif.

En 1931, le Parlement britannique promulgua le Statut de Westminster, qui donna le statut d'entité législative indépendante à toutes les colonies et à tous les dominions de l'Empire britannique, incluant le Canada, l'Australie, la Nouvelle-Zélande et l'Irlande. Cet acte permit à ces pays de rédiger leur propre constitution et supprima le pouvoir législatif qu'avait le gouvernement britannique dans ces régions, assurant ainsi l'indépendance de celles-ci tout en les incluant dans un Commonwealth britannique à l'échelle mondiale.

Lorsque le marché boursier américain connut son krach lors du mardi noir de 1929, événement qui marqua le début de la Grande dépression, l'économie canadienne ne tarda pas à en ressentir les effets. En 1933, le produit national brut canadien connut une baisse de 40 %. Les secteurs manufacturiers et agricoles furent le plus durement touchés, et le prix de blé, le principal produit d'exportation du Canada, chuta de moitié. Au creux de la vague, 30 % des Canadiens étaient sans emploi. Terre-Neuve, affirmant que les politiques du gouvernement canadien étaient la cause de ce creux économique, vota de quitter la Fédération canadienne pour rejoindre l'Empire britannique.

Après que les partis Libéral et Conservateur se soient montrés incapables de trouver des solutions à cette crise, beaucoup de Canadiens se tournèrent vers d'autres partis, comme la Fédération du Commonwealth coopératif et le Parti Crédit Social du Canada. Après que le gouvernement conservateur de R. B. Bennet ait placé des chômeurs dans des camps de travail pour pallier au coût élevé du système d'aide sociale, la Ligue d'unité ouvrière (LUO) organisa une importante manifestation appelée la « Marche sur Ottawa » dans le but d'obtenir des améliorations aux conditions et avantages dans les camps. La tentative de Bennett pour arrêter cette marche provoquera l'émeute de Regina et contribua en fin de compte à sa défaite aux élections de 1935. Le nouveau gouvernement libéral élimina les camps et institua des programmes sociaux pour diminuer les effets de la Dépression, mais ceci n'empêcha pas le Canada d'être fortement touché par cette dernière. Environ un cinquième de la population dépendait des allocations du gouvernement et du soutien des programmes sociaux. Même après le boom de l'économie canadienne causé par la Seconde Guerre mondiale, ces programmes restèrent en place et continuèrent d'évoluer.

La Seconde Guerre mondiale débuta le 1er septembre 1939. Puisque le Canada était de plus en plus indépendant de l'Angleterre, le pays n'entra pas en guerre immédiatement après la déclaration de la Grande-Bretagne comme il l'avait fait lors de la Première Guerre mondiale, mais décida plutôt de déclarer d'elle-même la guerre neuf jours plus tard. Alors que le massacre japonais et nazi était toujours à son comble, le ravitaillement et le matériel de guerre des Canadiens s'avérèrent d'une importance capitale pour permettre à la Grande-Bretagne de résister à l'invasion allemande. Une fois que les Alliés furent en position de contre-attaquer, les troupes canadiennes furent déployées partout dans le monde, et servirent vaillamment dans plusieurs batailles importantes, incluant l'invasion de la Sicile et de l'Italie en 1943, le débarquement allié en Normandie en 1944, la libération des Pays-Bas et la traversée de la France et de l'Allemagne pour mettre fin à la guerre. Un raid majoritairement canadien à Dieppe en France se solda par 3 000 morts, blessés et captifs, et les sous-marins allemands qui infestaient les eaux canadiennes coulèrent un grand nombre de navires de ravitaillement. En tout et partout, la Seconde Guerre mondiale entraînera la mort de 42 000 canadiens.

Lorsque les Japonais bombardèrent Pearl Harbor le 7 décembre 1941, les 22 000 Canadiens d'origine japonaise vivant alors en Colombie-Britannique durent composer avec les conséquences de la douleur et de la colère qui s'ensuivirent. Le sentiment anti-asiatique dans la province fut davantage attisé lorsque des milliers de Canadiens furent tués ou capturés durant l'invasion de Hong Kong par les Japonais. En 1942, toutes les personnes de descendance japonaise furent envoyées dans des camps d'internement, et après la fin de la guerre, tous les Canadiens d'origine japonaise furent déportés de la Colombie-Britannique. Ce n'est qu'en 1949 qu'ils furent libres de vivre n'importe où au Canada. En 1988, les Canadiens d'origine japonaise furent finalement indemnisés pour le tort qu'ils ont dû subir durant la guerre.

À la conclusion de la Seconde Guerre mondiale, le Canada et les États-Unis étaient les deux seuls pays à n'avoir pas eu de combats liés à cette guerre sur leur territoire. Cela permit à ces deux pays de profiter d'un contexte économique unique. Grâce à un secteur manufacturier en pleine relance, à la découverte de pétrole en Alberta et à sa position de partenaire commercial principal de la superpuissance économique juste au sud de la frontière, le Canada vit son économie exploser. Cette nouvelle prospérité favorisa la création d'un programme d'aide sociale radicalement amélioré. Grâce à l'aide sociale centralisée de la fin des années 1930 et du début des années 1940 ainsi qu'aux nombreuses politiques sociales de la Fédération du Commonwealth coopératif, les Canadiens profiteront de l'assurance-hospitalisation, d'un régime de pensions et des allocations familiales. Ces politiques sociales progressistes convainquirent Terre-Neuve de rejoindre le Canada suite à un référendum en 1949.

Le Canada consolida sa position lors de la Guerre froide grâce à son statut de membre fondateur de l'OTAN en 1949. L'économie du pays était directement liée à celle des États-Unis. Le Canada participa à la guerre de Corée, et ses troupes furent postées en Allemagne de l'Ouest, à la frontière du bloc communiste. Le vote canadien aux Nations Unies ne fut pas toujours identique à celui des États-Unis, mais il n'y avait aucun doute que le Canada était un allié des Américains dans sa guerre contre l'Union soviétique.

Le traitement que le Canada réserva à ses peuples autochtones au fil du temps présente une histoire peu reluisante. Si l'on recule à la fin des années 1800, lorsque le bison fut chassé au point d'être presque totalement exterminé et que les chemins de fer amenèrent davantage de colons dans les territoires autochtones, les membres des Premières nations furent traités comme des citoyens de second ordre. La famine, l'assimilation et une rébellion avortée mirent fin à la résistance autochtone, mais celle-ci reprit vigueur après la Seconde Guerre mondiale. La décolonisation et un esprit de démocratie renouvelé étaient mis de l'avant par les puissances occidentales dans leur lutte contre la tyrannie soviétique, mais la majorité des Premières nations n'obtinrent quand même le droit de vote qu'à la fin des années 1950. Pour pouvoir voter, les gens des Premières nations devaient renoncer à leur statut « d'Indien ». Ce n'est qu'en 1960 (1969 au Québec) que les gens des Premières nations obtinrent le droit de voter librement.

Au début des années 1960, le gouvernement canadien dut faire face à une croissance marquée du radicalisme et d'organisations populaires. Le mouvement nationaliste québécois n'avait cessé de prendre de l'ampleur depuis que les Britanniques avaient pris le contrôle du Canada aux dépens des Français en 1764. Les Canadiens français se considéraient comme une nation distincte, et étaient souvent en désaccord avec les politiques gouvernementales canadiennes. Les factions canadiennes-françaises les plus radicales avaient le sentiment d'être opprimées, et que leur langue et leur culture étaient menacées. Inspirés par les révolutions se déroulant partout dans le monde, les groupes de gauche nationalistes ou terroristes se multiplièrent, et le Canada ne fut pas épargné. Le Front de Libération du Québec commit plus de 200 attentats à la bombe, tuant ainsi cinq personnes dans sa quête d'un Québec indépendant. Bien que les actes de violence furent majoritairement condamnés par la population, un profond désir d'indépendance alimentait les protestations des Québécois. Lorsque Pierre Elliott Trudeau fut élu Premier ministre en 1968, il mit le Québec sous la loi martiale et procéda à l'arrestation de plusieurs membres du FLQ.

Pendant que la crise au Québec s'aggravait durant les années 1970, les États-Unis s'engagèrent dans un des conflits les plus controversés de l'histoire moderne : la guerre en Indochine. La guerre du Vietnam entraîna la mort de 1 500 000 personnes et radicalisa une génération entière. Le Canada ne fit pas exception. Les jeunes de tout le pays protestèrent contre ce qu'ils considéraient être l'impérialisme américain. Le gouvernement canadien refusa de participer à cette guerre, et accorda la citoyenneté à plus de 125 000 Américains réfractaires tout au long du conflit. Ceci mena à d'importantes frictions entre les gouvernements canadien et américain. Aujourd'hui encore, le Vietnam et le Canada jouissent d'une relation privilégiée, et des centaines de milliers de Vietnamiens ont immigré sur la côte Ouest du Canada. La guerre du Vietnam coïncida aussi avec l'ascension du Nouveau Parti Démocratique, le successeur de la Fédération du Commonwealth coopératif. Depuis ses débuts en 1962, le NPD changea le visage de la politique canadienne en obtenant régulièrement entre 10 et 20 % des votes et en formant une coalition majoritaire avec le parti vainqueur. Lors des élections fédérales de 2011, le NPD a obtenu son meilleur résultat à ce jour, en récoltant 30 % des voix et le rôle de l'opposition officielle pour la première fois. Il a combattu pour la sauvegarde du programme d'aide sociale du Canada, pour une politique étrangère humanitaire ainsi que pour les droits des Autochtones.

Les jeunes de tous les coins du Canada devinrent de plus en plus impliqués en politique après la guerre du Vietnam, et ce nouvel intérêt marqué pour la politique permit d'aborder la question de la souveraineté du Québec. Le Parti québécois fut formé en 1968, remporta les élections au Québec en 1976 et fit du français la langue officielle de la province en 1977. Finalement, le parti tint sa promesse et instaura un référendum pour décider de l'avenir du Québec. Ce référendum stipulait simplement que le Québec « négocierait une nouvelle entente avec le reste du Canada, entente fondée sur l'égalité des peuples, en vertu de laquelle le Québec aurait obtenu le pouvoir exclusif de faire ses lois, autrement dit, la souveraineté ». Le fait que le référendum ne garantissait pas une indépendance complète, combiné à un assaut du service des relations publiques du gouvernement, fit échouer le référendum.

Bien que le Canada devint une entité souveraine en 1867, et que son indépendance s'est accrue en 1931, techniquement, le pays n'était pas encore tout à fait une nation souveraine. Le Canada n'était pas en mesure d'apporter des amendements à sa propre constitution, et la capacité du Canada d'agir à l'encontre des désirs du gouvernement britannique était encore mise en doute. En 1982, Trudeau confirma le statut de nation souveraine du Canada en signant la loi constitutionnelle et la Charte canadienne des droits et libertés. Bien qu'il était encore membre du Commonwealth britannique, le Canada n'était plus sous le contrôle du parlement britannique.

Suite à l'indépendance complète du Canada par rapport à la Grande-Bretagne, la question du commerce avec les États-Unis devint la principale préoccupation de l'économie canadienne. L'Accord de libre-échange Canada-États-Unis rédigé en 1988 devint un modèle pour l'Accord de libre-échange nord-américain et l'Accord de libre-échange de l'Amérique centrale. Cet accord, de même que les accords de libre-échange subséquents, fut critiqué, car on considérait qu'éliminer les barrières commerciales ferait en sorte que les consommateurs canadiens seraient à la merci des puissantes corporations américaines. Cet accord fut au centre des élections de 1988 : le Parti libéral et le NPD s'y opposaient, alors que les progressistes conservateurs tentaient de le faire passer. Une majorité de 57 % vota contre les progressistes conservateurs, mais puisqu'ils reçurent néanmoins le plus grand nombre de votes pour un unique parti, ils obtinrent une majorité de sièges au parlement et conclurent l'accord de libre-échange.

Le Parti Québécois, suite à l'échec du référendum de 1980, forma un parti politique canadien, le Bloc Québécois, et poursuivit avec acharnement son échéancier pour un Québec indépendant. Un deuxième référendum, en 1995, occasionna un débat encore plus virulent que celui du référendum de 1980, avec des campagnes médiatiques massives de part et d'autres des deux camps. Le jour du scrutin, le référendum échoua par une mince marge de 54 000 votes, un résultat qui mit au jour la division du Québec sur cette question. Considérant que 86 000 bulletins avaient été rejetés comme invalides, le résultat sur la question de l'indépendance du Québec a été si près de la ligne décisive qu'il ne serait pas surprenant qu'un autre referendum ait lieu dans le futur.

En 1990, une révolte amérindienne dans une petite ville baptisée Oka, à l'ouest de Montréal, a mené à l'intervention de l'armée canadienne. Trois personnes moururent au cours de cette crise. Bien qu'il y ait précédemment eu de nombreux conflits violents entre les membres des Premières nations et le gouvernement du Canada, la situation à Oka marqua le début d'une nouvelle ère de résistance active des Autochtones. Comme le Canada compte plus d'un million d'habitants de descendance amérindienne, de nombreuses organisations autochtones ont réclamé un meilleur contrôle des ressources sur leurs terres, ce qui a causé des conflits violents entre les membres des Premières nations et les sociétés exploitant les ressources minières, maritimes ou forestières sur leurs territoires. L'une des conséquences de ces manifestations fut la création d'un nouveau territoire, le Nunavut en 1999, dans les régions de l'extrême nord du pays. Bien que ce territoire compte moins de 30 000 habitants, près de 85 % de sa population y possède le statut d'Inuit, et le territoire a été en mesure d'adopter de nombreuses lois assurant les droits des Inuits et donnant corps à leurs revendications concernant le territoire et ses ressources.

Aujourd'hui, le Canada doit continuer à gérer ses relations avec le Québec et les membres des Premières nations tout en faisant face à d'autres enjeux, comme la dépénalisation des drogues, l'immigration, sa participation aux missions de maintien de la paix, le réchauffement de la planète et le contrôle des bras de mer de l'Arctique.

National Anthem: O Canada

From "Chapter 5, Statutes of Canada 1980; proclaimed July 1, 1980." Composed by Calixa Lavallée; French lyrics written by Judge Adolphe-Basile Routhier; English lyrics written by Robert Stanley Weir (with some changes incorporated in 1967).

O Canada! Our home and native land!
True patriot love in all thy sons command.
With glowing hearts we see thee rise,
The True North strong and free!
From far and wide, O Canada, We stand on guard for thee.
God keep our land glorious and free!
O Canada, we stand on guard for thee.
O Canada, we stand on guard for thee.

O Canada! Terre de nos aïeux!
Ton front est ceint de fleurons glorieux!
Car ton bras sait porter l'épée, Il sait porter la croix!
Ton histoire est une épopée Des plus brillants exploits.
Et ta valeur, de foi trempée,
Protégera nos foyers et nos droits,
Protégera nos foyers et nos droits.

Emblems of Canada

The Beaver
Recognized as a symbol of Canada's sovereignty. Official status as an emblem of Canada as of May 24, 1975.
Maple Tree
Arboreal emblem of Canada, proclaimed April 25, 1996.
Official Colours
Red and white, as proclaimed in 1921.
Official Sports
Hockey (winter); Lacrosse (summer).

Full-colour images of Canadian and provincial flags, coats of arms, floral emblems, and selected honours start on page A-12.

Fathers of Confederation

Three conferences helped to pave the way for Confederation - those held at Charlottetown (September, 1864), Québec City (October, 1864) and London (December, 1866). As all the delegates who were at the Charlottetown conferences were also in attendance at Québec, the following list includes the names of all those who attended one or more of the three conferences.

*Hewitt Bernard was John A. Macdonald's private secretary. He served as secretary of both the Québec and London conferences.

DELEGATES TO THE CONFEDERATION CONFERENCES, 1864-1866

LEGEND:

Charlottetown, 1 September, 1864	C
Québec, 10 October, 1864	Q
London, 4 December, 1866	L

CANADA

John A. Macdonald	C Q L
George E. Cartier	C Q L
Alexander T. Galt	C Q L
William McDougall	C Q L
Hector L. Langevin	C Q L
George Brown	C Q
Thomas D'Arcy McGee	C Q
Alexander Campbell	C Q
Sir Etienne P. Taché	Q
Oliver Mowat	Q
J.C. Chapais	Q
James Cockburn	Q
W.P. Howland	L
*Hewitt Bernard	

NOVA SCOTIA

Charles Tupper	C Q L
William A. Henry	C Q L
Jonathan McCully	C Q L
Adams G. Archibald	C Q L
Robert B. Dickey	Q
J.W. Ritchie	L

NEW BRUNSWICK

Samuel L. Tilley	C Q L
J.M. Johnson	C Q L
William H. Steeves	C Q
E.B. Chandler	C Q
John Hamilton Gray	C Q
Peter Mitchell	Q L
Charles Fisher	Q L
R.D. Wilmot	L

PRINCE EDWARD ISLAND

John Hamilton Gray	C Q
Edward Palmer	C Q
William H. Pope	C Q
A.A. Macdonald	C Q
George Coles	C Q
T.H. Haviland	Q
Edward Whelan	Q

NEWFOUNDLAND

F.B.T. Carter	Q
Ambrose Shea	Q

PARTICIPANTS TO THE FIRST MINISTERS' CONSTITUTIONAL CONFERENCE ON PATRIATION OF THE CONSTITUTION

(Held in Ottawa from September 2 to 5, 1981)

- The Right Honourable Pierre Elliott Trudeau, P.C., Q.C., M.P., Prime Minister of Canada;
- The Honourable William G. Davis, Q.C., Premier of Ontario;
- The Honourable René Lévesque, Premier of Québec;
- The Honourable John M. Buchanan, Q.C., Premier of Nova Scotia;
- The Honourable Richard B. Hatfield, Premier of New Brunswick;
- The Honourable Sterling R. Lyon, Q.C., Premier of Manitoba;
- The Honourable W.R. Bennett, Premier of British Columbia;
- The Honourable J. Angus MacLean, P.C., D.F.C., C.D., Premier of Prince Edward Island;
- The Honourable Allan Blakeney, Q.C., Premier of Saskatchewan;
- The Honourable Peter Lougheed, Q.C., Premier of Alberta;
- The Honourable Brian Peckford, Premier of Newfoundland.

Timeline of Canadian History

- 12000 BC: Migration of natives across the Bering land bridge
- 2000 BC: Inuit arrive in North America
- 1000: Leif Erickson lands on Baffin Island
- 1497: John Cabot reaches Newfoundland
- 1534-1541: Jacque Cartier explores North America
- 1576-1578: Martin Frobisher searches for the Northwest Passage
- 1583: Humphrey Gilbert claims Newfoundland for England
- 1603: Samuel de Champlain's first voyage to New France. The fur trading monopoly Canada & Arcadia Company is formed.
- 1608: Champlain founds Quebec.
- 1609: The Battle of Ticonderoga. France allies with the Hurons to fight the Iroquois.
- 1610: Henry Hudson looks for the Northwest Passage. First European settlement in Newfoundland.
- 1629: Champlain surrenders New France to Great Britain.
- 1641: Village of Ville Marie (Montreal) is formed.
- 1649: The Iroquois destroy the missionary settlement of Huronia.
- 1663: France regains control of New France.
- 1670: Charles II forms the Hudson Bay Company. Fur trade attracts settlers to the Great Lakes area.
- 1682: LaSalle claims Louisiana for France.
- 1701: Peace is declared between native tribes and France.
- 1713: Nova Scotia's Acadian French population forced to swear allegiance to England.
- 1755-6: England deports the Acadians. Seven Years War begins.
- 1763: Seven Years War ends.
- 1766: Pontiac signs peace treaty with Great Britain.
- 1774: America's 13 Colonies urge Canada to join them against the English.
- 1776: American Loyalists flee to Canada.
- 1778: James Cook arrives on Vancouver Island.
- 1784: British divide Nova Scotia and create New Brunswick.
- 1791: King George II divides Quebec into Lower and Upper Canada.
- 1793: Alexander Mackenzie crosses the continent and reaches the Pacific Ocean.
- 1812: The War of 1812 begins when America declares war against Great Britain.
- 1814: The War of 1812 ends.
- 1834: The Patriotes of Lower Canada draw up a list of 92 grievances and deliver them to the government in England.
- 1841: United Canada created.
- 1849: The burning of Parliament in Montreal.
- 1858: Queen Victoria creates British Columbia. The gold rush begins.
- 1867: New Brunswick, Nova Scotia, and the Province of Canada were proclaimed the Dominion of Canada, with John A. Macdonald its first prime minister.
- 1885: Canadian Pacific Railway completed.
- 1896: Canada opens doors to European immigration.
- 1897-1899: Klondike gold rush. Canada enters Boer War.
- 1907: Chinese in Canada encounter violence.
- 1909: Coal miners strike in Cape Breton.
- 1914: Canada enters World War I.
- 1918: Spanish influenza kills millions. World War I ends. Women win vote.
- 1920: Bootlegging flourishes after America declares Prohibition.
- 1929: U.S. stock market crashes. Drought hits prairies.
- 1931: Ottawa outlaws Communist agitation. Socialist Party of Canada created.
- 1933: Unemployment crisis worsens.
- 1938: Canada rejects Jewish refugees escaping Nazi Germany.
- 1939: Canada enters World War II.
- 1945: World War II ends.
- 1947: First major oil find in Alberta.
- 1949: Newfoundland joins Canada.
- 1952: CBC television launched.
- 1956: Suez Canal crisis.
- 1960: Quebec's Quiet Revolution begins.
- 1965: New Maple Leaf flag raised.
- 1967: Expo in Montreal.
- 1970: Alberta aboriginals begin new era of native protests. British trade commissioner kidnapped by radical Quebec separatist group Front de Libération du Québec.
- 1971: Greenpeace begins in Vancouver.
- 1982: Trudeau brings home Canadian constitution.
- 1989: Free Trade with the US begins.
- 1999: New province of Nunavut separated from the Northwest Territories.
- 2001: Canada's border with the United States is on high alert in the aftermath of the September 11 Terrorist Attacks in the USA.
- 2002: G-8 leaders meet at Kananaskis, Alberta
- 2003: Health Canada announces 17 suspected SARS cases in Canada
- 2007: Canada Census data is released; the population of Canada in 2006 was 31,612,897
- 2007: Canadian dollar reaches parity with US greenback
- 2009: The 40th Canadian Parliament reopens, January 26, 2009, for its second session after a two-month prorogation.
- 2010: Toronto hosts G-20 Summit, June 26-27, 2010
- 2011: 41st Canadian federal election, May 2, 2011. Prime Minister Stephen Harper's Conservative Party wins a majority. New Democratic Party attains status of official opposition for the first time, led by Jack Layton.

Chronologie de l'histoire du Canada

- 12 000 av. J.-C. : Des peuples en migration traversent le pont continental de Béring.
- 2000 av. J.-C. : Arrivée des Inuits en Amérique du Nord.
- 1000 apr. J.-C. : Leif Erickson débarque sur l'Île de Baffin.
- 1497 : Jean Cabot atteint Terre-Neuve.
- 1534-1541 : Jacques Cartier explore l'Amérique du Nord.
- 1576-1578 : Martin Frobisher recherche le passage du Nord-Ouest.
- 1583 : Humphrey Gilbert revendique Terre-Neuve au nom de l'Angleterre.
- 1603 : Premier voyage de Samuel de Champlain en Nouvelle-France. La Canada & Arcadia Company, qui allait posséder le monopole du commerce des fourrures, voit le jour.
- 1608 : Champlain fonde la ville de Québec.
- 1609 : Bataille de Ticonderoga. La France s'allie aux Hurons pour combattre les Iroquois.
- 1610 : Henry Hudson recherche le passage du Nord-Ouest. Une première colonie européenne en Amérique du Nord est établie à Terre-Neuve.
- 1629 : Champlain cède la Nouvelle-France à la Grande-Bretagne.
- 1641 : Fondation du village de Ville-Marie (Montréal).
- 1649 : Les Iroquois détruisent la mission de Huronie.
- 1663 : La France reprend le contrôle de la Nouvelle-France.
- 1670 : Le roi Charles II forme la Compagnie de la Baie d'Hudson. Le commerce des fourrures attire des colons vers la région des Grands Lacs.
- 1682 : LaSalle revendique la Louisiane au nom de la France.
- 1701 : La paix est déclarée entre les tribus amérindiennes et la France.
- 1713 : La population acadienne francophone de la Nouvelle-Écosse est forcée de prêter serment d'allégeance à l'Angleterre.
- 1755-6 : L'Angleterre ordonne la déportation des Acadiens. Début de la guerre de Sept Ans.
- 1763 : Fin de la guerre de Sept Ans.
- 1766 : Pontiac signe un traité de paix avec la Grande-Bretagne.
- 1774 : Les 13 Colonies américaines recommandent vivement au Canada de se joindre à leur combat contre l'Angleterre.
- 1776 : Les loyalistes américains en fuite se réfugient au Canada.
- 1778 : James Cook découvre l'île de Vancouver.
- 1784 : L'Angleterre divise le territoire de la Nouvelle-Écosse et crée le Nouveau-Brunswick.
- 1791 : Le roi George II divise le Québec en deux parties : le Bas-Canada et le Haut-Canada.
- 1793 : Alexander Mackenzie traverse le continent et atteint l'océan Pacifique.
- 1812 : Les États-Unis déclarent la guerre à la Grande-Bretagne et déclenchent la guerre de 1812.
- 1814 : Fin de la guerre de 1812.
- 1834 : Les Patriotes du Bas-Canada dressent une liste de 92 griefs; elle est ensuite envoyée au gouvernement de l'Angleterre.
- 1841 : Création du Canada-Uni.
- 1849 : Incendie du Parlement à Montréal.
- 1858 : La reine Victoria crée la Colombie-Britannique. Début de la ruée vers l'or.
- 1867 : Le Nouveau-Brunswick, la Nouvelle-Écosse et la province du Canada deviennent le Dominion du Canada, et John A. Macdonald devient le premier Premier ministre du nouveau pays.
- 1885 : Le chemin de fer du Canadien Pacifique est complété.
- 1896 : Le Canada ouvre ses portes aux immigrants européens.
- 1897-1899 : Ruée vers l'or du Klondike. Participation du Canada à la guerre des Boers.
- 1907 : La population chinoise du Canada est victime d'actes de violence.
- 1909 : Grève du charbon au Cap-Breton.
- 1914 : Début de la participation du Canada à la Première Guerre mondiale.
- 1918 : La grippe espagnole fait des millions de victimes. Fin de la Première Guerre mondiale. Les femmes obtiennent le droit de vote.
- 1920 : Le commerce clandestin d'alcool devient florissant avec le début de la Prohibition aux États-Unis.
- 1929 : Aux États-Unis, le marché s'effondre. La sécheresse fait rage dans les Prairies.
- 1931 : Ottawa déclare l'agitation communiste illégale. Le Parti socialiste du Canada voit le jour.
- 1933 : La crise du chômage s'intensifie.
- 1938 : Le Canada refuse d'accueillir des réfugiés juifs ayant fui l'Allemagne nazie.
- 1939 : Début de la participation du Canada à la Deuxième Guerre mondiale.
- 1945 : Fin de la Deuxième Guerre mondiale.
- 1947 : Découverte d'un premier gisement de pétrole important en Alberta.
- 1949 : Terre-Neuve se joint au Canada.
- 1952 : Lancement de la télévision de Radio-Canada.
- 1956 : Crise du Canal de Suez.
- 1960 : Début de la Révolution tranquille au Québec.
- 1965 : Le nouveau drapeau unifolié est hissé pour la première fois.
- 1967 : L'Expo 67 bat son plein à Montréal.
- 1970 : Les Autochtones d'Alberta entament lune nouvelle ère de revendications autochtones. Un délégué commercial britannique est kidnappé par le Front de Libération du Québec, un groupe séparatiste radical.
- 1971 : Fondation de l'organisme Greenpeace à Vancouver.
- 1982 : Trudeau rapatrie la Constitution canadienne.
- 1989 : Début du libre-échange avec les États-Unis.
- 1999 : La nouvelle province du Nunavut se sépare des Territoires-du-Nord-Ouest.
- 2001 : La frontière du Canada et des États-Unis est sur un pied d'alerte par suite des attaques terroristes du 11 septembre chez nos voisins du sud.
- 2002 : Rencontre des dirigeants du G-8 à Kananaskis, en Alberta.
- 2003 : Santé Canada annonce 17 cas soupçonnés de grippe aviaire au Canada.
- 2007 : Les données du recensement de Statistique Canada sont rendues publiques; en 2006, la population du Canada atteignait 31 612 897 habitants.
- 2007 : Le dollar canadien atteint la même valeur que celle du dollar américain.
- 2009 : Réouverture de la 40e législature du Canada le 26 janvier 2009, après 2 mois de prorogation.
- 2010 : Sommet du G20 de Toronto, 26 et 27 juin 2010.
- 2011 : 41e élection fédérale, le 2 mai 2011. Le parti conservateur du premier ministre Stephen Harper remporte la majorité. Le nouveau parti démocratique, dirigé par Jack Layton, obtient le statut de l'opposition officielle pour la première fois dans son histoire.

THE ROYAL ARMS OF CANADA BY PROCLAMATION OF KING GEORGE V IN 1921

The Royal Arms of Canada were established by proclamation of King George V on 21 November, 1921. On the advice of the Prime Minister of Canada, Her Majesty the Queen approved, on 12 July, 1994, that the arms be augmented with a ribbon bearing the motto of the Order of Canada, DESIDERANTES MELIOREM PATRIAM - "They desire a better country".

This coat of arms was developed by a special committee appointed by Order in Council and is substantially based on a version of the Royal Arms of the United Kingdom, featuring the historic arms of England and Scotland. To this were added the old arms of Royal France and the historic emblem of Ireland, the harp of Tara, thus honouring many of the founding European peoples of modern Canada. To mark these arms as Canadian, the three red maple leaves on a field of white were added.

The supporters, and the crest, above the helmet, are also versions of elements of the Royal Arms of the United Kingdom, including the lion of England and unicorn of Scotland. The lion holds the Union Jack and the unicorn, the banner of Royal France. The crowned lion holding the maple leaf, which is the The Royal Crest of Canada, has, since 1981, also been the official symbol of the Governor General of Canada, the Sovereign's representative.

At the base of the Royal Arms are the floral emblems of the founding nations of Canada, the English Rose, the Scottish Thistle, the French Lily and the Irish Shamrock.

The motto - A MARI USQUE AD MARE - "From sea to sea" - is an extract from the Latin version of verse 8 of the 72nd Psalm - "He shall have dominion also from sea to sea, and from the river unto the ends of the earth."

THE NATIONAL FLAG

The National Flag of Canada, otherwise known as the Canadian Flag, was approved by Parliament and proclaimed by Her Majesty Queen Elizabeth II to be in force as of February 15, 1965. It is described as a red flag of the proportions two by length and one by width, containing in its centre a white square the width of the flag, bearing a single red maple leaf. Red and white are the official colours of Canada, as approved by the proclamation of King George V appointing Arms for Canada in 1921. The Flag is flown on land at all federal government buildings, airports, and military bases within and outside Canada, and may appropriately be flown or displayed by individuals and organizations. The Flag is the proper national colours for all Canadian ships and boats; and it is the flag flown on Canadian Naval vessels.

The Flag is flown daily from sunrise to sunset. However, it is not contrary to etiquette to have the Flag flying at night. No flag, banner or pennant should be flown or displayed above the Canadian Flag. Flags flown together should be approximately the same size and flown from separate staffs at the same height. When flown on a speaker's platform, it should be to the right of the speaker. When used in the body of an auditorium; it should be to the right of the audience. When two or more than three flags are flown together, the Flag should be on the left as seen by spectators in front of the flags. When three flags are flown together, the Canadian Flag should occupy the central position.

A complete set of rules for flying the Canadian Flag can be obtained from the Department of Canadian Heritage.

THE ROYAL UNION FLAG

The Royal Union Flag, generally known as the Union Jack, was approved by Parliament on December 18, 1964 for continued use in Canada as a symbol of Canada's membership in the Commonwealth of Nations and of her allegiance to the Crown. It will, where physical arrangements make it possible, be flown along with the National Flag at federal buildings, airports, and military bases and establishments within Canada on the date of the official observance of the Queen's birthday, the Anniversary of the Statute of Westminster (December 11th), Commonwealth Day (second Monday in March), and on the occasions of Royal visits and certain Commonwealth gatherings in Canada.

QUEEN'S PERSONAL CANADIAN FLAG

In 1962, Her Majesty The Queen adopted a personal flag specifically for use in Canada. The design comprises the Arms of Canada with The Queen's own device in the centre. The device - the initial "E" surmounted by the St. Edward's Crown within a chaplet of roses - is gold on a blue background.

When the Queen is in Canada, this flag is flown, day and night, at any building in which She is in residence. Generally, the flag is also flown behind the saluting base when She conducts troop inspections, on all vehicles in which She travels, and on Her Majesty's Canadian ships (HMCS) when the Queen is aboard.

FLAG OF THE GOVERNOR GENERAL

The Governor General's standard is a blue flag with the crest of the Arms of Canada in its centre. A symbol of the Sovereignty of Canada, the crest is made of a gold lion passant imperially crowned, on a wreath of the official colours of Canada, holding in its right paw a red maple leaf. The standard was approved by Her Majesty The Queen on February 23, 1981. The Governor General's personal standard flies whenever the incumbent is in residence, and takes precedence over all other flags in Canada, except The Queen's.

CANADIAN ARMED FORCES BADGE

The Canadian Armed Forces Badge was sanctioned by Her Majesty Queen Elizabeth II in May 1967. The description is as follows:

Within a wreath of 10 stylized maple leaves Red, a cartouche medium Blue edge Gold, charged with a foul anchor Gold, surmounted by Crusader's Swords in Saltire Silver and blue, pommelled and hilted Gold; and in front an eagle volant affront head to the sinister Gold, the whole ensigned with a Royal Crown proper.

The Canadian Forces Badge replaces the badges of the Royal Canadian Navy, the Canadian Army, and the Royal Canadian Air Force.

ALBERTA

The Arms of the Province of Alberta were granted by Royal Warrant on May 30, 1907. On July 30th, 1980, the Arms were augmented as follows: Crest: Upon a Helm with a Wreath Argent and Gules a Beaver couchant upholding on its back the Royal Crown both proper; Supporters: On the dexter side a Lion Or armed and langued Gules and on the sinister side a Pronghorn Antelope (Antilocapra americana) proper; the Compartment comprising a grassy mount with the Floral Emblem of the said Province of Alberta the Wild Rose (Rosa acicularis) growing therefrom proper; Motto: FORTIS ET LIBER (Strong and Free) to be borne and used together with the Arms upon Seals, Shields, Banners, Flags or otherwise according to the Laws of Arms.

In 1958, the Government of Alberta authorized the design and use of an official flag. A flag bearing the Armorial Ensign on a royal ultramarine blue background was adopted and the Flag Act proclaimed June 1st 1968. Proportions of the flag are two by length and one by width with the Armorial Ensign seven-elevenths of the width of the flag carried in the centre. The flag may be used by citizens of the Province and others in a manner befitting its dignity and importance but no other banner or flag that includes the Armorial Ensign may be assumed or used.

Floral Emblem: Wild Rose (Rosa Acicularis). Chosen in the Floral Emblem Act of 1930.

Provincial Bird: Great horned owl (budo virginianus). Adopted May 3, 1977.

BRITISH COLUMBIA

The shield of British Columbia was granted by Royal Warrant on March 31, 1906. On October 15th, 1987, the shield was augmented by Her Majesty Queen Elizabeth II. The crest and supporters have become part of the provincial Arms through usage. The heraldic description is as follows: Crest: Upon a Helm with a Wreath Argent and Gules the Royal Crest of general purpose of Our Royal Predecessor Queen Victoria differenced for Us and Our Successors in right of British Columbia with the Lion thereof garlanded about the neck with the Provincial Flower that is to say the Pacific Dogwood (Cornus nuttallii) with leaves all proper Mantled Gules doubled Argent; Supporters: On the dexter side a Wapiti Stag (Cervus canadensis) proper and on the sinister side a Bighorn Sheep Ram (Oviscanadensis) Argent armed and unguled Or; Compartment: Beneath the Shield a Scroll entwined with Pacific Dogwood flowers slipped and leaved proper inscribed with the Motto assigned by the said Warrant of Our Royal Predecessor King Edward VII that is to say SPLENDOR SINE OCCASU, (splendour without diminishment).

The flag of British Columbia was authorized by an Order-in-Council of June 27, 1960. The Union Jack symbolizes the province's origins as a British colony, and the crown at its centre represents the sovereign power linking the nations of the Commonwealth. The sun sets over the Pacific Ocean. The original design of the flag was located in 1960 by Hon. W.A.C. Bennett at the College of Arms in London.

Floral emblem: Pacific Dogwood (Cornus Nuttallii, Audubon). Adopted under the Floral Emblem Act, 1956.

Provincial Bird: Steller's jay. Adopted November 19, 1987.

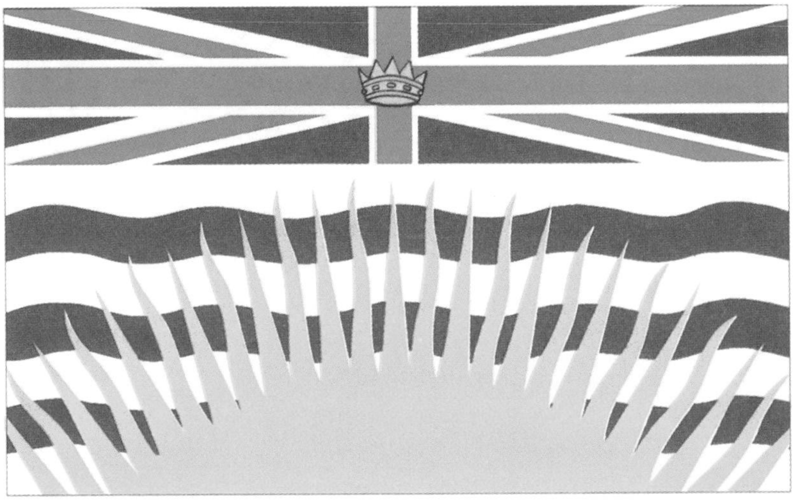

MANITOBA

The Arms of the Province of Manitoba were granted by Royal Warrant on May 10, 1905, augmented by warrant of the Governor General on October 23, 1992. The description is as follows: above the familiar shield of 1905 is a helmet and mantling; above the helmet is the Crest, including the beaver holding a prairie crocus, the province's floral emblem. On the beaver's back is the royal crown. The left supporter is a unicorn wearing a collar bearing a decorative frieze of maple leaves, the collar representing Manitoba's position as Canada's "keystone" province. Hanging from the collar is a wheel of a Red River cart. The right supporter is a white horse, and its collar of bead and bone honours First Peoples. The supporters and the shield rest on a compartment representing the province's rivers and lakes, grain fields and forests, composed of the provincial tree, the white spruce, and seven prairie crocuses. At the base is a Latin translation of the phrase "Glorious and Free."

The flag of the Province of Manitoba was adopted under The Provincial Flag Act, assented to May 11, 1965, and proclaimed into force on May 12, 1966. It incorporates parts of the Royal Armorial Ensigns, namely the Union and Red Ensign; the badge in the fly of the flag is the shield of the arms of the province.

Description: A flag of the proportions two by length and one by width with the Union Jack occupying the upper quarter next the staff and with the shield of the armorial bearings of the province centered in the half farthest from the staff.

Floral Emblem: Pasque Flower, known locally as Prairie Crocus (Anemone Patens). Adopted 1906.

Provincial Bird: Great gray owl. Adopted July 16, 1987.

NEW BRUNSWICK

The Arms of New Brunswick were granted by Royal Warrant on May 26, 1868. The motto SPEM REDUXIT (hope restored) was added by Order-in-Council in 1966. The description is as follows: The upper third of the shield is red and features a gold lion, symbolizing New Brunswick's ties to Britain. The lion is also found in the arms of the Duchy of Brunswick in Germany, the ancestral home of King George III. The lower part of the shield displays an ancient galley with oars in action. It could be interpreted as a reference to the importance of both shipbuilding and seafaring to New Brunswick in those days. It is also based on the design of the province's original great seal which featured a sailing ship on water. The shield is supported by two white-tailed deer wearing collars of Indian wampum. From one is suspended the Royal Union Flag (the Union Jack), from the other the fleur-de-lis to indicate the province's British and French background. The crest consists of an Atlantic Salmon leaping from a coronet of gold maple leaves and bearing St. Edward's Crown on its back. The base, or compartment, is a grassy mound with fiddleheads as well as purple violets, the provincial floral emblem. The motto "Spem Reduxit" is taken from the first great seal of the province and means "Hope restored.".

The flag of New Brunswick, adopted by Proclamation on February 24, 1965, is based on the Arms of the province. The chief and charge occupy the upper one-third of the flag, and the remainder of the armorial bearings occupy the lower two-thirds. The proportion is four by length and two and one half by width.

Floral Emblem: Purple Violet (Viola Cuculata). Adopted by Order-in-Council, December 1, 1936, at the request of the New Brunswick Women's Institute.

Provincial Bird: Black-capped chickadee. Adopted August 1983.

NEWFOUNDLAND & LABRADOR

The Arms of Newfoundland were granted by Royal Letters Patent dated January 1, 1637, by King Charles I. The heraldic description is as follows: Gules, a Cross Argent, in the first and fourth quarters a Lion passant guardant crowned Or, in the second and third quarters an Unicorn passant Argent armed and crined Or, gorged with a Coronet and a Chain affixed thereto reflexed of the last. Crest: on a wreath Or and Gules a Moose passant proper. Supporters: two Savages of the clime armed and apparelled according to their guise when they go to war. The motto reads QUAERITE PRIMEREGNUM DEI (seek ye first the kingdom of God).

The official flag of Newfoundland, adopted in 1980, has primary colours of Red, Gold and Blue, against a White background. The Blue section on the left represents Newfoundland's Commonwealth heritage and the Red and Gold section on the right represents the hopes for the future with the arrow pointing the way. The two triangles represent the mainland and island parts of the province.

Floral Emblem: Pitcher Plant (Sarracenia Purpurea). Adopted June 1954.

Provincial Bird: Atlantic puffin.

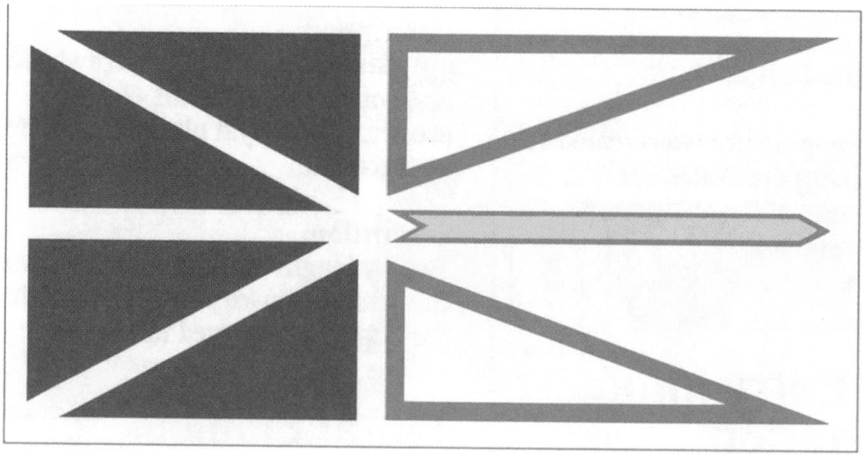

NORTHWEST TERRITORIES

The Arms of the Northwest Territories were approved by Her Majesty Queen Elizabeth II on February 24, 1956. The crest consists of two gold narwhals guarding a compass rose, symbolic of the magnetic north pole. The white upper third of the shield represents the polar ice pack and is crossed by a wavy blue line portraying the Northwest Passage. The tree line is reflected by a diagonal line separating the red and green segments of the lower portion of the shield: the green symbolizing the forested areas south of the tree line, and the red standing for the barren lands north of it. The important bases of northern wealth, minerals and fur, are represented by gold billets in the green portion and the mask of a white fox in the red.

The official flag of the Northwest Territories was adopted by the Territorial Council on January 1, 1969. Blue panels at either side of the flag represent the lakes and waters of the Territories. The white centre panel, equal in width to the two blue panels combined, symbolizes the ice and snow of the North. In the centre of the white portion is the shield from the Arms of the Territories.

Floral Emblem: Mountain Avens (Dryas Integrifolia). Adopted by the Council on June 7, 1957.

Territorial Bird: Gyrfalcon. Adopted June 1990.

NOVA SCOTIA

The Arms of the Province of Nova Scotia were granted to the Royal Province in 1625 by King Charles I. The complete Armorial Achievement includes the Arms, surmounted by a royal helm with a blue and silver scroll or mantling representing the Royal cloak. Above is the crest of heraldic symbols: two joined hands, one armoured and the other bare, supporting a spray of laurel for peace and thistle for Scotland. On the left is the mythical royal unicorn and on the right a 17th century representation of the North American Indian. The motto reads MUNIT HAEC ET ALTERA VINCIT (one defends and the other conquers). Entwined with the thistle of Scotland at the base is the mayflower, added in 1929, as the floral emblem of Nova Scotia.

The flag of the Province of Nova Scotia is a blue St. Andrew's Cross on a white field, with the Royal Arms of Scotland mounted thereon. The width of the flag is three-quarters of the length.

The flag was originally authorized by Charles I in 1625. In 1929, on petition of Nova Scotia, a Royal Warrant of King George V was issued, revoking the modern Arms and ordering that the original Arms granted by Charles I be borne upon (seals) shields, banners, and otherwise according to the laws of Arms.

Floral Emblem: Trailing Arbutus, also known as Mayflower (Epigaea Repens). Adopted April 1901.

Provincial Bird: Osprey. Adopted Spring, 1994.

NUNAVUT

The dominant colours blue and gold are the ones preferred by the Nunavut Implementation Commissioners to symbolize the riches of the land, sea and sky.

Red is a reference to Canada. In the base of the shield, the inuksuk symbolizes the stone monuments which guide the people on the land and mark sacred and other special places. The qulliq, or Inuit stone lamp, represents light and the warmth of family and the community. Above, the concave arc of five gold circles refers to the life-giving properties of the sun arching above and below the horizon, the unique part of the Nunavut year. The star is the Niqirtsuituq, the North Star and the traditional guide for navigation and more broadly, forever remains unchanged as the leadership of the elders in the community.

In the crest, the iglu represents the traditional life of the people and the means of survival. It also symbolizes the assembled members of the Legislature meeting together for the good of Nunavut; with the Royal Crown symbolizing public government for all the people of Nunavut and the equivalent status of Nunavut with other territories and provinces in Canadian Confederation. The tuktu (caribou) and qilalugaq tugaalik (narwhal) refer to land and sea animals which are part of the rich natural heritage of Nunavut and provide sustenance for people. The compartment at the base is composed of land and sea and features three important species of Arctic wild flowers.

Floral Emblem: Purple Saxifrage (Saxifraga oppositifolia). Adopted May 1, 2000.

Territorial Bird: Rock Ptarmigan.

ONTARIO

The Arms of the Province of Ontario were granted by Royal Warrants on May 26, 1868 (shield), and February 27, 1909 (crest and supporters). The heraldic description is as follows: Vert, a Sprig of three leaves of Maple slipped Or on a Chief Argent the Cross of St. George. Crest: upon a wreath Vert and Or a Bear passant Sable. The supporters are on the dexter side, a Moose, and on the sinister side a Canadian Deer, both proper. The motto reads: UT INCEPIT FIDELIS SIC PERMANET (loyal in the beginning, so it remained).

The flag of the Province of Ontario was adopted under the Flag Act of May 21, 1965. It incorporates parts of the Royal Armorial Ensigns, namely the Union and Red Ensign; the badge in the fly of the flag is the shield of the Arms of the province. The flag is of the proportions two by length and one by width, with the Union Jack occupying the upper quarter next the staff and the shield of the armorial hearings of the province centered in the half farthest from the staff.

Floral Emblem: White Trillium (Trillium Grandiflorum). Adopted March 25, 1937.

Provincial Bird: Common loon. Adopted June 23, 1994.

PRINCE EDWARD ISLAND

The Arms of the Province of Prince Edward Island were granted by Royal Warrant, May 30, 1905. The heraldic description is as follows: Argent on an Island Vert, to the sinister an Oak Tree fructed, to the dexter thereof three Oak saplings sprouting all proper, on a Chief Gules a Lion passant guardant Or. The motto reads: PARVA SUB INGENTI (the small under the protection of the great).

The flag of the Province of Prince Edward Island was authorized by an Act of the Legislative Assembly, March 24, 1964. The design of the flag is that part of the Arms contained within the shield, but is of rectangular shape, with a fringe of alternating red and white. The chief and charge of the Arms occupies the upper one-third of the flag, and the remainder of the Arms occupies the lower two-thirds. The proportions of the flag are six, four and one-quarter in relation to the fly, the hoist and the depth of the fringe.

Floral Emblem: Lady's Slipper (Cypripedium Acaule). Designated as the province's floral emblem by the Legislative Assembly in 1947. A more precise botanical name was included in an amendment to the Floral Emblem Act in 1965.

Provincial Bird: Blue Jay (cyanocitta cristata) was designated as avian emblem by the Provincial Emblems Acts, May 13, 1977.

QUÉBEC

The Arms of the Province of Québec were granted by Queen Victoria, May 26, 1868, and revised by a Provincial Order-in-Council on December 9, 1939. The heraldic description is as follows: Tierced in fess: Azure, three Fleurs-de-lis Or; Gules, a Lion passant guardant Or armed and langued Azure; Or, a Sugar Maple sprig with three leaves Vert veined Or. Surmounted with the Royal Crown. Below the shield a scroll Argent, surrounded by a bordure Azure, inscribed with the motto JE ME SOUVIENS (I remember) Azure.

The official flag of the Province of Québec was adopted by a Provincial Order-in-Council of January 21, 1948. It is a white cross on a sky blue ground, with the fleur-de-lis in an upright position on the blue ground in each of the four quarters. The proportion is six units wide by four units deep.

Floral Emblem: Iris Versicolor. Adopted November 5, 1999.

Provincial Bird: Snowy owl. Adopted December 17, 1987.

SASKATCHEWAN

The complete armorial bearings of the Province of Saskatchewan were granted by Royal Warrant on September 16, 1986, through augmentation of the original shield of arms granted by King Edward VII on August 25, 1906. The heraldic description is as follows: Shield: Vert three Garbs in fesse Or, on a Chief of the last a Lion passant guardant Gules. Crest: Upon a Helm with a Wreath Argent and Gules a Beaver upholding with its back Our Royal Crown and holding in the dexter fore-claws a Western Red Lily (Lilium philadelphicumandinum) slipped all proper Mantled Gules doubled Argent. Supporters: On the dexter side a Lion Or gorged with a Collar of Prairie Indian beadwork proper and dependent therefrom a six-pointed Mullet faceted Argent fimbriated and garnished Or charged with a Maple Leaf Gules and on the sinister side a White tailed deer (Odocoileus virginianus) proper gorged with a like Collar and dependent therefrom a like Mullet charged with a Western Red Lily slipped and leaved proper. Motto: Beneath the Shield a Scroll entwined with Western Red Lilies slipped and leaved proper inscribed with the motto MULTIS E GENTIBUS VIRES (From many peoples strength).

The official flag was dedicated on September 22, 1969, and features the Arms of the province in the upper quarter nearest the staff, with the Western Red Lily, in the half farthest from the staff. The upper green portion represents forests, while the gold symbolizes prairie wheat fields. The basic design was adopted from the prize-winning entry of Anthony Drake of Hodgeville from a province-wide flag design competition.

Floral Emblem: Western Red Lily (Lilium philadelphicum var. andinum). Adopted April 8, 1941.

Provincial Bird: Prairie sharp-tailed grouse. Adopted March 30, 1945.

YUKON

The Arms of the Yukon, granted by Queen Elizabeth II on February 24, 1956, have the following explanation: The wavy white and blue vertical stripe represents the Yukon River and refers also to the rivers and creeks where gold was discovered. The red spire-like forms represent the mountainous country, and the gold discs the mineral resources. The St. George's Cross is in reference to the early explorers and fur traders from Great Britain, and the roundel in vair in the centre of the cross is a symbol for the fur trade. The crest displays a Malamute dog, an animal which has played an important part in the early history of the Yukon.

The Yukon flag, designed by Lynn Lambert, a Haines Junction student, was adopted by Council in 1967. It is divided into thirds: green for forests, white for snow, and blue for water.

The flag consists of three vertical panels, the centre panel being one and one-half times the width of each of the other two panels. The panel adjacent to the mast is coloured green, the centre panel is coloured white and has the Yukon Crest disposed above a symbolic representation of the floral emblem of the territory, epilobium angustifolium, (fireweed), and the panel on the fly is coloured blue. The stem and leaves of the floral emblem are coloured green, and the flowers thereof are coloured red. The Yukon Crest is coloured red and blue, with the Malamute dog coloured black.

Floral Emblem: Fireweed (Epilobium Angustifolium). Adopted November 16, 1957.

Territorial Bird: Common raven. Adopted October 28, 1985.

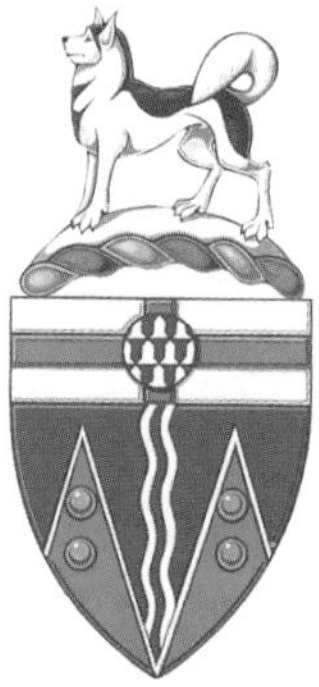

Geography

Land and Freshwater Areas

(in square kilometres)

Provinces and Territories	Land	Water	Total Area	Percentage of Canadian Total
Newfoundland and Labrador	373,872	31,340	405,212	4.06
Prince Edward Island	5,660	Not Available	5,660	0.06
Nova Scotia	53,338	1,946	55,284	0.55
New Brunswick	71,450	1,458	72,908	0.73
Quebec	1,365,128	176,928	1,542,056	15.44
Ontario	917,741	158,654	1,076,395	10.78
Manitoba	553,556	94,241	647,797	6.49
Saskatchewan	591,670	59,366	651,036	6.52
Alberta	642,317	19,531	661,848	6.63
British Columbia	925,186	19,549	944,735	9.46
Yukon Territory	474,391	8,052	482,443	4.83
Northwest Territories	1,183,085	163,021	1,346,106	13.48
Nunavut	1,936,113	157,077	2,093,190	20.96
Canada	9,093,507	891,163	9,984,670	100

Reproduced with the permission of Natural Resources Canada 2011, courtesy of the Atlas of Canada.

Largest Lakes Wholly or Partially in Canada

Name	Provinces and Territories	Area (square kilometres)
Superior	Ontario (and United States)	82,101 (total); 28,748 in Canada
Huron	Ontario (and United States)	59,569 (total); 36,000 in Canada
Great Bear	Northwest Territories	30,764
Great Slave	Northwest Territories	27,048
Erie	Ontario (and United States)	25,666 (total); 12,768 in Canada
Winnipeg	Manitoba	23,760
Ontario	Ontario (and United States)	19,554 (total); 10,334 in Canada

Reproduced with the permission of Natural Resources Canada 2011, courtesy of the Atlas of Canada.

Number of Lakes by Region (size classes are in square kilometres)

Region	3 to 99	100 to 199	200 to 399	400 to 999	1,000 to 2,499	2,500 to 9,999	10,000 to 36,000	Total
Atlantic Provinces[1]	1,761	19	5	4	1	2	0	1,792
Quebec	8,182	49	27	12	5	0	0	8,275
Ontario	3,837	34	12	9	1	2	4	3,899
Prairie Provinces[2]	5,245	65	39	18	8	5	1	5,381
British Columbia	838	6	12	4	1	0	0	861
Territories[3]	11,328	108	60	35	8	3	2	11,544
Canada	31,191	281	155	82	24	12	7	31,752

[1]Atlantic Provinces: Newfoundland and Labrador, Prince Edward Island, Nova Scotia, New Brunswick

[2]Prairie Provinces: Manitoba, Saskatchewan, Alberta

[3]Territories: Yukon Territory, Northwest Territories, Nunavut

Reproduced with the permission of Natural Resources Canada 2011, courtesy of the Atlas of Canada.

Longest Rivers in Canada

Rank	Name (at outflow)	Length (kilometres)	Outflow	Component Parts
1	Mackenzie	4,241	Beaufort Sea	Mackenzie - Slave - Peace - Findlay
2	Yukon	3,185 (1,143 kilometres in Canada)	Bering Sea	Yukon
3	St. Lawrence	3,058 (small part wholly in U.S.)	Gulf of St. Lawrence	St. Lawrence - Niagara - Detroit - St. Clair - St. Marys - St. Louis
4	Nelson	2,575	Hudson Bay	Nelson - Saskatchewan - South Saskatchewan - Bow
5	Columbia	2,000 (801 kilometres in Canada)	Pacific Ocean	Columbia
6	Churchill	1,609	Hudson Bay	Churchill [of Manitoba and Saskatchewan]
7	Fraser	1,370	Pacific Ocean	Fraser
8	North	1,287	Saskatchewan River	North Saskatchewan
9	Ottawa	1,271	St. Lawrence River	Ottawa
10	Athabasca	1,231	Slave River	Athabasca
11	Liard	1,115	Mackenzie River	Liard
12	Assiniboine	1,070	Red River (part of Nelson River drainage basin)	Assiniboine

Reproduced with the permission of Natural Resources Canada 2011, courtesy of the Atlas of Canada.

Largest Islands of Canada

Rank	Name	Provinces and Territories	Area (square kilometres)
1	Baffin (5th largest in the world)	Nunavut	507,451
2	Victoria	Nunavut and Northwest	217,291
3	Ellesmere	Nunavut	196,236
4	Island of Newfoundland	Newfoundland and Labrador	108,860
5	Banks	Northwest Territories	70,028
6	Devon	Nunavut	55,247
7	Axel Heiberg	Nunavut	43,178
8	Melville	Northwest Territories and	42,149
9	Southampton	Nunavut	41,214
10	Prince of Wales	Nunavut	33,339
11	Vancouver	British Columbia	31,285

Reproduced with the permission of Natural Resources Canada 2011, courtesy of the Atlas of Canada.

Selected Waterfalls in Canada

Name of Waterfall	Vertical Drop (metres)	Location
Della Falls	440	Della Lake, BC
Takakkaw Falls	254	Daly Glacier, BC
Hunlen Falls	253	Atnarko River, BC
Panther Falls	183	Nigel Creek, AB
Helmcken Falls	137	Murtle River, BC
Bridal Veil Falls	122	Bridal Creek, BC
Virginia Falls	90	South Nahanni River, NT
Chute Montmorency	84	Rivière Montmorency, QC
Twin Falls	80	Yoho National Park, BC
Chute Ouiatchouan	79	Rivière Ouiatchouan, QC
Brandywine Falls	61	Brandywine Creek, BC
Niagara Falls (American Falls)	59	(Niagara River, USA)
Niagara Falls (Horseshoe Falls)	57	Niagara River, ON
Wilberforce Falls	49	Hood River, NU
Dog Falls	47	Kaministiquia River, ON
Kakabeka Falls	47	Kaministiquia River, ON
Chute de Shawinigan	46	Rivière Saint-Maurice, QC
Grand Falls	43	Exploits River, NL
Parry Falls	40	Lockhart River, NT
Wawaitin Falls	38	Mattagami River, ON
Elizabeth Falls	34	Fond du Lac River, SK
Aubrey Falls	33	Mississagi River, ON
Alexandra Falls	32	Hay River, NT
Thomas Falls	31	Unknown River, NL
Marengo Falls	30	Marengo Creek, NT
Barrow Falls	27	Barrow River, NU
Pigeon Falls	27	Pigeon River, ON
Scott Falls	27	Unknown River, NL
Tyrrell Falls	26	Lockhart River, NT
High Falls	24	Onaping River, ON
Schist Falls	24	Pukaskwa River, ON
Smoky Falls	24	Mattagami River, ON
Christopher Falls	23	Opasatika River, ON
Chute du Calcaire	22	Rivière Caniapiscau, QC
Chute au Granite	21	Rivière Caniapiscau, QC
Partridge Falls	21	Pigeon River, ON
Steephill Falls	21	Magpie River, ON
Louise Falls	20	Hay River, NT
Muhigan Falls	19	Muhigan River, MB
Big Beaver Falls	18	Kapuskasing River, ON
Chutes aux Schistes	18	Rivière Caniapiscau, QC
Twin Falls	18	Abitibi River, ON
Lady Evelyn Falls	17	Kakisa River, NT
Muskrat Falls	15	Churchill River, NL
Taskinigup Falls	15	Burntwood River, MB
Kazan Falls	14	Kazan River, NU
Rideau Falls	12	Rideau River, ON

Reproduced with the permission of Natural Resources Canada 2011, courtesy of the Atlas of Canada.

Highest Points by Province and Territory

Provinces and Territories	Name of Highest Point	Height (metres)
British Columbia	Fairweather Mountain (on Alaska-British Columbia border)	4,663
Alberta	Mount Columbia (on Alberta-British Columbia border	3,747
Saskatchewan	Cypress Hills	1,392
Manitoba	Baldy Mountain	832
Ontario	Ishpatina Ridge	693
Quebec	Mont D'Iberville (on Quebec-Newfoundland and Labrador boundary; known as Mount Caubvick in Newfoundland and Labrador)	1,652
New Brunswick	Mount Carleton	817
Nova Scotia	White Hill	532
Prince Edward Island	Unnamed hill at 46 degrees 20 minutes North, 63 degrees 25 minutes West	142
Newfoundland and Labrador	Mount Caubvick (on Newfoundland and Labrador -Quebec boundary; known as Mont D'Iberville in Quebec)	1,652
Yukon Territory	Mount Logan (highest point in Canada)	5,959
Northwest Territories	Unnamed peak at 61 degrees 52 minutes North, 127 degrees 42 minutes West	2,773
Nunavut	Barbeau Peak (on Ellesmere Island)	2,616

Reproduced with the permission of Natural Resources Canada 2011, courtesy of the Atlas of Canada.

SYMBOLS OF CANADA

Provinces and Territories	Floral Emblem	Tree	Bird
Alberta	Wild Rose	Lodgepole Pine	Great Horned Owl
British Columbia	Pacific Dogwood	Western Red Cedar	Steller's Jay
Manitoba	Prairie Crocus	White Spruce	Great Gray Owl
New Brunswick	Purple Violet	Balsam Fir	Black-capped Chickadee
Newfoundland and Labrador	Pitcher Plant	Black Spruce	Atlantic Puffin
Northwest Territories	Mountain Avens	Tamarack	Gyrfalcon
Nova Scotia	Mayflower	Red Spruce	Osprey
Nunavut	Purple Saxifrage	Rock Ptarmigan	
Ontario	White Trillium	Eastern White Pine	Loon
Prince Edward Island	Lady's Slipper	Red Oak	Blue Jay
Quebec	Blue Iris Versicolor	Yellow Birch	Snowy Owl
Saskatchewan	Western Red Lily	Paper Birch	Sharp-tailed Grouse
Yukon	Fireweed	Subalpine Fir	Common Raven

Jasper National Park, Alberta

Moraine Lake near Lake Louise, Alberta

Banff, Alberta

Icefields Parkway in Jasper, Alberta

Beaver Creek, Yukon

Niagara Falls, Ontario

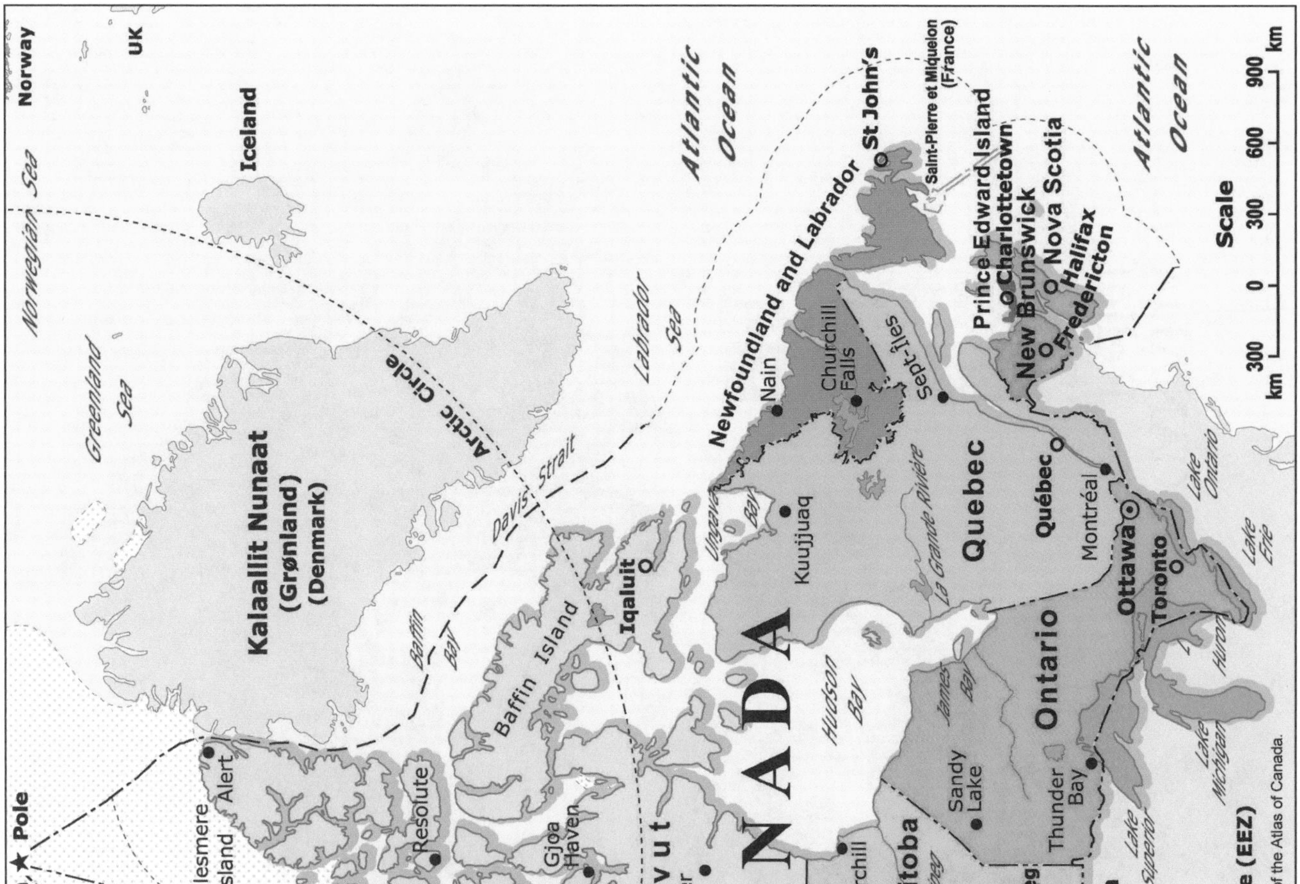
North Pole
Norway
UK
Iceland
Norwegian Sea
Atlantic Ocean
Kalaallit Nunaat (Grønland) (Denmark)
Greenland Sea
Arctic Circle
Davis Strait
Labrador Sea
Baffin Bay
St John's
Saint-Pierre et Miquelon (France)
Newfoundland and Labrador
Nain
Churchill Falls
Sept-Îles
Prince Edward Island
Charlottetown
Nova Scotia
Halifax
New Brunswick
Fredericton
Scale
300 0 300 600 900
km
Ellesmere Island
Alert
Resolute
Baffin Island
Iqaluit
Ungava Bay
Kuujjuaq
La Grande Rivière
Quebec
Québec
Montréal
Ottawa
Toronto
Lake Ontario
Lake Erie
Lake Huron
Lake Michigan
Lake Superior
CANADA
Hudson Bay
James Bay
Ontario
Sandy Lake
Thunder Bay
Churchill
Manitoba
L Winnipeg
Winnipeg
North Magnetic Pole
Gjoa Haven
Nunavut
Baker Lake
Victoria Island
Banks I
Polar Ice
Arctic Ocean
Beaufort Sea
Inuvik
Great Bear Lake
Northwest Territories
Yellowknife
Great Slave Lake
Mackenzie River
Saskatchewan
Saskatoon
Regina
Fort McMurray
Alberta
Edmonton
Calgary
Fort Nelson
British Columbia
Prince George
Kamloops
Fraser River
Vancouver
Victoria
Pacific Ocean
Yukon Territory
Dawson
Whitehorse
Russia
Alaska (USA)
Bering Strait
United States of America
LEGEND
National capital
Provincial or Territorial capital
Other populated places
International boundary
Provincial or Territorial boundary
Exclusive 200 nautical mile Economic Zone (EEZ)
Reproduced with the permission of Natural Resources Canada 2011, courtesy of the Atlas of Canada.

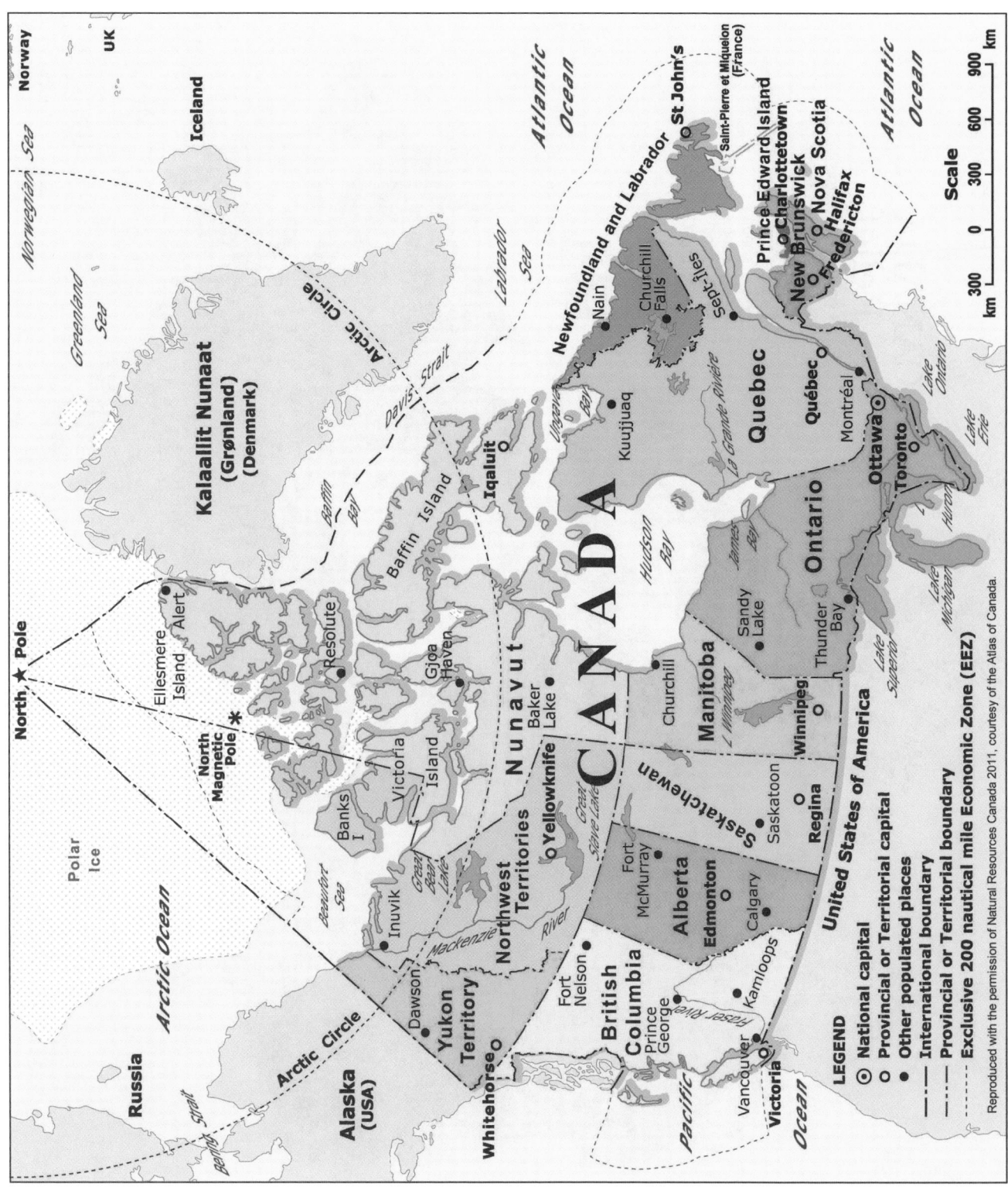

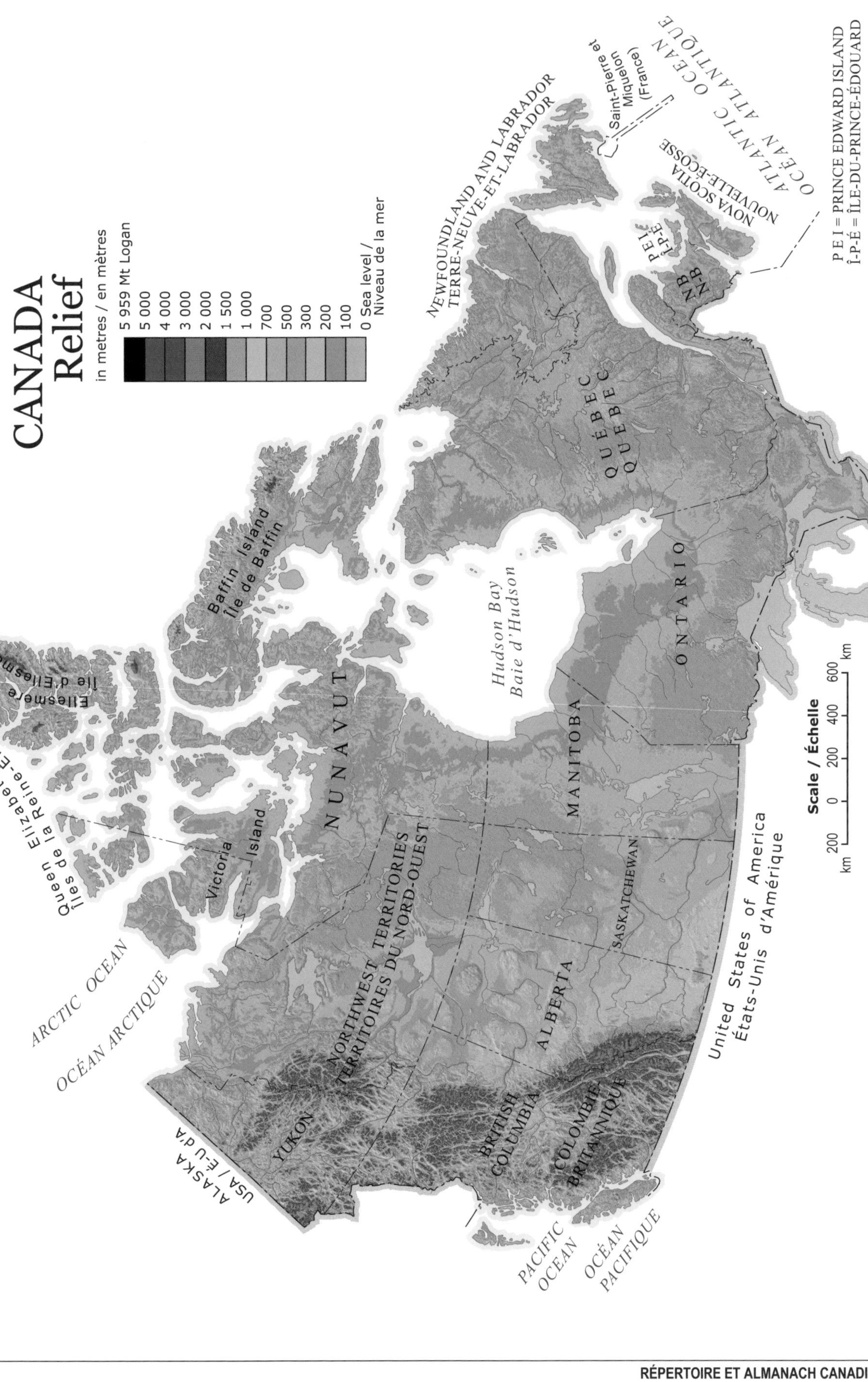
CANADA
Relief
in metres / en mètres
5 959 Mt Logan
5 000
4 000
3 000
2 000
1 500
1 000
700
500
300
200
100
0 Sea level / Niveau de la mer
Queen Elizabeth Islands
Îles de la Reine-Élisabeth
Ellesmere Island
Île d'Ellesmere
Baffin Island
Île de Baffin
Victoria Island
ARCTIC OCEAN
OCÉAN ARCTIQUE
ALASKA
USA / É-U d'A
YUKON
NORTHWEST TERRITORIES
TERRITOIRES DU NORD-OUEST
NUNAVUT
Hudson Bay
Baie d'Hudson
BRITISH COLUMBIA
COLOMBIE-BRITANNIQUE
ALBERTA
SASKATCHEWAN
MANITOBA
ONTARIO
QUÉBEC
QUÉBEC
NEWFOUNDLAND AND LABRADOR
TERRE-NEUVE-ET-LABRADOR
Saint-Pierre et Miquelon (France)
NB
N-B
PEI
Î-P-É
NOVA SCOTIA
NOUVELLE-ÉCOSSE
ATLANTIC OCEAN
OCÉAN ATLANTIQUE
PACIFIC OCEAN
OCÉAN PACIFIQUE
United States of America
États-Unis d'Amérique
Scale / Échelle
200 0 200 400 600
km km
atlas.gc.ca
P E I = PRINCE EDWARD ISLAND
Î-P-É = ÎLE-DU-PRINCE-ÉDOUARD
N B = NEW BRUNSWICK
N-B = NOUVEAU-BRUNSWICK

CLIMATE

Temperature Data for Representative Stations in Canada

Temperature in Degrees Celsius

Station (Airport)	Elevation (metres)	Mean Daily: Annual	Mean Daily: Jan.	Mean Daily: Apr.	Mean Daily: July	Mean Daily: Oct.	Extreme: Max.*	Extreme: Min.* (m)	Days with Measurable Rainfall	Total # of Sunshine Hours
Newfoundland:										
Goose Bay	46	-0.3	-17.3	-1.8	15.5	2.5	37.8	-39.4	109	1607.6
St. John's	134	4.7	-4.3	1.3	15.4	7.0	31.5	-23.8	217	-
Prince Edward Island:										
Charlottetown Int.	48	5.2	-7.7	2.3	18.4	8.0	34.4	-30.5	177	-
Nova Scotia:										
Halifax Int.	126	6.1	-5.8	3.6	18.3	8.5	34.4	-26.1	170	-
Sydney	55	5.5	-5.4	1.9	17.6	8.4	35.0	-25.6	189	1,804.6
Yarmouth	43	6.8	-3.0	4.7	16.3	9.3	30.0	-21.1	161	1,821.8
New Brunswick:										
Chatham	34	4.6	-10.4	2.8	19.1	6.8	37.8	-35.0	161	2,002.2
Fredericton	16	5.2	-9.6	4.1	19.3	7.3	37.2	-37.2	156	-
St. John	103	4.9	-8.2	3.2	16.9	7.5	34.4	-36.7	164	1,893.7
Quebec:										
Inukjuak	3	-6.8	-24.4	-11.2	9.1	-0.1	30.0	-49.4	151	1,457.4
Montréal Int. (Dorval)	31	6.1	-10.3	5.7	20.8	8.3	37.6	-37.8	162	-
Québec	70	4.0	-12.4	3.3	19.1	6.5	35.6	-36.1	178	1,910.4
Schefferville	522	-5.0	-23.4	-7.2	12.4	-1.4	34.3	-50.6	208	-
Sept-Iles	55	0.9	-14.6	0.0	15.2	3.4	32.2	-43.3	166	-
Sherbrooke	238	4.1	-11.6	3.9	18.0	6.4	33.7	-40.0	189	-
Ontario:										
Kapuskasing	226	0.5	-18.5	0.5	17.0	4.2	36.7	-45.3	190	-
Ottawa Int.	116	5.8	-10.8	5.6	20.8	7.9	37.8	-36.7	159	-
Thunder Bay	199	2.4	-15.0	2.7	17.7	5.4	40.3	-41.1	138	2,183.3
Toronto Int.	173	7.2	-6.7	6.0	20.5	8.9	38.3	-31.3	141	2,038.3
Windsor	190	9.1	-5.0	8.1	22.4	10.9	40.2	-27.2	143	-
Manitoba:										
Churchill	28	-7.1	-26.9	-10.0	11.8	-1.4	33.9	-45.4	148	1,820.7
The Pas	271	-0.3	-21.4	0.5	17.7	3.5	36.7	-49.4	127	2,203.2
Winnipeg Int.	239	2.4	-18.3	3.8	19.8	5.7	40.6	-45.0	119	2,377.3
Saskatchewan:										
Regina	577	2.6	-16.5	4.1	19.1	5.1	43.3	-50.0	109	2,364.6
Saskatoon	501	2.0	-17.5	3.9	18.6	4.8	40.6	-50.0	108	-
Alberta:										
Calgary Int.	1,077	3.9	-9.6	4.1	16.4	5.7	36.1	-45.0	111	2,394.6
Edmonton Int.	715	2.1	-14.2	3.7	16.0	4.6	35.0	-48.3	122	2,303.2
Grande Prairie	666	1.6	-15.4	3.3	16.0	4.4	34.5	-52.2	130	-
British Columbia:										
Kamloops	345	8.6	-4.8	9.4	20.8	8.5	40.6	-37.2	74	2,046.8
Prince George	676	3.7	-9.9	4.7	15.3	4.8	36.0	-50.0	107	1,942.4
Prince Rupert	34	6.9	0.8	5.5	12.9	7.8	28.7	-24.4	236	1,211.8
Vancouver Int.	3	9.9	3.0	8.8	17.2	10.0	33.3	-17.8	164	1,919.3
Victoria Int.	20	9.5	3.4	8.4	16.2	9.7	36.1	-15.6	153	2,081.9
Yukon Territory:										
Kamakuk Beach	14	-11.0	-24.0	-17.8	7.6	-9.4	30.0	-51.8	57	-
Whitehorse	703	-1.0	-18.7	0.3	14.1	0.7	34.4	-52.2	122	1,852.4
Northwest Territories:										
Alert	62	-18.1	-31.9	-25.1	3.4	-19.5	20.0	-50.0	100	-
Inuvik	59	-9.5	-28.8	-14.1	13.8	-8.2	31.7	-56.7	129	-
Yellowknife	205	-5.2	-27.9	-6.2	16.5	-1.4	32.5	-51.2	118	-
Nunavut:										
Iqaluit	34	-9.5	-25.8	-14.7	7.7	-4.9	24.4	-45.6	152	1,508.3

*Temperature extremes are for the total period of record 1961-1990.
*1 in. = 25.4 mm. = 2.54 cm.

Precipitation Data for Representative Stations in Canada

Station (Airport)	Average Total Precipitation (mm.): Jan.	Feb.	Mar.	Apr.	May	June	July	Aug.	Sept.	Oct.	Nov.	Dec.	Ann.	Aver. Ann. Snowfall (cm)
Newfoundland:														
Goose Bay	64.9	57.0	68.6	57.1	66.4	100.9	119.4	98.3	90.6	78.8	79.9	77.6	959.5	463.8
St. John's	147.8	133.6	126.7	110.4	100.9	96.9	77.9	121.8	125.0	151.7	144.7	144.2	1481.7	322.1
Prince Edward Island:														
Charlottetown Int.	106.3	91.5	92.2	91.8	96.8	91.1	81.6	88.6	94.1	111.7	121.9	133.2	1200.8	338.7
Nova Scotia:														
Halifax Int.	146.9	119.1	122.6	124.4	110.5	98.4	96.8	109.6	94.9	128.9	154.4	167.0	1473.5	261.4
Sydney	151.6	125.1	131.3	125.3	98.1	91.2	86.2	97.3	103.2	137.6	160.4	172.9	1480.1	329.5
Yarmouth	126.4	106.5	95.3	100.9	96.6	93.6	84.7	82.2	87.5	107.4	134.8	143.5	1259.4	205.3
New Brunswick:														
Chatham	85.2	69.5	86.6	86.3	88.1	84.5	97.8	95.9	87.8	95.2	104.4	105.5	1086.9	323.9
Fredericton	93.3	84.3	90.4	83.4	94.8	86.9	84.5	99.4	92.3	93.1	110.7	118.8	1131.0	294.5
St. John	128.3	102.6	109.9	109.7	123.1	104.8	103.7	103.0	111.3	122.5	146.2	167.6	1432.8	283.2
Quebec:														
Inukjuak	12.6	10.1	12.4	19.2	23.2	36.1	55.1	62.4	64.6	52.4	44.9	25.2	418.1	175.4
Montréal Int. (Dorval)	63.3	56.4	67.6	74.8	68.3	82.5	85.6	100.3	86.5	75.4	93.4	85.6	939.7	214.2
Québec	90.0	74.4	85.0	75.5	99.9	110.2	118.5	119.6	123.7	96.0	106.1	108.9	1207.7	337.0
Schefferville	48.8	38.9	47.8	52.6	51.0	70.0	103.3	89.4	94.3	75.7	68.2	53.4	793.6	415.0
Sept-Iles	86.8	68.9	80.9	93.4	96.3	92.4	90.8	99.6	111.5	100.8	99.6	107.0	1127.9	415.1
Sherbrooke	71.8	59.7	75.2	73.6	94.2	100.5	116.7	130.5	98.6	91.4	100.7	95.8	1108.9	288.2
Ontario:														
Kapuskasing	53.9	41.5	54.8	53.3	71.0	88.6	101.9	91.3	94.6	78.3	76.3	55.6	861.0	325.7
Ottawa Int.	58.0	58.6	64.8	69.0	76.4	76.9	88.1	92.0	82.9	74.8	86.4	82.5	910.5	221.5
Thunder Bay	32.4	25.6	40.9	47.1	69.3	84.0	79.9	88.5	86.4	60.9	49.4	39.3	703.5	195.5
Toronto Int.	45.6	45.5	56.9	64.0	66.0	68.9	76.6	84.2	74.2	63.0	70.3	65.5	780.8	124.2
Windsor	50.3	53.7	72.0	80.3	75.7	97.0	85.3	85.7	86.7	57.9	75.4	81.6	901.6	123.3
Manitoba:														
Churchill	17.3	12.8	18.3	22.6	30.5	44.5	50.7	60.5	52.6	46.5	35.5	19.7	411.6	200.1
The Pas	16.6	15.1	21.0	26.2	33.6	63.1	69.1	65.0	58.3	37.5	26.6	19.8	451.9	170.2
Winnipeg Int.	19.3	14.8	23.1	35.9	59.8	83.8	72.0	75.3	51.3	29.5	21.2	18.6	504.4	114.8
Saskatchewan:														
Regina	14.7	13.0	16.5	20.4	50.8	67.3	58.9	40.0	34.4	20.3	11.7	15.9	364.0	107.4
Saskatoon	15.9	12.9	16.0	19.7	44.2	63.4	58.0	36.8	32.1	16.9	14.1	17.2	347.2	105.4
Alberta:														
Calgary Int.	12.2	9.9	14.7	25.1	52.9	76.9	69.9	48.7	48.1	15.5	11.6	13.2	398.8	135.4
Edmonton Int.	22.9	15.5	15.9	21.8	42.8	76.1	101.0	69.5	47.5	17.7	16.0	19.2	465.8	127.1
Grande Prairie	32.7	20.5	18.6	19.8	35.3	74.2	67.9	61.8	42.2	21.7	28.6	26.9	450.2	174.6
British Columbia:														
Kamloops	26.1	13.8	9.6	14.8	21.8	28.6	27.9	30.2	27.6	14.4	22.0	32.6	269.5	86.2
Prince George	54.4	35.0	34.3	28.3	51.7	64.5	60.0	61.2	59.3	59.4	52.7	53.8	614.7	233.8
Prince Rupert	250.8	216.5	188.2	181.9	142.0	119.5	112.9	162.8	244.7	378.9	284.4	269.8	2551.6	142.6
Vancouver Int.	149.8	123.6	108.8	75.4	61.7	45.7	36.1	38.1	64.4	115.3	169.9	178.5	1167.4	54.9
Victoria Int.	141.1	99.3	71.9	41.9	33.4	27.3	17.6	23.7	36.6	74.4	139.2	151.6	857.9	46.9
Yukon Territory:														
Kamakuk Beach	5.3	4.1	2.9	4.2	4.4	15.5	29.6	36.0	19.7	18.7	8.3	5.4	154.0	68.9
Whitehorse	16.9	11.9	12.1	8.3	14.4	31.2	38.5	39.3	35.2	23.0	18.9	18.9	268.8	145.2
Northwest Territories:														
Alert	7.8	5.2	6.8	9.4	9.9	12.7	25.0	23.8	24.3	13.2	8.8	7.4	154.2	164.9
Inuvik	15.6	11.1	10.8	12.6	19.1	22.2	34.1	43.9	24.2	29.6	17.5	16.8	257.4	175.2
Yellowknife	14.9	12.6	10.6	10.3	16.6	23.3	35.2	41.7	28.8	34.8	23.9	14.7	267.3	143.9
Nunavut:														
Iqaluit	21.8	19.0	22.0	28.4	29.6	36.5	58.2	63.5	51.9	42.4	30.9	19.8	424.1	256.8

Reprinted with the permission of Environment Canada. Detailed climate information is available at www.climate.weatheroffice.ec.gc.ca/Welcome_e.html

KILOMETRES

MILES

	BANFF	BRANDON	CALGARY	CHARLOTTETOWN	CHICOUTIMI	CORNER BROOK	DAWSON CREEK	EDMONTON	FLIN FLON	FORT SMITH	FREDERICTON	GANDER	GASPÉ	HALIFAX	HAMILTON	JASPER	KENORA	LETHBRIDGE	LONDON	MONCTON	MONTRÉAL	NIAGARA FALLS	NORTH BAY
BANFF	•	782	80	3147	2702	3484	633	266	846	1094	2924	3725	2997	3225	2256	178	1037	216	2327	3047	2406	2299	2059
BRANDON	1259	•	702	2392	1920	2714	1082	715	451	1543	2142	2943	2215	2447	1474	944	255	622	1545	2292	1624	1517	1277
CALGARY	129	1130	•	3055	2622	3404	553	186	766	1011	2832	3633	2917	3133	2176	258	957	136	2247	2955	2326	2219	1979
CHARLOTTETOWN	5065	3850	4917	•	552	368	3442	3075	2787	3903	223	597	516	144	1143	3304	2105	3014	1184	100	736	1147	1083
CHICOUTIMI	4348	3090	4220	888	•	901	3002	2635	2347	3463	329	1130	402	544	673	2864	1665	2542	744	452	296	716	643
CORNER BROOK	5607	4368	5478	592	1450	•	3791	3424	3136	4252	572	229	865	402	1462	3653	2454	3336	1534	449	1085	1500	1432
DAWSON CREEK	1019	1741	890	5539	4831	6101	•	367	1020	640	3224	4020	3297	3525	2556	467	1337	689	2627	3342	2706	2599	2359
EDMONTON	428	1151	299	4949	4241	5510	591	•	653	828	2857	3653	2930	3158	2189	299	970	322	2260	2975	2339	2232	1992
FLIN FLON	1362	668	1233	4485	3777	5047	1642	1051	•	1481	2569	3365	2642	2870	1901	882	682	862	1972	2687	2051	1944	1704
FORT SMITH	1761	2483	1627	6281	5573	6843	1030	1333	2383	•	3685	4480	3758	3986	3017	995	1798	1150	3083	3803	3167	3055	2820
FREDERICTON	4706	3447	4558	359	529	921	5189	4598	4134	5930	•	801	435	215	895	3086	1887	2764	966	123	518	938	865
GANDER	5995	4736	5847	961	1819	369	6470	5879	5415	7210	1289	•	1094	631	1691	3882	2683	3560	1762	678	1314	1734	1661
GASPÉ	4823	3565	4694	830	647	1392	5306	4715	4252	6048	700	1761	•	587	968	3159	1960	2837	1039	416	591	1011	938
HALIFAX	5190	3938	5042	232	875	647	5673	5082	4619	6415	346	1015	945	•	1196	3387	2188	3065	1267	171	819	1239	1166
HAMILTON	3631	2372	3502	1839	1083	2353	4114	3523	3059	4855	1440	2721	1558	1925	•	2418	1219	2096	84	1013	377	43	250
JASPER	286	1519	415	5317	4609	5879	752	369	1419	1601	4966	6247	5084	5451	3891	•	1199	394	2489	3204	2568	2461	2221
KENORA	1669	410	1510	3388	2680	3949	2152	1561	1098	2894	3037	4318	3154	3521	1962	1930	•	877	1290	2005	1369	1262	1022
LETHBRIDGE	384	1001	219	4851	4091	5369	1109	518	1387	1851	4448	5729	4566	4933	3373	634	1411	•	2167	2882	2246	2139	1899
LONDON	3745	2486	3616	1905	1197	2469	4228	3637	3174	4962	1555	2836	1672	2039	135	4006	2076	3487	•	1084	448	126	321
MONCTON	4904	3689	4756	161	727	723	5378	4788	4324	6120	198	1091	669	275	1630	5156	3227	4638	1745	•	636	1056	983
MONTRÉAL	3872	2614	3743	1184	476	1746	4355	3764	3301	5097	834	2115	951	1318	607	4133	2203	3615	721	1024	•	420	347
NIAGARA FALLS	3700	2441	3571	1846	1152	2414	4183	3592	3129	4917	1510	2791	1627	1994	69	3961	2031	3442	203	1699	676	•	293
NORTH BAY	3314	2055	3185	1743	1035	2305	3796	3206	2742	4538	1392	2673	1510	1876	402	3574	1645	3056	517	1582	558	472	•
OTTAWA	3682	2424	3553	1374	666	1936	4165	3574	3111	4907	1024	2305	1141	1508	467	3943	2013	3425	581	1213	190	536	369
PORT AUX BASQUES	5401	4142	5253	367	1225	225	5876	5285	4822	6618	695	594	1167	422	2128	5654	3724	5135	2242	497	1521	2197	2079
PRINCE ALBERT	912	731	784	4529	3821	5090	1193	602	449	1934	4178	5459	4295	4662	3103	970	1141	1003	3233	4368	3344	3172	2786
PRINCE GEORGE	632	1865	761	5663	4955	6225	406	715	1765	1436	5312	6593	5430	5797	4237	346	2276	980	4352	5502	4479	4307	3920
PRINCE RUPERT	1373	2606	1502	6404	5695	6965	1146	1455	2506	2176	6053	7334	6170	6537	4978	1086	3016	1720	5092	6243	5219	5047	4661
QUÉBEC	4142	2884	4014	945	206	1506	4625	4035	3571	5367	586	1875	703	912	877	4403	2474	3885	991	784	270	946	829
REGINA	893	365	764	4163	3455	4725	1376	785	752	2118	3813	5094	3930	4297	2737	1154	776	636	2852	4002	2979	2807	2420
RIVIÈRE-DU-LOUP	4324	3066	4196	740	148	1302	4807	4216	3753	5549	381	1670	499	727	1059	4585	2655	4067	1173	579	452	1128	1011
ROUYN	3154	1896	3026	1828	1120	2390	3637	3046	2583	4379	1477	2758	1595	1962	694	3415	1485	2897	808	1667	644	763	291
SAINT JOHN	4812	3553	4664	309	616	871	5295	4704	4241	6037	106	1239	806	240	1547	5073	3143	4554	1661	148	940	1616	1498
ST. JOHN'S	6328	5073	6183	1294	2184	702	6803	6212	5749	7551	1622	333	2094	1349	3055	6581	4651	4453	3169	1424	2448	3124	3006
SASKATOON	748	623	620	4421	3713	4983	1118	528	613	1860	4070	5351	4188	4554	2995	896	1033	663	3109	4260	3236	3064	2678
SAULT STE. MARIE	2887	1629	2758	2169	1461	2731	3370	2779	2360	4112	1819	3100	1936	2303	744	3148	1218	2617	858	2008	985	813	426
SEPT-ÎLES	4796	3537	4667	855	620	1466	5279	4688	4225	6021	774	1835	481	1011	1530	5057	3127	4538	1645	744	924	1582	1482
SHERBROOKE	4028	2770	3899	1136	420	1698	4511	3920	3457	5253	777	2066	895	1123	763	4289	2359	3771	877	975	156	832	715
SUMMERSIDE	5039	3780	4910	63	863	655	5514	4923	4459	6256	333	1024	805	303	1765	5292	3362	4773	1876	135	1159	1835	1717
SYDNEY	5401	4142	5253	367	1225	225	5876	5285	4822	6618	695	594	1167	422	2128	5654	3724	5135	2242	497	1521	2197	2079
THE PAS	1481	575	1352	4424	3664	4942	1630	1040	151	2372	4022	5311	4139	4506	2947	1408	985	1236	3061	4263	3188	3016	2630
THUNDER BAY	2179	921	2050	2878	2169	3439	2662	2071	1608	3404	2527	3808	2644	3011	1452	2440	510	1922	1566	2717	1693	1521	1135
TORONTO	3563	2305	3434	1724	1015	2285	4046	3455	2992	4788	1373	2654	1490	1857	68	3824	1894	3306	182	1563	539	137	335
VANCOUVER	929	2187	1057	5985	5277	6547	1202	1244	2290	2232	5634	6915	5752	6119	4559	875	2597	1143	4674	5824	4801	4628	4242
VICTORIA	995	2253	1123	6051	5343	6613	1268	1310	2356	2298	5700	6981	5818	6185	4625	941	2663	1209	4740	5890	4867	4694	4308
WHITEHORSE	2514	3236	2385	7034	6326	7596	1495	2086	3137	2525	6684	7965	6801	7168	5609	2247	3647	2604	5710	6874	5850	5678	5279
WIINDSOR	3954	2699	3825	2097	1381	2659	4395	3804	3357	5137	1738	3027	1856	2223	319	4241	2260	3697	203	1936	904	388	700
WINNIPEG	1465	206	1336	3592	2884	4154	1947	1357	893	2689	3241	4522	3359	3726	2166	1725	204	1207	2280	3431	2408	2235	1849
YARMOUTH	4917	3658	4768	414	740	911	5380	4809	4345	6141	211	1279	911	349	1651	5177	3248	4670	1765	253	1044	1720	1603
YELLOWKNIFE	1939	2662	1811	6460	5752	7022	1209	1511	2562	713	6109	7390	6227	6593	5034	1780	3072	2029	5148	6299	5275	5103	4717

	OTTAWA	PORT AUX BASQUES	PRINCE ALBERT	PRINCE GEORGE	PRINCE RUPERT	QUÉBEC	REGINA	RIVIÈRE-DU-LOUP	ROUYN	SAINT JOHN	ST. JOHN'S	SASKATOON	SAULT STE. MARIE	SEPT-ÎLES	SHERBROOKE	SUMMERSIDE	SYDNEY	THE PAS	THUNDER BAY	TORONTO	VANCOUVER	VICTORIA	WHITEHORSE	WINDSOR	WINNIPEG	YARMOUTH	YELLOWKNIFE
BANFF	2288	3356	567	393	853	2574	555	2687	1960	2990	3932	465	1794	2980	2503	3131	3356	920	1354	2214	577	618	1562	2457	910	3055	1205
BRANDON	1506	2574	454	1159	1619	1792	227	1905	1178	2208	3152	387	1012	2198	1721	2349	2574	357	572	1432	1359	1400	2011	1677	128	2273	1654
CALGARY	2208	3264	487	473	933	2494	475	2607	1880	2898	3842	385	1714	2900	2423	3051	3264	840	1274	2134	657	698	1482	2377	830	2963	1125
CHARLOTTETOWN	854	228	2814	3519	3979	587	2587	460	1136	192	804	2747	1348	531	706	39	228	2749	1788	1071	3719	3760	4371	1303	2232	257	4014
CHICOUTIMI	414	761	2374	3079	3539	128	2147	92	696	383	1357	2307	908	385	261	536	761	2277	1348	631	3279	3320	3931	858	1792	460	3574
CORNER BROOK	1203	140	3163	3868	4328	936	2936	809	1485	541	436	3096	1697	911	1055	407	140	3071	2137	1420	4068	4109	4720	1652	2581	566	4363
DAWSON CREEK	2588	3651	741	252	712	2874	855	2987	2260	3290	4227	695	2094	3280	2803	3426	3651	1013	1654	2514	747	788	929	2731	1210	3343	751
EDMONTON	2221	3284	374	444	904	2507	488	2620	1893	2923	3860	328	1727	2913	2436	3059	3284	646	1287	2147	773	814	1296	2364	843	2988	939
FLIN FLON	1933	2996	279	1097	1557	2219	467	2332	1605	2635	3572	381	1439	2625	2148	2771	2996	94	999	1859	1423	1464	1949	2086	555	2700	1592
FORT SMITH	3049	4112	1202	892	1352	3335	1316	3448	2721	3751	4692	1156	2555	3741	3264	3887	4112	1474	2115	2975	1387	1428	1569	3192	1671	3816	443
FREDERICTON	636	432	2596	3301	3761	364	2369	237	918	66	1008	2529	1130	481	483	207	432	2499	1570	853	3501	3542	4153	1080	2014	131	3796
GANDER	1432	369	3392	4097	4557	1165	3165	1038	1714	770	207	3325	1926	1140	1284	636	369	3300	2366	1649	4297	4338	4949	1881	2810	795	4592
GASPÉ	709	725	2669	3374	3834	437	2442	310	991	501	1301	2602	1203	299	556	500	725	2572	1643	926	3574	3615	4226	1153	2087	566	3869
HALIFAX	937	262	2897	3602	4062	567	2670	452	1219	149	838	2830	1431	628	698	188	262	2800	1871	1154	3802	3843	4454	1381	2315	217	4097
HAMILTON	290	1322	1928	2633	3093	545	1701	658	431	961	1898	1861	462	951	474	1097	1322	1831	902	42	2833	2874	3485	198	1346	1026	3128
JASPER	2450	3513	603	215	675	2736	717	2849	2122	3152	4089	557	1956	3142	2665	3288	3513	875	1516	2376	544	585	1396	2635	1072	3217	1106
KENORA	1251	2314	709	1414	1874	1537	482	1650	923	1953	2890	642	757	1943	1466	2089	2314	612	317	1177	1614	1655	2266	1404	127	2018	1909
LETHBRIDGE	2128	3191	623	609	1069	2414	395	2527	1800	2830	2767	412	1626	2820	2343	2966	3191	768	1194	2054	710	751	1618	2297	750	2902	1261
LONDON	361	1393	2009	2704	3164	616	1772	729	502	1032	1969	1932	533	1022	545	1166	1393	1902	973	113	2904	2945	3548	126	1417	1097	3199
MONCTON	754	309	2714	3419	3879	487	2487	360	1036	92	885	2647	1248	462	606	84	309	2649	1688	971	3619	3660	4271	1203	2132	157	3914
MONTRÉAL	118	945	2078	2783	3243	168	1851	281	400	584	1521	2011	612	574	97	720	945	1981	1052	335	2983	3024	3635	562	1496	649	3278
NIAGARA FALLS	333	1365	1971	2676	3136	588	1744	701	474	1004	1941	1904	505	983	517	1140	1365	1874	945	85	2876	2917	3528	241	1389	1069	3171
NORTH BAY	229	1292	1731	2436	2896	515	1504	628	181	931	1868	1664	265	921	444	1067	1292	1634	705	208	2636	2677	3280	435	1149	996	2931
OTTAWA	•	1063	1960	2665	3125	286	1733	399	343	702	1639	1893	494	692	215	838	1063	1863	934	248	2865	2906	3517	475	1378	767	3160
PORT AUX BASQUES	1711	•	3023	3728	4188	796	2796	669	1345	401	576	2956	1557	771	915	267	129	2931	1997	1280	3928	3969	4580	1512	2441	426	4223
PRINCE ALBERT	3154	4865	•	818	1278	2246	227	2359	1632	2662	3599	102	1466	2652	2175	2798	3023	272	1026	1896	1144	1185	1670	2082	582	2727	1313
PRINCE GEORGE	4289	6000	1316	•	460	2951	932	3064	2337	3367	4304	772	2163	3357	2880	3503	3728	1090	1731	2591	495	536	1181	2850	1287	3432	1003
PRINCE RUPERT	5029	6740	2057	740	•	3411	1392	3524	2797	3827	4764	1232	2623	3817	3340	3963	4188	1550	2191	3051	955	996	1641	3310	1747	3892	1463
QUÉBEC	460	1281	3615	4749	5489	•	2019	127	568	418	1372	2179	780	406	133	571	796	2149	1220	503	3151	3192	3803	730	1664	495	3446
REGINA	2789	4500	365	1500	2240	3249	•	2132	1405	2435	3372	160	1231	2425	1948	2571	2796	373	799	1659	1132	1173	1784	1902	355	2507	1427
RIVIÈRE-DU-LOUP	642	1077	3796	4931	5671	204	3431	•	681	303	1245	2292	893	231	246	444	669	2262	1333	616	3264	3305	3916	843	1777	368	3559
ROUYN	552	2165	2626	3761	4501	914	2261	1096	•	984	1921	1565	446	974	497	1120	1345	1535	606	389	2537	2578	3189	616	1050	1049	2832
SAINT JOHN	1130	645	4284	5419	6159	673	3919	488	1584	•	977	2595	1196	547	537	176	401	2565	1636	919	3567	3608	4219	1146	2080	65	3862
ST. JOHN'S	2638	927	5792	6927	7667	2208	5427	2004	3092	1572	•	3532	2133	1347	1491	843	576	3507	2573	1856	4504	4545	5156	2088	3017	1012	4799
SASKATOON	3046	4757	164	1242	1983	3507	257	3689	2519	4176	5684	•	1391	2585	2108	2731	2956	346	959	1819	1042	1083	1624	2036	515	2660	1267
SAULT STE. MARIE	795	2506	2359	3481	4221	1255	1981	1437	718	1925	3422	2239	•	1186	709	1332	1557	1369	440	420	2363	2404	3015	647	884	1261	2666
SEPT-ÎLES	1114	1241	4268	5403	6143	653	3903	372	1568	880	2168	4160	1909	•	539	515	771	2555	1626	909	3557	3598	4209	1136	2070	612	3852
SHERBROOKE	346	1473	3500	4635	5375	214	3135	396	800	864	2400	3392	1141	867	•	690	915	2078	1149	432	3080	3121	3732	659	1593	614	3375
SUMMERSIDE	1349	430	4503	5638	6378	919	4138	715	1802	283	1357	4395	2144	829	1110	•	267	2706	1772	1053	3703	3744	4355	1287	2216	241	3998
SYDNEY	1711	207	4865	6000	6740	1281	4500	1077	2165	645	927	4757	2506	1241	1473	430	•	2931	1997	1280	3928	3969	4580	1512	2441	426	4223
THE PAS	2998	4717	438	1754	2494	3458	600	3640	2470	4128	5644	557	2203	4112	3344	4355	4717	•	929	1789	1388	1429	1942	2008	485	2630	1585
THUNDER BAY	1503	3214	1651	2786	3526	1963	1286	2145	975	2633	4141	1543	708	2617	1849	2852	3214	1495	•	860	1931	1972	2583	1087	444	741	2226
TORONTO	399	2060	3051	4170	4910	810	2670	991	626	1479	2987	2927	676	1463	695	1695	2060	2879	1384	•	2791	2832	3435	227	1304	984	3086
VANCOUVER	4611	6322	1841	797	1537	5071	1822	5253	4083	5741	7248	1677	3803	5724	4957	5959	6322	2234	3108	4492	•	41	1676	3034	1487	3632	1498
VICTORIA	4677	6387	1907	863	1603	5137	1818	5319	4149	5807	7314	1743	3869	5790	5023	6025	6387	2300	3174	4558	66	•	1717	3053	1528	3673	1539
WHITEHORSE	5660	7371	2688	1901	2641	6120	2871	6302	5132	6790	8298	2614	4852	6774	6006	7009	7371	3125	4157	5528	2697	2763	•	3660	2190	4284	1680
WIINDSOR	764	2433	3351	4587	5327	1175	3061	1357	991	1844	3360	3277	1041	1828	1061	2071	2433	3232	1749	365	4883	4913	5890	•	1547	1211	3303
WINNIPEG	2218	3928	937	2071	2812	2678	571	2860	1690	3347	4855	829	1423	3331	2564	3566	3928	781	715	2099	2393	2459	3524	2490	•	2145	1782
YARMOUTH	1234	686	4389	5523	6264	797	4035	592	1688	105	1629	4281	2029	985	988	388	686	4233	1193	1584	5845	5911	6894	1949	3452	•	3927
YELLOWKNIFE	5086	6796	2113	1614	2354	5546	2297	5728	4558	6215	7723	2039	4291	6199	5432	6418	6796	2551	3582	4966	2411	2477	2704	5316	2868	6320	•

Source: National Atlas Service, Natural Resources Canada

Science

Astronomical Calculations

Prepared for this publication by Duy C. Nguyen, Ph.D., Department of Astronomy and Astrophysics, University of Toronto.

ASTRONOMY IN CANADA

Astronomical research in Canada is carried out in universities, supported by the Natural Sciences and Engineering Research Council (NSERC) of Canada, and by the Canada Foundation for Innovation (CFI), and also in the National Research Council (NRC) — specifically by the Herzberg Institute of Astrophysics (HIA), which operates the following observatories: The Dominion Astrophysical Observatory (DAO) at Victoria, with optical telescopes of 1.8m and 1.2m aperture; and the Dominion Radio Astrophysical Observatory (DRAO) near Penticton, which has a 26m paraboloid and a 7-element array of 9m antennae. The National Research Council also maintains Canada's Time Service in its Institute of National Measurement Standards. The Canadian Astronomy Data Centre (CADC) is housed within HIA.

A number of Canadian universities offer graduate education in astronomy: Victoria, British Columbia (Vancouver), Alberta (Edmonton), Calgary, Saskatchewan (Saskatoon), Manitoba (Winnipeg), Western Ontario (London), Waterloo, McMaster (Hamilton), York (Toronto), Toronto, Queen's (Kingston), Montréal, McGill (Montréal), Laval (Québec), and St. Mary's (Halifax). Most of these have some local facilities for observational and theoretical studies, and all of them have access to national facilities in Canada and elsewhere. Among the major observatories operated by Canadian universities are: a 1.8m infrared telescope opened in 1987 by the University of Calgary; a 1.2m telescope at the University of Western Ontario; a 0.6m telescope now located in, and shared with, Argentina with access through the University of Toronto; and a 1.5m telescope at the Mont Mégantic Observatory operated by the University of Montréal, and Laval University. There is also a Canadian Institute for Theoretical Astrophysics hosted by the University of Toronto. Canadian astronomers have recently established the Association of Canadian Universities for Research in Astronomy (ACURA) to co-ordinate universities' participation in astronomy, especially in the development of large-scale facilities.

Through the National Research Council, Canadian astronomers also have access to excellent international facilities. One of these is the 3.6m Canada-France-Hawaii optical telescope atop Mauna Kea on the island of Hawaii, at an elevation of nearly 4200m. This telescope is shared, both as to cost and operation, by Canada, France, and the state of Hawaii. Canadian astronomers also share (with the Netherlands and the UK) in the operation of the James Clerk Maxwell telescope, a sophisticated millimetre-wave radio telescope at the same site. Canada also is a partner, along with several other countries, in the twin Gemini 8m telescopes, which are in operation in Hawaii and in Chile. Balloon-borne telescopes, Canada's first astronomical satellite MOST (Microvariability and Oscillations of STars), and participation in other space astronomy missions are funded through the Canadian Space Agency, and Canada is a partner in the James Webb Space Telescope, the planned successor to the Hubble Space Telescope. Canada is also a partner in the North American Program in Radio Astronomy, including the Atacama Large Millimetre Array, under contruction high in the Atacama Desert in Chile.

Astronomical education and outreach are carried out in a wide variety of settings. In the formal education system, astronomy is part of the elementary and secondary school science curriculum in most provinces, and is taught in most universities, most commonly in the form of introductory astronomy courses for non-majors. Canada's planetariums, science centres, and public observatories play a major role in communicating the nature and excitement of astronomy, as do science journalists, and the many professional and amateur astronomers who give public lectures, and organize open houses and star parties.

OBSERVATORIES

Observatories are open to the public as follows:

NEW Burke-Gaffney Observatory: St. Mary's University, Halifax NS B3H 3C3 - 902/420-5828; Info line: 902/496-8257; Fax: 902/496-8218; URL: www.smu.ca/academic/science/ap/bgo.html

Free public tours are held, weather permitting, on the 1st and 3rd Saturday of each month, except from June through September when they are held every Saturday. Tours begin at 7pm between November 1 and March 30 and at either 9pm or 10pm (depending on when it gets dark) between April 1 and October 31. On clear evenings, the 40-cm telescope is used to view the planets, the Moon, or other interesting celestial objects.

There will be no tour on cloudy or rainy nights. The decision to hold or cancel a tour is usually made by 6pm on Saturday. Always call the information line after 6pm to find out if the tour is on or off.

Groups wishing special tours can be accommodated on Monday evenings by reservation.

Canada Science & Technology Museum, Helen Sawyer Hogg Observatory: 1867 St. Laurent Blvd., Ottawa ON K1G 5A3 - 613/991-3044; Email: cts@technomuses.ca; URL: www.sciencetech.technomuses.ca

38-cm refractor (from the former Dominion Observatory). See website for details and special programs.

Canada-France-Hawaii Telescope: #65, 1238 Mamalahoa Hwy., Kamuela HI, 96743 - 808/885-7944; Fax: 808/885-7288; E-mail: outreach@cfht.hawaii.edu; URL: www.cfht.hawaii.edu

By appointment only.

Climenhaga Observatory: Dept. of Physics & Astronomy, University of Victoria, PO Box 3055, Station CSC, Victoria BC V8W 3P6 - 250/721-7700; Fax: 250/721-7715; URL: astrowww.phys.uvic.ca/events/

Daytime tours are open from the beginning of April until the end of June. The tour includes an entertaining educational presentation, a look through the big, fully automated telescope in the Climenhaga Observatory and weather permitting, an opportunity to search for sunspots using the smaller telescopes on the roof. The tours are free but space is limited. Interested parties are encouraged to book in advance.

Night time viewing sessions are open on Wednesdays from 8 p.m. (or sunset) until 10 p.m.

Gordon MacMillan Southam Observatory: H.R. MacMillan Space Centre, 1100 Chestnut St., Vancouver BC V6J 3J9 - 604/738-7827; Fax: 604/736-5665; E-mail: info@spacecentre.ca; URL: www.spacecentre.ca

Open Friday and Saturday starting at 8:30 p.m. To confirm observatory openings, please call 604/738-2855, or guest services at 604/738-7827 ext. 240 after 8:00 p.m. Admission is by donation.

Hume Cronyn Memorial Observatory: Dept. of Physics & Astronomy, University of Western Ontario, London ON N6A 3K7 - 519/661-2111, ext. 86708; URL: www.astro.uwo.ca/~dfgray/pub-nit.html

Public Nights run from late October through mid-December and mid-January through early April. This activity is oriented toward groups, and reservations must be made in advance.

Open House is run every Saturday evening during the months of June, July, and August. No reservations needed. Start time is 20:30 (8:30 p.m.). Closing time is 23:00 (11:00 p.m.).

National Research Council Canada, Centre of the Universe: Visitor Centre, 5071 West Saanich Rd., Victoria BC V9E 2E7 - 250/363-8262; Fax: 250/363-8290; E-mail: cu@nrc.gc.ca; URL: www.nrc-cnrc.gc.ca/eng/services/hia/centre-universe.html

Open for elementary, middle or high school class, or college or university students, for an exclusive daytime program for fall, winter and spring.

Open Tuesday to Saturday from 3:30 p.m. to 11:15 p.m. (last admission at 10:15 p.m.) during the summer, and 1:00 p.m. to 4:30 p.m. in September. See webpages for admission details.

National Research Council Canada, Dominion Astrophysical Observatory: 5071 West Saanich Rd., Victoria BC V9E 2E7 - 250/363-0001; Fax: 250/363-0045; E-mail: HIA-WWW@nrc-cnrc.gc.ca; URL: www.nrc-cnrc.gc.ca/eng/facilities/hia/astrophysical-observatory. html

Open every evening from April 1 up to and including October 31 to demonstrate the research telescope, regardless of the weather, and to offer a viewing of celestial objects, weather permitting. See website for details.

National Research Council Canada, Dominion Radio Astrophysical Observatory: 717 White Lake Road, PO Box 248, Penticton BC V2A 6J9 - 250/493-2300; Fax: 250/497-2355; E-mail: HIA-WWW@nrc-cnrc.gc.ca; URL: www.nrc-cnrc.gc.ca/eng/facilities/hia/radio-astrophysical.html

The Observatory grounds and Visitors' Centre are open year-round for self-guided tours between 10 a.m. and 5 p.m., Monday to Friday (except statutory holidays). The grounds are also open on weekends from Easter until Thanksgiving, between 10 a.m. and 5 p.m., with staff on duty in the Visitors' Centre. Guided tours led by Observatory staff are offered on Sundays in July and August, from 2 p.m. until 5 p.m. Tours typically take about 1 hour.

PRINCIPAL (MEAN) ELEMENTS OF THE SOLAR SYSTEM

Object	Equatorial Diameter (miles)	Equatorial Diameter (km)	Mass (earth=1)	Axial Rotation (days)	Magnitude at brightest	Mean Dist. from Sun (mill. miles)	Mean Dist. from Sun (mill. km)	Per. of Revol.	Eccentricity	Inclination (deg.)
Sun	865,000	1,392,000	332,946	24.7**	-26.8					
Moon	2,159	3,475	0.0123	27.3217	-12.6					
Mercury	3,032	4,879	0.0553	58.646	-2.0	36.0	57.9	88.0d	0.206	7.0
Venus	7,521	12,104	0.8150	243.019***	-4.7	67.2	108.2	224.7	0.007	3.4
Earth	7,926	12,756	1.0000	0.9973		93.0	149.6	365.3	0.017	(0.0)
Mars	4,222	6,794	0.1074	1.0260	-2.8	141.6	227.9	687.0	0.093	1.8
Jupiter	88,846*	142,984*	317.833	0.410**	-2.8	483.7	778	11.86y	0.048	1.3
Saturn	74,898*	120,536*	95.159	0.44401	-0.4	888	1,429	29.42	0.056	2.5
Uranus	31,763*	51,118*	14.500	0.71833***	5.7	1,786	2,875	83.75	0.046	0.8
Neptune	30,775*	49,528*	17.204	0.67125	7.8	2,799	4,504	163.7	0.009	1.8
Pluto	1,430	2,302	0.0025	6.3872***	13.8	3,676	5,916	248.0	0.249	17.1

at pressure 1 bar (101.325 kPa) ** at equator * retrograde*

PLANETARY CONFIGURATIONS, 2012

UNIVERSAL (GREENWICH) TIME

	d	*h*	
January	5	0	Earth at perihelion (147.1 million km)
	13	7	Venus 1.2° S. of Neptune
	25	1	Mars stationary
February	7	9	Mercury in superior conjunction
	8	12	Saturn stationary
	10	5	Venus 0.3° N. of Uranus
	19	21	Neptune in conjunction with Sun
March	3	20	Mars at opposition
	5	10	Mercury greatest elongation E. (18°)
	5	17	Mars closest approach
	11	21	Mercury stationary
	15	11	Venus 3° N. of Jupiter
	20	5	Vernal Equinox; spring begins in northern hemisphere
	21	19	Mercury in inferior conjunction
	24	18	Uranus in conjunction with Sun
	27	8	Venus greatest elongation E. (46°)
April	3	6	Mercury stationary
	10	15	Pluto stationary
	15	12	Mars stationary
	15	18	Saturn at opposition
	17	1	Venus 10° N. of Aldebaran
	18	17	Mercury greatest elongation W. (27°)
	22	2	Mercury 2° S. of Uranus
	30	8	Venus greatest illuminated extent
May	13	13	Jupiter in conjunction with Sun
	15	17	Venus stationary
	21	0	New Moon; Annular Eclipse of Sun (page A-33)
	27	11	Mercury in superior conjunction
June	4	11	Full Moon; Partial Eclipse of Moon (page A-33)
	5	6	Neptune stationary
	6	1	Venus in inferior conjunction, transit over Sun
	15	6	Venus 4° N. of Aldebaran
	20	23	Summer solstice; summer begins in northern hemisphere
	21	18	Mercury 5° S. of Pollux
	26	9	Saturn stationary
	27	4	Venus stationary
	29	15	Pluto at opposition
July	1	2	Mercury greatest elongation E. (26°)
	5	3	Earth at aphelion (152.1 million km)
	9	19	Venus 0.9° N. of Aldebaran
July *(cont.)*	12	16	Venus greatest illuminated extent
	13	17	Uranus stationary
	14	5	Mercury stationary
	28	20	Mercury in inferior conjunction
August	3	5	Jupiter 5° N. of Aldebaran
	7	17	Mercury stationary
	13	0	Mars 1.9° N. of Spica
	15	9	Venus greatest elongation W. (46°)
	16	12	Mercury greatest elongation W. (19°)
	17	9	Mars 3° S. of Saturn
	24	13	Neptune at opposition
September	1	22	Venus 9° S. of Pollux
	10	13	Mercury in superior conjunction
	17	21	Pluto stationary
	22	15	Autumnal Equinox; autumn begins in northern hemisphere
	29	7	Uranus at opposition
October	1	2	Mercury 1.8° N. of Spica
	3	8	Venus 0.1° S. of Regulus
	4	14	Jupiter stationary
	6	7	Mercury 3° S. of Saturn
	20	6	Mars 4° N. of Antares
	25	9	Saturn in conjunction with Sun
	26	22	Mercury greatest elongation E. (24°)
November	7	4	Mercury stationary
	11	11	Neptune stationary
	13	22	New Moon; Total Eclipse of Sun (page A-33)
	15	23	Venus 4° N. of Spica
	17	16	Mercury in inferior conjunction
	26	20	Mercury stationary
	27	5	Venus 0.6° S. of Saturn
	28	15	Full Moon; Penumbral Eclipse of Moon (page A-33)
December	3	2	Jupiter at opposition
	4	23	Mercury greatest elongation W. (21°)
	7	20	Jupiter 5° N. of Aldebaran
	13	20	Uranus stationary
	17	15	Mercury 6° N. of Antares
	21	11	Winter Solstice; winter begins in the northern hemisphere
	23	11	Venus 6° N. of Antares
	30	14	Pluto in conjunction with Sun

This table includes configurations involving the sun, planets, and bright zodiacal stars. The meaning of the terms is as follows:

Aphelion: the point in its orbit at which a planet is furthest from the sun.

Conjunction: in the same direction as another object (the sun, unless otherwise stated). Mercury and Venus can be at inferior conjunction (closer than the sun) or superior conjunction (beyond the sun).

Elongation: the angle between the planet and the sun.

Opposition: opposite another object (the sun, unless otherwise stated).

Perihelion: the point in its orbit at which a planet is closest to the sun.

Stationary: motionless relative to the background stars. Because of the orbital motions of the planet and the earth, the planet normally moves eastward or westward relative to the background stars. At the moment when its motion changes from eastward to westward, or vice versa, the planet is said to be stationary.

Observatoire Astronomique Du Mont Mégantic: 189 route du Parc, Notre-Dame-des-Bois QC J0B 2E0 - 819/888-2941; Fax 819/888-2943; E-mail: parc.mont-megantic@sepaq.com; URL: www.astro.umontreal.ca/omm/

The observatory hosts "Festival d'Astronomie Populaire du mont Mégantic" on the weekends in July. For other times of the year, visits including interactive exhibitions, high definition multimedia show, and tours of the observatories can be arranged through AstroLab du Mont Mégantic. See website for details on dates & times.

Rothney Astrophysical Observatory: Dept. of Physics & Astronomy, University of Calgary, 2500 University Dr. NW, Calgary AB T2N 1N4 - 403/931-2366; E-mail: rao@phas.ucalgary.ca; URL: www.ucalgary.ca/rao/

Day and evening programs are available for school groups which involve a grade appropriate presentation, tour of the observatory and skyviewing. Programs run from 7:00 pm to 9:00 pm. Free drop-in visits to the Interpretive Centre are available Monday, Tuesday, and Wednesday from noon - 4pm. Private tours are available on other evenings during the year. School group tours are also available. See website for details.

Telus World of Science - Edmonton Observatory: 11211 - 142 St., Edmonton AB T5M 4A1 - 780/452-9100; Fax: 780/455-5882; URL: www.edmontonscience.com/pages/PlanVisit/Observatory.aspx

Summer hours (July to Labour Day weekend) 1:00 p.m. - 5:00 p.m. and 6:30 p.m. - 10 p.m. 7 days a week. Fall/Winter/Spring hours (After Labour Day to the following summer) Saturdays, Sundays & holidays 1:00 p.m. - 4:00 p.m., and Fridays, Saturdays & Sundays 7:00 p.m. - 10:00 p.m. Open weather permitting.

University of Alberta Observatory: Dept. of Physics, University of Alberta, Edmonton AB T6G 2J1 - 780/492-5286; Email: stars@ualberta.ca; URL: www.ualberta.ca/stars

Open to the public Thursday nights from September through April (closed for final exams and winter holidays), weather permitting. School groups, youth groups and other groups can book a private visit free of charge. See website for exact hours and details.

University of Saskatchewan Observatory: Dept. of Physics & Engineering Physics, University of Saskatchewan, 116 Science Place, Saskatoon SK S7N 5E2 - 306/966-6396; URL: physics.usask.ca/observatory/

Saturday evening programs year round; times vary. Tours for school and community groups are arranged for Friday evenings (October - March). Special tours may be arranged during the summer months.

University of Toronto, St. George Campus Observatory: Dept. of Astronomy & Astrophysics, University of Toronto, 50 St. George Street, Toronto ON M5S 3H4 - 416/978-2016; URL: www1.astro.utoronto.ca/~gasa/public_talk/iWeb/index.php

Free tours are offered on the first Thursday of every month (excluding January). Tours start at 8 p.m. during winter months and 9 p.m. during summer months. Extra public tours may also be arranged. See website for details.

York University Observatory: 4700 Keele St., Toronto ON M3J 1P3 - 416/736-2100, ext. 77773 (voice mail); Email: pdelaney@yorku.ca; URL: www.physics.yorku.ca/observatory/

The observatory is open for online viewing Monday nights and public (in-person) viewing on Wednesday nights at the following times: October - March 7:30 p.m. - 9:30 p.m., and April - September 9:00 p.m. - 11:00 p.m. See website for further details.

PLANETARIUMS

A selection of planetaria with URL, phone number & related information:

ASTROLab du parc national du Mont-Mégantic: 189 route du Parc, Notre-Dame-des-Bois, QC J0B 2E0 - 819/888-2941; Toll Free: 1-800-665-6527; URL: www.astrolab-parc-national-mont-megantic.org

Cosmic Rhythms multimedia show; on-site lodging.

Doran Planetarium: Laurentian University, 935 Ramsey Lake Rd., Sudbury ON P3E 2C6 - 705/675-1151, ext. 2227, Fax: 705/675-4868; URL: www.oldwebsite.laurentian.ca/physics/planetarium/Planetarium.html

Largest planetarium in northern Ontario; programs.

The Lockhart Planetarium: 500 Dysart Rd., Winnipeg MB R3T 2M8 - 204/474-9785; URL: umanitoba.ca/faculties/science/astronomy/lockhart/

Dome seats 60; open year-round for public groups.

W.J. McCallion Planetarium: Dept. of Physics & Astronomy, McMaster University, 1280 Main St. West, Hamilton ON L8S 4M1 - 905/525-9140, ext. 27777; Fax: 905/546-1252; URL: physwww.physics.mcmaster.ca/planetarium

Planetarium has long history of support from RASC Hamilton Centre; first in Ontario open to the public. Public shows are Wednesdays (subject to change on occasion). See website for details.

MacMillan Planetarium: 1100 Chestnut St., Vancouver BC V6J 3J9. - 604/738-7827, Fax: 604/736-5665; URL: www.spacecentre.ca

Special laser shows in summer, numerous programs for school groups of all ages, teacher packages online.

Ontario Science Centre - CA Technologies Planetarium: 770 Don Mills Road, North York ON M3C 1T3 - 416/696-1000; URL: www.ontariosciencecentre.ca

Toronto's only public permanent planetarium. See website for details.

Planétarium de Montréal: 1000, rue St-Jacques Ouest, Montréal QC H3C 1G7 - 514/872-4530; Fax: 514/872-8102; E-mail: info@planetarium.montreal.qc.ca; URL: www.planetarium.montreal.qc.ca

Programs, activity sheets, classroom kits, advanced workshop for teachers & educators.

Royal Ontario Museum: Outreach Services, ROM, Royal Ontario Museum, 100 Queens Park, Toronto ON M5S 2C6 - 416/586-5681; Fax: 416/586-5832; E-mail: outreach@rom.on.ca; URL: www.rom.on.ca

Portable Starlab dome available for any location in Ontario.

Science North: 100 Ramsey Lake Road, Sudbury ON P3E 5S9 - 705/522-3701 or toll-free 1-800-461-4898; Fax: 705/522-4954; E-mail: contactus@sciencenorth.ca; URL: sciencenorth.ca

Digital planetarium with feature films about astronomy and other space topics.

Telus World of Science - Calgary: PO Box 2100, Station M, #73, Calgary AB T2P 2M5 - 403/268-8300; Fax: 403/237-0186; E-mail: discover@calgaryscience.ca; URL: www.calgaryscience.ca

Join "Seymour Sky" at the Planetarium dome, several programs, multimedia shows & kits available.

Telus World of Science - Edmonton: 11211 - 142 St., Edmonton AB T5M 4A1 - 780/451-3344; Fax: 780/455-5882; URL: www.edmontonscience.com

Mobile planetarium available. Gift shop, IMAX theatre, science programs & computer lab; observatory operated by RASC volunteers.

University of Toronto: Dept. Of Astronomy & Astrophysics, University of Toronto, 50 St. George Street, Toronto ON M5S 3H4 - 416/978-2016; URL: www1.astro.utoronto.ca/~gasa/public_talk/iWeb/index.php

Portable Starlab dome. Free tours offered on the first Thursday of most months. Tours start at 8 p.m. during winter months and 9 p.m. during summer months. Extra public tours may be also arranged. See website for details.

Winnipeg Planetarium: 190 Rupert Ave., Winnipeg MB R3B 0N2 - 204/956-2830; Fax: 204/942-3679; E-mail: info@manitobamuseum.ca; URL: www.manitobamuseum.ca/main

Science centre, museum & planetarium in one site; mobile planetarium.

Many of Canada's professional astronomers, & most of Canada's enthusiastic amateur astronomers are members of the Royal Astronomical Society of Canada (see index) which has 27 Centres across Canada. An extensive list of astronomy clubs in Canada has been published online by SkyNews and can be found at www.skynewsmagazine.com/pages/clubs.html. Many of these clubs have programs for the general public.

ECLIPSES AND TRANSITS IN 2012

In 2012, there will be four eclipses, two solar, and two lunar. Only one of the solar eclipses will be visible from North America.

1. An **annular eclipse** of the Sun on May 20-21, visible from North America.

2. A **partial eclipse** of the Moon on June 4, visible from North America.

3. A **total eclipse** of the Sun on November 13-14, not visible from North America.

4. A **penumbral eclipse** of the Moon on November 28, visible from North America.

There will be a transit of Venus over the disk of the Sun on June 5-6. The entire transit will be visible from northwestern North America, and the Arctic.

METEORS, METEORITES, AND METEOR SHOWERS

A *meteor* or "shooting star" appears momentarily in the sky when a particle from beyond the earth enters the earth's atmosphere at a high velocity. Most visible meteors are caused by particles smaller than a grape or marble, and these small particles are completely vaporized in the atmosphere at a height of about 80 km. A spectacular meteor, known as a *fire-ball*, is caused by a larger body which may fall to the earth's surface in one or more pieces. Particles seen thus to fall, or subsequently found by analysis to be of this nature, are called meteorites.

Meteorites may be divided into two main classes—the irons, which are almost pure nickel-iron, and the stones. Any freshly-fallen meteorite is characterized by a dark, smooth crust caused by the fusion of the outer part.

Meteors may be observed on any clear, moonless night at an average rate of about five an hour. At times *meteor showers* occur, when meteors are seen with much greater frequency and appear to radiate from a particular part of the sky which is called the *radiant*. This is an effect of perspective, the radiant being the vanishing point of the parallel tracks of the meteors. Meteor showers usually repeat themselves annually, and in some cases have been associated with the orbits of comets. When the earth passes through or near the orbit of a comet it can intercept the small particles (meteoroids) which cause meteors. The principal meteor showers for the northern hemisphere are listed below. The information is based on that in the annual *Observer's Handbook* of the Royal Astronomical Society of Canada.

The study of meteors and meteorites adds to our knowledge of the nature and origin of the solar system and also to our knowledge of the earth's outer atmosphere.

MAPS OF THE NIGHT SKY

The maps on the next six pages cover the northern sky. Stars are shown down to a magnitude of 4.5 or 5, i.e. those which are readily apparent to the unaided eye on a reasonably dark night.

The maps are drawn for 45°N latitude, but are useful for latitudes several degrees north or south of this. They show the hemisphere of sky visible to an observer at various times of the year. Because the aspect of the night sky changes continuously with both longitude and time, while time zones change discontinuously with both longitude and time of year, it is not possible to state simply when, in general, a particular observer will find that his or her sky fits exactly one of the six maps. The month indicated below each map is the time of year when the map will match the "late evening" sky. On any particular night, successive maps will represent the sky as it appears every four hours. For example, at 2 or 3 am on a March night, the May map should be used. Just after dinner on a January night, the November map will be appropriate. The centre of each map is the zenith, the point directly overhead; the circumference is the horizon. To identify the stars, hold the map in front of you so that the part of the horizon which you are facing (west, for instance) is downward. (The four letters around the periphery of each map indicate compass directions.)

On the maps, stars forming the usual constellation patterns are linked by straight lines, constellation names being given in upper case letters. The names in lower case are those of first magnitude stars, except Algol and Mira which are famous variable stars, and Polaris which is near the north celestial pole. Small clusters of dots indicate the positions of bright star clusters, nebulae, or galaxies. Although a few of these are just visible to the naked eye, and most can be located in binoculars, a telesope is needed for good views of these objects. The pair of wavy, dotted lines indicates roughly the borders of the Milky Way. Small asterisks locate the directions of the galactic centre (GC), the north galactic pole (NGP), and the south galactic pole (SGP). Two dashed lines appear on each of the six maps. The one with the more dashes is the celestial equator. Tick marks along this indicate hours of right ascension, the odd hours being labelled. The line with fewer dashes is the ecliptic, the apparent annual path of the Sun across the heavens. Letters along this line indicate the approximate position of the Sun at the beginning of each month. Also located along the ecliptic are the vernal equinox (VE), summer solstice (SS), autumnal equinox (AE), and winter solstice (WS). Moon and the other eight planets are found near the ecliptic, but since their motions are not related in a simple way to our year, it is not feasible to show them on a general set of maps.

The text above, and the six star charts on the following pages, were prepared by Professor Roy L. Bishop, former editor of the annual *Observer's Handbook* of the Royal Astronomical Society of Canada (RASC). They are copyright RASC 1996. They are used here with the kind permission of Professor Bishop and the RASC.

PRINCIPAL ANNUAL METEOR SHOWERS FOR THE NORTHERN HEMISPHERE

(UNIVERSAL TIME)

Shower	Location of Radiant	UT Date of Maximum Frequency	Zenithal Hourly Number	Duration (in days)
Quadrantids (2012)	Bootes	Jan. 4, 6h	120	1
Lyrids	Lyra	Apr. 22, 4h	20	1
Eta Aquarids	Aquarius	May 4, 17h	60	5
Delta Aquarids	Aquarius	July 27, 19h	20	8
Perseids	Perseus	Aug. 12, 11h	90	2
Orionids	Orion	Oct. 21, 3h	20	2
South Taurids	Taurus	Nov. 5, 4h	10	15
North Taurids	Taurus	Nov. 12, 3h	15	15
Leonids	Leo	Nov. 17, 9h	15	1
Geminids	Gemini	Dec. 13, 22h	120	1
Ursids	Ursa Minor	Dec. 22, 7h	10	1
Quadranids (2013)	Bootes	Jan. 3, 12h	90	1

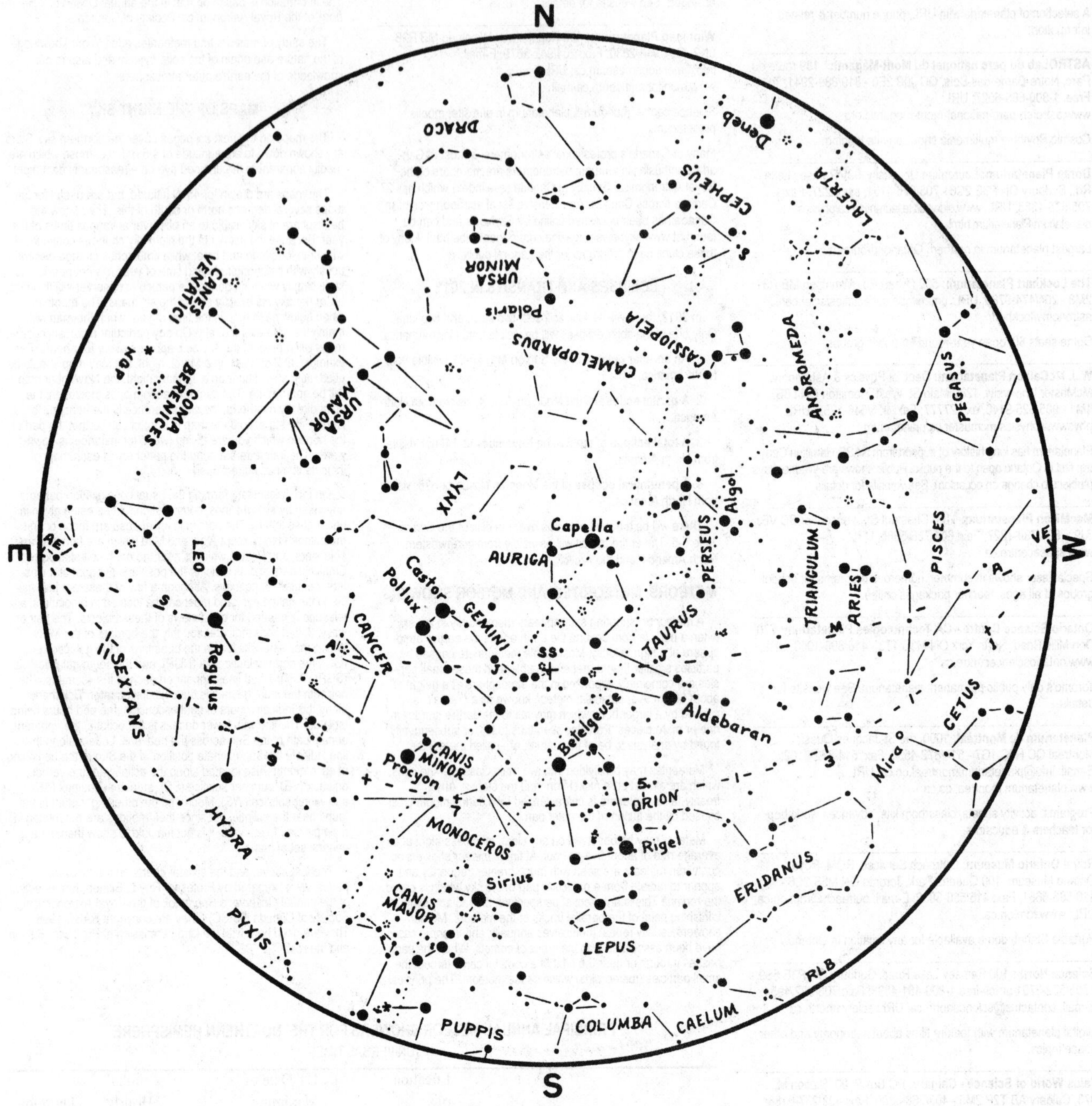

JANUARY

THE NAKED EYE PLANETS IN 2012

January

MERCURY is visible with some difficulty in the mornings until mid-month, low in the south-east, just before sunrise.

VENUS is a brilliant object in the south-western sky, just after sunset; it sets a few hours later. It passes just south of Neptune on the 13th.

MARS, moving from Leo to Virgo, rises shortly before midnight, and is visible high in the south-western sky at sunrise. It is stationary the night of the 24th, then moves slowly westward, against the background stars.

JUPITER, moving from Pisces to Aries, is visible high in the southern sky at sunset; it sets shortly after midnight.

SATURN, in Virgo, rises shortly after midnight, and is visible in the south at sunrise.

February

MERCURY is visible in the evenings by mid-month, low in the west, just after sunset.

VENUS is a brilliant object in the western sky, just after sunset; it sets a few hours later. It passes just south of Uranus on the 10th.

MARS, moving from Virgo to Leo, rises a few hours after sunset, and is visible low in the south-western sky at sunrise.

JUPITER, in Aries, is visible high in the southern sky at sunset; it sets shortly before midnight.

SATURN, in Virgo, rises around midnight, and is visible in the south-west at sunrise. It is stationary on the 8th, then moves slowly westward, against the background stars.SATURN, in Virgo, rises shortly before midnight, and is visible for the rest of the night.

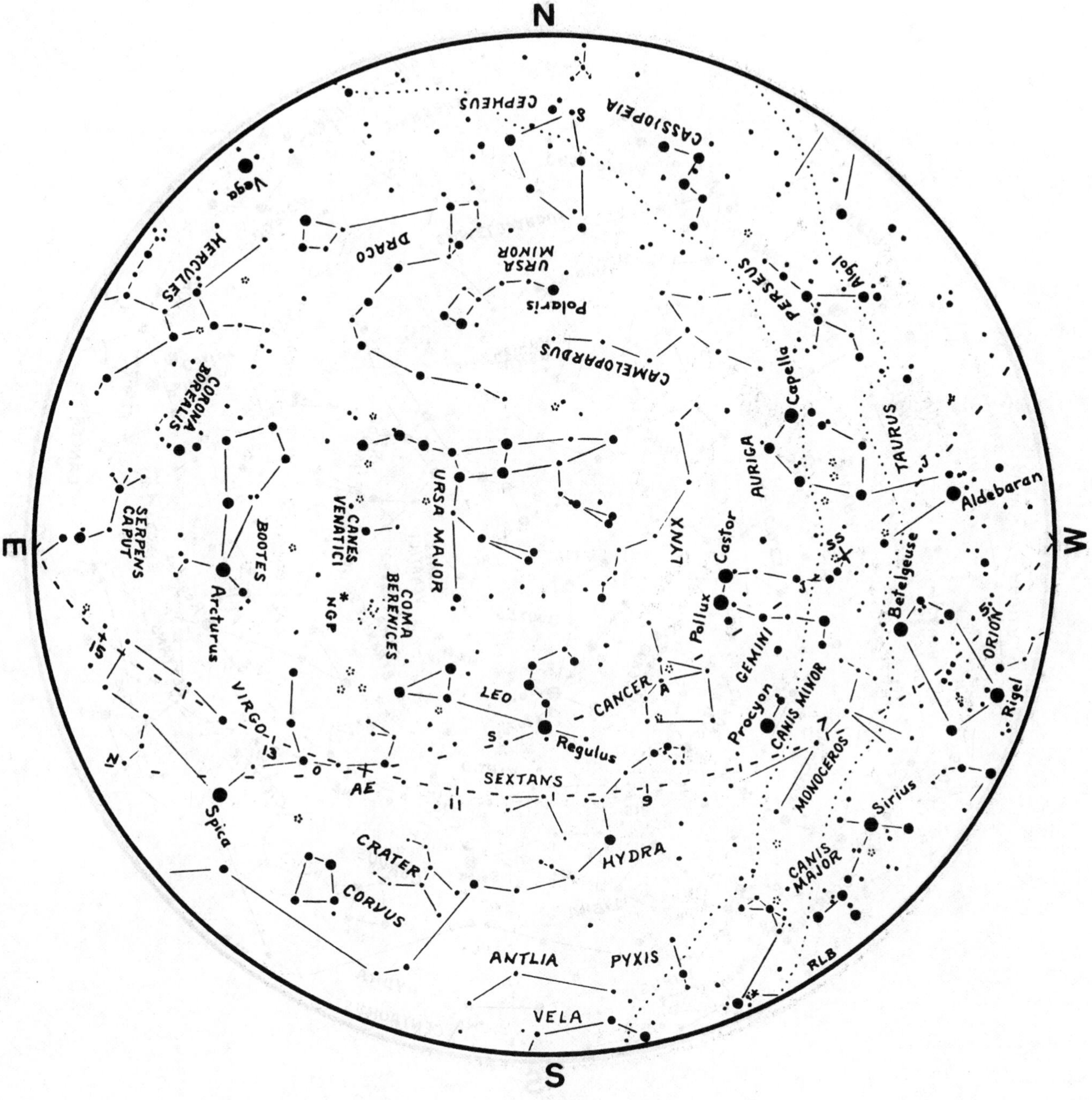

MARCH

THE NAKED EYE PLANETS IN 2012

March

MERCURY is visible in the evenings until mid-month, low in west, just after sunset; it is again visible with some difficulty at the end of the month, very low in the east, just before sunrise.

VENUS is a brilliant object in the western sky, just after sunset; it sets a few hours later. It passes just north of Jupiter on the 15th.

MARS, in Leo, is visible throughout the night as a bright, reddish object crossing the sky from east to west; it sets around sunrise time. It is at opposition with the Sun on the 3rd.

JUPITER, in Aries, is visible in the western sky at sunset; it sets a few hours later. It passes just south of Venus on the 15th. See also Venus, above.

SATURN, in Virgo, rises shortly before midnight, and is visible in the south-west at sunrise.

April

MERCURY is visible with some difficulty in the mornings this month, very low in the east, just before sunrise. It passes just south of Uranus on the night of the 21st.

VENUS is a brilliant object in the western sky, just after sunset; it sets a few hours later. It passes just north of Aldebaran on the night of the 16th.

MARS, in Leo, is visible high in the south-east at sunset; it sets in the west shortly before sunrise. It is stationary on the 15th, then resumes slow eastward motion, relative to the background stars.

JUPITER, in Aries, is visible in the evenings until mid-month, low in the west, just after sunset; it sets shortly afterwards.

SATURN, in Virgo, rises shortly after sunset, and is visible throughout most of the night; it sets around sunrise time.

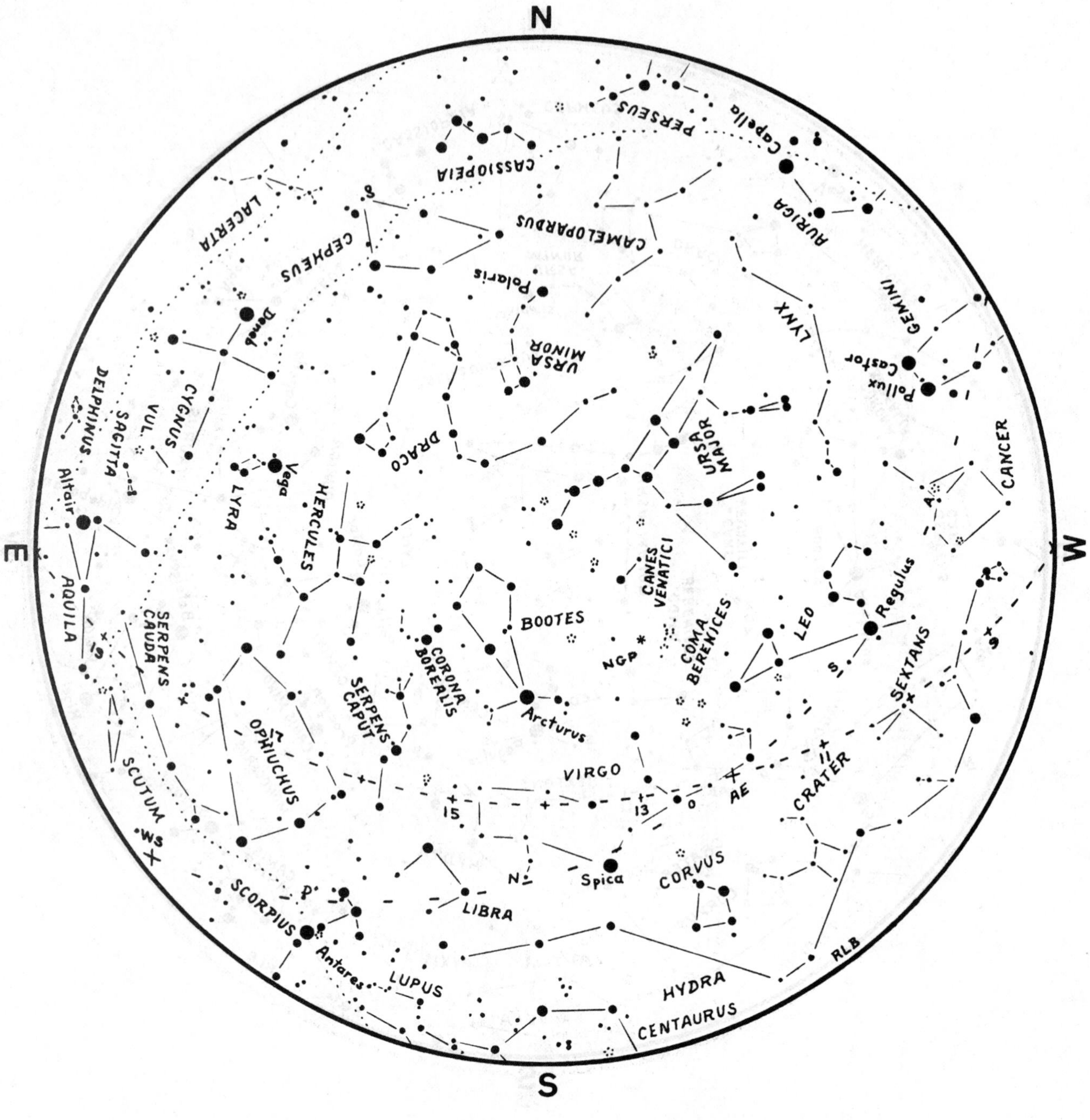

MAY

THE NAKED EYE PLANETS IN 2012

May

MERCURY is visible with considerable difficulty in the mornings until mid-month, very low in the east, just before sunrise.

VENUS is visible in the western sky, just after sunset; it sets soon afterwards.

MARS, in Leo, is visible high in the southern sky at sunset; it sets in the west a few hours before sunrise.

JUPITER, in Taurus, is visible in the mornings at the end of the month, low in the north-east, just before sunrise. It is in conjunction with the Sun on the 13th.SATURN, in Virgo, is visible in the south-eastern sky at sunset; it sets shortly before sunrise.

SATURN, in Virgo, is visible in the south-eastern sky at sunset; it sets shortly before sunrise.

June

MERCURY is visible in the evenings by the beginning of the month, low in the north-west, just after sunset. It passes just south of Pollux on the 21st.

VENUS is visible by mid-month, low in the eastern sky, just before sunrise. It transits the Sun's disk on the 5th at 10:10pm to the 6th at 4:50am, Greenwich Mean Time. It also passes just north of Aldebaran on the 15th.

MARS, moving from Leo to Virgo, is visible in the south-west at sunset, and sets in the west shortly after midnight.

JUPITER, in Taurus, is visible in the mornings, low in the east, just before sunrise.

SATURN, in Virgo, is visible in the southern sky at sunset; it sets a few hours before sunrise. It is stationary on the 26th, then resumes slow eastward motion, relative to the background stars.

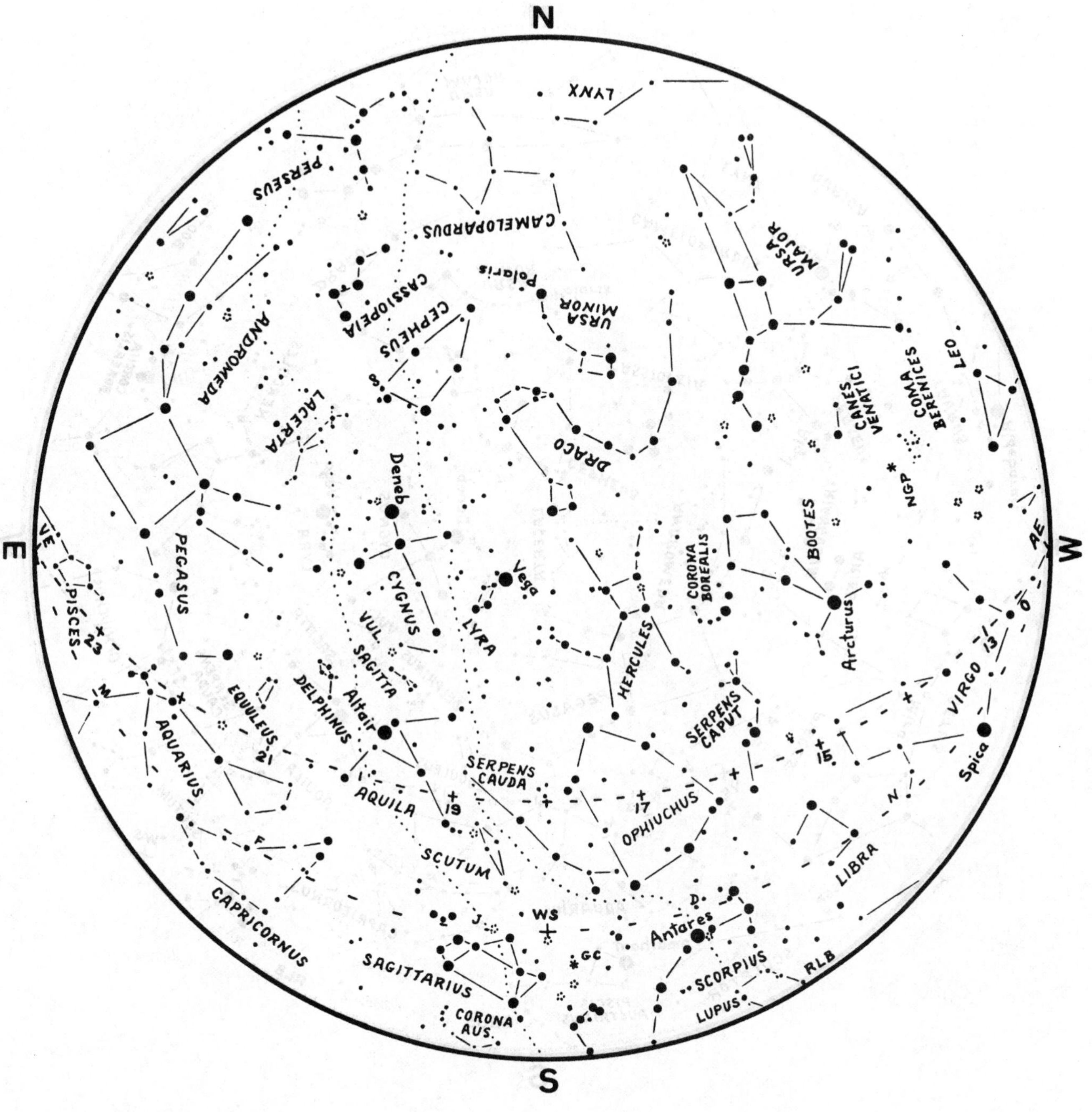

JULY

THE NAKED EYE PLANETS IN 2012

July

MERCURY is visible in the evenings until mid-month, low in the west, just after sunset.

VENUS is a brillant object in the eastern sky, rising a few hours before sunrise. It passes just north of Aldebaran on the 9th.

MARS, in Virgo, is visible in the south-west at sunset, and sets in the west around midnight.

JUPITER, in Taurus, rises a few hours before the Sun, and is visible in the eastern sky at sunrise.

SATURN, in Virgo, is visible in the south-western sky at sunset; it sets around midnight.

August

MERCURY is visible in the mornings by the beginning of the month, low in the east, just before sunrise. It passes just north of Spica on the night of the 12th.

VENUS is a brillant object in the eastern sky, rising a few hours before sunrise.

MARS, in Virgo, is visible, low in the south-west, just after sunset; it sets shortly afterwards. It passes just north of Spica on the 13th, and just south of Saturn on the 17th.

JUPITER, in Taurus, rises shortly after midnight, and is visible high in the south-eastern sky at sunrise. It passes just north of Aldebaran on the 3rd.

SATURN, in Virgo, is visible low in the south-western sky at sunset; it sets a few hours later. It passes just north of Mars on the 17th. See also Mars, above.

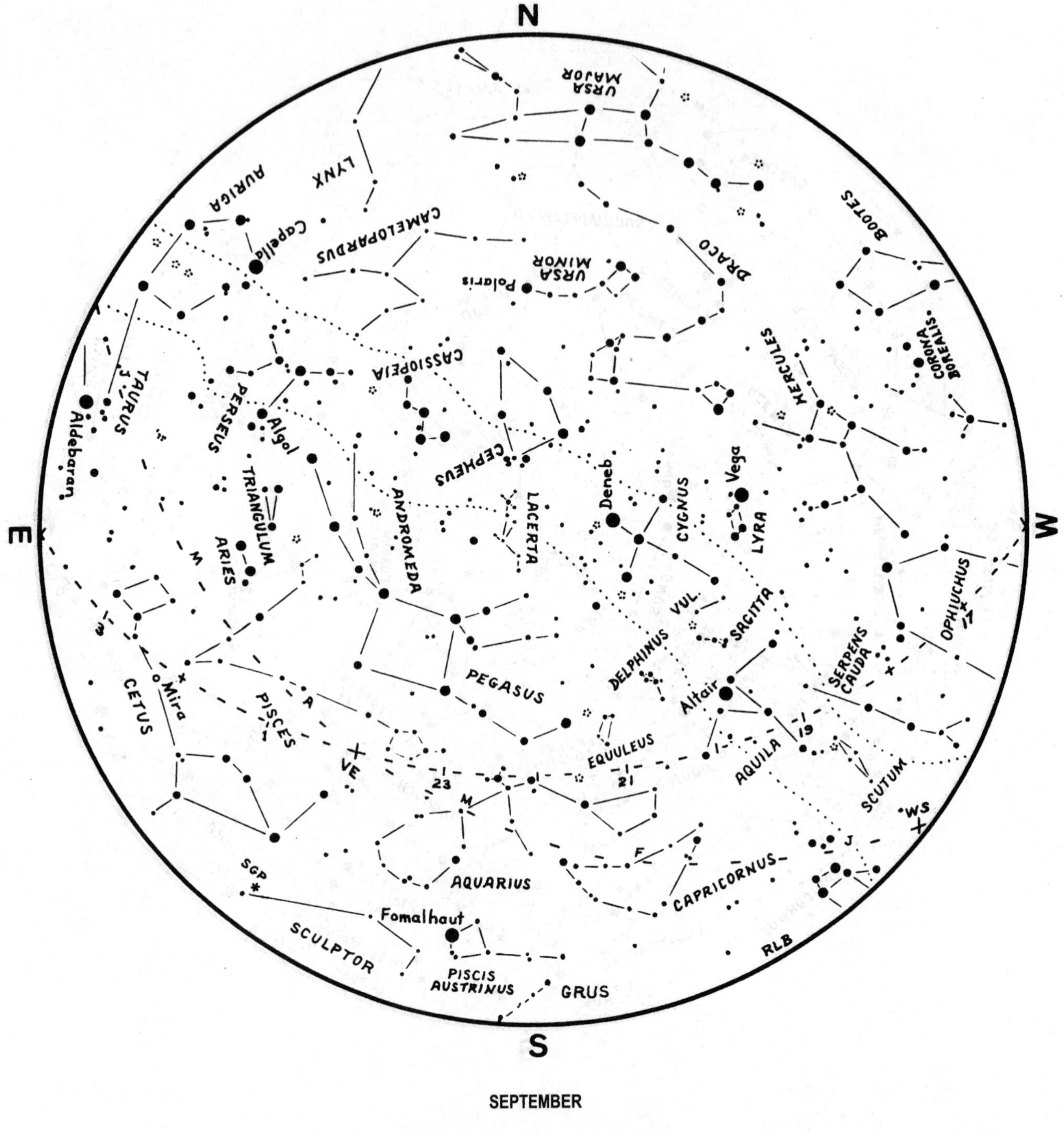

SEPTEMBER

THE NAKED EYE PLANETS IN 2012

September

MERCURY is visible with some difficulty in the mornings at the very beginning of the month, very low in the east, just before sunrise; it is again visible with considerable difficulty in the evenings by the end of the month, very low in the west, just after sunset. It passes just north of Spica on the night of the 30th.

VENUS is a brillant object in the eastern sky, rising a few hours before sunrise. It passes just south of Pollux on the 1st.

MARS, moving from Virgo to Libra, is visible, low in the south-west, just after sunset; it sets shortly afterwards.

JUPITER, in Taurus, rises shortly before midnight, and is visible high in the southern sky at sunrise.

SATURN, in Virgo, is visible, low in the south-west, just after sunset; it sets shortly afterwards.

October

MERCURY is visible with considerable difficulty in the evenings this month, very low in the south-west, just after sunset. It passes just south of Saturn on the 6th.

VENUS is a brillant object in the eastern sky, rising a few hours before sunrise. It passes just south of Regulus on the 3rd.

MARS, moving from Libra to Scorpius at the beginning of the month and into Ophiuchus by mid-month, is visible, very low in the south-west, just after sunset; it sets shortly afterwards. It passes just north of Antares on the 20th.

JUPITER, in Taurus, rises a few hours after sunset, and is visible high in the south-western sky at sunrise. It is stationary on the 4th, then moves slowly westward, against the background stars.

SATURN, in Virgo, is visible with some difficulty in the evenings until mid-month, very low in the south-west, just after sunset. It is in conjunction with the Sun on the 25th, and it passes just north of Mercury on the 6th. See also Mercury, above.

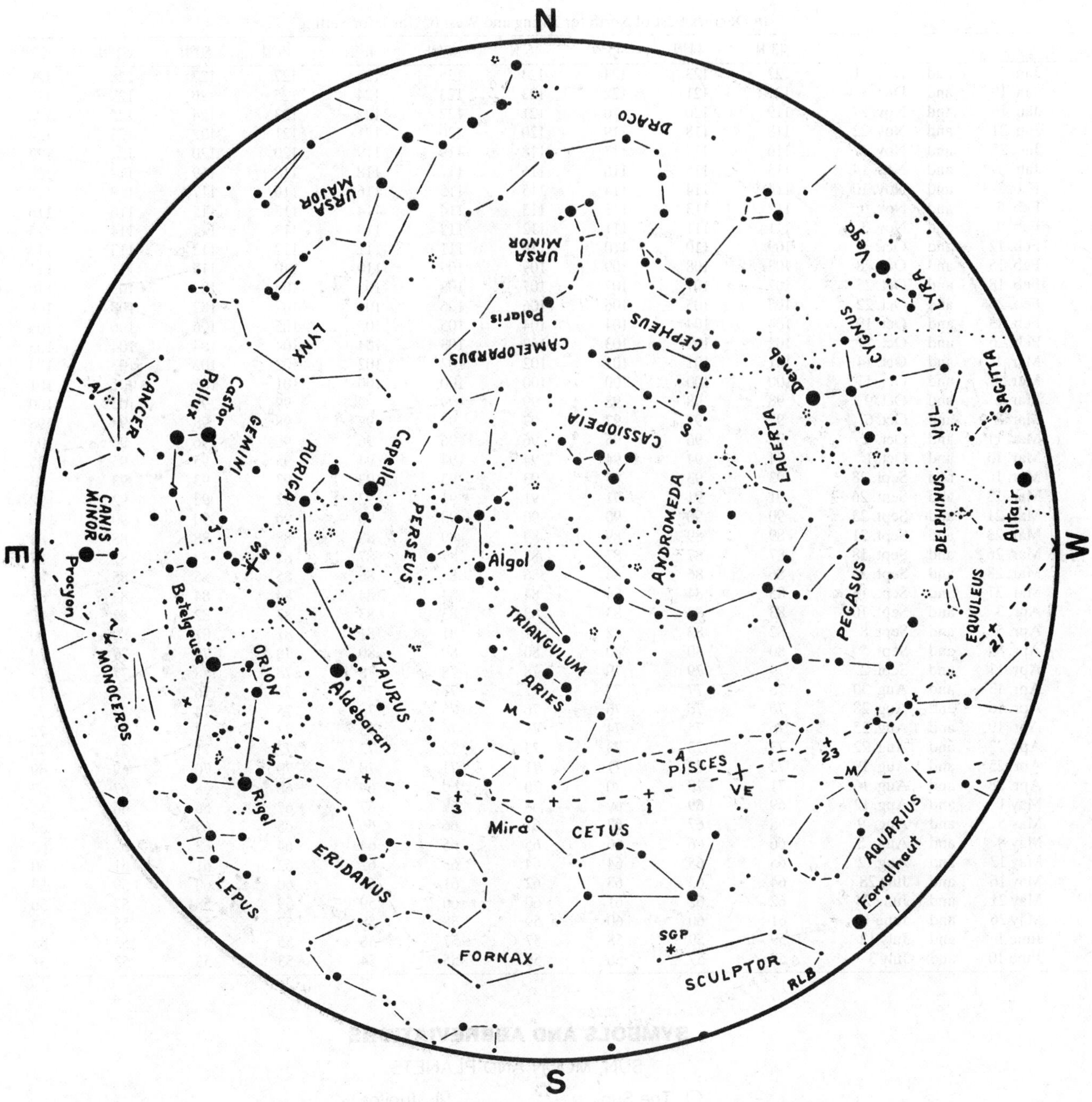

NOVEMBER

THE NAKED EYE PLANETS IN 2012

November

MERCURY is visible with considerable difficulty at the beginning of the month, very low in the south-west, just after sunset; it is again visible by the end of the month, low in the south-east, just before sunrise.

VENUS is a brilliant object in the south-eastern sky, rising shortly before sunrise. It passes just north of Spica on the 15th, and just south of Saturn on the 27th.

MARS, moving from Ophiuchus to Sagittarius, is visible, very low in the south-west, just after sunset; it sets shortly afterwards.

JUPITER, in Taurus, rises shortly after sunset, and is visible in the western sky at sunrise.

SATURN, in Virgo, is visible with some difficulty in the mornings by mid-month, very low in the south-east, just before sunrise. It passes just north of Venus on the 27th. See also Venus, above.

December

MERCURY is visible this month, low in the south-east, just before sunrise. It passes just north of Antares on the 17th.

VENUS is visible this month, low in the south-eastern sky, rising shortly before sunrise. It passes just north of Antares on the 23rd.

MARS, moving from Sagittarius to Capricornus, is visible, very low in the south-west, just after sunset; it sets shortly afterwards.

JUPITER, in Taurus, is visible in the north-eastern sky at sunset, and is visible for most of the night before setting in the north-west, just before sunset. It is at opposition with the Sun on the 3rd, and passes just north of Aldebaran on the 7th.

SATURN, moving from Virgo to Libra, rises a few hours before the Sun, and is visible in the south-eastern sky at sunrise.

AZIMUTHS OF THE POINTS OF RISING AND SETTING OF THE SUN FOR LATITUDES 43°N TO 52°N

In Degrees East of North for Rising and West of North for Setting

			43°N	44°N	45°N	46°N	47°N	48°N	49°N	50°N	51°N	52°N
Jan. 2	and	Dec. 11	122	123	124	124	125	126	127	127	128	129
Jan. 10	and	Dec. 3	121	121	122	123	123	124	125	126	127	127
Jan. 16	and	Nov. 27	119	120	120	121	122	122	123	124	125	126
Jan. 21	and	Nov. 22	118	118	119	120	120	121	121	122	123	124
Jan. 25	and	Nov. 17	116	117	117	118	119	119	120	120	121	122
Jan. 29	and	Nov. 14	115	115	116	116	117	118	118	119	119	120
Feb. 2	and	Nov. 10	114	114	114	115	115	116	116	117	118	118
Feb. 5	and	Nov. 6	112	113	113	113	114	114	115	115	116	116
Feb. 9	and	Nov. 3	111	111	111	112	112	113	113	114	114	115
Feb. 12	and	Oct. 31	109	110	110	110	111	111	112	112	113	113
Feb. 15	and	Oct. 28	108	108	109	109	109	110	110	110	111	111
Feb. 18	and	Oct. 25	107	107	107	107	108	108	108	109	109	110
Feb. 20	and	Oct. 22	105	105	106	106	106	106	107	107	108	108
Feb. 23	and	Oct. 19	104	104	104	104	105	105	105	106	106	106
Feb. 26	and	Oct. 17	102	103	103	103	103	104	104	104	104	105
Mar. 1	and	Oct. 14	101	101	101	102	102	102	102	102	103	103
Mar. 3	and	Oct. 11	100	100	100	100	100	100	101	101	101	101
Mar. 6	and	Oct. 9	98	98	98	99	99	99	99	99	100	100
Mar. 8	and	Oct. 6	97	97	97	97	97	97	98	98	98	98
Mar. 11	and	Oct. 4	95	96	96	96	96	96	96	96	96	96
Mar. 13	and	Oct. 1	94	94	94	94	94	94	95	95	95	95
Mar. 16	and	Sept. 28	93	93	93	93	93	93	93	93	93	93
Mar. 18	and	Sept. 26	91	91	91	91	91	92	92	92	92	92
Mar. 21	and	Sept. 23	90	90	90	90	90	90	90	90	90	90
Mar. 23	and	Sept. 21	89	89	89	89	89	88	88	88	88	88
Mar. 26	and	Sept. 18	87	87	87	87	87	87	87	87	87	87
Mar. 28	and	Sept. 16	86	86	86	86	86	86	85	85	85	85
Mar. 31	and	Sept. 13	85	84	84	84	84	84	84	84	84	84
Apr. 3	and	Sept. 10	83	83	83	83	83	83	82	82	82	82
Apr. 5	and	Sept. 8	82	82	82	81	81	81	81	81	80	80
Apr. 8	and	Sept. 5	80	80	80	80	80	80	79	79	79	79
Apr. 11	and	Sept. 2	79	79	79	78	78	78	78	78	77	77
Apr. 13	and	Aug. 30	78	77	77	77	77	76	76	76	76	75
Apr. 16	and	Aug. 28	76	76	76	76	75	75	75	74	74	74
Apr. 19	and	Aug. 25	75	75	74	74	74	73	73	73	72	72
Apr. 22	and	Aug. 22	73	73	73	73	72	72	72	71	71	70
Apr. 25	and	Aug. 19	72	72	71	71	71	70	70	70	69	69
Apr. 28	and	Aug. 16	71	70	70	70	69	69	68	68	67	67
May 1	and	Aug. 12	69	69	69	68	68	67	67	66	66	65
May 5	and	Aug. 9	68	67	67	67	66	66	65	65	64	63
May 8	and	Aug. 5	66	66	66	65	65	64	64	63	62	62
May 12	and	Aug. 2	65	65	64	64	63	62	62	61	61	60
May 16	and	July 28	64	63	63	62	61	61	60	60	59	58
May 21	and	June 24	62	62	61	60	60	59	59	58	57	56
May 26	and	June 19	61	60	60	59	58	58	57	56	55	54
June 1	and	July 12	59	59	58	57	57	56	55	54	53	53
June 10	and	July 3	58	57	56	56	55	54	53	53	52	51

SYMBOLS AND ABBREVIATIONS

SUN, MOON AND PLANETS

☉ The Sun	♃ Jupiter
☾ The Moon	♄ Saturn
☿ Mercury	⛢ Uranus
♀ Venus	♆ Neptune
⊕ The Earth	♇ Pluto
♂ Mars	

SIGNS OF THE ZODIAC

1. ♈ Aries	7. ♎ Libra	N. North	′ Minutes of Arc
2. ♉ Taurus	8. ♏ Scorpius	S. South	″ Seconds of Arc
3. ♊ Gemini	9. ♐ Sagittarius	E. East	h Hours
4. ♋ Cancer	10. ♑ Capricornus	W. West	m Minutes of Time
5. ♌ Leo	11. ♒ Aquarius	° Degrees	s Seconds of Time
6. ♍ Virgo	12. ♓ Pisces		

REFERENCES

The tables and charts in the Canadian Almanac are intended for simple astronomical observations. To make more extensive observations the following are recommended: The Observer's Handbook (obtainable from the Royal Astronomical Society of Canada, 136 Dupont St., Toronto, ON M5R 1V2); Astronomical Phenomena (obtainable from The Superintendent of Documents, U.S. Government Printing Office, Washington, D.C.).
See also "Suggestions for Further Reading".

AZIMUTH OF THE SUN AT RISING AND SETTING

Only twice a year, namely about March 21 and September 23, does the sun rise and set more or less exactly in the east and west respectively. It is of interest and sometimes of value to know the position of Sunrise and Sunset at other times. The table below tabulates these in degrees east of north and west of north for Sunrise and Sunset respectively for a selection of latitudes and dates. For latitudes and dates other than those tabulated take simple proportions. See table on page A-40.

SUGGESTIONS FOR FURTHER READING

There are many excellent astronomy books and materials. Here are some; the books are ones with a Canadian flavour.

Astronomical Society of the Pacific, 390 Ashton Ave., San Francisco CA USA 94112; URL: www.astrosociety.org. Excellent source of astronomical teaching resources, and other useful material; catalogue available. Also publish a free quarterly teachers' newsletter (available on-line).

Astronomy, PO Box 1612, Waukesha WI USA 53187; URL: www.astronomy.com. Popular non-technical monthly magazine for general astronomy readers.

The Backyard Astronomer's Guide, by Terence Dickinson & Alan Dyer. 2nd edition, Camden House Publishing, 2002. The best guide to equipment & techniques.

The Beginner's Observing Guide, by Leo Enright. Royal Astronomical Society of Canada, 136 Dupont St., Toronto ON M5R 1V2. A simple but serious introduction to the night sky. (5th edition: 2005-2010)

The Cold Light of Dawn, by Richard Jarrell. University of Toronto Press, 1988. An authoritative and comprehensive history of Canadian astronomy.

Exploring the Night Sky, by Terence Dickinson. Camden House Publishing, 1987. An award-winning guide, especially for young people.

Looking Up, by Peter Broughton. Dundurn Press, 1993. A history of the Royal Astronomical Society of Canada, illustrated.

Nightwatch, by Terence Dickinson. Camden House Publishing, (3rd revised edition, 1998). Excellent introduction to the night sky.

Observer's Handbook, edited by Patrick Kelly. Royal Astronomical Society of Canada, 136 Dupont St., Toronto ON M5R 1V2. Annual guide to sky phenomena & other astronomical information.

Sky Atlas 2000.0, by Wil Tirion. Sky Publishing. A popular sky atlas for amateur astronomers.

Sky & Telescope, PO Box 9111, Belmont MA USA 02178-9111; URL: skyandtelescope.com. A popular monthly magazine for amateur astronomers.

SkyNews. PO Box 1613, Belleville, ON K8N 9Z9; URL: www.skynews.ca. General astronomy from a Canadian perspective.

SkyWays, by Mary Lou Whitehorne. Royal Astronomical Society of Canada, 2003 (also available in French). A guide for Canadian schoolteachers.

Summer Stargazing, by Terence Dickinson. Firefly Books, 1996. A practical, user-friendly guide.

The Universe and Beyond, by Terence Dickinson, 4th Edition, Firefly Books, 2004. Excellent general book on Astronomy.

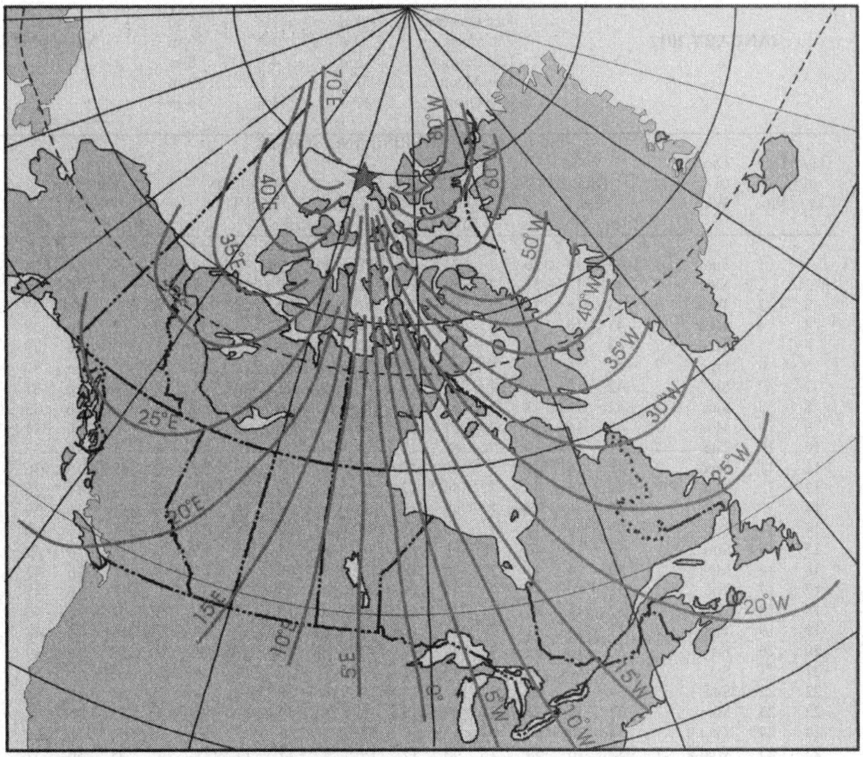

Reproduced with the permission of Natural Resources Canada 2011, courtesy of the Geological Survey of Canada.

The Universe at your Fingertips, and More Universe at Your Fingertips, edited by Andrew Fraknoi et al. Astronomical Society of the Pacific, 390 Ashton Avenue, San Francisco CA USA 94112. An excellent collection of teaching activities & resources.

The Universe on a T-Shirt, by Dan Falk, Arcade Publishing, 2005 (paperback). An excellent short introduction to our understanding of the universe.

CANADIAN ASTRONOMY WEBSITES

Most astronomical institutions and many of the branches of the Royal Astronomical Society of Canada have websites. They can be accessed from the following key sites:

- Canadian Astronomical Society: www.casca.ca
- Canadian Astronomy Education Website: www.cascaeducation.ca
- Canadian Space Agency: www.space.gc.ca
- Department of Astronomy and Astrophysics, University of Toronto: www.astro.utoronto.ca/home.html
- Herzberg Institute of Astrophysics: www.hia-iha.nrc-cnrc.gc.ca
- National Research Council Astronomy and Space Education: www.nrc-cnrc.gc.ca/education/skies/canadianskies_e.html
- Royal Astronomical Society of Canada: www.rasc.ca. Local branches of the RASC can be accessed through this site.

CHART OF MAGNETIC DECLINATION

A compass needle, even when unaffected by extraneous magnetic fields, does not in general point due north. The amount and direction by which its direction differs from true north is called magnetic declination or variation. The declination varies with the position of the observer and also varies slowly with time. The above chart gives the values of declination over Canada as of 2000. The chart is © Natural Resources Canada, and was kindly provided by Dr. Larry Newitt, National Geomagnetism Program, Geological Survey of Canada, Natural Resources Canada.

Example: What is the direction of the compass needle at the southern tip of Lake Manitoba?

That location is on the 5° east line; the declination is 5° east; the compass needle points 5° east of the true north.

For more information, see: http://gsc.nrcan.gc.ca/geomag; on the page http://geomag.nrcan.gc.ca/apps/mdcal-eng.php, you can do an online calculation of the magnetic declination for any place at any time.

NOTES ON THE ASTRONOMICAL TABLES

The purpose of the following notes is to explain the tables on pages A-42 to A-47 and to illustrate how they may be used for places other than those specified.

These tables give Standard Times of Sunrise and Sunset for Ottawa, Toronto, Winnipeg and Vancouver. When Daylight Saving Time is in effect, of course, one hour must be added to the listed times. The calculations are for the upper limb (edge) of the sun and for the astronomical (sea) horizon. Accordingly, the actual observation of Sunrise or Sunset will differ from the tabulated value if the observer is below or above the level of his visible horizon at the point of Sunrise or Sunset.

The listed times of Moonrise and Moonset have been calculated for places at the stated latitudes and for longitude 5 hours west.

To obtain the approximate times of Sunrise, Sunset, Moonrise and Moonset for other Canadian cities and towns proceed as indicated in the table on page A-48. The errors for Sunrise and Sunset by this approximate method will seldom exceed 10 minutes in winter and summer or 4 minutes in spring and fall, and for Moonrise and Moonset they will seldom exceed 15 minutes.

The tables have been calculated using a computer program written by Duy Cuong Nguyen based on modified algorithms from Astronomical Algorithms (second edition), by Jean Meeus (Willmann-Bell, 1999).

JANUARY 2012

Moon's Phases E.S.T.

First Quarter	1 d	1 h	15 m
Full Moon	9 d	2 h	30 m
Last Quarter	16 d	4 h	8 m
New Moon	23 d	2 h	39 m
First Quarter	30 d	23 h	10 m

			SUNRISE AND SUNSET								MOONRISE AND MOONSET Local Mean Time					
Day of Yr.	Day of Mo.	Day of Wk.	Ottawa E.S.T. Rises	Ottawa E.S.T. Sets	Toronto E.S.T. Rises	Toronto E.S.T. Sets	Winnipeg C.S.T. Rises	Winnipeg C.S.T. Sets	Vancouver P.S.T. Rises	Vancouver P.S.T. Sets	Lat. 45° Rises	Lat. 45° Sets	Lat. 50° Rises	Lat. 50° Sets	Day of Wk.	Day of Mo.
			h m	h m	h m	h m	h m	h m	h m	h m	h m	h m	h m	h m		
1	1	Sun	7 43	16 30	7 51	16 51	8 27	16 38	8 7	16 24	11 26	0 20	11 18	0 27	Sun	1
2	2	Mon	7 43	16 31	7 51	16 52	8 27	16 39	8 7	16 25	11 51	1 21	11 40	1 31	Mon	2
3	3	Tue	7 43	16 32	7 51	16 53	8 26	16 40	8 7	16 27	12 20	2 22	12 5	2 36	Tue	3
4	4	Wed	7 43	16 33	7 51	16 54	8 26	16 41	8 7	16 28	12 54	3 22	12 36	3 39	Wed	4
5	5	Thu	7 43	16 34	7 51	16 55	8 26	16 42	8 7	16 29	13 34	4 21	13 14	4 40	Thu	5
6	6	Fri	7 42	16 35	7 51	16 56	8 26	16 43	8 7	16 30	14 21	5 17	14 0	5 38	Fri	6
7	7	Sat	7 42	16 36	7 51	16 57	8 25	16 44	8 6	16 31	15 16	6 8	14 55	6 29	Sat	7
8	8	Sun	7 42	16 37	7 51	16 58	8 25	16 46	8 6	16 32	16 17	6 54	15 59	7 13	Sun	8
9	9	Mon	7 42	16 38	7 51	16 59	8 25	16 47	8 6	16 34	17 24	7 34	17 9	7 50	Mon	9
10	10	Tue	7 41	16 39	7 50	17 0	8 24	16 48	8 5	16 35	18 33	8 9	18 22	8 21	Tue	10
11	11	Wed	7 41	16 41	7 50	17 1	8 24	16 50	8 5	16 36	19 44	8 39	19 37	8 48	Wed	11
12	12	Thu	7 41	16 42	7 50	17 2	8 23	16 51	8 4	16 38	20 56	9 7	20 53	9 12	Thu	12
13	13	Fri	7 40	16 43	7 49	17 3	8 22	16 52	8 3	16 39	22 8	9 34	22 10	9 35	Fri	13
14	14	Sat	7 40	16 44	7 49	17 5	8 22	16 54	8 3	16 40	23 21	10 1	23 27	9 57	Sat	14
15	15	Sun	7 39	16 46	7 48	17 6	8 21	16 55	8 2	16 42	-- --	10 30	-- --	10 21	Sun	15
16	16	Mon	7 39	16 47	7 48	17 7	8 20	16 57	8 1	16 43	0 34	11 2	0 45	10 49	Mon	16
17	17	Tue	7 38	16 48	7 47	17 8	8 20	16 58	8 1	16 45	1 48	11 39	2 4	11 22	Tue	17
18	18	Wed	7 37	16 49	7 47	17 9	8 19	17 0	8 0	16 46	3 1	12 23	3 20	12 3	Wed	18
19	19	Thu	7 37	16 51	7 46	17 11	8 18	17 1	7 59	16 48	4 9	13 15	4 30	12 54	Thu	19
20	20	Fri	7 36	16 52	7 46	17 12	8 17	17 3	7 58	16 49	5 10	14 16	5 31	13 55	Fri	20
21	21	Sat	7 35	16 53	7 45	17 13	8 16	17 4	7 57	16 51	6 2	15 23	6 22	15 4	Sat	21
22	22	Sun	7 34	16 55	7 44	17 15	8 15	17 6	7 56	16 52	6 45	16 33	7 2	16 18	Sun	22
23	23	Mon	7 33	16 56	7 43	17 16	8 14	17 8	7 55	16 54	7 21	17 43	7 33	17 32	Mon	23
24	24	Tue	7 33	16 58	7 43	17 17	8 13	17 9	7 54	16 55	7 51	18 52	8 0	18 45	Tue	24
25	25	Wed	7 32	16 59	7 42	17 19	8 11	17 11	7 53	16 57	8 17	19 58	8 22	19 55	Wed	25
26	26	Thu	7 31	17 0	7 41	17 20	8 10	17 13	7 52	16 59	8 42	21 3	8 43	21 3	Thu	26
27	27	Fri	7 30	17 2	7 40	17 21	8 9	17 14	7 51	17 0	9 5	22 5	9 2	22 10	Fri	27
28	28	Sat	7 29	17 3	7 39	17 23	8 8	17 16	7 49	17 2	9 29	23 7	9 22	23 16	Sat	28
29	29	Sun	7 28	17 5	7 38	17 24	8 6	17 18	7 48	17 4	9 54	-- --	9 44	-- --	Sun	29
30	30	Mon	7 27	17 6	7 37	17 25	8 5	17 19	7 47	17 5	10 21	0 8	10 8	0 20	Mon	30
31	31	Tue	7 25	17 8	7 36	17 27	8 4	17 21	7 45	17 7	10 53	1 8	10 36	1 24	Tue	31

FEBRUARY 2012

Moon's Phases E.S.T.

Full Moon	7 d	16 h	54 m
Last Quarter	14 d	12 h	4 m
New Moon	21 d	17 h	35 m
First Quarter	29 d	20 h	21 m

			SUNRISE AND SUNSET								MOONRISE AND MOONSET Local Mean Time					
Day of Yr.	Day of Mo.	Day of Wk.	Ottawa E.S.T. Rises	Ottawa E.S.T. Sets	Toronto E.S.T. Rises	Toronto E.S.T. Sets	Winnipeg C.S.T. Rises	Winnipeg C.S.T. Sets	Vancouver P.S.T. Rises	Vancouver P.S.T. Sets	Lat. 45° Rises	Lat. 45° Sets	Lat. 50° Rises	Lat. 50° Sets	Day of Wk.	Day of Mo.
			h m	h m	h m	h m	h m	h m	h m	h m	h m	h m	h m	h m		
32	1	Wed	7 24	17 9	7 35	17 28	8 2	17 23	7 44	17 8	11 29	2 7	11 10	2 26	Wed	1
33	2	Thu	7 23	17 10	7 34	17 29	8 1	17 24	7 43	17 10	12 13	3 4	11 52	3 25	Thu	2
34	3	Fri	7 22	17 12	7 33	17 31	7 59	17 26	7 41	17 12	13 4	3 57	12 43	4 18	Fri	3
35	4	Sat	7 21	17 13	7 31	17 32	7 58	17 28	7 40	17 13	14 2	4 46	13 42	5 6	Sat	4
36	5	Sun	7 19	17 15	7 30	17 34	7 56	17 29	7 38	17 15	15 6	5 28	14 49	5 46	Sun	5
37	6	Mon	7 18	17 16	7 29	17 35	7 55	17 31	7 37	17 17	16 15	6 6	16 2	6 20	Mon	6
38	7	Tue	7 17	17 18	7 28	17 36	7 53	17 33	7 35	17 18	17 26	6 39	17 17	6 49	Tue	7
39	8	Wed	7 15	17 19	7 27	17 38	7 52	17 35	7 34	17 20	18 39	7 9	18 35	7 15	Wed	8
40	9	Thu	7 14	17 21	7 25	17 39	7 50	17 36	7 32	17 22	19 53	7 37	19 54	7 39	Thu	9
41	10	Fri	7 13	17 22	7 24	17 40	7 48	17 38	7 30	17 24	21 8	8 5	21 13	8 3	Fri	10
42	11	Sat	7 11	17 24	7 23	17 42	7 47	17 40	7 29	17 25	22 23	8 34	22 33	8 27	Sat	11
43	12	Sun	7 10	17 25	7 21	17 43	7 45	17 41	7 27	17 27	23 38	9 5	23 52	8 54	Sun	12
44	13	Mon	7 8	17 26	7 20	17 44	7 43	17 43	7 25	17 29	-- --	9 41	-- --	9 26	Mon	13
45	14	Tue	7 7	17 28	7 18	17 46	7 41	17 45	7 24	17 30	0 51	10 23	1 9	10 4	Tue	14
46	15	Wed	7 5	17 29	7 17	17 47	7 40	17 47	7 22	17 32	2 1	11 12	2 21	10 51	Wed	15
47	16	Thu	7 4	17 31	7 16	17 48	7 38	17 48	7 20	17 34	3 3	12 9	3 24	11 48	Thu	16
48	17	Fri	7 2	17 32	7 14	17 50	7 36	17 50	7 18	17 35	3 57	13 12	4 17	12 52	Fri	17
49	18	Sat	7 1	17 34	7 13	17 51	7 34	17 52	7 16	17 37	4 42	14 19	4 59	14 3	Sat	18
50	19	Sun	6 59	17 35	7 11	17 53	7 32	17 53	7 15	17 39	5 19	15 28	5 34	15 15	Sun	19
51	20	Mon	6 57	17 37	7 10	17 54	7 30	17 55	7 13	17 40	5 51	16 36	6 2	16 27	Mon	20
52	21	Tue	6 56	17 38	7 8	17 55	7 28	17 57	7 11	17 42	6 19	17 42	6 25	17 38	Tue	21
53	22	Wed	6 54	17 39	7 6	17 57	7 27	17 59	7 9	17 43	6 44	18 47	6 47	18 46	Wed	22
54	23	Thu	6 52	17 41	7 5	17 58	7 25	18 0	7 7	17 45	7 8	19 51	7 7	19 54	Thu	23
55	24	Fri	6 51	17 42	7 3	17 59	7 23	18 2	7 5	17 47	7 32	20 53	7 27	21 0	Fri	24
56	25	Sat	6 49	17 44	7 2	18 0	7 21	18 4	7 3	17 48	7 56	21 55	7 48	22 5	Sat	25
57	26	Sun	6 47	17 45	7 0	18 2	7 19	18 5	7 1	17 50	8 23	22 55	8 11	23 9	Sun	26
58	27	Mon	6 46	17 46	6 58	18 3	7 17	18 7	6 59	17 52	8 53	23 55	8 38	-- --	Mon	27
59	28	Tue	6 44	17 48	6 57	18 4	7 15	18 9	6 57	17 53	9 27	-- --	9 9	0 12	Tue	28
60	29	Wed	6 42	17 49	6 55	18 6	7 13	18 10	6 55	17 55	10 7	0 52	9 48	1 11	Wed	29

MARCH 2012

Moon's Phases E.S.T.

	d	h	m
Full Moon	8	4	39
Last Quarter	14	20	25
New Moon	22	9	37
First Quarter	30	14	41

Day of Yr.	Day of Mo.	Day of Wk.	SUNRISE AND SUNSET — Ottawa E.S.T. Rises h	m	Sets h	m	Toronto E.S.T. Rises h	m	Sets h	m	Winnipeg C.S.T. Rises h	m	Sets h	m	Vancouver P.S.T. Rises h	m	Sets h	m	MOONRISE AND MOONSET Local Mean Time — Lat. 45° Rises h	m	Sets h	m	Lat. 50° Rises h	m	Sets h	m	Day of Wk.	Day of Mo.
61	1	Thu	6	40	17	51	6	53	18	7	7	11	18	12	6	53	17	57	10	54	1	46	10	33	2	7	Thu	1
62	2	Fri	6	38	17	52	6	52	18	8	7	9	18	14	6	51	17	58	11	48	2	36	11	28	2	56	Fri	2
63	3	Sat	6	37	17	53	6	50	18	10	7	7	18	15	6	49	18	0	12	48	3	20	12	30	3	39	Sat	3
64	4	Sun	6	35	17	55	6	48	18	11	7	4	18	17	6	47	18	1	13	53	3	59	13	39	4	15	Sun	4
65	5	Mon	6	33	17	56	6	47	18	12	7	2	18	18	6	45	18	3	15	3	4	34	14	52	4	47	Mon	5
66	6	Tue	6	31	17	57	6	45	18	13	7	0	18	20	6	43	18	4	16	16	5	6	16	9	5	14	Tue	6
67	7	Wed	6	29	17	59	6	43	18	15	6	58	18	22	6	41	18	6	17	30	5	36	17	28	5	40	Wed	7
68	8	Thu	6	28	18	0	6	41	18	16	6	56	18	23	6	39	18	8	18	46	6	4	18	49	6	4	Thu	8
69	9	Fri	6	26	18	1	6	40	18	17	6	54	18	25	6	37	18	9	20	3	6	34	20	11	6	29	Fri	9
70	10	Sat	6	24	18	3	6	38	18	18	6	52	18	27	6	35	18	11	21	21	7	5	21	33	6	56	Sat	10
71	11	Sun	6	22	18	4	6	36	18	20	6	50	18	28	6	33	18	12	22	38	7	41	22	54	7	27	Sun	11
72	12	Mon	6	20	18	5	6	34	18	21	6	48	18	30	6	31	18	14	23	50	8	22	--	--	8	4	Mon	12
73	13	Tue	6	18	18	7	6	33	18	22	6	45	18	31	6	29	18	15	--	--	9	10	0	10	8	50	Tue	13
74	14	Wed	6	16	18	8	6	31	18	23	6	43	18	33	6	27	18	17	0	56	10	5	1	17	9	44	Wed	14
75	15	Thu	6	15	18	9	6	29	18	25	6	41	18	35	6	25	18	19	1	53	11	7	2	13	10	47	Thu	15
76	16	Fri	6	13	18	11	6	27	18	26	6	39	18	36	6	22	18	20	2	41	12	12	2	59	11	55	Fri	16
77	17	Sat	6	11	18	12	6	25	18	27	6	37	18	38	6	20	18	22	3	20	13	20	3	35	13	6	Sat	17
78	18	Sun	6	9	18	13	6	24	18	28	6	35	18	39	6	18	18	23	3	53	14	27	4	5	14	17	Sun	18
79	19	Mon	6	7	18	15	6	22	18	29	6	32	18	41	6	16	18	25	4	22	15	32	4	30	15	26	Mon	19
80	20	Tue	6	5	18	16	6	20	18	31	6	30	18	43	6	14	18	26	4	48	16	37	4	52	16	34	Tue	20
81	21	Wed	6	3	18	17	6	18	18	32	6	28	18	44	6	12	18	28	5	12	17	40	5	12	17	41	Wed	21
82	22	Thu	6	1	18	19	6	16	18	33	6	26	18	46	6	10	18	29	5	35	18	42	5	32	18	47	Thu	22
83	23	Fri	5	59	18	20	6	15	18	34	6	24	18	47	6	8	18	31	6	0	19	44	5	53	19	53	Fri	23
84	24	Sat	5	57	18	21	6	13	18	35	6	22	18	49	6	5	18	32	6	26	20	45	6	15	20	57	Sat	24
85	25	Sun	5	56	18	23	6	11	18	37	6	19	18	50	6	3	18	34	6	55	21	44	6	41	22	0	Sun	25
86	26	Mon	5	54	18	24	6	9	18	38	6	17	18	52	6	1	18	35	7	27	22	42	7	11	23	1	Mon	26
87	27	Tue	5	52	18	25	6	7	18	39	6	15	18	54	5	59	18	37	8	5	23	37	7	46	23	57	Tue	27
88	28	Wed	5	50	18	26	6	6	18	40	6	13	18	55	5	57	18	39	8	49	--	--	8	29	--	--	Wed	28
89	29	Thu	5	48	18	28	6	4	18	41	6	11	18	57	5	55	18	40	9	39	0	28	9	19	0	48	Thu	29
90	30	Fri	5	46	18	29	6	2	18	43	6	9	18	58	5	53	18	42	10	35	1	13	10	16	1	32	Fri	30
91	31	Sat	5	44	18	30	6	0	18	44	6	6	19	0	5	51	18	43	11	37	1	54	11	21	2	11	Sat	31

APRIL 2012

Moon's Phases E.S.T.

	d	h	m
Full Moon	6	14	19
Last Quarter	13	5	50
New Moon	21	2	18
First Quarter	29	4	57

Day of Yr.	Day of Mo.	Day of Wk.	SUNRISE AND SUNSET — Ottawa E.S.T. Rises h	m	Sets h	m	Toronto E.S.T. Rises h	m	Sets h	m	Winnipeg C.S.T. Rises h	m	Sets h	m	Vancouver P.S.T. Rises h	m	Sets h	m	MOONRISE AND MOONSET Local Mean Time — Lat. 45° Rises h	m	Sets h	m	Lat. 50° Rises h	m	Sets h	m	Day of Wk.	Day of Mo.
92	1	Sun	5	42	18	32	5	58	18	45	6	4	19	1	5	48	18	45	12	42	2	30	12	30	2	43	Sun	1
93	2	Mon	5	40	18	33	5	57	18	46	6	2	19	3	5	46	18	46	13	52	3	2	13	43	3	12	Mon	2
94	3	Tue	5	39	18	34	5	55	18	47	6	0	19	5	5	44	18	48	15	4	3	32	14	59	3	38	Tue	3
95	4	Wed	5	37	18	35	5	53	18	49	5	58	19	6	5	42	18	49	16	18	4	1	16	18	4	3	Wed	4
96	5	Thu	5	35	18	37	5	51	18	50	5	56	19	8	5	40	18	51	17	35	4	30	17	40	4	27	Thu	5
97	6	Fri	5	33	18	38	5	50	18	51	5	54	19	9	5	38	18	52	18	54	5	1	19	3	4	54	Fri	6
98	7	Sat	5	31	18	39	5	48	18	52	5	51	19	11	5	36	18	54	20	13	5	35	20	27	5	24	Sat	7
99	8	Sun	5	29	18	41	5	46	18	53	5	49	19	12	5	34	18	55	21	30	6	15	21	48	5	59	Sun	8
100	9	Mon	5	27	18	42	5	44	18	55	5	47	19	14	5	32	18	57	22	42	7	1	23	2	6	43	Mon	9
101	10	Tue	5	26	18	43	5	43	18	56	5	45	19	15	5	30	18	58	23	45	7	56	0	5	7	36	Tue	10
102	11	Wed	5	24	18	44	5	41	18	57	5	43	19	17	5	28	19	0	--	--	8	58	0	5	8	38	Wed	11
103	12	Thu	5	22	18	46	5	39	18	58	5	41	19	19	5	26	19	1	0	37	10	4	0	56	9	46	Thu	12
104	13	Fri	5	20	18	47	5	37	18	59	5	39	19	20	5	24	19	3	1	20	11	12	1	36	10	57	Fri	13
105	14	Sat	5	18	18	48	5	36	19	1	5	37	19	22	5	22	19	4	1	55	12	20	2	8	12	9	Sat	14
106	15	Sun	5	17	18	50	5	34	19	2	5	35	19	23	5	20	19	6	2	25	13	26	2	34	13	18	Sun	15
107	16	Mon	5	15	18	51	5	32	19	3	5	33	19	25	5	18	19	7	2	52	14	30	2	57	14	27	Mon	16
108	17	Tue	5	13	18	52	5	31	19	4	5	31	19	26	5	16	19	9	3	16	15	33	3	18	15	33	Tue	17
109	18	Wed	5	12	18	53	5	29	19	5	5	29	19	28	5	14	19	10	3	40	16	34	3	38	16	39	Wed	18
110	19	Thu	5	10	18	55	5	28	19	7	5	27	19	29	5	12	19	12	4	4	17	36	3	58	17	44	Thu	19
111	20	Fri	5	8	18	56	5	26	19	8	5	25	19	31	5	10	19	13	4	29	18	36	4	20	18	48	Fri	20
112	21	Sat	5	6	18	57	5	24	19	9	5	23	19	33	5	8	19	15	4	57	19	36	4	45	19	51	Sat	21
113	22	Sun	5	5	18	59	5	23	19	10	5	21	19	34	5	6	19	16	5	29	20	35	5	13	20	52	Sun	22
114	23	Mon	5	3	19	0	5	21	19	11	5	19	19	36	5	4	19	18	6	5	21	31	5	47	21	50	Mon	23
115	24	Tue	5	1	19	1	5	20	19	13	5	17	19	37	5	2	19	19	6	47	22	23	6	27	22	43	Tue	24
116	25	Wed	5	0	19	2	5	18	19	14	5	15	19	39	5	1	19	21	7	34	23	10	7	14	23	29	Wed	25
117	26	Thu	4	58	19	4	5	17	19	15	5	13	19	40	4	59	19	22	8	28	23	51	8	9	--	--	Thu	26
118	27	Fri	4	57	19	5	5	15	19	16	5	12	19	42	4	57	19	24	9	27	--	--	9	10	0	9	Fri	27
119	28	Sat	4	55	19	6	5	14	19	17	5	10	19	43	4	55	19	25	10	29	0	28	10	15	0	43	Sat	28
120	29	Sun	4	54	19	8	5	12	19	18	5	8	19	45	4	53	19	27	11	35	1	1	11	25	1	12	Sun	29
121	30	Mon	4	52	19	9	5	11	19	20	5	6	19	46	4	52	19	28	12	43	1	30	12	37	1	38	Mon	30

MAY 2012

Moon's Phases E.S.T.

Full Moon........	5 d	22 h	35 m
Last Quarter......	12 d	16 h	47 m
New Moon.......	20 d	18 h	47 m
First Quarter......	28 d	15 h	16 m

Day of Yr.	Day of Mo.	Day of Wk.	SUNRISE AND SUNSET: Ottawa E.S.T. Rises		Ottawa Sets		Toronto E.S.T. Rises		Toronto Sets		Winnipeg C.S.T. Rises		Winnipeg Sets		Vancouver P.S.T. Rises		Vancouver Sets		MOONRISE AND MOONSET Local Mean Time: Lat. 45° Rises		Lat. 45° Sets		Lat. 50° Rises		Lat. 50° Sets		Day of Wk.	Day of Mo.
			h	*m*	*h*	*m*	*h*	*m*	*h*	*m*	*h*	*m*	*h*	*m*	*h*	*m*	*h*	*m*	*h*	*m*	*h*	*m*	*h*	*m*	*h*	*m*		
122	1	Tue	4	51	19	10	5	9	19	21	5	4	19	48	4	50	19	30	13	54	1	59	13	52	2	2	Tue	1
123	2	Wed	4	49	19	11	5	8	19	22	5	3	19	49	4	48	19	31	15	8	2	26	15	10	2	26	Wed	2
124	3	Thu	4	48	19	13	5	7	19	23	5	1	19	51	4	47	19	33	16	24	2	56	16	31	2	51	Thu	3
125	4	Fri	4	46	19	14	5	5	19	24	4	59	19	53	4	45	19	34	17	42	3	28	17	54	3	19	Fri	4
126	5	Sat	4	45	19	15	5	4	19	25	4	58	19	54	4	43	19	36	19	2	4	4	19	18	3	51	Sat	5
127	6	Sun	4	43	19	16	5	3	19	27	4	56	19	56	4	42	19	37	20	18	4	48	20	37	4	31	Sun	6
128	7	Mon	4	42	19	18	5	1	19	28	4	54	19	57	4	40	19	39	21	27	5	40	21	48	5	20	Mon	7
129	8	Tue	4	41	19	19	5	0	19	29	4	53	19	58	4	39	19	40	22	26	6	41	22	46	6	20	Tue	8
130	9	Wed	4	39	19	20	4	59	19	30	4	51	20	0	4	37	19	41	23	15	7	48	23	32	7	29	Wed	9
131	10	Thu	4	38	19	21	4	58	19	31	4	50	20	1	4	36	19	43	23	54	8	58	--	--	8	42	Thu	10
132	11	Fri	4	37	19	22	4	56	19	32	4	48	20	3	4	34	19	44	--	--	10	8	0	8	9	56	Fri	11
133	12	Sat	4	36	19	24	4	55	19	33	4	47	20	4	4	33	19	46	0	27	11	16	0	37	11	8	Sat	12
134	13	Sun	4	34	19	25	4	54	19	35	4	45	20	6	4	31	19	47	0	55	12	22	1	1	12	18	Sun	13
135	14	Mon	4	33	19	26	4	53	19	36	4	44	20	7	4	30	19	48	1	21	13	26	1	23	13	25	Mon	14
136	15	Tue	4	32	19	27	4	52	19	37	4	42	20	8	4	29	19	50	1	45	14	28	1	43	14	31	Tue	15
137	16	Wed	4	31	19	28	4	51	19	38	4	41	20	10	4	27	19	51	2	8	15	29	2	4	15	36	Wed	16
138	17	Thu	4	30	19	29	4	50	19	39	4	40	20	11	4	26	19	52	2	33	16	30	2	25	16	40	Thu	17
139	18	Fri	4	29	19	31	4	49	19	40	4	38	20	13	4	25	19	54	3	0	17	30	2	49	17	43	Fri	18
140	19	Sat	4	28	19	32	4	48	19	41	4	37	20	14	4	24	19	55	3	30	18	29	3	16	18	45	Sat	19
141	20	Sun	4	27	19	33	4	47	19	42	4	36	20	15	4	22	19	56	4	5	19	26	3	48	19	44	Sun	20
142	21	Mon	4	26	19	34	4	46	19	43	4	35	20	17	4	21	19	58	4	45	20	19	4	26	20	39	Mon	21
143	22	Tue	4	25	19	35	4	45	19	44	4	34	20	18	4	20	19	59	5	31	21	8	5	11	21	27	Tue	22
144	23	Wed	4	24	19	36	4	44	19	45	4	33	20	19	4	19	20	0	6	23	21	51	6	4	22	9	Wed	23
145	24	Thu	4	23	19	37	4	44	19	46	4	32	20	20	4	18	20	1	7	20	22	29	7	3	22	45	Thu	24
146	25	Fri	4	22	19	38	4	43	19	47	4	31	20	21	4	17	20	2	8	21	23	3	8	7	23	15	Fri	25
147	26	Sat	4	22	19	39	4	42	19	48	4	30	20	23	4	16	20	4	9	25	23	33	9	14	23	42	Sat	26
148	27	Sun	4	21	19	40	4	42	19	49	4	29	20	24	4	15	20	5	10	31	24	0	10	24	--	--	Sun	27
149	28	Mon	4	20	19	41	4	41	19	50	4	28	20	25	4	14	20	6	11	39	0	0	11	36	0	6	Mon	28
150	29	Tue	4	19	19	42	4	40	19	50	4	27	20	26	4	14	20	7	12	49	0	27	12	50	0	29	Tue	29
151	30	Wed	4	19	19	43	4	40	19	51	4	26	20	27	4	13	20	8	14	1	0	55	14	7	0	52	Wed	30
152	31	Thu	4	18	19	44	4	39	19	52	4	25	20	28	4	12	20	9	15	16	1	24	15	26	1	17	Thu	31

JUNE 2012

Moon's Phases E.S.T.

Full Moon........	4 d	6 h	12 m
Last Quarter......	11 d	5 h	41 m
New Moon.......	19 d	10 h	2 m
First Quarter......	26 d	22 h	30 m

Day of Yr.	Day of Mo.	Day of Wk.	SUNRISE AND SUNSET: Ottawa E.S.T. Rises		Ottawa Sets		Toronto E.S.T. Rises		Toronto Sets		Winnipeg C.S.T. Rises		Winnipeg Sets		Vancouver P.S.T. Rises		Vancouver Sets		MOONRISE AND MOONSET Local Mean Time: Lat. 45° Rises		Lat. 45° Sets		Lat. 50° Rises		Lat. 50° Sets		Day of Wk.	Day of Mo.
			h	*m*	*h*	*m*	*h*	*m*	*h*	*m*	*h*	*m*	*h*	*m*	*h*	*m*	*h*	*m*	*h*	*m*	*h*	*m*	*h*	*m*	*h*	*m*		
153	1	Fri	4	18	19	44	4	39	19	53	4	25	20	29	4	11	20	10	16	33	1	57	16	47	1	46	Fri	1
154	2	Sat	4	17	19	45	4	38	19	54	4	24	20	30	4	11	20	11	17	50	2	36	18	8	2	21	Sat	2
155	3	Sun	4	17	19	46	4	38	19	54	4	23	20	31	4	10	20	12	19	3	3	23	19	24	3	5	Sun	3
156	4	Mon	4	16	19	47	4	37	19	55	4	23	20	32	4	10	20	13	20	9	4	19	20	29	3	59	Mon	4
157	5	Tue	4	16	19	48	4	37	19	56	4	22	20	33	4	9	20	13	21	4	5	24	21	22	5	4	Tue	5
158	6	Wed	4	15	19	48	4	37	19	57	4	22	20	34	4	9	20	14	21	49	6	35	22	4	6	17	Wed	6
159	7	Thu	4	15	19	49	4	36	19	57	4	21	20	34	4	8	20	15	22	25	7	48	22	37	7	34	Thu	7
160	8	Fri	4	15	19	50	4	36	19	58	4	21	20	35	4	8	20	16	22	56	8	59	23	4	8	49	Fri	8
161	9	Sat	4	14	19	50	4	36	19	58	4	21	20	36	4	7	20	16	23	23	10	8	23	27	10	2	Sat	9
162	10	Sun	4	14	19	51	4	36	19	59	4	20	20	37	4	7	20	17	23	48	11	14	23	49	11	12	Sun	10
163	11	Mon	4	14	19	51	4	36	20	0	4	20	20	37	4	7	20	18	--	--	12	18	--	--	12	20	Mon	11
164	12	Tue	4	14	19	52	4	35	20	0	4	20	20	38	4	7	20	18	0	13	13	20	0	9	13	26	Tue	12
165	13	Wed	4	14	19	52	4	35	20	1	4	20	20	38	4	7	20	19	0	37	14	22	0	30	14	31	Wed	13
166	14	Thu	4	14	19	53	4	35	20	1	4	20	20	39	4	7	20	19	1	3	15	22	0	53	15	35	Thu	14
167	15	Fri	4	14	19	53	4	35	20	1	4	19	20	39	4	6	20	20	1	32	16	21	1	19	16	37	Fri	15
168	16	Sat	4	14	19	54	4	35	20	2	4	19	20	40	4	6	20	20	2	5	17	19	1	49	17	37	Sat	16
169	17	Sun	4	14	19	54	4	35	20	2	4	19	20	40	4	7	20	21	2	43	18	14	2	25	18	34	Sun	17
170	18	Mon	4	14	19	54	4	36	20	2	4	20	20	40	4	7	20	21	3	28	19	5	3	8	19	25	Mon	18
171	19	Tue	4	14	19	55	4	36	20	3	4	20	20	41	4	7	20	21	4	18	19	50	3	58	20	9	Tue	19
172	20	Wed	4	14	19	55	4	36	20	3	4	20	20	41	4	7	20	21	5	14	20	30	4	55	20	47	Wed	20
173	21	Thu	4	15	19	55	4	36	20	3	4	20	20	41	4	7	20	22	6	14	21	6	5	59	21	19	Thu	21
174	22	Fri	4	15	19	55	4	36	20	3	4	20	20	41	4	7	20	22	7	18	21	37	7	6	21	47	Fri	22
175	23	Sat	4	15	19	55	4	37	20	3	4	21	20	41	4	8	20	22	8	24	22	5	8	15	22	12	Sat	23
176	24	Sun	4	15	19	55	4	37	20	3	4	21	20	41	4	8	20	22	9	31	22	32	9	26	22	35	Sun	24
177	25	Mon	4	16	19	55	4	37	20	4	4	21	20	41	4	8	20	22	10	39	22	59	10	38	22	57	Mon	25
178	26	Tue	4	16	19	55	4	38	20	4	4	22	20	41	4	9	20	22	11	48	23	26	11	52	23	21	Tue	26
179	27	Wed	4	17	19	55	4	38	20	4	4	22	20	41	4	9	20	22	13	0	23	57	13	8	23	47	Wed	27
180	28	Thu	4	17	19	55	4	39	20	3	4	23	20	41	4	10	20	22	14	14	--	--	14	26	--	--	Thu	28
181	29	Fri	4	18	19	55	4	39	20	3	4	23	20	41	4	10	20	21	15	28	0	32	15	45	0	18	Fri	29
182	30	Sat	4	18	19	55	4	40	20	3	4	24	20	41	4	11	20	21	16	41	1	13	17	1	0	56	Sat	30

JULY 2012

Moon's Phases E.S.T.	d	h	m
Full Moon	3 d	13 h	52 m
Last Quarter	10 d	20 h	48 m
New Moon	18 d	23 h	24 m
First Quarter	26 d	3 h	56 m

Day of Yr.	Day of Mo.	Day of Wk.	Ottawa E.S.T. Rises h	m	Sets h	m	Toronto E.S.T. Rises h	m	Sets h	m	Winnipeg C.S.T. Rises h	m	Sets h	m	Vancouver P.S.T. Rises h	m	Sets h	m	Moon Lat. 45° Rises h	m	Sets h	m	Moon Lat. 50° Rises h	m	Sets h	m	Day of Wk.	Day of Mo.
183	1	Sun	4	19	19	55	4	40	20	3	4	25	20	40	4	12	20	21	17	49	2	3	18	10	1	44	Sun	1
184	2	Mon	4	19	19	55	4	41	20	3	4	25	20	40	4	12	20	20	18	49	3	3	19	9	2	43	Mon	2
185	3	Tue	4	20	19	54	4	41	20	3	4	26	20	40	4	13	20	20	19	39	4	11	19	56	3	51	Tue	3
186	4	Wed	4	21	19	54	4	42	20	2	4	27	20	39	4	14	20	20	20	20	5	23	20	34	5	7	Wed	4
187	5	Thu	4	21	19	54	4	42	20	2	4	28	20	39	4	15	20	19	20	55	6	36	21	4	6	24	Thu	5
188	6	Fri	4	22	19	53	4	43	20	2	4	28	20	38	4	15	20	19	21	24	7	48	21	30	7	40	Fri	6
189	7	Sat	4	23	19	53	4	44	20	1	4	29	20	38	4	16	20	18	21	51	8	57	21	52	8	53	Sat	7
190	8	Sun	4	23	19	52	4	45	20	1	4	30	20	37	4	17	20	18	22	16	10	3	22	14	10	4	Sun	8
191	9	Mon	4	24	19	52	4	45	20	0	4	31	20	36	4	18	20	17	22	41	11	8	22	35	11	12	Mon	9
192	10	Tue	4	25	19	51	4	46	20	0	4	32	20	36	4	19	20	16	23	6	12	10	22	57	12	18	Tue	10
193	11	Wed	4	26	19	51	4	47	19	59	4	33	20	35	4	20	20	15	23	34	13	11	23	22	13	23	Wed	11
194	12	Thu	4	27	19	50	4	48	19	59	4	34	20	34	4	21	20	15	--	--	14	12	23	50	14	26	Thu	12
195	13	Fri	4	28	19	49	4	48	19	58	4	35	20	33	4	22	20	14	0	6	15	10	--	--	15	27	Fri	13
196	14	Sat	4	28	19	49	4	49	19	57	4	36	20	32	4	23	20	13	0	42	16	6	0	24	16	25	Sat	14
197	15	Sun	4	29	19	48	4	50	19	57	4	37	20	31	4	24	20	12	1	23	16	59	1	4	17	19	Sun	15
198	16	Mon	4	30	19	47	4	51	19	56	4	38	20	30	4	25	20	11	2	11	17	46	1	51	18	6	Mon	16
199	17	Tue	4	31	19	46	4	52	19	55	4	40	20	29	4	26	20	10	3	5	18	29	2	46	18	47	Tue	17
200	18	Wed	4	32	19	45	4	53	19	54	4	41	20	28	4	27	20	9	4	5	19	6	3	48	19	21	Wed	18
201	19	Thu	4	33	19	44	4	54	19	54	4	42	20	27	4	29	20	8	5	8	19	40	4	55	19	51	Thu	19
202	20	Fri	4	34	19	44	4	55	19	53	4	43	20	26	4	30	20	7	6	14	20	9	6	4	20	17	Fri	20
203	21	Sat	4	35	19	43	4	56	19	52	4	45	20	25	4	31	20	6	7	22	20	37	7	15	20	41	Sat	21
204	22	Sun	4	36	19	42	4	57	19	51	4	46	20	24	4	32	20	5	8	30	21	4	8	28	21	4	Sun	22
205	23	Mon	4	37	19	41	4	58	19	50	4	47	20	22	4	34	20	4	9	40	21	31	9	42	21	27	Mon	23
206	24	Tue	4	39	19	40	4	59	19	49	4	48	20	21	4	35	20	2	10	51	22	1	10	57	21	53	Tue	24
207	25	Wed	4	40	19	38	5	0	19	48	4	50	20	20	4	36	20	1	12	3	22	33	12	13	22	21	Wed	25
208	26	Thu	4	41	19	37	5	1	19	47	4	51	20	19	4	37	20	0	13	15	23	11	13	30	22	56	Thu	26
209	27	Fri	4	42	19	36	5	2	19	46	4	52	20	17	4	39	19	58	14	27	23	57	14	45	23	38	Fri	27
210	28	Sat	4	43	19	35	5	3	19	45	4	54	20	16	4	40	19	57	15	35	--	--	15	55	--	--	Sat	28
211	29	Sun	4	44	19	34	5	4	19	44	4	55	20	14	4	41	19	56	16	36	0	51	16	57	0	30	Sun	29
212	30	Mon	4	45	19	33	5	5	19	42	4	56	20	13	4	43	19	54	17	29	1	53	17	48	1	33	Mon	30
213	31	Tue	4	46	19	31	5	6	19	41	4	58	20	11	4	44	19	53	18	14	3	2	18	29	2	44	Tue	31

AUGUST 2012

Moon's Phases E.S.T.	d	h	m
Full Moon	1 d	22 h	27 m
Last Quarter	9 d	13 h	55 m
New Moon	17 d	10 h	54 m
First Quarter	24 d	8 h	54 m
Full Moon	31 d	8 h	58 m

Day of Yr.	Day of Mo.	Day of Wk.	Ottawa E.S.T. Rises h	m	Sets h	m	Toronto E.S.T. Rises h	m	Sets h	m	Winnipeg C.S.T. Rises h	m	Sets h	m	Vancouver P.S.T. Rises h	m	Sets h	m	Moon Lat. 45° Rises h	m	Sets h	m	Moon Lat. 50° Rises h	m	Sets h	m	Day of Wk.	Day of Mo.
214	1	Wed	4	48	19	30	5	7	19	40	4	59	20	10	4	45	19	51	18	51	4	14	19	3	4	0	Wed	1
215	2	Thu	4	49	19	29	5	8	19	39	5	1	20	8	4	47	19	50	19	23	5	26	19	31	5	16	Thu	2
216	3	Fri	4	50	19	27	5	9	19	38	5	2	20	7	4	48	19	48	19	51	6	37	19	55	6	31	Fri	3
217	4	Sat	4	51	19	26	5	10	19	36	5	3	20	5	4	49	19	46	20	17	7	45	20	17	7	43	Sat	4
218	5	Sun	4	52	19	25	5	11	19	35	5	5	20	3	4	51	19	45	20	43	8	51	20	39	8	53	Sun	5
219	6	Mon	4	53	19	23	5	13	19	34	5	6	20	2	4	52	19	43	21	9	9	55	21	1	10	1	Mon	6
220	7	Tue	4	55	19	22	5	14	19	32	5	8	20	0	4	54	19	42	21	36	10	58	21	25	11	8	Tue	7
221	8	Wed	4	56	19	20	5	15	19	31	5	9	19	58	4	55	19	40	22	6	11	59	21	52	12	12	Wed	8
222	9	Thu	4	57	19	19	5	16	19	29	5	11	19	56	4	56	19	38	22	40	12	59	22	24	13	15	Thu	9
223	10	Fri	4	58	19	17	5	17	19	28	5	12	19	55	4	58	19	36	23	20	13	56	23	1	14	14	Fri	10
224	11	Sat	4	59	19	16	5	18	19	27	5	14	19	53	4	59	19	35	--	--	14	50	23	45	15	9	Sat	11
225	12	Sun	5	1	19	14	5	19	19	25	5	15	19	51	5	1	19	33	0	5	15	39	--	--	15	59	Sun	12
226	13	Mon	5	2	19	13	5	20	19	24	5	17	19	49	5	2	19	31	0	56	16	24	0	36	16	42	Mon	13
227	14	Tue	5	3	19	11	5	22	19	22	5	18	19	47	5	4	19	29	1	53	17	4	1	35	17	20	Tue	14
228	15	Wed	5	4	19	9	5	23	19	21	5	19	19	46	5	5	19	27	2	55	17	39	2	40	17	52	Wed	15
229	16	Thu	5	5	19	8	5	24	19	19	5	21	19	44	5	6	19	26	4	0	18	11	3	49	18	20	Thu	16
230	17	Fri	5	7	19	6	5	25	19	17	5	22	19	42	5	8	19	24	5	8	18	40	5	0	18	45	Fri	17
231	18	Sat	5	8	19	4	5	26	19	16	5	24	19	40	5	9	19	22	6	17	19	8	6	14	19	9	Sat	18
232	19	Sun	5	9	19	3	5	27	19	14	5	25	19	38	5	11	19	20	7	28	19	36	7	28	19	33	Sun	19
233	20	Mon	5	10	19	1	5	28	19	13	5	27	19	36	5	12	19	18	8	40	20	5	8	45	19	58	Mon	20
234	21	Tue	5	12	18	59	5	29	19	11	5	28	19	34	5	14	19	16	9	52	20	37	10	2	20	26	Tue	21
235	22	Wed	5	13	18	58	5	31	19	9	5	30	19	32	5	15	19	14	11	6	21	14	11	19	20	59	Wed	22
236	23	Thu	5	14	18	56	5	32	19	8	5	31	19	30	5	17	19	12	12	18	21	56	12	34	21	39	Thu	23
237	24	Fri	5	15	18	54	5	33	19	6	5	33	19	28	5	18	19	10	13	26	22	47	13	45	22	27	Fri	24
238	25	Sat	5	16	18	52	5	34	19	4	5	34	19	26	5	19	19	8	14	29	23	45	14	49	23	25	Sat	25
239	26	Sun	5	18	18	51	5	35	19	3	5	36	19	24	5	21	19	6	15	23	--	--	15	42	--	--	Sun	26
240	27	Mon	5	19	18	49	5	36	19	1	5	37	19	22	5	22	19	4	16	10	0	50	16	26	0	31	Mon	27
241	28	Tue	5	20	18	47	5	37	18	59	5	39	19	20	5	24	19	2	16	49	1	59	17	2	1	43	Tue	28
242	29	Wed	5	21	18	45	5	38	18	58	5	40	19	18	5	25	19	0	17	22	3	9	17	32	2	57	Wed	29
243	30	Thu	5	22	18	43	5	40	18	56	5	42	19	15	5	27	18	58	17	52	4	19	17	57	4	11	Thu	30
244	31	Fri	5	24	18	41	5	41	18	54	5	43	19	13	5	28	18	56	18	19	5	28	18	20	5	24	Fri	31

SEPTEMBER 2012

Moon's Phases E.S.T.

Last Quarter......	8 d	8 h	15 m
New Moon.......	15 d	21 h	11 m
First Quarter......	22 d	14 h	41 m
Full Moon.......	29 d	22 h	19 m

Day of Yr.	Day of Mo.	Day of Wk.	SUNRISE AND SUNSET Ottawa E.S.T. Rises h	m	Sets h	m	Toronto E.S.T. Rises h	m	Sets h	m	Winnipeg C.S.T. Rises h	m	Sets h	m	Vancouver P.S.T. Rises h	m	Sets h	m	MOONRISE AND MOONSET Local Mean Time Lat. 45° Rises h	m	Sets h	m	Lat. 50° Rises h	m	Sets h	m	Day of Wk.	Day of Mo.
245	1	Sat	5	25	18	40	5	42	18	52	5	45	19	11	5	29	18	54	18	45	6	34	18	42	6	35	Sat	1
246	2	Sun	5	26	18	38	5	43	18	51	5	46	19	9	5	31	18	52	19	11	7	39	19	5	7	44	Sun	2
247	3	Mon	5	27	18	36	5	44	18	49	5	48	19	7	5	32	18	50	19	38	8	43	19	28	8	51	Mon	3
248	4	Tue	5	29	18	34	5	45	18	47	5	49	19	5	5	34	18	48	20	7	9	45	19	54	9	57	Tue	4
249	5	Wed	5	30	18	32	5	46	18	45	5	51	19	3	5	35	18	45	20	40	10	46	20	24	11	1	Wed	5
250	6	Thu	5	31	18	30	5	47	18	43	5	52	19	0	5	37	18	43	21	17	11	44	20	59	12	1	Thu	6
251	7	Fri	5	32	18	28	5	48	18	42	5	54	18	58	5	38	18	41	21	59	12	39	21	40	12	58	Fri	7
252	8	Sat	5	33	18	26	5	50	18	40	5	55	18	56	5	40	18	39	22	47	13	30	22	28	13	50	Sat	8
253	9	Sun	5	35	18	25	5	51	18	38	5	57	18	54	5	41	18	37	23	41	14	17	23	23	14	35	Sun	9
254	10	Mon	5	36	18	23	5	52	18	36	5	58	18	52	5	42	18	35	--	--	14	58	--	--	15	15	Mon	10
255	11	Tue	5	37	18	21	5	53	18	34	5	59	18	50	5	44	18	33	0	40	15	35	0	24	15	49	Tue	11
256	12	Wed	5	38	18	19	5	54	18	33	6	1	18	47	5	45	18	31	1	43	16	8	1	30	16	19	Wed	12
257	13	Thu	5	39	18	17	5	55	18	31	6	2	18	45	5	47	18	28	2	50	16	38	2	40	16	46	Thu	13
258	14	Fri	5	41	18	15	5	56	18	29	6	4	18	43	5	48	18	26	3	58	17	7	3	53	17	11	Fri	14
259	15	Sat	5	42	18	13	5	57	18	27	6	5	18	41	5	50	18	24	5	9	17	36	5	8	17	35	Sat	15
260	16	Sun	5	43	18	11	5	59	18	25	6	7	18	39	5	51	18	22	6	22	18	6	6	25	18	1	Sun	16
261	17	Mon	5	44	18	9	6	0	18	23	6	8	18	36	5	53	18	20	7	36	18	38	7	43	18	29	Mon	17
262	18	Tue	5	46	18	7	6	1	18	22	6	10	18	34	5	54	18	18	8	51	19	14	9	3	19	1	Tue	18
263	19	Wed	5	47	18	5	6	2	18	20	6	11	18	32	5	55	18	15	10	6	19	55	10	21	19	39	Wed	19
264	20	Thu	5	48	18	3	6	3	18	18	6	13	18	30	5	57	18	13	11	17	20	44	11	35	20	25	Thu	20
265	21	Fri	5	49	18	1	6	4	18	16	6	14	18	28	5	58	18	11	12	22	21	41	12	42	21	21	Fri	21
266	22	Sat	5	50	17	59	6	5	18	14	6	16	18	25	6	0	18	9	13	19	22	44	13	39	22	25	Sat	22
267	23	Sun	5	52	17	58	6	7	18	12	6	17	18	23	6	1	18	7	14	8	23	51	14	25	23	34	Sun	23
268	24	Mon	5	53	17	56	6	8	18	10	6	19	18	21	6	3	18	5	14	49	--	--	15	3	--	--	Mon	24
269	25	Tue	5	54	17	54	6	9	18	9	6	20	18	19	6	4	18	3	15	23	0	59	15	34	0	47	Tue	25
270	26	Wed	5	55	17	52	6	10	18	7	6	22	18	17	6	6	18	0	15	54	2	8	16	0	1	59	Wed	26
271	27	Thu	5	57	17	50	6	11	18	5	6	23	18	15	6	7	17	58	16	21	3	15	16	24	3	10	Thu	27
272	28	Fri	5	58	17	48	6	12	18	3	6	25	18	12	6	9	17	56	16	47	4	22	16	46	4	20	Fri	28
273	29	Sat	5	59	17	46	6	13	18	1	6	26	18	10	6	10	17	54	17	13	5	26	17	8	5	29	Sat	29
274	30	Sun	6	0	17	44	6	15	18	0	6	28	18	8	6	11	17	52	17	39	6	30	17	32	6	37	Sun	30

OCTOBER 2012

Moon's Phases E.S.T.

Last Quarter......	8 d	2 h	33 m
New Moon.......	15 d	7 h	3 m
First Quarter......	21 d	22 h	32 m
Full Moon........	29 d	14 h	49 m

Day of Yr.	Day of Mo.	Day of Wk.	SUNRISE AND SUNSET Ottawa E.S.T. Rises h	m	Sets h	m	Toronto E.S.T. Rises h	m	Sets h	m	Winnipeg C.S.T. Rises h	m	Sets h	m	Vancouver P.S.T. Rises h	m	Sets h	m	MOONRISE AND MOONSET Local Mean Time Lat. 45° Rises h	m	Sets h	m	Lat. 50° Rises h	m	Sets h	m	Day of Wk.	Day of Mo.
275	1	Mon	6	2	17	42	6	16	17	58	6	29	18	6	6	13	17	50	18	8	7	33	17	57	7	43	Mon	1
276	2	Tue	6	3	17	40	6	17	17	56	6	31	18	4	6	14	17	48	18	39	8	34	18	25	8	47	Tue	2
277	3	Wed	6	4	17	38	6	18	17	54	6	33	18	2	6	16	17	46	19	15	9	33	18	58	9	49	Wed	3
278	4	Thu	6	5	17	37	6	19	17	52	6	34	17	59	6	17	17	43	19	55	10	30	19	37	10	48	Thu	4
279	5	Fri	6	7	17	35	6	20	17	51	6	36	17	57	6	19	17	41	20	41	11	22	20	22	11	41	Fri	5
280	6	Sat	6	8	17	33	6	22	17	49	6	37	17	55	6	20	17	39	21	32	12	10	21	13	12	29	Sat	6
281	7	Sun	6	9	17	31	6	23	17	47	6	39	17	53	6	22	17	37	22	28	12	52	22	11	13	10	Sun	7
282	8	Mon	6	11	17	29	6	24	17	45	6	40	17	51	6	23	17	35	23	28	13	30	23	13	13	46	Mon	8
283	9	Tue	6	12	17	27	6	25	17	44	6	42	17	49	6	25	17	33	--	--	14	5	--	--	14	17	Tue	9
284	10	Wed	6	13	17	26	6	26	17	42	6	43	17	47	6	27	17	31	0	31	14	36	0	20	14	44	Wed	10
285	11	Thu	6	14	17	24	6	28	17	40	6	45	17	45	6	28	17	29	1	37	15	5	1	30	15	10	Thu	11
286	12	Fri	6	16	17	22	6	29	17	38	6	47	17	43	6	30	17	27	2	46	15	33	2	43	15	34	Fri	12
287	13	Sat	6	17	17	20	6	30	17	37	6	48	17	41	6	31	17	25	3	57	16	2	3	58	15	59	Sat	13
288	14	Sun	6	18	17	18	6	31	17	35	6	50	17	39	6	33	17	23	5	11	16	34	5	16	16	27	Sun	14
289	15	Mon	6	20	17	17	6	33	17	33	6	51	17	36	6	34	17	21	6	27	17	9	6	37	16	57	Mon	15
290	16	Tue	6	21	17	15	6	34	17	32	6	53	17	34	6	36	17	19	7	44	17	49	7	58	17	34	Tue	16
291	17	Wed	6	22	17	13	6	35	17	30	6	54	17	32	6	37	17	17	9	0	18	37	9	17	18	19	Wed	17
292	18	Thu	6	24	17	11	6	36	17	29	6	56	17	31	6	39	17	15	10	10	19	32	10	29	19	13	Thu	18
293	19	Fri	6	25	17	10	6	38	17	27	6	58	17	29	6	40	17	13	11	12	20	35	11	31	20	16	Fri	19
294	20	Sat	6	26	17	8	6	39	17	25	6	59	17	27	6	42	17	11	12	5	21	42	12	22	21	25	Sat	20
295	21	Sun	6	28	17	6	6	40	17	24	7	1	17	25	6	44	17	9	12	49	22	52	13	3	22	38	Sun	21
296	22	Mon	6	29	17	5	6	41	17	22	7	3	17	23	6	45	17	8	13	25	--	--	13	37	23	50	Mon	22
297	23	Tue	6	30	17	3	6	43	17	21	7	4	17	21	6	47	17	6	13	57	0	1	14	4	--	--	Tue	23
298	24	Wed	6	32	17	2	6	44	17	19	7	6	17	19	6	48	17	4	14	25	1	8	14	29	1	2	Wed	24
299	25	Thu	6	33	17	0	6	45	17	18	7	7	17	17	6	50	17	2	14	51	2	14	14	51	2	11	Thu	25
300	26	Fri	6	35	16	58	6	46	17	16	7	9	17	15	6	52	17	0	15	16	3	18	15	13	3	19	Fri	26
301	27	Sat	6	36	16	57	6	48	17	15	7	11	17	13	6	53	16	59	15	42	4	21	15	36	4	26	Sat	27
302	28	Sun	6	37	16	55	6	49	17	13	7	12	17	12	6	55	16	57	16	10	5	23	16	0	5	32	Sun	28
303	29	Mon	6	39	16	54	6	50	17	12	7	14	17	10	6	56	16	55	16	40	6	24	16	27	6	37	Mon	29
304	30	Tue	6	40	16	52	6	52	17	10	7	16	17	8	6	58	16	53	17	14	7	24	16	58	7	39	Tue	30
305	31	Wed	6	41	16	51	6	53	17	9	7	17	17	6	7	0	16	52	17	53	8	22	17	35	8	39	Wed	31

NOVEMBER 2012

Last Quarter.	6 d	19 h	36 m	
New Moon.	13 d	17 h	8 m	Moon's Phases E.S.T.
First Quarter.	20 d	9 h	31 m	
Full Moon.	28 d	9 h	46 m	

			SUNRISE AND SUNSET																MOONRISE AND MOONSET Local Mean Time									
Day of Yr.	Day of Mo.	Day of Wk.	Ottawa E.S.T. Rises		Sets		Toronto E.S.T. Rises		Sets		Winnipeg C.S.T. Rises		Sets		Vancouver P.S.T. Rises		Sets		Lat. 45° Rises		Sets		Lat. 50° Rises		Sets		Day of Wk.	Day of Mo.
			h	*m*	*h*	*m*	*h*	*m*	*h*	*m*	*h*	*m*	*h*	*m*	*h*	*m*	*h*	*m*	*h*	*m*	*h*	*m*	*h*	*m*	*h*	*m*		
306	1	Thu	6	43	16	49	6	54	17	8	7	19	17	5	7	1	16	50	18	37	9	16	18	18	9	34	Thu	1
307	2	Fri	6	44	16	48	6	55	17	6	7	21	17	3	7	3	16	48	19	26	10	5	19	7	10	24	Fri	2
308	3	Sat	6	46	16	47	6	57	17	5	7	22	17	1	7	4	16	47	20	19	10	49	20	2	11	7	Sat	3
309	4	Sun	6	47	16	45	6	58	17	4	7	24	17	0	7	6	16	45	21	17	11	28	21	2	11	44	Sun	4
310	5	Mon	6	48	16	44	6	59	17	3	7	26	16	58	7	8	16	44	22	18	12	3	22	6	12	16	Mon	5
311	6	Tue	6	50	16	43	7	1	17	1	7	27	16	57	7	9	16	42	23	21	12	34	23	12	12	45	Tue	6
312	7	Wed	6	51	16	41	7	2	17	0	7	29	16	55	7	11	16	41	--	--	13	3	--	--	13	10	Wed	7
313	8	Thu	6	53	16	40	7	3	16	59	7	31	16	54	7	12	16	39	0	27	13	31	0	21	13	34	Thu	8
314	9	Fri	6	54	16	39	7	5	16	58	7	32	16	52	7	14	16	38	1	34	13	59	1	33	13	58	Fri	9
315	10	Sat	6	55	16	38	7	6	16	57	7	34	16	51	7	16	16	37	2	45	14	28	2	48	14	24	Sat	10
316	11	Sun	6	57	16	37	7	7	16	56	7	36	16	49	7	17	16	35	3	59	15	1	4	6	14	52	Sun	11
317	12	Mon	6	58	16	35	7	9	16	55	7	37	16	48	7	19	16	34	5	15	15	38	5	26	15	25	Mon	12
318	13	Tue	7	0	16	34	7	10	16	54	7	39	16	47	7	20	16	33	6	32	16	23	6	47	16	6	Tue	13
319	14	Wed	7	1	16	33	7	11	16	53	7	40	16	45	7	22	16	31	7	47	17	16	8	5	16	57	Wed	14
320	15	Thu	7	2	16	32	7	13	16	52	7	42	16	44	7	24	16	30	8	55	18	17	9	15	17	58	Thu	15
321	16	Fri	7	4	16	31	7	14	16	51	7	44	16	43	7	25	16	29	9	55	19	26	10	13	19	8	Fri	16
322	17	Sat	7	5	16	30	7	15	16	50	7	45	16	42	7	27	16	28	10	44	20	37	11	0	20	22	Sat	17
323	18	Sun	7	6	16	29	7	16	16	49	7	47	16	41	7	28	16	27	11	25	21	49	11	37	21	38	Sun	18
324	19	Mon	7	8	16	29	7	18	16	48	7	48	16	40	7	30	16	26	11	59	22	59	12	8	22	51	Mon	19
325	20	Tue	7	9	16	28	7	19	16	48	7	50	16	39	7	31	16	25	12	28	--	--	12	33	--	--	Tue	20
326	21	Wed	7	10	16	27	7	20	16	47	7	51	16	38	7	33	16	24	12	55	0	6	12	57	0	2	Wed	21
327	22	Thu	7	12	16	26	7	21	16	46	7	53	16	37	7	34	16	23	13	21	1	11	13	19	1	11	Thu	22
328	23	Fri	7	13	16	25	7	23	16	46	7	54	16	36	7	36	16	22	13	46	2	14	13	41	2	18	Fri	23
329	24	Sat	7	14	16	25	7	24	16	45	7	56	16	35	7	37	16	21	14	13	3	16	14	4	3	24	Sat	24
330	25	Sun	7	16	16	24	7	25	16	44	7	57	16	34	7	39	16	20	14	42	4	17	14	30	4	28	Sun	25
331	26	Mon	7	17	16	24	7	26	16	44	7	59	16	33	7	40	16	19	15	15	5	17	15	0	5	31	Mon	26
332	27	Tue	7	18	16	23	7	27	16	43	8	0	16	32	7	41	16	19	15	52	6	15	15	35	6	32	Tue	27
333	28	Wed	7	19	16	22	7	29	16	43	8	2	16	32	7	43	16	18	16	34	7	10	16	15	7	29	Wed	28
334	29	Thu	7	20	16	22	7	30	16	42	8	3	16	31	7	44	16	17	17	21	8	1	17	2	8	21	Thu	29
335	30	Fri	7	22	16	22	7	31	16	42	8	4	16	30	7	45	16	17	18	14	8	48	17	55	9	6	Fri	30

DECEMBER 2012

Last Quarter	6 d	10 h	31 m	
New Moon	13 d	3 h	42 m	Moon's Phases E.S.T.
First Quarter	20 d	0 h	19 m	
Full Moon	28 d	5 h	21 m	

			SUNRISE AND SUNSET																MOONRISE AND MOONSET Local Mean Time									
Day of Yr.	Day of Mo.	Day of Wk.	Ottawa E.S.T. Rises		Sets		Toronto E.S.T. Rises		Sets		Winnipeg C.S.T. Rises		Sets		Vancouver P.S.T. Rises		Sets		Lat. 45° Rises		Sets		Lat. 50° Rises		Sets		Day of Wk.	Day of Mo.
			h	*m*	*h*	*m*	*h*	*m*	*h*	*m*	*h*	*m*	*h*	*m*	*h*	*m*	*h*	*m*	*h*	*m*	*h*	*m*	*h*	*m*	*h*	*m*		
336	1	Sat	7	23	16	21	7	32	16	42	8	6	16	30	7	47	16	16	19	10	9	28	18	54	9	45	Sat	1
337	2	Sun	7	24	16	21	7	33	16	41	8	7	16	29	7	48	16	16	20	10	10	5	19	56	10	19	Sun	2
338	3	Mon	7	25	16	21	7	34	16	41	8	8	16	29	7	49	16	15	21	11	10	37	21	1	10	48	Mon	3
339	4	Tue	7	26	16	20	7	35	16	41	8	9	16	29	7	50	16	15	22	14	11	6	22	8	11	14	Tue	4
340	5	Wed	7	27	16	20	7	36	16	41	8	11	16	28	7	52	16	15	23	19	11	33	23	16	11	38	Wed	5
341	6	Thu	7	28	16	20	7	37	16	41	8	12	16	28	7	53	16	15	--	--	12	0	--	--	12	1	Thu	6
342	7	Fri	7	29	16	20	7	38	16	41	8	13	16	28	7	54	16	14	0	26	12	27	0	27	12	24	Fri	7
343	8	Sat	7	30	16	20	7	39	16	41	8	14	16	27	7	55	16	14	1	36	12	57	1	41	12	50	Sat	8
344	9	Sun	7	31	16	20	7	40	16	41	8	15	16	27	7	56	16	14	2	48	13	30	2	57	13	19	Sun	9
345	10	Mon	7	32	16	20	7	41	16	41	8	16	16	27	7	57	16	14	4	3	14	10	4	16	13	55	Mon	10
346	11	Tue	7	33	16	20	7	42	16	41	8	17	16	27	7	58	16	14	5	18	14	57	5	35	14	39	Tue	11
347	12	Wed	7	34	16	20	7	42	16	41	8	18	16	27	7	59	16	14	6	30	15	54	6	49	15	34	Wed	12
348	13	Thu	7	35	16	20	7	43	16	41	8	19	16	27	8	0	16	14	7	35	17	0	7	55	16	41	Thu	13
349	14	Fri	7	35	16	20	7	44	16	41	8	20	16	27	8	0	16	14	8	31	18	12	8	49	17	55	Fri	14
350	15	Sat	7	36	16	20	7	45	16	41	8	21	16	28	8	1	16	14	9	18	19	27	9	32	19	13	Sat	15
351	16	Sun	7	37	16	21	7	45	16	42	8	21	16	28	8	2	16	15	9	56	20	40	10	7	20	31	Sun	16
352	17	Mon	7	38	16	21	7	46	16	42	8	22	16	28	8	3	16	15	10	29	21	51	10	36	21	46	Mon	17
353	18	Tue	7	38	16	21	7	47	16	42	8	23	16	29	8	3	16	15	10	58	22	59	11	1	22	58	Tue	18
354	19	Wed	7	39	16	22	7	47	16	43	8	23	16	29	8	4	16	16	11	24	--	--	11	24	--	--	Wed	19
355	20	Thu	7	39	16	22	7	48	16	43	8	24	16	29	8	5	16	16	11	51	0	4	11	46	0	7	Thu	20
356	21	Fri	7	40	16	23	7	48	16	44	8	24	16	30	8	5	16	17	12	17	1	8	12	9	1	14	Fri	21
357	22	Sat	7	40	16	23	7	49	16	44	8	25	16	30	8	6	16	17	12	45	2	10	12	34	2	19	Sat	22
358	23	Sun	7	41	16	24	7	49	16	45	8	25	16	31	8	6	16	18	13	17	3	10	13	3	3	23	Sun	23
359	24	Mon	7	41	16	24	7	50	16	45	8	26	16	32	8	6	16	18	13	52	4	9	13	35	4	25	Mon	24
360	25	Tue	7	41	16	25	7	50	16	46	8	26	16	32	8	7	16	19	14	32	5	5	14	13	5	23	Tue	25
361	26	Wed	7	42	16	26	7	50	16	47	8	26	16	33	8	7	16	20	15	17	5	57	14	58	6	16	Wed	26
362	27	Thu	7	42	16	27	7	51	16	48	8	26	16	34	8	7	16	21	16	8	6	45	15	49	7	4	Thu	27
363	28	Fri	7	42	16	27	7	51	16	48	8	27	16	35	8	7	16	22	17	4	7	28	16	47	7	46	Fri	28
364	29	Sat	7	42	16	28	7	51	16	49	8	27	16	36	8	7	16	22	18	3	8	6	17	48	8	22	Sat	29
365	30	Sun	7	43	16	29	7	51	16	50	8	27	16	37	8	7	16	23	19	4	8	40	18	53	8	52	Sun	30
366	31	Mon	7	43	16	30	7	51	16	51	8	27	16	37	8	7	16	24	20	7	9	10	19	59	9	19	Mon	31

TABLE FOR FINDING APPROXIMATE STANDARD TIME OF SUNRISE, SUNSET, MOONRISE, MOONSET, FOR CANADIAN CITIES AND TOWNS

PLACE	Time Zone	FOR SUNRISE OR SUNSET Take value for	and apply correction	FOR MOONRISE OR MOONSET Take value for	and apply correction
Brandon	C	Winnipeg	+11*m*	50°	+40*m*
Brantford	E	Toronto	+ 4	45	+21
Calgary	M	Winnipeg	+ 8	50	+36
Charlottetown	A	Ottawa	+10	45	+13
Cornwall	E	Ottawa	- 4	45	- 1
Edmonton	M	Winnipeg	+ 6	50	+34
Fredericton	A	Ottawa	+24	45	+27
Gander	N	Vancouver	- 4	50	+ 8
Glace Bay	A	Ottawa	- 3	45	0
Goose Bay	A	Winnipeg	-26	50	2
Granby	E	Ottawa	-12	45	- 9
Guelph	E	Toronto	+ 3	45	+21
Halifax	A	Ottawa	+11	45	+14
Hamilton	E	Toronto	+ 2	45	+21
Hull	E	Ottawa	0	45	+ 3
Kapuskasing	E	Vancouver	+17	50	+30
Kingston	E	Toronto	-12	45	+ 6
Kitchener	E	Toronto	+ 4	45	+22
London	E	Toronto	+ 8	45	+25
Medicine Hat	M	Winnipeg	- 4	50	+22
Moncton	A	Ottawa	+16	45	+19
Montréal	E	Ottawa	- 9	45	- 6
Moosonee	E	Winnipeg	- 6	50	+23
Moose Jaw	C	Winnipeg	+34	50	+62
Niagara Falls	E	Toronto	- 1	45	+16
North Bay	E	Ottawa	+14	45	+18
Ottawa	E	Ottawa	0	45	+ 3
Owen Sound	E	Ottawa	+21	45	+24
Penticton	P	Vancouver	-14	50	- 2
Peterborough	E	Toronto	- 4	45	+13
Prince Albert	C	Winnipeg	+36	50	+64
Prince Rupert	P	Winnipeg	+12	50	+40
Québec	E	Ottawa	-18	45	-15
Regina	C	Winnipeg	+30	50	+58
St. Catharines	E	Toronto	0	45	+17
St. Hyacinthe	E	Ottawa	-11	45	- 8
Saint John, NB	A	Ottawa	+22	45	+24
St. John's, NL	N	Vancouver	-11	50	+ 1
Sarnia	E	Toronto	+12	45	+30
Saskatoon	C	Winnipeg	+38	50	+66
Sault Ste. Marie	E	Ottawa	+34	45	+37
Shawinigan	E	Ottawa	-12	45	- 9
Sherbrooke	E	Ottawa	-14	45	-12
Stratford	E	Toronto	+ 6	45	+24
Sudbury	E	Ottawa	+21	45	+24
Sydney	A	Ottawa	- 2	45	+ 1
The Pas	C	Winnipeg	+16	50	+44
Trois-Rivières	E	Ottawa	-12	45	- 9
Thunder Bay	E	Vancouver	+44	50	+57
Timmins	E	Vancouver	+13	50	+25
Toronto	E	Toronto	0	45	+18
Trail	P	Vancouver	-22	50	-10
Truro	A	Ottawa	+10	45	+13
Vancouver	P	Vancouver	0	50	+12
Victoria	P	Vancouver	+2	50	+14
Windsor	E	Toronto	+14	45	+32
Winnipeg	C	Winnipeg	0	50	+28

PROMINENT CANADIAN SCIENTISTS

John F. Allen

Working with Pyotr Leonidovich Kapitsa and Don Misener, Allen discovered the superfluid phase of matter in 1937 at the Royal Society Mond Laboratory in Cambridge, England. A state achieved by a few liquids, such as helium, at extreme temperature where they become able to flow without friction, superfluids are used in high-precision devices, such as gyroscopes, which allow the measurement of some theoretically predicted gravitational effects. Allen along with Harry Jones also discovered the "fountain effect," in which superfluid helium flows up a tube and shoots into the air upon being exposed to a small heat source (the heat source in the original experiment was a flashlight that they were using to look at the apparatus). Allen was born in Winnipeg in 1908 and was professor of physics at St Andrews University, Scotland, from 1947 to 1978, and then emeritus professor until his death in 2001.

Sidney Altman

Born in 1939 in Montreal, the molecular biologist received a Nobel Prize in Chemistry in 1989 for his work with Thomas R. Cech on the catalytic properties of RNA. Their discovery, that ribonucleic acid in living cells is not only a molecule of heredity but also can function as a biocatalyst, affects fundamental aspects of the molecular basis of life. Virtually all chemical reactions taking place in a living cell require catalysts. Such biocatalysts are called enzymes and are determined by hereditary genes. Until the findings of Altman and Cech became known, all enzymes were considered to be proteins. The discovery of catalytic RNA will provide a new tool for gene technology, with potential to create defenses against viral infections. Altman is currently the Sterling Professor of Molecular, Cellular, and Developmental Biology and Professor of Chemistry at Yale University.

Frederick G. Banting

A doctor of orthopedic medicine and a decorated World War I veteran, Banting received a Nobel Prize in Medicine in 1923 for his discovery of insulin, a hormone that controls the metabolism of sugar. Early in his medical career, Banting became interested in diabetes, caused by a lack of insulin secreted by the pancreas. Before Banting's work, attempts to supply the missing insulin by feeding patients with fresh pancreas, or extracts of it, had failed. While working with his assistant Charles Best, Banting discovered how to extract insulin from the pancreas before it destroyed itself, thus birthing the first treatment for diabetes sufferers. The Banting and Best Diabetes Centre at the University of Toronto continues the work of the two doctors. The cause of diabetes remains a mystery. Banting was killed in an airplane disaster in 1941 in Newfoundland.

Bertram Brockhouse

Brockhouse was born in 1918 to homesteaders in Alberta and attended a one-room schoolhouse in Vancouver. During the Depression, the impoverished Brockhouses moved to Chicago, where, to help out with family finances, Brockhouse learned how to repair radios, and became involved in the socialist democratic movement. During World War II, he served six years in the Royal Canadian Navy repairing submarine-tracking equipment. At the war's end he attended the University of British Columbia, where he studied physics and mathematics, and received a PhD from the University of Toronto in the budding field of nuclear physics. In 1994 Brockhouse and Clifford G. Shull received a Nobel Prize in Physics for their contributions to the development of neutron scattering techniques for studies of condensed matter. Neutron scattering techniques are used in widely differing areas such as the study of the new ceramic superconductors, catalytic exhaust cleaning, elastic properties of polymers and virus structure.

H.S.M. Coxeter

Coxeter was born and educated in England. Shortly after finishing his doctoral studies at Cambridge University, he spent two years as a research visitor at Princeton University. In 1936 he joined the Faculty of the University of Toronto, where he remained as a mathematics professor until his death in 2003. Coxeter's work was mainly in geometry. In particular he made contributions of major importance in the theory of non-euclidean geometry, group theory, combinatorics, and polytopes or complicated geometric shapes of any number of dimensions that cannot be constructed in the real world but can be described mathematically and can sometimes be drawn. Much of Coxeter's time was devoted to group theory, or ways of measuring symmetry. This concerns the geometry of, for instance, kaleidoscopes and reflections in different planes, now known as Coxeter groups. Coxeter met the artist M.C. Escher, the master of depicting impossible reality, in 1954 and the two became lifelong friends. Coxeter also influenced Buckminster Fuller who used Coxeter's mathematical concepts of symmetry in his architecture. He attributed his long and productive life to vegetarianism and physical fitness.

J.C. Fields

John Charles Fields was born in Hamilton, Ontario, then Upper Canada, in 1863. He graduated with a degree in mathematics from the University of Toronto and was awarded a PhD from Johns Hopkins University in 1887. Dissatisfied with the state of mathematics in North America, Fields left for Europe, where he met the greatest mathematicians of the time, and changed his mathematical interests to algebraic functions. Fields worked tirelessly to raise the stature of mathematics within academic and public circles. He successfully lobbied the Ontario Legislature for an annual research grant of $75,000 for the university and helped establish the National Research Council of Canada, and the Ontario Research Foundation. Fields is best known for establishing what is now known as the Fields Medal, the premier award in mathematics, often called the Nobel Prize in Mathematics. It is awarded every four years to two to four mathematicians, under the age of 40, who have made important contributions to the field.

Sir Sandford Fleming

Fleming was born in Scotland in 1827, and at the age of 17, he emigrated to Ontario, where he was employed as a surveyor and map maker. In 1851 Fleming designed Canada's first postage stamp, which would do much to publicize the beaver as a distinctly Canadian emblem. In 1855 he became the chief engineer of the Northern Railway of Canada, where he instituted the construction of iron bridges instead of wood for safety reasons. Over the next few years he led a team of surveyors and engineers to investigate the first coast-to-coast railway line. Fleming was present in 1885 when the last spike was driven in Craigellachie, British Columbia. After missing a train in 1876 in Ireland because the printed schedule listed p.m. instead of a.m., he proposed Universal Time, a single 24-hour clock for the entire world, located in Greenwich, England, the center of the Earth and not linked to any surface meridian. He urged that standard time zones be used locally, but they were to be subordinate to his single world time. By 1929 all of the major countries of the world had accepted time zones. Fleming was knighted by Queen Victoria In 1897.

John Kenneth Galbraith

The economist's first major book, published in 1952, was American Capitalism: The Concept of Countervailing Power. In it he argued that giant firms had replaced small ones to the point where the competitive model no longer applied to much of the American economy. But, he argued, the muscle of large firms was offset by the power of large unions, so that consumers were protected by competing centres of power.

In his best-selling 1958 book The Affluent Society, Galbraith contrasted the affluence of the private sector with the squalor of the public sector. Galbraith's main argument is that as society becomes relatively more affluent, so private business must "create" consumer wants through advertising, and while this generates artificial affluence through the production of commercial goods and services, the "public sector" becomes neglected as a result. He proposed significant investment in parks, transportation, education, and other public amenities - what we now call infrastructure - to ameliorate these differences and postpone depression and revolution indefinitely.

Although born in Canada, Galbraith spent most of his life in the United States, namely as a professor at Harvard University. He was active in politics, serving four US presidents and was the US Ambassador to India under Kennedy. He was awarded the Order of Canada in 1997 and two Presidential Medals of Freedom. He died in 2006 at the age of 97.

William Francis Giauque

Born to American parents on the Canadian side of Niagara Falls, Giauque began his career at the Hooker Electro-Chemical Company in Niagara Falls, NY, as a chemical engineer. Soon after, he received a Ph.D. degree in chemistry with a minor in physics from the University of California, where he became a professor of chemistry in 1934. His principal objective was to demonstrate through a variety of accurate tests that the third law of thermodynamics is a basic natural law. In 1927 he proposed a new method of achieving extremely low temperatures using a process called adiabatic demagnetization. By 1933 he had a working apparatus that obtained a temperature within one-tenth of a degree of absolute zero. In the course of his low-temperature studies of oxygen, Giauque discovered with Herrick L. Johnston the oxygen isotopes of mass 17 and 18 in the Earth's atmosphere. He received the Nobel Prize in Chemistry in 1949.

James Gosling

The father of Java programming language was born in 1955 near Calgary, where he attended university. He received his PhD in Computer Science from Carnegie Mellon University. While at the college he built a multi-processor version of Unix, as well as several compilers and computer mail systems.

From 1984 to 2010, Gosling served Sun Microsystems as Vice President and Fellow. After spending six months at Google, Gosling moved to Liquid Robotics in August 2011, where he is chief software architect in the creation of robots that can explore the bottom of the ocean.

In February 2007, he was named an officer of the Order of Canada.

Gerhard Herzberg

Physicist Herzberg was born in Hamburg, Germany in 1904 but was forced to flee Nazi Germany in 1935, when he settled at the University of Saskatchewan. Herzberg's main contributions have enriched the fields of atomic and molecular spectroscopy for which he won a Nobel Prize in Chemistry in 1971. He and his associates determined the makeup of a large number of diatomic and polyatomic molecules, including the structures of many free radicals difficult to determine in any other way. Herzberg has also applied spectroscopic studies to the identification of certain molecules in planetary atmospheres, in comets, and in interstellar space. Herzberg was elected a Fellow of the Royal Society of Canada in 1939 and of the Royal Society of London in 1951. Herzberg died in 1999.

David Hubel

Hubel, along with Torsten Wiesel, greatly expanded the scientific knowledge of sensory processing, describing how signals from the eye are processed by the brain to generate edge detectors, motion detectors, stereoscopic depth detectors and color detectors, the building blocks of the visual scene. These studies opened the door for the understanding and treatment of childhood cataracts and strabismus. For their work the team was awarded the 1981 Nobel Prize in Physiology or Medicine. Hubel was born to American parents in Windsor, but spent his formative years in Montreal.

Rudolph Marcus

Born in Montreal in 1923, Marcus received the 1992 Nobel Prize in Chemistry for his theory of electron transfer. The Marcus theory, named after him, provides a thermodynamic and kinetic framework for describing one electron outer-sphere electron transfer. The Marcus theory describes, and makes predictions concerning, such widely differing phenomena as the fixation of light energy by green plants, photochemical production of fuel, chemiluminescence (cold light), the conductivity of electrically conducting polymers, corrosion, the methodology of electrochemical synthesis and analysis, and more.

Marcus developed his theory for what is perhaps the simplest chemical elementary process, the transfer of an electron between two molecules. No chemical bonds are broken in such a reaction, but changes take place in the molecular structure of the reacting molecules and their nearest neighbors. This molecular change enables the electrons to jump between the molecules. He is currently a professor at Caltech and is a member of the International Academy of Quantum Molecular Science.

Sir William Osler

Osler, often dubbed the father of modern medicine, grew up in Ontario, the son of an Anglican minister. After two years at the Toronto School of Medicine, Osler obtained his medical degree in 1872 from McGill University. Upon his death, Osler willed his library to the Montreal university where it forms the nucleus of McGill's Osler Library of the History of Medicine, which opened in 1929. Osler's greatest contribution to medicine was to insist that students learned from seeing and talking to patients and the establishment of the medical residency program. In 1889, Osler accepted the position of Physician-in-Chief at the recently founded Johns Hopkins Hospital in Baltimore where he refined the residency program. He died, at the age of 70, in 1919, during the Spanish influenza epidemic.

Wilder Penfield

The American-born Canadian neurosurgeon studied at Princeton before becoming a Rhodes Scholar at Oxford University where he studied neuropathology, the scientific study of diseases of the nervous system. With his colleague, Herbert Jasper, he invented what is now called the Montreal procedure for treating patients with severe epilepsy by destroying nerve cells in the brain where the seizures originated. Before operating, he stimulated the brain with electrical probes while the patients were conscious on the operating table and observed their responses. In this way he could more accurately target the areas of the brain responsible, reducing the side-effects of the surgery. His technique enabled him to map the sensory and motor parts of the brain, thus showing their connection to the various limbs and organs of the body. After studying epilepsy in New York, Penfield moved to Montreal where he taught at at McGill University and the Royal Victoria hospital, becoming the city's first neurosurgeon. He eventually became the director of the Montreal Neurological Institute and the associated Montreal Neurological Hospital, which was established with funding from the Rockefeller Foundation. In 1967 he was made a Companion of the Order of Canada. In 1994 he was inducted into the Canadian Medical Hall of Fame.

John Polanyi

After completing his undergraduate education at Manchester University, Polanyi moved to Canada in 1952 at the age of 23 to work for the for the National Research Council of Canada before moving to the University of Toronto, where he remains to this day. In 1986 Polanyi shared a Nobel Prize in Chemistry with Dudley R. Herschbach and Yuan T. Lee for their research in reaction dynamics, offering much more understanding into how energy disposal in chemical reactions takes place. Polanyi developed the method of infrared chemiluminescence, in which the extremely weak infrared emission from a newly formed molecule is measured and analyzed.

Arthur Schawlow

Schawlow grew up in Canada in a deeply religious family and studied at the University of Toronto. After World War II, he studied at Columbia University, spent a decade at Bell Labs, then left to become a professor at Stanford, where he remained as professor emeritus until his retirement in 1996. While at Stanford, he teamed up with Robert Hofstadter, who, like Schawlow, had an autistic child, to help each other find solutions to the condition. Later Schawlow spearheaded an institution to care for people with autism in Paradise, CA, named the Arthur Schawlow Center. Although his research focused on optics, in particular, lasers and their use in spectroscopy, he also pursued investigations in the areas of superconductivity and nuclear resonance. He and Nicolaas Bloembergen shared the 1981 Nobel Prize in Physics by using lasers to study the interactions of electromagnetic radiation with matter.

Myron Scholes

The 1997 winner of the Nobel Memorial Prize in Economics began his early years in Timmins. After the family moved to Hamilton, Scholes attended McMaster University and earned an MBA and PhD from the University of Chicago. He eventually put his name to the Black-Scholes model, which provides the fundamental conceptual framework for valuing options, such as calls or puts, and has become the standard in financial markets globally. All did not go well for Scholes, however. In 2005, Scholes was implicated in the case of Long-Term Capital Holdings v. United States, where he attempted to invest funds from his company, Long-Term Capital Holdings, in an illegal tax shelter in order to avoid having to pay taxes on profits from company investments. It was found that Scholes and his partners were not eligible for US$106 million in tax deductions they had claimed. They were fined more than US$40 million by the IRS. Scholes now runs the hedge fund Platinum Grove Asset Management and is the chairman of the Board of Economic Advisors for Stamos Partners. He was awarded the 2011 CME Group Fred Arditti Innovation Award for his co-creation of the Black-Scholes options pricing model.

Michael Smith

Born in 1932 in Blackpool, England, Smith attended the University of Manchester and soon after receiving his PhD accepted a fellowship in Vancouver to work on the synthesis of biologically important organo-phosphates. The 1992 Nobel Prize winner in chemistry didn't keep the money he was granted from the award. He gave half of it to researchers working on the genetics of schizophrenia and shared the other half between Science World BC and the Society for Canadian Women in Science and Technology. Smith could afford to be generous. He had made a small fortune in 1988 when he sold his share of Zymogenetics Incorporated, a Seattle-based biotechnology company that he co-founded in 1981.

Andrew Michael Spence

For his work on the dynamics of information flows and market development, Spence and his colleagues George A. Akerlof and Joseph E. Stiglitz, received the 2001 Nobel Memorial Prize in Economics. In his Job-Market Signaling model, employees convey their respective skills to employers by acquiring a certain degree of education, which is costly to them. Employers will pay higher wages to more educated employees, because they know that the proportion of employees with high abilities is higher among the educated ones, as it is less costly for them to acquire education than it is for employees with low abilities. For the model to work, it is not even necessary for education to have any intrinsic value if it can convey information about the sender (employee) to the recipient (employer) and if the signal is costly. Spence is currently a professor at the NYU Stern School of Business. He grew up in Canada, during and after the war, before leaving for college in the United States.

Henry Taube

For his work on the mechanisms of electron transfer reactions, especially in metal complexes, Taube won the 1983 Novel Prize in Chemistry. Born in Saskatchewan, Taube has published more than 350 articles and a book as a result of his research. A member of the Stanford University faculty since 1962, Taube was "one of the most creative contemporary workers in inorganic chemistry," according to the Nobel committee who rewarded him for his insights into how electrons are transferred from one molecule to another during chemical reactions. Taube maintained a lifelong interest in oxidation-reduction or redox reactions, in which electrons are lost and gained during a chemical reaction. He died in 2005 at the age of 89 at his home on the Stanford campus.

Richard E. Taylor

Born in 1929 in Medicine Hat, Alberta, Taylor received the 1990 Nobel Prize in Physics for his pioneering investigations concerning deep inelastic scattering of electrons on protons and bound neutrons, which have been of essential importance for the development of the quark model in particle physics. He shared the prize with Jerome Friedman and Henry Kendall. Taylor received his undergraduate degree from the University of Alberta and his PhD from Stanford, where he is a professor emeritus.

William Vickrey

Vickrey was born in Victoria, British Columbia, in 1914. His elementary and secondary education was in Europe and the United States, with graduation from Phillips Andover Academy in 1931. He received a B.S. in mathematics from Yale in 1935, followed by graduate work in economics at Columbia University from 1935 to 1937. A conscientious objector during World War II, he spent part of his alternate service designing a new inheritance tax for Puerto Rico. In 1946 he began his teaching career at Columbia University as a lecturer in economics. An essential part of Vickrey's research focused on the properties of different types of auctions, and how they can best be designed to generate economic efficiency. His work provided the basis for a field of research which has also been extended to practical applications such as auctions of treasury bonds and band spectrum licenses. He received the 1996 Nobel Prize in Economics for his endeavors.

John Tuzo Wilson

The Ottawa-born geologist achieved world-wide acclaim for his contributions to study of plate tectonics. Plate tectonics is the idea that the rigid outer layers of the Earth are broken up into numerous pieces that move independently over the weaker soft zone of the upper mantle. Wilson maintained that the Hawaiian Islands were created as a tectonic plate, extending across much of the Pacific Ocean, shifted slowly over a fixed hotspot, spawning a long series of volcanoes. He also conceived of the transform fault, a major plate boundary where two plates move past each other horizontally, such as the San Andreas Fault. The Wilson cycle of seabed expansion and contraction bears his name. He died in 1993 in Toronto.

CANADA'S ENERGY SOURCES

Canada is endowed with an abundant variety of energy resources. It ranks among top countries in the world for production of oil, natural gas, uranium and coal. Most of the country's energy is derived from hydrocarbons-coal, natural gas, and oil. These are used both as direct fuels and in the production of electricity. The only significant non-hydrocarbon energy sources are hydroelectricity and nuclear power. Canadians are the second-highest per capita consumers of energy in the world, doubling Japan and most of Europe. How will Canada cope with future energy needs and consumption?

Oil and Gas

Canada faces the same oil industry challenges as the rest of the world: recent crude oil prices have been high and volatile, and geopolitical uncertainty continues to be a threat to supply around the globe. The impact of severe weather on refining and production has resulted in higher crude oil and gasoline prices. Based on Canada's production rate, they have 10 years or less of proven reserves. This does not mean that Canada will run out of oil in 10 years. It means this is the size of its resource based on the oil pools today, production rates, and the portion that is recoverable using existing technology.

Canadian oil sands—a mixture of sand or clay, water, and extremely heavy crude oil—are estimated to contain 1.7 trillion barrels of oil, and based on today's technology, it's believed that 178 billion barrels can be recovered. To put this in perspective, the size of the recoverable resources ranks second only to Saudi Arabia. The oil sands currently account for approximately one-third of the 3.3 million barrels of oil produced per day in Canada. Conventional oil production in the Western Canada Sedimentary Basin peaked in 1973, but it still accounts for a significant portion of oil supply. There is call to slow the pace of oil sands development in order to allow for better understanding and assessment of the risks to the environment. This could mean temporarily halting further approvals of projects.

Natural Gas

Over the past decade, there has been a trend on the part of large energy consumers and the general public toward increased use of natural gas as the fuel of choice. This has been particularly noteworthy in the electricity generation industry. Canadian production of natural gas has probably already peaked, and will gradually decline as wells mature and become exhausted faster than new discoveries are made. In 2007, Canadian Liquefied Natural Gas production declined, but those deficiencies were offset by higher US imports. Drilling activity was weaker than it had been at the same time in each of the past three years. Annual increases in drilling activity and connection of new gas wells are necessary to maintain stable Canadian gas deliverability, because the productivity of new gas wells in the Western Canada Sedimentary Basin has lessened. In 2006, natural gas prices fell below the fuel oil range and competed with coal in the power generation market.

With North American natural gas supply expected to lag future increases in demand, imports of LNG from offshore sources are viewed as the largest source of additional natural gas to the continent. Over 40 import terminal projects have been proposed for North America and development of significant LNG trade could have implications for North American natural gas supply, demand and prices.

Canada will continue to research and develop gas hydrates, a form of natural gas found in the molecular structure of ice, in Northern provinces and offshore on both coasts. Canadian resource estimates are impressive: 1,500 to 28,000 trillion cubic feet of gas in place contained in hydrates, with 311 trillion cubic feet in the Beaufort/Mackenzie Delta region. Both the Pacific and Atlantic margins have confirmed gas hydrates deposits. If there was a system available to transport these deposits, hydrates would be as economical as gas. However, costs are not competitive with conventional gas at this time. Additional testing and modeling is required to ensure results. Plans are to have a full scale production test in about five years and first production by 2020.

Compressed natural gas seems to be a viable transportation option for stranded natural gas offshore Newfoundland, with possible development to occur by 2014 or later. Development still has a number of hurdles to overcome, including safety issues for the delivery to Boston or New York harbours.

Electricity and Coal

The size of Canada's coal resource dwarfs all other energy forms, even the oil sands. Based on current production rates, Canada has a 1,000-year reserve of coal. Currently about 60 percent of Canada's electricity comes from hydro projects, 18 percent from coal combustion, 13 percent from nuclear, 5 percent from natural gas, and the balance from oil and renewables. Coal-based generation became unpopular during the 1980s and 1990s because of its carbon emissions. Canada must develop ways to use coal in a manner that is environmentally acceptable. Until a few years ago, there were two ways to address the challenge of greenhouse gas management: to produce and use energy more efficiently or, to rely increasingly on low-carbon and carbon-free fuels. Unfortunately, energy efficiency and the use of alternative energy may not be enough to stabilize global concentrations of carbon dioxide. Carbon sequestration offers a third option that could, in tandem with the continued development of clean coal generation technologies, prove affordable, effective and environmentally safe.

Canadian metallurgical coal (coal consumed in making steel) is experiencing a comeback in Alberta and British Columbia, and opportunities for Canadian metallurgical coal are driven by demand in China, India and Brazil. Canadian steam coal (all non-metallurgical coal) production remains consistent with some export growth. Steam coal consumption is at risk in Ontario with projected plant shutdowns. Steam coal production remains strong in Alberta, Saskatchewan, New Brunswick and Nova Scotia. The government is to build and operate a full-scale clean coal demonstration plant by 2014.

A number of provinces have introduced or are in the process of introducing plans to address electricity needs by way of new generation and transmission projects. For example, British Columbia Transmission Corp. introduced a $3.2-billion 10-year transmission plan, Alberta Electric System Operator began a $3.5 billion 10-year transmission plan, Saskatchewan agreed to address its aging fleet of coal-fired generators, and the Ontario Power Authority moved on its Power System Plan.

Nuclear Energy

Ontario dominates Canada's nuclear industry, containing most of the country's nuclear power generating capacity. Ontario has 16 operating reactors—with another in the planning stage—providing about half of the province's electricity, plus two reactors undergoing refurbishment. Quebec and New Brunswick each have one reactor. Overall, nuclear power provides about 15.5 percent of Canada's electricity. The cost of nuclear power generation has been dropping over the last decade. This is because declining fuel (including enrichment), operating and maintenance costs, while the plant concerned has been paid for, or at least is being paid off. In general the construction costs of nuclear power plants are significantly higher than for coal- or gas-fired plants because of the need to use special materials, and to incorporate sophisticated safety features and back-up control equipment. These contribute much of the nuclear generation cost, but once the plant is built the cost variables are minor. Canada's nuclear plants, however, are quickly reaching the end of their operating lifespans and are entering the long and costly decommissioning phase.

Canada is one of the world's largest producers of uranium with about one third of world production coming from Saskatchewan mines. The country exports uranium and radioisotopes for medical and industrial purposes. These exports are subject to stringent nuclear non-proliferation policies.

Canada's used reactor fuel is now stored on an interim basis at licensed facilities located where the waste is produced. Like many other countries with nuclear power programs, Canada has yet to decide what to do with this used fuel over the long term. On site storage options are expected to perform well over the near term; however, existing reactor sites were not chosen for their suitability as permanent storage sites. Furthermore, the communities hosting the nuclear reactors have a reasonable expectation that used nuclear fuel will eventually be moved.

Alternative and Renewable Energy

Canadian energy development strategies traditionally focused on low-cost electric power, crude oil, and accessible energy resources. These strategies led to a strong energy industry that has contributed to Canadian prosperity. But today, the world's appetite for cheap energy is counterbalanced by climate change concerns and greenhouse gas emission restrictions. Canada has the potential to become a global leader in renewable energy given its abundant renewable energy resources such as solar, wind, earth, wave, water, tide and biomass. With its large forest and agricultural land base relative to its population, Canada is uniquely positioned to be a world leader in the production and use of biofuels derived from lignocellulose (forestry) biomass. However, renewable energy sources account for less than one percent of the total energy supply today. Utilization of these alternate sources will expand, but they will not become more than small, specialized niche contributors to Canada's energy supply for the foreseeable future.

A study by the Pembina Institute, a sustainable-energy think tank, concluded that smart, targeted investments in a diverse array of energy efficiency and renewable energy solutions over the next 20 years will achieve major cuts in greenhouse gas emissions, accelerate the closure of highly-polluting coal plants and avoid the need for new nuclear investments.

THE CALENDAR

The calendar is a method of identifying the passage of time and thereby regulating our civil life and religious observances.

Days, months and years are based on astronomical periods. The day is the time it takes the earth to make one revolution on its axis, the month is associated with the period of orbiting of the moon around the earth, while the year has to do with the orbiting of the earth around the sun.

Many religious ideas and observances have been connected with the changes of the moon, and in ancient times the calendar took account of the moon rather than the seasons. From new moon to new moon is 29.530 days, and from one spring equinox to the next is 365.24219 days. Since the two are incommensurable, the modern calendar disregards the moon, except insofar as our months are roughly equal to a lunation.

The Week

The division of the week is found only among Aryan nations and in nations and regions into which they have penetrated. The day is, for convenience, divided into 24 equal parts and is the period of a single rotation of the earth upon its own axis.

A solar or astronomical day commences at midnight, and is divided into two equal portions of 12 hours each - those before noon being termed (A.M.) those after noon (P.M.).

The Chinese week consists of 5 days, which are named after iron, wood, water, feathers and earth; they divide the day into 12 parts of 2 hours each.

The Anglo-Saxons named the days of the week after the following deities: Sunday, the Sun; Monday, the Moon; Tuesday, Tuesco (God of War); Wednesday, Woden (God of Storms); Thursday, Thor (God of Thunder); Friday, Freya (Goddess of Love); Saturday, Saturn (God of Time).

The word *week* is from Wikon (German); it means change, succession.

The Julian Calendar

When Julius Caesar came to power, the Roman Calendar was hopelessly confused. With the advice of the Alexandrian astronomer Sosigenes, Julius Caesar established the Julian Calendar. The length of the year was taken as 365 1/4 days, and in order to account for the 1/4 day, an extra day was added every fourth year. From 45 B.C. each month has had its present number of days. In the old Roman Calendar which was based on the moon an extra month was inserted to straighten out the difference between 12 lunations 354.37 days, and 355 days, which they called a year. This was inserted when necessary after February 23rd. In the Julian Calendar the extra day was added by repeating the sixth day before the Kalends (1st) of March, whence comes our word bissextile for leap year.

No very significant change was made until the reform by Pope Gregory XIII in A.D. 1582.

The Julian Calendar is known as the "Old Style" whereas the calendar as improved by Pope Gregory is known as the "New Style". The difference between the two is now 13 days.

The Gregorian Calendar

Because the Solar Year is 11 minutes, 12 seconds less than the Julian Year of 365 1/4 days, it followed in course of years that the Julian Calendar became inaccurate by several days, and in 1582 this difference amounted to 10 days. Pope Gregory XIII, at the suggestion of Aloysius Lilus, an astronomer of Naples, determined to rectify this, and devised the Calendar now known as the Gregorian Calendar. He dropped or cancelled these 10 days—October 5th being called October 15th—and made centurial years leap years only once in 4 centuries; so that whilst 1700, 1800 and 1900 were to be ordinary years, 2000 would be a leap year. This modification brought the Gregorian year into such close exactitude with the solar year that there is only a difference of 26 seconds, which amounts to a day in 3,323 years. This is the "New Style". The Gregorian Calendar was adopted in Italy, France, Spain, Portugal and Poland in 1582, by most of the German Roman Catholic states, Holland and Flanders in 1583, Hungary in 1587. The adoption in Switzerland began in 1584 and was not completed till 1812. The German and Dutch Protestant states generally, along with Denmark, adopted it in 1700, British dominions in 1752, Sweden in 1753, Japan in 1873, China in 1912, Bulgaria in 1915, Soviet Russia in 1918, Yugoslavia in 1919, Romania and Greece in 1924, Turkey in 1927. The rules for Easter have not, however, been adopted by those oriental churches that are not subject to the Papacy.

The difference between the two "Styles" will remain 13 days until A.D. 2100.

The Jewish Calendar

The Jewish Calendar from the institution of the Mosaic Law downward was a lunar one, consisting of 12 months. The cycles of religious feasts commencing with the Passover depended not only on the month but on the moon; the 14th of the month of Abid or Nisan was coincident with the full moon; and the new moons themselves were the occasions of regular festivals; the commencement of the month was generally determined by observations of the new moon, but 12 lunar months would make but 354 1/2 days, the years would be short 12 days of the true year and it was necessary that an additional month, Veader, be inserted about every third year.

The modern Jewish Calendar is based on fixed rules and not on observation. A common year may contain 353, 354 or 355 days and the leap year 383, 384 or 385 days. The intercalary month always contains 30 days and is inserted before the month Adar, the name and place of which it takes, Adar itself called second Adar or Veadar. Tishri 1 is the Jewish New Year and it cannot be a Sunday, Wednesday or Friday. Tishri 1 is not necessarily the day of new moon but is governed by a mean new moon which is calculated from the value of a mean lunation. It is complicated as compared with the Gregorian Calendar. The intercalary month is introduced seven times in every 19 years.

The identification of the Jewish months with our own cannot be effected with precision on account of the variations existing between the lunar and solar month.

The Muslim Calendar

The Muslim Calendar is called also the calendar of Hegira (i.e. Migration) and is attributed to the primary migration of Mohammed, the Prophet of Islam, on July 16, 622 A.D. from Mecca, his native city in the land of Hejaz, Arabia, to the city of Medina in the north of the same land. In Medina the Prophet and Founder of the Islamic Faith died and was buried.

Each year consists of 12 lunar months and, since no intercalation is made, the months go round the seasons in between 32 and 33 years.

Far Eastern Calendars

The ancient Chinese calendar is a lunar calendar, divided into 12 months of either 29 or 30 days. It is synchronized with the solar calendar by the addition of extra months as required. The four-day Chinese New Year (Hsin Nien) begins at the first new moon over China after the sun enters Aquarius, and may fall between January 21 and February 19. The calendar runs on a 60-year cycle, and each year has both a number and a name: 2012 (Dragon), 2013 (Snake), 2014 (Horse), 2015 (Ram), 2016 (Monkey). The three-day Vietnamese New Year (Tet) and the three-to-four-day Korean festival Suhl are set by the same new moon. The Japanese calendar uses the Gregorian date of new year, but with a different epoch.

The Hindu Calendar

The Hindu calendar contains both lunar and solar elements, and is therefore complex. Each lunar month is divided into two halves: the dark half (full moon to new moon) and the bright half (new moon to full moon). For some Hindus (primarily South Indian), the lunar month begins on the day following the new moon; for others (primarily North Indian), it begins on the day following the full moon. Likewise, the calculation of the date of New Year varies. There are some holidays which are set by the solar calendar, as well as several which are set by the lunar calendar.

The Indian Calendar

Various religious groups in India have their own calendars (see The Muslim Calendar, and The Hindu Calendar, above). The Indian civil calendar sets the New Year on March 22 in a common year, and on March 21 in a leap year. The years are reckoned according to the native Saka historical era.

The Zoroastrian Calendar

The Zoroastrian calendar is solar, and consists of 12 months of 30 days; five additional days called "gatha" bring the total days in a year to 365. The calculation of the date of the New Year varies among the various Zoroastrian groups.

The Baha'i Calendar

The Baha'i calendar is astronomically fixed, commencing at the vernal equinox. The calendar is solar, and consists of 19 months of 19 days, with the addition of four or five days to bring the total to 365 or 366.

US Civil Calendar 2012

New Year's Day	Sun. Jan. 1
Martin Luther King Day	Mon. Jan. 16
Presidents' Day	Mon. Feb. 20
Memorial Day	Mon. May 28
Independence Day	Weds. July 4
Labor Day	Mon. Sept. 3
Columbus Day	Mon. Oct. 8
Election Day	Tue. Nov. 6
Veterans' Day	Sun. Nov. 11
Thanksgiving Day	Thu. Nov. 22

PERPETUAL CALENDAR

(Table for Determining the Weekday of a Given Date)

In the YEAR table, locate the first two figures of the given year (lower left) and the last two figures (upper right) and take the number at the intersection.

With that number, enter the MONTH table, and take the number at the intersection with the given month. Note the special columns for January and February in the case of a bissextile (leap) year.

With that number, enter the DAY OF THE MONTH table. The weekday is found at the intersection with the given day of the month.

Example: 1970 March 7

YEAR					00 06 — 17 23 28 34 — 45 51 56 62 — 73 79 84 90 —	01 07 12 18 — 29 35 40 46 — 57 63 68 74 — 85 91 96	02 — 13 19 24 30 — 41 47 52 58 — 69 75 80 86 — 97	03 08 14 — 25 31 36 42 — 53 59 64 70 — 81 87 92 98	— 09 15 20 26 — 37 43 48 54 — 65 71 76 82 — 93 99	04 10 — 21 27 32 38 — 49 55 60 66 — 77 83 88 94	05 11 16 22 — 33 39 44 50 — 61 67 72 78 — 89 95
0	7	14	17	21	6	0	1	2	3	4	5
1	8	15 *J*			5	6	0	1	2	3	4
2	9		18	22	4	5	6	0	1	2	3
3	10				3	4	5	6	0	1	2
4	11	15 *G*	19	23	2	3	4	5	6	0	1
5	12	16	20	24	1	2	3	4	5	6	0
6	13				0	1	2	3	4	5	6

J: until 1582 October 4 inclusively (Julian Calendar)

G: from 1582 October 15 onwards (Gregorian Calendar)

Example: In the first table, we find 5 at the intersection of 19 and 70.

MONTH	May	Feb. *(B)* Aug.	Feb. March Nov.	June	Sept. Dec.	Jan. *(B)* April July	Jan. Oct.
1	2	3	4	5	6	0	1
2	3	4	5	6	0	1	2
3	4	5	6	0	1	2	3
4	5	6	0	1	2	3	4
5	6	0	1	2	3	4	5
6	0	1	2	3	4	5	6
0	1	2	3	4	5	6	0

(B) = Bissextile (leap) year

Example: In the second table, we find 1 at the intersection of 5 and March.

DAY OF MONTH	1 8 15 22 29	2 9 16 23 30	3 10 17 24 31	4 11 18 25	5 12 19 26	6 13 20 27	7 14 21 28
1	Sun.	Mon.	Tue.	Wed.	Thur.	Fri.	Sat.
2	Mon.	Tue.	Wed.	Thur.	Fri.	Sat.	Sun.
3	Tue.	Wed.	Thur.	Fri.	Sat.	Sun.	Mon.
4	Wed.	Thur.	Fri.	Sat.	Sun.	Mon.	Tue.
5	Thur.	Fri.	Sat.	Sun.	Mon.	Tue.	Wed.
6	Fri.	Sat.	Sun.	Mon.	Tue.	Wed.	Thu.
0	Sat.	Sun.	Mon.	Tue.	Wed.	Thu.	Fri.

Example: In the third table, we find *Saturday* at the intersection of 1 and 7.

FIXED AND MOVABLE FESTIVALS AND ANNIVERSARIES

(Gregorian Calendar)

	2012	2013	2014	2015	2016
JANUARY begins on	Sun.	Tue.	Wed.	Thu.	Sat.
New Year's Day	Su Jan. 1	Tu Jan. 1	We Jan. 1	Th Jan. 1	Fr Jan. 1
Circumcision	Su Jan. 1	Tu Jan. 1	We Jan. 1	Th Jan. 1	Fr Jan. 1
Gantan-sai (Shinto New Year)	Su Jan. 1	Tu Jan. 1	We Jan. 1	Th Jan. 1	Fr Jan. 1
Mary Mother of God	Su Jan. 1	Tu Jan. 1	We Jan. 1	Th Jan. 1	Fr Jan. 1
Twelfth Night	Th Jan. 5	Sa Jan. 5	Su Jan. 5	Mo Jan. 5	Tu Jan. 5
Epiphany	Fr Jan. 6	Su Jan. 6	Mo Jan. 6	Tu Jan. 6	We Jan. 6
Maghi	Fr Jan. 13	Su Jan. 13	Mo Jan. 13	Tu Jan. 13	We Jan. 13
New Year's Day (Orthodox Christian)	Sa Jan. 14	Mo Jan. 14	Tu Jan. 14	We Jan. 14	Th Jan. 14
Lunar New Year (Chinese, etc.)	Sa Jan. 23	Su Feb. 10	Fr Jan. 31	Th Feb. 19	Mo Feb. 8
FEBRUARY begins on	Wed.	Fri.	Sat.	Sun.	Mon.
Mawlid an Nabi	Sa Feb. 4	Th Jan. 24	Mo Jan. 13	Sa Jan. 3	We Dec. 14
				Fr Dec. 23	
Tu B'shvat	We Feb. 8	Sa Jan. 26	Th Jan. 16	We Feb. 4	Mo Jan. 25
St. Valentine's Day	Tu Feb. 14	Th Feb. 14	Fr Feb. 14	Sa Feb. 14	Su Feb. 14
Nirvana Day	We Feb. 15	Fr Feb. 15	Sa Feb. 15	Su Feb. 15	Mo Feb. 15
Ash Wednesday	We Feb. 22	We Feb. 13	We Mar. 5	We Feb. 25	We Feb. 10
First Sunday of Lent	Su Feb. 26	Su Feb. 17	Su Mar. 9	Su Mar. 1	Su Feb. 14
MARCH begins on	Thu.	Fri.	Sat.	Sun.	Tue.
St. David	Th Mar. 1	Fr Mar. 1	Sa Mar. 1	Su Mar. 1	Tu Mar. 1
World Day of Prayer	Fr Mar. 2	Fr Mar. 1	Fr Mar. 7	Fr Mar. 6	Fr Mar. 4
Purim	Th Mar. 8	Su Feb. 24	Su Mar. 16	Th Mar. 5	Th Mar. 24
Daylight Savings Time begins**	Su Mar. 12	Su Mar. 10	Su Mar. 9	Su Mar. 8	Su Mar. 13
	Su Apr. 2	Su Apr. 7	Su Apr. 6	Su Apr. 5	Su Apr. 3
St. Patrick	Sa Mar. 17	Su Mar. 17	Mo Mar. 17	Tu Mar. 17	Th Mar. 17
St. Joseph (Patron Saint of Canada)	Mo Mar. 19	Tu Mar. 19	We Mar. 19	Th Mar. 19	Sa Mar. 19
Naw Ruz (Baha'i New Year)	We Mar. 21	Th Mar. 21	Fr Mar. 21	Sa Mar. 21	Mo Mar. 21
Norouz (Persian/Zoroastrian New Year)	We Mar. 21	Th Mar. 21	Fr Mar. 21	Sa Mar. 21	Mo Mar. 21
Hindu New Year***	Fr Mar. 23	Th Apr. 11	Mo Mar. 31	Sa Mar. 21	Fr Apr. 8
Annunciation	Su Mar. 25	Mo Mar. 25	Tu Mar. 25	We Mar. 25	Fr Mar. 25
Passion Sunday	Su Mar. 25	Su Mar. 17	Su Apr. 6	Su Mar. 22	Su Mar. 13
Khordad Sal (Birth of Prophet Zaranhushtra)	We Mar. 28	Th Mar. 28	Fr Mar. 28	Sa Mar. 28	Mo Mar. 28
APRIL begins on	Sun.	Mon.	Tue.	Wed.	Fri.
Palm Sunday	Su Apr. 1	Su Mar. 24	Su Apr. 13	Su Mar. 29	Su Mar. 20
Good Friday	Fr Apr. 6	Fr Mar. 29	Fr Apr. 18	Fr Apr. 3	Fr Mar. 25
First Day of Passover (Pesach)	Sa Apr. 7	Tu Mar. 26	Tu Apr. 15	Sa Apr. 4	Sa Apr. 23
Easter Sunday	Su Apr. 8	Su Mar. 31	Su Apr. 20	Su Apr. 5	Su Mar. 27
Baisakhi	Fr Apr. 13	Sa Apr. 13	Mo Apr. 14	Tu Apr. 14	Th Apr. 14
Yom HaSho'ah	Th Apr. 19	Su Apr. 7	Su Apr. 27	Th Apr. 16	Th May 5
First Day of Ridvan	Sa Apr. 21	Su Apr. 21	Mo Apr. 21	Tu Apr. 21	Th Apr. 21
St. George	Mo Apr. 23	Tu Apr. 23	We Apr. 23	Th Apr. 23	Sa Apr. 23
St. James	Mo Apr. 30	Tu Apr. 30	We Apr. 30	Th Apr. 30	Sa Apr. 30
MAY begins on	Tue.	Wed.	Thu.	Fri.	Sun.
Buddha Day (Visakha Puja)	Mo May 6	Fr May 24	We May 14	Mo May 4	Su May 15
Rogation Sunday	Su May 13	Su May 5	Su May 25	Su May 10	Su May 1
Mother's Day	Su May 14	Su May 12	Su May 11	Su May 10	Su May 8
Ascension Thursday	Th May 17	Th May 9	Th May 29	Th May 14	Th May 5
Ascension Sunday	Su May 20	Su May 12	Su June 1	Su May 10	Su May 8
Victoria Day	Mo May 21	Mo May 20	Mo May 19	Mo May 18	Mo May 23
Pentecost (Shavuoth)	Su May 27	We May 15	We June 4	Su May 24	Su June 12
Pentecost (Whit Sunday)	Su May 27	Su May 19	Su June 8	Su May 24	Su May 15
Ascension of Baha'u'llah	Tu May 29	We May 29	Th May 29	Fr May 29	Su May 29
JUNE begins on	Fri.	Sat.	Sun.	Mon.	Wed.
Trinity Sunday	Su June 3	Su May 26	Su June 15	Su May 31	Su May 22
Corpus Christi (Thursday)	Th June 7	Th May 30	Th June 19	Th June 4	Th May 26
Corpus Christi (Sunday)	Su June 10	Su June 2	Su June 22	Su June 7	Su May 29
Sacred Heart of Jesus	Fr June 15	Fr June 7	Fr June 27	Fr June 19	Fr June 3
Father's Day	Su June 17	Su June 16	Su June 15	Su June 21	Su June 19
First Nations Day	Th June 21	Fr June 21	Sa June 21	Su June 21	Tu June 21
St. John Baptist	Su June 24	Mo June 24	Tu June 24	We June 24	Fr June 24
St. Peter and St. Paul	Fr June 29	Sa June 29	Su June 29	Mo June 29	We June 29
JULY begins on	Sun.	Mon.	Tue.	Wed.	Fri.
Canada Day	Su July 1	Mo July 1	Tu July 1	We July 1	Fr July 1
Martyrdom of the Bab	Mo July 9	Tu July 9	We July 9	Th July 9	Sa July 9
St. Benedict Day	We July 11	Th July 11	Fr July 11	Sa July 11	Mo July 11
Pioneer Day	Tu July 24	We July 24	Th July 24	Fr July 24	Su July 24
AUGUST begins on	Wed.	Thu.	Fri.	Sat.	Mon.
Lammas	We Aug. 1	Th Aug. 1	Fr Aug. 1	Sa Aug. 1	Mo Aug. 1
Transfiguration	Mo Aug. 6	Tu Aug. 6	We Aug. 6	Th Aug. 6	Sa Aug. 6
Assumption	We Aug. 15	Th Aug. 15	Fr Aug. 15	Sa Aug. 15	Mo Aug. 15
Eid al Fitr (Ramadan ends)	Su Aug. 19	Th Aug. 8	Tu July 29	Sa July 18	Th July 7
First Day of Ramadan*	Fr July 20	Tu July 9	Sa June 28	Th June 18	Mo June 6
Tisha B'Av	Su July 29	Tu July 16	Tu Aug. 5	Su July 26	Su Aug. 14

FIXED AND MOVABLE FESTIVALS AND ANNIVERSARIES *(continued)*

(Gregorian Calendar)

	2012	2013	2014	2015	2016
SEPTEMBER begins on	Sat.	Sun.	Mon.	Tue.	Thu.
Labour Day	Mo Sept. 3	Mo Sept. 2	Mo Sept. 1	Mo Sept. 7	Mo Sept. 5
Hebrew New Year (Rosh Hashanah)	Mo Sept. 17	Tu Sept. 5	Th Sept. 25	Fr Sept. 4	Mo Oct. 3
Day of Atonement (Yom Kippur)	We Sept. 26	Sa Sept. 14	Sa Oct. 4	We Sept. 23	We Oct. 12
St. Michael	Sa Sept. 29	Su Sept. 29	Mo Sept. 29	Tu Sept. 29	Th Sept. 29
OCTOBER begins on	Mon.	Tue.	Wed.	Thu.	Sat.
First Day of Feast of Tabernacles (Sukkoth)	Mo Oct. 1	Th Sept. 19	Th Oct. 9	Mo Sept. 28	Mo Oct. 17
St. Francis	Th Oct. 4	Fr Oct. 4	Sa Oct. 4	Su Oct. 4	Tu Oct. 4
Shemini Atzeret	Mo Oct. 8	Th Sept. 26	Th Oct. 16	Tu Oct. 13	Mo Oct. 24
Thanksgiving	Mo Oct. 8	Mo Oct. 7	Mo Oct. 13	Mo Oct. 12	Mo Oct. 10
Simhat Torah	Tu Oct. 9	Fr Sept. 27	Fr Oct. 17	We Oct. 14	Tu Oct. 25
Birth of the B'ab	Sa Oct. 20	Su Oct. 20	Mo Oct. 20	Tu Oct. 20	Th Oct. 20
Reformation Day	Sa Oct. 27	Su Oct. 27	Mo Oct. 27	Su Oct. 25	Mo Oct. 31
Daylight Savings Time ends**	Su Oct. 28	Su Oct. 27	Su Oct. 26	Su Oct. 25	Su Oct. 30
	Su Nov. 4	Su Nov. 3	Su Nov. 2	Su Nov. 1	Su Nov. 6
Mulvian Bridge Day	Su Oct. 28	Mo Oct. 28	Tu Oct. 28	We Oct. 28	Fr Oct. 28
All Hallows Eve	We Oct. 31	Th Oct. 31	Fr Oct. 31	Sa Oct. 31	Mo Oct. 31
NOVEMBER begins on	Thu.	Fri.	Sat.	Sun.	Tue.
All Saints' Day	Th Nov. 1	Fr Nov. 1	Sa Nov. 1	Su Nov. 1	Tu Nov. 1
All Souls' Day	Fr Nov. 2	Sa Nov. 2	Su Nov. 2	Mo Nov. 2	We Nov. 2
Remembrance Day	Su Nov. 11	Mo Nov. 11	Tu Nov. 11	We Nov. 11	Fr Nov. 11
Birth of Baha'u'llah	Mo Nov. 12	Tu Nov. 12	We Nov. 12	Th Nov. 12	Sa Nov. 12
Diwali	Tu Nov. 13	Su Nov. 3	Th Oct. 23	We Nov. 11	Su Oct. 30
Islamic New Year	Th Nov. 15	Tu Nov. 5	Sa Oct. 25	We Oct. 14	Su Oct. 2
Day of Covenant	Mo Nov. 26	Tu Nov. 26	We Nov. 26	Th Nov. 26	Sa Nov. 26
St. Andrew's Day	Fr Nov. 30	Sa Nov. 30	Su Nov. 30	Mo Nov. 30	We Nov. 30
DECEMBER begins on	Sat.	Sun.	Mon.	Tue.	Thu.
First Sunday in Advent	Su Dec. 2	Su Dec. 1	Su Nov. 30	Su Nov. 29	Su Nov. 27
Bodhi Day	Sa Dec. 8	Su Dec. 8	Mo Dec. 8	Tu Dec. 8	Th Dec. 8
First Day in Hanukah	Su Dec. 9	Th Nov. 28	We Dec. 17	Mo Dec. 7	Su Dec. 25
Feast day (Our Lady of Guadalupe)	We Dec. 12	Th Dec. 12	Fr Dec. 12	Sa Dec. 12	Mo Dec. 12
Christmas Day	Tu Dec. 25	We Dec. 25	Th Dec. 25	Fr Dec. 25	Su Dec. 25
Kwanzaa begins on	We Dec. 26	Th Dec. 26	Fr Dec. 26	Sa Dec. 26	Mo Dec. 26
Zarathosht Diso (Death of Prophet Zarathushtra)	We Dec. 26	Th Dec. 26	Fr Dec. 26	Sa Dec. 26	Mo Dec. 26
Last Day of Year	Mon.	Tue.	Wed.	Thu.	Sat.

*These are tabular dates; the festival begins at sunset on the day before. According to Islamic custom, the date is actually set by the direct observation of the new crescent moon.

Jewish holidays begin at sunset the previous evening.

**Alberta, British Columbia, Manitoba, New Brunswick, Northwest Territories, Nova Scotia, Ontario, Prince Edward Island and Quebec start Daylight Saving Time on the second Sunday in March and return to standard time on the first Sunday in November. Newfoundland, Nunavut and Yukon start Daylight Saving Time on the first Sunday in April and return to standard time on the last Sunday in October. Saskatchewan doesn't observe Daylight Saving Time.

*** Different branches of Hinduism celebrate the new year at different times

STANDARD HOLIDAYS in Canada include the following: New Year's Day, Good Friday, Victoria Day, Canada Day, Labour Day, Thanksgiving Day, Christmas Day, Boxing Day and any other day so proclaimed by the Governor General of Canada, or the Lieutenants Governor of the Provinces. Additionally, Provincial Holidays include:

ALBERTA: Alberta Family Day (3rd Monday in February), Heritage Day (1st Monday in August)

BRITISH COLUMBIA: British Columbia Day (1st Monday in August)

MANITOBA: Louis Riel Day (3rd Monday in February), Civic Holiday (1st Monday in August)

NEW BRUNSWICK: New Brunswick Day (1st Monday in August)

NEWFOUNDLAND: Regatta Day/Civic Holiday (by municipal orders); following celebrated on nearest Monday: St. Patrick's Day (Mar. 17), St. George's Day (Apr. 23), Discovery Day (June 24), Orangemen's Day (July 12)

NORTHWEST TERRITORIES: National Aboriginal Day (June 21), Civic Holiday (1st Monday in August)

NOVA SCOTIA: Natal Day (1st Monday in August, varies in Halifax)

NUNAVUT: Nunavut Day (July 9), 1st Monday in August (1st Monday in August)

ONTARIO: Family Day (3rd Monday in February), Civic Holiday (1st Monday in August)

PRINCE EDWARD ISLAND: Natal Day (by proclamation, usually 1st Monday in August)

QUEBEC: National Day (June 24)

SASKATCHEWAN: Family Day (3rd Monday in February), Civic Holiday (1st Monday in August)

YUKON: Discovery Day (3rd Monday in August)

United Kingdom Civil Calendar 2012

St. David (Wales)	Thurs. Mar. 1
Commonwealth Day	Mon. Mar. 12
St. Patrick (Ireland)	Sat. Mar. 17
Birthday of Queen Elizabeth II	Sat. Apr. 21
St. George (England)	Mon. Apr. 23
Queen's Diamond Jubilee (Coronation Day)	Tues. June 5
Remembrance Sunday	Sun. Nov. 11
St. Andrew (Scotland)	Fri. Nov. 30

For Canadian holidays and festivals, please see page A-53.

THE SEASONS 2012

Eastern Standard Time
- Spring begins March 20th 00 h 14 m
- Summer begins June 20th 18 h 9 m
- Autumn begins Sept. 22nd 09 h 49 m
- Winter begins Dec. 21st 6 h 12 m

Eastern Standard Time applies in Ontario and Québec. Newfoundland time is 1 1/2 hours later than Eastern Standard time; in the Maritime Provinces, on Atlantic time, time is 1 hour later; in Manitoba and Saskatchewan, on Central time, time is 1 hour earlier; in Alberta and the western half of Saskatchewan, on Mountain time, time is 2 hours earlier; in B.C., on Pacific time, time is 3 hours earlier.

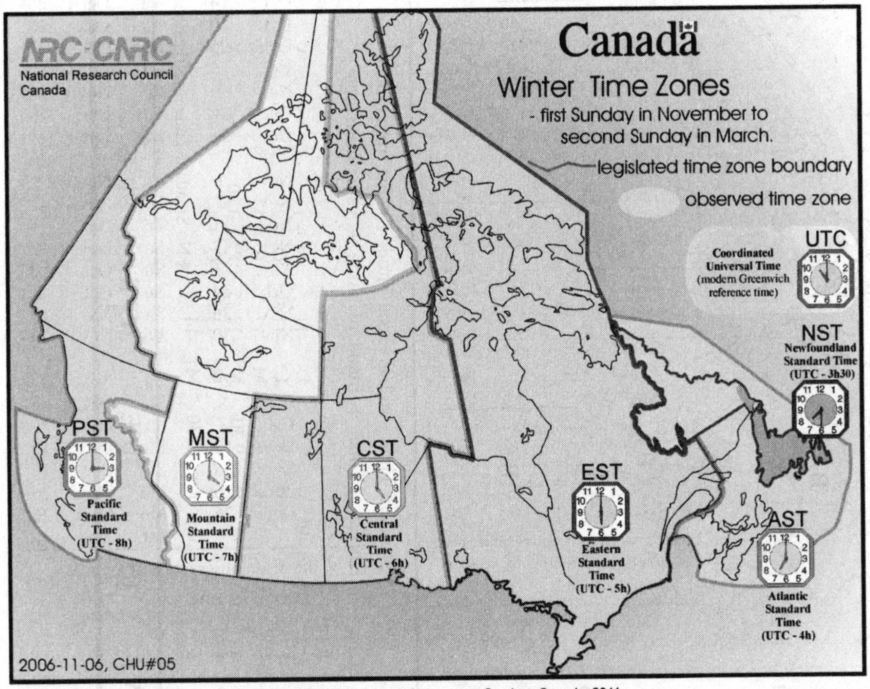

Reproduced with the permission of the Minister of Public Works and Government Services Canada, 2011.

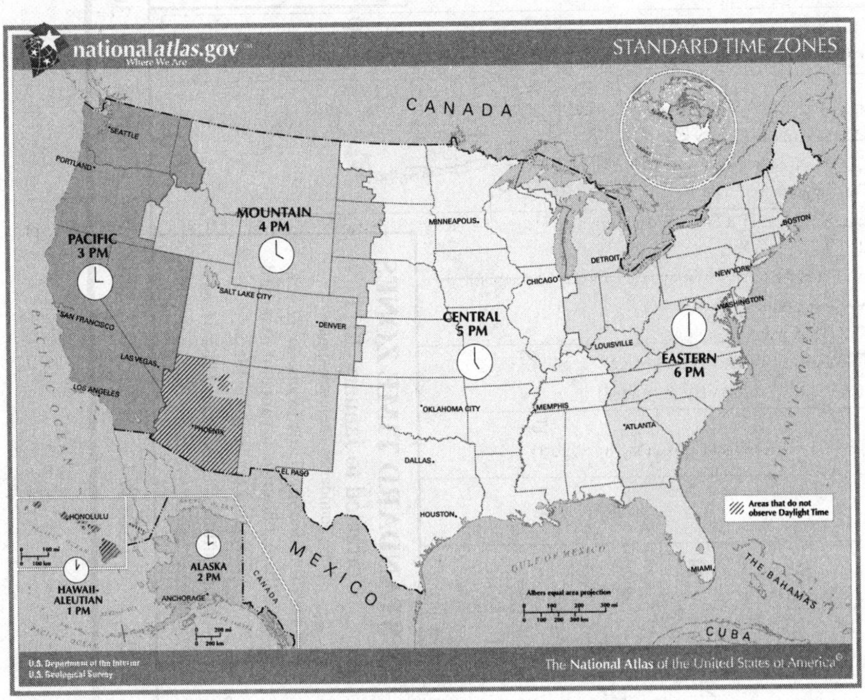

EPOCHS 2012

- The year 7521 of the Byzantine era begins on Fri., Sep. 14, 2012.
- The year 5773 of the Jewish era begins at sunset on Sun., Sep. 16, 2012.
- The New Year of the Chinese (ren chen) era begins on Mon., Jan. 23, 2012.
- The year 2765 of the Roman era begins on Sat., Jan. 14, 2012.
- The year 2761 of the Nabonassar era begins on Fri., Apr. 20, 2012.
- The year 2672 of the Japanese era begins on Sun., Jan. 1, 2012.
- The year 2324 of the Grecian (Seleucidae) era begins on Fri., Sep. 14, 2012 (or Sun., Oct. 14, 2012).
- The year 1934 of the Indian (Saka) era begins on Weds., Mar. 21, 2012.
- The year 1729 of the Diocletian era begins on Tues., Sep. 11, 2012.
- The year 1434 of the Islamic era (Hegira) begins at sunset on Weds., Nov. 14, 2012.
- January 1, 2012 of the Julian Calendar corresponds to Jan. 14, 2012 of the Gregorian Calendar.
- The 61st year of the reign of Queen Elizabeth II begins on Mon., Feb. 6, 2012.
- The 146th year of the Dominion of Canada begins Sun., July 1, 2012.
- The 237th year of the Independence of the United States of America begins Weds., July 4, 2012.
- The Julian Day 2,455,928 begins at Greenwich noon Jan. 1, 2012, Gregorian Calendar.

STANDARD TIME

Owing to the great breadth of Canada the difference in solar time in various parts of the country is adjusted by the creation of Standard Time Zones, one hour in width, fixed between arbitrary lines running approximately north and south, 15° of longitude apart, the time observed in each zone being an exact, except for Newfoundland, number of hours slow from Greenwich. Example: When it is 8 a.m. by Pacific Time it is 12 noon by Atlantic Time and 4 p.m. at Greenwich.

There are six zones divided as follows, reckoning from Greenwich:
- *Newfoundland Standard Time:* Newfoundland, excluding most of Labrador, 3 1/2 hours slow.
- *Atlantic Standard Time/60th Meridian Time:* most of Labrador, New Brunswick, Nova Scotia, Prince Edward Island, and those parts of Québec and Northwest Territories east of the 63rd Meridian, 4 hours slow.
- *Eastern Standard Time/75th Meridian Time:* Québec west of the 63rd Meridian and Ontario as far west as the 90th Meridian; Northwest Territories between the 68th and 85th Meridian, 5 hours slow.
- *Central Standard Time/90th Meridian Time:* Ontario west of the 90th Meridian, Manitoba, Saskatchewan and Northwest Territories between the 85th and 102nd Meridian, 6 hours slow.
- *Mountain Standard Time/105th Meridian Time:* Throughout Alberta and in Northwest Territories west of the 102nd Meridian, 7 hours slow.
- *Pacific Standard Time/120th Meridian Time:* Throughout most of British Columbia and in the Yukon, 8 hours slow.

Railways and airways make up their schedules according to Standard Time in winter and Daylight Saving Time in summer. Solar time around the globe varies four minutes with each degree of longitude.

WORLD MAP OF TIME ZONES

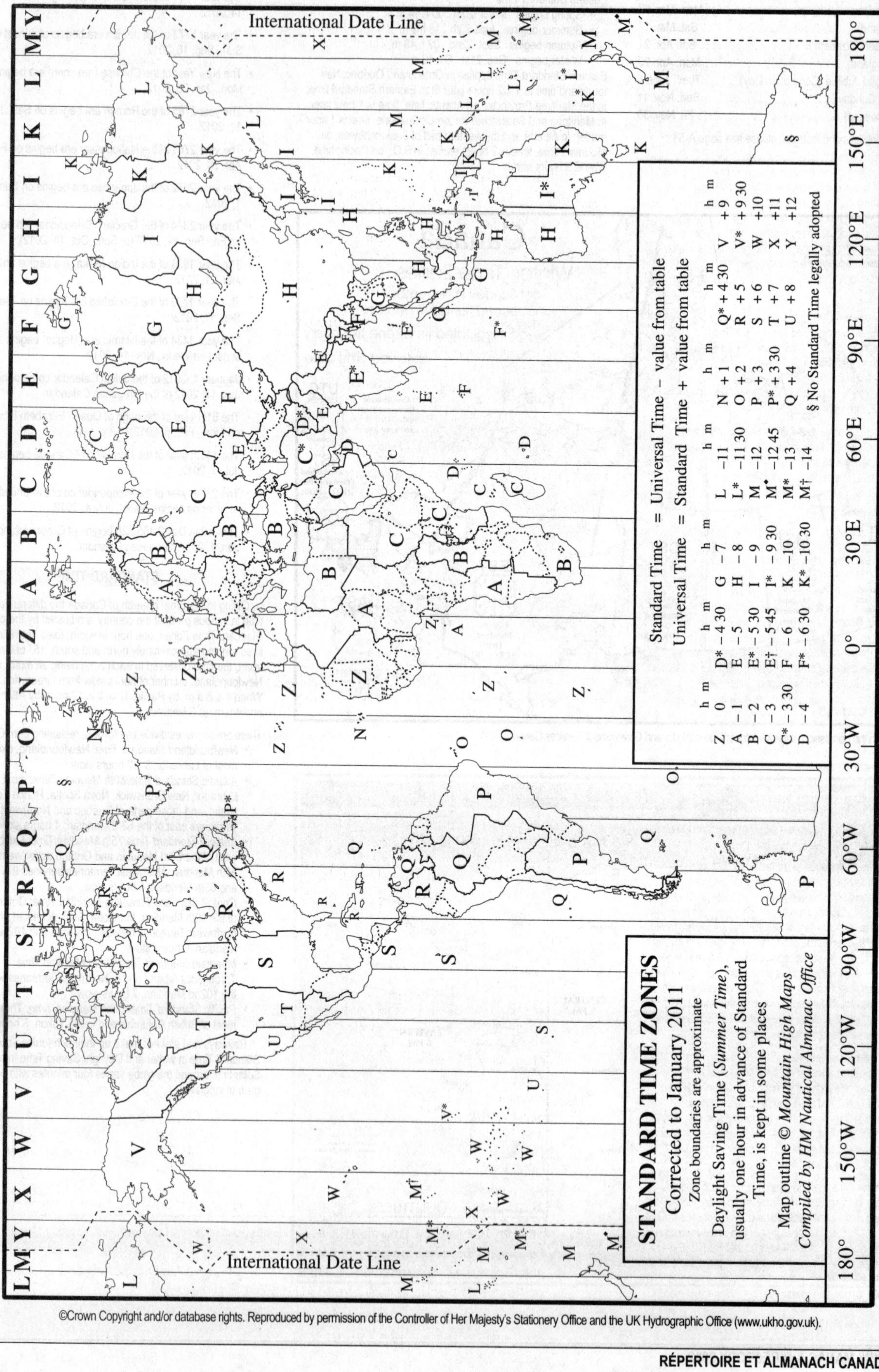
International Date Line
International Date Line
STANDARD TIME ZONES
Corrected to January 2011
Zone boundaries are approximate
Daylight Saving Time (Summer Time), usually one hour in advance of Standard Time, is kept in some places
Map outline © Mountain High Maps
Compiled by HM Nautical Almanac Office
Standard Time = Universal Time − value from table
Universal Time = Standard Time + value from table
Z 0; A −1; B −2; C −3; C* −3 30; D −4
D* −4 30; E −5; E* −5 30; E† −5 45; F −6; F* −6 30
G −7; H −8; I −9; I* −9 30; K −10; K* −10 30
L −11; L* −11 30; M −12; M* −12 45; M* −13; M† −14
N +1; O +2; P +3; P* +3 30; Q +4; Q* +4 30
R +5; S +6; T +7; U +8; V +9; V* +9 30
W +10; X +11; Y +12
§ No Standard Time legally adopted
180° 150°W 120°W 90°W 60°W 30°W 0° 30°E 60°E 90°E 120°E 150°E 180°
L M Y X W V U T S R Q P O N Z A B C D E F G H I K L M Y

Economics & Finance

Canada's Economy

Since World War II, the growth of Canada's manufacturing, mining and service sectors has transformed the economy of the world's second-largest nation from a largely rural model into one that is primarily industrial and urban. This transformation has been so progressive that Canada has long enjoyed top-level economic status within the G-7, the international grouping of seven leading industrial countries that also includes the United States, the United Kingdom, France, Germany, Italy and Japan.

The 1989 U.S.-Canada Free Trade Agreement and the 1994 North American Free Trade Agreement (which also includes Mexico) spurred a dramatic increase in trade and economic integration of the North American continent. Given its significant natural resources, skilled labor force and modern plants, Canada has benefited tremendously from the free-trade initiatives. Currently, some 79 percent of Canadian exports are absorbed by Canada's principal trading partner, making it the largest foreign supplier of energy, including oil, gas, uranium and electric power, to the U.S.

In general, Canada's overall economy is improving. After the recession, the economy returned to growth in the third quarter of 2009. Canada is the only G-7 country to have nearly recouped the loss incurred in the recession. The government plans to return to a budgetary surplus by 2015. Canada posted significant employment growth in 2010, with the national unemployment rate becoming 7.3 percent.

However, like any other allied country from World War II, Canada will soon see the baby-boom generation pass into retirement, causing the working-age proportion of its population to diminish. As well, there is continuing public debate regarding the rising cost of Canada's world-famous and well-regarded, publicly funded healthcare system.

In the last few decades, Canada's economic model has moved away from being natural-resource dependant to being service-based. While the production of goods remains significant, accounting for a third of the national economy, three out of four citizens are currently employed in service industries. Maintaining the transportation and storage of goods, along with servicing restaurants, shops, entertainment, healthcare, education, defense and government now occupies more Canadians than the actual manufacturing of materials. Canada's gross domestic product, being the balance between consumers' expenditures and income, has shown healthy progress, illustrating a growing demand for big-ticket items including houses, cars, furniture and electronics.

In 2007, the Canadian dollar had reached a 31-year high against the American dollar, achieving one-to-one parity with its neighbour's currency. Later that same year, Bloomberg reported that the dollar was approaching $1.10 U.S., the currency's all-time high since the information-service company began monitoring it in February 1971 (the Bank of Canada only let the currency float in 1970). The Canadian dollar continues to be strong, starying near parity with the U.S.

As a major international oil exporter, Canada has benefited from soaring crude prices, more than offsetting its declining conventional oil production. The country has equally profited from the export of nickel, copper, aluminum and zinc, commodities that all sit at or near record highs. Mineral prices are expected to remain elevated and oil sands production is projected to expand dramatically in coming years to reach close to 3.5 million barrels per day by 2015. With commodities accounting for 35 percent of Canada's exports, the loonie is finally being viewed around the world as a commodity-based currency and has been bid up accordingly. Since January 2002, Canada's dollar-coin has gained more than 40 percent against the buck.

Certainly, some economic sectors could be stronger. Performance in the high-tech sector has been weak, partially due to Canadian companies purchasing much of their software and machinery from the U.S. That said, the favourable exchange rate is expected to lead to improvement in this area. The challenges of adjusting to a higher Canadian dollar could additionally benefit other exporters, who have found it necessary to improve efficiency.

A decline in the American housing market has caused lumber prices to tumble, hurting British Columbia's forestry industry. However, strong domestic housing starts have boosted the overall production of lumber and other timber products, increasing forestry exports despite U.S. softwood lumber tariffs. (Every one-cent increase in the value of the loonie against the U.S. dollar translates to a loss of more than $150 million in annual revenue for the pulp, paper and forest industry.) Non-residential construction activity also increased in 2010, reflecting multi-billion dollar investments in projects in Canada's energy patch as well as increased investment in commercial building construction.

In May 2003, the discovery of Bovine Spongiform Encephalopathy (BSE), commonly known as mad-cow disease, in one cow from Alberta caused severe harm to Canada's beef-export market. Compounded by the advent of Severe Acute Respiratory Syndrome (SARS) in the late summer of that same year, Canada's growth forecast dampened from 3.4 percent to 2.3 percent, but the current outlook is improving. In September 2007, the U.S. Department of Agriculture (USDA) agreed to expand cattle trade with Canada, additionally urging beef-importing nations to eliminate unnecessary barriers erected after the mad-cow scare. More trade with the United States will help export-dependent Canadian ranchers recover from trade bans. The impact of the stronger Canadian dollar will also result in higher beef-processing costs relative to competitors in the U.S., which could offset more gains.

Canada's commercial ocean fisheries have experienced overall production decline, due in part to the 2003 closure of northern cod fishing grounds. The volume of production has been adversely affected by an average rate of 4 percent a year as a result of dwindling resources and problems caused by over-exploitation of some major species. West Coast over-fishing has led to a reduction in the size of the salmon fleet, as well as extensive government intervention in the fishing industry on both coasts. Meanwhile aquaculture, or fish farming, continues to thrive. In particular, Eastern Canada boasts extensive operations, growing predominantly Atlantic salmon and mussels. Other key species include bay and sea scallops, brook trout, oysters, bay quahogs, sea urchins, arctic char, haddock and bar clams, and significant progress has been made in the development of new species such as halibut, sturgeon, abalone and cod. That said, almost every province and territory in Canada, including the Yukon, runs commercial freshwater aquaculture operations, mostly raising rainbow and brook trout. Ontario and Québec are the dominant producers of freshwater fish in Canada, followed by Saskatchewan, Alberta and New Brunswick. As the Canadian freshwater aquaculture industry is young, it is also ideally poised for growth.

Always historically strong, the Canadian stock market has continued to thrive. The Toronto Stock Exchange (TSX) is the country's largest and the world's sixth largest by market capitalization. In addition, the TSX Group is the international leader in the oil and gas sector, boasting more oil and gas sector listings on the Toronto Stock Exchange and TSX Venture Exchange than any other exchange in the world (in 2010, 474 oil and gas companies were listed, with a total market capitalization of $425 billion). Oil and gas companies continue to raise equity on Canadian exchanges with $8 billion raised in 2010 and trading over 29.4 billion oil and gas shares.

Sourcing from China continues to offer an economically viable solution for Canadian companies. This option to reduce costs while growing wealth in major Chinese cities creates vast new opportunities for Canadian firms, particularly exporters of services. With a small domestic market, the steady expansion of multilateral trade is critical to the structure of the country's economy and the continued prosperity of its citizens. The rapid and ongoing industrialization of China has boosted the world price of Canadian oil, gas, mineral, metal and farm-product exports. Canadian exports to China in 2010 accounted for 3.3 percent of our total, up from 1.8 percent in 2006. However, Canadian sales to Japan have lagged. In 1996, Japan received 4.1 percent of Canada's exports, but only 2.3 percent in 2010.

Since the early 1990s, the focus of Canadian monetary policy on low, stable and predictable inflation has helped to both anchor inflation expectations and reduce the ups and downs in economic activity. Canadians have been able to make spending, saving and investment decisions with greater certainty, knowing that their central bank will hold the line on future inflation and that the economy will be more stable. Low interest rates and greater confidence about the future have encouraged Canadian firms to undertake important restructuring initiatives, stepping up to meet the challenges of sweeping worldwide technological change and intensely competitive global markets.

PRINCIPAL TRADING PARTNERS IN 2010

	Imports ($)	Exports ($)
United States (U.S.)	203,282,169,071	299,069,826,838
China	44,491,714,023	13,232,891,233
Mexico	22,108,275,581	5,009,854,421
Japan	13,449,917,049	9,194,095,416
Germany	11,281,181,632	3,937,321,259
United Kingdom (U.K.)	10,697,114,075	16,396,539,517
Korea, South	6,148,480,196	3,709,298,114
France (incl. Monaco, French Antilles)	5,428,160,362	2,349,610,500
Italy (includes Vatican City State)	4,646,975,353	1,923,993,390
Taiwan	3,969,819,676	1,289,097,243
Peru	3,644,040,139	479,022,314
Algeria	3,578,112,577	298,884,118
Brazil	3,287,106,441	2,567,269,370
Switzerland	2,944,871,867	1,535,797,114
Norway	2,845,961,985	2,528,640,504
Thailand	2,407,903,001	651,989,230
Kazakhstan	2,284,617,422	140,728,110
Malaysia	2,278,763,150	785,955,586
India	2,123,036,802	2,088,674,780
Sweden	2,095,215,626	473,053,443
Saudi Arabia	2,023,798,470	977,757,933
Iraq	1,912,946,303	236,578,223
Denmark	1,878,243,603	308,747,079
Chile	1,871,891,394	587,442,199
Belgium	1,719,301,457	2,154,524,884
TOTAL (ALL COUNTRIES)	399,562,532,547	399,383,209,353

Source: "International Trade data", based on Statistics Canada's International Trade Division, retrieved on Industry Canada's website: http://www.ic.gc.ca/sc_mrkti/tdst/tdo/tdo.php?lang=30&headFootDir=/sc_mrkti/tdst/headfoot&productType=HS6&cacheTime=962115865#tag, August 2011.

AVERAGE EARNINGS[1] OF MEN & WOMEN IN CANADA, 1993-2009

Work activity	All earners			Full-year full-time workers		
Earnings Date	Average earnings, females (dollars)	Average earnings, males (dollars)	Female-to-male earnings ratio (percent)	Average earnings, females (dollars)	Average earnings, males (dollars)	Female-to-male earnings ratio (percent)
1993	24,800	38,700	64.1	38,000	52,100	72.8
1994	24,800	40,100	61.9	37,700	53,800	70.2
1995	25,300	39,400	64.2	38,400	52,600	73.0
1996	25,500	40,100	63.6	38,700	53,100	72.8
1997	25,400	41,200	61.8	38,300	54,800	70.0
1998	26,600	42,400	62.8	40,600	56,400	71.9
1999	27,000	43,200	62.6	39,000	57,000	68.4
2000	27,500	44,600	61.7	40,300	57,000	70.6
2001	27,600	44,500	62.1	40,700	58,200	69.9
2002	28,000	44,500	62.8	40,900	58,300	70.2
2003	27,600	43,900	62.9	40,800	58,100	70.2
2004	28,000	44,100	63.5	42,100	60,000	70.1
2005	28,700	44,800	64.0	41,900	59,500	70.5
2006	29,100	44,900	64.7	43,300	60,200	71.9
2007	29,900	45,600	65.7	44,200	61,800	71.4
2008	30,300	47,000	64.5	44,800	62,800	71.3
2009	31,100	45,200	68.8	46,400	62,200	74.6

[1] 2009 Constant Dollars

Earnings ratio = (female earnings / male earnings) *100

Source: Adapted from Statistics Canada's CANSIM database http://www5.statcan.gc.ca/cansim/home-accueil?lang=eng, Table 202-0102, July 2011.

AVERAGE HOUSEHOLD EXPENDITURE, CANADA 2002 - 2009 ($)

	2002	2003	2004	2005	2006	2007	2008	2009
Total expenditure	59,439	60,088	62,464	65,575	67,736	69,946	71,364	71,117
Food	6,553	6,618	6,772	6,978	7,046	7,305	7,435	7,262
Shelter	11,079	11,419	11,987	12,376	12,986	13,643	14,183	14,095
Household operation	2,741	2,812	2,864	3,027	3,251	3,287	3,345	3,428
Household furnishings and equipment	1,810	1,779	1,871	1,954	2,131	1,964	1,967	1,896
Clothing	2,421	2,401	2,470	2,538	2,870	2,948	2,856	2,841
Transportation	8,337	8,179	8,476	8,914	9,240	9,395	9,722	9,753
Health care	1,561	1,553	1,653	1,755	1,867	1,932	2,044	2,004
Personal care	820	825	882	1,071	1,158	1,167	1,189	1,200
Recreation	3,520	3,533	3,619	3,850	3,975	3,976	4,066	3,843
Reading materials and other printed matter	280	278	278	278	264	260	253	232
Education	907	1,013	1,067	1,214	1,157	1,017	1,179	1,238
Tobacco products and alcoholic beverages	1,460	1,455	1,480	1,398	1,475	1,536	1,495	1,506
Games of chance (net)	302	262	258	271	258	251	260	255
Miscellaneous expenditures	875	870	1,000	987	1,087	1,081	1,075	1,180

Source: Adapted from Statistics Canada's CANSIM database http://www5.statcan.gc.ca/cansim/home-accueil?lang=eng, Table 203-0001, July 2011.

AVERAGE FAMILY INCOME[1], 1997- 2009

	1997	1998	1999	2000	2001	2002	2003	2004	2005	2006	2007	2008	2009
Canada	63,600	67,200	69,300	72,500	73,200	73,100	72,400	74,300	75,100	76,500	79,300	80,700	78,500
Newfoundland and Labrador	40,100	44,700	47,300	48,800	47,500	48,500	48,700	49,900	51,600	53,900	59,500	62,000	59,700
Prince Edward Island	45,900	50,900	51,300	52,600	52,400	53,100	54,200	55,600	55,800	57,800	57,900	60,800	59,400
Nova Scotia	49,100	53,000	56,100	57,800	59,800	61,000	57,800	59,800	63,000	64,800	65,400	64,600	66,000
New Brunswick	47,400	51,300	53,800	56,200	55,800	55,700	56,200	57,400	56,000	57,200	59,200	59,500	61,400
Quebec	55,100	58,700	60,400	63,600	64,100	64,500	63,600	65,600	64,800	65,700	66,300	66,700	66,400
Ontario	71,200	75,800	79,700	83,900	83,400	82,700	81,700	83,100	83,200	83,000	85,400	86,500	82,700
Manitoba	58,000	62,000	61,100	62,000	64,300	65,000	65,000	66,700	68,500	70,400	74,700	75,400	74,100
Saskatchewan	55,100	56,800	58,800	59,700	62,400	62,200	63,100	63,500	67,500	71,500	75,600	80,400	82,500
Alberta	72,800	76,100	74,900	78,200	82,300	79,600	82,200	84,600	87,200	93,500	100,300	103,300	100,600
British Columbia	65,500	66,000	66,800	68,100	69,300	70,600	68,600	71,100	74,100	76,300	80,300	82,900	79,000

[1] Average total income, economic families, 2 persons or more, 2009 contstant dollars.

Source: Adapted from Statistics Canada's CANSIM database http://www5.statcan.gc.ca/cansim/home-accueil?lang=eng, Table 202-0202, July 2011.

Current and Forthcoming Minimum Hourly Wage Rates for Experienced Adult Workers in Canada[1]

Jurisdiction	Effective Date	Wage	Note
Federal[2]	18-Dec-1996		The minimum wage rate applicable in regard to employees under federal jurisdiction is the general adult minimum rate of the province or territory where the employee is usually employed
Alberta	01-Apr-2009	$8.80	
Alberta	01-Sep-2011	$9.40	
British Columbia	01-May-2011	$8.75	
British Columbia	01-Nov-2011	$9.50	
British Columbia	01-May-2012	$10.25	
Manitoba	01-Oct-2010	$9.50	
Manitoba	01-Oct-2011	$10.00	
New Brunswick	01-Apr-2011	$9.50	
New Brunswick	01-Apr-2012	$10.00	
Newfoundland and Labrador	01-Jul-2010	$10.00	
Northwest Territories	01-Apr-2011	$10.00	
Nova Scotia[3]	01-Oct-2010	$9.65	
Nunavut	01-Jan-2011	$11.00	
Ontario	31-Mar-2010	$10.25	
Prince Edward Island	01-Jun-2011	$9.30	
Prince Edward Island	01-Oct-2011	$9.60	
Prince Edward Island	01-Apr-2012	$10.00	
Quebec	01-May-2011	$9.65	
Saskatchewan	01-May-2009	$9.25	
Saskatchewan	01-Sep-2011	$9.50	
Yukon	01-Apr-2011	$9.00	On April 1 of each year, this rate increases by an amount corresponding to the annual increase for the preceding year in the Consumer Price Index for the city of Whitehorse.

(1) In most jurisdictions, these rates also apply to young workers. More information is available on special rates for young workers under "Current and Forthcoming Minimum Wage Rates in Canada for Young Workers and Specific Occupations".

(2) The federal jurisdiction includes labour market sectors coming under federal authority by virtue of the Constitution, such as international and interprovincial transportation, telecommunication and banking.

(3) There is a special minimum wage rate for inexperienced employees. See "Current and Forthcoming Minimum Wage Rates in Canada for Young Workers and Specific Occupations".

Source: Reproduced with the permission of the Minister of Public Works and Government Services Canada, 2011.

CONSUMER PRICE INDEX, CANADA

2005 BASKET, 2002=100

Date	All-items	Food	Shelter	Household operations, furnishings and equipment	Clothing and footwear	Transportation	Health and personal care	Recreation, education and reading	Alcoholic beverages and tobacco products
2000	95.4	93.3	95.6	96.7	100.3	97.2	97.0	97.0	79.0
2001	97.8	97.4	99.1	98.6	100.7	97.3	98.9	98.4	85.0
2002	100.0	100.0	100.0	100.0	100.0	100.0	100.0	100.0	100.0
2003	102.8	101.7	103.2	100.7	98.2	105.2	101.4	100.8	110.1
2004	104.7	103.8	105.8	101.2	98.0	107.7	102.8	101.1	116.0
2005	107.0	106.4	109.2	101.7	97.6	112.0	104.6	100.8	119.1
2006	109.1	108.9	113.1	102.2	95.8	115.2	105.9	100.6	121.7
2007	111.5	111.8	116.9	103.2	95.7	117.1	107.3	101.8	125.5
2008	114.1	115.7	112.0	104.6	93.8	119.5	108.8	102.2	127.5
2009	114.4	121.4	121.6	107.3	93.4	113.1	112.1	103.1	130.7
2010	116.5	123.1	123.3	108.8	91.6	118.0	115.1	104.0	133.1
Jan-11	117.8	124.9	124.5	109.6	87.9	122.8	115.8	102.7	135.2
Feb-11	118.1	125.3	124.5	110.1	89.4	122.6	116.0	103.8	135.0
Mar-11	119.4	127.2	124.6	110.4	94.4	124.8	116.4	104.9	134.8
Apr-11	119.8	126.9	125.2	109.8	93.1	127.2	117.3	105.1	135.0
May-11	120.6	127.7	125.2	110.4	93.7	128.9	117.2	106.1	135.7

Source: Adapted from Statistics Canada's CANSIM database http://www5.statcan.gc.ca/cansim/home-accueil?lang=eng, Tables 326-0020 and 326-0021, July 2011.

New Housing Price Indexes, 1992 - 2010, Annual Averages[1]

2007=100

	Canada	Atlantic Region	Quebec	Ontario	Prairie Region	British Columbia
1992	65.9	75.2	64.5	71.6	38.2	90.7
1993	66.8	76.4	64.9	70.4	39.5	97.2
1994	66.9	77.6	65.1	70.1	40.3	96.6
1995	66.1	78.9	65.6	70.1	40.4	91.3
1996	64.9	79.0	65.3	69.4	40.6	85.7
1997	65.4	77.2	65.2	70.9	42.4	83.0
1998	66.0	76.9	65.6	72.6	44.9	78.8
1999	66.6	78.4	66.9	73.8	46.6	75.5
2000	68.1	79.9	69.2	76.1	47.6	74.6
2001	69.9	81.4	72.4	78.5	48.7	75.1
2002	72.8	83.9	76.5	81.4	51.3	77.1
2003	76.3	86.8	82.4	85.0	54.0	79.9
2004	80.5	89.4	87.6	89.8	56.9	84.1
2005	84.6	93.0	91.9	93.9	60.8	88.2
2006	92.8	96.4	95.9	97.4	81.7	93.9
2007	100.0	100.0	100.0	100.0	100.0	100.0
2008	103.4	109.5	105.0	103.5	102.5	102.1
2009	101.0	115.1	108.3	103.6	94.5	95.4
2010	103.2	118.3	111.6	106.1	95.6	97.9

[1]Total (house and land)

Source: Adapted from Statistics Canada's CANSIM database http://www5.statcan.gc.ca/cansim/home-accueil?lang=eng, Table 327-0046, July 2011.

HOUSEHOLD USE OF SELECTED MEDIA 2009 [1]

	Canada	N.L.	P.E.I.	N.S.	N.B.	Quebec	Ont.	Man.	Sask.	Alb.	B.C.
Telephones (includes business use)	11,987	196	52	357	286	3,100	4,515	403	363	1,202	1,486
Cellular Telephone	10,356	155	41	294	216	2,167	4,106	355	317	1,205	1,480
Compact disc player	10,616	168	45	316	253	2,685	3,872	365	323	1,143	1,420
Cablevision	8,865	141	28	246	160	2,304	3,229	309	230	843	1,357
Satellite dish	3,208	56	21	103	122	749	1,215	120	134	411	267
Colour televisions	13,264	207	56	387	309	3,356	4,907	462	399	1,366	1,781
Video cassette recorders	9,394	149	36	262	221	2,392	3,499	328	284	975	1,229
DVD player	11,737	176	49	337	264	2,931	4,338	406	344	1,251	1,612
Home computer	10,957	148	45	313	231	2,583	4,185	377	319	1,191	1,539
CD writer	7,355	112	28	211	153	1,657	2,779	263	223	852	1,060
DVD writer	6,256	98	22	172	128	1,473	2,392	227	189	666	873
Internet use from home	10,434	141	42	289	216	2,419	3,995	358	299	1,145	1,507
Type of Internet connection:											
Regular telephone connection to a computer	755	6	F	14	14	259	321	22	20	53	F
High-speed telephone connection to a computer	4,022	85	27	168	151	726	1,554	181	185	417	517
Cable connection to a computer	4,706	42	8	88	37	1,317	1,712	124	61	484	825

[1] Estimated number of households in thousands

F - Due to reliability concerns, the data in these tables have been replaced by an "F" for detailed spending categories reported by fewer than 30 households, since these would normally have coefficients of variation of 30% or more. This symbol should not be interpreted as zero. The expenditures are included in more reliable aggregates.

Source: Adapted from Statistics Canada's Survey of Household Survey, table 62F0041, 2009.

COUNTRIES VISITED BY CANADIANS, 2010

One or More Nights

	Country Visits	Spending Less Fares
United States	27,355,800	14,602,578,300
Mexico	1,354,100	1,426,611,800
Cuba	1,010,200	748,272,500
United Kingdom	880,200	1,010,506,100
Dominican Republic	753,300	663,813,900
France	739,700	913,736,500
Italy	375,800	483,105,800
Germany	328,600	276,466,000
Mainland China	300,000	506,039,800
Netherlands	225,000	167,944,000
Spain	216,600	272,027,300
Hong Kong	183,300	196,192,600
Jamaica	166,100	171,068,800
Republic of Ireland	160,400	191,460,700
Switzerland	143,500	110,989,300

Source: Statistics Canada, http://www40.statcan.gc.ca/l01/cst01/arts37a-eng.htm, August 2011.

LABOUR FORCE ESTIMATES, ANNUAL AVERAGES 1992-2010

	Population 15+	Labour Force	Employment	Unemployment	Unemployment rate (%)	Participation rate (%)	Employment rate (%)
1992	21,820	14,336	12,731	1,605	11.2	65.7	58.3
1993	22,093	14,435	12,793	1,642	11.4	65.3	57.9
1994	22,368	14,574	13,059	1,515	10.4	65.2	58.4
1995	22,660	14,689	13,295	1,394	9.5	64.8	58.7
1996	22,960	14,849	13,420	1,428	9.6	64.7	58.5
1997	23,247	15,081	13,708	1,372	9.1	64.9	59.0
1998	23,516	15,315	14,047	1,268	8.3	65.1	59.7
1999	23,781	15,584	14,402	1,182	7.6	65.5	60.6
2000	24,090	15,842	14,760	1,082	6.8	65.8	61.3
2001	24,439	16,105	14,941	1,164	7.2	65.9	61.1
2002	24,786	16,569	15,298	1,271	7.7	66.8	61.7
2003	25,099	16,948	15,663	1,285	7.6	67.5	62.4
2004	25,431	17,154	15,922	1,233	7.2	67.5	62.6
2005	25,780	17,294	16,125	1,169	6.8	67.1	62.5
2006	26,146	17,517	16,410	1,107	6.3	67.0	62.8
2007	26,520	17,884	16,806	1,079	6.0	67.4	63.4
2008	26,907	18,204	17,087	1,117	6.1	67.7	63.5
2009	27,298	18,329	16,813	1,516	8.3	67.1	61.6
2010	27,659	18,525	17,041	1,484	8.0	67.0	61.6

Labour force survey estimates (LFS), annual (persons unless otherwise noted)

Source: Adapted from Statistics Canada's CANSIM database http://www5.statcan.gc.ca/cansim/home-accueil?lang=eng, Table 282-0002, August 2011.

EMPLOYED LABOUR FORCE BY AGE, CANADA, 1992 - 2010
(in '000s)

	15 years +	15 - 24 years	25 years +	25 - 44 years	45 years +	25 - 54 years	55 years +	55 - 64 years	65 years +	Average Age at Retirement
1992	12,730.9	2,127.1	10,603.8	7,056.1	3,547.7	9,366.8	1,237.0	1,048.5	188.5	62.5
1993	12,792.7	2,072.3	10,720.5	7,079.4	3,641.0	9,499.2	1,221.3	1,038.1	183.2	62.0
1994	13,058.7	2,090.0	10,968.8	7,160.6	3,808.2	9,705.6	1,263.2	1,064.5	198.7	62.1
1995	13,295.4	2,096.9	11,198.5	7,260.1	3,938.3	9,941.3	1,257.1	1,064.1	193.1	61.9
1996	13,420.1	2,062.1	11,358.0	7,307.6	4,050.4	10,076.1	1,281.9	1,085.8	196.1	61.8
1997	13,708.2	2,029.6	11,678.6	7,423.8	4,254.8	10,339.9	1,338.7	1,130.8	207.9	61.2
1998	14,047.0	2,085.4	11,961.6	7,512.9	4,448.7	10,563.1	1,398.4	1,180.9	217.5	60.9
1999	14,402.0	2,192.3	12,209.7	7,548.3	4,661.3	10,743.1	1,466.6	1,255.0	211.7	61.0
2000	14,760.1	2,287.4	12,472.7	7,596.1	4,876.6	10,933.1	1,539.6	1,330.2	209.3	61.6
2001	14,940.9	2,322.5	12,618.4	7,566.2	5,052.2	11,019.6	1,598.8	1,386.1	212.7	61.5
2002	15,297.9	2,391.0	12,906.9	7,562.6	5,344.3	11,143.6	1,763.2	1,522.2	241.0	61.2
2003	15,662.9	2,440.5	13,222.4	7,556.3	5,666.2	11,254.1	1,968.3	1,695.6	272.7	61.7
2004	15,921.8	2,456.8	13,465.0	7,559.5	5,905.5	11,374.6	2,090.5	1,803.2	287.3	61.8
2005	16,124.7	2,480.8	13,643.9	7,535.1	6,108.8	11,424.4	2,219.5	1,910.6	308.9	61.4
2006	16,410.2	2,546.0	13,864.2	7,516.6	6,347.6	11,530.0	2,334.3	2,016.0	318.3	61.5
2007	16,805.6	2,615.1	14,190.5	7,556.6	6,633.9	11,687.2	2,503.3	2,146.9	356.4	61.6
2008	17,087.4	2,646.7	14,440.7	7,549.5	6,891.2	11,780.7	2,660.0	2,240.9	419.1	61.4
2009	16,813.1	2,471.9	14,341.2	7,359.2	6,982.0	11,574.3	2,766.9	2,325.2	441.6	61.9
2010	17,041.0	2,451.3	14,589.7	7,389.8	7,199.9	11,653.6	2,936.1	2,443.3	492.8	62.1

Source: Adapted from Statistics Canada's CANSIM database http://www5.statcan.gc.ca/cansim/home-accueil?lang=eng, Tables 282-0004 and 282-0051, August 2011

LABOUR FORCE BY DETAILED OCCUPATION, CANADA, ANNUAL AVERAGES, 2000-2010

('000)

Occupation	2000	2001	2002	2003	2004	2005	2006	2007	2008	2009	2010
Total, all occupations	15,841.9	16,104.9	16,569.1	16,948.0	17,154.3	17,293.5	17,516.7	17,884.2	18,203.9	18,329.0	18,525.1
Management occupations	1,448.7	1,365.8	1,388.1	1,400.4	1,473.4	1,484.3	1,531.8	1,522.9	1,595.5	1,574.8	1,566.4
Senior management occupations	88.2	72.3	72.5	82.4	105.6	92.5	92.7	85.4	78.9	84.6	79.1
Other management occupations	1,360.5	1,293.5	1,315.6	1,318.0	1,367.8	1,391.8	1,439.1	1,437.6	1,516.6	1,490.2	1,487.3
Business, finance and administrative occupations	2,689.7	2,800.9	2,846.2	2,913.6	3,001.6	2,995.6	3,071.4	3,127.6	3,228.0	3,191.0	3,190.8
Professional occupations in business and finance	416.9	437.2	469.9	460.5	476.6	486.9	506.0	529.9	546.3	583.4	590.1
Financial, secretarial and administrative occupations	779.4	773.5	770.0	795.0	804.3	817.8	818.9	833.7	909.9	859.3	876.2
Clerical occupations, including supervisors	1,493.4	1,590.1	1,606.3	1,658.1	1,720.7	1,690.9	1,746.6	1,763.9	1,771.9	1,748.3	1,724.5
Natural and applied sciences and related occupations	1,014.4	1,053.7	1,085.7	1,084.9	1,088.1	1,136.2	1,158.0	1,216.1	1,239.6	1,245.5	1,303.1
Health occupations	798.1	825.5	883.4	903.1	936.7	964.5	996.2	1,010.5	1,055.6	1,079.2	1,111.7
Professional occupations in health, nurse supervisors and registered nurses	390.6	397.3	434.2	430.7	447.1	454.4	465.4	482.1	498.2	504.3	502.9
Technical, assisting and related occupations in health	407.5	428.2	449.2	472.4	489.6	510.1	530.8	528.3	557.5	574.9	608.8
Occupations in social science, education, government service and religion	1,191.3	1,242.6	1,271.2	1,304.8	1,285.3	1,377.4	1,434.3	1,475.0	1,522.3	1,599.7	1,663.0
Occupations in social science, government service and religion	618.7	644.1	669.9	683.2	665.9	716.8	740.8	767.6	812.0	870.6	918.2
Teachers and professors	572.7	598.6	601.2	621.5	619.3	660.6	693.4	707.3	710.3	729.1	744.8
Occupations in art, culture, recreation and sport	438.7	463.1	469.0	498.6	492.7	521.5	510.2	529.3	552.5	572.5	581.6
Sales and service occupations	3,728.0	3,831.9	3,969.8	4,087.2	4,085.3	4,069.6	4,113.1	4,324.9	4,325.7	4,394.6	4,422.9
Wholesale, technical, insurance, real estate sales specialists, and retail, wholesale and grain buyers	480.5	515.4	493.3	527.5	510.3	545.3	542.5	573.0	548.5	589.8	587.8
Retail salespersons, sales clerks, cashiers, including retail trade supervisors	936.4	997.9	1,040.5	1,065.1	1,085.6	1,078.9	1,078.7	1,130.0	1,121.2	1,140.8	1,152.7
Chefs and cooks, and occupations in food & beverage service, incl. supervisors	514.3	539.6	554.8	564.5	570.0	532.4	558.3	596.3	585.5	572.8	575.3
Occupation in protective services	213.3	222.9	230.5	237.2	243.1	230.6	229.3	243.8	249.8	261.3	267.6
Childcare and home support workers	214.7	190.6	202.9	212.1	219.4	197.5	206.7	226.3	222.3	233.8	232.8
Sales and service occupations n.e.c., including occupations in travel and accommodation, attendants in recreation & sport as well as supervisors	1,368.7	1,365.5	1,447.8	1,480.9	1,456.9	1,484.9	1,497.7	1,555.4	1,598.4	1,596.0	1,606.6
Trades, transport and equipment operators and related occupations	2,356.4	2,374.5	2,436.6	2,509.3	2,554.4	2,555.1	2,608.9	2,677.7	2,777.6	2,741.1	2,711.0
Contractors and supervisors in trades and transportation	208.6	216.1	227.5	222.8	242.5	249.4	249.2	253.2	276.5	277.1	267.0
Construction trades	330.3	336.3	354.5	363.1	357.9	378.3	394.2	407.9	437.8	437.0	447.3
Other trades occupations	882.2	897.9	901.7	917.6	928.6	927.7	927.0	953.6	997.3	962.1	942.2
Transport and equipment operators	624.6	608.7	627.8	642.3	646.3	624.6	650.3	673.5	659.6	668.4	665.1
Trades helpers, construction, and transportation labourers & related occupations	310.7	315.6	325.0	363.5	379.1	375.0	388.2	389.5	406.5	396.5	389.4
Occupations unique to primary industry	627.1	580.9	586.5	603.9	615.3	632.1	637.1	626.3	593.0	595.8	583.0
Occupations unique to processing, manufacturing and utilities	1,178.1	1,187.4	1,234.7	1,241.4	1,231.6	1,177.5	1,103.1	1,052.4	982.4	901.7	866.6
Machine operators and assemblers in manufacturing, including supervisors	961.9	973.4	1,015.4	1,013.0	998.5	939.4	875.9	834.7	785.6	728.9	702.2
Labourer in processing, manufacturing and utilities	216.2	213.9	219.3	228.5	233.1	238.1	227.2	217.7	196.8	172.8	164.4
Unclassified occupations	371.4	378.7	397.8	400.7	390.0	379.8	352.4	321.7	331.7	433.2	525.1

Labour force survey estimates (LFS), by National Occupational Classification for Statistics (NOC-S)

Source: Adapted from Statistics Canada's CANSIM database http://www5.statcan.gc.ca/cansim/home-accueil?lang=eng, Table 282-0010, August 2011.

GROWTH STATISTICS: TRANSPORT/TRANSPORTATION

	Railway Gross Revenue ($000,000)	Railway Operating Expenses ($000,000)	Tonne Kilometres ('000,000)	Motor Vehicle Registration ('000)	Canadian Air Carriers' Revenues ('000,000)	Canadian Air Carriers' Expenses ('000,000)
1992	6,907	7,781	250,667	16,581	7,560	7,790
1993	6,992	6,601	256,134	16,718	7,480	7,493
1994	7,530	6,699	287,827	16,972	8,299	7,893
1995	7,210	8,461	280,477	17,048	9,372	8,989
1996	7,193	6,789	282,018	17,183	10,062	9,792
1997	7,903	6,719	305,635	17,478	11,056	10,420
1998	7,610	6,931	297,916	17,988	12,174	11,895
1999	7,717	6,728	300,140	17,534	13,306	12,733
2000	8,103	6,426	322,511	17,882	14,109	14,012
2001	8,156	6,594	323,211	18,102	13,156	13,800
2002	8,213	6,621	317,807	18,617	12,738	13,037
2003	8,307	6,713	318,263	18,883	11,695	12,435
2004	8,862	6,952	338,898	19,156	12,829	12,794
2005	9,822	7,506	352,140	19,515	14,009	13,274
2006	10,405	7,794	352,477	20,065	15,295	14,557
2007	10,481	7,989	358,832	20,593	16,261	15,127
2008	10,997	8,629	340,092	21,087	17,493	16,892
2009	9,410 [1]	7,783 [2]	299,646	21,387	15,399	15,250

[1] The derivation of this variable has changed as of reference year 2009 with branch line payments being removed from government payments. As a result, caution should be used in comparing year-over-year changes.

[2] The derivation of this variable has changed as of reference year 2009. An account related to roadway amortization was removed from ways and structures expenses, accounts related to roadway machinery and equipment maintenance were removed from equipment

For the years 1992 to 1999, the data are for Canadian air carriers, Levels I - IV.

For the years 2000 to 2009, the data are for Canadian air carriers, Levels I - III.

Source: Adapted from the Statistics Canada publication *Rail in Canada,* Catalogue 52-21XIE2008000; Statistics Canada's Aviation Statistics Internal Reports; and Statistics Canada's CANSIM Database http://www5.statcan.gc.ca/cansim/home-accueil?lang=eng, Tables 404-0016, 405-0001, 405-0004 and 401-0001, July 2011.

GROWTH STATISTICS: AGRICULTURE/FISHERIES

Year	Population[1]		Wheat '000 Bushels	Total Canadian Crops[2] '000 ACRES	Farm Cash for Total Crops $000,000	Farm Cash Receipts for Livestock and Livestock Products[3] $000,000	Shipments, Estimated Values of Goods of Own Manufacturing, Dairy Products $'000
1992	28,371,264	(ID)	1,097,806	100,905	8,551	11,388	7,502,142
1993	28,684,764	(ID)	1,000,387	102,612	9,046	12,300	7,361,334
1994	29,000,663	(ID)	842,154	102,771	11,543	12,514	7,458,679
1995	29,302,311	(ID)	918,197	102,553	13,114	12,704	7,856,580
1996	29,610,218	(ID)	1,095,008	100,567	14,016	13,857	8,228,177
1997	29,905,948	(ID)	892,846	110,319	14,094	14,633	8,177,141
1998	30,155,173	(ID)	884,866	100,832	13,642	14,442	8,619,947
1999	30,401,286	(ID)	990,598	100,902	13,121	15,160	8,756,324
2000	30,685,730	(ID)	975,014	100,727	12,970	17,101	9,068,182
2001	31,019,020	(ID)	755,722	100,016	13,505	18,973	9,876,082
2002	31,353,656	(ID)	595,143	99,791	14,412	18,130	9,748,671
2003	31,639,670	(ID)	865,402	99,485	13,312	16,085	10,725,376
2004	31,940,676	(ID)	950,204	99,715	14,420	17,056	10,897,547
2005	32,245,209	(ID)	983,821	99,006	13,526	18,354	11,365,203
2006	32,576,074	(ID)	1,002,240	99,335	14,784	17,753	12,579,043
2007	32,929,733	(ID)	736,856	96,529	18,520	18,267	11,912,997
2008	33,315,976	(PD)	1,051,282	94,305	22,959	18,846	12,793,635
2009	33,720,184	(PR)	974,249	93,210	23,182	18,074	13,220,393
2010	34,108,752	(PP)	851,232	92,138	22,426	18,880	13,394,071

(ID) Final intercensal estimates
(PD) Final Postcensal estimates
(PR) Updated Postcensal estimates
(PP) Preliminary Postcensal estimates

[1] Period from July 1 to June 30
[2] Includes grains, specialty crops, summerfallow and hay; excludes solin.
[3] Total livestock and livestock products (including poultry and animals on fur farms).
-- -- -- Not available

Source: adapted from the Statistics Canada publication 22-002-XIB, and CANSIM database http://www5.statcan.gc.ca/cansim/home-accueil?lang=eng, Tables 002-0001, 051-0001 and 304-0014, August 2011.

GROWTH STATISTICS: PRODUCTION OF SELECTED MINERALS/METALS

Year	Pig Iron Production ('000 metric tonnes)	Crude Oil & Equivalent ('000 cubic metres)	Copper (total production, metal content) ('000 tonnes)	Nickel (production) ('000 tonnes)	Natural Gas ('000,000	Iron Ore (producer's shipments) ('000 tonnes)	Zinc (total production, metal content) ('000 tonnes)	Cement ('000 tonnes)
1992	8,621	100,906	761.6	177.6	116,561	32,137.3	1,195.7	8,612
1993	8,633	105,780	711.2	178.4	128,817	33,774.3	990.6	9,284
1994	8,106	110,452	591.0	142.0	138,856	36,728.1	976.4	10,457
1995	8,464	114,372	700.9	172.2	148,203	37,023.6	1,094.9	10,600
1996	8,638	117,621	652.5	182.4	153,578	34,709.3	1,162.8	11,003
1997	8,669	123,827	647.9	180.6	156,171	39,292.9	1,026.8	11,790
1998	8,936	128,401	690.7	197.9	160,651	36,847.0	991.5	12,168
1999	8,856	122,287	581.5	176.9	162,219	33,990.0	963.3	12,643
2000	8,904	127,769	621.7	181.2	167,794	35,246.9	935.7	12,753
2001	8,302	128,951	614.2	184.2	171,351	27,119.3	1,012.2	12,793
2002	8,670	136,970	584.2	179.7	172,197	30,902.0	924.1	13,081
2003	8,554	144,813	541.0	155.4	166,457	33,322.4	757.4	13,418
2004	8,828	149,425	544.5	177.3	167,503	28,596.4	734.0	13,863
2005	8,274	146,221	577.2	192.9	170,740	30,386.5	618.8	14,179
2006	8,305	154,099	586.5	224.6	171,690	33,543.0	601.3	14,335
2007	8,579	161,276	577.4	244.5	167,195	32,774.2	594.1	15,078
2008	8,770	158,881	584.1	246.1	158,209	32,101.5	704.7	13,672
2009	4,573*	158,054	481.4	131.8	147,484	31,703.7	668.9	10,985
2010	7,666	167,775	508.2	159.2	144,406	36,058.5	606.4	12,431

* 2009 Pig Iron Production excludes data for July and August 2009, as the data for these months are suppressed for reasons of confidentiality under the Statistics Act

[1] Excludes oil and gas as of 2003

Source: adapted from the Statistics Canada publications *Primary Iron and Steel,* Catalogue 41-001, 41-019; Statistics Canada's Manufacturing and Energy Division; and from Statistics Canada's CANSIM database http://www5.statcan.gc.ca/cansim/home-accueil?lang=eng, Tables 152-0001, 152-0004, 303-0001, 303-0048 and 303-0060; August 2011.

GROWTH STATISTICS: IMPORTS & EXPORTS

Year	Total Exports+ ($000,000)	Total Imports ($000,000)	Imports of Raw Sugar Cane[1] ($,000)	Imports of Natural Rubber[2] ($,000)	Imports of Raw Cotton[3] ($,000)	Imports of Crude Petroleum[4] ($000,000)
1999	355,420	320,409	286,958	160,415	112,487	6,919
2000	413,215	356,992	288,573	164,913	153,731	13,673
2001	404,086	343,111	371,731	136,644	152,600	12,643
2002	396,382	348,957	291,055	189,228	119,890	12,007
2003	381,072	336,141	341,699	195,879	146,027	13,812
2004	412,290	355,886	304,851	228,334	130,528	16,063
2005	436,351	380,858	332,130	241,618	68,067	21,912
2006	440,365	397,044	439,943	301,508	48,696	23,361
2007	450,321	407,301	338,794	287,333	32,854	24,115
2008	483,488	433,999	425,641	341,329	7,793	33,954
2009	359,866	365,155	453,760	202,770	2,733	21,227
2010	399,434	403,713	553,224	391,829	4,335	23,855

Total Exports+ equals Domestic Exports plus Re-exports [1] HS code 1701.11 [2] HS codes 4001.21, 4001.22, 4001.29 [3] HS code 5201.00 [4] HS code 2709.00

Source: "International Trade data", based on Statistics Canada's International Trade Division, retrieved on Industry Canada's website: http://www.ic.gc.ca/sc_mrkti/tdst/tdo/tdo.php?lang=30&headFootDir=/sc_mrkti/tdst/headfoot&productType=HS6&cacheTime=962115865#tag, August 2011.

GROWTH STATISTICS: FINANCIAL

FEDERAL FINANCE

	Total Revenue[1] $000,000	Total Expenditure[1] $000,000	Net Worth[1,2] $000,000
1992	130,069	165,856	-1,619,360
1993	128,715	168,411	-1,836,651
1994	131,911	166,999	-1,927,463
1995	140,313	172,013	-2,113,483
1996	147,954	164,911	-2,248,051
1997	162,556	156,080	-2,253,546
1998	167,450	159,774	-2,231,509
1999	177,684	168,914	-2,183,389
2000	195,726	175,698	-2,078,221
2001	193,935	181,925	-1,980,901
2002	190,448	181,052	-1,974,943
2003	196,226	192,105	-1,975,074
2004	207,668	196,838	-1,933,707
2005	219,765	218,746	-1,953,126
2006	230,574	218,096	-1,895,417
2007	244,223	228,848	-1,818,295
2008	241,413	243,434	-1,830,072
2009	223,320	256,277	-1,934,832
2010	228,632	271,217	-2,100,580

[1] quarterly data aggregated on a calendar-year basis

[2] Total assets minus total liabilities

Source: Adapted from Statistics Canada's CANSIM database http://www5.statcan.gc.ca/cansim/home-accueil?lang=eng, Table 385-0032, August 2011.

GROWTH STATISTICS: FINANCIAL

BALANCE OF PAYMENTS, NET FLOWS BY INDUSTRY

Year	CANADIAN DIRECT INVESTMENT ABROAD (All Countries, $000,000) All industries	Wood and paper	Energy and metallic minerals	Machinery and transportation equipment	Finance and insurance	Services and retailing	Other industries	FOREIGN DIRECT INVESTMENT IN CANADA (All Countries, $000,000) All industries	Wood and paper	Energy and metallic minerals	Machinery and transportation equipment	Finance and insurance	Services and retailing	Other industries
1992	-4,339	12	-719	-406	-708	-741	-1,776	5,708	451	503	568	1,030	594	2,560
1993	-7,354	-84	-2,166	-649	-980	-1,510	-1,965	6,103	-240	1,208	2,108	330	681	2,014
1994	-12,694	-1,250	-4,500	-1,083	-906	-1,506	-3,448	11,206	745	-101	3,462	-420	2,944	4,577
1995	-15,732	-1,171	-5,669	-431	-817	-1,321	-6,322	12,703	647	-441	1,802	1,086	2,032	7,577
1996	-17,858	782	-9,125	-1,230	-3,813	-2,317	-2,155	13,137	15	3,249	729	2,443	2,659	4,040
1997	-31,937	-1,130	-8,728	-2,046	-8,320	-3,859	-7,853	15,958	282	3,566	2,304	4,054	1,606	4,146
1998	-50,957	-440	-4,915	-2,988	-13,287	-7,718	-21,610	33,828	2,847	9,104	2,185	5,931	2,796	10,965
1999	-25,625	-258	-5,964	-1,999	-11,809	-1,237	-4,357	36,762	2,280	4,362	1,447	12,633	3,033	13,008
2000	-66,352	82	-9,982	-12,532	-7,278	-3,033	-33,610	99,198	4,286	13,492	13,717	4,122	1,804	61,776
2001	-55,800	-2,469	-10,740	-5,161	-27,838	-3,566	-6,027	42,844	442	23,940	4,640	3,598	529	9,694
2002	-42,015	-555	-8,665	-3,913	-26,669	-1,592	-621	34,769	889	16,207	6,131	1,599	3,722	6,220
2003	-32,118	-647	-14,379	-2,670	-8,764	-971	-4,686	10,483	-45	2,782	-1,227	4,229	958	3,785
2004	-56,395	1,330	-16,118	-5,473	-24,627	-8,672	-2,835	-579	-1,010	3,392	-2,470	-6,212	1,569	4,151
2005	-33,370	-352	-11,133	234	-23,377	-1,532	2,789	31,132	62	22,157	-4,297	4,734	3,538	4,938
2006	-52,423	-2,498	-6,745	667	-34,098	-5,643	-4,104	68,395	850	45,166	5,477	-4,046	4,258	16,690
2007	-62,003	-1,177	-16,306	-120	-33,633	-1,198	-9,570	123,148	3,241	69,236	7,060	22,758	7,985	12,869
2008	-85,143	-437	-21,263	1,064	-53,212	-2,382	-8,913	61,010	-1,392	38,120	-1,619	6,938	4,995	13,969
2009	-47,627	-692	-3,815	-477	-29,176	-1,100	-12,368	24,469	-473	11,464	1,523	3,459	2,861	5,634
2010	-39,749	-2,852	-7,273	311	-26,891	-2,848	-196	24,119	662	11,627	255	5,217	2,875	3,483

Source: Adapted from Statistics Canada's CANSIM database http://www5.statcan.gc.ca/cansim/home-accueil?lang=eng, Table 376-0014, August 2011.

GROWTH STATISTICS: INDUSTRIAL/TELEPHONE/POSTAL

Year	Industry Price Index, All Manufacturing Industries (2002=100)	Average Weekly Earnings[1] ($CDN.)	Revenue From Postal Operations[2] ($'000,000)
1992	77.8	572.41	3,921
1993	80.6	582.87	4,118
1994	85.5	592.88	4,748
1995	91.9	598.67	4,953
1996	92.3	611.01	5,103
1997	92.9	623.43	5,088
1998	93.3	632.72	5,709
1999	94.9	640.47	5,638
2000	99.0	655.55	5,942
2001	100.0	657.01	4,441[3]
2002	100.0	672.85	6,154[4]
2003	98.8	690.87	6,344[4]
2004	102.0	709.37	6,651[4]
2005	103.6	737.39	6,945[4]
2006	106.0	755.53	7,265[4]
2007	107.6	788.18	7,474[4]
2008	112.3	810.96	7,729[4]
2009	108.4	823.88	7,312[4]
2010	109.5	853.19	7,453[4]

[1] Average weekly earnings (SEPH), unadjusted for seasonal variation, all employees, including overtime, industrial aggregate excluding unclassified (NAICS)

[2] Fiscal year ended March 31.

[3] Represents 9 months of revenue -- Canada Post's fiscal year now January - December.

[4] Fiscal year January - December data

Source: Adapted from Statistics Canada's CANSIM database http://www5.statcan.gc.ca/cansim/home-accueil?lang=eng, Tables 329-0057, 281-0027 and 356-0001; and Statistics Canada's Public Institutions Division (postal revenue), August 2011.

MANUFACTURING SALES, BY SUBSECTOR, CANADA
$ millions

	2006	2007	2008	2009	2010
All manufacturing industries	605526.9	597673.1	591969.7	486666.3	529847.0
Food	71713.7	71659.5	76608.0	78649.0	80493.1
Beverage and tobacco products	11329.2	10709.1	10307.0	10549.7	10686.0
Textile mills	2513.0	2088.4	1827.0	1502.7	1538.9
Textile product mills	2366.9	2347.3	2159.0	1583.2	1687.0
Leather and allied products	434.3	465.9	426.7	366.4	395.6
Paper	30645.2	29438.0	28636.8	24938.3	26470.1
Printing and related support activities	11286.1	10342.6	10283.4	9252.4	8749.0
Petroleum and coal products	61467.4	66870.8	82490.9	59093.7	68083.1
Chemicals	49234.9	47680.5	48638.8	41067.8	43883.3
Plastics and rubber products	27243.3	25653.3	23334.7	19061.8	20906.4
Clothing	4555.5	3610.1	2646.2	2213.2	2294.6
Wood products	30970.3	24806.4	21522.0	16703.8	18850.9
Non-metallic mineral products	14156.9	14410.1	14129.2	11638.2	12990.3
Primary metals	49834.4	51258.6	53840.6	33901.8	41963.2
Fabricated metal products	34868.9	36123.1	36439.0	29292.4	30645.0
Machinery	31359.3	32103.6	32260.3	27256.7	28888.7
Computer and electronic products	19268.5	18433.5	17278.4	15510.1	15491.6
Electrical equipment, appliances and components	10491.9	10780.2	10486.6	9404.2	9640.9
Transportation equipment	119387.2	116644.0	96403.1	74646.8	85293.4
Furniture and related products	13193.8	13169.1	12342.7	10427.7	10713.8
Miscellaneous manufacturing	9206.1	9078.8	9909.2	9606.3	10182.1

Source: Statistics Canada, http://www40.statcan.ca/l01/cst01/MANUF11-eng.htm, August 2011

IMPORTS AND EXPORTS FOR CANADA, 2010

	Imports ($)	Exports ($)		Imports ($)	Exports ($)		Imports ($)	Exports ($)
Afghanistan	1,741,805	100,781,938	France (incl. Monaco, Fr. Ant.)	5,428,160,362	2,349,610,500	Nigeria	1,668,721,103	222,843,439
Albania	5,361,595	34,688,411	French Polynesia	929,573	12,316,395	Niue	31,551	0
Algeria	3,578,112,577	298,884,118	French Southern Territories	0	76,023	Norfolk Island	1,217	88,202
American Samoa	301,144	1,449,754	Gabon	493,843	20,051,810	Norway	2,845,961,985	2,528,640,504
Andorra	451,842	88,412	Gambia	232,001	791,279	Oman (Muscat)	20,758,123	108,272,378
Angola	1,622,491,677	194,957,256	Georgia	128,937,605	19,075,962	Pakistan	271,053,799	549,195,628
Anguilla	320,166	916,317	Germany	11,281,181,632	3,937,321,259	Panama	84,208,655	129,501,107
Antartica	275,382	748,066	Ghana	20,592,081	179,122,010	Papua New Guinea	1,646,144	40,324,122
Antigua and Barbuda	420,336	20,085,284	Gibraltar	2,236,730	25,311,002	Paraguay	9,340,055	16,407,138
Argentina	1,555,361,636	283,911,952	Greece	142,460,002	114,837,952	Peru	3,644,040,139	479,022,314
Armenia	29,867,062	18,929,895	Greenland	488,962	14,555,790	Philippines	889,306,422	683,576,848
Aruba Island	139,282	27,630,441	Grenada	600,159	5,473,537	Pitcairn Island	33,092	81,154
Australia	1,618,749,700	1,751,792,124	Guam (U.S.)	112,756	2,087,632	Poland	992,365,754	219,696,718
Austria	1,176,383,699	368,498,339	Guatemala	323,423,101	90,685,745	Portugal	311,272,189	298,213,016
Azerbaijan	543,156,529	19,926,205	Guinea	48,280,798	10,395,187	Qatar	100,589,403	86,913,482
Bahamas	55,121,006	155,960,858	Guinea-Bissau	14,306	66,835	Romania	218,177,164	99,746,682
Bahrain	3,121,033	65,529,665	Guyana	290,735,641	29,548,602	Russia	1,641,877,497	1,190,100,640
Bangladesh	836,269,926	595,338,998	Haiti	26,063,577	47,963,439	Rwanda	455,476	1,217,454
Barbados	9,680,487	40,780,144	Heard/McDonald Island	13,530	1,800	Saint Lucia	203,676	8,430,780
Belarus (Byelorussia)	55,226,359	1,669,210	Honduras	151,244,693	40,780,922	Samoa (Western)	267,554	565,173
Belgium	1,719,301,457	2,154,524,884	Hong Kong	371,284,251	1,897,600,905	São Tomé and Principe	237,601	50,399
Belize	6,176,823	6,672,727	Hungary	344,801,639	165,912,800	Saudi Arabia	2,023,798,470	977,757,933
Benin	12,073	15,337,764	Iceland	32,825,420	106,387,337	Senegal	1,132,399	28,227,369
Bermuda	1,384,950	43,337,819	India	2,123,036,802	2,088,674,780	Serbia	12,837,221	8,506,011
Bhutan	45,171	1,565,651	Indonesia	1,260,324,950	1,061,462,651	Seychelles	274,923	1,062,654
Bolivia	143,209,890	48,900,789	Iran	38,040,863	118,949,818	Sierra Leone	1,805,791	10,652,733
Bosnia-Hercegovina	7,844,694	4,796,174	Iraq	1,912,946,303	236,578,223	Singapore	1,138,970,888	834,846,462
Botswana	6,921,703	3,742,185	Ireland	1,487,180,522	331,122,033	Slovakia	198,287,656	42,749,778
Bouvet Island	39	0	Israel	1,006,055,284	399,266,904	Slovenia	95,594,756	33,474,760
Brazil	3,287,106,441	2,567,269,370	Italy (incl. Vatican City State)	4,646,975,353	1,923,993,390	Solomon Islands	165,369	77,211
British Indian Ocean Terr.	22,291	2,191,402	Jamaica	161,933,973	130,149,013	Somalia	30,767	2,338,192
British Virgin Islands	622,083	22,399,631	Japan	13,449,917,049	9,194,095,416	South Africa	716,007,589	468,656,658
Brunei Darussalam	26,401	12,167,423	Jordan	19,867,065	66,038,197	Spain	1,462,913,658	981,094,288
Bulgaria	66,678,083	117,568,615	Kazakhstan	2,284,617,422	140,728,110	Sri Lanka	127,702,582	348,621,837
Burkina Faso	22,802,112	30,800,446	Kenya	18,095,736	73,555,261	St. Helena	31,333	2,949
Burma (Myanmar)	14,623	2,747,774	Kiribati (includes Tuvalu)	29,102	62,718	St. Kitts-Nevis	8,092,260	7,105,751
Burundi	51,937	927,032	Korea, North	122,584	12,304,345	St.Pierre-Miquelon	1,524,259	20,493,275
Cambodia (Kampuchea)	357,100,094	4,169,234	Korea, South	6,148,480,196	3,709,298,114	St.Vincent-Grenadines	161,792	11,363,928
Cameroon	6,203,778	29,672,433	Kuwait	31,538,562	97,051,917	Sudan	82,977,960	117,595,752
Cape Verde	71,249	1,099,581	Kyrgyzstan	554,862	6,566,851	Surinam	598,052,287	12,218,679
Cayman Islands	400,882	7,707,924	Laos	8,082,038	2,786,872	Swaziland	1,657,471	1,596,666
Central African Republic	111,459	129,484	Latvia	10,707,047	173,833,930	Sweden	2,095,215,626	473,053,443
Chad	1,083,458	6,858,010	Lebanon	17,214,515	83,168,709	Switzerland	2,944,871,867	1,535,797,114
Chile	1,871,891,394	587,442,199	Lesotho	16,838,798	85,040	Syria	16,731,777	59,950,742
China	44,491,714,023	13,232,891,233	Liberia	38,105,357	14,898,790	Taiwan	3,969,819,676	1,289,097,243
Christmas Island	143,189	918,393	Libya	24,613,563	246,143,860	Tajikistan	15,207	5,416,046
Cocos (Keeling) Islands	17,007	141,941	Lithuania	380,475,624	39,529,647	Tanzania	3,002,821	52,490,362
Colombia	717,269,421	644,371,917	Luxembourg	95,521,150	56,994,505	Thailand	2,407,903,001	651,989,230
Comoros	144,583	135,841	Macau (Macao)	8,989,565	3,807,684	Togo	3,174,405	13,023,590
Congo (Brazzaville)	47,252,229	18,790,186	Macedonia	7,983,608	11,114,873	Tonga	7,866	4,644,889
Congo (former Zaire)	755,143	13,988,358	Madagascar	50,477,186	85,152,102	Trinidad and Tobago	459,179,205	298,531,916
Cook Islands	122,101	82,251	Malawi	73,099,376	3,617,842	Tunisia	50,714,170	93,606,883
Costa Rica	436,092,625	108,791,577	Malaysia	2,278,763,150	785,955,586	Turkey	713,934,270	841,772,646
Côte-D'Ivoire (Ivory Coast)	420,026,413	22,265,540	Maldives	72,449	4,851,000	Turkmenistan	707,903	8,981,228
Croatia	65,800,280	94,331,679	Mali	603,231	9,176,706	Turks and Caicos Islands	112,127	5,729,937
Cuba	652,615,629	390,284,333	Malta	17,638,706	109,649,295	U.S. Minor Outlying Isl.	3,761,586	14,772,978
Cyprus	3,123,830	48,654,474	Mauritania	190,067	6,976,059	Uganda	3,832,777	11,730,856
Czech Republic	318,536,059	116,395,776	Mauritius	9,711,287	5,291,046	Ukraine	95,614,107	156,608,621
Denmark	1,878,243,603	308,747,079	Mexico	22,108,275,581	5,009,854,421	United Arab Emirates	153,334,633	1,137,884,843
Djibouti	10,877	6,116,871	Moldova	5,010,730	2,291,327	United Kingdom (U.K.)	10,697,114,075	16,396,539,517
Dominica	145,238	4,838,430	Mongolia	231,696,689	26,825,007	United States (U.S.)	203,282,169,071	299,069,826,838
Dominican Republic	143,766,060	200,575,419	Montenegro	449,989	1,971,088	Uruguay	51,864,486	115,040,189
East Timor	2,047,441	309,420	Montserrat	327,194	229,644	Uzbekistan	1,374,972	6,822,906
Ecuador	210,957,251	268,529,933	Morocco	141,242,879	186,908,486	Vanuatu (New Hebrides)	856,269	1,745,332
Egypt	298,172,953	628,347,639	Mozambique	1,411,967	12,774,844	Venezuela	784,314,057	559,223,548
El Salvador	87,012,670	36,289,373	Namibia	234,347,980	11,873,047	Vietnam	1,173,519,160	264,696,669
Equatorial Guinea	671,110,054	4,757,439	Nauru	61,094	1,307,701	Wallis and Futuna Islands	11,204	0
Eritrea	258,635	2,670,639	Nepal	15,380,313	5,496,537	Western Sahara	20	4,104
Estonia	39,248,171	23,323,206	Netherlands	1,667,103,388	3,246,601,602	Yemen	110,518	20,330,258
Ethiopia	15,095,467	175,462,736	Netherlands Antilles	289,456	46,290,832	Zambia (Zambi)	1,347,644	28,602,522
Faeroe Islands	5,594,003	475,863	New Caledonia	159,771	44,351,295	Zimbabwe	4,234,370	5,899,435
Falkland Islands	22,510	113,879	New Zealand	447,000,675	321,441,598			
Fiji	4,931,448	4,182,983	Nicaragua	215,083,409	40,024,510			
Finland	1,076,631,477	400,914,098	Niger	861,807	14,623,011	TOTAL (All Countries)	399,562,532,547	399,383,209,353

Note: excluding re-imports

Source: "International Trade data", based on Statistics Canada's International Trade Division, retrieved on Industry Canada's website: http://www.ic.gc.ca/sc_mrkti/tdst/tdo/tdo.php?lang=30&headFootDir=/sc_mrkti/tdst/headfoot&productType=HS6&cacheTime=962115865#tag, August 2011.

Exhibitions, Shows & Events

The following list includes Consumer & Trade Shows, Public Events, Conferences & Festivals arranged by category of interest. The addresses given are the addresses of associations/sponsors. Focus is on events of an ongoing annual or biennial nature. The lists are not complete but are fairly representative of shows held throughout Canada. Users are cautioned that dates or venues may vary.

ABORIGINAL *See* MULTICULTURAL

AGRICULTURE *See* FARM BUSINESS/AGRICULTURE

AIR SHOWS/AVIATION

15 Wing Armed Forces Day, 15 Wing, PO Box 5000, Moose Jaw, SK S6H 7Z8 - 306/694-2222; Fax: 306/694-2880; Email: 15wingpao@forces.gc.ca; URL: www.airforce.forces.gc.ca/15wing - Show Organizer, Major John Clowe - Static displays, plus ground & aerial demonstrations - Aug., Moose Jaw SK

17 Wing Manitoba Canadian Forces Day, 17 Wing, CFB Winnipeg, PO Box 17000, Stn. Forces, Winnipeg, MB R3J 3Y5 - 204/833-2500, ext. 6499; Fax: 204-833-2594; Email: Muralt.DA@forces.gc.ca; PubAffairs@forces.gc.ca; URL: www.17wingcfday.com - 17 Wing Public Affairs, Capt. Dave Muralt - Air & static display by Canadian Forces aircraft - May, Southport, MB

19 Wing Comox Armed Forces Day & Airshow, 19 Wing, CFB Comox, PO Box 1000, Stn. Main, Lazo BC V0R 2K0 - 250/339-8211; Fax (Media Information): 250/339-8120 - Celebrates Canadian Forces Day. Biennial - July or Aug.

Abbotsford International Airshow, Abbotsford International Airshow Society, #4, 1276 Tower St., Abbotsford, BC V2T 6H5 - 604/852-8511; Fax: 604/852-6093; Email: info@abbotsfordairshow.com; media@abbotsford airshow.com; URL: www.abbotsfordairshow.com - Large static display. Six hour flying show - Aug., Abbotsford International Airport, BC

Alberta International Airshow, Lethbridge International Airshow Association, PO Box 1315, Stn. Main, Lethbridge, AB T1K 4K1 - 403/380-4245; Toll Free (Ticketing Support): 1-888-695-0888; Email: info@albertaairshow.com; URL: www.albertaairshow.com - July, Lethbridge International Airport, AB

Borden Canadian Forces Day & Airshow, CFSTG/Base Borden Public Affairs Officer, Canadian Forces Base Borden, PO Box 1000 Stn. Main, 400 Cambrai Rd. Borden, ON L0M 1C0 - 705/424-1200, ext. 3162; Fax: 705/ 423-3385; Email: marion.jcn@forces.gc.ca; URL: www.airforce.forces.gc.ca/16wing - Military & civilian air demonstration & acrobatic teams. Ground displays - June, Canadian Forces Base Borden, Borden, ON

Canada Remembers Airshow, Saskatchewan Place, #101, 3515 Thatcher Ave., Saskatoon, SK S7R 1C4 - 306/975-2907; Email: b.swid@creditunioncentre.com; URL: www.canadaremembersairshow.com - Annual. Parade of Veterans. Active & static displays - Aug., Saskatoon, SK

Canadian International Airshow, Press Bldg., Exhibition Place, 210 Princes' Blvd., Toronto, ON M6K 3C3 - 416/263-3650; Fax: 416/263-3654 ; URL: www.cias.org - Annually, three days of the Labour Day Weekend. Best viewed from Canadian National Exhibition grounds - Sept., Over Lake Ontario, Toronto, ON

Festival of Flight, Festival of Flight Staff, Parks, Recreation & Tourism, Town of Gander, 100 Elizabeth Dr., Gander, NL A1V 1G7 - 709/651-5958; URL: www.gandercanada.com - Director, Parks, Recreation & Tourism, Kevin Waterman - Annual. A celebration of Gander's aviation history - 1st weekend in Aug.

Friendship Festival Air Show, Friendship Festival International Air Show, PO Box 1241, Fort Erie ON L2A 5Y2 - 905/871-6454; Fax: 905/871-1266; Tollfree: 1-888-333-1987; Email: info@friendshipfestival.com; URL: www.friendshipfestival.com - Annual - July London Airshow & Balloon Festival, 48 Crampton Dr., Belmont ON N0L 1B0 - 519/473-6444; Fax: 519/644- 1688; Email: info@londonairshow.com; URL: www.londonairshow.com

Nova Scotia International Airshow, Nova Scotia International Air Show Association (NSIASA), PO Box 218, Shearwater, NS B0J 3A0 - 902/465-2725; Fax: 902/484-3222; Email: info@nsairshow.ca; URL: www.nsairshow.ca - Executive Director, Colin Stephenson, Email: colin@nsairshow.ca - Aerial displays, including military & civilian aircraft. Ground displays - Sept., Halifax Stanfield International Airport, Halifax, NS

Saskatchewan Air Show, PO Box 1027, Moose Jaw SK S6H 4P8 - 306/692-4411; Fax: 306/692-2940; Email: info@saskatchewanairshow.com; URL: www.saskatchewanairshow.com - Executive Director, Clive Tolley, July, Moose Jaw SK

Yukon Sourdough Rendezvous Airshow, Yukon Sourdough Rendezvous Society, PO Box 31721, Whitehorse YT Y1A 6L3 - 867/393-4467; Fax: 867/668-6755; Email: ysr@polarcom.com; URL: www.yukonrendezvous.com - Vice-President, Public Relations, Anna Barron - Annual. Aerial & static displays - Feb., Whitehorse Airport, Whitehorse, YT

ANTIQUES

Carswell Collectables Antique Show, Carswell Collectables, PO Box 1036, Red Deer AB T4N 6S5 - 403/343-1614; Fax: 403/342-2943 - Rae Carswell - Nov., Red Deer, AB

The Toronto Toy & Doll Collectors' Show,PO Box 217, Grimsby, ON L3M 4G3 - 905/945-2775; Fax: 905/945-0197; Email: info@antiquetoys.ca; URL: www.antiquetoys.ca - Doug Jarvis, Email: dougjarvis@sympatico.ca - Annual antique & collectible childhood memorabilia - Nov., Mississauga, ON

The Toronto Christmas Train Show, PO Box 217, Grimsby, ON L3M 4G3 - 905/945-2775; Fax: 905/945-0197; Email: info@antiquetoys.ca; URL: www.antiquetoys.ca - Doug Jarvis, Email: dougjarvis@sympatico.ca - Layouts, exhibits, & clinics from railway historical associations & train vendors - Nov., Mississauga, ON

APPAREL *See* FASHION

ARCHITECTURE *See* CONSTRUCTION

ART/ARTS

***See Also* First Night; Crafts; Music; Events**

Arnold Mikelson Festival of Arts, Arnold Mikelson Mind and Matter Gallery, 13743 - 16 Ave., Surrey, BC V4A 1P7 - 604/536-6460; Email: mindandmatterart@aol.com; URL: www.mindandmatterart.com - Mary Mikelson - Featuring new & established artists offering their exhibits for sale - July

Artfocus Artist's Show, Artfocus Indoor Artists' Show, c/o Artfocus Communications, PO Box 1063, Stn F, Toronto ON M4Y 2T7 - 416/925-5564; Fax: 416/925- 2972; Email: info@artfocus.com; URL: www.artfocus.com/artfairs.htm - President, Pat Fleisher - Annual (fall) consumer show. Paintings, photography, sculpture, prints, drawings, electronic art, etc., Metro Hall Rotunda, Toronto ON

Atlantic Theatre Festival, 386 Main St., Wolfville, NS B4P 1C9 - 902/542-1515; Fax: 902/542-1526 - Classical theatre productions - July, Aug. & Sept.

Banff Summer Arts Festival, The Banff Centre, PO Box 1020, Banff AB T1L 1H5 - 403/762-6301; Fax: 403/762-6483; Tollfree: 1-800-413-8368; Email: box_office@banffcentre.ca; URL: www.banffcentre.ca - President & CEO, Mary E. Hofstetter

Bard on the Beach Shakespeare Festival, #301, 601 Cambie St., Vancouver, BC V6B 2P1 - 604/737-0625; Box Office: 604/739-0559; Fax: 604/737-0425; Tollfree: 1-877-739-0559; Email: info@bardonthebeach.org; URL: www.bardonthebeach.org - Artistic Director, Christopher Gaze; General Manager, Robert Barr - May - Sept., Vanier Park waterfront, Vancouver, BC

Blyth Festival, 423 Queen St., PO Box 10, Blyth, ON N0M 1H0 - 519/523-9300; Fax: 519/523-9804; Tollfree: 1-877-862-5984; Email: info@blythfestival.com; URL: www.blythfestival.com - Artistic Director, Eric Coates, Email: ecoates@blythfestival.com - June - Sept., Blyth Memorial Community Hall, Blyth, ON

Charlottetown Festival, Confederation Centre of the Arts, 145 Richmond St., Charlottetown PE C1A 1J1 - 902/628-1864; Fax: 902/566-4648; Tollfree: 1-800-565-0278; Email: info@confederationcentre.com; URL: www.confederationcentre.com - CEO, David MacKenzie, Email: dmack@confederationcentre.com; Artistic Director, Anne Allan, Email: aallan@confederationcentre.com - Annual. Musical & dramatic entertainment - June - Sept.

Dream in High Park, The Canadian Stage Company, 26 Berkeley St., Toronto, ON M5A 2W3 - 416/367-8243; Box Office: 416/368-3110; Fax: 416/367-1768; Email: general@canstage.com ; boxoffice@canstage.com; URL: www.canstage.com - Director, Production, Alistair Hepburn; Artistic Producer, Martin Bragg, July 1 - Labour Day, High Park, Toronto, ON

Edmonton International Fringe Theatre Festival, 10330 - 84 Ave., Edmonton AB T6E 2G9 - 780/448-9000; Box Office: 780/409-1910; Fax: 780/431-1893; URL: www.fringetheatreadventures.ca - Aug.

Festival Antigonish, Bauer Theatre, St. Francis Xavier University, PO Box 5000, Antigonish NS B2G 2W5 - 902/867-3333; Email: boxoffice@festivalantigonish.com; URL: www.festivalantigonish.com - Administrator, Madonna Van Vonderen; Artistic Producer Ed Thomason - July - Sept., Bauer Theatre, Antigonish, NS

Festival by the Sea, PO Box 6157, Saint John NB E2L 4R6 - 506/632-0086; Fax: 506/642-4644; Email: fbts@ nb.aibn.com - General Manager, Amy Wood - Annually, Performing arts - Aug.

Fringe Theatre Event, Fringe Theatre Festival, 10330 - 84 Ave., Edmonton AB T6E 2G9 - 780/448-9000; Fax: 780/431-1893; Email: fta@fringetheatreadventures. ca; URL: www.fringetheatreadventures.ca - Executive Director, Julian Mayne, Office Manager, Geralder Osborn - Aug.

Lunenburg Summer Festival of Crafts, 902/634-8511 - Contact, Robert Black - Annual - Features over 100 Nova Scotian crafters - July, Community Center Grounds, Lunenburg, NS

Manitoba Holiday Festival of the Arts, Margaret Laurence Home, PO Box 147, Neepawa, MB R0J 1H0 - 204/476-2927; Fax: 204/476-2927; Email: mhfa@mts.net; URL: www.mts.net/~mhfa - Administrator, Greg Heschuk - Annual. Programs for children, youth, & adults - July, Neepawa, MB

Nova Scotia Folk Art Festival - 902/640-2113; Email: info@nsfolkartfestival.com; URL: www.nsfolkartfestival.com - Contact, Nancy Wilson - Annual. Juried event, featuring an exhibition, workshops, speaker's corner, & sale of work by Nova Scotia folk artists - Aug., Lunenburg War Memorial Arena, Lunenburg, NS

Open Ears Festival of Music & Sound, c/o Kitchener-Waterloo Symphony, 101 Queen St. North, Kitchener, ON N2H 6P7 - 519/ 579-8564; Fax: 519/743-6773; Toll Free: 1-888-363-3591; Email: info@openears.ca; URL: www.openears.ca - Musical performances, music in alternative venues, sound poetry, sound installations, & conference activity - April / May, Kitchener, ON

Ottawa Fringe Theatre, Ottawa Fringe Festival, #100, 2 Daly Ave., Ottawa ON K1N 6E2 - 613/232-6162; Email: admin@ottawafringe.com; URL: www.ottawafringe.com

Saskatoon Fringe Theatre Festival, #9, 2404 Thayer Ave., Saskatoon, SK S7L 6B4 - 306/664-2239; Fax: 306/653-7701; URL: www.25thstreettheatre.org - Annual - July / Aug., 6 venues, Saskatoon, SK

Shakespeare by the Sea, 5799 Charles St., Halifax NS B3K 1K7 - 902/422-0295; Fax: 902/422-4250; Email: shakespeare@ns.aliantzinc.ca; URL: www.shakespearebythesea.ca - General Manager, Elizabeth Murphy Shakespeare by the Sea Festival, 11 Bavidge St., St. John's NL A1A 5B9 - 709/691-7287; Email: sbts@nfld.com; URL: www.nfld.com/~sbts

Shakespeare on the Saskatchewan Festival, PO Box 1646, Stn Main, Saskatoon SK S7K 3R8 - 306/653-2300; Fax: 306/653-2357; Email: shakespeare@sasktel.net; URL: www.shakespeareonthesaskatchewan.com - Executive & Artistic Director, Mark von Eschen, July/Aug.

Summerworks, 54 Wolseley St, 2nd Fl., PO Box 12, Stn C, Toronto ON M6J 3M7 - 416/410-1048; Email: info@summerworks.ca; URL: www.summerworks.ca - Artistic Producer, Kimahli Powell, Artistic Producer, Keira Loughran

Thunder Bay Fringe Festival, #15, 4A South Court St., Thunder Bay ON P7B 2W4 - 807/344-1343; Fax: 807/346-1855; Email: tbfringe@northroute.net; URL: www.tbfringe.com

Toronto Outdoor Art Exhibition, #264, 401 Richmond St. West, Toronto, ON M5V 3A8 - 416/408-2754; Fax: 416/408-2202; Email: toae@torontooutdoorart.org; URL: www.torontooutdoorart.org - Executive Director, Kelly Rintoul, Email: kelly@torontooutdoorart.org - Canada's largest oudoor art exhibition, held annually. Award program for participating artists - July, Nathan Phillips Square, Toronto ON

Vancouver Fringe Festival, 1398 Cartwright Street, Vancouver BC V6H 3R8 - 604/257-0350; Fax: 604/253-1924; Email: administration@vancouverfringe.com; URL: www.vancouverfringe.com - Executive Director, David Jordan - Annual - Sept.

Winnipeg Fringe Theatre Festival, Manitoba Theatre Centre, 174 Market Ave., Winnipeg MB R3B 0P8 - 204/956-1340; Fax: 204/947- 3741; Email: info@winnipegfringe.com; URL: www.winnipegfringe.com - Executive Producer, Bertram Schneider - Annual, July

World Stage, Harbourfront Centre, 235 Queens Quay West, Toronto ON M5J 2G8 - 416/973-4600; Fax: 416/973- 6055; Email: info@harbourfrontcentre.com; URL: www.harbourfrontcentre.com/worldstage - CEO, William J.S. Boyle - International theatre festival - April - Harbourfront Centre, Toronto ON

York Shakespeare Festival, Resurgence Theatre Company, 211 Main Street South, Newmarket ON L3Y 3Y9 - 905/953-2838;

Email: info@resurgence.on.ca; URL: www.resurgence.on.ca - General Manager, Anthony Leo

AUTOMOTIVE

Air Canada Grand Prix, Grand Prix of Canada, CP 340, Succ B, Montréal QC H3B 3J7 - 514/350-0000; Fax: 514/350-4709; URL: www.grandprix.ca - Vice-Présidente, Services corporatifs, Marie-Josée Labbé, - Annual international auto racing event - June - Gilles-Villeneuve Circuit, Montréal QC

Annual RV Camping & Leisure Show, Recreation Vehicle Dealers Association of Manitoba, 69 Morin Rd., St Francois Xavier MB R4L 1A8 - 204/864-2112; Fax: 204/864-2232; Email: rvdamb@mts.net; URL: www.manitoba.rvda.ca - Manager, Kim Wozniak - Annual consumer show - March, Winnipeg MB

Atlantic Truck Show, Master Promotions Ltd., PO Box 565, 48 Broad St., Saint John NB E2L 3Z8 - 506/658-0018; Fax: 506/658-0750; Tollfree: 1-888-454-7469; Email: info@masterpromotions.ca; URL: www.masterpromotions.ca - Annual - Show Manager, Mark Cusack, June - Coliseum, Moncton NB

Cam-Expo Québec, Pro-Expo Inc., #230, 1400, av St-Jean-Baptiste, Québec QC G2E 5B7 - 418/877-1919; Fax: 418/877-9292; Tollfree: 1-866-858-1919; Email: info@proexpo.qc.ca; URL: http://www.cam-expo.com - President, Roger Desrosiers - Biennial trade & consumer show - Nov.

Canadian International Motorcycle & Powersports Super Show, Bar Hodgson Productions Inc., 8780 Baldwin St., Ashburn ON L0B 1A0 - 905/655-5403; Fax: 905/655- 3812; Email: info@supershowevents.com; URL: www.supershowevents. com - President, Bar Hodgson - Annual consumer & trade show - Jan. - International Centre, Toronto ON

Edmonton Motor Show, Edmonton Motor Dealers' Association, 10310 - 39A Ave. NW, Edmonton AB T6H 5X9 - 780/423-2401; Fax: 780/423-2413; Email: contactemda@emdacars.com; URL: www.emdacars.com - Executive Manager, Robert Vilas - Annual consumer show

Expocam, dmg World Media, 180 Duncan Mills Rd., 4th Fl., Toronto ON M3B 1Z6 - 416/385-1880; Fax: 416/385-1855; Tollfree: 1-888-823-7469; URL: www.dmgworldmedia.com - Show Manager, Glen Chiasson - Biennial trade show. Trucks, trailers, bodies, heavy duty parts & services & accessories, engine & power train components, service shop equipment - Oct., Montréal QC

Halifax RV Show, Master Promotions Ltd., PO Box 565, Saint John NB E2L 3Z8 - 506/658-0018; Fax: 506/658- 0750; Tollfree: 1-888-454-7469; Email: info@masterpromotions. ca; URL: www.masterpromotions.ca - Annual consumer show - Show Manager, Scott Sprague, Feb., Halifax NS

Molson Indy Toronto, Molson Sports & Entertainment Inc., North Tower, #200, 175 Bloor St. East, Toronto ON M4W 3R8 - 416/922-7477; Fax: 416/922-8970; URL: www.molsonindy.com/toronto - President, Jo- Ann McArthur - Annual - July, Toronto ON

Moncton RV Show, Master Promotions Ltd., PO Box 565, Saint John NB E2L 3Z8 - 506/658-0018; Fax: 506/658- 0750; Tollfree: 1-888-454-7469; Email: info@masterpromotions. ca; URL: www.masterpromotions.ca - Annual consumer show - Show Manager, Scott Sprague, Feb., Moncton NB

Montréal International Auto Show, 2335, rue Guénette, Saint-Laurent QC H4R 2E9 - 514/331-6571; Fax: 514/331-7818; Email: communications@ccqm.qc.ca; URL: www.salonautomontreal.com - Executive Director, Francine St-Laurent - Annual consumer show. New cars, light trucks, accessories - Jan. - Palais des Congrès, Montréal QC

Performance World Custom Car Show, Pro-Sho Inc., 298 Sheppard Ave. East, Toronto ON M2N 3B1 - 416/229- 9919; Fax: 416/223-2826; Tollfree: 1-877-950-1500; Email: prosho@meteorshows.com; URL: www.performanceworldcarshow.com; www.llhashows. com - Annual consumer show - Contact, Larry King, March

RV Exposition & Sale, Recreation Vehicle Dealers Association of Alberta, #101, 10340 - 59th Ave., Edmonton AB T6H 1E6 - 780/455-8562; Fax: 780/453-3927; Tollfree: 1-888-858-8787; Email: rvda@rvda-alberta. org; URL: www.rvda-alberta.org - Executive Vice-President, Lori Auld - Annual consumer show held in Calgary, Edmonton & Red Deer

Salon de l'Auto, Club Optimiste de Rivière-du-Loup inc., CP 1344, Rivière-du-Loup QC G5R 4L9 - 418/862- 8454; Fax: 418/862-3366 - Jean-Louis Dorval - Annual. Cars & trucks - April - Motel Universel, Rivièredu-Loup QC

Salon de la Moto de Montréal/de Québec, ExpoMAX Canada Inc., CP 642, Succ B, Montréal QC H3B 3K3 - 514/285-2686; Fax: 514/282-4292; URL: www.salonmotomontreal.com - Executive Vice- President, Roger Saint-Laurent - Annual consumer show - Feb.

Spring Classic Car Auction, RM Classic Car Exhibit, One Classic Car Drive, Blenheim ON N0P 1A0 - 519/352- 2024 - Annual consumer show. Vintage cars, sale of parts & accessories - April - International Centre, Mississauga ON

Toronto International Spring Bike Show, Bar Hodgson Productions Inc., 8780 Baldwin St., Ashburn ON L0B 1A0 - 905/655-5403; Fax: 905/655-3812; Email: info@supershow events. com; URL: www.supershowevents.com - President, Bar Hodgson, April - International Centre, Toronto ON

Vancouver International RV Show, Recreation Vehicle Dealers Association of British Columbia, #201, 17700 - 56th Ave., Surrey BC V3S 1C7 - 604/575-3868; Fax: 604/575-3869; Email: admin@rvda.bc.ca; URL: www.rvda.bc.ca - Annual consumer show - Show Manager, Cathy James, March, Vancouver BC

Wheels, Master Promotions Ltd., PO Box 565, Saint John NB E2L 3Z8 - 506/658-0018; Fax: 506/658-0750; Tollfree: 1-888-454-7469; Email: info@masterpromotions. ca; URL: www.masterpromotions.ca - Marketing & Operations Manager, Jennifer Allaby, President, Wendell Howes - Annual consumer show

BLUEGRASS *See* MUSIC

BOATING

Classic Boat Festival, c/o Victoria Real Estate Board, 3035 Nanaimo St., Victoria BC V8T 4W2 - 250/385-7766; Fax: 250/385-8773; Email: vreb@vreb.org; URL: www.classic boatfestival.ca - Communications Manager, Michael Sampson - Annually, Labour Day weekend, Victoria BC

London International Boat Show, 395 Wellington Rd. South, PO Box 25354, London ON N6C 6B1 - 519/686- 3121; Fax: 519/680-0311; Email: jguy@london.com - General Manager, Jeff Guy - Consumer show - Feb., London ON

New Brunswick Boat & Outdoor Show, Master Promotions Ltd., PO Box 565, Saint John NB E2L 3Z8 - 506/658- 0018; Fax: 506/658-0750; Tollfree: 1-888-454-7469; Email: info@masterpromotions.ca; URL: www.masterpromotions.ca - Annual consumer show - Show Manager, Sydney Peacock, March - Exhibition Harbour Station, Saint John NB

Sudbury Boat & Sportsman Show, DAC Marketing Ltd., PO Box 2837, Stn A, Sudbury ON P3A 5J3 - 705/673- 5588; Fax: 705/525-0626; Email: dac@vianet.on.ca; URL: www.dacshows.com, Mar., Sudbury ON

Toronto International Boat Show, National Marine Manufacturers Association, #E9, 18 King St. East, Bolton ON L7E 1E8 - 905/951-0009; Email: lwaddell@nmma.org; URL: www.discoverboating.com/boatshows/toronto/home.asp - Show Manager, Linda Waddell, Jan. - National Trade Centre, Exhibition Place, Toronto ON

Victoria Boat & Outdoor Show, Canwest Shows Inc., 7 Panorama Bay SW, Calgary AB T3Z 3L6 - 403/686-9699; Fax: 403/246-3856; Email: info@canwestshows.com; URL: www.canwestshows.com - General Manager, Terra Connors - Annual consumer show - Feb. - Pearkes Recreation Centre, Victoria BC

BOOKS

BookExpo Canada, Reed Exhibition Companies Inc., #1, 3761 Victoria Park Ave., Toronto ON M1W 3S2 - 416/491-7565; Fax: 416/491-5088; Email: canada@reedexpo. com; URL: www.reedexpo.com - John Lewinski - Annual trade show - June, Toronto ON

International Festival of Authors, 235 Queen's Quay West, Toronto ON M5J 2G8 - 416/973-4760; Fax: 416/954- 4323; URL: www.readings.org - Director, Geoffrey E. Taylor - Interviews & readings by novelists, poets, playwrights & biographers - Oct. - Harbourfront Centre, Toronto ON

Montréal Book Fair/Salon du livre de Montréal, Salon du livre de Montréal, #403, 480, boul St-Laurent, Montréal QC H2Y 3Y7 - 514/845-2365; Fax: 514/845-7119; Email: slm.info@ videotron.ca; URL: www.salondulivredemontreal.com - Directrice Générale, Francine Bois - Annual consumer show - Nov., Montréal QC

Salon international du Livre de Québec, 26, rue Saint- Pierre, Québec QC G1K 8A3 - 418/692-0010; Fax: 418/692-0029; Email: info@silq.org; URL: www.silq.org - Annual consumer show - avril, Québec QC

The Word on the Street, The Word on the Street Book & Magazine Fair, #142, 67 Mowat Ave., Toronto ON M6K 3E3 - 416/504-7241; Fax: 416/504-7656; Email: toronto@theword onthestreet.ca; URL: www.thewordonthestreet.ca - Festival Coordinator, Maggie Rust - Annual celebration of literacy & the printed word; held in Toronto, Halifax, Calgary & Vancouver - Sept.

BRIDAL

Canada's Bridal Show, #10, 136 Winges Rd., 2nd Fl., Woodbridge ON L4L 6C4 - 905/264-7000; Fax: 905/264-7300; URL: www.canadasbridalshow.com - Lorie Sansone - Annual consumer show. Bridal fashion shows, gifts, florists, photography, entertainment, travel - Jan. & Oct., Toronto ON

Le Salon de la Mariée, Sheldon Kagan International Ltd., 35, McConnell, Dorval QC H9S 5L9 - 514/631-2160; Fax: 514/631-4430; Tollfree: 1-888-524-2648; Email: sheldon@sheldonkagan.com; URL: www.sheldonkagan.com - President, Sheldon Kagan - Annual consumer show - Nov. - Palais des Congrès, Montréal QC

The Total Wedding Show, Ten Star Productions Inc., 155 Castle Cres., Oakville ON L6J 5H4 - 905/845-2644; Fax: 905/845-8050; Email: info@totalweddingshow. com; URL: www.totalweddingshow.com - Janice Fernetti - Annual consumer show - Jan. - International Centre, Mississauga ON

Wedding Dreams, Bingemans Conference & Recreation Centre, 425 Bingemans Centre Dr., Kitchener ON N2B 3X7 - 519/744-1555; Fax: 519/744-1985; Tollfree: 1-800-667-0833; Email: dhauck@ringemans. com - Contact, Doris Hauck - Consumer show. Fashion shows, wedding exhibits; Jan. & Oct.

Wedding Wishes, Thunder Bay Chamber of Commerce Trade Show, #102, 200 Syndicate Ave. South, Thunder Bay ON P7E 1C9 - 807/624-2621; Fax: 807/622-7752; Email: nancy@tb-chamber.on.ca; URL: www.tbchamber. on.ca - Show Manager, Nancy Milani - Annual consumer show - Nov., Thunder Bay ON

BUSINESS

Business Showcase, Greater Saskatoon Chamber of Commerce, 345 - 3 Ave. South, Saskatoon SK S7K 1M6 - 306/244-2151; Fax: 306/244-8366; Email: chamber@ eboardoftrade.com; URL: www.eboardoftrade.com - Executive Director, Kent Smith-Windsor, President, C. Evans, Oct. - Centennial Auditorium, Saskatoon SK

Business World Exhibition, Martin International, #2910, 500, Place des Armes, Montréal QC H2Y 2W2 - 514/288-3931; Fax: 514/288-0641; Email: mbaudard@ martin-intl.com; URL: www.forum-export.ca - General Manager, Marc Baudard - Trade show. International showcase, e-commerce, transportation, export construction, digital office, finance, advertising, small business, home office - Sept.

Canadian Online Investing Forum, Diversified Business Communications Canada, #4, 800 Denison St., Markham ON L3R 5M9 - 905/948-0470; Fax: 905/479- 1364; Tollfree: 1-888-443-6486; URL: www.financialforum.ca/toronto/ visinfo.shtml

Cash & Treasury Management Conference, Treasury Management Association of Canada, #1010, 8 King St. East, Toronto ON M5C 1B5 - 416/367-8500; Fax: 416/367- 3240; Tollfree: 1-800-449-8622; Email: info@tmac.ca; URL: www.tmac.ca - Manager of Administration, Riina Koppel, Email: rkoppel@tmac.ca, President, Mike Whiston, Executive Director, Blair McRobie, Email: bmcrobie@tmac.ca, Director, Finance & Communication, Belinda Espley, Email: bespley@tmac.ca, Coordinator, Membership Development, Rose Ficco, Email: rficco@tmac.ca, Coordinator, Marketing Services, Jennifer Robb - Annual trade show. Bank products, communication systems, financial software, pension management, brokers, dealers, stock exchanges, commercial paper & computers - Oct.

Financial Forum, Diversified Business Communications Canada, #4, 800 Denison St., Markham ON L3R 5M9 - 905/948-0470; Fax: 905/479-1364; Tollfree: 1-888- 443-6786; URL: www.financialforum.ca - Show Manager, Bob McGregor - Annual consumer show

Island Trade Show, Greater Nanaimo Chamber of Commerce, 2133 Bowen Rd., Nanaimo BC V9S 1H8 - 250/756-1191; Fax: 250/756-1584; Email: info@nanaimochamber. bc.ca; URL: www.nanaimochamber.bc.ca - Executive Director, S.D. (Lee) Mason, President, Rick Thurmeier, Oct. - Woodgrove Mall

Quebec City Business & Computer Show, Martin International, #2910, 500, Place des Armes, Montréal QC H2Y 2W2 - 514/288-3931; Fax: 514/288-0641; Email: mbaudard@ martin-intl.com; URL: www.forum-export.ca - General Manager, Marc Baudard - Annual consumer show - May

Salon commerce-vacances de Ville-Marie, c/o Andr, Raymond enr., 147, rue de Montfort, Gatineau QC J8T 8A9 - 819/561-1992; Fax: 819/561-1992; Email: andre@ araymond.qc.ca; URL: araymond.qc.ca - Andr, Raymond - Annual, commercial consumer show - April - Olympia, Ville-Marie QC

Saving & Investment Marketplace, Martin International, #2910, 500, Place des Armes, Montréal QC H2Y 2W2 - 514/288-3931; Fax: 514/288-0641; Email: mbaudard@martin-intl.com; URL: www.forum-export.ca -

General Manager, Marc Baudard - Annual trade & consumer show. RRSPs, mutual funds, real estate tax shelters - Jan.

Sudbury Business & Computer Show, DAC Marketing Ltd., PO Box 2837, Stn A, Sudbury ON P3A 5J3 - 705/673-5588; Fax: 705/525-0626; Email: dac@vianet. on.ca; URL: www.dacshows.com, Sept., Sudbury ON

Thunder Bay Chamber of Commerce Trade Show, #102, 200 Syndicate Ave. South, Thunder Bay ON P7E 1C9 - 807/624-2621; Fax: 807/622-7752; Email: nancy@tbchamber.on.ca; URL: www.tb-chamber.on.ca - Show Manager, Nancy Milani - Annual trade & consumer show - May

CARS *See* AUTOMOTIVE

CHEMISTRY

Canadian Society of Clinical Chemists Annual Meeting, Events & Management Plus Inc., #310, 4 Cataraqui St., Kingston ON K7K 1Z7 - 613/531-9210; Fax: 613/531- 0626; Tollfree: 1-866-560-3838; Email: office@ eventsmgt.com; URL: www.eventsmgt.com - Owner, E. Hooper, June, Hamilton ON

CHILDREN

Calgary International Children's Festival, 205 - 8th Ave. SE, Calgary AB T2G 0K9 - 403/294-7414; Fax: 403/294-7425; Email: admin@calgarychildfest.org; URL: www.calgarychildfest.org - Producer, JoAnne James - Annual - May, Calgary AB

Celebration Jeunesse, Groupe Jeunesse, 7383, rue de la Roche, Montréal QC H2R 2T4 - 514/274-6124; Fax: 514/272-5939; Tollfree: 1-888-274-6124; Email: groupe.jeunesse@ comjeune.com; URL: www.groupejeunesse.com - Ginette Flynn - Children & parents products & services. Annual consumer show - May - Stade Olympique, Montréal QC

Milk International Children's Festival of the Arts, Harbourfront Centre, 235 Queens Quay West, Toronto ON M5J 2G8 - 416/973-3000; Fax: 416/973-6055; Email: info@harbourfront centre.com; URL: www.harbourfrontcentre.com - CEO, William J.S. Boyle - Annual - May - Harbourfront Centre, Toronto ON

Northern Alberta International Children's Festival, 5 St. Anne St., St. Albert AB T8N 3Z9 - 780/459-1542; Fax: 780/459-1726; URL: www.childfest.com - Festival Manager, Paul Moulton - June, St. Albert AB

Northern Saskatchewan International Children's Festival, PO Box 1642, Saskatoon SK S7K 3R8 - 306/664-3378; Fax: 306/664-2344; Email: cozens@sasktel.net; URL: www.saskatoonchildrensfestival.org - Artistic Director, Cass Cozens - Annually, June. Four-day international festival of the performing arts for children

Regina Children's Festival, PO Box 3813, Regina SK S4P 3N8 - 306/352-7655; Fax: 306/525-6947; Email: reginacf@sasktel. net; URL: www.reginachildrensfestival.com - Annually. Three-day festival & cultural activities for children - June

Winnipeg International Children's Festival, #201, One Forks Market Rd.., Winnipeg MB R3C 4L9 - 204/958- 4730; Fax: 204/943-7915; Tollfree: 1-800-527-1515; Email: kidsfest@kidsfest.ca; URL: www.kidsfest.ca - Neal Rempel - Annual - June, Winnipeg MB

CHRISTMAS CRAFTS *See* CRAFTS

COMMUNICATIONS

CTCA Conference & Trade Fair, Canadian Telecommunications Consultants Association, #310, 2175 Sheppard Ave., Toronto ON M2J 1W8 - 416/495-7761; Fax: 416/491-1670; Tollfree: 1-800-463-2569; Email: office@ ctca.ca; URL: www.ctca.ca - Contact, Cheryl Mottershead, 905/451-9819

EXPO COMM Canada Communications, Reed Exhibition Companies Inc., #1, 3761 Victoria Park Ave., Toronto ON M1W 3S2 - 416/491-7565; Fax: 416/491-5088; Email: canada@reedexpo.com; URL: www.reedexpo.com - John Lewinski - Annual trade show - May, Toronto ON

COMPUTERS

Computer Fest, Show Fest Productions Inc., #200, 175 Dufflaw Rd., Toronto ON M6A 2W4 - 416/782-0063; Fax: 416/564-9116; URL: www.compfest.ca - President, David Carter - Consumer show Feb. (Toronto), Apr. (Mississauga), Sept. (Toronto), Nov. (Mississauga). Computers & internet products, services, seminars, demonstrations & information for home, business & education

Exposition industrielle et commerciale, Chambre de Commerce de Sept-Iles, #237, 700, boul Laure, Sept-Iles QC G4R 1Y1 - 418/968-3488; Fax: 418/968-3432; Email: cadoretd@cgocable.ca - Directrice générale, Ginette Lehoux - Computer & small business consumer show

InfoSecurity Canada, Reed Exhibition Companies Inc., #1, 3761 Victoria Park Ave., Toronto ON M1W 3S2 - 416/491-7565; Fax: 416/491-5088; Email: canada@reedexpo. com; URL: www.reedexpo.com - John Lewinski - Annual trade show - June, Toronto ON

Multimedia International Market, Martin International, #2910, 500, Place des Armes, Montréal QC H2Y 2W2 - 514/288-3931; Fax: 514/288-0641; Email: mbaudard@martin-intl.com; URL: www.forum-export.ca - General Manager, Marc Baudard - Annual trade show. Multimedia & digital products

National Factory Automation Show, Reed Exhibition Companies Inc., #1, 3761 Victoria Park Ave., Toronto ON M1W 3S2 - 416/491-7565; Fax: 416/491-5088; Email: canada@reedexpo.com; URL: www.reedexpo.com - John Lewinski - Annual trade show alternating between Toronto & Montréal

CONSTRUCTION & BUILDING PRODUCTS

Atlantic Building Materials Show, Atlantic Building Supply Dealers Association, 70 Englehart St., Dieppe NB E1A 8H3 - 506/858-0700; Fax: 506/859-0064; Tollfree: 1-800-561-7114; Email: absda@nbnet.nb.ca; URL: www.absda.ca - President, Don Sherwood, Chair, David Pritchett - Annual trade show - March

Construct Canada, York Communications, #1000, 5255 Yonge St., Toronto ON M2N 6P4 - 416/512-1215; Fax: 416/512-1993; Tollfree: 1-800-660-7083; Email: jacqui@yorkcom.to; URL: www.yorkcommunications.ca - Principal, Jacqui Peake - Annual trade show. Products, technologies & systems for the design & construction of all building types - Dec. - Metro Toronto Convention Centre, Toronto ON

Homebuilder & Renovation Expo, York Communications, #1000, 5255 Yonge St., Toronto ON M2N 6P4 - 416/512-1215; Fax: 416/512-1993; Tollfree: 1-800-660- 7083; Email: jacqui@yorkcom.to; URL: www.yorkcommunications.ca - Principal, Jacqui Peake - Annual trade show - Dec. - Metro Toronto Convention Centre, Toronto ON

CRAFTS

Art Market, Art Market Productions, PO Box 190, Barriere BC V0E 1E0 - 250/672-2411; Fax: 250/672-9517; Tollfree: 1-877-929-9933; Email: info@artmarketcraftsale. com; URL: www.artmarketcraftsale.com - Marlene Loney - Annual consumer show; art & craft sale - Nov., Calgary AB

Atlantic Craft Trade Show, Nova Scotia Business Inc., PO Box 2374, Halifax NS B3J 3E4 - 902/424-8609; Fax: 902/424-6823; Email: acts@gov.ns.ca; URL: www.actshow.ca - Show Manager, Bernard Burton - Annual trade show. Juried craft & giftware products

Bazaart, MacKenzie Art Gallery, 3475 Albert St., Regina SK S4S 6X6 - 306/584-4250; Fax: 306/569-8191; Email: mackenzie@ uregina.ca; URL: www.mackenzieartgallery.sk.ca - Juried outdoor art show & sale; complete range of crafts - June

Big M Craft & Bake Sale, Manitoba Stampede & Exhibition, PO Box 849, Morris MB R0G 1K0 - 204/746- 2552; Fax: 204/746-2900 - General Manager, Ron Funk Christmas at the Forum - Festival of Crafts, Antiques, Art & Foods,

Christmas at the Forum Crafts Festival, PO Box 34, Annapolis Royal NS B0S 1A0; Tollfree: 1-866- 995-7469; Email: dmsshows@hotmail.com; URL: www.forumcrafts.com - Coordinator, Jason Susnick - Annual consumer show - Nov., Halifax NS

Craft-Ex, DAC Marketing Ltd., PO Box 2837, Stn A, Sudbury ON P3A 5J3 - 705/673-5588; Fax: 705/525-0626; Email: dac@vianet.on.ca; URL: www.dacshows.com - Annual consumer show in Timmins, Sault Ste Marie & Sudbury - April

CraftWorld, Fine Arts & Crafts Show, Cryderman Productions Inc., 136 Thames St., Chatham ON N7L 2Y8 - 519/351-8344; Fax: 519/351-8345; Tollfree: 1-866- 640-9663; Email: john@crydermanproductions.com; URL: www.crydermanproductions.com - John Cryderman - Semi-annual shows in Chatham (March & Oct.) & Kitchener (Mar. & Nov.)

Creative Stitches & Crafting Alive, Canwest Shows Inc., 7 Panorama Bay SW, Calgary AB T3Z 3L6 - 403/686- 9699; Fax: 403/246-3856; Email: info@canwestshows. com; URL: www.canwestshows.com - General Manager, Terra Connors - Annual consumer show in Calgary (Sept.) & Edmonton (April)

Metro Toronto Christmas Gift Show & Sale, Metro Toronto Christmas Show & Sale, Skydome, PO Box 54045, Toronto ON M6A 3B7 - 416/789-1925 - Lawrence Plaza - Annual consumer show - Dec. - Metro Toronto Convention Centre, Toronto ON

Na'Amat Craft & Gift Show, Na'Amat Canada, 272 Codsell Ave., Toronto ON M3H 3X2 - 416/636-5425; Fax: 416/636-5248; Tollfree: 1-888-622-6280; Email: naamatca@aol.com - Executive Director, Lorraine Levene - October

One of a Kind Christmas Canadian Craft Show & Sale, The Canadian Craft Show Ltd., #300, 717 Church St., Toronto ON M4W 2M4 - 416/960-3680; Fax: 416/923- 5624; Email: info@oneofakindshow.com; URL: www.oneofakindshow.com - Show Director, Patti Stewart - Annual consumer show - Nov./Dec. - National Trade Centre, Exhibition Place, Toronto ON

One of a Kind Springtime Canadian Craft Show & Sale, The Canadian Craft Show Ltd., #300, 717 Church St., Toronto ON M4W 2M4 - 416/960-3680; Fax: 416/923- 5624; Email: info@oneofakindshow.com; URL: www.oneofakindshow.com - Show Director, Patti Stewart - Annual consumer show - March/April - Automotive Building, Exhibition Place, Toronto ON

Originals Christmas Craft Show, Signatures Craft Shows Ltd., #810, 325 Dalhousie St., Ottawa ON K1N 7G2 - 613/241-5777; Fax: 613/241-5678; Tollfree: 1-800- 773-4444; Email: inf@signatures.ca; URL: www.signatures.ca, Dec.

Pine Tree Potters Sale, 22 Church St., Aurora ON L4G 1G4 - 905/727-1278 - May & Nov.

Saskatchewan Handcraft Festival, Saskatchewan Craft Council, 813 Broadway Ave., Saskatoon SK S7N 1B5 - 306/653-3616; Fax: 306/244-2711; Tollfree: 1-866- 653-3616; Email: saskcraftcouncil@shaw.ca; URL: www.saskcraftcouncil.org - Chair, Paula Cooley, Executive Director, Glenn Saganace, July, Battleford SK

Saskatchewan Handcraft Festival, 813 Broadway Ave., Saskatoon SK S7N 1B5 - 306/653-3616; Fax: 306/244- 2711; Email: saskcraftcouncil@shaw.ca; URL: www.saskcraft council.org - Marketing Coordinator, Chris Jones - Annual three-day festival - July, Battleford SK

Signatures London, Signatures Craft Shows Ltd., #810, 325 Dalhousie St., Ottawa ON K1N 7G2 - 613/241-5777; Fax: 613/241-5678; Tollfree: 1-800-773-4444; Email: inf@signatures.ca; URL: www.signatures.ca - Annual consumer show - Nov., London ON

Signatures Ottawa, Signatures Craft Shows Ltd., #810, 325 Dalhousie St., Ottawa ON K1N 7G2 - 613/241-5777; Fax: 613/241-5678; Tollfree: 1-800-773-4444; Email: inf@signatures.ca; URL: www.signatures.ca - Annual consumer show - Nov., Ottawa ON

Signatures Toronto, Signatures Craft Shows Ltd., #810, 325 Dalhousie St., Ottawa ON K1N 7G2 - 613/241-5777; Fax: 613/241-5678; Tollfree: 1-800-773-4444; Email: inf@signatures.ca; URL: www.signatures.ca - Annual consumer show - Nov., Toronto ON

Signatures Winnipeg, Signatures Craft Shows Ltd., #810, 325 Dalhousie St., Ottawa ON K1N 7G2 - 613/241- 5777; Fax: 613/241-5678; Tollfree: 1-800-773-4444; Email: inf@signatures.ca; URL: www.signatures.ca - Annual consumer show - Nov., Winnipeg MB

Sundog Handcraft Fair, PO Box 7183, Saskatoon SK S7K 4J1 - 306/384-7364; Fax: 306/384-7364; Email: sundoghand craftfaire@sasktel.net - Coordinator, Diane Boyko-Banda - Juried three-day craft market plus continuous stage acts & gourmet food court. Annually, first weekend of Dec.

Victoria Park Arts/Crafts Fair, PO Box 1394, Moncton NB E1C 8T6 - 506/386-1200; Fax: 506/857-0279; Email: oscar@nb.aibn.com; URL: www.victoriaparkcrafts. com - Annually - Aug.

Wintergreen, Saskatchewan Craft Council, 813 Broadway Ave., Saskatoon SK S7N 1B5 - 306/653-3616; Fax: 306/244-2711; Tollfree: 1-866-653-3616; Email: saskcraftcouncil@shaw.ca; URL: www.saskcraftcouncil.org - Chair, Paula Cooley, Executive Director, Glenn Saganace - Annual. Threeday Christmas craft market - Nov., Regina SK

DANCE *See* MUSIC

DECORATING *See* HOME SHOWS

ELECTRICAL/ELECTRONICS

Audio Thunder, Pro-Sho Inc., 298 Sheppard Ave. East, Toronto ON M2N 3B1 - 416/229-9919; Fax: 416/223- 2826; Tollfree: 1-877-950-1500; Email: prosho@meteorshows. com; URL: www.performanceworldcarshow.com; www.llhashows.com- Contact: Larry King, March - International Centre, Toronto ON

Canadian High Technology Show & Assembly Canada, Reed Exhibition Companies Inc., #1, 3761 Victoria Park Ave., Toronto ON M1W 3S2 - 416/491-7565; Fax: 416/491-5088; Email: canada@reedexpo.com; URL: www.reedexpo.com - John Lewinski - Annual trade show. Electronic components, robotics, communications systems

Electrical Showcase, Manitoba Electrical League, #104, 1780 Wellington Ave., Winnipeg MB R3H 1B3 - 204/783-4125; Fax: 204/783-4216; Email: office@meleague. net; URL: www.meleague.net - General Manager, Dave Foreman - Triennial trade show - April

Eptech, LVP Media Inc., #27, 1200 Aerowood Dr., Mississauga ON L4W 2S7 - 905/624-8100; Fax: 905/624- 1760; Email: info@ept.ca; URL: www.ept.ca - Trade show held in various locations. Electronic components, systems

Mechanical Electical Electronic Technology, Master Promotions Ltd., PO Box 565, Saint John NB E2L 3Z8 - 506/658-0018; Fax: 506/658-0750; Tollfree: 1-888- 454-7469; Email: info@masterpromotions.ca; URL: www.masterpromotions.ca - Marketing & Operations Manager, Jennifer Allaby, President, Wendell Howes - Bienniel show

La Salon de la Technologie Electronique au Québec/Quebec Electronics Technology Show, Reed Exhibition Companies Inc., #1, 3761 Victoria Park Ave., Toronto ON M1W 3S2 - 416/491-7565; Fax: 416/491-5088; Email: canada@ reedexpo.com; URL: www.reedexpo.com - John Lewinski - Biennial trade show

ENERGY

Enercom, York Communications, #1000, 5255 Yonge St., Toronto ON M2N 6P4 - 416/512-1215; Fax: 416/512- 1993; Tollfree: 1-800-660-7083; Email: jacqui@ yorkcom.to; URL: www.yorkcommunications.ca - Principal, Jacqui Peake - Annual conference & exposition focusing on major trends & emerging issues in the procurement, production & distribution of electricity, gas, oil & renewable energy - March - Metro Toronto Convention Centre, Toronto ON

ENVIRONMENT

National Conference on Drinking Water, Canadian Water & Wastewater Association, #11, 1010 Polytek Rd., Ottawa ON K1J 9H9 - 613/747-0524; Fax: 613/747-0523; Email: admin@cwwa.ca; URL: www.cwwa.ca - Executive Director, T. Duncan Ellison - Biennial - April, 2008, Québec QC

ETHNIC *See* MULTICULTURAL

EVENTS

***See Also* specific categories for events such as Winter Carnivals, Music Festivals, Rodeos, Exhibitions, etc.**

Ashkenaz: A Festival of New Yiddish Culture, #303, 455 Spadina Ave., Toronto ON M5S 2G8 - 416/979-9901; Email: info@ashkenazfestival.com; URL: www.ashkenazfestival.com - President, Judy Wolfe - Bienniel; Aug./Sept.

Atlantic Canada Bicycle Rally, c/o Atlantic Canada Cycling, PO Box 1555, Stn M, Halifax NS B3J 2Y3 - 902/423-2453; Fax: 902/423-2452; Email: acbr@atlanticcanadacycling. com; URL: www.atlanticcanadacycling.com - Largest bicycle event in Atlantic Canada - Aug.

Billy Barker Days, PO Box 4441, Quesnel BC V2J 3J4 - 250/992-1234; Fax: 250/992-5083; Email: billyb@ quesnelbc.com; URL: www.pgonline.com/billybarkerdays, July

Blossom Festival, PO Box 329, Creston BC V0B 1G0 - 250/428-2266; Fax: 250/428-3320 - Contact, Bernice Hamilton - May, long weekend

Brockville Riverfest, Waterfront, Brockville Riverfest, Blockhouse Island, PO Box 742, Brockville ON K6V 5V8 - 613/342-8975; Fax: 613/345-6174; Email: riverfest@ripnet.com; URL: www.brockvilleriverfest.ca, June

The Canadian Tulip Festival, Canadian Tulip Festival, #106, 112 Nelson St., Ottawa ON K1N 7R5 - 613/567- 5757; Fax: 613/567-6216; Tollfree: 1-800-668-8547; Email: info@tulipfestival.ca; URL: www.tulipfestival.ca - Executive Director, BemoOt Hubert, May

Canmore Highland Games, Three Sisters Scottish Festival Society, PO Box 8102, Canmore AB T1W 2T8 - 403/678-9454; Fax: 403/678-3385; Email: canmorehighlandgames@telus.net; URL: www.canmorehighlandgames.ca - Annually, Labour Day Sunday - Sept., Canmore AB

Charleswood In-Motion Days, 625 Municipal Rd., Winnipeg MB R3R 1J2 - 204/837-7356 - Annually, June. Business displays, stage performances, carnival, youth soccer tournament

CHIN International Picnic, Exhibition Place, Toronto ON M6K 3C3 - 416/531-9991; Fax: 416/531-5274; Email: info@chinradio.com; URL: www.chinradio.com - June/July

Chocolate Fest, Chocolate Festival, PO Box 5002, St. Stephen NB E3L 2X5 - 506/465-5616; Fax: 506/465- 5610; Email: info@chocolate-fest.ca; URL: www.chocolate-fest.ca - Coordinator, Roxanne Grant - Annual - Aug

Discovery Days, Discovery Days Festival, PO Box 389, Dawson YT Y0B 1G0 - 867/993-5575; Fax: 867/993- 6415; Email: kva@dawsoncity.net; URL: www.dawsoncity.ca - Aug.

Feast of St. Louis, 259 Park Service Rd., Louisbourg NS B1C 2L2 - 902/733-2280; Fax: 902/733-2362; Email: louisbourg.info@pc.gc.ca - Manager, Heritage Presentation, Anne O'Neill, Superintendent, Carol Whitfield - Eighteenth-century celebrations in honour of St. Louis - August, Louisbourg NS

Festival des peches et de l'aquaculture du Nouveau Brunswick, #200, 1 av Hotel de Ville, Shippagan NB E8S 1M1 - 506/336-8726; Fax: 506/336-3901; Email: festival@shippagan.com

Halifax Highland Games, 35 Clearview Cres., Dartmouth NS B3A 2M9 - 902/466-3778; Email: info@halifaxhighlandgames. com; URL: www.halifaxhighlandgames.com, July - Garrison Grounds, Halifax NS

Heritage Canoe Festival, (Lift Lock), c/o Friends of the Trent Severn Waterway, PO Box 572, Peterborough ON K9J 6Z6 - 705/742-2251; Fax: 705/750-4816; Tollfree: 1-800-663-2628; URL: www.ftsw.com - Mark Doherty - Annually, 2nd weekend in May

Icelandic Festival of Manitoba, #107, 94 - 1st Ave., Gimli MB R0C 1B0 - 204/642-7417; Fax: 204/642-9382; Email: icefest@mts.net; URL: www.icelandicfestival.com, Aug., Gimli MB

Just for Laughs Festival, 2101, boul Saint-Laurent, Montréal QC H2X 2T5 - 514/845-3155; Fax: 514/845-4140; Tollfree: 1-888-244-3155; Email: info@hahaha.com; URL: www.hahaha.com, July

Kitchener-Waterloo Oktoberfest, 17 Benton St., PO Box 1053, Kitchener ON N2G 4G1 - 519/570-4267; Fax: 519/742-3072; Tollfree: 1-888-294-4267; Email: info@oktoberfest.ca; URL: www.oktoberfest.ca - Executive Director, Larry Blundell - Annually, October. Bavarian festival: foods, entertainment, parades

Labrador Straits Bakeapple Folk Festival, PO Box 112, Forteau NL A0K 2P0 - 709/931-2013; Email: info@labradorcoastal drive.com - Director, Marketing, Bonnie Goudie - Annually, Aug.

Manitoba Sunflower Festival, PO Box 1630, Altona MB R0G 0B0 - 204/324-9005; Fax: 204/324-1550; Email: info@townofaltona.com; URL: www.town.altona.mb.ca - Annual, last weekend of July

Northern Manitoba Trappers' Festival, Inc., PO Box 475, The Pas MB R9A 1K6 - 204/623-2912; Fax: 204/623- 1974; URL: www.trappersfestival.com - Annually, Feb.; world championship sled dog race

Northwest Territorial Days, PO Box 668, North Battleford SK S9A 2Y9 - 306/445-2024; Fax: 306/445-3352; Email: b.agsociety@sasktel.net; URL: www.agsociety.com - Aug.

Nova Scotia Gaelic Mod, F,is A' MhThe Gaelic Mod, PO Box 80, Englishtown NS B0C 1H0 - 902/295-3411; Fax: 902/295-2912; Email: hector@gaeliccollege.edu; URL: www.gaeliccollege.edu - One-day festival - Aug. - Gaelic College, St. Ann's NS Nova Scotia International Tattoo, 1586 Queen St., Halifax NS B3J 2V1 - 902/420-1114; Fax: 902/423-6629; Tollfree: 1-800-563-1114; Email: info@nstattoo.ca; URL: www.nstattoo.ca - Ian Fraser - Annually, June/July

Penticton Peach Festival, #113, 437 Martin St., S343, Penticton BC V2A 5L1 - 250/492-9830; Fax: 250/492- 7980; Email: info@peachfest.com; URL: www.peachfest.com - Aug.

Peterborough Summer Festival of Lights, 610 Parkhill Rd., Peterborough ON K9J 6N6 - 705/755-1111; Fax: 705/755-0188; Email: info@festivaloflights.ca; URL: www.festivaloflights.ca - Special Events Coordinator, Emily Martin, General Manager, Kathy Kirkland - June to Aug. every Wednesday & Saturday evening at Del Crary Park

Pictou Lobster Carnival, PO Box 1480, Pictou NS B0K 1H0 - 902/485-5150; Fax: 902/485-4915; Email: picoulobstercarnival@hotmail.com; URL: www.townofpictou.com - Annual - July

Québec City Summer Festival, 226, rue St-Joseph est, Québec QC G1K 3A9 - 418/523-4540; Fax: 418/523- 0194; Tollfree: 1-888-992-5200; Email: infofestival@ infofestival.com; URL: www.infofestival.com - Entertainment in the streets & parks of Old Québec, July

Royal St. John's Regatta, PO Box 214, St. John's NL A1C 5J9 - 709/579-8921; Fax: 709/576-3315; Email: stjohnsregatta@nf.aibn.com; URL: www.stjohnsregatta.org - North America's oldest continuing sporting event - Aug., St. John's NL

Sam Steele Days, PO Box 115, Cranbrook BC V1C 4H6 - 250/426-4161; Fax: 250/426-3873; Tollfree: 1-800- 222-6174; Email: info@samsteeledays.org; URL: www.samsteeledays.org, June

Shediac Lobster Festival, 231A Belliveau Ave., Shediac NB E4P 1H4 - 506/532-1122; Fax: 506/532-7986; Tollfree: 1-888-707-1755; Email: lobsterf@ nbnet.nb.ca; URL: www.lobsterfestival.nb.ca - Guy Lavine - Annually, first week of July

Steinbach Pioneer Days, c/o Mennonite Heritage Village, 231, PTH 12 North, Steinbach MB R0A 2A0 - 204/326- 9661

Storytelling Festival, The Storytellers School of Toronto, 43 Queens Park Cres. East, Toronto ON M5S 2C3 - 416/656-2445; Fax: 416/656-8510; Email: admin@storytelling toronto.org; URL: www.storytellingtoronto.org - President, Michael Lobraico, Managing Director, Catherine Melville - Held annually, April

Summerside Lobster Carnival, PO Box 1295, Summerside PE C1N 4K2 - 902/436-4925; Fax: 902/436-0129; URL: www. exhibitions-festivalspeiae.com/summersidelobstercarnival, July

Threshermen's Show & Seniors' Festival, PO Box 98, Yorkton SK S3N 2V6 - 306/783-8361; Fax: 306/782- 1027; Email: yorkton@wdm.ca; URL: www.wdm.ca - Chair, Susan Mandzluk - Annually, Aug.

Trinity Conception Fair, c/o Harbour Grace Stadium, PO Box 365, Harbour Grace NL A0A 2M0 - 709/596-6201; Fax: 709/596-6261; Tollfree: 1-800-596-3233; Email: hgrecdept@nf.aibn.com - Fair Manager, Kevin Bennett - Annually, Sept.

Welland Rose Festival, 800 Niagara St. North, PO Box 23031, Welland ON L3C 5Z4 - 905/735-8696; Fax: 905/735-4832; URL: www.wellandrosefestival.on.ca - Director, Shane Sargant - Annually, June. Rose show, lobsterfest, sporting events, juried art show, seniors' events, day in the park, day-on-the-island, craft show, fishing derby, children's events, grand parade

Winnipeg Oktoberfest, Winnipeg Convention Centre, 375 York Ave., 3rd Fl., Winnipeg MB R3C 3J3 - 204/957- 4535; Fax: 204/943-0310; Email: oktoberfest@ wcc.mb.ca; URL: www.winnipegoktoberfest.com, Sept.

World's Invitational Class A Gold Panning Championships, Taylor Gold Panning Society, District of Taylor, PO Box 300, Taylor BC V0C 2K0 - 250/789-3004; Fax: 250/789-9076; URL: www.districtoftaylor.com - Director, Community Services, Natalie Poole-Moffat - Annually, Aug. long weekend Yukon Gold-Panning Championships, Klondike Visitors Association, PO Box 389, Dawson YT Y0B 1G0 - 867/993-5575; Fax: 867/993-6415; Email: kva@ dawson.net; URL: www.dawsoncity.org - On Canada Day - July, Dawson City YT

Yukon River Bathtub Race, Yukon Sourdough Rendezvous Society, PO Box 31721, Whitehorse YT Y1A 6L3 - 867/393-4467; Fax: 867/668-6755; Email: ysr@polarcom. com; URL: www.yukonrendezvous.com - Executive Director, Harold Sher, President, Marj Eschak - Longest & hardest bathtub race. Two days, 486 miles, Yukon River - Aug.

Yukon Sourdough Rendezvous, Yukon Sourdough Rendezvous Society, PO Box 31721, Whitehorse YT Y1A 6L3 - 867/393-4467; Fax: 867/668-6755; Email: ysr@polarcom.com; URL: www.yukonrendezvous.com - Executive Director, Harold Sher, President, Marj Eschak - Annually. Celebrates the gold rush times. Mad trapper, flour packing, tug-a-truck contests, fiddle show, lip sync & queen contests - Feb.

EXHIBITIONS

***See Also* Farm Business/Agriculture, Rodeos**

Buffalo Days Exhibition, Regina Exhibition Park, PO Box 167, Regina SK S4P 2Z6 - 306/781-9200; Fax: 306/565-3443; Tollfree: 1-888-734-3975; Email: info@reginaexhibition. com - Marketing Manager, Tom Mullin, General Manager, Douglas Cressman, July

Canadian Lakehead Exhibition, 425 Northern Ave., Thunder Bay ON P7C 2V7 - 807/622-6473; Fax: 807/623-5540; Email: clex@btbaytel.net; URL: www.cle.on.ca - Administrative Clerk, Dulcie Prystanski - Annually, Aug.

Canadian National Exhibition, Canadian National Exhibition Association, Exhibition Place, Toronto ON M6K 3C3 - 416/263-3800; Fax: 416/263-3838; Email: info@theex.com; URL: www.theex.com - Annual public show

Edmonton's Klondike Days Exposition, PO Box 1480, Edmonton AB T5J 2N5 - 780/471-7210; Fax: 780/471- 8176; Tollfree: 1-888-800-7275; Email: info@northlands. com; URL: www.northlands.com - Annual consumer show

Expo Québec, ExpoCit,, 250, boul Wilfrid-Hamel, Québec QC G1L 5A7 - 418/691-7110; Fax: 418/691-7249; Email: info@expocite.com - General Manager, Mark Sparrow - Annual exhibition. Industrial, agricultural, food - Aug. - City Fairgrounds, Québec QC

Fredericton Exhibition, PO Box 235, Stn A, Fredericton NB E3B 4Y9 - 506/458-9819; Fax: 506/458-9294; Email: frex@nb.net.nb.ca; URL: brentbriggs_frex@ nb.aibn.com - Annual, begins on Labour Day - Sept.

Home Town Fair, Hometown Fair, c/o Moose Jaw Exhibition Co. Ltd., 250 Thatcher Dr. East, Moose Jaw SK S6J 1L7 - 306/692-2723; Fax: 306/692-2762; Email: moosejawexh@sk.sympatico.ca - General Manager, Glen Lewis - Annually - June

Interior Provincial Exhibition, Interior Provincial Exhibition & Stampede, PO Box 490, Armstrong BC V0E 1B0 - 250/546-9406; Fax: 250/546-6181; Email: ipeandstampede@telus.net; URL: www.ipeandstampede.com - General Manager, Ken Mather - Annual consumer agricultural fair & show, Aug.-Sept. - Aug.

Lindsay Central Exhibition, 37 Adelaide St. North, Lindsay ON K9V 4K8 - 705/324-5551; Fax: 705/324-8111; Email: info@lindsayex.com; URL: www.lindsayex.com - Manager, Tom Saunders - Annual consumer agricultural fair & show - Sept.

Markham Agricultural Fair, 10801 McCowan Rd., Markham ON L3P 3J3 - 905/642-3247; Fax: 905/640- 8458; Tollfree: 1-800-450-3557; Email: office@ markhamfair.ca; URL: www.markhamfair.ca - Annual consumer show - Sept./Oct.

Medicine Hat Exhibition & Stampede, 2055 - 21st Ave. SE, PO Box 1298, Medicine Hat AB T1A 7N1 - 403/527- 1234; Fax: 403/529-6553; Email: mhstampede@mhstampede. com; URL: www.mhstampede.com/- General Manager, Jim MacArthur - Annual consumer show - July

New Atlantic National Exhibition, PO Box 284, Saint John NB E2L 3Y2 - 506/633-2020; Fax: 506/636-6958 - Annual - Aug.

Niagara Regional Exhibition, 1100 Niagara St. North, Welland ON L3C 1M6 - 905/735-6413; Fax: 905/735- 2317; Email: nreoffice@nre.ca; URL: www.nre.ca - Annual consumer agricultural fair & show, Sept. - Sept.

Nova Scotia Provincial Exhibition, PO Box 192, Truro NS B2N 5C5 - 902/893-9222; Fax: 902/897-0069; Email: nspe@eastlink.ca - David Coombes - Agricultural exhibition - August, Bible Hill NS

Pacific National Exhibition, 2901 East Hastings St., Stn Hastings Park, Vancouver BC V5K 5J1 - 604/253- 2311; Fax: 604/251-7768; Email: info@pne.ca; URL: www.pne.ca - President & CEO, Michael McDaniel - Annual event; agricultural competitions, parade

Paris Fall Fair, PO Box 124, Paris ON N3L 3E7 - 519/442- 2823; Fax: 519/442-5121; Email: parisfair@ on.aibn.com; URL: www.parisfair.com - Manager, Harry Emmott - Annual Labour Day weekend consumer show

Prince Albert Exhibition, Prince Albert Exhibition Association, PO Box 1538, Prince Albert SK S6V 5T1 - 306/764-1711; Fax: 306/764-5246; Email: paex@ sasktel.net; URL: www.paexhibition.com - Manager, Dave Young - Annual

Red River Exhibition, Red River Exhibition Association, Red River Exhibition Park, 3977 Portage Ave., Winnipeg MB R3K 2E8 - 204/888-6990; Fax: 204/888- 6992; URL: www.redriverex.com - Manitoba's largest fair & single-site entertainment event. Annually, 10 days, last two weeks in June

Thresherman's Reunion & Stampede, Central Canada's Fiddle Festival, PO Box 10, High Bluff MB R0H 0C0 - 204/637-2354; Fax: 204/637-2395; Email: info@agmuseum. mb.ca; URL: www.ag-museum.mb.ca - Contact, Sandra Head - Annual

Western Nova Scotia Exhibition, PO Box 425, Yarmouth NS B5A 4B3 - 902/742-8222; Fax: 902/742-5229; Email: frank@swsda.com; URL: yarmouthexhibition.com/index.html - Frank Anderson - Six-day agricultural fair & talent competition - July or Aug., Yarmouth NS

FARM BUSINESS/AGRICULTURE

See Also **Exhibitions, Rodeos**

Agribition Show & Rodeo, Canadian Western Agribition Show & Rodeo, c/o Public Relations Office, Canadian Western Agribition, PO Box 3535, Regina SK S4P 3J8 - 306/565-0565; Fax: 306/757-9963; Email: info@agribition. com; URL: www.agribition.com - General Manager, Leon Brin - Annually, Nov.

CAAR Convention, Canadian Association of Agri-Retailers, #107, 1090 Waverley St., Winnipeg MB R3T 0P4 - 204/989-9300; Fax: 204/989-9306; Tollfree: 1-800-463-9323; Email: info@caar.org; URL: www.caar.org - Executive Director, Jacqueline Ryrie, President, Bob Evans

Canadian National Hereford Show, c/o Canadian Hereford Association, 5160 Skyline Way NE, Calgary AB T2E 6V1 - 403/275-2662; Fax: 403/295-1333; Email: herefords@hereford.ca; URL: www.hereford.ca, Nov., Regina SK

Estevan Farmer's Day, c/o Estevan Chamber of Commerce, #303, 1133 Fourth St., Estevan SK S4A 0W6 - 306/634-2828; Fax: 306/634-6729 - Office Manager, Carol Gress - Annually, March

Farmers' Field Day & Open House, c/o St. John's Research Station, Agriculture Canada, Brookfield Rd., PO Box 39088, St. John's NL A1E 5Y7 - 709/772-4619; Fax: 709/772-6064; Email: henderf@em.agr.ca; URL: res.agr.ca/stjohns - Communications Advisor, Lesley Noftall - Annually, 4th Saturday in Aug.

Maritime Fall Fair, 200 Prospect Rd., Goodwood NS B3T 1P2 - 902/876-8221; Fax: 902/876-8551; URL: www.maritimefallfair.com - Annual consumer exhibition, Oct., over the Thanksgiving weekend

Norfolk County Fair & Horse Show, Norfolk County Agricultural Society, 172 South Dr., Simcoe ON N3Y 1G6 - 519/426-7280; Fax: 519/426-7286; URL: www.norfair.com - General Manager, Karen Matthews, Email: kmatthews@norfolkcountyfair.com - Annual consumer show

Northlands Farmfair, Farmfair International, PO Box 1480, Edmonton AB T5J 2N5 - 780/471-7210; Fax: 780/471- 8169; Tollfree: 1-888-800-7275; URL: www.farmfairinternational.com - Annually, Nov.

Nova Scotia 4-H Show, c/o NS Dept. of Agriculture & Fisheries, PO Box 550, Truro NS B2N 5E3 - 902/893-6587; Fax: 902/893-2757; Email: crouseea@gov.ns.ca; URL: www.gov.ns.ca/nsaf/4h - Manager, Elizabeth Crouse - Annual consumer show, Oct.

Poultry Industry Conference & Exhibition, Western Fair Association, 900 King St., PO Box 7550, London ON N5Y 5P8 - 519/438-7203; Fax: 519/679-3124; Tollfree: 1-800-619-4629; Email: gmcrae@westernfair. com; URL: www.westernfair.com - General Manager, Gary McRae - Annual trade show

Regional Potato Festival, #100, 1A Burgess St., Grand Falls NB E3Y 1C6 - 506/475-1816; Fax: 506/473-9091; Email: info@festivalregionaldelapatate.com; URL: www.festivalregionaldelapatate.com - President, John Bellefleur, June

Royal Agricultural Winter Fair, Royal Agricultural Winter Fair Association, The Coliseum, National Trade Centre, Exhibition Place, Toronto ON M6K 3C3 - 416/263- 3400; Fax: 416/263-3488; Email: information@royalfair. org; URL: www.royalfair.org - Annual consumer show. World's largest agricultural fair & equestrian event - Nov., Toronto ON

Salon de l'Agriculteur, #120, 2200, rue Pratte, Saint-Hyacinthe QC J2S 4B6 - 450/771-1226; Fax: 450/771- 6073; Email: info@salonagr.qc.ca; URL: salonagr.qc.ca - Annual trade show. Agricultural products - Jan., St-Hyacinthe QC

Western Canada Farm Progress Show, PO Box 167, Regina SK S4P 2Z6 - 306/781-9200; Fax: 306/781-9396; Tollfree: 1-888-734-3975; Email: wcfps@reginaexhibition. com; URL: www.wcfps.com - Show Manager, Rob O'Connor, Vice-President, Major Event Development, Darrell Komick - Annual consumer & trade show - June - Regina Exhibition Park, Regina SK

Western Fair, Western Fair Association, 900 King St., PO Box 7550, London ON N5Y 5P8 - 519/438-7203; Fax: 519/679-3124; Tollfree: 1-800-619-4629; Email: gmcrae@westernfair.com; URL: www.westernfair.com - General Manager, Gary McRae - Annual consumer show

Western Farm Show, Western Fair Association, 900 King St., PO Box 7550, London ON N5Y 5P8 - 519/438- 7203; Fax: 519/679-3124; Tollfree: 1-800-619-4629; Email: gmcrae@westernfair.com; URL: www.westernfair.com - General Manager, Gary McRae - Annual consumer show

FASHION

Luggage, Leathergoods, Handbags & Accessories, Pro-Sho Inc., 298 Sheppard Ave. East, Toronto ON M2N 3B1 - 416/229-9919; Fax: 416/223-2826; Tollfree: 1-877- 950-1500; Email: prosho@meteorshows.com; URL: www.performanceworldcarshow.com; www.llhashows. com - Annual trade show - Show Manager, Richard Swayze, April - International Centre, Mississauga ON

FESTIVALS *See* EVENTS

FILM & VIDEO FESTIVALS & SPECIAL EVENTS

Alberta Film & Television Awards, Alberta Motion Picture Industries Association, #401, 11456 Jasper Ave., Edmonton AB T5K 0M1 - 780/944-0707; Fax: 780/426- 3057; Email: info@ampia.org; URL: www.ampia.org - President, Connie Edwards, Executive Director, Richard Horne, Feb.

Le Carrousel international du film de Rimouski, 92, 2e rue ouest, Rimouski QC G5L 8B3 - 418/722-0103; Fax: 418/724-9504; Email: cifr@carrousel.qc.ca; URL: www.carrousel.qc.ca - Kathleen Aubry - Films for children. Competition, workshops - Sept., Rimouski QC

Cinéfest - The Sudbury International Film Festival, 45 Durham St., Sudbury ON P3E 3M2 - 705/688-1234; Fax: 705/688-1351; Tollfree: 1-877-212-3222; Email: cinefest@vianet.on.ca; URL: www.cinefest.com - Executive Director, Tammy Frick - Full-length feature festival with over 100 Canadian & international films, animations, shorts, Midnight Madness, documentary & children's film series - Sept., Sudbury ON

Festival du cinéma international en Abitibi-Témiscamingue, 215, av Mercier, Rouyn-Noranda QC J9X 5W8 - 819/762-6212; Fax: 819/762-6762; Email: info@festivalcinema. ca; URL: www.lino. com/festivalcinema - Executive Director, Jacques Matte - Features, mediumlength & short films. Competition; regional jury award for short or medium-length film; people's choice award for feature & animation - Oct., Rouyn-Noranda QC

Festival du film étudiant canadien/Canadian Student Film Festival, Festival du film ,tudiant canadien, 1432, rue de Bleury, Montréal QC H3A 2J1 - 514/848-7186; Fax: 514/848-3886; Email: info@ffm-montreal.org - Films & videos by Canadian students. Film competition - Aug., Montréal QC

Le Festival International du Film Scientifique du Québec, Téléscience, 15, rue de la Commune ouest, Montréal QC H2Y 2C6 - 514/849-1612; Fax: 514/281-0814; Email: dir@telescince.qc.ca; URL: www.telescience.qc.ca - Director, Lise Barrette

Festival international du nouveau Cinéma et des nouveaux M,dias de Montréal, Festival international du nouveau Cin,ma de Montréal, 3530, boul Saint-Laurent, Montréal QC H2X 2V1 - 514/847-9272; Fax: 514/847-0732; Email: info@fcmm.com - Directeur, Claude Chamberlan - New trends in new cinema, video & new media; non-competitive; people's choice award

Film Studies Association of Canada Conference, Film Studies Association of Canada, c/o Global Studies, Wilfrid Laurier Univ., Dr. Alvin Woods Bldg., 75 University Ave. West, Room 3-205, Waterloo ON N2L 3C5; Email: gekoff@contact.net; URL: www.filmstudies.ca - President, Brenda Austin-Smith, Vice-President, Janina Falkowska, Secretary, Christina Stojanowa - May/June annually, held at a different university each year

Flicks: Saskatchewan International Children's Film Festival, Flicks International Children's Film Festival, PO Box 9628, Saskatoon SK S7K 7G1 - 306/956-3456; Fax: 306/664-2344; Email: flicksfilmfestival@sasktel.net; URL: www.flicksfilmfest. org - Artistic Director, Cass Cozens - Annually in March, three day international film festival for children

Images Festival of Independent Film & Video, #448, 401 Richmond St. West, Toronto ON M5V 3A8 - 416/971- 8405; Fax: 416/971-7412; Email: images@imagesfestival. com; URL: www.imagesfestival.com/- Executive Director, Peter Chevrier - Annual. Independent films & videos. Workshops - April, Toronto ON

Les Journées africaines et créoles, Vues d'Afrique, 67, rue Ste-Catherine ouest, 5e étage, Montréal QC H2X 1Z7 - 514/284-3322; Fax: 514/845-0631; Email: info@vuesdafrique. org; URL: www.vuesdafrique.org - Gérard Le Chêne - Competition. Films by & about African & Creole peoples - April, Montréal QC

Les Rendez-vous du cinéma québécois, 1000, rue Fullum, Montréal QC H2K 3L7 - 514/526-9635; Fax: 514/526- 1955; Email: info@rvcq.com; URL: www.rvcq.com - Président, Denis Chouinard - Restrospective of recent Québec productions - Feb., Montréal QC

Ottawa International Animation Festival, #120, 2 Daly Ave., Ottawa ON K1N 6E2 - 613/232-8769; Fax: 613/232-6315; Email: info@animationfestival.ca; URL: www.awn.com/ottawa /- Annual. Animation films & videos. Television animation conference. Workshops & panels - Sept., Ottawa ON

St. John's Women's Film & Video Festival, PO Box 984, St. John's NL A1C 5M3 - 709/754-3141; Fax: 709/754- 3143; Email: womensfilmfestival@nfld.net; URL: www.womensfilmfestival.com - Festival Director, Katie Nicholson - Women's films & videos. Workshops & panels - Oct., St. John's NL Toronto International Film Festival,

Toronto International Film Festival Group, TIFF Bell Lightbox, Reitman Square, 350 King Street West, Toronto ON M5V 3X5 - 416/934-3200; Email:proffice@tiff.net; URL: tiff.net - Features & theatrical shorts. Competition. Awards for excellence in Canadian production. People's choice & film critics awards. Symposium, workshops, sales office - Sept., Toronto ON

Vancouver International Film Festival, #410, 1008 Homer St., Vancouver BC V6B 2X1 - 604/685-0260; Fax: 604/688-8221; Email: viff@viff.org; URL: www.viff.org - Festival Director, Alan Franey - Features, mediumlength & short films. Competition; juried awards for best western Canadian feature film, best young western Canadian director of a short film, best documentary feature & best film by a new director from Pacific Asia; people's choice award for most popular international film & for most popular Canadian film. Trade forum - Sept./Oct., Vancouver BC World Film Festival, Montréal

World Film Festival, 1432, rue de Bleury, Montréal QC H3A 2J1 - 514/848-3883; Fax: 514/848-3886; Email:

info@ffm-montreal.org; URL: www.ffm-montreal.org/- Features, mediumlength & short films. Competition, symposium, markets - Aug., Montréal QC

FIRST NIGHT CELEBRATIONS

First Night Labrador City, PO Box 280, Labrador City NL A2V 2K5 - 709/944-3602; Fax: 709/944-5277 First Night Toronto, 55 Mill St., Case Goods Warehouse 74, Studio 202, Toronto ON M5A 3C4 - 416/603-4778; Fax: 416/595-9651; Email: info@firstnighttoronto.ca; URL: www.firstnighttoronto.ca - Executive Director, Jeffrey Latimer, Dec.

First Night Whistler, 4010 Whistler Way, Whistler BC V0N 1B4 - 604/932-3928; Fax: 604/932-7231

FISHING/AQUACULTURE

Adams River Sockeye Salmon Run, PO Box 1563, Chase BC V0E 1M0 - 250/679-8315; URL: www.salmonsociety.com - Oct.

Atlantic Aquaculture Exposition, Master Promotions Ltd., PO Box 565, Saint John NB E2L 3Z8 - 506/658-0018; Fax: 506/658-0750; Tollfree: 1-888-454-7469; Email: info@masterpromotions.ca; URL: www.masterpromotions.ca - Marketing & Operations Manager, Jennifer Allaby, President, Wendell Howes - Canada's largest aquaculture event - June, St. Andrews NB

Eastern Canada Fisheries Exposition, Master Promotions Ltd., PO Box 565, Saint John NB E2L 3Z8 - 506/658- 0018; Fax: 506/658-0750; Tollfree: 1-888-454-7469; Email: info@masterpromotions.ca; URL: www.masterpromotions.ca - Annual commercial fishing show - Show Manager, Jeff Lacey, Feb - Mariner's Centre, Yarmouth NS

Fish Canada/Workboat Canada West, Master Promotions Ltd., PO Box 565, Saint John NB E2L 3Z8 - 506/658- 0018; Fax: 506/658-0750; Tollfree: 1-888-454-7469; Email: info@masterpromotions.ca; URL: www.masterpromotions.ca - Bienniel commercial fishing/boat show - Show Manager, Sydney Peacock, Nov., Vancouver BC

Flin Flon Trout Festival, PO Box 751, Flin Flon MB R8A 1N6 - 204/687-5166, June, Flin Flon MB

Great Northern Pike Festival, PO Box 863, Nipawin SK S0E 1E0 - 306/862-9866; Fax: 306/862-3076; Tollfree: 1-877-647-2946; Email: events@ nipawin.com; URL: www.nipawinpikefestival.com - June - Sept.

Lunenburg Fishermen's Picnic & Reunion, PO Box 308, Lunenburg NS B0J 2C0 - 902/634-8575; Fax: 902/634- 8575; Email: bacalao@tallships.ca - Chair, Barbara Zwicker, Aug., Lunenburg NS

Nova Scotia Smelt Tournament, 2228 Conquerall Rd., Bridgewater NS B4V 2W3 - 902/543-6453; Email: icefish@tallships.ca - Largest ice fishing tournament, Eastern Canada - Feb.

Salmon Festival, PO Box 24, Campbellton NB E3N 3G1 - 506/759-7997; Fax: 506/759-7403; Tollfree: 1-888- 813-4433; Email: tourism@campbellton.org; URL: www.campbellton.org - Contact, Gilbert Cyr, Email: gilbert.cyr@campbellton.org - June

FLOWERS/LANDSCAPING/GARDENING

Flower, Plant & Garden Show, dmg World Media, 180 Duncan Mills Rd., 4th Fl., Toronto ON M3B 1Z6 - 416/385-1880; Fax: 416/385-1855; Tollfree: 1-888-823- 7469; URL: www.dmgworldmedia.com - Show Manager, Glen Chiasson

Hamilton & Burlington Rose Society Show, Royal Botanical Gardens, 680 Plains Rd. West, Burlington ON L7T 4H4 - 905/527-1158; Fax: 905/577-0375, June Hamilton Orchid Show, Royal Botanical Gardens, 680 Plains Rd. West, Burlington ON L7T 4H4 - 905/527- 1158; Fax: 905/577-0375, March

Ikenobo Ikebana Japanese Flower Show, Royal Botanical Gardens, 680 Plains Rd. West, Burlington ON L7T 4H4 - 905/527-1158; Fax: 905/577-0375, Sept.

Ontario Garden Show, Town Media, 1074 Cooke Blvd., Burlington ON L7T 4A8 - 905/634-8003; Fax: 905/634-7661; URL: www.foodandwineshow.ca; ontariogardenshow. com - Annual - April - Royal Botanical Gardens Centre, Burlington ON

Provincial Rose Show, 1747 Summer St., Halifax NS B3H 3A6 - 902/423-4458 - Ann-Marie Clifford - Competitive show for rose growers in Nova Scotia - July - Nova Scotia Museum of Natural History, Halifax NS

Saskatoon Horticultural Society Annual Show, PO Box 161, Saskatoon SK S7K 3K4 - 306/373-7075; Email: sasktoonhortsociety@sasktel.net - Elsie, Aug.

FOOD & BEVERAGE

See Also **Hospitality Industry**

Canadian Natural Product Spring/Fall Show, Canadian Health Food Association, #205, 550 Alden Rd., Markham ON L3R 6A8 - 905/479-6939; Fax: 905/479- 1516; Tollfree: 1-800-661-4510, fax 1-888-2927; Email: admin@chfa.ca; URL: www.chfa.ca - Organic & natural products; homeopathy, food supplements & herbs. April & Oct.

The Good Food Festival & Market, 117 Evelyn Ave., Toronto ON M6J 4G7 - 416/766-2084; Fax: 416/762-9942; Email: info@goodfoodfestival.net; URL: www.goodfoodfestival.net - General Manager, Lynda Chubak - Annual consumer festival - April - International Centre, Hall 5, Mississauga ON

Gourmet Food & Wine Expo, Town Media, 1074 Cooke Blvd., Burlington ON L7T 4A8 - 905/634-8003; Fax: 905/634-7661; URL: www.foodandwineshow.ca; ontariogardenshow.com - Consumer show - Nov. - Metro Toronto Convention Centre, Toronto ON

Ottawa Wine & Food Show, Player Expositions International, 255 Clemow Ave., Ottawa ON K1S 2B5 - 613/567-6408; Fax: 613/567-2718; Email: rplayer@sympatico. ca; URL: www.playerexpo.com - Show Organizer, Halina Player - Annual trade & consumer show - Oct./Nov.

Salon des vins et spiritueux de Montréal, AFLD Consultants Inc., 3565, rue Edgar Leduc, Lachine QC H8T 3L5 - 514/639-6806; Fax: 514/639-6629; Email: afld@ videotron.ca - Show Manager, Lucie Desharnais, CDE - Biennial trade & public show

Salon Distal, Distal, 414, boul Raymond, Beauport QC GIC 7S4 - 418/666-5575; Fax: 418/666-8005 - Michel Renaud - Annual trade show. Food products & distributors. Held in Montréal & Québec - April

SSA International - Super Salon de l'alimentation, SIAL Montréal - Salon international de l'alimentation, #1100, 300, rue Léo Pariseau, CP 159, Montréal QC H2W 2M9 - 514/289-9669; Fax: 514/289-1034; Tollfree: 1-800- 281-7425; Email: info@sialmontreal.ca; URL: www.sial-montreal.com/- Directeur général, Alain Bellefeuille - Annual trade show for the food retail industry including food & beverage products & store equipment - April

Toronto Wine & Cheese Show, Premier Publications & Shows, 467 Speers Rd., Oakville ON L6K 3S4; Fax: 905/337-5570; Tollfree: 1-800-265-3673; URL: www.towineandcheese.com - Marti Milks, 905/815-0017, ext.426, Email: marti.milks@ sympatico.ca, Brad Dean, 416/365-1500, ext.41, Email: bdean@travelweek. ca, Christine Wong, 905/815-0017, ext.447, Email: cwong@metroland.com - Annual consumer show - March - International Centre, Toronto ON

FOREST INDUSTRY

DEMO International, Master Promotions Ltd., PO Box 565, Saint John NB E2L 3Z8 - 506/658-0018; Fax: 506/658- 0750; Tollfree: 1-888-454-7469; Email: info@masterpromotions. ca; URL: www.masterpromotions.ca - Active demonstrations of all types of industrial woodlands equipment. Harvesting, silviculture, transportation & handling, Sept. - Show Manager, Mark Cusack, Sept. - Laval University, Laval QC

Forest Expo, 850 River Rd., Prince George BC V2L 5S8 - 250/563-8833; Fax: 250/563-3697; Email: info@forestexpo. bc.ca; URL: www.forestexpo.bc.ca - General Manager, Trudy Swaan - Biennial - June 5-7, 2008, Prince George BC

InterSaw, Master Promotions Ltd., PO Box 565, Saint John NB E2L 3Z8 - 506/658-0018; Fax: 506/658-0750; Tollfree: 1-888-454-7469; Email: info@masterpromotions. ca; URL: www.masterpromotions.ca - Biennial show - Show Manager, Mark Cusack, May - Centre de foires, Québec QC

LogFor, Master Promotions Ltd., PO Box 565, Saint John NB E2L 3Z8 - 506/658-0018; Fax: 506/658-0750; Tollfree: 1-888-454-7469; Email: info@masterpromotions. ca; URL: www.masterpromotions.ca - Marketing & Operations Manager, Jennifer Allaby, President, Wendell Howes - Biennial logging & forestry show - Sept.

FUNERALS

Canadian Funeral Trade Show, PO Box 97507, Toronto ON M1C 4Z1 - 416/281-5460; Fax: 416/282-9095; Email: info@canadianfuneraltradeassociation.com; URL: www.canadianfuneraltradeassociation.com - Executive Director, Brenda Broughton - Annual trade show - June

FURNITURE *See* HOME SHOWS

GARDENING *See* FLOWERS

GIFTS & JEWELLERY

Expo Prestige, Corporation des bijoutiers du Québec, 868, rue Brisette, Sainte-Julie QC J3E 2B1 - 514/485-3333; Fax: 450/649-8984; Email: info@cbq.qc.ca; URL: www.cbq.qc.ca - Président, André Marchand, Directrice générale, Lise Petitpas, août - Palais des Congrès, Montréal QC

Jewellery World Expo, Reed Exhibition Companies Inc., #1, 3761 Victoria Park Ave., Toronto ON M1W 3S2 - 416/491-7565; Fax: 416/491-5088; Email: canada@ reedexpo.com; URL: www.reedexpo.com - John Lewinski - Annual trade show - Aug., Toronto ON

The Last Minute Christmas Show & Sale, Metro Toronto Christmas Show & Sale, Skydome, PO Box 54045, Toronto ON M6A 3B7 - 416/789-1925 - Lawrence Plaza - Annual consumer show - Dec. - Metro Toronto Convention Centre, Toronto ON

Montréal Gift Show/Le Salon du Cadeau - Montréal, dmg World Media, 180 Duncan Mills Rd., 4th Fl., Toronto ON M3B 1Z6 - 416/385-1880; Fax: 416/385-1855; Tollfree: 1-888-823-7469; URL: www.dmgworldmedia.com - Show Manager, Glen Chiasson - Annual trade show. Giftware, stationery, kitchenware, luggage & leathergoods, pottery, china, glass, jewellery - March, Montréal QC

North Bay Gift Show, North Bay & District Chamber of Commerce, 1375 Seymour St., PO Box 747, North Bay ON P1B 8J8 - 705/472-8480; Fax: 705/472-8027; Tollfree: 1-888-249-8998; Email: nbcc@northbaychamber. com; URL: www.northbay chamber.com - Manager, Patti Alcorn-Carr - Annual trade show. Giftware, fashion, food services & furniture - April - West Ferris Community Centre, North Bay ON

Toronto International Gift Fair, dmg World Media, 180 Duncan Mills Rd., 4th Fl., Toronto ON M3B 1Z6 - 416/385-1880; Fax: 416/385-1855; Tollfree: 1-888-823- 7469; URL: www.dmgworldmedia.com - Show Manager, Glen Chiasson

Vancouver Spring/Fall Gift Show, dmg World Media (Canada) Inc., #402, 4601 Canada Way, Burnaby BC V5G 4X7 - 604/433-5121; Fax: 604/434-6853; Tollfree: 1-800-633-8332; URL: www.dmgworldmedia.com - Exec. Vice-President, Gifts Sector, Fred Barnes - Annual trade show. Giftwares, housewares, luggage & leathergoods, jewellery. March & Sept.

GRAPHIC ARTS

Print Ontario, Print World, #8, 1606 Sedlescomb Dr., Mississauga ON L4X 1M6 - 905/625-7070; Fax: 905/625-4856; Tollfree: 1-800-331-7408 - Biennial trade show - Nov. - Exhibition Place, Toronto ON

HAIRDRESSING

Allied Beauty Show, Allied Beauty Association, #46/47, 450 Matheson Blvd. East, Mississauga ON L4Z 1R5 - 905/568-0158; Fax: 905/568-1581; Email: abacan@idirect. com; URL: www.abacanada.com - Executive Director, Marc Speir - Held in various locations

HEATING, PLUMBING & AIR CONDITIONING

See Also **Hardware**

CIPHEX, CIPH, #330, 295 The West Mall, Toronto ON M9C 4Z4 - 416/695-0447; Fax: 416/695-0450; Tollfree: 1-800-639-2474; Email: info@ciph.com; URL: www.ciph.com - Elizabeth McCullugh - Biennial trade show. Plumbing, heating, cooling & piping exhibits & conference (Calgary, Toronto & Montreal)

CMX, Shield Associates Ltd., 25 Bradgate Rd., Toronto ON M3B 1J6 - 416/444-5225; Fax: 416/444-8268; Tollfree: 1-800-282-0003; Email: sal@salshow.com; URL: www.cmxshow.com; www.windoorshow.com - Show Coordinator, Patrick Shield - Biennial trade show. Heating, ventilation, plumbing, air conditioning, ventilation & refrigeration - March

HOBBIES

See Also **Crafts**

Gem, Mineral & Fossil Show, Calgary Rock & Lapidary Club, 110 Lissington Dr. SW, Calgary AB T3E 5E3 - 403/287-1570; Email: martintm@telus.net; URL: www.crlc.ca - Director, Public Relations, Trudy Martin - Annual

Toronto Model Railway Show, 2938 Dundas St. West, PO Box 70618, Toronto ON M6P 4E7 - 416/249-4563 - Show Co-ordinator, Jack Bell - Annual consumer show held 3rd weekend of March

HOME ENTERTAINMENT *See* ELECTRICAL/ELECTRONICS

HOME SHOWS

Atlantic National Home Show, Master Promotions Ltd., PO Box 565, Saint John NB E2L 3Z8 - 506/658-0018; Fax: 506/658-0750; Tollfree: 1-888-454-7469; Email: info@masterpromotions.ca; URL: www.masterpromotions.ca -

Annual consumer show - Show Manager, Brian McKiel, March, Saint John NB

BC Home & Garden Show, dmg World Media (Canada) Inc., #402, 4601 Canada Way, Burnaby BC V5G 4X7 - 604/433-5121; Fax: 604/434-6853; Tollfree: 1-800- 633-8332; URL: www.dmgworldmedia.com - Annual consumer show - Show Manager, Trish Almeida, Feb.

Bridgewater Home & Leisure Show, Master Promotions Ltd., PO Box 565, Saint John NB E2L 3Z8 - 506/658- 0018; Fax: 506/658-0750; Tollfree: 1-888-454-7469; Email: info@masterpromotions.ca; URL: www.masterpromotions.ca - Annual consumer show. Home products, services & leisure products - Show Manager, Brian McKeil, April - Bridgewater Arena, Bridgewater NS

Burlington Fall Lifestyle Home Show, Jenkins Show Productions, 1076 Skyvalley Cres., Oakville ON L6M 3L2 - 905/827-4632; Fax: 905/827-8139; Tollfree: 1-800- 465-1073; Email: djenkins2@cogeco.ca; URL: www.jenkinsshow.com - President, Dave Jenkins - Annual consumer show - Sept., Burlington ON

Burlington Lifestyle Home Show, Jenkins Show Productions, 1076 Skyvalley Cres., Oakville ON L6M 3L2 - 905/827-4632; Fax: 905/827-8139; Tollfree: 1-800- 465-1073; Email: djenkins2@cogeco.ca; URL: www.jenkinsshow.com - President, Dave Jenkins - Annual consumer show - April, Burlington ON

Calgary Home & Interior Design Show, dmg World Media, #605, 999 - 8 St. SW, Calgary AB T2R 1N7 - 403/209- 3555; Fax: 403/245-8649; Tollfree: 1-888-799-2545; URL: www.dmgworldmedia.com - Annual consumer show - Show Manager, Lisa Macintosh, Sept. - Stampede Park, Calgary AB

Canadian Spa & Pool Conference & Expo, Pool & Hot Tub Council of Canada, #10B, 242 Applewood Cres., Vaughan ON L4K 4E5 - 905/761-7920; Fax: 905/761- 8837; Tollfree: 1-800-879-7066; Email: office@poolcouncil. ca; URL: www.poolcouncil.ca - Executive Director, Ken Tomihiro - Annual trade & consumer show - Dec. - Toronto Congress Centre, Toronto ON

Colchester County Home Show, Master Promotions Ltd., PO Box 565, Saint John NB E2L 3Z8 - 506/658-0018; Fax: 506/658-0750; Tollfree: 1-888-454-7469; Email: info@masterpromotions.ca; URL: www.masterpromotions.ca - Annual consumer show - Show Manager, Scott Sprague, April - Legion Stadium, Truro NS

Edmonton Home & Interior Design Show, dmg World Media, #605, 999 - 8 St. SW, Calgary AB T2R 1N7 - 403/209-3555; Fax: 403/245-8649; Tollfree: 1-888- 799-2545; URL: www.dmgworldmedia.com - Annual consumer show - Show Manager, Lisa Macintosh, Sept. - Northlands AgriCom, Edmonton AB

Expo Habitat de St-Hyacinthe, DBC Communications Inc. (Division Ev,nements), 655, av Ste-Anne, Saint-Hyacinthe QC J2S 5G4 - 450/773-3976; Fax: 450/773-3115 - Personne ressource, Pierre Charbonneau - Annual consumer show. Home construction & renovation products & services - April - Pavillion de Pionnieres, St-Hyacinthe QC

Fall Home & Outdoor Recreation Show, DAC Marketing Ltd., PO Box 2837, Stn A, Sudbury ON P3A 5J3 - 705/673-5588; Fax: 705/525-0626; Email: dac@vianet. on.ca; URL: www.dacshows.com, Sept., Sudbury ON

Fall Home Show, dmg World Media, 180 Duncan Mills Rd., 4th Fl., Toronto ON M3B 1Z6 - 416/385-1880; Fax: 416/385-1855; Tollfree: 1-888-823-7469; URL: www.dmgworldmedia.com - Show Manager, Glen Chiasson

Fredericton Lifestyles Show, Master Promotions Ltd., PO Box 565, Saint John NB E2L 3Z8 - 506/658-0018; Fax: 506/658-0750; Tollfree: 1-888-454-7469; Email: info@masterpromotions.ca; URL: www.masterpromotions.ca - Annual consumer show - Show Manager, Brian McKeil, March - Capital Exhibit Centre, Fredericton NB

Home - Health & Lifestyles Show, Cryderman Productions Inc., 136 Thames St., Chatham ON N7L 2Y8 - 519/351- 8344; Fax: 519/351-8345; Tollfree: 1-866-640-9663; Email: john@crydermanproductions.com; URL: www.crydermanproductions.com - John Cryderman - Annual - Jan. - Kinsmen Auditorium, Chatham ON

Home Show, Thunder Bay Chamber of Commerce Trade Show, #102, 200 Syndicate Ave. South, Thunder Bay ON P7E 1C9 - 807/624-2621; Fax: 807/622-7752; Email: nancy@tb-chamber.on.ca; URL: www.tbchamber. on.ca - Show Manager, Nancy Milani, Sept., Thunder Bay ON

Home, Garden & Leisure Show, Medicine Hat & District Chamber of Commerce, 413 - 6th Ave. SE, Medicine Hat AB T1A 2S7 - 403/527-5214; Fax: 403/527-5182; Email: mhchamber@monarch.net; URL: www.medicinehatchamber. com - President, Jason Mutschler, Executive Director, Mary Lou Hansen - Consumer show - March - Cypress Centre, Stampede Park, Medicine Hat AB

Home, Garden & Renovation, Cryderman Productions Inc., 136 Thames St., Chatham ON N7L 2Y8 - 519/351- 8344; Fax: 519/351-8345; Tollfree: 1-866-640-9663; Email: john@ crydermanproductions.com; URL: www.cryderman productions.com - John Cryderman - Annual - Feb. - Kinsmen Auditorium, Chatham ON

International Home & Garden Show, Showcase Marketing Ltd., #410, 1110 Sheppard Ave. East, Toronto ON M2K 2W2 - 416/512-1305; Email: homeshow@idirect. com - Paul Newdick - Annual consumer show - March - International Centre, Toronto ON

International Home Show, Showcase Marketing Ltd., #410, 1110 Sheppard Ave. East, Toronto ON M2K 2W2 - 416/512-1305; Email: homeshow@idirect.com - Paul Newdick - Annual consumer show - Oct. - International Centre, Toronto ON

London Home & Garden Show, London Show Productions, 2326 Fanshawe Park Rd. East, London ON N5X 4A2 - 519/455-5888; Fax: 519/455-7780 - Consumer show - April, London ON

Mall Home Shows, Jenkins Show Productions, 1076 Skyvalley Cres., Oakville ON L6M 3L2 - 905/827-4632; Fax: 905/827-8139; Tollfree: 1-800-465-1073; Email: djenkins2@cogeco.ca; URL: www.jenkinsshow.com - President, Dave Jenkins - Shows at shopping centres throughout Ontario in Feb., Mar., June, Oct., Nov.

Metro Home Show, dmg World Media, 180 Duncan Mills Rd., 4th Fl., Toronto ON M3B 1Z6 - 416/385-1880; Fax: 416/385-1855; Tollfree: 1-888-823-7469; URL: www.dmgworldmedia.com - Show Manager, Glen Chiasson - Annual consumer show - Jan. - National Trade Centre, Exhibition Place, Toronto ON

Miramichi Lifestyles Show, Master Promotions Ltd., PO Box 565, Saint John NB E2L 3Z8 - 506/658-0018; Fax: 506/658-0750; Tollfree: 1-888-454-7469; Email: info@masterpromotions.ca; URL: www.masterpromotions.ca - Annual consumer show - Show Manager, Brian McKeil, April - Miramichi Civic Centre, Miramichi NB

Moncton Kiwanis Lifestyles Show, Master Promotions Ltd., PO Box 565, Saint John NB E2L 3Z8 - 506/658- 0018; Fax: 506/658-0750; Tollfree: 1-888-454-7469; Email: info@masterpromotions.ca; URL: www.masterpromotions.ca - Annual consumer show - Show manager, Brian McKiel, April, Moncton NB

Montréal National Home Show, dmg World Media, 180 Duncan Mills Rd., 4th Fl., Toronto ON M3B 1Z6 - 416/385-1880; Fax: 416/385-1855; Tollfree: 1-888-823- 7469; URL: www.dmgworldmedia.com - Show Manager, Glen Chiasson

National Home Show, dmg World Media, 180 Duncan Mills Rd., 4th Fl., Toronto ON M3B 1Z6 - 416/385- 1880; Fax: 416/385-1855; Tollfree: 1-888-823-7469; URL: www.dmgworldmedia.com - Show Manager, Glen Chiasson - Annual consumer show - April - Coliseum Bldg., Exhibition Place, Toronto ON

Niagara Lifestyle Home Show, Jenkins Show Productions, 1076 Skyvalley Cres., Oakville ON L6M 3L2 - 905/827-4632; Fax: 905/827-8139; Tollfree: 1-800-465- 1073; Email: djenkins2@cogeco.ca; URL: www.jenkinsshow.com - President, Dave Jenkins - Annual consumer show - April - Garden City/Rex Stimers Arena, St Catharines ON

Nova Scotia Fall Ideal Home Show, Master Promotions Ltd., PO Box 565, Saint John NB E2L 3Z8 - 506/658- 0018; Fax: 506/658-0750; Tollfree: 1-888-454-7469; Email: info@masterpromotions.ca; URL: www.masterpromotions.ca - Annual consumer show - Show Manager, Bev Campbell, Oct., Halifax NS

Nova Scotia Spring Ideal Home Show, Master Promotions Ltd., PO Box 565, Saint John NB E2L 3Z8 - 506/658- 0018; Fax: 506/658-0750; Tollfree: 1-888-454-7469; Email: info@masterpromotions.ca; URL: www.masterpromotions.ca - Annual consumer show - Show Manager, Bev Campbell, April, Halifax NS

Oakville Lifestyle Home Show, Jenkins Show Productions, 1076 Skyvalley Cres., Oakville ON L6M 3L2 - 905/827-4632; Fax: 905/827-8139; Tollfree: 1-800-465- 1073; Email: djenkins2@cogeco.ca; URL: www.jenkinsshow.com - President, Dave Jenkins - Annual consumer show - April - Glen Abbey Recreation Centre, Oakville ON

Ottawa Spring/Fall Home Show, dmg World Media, #302, 260 Dalhousie St., Ottawa ON K1N 7E4 - 613/241- 2888; Fax: 613/241-4827; Tollfree: 1-877-241-0007; URL: www.ottawahomeshows.com - Show Manager, Chantale Boisvert - Annual consumer show. March & Sept.

PEI Provincial Home Show, Master Promotions Ltd., PO Box 565, Saint John NB E2L 3Z8 - 506/658-0018; Fax: 506/658-0750; Tollfree: 1-888-454-7469; Email: info@masterpromotions.ca; URL: www.masterpromotions.ca - Annual consumer show - Show Manager, Brian McKeil, March, Charlottetown PE

Red Deer Home Ideas, Home Ideas & Lifestyles, #10, 7895 - 49 Ave., Red Deer AB T4P 2B4 - 403/346-5321; Fax: 403/342-1301; Email: admin@cahb.ca; URL: www.cahba.ca - Contact, Joan Butler - Annual, Feb./March

Showcase, Medicine Hat & District Chamber of Commerce, 413 - 6th Ave. SE, Medicine Hat AB T1A 2S7 - 403/527-5214; Fax: 403/527-5182; Email: mhchamber@monarch.net; URL: www.medicinehatchamber.com - President, Jason Mutschler, Executive Director, Mary Lou Hansen - Annual consumer show - Nov.

Success With Gardening, Showcase Marketing Ltd., #410, 1110 Sheppard Ave. East, Toronto ON M2K 2W2 - 416/512-1305; Email: homeshow@idirect.com - Paul Newdick - Annual consumer show - Mar. - International Centre, Toronto ON

Sudbury Spring Home Show, DAC Marketing Ltd., PO Box 2837, Stn A, Sudbury ON P3A 5J3 - 705/673-5588; Fax: 705/525-0626; Email: dac@vianet.on.ca; URL: www.dacshows.com, March, Sudbury ON

Vancouver Home & Interior Design Show, dmg World Media (Canada) Inc., #402, 4601 Canada Way, Burnaby BC V5G 4X7 - 604/433-5121; Fax: 604/434-6853; Tollfree: 1-800-633-8332; URL: www.dmgworldmedia.com - Annual consumer show - Show Manager, Trish Almeida, Oct.

Western Canada Kitchen, Bath & Renovation Show, Manitoba Home Builders' Association, #1, 1420 Clarence Ave., Winnipeg MB R3T 1T6 - 204/925-2560; Fax: 204/925-2567; Email: mbhomebd@mb.sympatico. ca; URL: www.homebuilders.mb.ca - Show Manager, Danita Brisson - Annual consumer show

Win Door, Shield Associates Ltd., 25 Bradgate Rd., Toronto ON M3B 1J6 - 416/444-5225; Fax: 416/444-8268; Tollfree: 1-800-282-0003; Email: sal@salshow.com; URL: www.cmxshow.com; www.windoorshow.com - Show Coordinator, Patrick Shield - Trade, Windows & doors show, new products & technologies - Nov.

Windsor Home & Leisure Show, Cryderman Productions Inc., 136 Thames St., Chatham ON N7L 2Y8 - 519/351- 8344; Fax: 519/351-8345; Tollfree: 1-866-640-9663; Email: john@crydermanproductions.com; URL: www.crydermanproductions.com - John Cryderman - Annual - Feb. - University of Windsor, Windsor ON

Yarmouth Lifestyles Show, Master Promotions Ltd., PO Box 565, Saint John NB E2L 3Z8 - 506/658-0018; Fax: 506/658-0750; Tollfree: 1-888-454-7469; Email: info@masterpromotions.ca; URL: www.masterpromotions.ca - Marketing & Operations Manager, Jennifer Allaby, President, Wendell Howes, April, Yarmouth NS

HORSES

The Masters Show Jumping Tournament, Spruce Meadows, RR#9, Calgary AB T2J 5G5 - 403/974-4200; Fax: 403/974-4270; Email: information@sprucemeadows.com; URL: www.sprucemeadows.com - Annual tournament. Includes consumer/trade show Equi-Fair, & the Festival of Nations - Sept.

North American Tournament, RR#9, Calgary AB T2J 5G5 - 403/974-4249; Fax: 403/947-4266; Email: jack.hugill@ sprucemeadows.com; URL: www.sprucemeadows.com - Coordinator, Sales, Jack Hugill - Annual. Showcased through Sun Life Financials at Fort Meadows - July

Royal Red Arabian Horse Show, PO Box 167, Regina SK S4P 2Z6 - 306/781-9200; Fax: 306/781-9396; Email: roconnor@reginaexhibition.com - Facility Contact, Rob O'Connor - Annual - Aug.

HORTICULTURE *See* FLOWERS

HOSPITALITY INDUSTRY (HOTEL, MOTEL, RESTAURANT)

***See Also* Food & Beverage**

ApEx, Canadian Restaurant & Foodservices Association, 316 Bloor St. West, Toronto ON M5S 1W5 - 416/923- 8416; Fax: 416/923-1450; Tollfree: 1-800-387-5649; Email: info@crfa.ca; URL: www.crfa.ca - President, Douglas C. Needham, Senior Exec. Vice-President, David Harris - Annual trade show - April

ARFEX - Alberta Restaurant & Foodservices Exposition, Alberta Restaurant & Foodservices Association, #1003, 10080 Jasper Ave., Edmonton AB T5J 1V9 - 780/444- 9496; Fax: 780/481-8727; Tollfree: 1-800-461-9762; Email: lrollingson@arfa.net; URL: www.arfa.net - President, Lindy Rollingson, CPM CAE - Annual trade show - April - Northlands Agricom, Edmonton AB

Canadian Convenience Store Expo, Reed Exhibition Companies Inc., #1, 3761 Victoria Park Ave., Toronto ON M1W 3S2 - 416/491-7565; Fax: 416/491-5088; Email:

canada@reedexpo.com; URL: www.reedexpo.com - John Lewinski - Annual trade show - Sept., Mississauga ON

Grocery Showcase Canada, Canadian Federation of Independent Grocers, #902, 2235 Sheppard Ave. East, Toronto ON M2J 5B5 - 416/492-2311; Fax: 416/492-2347; Tollfree: 1-800-661-2344; Email: info@cfig.ca; URL: www.cfig.ca - President, John F.T. Scott, Chair, Mike Coleman, Vice-President, Gary Sanos - Annual trade show - Oct.

Grocery Showcase West, Canadian Federation of Independent Grocers, #902, 2235 Sheppard Ave. East, Toronto ON M2J 5B5 - 416/492-2311; Fax: 416/492-2347; Tollfree: 1-800-661-2344; Email: info@cfig.ca; URL: www.cfig.ca - President, John F.T. Scott, Chair, Mike Coleman, Vice-President, Gary Sanos - Annual trade show - March - Vancouver Trade & Convention Centre, Vancouver BC

HostEx, Canadian Restaurant & Foodservices Association, 316 Bloor St. West, Toronto ON M5S 1W5 - 416/923- 8416; Fax: 416/923-1450; Tollfree: 1-800-387-5649; Email: info@crfa.ca; URL: www.crfa.ca - President, Douglas C. Needham, Senior Exec. Vice-President, David Harris - Annual trade show

INDUSTRIAL

Atlantic Industrial Exhibition - Halifax, Reed Exhibition Companies Inc., #1, 3761 Victoria Park Ave., Toronto ON M1W 3S2 - 416/491-7565; Fax: 416/491-5088; Email: canada@reedexpo.com; URL: www.reedexpo.com - John Lewinski - Biennial trade show - Sept., Halifax NS

Atlantic Industrial Exhibition - Moncton, Reed Exhibition Companies Inc., #1, 3761 Victoria Park Ave., Toronto ON M1W 3S2 - 416/491-7565; Fax: 416/491-5088; Email: canada@reedexpo.com; URL: www.reedexpo.com - John Lewinski - Biennial trade show - Sept., Moncton NB

Montréal Fabricating & Machine Tool Show/Le Salon du Travail des M,taux et de la Machine Outil de Montréal, Reed Exhibition Companies Inc., #1, 3761 Victoria Park Ave., Toronto ON M1W 3S2 - 416/491-7565; Fax: 416/491-5088; Email: canada@reedexpo.com; URL: www.reedexpo.com - John Lewinski - Biennial trade show

Plant Maintenance & Engineering Show/Le Salon Industriel de la Maintenance et de l'Ingenierie, Reed Exhibition Companies Inc., #1, 3761 Victoria Park Ave., Toronto ON M1W 3S2 - 416/491-7565; Fax: 416/491- 5088; Email: canada@reedexpo.com; URL: www.reedexpo.com - John Lewinski - Bienniel trade show

Salon industriel de L'Estrie, Les Promotions André Pageau Inc., 1627, boul Bastien, Québec QC G2K 1H1 - 418/623-3383; Fax: 418/623-5033; Tollfree: 1-800-387- 3383; Email: info@promoapageau.com; URL: www.promoapageau.com - Pr,sident, Andr, Pageau, Sept., St-Hyacinthe QC

Salon Industriel de Québec, Les Promotions Andr, Pageau Inc., 1627, boul Bastien, Québec QC G2K 1H1 - 418/623-3383; Fax: 418/623-5033; Tollfree: 1-800-387- 3383; Email: info@promoapageau.com; URL: www.promoapageau.com - Président, André Pageau - Biennial trade show - Oct., Québec QC Salon Industriel du Saguenay/Lac-St-Jean, Les Promotions André Pageau Inc., 1627, boul Bastien, Québec QC G2K 1H1 - 418/623-3383; Fax: 418/623-5033; Tollfree: 1-800-387-3383; Email: info@promoapageau. com; URL: www.promoapageau.com - Président, André Pageau - Biennial - May, Chicoutimi QC

Weld Expo Canada, Reed Exhibition Companies Inc., #1, 3761 Victoria Park Ave., Toronto ON M1W 3S2 - 416/491-7565; Fax: 416/491-5088; Email: canada@reedexpo. com; URL: www.reedexpo.com - John Lewinski - Biennial trade show - Oct.

Western Manufacturing Technology Show - Edmonton, Reed Exhibition Companies Inc., #1, 3761 Victoria Park Ave., Toronto ON M1W 3S2 - 416/491-7565; Fax: 416/491-5088; Email: canada@reedexpo.com; URL: www.reedexpo.com - John Lewinski - Biennial trade show - June, Edmonton AB

Western Manufacturing Technology Show - Vancouver, Reed Exhibition Companies Inc., #1, 3761 Victoria Park Ave., Toronto ON M1W 3S2 - 416/491-7565; Fax: 416/491-5088; Email: canada@reedexpo.com; URL: www.reedexpo.com - John Lewinski - Biennial trade show - June, Abbotsford BC

JEWELLERY *See* GIFTS

LANDSCAPING *See* FLOWERS

LEGAL

Canadian Association of Law Libraries, Events & Management Plus Inc., #310, 4 Cataraqui St., Kingston ON K7K 1Z7 - 613/531-9210; Fax: 613/531-0626; Tollfree: 1-866-560-3838; Email: office@ eventsmgt.com; URL: www.eventsmgt.com - Owner, E. Hooper, May

LEISURE *See* SPORTS & RECREATION

MACHINERY & MANUFACTURING

***See Also* Industrial**

Assembly Québec, Reed Exhibition Companies Inc., #1, 3761 Victoria Park Ave., Toronto ON M1W 3S2 - 416/491-7565; Fax: 416/491-5088; Email: canada@reedexpo. com; URL: www.reedexpo.com - John Lewinski - Biennial trade show - April, Montréal QC

Atlantic Heavy Equipment Show, Master Promotions Ltd., PO Box 565, Saint John NB E2L 3Z8 - 506/658-0018; Fax: 506/658-0750; Tollfree: 1-888-454-7469; Email: info@masterpromotions.ca; URL: www.masterpromotions.ca - Biennial - Show Manager, Mark Cusack, April - Coliseum, Moncton NB

Canadian Machine Tool Show, Reed Exhibition Companies Inc., #1, 3761 Victoria Park Ave., Toronto ON M1W 3S2 - 416/491-7565; Fax: 416/491-5088; Email: canada@reedexpo.com; URL: www.reedexpo.com - John Lewinski - Biennial trade show - Sept., Toronto ON

Canadian Manufacturing Week, Reed Exhibition Companies Inc., #1, 3761 Victoria Park Ave., Toronto ON M1W 3S2 - 416/491-7565; Fax: 416/491-5088; Email: canada@reedexpo.com; URL: www.reedexpo.com - John Lewinski - Biennial trade show - Sept., Mississauga ON

National Heavy Equipment Show, Master Promotions Ltd., PO Box 565, Saint John NB E2L 3Z8 - 506/658-0018; Fax: 506/658-0750; Tollfree: 1-888-454-7469; Email: info@masterpromotions.ca; URL: www.masterpromotions.ca - Biennial - Show Manager, Mark Cusack, March - International Centre, Toronto ON

Toronto ISA Show, dmg World Media, 180 Duncan Mills Rd., 4th Fl., Toronto ON M3B 1Z6 - 416/385-1880; Fax: 416/385-1855; Tollfree: 1-888-823-7469; URL: www.dmgworldmedia.com - Show Manager, Glen Chiasson

MAGAZINES

Magazines, Print World, #8, 1606 Sedlescomb Dr., Mississauga ON L4X 1M6 - 905/625-7070; Fax: 905/625- 4856; Tollfree: 1-800-331-7408 - Annual conference & trade show for publishing professionals - June, Toronto ON

MARKETING *See* ADVERTISING

MATERIALS HANDLING *See* LOGISTICS

MEDICAL

Canadian Congress of Neurological Sciences, Venue West Conference Services Ltd., #645, 375 Water St., Vancouver BC V6B 5C6 - 604/681-5226; Fax: 604/681- 2503; Email: congress@venuewest.com; URL: www.venuewest.com

COS Annual Meeting & Exhibition, Canadian Ophthalmological Society, #610, 1525 Carling Ave., Ottawa ON K1Z 8R9 - 613/729-6779; Fax: 613/729-7209; Email: cos@eyesite.ca; URL: www.eyesite.ca - Executive Director, Hubert Drouin, June

Mayfest, The Canadian Hearing Society, 271 Spadina Rd., Toronto ON M5R 2V3 - 416/928-2500; Fax: 416/928- 2506; Tollfree: 1-877-347-3427; Email: info@chs.ca; URL: www.chs.ca - Executive Assistant, Mary Lumgair, President/CEO, Kelly Duffin, Vice-President, Regional Operations, Maribeth Meijer, President, Access, Counselling & Training, Katherine Hum-Antonopoulus, Vice-President Finance/CFO, Fred Enzel, Director, Human Resources, Lisa Smecca, Director, Marketing Communications, Susan Main, Director, External Affairs & Employment Development, Gary Malkowski - Latest innovations & access for deaf, deafened & hard of hearing people - May, Toronto ON

MINING & MINERALS

CIM Conference & Exhibition, Canadian Institute of Mining, Metallurgy & Petroleum, #855, 3400, boul de Maisonneuve ouest, Montréal QC H3Z 3B8 - 514/939- 2710; Fax: 514/939-2714; Email: cim@cim.org; URL: www.cim.org - Executive Director, Jean Vavrek - Annual consumers show. Mining industry, equipment & services - April-May - Palais des congrSs de Montréal, Montréal QC

Mines & Minerals Symposia, Ministry of Northern Development & Mines, 933 Ramsey Lake Rd., 6th Fl., Sudbury ON P3E 6B5 - 705/670-5838; Fax: 705/670-5807; URL: www.mndm.gov.on.ca/mndm/mines/- Annual trade show & seminar in April (Northern Ontario) & Dec. (Toronto)

MOTORCYCLES *See* AUTOMOTIVE

MULTICULTURAL

Canada's National Ukrainian Festival, 1550 Main St. South, PO Box 368, Dauphin MB R7N 2V2 - 204/622-4600; Fax: 204/622-4606; Tollfree: 1-877-474-2683; Email: cnuf@mts.net; URL: www.cnuf.ca - Annual. Three days of song, dance, music, costume, cuisine, culture - Aug.

Caravan, #503, 263 Adelaide St. West, Toronto ON M5H 1Y2; Email: kirk@caravan-org.com; URL: www.caravan-org.com - President, Kirk Jensen - Annual, mid-June. Nine days. Forty international pavilions

Celebration Multicultural Festival, Multicultural Association of Nova Scotia, 1113 Marginal Rd., Halifax NS B3H 4P7 - 902/423-6534; Fax: 902/422-0881; Email: admin@mans.ns.ca; URL: www.mans.ns.ca - Executive Director, Alexandra McCallum, President, Dr. Bridglal Pachai - Annual festival - June, Dartmouth NS

Le Festival de l'Escaouette, a/s Les Trois Pignons, PO Box 430, Cheticamp NS B0E 1H0 - 902/224-2612; Fax: 902/224-1579; Email: lestroispignons@ns.sympatico. ca; URL: www.lestroispignons.com - Assistant Manager, Daniel Aucoin - Annually. Acadian folklore, traditions, culture - Aug.

Foire Brayonne, 95 Victoria St., Edmundston NB E3V 3K8 - 506/739-6608; Fax: 506/739-9578; Email: info@ foirebrayonne.com; URL: www.foirebrayonne.com - July/Aug. Brayon heritage festival

Folkfest, #303, 506 - 25th St. East, Saskatoon SK S7K 4A7 - 306/931-0100; Fax: 306/665-3421; Email: info@ saskatoonfolkfest.com; URL: www.saskatoon.com/folkfest/- Coordinator, Deneen Gudjonson, Terri Rau - Annual. Three days. Twenty or more ethnic pavilions - Aug.

Folklorama - Canada's Cultural Celebration, 183 Kennedy St., Winnipeg MB R3C 1S6 - 204/982-6210; Fax: 204/943-1956; Tollfree: 1-800-665-0234; Email: folkarts@ folklorama.ca; URL: www.folklorama.ca - Executive Director, Ron Gauthier, Email: gauthierr@folklorama. ca - Annual. Fourteen days. More than forty ethnic pavilions - Aug.

Manitoba Highland Gathering, PO Box 59, Selkirk MB R1A 2B1 - 204/269-1304; Fax: 204/269-1304; Email: ccox@mts.net - Treasurer, John Cox - Annual - July

MOSAIC - Regina's Annual Festival of Cultures, Regina Multicultural Council, 2144 Cornwall St., Regina SK S4P 2K7 - 306/757-5990; Fax: 306/352-1977; Email: rmc.pa@sasktel.net; URL: www.reginamulticulturalcouncil.ca/mosaic.htm - Executive Director, Vivian Molnar - Annual. First weekend in June. Twenty ethno-cultural pavilions

Vesna Festival, PO Box 1592, Saskatoon SK S7K 3R3 - 306/657-4412; Fax: 306/657-4410; Email: dlalach@ wellwest.ca; URL: www.vesnafestival.com - Annual Spring celebration. Two days of entertainment, dancing, cultural demonstrations & displays. The World's Largest Ukrainian Cabaret - May

MUSIC

Atlantic Jazz Festival, PO Box 33043, Halifax NS B3L 4T6 - 902/492-2225; Fax: 902/425-7946; Tollfree: 1-800- 567-5277; Email: info@jazzeast.com; URL: www.jazzeast.com - Manager, Operations, Geoff Barnes - July

Beaches International Jazz Festival, 1998 Queen St. East, Toronto ON M4L 1G8 - 416/698-2152; Fax: 416/698- 2064; Email: infobeachesjazz@rogers.com; URL: www.beachesjazz.com - Executive Producer, Lido Chilelli, July, Toronto ON

Biennial Canada Dance Festival, Canada Dance Festival Society, PO Box 1376, Stn B, Ottawa ON K1P 5R4 - 613/947-7000, ext.576; Fax: 613/943-1399; Email: cdffdc@nac-cna.ca; URL: www.canadadance.ca - Artistic Producer, Brian H. Webb, Email: webb@shaw.ca, Chair, Myrna Barwin

Big Valley Jamboree, 4238 -37th St., Camrose AB T4V 4L6 - 780/672-0224; Fax: 780/672-9530; Tollfree: 1-888-404-1234; Email: bvj@bigvalleyjamboree. com; URL: www.bigvalleyjamboree.com - Country music - Aug.

Brandon Folk Music & Arts Festival, PO Box 22091, Brandon MB R7A 6Y9 - 204/727-3928; Fax: 204/571- 9243; Email: info@brandonfolkfestival.com; URL: www.brandonfolkfestival.com - Music Director, Jody Weger - Annually, last weekend in July

Canadian Open Old Time Fiddler's Contest, Canadian Open Old Time Fiddle Championship, Sports Complex, c/o, PO Box 27, Shelburne ON L0N 1S0 - 519/925- 3551; Fax: 519/925-1105; Email: cindy.sabo@sympatico. ca; URL: www.shelburnefiddlecontest.on.ca/, Aug.

Central Canada's Fiddle Festival, PO Box 10, High Bluff MB R0H 0C0 - 204/637-2354; Fax: 204/637-2395; Email: info@ag-museum.mb.ca; URL: www.ag-museum. mb.ca - Contact, Sandra Head - Held annually last weekend of July

Classical Music Festival, 4010 Whistler Way, Whistler BC V0N 1B0 - 604/932-3928; Fax: 604/932-7231 - Aug.

Dawson City Music Festival, PO Box 456, Dawson YT Y0B 1G0 - 867/993-5584; Fax: 867/993-5510; Email: info@dcmf.com; URL: www.dcmf.com - Producer, Dylan Griffith - Annually, second last weekend in July

Dockside Ceilidh, 89 King St., North Sydney NS B2A 2T3 - 902/794-3772; Fax: 902/539-7210; Email: 7batherson@ns.sympatico.ca - President, Northside Highland Dancers' Association, Kay Batherson, Secretary, Sheila Hall, Treasurer, Jeannie Niesten - Daily, July-Sept. Cultural music & entertainment at Marine Atlantic Ferry Terminal Downtown Jazz (Toronto), Toronto

Downtown Jazz Society, 82 Bleecker St., Toronto ON M4X 1L8 - 416/928- 2033; Fax: 416/928-0533; Email: tdjs@tojazz.com; URL: www.torontojazz.com - President/Executive Producer, Patrick Taylor, Artistic Director, Jim Galloway

Downtown Oakville Jazz Festival,Downtown Oakville BIA, 146 Lakeshore Rd. East, Oakville ON L6J 1H4 - 905/844-4520; Fax: 905/844-1154; Email: info@ oakvilledowntown.com; URL: www.oakvillejazz.com, Aug., Oakville ON

Edgefest, Edge 102, #1600, 1 Dundas St. West, Toronto ON M5T 1Z3 - 416/408-3343; Fax: 416/408-3300; URL: www.edge102.com, July

Elora Festival, 33 Henderson St., PO Box 370, Elora ON N0B 1S0 - 519/846-0331; Fax: 519/846-5947; Tollfree: 1-800-265-8977; Email: info@elorafestival. com; URL: www.elorafestival.com - Artistic Director, Noel Edison - July - Aug. Choral & contemporary Canadian & international music

Enbridge Symphony Under the Sky, Edmonton Symphony Orchestra, 9720 - 102 Ave., Edmonton AB T5J 4B2 - 780/428-1108; Fax: 780/425-0167; Tollfree: 1-800- 563-5081; Email: info@winspearcentre.com; URL: www.edmonton symphony.com - Managing Director, Elaine Calder, Music Director, Bill Eddins - Aug.-Sept.

Festival de LanaudiSre, 1500, boul Base-de-Roc, Joliette QC J6E 3Z1 - 450/759-7636; Fax: 450/759-3082; Email: festival@lanaudiere.org; URL: www.lanaudiere.org - Annually June-Aug.; biggest mostly classical festival in Canada

Festival International de Jazz de Montréal, 822, rue Sherbrooke est, Montréal QC H2L 1K4 - 514/523-3378; Fax: 514/525-8033; Tollfree: 1-888-515-0515; URL: www.montrealjazzfest.com - Senior Director, Communications & Advertising, Nathalie Carriere - Annual. Over 2,000 musicians & 450 shows - July, Montréal QC

Le Festival International du Domaine Forget, Le Festival International de Domaine Forget, 5, rang Saint-Antoine, Saint-Irénée QC G0T 1V0 - 418/452-8111; Fax: 418/452-3503; Tollfree: 1-888-336-7438; Email: info@domaineforget. com; URL: www.domaineforget.com - June-Aug.

Festival International Nuits d'Afrique de Montréal, 4374, boul St-Laurent, 1e ,tage, Montréal QC H2W 1Z5 - 514/499-9239, 9520; Fax: 514/499-9215; Email: info@festivalnuitsdafrique. com; URL: www.festivalnuitsdafrique.com, juil.

Festival of the Sound, 42 James St., PO Box 750, Parry Sound ON P2A 2Z1 - 705/746-2410; Fax: 705/746- 5639; Tollfree: 1-866-364-0061; Email: info@festivalofthesound. on.ca; URL: www.festivalofthesound.on.ca - July-Aug.

Festival Vancouver, The Vancouver Summer Festival Society, #400, 873 Beatty St., Vancouver BC V6B 2M6 - 604/688-1152; Fax: 604/688-8441; Email: music@festival vancouver. bc.ca; URL: www.festivalvancouver.bc.ca - Program Director, George Laverock, Administrative Director, Morna Edmundson

FFIDA Fringe Festival of Independent Dance Artists, FFIDA - 416/214-5854; Email: info@ffida.org; URL: www.ffida.org - Artistic Director, Michael Menegon

Folk on the Rocks, PO Box 326, Yellowknife NT X1A 2N3 - 867/920-7806; Fax: 867/873-6535; Email: info@ folkonthe rocks.com; URL: www.folkontherocks.com - Annual. Two days. Inuit, Dene, other northern & southern folk groups - July

Guelph Jazz Festival, 123 Woolwich St., 2nd Fl., Guelph ON N1H 3V1 - 519/763-4952; Fax: 519/763-3155; Email: info@guelphjazzfestival.com; URL: www.guelphjazz festival.com, Sept., Guelph ON

Harvest Jazz & Blues Festival, 65 York St., PO Box 20139, Fredericton NB E3B 6Y8 - 506/454-2583; Fax: 506/457-1815; Tollfree: 1-888-622-5837; Email: info@harvestjazzandblues. com; URL: www.harvestjazzandblues.com, Sept.

International Festival of Baroque Music, International Baroque Music Festival, #2, 28, rue de l'H"pital, Lameque NB E8T 1C3 - 506/344-5846; Fax: 506/344-5741; Tollfree: 1-800-320-2276; Email: baroque@ nbnet.nb.ca; URL: www.festivalbaroque.com - Executive Director, Claire Guimond - Early music festival with five productions, last week of July (Northeastern New Brunswick, on Lameque Island)

Jazz City International Music Festival, Jazz City Festival Society, #202, 10518 - 82 Ave. NW, Edmonton AB T6E 2A4 - 780/432-7166; Fax: 780/433-3779; Email: info@jazzcity.ca; URL: www.jazzcity.ca - Manager, Festival & Sponsorships, Lynda Jones, Contact, Media & Musicians, Kent Sutherland

JazzFest International, Victoria Jazz Society, #250, 727 Johnson St., PO Box 8542, Victoria BC V8W 3S2 - 250/388-4423; Fax: 250/388-4407; Tollfree: 1-888-671- 2112; Email: vicjazz@pacificcoast.net; URL: www.vicjazz.bc.ca/jazzfest/

Kinsmen International Band & Choral Festival, Moose Jaw Kinsmen Club, PO Box 883, Moose Jaw SK S6H 4P5 - 306/692-1291; Fax: 306/692-2091; Email: bl.mcdonald@ sasktel.net; URL: www.mjkinsmenfestival.com - Bill McDonald - 3,000 musicians, evening concerts. Annual - May, Moose Jaw SK

Kiwanis Music Festival of Greater Toronto, 330 Walmer Rd., Toronto ON M5R 2Y4 - 416/487-5885; Fax: 416/487-5784; Email: kiwanismusic@bellnet.ca; URL: www3.sympatico.ca/ kiwanismusicfest.toronto - Festival Coordinator, Pam Allen, General Manager, Pam Allen, Feb., Toronto ON

L'OFF Festival de Jazz, L'OFF Festival de Jazz de Montréal, 5101, rue St-Denis, CP 60150, Montréal QC H2J 4E1 - 514/570-0722; Email: info@lofffestivaldejazz. com; URL: www.lofffestivaldejazz.com

Mariposa Folk Festival, Mariposa Folk Foundation, 23 Peter St. South, PO Box 383, Orillia ON L3V 6J8 - 705/329-2333; Fax: 705/329-4099; Email: info@mariposafolk. com; URL: www.mariposafolkfestival.com - President, Chris Lusty Maritime Fiddle Fest,

Maritime Fiddle Festival, PO Box 3037, Stn DEPS, Dartmouth NS B2W 4Y3 - 902/434- 5466; Fax: 902/434-5466; Email: marfiddlefest@ ns.sympatico.ca; URL: www3.ns.sympatico.ca/marfiddlefest - Hon. Chair, James Delaney, Co-Chair, Betty Ann Chennell, 902/835-5988, Email: babm@ns.sympatico. ca, Co-Chair, Doug Morash, 902/435-4168, Email: rdouglas@ns.sympatico.ca, July

Markham Jazz Festival, #281, 4261 A-145, Hwy.#7, Unionville ON L3R 9W6 - 905/471-5299; Fax: 905/471- 7764; Email: info@guidingstar.ca; URL: www.guidingstar.ca/Markham_Jazz_Festival.htm, Aug., Markham ON

Miramichi Folk Song Festival, PO Box 13, Miramichi NB E1V 3M2 - 506/623-2150; Fax: 506/623-2261; Email: bb2@nb.sympatico.ca; URL: www.miramichifolksongfestival.com/- Susan Butler - Aug.

Newfoundland & Labrador Folk Festival, PO Box 6283, St. John's NL A1C 6J9 - 709/576-8508; Fax: 709/757- 8500; Tollfree: 1-866-576-8508; Email: office@ sjfac.nf.net; URL: www.sjfac.nf.net - Contact, Erin McArthur - Traditional Newfoundland & Labrador music & dance - Aug.

Northern Lights Festival BorSal, Northern Lights Festival Bor,al, 109 Elm St., Sudbury ON P3C 1T4 - 705/674- 5512; Fax: 705/671-1998; Email: info@nlfb.on.ca; URL: www.nlfb.on.ca - July

Nova Scotia Bluegrass Oldtime Music Festival, Annual Nova Scotia Bluegrass/Oldtime Music Festival, 1455 Hwy. 2, Lantz NS B2S 2A2 - 902/883-7189; Email: jerry@rushcomm.ca - Correspondent, Jerry Murphy - Annually, last weekend in July

Nova Scotia Kiwanis Music Festival, PO Box 22039, Halifax NS B3L 4T7 - 902/423-6147; Fax: 902/423-8668; URL: www.hfxmusicfest.com - Executive Director, Nancy Keating, Chair, Art Hood - Adjudicated music festival & closing concert - Feb., Halifax NS

Old Time Fiddle & Step Dancing Championships, PO Box 1329, Deep River ON K0J 1P0 - 613/584-3962 - Labour Day weekend, annually

Orford Festival, 3165, Parc Orford Rd., Orford QC J1X 7A2 - 819/843-9871; Fax: 819/843-7274; Tollfree: 1-800-567-6155; Email: centre@arts-orford. org; URL: www.arts-orford.org - June-Aug. Ottawa Bluesfest,

Ottawa BluesFest, 1810 St. Laurent Blvd., Ottawa ON K1G 1A2 - 613/247-1188; Fax: 613/247-2220; Tollfree: 1-866-258-3748; URL: www.ottawa-bluesfest.ca - Executive Director, Mark Monahan - Annual blues music & gospel festival - July

Ottawa Folk Festival, #107A, 858 Bank St., Ottawa ON K1S 3W3 - 613/230-8234; Fax: 613/230-7887; Email: festival@ottawafolk.ca; URL: www.ottawafolk.org, Aug.

Ottawa International Chamber Music Festival, Ottawa Chamber Music Society, PO Box 20583, Ottawa ON K1N 1A3 - 613/234-8008; Fax: 613/234-7692; Email: info@chamberfest. com; URL: www.chamberfest.com, July-Aug.

Ottawa International Jazz Festival, 61A York St., Ottawa ON K1N 5T2 - 613/241-2633; Fax: 613/241-5774; Email: info@ottawajazzfestival.com; URL: www.ottawajazzfestival.com - Manager, Programming, Jacques Emond - June-July

Regina Folk Festival, #101, 1855 Scarth St., PO Box 1203, Regina SK S4P 3B4 - 306/757-7684; Fax: 306/757- 7688; Email: info@reginafolkfestival.com; URL: www.reginafolk festival.com - Artistic Director, Sandra Butel - Annual three day folk-based music festival - Aug.

Scotia Festival of Music, 6181 Lady Hammond Rd., Halifax NS B3K 2R9 - 902/429-9467; Fax: 902/425-6785; Email: admin@scotiafestival.ns.ca; URL: www.scotiafestival.ns.ca - Contact, Christopher Wilcox - Annually, May. Chamber music

Stan Rogers Folk Festival, PO Box 46, Canso NS B0H 1H0 - 902/366-2475; Fax: 902/366-2978; Tollfree: 1-888- 554-7826; Email: info@stanfest.com; URL: www.stanfest.com - Artistic Director, Troy Greencorn

Summerfolk Music & Crafts Festival, Georgian Bay Folk Society, PO Box 521, Owen Sound ON N4K 5R1 - 519/371-2995; Fax: 519/371-2973; Email: gbfs@bmts.com; URL: www.summerfolk.org - President, David McLeish

Vancouver Chamber Music Festival, Vancouver Recital Society, #304, 873 Beatty St., Vancouver BC V6B 2M6 - 604/602-0363; Fax: 604/602-0364; URL: www.vanrecital.com - Artistic Director, Leila Getz, July

Vancouver Folk Music Festival, #1114, 207 West Hastings St., Vancouver BC V6B 1H7 - 604/602-9798; Fax: 604/602-9790; Tollfree: 1-800-883-3655; Email: info@ thefestival.bc.ca; URL: www.thefestival.bc.ca - Artistic Director, Dugg Simpson - Annual festival - July, Vancouver BC

Vancouver International Jazz Festival, Vancouver International Jazz Festival/Coastal Jazz & Blues Society, 316 West 6th Ave., Vancouver BC V5Y 1K9 - 604/872- 5200; Fax: 604/872-5250; Tollfree: 1-888-438-5200; Email: cjbs@coastaljazz.ca; URL: www.coastaljazz.ca - Executive Director, Robert Kerr, Artistic Director, Ken Pickering - June-July

Vancouver Island Music Fest, PO Box 338, Cumberland BC V0R 1S0 - 250/336-7981; Email: dougcox@shaw.ca; URL: www.islandmusicfest.com - Artistic Director, Doug Cox, July

Victoriaville International Festival of New Music, 82, rue Notre-Dame est, CP 460, Victoriaville QC G6P 6T3 - 819/752-7912; Fax: 819/758-4370; Email: info@ fimav.qc.ca; URL: www.fimav.qc.ca - 25 concerts in 5 days, musicians from 12 different countries - May

Western Canada Olde Tyme Fiddling Championship, Western Canada Amateur Olde Tyme Fiddling Championship, PO Box 2406, Swift Current SK S9H 4J8 - 306/773-4387; Fax: 306/773-9055 - Secretary, Alvina Kantrud - Annual - Sept.

Winnipeg Folk Festival, #203, 211 Bannatyne Ave., Winnipeg MB R3B 3P2 - 204/231-0096; Fax: 204/231- 0076; Email: info@winnipegfolkfestival.ca; URL: www.winnipegfolkfestival.ca - Annually, July

Winnipeg Jazz Festival, #501, 100 Arthur St., Winnipeg MB R3B 1H3 - 204/989-4650; Fax: 204/956-5280; URL: www.jazzwinnipeg.com, June

OKTOBERFESTS *See* EVENTS

PACKAGING

Pacex International, Packaging Association of Canada, #E330, 2255 Sheppard Ave. East, Toronto ON M2J 4Y1 - 416/490-7860; Fax: 416/490-7844; Email: info@ pac.ca; URL: www.pac.ca - President/CEO, Alan M. Robinson, Chair, Sylvia MacVey - Biennial trade show - May - National Trade Centre, Exhibition Place, Toronto ON

PARENTS *See* CHILDREN

PETROLEUM

Go-Expo Show, dmg World Media, #605, 999 - 8 St. SW, Calgary AB T2R 1N7 - 403/209-3555; Fax: 403/245- 8649; Tollfree: 1-888-799-2545; URL: www.dmgworldmedia.com - Pat Atkinson - Biennial trade show. Petroleum & natural gas products, services & technology; exploration, production, transmission, processing, marketing

Offshore Newfoundland Petroleum Show, dmg World Media, #605, 999 - 8 St. SW, Calgary AB T2R 1N7 - 403/209-3555; Fax: 403/245-8649; Tollfree: 1-888- 799-2545; URL: www.dmgworldmedia.com - Pat Atkinson

PETS

L'Exposition canine internationale de Montréal/Montreal International Dog Show, United Kennel Club Inc., c/o 1562, route 203, Howick QC J0S 1G0 - 450/825-2824; Email: info@ukc.ca; URL: www.ukc.ca - Show Secretary, Diana Edwards - Annual all breed dog exhibition

PetExpo Calgary, Canwest Shows Inc., 7 Panorama Bay SW, Calgary AB T3Z 3L6 - 403/686-9699; Fax: 403/246-3856; Email: info@canwestshows.com; URL: www.canwestshows. com - General Manager, Terra Connors - Annual consumer trade show - Sept. - Stampede Park, Calgary AB

Salon Canin Rive-Sud de Montréal, Club Canin de l'Estrie, 121, rue des Hirondelles, Sherbrooke QC J1R 0P3 - 819/346-4745

- Annual. All breed dog exhibition - April - Aréna régional, Iberville QC

Vancouver PetExpo, Canwest Shows Inc., 7 Panorama Bay SW, Calgary AB T3Z 3L6 - 403/686-9699; Fax: 403/246-3856; Email: info@canwestshows.com; URL: www.canwestshows.com - General Manager, Terra Connors - Annual consumer trade show - March - Vancouver Convention & Exhibition Centre, Vancouver BC

PLASTICS & RUBBER

Expoplast, Canadian Plastics Industry Association, #712, 5915 Airport Rd., Mississauga ON L4V 1T1 - 905/678- 7748; Fax: 905/678-0774; Email: national@cpia.ca; URL: www.plastics.ca - President & CEO, Serge Lavoie, Show Director, Sally Damstra - Triennial international trade show: plastics machinery, raw materials suppliers, mold makers, processors, fabricators, auxiliary equipment

Plast-Ex, Canadian Plastics Industry Association, #712, 5915 Airport Rd., Mississauga ON L4V 1T1 - 905/678- 7748; Fax: 905/678-0774; Email: national@cpia.ca; URL: www.plastics.ca - Triennial international trade show: plastics machinery, raw materials suppliers, mold makers, processors, fabricators, auxiliary equipment - Show Director: Sally Damstra, May - International Centre, Toronto ON

PSYCHIC PHENOMENA

ESP Psychic Expo, Impact Event Management, 358 Danforth Ave., PO Box 65060, Toronto ON M4K 3Z2 - 416/461-5306; Fax: 416/461-8460; Email: impactevent@ sympatico.ca - Donald Nausbaum - Annual consumer show. Psychics, astrologers, natural healing, crystals, books, tapes, computers - Feb. - International Centre, Toronto ON

Toronto Psychic Expo, Impact Event Management, 358 Danforth Ave., PO Box 65060, Toronto ON M4K 3Z2 - 416/461-5306; Fax: 416/461-8460; Email: impactevent@sympatico.ca - Donald Nausbaum - Consumer show. Psychics, astrologers, tarot card readers, holistic health, computers - Oct. - Exhibition Place, Toronto ON

REAL ESTATE

Leadership Conference, The Canadian Real Estate Association, Minto Place, The Canada Bldg., #1600, 344 Slater St., Ottawa ON K1R 7Y3 - 613/237-7111; Fax: 613/234-2567; Tollfree: 1-800-842-2732; Email: info@ crea.ca; URL: www.crea.ca - Annual trade show - Coordinator, Sherry Watson, March

Property Management Today, Master Promotions Ltd., PO Box 565, Saint John NB E2L 3Z8 - 506/658-0018; Fax: 506/658-0750; Tollfree: 1-888-454-7469; Email: info@masterpromotions.ca; URL: www.masterpromotions.ca - Annual trade show - Show Manager, Brian McKiel, Oct. - Trade & Convention Centre, Saint John NB

RECREATIONAL VEHICLES *See* AUTOMOTIVE

RODEOS

***See Also* Exhibitions, Farm Business/Agriculture**

Calgary Exhibition & Stampede, PO Box 1060, Stn M, Calgary AB T2P 2K8 - 403/261-0101; Fax: 403/265-7197; Tollfree: 1-800-661-1260; URL: www.calgarystampede.com - COO, Vern Kimball, Senior Manager, Corporate Communications, Lindsey Galloway - Annual city-wide festival; agricultural exhibits

CCA Finals Rodeo, RR#4, Site 412, PO Box 287, Saskatoon SK S7K 3J8 - 306/931-2700; Fax: 306/931-4480; Email: canadiancowboy@yourlink.ca; URL: www.canadiancowboys.sk.ca - Office Coordinator, Charlene Symington - Annually, Oct. Four days

Maple Creek Cowtown Rodeo, PO Box 1091, Maple Creek SK S0N 1N0 - 306/662-2673 - Tom Boychuk - Annually, May

Williams Lake Stampede, Williams Lake Stampede Association, PO Box 4076, Williams Lake BC V2G 2V2 - 250/392-6585; Fax: 250/398-7701; Tollfree: 1-800- 717-6336; Email: info@williamslakestampede.com; URL: www.williamslakestampede.com - President, Bob Breitkreutz, July

RVS *See* AUTOMOTIVE; SPORTS & RECREATION

SEWING *See* CRAFTS

SEX

The Everything to Do with Sex Show, Canwest Shows Inc., 7 Panorama Bay SW, Calgary AB T3Z 3L6 - 403/686- 9699; Fax: 403/246-3856; Email: info@canwestshows. com; URL: www.canwestshows.com - General Manager, Terra Connors

SPORTS & RECREATION

***See Also* Boating; Automotive, for combined auto/RV shows**

24 Hours of Adrenalin, #4, 160 Gibson Dr., Markham ON L3R 1K1 - 416/640-0824; Fax: 416/640-0825; Email: info@twenty4sports.com; URL: www.twenty4sports.com - Team & solo mountain biking events that take place in Alberta, Ontario & BC in June, July & Aug.

Atlantic Outdoor Sports & RV Show, PO Box 2968, Dartmouth NS B2W 4Y2 - 902/827-7469; Fax: 902/827- 1247; Email: dhubley@ns.sympatico.ca; URL: www.sportsandrvshow.com - Manager, Darrelyn Hubley - Annual consumer show. Trailer & motor homes, 4x4s, tent trailers, boats, motors, hunting, fishing & camping, tourism & sporting goods - March, Halifax NS

Bicycle Fall Blowout Sale, #1801, One Yonge St., Toronto ON M5E 1W7 - 416/363-1292; Fax: 416/369-0515; Email: josie@telsec.net; URL: www.bicycleshowtoronto.com - Marketing & Sales Manager, Josie Graziosi - Annual; fall - Oct., Toronto ON

Canadian Power Toboggan Championship, PO Box 22, Beausejour MB R0E 0C0 - 204/268-2049; Fax: 204/268-4209; URL: www.cptcracing.com/- Annual - March

Country Living Show, Square Feet Northwest Event Management Inc., PO Box 82550, Stn N, Burnaby BC V5C 5Z1 - 604/683-4766; Fax: 604/688-0270; Tollfree: 1-877-888-7111; Email: mgmt@ sqftevent.com; URL: www.reel-shows.com - Blaine Woit - Annual consumer show - March - Tradex, Abbotsford BC

Ironman Canada Triathlon Championship, 416 Westminster Ave. West, Penticton BC V2A 1K5 - 250/490-8787; Fax: 250/490-8788; Email: ironman@vip.net; URL: www.ironman.ca - Race Director, Dave Bullock - Annual four-day trade expo staged as part of the events prior to the Ironman race - Aug.

London Boat & Cottage Show, Western Fair Association, 900 King St., PO Box 7550, London ON N5Y 5P8 - 519/438-7203; Fax: 519/679-3124; Tollfree: 1-800-619- 4629; Email: gmcrae@westernfair.com; URL: www.westernfair.com - General Manager, Gary McRae - Annual consumer show

Motorhead Snowmobile, Watercraft & ATV Show, Marketer Shows Inc., 78 Main St. South, Newmarket ON L3Y 3Y6 - 905/898-8585; Fax: 905/898-8071; Tollfree: 1-888-661-7469; Email: rkehoe@bellnet.ca; URL: www.torontosnowmobileshows.com - Richard Kehoe - Annual consumer show - March - Toronto International Centre, Toronto ON

National Outfitter's Hunting & Fishing Show, Mobilvision Inc., 9200, boul Henri-Bourassa ouest, Montréal QC H4S 1L5 - 514/334-7277; Fax: 514/334-1180; Tollfree: 1-800-668-3976; Email: mobilvision@pourvoirie. net; URL: www.pourvoirie.net - Président, Jacques Forest, Feb. - Montréal Congress Centre

Ontario PGA Golf Merchandise Show, Reed Exhibition Companies Inc., #1, 3761 Victoria Park Ave., Toronto ON M1W 3S2 - 416/491-7565; Fax: 416/491-5088; Email: canada@reedexpo.com; URL: www.reedexpo.com - John Lewinski - Annual trade show - Oct., Toronto ON

Salon Camping, Plein Air, Chasse et Pêche de Montréal/Montréal Sportsmen's Show, Canadian National Sportsmen's Shows (1989) Ltd., #222, 980, St-Antoine ouest, Montréal QC H3C 1A8 - 514/866-5409; Fax: 514/866-4092; URL: www.sportsmensshows.com - Regional Manager, Francine St-Laurent - Annual consumer show: camping, fishing, hunting, RVs, tourism

Salon Camping, Plein Air, Chasse et Pêche de Québec/Québec City Sportsmen's Show, Canadian National Sportsmen's Shows (1989) Ltd., #222, 980, St-Antoine ouest, Montréal QC H3C 1A8 - 514/866-5409; Fax: 514/866-4092; URL: www.sportsmensshows.com - Regional Manager, Francine St-Laurent - Annual consumer show: camping, fishing, hunting, RVs, tourism

Sport Compact Challenge, Pro-Sho Inc., 298 Sheppard Ave. East, Toronto ON M2N 3B1 - 416/229-9919; Fax: 416/223-2826; Tollfree: 1-877-950-1500; Email: prosho@meteorshows.com; URL: www.performanceworldcarshow.com; www.llhashows. com, Mar. - International Centre, Toronto ON

Supertrax International Snowmobilers Show, Marketer Shows Inc., 78 Main St. South, Newmarket ON L3Y 3Y6 - 905/898-8585; Fax: 905/898-8071; Tollfree: 1-888-661-7469; Email: rkehoe@bellnet.ca; URL: www.torontosnowmobileshows.com - Richard Kehoe - Annual consumer show - Oct. - Toronto International Centre, Toronto ON

Toronto Ski & Snowboard Show, Canadian National Sportsmen's Shows (1989) Ltd., #202, 703 Evans Ave., Toronto ON M5C 5E9 - 416/695-0311; Fax: 416/695- 0381; Email: oster@sportshow.ca; URL: www.sportshow.ca - Annual consumer show - Show Manager, Harley Austin, Oct. - National Trade Centre, Exhibition Place, Toronto ON

Toronto Sportsmen's Show, Canadian National Sportsmen's Shows (1989) Ltd., #202, 703 Evans Ave., Toronto ON M5C 5E9 - 416/695-0311; Fax: 416/695- 0381; Email: oster@sportshow.ca; URL: www.sportshow.ca - Annual consumer show - Show Manager, Harley Austin, March - National Trade Centre, Exhibition Place, Toronto ON

The Toronto Star Golf & Travel Show, Premier Consumer Shows, 467 Speers Rd., Oakville ON L6K 3S4 - 905/815-0017; Fax: 905/337-5570; Tollfree: 1-800-265- 3673 - Show Manager, Jane Hills - Annual consumer show - March

STAMPEDES *See* RODEOS

THEATRE *See* ARTS

TOYS & GAMES

The Toronto Christmas Train Show, Toronto Show Promotions, PO Box 217, Grimsby ON L3M 4G3 - 905/945- 2775; Fax: 905/945-0197; Email: info@antiquetoys.ca; URL: www.antiquetoys.ca - Doug Jarvis - Annual; operating train layouts, memorabilia - Nov., Mississauga ON

TRANSPORTATION

***See Also* Automotive**

Annual Convention & Trade Show, Ontario School Bus Association, #304, 1 Eva Rd., Toronto ON M9C 4Z5 - 416/695-9965; Fax: 416/695-9977; Email: info@ osba.on.ca; URL: www.osba.on.ca - Coordinator of Communications, Jackie Laurie, Executive Director, Richard Donaldson - Annual conference & trade show. Safety, fuel economy, buses & accessories, computers

TRAVEL & TOURISM

Canadian Meetings & Incentive Travel Symposium & Trade Show, 1 Mount Pleasant Rd., Toronto ON M4Y 2Y5 - 416/764-1635; Fax: 416/764-1419; URL: www.meetingscanada.com - Annual trade show & conference - Aug.

Salon Industriel et Commercial, Chambre de Commerce de Manicouagan, #302, 67, Place Lasalle, Baie-Comeau QC G4Z 1K1 - 418/296-2010; Fax: 418/296-5397 - Directeur général, François Desy - Annual show. Recreational products & services - avril - Centre Léonard, Baie-Comeau QC

Summer Holiday Show, dmg World Media, 180 Duncan Mills Rd., 4th Fl., Toronto ON M3B 1Z6 - 416/385- 1880; Fax: 416/385-1855; Tollfree: 1-888-823-7469; URL: www.dmgworldmedia.com - Show Manager, Glen Chiasson

The Travel & Vacation Show, Player Expositions International, 255 Clemow Ave., Ottawa ON K1S 2B5 - 613/567-6408; Fax: 613/567-2718; Email: rplayer@sympatico. ca; URL: www.playerexpo.com - Show Organizer, Halina Player - Annual consumer & trade show - May - Lansdowne Park, Ottawa ON

Travel Technology Conference & Trade Show, Baxter Travel Group, 310 Dupont St., Toronto ON M5R 1V9 - 416/968-7252; Fax: 416/968-2377; Email: baxgroup@baxter.net; URL: www.baxter.net - Annual. Travel industry - March - Toronto Convention Centre, Toronto ON

TRUCKS *See* AUTOMOTIVE

TVS, STEREOS *See* ELECTRICAL/ELECTRONICS

VIDEO *See* COMMUNICATIONS

WINTER CARNIVALS

Banff/Lake Louise Winter Festival, PO Box 1298, Banff AB T0L 0C0 - 403/762-8421; Fax: 403/762-8163; Email: info@banfflakelouise.com; URL: www.banfflakelouise.com, Feb.

Carnaval de Québec M. Christie/Mr. Christie's Queb,c Winter Carnival, Carnaval de Québec, 290, rue Joly, Québec QC G1L 1N8 - 418/626-3716; Fax: 418/626- 7252; Tollfree: 1-866-422-7628; Email: comm@carnaval. qc.ca; URL: www.carnaval.qc.ca - Directeur général, Jean Pelletier, Directeur du marketing et des communications, Annick Marchand - 17 days, major winter event

Carnaval-Souvenir de Chicoutimi, 49, rue Lafontaine, CP 567, Chicoutimi QC G7H 5C8 - 418/543-4438; Fax: 418/543-4884; Tollfree: 1-877-543-4439; Email: info@carnavalsouvenir.qc.ca; URL: www.reseau.qc.ca/carnaval - Ten days, major winter event - Feb.

Charlottetown Winter Carnival, PO Box 98, Charlottetown PE C1A 7K2 - 902/892-5708, Feb.

Conception Bay South Winterfest, Conception Bay South NL - 709/834-6534, 834-6548, 682-0453; Fax: 709/834-8337, Feb.

Corner Brook Winter Carnival, PO Box 886, Corner Brook NL A2H 6H6 - 709/632-5343; Fax: 709/632-5344; Email: cbwc@nf.aibn.com; URL: www.cornerbrookwinercarnival.ca - General Manager, Shirley M. Brake - Annually, 10 days - Feb.
Elliot Lake Winterfest, Lester B. Pearson Civic Centre, Hwy.#108, Elliot Lake ON P5A 2T1 - 705/848-2084; Fax: 705/848-7121 - Donna Hennessy, Feb.
Fête des Neiges, Parc Jean-Drapeau, 1, circuit Gilles-Villeneuve, Montréal QC H3C 1A9 - 514/872-6120; Fax: 514/872-6779; Email: webmaster@fetedesneiges. com; URL: www.fetedesneiges.com - Marcel Caron - 6 day major winter event. Sports, cultural, ice sculptures - Jan.
Hamilton Winterfest, Culture & Recreation Division, Public Health & Community Services, 71 Main St. West, Hamilton ON L8P 4Y5 - 905/546-2424, ext.2747; Fax: 905/546-2338; URL: www.city.hamilton.on.ca/culture-and-rec/winterfest - Special Events Coordinator, Jim Moore, Feb.
Jasper in January, PO Box 98, Jasper AB T0E 1E0 - 780/852-3858; Fax: 780/852-4932; URL: www.jasperadventures.com, Jan.
Kapuskasing Winter Carnival, 88 Riverside Dr., Kapuskasing ON P5N 1B3 - 705/335-2341; URL: kapuskasing.com - Feb. & March
Kirkland Lake Winter Carnival, Kirkland Lake Festivals Committee, PO Box 277, Kirkland Lake ON P2N 3H7, March
Mount Pearl Frosty Festival, 3 Centennial St., Mount Pearl NL A1N 1G4 - 709/748-1008; Fax: 709/748-1150; Email: smoothsaleing@nl.rogers.com; URL: www.mtpearl.nf.ca - Contact, Karen Bowering, Feb.
Prince Albert Winter Festival, 1211 - 1 Ave. West, Prince Albert SK S6V 4T8 - 306/764-7595; Fax: 306/763- 3311; Email: pa.winterfestival@sasktel.net - Jane Smith, Feb.
Red Deer Family Winter Fest, c/o City of Red Deer, Recreation, Parks & Culture Dept., PO Box 5008, Red Deer AB T4N 3T4 - 403/309-8409; Fax: 403/342-6073; Email: suzanne.jubb@reddeer.ca; URL: www.reddeer.ca - Suzanne Jubb, Feb.
Regina Waskimo Winter Festival, City Hall, 2476 Victoria Ave., Regina SK S4N 6M5 - 306/777-7262; Email: cityhelp@regina.ca; URL: www.regina.ca - Executive Director, J.B. Paterson - Annual, third weekend in Feb.
Riverview Winter Carnival, 30 Honour House Court, Riverview NB E1B 3Y9 - 506/387-2028; Fax: 506/387- 7455 - Gina McNeil, Feb.
Vernon Winter Carnival, 3401 - 35th Ave., Vernon BC V1T 2T5 - 250/545-2236; Fax: 250/545-0006; Email: carnival@junction.net; URL: www.vernonwintercarnival.com - Chairman, Donna Hall, Feb.
Winterlude, #202, 40 Elgin St., Ottawa ON K1P 1C7 - 613/239-5555; Fax: 613/239-5063; Tollfree: 1-800-704- 8227; Email: info@ncc-ccn.ca; URL: www.canadascapital.gc.ca - Sr. Program Manager, Thérèse St-Onge, 613/239-5278 - Major winter festival, first three weekends of February. Skating on Rideau Canal, international ice & snow sculpture competitions, musical & figure skating shows, North America's largest winter playground for kids, various sporting & social events, fireworks, stage performances & buskers - Feb.
Winterlude, PO Box 439, Grand Falls-Windsor NL A2A 2J8 - 709/489-0450; Fax: 709/489-0454; URL: www.grandfallswindsor.com/centennial/events - Contact, Dave Nichols, Feb.

WOMEN

Calgary Woman's Show, The Calgary Woman's Show Ltd., #224, 1982 Kensington Rd. NW, Calgary AB T2N 3R5 - 403/270-7274; Fax: 403/270-3037; Email: calgary.woman.show@home.com; URL: www.calgarywomansshow.com - President, Judy Markle - Semi-annual consumer show in April & Oct.; Products & services.
Women's Conferences, PO Box 25125, London ON N6C 6A9 - 519/668-5677; Fax: 519/668-6883; Email: dianvail@execulink.com - Contact, Diann Vail - Bi-annual conference, spring & fall for business professional & corporate women
World of Women, 29 Fern Cres., Sylvan Lake AB T4S 1Y4 - 403/887-0111; Fax: 403/887-0133; Email: ptkennedy@shaw.ca; URL: www.worldofwomenshow.com - Event Marketing, Sherall Kennedy, Sept.

WOOD/WOODWORKING

Chatham Woodworking Show, Cryderman Productions Inc., 136 Thames St., Chatham ON N7L 2Y8 - 519/351- 8344; Fax: 519/351-8345; Tollfree: 1-866-640-9663; Email: john@crydermanproductions.com; URL: www.crydermanproductions.com - John Cryderman - Annual - Jan. - Kinsmen Auditorium
Salon Industriel du Bois Ouvre, Reed Exhibition Companies Inc., #1, 3761 Victoria Park Ave., Toronto ON M1W 3S2 - 416/491-7565; Fax: 416/491-5088; Email: canada@reedexpo.com; URL: www.reedexpo.com - John Lewinski - Biennial trade show - Sept., Montréal QC
Woodworking & Tool Show, Canwest Shows Inc., 7 Panorama Bay SW, Calgary AB T3Z 3L6 - 403/686-9699; Fax: 403/246-3856; Email: info@canwestshows.com; URL: www.canwestshows.com - General Manager, Terra Connors - Annual consumer show - Oct.

Awards & Honours

Canadian Awards

(Including Scholarships, Grants, Bursaries)

Awards are listed under the following categories:

ADVERTISING & PUBLIC RELATIONS

The Advertising & Design Club of Canada
#318, 160 Pears Ave., Toronto ON M5R 3P8
416/423-4113; Fax: 416/423-3362
Email: info@theadcc.ca; URL: www.theadcc.ca

The Advertising & Design Club of Canada Awards
Main categories of awards are: Advertising Print, Advertising Broadcast, Advertising Multiple Media, Graphic Design, Editorial Design & Interactive Design; winners receive gold, silver or merit awards

Association of Canadian Advertisers Inc. / Association canadienne des annonceurs
#1103, 95 St. Clair Ave. West, Toronto ON M4V 1N6
416/964-3805; Fax: 416/964-0771; Toll Free: 1-800-565-0109
Email: info@aca-online.com; URL: www.aca-online.com

ACA Gold Medal
Established in 1941 to encourage high standards of personal achievement in advertising - for introducing new concepts or techniques, for significantly improving existing practices, or for enhancing the stature of advertising

Canadian Marketing Association / Association canadienne du marketing
#607, One Concorde Gate, Toronto ON M3C 3N6
416/391-2362; Fax: 416/441-4062
Email: info@the-cma.org; URL: www.the-cma.org

CMA Awards
Celebrating the art and science of marketing, CMA has restructured its judging breakdown to 40%-Results, 40%-Creative, 20%-Production. Entries can be submitted under type of business, type of program or specialty, representing particularly innovative solutions. CMA also offers Student Awards to post secondary students enrolled in direct marketing, marketing or business programs.

Institute of Communication Agencies & Advertising / Institut des communications et de la publicité
#500, 2300 Yonge St., Toronto ON M4P 1E4
416/764-1608; Fax: 416/482-1856
Email: ica@ica-ad.com; URL: www.ica-ad.com

CASSIES Awards
Established 1993; CASSIES (Canadian Advertising Success Stories) are open to all channels of marketing communications. Eligible submissions must show impressive business results and convincingly prove results were a result of the advertising.

Marketing Magazine
1 Mount Pleasant Rd., 7th floor Toronto ON M4Y 2Y5
416/764-2000; Fax: 416/764-1519
URL: www.marketingmag.ca

The Marketing Awards
Annual advertising awards offering 40 Gold Awards in the following categories: television/cinema, radio, magazine, newspaper, transit, business press, direct mail, outdoor, point-of-purchase/interior store design, multimedia campaign, non-traditional & public service. Silver Awards, Bronze Awards, & Certificates of Excellence are also awarded. Entries must have run in the previous year & must have been conceived & created by people working in English in the Canadian advertising business

Publicité Club de Montréal
#200, 4316, boulevard St.-Laurent, Montréal QC H2W 1Z3
514/499-1391; Fax: 514/842-4886
Email: info@amm-pcm.ca; URL: www.pcm.qc.ca
Le Concourse Stratégics vise à mettre en valeur les réalisations des professionnels de l'industrie des communications et du marketing au Québec. Un jury selectionne une finalist pour chacune des cinq catégories du concours: Innovation, Créativité, Audace, Impacte et Efficience.

AGRICULTURE & FARMING

Canadian Society of Animal Science / Société canadienne de science animale
c/o Agriculture & Agri-Food Canada Research Station, PO Box 90, Lennoxville QC J1M 1Z3
819/565-9171; Fax: 819/564-5507
Email: info@csas.net; URL: www.csas.net
CSAS offers five prestigious awards:

Fellowship Award
Awarded to members who have made an outstanding contribution in any field of animal contribution

Award for Excellence in Nutrition and Meat Sciences

Award for Technical Innovation in Enhancing Production of Safe Affordable Food

Young Scientist Award

Animal Indutries Award in Extension & Public Service

International Development Research Centre / Centre de recherches pour le développement international
PO Box 8500, Ottawa ON K1G 3H9
613/236-6163; Fax: 613/238-7230
Email: info@idrc.ca; URL: www.idrc.ca
IRDC has five special awards awarded at the discretion of its Board of Governors. They are:

Journalism Award

Professional Development Award

Centre Sabbatical Award

Project-Related Award

Pearson Fellowship

Provincial Exhibition of Manitoba
#3, 1175 - 18 St., Brandon MB R7A 7C5
204/726-3590; Fax: 204/725-0202; Toll Free: 1-877-729-0001
Email: info@brandonfairs.com; URL: www.brandonfairs.com

Royal Manitoba Winter Fair Awards
Prizes given in various categories for best of show for agricultural products, animals & crops; several equestrian events offer prizes for best in competition

Royal Agricultural Winter Fair Association / Foire agricole royale d'hiver
The Ricoh Coliseum, Direct Energy Centre
Exhibition Place, Toronto ON M6K 3C3
416/263-3400; Fax: 416/263-3488
Email: info@royalfair.org; URL: www.royalfair.org

Agricultural Awards
Grand Champion is the highest honour in the following categories: dairy, beef, sheep, goats, swine, market livestock, field crops, vegetables, honey & maple, poultry, jams/jellies/pickles, dairy products, square dancing, fiddling, fleece wool, rabbits, & eight youth activities

Breeding Horse Awards
17 sections award prizes in this category

Performance Horse Awards
35 divisions & classes offer prizes; Leading International Rider is the highest honour in the horse show

BROADCASTING & FILM

Academy of Canadian Cinema & Television / Académie canadienne du cinéma et de la télévision
172 King St. East, Toronto ON M5A 1J3
416/366-2227; Fax: 416/366-8454; Toll Free: 1-800-644-5194
Email: info@academy.ca; URL: www.academy.ca

Gemini Awards
The nationally telecast awards for excellence & achievement in Canadian English-language television production are awarded annually & presented to winners in more than 80 categories covering Best Program, Best Performance & Best Craft, as well as special awards following nomination & voting by a peer group

Genie Awards
The nationally telecast Genie Awards celebrate excellence in Canadian cinema. The annual awards cover 21 categories from Best Picture to Best Sound, as well as the Golden Reel award for the top Canadian box office gross. Special achievement awards are voted by members of the Academy.

Prix Gémeaux
For excellence & achievement in French-language television production; held annually & presented in 70 categories covering Programs, Performance & Crafts; nominations & voting by peer groups composed of academy members

Alberta Motion Picture Industries Association
#318, 8944 - 182 Street NW, Edmonton AB T5T 2E3
780/944-0707; Fax: 780/426-3057
URL: www.ampia.org

Alberta Film & Television Awards
Awarded annually, the "Rosie Awards", are presented to producers and craftpeople, who reside in Alberta, in recognition of their outstanding film & television works. Awards are given in 22 class categories (ie. Best Documentary, Best Drama, Best Movie, Best Musical etc.) and 22 craft categories (ie. Best Director; Best Screenwriter, Cinematography etc.)

David Billington Awards
Awarded to a special individual in recognition of their incomparable dedication and contribution to the growth of Alberta's film and television industry.

The Alliance for Children & Television / Alliance pour l'enfant et la télévision
#713, 1400, boul René-Lévesque est, Montréal QC H2L 2M2
514/597-5417; Fax: 514/597-5205
Email: alliance@act-aet.tv; URL: www.act-aet.tv

The Award of Excellence
The Alliance for Children & Television has been recognizing the importance of quality television for Canadian children for over 30 years. This award is presented to a person or team for their exceptional work on a children's television show produced in Canada, which stands out for its excellence.

Banff World Television Festival
c/o Achilles Media Ltd., #202, 102 Boulder Cres., Canmore AB T1W 1L2
403/678-1216; Fax: 403/678-3357
Email: info@achillesmedia.com; URL: www.bwtvf.com/

Banff Rockie Awards
Annual television awards for: made-for-TV-movies; mini-series; continuing series; short dramas; comedies; social & political documentaries; original webcasts; popular science programs & natural history; arts documentaries; performance specials; animation; sports; children's programs; history & biography programs; & information programs. Also a grand prize winner, two special jury awards & best HDTV program. All entries must be made for television & either in English or French

Canadian Association of Broadcasters / Association canadienne des radiodiffuseurs
PO Box 627, Stn B, Ottawa ON K1P 5S2
613/233-4035; Fax: 613/233-6961
Email: cab@cab-acr.ca; URL: www.cab-acr.ca

Astral Media Scholarship
Established in 1975 by Astral Media with the association; awarded annually to French Canadian students who are members of a of visible minority or who are Aboriginals with broadcasting experience who are enrolled in, or wish to begin or complete a program of studies in communications at the university level
$5,000

BBM Scholarship
Established in 1986; awarded annually to a student in a graduate study program, or final year of an Honours degree with the intention of entering a graduate program at a Canadian university or post-secondary institution, who has demonstrated achievement in & knowledge of statistical &/or quantitative research methodology
$4,000

Jim Allard Broadcast Journalism Scholarship
Established 1983; awarded annually to an aspiring broadcaster enrolled in a broadcast journalism program at a Canadian col-

lege or university, who best combines academic achievement with natural talent
$2,500

Ruth Hancock Memorial Scholarships
Award established jointly in 1975 by the association, the Broadcast Executives Society & Canadian Association of Broadcast Representatives; presented annually to three Canadian students enrolled in recognized communications courses
$1,500 (x3)

Canadian Ethnic Media Association
24 Tarlton Rd., Toronto ON M5P 2M4
416/260-3625; Fax: 416/260-3810
Email: canscene@rogers.com; URL: www.canadianethnicmedia.com

Awards of Achievement
Up to nine plaques are offered annually to jounalists in print, radio, & television; awards are given to journalists for excellence in their field; competition is open to all journalists, in any language, whether or not they are members of the Club; a single award is also given to writers of a published work of fact, fiction or poetry in book form

Sierhey Khmara Ziniak Award
In honour of the Club's founder, award is presented to a single person, based on a body or work celebrating Canada's diversity

Canadian Film & Television Production Association / Association canadienne de production de film et télévision
#902, 151 Slater St., Ottawa ON K1P 5H3
613/233-1444; Fax: 613/233-0073; Toll Free: 1-800-656-7440
Email: ottawa@cftpa.ca; URL: www.cftpa.ca

CFTPA Producer's Award
Awarded to an independent producer of a Canadian feature being screened at the Toronto International Film Festival
The CFTDA - Kodak Canada Lifetime Achievement Award
Presented to an individual who has contributed to the success & progress of the Canadian film & television industry

The CFTPA Entrepreneur of the Year Award
Presented to an individual or company that has demonstrated private sector entrepreneurial achievement in the Canadian film & television industry

Canadian Society of Cinematographers
#131, 3007 Kingston Rd., Toronto ON M1M 1P1
416/266-0591; Fax: 416/266-3996
Email: admin@csc.ca; URL: www.csc.ca

Canadian Society of Cinematography Awards
16 Awards given annually for various genres and contributions.

Media Communications Association International - Toronto Chapter
PO Box 5822, Stn A, Toronto ON M5W 1P2
416/910-4776
Email: execdirect@mca-i.org; URL: www.mca-i.org

The Chuck Webb Award
This award recognizes and honours individuals who have demonstrated the highest level of involvement in, dedication and commmitment to the Association without regard for personal profit of gain. Candidates are nominated by the Board of Directors.

The Board of Directors Award
This award recognizes and honours members who have demonstrated outstanding service to the Association on a regional or national level. Candidates are nominated by the Board of Directors.

The President's Award
This prestigious recognition is not given annually, but allows the President to recognize individuals who have been of particular significance during his or her term.

Shining Star Award
This award was developed to recognize the special volunteers who give freely of their time and talents to the Association. The International Shining Star award recognizes chapter leaders who standout above all other member with their significant contributions to the chapter. The Chapter Shining Star recognizes chapter members who have gone above and beyond for the chapter.

G. Warren Scholarship Award
Presented annually, this $500 scholarship program was developed in memory of G. Warren. The only requirement is that the student will be returning for at least one more term of school

Société Saint-Jean-Baptiste de Montréal
82, rue Sherbrooke ouest, Montréal QC H2X 1X3
514/843-8851; Fax: 514/844-6369
Email: mbeaulieu@ssjb.com; URL: www.ssjb.com
Prix André-Guérin
Créé en 1990; décerné à une personnalité canadienne-française qui s'illustre dans le domaine du cinéma et vidéo

Toronto International Film Festival Group
2 Carlton St., Suite 1600., Toronto ON M5B 1J3
416/967-7371; Fax: 416/967-9477
Email: customerrelations@tiffg.ca; URL: www.tiffg.ca

AGF People's Choice Award
Sponsored by AGF & voted best film of the festival by festival audiences

Award for Best Canadian Short Film
CityTV Award for Best Canadian First Feature Film
Established by CityTV; awarded to a Canadian filmmaker whose first feature film is considered exemplary; award acknowledges the fresh new talent emerging within Canadian cinema
$15,000

FIPRESCI Award
Selected by an international FIPRESCI jury, awarded to a feature film by an emerging filmmaker having its world premiere at the festival

Toronto-City Award for Best Canadian Feature Film
Jointly sponsored by the City of Toronto & CityTV; awarded to the Best Canadian Feature Film
$25,000

BUSINESS & TRADE

Business Development Bank of Canada (BDC)
5, Place Ville-Marie, Suite 400, Montréal QC H3B 5E7
Fax: 1-877-329-9232; Toll Free: 1-877-232-2269
Email: yea@bdc.ca; URL: www.bdc.ca

BDC Ongoing Achievement Award
Introduced in 2003, this award is offered to an entrepreneur who received the a Yong Entrepreneur Award between 1988 and 2002 and whose business has since undergone sustained growth.

Laurentian Bank Export Achievement Award
This award is presented to the entrepreneurs to have most distinguished himself in the area of exports.

Bell Creative Mind Award
This award is presented to a company, in recognition of it's original approach and initiative that allows it to successfully differentiate itself from its competitors.

BDC Young Entrepreneur Awards
Awarded annually; honours outstanding entrepreneurs representing each province & territory

The Caldwell Partners
165 Avenue Rd., Toronto ON M5R 3S4
416/920-7702; Fax: 416/922-8646
Email: leaders@caldwell.ca; URL: www.caldwell.ca

Canada's Outstanding CEO of the Year
Sponsored by The Caldwell Partners, this annual award takes into consideration the candidate's leadership, innovation, business achievements, corporate performance, social responsibility, sense of vision & global competitiveness

Canada's Top 40 Under 40
Established & managed by The Caldwell Partners, celebrates Canadian leaders who have demonstrated remarkable success before the age of 40.

Canada's CFO of the Year
Founded in 2003 and sponsored by Financial Executives International, PricewaterhouseCoopers LLP and in association with The Caldwell Partners International, this annual award is designed to recognize the very highest level of financial leadership in the country. Winners are chosen by a distinguished panel of business leaders.

Certified General Accountants Association of Canada
#800, 1188 West Georgia St., Vancouver BC V6E 4A2
604/669-3555; Fax: 604/689-5845; Toll Free: 1-800-663-1529
Email: public@cga-canada.org; URL: www.cga-online.org/canada

Fellowship Award
This annual award was designed to recognize members who provide exemplary service to the Association, the profession or the public, or achiever prominence through a variety of means. Only members in good standing, who have been admitted into membership at least two year prior are eligible.

John Leslie Award
Given to a member who has achieved national recognition for exceptional service to business, the community, politics, & the arts, or who has overcome physical adversity

The Conference Board of Canada
255 Smyth Rd., Ottawa ON K1H 8M7
613/526-3280; Fax: 613/526-4857; Toll Free: 1-866-711-2262
Email: infoserv@conferenceboard.ca; URL: www.conferenceboard.ca

National Awards for Excellence in Business-Education Partnership
Awarded to partnerships that have a demonstrated record of success in promoting the importance of science, technology &/or mathematics; linking education & the world of work, promoting teacher development, encouraging students to stay in school, expanding vocational &/or apprenticeship training
- Mary Ann McLaughlin

National Awards in Governance
Awarded to boards of directors that have demonstrated excellence in governance & have implemented successful innovations in their governance practices; overall award for innovation & sector specific awards for public, private & not for profit sectors

Ernst & Young Entrepreneur of the Year Award
Ernst & Young Tower, TD Centre, 222 Bay St., PO Box 251, Toronto ON M5K 1J7
416/943-3785; Fax: 416/943-2207; Toll Free: 1-888-946-3694
Email: linda.moss@ca.ey.com; URL: www.eoy.ca

Ernst & Young Entrepreneur of the Year Award
Best entrepreneurs in 5 regions nationwide (Pacific Canada, The Prairies, Ontario, Québec, Atlantic Canada); other awards include Master Entrepreneur, Emerging Entrepreneur, Turnaround Entrepreneur, Young Entrepreneur, Supporter of Entrepreneurship. Awarded annually

Heritage Canada Foundation / Fondation Héritage Canada
5 Blackburn Ave., Ottawa ON K1N 8A2
613/237-1066; Fax: 613/237-5987
Email: heritagecanada@heritagecanada.org; URL: www.heritagecanada.org

The Prince of Wales Prize for Municipal Heritage Leadership
Established in 1999, The Prince of Wales agreed to lend his title to this annual award in recognition of the government of a municipality, which has demonstrated a strong and sustained commitment to the conservation of its historic places.

Gabrielle Léger Award for Lifetime Achievement in Heritage Conservation
Founded in 1978, this annual award is Canada's premier hounour fo individual achievement in heritage conservation

The Journalism Award
Presented annually to a journalist whose work has brought profile to Canadian communities' historic places.

Corporate Price
This annual award recognizes Canadian corporations, which have invested in the conservation of historic property of the purposes of restoration, rehabilitation, or reuse.

Achievement Awards
These awards honour individuals or groups for their achievement in heritage advocacy and volunteerism, and for projects that demonstrate a community's commitment to heritage conservation.

Information Highways Magazine
#102, 1999 Avenue Rd., Toronto ON M5M 4A5
416/488-7372; Fax: 416/488-7078
Email: info@econtentinstitute.org; URL: www.econtentinstitute.org

Canadian Online Product Awards
Honours online products designed for Canadian organizations & consumers; open to companies & individuals who develop or market products to Canadians in the following categories: general business, finance, legal, engineering, scientific, medical, consumer, library, internet search & retrieval technology & internet-enabled decision support products. Entry fee of $160.50 for each entry required

International Trade Canada
Canada Export Award Program, Team Canada Inc, 125 Sussex Dr., Ground Fl., Ottawa ON K1A 0G2

613/944-2395; Fax: 613/994-0120
Email: cea-peec@international.gc.ca; URL: www.infoexport.gc.ca/awards-prix

Canada Export Award
Honours those firms from across Canada who have demonstrated superior performance in the export arena. Open to all firms or divisions of firms resident in Canada, that have been exporting goods or services for three or more years; this includes trading houses & banks, as well as transport, market research, packaging & promotion firms; selection is based on but not limited to the extent to which the firm has shown significant increases in its export sales, success in breaking into new markets, success in introducing export products into world markets; other achievements by firms in export markets that contribute to Canada's economic well-being or to the reputation of the organization as a world-class exporter will also be considered.

National Quality Institute / Institut national de la qualité
#307, 2275 Lakeshore West Blvd., Toronto ON M8V 3Y3
416/251-7600; Fax: 416/251-9131; Toll Free: 1-800-263-9648
Email: info@nqi.ca; URL: www.nqi.ca

Canada Awards for Excellence
Previously called the Canada Awards for Business Excellence & established by the Government of Canada in 1984, the awards recognize outstanding continuous achievement in seven key areas: Leadership, Customer Focus, Planning for Improvement, People Focus, Process Optimization, Supplier Focus & Organizational Performance

National Transportation Week Inc.
Crowchild Square, #201, 5403 Crowchild Trail NW
Calgary AB T3B 4Z1
403/247-4115; Fax: 403/541-0915
Email: ntwsnt@igs.net

Transportation Person of the Year
This award is given annually to an individual who has assumed a leadership role that has contributed to significant improvements or advancements in the transportation industry in Canada.

Award of Achievement
Established 1987; awarded to those who have brought about positive & measurable developments of significant & lasting benefit to transportation in Canada

Award of Excellence
Established 1975; for an outstanding contribution to the betterment of the transportation industry

Skills/Compétences Canada
#205, 260, boul Saint Raymond, Gatineau QC J9A 3G7
819/771-7545; Fax: 819/771-5575; Toll Free: 1-877-754-5226
Email: skillscanada@skillscanada.com; URL: www.skillscanada.com

Canadian Skills Competition
Awarded annually; is an olympic-style skills competition in over 40 skilled trades, technology & leadership contests, representing 6 industry sectors, designed to test skills required in technology & trade occupations; allows students access to newest technologies & communicate with industry experts who serve as mentors Students compete at the local, regional & provincial levels to win the right to represent their province at the national level
Gold, silver & bronze medals

University of Alberta
School of Business, 3-23 Business Bldg.
Edmonton AB T6G 2R6
780/492-7676; Fax: 780/492-3325
URL: www.business.ualberta.ca

Canadian Business Leader Award
Annual award recognizes distinguished professional achievements & contributions to the community

CITIZENSHIP & BRAVERY

Alberta Order of Excellence
Executive Secretary, Alberta Order of Excellence Council
c/o Policy Coordination Office
Executive Council
1201 Legislature Annex
9718 - 107 Street., Edmonton AB T5K 1E4
780/427-7243; Fax: 780/427-0305
Email: aoe@gov.ab.ca; URL: www.lieutenantgovernor.ab.ca/aoe/

Alberta Order of Excellence
Established in 1979, the award recognizes those persons who have rendered service of the greatest distinction & of singular excellence for or on behalf of Albertans.

Bridgestone/Firestone Canada Inc.
#400, 5770 Hurontario St., Mississauga ON L5R 3G5
905/890-1990; Fax: 905/890-1991; Toll Free: 1-800-267-1318
URL: www.truckhero.ca

National Truck Hero Award
Established 1956; endorsed by the Canada Safety Council, the Traffic Injury Research Foundation & the trucking industry; designed to promote highway safety by focusing public attention on acts of bravery performed by professional Canadian truck drivers in the course of their daily work

The Canadian Council of Christians & Jews / Conseil canadien des chrétiens et des juifs
4211 Yonge St., PO Box 17, Toronto ON M2P 2A9
416/597-9693; Fax: 416/597-9775; Toll Free: 1-800-663-1848
Email: info@cccj.ca; URL: www.cccj.ca

Human Relations Award
This prestigious annual award recognizes outstanding contributions to Canadian society crossing cultural, religious, racial and ethnic lines.

Good Servant Medal
Created to commemorate the retirement of Richard D. Jones, O.C., LL.D., after 30 years of continuous service to CCCJ, as founder & principal officer, 1947-1977; recognizes individuals who have rendered extraordinary service to their community beyond the call of duty without seeking public recognition

Discovering Diversity Award
Established in 2004, this award is given to a student and his/her school who have made an outstanding effort to build community understanding and respect for others or different faiths and ethnic backgrounds.

The Canadian Council of the Blind / Le Conseil canadien des aveugles
#401, 396 Cooper St., Ottawa ON K2P 2H7
613/567-0311; Fax: 613/567-2728; Toll Free: 1-877-304-0968
Email: ccb@ccbnational.net; URL: ccbnational.net

Award of Merit
This award is bestowed in recognition of service to Canadians who are blind and vision impaired.

Book of Fame Citation
The Book of Fame was donated to the Council in 1958 by the disbanded Comrades Club of Toronto; it contains the names & citations of outstanding blind Canadians selected yearly by the eight divisions & the National Board of Directors of the Council; each recipient of a citation is presented with a framed photograph of the appropriate page in the book

Canadian Decorations for Bravery
c/o The Chancellory, Rideau Hall, One Sussex Drive
Ottawa ON K1A 0A1
613/991-0895; Fax: 613/991-1681; Toll Free: 1-800-465-6890
URL: www.gg.ca/honours/decorations/bra/bd-info_e.asp

Canadian Decorations for Bravery
Presented by the Governor General, Bravery decorations recognize people who have risked their lives to save or protect others; Three levels - the Cross of Valour, the Star of Courage & the Medal of Bravery - reflect the varying degrees of risk involved in any act of bravery

The Duke of Edinburgh's Award
#450, 207 Queen's Quay West, PO Box 124
Toronto ON M5J 1A7
416/203-0674; Fax: 416/203-0676
Email: sanderson@dukeofed.org; URL: www.dukeofed.org

Young Canadians Challenge
Established in Canada in 1963 with His Royal Highness Prince Philip as Patron, the award recognizes personal achievement in a voluntary program of activities by young people in the age range of 14-25.
Open to all Canadian youth; young people participate independently or through youth groups, clubs, schools, etc.; program is operated throughout Canada, with divisional offices located in each of the ten provinces.
Award is in the form of a pin & an inscribed certificate representing Gold, Silver, & Bronze levels; Gold awards are presented by Her Excellency The Governor General of Canada, or a member of the Royal Family, at national awards ceremonies

National Aboriginal Achievement Foundation
#450, 215 Spadina Ave., Toronto ON M5T 2C7
416/926-0775; Fax: 416/926-7554; Toll Free: 1-800-329-9780
Email: info@naaf.ca; URL: www.naaf.ca

National Aboriginal Achievement Awards
Established in 1993, this award recognizes the outstanding career achievemennts of First Nations, Inuit and Métis people, in diverse occupations.

Ontario Ministry of Citizenship & Immigration
Ontario Honours & Awards
400 University Ave. West, 6th Fl., Toronto ON M7A 2R9
416/327-2422; Fax: 416/314-4965; Toll Free: 1-800-267-7329

June Callwood Outstanding Achievement Award
Created in 2007 to commemorate the life of June Callwood CC, O.Ont, LL.D, a Canadian journalist whose life was marked by a strong concern for social justice, especially on issues affecting children and women. This annual award is given to 20 individual volunteers, volunteer groups, businesses and other organizations in recognition of their outstanding contributions to their communities ad the province.

Lieutenant Governor's Community Volunteer Award for Students
This award honours one graduating student from each of Ontario's post secondary schools who not only completed the number of volunteer hours required to graduate, but have gone above and byond.

Ontario Medal for Good Citizenship
This award recognizes residents of Ontario for outstanding achievement, whose lives serve as an example to all Ontarians. They are individuals who have made their communities better places to live.

Ontario Medal for Young Volunteers
Recognizes the outstanding achievements of 10 young volunteers, 15-24 who have made a difference to their communities

The Lincoln M. Alexander Award
Recognizes young people who have demonstrated exemplary leadership in eliminating racial discrimination; 3 student awards & 1 community award are offered yearly

The Ontario Medal for Firefighters Bravery
Established 1976 to recognize acts of superlative courage & bravery performed in the line of duty by members of Ontario's firefighting forces

The Ontario Medal for Good Citizenship
Established 1973 to recognize people who, through exceptional long-term efforts have made outstanding contributions to the well being of their communities

The Ontario Medal for Police Bravery
Established 1975 to recognize acts of superlative courage & bravery performed in the line of duty by members of Ontario's police forces

The Order of Ontario
Established 1986 to recognize those men & women who have rendered service of the greatest distinction & of singular excellence in all fields of endeavour benefiting society in Ontario & elsewhere

The Order of British Columbia
Honours & Awards Secretariat, PO Box 9422, Stn Prov Govt, Victoria BC V8W 9V1
250/387-1616; Fax: 250/356-2814
Email: protocol@gov.bc.ca; URL: www.protocol.gov.bc.ca

The Order of British Columbia
Established in 1989 to recognize individuals who have served with the greatest distinction & excelled in any field of endeavour benefiting the people of British Columbia or elsewhere.

Order of New Brunswick / Ordre du Nouveau-Brunswick
Intergovernmental & International Relations,
Office of Protocol
#274, 670 King St., PO Box 6000, Fredericton NB E3B 5H1
506/453-2671; Fax: 506/453-2995
URL: www.gnb.ca/lg/ONB/index-e.asp

Order of New Brunswick
Established in December, 2000 to recognize individuals who have demonstrated excellence & achievement & who have made outstanding contributions to the social, cultural or economic well-being of New Brunswick & its residents. Maximum of 10 recipients annually

The Order of Prince Edward Island
Legislative Assembly, Province House, PO Box 2000, Charlottetown PE C1A 7N8
902/368-5970; Fax: 902/368-5175
Email: chmackay@gov.pe.ca; URL: www.assembly.pe.ca

The Order of Prince Edward Island
Highest provincial honour that can be bestowed on a resident of the province; it is awarded in public recognition of individual Islanders whose efforts & accomplishments have been exemplary An enameled medallion, which incorporates the Provincial emblem against a blue background worn with a ribbon of rust, green & white. Recipients receive a stylized lapel pin & miniature medal, an official certificate & are entitled to use O.P.E.I. after their names

The Saskatchewan Order of Merit
Saskatchewan Honours & Awards Program
Office of Protocol & Honours
#1530 - 1855 Victoria Ave., Regina SK S4P 3T2
306/787-8965; Fax: 306/787-1269; Toll Free: 1-877-427-5505
Email: honours@gr.gov.sk.ca; URL: www.gr.gov.sk.ca/Protocol/Honours/SOM.htm

The Saskatchewan Order of Merit
This is a prestigious recognizes of excellence, achievement and contributions to the social, cultural and economic well-being of the province and its residence.

Secrétariat de l'Ordre national du Québec
Ministère du Conseil exécutif, #3.221, 875, Grande Allée Est, Québec QC G1R 4Y8
418/643-8895; Fax: 418/646-4307
Email: ordre-national@mce.gouv.qc.ca; URL: www.ordre-national.gouv.qc.ca/index.htm

Ordre national du Québec
L'Ordre national du Québec est la plus haute distinction décernée par le gouvernement du Québec. Il a été institué par la Loi sur l'Ordre national du Québec (L.R.Q., c. 0-7.01) sanctionnée le 20 juin 1984 par le Parlement de Québec.
L'Ordre national du Québec est composé de personnes à qui le gouvernement a conféré le titre de Grand Officier (G.O.) ou d'Officier (O.Q.) ou de Chevalier de l'Ordre national du Québec (C.Q.). La loi prévoit qu'une nomination puisse être faite à titre posthume. Elle accorde aussi au premier ministre du Québec le privilège exclusif de procéder à des nominations étrangères

Société Saint-Jean-Baptiste de Montréal
82, rue Sherbrooke Ouest, Montréal QC H2X 1X3
514/843-8851; Fax: 514/844-6369
Email: mbeaulieu@ssjb.com; URL: www.ssjb.com

Prix Bene Merenti De Patria
Créée en 1923, cette médaille souligne les mérites d'un compatriote ayant rendu des services exceptionnels à la patrie. La maquette est l'oeuvre d'un artiste qui a préparé les chars allégoriques de nos grands défilés pendant de nombreuses années
Médaille d'argent

Prix Chomedey-de-Maisonneuve
Créé en 1983; décerné à une personnalité dont les réalisations contribuent au rayonnement de Montréal

Prix Patriote de l'année
Décerné à une personnalité qui s'est distinguée dans la défense des intérêts du Québec et de la démocratie des peuples, en mémoire des Patriotes des années 1830; créé en 1975

Prix Séraphin-Marion
Créé en 1984; décerné à une personnalité qui défend les droits de la francophonie hors-Québec

St. John Ambulance / Ambulance Saint-Jean
#400, 1900 City Park Dr., Ottawa ON K1J 1A3
613/236-7461; Fax: 613/236-2425
Email: nhq@sja.ca; URL: www.sja.ca

Life-saving Awards of the Order of St. John
Instituted in 1874, recognizes those who risk their lives in unselfish acts of bravery & heroism when saving or attempting to save a life.

United Nations Association in Canada / Association canadienne pour les Nations-Unies
#300, 309 Cooper St., Ottawa ON K2P 0G5
613/232-5751; Fax: 613/563-2455
Email: info@unac.org; URL: www.unac.org

Pearson Peace Medal
Awarded to a Canadian who has contributed significantly to humanitarian causes

CULTURE, VISUAL ARTS & ARCHITECTURE

The Canada Council for the Arts / Conseil des Arts du Canada
350 Albert St., PO Box 1047, Ottawa ON K1P 5V8
613/566-4414; Fax: 613/566-4390; Toll Free: 1-800-263-5588
Email: info@canadacouncil.ca; URL: www.canadacouncil.ca

Bell Canada Award in Video Art
$10,000 awarded annually to a Canadian video artist who has made an exceptional contribution to the advancement of video art in Canada through his/her video tapes or video installations; candidates are nominated by three professional curators &/or critics who are specialists in Canadian video art; the winner is selected by the committee of professional video artists

Duke & Duchess of York Prize in Photography
Endowed by the Government of Canada in 1986 on the occasion of Prince Andrew's marriage; $8,000 prize awarded annually to the best candidate in the competition for the Grants to Professional Artists in visual arts; prize is given in addition to the arts grant received

Governor General's Medals in Architecture
Awarded every two years; recognizes excellence in the art of architecture in completed projects; Canada Council adminsters the jurying of the awards & contributes $20,000 to the Royal Architectural Institute of Canada towards the publication of a book/catalogue on the winning projects

Governor-General's Awards for Visual & Media Arts
Six $15,000 prizes awarded annually for distinguished career achievement in visual & media arts, plus one $15,0000 prize for distinguished contributions to the visual & media arts through voluntarism, philanthropy, board governance or community outreach activities.
Nominees must be Canadian Citizens or permanent residents of Canada, & they may not apply for an award. They must be nominated by specialist in the field. To be nominated for one of the six awards in the artistic category, candidates must have created an outstanding, distinguished body of work in visual or media arts & have made a substantial contribution to the development of visual or media arts in Canada over a significant period of time. A peer assessment committee selects the winners

J.B.C. Watkins Award
A bequest from the estate of the late John B.C . Watkins, provides special fellowships of $5,000 to Canadian artists in any field, who are graduates of a Canadian university or post-secondary art institution or training school. Preference is given to those who wish to carry out their post-graduate studies in Denmark, Norway, Sweden or Iceland, but applications are accepted for studies in any country other than Canada. Post-graduate schools include post-secondary institutions or training schools, whether or not these are degree-granting institutions; fellowships are normally awarded in music, visual arts (architecture only), theatre & media arts

Joseph S. Stauffer Prizes
Each year the Canada Council designates up to three Canadians who have been awarded an arts grant in the fields of music, visual arts or literature as winners; the prizes, which provide an additional $5,000 each, honour the memory of the benefactor whose bequest to the Canada Council enables it to "encourage young Canadians of outstanding promise or potential"
Molson Prizes.
Two prizes of $50,000 each are awarded annully to distinguished Canadians, one in the arts and the other in the social sciences and humanities.

Petro-Canada Award in New Media
Endowed by Petro-Canada in 1987 to celebrate the centenary of engineering in Canada, $10,000 awarded approximately every three years to a professional Canadian artist. The recipient must demonstrate outstanding & innovative use of new technology in the media arts. Candidates are nominated by a committee of three professional curators &/or critics who are specialists in new media & audio arts; winner is selected by a committee of professional new media & audio artists

Prix de Rome in Architecture
Established 1987; designed to recognize the work of a Canadians actively engaged in the field of contemporary architecture whose career is well under way & whose personal work shows exceptional talent. Winner is chosen by a peer assesment committee convened by the Canada Council for the Arts

Ronald J. Thom Award for Early Design Achievement
$10,000 awarded every two years to a Canadian in the early stages of his/her career in architecture who must demonstrate both outstanding creative talent & exceptional potential in architectural design.
Sensitivity to architecture's allied arts, crafts & professions in the context of the integrated building environment must be evident in all work. Winner is chosen by the peer assessment committee for the Creation/Production Grants to Professional Artists in architecture

Saidye Bronfman Awards
Funded by the Samuel & Saidye Bronfman Family Foundation, $25,000 prize is awarded annually to an exceptional craftsperson for excellence in the fine crafts; in addition to the cash award, works by the recipient are acquired by the Canadian Museum of Civilization.
Candidates must be nominated by the national or provincial crafts council, a previous recipient of the awards, a member association of the Canadian Craft Council or a single media guild. Laureates are chosen by a peer assessment committee of distinguished craftspersons & experts in the fine crafts

Victor Martyn Lynch-Staunton Awards
Each year the Canada Council designates several Canadian artists who have been awarded grants in music & visual arts as holders of Victor Martyn Lynch-Staunton Awards; this designation is made to honour the memory of the benefactor whose bequest to the Council enables it to increase the number of grants available to senior or established artists; the awards provide each recipient with $4,000 in addition to the arts grant, which is also provided by the income from this bequest

York Wilson Endowment Awards
$30,000 awarded annually; enables Canadian art museums & public art galleries to purchase original works by living, contemporary Canadian painters & sculptors; awarded through a Canada Council for the Arts competition, to an eligible Canadian institution to allow it to purchase an original artwork that would significantly enhance its collection of contemporaray Canadian painting or sculpture. Winner is chosen by a peer assessment committee of Canadian curators of contemporary art or other appropriate peers

Canadian Conference of the Arts / Conférence canadienne des arts
#804, 130 Albert St., Ottawa ON K1P 5G4
613/238-3561; Fax: 613/238-4849
Email: info@ccarts.ca; URL: www.ccarts.ca

Diplôme d'honneur
Established in 1954; presented annually to Canadians who have contributed outstanding service to the arts; recipients have included Vincent Massey, Wilfrid Pelletier, Maureen Forrester, Floyd Chalmers, Gabrielle Roy, Glenn Gould, Alfred Pellan, Bill Reid, Antonine Maillet

Canadian Historical Association / Société historique du Canada
395 Wellington St., Ottawa ON K1A 0N3
613/233-7885; Fax: 613/567-3110
Email: cha-shc@lac-bac.bc.ca; URL: www.cha-shc.ca

Albert B. Corey Prize
Established 1966 & jointly sponsored by the CHA & the American Historical Association; awarded every two years to the best book dealing with the history of Canadian-American relations or the history of both countries
$1,000

The Wallace K. Ferguson Prize
Established 1979; awarded annually for outstanding work in a field of history other than Canadian
$1,000

The City of Toronto
Chief Administrator's Office, City Hall, 100 Queen St. West, 11th Fl., East Tower, Toronto ON M5H 2N2
416/392-8592; Fax: 416/696-3645

Architecture & Urban Design Awards
Awarded every two years, this award recognizes and celebrates design excellence and in turn elevates public awareness of the vital role that design plays in Toronto

Conseil de la vie française en Amérique
#201, 5350, boul Henri-Bourassa, Québec QC G1H 6Y8
418/626-5665; Fax: 418/626-5663
Email: cvfa@cvfa.ca; URL: www.cvfa.ca/

L'Ordre du Conseil de la vie française en Amérique
Destiné à reconnaître les mérites exceptionnels d'un francophone ayant apporté une contribution significative au progrès des francophones et à la promotion des facteurs de vie et de la culture française en Amérique du Nord

Prix littéraire Champlain
1 500 $; vise à encourager en Amérique du Nord la production littéraire chez les francophones qui vivent à l'extérieur du Québec, d'une part, et à susciter chez les Québécois un intérêt pour les francophones qui sont en situation de minorité hors du Québec en Amérique du Nord

Fondation Émile-Nelligan
261, rue Bloomfield, Outremont QC H2V 3R6
514/278-4657; Fax: 514/271-6369
Email: info@fondation-nelligan.org; URL: www.fondation-nelligan.org

Prix Émile-Nelligan
Ce prix annuel date de 1979, année de la création de la Fontation Émile-Nelligan. C'est un prix de poésie décerné à des poètes de 35 ans ou moins, pour un recueil publié au cours de l'année.
7 500$

Prix Ozias-Leduc
Prix triennal en arts visuels (peinture, sculpture, gravure, installations, 'land art'). Décerné à un artiste citoyen du Canada né au Québec ou à un artiste citoyen du Canada ayant sa résidence principale au Québec depuis au moins dix ans
25 000$

Prix Gilles-Corbeil
Le prix Gilles-Corbeil est un prix de littérature. C'est un prix triennal et is al été décerné pour la première fois en 1990.
100 000$

Prix Serge-Garant
Le prix Serge-Garant est un prix de compostiion musicale. C'est un prix triennal qui a été décerné pour le première fois en 1991.
25 000$

The Gershon Iskowitz Foundation
#302, 862 Richmond St. West, Toronto ON M6J 1C9
416/351-0216; Fax: 416/351-0217

Gershon Iskowitz Prize
$25,000 to recognize achievements in visual art

Heritage Canada Foundation / Fondation Héritage Canada
5 Blackburn Ave., Ottawa ON K1N 8A2
613/237-1066; Fax: 613/237-5987
Email: heritagecanada@heritagecanada.org; URL: www.heritagecanada.org

Achievement Awards
Established 1989, these awards honour individuals or groups for their achievement in heritage advocacy and volunteerism, and for projects that demonstrate a community's commitment to heritage conservation. Local Heritage organizations are encouraged to submit nominations within prescribed criteria and eligibility rules. Each award is given jointly by the Heritage Canada Foundation and the heritage organization making the nomination. In this way, the Heritage Canada Foundation also recognizes the nominating organizations for their dedication and commitment to excellence in heritage conservation.

Gabrielle Léger Award
Recognizes outstanding work in architectural conservation in Canada; this is an annual national award to an individual who has contributed outstanding community service in the cause of heritage conservation

Lieutenant Governor's Award
Established 1979 to recognize outstanding work in architectural conservation on a provincial level by an individual or group
It must be demonstrated that the applicant's continuous efforts in the field of heritage conservation have benefited the province where the foundation's annual meeting is being held; applicants must be sponsored by an organized heritage group &/or elected officials at any level of government

Prince of Wales Prize
Established in 1999, awarded annually to a municipal government which has shown exemplary commitment to heritage preservation within its jurisdiction

Ontario Arts Council / Conseil des arts de l'Ontario
151 Bloor St. West, 5th Fl., Toronto ON M5S 1T6
416/961-1660; Fax: 416/961-7796; Toll Free: 1-800-387-0058
Email: info@arts.on.ca; URL: www.arts.on.ca
The Ontario Arts Council provides a variety of Funds and Scholarships for different studies and careers in the arts. For more information visit their website.

PEI Council of the Arts
115 Richmond St., Charlottetown PE C1A 1H7
902/368-6176; Fax: 902/368-4418 Toll Free: 1-888-734-2784
Email: info@peiartscouncil.com; URL: www.peica.ca

Father Adrien Arsenault Senior Arts Awards
The Price Edward Island Council of the Arts recognizes the achievements of artists on Prince Edward Island through a program of annual and bi-annual awards and prizes.

Island Literary Awards
These awards are given annually to Prince Edward Island's writers. Awards are made to all levels of the discipline from students, through senior memebers of the writing community.

Québec Ministère de la culture et des communications
225, Grande Allée est, Québec QC G1R 5G5
418/380-2300; Fax: 418/080-2364
Email: DC@mcc.gouv.qc.ca; URL: www.mcc.gouv.qc.ca

Les Prix du Québec:

Prix d'excellence en architecture
Ce prix souligne, depuis 1978, la contribution essentielle des architectes québecois au cadre bâti. Les prix accordés par l'Order des architectres du Québec permettent d'identifier et de valoriser les meilleures réalisations architecturales au Québec et ailleurs dans le monde.

Prix Paul-Émile-Borduas
Accordée à un artisan ou un artiste pour l'ensemble de son oeuvre dans le domaine des arts visuels, des métiers d'art, de l'architecture et du design

Royal Architectural Institute of Canada / Institut royal d'architecture du Canada
#330, 55 Murray St., Ottawa ON K1N 5M3
613/241-3600; Fax: 613/241-5750
Email: info@raic.org; URL: www.raic.org

Awards of Excellence
These awards are bestowed every two years, recognizing the greatest achievement in several different categories.

RAIC Gold Medal
Established 1930; this medal is awarded annually in recognition of an individual whose personal work has demonstrated exceptional excellence in the design and practice of architecture; and/or, whose work related to architecture, has demonstrated exceptional excellence in research or education.

The Royal Society of Canada / La Société royale du Canada
170 Waller St., Ottawa ON K1N 9B9
613/991-6990; Fax: 613/991-6996
Email: info@rsc.ca; URL: www.rsc.ca

Centenary Medal
Established 1982; awarded at irregular intervals in recognition of outstanding contributions to the object of the society & to recognize links to international organizations

Sir John William Dawson Medal
Established 1985; awarded for important & sustained contributions by one individual in at least two different fields in the general areas of interest of the Society or in a broad domain that transcends the usual disciplinary boundaries
$2,500 & a silver medal

The J.B. Tyrrell Historical Medal
Established 1927; awarded at least every two years for outstanding work in the history of Canada

Sobey Art Foundation
c/o Art Gallery of Nova Scotia
1723 Hollis Street, PO Box 2262, Halifax NS B3J 3C8
902/424.5169;
Email: fillmose@gov.ns.ca URL: www.sobeyartaward.ca

Sobey Art Award
Awarded every year to an artist 39 years old or younger who has shown their work in a public or commercial art gallery in Canada in the past 18 monthe.
$50 000

Social Sciences & Humanities Research Council of Canada
350 Albert St., PO Box 1610, Ottawa ON K1P 6G4
613/992-0691; Fax: 613/992-1787
Email: info@sshrc.ca; URL: www.sshrc.ca

Doctoral Fellowships
Must have completed one year of doctoral study or a master's degree leading to a Ph.D. or equivalent; disciplines include: Geography, Health Studies, Applied Health Studies & Environmental Studies
Approx. $14,400 per year

Postdoctoral Fellowships
To support a core of the most promising new scholars in the social sciences & humanities & to assist them in establishing a research base at an important time in their research career; provides stipendiary support to non-tenured PhD graduates who are undertaking new research, publishing research findings, developing & expanding personal research networks, broadening teaching experience & preparing to become competitive in national research competitions.
Approximately $38,000 per year (for a maximum of two years) plus a $5,000 accountable research allowance

The Bora Laskin National Fellowship in Human Rights Research
To support interdisciplinary or multidisciplinary research & the development of expertise in the field of human rights, with emphasis on Canadian human rights issues
$45,000 stipend plus $10,000 for research & research-related travel expenses

The Jules & Gabrielle Léger Fellowship
Awarded to promote research & writing on the historical contribution of the Crown & its representatives, federal & provincial, to the political, constitutional, cultural, intellectual & social life of the country.
Award is for $40,000, plus $10,000 for research & research -travel expenses

Société Saint-Jean-Baptiste de Montréal
82, rue Sherbrooke Ouest, Montréal QC H2X 1X3
514/843-8851; Fax: 514/844-6369
Email: mbeaulieu@ssjb.com; URL: www.ssjb.com

Prix Esdras-Minville
Créé en 1978; décerné à une personnalité canadienne-française qui s'illustre dans le domaine des sciences humaines

Prix Louis Philippe-Hébert
Créé en 1971; décerné à une personnalité canadienne-française qui s'illustre dans le domaine des arts plastiques

Prix Victor-Morin
Créé en 1962; décerné à une personnalité canadienne-française qui s'illustre dans le domaine des arts de la scène

Toronto Arts Council Foundation
141 Bathurst St., Toronto ON M5V 2R2
416/392-6800; Fax: 416/392-6920
Email: mail@torontoartscouncil.org; URL: www.torontoartscouncil.org

Margo Bindhardt Award
$10,000 cash prize presented every second year to Toronto artist or administrator whose leadership & vision, whether through their creative work or cultural activism, have had a significant impact on the arts in Toronto & for whom the cash prize will make a difference

Marilyn Lastman Award
$5,000 cash prize presented to a professional artist or arts administrator who is a Toronto resident & who has made a significant contribution in the field of arts education. Awarded every second year

Muriel Sherrin Award
$10,000 cash prize presented to an artist or creator who has made a contribution to the cultural life of Toronto through outstanding achievement in music. The recipient will also have participated in international initiatives, including touring, study abroad & artist exchanges. Awarded every second year

Rita Davies Award
$5,000 cash prize presented to a Toronto artist, volunteer or administrator who has demonstrated creative leadership in the development of arts & culture in Toronto. Awarded every second year

William Kilbourn Award
$5,000 cash prize presented to an individual performer, teacher, administrator or creator in any arts discipline, including architecture & design, whose work is a celebration of life through the arts in Toronto. Awarded every second year

Ville de Montréal
Service du développement culturel
5650, d'Iberville, 4e étage, Montréal QC H2G 3E4
514/872-1156
URL: www.ville.montreal.qc.ca/culture/culture.htm

Prix François-Houdé
La Ville de Montréal, en collaboration avec le Conseil des métiers d'art du Québec décerne annuellement ce Prix afin de promouvoir l'excellence de la nouvelle création montréalaise en métiers d'art et de favoriser la diffusion d'oeuvres des jeunes artisans créateurs. Bourse de 3000$ et 2 500$ pour organiser une exposition

Prix Louis-Comtois
La Ville de Montréal, en collaboration avec l'Association des galeries d'art contemporain, décerne annuellement ce Prix qui vient apppuyer et promouvoir le travail d'un artiste en mi-carrière qui s'est distingué dans le domaine de l'art contemporain à Montréal depuis les 15 dernières années. Bourse 5000$ et 2 500$ pour organiser une exposition solo

Prix Pierre-Ayot
La Ville de Montréal, en collaboration avec l'Association des galeries d'art contemporain, décerne annuellement ce Prix qui souligne la facture exceptionnelle et l'apport original de la production des jeunes artistes en peinture, en estampe, en dessin, en illustration, en photographie ou tout autre médium. Bourse 3000$ et 2 500$ pour organiser une exposition solo

EDUCATIONAL

Alberta Scholarship Programs
PO Box 28000, Stn Main, Edmonton AB T5J 4R4
780/427-8640; Fax: 780/427-1288
Email: scholarships@gov.ab.ca; URL: www.alis.gov.ab.ca/scholarships/main.asp

Alberta Scholarships Program
32 scholarships & awards are available in various fields of study

Association for Media & Technology in Education in Canada / Association des médias et de la technologie en éducation au Canada
#1318, 3-1750 The Queensway, Etobicoke ON M9C 5H5
URL: www.amtec.ca

AMTEC Leadership Award
Two awards recognize outstanding individual achievement & leadership in the field of educational media & technology
Association of Canadian Universities for Northern Studies / Association universitaire canadienne d'études nordiques
#405, 17 York St., Ottawa ON K1N 9J6
613/562-0515; Fax: 613/562-0533
Email: awards@acuns.ca; URL: www.acuns.ca/

Studentships in Northern Studies
Research culminating in a thesis or similar document involving direct northern experience; for students enrolled in graduate & undergraduate degree programs or other courses of study recognized at a Canadian university with special relevance to Canada's northern territories & adjacent regions
$10,000

Association of Universities & Colleges of Canada / Association des universités et collèges du Canada
#600, 350 Albert St., Ottawa ON K1R 1B1
613/563-1236; Fax: 613/563-9745
Email: awards@aucc.ca; URL: www.aucc.ca

AUCC Scholarship for Students with Disabilities
Scholarships open to students entering full-time studies leading to a first undergraduate degree
Up to ten $5,000

Bowater Maritimes Scholarship Program
Scholarships open to grade 12 New Brunswick students
Three $1,500 for undergraduate studies

CATSA - Brian Flemming Research Fellowship and Security Award
Scholarship open to doctoral or post-doctoral research relating to tactical and strategic issues of Canadian aviation security screening
$15,000

C.D. Howe Memorial Foundation Engineering Awards
(One male, one female) for students who have completed the first year of an engineering program
Two $7,500 scholarships

C.D. Howe Scholarship Program
Scholarships open to all disciplines but for students from Thunder Bay or the following school boards: Lakehead, Lakehead District R.C., Lake Superior, North of Superior District R.C., Geraldton, Geraldton District R.C., Nipigon-Red Rock, & Hornepayne
Two $5,500

Cable Telecommunications Research Fellowship (Canadian Cable Telecommunications Association)
Scholarship awarded annually to students pursuing a master's degree in any discipline directly related to the development & delivery of cable in Canada
$5,000

CIBC Youthvision Scholarship
Must be enrolled in Big Brothers/Big Sisters of Canada
30 scholarships: $4,000 or actual tuition fees, plus paid summer employment with YMCA Canada

Conocophillips Canada Centennial Scholarship
Scholarship program encourages individuals with academic excellence and demonstrated leadership.
Three scholarships of up to $10,000 per year for a maximum of 2 consecutive years

Department of National Defence Security & Defence Forum
Eight $8,000 (master's), four $16,000 (doctorate) scholarships & two $35,000 (post-doctoral) fellowships in studies relating to current & future Canadian natural security & defence issues. Three internships of up to 12 months worth $32,000 to help recent MA graduates obtain work experience in security & defence studies by working in this field in the non-governmental or private sectors.

Fessenden-Trott Awards
Scholarships open to all disciplines; restricted to Ontario in 2005
Four $9,000

Frank Knox Memorial Fellowship Program
Awards, plus tuition fees & health insurance for Canadian citizens or permanent residents who have graduated from a AUCC member institution before Sept. 2005 & wish to study at Harvard in the following disciplines: arts & sciences (including engineering), business administration, design, divinity studies, education, law, public administration, medicine, dental medicine & public health; applications for students currently studying in the US will not be considered
Up to three US$18,500

Mattinson Endowment Fund Scholarship for Disabled Students
For undergraduate study, all disciplines
$2,500

Programme canadien de bourses de la Francophonie
Scholarship based on merit for especially deserving and motivated applicants, funded by the Canadian International Development Agency. Awarded by competition for professional training in leading-edge technologies at the college level (certificate or diploma) or for undergraduate, master's or doctoral studies at a university

Public Safety & Emergency Prepardeness Canada Research Fellowship in Honour of Stuart Nesbitt White
For research in the area of disaster/emergency research & planning; preference is given to applicants who hold a Master's degree & who are planning research in the following fields: Urban & Regional Planning, Economics, Earth Sciences, Risk Analysis & Management, Systems Science, Social Sciences, Business Administration & Health Administration
Eight up to $19,250

Queen Elizabeth Silver Jubilee Endowment Fund for Study in a Second Official Language Award Program
Scholarships open to all disciplines, except translations, for students studying in their second language
Three $5,000 (plus travel costs)

TD Canada Trust Scholarship for Outstanding Community Leadership
All disciplines, undergraduate degrees
20 renewable scholarships for $5,000 living stipend, plus all tuition & compulsory fees, plus summer employment

BC Ministry of Advanced Education
PO Box 9173, Stn Prov Govt, Victoria BC V8W 9H7
250/387-6100; Fax: 250/356-9455; Toll Free: 1-800-561-1818
URL: www.bcsap.bc.ca

Governor General's Academic Medal Award
Awards medals to college & university students achieving the highest academic standing upon graduation

Irving K. Barber Scholarship
Up to 150 scholarships worth $5,000 annually; open to students who have completed two years at a BC community college, university college or institute & must transfer to a public degree-granting institution in BC in order to complete their degrees

Lieutenant Governor's Silver Medal Award
Honours students registered in a vocational or career program of less than two years duration, who have excelled academically, & have contributed to the life of the college or institute or their community

Premier's Excellence Award
Recognizes the top all-around graduating secondary students, from the 15 college regions in BC, who are proceeding to full-time post secondary education in BC

United World College Scholarships
Valued at approximately $60,000, the award covers full tuition & residence for two years at the Lester B. Pearson College of the Pacific; the International Baccalaureate allows students to finish their final year of high school & earn credit towards the first year of university

Black Business & Professional Association
#210, 675 King St. West, Toronto ON M5V 1M9
416/504-4097; Fax: 416/504-7343
Email: bbpa@bellnet.ca; URL: www.bbpa.org

Harry Jerome Scholarships
Scholarship celebrates excellence in achievement in the Black community. Award recipients are selected from among Canada-wide nominees recommended by business and professional colleagues, teachers, relatives and friends.
Five $2,000 annual awards

The Canada Council for the Arts / Conseil des Arts du Canada
350 Albert St., PO Box 1047, Ottawa ON K1P 5V8
613/566-4414; Fax: 613/566-4390; Toll Free: 1-800-263-5588
Email: info@canadacouncil.ca; URL: www.canadacouncil.ca

Coburn Fellowships
Up to three $20,000 fellowships are awarded annually to a Canadian student (at Victoria University or the University of Toronto) & an Israeli student, in the fields of fine arts or humanities, to study on a reciprocal basis; they are intended to cover travel expenses, tuition & accommodation costs for a year; winners are chosen by Victoria University

John G. Diefenbaker Award
Funded by the Government of Canada, this annual award honours the memory of former Prime Minister John G. Diefenbaker; it enables a German scholar to spend up to 12 months in Canada to pursue research in any of the disciplines in the social sciences & humanities; candidates must be nominated by university departments or research institutes in Canada. Value of full award is $75,000; in addition, the Social Sciences & Humanities Research Council of Canada provides a travel allowance of up to $20,000

Canadian Association of University Business Officers / Association canadienne du personnel administratif universitaire
#320, 350 Albert St., Ottawa ON K1R 1B1
613/230-6760; Fax: 613/563-7739
Email: cworkman@caubo.ca; URL: www.caubo.ca

CAUBO Quality & Productivity Awards
Designed to recognize, reward & share university achievements in improving the quality & reducing the cost of higher education programs & services; National & Regional categories
Awards evaluated on portability, originality, quality impact, productivity impact, & involvement
National: first prize $10,000; second prize $5,000; third prize $3,000

Canadian Mathematical Society / Société mathématique du Canada
#109, 577 King Edward St., Ottawa ON K1N 6N5
613/562-5702; Fax: 613/565-1539
Email: office@cms.math.ca; URL: www.cms.math.ca

Canadian Mathematical Olympiad
Annual mathematics competition established to provide an opportunity for students to perform well on the Canadian Open Mathematics Challenge & to complete on a national basis.
Fifteen cash prizes

Canadian Merit Scholarship Foundation
#502 - 460 Richmond Street West St., Toronto ON M5V 1Y1
416/646-2120; Fax: 416/646-0846; Toll Free: 1-866-544-2673
URL: www.cmsf.ca

Finalist Award
Given to every finalist who is selected for & attends, National Selections
$2,500 awarded to outstanding students from across the country as one-time entrance awards to be used at any accredited Canadian university

National Award
Up to $8,000 per year plus a tuition stipend, for up to four years of full-time undergraduate study at any one of our participating Canadian universities

Provincial Award
One-time entrance award tenable at any accredited university in Canada at which the recipient gains admission & enrolls in a full-time program of study
$1,500

Regional Award
One-time entrance award tenable at any accredited university in Canada at which the recipient gains admission & enrolls in a full-time program of study
$1,500

Canadian Sociology & Anthropology Association / Société canadienne de sociologie et d'anthropologie
Université Concordia University SB-323
1455, De Maisonneuve Ouest, Montréal QC H3G 1M8
514/848-8780; Fax: 514/848-8780
Email: info@csaa.ca; URL: www.csaa.ca

John Porter Award
Recognizes outstanding published scholarly contributions within the "John Porter Tradition" to the advancement of sociological and/or anthropological knowledge in Canada
Outstanding Contribution Award
Given to recognize the work of eminent sociologists & anthropologists

Best Student Paper Award
Recognizes the best paper among those received for adjudication, written by a graduate student

CIDA Awards Program
Canadian Bureau for International Education
#1550, 220 Laurier Ave. West, Ottawa ON K1P 5Z9
613/237-4820; Fax: 613/237-1073
Email: info@cbie.ca; URL: www.cbie.ca

Awards for Canadians
A program funded by CIDA & managed by the Canadian Bureau for International Education; CIDA wishes to increase the number of Canadian professionals capable of working in the international arena by providing funding up to $15,000 for short-term, overseas work experiences
Must possess a university degree, college diploma or professional designation, have substantial work experience, two years of which have involved using specific skills necessary to undertake the proposed project. For information on fields of specialization & eligible countries, contact CIDA Communications Branch, 200 Promenade du Portage, Hull PQ K1A 0G4; 819/997-5006; Fax: 819/953-6088. Other information & applications should be sent to the CBIE at the above address

Foundation for Educational Exchange Between Canada & the United States of America
#2015, 350 Albert St., Ottawa ON K1R 1A4
613/688-5540; Fax: 613/237-2029
Email: info@fulbright.ca; URL: www.fulbright.ca

Canada-US Fulbright Program
To expand research, teaching & study opportunities for Canadian & American faculty & students engaged in the study of Canada, the United States & the relationship between the two countries; based on academic excellence & the merit of the applicant's proposed project, awards given annually for study in a number of different fields including conservation, ecology, environmental management, resource analysis & environmental policy. Applicants must relocate from the U.S. to Canada, or Canada to the U.S.
$15,000 US for graduate students; $25,000 US for faculty

International Development Research Centre / Centre de recherches pour le développement international
250 Albert St., Ottawa ON K1G 3H9
613/236-6163; Fax: 613/238-7230
Email: info@idrc.ca; URL: www.idrc.ca

Canadian Window on International Development Awards
Award offered for doctoral research that explores the relationship between Canadian aid, trade, immigration & diplomatic policy, & international development & the alleviation of global policy
Applicants must hold Canadian citizenship or permanent residency status; be registered at a Canadian university; be conducting the proposed research for a doctoral dissertation & have completed course work & passed comprehensive examinations by the time of the award tenure
$20,000 per year - Centre Training & Awards Unit, 613/236-6163 ext 2098; Fax: 613/563-0815; Email: cta@idrc.ca

Centre Internships
These awards provide exposure to research for international development through program work & research under the guidance of IDRD program staff. Internships will be considered for a program of work & research responding to IDRC's current Program Initiatives
The program is aimed at candidates who, through demonstrated achievements in academic studies, work or research, have shown interest in the creation & utilization of knowledge from an international perspective. Candidates can be both Canadians (or permanent residents) or citizens of developing countries, & will have had some training at the master's level. Candidates need not be affiliated with an institution. They may participate in internships as part of an academic requirement
Stipend $2,500 - $28,000 per year - Centre Training & Awards Unit, 613/236-6163 ext 2098; Fax: 613/563-0815; Email cta@irdc.ca

The Japan Foundation, Toronto / Kokosai Koryu Kikin Toronto Nihon Bunka Centre
#213, 131 Bloor St. West, Toronto ON M5S 1R1
416/966-1600; Fax: 416/966-9773
Email: info@jftor.org; URL: www.japanfoundationcanada.org

The Japan Foundation Fellowships
Scholars, researchers, artists & other professionals are provided an opportunity to conduct research or pursue projects in Japan. Term of award is from two to 14 months, depending on category; annual application deadline is Dec. 1 for funding year beginning the following April 1

The Japan Foundation Scholarships & Programs
The Foundation offers a wide range of programs in more than 180 countries, including the following: exchange of persons (fellowships); support for Japanese-language instruction; support for Japanese studies; support for arts-related exchange; support for media exchange

National Aboriginal Achievement Foundation
#450 - 215 Spadina Ave., Toronto ON M5T 2C7
416/926-0775; Fax: 416/926-7554; Toll Free: 1-800-329-9780
Email: info@naaf.ca; URL: www.naaf.ca

National Aboriginal Achievement Foundation Scholarships
Established 1985; provides scholarships to Aboriginal students for post-secondary education

Northern Enterprise Fund Inc.
PO Box 220, Beauval SK S0M 0G0
306/288-2258; Fax: 306/288-4667; Toll Free: 1-800-864-3022
Email: info@nefi.ca; URL: www.nefi.ca

Northern Spirit Scholarship Program
To promote entrepreneurial spirit in Northern Saskatchewan by providing scholarships to students enrolled in courses related to business or based on occupational shortages in the north
Ten $2,500 scholarships are awarded to full-time students who are permanent northern residents of the Northern Administration District; priority will be given to applicants showing intention of returning to, or remaining in the north; with an academic record of 70% average in most recent year completed

Ontario Council on Graduate Studies / Conseil ontarien des études supérieures
#1100, 180 Dundas St. West, Toronto ON M5G 1Z8
416/979-2165; Fax: 416/595-7392
Email: kpanesar@cou.on.ca; URL: ocgs.cou.on.ca/

John Charles Polanyi Prizes
In honour of the achievement of John Charles Polanyi, co-recipient of the 1986 Nobel Prize in Chemistry, the Government of Ontario has established a fund to provide annually up to five prizes to persons continuing to post-doctoral studies at an Ontario university; prizes available in the areas of Physics, Chemistry, Physiology or Medicine, Literature & Economic Science
$15,000

Ordre des conseillers en ressources humaines et en relations industrielles agréés du Québec
#1400, 1200, av McGill College, Montréal QC H3B 4G7
514/879-1636; Fax: 514/879-1722; Toll Free: 1 (800) 214-1609
Email: info@orhri.org; URL: www.orhri.org

EXCALIBUR: Le tournoi universitaire canadien en ressources humaines
Promouvoir un enseignement de la gestion des ressources humaines dans les universités canadiennes préparant les étudiants au marché du travail
3 000$; 2 250$; 1 500$

The Royal Society of Canada / La Société royale du Canada
170 Waller St., Ottawa ON K1N 9B9
613/991-6990; Fax: 613/991-6996
Email: info@rsc.ca; URL: www.rsc.ca

Innis-Gérin Medal
Established 1966; awarded every two years for a distinguished & sustained contribution to the literature of the social sciences including human geography & social psychology

Pierre Chauveau Medal
Established 1951; awarded every two years (since 1966) for a distinguished contribution to knowledge in the humanities other than Canadian literature & Canadian history

Social Sciences & Humanities Research Council of Canada
350 Albert St., PO Box 1610, Ottawa ON K1P 6G4
613/992-0691; Fax: 613/992-1787
Email: info@sshrc.ca; URL: www.sshrc.ca

The Thérèse F.-Casgrain Fellowship
$40,000 stipend awarded every second year (2004, 2006, etc.) to support research on women & social change in Canada

Yukon Government
PO Box 2703, Whitehorse YT Y1A 2C6
867/667-5811; Fax: 867/393-6339
Email: information@gov.yk.ca

Excellence in Education Award
Awarded to individuals or groups that have demonstrated innovation, superior dedication or outstanding service to public school education in the Yukon; winners receive a specially commissioned artwork created by Ted Harrison

ENVIRONMENTAL

Alberta Emerald Foundation for Environmental Excellence
c/o McLennan Ross LLP, #400, 12220 Stony Plain Rd., Edmonton AB T5N 3Y4
780/413-9629; Fax: 780/482-9100; Toll Free: 1-800-219-8329
Email: info@emeraldawards.com; URL: www.emeraldawards.com

Emerald Awards
Awarded to Albertans who have made a significant contribution to the protection or enhancement of the environment
Nominations are open to individual, not-for-profit organizations, business & industry, communities & government, educational institutions & volunteer organizations excelling in environmental achievements

Alberta Sustainable Resource Development
Fish & Wildlife Division
Information Centre, Main Floor, 9920 - 108 St. Edmonton AB T5K 2M4
780/944-0313; Fax: 780/427-4407
URL: www.srdgov.ab.ca

Order of the Bighorn
Fish & wildlife conservation awards presented every other year, to individuals, organizations & corporations for their outstanding contributions to fish & wildlife conservation in Alberta - Program Manager, Dave England

Association of Universities & Colleges of Canada / Association des universités et collèges du Canada
#600, 350 Albert St., Ottawa ON K1R 1B1
613/563-1236; Fax: 613/563-9745
Email: info@aucc.ca; URL: www.aucc.ca

Cement Association of Canada Environmental Scholarship Program
Open to students in Alberta, British Columbia, Newfoundland, Nova Scotia, Ontario & Quebec who have fully completed the two years of course work in an environmental science or environmental engineering program that is required to continue a third year of their eligible program
Six $2,000

Atlantic Salmon Federation / Fédération du saumon atlantique
15 Rankine Mill Road, Chamcook NB E5B 3A9
506/529-1033; Fax: 506/529-4438; Toll Free: 1-800-565-5666
Email: tiffinic@nb.aibn.com; URL: www.asf.ca

Affiliate of the Year
Recognizes outstanding leadership & achievement in Atlantic salmon conservation within the federation's affiliate structure
Engraved plaque & a cheque for $500 to be used toward its conservation programs - Muriel Ferguson, Manager, Public Information

Olin Fellowship
Fellowships offered annually to individuals seeking to improve their knowledge or skills in fields dealing with current problems in biology, management, or conservation of Atlantic salmon & its habitat; the fellowship may be applied toward a wide range of endeavours such as salmon management, graduate study, & research.

Applicants need not be enrolled in a degree program, but must be legal residents of the US or Canada
$1,000-$3,000 - Ellen Merrill

Roll of Honour
Presented annually to individuals who exhibit outstanding commitment to salmon conservation at the grassroots level
ASF member in good standing - Muriel Ferguson, Manager, Public Information

T.B. (Happy) Fraser Award
Presented annually to an individual who has made outstanding long-term contributions to Atlantic salmon conservation in Canada. The award reflects efforts on a regional or national level - Muriel Ferguson, Manager, Public Information

BC Ministry of Environment
PO Box 9339, Stn Prov Govt, Victoria BC V8W 9M1
250/387-9422
URL: www.gov.bc.ca/wlap/

Minister's Environmental Awards
Awarded for identifying, reducing, solving or avoiding an environmental problem; demonstrating consistently responsible environmental management practices; &/or promoting public awareness, understanding & active concern for the enhancement & protection of the environment
Categories include individual citizen, youth, government, community or non-profit organization, business, industry or labour, environmental educator, scientist or innovator, environmental steward by nomination

Canadian Land Reclamation Association / Association canadienne de réhabilitation des sites dégradés
PO Box 61047, RPO Kensington, Calgary AB T2N 4S6
403/289-9435; Fax: 403/289-9435
Email: clra@telusplanet.net; URL: www.clra.ca

Dr. Edward M. Watkin Award
Presented annually to an association member in recognition of outstanding contribution to the field of reclamation, through research, field work, teaching or innovation, or distinguished service to the association through active participation & leadership

The Noranda Land Reclamation Award
Presented annually by the association on behalf of Noranda Mines Inc. in recognition of superior research or field work in reclamation; not restricted to members

Canadian Wildlife Federation / Fédération canadienne de la faune
350 Michael Cowpland Dr., Kanata ON K2M 2W1
613/599-9594; Fax: 613/599-4428; Toll Free: 1-800-563-9453
Email: info@cwf-fcf.org; URL: www.cwf-fcf.org

Canadian Conservation Achievement Awards Program:

Roderick Haig-Brown Memorial Award
Awarded annually to an individual who has made a significant contribution to furthering the sport of angling &/or conservation & wise use of Canada's recreational fisheries resources

Roland Michener Conservation Award
A trophy is given annually in recognition of an individual's outstanding achievement in the field of conservation in Canada

Stan Hodgkiss Outdoorsman of the Year Award
Presented annually to an outdoorsperson who has demonstrated an active commitment to conservation in Canada

Centre for Environment
University of Toronto, #1016, 33 Wilcocks St.
Toronto ON M5S 3E8
416/978-7077; Fax: 416/978-3884
Email: centre.environment@utoronto.ca; URL: www.environment.utoronto.ca/

Adaptation & Impacts Research Group (AIRG) Annual Prize
Awarded to a qualified graduate student for the best research paper addressing one or more of AIRG's reseach directions. This includes impacts of, & adaptation to, climate change/variability & extreme events; atmospheric natural hazards/disasters & societal adjustment; & integrated assessment of multiple atmospheric issues (climate change, stratospheric ozone depletion, acidic deposition & air quality), particularly in terms of their cumulative effects on human health

Energy Probe Research Foundation
225 Brunswick Ave., Toronto ON M5S 2M6
416/964-9223; Fax: 416/964-8239
Email: webadmin@eprf.ca; URL: www.eprf.ca/eprf/index.html

The Margaret Laurence Fund
Grants & scholarships are made to foster an understanding of peace & the environment upon which the fate of the planet rests
Recipients of the grants & scholarships are limited to students, authors, researchers, & publishers, working with the foundation in collaborative projects approved by the directors

Environment Canada
70 Crémazie St., Gatineau QC K1A 0H3
819/997-2800; Fax: 819/994-1412; Toll Free: 1-800-668-6767
Email: enviroinfo@ec.gc.ca; URL: www.ec.gc.ca

Canadian Environment Awards
Annual awards to honour initiatives in the areas of clean air, environmental learning, sustainable living, climate change, clean water, environmental health, lands & forests, wildlife & nature

International Development Research Centre / Centre de recherches pour le développement international
250 Albert St., Ottawa ON K1P 6M1
613/236-6163; Fax: 613/238-7230
Email: info@idrc.ca; URL: www.idrc.ca

Ecosystem Approaches to Human Health Training Awards
Supports research that focuses on ecosystem management interventions leading to the improvement of human health & well-being while simultaneously maintaining or improving the condition of the ecosystem as a whole. Awards will be granted for training & research linked to the Ecosystem Approaches to Human Health Program Initiatives of the Centre. Priority will be give to proposals for research on ecosystems that are stressed through agriculture, urbanization or mining activities.
Citizens of developing countries &/or Canadian citizens or landed immigrants students currently enrolled in a graduate programme at a recognized university in Canada or in a developing country. Relevant language proficiency for site of study
Up to 6 awards for a maximum of $15,000 - Centre Training & Awards Unit, 613/236-6163 ext 2098; Fax: 563-0815; Email: cta@idrc.da

IDRC Doctoral Research Awards (IDRA)
Supports the field research of Canadian graduate students enrolled in a Canadian university for doctoral research on a topic of relevance to sustainable & equitable development
Applicants must hold Canadian citizenship or permanent residency status; be registered at a Canadian university; research proposal is for a doctoral thesis; provide evidence of affiliation with an institution or organization in the region in which the research will take place; have completed course work & passed comprehensive examinations by the time of award tenure
Maximum of $20,000 per year - Centre Training & Awards Unit, 613/236-6163 ext 2098; Fax: 613/563-0815; Email: cta@irdc.ca

John G. Bene Fellowship: Community Forestry, Trees & People
Contributes to the expenses of Canadian graduate students undertaking field research in social forestry in a developing country
Applicants must be Canadian citizens or hold permanent residency status; be registered in a Canadian university at the master's or doctoral level; have an academic background that combines forestry or agroforestry with social sciences. Applicants from interdisciplinary programs (e.g. environmental studies) may also be eligible, provided their programs contain the specified elements
$15,000 per year - Centre Training & Awards Unit, 613/236-6163 ext. 2098; Fax: 613/563-0815; Emails cta@irdc.ca

Newfoundland & Labrador Department of Environment & Conservation
Confederation Bldg., West Block, 4th Fl., PO Box 8700, St. John's NL A1B 4J6
709/729-2664; Fax: 709/729-6639
Email: info@gov.nl.ca; URL: www.env.gov.nl.ca/env/

The Newfoundland & Labrador Environmental Awards Program
Established in partnership with the Newfoundland & Labrador Women's Institutes Multi-Materials Stewardship Board & the Dept. of Environment to create public awareness for the proactive environmental actions being taken by Newfoundlanders & Labradorians; the object is to demonstrate the contributions people are making to create a healthier environment & through their efforts, encourage others to do the same; awards are given in seven categories: individual, citizen's group or organization, educator, youth, school, business, & municipal - Newfoundland & Labrador Women's Institutes, Executive Director, Sylvia Manning, 709/753-8780; email nlwi@nfld.com

Recycling Council of Ontario / Conseil du recyclage de l'Ontario
#407 - 215 Spadina Av., Toronto ON M5T 2C7
416/657-2797; Fax: 416/960-8053
Email: rco@rco.on.ca; URL: www.rco.on.ca

Ontario Waste Minimization Awards
A series of awards for outstanding achievement in recycling: includes 3Rs initiatives in commercial, industrial & institutional settings; Outstanding Municipal, Non-profit Organization, Recycling Program Operator; Outstanding School Program, & Media Contribution Award - Tracy Sakamoto

The Royal Society of Canada / La Société royale du Canada
170 Waller St., Ottawa ON K1N 9B9
613/991-6990; Fax: 613/991-6996
Email: info@rsc.ca; URL: www.rsc.ca

Miroslaw Romanowski Medal
Established in 1994; awarded every year in recognition of significant contributions to the resolution of scientific aspects of environmental problems or for important improvements to the quality of an eco-system in all aspects, terrestrial, atmospheric & aqueous brought about by scientific means.
$3,000 & a medal - Geneviève Gouin, Awards Coordinator, 613/991-5760

HEALTH & MEDICAL

Canadian Association of Medical Radiation Technologists / Association canadienne des technologues en radiation médicale
#500, 1095 Carling Ave., Ottawa ON K1Y 4P6
613/234-0012; Fax: 613/234-1097; Toll Free: 1-800-463-9729
Email: lgoulet@camrt.ca; URL: www.camrt.ca

CAMRT Awards
Administers awards for students & registered technologists including: Dr. M. Mallett Student Award, Dr. Petrie Memorial Award, George Reason Memorial Cup, E.I. Hood Award, CAMRT Student Achievement Award, Philips Rose Bowl, PACS Technology Award

Canadian Association on Gerontology / Association canadienne de gérontologie
#106 - 222 College St., Toronto ON M5T 3J1
416/978-7977; Fax: 416/978-4771
Email: contact@cagacg.ca; URL: www.cagacg.ca

CAG Award for Contribution to Gerontology
To recognize an individual who has recently made an outstanding contribution to the field of aging
Certificate

Canadian Federation for Sexual Health / Fédération canadienne pour la santé sexuelle
#430, One Nicholas St., Ottawa ON K1N 7B7
613/241-4474; Fax: 613/241-7550; Toll Free: 1-888-270-7444
Email: admin@cfsh.ca; URL: www.cfsh.ca

John & Lois Lamont Scholarship
Established 2004; awarded to a full-time graduate student in the field of sexual & reproductive health
$2,600

Phyllis P. Harris Scholarship
Endowed in the memory of Phyllis P. Harris, who for over thirty years was an inspiring presence in the world of family planning. This scholarship is awarded to a volunteer or individual currently enrolled in undergraduate studies in the general field of human sexuality, family planning or population including: biology, education, history, medicine, political science, psychology.
$2,600

Canadian Institutes of Health Research
160 Elgin St., 9th Floor; Address Locator 4809A, Ottawa ON K1A 0W9
613/941-2672; Fax: 613/954-1800; Toll Free: 1-888-603-4178
Email: info@cihr-irsc.gc.ca; URL: www.cihr-irsc.gc.ca

Michael Smith Prize in Health Research
A medal plus $50,000 research grant awarded annually to an outstanding Canadian researcher who has demonstrated innovation, creativity & dedication to health research

Canadian Nurses Association / Association des infirmières et infirmiers du Canada
50 Driveway, Ottawa ON K2P 1E2
613/237-2133; Fax: 613/237-3520; Toll Free: 1-800-361-8404
Email: info@cna-aiic.ca; URL: www.cna-aiic.ca

Jeanne Mance Awards
Established in 1971, this award is named after one of Canada's most inspirational nurses. Awarded every other year, Nurses nominated for this have have made significant and innovative contributions to the health of Canadians.

Canadian Orthopaedic Foundation / Fondation orthopédique du Canada
PO Box 7029, Innisfil ON L9S 1A8
416/410-2341; Toll Free: 1-800-461-3639
Email: mailbox@canorth.org; URL: www.canorth.org

I. Edouard Samson Award
Medal & $15,000 awarded for outstanding orthopaedic research by a young investigator; paper presented at the annual meeting of the Canadian Orthopaedic Research Society

Canadian Society for Medical Laboratory Science / Société canadienne de science de laboratoire médical
PO Box 2830, Stn LCD 1, Hamilton ON L8N 3N8
905/528-8642; Fax: 905/528-4968; Toll Free: 1-800-263-8277
Email: michellee@csmls.org; URL: www.csmls.org

CSMLS Student Scholarship Program
Awarded to the best students who are enrolled in general medical laboratory technology, cytotechnology, or cytogenetics studies
Five scholarships of $500 each

E.V. Booth Scholarship Award
Awarded to certified medical laboratory technologists who are enrolled in studies leading to a degree in medical laboratory science
Two awards of $500

Canadian Veterinary Medical Association / Association canadienne des médecins vétérinaires
339 Booth St., Ottawa ON K1R 7K1
613/236-1162; Fax: 613/236-9681; Toll Free: 1-800-567-2862
Email: admin@cvma-acmv.org; URL: www.canadianveterinarians.net; www.veterinairesaucanada.net

The CVMA Humane Award
Established 1986 to encourage care & well-being of animals; awarded to an individual (veterinarian or non-veterinarian) whose work is judged to have contributed significantly to the welfare & well-being of animals; $1,000 & a plaque awarded

The Schering Veterinary Award
Established 1985 to enhance progress in large animal medicine & surgery; award made to a veterinarian whose work in large animal practice, clinical research or basic sciences is judged to have contributed significantly to the advancement of large animal medicine, surgery & theriogenology, including herd health management; $1,000 & a plaque awarded

The Small Animal Practitioner Award
Established 1987 to encourage progress in the field of small animal medicine & surgery; awarded to a veterinarian whose work in small animal practice, clinical research or basic sciences is judged to have contributed significantly to the advancement of small animal medicine, surgery, or the management of small animal practice, including the advancement of the public's knowledge of the responsibilities of pet ownership; $1,000 & a plaque awarded

Catholic Health Association of Canada / Association catholique canadienne de la santé
1247 Kilborn Pl., Ottawa ON K1H 6K9
613/731-7148; Fax: 613/731-7797
Email: info@chac.ca; URL: www.chac.ca

Performance Citation Award
Established 1981; awarded annually to an individual who makes an outstanding contribution to health care in a Christian context, who exhibits exemplary leadership of a national effort at building the Christian community & unselfish dedication to others

College of Family Physicians of Canada / Collège des médecins de famille du Canada
2630 Skymark Ave., Mississauga ON L4W 5A4
905/629-0900; Fax: 905/629-0893; Toll Free: 800/387-6197
Email: info@cfpc.ca; URL: www.cfpc.ca

D.I. Rice Merit Award
Awarded annually to a renowned leader in family medicine to allow travel for a period of approximately one month in order to engage in educational activities
$10,000 plus travel expenses

Family Physician of the Year Award
Sponsored by Janseen Ortho; awarded to physicians who have been in family practice for a minimum of 15 years & members of the college for at least 10 years, & who have made outstanding contributions to family medicine, to their communities & to the college

Family Medicine Researcher of the Year Award
Sponsored by the CFPC'S Research & Education Foundation, this award recognizes a Family Medicine researcher who has been a pivotal force in the definition, development and dissemination of concepts central to the discipline of family medicine.

Easter Seals Canada / Timbres de Pâques Canada
#208, 90 Eglinton Ave. East, Toronto ON M4P 2Y3
416/932-8382; Fax: 416/932-9844
Email: info@easterseals.ca; URL: www.easterseals.ca

The Easter Seals Canada Leadership Award
Established in 1959 as the Timmy Award, is intended to celebrate & recognize outstanding leadership & dedication by a volunteer to children with disabilities, through involvement with Easter Seals

Epilepsy Canada / Épilepsie Canada
#336, 2255B Queen St. East, Toronto ON M4E 1G3
Toll Free: 1-877-734-0873
Email: epilepsy@epilepsy.ca; URL: www.epilepsy.ca

Epilepsy Canada Research Fellowships
To develop expertise in clinical or basic epilepsy research & to enhance the quality of care for epilepsy patients in Canada; awarded annually to a Ph.D. or M.D. for clinical research at a Canadian institution; designed as a training program & not intended for those holding faculty appointments

The Royal College of Physicians & Surgeons of Canada / Le Collège royal des médecins et chirurgiens du Canada
774 Echo Dr., Ottawa ON K1S 5N8
613/730-8177; Fax: 613/730-8830; Toll Free: 1-800-668-3740
Email: infos@rcpsc.edu; URL: medical.org
The Office of Fellowship Affairs administers an annual competition for five Fellowship grants, three Awards that recognize original research, and three faculty development projects.

The Royal Society of Canada / La Société royale du Canada
170 Waller St., Ottawa ON K1N 9B9
613/991-6990; Fax: 613/991-6996
Email: info@rsc.ca; URL: www.rsc.ca

Jason A. Hannah Medal
Established 1976; awarded annually for an important publication in the history of medicine
$1,500 & a bronze medal

The McLaughlin Medal
Awarded annually for important research of sustained excellence in any branch of medical science
$2,500 & a medal

JOURNALISM

Atlantic Journalism Awards
46 Swanton Dr., Dartmouth NS B3W 2C5
902/425-2727; Fax: 902/462-1892
Email: office@ajas.ca; URL: ajas.ca

Atlantic Journalism Awards
Originally a program of the University of King's College School of Journalism established in 1981, is now a non-profit organization to recognize excellence & achievement in work by Atlantic Canadian journalists; covers work in English or French; 23 award categories featuring work published or broadcast in the news media of Atlantic Canada.
Winners in individual categories will receive framed certificate presented at the Awards dinner.

Journalistic Achievement Award
An award which recognizes outstanding work in Atlantic Canada by an individual journalist, team of journalists, or a media organization, presented at the Awards dinner

Canadian Association of Journalists / L'Association canadienne des journalistes
c/o Algonquin College, #B224, 1385 Woodroffe Ave., Ottawa ON K2G 1V8
613/526-8061; Fax: 613/521-3904
Email: canadianjour@magma.ca; URL: www.caj.ca

The CAJ Awards
Awards presented for the top investigative report published or broadcast in the following media: Newspaper/Newswire (open category), Newspaper (circulation under 25,000), Magazine, TV, Radio, Faith & Spirituality, Photojournalism, Computer assisting reporting & the Don McGillivray award for Best Investigative Report
$1,000 - John Dickins

Canadian Business Press / La Presse spécialisée du Canada
#346, 4195 Dundas St. West, Toronto ON M8X 1Y4
416/239-1022; Fax: 416/239-1076
Email: admin@cbp.ca; URL: www.cbp.ca

Kenneth R. Wilson Awards
Recognize excellence in writing & graphic design (17 categories) in specialized business/professional publications; open to all business publications, regardless of CBP membership, that are published in English &/or French; all awards, except the Harvey Southam Editorial Career Award, require an entry fee - krwawards@cbp.ca

Canadian Newspaper Association / Association canadienne des journaux
#200, 890 Yonge St., Toronto ON M4W 3P4
416/923-3567; Fax: 416/923-7206
Email: info@cna-acj.ca; URL: www.cna-acj.ca

National Newspaper Awards/Concours canadien de journalisme
Awards are presented annually in early spring in 16 categories: Spot News Reporting, Enterprise Reporting, Special Project, Layout & Design, Critical Writing, Sports Writing, Feature Writing, Cartooning, Columns, Business Reporting, International Reporting, Spot News Photography, Feature Photography, Sports Photography, Editorial Writing, Local Reporting.
Eligible are those employed by or freelance for daily newspapers or wire services in French or English; awards are governed by an independent board of governors consisting of newspaper & public representatives.
Winners receive $2,500 plus certificates; two runners-up in each category receive citations of merit & $250

Canadian Science Writers' Association / Association canadienne des rédacteurs scientifiques
PO Box 75, Stn A, Toronto ON M5W 1A2
Toll Free: 1-800-796-8595
Email: office@sciencewriters.ca; URL: www.sciencewriters.ca

Canadian Forest Service-Ontario Journalism Award
Open to print journalists who have published an article concerning some aspect of forestry in Ontario during the previous calendar year in either a newspaper or magazine published in Ontario

Science in Society Journalism Awards
Open to Canadian journalists in all media for work appearing in the previous calendar year; 14 categories include newspapers, magazines, trade publications, radio, television, children's books & general books; awards total $14,000

L'Oreal Excellence In Science Journalism Award

Heritage Canada Foundation / Fondation Héritage Canada
5 Blackburn Ave., Ottawa ON K1N 8A2
613/237-1066; Fax: 613/237-5987
Email: heritagecanada@heritagecanada.org; URL: www.heritagecanada.org

The Heritage Canada Journalism Prize
Awarded annually to a journalist, working in either the print or electronic media, whose coverage of heritage issues is judged to be outstanding

National Magazine Awards Foundation / Fondation nationale des prix du magazine canadien
#700, 425 Adelaide St. West, Toronto ON M5V 3C1
416/828-9011; Fax: 416/504-0437
Email: staff@magazine-awards.com; URL: www.magazine-awards.com

National Magazine Awards
Awards are presented annually in 26 categories including Personal Journalism, Arts & Entertainment, Humour, Business, Science, Health & Medicine, Sports & Recreation, Fiction, Poetry, Travel, Magazine Illustration, Photojournalism, Art Direction, Magazine Covers, & Photography; all above awards go to individual magazine writers, photographers, illustrators, or art directors; Magazine of the Year recognizes continual overall excellence, The President's Medal is awarded to an article from the text categories & offers a prize of $3,000; The Foundation Award for Outstanding Achievement was introduced in 1990 & recognizes an individual's innovation & creativity through career-long contributions to the magazine industry
Awards are gold or silver scrolls with $1,500 & $500 cash prizes respectively; President's Medal $3,000

Ontario Newspaper Awards
c/o The Record, 160 King St. East, Kitchener ON N2G 4E5
519/894-2231
Email: lwilson@therecord.com
Celebrated annually and available in a variety of journalism categories such as: Novice Reporting; Sports Writing; Sports Photography, Humour Writing.

Société Saint-Jean-Baptiste de Montréal
82, rue Sherbrooke Ouest, Montréal QC H2X 1X3
514/843-8851; Fax: 514/844-6369
Email: mbeaulieu@ssjb.com; URL: www.ssjb.com

Prix Olivar-Asselin
Established 1955; $1,500 & a medal awarded annually to a French Canadian in recognition of outstanding achievement in journalism in serving the higher interests of the French Canadian people

Western Magazine Awards Foundation
1506 East 11th Ave., Garden Unit, Vancouver BC V5N 1Y7
604/669-3717;
URL: www.westernmagazineawards.com

The Western Magazine Awards
Editorial excellence in western Canadian magazine writing, photography, illustration & art direction

LEGAL, GOVERNMENTAL, PUBLIC ADMINISTRATION

Alberta Solicitor General and Public Security
Communications, 10365 - 97 St., 10th Fl., Edmonton AB T5J 3W7
780/427-3441; Fax: 780/427-1903
URL: www.solgen.gov.ab.ca/crime_prev/awards.aspx

Crime Prevention Awards
Awards highlight the activities & accomplishments of special Albertans who prove that preventing crime is everyone's responsibility; awards are presented to an individual, for youth leadership, business, community program or organization & police member for efforts beyond regular duties

Canadian Society of Association Executives / Société canadienne des directeurs d'association
#1100, 10 King St. East, Toronto ON M5C 1C3
416/363-3555; Fax: 416/363-3630; Toll Free: 1-800-461-3608
Email: csae@csae.com; URL: www.csae.com

Pinnacle Award
Recognizes the association executive who has demonstrated exceptional & outstanding leadership qualities within their organization, has contributed to other voluntary organizations & the community at large, to CSAE at local & national levels

Institute of Public Administration of Canada / Institut d'administration publique du Canada
#401, 1075 Bay St., Toronto ON M5S 2B1
416/924-8787; Fax: 416/924-4992
URL: www.ipac.ca

IPAC Award for Innovative Management
Awarded in recognition of outstanding organizational achievement in the public sector

Vanier Medal
A gold medal is awarded annually as a mark of distinction & exceptional achievement to a person who has shown outstanding leadership in public administration in Canada

Justice Canada
Legal Studies for Aboriginal People Program, Department of Justice Canada, Programs Branch, 284 Wellington St., 6th Fl., Ottawa ON K1A 0H8
613/941-0388; Fax: 613/941-2269; Toll Free: 1-888-606-5111
Email: LSAP@justice.gc.ca; URL: canada.justice.gc.ca/en/ps/pb/prog/legal_sap.html

Legal Studies for Aboriginal People Program
A scholarship program to encourage Métis & Non-Status Indians to enter the legal profession by providing financial assistance through a pre-law orientation course & an annual scholarship program for a maximum of 3 years
Open to Aboriginal People (Métis & Non-Status Indians)

The Professional Institute of the Public Service of Canada / Institut professionnel de la fonction publique du Canada
250 Tremblay Rd., Ottawa ON K1G 3J8
613/228-6310; Fax: 613/228-9048; Toll Free: 1-800-267-0446
URL: www.pipsc.ca

Gold Medal Awards
Established 1937; the gold medals are presented biennially. Those eligible are scientific, professional, or technical workers or groups of workers employed by the federal, provincial, or municipal government services of Canada who have made a contribution of outstanding importance to national or world well-being in either pure or applied science or in some field outside pure or applied science

LITERARY ARTS, BOOKS & LIBRARIES

Book Publishers Association of Alberta
10523 - 100 Ave., Edmonton AB T5J 0A8
780/424-5060; Fax: 780/424-7943
Email: info@planet.eon.net; URL: www.bookpublishers.ab.ca

Alberta Book Awards
To recognize outstanding achievements in Alberta publishing; nine awards are given - Alberta Publisher of the Year, Alberta Trade Book of the Year, Alberta Book Design Award, Alberta Book Cover Design Award, Alberta Educational Book of the Year, Alberta Childrens' Book of the Year, Alberta Book Illustration Award, Alberta Scholarly Book, Alberta Emerging Publisher of the Year.
Stone carvings by Brian Clark are presented & kept by the winner in the award year & exchanged for plaques the following year.

Lois Hole Award for Editorial Excellence
Established in honour of Lois Hole's dedication to books, libraries, literacy and respect for editors.

Alberta Book Publishing Achievement Award
Established to recognize long-standing contributions made to Alberta book publishing.

British Columbia Historical Federation
PO Box 5254, Stn B, Victoria BC V8R 6N4
604/277-2627; Fax: 604/277-2657
Email: info@bchistory.ca; URL: www.bchistory.ca
W. Kaye Lamb Essay Scholarships
Awarded for essays written by students at BC colleges or universities on a topic related to BC history

Writing Awards
Established 1983; Lieutenant-Governor's Medal for Historical Writing, three Certificates of Merit, & cash awards given annually to authors of best books on any facet of BC history

The Canada Council for the Arts / Conseil des Arts du Canada
350 Albert St., PO Box 1047, Ottawa ON K1P 5V8
613/566-4414; Fax: 613/566-4390; Toll Free: 1-800-263-5588
Email: info@canadacouncil.ca; URL: www.canadacouncil.ca

Canada-Japan Literary Awards
Two awards valued at $10,000 awarded every two years in recognition of literary excellence by Canadian writers writing about Japan, Japanese themes or themes that promote mutual understanding between Japan & Canada, or by Canadian translators of such books from Japanese into English or French

CBC Literary Awards
A joint presentation of CBC, enRoute magazine & the Canada Council for the Arts; two prizes of $6,000 & $4,000 given in each of three categories in English & French: poetry, travel literature & short fiction. CBC selects the jury & administers the adjudication process, enRoute publishes the winning entries & the Canada Council provides the cash prizes to the six winners in French & English

The Governor General's Literary Awards
$15,000 each awarded annually to the best English-language & best French-language work in each of the following categories: children's literature (text & illustration), drama, fiction, poetry, literary non-fiction, & translation.
Books must be by Canadian authors, illustrators & translators, published in Canada or abroad. In the case of translation, the original work must also be a Canadian-authored title. Peer assessment committees select the winning titles from the books formally nominated by publishers.

Canadian Association for School Libraries
c/o Canadian Library Association, 328 Frank St., Ottawa ON K2P 0X8
613/232-9625; Fax: 613/563-9895
URL: www.cla.ca/casl.html

The Angela Thacker Memorial Award
Established in memory of Angela Thacker, teacher-librarian, library coordinator, this award honours teacher-librarians who have made contributions to the profession through publications, productions or professional development activities that deal with topics relevant to teacher-librarianship and/or information literacy.

Margaret B. Scott Award of Merit
Awarded annually to recognize outstanding achievement in school librarianship in Canada

National Book Service Teacher-Librarian of the Year Award
To honour a school-based teacher-librarian who has made an outstanding contribution to school librarianship by planning & implementing an exemplary school library program based on a collaborative model; award is sponsored by National Book Service

Canadian Association of Children's Librarians
c/o Canadian Library Association, 328 Frank St., Ottawa ON K2P 0X8
613/232-9625; Fax: 613/563-9895
Email: info@cla.ca; URL: www.cla.ca/divisions/capl/cacl.htm

Amelia Frances Howard-Gibbon Illustrators Medal
Established 1971; a silver medal awarded annually for outstanding illustrations in a children's book published in Canada; the illustrator must be a Canadian or a Canadian resident - Brenda Shield

Book of the Year for Children Medal
A silver medal awarded annually for the outstanding children's book published during the calendar year; book must have been written by a Canadian or a resident of Canada - Brenda Shield

Canadian Association of College & University Libraries
c/o Canadian Library Association, 328 Frank St., Ottawa ON K2P 0X8
613/232-9625; Fax: 613/563-9895
Email: info@cla.ca; URL: www.cla.ca/divisions/cacul/ctcl.htm

Innovation Achievement Award
To recognize academic libraries which, through innovation in ongoing programs/services or in a special event/project, have contributed to academic librarianship & library development; a framed acknowledgement & a $1,500 gift certificate is offered for the vendor of the institution's choice

Miles Blackwell Award for Outstanding Academic Librarian
Awarded to a librarian who has made a notable contribution to the field of academic librarianship

Canadian Association of Public Libraries
c/o Canadian Library Association, 328 Frank St., Ottawa ON K2P 0X8
613/232-9625; Fax: 613/563-9895
Email: info@cla.ca; URL: www.cla.ca/divisions/capl/

CAPL/Brodart Outstanding Public Library Service Award
The Canadian Association of Public Libraries, in partnership with Brodart, is please to offer this prestigious award offered annually for outstanding service in the field of Canadian public librarianship.

Canadian Authors Association
320 South Shores Rd., PO Box 419, Campbellford ON K0L 1L0
705/653-0323; Fax: 705/653-0593; Toll Free: 1-866-216-6222
Email: admin@canauthors.org; URL: www.canauthors.org

CAA Award for Fiction
$2,500 & a silver medal

CAA Carol Bolt Award
$1,000 & a silver medal

CAA Jack Chalmers Poetry Award
$1,000 & a silver medal

Lela Common Award for Canadian History
$2,500 & a silver medal

The Canadian Children's Book Centre
#101, 40 Orchard View Blvd., Toronto ON M4R 1B9
416/975-0010; Fax: 416/975-8970
Email: info@bookcentre.ca; URL: www.bookcentre.ca

The Geoffrey Bilson Award for Historical Fiction
Rewards excellence in outstanding work of historical fiction for young people by a Canadian author, published in previous calendar year; judges are: a writer, bookseller, children's books specialist, historian, librarian
$1,000

The Norma Fleck Award for Non-Fiction
Rewards excellence in outstanding work of non-fiction for young people by a Canadian author, published in previous calendar year; jury members include a teacher, a librarian, a reviewer & a bookseller
$10,000

Canadian Historical Association / Société historique du Canada
395 Wellington St., Ottawa ON K1A 0N3
613/233-7885; Fax: 613/567-3110
Email: cha-shc@lac-bac.gc.ca; URL: www.cha-shc.ca
10 Awards available for outstanding nonfiction publications in the field of history.
Prizes also available for High School and University levels as well as Research Work and Popular Work.

Canadian Library Association
328 Frank St., Ottawa ON K2P 0X8
613/232-9625; Fax: 613/563-9895
Email: info@cla.ca; URL: www.cla.ca

Dafoe Scholarship
$3,000 awarded annually to a student entering an accredited Canadian library school

H.W. Wilson Scholarship
$2,500 presented annually to a student entering an accredited Canadian library school

World Book Scholarship in Library Science & Information Studies
$2,500 scholarship given annually to be used for a program of study or series of courses either leading to a further library degree or related library work in which the candidate is currently engaged

Young Adult Canadian Book Award
Presented to recognize the best English-language fiction for young adults by a Canadian author

Canadian Library Trustees Association
c/o Canadian Library Association, 328 Frank St., Ottawa ON K2P 0X8
613/232-9625; Fax: 613/563-9895
Email: info@cla.ca; URL: www.cla.ca/divisions/clta/clta.htm

CLTA/Stan Heath Achievement in Literacy Award
Through this award, CLTA endorses the initiatives of the public library systems, which have structured literacy programs as a component of library services to the community

CLTA Merit Award for Distinguished Service as a Public Library Trustee
The CLTA Merit Award is presented annually to a library trustee who has demonstrated outstanding leadership in the advancement of trusteeship and public library service in Canada.

CBC Literary Awards/Prix Littéraires Radio-Canada
CBC Radio, PO Box 6000, Montréal QC H3C 3A8
Toll Free: 1-877-888-6788
URL: www.radio-canada.ca/prixlitteraires/

CBC Literary Awards/Prix Littéraires Radio-Canada
The only literary competition that celebrates original, unpublished works, in Canada's two official languages. Prizes are available in three categories: short story, poetry and creative nonfiction. Winning entries are published in Air Canada's enRoute magazine.

Corporation des bibliothécaires professionnels du Québec / Corporation of Professional Librarians of Québec
#103, 353, rue St. Nicolas, Montréal QC H2Y 2P1
514/845-3327; Fax: 514/845-1618
Email: info@cbpq.qc.ca; URL: www.cbpq.qc.ca

Annuel de la CBPQ - Bibliothécaire de l'année
Stimuler et reconnaître l'excellence parmi les membres; attirer l'attention des médias sur les récipiendaires de cette distinction honorifique et sur la nature des réalisations primées; orienter des perceptions; le prix comporte les volets suivants: distinction honorifique, remise d'une épinglette en or, publicité entourant l'événement

The Crime Writers of Canada
3007 Kingston Rd., PO Box 113, Toronto ON M1M 1P1
416/597-9938
Email: info@crimewriterscanada.com; URL: www.crimewriterscanada.com

The Arthur Ellis Awards
Established 1984; awarded annually in the following categories: best crime novel (by a previously published novelist), best crime non-fiction, best first crime novel (by a previously unpublished novelist), best crime short story, best juvenile crime book, & best crime writing in French

Donner Canadian Foundation
c/o Meisner Publicity & Promotion, 394A King St. East, Toronto ON M5A 1K9
416/368-8253; 368-3763; Fax: 416/363-1448
Email: meisnerpublicity@sympatico.ca; URL: www.donnerbookprize.com

The Donner Prize
Award of $35,000 for the best book on Canadian public policy; five runners-up prizes of $5,000 each

Fondation Émile-Nelligan
261, rue Bloomfield, Outremont QC H2V 3R6
514/278-4657; Fax: 514/271-6369
Email: info@fondation-nelligan.org; URL: www.fondation-nelligan.org

Prix Émile-Nelligan
Prix annuel. Il s'agit d'un prix de poésie décerné à un poète de moins de 35 ans, pour un recueil publié au cours de l'année 7 500$ et une médaille en bronze frappée à l'effigie d'Émile Nelligan

Prix Gilles-Corbeil
Prix triennal en littérature (poésie, roman, nouvelles, récits, théâtre ou essai littéraire). Décerné à un écrivain citoyen du Canada ou des États-Unis, pour une oeuvre écrite en langue française
100 000$

Fondation Les Forges
1497, rue Laviolette, CP 335, Trois-Rivières QC G9A 5G4
819/379-9813; Fax: 819/376-0774
Email: info@fiptr.com; URL: www.fiptr.com

Grand Prix du Festival International de la Poésie
Le Festival International de la Poésie remet une bourse de 5 000 $ au lauréat lors de l'ouverture officielle du festival; le candidat doit: être de citoyenneté canadienne et avoir déjà publié trois ouvrages de poésie chez un éditeur reconnu

Prix Félix-Antoine-Savard de poésie
Décerné annuellement lors des cérémonies d'ouverture du Festival International de la Poésie; vise à honorer, tout en les respectant, la mémoire, l'esprit et l'oeuvre poétique de cet écrivain; une bourse de 250$ y est rattachée et le contenant de 100 feuilles de papier Saint-Gilles sont remis à St-Joseph-de-la-Rive, le jour de l'Action de Grâce
Prix Félix-Leclerc de poésie
Créé en octobre 1997, à l'occasion du 10e anniversaire de la mort du poète; décerné tous les 2 ans lors des cérémonies d'ouverture du Festival International de la Poésie; prix de 1000$
Prix Piché de poésie
Les bourses sont offertes par le Festival International de la Poésie; 1er prix, 2 000 $, 2e prix, 500 $; le candidat doit être de citoyenneté canadienne et n'avoir jamais publié d'ouvrage de poésie chez un éditeur reconnu
The Griffin Trust for Excellence in Poetry
6610 Edwards Blvd., Mississauga ON L5T 2V6
905/565-5993
Email: info@griffinpoetryprize.com; URL: www.griffinpoetryprize.com/home.php
The Griffin Prize
Established in 2000, two prizes of $50,000 each awarded annually for collections of poetry published in English during the preceding year; one will go to a living Canadian poet; the other to a living poet or translator from any other country which may include Canada
International Board on Books for Young People - Canadian Section / Union internationale pour les livres de jeunesse
c/o Canadian Children's Book Centre, #101, 40 Orchard View Blvd., Toronto ON M4R 1B9
416/975-0010; Fax: 416/975-8970
Email: info@ibby-canada.org; URL: www.ibby-canada.org
Claude Aubry Award
Awarded biennially for distinguished contributions to Canadian children's literature by a librarian, teacher, author, illustrator, publisher, bookseller, or editor
$1,000
Elizabeth Mrazik-Cleaver Picture Book Award
Awarded for distinguished Canadian picture book illustration; submissions to Children's Literature Service, National Library of Canada, 395 Wellington St., Ottawa, ON K1A 0N4
$1,000
Frances E. Russell Award
Awarded to initiate & encourage research in children's literature in Canada
$1,000
The League of Canadian Poets
#608, 920 Yonge St., Toronto ON M4W 3C7
416/504-1657; Fax: 416/504-0096
Email: info@poets.ca; URL: www.poets.ca
Gerald Lampert Memorial Award
Established 1979; awarded annually for excellence in a first book of poetry, written by a Canadian citizen or landed immigrant, & published in the preceding year
$1,000
Pat Lowther Memorial Award
$1,000 awarded annually for excellence in a book of poetry, written by a Canadian female citizen or landed immigrant, & published in the preceding year
The Lionel Gelber Prize
c/o Prize Administrator, Munk Centre for International Studies, University of Toronto, 1 Devonshire Pl., Toronto ON M5S 3K7
416/946-8901; Fax: 416/946-9815
Email: gelberprize.munk@utoronto.ca; URL: www.utoronto.ca/mcis/gelber
The Lionel Gelber Prize
This $15,000 prize is the largest of its kind in the world; a legacy of Lionel Gelber, international writer who died in 1989 & who was much acclaimed for his service to Canada; the prize is "designed to stimulate authors of any nationality who write about international relations, & to encourage the audience for these books to grow"
Books published in English or English translation, must be copyrighted in the year in which the prize is awarded; books must be published or distributed in Canada; submissions by publishers only
Literary Translators' Association of Canada / Association des traducteurs et traductrices littéraires du Canada
Concordia University LB 631, 1455, boul de Maisonneuve ouest, Montréal QC H3G 1M8
514/848-2424, ext. 8702; Fax: 514/848-4514
Email: info@attlc-ltac.org; URL: www.attlc-ltac.org
Glassco Translation Prize
Awarded annually for a translator's first work in book-length literary translation into French or English, published in Canada during the previous calendar year
$1,000 & one year's membership in the association

Manitoba Writers' Guild Inc.
#206, 100 Arthur St., Winnipeg MB R3B 1H3
204/942-6134; Fax: 204/942-5754; Toll Free: 1-888-637-5802
Email: info@mbwriter.mb.ca; URL: www.mbwriter.mb.ca

Alexander Kennedy Isbister Award for Non-Fiction
Presented to the Manitoba writer whose book is judged the best book of adult non-fiction written in English
$3,500

Carol Shields City of Winnipeg Award
To honour books that evoke the special caracter of & contribute to the appreciation & understanding of the City of Winnipeg
$5,000

Eileen McTavish Sykes Award for Best First Book
Awarded annually to a Manitoba author whose first professionally published book is deemed the best written
Must have been written in the previous year
$1,500

John Hirsch Award for Most Promising Manitoba Writer
Awarded annually to the most promising Manitoba writer working in poetry, fiction, creative non-fiction or drama
$2,500

Le Prix littéraire Rue des Chambeault
Biennial award presented to the author whose published book or play is judged to be the best French language work by a Manitoba author
$3,500

Manitoba Book Design of the Year Awards
For the best overall design in Manitoba book publishing in two categories: book design & best illustration

Margaret Laurence Award for Fiction
Presented to the Manitoba writer whose book is judged the best book of adult fiction written in English
$3,500

Mary Scorer Award for Best Book by a Manitoba Publisher
Awarded to the best book published by a Manitoba publisher & written for the trade, bookstore, educational, academic or scholarly market
$1,000

McNally Robinson Book for Young People Awards
Awarded annually to the writer whose young person's book is judged the best written by a Manitoba author; two categories: children's & young adult
$2,500

McNally Robinson Book of the Year
To the Manitoba author judged to have written the best book in the calendar year
$5,000

McClelland & Stewart
c/o McClelland & Stewart Ltd., #900 - 481 University Ave., Toronto ON M5G 2E9
416/598-1114; Fax: 416/598-7764
Email: journeyprize@mcclelland.com; URL: www.mcclelland.com/jpa

The Writers' Trust of Canada/McClelland & Stewart Journey Prize
$10,000 awarded annually to a new & developing writer of distinction for a short story published in a Canadian literary journal. The shortlisted stories are selected from journal submissions & published annually by McClelland & Stewart as The Journey Prize Anthology. M&S presents its own award of $2,000 to the literary journal that originally published the winning story. Only submissions from Canadian literary journals are accepted. Stories must have had original publication in the nominating journal during the previous year.

The Municipal Chapter of Toronto IODE
#205, 40 St. Clair Ave. East, Toronto ON M4T 1M9
Phone: 416/925-5078; Fax: 416/925-5127
Email: iodetoronto@bellnet.ca

IODE Book Award
Established in 1975; an inscribed scroll & not less than $1,000 awarded annually to the author or illustrator of the best children's book written or illustrated by a Canadian resident in Toronto or surrounding area & published by a Canadian publisher within the preceding 12 months

The National Chapter of Canada IODE
#254, 40 Orchard View Blvd., Toronto ON M4R 1B9
416/487-4416; Fax: 416/487-4417; Toll Free: 1-866-827-7428
Email: iodecanada@bellnet.ca

The National Chapter of Canada IODE Violet Downey Book Award
Awarded annually for the best English-language book, containing at least 500 words of text, preferably with Canadian content, in any category suitable for children aged 13 & under
$3,000

Nova Scotia Library Association
c/o Nova Scotia Provincial Library, 3770 Kempt Rd., Halifax NS B3K 4X8
902/742-2486; Fax: 902/742-6920
Email: mlandry@nsme.library.ns.ca; URL: www.nsla.ns.ca

Ann Connor Brimer Award
Awarded to the author of fiction or non-fiction books published in Canada currently in print & intended for children up to the age of 15; writer must be residing in Atlantic Canada
$1,000 - Heather Mackenzie, Halifax Regional Library, 5381 Spring Garden Rd., Halifax NS B3J 1E9; Email: mahm1@nsh.library.ns.ca

Norman Horrocks Award for Library Leadership
Honours leadership in the Nova Scotia Library community & is awarded for distinguished contributions to the promotion & development of library service in Nova Scotia - Trudy Amirault, Western Counties Regional Library, 405 Main St., Yarmouth NS B5A 1G3, Email: tamiraul@nsy.library.ns.ca

Ontario Arts Council / Conseil des arts de l'Ontario
151 Bloor St. West, 5th Fl., Toronto ON M5S 1T6
416/961-1660; Fax: 416/961-7796; Toll Free: 1-800-387-0058
Email: info@arts.on.ca; URL: www.arts.on.ca

Ruth Schwartz Children's Book Award
Two awards presented annually; $3,000 for best picture book & $2,000 for best young adult/middle reader book; in conjunction with the Canadian Booksellers Association

Ontario Library Association
50 Wellington St. East, Suite 201, Toronto, ON M5E 1C8
416/363-3388; Fax: 416/941-9581
Email: info@accessola.com; URL: www.accessola.com

Blue Spruce(tm) Award Program
The Blue Spruce Award(tm) is a provincial primary reading program which brings recently published Canadian children's picture books to Ontario children ages 4 to 7 in kindergarten through to grade two. Award given out in May every year.

Silver Birch(r) Fiction, Non-Fiction And Express Award Program
The Silver Birch Award(r) is given by Grade 3, 4, 5 and 6 students in a spectacular ceremony held annually in May before fifteen hundred of their peers. The children choose winners in Fiction, Non-Fiction and Express when they cast their ballots on the province-wide Voting Day earlier in the same month. It is the most democratic and unbiased process possible when the children make their choice. The program is administered by the Ontario Library Association and run by teacher-librarians and teachers in schools and by children's librarians in public libraries. But the choice belongs to the children. And, in their tens of thousands, they know what they are doing.

Red Maple(tm) Award Program
The Red Maple Award(tm) reading program is offered for the enjoyment of students in Grades 7 and 8. The program, like the Association's Silver Birch Awards(tm) reading program, gives students who have read a minimum number of nominated titles the opportunity to vote with a large group of their peers for the nominated title that they feel should win the Red Maple Award(tm) each year.

White Pine(tm) Award Program
The White Pine Award(tm) reading program offers high school-aged teens at all grade levels the opportunity to read the best of Canada's recent young adult fiction titles. All of these 10 books for Young Adults on this list are accessible and will allow all readers to be successful participants/voters. As in all of the independent reading programs, a reader only needs to read 5 books out of a list of 10 to qualify to vote. Based on student voting across the province, the most popular book is then selected and author is honoured with the White Pine Award(tm).

The Evergreen(r) Award Program
The Evergreen Award(tm) is OLA's newest addition to the Forest of Reading(r). It was introduced at Super Conference 2005 for adults of any age. It gives adult library patrons the opportunity to vote for a work of Canadian fiction or non-fiction that they have liked the most.

Ontario Media Development Corporation
c/o OMDC, North Tower, #501, 175 Bloor St. East, Toronto ON M4W 3R8
416/314-6858; Fax: 416/314-6876
Email: mail@omdc.on.ca; URL: www.omdc.on.ca

Trillium Book Award for Poetry
Awarded in both English & French
$10,000

Trillium Book Award/Prix Trillium
Awarded annually to an Ontario author of a book of excellence; the winning book must have been published within the preceding 12 months; books in English or French in any genre are eligible; winner receives $12,000 & the publisher receives $2,500

PEI Council of the Arts
115 Richmond St., Charlottetown PE C1A 1A7
902/368-4410; Fax: 902/368-4418; Toll Free: 1-888-734-2784
Email: info@peiartscouncil.com; URL: www.peiartscouncil.com

Island Literary Awards
Established in 1987 in recognition of Island writers in six categories: Short Story, Poetry, Children's Literature, Feature Article, Creative Writing for Children, Playwriting; an additional award is made "for distinguished contribution to the literary arts"
$500, $200 & $100

Periodical Marketers of Canada
South Tower, #1007, 175 Bloor St. East, Toronto ON M4W 3R8
416/968-7311; Fax: 416/968-6281

Canadian Letters Awards
Established 1996; recognizes an individual who has made an outstanding contribution to writing, publishing, teaching or literary administration; award consists of a statuette & a $5,000 donation to the charitable literary organization or educational institution of the winner's choice

Phoenix Community Works Foundation
316 Dupont St., Toronto ON M5R 1V9
416/964-7919; Fax: 416/964-8516
Email: info@pcwf.ca; URL: www.pcwf.ca

The Chap-Book Award
Awarded for the best poetry chap-book in English, published in Canada; entries must be from 10-48 pages in length
$1,000

PriceWaterhouseCoopers
Royal Trust Tower, #3000, 77 King St. West, Toronto ON M5K 1G8
416/869-1130; Fax: 416/941-8345
URL: www.pwcglobal.com/ca/eng/about/events/nbba.html

National Business Book Award
Established 1985; annual prize of $20,000 awarded to author of book containing key material on business in Canada - Mary Ann Freedman

Prism International
Creative Writing Program, UBC, Buch. E462 - 1866 Main Mall, Vancouver BC V6T 1Z1
604/822-2514; Fax: 604/822-3616
Email: prism@interchange.ubc.ca; URL: prism.arts.ubc.ca

Earle Birney Prize for Poetry
Awarded annually to an outstanding poetry contributor published in Prism International
$500

Literary Non-Fiction Contest
$1,500

Prism Short Fiction Contest
$3,000 in prizes for annual short fiction contest

Prix Aurora Awards
#501, 88 Bruce St., Kitchener ON N2B 1Y8
Email: prix.aurora.awards@gmail.com; URL: www.sentex.net/~dmullin/aurora

Prix Aurora Awards
Awards presented annually for the best in Canadian Science Fiction & Fantasy; 10 categories: six professional awards (three English & three French), three fan awards & the artistic achievement award

Québec Ministère de la culture et des communications
225, Grande Allée est, Québec QC G1R 5G5
418/380-2300; Fax: 418/080-2364
Email: DC@mcc.gouv.qc.ca; URL: www.mcc.gouv.qc.ca

Les Prix du Québec
Founded in 1977, these awards are given annually by the Government of Quebec to individuals for cultural and scientific achievements. There are six awards in the cultural field.

Québec Ministère des Relations internationales
Édifice Hector-Fabre, 525, boul René-Lévesque est, Québec QC G1R 5R9
418/649-2300; Fax: 418/649-2656
Email: francine.marcotte@mri.gouv.qc.ca; URL: www.mri.gouv.qc.ca

Prix Québec Wallonie-Bruxelles de littérature de jeunesse
Créé en 1978; vise à encourager le développement de la littérature de jeunesse de langue fran‡aise et à faire la promotion des lauréats. Décerné conjointement par le ministère des Relations internationales et ministère de la Culture et des Communications

Québec Writers' Federation / Fédération des Écrivaines et Écrivains du Québec
1200 Atwater av., Montréal QC H3Z 1X4
514/933-0878; Fax: 514/933-0878
Email: info@qwf.org; URL: www.qwf.org

QWF Prizes
Established 1988; awards five annual prizes of $2,000 each to honour literary excellence: The A.M. Klein poetry prize, The Hugh MacLennan fiction prize, Mavis Gallant prize for non-fiction, The McAuslan First Book Award & Translation award Books can be submitted for prizes in five categories by publishers or authors; four copies, accompanied by entry form & $10 registration fee per submission; authors must have lived in Québec three of the past five years

The Royal Society of Canada / La Société royale du Canada
170 Waller St., Ottawa ON K1N 9B9
613/991-6990; Fax: 613/991-6996
Email: info@rsc.ca; URL: www.rsc.ca

Lorne Pierce Medal
Established 1926; awarded every two years for an achievement of special significance & conspicuous merit in imaginative or critical literature written in either English or French, preferably dealing with a Canadian subject

Salon International du livre de Québec
26, rue Saint-Pierre, Québec QC G1K 8A3
418/692-0010; Fax: 418/692-0029
Email: info@silq.org; URL: www.silq.org

Prix des libraires du Québec
Ce prix fut créé en 1994 par l'Association des libraires du Québec et le Salon international du livre de Québec; il souligne

l'excellence d'un roman québécois par sa qualité d'écriture et son originalité; une bourse de 2 000 $ est offerte en 2005 par le Conseil des Arts et des Lettres du Québec

Saskatchewan Book Awards

#205B, 2314 - 11th Ave., Regina SK S4P 0K1
306/569-1585; Fax: 306/569-4187
Email: director@bookawards.sk.ca; URL: www.bookawards.sk.ca

Anne Szumigalski Poetry Award
$2,000 awarded for the best book of poetry by a Saskatchewan author; sponsored by the Saskatchewan Arts Board

Award for Publishing
A commemorative plaque for the publisher & a certificate for the author presented to the best book published in Saskatchewan; judged on overall quality of design, production, content & significance; sponsored by Saskatchewan Culture, Youth & Recreation

Book of the Year Award
$2,000 awarded for the best book (any genre) by a Saskatchewan author

Brenda MacDonald Riches First Book Award
$2,000 for the best first book by a Saskatchewan writer; sponsored by Agrium Inc.

Children's Literature Award
$2,000 awarded for the best book of children's literature by a Saskatchewan author; sponsored by SaskEnergy

Fiction Award
$2,000 awarded for the best book of fiction (novel or short fiction) by a Saskatchewan author; sponsored by SaskPower

First Peoples Publishing Award
Commemorative certificate for the publisher & for the writer of the best book with First Nations, Metis, or non-status Indian content written, or in the case of an anthology, edited by a person of First Nations, Metis, or non-status Indian descent; based on the quality of publisher's craft, editing, & literary or artistic value; sponsored by the University of Saskatchewan

Non-Fiction Award
$2,000 award awarded for the best book of non-fiction by a Saskatchewan author; sponsored by the University of Saskatchewan

Prix du livre français
$2,000 awarded biennially for the best book written in French by a Saskatchewan author; sponsored by Fondation fransaskoise

Publishing in Education Award
Commemorative plaque for the publisher & certificates for the writer or editor & publisher of the best book produced as an educational resource, judged on the quality of the publisher's craft, editing & its value to educators at primary, secondary or post secondary levels; sponsored by the University of Regina Bookstore

Regina Book Award
$2,000 to the author of the best book by a Regina writer; sponsored by the City of Regina & Regina Public Library

Saskatoon Book Award
$2,000 awarded to the best book written by a Saskatoon author; sponsored jointly by the Saskatoon Public Library & the City of Saskatoon

Scholarly Writing Award
$2,000 awarded for the book making the best contribution to scholarship by a Saskatchewan author; sponsored by Luther College

Saskatchewan Library Association

#15, 2010 - 7th Ave., Regina SK S4R 1C2
306/780-9413; Fax: 306/780-9447
Email: slaexdir@sasktel.net; URL: www.lib.sk.ca/sla/

The Mary Donaldson Award of Merit
Awarded for excellence to a student studying at a library education institution in Saskatchewan

The SLA Frances Morrison Award
Awarded for outstanding service to libraries

Saskatchewan Writers Guild Inc.

#205, 2314 - 11th Ave., Regina SK S4P 0K1
306/757-6310; Fax: 306/565-8554; Toll Free: 1-800-667-6788
Email: swg@sasktel.net; URL: www.skwriter.com

City of Regina Writing Award
To a Regina writer to reward merit & enable a writer to work on a specific writing project; funded by the City of Regina Arts Commission & administered by the SWG
$4,000

The Scotiabank Giller Prize

c/o Elana Rabinovitch, 576 Davenport Rd., Toronto ON M5R 1K9
416/934-0755
Email: contact@scotiabankgillerprize.ca; URL: www.scotiabankgillerprize.ca/

The Giller Prize
$25,000 award to the author of the best Canadian novel or collection of short stories published in English

Société Saint-Jean-Baptiste de Montréal

82, rue Sherbrooke ouest, Montréal QC H2X 1X3
514/843-8851; Fax: 514/844-6369
Email: mbeaulieu@ssjb.com; URL: www.ssjb.com

Prix Ludger-Duvernay
Le prix a été crée en 1944 afin de signaler les mérites d'un compatriote dont la compétence et le rayonnement dans le domaine intellectuel et littéraire servent les intérêts supérieurs de la nation québécoise; le prix est de 3 000 $, accompagne une médaille, et est attribué à tous les trois ans

Stephen Leacock Association Inc.

PO Box 854, Orillia ON L3V 6K8
705/835-7061; Fax: 705/835-7062
Email: info@leacock.ca; URL: www.leacock.ca

Stephen Leacock Memorial Medal
Established 1946 to encourage the writing & publishing of humorous works in Canada; given annually for the best Canadian book of humour published in the preceding year
Winner receives the medal & a cash award of $10,000 donated by TD Canada Trust

The Order of Mariposa
Awarded occasionally to someone who has contributed significantly to humour in Canada, in other than the written word

University of British Columbia

President's Office, 6328 Memorial Rd., Vancouver BC V6T 1Z2
604/822-4439; Fax: 604/822-6906
Email: jflick@interchange.ubc.ca

Medal for Canadian Biography
Established 1952; awarded annually for the best biography written either about or by a Canadian & published in the preceding year - Jane Flick

Ville de Montréal

Service du développement culturel
5650, d'Iberville, 4e étage, Montréal QC H2G 3E4
514/872-1156
URL: www.ville.montreal.qc.ca/culture/culture.htm

Grand Prix du livre de Montréal
Le prix est offert par la Ville de Montréal à l'auteur ou aux co-auteurs d'un ouvrage de langue française ou anglaise, pour la facture exceptionnelle et l'apport original de cette publication; le prix consiste en une bourse de 15 000 $, ount admissibles un auteur ou un éditeur qui habite sur le territoire de la Ville de Montréal

West Coast Book Prize Society

#902, 207 West Hastings St., Vancouver BC V6B 1H7
604/687-2405; Fax: 604/669-3701
Email: info@bcbookprizes.ca; URL: www.bcbookprizes.ca

BC Book Prizes:
Established 1985; awards of $2,000 presented to winners in each of six categories; the book may have been published anywhere in the world; $25 fee per entry:

Dorothy Livesay Poetry Prize
Awarded to the author of the best work of poetry; the writer must have lived in BC for three of the preceding five years

Lieutenant Governor's Award of Literary Excellence

The Bill Duthie Booksellers' Choice Prize
Awarded for the best book in terms of public appeal, initiative, design, production & content; the book must have been published in BC
The Christie Harris Illustrated Children's Literature Prize

The Ethel Wilson Fiction Prize
Awarded to the author of the best work of fiction; the writer must have lived in BC for three of the preceding five years

The Hubert Evans Non-Fiction Prize
Awarded to the author of the best original non-fiction literary work (philosophy, belles lettres, biography, history, etc.); the writer must have lived in BC for three of the preceding five years

The Haig-Brown Regional Prize
Awarded to the author of the book that contributes most to the enjoyment & understanding of BC; the book may deal with any aspect of the province & should epitomize the BC experience

The Sheila A. Egoff Children's Prize
Awarded to the author of the best book for young people aged 16 & under; the author or illustrator must have lived in BC for three of the preceding five years

Writers Guild of Alberta

11759 Groat Rd., Edmonton AB T5M 3K6
780/422-8174; Fax: 780/422-2663; Toll Free: 1-800-665-5354
Email: mail@writersguild.ab.ca; URL: www.writersguild.ab.ca

Annual Awards Program
Established 1982 to recognize excellence in writing by Alberta authors; published books may be entered in any of the following categories: Children's Literature (any genre), Drama, Novel, Non-Fiction, Poetry, Short Fiction, Best First Book; winners receive $1000 cash award

Writers' Federation of Nova Scotia

1113 Marginal Rd., Halifax NS B3H 4P7
902/423-8116; Fax: 902/422-0881
Email: talk@writers.ns.ca; URL: www.writers.ns.ca

Atlantic Poetry Prize
$2,000

Evelyn Richardson Memorial Literary Trust Award
Award was established in 1978 to recognize outstanding work in non-fiction by a Nova Scotian writer (native or resident)
$2,000

Thomas H. Raddall Atlantic Fiction Prize
Honours the best fiction writing by an Atlantic Canadian writer
$10,000

The Writers' Trust of Canada

#200, 90 Richmond St. East, Toronto ON M5C 1P1
416/504-8222; Fax: 416/504-9090
Email: info@writerstrust.com; URL: www.writerstrust.com

The Bronwen Wallace Memorial Award
Awarded annually to a Canadian writer under the age of 35 who is not yet published in book form; award alternates each year between poetry & short fiction
$1,000

McClelland & Stewart Journey Prize
Awarded annually to a new & developing writer
$10,000

The Marian Engel Award
Established 1986; awarded annually to a female Canadian writer, for a body of work & in hope of future contributions
$15,000

Matt Cohen Award
For a lifetime of distinguished work by a Canadian writer, working in either poetry or prose, writing in either French or English who has dedicated their life to writing as a primary pursuit
$20,000

Rogers Writers' Trust Fiction Prize
Annually to the author of the work of fiction published in the previous year that in the opinion of the judges, shows the best literary merit
$15,000

Nereus Writers' Trust Non-Fiction Prize
Awarded annually to the author of the work of non-fiction published in the previous year that, in the opinion of the judges, shows the best literary merit
$15,000

The Writers Trust of Canada's Shaughnessy Cohen Award for Political Writing
Sponsored by CTV awarded to a non-fiction book of outstanding literary merit that enlarges our understanding of contemporary Canadian political & social issues
$10,000

The Timothy Findley Award
Awarded annually to a male Canadian writer for a body of work & in hope of future contributions
$15,000

Vicky Metcalf Prize for Children's Literature
Awarded annually to an author of children's literature, either fiction, non-fiction, picture books or poetry, not for a single book, but for a body of work, unless, in the opinion of the jury, there is no author worthy of the award that year
$15,000

The W.O. Mitchell Literary Prize
Presented annually to a writer who has produced an outstanding body of work, has acted during his/her career as a "caring mentor" for writers, & has published a work of fiction or had a new stage play produced during the three-year period specified for each competition; every third year the prize will be awarded to a writer who works in French
$15,000

The Writers' Union of Canada
#200, 90 Richmond St. East, Toronto ON M5C 1P1
416/703-8982; Fax: 416/504-9090
Email: info@writersunion.ca; URL: www.writersunion.ca

Danuta Gleed Literary Award
Awarded to a Canadian writer for the best first collection of published short stories in the English language
$10,000

Postcard Story Competition
$500

Short Prose Competition for Developing Writers
$2,500

Writing for Children Competition
$1,500

PERFORMING ARTS

Alberta Scholarship Programs
PO Box 28000, Stn Main, Edmonton AB T5J 4R4
780/427-8640; Fax: 780/427-1288
Email: scholarships@gov.ab.ca; URL: www.alis.gov.ab.ca/scholarships/main.asp

Arts Graduate Scholarships
Five awards of $5,000 at graduate level for study in music, drama, dance & the visual arts & up to $50,000 is available to assist Alberta artists to further their training through non-academic short-term courses & internship or apprenticeship programs

Association québécoise de l'industrie du disque, du spectacle et de la vidéo
6420, rue Saint-Denis, Montréal QC H2S 2R7
514/842-5147; Fax: 514/842-7762
Email: info@adisq.com; URL: www.adisq.com

ADISQ Awards
The event honours the best musical achievement produced in Québec during the past year

The Banff Centre
PO Box 1020, Banff AB T1L 1H5
403/762-6180; Fax: 403/762-6345
Email: arts_info@banffcentre.ca; URL: www.banffcentre.ca

The Clifford E. Lee Choreography Award
Established 1978; awarded annually in recognition of outstanding Canadian choreography & jointly sponsored by the Banff Centre & the Edmonton-based Clifford E. Lee Foundation. Winner receives a $5,000 cash prize & a commission to mount a new work for premiere at the Banff Festival of the Arts - George Ross.

The Canada Council for the Arts / Conseil des Arts du Canada
350 Albert St., PO Box 1047, Ottawa ON K1P 5V8
613/566-4414; Fax: 613/566-4390; Toll Free: 1-800-263-5588
Email: info@canadacouncil.ca; URL: www.canadacouncil.ca

Bernard Diamant Prize
Offers professional Canadian classical singers under 35 an opportunity to pursue their career through further studies. $5,000 awarded in addition to the regular grant to an outstanding young classical singer in the annual competition for Grants to Professional Musicians

Canada Council for the Arts Grand Prize for the CBC Young Composers Competition
$10,000 grand prize awarded every two years to the winner of the CBC Young Composers Competition

Canada Council for the Arts/CBC First Prizes for the CBC Radio National Young Performers Competition
Every two years; two first prizes of $15,000 is awarded to the winners of each of the two categories

Canada Council Musical Instrument Bank
Created in 1987 as a means of acquiring exceptional instruments to be loaned to established Canadian musicians or gifted young musicians who are about to embark on an international solo career, following a national jured competition; collection includes the 1827 McConnel Nicolaus Gagliano cello & the 1717 Windsor-Weinstein Stradivarius violin

Eckhardt-Gramatté National Music Competition
Provides assistance in the amount of $9,000 towards the cost of administering the competiton

Healey Willan Prize
$5,000 awarded every two years to the Canadian amateur choir that gives the best performance in terms of musicianship, technique & program in the CBC National Radio Competition for Amateur Choirs

Jacqueline Lemieux Prize
$6,000 awarded annually to the most talented Canadian candidate in the Grants to Dance Professionals competition

Japan-Canada Fund
Supports performance, exhibitions, distribution networks, etc. of Japanese performing artists, media artists, visual artists through established, professional Canadian presenters, as well as for the translations of Canadian & Japanese literary works

Jean-Marie Beaudet Award in Orchestra Conducting
$1,000 awarded annually to a young Canadian conductor, is adjudicated by a committee of music professionals convened by the Canada Council

John Hirsh Prize
$6,000 awarded to a new & developing theatre director who has demonstrated great potential for future excellence & exciting artistic vision; awarded every two years, one in each of the Anglophone & Francophone theatre communites; nominations are made by the professional theatre community & the winners are chosen by a peer assessment committee for the Canada Council Grants to Theatre Artists program

Jules Léger Prize for New Chamber Music
Established in 1978; annual $7,500 prize designed to encourage Canadian composers to write for chamber music groups & to foster the performance of Canadian chamber music by these groups; the Canadian Music Centre administers the award, the Canada Council funds the award & selects the assessment committee of musicians to study the submitted scores; the CBC Radio Two & La Chaîne culturelle de Radio-Canada broadcasts the winning work on the English- & French-language stereo networks

Robert Fleming Prizes
The annual $2,000 prize in memory of Robert Fleming is intended to encourage the career development of young composers & is awarded to the most talented Canadian music composer in the competition for Canada Council Grants to Professional Musicians in classical music

Sylva Gelber Foundation Award
Established 1981; $15,000 awarded annually to the most talented Canadian artist under the age of 30 in the "Grants to Musicians" competition for performers in classical music

Virginia Parker Award
Approximately $25,000 awarded annually to a young Canadian classical musician, instrumentalist, or conductor who has received at least one Canada Council grant awarded by a peer assessment committee; the prize is intended to assist a young performer in furthering his/her career

Peter Dwyer Scholarships
Annual scholarships totalling $20,000 awarded to the most promising Canadian students at the National Ballet School & the National Theatre School; each school is awarded $10,000 & chooses the winner on behalf of the Canada Council

Walter Carsen Prize for Excellence in the Performing Arts
Awarded annually, $50,000 prize recognizes the highest level of artistic excellence & distinguished career in the performing arts; awarded to a Canadian artist who is actively performing or who has spent the major part of his/her career in Canada in dance, theatre, or music - in creation or interpretation; prize will be presented on a four-year cycle - dance, theatre, dance, music

Canadian Academy of Recording Arts & Sciences / Académie canadienne des arts et des sciences de l'enregistrement
345 Adelaide Street West, 2nd Floor, Toronto ON M5V 1R5
416/485-3135, ext.227; Fax: 416/485-4978; Toll Free: 1-888-440-5866
Email: info@carasonline.ca; URL: www.carasonline.ca

Juno Awards
Annual awards for: Canadian Hall of Fame Award, Walt Grealis Special Achievement Award, Juno Fan Choice (presented by Doritos), Single of the Year, International Album of the Year, Francophone Album of the Year, Artist of the Year, Group of the Year, Instrumental Album of the Year, New Artist of the Year (sponsored by FACTOR & Canada's Private Radio Broadcasters), New Group of the Year (sponsored by FACTOR & Canada's Private Radio Broadcasters), Songwriter of the Year, Country Recording of the Year, Rap Recording of the Year, Pop Album of the Year, Rock Album of the Year, Vocal Jazz Album of the Year, Contemporary Jazz Album of the Year, Traditional Jazz Album of the Year, Children's Album of the Year, Classical Album of the Year: Solo or Chamber Ensemble, Classical Album of the Year: Large Ensemble or Soloist(s) with Large Ensemble Accompaniment, Classical Album of the Year: Vocal or Choral Performance, Classical Composition of the Year, Alternative Album of the Year, Dance Recording of the Year,
Also: Reggae Recording of the Year, Roots & Traditional Album of the Year-Solo, Roots & Traditional Album of the Year-Group, Blues Album of the Year, Jack Richardson Producer of the Year, Recording Engineer of the Year, Album Design of the Year (sponsored by Ever-Reddy Packaging Ltd.), Video of the Year, Music DVD of the Year

Canadian Broadcasting Corporation
CBC Radio Music, PO Box 500, Stn A, Toronto ON M5W 1E6
416/205-3311; Fax: 416/205-6040
URL: www.radio.cbc.ca

National Radio Competition for Amateur Choirs
Established 1975; awarded biennially; prizes offered in following categories: Children's, Youth, Large, Adult Mixed Chamber, Adult Equal Voice, Church, Traditional & Ethno-Cultural, & Contemporary Choral Music.
Eight first prizes of $3,000 each; eight 2nd prizes of $2,000 each; $1,000 for best performance of a Canadian work.

National Radio Competition for Young Composers
Established 1973; competition sponsored every two years by CBC & the Canada Council; entrants must be Canadian citizens or landed immigrants, 30 years of age or under, & must not be employees of the CBC.
Up to 10 prizes are given: three 1st prizes of $5,000 each; three 2nd prizes of $4,000 each; three 3rd prizes; a $5,000 Grand Prize; a performance of the winning works is given on CBC English & French radio networks.

National Radio Competition for Young Performers
Established 1960; competition sponsored every two years by CBC/Radio-Canada & the Canada Council for the Arts; entrants must be Canadian citizens or landed immigrants, 30 years of age or under (32 for singers); categories rotate among strings, piano, voice, winds & brass; finals of competiton heard live on CBC Radio Two & La Chaîne culturelle.
First prize $15,000; 2nd prize $10,000; 3rd prize $5,000; prizes also include recital & concert engagements across Canada - URL: www.cbc.ca/ypc.

Canadian Country Music Association / Association de la musique country canadienne
#203, 626 King St. West, Toronto ON M5V 1M7
416/947-1331; Fax: 416/947-5924
Email: country@ccma.org; URL: www.ccma.org

Music Awards
Awards in 10 categories are presented annually to outstanding performers; 35 citations honour individuals & organizations which, have made a significant contribution to country music

Canadian Theatre Critics Association / Association des critiques de théâtre du Canada
#700, 250 Dundas St. West, Toronto ON M5T 2Z5
416/782-0966; Fax: 416/782-0366
Email: aruprech@ccs.carleton.ca; URL: www.canadiantheatrecritics.ca

The Herbet Whittaker/Drama Bench Award for Outstanding Contribution to Canadian Theatre
Presented annually to Canadian citizen or permanent resident working in any theatrical discipline who has demonstrated distinguished contribution in playwriting, performance, direction or design; named after Herbert Whittaker Founding Chairman of the Canadian Theatre Critics Assoc.

Council for Business & the Arts in Canada / Conseil pour le monde des affaires et des arts du Canada
#903, 165 University Ave., Toronto ON M5H 3B8
416/869-3016; Fax: 416/869-0435
Email: info@businessforarts.org; URL: www.businessforarts.org

Globe and Mail Business for the Arts Awards
These awards honour businesses in the categories of Best Arts/Entrepreneur Partnership, Most Effective Corporate Program, Most Innovative Marketing Sponsorship and The First Dance Award.

Edmund C. Bovey Award
To recognize individual members of the business community who contribute leadership, time, money & expertise to the arts
A sculpture to the winner & $20,000 distributed to the arts in a way specified by the winner

Dance Ontario Association / Association Ontario Danse

Case Goods Bldg., #304, 55 Mill St., Toronto ON M5A 3C4
416/204-1083; Fax: 416/204-1085
Email: contact@danceontario.ca; URL: www.danceontario.ca

Dance Ontario Award
Recognizes a lifetime commitment to dance - Peter Ryan

Dancer Transition Resource Centre / Centre de ressources et transition pour danseurs

The Lynda Hamilton Centre, #500, 250 The Esplanade, Toronto ON M5A 1J2
416/595-5655; Fax: 416/595-0009; Toll Free: 1-800-667-0851
Email: nationaloffice@dtrc.ca; URL: www.dtrc.ca

Anne M. Delicaet Bursary
To help fund tuition, books &/or supplies for applicant in their third year of full-time retraining/grants received from the DTRC
Award amount is discretionary

Karen Kain Award
Given to a dancer entering a second or subsequent year of full-time retraining
Award is discretionary

Lynda Hamilton Award
Awarded annually to a dancer in transition who has completed two years of study & requires a third to complete or continue the proposed course of study
$18,000 subsistence & $4,000 for tuition & supplies

Peter F. Bronfman Memorial Award
It is earmarked for a second or third year of retraining & subsistence & may be only awarded for the full amount
$18,000 subsistence & $4,000 for tuition & supplies

Sara Symons Bursary
Open to all recipients of at least one year of funding under type C grant who are continuing their studies
Amount is discretionary

Zella Wolofsky/Doug Wright Bursary
Awarded to a dancer with a degree from a recognized university & who is in second or subsequent year of professional program or doing graduate studies or second degree
$2,000 for any purpose

East Coast Music Association / Association de la musique de la côte est

145 Richmond St., Charlottetown PE C1A 1J1
902/892-9040; Fax: 902/892-9041
Email: ecma@ecma.ca; URL: www.ecma.ca

East Coast Music Awards
General Categories: Male Artist of the Year, Female Artist of the Year, Group of the Year, Songwriter of the Year, Single of the Year, Video of the Year, Album of the Year, New Artist(s) of the Year, Entertainer of the Year; Genre Specific Categories: Country Recording of the Year, Pop Recording of the Year, Rock Recording of the Year, Instrumental Recording of the Year, Alternative Recording of the Year, Jazz Recording of the Year, Blues Recording of the Year, Gospel Recording of the Year, Children's Recording of the Year, Bluegrass Recording of the Year, Urban Recording of the Year, Classical Recording of the Year, Roots/Traditional Recording of the Year, Folk Recording of the Year; Cultural Categories: Francophone Recording of the Year, Aboriginal Recording of the Year, African-Canadian Recording of the Year

Elinore & Lou Siminovitch Prize in Theatre

c/o BMO Financial Group, 55 Bloor St. West, 4th Fl., Toronto ON M4W 3N5
(416) 9927-2771
Email: andrew.soren@bmo.com; URL: www.siminovitchprize.com

Elinore & Lou Siminovitch Prize
Awarded annually; honours a director, playwright, or designer who in mid-career has made a significant contribution through a body of work to the theatre in Canada; direction, playwriting & design will be honoured on a three year cycle.
$100,000; the winner will receive an immediate cash prize of $75,000, in addition the honoured artist will be invited to designate $25,000 to a protegé of his/her choice who is involved in direction, playwriting or design in theatre in Canada or to an institution (theatre or educational facility) that contributes to better & more successful theatre in Canada

Fondation Émile-Nelligan
261, rue Bloomfield, Outremont QC H2V 3R6
514/278-4657; Fax: 514/278-1943
Email: info@fondation-nelligan.org; URL: www.fondation-nelligan.org

Prix Serge-Garant
Prix triennal de composition musicale décerné à un compositeur citoyen du Canada né au Québec ou à un compositeur citoyen du Canada ayant sa résidence principale au Québec depuis au moins dix ans
25 000$

Governor General's Performing Arts Awards Foundation

#113, 24 York St., Ottawa ON K1N 1K2
613/241-5297; Fax: 613/241-4677
URL: www.bce.ca/ggawards

Governor General's Performing Arts Awards
Established in 1992; honours six performing artists for their lifetime achievement & contribution to the cultural enrichment of Canada; each recipient is awarded $15,000 & a commemorative medal

Ramon John Hnatyshyn Award for Voluntarism in the Performing Arts
Recognizes outstanding service to the performing arts; the recipient is presented with a specially commissioned artwork by Canadian glass artist Naoko Takenouchi

The Jazz Report

#7, 592 Markham St., Toronto ON M6G 2L8
Email: jazzreport@sympatico.ca; URL: www.nationaljazzawards.com

The National Jazz Awards
Established in 2001; annual awards in 26 categories determined by readers & contributors to the quarterly; voting done online, through website
Open to all Canadian residents

Ontario Arts Council / Conseil des arts de l'Ontario

151 Bloor St. West, 5th Fl., Toronto ON M5S 1T6
416/969-7422; Fax: 416/961-7796;
Toll Free: 1-800-387-0058 ext. 7422
Email: mwarren@arts.on.ca; URL: www.arts.on.ca

John Adaskin Memorial Fund
Established in memorial of the Canadian Music Centre's first executive secretary; supports a project that encourages the promotion & development of Canadian music in the school system

Colleen Peterson Songwriting Award
Established in 2003, in honour of Colleen Peterson's contribution to Canadian folk and country music. This annual award was designed to support and promote the work of an emerging professional singer/songwriter in the genres of roots, traditional, folk and country music
$1,000

Heinz Unger Award for Conducting
Awarded every two years; Established 1968 & awarded biennially to honour the memory of the York Concert Society music director; administered by the Music Office of the Ontario Arts Council in cooperation with the Association of Canadian Orchestras
Up to $9,000

John Hirsch Director's Award
Established by a bequest to the Ontario Arts Council from the late John Hirsch; presented every three years to a promising theatre director in Ontario
$5,000

Leslie Bell Scholarship for Choral Conducting
Established 1973; awarded biennially in competition; the purpose of the award is to help young emerging choral conductors in Ontario further their studies in the choral music field either in Canada or abroad; competition organized by the Ontario Choral Federation
Up to $2,000

Pauline McGibbon Award
Annual award alternates between designers, directors & production crafts persons
$7,000

Premier's Award for Excellence in the Arts
Established in 2006, the Government of Ontario created this award to recognize outstanding achievement in the professional arts by an individual and a group.
Up to $50,000

The Vida Peene Fund
Provides assistance to projects which benefit the orchestra community as a whole

Tim Sims Encouragement Fund Award
Established in 1995; to be awarded annually to a promising young comedic performer or troupe
$1,000

Québec Ministère de la culture, des communications et de la condition féminine

Direction générale du secrétariat et des sociétés d'Etat
225, Grande Allée est, Québec QC G1R 5G5
418/380-2358 ext. 7220; Fax: 418/080-2364
Email: claude.janelle@mcc.gouv.qc.ca; URL: www.prixduquebec.gouv.qc.ca

Prix Denise-Pelletier
Prix réservé aux domaines de la chanson, de la musique, de l'art lyrique, du théâtre et de la danse

Québec Ministère des Relations internationales

Édifice Hector-Fabre, 525, boul René-Lévesque est, Québec QC G1R 5R9
418/649-2300; Fax: 418/649-2656
URL: www.mri.gouv.qc.ca

Prix Québec-Flandre de musique contemporaine
Créé en 1988; récompense les compositeurs flamands et interprètes québecois; décerné aux deux ans et en alternance, ce prix est constitué d'une bourse pour le compositeur et l'exécution de l'ouvre devant le public de l'autre communauté

Prix Rapsat-Lelièvre du disque de chanson
Initialement connu sous le nom Prix Québec/Wallonie-Bruxelles du disque de chanson; vise à encourager le développement et la promotion de la langue française, à stimuler la production et la diffusion de disques francophones

Société Saint-Jean-Baptiste de Montréal

82, rue Sherbrooke ouest, Montréal QC H2X 1X3
514/843-8851; Fax: 514/844-6369
Email: mbeaulieu@ssjb.com; URL: www.ssjb.com

Prix Calixa-Lavallée
Established 1959; $1,500 & a medal awarded annually to a French Canadian in recognition of outstanding achievement in music in serving the higher interests of the French Canadian people

Toronto Alliance for the Performing Arts

#210, 215 Spadina Ave., Toronto ON M5T 2C7
416/536-6468; Fax: 416/536-3463; Toll Free: 1-800-541-0499
URL: www.tapa.ca

Dora Mavor Moore Awards
Established 1979; celebrating excellence in Toronto theatre, 33 awards in large, medium & small theatre divisions, Theatre for Young Audiences & New Choreography

Western Canadian Music Alliance

#637, 776 Corydon Ave., Winnipeg MB R3M 0Y1
204/943-8485; Fax: 204/453-1594
Email: info@wcmw.ca; URL: www.wcmw.ca

Prairie Music Awards
Annual Awards in the following categories: Recording Engineer of the Year, Record Producer of the Year, Recording Studio of the Year, Record Company of the Year, Publishing Company of the Year, Best Compilation Album of the Year, Best Album Design of the Year, Best Music Score of the Year, Best Music Video, Best Booking Agent, Manager of the Year, & Musician of the Year; also Annual Awards for Prairie artists in the following categories: People's Choice Award, Female/Male Recording Artist of the Year, Group Recording of the Year, Most Promising Artist, Best Pop/Light Rock, Best Rock/Heavy Metal, Best Alternative, Best Country, Best Blues/R&B/Soul, Best Roots/Traditional/Ethnic, Best Rap/Dance/Rhythm, Best Jazz, Best Classical Performance

PUBLIC AFFAIRS

B'nai Brith Canada

15 Hove St., Toronto ON M3H 4Y8
416/633-6224; Fax: 416/630-2159
Email: bnb@bnaibrith.ca; URL: www.bnaibrith.ca

Award of Merit & Humanitarian Awards
Established 1981; presented annually at gala events in major communities across Canada

Selection of honourees based on outstanding achievement in their chosen fields as well as personal commitment to the overall betterment of Canadian society - Sharon Anisman

Canadian Association on Gerontology / Association canadienne de gérontologie

#106, 222 College St., Toronto ON M5T 3J1
416/978-7977; Fax: 416/978-4771
Email: contact@cagacg.ca; URL: www.cagacg.ca

The CAG Donald Menzies Bursary
To support post-baccalaureate students registered in a program of study focused on aging or the aged
$1,500

The CAG Margery Boyce Bursary
To support post-baccalaureate students who have made a significant contribution to their community through volunteer activities with or on behalf of seniors & who are registered in a program of study focused on aging or the aged
$500

The Canadian Council of Christians & Jews / Conseil canadien des chrétiens et des juifs

4211 Yonge St., PO Box 17, Toronto ON M2P 2A9
416/597-9693; Fax: 416/597-9775; Toll Free: 1-800-663-1848
Email: info@cccj.ca; URL: www.cccj.ca

Human Relations Award
Made to outstanding Canadians who have made a significant contribution towards bringing people together regardless of race, religion, or social status, in an atmosphere of understanding & respect; the award is made annually & is approved by a National Nominating Committee from the Board of Directors of CCCJ

Canadian Council of Professional Engineers / Conseil canadien des ingénieurs

#1100, 180 Elgin St., Ottawa ON K2P 2K3
613/232-2474; Fax: 613/230-5759
Email: info@engineerscanada.ca; URL: www.engineerscanada.ca

Meritorious Service Award for Community Service
Awarded for exemplary voluntary contribution to a community organization or humanitarian endeavour

The Canadian Council of the Blind / Le Conseil canadien des aveugles

#401, 396 Cooper St., Ottawa ON K2P 2H7
613/567-0311; Fax: 613/567-2728; Toll Free: 1-877-304-0968
Email: ccb@ccbnational.net; URL: ccbnational.net

Award of Merit
Established 1952; presented to a Canadian, blind or sighted, who has rendered outstanding work for the blind
A gold medal & clasp, a specially printed & bound citation & honorary life membership in the CCB

Canadian Federation for Sexual Health / Fédération canadienne pour la santé sexuelle

#430, One Nicholas St., Ottawa ON K1N 7B7
613/241-4474; Fax: 613/241-7550
Email: admin@cfsh.ca; URL: www.cfsh.ca

Phyllis P. Harris Scholarship
For students who have worked or volunteered in the general field of human sexuality who intend to work for a degree in the field of family planning or population issues
$2,500 towards full-time study at a Canadian university

The City of Toronto

Diversity Management and Community Engagement, Strategic and Corporate Policy/Healthy City Office, Manager's Office, City Hall, 100 Queen St. West, 11th Fl., East Tower, Toronto ON M5H 2N2
416/392-8592; Fax: 416/696-3645
Email: diversity@toronto.ca; URL: www.toronto.ca/civicawards/

Aboriginal Affairs Award
Est. 2003, given to a person(s) or organization whose volunteer efforts have made or are making a significant or ongoing contribution to the well-being & advancement of the Aboriginal community in Toronto

Access Award for Disability Issues
Established 1982; honours people or organizations that have made or are making a significant or ongoing contribution, beyond legislated requirements, to the well-being & advancement of people with disabilities; the award honours those who are sensitive to the access needs of persons with disabilities when planning structures or programs (this could include consideration of access requirements in the design of new or renovated buildings, a job creation campaign, a transportation system, recreational program, etc.)

Constance E. Hamilton Award on the Status of Women
This award commemorates the Privy Council of Great Britain granting women status as persons in 1929; award is named after the first woman member of City Council; recipients are persons who have made a significant contribution to securing equitable treatment for Toronto women

Pride Award for Lesbian Gay Bisexual Transgender Transsexual Two Spirited Issues
Est. 2003, the Pride Award honours individuals &/or organizations that have made or are making a significant or ongoing contribution to the well-being & advancement of these communities in Toronto

William P. Hubbard Race Relations Award
Named for Toronto's first visible minority Member of Council & Acting Mayor, this award honours persons with outstanding achievement & commitment to this field in Toronto; award was presented for the first time in 1990

Ethics in Action Awards

c/o VanCity, 183 Terminal Ave., PO Box 2120, Stn Terminal, Vancouver BC V6B 5R8
604/877-7000; Toll Free: 1-800-826-2489
Email: eia@ethicsinaction.com; URL: www.ethicsinaction.com

Ethics in Action Awards
Awards recognize businesses & individuals in business, whose actions & decisions have made a positive impact on our communities

Ontario Ministry of Citizenship & Immigration

Ontario Honours & Awards
Secretariat Ministry of Citizenship and Immigration, 400 University Ave., 4th Fl., Toronto ON M7A 2R9
416/314-7526; Fax: 416/314-7743
Email: ontariohonoursandawards@ontario.ca; URL: www.citizenship.gov.on.ca/english/honours

Ontario Senior Achievement Award
Presented annually to Ontario residents who have made a significant contribution to their communities after reaching 65 years of age; nominations may be made by any individual or organization

Status of Women Canada

Ottawa ON K1P 1H9
613/995-7835; Fax: 613/943-2386
URL: www.swc-cfc.gc.ca

Governor General's Award in Commemoration of Persons Case
Established 1979 to celebrate the 50th anniversary of the "Persons Case" which resulted in women being declared eligible for appointment to the Senate; annual awards recognize contributions by individuals toward promoting the equality of women in Canada

SCIENTIFIC, ENGINEERING, TECHNICAL

Association of Universities & Colleges of Canada / Association des universités et collèges du Canada

#600, 350 Albert St., Ottawa ON K1R 1B1
613/563-1236; Fax: 613/563-9745
Email: awards@aucc.ca; URL: www.aucc.ca

Fairfax Financial Holdings Limited Program
Undergraduate students of all disciplines
36 university undergraduate scholarships of $5,000; 24 college diploma scholarships of $3,500

BC Innovation Council

1188 West Georgia St., 9th Fl., Vancouver BC V6E 4A2
604/438-2752; Fax: 604/438-6564; Toll Free: 1-800-665-7222
Email: info@bcinnovationcouncil.com; URL: www.bcinnovationcouncil.com

BC Innovation Council Awards
Up to six gold medals awarded each year for outstanding achievements by BC scientists, engineers, industrial innovators & science communicators. The awards are: BC Science & Technology Champion of the Year, Young Innovator Award, Frontiers in Research, Cecil Green Award for Technology Entrepreneurship, Chairman's Award for Career Achievement, Lieutenant Govenor's Technology Innovation Award & Eve Savory Award for Science Communication

The Canada Council for the Arts / Conseil des Arts du Canada

350 Albert St., PO Box 1047, Ottawa ON K1P 5V8
613/566-4414; Fax: 613/566-4390; Toll Free: 1-800-263-5588
Email: info@canadacouncil.ca; URL: www.canadacouncil.ca

Killam Prizes
Up to five prizes of $100,000 each are given annually to eminent Canadian scholars in recognition of a distinguished career achievement in the natural sciences, health sciences, engineering, social sciences & humanities. Candidates must be nominated by three experts in their field. Chosen by Killam Selection

Killam Research Fellowships
Fellowships offered on a competitive basis to support specific research projects by distinguished Canadian researchers in any of the following broad fields: humanities, social sciences, natural sciences, health sciences, engineering & studies linking any of the disciplines within these broad fields; provide release time to individual scholars, normally full professors in Canadian universitites, who wish to pursue individual research; provides two years of teaching replacement to a maximum of $53,000 per year, plus the cost of fringe benefits of the Fellow, based on actual salary for the year before the tenure of the award; application must be made by individuals, not by institutions, universities or organizations

Canadian Aeronautics & Space Institute / Institut aéronautique et spatial du Canada

#104, 350 Terry Fox Drive., Kanata ON K2K 2W5
613/591-8787; Fax: 613/591-7291
Email: casi@casi.ca; URL: www.casi.ca

C.D. Howe Award
Established 1966; a silver plaque presented annually for achievement in the fields of planning, policy making & overall leadership in Canadian aeronautics & space activities

McCurdy Award
Established 1954; a silver medal & trophy presented annually for outstanding achievement in art, science & engineering relating to aeronautics & space

Romeo Vachon Award
Established 1969; bronze plaque awarded annually for outstanding contribution of a practical nature to the art, science, & engineering of aeronautics & space in Canada

Trans-Canada (McKee) Trophy
Canada's oldest aviation award established 1927; presented annually except when no qualified recipient is nominated for outstanding achievement in the field of air operations

Canadian Council of Professional Engineers / Conseil canadien des ingénieurs

#1100, 180 Elgin St., Ottawa ON K2P 2K3
613/232-2474; Fax: 613/230-5759

Email: info@engineerscanada.ca; URL: www.engineerscanada.ca
Gold Medal Award
Awarded for exceptional individual achievement & distinction in a field of engineering

Medal for Distinction in Engineering Education
Awarded for exemplary contribution to engineering teaching at a Canadian University

The Young Engineer Achievement Award
Awarded for outstanding contribution in a field of engineering by an engineer 35 years of age or younger

Canadian Institute of Forestry / Institut forestier du Canada

#504, 151 Slater St., Ottawa ON K1P 5H3
613/234-2242; Fax: 613/234-6181
Email: cif@cif-ifc.org; URL: www.cif-ifc.org

Canadian Forest Management Group Achievement Award
Established 1998; to recognize outstanding achievement by teams in groups of Natural Resource managers, researchers and NGO groups in forest resources related activities in Canada.

Canadian Forestry Achievement Award
Established 1966 & presented annually in recognition of superior accomplishments in forestry research &/or in recognition of outstanding administrative leadership in management, education, research & affairs of professional & scientific societies

Canadian Forestry Scientific Achievement Award
Established 1980; presented annually in recognition of superior accomplishments in scientific forestry

International Forestry Achievement Award
Established 1980; presented in recognition of outstanding achievement in international forestry

James M. Kitz Award
Awarded to a person who has made outstanding contributions to the practice of forestry, including: superior personal accomplishments; outstanding leadership in education, management re-

search or professional association work; promotion of forestry to various audiences
Open to anyone involved in forestry

Canadian Institute of Mining, Metallurgy & Petroleum / Institut canadien des mines, de la métallurgie et du pétrole

#855, 3400, boul de Maisonneuve ouest, Montréal QC H3Z 3B8
514/939-2710; Fax: 514/939-2714
Email: cim@cim.org; URL: www.cim.org

CIM Awards
The institute administers 26 awards recognizing achievement in mining, metallurgy & petroleum industries

CANARIE Inc.: Canada's Advanced Internet Development Organization

110 O'Connor St., Ottawa ON K1P 1H1
613/943-5454; Fax: 613/943-5443
Email: info@canarie.ca; URL: www.canarie.ca

Iway Awards
The Canarie !WAY Awards honors individuals or group & organizations who have made outstanding contributions to Canada's information society; focuses on R&D, advancements in internet technology providing cultural, social & economic benefits; five categories: New Technology Development; Application of Technology; Public Leadership; Community Service; Adaptive Technologies; Judges Award

The Chemical Institute of Canada / Institut de chimie du Canada

#550, 130 Slater St., Ottawa ON K1P 6E2
613/232-6252; Fax: 613/232-5862; Toll Free: 1-888-542-2242
Email: info@cheminst.ca; URL: www.cheminst.ca

Chemical Institute of Canada Awards
The institute administers several awards & scholarships in chemistry, chemical engineering, & macromolecular science or engineering

E.W.R. Steacie Memorial Fund / Fondation E.W.R. Steacie

100 Sussex Dr., Ottawa ON K1A 0R6
613/993-1212; Fax: 613/954-5242
Email: PrixSteaciePrize.SIMS@nrc-cnrc.gc.ca; URL: www.steacieprize.ca/index_e.html

The Steacie Prize
Canada's most prestigious award for young scientists & engineers; named to honour the memory of Edgar William Richard Steacie, a physical chemist & former President of the National Research Council of Canada; established 1963; awarded annually to a young scientist or engineer up to 40 years of age for outstanding scientific work in a Canadian context; winner receives a certificate & $10,000
$15,000

The Engineering Institute of Canada / Institut canadien des ingénieurs

1295 Hwy. 2 East, Kingston ON K7L 4V1
613/547-5989; Fax: 613/547-0195
Email: jplant1@cogeco.ca; URL: www.eic-ici.ca

The Sir John Kennedy Medal
Established in 1927 in commemoration of the great services rendered in the field of engineering by Sir John Kennedy, a past president of the EIC; medal is awarded every two years by the council in recognition of outstanding merit in the profession or of noteworthy contributions to the science of engineering or to the benefit of the institute

Ernest C. Manning Awards Foundation

#421 - 7th Ave. SW, 38th floor, Calgary AB T2P 4K9
403/645-8277; Fax: 403/645-8320
Email: manning@encana.com; URL: www.manningawards.ca

The Manning Awards
Given annually to Canadian innovators who have conceived & developed new concepts, procedures, processes or products of benefit to Canada; awards may be in any area of activity.
One $100,000 Principal Award; one $25,000 Award of Distinction; two $10,000 Innovation prizes, & four $4,000 Young Canadian Innovation Awards.

Natural Sciences & Engineering Research Council of Canada / Conseil de recherches en sciences naturelles et en génie

350 Albert St., Ottawa ON K1A 1H5
613/995-5992; Fax: 613/992-5337
URL: www.nserc.ca

Gerhard Herzberg Gold Medal for Science & Engineering
Awarded annually to an individual who has made outstanding & sustained contributions to Canadian research in natural sciences & engineering; the gold medal will be awarded for any activity of exceptional importance & impact that leads to the enhancement of the research enterprise in Canada - such activities may include contributions to knowledge, the application of existing knowledge, to the novel solution of practical problems, the promotion or management of research activity, the leadership in the transfer of knowledge.
The accomplishments for which the award is given must have been carried out in Canada & achieved over a substantial period of time; persons from any sector (academic, business & industry, or government) are eligible; current members of council are not eligible; awardee's performance in relation to the cited achievement must demonstrate an unusually high degree of ability & the application of such qualities as expertise, creativity, imagination, leadership, perseverance & dedication.

The E.W.R. Steacie Memorial Fellowships
Awarded to enhance the career development of outstanding & highly promising scientists & engineers who are staff members of Canadian universities; successful fellows are relieved of any teaching & administrative duties, enabling them to devote all their time & energy to research; up to four fellowships are awarded annually for a one or two-year period; fellowships are held at a Canadian university or affiliated research institution
Set at $90,000 to be paid to the university by NSERC to cover the cost of replacing the Steacie Fellow's teaching & administrative responsibilities

Prix Galien Canada

#800, 1200, av McGill College, Montréal QC H3B 4G7
514/843-2535; Fax: 514/843-2183
Email: christiane.bordeleau@groupesante.rogers.com; URL: htt://fgic-gfci.scitech.gc.ca/

Belleau-Nickerson Prize
Awarded in recognition of a drug that has been on the market for the past 10 years anywhere in the world & for at least three years in Canada

MacLean Hunter Health Fellowship
Awarded to a deserving young Canadian researcher
$15,000

Prix Galien - Innovative Drug
Awarded to a company that has developed & marketed a drug that has made the most significant contribution to the well-being of the general public, in terms of efficacy, safety & innovation

Prix Galien - Research
Awarded to a scientist who is known for his/her contribution to pharmaceutical research in Canada

Québec Ministère du Développement économique, de l'Innovation et de l'Exportation

710, place D'Youville, 3e étage, Québec QC G1R 4Y4
418/691-5950; Fax: 418/644-0118
URL: www.mdeie.gouv.qc.ca/

Prix Armand-Frappier
Décerné pour la création ou le développement d'institutions de recherche, ou pour l'administration et la promotion de recherche

Prix Lionel-Boulet
Décerné au chercheur qui s'est distingué par ses inventions, ses innovations scientifiques et technologiques, son leadership dans le développement scientifique et sa contribution à la croissance économique du Québec

Prix Marie-Victorin
Décerné aux chercheurs de sciences exactes et naturelles, les sciences de l'ingénierie et technologiques ainsi que les sciences agricoles

Prix Wilder-Penfield
Décerné aux scientifiques dont l'objet de recherche appartient au domaine biomédical

Royal Astronomical Society of Canada / Société royale d'astronomie du Canada

136 Dupont St., Toronto ON M5R 1V2
416/924-7973; Fax: 416/924-2911; Toll Free: 1-888-924-7272
Email: nationaloffice100000@rasc.ca; URL: www.rasc.ca

Chant Medal
Established 1940 in appreciation of the great work of the late Prof. C.A. Chant in furthering the interests of astronomy in Canada; silver medal is awarded no more than once a year to an amateur astronomer resident in Canada on the basis of the value of the work which he/she has carried out in astronomy & closely allied fields of original investigation

Ken Chilton Prize
Established 1977; plaque awarded annually to an amateur astronomer resident in Canada, in recognition of a significant piece of work carried out or published during the year

Simon Newcomb Award
Established 1978; trophy awarded annually for the best article on astronomy, astrophysics or space sciences submitted by a member of the society during the year

The Plaskett Medal
Presented jointly with CASCA for an outstanding doctoral thesis

The Royal Canadian Geographical Society / Société géographique royale du Canada

39 McArthur Ave., Vanier ON K1L 8L7
613/745-4629; Fax: 613/744-0947; Toll Free: 1-800-267-0824
Email: rcgs@rcgs.org; URL: www.rcgs.org

The Gold Medal
Established 1972; to recognize a particular achievement of one or more individuals in the field of geography, or a significant national or international event - Coordinator, Society Programs, Carolyn Milano

The Massey Medal
Established 1959; awarded annually for outstanding personal achievement in the exploration, development, or description of the geography of Canada

The Royal Society of Canada / La Société royale du Canada

170 Waller St., Ottawa ON K1N 9B9
613/991-6990; Fax: 613/991-6996
Email: info@rsc.ca; URL: www.rsc.ca

Bancroft Award
Established 1968; awarded every two years for publication, instruction & research in the earth sciences that have conspicuously contributed to public understanding & appreciation of the subject
$2,500 & a presentation scroll - Geneviève Gouin, Awards Coordinator, 613/991-5760

Eadie Medal
Established 1975; awarded annually in recognition of major contributions to any field in engineering or applied science with preference given to those having an impact on communications.
$3,000 & a bronze medal - Génèvieve Gouin, Awards Coordinator, 613/991-5760

John L. Synge Award
Established 1986; awarded at irregular intervals for outstanding research in any of the branches of mathematics
$2,500 & a diploma

Rutherford Memorial Medals: Chemistry & Physics
Established 1980; awarded annually for outstanding research, one in chemistry, one in physics
Two medals & $2,500 each

The Flavelle Medal
Established 1924; awarded every two years (since 1966) for an outstanding contribution to biological science during the preceding 10 years or for significant additions to a previous outstanding contribution to biological science

The Henry Marshall Tory Medal
Established 1941; awarded every two years (since 1947) for outstanding research in a branch of astronomy, chemistry, mathematics, physics, or an allied science

The McNeil Medal
Awarded to encourage communication of science to students & the public
$1,500 bursary & a medal

Willet G. Miller Medal
Established 1943; awarded every two years for outstanding research in any branch of the earth sciences - Génèvieve Gouin, Awards Coordinator, 613/991-5760

Société Saint-Jean-Baptiste de Montréal

82, rue Sherbrooke ouest, Montréal QC H2X 1X3
514/843-8851; Fax: 514/844-6369
Email: mbeaulieu@ssjb.com; URL: www.ssjb.com

Prix Léon-Lortie
Established 1987; awarded for achievement in the area of pure & applied sciences

Society of Chemical Industry - Canadian Section

#550, 130 Slater St., Ottawa ON K1P 6E2
Email: communications@soci.org; URL: www.soci.org

Canada Medal Award
Established 1939; awarded every two years for outstanding services in the Canadian chemical industry; recipient delivers an address at a meeting of the society

International Award
Established 1976; award is presented in recognition of outstanding service in the chemical industry in the international sphere, preferably to Canadians or persons who have contributed measurably to the Canadian chemical scene

Le Sueur Memorial Award
Established 1955 to commemorate Ernest A. Le Sueur; award is presented in recognition of outstanding innovation in the Canadian chemical industry

SPORTS & RECREATION

Canadian Association for Health, Physical Education, Recreation & Dance / Association canadienne pour la santé, l'éducation physique, le loisir et la danse
#301, 2197 Riverside Dr., Ottawa ON K1H 7X3
613/523-1348; Fax: 613/523-1206; Toll Free: 1-800-663-8708
Email: info@cahperd.ca; URL: www.cahperd.ca

R. Tait McKenzie Award of Honour
Instituted at the Montreal Convention in 1948, this is the most prestigious award presented by CAHPERD; named after the distinguished Canadian physician, sculptor & physical educator, Dr. Robert Tait McKenzie; candidate shall have performed distinguished, meritorious service as a recognized leader regionally & nationally in his/her field

Canadian Association for the Advancement of Women & Sport & Physical Activity / Association canadienne pour l'avancement des femmes du sport et de l'activité physique
#N202, 801 King Edward Ave., Ottawa ON K1N 6N5
613/562-5667; Fax: 613/562-5668
Email: caaws@caaws.ca; URL: www.caaws.ca

Breakthrough Awards
Presented annually to outstanding nominees who have used innovative ideas & alternative approaches to encourage & enable more girls & women to participate/lead/coach in sport & physical activity - Karin Lofstrom

CAAWS/Nike Girls@Play MVP Grant
Monthly grant awarded to a female athlete, coach, official or sport/recreation organization to help make their sporting goals & dreams - URL: www.caaws.ca/girlsatplay/grants/index.htm

Girls@Play Nike Youth Award

Stacey Levitt Scholarships
Awarded each year on behalf of the Levitt family & in memory of Stacey Levitt, who was killed while jogging in 1995 after being hit by a car.
$500 & a copy of "I am a Rose," a collection of poetry written by Stacey is given to a young woman, a girl's team or a sport organization that exemplifies Stacey's ideals & qualities.

Canadian Curling Association / Association canadienne de curling
1660 Vimont Ct., Cumberland ON K4A 4J4
613/834-2076; Fax: 613/834-0716; Toll Free: 1-800-550-2875
Email: info@curling.ca; URL: www.curling.ca

Award of Achievement
Commemorative plaque presented in recognition of individuals who have contributed significantly to any aspect of Canadian curling operations

Ray Kingsmith Award
Awarded to an individual who parallels the level of involvement & commitment exemplified by Ray Kingsmith

Volunteer of the Year Award
Based on contributions from the previous curling season; national volunteer of the year receives an all-expense paid weekend trip to Nokia Brier or Scott Tournament of Hearts, where they will be recognized during a playoff game

Ontario Ministry of Tourism & Recreation
Ontario Sport Awards
900 Bay St., 9th Fl., Toronto ON M7A 2R9
416/326-9326
URL: www.tourism.gov.on.ca/english/sportdiv/sport/sports-awards.htm

Ontario Sports Awards
Awards for Athlete of the Year (Male & Female), Coach of the Year (Male & Female), Athlete with a Disability of the Year (Male & Female), Team of the Year, Special Achievement Award for Volunteers, Corporate Sport Citation

Société Saint-Jean-Baptiste de Montréal
82, rue Sherbrooke ouest, Montréal QC H2X 1X3
514/843-8851; Fax: 514/844-6369
Email: mbeaulieu@ssjb.com; URL: www.ssjb.com

Prix Maurice-Richard
Established 1979; $1,500 & a medal awarded annually to a French Canadian in recognition of outstanding achievement in sports & athletics in serving the higher interests of the French Canadian people

Swimming/Natation Canada
#700, 2197 Riverside Dr., Ottawa ON K1H 7X3
613/260-1348; Fax: 613/260-0804
Email: natoffice@swimming.ca; URL: www.swimming.ca

Administrator of the Year Award
Annual award presented to a volunteer, who has demonstrated outstanding commitment to the organization

Club of the Year Award
Awards presented annually to three clubs

Coach of the Year
Annual awards recognize coaches of swimmers in the following categories: 1) able-bodied athletes; 2) athletes with a disability, & 3) long distance competitors; each winner receives a plaque & gift

Female/Male Swimmer of the Year
Annual awards recognize best international swimmers in the following categories: 1) able-bodied athletes, 2) athletes with a disability, & 3) long distance competitors; each winner receives a plaque & gift

Official of the Year Award
Annual award recognizes outstanding service to Canadian swimming

Victor Davis Memorial Award
Annual awards from the Victor Davis Memorial Fund assist young Canadian swimmers to continue their training, education & pursuit of excellence at the international level of competition; recipients are determined by the Victor Davis Memorial Fund Awards Committee

Canadian Honours System

For some years after Confederation, awards were made of a few hereditary honours and some knighthoods and companionships in orders of chivalry, and this policy continued until the end of the first World War.

From 1919 until 1933 no titular honours were granted. There was a brief revival of the defunct honours policy during the Conservative administration of R.B. Bennett, and several distinctions were awarded from 1934 to 1935, but the prohibition was reinstated with the return of the Liberals to office in 1935. Consequently, at the outset of the second World War, Canadians in the armed services were not entitled to receive awards in the order of chivalry for which other Commonwealth personnel were eligible. A parliamentary committee appointed in 1943 recommended that the ban on nontitular honours be lifted, clearing the way for members of the military and civilians to receive recognition for wartime services.

The hundredth anniversary of Confederation, July 1st, 1967, was the occasion on which the Order of Canada was created as the first component of a distinctly Canadian honours system. More information concerning Orders, Decorations and Medals (as well as various Governor General's awards) may be obtained by writing to: Public Information Directorate, Government House, 1 Sussex Dr., Ottawa ON K1A 0A1.

HERALDRY
Coats-of-arms, flags, badges and other heraldic devices are marks of honour and symbols of identity, authority and, in some cases, sovereignty. Each is granted by the Crown under an exercise of the Sovereign's prerogative to create heraldic honours.

Until June 4, 1988, Canadian corporations and individuals wishing to bear lawful arms petitioned the Sovereign's traditional heraldic officers in London and Edinburgh. On that date, by Royal Letters Patent, the Queen transferred the exercise of her heraldic prerogative, as Queen of Canada, to the Governor General who now heads a new office, the Canadian Heraldic Authority. With the act, heraldry, which has a long history in Canada, has been fully patriated.

These vice-regal responsibilities are administered by Canadian officers of arms appointed by commission under the Governor General's privy seal: the Herald Chancellor (the Secretary to the Governor General), the Deputy Herald Chancellor (the Deputy Secretary, Chancellery) and the Chief Herald of Canada (Director, Heraldry). He is assisted by three officers of arms: Saint-Laurent, Athabaska, and Fraser heralds, and one officer of arms extraordinary, Dauphin Herald.

New heraldic emblems are granted, and existing ones registered, by the Chief Herald upon receipt of an enabling Warrant from the Herald Chancellor or the Deputy Herald Chancellor acting on behalf of the Governor General. Grants and registrations are made by Letters Patent, documents that set out the Governor General's heraldic responsibilities, describe the emblem granted, and feature a representation of the Governor General's personal arms. To ensure a lasting record, the newly granted and registered emblems are entered in Canada's national armorial, the Public Register of Arms, Flags and Badges of Canada. Since the Authority was created, hundreds of petitions have been received from every part of the country, most for new grants of arms.

Canadian Honours List

ORDER OF CANADA
As mentioned above, the Order of Canada was created July 1, 1967. Her Majesty The Queen is Sovereign of the Order of Canada and the Governor General is, by virtue of that office, Chancellor and Principal Companion. He/She is assisted in the administration of the Order by an Advisory Council which comprises of:

a) the Chief Justice of Canada (Chair)
b) the Clerk of the Privy Council
c) the Deputy Minister, Canadian Heritage
d) the Chair of the Canada Council
e) the President of the Royal Society of Canada
f) the Chair of the Board of the Association of Universities and Colleges of Canada
g) not more than five other members, when considered appropriate by the Governor General, can be appointed for three-year terms.

The Secretary to the Governor General is, by his/her office, Secretary General of the Order.

The Order of Canada is designed to honour Canadian citizens for outstanding achievement and service to the country or to humanity at large and also for distinguished service in particular localities and fields of activity. The Order comprises three levels of membership: Companion, Officer, and Member. Up to 15 Companions may be appointed annually, but the total number of living Companions may not exceed 165. Up to 64 Officers and 136 Members may be appointed annually with no over-all limit.

The Order includes no titles of honour and confers no special privileges, hereditary or otherwise. Awards are made solely on the basis of merit. Members of the Order are entitled to place after their names the letters "C.C." for Companions, "O.C." for Officers, and "C.M." for Members.

Any person or organization may make nominations for appointment to the Order by writing to the Chancellery, Rideau Hall, Ottawa. The Advisory Council submits to the Governor General lists of those nominees who, in the opinion of the Council, are of greatest merit. Appointments to the Order are made by the Sovereign of the Order on the recommendation of the Governor General as Chancellor of the Order, under an instrument sealed with the Seal of the Order.

Non-Canadians whom the Government desires to honour may be accorded honourary membership in the Order.

Companions of the Order of Canada/ Compagnons de l'Ordre du Canada (C.C.) (Announced November 12, 2010)
Willard S. Boyle, C.C., Halifax, NS
Joseph A. Rouleau, C.C., G.O.Q., Montréal, QC
The Honourable Michael H. Wilson, P.C., C.C., Toronto, ON

Officers of the Order of Canada/ Officiers de l'Ordre du Canada (O.C.) (Invested September 14, 2011)
Richard B. Baltzan, O.C., Saskatoon, SK
James A. Dosman, O.C., S.O.M., Saskatoon, SK
René Dussault, O.C., O.Q., Québec, QC
Angela Enright, O.C., Victoria, BC
John Furlong, O.C., Vancouver, BC
Clément Gosselin, O.C., Québec, QC
R. Brian Haynes, O.C., Dundas, ON
Linda Hutcheon, O.C., Toronto, ON
Anthony Lang, O.C., Toronto, ON
Terence Macartney-Filgate, O.C., Toronto, ON
James Orbinski, O.C., O.Ont., M.S.C., Toronto, ON
Julie Payette, O.C., C.Q., Montréal, QC
Shelagh Rogers, O.C., Vancouver, BC

(Announced June 30, 2011)
André Bandrauk, O.C., North Hatley, QC
William Buyers, O.C., Deep River, ON
The Honourable Herménégilde Chiasson, O.C., Grand-Barachois, NB
Lorna Crozier, O.C., Saanich, BC
Alain Lefèvre, O.C., C.Q., Montréal, QC
Terence Macartney-Filgate, O.C., Toronto, ON
Denis Marleau, O.C., C.Q., Montréal, QC
Bob McDonald, O.C., Toronto, ON
Maureen O'Neil, O.C., Ottawa, ON
Viola Robinson, O.C., O.N.S., Yarmouth, NS
Maureen Sabia, O.C., Toronto, ON
Peter Alexander Singer, O.C., Toronto, ON
Annette Verschuren, O.C., Toronto, ON
Hayley Wickenheiser, O.C., Calgary, AB
Ronald G. Worton, O.C., Ottawa, ON *
** Indicates a promotion within the Order.*

(Invested May 25, 2011)
Raymond Chrétien, O.C., Montréal, QC
Sylvia Cruess, O.C., Montréal, QC
Claudio Cuello, O.C., Westmount, QC
Hélène Dorion, O.C., C.Q., Sherbrooke and Montréal, QC
The Honourable Arthur Jacob (Jake) Epp, P.C., O.C., Calgary, AB and St. Boniface, MB
Michael J. Fox, O.C., New York, NY, USA and Vancouver, BC
Margaret Lock, O.C., O.Q., Westmount, QC
Maurice McGregor, O.C., C.Q., Montréal, QC
The Honourable A. Anne McLellan, P.C., O.C., Edmonton, AB
Earl Muldon, O.C., Hazelton, BC
Robbie Robertson, O.C., Los Angeles, CA, USA and Toronto, ON
Nahum Sonenberg, O.C., Montréal, QC
Mary Vingoe, O.C., Dartmouth, NS
Harry Walsh, O.C. (*deceased*), Winnipeg, MB

(Announced December 30, 2010)
Nicole Brossard, O.C., Montréal, QC
Sylvia R. Cruess, O.C., Montréal, QC
James A. Dosman, O.C., S.O.M., Saskatoon, stock
The Honourable René Dussault, O.C., O.Q., Québec, QC
Angela Enright, O.C., Victoria, B.C.Clément Gosselin, O.C., Québec, QC
Linda Hutcheon, O.C., Toronto, ON
Anthony Edward Thomas Lang, O.C., Toronto, ON
Maurice McGregor, O.C., C.Q., Montréal, QC
Shelagh Rogers, O.C., Vancouver, BC
Mary Vingoe, O.C., Dartmouth, NS
Harry Walsh, O.C., Winnipeg, MB

(Announced November 12, 2010)
The Honourable David A. Anderson, P.C., O.C., Victoria, BC
Raymonde April, O.C, Montréal, QC
Michael J. Audain, O.C., O.B.C., West Vancouver, BC
Peter Hinton, O.C., Ottawa, ON
The Honourable Philippe Kirsch, O.C., The Hague, Netherlands and Montréal, QC
Shrawan Kumar, O.C., Fort Worth, Texas, USA and Edmonton, AB
Carol L. Richards, O.C., Québec, QC
Alvin Segal, O.C., Westmount, QC
Carol Stephenson, O.C., London, ON
Mladen Vranic, O.C., O.Ont., Toronto, ON

Honorary Officer of the Order of Canada/ Officier honorifique de l'Ordre du Canada (Announced November 12, 2010)
Sima Samar, O.C., Kabul, Afghanistan

Honorary Member of the Order of Canada/ Membre honorifique de l'Ordre du Canada
None awarded since last edition.

Members of the Order of Canada/ Membres de l'Ordre du Canada (C.M.) (Invested September 14, 2011)
Marthe Asselin-Vaillancourt, C.M., C.Q., Saguenay, QC
Robert Bourdeau, C.M., Ottawa, ON
The Honourable Patricia Carney, P.C., C.M., Saturna Island, BC
Marc Chouinard, C.M., Memramcook, NB
Paul D. Copeland, C.M., Toronto, ON
Ollie Currie, C.M., Edmonton, AB
Vera Elizabeth Dewar, C.M., Stratford, PEI
Pierre Fréchette, C.M., C.Q., Québec, QC
David Halliday, C.M., Maple Ridge, BC
Robert D. Hare, C.M., Surrey, BC
Hanny Hassan, C.M., London, ON
Ellis Jacob, C.M., Toronto, ON
Gilles Julien, C.M., Montréal, QC
Ruth E. Kajander, C.M., Thunder Bay, ON
Josef Kates, C.M., North York, ON
Jamie Kennedy, C.M., Toronto, ON
Jeffrey C. Lozon, C.M., Toronto, ON
Pierre Maranda, C.M., Québec, QC
John McLaughlin, C.M., O.N.B., Fredericton, NB
Rudolph (Rudy) North, C.M., Vancouver, BC
Gilles G. Patry, C.M.,O.Ont., Ottawa, ON
Shirley Post, C.M., Peterborough, ON
Terrence Punch, C.M., Halifax, NS
Charlene M. T. Robertson, C.M., Edmonton, AB
Bernard Saladin d'Anglure, C.M., Québec, QC
Jennifer Simons, C.M., Vancouver, BC
Ann Southam, C.M. (*deceased*), Toronto, ON
Beth Symes, C.M., Toronto, ON
Louis Taillefer, C.M., Sherbrooke, QC
Robert C. P. Westbury, C.M., Edmonton, AB
Edwina Wetzel, C.M., Conne River, NL
Christopher Wiseman, C.M., Calgary, AB

(Announced July 28, 2011)
Jean Roberts, C.M., Bagnols-en-Forêt, France and Montréal, QC

(Announced June 30, 2011)
Arnold Aberman, C.M., Toronto, ON
Shirley Bear, C.M., Perth-Andover, NB
Jeanne Besner, C.M., Calgary, AB
Anita Best, C.M., Norris Point, NL
John M. W. Bradford, C.M., Brockville, ON
The Honourable Patricia Carney, P.C., C.M., Vancouver, BC
Vera Dewar, C.M., Stratford, PE
Joan Donald, C.M., Red Deer, AB
Frank Fagan, C.M., St. John's, NL
Mary Lou Fallis, C.M., Toronto, ON
Edra Sanders Ferguson, C.M., Toronto, ON
Jean-Claude Fouron, C.M., Montréal, QC
Marie Gignac, C.M., Québec, QC
John H. V. Gilbert, C.M., Vancouver, BC
Malcom Gladwell, C.M., New York, NY, U.S.A. and Elmira, ON
Dorothy Griffiths, C.M., O.Ont., Welland, ON
Paul Valdemar (Valdy) Horsdal, C.M., Salt Spring Island, BC
Frederick Hyndman, C.M., Charlottetown, PE
Frederic (Eric) Jackman, C.M., O.Ont., Toronto, ON
Ruth E. Kajander, C.M., Thunder Bay, ON
Josef Kates, C.M., Toronto, ON
Pierre Lavoie, C.M., C.Q., M.S.M., Saguenay, QC
Eugene Levy, C.M., Toronto, ON
Pierre Maranda, C.M., Québec, QC
Robert Y. McMurtry, C.M., Picton, ON
Alvaro Morales, C.M., Kingston, ON
Larry Nelson, C.M., Moncton, NB
Pierre Nepveu, C.M., Montréal, QC
Samantha Joan Nutt, C.M., O.Ont., Toronto, ON
Nino Ricci, C.M., Toronto, ON
Bernard Saladin-d'Anglure, C.M., Québec, QC
David William Shannon, C.M., O.Ont., Thunder Bay, ON
David Staines, C.M., O.Ont., Ottawa, ON
F. Thomas Stanfield, C.M., Truro, NS
W. Brett Wilson, C.M., Calgary, AB

(Invested May 25, 2011)
Georges A. Arès, C.M., Edmonton, AB
Michel G. Bergeron, C.M., O.Q., Québec, QC
Bernard Blishen, C.M., Ottawa, ON
W. Edmund Clark, C.M., Toronto, ON
Stephen Clarkson, C.M., Toronto, ON
The Honourable Erminie J. Cohen, C.M., Saint John, NB
Phil Comeau, C.M., Saulnierville, N.S. and Montréal, QC
Abraham (Braam) de Klerk, C.M., Victoria, B.C. and Inuvik, NWT
René Derouin, C.M., C.Q., Val-David, QC
Mary Jo Haddad, C.M., Oakville, ON
Martha Lou Henley, C.M., Vancouver, BC
Mary-Ellen Jeans, C.M., Ottawa, ON
Donald Julien, C.M., O.N.S., Truro, NS
Derek Key, C.M., O.P.E.I., Summerside, PEI
Claude Laberge, C.M., Westmount, QC
Louise Lévesque, C.M., C.Q., Hudson, QC
Andrée Lortie, C.M., Ottawa, ON
Pierre Lucier, C.M., Québec, QC
James (Jamie) C. MacDougall, C.M., Westmount, QC
Joy Harvie Maclaren, C.M., Ottawa, ON
Howard (Howie) W. Meeker, C.M., Waterloo, ON and Parksville, BC
Alex C. Michalos, C.M., Brandon, MB and Prince George, BC
Rita Mirwald, C.M., Saskatoon, SK
Aftab A. Mufti, C.M., North Vancouver, BC and Winnipeg, MB
Harold (Hal) O'Leary, C.M., Winter Park, CO, USA and Fredericton, NB
Rosalind Prober, C.M., Winnipeg, MB
Ernesto L. Schiffrin, C.M., Montréal, QC
David H. Turpin, C.M., Victoria, BC
Kue Young, C.M., Toronto, ON

(Announced December 30, 2010)
Patricia Aldana, C.M., Toronto, ON
Marthe Asselin-Vaillancourt, C.M., C.Q., Saguenay, QC
Bernard Blishen, C.M., Ottawa, ON
Robert Bourdeau, C.M., Ottawa, ON
Ronald Caplan, C.M., Sydney, NS
Marc Chouinard, C.M., Memramcook, NB
The Honourable Erminie J. Cohen, C.M., Saint John, NB
Anthony Comper, C.M., Toronto, ON
Elizabeth Comper, C.M., Toronto, ON
Paul D. Copeland, C.M., Toronto, ON
Ollie Currie, C.M., Edmonton, AB
Pierre Fréchette, C.M., C.Q., Lévis, QC
Monique Giroux, C.M., Montréal, QC
David Halliday, C.M., Maple Ridge, BC
Robert D. Hare, C.M., White Rock, BC
Hanny A. Hassan, C.M., London, ON
Michael Hayden, C.M., O.B.C., Vancouver, BC
Martha Lou Henley, C.M., Vancouver, BC
Ellis Jacob, C.M., Toronto, ON
Gilles Julien, C.M., Montréal, QC
Jamie Kennedy, C.M., Toronto, ON
Derek Key, C.M., O.P.E.I, Summerside, PE
Camille Limoges, C.M., Montréal, QC
Trevor Linden, C.M., O.B.C., Vancouver, BC
M. Joy Maclaren, C.M., Ottawa, ON
John McLaughlin, C.M., O.N.B., Fredericton, NB
Howard (Howie) W. Meeker, C.M., Kitchener-Waterloo, ON and Parksville, BC
Gwyn Morgan, C.M., Calgary, AB and North Saanich, BC
Daniel Nestor, C.M., Toronto, ON and Nassau, Bahamas
Rudolph (Rudy) North, C.M., Vancouver, BC
Eric Peterson, C.M., Toronto, ON
Shirley Post, C.M., Peterborough, ON
Terrence Punch, C.M., Halifax, NS
Charlene M.T. Robertson, C.M., Edmonton, AB
Jennifer Simons, C.M., Vancouver, BC
Tricia Smith, C.M., Vancouver, BC
Mavis Staines, C.M., Toronto, ON
Beth Symes, C.M., Toronto, ON
Robert H. Taylor, C.M., Vancouver, BC
Robert C.P. Westbury, C.M., Edmonton, AB
Edwina Wetzel, C.M., Conne River, NL
Christopher Wiseman, C.M., Calgary, AB

(Announced November 19, 2010)
F. Richard Matthews, C.M., Calgary, AB

(Announced November 12, 2010)
Herbert (Herb) C. Belcourt, C.M., Edmonton, AB
Alice Chan-Yip, C.M., Montréal, QC
Adriana A. Davies, C.M., Edmonton, AB
Marq de Villiers, C.M., Eagle Head, NS
Calixte Duguay, C.M., Caraquet, NB
Marlys A. Edwardh, C.M., Toronto, ON
James Ehnes, C.M., Brandon, MB and Bradenton, Florida, USA
Étienne Gaboury, C.M., Winnipeg, MB
Joan Glode, C.M., Shubenacadie, NS
S. Larry Goldenberg, C.M., O.B.C., Vancouver, BC
Bernard S. Goldman, C.M., Toronto, ON
Clarence A. Guenter, C.M., Canmore, AB
Patrick J. Gullane, C.M., Toronto, ON
Garry Hilderman, C.M., Dugald, MB
Karen Minden, C.M., Toronto, ON
Bonnie Patterson, C.M., O.Ont., Toronto, ON
Ross H. Paul, C.M., Vancouver, BC and Windsor, ON
David K. Pecaut, C.M. (*deceased*), Toronto. ON
Ches D. Penney, C.M., Conception Bay South, NL
Gordon Porter, C.M., Woodstock, NB
Pierre Rolland, C.M., Montréal, QC
Walter Rosser, C.M., Kingston, ON
Robert W. Slater, C.M., Ottawa, ON
Glen Sorestad, C.M., Saskatoon, SK
John Stanton, C.M., Edmonton, AB
Irene (Orysia) Sushko, C.M., Hamilton, ON

ORDER OF MILITARY MERIT

The Order of Military Merit was created on July 1, 1972 to recognize meritorious service and devotion to duty by members of the Canadian Forces. The Order has three grades of membership: Commander (C.M.M.), Officer (O.M.M.) and Member (M.M.M.). The annual number of appointments is limited to one-tenth of one percent of the number of persons in the Canadian Forces in the preceding year.

Commanders of the Order of Military Merit/
Commandeurs de l'Ordre du mérite militaire (C.M.M.)
(Announced January 25, 2011)

Rear-Admiral Nigel Stafford Greenwood, C.M.M., C.D., Victoria, BC*
Major-General Joseph Marcel Marquis Hainse, C.M.M., C.D., Ottawa, ON*
Major-General Tom James Lawson, C.M.M., C.D., Ottawa, ON*
Rear-Admiral Paul Andrew Maddison, C.M.M., M.S.M., C.D., Ottawa, ON*
Major-General Mark Edmund McQuillan, C.M.M., C.D., Ottawa, ON
Major-General Guy Robert Thibault, C.M.M., C.D., Ottawa, ON
** Indicates a promotion within the Order.*

(Announced December 7, 2010)

Rear-Admiral Robert Andrew Davidson, C.M.M., C.D., Ottawa, ON
Major-General David A. Fraser, C.M.M., M.S.C., M.S.M., C.D., Kingston, ON*
** Indicates a promotion within the Order.*

Officers of the the Order of Military Merit/
Officiers de l'Ordre du mérite militaire (O.M.M.)
(Announced January 25, 2011)

Captain(N) Scott Edward George Bishop, O.M.M., C.D., Ottawa, ON
Lieutenant-Colonel Allan Eric Bratland, O.M.M., C.D., Winnipeg, MB
Lieutenant-Colonel Kevin Francis Bryski, O.M.M., C.D., Ottawa, ON
Major James Randall Burton, O.M.M., C.D., Hornell Heights, ON
Colonel Kenneth André Corbould, O.M.M., C.D., Belleville, ON
Commander Anthony Robert Evans, O.M.M., C.D., Victoria, BC
Lieutenant-Commander Cindy Bernadette Galt, O.M.M., C.D., Summerside, PEI
Colonel Martin Girard, O.M.M., C.D., Ottawa, ON
Brigadier-General Paul-Émilien Richard Simon Hébert, O.M.M., C.D., Montréal, QC
Colonel David Gerald Henley, O.M.M., C.D., Halifax, NS
Lieutenant-Colonel Patricia Henry, O.M.M., C.D., Ottawa, ON
Colonel Jean-Marc Lanthier, O.M.M., M.S.C., C.D., Courcelette, QC
Commander Robert Lewis-Manning, O.M.M., C.D., Esquimalt, BC
Lieutenant-Colonel Deborah Lynn McKenzie, O.M.M., C.D., Lazo, BC
Lieutenant-Colonel Shawn Darric McKinstry, O.M.M., C.D., Kingston, ON
Lieutenant-Colonel Darryl Albert Mills, O.M.M., M.S.C., C.D., Meaford, ON
Colonel Richard Francis Pucci, O.M.M., C.D., Ottawa, ON
Lieutenant-colonel Joseph Joël Roy, O.M.M., C.D., Astra, ON
Colonel James Baxter Simms, O.M.M., C.D., Oromocto, NB
Captain(N) Martin William Teft, O.M.M., C.D., Ottawa, ON
Lieutenant-Colonel Homer Chin-nan Tien, O.M.M., C.D., Petawawa, ON
Chief Warrant Officer Bernard Joseph Noël Verreault, O.M.M., C.D., Winnipeg, MB*
Lieutenant-Colonel Lawrence James Zaporzan, O.M.M., C.D., Ottawa, ON
** Indicates a promotion within the Order.*

(Announced December 7, 2010)

Captain(N) Richard Bergeron, O.M.M., C.D., Colorado Springs, Colorado, U.S.A
Major Steven Card, O.M.M., C.D., Moncton, NB
Colonel F. Paul Crober, O.M.M., C.D., Victoria, BC
Commander Christopher Deere, O.M.M., C.D., Chief of the Maritime Staff, Ottawa, ON
Colonel Derek W. Joyce, O.M.M., C.D., Greenwood, NS
Colonel Craig King, O.M.M., C.D., M.B.E., Denwood, AB
Captain(N) Colin Plows, O.M.M., C.D., Chief of the Maritime Staff, Ottawa, ON
Captain(N) Daniel Sing, O.M.M., C.D., Ottawa, ON
Colonel Pierre St-Amand, O.M.M., C.D., Cold Lake, AB
Colonel Christopher Thurrott, O.M.M., M.S.M., C.D., Kingston, ON

Members of the Order of Military Merit/
Membres de l'Ordre du mérite militaire (M.M.M.)
(Announced January 25, 2011)

Sergeant Jorgan Aitaok, M.M.M., Yellowknife, NWT
Chief Warrant Officer Mark Arden, M.M.M., C.D., Vancouver, BC
Chief Warrant Officer Denise Aimee Ballermann, M.M.M., C.D., Edmonton, AB
Master Warrant Officer Robert Paul Bartlett, M.M.M., C.D., Oromocto, NB
Chief Warrant Officer Joseph Yvan Denis Bédard, M.M.M., C.D., Québec, QC
Chief Warrant Officer Joseph Bernard Alain Bergeron, M.M.M., C.D., Ottawa, ON
Chief Warrant Officer Gerard Joseph Brennan, M.M.M., C.D., Halifax, NS
Major Patrick Albert Denis Brizay, M.M.M., C.D., Astra, ON
Master Warrant Officer Kirby Vincent Burgess, M.M.M., C.D., Belleville, ON
Chief Petty Officer 1st Class Joseph François Luc Champagne, M.M.M., C.D., Shearwater, NS
Sergeant Joseph Jacques Mario Charette, M.M.M., M.B., C.D., Borden, ON
Chief Petty Officer 1st Class Malcolm Derek Conlon, M.M.M., C.D., Victoria, BC
Captain Joseph Charles Serge Côté, M.M.M., C.D., Richelain, QC
Sergeant Russell Wayne Coughlin, M.M.M., C.D., Petawawa, ON
Chief Warrant Officer Bernard Joseph Curtis, M.M.M., C.D., Sydney, NS
Chief Warrant Officer William Darling, M.M.M., C.D., Toronto, ON
Warrant Officer Robert Allan David, M.M.M., C.D., Petawawa, ON
Master Warrant Officer Joseph Raymond Yves Demers, M.M.M., C.D., Courcelette, QC
Master Warrant Officer Stephen Christopher Downey, M.M.M., C.D., Edmonton, AB
Warrant Officer William Francis Doupe, M.M.M., C.D., Petawawa, ON
Chief Petty Officer 1st Class Walter Joseph Bernard Dubeau, M.M.M., C.D., Victoria, BC
Chief Warrant Officer Joseph Peter Dulong, M.M.M., C.D., Halifax, NS
Captain Sylvain Charles Falle, M.M.M., C.D., Kingston, ON
Chief Petty Officer 1st Class Michael Craig Feltham, M.M.M., C.D., Shearwater, NS
Chief Petty Officer 2nd Class Richard Alton Fisher, M.M.M., C.D., Astra, ON
Sergeant Lorne Emerson Lionel Ford, M.M.M., C.D., Edmonton, AB
Warrant Officer Melina Dorothy Ann Fournier, M.M.M., C.D., Ottawa, ON
Major Carl Gauthier, M.M.M., C.D., Ottawa, ON
Chief Warrant Officer Daphine Viola Germain, M.M.M., C.D., Hornell Heights, ON
Lieutenant(N) Corey Lloyd Ellis Gleason, M.M.M., C.D., Esquimalt, BC
Chief Warrant Officer Joseph Ernest Gilles Godbout, M.M.M., C.D., Courcelette, QC
Chief Warrant Officer Joseph Lucien Éric Gravel, M.M.M., C.D., Courcelette, QC
Chief Warrant Officer Gerald Olympe Gravelle, M.M.M., C.D., Kingston, ON
Chief Warrant Officer Alain Grenier, M.M.M., C.D., Courcelette, QC
Warrant Officer Sean Michael Hansen, M.M.M., C.D., Denwood, AB
Captain Paul Henry Hartinger, M.M.M., C.D., Oromocto, NB
Captain John Douglas Hill, M.M.M., C.D., Oromocto, NB
Master Warrant Officer Richard David Hills, M.M.M., C.D., Kingston, ON
Warrant Officer Murray Clair Hiltz, M.M.M., C.D., Greenwood, NS
Warrant Officer Kevin Thomas Johnson, M.M.M., M.S.M., C.D., Kingston, ON
Master Warrant Officer Edward James Kilcup, M.M.M., C.D., Ottawa, ON
Master Warrant Officer Marc Daniel Lafontaine, M.M.M., C.D., Ottawa, ON
Master Warrant Officer William Kenneth Laing, M.M.M., C.D., Kingston, ON
Chief Petty Officer 2nd Class Stephen Joseph Lamarche, M.M.M., C.D., Windsor, ON
Sergeant Frédéric Gilles Joseph Lavoie, M.M.M., C.D., Kingston, ON
Warrant Officer Robert Ronald Leblanc, M.M.M., C.D., Vancouver, BC
Petty Officer 2nd Class James Anthony Leith, M.M.M., S.C., M.S.M., C.D., Shearwater, NS
Chief Warrant Officer Robert Colin MacDonald, M.M.M., C.D., Greenwood, NS
Master Warrant Officer Donald Nolan MacIntyre, M.M.M., C.D., Shearwater, NS
Petty Officer 1st Class Arthur Wilberforce MacLeod, M.M.M., C.D., Shearwater, NS
Warrant Officer Patricia Susan MacWilliams, M.M.M., C.D., Edmonton, AB
Captain William McAuley, M.M.M., C.D., Calgary, AB
Chief Petty Officer 1st Class Michael Daniel McCallum, M.M.M., C.D., Victoria, BC
Warrant Officer Craig Richard McKay, M.M.M., C.D., Cold Lake, AB
Major Wendy Mae McKenzie, M.M.M., C.D., Vancouver, BC
Warrant Officer David Francis McLaughlin, M.M.M., C.D., Borden, ON
Master Warrant Officer Shawn Anthony Mercer, M.M.M., M.S.M., C.D., Ottawa, ON
Master Warrant Officer Kenneth Miles, M.M.M., C.D., Petawawa, ON
Chief Warrant Officer Steven Maurice Milton, M.M.M., C.D., Shilo, MB
Captain William English Moore, M.M.M., C.D., Oromocto, NB
Master Warrant Officer Marie Rose Christine Ouellet, M.M.M., C.D., Ottawa, ON
Warrant Officer Bryan Keith Pierce, C.V., M.M.M., M.S.C., C.D. , Winnipeg, MB
Master Warrant Officer Roy Harold Pugh, M.M.M., C.D., Halifax, NS
Chief Warrant Officer Joseph Vernon Pynn, M.M.M., C.D., Petawawa, ON
Major Douglas Reid, M.M.M., C.D., Kingston, ON
Chief Petty Officer 1st Class Thomas Christopher Riefesel, M.M.M., C.D., Halifax, NS
Master Warrant Officer Joseph Henry Sampson, M.M.M., C.D., Winnipeg, MB
Chief Warrant Officer Joseph Normand Yvon Sauvageau, M.M.M., C.D., Richelain, QC
Chief Warrant Officer Jean-Paul Savoie, M.M.M., C.D., Saint John, NB
Chief Petty Officer 2nd Class Angela Lynne Schenkers, M.M.M., C.D., Esquimalt, BC
Warrant Officer Marie Lucette Sylvie Seaward, M.M.M., C.D., Shilo, MB
Master Warrant Officer Patrick Henry Simms, M.M.M., C.D., Edmonton, AB
Warrant Officer Wayde Lee Simpson, M.M.M., M.B., C.D., Astra, ON
Master Warrant Officer Carol Snow, M.M.M., C.D., Ottawa, ON
Chief Warrant Officer Andrew Peter Stapleford, M.M.M., C.D., Toronto, ON
Captain Terrence Gordon Stead, M.M.M., C.D., Gander, NL
Master Warrant Officer Keith Charles Thibault, M.M.M., C.D., Cold Lake, AB
Chief Warrant Officer David Charles Tofts, M.M.M., C.D., Courcelette, QC
Master Warrant Officer Guy Tremblay, M.M.M., C.D., Hornell Heights, ON
Chief Warrant Officer Joseph Louis Philippe Turbide, M.M.M., C.D., Richelain, QC
Captain Joseph Napoléon Denis Veilleux, M.M.M., C.D., Sherbrooke, QC
Master Warrant Officer Lise Marie Juliette Ward, M.M.M., C.D., Richelain, QC
Petty Officer 1st Class Paul Joseph Walsh, M.M.M., C.D., Shearwater, NS
Captain Shannon Marie Wills, M.M.M., C.D., Victoria, BC
Master Warrant Officer John Cameron Winters, M.M.M., C.D., Hornell Heights, ON

Members of the Order of Military Merit/
Membres de l'Ordre du mérite militaire (M.M.M.)
(Announced December 7, 2010)

Chief Warrant Officer David Alex, M.M.M., C.D., Winnipeg, MB
Warrant Officer Charles Brady, M.M.M., C.D., Toronto, ON
Warrant Officer Linda Chassé, M.M.M., C.D., Courcelette, QC
Master Warrant Officer Dale Coble, M.M.M., C.D., Edmonton, Edmonton, AB
Chief Warrant Officer William Dalke, M.M.M., C.D., Borden, ON
Warrant Officer Edward Dallow, M.M.M., C.D., Petawawa, ON
Chief Warrant Officer Kirk Drew, M.M.M., C.D., Windsor, ON
Master Warrant Officer Elizabeth Dunsmore, M.M.M., C.D., Lazo, BC
Master Warrant Officer Pierre Frenette, M.M.M., C.D., Montréal, QC
Captain Douglas Gayton, M.M.M., C.D., Vancouver, BC
Chief Petty Officer 2nd Class Gilles Grégoire, M.M.M., C.D., Halifax, NS
Chief Warrant Officer Stéphane Guy, M.M.M., C.D., Kingston, ON
Major Carmen Hamel, M.M.M., C.D., Richelain, QC
Master Warrant Officer James Jeckell, M.M.M., C.D., Astra, ON
Captain Lennard Johnston, M.M.M., C.D., Borden, ON
Master Warrant Officer Roger King, M.M.M., C.D., Ottawa, ON
Master Warrant Officer J. S. Michel Lavallée, M.M.M., C.D., Oromocto, NB
Captain Patrick Lee, M.M.M., C.D., Halifax, NS

Chief Petty Officer 2nd Class Thomas Lizotte, M.M.M., C.D., Halifax, NS
Chief Warrant Officer Donald MacIsaac, M.M.M., C.D., Brunssum, Netherlands
Chief Warrant Officer Michael Lawrence McDonald, M.M.M., M.S.C., C.D., Kingston, ON
Sergeant Sandra Melanson, M.M.M., C.D., Astra, ON
Chief Petty Officer 2nd Class Eric Meredith, M.M.M., C.D., Victoria, BC
Chief Warrant Officer Mark Miller, M.M.M., C.D., 1st Battalion, Petawawa, ON
Master Warrant Officer Carol Monsigneur, M.M.M., C.D., Richelain, QC
Warrant Officer Russell Mullen, M.M.M., C.D., Denwood, AB
Master Warrant Officer Sean Murphy, M.M.M., C.D., Headquarters, California, USA
Petty Officer 2nd Class Peter Neville, M.M.M., C.D., NS
Chief Warrant Officer Marc Pelletier, M.M.M., C.D., Astra, ON
Warrant Officer Stephen Piccolo, M.M.M., C.D., Edmonton, AB
Captain Lorne Plemel, M.M.M., C.D., Moncton, NB
Chief Petty Officer 2nd Class Christopher Radimer, M.M.M., C.D., Halifax, NS
Petty Officer 1st Class Patrick J. J. Saunders, M.M.M., C.D., Halifax, NS
Master Warrant Officer Marco Séguin, M.M.M., C.D., Courcelette, QC
Master Warrant Officer Sharman Thomas, M.M.M., C.D., Chilliwack, BC
Captain Darren Turner, M.M.M., C.D., Petawawa, ON
Chief Warrant Officer Armand Vinet, M.M.M., C.D., Oromocto, NB
Chief Petty Officer 2nd Class Kevin Woods, M.M.M., C.D., Victoria, BC
Captain Gregory Zwicker, M.M.M., C.D., Edmonton, AB

ORDER OF MERIT OF THE POLICE FORCES

In October 2000, Her Majesty The Queen approved the creation of the Order as a means of recognizing conspicuous merit and exceptional service by members and employees of the Canadian police forces whose contributions extend beyond protection of the community. There are three levels of membership - Commander, Officer and Member - that reflect long-term, outstanding service in varying degrees of responsibility. Each level has corresponding nominal letters: C.O.M., O.O.M. and M.O.M.

Commander of the Order of Merit of the Police Forces/ Commandeur de l'Ordre du mérite des corps policiers (C.O.M.)
None awarded since last edition.

Officers of the the Order of Merit of the Police Forces/ Officiers de l'Ordre du mérite des corps policiers (O.O.M.) (Announced May 16, 2011)
Assistant Commissioner Line Carbonneau, Royal Canadian Mounted Police, Westmount, QC
Director General Robert Fahlman, Royal Canadian Mounted Police, Ottawa, ON
Chief Robert Herman, Thunder Bay Police Service, ON
Deputy Chief Constable Warren Lemcke, Vancouver Police Department, BC
Chief Dale R. McFee, Prince Albert Police Service, SK*
Superintendent Brian Simpson, Royal Canadian Mounted Police, Red Deer, AB
Chief A. Paul Smith, Charlottetown Police Services, PEI
Chief Wendy Southall, Niagara Regional Police Service, ON
** Indicates promotion within the Order.*

Members of the the Order of Merit of the Police Forces/ Membres de l'Ordre du mérite des corps policiers (M.O.M.) (Announced on May 16, 2011)
Deputy Chief Danny Aikman, Cornwall Community Police Service, ON
Director Serge Bélisle, Service de police de la Ville de Québec, QC
Deputy Chief Gary Broste, Saskatoon Police Service, SK
Assistant Commissioner J.G.P. Michel Cabana, Royal Canadian Mounted Police, Ottawa, ON
Staff Sergeant Jean-Marc Collin, Royal Canadian Mounted Police, Moncton, NB
Deputy Chief Troy Cooper, Prince Albert Police Service, SK
Superintendent Robert Davis, Royal Canadian Mounted Police, Newmarket, ON
Chief Glenn De Caire, Hamilton Police Service, ON
Chief Henry DeLaronde, Treaty Three Police Service, ON
Chief Frank Elsner, Greater Sudbury Police Service, ON
Deputy Chief Eric Girt, Hamilton Police Service, ON
Chaplain R.A. (Bob) Harper, Royal Canadian Mounted Police, Edmonton, AB
Superintendent Timothy Head, Royal Canadian Mounted Police, Ottawa, ON
Sergeant Toby Hinton, Vancouver Police Department, BC
Superintendent Andrew Hobbs, Vancouver Police Department, BC
Superintendent Jamie Jagoe, Royal Canadian Mounted Police, Kitchener, ON
Director Kristine Kijewski, Toronto Police Service, ON
Chief Superintendent Alphonse MacNeil, Royal Canadian Mounted Police, Ottawa, ON
Ms. Sylvie Mantha, Service de police de la Ville de Gatineau, QC
Superintendent Kathryn Martin, Toronto Police Service, ON
Assistant Commissioner Dale McGowan, Royal Canadian Mounted Police, Regina, SK
Staff Superintendent Jeffrey McGuire, Toronto Police Service, ON
Chief Stephen McIntyre, Rothesay Regional Police Force, NB
Chief Superintendent Blair McKnight, Royal Canadian Mounted Police, Halifax, NS
Staff Sergeant Terry McLachlan, Royal Canadian Mounted Police, Kelowna, BC
Detective Raymond Wai-Sang Miu, Toronto Police Service, ON
Deputy Chief Robert Napier, Kingston Police, ON
Chief Superintendent Richard Noble, Royal Canadian Mounted Police,
St. John's, NL
Detective Inspector Dennis J. Olinyk, Ontario Provincial Police, Kenora, ON
Deputy Chief Bernard Pannell, Saskatoon Police Service, SK
Staff Sergeant Stephen Patterson, Saint John Police Force, NB
Assistant director Marc Parent, Service de police de la Ville de Montréal, QC
Assistant director Mario Plante, Service de police de la Ville de Montréal, QC
Chief Murray Rodd, Peterborough Lakefield Community Police, ON
Staff Sergeant Joseph Roch Stéphane St-Jacques, Royal Canadian Mounted Police, Ottawa, ON
Chief Joseph Tomei, Orangeville Police Service, ON

MILITARY VALOUR DECORATIONS/DÉCORATIONS DE LA VAILLANCE MILITAIRE

Military Valour Decorations are national honours awarded to recognize acts of valour, self-sacrifice or devotion to duty in the presence of the enemy. The decorations were approved by Her Majesty Queen Elizabeth II in 1993. They consist of the Victoria Cross, the Star of Military Valour and the Medal of Military Valour.

Victoria Cross/La Croix de Victoria (C.V.)
None awarded since last edition.

Star of Military Valour/Étoile de la vaillance militaire (É.V.M.) (Announced September 8, 2011)
Master Corporal Paul D. Rachynski, M.M.V., Edmonton and Bonnyville, AB

(Announced June 2, 2011)
Lieutenant Gabriel Chassé-Jean, S.M.V., Alma, QC
Master Warrant Officer Richard Stacey, S.M.V., C.D., Edmonton, AB

Medal of Military Valour/ Médaille de la vaillance militaire (M.V.M) (Announced September 9, 2011)
Lieutenant Guillaume Frédéric Caron, M.M.V., C.D., Rimouski, QC
Corporal Bradley D. Casey, M.M.V., Pugwash, NS
Private Tony Rodney Vance Harris, M.M.V., Penfield, NB
Captain Michael A. MacKillop, M.M.V., C.D., Calgary, AB
Master Corporal Gilles-Remi Mikkelson, M.M.V., Bella Coola, BC
Master Corporal Marc-André J. M. Rousseau, M.M.V., La Sarre, QC

(Announced June 2, 2011)
Sergeant T. David Bérubé, M.M.V., C.D., Québec, QC
Master Corporal Simon R. Frigon, M.M.V., Québec, QC
Sergeant Joseph Martin Stéphane Mercier, M.M.V., C.D., La Sarre, QC
Leading Seaman Pier-Vincent Michaud, M.M.V., Trois-Rivières, QC
Sergeant Joseph Denis François Ranger, M.M.V., C.D., Vaudreuil, QC

CANADIAN BRAVERY DECORATIONS/DÉCORATIONS CANADIENNES POUR ACTES DE BRAVOURE

The Decorations for Bravery, consisting of the Cross of Valour, the Star of Courage, and the Medal of Bravery, were instituted and created on May 10, 1972. They may be awarded to Canadian citizens or to non-Canadians who have performed an act of bravery in Canada, or outside Canada if the act was in Canada's interest. The Decorations for Bravery may be awarded posthumously.

The Cross of Valour is awarded for acts of the most conspicuous courage in circumstances of extreme peril. The Star of Courage is awarded for acts of conspicuous courage in circumstances of great peril. The Medal of Bravery is awarded for acts of bravery in hazardous circumstances.

Cross of Valour/Croix de Valeur (C.V.)
None awarded since last edition.

Star of Courage/Étoile du courage (S.C.) (Announced September 8, 2011)
Private Adam J. P. Fraser, S.C., Saint-Jean-sur-Richelieu and Courcelette, QC
Corporal Déri J. G. Langevin, S.C., Chicoutimi and Québec, QC
Corporal Marc-André Poirier, S.C., Amos and Québec, QC

(Announced June 23, 2011)
Angela Jeannette Stirk, S.C., Norland and Oro-Medonte, ON
Fontella Twoyoungmen, S.C. (*posthumous*), Morley, AB

(Invested May 4, 2011)
Miranda Suggitt, S.C., Lindsay, ON
Michael Thomas Westwell, S.C., C.D., Winnipeg, MB

(Announced February 2, 2011)
Miguel Gonzalez, S.C., Montréal, QC
Luc Paquette, S.C., Montréal, QC

Medal of Bravery/Médaille de la bravoure (M.B.) (Announced September 8, 2011)
Maxime Bondu, M.B., Notre-Dame-de-Pontmain, QC
Sergeant André Coallier, M.B., Montréal, QC
Steve Degrace, M.B., Beresford, NB
Denis Diotte, M.B., Notre-Dame-de-Pontmain, QC
Monique Gagnon, M.B., Petit-Rocher, NB
Constable Karine Giroux, M.B., Montréal, QC
Kevin Gooding, M.B., Stoney Creek, ON
Bernard Keetash, M.B., Mishkeegogamang, ON
Lana Mae Krieser, M.B., Brandon, MB
André J. Maillet, M.B., Saint-Thomas-de-Kent, NB
J. Robert Maillet, M.B., Saint-Thomas-de-Kent, NB
William Edward Lance Matthews, M.B., Mansfield, ON
Mark Montour, M.B., Mishkeegogamang, ON
Ross P. Moore, M.B., Dwight, ON
Jeffrey Neekan, M.B., Mishkeegogamang, ON
Geneviève Otis-Leduc, M.B., Montréal, QC
Alexandre Phaneuf, M.B., Laval, QC
Constable David Pilote, M.B., Montréal, QC
Jean-François Renault, M.B., Mirabel, QC
Tyler Glenn Sampson, M.B. (*posthumous*), Halifax, NS
Madden Sarver, M.B., 100 Mile House, BC
Constable Daniel Tétreault, M.B., Montréal, QC
Philbert Truong, M.B. (*posthumous*), Victoria, BC
Kathryn Whittaker, M.B., Ottawa, ON

(Announced June 23, 2011)
Michael Lee Anderson, M.B., Vancouver, BC
RCMP Constable Andrew Ashton, M.B., Edmonton and Morinville, AB
Brent Michael Blackmore, M.B., Nanaimo, BC
Robert C. Bombardir, M.B., Powell River, BC
Leading Seaman Cory K. Bond, M.B., La Poile, N.L. and Halifax, NS
Darryl Fabian Boone, M.B., Marion Bridge, NS
Kingsley Cheung, M.B., Williams Lake, BC
Darren Coogan, M.B., Orangeville, ON
Archie L. Coughlin, M.B., Ellerslie and Conway, PE
Sergeant Delkie Curtis, M.B., Cobourg, ON
Jubal Daley, M.B., Negril, Jamaica
Jewel Denison, M.B., Verona, ON
Lieutenant(N) Christopher Michael Devita, M.B., C.D., Richmond Hill, Ont. and Bedford, NS
Ratko Ray Djuric, M.B., Prince George and Bear Lake, BC
Constable Patrick Duerden, M.B., Oakville and Milton, ON
Brian Dean Fowlow, M.B., Happy Valley-Goose Bay, NL
Dennis William Robert Fowlow, M.B., Buchans, NL
Bonnie Gamble, M.B., Calgary, AB
Gordon Joseph Gamble, M.B., Calgary, AB
Krista Dorothy Girvan, M.B., Edmonton, AB and Riverview, NB
Donald George Gough, M.B., Summerland, BC
Donald Neil Harper, M.B. (*posthumous*), Odessa, ON
Jeremy Hodder, M.B., Toronto, ON
Justin Kenneth Darwin Ilnicki, M.B., Williams Lake, BC
Matthew Michael Jackson, M.B., Kelowna, BC
Jewel James, M.B., Swastika and Kirkland Lake, ON
Tara Michelle Josey, M.B., Ottawa, ON
Nadine Anik Leduc, M.B., Ottawa, ON
Tamsen Laine Lahnalampi, M.B., Onaping, ON
Kevin Joseph Leski, M.B., Langley and Squamish, BC

Tyler Norman David Lockerby, M.B., Kelowna, BC
Dean Lucas, M.B., Edmonton, AB
Tina Maryann Moores, M.B. (*posthumous*), Grand Falls-Windsor, NL
RCMP Constable Shane Douglas Nicoll, M.B., Terrace and Surrey, BC
Barry Ryder Nilsen, M.B., Bear Lake, B.C. and Kelvington, SK
Patrick Robert O'Connor, M.B., Calgary, AB
Sergeant John K. Potts, M.B., Larder Lake and Hastings, ON
Steven C. Reynolds, M.B., Milton, ON
Wayne Reynolds, M.B., Negril, Jamaica
Timothy Andrew Rider, M.B., Kincardine, ON
Sharon Yvonne Rider, M.B., Kincardine, ON
Eric Roy, M.B. (*posthumous*), Boucherville, QC
Vince P. Sharpe, M.B., Inuvik, NT
Sharon Rose Sparks, M.B., Grand Falls-Windsor, NL
Chance Stewart, M.B., Vancouver, BC
Constable Michelle Stinson, M.B., La Ronge, SK and Kirkland Lake, ON
James Jacob Daniel Thede, M.B., Port Elgin, ON
Sergeant Roger Thomas, M.B., Cobourg, ON
Pazia Toyne, M.B., Lorette, MB
Vanna Jade Twoyoungmen, M.B., Morley, AB
Major Frank Wagener, M.B., Siegen, Germany and Moose Jaw, SK
Glen William Watts, M.B., Nanaimo, BC
Constable Christopher C. Wells, M.B., Wetaskiwin, AB
Russell Ryan Werner, M.B., Powell River, BC
Sheldon Steven Willier, M.B., Rocky Mountain House, AB
Twain Wright, M.B., New York, NY, USA

(Invested May 4, 2011)
Norman Anderson, M.B. (*posthumous*), Trenton, ON
Constable Patrick Benoit, M.B., Amherstview, ON
Scott Borlase, M.B., Winnipeg, MB
Joseph Henry Roland Bouliane, M.B., Winnipeg, MB
John Peter Chatterton, M.B., Richmond, ON
Richard K. Colbourne, M.B., Edmonton, AB
Thomas James Dodd, M.B. (*posthumous*), Chilliwack, BC
Daisy Flamand, M.B., Manawan, QC
Richard C. Frauley, M.B., Saint John, NB
Jared Douglas Gagen, M.B., Cobble Hill, BC
Master Corporal Julien Gauthier, M.B., Alouette, QC
Major William Robertson Green, M.B., C.D., Caronport, SK
Blair William Allan Hockin, M.B., Portage la Prairie, MB
Sergeant Joseph André Hotton, M.B., C.D., Kingston, NS
RCMP Constable Michelle Allison Howey, M.B., Calgary, AB
Ernest Jean, M.B., Montréal, QC
John Jew, M.B., Seaforth, ON
Timothy Sigluk Kautaq, M.B., Hall Beach, NU
RCMP Constable Alfred Douglas Lavallee, M.B., C.D., St. Ambroise, MN
Able Seaman Jaret A. McQueen, M.B., Hamilton, ON
Warren Bruce Miller, M.B., Victoria, BC
Sergeant Joseph Kenneth Penman, M.B., Winnipeg, MB
Stephen Power, M.B., Charlottetown, PEI
Constable Alain Rochette, M.B., Fournier, ON
Warrant Officer Shaun Spence, M.B., C.D., Winnipeg, MB
Master Warrant Officer Hamish Jackson Seggie, M.B., C.D., Winnipeg, MB
Edward Stirling, M.B., Ladysmith, BC
Tami Elizabeth Strickland, M.B., Charlottetown, PEI
Constable Wayne Thompson, M.B., Delta, BC
Michael André Toupin, M.B., St. Margarets, NB
Philippe Tremblay, M.B., Bathurst, NB
Art Unruh, M.B., Abbotsford, BC
Chad Verch, M.B., Victoria, BC
Provincial Constable of the OPP Darrell Wagner, M.B., Petawawa, ON
William Watt, M.B., Victoria, BC
Abebe Yohannes, M.B., Brandon, MB
Hermann Zarbl, M.B., Winnipeg, MB

(Announced April 20, 2011)
Norman Anderson, M.B. (posthumous), Trenton, ON

(Invested February 2, 2011)
Constable Robert Bérubé, M.B., Montréal, QC
Constable Benoit Brissette, M.B., Montréal, QC
Sergeant Steve Desgagné, M.B., Montréal, QC
Isabelle Gagnon, M.B., Saint-Hubert, QC
Marjorie Jean-Baptiste, M.B., Joliette, QC
Pascale Pelletier, M.B., Mercier, QC

(Announced January 18, 2011)
Clermont Bélanger, M.B., Pointe-à-la-Frégate, QC
Jean-Louis Clavet, M.B., Cloridorme, QC
Marie-Claude Élie, M.B., Montréal, QC
Serge Fournier, M.B., Cloridorme, QC
Robert Francoeur, M.B., Pointe-à-la-Frégate, QC
Yvon Lévesque, M.B., Salaberry-de-Valleyfield, QC
Yvan Pruneau, M.B., Cloridorme, QC
Constable Jean-François Rousselle, M.B., Montréal, QC

(Announced November 26, 2010)
Leading Seaman Robert T. Binder, M.B. *(deceased)*, Toronto, ON

MERITORIOUS SERVICE DECORATIONS/DÉCORATIONS POUR SERVICE MÉRITOIRE

Approved by Her Majesty the Queen on July 10, 1991, the Meritorious Service Decorations were created to honour Canadians & foreigners (military) for commendable actions performed on or after June 11, 1984.

The Meritorious Service Cross (Military Division) is awarded for the performance of a military deed or a military activity in an outstandingly professional manner or of a rare high standard that brings considerable benefit or great honour to the Canadian Forces.

The Meritorious Service Medal (Military Division) is awarded for the performance of a military deed or a military activity in a highly professional manner or of a very high standard that brings benefit or honour to the Canadian Forces.

Meritorious Service Cross/M.S.C. (Military)/ La Croix du service méritoire (militaire)
(Announced July 27, 2011)
Chief Warrant Officer Jules Joseph Moreau, M.M.M., M.S.C., C.D., Saint-Pamphile, QC
Lieutenant-Colonel Jocelyn. J.M.J. Paul, M.S.C., C.D., Wendake, QC
General David H. Petraeus, M.S.C. (United States Army), Cornwall-on-Hudson, NY, USA
Sergeant Michael Adam Smith, M.S.C., C.D., Ste-Thérèse, QC
Lieutenant-Colonel Gilbert Clement Thibault, M.S.C., C.D., Gaspé, QC
Lieutenant-Colonel Carl Jean Turenne, M.S.C., C.D., Kingston, ON
Brigadier-General Jonathan Holbert Vance, O.M.M., M.S.C., C.D., Tweed, ON

(Announced June 2, 2011)
Major Timothy Maurice Arsenault, M.S.C., C.D., Sudbury, ON
Petty Officer 2nd Class Martin Joseph Claude Bédard, M.S.C., C.D., Valcourt, QC
Lieutenant-Colonel Marc Joseph André Bigaouette, M.S.C., C.D., Québec, QC
Rear-Admiral Tyrone Herbert William Pile, C.M.M., M.S.C., C.D., Geraldton, ON and Victoria, BC

(Announced May 21, 2011)
General Franciszek Gągor, M.S.C. *(Posthumous)*, Koniuszowa, Poland

(Invested November 2, 2010)
Sergeant Joseph Martin Brink, M.S.C., Sylvan Lake, AB

(Announced October 28, 2010)
Brigadier-General Joseph René Marcel Guy Laroche, O.M.M., M.S.C., C.D., Québec, QC

Meritorious Service Medal M.S.M. (Military)/ La Médaille du service méritoire (militaire)
(Announced July 27, 2011)
Colonel Gregory C. Bilton, M.S.M. (Australian Army), Wanniassa, Australia
Major Emanuel Jeannot Boucher, M.S.M., C.D., Granby, QC
Major General Mart C. de Kruif, M.S.M. (Royal Netherlands Army), Apeldoorn, Netherlands
Major Jean-François Duval, M.S.M., C.D., Québec, QC
Corporal François-Jonathan Gilles Michel Hébert, M.S.M., Montréal, QC
Sergeant William Joseph Kelland, M.S.M., C.D., St. John's, NL
Sergeant Charles Andrew McLean, M.M.M., M.S.M., C.D., Ottawa, ON
Captain Andrew John Mercer, M.S.M., C.D., Toronto, ON
Warrant Officer Keith Paul Mitchell, C.V., M.S.M., C.D., Lasalle, QC
Major Joseph Serge Raynald Morin, M.S.M., C.D., Lac Mégantic, QC
Sergeant David Michael Pawulski, S.C., M.S.M., C.D., Calgary, AB
Major Yannick Pépin, M.S.M., C.D. *(posthumous)*, Arthabaska, QC
Sergeant Joseph François Colin Piché, M.S.M., C.D., St-Basile-de-Portneuf, QC
Colonel John Bruce Ploughman, M.S.M., C.D., St. John's, NL
Chief Warrant Officer Joseph Gerard Gilbert Poirier, M.M.M., M.S.M., C.D., Verdun, QC
Chief Warrant Officer Ernest Gérard Joseph Poitras, M.S.M., C.D., Tracadie, NB
Colonel Marie Céline Danielle Savard, M.S.M., C.D., Chicoutimi, QC
Major Paul Scannell, M.S.M. (British Army), Ruislip, United Kingdom
Chief Warrant Officer Andrew Peter Stapleford, M.S.M., C.D., Halifax, NS
Lieutenant-Colonel Ann-Marie Brigitte Tardif, M.S.M., C.D., Plessisville, QC
Lieutenant-Colonel John Tringali, M.S.M. (United States Air Force), Charleston, SC, USA
Major Joseph Richard Marc Verret, M.S.M., C.D., Ottawa, ON
Lieutenant-Colonel Michael Whited, M.S.M. (United States Army), Colorado Springs, CO, USA

(Invested June 8, 2011)
Corporal Derick R. Lewis, M.S.M., Kentville, NS
Master Warrant Officer Robert Joseph Montague, M.M.M., M.S.M., C.D., Deep River, ON
Colonel Theodore E. Osowski, M.S.M. (United States Air Force), Flushing, MI, USA
Major Russell Neal Washburn, M.S.M., C.D., St. George, NB
Sergeant Christopher Stuart Whalen, M.S.M., St. John's, NL

(Announced June 2, 2011)
Major Darryl Gordon Adams, M.S.M., C.D., Antigonish, NS
Colonel Anthony Joseph Mark Hilaire Ashfield, M.S.M., C.D., Montréal, QC
Brigadier-General Robert J. Beletic, M.S.M. (United States Air Force), Cleveland, OH, USA
Sergeant Lee William Edward Bibby, M.S.M., C.D., Prince Albert, SK
Corporal Mathieu S. Boulay-Paillé, M.S.M., Trois-Rivières, QC
Colonel Gregory Dawson Burt, O.M.M., M.S.M., C.D., Corner Brook, NL
Major Trevor John Cadieu, M.S.M., C.D., Vernon, BC
Major Luis C. Carvallo, M.S.M., C.D., Windsor and Essex, ON
Sergeant Patrice Pascal Chartrand, M.S.M., C.D., Montréal, QC
Lieutenant Gabriel Chassé-Jean, S.M.V., Alma, QC
Lieutenant-Colonel Scott Norman Clancy, M.S.M., C.D., Ottawa, ON
Captain Marc A. Dauphin, M.S.M., C.D., Sherbrooke, QC
Lieutenant-Colonel Roland Grant Delaney, M.S.M., C.D., Kingston, ON
Master Corporal Jonathan D.J. Déziel, M.S.M., Shawinigan, QC
Chief Warrant Officer Joseph Richard Denis Dompierre, M.S.M., C.D., Ottawa, ON
Major J. R. Mario Ferland, M.S.M., C.D., Baie St-Paul and Québec, QC
Lieutenant-Colonel Gyula John Joseph Gergely, M.S.M., C.D., Winnipeg, MB
Lieutenant-Colonel Lee John Hammond, M.S.M., C.D., North Vancouver, BC and St. Albert, AB
Commander Christopher John Hargreaves, O.M.M., M.S.M., C.D., Victoria, BC
Lieutenant-Colonel Joseph Jean-Paul Christian Labrosse, M.S.M., C.D., Montréal, QC
Chief Warrant Officer Grégoire Raymond Lacroix, M.M.M., M.S.M., C.D., Orléans, ON and Saint-Mard, Belgium
Colonel Joseph Conrad Roch Lacroix, M.S.M., C.D., Gimli, MB
Captain Francis Joseph Michel Mallet, M.S.M., C.D., LaSalle, QC
Master Corporal Stéphane Joseph Michel Richard, M.S.M., C.D., Val d'Or, QC
Lieutenant-Colonel James Joseph Raoul Normand Richardson, M.S.M., C.D., Laval, QC
Master Warrant Officer Richard Stacey, S.M.V., C.D., Edmonton, AB
Honorary Captain (N) Cedric Steele, M.S.M., C.D., Victoria, BC

(Announced November 2, 2010)
Major Geoffrey Arthur Abthorpe, M.S.M., C.D., Thunder Bay, ON
Lieutenant-Colonel Roger Ronald Barrett, M.S.M., C.D., Ottawa, ON
Colonel Tony Battista, M.S.M., C.D., Montréal, QC
Corporal Joseph Rudolf Éric Beauclair, M.S.M., C.D., Trenton, ON
Petty Officer 2nd Class Barbara Agnes Benson, M.S.M., C.D., Isle aux Morts, NL
Major Timothy Charles Byers, M.S.M., C.D., Belleisle Creek, NB
Lieutenant-Colonel Scott Norman Clancy, M.S.M., C.D., Ottawa, ON
Lieutenant-Colonel Gordon David Corbould, M.S.M., C.D., Belleville, Ont. and Bella Coola, BC
Chief Warrant Officer Robert Daly, M.S.M., C.D., Lincoln, NB
Captain Wayne Craig Desjardins, M.B., M.S.M., C.D., North Bay, ON
Chief Warrant Officer Patrick Joseph Earles, M.S.M., C.D., Mount Pearl, NL
Colonel Richard Gervais, M.S.M., C.D., Ottawa, ON
Colonel J. J. Martin Girard, M.S.M., C.D., Gatineau, QC

ORDER OF CANADA

Companions of the Order of Canada

Members of the Order of Canada

Officers of the Order of Canada

ORDER OF MILITARY MERIT

Officers of the Order of Military Merit

Commanders of the Order of Military Merit

Members of the Order of Military Merit

Commodore Richard Weston Greenwood, O.M.M., M.S.M., C.D., Powell River, BC
Sergeant Renay Marie Groves, M.S.M., C.D., St. John's, NL
Master Warrant Officer John William Hooyer, M.S.M., C.D., Brantford, ON
Lieutenant-Colonel James Andrew Irvine, M.S.M., C.D., Belleville, ON
Chief Warrant Officer Michael Raymond Lacharite, M.S.M., C.D., Edmonton, AB
Colonel Jean-Marc Lanthier, M.S.C., M.S.M., C.D., Québec, QC
Captain Tyler Lavigne, M.S.M., Bathurst, NB
Major Martin Andre Lipcsey, M.S.M., C.D., Ottawa, ON
Captain Steven E. Luce, M.S.M. (United States Navy), Las Vegas, Nevada, USA
Major Joseph Gilbert Léon McCauley, M.S.M., C.D., Sherbrooke and Gatineau, QC
Captain(N) Arthur Gerard McDonald, M.S.M., C.D., New Waterford, NS
Chief Warrant Officer Mark Henry Miller, M.M.M., M.S.M., C.D., Minto, NB
Lieutenant-Colonel Scott Miller, M.S.M. (United States Air Force), Las Vegas, Nevada and Los Angeles, California, USA
Major Steven John Vincent Nolan, M.S.M., C.D., Whitby and Scarborough, ON
Lieutenant-Colonel Christopher Kenneth Penny, M.S.M., Ottawa, ON
Captain Jeffrey Middleton Powell, M.S.M., Clinton, ON
Lieutenant-Colonel Joseph Stephen Shipley, M.S.M., C.D., Windsor Junction and Halifax, NS
Corporal Curtis J. Stephens, M.S.M., Victoria, BC
Lieutenant-Colonel Duart Paul Townsend, M.S.M., C.D., Toronto, ON
Captain(N) Thomas Charles Tulloch, M.S.M., C.D., Peterborough, ON
Captain Connie Noreen Watson, M.S.M., C.D., Winnipeg, MB

(Announced October 28, 2010)
Master Corporal Joseph Léonard Arsenault, M.S.M., C.D., Antigonish, N.S
Colonel Tony Battista, M.S.M., C.D., Montréal, QC
Corporal Joseph Rudolf Éric Beauclair, M.S.M., C.D., Trenton, ON
Major Jonathan Claude Yvon Bouchard, M.S.M., C.D., Montréal, QC
Lieutenant-Colonel Scott Norman Clancy, M.S.M., C.D., Ottawa, ON
Captain Wayne Craig Desjardins, M.B., M.S.M., C.D., North Bay, ON
Chief Petty Officer 1st Class Jocelyn Joseph René Fréchette, M.S.M., C.D., Sainte-Foy, QC
Commodore Richard Weston Greenwood, O.M.M., M.S.M., C.D., Powell River, BC
Lieutenant-Colonel James Andrew Irvine, M.S.M., C.D., Belleville, ON
Colonel Jean-Marc Lanthier, M.S.C., M.S.M., C.D., Québec, QC
Captain(N) Arthur Gerard McDonald, M.S.M., C.D., New Waterford, NS
Lieutenant-Colonel Christopher Kenneth Penny, M.S.M., Ottawa, ON
Corporal Emelie Pilon, M.S.M., Mississauga, ON
Captain Jeffrey Middleton Powell, M.S.M., Clinton, ON
Master Corporal Jeffrey Gordon Spence, M.S.M., C.D., Kamloops, BC
Captain(N) Thomas Charles Tulloch, M.S.M., C.D., Peterborough, ON
Captain Connie Noreen Watson, M.S.M., C.D., Winnipeg, MB

GENERAL SERVICE AWARDS

Rather than creating a new honour for each new Canadian Forces operation as it arises, in July of 2004, Her Majesty the Queen approved the creation of the following:

The General Campaign Star (G.C.S.) recognizes military service in a theatre of operations in the presence of an armed enemy.

The General Service Medal (G.S.M.) acknowledges civilian and military service in direct support of operations in the presence of an armed enemy.

General Campaign Star/Étoile de campagne générale (G.C.S.)
None awarded since last edition.

General Service Medal/Médaille du service général (G.S.M.)
None awarded since last edition.

British & Commonwealth Honours

In earlier times Canadians could receive hereditary titles, knighthoods and other such honours under the British system of honours, and this is still the case with Canadians who pursue careers in the United Kingdom. Furthermore, the Canadian military system of decorations was based on the British system and many Canadians hold British honours as a result of service in Canadian, British or other Commonwealth forces. While Canada has developed its own honours system, honours are still from time to time granted by the Sovereign to Canadians for, among other things, service to the Commonwealth.

VICTORIA CROSS (V.C.)

The Victoria Cross was founded by Queen Victoria at the close of the Crimean War in 1856, but made retroactive to 1854. It is described as a Maltese cross, made of gun metal, with a Royal Crest in the centre and underneath it an escroll bearing the inscription "For Valour". It is awarded, irrespective of rank, to members of any branch of Her Majesty's services, either in the British Forces or those of any Commonwealth realm, dominion, colony or dependency, the Mercantile Marine, nurses or staffs of hospitals, or to civilians of either sex while serving in either regular or temporary capacity during naval, military, or air force operations. It is awarded only "for most conspicuous bravery or some daring or pre-eminent act of valour or self-sacrifice or extreme devotion to duty in the presence of the enemy." For additional conduct of similar bravery, a Bar is added. The ribbon was for-

CANADIAN BRAVERY DECORATIONS

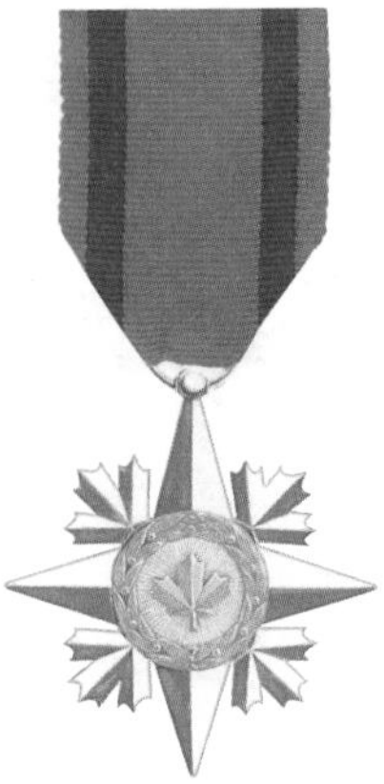
Star of Courage

Cross of Valour

Medal of Bravery

MERITORIOUS SERVICE DECORATIONS

Meritorious Service Cross
Obverse (Military Version)

Meritorious Service Medal
Reverse (Civil Version)

merly red for the Army and blue for the Navy, but it is now red (a dull crimson) for all services. Since June 17th, 1943, the financial responsibility for a stipend to Canadian recipients has been assumed by the Canadian Government. Ninetysix V.C.s have been awarded to Canadians or to foreigners serving in Canadian or Commonwealth forces.

GEORGE CROSS (G.C.)

Arthur Richard Cecil Butson, G.C., O.M.M., C.St.J., C.D., M.A., M.D., F.R.C.S. (Eng.), F.R.C.S.C.C. In 1940, King George VI instituted the George Cross for civilians and members of the services alike, male or female, who performed "acts of the greatest heroism or of the most conspicuous courage in circumstances of extreme danger." This decoration - the second highest Commonwealth award for bravery - is a plain silver cross bearing in the centre a representation of Saint George slaying the dragon and the words: "For Gallantry". The ribbon is garter blue. Eleven Canadians, and a Bermudian serving in a Canadian unit, have won the G.C. Not all were members of the armed forces.

ALBERT MEDAL (A.M.)

Ernest Alfred Wooding, A.M., R.C.N.V.R. Queen Elizabeth II requested that all living Albert Medal recipients convert their Albert Medal to a George Cross. For some reason Mr. Wooding did not convert his Albert Medal.

ROYAL HONOURS (COMMONWEALTH)

The Order of Baronets, the lowest Hereditary rank, was instituted in 1611; a Baronet is designated "Sir John Smith, Baronet." The abbreviation Bt. is used in Court Circulars and has been generally adopted in lieu of "Bart." Taking precedence to Baronets are members of The Most Honourable Privy Council, who are addressed "Right Honourable."

The Most Noble Order of the Garter, instituted 1349. - K.G.

The Most Ancient and Most Noble Order of the Thistle, instituted 1687. - K.T.

The Most Honourable Order of the Bath, instituted in 1399, and revived in 1725, is divided into three classes - Knights Grand Cross, G.C.B.; Knights Commanders, K.C.B.; and Companions, C.B.

The Order of Merit, O.M., carries no title.

The Most Distinguished Order of St. Michael and St. George, instituted in 1818, has three classes - Knights Grand Cross, G.C.M.G.; Knights Commanders, K.C.M.G.; Companions, C.M.G.

The Most Eminent Order of the Indian Empire instituted 1877, has three classes - Knights Grand Commanders, G.C.I.E.; Knights Commanders, K.C.I.E.; Companions, C.I.E. (This Order has not been conferred since 1947.)

The Royal Victorian Order, instituted in 1896, has five classes - Knights Grand Cross, G.C.V.O.; Knights Commanders, K.C.V.O.; Commanders, C.V.O.; Members 4th and 5th classes - M.V.O. Ribbon, blue with red and white edges.

The Most Excellent Order of the British Empire, instituted in 1917, has five classes - Knights (or Dames) Grand Cross, G.B.E.; Knights Commanders, K.B.E.; Dames Commanders, D.B.E.; Commanders, C.B.E.; Officers, O.B.E.; and Members, M.B.E. Ribbon (Military) rose pink, pearl grey edging, vertical pearl stripe in centre; (Civil) rose pink, pearl grey edging, and no central vertical stripe.

Knights Bachelors are gentlemen unconnected with any order who have received the honour of Knighthood, and are entitled to the prefix "Sir". They rank immediately after Knights Commanders of the British Empire.

The Companions of Honour, C.H., instituted in 1917 rank immediately after Knights (Dames) Grand Cross of the Order of the British Empire. Membership is limited and carries no title.

In all Orders of Knighthood the Knights Grand Cross and the Knights Commanders have the prefix "Sir" with the initials of their class following the name. Companions and Members bear no title, but have the letters C.B., C.M.G., L.V.O., M.V.O., as the case may be, attached to their names.

The Garter, the Thistle, The Order of Merit and the Royal Victorian Order are all in the personal bestowal of the Sovereign. Appointments to the other Orders are made by Her Majesty on recommendation of the Prime Ministers of Commonwealth countries who wish to secure such appointments. Premiers of individual Australian states may also make recommendations.

MARQUESS

The Most Hon. the Marquess of Exeter, Michael Anthony Cecil, 8th Marquess

The Most Hon. the Marquess of Ely, Charles John Tottenham, 9th Marquess

EARLS

The Right Hon. the Earl of Egmont, Thomas Frederick Gerald Perceval, 12th Earl and 16th Baronet

The Right Hon. the Earl Grey, Richard Fleming George Charles Grey, 6th Earl

The Right Hon. the Earl of Orkney, Peter St. John, 9th Earl

The Right Hon. the Earl Winterton, Donald David Turnour, 8th Earl

VISCOUNTS

The Right Hon. the Viscount Charlemont, John Dodd Caulfield, 15th Viscount

The Right Hon. the Viscount Galway, L.Cdr. George Rupert Monckton, R.C.N. (Ret'd), 12th Viscount

The Right Hon. the Viscount Hardinge, Andrew Hartland Hardinge, 7th Viscount

OLD CANADIAN TITLE
The title of Baron de Longueuil existed prior to the Treaty of Paris (1763), and was duly recognized by Queen Victoria pursuant to that treaty.

BARONS
The Right Hon. the Lord Beaverbrook, Maxwell William Henry Aitken, 3rd Baron and 3rd Baronet
The Right Hon. the Lord Cullen of Ashbourne, Edmund Willoughby Marsham Cokayne, 3rd Baron
The Right Hon. the Lord Lucas of Chilworth, Simon William Lucas, 3rd Baron
The Right Hon. the Lord Martonmere, John Stephen Robinson, 2nd Baron
The Right Hon. the Lord Morris, Michael David Morris, 3rd Baron
The Right Hon. the Lord Rodney, George Brydges Rodney, 10th Baron and 10th Baronet
The Right Hon. the Lord Sanford, James, John, Mowbray Edmonton Sanford, 3rd Baron
The Right Hon. The Lord Shaughnessy, Charles George Patrick Shaughnessy, 5th Baron
The Right Hon. the Lord Strathcona and Mount Royal, Hon. Col. Donald Euan Palmer Howard, 4th Baron
The Right Hon. the Lord Thomson of Fleet David Kenneth Roy Thomson, 3rd Baron

BARONETS
Sir Richard Aylmer (16th Bt.)
Sir Christopher Hilaro Barlow (7th Bt.)
Sir James Barlow (4th Bt.)
Sir Benjamin Barrington (8th Bt.)
Sir James Bates (7th Bt)
Sir John Irving Bell, (1st Bt.)
Sir Alexander Boyd (3rd Bt.)
Sir Theodore Brinckman (6th Bt.)
Sir James Brunton (4th Bt.)
Sir Peter Burbidge (6th Bt.)
Sir Michael Butler (3rd Bt.)
Sir Robert Cave-Brown-Cave (16th Bt.)
Sir Bruce Chaytor (9th Bt.)
Sir Robin Chetwynd (9th Bt.)
Sir John Davis (3rd Bt.)
Sir David Dyke (10th Bt.)
The Revd. Sir Christopher Gibson, Bt., C.P. (4th Bt.)
Sir James Grant-Suttie (9th Bt.)
Sir Philip Grotrian (3rd Bt.)
Sir Charles Gunning C.D., (8th Bt.)
Sir Wayne King (8th Bt,)
Sir Charles Knowles (7th Bt.)
Sir Colpoys Johnson (8th Bt.)
Sir Peter Lambert (10th Bt.)
Sir Richard Latham (3rd Bt.)
Sir Ian McGregor (8th Bt.)
Sir Roderick McQuhae MacKenzie (12th Bt.)
Sir Allan Morris (11th Bt.)
Sir Christopher Oakes (3rd Bt.)
Sir Mathew Philipson-Stow (6th Bt.)
Sir James Piers (11 Bt.)
Sir Francis Price, Bt. (7th Bt.)
Sir Christopher Robinson (8th Bt.)
Sir John James Michael Laud Robinson (11th Bt.)
Sir Julian Rose (5th Bt.)
Sir James Rugge-Price (10th Bt.)
Sir John Samuel (5th Bt.)
Sir Adrian Sharp (4th Bt.)
Sir Richard Simeon (8th Bt.)
The Rev. Sir Michael Stonhouse (19th Bt.)
Sir Adrian Stott (4th Bt.)
Sir John Stracey (9th Bt.)
Sir Philip Stuart (9th Bt.)
Sir Richard Sullivan (9th Bt.)
Sir Robert Synge (8th Bt.)
Sir Rodney Touche (2nd Bt.)
Sir Charles Hibbert Tupper (5th Bt.)
Sir Christopher Wells, M.D. (3rd Bt.)
Sir Donald Williams (10th Bt.)

Knight Grand Cross of the Most Honourable Order of the Bath (G.C.B.)
Air Chief Marshal Sir David Evans, G.C.B., C.B.E.

The Order of Merit (O.M.)
The Right Honourable Jean Chrétien, PC, OM, CC.

Knight Grand Cross or Dame Grand Cross of the Most Excellent Order of the British Empire (G.B.E.)

Member of the Order of the Companions of Honour (C.H.)
General John de Chastelaine, O.C., C.M.M., C.H., E.D.
Dr. Anthony Pawson, C.H., O.C., O.Ont.

Knight Commander of the Most Distinguished Order of St. Michael and St. George (K.C.M.G.)

Knight Commander of the Royal Victorian Order (K.C.V.O.)
Sir Conrad Swan, K.C.V.O.

Knight Commander of the Most Excellent Order of the British Empire (K.B.E.)
Sir David Bate, K.B.E.

Knight Commander or Dame Commander of the Most Excellent Order of the British Empire (K.B.E. or D.B.E.)
Dame Clara Furse, D.B.E.

KNIGHT BACHELOR
Sir George Bain
Sir Graham Day
Sir John Reginald Gorman, C.V.O., C.B.E., M.C
Sir Terence Matthews, O.B.E.
Sir Christopher Ondaatje, C.B.E.
Sir Neil Shaw

Companion of the Most Honourable Order of the Bath (C.B.)
Air Vice-Marshal George Brookes, C.B., O.B.E.

Companion of the Most Distinguished Order of St. Michael and St. George (C.M.G.)
H.J. Carmichael, C.M.G.
Edmond Cloutier, C.M.G., B.A., L.Ph.
Donovan Bartley Finn, C.M.G., M.Sc., Ph.D., F.R.S.C., F.C.I.C.
George H. McIvor, C.M.G.
Hector Brown McKinnon, C.C., C.M.G.
William Andrew O'Neil, C.M.G.
Alexander Ross, C.M.G.
Joseph Emile St. Laurent, C.M.G.
Ivor Otterbein Smith, C.M.G., O.B.E.

Companion of the Most Eminent Order of the Indian Empire (C.I.E.)
Maj. Frederick Wernham Gerrard, C.I.E.
Capt. John Ryland, C.I.E., R.C.N.
Maj. Frederick Augustus Berrill Sheppard, C.I.E., O.B.E.

Commander of the Royal Victorian Order (C.V.O.)
Leopold Henry Amyot, C.V.O.
Dr. Michael Jackson, C.V.O., C.D.
The Hon. David C. Lam, C.V.O., C.M., K.St.J., O.B.C., B.A.(Econ.), M.B.A., L.L.D., D.Mil.Sc., D.H.L., D.H.
Veronica Jane Langton, C.V.O.
Judith A. LaRocque, C.V.O.
Kevin Stewart MacLeod, C.V.O.
Cdr. G.J. Manson, C.V.O., C.D., R.C.N.
John Crosbie Perlin, C.V.O.
Peter Michael Pitfield, C.V.O., P.C., Q.C.
M.Gen. Roy A. Reid, C.V.O., C.M., M.C., C.D.
L.Cdr. Lawrence James Wallace, C.V.O., O.C., O.B.C., R.C.N.V.R.

Commander of the Order of the British Empire (C.B.E.)
William Eric Adams, C.B.E.
James Pomeroy Anderson, C.B.E.
Brig. Gerald Gardiner Anglin, C.B.E., M.C., E.D.
Brig. Walter A. Bean, C.B.E., E.D., C.D.
Brig. John Arthur Watson Bennett, C.B.E., C.D.
Brig. John Francis Bingham, C.B.E.
Brig. Dudley Kingdon Black, C.B.E., D.S.O.
George Herbert Bowler, C.B.E.
Garrett Brownrigg, C.B.E.
John Burke, C.B.E.
Alfred Charpentier, C.B.E.
Howard Brown Chase, C.B.E.
Brig. Frederick Graham Coleman, C.B.E.
Brig. J. A. de Lalanne, C.B.E., M.C., E.D.
Conrad Trelawny Fitz-Gerald, C.B.E., M.D.
Charles Gavsie, C.B.E., Q.C.
Gerald Godsoe, C.B.E., Q.C.
Alexander Grant, C.B.E.
Joseph Ernest Gregoire, C.B.E.
Frank Sydney Grisdale, C.B.E.
Raymond Gushue, O.C., C.B.E., Q.C.
Wallace Bruce Haughan, C.B.E.
Brig. Robert James Henderson, C.B.E.
Harold Ferguson Hodgson, C.B.E.
Capt. Francis Deschamps Howie, C.B.E., D.S.O., R.N.
Alexander George Irvine, C.B.E.
Lester Millman Keachie, C.B.E., Q.C.
Capt. Thomas Douglas Kelly, C.B.E., R.C.N.R.
Allan Collingwood Travers Lewis, C.B.E., Q.C.
Col. Edward Raymond Lewis, C.B.E.
Wilfrid Bennett Lewis, C.O., C.B.E., Ph.D
Gordon Clapp Lindsay, C.B.E.
John Struthers McNeil, C.B.E.
E.J. Mackie, C.B.E.
Raymond Charles Manning, C.B.E.
Walter Melvill Marshall, C.B.E.
James Matson, C.B.E.
Ronald Henry Moray Mavor, C.B.E.
Air Vice-Marshal Walter Alyn Orr, C.B.E., C.D., R.C.A.F.
Luke William Pearsall, C.B.E.
M.Gen. Matthew Howard Somers Penhale, C.B.E., C.D.
Cyril Horace Frederick Pierrepont, C.B.E., E.D.
M.Gen. Norman Elliott Rodger, C.B.E.
James Joseph Alexander Ross, C.B.E., C.D.
T.H. Savage, C.B.E.
Lynn Seymour, C.B.E.
Air Vice-Marshal Douglas McCully Smith, C.B.E., C.D.
Brig. Gerald Lucian Morgan Smith, C.B.E., C.D.
George Spence, C.B.E., LL.D.
William Leonard O'Brien Stallard, C.B.E.
Basil Otto Stevenson, C.B.E.
Air Cdre. Stanley Gibson Tackaberry, C.B.E.
Kenneth Wiffin Taylor, O.C., C.B.E.
George Gamlin Thomas, C.B.E.
Lyman Trumbull, C.B.E.
M.Gen. Arthur Egbert Wrinch, C.B.E., C.D.
Henry Wrong, C.B.E.

IMPERIAL SERVICE ORDER (I.S.O.)
George Clayton Anderson
Robert Albert Andison
Arthur Barnstead
Avila Bedard
Peter Cooligan
Henri Fortier
Frank Henry French
Arthur Leigh Jolliffe
Edward Jost
Louis MacMillan
Walter Clifton Ronson
David John Scott
Ivan Vallee

ROYAL VICTORIAN CHAIN
Bestows no precedence; currently not held by anyone.

Order of Precedence for Orders, Decorations and Medals

The following is the approved order of predence as of April 2, 1998. The asterisk indicates honours added since that date.

SEQUENCE 1
1. The sequence for wearing the insignia of Canadian orders, decorations and medals, and the post-nominal letters associated with such orders, decorations and medals are the following:
Victoria Cross (V.C.)
Cross of Valour (C.V.)

NATIONAL ORDERS
Companion of the Order of Canada (C.C.)
Officer of the Order of Canada (O.C.)
Member of the Order of Canada (C.M.)
Commander of the Order of Military Merit (C.M.M.)
*Commander of the Order of Merit of the Police Forces (C.O.M.)
Commander of the Royal Victorian Order (C.V.O.)
Officer of the Order of Military Merit (O.M.M.)
*Officer of the Order of Merit of the Police Forces (O.O.M.)
Lieutenant of the Royal Victorian Order (L.V.O.)
Member of the Order of Military Merit (M.M.M.)
*Member of the Order of Merit of the Police Forces (M.O.M.)
Member of the Royal Victorian Order (M.V.O.)
The Most Venerable Order of the Hospital of St. John of Jerusalem (all grades) (post-nominal letters only for internal use by the Order of St. John)

PROVINCIAL ORDERS
*Ordre national du Québec (G.O.Q., O.Q., C.Q.)
Saskatchewan Order of Merit (S.O.M.)
Order of Ontario (O.Ont.)
Order of British Columbia (O.B.C.)
Alberta Order of Excellence (A.O.E.)
Order of Prince Edward Island (O.P.E.I.)
Order of Manitoba (O.M.)
Order of New Brunswick (O.N.B.)
Order of Nova Scotia (O.N.S.)
Order of Newfoundland & Labrador (O.N.L.)

DECORATIONS
Star of Military Valour (S.M.V.)
Star of Courage (S.C)
Meritorious Service Cross (M.S.C.)
Medal of Military Valour (M.M.V.)

Medal of Bravery (M.B.)
Meritorious Service Medal (M.S.M.)
Royal Victorian Medal (R.V.M.)

WAR AND OPERATIONAL SERVICE MEDALS
Korea Medal
Canadian Volunteer Service Medal for Korea
Gulf and Kuwait Medal
Somalia Medal
*South-West Asia Service Medal
*General Campaign Star
*General Service Medal

SPECIAL SERVICE MEDALS (S.S.M.)
S.S.M. with bars for:
Pakistan (1989-1990)
Alert
Humanitas
NATO/OTAN
Peace/Paix
*Ranger
*Canadian Peacekeeping Service Medal (C.P.S.M.)

UNITED NATIONS MEDALS
Service (Korea) (1950-1954)
Emergency Force (Egypt/Sinai) (1956-67)
Truce Supervision Organization in Palestine (1948-) and Observer Group in Lebanon (1958)
Military Observation Group in India and Pakistan (1948-)
Operation in Congo (1960-64)
Temporary Executive Authority in West New Guinea (1962-63)
Yemen Observation Mission (1963-64)
Force in Cyprus (1964-)
India/Pakistan Observation Misison (1965-66)
Emergency Force Middle East (1973-79)
Disengagement Observation Force Golan Heights (1974-)
Interim Force in Lebanon (1978-)
Military Observation Group in Iran/Iraq (1988-91)
Transition Assistance Group (Namibia) (1989-90)
Observer Group in Central America (1989-92)
Iraq/Kuwait Observer Mission (1991-)
Angola Verification Mission (1988-97)
Mission for the Referendum in Western Sahara (1991-)
Observer Mission in El Salvador (1991-95)
Protection Force (Yugoslavia) (1992-95)
Advance Mission in Cambodia (1991-92)
Transitional Authority in Cambodia (1992-93)
Operation in Somalia (1992-93)
Operation in Mozambique (1992-94)
Observation Mission in Uganda/Rwanda (1993-94)
Assistance Mission in Rwanda (1993-96)
Mission in Haïti (1993-)
Verification of Human Rights and Compliance with the Comprehensive Agreement on Human Rights in Guatemala (1997-98)
*Mission in the Central African Republic (1998-2000)
*Preventive Deployment Force (Macedonia) (1995- 99)
*Mission in Bosnia and Herzegovina (1995-) *Mission of Observers in Prevlaka (Croatia) (1996-)
*Interim Administration Mission in Kosovo (1999-)
*Observer Mission in Sierra Leone (1999-)
*Mission in East Timor and Transitional Administration in East Timor (1999-)
*Mission in the Democratic Republic of the Congo (1999-)
*Mission in Ethiopia and Eritrea (2000-)
Special Service (1995-)
*Headquarters

NATO MEDALS
*North Atlantic Treaty Organization (NATO) Medal for the Former Yugoslavia (1992-2002)
*NATO Medal for Kosovo (1999-)
*NATO Medal for the Former Yugoslav Republic of Macedonia (2001-02)
*Article 5 NATO Medal for Operation "Eagle Assist" (2001-02)
*Article 5 NATO Medal for Operation "Active Endeavour" (2001-)
*Non-Article 5 NATO Medal for Operations in the Balkans (2003-)

INTERNATIONAL MISSION MEDALS
International Commission for Supervision and Control (Indo-China) (1954-74)
International Commission for Control and Supervision (Vietnam) (1973)
Multinational Force and Observers (Sinai) (1982-)
European Community Monitor Mission (Yugoslavia) (1991-)
*International Force East Timor (1999-)
*European Security and Defence Policy Service Medal

COMMEMORATIVE MEDALS
Canadian Centennial Medal (1967)
Queen Elizabeth II's Silver Jubilee Medal (1977)
125th Anniversary of the Confederation of Canada Medal (1992)
*Queen Elizabeth II's Golden Jubilee Medal (2002)

LONG SERVICE AND GOOD CONDUCT MEDALS
R.C.M.P. Long Service Medal
Canadian Forces Decoration (C.D.)

EXEMPLARY SERVICE MEDALS
Police Exemplary Service Medal
Corrections Exemplary Service Medal
Fire Services Exemplary Service Medal
Canadian Coast Guard Exemplary Service Meda
Emergency Medical Services Exemplary Service Medal
*Peace Officer Exemplary Service Medal

SPECIAL MEDAL
Queen's Medal for Champion Shot

OTHER DECORATIONS AND MEDALS
Ontario Medal for Good Citizenship (O.M.C.)
Ontario Medal for Police Bravery
Ontario Medal for Firefighters Bravery
Saskatchewan Volunteer Medal (S.V.M.)
Ontario Provincial Police Long Service and Good Conduct Medal
Service Medal of the Most Venerable Order of the Hospital of St. John of Jerusalem
Commissionaire Long Service Medal
*Newfoundland and Labrador Bravery Award
*Newfoundland and Labrador Volunteer Service Medal
*British Columbia Fire Services Long Service and Bravery Medals
*Commemorative Medal for the Centennial of Saskatchewan
*Alberta Centennial Medal

2. The Bar to the Special Service Medal is worn centred on the ribbon. If there is more than one Bar, they are spaced evenly on the ribbon with the most recent uppermost.

3. Commonwealth orders, decorations and medals, the award of which is approved by the Government of Canada, are worn after Canadian orders, decorations and medals listed in Section 1, the precedence in each category being set by the date of appointment or award.

4. Foreign orders, decorations and medals, the award of which is approved by the Government of Canada, are worn after those referred to in Sections 1 and 3, the precedence in each category being set by the date of appointment or award.

5. Notwithstanding Sections 1, 3 and 4, a person who, **prior to 1 June, 1972,** was a member of a British Order or the recipient of a British decoration or medal referred to in this section, may wear the insignia of the decoration or medal together with the insignia of any Canadian order, decoration or medal that the person is entitled to wear, the proper sequence being the following:
Victoria Cross (V.C.)
George Cross (G.C.)
Cross of Valour (C.V.)
Order of Merit (O.M.)
Order of the Companions of Honour (C.H.)
Companion of the Order of Canada (C.C.)
Officer of the Order of Canada (O.C.)
Member of the Order of Canada (C.M.)
Commander of the Order of Military Merit (C.M.M.)
*Commander of the Order of Merit of the Police Forces (C.O.M.)
Companion of the Order of the Bath (C.B.)
Companion of the Order of St. Michael and St. George (C.M.G.)
Commander of the Royal Victorian Order (C.V.O.)
Commander of the Order of the British Empire (C.B.E.)
Distinguished Service Order (D.S.O.)
Officer of the Order of Military Merit (O.M.M.)
*Officer of the Order of Merit of the Police Force (O.O.M.)
Lieutenant of the Royal Victorian Order (L.V.O.)
Officer of the Order of the British Empire (O.B.E.)
Imperial Service Order (I.S.O.)
Member of the Order of Military Merit (M.M.M.)
*Member of the Order of the Police Forces (M.O.M.)
Member of the Royal Victorian Order (M.V.O.)
Member of the Order of the British Empire (M.B.E.)
Member of the Royal Red Cross (R.R.C.)
Distinguished Service Cross (D.S.C.)
Military Cross (M.C.)
Distinguished Flying Cross (D.F.C.)
Air Force Cross (A.F.C.)
Star of Military Valour (S.M.V.)
Star of Courage (S.C.)
Meritorious Service Cross (M.S.C.)
Medal of Military Valour (M.M.V.)
Medal of Bravery (M.B.)
Meritorious Service Medal (M.S.M.)
Associate of the Royal Red Cross (A.R.R.C.)
The Most Venerable Order of St. John of Jerusalem (all grades) (post-nominal letters only for internal use by the Order of St. John)
Provincial Orders (order of precedence as set out in Section 1)
Distinguished Conduct Medal (D.C.M.)
Conspicuous Gallantry Medal (C.G.M.)
George Medal (G.M.)
Distinguished Service Medal (D.S.M.)
Military Medal (M.M.)
Distinguished Flying Medal (D.F.M.)
Air Force Medal (A.F.M.)
Queen's Gallantry Medal (Q.G.M.)
Royal Victorian Medal (R.V.M.)
British Empire Medal (B.E.M.)

WAR AND OPERATIONAL SERVICE MEDALS
Africa General Service Medal (1902-1956)
India General Service Medal (1908-1935)
Naval General Service Medal (1915-1962)
India General Service Medal (1936-39)
General Service Medal - Army and Air Force (1918- 1962)
General Service Medal (1962-)
1914 Star
1914-15 Star
British War Medal (1914-18)
Mercantile Marine War Medal (1914-18)
Victory Medal (1914-18)
Territorial Force War Medal (1914-19)
1939-45 Star
Atlantic Star
Air Crew Europe Star
Africa Star
Pacific Star
Burma Star
Italy Star
France and Germany Star
Defence Medal
Canadian Volunteer Service Medal
Newfoundland Second World War Volunteer Service Medal (see Section 6)
War Medal (1939-45)
Korea Medal
Canadian Volunteer Service Medal for Korea
Gulf and Kuwait Medal Somalia Medal
*South-West Asia Service Medal
*General Campaign Medal
*General Service Medal

SPECIAL SERVICE MEDALS
(The order of precedence is as set out for Special Service Medals in Section 1.)

UNITED NATIONS MEDALS
(The order of precedence is as set out for United Nations Medals in Section 1.)

INTERNATIONAL COMMISSION AND ORGANIZATION MEDALS
(The order of precedence is as set out for International Commission and Organization Medals in Section 1.)

POLAR MEDALS
(The order of precedence is by order of date awarded.)

COMMEMORATIVE MEDALS
King George V's Silver Jubilee Medal (1935)
King George VI's Coronation Medal (1937)
Queen Elizabeth II's Coronation Medal (1953)
Canadian Centennial Medal (1967)
Queen Elizabeth II's Silver Jubilee Medal (1977)
125th Anniversary of the Confederation of Canada Medal (1992)
*Queen Elizabeth II's Golden Jubilee Medal (2002)

LONG SERVICE AND GOOD CONDUCT MEDALS
Army Long Service and Good Conduct Medal
Naval Long Service and Good Conduct Medal
Air Force Long Service and Good Conduct Medal
RCMP Long Service Medal
Volunteer Officer's Decoration (V.D.)
Volunteer Long Service Medal
Colonial Auxiliary Forces Officer's Decoration (V.D.)
Colonial Auxiliary Forces Long Service Medal
Efficiency Decoration (E.D.)
Efficiency Medal
Naval Volunteer Reserve Decoration (V.R.D.)
Naval Volunteer Reserve Long Service and Good Conduct Medal

Air Efficiency Award Canadian Forces Decoration (C.D.)

EXEMPLARY SERVICE MEDALS

(The order of precedence is as set out for Exemplary Service Medals in Section 1.)

SPECIAL MEDAL

Queen's Medal for Champion Shot

OTHER DECORATIONS AND MEDALS

(The order of precedence is as set out for Other Decorations and Medals in Section 1.)

6. The Newfoundland Volunteer War Service Medal has the same precedence as the Canadian Volunteer Service Medal.

7. The insignia of orders, decorations and medals not listed above, as well as foreign awards, the award of which has not been approved by the Government of Canada, shall not be mounted or worn in conjunction with orders, decorations and medals listed above.

8. The insignia of orders, decorations and medals shall not be worn by anyone other than the recipient of the orders, decorations or medals.

NOTE: Policy regarding the wearing on non-authorized awards Only the insignia of orders, decorations and medals officially awarded under the authority of the Crown or that the wearing of which has been authorized by the Crown may be worn. Only the actual recipient of an honour can wear its insignia; no family member or any person other than the original recipient may wear the insignia of an order, decoration or medal. Insignia that are purchased or otherwise acquired may be used for display purpose only and cannot be worn on the person in any form or manner.

Abbreviations Indicating Honours and Decorations

A.F.C. - Air Force Cross. Ribbon, wide diagonal stripes of white and red.

A.F.M. - Air Force Medal. Ribbon, narrow diagonal stripes of white and red.

A.M. - Albert Medal, gold (Sea). Ribbon, nine alternate narrow stripes of blue and white.

Albert Medal, gold (Land). Ribbon, nine alternate narrow stripes of red and white.

Albert Medal, bronze (Sea). Ribbon, blue ground with two wide stripes of white.

Albert Medal, bronze (Land). Ribbon, red ground with two wide stripes of white.

B.E.M. - British Empire Medal.

Bt. - Baronet

C.B. - Companion of the Most Honourable Order of the Bath.

C.B.E. - Commander of the Order of the British Empire.

C.C. - Companion of the Order of Canada.

C.D. - Canadian Forces Decoration.

C.G.M. - Conspicuous Gallantry Medal; Navy and Air Force. It carries a cash grant. The Navy Medal ribbon is white with dark blue edges; the Air Force ribbon is light blue with dark blue edges.

C.H. - Member of the Order of the Companions of Honour.

C.I.E. - Companion of the Most Eminent Order of the Indian Empire.

C.M. - Member of the Order of Canada. C.M.G. - Companion of the Most Distinguished Order of St. Michael and St. George.

C.M.M. - Commander of the Order of Military Merit.

C.P.S.M. - Canadian Peacekeeping Service Medal.

C.S.I. - Companion of the Most Exalted Order of the Star of India.

C.V. - Cross of Valour. C.V.O. - Commander of the Royal Victorian Order.

D.C.M. - Distinguished Conduct Medal. Ribbon, red ground, dark blue stripe in centre.

D.F.C. - Distinguished Flying Cross. Ribbon, wide diagonal stripes of violet and white.

D.F.M. - Distinguished Flying Medal. Ribbon, narrow diagonal stripes of white and violet.

D.S.C. - Distinguished Service Cross. Ribbon, three broad bands, dark blue, white, dark blue.

D.S.M. - Distinguished Service Medal.

D.S.O. - Companion of the Distinguished Service Order. Instituted 1886. Ribbon, dark red with dark blue stripe at each end.

E.D. - Canadian Efficiency Decoration for Officers of Military Auxiliary Forces.

E.M. - Edward Medal. Posthumous award.

E.M. - Efficiency Medal.

G.B.E. - Knight Grand Cross or Dame Grand Cross of the Most Excellent Order of the British Empire.

G.C. - George Cross.

G.C.B. - Knight Grand Cross of the Most Honourable Order of the Bath.

G.C.I.E. - Knight Grand Commander of the Most Eminent Order of the Indian Empire.

G.C.M.G. - Knight Grand Cross of the Most Distinguished Order of St. Michael and St. George.

G.C.S.I. - Knight Grand Commander of the Most Exalted Order of the Star of India.

G.C.V.O. - Knight Grand Cross of the Royal Victorian Order.

G.M. - George Medal.

I.S.M. - Imperial Service Medal.

I.S.O. - Companion of the Imperial Service Order. Instituted 1902.

K.B.E. - Knight Commander of the Most Excellent Order of the British Empire.

K.C.B. - Knight Commander of the Most Honourable Order of the Bath.

K.C.I.E. - Knight Commander of the Most Eminent Order of the Indian Empire.

K.C.M.G. - Knight Commander of the Most Distinguished Order of St. Michael and St. George.

K.C.S.I. - Knight Commander of the Most Exalted Order of the Star of India.

K.C.V.O. - Knight Commander of the Royal Victorian Order.

K.G. - Knight of the Most Noble Order of the Garter.

K.P. - Knight of the Most Illustrious Order of St. Patrick.

Kt. - Knight Bachelor.

K.T. - Knight of the Most Ancient and Most Noble Order of the Thistle.

L.V.O. - Lieutenant of the Royal Victorian Order.

M.B. - Medal of Bravery.

M.B.E. - Member of the Order of the British Empire.

M.C. - Military Cross. Instituted 1915. Ribbon, white with broad band of blue in centre.

M. du C. - Canada Medal.

M.M. - Military Medal.

M.M.M. - Member of the Order of Military Merit.

M.V.O. - Member of the Royal Victorian Order.

M.S.C. - Meritorous Service Cross.

M.S.M. - Meritorious Service Medal.

O.B.E. - Officer of the Order of the British Empire.

O.B. - Order of the Beaver (Award of the BNAPS).

O.C. - Officer of the Order of Canada.

O.M. - Member of the Order of Merit.

O.M.M. - Officer of the Order of Military Merit.

P.C. - Privy Counsellor.

R.R.C. - Royal Red Cross. Instituted 1883. Ribbon, dark blue with narrow band of dark red at each end.

R.V.M. - Royal Victorian Medal.

S.C. - Star of Courage.

S.S.M. - Special Service Medal

U.E. - Unity of Empire. Descendants of United Empire Loyalists.

V.C. - Victoria Cross.

V.D. - Auxiliary Forces (Volunteer) Officers' Decoration.

V.R.D. - Naval Volunteer Reserve Decoration.

Government

Table of Precedence for Canada

1. The Governor General of Canada or the Administrator of the Government of Canada. (Notes 1, 2 & 2.1).
2. The Prime Minister of Canada. (Note 3).
3. The Chief Justice of Canada. (Note 4).
4. The Speaker of the Senate.
5. The Speaker of the House of Commons.
6. Ambassadors, High Commissioners, Ministers Plenipotentiary. (Note 5).
7. Members of the Canadian Ministry:
   a. Members of the Cabinet; and
   b. Secretaries of the State; with relative precedence within sub-categories (a) and (b) governed by the date of their appointment to the Queen's Privy Council for Canada.
8. The Leader of the Opposition. (Subject to Note 3).
9. The Lieutenant Governor of Ontario;
   The Lieutenant Governor of Québec;
   The Lieutenant Governor of Nova Scotia;
   The Lieutenant Governor of New Brunswick;
   The Lieutenant Governor of Manitoba;
   The Lieutenant Governor of British Columbia;
   The Lieutenant Governor of Prince Edward Island;
   The Lieutenant Governor of Saskatchewan;
   The Lieutenant Governor of Alberta;
   The Lieutenant Governor of Newfoundland
   (Note 6).
10. Members of the Queen's Privy Council for Canada, not of the Canadian Ministry, in accordance with the date of their appointment to the Privy Council.
11. Premiers of the Provinces of Canada in the same order as Lieutenant Governors. (Note 6).
12. The Commissioner of the Northwest Territories; The Commissioner of the Yukon Territory; The Commissioner of Nunavut
13. Government Leader of the Northwest Territories; The Government Leader of the Yukon Territory; The Government Leader of Nunavut
14. Representatives of faith communities. (Note 7).
15. Puisne Judges of the Supreme Court of Canada.
16. The Chief Justice and the Associate Chief Justice of the Federal Court of Canada.
17. (a) Chief Justices of the highest court of each Province and Territory; and
    (b) Chief Justices and Associate Chief Justices of the other superior courts of the Provinces and Territories; with precedence within sub-categories (a) and (b) governed by the date of appointment as Chief Justice.
18. (a) Judges of the Federal Court of Canada.
    (b) Puisne Judges of the superior courts of the Provinces and Territories.
    (c) the Chief Judge of the Tax Court of Canada;
    (d) the Associate Chief Judge of the Tax Court of Canada; and
    (e) Judges of the Tax Court of Canada; with precedence within each sub-category governed by date of appointment.
19. Senators of Canada.
20. Members of the House of Commons.
21. Consuls General of countries without diplomatic representation.
22. The Chief of the Defence Staff and the Commissioner of the Royal Canadian Mounted Police.
    (Note 8).
23. Speakers of Legislative Assemblies, within their Provinces and Territory.
24. Members of the Executive Councils, within their Provinces and Territory.
25. Judges of Provincial and Territorial Courts, within their Province and Territory.
26. Members of Legislative Assemblies, within their Provinces and Territory.

NOTES

1. The presence of the Sovereign in Canada does not impair or supersede the authority of the Governor General to perform the functions delegated to him under the Letters Patent constituting the office of the Governor General. The Governor General, under all circumstances, should be accorded precedence immediately after the Sovereign.
2. Precedence to be given immediately after the Chief Justice of Canada to former Governors General, with relative precedence among them governed by the date of their leaving office.

2.1 Precedence to be given immediately after the former Governors General to surviving spouses of deceased former Governors General (applicable only where the spouse was married to the Governor General during the latter's term of office), with relative precedence among them governed by the dates on which the deceased former Governor General left office.

3. Precedence to be given immediately after the surviving spouses of deceased former Governors General referred to in Note 2.1 to former Prime Ministers, with relative precedence among them governed by the dates of their first assumption of office.
4. Precedence to be given immediately after former Prime Ministers to former Chief Justices of Canada, with relative precedence among them governed by the dates of their appointment as Chief Justice of Canada.
5. Precedence among Ambassadors and High Commissioners, who rank equally, to be determined by the date of the presentation of their credentials. Precedence to be given to Chargés d'Affaires immediately after Ministers Plenipotentiary.
6. This provision does not apply to such ceremonies and occasions which are of a provincial nature.
7. The religious dignitaries will be senior Canadian representatives of faith communities having a significant presence in a relevant jurisdiction. The relevant precedence of the representatives of faith communities is to be governed by the date of their assumption in their present office, their representatives being given the same relative precedence.
8. This precedence to be given to the Chief of the Defence Staff and the Commissioner of the R.C.M.P. on occasions when they have official functions to perform, otherwise they are to have equal precedence with Deputy Ministers, with their relative position to be determined according to the respective dates of their appointments to office. The relative precedence of Deputy Ministers and other high officials of the public service of Canada is to be determined from time to time by the Minister of Canadian Heritage in consultation with the Prime Minister.

Table of Titles to Be Used in Canada

1. The Governor General of Canada to be styled "Right Honourable" for life and to be styled "His Excellency" and his wife "Her Excellency", or "Her Excellency" and her husband "His Excellency", as the case may be, while in office.
2. The Lieutenant Governor of a Province to be styled "Honourable" for life and to be styled "His Honour" and his wife "Her Honour", or "Her Honour" and her husband "His Honour", as the case may be, while in office.
3. The Prime Minister of Canada to be styled "Right Honourable" for life.
4. The Chief Justice of Canada to be styled "Right Honourable" for life.
5. Privy Councillors of Canada to be styled "Honourable" for life.
6. Senators of Canada to be styled "Honourable" for life.
7. The Speaker of the House of Commons to be styled "Honourable" while in office.
8. The Commissioner of a Territory to be styled "Honourable" while in office.
9. Puisne Judges of the Supreme Court of Canada and Judges of the Federal Courts and the Tax Court of Canada as well as the Judges of the undermentioned Courts in the Provinces and Territories:
   Ontario - Court of Appeal and the Ontario Court of Justice (General Division)
   Québec - The Court of Appeal and the Superior Court of Québec
   Nova Scotia - The Court of Appeal and the Supreme Court of Nova Scotia
   New Brunswick - The Court of Appeal and the Court of Queen's Bench of New Brunswick
   Manitoba - The Court of Appeal and the Court of Queen's Bench of Manitoba
   British Columbia - The Court of Appeal and the Supreme Court of British Columbia
   Prince Edward Island - The Supreme Court of Prince Edward Island

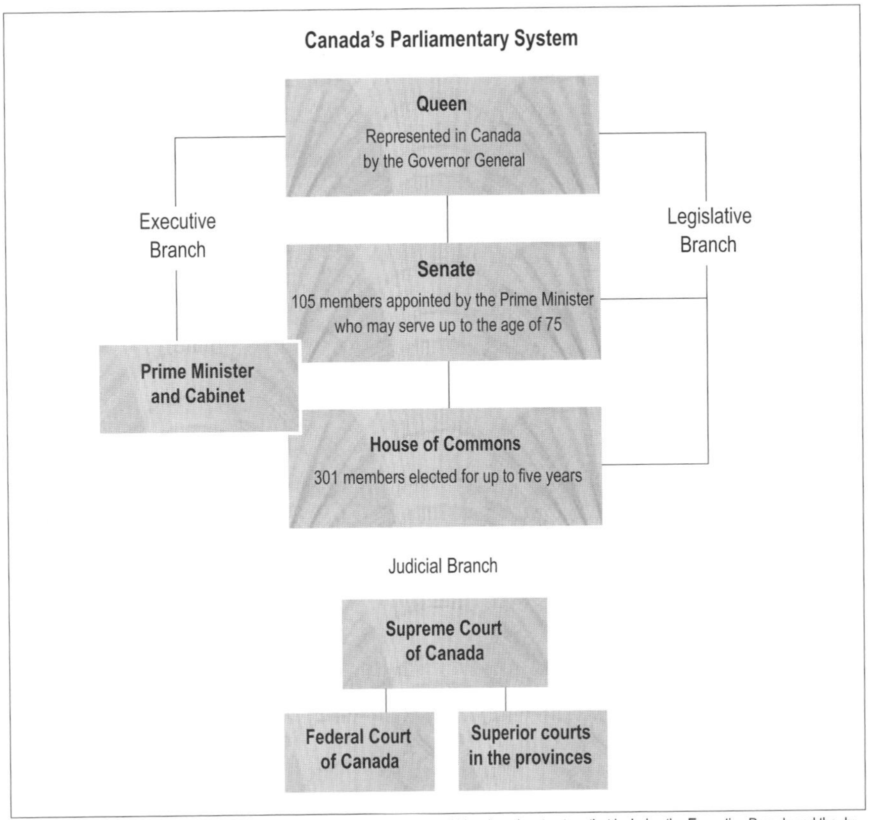

Parliament as a legislative body functions as an instrument of government within a broader structure that includes the Executive Branch and the Judicial Branch. In the Westminster-based model of parliamentary government, the Executive, comprised of the Prime Minister and the Cabinet, is incorporated into Parliament, while retaining a separate sphere of authority and autonomy. The Judiciary, consisting of the Supreme Court and all the other courts of the land, is the third branch of government that is also independent of either Parliament or the Executive.

Saskatchewan - The Court of Appeal and the Court of Queen's Bench of Saskatchewan
Alberta - The Court of Appeal and the Court of Queen's Bench of Alberta
Newfoundland - The Supreme Court of Newfoundland
Northwest Territories - The Supreme Court of Northwest Territories
Yukon Territory - The Supreme Court of Yukon
Nunavut Territory - The Nunavut Court of Justice
to be styled "The Honourable" while in office.

10. Presidents and Speakers of the Legislative Assemblies of the Provinces and Territories to be styled "Honourable" while in office.
11. Members of the Executive Councils of the Provinces and Territories to be styled "Honourable" while in office.
12. Judges of Provincial and Territorial Courts (appointed by the Provincial and Territorial Governments) to be styled "Honourable" while in office.
13. The following are eligible to be granted permission by the Governor General, in the name of Her Majesty The Queen, to retain the title of "Honourable" after they have ceased to hold office: (a) Speakers of the House of Commons; (b) Commissioners of Territories; (c) Judges designated in item 9.
14. The title "Right Honourable" is granted for life to the following eminent Canadians: The Right Honourable Martial Asselin The Right Honourable Ellen L. Fairclough The Right Honourable Francis Alvin George Hamilton The Right Honourable Donald F. Mazankowski The Right Honourable Robert Lorne Stanfield The Right Honourable Herb Eser Grey
15. Mayors of Area Municipalities to be styled "His Worship" or "Her Worship", as the case may be, while in office.
16. Visiting Heads of State to be styled:
    • "His Excellency The Honourable" or "Her Excellency The Honourable", as the case may be, if the President of the United States,
    • "His Excellency" or "Her Excellency" as the case may be, for all other visiting Heads of State.

GOVERNORS GENERAL OF CANADA SINCE CONFEDERATION
(WITH DATE APPOINTED)

**The Viscount Monck,
G.C.M.G.**
June 1, 1867

**Lord Lisgar,
G.C.M.G.**
Dec. 29, 1868

**The Earl of Dufferin,
K.P., G.C.B., G.C.S.I., G.C.M.G., G.C.I.E**
May 22, 1872

**The Marquess of Lorne,
K.T., G.C.M.G., G.C.V.O.**
Oct. 5, 1878

**The Marquess of Lansdowne,
K.G., G.C.S.I., G.C.M.G., G.C.I.E.**
Aug. 18, 1883

**Lord Stanley of Preston,
K.G., G.C.B., G.C.V.O.**
May 1, 1888

**The Earl of Aberdeen,
K.T., G.C.M.G., G.C.V.O.**
May 22, 1893

**The Earl of Minto,
K.G., G.C.S.I., G.C.M.G., G.C.I.E.**
July 30, 1898

**The Earl Grey,
G.C.B., G.C.M.G., G.C.V.O.**
Sept. 26, 1904

**H.R.H. The Duke of Connaught,
K.G., K.T., K.P., G.M.B., G.C.S.I., G.C.M.G., G.C.I.E., G.C.V.O., G.B.E., T.D.**
Mar. 21, 1911

**The Duke of Devonshire,
K.G., G.C.M.G., G.C.V.O., T.D.**
Aug.. 19, 1916

**Lord Byng of Vimy,
G.C.B., G.C.M.G., M.V.O.**
Aug. 2, 1921

**The Viscount Willingdon of Ratton,
G.C.S.I., G.C.M.G., G.C.I.E., G.B.E.**
Aug. 5, 1926

**The Earl of Bessborough,
G.C.M.G.**
Feb. 9, 1931

Baron Tweedsmuir of Elsfield, G.C.M.G., G.C.V.O., C.H.
Aug. 10, 1935

Major-General The Earl of Athlone, K.G., G.C.B., G.C.M.G., G.C.V.O., D.S.O.
Apr. 3, 1940

Field Marshal The Viscount Alexander of Tunis, K.G., G.C.B., O.M., G.C.M.G., C.S.I., D.S.O., M.C., A.D.C.
Aug. 1, 1945

The Rt. Hon. Vincent Massey, P.C., C.C., C.H.
Jan. 24, 1952

Major General The Rt. Hon. Georges-P. Vanier, D.S.O., M.C., C.D.
Aug. 1, 1959

The Rt. Hon. Roland Michener, P.C., C.C., C.M.M., C.D., Q.C.
Mar. 25, 1967

The Rt. Hon. Jules Léger P.C., C.C., C.M.M., C.D.
Oct. 5, 1973

The Rt. Hon. Edward Richard Schreyer, P.C., C.C., C.M.M., C.D.
Dec. 7, 1978

The Rt. Hon. Jeanne Sauvé, P.C., C.C., C.M.M., C.D.
Dec. 23, 1983

Photo Credit: Yousuf Karsh

The Rt. Hon. Ramon John Hnatyshyn, P.C., C.C., C.M.M., C.D., Q.C.
Oct. 6, 1989

Photo Credit: Rideau Hall

The Rt. Hon. Roméo LeBlanc, P.C., C.C., C.M.M., C.D.
Nov. 22, 1994

Photo Credit: Rideau Hall

Her Excellency, the Rt. Hon.
Adrienne Clarkson,
C.C., C.M.M., C.O.M., C.D.
Oct. 7, 1999

Photo Credit: Andrew MacNaughtan
© Her Majesty The Queen in Right of Canada represented by the Office of the Secretary to the Governor General (1999)

Her Excellency, the Rt. Hon.
Michaëlle Jean,
C.C., C.M.M., C.O.M., C.D.
Sept. 27, 2005

Photo Credit: Sgt Eric Jolin, Rideau Hall
© Her Majesty The Queen in Right of Canada represented by the Office of the Secretary to the Governor General (2006)

His Excellency, the Rt. Hon.
David Johnston,
C.C., C.M.M., C.O.M., C.D.
Oct. 1, 2010

Photo Credit: Sgt Serge Gouin, Rideau Hall
© Her Majesty The Queen in Right of Canada represented by the Office of the Secretary to the Governor General (2010)

CANADIAN PRIME MINISTERS

(WITH PARTY AFFILIATION AND TIME IN OFFICE)

Rt. Hon. Sir John A. Macdonald (Conservative)
July 1, 1867 to Nov. 5, 1873
Oct. 17, 1878 to June 6, 1891
Photo credit: William James Topley/National Archives of Canada/PA-027013

Hon. Alexander MacKenzie (Liberal)
Nov. 7, 1873 to Oct. 16, 1878
Photo credit: William James Topley/National Archives of Canada/PA-026308

Hon. Sir John J. Abbott (Conservative)
June 16, 1891 to Nov. 24, 1892
Photo credit: William James Topley/National Archives of Canada/PA-033933

Rt. Hon. Sir John S. D. Thompson (Conservative)
Dec. 5, 1892 to Dec. 12, 1894
Photo Credit: National Archives of Canada/C-000698

Hon. Sir Mackenzie Bowell (Conservative)
Dec. 21, 1894 to April 27, 1896
Photo Credit: William James Topley/National Archives of Canada/PA-027159

Rt. Hon. Sir Charles Tupper (Conservative)
May 1, 1896 to July 8, 1896
Photo Credit: National Archives of Canada/PA-027743

Rt. Hon. Sir Wilrid Laurier (Liberal)
July 11, 1896 to Oct. 6, 1911
Photo Credit: William James Topley/National Archives of Canada/C-001971

Rt. Hon. Sir Robert L. Borden
Oct. 10, 1911 to Oct. 12, 1917
(Conservative Administration)
Oct. 12, 1917 to July 10, 1920
(Unionist Administration)
Photo Credit: William James Topley/National Archives of Canada/PA-028128

Rt. Hon. Arthur Meighen
July 10, 1920 to Dec. 29, 1921
(Unionist "National Liberal and Conservative Party")
June 29, 1926 to Sept. 25, 1926
(Conservative)
Photo Credit: William James Topley/National Archives of Canada/PA-026987

Rt. Hon. William Lyon Mackenzie King (Liberal)
Dec. 29, 1921 to June 28, 1926
Sept. 25, 1926 to Aug. 6, 1930
Oct. 23, 1935 to Nov. 15, 1948
Photo Credit: National Archives of Canada/C-027645

Rt. Hon. Richard Bedford Bennett (Conservative) (Became Viscount Bennett, 1941)
Aug. 7, 1930 to Oct. 23, 1935
Photo Credit: National Archives of Canada/C-000687

Rt. Hon. Louis Stephen St. Laurent (Liberal)
Nov. 15, 1948 to June 21, 1957
Photo Credit: National Archives of Canada/C-010461

Rt. Hon. John G. Diefenbaker (Progressive Conservative)
June 21, 1957 to April 22, 1963
Photo Credit: Paul Horsdal/National Archives of Canada/PA-130070

Rt. Hon. Lester Bowles Pearson (Liberal)
April 22, 1963 to April 20, 1968
Photo Credit: Ashley-Crippen Studio/National Archives of Canada/PA-126393

Rt. Hon. Pierre Elliott Trudeau (Liberal)
April 20, 1968 to June 4, 1979
Mar. 3, 1980 to June 30, 1984
Photo Credit: National Archives of Canada/C-046600

Rt. Hon. Charles Joseph Clark (Progressive Conservative)
June 4, 1979 to Mar. 3, 1980
Photo Credit: House of Commons, Ottawa

Rt. Hon. John Napier Turner (Liberal)
June 30, 1984 to Sept. 17, 1984
Photo Credit: Jean-Marc Carisse

Rt. Hon. Martin Brian Mulroney (Progressive Conservative)
Sept 17, 1984 to June 25, 1993
Photo Credit: Robert Cooper/National Archives of Canada/PA-152416

Rt. Hon. Kim Campbell (Progressive Conservative)
June 25, 1993 to Nov. 4, 1993
Photo Credit: Courtesy of the Office of Rt. Hon. Kim Campbell

Rt. Hon. Jean Chrétien (Liberal)
Nov. 4, 1993 to Dec. 11, 2003
Photo Credit: Jean-Marc Carisse

Rt. Hon. Paul Edgar Philippe Martin (Liberal)
Dec. 12, 2003 to Feb. 6, 2006
Photo Credit: Dave Chan

Rt. Hon. Stephen Joseph Harper (Conservative)
Feb. 6, 2006 to —
Photo Credit: Courtesy of The Office of the Prime Minister

PORTRAITS OF PRIME MINISTERS IN THE HOUSE OF COMMONS

Reproduced with the permission of the Curator, House of Commons

Sir John Alexander Macdonald
Credit: Henry Sandham
National Archives of Canada C-025743

Hon. Alexander Mackenzie
Credit: John Wycliffe Lowes Forster
National Archives of Canada C-116811

Hon. Sir John J. Abbott
Credit: Muli Tang
House of Commons Collection

Sir John Thompson
Credit: John Wycliffe Lowes Forster
National Archives of Canada C-116812

Hon. Sir Mackenzie Bowell
Credit: Joanne Tod
House of Commons Collection

Sir Charles Tupper
Credit: Victor A. Long
National Archives of Canada C-116813

Sir Wilfrid Laurier
Credit: John Wentworth Russell
National Archives of Canada C-116814

Sir Robert Borden
Credit: Kenneth Keith Forbes
National Archives of Canada C-116815

Rt. Hon. Arthur Meighen
Credit: George Ernest Fosbery
National Archives of Canada C-116816

Rt. Hon. William Lyon Mackenzie King
Credit: Frank O. Salisbury
National Archives of Canada C-116818

Rt. Hon. Richard Bedford Bennett
Credit: Kenneth Keith Forbes
National Archives of Canada C-116817

Rt. Hon. Louis St. Laurent
Credit: Audrey Watts McNaughton
National Archives of Canada C-116819

Rt. Hon. John G. Diefenbaker
Credit: Arthur Edward Cleeve Horne
National Archives of Canada C-116820

Rt. Hon. Lester Bowles Pearson
Credit: Hugh Seaforth MacKenzie
National Archives of Canada C-116821

Rt. Hon. Pierre Elliott Trudeau
Credit: Myfanwy Pavelic
House of Commons Collection

Rt. Hon. Charles Joseph Clark
Credit: Patrick Douglass Cox
House of Commons Collection

Rt. Hon. John Napier Turner
Credit: Brenda Bury
House of Commons Collection

Rt. Hon. Brian Mulroney
Credit: Igor Babailov
House of Commons Collection

Rt. Hon. Kim Campbell
Credit: David Goatley
House of Commons Collection

Rt. Hon. Jean Chrétien
Credit: Christian Nicholson
House of Commons Collection

Regulations & Abbreviations

Forms of Address

The following are reprinted with the permission of Canadian Heritage.

The Royal Family/La Famille Royale

THE QUEEN:
Her Majesty The Queen, Buckingham Palace, London SW1A 1AA United Kingdom
Salutation - Your Majesty:
Final Salutation - I remain Your Majesty's faithful and devoted servant,
In Conversation - "Your Majesty" first then "Ma'am"
Note: The Queen's full title is "Her Majesty Queen Elizabeth II, Queen of Canada" Normally one refers to "Her Majesty The Queen" or "The Queen"

LA REINE:
Sa Majesté la Reine, Palais de Buckingham, Londres SW1A 1AA Royaume-Uni
Appel - Majesté,
Salutation - Je prie Votre Majesté d'agréer l'expression de ma très haute considération.
Conversation - ‹‹Majesté››
Remarques: Le titre complet de la Reine est le suivant: ‹‹Sa Majesté la reine Ellizabeth II, Reine du Canada›› On parle normalement de ‹‹Sa Majesté›› ou de ‹‹la Reine››

THE PRINCE OF WALES:
His Royal Highness The Prince of Wales, St. James's Palace, London SW1A 1BS United Kingdom
Salutation - Your Royal Highness:
Final Salutation - Yours very truly,
In Conversation - "Your Royal Highness" first then "Sir"
Note: Should never be referred to as: "Charles, Prince of Wales" or Prince Charles.

LE PRINCE DE GALLES:
Son Altesse Royale le prince de Galles, Palais de St. James, Londres SW1A 1BS Royaume-Uni
Appel - Altesse Royale,
Saluation - Je prie Votre Altesse Royal d'agréer l'expression de ma très haute considération.
Conversation - ‹‹Altesse Royale››
Remarques: Il ne faut jamais dire: ‹‹Charles, prince de Galles›› ou ‹‹le prince Charles››

Government/Gouvernement

GOVERNOR GENERAL OF CANADA:
His/Her Excellency the Right Honourable (full name), C.C., C.M.M., C.D., Governor General of Canada, Rideau Hall, 1 Sussex Dr., Ottawa ON K1A 0A1
Salutation - Excellency:
Final Salutation - Yours truly,
In Conversation - "Your Excellency" or "Excellency" first then "Sir" or "Madam"
Note: The Governor General may have other postnominal letters, such as P.C., Q.C.

GOVERNEUR GÉNÉRAL DU CANADA:
(homme) Son Excellence le très honorable (prénom et nom), C.C., C.M.M., C.O.M., C.D., Gouverneur général du Canada, Rideau Hall, 1, promenade Sussex, Ottawa ON K1A 0A1
(femme) Son Excellence la très honorable (prénom et nom), C.C., C.M.M., C.O.M., C.D., Gouverneure générale du Canada, Rideau Hall, 1, promenade Sussex, Ottawa ON K1A 0A1
Appel - (homme) Monsieur le Gouverneur général,
(femme) Madame la Gouverneure générale,
Saluation - (homme) Je vous prie d'agréer, Monsieur le Gouverneur général, l'expression de ma très haute considération.
(femme) Je vous prie d'agréer, Madame la Gouverneure générale, l'hommage de mon profond respect.
Remarques: D'autres initiales peuvent suivre le nom du gouverneur général, comme C.P. et C.R.

LIEUTENANT GOVERNOR OF A PROVINCE:
His/Her Honour the Honourable (full name) Lieutenant Governor of (Province), Address
Salutation - Your Honour or My dear Lieutenant Governor:
Final Salutation - Yours sincerely,
In Conversation - "Your Honour" first then "Sir" or "Madam" or "Mr./Mrs./Ms./Miss (name)"
Note: The Lieutenant Governor of a province has the title "Honourable" for life; the courtesy title "His/ Her Honour" is used only while in office.

LIEUTENANT-GOUVERNEUR
(homme) Son Honneur l'honorable (prénom et nom) Lieutenant-gouverneur de (province), Adresse
(femme) Son Honneur l'honorable (prénom et nom) Lieutenante-gouverneure de (province), Adresse
Appel - (homme) Monsieur le Lieutenant-Gouverneur,
(femme) Madame la Lieutenante-Gouverneure,
Salutation - (homme) Je vous prie d'agréer, Monsieur le Lieutenant-Gouverneur, l'expression de ma haute considération.
(femme) Je vous prie d'agréer, Madame la Lieutenante-Gouverneure, l'hommage de mes respectueux hommages.
Conversation - On commence par ‹‹Votre Honneur››. On poursuit avec ‹‹Monsieur›› ou ‹‹Madame››
Remarques: Le titre ‹‹honorable›› est accordé à vie au lieutenant-gouverneur; le titre de courtoisie ‹‹Son Honneur›› n'est utilisé que pendant la durée du mandat.

THE PRIME MINISTER OF CANADA:
The Right Honourable (full name), P.C., M.P., Prime Minister of Canada, Langevin Block, Ottawa, ON K1A 0A2
Salutation - Dear Prime Minister: or Prime Minister:
Final Salutation - Yours sincerely,
In Conversation - "Prime Minister" first then "Mr./ Mrs./Ms./Miss (name)"
Note: The term "Mr. Prime Minister" should not be used. The Prime Minister may have other post-nominal letters, such as Q.C.

PREMIER MINISTRE DU CANADA
(homme) Le très honorable (prénom et nom), C.P., député Premier Ministre du Canada, Édifice Langevin, Ottawa ON K1A 0A2
(femme) La très honorable (prénom et nom), C.P., députée Première Ministre du Canada, Édifice Langevin, Ottawa ON K1A 0A2
Appel - (homme) Monsieur le Premier Ministre,
(femme) Madame la Première Ministre,
Salutation -
(homme) Je vous prie d'agréer, Monsieur le Premier Ministre, l'expression de ma très haute considération.
(femme) Je vous prie d'agréer, Madame la Première Ministre, l'hommage de mon profond respect. Conversation -
(homme) On commence par ‹‹Monsieur le Premier Ministre››. On poursuit avec ‹‹Monsieur››
(femme) On commence par ‹‹Madame la Première Ministre››. On pousuit avec ‹‹Madame››
Remarques: D'autres initiales peuvent suivre le nom, comme C.R.

THE PREMIER OF A PROVINCE OF CANADA:
The Honourable (full name), M.L.A. or (M.P.P., M.N.A., or M.H.A.), Premier of (Province), Address
Salutation - Dear Premier:
Final Salutation - Yours sincerely,
In Conversation - "Premier" first then "Mr./Mrs./Ms./ Miss (name)"
Note: The title "Honourable" is used only while in office, unless he/she is a member of the Privy Council. The term "Mr./Madam Premier" should not be used.

LE PREMIER MINISTRE D'UNE PROVINCE
(homme) L'honorable (prénom et nom) M.A.L ou (M.A.N., M.P.P. ou M.C.A) Premier Ministre de (province), Adresse
(femme) L'honorable (prénom et nom) M.A.L ou (M.A.N., M.P.P. ou M.C.A) Première Ministre de (province), Adresse
Appel - (homme) Monsieur le Premier Ministre,
(femme) Madame la Première Ministre,
Salutation - (homme) Je vous prie d'agréer, Monsieur le Premier Ministre, l'expression de ma haute considération.
(femme) Je vous prie d'agréer, Madame la Première Ministre, l'hommage de mon profond respect.
Conversation - On commence par ‹‹Monsieur le Premier Ministre››. On poursuit avec ‹‹Monsieur››
(femme) On commence par ‹‹Madame la Première Ministre››. On poursuit avec ‹‹Madame››
Remarques: Les premiers ministres ne conservent pas le titre ‹‹honorable›› après la fin de leur mandat, à moins qu'ils ne soient membres du Conseil privé.

COMMISSIONER OF A TERRITORY:
The Honourable (full name), Commissioner of (Territory), Address
Salutation - Commissioner (name):
Final Salutation - Yours sincerely,
In Conversation - "Sir" or "Madam" or "Mr./Mrs./ Ms./Miss (name)"

COMMISSAIRE DU TERRITOIRE
(homme/femme) L'honorable (prénom et nom) Commissaire du (territoire), Adresse
Appel - (homme) Monsieur le Commissaire,
(femme) Madame la Commissaire,
Salutation - Je vous prie d'agréer, Monsieur le Commissaire, l'expression de ma haute considération.
(femme) Je vous prie d'agréer, Madame la Commissaire, l'expression de mes respectueux hommages. Conversation -
(homme) ‹‹Monsieur››
(femme) ‹‹Madame››
Remarques: Le titre ‹‹honorable›› n'est utilisé que pendant la durée de ses fonctions.

GOVERNMENT LEADER OF A TERRITORY:
The Honourable (full name), M.L.A., Government Leader of (Territory), Address
Salutation - Dear Mr./Mrs./Ms./Miss (name):
Final Salutation - Yours sincerely,
In Conversation - "Mr./Mrs./Ms./Miss (name)"
Note: The title "Honourable" is used only while in office, unless he/she is a member of the Privy Council. The term "Mr./Madam Leader" should not be used.

LE LEADER DU GOUVERNEMENT D'UN TERRITOIRE
(homme/femme) L'honorable (prénom et nom), M.A.L. Leader du gouvernement du (territoire), Adresse
Appel - (homme) Monsieur le leader du gouvernement,
(femme) Madame la leader du gouvernement,
Salutation - (homme) Je vous prie d'agréer, Monsieur le Leader du gouvernement, l'expression de ma haute consideration.
(femme) Je vous prie d'agréer, Madame la Leader du gouvernement, l'hommage de mon profond respect.
Conversation - On commence par ‹‹Monsieur le Leader du gouvernement››. On poursuit avec ‹‹Monsieur››
(femme) On commence par ‹‹Madame la Leader du gouvernement››. On poursuit avec ‹‹Madame››
Remarques: Les leaders ne conservent pas le titre ‹‹honorable›› après la fin de leur mandat, à moins qu'ils ne soient membres du Conseil privé.

CABINET MINISTERS:
Member of the House of Commons: The Honourable (full name), P.C., M.P., Minister of ________, House of Commons, Ottawa ON K1A 0A6
Salutation - Dear Minister: or Dear Colleague: (between colleagues)
Final Salutation - Yours sincerely,
In Conversation - "Minister" first then "Mr./Mrs./ Ms./Miss (name)"
For a Senator: Senator the Honourable (full name), P.C., Minister of ________, The Senate, Ottawa, ON K1A 0A4
Salutation - Dear Minister: or Dear Colleague: (between colleagues)
Final Salutation - Yours sincerely,
In Conversation - "Minister" first then "Mr./Mrs./ Ms./Miss (name)"

CONSEIL DES MINISTRES DU CANADA
(homme) L'honorable (prénom et nom), C.P. député Ministre de ________, Chambre de communes, Ottawa ON K1A 0A6
(femme) L'honorable (prénom et nom), C.P. députée Ministre de ________, Chambre de communes, Ottawa ON K1A 0A6
Appel - (homme) Monsieur le Ministre, ou Cher collègue, (Entre collègues)
(femme) Madame la Ministre, ou Chère collègue, (Entre collègues)
Salutation -
(homme) Je vous prie d'agréer, Monsieur le Ministre, l'expression de ma considération respectueuse.
(femme) Je vous prie d'agréer, Madame la Ministre, l'hommage de mon profond respect. Conversation -
(homme) On commence par ‹‹Monsieur le Ministre››. On poursuit avec ‹‹Monsieur››
(femme) On commence par ‹‹Madame la Ministre››. On poursuit avec ‹‹Madame››
Remarques: Les ministres fédéraux sont membres du Conseil privé de la Reine pour le Canada et conservent le titre ‹‹honorable›› à vie. On place les initiales C.P. après leur nom.

SECRETARIES OF STATE:
The Honourable (full name), P.C., M.P., Secretary of State (Portfolio), House of Commons, Ottawa, ON K1A 0A6
Salutation - Dear Secretary of State: or Dear Colleague: (between colleagues)
Final Salutation - Yours sincerely,
In Conversation - "Secretary of State" first then "Mr./ Mrs./Ms./Miss (name)"
Note: Members of the Ministry are members of the Queen's Privy Council for Canada and retain the title "Honourable" for life, using the initials P.C. after their name. The term "Mr. Minister" or "Madame Minister" should not be used. The term "Mr. Secretary of State" or "Madame Secretary of State" should not be used.

SECRÉTAIRES D'ÉTAT

(homme) L'honorable (prénom et nom), C.P. député Secrétaire d'État (Portefeuille), Chambre des communes, Ottawa ON K1A 0A6

(femme) L'honorable (prénom et nom), C.P. députée Secrétaire d'État (Portefeuille), Chambre des communes, Ottawa ON K1A 0A6

Appel - (homme) Monsieur le Secrétaire d'État, ou Cher collègue, (Entre collègues)

(femme) Madame la Secrétaire d'État, ou Chère collègue, (Entre collègues)

Salutation - (homme) Je vous prie d'agréer, Monsieur le Secrétaire d'État, l'expression de ma considération respectueuse. Ou Je vous prie, cher collègue, de recevoir mes cordiales salutations. (Entre collègues)

(femme) Je vous prie d'agréer, Madame la Secrétaire d'État, l'hommage de mon profond respect. Ou Je vous prie, chère collègue, de recevoir mes cordiales salutations. (Entre collègues) Conversation -

(homme) On commence par «Monsieur le Secrétaire d'État». On poursuit avec «Monsieur»

(femme) On commence par «Madame la Secrétaire d'État». On poursuit avec «Madame»

Remarques: Les secrétaires d'État sont membres du Conseil privé de la Reine pour le Canada et conservent le titre «honorable» à vie. On place les initiales C.P. aprés leur nom.

SPEAKER OF THE SENATE:

The Honourable (full name), Senator, Speaker of State, The Senate, Ottawa, ON K1A 0A4

Salutation - Dear Mr./Madam Speaker:

Final Salutation - Yours sincerely,

In Conversation - "Mr. Speaker" or "Madam Speaker"

Note: A senator who is a member of the Canadian Privy Council is addressed as "Senator the Honourable (name), P.C. " After a Senator retires, he/she retains the title "Honourable" but the salutation is "Dear Sir/ Madam" or "Dear Mr./Mrs./Ms./Miss (name)"

PRÉSIDENT OU PRÉSIDENTE DU SÉNAT

(homme) L'honorable (prénom et nom), sénateur Président du Sénat, Le Sénat, Ottawa ON K1A 0A4

(femme) L'honorable (prénom et nom), sénatrice Présidente du Sénat, Le Sénat, Ottawa ON K1A 0A4

Appel - (homme) Monsieur le Président,

(femme) Madame la Présidente,

Salutation - (homme) Je vous prie d'agréer, Monsieur le Président, l'expression de ma haute considération.

(femme) Je vous prie d'agréer, Madame la Présidente, l'hommage de mon profond respect. Conversation -

(homme) «Monsieur le Président»

(femme) «Madame la Présidente»

Remarques: Dans le cas d'un sénateur ou d'une sénatrice qui est membre du Conseil privé, la formule d'appel à utiliser est «L'honorable (nom), C.P., sénateur(trice)». Après leur retraite, les sénateurs conservent le titre «honorable» mais la formule d'appel devient: «Monsieur/Madame».

SPEAKER OF THE HOUSE OF COMMONS:

The Honourable (full name), M.P., Speaker of the House of Commons, House of Commons, Ottawa, ON K1A 0A6

Salutation - Dear Mr./Madam Speaker:

Final Salutation - Yours sincerely,

In Conversation - "Mr. Speaker" or "Madam Speaker"

PRÉSIDENT OU PRÉSIDENTE DE LA CHAMBRE DES COMMUNES

(homme) L'honorable (prénom et nom) député Président de la Chambre des communes, Chambre des communes, Ottawa ON K1A 0A6

(femme) L'honorable (prénom et nom) députée Présidente de la Chambre des communes, Chambre des communes, Ottawa ON K1A 0A6

Appel - (homme) Monsieur le Président,

(femme) Madame la Présidente,

Salutation - (homme) Je vous prie d'agréer, Monsieur le Président, l'expression de ma haute considération.

(femme) Je vous prie d'agréer, Madame la Présidente, l'hommage de mon profond respect. Conversation -

(homme) «Monsieur le Président»

(femme) «Madame la Présidente»

SENATORS:

The Honourable (full name), Senator, The Senate, Ottawa, ON K1A 0A1

Salutation - Dear Senator (name):

Final Salutation - Yours sincerely,

In Conversation - "Senator (name)"

Note: A senator who is a member of the Queen's Privy Council is addressed as "Senator the Honourable (full name), P.C." After a Senator retires, he/she retains the title "Honourable" for life but the salutation is "Dear Sir/Madam" or "Dear Mr./Mrs./Ms./Miss (name)".

SÉNATEURS:

(homme) L'honorable (prénom et nom) sénateur, Le Sénat, Ottawa ON K1A 0A4

(femme) L'honorable (prénom et nom) sénatrice, Le Sénat, Ottawa ON K1A 0A4

Appel - (homme) Monsieur le Sénateur,

(femme) Madame la Sénatrice,

Salutation - (homme) Je vous prie d'agréer, Monsieur le Sénateur, l'expression de mes meilleurs sentiments.

(femme) Je vous prie d'agréer, Madame la Sénatrice, mes hommages respectueux. Conversation -

(homme) «Monsieur le Sénateur». On poursuit avec «Monsieur»

(femme) «Madame la Sénatrice». On poursuit avec «Madame»

Remarques: Après leur retraite, les sénateurs conservent le titre «honorable», mais la formule d'appel devient: «Monsieur» ou «Madame».

MEMBERS OF THE HOUSE OF COMMONS:

Mr. John Smith, M.P. or The Honourable John Smith, P.C., M.P., House of Commons, Ottawa, ON K1A 0A6

Salutation - Dear Mr./Mrs./Ms./Miss (name):

Final Salutation - Yours sincerely,

In Conversation - "Mr./Mrs./Ms./Miss (name)"

Note: The members of the House of Commons who are members of the Queen's Privy Council retain the title "Honourable" for life and use the initials "P.C." after their name. M.P.: Member of the House of Commons P.C., M.P.: Member of the Privy Council and Member of the House of Commons

DÉPUTÉS FÉDÉRAUX

(homme) Monsieur (prénom et nom), député ou L'honorable (prénom et nom), C.P., député Chambre des communes, Ottawa ON K1A 0A6

(femme) Madame (prénom et nom), députée ou L'honorable (prénom et nom), C.P., députée Chambre des communes, Ottawa ON K1A 0A6

Appel - (homme) Monsieur le Député,

(femme) Madame la Députée,

Salutation - (homme) Je vous prie d'agréer, Monsieur le Député, l'expression de mes meilleurs sentiments.

(femme) Je vous prie d'agréer, Madame la Députee, mes respectueux hommages. Conversation -

(homme) On commence par «Monsieur le Député». On poursuit avec «Monsieur»

(femme) On commence par «Madame la Députee». On poursuit avec «Madame»

Remarques: Les députés qui sont membres du Conseil privé de la Reine pour le Canada ont le «honorable» à vie et portent les initiales «C.P.» après leur nom.

MEMBER OF THE PROVINCIAL/TERRITORIAL CABINET:

The Honourable (full name), M.L.A. or (M.P.P., M.N.A. or M.H.A.), Minister of ________, Address

Salutation - Dear Minister: or Dear Colleague: (between colleagues)

Final Salutation - Yours sincerely,

In Conversation - "Minister" first then "Mr./Mrs./ Ms./Miss (name)"

Note: A provincial/territorial cabinet minister does not retain the title "Honourable" after tenure of office unless he/she is a member of the Privy Council. M.L.A.: all provinces/territories except for: Ontario (M.P.P.); Québec (M.N.A.); Newfoundland (M.H.A.). The term "Mr./Madam Minister" should not be used.

MINISTRES PROVINCIAUX/TERRITORIAUX

(homme/femme) L'honorable (prénom et nom), M.A.L. ou (M.A.N., M.P.P. ou M.C.A.) Ministre de ________, Adresse

Appel - (homme) Monsieur le Ministre, ou Cher collègue, (Entre collègues)

(femme) Madame la Ministre, ou Chère collègue, (Entre collègues)

Salutation - (homme) Je vous prie d'agréer, Monsieur le Ministre, l'expression de ma considération respectueuse. Ou Je vous prie, cher collègue, de recevoir mes cordiales salutations. (Entre collègues)

(femme) Je vous prie d'agréer, Madame la Ministre, l'expression de ma considération respectueuse. Ou Je vous prie, chère collègue, de recevoir mes cordiales salutations. (Entre collègues) Conversation -

(homme) On commence par «Monsieur le Ministre». On poursuit avec «Monsieur»

(femme) On commence par «Madame la Ministre». On poursuit avec «Madame»

Remarques: Les ministres provinciaux/territoriaux ne conservent pas le titre «honorable» après la fin de leur mandat à moins qu'ils ne soient membres du Conseil privé. M.A.L.: toutes les provinces et les territoires, sauf: - l'Ontario (M.P.P.) - le Québec (M.A.N.) - Terre- Neuve (M.C.A.)

MEMBER OF A PROVINCIAL/TERRITORIAL LEGISLATIVE ASSEMBLY:

Mr. John Smith, M.L.A. or (M.P.P., M.N.A., or M.H.A.)

Salutation - Dear Mr./Mrs./Ms./Miss (name),

Final Salutation - Yours sincerely,

In Conversation - "Mr./Mrs./Ms./Miss (name)"

Note: Members of the Queen's Privy Council retain the title "Honourable" for life and use the initials "P.C." after their name. M.L.A.: all provinces/territories except for: Ontario (M.P.P.); Quebec (M.N.A.); Newfoundland (M.H.A.) P.C., M.L.A.: Member of the Privy Council and Member of the Legislative Assembly

DÉPUTÉS PROVINCIAUX/TERRITORIAUX

(homme) Monsieur (prénom et nom), M.A.L. ou (M.P.P., M.A.N. ou M.C.A.), Adresse

(femme) Madame (prénom et nom), M.A.L. ou (M.P.P., M.A.N. ou M.C.A.), Adresse

Appel - (homme) Monsieur le Député,

(femme) Madame la Députée,

Salutation - (homme) Je vous prie d'agréer, Monsieur le Député, l'expression de mes meilleurs sentiments.

(femme) Je vous prie d'agréer, Madame la Députee, mes respectueux hommages. Conversation -

(homme) «Monsieur»

(femme) «Madame»

Remarques: Les membres du Conseil privé de la Reine conservent le titre «honorable» à vie et placent les initiales C.P. après leur nom. M.A.L.: toutes les provinces et les territoires sauf: - l'Ontario (M.P.P.) - le Québec (M.A.N.), Terre-Neuve (M.C.A.) C.P., M.A.L.: Membre du Conseil privé et membre de l'Assemblée législative.

MAYOR OF A CITY OR TOWN:

His/Her Worship (full name), Mayor of (name), Address

Salutation - Dear Sir/Madam: or Dear Mr./Madam Mayor:

Final Salutation - Yours sincerely,

In Conversation - "Your Worship" first then "Mayor (name)"

MAIRE/MAIRESSE

(homme) Son Honneur monsieur (prénom et nom), Maire de (Ville), Adresse

(femme) Son Honneur madame (prénom et nom), Mairesse de (Ville), Adresse Appel - Monsieur le Maire,

(femme) Madame la Mairesse,

Salutation - (homme) Je vous prie d'agréer, Monsieur le Maire, l'expression de mes meilleurs sentiments.

(femme) Je vous prie d'agréer, Madame la Mairesse, mes hommages respectueux. Conversation -

(homme) On commence par «Votre Honneur». On poursuit avec «Monsieur le Maire»

(femme) On commence par «Votre Honneur». On poursuit avec «Madame la Mairesse»

JUDGES/JUGES

CHIEF JUSTICE: The Right Honourable (full name), P.C., Chief Justice of Canada, Supreme Court of Canada, Ottawa, ON K1A 0J1

Salutation - Dear Chief Justice:

Final Salutation - Yours sincerely,

In Conversation - "Mr./Madam Chief Justice" first then "Sir/Madam" or "Mr./Mrs./Ms./Miss (name)"

JUGE EN CHEF DU CANADA

(homme) Le très honorable (prenom et nom), C.P. Juge en chef du Canada, Cour suprême du Canada, Ottawa ON K1A 0J1

(femme) La très honorable (prenom et nom), C.P. Juge en chef du Canada, Cour suprême du Canada, Ottawa ON K1A 0J1

Appel - (homme) Monsieur le Juge en chef,

(femme) Madame la Juge en chef,

Salutation - (homme) Je vous prie d'agréer, Monsieur le Juge en chef, l'expression de ma très haute considération.

(femme) Je vous prie d'agréer, Madame la Juge en chef, l'hommage de mon profond respect. Conversation -

(homme) On commence par «Monsieur le Juge en chef». On poursuit avec «Monsieur»

(femme) On commence par «Madame la Juge en chef». On poursuit avec «Madame»

JUDGES OF SUPERIOR COURTS:

Supreme Court of Canada & Federal Court of Canada: The Honourable (full name), Judge of the ________ Court of Canada, Address.

Salutation - Dear Mr./Madam Justice (name):

Final Salutation - Yours sincerely,

In Conversation - "Mr./Madam Justice" Appeal Court, Superior Court, Court of the Queen's Bench: The Honourable (full name), Judge of ________, Address

Salutation - Dear Mr./Madam Justice (name):

Final Salutation - Yours sincerely,

In Conversation - "Mr./Madam Justice (name)"

JUGES DES COURS SUPÉRIEURES
Cour suprême, Cour fédérale et Cour de l'impôt: L'honorable (prénom et nom), Titre, Adresse
Appel - (homme) Monsieur le Juge,
(femme) Madame la Juge,
Salutation - (homme) Je vous prie d'agréer, Monsieur le Juge, l'expression de ma haute considération.
(femme) Je vous prie d'agréer, Madame la Juge l'hommage de mon profond respect. Conversation -
(homme) ‹‹Monsieur le Juge››
(femme) ‹‹Madame la Juge›› Cour d'appel, Cour supérieure, Cour du Banc de la Reine, L'honorable (prénom et nom) Juge de ________, Adresse
Appel - (homme) Monsieur le Juge,
(femme) Madame la Juge,
Salutation -
(homme) Je vous prie d'agréer, Monsieur le Juge, l'expression de ma haute considération.
(femme) Je vous prie d'agréer, Madame la Juge, l'hommage de mon profond respect. Conversation -
(homme) ‹‹Monsieur le Juge››
(femme) ‹‹Madame la Juge››

JUDGES OF THE TAX COURT:
The Honourable (full name), Judge of the Tax Court of Canada, Address
Salutation - Dear Chief Judge/Judge (name):
Final Salutation - Yours sincerely,
In Conversation - "Chief Judge/Judge (name)"
Remarques: En français, voir ci-dessus.

CHIEF JUDGES/JUDGES OF PROVINCIAL/TERRITORIAL COURTS:
The Honourable (full name), Provincial/Territorial Court of ________, Address
Salutation - Dear Chief Judge/Judge (name):
Final Salutation - Yours sincerely,
In Conversation - "Judge (name)"
Note: The titles to be used in Canada now recognize the title"Honourable" for provincially/territorially appointed judges. The courtesy title "His/Her Honour" is no longer appropriate given an official title has been granted.

JUGES EN CHEF/JUGES DES COURS PROVINCIALES/ TERRITORIALES
L'honorable (prénom et nom), Cour provinciale de ________, Adresse
Appel - (homme) Monsieur le Juge en chef/le Juge,
(femme) Madame la Juge en chef/la Juge,
Salutation -
(homme) Je vous prie d'agréer, Monsieur le Juge en chef/le Juge, l'expression de mon profond respect.
(femme) Je vous prie d'agréer, Madame la Juge en chef//la Juge, l'hommage de mon profond respect. Conversation -
(homme) ‹‹Monsieur le Juge en chef/ le Juge››
(femme) ‹‹Madame la Juge en chef/la Juge››
Remarques: Le tableau des titres pour le Canada reconnaît le titre ‹‹honorable›› aux juges des cours provinciales/ territoriales; le titre de courtoisie ‹‹Son Honneur›› n'est plus de mise maintenant qu'un titre officiel est utilisé.

Religion

Anglican Church of Canada/ Église anglicane du Canada

PRIMATE:
The Most Reverend (full name), Primate of the Anglican Church of Canada, Address
Salutation - Dear Archbishop (name):
Final Salutation - Yours sincerely,
In Conversation - "Archbishop"

PRIMAT:
Le révérendissime (prénom et nom), Primate de l'Église anglicane du Canada, Adresse Appel - Monsieur le Primat,
Salutation - Je vous prie d'agréer, Monsieur le Primat, l'expression de mes sentiments les plus respectueux.
Conversation - ‹‹Monsieur l'Archevêque››

ARCHBISHOP:
The Most Reverend (full name), D.D., Archbishop of (name of Diocese), Address
Salutation - Dear Archbishop (name):
Final Salutation - Yours very truly,
In Conversation - "Archbishop"
ARCHEVÊQUE:
Le révérendissime (prénom et nom), Archevêque de (nom du diocèse), Adresse Appel - Monsieur l'Archevêque,
Salutation - Je vous prie d'agréer, Monsieur l'Archevêque, l'expression de mes sentiments les plus respectueux.
Conversation - ‹‹Monsieur l'Archevêque››

BISHOP:
The Right Reverend (full name), Bishop of (name of Diocese), Address
Salutation - Dear Bishop (name):
Final Salutation - Yours very truly,
In Conversation - "Bishop (name)" or "Bishop"

ÉVÊQUE:
(homme) Le très révérend (prénom et nom), Évêque de (nom du diocèse), Adresse
(femme) La très révérende (prénom et nom), Évêque de (nom du diocèse), Adresse
Appel - (homme) Monsieur l'Évêque,
(femme) Madame l'Évêque,
Salutation - (homme) Je vous prie d'agréer, Monsieur l'Évêque, l'expression de mes sentiments les plus respectueux.
(femme) Je vous prie d'agréer, Madame l'Évêque, l'hommage de mon profond respect. Conversation -
(homme) ‹‹Monsieur l'Évêque››
(femme) ‹‹Madame l'Évêque››

ARCHDEACON:
The Venerable (full name), Archdeacon, Address
Salutation - Dear Archdeacon (name):
Final Salutation - Yours sincerely,
In Conversation - "Archdeacon (name)"

ARCHIDIACRE:
(homme) Le vénérable (prénom et nom), Archidiacre, Adresse
(femme) La vénérable (prénom et nom), Archidiacre, Adresse
Appel - (homme) Monsieur l'Archidiacre,
(femme) Madame l'Archidiacre,
Salutation - (homme) Je vous prie d'agréer, Monsieur l'Archidacre, l'expression de mes sentiments les plus respectueux.
(femme) Je vous prie d'agréer, Madame l'Archidacre, l'hommage de mon profond respect. Conversation -
(homme) ‹‹Monsieur l'Archidiacre››
(femme) ‹‹Madame l'Archidiacre››

DEAN:
The Very Reverend (full name), Dean of (name of Cathedral), Address
Salutation - Dear Dean (name):
Final Salutation - Yours sincerely,
In Conversation - "Dean (name)" or "Mr./Mrs./Ms./ Miss (name)"

DOYEN:
(homme) Le très révérend (prénom et nom), Doyen de (nom de la cathédrale), Adresse
(femme) La très révérende (prénom et nom), Doyenne de (nom de la cathédrale), Adresse
Appel - (homme) Monsieur le Doyen,
(femme) Madame la Doyenne,
Salutation - (homme) Je vous prie d'agréer, Monsieur le Doyen, l'expression de mes sentiments les plus respectueux.
(femme) Je vous prie d'agréer, Madame la Doyenne, l'hommage de mon profond respect. Conversation -
(homme) ‹‹Monsieur le Doyen›› ou ‹‹Monsieur››
(femme) ‹‹Madame la Doyenne›› ou ‹‹Madame››

CANON:
The Reverend Canon (full name), Address
Salutation - Dear Canon (name):
Final Salutation - Yours sincerely,
In Conversation - "Canon (name)"

CHANOINE:
(homme) Le chanoine, (prénom et nom), Adresse
(femme) La chanoinesse, (prénom et nom), Adresse
Appel - (homme) Monsieur le Chanoine,
(femme) Madame la Chanoinesse,
Salutation - (homme) Je vous prie d'agréer, Monsieur le Chanoine, l'expression de mes sentiments les plus respectueux.
(femme) Je vous prie d'agréer, Madame La Chanoinesse, l'hommage de mon profond respect. Conversation -
(homme) ‹‹Monsieur le Chanoine››
(femme) ‹‹Madame la Chanoinesse››

PRIEST:
The Reverend (full name), Address
Salutation - Dear Father (name) or Dear Mr. (name): or Dear Mrs./Ms./Miss (name)
Final Salutation - Yours sincerely,
In Conversation - "Father" or "Father (name)" or "Mrs./Ms./Miss (name)"
Note: "Reverend" is an adjective which is never used without the full name.

PRÊTRE:
(homme) Le révérend père (prénom et nom), Adresse
(femme) La révérende (prénom et nom), Adresse
Appel - (homme) Monsieur le Curé, Monsieur l'Abbé,
(femme) Madame,
Salutation - (homme) Je vous prie d'agréer, Monsieur le Curé, l'expression de mes sentiments respectueux.
(femme) Je vous prie d'agréer, Madame, l'expression de mes sentiments respectueux. Conversation -
(homme) ‹‹Monsieur le Curé/Monsieur l'Abbé››
(femme) ‹‹ Madame››

RELIGIOUS:
(man) The Reverend Father (full name), Address
Salutation - Dear Father (name):
Final Salutation - Yours sincerely,
In Conversation - "Reverend Father" (woman) Reverend Mother (full name)/Reverend Sister (full name)
Salutation - Dear Reverend Mother/Sister:
Final Salutation - Yours sincerely,
In Conversation - "Reverend Mother (name)/Reverend Sister (name)"

RELIGIEUX/RELIGIEUSE:
(homme) Le révérend père (prénom et nom), Adresse
(femme) La révérende mère/ soeur (prénom et nom), Adresse
Appel - (homme) Révérend père/Mon père,
(femme) Révérende mère/Ma soeur
Salutation - (homme) Je vous prie d'agréer, Révérend père/Mon père, l'expression de mes sentiments les plus respectueux.
(femme) Je vous prie d'agréer, Révérende mère/ Ma soeur, l'hommage de mon profond respect. Conversation -
(homme) ‹‹Révérend père/Mon père››
(femme) ‹‹Révérende mère/Ma soeur››

Roman Catholic Church/Église catholique romaine

THE POPE:
His Holiness Pope Benedict XVI, Address
Salutation - Your Holiness:
Final Salutation - I have the honour to remain Your Holiness's obedient servant,
In Conversation - "Your Holiness"

LE PAPE:
Sa Sainteté le pape Benedict XVI, Adresse Appel - Très Saint-Père,
Salutation - Je vous prie d'agréer, Très Saint-Père, l'expression de mon profond respect et de ma très haute considération.
Conversation - ‹‹Votre Sainteté›› ou ‹‹Très Saint- Père››

CARDINAL:
His Eminence John Cardinal Smith, Address
Salutation - Your Eminence: or Dear Cardinal (name):
Final Salutation - Yours very truly,
In Conversation - "Your Eminence"

CARDINAL:
Son Éminence le cardinal (prénom et nom), Adresse Appel - Monsieur le Cardinal,
Salutation - Je vous prie d'agréer, Monsieur le Cardinal, l'expression de mon profond respect.

Conversation - ‹‹Éminence››
ARCHBISHOP/BISHOP:
The Most Reverend (full name), Archbishop/Bishop of (name of Diocese). Address
Salutation - Dear Archbishop/Bishop (name):
Final Salutation - Yours very truly,
In Conversation - "Archbishop/Bishop"
Note: The Holy See accorded the courtesy title "His Excellency" to Roman Catholic Archbishops and Bishops; that title is not recognized by Canadian civil authorities.

ARCHEVÊQUE/ÉVÊQUE:
Monseigneur (prénom et nom), Archevêque ou Évêque de (nom du diocèse), Adresse Appel - Monseigneur,
Salutation - Je vous prie d'agréer, Monseigneur , l'expression de mes sentiments les plus respectueux.
Conversation - ‹‹Monseigneur››
Remarques: Le titre ‹‹Son Excellence›› est utilisé par le Saint-Siège pour les archevêques et évêques catholiques; il n'est toutefois pas reconnu par les autorités civiles canadiennes.

ABBOT:
The Right Reverend (full name), Abbot of (name of ________), Address
Salutation - Right Reverend Father: or Dear Abbott (name):
Final Salutation - Yours sincerely,
In Conversation - "Father Abbott"

ABBÉ:
Le révérend père (prénom et nom), Adresse Appel - Monsieur l'Abbé,

Salutation - Je vous prie d'agréer, Monsieur l'Abbé, l'expression de mes sentiments les plus respectueux.
Conversation - ‹‹Monsieur l'Abbé››

CANON:
The Very Reverend (full name), Address
Salutation - Dear Canon (name):
Final Salutation - Yours sincerely,
In Conversation - "Canon (name)"

CHANOINE:
Le chanoine (prénom et nom), Adresse Appel - Monsieur le Chanoine,
Salutation - Je vous prie d'agréer, Monsieur le Chanoine, l'expression de mes sentiments respectueux.
Conversation - ‹‹Monsieur le Chanoine››

PRIEST
The Reverend (full name), Address
Salutation - Dear Father:
Final Salutation - Yours sincerely,
In Conversation - "Father" or "Father (name)"
Note: "Reverend" is an adjective which is never used without the full name.

PRÊTRE:
Le révérend père (prénom et nom), Adresse Appel - Monsieur le Curé/l'Abbé,
Salutation - Je vous prie d'agréer, Monsieur le Curé, l'expression de mes sentiments respectueux.
Conversation - ‹‹Monsieur le Curé/l'Abbé››

SULPICIAN:
Mr. (full name), Address
Salutation - Dear Mr. (name):
Final Salutation - Yours truly,
In Conversation - "Mr. (name)"

SULPICIEN:
Monsieur (prénom et nom), Adresse Appel - Monsieur,
Salutation - Je vous prie d'agréer, Monsieur, l'expression de mes sentiments respectueux.
Conversation - ‹‹Monsieur››

RELIGIOUS:
(man) The Reverend Father (full name), Address
Salutation - Dear Father (name):
Final Salutation - Yours sincerely,
In Conversation - "Reverend Father" (woman) Reverend Mother (full name)/Reverend Sister (full name)
Salutation - Dear Reverend Mother/Sister:
Final Salutation - Yours sincerely,
In Conversation - "Reverend Mother/Sister (name)"

RELIGIEUX/RELIGIEUSE:
(homme) Le révérend père (prénom et nom), Adresse
(femme) La révérende mère/soeur (prénom et nom), Adresse
Appel - (homme) Révérend père/Mon père,
(femme) Révérende mère/Ma soeur,
Salutation - (homme) Je vous prie d'agréer, Révérend père/Mon père, l'expression de mes sentiments respectueux.
(femme) Je vous prie d'agréer, Révérende mère/Ma soeur, l'hommage de mon profond respect. Conversation -
(homme) ‹‹Révérend père ou Mon père››
(femme) ‹‹Révérende mère/Ma soeur››

Other Religious Denominations/ Autres dénominations:

MODERATOR:
(United Church of Canada and Presbyterian Church in Canada) A present ordained Moderator: The Right Reverend (full name), Moderator of (name of Church), Address
Salutation - Dear Mr./Mrs./Ms./Miss (name):
Final Salutation - Yours sincerely,
In Conversation - "Mr./Mrs./Ms./Miss (name)" A past ordained Moderator: The Very Reverend (full name), Moderator of (name of Church), Address
Salutation - Dear Mr./Mrs./Ms./Miss (name):
Final Salutation - Yours sincerely,
In Conversation - "Mr./Mrs./Ms./Miss (name)"

MODÉRATEURS:
(Église unie du Canada et Église presbytérienne au Canada)
(homme) Le très révérend (prénom et nom), Modérateur de (nom de l'Église), Adresse
(femme) La très révérende (prénom et nom), Modératrice de (nom de l'Église), Adresse
Appel - (homme) Monsieur le Modérateur,
(femme) Madame la Modératrice,
Salutation - (homme) Je vous prie d'agréer, Monsieur le Modérateur, l'expression de mes sentiments respectueux.
(femme) Je vous prie d'agréer, Madame la Modératrice, l'hommage de mon profond respect. Conversation -
(homme) ‹‹Monsieur le Modérateur››
(femme) ‹‹Madame la Modératrice››

MINISTER:
The Reverend (full name), Address
Salutation - Dear Mr./Mrs./Ms./Miss (name):
Final Salutation - Yours sincerely,
In Conversation - "Mr./Mrs./Ms./Miss (name)"
Note: "Reverend" is an adjective which is never used without the full name.

MINISTRE:
(homme) Le révérend (prénom et nom), Adresse
(femme) La révérende (prénom et nom), Adresse
Appel - (homme) Monsieur le Pasteur,
(femme) Madame,
Salutation - (homme) Je vous prie d'agréer, Monsieur le Pasteur, l'expression de mes sentiments respectueux.
(femme) Je vous prie d'agréer, Madame, l'hommage de mon profond respect.
Conversation - (homme) ‹‹Monsieur le Pasteur››
(femme) ‹‹Madame››

RABBI:
Rabbi (full name), Address
Salutation - Dear Rabbi (name):
Final Salutation - Yours sincerely,
In Conversation - "Rabbi (name)"

RABBIN:
Le rabbin (prénom et nom), Adresse Appel - Monsieur le Rabbin,
Salutation - Je vous prie d'agréer, Monsieur le Rabbin, l'expression de mes sentiments respectueux.
Conversation - ‹‹Monsieur le Rabbin››

Diplomatic/Diplomates

AMBASSADORS/HIGH COMMISSIONERS of foreign countries in Canada:
His/Her Excellency (full name), Ambassador of Canada to ________ /High Commissioner for ________ , Address
Salutation - Dear Ambassador/High Commissioner:
Final Salutation - Yours sincerely,
In Conversation - "Your Excellency" or "Excellency"
Note: British High Commissioner and not High Commissioner for Britain

AMBASSADEURS/HAUTS-COMMISSAIRES de pays étrangers au Canada:
(homme) Son Excellence monsieur (prénom et nom), Ambassadeur de ________/Haut-Commissaire de ________, Adresse
(femme) Son Excellence madame (prénom et nom), Ambassadrice de ________/Haute-Commissaire de ________, Adresse
Appel - (homme) Monsieur/l'Ambassadeur/le Haut-Commissaire,
(femme) Madame l'Ambassadrice/la Haute-Commissaire,
Salutation - (homme) Je vous prie d'agréer, Monsieur l'Ambassadeur/le Haut-Commissaire, l'expression de ma haute considération.
(femme) Je vous prie d'agréer, Madame l'Ambassadrice/ la Haute-Commissaire, l'expression de mes respectueux hommages.
Conversation - ‹‹Excellence››

CANADIAN AMBASSADORS/HIGH COMMISSIONERS abroad:
Mr./Mrs. (full name), Ambassador of Canada to ________ /High Commissioner for Canada to ________ , Address
Salutation - Dear Ambassador/High Commissioner:
Final Salutation - Yours sincerely,
In Conversation - "Mr./Madam Ambassador/High Commissioner"
AMBASSADEURS DU CANADA/HAUTS-COMMISSAIRES à l'étranger
(homme) Monsieur (prénom et nom) Ambassadeur du Canada/Haute-commissaire du Canada au ________, Adresse
(femme) Madame (prénom et nom) l'Ambassadrice du Canada/Haute-commissaire du Canada au ________, Adresse
Appel - (homme) Monsieur l'Ambassadeur/le Haut-Commissaire,
(femme) Madame l'Ambassadrice/la Haute-Commissaire,
Salutation - (homme) Je vous prie d'agréer, Monsieur l'Ambassadeur/le Haut-commissaire, l'expression de ma haute considération.
(femme) Je vous prie d'agréer, Madame l'Ambassadrice/ la Haute-commissaire, l'expression de mes respectueux hommages.
Conversation - (homme) ‹‹Monsieur l'Ambassadeur/ le Haut-Commissaire››
(femme) ‹‹Madame l'Ambassadrice/la Haut-Commissaire››
Remarques: Si un ambassadeur du Canada ou un haut-commissaire du Canada se trouve au Canada ou à l'étranger, la formule à employer est simplement ‹‹Ambassadeur›› ou ‹‹Haut-commissaire››. Le titre ‹‹Excellence›› n'est pas accordé par un citoyen canadien à un ambassadeur du Canada ou à un haut-commissaire du Canada, mais par le gouvernement et les citoyens du pays auprès duquel l'ambassadeur ou le haut-commissaire est accédité.

Armed Forces/Forces Armeés

OFFICER RANK:
Brigadier General/Major General/Lieutenant General/General (full name), Address
Salutation - Dear General:
Final Salutation - Yours sincerely,
In Conversation - "General (name)"
Colonel (full name), Address
Salutation - Dear Colonel:
Final Salutation - Yours sincerely,
In Conversation - "Colonel (name)"
Lieutenant Colonel (full name), Address
Salutation - Lieutenant Colonel:
Final Salutation - Yours sincerely,
In Conversation - "Lieutenant Colonel (name)"
Major (full name), Address
Salutation - Dear Major:
Final Salutation - Yours sincerely,
In Conversation - "Major (name)"
Captain (full name), Address
Salutation - Dear Captain:
Final Salutation - Yours sincerely,
In Conversation - "Captain (name)"
Lieutenant (full name), Address
Salutation - Dear Lieutenant:
Final Salutation - Yours sincerely,
In Conversation - "Lieutenant (name)"

AVEC GRADE:
(homme) Le brigadier-général/major-général/lieutenant- général (prénom et nom), Adresse
(femme) La brigadière-générale/majore-générale/lieutenante-générale (prénom et nom), Adresse
Appel - (homme) Général,
(femme) Générale,
Salutation - (homme) Je vous prie d'agréer, Général, l'expression de mes meilleurs sentiments.
(femme) Je vous prie d'agréer, Générale, l'expression de mes hommages respectueux.
Conversation - (homme) ‹‹Général››
(femme) ‹‹Générale››
(homme) Le colonel (prénom et nom), Adresse
(femme) La colonelle (prénom et nom), Adresse
Appel - (homme) Colonel,
(femme) Colonelle,
Salutation - (homme) Je vous prie d'agréer, Colonel, l'expression de mes meilleurs sentiments.
(femme) Je vous prie d'agréer, Colonelle, l'expression de mes hommages respectueux.
Conversation - (homme) ‹‹Colonel››
(femme) ‹‹Colonelle››
(homme) La lieutenant-colonel, (prénom et nom), Adresse
(femme) La lieutenante-colonelle, (prénom et nom), Adresse
Appel - (homme) Lieutenant-Colonel,
(femme) Lieutenante-Colonelle,
Salutation - (homme) Je vous prie d'agréer, Lieutenant- Colonel, l'expression de mes meilleurs sentiments.
(femme) Je vous prie d'agréer, Lieutenante-Colonelle, l'expression de mes meilleurs hommages respectueux.
Conversation - (homme) ‹‹Lieutenant-Colonel››
(femme) ‹‹Lieutenante-Colonelle››
(homme) Le major (prénom et nom), Adresse
(femme) La majore (prénom et nom), Adresse
Appel - (homme) Major,
(femme) Majore,
Salutation - (homme) Je vous prie d'agréer, Major, l'expression de mes meilleurs sentiments.
(femme) Je vous prie d'agréer, Majore, l'expression de mes hommages respectueux.
Conversation - (homme) ‹‹Major››
(femme) ‹‹Majore››
(homme) Le capitaine (prénom et nom), Adresse
(femme) La capitaine (prénom et nom), Adresse
Appel - Capitaine,
Salutation - (homme) Je vous prie d'agréer, Capitaine, l'expression de mes meilleurs sentiments.
(femme) Je vous prie d'agréer, Capitaine, l'expression de mes hommages respectueux.
Conversation - ‹‹Capitaine››
(homme) Le lieutenant (prénom et nom), Adresse

(femme) La lieutenante (prénom et nom), Adresse
Appel - (homme) Lieutenant,
(femme) Lieutenante,
Salutation - (homme) Je vous prie d'agréer, Lieutenant, l'expression de mes meilleurs sentiments.
(femme) Je vous prie d'agréer, Lieutenante, l'expression de mes hommages respectueux.
Conversation - (homme) «Lieutenant»
(femme) «Lieutenante»

NCO and other ranks:
Chief Warrant Officer (full name)
Salutation - Dear Chief Warrant (name)
Final Salutation - Yours sincerely,
In Conversation - "Mr./Mrs./Ms./Miss (name)"
Master Warrant Officer (full name)
Salutation - Dear Master Warrant (name):
Final Salutation - Yours sincerely,
In Conversation - "Mr./Mrs./Ms./Miss (name)"
Warrant Officer (full name)
Salutation - Dear Warrant (name):
Final Salutation - Yours sincerely,
In Conversation - "Mr./Mrs./Ms./Miss (name)"
Sergeant (full name)
Salutation - Dear Sergeant (name):
Final Salutation - Yours sincerely,
In Conversation - "Mr./Mrs./Ms./Miss (name)"
Corporal (full name)
Salutation - Dear Corporal (name):
Final Salutation - Yours sincerely,
In Conversation - "Mr./Mrs./Ms./Miss (name)"
Private (full name)
Salutation - Dear Private (name):
Final Salutation - Yours sincerely,
In Conversation - "Mr./Mrs./Ms./Miss (name)"

SOUS OFFICIERS ET AUTRES GRADES:
(homme) L'adjudant-chef (prénom et nom)
(femme) L'adjudante-chef (prénom et nom)
Appel - (homme) Adjudant-chef,
(femme) Adjudante-chef,
Salutation - (homme) Je vous prie d'agréer, Adjudant-chef, l'expression de mes meilleurs sentiments.
(femme) Je vous prie d'agréer, Adjudante-chef, l'expression de mes hommages respectueux.
Conversation - Le qualificatif du grade «Monsieur/ Madame/Mademoiselle»
(homme) L'adjudant-maître (prénom et nom)
(femme) L'adjudante-maîtresse (prénom et nom)
Appel - (homme) Adjudant-maître,
(femme) Adjudante-maîtresse,
Salutation - (homme) Je vous prie d'agréer, Adjudant-maître, l'expression de mes meilleurs hommages respectueux.
(femme) Je vous prie d'agréer, Adjudantemaîtresse, l'expression de mes hommages respectueux.
Conversation - Le qualificatif du grade «Monsieur/ Madame/Mademoiselle»
(homme) L'adjudant (prénom et nom)
(femme) L'adjudante (prénom et nom)
Appel - (homme) Adjudant,
(femme) Adjudante,
Salutation - (homme) Je vous prie d'agréer, Adjudant, l'expression de mes meilleurs sentiments.
(femme) Je vous prie d'agréer, Adjudante, l'expression de mes hommages respectueux.
Conversation - Le qualificatif du grade «Monsieur/ Madame/Mademoiselle»
(homme) Le sergent (prénom et nom)
(femme) La sergente (prénom et nom)
Appel - (homme) Sergent,
(femme) Sergente,
Salutation - (homme) Je vous prie d'agréer, Sergent, l'expression de mes meilleurs sentiments.
(femme) Je vous prie d'agréer, Sergente, l'expression de mes hommages respectueux.
Conversation - Le qualificatif du grade «Monsieur/ Madame/Mademoiselle»
(homme) Le caporal (prénom et nom)
(femme) La caporale (prénom et nom)
Appel - (homme) Caporal,
(femme) Caporale,
Salutation - (homme) Je vous prie d'agréer, Caporal, l'expression de mes meilleurs sentiments.
(femme) Je vous prie d'agréer, Caporale, l'expression de mes hommages respectueux.
Conversation - Le qualificatif du grade «Monsieur/ Madame/Mademoiselle»
(homme) Le soldat (prénom et nom)
(femme) La soldate (prénom et nom)
Appel - Monsieur/Madame/Mademoiselle,
Salutation - (homme) Je vous prie d'agréer, Monsieur, l'expression de mes meilleurs sentiments.
(femme) Je vous prie d'agréer, Madame/Mademoiselle, l'expression de mes hommages respectueux.
Conversation - Le qualificatif du grade «Monsieur/ Madame/Mademoiselle»

Foreign Dignitaries/Les Dignitaires Étrangers

AN EMPEROR:
His Imperial Majesty Akihito, Emperor of Japan, Address
Salutation - Your dignified Majesty:
Final Salutation - I have the honour to remain, Your Imperial Majesty's obedient servant,
In Conversation - "Your Majesty" first then "Sire"

EMPEREUR:
Sa Majesté Impériale (Nom) ________, Empereur du ________, Adresse Appel - Votre Majesté Impériale,
Salutation - Je prie Votre Majesté Impériale d'agréer l'hommage de mon profond respect et de ma très haute considération.
Conversation - On commence par «Majesté». On poursuit avec «Sire»

A KING:
His Majesty Juan Carlos, King of Spain, Address
Salutation - Your Majesty/Sire:
Final Salutation - I have the honour to remain, Your Majesty's obedient servant,
In Conversation - "Your Majesty" first then "Sire"

UN ROI:
Sa Majesté (Nom) ________, Roi de ________, Adresse Appel - Majesté/Sire,
Salutation - Je prie Votre Majesté d'agréer l'hommage de mon profond respect et de ma très haute considération.
Conversation - On commence par «Majesté». On poursuit avec «Sire»

A QUEEN:
Her Majesty Queen Sophia, Queen of Spain, Address
Salutation - Your Majesty/Madame:
Final Salutation - I have the honour to remain, Your Majesty's obedient servant,
In Conversation - "Your Majesty" first then "Ma'am"

UNE REINE:
Sa Majesté la reine (Nom) ________, Reine de ________, Adresse Appel - Majesté/Madame,
Salutation - Je vous prie d'agréer Madame, l'hommage de mon profond respect et de ma très haute considération.
Conversation - On commence par «Majesté». On poursuit avec «Madame»

A PRESIDENT OF A REPUBLIC:
His/Her Excellency (full name), President of the Republic of (name), Address
Salutation - Excellency:
Final Salutation - Yours sincerely
In Conversation - "Excellency" first then "President" or "Sir/Madam"
UN PRÉSIDENT DE RÉPUBLIQUE:
(homme) Son Excellence monsieur (prénom et nom) Président de la République (nom), Adresse
(femme) Son Excellence madame (prénom et nom) Présidente de la République (nom), Adresse
Appel - (homme) Monsieur le Président,
(femme) Madame la Présidente,
Salutation - (homme) Je vous prie d'agréer Monsieur le Président, l'expression de ma très haute considération.
(femme) Je vous prie d'agréer Madame la Présidente, l'hommage de mon profond respect. Conversation -
(homme) On commence par «Excellence». On poursuit avec «Monsieur le Président» ou «Monsieur»
(femme) On commence par «Excellence». On poursuit avec «Madame la Présidente» ou «Madame»

THE PRESIDENT OF THE UNITED STATES:
The Honourable (full name), President of the United States, The White House, Washington, D.C.
Salutation - Dear Mr. President:
Final Salutation - Yours sincerely,
In Conversation - "Mr. President" first then "Sir"

PRÉSIDENT DES ÉTATS-UNIS D'AMÉRIQUE:
Son Excellence l'honorable (prénom et nom) Président de États-Unis d'Amérique, The White House, Washington D.C. Appel - Monsieur le Président,
Salutation - Je vous prie d'agréer Monsieur le Président, l'expression de ma très haute considération.
Conversation - On commence par «Monsieur le Président» ou «Excellence»

A PRIME MINISTER:
His/Her Excellency (full name), Prime Minister of (name), Address
Salutation - Dear Prime Minister:
Final Salutation - Yours sincerely,
In Conversation - "Prime Minister" or "Excellency" first then "Sir/Madam" or "Mr./Mrs./Ms./Miss (name)"

PREMIER MINISTRE:
(homme) Son Excellence monsieur (prénom et nom) Premier Ministre de ________, Adresse
(femme) Son Excellence madame (prénom et nom) Première Ministre de ________, Adresse
Appel - (homme) Monsieur le Premier Ministre,
(femme) Madame la Première Ministre,
Salutation - (homme) Je vous prie d'agréer Monsieur le Premier Ministre, l'expression de ma haute considération.
(femme) Je vous prie d'agréer Madame la Première Ministre, l'hommage de mon profond respect. Conversation -
(homme) On commence par «Monsieur le Premier Ministre» ou «Excellence». On poursuit par «Monsieur»
(femme) On commence par «Madame la Première Ministre» ou «Excellence». On poursuit par «Madame»

Others/Autres

LAWYERS/NOTARIES:
Mr./Mrs./Ms./Miss (full name) or Mr./Mrs./Ms./Miss, Q.C.
Salutation - Dear Mr./Mrs./Ms./Miss (name):
Final Salutation - Yours sincerely,
In Conversation - "Mr./Mrs./Ms./Miss (name)"

AVOCATS/NOTAIRES:
Me (prénom et nom) Appel - Maître,
Salutation - Je vous prie d'agréer, Maître, l'expression de mes meilleurs sentiments.
Conversation - «Maître»

AIDE-DE-CAMP:
Military: (See Armed Forces) Civilian (according to their title), Mr./Mrs./Ms./Miss (full name)
Salutation - Dear Mr./Mrs./Ms./Miss (name):
Final Salutation - Yours sincerely,
In Conversation - "Mr./Mrs./Ms./Miss (name)"
Note: Post nominals "A. de C." have been authorized for Aides-de-camps to the Governor General and Lieutenant Governors. Militaire: (voir la rubrique «Forces armées») Civil (selon le titre), Monsieur/Madame/Mademoiselle (prénom et nom) Appel - Monsieur/Madame/Mademoiselle,
Salutation - Je vous prie d'agréer, Monsieur/Madame/ Mademoiselle, l'expression de mes sentiments les meilleurs.
Conversation - «Monsieur/Madame/Mademoiselle» Remarque: Les initiales «A. de C.» sont autorisées pour les aides de camp du Governeur général et des lieutenants-gouverneurs.

NATIVE CITIZENS/AUTOCHTONES:

Indian Chiefs:
Chief (full name), Chief of (name), Address
Salutation - Chief (name):
Final Salutation - Yours sincerely,
In Conversation - "Chief (name)"

Chefs indiens:
Chef (prénom et nom), Chef de (nom), Adresse Appel - Chef,
Salutation - Je vous prie d'agréer, Chef, l'expression de mes sentiments les meilleurs.
Conversation - «Chef»

Band Councillors:
Mr./Mrs./Ms./Miss (full name):
Salutation - Mr./Mrs./Ms./Miss (name):
Final Salutation - Yours sincerely,
In Conversation - "Mr./Mrs./Ms./Miss (name)"

Conseillers de bandes:
Monsieur/Madame/Mademoiselle (prénom et nom), Adresse Appel - Monsieur/Madame/Mademoiselle,
Salutation - Je vous prie d'agréer, Monsieur/Madame/ Mademoiselle, l'expression de mes sentiments les meilleurs.
Conversation - «Monsieur/Madame/Mademoiselle»

Abbreviations

Indicating Academic, Ecclesiastical and other Degrees, membership in Societies and Institutions, military ranks, etc., appearing in the Canadian Almanac and Directory. For other lists of abbreviations, see Index.

AACCA .... Associate of Association of Certified Accountants & Corporate Accountants (British)
AACI .... Accredited Appraiser Canadian Institute
AAE .... Associate of Accountants' & Executives' Corp. of Canada
AAGO .... — of the American Guild of Organists
AASA .... — of the Alberta Society of Artists
AB .... Bachelor of Arts, American (Artium Baccalaureus)
AC .... "Advanced Certification" Canadian Association of Medical Radiation Technologists
ACA .... Associate of Institute of Chartered Accountants (Eng.)
ACAM .... Associate Certified Administrative Manager
ACCO .... — of Canadian College of Organists
AccSCRP .... — of Canadian Public Relations Society Inc.
ACD .... Archaeologiae Christianae Doctor
ACGI .... Associate of the City & Guilds of London Institute
ACIC .... — of Canadian Institute of Chemistry
ACInstM .... — of the Institute of Marketing
ACIS .... — of Chartered Institute of Secretaries (British)
ACSM .... — of Cambourne School of Mines
Adm. .... Admiral
Adm. A. Pl.Fin. .... Administrateur agréé en planification financière
AFC .... Accredited Financial Counsellor
AFRAS (AFRAeS) ..... Fellow of the Royal Aeronautical Society
Ag de l'U (Paris) .... Honorary Professor of University of Paris (Agrégé de l'Université Paris)
Ag. de Phil. .... Professor of Philosophy (Agrégé en Philosophie Louvain)
AGSM .... Associate of the Guildhall School of Music (British)
AIC .... — of the Institute of Chemistry (British)
AICB .... Associate of the Institute of Canadian Bankers
AIIC .... — of the Insurance Institute of Canada
AKC .... — of King's College (London)
ALCM .... — of London (Canada) Conservatory of Music
ALS .... Commissioned Alberta Land Surveyor
AM .... Master of Arts (Artium Magister)
AMEIC .... Associate Member of the Engineering Institute of Canada
AMICE .... — Member of the Institution of Civil Engineers (British)
AMIEE .... — Member of the Institute of Electrical Engineers
AMIMechE .... — Member of the Institution of Mechanical Engineers (British)
A.Mus. .... — of Music
APA .... — Member of the Institute of Accredited Public Accountants (British)
APHA .... — Member of the Public Health Association (British)
APR .... Accredited Member of the Canadian Public Relations Society
ARA .... Associate of the Royal Academy (honorary)
ARCD .... — of the Royal College of Dancing
ARCM .... — of the Royal College of Music
ARCO .... — of the Royal College of Organists (Canadian)
ARCS (A.R.C.Sc.) ..... — of the Royal College of Science
ARCT .... — of the Royal Conservatory of Music of Toronto
ARCVS .... — of the Royal College of Veterinary Surgeons
ARDIO .... — of Registered Interior Designers of Ontario
ARDS .... — of the Royal Drawing Society (London, Eng.)
ARIBA .... — of the Royal Institute of British Architects
ARIC .... — of the Royal Institute of Chemistry
ARSH .... — of the Royal Society of Health
ARSM .... — of the Royal School of Mines
ARSM .... — of the Royal School of Music
AScT .... Applied Science Technologist
Assoc. Inst. M.M. .... Associate of the Institute of Mining and Metallurgy (British)
ATCL .... — of Trinity College, London (Eng.)
ATCM .... — of the Toronto Conservatory of Music
A.Th. .... — in Theology
BA .... Bachelor of Arts
BAA .... — of Applied Arts
B.Acc. .... — of Accountancy
B.Adm. (B.Admin.) ..... — of Administration
B.Adm.Pub. .... — Baccalauréat spécialisé en administration publique
BAeE (BAeroE) .... Bachelor of Aeronautical Engineering
BAI .... — of Engineering (U. of Dublin)
BALS .... — of Arts in Library Science
BAO .... — of Obstetrics
B.Arch. .... — in Architecture
BAS (B.A.Sc.) .... — of Applied Science
BASM. .... — of Arts, Master of Science
B.A.Theo. .... — of Arts in Theology
BBA .... — of Business Administration
BCD .... Bachelier en Chirurgie Dentale
BCE .... Bachelor of Civil Engineering
B.Ch. (ChB) .... — in Surgery (British)
BChE .... — in Chemical Engineering (American)
BCL .... — of Civil Law (or Canon Law)
B.Com. (B. Comm.) .... — of Commerce
B.Comp.Sc. .... — of Computer Science
BD .... — of Divinity
BDC .... Bachelier en droit canonique
B.Des. .... Bachelor of Design
BDS .... — of Dental Surgery (British)
BE (B.Eng.) .... — of Engineering
B.Ed. (BEAD) .... — of Education
BEDS .... — of Environmental Design Studies
BEE .... — of Electrical Engineering (American)
B. en Ph. .... Bachelier en Philosophie
B. en Sc. Com. .... — en Science Commerciale
BES .... Bachelor of Environmental Sciences (or Studies)
B ès A .... Bachelier ès Arts
B ès L. .... — ès Lettres
B. ès Sc. .... — ès Science
B. ès Sc. App. .... — ès Science Appliquée
BF .... Bachelor of Forestry (American)
BFA .... — of Fine Arts
B.Gen. .... Brigadier-General
BHE (B.H.Ec.) .... Bachelor of Home Economics
B.H.Sc. .... — of Household Science
BJ .... — of Journalism
BJC .... — in Canon Law
BL .... — in Literature (or of Laws)
BLA .... — of Landscape Architecture
B.Litt. .... — of Literature (American & British)
BLS .... — of Library Science
BM .... — of Medicine
B.Mus. .... — of Music
BMV .... Bachelier en Médecine Vetérinaire
BN .... Bachelor of Nursing
B.N.Sc. .... — of Nursing Science
B. Paed. (Péd.) .... — of Pedagogy
BPA .... — of Public Administration
BPE .... — of Physical Education
B.Ph. (B.Phil.) .... — of Philosophy
BPHE .... — of Physical & Health Education
B.Ps. .... Baccalauréat en Psychologie
Br. .... Brother
BS .... Bachelor of Science (or of Surgery) (American)
BSA .... — of Science in Agriculture (or in Accounting, or in Administration)
B.Sc. .... — of Science
BScA .... Bachelier ès science appliquées
BScB .... — en Bibliothéconomie
B.Sc.(CE) .... Bachelor of Science in Civil Engineering
B.Sc.Com. .... — of Commercial Science
B.Sc.Dom. .... Baccalauréat en Sciences Domestiques
BScF (BSF) .... Bachelor of Science in Forestry
BScFE .... — of Science in Forestry Engineering
BScH .... Bachelier en Sciences Hospitalières
BScN .... Bachelor of Science in Nursing
B.Sc.(Nurs.) .... — of Science in Nursing
B.Sc.(Occ.Ther.) .... — of Science in Occupational Therapy
B.Sc.(OT) .... — of Science in Occupational Therapy
B.Sc.Phm.(BSP) .... — of Science in Pharmacy
B.Sc.Soc. .... — of Social Science
BSCE .... — of Science in Civil Engineering
B.S.Ed. .... — of Science in Education
BSEE .... — of Science in Electrical Engineering
BSN .... — of Science in Nursing
BSS .... — of Social Sciences
BSW. .... — of Social Work (or Welfare)
B.Tech. .... — of Technology
B.Th. .... — of Theology
BTS .... — of Technological Science (Edinburgh)
B.V.Sc. .... — of Veterinary Science
CA .... Chartered Accountant
C. Adm., F.P. .... Chartered Administrator in Financial Planning
CAAP .... Certified Advertising Agency Practitioner
CAE .... — Association Executive
CAE/c.a.é. .... Chartered Account Executive
CAM .... Certified Administrative Manager
CAP .... Certificat d'Aptitude Pedagogique
Capt. (or Capt.(N)) .... Captain (or Captain (Naval))
CBE .... Commander, Order of the British Empire
CBV .... Chartered Business Valuator

CC	Chartered Cartographer
CC	Companion, Order of Canada
CD	Canadian Forces Decoration
Cdr.	Commander
CE	Civil Engineer
CEA	Certified Environmental Administrator
CEA	Certified Environmental Auditor
CEBS	Certified Employee Benefit Specialist
Cer.E.	Ceramic Engineer
Cert. Bus. Admin.	Doctor of Applied Science Diploma Business Administration
CES	Certificat d'Études Secondaires (La Sorbonne)
CFA	Chartered Financial Analyst
CFP	Chartered Financial Planner
CGA	Certified General Accountant
CHA	Certified Housing Administrator
Chan.	Chanoine (Canon)
Ch.E.	Chartered Executive
CHE	Certified Health Executive
Chem. Ing.	Ingénieur Chimiste Diplomé (Swiss Fed. Inst. Technology)
CHFC	Chartered Financial Consultant
CIF	Canadian Institute of Forestry
CIM	Certificate in Management
CIM	Certified Industrial Manager
CIM	Certified Investment Manager
CIS&P	Canadian Inst. of Surveying & Photogrammetry
CLA	Canadian Library Association
CLS	Canada Land Surveyor
CLU	Chartered Life Underwriter
CM	Master in Medicine (British)
CM	Member, Order of Canada
CMA	Certified Management Accountant (or Canadian Medical Association or Canadian Management Association)
CMC	Certified Management Consultant
CmdO	Commissioned Officer
Cmdre.	Commodore
CMM	Certified Municipal Manager (Ontario)
CMM	Commander, Order of Military Merit
COM	Commander of the Order of Merit (Police Forces)
Col.	Colonel
CPA	Certified Public Accountant
CPC	— Personnel Consultant
CPM	Certificate in Personnel Management
CPPMA	— in Public Personnel Management Association
CPPO	Certified Public Purchasing Officer
CPP	— Professional Purchaser
CR (c.r.)	Conseiller de la Reine (Queen's Counsel)
CRA	Canadian Residential Appraiser
CSC	Canadian Securities Course
CSR	Chartered Stenographic Reporter
CTC	Certified Travel Counsellor
C.Tech.	— Technician
CWO	Chief Warrant Officer
DA	Doctor of Arts (honorary)
DA	— of Archaeology (Laval)
D.Arch.	— of Architecture
D.A.Sc.	— in Applied Sciences
DC	— of Chiropractic
DCD	Docteur en Chirurgie Dentale
D.Ch.	Doctor of Surgery (British)
DChE	— of Chemical Engineering (American)
DCL	— of Civil Law (or Canon Law)
DD	— of Divinity
DDC	Doctorat Droit Canonique
D. de l'Un.	— Docteur de l'Université
DDS	Doctor of Dental Surgery (British)
DDT	— of Drugless Therapy
D.Ed.	— of Education
D.Eng.	— of Engineering
D. en Méd. Vet.	Docteur en Médecine Vetérinaire
D. en Ph.	— en Philosophie
D ès L	— ès Lettres (Doctor of Letters)
D. ès Sc. App.	Doctor of Applied Science
DF	— of Forestry (American)
DFA	— of Fine Arts (often honorary)
D.F.Sc.	— of Financial Science (Laval)
DIC	Diploma of Membership of Imperial College of Science & Technology (British)
Dip. Bact.	— in Bacteriology
Dip d'É	Diplome d'Études
Dip de l'U (P)	Diploma of the U. of Paris
Dip. d'É. Sup. or DipES	Diplome d'Études Supérieures, Paris
Dip. Ing.	Diploma in Engineering
Dipl. Bus. Admin.	Diploma Business Administration
D.Jour	Doctor of Journalism
D. Lit. (D. Litt.)	— of Letters (or Literature)
DLO	Diploma in Laryngology & Otology
DLS	Dominion Land Surveyor (or Doctor of Library Science)
DM	Doctorat Médecine
DMD	Doctor of Dental Medicine
D.Ms.	— in Missionology
D.Mus.	Doctorat en Musique
DMR (D or T)	Diploma in Medical Radiology (Royal Coll. of Surgeons, London)
DMT	— in Tropical Medicine
DMT & H (Eng.)	— in Tropical Medicine & Hygiene
D.N.S (D.N.Sc.)	Doctor of Nursing Science
DO	— of Osteopathy
Doct.Arch.	— of Christian Archaeology (Pontifical Institute, Rome)
D.Paed. (Péd.)	— of Paedagogy
DPE	Diploma in Physical Education
D.Ph. (D.Phil. or PhD)	Doctor of Philosophy
D.P.Ec.	— of Political Economy
DPH	— (or Diploma) in Public Health
D.Ps. (D.Psy.)	— of Psychologie
D.P.Sc.	— of Political Science
D.Psych.	— (or Diploma) in Psychiatry
DPT	— of Physio-Therapy
Dr.	Doctor
DR	Doctor of Radiology
Dr.Com.Sc.	— of Commercial Science
Dr de l'U (P)	— of the U. of Paris
Dr. ès Lettres	— of Letters (History of Literature)
Dr. jur.	— of Law (Dr. Juris)
Dr. rer. pol.	— of Political Economy (Dr. Rerum Politicarum) (Docteur des Sciences Politiques)
DSA (DScA)	Docteur ès science appliqués
D.Sc.	Doctor of Science
D.Sc.Mil.	— of Military Science
DSL	— of Sacred Letters
D.Sc.Com.	— of Commercial Science
D.Sc.Fin.	— of Financial Science
D.Sc.Nat.	— in Natural Science
D.Sc.Soc.	— of Social Science
D.Th.	— of Theology
DVM (DMV)	— of Veterinary Medicine
D.V.Sc.	— of Veterinary Science
E.C.E.	Early Childhood Educator
EdD	Doctor of Education
EdM	Master of Education (Harvard)
EE	Electrical Engineer
EM	Mining Engineer
ETCM	Graduate of Eastern Townships Conservatory of Music
FAAO	Fellow of the American Academy of Optometry
F.A.A.O.Dip.	Diplomatic Fellow of the American Academy of Optometry
FACD	Fellow of the American College of Dentists
FACO	— of the American College of Organists
FACP	— of the American College of Physicians
FACR	— of the American College of Radiology
FACS	— of the American College of Surgeons
FAE	— of the Accountants' & Executives' Corp. of Canada
FAGS	— of the American Geographical Society
FAIA	— of the American Institute of Actuaries
	— of the American Institute of Architects
FAIA	Association of International Accountants
FAOU	Fellow of the American Ornithologists Union
FAPHA	— of the American Public Health Association
FAPS	— of the American Physical Society
FAS	— of the Actuarial Society
FBA	— of the British Academy (honorary)
FBOA	— of British Association of Optometrists
FCA	— of the Institute of Chartered Accountants (British)
FCAM	— of the Certified Administrative Manager
FCBA	— of Canadian Bankers' Association
FCCA	— of the Association of Certified Accountants
FCCO	— of the Canadian College of Organists
FCCT	— of the Canadian College of Teachers
FCCUI	— of the Canadian Credit Union Institute
FCGI	— of the City & Guilds of London Institute
FCI	— of the Canadian Credit Institute
FCIC	— of the Chemical Institute of Canada
FCII	— of the Chartered Insurance Institute (British)

FCIS	— of the Chartered Institute of Secretaries (British)
FCOG	— of the College of Obstetricians & Gynaecologists (British)
FCAMRT	— of Canadian Association of Medical Radiation Technologists
FCIA	— of the Canadian Institute of Actuaries
FCMA	— of the Society of Management Accountants of Canada
FCSI	— of the Canadian Securities Institute
FCTC	— of the Canadian Institute of Travel Counsellors
FCUIC	— of the Credit Union Institute of Canada
FE	Forest Engineer
FEIC	Fellow of the Engineering Institute of Canada
FFA	— of the Faculty of Actuaries (Scotland)
FFR	— of the Faculty of Radiologists (British)
FGS	— of the Geological Society (British)
FGSA	— of the Geological Society of America
FIA	— of the Institute of Actuaries (British)
FIC	— of the Institute of Chemistry
FICB	— of the Institute of Canadian Bankers
FICE	— of the Institution of Civil Engineers
FIEE	— of the Institution of Electrical Engineers
FIIC	— of the Insurance Institute of Canada
FIL	— of the Institute of Linguists (British)
FLA	— of the Library Association (England)
FMA	Financial Management Advisor
FMSA	— of the Mineralogical Society of America
Fr.	Father
FRAI	Fellow of the Royal Anthropological Institute
FRAIC	— of the Royal Architectural Institute of Canada
FRAM	— of the Royal Academy of Music
FRAS	— of the Royal Astronomical Society
FRCCO	— of the Royal Canadian College of Organists
FRCM	— of the Royal College of Music
FRCO	— of the Royal College of Organists
FRCOG	— of the Royal College of Obstetricians & Gynaecologists
FRCP	— of the Royal College of Physicians of London
FRCP(C)	— of the Royal College of Physicians of Canada
FRCP(E)	— of the Royal College of Physicians of Edinburgh
FRCP(I)	— of the Royal College of Physicians of Ireland
FRCP(Glas)	— of the Royal College of Physicians of Glasgow
FRCS	— of the Royal College of Surgeons of England
FRCS(C)	— of the Royal College of Surgeons of Canada
FRCS(E)	— of the Royal College of Surgeons of Edinburgh
FRCS(I)	— of the Royal College of Surgeons of Ireland
FRCS(Glas)	— of the Royal College of Surgeons of Glasgow
FRGS	— of the Royal Geographical Society
FRHistS	— of the Royal Historical Society
FRHortS	— of the Royal Horticultural Society
FRIBA	— of the Royal Institute of British Architects
FRIC	— of the Royal Institute of Chemistry
FRICS	— of the Royal Institution of Chartered Surveyors
FRMCM	— of Royal Manchester College of Music
FRMS (FRMetS)	— of the Royal Meteorological Society
FRS	— of the Royal Society (honorary)
FRSA	— of the Royal Society of Arts
FRSC	— of the Royal Society of Canada
FRSE	— of the Royal Society of Edinburgh
FRSH	— of the Royal Society of Health
FRSL	— of the Royal Society of Literature
FSA	— of the Society of Actuaries (or of Antiquaries) (honorary)
FSMAC	— of the Society of Management Accountants of Canada
FSS	— of the Royal Statistical Society
FTCL	— of Trinity College of Music (London)
FZS	— of the Zoological Society (British)
Gen.	General
GJ	Graduate Jeweller
HARCVS	Honorary Associate of Royal College of Veterinary Surgeons
IA	Investment Advisor
IC	Investment Counsellor
IngETP	Diplome de l'École Spéciale des Travaux Publiques
JCB	Bachelor of Canon Law
JCD	Doctor of Canon Law (or of Civil Law)
JCL	Licentiate in Canon Law (Juris Canonici Licentiatus)
JD	Doctor of Jurisprudence
JDS	— of Jurisdical Science
Jr.	Junior
JUL	Licentiate of Law in Utroque (both Civil & Canon Law)
JurM	Master of Jurisprudence
Jur. utr. Dr.	Juris utriusque doctor, Equiv. to LL.D.
LAB	Licentiate of the Assoc. Bd. of Royal Schools of Music (London, Eng.)
L.Cdr.	Lieutenant-Commander
LCL	Licentiate in Canon Law
LCMI	— of the Cost & Management Institute
L.Col.	Lieutenant-Colonel
LDC	Licencié ès Droit Canonique
LDS	Licentiate in Dental Surgery (British)
L ès L	Licencié ès Lettres
L. ès Sc.	— ès Sciences
L.Gen.	Lieutenant-General
LGSM	Licentiate of the Guildhall School of Music & Drama (London, Eng.)
LittD	Doctor of Letters (or Literature)
LittL	Licence ès Lettres
Litt.M.	Master of Letters (or Literature)
LJC	Licentiatus Juris Canonici
LL	License in Civil Law
LLB	Bachelor of Laws (Legum Baccalaureus)
LLD	Doctor of Laws (usually honorary)
LLL	Licence en droit
LLM	Master of Law
L. Mus.	Licentiate in Music
LMUS	— in Music of the Univ. of Saskatchewan
L Mus TCL	— in General Musicianship of Trinity College, London
L.Péd.	Licence en Pédagogie
L.Ph.	— en Philosophie
L.Psych.	Licencié en Psychologie
LRAM	Licentiate of the Royal Academy of Music (London)
LRCM	— of the Royal College of Music (London)
LRCP	— of the Royal College of Physicians
LRCS	— of the Royal College of Surgeons
LRCT	— of the Royal Conservatory of Toronto
LRE	— in Religious Education
LRSM	— of the Royal Schools of Music (London)
LS	Land Surveyor
LSA	Licentiate in Agricultural Science
L.Sc.Com.	— in Commercial Science
LScO	Licence en optométrie
L.S.Sc.	Licentiate in Sacred Scriptures
L.Sc.Soc.	Licence in Social Science
LST	Licentiate in Sacred Theology
Lt. (or Lt(N))	Lieutenant (or Lieutenant (Naval))
LTCL	Licentiate of Trinity College of Music (London)
LTCM	— of the Toronto Conservatory of Music
L.Th	Licentiate in Theology
M.	Monsieur
MA	Master of Arts
M.Acc.	— of Accountancy
MACF	Membre de l'Académie canadiennefrançaise
MAeE	Master of Aeronautical Engineering
MAIEE	Member of American Institute of Electrical Engineers
MAIME	— of American Institute of Mining Engineers
Maj.	Major
MALS	Master of Arts in Library Science
MAP	Maîtrise en administration publique
M.Arch.	Master of Architecture
MAS	— of Archival Studies
M.A.Sc. (MAS)	— of Applied Science
MASCE	Member of the American Society of Civil Engineers
MASME	— of the American Society of Mechanical Engineers
MAust IM	— of the Australian Institute of Mining & Metallurgy
MB	Bachelor of Medicine (British)
MBA	Master in Business Administration
MCE	— of Civil Engineering
M.Ch. (ChM)	— of Surgery (British)
MChE	— of Chemical Engineering (American)
MCI	Member of the Credit Institute
MCIC	— of the Chemical Institute of Canada
MCIF	— of the Canadian Institute of Forestry
MCIM	— of the Canadian Institute of Mining
MCIMM	— of the Canadian Institute of Mining & Metallurgy
MCInstM	— of the Canadian Institute of Marketing
MCL	Master of Civil Law
M.Com.	— of Commerce
M.Comp.	— of Canon Law
M.Comp.Sc.	— of Computer Science
MD	Doctor of Medicine
MDC	Master of Canon Law
MDCM	Doctor of Medicine & Master of Surgery
M.Des.	Master of Design
M.Div.	— of Divinity
MDS	— of Dental Surgery (British)
MDV	Doctor of Veterinary Medicine
Me	Maître

ME .... Master of Mechanical Engineering
M.Ed. (M.A.Ed.) .... — of Education
MEDS .... — of Environmental Design Studies
MEE................ — of Electrical Engineering (American)
MEIC .... Member of the Engineering Institute of Canada
M.Eng. .... Master of Engineering
MF .... — of Forestry
MFA................ — of Fine Arts
M.Gen. .... Major-General
Mgr................. Monsignor (or Manager or Monseigneur)
MHA .... Master of Health (or Hospital) Administration
MHE (M.H.Ec.)........ — of Home Economics
MICE .... Member of the Institution of Civil Engineers (British)
MICIA............... — of Industrial, Commercial & Institutional Accountants
MIEE .... — of the Institution of Electrical Engineers (British)
MIMM............... — of the Institute of Mining & Metallurgy (British)
MINA .... — of the Institute of Naval Architects
MIRE .... — of the Institute of Radio Engineers
M.I.St. .... Master of Information Studies
MJ .... — of Journalism
M.Litt................ — of Letters (or Literature)
MLIS .... — of Library & Information Science
MLS................ — of Library Science (or Licentiate in Medieval Studies)
MM (M.Mus.) .... — of Music
MMM .... Member, Order of Military Merit
MOM .... Member of the Order of Merit (Police Forces)
MN (M.Nurs.) .... Master of Nursing
MP................. — of Planning
MP .... Member of Parliament
MPE .... Master of Physical Education
M.Ph. (M.Phil.)........ — of Philosophy
MPM .... — of Pest Management
MPP .... Member of Provincial Parliament
M.Ps. (M.Psy.) .... Master of Psychology
MRAIC .... Member of the Royal Architectural Institute of Canada
MRCOG.............. — of the Royal College of Obstetricians & Gynaecologists
MRCP .... — of the Royal College of Physicians
MRCP(E)............ — of the Royal College of Physicians of Edinburgh
MRCP(I)............. — of the Royal College of Physicians of Ireland
MRCP(Glas).......... — of the Royal College of Physicians of Glasgow
MRCS .... — of the Royal College of Surgeons
MRCS(E)............ — of the Royal College of Surgeons of Edinburgh
MRCVS .... — of the Royal College of Veterinary Surgeons
MRM .... Master of Resource Management
MRSC .... Member of the Royal Society of Canada
MRSH .... — of the Royal Society of Health
MRST............... — of the Royal Society of Teachers
MS .... Master of Surgery (British)
MSA................ — of Science in Agriculture
M.Sc................ — of Science
MScA............... — of Applied Science
MSCE .... — of Science in Civil Engineering
MScF............... — of Science in Forestry
M.Sc.(Med.).......... — of Science in Medicine
MScN (MSN) .... — of Science in Nursing
M.Sc.Phm............ — of Science in Pharmacy
M.Sc.Soc. .... — in Social Sciences
M.S.Ed.............. — of Science in Education
M.S.Litt.............. — of Sacred Letters
MSPE .... McGill School of Physical Education
MSRC .... Membre Société Royale du Canada
MSS .... Master of Social Science
MSW .... — of Social Work
MTCI .... Member of Trust Companies Institute
M.U.Dr. .... Medecinae Universae Doctor (Prague) (Dentistry & Medicine)
MUP .... Master of Planning
MURP .... — of Urban & Rural Planning
Mus. Bac. (Mus.B.) .... Bachelor of Music
Mus. Doc. (Mus.D.) .... Doctor of Music
Mus. G. Paed.......... Musicae Graduatus Paedagogus (Graduate Teacher in Music)
MusM .... Master of Music
MV .... Médécin Vétérinaire
M.V.Sc. .... Master of Veterinary Science
NDA .... National Diploma in Agriculture (Royal Ag. Soc. of Engineering)
NDD .... National Diploma in Dairying (Scotland)
NP................. Notary Public
OA................. Officier d'Académie (France)
OC .... Order of Canada
OD .... Doctor of Optometry
OIP .... Officier de l'Instruction Publique
OLS................ Ontario Land Surveyor
OMM .... Officer, Order of Military Merit
OOM .... Officer of the Order of Merit (Police Forces)
OSA .... Ontario Society of Artists
PC .... Privy Councillor
PD .... Doctor of Parapsychology
PE .... Professional Engineer
P.Eng. .... Registered Professional Engineer
PFC .... Planificateur Financier Certifié
PFP .... Personal Financial Planner
PhB .... Bachelor of Philosophy
PhC .... Philosopher of Chiropractic
PhD .... Doctor of Philosophy
PhTD .... Physical Therapy Doctor
PhL .... Licentiate in Philosophy
PLS .... Professional Legal Secretary
P.Mgr................ — Manager
PP .... — Purchaser
PPB................. — Public Buyer
Prof................. Professor
PTIC .... Patent & Trade Mark Institute of Canada
QAA .... Qualified Administrative Assistant
QC .... Queen's Counsel
QLS .... Québec Land Surveyor
RA .... Royal Academy (honorary)
R.Adm. .... Rear-Admiral
RAM .... Royal Academy of Music (Budapest)
RAS .... Royal Aeronautical Society
RBA .... Royal Society of British Artists
RCA .... Royal Canadian Academy of Arts
RCAM .... Royal College & Academy of Music (Budapest)
RCM .... Royal Conservatory of Music (Leipzig)
RE .... Royal Engineers
REBC .... Registered Employee Benefits Consultant
Rev. .... Reverend
RFP .... Registered Financial Planner
RHU .... Registered Health Underwriter
RMS .... Royal Society of Miniature Painters
RMT .... Registered Music Teacher
RN .... — Nurse
ROI .... Royal Institute of Oil Painters
RP .... Member of the Royal Society of Portrait Painters
RP .... Révérend Père (Reverend Father)
RPA .... Registered Professional Accountant
R.P.Bio. .... — Professional Biologist
R.P.Dt. .... — Professional Dietitian
RPF .... — Professional Forester
RRL .... — Record Librarian
RSH .... Royal Society of Health
RSW .... Registered Specification Writer
RT .... — Technician of the Cdn. Association of Medical Radiation Technologists
SC .... Senior Counsel (Eire) equivalent of Q.C.
ScD .... Doctorat ès Sciences
ScL .... Licence ès Sciences
Sc Soc B .... Bachelier Science Sociale
Sc Soc D .... Doctor of Social Science
Sc Soc L .... License in Social Science
SFC .... Specialist in Financial Counselling
SJ .... Society of Jesus
SLS .... Saskatchewan Land Surveyor
S.Lt. .... Sub-Lieutenant
SM .... Master of Science
Sr. .... Senior
Sr. .... Sister
SSB .... Bachelier en Science Sacrée
SSC .... Sculptors' Society of Canada
SSL .... Licentiate in Sacred Scripture
STB (SThB) .... Bachelor of Sacred Theology
STD (SThD) .... Doctor of Sacred Theology
STL (SThL) .... Sacrae Theologiae Licentiatus (Licentiate in Sacred Theology)
STM .... Master of Sacred Theology
TCL .... Trinity College, London
TMMG .... Teacher, Massage & Medical Gymnastics
ThD .... Doctor of Theology
V.Adm. .... Vice-Admiral
VG .... Vicar-General
VS .... Veterinary Surgeon

Business & Shipping Abbreviations

As shipping terms vary in different countries, insurance or shipping agents should be consulted. For other lists of abbreviations, academic, etc., see Index.

a/c	Account
Ad val.	Ad valorem
avoir	Avoirdupois
bbl.	Barrel
B/L.	Bill of Lading
b.m.	Board Measure
B.O.	Buyer's Option
B/P.	Bills Payable
B/R.	Bills Receivable
B/S.	Bill of Sale
c.	Hundred
C or Cent.	Centigrade
cf.	Compare
C. and F.	Cost & Freight
Cie	Compagnie
c.i.f.	Cost insurance & freight
C.L.	Car Load (of freight)
Co.	Company
C.O.D.	Cash on Delivery
C. of F.	Cost of Freight
Cr.	Credit
C.W.O.	Cash with Order
Cwt.	Hundredweight
D/A.	Documents Attached, also Deposit Account
Dis. (Disct.)	Discount
Dl. (or Tl.)	Double (or triple) first class
D.O.A.	Deliver Documents on Acceptance of Draft
D.O.P.	Deliver Documents on Payment of Draft
Dr.	Debit
D.V.	God willing (Deo volente)
e.g.	For example (exempli gratia)
E.&.O.E.	Errors & omissions excepted
Est. Wt.	Estimated Weight
et seq.	And the following (et sequens)
Ex. Div.	Without Dividend
Ex-Warehouse	Purchaser pays carriage charges & assumes risks from seller's warehouse
F.	Fahrenheit
F.a.a.	Free of Average (marine insurance)
F.A.S.	Free Alongside (Seller assumes risks & delivers goods to alongside of steamer free of carriage charges)
F.O.B.	Free on Board (Purchaser pays carriage charges & assumes risks from point specified)
F.P.A.	Free of Particular Average (Insured can recover only for a total loss, subject to other conditions of the contract)
Franco.	Pre-paid free of expense to point specified
G.A.	General Average (All owners of cargo & vessel share in any loss arising from expense incurred to preserve ship & contents from greater loss)
gm.	Grammes
gr.	Grain; grains, or gross
ibid.	In the same place (ibidem)
i.e.	That is (id est)
Inc.	Incorporated
Int.	Interest
K.D.	Knocked down
lb. (libra)	Pound
L/C.	Letter of Credit
L.C.L.	Less than Car Load (of freight)
Limited; Ltd.	Limited Liability (Shareholders are "limited" in liability to the amount of their subscribed stock in certain companies)
L.P.	List Price
M.	Thousand (Mille)
MS., MSS.	Manuscript(s)
N.E.S. (N.O.P.)	Not Otherwise Provided For (Customs)
N.O.S.	Not Otherwise Specified
N.S.F.	Not Sufficient Funds (re cheques)
Nstd.	Nested
O.K.	Correct
op. cit.	In the work quoted (opere citato)
O.R.	At Owner's Risk
O.R.B.	At Owner's Risk of Breakage
oz.	Ounce
P.A.	Particular Average (As used in Marine Insurance, means damage to the goods caused by perils insured against & named in the contract. This form is often written with a Franchise Clause, & means there will be no claim unless the loss exceeds the percentage named)
P/A.	Power of Attorney
P & D.	Pick Up & Deliver
pp.	Pages
Pro forma	As a Matter of Form
P.S.	Postscript
q.v.	Which see (quod vide)
R.R.	Rural Route (Postal delivery)
S.B.	Shipping Bill
s.s.	Steamship
s/o	Ship's Option, weight or measurement
S.U.	Set Up (meaning article is complete)
T.B.L.	Through Bill of Lading
Tare	Weight of Container (Deducting tare from "gross weight" gives "net weight")
Ton	2,000 (short ton) or 2,240 (long ton) lbs. avoirdupois. A cubic ton in marine freight = 40 cubic feet
Ton wt/M.	Ton, weight or measurement (ship's option)
vide	See
viz	Namely; to wit (videlicet)

Border Services, Customs Regulations for Canadians Returning from Abroad

Note: The Canada Border Services Agency (CBSA) operates as an agency under the Public Safety and Emergency Preparedness (PSEP) portfolio, and its mission is to ensure the security and prosperity of Canada by managing the access of people and goods to and from Canada. With a workforce of approximately 12,000 public servants, the Canada Border Services Agency (CBSA) provides services at 1,200 points across Canada and over 30 locations abroad. At over 100 land border crossings and nine international airports, it operates on a 24/7 basis. It administers more than 90 acts and regulations on behalf of other Government of Canada departments and agencies, and international agreements.

It integrates several key functions previously spread among three organizations: the Customs program from the Canada Customs Revenue Agency, the Intelligence, Interdiction and Enforcement program from Citizenship and Immigration Canada, and the Import Inspection at Ports of Entry program from the Canadian Food Inspection Agency.

If you have information about suspicious cross-border activity, please call the CBSA Border Watch tollfree line at 1-888-502-9060.

Canadians returning to Canada may bring any amount of goods into the country subject to duties and any provincial or territorial assessments, with the exception of restricted items. This applies even if you do not qualify for a personal exemption. The term duty can include Goods and Services. Duties represent duty, excise taxes and the Goods & Services Tax (GST) or Harmonized Sales Tax (HST). In addition to duties, provincial and territorial taxes (PST) are assessed if an agreement has been signed between the federal government and a province or territory whereby the federal government collects the PST, levies and fees on their behalf.

Goods included in personal exemptions must be for personal or household use, souvenirs or gifts. Goods brought in for commercial use, or on behalf of another person do not qualify and are subject to full duties.

On your return to Canada, you must declare to the Canada Border Services Agency (CBSA) all goods acquired (purchases, gifts, awards, prizes, and purchases made at Canadian or foreign duty-free shops and still in your possession) and repairs or modifications you made to your vehicle, vessel or aircraft while outside Canada.

Personal Exemptions

To qualify for personal exemptions you must be:

- Canadian resident returning from a trip abroad;
- former resident of Canada returning to live in Canada; or
- temporary resident of Canada.

Children and infants qualify for personal exemptions as long as the goods are for the use of the child or infant. The parent or guardian makes the customs declaration for the child.

Personal exemptions are applicable after the following minimum absences:

1. After an absence of 24 hours but less than 48 hours: up to a value of $50 (Canadian) in total (with the exception of tobacco products and alcoholic beverages) any number of times a year. If the value of the goods exceeds $50, you pay duties and PST on the full value (exemption cannot be claimed). The goods must accompany you on your return to Canada.

2. After an absence of 48 hours but less than seven days: up to $400 (Canadian) in total any number of times in a year. The goods must accompany you on your return to Canada.

3. After an absence of seven days or more: up to $750 (Canadian) any number of times in a year. You may have to make a written declaration. Goods you claim under this exemption may follow you by mail or other means, with the exception of alcoholic beverages and tobacco products. You require a Form E24, Personal Exemption Customs Declaration, which is to be completed at the time of arrival and can be obtained from a customs officer. To claim your goods when they arrive, present your copy of the E24 to the CBSA for clearance. Goods must be claimed within 40 days of their arrival in Canada; duties and taxes are then payable, along with a Canada Post Corporation processing fee. You may pay the duties and then apply to the CBSA for a refund (if the personal exemption applies) or refuse delivery; following a review that determines if the goods are eligible for free importation, the goods will be released to you without an assessment.

Persons residing outside Canada for part of the year are considered to be residents of Canada and are entitled to the above personal exemptions.

Exemptions cannot be transferred to another person or combined with another person's personal exemption. You cannot combine a 24-hour ($50) or 48- hour ($400) or the seven-day ($750) exemption when claiming an exemption, nor can you carry over an unused portion of an exemption for another period of absence.

Tobacco & Alcohol

Tobacco products and alcoholic beverages must accompany you in your hand or checked luggage and may be included in the 48-hour ($400) or the seven-day ($750) exemptions, but not in the 24-hour ($50) exemption. You must meet the age requirements set by the province or territory where you enter Canada. In addition the following conditions apply:

1. You may bring in up to 200 cigarettes, 50 cigars or cigarillos, 200 tobacco sticks **and** 200 grams of manufactured tobacco. Duties must be paid on anything above this allowance, plus any applicable provincial or territorial limits or assessments.

If you include cigarettes, tobacco sticks, or manufactured tobacco in your personal allowance, only a partial exemption will apply. You will have to pay a special duty on these products **unless** they are marked "CANADA DUTY-PAID — DROIT ACQUITTÉ." You will find Canadian-made products sold at a duty-free shop marked this way. You can speed up your clearance by having your tobacco products available for inspection when you arrive.

2. You may include up to 1.5 litres of wine, or 1.14 litres (40 ounces) of liquor, or a total of 1.14 litres (40 ounces), or 24 x 335 ml (12-ounce) cans or bottles (8.5 litres) of beer or ale. Wine coolers are classified as wine; beer coolers are classified as beer. Beer or wine that contains 0.5% alcohol by volume or less is not classified as an alcoholic beverage, so no quantity limits apply. You may bring in more than this allowance of alcohol anywhere in Canada (with the exception of the Northwest Territories and Nunavut) as long as the quantities are within the limits set by the province or territory. If bringing in more than the free allowance, you must pay customs and provincial/territorial assessments. For more information, check with the appropriate provincial/ territorial liquor control agency prior to leaving Canada.

Gifts

While abroad, you may send gifts duty- and tax-free to recipients in Canada. To qualify, the gift must be valued at $60 CAN or less and cannot be an alcoholic beverage, tobacco product, or advertising material. Gifts in excess of $60 CAN require duty payment by the recipient on the excess amount. Gifts that accompany you on your return to Canada must be included in your personal exemption, while gifts you send from abroad are not included. Some conditions apply - for additional information, contact the CBSA Border Information Service (BIS) at one of the numbers listed at the end of this section.

Prizes & Awards

In most cases, you pay regular duties on prizes or awards received outside Canada. Contact the BIS line for more information.

Paying Duties

Duties may be paid by cash or travellers' cheques. Personal cheques are also acceptable (for amounts of $2,500 or less and with proper identification); VISA, American Express and MasterCard are accepted at most border services locations and Debit Cards at many locations.

For information on duty rates for particular items, contact the BIS line.

Special Duty Rate

After any trip abroad of 48 hours or longer you are entitled to a special duty rate on goods worth up to $300 more than your personal exemption of $400 or $750. The goods must accompany you. The special duty rate does not apply to tobacco or alcoholic beverages. The special duty rate for goods not eligible under NAFTA, when combined with the GST, is about 14% or 22% when combined with the HST.

NAFTA Special Duty Rate

Goods qualify for a lower U.S. duty rate under NAFTA if they are:

- for personal use; and
- marked as made in the U.S. or Canada; or
- not marked or labelled to indicate they were made anywhere other than in the U.S. or Canada.

Your goods qualify for the lower Mexican duty rate in a similar way.

If you do not qualify for a personal exemption, or if you exceed your exemption limit, you will have to pay GST or HST over and above applicable duties or taxes on the portion not eligible under your exemption. The rates vary according to the goods, their country of origin, and the country from which you are importing them.

For information on goods eligible for the special duty rate under NAFTA, contact your nearest CBSA office and ask for a copy of Memorandum D11-4-13, Rules of Origin for Casual Goods Regulations.

Regular Duty Rates

If you do not qualify for a personal exemption, or you exceed your exemption limit, you will pay GST or HST over and above all duties, taxes, and assessments that apply on the portion not eligible under your exemption. The rates vary according to the goods, their country of origin, and the country from which you are importing them. You may also have to pay provincial sales tax if you live in a province where we have an agreement to collect the tax and you return from your trip through your province.

World Trade Organization (WTO) Agreement

The duty on a wide range of products originating in non-NAFTA countries has been eliminated or will be reduced to zero within the next few years. NAFTA goods also qualify for the WTO rate, so if the rate on the goods you are importing is lower under WTO than under NAFTA, the lower rate will automatically be applied.

Value for Duty/Foreign Sales Tax

Value for duty is the amount used to calculate duty and is generally the price you paid for the item. Foreign sales tax is included in the price and forms part of the value of the item.

Some foreign governments will refund sales tax to you if you export the items you bought. If this is the case, you do not include the amount of the foreign sales tax that was or will be refunded to you.

Declaration

When returning to Canada by commercial aircraft, a Canada Border Services Agency (CBSA) declaration card is distributed for completion before arrival. The cards are also used at some locations for people arriving by train, vessel or bus. If arriving by a private vehicle (e.g., automobile), you must make an oral declaration unless you are claiming goods that preceded or will follow your arrival in Canada as part of your $750 exemption. If this is the case, ask the border services officer for Form E24, Personal Exemption Customs Declaration. You will need your copy of this form to claim your goods. Otherwise, you may have to pay regular duty on them.

CBSA officers are legally entitled to examine luggage; you are responsible for opening, unpacking and repacking the luggage. Retain receipts of purchases and repairs made to verify length of stay and value of goods or repairs. Failure to declare or a false declaration may result in the seizure of goods. Penalties range from 25 to 80% of the value of the seized goods. Vehicles used to transport unlawfully imported goods may also be seized, with a penalty imposed before the vehicle can be returned. Commodities such as alcohol and tobacco are seized and not returned.

Currency and Monetary Instruments

If you are importing or exporting monetary instruments equal to or greater than CAN$10,000 (or its equivalent in a foreign currency), whether in cash or other monetary instruments, you must report it to the CBSA when you arrive or before you leave Canada. For more information, ask for a copy of the publication called "Crossing the Border with $10,000 or More?" or select "Publications and forms" on our Web site at www.cbsa.gc.ca.

Restrictions

Firearms: Contact the Canadian Firearms Program at:(613) 993 7267, Fax: (613) 993-0260, Website: www.rcmp-grc.gc.ca/cfp-pcaf.

Replica firearms are designed or intended to resemble a firearm with near precision. They are classified as prohibited devices and you cannot import them into Canada.

Mace or pepper spray that is used for the purpose of injuring, immobilizing or otherwise incapacitating any person is considered a prohibited weapon. You cannot import it into Canada. Aerosol or similar dispensers that contain substances capable of repelling or subduing animals are not considered weapons if the label of the container specifically indicates that they are for use against animals.

Explosives, fireworks, certain types of ammunition: You require written authorization and permits. Contact Chief Inspector of Explosives Regulatory Division, Natural Resources Canada, 1431 Merivale Rd., Ottawa ON K1A 0G1, 613/948-5200.

Vehicles: Vehicles must meet the requirements of the CBSA, Transport Canada and the Canadian Food Inspection Agency before they can be imported. Transport Canada defines a vehicle as any vehicle that is capable of being driven or drawn on roads, by any means other than muscular power exclusively, but does not run exclusively on rails. It considers trailers such as recreational, camping, boat, horse and stock trailers as vehicles, as well as woodchippers, generators and any other equipment mounted on rims and tires.

CBSA import restrictions apply to most used or second- hand vehicles that are not manufactured in the current year. Transport Canada requirements apply to vehicles that are less than fifteen years old. All imported vehicles less than fifteen years old must comply with Canadian federal safety and emission standards. The person importing the vehicle is responsible for ensuring it meets the Canadian safety standards.

If you have acquired a vehicle from the United States, you must contact the Transport Canada's Registrar of Imported Vehicle (RIV) before you import your vehicle, to ensure that it is admissible for importation and can be modified to meet the Canadian standards after you import it.

Registrar of Imported Vehicles: Telephone: 1-888- 848-8240 (toll free in Canada, the United States and Mexico); (416) 626-6812 (from all other countries), Fax: 1-888-346-8235, Website: www.riv.ca.

Import restrictions apply to most used or secondhand cars, generally from countries other than the United States. Under NAFTA, restrictions do not apply to vehicles imported from the U.S., however, not all vehicles that are manufactured for sale in the U.S. can be imported because they do not meet the Transport Canada requirements; special duty rates, as outlined above, apply. Excise tax and GST continue to apply in the usual way. Under NAFTA, customs restrictions continue to apply to vehicles imported from Mexico until 2009, when you will be able to import vehicles ten years or older. The age restriction will drop every second year until the restriction is dropped altogether in 2019.

In most instances, Canadian residents are not allowed to import vehicles into Canada that have been purchased or obtained in countries other than the United States. If you have acquired a vehicle from a country other than the United States, before importing it, contact: Transport Canada, Road Safety & Motor Vehicle Regulation, Place de Ville, Tower C, 330 Sparks St., 8th Fl., Ottawa ON K1A 0N5, 613/998-8616, or 1-800-333- 0371 (toll free from Canada and the U.S.); Fax: 613/998- 4831; Website: www.tc.gc.ca.

Your vehicle may be subject to provincial or territorial sales tax; contact your provincial or territorial department of motor vehicles for information. In addition, you may need to meet some requirements in the country which the vehicle is being exported.

Import Controls: Importations of certain goods are controlled. You may need a permit to import, even for personal and household use. For information, contact: Export & Import Controls Bureau, International Trade Canada (ITCan) , Tower C, 4th Floor, 125 Sussex Drive, Ottawa ON K1A 0G2, Website: www.international. gc.ca.

Meat, dairy products, wheat, barley, and their products: Complex requirements and restrictions exist; importation of certain meat and dairy products from certain U.S. states is allowed. All meat and meat products have to be identified as products of the United States. Limits exist for amounts or dollar value in certain foodstuffs you can import for personal use; if above those limits, duty ranges from 150 to 300% and you may also require an agricultural inspection certificate. For more information, contact the CBSA BIS line.

Agricultural products: Restrictions exist on live animals and animal products, meat and poultry products, dairy products, egg and egg products, honey and fresh fruits and vegetables, seeds and grains, animal feeds, plant and plant products, forestry products, soil and fertilizers, pest control products, biological products. For information on these products, refer to the Automated Import Reference System (AIRS) on the CFIA Website at www.inspection.gc.ca or call the CBSA BIS line.

Cultural property: Antiquities or cultural objects of significance in the country of origin cannot be imported into Canada. For information, contact Movable Cultural Property, Canadian Heritage, 15 Eddy St., 3rd Fl., Gatineau, QC K1A 0M5, 819/997-7761, Fax: 613/997- 7757.

Endangered species: Canada has signed an international agreement restricting the sale, trade or movement of endangered animals, birds, reptiles, fish, insects and certain forms of plant life; the restrictions also apply to their parts or products made from their parts. Before you bring back any of these products, you should contact CITES Administrator, Canadian Wildlife Service, Environment Canada, Ottawa ON K1A 0H3, 1-800-668-6767 (toll-free number in Canada), 819/ 997-1840 (local calls and from all other countries).

Appeals

If you disagree with the amount of duty and taxes that you had to pay, please ask to speak with the superintendent on duty. A consultation can often resolve the issue quickly and without cost. If you are still not satisfied, our officers can tell you how to make a formal appeal. If you do not declare goods, or if you falsely declare them, we can seize the goods. This means that you may lose the goods permanently, or that you may have to pay a penalty to get them back.

If you do not declare tobacco products and alcoholic beverages at the time of importation, we will seize them permanently.

Depending on the type of goods and the circumstances involved, we may impose a penalty that ranges from 25% to 80% of the value of the seized goods.

In addition, the *Customs Act* provides CBSA officers with the authority to seize all vehicles that were used unlawfully to import goods. When this happens, we impose a penalty you have to pay before we return the vehicle.

If goods have been seized and you disagree with the action taken, you must notify the CBSA in writing within 90 days of the seizure date of your intention to appeal. You should send your appeal to the CBSA Office where the seizure took place. You can find more information about this process on the front of your seizure receipt form.

In addition to the activities mentioned above, designated CBSA officers may arrest for a criminal offence under the *Criminal Code* or any other Act of Parliament. This includes the offences of impaired driving, outstanding arrest warrants, stolen property, and abductions/kidnappings. If you are arrested, you may be compelled to attend court in Canada. You should note that all persons arrested in Canada are protected by, and will be treated in accordance with, the *Canadian Charter of Rights and Freedoms*.

A record of infractions is kept in the CBSA computer system. If you have an infraction record, you may have to undergo a more detailed examination on future trips.

Precautions

Carry proper identification.

Traveling with Children

Border services officers are on alert for children who need protection. Children under the age of 18 are classified as minors and are subject to the same entry requirements as any other visitor to Canada.

We will conduct a more detailed examination of minors entering Canada without proper identification or those traveling in the company of adults other than their parents or legal guardian(s). This additional scrutiny helps ensure the safety of the children.

Minors traveling alone must have proof of citizenship and a letter from both parents detailing the length of stay, providing the parents' telephone number and authorizing the person waiting for them to take care of them while they are in Canada.

If you are traveling with minors, you must carry proper identification for each child such as a birth certificate, passport, citizenship card, permanent resident card or Certificate of Indian Status.

If you are a parent traveling alone with your child, it is recommended that you have a letter of authorization from your spouse. If you are divorced or separated, you should carry with you copies of the legal custody agreements for your children. If you are traveling with minors and you are not their parent/guardian, you should have written permission from the parent/guardian authorizing the trip. The letter should include addresses and telephone numbers of where the parents or guardian can be reached and identify a person who can confirm that the children are not being abducted or taken against their will.

If you are traveling with a group of vehicles, make sure you arrive at the border in the same vehicle as your children, to avoid any confusion.

"Identification of Articles for Temporary Exportation": CBSA offices offer a free identification program for valuables; a list of your valuables (excluding jewellery) and their serial numbers on a wallet-sized form will show border services officers that the items were previously purchased in Canada or that you lawfully imported them prior to your current time abroad. In the case of jewellery, carry an appraisal of the item(s) from a gemmologist, jeweller or insurance agent, together with a signed and dated photograph and a written declaration that the items in the photograph are those described in the appraisal report. If previously imported, carry a copy of the customs receipt.

If you take any item outside Canada and modify it, it is considered to be a new item and its full value will need to be declared. Similarly, under Canadian law, any repairs or modifications to a vehicle that increase its value, improve its condition or modify it while abroad may require that you pay duties on its full value on your return to Canada. This does not apply to incidental repairs to keep the car in operational condition while abroad, although you may be required to pay duties on the repairs and parts. A special provision is available that waives duties payable in such cases. Contact the CBSA for information.

Additional Information

If you have any other questions, contact the Border Information Service (BIS) line. This is a 24-hour telephone service that automatically answers all incoming calls and provides general border services information. If you call during regular business hours (8:00 a.m. to 4:00 p.m. local time, Monday to Friday, except holidays), you can speak directly to an agent by pressing "0" at any time.

English Enquiries: 1-800-461-9999 (toll-free in Canada)
French Enquiries: 1-800-959-2036 (toll-free in Canada)
Out-of-Canada callers can reach BIS by calling:

Western Sites
English: . . . . . . 204/983-3500 (long-distance charges will apply)
French . . . . . . : 204/983-3700 (long-distance charges will apply)

Eastern Sites
English: . . . . . . 506/636-5064 (long-distance charges will apply)
French . . . . . . : 506/636-5067 (long-distance charges will apply)
Website: . . . . www.cbsa-asfc.gc.ca

Election Regulations

According to the Canada Elections Act, and subject to certain exceptions, the general rule as to the franchise of electors at a federal election is that every person is qualified as an elector if such person

(a) is of the full age of 18 years on election day;

(b) is a Canadian citizen.

Among persons disqualified are certain officials charged with administering the elections, and, individuals who have lost their right to vote for a specified period for the commission of an election-related offence.

Writs for an election (general or by-election) are issued at least 36 days before the date fixed for election day.

Similar qualifications apply in the Provinces and Territories, although for provincial and territorial elections there is usually a residence requirement of either six or twelve months before the date of the issue of the writ of election. The age requirement is 18 years.

To contact election officers see Index, "Elections, Govt. Info. Sources".

Elections Canada - 613/993-2975; Toll Free: 1-800-463-6868; TTY: 1-800-361-8935; Fax: 1-888-524-1444; URL: www.elections.ca.

Liquor Regulations

For names of personnel of the various Liquor Control Boards see index "Liquor Board, Commission, or Control."

Alberta

- Ensure integrity, transparency, disclosure, public consultation & accountability in Alberta's gaming & liquor industries;
- Administer the Alberta Lottery Fund with full public disclosure & continue to support communities & charitable organizations;
- License, regulate & monitor liquor & gaming activities, as well as certain aspects of tobacco sales;
- Implement & account for specific lottery fund programs administered by Alberta Gaming;
- Develop & communicate provincial gaming & liquor policy;
- Responsible for the Department of Gaming, the Alberta Gaming & Liquor Commission (AGLC), the Alberta Gaming Research Council.

Alberta Gaming & Liquor Commission, 50 Corriveau Ave., St. Albert AB T8N 3T5 - 780/447-8600; Fax: 780/447-8918; Toll Free: 1-800-272-8876; URL: www.aglc.ca

British Columbia

The Liquor Control & Licensing Branch is responsible for issuing licences to:

- pubs, bars, lounges, stadiums, nightclubs & restaurants to sell liquor by the glass, & cold beer & wine stores to sell liquor by the bottle
- breweries, distilleries & wineries to manufacture liquor, &
- UBrews/UVins to sell their customers the ingredients, equipment & advice they need to make their own beer, wine cider or coolers

In addition, the branch:

- regulates both Serving It Right: The Responsible Beverage Service Program & Special Occasion Licences for the events such as community celebrations, weddings or banquets
- educates those who hold liquor licences (called licensees) about the laws & rules that may affect them inspects licensed establishments, &
- takes enforcement action when licensees do not follow the *Liquor Control & Licensing Act*, Regulations, &/or the specific terms & conditions of their licences British Columbia Liquor Control & Licensing

Branch, PO Box 9292, Stn Prov Govt, Victoria BC V8W 9J8; street address: 1019 Wharf St., 250/387-1254; Fax: 250/387-9184; Toll Free: 1-866-209-2111; Email: lclb.lclb@gems4.gov.bc.ca; URL: www.pssg.gov.bc.ca/lclb

Manitoba

Persons over the age of 18 years and who are not otherwise prohibited may purchase and consume spirits, wine and beer in premises licensed by the Liquor Control Commission. Further, those persons may purchase from a MLCC liquor mart, liquor vendor or specialty wine store for consumption in a residence.

Beer may also be purchased from beer vendor depots located in most hotels throughout the province.

Parents dining with their children may purchase alcoholic beverages for the latter, for consumption with meals, only in licensed restaurants, dining rooms, cocktail lounges or cabarets.

Beverage rooms and cocktail rooms must be vacated within 30 minutes after the hour at which sale of liquor must cease.

Manitoba Liquor Control Commission, 1555 Buffalo Place, PO Box 1023, Winnipeg MB R3C 2X1 - 204/ 284-2501; Fax: 204/453-5254; URL: www.liquormartsonline.com

New Brunswick

Intoxicating liquor is sold in sealed packages at Liquor Stores and agency stores. Where a permit and/or a license has been obtained, liquor may be sold by the glass in dining rooms, restaurants, taverns, cabarets, lounges, beverage rooms, and clubs. Age of majority is 19.

New Brunswick Liquor Corp., PO Box 20787, Fredericton NB E3B 5B8 - 506/452-6826; Fax: 506/462- 2024; Email: info@anbl.com; URL: www.anbl.com

Newfoundland & Labrador

The importation, manufacture, and sale of alcoholic beverages through Retail Liquor outlets is the responsibility of the Newfoundland Liquor Corp.

The Newfoundland Liquor Corporation is also responsible for the issuing of all licenses, including those to manufacture and to sell packaged beer, and enforcement of regulations including, but not limited, to the following:

- All liquor sold upon licensed premises shall be consumed thereon.
- All liquor served in licensed premises shall be dispensed from the original container in which the liquor is purchased from or under the authority of the Liquor Corp.
- The drinking age in Newfoundland is 19 years.

Nfld. Liquor Corp., PO Box 8750, Stn A, St. John's NL A1B 3V1 - 709/724-1100; Fax: 709/754-0321; URL: www.nlliquor.com

Northwest Territories

The *Northwest Territories Act*, Chapter 331 of the Revised Statutes of Canada, 1952, authorizes the Commissioner in Council of the Northwest Territories to make acts respecting intoxicants.

The Liquor Licensing Board, established under Part I of the *Liquor Act*, controls the conduct of licensees and operation of licensed premises; grants, renews and transfers licenses and, after a hearing, may cancel or suspend licenses. There are presently twelve types of licenses issued by the Board. Part I also provides for plebiscites to be held concerning new liquor license applications and also concerning restriction or prohibition in a community.

Part II of the *Liquor Act* establishes a Liquor Commission. The Minister responsible for this Part may designate his powers to the Liquor Commission to operate liquor stores and to purchase, sell and distribute liquor in the Northwest Territories. Through agency agreements, private contractors operate retail liquor stores on behalf of the Liquor Commission in Fort Simpson, Fort Smith, Hay River, Inuvik, Yellowknife, Norman Wells and liquor warehouses in Hay River and Yellowknife.

Northwest Territories Liquor Commission, #201, 31 Capital Dr., Hay River NT X0E 1G2 - 867/874-2100; Fax: 867/874-2180; URL: www.fin.gov.nt.ca/liquor

Northwest Territories Liquor Licensing Board, #210, 31 Capital Dr., Hay River NT X0E 1G2 - 867/874- 2906; Fax: 867/874-6011

Nova Scotia

All liquor is sold through Government Stores.

Generally local option vote applies.

Eating establishment liquor licenses, lounges, clubs and cabarets serve spirits, draught beer, bottled beer and wine.

The legal minimum drinking age is 19 years.

Nova Scotia Alcohol & Gaming Authority, PO Box 545, Alderney Gate, 40 Alderney Dr., Dartmouth NS B2Y 3Y8 - 902/424-6160; Fax: 902/424-4942; Toll Free: 1-877-565-0556; URL: www.mynslc.ca

Nova Scotia Liquor Corporation, PO Box 8720, Stn A, Halifax NS B3K 5M4 - 902/450-6752; Fax: 902/453-1153

Nunavut

Nunavut Liquor Management is a Branch of the Department of Finance within the Government of Nunavut. Nunavut Liquor Management has two sections, referred to as the Nunavut Liquor Commission and the Nunavut Liquor Licensing Board.

The Nunavut Liquor Commission is responsible for, as first receiver, the purchasing, storage and distribution of alcohol products within the Nunavut Territory.

The Nunavut Liquor Licensing Board deals with the issuance of liquor licenses, liquor permits, inspection and enforcement under the *Nunavut Liquor Act.*

Communities in Nunavut are empowered and are enabled to establish their own liquor controls through the *Nunavut Liquor Act.* They are prohibited, restricted (variety) and unrestricted (only Liquor Act applies). The age of majority in Nunavut is nineteen.

Nunavut Liquor Commission, Bag 002, Rankin Inlet, NU X0C 0G0 - 867/645-3148; 867/645-3327

Nunavut Liquor Licensing Board, Bag 002, Rankin Inlet, NU X0C 0G0 - 867/645-3302; 867/645-3327

Ontario

In accordance with the provisions of the *Liquor Control Act* of Ontario, the Liquor Control Board buys wine, spirits and beer from all over the world for distribution and sale to Ontario consumers and licensed establishments. To provide this service, the

LCBO operates five major regional storage and distribution centres which supply more than 600 retail liquor stores.

In the interests of consumer protection, the LCBO also regularly tests all alcoholic beverages sold in Ontario. This "quality control" testing ensures that all products carried by LCBO stores, Ontario winery stores and Brewers Retail outlets comply with the standards required under the Federal *Food & Drug Act* and Regulations.

The Alcohol and Gaming Commission of Ontario (AGCO) is a Provincial agency that was established on February 23, 1998 after legislation was tabled to merge the Liquor Licence Board of Ontario (LLBO) with the Gaming Control Commission (GCC). The AGCO is responsible for administering the *Liquor Licence Act*, the *Gaming Control Act*, 1992, and the *Wine Content Act*. The AGCO conducts hearings as required: to determine the eligibility for liquor licences or gaming registration; to determine the eligibility for, or the revocation of liquor licences in public interest cases; and, in disciplinary cases involving liquor licensees or gaming registrants.

Liquor-related responsibilities include: licensing of public places which serve beverage alcohol for on-premises consumption; licensing of Ontario liquor manufacturers and the sales representatives of foreign manufacturers; promoting moderation and the responsible use of beverage alcohol.

Gaming-related responsibilities include: regulating charitable and casino gambling in Ontario; ensuring that games of chance are conducted fairly in compliance with the *Gaming Control Act*, regulations, and the terms and conditions that are imposed with charity gaming licences; ensuring that the people and the companies involved in casino and charitable gaming satisfy high standards of honesty, integrity and financial responsibility; registering commercial suppliers and gaming assistants of charitable gaming events and administering the issuance of charity gaming licences in partnership with municipalities.

Alcohol and Gaming Commission of Ontario, 20 Dundas St. W., Toronto ON M5G 2N6; Enquiries: 416/326-8700, or 1-800-522-2876 (toll-free in Ontario); Fax: 416/326-5555 (liquor), 416/326-8711 (gaming); URL:www.agco.on.ca

Prince Edward Island

Beverage alcohol sealed packages may be purchased at Commission Stores throughout the Province by any person 19 or older who is not otherwise disqualified.

Spirits by the glass, and beer and wine by the open bottle or glass, may be purchased in dining rooms, lounges, clubs and military canteens licensed by the Commission.

Prince Edward Island Liquor Control Commission, 3 Garfield St., PO Box 967, Charlottetown, PE C1A 7M4 - 902/368-5710; Fax: 902/368-5735; URL: www.peilcc.ca

Québec

Spirits and wines are sold by Québec Liquor Corporation (Société des alcools du Québec) stores only.

Spirits, beer and wine may be sold to the public by restaurants, bars and clubs under permit for consumption on the premises. Taverns may sell beer and cider. Pubs may sell beer, draught wine and cider.

A licensed grocery store may sell beer and certain designated wines and the product must not be consumed on the premises.

Persons under the age of 18 years old cannot be admitted into bars, pubs and taverns and at no time may alcoholic beverages be sold to them in other establishments.

Régie des Alcools, des courses et des jeux, 1, rue Notre-Dame est, Montréal PQ H2Y 1B6 - 514/873- 3577; 560, boul Charest est, Québec PQ G1K 3J3 - 418/643-7667; URL: www.saq.com

Saskatchewan

The Saskatchewan Liquor & Gaming Authority, a Treasury Board Crown corporation, regulates liquor and gaming activities and conducts and manages gaming in the Saskatchewan Indian Gaming Authority Casinos and the Video Lottery Terminals throughout the province. It is responsible for the control, sale and distribution of liquor in the province, and also licenses and regulates bingos, raffles, casinos, and breakopen tickets.

The minimum drinking age is 19.

Saskatchewan Liquor & Gaming Authority, PO Box 5054, Regina SK S4P 3M3 -306/787-4213; Fax: 306/798-2252; www.saskliquor.com

Yukon Territory

The *Yukon Act*, Chapter Y-2 of the Revised Statutes of Canada, 1970, authorizes the Commissioner in Executive Council, Yukon Territory, to make acts respecting intoxicants.

By virtue of Chapter 105 cited as the *Liquor Act*, established the laws governing the importation, distributing, licensing and retailing of alcoholic beverages in Yukon.

The formation of the Yukon Liquor Corporation by means of amendments to the *Liquor Act* came into force on April 1st, 1977. The separation as a Corporate entity resulted in increased responsibility and full accountability in all areas except major government policy.

The five members of the Board of Directors are appointed by the Commissioner in executive council to hold office at pleasure.

The President and Chief Executive Officer of the Corporation, is charged with the general direction, supervision and control of the Corporation and the administration of the Act.

Yukon Liquor Corp., 9031 Quartz Road, Whitehorse YT Y1A 4P9 - 867/667-5245; Fax: 867/393-6306; URL: www.ylc.yk.ca

Legal Age of Consent to Sexual Activity

Age of Consent, under the *Tackling Violent Crime Act, 2008*:

Raises the age at which youths can consent to non-exploitative sexual activity from 14 to 16 years of age;

Maintains the existing age of protection of 18 years for exploitative sexual activity (i.e. sexual activity involving prostitution, pornography, or a relationship of trust, authority or dependency or that is otherwise exploitative); and

Includes a close-in-age exception which permits 14- and 15-year old youths to engage in consensual, non-exploitative sexual activity with a partner who is less than five years older. Another exception will be available for marriages and for pre-existing common-law relationships.

Marriage Regulations

Divorce Act in Canada

Divorce grounds in Canada, under the *Divorce Act, 1985:*

Breakdown of marriage, established by:
- Spouses intentionally living separate and apart at least one year with the idea that the marriage is over, or

Since the marriage, either spouse has:
- Committed adultery, or
- Treated the other spouse with physical or mental cruelty rendering continued cohabitation intolerable.

Alberta

Marriageable age:
- Without parental consent: 18 years
- With parental consent: 16 years
- A female, under the age of 16, may be married with parental consent & proof that she is the mother of a living child or proof that she is expecting a child.

Blood Test: not required
Waiting Period: None. Marriage Licence is valid immediately & is valid for 3 months (from date of issuance).
Licence fee: $40 + agent
Civic Marriage ceremony fee: uncapped

British Columbia

Marriageable age:
- Without parental consent: 19 years
- With parental consent: 16 to 18 years
- A court order of consent: under 16 years

Blood test: not required
Waiting period for licence: none
Marriage Licence: $100
Civil Marriage Ceremony: $80.25

Manitoba

Marriageable age:
- Without parental consent: 18 years
- With parental consent: 16 years (Persons under 16 years of age can be married only with the consent of a judge of the Family Court.)

Blood test: not required
Waiting period for licence: none
Waiting period after issuance of licence: 24 hours (This may be waived in exceptional circumstances by person performing ceremony.)
Licence fee: $90. Licence valid for 3 months (from date of issuance).

New Brunswick

Marriageable age:
- Without parental consent: 18 years
- With parental consent: under 18 years
- Under 16 years: a declaration of a Judge of the Court of Queen's Bench that the proposed marriage may take place is necessary.

Blood test: not required
Waiting period for licence: none
Licence fee: none
Vital Statistics, Dept. of Health & Wellness - 506/ 453-7411; Fax: 506/453-3245; URL: www.gov.nb.ca/en/ index.htm

Newfoundland & Labrador

Marriageable age:
- Greater than or equal to 19 years: without parental consent
- Greater than or equal to 18 years: without parental consent in certain circumstances
- Greater than or equal to 16 years and less than 19 years: with the applicable parental, guardian or Director of Child Welfare consent (Consent may be dispensed within exceptional cases.)
- Less than 16 years: where by reason of pregnancy a judge issues a licence

Blood test: not required
Licence fee: $50

Northwest Territories

Marriageable age:
- Without parental consent: 19 years
- Under the age of 19 years and declares via statutory declaration that:
  - (a) that no person has lawful custody of the minor; or
  - (b) that any person who has lawful custody of the minor not a resident of the Territories & that the minor has been a resident of the Territories for not less than 12 months immediately preceding the date of the declaration; or
  - (c) that any person who has lawful custody of the minor is unable to consent by reason of disability; or
  - (d) that the minor has, for not less than six months immediately preceding the date of the declaration, withdrawn from the charge of the persons who have lawful custody of the minor & that the minor has not returned to such charge
- With parental consent: 15 years, or under 15 years & pregnant

Blood test: not required
Waiting period for licence: none
Licence fee: $50

Nova Scotia

Marriageable age:
- Without parental consent: 19 years or over
- With parental consent, or if a widow, widower, or divorcee: 16 years
- With court order: under 16 years

Blood test: not required
Waiting period for licence: 5 days
Licence fee: $106.50

Nunavut

Marriageable age:
- Without parental consent: 19 years
- At least 18 years of age

Blood test: not required
Waiting period for licence: none
Licence fee: $25

Ontario

Marriageable age:
- Without parental consent: 18 years
- With parental consent: 16 years

Blood test: not required
Waiting period after issuance of licence: none
Licence fee: $75-$100
Fee for solemnization of marriage by judge or justice of the peace: $75
Purchased marriage licence must be used within 3 months.

Prince Edward Island

Marriageable age:
- Without parental consent: 18 years
- With parental consent: under 18 years

Other requirements: birth certificates and Social Insurance Numbers; in the case of a widow or widower, death certificate; in the case of a divorced person, certified copy of the Decree Absolute or Certificate of Divorce

Waiting period for licence: none
Licence fee: $100

Québec

Marriageable age:

- Minimum age: 16 years (ref.: art. 373, Code Civil du Québec)
- Moreover, a minor (under 18 years of age) must have the authorization of his or her parent(s) or tutor to get married.

Blood test: not required
Waiting period for licence: none
Fee for civil marriage: $186.89 (taxes included)

Saskatchewan

Marriageable age:

- Without parental consent: 18 years
- With parental consent: 16 to 18 years
- With parental and court consent: under 16 years

Blood test: not required
Licence fee: $50

Yukon Territory

Marriageable age:

- Without parental consent: 19 years (In the case of an 18 year old person who has lived apart from his parents/guardians for at least 6 months & received no financial aid from them during that time, no consent is needed.)

A certificate of divorce or death must be produced if previously married
Blood test: not required
Waiting period for licence: none
Waiting period after issuance of licence: 24 hours
Licence fee: $20
Vital Statistics - Email: vital.statistics@gov.yk.ca; URL: www.hss.gov.yk.ca

Postal Information

Services and rates quoted are subject to change. For complete and up-to-date information you may: consult a local Canada Post retail outlet; call 1-800-267-1177, TTD 1-800-267-2797; or refer to the Canada Post website at www.canadapost.ca. For distribution services, call 1-888-550-6333, and for Postal Code information (fees apply) call 1-900-565-2633 (English) or 1-900-565- 2634 (French).

Communications Services

LETTERMAIL RATES FOR DELIVERY IN CANADA

Includes letters, postcards, greeting cards and business correspondence.

Standard Lettermail:

Up to 30 g	$0.59
Over 30 g to 50 g	$1.03

Other Lettermail Incl. Non-Standard & Oversize:

Up to 100 g	$1.25
Over 100 g to 200 g	$2.06
Over 200 g to 300 g	$2.85
Over 300 g to 400 g	$3.25
Over 400 g to 500 g	$3.50

For cards and postcards, the maximum dimensions are 23.5 cm (length) x 12 cm (width). Oversize Letter Rates apply to all letters with any dimension greater than 24.5 cm (length) x 15 cm (width) x .5 mm (thickness), but not greater than 38 cm (length) x 27 cm (width) x 2 cm (thickness). Maximum weight for Standard Lettermail and Other Lettermail is 500g. Items with any dimension exceeding the maximum dimension for Oversize Lettermail or exceeding 500g must be paid at parcel rates. Incentive Rates are available under sales agreements for customers whose mailing meets volume, frequency and mail preparation requirements. For details, please contact a Canada Post Corp. representative. Canada Post is committed to consistently deliver properly prepared lettermail as follows: two business days within the same metropolitan area/community; three business days within the same province; four business days between provinces.

Distribution Services

PRIORITY NEXT AM™

Priority Next AM is an overnight domestic courier service providing next business day noon delivery of your items for local and regional destinations and next business day noon to three day delivery nationally between major Canadian centres. This service comes with an on-time delivery guarantee, an acceptance scan, delivery confirmation, free insurance up to $100 and a no-charge signature-on-delivery option. Prepaid envelopes are available in two sizes and prepaid labels are available to business customers in 4 weight increments. For item delivery status or product information, customers can call 1-888-550-6333 or visit the website at www.canadapost.ca.

XPRESSPOST™

XPRESSPOST is an affordable, simple to use delivery service for packages and documents which provides an on-time service guarantee and confirmation of delivery. Positioned right in the middle between Priority Next AM and Regular Post in terms of price, service and features, XPRESSPOST offers next business day locally and regionally, and 2 days national between most major urban centres. Customers can verify delivery of their items or obtain product information by calling 1- 888-550-6333, or by accessing the Internet.

EXPEDITED PARCEL™

Expedited Parcel is the fastest ground service providing next business day local, 1-3 business day regional and 2-7 business day national delivery and a no-charge delivery confirmation/guarantee option. A full range of prepaid labels are also available to business customers.

REGULAR PARCEL™

Regular Parcel is the most economical, domestic, ground parcel service. Service is 3 business days local, 4-6 business days regional and 5-10 business days national between most major urban centres.

ADVICE OF RECEIPT (USA/INTERNATIONAL ONLY)

The Advice of Receipt (AR) service provides mailers with the actual signature of the addressee. An Advice of Receipt card is purchased at the time of mailing. The addressee's signature is obtained on the AR card and returned to the sender, thus providing the mailer with a Delivery Confirmation.

To international and USA destinations, AR can be used only with Registered Mail and only at the time of mailing, for a fee of $1.75.

AIR STAGE SERVICE (LESS THAN 5 ITEMS)

Canada Post services many communities where the only access to the community is by air. These communities are called Air Stage Offices.

The casual mailer who sends the occasional letter and parcel to these isolated communities pays the normal rate outlined in the various rate charts for Lettermail, Parcel Post, XPRESSPOST & Priority Next AM.

Any customer (individual or business) who ships more than 5 parcels or more than 20 kg of parcels on any day or more than 20 parcels or more than 80 kg of parcels in any month is considered an Air Stage Service Shipper and must pay Air Stage Freight Service rates. These shippers must also sign an agreement with CPC in order to use this service. An infrequent mailer who meets the volume or weight criteria can use the Air Stage Freight Service rates providing the goods shipped are not for resale. There are various rate levels based on the type of goods shipped.

Air Stage Freight Service rates apply whether the mailer is a business or an individual. Appropriate Regular Post zoned parcel rates apply for all other shippers, and appropriate Priority Next AM or Xpresspost Rates apply.

CANADIAN FORCES MAIL SERVICE

Canadian Forces Mail is mail sent to or by Canadian Forces personnel, their dependents and the civilians attached to the Canadian Forces served through the Canadian Forces Post Office (CFPO) or the Fleet Mail Office (FMO).

The rate charged for domestic mail is applicable for mail sent to Canadian Forces personnel providing it is sent through a CFPO or an FMO.

All parcels must include an International Customs Declaration form (CP72) and are subject to customs inspection in the country of destination. Oversize parcels and parcels over 20 kg are not acceptable.

COLLECT ON DELIVERY (COD)

COD is a service for domestic mail for which an amount due to the sender, up to $1,000 where the amount to be collected is in cash and $25,000 where the amount to be collected is by cheque, is collected from the addressee before delivery and returned to the mailer. It is a service available to consumer and business mailers. COD is available for parcels only or items mailed at parcel rates. The amount collected from the addressee can include:

1. Amount representing the value of the item.
2. Service charge in the case of repairs.
3. Sales tax.
4. Postage.
5. COD fee & special service fees.

COD cannot be used to collect on items not ordered or requested by the addressee or to collect money owing on previous accounts. Insurance is available up to $5,000. Items sent COD must abide by Canada Post mail preparation requirements. The amount of the COD collected from the addressee will be forwarded to the sender by Postal Money Order when payment is made by cash or by cheque drawn up by the addressee payable to the sender.

PRIORITY™ WORLDWIDE

International shipping service to the USA and destinations around the world. International shipping by FedEx Express.

DEFICIENT POSTAGE FEE

Unpaid or shortpaid mail is mail for which the postage or fees have not been paid or have been partially paid. Lettermail and Parcelmail is returned to the sender for the collection of the postage.

When there is no return address on the item, the item is forwarded to the addressee for the collection of the postage plus an administrative charge. All postage due charges must be paid before delivery.

DO NOT FORWARD SERVICE

Do Not Forward is a service for Lettermail, mailed in Canada for delivery in Canada. Mail that cannot be delivered as addressed because the addressee has filed a Change Of Address Notification will be returned to the sender rather than being forwarded to the addressee.

FRANKED MAIL

Canada Post provides free mailing privileges to the following:

1. Governor General or Secretary to the Governor General;
2. Speaker or Clerk of the Senate or House of Commons;
3. Parliamentary Librarian or Associate Parliamentary Librarian;
4. Members of the Senate;
5. Members of the House of Commons.

In addition, anyone mailing an item to the above in Canada receives free postage. As a general rule, only Lettermail, Publications Mail and Addressed Admail are acceptable. Parcels and add-on services are not acceptable as part of this service. As long as the letters M.P. appear on the mailing, it can be sent free of postage.

COLLECTION OF THE GST

The Goods & Service Tax (GST) is a value added consumption tax instituted by the Federal Government. By law, businesses must charge 5% on most goods and services provided.

Most postal services and products are subject to the GST, such as stamps, Advance Purchase Products, all add-on options (e.g., Insurance, Trace Mail, COD), optional Postal Box rentals, and postage meter fill-ups.

There are certain items sold by Canada Post that are not taxable such as Postal Money Orders, the fee on a Money Order and the exchange on a Money Order. Provincial governments are exempt from paying the GST.

Mail addressed to foreign destinations requiring total shipping charges of $5 or more (single item or a cumulative purchase) and products ordered from and shipped directly by Canada Post to a foreign destination, such as Philatelic and Retail products, are not subject to the GST. The 5% tax is calculated on the total taxable purchased and rounded up or down to the nearest cent.

HOLD MAIL

Many Canadians wish to have their mail held because they are going on an extended holiday or will be away from their home or their business for a period of time. Customers must complete a "Hold Mail" form which can be obtained from a postal outlet, or online. The completed card, which indicates the period of time that the mail should be held, is sent to the customer's normal delivery office to inform the postal employees to hold the mail. The held mail will be delivered on the "resume service" date indicated on the card.

HUNTING PERMITS

Prior to hunting season, hunting permits can be purchased from a postal outlet. The rules, regulations and fees pertaining to these permits are provided to the outlets by the Provincial and Federal bodies responsible for these permits. Unsold permits can be returned by the postal outlet to the depot from where they were originally ordered at the end of the hunting season for a refund.

INSURANCE

Insurance is available from Canada Post to provide compensation for the loss or damage of mailable items if the require-

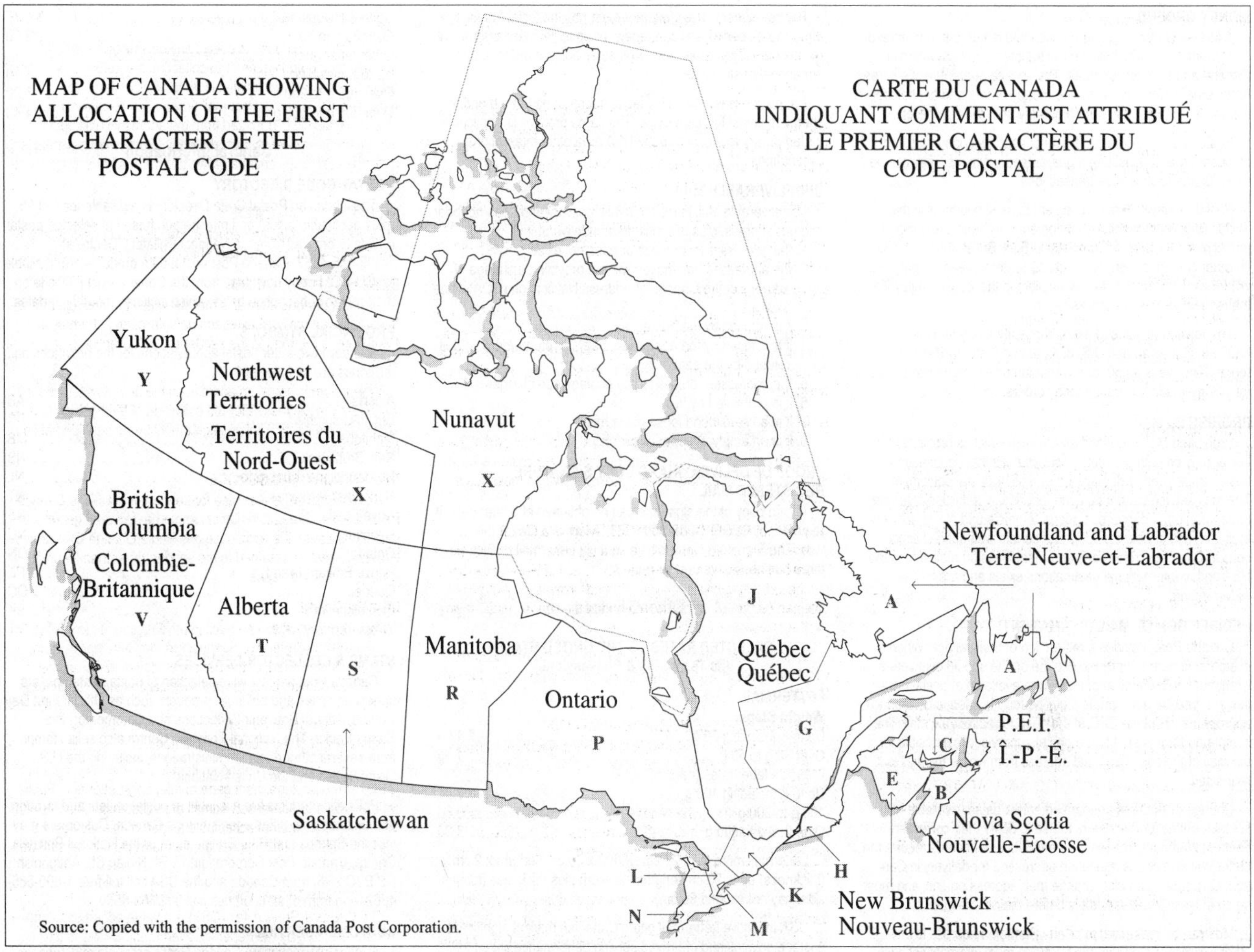

Source: Copied with the permission of Canada Post Corporation.

ments are met. Coverage for up to $100 is included for Registered Mail services; however, Canada Post shall have no liability for loss or damage of Registered Mail items containing:

1. Bank notes, travellers' cheques & coins;
2. Stocks, bonds, coupons, & other securities negotiable by bearer;
3. Lottery tickets;
4. Jewellery;
5. Manufactured & non-manufactured precious metals, precious stones, gold bullion & gold dust;
6. Canceled or uncanceled postage stamps.

Additional coverage is available, for a fee, for domestic Registered Mail items up to $5,000.

To USA destinations, coverage for up to $100 is included for Registered Mail services, with the same exceptions as above. Additional coverage is available for USA Registered Mail up to $1000.

KEY SERVICE™

Hotel, motel and automobile keys can be mailed without postage at any postal outlet in Canada for delivery in Canada if the keys have a tag clearly showing the complete address of the addressee. They can also be dropped in a street letter box.

LIBRARY BOOKS

Available to Public Libraries, University Libraries, and Libraries maintained by non-profit organizations for use by the general public in Canada to mail library books to their Canadian patrons. This service is for books only (not CDs, DVDs or other recordings). The library completes an "Application for Mail Privileges" form and be authorized by Canada Post to use this service. The maximum weight per shipment is 5 kg.

The maximum weight for sewn or bound books is 5 kg and 3 kg for books that are not sewn or bound. The rates are based on a per item cost plus weight and destination. Postage paid by the library at the time of mailing covers both the outgoing and the return postage.

LITERATURE FOR THE BLIND

Literature for the Blind is a service available free of charge from Canada Post allowing blind persons and recognized institutions for the blind to mail free of postage specific items used by blind persons.

Admissible items in Canada include items impressed in Braille or similar raised type, plates for printing literature for the blind, tapes and records posted by the blind in Canada for delivery in Canada and recording tapes, records and special writing paper intended solely for the use of the blind-when mailed by or addressed to a recognized institution for the blind.

The maximum weight in Canada is 7 kg. Add on services such as Registered (500 g), and Advice of Receipt (USA/International only), which should be endorsed "Braille Free" can be applied to Literature for the Blind at no charge.

This service is available to the USA and to international destinations at no charge. There is a charge for Literature for the Blind mailed to international destinations using Air mail service. Although the objective of the service is the same for Canada, the USA, and international destinations, some minor variations exist in the rules and conditions.

MAILING LISTS

Some Canadians may object to receiving Addressed Admail and would like their name removed from all mailing lists. Canadians are advised to contact the sender of the Admail to request that his or her name be removed from their mailing list.

If any recipient of this type of mail wishes to have all Addressed Admail stopped, the customer should write to the following addresses asking them to have their members delete his or her name from their mailing lists.

In Canada:
Canadian Direct Marketing Association
Do Not Mail Service
#607, 1 Concorde Gate, Don Mills ON M3C 3N6
416/391-2362; Fax: 416/441-4062

In the United States:
Direct Marketing Association
Mail Preference Service
PO Box 9008, Farmingdale NY 11735-9008, USA.
212/768-7277

PHILATELIC PRODUCTS

Canada Post offers stamp collectors, ranging from the person with a passing interest in stamps to a very serious collector, a complete range of philatelic products. Stamp collectors are concerned with product quality. It is for this reason that we have set up philatelic centres within specific postal outlets across the country. It is from these centres that the philatelist can more easily obtain the product and information required. There is also a National Philatelic Centre in Antigonish, Nova Scotia, from which any collector can get access to information and products by mail or by telephone.

POSTAL BOXES/CONTAINERS/BAG SERVICE/GENERAL DELIVERY

A postal box is a numbered compartment in a post office that is kept locked, and to which the boxholder and postal employee have access.

The container/bag service is a service whereby containers or bags are assigned to a customer for the delivery of mail, either because postal boxes are not available or because the size of the postal boxes cannot accommodate the volume of mail addressed to this particular customer.

The General Delivery service at post offices is offered to the travelling public, customers with no fixed address within the letter carrier delivery area, or to anyone who cannot receive their mail from the normal delivery modes.

MONEY ORDERS

A Money Order is a secured cashable document, guaranteed by Canada Post, which is used to transfer funds anywhere in Canada and to most countries. The service guarantee offers free replacement of lost or destroyed money orders and/or photocopies of paid money orders upon enquiry from the purchaser.

Postal money orders can be purchased by consumers and businesses, and constitute a guaranteed payment. They can be used for financial or retail transactions.

Postal money orders can be sent to most countries in the world. To several countries, customers may send Canadian postal money orders in Canadian, U.S. or British funds directly. To other countries there is an advice system, meaning that CPC will forward the amount to the recipient in the local currency via the respective Postal Administration.

The maximum value of a single postal money order is $999.99 (Canadian and U.S. dollars) and £100. (British currency). The fee is $5.50 for a Canadian postal money order. and for US/International postal money orders.

PROHIBITED MAIL

Prohibited Mail is defined as any mail which is prohibited by law or may contain products or substances that could harm postal employees or damage other mail or postal equipment. The mail service cannot be used for criminal activities or for the transportation of dangerous goods. Animals and plants are generally not acceptable except under certain well-defined conditions in Canada. Prohibitions and restrictions on mail sent to the USA and to international destinations exists and are wide-ranging.

REDIRECTION OF MAIL (PERMANENT)

Canada Post provides a redirection of mail service. When a customer is permanently moving, he or she should complete a "Request for Redirection of Mail" form available at postal facilities and pay the appropriate fee. The form is used to advise the appropriate people at CPC of the need to redirect the mail. The completed form is sent to the postal supervisor responsible for the mail at the customer's old address from where the mail is redirected.

Change of Address announcement cards are available at postal facilities for customers to use to notify their correspondents of their new address. The announcement cards require the Lettermail rate of postage when addressed for delivery in Canada. Customers can also change their address on-line, and must do so at least 3 business days before their move date.

Mail can be redirected from any Canadian address to any other address in Canada, the USA and most international destinations. The service is available for a six-month period. The service can be extended, providing the extension is requested before the expiry date of the service. There are no limitations on the additional periods of extension, although the extension price will be the current price at the time the application is filed.

Redirection of mail to the USA and to international destinations is also available for six-month renewable periods for both consumers and businesses.

REDIRECTION OF MAIL (TEMPORARY)

Temporary redirection of mail is also available from a Canadian address to another address in Canada, the USA and international destinations. The customer must complete a "Request for Temporary Redirection of Mail" card and pay the required fee. The card is sent by the postal authorities to the postal supervisor responsible for the mail at the customer's old address.

For consumers: The customer must pay the initial fee for a three-month period and can renew for up to six months for a monthly fee. The same process is applicable for the U.S. and international destinations.

For businesses: The initial fee is not required but a monthly charge is levied for the service. The same process is applicable for temporary redirection to the USA or to other international destinations.

UNDELIVERABLE MAIL

Undeliverable Mail is mail that fails delivery and does not bear a return address. Mail is considered undeliverable if:

1. the address is incomplete or does not exist
2. the addressee has moved without providing a change of address or the Change of Address Notification (COAN) has expired
3. it is refused by the addressee
4. it is refused by the addressee, bears a return address, & is refused by the sender
5. the addressee refuses to pay postage due charges
6. it is prohibited by law
7. it is an item found loose in the mail
8. it is an empty wrapper or carton.

PROOF OF DELIVERY/HARD COPY SIGNATURE - REGISTERED MAIL

A hard copy of the signature can be obtained at a later date, if required, by calling 1-888-550-6333. There is a fee for this service. The Signature Copy will be sent via Lettermail or Fax within three business days of your request.

Other Services

SELECTED RATES TO THE UNITED STATES (its Territories & Possessions):

LETTERMAIL

Weight Steps:

Up to & including 30 g	$ 1.03
Over 30 g to 50 g	1.25
Oversize letter rates (max. 500g)	
Up to & including 100 g	2.06
100 g to 200 g	3.60
Over 200 g to 500 g	7.20

Lettermail more than 27 cm (width) x 38 cm (length) x 2 cm (thickness) up to 90 cm length plus width plus thickness (longest side may not exceed 60 cm).

USA Incentive Lettermail offers Canadian mailers significant postage savings and improved service performance linked to volume, and quality of mail preparation. For various USA Incentive Lettermail rates, please inquire at a postal outlet.

XPRESSPOST™ - USA

Xpresspost service is now available to the USA providing 3-5 days service for documents and packages to major centres.

REGISTERED MAIL

Available for airmail lettermail items. Fees to the USA- $13.95 plus the applicable postage.

SELECTED INTERNATIONAL RATES

All countries except the USA, its Territories and Possessions, Canadian Forces post offices and Fleet Mail Offices.

LETTERMAIL

Weight Steps	Air Mail
Up to & including 30 g	$ 1.75
Over 30 g to 50 g	2.50
Other letter rates, including Oversize (max. 500g)	
Up to & including 100g	4.10
Over 100 g to 200 g	7.20
Over 200 g to 500 g	14.40

General Information

POSTAL CODE DIRECTORY

The Canadian Postal Code Directory is available for $49.95 (plus applicable taxes) and may be purchased at selected postal outlets or ordered from the National Philatelic Centre at 1-800-565-4362. Canada Post postal data products are available on CD-ROM or by download from the Canada Post FTP site on a 12-month subscription basis, which includes monthly updates.

PROVINCIAL SYMBOLS

Standard two-letter postal abbreviations for the provinces and territories are as follows:

Alberta	AB
British Columbia	BC
Manitoba	MB
New Brunswick	NB
Newfoundland & Labrador	NL
Northwest Territories	NT
Nova Scotia	NS
Nunavut	NU
Ontario	ON
Prince Edward Island	PE
Québec	QC
Saskatchewan	SK
Yukon Territory	YT

STAMP & COLLECTOR SERVICES

Canada Post offers a wide selection of postage stamps, stationery, supplies and philatelic products such as Official First Day Covers, Annual Souvenir Collections and Commemorative Stamp Packs. The National Philatelic Centre also sells stamps from several other postal administrations, including the U.S., Great Britain and the United Nations.

Philatelic products are available at postal outlets and through authorized stamp sales agents across Canada. Customers may visit the Stamps and Gifts On-line store or the National Philatelic Centre, Canada Post Corporation, 75 St. Ninian St., Antigonish NS B2G 2R8; from Canada and the USA call toll-free 1-800-565-4362, and from other countries call 902/863-6550.

CUSTOMER SERVICE

Further information on Canada Post's products and services can be obtained through your local postal outlets, postal directory, your local customer service representative, or by calling one of the following numbers:

Toll Free (Canada)	1-800-267-1177
(8 a.m. to 6 p.m. local time)	
Outside of Canada	416/979-8822
Hearing Impaired with TTY-Teletyping	1-800-267-2797

Customers may also contact Canada Post via the Internet: www.canadapost.ca or mail: Canada Post Corporation, 2701 Riverside Dr., Ottawa ON K1A 0B1.

Vital Statistics

CANADIAN POPULATION AND PERCENTAGE DISTRIBUTION
PROVINCES AND TERRITORIES, 1971-2006 (CENSUS)

	1971 %	1981 %	1991 %	2001 %	2006 %
Newfoundland & Labrador	522,104	567,681	568,474	512,930	505,469
	2.42	2.33	2.08	1.71	1.60
Prince Edward Island	111,641	122,506	129,765	135,294	135,851
	0.52	0.50	0.46	0.45	0.43
Nova Scotia	788,960	847,442	899,942	908,007	913,462
	3.66	3.48	3.30	3.03	2.89
New Brunswick	634,557	696,403	723,900	729,498	729,997
	2.94	2.86	2.65	2.43	2.31
Québec	6,027,764	6,438,403	6,895,963	7,237,479	7,546,131
	28.00	26.40	25.30	24.10	23.87
Ontario	7,703,106	8,625,107	10,084,885	11,410,046	12,610,282
	35.70	35.40	36.90	38.00	38.47
Manitoba	988,247	1,026,241	1,091,942	1,119,583	1,148,401
	4.58	4.21	4.00	3.73	3.63
Saskatchewan	926,242	968,313	988,928	978,933	968,157
	4.29	3.97	3.62	3.26	3.06
Alberta	1,627,874	2,237,724	2,545,553	2,974,807	3,290,350
	7.55	9.19	9.33	9.91	10.41
British Columbia	2,184,621	2,744,467	3,282,061	3,907,738	4,113,487
	10.10	11.30	12.00	13.00	13.01
Yukon	18,388	23,153	27,797	28,674	30,372
	0.09	0.09	0.10	0.10	0.10
Northwest Territories	34,807	45,741	57,649	37,360	41,464
	0.16	0.18	0.21	0.13	0.13
Nunavut	-	-	-	26,745	29,474
	-	-	-	0.09	0.09
Totals	21,568,311	24,343,181	27,296,859	30,007,094	31,612,897
	100.00	100.00	100.00	100.00	100.00
Rural	5,157,525	5,907,254	6,389,724	6,098,883	6,262,154
	23.90	24.30	23.40	20.30	19.81
Urban	16,410,785	18,435,927	20,907,135	23,908,211	25,350,743
	76.10	75.70	76.60	79.70	80.19

Source: Adapted from the Statistics Canada publications *A National Overview: Population and Dwelling Counts, 2001 Census* Catalogue 93-360-XPB and *A National Overview: Population and Dwelling Counts, 2006 Census,* Catalogue 92-200-XPB.

POPULATION OF CANADA, PROVINCES AND TERRITORIES, BY AGE GROUPS
2006 CENSUS OF POPULATION

Age groups	Total	< 5 years	5 to 9	10 to 14	15 to 24	25 to 34	35 to 44	45 to 54	55 to 64	65 to 74	75 to 84	85 +
Canada	31,612,895	1,690,540	1,809,370	2,079,925	4,220,875	4,005,805	4,818,730	4,977,905	3,674,490	2,288,360	1,526,280	520,605
Newfoundland and Labrador	505,465	22,860	25,905	29,460	65,295	58,370	78,200	85,575	69,540	39,685	22,930	7,645
Prince Edward Island	135,850	6,690	7,920	9,375	18,530	15,205	19,435	21,070	17,440	10,810	6,685	2,690
Nova Scotia	913,460	42,040	48,145	56,245	118,210	105,235	136,660	148,910	119,805	73,300	46,310	18,610
New Brunswick	729,995	34,430	38,875	44,945	92,330	87,495	109,445	120,070	94,760	56,845	36,685	14,105
Quebec	7,546,130	375,270	398,980	478,255	947,175	960,190	1,121,420	1,232,120	952,425	583,710	377,300	119,285
Ontario	12,160,285	670,770	721,590	818,440	1,630,370	1,535,645	1,916,400	1,861,370	1,356,510	868,190	589,180	191,810
Manitoba	1,148,400	68,100	73,835	83,235	161,575	140,970	161,740	171,570	125,480	78,930	59,045	23,910
Saskatchewan	968,155	57,495	61,070	69,135	142,145	113,180	127,875	146,015	101,935	70,885	54,595	23,820
Alberta	3,290,350	202,600	204,110	224,810	489,285	474,830	506,135	512,205	322,970	189,330	121,795	42,295
British Columbia	4,113,485	201,880	220,700	257,020	539,465	499,855	625,480	664,255	505,010	313,400	210,365	76,050
Yukon Territory	30,370	1,740	1,830	2,145	4,160	3,785	4,960	5,820	3,635	1,475	635	180
Northwest Territories	41,460	3,220	3,095	3,605	6,725	6,445	6,905	6,150	3,345	1,235	580	165
Nunavut	29,475	3,430	3,315	3,260	5,615	4,590	4,070	2,760	1,630	580	180	45

Source: Adapted from the Statistics Canada publication *Age and Sex - 2006 Census,* Catalogue 97-551-X, Issue 2006005.

POPULATION OF CANADA, PROVINCES AND TERRITORIES, BY SEX

2006 CENSUS OF POPULATION

	Total	Male	Female
Canada	31,612,895	15,475,970	16,136,930
Newfoundland and Labrador	505,465	245,730	259,735
Prince Edward Island	135,850	65,595	70,255
Nova Scotia	913,460	439,830	473,630
New Brunswick	729,995	355,500	374,495
Quebec	7,546,130	3,687,695	3,858,435
Ontario	12,160,285	5,930,705	6,229,580
Manitoba	1,148,400	563,275	585,125
Saskatchewan	968,155	475,235	492,920
Alberta	3,290,350	1,646,795	1,643,550
British Columbia	4,113,485	2,013,985	2,099,500
Yukon Territory	30,370	15,280	15,090
Northwest Territories	41,460	21,225	20,235
Nunavut	29,475	15,110	14,365

Source: Adapted from the Statistics Canada publication *Age and Sex - 2006 Census,* Catalogue 97-551-X, Issue 2006005.

POPULATION OF CENSUS METROPOLITAN AREAS

1996 - 2006

	1996	2001	2006
Abbotsford, BC	136,48	147,370	159,020
Calgary, AB	821,628	951,395	1,079,310
Saguenay[1], PQ	160,454	154,938	151,643
Edmonton, AB	862,597	937,845	1,034,945
Greater Sudbury, ON	165,618[A]	155,601	158,258
Halifax, NS	342,966[A]	359,183	372,858
Hamilton, ON	624,360	662,401	692,911
Kingston, ON	144,528	146,838	152,358
Kitchener, ON	382,940[A]	414,284	451,235
London, ON	416,546[A]	432,451	457,720
Montréal, PQ*	3,326,447[A]	3,426,350	3,635,571
Oshawa, ON	268,773	296,298	330,594
Ottawa-Gatineau[2], ON, PQ	998,718[A]	1,063,664	1,130,761
Ontario (part)	751,646[A]	806,096	846,802
Québec (part)	247,072	257,568	283,959
Québec, PQ	671,889	682,757	715,515
Regina, SK	193,652	192,800	194,971
St John, NB	125,705	122,678	122,389
Saskatoon, SK	219,056	225,927	233,923
Sherbrooke, PQ	149,569[A]	153,811	186,952
St Catharines-Niagara, ON	372,406	377,009	390,317
St John's, NF	174,051	172,918	181,113
Thunder Bay, ON	126,643[A]	121,986	122,907
Toronto, ON	4,263,759[A]	4,682,897	5,113,149
Trois-Rivières, PQ	139,956	137,507	141,529
Vancouver, BC	1,831,665	1,986,965	2,116,581
Victoria, BC*	304,287	311,902	330,088
Windsor, ON	286,811[A]	307,877	323,342
Winnipeg, MB	667,093[A]	671,274	694,668
New 2006 Census CMAs:			
Barrie, ON	-	148,480	177,061
Brantford, ON	-	118,086	124,607
Guelph, ON	-	117,344	127,009
Kelowna, BC	-	147,739	162,276
Moncton, NB	-	118,678	126,424
Peterborough, ON	-	110,876	116,570

* Excludes census data for one or more incompletely enumerated Indian reserves or Indian settlements

[A] Adjusted figure due to boundary change

[1] Formerly Chicoutimi-Jonquière

[2] Formerly Ottawa-Hull

Source: Adapted from the Statistics Canada publications *A National Overview: Population and Dwelling Counts, 2001 Census* Catalogue 93-360-XPB and *A National Overview: Population and Dwelling Counts, 2006 Census* Catalogue 92-200-XPB.

Estimates of Population by Age & Sex for Canda, 1996 - 2010

	1996	1997	1998	1999	2000	2001	2002	2003	2004	2005	2006	2007	2008	2009	2010
Both Sexes															
All ages	29,610,218	29,905,948	30,155,173	30,401,286	30,685,730	31,019,020	31,353,656	31,639,670	31,940,676	32,245,209	32,576,074	32,929,733	33,315,976	33,720,184	34,108,752
0 to 14 years	5,985,792	5,977,731	5,958,400	5,918,977	5,883,508	5,854,321	5,829,983	5,795,726	5,754,660	5,698,605	5,651,798	5,619,684	5,608,141	5,610,101	5,616,670
0 to 17 years	7,198,564	7,202,273	7,189,688	7,157,153	7,137,692	7,121,079	7,095,985	7,053,939	7,023,932	7,005,983	6,996,462	6,970,481	6,941,983	6,922,221	6,912,198
15 to 64 years	20,045,149	20,273,661	20,472,300	20,696,249	20,950,263	21,242,401	21,532,363	21,779,619	22,044,570	22,326,765	22,599,461	22,877,927	23,152,366	23,424,059	23,672,481
18 years and over	22,411,654	22,703,675	22,965,485	23,244,133	23,548,038	23,897,941	24,257,671	24,585,731	24,916,744	25,239,226	25,579,612	25,959,252	26,373,993	26,797,963	27,196,554
18 to 64 years	18,832,377	19,049,119	19,241,012	19,458,073	19,696,079	19,975,643	20,266,361	20,521,406	20,775,298	21,019,387	21,254,797	21,527,130	21,818,524	22,111,939	22,376,953
18 to 24 years	2,798,097	2,810,699	2,834,012	2,875,149	2,909,950	2,956,778	2,999,724	3,044,806	3,081,998	3,100,719	3,118,696	3,159,018	3,209,584	3,259,591	3,296,159
25 to 44 years	9,713,951	9,729,837	9,697,095	9,650,065	9,616,676	9,605,618	9,581,708	9,525,469	9,479,900	9,438,961	9,393,924	9,379,069	9,374,604	9,386,438	9,411,643
45 to 64 years	6,320,329	6,508,583	6,709,905	6,932,859	7,169,453	7,413,247	7,684,929	7,951,131	8,213,400	8,479,707	8,742,177	8,989,043	9,234,336	9,465,910	9,669,151
65 years and over	3,579,277	3,654,556	3,724,473	3,786,060	3,851,959	3,922,298	3,991,310	4,064,325	4,141,446	4,219,839	4,324,815	4,432,122	4,555,469	4,686,024	4,819,601
Males															
All ages	14,650,326	14,806,491	14,925,201	15,048,761	15,193,958	15,365,609	15,533,158	15,675,460	15,825,754	15,979,800	16,147,873	16,324,732	16,519,001	16,723,138	16,917,282
0 to 14 years	3,068,454	3,065,381	3,054,035	3,032,746	3,012,946	2,997,037	2,985,215	2,968,334	2,947,720	2,919,903	2,898,453	2,883,579	2,878,510	2,880,211	2,883,892
0 to 17 years	3,691,878	3,694,527	3,686,460	3,669,084	3,658,463	3,649,014	3,636,266	3,614,557	3,599,729	3,592,181	3,589,283	3,575,395	3,560,261	3,550,499	3,546,792
15 to 64 years	10,068,025	10,189,782	10,285,595	10,400,140	10,532,534	10,684,572	10,829,898	10,952,582	11,084,776	11,226,895	11,363,110	11,499,753	11,636,154	11,772,217	11,895,354
18 years and over	10,958,448	11,111,964	11,238,741	11,379,677	11,535,495	11,716,595	11,896,892	12,060,903	12,226,025	12,387,619	12,558,590	12,749,337	12,958,740	13,172,639	13,370,490
18 to 64 years	9,444,601	9,560,636	9,653,170	9,763,802	9,887,017	10,032,595	10,178,847	10,306,359	10,432,767	10,554,617	10,672,280	10,807,937	10,954,403	11,101,929	11,232,454
18 to 24 years	1,427,462	1,437,061	1,450,030	1,472,328	1,490,651	1,514,524	1,535,879	1,559,934	1,579,333	1,588,650	1,599,104	1,621,320	1,648,176	1,674,697	1,691,915
25 to 44 years	4,877,603	4,890,769	4,872,381	4,852,544	4,841,436	4,843,176	4,833,847	4,805,459	4,781,919	4,759,831	4,734,782	4,724,560	4,720,045	4,724,162	4,735,532
45 to 64 years	3,139,536	3,232,806	3,330,759	3,438,930	3,554,930	3,674,895	3,809,121	3,940,966	4,071,515	4,206,136	4,338,394	4,462,057	4,586,182	4,703,070	4,805,007
65 years and over	1,513,847	1,551,328	1,585,571	1,615,875	1,648,478	1,684,000	1,718,045	1,754,544	1,793,258	1,833,002	1,886,310	1,941,400	2,004,337	2,070,710	2,138,036
Females															
All ages	14,959,892	15,099,457	15,229,972	15,352,525	15,491,772	15,653,411	15,820,498	15,964,210	16,114,922	16,265,409	16,428,201	16,605,001	16,796,975	16,997,046	17,191,470
0 to 14 years	2,917,338	2,912,350	2,904,365	2,886,231	2,870,562	2,857,284	2,844,768	2,827,392	2,806,940	2,778,702	2,753,345	2,736,105	2,729,631	2,729,890	2,732,778
0 to 17 years	3,506,686	3,507,746	3,503,228	3,488,069	3,479,229	3,472,065	3,459,719	3,439,382	3,424,203	3,413,802	3,407,179	3,395,086	3,381,722	3,371,722	3,365,406
15 to 64 years	9,977,124	10,083,879	10,186,705	10,296,109	10,417,729	10,557,829	10,702,465	10,827,037	10,959,794	11,099,870	11,236,351	11,378,174	11,516,212	11,651,842	11,777,127
18 years and over	11,453,206	11,591,711	11,726,744	11,864,456	12,012,543	12,181,346	12,360,779	12,524,828	12,690,719	12,851,607	13,021,022	13,209,915	13,415,253	13,625,324	13,826,064
18 to 64 years	9,387,776	9,488,483	9,587,842	9,694,271	9,809,062	9,943,048	10,087,514	10,215,047	10,342,531	10,464,770	10,582,517	10,719,193	10,864,121	11,010,010	11,144,499
18 to 24 years	1,370,635	1,373,638	1,383,982	1,402,821	1,419,299	1,442,254	1,463,845	1,484,872	1,502,665	1,512,069	1,519,592	1,537,698	1,561,408	1,584,894	1,604,244
25 to 44 years	4,836,348	4,839,068	4,824,714	4,797,521	4,775,240	4,762,442	4,747,861	4,720,010	4,697,981	4,679,130	4,659,142	4,654,509	4,654,559	4,662,276	4,676,111
45 to 64 years	3,180,793	3,275,777	3,379,146	3,493,929	3,614,523	3,738,352	3,875,808	4,010,165	4,141,885	4,273,571	4,403,783	4,526,986	4,648,154	4,762,840	4,864,144
65 years and over	2,065,430	2,103,228	2,138,902	2,170,185	2,203,481	2,238,298	2,273,265	2,309,781	2,348,188	2,386,837	2,438,505	2,490,722	2,551,132	2,615,314	2,681,565

Source: Adapted from Statistics Canada's CANSIM database http://www5.statcan.gc.ca/cansim/home-accueil?lang=eng, Table 051-0001, July 2011.

Population of Canada, Projections, 2010-2061
(in thousands)

Year	Projection Scenario								
	L: low-growth	M1: medium-growth, historical trends (1981 to 2008)	M2: medium-growth, 2006 to 2008 trends	M3: medium-growth, 1988 to 1996 trends	M4: medium-growth, 2001 to 2006 trends	H: high-growth	A1: replacement fertility	A2: zero immigration	A3: 1% immigration
2010	34,103.4	34,138.2	34,138.2	34,138.1	34,138.2	34,163.9	34,161.4	33,883.1	34,224.5
2011	34,454.5	34,532.2	34,532.4	34,532.0	34,532.4	34,594.6	34,596.3	34,016.8	34,711.9
2012	34,792.4	34,921.9	34,922.3	34,921.4	34,922.3	35,031.8	35,044.8	34,141.1	35,202.1
2013	35,086.3	35,317.5	35,318.1	35,316.8	35,318.2	35,527.5	35,518.4	34,255.6	35,695.0
2014	35,367.6	35,711.7	35,712.5	35,710.6	35,712.5	36,035.2	36,009.5	34,360.2	36,190.3
2015	35,643.2	36,103.9	36,105.0	36,102.4	36,105.1	36,545.2	36,500.4	34,454.6	36,687.7
2016	35,912.8	36,493.8	36,495.3	36,491.9	36,495.4	37,057.1	36,990.3	34,538.5	37,186.7
2017	36,176.1	36,881.0	36,882.8	36,878.6	36,882.9	37,570.6	37,478.8	34,611.8	37,686.9
2018	36,432.5	37,264.8	37,266.9	37,261.8	37,267.0	38,084.8	37,965.0	34,674.1	38,187.7
2019	36,681.7	37,644.6	37,647.2	37,641.1	37,647.3	38,599.2	38,448.4	34,725.0	38,688.5
2020	36,928.1	38,025.1	38,028.0	38,021.0	38,028.1	39,118.2	38,933.2	34,769.4	39,193.7
2021	37,171.2	38,405.5	38,408.9	38,400.9	38,409.0	39,641.2	39,418.8	34,806.8	39,702.9
2022	37,410.6	38,785.5	38,789.2	38,780.3	38,789.3	40,167.4	39,904.6	34,837.1	40,215.3
2023	37,645.6	39,164.3	39,168.4	39,158.5	39,168.4	40,696.3	40,389.8	34,859.7	40,730.5
2024	37,875.9	39,541.3	39,545.7	39,535.0	39,545.8	41,227.1	40,873.7	34,874.2	41,247.7
2025	38,100.7	39,915.9	39,920.7	39,909.1	39,920.7	41,759.4	41,355.9	34,880.3	41,766.5
2026	38,319.6	40,287.7	40,292.8	40,280.4	40,292.7	42,292.6	41,835.7	34,877.5	42,286.2
2027	38,532.3	40,656.2	40,661.5	40,648.4	40,661.5	42,826.5	42,313.2	34,865.6	42,806.5
2028	38,738.3	41,021.1	41,026.8	41,012.8	41,026.6	43,360.9	42,788.1	34,844.5	43,327.3
2029	38,937.5	41,382.4	41,388.3	41,373.6	41,388.1	43,895.8	43,260.9	34,814.0	43,848.3
2030	39,129.6	41,740.0	41,746.1	41,730.7	41,745.9	44,431.3	43,732.1	34,774.2	44,369.6
2031	39,314.5	42,093.9	42,100.3	42,084.1	42,100.0	44,968.0	44,202.3	34,725.2	44,891.3
2032	39,492.5	42,444.6	42,451.1	42,434.2	42,450.8	45,506.4	44,672.6	34,667.4	45,413.8
2033	39,664.0	42,792.2	42,799.0	42,781.3	42,798.6	46,046.6	45,144.0	34,601.1	45,937.5
2034	39,829.3	43,137.3	43,144.4	43,125.8	43,143.9	46,589.4	45,617.6	34,526.6	46,462.9
2035	39,988.7	43,480.4	43,487.6	43,468.2	43,487.1	47,135.7	46,094.6	34,444.5	46,990.6
2036	40,142.4	43,821.7	43,829.3	43,808.9	43,828.7	47,686.0	46,576.1	34,355.3	47,521.0
2037	40,290.8	44,162.0	44,169.8	44,148.4	44,169.2	48,241.2	47,063.2	34,259.2	48,054.6
2038	40,434.6	44,501.4	44,509.5	44,487.0	44,508.9	48,801.5	47,557.0	34,156.7	48,592.1
2039	40,573.9	44,840.5	44,848.9	44,825.3	44,848.3	49,367.6	48,058.6	34,048.2	49,133.8
2040	40,708.9	45,179.6	45,188.3	45,163.4	45,187.6	49,940.2	48,568.9	33,933.9	49,680.3
2041	40,839.8	45,518.8	45,527.9	45,501.7	45,527.2	50,519.6	49,088.5	33,814.1	50,231.7
2042	40,966.6	45,858.5	45,868.0	45,840.3	45,867.2	51,106.4	49,617.9	33,688.8	50,788.4
2043	41,089.4	46,198.7	46,208.6	46,179.5	46,207.9	51,700.8	50,157.3	33,558.3	51,350.7
2044	41,208.5	46,539.6	46,550.0	46,519.3	46,549.2	52,302.8	50,706.7	33,422.6	51,918.7
2045	41,324.2	46,881.3	46,892.1	46,859.8	46,891.3	52,912.5	51,265.8	33,282.0	52,492.7
2046	41,436.5	47,224.0	47,235.2	47,201.1	47,234.4	53,529.9	51,834.0	33,136.6	53,072.7
2047	41,546.0	47,567.5	47,579.3	47,543.4	47,578.5	54,154.9	52,411.1	32,986.5	53,659.0
2048	41,652.9	47,912.3	47,924.5	47,886.8	47,923.7	54,787.3	52,996.3	32,832.0	54,251.7
2049	41,757.8	48,258.3	48,271.1	48,231.4	48,270.2	55,427.2	53,589.3	32,673.5	54,851.0
2050	41,860.9	48,605.9	48,619.2	48,577.6	48,618.3	56,074.4	54,189.5	32,511.3	55,457.2
2051	41,962.9	48,955.2	48,969.1	48,925.4	48,968.2	56,729.1	54,796.8	32,345.8	56,070.5
2052	42,064.1	49,306.6	49,320.9	49,275.2	49,320.0	57,391.3	55,410.7	32,177.6	56,691.1
2053	42,164.9	49,660.2	49,675.1	49,627.3	49,674.2	58,061.2	56,031.3	32,007.0	57,319.5
2054	42,265.7	50,016.5	50,032.0	49,982.0	50,031.0	58,739.1	56,658.8	31,834.8	57,955.9
2055	42,367.1	50,375.9	50,391.9	50,339.8	50,390.9	59,425.5	57,293.6	31,661.6	58,600.9
2056	42,469.4	50,738.9	50,755.5	50,701.1	50,754.4	60,121.0	57,936.0	31,487.9	59,254.8
2057	42,572.9	51,105.8	51,122.9	51,066.3	51,121.8	60,826.1	58,586.8	31,314.5	59,918.1
2058	42,677.8	51,477.1	51,494.8	51,435.8	51,493.5	61,541.5	59,246.5	31,141.9	60,591.2
2059	42,784.4	51,853.2	51,871.4	51,810.1	51,870.1	62,267.8	59,915.9	30,970.7	61,274.5
2060	42,892.8	52,234.3	52,253.1	52,189.4	52,251.7	63,005.7	60,595.9	30,801.4	61,968.4
2061	43,003.1	52,620.8	52,640.2	52,573.9	52,638.6	63,755.9	61,287.2	30,634.5	62,673.2

Source: Adapted from Statistics Canada's CANSIM database http://www5.statcan.gc.ca/cansim/home-accueil?lang=eng, Table 052-0005, August 2010.

VITAL STATISTICS COMPARED WITH MACROREGIONS & REGIONS 1995-2000

MACRO REGIONS AND REGIONS	BIRTH RATE 0/000	DEATH RATE 0/000
World	**22**	**9**
Africa	**38**	**14**
Eastern Africa	42	18
Middle Africa	45	15
Northern Africa	28	7
Southern Africa	28	12
Western Africa	40	15
Northern America	**14**	**8**
Latin America	**23**	**6**
Caribbean	21	8
Central America	27	5
South America	22	7
Asia	**22**	**8**
Eastern Asia	16	7
South Central Asia	27	9
South Eastern Asia	23	7
Western Asia	30	7
Europe	**10**	**11**
Eastern Europe	10	13
Northern Europe	12	11
Southern Europe	10	10
Western Europe	11	10
Oceania	**18**	**8**
Australia and New Zealand	14	8
Melanesia	31	9
Micronesia	36	5
Polynesia	25	5

Source: United Nations Statistical Yearbook, 45th issue, Perm. No. 2011-278

BIRTHS & DEATHS, NUMBER AND RATES, 2008

Province	Live Births Number	Live Births Rate[2]	Deaths Number	Deaths Rate[2]	Infant Deaths[1] Number	Infant Deaths[1] Rate[3]
Newfoundland and Labrador	4,898	9.7	4,539	9.0	25	5.1
Prince Edward Island	1,483	10.6	1,201	8.6	3	2.0
Nova Scotia	9,188	9.8	8,220	8.8	32	3.5
New Brunswick	7,402	9.9	6,450	8.6	24	3.2
Quebec	87,870	11.3	57,106	7.4	379	4.3
Ontario	140,791	10.9	88,041	6.8	753	5.3
Manitoba	15,485	12.8	10,073	8.4	101	6.5
Saskatchewan	13,737	13.6	9,243	9.1	85	6.2
Alberta	50,856	14.2	21,079	5.9	317	6.2
British Columbia	44,276	10.1	32,095	7.3	166	3.7
Yukon	373	11.3	198	6.0	2	5.4
Northwest Territories	721	16.5	201	4.6	7	9.7
Nunavut	805	25.5	147	4.7	13	16.1
TOTALS	377,886	11.3	238,617	7.2	1,911	5.1

[1] Children under one year of age.
[2] Rate per 1,000 population.
[3] Rate per 1,000 live births.

Source: Adapted from Statistics Canada's CANSIM database http://www5.statcan.gc.ca/cansim/home-accueil?lang=eng, Tables 102-4502, 102-4505, 102-0504, 102-0507, September 2011.

DEATHS, CANADA, 2008

	Number of deaths Both sexes	Number of deaths Males	Number of deaths Females	Mortality rate* Both sexes	Mortality rate* Males	Mortality rate* Females
Canada	238,617	120,426	118,191	7.2	7.3	7.0
Newfoundland and Labrador	4,539	2,315	2,224	9.0	9.3	8.6
Prince Edward Island	1,201	603	598	8.6	8.9	8.4
Nova Scotia	8,220	4,093	4,127	8.8	9.0	8.6
New Brunswick	6,450	3,256	3,194	8.6	8.9	8.4
Quebec	57,106	28,430	28,676	7.4	7.4	7.3
Ontario	88,041	44,153	43,888	6.8	6.9	6.7
Manitoba	10,073	5,050	5,023	8.4	8.4	8.3
Saskatchewan	9,243	4,747	4,496	9.1	9.4	8.8
Alberta	21,079	11,000	10,079	5.9	6.0	5.7
British Columbia	32,095	16,420	15,675	7.3	7.6	7.1
Yukon Territory	198	120	78	6.0	7.1	4.8
Northwest Territories	201	127	74	4.6	5.6	3.5
Nunavut	147	92	55	4.7	5.6	3.6

*per 1,000 population

Source: Adapted from Statistics Canada's CANSIM database http://www5.statcan.gc.ca/cansim/home-accueil?lang=eng, Table 102-0504, September 2011.

LEADING CAUSES OF DEATH, CANADA, 2007

MALES	Number of Deaths	Mortality Rate[1]	FEMALES	Number of Deaths	Mortality Rate[1]
Malignant neoplasms	36,569	224.0	Major cardiovascular diseases	34,995	210.8
Major cardiovascular diseases	34,508	211.4	Malignant neoplasms	33,026	198.9
All other diseases (residual)	10,672	65.4	All other diseases (residual)	15,306	92.2
Accidents (unintentional injuries)	6,015	36.8	Chronic lower respiratory diseases	5,087	30.6
Chronic lower respiratory diseases	5,572	34.1	Alzheimer's disease	4,164	25.1
Diabetes mellitus	3,906	23.9	Accidents (unintentional injuries)	3,936	23.7
Intentional self-harm (suicide)	2,727	16.7	Diabetes mellitus	3,488	21.0
Influenza and pneumonia	2,438	14.9	Influenza and pneumonia	3,014	18.2
Nephritis, nephrotic syndrome and nephrosis	1,877	11.5	Nephritis, nephrotic syndrome and nephrosis	1,926	11.6
Chronic liver disease and cirrhosis	1,756	10.8	Other diseases of respiratory system	1,184	7.1
Alzheimer's disease	1,739	10.7	Septicaemia	1,008	6.1
Other diseases of respiratory system	1,419	8.7	Chronic liver disease and cirrhosis	895	5.4
Parkinson's disease	1,073	6.6	Intentional self-harm (suicide)	884	5.3
Pneumonitis due to solids and liquids	839	5.1	Parkinson's disease	817	4.9
Total, all causes of death	118,681	726.9	Total, all causes of death	116,536	702.0

[1] per 100,000 population

Source: Adapted from Statistics Canada's CANSIM database http://www5.statcan.gc.ca/cansim/home-accueil?lang=eng, Table 102-0551, August 2011.

IMMIGRANTS TO CANADA, BY CLASS, 1992 - 2010

Year	Economic	Family	Refugees	Others [1]	Total
1992	95,796	101,112	52,345	5,544	254,797
1993	105,653	112,647	30,600	7,751	256,651
1994	102,309	94,193	20,435	7,455	224,392
1995	106,626	77,386	28,093	761	212,866
1996	125,370	68,359	28,478	3,866	226,073
1997	128,350	59,979	24,308	3,400	216,037
1998	97,912	50,896	22,843	2,547	174,198
1999	109,249	55,274	24,397	1,031	189,951
2000	136,287	60,616	30,092	460	227,455
2001	155,718	66,795	27,919	207	250,639
2002	137,863	62,292	25,114	3,780	229,049
2003	121,047	65,120	25,983	9,199	221,349
2004	133,748	62,269	32,687	7,121	235,825
2005	156,312	63,367	35,776	6,786	262,241
2006	138,251	70,517	32,499	10,375	251,642
2007	131,245	66,242	27,954	11,313	236,754
2008	149,071	65,580	21,860	10,736	247,247
2009	153,492	65,206	22,846	10,628	252,172
2010 [2]	186,881	60,207	24,693	8,848	280,636
		%			
1992	37.6	39.7	20.5	2.2	100.0
1993	41.2	43.9	11.9	3.0	100.0
1994	45.6	42.0	9.1	3.3	100.0
1995	50.1	36.4	13.2	0.4	100.0
1996	55.5	30.2	12.6	1.7	100.0
1997	59.4	27.8	11.3	1.6	100.0
1998	56.2	29.2	13.1	1.5	100.0
1999	57.5	29.1	12.8	0.5	100.0
2000	59.9	26.6	13.2	0.2	100.0
2001	62.1	26.6	11.1	0.1	100.0
2002	60.2	27.2	11.0	1.7	100.0
2003	54.7	29.4	11.7	4.2	100.0
2004	56.7	26.4	13.9	3.0	100.0
2005	59.6	24.2	13.6	2.6	100.0
2006	54.9	28.0	12.9	4.1	100.0
2007	55.4	28.0	11.8	4.8	100.0
2008	60.3	26.5	8.8	4.3	100.0
2009	60.9	25.9	9.1	4.2	100.0
2010 [2]	66.6	21.5	8.8	3.2	100.0

[1] Includes defered removal order class, post determination refugee claimant class, temporary resident permit holders and humanitarian and compassionate/public policy cases.
[2] Observed data are preliminary

Source: Adapted from the Statistics Canada publication *Report on the demographic situation in Canada,* Catalogue 91-209-X, Issue 2011001, http://www.statcan.gc.ca/bsolc/olc-cel/olc-cel?catno=91-209-XWE&lang=eng

MOTHER TONGUE[1]
2006 CENSUS (TOP 25)

Language	Total Responses
English	18,232,200
French	6,970,405
Italian	476,905
Chinese, n.o.s.	467,235
German	466,655
Panjabi (Punjabi)	382,585
Cantonese	369,645
Spanish	362,120
Arabic	286,790
Tagalog (Pilipino, Filipino)	266,445
Portuguese	229,280
Polish	217,605
Mandarin	173,730
Urdu	156,420
Vietnamese	146,410
Ukrainian	141,805
Persian (Farsi)	138,075
Russian	136,235
Dutch	133,240
Korean	128,120
Greek	123,575
Tamil	122,020
Gujarati	86,285
Hindi	85,500
Cree	84,905

[1] Total Single and Multiple Responses

Source: Adapted from the Statistics Canada publication *Language, 2006 Census,* Catalogue 97-555-X, Issue 2006007.

Net Migration for Provinces and Territories, 1992-2010

Year [1]	N.L.	P.E.I.	N.S.	N.B.	Que.	Ont.	Man.	Sask.	Alta.	B.C.	Y.T.	N.W.T.	Nvt.
1992/1993	-3,078	654	96	-1,402	-8,420	-14,189	-5,544	-6,348	-1,181	40,099	-265	-330	-92
1993/1994	-4,952	622	-1,887	-671	-8,758	-9,420	-4,614	-5,431	-1,630	37,871	-1,094	-19	-17
1994/1995	-6,974	349	-2,741	-813	-8,947	-2,841	-3,220	-3,652	-556	29,291	269	78	-243
1995/1996	-7,436	638	-1,245	-369	-12,626	-2,822	-3,566	-2,161	7,656	22,025	564	-554	-104
1996/1997	-8,134	136	-1,648	-1,263	-17,436	1,977	-5,873	-2,794	26,282	9,880	-54	-696	-377
1997/1998	-9,490	-416	-2,569	-3,192	-16,958	9,231	-5,276	-1,940	43,089	-10,029	-1,024	-1,316	-110
1998/1999	-5,695	193	201	-1,244	-13,065	16,706	-2,113	-4,333	25,191	-14,484	-747	-555	-55
1999/2000	-4,263	104	-270	-1,183	-12,146	22,369	-3,456	-7,947	22,674	-14,610	-691	-651	70
2000/2001	-4,493	165	-2,077	-1,530	-9,442	18,623	-4,323	-8,410	20,457	-8,286	-572	-160	48
2001/2002	-3,352	62	-898	-1,218	-4,350	5,354	-4,344	-8,820	26,235	-8,556	-221	84	24
2002/2003	-1,683	165	510	-843	-1,829	637	-2,875	-5,141	11,903	-1,037	149	242	-198
2003/2004	-2,027	144	-772	-760	-822	-6,935	-2,565	-4,521	10,606	7,865	27	-105	-135
2004/2005	-3,710	-139	-3,041	-2,074	-4,963	-11,172	-7,227	-9,515	34,423	8,214	53	-668	-181
2005/2006	-4,342	-639	-3,024	-3,487	-9,411	-17,501	-7,881	-7,083	45,795	8,800	-73	-954	-200
2006/2007	-4,067	-849	-4,126	-2,632	-12,865	-20,047	-5,500	1,549	33,809	15,005	101	-221	-157
2007/2008	-528	-291	-1,794	-908	-11,682	-14,750	-3,703	4,171	15,317	14,643	235	-420	-290
2008/2009 (Final)	1,877	-536	-751	-237	-7,419	-15,601	-3,111	2,983	13,184	9,995	228	-577	-35
2009/2010 (Preliminary)	1,309	-876	205	722	-3,252	-7,275	-2,182	3,909	-2,183	9,367	332	-477	401
Average (1999/2000 - 2009/10)	-2,298	-245	-1,458	-1,286	-7,107	-4,209	-4,288	-3,530	21,111	3,764	-39	-355	-59
Total (1992/93 - 2009/10)	-71,038	-514	-25,831	-23,104	-164,391	-47,656	-77,373	-65,484	331,071	156,053	-2,783	-7,299	-1,651

[1] the period beginning July 1 of a given year and ending June 30 of the following year.

Source: Adapted from Statistics Canada's CANSIM database http://www5.statcan.gc.ca/cansim/home-accueil?lang=eng, Table 051-0018, August 2011.

MARRIAGES, 2004-2008

	Canada	N.L.	P.E.I.	N.S.	N.B.	Que.	Ont.	Man.	Sask.	Alta.	B.C.	Yukon	N.W.T.	Nvt.
2004														
Marriages	146,242	2,848	851	4,609	3,589	21,281	62,425	5,706	5,050	17,457	22,076	150	131	69
Crude Marriage Ratio[1]	4.6	5.5	6.2	4.9	4.8	2.8	5.0	4.9	5.1	5.4	5.3	4.9	3.1	2.3
Mean Age at Marriage: [2]														
Males	34.9	33.9	34.1	35.1	34.7	36.8	*	33.3	32.5	33.0	35.8	37.7	35.8	32.3
Females	32.4	31.4	31.8	32.8	32.2	34.0	*	30.9	30.2	30.6	33.3	33.8	32.7	30.1
2005														
Marriages	147,908	2,771	892	4,863	3,758	22,260	61,657	5,725	5,125	17,905	22,644	145	122	41
Crude Marriage Ratio[1]	4.6	5.4	6.5	5.2	5.0	2.9	4.9	4.9	5.2	5.5	5.3	4.7	2.9	1.4
Mean Age at Marriage: [2]														
Males	35.1	33.9	34.7	35.7	35.2	37.2	*	33.2	32.4	33.1	35.6	38.9	34.7	29.6
Females	32.6	31.5	32.1	33.3	32.7	34.5	*	30.9	30.2	30.8	33.2	38.2	32.4	27.6
2006														
Marriages	150,505	2,662	843	4,756	3,845	21,968	62,930	5,776	5,160	18,723	23,521	154	107	60
Crude Marriage Ratio[1]	4.6	5.2	6.1	5.1	5.1	2.9	5.0	4.9	5.2	5.6	5.4	4.9	2.5	2.0
Mean Age at Marriage: [2]														
Males	35.3	34.4	35.1	35.6	34.8	37.5	*	33.4	*	33.0	35.6	36.9	*	*
Females	32.8	31.9	32.8	33.2	32.7	34.7	*	31.1	*	30.8	33.1	34.2	*	*
2007														
Marriages	148,957	2,754	883	4,769	3,761	22,180	61,155	5,794	5,239	19,093	22,971	174	114	70
Crude Marriage Ratio[1]	4.5	5.4	6.4	5.1	5.0	2.9	4.8	4.9	5.3	5.5	5.2	5.7	3.0	2.3
Mean Age at Marriage: [2]														
Males	35.4	34.5	35.0	35.9	35.5	37.7	*	33.5	*	33.3	35.5	38.8	*	*
Females	32.9	32.1	32.5	33.7	33.1	34.9	*	31.2	*	30.9	33.0	35.6	*	*
2008														
Marriages	147,288	2,699	942	4,622	3,624	22,064	60,334	5,609	5,338	18,757	22,974	133	120	78
Crude Marriage Ratio[1]	4.4	5.3	6.8	4.9	4.9	2.9	4.7	4.7	5.3	5.3	5.2	4.0	2.7	2.5
Mean Age at Marriage: [2]														
Males	35.5	34.1	35.3	35.8	35.3	37.7	*	33.3	*	33.3	35.5	37.7	35.8	*
Females	32.9	31.9	32.7	33.5	32.7	34.9	*	30.9	*	30.8	32.9	35.2	33.2	*

* Data not available for this reference period

[1] Per 1,000 population.

[2] Total Marital Status

Source: Adapted from Statistics Canada's CANSIM database http://www5.statcan.gc.ca/cansim/home-accueil?lang=eng, Tables 101-1001, 101-1002 and 101-1004 (2004 data), Statistics Canada's Health Statistics Division (2005-2008 data), September 2011.

RELIGION

2001 CENSUS OF POPULATION

	Population	% of Total Population
All Religions	29,639,030	100.0
Catholic[1]	12,936,910	43.6
Protestant[2]	8,654,850	29.2
United Church	2,839,125	9.6
Anglican	2,035,500	6.9
Baptist	729,475	2.5
Lutheran	606,590	2.0
Protestant, n.o.s.	549,205	1.9
Presbyterian	409,830	1.4
Pentecostal	369,480	1.2
Christian, n.i.e.[3]	780,450	2.6
Eastern religions[4]	37,545	0.1
Muslim	579,640	2.0
Buddhist	300,345	1.0
Hindu	297,200	1.0
Sikh	278,410	0.9
Jewish[5]	329,995	1.1
Christian Orthodox[6]	479,620	1.6
Para-religious[7]	63,975	0.2
No religious affiliation	4,900,095	16.5

[1] Catholic includes Eastern Catholic groups in 2001, which were previously included in the "Eastern Orthodox" group in 1991

[2] in 2001, Protestant does not include "Other Christian" and "Christian n.o.s." as it did in 1991.

[3] Christian, n.i.e. is separate in 2001, but was previously included in "Protestant" in 1991.

[4] in 1991, "Eastern non-Christian" included Hindu, Islam, Sikh and Buddist. They are reported separately in 2001.

[5] Jewish includes Kalabarian or Kabbalah which were included in Para-religious groups in 1991

[6] was "Eastern Orthodox" in 1991. Does not include Eastern Catholic groups, which were reassigned to "Other Catholics" in 2001.

[7] Religions listed in "Para-religions groups" in 1991 are listed separately in 2001, but aggregated here for comparison.

Source: Adapted from the Statistics Canada publication *Religions in Canada, 2001 Census,* Catalogue 97F0022X, Issue 2001001.

EDUCATION STATISTICS, CANADA

	2001/2002	2002/2003	2003/2004	2004/2005	2005/2006	2006/2007	2007/2008	2008/2009
Elementary and Secondary Education (public)								
Enrolment (Full-time equivalent)	5,035,949	5,024,286	4,963,209	4,926,376	4,889,303	4,836,484	4,781,704	4,735,467
Enrolment (Headcount)	5,360,788	5,352,040	5,293,261	5,255,616	5,213,457	5,169,516	5,116,727	5,088,789
Graduates	331,070	329,221	310,519	313,899	310,474	320,438	330,932	341,744
Educators (Headcount)	350,206	351,567	353,767	358,196	365,374	381,859	387,676	392,632
Educators (Full-time equivalent)	316,574	317,612	316,698	320,295	325,056	333,076	336,470	339,361
Expenditure (current $ per student)	7,897	8,244	8,656	9,136	9,745	10,308	10,740	11,614
University Institutions								
Enrolment[1]	886,665	936,393	993,714	1,021,521	1,050,225	1,066,905	1,072,488	1,112,370
Graduates[1]	178,098	186,462	199,137	211,902	216,240	227,085	242,787	244,380
Educators	35,113	36,053	37,204	38,572	39,615	40,567	31,286	30,837
Domestic Tuition Fees[2]	3,577	3,711	3,975	4,141	4,211	4,400	4,558	4,747
Number of Institutions[3]	80	81	82	83	84	84	83	81

[1] Excludes University of Regina for 2005/2006, 2006/2007, 2007/2008 and 2008/2009.

[2] Weighted average undergraduate domestic tuition fees for full-time students in current dollars

[3] Reporting based on enrolment - parent institutions

Source: Adapted from Statistics Canada, 81C9996, Culture, Tourism and Education Statistics Division, various education surveys, 2008/2009.

Selected Criminal Code Incidents, Canada, 2009 and 2010

	2009[r] Number	2009[r] Rate[1]	2010 Number	2010 Rate
Homicide	610	2	554	2
Assault (Levels 1, 2, & 3)	237,566	704	228,593	671
Sexual Assault (Levels 1, 2 & 3)	20,921	62	22,180	65
Robbery	32,463	96	30,405	89
Total Crimes of Violence	444,533	1,318	437,316	1,282
Breaking and Entering	206,069	611	196,881	577
Motor Vehicle Theft	107,992	320	92,683	272
Mischief Under $5,000 (property damage)	362,326	1,075	339,831	996
Total Property Crimes	1,386,184	4,111	1,311,891	3,846
Total Other Criminal Code Offences (Excluding Traffic)	342,243	1,015	346,714	1,016
TOTAL - CRIMINAL CODE OFFENCES (Excluding Traffic)	2,172,960	6,444	2,095,921	6,145

[1] per 100,000 population

[r] - revised 2008 data

Source: adapted from the Statistics Canada publication, *Juristat,* Catalogue 85-002-XIE2011001, July 2011, http://www.statcan.gc.ca/bsolc/olc-cel/olc-cel?catno=85-002-XIE&lang=eng

Internet use by individuals, Internet shopping, by type of product and service

	2005 %	2007 %	2009 %
On-line consumers[1] ordering			
Computer software	20.2	19.7	21.8
Computer hardware	12.1	13.4	13.2
Music[3]	16.4	22.1	25.9
Books, magazines and online newspapers	35.4	36.8	35.4
Videocassettes and digital videodiscs (DVD)	13.5	13.8	14.5
Other entertainment products[4]	25.0	32.5	39.7
Food, condiments and beverages	3.4	4.5	5.6
Prescription drugs	1.3^E	1.0	1.4
Other health products, beauty and vitamins	8.1	8.6	10.6
Clothing, jewellery and accessories	24.8	29.5	32.8
Housewares[5]	8.3	10.8	12.0
Consumer electronics[6]	15.9	19.6	20.8
Automotive products[7]	5.6	8.2	8.3
Travel arrangements[8]	36.4	44.5	48.8
Flowers, gifts	13.2	15.9	18.0
Sports equipment	6.6	9.2	9.6
Toys and games	11.7	14.6	19.0
Real estate	1.1^E	1.3^E	1.5
Window shoppers[2] browsing for			
Computer software	18.6	18.5	20.0
Computer hardware	19.8	20.5	20.8
Music[3]	21.5	23.7	24.6
Books, magazines and online newspapers	28.3	30.6	34.8
Videocassettes and digital videodiscs (DVD)	17.7	18.8	20.3
Other entertainment products[4]	22.5	26.4	33.2
Food, condiments and beverages	7.5	8.2	11.3
Prescription drugs	2.4	2.7	2.3
Other health products, beauty and vitamins	11.0	12.8	14.9
Clothing, jewellery and accessories	36.9	40.6	45.2
Housewares[5]	39.0	42.8	45.2
Consumer electronics[6]	42.4	43.7	48.3
Automotive products[7]	25.8	28.0	30.8
Travel arrangements[8]	36.7	41.5	45.7
Flowers, gifts	11.9	13.4	16.9
Sports equipment	15.7	16.6	18.5
Toys and games	18.3	21.2	26.5
Real estate	16.2	18.7	22.1

E : use with caution.

Notes: The target population for the Canadian Internet use survey has changed from individuals 18 years of age and older in 2005 to individuals 16 years of age and older in 2007.

Internet shopping refers to the activities of window shopping and/or ordering and/or paying for products and services on-line, for personal or household consumption.

Respondents were asked to indicate all categories that applied to them.

1. On-line consumers: Refers to individuals who reported to having ordered at least one product or service using the Internet, for personal or household consumption, during the preceding twelve months, whether or not the payment was made on-line. The users may or may not have been window-shoppers.
2. Window shoppers: Refers to Internet users who reported, during the preceding twelve months, having used the Internet to browse for goods or services without placing an order directly over the Internet for that product.
3. Music (such as compact discs, tapes or audio files (MP3s, etc.)).
4. Other entertainment products (such as concert or theatre tickets).
5. Housewares (such as large appliances or furniture).
6. Consumer electronics (such as cameras, computers, stereos, televisions or digital video disc system or videoplayer).
7. Automotive (such as cars, trucks, or recreational vehicles).
8. Travel arrangements (such as hotel reservations, travel tickets or rental cars).

Source: Statistics Canada, http://www40.statcan.gc.ca/l01/cst01/comm24-eng.htm, August 2011.

Weights & Measures

THE INTERNATIONAL SYSTEM OF UNITS (SI) (BASE & SUPPLEMENTARY UNITS)

With the permission of the Canadian Standards Association, material is reproduced from CSA Standard CAN/CSA-Z234.1-89 (Canadian Metric Practice Guide), which is copyrighted by CSA, 178 Rexdale Blvd., Etobicoke, ON M9W 1R3. While use of this material has been authorized, CSA shall not be responsible for the manner in which the information is presented, nor for any interpretations thereof.

BASE UNITS

The International System of Units includes two classes of units: seven base units, and derived units. The base units are seven precisely defined units used internationally for teaching and scientific research.

SI BASE UNITS

Quantity	Name	Symbol
length	metre	m
mass	kilogram	kg
time	second	s
electric current	ampere	A
thermodynamic temperature	kelvin	K
amount of substance	mole	mol
luminous intensity	candela	cd

SI PREFIXES

Multiplying Factor	Prefix	Symbol
1 000 000 000 000 000 000 = 10^{18}	exa	E
1 000 000 000 000 000 = 10^{15}	peta	P
1 000 000 000 000 = 10^{12}	tera	T
1 000 000 000 = 10^{9}	giga	G
1 000 000 = 10^{6}	mega	M
1 000 = 10^{3}	kilo	k
100 = 10^{2}	hecto	h
10 = 10^{1}	deca	da
0.1 = 10^{-1}	deci	d
0.01 = 10^{-2}	centi	c
0.001 = 10^{-3}	milli	m
0.000 001 = 10^{-6}	micro	µ
0.000 000 001 = 10^{-9}	nano	n
0.000 000 000 001 = 10^{-12}	pico	p
0.000 000 000 000 001 = 10^{-15}	femto	f
0.000 000 000 000 000 001 = 10^{-18}	atto	a

SI Prefixes and their symbols given in the above table are used to form names and symbols of decimal multiples or sub-multiples of SI units.

SI DERIVED UNITS WITH SPECIAL NAMES

Name	Symbol	Typical Form [1]	In Base Units	Quantity
becquerel	Bq	s^{-1}	s^{-1}	activity of radionuclides
coulomb	C	s•A	s•A	quantity of electricity, electric charge
degree Celsius	°C	K	K	Celsius Temperature [2]
farad	F	C/V	$m^{-2}•kg^{-1}•s^{4}•A^{2}$	electric capacitance
gray	Gy	J/kg	$m^{2}•s^{-2}$	absorbed dose of ionizing radiation
henry	H	Wb/A	$m^{2}•kg•s^{-2}•A^{-2}$	inductance
hertz	Hz	s^{-1}	s^{-1}	frequency [3]
joule	J	N•m	$m^{2}•kg•s^{-2}$	energy, work, quantity of heat
lumen	lm	cd•sr	cd	luminous flux
lux	lx	lm/m^{2}	$m^{-2}•cd$	illuminance
newton	N	$m•kg/s^{2}$	$m•kg•s^{-2}$	force
ohm	Ω	V/A	$m^{2}•kg•s^{-3}•A^{-2}$	electric resistance
pascal	Pa	N/m^{2}	$m^{-1}•kg•s^{-2}$	pressure, stress
radian	rad	m/m	$m•m^{-1} = 1$	plane angle
siemens	S	A/V	$m^{-2}•kg^{-1}•s^{3}•A^{2}$	electric conductance
sievert	Sv	J/kg	$m^{2}•s^{-2}$	dose equivalent of ionizing radiation
steradian	sr	m^{2}/m^{2}	$m^{2}•m^{-2} = 1$	solid angle
tesla	T	Wb/m^{2}	$kg•s^{-2}•A^{-1}$	magnetic flux density
volt	V	W/A	$m^{2}•kg•s^{-3}•A^{-1}$	electric potential, potential difference, electromotive force
watt	W	J/s	$m^{2}•kg•s^{-3}$	power, radiant flux
weber	Wb	V•s	$m^{2}•kg•s^{-2}•A^{-1}$	magnetic flux

1. The formulae for derived units are not necessarily unique. For example, the volt may be defined as one joule per coulomb.
2. The Celsius temperature scale (previously called Centigrade, but renamed to avoid confusion with "centigrade", associated with the centesimal system of angular measurement) is the commonly used scale, except for certain scientific and technological purposes where the thermodynamic temperature scale is preferred. Note the use of uppercase C for Celsius.
3. The SI unit of frequency, the hertz, is one cycle per second. The reciprocal of the frequency is the period. The hertz should not be used as a measure of discrete items per unit of time, e.g. 5 boxes per second on an assembly line would not be referred to as 5 hertz, but may be referred to in terms of the reciprocal second i.e. $5s^{-1}$.

EXAMPLE OF SI DERIVED UNITS WITHOUT SPECIAL NAMES

Name	Typical Form	In Base Units	Quantity
ampere per metre	A/m	$A \bullet m^{-1}$	magnetic field strength
ampere per square metre	A/m^2	$A \bullet m^{-2}$	current density
candela per square metre	cd/m^2	$cd \bullet m^{-2}$	luminance
coulomb per cubic metre	C/m^3	$m^{-3} \bullet s \bullet A$	electric charge density
coulomb per kilogram	C/kg	$A \bullet s \bullet kg^{-1}$	exposure
coulomb per square metre	C/m^2	$m^{-2} \bullet s \bullet A$	surface density of charge, flux density
cubic metre	m^3	m^3	volume
cubic metre per kilogram	m^3/kg	$m^3 \bullet kg^{-1}$	specific volume
farad per metre	F/m	$m^{-3} \bullet kg^{-1} \bullet s^4 \bullet A^2$	permittivity
gray per second	Gy/s	$m^2 \bullet s^{-3}$	absorbed dose rate
henry per metre	H/m	$m \bullet kg \bullet s^{-2} \bullet A^{-2}$	permeability
joule per cubic metre	J/m^3	$m^{-1} \bullet kg \bullet s^{-2}$	energy density
joule per kelvin	J/K	$m^2 \bullet kg \bullet s^{-2} \bullet K^{-1}$	heat capacity, entropy
joule per kilogram kelvin	J/(kg•K)	$m^2 \bullet s^{-2} \bullet K^{-1}$	specific heat capacity, specific entropy
joule per kilogram	J/kg	$m^2 \bullet s^{-2}$	specific energy
joule per mole	J/mol	$m^2 \bullet kg \bullet s^{-2} \bullet mol^{-1}$	molar energy
joule per mole kelvin	J/(mol•K)	$m^2 \bullet kg \bullet s^{-2} \bullet K^{-1} \bullet mol^{-1}$	molar entropy, molar heat capacity
kilogram per cubic metre	kg/m^3	$kg \bullet m^{-3}$	density, mass density
metre per second	m/s	$m \bullet s^{-1}$	speed - linear
metre per second squared	m/s^2	$m \bullet s^{-2}$	acceleration - linear
mole per cubic metre	mol/m^3	$mol \bullet m^{-3}$	concentration (of amount of substance)
newton metre	N•m	$m^2 \bullet kg \bullet s^{-2}$	moment of force
newton per metre	N/m	$kg \bullet s^{-2}$	surface tension
pascal second	Pa•s	$m^{-1} \bullet kg \bullet s^{-1}$	dynamic viscosity
radian per second	rad/s	s^{-1}	speed- angular
radian per second squared	rad/s^2	s^{-2}	acceleration- angular
reciprocal metre	m^{-1}	m^{-1}	wave number*
square metre	m^2	m^2	area
square metre per second	m^2/s	$m^2 \bullet s^{-1}$	kinematic viscosity
volt per metre	V/m	$m \bullet kg \bullet s^{-3} \bullet A^{-1}$	electric field strength
watt per metre kelvin	W/(m•K)	$m \bullet kg \bullet s^{-3} \bullet K^{-1}$	thermal conductivity
watt per square metre	W/m^2	$kg \bullet s^{-3}$	heat flux density, irradiance
watt per square metre steradian	$W/(m^2 \bullet sr)$	$kg \bullet s^{-3}$	radiance
watt per steradian	W/sr	$m^2 \bullet kg \bullet s^{-3}$	radiant intensity

UNITS PERMITTED FOR USE WITH THE SI

Quantity	Name	Unit Symbol	Definition [1]
time	minute	min	1 min = **60** s [2]
	hour	h	1 h = **3600** s [2]
	day	d	1 d = **86 400** s [2]
	year	a	
plane angle	degree	°	1° = (π/**180**) rad [3]
	minute	'	1' = (π/**10 800**) rad [3]
	second	"	1" = (π/**648 000**) rad [3]
	revolution	r	1 r = **2**π rad [4]
area	hectare	ha	1 ha = **1** hm^2 = **10 000** m^2 [5]
volume	litre	L	1 L = **1** dm^3 [6]
mass	metric ton or tonne	t	1 t = **1000** kg [7] = **1** Mg
linear density	tex	tex	1 tex = **1 x** $\mathbf{10^{-6}}$ kg/m [8]
energy	electronovolt	eV	* [9]
mass of atom	unified atomic mass unit	u	* [10]
length	astronomical unit parsec	pc	* [11, 12]

1. Conversion factors that are exact are shown in boldface.
2. These sysmbols are used only in the sense of duration of time & not for expressing the time of day.
3. No space is left between these symbols & the last digit of a number. The unit "degree", with its decimal subdivisions, is used when the unit "radian" is not suitable.
4. The designations revolution per minute (r/min) and revolution per second (r/s) are widely used in connection with rotating machinery.
5. Because of the need for a unit similar to the acre, the hectare will continue to be recognized as a unit for use in surveying & agriculture.
6. The international symbol for litre is L or l. In order to avoid possible confusion with the number one, the "L" is preferred in Canada.
7. Care must be taken in the interpretation of the word "tonne" when it occurs in French text of Canadian origin, where the meaning may be a "ton of 2000 pounds".
8. The tex is used only in the textile industry.
9. One electronvolt is the kinetic energy acquired by an electron in passing through a potential difference of 1V in vacuum.
10. The unified atomic mass unit is equal to the fraction 1/12 of the mass of an atom of the nuclide ^{12}C.
11. The astronomical symbol does not have an international symbol; abbreviations are used (e.g. AU in English, UA in French). The astronomical unit of distance is the length of the radius of the unperturbed circular orbit of a body of negligible mass moving around the sun with a sidereal angular velocity of 0.017 202 098 950 radian per day of 86 400 ephemeris seconds.
12. 1 parsec (pc) is the distance at which 1 astronomical unit subtends an angle of 1 second of arc.

CONVERSION OF UNITS TO THE INTERNATIONAL SYSTEM OF UNITS (SI)

Area

1 acre	=0.404 685 6 ha
1 arpent (French measure)*	=0.341 889 4 ha
1 circular mil	=506.7 x 10^{-6} or μm^2
1 legal subdivision (40 acres)	=0.161 874 2 km^2
1 perch (French measure)*	=34.188 94 m^2
1 rood (1210 square yards)	=0.101 171 4 ha
1 section (1 mile square, 640 acres)	=2.589 988 km^2
1 square foot	=929.030 4 cm^2
1 square foot (French measure)*	=1 055.214 cm^2
1 square inch	=645.16 mm^2
1 square mile	=2.589 988 km^2
1 square yard	=0.836 127 4 m^2
1 township (36 sections)	=93.239 57 km^2

* Measures formerly used to describe certain land in the Province of Québec

Energy

1 British thermal unit (Btu) (International Table)	= 1.055 056 kJ
1 British thermal unit (Btu) (mean)	= 1.055 87 kJ
1 British thermal unit (Btu) (thermochemical)	= 1.054 35 kJ
1 British thermal unit (Btu) (39° F)	= 1.059 67 kJ
1 British thermal unit (Btu) (59° F, 15° C)	= 1.054 80 kJ
1 British thermal unit (Btu) (60.5° F)	= 1.054 615 kJ
1 Calorie (dietetic)	= 4.185 5 kJ
1 calorie (International Table)	= 4.186 8 J
1 calorie (thermochemical)	= 4.184 J
1 calorie (15° C)	= 4.185 5 J
1 calorie (15° C)	= 4.185 8 J
1 electronovolt	= 0.160 217 7 aJ
1 erg	= 0.1 µJ
1 foot poundal	= 42.140 11 mJ
1 foot pound-force	= 1.355 818 J
1 horsepower hour	= 2.684 520 MJ
1 kilowatt hour	= 3.6 MJ
1 therm	= 105.506 MJ
1 ton (nuclear equivalent of TNT)	= 4.2 GJ
1 watt hour	= 3.6 kJ
1 watt second	= 1 J

Force

1 dyne	=10 µN
1 kilogram-force	= 9.806 65 N
1 kilopond	= 9.806 65 N
1 kip (thousand pounds force)	= 4.448 222 kN
1 ounce-force	= 0.278 013 9 N
1 poundal	= 0.138 255 0 N
1 pound-force	= 4.448 222 N

Length

1 angstrom	=0.1 nm
1 arpent (French measure)*	=58.471 31 m
1 astronomical unit	=149.597 870 Gm
1 chain (66 feet)	=20.116 8 m
1 ell (45 inches)	=1.143 m
1 fathom	=1.828 8 m
1 fermi	=1 fm
1 foot	=0.304 8 m
1 foot (French measure)*	=0.324 840 6 m
1 foot (US survey, limited usage)	=0.304 800 6 m
1 furlong	=0.201 168 km
1 inch	=25.4 mm
1 league (Intl. nautical)	=5.556 km
1 league (UK nautical)	=5.559 552 km
1 league (US)	=4.828 032 km
1 light year	=9.460 528 Pm
1 link (1/100 chain)	=0.201 168 m
1 microinch	=25.4 nm
1 micron	=1 µm
1 mil (0.001 inch)	=25.4 µm
1 mile	=1.609 344 km
1 mile (Intl. nautical)	=1.852 km
1 mile (UK nautical)	=1.853 184 km
1 mile (US nautical)	=1.852 km
1 parsec	=30.856 78 Pm
1 perch	=5.029 2 m
1 perch (French measure)*	=5.847 130 8 m
1 pica (printers)	=4.217 518 mm
1 point (printers)	=0.351 459 8 mm
1 pole	=5.029 2 m
1 rod	=5.029 2 m
1 yard	=0.914 4 m

Mass

1 carat	=200 mg
1 cental (100 lb)	=45.359 237 kg
1 coal tub (100 lb, Newfoundland)	=45.359 237 kg
1 drachm (apothecary)	=3.887 935 g
1 dram (apothecary, US)	=3.887 935 g
1 dram (avoirdupois)	=1.771 845 g
1 gamma	=1 µg
1 grain	=64.798 91 mg
1 hundredweight (100 lb)	=45.359 237 kg
1 hundredweight (long 112 lb, UK)	=50.802 35 kg
1 ounce (avoirdupois)	=28.349 523 g
1 ounce (troy or apothecary)	=31.103 476 8 g
1 metric carat	=200 mg
1 pennyweight	=1.555 174 g
1 pound (avoirdupois)	=0.453 592 37 kg
1 pound (troy or apothecary)	=373.241 721 6 g
1 quarter (28 lb, UK)	=12.700 58 kg
1 scruple (apothecary, 20 grains)	=1.295 978 g
1 slug	=14.593 90 kg
1 stone (14 lb, UK)	=6.350 293 kg
1 ton (2240 lb, UK)	=1.016 046 908 8 Mg
1 ton (short, 2000 lb)	=0.907 184 74 Mg
1 unified atomic mass	=1.660 540 x 10^{-27} kg

Power

1 Btu (IT) per hour	=0.293 071 1 W
1 Btu (thermochemical) per hour	=0.292 875 1 W
1 Btu (thermochemical) per minute	=17.572 50 W
1 Btu (thermochemical) per second	=1.054 350 kW
1 foot pound-force per hour	=0.376 616 1 mW

1 foot pound-force per second	=1.355 818 W
1 horsepower (boiler)	=9.809 50 kW
1 horsepower (electric)	=746 W
1 horsepower (metric, cheval vapeur)	=735.498 75 W
1 horsepower (water)	=746.043 W
1 horsepower (550 ft•lbf/s)	=745.699 9 W

Pressure or Stress (Force per Area)

1 atmosphere, standard	=101.325 kPa (=760 torr)
1 atmosphere, technical	=98.066 5 kPa (=1 kgf/cm^2)
1 bar	=100 kPa
1 foot of water (39.2° F, 4° C)	=2.988 98 kPa
1 inch of mercury (conventional 32° F)	=3.386 39 kPa
1 inch of mercury (60° F)	=3.376 85 kPa
1 inch of mercury (68° F, 20° C)	=3.374 11 kPa
1 inch of water (conventional)	=249.088 9 Pa
1 inch of water (39.2° F, 4° C)	=249.082 Pa
1 inch of water (60° F)	=248.843 Pa
1 inch of water (68° F, 20° C)	=248.641 Pa
1 ksi (1000 lbf/in^2)	=6.894 757 MPa
1 poundal /square foot	=1.488 164 Pa
1 pound-force/square foot	=47.880 26 Pa
1 pound-force/square inch (psi)	=6.894 757 kPa
1 ton-force/square inch	=13.789 514 MPa
1 ton-force (UK)/square inch	=15.444 3 MPa
1 torr	=133.322 4 Pa

Temperature

Celsius temperature	= temperature in kelvins - 273.15
Fahrenheit temperature	= 1.8 (Celsius temperature) + 32
Fahrenheit temperature	= 1.8 (temperature in kelvins) - 459.67
Rankine temperature	= 1.8 (temperature in kelvins)

Velocity (Speed)

1 foot per hour	=84.666 67 µm/s
	=304.8 mm/h
1 foot per minute	=5.08 mm/s
	=304.8 mm/min
1 foot per second	=304.8 mm/s
1 inch per minute	=25.4 mm/min
1 inch per second	=25.4 mm/s
1 knot (International)	=1.852 km/h
	=0.514 444 4 m/s
1 knot (UK)	=1.853 184 km/h
1 mile per hour	=0.447 04 m/s
	=1.609 344 km/h
1 mile per minute	=26.822 4 m/s

Volume

1 acre foot	=1233.482 m^3
1 barrel (oil, 42 US gallons)	=0.158 987 3 m^3
1 barrel (US dry, 7056 in^3)	=0.115 627 1 m^3
1 barrel (US dry, cranberries, 5826 in^3)	=95.471 03 dm^3
1 barrel (36 UK gallons)	=0.163 659 2 m^3
1 board foot [a]	=2.359 737 dm^3
1 bushel	=36.368 72 dm^3
1 bushel (US dry, 2150.42 in^3)	=35.239 07 dm^3
1 cord (128 ft^3, 4 ft x 4 ft x 8 ft, stacked wood)	=3.624 556 m^3
1 cubic foot	=28.316 85 dm^3
1 cubic inch	=16.387 064 cm^3
1 cubic yard	=0.764 554 9 m^3
1 cunit (100 ft^3, solid wood)	=2.831 685 m^3
1 cup	=250 cm^3
1 demiard	=0.284 130 6 dm^3
1 drop (1/100 teaspoon)	=0.05 cm^3
1 fluid dram	=3.551 633 cm^3
1 fluid dram (US measure)	=3.696 691 cm^3
1 fluid ounce	=28.413 062 cm^3
1 fluid ounce (US)	=29.573 53 cm^3
1 gallon	=4.546 09 dm^3
1 gallon (US)	=3.785 412 dm^3
1 gill	=0.142 065 dm^3
1 gill (US)	=0.118 294 dm^3
1 herring barrel	=145.474 9 dm^3
1 herring tub	=72.737 44 dm^3
1 hogshead	=245.488 9 dm^3
1 lambda	=1 mm^3
1 minim	=59.193 9 mm^3
1 minim (US)	=61.611 52 mm^3
1 peck	=9.092 180 dm^3
1 peck (US dry)	=8.809 768 dm^3
1 Petrograd standard (165 ft^3, sawn timber)	=4.672 280 m^3
1 pint	=0.568 261 2 dm^3
1 pint (US dry)	=0.550 610 5 dm^3
1 pint (US liquid)	=0.473 176 5 dm^3
1 quart	=1.136 522 dm^3
1 quart (US dry)	=1.101 221 dm^3
1 quart (US liquid)	=0.946 352 9 dm^3
1 salt cart	=490.977 7 dm^3
1 salt tub	=81.829 62 dm^3
1 sand barrel	=81.829 62 dm^3
1 tablespoon	=15 cm^3
1 teaspoon	=5 cm^3
1 ton (register)	=2.831 685 m^3

a. The board foot is nominally 1x12x12 = 144 in^3. However, the actual volume of wood is about 2/3 of the nominal quality.

b. This applies to stacked wood, comprising wood, bark, & arispace, to a total volume of 128 ft^3.

c. Also referred to as the "imperial gallon".

MEASURES HAVING FORMER HOUSEHOLD USAGE

1 cup (Canadian, 8 fluid ounces)	=227 cm^3
1 cup (US, 8 fluid ounces)	=236 cm^3
1 cup (UK, 10 fluid ounces)	=284 cm^3
1 tablespoon (Canadian, 1/2 fluid ounce)	=14.21 cm^3
1 tablespoon (UK, 5/8 fluid ounce)	=17.8 cm^3
1 tablespoon (US, 1/2 fluid ounce)	=14.8 cm^3
1 teaspoon (1/6 fluid ounce)	=4.74 cm^3
1 teaspoon (UK, 5/24 fluid ounce)	=5.92 cm^3
1 teaspoon (US, 1/6 fluid ounce)	=4.93 cm^3
*1 cm^3	=1 ml

SECTION 2

ARTS & CULTURE

Many of the following categories are also represented in Section 3: Associations.

Art Galleries

National Art Galleries

National Gallery of Canada (NGC) / Musée des beaux-arts du Canada (MBAC)
PO Box 427 A, 380 Sussex Dr., Ottawa, ON K1N 9N4
Tel: 613-990-1985; *Fax:* 613-993-4385
Toll-Free: 800-319-2787
info@gallery.ca
national.gallery.ca
The permanent collection of the National Gallery comprises paintings, sculpture, prints & drawings, photographs, film & video art from the Canadian, European, American & Asian schools. Special exhibitions as well as permanent installations of the gallery's collections are on display. The gallery also sends its exhibitions on tour across the country & participates in international exhibitions.
Marie Claire Morin, Director, Development
Mayo Graham, Director, Outreach & International Relations
Dr. David Franklin, Deputy Director/Chief Curator
Alain Boivert, Chief, Communications & Marketing
Lise Labine, Director, Human Resources
Daniel Amadei, Director, Exhibitions & Installations
Charles Hill, Curator, Canadian Art
Ann Thomas, Curator, Photographs
Graham Larkin, Curator, European Art
Stephen Gritt, Chief, Restoration & Conservation Laboratory
Murray Waddington, Chief Librarian
Serge Thériault, Chief, Publications
Louise Filiatrault, Chief, Education & Public Programs
Delphine Bishop, Chief, Collections Management
Pierre Théberge, Director O.C., C.Q.
David Baxter, Deputy Director, Administration & Finance
Joanne Charette, Director, Public Affairs
Kitty Scott, Curator, Contemporary Art

Alberta

Provincial Art Galleries

The Edmonton Art Gallery (EAG)
2 Sir Winston Churchill Sq., Edmonton, AB T5J 2C1
Tel: 780-422-6223; *Fax:* 780-426-3105
info@artgalleryalberta.com
www.artgalleryalberta.com
Collections include: Canadian & international contemporary & historical paintings, sculpture, photography, video & graphic art. Research fields: Western Canadian art, historical & contemporary art; painting; sculpture; photography; graphics. Activities: Guided tours; lectures; films; gallery talks; art rental & sales gallery; studio art classes for children & adults; program workshops & seminars
Catherine Crowston, Deputy Director & Senior Curator
Ron Gregg, Director, Administration
Tony Luppino, Executive Director
Catrin Owen, Director, Development & Marketing

Local Art Galleries in Alberta

***Banff:* Walter Phillips Gallery (WPG)**
The Banff Centre, PO Box 1020 14, 107 Tunnel Mountain Dr., Banff, AB T1L 1H5
Tel: 403-762-6281; *Fax:* 403-762-6659
walter_phillipsgallery@banffcentre.ca
www.banffcentre.ca/WPG
Contemporary, national & international fine arts; open year round
Anthony Kiendl, Director
Sylvie Gilbert, Senior Curator

***Brocket:* Oldman River Cultural Centre**
PO Box 70, Brocket, AB T0K 0H0
Tel: 403-965-3939
oldmancc@telusplanet.net
Aboriginal history
Jo-Ann Yellow Horn, Director

***Calgary:* Art Gallery of Calgary**
117 - 8th Ave. SW, Calgary, AB T2P 1B4
Tel: 403-770-1350; *Fax:* 403-264-8077
artinfo@artgallerycalgary.org
www.artgallerycalgary.org
Non-profit public gallery, exhibiting works by contemporary Canadian artists; travelling exhibitions & education programs
Valerie Cooper, President & Chief Executive Officer

***Calgary:* Illingworth Kerr Gallery (IKG)**
Alberta College of Art & Design, 1407 - 14 Ave. NW, Calgary, AB T2N 4R3
Tel: 403-284-7680; *Fax:* 403-289-6682
gallery@acad.ab.ca
www.acad.ca
Contemporary art exhibitions, publications, lectures, screenings & related events
Ron Moppett, Director/Curator
Richard Gordon, Curator

***Calgary:* Leighton Foundation Collection**
Box 9, Site 31, RR#8, Calgary, AB T2J 2T9
Tel: 403-931-3633; *Fax:* 403-931-3633
www.sharecom.ca/leighton
A.C. Leighton's paintings; open year round
Lorna Johnson, Director

***Edmonton:* Front Gallery**
12312 Jasper Ave., Edmonton, AB T5N 3K5
Tel: 780-488-2952

***Edmonton:* Latitude 53**
10248 - 106 St., Edmonton, AB T5J 1H5
Tel: 780-423-5353; *Fax:* 780-424-9117
info@latitude53.org
www.latitude53.org
Contemporary artistic projects, experimental cultural development; performance art; literary projects; interdisciplinary art
Todd Janes, Executive Director

***Edmonton:* West End Gallery**
12308 Jasper Ave., Edmonton, AB T5N 3K5
Tel: 780-488-4892; *Fax:* 780-488-4893
info@westendgalleryltd.com
www.westendgalleryltd.com
Fine art gallery representing Canadian paintings & sculpture; the largest representation of glass artists in Canada
Daniel Hudon
Lana Hudon

***Grande Prairie:* The Prairie Art Gallery**
#103, 9856-97 Ave., Grande Prairie, AB T8V 7K2
Tel: 780-532-8111; *Fax:* 780-539-9522
info@prariegallery.com
www.prairiegallery.com
Public art gallery. The Gallery's collection currently stands at approximately 600 works of art, almost exclusively created in Alberta in the midto late 20th Century.
Robert Steven, Curator

***Lethbridge:* Southern Alberta Art Gallery (SAAG)**
601 - 3 Ave. South, Lethbridge, AB T1J 0H4
Tel: 403-327-8770; *Fax:* 403-328-3913
info@saag.ca
www.saag.ca
Fosters the work of contemporary visual artists who challenge the boundaries of their discipline & advance their work in a larger public realm
Joan Stebbins, Curator
Marilyn Smith, Director

***Lethbridge:* University of Lethbridge Art Gallery**
W600, Centre for the Arts, 4401 University Dr., Lethbridge, AB T1K 3M4
Tel: 403-329-2666; *Fax:* 403-382-7115
www.uleth.ca/artgallery/
Josephine Mills, Director & Curator

British Columbia

Provincial Art Galleries

Vancouver Art Gallery
750 Hornby St., Vancouver, BC V6Z 2H7
Tel: 604-662-4700; *Fax:* 604-682-1086
www.vanartgallery.bc.ca
Other contact information: Info Line: 604/662-4719
Largest gallery in western Canada; presents major exhibitions from contemporary art to historical masters; founded in 1931, has over 7,800 works in its collection, 41,400 sq. ft. of exhibition space & is located in the former provincial courthouse in downtown Vancouver; collection includes acclaimed Canadian artists such as Stan Douglas, Jeff Wall & Ian Wallace.
Kathleen Bartels, Director
Paul Larocque, Associate Director

Local Art Galleries in British Columbia

***Burnaby:* Burnaby Art Gallery**
***Also known as:* Visual Arts Burnaby**
6344 Deer Lake Ave., Burnaby, BC V5G 2J3
Tel: 604-205-7332; *Fax:* 604-205-7339
darrin.martens@city.burnaby.bc.ca
www.city.burnaby.bc.ca
Services include educational programs for children, adults & seniors; community projects & exhibitions in libraries & recreational centres; school programs support the exhibitions & take works of art into the schools
Darrin Martens, Director/Curator

***Burnaby:* The Simon Fraser University Gallery**
AQ 3004, Simon Fraser University, 8888 University Dr., Burnaby, BC V5A 1S6
Tel: 604-291-4266; *Fax:* 604-291-3029
gallery@sfu.ca
www.sfu.ca/gallery
Hosts six or seven exhibitions a year, both historical & contemporary, covering the full range of media; serves the SFU community directly by providing an occasional platform for student, staff & faculty work to be shown; The Gallery also administers the Teck Gallery at the SFU Vancouver Campus, a small space used to show work that deals with social & environmental issues
Bill Jeffries, Director/Curator
Veronika Klaptoez, Coordinator

***Campbell River:* Campbell River & District Public Art Gallery**
1235 Shoppers Row, Campbell River, BC V9W 2C7
Tel: 250-287-2261; *Fax:* 250-287-2268
art.gallery@crcn.net
crartgal.ca
Contemporary work from both local & visiting artists; classes, lectures & workshops throughout the year; open Tue.-Sat., 12-5; June & Aug. Mon.-Sat., 10-5
Jeanette Taylor, Director
Manon Staiger, Curator

***Castlegar:* Kootenay Gallery of Art, History & Science**
***Also known as:* Kootenay Gallery**
120 Heritage Way, Castlegar, BC V1N 4M5
Tel: 250-365-3337; *Fax:* 250-365-3822
info@kootenaygallery.com
www.kootenaygallery.com
Exhibits on art, history & science, from international to local sources; offers workshops, performances, lectures & classes; gift shop
Val Field, Executive Director
Marilyn Luscombe, Chair

***Dawson Creek:* Dawson Creek Art Gallery**
#101, 816 Alaska Ave., Dawson Creek, BC V1G 4T6
Tel: 250-782-2601; *Fax:* 250-782-8801
www.dcartgallery.ca
Open year round
Ellen Corea, Curator

***Grand Forks:* Grand Forks Art Gallery**
PO Box 2140, Grand Forks, BC V0H 1H0
Tel: 250-442-2211; *Fax:* 250-442-0099
gfagchin@direct.ca
www.galleries.bc.ca/grandforks
Historical & contemporary works by established & emerging regional, national & international artists
Paul Crawford, Director

***Hope:* John Weaver Sculpture Museum**
PO Box 1723, 19225 Silverhope Rd., Hope, BC V0X 1L0
Tel: 604-869-5312; *Fax:* 604-869-5117
johnweaver@johnweaverfinearts.com
Founded: 1977 John Weaver's work of bronzes based on historical, anthropological, & charity-work themes can be viewed by those wishing to learn about bronze sculpture & by those who wish to be commissioners of work; collection of over 60 years of work
Henry Weaver, Director
Sara M. Lesztak, Chief Information Officer & Director
Elizabeth Lesztak, Director
Richard Roles, Computer Expert

***Kamloops:* Kamloops Art Gallery**
#101, 465 Victoria St., Kamloops, BC V2C 2A9
Tel: 250-377-2400; *Fax:* 250-828-0662
kamloopsartgallery@kag.bc.ca
www.kag.bc.ca
Changing exhibits of contemporary & historical art; permanent collection of Canadian art
Jann L.M. Bailey, Director

***Kaslo:* Langham Cultural Centre**
PO Box 1000, Kaslo, BC V0G 1M0
Tel: 250-353-2661; *Fax:* 250-353-2671
langham@netidea.com
www.thelangham.ca
Founded: 1975 Art exhibits; theatre; music; workshops; The Japanese Canadian Museum. Street address: 447 A Ave., Kaslo, BC
Alice Windsor, Executive Director

***Kelowna:* Kelowna Art Gallery**
1315 Water St., Kelowna, BC V1Y 9R3
Tel: 250-762-2226; *Fax:* 250-762-9875
kelowna.artgallery@shaw.ca
www.kelownaartgallery.com
Historical & contemporary fine art; extensive education programs; open year round

Dona Moore, Executive Director
Ms Liz Wylie, Curator

Maple Ridge: **Maple Ridge Art Gallery Society**
11944 Haney Pl., Maple Ridge, BC V2X 6G1
Tel: 604-467-5855; *Fax:* 604-466-5852
gallery@mrag.ca
www.theactmapleridge.org
Exhibition of local, amateur & professional artists; art rental program for patrons
Ms Laura Moodie, Curator

Nakusp: **Bonnington Arts Centre**
6th Ave. West & 4th St. North, Nakusp, BC V0G 1R0
Tel: 250-265-4234; *Fax:* 250-265-3808
Open Sept. - June

Nanaimo: **Nanaimo Art Gallery**
c/o Malaspina University College, 900 - Fifth St., Nanaimo, BC V9R 5S5
Tel: 250-740-6350; *Fax:* 250-740-6475
Info@nanaimogallery.ca
www.nanaimogallery.ca
Celebrating art on the west coast; art central & sales program; gift shop full of elegant & eclectic gifts; inspiring & thought provoking exhibitions
Chris Kuderle, Administrative Director
Gregory Ball, Curator

New Westminster: **Amelia Douglas Gallery**
PO Box 2503, New Westminster, BC V3L 5B2
Tel: 604-527-5465; *Fax:* 604-527-5528
lmccallum@douglas.bc.ca
www.douglas.bc.ca/artscomm
A non-profit organization run by members of the Arts Exhibition Committee at Douglas College; mandate is to feature new & established BC artists & to enhance the educational offerings of the College
Lorna McCallum, Representative

North Vancouver: **Presentation House Museum Galleries**
209 West 4th St., North Vancouver, BC V7M 1H8
Tel: 604-987-5612; *Fax:* 604-987-5609
www.presentationhousegall.com
Celebrates & preserves North Vancouver's social, industrial & cultural history
Robin Inglis, Director

North Vancouver: **Seymour Art Gallery**
4360 Gallant Ave., North Vancouver, BC V7G 1L2
Tel: 604-924-1378; *Fax:* 604-924-3786
seymourartgallery@shawcable.com
seymourartgallery.com
Open year round
Jacquie Morgan, Director/Curator

Osoyoos: **Osoyoos Art Gallery**
PO Box 256, 8713 Main St., Osoyoos, BC V0H 1V0
Tel: 250-495-2800
Ivana Zita, Director

Penticton: **Penticton Art Gallery (AGSO)**
199 Marina Way, Penticton, BC V2A 1H3
Tel: 250-493-2928; *Fax:* 250-493-3992
agso@shawbiz.ca
www.galleries.bc.ca/agso
Founded: 1972 The Penticton Art Gallery offers in-house & touring exhibitions from local, regional & national sources.

Port Alberni: **Rollin Art Centre**
Also known as: **Community Arts Council of the Alberni Valley**
3061 - 8th Ave., Port Alberni, BC V9Y 2K5
Tel: 250-724-3412; *Fax:* 250-724-3472
communityarts@alberni.net
www.alberni.net/communityarts
Gareth Flostrand, Arts Administrator
Liisa McInnis, Co-ordinator, Gallery & Gift Shop

Prince George: **Two Rivers Gallery**
Prince George Art Gallery Association, 725 Civic Plaza, Prince George, BC V2L 5T1
Tel: 250-614-7800; *Fax:* 250-563-3211
Toll-Free: 888-221-1155
art@tworiversartgallery.com
www.tworiversartgallery.co m
The Two Rivers Gallery is a vital centre for visual art in Prince George and the central interior of British Columbia, Canada. It is run by the nonprofit Prince George Regional Art Gallery Association with a mission to: encourage lifelong learning through the arts, create an environment for vigorous artistic and cultural expression, provide opportunities for diverse experiences through participation and exhibition.
George Harris, Curator
Peter L. Thompson, Managing Director

Prince Rupert: **CHTK**
Also known as: **Standard Radio Inc.**
#212, 215 Cow Bay Rd., Prince Rupert, BC V8J 1A2
Tel: 250-624-9111; *Fax:* 250-624-3100
Toll-Free: 800-668-6330
smenhinick@srt.ca
wwww.themix.com
Brian Langston

Qualicum Beach: **The Old School House Arts Centre (TOSH)**
PO Box 791, 122 Fern Rd. West, Qualicum Beach, BC V9K 1T2
Tel: 250-752-6133; *Fax:* 250-752-2600
Toll-Free: 800-661-3211
qbtosh@shaw.ca
www.theoldschoolhouse.org
Fifteen resident artists; 3 exhibition galleries; concert series; classrooms; gift shop
Greg Sabo, President

Richmond: **Richmond Art Gallery**
#180, 7700 Minoru Gate, Richmond, BC V6Y 1R9
Tel: 604-247-8300; *Fax:* 604-247-8301
gallery@richmond.ca
www.richmondartgallery.org
Presents a diverse program of exhibitions, workshops, lectures & special events, as well as outreach programs which focus on contemporary art & art issues
Corinne Currie, Director/Curator

Smithers: **Smithers Gallery Association & Public Art Gallery**
Central Park Bldg., PO Box 122, Smithers, BC V0J 2N0
Tel: 250-847-3898
Public gallery, admission by donation; monthly exhibition rotation; workshops & artcamps for young & old, all artisan levels & mediums; call for a current listing
Sue Brookes, President
Pam Allen, Secretary

South Surrey: **Arnold Mikelson Mind & Matter Gallery**
13743 -16 Ave., South Surrey, BC V4A 1P7
Tel: 604-536-6460
mindandmatterart@aol.com
www.mindandmatterart.com
Wood sculptures of the late Arnold Mikelson
Mary Mikelson, Owner/Director

Vancouver: **Charles H. Scott Gallery**
Emily Carr College of Art & Design, 1399 Johnston St., Granville Island, Vancouver, BC V6H 3R9
Tel: 604-844-3809; *Fax:* 604-844-3801
scottgal@eciad.ca
www.eciad.ca/www/whatson/chs_index.html
Greg Bellerby, Curator

Vancouver: **Circle Craft Gallery**
1-1666 Johnston St., Net Loft Granville Island, Vancouver, BC V6H 3S2
Tel: 604-669-8021; *Fax:* 604-669-8585
shop@circlecraft.net
www.circlecraft.net
Features over 200 works of BC artists
Ron Kong, Store Manager

Vancouver: **Contemporary Art Gallery**
555 Nelson St., Vancouver, BC V6B 6R5
Tel: 604-681-2700; *Fax:* 604-683-2710
info@contemporaryartgallery.ca
www.contemporaryartgallery.ca
Promotes knowledge & understanding of contemporary visual art through: exhibitions that address current issues in contemporary art; educational programs in the form of artist & curator talks, student tours, high school projects, public symposia; publications; visiting artist/curator programs; information & resource services; The City of Vancouver Art Collection of 3,000 works of art
Christina Ritchie, Director/Curator

Vancouver: **Exposure Gallery (VAPA)**
Also known as: **Vancouver Association for Photographic Art**
851 Beatty St., Vancouver, BC V6B 2M6
Tel: 604-688-9501
exposuregallery@shaw.ca
www.exposure-gallery.com
Photographic & photo-based medium
Ian McGuffie, President/Curator

Vancouver: **grunt gallery**
#116, 350 - East 2nd Ave., Vancouver, BC V5T 4R8
Tel: 604-875-9516; *Fax:* 604-877-0073
grunt@telus.net
www.grunt.bc.ca
Open Wed. - Sat., 12-6
Glenn Alteen, Director

Vancouver: **Heffel Gallery Limited**
2247 Granville St., Vancouver, BC V6H 3G1
Tel: 604-732-6505; *Fax:* 604-732-4245
mail@heffel.com
www.heffel.com
Fine art auction house.
Mr. David Heffel, Director

Vancouver: **Marion Scott Gallery**
308 Water St., Vancouver, BC V6B 1B6
Tel: 604-685-1934; *Fax:* 604-685-1890
art@marionscottgallery.com
www.marionscottgallery.com
Established in 1975, & one of the leading galleries dealing with Canadian Inuit art
Judy Kardosh, Director

Vancouver: **Morris & Helen Belkin Art Gallery**
University of British Columbia, 1825 Main Mall, Vancouver, BC V6T 1Z2
Tel: 604-822-2759; *Fax:* 604-822-6689
belkin@interchange.ubc.ca
www.belkin-gallery.ubc.ca
Specializes in exhibiting contemporary work by national & international artists; programming includes exhibitions, artists' talks, publications & collaborative projects with other galleries/organizations; masters program in Critical Curatorial Studies; archival collections focus on Vancouver Canadian avant garde in 1960s-70s
Scott Watson, Director/Curator

Vancouver: **Wickaninnish Gallery**
#14, 1166 Johnston St., Vancouver, BC V6H 3S2
Tel: 604-681-1057
info@wickaninnishgallery.com
www.wickaninnishgallery.com
Patricia Rivard, Owner

Vernon: **Vernon Public Art Gallery (VPAG)**
3228 - 31st Ave., Vernon, BC V1T 2H3
Tel: 250-545-3173; *Fax:* 250-545-9096
vernonartgallery@shawbiz.ca
www.galleries.bc.ca/vernon
Community programming; local, regional, national & international exhibitions; gift shop; art & video rentals; group tours
Paula Burns Resch, Executive Director
Marion Morrison, President

Victoria: **Art Gallery of Greater Victoria (AGGV)**
1040 Moss St., Victoria, BC V8V 4P1
Tel: 250-384-4101; *Fax:* 250-361-3995
aggv@aggv.bc.ca
aggv.bc.ca
Canadiana 1860 to present; work of Emily Carr; one of Canada's finest collections of Asian art
Donna McAlear, Director/CEO

Victoria: **Maltwood Art Museum & Gallery (MAMAG)**
PO Box 3025 CSC, Victoria, BC V8W 3P2
Tel: 250-721-8298; *Fax:* 250-721-8997
msegger@uvic.ca
www.maltwood.uvic.ca
Named after the collection of fine, decorative & applied arts of English sculptress & antiquarian Katherine Emma Maltwood, F.R.S.A. (1878-1961); over 6,000 items representing the work of contemporary Western Canadian artists
Martin Segger, Director

Wells: **Island Mountain Gallery**
PO Box 65, Wells, BC V0K 2R0
Tel: 250-994-3466; *Fax:* 250-994-3433
Toll-Free: 800-442-2787
info@imarts.com
www.imarts.com
Provides visual, literary & performing arts instruction; presents contemporary art exhibitions; concert venue in summer; also holds workshops
Julie Fowler, Artistic Director

Williams Lake: **Stationhouse Gallery & Gift Shop**
1 North Mackenzie Ave., Williams Lake, BC V2G 1N4
Tel: 250-392-6113; *Fax:* 250-392-6184
manager@stationhousegallery.com
www.stationhousegallery.com
Monthly exhibitions; gift shop
Diane Koebel, Gallery Manager

Manitoba

Provincial Art Galleries

The Winnipeg Art Gallery (WAG)
300 Memorial Blvd., Winnipeg, MB R3C 1V1
Tel: 204-786-6641; *Fax:* 204-788-4998
inquiries@wag.mb.ca
www.wag.mb.ca

Founded in 1912, the WAG is Western Canada's oldest civic art gallery. With over 23,000 works in its collection, the WAG features 9 galleries of contemporary & historical works (fine arts, decorative arts & photography) by Manitoban, Canadian & international artists. A highlight is the Gort Collection of Northern Gothic & Renaissance paintings & altar panels.
Eva Rempel, Deputy Director
Pierre Arpin, Director

Local Art Galleries in Manitoba

***Brandon:* The Art Gallery of Southwestern Manitoba / Le Musé D'art du Sud-ouest du Manitoba**
***Also known as:* Art Gallery of Southwestern Manitoba**
#2, 710 Rosser Ave., Brandon, MB R7A 0K9
Tel: 204-727-1036; *Fax:* 204-726-8139
info@agsm.ca
www.agsm.ca
Contemporary Manitoban art; approximately 16 exhibitions a year; open year round
Jenny Western, Curator, Contemporary & Aboriginal Art

***Saint Boniface:* Centre culturel franco-manitobain (CCFM)**
340, boul Provencher, Saint Boniface, MB R2H 0G7
Tél: 204-233-8972; *Téléc:* 204-233-3324
ccfm@ccfm.mb.ca
www.ccfm.mb.ca
Le Centre culturel franco-manitobain a un rôle de premier plan comme maison de la culture et carrefour de la vie culturelle et artistique en français à Winnipeg et au Manitoba/The Centre culturel franco-manitobain is the focal point of French cultural life in Winnipeg & Manitoba
Agnès Champagne, Executive Director

***Winnipeg:* aceartinc.**
290 McDermot Ave., 2nd Fl., Winnipeg, MB R3B 0T2
Tel: 204-944-9763; *Fax:* 204-944-9101
gallery@aceart.org
www.aceart.org
aceartinc. is an artist-run centre dedicated to the development, exhibition & dissemination of contemporary art by cultural producers; dedicated to cultural diversity
Theo Sims, Programmer

***Winnipeg:* Gallery 1.1.1.**
211 FitzGerald Bldg., School of Art, University of Manitoba, Winnipeg, MB R3T 2N2
Tel: 204-474-9322; *Fax:* 204-474-7605
umanitoba.ca/schools/art/galleryoneoneone/info111.html
Prof. Cliff Eyland, Gallery Director, eylandc@cc.umanitoba.ca
Robert Epp, Coordinator, epp@ms.umanitoba.ca

***Winnipeg:* University of Winnipeg Fine Art Collection & Gallery 1C03**
515 Portage Ave., Winnipeg, MB R3B 2E9
Tel: 204-786-9253; *Fax:* 204-774-4134
j.gibson@uwinnipeg.ca
gallery1c03.uwinnipeg.ca
19th & 20th century paintings, drawings, prints, photographs & sculptures; open year round

***Winnipeg:* Upstairs Gallery**
266 Edmonton St., Winnipeg, MB R3C 1R9
Tel: 204-943-2734; *Fax:* 204-943-7726
upstairs@mts.net
Inuit Contemporary & early 20th-century Canadian art; prints, sculptures, wall-hangings & drawings
Faye Settler, Director

New Brunswick

Provincial Art Galleries

Owens Art Gallery
c/o Mount Allison University, 61 York St., Sackville, NB E4L 1E1
Tel: 506-364-2574; *Fax:* 506-364-2575
owens@mta.ca
www.mta.ca/owens
Permanent collection of over 2500 works, dating from the 18th century; 30 exhibitions yearly
Gemey Kelly, Director

Local Art Galleries in New Brunswick

***Campbellton:* Galerie Restigouche Gallery**
PO Box 674, 39 Andrew St., Campbellton, NB E3N 3H1
Tel: 506-753-5750; *Fax:* 506-759-9601
rgaleri@nbnet.nb.ca
Charline Lanteigne, Director

***Edmundston:* Gallerie Colline**
195, boul Hébert, Edmundston, NB E3V 2S8
Tel: 506-737-5282; *Fax:* 506-737-5373
galerie@umce.ca
www.umce.ca/galerie
Trente ans d'expositions d'artistes amateurs et professionnels qui ont aidé à l'appréciation de l'art dans notre milieu.
Ms Elisabeth Hubault, Présidente

***Fredericton:* The Beaverbrook Art Gallery / La galerie d'art Beaverbrook**
PO Box 605, 703 Queen St., Fredericton, NB E3B 5A6
Tel: 506-458-8545; *Fax:* 506-459-7450
Toll-Free: 888-458-8545
emailbag@beaverbrookartgallery.org
www.beaverbrookartg allery.org
Founded: 1959 Atlantic Canadian art & historical British art; open year round
Bernard Riordon, Director/CEO O.C., briordon@beaverbrookartgallery.org, 506-458-2030

***Fredericton:* Gallery Connexion**
Justice Bldg. Annex, PO Box 696, 453 Queen St., Fredericton, NB E3B 5B4
Tel: 506-454-1433; *Fax:* 506-454-1401
connex@nbnet.nb.ca
galleryconnexion.ca
Artist-run centre, non-profit & non commercial; gallery exists for the purpose of exhibiting, supporting, & promoting the development & understanding of all forms of contemporary art practice of local, national & international significance
Ms Meredith Snider, Director

***Fredericton:* UNB Art Centre**
Memorial Hall, PO Box 4400, University of New Brunswick, Fredericton, NB E3B 5A3
Tel: 506-453-4623; *Fax:* 506-453-5012
mem@unb.ca
www.unb.ca/web/FineArts
Historical & contemporary exhibitions; interpretive programs; Atlantic art collection
Marie Maltais, Director

***Moncton:* Atelier IMAGO**
#35, 140 Botsford St., Moncton, NB E1C 4X5
Tel: 506-388-1431; *Fax:* 506-857-2064
imago@nb.aibn.com
www.atelierimago.com
Artist-run not-for-profit printmaking studio

***Moncton:* Galerie d'art de l'Université de Moncton (GAUM)**
***Also known as:* Galerie d'art Louise-et-Reuben-Cohen**
Pavillon Clément-Cormier, Centre universitaire de Moncton, 10, av Université, Moncton, NB E1A 3E9
Tél: 506-858-4088; *Téléc:* 506-858-4043
galrc@umoncton.ca
www.umoncton.ca/gaum/
Founded: 1964 La Galerie a pour mission encourager la créativité des artistes acadiens/acadiennes, et collectioner et documenter les oeuvres d'art; centre de documentation; programmation.
Luc A. Charette, Directeur-conservateur

***Moncton:* Galerie Georges-Goguen SRC**
***Also known as:* Mini Galerie Radio-Canada**
CP 950, 250, av Université, Moncton, NB E1C 8N8
Tél: 506-382-8326; *Téléc:* 506-853-6739
ghg@nbnet.nb.ca
Primarily promotes the works of Atlantic artists
Georges Goguen

***Moncton:* Galerie Sans Nom Coop Ltée**
***Also known as:* GSN Coopérative**
Centre Culturel Aberdeen, #16, 140 Botsford St., Moncton, NB E1C 4X4
Tel: 506-854-5381; *Fax:* 506-857-2064
ash@fundy.net
www.galeriesansnom.org
Galerie Sans Nom (GSN) is a non-profit, artist-run centre involved in the promotion, production & exhibition of contemporary art. GSN is a venue for creative expression of the artistic community & acting as a vital communication vehicle, provides an impetus for innovation & creativity
Nisk Imbeault, Directrice
André Gorin, Président

***Sackville:* Struts Gallery & Faucet Media Arts Centre: An Artist-Run Centre**
7 Lorne St., Sackville, NB E4L 3Z6
Tel: 506-536-1211; *Fax:* 506-536-4565
info@strutsgallery.ca
www.strutsgallery.ca
Presenting local, regional & national contemporary artist-initiated activities: expositions, performances, demonstrations, workshops, symposia, residencies & digital video production facilities
Paul Henderson, Faucet Manager
John Murchie, Coordinator

***Saint John:* City of Saint John Gallery**
Saint John Arts Centre, 20 Hazen Ave., Saint John, NB E2L 3G8
Tel: 506-649-6040; *Fax:* 506-632-6118
info@saintjohnartscentre.com
www.saintjohnartscentre.com
First municipally funded art gallery in Atlantic Canada; features monthly exhibitions of local & regional art works
Bernard J. Cormier

***St Andrews:* Sunbury Shores Arts & Nature Centre**
139 Water St., St Andrews, NB E5B 1A7
Tel: 506-529-3386; *Fax:* 506-529-4779
info@sunburyshores.org
www.sunburyshores.org
Provides facilities for the study, practice & appreciation of the art, crafts & environmental sciences; stresses the aesthetic appreciation of nature & the importance of its use
Debbie Nielsen, Director

Newfoundland & Labrador

Provincial Art Galleries

The Rooms Provincial Art Gallery
The Rooms Corporation of Newfoundland & Labrador, PO Box 1800 C, 9 Bonaventure Ave., St. John's, NL A1C 5P9
Tel: 709-757-8040; *Fax:* 709-757-8041
www.therooms.ca/artgallery/
Regularly changing exhibitions of all media, chiefly contemporary Canadian, with some international, historic Canadian & Newfoundland folk art & traditional crafts; permanent collection of contemporary Canadian art in many media, with strong holdings of Newfoundland work; art slide library. Extensive public programming & special projects with emphasis on collaboration with professional artists.
Dr. Shauna McCabe, Director

Local Art Galleries in Newfoundland & Labrador

***Corner Brook:* Sir Wilfred Grenfell College Art Gallery (SWGC)**
Memorial University of Newfoundland, Corner Brook, NL A2H 6P9
Tel: 709-637-6209; *Fax:* 709-637-6203
gtuttle@swgc.ca
www.swgc.ca/artgallery
Contemporary art
Gail Tuttle, Director

***St. John's:* Eastern Edge Art Gallery**
72 Harbour Dr., PO Box 2641 C, St. John's, NL A1C 6K1
Tel: 709-739-1882; *Fax:* 709-739-1866
egallery@nfld.net
www.easternedge.ca
Not-for-profit, artist-run centre dedicated to exhibiting contemporary art in diverse media; exhibitions include work by Newfoundland artists & artists from the rest of Canada
Michelle Bush, Director

Northwest Territories

Territorial Art Galleries

Gallery of the Midnight Sun
5005 Bryson Dr., Yellowknife, NT X1A 2A3
Tel: 867-873-8064; *Fax:* 867-873-8065
galleryofthemidnightsun@canada.com
www.gallerymidnightsun.com
NWT's largest selection of Inuit & Dene arts & crafts
Lisa Seagrave, Contact

Nova Scotia

Provincial Art Galleries

Art Gallery of Nova Scotia (AGNS)
PO Box 2262, 1723 Hollis St., Halifax, NS B3J 3C8
Tel: 902-424-7542; *Fax:* 902-424-7359
spaldiij@gov.ns.ca
www.agns.gov.ns.ca
Housed in 1868 heritage building. The Gallery has over 13,000 peices in its permanent collection.
Jeffrey Spalding, Director/Chief Curator

Local Art Galleries in Nova Scotia

***Chéticamp:* Les Trois Pignon**
La Société St-Pierre, CP 430, 15584 Cabot Trail, Chéticamp, NS B0E 1H0
Tél: 902-224-2642; *Téléc:* 902-224-1579
lestroispignons@ns.sympatico.ca
www.lestroispignons.com

Les tapisseries du Dr. Elizabeth LeFort ainsi que d'autres tapis historiques de la région; le musée d'antiquité à Marguerite Gallant est attaché sur la Galerie aussi que centre généalogique
Lisette Aucoin-Bourgeois, Director

***Halifax:* Centre for Art Tapes**
#207, 5600 Sackville St., Halifax, NS B3J 1L2
Tel: 902-420-4002; *Fax:* 902-420-4581
www.centreforarttapes.ca
An artist-run centre that facilitates & supports emerging, intermediate & established artists working with electronic media, such as video, audio & new media; strives to provide production facilities, ongoing programming & training to a diverse membership whose creative abilities contribute to social & artistic goals
Ilan Sandler, Executive Director,
cfat.operations@ns.sympatico.ca

***Halifax:* Dalhousie Art Gallery (DAG)**
6101 University Ave., Halifax, NS B3H 3J5
Tel: 902-494-2403; *Fax:* 902-423-0591
art.gallery@Dal.ca
www.artgallery.Dal.ca
The Dalhousie Art Gallery is a public art gallery, an academic support unit within the educational and research context of Dalhousie University, and a cultural resource for the whole community.
Susan Gibson Garvey, Director/Curator

***Halifax:* Eye Level Gallery**
2128 Gottingen St., Halifax, NS B3K 3B3
Tel: 902-425-6412; *Fax:* 902-425-0019
director@eyelevelgallery.ca
www.eyelevelgallery.ca
Eryn Foster, Director

***Halifax:* MSVU Art Gallery, Mount Saint Vincent University**
166 Bedford Hwy., Halifax, NS B3M 2J6
Tel: 902-457-6160; *Fax:* 902-457-2447
info@msvuart.ca
msvuart.ca
Open daily except Mondays; exhibition program emphasizes women as cultural subjects & producers, new Nova Scotia artists, & themes relevant to the university's academic programs; admission free
Stephen Fisher, Gallery Technician
Ingrid Jenkner, Director

***Halifax:* Nova Scotia Centre for Craft & Design & Maray E. Black Gallery (NSCCD)**
1683 Barrington St., Halifax, NS B3J 1Z9
Tel: 902-424-4062; *Fax:* 902-492-2526
info@craft-design.ns.ca
www.craft-design.gov.ns.ca
Develops & promotes crafts & design in Nova Scotia; includes the Mary E. Black Gallery, a craft showroom, an info. centre, & 5 studios; open year round
Susan MacAlpine Foshay, Director

***Halifax:* Saint Mary's University Art Gallery**
Saint Mary's University, Halifax, NS B3H 3C3
Tel: 902-420-5445; *Fax:* 902-420-5060
gallery@smu.ca
www.smu.ca/administration/externalaffairs/artgallery
Contemporary visual arts by artists within & outside the region; lectures, publications & performing arts program; permanent collection of over 1,800 works
Robin Metcalfe, Director/Curator

***Lunenburg:* Lunenburg Art Gallery (L.A.G.S)**
PO Box 1418, 79-81 Pelham St., Lunenburg, NS B0J 2C0
Tel: 902-640-4044; *Fax:* 902-640-3035
lag@eastlink.ca
www.lunenburgartgallery.com
Founded: 1972 The gallery promotes the works of local, provincial & international artists, sponsors workshops & raises funds; houses the Meldrum collection by the late Earl Bailly; month-long solo exhibitions & ongoing Members Gallery; open seasonally: Mar.-Oct., Tues-Sat 10-5 & Sun 1-5.
Doug Cooke, President
Jim Hannaford, Treasurer
Christine Hurlburt, Gallery Attendant

***Pictou:* Hector Exhibit Centre**
***Also known as:* Hector Centre**
PO Box 1210, 86 Haliburton Rd., Pictou, NS B0K 1H0
Tel: 902-485-4563; *Fax:* 902-485-5213
pcghs@gov.ns.ca
www.rootsweb.com/~nspcghs/
Genealogical & historical archives for Pictou County - census records, cemetery records, shipping lists, newspapers, etc.; local historical, cultural, genealogical & craft exhibits
Katherine Chaisson, Site Manager

***Sydney:* Cape Breton University Art Gallery**
PO Box 5300, Sydney, NS B1P 6L2
Tel: 902-563-1342; *Fax:* 902-563-1142
suzanne_crowdis@capebretonu.ca
capebretonartgallery.blogspot.com;
www.capebretonu.ca/artgalley/
First & only full-time public art gallery on Cape Breton Island; acquires & presents art with emphasis on contemporary Canadian works & the artistic traditions of Cape Breton Island; offers educational & research facilities; a major cultural resource within the educational & research context of the university
Suzanne A. Crowdis, Director/Curator

***Wolfville:* Acadia University Art Gallery**
Highland Ave., Wolfville, NS B4P 2R6
Tel: 902-585-1373; *Fax:* 902-585-1070
fran.kruschen@acadiau.ca
ace.acadiau.ca/arts/artgal/home.htm
The University Gallery serves both as a public gallery and as a teaching facility within Acadia's Faculty of Arts. Its purpose in the community and on the campus is to enrich visual experience through showcasing original works of historical or contemporary importance. The Gallery looks after Acadia's collection of art.
Franziska Kruschen, Director

Ontario

Provincial Art Galleries

Art Gallery of Hamilton (AGH)
123 King St. West, Hamilton, ON L8P 4S8
Tel: 905-527-6610; *Fax:* 905-577-6940
larissa@artgalleryofhamilton.com
www.artgalleryofhamilton.com
Collection of 8,000 art objects; holds one of Canada's most comprehensive collections of Canadian historical, modernist & contemporary art; British, American & European works
Louise Dompierre, President/CEO

Art Gallery of Ontario (AGO)
317 Dundas St. West, Toronto, ON M5T 1G4
Tel: 416-979-6648; *Fax:* 416-204-2713
Toll-Free: 877-225-4246
ticketing@ago.net
www.ago.net
Visit the AGO, located in the heart of Toronto, for an experience of art that includes European Old Masters, Group of Seven, & Canadian & international contemporary works — plus the world's largest public collection of sculptures by Henry Moore.
Dennis Reid, Chief Curator
Matthew Teitelbaum, Director/CEO

Art Gallery of Windsor (AGW)
401 Riverside Dr. West, Windsor, ON N9A 7J1
Tel: 519-977-0013; *Fax:* 519-977-0776
email@artgalleryofwindsor.com
www.artgalleryofwindsor.com
One of the larger, non-government run galleries in Ontario; focus is on Canadian art in an international context; permanent collection of 2,500 paintings & sculptures; resource centre & gift shop; closed Mon., Tue.
Merry Ellen Scully Mosna, President

McMichael Canadian Art Collection
10365 Islington Ave., Kleinburg, ON L0J 1C0
Tel: 905-893-1121; *Fax:* 905-893-0692
Toll-Free: 888-213-1121
info@mcmichael.com
www.mcmichael.com
Founded: 1965 The collection features works of art created by First Nations & Inuit artists, the artists of the Group of Seven & their contemporaries, & other artists who have contributed to the development of Canadian art. Comprehensive education program at kindergarten, elementary & secondary school levels; guided group tours by appt.; extension program & temporary exhibition program. Also programs for adults
Thomas Smart, Executive Director/CEO
Mary Benvenuto, CFO

Local Art Galleries in Ontario

***Bancroft:* The Art Gallery of Bancroft**
PO Box 1360, 8 Hastings Heritage Way, Bancroft, ON K0L 1C0
Tel: 613-332-1542; *Fax:* 613-332-2119
artgallerybancroftont@bellnet.ca
www.algonquinarts.ca
Local & other Ontario artists; gift shop for area artists only; open year round
Diana Gurley, Director
Mr. Wayne Link, Curator

***Barrie:* MacLaren Art Centre**
37 Mulcaster St., Barrie, ON L4M 3M2
Tel: 705-721-9696; *Fax:* 705-735-6935
maclaren@maclarenart.com
www.maclarenart.com
Open Tue.-Fri. 10-5, Sat. 10-4
John Lister, Interim Director

***Bracebridge:* Chapel Gallery**
c/o Muskoka Arts & Crafts Inc., PO Box 376, 15 King St., Bracebridge, ON P1L 1T7
Tel: 705-645-5501; *Fax:* 705-645-0385
info@muskokaartsandcrafts.com
www.muskokaartsandcrafts.com
Open Tue.-Sat.
Elene J. Freer, Curator

***Bracebridge:* Ziska Gallery Muskoka**
RR#1, Bracebridge, ON P1L 1W8
Tel: 705-645-2587
The beauty of nature in paintings & sculpture; open June to Oct.
Jack MacCallum, Curator

***Brampton:* Art Gallery of Peel**
Peel Heritage Complex, 9 Wellington St. East, Brampton, ON L6W 1Y1
Tel: 905-791-4055; *Fax:* 905-451-4931
david.somers@peelregion.ca
www.peelheritagecomplex.org
Located within a cluster of 19th century buildings; features the works of local artists in Peel & contemporary art from across Canada; collection of over 1,500 works consists of contemporary & historic Canadian works with a special emphasis on artists from Peel
David Somers, Curator

***Brantford:* Glenhyrst Art Gallery of Brant**
20 Ava Rd., Brantford, ON N3T 5G9
Tel: 519-756-5932; *Fax:* 519-756-5910
info@glenhyrstartgallery.ca
www.glenhyrst.ca
Permanent collection comprises contemporary works on paper & paintings by Robert Reginald Whale & his descendants; offers a rotating schedule of art exhibitions, an art rental & sales showroom, giftshop & a variety of classes & programmes
James M. Stowe, President, Board of Govenors

***Burlington:* Burlington Art Centre (BAC)**
1333 Lakeshore Rd., Burlington, ON L7S 1A9
Tel: 905-632-7796; *Fax:* 905-632-0278
info@BurlingtonArtCentre.on.ca
www.BurlingtonArtCentre.on.ca
Exhibitions of regional & nationally recognized Canadian artists; a permanent collection of contemporary Canadian ceramic art & a gallery shop, art rental & sales & studios; open daily
Ian D. Ross, Executive Director MFA

***Caledon East:* Yaneff International Art**
18949 Centreville CRK. Rd., Caledon East, ON L0N 1E6
Tel: 905-584-9398; *Fax:* 905-584-9569
posters@yaneff.com
www.yaneff.com
Specializes in rare, 19th-century, 20th century & modern posters online
Chris Yaneff, Director R.C.A., R.GDC, F.GDC
Greg Yaneff, Director/Curator

***Cambridge:* Cambridge Galleries**
Queen's Square, 1 North Square, Cambridge, ON N1S 2K6
Tel: 519-621-0460; *Fax:* 519-621-2080
mmisner@cambridge.galleries.ca
www.cambridgegalleries.ca
Exhibitions offered at 3 locations within Cambridge reflect a range of local & international developments in contemporary & historical visual arts & architecture; collection of contemporary Canadian fibre art; studio courses for all ages; concerts; Canadian international film series
Mary Misner, Gallery Director
Ivan Jurakic, Curator
Sascha Hastings, Curator, Design at Riverside

***Chatham:* Thames Art Gallery (TAG)**
Chatham Cultural Centre, 75 William St. North, Chatham, ON N7M 4L4
Tel: 519-360-1998; *Fax:* 519-354-4170
carll@chatham-kent.ca
www.chatham-kent.ca/ccc
Historical & contemporary artwork by local, national & international artists; hosts 12-15 exhibitions a year; guided tours available with advanced bookings; art lectures & workshops for children & adults; open daily 1-5; admission by donation
Carl L. Lavoy, Curator

Cobourg: **Art Gallery of Northumberland**
55 King St. West, Cobourg, ON K9A 2M2
Tel: 416-372-0333; *Fax:* 416-372-1587
agn@eagle.ca
www.artgalleryofnorthumberland.com
Maintains a permanent collection of more than 600 works of art; changing exhibitions are displayed throughout the year; lectures; education trips; workshops & special events
Dorette E. Carter, Director/Curator

Cornwall: **Cornwall Regional Art Gallery (CRAG) / Galerie régionale des arts de Cornwall**
168 Pitt St., Cornwall, ON K6J 6P4
Tel: 613-938-7387; *Fax:* 613-938-9619
info@cornwallregionalartgallery.ca
www.cornwallregionalartgallery.ca
Promotes and stimulates interest in and the study of the visual arts; advances knowledge and appreciation of the visual arts; provides improved opportunities for Canadian artistic talent; advances the development of the visualarts in Canada.

Curve Lake: **Whetung Craft Centre & Art Gallery**
Curve Lake, ON K0L 1R0
Tel: 705-657-3661; *Fax:* 705-657-3412
mwhetung@whetung.com
www.whetung.com
Authentic works by Indian artists from across Canada.
Michael Whetung, Owner

Durham: **Durham Art Gallery**
PO Box 1021, Durham, ON N0G 1R0
Tel: 519-369-3692; *Fax:* 519-369-3120
info@durhamart.on.ca
www.durhamart.on.ca
Located at 251 George St. East
Ilse Gassinger, Executive Director

Etobicoke: **The Art Gallery, Neilson Park Creative Centre**
56 Neilson Dr., Etobicoke, ON M9C 1V7
Tel: 416-622-5294; *Fax:* 416-622-0892
info@neilsonparkcreativecentre.com
www.neilsonparkcreativecentre.com
Provides a community focus for creative visual arts; variety of exhibitions with strong emphasis on local & contemporary artists
Denise Rainville, Executive Director

Grimsby: **Grimsby Public Art Gallery**
18 Carnegie Lane, Grimsby, ON L3M 1Y1
Tel: 905-945-3246; *Fax:* 905-945-1789
gpag@town.grimsby.on.ca
www.grimsby.ca
Permanent collection of 1,000+ works; contemporary exhibitions & programmes year round
Rhona Wenger, Director

Guelph: **Macdonald Stewart Art Centre (MSAC)**
358 Gordon St., Guelph, ON N1G 1Y1
Tel: 519-837-0010; *Fax:* 519-767-2661
info@msac.ca
www.uoguelph.ca/msac
Permanent collection of over 4,000 works; contemporary Inuit drawings & the Donald Forster Sculpture Park
Judith Nasby, Director

Haileybury: **Temiskaming Art Gallery**
Hailebury Public Library Bldg., PO Box 1090, 545 Lakeshore Rd., Haileybury, ON P0J 1K0
Tel: 705-672-3706; *Fax:* 705-672-5966
tag@ntl.sympatico.ca
www.museumnorth.org/temiskaming_art_gallery
Public gallery; open year round
Maureen Steward, Director/Curator

Haliburton: **Rails End Gallery & Arts Centre**
PO Box 912, 23 York St., Haliburton, ON K0M 1S0
Tel: 705-457-2330; *Fax:* 705-457-2338
hhgfa.railsend@on.aibn.com
www.railsendgallery.com
Open year round
Saskiatent Rees, Executive Director

Kingston: **Agnes Etherington Art Centre (AEAC) / Centre d'art Agnes Etherington**
Queen's University, Kingston, ON K7L 3N6
Tel: 613-533-2190; *Fax:* 613-533-6765
aeac@post.queensu.ca
www.queensu.ca/ageth/
Contemporary & historical art collections & exhibitions; gallery shop, art rental & sales gallery, facility rentals; open year round
Janet M. Brooke, Director

Kingston: **St. Lawrence College Art Gallery**
Portsmouth Ave., Kingston, ON K7L 5A6
D. Gordon, Director

Kitchener: **Homer Watson House & Gallery**
1754 Old Mill Rd., Kitchener, ON N2P 1H7
Tel: 519-748-4377; *Fax:* 519-748-6808
programs@homerwatson.on.ca
www.homerwatson.on.ca
Open Jan. - Dec.
Faith Hieblinger, Director/Curator

Kitchener: **Kitchener-Waterloo Art Gallery (KWAG)**
101 Queen St. North, Kitchener, ON N2H 6P7
Tel: 519-579-5860; *Fax:* 519-578-0740
mail@kwag.on.ca
www.kwag.ca
Founded: 1956 Open year round; Monday - Wednesday: 9:30-5:00; Thursday: 9:30-9:00; Saturday: 10:00-5:00; Sunday 1:00-5:00.
Alf Bogusky, Director General
Caroline Oliver, Director, Development & Marketing

Leamington: **Leamington Art Centre**
72 Talbot St. West, Leamington, ON N8H 1M4
Tel: 519-326-2711; *Fax:* 519-326-6491
artcentr@mnsi.net
www.leamingtonartscentre.com
The Leamington Arts Centre, run by the South Essex Arts Association, is a charitable, not-for-profit organization. Its purpose is to serve the community through arts & culture. The Leamington Arts Centre includes a main gallery, which exhibits the work of local artists. Heinz Memorabilia explains the history of the Heinz Co.. The Centre also features the Marine Heritage Interpretive Centre, Signature Gifts, & several educational programs throughout the year for both adults & children.
Tamsen Dippel, Gallery Coordinator

Lindsay: **The Lindsay Gallery**
190 Kent St. West, Lindsay, ON K9V 2Y6
Tel: 705-324-1780; *Fax:* 705-324-1780
lind.gall@on.aibn.com
www.thelindsaygallery.com
Not-for-profit gallery offering regular exhibitions, art classes & a boutique
Margot J. Fawcett, Marketing Co-chair
Janet Smith, Chair

London: **McIntosh Gallery**
The University of Western Ontario, London, ON N6A 3K7
Tel: 519-661-3181; *Fax:* 519-661-3059
akenned4@uwo.ca
www.mcintoshgallery.ca
Exhibitions featuring local, national, & international artists working in various media; exhibitions change every 6 weeks & are accompanied by art-related videos, films & lectures; art collection & gallery's records, some artist archives & periodical library available as resources to students for research purposes; open 6 days/week
Arlene Kennedy, Director

Minden: **Agnes Jamieson Gallery**
PO Box 648, 176 Bobcaygeon Rd. North, Minden, ON K0M 2K0
Tel: 705-286-3763; *Fax:* 705-286-4917
gallery@minden.on.ca
Laurie Carmount, Administrator

Mississauga: **Art Gallery of Mississauga (AGM)**
300 City Centre Dr., Mississauga, ON L5B 3C1
Tel: 905-896-5088; *Fax:* 905-615-4167
fred.troughton@mississauga.ca
www.artgalleryofmississauga.com
A public art gallery providing state of the art exhibitions by local, national & international artists; exhibits change every 7 weeks; admission is free; open Mon.-Fri. 9 am to 5 pm, weekends: noon to 4 pm
Fred Troughton, Executive Director

Mississauga: **Blackwood Gallery**
University of Toronto, 3359 Mississauga Rd. North, Mississauga, ON L5L 1C6
Tel: 905-828-3789; *Fax:* 905-569-4262
blackwood.gallery@utoronto.ca
www.blackwoodgallery.ca
Founded: 1992 Presents exhibitions of contemporary art in all media.
Carmen Victor, Curatorial Assistant
Christof Migone, Director/Curator

Mississauga: **Harbour Gallery**
1697 Lakeshore Rd. West, Mississauga, ON L5J 1J4
Tel: 905-822-5495; *Fax:* 905-822-5578
info@harbourgallery.com
www.harbourgallery.com
Rotating collection of over 30 accredited Canadian artists in a variety of mediums.
Jacqueline Bryant, Director

Niagara-on-the-Lake: **RiverBrink: Home of the Weir Collection**
116 Queenston St., RR#1, Niagara-on-the-Lake, ON L0S 1J0
Tel: 905-262-4510; *Fax:* 905-262-4477
weirlib@becon.org
www.riverbrink.org
Open Victoria Day - Thanksgiving
Karin Jahnke-Haslam, Managing Director
Gary Essar, Curator/Artistic Director

North Bay: **W.K.P. Kennedy Gallery**
150 Main St. East, North Bay, ON P1B 1A8
Tel: 705-474-1944; *Fax:* 705-474-8431
gallery@capitolcentre.ca
www.kennedygallery.org
A changing program of historical & contemporary visual art; free
Dermot Wilson, Director/Curator

North Bay: **White Water Gallery**
PO Box 1491, 147 Worthington St. East, North Bay, ON P1B 8K6
Tel: 705-476-2444; *Fax:* 705-476-9243
info@whitewatergallery.com
whitewatergallery.com
Artist-run centre for contemporary art

Oakville: **Oakville Galleries**
1306 Lakeshore Rd. East, Oakville, ON L6J 1L6
Tel: 905-844-4402; *Fax:* 905-844-7968
info@oakvillegalleries.com
www.oakvillegalleries.com
Contemporary art gallery with 2 exhibition spaces: Oakville Galleries at Centennial Square, 120 Navy St. & Oakville Galleries in Gairloch Gardens, 1306 Lakeshore Rd. East
Francine Périnet, Director
Marnie Fleming, Curator, Contemporary Art

Orillia: **Orillia Museum of Art & History**
30 Peter St. South, Orillia, ON L3V 5A9
Tel: 705-326-2159; *Fax:* 705-326-7828
info@orilliamuseum.org
www.orilliamuseum.org
Public art gallery & museum; gift shop; open Mon. - Sat.
Sim Salata, Director/Curator

Orton: **Burdette Gallery Ltd.**
111212 - 11th Line, East Garafraxa, RR#2, Orton, ON L0N 1N0
Tel: 519-928-5547; *Fax:* 519-928-2349
art@burdettegallery.com
www.burdettegallery.com
The Gallery represents approximately 100 artists who are locally, nationally, and internationally renowned.
Dr. George R. Cormack, Owner

Oshawa: **The Robert McLaughlin Gallery**
Civic Centre, 72 Queen St., Oshawa, ON L1H 3Z3
Tel: 905-576-3000; *Fax:* 905-576-9774
communications@rmg.on.ca
www.rmg.on.ca
Permanent exhibitions include masterpieces of Canadian Art: Emily Carr, members of the Group of Seven, Painters Eleven
David Aurandt, Executive Director

Oshweken: **Two Turtle Iroquois Fine Art Gallery**
Middleport Plaza, 1180 Hwy. 54, Oshweken, ON N3W 2G9
Tel: 519-751-2774; *Toll-Free:* 877-264-6651
arnold@twoturtle.com
www.twoturtle.com
Showcasing the art of the Hodenosaunee and Arnold Jacobs.
Arnold Aron Jacobs, Owner

Ottawa: **Artists' Centre d'Artistes Ottawa Inc.**
Also known as: **Gallery 101**
236 Nepean St., Ottawa, ON K2P 0B8
Tel: 613-230-2799; *Fax:* 613-230-3253
info@gallery101.org
www.gallery101.org
A non-profit artist operated centre dedicated to the professional presentation & circulation of visual & media arts; solo & curated group exhibitions by local Canadian & international contemporary artists
Leanne L'Hirondelle, Director

Ottawa: **Carleton University Art Gallery (CUAG)**
Carleton University, St. Patrick's Bldg., 1125 Colonel By Dr., Ottawa, ON K1S 5B6
Tel: 613-520-2120; *Fax:* 613-520-4409
www.carleton.ca/gallery
27,000 works in contemporary Canadian art, European prints & drawings from the 16th to 19th centuries, Inuit prints & sculpture
Sandra Dyck, Curator

Owen Sound: **Tom Thomson Memorial Art Gallery**
840 First Ave. West, Owen Sound, ON N4K 4K4
Tel: 519-376-1932; *Fax:* 519-376-3037
ttmag@city.owen-sound.on.ca
www.tomthomson.org
Public art gallery featuring an extensive collection of Canadian art, historical & contemporary, with a focus on Thomson & the Group of Seven; full range of educational activities including lectures, workshops, & tours; gallery shop
Stuart Reid, Director/Curator

Peterborough: **Art Gallery of Peterborough**
250 Crescent St., Peterborough, ON K9J 2G1
Tel: 705-743-9179; *Fax:* 705-743-8168
gallery@agp.on.ca
www.agp.on.ca
Public art gallery with changing exhibitions
Curtis Joseph Collins, Director
Pamela Edmonds, Curator/Arts Coordinator

Peterborough: **Artspace**
PO Box 1748, 378 Aylmer St. North, Peterborough, ON K9J 7X6
Tel: 705-748-3883; *Fax:* 705-748-3224
info@artspace-arc.org
www.artspace-arc.org
Committed to supporting the growth & development of contemporary artists & related-art practices; dedicated to artistic freedom & exploration
Iga Janik, Director

Peterborough: **The Russell Gallery of Fine Art**
165 King St., Peterborough, ON K9J 2R8
Tel: 705-743-0151
info@russellgallery.com
www.russellgallery.com
Representing leading Canadian & international contemporary artists
Bruce Rapp, Co-Director
Sally Rapp, Co-Director

St Catharines: **Rodman Hall Arts Centre**
109 St. Paul Cres., St Catharines, ON L2S 1M3
Tel: 905-684-2925; *Fax:* 905-682-4733
rodmanhall@brocku.ca
www.brocku.ca/rodmanhall/
Collection of about 1000 works of art, contemporary & historical, majority by Canadian artists; closed Mon.
Gordon Hatt, Director

St Thomas: **St Thomas-Elgin Public Art Centre**
301 Talbot St., St Thomas, ON N5P 1B5
Tel: 519-631-4040; *Fax:* 519-631-4057
info@stepac.ca
www.stepac.ca
Promotion of visual arts by a permanent collection of over 800 artworks, exhibitions by current artists, & a variety of art education programs; volunteers & new members welcome; facility rental available; open Tue. - Sun.
David Bobier, Executive Director
Barbara Hodge, Admin. Asst/Volunteer Coordinator
Sherri Howard, Education Coordinator/Events Coordinator

Sarnia: **Gallery Lambton**
Bayside Mall, 150 Christina St. North, Sarnia, ON N7T 2M6
Tel: 519-336-8127; *Fax:* 519-336-8128
david.talyor@county-lambton.on.ca
www.lclmg.org
Other contact information:
holly.rutherford@county-lambton.on.ca
Exhibitions of contemporary art, featuring some of the best artists working in Ontario today, many with national & international reputations; collection contains paintings by the Group of Seven, & others, which are important to Canadian art history & are considered national treasures; wide range of changing exhibitions, tours for adults & school groups, education services, artist talks, films, pub
David G. Taylor, Curator

Sault Ste Marie: **Art Gallery of Algoma**
10 East St., Sault Ste Marie, ON P6A 3C3
Tel: 705-949-9067; *Fax:* 705-949-6261
aga@shaw.ca
www.artgalleryofalgoma.on.ca
Dedicated to cultivating & advancing the awareness of visual arts in Sault Ste Marie & the district of Algoma
Michael Burtch, Director/Curator

Simcoe: **Norfolk Arts Centre**
Lynnwood National Historic Site, PO Box 67, 21 Lynnwood Ave., Simcoe, ON N3Y 4K8
Tel: 519-428-0540; *Fax:* 519-428-0549
artscentre@norfolkcounty.on.ca
www.norfolkcounty.on.ca
Norfolk county's only arts centre, located in downtown Simcoe; programming includes exhibitions, kids studio, adult art workshops, Lynnwood's Film Simcoe, annual drive-thru art gallery exhibition
Robert Missen, Curator/Director

Stouffville: **The Latcham Gallery**
PO Box 3, 6240 Main St., Stouffville, ON L4A 7Z4
Tel: 905-640-8954; *Fax:* 905-640-6246
Public art gallery
Roz Pritchard, Director
Maura Broadhurst, Curator

Stratford: **Gallery Stratford**
54 Romeo St. South, Stratford, ON N5A 4S9
Tel: 519-271-5271; *Fax:* 519-271-1642
clee@gallerystratford.on.ca
www.gallerystratford.on.ca
A non-profit, public art gallery open year round; contemporary, historical, local, national & international artists are highlighted annually in the heritage building; offers educational programs, workshops & fundraisers
Jennifer Rudder, Executive Director

Sudbury: **Art Gallery of Sudbury / Galerie d'art de Sudbury**
251 John St., Sudbury, ON P3E 1P9
Tel: 705-675-4871; *Fax:* 705-674-3065
gallery@artsudbury.org
www.artsudbury.org
Historical & contemporary Canadian art; open Tue.-Sat. 10-5, Sun. 12-5
Celeste Scopelites, Director/Curator

Thunder Bay: **Thunder Bay Art Gallery**
Also known as: **Thunder Bay National Exhibition Centre & Centre for Indian Art**
PO Box 10193 F, 1080 Keewatin St., Thunder Bay, ON P7B 6T7
Tel: 807-577-6427; *Fax:* 807-577-3781
info@tbag.ca
www.tbag.ca
Collection & exhibition of contemporary First Nations art, regional & international exhibits
Sharon Godwin, Director
Glenn Allison, Curator

Toronto: **Academy of Spherical Arts**
38 Hanna Ave., Toronto, ON M6K 1X5
Tel: 416-532-2782; *Fax:* 416-532-3075
Toll-Free: 866-532-2782
info@sphericalarts.com
www.sphericalarts.com
Four room gallery displaying Canada's oldest collection of billiard tables, as well as billiard related accessories. Also hosts yearly art exhibitions for emerging Canadian artists, and includes Canadian art in its permanent collection.
Rick Williams, Founder

Toronto: **Angell Gallery**
890 Queen St. West, Toronto, ON M6J 1G3
Tel: 416-530-0444
info@angellgallery.com
www.angellgallery.com
Wed.-Sat. 12-5
Jamie Angell, Director

Toronto: **Annex Art Centre**
1073 Bathurst St., Toronto, ON M5R 3G8
Tel: 416-516-0110
info@annexartcentre.com
www.annexartcentre.com
An art gallery and teaching studio located in Toronto's Annex. We offer visual art, drama for kids, teens, and adults.

Toronto: **Art Dialogue Gallery**
#501, 900 Yonge St., Toronto, ON M4W 3P5
Tel: 416-928-5904; *Fax:* 416-928-6515
Provides educated information & guidance in acquiring fine art; exhibitions & consultations for the display of artwork; lectures on various topics of contemporary art
Luciana Benzi, Director

Toronto: **Art Gallery of York University**
Accolade East, 4700 Keele St., Toronto, ON M3J 1P3
Tel: 416-736-5169; *Fax:* 416-736-5985
AGYU@yorku.ca
www.yorku.ca/agyu
Devoted to the presentation of innovative contemporary art; aims to situate Canadian art within an international context & to introduce Canadian audiences to important artists working abroad
Philip Monk, Director

Toronto: **Art Metropole**
Also known as: **Art Official Inc.**
788 King St. West, Toronto, ON M5V 1N6
Tel: 416-703-4400; *Fax:* 416-703-4404
info@artmetropole.com
www.artmetropole.com
Specializes in contemporary art in multiple formats; offers artists' products for sale on premises & through web site as well as publishes, promotes, exhibits & distributes artists' products in various formats
Ann Dean, Director

Toronto: **The Bluffs Gallery**
Scarborough Arts Council, 1859 Kingston Rd., Toronto, ON M1N 1T3
Tel: 416-698-7322; *Fax:* 416-698-7972
info@scarborougharts.com
www.scarborougharts.com
Founded: 1979 The Bluffs Gallery is dedicated to the exhibition & sale of artwork by Scarborough Arts Council members. The Gallery offers solo & group exhibitions of all arts media, special events, workshops, & city-wide programs to promote the arts. Open Monday - Saturday; Closed on long weekends.
Tim Whalley, Executive Director

Toronto: **Corkin Shopland Gallery**
Bldg. 61, 55 Mill St., Toronto, ON M5A 3C4
Tel: 416-979-1980; *Fax:* 416-979-7018
info@corkinshopland.com
www.corkinshopland.com
Eclectic works by contemporary artists in all media
Jane Corkin

Toronto: **Creative Spirit Art Centre (CSAC)**
PO Box 16 P, 122 Wells St., Toronto, ON M5S 2S6
Tel: 416-588-8801; *Fax:* 416-588-8966
csac@creativespirit.on.ca
creativespirit.on.ca
Founded: 1992 Arts & Disabilities - Public Art Gallery/Studio, resource and information centre. Monthly exhibitions - Special area of collection of Art Brut, Outsider Art, Folk Art - Integrated exhibitions of Art produced by Artists with disabilities and Artists without disabilities. Closed August.
Ellen Anderson, Director

Toronto: **Drabinsky Gallery**
122 Scollard St., Toronto, ON M5R 1G2
Tel: 416-324-5766; *Fax:* 416-324-5770
info@drabinskygallery.com
www.drabinskygallery.com
Presents & promotes contemporary Canadian art in all media, representing the estate of Harold Town; located in Toronto's Yorkville district
Linda Book, Director
Garth Drabinsky, Principal

Toronto: **Edward Day Gallery**
952 Queen St. West, Toronto, ON M6J 1G8
Tel: 416-921-6540; *Fax:* 416-921-6624
eddaygal.toronto@sympatico.ca
www.edwarddaygallery.com
Mary Sue Rankin, Director

Toronto: **Gabor Mezei Studio**
587 Markham St., Toronto, ON M6G 2L7
Tel: 416-534-9800
www.gallerygabor.com
Other contact information: Mobile: 416/319-0914
Small art gallery showing mainly the owner's work & a small selection of Canadian & international artists; approximately four exhibitions per year; by appt.
Gabor P. Mezei, Director/Curator

Toronto: **Gallery Arcturus**
80 Gerrard St. East, Toronto, ON M5B 1G6
Tel: 416-977-1077; *Fax:* 416-977-1066
ob-art@arcturus.ca
www.arcturus.ca
Contemporary art gallery.
Cathy Stilo, Curator

Toronto: **Gallery TPW**
Also known as: **Toronto Photographers Workshop**
56 Ossington Ave., Toronto, ON M6J 2Y7
Tel: 416-645-1066; *Fax:* 416-645-1681
info@gallerytp.ca
gallerytpw.ca
Contemporary photography by Canadian & international artists.
Gary Hall, Executive Director
Kim Simon, Programming Director

Toronto: **Glendon Gallery / Galerie Glendon**
Glendon College, York University, 2275 Bayview Ave., Toronto, ON M4N 3M6
Tel: 416-487-6721; *Fax:* 416-487-6779
gallery@glendon.yorku.ca
www.glendon.yorku.ca/gallery
University-affiliated public art gallery that focuses on contemporary Canadian art of merit with an added interest in francophone artistic expression; literature in French & English; guided tours & lectures
Martine Rheault, Director, 416/487-6859

Toronto: **The Isaacs/Innuit Gallery**
PO Box 84, 401 Richmond St. West, Toronto, ON M5V 3A8
Tel: 416-921-9985; *Fax:* 416-921-9530
Contemporary Inuit art, Inuit antiquities & early North American Indian art; contemporary Canadian artists
A. Isaacs

Toronto: **Joseph D. Carrier Art Gallery**
Columbus Centre, 901 Lawrence Ave. West, Toronto, ON M6A 1C3
Tel: 416-789-7011; *Fax:* 416-789-3951
jdcarrier@villacharities.com
www.villacharities.com
Flavio Belli, Curator/Director

Toronto: **The Justina M. Barnicke Gallery**
Hart House, University of Toronto, 7 Hart House Circle, Toronto, ON M5S 3H3
Tel: 416-978-8398; *Fax:* 416-978-8387
barbara.fischer@utoronto.ca
www.utoronto.ca/gallery/
Each year, 8-10 exhibitions are mounted featuring contemporary Canadian artists as well as historical exhibitions
Barbara Fischer, Director/Curator

Toronto: **Knight Galleries International**
472 Coldstream Ave., Toronto, ON M5N 1Y5
Tel: 416-923-0836; *Fax:* 416-923-8985
knight@knightgall.com
www.knightgall.com
Julian Liknaitzky, President

Toronto: **Koffler Gallery/Koffler Centre of the Arts**
4588 Bathurst St., Toronto, ON M2R 1W6
Tel: 416-636-1880; *Fax:* 416-636-5813
koffler@bjcc.ca
www.bjcc.ca
The Koffler Gallery maintains a year-round exhibition program of contemporary art; programming emphasizes new work by mid-career & more senior Canadian artists, & within this context, work of special interest to the Jewish community
Carolyn Bell Farrell, Senior Curator
Diane Uslaner, Director

Toronto: **The Market Gallery**
South St. Lawrence Market, 95 Front St. East, Toronto, ON M5E 1C2
Tel: 416-392-7604; *Fax:* 416-392-0572
marketgallery@toronto.ca
www.toronto.ca/culture/the_market_gallery.htm
A focus on the art & history of Toronto
Pamela Wachna, Curator

Toronto: **Mercer Union, A Centre for Contemporary Visual Art**
37 Lisgar St., Toronto, ON M6J 3T3
Tel: 416-536-1519
info@mercerunion.org
www.mercerunion.org
An artist-run centre dedicated to the existence of contemporary art; provides a forum for the production & exhibition of Canadian & international conceptually & aesthetically engaging art & related cultural practices; pursues primary concerns through critical activities that include exhibitions, lectures, screenings, performances, publications, events & special projects; non-profit, charitable organization.
Dave Dyment, Co-Director

Toronto: **Museum of Contemporary Canadian Art**
952 Queen St. West, Toronto, ON M6J 1G8
Tel: 416-395-0067; *Fax:* 416-395-7598
mocca@toronto.ca
www.mocca.toronto.ca
Contemporary Canadian artists' works, including traditional & new media; six exhibitions a year showcase established & emerging artists from across Canada; exhibition based programming; open Tue.-Sun., 11-6; free admission; groups & tours by appt.
David Liss, Director/Curator

Toronto: **Odon Wagner Gallery**
196 Davenport Rd., Toronto, ON M5R 1J2
Tel: 416-962-0438; *Fax:* 416-962-1581
Toll-Free: 800-551-2465
info@odonwagnergallery.com
www.odonwagnergallery.com
Fine art gallery featuring masterpieces of past & present; sale & purchase of quality paintings, restoration, appraisal, consultation & framing services
Odon Wagner, Director

Toronto: **Odon Wagner Gallery & Odon Wagner Contemporary**
172 Davenport Rd., Toronto, ON M5R 1J2
Tel: 416-962-0438; *Fax:* 416-962-1581
Toll-Free: 800-551-2465
info@odonwagnergallery.com
www.odonwagnergallery.com
Features an ensemble of historic, modern & contemporary painting, representing the many periods & schools from the last three centuries
Odon Wagner, Director

Toronto: **Olga Korper Gallery**
17 Morrow Ave., Toronto, ON M6R 2H9
Tel: 416-538-8220; *Fax:* 416-538-8772
info@olgakorpergallery.com
www.olgakorpergallery.com
Established in 1973, the gallery is committed to the exhibition & promotion of Canadian & international contemporary art
Olga Korper, Director

Toronto: **A Space Gallery**
#110, 401 Richmond St. West, Toronto, ON M5V 3A8
Tel: 416-979-9633; *Fax:* 416-979-9683
info@aspacegallery.org
www.aspacegallery.org
A Space has a thirty year history of multi-disciplinary artist-run activity. The organizations' mandate encompasses the investigation, presentation and interpretation of contemporary art forms, different disciplines and theories. A Space maintains a politically engaged issue oriented programming that is inclusive of a wide range of media, disciplines and views.
Michelle LaVallee, Curatorial Resident

Toronto: **Susan Hobbs Gallery**
137 Tecumseth St., Toronto, ON M6J 2H2
Tel: 416-504-3699; *Fax:* 416-504-8064
info@susanhobbs.com
www.susanhobbs.com
Exhibition & sales of contemporary Canadian art; artists represented include Ian Carr-Harris, Magdalen Celestino, Robin Collyer, Max Dean, Brian Groombridge, Scott Lyall, Arnaud Maggs, Liz Magor, Sandra Meigs, Colette Whiten, Robert Wiens, Shirley Wiitasalo, & Kevin Yates
Susan Hobbs

Toronto: **University of Toronto Art Centre**
University College, 15 King's College Circle, Toronto, ON M5S 3H7
Tel: 416-978-1838; *Fax:* 416-971-2059
niamh.olaoghaire@utoronto.ca
www.utoronto.ca/artcentre
Housing galleries with selections from university collections as well as a schedule of changing exhibitions
Dr. Niamh O'Laoghaire, Director, 416/946-7015
Dr. Dawn Cain, Malcove Curator, 416/978-6596
Liz Wylie, University of Toronto Art Curator, 416/946-3029

Toronto: **Ydessa Hendeles Art Foundation (YHAF)**
778 King St. West, PO Box 757 F, Toronto, ON M4Y 2N6
Tel: 416-413-9400; *Fax:* 416-969-9889
ydessa@yhaf.org
Contemporary art collection; features work of international artists; works on display include paintings, photography, and multimedia projects.
Ydessa Hendeles

Toronto: **York Quay Gallery**
Harbourfront Centre, 235 Queen's Quay West, Toronto, ON M5J 2G8
Tel: 416-973-4000; *Fax:* 416-973-4859
info@harbourfront.on.ca
www.harbourfront.on.ca
Contemporary art.

Toronto: **YYZ Artists' Outlet**
#140, 401 Richmond St. West, Toronto, ON M5V 3A8
Tel: 416-598-4546; *Fax:* 416-598-2282
yyz@yyzartistsoutlet.org
www.yyzartistsoutlet.org
YYZ is dedicated to the support of work by contemporary artists working in all media, and to the provision of a venue for the exhibition of this work through on-going programs in both visual and time-based arts - video, film and performance.
Gregory Elgstrand, Director of Programming
Jeffrey Matt, Director of Operations

Waterloo: **Canadian Clay & Glass Gallery / Galerie Canadienne de la Céramique et du Verre**
25 Caroline St. North, Waterloo, ON N2L 2Y5
Tel: 519-746-1882; *Fax:* 519-746-6396
info@canadianclayandglass.ca
www.canadianclayandglass.ca
Exhibits contemporary artworks executed in clay, glass, stained glass & enamel for public education & enjoyment
Robert Achtemichuk, Director

Waterloo: **Robert Langen Gallery**
Wilfrid Laurier University, Waterloo, ON N2L 3C5
Tel: 519-884-1970; *Fax:* 519-888-9721
sluke@wlu.ca
www.wlu.ca
The University's visual arts centre, since 1989; provides knowledge, stewardship, appreciation & enjoyment of Canadian art & culture to members of the Laurier community & the community at large
Suzanne Luke, Curator/Art Gallery Coordinator
Deborah Currie, Manager, Cultural Affairs

Waterloo: **University of Waterloo Art Gallery**
University of Waterloo, 200 University Ave. West., ECH, Waterloo, ON N2L 3G1
Tel: 519-888-4567; *Fax:* 519-746-4982
cpodedwo@uwaterloo.ca
www.artgallery.uwaterloo.ca
Produces exhibitions of contemporary Canadian art in all media; holds a collection of contemporary Canadian art since 1960; open Tue. - Sat. during academic year at two sites: Modern Languages Building & the main gallery in East Campus Hall
Andrew Hunter, Director/Curator
Bruce Taylor, Chair, Board

Whitby: **The Station Gallery**
1450 Henry St., Whitby, ON L1N 0A8
Tel: 905-668-4185; *Fax:* 905-668-1934
stationgallery@whitby.ca
www.whitbystationgallery.com
The gallery's Permanent Collection exceeds 300 original prints, paintings, sculpture, and mixed media works.
Donna Raetsen-Kemp, Director

Woodstock: **Woodstock Art Gallery (WAG)**
447 Hunter St., Woodstock, ON N4S 4G7
Tel: 519-539-2382; *Fax:* 519-539-2564
gallery@city.woodstock.on.ca
www.city.woodstock.on.ca
Features contemporary & historical exhibitions; wide range of classes & workshops for adults & children; focuses on local painter Florence Carlyle through an extensive permanent collection & family artifacts
Maria Ricker, Curator

Prince Edward Island

Provincial Art Galleries

Confederation Centre Art Gallery (CCAG) / Le Musée d'Art du Centre de la Confédération
145 Richmond St., Charlottetown, PE C1A 1J1
Tel: 902-628-6111; *Fax:* 902-566-4648
jsimpson@confederationcentre.com
www.confederationcentre.com
Critical inquiry into 200 years of Canadian art; 28 annual exhibitions; 15,000 work collection
Jon L. Tupper, Director

Quebec

Provincial Art Galleries

Musée d'art contemporain de Montréal (MACM)
185, rue Ste-Catherine ouest, Montréal, QC H2X 3X5
Tél: 514-847-6226; *Téléc:* 514-847-6292
info@macm.org
www.macm.org
Collection of over 6,000 works dating from 1939 by artists from Québec, Canada & around the world; a specialized reference centre is available for research; various performances, lectures & educational programs are offered by the museum throughout the year; restaurant, boutique & bookstore
Marc Mayer, Directeur
Paulette Gagnon, Curator-in-Chief

Musée des beaux-arts de Montréal / Montreal Museum of Fine Arts
CP 3000 A, #1379, 1380, rue Sherbrooke ouest, Montréal, QC H3G 2T9
Tél: 514-285-2000; *Téléc:* 514-844-6042
Ligne sans frais: 800-899-6873
webmaster@mbamtl.org
www.mmfa.qc.ca
The Museum houses an encyclopaedic collection that includes Canadian Art, Contemporary Art, European Art, Decorative Arts, Ancient Cultures, & Mediterranean Archeology; access to the permanent collection is free
Guy Cogeval, Director
Wanda Palma, Public Relations

Musée national des beaux-arts du Québec
Parc des Champs-de-Bataille, Québec, QC G1R 5H3
Tél: 418-643-2150; *Téléc:* 418-646-3330
Ligne sans frais: 866-220-2150
info@mnba.qc.ca
www.mnba.qc.ca
Founded: 1933 The museum, situated on the Plains of Abraham, houses prestigious collections of 17th, 18th, & 19th century art, plus a collection of contemporary art. Various temporary exhibitions are also held. Open year round, the museum also features a library, a bookstore, & an educational service.
Esther Trépanier, Director

Local Art Galleries in Quebec

***Alma:* Langage Plus**
CP 518, #102, 414, rue Collard, Alma, QC G8B 5W1
Tél: 418-668-6635; *Téléc:* 418-668-3263
langageplus@cgocable.ca
www.langageplus.com

***Amos:* Centre d'exposition d'Amos**
222, 1e av est, Amos, QC J9T 1H3
Tel: 819-732-6070; *Fax:* 819-732-3242
exposition@ville.amos.qc.ca
www.ville.amos.qc.ca
L'art actuel et traditionnel; les sciences et l'histoire
Marianne Trudel, Directrice

***Aylmer:* Centre d'exposition l'Imagier**
9, rue Front, Aylmer, QC J9H 4W8
Tél: 819-684-1445; *Téléc:* 819-684-4058
info@limagier.qc.ca
www.limagier.qc.ca
Gallery & sculpture garden
Yvette Debain, Directrice

***Baie-Saint-Paul:* Centre d'Art**
4, boul Fafard, Baie-Saint-Paul, QC G3Z 2J3
Tél: 418-435-3681; *Téléc:* 418-435-6269
cartbstp@charlevoix.net
www.centredart-bsp.qc.ca

***Baie-Saint-Paul:* Centre d'Exposition de Baie-St-Paul**
23, rue Ambroise-Fafand, Baie-Saint-Paul, QC G3Z 2J2
Tél: 418-435-3681; *Téléc:* 418-435-6269
cexpo@bellnet.ca
centredart-bsp.qc.ca/cexpo/centrexpo.htm
Françoise Labbé

***Carleton:* Centre d'Artistes Vaste et Vague**
774, boul Perron est, Carleton, QC G0C 1J0
Tél: 418-364-3123; *Téléc:* 418-364-6822
cvaste.communication@globetrotter.net
Centre de production et de diffusion en art actuel et contemporain Expositions, résidences d'artiste, atelier de production, production d'événements majeurs (Symposium)
Guylaine Langlois

***Chicoutimi:* Espace Virtuel**
534, rue Jacques-Cartier est, Chicoutimi, QC G7H 1Z6
Tél: 418-698-3873; *Téléc:* 418-698-3874
espacevirtuel@cybernaute.com
espacevirtuel.ca/centre.html

***Drummondville:* Galerie d'art l'Union-Vie du Centre Culturel de Drummondville**
175, rue Ringuet, Drummondville, QC J2C 2P7
Tél: 819-477-5416; *Téléc:* 819-477-5723
nblanchette@centre-culturel.qc.ca
www.centre-culturel.qc.ca
Open year round
Normand Blanchette, Directeur

***Gatineau:* Axe Néo-7 Art Contemporain**
80, rue Hanson, Gatineau, QC J8Y 3M5
Tél: 819-771-2122; *Téléc:* 819-771-0696
axeneo7@axeneo7.qc.ca
www.axeneo7.qc.ca
Artist run centre; contemporary art gallery

***Gatineau:* Centre d'exposition Art-Image et espace Odyssée Maison de la Culture de Gatineau**
855, boul de la Gappe, Gatineau, QC J8T 8H9
Tél: 819-243-2325; *Téléc:* 819-243-2527
art_image@gatineau.ca
www.ville.gatineau.qc.ca/artimage
To increase communication between the artistic fields & the general public

***Gatineau:* Galerie Montcalm**
Maison du Citoyen, CP 1970 Hull, 25, rue Laurier, Gatineau, QC J8X 3Y9
Tél: 819-595-7488; *Téléc:* 819-595-7492
galeriemontcalm1@gatineau.ca
www.gataineau.ca/galerie
Open year round; free
Dominique Laurent, Responsable

***Jonquière:* Centre national d'exposition**
CP 605 A, 4160, rue du Vieux Pont, Jonquière, QC G7X 7W4
Tél: 418-546-2177; *Téléc:* 418-546-2180
cne@videotron.ca
pages.infinit.net/cne
Presents exhibitions of the works of professional artists & several travelling shows; demonstrates richness of the collections of Québec & other Canadian & international museums; guided tours, workshops, demonstrations & edukits available
Jacqueline Caron, Directrice

***Laval:* Salle Alfred Pellan, Maison des arts de Laval**
1395, boul de la Concorde ouest, Laval, QC H7N 5W1
Tél: 450-662-4440; *Téléc:* 450-662-4428
sallealfredpellan@ville.laval.qc.ca
www.ville.laval.qc.ca
Arts visuels à caractère contemporain
Ginette Beaunoyer, Contact

***Lennoxville:* Foreman Art Gallery of Bishop's University**
***Also known as:* Galerie d'art Foreman de l'Université Bishop's**
Bishop's University, 2600 College St., Lennoxville, QC J1M 0C8
Tel: 819-822-9600; *Fax:* 819-822-9703
gallery@ubishops.ca
www.ubishops.ca/artgallery.htm
To serve as a forum for the presentation & examination of the visual arts through the programming of contemporary & historical exhibitions as well as lecture series, workshops & films; open Tues. - Sat. 12-5, evenings when Centennial Theatre open; admission free
Vicky Chainey Gagnon, Curator

***Longueuil:* Plein sud, centre d'exposition en art actuel à Longueuil**
100, rue de Gentilly est, espace D-0626, Longueuil, QC J4H 4A9
Tél: 450-679-2966; *Téléc:* 450-679-4480
plein-sud@plein-sud.org
www.plein-sud.org
Diffuse la production d'artistes professionnels dont les recherches s'inscrivent en art actuel; présente des expositions temporaires et offre des activités qui visent à familiariser le public avec les différentes avenues proposées par cet art

***Matane:* Galerie d'art de Matane**
#3, 520, av Saint-Jérôme, Matane, QC G4W 3B5
Tél: 418-566-6687; *Téléc:* 418-562-6675
gartm@globetrotter.qc.ca
www.rcaaq.org/membres/profil/34
Présenter environ 8 expositions d'artistiques du Québec, du Canada et de l'étranger

***Mont-Laurier:* Centre d'exposition Mont-Laurier**
CP 323, 385, rue Du Pont, Mont-Laurier, QC J9L 3N7
Tél: 819-623-2441; *Téléc:* 819-623-3007
ceml@lino.sympatico.ca
Le Centre d'exposition de Mont-Laurier est une institution muséale dont la mission est la diffusion, l'éducation et l'action culturelle en arts visuels et en patrimoine

***Montréal:* Artothèque**
5720, rue St-André, Montréal, QC H2S 2K1
Tél: 514-278-8181; *Téléc:* 514-278-3044
info@artotheque.ca
www.artotheque.ca/

***Montréal:* La Centrale (Galerie Powerhouse)**
4296, boul Saint-Laurent, Montréal, QC H2W 1Z3
Tél: 514-871-0268; *Téléc:* 514-871-9830
galerie@lacentrale.org
www.lacentrale.org
Artist-run centre dedicated to the presentation of women's contemporary art

***Montréal:* Centre international d'art contemporain de Montréal**
CP 760 Place du Parc, Montréal, QC H2X 4A6
Tél: 514-288-0811; *Téléc:* 514-288-5021
ciac@ciac.ca
www.ciac.ca
Centre international d'art contemporain de Montréal is an office for contemporary art producing exhibitions, La Biennale de Montréal, an electronic art magazine, publications, & events.
Claude Gosselin, Director

***Montréal:* Galerie de l'UQAM**
Université du Québec à Montréal, CP 8888 Centre-ville, Montréal, QC H3C 3P8
Tél: 514-987-6150; *Téléc:* 514-987-6897
galerie@uqam.ca
www.galerie.uqam.ca

***Montréal:* Leonard & Bina Ellen Art Gallery / Galerie Leonard et Bina Ellen**
Concordia University, 1455, boul de Maisonneuve ouest, Montréal, QC H3G 1M8
Tel: 514-848-2424
ellengallery.concordia.ca
Committed to researching, collecting & interpreting Canadian art; programming centres on exhibitions that help advance knowledge in the visual arts; in keeping with Concordia's academic mission, the Gallery is committed to the enhancement of the University's educational programmes & cultural environment
Michèle Thériault, Director

***Montréal:* Segal Centre for Performing Arts**
5170, côte Sainte-Catherine, Montréal, QC H3W 1M7
Tel: 514-739-2301; *Fax:* 514-739-9340
info@segalcentre.org
www.segalcentre.org
Alvin Segal, President
Joel Segal, Vice-President
Bryna Wasserman, Artistic & Executive Director
Barry Taggart, Director, Finance & Operations
Michael Blumenstein, Secretary
Tasso Lagios, Treasurer

***Mont-Saint-Hilaire:* Musée d'art de Mont-Saint-Hilaire**
150, rue du Centre-Civique, Mont-Saint-Hilaire, QC J3H 5Z5
Tél: 450-536-3033; *Téléc:* 450-536-3032
mamsh@mamsh.qc.ca
mamsh.qc.ca
Promotes work of local artists Ozias Leduc, Paul-Émile Borduas & Jordi Benet; works of contemporary artists

***Pointe-Claire:* La Galerie d'art Stewart Hall Art Gallery**
Centre culturel de Pointe-Claire Stewart Hall, 176, ch Bord-du-Lac, Pointe-Claire, QC H9S 4J7
Tél: 514-630-1254; *Téléc:* 514-630-1285
millarj@ville.pointe-claire.qc.ca
Open year round; exhibitions from local, national & international sources; paintings, photographs, sculptures, graphics & theme exhibitions; free admission; wheelchair access

***Québec:* VU centre de diffusion et de production de la photographie**
***Also known as:* Centre VU**
523, Saint-Vallier est, Québec, QC G1K 3P9
Tél: 418-640-2558; *Téléc:* 418-640-2586
vuphoto@meduse.org
www.meduse.org/vuphoto/
VU se consacre à la promotion et au développement de la photographie d'auteur. Son mandat vise principalement le soutien aux activités de recherche et de création en photographie à travers des expositions, des résidences d'artistes, des publications et des événements spéciaux. VU offre un accès privilégié à une vaste gamme d'équipements de production en photographie argentique et numérique
André Gilbert, Directeur

***Rimouski:* Galerie Coup d'Oeil**
CP 710, Rimouski, QC G5L 7C7
Tél: 418-724-3235; *Téléc:* 418-724-3139

***Rouyn-Noranda:* Centre d'exposition de Rouyn-Noranda inc.**
Cégep de l'Abitibi-Témiscamingue, CP 415, 425, boul du Collège, Rouyn-Noranda, QC J9X 6C4
Tél: 819-762-6600; *Téléc:* 819-762-9425
cern@cegepat.qc.ca
www.cern.ca
Louise Boudreault, Directrice générale

***Saint-Hyacinthe:* Expression, Centre d'exposition de Saint-Hyacinthe**
495, rue Saint-Simon, Saint-Hyacinthe, QC J2S 5C3
Tél: 450-773-4209; *Téléc:* 450-773-5270
expression@expression.qc.ca
www.expression.qc.ca
Une institution muséale dont la mission est de promouvoir et de diffuser l'art contemporain et actuel. Depuis 1985, Expression présente au public, dans une salle magnifique et spacieuse, des expositions réputées pour leur qualité artistique. A ces expositions, s'ajoutent un service d'animation, des conférences et des publications. De plus, Expression insère ponctuellement des activités satellites

***Saint-Jean-Port-Joli:* Maison Médard-Bourgault**
322, av de Gaspé ouest, Saint-Jean-Port-Joli, QC G0R 3G0
Tél: 418-598-3880

***Saint-Laurent:* Musée des maîtres et artisans du Québec (MMAQ)**
615, av Sainte-Croix, Saint-Laurent, QC H4L 3X6
Tél: 514-747-7367; *Téléc:* 514-747-8892
m.dube@mmaq.qc.ca
www.mmaq.qc.ca

Chefs d'oeuvres de grands maîtres et pièces exceptionnelles d'artisans anonymes présentent un panorama de la culture traditionnelle québécoise dans une église néo-gothique de 1867
Pierre Wilson, Directeur-conservateur

***Saint-Léonard:* Galerie Port-Maurice**
8420, boul Lacordaire, Saint-Léonard, QC H1R 3G5
Tél: 514-328-8514
Crée en 1979; sensibilise la population aux différents courants contemporains d'arts visuels

***La Sarre:* Centre d'art Rotary**
195, rue Principale, La Sarre, QC J9Z 1Y3
Tél: 819-333-2294; *Téléc:* 819-333-2296
llafreniere@ville.lasalle.qc.ca
www.ville.lasarre.qc.ca/Loisir/Plan.htm
Susy Tousignant

***Shawinigan:* Centre d'exposition de Shawinigan**
***Also known as:* Centre des Arts de Shawinigan**
c/o Corporation culturelle de Shawinigan, 2100, boul Des Hêtres, Shawinigan, QC G9N 8R8
Tél: 819-539-1888; *Téléc:* 819-539-2400
corporationculturelle@shawinigan.ca
www.cdas.ca
Louise Martin, Directrice générale

***Sherbrooke:* Galerie d'art du Centre culturel de l'Université de Sherbrooke**
2500, boul Université, Sherbrooke, QC J1K 2R1
Tél: 819-821-7000
www.usherbrooke.ca/galerie/

***Sherbrooke:* Musée des beaux-arts de Sherbrooke**
241, rue Dufferin, Sherbrooke, QC J1H 4M3
Tél: 819-821-2115; *Téléc:* 819-821-4003
mbas@interlinx.qc.ca
www.mbas.qc.ca
Plusieurs expositions temporaires ainsi que la collection du Musée, notamment les oeuvres de Frederick Simpson Coburn et la collection Luc LaRochelle
Cécile Gélinas, Directrice

***St-Georges:* Centre d'Art de St-Georges**
c/o Centre culturel Marie-Fitzbach., 250, 18e rue ouest, St-Georges, QC G5Y 4S9
Tél: 418-226-2271; *Téléc:* 418-228-1321
Open year round
Marie Tanguay, Chef de division

***Trois-Rivières:* Galerie d'art du Parc et Manoir de Tonnancour**
CP 871, 864, rue des Ursulines, Trois-Rivières, QC G9A 5J9
Tél: 819-374-2355; *Téléc:* 819-374-1758
www.galeriedartduparc.qc.ca
Drawings, paintings, sculptures, stamps, photos, videos & mixed-media exhibitions; permanent exhibition on the history of the Manoir de Tonnancour

***Valcourt:* Centre culturel Yvonne L. Bombardier**
1002, av J.-A.-Bombardier, Valcourt, QC J0E 2L0
Tél: 450-532-3033
ccylb@fjab.qc.ca
www.centreculturelbombardier.com/accueil.htm

***Val-d'Or:* Centre d'exposition de Val d'Or inc.**
600, 7e rue, Val-d'Or, QC J9P 3P3
Tél: 819-825-0942; *Téléc:* 819-825-3062
expovd@ville.valdor.qc.ca
membres.lycos.fr/centreexpositionvd/
Ginette Vézina, Présidente

***Verdun:* Centre culturel de Verdun**
5955, rue Bannantyne, Verdun, QC H4H 1H6
Tel: 514-765-7170; *Fax:* 514-765-7263
nancy.raymond@verdun.ca

Saskatchewan

Provincial Art Galleries

MacKenzie Art Gallery (MAG)
T.C. Douglas Bldg., 3475 Albert St., Regina, SK S4S 6X6
Tel: 306-584-4250; *Fax:* 306-569-8191
mackenzie@uregina.ca
www.mackenzieartgallery.sk.ca
Founded: 1953 Historical & contemporary Canadian, American & European works; special emphasis on western Canadian art; works on paper, contemporary photography, major touring exhibits; facilities include learning centre, studios, theatre, gift shop; sculpture court; outdoor sculpture garden; open daily year round
Stuart Reid, Director
Timothy Long, Curator

Mendel Art Gallery & Civic Conservatory (MAG)
PO Box 569, 950 Spadina Cres. East, Saskatoon, SK S7K 3L6
Tel: 306-975-7610; *Fax:* 306-975-7670
info@mendel.ca
www.mendel.ca
Historical & contemporary Canadian & international art; 5 exhibition periods/year; open year-round
Terry Graff, Director

Local Art Galleries in Saskatchewan

***North Battleford:* Allen Sapp Gallery**
***Also known as:* Allen Sapp Gallery - The Gonor Collection**
PO Box 460, 1 Railway Ave. East, North Battleford, SK S9A 2Y6
Tel: 306-445-1760; *Fax:* 306-445-1694
sapp@accesscomm.ca
www.allensapp.com
Cree art & interpretive centre; open year round
Dean Bauche, Curator

***North Battleford:* The Chapel Gallery**
PO Box 460, 891 - 99 St., North Battleford, SK S9A 2Y6
Tel: 306-445-1757; *Fax:* 306-445-1009
chapelgallery@sasktel.net
www.nbleisure.com/galleries
Exhibition of local to international artists, permanent collection of the city of North Battleford
Michael Brukop, Curator
Dean Bauche, Director

***Prince Albert:* Grace Campbell Gallery**
c/o John M. Cuelenaere Public Library, 125 - 12 St. East, Prince Albert, SK S6V 1B7
Tel: 306-763-8496; *Fax:* 306-763-3816
bmazurkewich@jmcpl.ca
www.jmcpl.ca
Local, provincial & national exhibitions; no permanent collection
Eleanor Acorn, Library Director
Beverley Mazurkewich, Gallery Coordinator

***Regina:* Dunlop Art Gallery**
Regina Public Library, PO Box 2311, 2311 - 12th Ave., Regina, SK S4P 3Z5
Tel: 306-777-6040; *Fax:* 306-949-7264
bantal@rpl.regina.sk.ca
www.dunlopartgallery.org
Permanent art collection of contemporary & historical significance by Saskatchewan artists

***Regina:* McIntyre Gallery**
2347 McIntyre St., Regina, SK S4P 2S3
Tel: 306-757-4323
mcintyre.gallery@sasktel.net
www.mcintyregallery.com
Contemporary Saskatchewan art; open year round
Louise Durnford, Director

***Regina:* Rosemont Art Gallery**
Neil Balkwill Civic Arts Centre, PO Box 1790, 2420 Elphinstone St., Regina, SK S4P 3C8
Tel: 306-522-5940

***Saskatoon:* A.K.A. Gallery**
424 - 20th St. West, Saskatoon, SK S7M 0X4
Tel: 306-652-0044; *Fax:* 306-652-0534
aka@sasktel.net
www.akagallery.org
Artist-run centre; membership open to all
Clark Ferguson, Administrative Coordinator
Cindy Baker, Programme Coordinator

***Saskatoon:* Gordon Snelgrove Art Gallery**
191 Murray Bldg., University of Saskatchewan, 3 Campus Dr., Saskatoon, SK S7N 5A4
Tel: 306-966-4208; *Fax:* 306-966-4266
gary.young@usask.ca
www.usask.ca/snelgrove
The gallery, managed by the Univ. of Sask. department of Art & Art History, supports program & course instruction, student shows & exhibitions, & community outreach.
Gary Young, Coordinator

***Saskatoon:* Kenderdine Art Gallery/University of Saskatchewan Permanent Art Collection**
University of Saskatchewan, #12, College Bldg., 107 Administration Pl., Saskatoon, SK S7N 5A2
Tel: 306-966-4571; *Fax:* 306-978-8340
kenderdine.artgallery@usask.ca
www.usask.ca/kenderdine
Open year round
Kent Archer, Director/Curator

***Saskatoon:* St. Thomas More Art Gallery**
St. Thomas More College, 1437 College Dr., Saskatoon, SK S7N 0W6
Tel: 306-966-8900; *Fax:* 306-966-8904
Toll-Free: 800-667-2019
lstark@stmcollege.ca
www.stmcollege.ca
Founded: 1964 Located on the 2nd floor of the College, next to the Library. Exhibitions from Sept. through April, featuring local & regional artists with a university level studio background or extensive formal training. Submissions accepted year round.
Linda Stark, Curator

***Weyburn:* Allie Griffin Art Gallery (AGAG)**
45 Bison Ave., Weyburn, SK S4H 1L8
Tel: 306-848-3278; *Fax:* 306-848-3271
weyburnartscouncil@live.ca
www.weyburnartscouncil.ca
Founded: 1964 Features touring exhibitions from the Mendel Art Gallery, the Mackenzie Art Gallery, the Saskatchewan Craft Council, the Saskatchewan Arts Board through OSAC, and many locally curated shows. The exhibitions feature the work of well-known as well as emerging Saskatchewan artists.
Marnie Bernard, Gallery Curator
Alice Neufeld, Arts Director

***Weyburn:* Signal Hill Arts Centre**
424 - 10 Ave. South, Weyburn, SK S4H 2A1
Tel: 306-848-3278; *Fax:* 306-848-3271
aneufeld@weyburn.ca
Founded: 1985 The Signal Hill Arts Centre is located in a five storey multi-purpose civic heritage facility, which also houses a pottery studio, gallery, gift shop, kitchen, dance studio, an office, & meeting rooms.
Alice Neufeld, Arts & Cultural Director

***Yorkton:* Godfrey Dean Art Gallery**
Yorkton Arts Council, 49 Smith St. East, Yorkton, SK S3N 0H4
Tel: 306-786-2992; *Fax:* 306-782-2767
gdag@sasktel.net
www.deangallery.ca
Founded: 1981 Devoted to the exhibition of visual art that reflects contemporary issues relevant to the Yorkton region; classes & special events programming.
Donald Stein, Director

Yukon Territory

Territorial Art Galleries

Yukon Arts Centre
Yukon Place, PO Box 16, 300 College Dr., Whitehorse, YT Y1A 5X9
Tel: 867-667-8485; *Fax:* 867-393-6300
info@yac.ca
www.yukonartscentre.org
Yukon Arts Centre is the territory's premier venue for performing and visual arts. The Gallery hosts 10-14 contemporary art exhibitions per year. Emphasis is to showcase work of professional Yukon artists & to bring exhibitions of national importance to the Yukon. The Theatre is a 428-seat proscenium theatre, boasting outstanding acoustics and top-of-the-line technical support.
Scott Marsden, Curator, Public Art Gallery
Al Cushing, Executive Director

Aquaria

British Columbia

Local Aquaria in British Columbia

***Sidney:* Marine Ecology Station**
Port Sidney Marina, 9835 Seaport Pl., Sidney, BC V8L 4X3
Tel: 250-655-1555; *Fax:* 250-655-1573
info@mareco.org
mareco.org
Dedicated to marine education, awareness & stewardship; open year round
Dr. Bill Austin, Director

***Vancouver:* Vancouver Aquarium**
Stanley Park, PO Box 3232, Vancouver, BC V6B 3X8
Tel: 604-659-3474; *Fax:* 604-659-3515
Toll-Free: 800-931-1186
information@vanaqua.org
www.vanaqua.org
The largest in Canada & one of the five largest in North America; a self-sufficient, non-profit organization, the Aquarium is internationally recognized for display & interpretation excellence & was the first facility to incorporate professional Naturalists into the galleries to complement interpretive graphics; research

projects extend world wide & it is internationally recognized for its success
Dr. John Nightingale, President

New Brunswick

Local Aquaria in New Brunswick

***St Andrews:* Huntsman Marine Science Centre**
1 Lower Campus Rd., St Andrews, NB E5B 2L7
Tel: 506-529-1200; *Fax:* 506-529-1212
aquarium@huntsmanmarine.ca
www.huntsmanmarine.ca
Public aquarium/museum with local flora & fauna, & the Atlantic Reference Centre which houses a zoological & botanical museum reference collection; research & teaching in marine sciences & coastal biology; marine education courses for elementary, high school & university groups; aquaculture research & development facilities
William Robertson, Executive Director

***Shippagan:* Aquarium et Centre Marin de Shippagan (ACM)**
100, rue Aquarium, Shippagan, NB E8S 1H9
Tél: 506-336-3013; *Téléc:* 506-336-3057
aquarium@gnb.ca
www.gnb.ca/aquarium
Aquarium publique qui expose un nombre impressionnant d'espèces de poissons qui vivent dans les eaux du golfe St-Laurent ainsi que dans les lacs et rivières de l'est du Canada. L'Attraction vedette est une famille de phoque communs; présentation audio-visuelle; bassin touchez-y; ouvert de mai á sept.; acceptons réservations de groups hors saison
Robert Rioux, Directeur

Newfoundland & Labrador

Local Aquaria in Newfoundland & Labrador

***St. John's:* The Fluvarium**
Nagle's Place, Box 5, St. John's, NL A1B 2Z2
Tel: 709-754-3474; *Fax:* 709-754-5947
info@fluvarium.ca
www.fluvarium.ca
Delivers an environmental education program to over 10,000 school children annually; houses interactive fresh water exhibits & nine underwater viewing windows into Nagle's Hill Brook
Jane Smith-Parsons, Executive Director

Ontario

Local Aquaria in Ontario

***Niagara Falls:* Marineland**
7657 Portage Rd., Niagara Falls, ON L2E 6X8
Tel: 905-356-9565
www.marinelandcanada.com
Interactive marina and amusement park; facility for animal and marine mammal care, where guests can learn about animals through an exciting mix of entertainment and education. Contains the largest whale habitat in the world. Open May - Oct.
John Holer, President

Prince Edward Island

Local Aquaria in Prince Edward Island

***Stanley Bridge:* Stanley Bridge Marine Aquarium**
Rte. 6, Stanley Bridge, PE C0A 1E0
Tel: 902-886-3355
www.kata.pe.ca/attract/marine/marine.htm
With live fish aquariums and touch tanks, North America's largest collection of mounted birds - over 700 specimens - the World of Butterflies display, and a history of Malpeque oysters, the Irish moss and shellfish industries, it's an educational experience for the whole family. Open June - Oct.
John Holer, President

Quebec

Local Aquaria in Quebec

***Sainte-Flavie:* Parc de la rivière Mitis (CISA)**
900, route de la Mer, Sainte-Flavie, QC G0J 2L0
Tél: 418-775-2969; *Téléc:* 418-775-9466
info@parcmitis.com
www.parcmitis.com
Le Parc de la rivière Mitis est situé à Saint-Flavie et se veut un site écotouriste qui amène les gens à porter un nouveau regard sur l'interprétation et la préservation du patrimonie naturel et culturel. Ouvert mi-juin - sept.
Julie Isabel

***Sainte-Foy:* Parc aquarium du Québec**
1675, av des Hôtels, Sainte-Foy, QC G1W 4S3
Tel: 418-659-5264; *Fax:* 418-646-9238
Toll-Free: 866-659-5264
aquarium@sepaq.com
www.sepaq.com
16 hectare park encompassing aspects of the northern ecosystem and marine life. Observe and interact with over 10,000 fresh and salt-water fish specimens, reptiles, amphibians, invertebrates, as well as marine mammals, such as Atlantic and Pacific walruses, seals and polar bears.

Saskatchewan

Local Aquaria in Saskatchewan

***Fort Qu'appelle:* Fish Culture Station**
PO Box 190, Fort Qu'appelle, SK S0G 1S0
Tel: 306-332-3200; *Fax:* 306-332-3203
Jerry Banks, Manager

Botanical Gardens

Alberta

Local Botanical Gardens in Alberta

***Brooks:* Golden Prairie Arboretum**
Alberta Agriculture, Food & Rural Development, Crop Diversification Centre South, SS#4, Brooks, AB T1R 1E6
Tel: 403-362-1300; *Fax:* 403-362-1306
christine.murray@gov.ab.ca
Collection of deciduous trees & shrubs
Dr. Christine Murray
Nigel Seymour

***Calgary:* University of Calgary Herbarium**
Dept. of Biological Sciences, 2500 University Dr. NW, Calgary, AB T2N 1N4
Tel: 403-220-5262; *Fax:* 403-289-9311
ccchinna@ucalgary.ca
Vascular plants
C.C. Chinnappa, Curator

***Edmonton:* Devonian Botanic Garden**
University of Alberta, Edmonton, AB T6G 2E1
Tel: 780-987-3054; *Fax:* 780-987-4141
www.devonian.ualberta.ca
80 acres of cultivated gardens & 110 acres of natural area; native & alpine plants, ecological reserves, Kurimoto Japanese Garden & Orchid House & a Butterly House; picnic area, patio cafe & gift shop; open daily, Apr.-Dec.
Dr. Michael Hickman, Associate Director
Bruce Dancik, Director
Dionne Allen, General Manager

***Edmonton:* Muttart Conservatory**
9626 - 96A St., Edmonton, AB T6C 4L8
Tel: 780-496-8735; *Fax:* 780-496-8747
muttartquestions@edmonton.ca
www.edmonton.ca/muttart
Four pyramids house flora of different world climatic zones, including arid, temperate, & tropical; Show Pyramid features 6 different floral shows per year; species orchid greenhouse; outdoor trail gardens in summer
Judith Rohovie, Director

***Lethbridge:* Nikka Yuko Japanese Garden**
c/o Lethbridge & District Japanese Garden Society, PO Box 751, Lethbridge, AB T1J 3Z6
Tel: 403-328-3511; *Fax:* 403-328-0511
info@nikkayuko.com
www.japanesegarden.ab.ca
The Nikka Yuko Japanese Garden is a mature four acre garden providing a quiet, serene place for the appreciation of nature and discovery of inner peace. Includes dry rock garden, mountain and waterfall, streams and bridges, ponds and islands, flat prarie garden.

***Trochu:* Trochu Arboretum & Gardens**
***Also known as:* The Arboretum at Trochu**
PO Box 340, Trochu, AB T0M 2C0
Tel: 403-442-2111; *Fax:* 403-442-2528
Open Victoria Day to Thanksgiving
Roy Ashcroft, President
Judy Reeds, Curator

British Columbia

Local Botanical Gardens in British Columbia

***Burnaby:* Simon Fraser University Arboretum**
Dept. of Biological Sciences, Simon Fraser University, Burnaby, BC V5A 1S6
Tel: 604-291-4475; *Fax:* 604-291-3496

***Kimberley:* Cominco Gardens**
340 Spokane St., Kimberley, BC V1A 2E8
Tel: 250-427-5160
kcds@kimberley.ca
Open May - Oct.
Ginnesa Clive, Manager

***North Vancouver:* Park & Tilford Gardens**
Park & Tilford Centre, #440, 333 Brookbank Ave., North Vancouver, BC V7J 3S8
Tel: 604-984-8200; *Fax:* 604-984-6099
bfielding@bentall.com
www.parkandtilford.ca
10 themed public gardens; free admission; open dawn to dusk
Bernice Fielding, Garden Director

***Richmond:* Fantasy Garden World**
10800 No. 5 Rd., Richmond, BC V7A 4E5
Tel: 604-277-7777; *Fax:* 604-274-1212
An amusement park with gardens, rides, a miniature train, a "castle" from Coevorden, Holland and an Olde World Village

***Rosedale:* Minter Gardens**
52892 Bunker Rd., Rosedale, BC V0X 1X0
Tel: 604-792-3799; *Toll-Free:* 888-646-8377
mail@mintergardens.com
www.mintergardens.com
Founded: 1980 Open Apr. - mid-Oct.; located at 52892 Bunker Rd., Rosedale BC; take exit #135 of the Trans Canada Hwy #1
Brian Minter
Faye Minter

***Surrey:* Surrey Art Gallery**
Surrey Arts Centre, 13750 - 88 Ave., Surrey, BC V3W 3L1
Tel: 604-501-5566; *Fax:* 604-501-5581
artgallery@city.surrey.bc.ca
www.arts.surrey.ca
Promotes contemporary BC & Canadian artists; exhibitions & public programs encourage community appreciation of contemporary visual art; open year round
Liane Davison, Curator, Exhibitions
Ingrid Kolt, Curator, Visual Arts Programs

***Vancouver:* Bloedel Conservatory**
Queen Elizabeth Park, c/o Van. Bd. of Parks & Recreation, 2099 Beach Ave., Vancouver, BC V6G 1Z4
Tel: 604-257-8584; *Fax:* 604-257-8427
www.vancouver.parks.ca
Canada's largest single-structure tropical conservatory featuring over 500 species in simulated rain-forest, subtropic & desert environments; also features tropical birds, parrots & a Japanese Koi fish collection

***Vancouver:* Dr. Sun Yat-Sen Classical Chinese Garden**
578 Carrall St., Vancouver, BC V6B 5K2
Tel: 604-662-3207; *Fax:* 604-682-4008
sunyatsen@telus.net
www.vancouverchinesegarden.com
The first authentic, full-scale, classical Chinese garden built outside China; museum, garden & cultural attraction
Kathy Gibler, Executive Director

***Vancouver:* Nitobe Memorial Garden**
c/o UBC Botanical Garden and Centre for Plant Research, 6804 Southwest Marine Dr., Vancouver, BC V6T 1Z4
Tel: 604-822-9666; *Fax:* 604-822-2016
botg@interchange.ubc.ca
www.nitobe.org
Authentic Japanese tea & stroll garden; cherry blossoms; Japanese Irises, Japanese Maples; Koi; lanterns & much more
Quentin Cronk, Director
Douglas Justice, Associate Director

***Vancouver:* Queen Elizabeth Park & Arboretum**
30 East 30th Ave., Vancouver, BC V5V 2T9
Tel: 604-257-8373
A 125 acre public park with extensive floral display gardens, naturalized areas, arboretum, golf course, tennis courts, roller hockey rinks & basketball courts

***Vancouver:* UBC Botanical Garden**
University of British Columbia, 6804 Southwest Marine Dr., Vancouver, BC V6T 1W5
Tel: 604-822-9666; *Fax:* 604-822-2016
botg@interchange.ubc.ca
www.ubcbotanicalgarden.org
Living museum of plants in 110 acres of BC coastal native forest; over 10,000 assorted trees, shrubs, flowers; divided into various components
Quentin Cronk, Director
Douglas Justice, Associate Director

***Vancouver:* VanDusen Botanical Garden**
5251 Oak St., Vancouver, BC V6M 4H1
Tel: 604-878-9274; *Fax:* 604-266-2436
jill.cherry@vancouver.ca
www.vandusengarden.org

22-hectare garden comprised of over 255,000 plants. Open year-round.
Chris Woods, Garden Director

***Victoria:* The Butchart Gardens Ltd.**
PO Box 4010, Victoria, BC V8X 3X4
Tel: 250-652-4422; *Fax:* 250-652-7751
Toll-Free: 866-652-4422
email@butchartgardens.com
www.butchartgardens.com
55 acres of manicured gardens on a 130 acre private estate; open year-round

***Victoria:* Horticulture Centre of the Pacific**
505 Quayle Rd., Victoria, BC V6E 2J7
Tel: 250-479-6162; *Fax:* 250-479-6047
info@hcp.bc.ca
www.hcp.bc.ca
A nonprofit organization founded in 1979 as The Horticulture Centre of the Pacific or HCP, it manages 103 acres to demonstrate sound gardening practices using the diversity of plants that can be grown in this area, to preserve natural plant and animal habitat, and to provide a unique environment for preparing students for careers in horticulture. It relies on public funding, on local businesses, and on its own fundraising activities to support these activities.

***Victoria:* Royal Roads Botanical Garden**
***Also known as:* Hatley Park Gardens**
c/o Royal Roads University, 2005 Sooke Rd., Victoria, BC V9B 5Y2
Tel: 250-391-2617; *Fax:* 250-391-2622
www.hatleypark.ca
Native coastal forest & formal gardens

Manitoba

Local Botanical Gardens in Manitoba

***Boissevain:* International Peace Garden**
PO Box 419, Boissevain, MB R0K 0E0
Tel: 204-534-2510; *Toll-Free:* 888-432-6733
kathy@peacegarden.com
www.peacegarden.com
2300-acre park located on the North Dakota & Manitoba boarders; tribute to peace & friendship between the people of Canada & the United States of America; maintains extensive gardens containing a wide variety of shrubs, perennials, & annual plants; souvenir shop, interpretative centre, picnic sites, hiking trails, International music camp, Royal Canadian Legion sports camp, 9/11 Memorial Site
Doug Hevenor, CEO

***Leaf Rapids:* Leaf Rapids National Exhibition Centre**
***Also known as:* Societé des Arts of Leaf Rapids, Inc.**
Town Centre Complex, PO Box 220, Leaf Rapids, MB R0B 1W0
Tel: 204-473-8682; *Fax:* 204-473-2707
excentre@mts.net
The Exhibition Centre features traveling displays and local and regional artists exhibits. Each year, two to four live performances are offered for youth and adults.
Joan Seddon, Director

***Morden:* Morden Arboretum**
Morden Research Centre, Agriculture & Agri-Food Canada, #100-101, Rte. 100, Morden, MB R6M 1Y5
Tel: 204-822-4471; *Fax:* 204-822-7207
res2.agr.ca/winnipeg/index_e.htm
A federal government research centre; variety of programs including breeding & development of trees, shrubs, roses & herbaceous perennials; improvement & agronomic research programs carried out on linseed flax, field peas & dry edible beans
Dr. Campbell G. Davidson

***Winnipeg:* Assiniboine Park**
***Also known as:* City Park**
c/o Community Services Dept., 395 Main St., 6th Fl., Winnipeg, MB R3B 3N8
Tel: 204-986-4208; *Fax:* 204-986-8112
www.winnipeg.ca/cms/ape
Includes Assiniboine Park Zoo, Assiniboine Park Conservatory, Leo Mol Sculpture Garden, Pavillion Art Gallery, English & Formal Gardens, Assiniboine Forest Natural Area
Patti Sullivan, COO, Assiniboine Park Enterprise, City of Winnipeg Community Services Dept.

***Winnipeg:* Living Prairie Museum**
2795 Ness Ave., Winnipeg, MB R3J 3S4
Tel: 204-832-0167; *Fax:* 204-986-4172
www.winnipeg.ca/publicworks/naturalist/livingprairie/
38-hectare preserve of original tall grass; interpretive centre; open Apr. 15 - Aug.; Sept - April by appt.

***Winnipeg:* Sandilands Forest Centre, Hadashville, MB**
c/o 900 Corydon Ave., Winnipeg, MB R3M 0Y4
Tel: 204-453-3182; *Fax:* 204-477-5765
mfainc@mts.net
www.mbforestryassoc.ca
125 hectares of forests; artifacts in the museum; open May - Oct.
Dianne Beaven, President

New Brunswick

Local Botanical Gardens in New Brunswick

***Saint-Jacques:* New Brunswick Botanical Garden**
PO Box 1629, 33 Principale St., Saint-Jacques, NB E7B 1A3
Tel: 506-737-4444; *Fax:* 506-737-5389
jardin@umce.ca
www.umce.ca/jardin
7 hectares; over 50,000 plants.

Newfoundland & Labrador

Local Botanical Gardens in Newfoundland & Labrador

***St. John's:* The Memorial University of Newfoundland Botanical Garden**
306 Mt. Scio Rd., St. John's, NL A1C 5S7
Tel: 709-737-8590; *Fax:* 709-737-8596
garden@mun.ca
www.mun.ca/botgarden
The Memorial University of Newfoundland Botanical Garden maintains cultivated gardens and natural habitats for public display and is a centre for botanical, horticultural and environmental research and education.
Dr. K. Wilf Nicholls, Director

Nova Scotia

Local Botanical Gardens in Nova Scotia

***Annapolis Royal:* Annapolis Royal Historic Gardens**
PO Box 278, 441 Saint George St., Annapolis Royal, NS B0S 1A0
Tel: 902-532-7018; *Fax:* 902-532-7445
www.historicgardens.com
Theme gardens, collections & displays reflect historical periods - Open May - Oct.
Dr. K.W. Nicholls, Director

***Halifax:* Halifax Public Gardens**
1606 Bell Rd., Halifax, NS B3H 2Z3
Tel: 902-423-9865; *Fax:* 902-446-4002
www.halifaxpublicgardens.ca
Formal Victorian Garden, located at Summer St. & Spring Garden Rd.
, Parks

Ontario

Local Botanical Gardens in Ontario

***Burlington:* Royal Botanical Gardens (RBG)**
680 Plains Rd. West, Burlington, ON L7T 4H4
Tel: 905-527-1158; *Fax:* 905-577-0375
Toll-Free: 800-694-4769
info@rbg.ca
www.rbg.ca
A living museum which serves local, regional and global communities while developing and promoting public understanding of the relationship between the plant world, humanity and the rest of nature. 1,100 hectares of land: 120 cultivated hectares, while the rest remains a managed natural area including marshlands and walking trails.
Mark Runciman, Director

***Guelph:* The Arboretum**
University of Guelph, Guelph, ON N1G 2W1
Tel: 519-824-4120; *Fax:* 519-763-9598
arbor@uoguelph.ca
www.uoguelph.ca/arboretum
Environmental education & research activities; plant collections; formal gardens; recreational workshops; dinner theatre; meeting & banquet facilities
Prof. Alan Watson, Director, awatson@uoguelph.ca

***Hamilton:* Centre for Canadian Historical Horticultural Studies (CCHHS)**
PO Box 399, Royal Botanical Gardens, Hamilton, ON L8N 3H8
Tel: 905-527-1158; *Fax:* 905-577-0375
Toll-Free: 800-668-9449
library@rbg.ca
Vicki DeNardis, Contact

***Kingsville:* Colasanti's Tropical Gardens**
1550 Rd. 3 East, Kingsville, ON N9Y 2E5
Tel: 519-326-3287; *Fax:* 519-322-2302
tropical@colasanti.com
www.colasanti.com
Founded: 1941 Colasanti's Tropical Gardens features over 3.5 acres of tropical greenhouses. It is open 363 days each year. Attractions include exotic plants, animals, indoor miniature golf, children's rides, an indoor playground, an arcade, a restaurant, plus home decor & collectables.
Joe Colasanti, Contact
Terry Colasanti

***London:* Sherwood Fox Arboretum**
University of Western Ontario, Richmond St. North, London, ON N6A 5B7
Tel: 519-661-2111; *Fax:* 519-661-3935
arboretum@uwo.ca
www.uwo.ca/biology/arboretum
The arboretum includes the trees planted on the campus of the university
Dr. Jane Bowles

***Miller Lake:* Larkwhistle Garden**
191 Lindsay Rd. 40, Miller Lake, ON N0H 1Z0
Tel: 519-795-7763
larkwhistle@amtelecom.net

***Niagara Falls:* Niagara Parks Botanical Gardens & School of Horticulture**
c/o Niagara Parks Commission, PO Box 150, Niagara Falls, ON L2E 6T2
Tel: 905-356-8554; *Fax:* 905-356-5488
schoolofhorticulture@niagaraparks.com
www.schoolofhorticulture.com
Includes the Niagara Parks Butterfly Conservatory
Tom Laviolette, Superintendent, Botanical Gardens & Butterfly Conservatory
Liz Klose, Superintendent, School of Horticulture

***Ottawa:* Central Experimental Farm**
c/o Bldg. 72, Arboretum, Ottawa, ON K1A 0C6
Tel: 613-230-3276; *Fax:* 613-230-1238
thefarm@cyberus.ca
www.friendsofthefarm.ca

***Ridgetown:* J.J. Neilson Arboretum**
120 Main Street East, Ridgetown, ON N0P 2C0
Tel: 519-674-1570; *Fax:* 519-674-1600
arboretu@ridgetownc.uoguelph.ca
www.ridgetownc.uoguelph.ca
Includes upwards of 500 taxa., including Carolinian trees & shrubs, & collections of Viburnum & Dogwood, along with perennial & annual displays, & theme landscape areas
Mike Gladstone, Contact

***Sault Ste Marie:* Great Lakes Forestry Centre Arboretum**
Canadian Forest Service, 1219 Queen St. East, Sault Ste Marie, ON P6A 2E5
Tel: 705-949-9461; *Fax:* 705-541-5700
www.glfc.cfs.nrcan.gc.ca/arboretum/index_e.html
Two hectares of natural land and forest.
D.J. Kennington, Arboretum Manager

***Thunder Bay:* Centennial Conservatory**
c/o Parks & Recreation Dept., 1601 Dease St. North, Thunder Bay, ON P7B 4A2
Tel: 807-622-7036; *Fax:* 807-622-7602
Toll-Free: 807-622-7036
Four seasonal flower displays; cactus & tropical displays year round; open year round, 1-4 pm daily; free admission

***Thunder Bay:* Soroptimist International Friendship Garden**
Parks Division, Victoriaville Civic Centre, 111 South Syndicate Ave., Thunder Bay, ON P7E 6S4
Tel: 807-625-3166; *Fax:* 807-625-3258
Soroptimist International Friendship Garden was created by Canadians of varied ethnic origins as a centennial gift to Canada & the community. Individual gardens have been planned, designed, constructed, & financed by the respective groups; Each group has created a garden typical of their culture & homeland.
Don Vezina, Coordinator, Parks Services, dvezina@thunderbay.ca

***Toronto:* Allan Gardens Conservatory**
19 Horticultural Ave., Toronto, ON M5A 2P2
Tel: 416-392-7288; *Fax:* 416-392-0318
ckenned1@toronto.ca
collections.ic.gc.ca/gardens
Permanent plant collection of tropical & sub-tropical plants; seasonal plant displays; open daily 10-5
Chris Kennedy, Superintendent

Toronto: **Edwards Gardens**
Civic Garden Centre, 777 Lawrence Ave. East, Toronto, ON M3C 1P2
Tel: 416-392-8188
A former Estate garden featuring perennials and roses on the uplands and wildflowers, rhododendrons and an extensive rockery in the valley.

Toronto: **Humber Arboretum**
205 Humber College Blvd., Toronto, ON M9W 5L7
Tel: 416-675-6622; *Fax:* 416-255-6876
steve.bodsworth@humber.ca
www.humberarboretum.on.ca
100 hectares of ornamental gardens & green space on the west branch of the Humber River
Stephen Bodsworth, Director

Toronto: **The Power Plant Contemporary Art Gallery at Harbourfront Centre**
231 Queens Quay West, Toronto, ON M5J 2G8
Tel: 416-973-4949; *Fax:* 416-973-4933
thepowerplant@harbourfrontcentre.com
www.thepowerplant.org
New work by today's best artists
Helena Reckitt, Curator

Toronto: **Toronto Sculpture Garden**
#713, 38 Avenue Rd., Toronto, ON M5R 2G2
Tel: 416-515-9658; *Fax:* 416-515-9655
www.torontosculpturegarden.com
Semi-annual exhibitions of contemporary sculpture in a park, 115 King St. East
Rina Greer, Director

Windsor: **Fogolar Furlan Botanic Garden**
1800 E.C. Row, North Service Rd., Windsor, ON N8W 1Y3

Windsor: **Jackson Park Queen Elizabeth II Garden**
c/o Parks & Recreation Dept., 2450 McDougall Rd., Windsor, ON N8X 3N6
Tel: 519-253-2300; *Fax:* 519-255-7990
parkrec@city.windsor.on.ca
www.city.windsor.on.ca
More than 10,000 plants, formal gardens, fountains, and sports park.

Prince Edward Island

Local Botanical Gardens in Prince Edward Island

Kensington: **Malpeque Gardens**
RR#1, Blue Heron Dr., Kensington, PE C0B 1M0
Open June 15 - Aug. 15
George MacKay

Quebec

Local Botanical Gardens in Quebec

Grand-Métis: **Jardin de Métis / Reford Gardens**
200, rte 132, Grand-Métis, QC G0J 1Z0
Tél: 418-775-2222; *Téléc:* 418-775-6201
reford@refordgardens.com
www.jardinsmetis.com
3,000 species; native & exotic plants
Brigitte Bourdages, Office Co-ordinator

Montréal: **Jardin botanique de Montréal / Montréal Botanical Garden**
4101, rue Sherbrooke est, Montréal, QC H1X 2B2
Tel: 514-872-1400; *Fax:* 514-872-4917
jardin_botanique@ville.montreal.qc.ca
www.ville.montreal.qc.ca/jardin
Collection of 22,000 plant species & varieties, 10 exhibition greenhouses & 30 thematic gardens from around the world; Insectarium; covers 75 hectares
Gilles Vincent, Director

Sainte-Anne-de-Bellevue: **Morgan Arboretum**
Macdonald Campus, McGill University, PO Box 186, Sainte-Anne-de-Bellevue, QC H9X 3V9
Tel: 514-398-7811; *Fax:* 514-398-7959
morgan.arboretum@mcgill.ca
www.morganarboretum.org
Situated at the western tip of the island of Montreal; trees grow in forests, experimental plantations & ornamental collections
Leslie Ann LaDuke, Financial Administrator
Christina Idziak, Curator

Sainte-Foy: **Jardin Roger-Van den Hende**
Université Laval, Pavillon de L'Envirotron, 2480 Hochelaga, Sainte-Foy, QC G1K 7P4
Tél: 418-656-3742; *Téléc:* 418-656-3515
jardin@fsaa.ulaval.ca
www.jardin.ulaval.ca

More than 4000 species and cultivars arranged in order of botanical family. Open April - Oct.; free admission
Simon Chrétien
Hélène Corriveau

Saskatchewan

Local Botanical Gardens in Saskatchewan

Estevan: **Shand Greenhouse**
PO Box 280, Estevan, SK S4A 2A3
Tel: 306-634-9771; *Fax:* 306-634-6682
Toll-Free: 866-778-7337
greenhouse@saskpower.com
www.saskpower.com
Greenhouse, shade houses, nursery, display area; uses by-products of energy generation from the Shand Power Station; open year round
Martin Lelliott, Manager

Indian Head: **Prairie Farm Rehabilitation Administration (PFRA)**
Also known as: **Shelterbelt Centre**
PO Box 940, Hwys. 1 & 56, Indian Head, SK S0G 2K0
Tel: 306-695-2284; *Fax:* 306-695-2568
pfratree@agr.gc.ca
www.agr.ca/pfra/shelterbelt.htm
Arboretum, nursery, horticultural displays; open daily
Dr. G.B. Neill, Manager

Saskatoon: **Patterson Gardens**
Dept. of Plant Sciences, University of Saskatchewan, 51 Campus Dr., Saskatoon, SK S7N 5A8
Tel: 306-966-5855; *Fax:* 306-966-5015
www.usask.ca/agriculture/plantsci/facilities.html
Patterson Gardens are a 5 acre plot of mature trees & shrubs which are open to the public at anytime; it represents many of our hardy good quality landscape materials
B. E. Coulman, Dept. Head

Swift Current: **Art Gallery of Swift Current NEC**
411 Hebert St. East, Swift Current, SK S9H 1M5
Tel: 306-778-2736; *Fax:* 306-773-8769
k.houghtaling@swiftcurrent.ca
www.artgalleryofswiftcurrent.org
Non-profit public art gallery & national standard art museum offering exhibitions of provincial, national & international artwork; provides access to & education in visual art culture for Southwest Saskatchewan
Laurie Wagner, Education Coordinator, l.wagner@swiftcurrent.ca
Kim Houghtaling, Director/Curator, k.houghtaling@swiftcurrent.ca

Museums

National Museums

Canada Aviation Museum / Musée de l'aviation du Canada
PO Box 9724 T, 11 Aviation Pkwy., Ottawa, ON K1G 5A3
Tel: 613-993-2010; *Fax:* 613-990-3655
Toll-Free: 800-463-2038
aviation@technomuses.ca; member@technomuses.ca
www.aviation.technomuses.ca
Other contact information: TDD: 613-990-7530; Phone, Library & Archives: 613-993-2303
As a component of the Canada Science and Technology Museum Corporation, the Canada Aviation Museum collects, preserves, & displays aviation-related objects, from the pioneer era, through war & peace, & to the present time.
Denise Amyot, President & Chief Executive Officer, Canada Science & Technology Museum Corporation
Anthony P. Smyth, Director General, Canada Aviation Museum

Canada Science & Technology Museum Corporation (CSTMC/SMSTC) / Société du Musée des Sciences et de la technologie du Canad
PO Box 9724 T, 1867 St. Laurent Blvd., Ottawa, ON K1G 5A3
Tel: 613-991-3044; *Fax:* 613-990-3636
Toll-Free: 866-442-4416
info@technomuses.ca
www.sciencetech.technomuses.ca
Other contact information: TDD: 613-991-9207; E-mail, Library: library@technomuses.ca
Exhibits at the Canada Science & Technology Museum include astronomy, space, marine & land transportation, communications, computer technology, & domestic technology. The library of the Canada Science & Technology Museum contains material about the history & development of science & technology, with an emphasis upon Canada.
Denise Amyot, President & Chief Executive Officer
James Paul, Chair

Michèle Desloges, Corporate Secretariat, 613-990-6352

The Canadian Museum of Civilization Corporation (CMCC) / Société du Musée canadien des civilisations
100, rue Laurier, Gatineau, QC K1A 0M8
Tel: 819-776-7000; *Fax:* 819-776-8300
Toll-Free: 800-555-5621
web@civilization.ca
www.civilization.ca
The Canadian Museum of Civilization conducts research in Canadian studies & collects, preserves & displays objects which reflect Canada's cultural heritage. Its activities extend across the country through field research programs, publications & loans to various groups & institutions. Through permanent & changing exhibitions, public programs, film & theatre programs, the museum unfolds the storie
Victor Rabinovitch, President & CEO, victor.rabinovitch@civilization.ca
Chantal Schryer, Vice-President, Public Affairs & Publishing, chantal.schryer@civilization.ca

Canadian Museum of Contemporary Photography (CMCP / MCPC) / Musée canadien de la photographie contemporaine
PO Box 465 A, 380 Sussex Dr., Ottawa, ON K1N 9N6
Tel: 613-990-1985; *Fax:* 613-993-4385
Toll-Free: 800-319-2787
cmcp@gallery.ca
www.cmcp.gallery.ca
Other contact information: TTD: 613-990-0777
Founded: 1985 Affiliated with the National Gallery of Canada, the collection of the Canadian Museum of Contemporary Photography dates from the early 1960s to the present. Photographic works include prints, negatives, transparencies, books, filmstrips, video art, audio-visual presentations, mixed media works, assemblages, & installation pieces.
Martha Hanna, Director
Joanne Charette, Director, Public Affairs, 613-990-5050, Fax: 613-990-9824, jcharette@gallery.ca

Canadian Museum of Nature / Musée canadien de la nature
PO Box 3443 D, Ottawa, ON K1P 6P4
Tel: 613-566-4700; *Fax:* 613-364-4021
Toll-Free: 800-263-4433
questions@mus-nature.ca; cmnlib@mus-nature.ca
www.nature.ca
Other contact information: TDD: 613-566-4770; 1-866-600-8801
The natural sciences & natural history museum features specimens, such as fossils, horned dinosaurs, fish, freshwater mussels, tropical beetles, animals, lichens, plants, & minerals from Canada & around the world.
Joanne DiCosimo, President & Chief Executive Officer, 613-566-4733, Fax: 613-364-4020, jdicosimo@mus-nature.ca
Maureen Dougan, Vice-President & Chief Operating Officer, 613-566-4732, Fax: 613-364-4020, mdougan@mus-nature.ca
Roger Baird, Director, Collection Services, 613-364-4138, Fax: 613-364-4022, rbaird@mus-nature.ca
Kim Curran, Director, Development & Fundraising Services, 613-566-4790, Fax: 613-364-4021, kcurran@mus-nature.ca
Mark S. Graham, Director, Research, 613-566-4743, Fax: 613-364-4022, mgraham@mus-nature.ca
Denyse Jomphe, Director, Human Resources Management Services, 613-566-4294, Fax: 613-364-4028, djomphe@mus-nature.ca
Lynne Ladouceur, Director, Financial Management Services, 613-566-4253, Fax: 613-364-4025, lladouceur@mus-nature.ca
Marie Lasnier, Director, Community Services, 613-364-4101, Fax: 613-566-4746, mlasnier@mus-nature.ca
Jennifer Doubt, Chief Collection Manager, Botany, 613-364-4076, Fax: 613-364-4027, jdoubt@mus-nature.ca
Jean-Marc Gagnon, Chief Collection Manager, Invertebrates, 613-364-4066, Fax: 613-364-4027, jmgagnon@mus-nature.ca
Kamal Khidas, Chief Collection Manager, Vertebrates, 613-364-4098, Fax: 613-364-4027, kkhidas@mus-nature.ca
Kieran Shepherd, Chief Collection Manager, Earth Sciences, 613-364-4054, Fax: 613-364-4027, kshepherd@mus-nature.ca
Elizabeth McCrea, Manager, Communications Services, 613-566-4249, Fax: 613-364-4021, emccrea@mus-nature.ca

The Canadian War Museum (CWM) / Musée canadien de la guerre
1 Vimy Place, Ottawa, ON K1A 0M8
Tel: 819-776-8600; *Fax:* 819-776-8623
Toll-Free: 800-555-5621
info@warmuseum.ca
www.warmuseum.ca
Affiliated museum of the Canadian Museum of Civilization; war art; uniforms & accoutrements; medals; weapons & small arms; archives; the Hartland Molson library; vast collection of military vehicles & artillery

Dr. Victor Rabinovitch, President/CEO, mark.oneill@warmuseum.ca
Mark O'Neill, Director General, mark.oneill@warmuseum.ca
Chantal Schryer, Public Affairs & Publishing

Currency Museum of the Bank of Canada / Musée de la monnaie de la Banque du Canada
245 Sparks St., Ottawa, ON K1A 0G9
Tel: 613-782-8914; *Fax:* 613-782-7761
museum-musee@bank-banque-canada.ca
www.currencymuseum.ca; www.museedelamonnaie.ca
The most complete collection of Canadian notes & coins in the world, plus representative collections of world coins & paper money, including whales' teeth, glass pearls, elephant-hair bracelets, shells & copper axes
Paul S. Berry, Chief Curator
Henriette Riegel, Director, Visitor Services
Enrica Schwilden, Manager, Marketing & Communications

Alberta

Provincial Museums

Glenbow Museum, Art Gallery, Library & Archives
130 - 9 Ave. SE, Calgary, AB T2G 0P3
Tel: 403-268-4100; *Fax:* 403-265-9769
glenbow@glenbow.org
www.glenbow.org
Glenbow documents the settlement of western Canada with exhibits tracing the lives & traditions of native peoples, the development of the railway, ranching, farming & growing up in the West. A large art gallery highlights historical & contemporary art from Glenbow's own collections as well as from national & international collections.
Kristin Evenden, President & CEO
Lauchlan Currie, Chair

Royal Alberta Museum
12845 - 102 Ave., Edmonton, AB T5N 0M6
Tel: 780-453-9100; *Fax:* 780-454-6629
www.royalalbertamuseum.ca
Major collections & exhibits of Alberta's natural & human history, including habitat groups, geology, palaeontology, archaeology, & western Canadian history & the Syncrude Gallery of Aboriginal Culture; feature exhibitions, museum shop, café, films, lectures, live demonstrations & cultural performances; special programs for schools & other groups; discovery room
Chris Robinson, Acting Executive Director, 780-453-9168, chris.robinson@gov.ab.ca
Albert Finnamore, Director, Curatorial & Collections Preservation, 780-453-9177, Fax: 780-454-6629, albert.finnamore@gov.ab.ca
Chris Robinson, Director, Marketing, Communications & Education, 780-453-9168, chris.robinson@gov.ab.ca
Bruce Bolton, Director, Business Operations, 780-453-9130, Fax: 780-454-6629, bruce.bolton@gov.ab.ca
Tom Thurston, Director, Renewal Project, 780-453-9105, Fax: 780-454-9105, tom.thurston@gov.ab.ca

Royal Tyrrell Museum
PO Box 7500, Drumheller, AB T0J 0Y0
Tel: 403-823-7707; *Fax:* 403-823-7131
Toll-Free: 888-440-4240
tyrrell.info@gov.ab.ca
www.tyrrellmuseum.com
Founded: 1985 Located in Midland Provincial Park, on Hwy #838 in Drumheller, the internationally recognized Royal Tyrrell Museum is in the heart of one of the richest fossil localities in the world. The Museum is Canada's only museum dedicated exclusively to palaeontology & showcases Alberta's abundant & diverse fossil record, featuring more than 800 fossils & 35 dinosaur skeletons on display. Other highlights include dramatic dioramas, interactive exhibits, computer stations & mini-theatre, special events & programming, gift shop & cafeteria
Andrew Neuman, Executive Director M.Sc.

Local Museums in Alberta

***Airdrie:* Nose Creek Valley Museum**
1701 Main St. SW, Airdrie, AB T4B 1C5
Tel: 403-948-6685
ncvm@telus.net
www.nosecreekvalleymuseum.com
Nose Creek Valley Museum offers the history of Airdrie & the surrounding region. Visitors will learn about the geology & natural history of the area, the First Nations & pioneers, farming, antique automobiles, & military history. A Canadian Pacific caboose is also on display. The museum is open year-round.
Laurie Harvey, Curator

***Alberta Beach:* Alberta Beach & District Museum**
PO Box 68, 4823 - 50 Ave., Alberta Beach, AB T0E 0A0
Tel: 780-924-2140
abmuseum@netscape.ca
History of the Lac Ste Anne area; open year round, weekends only in winter
Leanne Knysh, President

***Alberta Beach:* Garden Park Farm Museum**
PO Box 639, Alberta Beach, AB T0E 0A0
Tel: 780-924-3391
David Oselies

***Alix:* Alix Wagon Wheel Museum**
PO Box 245, Alix, AB T0C 0B0
Tel: 403-747-3119
alixwagonwheelmuseum@live.ca
alixwagonwheelmuseum.wordpress.com
Local history and artifacts; souvenir shop. Open year round, but by appointment from Oct. through May.
Eve Keates, Curator

***Andrew:* Andrew & District Local History Museum**
PO Box 180, Andrew, AB T0B 0C0
Tel: 403-365-3687
Local artifacts & records; open year round

***Banff:* Banff Park Museum National Historic Site**
PO Box 900, Banff, AB T1L 1K2
Tel: 403-762-1558; *Fax:* 403-762-1565
banff.vrc@pc.gc.ca
www.pc.gc.ca/lhn-nhs/ab/banff/index_e.asp
Founded: 1895 The Banff Park Museum is a natural history museum. The collection is located in a 1903 building.

***Banff:* Buffalo Nations Luxton Museum**
PO Box 850, 1 Birch Ave., Banff, AB T1L 1A8
Tel: 403-762-2388; *Fax:* 403-760-2803
buffalonations@telus.net
www.buffalonationsmuseum.ca
The Buffalo Nations Luxton Museum depicts the cultures & traditions of the First Nations people of the Plains. Artifacts date back over 100 years.
Joseph Yellowhorn, President
Anthony Starlight, Vice-President
Roy Louis, Secretary
Stewart Breaker, Treasurer
Estelle Guthro, General Manager
Ray Cowley, Head, Buildings & Installations

***Banff:* Whyte Museum of the Canadian Rockies**
PO Box 160, 111 Bear St., Banff, AB T1L 1A3
Tel: 403-762-2291; *Fax:* 403-762-8919
info@whyte.org; archives@whyte.org
www.whyte.org
Other contact information: Phone, Archives: 403-762-2291, ext. 335
Visitors to the Whyte Museum discover the history, art, & social & cultural past of the Canadian Rockies. Guided tours are provided of the heritage gallery, the art gallery, heritage homes, the Luxton home & garden, & historic Banff. The Archives & Library, located at the museum, collects books, journals, maps, newspaper clippings, microforms, textual records, photographs, & audio-visual materials related to the Canadian Rockies.
Michale Lang, Executive Director & Chief Curator
Graeme Nunn, Chief Financial & Operating Officer & Executive Director, Whyte Foundation
Natalie Fedrau, Manager, Visitor Services
Elizabeth Kundert-Cameron, Manager, Archives & Library, Fax: 403-762-2339, archives@whyte.org
Craig Richards, Curator, Photography
Jennifer Rutkair, Archivist
Lena Goon, Reference Archivist
Catherine Hawkins, Coordinator, Education & Interpretation
Katie Daniel, Specialist, Marketing & Communications

***Barrhead:* Barrhead Centennial Museum & Visitor Information Center**
PO Box 4122, 5629 - 49th St., Barrhead, AB T7N 1A1
Tel: 780-674-5203
barrheadmuseum@lycos.ca
Other contact information: Phone, Appointments: 780-674-3513
Founded: 1967 The Barrhead Centennial Museum is operated by the Barrhead & District Historical Society. Exhibits at the Barrhead Centennial Museum & Visitor Information Center include Barrhead settlers' furniture, pioneer farm equipment, & tools. The complete local newspaper is also available at the museum, plus a large collection of African artifacts. The museum is open from the Victoria Day weekend in May to the Labour Day weekend in September.

***Beaverlodge:* South Peace Centennial Museum**
PO Box 493, Beaverlodge, AB T0H 0C0
Tel: 780-354-8869; *Fax:* 780-354-8068
sitemanager@spcm.ca
www.spcm.ca
Pioneer equipment & buildings; open mid-May - Sept. 1
Lois Dueck, President

***Bowden:* Bowden Pioneer Museum**
PO Box 576, 2201 - 19th Ave., Bowden, AB T0M 0K0
Tel: 403-224-2122
bhs@shawbiz.ca
museum.anwc.net
Founded: 1967 Goverened by the Bowden Historical Society, the Bowden Pioneer Museum is located in the old Bowden curling rink. The museum contains the following artifacts & exhibits: The Bob Hoare Photography Exhibit; The Eastern Star Exhibit; The Irene M. Wood Avon Collection, The Women of Aspenland Lives & Works; a hardware & general store display; military artifacts; geological collections, decorative arts, such as musical instruments; fine arts of First Nations & European origins; & human hisotry artifacts, such as religious objects, household items, & sports equipment. The museum also conducts research services. It is open from the long weekend in May to September.

***Brooks:* Brooks Aqueduct National & Provincial Historic Site**
c/o Eastern Irrigation District, PO Box 8, 550 Industrial Rd., Brooks, AB T1R 1B2
Tel: 403-653-5139
eid@eid.ab.ca
www.eidnet.org/local/aqueduct
Other contact information: Phone, Information Kiosk: 403-362-4451
The Brooks Aqueduct is located 8 km southeast of Brooks, Alberta. The structure was completed in 1914 by the irrigation division of the Canadian Pacific Railway. It has been preserved by the Government of Alberta, Environment Canada, the Prairie Farm Rehabilitation Administration, & the Eastern Irrigation District. The interpretive center at the aqueduct is open from May 15th to Labour Day.

***Brownvale:* Brownvale North Peace Agricultural Museum**
PO Box 186, Brownvale, AB T0H 0L0
Tel: 780-597-3934; *Fax:* 780-597-3950
The Brownvale North Peace Agricultural Museum features artifacts such as historic farm machinery, horse-powered equipment, & construction equipment. The museum is open during July & August.

***Calgary:* Aero Space Museum of Calgary**
4629 McCall Way NE, Calgary, AB T2E 8A5
Tel: 403-250-3752; *Fax:* 403-250-8399
info@asmac.ab.ca
www.asmac.ab.ca
With over 20 historical aircrafts on display, guests can explore Canadian achievements in aviation & space. Aircraft engines, extensive aviation library & interactive exhibits; educational programs & tours; gift shop; meeting/function room rentals. Open year round.
Steven Ogle, CEO
Jennifer Herrick, Executive Director
Sara Bateman, Marketing & Development
Anthony Worman, Curator

***Calgary:* Calgary Chinese Cultural Centre**
197 - First St. SW, Calgary, AB T2P 4M4
Tel: 403-262-5071; *Fax:* 403-232-6387
info@culturalcentre.ca
www.culturalcentre.ca
Founded: 1992 The Calgary Chinese Cultural Centre promotes Chinese heritage, history, & culture, as well as cultural diversity.
Victor Mah, Chair
Malcolm Chow, Vice-President
Samantha Yang, Executive Administrator
Tony Wong, Secretary
Leonard Chow-Wah, Treasurer

***Calgary:* The Calgary Highlanders Museum & Archives**
4520 Crowchild Trail SW, Calgary, AB T3E 1T8
Tel: 403-974-2855; *Fax:* 403-974-2855
highrs@nucleus.com
www.calgaryhighlanders.com
A history and recollection of the Calgary Highlanders
Barry Agnew, Curator Lt. Ret'd

***Calgary:* Fort Calgary**
***Also known as:* Fort Calgary Historic Park**
PO Box 2100 M, #106, 750 - 9th Ave. SE, Calgary, AB T2P 2M5
Tel: 403-290-1875; *Fax:* 403-265-6534
info@fortcalgary.com
www.fortcalgary.com
40-acre park; interpretive centre; 1875 fort reconstruction project; guided tours; open year round
Sara Jane Gruetzner, Executive Director

Calgary: The Grain Academy
Plus 15 Level, Roundup Centre, Stampede Park, PO Box 1060 M, Calgary, AB T2P 2K8
Tel: 403-263-4594; *Fax:* 403-233-9500
grainacademy@nucleus.com
www.grainacademymuseum.com
Founded: 1981 Grain elevator; grain transportation exhibit

Calgary: Heritage Park Historical Village
1900 Heritage Dr. SW, Calgary, AB T2V 2X3
Tel: 403-268-8500; *Fax:* 403-268-8501
info@heritagepark.ab.ca
www.heritagepark.ca
Founded: 1964 Billed as a living history museum, the expansive site offers a wide range of exhibits and activities, most notably the exploration of a village of historical, "old west" buildings replete with antiques, artifacts and costumed guides. Gasoline Alley Museum focuses on the history of the automobile. There is a steam train, antique midway and Haskayne Mercantile Block of shops. Open May - Sept.
Ms Alida Visbach, President/CEO

Calgary: King's Own Calgary Regiment (RCAC) Museum
***Also known as:* Museum of the Regiments**
CFB Calgary, 4520 Crowchild Trail South West, Calgary, AB T2P 5J4
Tel: 403-974-2856
Robertson.DB@kingsown.org
www.kingsown.org
Depicts the history of the four regiments of Calgary; art gallery; open all year. Artifacts and pictures of regimental "family tree"; permanent displays of the 50th Battalion C.E.F. which deature The Deadly Sniper; Cpl. Henry Norwest; M.M. Vimy; Pte. John George Pattison V.C.; non-permanent active militial Dieppel The Prisoner of War Room; Sicily, Italy, including the Kingsmill Bridge and the Battle of Cassino. Special film and military documentaties in the Amoco Theatre.
Col. Ian Gray, Executive Director CD (Ret'd)
Jan Roseneder, Librarian/Archivist
Noel Ratch, Curator

Calgary: Lord Strathcona's Horse (Royal Canadians) Regimental Museum
4520 Crowchild Trail SW, Calgary, AB T2T 5J4
Tel: 403-974-2854; *Fax:* 403-974-2858
museum@strathconas.ca; archives@strathconas.ca
www.strathconas.ca
Founded: 1990 Museum relates the history of the Regiment from 1900 to present. The collection holds many artifacts yet undisplayed. The Archives store photographs, records, documents and diaries and research is conducted for personal and professional institutions. Open year round.
Warrant Officer D.E. (Ted) MacLeod, Curator

Calgary: Naval Museum of Alberta
1820 - 24 St. SW, Calgary, AB T2T 0G6
Tel: 403-242-0002; *Fax:* 403-240-1966
info@navalmuseum.ab.ca
www.navalmuseum.ab.ca
Other contact information: Information line: 403/974-2853
Collection includes one each of the 3 naval aircraft (fighter planes) used by RCN; naval armament including guns, torpedos, anti-submarine equipment, clothing etc. Part of The Military Museums
Glen Hardie, President

Calgary: The Nickle Arts Museum
The University of Calgary, 2500 University Dr. NW, Calgary, AB T2N 1N4
Tel: 403-220-7234; *Fax:* 403-282-4742
nickle@ucalgary.ca
www.ucalgary.ca/~nickle
Founded in 1979 through a donation from Sam Nickle & a Province of Alberta grant; champions contemporary Canadian art, numismatics & Oriental carpets; changing exhibitions & programs
Dr. Ann Davis, Director

Calgary: Olympic Hall of Fame & Museum
c/o Canada Olympic Park, 88 Canada Olympic Rd. SW, Calgary, AB T3B 5R5
Tel: 403-247-5452
info@winsportcanada.ca; groups@winsportcanada.ca
www.winsportcanada.ca/cop
Other contact information: Phone, School Department, Outdoor Education Programming: 403-202-6577
The Olympic Hall of Fame & Museum honours past & present Canadian Olympians & Paralympians. A large collection of Olympic artifacts is featured, such as Olympic torches. Visitors can test their skills with interactive simulators of Olympic sports, including alpine skiing. The Olympic Hall of Fame & Museum is open year-round.
Gordon Ritchie, Chair, WinSport Canada Board of Directors
Tracy Cobb, National Director, Communications & Fund Development, WinSport Canada, 403-247-5954, tracy.cobb@winsportcanada.ca

Calgary: Princess Patricia's Canadian Light Infantry Regimental Museum & Archives
4520 Crowchild Trail SW, Calgary, AB T2T 5J4
Tel: 403-974-2862; *Fax:* 403-974-2864
ppcli@nucleus.com
www.archivesalberta.org/place/ppcli.htm
Other contact information: Phone, Archives: 403-974-2867
Princess Patricia's Canadian Light Infantry Regimental Museum & Archives collects & preserves items that cover the dates from 1914, when Princess Patricia's Canadian Light Infantry was founded, to the present day. The Infantry is known for its service in both World Wars, Korea, & Afghanistan, & during other operations for the United Nations & NATO. Holdings include war journals, photographs, training manuals, cartographic materials, & audio-visual resources, especially related to the Princess Patricia's Canadian Light Infantry, & to the Canadian Army in general. The museum is open year-round.
Ronald B. Gallant, Curator
Bruce A. Graham, Archivist

Calgary: Sarcee Tsuu T'ina People's Museum
#135, 3700 Anderson Rd. SW, Calgary, AB T2W 3C4
Tel: 403-238-2677
Located on Sarcee (Tsuu T'ina) Reserve, the museum features artifacts such as headdresses from around 1938 & a model tipi.

Calgary: University of Calgary, Museum of Zoology
2500 University Dr., Calgary, AB T2N 1N4
Tel: 403-220-5269; *Fax:* 403-289-9311
fitch@ucalgary.ca
Teaching museum used for zoology & ecology courses
Warren Fitch, Curator

Calgary: Youthlink Calgary: Calgary Police Service Interpretive Centre
133 - 6th Ave. SE, Calgary, AB T2G 4Z1
Tel: 403-206-4566
www.youthlinkcalgary.com
Interactive exhibits & programs educate youth about life, crime, & law enforcement.
Janet Pieschel, Executive Director, janet.pieschel@calgarypolice.ca
Gail Niinimaa, Administrator, 403-206-8927, gail.niinimaa@calgarypolice.ca
Lindsie Bruns, Technician, Historical Collections, 403-206-8691, lbruns@calgarypolice.ca
Colleen Acheson, Coordinator, Booking, 403-206-8950, colleen.acheson@calgarypolice.ca
Rachel Joo, Coordinator, Outreach Programs, 403-206-8691, rachel.joo@calgarypolice.ca

Camrose: Camrose & District Centennial Museum
PO Box 1622, Camrose, AB T4V 1X6
Tel: 780-672-3298
www.camrosemuseum.ca
Founded: 1967 Buildings on the museum grounds include a pioneer home, The Likeness School, the St. Dunstan's Church, a firehall, the local newspaper building, a blacksmith shop, the Mona Sparling Building, the Oldtimers Hut, & the R.C.M.P. Machine Building. The musuem is open from Victoria Day weekend to Labour Day weekend. Appointments may be arranged at other times of the year.

Canmore: Canmore Museum & Geoscience Centre
Civic Centre, 902B - 7th Ave., Canmore, AB T1W 3K1
Tel: 403-678-2462; *Fax:* 403-678-2216
info@cmags.org
www.cmags.org
Other contact information: Phone, 1893 North West Mounted Police Barracks: 403-678-1955
The Canmore Museum & Geoscience Centre features historical artifacts, geological collections, & information about the heritage of Canmore & the surrounding mountainous area. The museum also operates the 1893 North West Mounted Police Barracks, which is situated on 609 Main Street.
V. Richard (Rick) Green, President
Ian Schofield, Vice-President, Heritage
Edward van Vliet, Director & Curator
Lindsay Walker, Coordinator, Earth Science
David Moore, Treasurer

Cardston: C.O. Card Pioneer Home & Museum
PO Box 1830, 337 Main St., Cardston, AB T0K 0K0
Tel: 403-653-4322
Other contact information: Phone, Off Season: 403-653-3366
C.O. Card Home & Museum is a Provincial Historic Site. It features the log cabin built by Charles Ora Card, who was the founder of Cardston. The museum is open during July & August. During the off season, appointments may be arranged.

Cardston: Courthouse Museum
89 - 3rd Ave. West, Cardston, T0K 0K0
Tel: 403-653-4322
Other contact information: Phone, Off Season: 403-653-3366
The Courthouse is a Provincial Historic Site, which was constructed in 1907 from local sandstone. Court artifacts are on display, including the witness stand, judge's bench, & orginal jail cells. The musuem is open during July & August. During the off season, appointments may be arranged.

Cardston: Remington Carriage Museum
PO Box 1649, Cardston, AB T0K 0K0
Tel: 403-653-5139; *Fax:* 403-653-5160
info@remingtoncentre.com
www.remingtoncarriagemuseum.com
Founded: 1993 The Remington Carriage Museum features the largest collection of horse-drawn vehicles in North America, such as carriages, sleighs, & wagons. The facility also contains a working stable, a carriage factory, & a restoration shop. Educational programs are offered. The museum is open year-round.

Carstairs: Roulston Museum
***Also known as:* Carstairs Museum**
PO Box 1067, Carstairs, AB T0M 0N0
Tel: 403-337-3710; *Fax:* 403-337-3343
Founded: 1988 Located at 1138 Nanton St. in Carstairs. Main collection housed in the hall of Knox Presbyterian Church (1901), a registered historic site; church records; pictures & artifacts of local life from early settlement to present; McCaig House (1901); archives; new library research room; new farm implement display building
Betty Ayers, Curator
Robert Disney, President

Cereal: Cereal Prairie Pioneer Museum
PO Box 131, Cereal, AB T0J 0N0
Tel: 403-326-3899
Museum of artifacts from Pioneer days; pictures, papers & cards of the period; museum was once old CN Railway Station with living quarters; yard includes old jail house & restoration of old Cereal Town Office

Claresholm: Appaloosa Horse Club of Canada Senior Citizens Museum & Archives
PO Box 940, Claresholm, AB T0L 0T0
Tel: 403-625-3326; *Fax:* 403-625-2274
museum@appaloosa.ca
www.appaloosa.ca/museum.htm
History of Appaloosa horse

Claresholm: Claresholm Museum
PO Box 1000, 5126 1st St. W., Claresholm, AB T0L 0T0
Tel: 403-625-3131; *Fax:* 403-625-3869
claresholmmuseum@gmail.com
www.town.claresholm.ab.ca
Founded: 1969 Local history museum in the old Sandstone Railway Station; Claresholm was home to Louise C. McKinney, a social activist for the cause of women's welfare and legal status, and the first woman parliamentarian in the British Empire; open daily May-Sept; admission by donation
Jo-Ann Peach, Collections Assistant

Cochrane: Cochrane Ranche Historic Site
PO Box 1522, Cochrane, AB T4C 1A7
Tel: 403-932-2902; *Fax:* 403-932-2578
www.cochrane.ca
Located off Hwy #22, north of downtown Cochrane, The Cochrane Ranche is Alberta's first large-scale livestock ranch, comprising approx. 136 acres; open May 15 - Labour Day; hiking & picnic areas open year round

Coleman: Crowsnest Museum
PO Box 306, 7701 - 18 Ave., Coleman, AB T0K 0M0
Tel: 403-563-5434; *Fax:* 403-563-5434
cnmuseum@shaw.ca
www.crowsnestmuseum.ca
Over 25,000 artifacts on display interpreting the history of the Crowsnest Pass & its people; themed galleries include pioneers, underground mining, general store/blacksmith shop, Legends of Prohibition, Gushul Studio. Veterans' exhibit, wildlife diorama; open year round
Wendy Zack, Manager, Operations

Crowsnest Pass: The Frank Slide Interpretive Centre (FSIC)
PO Box 959 Blairmore, Crowsnest Pass, AB T0K 0E0
Tel: 403-562-7388; *Fax:* 403-562-8635
info@frankslide.com
www.frankslide.com
Site of the 1903 rockslide avalanche; visual presentation "In the Mountain's Shadow" shown daily; open year-round.
Monica Field, Manager

***Crowsnest Pass:* Leitch Collieries Provincial Historic Site**
PO Box 959 Blairmore, c/o Frank Slide Interpretive Centre, Crowsnest Pass, AB T0K 0E0
Tel: 403-562-7388; *Fax:* 403-562-8635
Toll-Free: 310-000-0 in
info@frankslide.com
tprc.alberta.ca/museums/historicsiteslisting/leitchcollieries
Ruin of coal mining operation; staffed May 15 - Labour Day
Monica Field, Manager

***Czar:* Prairie Panorama Museum**
PO Box 149, Czar, AB T0B 0Z0
Tel: 780-857-3778; *Fax:* 782-857-2239
Displays many historical artifacts; includes a school section
Julie Anne Adams, Sec.-Treas.

***DeBolt:* DeBolt & District Pioneer Museum**
311 - 1st St. West, DeBolt, AB T0H 1B0
Tel: 780-957-3957; *Fax:* 780-957-2934
www.albertasource.ca/spiritofthepeace/collections/
Founded: 1975 The museum comprises 8 heritage buildings with displays: in Hubert Memorial Park on Viriginia Ave., in the community church & Legion Hall; collections include the Bickell Fossil Collection. Open summer.
Fran Moore, Curator, franmoore@iwantwireless.ca

***Delburne:* Anthony Henday Museum**
PO Box 374, Delburne, AB T0M 0V0
Tel: 403-749-2711; *Fax:* 403-749-2800
Housed in the former CNR train station; water tank tower, caboose, machine shed & pioneer cabin replica on site; depicts history of Delburne & district with emphasis on agriculture, households & coal mining. Open June M-F, 9-5. From July to Labour Day open daily 9-5.

***Didsbury:* Didsbury & District Museum**
PO Box 1175, 2118 - 21st Ave., Didsbury, AB T0M 0W0
Tel: 403-335-9295
ddhs@telusplanet.net
1906 building; local history; open year round; Tue.-Wed. 1-4:30; Sat. 1-5
Tyrone Patten, President
Joan Court, Secretary

***Donalda:* Donalda & District Museum**
PO Box 179, Donalda, AB T0B 1H0
Tel: 403-883-2100; *Fax:* 403-883-2022
info@donaldamuseum.com
www.donaldamuseum.com
Over 850 lamps; Whitford Collection of Métis artifacts from the late 1800's; native tools; artifacts; open year round
Gail Kerr, Manager

***Drayton Valley:* Drayton Valley & District Historical Society**
PO Box 5099, Drayton Valley, AB T7A 1R3
Tel: 780-542-5482
Local history; open Wed. & Sat. 1-4
Fred Cox, Vice-President
Vi Koehmstedt, President
Charlie Miner, Secretary

***Drumheller:* Drumheller & District Museum**
PO Box 2135, 335 - 1st St., Drumheller, AB T0J 0Y0
Tel: 403-823-2593; *Fax:* 403-823-4737
stego@telusplanet.net
Fossil remains; interpretive displays; Aboriginal artifacts & items of local historical interest

***Drumheller:* Homestead Pioneer Museum**
PO Box 3154, 901 North Dinosaur Trail, Drumheller, AB T0J 0Y0
Tel: 403-823-2600; *Fax:* 403-823-5411
www.traveldrumheller.com/homestead-museum.html
Founded: 1965 Situated in the Canadian Badlands, the Homestead Pioneer Museum presents exhibits from the Drumheller Valley, including farm machinery & tools, vehicles, & a 1919 house. The museum is open from mid May to mid October.

***East Coulee:* Atlas Coal Mine National Historic Site**
PO Box 521, 110 Century Ave., East Coulee, AB T0J 1B0
Tel: 403-822-2220; *Fax:* 403-822-2225
info@atlascoalmine.ab.ca
www.atlascoalmine.ab.ca
Founded: 1989 Located in the Canadian Badlands, the Atlas Coal Mine National Historic Site offers tours & educational programs. Visitors can go underground, explore the last wooden tipple in Canada, see the blacksmith shop, & ride an authentic mine locomotive. The site is open from the beginning of May to mid-October.
Linda Digby, Director

***East Coulee:* East Coulee School Museum**
PO Box 539, East Coulee, AB T0J 1B0
Tel: 403-822-3970; *Fax:* 403-922-2111
info@ecsmuseum.ca
www.ecsmuseum.ca
Open year round
Heather Farquherson, Museum Administrator

***Edmonton:* Alberta Aviation Museum**
11410 Kingsway Ave., Edmonton, AB T5G 0X4
Tel: 780-451-1175; *Fax:* 780-451-1607
info@albertaaviationmuseum.com
www.albertaaviationmuseum.com
Tells & interprets the story of aviation & its importance to Edmonton & Northern Alberta; displays & exhibits allow visitors to embrace the spirit of those involved in early aviation endeavours that helped Edmonton establish its title as "Gateway to the North". Flight simulators, aircraft restoration area, activities for children, guided tours, special events. Space rentals, with theatre projection & sound system, wireless Internet available. Open year round.
Jim Salzman, President

***Edmonton:* Alberta Railway Museum**
PO Box 70014 LRPO, 24215 - 34th St., Edmonton, AB T5C 3R6
Tel: 780-472-6229; *Fax:* 780-968-0167
hdixon@incentre.net
www.railwaymuseum.ab.ca
Founded: 1968 The Alberta Railway Museum features over sixty railway cars & locomotives, interpretive displays, a Morse telegraph demonstration, tours, & train rides on selected long weekends. The museum is open on weekends only from Victoria Day (the long weekend in May) to Labour Day (the long weekend in September).

***Edmonton:* Calgary & Edmonton (1891) Railway Museum**
10447 - 86th Ave., Edmonton, AB T6E 2M4
Tel: 780-433-9739; *Fax:* 780-431-0138
jledm@ecn.ab.ca
Visitors to the Calgary & Edmonton (1891) Railway Museum can see a replica railway station, which served the area from 1891 to 1907. Train & station artifacts are on display, including a working telegraph service. The museum is open from June to August. At other times, appointments may be arranged.

***Edmonton:* College & Association of Registered Nurses Of Alberta Museum & Archives**
11620 - 168 St., Edmonton, AB T5M 4A6
Tel: 780-453-0534; *Fax:* 780-482-4459
Toll-Free: 800-252-9392
www.nurses.ab.ca
Items related to the founding & development of the AARN, as well as the early history of professional nursing in Alberta; Collection includes caps, pins, uniforms, yearbooks, original diplomas, & photographs from early days of nurses' education in Alberta to present; Scrapbooks, uniforms, & military medals (WWI & WWII) from the Nursing Sisters Association; Records of various nursing interest groups
Lorraine Mychajlunow, Curator & Archivist, 780-453-0534, lmychajlunow@nurses.ab.ca

***Edmonton:* Edmonton Public Schools Archives & Museum**
10425 - 99 Ave., Edmonton, AB T5K 0E5
Tel: 780-422-1970; *Fax:* 780-426-0192
archives@epsb.ca
archives.epsb.net
Located in historic McKay Ave. School, site of the first session of the Alberta Legislature; 1905 restored brick building & features the restored 1906 legislative Chamber; holdings include Edmonton Public School Board District #7 & individual school records from 1885 to present
Catherine Luck, Supervisor

***Edmonton:* Edmonton Radial Railway Society**
PO Box 45040 Lansdowne PO, Edmonton, AB T6H 5Y1
Tel: 780-437-7721; *Fax:* 780-437-3095
info@edmonton-radial-railway.ab.ca
edmonton-radial-railway.ab.ca
Other contact information: Park Line: 780/496-1464
Vintage 3 km streetcar ride from Strathcona to downtown Edmonton along former CPR right of way & across the High Level Bridge; restored streetcar rides for visitors to Fort Edmonton Park
Robert Clark, President

***Edmonton:* Father Lacombe Chapel - Provincial Historic Site / La Chapelle du Père Lacombe**
8820 -112 St., Edmonton, AB T6G 2P8
Tel: 780-459-7663; *Fax:* 780-427-0808
father-lacombe@gov.ab.ca
www.cd.gov.ab.ca/flc
Alberta's oldest building; Located on St. Vital Ave., St. Albert; open May 15 - Labour Day
Marianne Mack, Facility Supervisor

***Edmonton:* Fort Edmonton Park**
c/o City of Edmonton Community Services, PO Box 2359, Edmonton, AB T5J 2R7
Tel: 780-442-5311; *Fax:* 780-496-8797
attractions@edmonton.ca
www.fortedmontonpark.ca
Canada's largest living history park; a complete 1846 fur-trading fort & 1885, 1905 & 1920 costumed interpreters; steam train & street car; giftshops & restaurants; fully operational hotel on site
Roger Jevne, Director

***Edmonton:* John Janzen Nature Centre**
PO Box 2359, Edmonton, AB T5J 2R7
Tel: 780-428-7900; *Fax:* 780-496-4701
Sandra Opdenkamp

***Edmonton:* John Walter Museum**
10661 - 91A Ave., Edmonton, AB T5K 0B3
Tel: 780-496-8787; *Fax:* 780-496-4701
attractions@edmonton.caton.ca
www.edmonton.ca/johnwalter
Other contact information: E-mail, School Programs: cmsschoolbookings@edmonton.ca
The museum consists of houses from 1874, 1886, & 1901. A variety of group programs are available. John Walter Museum is open from mid March to mid December.

***Edmonton:* The Loyal Edmonton Regiment Military Museum**
Prince of Wales Armouries, #118, 10440 - 108 Ave., Edmonton, AB T5H 3Z9
Tel: 780-421-9943; *Fax:* 780-421-9943
lermus1@telus.net
www.lermuseum.org
Military museum focusing on history of The Loyal Edmonton Regiment & other military service branches from Northern Alberta
David Haas, Curator

***Edmonton:* Rutherford House Provincial Historic Site**
11153 Saskatchewan Dr., Edmonton, AB T6G 2S1
Tel: 780-427-3995; *Fax:* 780-422-4288
info@rutherfordhouse.ca
www.rutherfordhouse.ca
Home of Alberta's first premier; gift shop, tea room, tours & special events; open year round

***Edmonton:* Stephansson House Provincial Historic Site**
8820 - 112 St., Edmonton, AB T6G 2P8
Tel: 780-427-3995
Icelandic poet's pioneer home; open May 15 - Labour Day; located 7 km. north of Markerville off Hwy. 592 or 781

***Edmonton:* The Telephone Historical Centre (THC)**
PO Box 188 Main, 10440 - 108 Ave., Edmonton, AB T5J 2J1
Tel: 780-433-1010; *Fax:* 780-426-1876
bertyeudall@hotmail.com
www.telephonehistoricalcentre.com
Open year round; Canada's largest independent telephone museum
Bert Yeudall, Executive Director

***Edmonton:* Ukrainian Canadian Archives & Museum of Alberta**
9543 - 110 Ave., Edmonton, AB T5H 1H3
Tel: 780-424-7580; *Fax:* 780-420-0562
ucama@shaw.ca
www.ucama.ca
The Ukrainian Canadian Archives & Museum of Alberta is dedicated to preserving Ukrainian-Canadian history & culture. Collections include Ukrainian-Canadian military memorabilia such as uniforms, textiles made by Ukrainian pioneers in Alberta, as well as ecclesiastical artifacts. The museum is open year-round, from Tuesday to Friday.
Khrystyna Kohut, President
Michelle Tracy, Vice-President
Christina Scharabun, Secretary

***Edmonton:* Ukrainian Catholic Women's League of Canada Arts & Crafts Museum**
10825 - 97th St., Edmonton, AB T5H 2M4
Tel: 780-474-0846
cyncarno@shaw.ca
Open by appt.
Nadia Cyncark, President
Elizabeth Holinaty, Corresponding Secretary

***Edmonton:* Ukrainian Cultural Heritage Village**
8820 - 112 St. NW, Edmonton, AB T6G 2P8
Tel: 780-662-3640; *Fax:* 780-662-3273
uchv@gov.ab.ca
www.ukrainianvillage.ca
The provincial historic site presents Ukrainian settlement in east central Alberta between 1892 & 1930. The Ukrainian Cultural Heritage Village has over thiry historic buildings for visitors to explore, including a grain elevator, a budei (a sod hut), & three churches of Eastern Byzantine Rite. The village is open from the

May long weekend to Labour Day. School groups may book a tour at other times of the year.
Arnold Grandt, Acting Director, Arnold.Grandt@gov.ab.ca
Becky Dahl, Curator, Becky.Dahl@gov.ab.ca
Shirley Hauck, Head, Special Events, Shirley.Hauck@gov.ab.ca
Pamela Trischuk, Head, Education & Interpretation Services, Pamela.Trischuk@gov.ab.ca
Radomir Bilash, Senior Historian & Project Manager, Alberta-Ukraine Genealogical Project, Radomir.Bilash@gov.ab.ca
Bruce McGregor, Coordinator, Historic Farm Program, Bruce.McGregor@gov.ab.ca

***Edmonton:* University of Alberta Dental Museum**
Dentistry Pharmacy Centre, University of Alberta, Edmonton, AB T6G 2N8
Tel: 780-492-5194; *Fax:* 780-492-1624
gsperber@ualberta.ca
Collection of antique dental instruments & furniture; natural history collection of animal skulls & fossil hominid models
Dr. G. Sperber, Curator

***Edmonton:* University of Alberta Museum of Paleontology**
University of Alberta - B-01 Earth Sciences Building, Edmonton, AB T6G 2E3
Tel: 780-492-3265; *Fax:* 780-492-8190
eas-inquiries@ualberta.ca
www.ualberta.ca/EAS
The museum presents the history of life over the course of geological time, starting with PreCambrian stromatolites and ending with Pleistocene megafauna; open during business hours Mon.-Fri.
M. Sharp, Chair
A. Locock, Collections Manager

***Edmonton:* University of Alberta Museum of Zoology**
#Z1011, Biological Sciences Bldg., University of Alberta, Edmonton, AB T6G 2E9
Tel: 780-492-4622; *Fax:* 780-492-9234
uamz@odum.biology.ualberta.ca
www.biology.ualberta.ca/uamz.hp/uamz.html
Open year round

***Edmonton:* University of Alberta Museums**
c/o Museums & Collections Services, Ring House #1, Edmonton, AB T6G 2E1
Tel: 780-492-5834; *Fax:* 780-492-6185
museums@ualberta.ca
www.museums.ualberta.ca
Museum services & expertise are provided to more than 35 teaching & research collections at the University; human history, fine art, natural & applied science collections, public programs, educational outreach & other community service programs offered
Janine Andrews, Executive Director
Frannie Blondheim, Manager, Communications Program
Pauline Rennick, Manager, Collections Program
Jim Corrigan, Curator, Univ. of Alberta Art & Artifact Collection

***Edmonton:* University of Alberta Vascular Plant Herbarium**
Dept. of Biological Sciences, University of Alberta, B-414, Biological Sciences, Edmonton, AB T6G 2E1
Tel: 780-492-3308; *Fax:* 780-492-9234
dorothy.fabijan@ualberta.ca
www.biology.ualberta.ca
Dorothy Fabijan, Assistant Curator

***Edmonton:* Victoria School Archives & Museum**
10210 - 108 Ave., Edmonton, AB T5H 1A8
Tel: 780-426-3010; *Fax:* 780-498-8727
jack.calkins@epob.ca
www.virtualmuseum.ca
Artifacts that relate to the school from 1903 to present; student & teacher records from 1911; books, playbills, posters, uniforms, photos, sweaters
Jack Calkins, Director, Cell: 780-862-0644
Michael Calkins, Archivist

***Edson:* Galloway Station Museum**
5425A - 3 Ave., Edson, AB T7E 1L5
Tel: 780-723-5696
Forestry; coal mining; railway
Jean Hatlen

***Edson:* Red Brick Arts Centre & Museum**
4818 - 7 Ave., Edson, AB T7E 1K8
Tel: 780-723-3582; *Fax:* 780-723-3582
Art gallery, theatre, school room museum, dance studio & gift shop
Betty Stitzenberger, President

***Elk Point:* Fort George Museum**
PO Box 66, Elk Point, AB T0A 1A0
Tel: 780-645-6256; *Fax:* 780-645-4760
Historical & archaeological material of a local nature; located 13 km SE of Elk Point on Secondary Rd. #646

***Etzikom:* Heritage Museum & Historic Windmill Centre**
PO Box 585, Etzikom, AB T0K 0W0
Tel: 403-666-3737; *Fax:* 403-666-2002
Canadian national historic windmill centre; open May long weekend - Sept. long weekend Mon-Sat 10-5, Sun. 12-6
June Mitzel, Director
Harold Halvorson, President

***Evansburg:* Pembina Lobstick Historical Museum**
PO Box 85, Evansburg, AB T0E 0T0
Artifacts of local historical interest

***Fairview:* RCMP Centennial Celebration Museum**
PO Box 1994, Fairview, AB T0H 1L0
Tel: 780-835-4815
Original barracks; also 2nd museum on a 10-acre site; open summer
Jean Bartlett, 780/835-4715
Robert Keddie, 780/835-2847
Marshall Rolling, 780/835-2392

***Forestburg:* Forestburg & District Museum**
PO Box 46, 4707 - 50 St., Forestburg, AB T0B 1N0
Tel: 780-582-2165; *Fax:* 780-582-4203
Housed in former Masonic Hall; displays relevant to the area; open by appt.

***Fort Chipewyan:* Fort Chipewyan Bicentennial Museum**
PO Box 203, Fort Chipewyan, AB T0P 1B0
Tel: 780-697-3844; *Fax:* 780-697-2389
fortchipmuseum@telus.net
www.woodbuffalo.ab.ca
Founded: 1991 The museum is a replica of the Hudson's Bay Store; local artifacts & archives; library reference collection; classes. Located on Mackenzie Ave. in Fort Chipewyan.
Oliver Glanfield, Chair
Maureen Clarke, Vice-Chair

***Fort MacLeod:* The Fort Museum**
PO Box 776, Fort MacLeod, AB T0L 0Z0
Tel: 403-553-4703; *Fax:* 403-553-3451
Toll-Free: 866-273-6841
info@nwmpmuseum.com
www.nwmpmuseum.com
Tells the story of the arrival of the NWMP into Western Canada, & the Natives & Pioneers of that time

***Fort MacLeod:* Head-Smashed-In Buffalo Jump**
PO Box 1977, Fort MacLeod, AB T0L 0Z0
Tel: 403-553-2731; *Fax:* 403-553-3141
info@head-smashed-in.com
www.head-smashed-in.com
Founded: 1987 Designated a UNESCO World Heritage Site in 1981, this jump is a testimony to the hunting customs of native peoples, particularly the Blackfoot, for thousands of years. The Interpretive Centre, blending into a sandstone cliff, explores the lives of the Blackfoot peoples from the geography of the region to the family life and ceremonies. Open year round.
Terry Malone, Facility Manager

***Fort McMurray:* Fort McMurray Oil Sands Discovery Centre**
515 MacKenzie Blvd., Fort McMurray, AB T9H 4X3
Tel: 780-743-7167; *Fax:* 780-791-0710
osdc@gov.ab.ca
www.oilsandsdiscovery.com
Open year round
Nancy Dodsworth, Facility Supervisor

***Fort McMurray:* Heritage Park**
1 Tolen Dr., Fort McMurray, AB T9H 1G7
Tel: 780-791-7575; *Fax:* 780-791-5180
heritage@fortmcmurrayhistory.com
www.fortmcmurrayhistory.com
Founded: 1974 The park is a village of 17 historic buildings from a trapper's cabin to a Catholic Mission celebrating the history of Ft. McMurray and the region. On site are 2 railway cars. Exhibits cover the logging, fishing and trapping industries. There is an extensive archive of photographs and historical documents.
Ms Roseann Davidson, Executive Director, 780-791-7575, X-228

***Fort Saskatchewan:* Fort Saskatchewan Museum**
10006 - 101 St., Fort Saskatchewan, AB T8L 1V9
Tel: 780-998-1783
info@fortsask.ca
www.fortsask.ca
Kris Nygren, Curator

***Girouxville:* Musée Girouxville Museum**
Village of Girouxville, PO Box 276, Girouxville, AB T0H 1S0
Tel: 780-323-4252; *Fax:* 780-323-4110
Located in the heart of Girouxville, museum offers visitors a glimpse back into a time when pioneers first settled in the Smoky River Region; more than 6,000 pieces on display; collections includes: Religion, Native history, Natural history, Pioneer life, Hunting & Trapping, Transportation, Fur trade, Domestic history, Communications, Agriculture, Photography, Education, Geology & Palaeontology

***Grande Prairie:* Grande Prairie Museum**
Pioneer Museum Society of Grande Prairie & District, PO Box 687, Grande Prairie, AB T8V 3A8
Tel: 780-532-5482; *Fax:* 780-831-7371
info@grandeprairiemuseum.org
www.grandeprairiemuseum.org
Dinosaur bones; arrowheads; wildlife exhibits; pioneer artifacts; heritage village; archives; open daily, closed on holidays
Peter Goertzen, Manager/Curator

***Grande Prairie:* The Heritage Discovery Centre (HDC)**
Centre 2000 Building, PO Box 687, Grande Prairie, AB T8V 3A8
Tel: 780-532-5790; *Fax:* 780-831-7371
pgoertzen@grandeprairiemuseum.org
Located at Centre 2000 in the Tourist Information Bldg.; includes a main exhibit gallery, a Rotary Learning Theatre, & the Kin Gallery. Also includes dinosaur exhibit, survivor games, mini-theatres, and hands-on display.
Peter Goertzen

***Hanna:* Hanna Museum & Pioneer Village**
PO Box 1528, Pioneer Trail, Hanna, AB T0J 1P0
Tel: 403-854-4244
www.hanna.ca
Historic buildings at the pioneer village include a ranch house, a one room schoolhouse, a store, a church, a hospital, a dental office, & a power mill. Archives are also available for research. The museum & pioneer village is open from June to August, & in May & September by appointment.
Vic Mohl, Secretary-Treasurer

***High Prairie:* High Prairie & District Museum & Historical Society**
PO Box 1442, High Prairie, AB T0G 1E0
Tel: 780-523-2601; *Fax:* 780-523-2633
hpdmhs@telusplanet.net
www.highprairiemuseum.com
Founded: 1967 The museum preserves the history of High Prairie & surrounding area by conserving artifacts used by homesteaders from the early 1900s. Stories of the settlers are also archived. Programs offered to children include butter-making, bread-making and sewing lessons. Open year round, with summer & winter hrs.

***High River:* Museum of the Highwood**
309B Macleod Trail SW, High River, AB T1V 1Z5
Tel: 403-652-7156; *Fax:* 403-652-2396
museumofthehighwood@highriver.ca
www.highriver.ca
Located in the historic sandstone Canadian Pacific Railway Station on 1st Street Southwest in High River, the Museum of the Highwood exhibits the history of the Highwood River basin. The museum features a family discovery room, which is a hands-on space with old fashioned games & toys. Programs & tours are available upon request.

***Hines Creek:* End of Steel Heritage Society**
PO Box 686, Hines Creek, AB T0H 2A0
Tel: 403-494-3522
Former Northern Alberta Railway cars; homes & church circa. 1930; pioneering artifacts; trapper's cabin; community hall

***Hinton:* Alberta Forest Service Museum**
1176 Switzer Dr., Hinton, AB T7V 1V3
Tel: 780-865-8200; *Fax:* 780-865-8266
envtrain@gov.ab.ca
tpr.alberta.ca/parks/switzer/attractions
Established to preserve a history of forestry in the province of Alberta; displays reflect work performed by the early rangers & provide an appreciation of their accomplishments achieved without benefit of modern transportation, tools & technology; "compact disk" guided tour; ranger headquarters cabin built in 1922; open daily; weekends by appt
Rob Thorburn

***Holden:* Holden Historical Society Museum**
PO Box 32, 4920 - 50 Holden Ave., Holden, AB T0B 2C0
Tel: 780-688-2464; *Fax:* 780-688-2464
dmarus@telus.net
The collection is of the local farming community with objects pertaining to pioneer life. Open Wed., Fri., & Sun. in summer, 2-4
Dave Maruszeczka

***Iddesleigh:* Rainy Hills Historical Society Pioneer Exhibits (RHHS)**
***Also known as:* Rainy Hills Historical Society**
c/o Margaret Harahue, Iddesleigh, AB T0J 1T0
Tel: 403-898-2443
Community museum exhibiting homestead items including furnishings, clothing, farm equipment & photographs; also features a blacksmith shop, school room, general store, an

old-time kitchen & the original Iddlesleigh Alberta Wheat Post Office building
Margaret Harahue, Sec.-Treas.

***Innisfail:* Innisfail Historical Village**
52nd Ave. & 42nd St., Innisfail, AB T0M 1A0
Tel: 403-227-2906; *Fax:* 403-227-2901
idhs@telus.net
www.innisfailhistory.com
Promote the preservation, interpretation, enjoyment of the history of Innisfail & District; village is made up of seventeen buildings on two acres of land; farm machinary and picnic area.

***Irvine:* Prairie Memories Museum**
PO Box 245, Irvine, AB T0J 1V0
Tel: 403-834-2646
Local history; open June 30 - Sept.

***Islay:* Morrison Museum of the Country School**
PO Box 120, Islay, AB T0B 2J0
Tel: 780-744-2271
Contains a collection of the artifacts to be found in a western Canadian country school of the 1930s & 1940s
Allen Ronaghan, Curator

***Jasper:* Jasper Yellowhead Museum & Archives (JYHS)**
PO Box 42, 400 Pyramid Lake Rd., Jasper, AB T0E 1E0
Tel: 780-852-3013
webadministrator@jaspermuseum.org
www.jaspermuseum.org
Other contact information: Phone, Archives: 780-852-3240
The Jasper Yellowhead Museum & Archives collects, preserves, & exhibits artifacts & documents related to the human history of Jasper National Park & the Yellowhead corridor. Displays in the historical gallery tell the story of the fur trade, the railway, & early tourism. The area has been designated as part of a World Heritage Site. The Jasper Yellowhead Museum & Archives is open year-round. Visits to the archives are by appointment only.
B. Bell, President
Karen Byers, Manager, manager@jaspermuseum.org
J. Couture, Historian
Dee Dee Bartlett, Contact, Collections, collections@jaspermuseum.org
Val Delill, Contact, Exhibits, exhibits@jaspermuseum.org
Lucie Doucet, Contact, Gift Shop, giftshop@jaspermuseum.org
Meghan Power, Contact, Archives, archives@jaspermuseum.org

***Leduc:* Dr. Woods House Museum**
4801 - 49 Ave., Leduc, AB T9E 6L6
Tel: 780-986-1517
Restored 1920s house with attached garage & medical wing

***Lethbridge:* Fort Whoop-Up**
***Also known as:* Fort Hamilton**
PO Box 1074, Lethbridge, AB T1J 4A2
Tel: 403-329-0444; *Fax:* 403-329-0645
info@fortwhoopup.ca
www.fortwhoopup.ca
Located in Indian Battle Park, west end of 3rd Ave. As an Interpretive Centre, "the Fort" has been reconstructed and interpreted to be the norotirious whiskey fort: as such is has electronic displays, historical sights, and sounds to pay tribute to and commentorate the legact of the NMMP, Aboriginal People, and pioneers that shaped Western Canada. Open year round
Doran Degenstein, Curator and Director, 403-329-0444

***Lethbridge:* Sir Alexander Galt Museum & Archives**
910 - 4 Ave. South, Lethbridge, AB T1J 0P6
Tel: 403-320-3898; *Fax:* 403-329-4958
info@galtmuseum.com
www.galtmuseum.com
The human history of Lethbridge & southern Alberta in 5 galleries & an outdoor courtyard; free admission
Wendy Aitkens, Curator

***Lloydminster:* Barr Colony Heritage Cultural Centre**
4420 - 50th Ave., Lloydminster, AB T9V 0W2
Tel: 306-825-5655; *Fax:* 306-825-9070
bchcc@lloydminster.ca
142.179.207.186/bchcc
Other contact information: Phone, City of Lloydminster: 780-875-6184; Fax: 780-871-8345
Located at Highway 16 & 45th Avenue, the Barr Colony Heritage Cultural Centre consists of an antique museum, the Imhoff art collection, the OTS Heavy Oil Science Centre, & the Fuchs wildlife exhibit. The Richard Larsen Museum presents antiques of the Barr Colonists. Artifacts include funiture & agricultural equipment. Visitors can also see Lloydminster's first church, a log cabin, a filling station, & a 1906 schoolhouse. The centre is open year-round.

***Longview:* Bar U Ranch National Historic Site of Canada**
PO Box 168, Longview, AB T0L 1H0
Tel: 403-395-2212; *Fax:* 403-395-2331
Toll-Free: 888-773-8888
BarU.info@pc.gc.ca
www.pc.gc.ca/lhn-nhs/ab/baru/index_ e.asp
Other contact information: TDD: 866-787-6221
With 35 buildings & structures, the Bar U Ranch commemorates the history of ranching in Canada. The Ranch is open from late May to the end of September. Visits can be arranged during the off season.

***Lougheed:* Iron Creek Museum**
PO Box 249, Lougheed, AB T0B 2V0
Tel: 780-386-3787
Two one-room school houses; church; blacksmith & shoe repair shop; log hall housing artifacts & farm machinery

***Markerville:* Historic Markerville Creamery**
PO Box 837, Markerville, AB T0M 1M0
Tel: 403-728-3006; *Fax:* 403-728-3225
creamery@touralberta.com
Creamery museum restored to 1930s profiles Icelandic settlement of central Alberta; "Kaffistofa" features Icelandic menu
Kathleen Raines, Manager

***Medicine Hat:* Esplanade Arts & Heritage Centre (MHM&AG)**
401 First St. SE, Medicine Hat, AB T1A 8W2
Tel: 403-502-8580; *Fax:* 403-502-8589
esplanade@medicinthat.ca
www.esplanade.ca
Museum: Permanent Gallery featuring the history of Medicine Hat & area using pieces from vast collection, including pioneer home funishings, Victorian period artifacts, archaeological artifacts, military, sporting & Native artifacts, business & industry equipment, clothing & more; Archives: database of manuscripts, extensive black & white photographic collection, genealogical information & more; A
Carol Beatty, Manager

***Medicine Hat:* Medicine Hat Clay Industries National Historic District**
713 Medalta Ave. SE, Medicine Hat, AB T1A 3K9
Tel: 403-529-1070; *Fax:* 403-580-5868
Toll-Free: 866-526-2777
info@medalta.org
www.medalta.org
The 150-acre Historic Clay District preserves the history of the region's pottery industry. With working, circular kilns and original factory, it is living museum. The Medalta International Artists in Residence (MIAIR) program hosts contemporary ceramic artists. An interactive clay area and education programs are available for children.
Mr. Barry G. Finkelman, General Manager/Executive Director, barry@medalta.org

***Millet:* Millet & District Museum & Archives**
PO Box 178, 5120 - 50 St., Millet, AB T0C 1Z0
Tel: 780-387-5558; *Fax:* 780-387-5548
info@milletmuseum.ca
www.milletmuseum.ca
Founded: 1985 Exhibits incude archives on local history, home settings from 1900-1950 and portraits of over 200 local veterans of World Wars I, II. Building also houses the Millet Visitor Information Centre; open to the public Tues. - Sat. in summer
Ms Tracey Leavitt, Executive Director/Curator

***Mirror:* Mirror & District Museum**
PO Box 246, 4910 - 53 St., Mirror, AB T0B 3C0
Tel: 403-788-3828
mmuseum@telus.net
Other contact information: Phone, Off season: 403-788-3094
Settler & railway artifacts are presented at the Mirror & District Museum. The museum if open from mid May to the beginning of September. Appointments may be arranged at other times.

***Mundare:* Basilian Fathers Museum**
PO Box 386, Mundare, AB T0B 3H0
Tel: 780-764-3887; *Fax:* 780-764-3825
curator@basilianmuseum.org
www.basilianmuseum.org
Ukrainian culture & religion
Karen Lemiski, Associate Director/Curator

***Nanton:* Bomber Command Museum of Canada**
PO Box 1051, Nanton, AB T0L 1R0
Tel: 403-646-2270; *Fax:* 403-646-2214
office@bombercommandmuseum.ca
www.bombercommandmuseum.ca
Other contact information: Twitter: www.twitter.com/BCMofCanada
The Bomber Command Museum of Canada honours persons associated with Bomber Command during World War II. It also commemorates the operations of the British Commonwealth Air Training Plan. The Museum's library & archives may be contacted at the following e-mail address: library@bombercommandmuseum.ca. School & group visits may be organized by contacting the following e-mail address: visitorservices@bombercommandmuseum.ca.
Bob Evans, Curator, curator@bombercommandmuseum.ca
Robert Pedersen, President

***Olds:* Mountain View Museum & Archives**
PO Box 3882, 5038 - 50th St., Olds, AB T4H 1P6
Tel: 403-556-8464
info@oldsmuseum.ca
www.oldsmuseum.ca
Founded: 1972 The Olds Historical Society preserves artifacts, textual documents, & photographs, which depict the history & heritage of Olds & its surrounding area. Items are displayed & research services are available at the Mountain View Museum & Archives, which is located in the 1920 Olds AGT building. The museum is open from Monday to Friday. Guided tours & educational programs are offered.
Michael Dougherty, Museum Manager, manager@oldsmuseum.ca
Jeffery Kearney, Archivist, archives@oldsmuseum.ca

***Oyen:* Crossroads Museum**
PO Box 563, 310 1st Avenue East, Oyen, AB T0J 2J0
Tel: 403-664-2330
www.virtualmuseum.ca
Buildings include a period house (1918); cook car; blacksmith shop; tractor & truck building; a 120x40 Quonset; 1912 schoolhouse; former community hall; "teepee" type building containing archaeological artifacts; season May-Aug.
Nellie Eaton, President

***Peace River:* Peace River Centennial Museum & Archives (PRMCAA)**
***Also known as:* Peace River Museum**
10302 - 99 St., Peace River, AB T8S 1K1
Tel: 780-624-4261; *Fax:* 780-624-2470
prcma@telusplanet.net
Displays include: Sir Alexander Mackenzie, fur trade, town of Peace River

***Pincher Creek:* Kootenai Brown Pioneer Village**
PO Box 1226, Pincher Creek, AB T0K 1W0
Tel: 403-627-3684; *Fax:* 403-627-5850
Toll-Free: 888-298-5855
kootenai@telusplanet.net
telusplanet.net/public/kooten ai
Open year round
George Sinnott, President

***Plamondon:* Plamondon & District Museum**
c/o Emilie Chevigny, PO Box 119, Plamondon, AB T0A 2T0
Tel: 403-798-3193
www.plamondonalberta.ca
Operated by the Plamondon & District Museum Society, the Plamondon & District Museum features local cultural artifacts from early pioneers. The museum is open from June to August.
Bonita Marchand, Contact

***Ponoka:* Fort Ostell Museum**
5320 - 54 St., Ponoka, AB T4J 1L8
Tel: 403-783-5224
fomol@telus.net
www.ponoka.org
Founded: 1967 Open May 24-Sept. 4, winter special occasions or by appt.
Barb Greshner, Chair

***Red Deer:* Alberta Sports Hall of Fame & Museum**
30 Riverview Park, Red Deer, AB T4N 1E3
Tel: 403-341-8614; *Fax:* 403-341-8619
postmaster@albertasportshalloffame.com
www.albertasportshalloffame.com
Founded: 1957 To preserve artifacts & archival material that are significant in Alberta's sporting history; 7 Honoured Members are inducted into the Sports Hall of Fame each year, plus 3 award recipients; interactive multisport virtual game system & a curriculum based education program; theatre; boardroom rental.
Donna Hately, Managing Director

***Red Deer:* Kerry Wood Nature Centre**
6300 - 45 Ave., Red Deer, AB T4N 3M4
Tel: 403-346-2010; *Fax:* 403-347-2550
general@waskasoopark.ca
www.waskasoopark.ca
Central Alberta's year-round home of entertaining & informative nature activities & exhibits; gateway to Gaetz Lakes Sanctuary; features art gallery, bookshop, A/V theatre, meeting rooms, children's Discovery Room & exhibits; extensive programs, courses, field trips for all ages; open daily except Christmas; admission by donation
Jim Robertson, Manager
Paul Gowans, Executive Director

Red Deer: **Red Deer Museum & Art Gallery**
4525 - 47A Ave., Red Deer, AB T4N 6Z6
Tel: 403-309-8405; *Fax:* 403-342-6644
museum@reddeer.ca
www.reddeermuseum.com
Founded: 1973 The Red Deer Museum & Art Gallery tells the story of the people, history, & culture of central Alberta, through its collections, exhibitions, & programs. The museum's more than 85,000 objects include clothing & First Nations & Inuit art. A library on the site houses artifact books, catalogues, & other printed material.
Lorna Johnson, Executive Director BFA, M.ED, lorna.johnson@reddeer.ca
Michael Dawe, Curator, History, michael.dawe@reddeer.ca
Valerie Miller, Coordinator, Collections, valerie.miller@reddeer.ca
Lynn Norman, Coordinator, Communications & Marketing, lynn.norman@reddeer.ca

Redcliff: **Redcliff Historical & Museum Society**
Also known as: **Redcliff Museum**
PO Box 758, Redcliff, AB T0J 2P0
Tel: 403-548-6260
Exhibits showing the commercial & recreational aspect of Redcliff citizens; extensive drug store, domestic, school, toy & organizational exhibits; history of past industries with manufactured artifacts; weekly newpaper on microfilm 1910-1939; open May-Aug., Tue.-Sat., Sun., Oct.-Apr. by appt.

Rocky Mountain House: **Rocky Mountain House National Historic Site of Canada**
Comp. 6, Site 127, RR#4, Rocky Mountain House, AB T4T 2A4
Tel: 403-845-2412; *Fax:* 403-845-5320
rocky.info@pc.gc.ca
www.pc.gc.ca/rockymountainhouse
Site of four fur trading posts dating back to 1799; Commemorates the fur trade & the role of Native peoples in the fur trade & western exploration (David Thompson); Over 500 acres; Hiking trails, displays, herd of bisons; Exhibits; 3/4 size playfort; Eight trailside listening stations; Heritage demonstrations & presentations; Open Victoria Day weekend - Labour Day
Scott Whiting, Site Operations Supervisor

Rosebud: **Rosebud Historical Society**
PO Box 601, Rosebud, AB T0J 2T0
Tel: 403-677-2208; *Fax:* 403-533-2243
A collection of pioneer tools, etc. that have been donated to the museum; open year round

Rowley: **Yester-Year Artifacts Museum**
General Delivery, Rowley, AB T0J 2X0
Tel: 403-368-3816; *Fax:* 403-368-2239
Early settlers artifacts housed in original buildings

St Albert: **Musée Héritage Museum & Archives**
Also known as: **St. Albert Museum**
5 Ste-Anne St., St Albert, AB T8N 3Z9
Tel: 780-459-1528; *Fax:* 780-459-1546
museum@compusmart.ab.ca
History of St. Albert & surrounding area
Alexandra Hatcher, Director

St Paul: **Fort George & Buckingham House Provincial Historic Site (FGBH)**
#318, Provincial Bldg., 5025, 49th Ave., St Paul, AB T0A 3A4
Tel: 403-645-6256; *Fax:* 403-645-4760
ross.stromberg@gov.ab.ca
Archaeological remains of 2 fur trade forts; interpretive centre & gift shop; open May 15 - Labour Day; located 13 km SE of Elk Point on Hwy. 646

Saint-Paul: **Musée historique de Saint-Paul**
CP 1925, Saint-Paul, AB T0A 3A0
Tél: 780-645-4800; *Téléc:* 780-645-5959
Founded: 1984 Relever l'histoire de la communauté de Saint-Paul; expositions; cours d'histoire aux élèves; projets spécials.
Jeannette Létourneau, Trésorière

St Paul: **Victoria Settlement Provincial Historic Site**
Also known as: **Fort Victoria**
#318, Provincial Bldg., St Paul, AB T0A 3A4
Tel: 403-645-6256; *Fax:* 403-645-4760
Located 10 km south of Smoky Lake on Hwy. 855, 6 km east along Victoria Trail; Hudson Bay Company post & settlement; open May 15-Labour Day

Sangudo: **Lac Ste-Anne Historical Society Pioneer Museum**
PO Box 525, Sangudo, AB T0E 2A0
Tel: 403-785-2674
Ed Liss, President

Seba Beach: **Seba Beach Heritage Museum**
General Delivery, Seba Beach, AB T0E 2B0
Tel: 403-420-6704
Summer resort themed artifacts, such as regatta trophies & photographs; historical material related to Seba Beach; located at Main Ave. & 101 St. North

Sedgewick: **Sedgewick Archives, Gallery & Museum**
PO Box 538, Sedgewick, AB T0B 4C0
Tel: 780-384-3741
www.sedgewick.ca
Founded: 1989 Clothing, jewelry, books, photographs, tools; open Tues-Fri, 1:30-4:30; located in the historic Bank of Montreal building on Main St. in Sedgewick
Lorne Abre, President
Myrtle Matthews, Secretary

Sherwood Park: **Strathcona County Heritage Museum**
913 Ash St., Sherwood Park, AB T8A 2G3
Tel: 780-467-8189; *Fax:* 780-467-8189
Local history; open year round

Siksika: **Siksika Nation Museum**
PO Box 1730, Siksika, AB T0J 3W0
Tel: 403-734-5361; *Fax:* 403-264-9659
Floria Duckchief, Manager

Stettler: **Stettler Town & Country Museum**
PO Box 2118, Stettler, AB T0C 2L0
Tel: 403-742-4534
stcmuse@telus.net
A village replica housing artifacts from the local & surrounding areas; includes a courthouse, schools, church, CN station, pioneer homes & barns, agricultural items as well as a local sports museum; also an original Estonian Grist mill & log cabin of the early twenties constructed by early Estonian pioneers; situated on 10 acres in SW Stettler; open daily May-Aug. or by appt.
Wilda V. Gibbon, Curator
Karen Wahlund, Assistant

Stony Plain: **Multicultural Heritage Centre**
PO Box 5411, 51 Street, Stony Plain, AB T7Z 1X7
Tel: 780-963-2777; *Fax:* 780-963-0233
The Heritage Centre includes restored buildings including a 1925 high school, a settler's cabin, and a homestead's kitchen. This living history museum offers entertainment and weekend demos. Open M-Sa 10-6, Su 10-6:30
Judy Unterschultz, Executive Director

Stony Plain: **Stony Plain & District Pioneer Museum**
5120 - 43 Ave., Stony Plain, AB T7Z 1X2
Tel: 780-963-9825
Open April 1 - Oct. 31

Strome: **Sodbuster Archives Museum**
PO Box 151, Strome, AB T0B 4H0
Tel: 780-376-3546
sodbustersarchivesmuseum@telus.net
Other contact information: Tel. 780/376-3688 (summer)
Shows the development of the West & of the Strome & district community from 1900 to the 1950s
Joan Brockhoff, Sec.-Treas., joanbl@telusplanet.net

Sundre: **Sundre Pioneer Village Museum**
PO Box 314, 211, 1st Ave. SW, Sundre, AB T0M 1X0
Tel: 403-638-3233
sundremuseum@telus.net
www.museum.sundre.com
Located at 130 Centre St. South; open May-Sept.
Darleen Smee, Secretary

Taber: **Taber & District Museum**
4702 - 50 St., Taber, AB T1G 2B6
Tel: 403-223-5708; *Fax:* 403-223-0529
tiimchin@telusplanet.net
Open year round, closed in Aug.

Three Hills: **Knee Hill Historical Museum**
PO Box 653, 1301-2nd St.N, Three Hills, AB T0M 2A0
Tel: 403-443-2092; *Fax:* 403-443-7941
www.threehills.ca
Pioneer Museum and tourist information centre.

Tofield: **Beaverhill Lake Nature Centre & Tofield Museum**
PO Box 30, 5020 - 48th Ave., Tofield, AB T0B 4J0
Tel: 780-662-3269
Founded: 1985 The Beaverhill Lake Nature Centre presents information about Beaverhill Lake & its wildlife. The lake is a federally recognized bird sanctuary. Located in the Beaverhill Lake Nature Centre facility is the Tofield Museum. The museum features the history of the community since 1882. The Tofield Museum is open from mid-April to Labour Day. Appointments may be arranged at other times of the year.

Trochu: **Trochu & District Museum**
PO Box 538, Trochu, AB T0M 2C0
Tel: 403-442-2220
Displays on the early pioneers including a kitchen, blacksmith shop, general store, schools, coal mining & an extensive collection of WW I & II pictures & uniforms; open May to Aug.
George O. Braham

Two Hills: **Two Hills & District Historical Museum**
PO Box 566, 5910-51 St., Two Hills, AB T0B 4K0
Tel: 403-657-2461
Houses 4,000 artifacts pertaining to the area; collection of steamers, automobiles, farm equipment, farm tools, early household artifacts, buildings, railways caboose, etc.

Valhalla Centre: **Melsness Mercantile**
PO Box 52, Valhalla Centre, AB T0H 3M0
Tel: 780-356-2403; *Fax:* 780-356-2007
loberg@gpwins.ca
Provincial historic site; museum displays, deli café, gift shop
E. Loberg, President

Vegreville: **Vegreville Regional Museum**
PO Box 328, Vegreville, AB T9C 1R3
Tel: 780-632-7650
museum@digitalweb.net
www.vegreville.com
Located on the site of the solonetzic soils research station of Agriculture Canada, The Vegreville Regional Museum depicts the history of Vegreville & its agricultural & business development. A special collection is The Right Honourable Donald Mazankowski, P.C. Collection. Mazankowski was the former Deputy Prime Minister of Canada. The regional museum also houses the Vegreville & District Sports Hall of Fame. The museum is open year-round.

Viking: **Viking Historical Museum**
PO Box 270, Viking, AB T0B 4N0
Tel: 780-336-3066
Displays various facets of pioneer life; includes 1907 school, 1903 log store, 1938 church & 1919 farm house; open summer; May 15 - Thanksgiving
J.H. Roddick, Director

Wainwright: **Wainwright Museum**
PO Box 2994, Wainwright, AB T9W 1S9
Tel: 403-842-3115; *Fax:* 403-842-4910
battleriverhs@cablerocket.com
Open year round
Billie Patterson

Wanham: **Grizzly Bear Prairie Museum**
PO Box 68, Wanham, AB T0H 3P0
Tel: 780-694-3933
jesather@telusplanet.net
Several buildings including 1920s log house, Presbyterian church & storage building; displays of agricultural machinery & artifacts used by the pioneers of the area; forestry tower; forestry cabin containing schoolroom, toolroom & pioneer kitchen displays; 1920 era hiproof barn; CNR rail display: building to store two handcars; two handcars; various tools related to work on CNR
Stan Sather

Warner: **Devil's Coulee Dinosaur Heritage Museum**
PO Box 156, 300 County Rd., Warner, AB T0K 2L0
Tel: 403-642-2118; *Fax:* 403-642-3660
dinoegg@telusplanet.net
www.devilscoulee.com
Dinosaur eggs; local fossils; local history
Suzanne Lodermeier, Manager

Wetaskiwin: **Alberta Central Railway Museum**
RR#2, Wetaskiwin, AB T9A 1W9
Tel: 780-352-2257; *Fax:* 780-352-3202
abcentral@incentre.net
www.abcentralrailway.com
Collection of early heavy weight cars from the passenger era, as well as fright equipment, cabooses, freight cars, and a snowplow. They also house the second oldest standing grain elevator in Alberta built by the Alberta Grain Company in 1906. Located southeast of Westaskiwin. Open from Victoria Day until Labour Day.
W.G. Wilson, Operations Manager
Ellen Wilson, Customer Services Manager

Wetaskiwin: **Canada's Aviation Hall of Fame / Panthéon de l'Aviation du Canada**
PO Box 6360, Hwy. 13, Wetaskiwin, AB T9A 2G1
Tel: 780-361-1351
cahf@telusplanet.net
www.cahf.ca
Founded: 1973 Canada's Aviation Hall of Fame collects, preserves, & exhibits material related to individuals & organizations that have made outstanding contributions to aviation & aerospace in Canada.
John Holding, Chair
Brian Fowler, Chair, Operations
Rosella Bjornson, Secretary-Treasurer

Wetaskiwin: **Reynolds Museum Ltd.**
4110 - 57 St., Wetaskiwin, AB T9A 2B6
Tel: 780-352-5201; *Fax:* 780-352-4666
rml@incentre.net

800 surplus antique cars, trucks, fire engines, tractors plus machinery for sale to allow for expansion of our displays of aircraft & military vehicles
Stanley G. Reynolds, President
Bruce A. Olson, Manager

Wetaskiwin: **Wetaskiwin & District Heritage Museum**
5007 - 50th Ave., Wetaskiwin, AB T9A 0S3
Tel: 780-352-0227; *Fax:* 780-352-0226
wdhm@persona.ca
www.wetaskiwinmuseum.com

Founded: 1986 The Wetaskiwin & District Heritage Museum presents the history of Wetaskiwin, Alberta & the surrounding area, from dinosaur fossils, to First Nations' history, to the war years. Visitors can also learn about life on a Hutterite colony. A resource library is part of the museum. The museum is open year-round.
Sylvia Larson, Chief Executive Officer & Manager
Brianne Stone, Museum Administrator
Gillian Furuness, Manager, Collections
Helmer Larson, Manager, Projects

Willingdon: **Historic Village & Pioneer Museum at Shandro**
PO Box 102, Willingdon, AB T0B 4R0
Tel: 780-367-2452
mereska@vegnet.com

Ukrainian architecture & artifacts; open summer, other seasons by appt.

British Columbia

Provincial Museums

Museum of Anthropology
University of British Columbia, 6393 Marine Dr. NW, Vancouver, BC V6T 1Z2
Tel: 604-822-5950; *Fax:* 604-822-2974
jenwebb@interchange.ubc.ca
www.moa.ubc.ca

Art & objects from around the world, with emphasis on First Nations cultures of the Northwest Coast; displayed in architect Arthur Erickson's award-winning building overlooking Howe Sound
Dr. Anthony A. Shelton, Director

Museum of Vancouver (MOV)
1100 Chestnut St., Vancouver, BC V6J 3J9
Tel: 604-736-4431
guestservices@museumofvancouver.ca
www.museumofvancouver.ca

The Museum of Vancouver offers permanent displays, exhibitions, & educational programs about the human, cultural, & natural history of the city of Vancouver & the surrounding area. The Local History Lab & the Archaeology Education Centre contribute to the museum's school programs. The museum is open year-round.
Nancy Noble, Chief Executive Officer, 604-730-5323, nnoble@museumofvancouver.ca
Amanda Gibbs, Director, Audience Engagement, 604-730-5317, agibbs@museumofvancouver.ca
Joan Seidl, Director, Collections & Exhibitions, 604-730-5316, jseidl@museumofvancouver.ca
Viviane Gosselin, Curator, Contemporary Issues, 604-730-5318, vgosselin@museumofvancouver.ca
Wendy Nichols, Curator, Collections, 604-730-5312, wnichols@museumofvancouver.ca
Genny Krikorian, Officer, Marketing, 604-730-5309, gkrikorian@museumofvancouver.ca
Jane Lougheed, Officer, Education Program, 604-730-5307, jlougheed@museumofvancouver.ca

Royal BC Museum Corp.
675 Belleville St., Victoria, BC V8W 9W2
Tel: 250-356-7226; *Fax:* 250-387-5674
Toll-Free: 888-447-7977
reception@royalbcmuseum.bc.ca
www.royalbcmuseum.bc.ca

Founded in 1886, the RBCM specializes in the natural & human history of British Columbia
Pauline Rafferty, CEO
Grant Hughes, Director, Curatorial Services
Cynthia Wrate, Director, Marketing & Communications
Angela Williams, Director, Visitor & Human Resource Services
Gary Mitchell, Director, Access & Information Management
Faye Zinck, CFO

Local Museums in British Columbia

108 Mile Ranch: **100 Mile & District Historical Society**
PO Box 225, 108 Mile Ranch, BC V0K 2Z0
Tel: 250-791-5288; *Fax:* 250-791-1947
historical@bcinternet.net
www.historical.bc.ca

The 108 Mile Ranch Heritage Site comprises 11 historical buildings dating from the Gold Rush era; largest log barn in Canada; open May long weekend to Labour Day
Tom Rutledge, President

108 Mile Ranch: **108 Mile House Heritage Site & Museum**
100 Mile & District Historical Society, Hwy. 97, Box 225, 108 Mile Ranch, BC V0K 2Z0
Tel: 250-791-5288; *Fax:* 250-791-1947
historical@bcinternet.net
www.historical.bc.ca

Original 105 Mile Roadhouse along the Cariboo Gold Rush Trail, 10 other historical buildings including the largest log barn in Canada (circa 1908), also mill equipment display
Marianne Rutledge, Director

Abbotsford: **Matsqui-Sumas-Abbotsford Museum - Trethewey House**
Also known as: **MSA Museum**
2313 Ware St., Abbotsford, BC V2S 3C6
Tel: 604-853-0313; *Fax:* 604-853-0326
mail@MSA.Museum.bc.ca
www.abbotsford.net/msamuseum

Trethewey House was built in 1920 by B.C. timber baron, J.O. Trethewey and has been restored to period style, incuding its gardens and grounds. Also on site are the Playhouse and the Carriage House with the museum offices. Exhibits include an extensive collection of historical photographs of the region, in addition to an array of artifacts from local home life and businesses, particularly, the lumber industry. Tours are available.
Ms Dorothy Van der Ree, Executive Director
Ms Christina Reid, Collections Manager

Ainsworth Hot Springs: **Silver Ledge Hotel Museum**
PO Box 1314, Ainsworth Hot Springs, BC V0G 1A0
Tel: 403-243-6302; *Fax:* 403-243-3672
silverledge@shaw.ca
www.members.shaw.ca/silverledge

Photographic history of the first community in the west Kootenays & the Ainsworth Mining District housed in the Silver Ledge Hotel built in 1896
J.E Duff, President, 604/221-7605

Alert Bay: **Alert Bay Library & Museum**
PO Box 440, 118 Fir St., Alert Bay, BC V0N 1A0
Tel: 250-974-5721; *Fax:* 250-974-5026
abplb@island.net
www.alertbay.bclibrary.ca; www.alertbay.ca

Ethnographic material; artifacts related to the fishing industry, local history; gift shop
Joyce Wilby, Head Librarian/Archivist

Alert Bay: **U'Mista Cultural Centre**
PO Box 253, Front St., Alert Bay, BC V0N 1A0
Tel: 250-974-5403; *Fax:* 250-974-5499
umista@north.island.net

Kwakwaka'wakw masks depicting the Potlatch ceremony; traditional & contemporary arts & crafts

Armstrong: **Armstrong Spallumcheen Museum & Arts Society**
PO Box 308, 3415 Pleasant Valley Rd., Armstrong, BC V0E 1B0
Tel: 250-546-8318
www.asmas.ca
Other contact information: asmas@telus.net

Founded: 1974 The Armstrong Spallumcheen Museum and Arts Society features a museum, archives, & an art gallery. Visitors are educated about the history of the local region. Genealogy & art workshops are conducted.

Ashcroft: **Ashcroft Museum & Archives**
PO Box 129, Ashcroft, BC V0K 1A0
Tel: 250-453-9161; *Fax:* 250-453-9664
admin@village.ashcroft.bc.ca
www.village.ashcroft.bc.ca

Founded: 1935 History of the Southern Cariboo region, & the farming & ranching communities of Hat Creek Valley. Open 5 days a week, Apr.-Nov.; open 7 days a week July & Aug. Admission by donation. Located at the corner of Brink & Fourth streets in Ashcroft.
Kathy Paulos, Curator

Atlin: **Atlin Historical Museum (AHS)**
Also known as: **Atlin Historical Society**
PO Box 111, Atlin, BC V0W 1A0
Tel: 250-651-7522; *Fax:* 250-651-7522
heritage@atlin.net

Open May 15 - Labour Day. Closed on Mondays.

Barkerville: **Barkerville Historic Town**
PO Box 19, Barkerville, BC V0K 1B0
Tel: 250-994-3332; *Fax:* 250-994-3435
Toll-Free: 888-994-3332
barkerville@barkerville.ca
www.barkerville.ca
Other contact information: Info Email: barkerville@gems8.gov.bc.ca

Restored Cariboo Gold Rush town; Blessing's Grave; Richfield Court House; open year round; peak season from early May to late Sept.
William Quackenbush, Curator
Judy Campbell, CEO
Reuben Berlin, Manager, Operations

Bella Coola: **Bella Coola Museum**
PO Box 726, 269 Hwy. 20, Bella Coola, BC V0T 1C0
Tel: 250-799-5767
info@bellacoolamuseum.ca
www.bellacoolamuseum.ca
Other contact information: Phone, Archives: 250-982-2130

Founded: 1963 Owned & operated by the Bella Coola Valley Museum Society, the Bella Coola Valley Museum depicts the human history of the Bella Coola Valley. Exhibits present the history of the area from European contact to 1955. The museum's historic building is open from June to September. School presentations can be arranged at other times of the year. The British Columbia Central Coast Archives is open year-round, from Tuesday to Thursday.
Wendy Kingsley, Manager

Bralorne: **Bralorne Pioneer Museum**
PO Box 40, 400 Hawkes Ave., Bralorne, BC V0K 1P0
Tel: 250-238-2349; *Fax:* 250-238-2349
bralornepioneermuseum@telus.net

Founded: 1977 Bralorne Pioneer Museum depicts the history of a community which is known as the home of the Bralorne Mine, a productive gold mine during the gold mining era. Mining artifacts are part of the museum's collection, as well as general historical information about the local Bridge River Valley area. The museum is situated in the industrial education shop of the Bralorne High School. It is open during the summer & on weekends.

Britannia Beach: **British Columbia Museum of Mining**
PO Box 188, Britannia Beach, BC V0N 1J0
Tel: 604-896-2233; *Fax:* 604-896-2260
Toll-Free: 800-896-4044
general@bcmuseumofmining.org
www.bcmuseumofmining.org

Founded: 1971 Governed by the Britannia Beach Historical Society, the British Columbia Museum of Mining preserves the material & social history of mining in British Columbia.
Mark Germyn, President, Britannia Beach Historical Society, mark@bcmuseumofmining.org
Kirsten Clausen, Executive Director, kclausen@bcmuseumofmining.org
Diane Mitchell, Curator, Education & Collections, diane@bcmuseumofmining.org
Henry Gottardi, Site Manager & Coordinator, Filming, henry@bcmuseumofmining.org
Carol Watts, Manager, Visitor Services, Retail Operations, & Tour Buses, carol@bcmuseumofmining.org
Katherine Flett, Director, Marketing, 604-924-5542
Robin MacDonald, Coordinator, Bookings & Communications, robin@bcmuseumofmining.org
Rory Odenbach, Coordinator, Programmes & Head Tour Guide, rory@bcmuseumofmining.org

Burnaby: **Burnaby Village Museum**
6501 Deer Lake Ave., Burnaby, BC V5G 3T6
Tel: 604-297-4565; *Fax:* 604-297-4557
bvm@burnaby.ca
www.burnabyvillagemuseum.ca
Other contact information: Phone, Schools: 604-297-4558; Phone, Rentals: 604-297-4552

The Burnaby Village Museum consists of heritage & replica buildings from the 1920s, such as a blacksmith shop, a general store, a print shop, a farmhouse, a restored interurban tram & a carousel.
Lisa Codd, Curator, lisa.codd@burnaby.ca
Elisabeth Czerwinski, Conservator, elisabeth.czerwinski@burnaby.ca
Maurice Guibord, Coordinator, Programs, maurice.guibord@burnaby.ca
Nancy Stagg, Coordinator, Marketing, nancy.stagg@burnaby.ca

Burnaby: **Canadiana Costume Society of British Columbia & Western Canada**
6501 Deer Lake Ave., Burnaby, BC V8Z 1G1
Tel: 604-293-6520; *Fax:* 604-293-6525
CanadianaCostume@hotmail.com
www.vcn.bc.ca/ccs

Founded: 1976 The Canadiana Costume Society of British Columbia & Western Canada collects, conserves, researches, & displays British Columbia's costume heritage. The collection dates from the late 1700s to the 1980s. The Society's members create displays & provide lectures.

Burnaby: **Simon Fraser University Museum of Archaeology & Ethnology**
c/o Dept. of Archaeology, Simon Fraser University, 8888 University Dr., Burnaby, BC V5A 1S6
Tel: 604-291-3325; *Fax:* 604-291-5666
bwinter@sfu.ca
www.sfu.museum
Major emphasis on the Pacific Northwest coast; open year round
Dr. Barbara J. Winter, Curator

Burns Lake: **Lakes District Museum Society**
PO Box 266, Burns Lake, BC V0J 1E0
Tel: 250-692-7450
Artifacts, archival records, and historical reference material relation to the Lakes District of northwestern B.C., including Burns Lake, Palling, Francois Lake, Babine Lake, Ootsa Lake, and Tweedsmuir Provinvial Park. Includes interviews with early settlers (and descendants) in the Lakes District.

Cache Creek: **Historic Hat Creek Ranch**
PO Box 878, Junction Hwy. 97-99, Cache Creek, BC V0K 1H0
Tel: 250-457-9722; *Fax:* 250-457-9311
Toll-Free: 800-782-0922
contact@hatcreekranch.com
www.hatcreekranch.com
Founded: 1984 Offering a blend of cultures, on site are an 1860 roadhouse with gold rush era artifacts and a traditional kekuli, or pit house, used as a winter home by people of the Shuswap Nation. Costumed guides explain the life of area's history & culture and visitors can experience firsthand a stagecoach ride. Other activities include gold panning and archery. There are a gift shop, food services, as well as cabins & campground facilities. Open daily, May to Sept.
Mr. Ken Mather, General Manager, kenm@hatcreekranch.com

Campbell River: **Museum at Campbell River (MCR)**
Also known as: **Campbell River Museum & Archives**
PO Box 70 A, 470 Island Hwy., Campbell River, BC V9W 4Z9
Tel: 250-287-3103; *Fax:* 250-286-0109
general.inquiries@crmuseum.ca
www.crmuseum.ca
Founded: 1958 Exhibits include First Nations ceremonial masks & regalia, coastal logging, fishing history & settler development; archives & research centre; gift shop
Lesia Davis, Executive Director, lesia.davis@crmuseum.ca

Castlegar: **Castlegar & District Heritage Society**
400 - 13th Ave., Castlegar, BC V1N 1G2
Tel: 250-365-6440
www.stationmuseum.ca/museum/
The Society operates the CPR Museum, housed in a 99 year old station, and Zuckerberg Island park; newspaper archives; gift shop featuring local artisans; special events and programming.

Chetwynd: **Little Prairie Heritage Museum**
PO Box 1777, Chetwynd, BC V0C 1J0
Tel: 250-788-3358
lphs@pris.ca
Open July & Aug.
Shirley Weeks, President

Chilliwack: **Chilliwack Museum & Archives**
45820 Spadina Ave., Chilliwack, BC V2P 1T3
Tel: 604-795-5210; *Fax:* 604-795-5291
cm_chin@smartt.com
www.chilliwack.museum.bc.ca/museum
Founded: 1957 The Archives are located at 9291 Corbould St. in Chilliwack, phone 604-795-9255; newspapers, photographs, books, DVDs, maps relating to the flood history of Chilliwack; special exhibits; programming; gift shop; open year round.
Ron Denman, Director
Brenda Paterson, Education Co-ordinator
Paul Ferguson, Manager, Heritage Collections

Clearbrook: **Fraser Valley Antique Farm Machinery Association**
PO Box 2234, Clearbrook, BC V2T 3X8
Tel: 604-856-4571
johnbateman@telus.net
To collect & restore to working condition antique farm & household machinery; displays annually at Agrifair; visitors welcome to building any time of year; call for appt.
Phil Chapman, President

Clinton: **South Cariboo Historical Museum Society**
1419 Cariboo Hwy., Clinton, BC V0K 1K0
Tel: 250-459-2442; *Fax:* 250-459-0058
Open daily June - Sept.

Courtenay: **Courtenay & District Museum & Palaeontology Centre**
207 - 4th St., Courtenay, BC V9N 1G7
Tel: 250-334-0686; *Fax:* 250-338-0619
museum@island.net
www.courtenaymuseum.ca
Includes archives; open year round
Deborah Griffiths, Curator

Cowichan Bay: **Cowichan Bay Maritime Centre**
PO Box 22, 1761 Cowichan Bay Rd., Cowichan Bay, BC V0R 1N0
Tel: 250-746-4955; *Fax:* 250-746-9989
cwbs@island.net
www.classicboats.org
Exhibits housed in unique pods designed to reflect the surrounding landspace & reveal the rich maritime history of Cowichan Bay; offers classic wooden boat building programs & undertakes restoration projects; open daily
Eric Sandilands, Manager

Cranbrook: **Aasland Museum Taxidermy**
3700 Collinson Rd., Cranbrook, BC V1C 7B8
Tel: 250-426-3566; *Fax:* 250-426-3574
www.aasland@shaw.ca
Small natural history museum displaying mounted birds & animals for the public; admission free; a lecture accompanies the visit if prior arrangements are made; school groups, handicapped, adult groups & individual visitors welcome; Mon.-Sat.
Odd Aasland, Director

Cranbrook: **Canadian Museum of Rail Travel**
Also known as: **The Cranbrook Archives, Museum & Landmark Foundation**
PO Box 400, 57 Van Horne St. South, Cranbrook, BC V1C 4H9
Tel: 250-489-3918; *Fax:* 250-489-5744
mail@trainsdeluxe.com
www.trainsdeluxe.com
The Canadian Museum of Rail Travel depicts the story of rail travel in Canada, through the collection, restoration, & display of historic rail equipment from various eras. The museum features a large historic railcar collection. Other sights at the museum include the Royal Alexandra Hall, which was the former cafe from the Canadian Pacific Railway's 1906 Royal Alexandra Hotel in Winnipeg, an 1898 railway freight shed, & a wooden railway water tower.
Garry W. Anderson, Executive Director
Brian Dees, Office Manager

Creston: **Creston & District Museum**
Also known as: **Stone House Museum**
219 Devon St., Creston, BC V0B 1G3
Tel: 250-428-9262; *Fax:* 250-428-3324
mail@creston.museum.bc.ca
www.creston.museum.bc.ca
Guided tours, permanent & temporary exhibits; open spring, summer, fall; in winter by appt.
Fred Ryckman, President
Tammy Hardwick, Manager

Crofton: **Old Crofton School Museum Society**
Also known as: **Crofton Old School Museum Society**
PO Box 49, 1507 Joan St., Crofton, BC V0R 1R0
Tel: 250-246-2456; *Fax:* 250-246-2778
History of old schools, Crofton & area; open June-Sept.
Pat Montgomery, President

Cumberland: **Cumberland Museum & Archives**
Also known as: **Cumberland & District Historical Society**
PO Box 258, 2680 Dunsmuir Ave., Cumberland, BC V0R 1S0
Tel: 250-336-2445; *Fax:* 250-336-2321
info@cumberland.museum.bc.ca
www.museum.bc.ca/cma
Open year round

Dawson Creek: **Dawson Creek Station Museum**
900 Alaska Ave., Dawson Creek, BC V1G 4T6
Tel: 250-782-9595; *Fax:* 250-782-9538
Toll-Free: 866-645-3022
frontoffice@tourismdawsoncreek.com
www.pris.bc.ca/dcsm /
Two galleries, the Northern Alberta Railway and the Natural History Gallery. Open year round
Dan Bastiansen, President, 250-782-5408, museum@pris.ca

Dawson Creek: **Walter Wright Pioneer Village & Sudeten Hall**
1901 Alaska Hwy., Dawson Creek, BC V1G 1P7
Tel: 250-782-7144
info@tourismdawsoncreek.com
www.dawsoncreek.ca/life/recreation/walter.asp
The Walter Wright Pioneer Village presents life in Dawson Creek, before the construction of the Alaska Highway. Historic buildings include the Pouce Coupe School, the W.O. Harper General Store, & the St. Paul's Anglican Church. The Sudeten Hall honours Germany's Sudeten people who arrived in the area in 1939.

Delta: **Delta Museum & Archives**
4858 Delta St., Delta, BC V4K 2T8
Tel: 604-946-9322; *Fax:* 604-946-5791
info@deltamuseum.ca
www.deltamuseum.ca
1912 heritage building; archives; exhibitions on pioneer homelife, village life, farming, fishing, duck decoys, First Nations archeology, basketry
Mark Sakai, Executive Director
Jordana Feist, Curator
Carol Ballard, Program Coordinator
Kathy Bossort, Archivist

Denman Island: **Denman Island Museum**
PO Box 28, Denman Island, BC V0R 1T0
Tel: 250-335-0880
Collection houses NW Coast artifacts from the Salish; natural history specimens; European settlement items; photographs & maps

Duncan: **British Columbia Forest Discovery Centre**
2892 Drinkwater Rd., Duncan, BC V9L 6C2
Tel: 250-715-1113; *Fax:* 250-715-1170
info.bcfdc@shawlink.ca; manager.bcfdc@shawlink.ca
www.discoveryforest.com
Other contact information: E-mail, Volunteering & Education: education.bcfdc@shawlink.ca
The BC Forest Discovery Centre is a 100-acre, open air museum, which features forest & marsh trails, logging artifacts, & heritage buildings.
Vicki Holman, Manager
Aimee Greenaway, Coordinator, Program & Collections

Duncan: **Cowichan Valley Museum**
PO Box 1014, Duncan, BC V9L 3Y2
Tel: 250-746-6612; *Fax:* 250-746-6612
cvmuseum.archives@shaw.ca
www.cowichanvalleymuseum.bc.ca
Local history museum; includes archives; open year round
Priscilla Lowe, Curator/Manager

Enderby: **Enderby & District Museum Society**
901 George St., Enderby, BC V0E 1V0
Tel: 250-838-7170; *Fax:* 250-838-9641
edms@jetstream.net
www.enderbymuseum.ca
Founded: 1973 Open year round
Joan Cowan, Curator, 250-838-7171

Fernie: **Fernie & District Historical Society Museum**
PO Box 1527, Fernie, BC V0B 1M0
Tel: 250-423-7016; *Fax:* 250-423-7461
history@ferniemuseum.com
www.ferniemuseum.com
Coal mining history museum; local history & early families research

Fort Langley: **British Columbia Farm Machinery & Agricultural Museum Association**
PO Box 279, 9131 King St., Fort Langley, BC V1M 2R6
Tel: 604-888-2273
bcfm@telus.net
www.bcfma.com
British Columbia Farm Machinery & Agricultural Museum Association presents the history of farming in British Columbia. Displays include horse drawn carriages & wagons, steam, gas & diesel powered grinders & tractors, an 1890s sawmill, a blacksmith shop, & British Columbia's first crop duster, the Tiger Moth airplane. The museum is open seven days a week from April 1st to Thanksgiving Day.

Fort Langley: **Fort Langley National Historic Site of Canada (FLNHSC) / Lieu historique national du Canada Fort-Langley**
PO Box 129, 23433 Mavis Ave., Fort Langley, BC V1M 2R5
Tel: 604-513-4777; *Fax:* 604-513-4798
fort.langley@pc.gc.ca
www.pc.gc.ca/fortlangley
Birthplace of British Columbia; 19th century Hudson's Bay Co. trading post; Open year round
John Aldag, Contact

Fort Langley: **Langley Centennial Museum & National Exhibition Centre**
PO Box 800, 9135 King St., Fort Langley, BC V1M 2S2
Tel: 604-888-3922; *Fax:* 604-888-7291
info@langleymuseum.org
www.langleymuseum.org
Art, history & science exhibits; open year round
John Robertson, Manager, Community & Heritage Services

Fort Nelson: **Fort Nelson Heritage Museum**
PO Box 716, Fort Nelson, BC V0C 1R0
Tel: 250-774-3536
info@fortnelsonmuseum.ca
www.fortnelsonmuseum.ca
Artifacts related to the construction of the Alaska Highway; open mid-May - mid-Sept.
Marlin Brown, Curator

Fort St. James: **Fort St. James National Historic Site of Canada**
280 Kwah Rd. West, Fort St. James, BC V0J 1P0
Tel: 250-996-7191; *Fax:* 250-996-8566
bob_grill@pch.gc.ca
The Fort St James National Historic Site offers the largest collection of original wooden buildings, representing the fur trade in Canada. The following buildings are located at the site: Fur WareHouse (1888-1889); Fish cache (1889); Men's House (1884); Trade Store & Office (1884); Murray House (1883-1884); Dairy (1884); & Wharf & Tramway (1894-1914). The Historic Site is open daily from 9:00 to 5:00, from the long weekend in May to the end of September.
Alan Latourelle, Chief Officer

Fort St John: **Fort St. John-North Peace Museum**
9323 - 100 St., Fort St John, BC V1J 4N4
Tel: 250-787-0430; *Fax:* 250-787-0405
fsjnpmuseum@solarwinds.com
Open year round
Larry Evans, President

Fort Steele: **Fort Steele Heritage Town**
9851 Hwy. 93/95, Fort Steele, BC V0B 1N0
Tel: 250-417-6000; *Fax:* 250-489-2624
info@FortSteele.bc.ca
www.FortSteele.bc.ca
Restored 1890s mining boom town of the East Kootenay; open year round with varying program levels each season, call for details
David Stokes, General Manager

Fraser Lake: **Fraser Lake Museum**
PO Box 430, Fraser Lake, BC V0J 1S0
Tel: 250-699-6257; *Fax:* 250-699-6469
village@fraserlake.ca
Open summer
Donna Ward, Clerk/Treas.

Gibsons: **Sunshine Coast Museum & Archives**
PO Box 766, 716 Winn Rd., Gibsons, BC V0N 1V0
Tel: 604-886-8232; *Fax:* 604-886-8232
scm_a@dccnet.com
www.sunshinecoastmuseum.ca
Collection of historical documents & artifacts pertaining to the Sunshine Coast of BC; open year round; closed Sun. & Mon.

Golden: **Golden & District Museum**
PO Box 992, 1302 - 11 Ave., Golden, BC V0A 1H0
Tel: 250-344-5169; *Fax:* 250-344-5169
museum@redshift.bc.ca
Open May-Sept.
Colleen Palumbo, Curator

Grand Forks: **Boundary Museum**
Boundary Museum Society, PO Box 817, 6145 Reservoir Rd., Grand Forks, BC V0H 1H0
Tel: 250-442-3737; *Fax:* 250-442-3737
boundarymuse@shaw.ca
www.boundarymuseum.com
The Boundary Museum is situated in a former schoolhouse, which was built in 1929 by the Christian Communities of Universal Brotherhood Doukhobors. The grounds of the restored schoolhouse feature a fruit drying facility & a bread oven which were also built by the society.

Grand Forks: **Mountain View Doukhobor Museum**
PO Box 1235, 3655 Hardy Mountain Rd., Grand Forks, BC V0H 1H0
Tel: 250-442-8855

Greenwood: **Greenwood Heritage Society**
PO Box 399, 214 South Copper St., Greenwood, BC V0H 1J0
Tel: 250-445-6355; *Fax:* 250-445-6355
museum@shaw.ca
www.greenwoodmuseum.com
Mining, forestry, ranching & the internment of Japanese Canadians; Greenwood was an internment camp during WW II
Marge Maclean, Chair

Groundbirch: **Groundbirch Museum**
PO Box 124, Groundbirch, BC V0C 1T0
Tel: 250-780-2383
Open summer

Harrison Mills: **Kilby Museum & Farm**
PO Box 55, 215 Kilby Rd., Harrison Mills, BC V0M 1L0
Tel: 604-796-9576; *Fax:* 604-796-9592
info@kilby.ca
www.kilby.ca
Open daily May-Sept. 11-5, then seasonal hours

Hazelton: **'Ksan Historical Village & Museum**
PO Box 326, Hazelton, BC V0J 1Y0
Tel: 250-842-5544; *Fax:* 250-842-6533
Toll-Free: 877-842-5518
ksan@ksan.org
www.ksan.org
Replica Gitxkan Indian Village; museum has approx. 600 items on display, including ceremonial artifacts, hunting and fishing tools, masks and shaman's regalia; open year round

Hope: **Hope Museum**
PO Box 26, 919 Water Ave., Hope, BC V0X 1L0
Tel: 604-869-7322; *Fax:* 604-869-2160
Toll-Free: 866-467-3842
destinationhope@telus.net
Open summer; off-season tours by request
Inge Wilson, Manager

Horsefly: **Jack Lynn Memorial Museum**
c/o Horsefly Historical Society, PO Box 11, Horsefly, BC V0L 1L0
Tel: 250-620-3440
www.horsefly.bc.ca/community/virtualvillage/museum.html
Open daily July to Aug. anually; Sept. to June by appointment only; small museum run by volunteers; features artifacts, photos & paper archives, all relating to Horsefly

Hudson's Hope: **Hudson's Hope Museum & Historical Society**
PO Box 98, 9510 Beattie Dr., Hudson's Hope, BC V0C 1V0
Tel: 250-783-5735; *Fax:* 250-783-5770
hhmuseum@pris.ca
www.hhmuseum.com
Hudson's Bay Company store of 1942; archives; fossil collection; Aboriginal display; North West & Hudson's Bay Company artifacts; North West Mounted Police, trapping, coal mining, gold mining, pioneer, logging & World War memorabilia & photographic history of W.A.C. Bennett dam
Melodie Godsma, Coordinator/Administrator
Fay Lavallee, President

Invermere: **Windermere Valley Museum & Archives**
PO Box 2315, Invermere, BC V0A 1K0
Tel: 250-342-9769
wvmuseum@cyberlink.bc.ca
Open Mon. - Fri. June & Sept.; Tue.-Sat. July & Aug.; Oct. - May by appt.
Jaryl McIsaac, Archivist
Dorothy Blunden, Curator, 250/342-2005

Kamloops: **Kamloops Museum & Archives**
207 Seymour St., Kamloops, BC V2C 2E7
Tel: 250-828-3576; *Fax:* 250-314-2016
museum@city.kamloops.bc.ca
Open year round

Kamloops: **Rocky Mountain Rangers Museum & Archives**
PO Box 3250, 1221 McGill Rd., Kamloops, BC V2C 6B8
Tel: 250-372-7424

Kamloops: **Secwepemc Museum & Heritage Park (SCES)**
#311, 355 Yellowhead Hwy., Kamloops, BC V2H 1H1
Tel: 250-828-9778; *Fax:* 250-372-1127
museum@secwepemc.org
www.secwepemc.org
Museum is located on 12 acres & exhibits artifacts, photographs & histories of the Secwepemc people; displays include canoes, hunting & fishing objects, clothing, games; the Heritage Park complements the Museum with outdoor displays & reconstructed winter pit houses. lean-tos, smoke house & traditional plant foods; trails, gardens; giftshop (seasonal); museum open year round
Daniel Saul, Museum Manager

Kaslo: **Kaslo Village**
PO Box 576, 413 - 4th St., Kaslo, BC V0G 1M0
Tel: 250-353-2311; *Fax:* 250-353-7767
village@netidea.com
www.kaslo.ca
Designated National Historic Site; open Mon. - Fri.
Rae Sawyer, CAO

Kaslo: **S.S. Moyie National Historic Site**
PO Box 537, Kaslo, BC V0G 1M0
Tel: 250-353-2525; *Fax:* 250-353-2525
ssmoyie@klhs.bc.ca
www.klhs.bc.ca
Moored in the town of Kaslo, this is the oldest intact passenger sternwheeler in the world; gift shop; operated by the Kootenay Lake Historical Society; open daily mid-May to mid-Oct.

Ken Butler, Manager
Jack Morris, President
Mark Gordon, Manager

Kelowna: **Benvoulin Heritage Park & Benvoulin Heritage Church**
c/o Central Okanagan Heritage Society, 1060 Cameron Ave., Kelowna, BC V1Y 8V3
Tel: 250-861-7188; *Fax:* 250-868-1392
cohs@telus.net
www.okheritagesociety.com
Located at 2279 Benvoulin Road in Kelowna, the Benvoulin Church was built in 1892 in the Gothic Revival style. The pioneer church was restored by the Central Okanagan Heritage Society, which owns & operates Benvoulin Heritage Park.
Janice Henry, Executive Director, Central Okanagan Heritage Society

Kelowna: **British Columbia Orchard Industry Museum**
1304 Ellis St., Kelowna, BC V1Y 1Z8
Tel: 250-763-0433; *Fax:* 250-868-9272
orchard@kelownamuseum.ca
www.kelownamuseum.ca
Founded: 1989 The BC Orchard Industry Museum is located in the historic, restored Laurel Packinghouse. The museum features exhibits about the Okanagan Valley's orchard industry, including picking, processeing, packing, preserving, & marketing. The museum is open year round.
Wayne Wilson, Director
Nathalie Limbos-Bomberg, Associate Director
Colleen Cornock, Program Assistant

Kelowna: **Central Okanagan Heritage Society**
1060 Cameron Ave., Kelowna, BC V1Y 8V3
Tel: 250-861-7188; *Fax:* 250-868-0391
cohs@telus.net
www.okheritagesociety.com
Founded: 1982 The Society promotes & participates in the preservation of the Central Okanagan region's natural, cultural & horticultural heritage; operates the Guisachan Heritage Park, the Benvoulin Heritage Park, Brent's Grist Mill Park.
Janice Henry, Executive Director

Kelowna: **Father Pandosy Mission**
Box 22105, Capri PO, Kelowna, BC V1Y 9N9
Tel: 250-860-8369
www.okanaganhistoricalsociety.org/pandosy_mission.html
Oblate Mission, 1859
John Sugars, Contact

Kelowna: **Kelowna Museum**
470 Queensway, Kelowna, BC V1Y 6S7
Tel: 250-763-2417; *Fax:* 250-763-5722
info@kelownamuseum.ca
www.kelownamuseum.ca
Open Tue.-Sat. 10-5; admission by donation
Nathalie Limbos-Bomberg, Associate Director
Wayne Wilson, Director

Kelowna: **Silver Lake Forestry Centre**
PO Box 20023, Kelowna, BC V1Y 9H2
Tel: 250-717-0033; *Fax:* 250-717-3231
info@silverlakekidscamp.com
www.silverlakekidscamp.com/society.html
Other contact information: E-mail, Board of Directors: directors@silverlakekidscamp.com
Founded: 1971 The Silver Lake Forestry Centre is owned & managed by the Silver Lake Forest Education Society. Year-round outdoor environmental education is available for youth, adults, & educators. The society is also engaged in the collection, restoration, & display of logging & forestry artifacts.

Keremeos: **The Grist Mill at Keremeos**
Upper Bench Rd., RR#1, Keremeos, BC V0X 1N0
Tel: 250-499-2888
Designated British Columbia Heritage Site; open May - Oct & by appt.

Keremeos: **South Similkameen Museum**
PO Box 135, Keremeos, BC V0X 1N0
Tel: 250-499-5445; *Fax:* 250-499-5746
Restored gaol-house with B.C. provincial police displays, pioneer artifacts

Kimberley: **Kimberley Heritage Musuem**
PO Box 144, 105 Spokane St., Kimberley, BC V1A 2Y5
Tel: 250-427-7510
kdhs@telus.net
Early Kimberley History; Sullivan Mine display; open year round; admission by donation; archives available for research, by request, at a nominal fee
Marie Stang, Administrator

Kitimat: **Kitimat Centennial Museum**
293 City Centre, Kitimat, BC V8C 1T6
Tel: 250-632-8950; *Fax:* 250-632-7429
kitimatmuseum@telus.net
www.kitimatmuseum.ca
Natural history; homesteader & Haida histories; Kemano-Kitimat Project history; temporary exhibitions; giftshop; open year round
Louise Avery, Curator

Kitwanga: **Meanskinisht Village Historical Association, Cedarvale**
Also known as: **Cedarvale Museum**
PO Box 183, Kitwanga, BC V0J 2A0
Tel: 250-849-5732
Houses the history & remnants of ancient village of Gitlusec, Meanskinisht village & Cedarvale; also looks after the graveyard (private); Cedarvale Museum open by appt.
Mary G. Dalen, Director

Ladysmith: **Black Nugget Museum**
PO Box 1449, 12 Gatacre St., Ladysmith, BC V0R 2E0
Tel: 250-245-4846
Formerly the Jones Hotel, the Black Nugget Museum depicts the history of Ladysmith, through antiques & memorabilia dating back to the late 1800s. The hotel's barroom & lobby have been restored. The museum is open during the summer, and at other times when requested by groups.
Kurt Guilbride, Owner

Lake Cowichan: **Kaatza Station Museum & Archives**
PO Box 135, Lake Cowichan, BC V0R 2G0
Tel: 250-749-6142; *Fax:* 250-749-3900
kaatzamuseum@shaw.ca
Open year round

Langley: **Canadian Museum of Flight (CMF)**
Hangar 3, Langley Airport, 5333 - 216th St., Langley, BC V2Y 2N3
Tel: 604-532-0035; *Fax:* 604-532-0056
cmflight@telus.net
www.canadianflight.org
Founded: 1977 The Canadian Museum of Flight restores, preserves, & displays Canada's aviation heritage. The museum & restoration site features more than twenty-five aircraft, such as a World War II Handley Page Hampden & a T-33 Silver Star. The Millennium Kids Room ia a "hands-on" facility for young visitors.
Gord Wintrup, President
George Miller, Vice-President
Terry Brunner, General Manager, tbrunner@telus.net
Paul de Lange, Treasurer
Matt Offer, Secretary

Lazo: **Comox Air Force Museum (CAFM)**
PO Box 1000 Forces, 19 Wing Comox, Lazo, BC V0R 2K0
Tel: 250-339-8162; *Fax:* 250-339-8162
info@comoxairforcemuseum.ca
www.comoxairforcemuseum.ca
History of CFB Comox & West Coast aviation
Capt. John Low, Executive Director
Lorraine Analy, Curator

Lillooet: **Lillooet District Historical Society & Museum**
PO Box 441, Lillooet, BC V0K 1V0
Tel: 250-256-4308; *Fax:* 250-256-0043
lillmuseum@cablelan.net
www.lillooetbc.com
Open May-Oct., Tue.-Sat., 10-4; daily July & Aug. 9-7
Susan H. Bell, Manager

Lytton: **Lytton Museum & Archives**
420 Fraser St., Lytton, BC V0K 1Z0
Tel: 250-455-2254; *Fax:* 250-455-2394
curator@lyttonmuseum.ca
www.botaniecreek.com/museum
Founded: 1995 Built by the Canadian National Railway as a residence in 1942, the museum is filled with local artifacts and archives, including pieces formally used at the C.N. station.
Mr. Richard Forrest, President, Lytton Museum and Archives Commission
Dorothy Dodge, Curator

Mackenzie: **Mackenzie & District Museum**
PO Box 934, Mackenzie, BC V0J 2C0
Tel: 250-997-3021
museum@mackbc.com

Maple Ridge: **Haney House Museum**
11612 - 224th St., Maple Ridge, BC V2X 5Z7
Tel: 604-463-1377; *Fax:* 604-463-5317
haneyhouse@telus.net
www.mapleridgemuseum.org
Founded: 1981 Haney House was the residence of pioneer Thomas Haney, who came to Maple Ridge, British Columbia in 1876. Guided tours are available year-round.

Maple Ridge: **Maple Ridge Museum & Archives**
22520 - 116th Ave., Maple Ridge, BC V2X 0S4
Tel: 604-463-5311; *Fax:* 604-463-5317
mrmuseum@telus.net
Open year round

Mayne Island: **Mayne Island Museum**
Comp. 4, Site 1, RR#1, Mayne Island, BC V0N 2J0
Tel: 250-539-5286

McBride: **Valley Museum & Archives**
PO Box 775, 241 Dominion St., McBride, BC V0J 2E0
Tel: 250-569-2411
Displays within McBride & District Public Library

Merritt: **Nicola Valley Museum & Archives**
PO Box 1262, 1675 Tutill Court, Merritt, BC V1K 1B8
Tel: 250-378-4145; *Fax:* 250-378-4145
nvm@uniserve.com
www.nicolavalleymuseum.org
Founded: 1976 The museum houses an extensive collection of artifacts & photographs of various aspects of Nicola Valley's history, including churches, the general hospital, rail travel & other transportation, Craigmont mine history, Judge Henry Castillou, ranching & mining displays; James Teit Gallery & First Nations displays; Merritt Model Railway club display; the Archives preserves the James Teit First Nations reference material, early newspapers, mining reports, cemetery information, early maps & hundreds of photopgraphs. Open year round.
Barbara Watson, Office Manager

Midway: **Kettle River Museum Society**
PO Box 149, Midway, BC V0H 1M0
Tel: 250-449-2614; *Fax:* 250-449-2614
midwaybc@sunshinecable.com
Mile of Kettle Valley Railway; restored 1900s CPR Station; B.C. Provincial Police display
Tannis Killough, President
Helen Schultheiss, Manager

Mission: **Fraser River Heritage Park**
PO Box 3341, 7494 Mary St., Mission, BC V2V 4J5
Tel: 604-826-0277; *Fax:* 604-826-0333
mhadmin@direct.ca
www.heritagepark-mission.ca
Original site of St. Mary's Mission & Indian Residential School, founded in 1861; park features foundations of mission

Mission: **Mission District Historical Society & Museum**
33201 - 2nd Ave., Mission, BC V2V 1J9
Tel: 604-826-1011; *Fax:* 604-826-1017
muse@mission.museum.bc.ca
www.mission.museum.bc.ca
Founded: 1972 Permanent exhibits include Sto:lo First Nations display, the history of settlement with pioneers, rails, rivers, and items from business and home life, notably period 1920s rooms. Also featured are items from Mission's old Chinatown. Museum is housed in a 1907 B.C. Mills, prefabricated, Canadian Bank of Commerce Bldg. Gift shop offers books on Mission's history. There is a selection of school tours.
Kim Allen, Curator

Mission: **Xá:ytem Longhouse Interpretive Centre**
35087 Lougheed Hwy., Mission, BC V2V 6T1
Tel: 604-820-9725; *Fax:* 604-820-9735
info@xaytem.ca
www.xaytem.ca
On the coast of British Columbia, Xá:ytem has been an important Salish spiritual site. Today, Xá:ytem is a National Historic Site, where visitors discover a traditional Salish cedar longhouse & two pit houses. The site is open year-round.

Nanaimo: **The Bastion**
#211, 450 Stewart Ave., Nanaimo, BC V9S 5E9
Tel: 250-755-1047; *Fax:* 250-740-0125
www.nanaimomuseum.ca
1853 Hudson's Bay Co. log fortification

Nanaimo: **Centennial Museum of the Nanaimo Regional General Hospital**
Nanaimo Regional General Hospital, 1200 Dufferin Cres., Nanaimo, BC V9S 2B7
Tel: 250-755-7637; *Fax:* 250-755-7947
www.viha.ca
Health care records & artifacts
Lynne Tourond, Manager, Volunteer Resources, lynne.tourond@viha.ca

Nanaimo: **Nanaimo District Museum (NDM)**
100 Cameron Rd., Nanaimo, BC V9R 2X1
Tel: 250-753-1821; *Fax:* 250-740-0125
debbie@nanaimomuseum.ca
www.nanaimomuseum.ca
Open year round
Debbie Trueman, General Manager

Naramata: **Naramata Heritage Museum**
PO Box 95, Naramata, BC V0H 1N0
Tel: 250-496-5866
Local history; 3 permanent displays
Berte Berry, Chair

Nelson: **Touchstones Nelson: Museum of Art & History**
Also known as: **Nelson & District Museum, Archives, Art Gallery & Historical Soc.**
502 Vernon St., Nelson, BC V1L 4E7
Tel: 250-352-9813; *Fax:* 250-352-9810
info@touchstonesnelson.ca
www.touchstonesnelson.ca
Other contact information: E-Mail, Exhibitions: exhibitions@touchstonesnelson.ca
The museum displays the history & culture of Nelson, British Columbia. Archives & an art gallery are also part of the museum.
Best Leah, Executive Director, director@touchstonesnelson.ca
Rod Taylor, Co-Curator, rod@touchstonesnelson.ca
Deborah Thompson, Co-Curator, deborah@touchstonesnelson.ca
Alex Dudley, Manager, Visitor Services, shop@touchstonesnelson.ca
Laura Fortier, Archivist & Manager, Collections, collections@touchstonesnelson.ca

New Denver: **Sandon Historical Society Museum & Visitors' Centre**
PO Box 52, New Denver, BC V0G 1S0
Tel: 250-358-7920
shs@slocanlake.com
www.slocanlake.com/sandon/
Historic museum & archives of Sandon & area; heritage photographs, artifacts, guided tours
Lorna Obermayr, Contact, 250-358-7965

New Denver: **Silvery Slocan Historical Museum**
PO Box 301, New Denver, BC V0G 1S0
Tel: 250-358-2201; *Fax:* 250-358-7251
sgn@netidea.com
Cultural & economic history of the Slocan Lake area; open July & Aug.
Webb Cummings, President

New Westminster: **Canadian Lacrosse Hall of Fame**
PO Box 308, 302 Royal Ave., New Westminster, BC V3L 4Y6
Tel: 604-527-4640; *Fax:* 604-527-4641
allan@lacrosse.ca
www.lacrosse.ca
Founded: 1965 Inductees to the Canadian Lacrosse Hall of Fame are featured in the following categories: builders, box players, field players, veteran players, & teams.

New Westminster: **Museum of the Royal Westminster Regiment Historical Society**
The Armouries, 530 Queens Ave., New Westminster, BC V3L 1K3
Tel: 604-526-5116; *Fax:* 604-666-4042
Permanent collection of military artifacts & memorabilia from the experience of The Royal Westminster Regiment & its antecedents; open every Tue. & Thurs.
Lt.Col. B.V. Morgan, Curator (Ret'd)
B. Gen. H.E. Hamm, Chair C.D., (Ret'd)

New Westminster: **New Westminster Museum & Archives**
302 Royal Ave., New Westminster, BC V3L 1H7
Tel: 604-527-4640; *Fax:* 604-527-4641
www.nwpr.bc.ca
The New Westminster Museum, with more than 30,000 items in its collection, depicts the history of British Columbia's first capital. The New Westminster Archives, which contains 13,000 archival items, preserves the documentary heritage of the city from its time as a Royal Engineers' settlement camp. Irving House is an 1865 colonial period house. Guided tours are given of the home.
Colin Stevens, Manager, cstevens@newwestcity.ca
Cynthia Bronaugh, Coordinator, Tour Groups, cbronaugh@city.new-westminster.bc.ca
Barry Dykes, Archivist, 604-527-4642, bdykes@newwestcity.ca

New Westminster: **Samson V Maritime Museum**
c/o Royal Agricultural & Industrial Society of BC, PO Box 42516, #105, 1005 Columbia St., New Westminster, BC V3M 6H5
Tel: 604-522-6894; *Fax:* 604-522-6094
hyackfst@direct.ca
www.nwheritage.org/heritagesite/orgs/samson/
A restored sternwheel snagpuller, moored on the Fraser River at the Westminster Quay Market; history of the vessel, educational programming
Valerie Francis, Manager

North Vancouver: **Lynn Canyon Ecology Centre**
3663 Park Rd., North Vancouver, BC V7J 3G3
Tel: 604-981-3103; *Fax:* 604-981-3154
kissings@district.north-van.bc.ca

Open year round

North Vancouver: **North Vancouver Museum & Archives**
Community History Centre, 3203 Institute Rd., North Vancouver, BC V7K 3E5
Tel: 604-990-3700; *Fax:* 604-987-5688
nvmac@dnv.org
www.dnv.org/nvma
Celebrates & preserves North Vancouver's social, industrial & cultural history; WWII shipbuilding; P.G.E. Railway; logging; Archives Reading Room & Archives Collection
Nancy L. Kirkpatrick, Director

North Vancouver: **Pacific Great Eastern Railway Station**
107 Carrie Cates Ct., North Vancouver, BC V7M 3J4
Tel: 604-984-8588
Restored station building with railway exhibits
Robin Inglis, Director

Okanagan: **Lake Country Museum**
11255 Okanagan Centre Rd. West, Okanagan, BC V4V 2J7
Tel: 250-766-0111; *Fax:* 250-766-2844
lcmuseum@cablelan.net
www.lakecountrymuseum.com/
Open Mid-May - Aug.
Felena Sigal

Okanagan Falls: **Okanagan Falls Heritage House & Museum**
Also known as: **Bassett House**
Okanagan Falls Heritage & Museum Society, PO Box 323, 1145 Main St., Okanagan Falls, BC V0H 1R0
Tel: 250-497-7047
ofhms@uniserve.com
www3.telus.net/okmuseum
The Bassett House is a prefabricated house. Ordered from the T. Eaton & Company catalogue, the house was shipped by rail from the east, and then by sternwheeler, & horse-drawn wagon to Okanagan Falls. The pioneer Bassett family lived in the home from 1909.

Osoyoos: **Osoyoos Desert Society & Osoyoos Desert Centre**
PO Box 123, Osoyoos, BC V0H 1V0
Tel: 250-495-2470; *Fax:* 250-495-2474
mail@desert.org
www.desert.org
Founded: 1991 The Osoyoos Desert Society is a non-profit society that was founded in 1991 to conserve the biologically rich and diverse habitats of British Columbia's southern interior. The south Okanagan is home to one of the largest concentrations of rare and at-risk species in all of Canada. Through conservation and education, the society strives to generate public knowledge, respect and active concern for these fragile and endangered ecosystems. In 1998, as part of it's effort to conserve the Southern Okanagan's unique habitats, the Desert Society opened an interpretive facility - the Osoyoos Desert Centre. In addition to an interpetive centre with hands-on exhibits, the Desert Centre also features a 1.5 km elevated wooden walkway. Visitors are invited to explore Canada's desert while enjoying a guided or self-guided tour along the boardwalk. The Desert Centre, located 3 km north of Osoyoos off Highway 97, is open annually from April through October
Marlin Clapson, Treasurer
Leslie Plaskett, President

Parksville: **Craig Heritage Park Museum**
PO Box 1452, Parksville, BC V9P 2H4
Tel: 250-248-6966
parksvillemuseum@shaw.ca
www.parksvillemuseum.ca
Open mid-May - Sept. 30
J. Tryon, Museum Manager
P. Cardwell, Archives

Pemberton: **Pemberton & District Museum**
PO Box 267, Pemberton, BC V0N 2L0
Tel: 604-894-6765
Three heritage buildings decorated with artifacts depicting local history dating back to 1850s

Penticton: **Penticton R.N. Atkinson Museum & Archives**
785 Main St., Penticton, BC V2A 5E3
Tel: 250-490-2451; *Fax:* 250-490-2442
museum@city.penticton.bc.ca
Museum & archives open July & Aug. Mon.-Sat. 10-5; Oct., Apr., May & June Tue.-Sat. 10-5; Nov., Dec., Jan., Feb. & Mar. Tue.-Sat. 10-4
R. Manuel, Director
Jeanne Boyle, Museum Assistant

Pitt Meadows: **Pitt Meadows Museum**
12294 Harris Rd., Pitt Meadows, BC V3Y 2E9
Tel: 604-465-4322; *Fax:* 604-465-4322
pittmeadowsmuseum@telus.net
www.pittmeadows.bc.ca
Founded: 1997 Located in an 1885 general store, which was later used as a post office & a residence, the Pitt Meadows Museum relates the pioneer & agricultural history of the Pitt Meadows community. An archives is also situated at the museum. The Hoffmann & Son machine shop & ditching business was donated to the Pitt Meadows Heritage & Museum Society. Hoffmann & Son Ltd. had been in business since the 1920s. The museum is open year-round.

Port Alberni: **Alberni Valley Museum**
4255 Wallace St., Port Alberni, BC V9Y 3Y6
Tel: 250-723-2181; *Fax:* 250-723-1035
info@alberniheritage.com
www.alberniheritage.com
History & culture of Alberni Valley & West Coast of Vancouver Island; exhibits include aboriginal artifacts, particularly the Nuu chah Nulth basketry; clothing and textiles; household implements and tools; agricultural equipment; local memorabilia; and 17,0000 historic photographs available for research purposes or reproduction on request. Open year round

Port Alberni: **McLean Mill National Historic Site**
5633 Smith Rd., Comp. 14, Site 125, Port Alberni, BC V9Y 7L5
Tel: 250-723-1376; *Fax:* 250-723-5910
email@alberniheritage.com
www.alberniheritage.com/mill/
Founded: 1989 Operated by R.B. McLean and his three sons from 1926 to 1965, the site commemorates the history of logging and saw milling in British Columbia. As well as the steam sawmill, typical remote coastal lumber camp buildings are being restored. A resident troupe of interpretive actors called the Tin Pants Theatre Company perform original stage shows and offer guided tours. There is also a cafe and gift shop.
Mr. Neil Malbon, General Manager

Port Clements: **Port Clements Museum**
PO Box 417, Port Clements, BC V0T 1R0
Tel: 250-557-4576; *Fax:* 250-557-4576
pcmuseum@island.net
www.portclementsmuseum.org
The Port Clements Museum contains artifacts of pioneer life on the Queen Charlotte Islands, including information & photographs about the logging, farming, fishing, & mining industries. The museum grounds display early machinery from the logging industry.

Port Edward: **North Pacific Cannery Historic Site and Museum**
PO Box 1109, 1889 Skeena Dr., Port Edward, BC V0V 1G0
Tel: 250-628-3538; *Fax:* 250-628-3540
northpac@citytel.net
www.cannery.ca
National historic site; oldest & most complete cannery village in BC; guided tours, gift shop, café; open May-Sept.

Port Hardy: **Port Hardy Museum & Archives**
c/o Port Hardy Heritage Society, PO Box 2126, 7110 Market St, Port Hardy, BC V0N 2P0
Tel: 250-949-8143
phmachin@island.net
www.northislandmuseums.org
The Port Hardy Museum & Archives houses geological & First Nations displays, as well as exhibits of settlers' history. The story of the fishing & logging industries in Port Hardy, Port Alice, Cape Scott, & Quatsino is also depicted at the museum. The museum is open year-round.

Port McNeill: **Port McNeill Museum**
351 Shelley Cres., Port McNeill, BC V0N 2R0
Tel: 250-956-9898
Hornsby steam tractor located at Seven Hills Golf Course
Margaret Hanuse, Chair

Port Moody: **Port Moody Station Museum**
2734 Murray St., Port Moody, BC V3H 1X2
Tel: 604-939-1648; *Fax:* 604-939-1647
pmmuseum@telus.net
www.vcn.bc.ca/pmmuseum
Exhibits & programs about the heritage of Port Moody & the surrounding area are presented at the Port Moody Station Museum. The museum is located in the Port Moody Station, which was built by the Canadian Pacific Railway Company in 1905. The Port Moody Heritage Society is the owner & operator of the museum.
Jim Millarn, Manager & Curator
Rebecca Clarke, Coordinator, Events
Deb Naso, Bookkeeper

Pouce Coupe: **Pouce Coupe Museum**
PO Box 293, 49th Ave., Pouce Coupe, BC V0C 2C0
Tel: 250-786-5555; *Fax:* 250-786-5216
Pioneer artifacts & archives
Ellen DeWetter, President

Powell River: **Powell River Historical Museum & Archives**
PO Box 42, 4798 Marine Ave., Powell River, BC V8A 4Z5
Tel: 604-485-2222; *Fax:* 604-485-2327
museum@powellrivermuseum.ca
www.powellrivermuseum.ca
Open year-round, exhibits at the Powell River Historical Museum & Archives include the local First Nation culture, logging at the Powell River Mill, & the war years.
Don Allan, President
Teedie Kagume, Coordinator
Debbie Dan, Curator
Frances Cudworth, Bookkeeper

Prince George: **The Exploration Place at the Fraser-Fort George Regional Museum (FFGRM)**
PO Box 1779, 333 Becott Pl., Prince George, BC V2L 4V7
Tel: 250-562-1612; *Fax:* 250-562-6395
Toll-Free: 866-562-1612
info@theexplorationplace.com
www.theexplorationplace.c om
Children's gallery; hands-on Explorations Gallery of Science & Natural History; History Hall of regional development; photo archives; motion simulator ride; Nature Exchange; Sports Hall of Fame Gallery with interactive sports machine
Tracy Calogheros, Executive Director

Prince George: **Huble Homestead/Giscome Portage Heritage Society**
#202, 1685 Third Ave., Prince George, BC V2L 3G5
Tel: 250-564-7033; *Fax:* 250-564-7040
hublehomestead@shaw.ca
www.huble.ca
A living heritage site with over one dozen historic buildings

Prince George: **The Railway & Forestry Museum, Prince George & Region**
850 River Rd., Prince George, BC V2L 5S8
Tel: 250-563-7351; *Fax:* 250-563-3697
trains@pgrfm.bc.ca
www.pgrfm.bc.ca
1913 100-tonne steam wrecking crane; wooden 1903 Ruissell snowplow

Prince Rupert: **Kwinitsa Station Railway Museum**
PO Box 669, Prince Rupert, BC V8J 3S1
Tel: 250-624-3207; *Fax:* 250-627-8009
mnbc@citytel.net
www.museumofnorthernbc.com
Depicts the life of early station agents & linemen who worked the Grand Trunk Railway at the turn of the 20th century; located at the Prince Rupert waterfront next to Rotary Waterfront Park; June - Aug.
Susan Marsden, Curator

Prince Rupert: **Museum of Northern British Columbia**
100 First Ave. West, Prince Rupert, BC V8J 1A8
Tel: 250-624-3207; *Fax:* 250-627-8009
mnbc@citytel.net
www.museumofnorthernbc.com
Exhibits artifacts depicting 12,000 years of human & natural history of the Northwest Coast of BC
Robin R. Weber, Director
Susan Marsden, Curator

Prince Rupert: **Prince Rupert Fire Museum Society**
200 - 1st Ave. West, Prince Rupert, BC V8J 1A8
Tel: 250-624-2211; *Fax:* 250-624-3407
Firefighting in Prince Rupert since 1908; restored 1925 fire engine; old fire alarm system

Princeton: **Princeton & District Museum & Archives Society**
PO Box 281, 167 Vermilion Ave., Princeton, BC V0X 1W0
Tel: 250-295-7588; *Fax:* 250-295-3477
Founded: 1958 The museum's collection features fossils & mining artifacts, as well as Aboriginal, Chinese, & pioneer items. Archives collected include records of Princeton & surrounding area organizations, land assessment rolls, court information, photographs, historical newspapers, postcards, posters, & personal papers.

Qualicum Beach: **Vancouver Naval Museum & Heritage Society**
771 Chartwest Ct., Qualicum Beach, BC V9K 2P9
Tel: 250-752-1291; *Fax:* 250-752-1292
fosterdennison@shaw.ca
Depicts the history of the Royal Canadian Navy since its inception: uniforms, medals & decorations, 3D artifacts, pictorial displays, including naval library & archives
Foster K. Dennison, Curator/Director
Roderick H. Macloy, President

Quathiaski Cove: **Kwagiulth Museum & Cultural Centre**
PO Box 8, Quathiaski Cove, BC V0P 1N0
Tel: 250-285-3733; *Fax:* 250-285-3753
kmccchin@island.net
Potlatch collection of Kwakwaka'wakw (Kwagiulth) ceremonial artifacts

***Queen Charlotte:* Kitwanga Fort National Historic Site c/o Gwaii Haanas National Park Reserve, Haida Heritage Site, PO Box 37, Queen Charlotte, BC V0T 1S0**
Tel: 250-559-8818; *Fax:* 250-559-8366
gwaii.haanas@pc.gc.ca
www.pc.gc.ca/lhn-nhs/bc/kitwanga/index_e.asp
Other contact information: TDD: 250/559-8139
Commemorates the culture of the Tsimshian people & their history; located near an important native trade route between the Skeena & Nass Rivers; Battle Hill features archaeological evidence from the 1750-1835 period
Ernie Gladstone, Field Unit Superintendent

***Quesnel:* Quesnel & District Museum & Archives (QDMA) 705 Carson Ave., Quesnel, BC V2J 2B6**
Tel: 250-992-9580; *Fax:* 250-992-9680
ehunter@city.quesnel.bc.ca
www.quesnelmuseum.ca
Artifacts & archival items include Chinese artifacts, pioneer items, medical instruments, World War II letters from service men & women, & photographs from Quesnel & the surrounding area. Quesnel & District Museum & Archives is open year-round.
Elizabeth Hunter, Manager, Museum & Heritage

***Revelstoke:* Revelstoke Court House 1123 - 2nd St. West, Revelstoke, BC V0E 2S0**
Tel: 250-837-6981; *Fax:* 250-837-4669
Courthouse built in 1913; no tours & no collections

***Revelstoke:* Revelstoke Museum & Archives PO Box 1908, 315 First St. West, Revelstoke, BC V0E 2S0**
Tel: 250-837-3067; *Fax:* 250-837-3094
Revelstokemuseum@telus.net
www.revelstoke-museums-gallery.com
The Revelstoke Museum & Archives is situated in Revelstoke's former post office & customs building, where the history of Revelstoke & the surrounding district is presented. The museum organizes exhibits, programs, heritage walks, & cemetery tours. The archives, consisting of photographs, newspapers, assessment rolls, & records of local businesses & organizations, are housed on the second floor of the building. There, visitors will find a microform reader/printer to facilitate their research.
Cathy English, Curator

***Revelstoke:* Revelstoke Railway Museum (RRM) PO Box 3018, 719 Track St. West, Revelstoke, BC V0E 2S0**
Tel: 250-837-6060; *Fax:* 250-837-3732
Toll-Free: 877-837-6060
railway@telus.net; finance.railway@telus.net
www.railwaymuseum.com
Other contact information: E-mail, Gift Shop: giftshop.railway@telus.net
Visitors to the Revelstoke Railway Museum will learn about the challenges of building the Canadian Pacific Railway through British Columbia. Displays include survey & railway tools, CPR china & silverware, a locomotive, a car, a CPR telegraph service office, & a CPR weight scale shack. The museum also collects & organizes photographic archives. The museum is open year-round.
Jennifer Dunkerson, Executive Director, director.railway@telus.net

***Revelstoke:* Rogers Pass Information Centre Glacier National Park, PO Box 350, Revelstoke, BC V0E 2S0**
Tel: 250-837-6274
Natural & human history of Mount Revelstoke & Glacier National Park

***Revelstoke:* Three Valley Gap Heritage Ghost Town PO Box 860, Revelstoke, BC V0E 2S0**
Tel: 250-837-2109; *Fax:* 250-837-5220
Toll-Free: 888-667-2109
hello@3valley.com; 3valley@revelstoke.net
www.3valleyroundhouse.com
Guided tours of historic town of late 1800s; open mid April - mid Oct.

***Richmond:* Britannia Heritage Shipyard Britannia Heritage Shipyard Site Office, 5180 Westwater Dr., Richmond, BC V7E 6P3**
Tel: 604-718-8050; *Fax:* 604-718-8040
britannia@richmond.ca
www.britannia-hss.ca
Britannia Heritage Shipyard is a National Historic Site, which depicts Canada's west coast marine history. It is an example of a village which served the fishing industry. Many buildings date back to 1885. The Britannia Heritage Shipyard Society works to preserve the history of commercial boat building in Steveston. The shipyard is open from the beginning of May to the end of September. From October to April, the shipyard is open on weekends.
Bryan Klassen, Site Supervisor, 604-718-8044
Brooke Lees, Coordinator, Heritage, 604-718-8043
Angela Soon, Coordinator, Special Projects, 604-718-8037

***Richmond:* Deeley Motorcycle Exhibition 1875 Boundary Rd., Richmond, BC V6V 1V2**
Tel: 604-293-2221; *Fax:* 604-909-6232
info@deeleymotorcycleexhibition.ca
www.deeleymotorcycleexhibition.ca
Display of over 250 classic & antique motorcycles; open year round Mon.-Fri., 10-4.

***Richmond:* Gulf of Georgia Cannery National Historic Site 12138 - 4th Ave., Richmond, BC V7E 3J1**
Tel: 604-664-9009; *Fax:* 604-664-9008
gog.info@pc.gc.ca
www.gulfofgeorgiacannery.com
History of the west coast fishing industry; open May-Oct..
Mark Sakai, Manager

***Richmond:* Richmond Museum Richmond Cultural Centre, 7700 Minoru Gate, Richmond, BC V6Y 1R9**
Tel: 604-247-8300; *Fax:* 604-247-8341
museum@richmond.ca
www.richmond.ca
The mission of the Richmond Musuem is to collect, research, document, preserve, exhibit, & interpret items of significance to the history of the community.
Connie Baxter, Supervisor, Museum & Heritage Services
Rebecca Forrest, Curator
Peter Harris, Coordinator, Exhibits & Programs
Emily So, Coordinator, Educational Programs
Bill Jones, Treasurer

***Richmond:* Steveston Museum 3811 Moncton St., Richmond, BC V7E 3A7**
Tel: 604-271-6868
steveston@telus.net
www.steveston.bc.ca/online/museum.html
Founded: 1976 Housed in a 1905 bank building, currently a post office; summer music series on the museum grounds; music & craft programs; museum tours; walking tours of Steveston Village.
Karen Schiefner, Chair

***Richmond:* 12 (Vancouver) Service Battalion Museum The Sherman Armoury, 5500 - No. 4 Rd., Richmond, BC V6X 3L5**
Tel: 604-666-4097; *Fax:* 604-666-4040
info@12servicebattalion.com
www.12servicebattalion.com/museum.htm
Founded: 1990 An accredited Canadian Forces museum; military artifacts, with particular emphasis on the 12 Service Battalion and it's predecessor corps; small reference library of military-related materials; open Tue. & Thu. evenings
J.B. Dutton C.W.O.(R), 604/940-9812, jdutt@oanet.com

***Rossland:* Rossland Historical Museum PO Box 26, Rossland, BC V0G 1Y0**
Tel: 250-362-7722; *Fax:* 250-362-5379
Toll-Free: 888-448-7444
museum@rossland.com
www.rosslandmuseum.ca
Local pioneer & mining history; Western Canada Ski Hall of Fame; underground mine tour; open daily mid-May - mid-Sept.; in winter by appt.
Joyce Austin, Manager

***Saanichton:* Log Cabin Museum & Archives c/o Saanich Pioneer' Society, 7910 East Saanich Rd., Saanichton, BC V8M 1T4**
Tel: 250-658-8347; *Fax:* 250-479-8580
spsma@shaw.ca; bbjohnson@shaw.ca
victoria.tc.ca/Community/Spsma
Artifacts & archives from the early days of the Saanich Peninsula pioneer families; operates in the log cabin built for this purpose in 1933
Beatrice Johnson, President
Edna Ralston, Secretary

***Saanichton:* Saanich Historical Artifacts Society (SHAS) 7321 Lochside Dr., Saanichton, BC V8M 1W4**
Tel: 250-652-5522; *Fax:* 250-652-5999
heritageacres@shas.ca
www.shas.ca
Collects & preserves artifacts from Saanich's rural past, including household & industrial objects, working steam engines, tractors & other agricultural machinery; chapel, school house & other buildings on site; trails & picnic area; open year round
Brian Bevan, President

***Salmo:* Salmo Museum PO Box 69, 100 - 4th St., Salmo, BC V0G 1Z0**
Tel: 250-357-2200; *Fax:* 250-357-2596
salmomus@telus.net
www.virtualmuseum.ca; www.salmovillage.ca
Local histories, photographs, mining/logging/farming artifacts; household objects & clothing; tours; educational programming; annual Heritage Tea & annual Dinner Evening; admission by donation; open May-Sept.

***Salmon Arm:* R.J. Haney Heritage Village & Museum (SAM) PO Box 1642, 751 Hwy. 97B NE, Salmon Arm, BC V1E 4P7**
Tel: 250-832-5243; *Fax:* 250-832-5291
hpark@sunlite.ca
www.salmonarmmuseum.org
Other contact information: Archives phone: 250/832-5289; Email: samha@sunlite.ca
40-acre parcel of land with a municipally designated heritage home; 10 relocated, replicated & restored buildings from the village depict thematic displays on the history of Salmon Arm; 2 km nature trail; majority of collection housed in Salmon Arm Museum; Ernie Doe Archives Room also on site, with 111 linear feet of records dating from turn of 20th century; Museum open May-Sept., W-Su, 10-5, May & Oct., M-F, 9-4. Archives open all year round, W & Th, 10-4.
Gary Cruikshank, General Manager
Colleen McLellan, Coordinator, Visitor Services

***Scotch Creek:* Shuswap Lake Provincial Park Nature House PO Box 24108, Scotch Creek, BC V0E 3L0**
Tel: 250-955-0861
peg@mail.ocis.net
Natural history

***Sechelt:* Téms Swiya Museum PO Box 740, Sechelt, BC V0N 3A0**
Tel: 604-885-2273; *Fax:* 604-885-3490
Bee Jackson, Curator

***Sicamous:* Sicamous & District Museum & Historical Society PO Box 944, Sicamous, BC V0E 2V0**
Tel: 250-836-4456
Museum & archives; collects, preserves, records, exhibits & promotes information, of artifacts & archival, historical & cultural value associated with the Columbia Shuswap Regional District Electoral Area E; open July & Aug.; located in Finlayson Park
Betty Durocher, President

***Sidney:* A.N.A.F. Vets Sidney No. 302 Museum Unit 9831 4th St., Sidney, BC V8L 3S3**
Tel: 250-656-3777; *Fax:* 250-656-6410
info@unit302.ca
www.unit302.ca
Military artifacts
Shane Holwell, President, Unit 302

***Sidney:* British Columbia Aviation Museum 1910 Norseman Rd., Sidney, BC V8L 5V5**
Tel: 250-655-3300; *Fax:* 250-655-1611
bcam@bcam.net
www.bcam.net
Located beside Victoria International Airport, the British Columbia Aviation Museum preserves & displays aircraft & aviation artifacts, with an emphasis on the history of aviation in British Columbia. Aircraft on display include the Avro Anson MK II, the Eastman E2 Sea Rover, & the Bristol Bolingbroke MK IV. The museum is open year-round.

***Silverton:* Silverton Outdoor Mining Exhibit PO Box 69, Silverton, BC V0G 1S0**
Tel: 250-358-2485; *Fax:* 250-358-2485
Open May - Sept.

***Skidegate:* Haida Gwaii Museum at Qay'llnagaay PO Box 1373, Skidegate, BC V0T 1S1**
Tel: 250-559-4643; *Fax:* 250-559-4662
muse@haidagwaii.net
www.haidagwaiimuseum.com
History collections of the Queen Charlotte Islands; open year round
Nathalie Macfarlane, Director
Nika Collison, Curator

***Smithers:* Adams Igloo Wildlife Museum 11955 Yellowhead Hwy., Smithers, BC V0J 2N2**
Tel: 250-847-3188; *Fax:* 250-847-3188
Display of area wildlife, including bear & cougar.

***Smithers:* Bulkley Valley Museum**
***Also known as:* BV Museum**
PO Box 2615, 1425 Main St., Smithers, BC V0J 2N0
Tel: 250-847-5322; *Fax:* 250-847-5363
info@bvmuseum.com
www.bvmuseum.com
Founded: 1976 The Bulkley Valley Museum's collection showcases the social & technological development of the Bulkley Valley. Exhibits include the Bulkley Valley First Nations, the Grand Trunk Pacific Railway in Smithers, & the forestry & mining industries in the area. The museum, operated under the Bulkley Valley Historical & Museum Society, is open year-round.

***Sooke:* Sooke Region Museum, Gallery, Historic Cottage & Lighthouse**
PO Box 774, 2070 Phillips Rd., Sooke, BC V0S 1N0
Tel: 250-642-6351; *Fax:* 250-642-7089
Toll-Free: 866-888-4748
info@sookeregionmuseum.com
www.sookeregionmuseum.com
Extensive archive and significant collection of photographs from Sooke's past. Aritfacts include a restored steam engine yarder, blacksmith shop, and a rotating lighthouse light.
Elida Peers, Executive Director

***Squamish:* West Coast Railway Heritage Park**
39645 Government Rd., Squamish, BC V8B 0B6
Tel: 604-898-9336; *Toll-Free:* 800-722-1233
park@wcra.org; info@wcra.org; tours@wcra.org
www.wcra.org
Other contact information: E-mail, Archives: archives@wcra.org; Twitter: twitter.com/WCRailway
The mission of the West Coast Railway Association is the collection & preservation of British Columbia's railway heritage. Visitors to the West Coast Railway Heritage Park have the opportunity to view authentic railway equipment, including seventy locomotives & cars. The site also features the 1914 Pacific Great Eastern carshop & a railway station, built to 1915 Pacific Great Eastern plans. The heritage park is open year-round.

***Stewart:* Stewart Historical Museum**
PO Box 402, 603 Columbia St., Stewart, BC V0T 1W0
Tel: 250-636-2568

***Summerland:* Summerland Museum & Heritage Society**
PO Box 1491, 9521 Wharton St., Summerland, BC V0H 1Z0
Tel: 250-494-9395; *Fax:* 250-494-9326
info@summerlandmuseum.org
www.summerlandmuseum.org
Collections and displays devoted to Summerland's history.

***Surrey:* Historic Stewart Farmhouse**
13723 Crescent Rd., Surrey, BC V4A 2W3
Tel: 604-592-6956; *Fax:* 604-591-4789
heritage@surrey.ca
www.surrey.ca/Living+in+Surrey/Heritage/default.htm
This restored Victorian farmhouse was originally built in 1894 and features a parlor, dining room and kitchen with working wood-burning stove. Also on site are a circa-1900 pole barn which used to house 6 draft horses and other animals, as well as a fully loaded hay wagon. A team of staff and volunteers tend the heritage gardens of period flowers, vegetables and herbs, and to the orchards with trees of apple, pear and plum. Tours and school programs are also available. Open mid-Feb. - mid-Dec.

***Surrey:* Surrey Museum**
17710 - 56A Ave., Surrey, BC V3S 5H8
Tel: 604-592-6956; *Fax:* 604-592-6957
City Museum; Local history collections; Textile studio; open Tuesdays to Saturdays; admission free
Jacqueline O'Donnell, Manager
Robert McCullough, Public Programs
Oana Capota, School Programs
Dennis Oomen, Exhibits Technician

***Telkwa:* Telkwa Museum**
PO Box 595, Telkwa, BC V0J 2X0
Tel: 250-846-9656
Open May - Sept.
Joanne Cattle

***Terrace:* Heritage Park Museum**
PO Box 512, 4702 Kerby Ave., Terrace, BC V8G 4B5
Tel: 250-635-4546; *Fax:* 250-635-4536
hpmuseum@telus.net
Contains historic log buildings, depicting the history of the pioneers in the region; guided tours offered; open May - Aug.

***Trail:* Trail Museum**
PO Box 405, 1051 Victoria St., Trail, BC V1R 4L7
Tel: 250-364-1262; *Fax:* 250-364-0830
jforbes@trail.ca
www.trailhistory.com
Open June - Aug.
Jamie Forbes, Curator

***Valemount:* Valemount Museum & Archives**
1090 Main St., Valemount, BC V0E 2Z0
Tel: 250-566-4177; *Fax:* 250-566-8428
museum@valemount.com
www.valemountmuseum.ca
Founded: 1992 The Valemount Museum & Archives is housed in the original train station, where visitors learn about the history of the community. Exhibits include information about trapping, the railroad, early settlers, & the Japanese internment camps. The museum is open from May to September.

***Vancouver:* Biblical Museum of Canada**
#70, 3180 East 58th Ave., Vancouver, BC V5S 3S8
Tel: 604-432-6122
fwmetzger@telus.net
www.biblicalmuseum.com
The Biblical Museum of Canada is a teaching museum. It features items from Sumerian, Egyptian, Biblical, & classical times. Also part of the museum's collections are documentations & art objects from the Middle Ages, the Renaissance, the Industrial Revolution, & modern history.
Hon. Garde G. Gardom, Honorary Chair
Rev. John Opmeer, President
Rev. Dr. Frederick W. Metzger, Executive Director & Curator
Florence Metzger, Secretary

***Vancouver:* British Columbia Golf Museum & Hall of Fame**
University Golf Club, 2545 Blanca St., Vancouver, BC V6R 4N1
Tel: 604-222-4653
office@bcgolfmuseum.org
www.bcgolfmuseum.org
Founded: 1986 The BC Golf Museum & Hall of Fame collects, preserves, & displays the history of golf & golfers in British Columbia. A collection of golf clubs dates back to 1790. The reference library houses a collection of over 5,000 books, plus player biographies & tournament records. The museum is open year round.
Barrie McWha, Executive Director
Peter Young, Treasurer

***Vancouver:* British Columbia Medical Association Medical Museum**
c/o British Columbia Medical Association Archives Department, #1665, 1665 West Broadway, Vancouver, BC V6J 5A4
Tel: 604-736-5551; *Fax:* 604-736-4566
museum@bcma.bc.ca
www.bcmamedicalmuseum.org
Founded: 1962 The BCMA Medical Museum holdings include instruments & other equipment used by physicians in British Columbia throughout the past 150 years.

***Vancouver:* British Columbia Sports Hall of Fame & Museum**
Gate A, BC Place Stadium, 777 Pacific Blvd. South, Vancouver, BC V6B 4Y8
Tel: 604-687-5520; *Fax:* 604-687-5510
sportinfo@bcsportshalloffame.com
www.bcsportshalloffame.com
The BC Sports Hall of Fame & Museum contains interactive displays about British Columbia's world-class athletes. In addition to its history galleries, the Hall of Fame & Museum features galleries devoted to Terry Fox & Rick Hansen, a Greg Moore gallery, & a participation gallery.
Bill Maclagan, Chair
Jason Beck, Curator
John Ormiston, Treasurer

***Vancouver:* Cowan Vertebrate Museum**
Dept. of Zoology, University of British Columbia, #4349, 6270 University Blvd., Vancouver, BC V6T 1Z4
Tel: 604-822-4665; *Fax:* 604-822-2416
vertmus@zoology.ubc.ca
www.zoology.ubc.ca/~vertmus
Natural history collection with bird, mammal & herpetological specimens; open year round, by appt.
Dr. D. Irwin, Director
Dr. R. Kenner, Curator

***Vancouver:* 15th Field Artillery Regiment Museum & Archives Society**
2025 - 11th Ave. West, Vancouver, BC V6J 2C7
Tel: 604-666-4370; *Fax:* 604-666-4083
Equipment of artillery units from Vancouver area; open year round

***Vancouver:* Old Hastings Mill Store Museum**
1575 Alma Rd., Vancouver, BC V6R 3P3
Tel: 604-734-1212; *Fax:* 604-876-9779
eandelockhart@shaw.ca
www.findfamilyfun.com/hastingsmill.htm
Founded: 1919 Oldest building in Vancouver owned by The Native Daughters of British Columbia Post No. 1; houses artifacts pertaining to the pioneers of the city and Native peoples; open Tue.-Sun., June 15 - Sept. 15, 1-4; weekends in winter months, closed Dec. & Jan.
Jacqui Underwood, Chief Factor
Elsie Lockhart, Corresponding Secretary

***Vancouver:* The Pacific Museum of the Earth**
Dept. of Earth & Ocean Sciences, University of British Columbia, 6339 Stores Rd., Vancouver, BC V6T 1Z4
Tel: 604-822-6992; *Fax:* 604-228-6088
mparker@eos.ubc.ca
www.eos.ubc.ca/resources/museum
Includes mounted dinosaur, insects in amber, wide variety of fossils & minerals
Kirsten Parker, Curator

***Vancouver:* Roedde House Museum**
1415 Barclay St., Vancouver, BC V6G 1J6
Tel: 604-684-7040
roeddehs@roeddehouse.org
www.roeddehouse.org
Founded: 1990 Roedde House is a late-Victorian home, built in 1893. Today, the house reflects the life of an immigrant, middle class family around 1900. The museum provides guided tours & educational & cultural programs.
Anthony Norfolk, President
Helene Perndl, Manager
Susan Erb, Secretary
Sharon Sprinkhuysen, Treasurer

***Vancouver:* St. Roch National Historic Site**
c/o Vancouver Maritime Museum, 1095 Ogden Ave., Vancouver, BC V6J 1A3
Tel: 604-257-8300; *Fax:* 604-737-2621
info@vancouvermaritimemuseum.com
www.vancouvermaritimemuseum.com
Arctic patrol vessel & 1944 RCMP memorabilia
Simon Robinson, Executive Director

***Vancouver:* Seaforth Highlanders Regimental Museum**
Seaforth Armoury, 1650 Burrard St., Vancouver, BC V6J 3G4
Tel: 604-733-3836; *Fax:* 604-666-4078
seaforthmuseum@gmail.com
bcoy1cpb.pacdat.net/museum.htm
Founded: 1972 Artifacts pertaining to the Seaforth Highlanders of Canada & affiliated regiments
Colin Stevens, Curator

***Vancouver:* Spencer Entomological Museum (SEM)**
Dept. of Zoology, University of British Columbia, 6270 University Blvd., Vancouver, BC V6T 1Z4
Tel: 604-822-3379; *Fax:* 604-822-2416
needham@zoology.ubc.ca
www.insecta.com
Largest collection of BC insects in the world containing 700,000 specimens; museum closed to public
Karen Needham, Curator
G.G.E. Scudder, Director

***Vancouver:* Vancouver Holocaust Education Centre (VHEC)**
#50, 950 - 41st Ave. West, Vancouver, BC V5Z 2N7
Tel: 604-264-0499; *Fax:* 604-264-0497
info@vhec.org; library@vhec.org
www.vhec.org
Founded: 1994 The Vancouver Holocaust Education Centre is a teaching museum which provides Holocaust based anti-racism education. It aims to promote human rights, genocide awareness, & social justice. The causes & consequences of discrimination, racism, & antisemitism are explored. The centre includes a museum collection, archives, a library, & a resource centre. The education centre is also engaged in a survivor testimony project. School programs & outreach speakers are available. Exhibits are not recommended for children under the age of ten. The education centre is open year-round.
Frieda Miller, Executive Director
Nina Krieger, Education Director
Shannon LaBelle, Librarian
Elizabeth Shaffer, Archivist
Gisella Levitt, Coordinator, Suvivivor Services
Marla Guralnick Pekarsky, Secretary
Robbie Waisman, Treasurer

***Vancouver:* The Vancouver Maritime Museum Society (VMM)**
1905 Ogden Ave., Vancouver, BC V6J 1A3
Tel: 604-257-8300; *Fax:* 604-737-2621
info@vancouvermaritimemuseum.com
www.vancouvermaritimemuseum.com
Includes National Historic Site St. Roch, RCMP Schooner
Simon Robinson, Executive Director

***Vancouver:* Vancouver Police Museum**
240 Cordova St. East, Vancouver, BC V6A 1L3
Tel: 604-665-3346; *Fax:* 604-665-3585
info@vancouverpolicemuseum.ca
www.vancouverpolicemuseum.ca
Other contact information: Twitter: www.twitter.com/policemuseum
Founded: 1986 Located in the historic City Morgue & Coroner's Court in Vancouver, the Vancouver Police Museum presents a collection of artifacts, papers, photographs, & published materials related to the history of the Vancouver Police Department. The museum is open year-round.

***Vanderhoof:* Vanderhoof Heritage Museum**
c/o Nechako Valley Historical Society, PO Box 1515, Vanderhoof, BC V0J 3A0
Tel: 250-567-2991; *Fax:* 250-567-2931

1920's heritage village & community museum with restaurant café serving old-fashioned food
Stephen Flagg, President
Shelley Olson, Curator/Manager

***Vernon:* Greater Vernon Museum & Archives**
3009 - 32 Ave., Vernon, BC V1T 2L8
Tel: 250-542-3142; *Fax:* 250-542-5358
mail@vernonmuseum.ca
www.vernonmuseum.ca
Open year round
Ron Candy, Curator

***Vernon:* O'Keefe Ranch**
***Also known as:* Historic O'Keefe Ranch**
9380 Hwy. 97, Vernon, BC V1H 1W9
Tel: 250-542-7868
www.okeeferanch.ca
Founded: 1867 Founded in 1867, the O'Keefe Ranch operated when thousands of cattle grazed in the Okanagan, Thompson, & Cariboo regions. Today, Historic O'Keefe Ranch depicts the story of early ranching in British Columbia. The ranch offers an informative & entertaining school program. Each summer the ranch hosts a Cowboy Festival.

***Victoria:* Canadian Forces Base Esquimalt Naval & Military Museum**
Canadian Forces Base Esquimalt, PO Box 17000 Forces, Victoria, BC V9A 7N2
Tel: 250-363-4312; *Fax:* 250-363-4252
info@NavalandMilitaryMuseum.org
www.navalandmilitarymuseum.org
Other contact information: E-mail, Curator: curator@NavalandMilitaryMuseum.org
The CFB Esquimalt Naval & Military Museum collects, preserves, & displays the history of naval presence on the Canadian west coast. In addition, the history of the military on southern Vancouver Island is also depicted. The musuem features an archive & research library. Reproductions of photographs in the archive are available.
Debbie Towell, Curator, nadenmuseum@pacificcoast.net
Joseph Lenarcik, Assistant Curator, 250-363-5655
Clare Sugrue, Coordinator, Museum Volumteers

***Victoria:* The Canadian Scottish Regiment (Princess Mary's) Regimental Museum**
Bay Street Armoury, 715 Bay St., Victoria, BC V8T 1R1
Tel: 250-363-8753; *Fax:* 250-363-3593
csrmuse@islandnet.com
www.islandnet.com/~csrmuse
Items of historical significance to the regiment; located in the Bay Street Armoury, a National Historic Site built in 1915

***Victoria:* Craigdarroch Castle**
1050 Joan Cres., Victoria, BC V8S 3L5
Tel: 250-592-5323; *Fax:* 250-592-1099
info@thecastle.ca
www.craigdarrochcastle.com
Historic house museum, built in 1890 by Robert Dunsmuir, wealthy coal baron; 39 rooms, 87 stairs to tower, lavish Victorian era furnishings, woodwork, stained glass
C. Williams, Executive Director

***Victoria:* Emily Carr House**
207 Government St., Victoria, BC V8V 2K8
Tel: 250-383-5843; *Fax:* 250-356-7796
ecarr@shaw.ca
www.emilycarr.com
Birthplace of Emily Carr; People's Gallery; open May-Oct. & Dec. or by appointment

***Victoria:* Fort Rodd Hill & Fisgard Lighthouse National Historic Sites**
603 Fort Rodd Hill Rd., Victoria, BC V9C 2W8
Tel: 250-478-5849; *Fax:* 250-478-2816
fort.rodd@pc.gc.ca
www.fortroddhill.com
Turn of the century coastal defence gun batteries & first permanent lighthouse (1860) on Canada's west coast

***Victoria:* Goldstream Regional Museum**
#2, 697 Goldstream Ave., Victoria, BC V9B 2X2
Tel: 250-474-6113
History of region; WWI & WWII displays; open year round

***Victoria:* Helmcken House**
Royal BC Museum, 675 Belleville St., Victoria, BC V8W 9W2
Tel: 250-356-7226; *Fax:* 250-387-5674
Toll-Free: 888-447-7977
reception@royalbcmuseum.bc.ca
www.royalbcmuseum.bc.ca
Home of Dr. John Sebastian Helmcken built in 1852; medical & domestic collections; managed by the Royal BC Museum
Pauline Rafferty, CEO

***Victoria:* Lt. General Ashton Armoury Museum**
724 Vanalman Ave., Victoria, BC V8Z 3B5
Tel: 250-363-8346; *Fax:* 250-363-8326
Army service support
Maj. Derek Brown

***Victoria:* Maritime Museum of British Columbia**
28 Bastion Sq., Victoria, BC V8W 1H9
Tel: 250-385-4222; *Fax:* 250-382-2869
info@mmbc.bc.ca
www.mmbc.bc.ca
Founded: 1954 This extensive museum of 3 floors covers the history of marine navigation on the BC coast from First Nation cultures through to European explorers and territorial tussles. Interactive displays include a mock-up of a ship's deck complete with climbable crow's nest & ratlines. The 2nd floor offers model ships for viewing, while the 3rd floor houses a library. Open all year, with winter & summer hrs.
Ms Shirley Vickers, Executive Director, 250-385-4222, X-104, svickers@mmbc.bc.ca

***Victoria:* Metchosin School Museum**
4475 Happy Valley Rd., Victoria, BC V9C 3Z3
Tel: 250-478-3451
roper@pacificcoast.net
www.metchosinmuseum.org
Founded: 1972 School, household & agricultural exhibits/archives pertaining to the School and the area; operated by a society of volunteers; open April-Oct.

***Victoria:* Museum & Archives of 5 (BC) Regiment, Royal Canadian Artillery**
The Armoury, #304, 715 Bay St., Victoria, BC V8T 1R1
Tel: 250-363-3814; *Fax:* 250-363-3512
info@5rcamuseum.ca; curator@5rcamuseum.ca
www.5rcamuseum.ca
Other contact information: E-mail, Archives: archivist@5rcamuseum.ca; Gifts: shop@5rcamuseum.ca
Founded: 1996 The Museum & Archives of 5 (BC) Regiment depicts the history of coast artillery & associated units. Displays date from 1861 to the present. Examples of artifacts include a rifled muzzle loading gun & a vintage cannon. An archives & reference library are also available for research. The museum is open year-round, two days each week. For visits outside regular hours, please call 250-363-8270.

***Victoria:* Point Ellice House & Gardens**
2616 Pleasant St., Victoria, BC V8T 4V3
Tel: 250-380-6506; *Fax:* 250-381-2338
reservations@pointellicehouse.ca
www.tca.gov.bc.ca/heritage/historic_sites/point_ellice_house.htm
Other contact information: Alternative URL: www.pointellicehouse.ca
Point Ellice House was owned by Magistrate & Gold Commissioner Peter O'Reilly, starting in 1867. The home & garden are open from May to September.

***Victoria:* Royal London Wax Museum**
470 Belleville St., Victoria, BC V8V 1W9
Tel: 250-388-4461; *Fax:* 250-388-4493
Toll-Free: 877-929-3228
info@waxmuseum.bc.ca
www.waxmuseum.bc.ca
Houses over 300 wax sculptures; group tours available; open daily
Dr. Arne H. Lane, President
Ken H. Lane, General Manager

***Victoria:* Victoria Police Historical Society**
850 Caledonia Ave., Victoria, BC V8T 5J8
Tel: 250-995-7654; *Fax:* 250-995-7450
museum@police.victoria.bc.ca
History of the Victoria police, est. 1858; exhibits include 1921 "Commerce" Patrol Wagon, 1938 UL Harley Davidson motorcycle & sidecar, 1940 Dodge police car
Cst. Bob Raappana, Curator

***Wells:* Wells Museum**
PO Box 244, Wells, BC V0K 2R0
Tel: 250-994-3422
museum@wellsbc.come
www.wellsmuseum.ca
Wells Museum is located within the Island Mountain Mine office, which was built during the 1930s when Wells was established as a company town for the Cariboo Gold-Quartz Mine. The museum features displays about the mining history in the area. It is open from May to September.
William (W.G) (W.G) Quackenbush, Contact

***West Vancouver:* West Vancouver Museum**
680 - 17th St., West Vancouver, BC V7V 3T2
Tel: 604-925-7295
www.westvancouvermuseum.ca
The West Vancouver Museum offers exhibitions & educational programs to increase awareness of the history, culture, & art of the West Vancouver region & the country. The museum is open year-round.
Darrin Morrison, Curator, 604-925-7296, dmorrison@westvancouver.ca
Carol Howie, Coordinator, Collections, 604-925-7294, chowie@westvancouver.ca
Isaac Vanderhorst, Coordinator, Education, 604-925-7297, ivanderhorst@westvancouver.ca

***White Rock:* White Rock Museum & Archives**
14970 Marine Drive, White Rock, BC V4B 1C4
Tel: 604-541-2222; *Fax:* 604-541-2223
whiterockmuseum@telus.net
www.whiterock.museum.bc.ca
Located in the White Rock Train Station; collections include artifacts relating to the history & families of White Rock, documentation relating to the civic, political & business life of the community, objects relating to the Great Northern Railway & rail history of the area, and natural history objects of the locality.
Shelly Copping, Manager

***Williams Lake:* Museum of the Cariboo-Chilcotin**
113 - 4th Ave. North, Williams Lake, BC V2G 2C8
Tel: 250-392-7404; *Fax:* 250-392-7404
mccwl@uniserve.com
cowboy-museum.com
Displays focusing on the ranching & rodeo history of the Cariboo Chilcotin area; home of the BC Cowboy Hall of Fame; Shuswap First Nation, Chinese & Chilcotin materials; open June-Aug., Mon.-Sat. 10-4; Sept.-May, Tues.-Sat. 11-4
Pat Skoblanuik, Manager

***Yale:* Historic Yale Museum**
PO Box 74, 31187 Douglas St., Yale, BC V0K 2S0
Tel: 604-863-2324; *Fax:* 604-863-2495
yahs@uniserve.com
First Nations; Gold Rush; Railway Era

***Ymir:* Ymir Arts & Museum Society**
PO Box 65, Ymir, BC V0G 2K0
Tel: 250-357-9262
ymirartsandmuseumsociety@hotmail.com
www.ymirbc.com/yams
The Ymir Arts & Museum Society preserves the Ymir Schoolhouse, where arts & culture in Ymir are promoted. Located in the West Kootenays of British Columbia, Ymir was an active mining town in the late 1800s.
Robyn Balaski, Arts & Museum Contact, rainspirit13@hotmail.com

Manitoba

Provincial Museums

The Manitoba Museum / Le Musée du Manitoba
190 Rupert Ave., Winnipeg, MB R3B 0N2
Tel: 204-956-2830; *Fax:* 204-942-3679
Toll-Free: 888-231-9739
info@manitobamuseum.ca
www.manitobamuseum.ca
Other contact information: Info Line: 204/943-3139
Nine permanent galleries & Alloway Hall which houses temporary & travelling exhibitions. Permanent galleries are: Orientation (in which the main theme of the Museum is explained), Earth History, Grasslands, Urban (a section of Winnipeg, reconstructed as it might have been in 1920), Nonsuch (a replica of the 17th-century Ketch), Arctic-Subarctic & Boreal Forest. The Hudson's Bay Company Gallery reflects the legacy of the Company & the people whose daily activities & legendary deed bring to life the drama & history of Canada's fur trade. The all new Parklands/mixed woods Gallery, representing the most natural & culturally diverse region of the province. The Planetarium provides educational & entertaining programs for the general public & school groups in the 287-seat Star Theatre; feature presentations touch all aspects of astronomy, science facts/science fiction, as well as present day space programs & technology
Claudette Leclerc, Chief Executive Officer
C. Ellis, Director, Operations
J. Schwersensky, Director, Marketing
Mike Jensen, Supervisor, Planetarium Programs

Local Museums in Manitoba

***Alonsa:* Alex Robertson Museum**
Alonsa, MB R0H 0A0
Tel: 204-767-2101; *Fax:* 204-767-2004
alonsa@mts.net
Antique guns; pioneer tools & artifacts; 1939 fire engine; open year round

***Anola:* Anola & District Museum**
PO Box 153, Anola, MB R0E 0A0
Tel: 204-866-2922
Open May - Sept., Sun. or by appt.

Jack Mavins, Treasurer

Ashern: **Ashern Pioneer Museum**
PO Box 642, 36 - 1st St. South, Ashern, MB R0C 0E0
Tel: 204-768-3147; *Fax:* 204-768-3051
Other contact information: Phone, appointments: 204-768-2394
The Ashern Museum features the following restored buildings: St Michael's Anglican Church, the CNR station, the Ashern Post Office, the Hoffman Log House, the Darwin School House, & Ashern's first Rural Municipality of Siglunes Office. Artifacts include a threshing machine, tractor, bailer, & plow. The museum is open from May to September. At other times, tours can be arranged.

Austin: **Manitoba Agricultural Museum**
PO Box 10, Austin, MB R0H 0C0
Tel: 204-637-2354; *Fax:* 204-637-2395
agmuseum@mts.net; info@ag-museum.mb.ca
www.ag-museum.mb.ca
Founded: 1953 Located 3 km south of Hwys. 1 & 34, the site boasts Canada's largest collection of vintage agricultural equipment from 1900 on. There is also a pioneer village with over 20 buildings from log cabins to mills & mansions. The Manitoba Amateur Radio Museum is also housed on site. Events include the annual Thresherman's Reunion & Stampede last week in July. Open daily 9:00-5:00, May 12 - Oct. 5.
Diane Nesbitt, Administrator

Austin: **Manitoba Amateur Radio Museum Inc. (MARM)**
PO Box 10, Austin, MB R0H 0C0
Tel: 204-728-2463; *Fax:* 204-728-2463
ve4arm@mts.net
www.marminc.ca
Located on the grounds of the Manitoba Agricultural Museum, Hwy. #34 in Austin; Canada's only amateur radio museum; home of amateur radio station VE4ARM/VE4MTR.
Dave Snydal, Curator, dsnydal@mts.net

Beausejour: **Pioneer Village Museum**
PO Box 310, 7th St. North, Beausejour, MB R0E 0C0
Tel: 204-268-3048; *Fax:* 204-268-3048
Open July & Aug.
Peter H. Kozyra, President

Belmont: **Belmont & District Museum**
PO Box 69, 202 - 5th St., Belmont, MB R0K 0C0
Tel: 204-528-3300
Other contact information: Phone, Off-season: 204-537-2405; 204-537-2474
The Belmont & District Museum features a CNR caboose, plus displays of medical equipment, sports memorabilia, military uniforms, & printing equipment for the Belmont News. The museum is open during July & August, & by appointment at other times of the year.

Belmont: **Evergreen Firearms Museum Inc.**
PO Box 57, Belmont, MB R0K 0C0
Tel: 204-537-2647
www.museumsmanitoba.com/dir/western/95.html
Military & non-military historical firearms; open year round

Binscarth: **Binscarth & District Gordon Orr Memorial Museum**
PO Box 239, 162 - 2nd Ave., Binscarth, MB R0J 0G0
Tel: 204-532-2217; *Fax:* 204-532-2153
vilbins@mts.net
www.binscarthmb.com/museum.html
The Binscarth & District Gordon Orr Memorial Museum contains displays such as Native artifacts, a chapel, a general store, a school room, & large agricultural machinery. The museum is open during July & August.
Rita Wasslen, Contact

Birtle: **Birdtail Country Museum**
PO Box 508, 738 Main St., Birtle, MB R0M 0C0
Tel: 204-842-5342
birdtailcm@hotmail.com
Other contact information: Alternative Phone: 204-842-3363; 204-842-5350
The Birdtail Country Museum is housed in the former Union Bank Building in Birtle. It contains a variety of objects from pioneer days in the Birtle area. The museum also holds local newspapers on microfilm. Birdtail Country Museum is open from mid-May to the end of August.

Boissevain: **Beckoning Hills Museum**
PO Box 389, 425 Mill Rd. South, Boissevain, MB R0K 0E0
Tel: 204-534-6544
bhmuseum@mts.net
The Beckoning Hills Museum presents historical displays from Boissevain & the surrounding area. Exhibits include pioneer household items, agricultural tools & implements, native artifacts, & military items. The museum is open from June until September. Appointments can be arranged at other times of the year.

Boissevain: **Moncur Gallery**
PO Box 1241, Civic Centre, Boissevain, MB R0K 0E0
Tel: 204-534-6478; *Fax:* 204-534-3710
info@moncurgallery.org
www.moncurgallery.org
Founded: 1984 Gallery showcases an extensive collection of ancient artifacts portraying the earliest history of the Turtle Mountain and surrounding prairie area in southwestern Manitoba. Exhibits include lifestyle artifacts of nomadic peoples which predate the written record, such as ceremonial items, food preparation utensils & tools. Open Tue.-Sat., 10:00-5:00.
Shannon Moncur, Chair
Phyllis Hallett, Secretary

Brandon: **B.J. Hales Museum of Natural History**
George T. Richardson Library, Lower Level, Brandon University, 270 - 18th St., Brandon, MB R7A 6A9
Tel: 204-727-7307; *Fax:* 204-728-7346
jacksonk@brandonu.ca
www2.brandonu.ca/bjhales
The B.J. Hales Museum of Natural History collects, preserves, & presents artifacts of the natural heritage of Manitoba. Collections include bird & mammal specimens & a geological display. The museum is open year-round, Monday to Friday.

Brandon: **Chapman Museum**
PO Box 43, RR#2, Brandon, MB R7A 5Y2
Tel: 204-728-7396
www.brandon.com; www.virtualmuseum.ca
Village-type museum setting with 16 historic buildings, among them the Roseville Church, Harrow School, Pendennis Rail Station, Robinville School, and various shops; guided tours; special needs facilities & wheelchair access; picnic area; open during the summer, free admission or donations appreciated.
Albert T. Chapman, Director

Brandon: **Commonwealth Air Training Plan Museum**
PO Box 3, Group 520, RR#5, Brandon, MB R7A 5Y5
Tel: 204-727-2444; *Fax:* 204-725-2334
airmuseum@inetlink.ca
www.airmuseum.ca
Canada's only air museum dedicated to those who trained & fought for the British Commmonwealth during WW II; artifacts include photographs, uniforms & clothing, personal papers, logbooks, station magazines, tools, equipment, trade badges, & medals; display of training aircraft
Stephen Hayter, Executive Director
John McNarry, President

Brandon: **Daly House Museum & Steve Magnacca Research Centre**
122 - 18 St., Brandon, MB R7A 5A4
Tel: 204-727-1722; *Fax:* 204-727-1722
dalymus@mts.net
www.mts.net/~dalymus
Period home of the 1880s; 1903 grocery store; 1892 council chambers; open daily in the summer; Tue.-Sun. winter
Eileen Trott, Curator

Brandon: **Manitoba Agricultural Hall of Fame**
1129 Queens Ave., Brandon, MB R7A 1L9
Tel: 204-728-3736; *Fax:* 204-726-6260
info@manitobaaghalloffame.com
www.manitobaaghalloffame.com
Recognizing those who improved agricultural & rural living; plaques are at the Keystone Centre in Brandon (1175 - 18th St.); open daily
Robert G. (Bob) Roehle, President
Allan Chambers, Treasurer
Patricia Bailey, Office Manager, info@manitobaaghalloffame.com

Brandon: **XII Manitoba Dragoons/26 Field Regiment Museum**
Brandon Armoury, 1116 Victoria Ave., Brandon, MB R7A 1B2
Tel: 204-726-3498; *Fax:* 204-725-1766
sim.gordo@gmail.com
www.12mbdragoons.com
Founded: 1979 The museum has a wide range of military memorabilia and artifacts on display, including photos, uniforms and equipment; small research library; archival materials; regimental button collection; open Tuesdays throughout the year
Mr. Ed McArthur, Curator

La Broquerie: **Musée Saint Jachim**
PO Box 66, La Broquerie, MB R0A 0W0
Tel: 204-424-5232

Carberry: **Carberry Plains Museum**
PO Box 1072, 520 - 4th Ave., Carberry, MB R0K 0H0
Tel: 204-834-6609; *Fax:* 204-834-2795
www.townofcarberry.ca
Other contact information: Phone, Off Season: 204-834-2284
The Carberry Plains Museum reflects early prairie life, through its collections from former residents, including a First World War pilot & Ernest Thompson Seton, a well-known naturalist. The museum is open during July & August. Appointments may be made during June & September.
Rae Anderson, Contact, 204-834-2284

Carberry: **The Seton Centre**
PO Box 408, 116 Main St., Carberry, MB R0K 0H0
Tel: 204-834-2509
Materials by & about Ernest Thompson Seton, 1860-1946; open June - Sept. long weekend
Cheryl Orr, Contact

Carberry: **Spruce Woods Provincial Heritage Park**
Park Centre, PO Box 900, Carberry, MB R0K 0H0
Tel: 204-827-8950; *Fax:* 204-827-8852
swppterp@mts.net
Northwest Co. fur-trading artifacts
Madelyn Robinson, Interpreter

Carman: **Dufferin Historical Museum**
PO Box 1646, 44 King's Park Ed., Carman, MB R0G 0J0
Tel: 204-745-3597; *Fax:* 204-828-3698
www.cici.mb.ca/mmedia/dufferin.html
Other contact information: Off-season phone: 204/745-2443
An early 20th century home. Open Mid-June - September.
Shirley Snider, President

Carman: **Heaman's Antique Autorama**
PO Box 105, Hwy. 3, Carman, MB R0G 0J0
Tel: 204-745-2981
Canadian & American automobiles dating back to 1902

Cartwright: **Heritage Village Museums**
PO Box 9, Cartwright, MB R0K 0L0
Tel: 204-529-2047
edocart@hotmail.com
www.cartwrightmb.ca
This is a collection of historic buildings representing village life in pioneer days. The Blacksmith Museum is a fully restored, functional smithy. Todds Shoe Repairs has authentic cobbling equipment. Badger Creek Museum conserves artifacts of rural family life. There are also a schoolhouse, post office and telephone office.

Churchill: **Eskimo Museum**
PO Box 10, 242 La Verendrye Ave., Churchill, MB R0B 0E0
Tel: 204-675-2030; *Fax:* 204-675-2140
chhbay@mts.net
Open Mon.-Sat., year-round
Lorraine Brandson, Curator
Cathy Widdowson, Asst. Curator

Churchill: **Manitoba North National Historic Sites & Wapusk National Park of Canada**
Parks Canada Visitor Centre, PO Box 127, 1 Manteyo Seepee, Churchill, MB R0B 0E0
Tel: 204-675-8863; *Fax:* 204-675-2026
mannorth.nhs@pc.gc.ca; wapusk.np@pc.gc.ca
www.pc.gc.ca/eng/lhn-nhs/mb/prince/index.aspx
Guided tours are offered to Prince of Wales Fort, Cape Merry Battery, Sloop Cove & York Factory by contacting the Parks Canada Visitor Centre in Churchill which houses exhibits introducing the history of the Hudson's Bay Company and the fur trade of the 1700s. Open year round.

Crystal City: **Crystal City Community Printing Museum**
PO Box 302, 218 Broadway, Crystal City, MB R0K 0N0
Tel: 204-873-2260
btreble@mts.net
Newspaper print shop started by Thomas Greenway (7th premier of Manitoba) in 1881; tours on request
B. Treble

Darlingford: **Darlingford School Heritage Museum**
PO Box 98, 197 Bradburn St., Darlingford, MB R0G 0L0
Tel: 204-246-2015
School built in 1910; open by appointment
Robert Jordan

Dauphin: **Cross of Freedom Historical Site & Museum**
Also known as: **Trembowla Cross of Freedom**
121 - 7 Ave. SE, Dauphin, MB R7N 2E3
Tel: 204-638-9641; *Fax:* 204-638-9963
The history & culture of Ukrainian pioneers; Cross of Freedom site of first Ukrainian Catholic Divine Liturgy & first Ukrainian Catholic Church St. Michael's, the oldest such church in Canada & dedicated as an Heritage site building in 2000; monuments include a large granite cross, bronze bust of Rev. Nestor Dmytriw, a grotto & monument of the first Ukrainian Catholic Bishop in Canada, Bishop Nyky
Kay Slobodzian, Secretary
Stella Sapach, Treasurer
John Slobodzian, President

Dauphin: **Fort Dauphin Museum**
PO Box 181, 140 Jackson Ave., Dauphin, MB R7N 2V1
Tel: 204-638-6630; *Fax:* 204-629-2327
fortdphn@mts.net
www.dauphin.ca; fortdauphinmuseum.wordpress.com

Fur trade history, pioneer history, local history, the Parkland Archaeological Laboratory; open mid-May - early Sept. & by appt. early Sept.-mid May
Heidi Husband, Curator/Manager

***Dufresne:* Aunt Margaret's Museum of Childhood Inc.**
Trans-Canada Hwy., Dufresne, MB R0A 0J0
Tel: 204-422-8426
Aunt Margaret's Museum of Childhood includes a collection of antique furniture & artifacts.

***Dugald:* Cook's Creek Heritage Museum**
Group 22, Box 6, RR#2, Dugald, MB R0E 0K0
Tel: 204-444-4448; *Fax:* 204-444-4224
cchm@mts.net
www.stmichaelsrc.mb.ca
Open daily, except Wed. May-Aug. 11-5
Jane Burpee, President

***Elkhorn:* Manitoba Antique Automobile Museum**
PO Box 477, Elkhorn, MB R0M 0N0
Tel: 204-845-2604; *Fax:* 204-845-2312
info@elkhorn.mb.ca
www.mbautomuseum.com
Founded: 1961 Donated to the community by local farmer, Isaac "Ike" Clarkson, the collection began with a hand-restored 1909 Hupmobile to a sizeable array of vintage automobiles. The site also includes exhibits of agricultural machinery and household articles. Open May - Sept., 9:00-6:00.
Agnes Wolfe, Curator
Roland Gagnon, Chair
Garth Mitchell, Sec.-Treas.

***Erickson:* The Erickson Museum**
Erickson, MB R0J 0P0
Tel: 204-636-2431
The Parsonage, built in 1897-98 & the Nedrob School feature period artifacts; open by appt.

***Eriksdale:* Eriksdale Museum**
PO Box 71, Eriksdale, MB R0C 0W0
Tel: 204-739-2621; *Fax:* 204-739-2073
dmysmith@mts.net
www.eriksdale.com
Open mid-May - Sept., excluding Thurs. & Sun.; Eriksdale Creamery Museum now open
Elaine Henrotte, Secretary
Donna Smith, Chair

***Flin Flon:* Flin Flon Station Museum**
CN Building, PO Box 160, Highway 10, Flin Flon, MB R8A 1M6
Tel: 204-687-2946; *Fax:* 204-687-4456
www.cityofflinflon.com
Household artifacts from the late 1920s; mining; open Victoria Day - Labour Day
Ron Dodds

***Gardenton:* Ukrainian Museum & Village Society**
***Also known as:* Gardenton Park**
Gardenton, MB R0A 0M0
Tel: 204-425-3501
Clothing, icons & many articles from the early settlers; an exhibit of churches & photos of early pioneer life; clay thatched roof house & a one-room school; picnic facilities; tours & meals upon request
Linda Shewchuk, President

***Gilbert Plains:* Gilbert Plains & District Historical Society**
PO Box 662, Gilbert Plains, MB R0L 0X0
Tel: 204-548-4448; *Fax:* 204-548-2564
rmofgilbertplains@mts.net
10 log buildings; Ukrainian artifacts; open July & Aug.
Susan Boyachek, Sec.-Treas.
Eugene Dedio, President
Jim Michaluk, Vice-President

***Gimli:* New Iceland Heritage Museum**
The Waterfront Centre, #108, 94 - 1st Ave., Gimli, MB R0C 1B1
Tel: 204-642-4001; *Fax:* 204-642-9382
nihm@mts.net
www.nihm.ca
The New Iceland Heritage Museum preserves & interprets the history of New Iceland & Lake Winnipeg & its fishing industry.
Tammy Axelsson, Executive Director

***Gladstone:* Gladstone & District Museum**
PO Box 651, 49 - 6th St., Gladstone, MB R0J 0T0
Tel: 204-385-2551; *Fax:* 204-385-2391
Local pioneer artifacts

***Grandview:* The Watson Crossley Community Museum**
PO Box 396, Grandview, MB R0L 0Y0
Tel: 204-546-2661; *Fax:* 204-546-3310
guards45@mts.net
Facility includes museum display of local area pioneer artifacts, shedded display of antique farm machinery, tractors & automobiles; also included is a pioneer homestead building (1896), pioneer house (1918), rural one-room schoolhouse & a pioneer Ukrainian Orthodox church; open June-Sept. & year round by appt.
Gerald Morran
Mervin Mitchell
Allan Yuihl

***Hamiota:* Hamiota Pioneer Club Museum**
PO Box 279, Hamiota, MB R0M 0T0
Tel: 204-764-2552
Open Sundays in July & Aug. & by appt.
R. Neil McDonald, Secretary
John L. Rankin, President

***Hartney:* Hart-Cam Museum**
PO Box 399, Hartney, MB R0M 0X0
Tel: 204-858-2590; *Fax:* 204-858-2681
hartney@mts.net
Artifacts from Aboriginal to post-settlement times

***Inglis:* St. Elijah 1908 Pioneer Church Museum**
Inglis, MB R0J 0X0
Tel: 204-564-2228; *Fax:* 204-564-2643
Designated provincial historic site
Barry Sawchuk, President

***Killarney:* J.A.V. David Museum**
PO Box 1451, 414 Williams Ave., Killarney, MB R0K 1G0
Tel: 204-523-8836; *Fax:* 204-523-8740
Museum of artifacts, clothing & memorabilia associated with Killarney & area history
Mark Witherspoon, Chair

***Lac du Bonnet:* Lac du Bonnet & District Historical Society**
PO Box 658, 578 Riverland, Lac du Bonnet, MB R0E 1A0
Tel: 204-345-2726; *Fax:* 204-345-9787
memories@granite.mb.ca
Louis Bruneau, President

***Ladywood:* Atelier Ladywood Museum**
PO Box 14, RR#3, Ladywood, MB R0E 0C0
Tel: 204-265-3226
Atelier Ladywood Museum features the former H. Gabel's General Store, with items from the 1930s to the 1950s.

***Lundar:* Lundar Museum Society**
PO Box 265, Lundar, MB R0C 1Y0
Tel: 204-739-0147
Open mid-June - Sept.
Harold Hallson, Director

***Lynn Lake:* Lynn Lake Mining Town Museum**
PO Box 847, 470 Cobalt Pl., Lynn Lake, MB R0B 0W0
Tel: 204-356-8302
Open May 24 - Aug. 31

***Melita:* Antler River Historical Society Museum**
Townsend Dr., Melita, MB R0M 1L0
Tel: 204-522-3103; *Fax:* 204-522-8387
Local history
W.H. Critchlow, President

***Miami:* Miami Museum**
PO Box 153, Miami, MB R0G 1H0
Tel: 204-435-2305; *Fax:* 204-435-2067
Fossils; souvenirs of WWI & WWII; wedding dresses from 1896-1900

***Miniota:* Miniota Municipal Museum Inc.**
PO Box 59, 110 Stewart Ave., Miniota, MB R0M 1M0
Tel: 204-567-3675; *Fax:* 204-567-3505
Open May - Oct.; pioneer & Aboriginal artifacts
R. Moorehead, President
S. Moorehead, Secretary

***Minnedosa:* Minnedosa Heritage Museum**
PO Box 2005, 100 Heritage Park Cres., Minnedosa, MB R0J 1E0
Tel: 204-867-3542
Local history includes Cadurcis House, Hunterville Church, Havelock School, McManus Trappers' Cabin, Munro Blacksmith Shop, Minnedosa Power House, Hopkins Log Barn & operating windmill & waterwheel; museum open July 1st - Sept. long weekend; group tours by appt.
Earl Thompson, Vice-President, 204/867-2050
Charlie Kingdon, President, 204/867-2027

***Moosehorn:* Moosehorn Heritage Museum Inc.**
PO Box 28, Moosehorn, MB R0C 2E0
Tel: 204-768-3305
Local pioneer history; radar equipment

***Morden:* Canadian Fossil Discovery Centre**
111B Gilmour St., Morden, MB R6M 1N9
Tel: 204-822-3406; *Fax:* 204-272-3303
info@discoverfossils.com
www.discoverfossils.com
Housing an extensive collection of marine reptile fossils, the galleries of the Canadian Fossil Discovery Centre interpret life in the Western Interior Seaway during the cretaceous period. The museum is open year round.
Tyler Schroeder, General Manager, gm@discoverfossils.com
Anita-Maria Janzic, Curator, curator@discoverfossils.com

***Morris:* Morris & District Centennial Museum Inc.**
PO Box 344, Morris, MB R0G 1K0
Tel: 204-746-2169
morrismuseum@mts.net
Exhibits artifacts which depict pioneer life in the Red River Valley
Larry McCrady, Director

***Neepawa:* Beautiful Plains Museum**
PO Box 1732, 91 Hamilton St. West, Neepawa, MB R0J 1H0
Tel: 204-476-3896
www.neepawa.ca/museum
Other contact information: Phone, September - May: 204-476-3232
The Beautiful Plains Museum features the following attractions: a military room; costume rooms; a medical hall; jewellery & general store displays; a post office exhibit; a local history room; office equipment; farm & home tools; information about local lodges; sports memorabilia; information about the local Ukranian Polish culture; & a chapel room, which depicts the history of religious settlement in the Neepawa area. The museum is house in the CNR station, which was built in 1902. Neepawa's Beautiful Plains Museum is open from Victoria Day to Labour Day.

***Neepawa:* The Margaret Laurence Home**
PO Box 2099, 312 - 1st Ave., Neepawa, MB R0J 1H0
Tel: 204-476-3612
mlhome@mts.net
www.mts.net/~mlhome/
Birthplace of Margaret Laurence; includes research area, meeting room & modern artwork; open daily in summer, other times by appt.
Lane England

***Notre Dame de Lourdes:* Pioneers & Chanoinesses Museum / Musée des Pionniers et des Chanoinessess**
PO Box 186, 55 Rogers St., Notre Dame de Lourdes, MB R0G 1M0
Tel: 204-248-2687; *Fax:* 204-248-2049
museend@mts.net
The first pioneers in Notre Dame de Lourdes arrived from Quebec in 1880, & soon after pioneers came from France & Switzerland. The Chanoinesses Regulieres des Cinq-Plaies du Sauveur came to Notre Dame de Lourdes from Lyon, France in 1895. The Pioneers & Chanoinesses Museum houses artifacts of the pioneers & Chanoinesses in the community. The museum is open year round.

***The Pas:* The Sam Waller Museum**
PO Box 185, 306 Fischer Ave., The Pas, MB R9A 1K4
Tel: 204-623-3802; *Fax:* 204-623-5506
samwallermuseum@mts.net
www.samwallermuseum.ca
Permanent collection comprises some 70,000 items of natural history specimens, historical artifacts, books & other library materials, photographs & negatives, fine art objects, & archival resources of the Town of The Pas; temporary exhibits; special events & programming
David Raitt, Director
Sharain Jones, Curator

***Pilot Mound:* Marringhurst Pioneer Park Museum**
PO Box 58, RR#2, Pilot Mound, MB R0G 1P0
Tel: 204-825-2102; *Fax:* 204-825-2391
Schoolhouse with original furnishings; open year round

***Pilot Mound:* Pilot Mound Museum**
Centennial Bldg., PO Box 126, Broadway St., Pilot Mound, MB R0G 1P0
Tel: 204-825-2035
amdata@hotmail.com
Pioneer household & agricultural items; natural history artifacts; open year round

***Plum Coulee:* Plum Coulee & District Museum**
PO Box 36, 277 Main Ave., Plum Coulee, MB R0G 1R0
Tel: 204-829-3419; *Fax:* 204-829-3436
pcoulee@mts.net
Artifacts & photographs portray the Ukrainian, Mennonite, Jewish, & Ukrainian pioneer history of Plum Coulee & the surrounding area. The Plum Coulee & District Museum is open during the summer, or by appointment.

***Portage la Prairie:* The Fort-La-Reine Museum & Pioneer Village**
PO Box 744, 2652 Saskatchewan Ave. East, Portage la Prairie, MB R1N 3C2
Tel: 204-857-3259; *Fax:* 204-239-4917
enquiries@fortlareinemuseum.ca
www.fortlareinemuseum.ca
Depicts native & pioneer life in the 1800s & includes a fort, trading post, village store, country church, schoolhouse, print shop, fire hall, stable, trapper's cabin & several heritage homes;

also includes a railway display of a caboose, 1882 official private railcar of Sir William Van Horne, several maintenance railroad vehicles & railway crossing; Muskateer Aircraft & Allis Chalmers Museum hous
John L. Bjore, Sec.-Manager/Curator

Rapid City: **Rapid City Museum**
PO Box 271, Rapid City, MB R0K 1W0
Tel: 204-826-2043
hhaslen@yahoo.ca
Cundy watch display; Frederick Philip Grove display; old school building; old Rapid City Reporter building with press & back copies; open July & Aug., other times by appt.
Howard Haslen, Contact

Reston: **Reston & District Historical Museum**
PO Box 304, Reston, MB R0M 1X0
Local artifacts & archival material

Riverton: **Hecla Island Heritage Home Museum**
c/o Manitoba Conservation, Riverton, MB R0C 2R0
Tel: 204-279-2056
Depiction of the life of an Icelandic family, 1920-1940s

La Riviere: **Archibald Historical Museum**
Also known as: **Archibald Museum**
PO Box 97, La Riviere, MB R0G 1A0
Tel: 204-242-2825
1878 log house furnished as it was during Nellie McClung's residency plus large frame home (furnished) where she lived, had the first of her family & wrote her first books; also La Rivière C.P.R. Station & more; open mid-May - Labour Day, closed Wed. & Thu. unless by appt.
R.K. Wallcraft, President

Roblin: **Keystone Pioneers Museum Inc.**
PO Box 10, Roblin, MB R0L 1P0
Tel: 204-937-2935
Agricultural equipment & artifacts; Elaschuk House; Makaroff Church; Sawmill
Len Curle, President, 204/934-2602
Gladys Ludwig, Sec.-Treas., 204/937-2863
Art McIntyre, Director

Rossburn: **Rossburn Museum**
c/o Town of Rossburn, PO Box 70, 43 Main St. North, Rossburn, MB R0J 1V0
Tel: 204-859-2762; *Fax:* 204-859-2959
town.rsb@mts.net
www.town.rossburn.mb.ca
The Rossburn Museum features rooms representing a pioneer kitchen, a classroom, a hospital room, a print shop, & a hairdressing salon. The museum also displays a miniature Ukrainian village, plus Ukrainian artifacts.

St Andrews: **Lower Fort Garry National Historic Site of Canada**
5925 Hwy. 9, St Andrews, MB R1A 4A8
Tel: 204-785-6050; *Fax:* 204-482-5887
Toll-Free: 888-773-8888
LFGNHS.Info@pch.gc.ca
pc.gc.ca/garry
1830s stone Hudson's Bay Co. fort; costumed interpreters, visitor centre, gift store, restaurant; open May 15 - Labour Day, daily from 9-5
Tom Kynman, Superintendent

Saint-Boniface: **Le Musée de Saint-Boniface / Saint Boniface Museum**
494, av Taché, Saint-Boniface, MB R2H 2B2
Tél: 204-237-4500; *Téléc:* 204-986-7964
info@msbm.mb.ca
www.msbm.mb.ca
Logé dans l'ancien couvent des Soeurs Grises, le musée a pour mission d'effectuer des recherches sur des objets reliés au patrimoine canadien-français et métis de l'Ouest canadien; préservation et interprétation; expositions thématiques; plus de 30 000 objets historiques et ethnologiques dans la collection; programmation; boutique.
Dr. Philippe R. Mailhot, Directeur
Pierrette Boily, Conservatrice

St Claude: **Manitoba Dairy Museum**
PO Box 131, St Claude, MB R0G 1Z0
Tel: 204-379-2156; *Fax:* 204-379-2156
Artifacts from settlers, many of whom came from France; variety of dairy artifacts
Raymond Philippot, Contact

St George: **Musée St-Georges**
CP 171, St George, MB R0E 1V0
Tél: 204-367-8801
Open May - Sept.
Jean Dupont, Conservateur

St Joseph: **Musée St-Joseph Museum Inc.**
PO Box 8096, St Joseph, MB R0G 2C0
Tel: 204-737-2397; *Fax:* 204-737-2248
stm@stjosephmuseum.org
Domestic & agricultural artifacts; the oldest timber house in southern Manitoba; antique tractors. Open May 15 - Sept. 15
George Perron, Vice-President
Renald Parent, President

Sandy Lake: **Ukrainian Cultural Heritage Museum**
Sandy Lake, MB R0J 1X0
Tel: 204-585-2168
1899 Ukrainian settlement; traditional Ukrainian arts & crafts; open June - Sept. & by appt.
S. Liebing, President
H. Lewandoski, Secretary
M. Solonyczny, Treasurer

Selkirk: **Marine Museum of Manitoba (Selkirk) Inc.**
PO Box 7, 490 Eveline St., Selkirk, MB R1A 2B1
Tel: 204-482-7761
marinemuseum@mts.net
www.marinemuseum.ca
Founded: 1973 The museum gathers and restores marine vessels related to Manitoba's Lake Winnipeg and the Red River from about 1850 to the present. Storehouses of artifacts and records are located aboard historic vessels, including the S.S. Keenora and the C.G.S. Bradbury. Open May - Sept.; school/group tours available.
Ms Shaylene Nordal, Museum Manager
Don Gordon, Chair

Selkirk: **St. Andrews' Rectory National Historic Site**
374 River Rd., Selkirk, MB R1A 2Y1
Tel: 204-785-6050; *Fax:* 204-482-5887
Toll-Free: 800-442-0600
Collection of panels & antiques; open May - Sept.

Seven Sisters: **Whiteshell Natural History Museum**
c/o Manitoba Conservation, Seven Sisters, MB R0E 1Y0
www.gov.mb.ca/conservation/parks/popular_parks/whiteshell
Founded: 1960 Located in the Whiteshell Provincial Park, the natural history museum contains informative displays about the wildlife in the park, the boreal forest, sturgeon & the Winnipeg River, petroforms, & the Aborignal people. The Whiteshell Natural History Museum, located in a log building at Nutimik Lake, is open from the long weekend in May to the long weekend in September.

Shilo: **Royal Canadian Artillery Museum / Le Musée national de l'Artillerie du Canada; Le Musée de l'**
Also known as: **The National Artillery Museum of Canada; The RCA Museum**
CFB Shilo, Shilo, MB R0K 2A0
Tel: 204-765-3000; *Fax:* 204-765-5289
stag@mts.net
www.rcamuseum.com
Three permanent galleries, one temporary exhibits gallery; archives; library; kit shop; 109 major pieces of equipment; largest collection of Canadian military-pattern vehicles; open year round
K. Christensen, Curator
R. Sanderson, Director

Shoal Lake: **The Clack Family Heritage Museum**
c/o Don Yanick, PO Box 568, Shoal Lake, MB R0J 1Z0
Tel: 204-759-2368; *Fax:* 204-759-2484
dsyanick@inethome.ca
www.shoallake.ca/prairiemountain
Antique cars, tractors, trucks & farm implements; Victorian china & clothing; railway, RCMP military & native artifacts; open June-Sept.

Shoal Lake: **Clegg Carriage Museum**
c/o Prairie Mountain Regional Museums Collection Inc., PO Box 568, Shoal Lake, MB R0J 1Z0
Tel: 204-759-2368; *Fax:* 204-759-2484
dsyanick@inethome.ca
www.shoallake.ca/prairiemountain; www.museumsmanitoba.com
Located 3 miles south of Hwy #24 in Arrow River; collection of 90 completely restored horse-drawn vehicles, including a WW1 ambulance, a covered wagon, peddlar's wagon and hearse
Don Yanick, President, Prairie Mountain Regional Museums Collection Inc.

Shoal Lake: **Shoal Lake Police & Pioneer Museum**
PO Box 233, Shoal Lake, MB R0J 1Z0
Tel: 204-759-2429; *Fax:* 204-759-2704
Other contact information: Summer phone: 204/759-3326
A replica of an 1875 NWMP building; it houses a collection of North West Mounted Police & Royal Canadian Mounted Police displays; official Museum for the Mounted Police in Manitoba; open June-Sept. by summer staff, other times by appt.; school talks & presentations available
Ewen Booth, Museum Manager
Barb Pettinger, Secretary/Treasurer

Snowflake: **Star Mound School Museum Park**
General Delivery, Snowflake, MB R0G 2K0
Tel: 204-876-4749
One-room country school c. 1886

Souris: **Hillcrest Museum**
PO Box 662, Souris, MB R0K 2C0
Tel: 204-483-2008
souris.cimnet.ca
Includes agricultural museum & CPR caboose; open May - Sept.; collection of over 5000 butterflies on display
Donna Russell, President
Laura Horn, Secretary

Ste Anne des Chênes: **Musée Pointe des Chênes**
208 Centrale Ave., Ste Anne des Chênes, MB R5H 1C9
Tel: 204-422-5639; *Fax:* 204-422-5514
Situated in a park next to the Villa Youville; museum features old pioneer artifacts of the region
Louis Bernardin, Responsable

Steinbach: **Mennonite Heritage Village (Canada) Inc.**
231 PTH 12 N, Steinbach, MB R5G 1T8
Tel: 204-326-9661; *Fax:* 204-326-5046
Toll-Free: 866-280-8741
info@mhv.ca
www.mennoniteheritagevillage.com
Includes J.J. Reimer Historical Library & Archives; historical village with traditional housebarns, semlin, blacksmith shop, printery, general store, operating windmill, farm fields, exihibition gallery; livery barn restaurant serving ethnic Mennonite food; library; gift shop; special events throughout the summer; educational programming; online bookstore on the website. Open May through September.
Barry Dyck, Executive Director, barryd@mhv.ca
Dr. Roland Sawatzky, Senior Curator, rolands@mhv.ca
John Milinkovic, Manager, Fundraising, johnm@mhv.ca
Anne Toews, Program Director, annet@mhv.ca

St-Malo: **Le Musée Pionnier St Malo**
PO Box 328, Hwy. 59 South, St-Malo, MB R0A 1T0
Tel: 204-347-5102; *Fax:* 204-347-5307
pmaynard@conexe.ca
Depiction of early settlers' lives

Stonewall: **Stonewall Quarry Park**
PO Box 250, Stonewall, MB R0C 2Z0
Tel: 204-467-5354; *Fax:* 204-467-5260
stoneqp@stonewall.ca
www.stonewall.ca
Exhibits pertain to the limestone quarries & their role in the development of the community of Stonewall

St-Pierre-Jolys: **Musée de St-Pierre-Jolys**
CP 321, 432, rue Joubert nord, St-Pierre-Jolys, MB R0A 1V0
Tél: 204-433-7635
froy@hsd.ca
www.museestpierrejolys.ca
Le musée est un ancien couvent et sert à se rappeler le patrimoine et les contributions des religieuses au développement du village de Saint-Pierre-Jolys; on retrouve aussi la Maison Goulet, et un cabane à sucre.

Strathclair: **Strathclair Museum**
PO Box 383, Main St., Strathclair, MB R0J 2C0
Tel: 204-365-5201
www.museumsmanitoba.com/dir/western/68.html
In a restored CPR station and residence, the museum contains material relating to the district, which includes geneaology and information on Lord Elphinstone; replica blacksmith shop and machine shed; Open July & August or by appt.
Helga Gerrard, Sec.-Treas.

Swan River: **Swan Valley Historical Museum & Archives**
PO Box 2078, Swan River, MB R0L 1Z0
Tel: 204-734-3585
History of Swan River Valley, Ice Age to settlement; open mid-May - mid-Sept.; archives open by appt. Tues. 9-2, summer
Niel Brown, President
Gwen Palmer, Secretary

Teulon: **Teulon & District Museum**
PO Box 44, Teulon, MB R0C 3B0
Tel: 204-886-2098; *Fax:* 204-886-3787
jtrombo@mts.net
Site includes a log house, a caboose, two schoolhouses, a small church, a large machine shed, old shoe shop, outside bake oven & the Dr. Hunter Home, 1918 Ford car, doll house with over 300 dolls; open June - Sept., Tues. to Sun., or by appt.
Joan Trombo, Treasurer

Thompson: **Heritage North Museum**
162 Princeton Dr., Thompson, MB R8N 2A4
Tel: 204-677-2216; *Fax:* 204-677-8953
hnmuseum@mts.net
www.heritagenorthmuseum.ca

Founded: 1990 The museum preserves the heritage & history of Thompson & area, where in 1956 nickel was discovered. One of the log buildings displays a taxidermy array of animals native to the region, hides, furs and fossils, while the other building focuses on the mining industry. There is a gift shop.
Tanna Teneycke, Executive Director
Sharon McLeod, President
Valerie Little, Vice-President

***Treherne:* Treherne Museum**
PO Box 30, 183 Vanzile St., Treherne, MB R0G 1H0
Tel: 204-723-2621

***Virden:* Currahee Military Museum**
PO Box 729, Virden, MB R0M 2C0
Tel: 204-748-1461; *Fax:* 204-748-1805
john@wolverinesupplies.com
Open by appt. only
John Hipwell

***Virden:* Pioneer Home Museum of Virden & District**
***Also known as:* Virden Pioneer Home Museum Inc.**
PO Box 29, 390 King St. West, Virden, MB R0M 2C0
Tel: 204-748-1659
virden.cimnet.ca/cim/187C1_4T421T3T168.dhtm
Open summer daily
F. Eleanor McIntosh, Secretary
Helen Boulton-Elliott, President

***Virden:* River Valley School Museum**
PO Box 2048, Virden, MB R0M 2C0
Tel: 204-748-3920; *Fax:* 204-748-3920
Country school furnishings & library 1896-1955
Lawrence Anderson, President
Alene R. Welch, Treasurer

***Wabowden:* Wabowden Historical Museum**
c/o Wabowden Community Council, PO Box 130, Wabowden, MB R0B 1S0
Tel: 204-689-2362; *Fax:* 204-689-2355
wabcouncil@digistar.mb.ca
wabowden.cimnet.ca/cim/83C150_239T6744T238T613 6.dhtm
The Wabowden Historical Museum preserves & displays artifacts from Wabowden & the surrounding region, such as mining, logging, fishing, & trapping items. The museum is open from Canada Day until the Labour Day weekend.

***Wasagaming:* Riding Mountain Historical Society & Pinewood Museum**
PO Box 254, Wasagaming, MB R0J 2H0
Tel: 204-848-2310
Records & preserves the history of humans in the Riding Mountain National Park; open daily 2-5pm in July & Aug.
Cathy Chalmers, President

***Wasagaming:* Riding Mountain National Park of Canada (RMNPC) / Parc national du Canada du Mont-Riding**
General Delivery, Wasagaming, MB R0J 2H0
Tel: 204-848-7275; *Fax:* 204-848-2596
rmnp.info@pc.gc.ca
www.pc.gc.ca/ridingmountain
Other contact information: TDD: 1-866-787-6221; E-mail, Friends of RMNP: friends.rmnp@pc.gc.ca
The Riding Mountain National Park of Canada covers 3,000 km2 of the Manitoba prairie & escarpment. The park provides a variety of school & interpretation programs. The Visitor Centre is open from mid May to mid October.
Scot Shellborn, Officer, Visitor Experiences, 204-848-7284

***Waskada:* Waskada Museum**
c/o Village of Waskada, PO Box 40, 103 - 2nd St., Waskada, MB R0M 2E0
Tel: 204-673-2503
www.waskada.ca/pages/Museum.htm
Other contact information: Phone, Appointments: 204-673-2557
The Waskada Museum features the following buildings: the 1914 Anglican Church, the 1906 Union (Royal) Bank, a 1927 blacksmith shop, the 1896 Menota country school, a vehicle display building, & a display building. The museum is open during July & August.

***Wawanesa:* Sipiweske Museum**
PO Box 116, 102 - 4th St., Wawanesa, MB R0K 2G0
Tel: 204-824-2289; *Fax:* 204-824-2008
wawanesacap@yahoo.com
www.wawanesa.ca/Sipiweske Museum.htm
Memorabilia from pioneers, Nellie McClung, Native people & 1903 insurance company; open July-Aug.; by appointment other times

***Whitemouth:* Whitemouth Municipal Museum**
PO Box 294, Whitemouth, MB R0E 2G0
Tel: 204-348-2641; *Fax:* 204-348-7731
Museum depicting the different ways of life in the area - farming, railway, forestry, trapping, peat moss plants, hydro, AECL, fishing, brickyard, flour mill; artifacts housed in six buildings & two pole sheds; cairn honouring Dr. Charlotte Ross (The Iron Rose), first female to practice medicine in Manitoba; turn of the century house; 1905 Anglican Church; CPR Caboose; seasonal hours.
Sheilagh Wardrop, Secretary
Gloria Henderson, Treasurer
David King, President

***Winkler:* Pembina Threshermen's Museum Inc.**
PO Box 1103, Winkler, MB R6W 4B2
Tel: 204-325-7497; *Fax:* 204-331-3733
info@threshermensmuseum.com
www.threshermensmuseum.com
The Pembina Threshermen's Museum preserves the area's agricultural & Mennonite heritage. The grounds of the museum feature several heritage buildings, such as the 1909 Pomeroy School, the 1905-1906 Morden CPR Sation, an 1885 log house, plus a sawmill, windmill, blacksmith shop, barbershop, & post office. The museum is open from the beginning of May to the end of September.

***Winnipeg:* Air Force Heritage Museum & Air Park / Le Musée du patrimoine de la force aérienne et du parc aéri**
1 Canadian Air Division Headquarters, PO Box 17000 Forces, 17 Wing, Winnipeg, MB R3J 3Y5
Tel: 204-833-2500; *Fax:* 204-833-2512
pearsons@mts.net
www.airforce.dnd.ca
The museum, located in the Billy Bishop building, is part of a complex that consists of an outdoor air park showcasing 14 aircraft. The air park is open year round. Museum is open daily Mon-Fri throughout the summer from 8:00-4:00 BY APPOINTMENT. Guided tours, with services in English and French; wheelchair accessible; food service and restrooms. Located on Air Force Way, north off Ness Ave. on Sharp Blvd.
Maj. Guy Trudeau, Contact
Don Pearsons, Contact

***Winnipeg:* Aquatic Hall of Fame & Museum of Canada, Inc.**
25 Poseidon Way, Winnipeg, MB R3M 3E4
Tel: 204-986-5890
Aquatic art & memorabilia on display; Olympics, Commonwealth, Pan-Am & posters; open year round
Vaughan L. Baird, President/Chair

***Winnipeg:* Costume Museum of Canada**
109 Pacific Ave., Winnipeg, MB R3B 0M1
Tel: 204-989-0072; *Fax:* 204-853-2077
Toll-Free: 866-853-2166
info@costumemuseum.com
www.costumemuseum.com
Over 35,000 artifacts spanning over 400 years; collection of costumes, textiles & related accessories
Brenda Hamer, Curator
Garth Rogerson, Executive Director

***Winnipeg:* Dalnavert Museum**
61 Carlton St., Winnipeg, MB R3C 1N7
Tel: 204-943-2835; *Fax:* 204-943-2565
dalnavert@mhs.mb.ca
www.mhs.mb.ca/info/museums/dalnavert/index.shtml
1895 restored Victorian home of Hugh John Macdonald, son of Sir John A. Macdonald
Tim Worth, Curator

***Winnipeg:* Fort Garry Horse Regimental Museum & Archives Inc.**
c/o McGregor Armoury, 551 Machray Ave., Winnipeg, MB R2W 1A8
Tel: 204-586-6298; *Fax:* 204-582-0370
museum12009@fortgarryhorse.ca
www.fortgarryhorse.ca
Depicts the history of the Fort Garry Horse from 1912 to present; open Mon. evenings 7:30-10:30; other times by appt.
Larry Lajeunesse, Chair

***Winnipeg:* Fort Whyte Centre**
1961 McCreary Rd., Winnipeg, MB R3P 2K9
Tel: 204-989-8355; *Fax:* 204-895-4700
info@fortwhyte.org
www.fortwhyte.org
74 hectares of lakes, marshes aspen parkland for environmental education; exhibit building

***Winnipeg:* 402 Squadron Association**
PO Box 42202 St. James, Winnipeg, MB R3J 0X7
Tel: 204-786-5503
Archives, photographs of #402 City of Winnipeg Squadron
Jim Bell, Director

***Winnipeg:* Historical Museum of St. James-Assiniboia**
3180 Portage Ave., Winnipeg, MB R3K 0Y5
Tel: 204-888-8706
bonitah@mts.net
Open year round

***Winnipeg:* Ivan Franko Museum**
200 Mc Gregor St., 595 Pritchard Ave., Winnipeg, MB R2W 2K4
Tel: 204-589-4397; *Fax:* 204-589-3404
History of Ivan Franko, Ukrainian poet, novelist, and social activist & Ukrainian pintings; ceramics, woodcarving, glassware, embroidery, and weaving.

***Winnipeg:* J.B. Wallis Museum of Entomology**
Dept. of Entomology, University of Manitoba, Winnipeg, MB R3T 2N2
Tel: 204-474-9257; *Fax:* 204-474-7628
head_entomo@umanitoba.ca
250,000 species of insects

***Winnipeg:* Manitoba Children's Museum**
The Forks, 45 Forks Market Rd., Kinsmen Building, Winnipeg, MB R3C 4T6
Tel: 204-924-4000; *Fax:* 204-956-2122
general@childrensmuseum.com
www.childrensmuseum.com
Founded: 1983 Catering to children, the site includes such hands-on exhibits as a 1950s train station with CNR diesel locomotive. Open daily, year round.
Diane Doth, Executive Director

***Winnipeg:* Manitoba Crafts Museum & Library**
#1B, 183 Kennedy St., Winnipeg, MB R3C 1S6
Tel: 204-487-6117
mcml1@mts.net
www.mts.net/~mcml
Founded: 1986 The museum's collection focuses on the development of Canadian, and particularly Manitoban, crafts since the 1920s. The library houses about 2,500 titles pertaining to crafts, including scrapbooks and design patterns. Open year round
Ms Andrea Reichert, Curator

***Winnipeg:* Manitoba Electrical Museum & Education Centre**
PO Box 815, 680 Harrow St., Winnipeg, MB R3C 2P4
Tel: 204-477-7905
www.hydro.mb.ca/about_us/electrical_museum.shtml
Founded: 1971 The museum explores the history of electricity in Manitoba from the 1800s. Exhibits include archival photographs, documents and electrical artifacts, including vintage household appliances and an electric streetcar. In the lower level is an interactive section with Hazard Hamlet where, children can learn about potentially hazardous situations if electricity is not used properly.

***Winnipeg:* Manitoba Sports Hall of Fame & Museum Inc. (MSHOF)**
Offices, #210, 200 Main St., Winnipeg, MB R3C 4M2
Tel: 204-925-5736; *Fax:* 204-925-5792
halloffame@sport.mb.ca
www.halloffame.mb.ca
Founded: 1993 The museum aims to honour those people who have contributed significantly to Manitoba's rich sports history. The exhibits use various memorabilia and photos to cover such sports as athletics, basketball, baseball/softball, curling, football, golf, hockey, and the Winter Olympics. The museum is closed until Nov., 2010, when it will open in a new location at in the Sport for Life Centre, 145 Pacific Ave.
Rick D. Brownlee, Sport Heritage Manager, Sport Manitoba

***Winnipeg:* Ogniwo Polish Museum Society Inc.**
1417 Main St., Winnipeg, MB R2W 3V3
Tel: 204-586-5070
ogniwo@mb.sympatico.ca
Artifacts related to Polish immigrants in Canada; open year round
Christine Tabbernor

***Winnipeg:* Queen's Own Cameron Highlanders of Canada Regimental Museum Inc.**
Minto Armoury, #230, 969 St. Matthew's Ave., Winnipeg, MB R3G 0J7
Tel: 204-786-4330
Regimental dress, equipment & archives from 1910 to present

***Winnipeg:* Riel House National Historic Site of Canada / Parc historique national du Canada de la Maison-Riel**
PO Box 73, Winnipeg, MB R2M 4A5
Tel: 204-257-1783; *Fax:* 204-254-8331
Riel family home, depicts life of Métis family in St. Vital during the 1880s; open daily mid-May - Labour Day
Vania Gagnon

***Winnipeg:* Ross House Museum**
Joe Zuken Heritage Park, 140 Meade St. North, Winnipeg, MB R2W 3K5
Tel: 204-943-3958
rosshouse@mhs.mb.ca
www.mhs.mb.ca
Ross House was the first post office in western Canada. It is now a museum, owned by the City of Winnipeg & operated by the Manitoba Historical Society. The museum depicts the

operation of early postal service & the life of the Ross family around 1850. Ross House is open from the beginning of June to the end of August. Schools & large groups may arrange appointments at other times of the year.
Dr. Simon Lucy, Chair, Ross House Community Committee
Victor Sawelo, Museum Manager

***Winnipeg:* Royal Canadian Mint - Winnipeg Facility**
520 Lagimodiere Blvd., Winnipeg, MB R2J 3E7
Tel: 204-983-6400; *Fax:* 204-255-5203
www.mint.ca
Tours of the mint available year round; call for reservations
Christian Robin, Supervisor, Tour Operations, robin@mint.ca

***Winnipeg:* Royal Winnipeg Rifles Regimental Museum**
Minto Armoury, #208, 969 St. Matthews Ave., Winnipeg, MB R3G 0J7
Tel: 204-786-4300; *Fax:* 204-786-4384
riflesmuseum@shaw.ca
www.mts.net
Founded: 1970 Collects & preserves the history of the Regiment, & also houses displays relevant to the Winnipeg Light Infantry & the Winnipeg Grenadiers; military artifacts & memorabilia, pictures, books & other documents; open Tues. & by appt.; closed Sat. June - Aug
Dave Wawryk, Archivist
Win Anders, Curator

***Winnipeg:* St. Norbert Provincial Heritage Park**
PO Box 53, 200 Saulteaux Cres., Winnipeg, MB R3J 3W3
Tel: 204-945-4375; *Fax:* 204-945-0012
kporteous@gov.mb.ca
manitobaparks.com
Illustrates how a natural landscape used for hunting, fishing & camping by Aboriginal peoples evolved into a French-speaking Métis settlement, then a French-Canadian agricultural community of the pre-World War I period; guided tours of restored Turenne & Bohémier houses; open daily May long weekend to Labour Day weekend.
Ken Porteous

***Winnipeg:* St. Vital Historical Society**
600 St. Mary's Rd., Winnipeg, MB R2M 3L5
Tel: 204-255-2864; *Fax:* 204-256-6892
info@svhs.ca
www.svhs.ca/
Educational centre, bringing "the history of St. Vital" to the community by way of shows & displays; museum holds artifacts
Lorna Miner, President

***Winnipeg:* Sandilands Forest Centre**
c/o The Manitoba Forestry Association, 900 Corydon Ave., Winnipeg, MB R3M 0Y4
Tel: 204-453-3182; *Fax:* 204-477-5765
mfainc@mts.net
www.mbforestryassoc.ca
The Centre is sited on 122 hectares of land granted to the Manitoba Forestry Ass'n, and located near Hadashville, just south of the Trans Canada Hwy, east of Winnipeg; information on biodiversity, forest ecology, sustainable management of forest resources, fire prevention and management; nature trails, museum, fire tower & picnic area; educational programming; commemorative tree planting
Bill Baker, Education Director

***Winnipeg:* Seven Oaks House Museum**
PO Box 25176, 1650 Main St., Winnipeg, MB R2V 4C8
Tel: 204-339-7429; *Fax:* 204-334-8516
Seven Oaks House is a log residence, which was built between 1851 & 1853. It has been restored to reflect life during the Red River settlement in the 19th century. The museum is open from mid May to Labour Day.

***Winnipeg:* Stewart Hay Memorial Museum**
Duff Roblin Bldg., Dept. of Zoology, University of Manitoba, Winnipeg, MB R3T 2N2
Tel: 204-474-9245; *Fax:* 204-474-7588
hann@ms.umanitoba.ca
Mounted & study specimens of mammals, birds, fish, reptiles, amphibians, crustaceans, mollusks & other invertebrates; casts of fossils; open year round

***Winnipeg:* Transcona Historical Museum**
141 Regent Ave. West, Winnipeg, MB R2C 1R1
Tel: 204-222-0423; *Fax:* 204-222-0208
info@transconamuseum.mb.ca
www.transconamuseum.mb.ca
Archives, photographs, rare books, reference files, natural history (including an 8,000 specimen lepidoptera collection), First Nations cultural artifacts (3,500 items), Euro-Canadian cultural artifacts & a clothing & textile collection
Alanna Horejda, Curator

***Winnipeg:* Ukrainian Cultural & Educational Centre**
***Also known as:* Oseredok Archives and Museum**
184 Alexander Ave. East, Winnipeg, MB R3B 0L6
Tel: 204-942-0218; *Fax:* 204-943-2857
uce@mts.net
www.oseredok.org
Library & historical & archival collections dealing with the history of Ukrainians in Canada & the history of Ukraine; open Tues. - Sat. year round

***Winnipeg:* University of Manitoba: Fitzgerald Study Collection**
School of Art, Fitzgerald Bldg., Main Fl., Winnipeg, MB R3T 2N2
Tel: 204-474-9367
Papers, drawings & watercolours of L.L. Fitzgerald; open year round

***Winnipeg:* University of Winnipeg Geography Museum**
515 Portage Ave., Winnipeg, MB R3B 2E9
Tel: 204-786-9485; *Fax:* 204-774-4134
kmonson@uwinnipeg.ca
Teaching & reference collection of rocks, minerals & fossils, with a Manitoba focus; open year round

***Winnipeg:* UVAN Historical Museum & Archives**
#203, 456 Main St., Winnipeg, MB R3B 1B6
Tel: 204-942-5861
Historical, ethnological & archival material

***Winnipeg:* Western Canada Aviation Museum (WCAM) / Musée de l'aviation de l'ouest du Canada**
Hangar T-2, 958 Ferry Rd., Winnipeg, MB R3H 0Y8
Tel: 204-786-5503; *Fax:* 204-775-4761
info@wcam.mb.ca; events@wcam.mb.ca
www.wcam.mb.ca
Other contact information: E-mail, School Tours: programs@wcam.mb.ca; Gifts: giftshop@wcam.mb.ca
The Western Canada Aviation Museum's recovery & restoration department works to prepare aircraft for display. The museum features sights such as Canada's first helicopter, bushplanes, historic military jets, & commercial aircraft. The museum also contains an aviation reference library, with collections of books, magazines, manuals, photographs, drawings, & audio-visual materials. The library is open to the public by appointment. The museum is open year-round.

***Winnipeg:* Winnipeg Police Museum**
PO Box 1680, 130 Allard Ave., Winnipeg, MB R3C 2Z7
Tel: 204-986-3976
wps-museum@winnipeg.ca
www.winnipeg.ca
Founded: 1974 The Winnipeg Police Museum exhibits items related to the Winnipeg Police Force, which formed in 1874. Objects on display include early handcuffs,& identification cameras, & a jail cell which was built in 1911. There are also exhibits surrounding the 1919 Winnipeg General Strike & Earle "The Strangler" Nelson. Located at the Winnipeg Police Academy, the Winnipeg Police Museum is open daily. Conducted group tours can be arranged.

***Winnipeg Beach:* Winnipeg Beach Ukrainian Homestead**
PO Box 396, Winnipeg Beach, MB R0C 3G0
Tel: 204-389-4079
Artifacts of Ukrainian origin & tradition; historic house with furnishings; clay-bake oven; grist mill; open weekends Victoria Day - July 1; daily, July 1 - Labour Day weekend; closed Wed.
Vic Siran

***Winnipegosis:* Winnipegosis Museum**
Winnipegosis, MB R0L 2G0
Tel: 204-656-4791; *Fax:* 204-656-4947
Housed in former CNR Railway Station (c.1897); 65-foot freighter, the "Myrtle M"; artifacts; CNR historical material; War Memorial items; native handiwork
Edna Medd, Curator

***Woodlands:* Woodlands Pioneer Museum**
General Delivery, Woodlands, MB R0C 3H0
Tel: 204-383-5554
Post office; municipal office; doctor's office; church; school; log house; open July-Aug.

New Brunswick

Provincial Museums

Kings Landing Historical Settlement
20 Kings Landing Rd., Kings Landing Historical, NB E6K 3W3
Tel: 506-363-4999; *Fax:* 506-363-4989
info@kingslanding.nb.ca
www.kingslanding.nb.ca
Historical settlement on the St. John River with more than 100 costumed interpreters depicting rural life from 1790-1910; 65,000 artifacts; open June - Oct.

Musée Acadien (MAUM)
c/o Pavillon Clément-Cormier, Université de Moncton, Moncton, NB E1A 3E9
Tél: 506-858-4088; *Téléc:* 506-858-4043
maum@umoncton.ca
www.umoncton.ca/maum
Founded: 1886 Le plus ancien musée acadien au monde est fondé par le père Camille Lefebvre. La collection dépasse 35,000 objets et photographies et représente tous les aspects de la vie acadienne. Exposition permanente; expositions temporaires; expositions virtuelles.
Isabelle Cormier, Directrice
Nicole LeBlanc, Secrétaire administrative
Jeanne Mance Cormier, Conservatrice
Bernard LeBlanc, Conservateur

New Brunswick Museum (NBM/MNB) / Musée du Nouveau-Brunswick
277 Douglas Ave., Saint John, NB E2K 1E5
Tel: 506-643-2300; *Fax:* 506-643-2360
Toll-Free: 888-268-9595
nbmuseum@nbm-mnb.ca
www.nbm-mnb.ca
Founded: 1934 Collections at the provincial museum of New Brunswick include human history, marine & technology, prints, fine & decorative arts, botany, zoology, & geology; A full range of exhibitions & programs are offered daily; Closed Christmas Day & Good Friday
Jane Fullerton, Director & Chief Executive Officer, 506-643-2346

Local Museums in New Brunswick

***Aulac:* Fort Beauséjour National Historic Site**
111 Fort Beauséjour Rd., Aulac, NB E4L 2W5
Tel: 506-364-5080; *Fax:* 506-536-4399
fort.beausejour@pc.gc.ca
www.pc.gc.ca/lhn-nhs/nb/beausejour/index_E.asp
Built in 1751 by the French; star-shaped fort overlooking the Bay of Fundy
Pierrette Robichaud, Manager

***Boiestown:* Central New Brunswick Woodmen's Museum Inc.**
6342 Rte. 8, Boiestown, NB E6A 1Z5
Tel: 506-369-7214; *Fax:* 506-369-9081
woodmen@nb.aibn.com
www.woodmenmuseum.com
Founded: 1979 16 exhibit buildings, depicts life of Central New Brunswick lumberjack & culture of Miramichi people
Megan Scammell, Executive Director

***Caraquet:* Musée Acadien de Caraquet/Caraquet Acadian Museum**
15, boul St-Pierre est, Caraquet, NB E1W 1B6
Tél: 506-726-2682; *Téléc:* 506-726-2660
Promotes the history & culture of the Acadian people from the Acadian Peninsula using its own collection as well as other collections & regional archives
Mrs. Graham LeBlanc, Trésorière

***Clair:* Société historique de Clair Inc.**
724, rue Principale, Clair, NB E7A 2H4
Tel: 506-992-3637; *Fax:* 506-992-6247
sochclair@nb.aibn.com
Museum & historic site guided tours; Beaux-arts, Historie humaine; visites guidées; open June to Labour Day
Betty Levasseur, Président
Lyne Bard, Trésorière

***Connors:* Connors Museum**
3614 Rte. 205, Connors, NB E7A 1S3
Tel: 506-992-2500; *Fax:* 506-992-2500
armandb@nb.sympatico.ca
Items used in general store; blacksmith shop; Victorian mansion
Rachel Bernier, Director

***Dalhousie:* Musée Restigouche Regional Museum**
115 George St., Dalhousie, NB E8C 1R6
Tel: 506-684-7490; *Fax:* 506-684-7613
qurrm@nbnet.nb.ca
Local history museum, archives, gallery
Bill Clarke, Director

***Doaktown:* Atlantic Salmon Museum**
***Also known as:* Miramichi Salmon Museum**
263 Main St., Doaktown, NB E9C 1A9
Tel: 506-365-7787; *Fax:* 506-365-7359
museum@nbnet.nb.ca
www.atlanticsalmonmuseum.com
Founded: 1982 Through interpretive displays, the Atlantic Salmon Museum shows the history of the life of the Atlantic salmon, as well as the cultural & economic value of the Atlantic salmon to the Miramichi River & New Brunswick. Conservation is also emphasized. The museum is open from June to October. Appointments for rentals can be made during other times.

Linda Gaston, Executive Director

***Doaktown:* Doak House Historic Site**
386 Main St., Doaktown, NB E9C 1E4
Tel: 506-453-2324; *Fax:* 506-453-2416
guy.tremblay@gnb.ca
Open end June - Early Sept.
Glen Harding, Site Manager

***Dorchester:* Dorchester Heritage Properties Committee**
#5, 3497 Cape Rd., Dorchester, NB E4K 2X2
Tel: 506-379-6633; *Fax:* 506-379-3033
Toll-Free: 800-822-6633
keillorhouse@nb.aibn.com
www.keillorhousemuseum.com
Operating: The Keillor House (Westmorland Centennial Museum, c. 1813), 506/379-6633; open June - Sept. or by appt.; Bell Inn (c.1811), 506/379-2580; open Apr. - Oct.; St. James Presbyterian Church Museum, 506/379-6633; Beachkirk Collection (c. 1884); open June - Sept. or by appt.; The Maritime Penetentiary Museum, 506/379-6633; open June - Sept.
Alice Folkins, Manager

***Edmundston:* Antique Automobile Museum**
35, Principale St., Edmundston, NB E7B 1V6
Tél: 506-737-2637
Open June - Sept.
Jocelyne Michaud

***Edmundston:* Musée historique du Madawaska**
195, boul Hébert, Edmundston, NB E3V 2S8
Tel: 506-737-5282; *Fax:* 506-737-5373
Gilbert Lavoie, Director

***Fredericton:* Brydone Jack Observatory Museum**
University of New Brunswick, PO Box 4400, Fredericton, NB E3B 5A3
Tel: 506-453-4723
The first astronomical observatory in Canada was built in 1851. The building is now a Nnational Historic Site & a museum on the campus of the University of New Brunswick. It houses tools & equipment used by Dr. William Brydone Jack, who was a professor of mathematics, natural philosophy, & astronomy.

***Fredericton:* Electrical Engineering Museum**
University of New Brunswick, Dept. of Electrical Engineering, Fredericton, NB E3B 5A3
Tel: 506-453-4561; *Fax:* 506-453-3589

***Fredericton:* Guard House & Soldiers' Barracks**
c/o Fredericton Tourism, PO Box 130, 11 Carleton St., Fredericton, NB E3B 4Y7
Tel: 506-460-2041; *Fax:* 506-460-2474
Toll-Free: 888-888-4768
tourism@fredericton.ca
www.tourismfredericton.ca
Historic military buildings 1828-1866

***Fredericton:* New Brunswick Sports Hall of Fame / Temple de la renommée sportive du Nouveau-Brunswick**
PO Box 6000, 503 Queen St., Fredericton, NB E3B 5H1
Tel: 506-453-3747; *Fax:* 506-459-0481
deborah.williams@gnb.ca
www.nbsportshalloffame.nb.ca
Open year round, hours vary; recognizes, collects, preserves, exhibits & promotes New Brunswick's sports heroes & sports heritage. Street address is 503 rue Queen St., Frederiction, NB, E3B 1B8.
Jamie Wolverton, Executive Director, jamie.wolverton@gnb.ca
Deborah Williams, Executive Assistant, deborah.williams@gnb.ca
Kelly Ross, Curator/Exhibits Director, curator@gnb.ca

***Fredericton:* Old Government House**
PO Box 6000, 51 Woodstock Rd., Fredericton, NB E3B 5H1
Tel: 506-453-2505; *Fax:* 506-453-2416
ogh@gnb.ca
www.gnb.ca/lg/ogh/index-e.asp
Constructed from 1826 to 1828, Government House was the residence of New Brunswick's Governors & Lieutenant-Governors. Government House also served as a school for hearing impaired students, a military barracks during World War I, a hospital for returning soldiers, & an RCMP headquarters. Since 1999, the House has been open to the public, featuring restored rooms, exhibits, & bilingual tours during the summer. Government House still contains the Lieutenant-Governor's office & residence.

***Fredericton:* 'School Days' Museum**
PO Box 752, Fredericton, NB E3B 5R6
Tel: 506-459-3738; *Fax:* 506-459-3738
sdmuseum@nb.sympatico.ca
museum.nbta.ca
NB's educational heritage from 19th century; located in Justice Bldg. ANNEX, off Queen St.; artifacts pertaining to NB schools & teacher training
David McCormack, President

***Fredericton:* Wulastook Museums**
PO Box 700, 108 Queen St., Fredericton, NB E3B 5B4
Tel: 506-451-7777; *Fax:* 506-451-1029
Francis Atkinson, Owner

***Fredericton:* York Sunbury Museum**
PO Box 1312, Fredericton, NB E3B 5C8
Tel: 506-455-6041; *Fax:* 506-458-8741
yorksun@nbnet.nb.ca

***Fredericton Junction:* Currie House**
110 Currie Lane, Fredericton Junction, NB E5L 1X7
Tel: 506-368-2818; *Fax:* 506-368-1900
ddupl@nbnet.nb.ca
www.tourismnewbrunswick.ca/en-CA/Product/Museum.htm?pi d=401
Museum with displays of antiques and artifacts, history of area and local families. Large picnic area, nature trails through woods and by river.
Don Duplisea, Contact, 506-368-2818, Fax: 506-422-1223, ddupl@nbnet.nb.ca

***Gagetown:* Queens County Museum**
69 Front St., Gagetown, NB E5M 1A4
Tel: 506-488-2966
Gagetown's Queens County Museum is located in the Tilley Home, which was the home of Sir Leonard Tilley, a Father of Confederation, & the 1836 Queens County Courthouse. The museum contains furnishings of the Loyalist & Victorian periods, plus historical exhibits. It is open from mid June to mid September.

***Grand Falls:* Grand Falls Museum / Musée de Grand-Sault**
#103, 142 Court St., Grand Falls, NB E3Z 2R2
Tel: 506-473-5265; *Fax:* 506-473-7160
Local artifacts; Extensive collection of church records, genealogies, etc.; Open mid-June to end of Aug. or by appt.
Patrick McCooey, President

***Grand Manan:* Grand Manan Museum**
1141 Rte. 776, Grand Manan, NB E0G 1X0
Tel: 506-662-3524
gmadmin@grandmananmuseum.ca
www.grandmananmuseum.ca
Open June - Sept.; in winter by appt.

***Grand-Anse:* Musée des Papes**
184 Acadie St., Grand-Anse, NB E8N 1A6
Tel: 506-732-3003; *Fax:* 506-732-5491
museedespapes@nb.aibn.com
Relates the evolution of Christianity to the present religious congregations; open mid-June to end of Aug.
Edmond Landry, Directeur

***Hampton:* Kings County Museum**
c/o Kings County Historical & Archival Society Inc., PO Box 1813, 27 Centennial Rd., Hampton, NB E5N 6N3
Tel: 506-832-6009; *Fax:* 506-832-6409
kingscm@nbnet.nb.ca
www3.nbnet.nb.ca/kingscm
Founded: 1968 Artifacts include textiles, clothing, china, guns, glassware, military, royalty, art & archival material
A. Faye Pearson, Director

***Hillsborough:* Hon. William Henry Steeves House**
40 Mill St., Hillsborough, NB E4H 2Z8
Tel: 506-734-3102; *Fax:* 506-734-3452
steevesmuseum@nb.aibn.com
www.steeveshousemuseum.ca
Founded: 1971 Operated by Heritage Hillsborough Inc.; birthplace of William Henry Steeves, a Father of Confederation; open every day July 1 to Labour Day
Lois Snider, President

***Hillsborough:* New Brunswick Railway Museum**
2847 Main St., Hillsborough, NB E4H 2X7
Tel: 506-734-3195; *Fax:* 506-734-3711
info@nbrm.ca
www.nbrm.ca/en/index.shtml
Founded: 1993 Dedicated to preserving the history of train travel in New Brunswick, the museum has on site an extensive collection of full-sized railway cars. This is the province's only operating railway museum, with excursion trains 4 days a week along the Petitcodiac River & southeastern New Brunswick. Displays of equipment & artifacts highlight the local & area railway history. There is a gift shop. Open daily, June - Sept.
Patrick McKinley, President
J.A. Clowes, Secretary & Director

***Hopewell Cape:* Albert County Museum**
3940 Rte 114, Hopewell Cape, NB E4H 3J8
Tel: 506-734-2003; *Fax:* 506-734-3291
albertcountymuseum@nb.aibn.com
www.albertcountymuseum.ca
The museum is located in the UNESCO Fundy Biosphere Reserve. Experience early life in Albert County & the Shepody Bay region by visiting the original Shire Town buildings, circa 1845. Explore the former County Jail complete with cells, displays & collections relating to the early history of the area. Visit the magnificent County Courthouse & ask about the project to commemorate R.B. Bennett, Canada's 11th Prime Minister. Displays on shipbuilding, farming; gift shop; meeting rooms; research resources room.
Donald Alward, Manager/Curator

***Kingston:* John Fisher Memorial Museum**
129 Gorhams Bluff Rd., Kingston, NB E5N 1A7
Tel: 506-763-2561; *Fax:* 506-763-2632
gbaxter@nb.sympatico.ca
macdonald.nbed.nb.ca/johnfisher1.htm
Located in MacDonald Consolidated School

***Kouchibouguac:* Saint Croix Island International Historic Site / Lieu historique international de l'Ile-Sainte-Croix**
c/o Kouchibouguac National Park of Canada, 186, Rte. 117, Kouchibouguac, NB E4X 2P1
Tel: 506-876-2443; *Fax:* 506-876-4802
kouch.info@pc.qc.ca
www.pc.gc.ca
Founded: 1984 Located on Rte. 127 Bayside, with a view of Saint Croix Island; site of Pierre Dugua's first attempt to found a settlement in N. America; viewing deck & self-guided interpretive trail; picnic area. The site is also a U.S. National Monument
Carole Loiselle, Unit Superintendent

***Lower Newcastle:* MacDonald Farm Historic Site**
600 Rte. 11, Lower Newcastle, NB E1V 7G1
Tel: 506-453-2324; *Fax:* 506-453-2416
www.gnb.ca/0007/heritage/Macdonald.asp
Founded: 1970 Constructed by Scottish settler, Lt. Col. Alexander MacDonald of Bartibog, between 1815 and 1820 in Georgian style, the site includes a barn, 4 outbuildings, as well as a wharf and boat house. Costumed guides demonstrate cooking, crafts and care of animals.
Mr. Guy Tremblay, Manager, Museum Services, Government of New Brunswick, 506-444-5892, guy.tremblay@gnb.ca

***Memramcook:* Monument Lefebvre National Historic Site / Lieu historique national du Monument-Lefebvre**
480, rue Centrale, Memramcook, NB E4K 3S6
Tél: 506-758-9783; *Téléc:* 506-758-9813
Ligne sans frais: 877-765-1896
monument@nbnet.nb.ca
www.pc.gc.ca/lhn-nhs/nb/lefebvre/index_e.asp
Founded: 1982 Located in the Monument LeFebvre building, in cooperation with Parks Canada, the centre focuses on the survival of the Acadian people from 1755 to present. Shows are performed in the theatre. There is a gift shop with a variety of Acadian products. Guided tours are offered.
Conrad LeBlanc, President, Monument LeFebvre Society
Hermance LeBlanc, Directrice générale

***Minto:* Minto Museum & Information Centre**
420 Pleasant Dr., Minto, NB E4B 2T3
Tel: 506-327-3383; *Fax:* 506-327-3041
Open July 1 - Sept. 1
Rose Collette, Clerk Administrator

***Minto:* New Brunswick Internment Camp Heritage Museum**
#1, 420 Pleasant Dr., Minto, NB E4B 2T3
Tel: 506-327-3573; *Fax:* 506-327-6008
Artifacts & model of the Ripples Internment Camp
Ed Caissie, Director, 506/450-9666

***Miramichi:* Miramichi Natural History Museum**
PO Box 162, 149 Wellington St., Miramichi, NB E1N 2B5
Tel: 506-773-7305
Natural history museum built in 1909, the oldest museum of its kind in New Brunswick and the third oldest in Canada; houses the Dr. Henri Marc Ami Collection; leased to the Miramichi Natural History Association

***Miramichi:* Rankin House Museum**
2224 King George Hwy., Miramichi, NB E1V 6N3
Tel: 506-773-3448
1837; example of mansions built by the early lumber & shipping barons; unique collection of historic items; tourist information centre; open July & Aug.
Jack Ullock, Director

***Miramichi:* St. Michael's Museum Association Inc.**
PO Box 368, 10 Howard St., Miramichi, NB E1N 3A7
Tel: 506-778-5152; *Fax:* 506-778-5156
mmuseum@nbnet.nb.ca; connejof@nbed.nb.ca
www.saintmichaelsmuseum.com
Miramichi history & extensive civil & church records for most denominations; geneology; tours in June-Aug.
John Connell, Curator

***Miramichi:* W.S. Loggie Cultural Centre**
222 Wellington St., Miramichi, NB E1N 1M9
Tel: 506-773-7645

Moncton: Free Meeting House
c/o Moncton Museum, 20 Mountain Rd., Moncton, NB E1C 2J8
Tel: 506-856-4383; *Fax:* 506-856-4355
info.museum@moncton.ca
www.moncton.ca

Moncton: Lutz Mountain Meeting House
Lutz Mountain Heritage Foundation, 3143 Mountain Rd., Moncton, NB E1G 2X1
Tel: 506-384-7719; *Fax:* 506-854-8051
lutzmtnheritage@rogers.com
www.lutzmtnheritage.ca
Founded: 1975 The Lutz Mountain Meeting House is open during the summer only, or by appointment.
Gerry Gillcash, President

Moncton: Moncton Museum / Musée de Moncton
20 Mountain Rd., Moncton, NB E1C 2J8
Tel: 506-856-4383; *Fax:* 506-856-4355
info.museum@moncton.org
www.moncton.ca/Residents/Recreation_Parks_and_Culture/Museums_and_Heritage
Founded: 1974 The permanent exhibits showcase Moncton's history from the time of the Micmacs to the period preceding the Deportation of Acadians, when agriculture was Moncton's primary economic engine, to the golden shipbuilding years and the railway era. There are also temporary and travelling exhibits. A research library and educational programs are offered. Open year round.
Brenda Orr, Sr. Heritage Officer, Recreation, Parks & Culture Dept., City of Moncton, 506-856-4383, brenda.orr@moncton.ca

New Denmark: New Denmark Memorial Museum
6 Main Rd., New Denmark, NB E7G 2B7
Tel: 506-553-6724
newdenmarkmuseum@live.com
www.republiquemadawaska.com
New Denmark Memorial Museum honours the Danish immigrants who settled in the New Denmark area of New Brunswick in 1872. It is the oldest Danish settlement in Canada. Exhibits include books, china, & farm machinery. The museum is open from mid June to the beginning of September.

Oromocto: Canadian Forces Base Gagetown Military Museum / Musée militaire de la BFC Gagetown
Bldg. A-5, PO Box 17000 Forces, Oromocto, NB E2V 4J5
Tel: 506-422-1304; *Fax:* 506-422-1304
museumgagetown@nb.aibn.com
www.museumgagetown.ca
Visitors to the Canadian Forces Base Gagetown Military Museum may visit the following rooms: Royal Canadian Dragoons \ 8th Canadian Hussars; 403 Squadron Air Force; Black Watch; MacGillivray; Naval; Barrack; & Weapons.

Oromocto: Canadian Military Engineering Museum
Also known as: CME Museum
Canadian Forces School of Military Engineering, CFB / ASG Gagetown, #J-10, D215, Mitchell Bldg., Oromocto, NB E2V 4J5
Tel: 506-422-2000; *Fax:* 506-422-1220
cmemuseum@forces.gc.ca (Museum Staff)
www.cmemuseum.ca
Other contact information: E-mail, Research Inquiries: cme.research@sympatico.ca
Founded: 1957 Displays at the Canadian Military Engineering Museum date back before the 1800s, with drawings, plans, & photographs of forts built by engineers, such as the Citadel in Nova Scotia. Displays also depict trench life during World War I. Weapons & uniforms from World War II, artifacts from the Korean War, & a United Nations display are also part of the museum. A research library houses photographs, reference books, training manuals, & personal diaries. The museum is open year round.
Col. John Tattersall, Chair
Maj. Joe Gale, Museum Executive Officer
CWO Blaine Thurston, Vice-President, History & Heritage
Sgt John Wilt, Curator & Treasurer

Oromocto: Fort Hughes Military Blockhouse
1 Wharf Rd., Oromocto, NB E2V 1S2
Tel: 506-357-3333; *Fax:* 506-357-2266
bjarratt@town.oromocto.nb.ca
Located in Sir Douglas Hazen Park
James Arbeau, Director

Petit-Rocher: New Brunswick Mining & Mineral Interpretation Centre (CIMMNB) / Centre d'interprétation des mines & minerais du Nouveau-Bru
397, rue Principale, Petit-Rocher, NB E8J 1L9
Tel: 506-542-2672; *Fax:* 506-542-2708
The Mining & Mineral Interpretation Centre features exhibitions about the mining heritage of New Brunswick, plus a simulation of an underground descent.
Marc-André Godin, Contact

Plaster Rock: Plaster Rock Museum & Information Centre
81 Ridgewell St., Plaster Rock, NB E7G 2N6
Tel: 506-356-6077
Plaster Rock Museum & Information Centre features exhibits about the community's past, including the lumbering & farming activities in Plaster Rock & the surrounding region.

Riverside-Albert: Old Bank Museum
Also known as: Albert County Heritage Trust
5985 Rte. 114, Riverside-Albert, NB E4H 4B8
Tel: 506-882-2015
maryspt@nbnet.nb.ca
Historic bank building now a museum & information centre
Mary Majka, President

Sackville: Mary's Point Shorebird Reserve & Interpretive Centre
Also known as: Shepody National Wildlife Area, Mary's Point Section
PO Box 6227, Sackville, NB E4L 1G6
Tel: 506-882-2544
maryspt@nbnet.nb.ca
www.naturenb.ca/Eng/maryspoint.aspx
Founded: 1992 Located in the Shepody National Wildlife Area and administered by both Nature NB and Environment Canada's Canadian Wildlife Service, these wetlands protect large numbers of shorebird species. The Interpretation Centre educates the public on the shorebirds' habitats and their hemispheric migrations over the Bay of Fundy region.

Sackville: Struts Gallery
7 Lorne St., Sackville, NB E4L 3Z6
Tel: 506-536-1211; *Fax:* 506-536-4565
info@strutsgallery.ca
www.strutsgallery.ca
An artist-run centre dedicated to presenting regional & national contemporary artist-initiated activities
Leah Garnett, President

Saint John: Barbour's General Store
St. Andrew's Sq., PO Box 1971, King St., Saint John, NB E2L 4L1
Tel: 506-658-2939
www.tourismsaintjohn.com
Other contact information: Phone, Off season: 506-658-2855
Artifacts housed at Barbour's General Store include authentic grocery items, pharmaceutical items, cooking utensils, china, farm implements, & yard goods. The restored nineteenth-century country general stored is open from mid-June to mid-September.

Saint John: Loyalist House Museum
Also known as: Merritt House
120 Union St., Saint John, NB E2L 1A3
Tel: 506-652-3590; *Fax:* 506-637-9163
info@loyalisthouse.com
www.loyalisthouse.com
Founded: 1960 Operated by the New Brunswick Historical Society as a national historic site, Loyalist House was built in 1817 by David Daniel Merritt, a United Empire Loyalist from Rye, NY. The house remains very much as it was built & still displays its original furniture: piano-organ, swooning divans, 'yoke-back' chairs, four-poster bed, etc. This buiding is one of the few surviving buildings of the Great Saint John Fire in 1877.
Ms Kathy Wilson, President, New Brunswick Historical Society

Saint John: Saint John Firefighters Museum
24 Sydney St., Saint John, NB E2L 3X1
Tel: 506-633-1840; *Fax:* 506-633-1840
www.tourismsaintjohn.com
The museum is the site of the No. 2 Engine house, built in 1840; a collection of firefighting artifacts & photographs; includes an entire room dedicated to the Great Saint John Fire of 1877, an authentic hand pump, a 1956 LaFrance Fire Engine, a Junior Firefighters play room & much more!

Saint John: Saint John Jewish Historical Museum
91 Leinster St., Saint John, NB E2L 1J2
Tel: 506-633-1833; *Fax:* 506-642-9926
sjjhm@nbnet.nb.ca
personal.nbnet.nb.ca/sjjhm
Founded: 1986 Housed in the same building with the Shaarei Zedek Synagogue, the museum collects, displays & preserves articles related specifically to the Saint John Jewish community; provides a research facility for genealogists, historians & religious scholars; 7 display areas; Jewish education outreach kits, membership program
Katherine Biggs-Craft, Curator

Saint John: Saint John Sports Hall of Fame
PO Box 1971, Saint John, NB E2L 4L1
Tel: 506-658-2909; *Fax:* 506-658-2902
recandparks@saintjohn.ca
www.cityofsaintjohn.com/services_recreation_hall-of-fame.cfm
Located in Harbour Station
Ian Polley, Chair

Saint John: St. Andrews Blockhouse National Historic Site
454 Whipple St., Saint John, NB E2M 2R3
Tel: 506-529-4270; *Fax:* 506-636-4574
fundy.info@pc.gc.ca
www.pc.gc.ca
Other contact information: Off-season Tel: 506/636-4011
Blockhouse built for border defence during the War of 1812; contains elements of the oldest blockhouse in New Brunswick; located at 23 Joe's Point Rd., St. Andrews NB E5B 2J7
Anne Bardou

St Andrews: Ross Memorial Museum / Musée mémorial Ross
188 Montague St., St Andrews, NB E5B 1J2
Tel: 506-529-5124; *Fax:* 506-529-5183
rossmuse@nb.aibn.com
www.townsearch.com/rossmuseum
Decorative arts museum in one of St. Andrews' finest early houses; open June - Oct.
Margot Magee Sackett, Director

St Martins: Quaco Museum & Archives
236 Main St., St Martins, NB E5R 1B8
Tel: 506-833-4740; *Fax:* 506-833-2594
quaco@nbnet.nb.ca
www.quaco.ca
Founded: 1970 Displays the history & heritage of the Quaco-St. Martins area with a specific focus on the shipbuilding heritage of the region; archives available for historical/genealogical research; the Carson Memorial Library, located behind the museum, is a volunteer-run public reading/lending library; gift shop. Museum & archives open June-Sept., other times by apppointment. Library is open Wednesdays & Saturdays throughout the year.
Barbara McIntyre, Curator, 506-833-4768, curator@quaco.ca
Faye Marks, Archivist, 506-833-2553, archivist@quaco.ca
Elizabeth Thibodeau, Librarian, 506-833-2553, librarian@quaco.ca

St Stephen: Charlotte County Museum Inc.
443 Milltown Blvd., St Stephen, NB E3L 1J9
Tel: 506-466-3295; *Fax:* 506-466-6606
charlotteco.museum@nb.aibn.com
www.town.ststephen.nb.ca
Founded: 1977 Exhibits on 3 floors of the 1864 James Murchie Home; collection includes china, including early Chinese porcelain dating to the 17th century; hand-crafted articles, quilts, samplers; costumes; early tools & furniture; theme rooms portray area from the late 18th - early 20th century.
Irene Ritch, Executive Director

Shippagan: Societé historique Nicolas-Denys
218, boul J.D. Gauthier, Shippagan, NB E8S 1P6
Tel: 506-336-3461; *Fax:* 506-336-3434
shnd@umcs.ca
www.acadie.net/guide/organismes3.cfm?id=40
Heures d'ouvertures et les différentes coordonnées comment nous joindre pour le centre de documentation: mardi, mercredi et jeudi de 9 h 00 à 12 h et de 13 h à 16 h, mercredi soir de 19 à 21 h.
Ivan Robichaud, Président, 506-336-0400
Nathalie M. Lanteigne, Secrétaire, 506-336-3461

St-Isidore: St-Isidore Museum Inc.
3942, boul des Fondateurs, St-Isidore, NB E8M 1C2
Tel: 506-358-2983; *Fax:* 506-358-6610
Exhibits depict agricultural & forestry background of the region; open in July & Aug., Thu.-Sun.

Sussex: Agricultural Museum of New Brunswick
28 Perry St., Sussex, NB E4E 2N7
Tel: 506-433-6799; *Fax:* 506-433-2829
www.agriculturalmuseumofnb.com
The museum houses agricultural equipment, military memorabilia, and furniture and housewares. Open mid-June - mid-Sept.
Judy Ross, Secretary

Tabusintac: Tabusintac Centennial Memorial Library & Museum
4490 Rte. 11, Tabusintac, NB E9H 1J3
Tel: 506-779-9261
Houses historical artifacts & memorabilia from the Tabusintac area

Tracadie-Sheila: Musée Historique de Tracadie Inc.
#399, 222, rue du Couvent, Tracadie-Sheila, NB E1X 1E1
Tél: 506-393-6366; *Téléc:* 506-395-6355
museehis@nb.sympatico.ca
Founded: 1978 Leprosy in the 19th century; also history of Tracadie, artifacts dating several centuries before the arrival of the white colonists, articles relating to the life of the Acadians
Zélica Daigle, President, 506-393-6366, museums@nb.sympatico.ca

Welshpool: **Roosevelt Campobello International Park / Parc international Roosevelt de Campobello**
459 Rte. 774, Welshpool, NB E5E 1A4
Tel: 506-752-2922; *Fax:* 506-752-6000
info@fdr.net
www.fdr.net
The Roosevelt Campobello International Park, located on Campobello Island in New Brunswick's Bay of Fundy, features the 34-room summer residence of Franklin D. Roosevelt & his wife Eleanor. Guided tours are given of the home. The park also contains the Edmund S. Muskie Visitor Center, where visitors learn the story of the former president of the United States, through displays & a film. The Roosevelt Cottage & Visitor Centre are open from mid May to mid October. The park is open year-round.

Woodstock: **Old Carleton County Court House**
c/o Carleton County Historical Society, 128 Connell St., Woodstock, NB E7M 1L5
Tel: 506-328-9706; *Fax:* 506-328-2942
cchs@nb.aibn.com
www.cchs-nb.ca
Founded: 1986 The Carleton County Historical Society restored the Old County Court House which was built in 1833. The court house originally served as the County seat of justice & was also the meeting place for the first County Council in New Brunswick. Guided tours are available during the summer & by appointment at other times.

Newfoundland & Labrador

Provincial Museums

The Rooms
PO Box 1800 C, 9 Bonaventure Ave., St. John's, NL A1C 5P9
Tel: 709-757-8000; *Fax:* 709-757-8017
information@therooms.ca
www.therooms.ca
Other contact information: Archives: 709-757-8030; Museum: 709-757-8020; Gallery: 709-757-8040
The Rooms consists of the Newfoundland & Labrador Provincial Archives, Art Gallery, & Museum. The Archives collects records of the Government of Newfoundland & Labrador, as well as records from private sources which have value to the history of the province. Permanent exhibits at the museum depict Newfoundland & Labrador's early people, as well as Fort Townsend, the home of British soldiers &, since 1870, the Royal Newfoundland Constabulary. One level of the museum is dedicated to the birds of Newfoundland & Labrador. The Rooms Provincial Art Gallery presents more than 7,000 historical & contemporary works.
Dean Brinton, Chief Executive Officer, 709-757-8012, Fax: 709-757-8017
Anne Chafe, Director, The Rooms Provincial Museum, 709-757-8077, Fax: 709-757-8021, annechafe@therooms.ca
Deanne Fisher, Director, Marketing & Development, 709-757-8070, Fax: 709-757-8017, deannefisher@therooms.ca
Penny Houlden, Director, The Rooms Regional Museums, 709-757-8022, Fax: 709-757-8021, phoulden@therooms.ca
Vicky Lewis, Director, Finance & General Operations, 709-757-8015, Fax: 709-757-8017, vlewis@therooms.ca
Sheila Perry, Director, The Rooms Provincial Art Gallery, 709-757-8042, Fax: 709-757-8041, sheilaperry@therooms.ca
Greg Walsh, Director, Provincial Archives, 709-757-8032, Fax: 709-757-8031
Gillian Davidge, Manager, Education & Public Programming, 709-757-8109, gilliandavidge@therooms.ca

Local Museums in Newfoundland & Labrador

L'Anse au Loup: **Labrador Straits Museum**
PO Box 98, L'Anse au Loup, NL A0K 3L0
Tel: 709-927-5659
Hunting & fishing collections, household communication & religious items

Baie Verte: **Baie Verte Peninsula Miners' Museum**
PO Box 122, Hwy. 410, Baie Verte, NL A0K 1B0
Tel: 709-532-8090; *Fax:* 709-532-4166
baievertpeda@nf.aibn.com
Founded: 1975 The Miners' Museum presents a replica of life & work during the mining years (1860 - 1864 & 1901-1915) on the Baie Verte Peninsula.
Frank Clarke, President
Gail Goudie, Administrator
Jennifer Whelan, Treasurer

Bonavista: **Bonavista Historical Society Museum**
Ryan Premises National Historic Site, PO Box 295, 10 Ryan's Hill, Bonavista, NL A0C 1B0
Tel: 709-468-2920; *Fax:* 709-468-2495
Founded: 1969 The Bonavista Historical Society Museum is situated in the restored turn-of-the-century Ryan Retail Store at the Ryan Premises National Historic Site. The collection reflects local life in the late 19th century in one of Newfoundland's inshore fishing communities. The musuem also holds a collection of medical artifacts from the early twentieth century. Bonavista Museum is open from mid-June to mid-October.

Bonne Bay: **Wiltondale Pioneer Village**
PO Box 159, Woody Point, Bonne Bay, NL A0K 1P0
Tel: 709-453-2470; *Fax:* 709-453-7214
Recreated turn-of-the-century logging community; museum; one-room schoolhouse; church; log barn; original home; general store, craft store & tearoom

Botwood: **Botwood Heritage Centre**
12 Airbase Pl., Botwood, NL A0H 1E0
Tel: 709-257-4612; *Fax:* 709-257-3022
bhsa@nf.aibn.com
town.botwood.nl.ca
The Botwood Heritage Centre depicts the time of the Beothuk, the European exploration era in the Exploits Valley, & the early railway & shipping period of Abitibi.

Burin: **Burin Heritage House**
Also known as: **Reddy House**
PO Box 500, Seaview Dr., Burin, NL A0E 1E0
Tel: 709-891-2217; *Fax:* 709-891-2358
burinheritagemuseum@nf.aibn.com
www.burincanada.com
Other contact information: Phone, Off Season: 709-891-1760; Fax, Off Season: 709-891-2069
The Burin Heritage House features artifacts related to the history of Burin, including the fishery & the tidal wave. The museum is open from mid May to the beginning of October.
Claudine Prior, Contact

Carbonear: **Baccalieu Trail Heritage Corporation**
#2, 4 Pike's Lane, Carbonear, NL A1Y 1A7
Tel: 709-596-1906
www.baccalieudigs.ca
Founded: 1993 The corporation preserves, protects, & promotes the heritage of the Baccalieu Trail Region, which consists of approximately seventy communities along 240 km of coastline on Newfoundland & Labrador's Avalon Peninsula.

Carbonear: **Carbonear C.N. Railway Station**
PO Box 64, Water St. West, Carbonear, NL A1Y 1B5
Tel: 709-596-2532; *Fax:* 709-596-2582
www.heritage.nf.ca/society/rhs
Other contact information: Phone, Off Season: 709-596-2849
The Carbonear Railway Station is one of Newfoundland & Labrador's Resgistered Heritage Structures. Built around 1917, the building exemplifies a station during the one hundred year era of the Newfoundland railroad. Operated by the Carbonear Heritage Society, the station contains railway artifacts, exhibits about the history of Carbonear, genealogical information, & a tourist information centre. The Carbonear C.N. Railway Station is open from June to September. Appointments may be arranged during the off season.

Cow Head: **Dr. Henry N. Payne Community Museum**
Conservation & Heritage Inc., PO Box 238, Cow Head, NL A0K 2A0
Tel: 709-243-2466
cowhead.ca/heritage/index.htm
Restored theme home; artifacts tell story of Dr. Henry N. Payne & cultural heritage of area; gift shop. Located at the northern tip of Gros Morne National Park.
Ms Glenda Reid Bavis, Staff contact, 709-243-2466, g.bavis@nf.sympatico.ca

Cupids: **Cupids Museum**
PO Box 200, Cupids, NL A0A 2B0
Tel: 709-528-3500
cupidshistorical@nf.sympatico.ca
www3.nf.sympatico.ca/cupidshistorical
Located on Seaforest Dr.; open June 15-Sept. 30
Linda Kane, Curator

Deer Lake: **Heritage Museum**
PO Box 989, Rte. 1, Deer Lake, NL A0K 2E0
Tel: 709-635-4440; *Fax:* 709-635-5103
www.town.deerlake.nf.ca
Founded: 1988 The museum preserves the local history with displays related to logging, agriculture and the settlers' lives in the Humber Valley. Open May-Dec.

Durrell: **Durrell Museum & Crafts**
PO Box 83, Durrell, NL A0G 1Y0
Tel: 709-884-2780
lbulgin@nf.sympatico.ca
Other contact information: 709/884-5391/5537
Open end of May - end of Sept.; mounted polar bear exhibit & crafts
Lloyd Bulgin, President

Ferryland: **Historic Ferryland Museum**
PO Box 7, Ferryland, NL A0A 2H0
Tel: 709-432-2711
Other contact information: Off Season: 709/432-2155
Located in the old Courthouse; exhibits depicting community life & Ferryland's role in colonization of North America; open mid-June - Labour Day
Maxine Dunne, Curator

Flatrock: **Flat Rock Museum**
663 Windgap Rd., Flatrock, NL A1K 1C7
Tel: 709-437-6312; *Fax:* 709-437-6311
Open July - Sept. or by appt.

Fogo: **Bleak House Museum**
PO Box 57, Fogo, NL A0G 2B0
Tel: 709-266-2237
Other contact information: Alternative Phone: 709-266-2487
Founded: 1988 Bleak House was built around 1816 for the Slade family, who were involved in the Fogo Island fish trade. The home was restored & made into a museum. The home features items that belonged to owners of the home, plus artifacts that depict the history of Fogo. Bleak House Museum is open from July to September.

Forteau: **Point Amour Lighthouse**
c/o Labrador Straits Historical Development Corporation, PO Box 112, Forteau, NL A0K 2P0
Tel: 709-927-5825; *Fax:* 709-656-3150
Toll-Free: 800-563-6353
lshdc@labradorstraits.net; tourisminfo@gov.nl.ca
www.pointamourlighthouse.ca
Other contact information: Alternative Phone: 709-931-2013; 709-927-5826
Consisting of several buildings, the Point Amour Light station dates back to the 1850s. The Provincial Historic Site in Newfoundland & Labrador has been restored, & now features displays that depict the maritime history of the Labrador Straits. An interpretive trail at the site takes visitors to the site of the HMS Raleigh & HMS Lily shipwrecks. The site is open from mid May to the beginning of October.
Linda Badcock, Historic Sites Officer, 709-729-0592, Fax: 709-729-7989, lbadcock@gov.nl.ca

Gander: **North Atlantic Aviation Museum**
PO Box 234, Trans Canada Hwy., Gander, NL A1V 1W6
Tel: 709-256-2923
naam@nf.aibn.com
www.naam.ca
Founded: 1996 The North Atlantic Aviation Museum depicts important aviation moments over the North Atlantic, from the war years to commercial flying. The focus is upon Gander's involvement in aviation history. The Museum features six aircraft.
Bob Briggs, President
Brian Williams, Vice-President
Jonathan Waterman, Secretary
Harold Penney, Treasurer

Grand Bank: **Southern Newfoundland Seamen's Museum (SNSM)**
PO Box 1109, 54 Marine Dr., Grand Bank, NL A0E 1W0
Tel: 709-832-1484; *Fax:* 709-832-2053
gwcrews@nf.aibn.com
Artifacts pertaining to the banks fishery

Grand Falls-Windsor: **Beothuk Village**
PO Box 222, Grand Falls-Windsor, NL A2A 2J7
Tel: 709-489-3559; *Fax:* 709-489-0465
Toll-Free: 888-491-9453
evta@nf.sympatico.ca
Other contact information: Phone, Off Season: 709-489-9629
Beothuk Village is a replica of a Beothuk village, where visitors can discover the lifestyle of people who lived in the Exploits Valley. The village features reconstructed mamateek dwellings, a smokehouse, a storage pit, & a burial place. The site is open from mid June to early September.

Grand Falls-Windsor: **Logger's Life Provincial Museum**
Provincial Bldg., Grand Falls-Windsor, NL A2A 1W9
Logging exhibit is a replica of 1920s logging camp; displays tools & clothing representative of that era; located west of Grand Falls-Windsor on Trans Canada Hwy.

Grand Falls-Windsor: **Mary March Provincial Museum**
Provincial Building, Cromer Ave., Grand Falls-Windsor, NL A2A 1W9
Tel: 709-292-4522; *Fax:* 709-292-4526
information@therooms.ca
www.therooms.ca/museum/mary_march_museum.asp
Founded: 1988 From the European name of one of the last Beothuks, the aboriginal people of the island of Newfoundland, the Mary March Museum traces the Aboriginal, European, natural & geological history of the Central Newfoundland Region. Open daily 9am-4:45pm, May-Oct. The museum is located at 24

St. Catherine St. It is part of The Rooms Regional Museums network.
Ms Deanne Fisher, Director, Marketing and Development, The Rooms, 709-757-8070, deannefisher@therooms.ca

***Greenspond:* Greenspond Court House**
PO Box 119, Greenspond, NL A0G 3L0
Tel: 709-536-3220
lindaw@morgan.ucs.mun.ca
Open June - Sept.
Frank E. Blackwood, Director
Roland Burry

***Happy Valley-Goose Bay:* Northern Lights Military Museum**
PO Box 2168 B, Happy Valley-Goose Bay, NL A0P 1E0
Tel: 709-896-5939

***Harbour Grace:* Conception Bay Museum**
PO Box 298, Water St., Harbour Grace, NL A0A 2M0
Tel: 709-596-5465; *Fax:* 709-596-5465
pfahey@conceptionbaymuseum.nf.ca
Open June - Aug; off season by appt.

***Hopedale:* National Historic Site: Agvituk Historical Society Museum**
PO Box 12, Hopedale, NL A0P 1G0
Tel: 709-933-3777; *Fax:* 709-933-3746
Moravian Mission House; archaeology artifacts from 1500-2000 years ago; items related to Labrador Inuit; European medical supplies & furniture

***Lewisporte:* By The Bay Museum & Craft Shop**
PO Box 569, 235 Main Rd., Lewisporte, NL A0G 3A0
Tel: 709-535-8555
lada@nf.aibn.com; btbmuseum@nf.aibn.com
Other contact information: Alternative Phone: 709-535-3900
Founded: 1872 Exhibits at the Bye The Bay Museum show the history of Lewisporte & its surrounding region, including Beothuk artifacts, the shipbuilding & logging industries & World War I & World War II. Owned & operated by the Lewisporte Area Development Association, the museum is open from the end of May to the end of August.
Pat Martin, Contact
Barry Porter, Contact

***Little Catalina:* Mockbeggar Plantation Provincial Historic Site**
***Also known as:* Bradley House**
PO Box 128, Little Catalina, NL A0C 1W0
Tel: 709-468-7300; *Fax:* 709-468-5044
Toll-Free: 800-563-6353
mockbeggar@nf.aibn.com
www.tcr.gov.nl.ca/tcr/heritage/ historicsites/mockbeggar.html
Other contact information: In Season Tel: 709-468-7300; Fax: 709-468-5044
Founded: 1990 Built in the 1870s, the museum was the home of Newfoundland statesman, Senator F. Gordon Bradley and is restored to that 1939 period. Other buildings include a carpenter shop, fish store and cod-liver oil factory from the 18 century. Museum is located on Roper St., Bonavista, NL, A0C 1B0.
Ms Linda Badcock, Historic Sites Officer, 709-729-0592, Fax: 709-729-7989
Don Johnson, Site Supervisor

***Marystown:* Marystown Heritage Museum Corporation**
PO Box 688, Ville Marie Dr., Marystown, NL A0E 2M0
Tel: 709-279-2463; *Fax:* 709-276-5116
heritagemuseum@nf.aibn.com
www.marystownheritagemuseum.com/
The museum exhibits include everyday articles from the town's historic past, from squid jiggers to priests. Open daily mid-June - Aug.; Jan.-May, Sept.-Dec. Mon.-Fri 9-5
Albert Dober

***Moreton's Harbour:* Moreton's Harbour Community Museum**
PO Box 28, Main Rd., Moreton's Harbour, NL A0G 3H0
Tel: 709-684-2355
Operated by the Moreton's Harbour Women's Institute, the Moreton's Harbour Community Museum is situated in a house which was built in 1916. The museum features various artifacts, including agricultural implements & equipment used during the inshore fishery. Archives include census records, diaries, & school minute books. The community museum is open from mid June to the beginning of September. Tours may be arranged during the off season.

***Mount Arlington Heights:* St. Bartholomew's Church**
c/o Mt. Arlington Hts., PO Box 25, Mount Arlington Heights, NL A0B 2L0
Tel: 709-228-2583
Church built in 1930 by parishoners

***Musgrave Harbour:* Fishermen's Museum**
PO Box 159, 4 Marine Dr., Musgrave Harbour, NL A0G 3J0
Tel: 709-655-2162
Ship models, engines, photographs, accounts of local shipwrecks

***Nain:* Piulimatsivik - Nain Museum**
c/o Moravian Mission, General Delivery, Nain, NL A0P 1L0
Tel: 709-922-2821
Moravian & Inuit artifacts are on display at Piulimatsivik, the Nain Museum.

***North West River:* Labrador Heritage Museum**
PO Box 99, North West River, NL A0P 1M0
Tel: 709-492-8282; *Fax:* 709-497-8856
lab.heritage@nf.sympatico.ca
www3.nf.sympatico.ca/lab.heritage/museum.ht m
Exhibit includes arifacts & infomation about the Hudson Bay Company store, trapping, exploration of Labrador & the International Grenfell Association in North West River

***Old Perlican:* Howard House of Artifacts**
PO Box 100, Old Perlican, NL A0A 3G0
Tel: 709-587-2022
Located 3 miles from Old Perlican on Shore Line country road at Daniel's Cove; artifacts represent the 1890s & 1900 to 1945; collection of Newfoundland homemade furniture of the 1930s; open daily
Jerome Howard, Owner

***Placentia:* O'Reilly House Museum**
c/o Placentia Area Historical Society, PO Box 233, 48 Orcan Dr., Placentia, NL A0B 2Y0
Tel: 709-227-5568
pahs37@hotmail.com
www.placentia.20m.com/mainframe2.htm
Founded: 1989 Built in 1902 as a residence for magistrate, William O'Reilly, O'Reilly House is now a museum operated by the Placentia Area Historical Society. The Victorian home displays many items from Placentia' past. The museum is open from the beginning of June to mid October.

***Placentia Bay:* Castle Hill National Historic Site of Canada**
PO Box 10 Jerseyside, Placentia Bay, NL A0B 2G0
Tel: 709-227-2401; *Fax:* 709-227-2452
castle.hill@pc.gc.ca
www.pc.gc.ca
17th & 18th century remains of French & English fortifications; picnic areas & hiking trails; special events & programming; Visitor Centre with gift shop
Jewel Cunningham, Acting Superintendent

***Port au Choix:* Port au Choix National Historic Park Site**
PO Box 140, Port au Choix, NL A0K 4C0
Tel: 709-861-3522; *Fax:* 709-861-3827
pac-historic-site@pch.gc.ca
parkscanada.pch.gc.ca
Commemorates area's rich aboriginal history dating back 5400 years; visitors can view artifacts & exhibits on the four prehistoric cultures that occupied area; walking trails, archaeological sites, lighthouse & fossils
Millie Spence, Site Supervisor

***Port au Port:* Our Lady of Mercy Museum**
PO Box 239, Port au Port, NL A0N 1T0
Tel: 709-648-2632
Open May - Sept.
Margaret Lawler, Chair

***Port aux Basques:* Gulf Museum**
c/o South West Coast Historical Society, PO Box 1299, Port aux Basques, NL A0M 1C0
Tel: 709-695-7604
Nautical items & the astrolabe (dated 1628) an instrument used by early navigators to determine latitude; society operates a refurbished train site facility consisting of a railway station & nine rail cars

***Port aux Basques:* Port aux Basques Railway Heritage Centre**
PO Box 1299, Port aux Basques, NL A0M 1C0
Tel: 709-695-7560
The Port aux Basques Railway Heritage Centre depicts the significance of the railway to Newfoundland's history. In the late 1890s, Port aux Basques became the western terminus of the Newfoundland Railway, where the railway schedule connected with steamers. Open from June to October, the heritage centre features the train station & various rail cars.

***Port de Grave:* Fishermen's Museum, Porter House & School**
Port de Grave, NL A0A 3J0
Tel: 709-786-3912
hermanporter@personainternet.com
Founded: 1979 Museum contains artifacts depicting life & times of Newfoundland fishermen; Porter House is a traditional fisherman's house restored to early 1900s; Hibbs' Hole Schoolhouse, a restored one-room school
Herman Porter, Curator

***Port Union:* Port Union Museum**
PO Box 98, Port Union, NL A0C 2J0
Tel: 709-469-2304
thebungalow@nf.aibn.com
Includes estate of the late Sir Wm. F. Coaker, founder of Port Union & Sir Wm. F. Coaker Memorial Cemetery; open mid June - Sept.; small admission fees apply
Rosella Hiscock, Curator

***Pouch Cove:* Pouch Cove Museum**
PO Box 59, 660 Main Rd., Pouch Cove, NL A0A 3L0
Tel: 709-335-2848; *Fax:* 709-335-2840
pouchcove@nf.aibn.com
pouchcove.ca
Open year round
Wavy Ellsworth, Town Clerk/Manager

***Red Bay:* Red Bay National Historic Site of Canada**
PO Box 103, Red Bay, NL A0K 4K0
Tel: 709-920-2142; *Fax:* 709-920-2144
redbay.info@pc.gc.ca
www.pc.gc.ca/lhn-nhs/nl/redbay/natcul/basque.aspx
Other contact information: Phone, Summer: 709-920-2051
During the 16th century, Basque merchants & ship owners from France & Spain planned seasonal expeditions to the south coast of Labrador & the north shore of Quebec to hunt whales. The port they used most often was called Butus, which is now Red Bay. Red Bay is now a National Historic Site with a Visitor Centre. The Visitor Centre features discoveries from a marine archaeology project in the Red Bay area. Visitors learn about Labrador's 16th century history, through displays of original artifacts recovered from archaeological excavations, plus reproductions. The site is open from June to October.

***Rocky Harbour:* L'Anse aux Meadows National Historic Site**
Parks Canada, PO Box 70, Rocky Harbour, NL A0K 4N0
Tel: 709-623-2608; *Fax:* 709-623-2028
viking_lam@pch.gc.ca
www.pc.gc.ca/lhn-nhs/nl/meadows/index_E.asp
Other contact information: TTD: 709/772-4564
UNESCO World Heritage Site depicting first authenticated European presence in North America; the focal point are the reconstructions of three Norse buildings of this archaeological site. There are also exhibits the Viking lifestyle, artifacts, and the archaeological discovery of the site. Visitor centre open mid-June - early Oct.

***Rocky Harbour:* Gros Morne National Park Visitor Reception Centre**
PO Box 130, Rocky Harbour, NL A0K 4N0
Tel: 709-458-2417; *Fax:* 709-458-2059
grosmorner.info@pc.gc.ca
www.parkscanada.gc.ca/grosmorne
Other contact information: TDD: 709/772-4564
Gros Morne was declared a UNSESCO World Heritage site in 1987. GM discovery centre looks at the forces of nature. The centre looks at geology, plant and animal life, marine story and human history. It is located on the south side of Bonne Bay, one hour from Deer Airport and the Trans Canada Highway.

***St Anthony:* Grenfell House Museum**
PO Box 93, St Anthony, NL A0K 4S0
Tel: 709-454-4010; *Fax:* 709-454-4047
info@grenfell-properties.com
www.grenfell-properties.com
Dr. Wilfred Grenfell's former home restored circa 1920; open May to Oct.

***St. John's:* Anglican Cathedral of St. John the Baptist Parish House, 9 Cathederal St., St. John's, NL A1C 3Y4**
Tel: 709-726-5677; *Fax:* 709-726-2053
cathedral@nf.aibn.com
www.infonet.st-johns.nf.ca/cathedral
Pictures, artifacts, records, documents & books related to the history of the Cathedral & Parish; established in 1699, the parish is the oldest non-Roman Catholic religious foundation in Canada; Cathedral building is one of the finest examples of English neo-Gothic architecture in North America
Donna Hiscock, Cathederal Archivist
Very Rev. Josiah Noel, Dean

***St. John's:* Boyd's Cove Beothuk Site & Interpretation Centre**
PO Box 8700, St. John's, NL A1B 4J6
Tel: 709-656-3114; *Fax:* 709-656-3150
Toll-Free: 800-563-6353
boydscove@nf.aibn.com
Founded: 1981 The Beothuk site at Boyd's Cove dates back to the late 17th & early 18th centuries. The site features the archaeological remains of Beothuk life, including their house pits. Visitors can learn about these extinct people at the interpretive centre, where several artifacts from the site are displayed & on the interpretive trail. The centre is open from mid June to mid October.
Linda Badcock, Historic Sites Officer
Karen Le Drew Day, Site Supervisor

St. John's: **Cape Bonavista Lighthouse Provincial Historic Site**
Department of Tourism, Culture & Recreation, Heritage Division, PO Box 8700, Hwy. 230, St. John's, NL A1B 4J6
Toll-Free: 800-563-6353
tourisminfo@gov.nl.ca
www.tcr.gov.nl.ca/tcr/heritage/historicsites/capebonavista.html
The Cape Bonavista Lighthouse was built in 1843. The site features guided tours & a walking trail. The lighthouse is open from mid May to the beginning of October.
Linda Badcock, Historic Sites Officer (Year Round Contact), 709-729-0592, Fax: 709-729-7989, lbadcock@gov.nl.ca
Don Johnson, Site Supervisor (Seasonal Contact), 709-468-7444, Fax: 709-468-5426, capebonavista@nf.aibn.com

St. John's: **Cape Spear National Historic Site of Canada / Lieu historique national du Canada du Cap-Spear**
PO Box 1268 C, St. John's, NL A1C 5M9
Tel: 709-772-5367; *Fax:* 709-772-6302
cape.spear@pc.gc.ca
www.pc.gc.ca/eng/lhn-nhs/nl/spear/index.aspx
Located at most easterly point in North America, the Cape Spear lighthouse is the oldest in Newfoundland & Labrador. The lighthouse has been restored to reflect 1839. Visitors can view displays about the history of lighthouses & lightkeeping. The grounds are open year round, & the lighthouse, Visitor Interpretation Centre & the Heritage Gift Shop are open from mid May to mid October.

St. John's: **Commissariat House Provincial Historic Site, St. John's, NF**
Dept. of Tourism, Culture & Recreation, Culture & Heritage Division, PO Box 8700, King's Bridge Rd., St. John's, NL A1B 4J6
Tel: 709-729-6730; *Fax:* 709-729-6745
Toll-Free: 800-563-6353
commissariat@nf.aibn.com
www.explorenewfoundlandandlab rador.com
Other contact information: Year-round Email: tourisminfo@gov.nl.ca
This building, one of the oldest buildings in NFLD, was built especially for the Commissariat to supply the city's garrison and has been restored back to the 1830's era complete with tradtionally dressed maids and clerks to help answer questions.
Linda Badcock, Historic Sites Officer

St. John's: **Heart's Content Cable Station Provincial Historic Site, Heart's Content NF**
Provincial Historic Sites, Arts & Culture Centre, PO Box 8700, St. John's, NL A1B 4J6
Tel: 709-583-2160; *Fax:* 709-583-2373
Toll-Free: 800-563-6353
heartscontent@nf.aibn.com
www.tcr.gov.nl.ca/tcr/herita ge/historicsites/heartscontentcablestation.html
Other contact information: Year-round Email: tourisminfo@gov.nf.ca
Founded: 1974 Located on Hwy. 80, this cable station marks the first successful transatlantic telegraph cable landing in 1866. Displays focus on the history of cable, with equipment and instrumentation on exhibit. Open May-Oct., 10:00-5:30 daily.
Scott Andrews, Historic Sites Officer, Tourism, Culture & Recreation, 709-729-0592, Fax: 709-729-7989, tourisminfo@gov.nl.ca
Bob Balsom, Site Supervisor

St. John's: **Hiscock House Provincial Historic Site, Trinity NL**
Also known as: **Mountain Ash Villa**
Dept. of Tourism, Culture & Recreation, PO Box 8700, St. John's, NL A1B 4J6
Tel: 709-464-2042; *Fax:* 709-464-2349
Toll-Free: 800-563-6353
trinity@nf.aibn.com
www.tcr.gov.nl.ca/tcr/heritage/his toricsites/thehiscockhouse.html
Other contact information: In Season Tel: 709/464-2042; Fax: 709/464-2349
Founded: 1982 Owned solely by the Hiscock family until it was reborn as a museum, the house has been restored to its 1910 style. Located on Church St., it is open late spring to early autumn, 10:00-5:30 daily.
Ms Linda Badcock, Historic Sites Officer, Tourism, Culture & Recreation, 709-729-0592, Fax: 709-729-7989, tourisminfo@gov.nl.ca
Joan Kane, Site Supervisor

St. John's: **James J. O'Mara Pharmacy Museum**
Apothecary Hall, 488 Water St., St. John's, NL A1E 1B3
Tel: 709-753-5877; *Fax:* 709-753-8615
jomara@nlpb.ca
www.nlpb.ca
Drug store c. 1895; open end-June - end-Aug. or by appt.
Donald F. Rowe, Secretary-Registrar

St. John's: **Lester-Garland Premises Provincial Historic Site, Trinity NL**
Also known as: **The Ryan Shop**
c/o Dept of Tourism, Culture & Recreation, Culture & Heritage, PO Box 8700, St. John's, NL A1B 4J6
Tel: 709-464-2042; *Fax:* 709-729-7989
Toll-Free: 800-563-6353
trinity@nf.aibn.com
www.tcr.gov.nl.ca/tcr/historicsite s
Mercantile bldg. including counting house restored to 1820 & retail shop restored to 1910; open daily June - Sept.
Linda Badcock, Historic Sites Officer
Joan Kane, Site Supervisor

St. John's: **Quidi Vidi Battery Provincial Historic Site**
PO Box 8700, St. John's, NL A1B 4J6
Tel: 709-729-0592; *Fax:* 709-729-6745
commissariat@nf.aibn.com
The Quidi Vidi Battery was built by the French in the 1700s. It was later taken over by the British, who rebuilt the guardhouse. The site is now restored to the era of 1812, when it was used to ward off a possible American attack. The Quidi Vidi Battery is located on Cuckhold's Cove Road in Quidi Vidi Village, Newfoundland & Labrador. Tours are available from guides dressed in period costumes, from late June until September.
Andrea van Nostrand, Seasonal Contact, 709-729-6745, quidividi@nf.aibn.com

St. John's: **Royal Newfoundland Constabulary Historical Society Archives & Museum**
Royal Newfoundland Constabulary Bldg., 1 Fort Townshend, St. John's, NL A1C 2G2
Tel: 709-729-8000; *Fax:* 709-729-8214
contactrnc@rnc.gov.nl.ca
www.rnc.gov.nl.ca
Collects & preserves early police records; 48+ audio tapes of oral history interviews, as well as 10,000+ photographs; researchers may contact the office of the Chief of Police, indicating their area of interest, to arrange for access to the archives; photocopying available upon request, subjet to copyright protocols; open year round

St. John's: **The Royal St. John's Regatta Museum**
PO Box 214, Clancy Dr., St. John's, NL A1C 5J2
Tel: 709-576-8921; *Fax:* 709-576-3315
stjohnsregatta@nf.aibn.com
www.stjohnsregatta.org
The long history of rowing competition in St. John's, dating back to the early 1800s, is depicted at the Regatta Museum, through photographs, trophies, & other memorabilia. Please contact the Regatta Museum to arrange an appointment to visit.
Wayne Young, President, Regatta Committte
Paul Rogers, Secretary, Regatta Committte

St. John's: **St. Thomas' Old Garrison Church Museum**
8 Military Rd., St. John's, NL A1C 2C4
Tel: 709-576-6632; *Fax:* 709-576-2541
office@st-thomaschurch.com
www.st-thomaschurch.com
c. 1836
Jean E.C. Lewis, Archival Committee Member
David Edwards, Archival Committee Member
Rev. Robert Chafe, Archival Committee Member

St. John's: **Signal Hill National Historic Site of Canada / Lieu historique national du Canada de Signal Hill**
PO Box 1268, St. John's, NL A1C 5M9
Tel: 709-772-5367; *Fax:* 709-772-6302
Toll-Free: 888-773-8888
signal.hill@pc.gc.ca
www.pc.gc.ca/lhn-nhs/nl/signalhil l/index.aspx
In 1901, Signal Hill was the reception point of the first transatlantic wireless signal. From the 18th century to World War II, Signal Hill was also the site of harbour defence for St. John's, Newfoundland. Today, visitors can tour the Visitor Interpretation Centre & visit Cabot Tower to view the Marconi exhibit. The site is open year-round.

St. John's: **Trinity Interpretation Centre, Trinity NL**
Dept. of Tourism, Culture & Recreation, Culture & Heritage Division, PO Box 8700, St. John's, NL A1B 4J6
Tel: 709-464-2042; *Fax:* 709-729-7989
Toll-Free: 800-563-6353
trinity@nf.aibn.com
www.tcr.gov.nl.ca/tcr/heritage/his toricsites/index.html
Exhibits on the commercial & social history of Trinity; open June - Sept.
Linda Badcock, Historic Sites Officer
Joan Kane, Site Supervisor

St Lawrence: **St. Lawrence Miner's Memorial Museum**
PO Box 128, St Lawrence, NL A0E 2V0
Tel: 709-873-2222; *Fax:* 709-873-3352
townofstlawrence@nf.aibn.com
Open daily in summer
Mayor Wayde Rowsell
Gregory Quirke, Clerk/Manager

Salvage: **Salvage Fishermens' Museum**
General Delivery, Salvage, NL A0G 3X0
Tel: 709-677-2414
gmheffen@hotmail.com
www.explorenewfoundlandandlabrador.com
The museum building, a home once owned by the Lane family, dates from 1860 and is the oldest dwelling in the area; collection of fishing & domestic artifacts relates to the history and cultural life of Salvage, from the late 19th c. to the present; open daily, mid-June to Labour Day; wheelchair accessible; archive; gift shop
Marion Heffern, Contact

Springdale: **Harvey Grant Heritage Centre Community Museum**
Also known as: **H.C. Grant Heritage Museum**
PO Box 57, 50 Main St., Springdale, NL A0J 1T0
Tel: 709-673-4313; *Fax:* 709-673-4969
Artifacts from 1940s, 50s & 60s, related to life of Harvey Grant; open July & Aug.

Torbay: **Torbay Museum**
Torbay Municipal Centre, PO Box 1160, 1288 Torbay Rd., Torbay, NL A1K 1K4
Tel: 709-437-6534; *Fax:* 709-437-1309
torbayheritage@nfmail.net
torbay.museum.tripod.com
Over 500 artifacts dating from early 1800s; the collection is dedicated to produce a display of historical artifacts for public viewing, and the preservation and promotion of the heritage of Torbay. Open Mon. - Fri. 9-4, Tues. & Thu. 6:30-8:30 in summer; Tue. & Thu. 6:30-8:30 off season; otherwise by appt.
Jerri Pellegrinetti, Curator

Trepassey: **Trepassey Area Museum**
PO Box 63, Trepassey, NL A0A 4B0
Tel: 709-436-2044
Open July & Aug.

Trinity: **Trinity Museum**
PO Box 8, Trinity, NL A0C 2S0
Tel: 709-464-3599; *Fax:* 709-464-3599
info@trinityhistoricalsociety.com
www.trinityhistoricalsociety.com
Founded: 1967 The artifacts of Trinity Museum are displayed in a salt box style house, which was built in the 1880s. The collection reflects the history of Trinity, & includes fishing, boat building, commercial, & domestic items. The site also features a fire engine shed, which displays an 1811 fire pump. Trinity Museum is owned & operated by the Trinity Historical Society. The museum is open from mid June to mid October, & by appointment at other times during the year.

Twillingate: **Twillingate Museum & Craft Shop**
PO Box 369, Twillingate, NL A0G 4M0
Tel: 709-884-2825
info@tmacs.ca
www.tmacs.ca
Other contact information: Phone, After Hours: 709-884-2044
Founded: 1973 Twillingate Museum is located in the former Anglican Church Rectory, which was built around 1900. Furnishings in the museum reflect the Victorian era. Examples of exhibits include Inuit, Dorset, & Beothuk First Nations artifacts. Archives include photographs, family histories, & cemetery data. The museum is open from May to October.
Linda Blondin, Contact

Wesleyville: **Bonavista North Museum & Gallery**
PO Box 257, 12 Memorial Dr, Wesleyville, NL A0G 4R0
Tel: 709-536-2110
museum@nf.aibn.com
www.bonavistanorth.blogspot.com
The Bonavista North Museum & Gallery contains photographs, artifacts, & artwork from the local area. The museum is open daily from the beginning of July to the end of August. Appointments can be arranged during the off season.

Whitbourne: **Whitbourne Heritage Society, Inc.**
PO Box 166, Station Rd., Whitbourne, NL A0B 3K0
Tel: 709-759-2345; *Fax:* 709-759-2242
Founded: 1991 Open July 1 - Labour Day.
Judy Gosse, President
Curtis Sheppard, Vice-President
Susan George, Secretary
Mary Gosse, Treasurer

Northwest Territories

Territorial Museums

Prince of Wales Northern Heritage Centre (PWNHC)
PO Box 1320, 4750 48th St., Yellowknife, NT X1A 2L9
Tel: 867-873-7551; *Fax:* 867-873-0205
www.pwnhc.ca
Other contact information: Phone, NWT Archives: 867-873-7698; Fax, NWT Archives: 867-873-0660
Located on the shores of Frame Lake, the Prince of Wales Northern Heritage Centre is open year-round. Visitors to the centre will discover various exhibits about the people, places, & natural history of the Northwest Territories.
Barb Cameron, Director, 867-873-7551, barb_cameron@gov.nt.ca
Joanne Bird, Curator of Collections, 867-873-7668, joanne_bird@gov.nt.ca
Rosalie Scott, Conservator, 867-873-7664, rosalie_scott@gov.nt.ca
Richard Valpy, Territorial Archivist, 867-873-7657, richard_valpy@gov.nt.ca

Local Museums in Northwest Territories

***Colville Lake:* Colville Lake Museum**
General Delivery, Colville Lake, NT X0E 1L0
Tel: 867-709-2500; *Fax:* 867-709-2500
www.virtualmuseum.ca
Museum housing ethnographic artifacts, art gallery & archives; discovery centre; guided tours; gift shop; part of Colville Lake Lodge, a log cabin facility in a Dene community
Bern Will Brown, Curator

***Fort Smith:* Northern Life Museum**
PO Box 420, Fort Smith, NT X0E 0P0
Tel: 867-872-2859; *Fax:* 867-872-5808
nlmmanager@hughes.net
Collection, preservation & presentation of NWT culture & history; open year round
Kevin Brunt, Curator

***Norman Wells:* Norman Wells Historical Centre**
PO Box 56, Norman Wells, NT X0E 0V0
Tel: 867-587-2415; *Fax:* 867-587-2469
Dene cultural artifacts; geological history; WWI & Canol Project interpretation; Great Bear Lake & MacKenzie River explorers; local archives

Nova Scotia

Provincial Museums

Fisheries Museum of the Atlantic
Lunenburg Waterfront, PO Box 1363, 68 Bluenose Dr., Lunenburg, NS B0J 2C0
Tel: 902-634-4794; *Fax:* 902-634-8990
Toll-Free: 866-579-4909
fma@gov.ns.ca
museum.gov.ns.ca/fma/
Historic buildings featuring 3 floors of exhibits & activities: Millenium Aquarium; Bluenose Memorabilia; Fishermen's Memorial Room; August Gales 1926-1927; Bank Fishery Gallery; Rum Running; life in fishing communities; Hall of Inshore Fisheries; fisherman's store; Marine Engine Room, whales, boat shop; schooner Theresa E. Connor; side trawler Cape Sable; part of the Nova Scotia Museum
Jim Tupper, General Manager
Felicia Knock, Secretary-Bookkeeper
Ralph Getson, Curator, Education

Maritime Museum of the Atlantic (MMA) / Musée Maritime d'Atlantique
1675 Lower Water St., Halifax, NS B3J 1S3
Tel: 902-429-7490; *Fax:* 902-424-0612
hennigsj@gov.ns.ca
museum.gov.ns.ca/mma/
Marine history branch of the Nova Scotia Museum; on waterfront; marine artifacts, memorabilia from the Titanic, Halifax explosion exhibit, restored ship chandlery, extensive small craft collection; library & gift shop; Vessel CSS Acadia at museum wharf; open year round
John Hennigar-Shuh, General Manager

Nova Scotia Museum
Heritage Division, NS Dept. of Tourism, Culture & Heritage, 1747 Summer St., Halifax, NS B3H 3A6
Tel: 902-424-7344; *Fax:* 902-424-0560
Toll-Free: 800-632-1114
museum.gov.ns.ca
The Nova Scotia Museum family includes 27 museums across the province, including Museum of Natural History, Halifax; Maritime Museum of the Atlantic, Halifax; Haliburton House, Windsor; Uniacke Estate Museum Park, Mount Uniacke; Prescott House, Starr's Point; Lawrence House, Maitland; Balmoral Grist Mill, Balmoral; Sutherland Steam Mill, Denmark; Fisherman's Life Museum, Jeddore; & Shand House, Windsor.
Bill Greenlaw, Executive Director

Local Museums in Nova Scotia

***Amherst:* Cumberland County Museum & Archives**
150 Church St., Amherst, NS B4H 3C4
Tel: 902-667-2561; *Fax:* 902-667-0996
ccmuseum@ns.aliantzinc.ca
www.cumberlandcountymuseum.com
Founded: 1973 Exhibits & archives on the natural, social & industrial heritage of Cumberland County; located in the 1838 heritage home of Robert Barry Dickey, a Father of Confederation; the archives houses genealogical & other material; fine art collection by County artists; well maintained gardens surround the museum. Open year round.
Shirley Nickerson, Manager/Curator

***Annapolis Royal:* Fort Anne National Historic Site / Lieu historique national du Fort-Anne**
PO Box 9, Annapolis Royal, NS B0S 1A0
Tel: 902-532-2397; *Fax:* 902-532-2232
information@pc.gc.ca
www.pc.gc.ca
Other contact information: Off-Season Phone: 902/532-2321
French & English period fortifications, 1629-1854; exhibits; open May 15 - Oct. 15
Theresa Bunbury, Supt., Operations

***Annapolis Royal:* Fort Edward National Historic Site / Lieu historique national du Fort Édouard**
PO Box 9, Annapolis Royal, NS B0S 1A0
Tel: 902-532-2321; *Fax:* 902-532-2232
www.parkscanada.gc.ca
Built in 1750 by Major Charles Lawrence, this Fort protected the route from Halifax to the Annapolis Valley and remains one of Nova Scotia's oldest buildings.
Theresa Bunbury, Director

***Annapolis Royal:* North Hills Museum**
PO Box 503, 5065 Granville Rd., Annapolis Royal, NS B0S 1A0
Tel: 902-532-7754; *Fax:* 902-532-0700
scrantrg@gov.ns.ca
museum.gov.ns.ca/nhm/
Other contact information: Tel.: 902/532-7754 (late Oct.-late May)
Late 18th-century farmhouse which serves as the setting for the collection of Georgian furniture, ceramics, glass, silver & paintings of former owner Robert Patterson
Ryan Scranton, Executive Director

***Annapolis Royal:* O'Dell House Museum**
136 Saint George St., Annapolis Royal, NS B0S 1A0
Tel: 902-532-7754
historic@ns.aliantzinc.ca
www.annapolisheritagesociety.com/odell.htm
The museum is housed in a stagecoach inn & tavern from around 1869. O'Dell House is the former home of Nova Scotia Pony Express rider, Corey O'Dell & his family. Among the displays are items from Annapolis Royal's ship-building & sea-faring history. The Annapolis Heritage Society's Genealogy Centre's Archives & Collections Centre is also located at O'Dell House Museum. The Centre contains local histories, vital statistics for Annapolis & Digby counties, deeds, & church, cemetery, & probate records.
Barry Moody, Chair, Annapolis Heritage Society
Frances Rafuse, Secretary, Annapolis Heritage Society
Jane Dewolfe, Treasurer, Annapolis Heritage Society

***Annapolis Royal:* Port-Royal National Historic Site of Canada / Lieu historique national de Port-Royal**
PO Box 9, Annapolis Royal, NS B0S 1A0
Tel: 902-532-2898; *Fax:* 902-532-2232
information@pc.gc.ca
www.pc.gc.ca/lhn-nhs/ns/portroyal/index.aspx
Other contact information: Phone, Off-Season: 902-532-2321 (mid October to mid May)
The national historic site on the coast of Nova Scotia is a reconstruction of early 17th-century buildings. The buildings represent a French colony from the era. The site features costumed interpreters & demonstrations to reflect life in one of the earliest settlements in North America.

***Antigonish:* Antigonish Heritage Museum**
20 East Main St., Antigonish, NS B2G 2E9
Tel: 902-863-6160
antheritage@auracom.com
Open year round

***Arichat:* Lenoir Forge Museum**
PO Box 223, General Delivery, Arichat, NS B0E 1A0
Tel: 902-226-9364; *Fax:* 902-226-1919
Community museum; local artifacts; local artisan blacksmith

***Baddeck:* Alexander Graham Bell National Historic Site of Canada / Lieu historique national Alexander-Graham-Bell du Canada**
PO Box 159, Baddeck, NS B0E 1B0
Tel: 902-295-2069; *Fax:* 902-295-3496
information@pc.gc.ca
www.parkscanada.gc.ca; capebretonisland.com/AGBell.html
Presents Dr. Bell's life & work, with emphasis on his accomplishments in Baddeck; open year round; Nov. 1 - Apr. 30 site visits by arrangement. The site is located on Chebucto St. (Rte 205), on the eastern edge of Baddeck.
Aynsley MacFarlane, Site Manager
Carol Whitfield, Field Unit Supt.

***Baddeck:* Canso Islands & Grassy Island Fort National Historic Sites of Canada / Iles-Canso et Fort-de-l'Ile-Grassy Lieux historiques du Can**
PO Box 159, Baddeck, NS B0E 1B0
Tel: 902-295-2069; *Fax:* 902-295-3496
information@pc.gc.ca; atlantic.parksinfo@pc.gc.ca
www.pc.gc.ca/eng/lhn-nhs/ns/canso/index.aspx
Other contact information: Alternative Phone, Summer: 902-366-3136
The Canso Islands were a fishing base for the French during the 16th & 17th centuries. The British used the fishing port during the first half of the 18th century. The Islands were the scene of several battles between the French & English & the Mi'kmaq. In 1744, the Canso settlement was destroyed by the French. The visitor centre & interpretive trail are open from June 1st to September 15th.

***Baddeck:* Marconi National Historic Site of Canada / Lieu historique national Marconi du Canada**
c/o Alexander Graham Bell National Historic Site, PO Box 159, Baddeck, NS B0E 1B0
Tel: 902-295-2069; *Fax:* 902-295-3496
information@pc.qc.ca
parkscanada.gc.ca/marconi
The site marks where Guglielmo Marconi initiated the age of global communications in 1902 by transmitting the first wireless message across the Atlantic Ocean. Visitors can see the Wireless Hall of Fame and walk to the original transmission station. Open June 1 - Sept.
Aynsley MacFarlane, Site Manager
Carol Whitfield, Field Unit Supt.

***Barrington:* Cape Sable Historical Society Centre**
Old Court House, PO Box 67, 2401 Hwy. 3, Barrington, NS B0W 1E0
Tel: 902-637-2185; *Fax:* 902-637-2185
barmusuemcomplex@eastlink.ca
Founded: 1937 The Cape Sable Historical Society illustrates the history of Shelburne & Yarmouth Counties by collecting historical documents, genealogical records, & other items, & preserving historical sites. The Cape Sable Historical Society Centre is open year round.
Brenda Maxwell, Manager

***Barss Corners:* Parkdale Maplewood Community Museum**
3005 Barss Corner Rd., RR#1, Barss Corners, NS B0R 1A0
Tel: 902-644-2893; *Fax:* 902-644-3422
p-mcm@hotmail.com.ca
parkdale.ednet.ns.ca
Founded by Thomas I. Spidell, a missionary-salesman for the New & Latter House of Israel
Donna M. Smith, Administrator

***Bear River:* Riverview Ethnographic Museum**
18 Chute Rd., Box 3, RR#1, Bear River, NS B0S 1B0
Tel: 902-467-4321
Folk costumes & early Americana, open year round
Sarah Elizabeth Glover, Owner & Curator

***Bedford:* Atlantic Canada Aviation Museum (ACAM) / Musée D'aviation des provinces Atlantique**
PO Box 44006, 1658 Bedford Hwy., Bedford, NS B4A 3X5
Tel: 902-873-3773
info@atlanticcanadaaviation.com
www.atlanticcanadaaviation.com
Founded: 1977 Located at the Halifax International Airport (20 Sky Blvd.), the Atlantic Canada Aviation Museum preserves the aviation heritage of Atlantic Canada. The aircraft collection includes the Bell 47-J-2 Ranger Helicopter, the CF-5A Freedom Fighter, a Harvard Mk II, & a CF-104 Starfighter. The museum is open from mid-May to mid-October. At other times, tours can be arranged.
Michael White, Public Affairs Officer, 902-446-7606, mga1937@hotmail.com

***Bridgetown:* James House**
c/o The Bridgetown & Area Historical Society, PO Box 645, 12 Queen St., Bridgetown, NS B0S 1C0
Tel: 902-665-4530
james.house.museum@gmail.com
Founded: 1979 James House was built in 1835 by Richard James, a member of the British Army who served in England &

India. The house was donated to the Bridgetown & Area Historical Society. It became a Provincial Heritage Building, & now operates as the museum for the town of Bridgetown. James House features the Memorial Military Museum, which is sponsored by the Royal Canadian Legion, Branch 33. The museum is open from June to October.

Bridgetown: Tupperville School Museum
RR#3, Bridgetown, NS B0S 1C0
Tel: 902-665-2427; *Fax:* 902-665-4890
Open daily mid-May - mid-Sept.
Marion Inglis, Chair

Bridgewater: DesBrisay Museum & Exhibition Centre
c/o 60 Pleasant St., Bridgewater, NS B4V 3X9
Tel: 902-543-4033; *Fax:* 902-543-4713
museum@bridgewater.ca
www.bridgewater.ca/desbrisay-museum
Founded: 1902 Home of famed porcupine quill-decorated cradle; parkland & trails; open year round; located 130 Jubilee Rd., Bridgewater; admission fee
Linda Bedford, Curator
Barbara Thompson, Director

Bridgewater: Wile Carding Mill
c/o 60 Pleasant St., Bridgewater, NS B4V 3X9
Tel: 902-543-8233; *Fax:* 902-543-4713
museum@town.bridgewater.ns.ca
cardingmill.museum.gov.ns.ca
Other contact information: Off season: 902/543-4033
Last surviving plant of a 19th-century water-powered industrial park; part of Nova Scotia Museum; open June 1 - Sept. 30; located at 242 Victoria Rd., Bridgewater; admission fee
Gary Selig, Manager

Canso: Whitman House Museum & Tourist Bureau
Canso Historical Society, PO Box 128, 1297 Union St., Canso, NS B0H 1H0
Tel: 902-366-2170; *Fax:* 902-366-3093
cansotouristbureau@ns.sympatico.ca
Founded: 1975 Whitman House was built in 1885. The first resident was C.H. Whitman, a Baptist minister. The operation of the Whitman House Museum is now overseen by the Canso Historical Society. Exhibits at the Whitman House Museum depict the history of the town of Canso & eastern Guysborough County, & Canso Harbour. The museum is open from June 1st to September 30th. At other times of the year, appointments may be arranged.

Cheticamp: Musée Acadien
CP 98, Cheticamp, NS B0E 1H0
Tél: 902-224-3463; *Téléc:* 902-224-2170
Open May - Oct.

Church Point: Le Musée Sainte-Marie
PO Box 28, Church Point, NS B0W 1M0
Tel: 902-769-2832; *Fax:* 902-769-0048
stmarysmuseum@hotmail.com
Largest wooden church in North America; open June - Oct.
André Valotaire, Président

Clarks Harbour: Archelaus Smith Museum & Historical Society
PO Box 190, Clarks Harbour, NS B0W 1P0
Tel: 902-745-3361
bryant.newell@ns.sympatico.ca
Portrays the history of Cape Sable Island including fishing techniques & gear, the Cape Island boat, shipwrecks, lives of sea captains, items from old kitchens, paintings by local artists, geneological & other historical records. The collection illustrates the background & growth of a pre-Loyalist fishing community
Bryant Newell, Secretary

Clementsport: Old St. Edward's Anglican Loyalist Church
PO Box 171, Clementsport, NS B0S 1E0
Original Loyalist, Old St. Edward's Anglican Church & Cemetery consecrated 1797; managed by volunteers; situated at 34 Old Post Rd., Clementsport, Annapolis County, NS

Cole Harbour: Cole Harbour Heritage Farm Museum
471 Poplar Dr., Cole Harbour, NS B2W 4L2
Tel: 902-434-0222
farm.museum@ns.aliantzinc.ca
www.coleharbourfarmmuseum.ca
Open daily from May 15 - Oct.15; or by appt.
Elizabeth Corser

Dartmouth: Black Cultural Centre for Nova Scotia
1149 Main St., Dartmouth, NS B2Z 1A8
Tel: 902-434-6223; *Fax:* 902-434-2306
Toll-Free: 800-465-0767
contact@bccns.com
www.bccns.com
Founded: 1983 Programs at the cultural education centre have include guided tours, music, plays, workshops, & lectures.
Dr. Henry V. Bishop, Chief Curator
Russell Grosse, Manager, Operations

Digby: Admiral Digby Museum
PO Box 1644, 95 Montague Row, Digby, NS B0V 1A0
Tel: 902-245-6322; *Fax:* 902-245-5196
admuseum@ns.sympatico.ca
www.admuseum.ns.ca
Museum is housed in a Georgian-style home and is named for Rear Admiral Robert Digby. On display are period rooms, furnishings and artifacts relating to the history of Digby; costumes; Marine Room with charts, ship models, and navigational equipment; photographs; online gift shop; online archives which include family registers and other items of interest to genealogical and historical researchers. Open mid-June - mid-Oct.; two days a week in winter
Sheryl Stanton, Curator

Dingwall: North Highlands Community Museum & Culture Centre
PO Box 3, Dingwall, NS B0C 1G0
Tel: 902-383-2579
community@northhighlandsmuseum.ca
www.northhighlandsmuseum.ca
The history & culture of northern Cape Breton Island is celebrated at the North Highlands Community Museum & Culture Centre, through artifacts & documents. The collection includes maritime artifacts, such as shipwreck booty, schoolroom materials, doctor's instruments, & farming tools.
Rob Macdonald, Co-Chair
David Rasmussen, Co-Chair
Deidre Fraser, Coordinator
Esther Danielson, Secretary
Maureen Grover, Treasurer

Englishtown: Great Hall of The Clans, Highland Pioneers Museum
PO Box 80, Englishtown, NS B0C 1H0
Tel: 902-295-3411; *Fax:* 902-295-2912
info@gaeliccollege.edu
www.gaeliccollege.edu
Open daily June - Sept.
Beth Anne MacEachen, Manager

Glace Bay: Cape Breton Miners' Museum
PO Box 310, 42 Birkley St., Glace Bay, NS B1A 5T8
Tel: 902-849-4522; *Fax:* 902-849-8022
info@minersmuseum.com
www.minersmuseum.com
The Cape Breton Miners' Museum tells the story of the area's history of coal mining. Visitors may tour the Ocean Deeps Colliery, which is a coal mine situated beneath the museum building. Exhibits include coal mining equipment. Research inquiries will be responded to by museum staff. The museum also features the Men of the Deeps Theatre.

Grand Pre: Grand-Pré National Historic Site of Canada
PO Box 150, Grand Pre, NS B0P 1M0
Tel: 902-542-3631; *Fax:* 902-542-1691
Toll-Free: 866-542-3631
contact@grand-pre.com
www.grand-pre.com
Bilingual guides interpret history of the Acadians; open daily May 1 - Oct. 30; entrance fee
Victor Tétrault, Executive Director

Greenwood: Greenwood Military Aviation Museum
PO Box 786, Greenwood, NS B0P 1N0
Tel: 902-765-1494; *Fax:* 902-765-1261
gmam001@hotmail.com
gmam.ca
Founded: 1995 Recording the history of RAF/RCAF/CF station 1942 to present
Maj. R. Leblanc, General Manager
Bryan Nelson, Curator

Guysborough: Old Court House Museum
PO Box 232, Guysborough, NS B0H 1N0
Tel: 902-533-4008
guysborough.historical@ns.sympatico.ca
Open June - Oct.

Halifax: Africville National Historic Site
PO Box 392 CBO, Halifax, NS B3J 3P8
Tel: 902-492-0253; *Fax:* 902-420-2816
Accessible year round
Irvine Carvery, President

Halifax: Army Museum
Cavalier Bldg., Halifax Citadel National Historic Site, PO Box 9080 A, Halifax, NS B3K 5M7
Tel: 902-422-5979; *Fax:* 902-426-4228
armymuseum@ns.aliantzinc.ca
Founded: 1953 The Army Museum preserves & promotes the military heritage of Atlantic Canada. Displays, including uniforms, decorations, weapons, & firearms, are related to the British, Canadian Regular Force, & Militia. The museum is open from May to October.

Halifax: Fisherman's Life Museum (FLM)
Jeddore, Oyster Pond, 58 Navy Pool Loop, Halifax, NS B0J 1W0
Tel: 902-772-2344; *Fax:* 902-772-2344
monkma@gov.ns.ca
museum.gov.ns.ca/flm/
Other contact information: Summer Tel: 902/889-2053, Fax: 902/889-2053
Open daily June 1 - Oct. 15
Martha Monk, Site Manager
Judith Shiers Milne, Public Information Officer, 902/424-7398, shiersjl@gov.ns.ca

Halifax: Halifax Citadel National Historic Site of Canada
PO Box 9080 A, Halifax, NS B3K 5M7
Tel: 902-426-5080; *Fax:* 902-426-4228
denise.graham@pc.gc.ca
www.pc.gc.ca/lhn-nhs/ns/halifax/index_e.asp
Present Citadel was completed in 1856 & was the fourth in a series of British forts on this site; a national landmark commemorating Halifax's role as a key naval station in the British Empire; living history program featuring the 78th Highlanders & the precision of the Royal Artillery
Linda Frank, Field Unit Superintendent

Halifax: Halifax Police Museum
1975 Gottingen St., Halifax, NS B3J 2H1
Tel: 902-421-6595

Halifax: HMCS Sackville
***Also known as:* Canadian Naval Memorial Trust (CNMT)**
PO Box 99000 Forces, Halifax, NS B3K 5X5
Tel: 902-429-2132; *Fax:* 902-427-1346
rasoucie@ns.sympatico.ca
www.hmcssackville-cnmt.ns.ca
Canada's Naval Memorial; WWII corvette museum; open summer, downtown Halifax, open winter, HMCS Dockyard
Vice-Admiral Duncan Miller, Chair
Cdr. Wendall Brown, Commanding Officer

Halifax: Maritime Command Museum / Musée du Commandement Maritime
***Also known as:* Marcom Museum**
Admiralty House, PO Box 99000 Forces, 2725 Gottingen St., Halifax, NS B3K 5X5
Tel: 902-721-8250; *Fax:* 902-721-8541
marcommuseum@forces.gc.ca
www.pspmembers.com/marcommuseum
Founded: 1974 Of the Dept. of National Defence's 55 museums, this is the largest. Housed within 30 rooms of Admiralty House, a Georgian mansion, are displays representing facets of the Canadian Military. The collection consists of a research library, uniforms, model ships, medals, badges, ships' bells and other memorabilia associated with naval life. Open year round
Marilyn Gurney, Director

Halifax: Nova Scotia Sport Hall of Fame
#446, 1800 Argyle St., Halifax, NS B3J 3N8
Tel: 902-421-1266; *Fax:* 902-425-1148
sporthalloffame@eastlink.ca
www.novascotiasporthalloffame.com
The Hall of Fame honours Nova Scotians who have made an impact on sports during the past 100 years. Inductees are addeed to the Hall of Fame each year, during The Hall of Fame Induction Night.
Bill Robinson, Executive Director, billr@eastlink.ca
Shane Mailman, Manager, Facility & Communications
Karolyn Sevcik, Coordinator, Administration & Special Events, halloffameevents@eastlink.ca
Rob Randall, Treasurer

Halifax: Prince of Wales Tower National Historic Site of Canada
c/o Halifax Citadel National Historic Site, PO Box 9080 A, Halifax, NS B3K 5M7
Tel: 902-426-5080; *Fax:* 902-426-4228
halifax.citadel @pc.gc.ca
www.pc.gc.ca/lhn-nhs/ns/prince/index.aspx
The Prince of Wales Tower was built in 1796 & 1797. Its purpose was to protect the British from Fench attack. Over 200 years later, visitors will discover exhibits which show the tower's history. The Tower is open from the beginning of July to the end of August.
Linda Frank, Field Unit Superintendent, Mainland Nova Scotia Field Unit, Parks Canada
Dave Danskin, Manager, Heritage Presentation & Visitor Services, Mainland Nova Scotia Field Unit, Parks Canada
Tanya Taylor White, Manager, External Relations, Mainland Nova Scotia Field Unit, Parks Canada

Halifax: Thomas McCulloch Museum
Biology Dept., Dalhousie University, 1355 Oxford St., Halifax, NS B3H 4J1
Tel: 902-494-3515; *Fax:* 902-494-3736
biology@dal.ca
biotype.biology.dal.ca/museum/

Founded: 1883 Collection of mounted birds, artifacts, Lorenzen ceramic mushrooms, shells & insects; marine & freshwater aquaria; occasional temporary exhibits; open weekdays; free admission
Stephen Fry, Chief Curator, 902-494-3530, steve.fry@dal.ca
Karen Smith, Curator, 902-494-2785, karen.smith@dal.ca
Julie Walker, Director

***Halifax:* York Redoubt National Historic Site of Canada**
c/o Halifax Citadel National Historic Site, PO Box 9080 A, Halifax, NS B3K 5M7
Tel: 902-426-5080; *Fax:* 902-426-4228
halifax.citadel@pc.gc.ca
www.pc.gc.ca/lhn-nhs/ns/york/index.aspx
York Redoubt was established in 1793 to defend the Halifax Harbour. Today, it is a National Historic Site of Canada, which is part of the Halifax Defence Complex. The site is open year-round.
Linda Frank, Field Unit Superintendent, Mainland Nova Scotia Field Unit

***Hantsport:* Churchill House & Marine Memorial Room**
c/o Town of Hantsport, PO Box 399, Hantsport, NS B0P 1P0
Tel: 902-684-3461; *Fax:* 902-684-3227
susan@hantsportnovascotia.com
www.hantsportnovascotia.com;
nsgna.ednet.ns.ca/hantsport/churchl.htm
Other contact information: (off season) 902/684-9068
Located at 6 Main St., Hantsport; open daily July - Sept., or by appt.; classic Victorian architecture; documents local shipbuilding history
Susan Carey, Tourism Manager, Hantsport

***La Have:* Fort Point Museum**
c/o Lunenburg County Historical Society, PO Box 99, La Have, NS B0R 1C0
Tel: 902-688-2696
lchs-fortpoint@ns.sympatico.ca
www3.ns.sympatico.ca/lchs-fortpoint/
On National Historic Site of Fort Ste. Marie de Grâce, 1632

***La Have:* La Have Island Marine Museum**
PO Box 69, La Have, NS B0R 1C0
Tel: 902-688-3192
limms@auracom.com
www.lahaveislandsmarinemuseum.ca
Historical treasures from a community that derived its life & livelihood from the sea
Douglas Berrigan, President
Sheila Chambers, Contact

***Inverness:* Inverness Miners Museum**
PO Box 598, Inverness, NS B0E 1N0
Tel: 902-258-3822
invhistsoc@ns.sympatico.ca
Location: 62 Lower Railway St.
Ned MacDonald, Director

***Iona:* Highland Village Museum / An Clachan Gàidhealach**
4119 Hwy. 223, Iona, NS B2C 1A3
Tel: 902-725-2272; *Fax:* 902-725-2227
Toll-Free: 866-442-3542
highlandvillage@gov.ns.ca
www.museum.gov.ns.ca/hv
Founded: 1959 The museum's mission is to collect & preserve the Gaelic heritage of Nova Scotia, with a focus on advancing the language. Included on site are: interpretation centre & museum, carding mill, 1880-1900 frame house, schoolhouse, forge, country store, barn, frame house (1830-1875), log cabin, stone (black) house, outdoor performance centre. There is also an extensive database of genealogical information. The museum is open June - Oct., 9:30-5:30 daily.
Mr. Rodney Chaisson, Director, chaissrs@gov.ns.ca

***Kentville:* Blair House Museum**
c/o N.S. Fruit Growers' Association, Kentville Agricultural Centre, 32 Main St., Kentville, NS B4N 1J5
Tel: 902-678-1093; *Fax:* 902-678-1567
www.nsapples.com/museumb.htm
Founded: 1981 The Blair House Museum was opened by the Nova Scotia Fruit Growers' Association. The purpose of the museum is the preservation & presentation of the history of the apple growing industry. The Agriculture Canada wing of the museum displays past & present research conducted at the station. The museum is located in a 1911 building, which was the residence of the research station's first superintendent, Dr. William Saxby Blair.
Dela Erith, Executive Director, Nova Scotia Fruit Growers' Association, derith@nsapples.com
Helen Arenburg, Inspector, & Contact, Public Relations, harenburg@nsapples.com

***Kentville:* Kings County Museum**
37 Cornwallis St., Kentville, NS B4N 2E2
Tel: 902-678-6237; *Fax:* 902-678-2764
curator@okcm.ca
www.okcm.ca
Cultural & natural history of Kings County; Parks Canada commemorative exhibit to the New England Planters; genealogy & community history archives
Cathy Margeson, Office Manager
Bria Stokesbury, Curator

***Liverpool:* Hank Snow Country Music Centre**
PO Box 1419, 148 Bristol Ave., Liverpool, NS B0T 1K0
Tel: 902-354-4675; *Fax:* 902-354-5199
Toll-Free: 888-450-5525
info@hanksnow.com
www.hanksnow.com
Founded: 1996 A tribute to Hank Snow, legendary country/folk singer from "down east," the displays include a plethora of photos and memorabilia, from his guitar strings to his iconic toupées to his yellow 1947 Cadillac. The centre also houses the Nova Scotia Country Music Hall of Fame.

***Liverpool:* Perkins House**
Queen's County Museum, PO Box 1078, 105 Main St., Liverpool, NS B0T 1K0
Tel: 902-354-4058; *Fax:* 902-354-2050
rafusela@gov.ns.ca
museum.gov.ns.ca/peh/
Connecticut style cottage built by merchant & diarist Simeon Perkins in 1766; open June - Oct. 15
Linda Rafuse, Curator, rafusel@gov.ns.ca

***Liverpool:* Queens County Museum**
PO Box 1078, 109 Main St., Liverpool, NS B0T 1K0
Tel: 902-354-4058; *Fax:* 902-354-2050
www.queenscountymuseum.com
Founded: 1980 The Queens County Museum depicts the cultural history of Nova Scotia's Queens County. The south shore of the province has a strong history related to the Mi'kmaq culture, fishing, & the forest. Programs are available for schools & the public.
Linda Rafuse, Director, rafusela@gov.ns.ca

***Lockeport:* Little School Museum**
PO Box 69, Lockeport, NS B0T 1L0
Tel: 902-656-2238
townoflockeport@aura.com
Replica of a former school room & a marine room; historical artifacts of local area

***Louisbourg:* Fortress of Louisbourg National Historic Site / Forteresse-de-Louisbourg, Lieu historique national**
259 Park Service Rd., Louisbourg, NS B1C 2L2
Tel: 902-733-2280; *Fax:* 902-733-2423
lhs.library@pc.gc.ca
fortress.uccb.ns.ca/parks/gal_e.html
Other contact information: TDD: 902/733-3607
Carol Whitfield, Field Unit Manager, Parks Canada, Cape Breton District

***Louisbourg:* Louisbourg Marine Interpretive Centre**
7548 Main St., Louisbourg, NS B1C 1J4
Tel: 902-733-2252; *Fax:* 902-733-2053
e.p@seascape.ns.ca
Open June- Sept.
Ernie Parsons, Director

***Louisbourg:* S&L (Sydney & Louisburg) Railway Museum**
7330 Main St., Louisbourg, NS B1C 1P5
Tel: 902-733-2720
fortress.uccb.ns.ca/historic/s_l.html
Exhibits include railroad artifacts, models, photographs & other documentation; paintings; rolling stock, model railroad, souvenirs; open June 1 - Oct. 15; tourist information centre
Eugene Magee, Curator

***Lower Sackville:* Fultz House Museum**
PO Box 124, 33 Sackville Dr., Lower Sackville, NS B4C 2S8
Tel: 902-865-3794; *Fax:* 902-865-6940
fultz.house@ns.sympatico.ca
www.fultzhouse.ca
1860s home which belonged to the Fultz family of Sackville, NS; contains many artifacts & photographs from the Sackville area; blacksmith shop & cooperage shop from 1800s
Gail Hagee, Vice-President
Wilma Treen, President

***Mabou:* An Drochaid**
PO Box 175, Mabou, NS B0E 1X0
Tel: 902-945-2311
androchaid@ns.sympatico.ca
Mabou Gaelic and Historical Society. Open July & Aug.
Margie Beaton, Director, 902/945-2790
Effie Rankin, Director, 902/945-2279

***Mahone Bay:* Mahone Bay Settlers Museum**
PO Box 583, 578 Main St., Mahone Bay, NS B0J 2E0
Tel: 902-624-6263; *Fax:* 902-624-0646
info@settlersmuseum.ns.ca
www.settlersmuseum.ns.ca
Community Museum which provides vistors with a local history of the area; Open June to Sept.
Wilma Stewart-White, Curator

***Maitland:* East Hants Historical Museum**
PO Box 51, Maitland, NS B0N 1C0
Tel: 902-261-2796
ehhs.weebly.com
Small museum containing historical Nova Scotian artifacts with local connections, historical documents, military records & cemetary records
Nancy Doane, President, East Hants Historical Society
Glenys Leck, Secretary
Olive Terris, Treasurer

***Maitland:* Lawrence House Museum**
8660 rte. 215, RR #1, Maitland, NS B0N 1T0
Tel: 902-424-6478; *Fax:* 902-424-0560
lawrence.museum.gov.ns.ca
c.1865 home of William D. Lawrence, shipwright; open June 1 - Oct. 15
Marvan Moore, Director

***Middleton:* Annapolis Valley Macdonald Museum**
PO Box 925, 21 School St., Middleton, NS B0S 1P0
Tel: 902-825-6116; *Fax:* 902-825-0531
info@macdonaldmuseum.ca
www.macdonaldmuseum.ca
Features antique clocks and pocket watches; Art Gallery featuring local artists; historical artifacts, household items, tools; recreated classroom and general store; sports heritage wall of fame; gift shop.
Sherry Griffin, Director

***Milton:* Milton Blacksmith Shop Museum**
PO Box 572, 351 West St., Milton, NS B0T 1P0
Tel: 902-350-0268
www.qcis.ns.ca/blacksmith
Managed by the Milton Heritage Society, the museum is a 1903 smithy, complete with forge, ox sling & original workbenches, as well as a wide array of tools of the trade; also large display of photographs of historical Milton, NS
Ms Christine Tupper, Curator, 902-354-2550

***Mount Uniacke:* Uniacke Estate Museum Park**
PO Box 12, 758 Hwy. #1, Mount Uniacke, NS B0N 1Z0
Tel: 902-866-0032; *Fax:* 902-866-2560
c.1813; open June - Oct. 15
Martina Murphy, Supervisor

***Musquodoboit Harbour:* Musquodoboit Railway Museum**
PO Box 303, Musquodoboit Harbour, NS B0J 2L0
Tel: 902-889-2689
Open May 16 - Oct.

***New Glasgow:* Carmichael Stewart House**
86 Temperance St., New Glasgow, NS B2H 3A7
Tel: 902-752-5583
pictoucounty@ns.sympatico.ca
www.parl.ns.ca/csmuseum
Founded: 1965 Operated by the Pictou County Historical Society, the Carmichael Stewart House Museum is a late Victorian home which contains collections such as photographs, clothing, & Trenton Glassware. The museum is open during the summer.
Fergie MacKay, President
Jessica MacNeil, Treasurer
George McKay, Secretary

***New Glasgow:* Pictou County Historical Museum**
86 Temperance St., New Glasgow, NS B2H 3A7
Tel: 902-752-5583
pictoucounty@ns.sympatico.ca
Fergie MacKay, President

***New Ross:* Ross Farm Museum**
4568 Hwy. 12, New Ross, NS B0J 2M0
Tel: 902-689-2210; *Fax:* 902-689-2264
rossfarm@gov.ns.ca
rossfarm.museum.gov.ns.ca
Ross family farm 1817
Lisa Wolfe, Director

***North East Margaree:* Margaree Salmon Museum**
PO Box 21, North East Margaree, NS B0E 2H0
Tel: 902-248-2848
Exhibits relate to salmon angling on the Margaree River. In a former schoolhouse excellent collections of fishing tackle, photos & memorabilia of famous anglers

***Orangedale:* Orangedale Railway Museum**
PO Box 16, Orangedale, NS B0E 2K0
Tel: 902-756-3384; *Fax:* 902-756-2547

Open June - mid-Oct.; railway station built in 1911
Martin Boston

***Parrsboro:* Fundy Geological Museum**
PO Box 640, 162 Two Island Rd., Parrsboro, NS B0M 1S0
Tel: 902-254-3814; *Fax:* 902-254-3666
Toll-Free: 866-856-9466
fundygeo@gov.ns.ca
fundygeo.museum.gov.ns.ca
Open daily in summer; Tues.-Sat. in winter
Carol Corbett, Education Coordinator
Kenneth Adams, Director/Curator

***Pictou:* McCulloch House Museum (MCH)**
PO Box 1210, 100 Old Haliburton Rd., Pictou, NS B0K 1H0
Tel: 902-485-4563; *Fax:* 902-485-5213
nsmwebmaster@gov.ns.ca
www.rootsweb.ancestry.com/~nspcghs
Founded: 1972 Administered by the Pictou County Genealogy and Heritage Society, the museum was built in 1805 as home to Rev. Dr. McCulloch, the founder of Pictou Academy & first president of Dalhousie University. The exhibits reflect the life & times of the Scottish immigrants and their influence on today's Nova Scotia.
Ms Dayle Crouse, Director

***Pictou:* Northumberland Fisheries Museum & Heritage Association (NFM)**
PO Box 1489, 71 Front St., Pictou, NS B0K 1H0
Tel: 902-485-4972; *Fax:* 902-485-6586
northumberlandmuseum@ns.sympatico.ca
www.northumberlandfisheriesmuseum.c om
Founded: 1978 Located in the historic C.N. Station; fishing artifacts from the late 1800s to present day; original fisherman's Bunkhouse; The "Silver Bullet"; photographs; boat models; fishing tools; artifacts on lobster processing; shell fish/live fish displays; sea heritage education for schools & seniors; education is based on fact & scientific data from Northumberland Strait area; local research conducted on fishing & sea heritage; recent additions to the museum include a lobster hatchery & lighthouse museum & research centre.
David MacKeil, Chairman, dave_mackeil@hotmail.com
Michelle Davey, Business Manager

***Port Hastings:* Port Hastings Museum & Archives**
9 Church St., Port Hastings, NS B9A 1N5
Tel: 902-625-1295
gutofcanso@ns.sympatico.ca
fortress.uccb.ns.ca/historic/port.html
Located in 100-year-old Cape Breton house; displays include pioneer artifacts, photographic displays & exhibits on construction of causeway; genealogical records available
Dernie Gillis, President
Beryl MacDonald-MacLeod, Curator

***Port Hood:* Chestico Museum & Historical Society**
PO Box 144, Port Hood, NS B0E 2W0
Tel: 902-787-2244
chesticoplace.com
Founded: 1986 Located in Harbourview, on Rte 19 on the outskirts of Port Hood, the museum houses artifacts from the local community; house histories, historical events, people of the Port Hood area; gift shop; tea room; special programming. The museum will be housed in a new facility, Chestico Place, located in the centre of Port Hood, in the near future.
Susan Mallette, Director

***Port Williams:* Prescott House**
1633 Starr's Point Rd., Port Williams, NS B0P 1T0
Tel: 902-542-3984; *Fax:* 902-542-3984
mortonnl@gov.ns.ca
museum.gov.ns.ca/prh/
c.1814 Georgian house, open June 1 - Oct. 15; museum shop; bus tours welcome
Nancy Morton, Caretaker

***Pubnico-Ouest:* Musée des Acadiens des Pubnicos et Centre de recherche**
CP 92, Pubnico-Ouest, NS B0W 3S0
Tél: 902-762-3380; *Téléc:* 902-762-0726
musee.acadien@ns.sympatico.ca
www.museeacadien.ca
Le Musée: #898, autoroute 335; consacré au patrimoine des Acadiens/Acadiennes de Pubnico-Ouest; articles de maison; documents; photographies; archives; potager traditionnel; boutique de souvenirs.
Paul d'Entremont, Président

***Riverport:* Ovens Natural Park & Museum**
326 Ovens Rd., Riverport, NS B0J 2W0
Tel: 902-766-4621; *Fax:* 902-766-4344
info@ovenspark.com
www.ovenspark.com
Located on the Atlantic coast of Nova Scotia, Ovens Natural Park is a reserve of coastal forest, featuring the sea caves or "Ovens". The area became known internationally during th 1861 gold rush. The Gold Rush Museum contains artifacts from that era.
Angel Chapin, Director

***St Peters:* Nicolas Denys Museum**
PO Box 249, St Peters, NS B0E 3B0
Tel: 902-535-2175
nicolasdenysmuseum@ns.aliantzinc.ca
fortress.uccb.ns.ca/historic/deny s.html
Micmac, Acadien, Scottish & Irish artifacts

***Shag Harbour:* Chapel Hill Museum**
PO Box 46, 5492 Hwy #3, Shag Harbour, NS B0W 3B0
Tel: 902-723-1313
chapelhillhistory@aliantzinc.ns.ca
chapelhill.webs.com
Located in former Baptist Church; features various displays related to local area including tools for ship building, genealogical research materials, various fishing exhibits; able to view 4 local lighthouses from observation tower; open June 1 - Sept. 15 daily; rest of the year by appt.
Douglas Shand, President, Chapel Hill Historical Society, 902-723-2949, shawimm@ns.sympatico.ca
Veronica Hopkins, Vice President/Treasurer, Chapel Hill Historical Society, vhopkins@ns.sympatico.ca

***Shelburne:* John C. Williams Dory Shop**
PO Box 39, 11 Dock St., Shelburne, NS B0T 1W0
Tel: 902-875-4003; *Fax:* 902-875-4141
shelburne.museum@ns.sympatico.ca
www.historicshelburne.com
Restored dory factory, est. 1880; open June 1 - Sept. 30; dories still built to order
Kim Truchan, Complex Manager, shs.kimtruchan@ns.aliantzinc.ca

***Shelburne:* Ross Thomson House & Store Museum**
PO Box 39, Shelburne, NS B0T 1W0
Tel: 902-875-3141; *Fax:* 902-875-4141
shelburne.museum@ns.sympatico.ca
www.historicshelburne.com
Located on Charlotte St. in Shelburne; 1785 Loyalist house & garden; 18th-century store & chandlery; 19th-century military artifacts; open June 1 - Oct. 15
Kim Truchan, Complex Manager, shs.kimtruchan@ns.aliantzinc.ca

***Shelburne:* Shelburne County Museum**
PO Box 39, 20 Dock St., Shelburne, NS B0T 1W0
Tel: 902-875-3219; *Fax:* 902-875-4141
shelburne.museum@ns.sympatico.ca
www.historicshelburne.com
Cultural & economic history of Shelburne from 1783; genealogy information; open year round
Finn Bower, Curator

***Sherbrooke:* Sherbrooke Village**
PO Box 295, 42 Main St., Sherbrooke, NS B0J 3C0
Tel: 902-522-2400; *Fax:* 902-522-2974
svillage@gov.ns.ca
sherbrookevillage.museum.gov.ns.ca
Open June - mid-Oct.
Craig MacDonald, Project Director

***Smiths Cove:* Old Temperance Hall Museum**
Smiths Cove, NS B0S 1S0
Tel: 902-245-4315
Exhibits of the 19th and 20th century pertaining to the local community including the earliest inhabitants, the Mi'kmaq; history of the Sons of Temperance.
Dorothy Gray, President, 902/245-4665

***Springhill:* The Anne Murray Centre**
36 Main St., Springhill, NS B0M 1X0
Tel: 902-597-8614; *Fax:* 902-597-2001
info@annemurraycentre.com
www.annemurraycentre.com
Founded: 1989 Pays tribute to the achievements of Springhill's internationally acclaimed singing superstar; open May - Oct., otherwise by appt. or by chance.

***Springhill:* Springhill Miner's Museum**
PO Box 610, Black River Rd., Springhill, NS B0M 1X0
Tel: 902-597-3449; *Fax:* 902-597-2001
museum.gov.ns.ca/musdir/springhillminersmuseum.htm
Tours of the Springhill coal mine, famous in song & legend; gift shop & picnic area; open May - Oct.

***Stellarton:* The Museum of Industry**
PO Box 2590, 147 North Foord St., Stellarton, NS B0K 1S0
Tel: 902-755-5425; *Fax:* 902-755-7045
industry@gov.ns.ca
museum.gov.ns.ca/moi/index.html
Atlantic Canada's largest museum; chronicles the impact of industrialization on the people, economy & landscape of Nova Scotia; features Canada's oldest steam locomotives, an historic model railway layout, a belt-driven working machine shop & a collection of Nova Scotia's Trenton glass
Debra McNabb, Director

***Sydney:* Cape Breton Centre for Heritage & Science**
***Also known as:* The Lyceum Museum**
225 George St., Sydney, NS B1P 1J5
Tel: 902-539-1572; *Fax:* 902-539-1572
fortress.uccb.ns.ca/historic/oldsyd.html
The Lyceum was built in 1904 by the Roman Catholic diocese. The Opera House contained a 900 seat theatre, as well as a library, gymnasium, billiards room, & clubrooms. Today, the Lyceum houses the Cape Breton Centre for Heritage & Science. The Old Sydney Society provides tours of the Colonial Town of Old Sydney, which was first the home to Mi'Kmaq people, then Basque fishermen, Loyalists, & later immigrating Scots. In the Cape Breton Centre for Heritage & Science, visitors will discover the natural & social histories of Cape Breton County. The museum is open year round.
Dr. Robert Morgan, President, 902-539-3951
J. Peyton Chisholm, Curator
Elaine Hummer, Bookkeeper

***Tatamagouche:* Balmoral Grist Mill**
RR#4, Tatamagouche, NS B0K 1V0
Tel: 902-657-3016; *Fax:* 902-657-2606
www.museum.gov.ns.ca/bgm
Located at 660 Matheson Brook Road in Balmoral Mills, the 1874 three-storey grist mill is still operational. The grist mill is open from June 1st to October 15th.
Darrell Burke, Site Manager, 902-657-3016, burked@gov.ns.ca

***Tatamagouche:* Sunrise Trail Museum**
216 Main St., Tatamagouche, NS B0K 1V0
Tel: 902-657-2689
Open daily mid-June - Labour Day

***Tatamagouche:* Sutherland Steam Mill Museum**
RR#5, Tatamagouche, NS B0K 1V0
Tel: 902-657-3365; *Fax:* 902-657-3016
museum.gov.ns.ca/ssm/
Open June 1 - Oct. 15
John Taylor, Superintendent, 902/657-3016

***Truro:* Colchester Historical Society Museum**
***Also known as:* Colchester Historical Museum**
PO Box 412, 29 Young St., Truro, NS B2N 5C5
Tel: 902-895-6284; *Fax:* 902-895-9530
colchestermuseum@ns.aliantzinc.ca
www.genealogynet.com/Colchester/
Founded: 1954 Open year round
Aidan Norton, Curator
Nan Harvey, Archivist, colchesterarchives@ns.aliantzinc.ca

***Truro:* The Little White Schoolhouse**
PO Box 1252, 20 Arthur St., Truro, NS B2N 5N2
Tel: 902-895-5170
lwsm1979@msn.com
lwsm.ednet.ns.ca
Original Riverton School; commemorates schoolhouses in Nova Scotia from Confederation to the 1950s; contains books & artifacts from the era of one-room schoolhouse; requests for research on the graduates of the Provincial Normal School & College & in old copies of the NS Journal of Education, accepted; open early June - Aug. & by appt.
Tom Acker, Curator

***Wallace:* Wallace Area Museum**
PO Box 179, 13440 Rte. 6, Wallace, NS B0K 1Y0
Tel: 902-257-2191; *Fax:* 902-257-2191
wallacemuseum@ns.aliantzinc.ca
www.wallaceandareamuseum.com
Founded: 1984 The museum collect, preserves, & displays the history of Wallace & the surrounding region. Artifacts include nineteenth century marine charts & maps, the United Empire Loyalist grant, pre-Confederation letters, & items about shipbuilding in Wallace & the Wallace sandstone quarries.
Doris Purdy, President
Glenda Dewaugh, Vice-President
David Dewar, Curator
Doug Perry, Secretary

***West Bay:* Marble Mountain Library & Museum**
RR#1, West Bay, NS B0E 3K0
Tel: 902-756-3289
Wendy MacDonald, Curator

***Windsor:* The Haliburton**
PO Box 2683, 414 Clifton Ave., Windsor, NS B0N 2T0
Tel: 902-798-2915
dauphiar@gov.ns.ca
museum.gov.ns.ca/hh/
Open June 1 - Oct. 15
Alan Dauphinee, Superintendent

Windsor: **Shand House**
PO Box 2683, 389 Avon St., Windsor, NS B0N 2T0
Tel: 902-798-8213; *Fax:* 902-798-5619
dauphiar@gov.ns.ca
museum.gov.ns.ca/sh/

Open June 1 - Oct. 15
Alan Dauphinee, Superintendent

Windsor: **West Hants Historical Society Museum**
PO Box 2335, 281 King St., Windsor, NS B0N 2T0
Tel: 902-798-4706
whhs@ns.aliantzinc.ca
www.westhantshistoricalsociety.ca
Artifacts related to the history of Hants County in Nova Scotia are collected & preserved by the West Hants Historical Society & displayed at its museum. Visitors will find information about the Mi'kmaq, the Acadians, the Loyalists, the Great Windsor Fire of 1897, & the local shipbuilding industry. The society also operates a genealogy department. The museum is open five days a week from mid June to the end of August, & one day a week from September to June. Summer tours are available of the Fort Edward Blockhouse. Appointments may be arranged for times when the museum is closed.

Wolfville: **Randall House Museum**
c/o Wolfville Historical Society, 259 Main St., Wolfville, NS B4P 1C6
Tel: 902-542-9775
randallhouse@live.ca
www.wolfvillehs.ednet.ns.ca
The Randall House is an historic farmhouse, from around 1800, which is owned & operated by the Wolfville Historical Society. The Randall House Museum reflects life in Wolfville & the surrounding area during the 18th & 19th centuries. On display are furniture, clothing, china, & a collection of Victorian greeting cards. A library is located in The Randall House for persons researching local history & genealogy.
John Whidden, President
Heather Watts, Archivist, 902-542-0307
William Bishop, Historian

Yarmouth: **Firefighters' Museum of Nova Scotia**
Nova Scotia Museum Complex, 451 Main St., Yarmouth, NS B5A 1G9
Tel: 902-742-5525
darbydl@gov.ns.ca
museum.gov.ns.ca/fm/
Artifacts date to the early 1800s; open year round
David Darby, Curator

Yarmouth: **Yarmouth County Museum & Archives**
c/o Yarmouth County Historical Society, 22 Collins St., Yarmouth, NS B5A 3C8
Tel: 902-742-5539; *Fax:* 902-749-1120
ycmuseum@eastlink.ca
yarmouthcountymuseum.ednet.ns.ca
Also operates the Pelton-Fuller House in Yarmouth, the historic summer home of A.C. Fuller, the Fuller Brush Man & the Killam Brothers' shipping office, the oldest in Canada, during the summer months
Nadine Gates, Curator
Adèle Hampel, Director
J. Stuart McLean, Archivist MLIS

Nunavut

Local Museums in Nunavut

Arctic Bay: **Sod House Museum**
c/o Innumariit Committee, Arctic Bay, NU X0A 0A0

History & traditions of the Inuit of Admiralty Inlet

Iqaluit: **Nuantta Sunaqutangit Museum**
PO Box 1900, Iqaluit, NU X0A 0H0
Tel: 867-979-5537; *Fax:* 867-979-4533
museum@nunanet.com
Founded in 1969; housed in a historic Hudson Bay Company warehouse building; collections focus on Inuit culture & history from the Baffin region, including historical & archeological artifacts, tools, clothing, & equipment as well as arts & crafts; also maintains a collection of archival photographs, publications & documents for exhibition & research purposes; open Tues.-Sun.
Brian Lunger, Manager/Curator

Pangnirtung: **Auyuittuq National Park of Canada (ANPR)**
Parks Canada, PO Box 353, Pangnirtung, NU X0A 0R0
Tel: 867-473-3500; *Fax:* 867-473-8612
nunavut.info@pch.gc.ca
www.pc.gc.ca/pn-np/nu/auyuittuq/index_e.asp
Other contact information: Phone, Communications: 867-975-4673; Fax: 867-975-4674
Founded: 1976 Located in the eastern Arctic, on Baffin Island, Auyuittuq National Park of Canada protects 19,089 km2 of terrain.
Maryse Mahy, Planner, Nunavut Field Unit, 867-975-4673, Fax: 867-975-4674, Maryse.Mahy@pc.gc.ca

Pangnirtung: **Sipalaseequtt Museum Society**
Angmarlik Visitor Centre, PO Box 227, Pangnirtung, NU X0A 0R0
Tel: 867-473-8737; *Fax:* 867-473-8685
oarnaqaq1@gov.nu.ca
Inuit artifacts; whaling history in Cumberland Sound Baffin Island; Elders' meetings; craft production; tours
Ooleepeela Arnaqaq, Manager

Ontario

Provincial Museums

Hockey Hall of Fame (HHOF) / Le Temple de la Renommée du Hockey
Brookfield Place, 30 Yonge St., Toronto, ON M5E 1X8
Tel: 416-360-7765; *Fax:* 416-360-1501
info@hhof.com
www.hhof.com
Founded: 1961 The museum holds a veritable treasure of artifacts, memorabilia, films and photos, displayed in multi-media exhibits, all on a hockey theme. Also on site is the D.K. (Doc) Seaman Hockey Resource Centre which stores a vast archive. The museum offers a variety of educational programs. Visitors can also enjoy interactive games. This is the home of hockey's ultimate trophy, Lord Stanley's Cup.
Mr. William C. Hay, Chair/CEO, Board of Directors, bhay@hhof.com
Mr. Philip Pritchard, Vice-President/Curator, ppritchard@hhof.com

Royal Ontario Museum (ROM)
100 Queen's Park, Toronto, ON M5S 2C6
Tel: 416-586-8000
info@rom.on.ca
www.rom.on.ca
Founded: 1912 The Royal Ontario Museum (ROM) is Canada's largest museum, an internationally renowned facility & popular public attraction. Created in 1912, the ROM has an unusually broad dual mandate of collecting & preserving in the areas of natural history & human cultures, & communicating its research to the world. Today, the ROM holds in excess of 6 million objects in its collections, which include galleries of art, archaeology & science.
William Thorsell, Director & CEO
Glenn Dobbin, Deputy Director, Operations
Dr. Mark Engstrom, Deputy Director, Collections & Research
James Temerty, Chair, Board of Governors

Local Museums in Ontario

Alliston: **Museum on the Boyne**
PO Box 910, Alliston, ON L9R 1A1
Tel: 705-435-0167; *Fax:* 705-434-3006
boynemuseum@town.newtecumseth.on.ca
www.town.newtecumseth.on.ca/museum.c fm
Community museum displaying household, agricultural & industrial artifacts from 1840's to present; site features 1850's log cabin, 1860 English barn & 1915 fair building
Rachelle Clayton, Curator

Almonte: **J.H. Naismith Museum & Hall of Fame**
c/o Dr. James Naismith Basketball Foundation, PO Box 1991, 14 Bridge St., Almonte, ON K0A 1A0
Tel: 613-256-0492
info@naismithmuseum.com
www.naismithmuseum.com
Artifacts related to life of Dr. James Naismith, originator of game of basketball; Canadian Basketball Hall of Fame exhibits & archives
John Gosset, Executive Director
Phil Wood, President

Almonte: **Mill of Kintail Conservation Area**
4175 Hwy 511, RR#2, Almonte, ON K0G 1K0
Tel: 613-259-2421; *Fax:* 613-259-3468
info@mvc.on.ca
www.mvc.on.ca/index.php/conservation-areas/mill-of-kintai l
Kintail Museum, housed in a heritage grist mill, is a collection and a conservation site on the Indian River in Lanark County. The museum showcases the life and works of Robert Tait McKenzie as the mill was his summer home and sculpture studio; the museum showcases the largest collection of McKenzie's sculptures and memorabilia in Canada.
Stephanie Kolsters, Museum Manager, 613-256-3610, ext. 2, skolsters@mvc.on.ca

Almonte: **Mississippi Valley Textile Museum**
PO Box 784, 3 Rosamond St. East, Almonte, ON K0A 1A0
Tel: 613-256-3754; *Fax:* 613-256-3754
mvtm@magma.ca
www.textilemuseum.mississippimills.com
Founded: 1985 Museum is located in the annex of the former Rosamond Woolen Company constructed in 1867; houses information on the early mills & their owners, displays of period offices, artifacts & machinery related to the beginnings of the textile industry, and a gift shop.
Mr. Martin Ruben, President

Almonte: **North Lanark Regional Museum**
Appleton Ramsay Township, Almonte, ON K0A 1A0
Tel: 613-256-1805
jeandawn@comnet.ca
Operates a small regional museum; open May 22nd to Thanksgiving, Wed.-Sun., 10-4; admission $2
Dawn Leduc, Curator

Ameliasburg: **Ameliasburgh Historical Museum**
PO Box 67, Ameliasburg, ON K0K 1A0
Tel: 613-968-9678; *Fax:* 613-966-1599
amelmuseum@pecounty.on.ca
www.pec.on.ca/ameliasburghmuseum/index.html
Founded: 1968 Household items, quilts, crafts, agricultural machinery & tools & a 1910 Goldie Corlis engine with an 18-foot flywheel in a village setting; lots of events during season; tea room. Located at 517 County Rd. 19, Ameliasburgh.
Janice Hubbs, Curator

Ameliasburgh: **Quinte Educational Museum & Archives**
14 Coleman St., Ameliasburgh, ON K0K 1A0
Tel: 613-966-5501
qema@bellnet.ca
www.pec.on.ca/victoriaschoolhouse
The history of education in Prince Edward County & Ontario is preserved at the Quinte Educational Museum & Archives, through educational artifacts & archival material.

Amherstburg: **Fort Malden National Historic Site of Canada (FMNHS) / Lieu historique national du Canada du Fort-Malden**
PO Box 38, 100 Laird Ave., Amherstburg, ON N9V 2Z2
Tel: 519-736-5416; *Fax:* 519-736-6603
ont.fort-malden@pc.gc.ca
www.parkscanada.gc.ca/malden
Riverfront site includes original earthworks, a restored soldier's barrack & a museum
John MacLeod, Resource Centre Specialist
Jennifer Duquette, Site Manager

Amherstburg: **North American Black Historical Museum**
277 King St., Amherstburg, ON N9V 2C7
Tel: 519-736-5433; *Fax:* 866-622-4672
Toll-Free: 800-713-6336
nabhm@mnsi.net
www.blackhistoricalmuseum.org
The Museum allows visitors to experience Black history through the Taylor Log Cabin, a home of escaped slaves from the United States, the Nazrey African Methodist Episcopal Church, & a Cultural Centre.
Kenn Stanton, Curator & Administrator
Lyle Browning, President
Paul Hertel, Secretary
Wava Jackson, Treasurer

Amherstburg: **Park House Museum**
Kings Navy Yard, 214 Dalhousie St., Amherstburg, ON N9V 1W4
Tel: 519-736-2511; *Fax:* 519-736-2511
info@ParkHouseMuseum.com
www.parkhousemuseum.com
Other contact information: E-mail, Tours: order@ParkHouseMuseum.com
Built during the 1790s by a family of Loyalists, Park House is an example of Pièce sur Pièce log construction. The Park House Museum is open year-round to display items of historical significance to the town of Amherstburg & the surrounding area. During the summer, tinsmithing is demonstrated in the pensioner's cottage.

Ancaster: **Fieldcote Memorial Park & Museum**
64 Sulphur Springs Rd., Ancaster, ON L9G 1L8
Tel: 905-648-8144; *Fax:* 905-648-4857
fieldcote@hamilton.ca
Collection, preservation & exhibition of local history; landscaped gardens & walking trails
Lois Corey

Ancaster: **Ingledale**
c/o Hamilton Region Conservation Authority, PO Box 7099, Ancaster, ON L9G 3L3
Tel: 416-643-2103
c. 1812 home of Inglehart family; located at Fifty Point Conservation Area, Stoney Creek

***Ancaster:* Sulpher Springs Station/Dundas Valley Trail Centre**
c/o Hamilton Conservation Authority, PO Box 7099, Ancaster, ON L9G 3L3
Tel: 905-627-1233; *Fax:* 905-627-9722
Toll-Free: 888-319-4722
dvalley@conservationhamilton.ca
www.conservationhamilt on.ca
Centre is a replica of an 1800-era train station; displays/exhibits on the Niagara Escarpment, local cultural heritage & trail etiquette governing the valley's extensive, multi-use trail network; bird watching, cycling or historical tours
Paul Piett, Supt.

***Ancaster:* Valens Log Cabin Museum**
PO Box 7099, Ancaster, ON L9G 3L3
Tel: 905-659-7715
C. 1836 restored homestead located at Valens Conservation Area, 1691 Regional Rd. 97, RR#6, Cambridge ON N1R 5S7

***Appin:* Ekfrid Community Museum**
48 Wellington St., Appin, ON N0L 1A0
Tel: 519-289-2015; *Fax:* 519-287-2359
Located in the former Appin Post Office & Orange Hall; artifacts from late 1800s; open May-Aug., weekends & by request

***Arnprior:* Arnprior & District Museum / Musée d'Arnprior et Région**
35 Madawaska St., Arnprior, ON K7S 1R6
Tel: 613-623-4902; *Fax:* 613-623-4902
www.arnpriormuseum.org/Museum.htm
Located in the former post office, which was built in 1896, the Arnprior & District Museum features local artifacts & photograpsh, a 1928 fire engine, a lumbering exhibit, & an early 19th century canon. The museum is open Monday to Saturday.
Janet Carlile, Curator, jcarlile@arnprior.ca

***Astra:* RCAF Memorial Museum / ARC Musée Commémoratif**
PO Box 1000 Forces, Astra, ON K0K 3W0
Tel: 613-965-7223; *Fax:* 613-965-7352
Toll-Free: 866-701-7223
director@rcafmuseum.on.ca
rcafmuseum.on.ca
Social history museum dedicated to the airmen & airwomen who served in Canada's Air Force; features daily viewing of the on-going restoration of the world's only fully restored Halifax bomber aircraft; an Air Park displays 14 aircraft, 21 commemorative cairns & 5,600 "ADASTRA" granite stones; a large collection of artifacts; & a specialty gift shop; open daily May 1 - Sept. 30 Wed. - Sun.
Jodi Ann Eskritt, Curator
Chris Colton, Executive Director

***Atikokan:* Atikokan Centennial Museum & Historical Park**
204 East Main St., Atikokan, ON P0T 1C0
Tel: 807-597-6585; *Fax:* 807-597-6585
atikokancentennialmuseum@bellnet.ca
Restored logging engine & train; mining & logging exhibits; Steep Rock & Caland Iron Ore Mines; local archival & art collections
Catherine Reilly, Museum Curator
Janis McIntyre, Museum Assistant

***Aurora:* Aurora Historical Society & Hillary House, National Historic Site**
15372 Yonge St., Aurora, ON L4G 1N8
Tel: 905-727-8991
ahs@aurorahs.com
www.hhahs.space4art.biz
Founded: 1963 Heritage artifacts held by the Aurora Historical Society date back over 200 years. The collections are related to the history of Aurora & to Hillary House. Hillary House, the Koffler Museum of Medicine, contains a significant collection of medical instruments.
Jennifer Steen, Manager & Curator, jennifer@aurorahs.com

***Aurora:* Hillary House, Koffler Museum of Medicine**
15372 Yonge St., Aurora, ON L4G 1N8
Tel: 905-727-8991
ahs@aurorahs.com
www.hillaryhouse.ca
Built in 1862, the house was home to 3 generations of medical doctors and their families, covering the evolution of medicine from the era of leeches and bleeding to the discovery of penicillin. Exhibits include: medicial instruments, books, papers, household furnishings, and equipment dating from the early 19th century. Open May - Aug., 9:30-4:30 daily; Sept. - Apr. by appointment only.

***Aylmer:* Aylmer & District Museum Association**
14 East St., Aylmer, ON N5H 1W2
Tel: 519-773-9723; *Fax:* 519-773-3445
aylmermuseum@amtelecom.net
www.amtelecom.net/~aylmermuseum
The Aylmer & District Museum Association preserves & promotes the history of Aylmer & Malahide. The museum is open from the beginning of March to the end of November.
Pat Zimmer, Curator
Jacquie Jeffery, Chair

***Aylmer:* Ontario Police College Museum**
PO Box 1190, 10716 Hacienda Rd., Aylmer, ON N5H 2T2
Tel: 519-773-5361; *Fax:* 519-773-5762
Founded: 1962 Small display of police related items including speed measuring devices, breath collection & testing equipment, handcuffs & batons, police uniforms & hats, First Nations Police display, Forensics Investigative display
Rudy Gheysen, Director, 519-773-4200, rudy.gheysen@ontario.ca
Bill Stephens, Deputy Director, 519-773-4516, bill.stephens@ontario.ca

***Bancroft:* Bancroft Mineral Museum**
c/o Bancroft and District Chamber of Commerce, PO Box 539, Bancroft, ON K0L 1C0
Tel: 613-332-1513; *Fax:* 613-332-2119
Located at 30 Station Street in Bancroft, the Bancroft Mineral Museum is a natural science museum which features mineral specimens collected from the local area. The museum is open year-round.

***Bancroft:* North Hastings Heritage Museum**
PO Box 239, Station Street, Bancroft, ON K0L 1C0
Tel: 613-332-1884
Log house built in 1859; documents of North Hastings area

***Barriefield:* Frontenac County Schools Museum**
***Also known as:* Schools Museum**
414 Regent St., Barriefield, ON K7K 5R1
Tel: 613-544-9113
www.fcsmuseum.com/MuseumInfo.html
This community museum and archives has a geographical focus on Frontenac County and the City of Kingston, with a heritage schoolroom (1900-1920), a late 19th- and 20th-century archival collection and public elementary school records. Public programming includes costumed interpretive tours, educational programs and research assistance.

***Bath:* United Empire Loyalist Heritage Centre & Park**
54 Adolphustown Park Rd., Bath, ON K0K 2S0
Tel: 613-373-2196
1784@uel.ca
www.uel.ca
The United Empire Loyalist Heritage Centre houses the H.C. Burleigh Archives. The Heritage Centre is owned & operated by the Bay of Quinte Branch of the United Empire Loyalist Association of Canada. It is open from April to October, & by appointment at other times of the year.
Brian Tackaberry, Bay of Quinte Branch President, United Empire Loyalist Association
June Dafoe, Bay of Quinte Branch Board Governor, United Empire Loyalist Association, adafoe1@cogeco.ca
Tom Riddolls, Curator, tom@uel.ca

***Beachville:* Beachville District Museum**
PO Box 220, 584371 Beachville Rd., Beachville, ON N0J 1A0
Tel: 519-423-6497; *Fax:* 519-423-6935
bmchin@execulink.com
www.beachvilledistrictmuseum.ca
The Beachville District Museum features artifacts, such as Mastadon bones found on the O.J. Bond farm. The history of limestone quarries is also depicted at the museum, since the area is home to the largest open face quarries in Canada. A baseball display is featured because Beachville is the place where the first recorded baseball game in North America took place. The museum is open year round.

***Beaverton:* Beaver River Museum**
PO Box 314, 284 Simcoe St., Beaverton, ON L0K 1A0
Tel: 705-426-9641
bte.hist.soc@on.aibn.com
www.btehs.com
Founded: 1976 The Beaver River Museum consists of the Old Stone Jail, a settlers' log cabin (c.1850), & a brick house (c.1900). The museum is open during weekends in May, June, & September, & daily, except on Tuesdays, in July & August.
Julie Everett, Curator
Ken Alsop, Archivist

***Belleville:* Glanmore National Historic Site**
257 Bridge St. East, Belleville, ON K8N 1P4
Tel: 613-962-2329; *Fax:* 613-962-6340
mwakeling@city.belleville.on.ca
www.quinte.net/glanmore/
The restored Victoria home of the Phillips-Burrows-Faulkner families; original & period furnishings displayed in principal rooms; paintings & decorative art from the Couldery Collection on permanent exhibit; lamps from the Paul Lamp Collection, as well as other exhibits; special exhibits/events held throughout the year
Rona Rustige, Curator

***Blind River:* Timber Village Museum**
PO Box 628, 180 Leacock St., Blind River, ON P0R 1B0
Tel: 705-356-7544; *Fax:* 705-356-7343
museum@blindriver.ca
www.blindriver.com/museum
Other contact information: Year round: 705/356-2251
Provides guest with a sense of what a lumberjack's life was like at the turn of the last century; displays include axes, saws, logging tools & a portable forge; art gallery which exhibits works of contemporary local artists & artisans; workshops, children's educational programmes; lumberjack dinner, 1st Sat. in Oct.; open all year round.
Christine Clark, Curator/Manager
Ken Corbiere, Clerk Administrator/Treasurer

***Bobcaygeon:* Kawartha Settlers' Village**
85 Dunn St., Bobcaygeon, ON K0M 1A0
Tel: 705-738-6163
settlersvillage@nexicom.net
www.kawartha.net/~bobcom/ksv.htm
Twelve historic homes & buildings collected on former Kawartha farm; regional arts & heritage centre offering courses in the Arts
Shane Maclean, President

***Borden:* Base Borden Military Museum**
Canadian Forces Base Borden, PO Box 1000 Main, 27 Ram St., Borden, ON L0M 1C0
Tel: 705-423-3531; *Fax:* 705-423-3623
beaton.sl@forces.gc.ca
www.borden.forces.gc.ca/998/89/46/91-eng.asp
The Base Borden Military Museum consists of several buildings & a memorial park. It features the history of CFB Borden, with a collection of armoured vehicles, artillery pieces, trucks, & aircraft from World War I, World War II, & the present. As the birthplace of the Canadian Air Force, Base Borden also displays the Avro 504 K aircraft, a Tiger Moth, a Silver Star, & a Tutor aircraft.

***Bothwell:* Fairfield Museum**
14878 Longwoods Rd., RR#3, Bothwell, ON K0P 1C0
Tel: 519-692-4397
fairfield.museum@sympatico.ca
Site of Moravian Delaware mission, est. 1792, destroyed 1813 by US soldiers; artifacts from burnt village

***Bowmanville:* Clarington Museums & Archives**
Municipality of Clarington, 62 Temperance St., Bowmanville, ON L1C 3A8
Tel: 905-623-2734; *Fax:* 905-623-5684
info@claringtonmuseums.com
www.claringtonmuseums.com
Comprised of Bowmanville Museum, Clarke Museum, Sarah Jane Williams Heritage Centre; depicts the early urban & rural roots of the Municipality of Clarington; special collections including Dominion Pianos & Organs; one of the largest doll collections in Canada
Martha Rutherford Conrad, Administrator, claringtonmuseums@rogers.com

***Bracebridge:* Woodchester Villa**
PO Box 376, 15 King St., Bracebridge, ON P1L 1T7
Tel: 705-645-5501; *Fax:* 705-645-0385
info@octagonalhouse.com
www.octagonalhouse.com
Woodchester Villa is an octagonal house museum, which dates back to 1882. The house is designated as a historic site, under the Ontario Heritage Act. Woodchester Villa is open from Canada Day to Labour Day.

***Brampton:* Lorne Scots Regimental Museum**
The Armoury, 2 Chapel St., Brampton, ON L6W 2H1
Tel: 905-451-5724; *Fax:* 905-454-1533
goodmanav@sweb.net
Located at 48 John St.

***Brantford:* Bell Homestead National Historic Site**
94 Tutela Heights Rd., Brantford, ON N3T 1A1
Tel: 519-756-6220; *Fax:* 519-759-5975
bellhomestead@brantford.ca
www.bellhomestead.ca
Displays at the Bell Homestead National Historic Site depict the 1870 to 1881 household of Alexander Graham Bell, the invention of the telephone, & the origins of Canadian telephone operations.
Brian Wood, Curator
Lorie Steiner, Chair

***Brantford:* Brant Museum & Archives**
c/o Brant Historical Society, 57 Charlotte St., Brantford, ON N3T 2W6
Tel: 519-752-2483; *Fax:* 519-752-1931
information@brantmuseums.ca
www.brantmuseum.ca
Operated by the Brant Historical Society, the Brant Museum & Archives collects, preserves, researches, & exhibits items related to the founding, settlement, & diversity of Brant County &

the surrounding area. Researchers will discover items such as photographs, diaries, letters, & maps in the archive collection. Open year round.
Stacey McKellar, Curator

***Brantford:* Myrtleville House Museum**
34 Myrtleville Dr., Brantford, ON N3V 1C2
Tel: 519-752-3216; *Fax:* 519-752-0396
myrtleville@myrtleville.ca
www.myrtleville.ca
One of the oldest homes in Brant County (1837); the museum also promotes interactive learning and provide hands-on activities to aid students in explore the heritage of the county. Open year-round Monday-Friday 9-4 and Sat/Sun 1-4 in July and August.

***Brighton:* Presqu'ile Provincial Park**
RR#4, Brighton, ON K0K 1H0
Tel: 613-475-2204; *Fax:* 613-475-4324
One of Ontario's oldest provincial parks (1922); displays & programs of early history of the area; working lighthouse

***Brighton:* Proctor House Museum (SOHO)**
***Also known as:* Save Our Heritage Organization**
PO Box 578, 96 Young St., Brighton, ON K0K 1H0
Tel: 613-475-2144; *Fax:* 613-475-2144
proctorhousemuseum@sympatico.ca
www3.sympatico.ca/proctorhousemuseum/
Living museum: 1860s gentleman's home, completely furnished; open daily July & August for tours; or by appt. The Brighton Barn Theatre is housed in the Proctor-Simpson Barn adjacent to the property.
Anna Rittwage, President

***Brockville:* Brockville Museum**
5 Henry St., Brockville, ON K6V 6M4
Tel: 613-342-4397; *Fax:* 613-342-7345
info@brockvillemuseum.com
www.brockvillemuseum.com
Founded: 1981 The Brockville Museum is committed to preserving and promoting the history of Brockville through quality exhibits and education programs.
Bonnie Burke, Director, 613-342-4397, bburke@brockville.com

***Bruce Mines:* Bruce Mines Museum**
PO Box 220, 75 Taylor St, Bruce Mines, ON P0R 1C0
Tel: 705-785-3426; *Fax:* 705-785-3170
www.brucemines.ca
Founded: 1961 Situated in a church built in 1894, the Bruce Mines Museum features pioneer items such as an 1876 slot machine, a Victorian doll house, & a Yakaboo canoe.

***Burgessville:* Thames Valley Museum School**
PO Box 37, 656 Main St. North, Burgessville, ON N0J 1C0
Tel: 519-424-9964; *Fax:* 519-242-9964
info@museumschool.ca
www.museumschool.ca
1905 Baronial-style two-room schoolhouse; one classroom is restored to reflect the first quarter of the 20th century; the other is a gallery for changing exhibits on educational history; tours, educational programs, archives
Sharon Meek, Curator
Ken Riehl, Chair

***Burlington:* Ireland House at Oakridge Farm (Museums)**
2168 Guelph Line, Burlington, ON L7P 5A8
Tel: 905-332-9888; *Fax:* 905-332-1714
Toll-Free: 800-374-2099
www.museumsofburlington.com
Home of Joseph Ireland, built between 1835 & 1837; open year round
Barbara Teatero

***Burlington:* Joseph Brant Museum**
1240 North Shore Blvd. East, Burlington, ON L7S 1C5
Tel: 905-634-3556; *Fax:* 905-634-4498
Toll-Free: 888-748-5386
www.museumsofburlington.com
Founded: 1942 The museum is a replica of the original 1800 home of Mohawk, Captain Joseph Brant, "Thayendanegea"; exhibits relating to indigeneous culture, with emphasis on the Iroquois; history of Burlington; historical costume exhibit, one of Ontario's finest collection of Victorian clothing & accessories; open year round
Barbara Teatero, Director of Museums, teaterob@burlington.ca

***Caledonia:* Edinburgh Square Heritage & Cultural Centre**
***Also known as:* Edinburgh Square**
PO Box 2056, 80 Caithness St. East, Caledonia, ON N3W 2G6
Tel: 905-765-3134; *Fax:* 905-765-3009
esquare.centre@haldimandcounty.on.ca
Artifacts relating to Town of Haldimand, from pioneer times to 1970s; open year round
Anne Unyi, Curator

***Campbellford:* Campbellford-Seymour Heritage Centre**
Campbellford-Seymour Heritage Society, PO Box 1294, 113 Front St. North, Campbellford, ON K0L 1L0
Tel: 705-653-2634
csheritage@persona.ca
www.csheritage.org
Founded: 1989 The Campbellford-Seymour Heritage Centre is the home of the Campbellford-Seymour Heritage Society. The Society preserves & communicates the history of Campbellford / Seymour, maintains local archives, & assists with genealogical research.
Anne Linton, Contact

***Cannington:* Cannington Historical Museum**
c/o Cannington Historical Society, Cannington Town Hall, PO Box 196, 38 Laidlaw St. South, Cannington, ON L0E 1E0
Tel: 705-432-3136
canningtonsecretary@brockhistoricalsocieties.ca
www.brockhistoricalsocie ties.ca
Other contact information: E-mail, President: canningtonpresident@brockhistoricalsocieties.ca
Located in Cannington's MacLeod Park on Peace Street, the Cannington Historical Museum features the following buildings: log homes (circa 1827 & 1857), an 1871 Canadian Northern Railway station, a 1929 Canadian National Railway caboose, the 1934 Derryville (LOL) Hall, & a driving shed. The museum is open from Victoria Day to Labour Day, or by appointment.
Ted Foster, President
Ray Lush, Vice-President
Margaret Crammond, Secretary
Cheryl Dillon, Publicist

***Carleton Place:* Victoria School Museum**
267 Edmund St., Carleton Place, ON K7C 3E8
Tel: 613-253-1395
Local history of Carleton Place & Beckwith Township

***Cayuga:* Haldimand County Museum & Archives**
PO Box 38, 8 Echo St., Cayuga, ON N0A 1E0
Tel: 905-772-5880; *Fax:* 905-772-1725
museum.archives@haldimandcounty.on.ca
tourism.haldimandcounty.on.ca/muse ums/hcmuseum.html
Temporary & permanent exhibits; 1835 log cabin on site; regional & genealogical archives
Jennifer Tigert, Curator

***Chapleau:* Chapleau Centennial Museum**
***Also known as:* Chapleau Museum & Tourist Information Centre**
PO Box 129, 94 Monk St., Chapleau, ON P0M 1K0
Tel: 705-864-1122; *Fax:* 705-864-2138
salvador@township.chapleau.on.ca
www.chapleau.ca
Founded: 1967 Located in Centennial Park, on Monk St. in Chapleau; tourist information centre; mineral collection, mounted animals, material related to Chapleau & area; archives; educational programming; bilingual services; special needs facilities; picnic area; open May 15 - Oct. 15

***Chatham:* Chatham Railroad Museum**
PO Box 434, 2 McLean St., Chatham, ON N7M 5K5
Tel: 519-352-3097
CKtourism@chatham-kent.ca
www.chatham-kent.ca
Located in a CN baggage car built in 1955; contains early railroad equipment, several model trains & other memorabilia; open May through Labour Day, with group tours available all year round
Gary Shurgold

***Chatham:* Chatham-Kent Museum**
Chatham Cultural Centre, 75 William St. North, Chatham, ON N7M 4L4
Tel: 519-360-1998; *Fax:* 519-354-4170
CKccc@chatham-kent.ca
www.chatham-kent.ca
Local history museum & archives; features a retrospective of Chatham-Kent during first half of 20th century; special exhibitions gallery with changing displays throughout year; open daily
David Benson, Heritage Co-ordinator

***Chatham:* Milner Heritage House**
c/o Chatham-Kent Museum, 75 William St. North, Chatham, ON N7M 4L4
Tel: 519-360-1998; *Fax:* 519-354-4170
ckccc@chatham-kent.ca
www.chatham-kent.ca
Founded: 1943 Museum depicts the turn-of-the-century lifestyle of Robert Milner,a successful, local industrialist and carriage maker; also features award-winning artwork by Robert's wife Emma; second floor features the Rev. Sandys bird collection & the MacPhail exotic animal collection
Ms Stephanie Suitor, Curator

***Cheltenham:* The Great War Flying Museum**
Brampton Airport, PO Box 27, 13691 McLaughlin Rd., RR#1, Cheltenham, ON L7C 3L7
Tel: 905-838-4936
info@GreatWarFlyingMuseum.com
www.greatwarflyingmuseum.com
Volunteer group builds, maintains & flies WWI replica fighter aircraft; artifacts from WWI

***Cloyne:* Cloyne Pioneer Museum**
PO Box 228, Hwy. 41, Cloyne, ON K0H 1K0
Tel: 613-336-2203
pioneer@mazinaw.on.ca
www.mazinaw.on.ca/pioneerclub/
Artifacts from the pioneer days of the area including tools, clothing, kitchen and other households effects, glass bottles, flat irons, a rolling pin made from a block of solid maple, photos and old catalogues; genealogical archive. Located across from the Post Office in Cloyne
Margaret Axford, Co-Chair
Carolyn McCulloch, Co-Chair

***Cobalt:* Cobalt Mining Museum**
***Also known as:* Northern Ontario Mining Museum**
PO Box 215, 24 Silver St., Cobalt, ON P0J 1C0
Tel: 705-679-8301; *Fax:* 705-679-1151
cnomchin@ntl.sympatico.ca
www.museumsnorth.org/cobalt_mining/
Founded: 1953 The museum preserves the world's largest collection of native silver ore, mining & prospecting equipment & artifacts, & fluorescent rock; other displays highlight the early cultural & social life of Cobalt; unique, handcrafted silver jewelry available in the gift shop; underground tours of the Colonial Adit can be arranged. Open all year.
R.M. Holdsworth, Chairman

***Cochrane:* Cochrane Railway & Pioneer Museum**
PO Box 490, 210 Railway St., Cochrane, ON P0L 1C0
Tel: 705-272-4361; *Fax:* 705-272-6068
lise@puc.net
www.town.cochrane.on.ca
Located across from the train station in Cochrane; railway artifacts & memorabilia, photographs, displays
Paul Latondress, Curator

***Coldwater:* Coldwater Canadiana Heritage Museum**
***Also known as:* Woodrow Homestead**
PO Box 125, 1474 Woodrow Rd., Coldwater, ON L0K 1E0
Tel: 705-835-5032
dougbi@sympatico.ca
www.coldwaterheritagemuseum.com
1840s log house & other buildings; open May - Oct.
Richard Jolliffe, President

***Collingwood:* The Collingwood Museum**
PO Box 556, 45 St. Paul St., Collingwood, ON L9Y 4B2
Tel: 705-445-4811; *Fax:* 705-445-9004
museum@collingwood.ca
www.collingwood.ca/museum
Located in the "Station"; large collection relating to history of Collingwood & area; exhibits showcasing shipping & shipbuilding & early history; archival materials & special events & activities throughout the year
Anita Miles, Manager

***Comber:* Comber & District Historical Society**
PO Box 158, RR#2, 8840 Hwy. 77, Comber, ON N0P 1J0
Tel: 519-687-3332
Pioneer articles & agricultural items; admission by donation; open Thu.-Mon.
Lila McFadden, Sec.-Treas.
Ralph Mellow, President
Kenneth Cranston, Vice-President

***Combermere:* Madonna House Pioneer Museum**
2888 Dafoe Rd., RR#2, Combermere, ON K0J 1L0
Tel: 613-756-3713; *Fax:* 613-756-0211
combermere@madonnahouse.org
www.madonnahouse.org
Founded: 1967 History of early settlers in the area; located in century-old barn
Carolyn Desch, Contact, registrar@madonnahouse.org

***Commanda:* Commanda Heritage Centre**
4077 Hwy. 522, Commanda, ON P0H 1J0
Tel: 705-729-2113
commplex@vianet.ca
www.visitamuseum.com
Complete with original shelves, counter & floor from the 1870s; features artifacts from 1870s - 1930s as well as a gift shops which features work from the region; tea room; open daily mid-June - mid-Oct.

***Cornwall:* Cornwall Community Museum**
PO Box 773, 160 Water St. West, Cornwall, ON K6H 5T5
Tel: 613-936-0842
ian10@bellnet.ca

Loyalist & local history archives, local domestic manufacturing; open year round, Wed.-Sun.
Ian Bowering, Curator

***Cornwall Island:* Ronathahon:ni Cultural Centre**
RR#3, Cornwall Island, ON K6H 5R7
Tel: 613-932-9452; *Fax:* 613-932-0092
nnate@glen-net.ca
Iroquois, Cree & Ojibwa artifacts

***Cumberland:* Cumberland Heritage Village Museum**
PO Box 159, 2940 Queen St., Cumberland, ON K4C 1E6
Tel: 613-833-3059; *Fax:* 613-830-3061
cumberlandmuseum@ottawa.ca
Representation of a rural village in the Lower Ottawa Valley, with artifacts related to period of 1880-1935; open year round

***Delhi:* Delhi Ontario Tobacco Museum & Heritage Centre**
200 Talbot Rd., Delhi, ON N4B 2A2
Tel: 519-582-0278; *Fax:* 519-582-0122
tobacco.museum@norfolkcounty.on.ca
www.norfolkcounty.on.ca
Tobacco-related machinery; a ginseng exhibit; multicultural exhibits & street scene depicting five historic buildings at turn of the 20th century; a large pavilion complete with barbecues is available in Quance Park nearby
Judy A. Livingstone, Curator/Director
Tanya Zajac, Asst. Curator

***Delhi:* Teeterville Pioneer Museum**
c/o Delhi Ontario Tobacco Museum & Heritage Centre, 200 Talbot Rd., Delhi, ON N4B 2A2
Tel: 519-582-0278; *Fax:* 519-582-0122
teeterville.museum@norfolkcounty.on.ca
Other contact information: Victoria Day - Labour Day: 519/443-4400
Site location: 194 Teeter St., Teeterville ON
Judy A. Livingstone, Curator/Director
Tanya Zajac, Asst. Curator

***Delta:* The Old Stone Mill, National Historic Site (DMS)**
***Also known as:* The Delta Mill Society**
PO Box 172, Delta, ON K0E 1G0
Tel: 613-928-2584; *Fax:* 613-928-2584
info@deltamill.org
www.deltamill.org
Stone mill c. 1810. Part of the Family of National Historic Sites;the oldest surviving automatic stone grist mill in Ontario; showcases milling technology and 1800s industrial heritage; artifacts include buhr millstones, 48 inch Swain turbines, roller mills.
Dr. Paul Fritz, President

***Dresden:* Uncle Tom's Cabin Historic Site (UTCHS)**
***Also known as:* Uncle Tom's Cabin**
29251 Uncle Tom's Rd., Dresden, ON N0P 1M0
Tel: 519-683-2978; *Fax:* 519-683-1256
utchs@heritagetrust.on.ca
www.uncletomscabin.org
Uncle Tom's Cabin educates visitors about fugitive slaves in the Dresden area. The site focuses on the life of the Reverend Josiah Henson, a slave who escaped with his family to Upper Canada via the Underground Railroad. The grounds feature the following attractions: the Josiah Henson Interpretive Centre, the North Star Theatre, the Underground Railroad Freedom Gallery, the Harris House, a smokehouse, a sawmill, the Josiah Henson House, a pioneer church, & the Henson Family Cemetery. Open from mid May to the end of October. At other times of the year, groups of twenty or more may make an appointment.
Steven Cook, Curator

***Dryden:* Dryden & District Museum**
15 Van Horne Ave., Dryden, ON P8N 2A5
Tel: 807-223-4671; *Fax:* 807-223-7354
lgardner@dryden.ca
First Nations & pioneer artifacts; minerals; archival material

***Dundas:* Dundas Historical Society Museum**
139 Park St. West, Dundas, ON L9H 1X8
Tel: 905-627-7412; *Fax:* 905-627-4872
mail@dundasmuseum.ca
www.dundasmuseum.ca
Celebrates & preserves the story of the Dundas community; museum features true to life displays, & a diversified collection of exhibits reflecting the varied occupations & activities of those who have contributed to the development of the community
Carolyn Westoby, Curator

***Dunvegan:* The Glengarry Pioneer Museum**
***Also known as:* Dunvegan Museum**
#30, 1645 County Rd., RR#1, Dunvegan, ON K0C 1J0
Tel: 613-527-5230
info@glengarrypioneermuseum.ca
www.glengarrypioneermuseum.ca
1840 log inn; miniature cheese factory; 1869 municipal hall; carriage shed & log barn; blacksmith shop
Jennifer Black, Curator

***Ear Falls:* Ear Falls District Museum**
PO Box 309, Ear Falls, ON P0V 1T0
Tel: 807-222-3624; *Fax:* 807-222-2384
eftownship@ear-falls.com
www.ear-falls.com
Dedicated to the history of exploration, transportation, & the settlement of the area

***Egmondville:* The Van Egmond House**
***Also known as:* The Van Egmond Foundation**
PO Box 1033, 80 Kippen Rd., Egmondville, ON N0K 1W0
Tel: 519-522-0413
vanegmondfd@tcc.on.ca
www.huroneast.com/images/doorsopen/Egmondville/VanEgmondHouse.pdf
Restored & furnished Georgian county-manor house dating to the mid-19th century with antiques indicitive of the time; founded by Constant Van Egmond.

***Elgin:* Jones Falls Defensible Lockmaster's House & Blacksmith Shop**
PO Box 10, Elgin, ON K0G 1E0
Tel: 613-359-5377; *Fax:* 613-359-6042
Lockmaster's house c. 1841; blacksmith shop produces hardware c. 1843
Sandy Haining, Sector Supervisor

***Elgin:* Kingston Mills Blockhouse**
PO Box 10, Elgin, ON K0G 1E0
Tel: 613-359-5377; *Fax:* 613-359-6042
Toll-Free: 800-230-0016
1840s animated militia barracks
A.J. \Sandy\"""" Haining, Sector Supervisor

***Elk Lake:* Elk Lake Heritage Museum**
c/o Corporation of Township of James, PO Box 70, Elk Lake, ON P0J 1G0
Tel: 705-678-2237; *Fax:* 705-678-2495
History of area, in particular, mining, lumbering, agriculture
Lionel Venne, Chair

***Elliot Lake:* Elliot Lake Nuclear & Mining Museum**
Lester B. Pearson Centre, Hwy. 108, Elliot Lake, ON P5A 2T1
Tel: 705-848-2084; *Fax:* 705-848-0545
darla.hennessey@city.elliotlake.on.ca
Mining heritage; northern home of the Canadian Mining Hall of Fame; Dr. Franc Joubin Mineral Collection; open Sept. - June, Mon.-Fri.; July - Aug., daily

***Emo:* Rainy River District Women's Institute Museum**
***Also known as:* Emo Women's Institute Museum**
PO Box 511, Emo, ON P0W 1E0
Tel: 807-482-2007; *Fax:* 807-482-2556
Small pioneer museum; open mid May - Oct.; other times by appointment

***Englehart:* Englehart & Area Historical Museum**
PO Box 444, 67 - 6th Ave., Englehart, ON P0J 1H0
Tel: 705-544-2400; *Fax:* 705-544-8737
eahmchin@ntl.sympatico.ca
museumsnorth.org
Exhibits show how settlement along the Temiskaming & Northern Ontario railway created town of Englehart & brought homesteaders to the claybelt's rural communites, 1900-1950; open May 1 - Dec. 1 & exhibition room
Bonnie Rozell-Shortt, Manager, 705-544-2400

***Exeter:* Arkona Lions Museum & Information Centre**
c/o Ausable Bayfield Conservation Authority, 71108 Morrison Line, RR#3, Exeter, ON N0M 1S5
Tel: 519-828-3071; *Fax:* 519-235-1963
info@abca.on.ca
www.abca.on.ca
Arkona Lions Museum & Information Centre features local First Nations artifacts, Devonian era fossils, minerals, & semi-precious stone.
Tom Prout, General Manager, tprout@abca.on.ca

***Fenelon Falls:* Fenelon Falls Museum**
PO Box 179, 50 Oak St., Fenelon Falls, ON K0M 1N0
Tel: 705-887-1044; *Fax:* 705-887-1532
maryboro2003@yahoo.ca
www.maryboro.ca
Open daily June 15 - Labour Day; weekends only May 20-June 15 & Labour Day to Thanksgiving
Ali Scott, Curator

***Fergus:* Wellington County Museum & Archives**
RR#1, 0536 County Rd. 18, Fergus, ON N1M 2W3
Tel: 519-846-0916; *Fax:* 519-846-9630
Toll-Free: 800-663-0750
info@wcm.on.ca
www.wcm.on.ca
Other contact information: Museum: 519-846-0916, ext. 5221; Archives: 519-846-0916, ext. 5225
The Wellington County Museum reflects the history of Wellington County people. The museum is housed in the former House of Industry & Refuge, which was built in 1877. Permanent exhibits include a World War I military exhibit, a pioneer log cabin, a 1920s kitchen, & textiles. The archives feature historical & genealogical records which date back to the first settlement in Wellington County. The Couling Collection consists of architectural information.
Bonnie Callen, Administrator, bonniec@wcm.on.ca
Susan Dunlop, Curator MA, susan@wcm.on.ca
Karen Wagner, Archivist BA, MLS, karen@wcm.on.ca
Patty Whan, Conservator, patty@wcm.on.ca
Libby Walker, Coordinator, Activities, libbyw@wcm.on.ca

***Flesherton:* South Grey Museum & Historical Library**
PO Box 299, Flesherton, ON N0C 1E0
Tel: 519-924-2843; *Fax:* 519-986-3643
museum@greyhighlands.ca
www.greyhighlandsmuseum.com
Open Tues. - Sat. end of June - Labour Day, or by appt; Open Thurs. - Sat. Labour Day - June.
Sarah Redmond, Curator

***Forest:* Forest-Lambton Museum**
PO Box 707, 59 Broadway St., Forest, ON N0N 1J0
Tel: 519-786-3239
www.lambtononline.com/forest_lambton
Local artifacts including doll collection; flax industry; early telephone equipment; Grand Truck Railroad; First Nation's Artifacts; pictures & documents from the 1800s
Sylvia Freeman, Secretary
Ken Kingdon, President

***Fort Erie:* Mildred M. Mahoney Silver Jubilee Dolls' House Gallery**
657 Niagara Blvd., Fort Erie, ON L2A 3H9
Tel: 905-871-5833; *Fax:* 905-871-2447
mahoneydollhouse@bellnet.ca
www.mahoneydollhouse.com
Founded: 1983 Collection of miniatures & dollhouses spanning from 1730-1990; housed in historic Bertie Hall which was part of the Underground Railroad
Ms Julie Rivet, Assistant Curator

***Fort Frances:* Fort Frances Museum & Cultural Centre**
259 Scott St., Fort Frances, ON P9A 1G8
Tel: 807-274-7891; *Fax:* 807-274-4103
phawley@fort-frances.com
www.fort-frances.com/museum
The community museum is housed in an 1898 school house. The exhibits of the Fort Frances Museum & Cultural Centre reflect the development of Fort Frances & the Rainy River District from pre-contact to present day.
Pam Hawley, Curator

***Frankville:* Maple Sugar House & Museum**
41 Leacock Rd., RR#1, Frankville, ON K0E 1H0
Tel: 613-275-2893; *Fax:* 613-275-1839
Toll-Free: 877-440-7887
mail@gibbonsmaple.com
www.gibbonsmaple.com
The House produces & sells maple syrup, maple sugar, maple butter & other maple products. As well, there displays from the past and present of maple syrup making equipment. Tours are offered.

***Gananoque:* Gananoque Museum**
PO Box 100, 30 King St. East, Gananoque, ON K7G 2T6
Tel: 613-382-4024; *Fax:* 613-382-8587
Open mid-June - mid-Sept., Mon. - Sun.

***Gloucester:* Gloucester Museum**
4550B Bank St., Gloucester, ON K1G 3W6
Tel: 613-822-2076
Domestic ware; agricultural implements; Gloucester History Society archives; City of Gloucester archives

***Goderich:* Huron County Museum & Historic Gaol**
110 North St., Goderich, ON N7A 2T8
Tel: 519-524-2686; *Fax:* 519-524-1922
mail@huroncountymuseum.on.ca
www.huroncounty.ca/museum
Local history including transportation, military, agriculture & furniture
Claus Breede

***Golden Lake:* Golden Lake Algonquin Museum**
PO Box 1657A Mishomis Inamo, Golden Lake, ON K0J 1X0
Tel: 613-625-2823; *Fax:* 613-625-2332
mgr.economicdevelopment@pikwakanagan.ca
Algonquin artifacts; domestic & ornamental artifacts of the early settlers

***Gore Bay:* Western Manitoulin Island Historical Society Museum**
PO Box 298, Gore Bay, ON P0P 1H0
Tel: 705-282-2420
Canadian 19th century artifacts, including historical & documentary art; open Mar.-Nov.

***Gormley:* Whitchurch-Stouffville Museum**
14732 Woodbine Ave., Gormley, ON L0H 1G0
Tel: 905-727-8954; *Fax:* 905-727-1282
Toll-Free: 888-290-0337
wsmuseum@townofws.com
www.townofws.com/museum
Founded: 1971 The museum is located in the hamlet of Vandorf & includes the Bogarttown Schoolhouse, a restored 1850 log cabin, the Brown House, barn, & the Vandorf Public School; special events & programming, tours, craft workshops, & research material. Open year round.
Stephanie Foley, Curator

***Gowganda:* Gowganda & Area Museum**
Lot 12, Third St., Gowganda, ON P0J 1J0
Tel: 705-624-3171
Silver mining displays; log cabin; research library & resource centre; open mid-May - mid-Sept.

***Grafton:* Barnum House Museum**
PO Box 161, 10568 Country Rd. 2, Grafton, ON K0K 2G0
Tel: 905-349-2656; *Fax:* 905-349-3357
barnum@heritagetrust.on.ca
www.heritagefdn.on.ca
Owned by the Ontario Heritage Trust, Barnum House was built in 1819. The home is an example of Neo-Classical architecture. The decor of Barnum House reflects an Upper Canada home between 1820 & 1840. Barnum House Museum is open from June to Labour Day.
Wayne Kelly, Manager, Public Education & Community Development, 416-314-4913

***Grand Bend:* Lambton Heritage Museum**
RR#2, 10035 Museum Rd., Grand Bend, ON N0M 1T0
Tel: 519-243-2600; *Fax:* 519-243-2600
heritage.museum@county-lambton.on.ca
Eight buildings on a 30 acre site; extensive collection of pressed glass & Currier & Ives prints; features history of Sarnia-Lambton area including large collection of agricultural implements

***Gravenhurst:* Bethune Memorial House National Historic Site**
235 John St. North, Gravenhurst, ON P1P 1G4
Tel: 705-687-4261; *Fax:* 705-687-4935
ont-bethune@pch.gc.ca
www.pc.gc.ca/bethune
At the Bethune Memorial House National Historic Site, the life & achievements of Dr. Henry Norman Bethune are commemorated. The house is his birthplace. Dr. Bethune is recognized for his time in China, where he served as a surgeon & a teacher. The site is open from June 1st to October 31st. At other times, group tours may be arranged by phone.
Scott Davidson, Site Manager

***Gravenhurst:* Muskoka Boat & Heritage Centre**
275 Steamship Bay Rd., Gravenhurst, ON P1P 1Z9
Tel: 705-687-2115; *Fax:* 705-687-9408
Toll-Free: 866-687-6667
Muskoka Boat & Heritage Centre
www.segwun.com
The Muskoka Boat & Heritage Centre presents the history of boat-building, Muskoka's steamship era, & life on the water in Muskoka. At the site is a large in water collection of antique boats. The RMS Segwun is the oldest operating steamship in North America. The Muskoka Boat & Heritage Centre is open year-round.

***Grimsby:* Grimsby Museum**
PO Box 244, 6 Murray St., Grimsby, ON L3M 4G5
Tel: 905-945-5292; *Fax:* 905-945-0715
museum-public@town.grimsby.on.ca
www.town.grimsby.on.ca
Founded: 1984 Owned & operated by the Town of Grimsby, the museum interprets the history of Grimsby from prehistoric times. The Gallery of the Forty explores the settlement of the United Empire Loyalists in 1787. The Grimsby museum provides educational programs, as well as local history & genealogical information. It is open year-round.
Janet Cannon, Curator

***Guelph:* Guelph Civic Museum**
6 Dublin St. South, Guelph, ON N1H 4L5
Tel: 519-836-1221; *Fax:* 519-836-5280
museum@guelph.ca
www.guelph.ca/museum
Founded: 1967 The museum is housed in a c. 1850 limestone building and features over 30,000 artifacts and 4,000 photos relating to the istory of Guelph and area; special events and programming for children.
Katherine McCracken, Director,
katherine.mccracken@guelph.ca
Bev Dietrich, Curator, bev.dietrich@guelph.ca

***Guelph:* McCrae House**
108 Water St., Guelph, ON N1G 1A6
Tel: 519-836-1482; *Fax:* 519-836-5280
museum@guelph.ca
www.guelph.ca/museum
Founded: 1968 The house, built in 1858, is the 1872 birthplace of John McCrae, author of "In Flanders Fields", and a National Historic Site. Exhibitions interpret McCrae's life and times, and an award-winning historic garden is maintained by volunteers. Activities include garden teas, the Poppy Push, Teddy Bear Picnic and Canada Day celebration.
Katherine McCracken, Director

***Haileybury:* Haileybury Heritage Museum**
PO Box 911, 575 Main St., Haileybury, ON P0J 1K0
Tel: 705-672-1922; *Fax:* 705-672-2551
hhmuseum@onlink.net
Haileybury Heritiage Museum is focused on one of Canada's ten worst natural disasters, the Great Fire of 1922 which destroyed 90 percent of the Town of Haileybury & communities in 18 surrounding townships in South Temiskaming; features a restored 1904 Toronto Railway Company streetcar (used as housing after the '22 fire); a 1922 Ruggles Fire Pumper; & the tugboat M.V. Beauchene.
Sarah Bowdidge, Curator

***Haliburton:* Haliburton Highlands Museum**
PO Box 535, Haliburton, ON K0M 1S0
Tel: 705-457-2760
haliburtonmuseum@halhinet.on.ca
www.haliburtonhighlands.com/museum/
Local domestic, lumbering & agricultural history; open year round

***Hamilton:* Canadian Football Hall of Fame & Museum**
58 Jackson St. West, Hamilton, ON L8P 1L4
Tel: 905-528-7566; *Fax:* 905-528-9781
info@cfhof.ca; store@cfhof.ca
www.cfhof.ca
Founded: 1962 The Canadian Football Hall of Fame & Museum features exhibits which depict the history of the game at all levels. A special section is dedicated to the Hall of Famers.
Steve Howse, Chair
George Black, Chair, Selection Committee
Mark DeNobile, Executive Director, mark@cfhof.ca
Meghan Sturgeon, Curator, meg@cfhof.ca
Bob Morreale, Treasurer & Office Manager, rob@cfhof.ca

***Hamilton:* Dundurn Castle**
610 York Blvd., Hamilton, ON L8R 3H1
Tel: 905-546-2872; *Fax:* 905-546-2875
dundurn@hamilton.ca
www.dundurncastle.com
Restored home of Sir Allan MacNab, one of Canada's first premiers; depiction of mid-19th century life in over 40 rooms; open year round

***Hamilton:* Hamilton Children's Museum**
1072 Main St. East, Hamilton, ON L8M 1N6
Tel: 905-546-4848; *Fax:* 905-546-4851
childrensmuseum@hamilton.ca
www.hamilton.ca/CultureandRecreation/Arts_Culture_And_Museums
Founded: 1978 This is an interactive, hands-on learning centre that offers children the opportunity to explore a wide variety of themes from the natural sciences and arts. Closed on Mondays.
Ms Karen McCartney, Curator/Site Supervisor, Education, 905-546-2424, X-1886, kmccartn@hamilton.ca

***Hamilton:* Hamilton Military Museum / Le musée militaire de Hamilton**
610 York Blvd., Hamilton, ON L8R 3H1
Tel: 905-546-2872; *Fax:* 905-546-2875
dcchin@interlynx.net
Uniforms, weapons & lifestyle from War of 1812, Rebellion of 1837-38, the Victorian era, Boer War, & WWI; open year round

***Hamilton:* Hamilton Museum of Steam & Technology**
900 Woodward Ave., Hamilton, ON L8H 7N2
Tel: 905-546-4797; *Fax:* 905-546-4798
steammuseum@hamilton.ca
www.hamilton.ca
Housed in a 19th century public works building. The facility is a Civil & Power Engineering Landmark & a National Historic Site. It contains two steam engines that pumped water to Hamilton more than 140 years ago. Open year-round.

***Hamilton:* Hamilton Psychiatric Hospital Museum**
c/o St. Joseph's Mountain Health Services, PO Box 585, Hamilton, ON L8N 3K7
Tel: 905-388-2511; *Fax:* 905-381-5601
lmuirhea@stjosham.on.ca
www.stjosham.on.ca
With a variety of artifacts and photographs, the museum preserves the history of psychiatric care & treatment in Ontario with an emphasis on events at the Hamilton Psychiatric Hospital & in the regions it serves.
Ms Betty Laird, Coordinator, Volunteer Services, 905-522-1155, x35561

***Hamilton:* Hamilton-Scourge Project**
Dept. of Culture & Recreation, City Hall, 72 Main St. West, Hamilton, ON L8P 3T4
Tel: 905-546-3967; *Fax:* 905-546-2338
Research files on the Hamilton & Scourge, armed merchant schooners from the War of 1812, which capsized & lie in water off Port Dalhousie

***Hamilton:* HMCS Haida National Historic Site of Canada**
658 Catharine St. North (Pier 9), Hamilton, ON L8L 4V7
Tel: 905-526-0911; *Fax:* 905-526-9734
haida.info@pc.gc.ca
www.pc.gc.ca/haida
Commissioned in 1943, and dubbed "the fightingest ship in the Royal Canadian Navy", HMCS Haida saw service in WWII and the Korean War. Canada's most famous warship and the last of the Tribal Class destroyers left in the world is berthed at Hamilton.

***Hamilton:* Royal Hamilton Light Infantry Heritage Museum**
John Weir Foote VC Armoury, 200 James St. North, Hamilton, ON L8R 2L1
Tel: 905-528-2945
www.rhli.ca/museum/
Military artifacts from 1830 to present, with specific reference to the Royal Hamilton Light Infantry; library
Ed Newman, Museum Administrator

***Hamilton:* Whitehern Historic House & Garden**
The McQuesten Residence, 41 Jackson St. West, Hamilton, ON L8P 1L3
Tel: 905-546-2018; *Fax:* 905-546-4933
whitehern@city.hamilton.on.ca
Former home of the McQuesten family from 1852 - 1968; period rooms feature original furnishings
Ken Heaman, Curator

***Hamilton:* Workers Arts & Heritage Centre (WA&HC)**
51 Stuart St., Hamilton, ON L8L 1B5
Tel: 905-522-3003; *Fax:* 905-522-5424
wahc@wahc-museum.ca
www.wahc-museum.ca
Other contact information: Twitter: www.twitter.com/WAHC
Located at Hamilton's former Custom House, which was built in 1860, the Workers Arts & Heritage Centre celebrates the history & culture of all working people in Canada. Exhibits include the labour movement in the Hamilton area, a history of office work, & the history of life on the shop floor, which explores Canada's early industrial days to the rise of automation in the workplace. The museum is open year-round.
Elizabeth McLuhan, Executive Director,
executivedirector@wahc-museum.ca
Fabiola De Vierna, Coordinator, Administration & Finance,
fabiola@wahc-museum.ca
Brian Kelly, Coordinator, Building & Exhibitions,
brian@wahc-museum.ca
Andrew Lochhead, Coordinator, Labour Arts,
andrew@wahc-museum.ca
Ian Walker, Coordinator, Labour Heritage,
ian@wahc-museum.ca

***Harrow:* John R. Park Homestead**
915 County Rd. 50 East, RR#1, Harrow, ON N0R 1G0
Tel: 519-738-2029; *Fax:* 519-776-8688
Toll-Free: 888-487-4760
jrph@erca.org
www.erca.org
Living history museum; open year round
Janet Cobban, Curator

***Holland Centre:* Comber Pioneer Village**
Rte. 3, Holland Centre, ON N0H 1R0
Tel: 519-794-3467
First log school of Holland Township; settler's cabin; log barn; replica of Martins Inn; log smoke house

***Ignace:* Ignace Heritage Centre**
PO Box 480, 36 Main St., Ignace, ON P0T 1T0
Tel: 807-934-2280; *Fax:* 807-934-6452
Local artifacts

***Ingersoll:* Ingersoll Cheese Factory Museum / Musée de la fabrique de fromage d'Ingersoll**
130 Oxford St., Ingersoll, ON N5C 2V5
Tel: 519-485-0120; *Fax:* 519-485-3543
curator@ingersoll.ca
Located in Centennial Park; 6 buildings including cheese factory museum, blacksmith shop; barn; community museum featuring spectacular woodcarved scene "pathway of the giants" & Ingersoll Sports Hall of Fame houses Harold Wilson's Miss Canada IV Speedboat; open daily July - Aug.; open weekends through May & June to Thanksgiving

Shirley Lovell, Curator

***Iron Bridge:* Iron Bridge Historical Museum**
PO Box 460, Iron Bridge, ON P0R 1H0

Pioneer artifacts

***Iroquois:* Carman House Museum**
PO Box 249, Carman Rd., Iroquois, ON K0E 1K0
Tel: 613-652-4422; *Fax:* 613-652-4636
mornet94@mor-net.on.ca
Other contact information: Phone, Summertime: 613-652-4808
Carman House is a United Empire Loyalist home, which was built in 1815. It is a living history museum, which reflects life in 1835. The museum is open from late June to Labour Day.

***Iroquois Falls:* Iroquois Falls Pioneer Museum**
PO Box 448, 245 Devonshire Ave., Iroquois Falls, ON P0K 1E0
Tel: 705-258-3730; *Fax:* 705-258-3730
akw_1594@hotmail.com
Other contact information: Phone, Tours by appointment during the off season: 705-258-3409
Founded: 1970 The Garden Town of the North is home of the Shay Train Engine, the workhorse of the logging industry. The Iroquois Falls Pioneer Museum offers many displays, including the history of a company which became the world's largest producer of pulp & paper, the general store, a telephone exhibit, a hands-on display for children, the 1916 fire, a replica of a tug boat, & the Iroquois Hotel, which was built by the company.
Alexa Wollan, President, Iroquois Falls Historical Society Bd., & Director
Michael Shea, Secretary
Ramona Pepin, Treasurer

***Kakabeka Falls:* Hymers Museum**
RR#1, Kakabeka Falls, ON P0T 1W0
Tel: 807-577-4787; *Fax:* 807-577-4459
lindat@tbaytel.net
Local history
Linda Turk, Contact

***Kapuskasing:* Ron Morel Memorial Museum**
88 Riverside Dr., Kapuskasing, ON P5N 1B3
Tel: 705-337-4274; *Fax:* 705-337-1741
Museum is housed in two railway cars & a caboose headed by steam locomotive 5107; changing seasonal exhibits & permanent displays; one railway car is devoted to trains & railway history, with a large working HO-gauge model; the Heritage Caravan with its clay sculptures depict Northern Ontario history; open daily from early June to Labour Day

***Kars:* Swords & Ploughshares Museum**
7500 Reeve Craig Rd. North, RR#1, Kars, ON K0A 2E0
Tel: 613-489-3447; *Fax:* 613-489-1166
swords@calnan.com
www.calnan.com/swords/
Military artifacts, 1914-present; agricultural machinery & implements, 1840-1940; open May - Oct. & by appt.

***Kenora:* Lake of the Woods Museum**
PO Box 497, 300 Main St. South, Kenora, ON P9N 3X5
Tel: 807-467-2105; *Fax:* 807-467-2109
museum@kmts.ca
www.lakeofthewoodsmuseum.ca
Collection of more than 20,000 articles; displays feature native & pioneer artifacts, natural history, minerals, textiles, pictorial & archival material illustrating the history of the Lake of the Woods & surrounding area
Lori Nelson, Director

***Keswick:* Georgina Pioneer Village & Archives**
26557 Civic Centre Rd., RR#2, Keswick, ON L4P 3G1
Tel: 905-476-4305; *Fax:* 905-476-7492
georginapioneervillage@georgina.ca
www.town.georgina.on.ca
Late 19th century historic village; interpreters & demonstrators; special exhibitions, events, tours, workshops & genealogical archives; open June-Sept., Thur.-Sun., 10-5 or by appt.
Phillip Rose-Donahoe, Manager/Curator

***Killarney:* Killarney Centennial Museum**
32 Commissioners St., Killarney, ON P0M 2A0
Tel: 705-287-2424; *Fax:* 705-287-2660
Toll-Free: 888-597-2721
townkill@vianet.on.ca
www.municipality.killarney.on.ca
Founded: 1967 The museum preserves historical artifacts from the time of the fur trade to the present; collection includes household items, objects from local commercial fishing, logging, mining & tourism industries, & photographs. Located at 29 Commissioners St. in Killarney. Open 6 days per week from late June to early September.
Laurier Low
Rosemarie Roque

***King City:* King Township Museum**
2920 King Rd., King City, ON L7B 1L6
Tel: 905-833-2331; *Fax:* 905-833-2331
kingmuseum@township.king.on.ca

***Kingston:* Bellevue House National Historic Site (BHNHS)**
35 Centre St., Kingston, ON K7L 4E5
Tel: 613-545-8666; *Fax:* 613-545-8721
bellevue.house@pc.gc.ca
www.pc.gc.ca/lhn-nhs/on/bellevue/index_e.asp
Other contact information: TDD: 613-545-8668
Built in the early 1840s, Bellevue House was the home of Sir John A. Macdonald. The site is closed from November to March, but groups may make reservations.

***Kingston:* Canada's Penitentiary Museum (CPM) / Musée du service correctionnel du Canada**
***Also known as:* Canada's Penitentiary Museum/Musée pénitentiaire du Canada**
PO Box 260, 555 King St. West, Kingston, ON K7L 4V8
Tel: 613-530-3122; *Fax:* 613-536-4815
fpm@cogeco.net
www.penitentiarymuseum.ca
To preserve & interpret the past & contemporary experiences of the people & places associated with the history of corrections in Canada; located at 555 King St. West
Dave St. Onge, Curator

***Kingston:* Cataraqui Archaeological Research Foundation/Kingston Archaeological Centre**
611 Princess St., Kingston, ON K7L 1E1
Tel: 613-542-3483
carf@carf.info
www.carf.info
Founded: 1986 The Foundation was established to oversee the excavation of Fort Frontenac, and to collect and preserve artifacts from the site. It is now involved in numerous archaeological projects at sites in Eastern Ontario, and operates the Kingston Archaeological Centre; educational programming and research collection. Open Mon to Fri, 9:30-4:00.
Sue Bazely, Executive Director

***Kingston:* City of Kingston Fire Department Museum**
271 Brock St., Kingston, ON K7L 1S5
www.virtualmuseum.ca
Antique firefighting equipment, photographs & models

***Kingston:* Fort Henry**
***Also known as:* The Citadel of Upper Canada**
PO Box 213, Kingston, ON K7L 4V8
Tel: 613-542-7388; *Fax:* 613-542-3054
Toll-Free: 800-437-2233
john.robertson@forthenry.com, getaway@parks.on.ca
www.forthenry.com
The Citadel of Upper Canada, brought to life by the Fort Henry Guard; restaurant; gift stores; children's muster parades; festivals, events, historic dining
John Robertson, Manager

***Kingston:* International Hockey Hall of Fame & Museum**
PO Box 82, 277 York St., Kingston, ON K7L 4V6
Tel: 613-544-2355; *Fax:* 613-544-2844
info@ihhof.com
www.ihhof.com
Home to 10,000 sq. feet of hockey memories; open mid-June - Labour Day, daily 10-3; off-season group tours by appt.
Larry Paquette, Vice-President
Mark Potter, President

***Kingston:* MacLachlan Woodworking Museum**
2993 Hwy. 2 East, Kingston, ON K7L 4V1
Tel: 613-542-0543; *Fax:* 613-547-5968
mwmuseum@cityofkingston.ca
www.cityofkingston.ca/museum
Founded: 1967 Exhibits include tools & lifestyles of 19th century tradespeople; hands-on workshops, educational programs & demonstrations are offered. The gift shop stocks handmade wooden kitchenware, linen, toys and wooden ornaments.
Annabelle Girard, Program Coordinator
Caroline Petznick, Curator

***Kingston:* Marine Museum of the Great Lakes at Kingston**
55 Ontario St., Kingston, ON K7L 2Y2
Tel: 613-542-2261; *Fax:* 613-542-0043
marmus@marmuseum.ca
www.marmuseum.ca
Founded: 1976 The museum showcases an original pumping station and steam engines built in 1891. Exhibits include the history of boat building, as well as Kingston's maritime history on the Great Lakes. An Eco Gallery focuses on environmental issues related to the Great Lakes. At dock is the Alexander Henry, a icebreaking ship built in 1959.

***Kingston:* Military Communications & Electronics Museum**
PO Box 17000 Station Forces, 95 Craftsman Blvd., Highway #2, Kingston, ON K7K 7B4
Tel: 613-541-4675; *Fax:* 613-540-8111
staff@c-and-e-museum.org
www.c-and-e-museum.org
Preserves & interprets the Communications & Electronics Branch military history; provides group & individual tours; responds to research requests & is available to provide expert artifact appraisals; supports community activities with mobile displays & temporary loans of artifacts
Maj. (Ret'd) Mike DeNoble, Director, 613-541-4211, denoble.mp@forces.gc.ca

***Kingston:* Miller Museum of Mineralogy & Geology**
Miller Hall, Queen's University, Kingston, ON K7L 3N6
Tel: 613-533-6767; *Fax:* 613-533-6592
badham@geol.queensu.ca
geol.queensu.ca/museum/
Collection of rocks, minerals & fossils from around the world; education tour programs available by request
Mark Badham, Curator

***Kingston:* Murney Tower Museum**
PO Box 54, Kingston, ON K7L 4V6
Tel: 613-544-9925
Tower, built in 1846, now houses military, agricultural, Aboriginal & early settlers' artifacts; open summer

***Kingston:* Pump House Steam Museum**
23 Ontario St., Kingston, ON K7L 2Y2
Tel: 613-546-4696
Former pumping station with artifacts relating to steam power; operating steam & pump engines

***Kingston:* The Royal Military College Museum / Le musée du Collège militaire royal du Canada**
***Also known as:* RMC Museum**
PO Box 17000 Forces, Kingston, ON K7K 7B4
Tel: 613-541-6000; *Fax:* 613-542-3565
mckenzie-r@rmc.ca
Housed in the Fort Frederick Martello Tower on the College grounds; holdings relate to the history of the College, the achievements of its ex-cadets & to the history of the Royal Navy Dockyard which once occupied the site; amongst the Museum's most treasured possessions is the superb Douglas Arms Collection; open daily last Sat. in June - Labour Day
Ross McKenzie, Curator
Dr. J.G. Pike, Committee Chair

***Kingsville:* Canadian Transportation Museum & Heritage Village**
6155 Arner Townline, RR#2, Kingsville, ON N9Y 2E5
Tel: 519-776-6909; *Fax:* 519-776-8321
Toll-Free: 866-776-6909
info@ctmhv.com
www.ctmhv.com
Located on Country Road #23 in Kingsville, Ontario, the Canadian Transportation Museum collects, restores, & exhibits modes of transportation from the mid 1800s to 1992. Examples of displays include horse drawn carts, fire trucks, & Ford Model Ts. The Heritage Village contains buildings, such as a one room schoolhouse, a train station, a log home, & a general store.
Harry Bergman, Chair

***Kingsville:* Jack Miner Bird Sanctuary & Museum**
PO Box 39, Kingsville, ON N9Y 2E8
Tel: 519-733-4034; *Toll-Free:* 877-289-8328
info@jackminer.com
www.jackminer.com
Founded: 1904 Known as "Wild Goose Jack", Jack Miner founded the bird sanctuary in 1904 and stipulated that admission would remain free. In addition to the sanctuary and grounds, the museum holdings include memorabilia, wildlife prints, medals, manuscripts & newspaper clippings, books, a bust of Jack Miner and letter from friend Henry Ford, and baseball bats from Ty Cobb. Located at 322 Road 3 West, off Division Road in Kingsville.

***Kirkland Lake:* Museum of Northern History at the Sir Harry Oakes Chateau**
PO Box 1148, 2 Chateau Dr., Kirkland Lake, ON P2N 3M7
Tel: 705-568-8800; *Fax:* 705-567-6611
museum@tkl.ca
www.town.kirklandlake.ca
The Chateau, built by Sir Henry Oakes and has been preserved as a museum exhibit and is also a space to preserve northern history.
Robin Ormerod, Director/Curator
Darren Sutherland, Director, gsutherland@ns.sympatico.ca
Brian Kellock, Director, rbak@gmail.com
Allen Tobey, Director, atobey@eastlink.ca
Gerard MacIsaac, Director, gerard.macisaac@ns.sympatico.ca
Hal Maybe, Director, haroldmaybe@eastlink.ca
Kirk Munro, Director, kmunro@hotmail.com
Robert Mills, Director

Charlie Clarke, Director
Donnie Chaisson, Director
Danny Rankin, Director

***Kitchener:* Doon Heritage Crossroads**
***Also known as:* Doon Pioneer Village**
10 Huron Rd., Kitchener, ON N2P 2R7
Tel: 519-748-1914; *Fax:* 519-748-0009
rtom@region.waterloo.on.ca
www.region.waterloo.on.ca
Other contact information: TDD: 519/748-0537
Turn of the century living history village; open daily May - Dec.
Thomas A. Reitz, Curator/Manager

***Kitchener:* Joseph Schneider Haus Museum**
466 Queen St. South, Kitchener, ON N2G 1W7
Tel: 519-742-7752; *Fax:* 519-742-0089
www.region.waterloo.on.ca
Traces back to the Schneider family, one of the first group of Pennsylvania German Mennonites in the area

***Kitchener:* Woodside National Historic Site of Canada / Lieu historique national de Woodside**
528 Wellington St. North, Kitchener, ON N2H 5L5
Tel: 519-571-5684; *Fax:* 519-571-5686
Toll-Free: 888-773-8888
ont-woodside@pc.gc.ca
www.pc.gc.ca/lhn-nhs/on/woodside /index.aspx
Woodside National Historic Site was the childhood home of Canada's longest-serving Prime Minister, William Lyon Mackenzie King. Today, the house is restored to the Victorian era of the 1890s. The site is open from mid May to late December. Groups may reserve tours during the off season.
Kim Seward-Hannam, Supt.

***Komoka:* Komoka Railway Museum Inc.**
PO Box 22, 133 Queen St., Komoka, ON N0L 1R0
Tel: 519-657-1912; *Fax:* 519-657-6791
komokarailmuseum@aol.com
www.komokarailmuseum.ca
Restored railroad station; site includes 1913 Shay logging locomotive, 1939 CN baggage car, 1972 caboose & a collection of CN maintenance jiggers

***Lakefield:* Christ Church Community Museum**
c/o St. John the Baptist Anglican Church, PO Box 217, Lakefield, ON K0L 2H0
Tel: 705-652-8302; *Fax:* 705-652-8702
stjohnslakefield@nexicom.net
stjohnslakefield.ca
History of Lakefield, & the Strickland family; The Bill Twist Collection; display of old toys, dolls & doll furniture, cards; open 1:00-4:00 daily

***Lanark:* Lanark & District Museum**
80 George St., Lanark, ON K0G 1K0
Tel: 613-259-5350
www.lanarkhighlands.ca/Community/Museums/Lanark.htm
Open weekends, mid-May to mid-Oct.

***Lanark:* Middleville & District Museum**
PO Box 6, Wolf Grove Rd (city rd.16), Lanark, ON K0G 1K0
Tel: 613-259-5462; *Fax:* 613-259-2291
alice006@sympatico.ca
Local pioneer artifacts including items for the maple syrup, cheese & lumbering industries; open May 24-Thanksgiving
Mary Dixon, Chairperson, gdixon@perth.igs.net

***Latchford:* House of Memories**
PO Box 82, Latchford, ON P0J 1N0
Tel: 705-676-2417
Local artifacts from 1900-1940; WWI & WWII items; natural history exhibits

***Leamington:* Point Pelee National Park of Canada, Visitor Centre, DeLaurier Historical House, & Trail / Parc national du Canada de la Pointe-Pelée**
407 Monarch Lane, RR#1, Leamington, ON N8H 3V4
Tel: 519-322-2365; *Fax:* 519-322-1277
Toll-Free: 888-773-8888
pelee.info@pc.gc.ca
www.pc.gc.ca./pelee
Other contact information: TDD: 1-866-787-6221
Located at the southern tip of Canada, Point Pelee National Park features the DeLaurier Historical House. The homestead & barn depict the park's human & cultural heritage. The Visitor Centre houses exhibits, a children's discovery room, & theatre programs about the area's natural & cultural heritage.

***Limehouse:* Canadian Military Studies Museum**
Lot 23, Conc. 6, RR#1, Limehouse, ON L0P 1H0
Tel: 905-877-6522
durangedhemi@sympatico.ca
The Canadian Military Studies Museum features artifacts from the mid-17th century, the Boer War, World War I, & World War II, to the Korean & Vietnam Wars.

***Lindsay:* Old Lindsay Jail**
PO Box 187, 50 Victoria Ave. North, Lindsay, ON K9V 4S1
Tel: 705-324-3404; *Fax:* 705-324-1805
info@oldejailmusem.ca
www.oldejailmuseum.com
The Lindsay Jail, built in 1863, was historically known as the County Gaol. The Victoria County Historical Society collects, preserves, & exhibits the history of the County of Victoria.
John Macklem, President

***Little Current:* Centennial Museum of Sheguiandah**
Postal Bag 2000, Little Current, ON P0P 1K0
Tel: 705-368-2367; *Fax:* 705-368-0761
shegmus@vianet.ca
Founded: 1967 pioneer culture & history on Manitoulin Island
Heidi Ferguson, Curator

***London:* Eldon House**
481 Ridout St. North, London, ON N6A 2P8
Tel: 519-661-0333; *Fax:* 519-661-2559
ramurray@museumlondon.ca
www.londonmuseum.on.ca
House of the Harris family from 1834-1959
Brian Meehan, Executive Director

***London:* Fanshawe Pioneer Village (FPV)**
2609 Fanshawe Park Rd. East, London, ON N5X 4A1
Tel: 519-457-1296; *Fax:* 519-457-3364
info@fanshawepioneervillage.ca
www.fanshawepioneervillage.ca
Costumed interpreters demonstrate life in mid-1800s to early 1900s rural Ontario crossroads community
Sheila A. Johnson, Executive Director
Shanna Dunlop, Curator & Head of Operations

***London:* First Hussars: Citizen Soldiers Museum**
399 Ridout St. North, London, ON N6A 2P1
Tel: 519-471-1538
www.firsthussars.ca/museum.html
Follows the history of the 1st Hussars from 1856 until today; includes material on the Boer War, the Great War & WWII
Alastair Neely, Curator

***London:* Grosvenor Lodge**
1017 Western Rd., London, ON N6G 1G5
Tel: 519-645-2845; *Fax:* 519-645-0981
hlfgl@golden.net
www.grosvenorlodge.com
1853 estate; operates as London Regional Resource Centre for Heritage & the Environment, administered by the Heritage London Foundation; resources available on heritage & environmental issues; venue for meetings, seminars & social events; library & display areas open to public; open Mon.-Fri. 9-4

***London:* Guy Lombardo Music Centre**
205 Wonderland Rd. South, London, ON N6K 3T3
Tel: 519-473-9003; *Fax:* 519-473-9003
seventyeights@aol.com
Memorabilia relating to bandleader & his band, the Royal Canadians, including original recordings & videotapes; open June-Aug., Wed.-Sun., 11-7; Sept. 12:30-4:30 or by appt.

***London:* London Regional Children's Museum**
21 Wharncliffe Rd. South, London, ON N6J 4G5
Tel: 519-434-5726; *Fax:* 519-434-1443
info@londonchildrensmuseum.ca
www.londonchildrensmuseum.ca
Hands-on, interactive museum; features ten themed galleries, school programs, outreach programs, day camps, workshops, birthday parties & membership programs

***London:* Museum London**
421 Ridout St. North, London, ON N6A 5H4
Tel: 519-661-0333; *Fax:* 519-661-2559
info@museumlondon.ca
www.londonmuseum.on.ca
Operates Eldon House; exhibits include family life, historical & contemporary art & historical artifacts from the London area from 1834 to 1960
Brian Meehan, Executive Director & Chief Curator
Cydna Mercer, Head of Administration
Melanie Townsend, Head of Exhibitions & Collections

***London:* Museum of Ontario Archaeology & Iroquoian Village Site**
Lawson-Jury Bldg., University of Western Ontario, 1600 Attawandaron Rd., London, ON N6G 3M6
Tel: 519-473-1360; *Fax:* 519-473-1363
museum.of.archaeology@uwo.ca
www.uwo.ca/museum
Archaeological & ethnographical collection; prehistoric archaeological Iroquois village site; museum open year round with reduced hours in fall & winter
Cindy Barrett, Manager
Dr. Robert Pearce, Executive Director

***London:* The Royal Canadian Regiment Museum**
Wolseley Barracks, 701 Oxford St. East, London, ON N5Y 4T7
Tel: 519-660-5102; *Fax:* 519-660-5344
Breede.C@forces.gc.ca
www.theroyalcanadianregiment.ca/thercrmuseum/thercrmuseum.htm
To serve as a training medium to teach regimental history; to preserve regimental history through the collection of documents, pictures, books & artifacts with emphasis on the RCR; to serve as a place of military interest for the public & Canadian Forces personnel; to provide research facilities for the study of Canadian military history.
Claus Breede, Curator
Maj. R.A. Smyth, Director

***Lucan:* Donnelly Homestead**
34937 Roman Line, RR#3, Lucan, ON N0M 2J0
Tel: 519-227-1244
rsalts@quadro.net
www.quadro.net/~donnelly
Historical on-site tours given on the original Donnelly property by current owner; artifacts & photographs; tours preferably by appt., year round; private residence
Robert Salts, Contact

***Madoc:* O'Hara Mill Pioneer Homestead**
PO Box 56, 638 Mill Rd., Madoc, ON K0K 2K0
Tel: 613-473-2084
www.ohara-mill.org
Other contact information: Phone, Membership Services: 413-473-1015
Attractions include O'Hara House, a log house, a saw mill, & a one room log schoolhouse. O'Hara House is restored to represent the Victorian era around 1840. The saw mill is a rare working English Gate or Reciprocating Frame saw mill.
Dave Little, Chair, 613-967-2466
Clara Hopkins, Vice-Chair, 613-473-2084
Karen Maguire, Secretary, 613-473-2177
Gayle Ketcheson, Treasurer, 613-473-4680

***Magnetawan:* Magnetawan Historical Museum**
PO Box 263, Magnetawan, ON P0A 1P0
Tel: 705-387-3308
gomon@vianet.on.ca.
Restored plant & turbine that supplied first electricity for village; log cabin

***Manitowaning:* Assiginack Museum & Heritage Park**
PO Box 147, 125 Arthur St., Manitowaning, ON P0P 1N0
Tel: 705-859-3732; *Fax:* 705-859-2416
assigmuse@amtelecom.net
www.manitoulin-island.com/museums/assiginack_com plex.htm
The Assiginack Museum & Heritage Park is a community & marine museum. Artifacts are from the mid-1800s to the mid-1900s. Visitors can see a pioneer home & school, a 19th century grist mill, plus the Great Lakes steamship, S.S. Norisle, which was built in 1946. The museum is open from June to October.
Jeanette Allen, Curator, 705-859-3905

***Manotick:* Watson's Mill**
***Also known as:* Manotick Mill**
PO Box 145, 5525 Dickinson St., Manotick, ON K4M 1A3
Tel: 613-692-6455; *Fax:* 613-692-5486
Toll-Free: 800-267-3504
watsonsmillmanotick@rogers.com
www.watsonsmill.com
Founded: 1860 19th century working gristmill, built 1860; gift shop; tours; picnic area; live interpretation, gossip tours
Bonnie Gray, President, Board of Directors
Isabelle Geoffrion, Manager, 613-692-6455
Cam Trueman, Interpretation & Education Officer, 613-692-6455

***Markham:* Markham Museum & Historic Village**
9350 Hwy. 48, Markham, ON L3P 3J3
Tel: 905-294-4576; *Fax:* 905-294-4590
museuminfo@markham.ca
www.markham.ca/markham/channels/museum/overview.ht m
Buildings, vehicles, furnishing & agricultural & industrial equipment that relate to Markham Township's history, from native presence to the 20th century; open year round
George Phillips, Manager

***Marten River:* Marten River Provincial Park Logging Museum**
c/o Marten River Provincial Park, Marten River, ON P0H 1T0
Tel: 705-892-2200
Artifacts for early logging era in Northern Ontario

***Massey:* Massey Area Museum**
160 Sauble St., Massey, ON P0P 1P0
Tel: 705-865-2266; *Fax:* 705-865-2266
info@masseyareamuseum.com
www.masseyareamuseum.com

Founded: 1967 The Massey Area Museum is housed in the original Bretzlaff General Store, which was built in 1909. The museum details logging history, as well as Aboriginal, Fort LaCloche, mining, farming, & early settler history. Model rooms, a chapel, a general store, & Massey's first horse-drawn fire engine are featured at the museum. There is also an historical & genealogical research centre, which includes records of the Township of Sables-Spanish River's ten cemeteries.
Carolyn Hein, Curator

Matheson: **Thelma Miles Historical Museum**
PO Box 601, Matheson, ON P0K 1N0
Tel: 705-273-2325; *Fax:* 705-273-1731
tmhm@ntl.sympatico.ca
History of the communities of Val Gagné, Shillington, Wavel, Ramore, Holtyre & Matheson from 1900-1945
Dianne Bush, Director/Curator

Mattawa: **Mattawa & District Museum**
PO Box 9, 285 First St., Mattawa, ON P0H 1V0
Tel: 705-744-5495
mmuseum@vianet.ca
Open daily July - Aug.; weekends in May, June, Sept., Oct.
Bob Einboden, Vice-President
Claudette DesRoches, President of Board

Mattawa: **Voyageur Heritage Centre**
Samuel de Champlain Provincial Park, PO Box 147, Hwy. 17 East, Mattawa, ON P0H 1V0
Tel: 705-744-2276
www.ontarioparks.com/english/samu.html
The Voyageur Heritage Centre tells the story of the Mattawa River & the lives of the voyageurs. The centre features one of the largest reproduced birch bark canoes.

Maxville: **Glengarry Sports Hall of Fame**
PO Box 282, Maxville, ON K0C 1T0
Tel: 613-527-1044
www.glengarrysports.com

Meaford: **Meaford Museum**
111 Bayfield St., Meaford, ON N4L 1N4
Tel: 519-538-5974; *Fax:* 519-538-5974
meafordmuseum@meaford.ca
www.meafordmuseum.ca
Founded: 1961 The Meaford Museum aims to collect, educate, display, conserve and feature the history of the former Town of Meaford and the surrounding area, from early settlements to the present.
Pam Woolner, Curator

Meldrum Bay: **Mississagi Strait Lighthouse Museum**
General Delivery, Meldrum Bay, ON P0P 1R0
Tel: 705-282-7258
Lighthouse built in 1873, includes artifacts related to seafaring & fishing; keeper's house features 19th-century furnishings; open mid-May - Sept.

Meldrum Bay: **The Net Shed Museum**
Water St., Meldrum Bay, ON P0P 1R0
Tel: 705-283-1818
jan.island@onlink.net
Open June - Labour Day; artifacts of pioneer fishing, lumbering & farming; display of nursing in WWII
Jan Laurin, Sec.-Treas./Director

Merrickville: **The Blockhouse Museum**
PO Box 294, Merrickville, ON K0G 1N0
Tel: 613-269-4034
info@merrickvillehistory.org
www.merrickvillehistory.org
Built as a defence for the Rideau Canal built in 1830. Contains local pioneer artifacts.
Gillian Hammonds, Manager, The Blockhouse Museum

Midland: **Huronia Museum**
PO Box 638, Midland, ON L4R 4P4
Tel: 705-526-2844; *Fax:* 705-527-6622
Toll-Free: 800-263-7745
director@huroniamuseum.com
www.huroniamuseum.com;
collections.ic.gc.ca/huronia/huronia.htm
Recreated Huron Village represents one of hundreds that existed in the Georgian Bay area, representing a unique & sophisticated society which lasted nearly 1,000 years; Canada's first recreated Native village; extensive exhibits on regional history, art gallery, archives & Mundys Bay Store; a large selection of native & historical books
Jamie Hunter, Director/Curator

Midland: **Martyrs' Shrine**
PO Box 7, 16163 Hwy. 12 West, Midland, ON L4R 4K6
Tel: 705-526-3788; *Fax:* 705-526-1546
shrine@jesuits.ca
www.martyrs-shrine.com
Founded: 1926 Built in 1926 in tribute to the Jesuit missionaries who laboured among the Huron, 1625-50, and to the eight who were martyred, the interior of this church with its wooden walls and canoe-like ceiling celebrates the melding of historical cultures. Open daily, Victoria Day weekend through Thanksgiving weekend; tours &/or talks given on request.
Rev. Alex F. Kirsten, Director S.J.

Midland: **Sainte-Marie among the Hurons / Sainte-Marie-au-Pays-des-Hurons**
PO Box 160, Hwy. 12 East, Midland, ON L4R 4K8
Tel: 705-526-7838; *Fax:* 705-526-9193
hhp@hhp.on.ca
www.saintemarieamongthehurons.on.ca
Other contact information: TDD: 705-528-7697; E-mail, Friends of Sainte-Marie: friends@csolve.net
During the 17th century, Sainte-Marie served as the fortress & headquarters for the French Jesuit mission to the Huron nation. Based upon archaeological & historical research, Sainte-Marie was recreated on its original site. Special programs & courses are offered about the first European community in Ontario. The site is open from the end of April to the end of October.

Milford: **Mariners Park Museum**
PO Box 12, 2065 County Rd. 13, Milford, ON K0K 2P0
Tel: 613-476-8392
marinersmuseum@pecounty.on.ca
pecounty.on.ca/government/rec_parks_culture/rec_culture/museums/index.php
Founded: 1967 Indoor and outdoor exhibits distinguish the site, with displays of various artifacts from marine activity in the area, including treasures from diving expeditions, as well as pieces related to local fishing, ship building, ice harvesting and rum running days. The False Duck Lighthouse has become a memorial to the County's sailors.
Ms. Jennifer Lyons, Head Curator, Recreation, Parks & Culture, Prince Edward County, 613-476-2148, X-426, Fax: 613-476-9835, museums@pecounty.on.ca

Milton: **Country Heritage Park**
PO Box 38, Milton, ON L9T 2Y3
Tel: 905-878-8151; *Fax:* 905-876-4530
Toll-Free: 888-307-3276
information@countryheritagepark.com
www.countryheritag epark.com
Display of machinery & tools related to all aspects of agricultural industry in Ontario

Milton: **Halton Region Museum**
5181 Kelso Rd., RR#3 (Kelso Conservation Area), Milton, ON L9T 2X7
Tel: 905-875-2200; *Fax:* 905-876-4322
Toll-Free: 866-442-5866
museum@halton.ca
www.halton.ca/museum
Founded: 1962 Focusing on Halton's natural & cultural heritage, the main exhibits are located in Alexander Barn and in the Visitor Centre on the main floor. Both Heritage and Environmental Programmes are offered. The Reference Library stores various regional, historical records available for research purposes. Open year round.
Ms. Nancy Field, Manager, Heritage Services, Halton Region, 905-875-2200, X-22, nancy.field@halton.ca

Milton: **Streetcar & Electric Railway Museum**
c/o Ontario Electric Railway Historical Association Inc., PO Box 578, Milton, ON L9T 5A2
Tel: 519-856-9802; *Fax:* 519-856-1399
streetcar@hcry.org
www.hcry.org
Operating streetcar & electric railway museum
Gord McOuat, Vice-President
J. Borland, President

Minesing: **Simcoe County Museum**
1151 Hwy. 26, Minesing, ON L0L 1Y0
Tel: 705-728-3721; *Fax:* 705-728-9130
museum@simcoe.ca
www.county.simcoe.on.ca
Open daily; 9:00-4:30 Monday to Saturday and 1:00-4:30 Sunday. Admission $6.00 adults, $4.00 seniors/students

Mississauga: **Benares Historic House & Visitor Centre**
1507 Clarkson Rd. North, Mississauga, ON L5J 2W8
Tel: 905-822-2347; *Fax:* 905-822-5372
scott.gillies@city.mississauga.on.ca
www.mississauga.ca/portal/discover/ benareshistorichouse
Founded: 1995 Owned & operated by the City of Mississauga, Community Services Department, the Benares Historic House is a Georgian style home, which was built in 1857. The home has been restored to reflect the early 20th century & displays original artifacts from the Harris family & home. The Benares House is believed to be the inspiration for Mazo de la Roche's Jalna novels.

Mississauga: **Bradley House Museum**
1620 Orr Rd., Mississauga, ON L5J 4T2
Tel: 905-822-1569; *Fax:* 905-823-3591
scott.gillies@mississauga.ca
www.mississauga.ca/portal/discover/bradleym useum
The Bradley Museum is owned & operated by the City of Mississauga, Community Services Department. The museum grounds feature an early 19th century home known as The Anchorage, a farmhouse which was built in 1830, & a log cabin. The farmhouse was owned by the Bradleys, who were a United Empire Loyalist couple. The museum is open year round.

Mississauga: **Lithuanian Museum/Archives of Canada**
2185 Stavebank Rd., Mississauga, ON L5C 1T3
Tel: 905-566-8755; *Fax:* 905-275-1336
litharch@the-wire.com
To collect, display, organize & preserve documents, photographs, fine art, textiles, memorabilia, souvenirs of community events, uniforms, medals, coins, maps, flags, videos, audio tapes & rare books or periodicals which pertain to Lithuania & Lithuanian Canadians; small lending library
Dr. Rasa Mazeika, Director

Mooretown: **Moore Museum**
94 Moore Line, Mooretown, ON N0N 1M0
Tel: 519-867-2020; *Fax:* 519-867-2020
lmason@twp.stclair.on.ca
www.lambtononline.com/moore_museum
Founded: 1975 Open year round; Jan. - Feb. by appt.
Laurie Mason, Curator

Morpeth: **Rondeau Provincial Park Visitor Centre**
RR#1, Morpeth, ON N0P 1X0
Tel: 519-674-1768; *Fax:* 519-674-1755
Herbarium, egg, mammal, insect, archaeological, photographic & bird collection

Morrisburg: **Upper Canada Village**
13740 County Rd. 2, Morrisburg, ON K0C 1X0
Tel: 613-543-4328; *Toll-Free:* 800-437-2233
www.uppercanadavillage.com
Other contact information: Phone, Village Library Appointments: 613-543-3704
Upper Canada Village features more than forty heritage buildings. The village depicts daily life in the 1860s, through demonstrations, talks, & hands-on activities. The site also has a library & research facility. Upper Canada Village is open from mid May to mid October.

Mount Brydges: **Ska-Nah-Doht Iroquoian Village & Museum**
8449 Irish Dr., RR#1, Mount Brydges, ON N0L 1W0
Tel: 519-264-2420; *Fax:* 519-264-1562
lowerthames@odyssey.on.ca
www.lowerthames-conservation.on.ca/SkaNahDoht. htm
This recreated Iroquoian village of 1,000 years ago has 18 outdoor exhibits including a palisade with maze & longhouses; museum in resource centre; displays on nature & conservation; trails, wetland boardwalks & picnic areas.There are hands on exhibits and an archaeological collection.
Karen Mattila, Curator

Mount Hope: **Canadian Warplane Heritage Museum (CWH)**
Hamilton Airport, 9280 Airport Rd., Mount Hope, ON L0R 1W0
Tel: 905-679-4183; *Fax:* 905-679-4186
Toll-Free: 877-347-3359
museum@warplane.com
www.warplane.com
Founded: 1971 The museum is dedicated to the acquisition & preservation of aircraft flown by Canadians from WWII to the present, & the collection of related aviation artifacts & memorabilia; library & archival resources; meeting room & hangar rental; special events & programming; group tours available. Open daily 9-5, year round.
David G. Rohrer, CEO/Director

Napanee: **Allan Macpherson House**
180 Elizabeth St., Napanee, ON K7R 1B5
Tel: 613-354-5982; *Fax:* 613-354-5285
machouse@kingston.net
www.macphersonhouse.ca
Founded: 1967 1826 mansion of Allan Macpherson, one of Napanee's leading citizens; reflects the taste, public & private activities of an entrepreneurial Scottish immigrant. Open May-Dec. School programs; bridal party rentals; children's summer activity days; annual whiskey tasting.
Sandra Penney, Managing Director

Napanee: **Lennox & Addington County Museum & Archives**
97 Thomas St. East, PO Bag 1000, Napanee, ON K7R 3S9
Tel: 613-354-3027; *Fax:* 613-354-1005
nmuseum@lennox-addington.on.ca
www.lennox-addington.on.ca
Located in former County jail (1864); genealogy & historical research centre, county's origins, Loyalist settlement &

development from 1784 to present, displays & extensive archives; open year round
Jane Foster, Manager
Shelley Respondek, Archivist, archives@lennox-addington.on.ca

***Napanee:* Old Hay Bay Church**
c/o 304 Staples Lane, Napanee, ON K7R 3K7
Tel: 613-373-2877; *Fax:* 613-373-8816
www.oldhaybaychurch.org
A National Historic Site, Old Hay Bay Church was erected in 1792. Located at 2365 South Shore Road in Adolphustown, Ontario, the church is the oldest Methodist building in Canada.
Katherine Staples, Contact

***Nepean:* Algonquin College Museum**
Applied Museum Studies Program, Algonquin College, 1385 Woodroffe Ave., Nepean, ON K2G 1V8
Tel: 613-727-4723; *Fax:* 613-727-7786
pattilk@algonquincollege.com
Teaching collection
Katherine Pattillo, Coordinator

***Nepean:* Nepean Museum Inc.**
16 Rowley Ave., Nepean, ON K2G 1L9
Tel: 613-723-7936; *Fax:* 613-723-7936
reception@nepeanmuseum.ca
www.nepeanmuseum.ca
Founded: 1983 Housed in the first Nepean Library, the museum displays historical objects related to Nepean's past & present. Nepean Museum contains two meeting rooms.
Lindsay MacDonald, Director & Curator, curator@nepeanmuseum.ca
Kalle Boucher, Manager, Education & Volunteers, educationservices@nepeanmuseum.ca
Emily Bracewell, Manager, Collections, collections@nepeanmuseum.ca

***New Liskeard:* Little Claybelt Homesteaders Museum**
PO Box 1718, New Liskeard, ON P0J 1P0
Tel: 705-647-9575
lchmuse@ntl.sympatico.ca
www.museumsnorth.org/new_liskeard/
Displays of geological origin of Little Claybelt, pioneer activities, historical documents, artifacts & agricultural implements, pioneer family histories
Clair Shepherdson, President

***Newmarket:* Elman W. Campbell Museum**
***Also known as:* Newmarket Museum**
134 Main St. South, Newmarket, ON L3Y 3Y7
Tel: 905-953-5314; *Fax:* 905-898-2083
Toll-Free: 877-550-5575
elmanmuseum@rogers.com
www.newmarket.ca
Exhibits trace the development of Newmarket from the time of the first settlers
Elizabeth Sinyard, Curator

***Niagara Falls:* Daredevil Gallery**
6170 Fallsview Blvd., Niagara Falls, ON L2G 7T8
Tel: 905-358-3611; *Fax:* 905-358-3613
Toll-Free: 866-405-4629
info@imaxniagara.com
www.imaxniagara.com/daredevil-gal lery
Only collection of original daredevil barrels found in Niagara Falls

***Niagara Falls:* Guinness World Records Museum**
4943 Clifton Hill, Niagara Falls, ON L2G 3N5
Tel: 905-356-2299; *Fax:* 905-356-8614
info@guinnessniagarafalls.com
www.guinnessniagarafalls.com
Displays of human achievements; models of the extraordinary; computer databanks & videos; open year round

***Niagara Falls:* Laura Secord Homestead**
c/o, PO Box 150, Niagara Falls, ON L2E 6T2
Tel: 905-262-4851
Open May-Sept. in Queenston ON

***Niagara Falls:* Louis Tussaud's Waxworks**
5907 Victoria Ave., Niagara Falls, ON L2G 3L5
Tel: 905-374-6601; *Fax:* 905-374-7345
www.cliftonhill.com/attractions
Founded: 1953 Museum displays wax models of famous and infamous people, such as artists, musicians, celebrities, politicians and religious & historical figures. Open year round.
Mr. Tim Parker, Gneral manager Manager, parker@ripleys.com
André Ross

***Niagara Falls:* McFarland House**
c/o Niagara Parks Commission, PO Box 150, Niagara Falls, ON L2E 6T2
Tel: 905-295-4377; *Fax:* 905-295-4142
Toll-Free: 877-642-7275
www.niagaraparks.com/heritage-trail/mcfarland-house.html
Founded: 1959 Built in 1800 and home to John McFarland and his family for 150 years, the house served as a hospital for both the British & American wounded during the War of 1812. Restored by the Niagara Parks Commission in period style, there are also traditional grounds and the McFarland Tea Garden to enjoy refreshments. Nature trails can be accessed from the park. The house is located at 15927 Niagara Parkway, Niagara-on-the-Lake.
Ms April Petrie, Manager, Heritage & Educational Services

***Niagara Falls:* Movieland Wax Museum**
4950 Clifton Hill, Niagara Falls, ON L2G 3N4
Tel: 905-358-3061
Open year round

***Niagara Falls:* Niagara Falls History Museum**
5810 Ferry St., Niagara Falls, ON L2G 1S9
Tel: 905-358-5082; *Fax:* 905-358-0920
llmuseum@niagarafalls.ca
www.niagarafallsmuseum.ca/lundyslanehistoricalm useum.html
Founded: 1961 The 1874 museum was originally located on Drummond Rd., the site of the Battle of Lundy's Lane, July 25, 1814, but was moved to its present site in 1970. Exhibits include a significant collection of War of 1812 artifacts, as well as historic prints of Niagara Falls. The Museum also houses a variety of artifacts relating to all aspects of the founding and development of the City of Niagara Falls.
Mr. Gordon West, Board Chair
Kathleen Powell, Manager

***Niagara Falls:* Old Fort Erie**
PO Box 150, Niagara Parks Commission, 350 Niagara Pkwy., Niagara Falls, ON L2E 6T2
Tel: 905-356-2241
Collection of military equipment housed in a reconstructed fort

***Niagara Falls:* Ripley's Believe It or Not! Museum**
4960 Clifton Hill, Niagara Falls, ON L2G 3N4
Tel: 905-356-2238; *Fax:* 905-374-7345
www.ripleysniagara.com
Founded: 1963 Ripley's Believe It or Not! in Niagara Falls presents strange & bizarre exhibits. The museum is open year-round.
Tim Parker, General Manager

***Niagara Falls:* Willoughby Historical Museum**
9935 Niagara Pkwy., Niagara Falls, ON L2E 6S6
Tel: 905-295-4036; *Fax:* 905-295-4036
whmuseum@niagarafalls.ca
www.niagarafallsmuseum.ca/willoughby.html
The Willoughby Historical Museum collects, preserves, interprets, & displays items related to Ontario's former Township of Willoughby, the Village of Chippawa, & the surrounding region. Examples of artifacts include household objects, school materials, toys, telephones, & a functioning magneto switchboard. The museum is open year-round. Tours & research can be arranged by phoning the museum.

***Niagara-on-the-Lake:* Niagara Apothecary**
PO Box 903, 5 Queen St., Niagara-on-the-Lake, ON L0S 1J0
Tel: 905-468-3845
niagaraapothecary@ocpinfo.com
www.niagaraapothecary.ca
The Niagara Apothecary depicts an 1869 pharmacy. Artifacts include the Harvey bottles & jars, which were imported from Britain around 1830, mortars & pestles, a 19th century leech jar, & an early cash register.

***Niagara-on-the-Lake:* Niagara Fire Museum**
PO Box 498, Niagara-on-the-Lake, ON L0S 1J0
Tel: 905-468-7279
Fire-fighting equipment dating back 140 years

***Niagara-on-the-Lake:* Niagara Historical Society & Museum**
***Also known as:* Niagara Historical Museum**
PO Box 208, 43 Castlereagh St., Niagara-on-the-Lake, ON L0S 1J0
Tel: 905-468-3912; *Fax:* 905-468-1728
contact@niagarahistorical.museum
www.niagarahistorical.museum
Founded: 1895 Ontario's first purpose-built museum; artifacts from Niagara's social & military history
Clark Bernat, Managing Director
Amy Klassen, Administrator, Niagara Historical Society

***Niagara-on-the-Lake:* Niagara-on-the-Lake Fort George National Historic Site**
***Also known as:* Fort George**
Parks Canada, PO Box 787, Niagara-on-the-Lake, ON L0S 1J0
Tel: 905-468-4257
Recontructed fort built in 1799

***Nipigon:* Nipigon Museum**
PO Box 208, Nipigon, ON P0T 2J0
Tel: 807-887-2727
Artifacts relating to local lumbering & fur trading; rocks & minerals; bottles

***Nipissing:* Nipissing Township Museum**
General Delivery, Nipissing, ON P0H 1W0
Tel: 705-724-2938; *Fax:* 705-724-5385
Housed in a former Anglican church built in late 1800s of logs; displays mostly of tools, clothing & photos pertaining to the families who first settled in the area
Joe Steele, Curator

***North Bay:* Callander Bay Heritage Museum**
PO Box 100, 107 Lansdowne St. East, North Bay, ON P0H 1H0
Tel: 705-752-2282; *Fax:* 705-752-3116
museum@callander.ca
www.mycallander.ca/museum
The Callander Bay Heritage Museum was the home & office of Dr. Allan R. Dafoe from 1914 to 1943. Dr. Dafoe was the doctor for the Dionne Quintuplets. The museum contains exhibits about the doctor & the quintuplets. The Alex Dufrense Gallery features the work of local artists. The museum also houses local genealogical sources & historical records for research.
Tom Fletcher, Chair

***North Bay:* Dionne Quints Museum**
c/o North Bay & District Chamber of Commerce, 1375 Seymour St., North Bay, ON P1B 9V6
Tel: 705-472-8480; *Fax:* 705-472-8027
Toll-Free: 888-249-8998
nbcc@northbaychamber.com
www.northbaychamber.com
The Quints Museum is a not for profit institution dedicated to the Dionne Quintuplets; artifacts from the Quints's early days and their growing up years; baby buggies, baby dresses, books, newspaper and magazine articles, artisitic reproductions, postcards. Located at Hwys 11 and 17 at Seymour Street in North Bay.
Amy Bennett, Director

***North Bay:* North Bay & Area Museum**
100 Main St. East, North Bay, ON P1B 1A8
Tel: 705-476-2323; *Fax:* 705-476-9300
nbamchin@vianet.on.ca
10,000 domestic & business objects related to settling & development of local region; open year round

***North Buxton:* Buxton National Historic Site & Museum**
21975 A.D. Shadd Rd., North Buxton, ON N0P 1Y0
Tel: 519-352-4799; *Fax:* 519-352-8561
buxton@ciaccess.com
www.buxtonmuseum.com
Founded: 1967 The site is a memorial to the Elgin Settlement, which was the last stop on the Underground Railroad for many fugitives of the American system of slavery in the pre-Civil War years. The Raleigh (Buxton) Schoolhouse of 1861 & a settlement cabin from 1854 are now part of the museum. The museum preserves the artifacts of the original settlers of the Elgin Settlement & their descendants.
Shannon Prince, Curator

***Norwich:* The Norwich & District Museum & Archives**
89 Stover St. North, RR#3, Norwich, ON N0J 1P0
Tel: 519-863-3101; *Fax:* 519-863-2343
norwichdhs@execulink.com
www.ocl.net/projects/norwich_historical/museum/
1889 Quaker Meeting House; archives & genealogical library
Janet Hilliker, Archivist
Kerrie Gill, Curator

***Oakville:* Canadian Golf Hall of Fame & Museum (CGHF)**
Glen Abbey Golf Club, 1333 Dorval Dr., Oakville, ON L6J 4Z3
Tel: 905-849-9700
cghf@rcga.org
www.rcga.org
Founded: 1971 Located at Glen Abbey, the Canadian Golf Hall of Fame & Museum tells the history of golf in Canada. The Hall of Fame honours amateur & professional golfers & builders of the sport, who have made extraordinary contributions to the game of golf in Canada. The archives & library collects photographs & documents, as well as golf publications about the game, golf courses & golfers. Staff are available to assist with research. The museum also arranges travelling exhibitions. The Canadian Golf Hall of Fame & Museum is open year round.
Karen Hewson, Director, CGHF, & Executive Director, Royal Canadian Golf Association Foundation, 1-800-263-0009, khewson@rcga.org
Meggan Gardner, Curator, mgardner@rcga.org
Jordan Diacur, Museum Assistant, jdiacur@rcga.org

***Oakville:* Oakville Museum at Erchless Estate**
8 Navy St., Oakville, ON L6J 2Y5
Tel: 905-338-4400; *Fax:* 905-815-5973
www.oakvillemuseum.com
The Oakville Museum at Erchless Estate features the following historical buildings: Erchless Estate (c. 1858), The Custom

House & Toronto Bank (c. 1856), & The Old Post Office (c. 1835). The Thomas Museum is operated by the Oakville Historical Society.
Claire Loughheed, Senior Manager, Culture Services, cloughheed@oakville.ca
Bill Nesbitt, Museum Supervisor, bnesbitt@oakville.ca
Carolyn Cross, Curator, Collections, ccross@oakville.ca
Susan Crane, Officer, Learning & Community Development, scrane@oakville.ca
Julie Hawryszko, Mueum Programmer, Public Programs, jhawryszko@oakville.ca
Preeya Nayee, Mueum Programmer, Education Programs, pnayee@oakville.ca

Odessa: Historic Babcock Mill
100 Bridge St., Odessa, ON K0H 2H0
Tel: 613-386-7351; *Fax:* 613-386-3833
clawson@loyalist.ca
Restored, fully operational water-powered 1856 mill
Patrick Beyer, Contact

Ohsweken: Chiefswood National Historic Site
***Also known as:* Pauline Johnson House**
PO Box 640, Ohsweken, ON N0A 1M0
Tel: 519-752-5005; *Fax:* 519-752-9578
chiefswood@execulink.com
www.chiefswood.com
The site is the location of the Chiefswood Museum, birthplace and childhood home of poet Emily Pauline Johnson (Tekahionwake); educational programming; tours; gift shop; "The Homing Bee" newsletter. Open Tues. through Sunday, 10:00-3:00, May-Oct. Open by appointment Oct.-May.
Paul Whitlow, Curator, Chiefswood Museum

Oil Springs: Oil Museum of Canada
PO Box 16, 2423 Kelly Rd., Oil Springs, ON N0N 1P0
Tel: 519-834-2840; *Fax:* 519-834-2840
oil.museum@county-lambton.on.ca
www.lambtononline.com/oil_museum
Situated in Oil Springs, Ontario, The Oil Museum of Canada preserves the site of the first commercial oil well in North America. Visitors learn the story of Canadian oil pioneers, through petroleum industry artifacts, working exhibits, & photographs. Visitors can also see original oil wells, which continue to produce oil.
Connie Bell, Supervisor

Orillia: Stephen Leacock Museum
PO Box 625, 50 Museum Dr., Orillia, ON L3V 6K5
Tel: 705-329-1908; *Fax:* 705-326-5578
lmcurator@rogers.com
www.leacockmuseum.com
Fred Addis, Curator

Oshawa: Canadian Automotive Museum
99 Simcoe St. South, Oshawa, ON L1G 4G7
Tel: 905-576-1222; *Fax:* 905-576-1223
infoservices@oshawa.ca
www.oshawa.ca
Founded: 1961 The Canadian Automotive Museum depicts the history & future plans of the Canadian automotive industry. More than sixty vehicles, dating from 1898 to 1981 are on display. Items related to the era of the vehicles are also displayed.

Oshawa: Oshawa Sydenham Museum
1450 Simcoe St. South, Oshawa, ON L1H 8S8
Tel: 905-436-7624; *Fax:* 905-436-7625
Henry House c1849; Robinson House c1846; Guy House c1835

Oshawa: Parkwood National Historic Site, The R.S. McLaughlin Estate
270 Simcoe St. North, Oshawa, ON L1G 4T5
Tel: 905-433-4311
info@parkwoodestate.com
www.parkwoodestate.com
Built between 1915 & 1917, Parkwood was the grand estate of R. Samuel McLaughlin, who was the founder of General Motors of Canada. The McLaughlin family lived at the home from 1917 to 1972. Today, it is furnished to reflect the 1920s & 1930s. The National Historic Site is open year-round.

Ottawa: The Billings Estate National Historical Site / Lieu historique national du domaine Billings
2100 Cabot St., Ottawa, ON K1H 6K1
Tel: 613-247-4830; *Fax:* 613-247-4832
museums@ottawa.ca
www.ottawa.ca/museums;
www.friendsofbillingsestatemuseum.org
Home & property of Braddish & Lamira Billings, two of Ottawa's earliest settlers, c. 1828; exhibits highlight 5 generations of family & community history
Anik Després, Education Officer
Brahm Lewandowski, Education Officer

Ottawa: Bytown Museum / Musée Bytown
PO Box 523 B, Ottawa, ON K1P 5P6
Tel: 613-234-4570; *Fax:* 613-234-4846
program@storm.ca (Appointments)
www.bytownmuseum.com
Bytown Museum is situated in the oldest stone building in Ottawa, which was a treasury & storehouse during the construction of the Rideau Canal. Within the museum, the history of Bytown & the nation's capital is traced. The museum is open from the beginning of April to the end of November, & during March Break. From December to March, the museum is open by appointment only.
Mike Steinhauer, Director, mikesteinhauer@bytownmuseum.ca

Ottawa: Cameron Highlanders of Ottawa Regimental Museum
Cartier Sq. Drill Hall, 2 Queen Elizabeth Dr., Ottawa, ON K1A 0K2
www.camerons.ca/Org_Museum.html
The Regimental Museum contains memorabilia of the Cameron Highlanders of Ottawa. It is open one evening each week.

Ottawa: Canada Agriculture Museum / Musée de l'agriculture du Canada
Prince of Wales Dr., PO Box 9724 T, Ottawa, ON K1G 5A3
Tel: 613-991-3044; *Fax:* 613-993-7923
Toll-Free: 866-442-4416
www.agriculture.technomuses.ca
Other contact information: TDD: 613-991-9207; Phone, Media: 613-996-7812
The Canada Agriculture Museum is a demonstration farm & research station, which features animal barns, the Dominion Arboretum, ornamental gardens, & special exhibitions.
David Sutin, Manager, Communications & Marketing, 613-996-7812, dsutin@technomuses.ca

Ottawa: The Canadian Museum of Scouting
1345 Baseline Rd., Ottawa, ON K2C 0A7
Tel: 613-224-5131; *Fax:* 613-224-3571
mailbox@scouts.caca
www.scouts.ca
Founded: 1907 Scouting artifacts and historical memorobilia (Canada/UK/World); Open by appointment only
Robert Stewart, Exec. Commissioner & CEO, Scouts Canada
Stephen Kant, Chief Commissioner & Chair of the Board
Gary Boutilier, Director, Financial Services
John Singleton, Vice-President, Finance, Board of Governors
Lisa Nowlan, Director, Communication Services

Ottawa: Canadian Ski Museum & Canadian Ski Hall of Fame (CSMus) / Musée canadien du ski et Temple de la renommée du ski canad
#301, 1960 Scott St., Ottawa, ON K1Z 8L8
Tel: 613-722-3584; *Fax:* 613-722-2914
info@skimuseum.ca
www.skimuseum.ca
The Canadian Ski Museum & Canadian Ski Hall of Fame preserves Canadian skiing history & celebrates Canadian skiing & snowboarding traditions & achievements. The Hall of Fame honours Canada's accomplished skiers, snowboarders, coaches, officials, & builders of the sport.
Ivo Krupka, Chair
Walter Boyce, Director, Fundraising
Ron Crook, Director, Communications
Trevor Klotz, Director, Legal
Bruce Meredith, Director & Treasurer
Don Runge, Director, Publications

Ottawa: The Canadian Wildlife & Wilderness Art Museum (CWWAM) / Musée canadien d'art naturaliste
PO Box 98 B, Ottawa, ON K1P 6C3
Tel: 613-237-1581; *Fax:* 613-237-1581
cawa@magma.ca
www.magma.ca/cawa
Established by the Canadian Academy of Wilderness Artists (CAWA) "Hall of Fame" Art Foundation; 9,500 artifacts, drawings, prints, lithographs, carvings, sculpture & paintings. Coupled with major Canadian artists from the present and the past: Robert Bateman, Glen Loates, Ely Kish, Neil Blackwell, Norval Morriseau, A.J. Casson, Bernard Loates & many more; are several important American & European artists including Frederic Remington, Charles Marion Russell, Georgia O'Keefe, Eanger Irving Couse, Albert Bierstadt, Manfred Schatz & many more; some pieces are privately held & are on loan
Maria Amati, Executive Director
Gary Slimon, Director

Ottawa: Governor General's Foot Guards Museum
Drill Hall, Cartier Sq., Ottawa, ON K1A 0K2
Tel: 613-990-0620
elane22@rogers.com
www.ggfg.ottawa.on.ca
Regimental museum; brief history of regiment from 1872 to present by way of artifacts
Martin J. Lane, Curator CD

Ottawa: Laurier House National Historic Site
335 Laurier Ave. East, Ottawa, ON K1N 6R4
Tel: 613-992-8142; *Fax:* 613-947-4851
laurier.house@pc.gc.ca
Residence of Sir Wilfrid Laurier & the Right Honourtable William Lyon MacKenzie King, built in 1878

Ottawa: Mackenzie King Estate / Domaine Mackenzie-King
National Capital Commission, #202, 40 Elgin St., Ottawa, ON K1P 1C7
Tel: 819-827-6026; *Fax:* 819-827-3337
Toll-Free: 800-465-1867
dmessier@ncc-ccn.ca
Located in Gatineau Park; open daily from mid-May to the end of Oct.
Denis Messier, Manager

Owen Sound: Grey Roots Museum & Archives
102599 Grey Rd. 18, RR#4, Owen Sound, ON N4K 5N6
Tel: 519-376-3690; *Fax:* 519-376-4654
Toll-Free: 877-473-9766
info@greyroots.com
www.greyroots.com
Collects, preserves, restores, documents, interprets & displays the material culture of Grey County & the city of Owen Sound, c. 1815 - present; research, interpretive programs, tours; gift shop
Brian Manser, Manager, brian.manser@greyroots.com

Parry Sound: West Parry Sound District Museum (WPSDM)
***Also known as:* Museum on Tower Hill**
PO Box 337, 17 George St., Parry Sound, ON P2A 2X4
Tel: 705-746-5365; *Fax:* 705-746-8775
info@wpsdm.com
www.wpsdm.com
Founded: 1983 Situated in Tower Hill Park, the West Parry Sound District Museum displays items related to the First Nations, settlement, logging, shipping, agriculture, recreation, & natural history. The museum is open year-round.
Darcy Yanni, Museum Director, darcy@wpsdm.com
Tanya Bolwerk, Bookkeeper, accounting@wpsdm.com

Pelee Island: Pelee Island Heritage Centre
West Dock, Pelee Island, ON N0R 1M0
Tel: 519-724-2291; *Fax:* 519-724-2470
pimuseum@mnsi.net
Rare Flora & fauna exhibits; early navigation displays; local shipwreck information

Pembroke: Champlain Trail Museum & Pioneer Village
PO Box 985, 1032 Pembroke St. East, Pembroke, ON K8A 7M5
Tel: 613-735-0517; *Fax:* 613-629-5067
pembrokemuseum@nrtco.net
www.champlaintrailmuseum.com
Economic, political & social history of upper Ottawa Valley & Renfrew County; archival & genealogical material
Tony Cowan, Manager

Penetanguishene: Discovery Harbour / Havre de la Découverte
Ministry of Tourism, 93 Jury Dr., Penetanguishene, ON L9M 1G1
Tel: 705-549-8064; *Fax:* 705-549-4858
Toll-Free: 705-526-7697
hhp@hhp.on.ca
www.discoveryharbour.on.ca
Ontario's leading Marine Heritage Site; orginally built as a military base with its roots tracing back to the War of 1812. Tours, interactive daily activies in the summer. Open weekdays late-May to July 1; open daily July 1 to Labour Day weekend
Jan Gray, General Manager

Penetanguishene: Penetanguishene Centennial Museum & Archives
13 Burke St., Penetanguishene, ON L9M 1C1
Tel: 705-549-2150; *Fax:* 705-549-7542
info@pencenmuseum.com
www.pencenmuseum.com
Other contact information: E-mail, Genealogy & History Research Ctr.: genealogy@pencenmuseum.com
Penetanguishene's museum is housed in the former C. Beck Lumber Office & General Store which was built in 1875. The location also features a Genealogy & History Research Center & Archives, which houses the the Georgian Bay Heritage League Collection with more than 500 genealogical files & local history books. Penetanguishene Centennial Museum & Archives is open year-round.
Nicole Jackson, Curator, njackson@pencenmuseum.com
Pam Tessier, Coordinator, Research, ptessier@pencenmuseum.com
Janice Gadsdon, Curatorial Assistant, jgadsdon@pencenmuseum.com

Perth: **Innisville & District Museum**
c/o Willard Shaw, RR#6, Perth, ON K7H 3C8
Tel: 613-267-6500; *Fax:* 613-267-2083
lindav@drummondnorthelmsley.com
Country-style museum
George Jackson

Perth: **The Perth Museum**
Also known as: **Matheson House**
11 Gore St. East, Perth, ON K7H 1H9
Tel: 613-267-1947; *Fax:* 613-267-5635
perthmuseum@town.perth.on.ca
www.perthcanada.com
1840 stone home of Senator Matheson; open year round; National Historic Site; 2 galleries; historic gardens
Karen Rennie, Curator

Petawawa: **Canadian Airborne Forces Museum / Musée des Forces aéroportées canadiennes**
Canadian Forces Base Petawawa, PO Box 9999 Main, 63 Colborne Rd., Petawawa, ON K8H 2X3
Tel: 613-588-6238
info@petawawamuseums.com
www.petawawamuseums.com
Other contact information: E-mail, Volunteer Coordinator: volunteers@petawawamuseums.com
The Canadian Airborne Forces Museum preserves & honours the memory of airborne forces that served Canada since World War II. Their history is presented through historical artifacts, dioramas, videos, & a large screen mini-theatre. The museum is a member of the following organizations: the Organization of Military Museums of Canada, the Canadian Museums Association, the Ontario Museums Association, the Ottawa Valley Tourist Association, & the Renfrew County Museums Network. The Canadian Airborne Forces Museum is open year-round.
Anne Lindsay, Museologist, Lindsay.A@forces.gc.ca
Ainsley Greenfield, Manager, Collections

Petawawa: **Canadian Forces Base Petawawa Military Museum**
Canadian Forces Base Petawawa, PO Box 9999 Main, 63 Colborne Rd., Petawawa, ON K8H 2X3
Tel: 613-588-6238
info@petawawamuseums.com
www.petawawamuseums.com
Other contact information: E-mail, Volunteer Coordinator: volunteers@petawawamuseums.com
The Canadian Forces Base Petawawa Military Museum collects, preserves, & interprets items related to the history of individuals & units of CFB Petawawa since 1905. Museum staff also assist with research requests.
Anne Lindsay, Museologist, Lindsay.A@forces.gc.ca
Ainsley Greenfield, Manager, Collections

Peterborough: **The Canadian Canoe Museum**
910 Monaghan Rd., Peterborough, ON K9J 5K4
Tel: 705-748-9153; *Fax:* 705-748-0616
Toll-Free: 866-342-2663
inquiries@canoemuseum.net
www.canoemuseum.net
Collection of over 600 canoes & kayaks, plus related artifacts; open year round

Peterborough: **Hope Water-Powered Saw Mill**
Also known as: **Hope Mill**
c/o Otonabee Region Conservation Authority, 250 Milroy Dr., Peterborough, ON K9H 7M9
Tel: 705-745-5791; *Fax:* 705-745-7488
otonabeeca@otonabee.com
www.otonabee.com/orcf/news/events/hope_mill.htm
Built in 1835 by Scottish immigrant Squire William Lang, the Otonabee Conservation Authority purchased the mill from his great grandson in 1966. The saw-powered Hope Mill has been restored to its original charm and is fully functional. Demonstrations and tours are offered. A collection of 19th-century carpentry tools, as well as larger pieces of equipment (lathe, planer, drill-press), are on exhibit. The mill is located at 3414 Hope Mill Rd. on the banks of the Indian River in Lang, ON.
Richard Hunter, CAO
John Williams, Coordinator, Conservation Lands

Peterborough: **Hutchison House Museum**
270 Brock St., Peterborough, ON K9H 2P9
Tel: 705-743-9710; *Fax:* 705-740-0395
Toll-Free: 866-743-9710
hutchisonhouse@nexicom.net
www.nexicom.net/~history
Living history museum owned & operated by the Peterborough Historical Society open to all interested in the history of Upper Canada in the 1800s
Gale Fewings, Administrator/Curator

Peterborough: **Lang Pioneer Village**
470 Water St., Peterborough, ON K9H 3M3
Tel: 705-295-6694; *Fax:* 705-295-6644
Toll-Free: 866-289-5264
jcorrigan@county.peterborough.on.ca
langpioneervillage .ca
Living history museum from 1800-1900; over 20 restored buildings with costumed interpreters; open Mon.-Fri. May 15-June 30, Sat.-Fri. July 1 to Labour Day; call or see website for hours of operation, admission prices & list of special events
Joe Corrigan, Manager

Peterborough: **Lang Water Powered Grist Mill**
Also known as: **Lang Mill**
c/o Otonabee Region Conservation Authority, 250 Milroy Dr., Peterborough, ON K9H 7M9
Tel: 705-745-5791; *Fax:* 705-745-7488
otonabeeca@otonabee.com
www.otonabee.com
Fully operational water-powered grist mill located on the west bank of the Indian River at Lang Pioneer Village (Otonabee-South Monaghan Township-County of Peterborough).
John DuChene, CAO
John Williams, Coordinator, Conservation Lands

Peterborough: **Peterborough Museum & Archives**
Ashburnham Memorial Park, PO Box 143, Peterborough, ON K9J 6Y5
Tel: 705-743-5180; *Fax:* 705-743-2614
administration@peterboroughmuseumandarchives.ca
www.peterboroughmuseuman darchives.ca
Other contact information: E-mail, Artifacts: collections@peterboroughmuseumandarchives.ca
The heritage & culture of Peterborough & the surrounding area is preserved & presented at Peterborough Museum & Archives. The Museum houses a variety of artifacts, such as archaeological collections, technological artifacts, & military collections. The Archives holds over 2,000 fonds, including personal letters, maps, photographs, association records, early Peterborough Examiner newspapers, & the early records of Peterborough County Court. The Museum & Archives is open year-round. Appointments are required to visit the Archives (archives@peterboroughmuseumandarchives.ca).
Jon Oldham, Media Contact, joldham@peterborough.ca

Peterborough: **Trent-Severn Waterway National Historic Site of Canada, Lock 21 - Peterborough Lift Lock**
PO Box 567, Peterborough, ON K9J 6Z6
Tel: 705-750-4900; *Fax:* 705-742-9644
Toll-Free: 888-773-8888
Ont.Trentsevern@pc.gc.ca
www.pc.gc.ca/eng/lhn-nhs/on/t rentsevern/visit/visit6/lock21.aspx
Other contact information: Phone, Group Tours: 705-750-4950; Teletypewriter (TDD): 705-750-4949
Opened in 1904, the Peterborough Lift Lock is the highest hydraulic lift lock in the world. Located next to Lock 21 is the Peterborough Lift Lock Visitor Centre, which contains exhibits & films. The Peterborough Lift Lock Visitor Centre is open during the navigation season.
Peter Frood, Field Unit Superintendent, Parks Canada Central Ontario Field Unit
Sara Atkins, Manager, External Relations & Communications, Parks Canada Central Ontario Field Unit

Petrolia: **Petrolia Discovery**
PO Box 1480, Petrolia, ON N0N 1R0
Tel: 519-882-0897; *Fax:* 519-882-4209
petdisc@xcelco.on.ca
www.petroliadiscovery.com
Petrolia Discovery depicts the history of the pioneer oil men of Lambton County, Ontario. The museum is located at an oilfield which was established in the 1870s. This 19th century oilfield has been restored & is still operational. Petrolia Discovery is open from Victoria Day until Labour Day. School & educational tours may be arranged after the summer season.

Pickering: **Pickering Museum Village**
c/o City of Pickering, One The Esplanade, Pickering, ON L1V 6K7
Tel: 905-683-8401; *Fax:* 905-686-4079
museum@city.pickering.on.ca
www.cityofpickering.com/museum
Located at 2365 Concession Road #6 in Pickering, Ontario, the Pickering Museum Village features fifteen restored heritage buildings, including a schoolhouse, churches, a blacksmith shop, houses, & barns.

Picton: **Macaulay Heritage Park**
Also known as: **Prince Edward County Museum**
PO Box 2150, 35 Church St., Picton, ON K0K 2T0
Tel: 613-476-3833; *Fax:* 613-476-9835
macmuseum@pecounty.on.ca
www.pec.on.ca/macaulay
Founded: 1973 The site encompasses the 1830 Macaulay House, home of the Rev. William Macaulay, carriage house, heritage gardens & former St. Mary Magdalene Church and cemetary; open Tues.-Sun. 1-4:30 from long weekend in May to Thanksgiving; 10-4:30 (July & Aug.)
Ms Jennifer Lyons, Head Curator, 613-476-2148 ext 426, museums@pecounty.on.ca
Elizabeth Hunter, Museum Manager

Picton: **Rose House Museum**
PO Box 3530, Picton, ON K0K 2T0
Tel: 613-476-5439
rosemuseum@pecounty.on.ca
1804 original homestead; home to five generations of the Rose family; living history depicting life in 1800s; guided tours
Susan Rose, Curator

Port Carling: **Muskoka Lakes Museum**
PO Box 432, 1 Joseph St., Port Carling, ON P0B 1J0
Tel: 705-765-5367; *Fax:* 705-765-7682
mlmchin@muskoka.com
www.muskoka.com/tourism/mlm/
Log home from 1875; artifacts of early settlers & lumber industry; displays related to boat building & water transportation; archives of Muskoka region; open May 19 - Thanksgiving
Doug Smith, Director/Curator

Port Colborne: **Port Colborne Historical & Marine Museum**
PO Box 572, 280 King St., Port Colborne, ON L3K 5X8
Tel: 905-834-7604; *Fax:* 905-834-6198
museum@portcolborne.ca
www.portcolborne.ca/page/museum
The Port Colborne Historical & Marine Museum depicts the history of Port Colborne & the Welland Canala. The museum features heritage buildings, such as an 1869 home & carriage house, a log schoolhouse, & an 1850 marine blacksmith shop. A reproduction of the parapet of Port Colborne's Lighthouse contains ship models & marine artifacts. The museum, heritage village, & gift shop are open from May to December.
Stephanie Powell Baswick, Director & Curator
Lynn van Dillen, Assistant Curator, lynnvandillen@portcolborne.ca
Glenn Walker, Technician, Heritage Research, archives@portcolborne.ca

Port Dover: **Port Dover Harbour Museum**
PO Box 1298, 44 Harbour St., Port Dover, ON N0A 1N0
Tel: 519-583-2660
portdover.museum@norfolkcounty.ca
www.norfolkcounty.ca
The Port Dover Harbour Museum tells the story of Port Dover's fishing industry, ship building, Lake Erie shipwrecks, rum running, & other parts of lakeside life. The museum is open year round.

Port Hope: **Dorothy's House Museum (EDHS)**
Also known as: **East Durham Historical Society**
PO Box 116, 3632 Ganaraska Rd., Port Hope, ON L1A 3V9
Tel: 905-797-2247
info@porthopehistorical.ca
www.porthopehistorical.ca
Artifacts from the Port Hope & Hope Township area; house built around 1869; barn; driveshed; open May - Aug.
Ron Getz, President

Port Perry: **Scugog Shores Historical Museum**
Also known as: **Scugog Shores Museum Village & Archives**
16210 Island Rd., Port Perry, ON L9L 1B4
Tel: 905-985-3589; *Fax:* 905-985-3492
cbelfry@scugogshoresmuseum.com
www.scugogshoresmuseum.com
Historic village, comprising a log cabin, Lee House, blacksmith & woodright shops, print shop, school, church, barns, heritage flower, herb & dye plant gardens, & Ojibway Heritage Interpretive Lands; museum archives houses genealogical resources; special events & programming, themed artifact kits for rent, tours, building rentals
Craig Belfry, Manager, Culture & Heritage, Township of Scucog

Port Rowan: **Backus Heritage Conservation Area & Village (BHCA)**
c/o Long Point Region Conservation Authority, RR#1, Port Rowan, ON N0E 1M0
Tel: 519-586-2201
www.lprca.on.ca
Other contact information: Phone, Administration Office: 519-428-4623
Owned & operated by the Long Point Region Conservation Authority, the Backus Heritage Conservation Area features a conservation education centre & a heritage village. The village consists of restored & reconstructed buildings, including the John C. Backhouse Mill, the Teeterville Baptist Church, the Vittoria Carriage Shop, & the Forbes Barn. The history of the Long Point Region Watershed is depicted through exhibits & artifacts.

Prescott: **Fort Wellington National Historic Site of Canada**
PO Box 479, Prescott, ON K0E 1T0
Tel: 613-925-2896; *Fax:* 613-925-1536
ont-wellington@pc.gc.ca
www.pc.gc.ca/eng/lhn-nhs/on/wellington/ne/ne3.as px
Built during the War of 1812, Fort Wellington defended the St. Lawrence River shipping route between Kingston & Montréal. It was rebuilt in 1838 to once again defend against possible attack by the United States. Today, the Visitor Centre at the site displays exhibits related to the War of 1812 & the Upper Canada Rebellion. The site is open from Victoria Day weekend to the end of September. During the off-season, groups of ten or more may make an appointment.

Prescott: **The Forwarders' Museum**
PO Box 2179, 201 Water St., Prescott, ON K0E 1T0
Tel: 613-925-1861; *Fax:* 613-925-4381
Toll-Free: 800-218-1131
tourism@prescott.ca
www.prescott.ca
Forwarding trade; St Lawrence River & local history; open June-Labour Day

Red Lake: **Red Lake Regional Heritage Centre**
PO Box 64, 51A Hwy. 105, Red Lake, ON P0V 2M0
Tel: 807-727-3006; *Fax:* 807-727-2686
heritage@redlake.ca
www.redlakemuseum.com
At the Red Lake Regional Heritage Centre, visitors will discover Aboriginal, fur trade, gold mining, & immigration history. The centre also provides information about Woodland Caribou Park. The Red Lake Regional Heritage Centre is open year-round.
Richard Pasloski, Chair
Michele Alderton, Curator
Sara Cuthbertson, Assistant Curator

Renfrew: **McDougall Mill Museum**
Also known as: **Renfrew Museum**
PO Box 554, Arthur Ave., Renfrew, ON K7V 4B1
Tel: 613-432-2129
museum@renfrewmuseum.ca
www.renfrewmuseum.ca
Other contact information: Tel. (Off-season) 613/432-7015
Founded: 1969 Housed in a stone, 1855 grist mill built on the Bonnechere River by Hudson's Bay Company agent, John Lorne McDougall, the museum displays 3 floors of artifacts, including early appliances from Renfrew's industrial days. There are also exhibits of military articles, Victorian clothing and a wedding dress gallery. The museum is run by the Renfrew And District Historical And Museum Society.

Richards Landing: **Fort St. Joseph National Historic Site of Canada**
PO Box 220, Richards Landing, ON P0R 1J0
Tel: 705-246-2664; *Fax:* 705-246-1796
fortstjoseph-info@pc.gc.ca
www.pc.gc.ca/lhn-nhs/on/stjoseph/index_e.asp
Ruins of a fort erected after 1796 to serve as a fur trade centre; artifacts from excavation of site

Richards Landing: **St. Joseph Island Museum Complex**
Also known as: **St. Joseph Island Museum Village**
RR#2, Richards Landing, ON P0R 1J0
Tel: 705-246-2672
Six artifact buildings represent the pioneer era (1820-1880) & the settlement era after the Homestead Act of 1868; over 6,000 artifacts; farming, lumbering, maple syruping & early navigation displays; 2 schools, a church, a store, a barn, an 1880 log cabin & a general store
Pat Fleming, Curator
Micheline Yandeau, Chair

Ridgetown: **Ridge House Museum**
PO Box 550, 53 Erie St. South, Ridgetown, ON N0P 2C0
Tel: 519-674-2223; *Fax:* 519-674-3747
ckridgehouse@chatham-kent.on.ca
www.chatham-kent.ca/ridgehouse
Founded: 1975 The Ridge Hose Museum depicts the life of a middle class family in Ridgetown around 1875. Interactive tours & interpretive programs are provided.
Nicole Gignac, Curator

Ridgeway: **Fort Erie Historical Museum**
c/o Fort Erie Museum Board, PO Box 339, 402 Ridge Rd., Ridgeway, ON L0S 1N0
Tel: 905-894-5322; *Fax:* 905-894-6851
museum@forterie.on.ca
www.museum.forterie.ca/historical.html
Exhibits on archaelogy, genealogy, Fenian Raids, local history & archives; open year-round Sun.-Fri.; daily in July & Aug.
Jane Davies, Curator

Ridgeway: **Fort Erie Railroad Museum**
Fort Erie Museum Board, PO Box 339, 400 Central Ave., Ridgeway, ON L0S 1N0
Tel: 905-871-1412; *Fax:* 905-894-6851
museum@forterie.on.ca
Located on Central Ave.; includes Steam engine #6218, caboose & 2 train stations; open daily Victoria Day - Labour Day; open weekends until Thanksgiving
Jane Davies, Curator

Ridgeway: **Ridgeway Battlefield National Historic Site**
c/o Fort Erie Historical Museum, PO Box 339, 402 Ridge Rd., Ridgeway, ON L0S 1N0
Tel: 905-894-5322; *Fax:* 905-894-6851
museum@forterie.on.ca
www.museum.forterie.ca/battlefield.html
The Ridgeway Battlefield national historic site site marks the location where in 1866 Irish-American soldiers, known as Fenians, fought Canadian forces in an attempt to gain Ireland's independence of England. The Fort Erie Museum maintains the original cabin at the battle site, where visitors can see a visual account of the Battle of Ridgeway.

Rockton: **Westfield Heritage Village (WHV)**
1049 Kirkwall Rd., Rockton, ON L0R 1X0
Tel: 519-621-8851; *Fax:* 519-621-6897
Toll-Free: 800-883-0104
westfield@speedway.ca
www.westfieldheritage.ca
The Heritage Village presents more than thirty-five historical & reproduction buildings. The site also features Ontario's oldest log cabin & a T.H. & B. steam locomotive.

Rosemont: **Dufferin County Museum & Archives**
PO Box 120, 936029 Airport Rd., Rosemont, ON L0N 1R0
Tel: 705-435-1881; *Fax:* 705-435-9876
Toll-Free: 877-941-7787
info@dufferinmuseum.com
www.dufferinmuseum.com
Two log structures; CPR flagging station; historic church; changing exhibits; archives
Wayne Townsend, Director/Curator
Darrell Keenie, General Manager

St Catharines: **Morningstar Mill (Mountain Mills Museum)**
22 Cliff Rd., St Catharines, ON L2R 3W1
Tel: 905-688-6050
info@morningstarmill.ca
www.morningstarmill.ca
Founded: 1962 Museum site is made up of a number of buildings: the water-powered gristmill (built in 1872 & known as Morningstar Mill), the turbine shed, the millers house, the icehouse, sawmill and the barn which houses the blacksmith shop and carpentry shop. School tours are welcome. Admission by donation.
Tom Wilson, St. Catharines, Recreation & Community Services, 905-688-5601 X-3134, Fax: 905-646-9262

St Catharines: **St. Catharines Museum**
PO Box 3012, 1932 Welland Canals Pkwy., St Catharines, ON L2R 7C2
Tel: 905-984-8880; *Fax:* 905-984-6910
Toll-Free: 800-355-134
museuminfo@stcatharines.ca
www.stcatharineslock3museum. ca
Founded: 1965 Major collection of artifact, archival & art material related to the history of St. Catharines & the Welland Canal; collections include Girl Guides, Fred Pattison Aviation Collection (BCATP), St. Lawrence Seaway, family papers, marine photographs, Ferranti-Packard & the DeCew Falls Waterworks Collection; guided tours; summer camps, edu-fun camps; guest speakers; tours & special events
Anne Crawford, Administrative Co-ordinator, acrawford@stcatharines.ca

St. George: **Adelaide Hunter Hoodless Homestead**
PO Box 209, 359 Blue Lake Rd., RR#1, St. George, ON N0E 1N0
Tel: 519-448-1130; *Fax:* 519-448-1150
hoodlesshomestead@gmail.com
www3.sympatico.ca/hoodlesshomestead1/AHH.htm
Birthplace of Adelaide Hunter Hoodless, an educational reformer, one of Canada's early feminists and a co-founder of a number of organizations promoting the cause of women's well-being, including: the Women's Institute, the Victorian Order of Nurses, the YWCA, and the National Council of Women. Hunter Hoodless was instrumental in establishing domestic science on the curriculum of Ontario schools, and wrote the first textbook to be used. Before her untimely death at the age of 53, she was engaged in the cause of promoting technical trades education for women. Her childhood home, built in 1830, is an example of mid-nineteenth century Ontario Neo Gothic style. The homestead property includes picnic facilities and grounds that can be rented for gatherings and other special occasions. Guided tours, and school programs available. Open year round.

St Jacobs: **The Maple Syrup Museum**
Also known as: **Maple Syrup Museum of Ontario**
Country Mill, PO Box 701, 1441 King St. North, St Jacobs, ON N0B 2N0
Tel: 519-664-1232; *Fax:* 519-669-4259
www.stjacobs.com
History of maple syrup production; artifacts; photographs
Albert Martin, Contact, 519-669-2423

St Marys: **Canadian Baseball Hall of Fame & Museum**
PO Box 1838, 140 Queen St., St Marys, ON N4X 1C2
Tel: 519-284-1838; *Fax:* 519-284-1234
Toll-Free: 877-250-2255
baseball@baseballhalloffame.ca
www.baseballhalloffame. ca
Open May - Thanksgiving; displays include exclusive collection of Ferguson Jenkins memorabilia & artifacts of the Montreal Expos & Toronto Blue Jays

St Marys: **St Marys Museum**
PO Box 98, 177 Church St. South, St Marys, ON N4X 1A9
Tel: 519-284-3556; *Fax:* 519-284-2881
museum@town.stmarys.on.ca
www.stmarysmuseum.ca
Changing exhibits; seasonal activities; research facilities for genealogy & area history in 1850s limestone house
Mary Smith, Manager
Trisha McKibbin, Curator

St Thomas: **Elgin County Museum**
450 Sunset Dr., St Thomas, ON N5R 5V1
Tel: 519-631-1460; *Fax:* 519-631-9209
museum@elgin-county.on.ca
www.eglinconnects.ca
Founded: 1957 History of Elgin County; changing exhibits in gallery, workshops & special events
Mike Baker, Curator

St Thomas: **The Elgin Military Museum**
30 Talbot St., St Thomas, ON N5P 1A3
Tel: 519-633-7641; *Fax:* 519-637-0580
emm@exculink.com
Information on veterans from Elgin County; archive collection with military documents & publications

Sault Ste Marie: **Ermatinger-Clergue National Historic Site**
c/o Historic Sites Board, PO Box 580, Sault Ste Marie, ON P6A 5X6
Tel: 705-759-5443; *Fax:* 705-541-7023
old.stone.house@cityssm.on.ca
1814 stone house: features historic crop gardens, recreated rooms, costumed interpreters, hands-on activities; Blockhouse: exhibits & period furnishings; open Mid-Apr. - Nov.
Kathryn Fisher, Curator

Sault Ste Marie: **St. Mary's River Marine Centre**
Also known as: **Museum Ship \Norgoma\"""**
PO Box 23099 Mall, Sault Ste Marie, ON P6A 6W6
Tel: 705-942-2919; *Fax:* 705-942-2093
marineheritagecentre@shaw.ca
Other contact information: Seasonal Phone: 705/256-7447
An 188-foot passenger/cargo vessel built in 1950; open June - Oct.

Sault Ste Marie: **Sault Ste Marie Canal National Historic Site of Canada**
1 Canal Dr., Sault Ste Marie, ON P6A 6W4
Tel: 705-941-6262; *Fax:* 705-941-6206
info-saultcanal@pc.gc.ca
www.pc.gc.ca/sault
Operates a recreational lock between May & Oct. & offers school programming, guided tours & a large open space for the enjoyment of visitors (boat watching, nature trail, birdwatching, cycling, fishing)
Louise Robillard, Chief, Visitor Activities, louise.robillard@pc.gc.ca

Sault Ste Marie: **Sault Ste Marie Museum**
690 Queen St. East, Sault Ste Marie, ON P6A 2A4
Tel: 705-759-7278; *Fax:* 705-759-3058
heritage@saultmuseum.com
www.saultmuseum.com
Maintained by the Sault St. Marie & 49th Field Regiment R.C.A. Historical Society; the museum collects & preserves artifacts & archival material illustrating the history of Sault Ste Marie & area
Kim Forbes, Curator & Administrator

Selkirk: **Wilson MacDonald Memorial School Museum**
3513 Rainham Rd., Selkirk, ON N0A 1P0
Tel: 905-776-3319; *Fax:* 905-776-0683
wmacdonald.museum@haldimandcounty.on.ca
www.haldimandcounty.on.ca
Wilson MacDonald Memorial School Museum presents the story of poet Wilson Pugsley MacDonald, rural education, & Selkirk, Ontario & its surrounding area. Archival research is available for a fee. The museum is open from mid March to mid December.
Dana B. Stavinga, Curator

***Sharon:* Sharon Temple National Historic Site & Museum**
18974 Leslie St., Sharon, ON L0G 1V0
Tel: 905-478-2389
info@sharontemple.ca
www.sharontemple.ca
The Sharon Temple National Historic Site features nine historic buildings. The centerpiece of the site is the Temple of the Children of Peace, which was completed in 1832. Sharon Temple is open from mid May to mid October. Group & scholars may make appointments at other times of the year.

***Simcoe:* Eva Brook Donly Museum & Archives**
109 Norfolk St. South, Simcoe, ON N3Y 2W3
Tel: 519-426-1583; *Fax:* 519-426-1584
office@norfolklore.com; genealogy@norfolklore.com
www.norfolklore.com
The Museum & Archives feature information about the people, heritage, & history of Norfolk County. Museum artifacts are housed in a two storey brick home which was erected in the 1840s. Archives include family histories, documents, records, & phototgraphs.
Scott Gillies, Curator & Marager, marketing@norfolklore.com
Jo-Anne Barber, President, Norfolk Historical Society

***Sioux Lookout:* Sioux Lookout Museum**
PO Box 1377, Sioux Lookout, ON P8T 1B9
Tel: 807-737-1562; *Fax:* 807-737-4624
slrec@slkt.net
First Nations artifacts; pioneer artifacts related to logging, mining, aviation & the Canadian National Railway

***Smiths Falls:* Heritage House Museum / Musée de la maison du patrimoine**
PO Box 695, 11 Old Slys Rd., Smiths Falls, ON K7A 4T6
Tel: 613-283-8560; *Fax:* 613-283-4764
heritagehouse@smithsfalls.ca
www.smithsfalls.ca/heritagehouse
Founded: 1981 Built in 1860-1861 by Joshua Bates, the house is located near the Rideau River and displays 7 rooms, including kitchen, parlor and bedroom, all restored to Victorian style. Workshops and programs for children are offered. There is a gift shop. Tours available; open year round.
Carol Miller, Curator

***Smiths Falls:* Industrial Heritage Complex Merrickville Lockstation**
34A Beckwith St. South, Smiths Falls, ON K7A 2A8
Tel: 613-283-5170
19th century construction on Rideau Canal, with emphasis on Merrickville; collection includes power generation machinery

***Smiths Falls:* Rideau Canal Museum**
34 Beckwith St. South, Smiths Falls, ON K7A 2B3
Tel: 613-284-0505
High-tech displays; artifacts

***Smiths Falls:* Smiths Falls Railway Museum of Eastern Ontario**
PO Box 962, 90 William St. West, Smiths Falls, ON K7A 5A5
Tel: 613-283-5696; *Fax:* 613-283-7211
sfrmchin@superaje.com
www.sfrmeo.ca
Railway Museum at the historic CNR station
Robert A. Moore, Vice-President
John Saunders, Treasurer
John Weir, Secretary
George R. Ward, President

***Sombra:* Sombra Museum**
3470 St. Clair Parkway, Sombra, ON N0P 2H0
Tel: 519-892-3982; *Fax:* 519-892-3982
www.lambtononline.com/sombra_museum
Local historical artifacts housed in 1881 Victorian frame home; stories of the St. Clair River illustrated through photos & artifacts in 3 rooms; log cabin circa 1830; reference collection & family archives; marine room featuring nautical equipment & photos relating to the St. Clair River & the Great Lakes; special events & programming.
Shelley Lucier, Curator, shelleylucier@hotmail.com

***South Baymouth:* Little Schoolhouse & Museum South Baymouth**
General Delivery, South Baymouth, ON P0P 1Z0
Tel: 705-859-2344
Trace the history of Tehkummah Township, one of Ontario's ghost towns, Michael's Bay, and the development of South Baymouth and includes one of the pioneer one room schools. Displays the history of this fishing village through artifacts and pictures.
Bryan Gleason, Contact, 705-859-2344

***South Porcupine:* Timmins Museum: National Exhibition Centre / Musée de Timmins: Centre national d'exposition**
70 Legion Dr., South Porcupine, ON P0N 1H0
Tel: 705-235-5066; *Fax:* 705-235-9631
tmnec@city.timmins.on.ca
Preserves, presents & studies the history of the Porcupine Gold Camp, Timmins Ontario

***Southampton:* Bruce County Museum & Cultural Centre**
PO Box 180, 33 Victoria St. North, Southampton, ON N0H 2L0
Tel: 519-797-2080; *Fax:* 519-797-2191
Toll-Free: 866-318-8889
collections@brucecounty.on.ca
www.brucemuseum.ca
Other contact information: E-mail, Archival Information: archives@brucecounty.on.ca
Permanent galleries at the Bruce County Museum & Cultural Centre include the following: Creation Stories; Our Tropical Past; Geology & The Ice Ages; First People's Gallery; A Time To Remember, featuring military exhibits; Telephone Beginnings, depicting the history of telephone service in Bruce County; Living On The Land, showcasing the area's agricultural history; The Land; Living On The Water, with information about lighthouses, shipbuilding, fishing, & shipwrecks; & Living in Balance, with information about resources & industries.
Barbara Ribey, Director & Curator

***Stittsville:* Goulbourn Museum**
PO Box 621, 2064 Huntley Rd., RR#3, Stittsville, ON K2S 1A7
Tel: 613-831-2393
goulbmus@rogers.com
www.goulbournmuseum.ca
Collection housed in 1873 Township Hall & 1961 Clerk's Building; displays about a family farms & rural schools; exhibit of military service from 1812 to present; genealogical data & library; open year round

***Stoney Creek:* Battlefield House Museum & Park**
PO Box 66561, 77 King St. West, Stoney Creek, ON L8G 3X9
Tel: 905-662-8458; *Fax:* 905-662-0529
battlefield@hamilton.ca
www.battlefieldhouse.ca
The Gage Homestead was built in 1796. During the War of 1812 & the Battle of Stoney Creek, the Gage family fled to the cellar of the home. The Battlefield Monument commemorates the soldiers who died during the battle. Each June, the Battlefield House Museum & Park is the site of a military re-enactment of the Battle of Stoney Creek. The site is open from July 1st to Labour Day.
Susan Ramsay, Curator

***Stoney Creek:* Erland Lee Museum**
***Also known as:* The Women's Institutes Museum**
552 Ridge Rd., Stoney Creek, ON L8J 2Y6
Tel: 905-662-2691; *Fax:* 905-662-2045
erlandlee@interlynx.net
www.erlandlee.com
Museum, carriagehouse & gardens; site of the 1897 founding of the Women's Institutes organization; home of the Lee family 1790-1970; guided tours, education programs, special events, picnic area & gift shop, room rentals
Meaghan FitzGibbon, Curator

***Stratford:* Brocksden Country School Museum**
2719 Perth Line 37, RR#1, Stratford, ON N5A 4C7
Tel: 519-271-0499; *Fax:* 519-271-1978
The school which opened in 1853 presents a living history program for classes.
Wilma McCaig, Secretary

***Stratford:* Fryfogel Tavern**
Perth County Historical Foundation, 1931 Line 34, Stratford, ON N0B 2P0
Stagecoach stop & resting place 1844-45; history of Perth County's settlers; open by appt.

***Strathroy:* A.W. Campbell House Museum**
c/o St. Clair Region Conservation Authority, 205 Mill Pond Cres., Strathroy, ON N7G 3P9
Tel: 519-245-3710; *Fax:* 519-245-3348
stclair@scrca.on.ca
www.scrca.on.ca
The museum is located in the A.W. Campbell Conservation Area, R.R.#2 Alvinston, ON, off Nauvoo Rd. A typical 1890s southwestern Ontario rural home comprises the museum, and the conservation area also includes a campground and walking trails.
Rick Battson, Director of Communications, rbattson@scrca.on.ca

***Strathroy:* Strathroy Middlesex Museum**
34 Frank St., Strathroy, ON N7G 2R4
Tel: 519-245-0492; *Fax:* 519-245-1073
info@strathroymuseum.ca
www.strathroymuseum.ca
Open year round; medical theme room; military display; 1930s electric kitchen; printing shop; archival material

***Sturgeon Falls:* Musée Sturgeon River House Museum**
250 ch Fort Rd., Sturgeon Falls, ON P2B 2N7
Tél: 705-753-4716; *Téléc:* 705-753-5476
info@sturgeonriverhouse.com
www.sturgeonriverhouse.com
Le musée se trouve sur un site de la Compagnie de la Baie d'Hudson; l'exposition traite de fourrure et les animaux de la région.
Serge Ducharme, Directeur

***Sudbury:* Anderson Farm Museum**
PO Box 6400, Sudbury, ON P3A 3B7
Tel: 705-692-4448
jim.fortin@city.greatersudbury.on.ca
Open year round

***Sudbury:* Centre franco-ontarien de folklore (CFOF)**
1169, rue Dollard, Sudbury, ON P3A 4G7
Tél: 705-675-8986; *Téléc:* 705-675-5809
cfof@cfof.on.ca
www.cfof.on.ca
Founded: 1972 A pour mission de mettre en valeur le folklore et le patrimoine franco-ontarien; musée; activités éducatives; bibliothèque; archives; publications; magasin virtuel
Diane Charette-Lavoie, Présidente, Conseil d'administration

***Sudbury:* Copper Cliff Museum**
PO Box 6400 A, Sudbury, ON P3A 3B7
Tel: 705-692-4448
Founded: 1901 Located in 1890 log house; contains artifacts pertaining to the lifestyle of residents of a mining community; photographs & documents leading back to establishment of Copper Cliff

***Sutton West:* Eildon Hall Sibbald Memorial Museum**
Sibbald Point Provincial Park, RR#2, Sutton West, ON L0E 1R0
Tel: 905-722-8061; *Fax:* 905-722-5416
Situated by the shore of Lake Simcoe, Eildon Hall was the Sibbald family home

***Thunder Bay:* Centennial Park 1910 Logging Camp and Museum**
Parks Division, Victoria Ville Civic Centre, 111 Syndicate Ave. South, Thunder Bay, ON P7E 6S4
Tel: 807-625-2351; *Fax:* 807-625-3528
www.thunderbay.ca/parks
Full scale replica of a 1910 logging camp re-creates the early history of Northern Ontario's forest industry; park open year round; logging camp and museum open mid-June to Labour Day, 8:00 am.m to 8:00 p.m.; Muskeg Express logging train; Winter sleigh rides; craft shop; picnic area; trails
Bruce Phillips

***Thunder Bay:* Fort William Historical Park (FWHP)**
Vickers Heights PO, Thunder Bay, ON P0T 2Z0
Tel: 807-577-8461; *Fax:* 807-473-2327
info@fwhp.ca
www.fwhp.ca
A living history site that depicts the fur trade activities of the North West Company in the early 1800s; 42 reconstructed buildings on a 225-acre site. Touts that it is the largest Fur Trade Post.
Sergio Buonocore, General Manager, sergio.buonocore@mtr.gov.on.ca

***Thunder Bay:* Northwestern Ontario Sports Hall of Fame**
219 May St. South, Thunder Bay, ON P7E 1B5
Tel: 807-622-2852; *Fax:* 807-622-2736
nwosport@tbaytel.net
www.nwosportshalloffame.com
Founded: 1978 The Hall's mission is to preserve and honour Northwestern Ontario's sports heritage, with displays, photos, archival material, artifacts and other documentation on over 200 athletes; reference library; educational programming. Open all year.
Diane Imrie, Executive Director

***Thunder Bay:* Paipoonge Historical Museum**
RR#6, Thunder Bay, ON P7C 5N5
Tel: 807-939-1262; *Fax:* 807-577-3888
lgarrity@tbaytel.net
Founded: 1952 Reflecting the history of the Municipality of Oliver/Paipoonge & area during the late 1800s & early 1900s. Collection of pioneer material and farm machinery, old school room, kitchen and bedroom displays.
Lois Garrity, Curator & Director

***Thunder Bay:* Thunder Bay Military Museum**
The Armoury, 317 Park Ave., Thunder Bay, ON P7B 1C7
Tel: 807-343-5175; *Fax:* 807-346-4022
jjyoung@vianet.ca
Georg Hoegel Art Collection - paintings & drawings done by Mr. Hoegel when he was a prisoner of war in Canada from 1941-1946; other military art; tri-service collection, representing all three services, rotated regularly; open 4 afternoons, 2 evenings & by request

Lt.(N) Ken MacAskill, Chair
Lt.Col. John J. Young, Curator

***Thunder Bay:* Thunder Bay Museum**
***Also known as:* Thunder Bay Historical Museum Society**
425 East Donald St., Thunder Bay, ON P7E 5V1
Tel: 807-623-0801; *Fax:* 807-622-6880
info@thunderbaymuseum.com
www.thunderbaymuseum.com
A museum, historical society & archives for Thunder Bay & Northwestern Ontario
Dr. Tory Tronrud, Curator

***Tillsonburg:* Annandale National Historic Site**
***Also known as:* Tillsonburg Museum**
30 Tillson Ave., Tillsonburg, ON N4G 2Z8
Tel: 519-842-2294; *Fax:* 519-842-9431
rcorner@tillsonburg.ca
www.tillsonburg.ca
Nationally designated for its Aesthetic *interior, Annandale House is restored to the 1880's period; location of tourist information for Tillsonburg; open year round*
Rita Corner, Curator

***Tobermory:* The Peninsula & St. Edmunds Township Museum**
RR#1, Tobermory, ON N0H 2R0
Tel: 519-596-2479
Founded: 1967 Housed in the former St. Edmunds Settlement School (ca. 1898), the museum's holdings include land deeds and registers, photographs, and exhibits on lumbering, fishing, and hunting activities; the upper floor of the museum is dedicated to area marine history and includes maps, tools, and relics from shipwrecks. An 1875 furnished log house is located on the grounds and is open by appointment only. Located south of Tobermory Harbour, on the east side of Hwy 6. Open weekends from Victoria Day to Thanksgiving, and weekdays from July 1 to Labour Day.

***Toronto:* The Bata Shoe Museum (BSM)**
327 Bloor St. West, Toronto, ON M5S 1W7
Tel: 416-979-7799; *Fax:* 416-979-0078
www.batashoemuseum.ca
Explores footwear in the social & cultural life of humankind from ancient times to present. Exhibits vary but there is a permanant exhibit which includes a pair of Elton John platform shoes and shoes which date back hundreds of years.
Sonja Bata, Chair

***Toronto:* Baycrest Heritage Museum**
***Also known as:* The Morris and Sally Justein Heritage Museum**
Baycrest Hospital, 3560 Bathurst St., Main Fl., Toronto, ON M6A 2E1
Tel: 416-785-2500; *Fax:* 416-785-2378
www.baycrest.org
The Morris and Sally Justein Heritage Museum displays Judaica exhibits. The historical & cultural Judaica exhibits & permanent collections are designed for Baycrest Hospital & Home's elderly clients.
Lois Buckstein, Chair

***Toronto:* Beth Tzedec Reuben & Helene Dennis Museum**
c/o Beth Tzedec Synagogue, 1700 Bathurst St., Toronto, ON M5P 3K3
Tel: 416-781-3514; *Fax:* 416-781-0150
museum@beth-tzedec.org
www.beth-tzedec.org/museum
Founded: 1965 The museum features a major Judaica collection, including Jewish art & history from ancient times to the present. Appointments may be made for tours.
Dorion Liebgott, Curator

***Toronto:* Black Creek Pioneer Village**
1000 Murray Ross Pkwy., Toronto, ON M3J 2P3
Tel: 416-736-1733
bcpvinfo@trca.on.ca
www.blackcreek.ca
Operated by the Toronto & Region Conservation Authority (TRCA), Black Creek Pioneer Village is a living history experience, which spans over 30 acres. It exemplifies a small south central Ontario community between the 1790s & the 1860s. Demonstrations & special activities depict rural life. Black Creek Village also features the historic Black Creek Historic Brewery. The village is open from the beginning of May to the end of December.
Rick Sikorski, Manager, Marketing & Communications, TRCA

***Toronto:* Campbell House**
160 Queen St. West, Toronto, ON M5H 3H3
Tel: 416-597-0227; *Fax:* 416-597-0750
info@campbellhousemuseum.ca
www.campbellhousemuseum.ca
Built in 1822, the Campbell House is the oldest remaining building from the original town of York. The Sir William Campbell Foundation operates the museum. Special programs are available for groups. The Home is open from the beginning of May until Thanksgiving.

***Toronto:* Canada's Sports Hall of Fame (CSHOF) / Panthéon des Sports Canadiens**
Exhibition Place, 115 Prince's Blvd., Toronto, ON M6K 3C3
Tel: 416-260-6789; *Fax:* 416-260-9347
info@cshof.ca; events@cshof.ca
www.cshof.ca
Canada's Sports Hall of Fame tells the stories of Canadian amateur & professional athletes, as well as sport builders, who have made outstanding achievements thoughout sports history.
Janice Smith, Executive Director
Sheryn Posen, Chief Operating Officer
Nick Brentanos, Photo Archivist
Kathy Dostaler, Translator

***Toronto:* Canadian Air & Space Museum (TAM)**
PO Box 1, 65 Carl Hall Rd., Toronto, ON M3K 2E1
Tel: 416-638-6078; *Fax:* 416-638-5509
casm@casmuseum.org
www.casmuseum.org
Aviation industry & history in the Toronto region

***Toronto:* Canadian Broadcasting Corporation Museum & & Graham Spry Theatre**
PO Box 500 A, 250 Front St. West, Toronto, ON M5W 1E6
Tel: 416-205-5574
www.cbc.ca/museum
The CBC Museum presents the story of CBC's broadcasting history, since 1936.

***Toronto:* The Canadian Business Hall of Fame / Le Temple de la renommée de l'entreprise canadienne**
#306, 2275 Lakeshore Blvd. West, Toronto, ON M8V 3Y3
Tel: 416-622-4602; *Fax:* 416-622-6861
rmaund@jacan.org
cbhof.org
Located in The Galleria, BCE Place
Ross Maund, President & CEO

***Toronto:* Casa Loma**
1 Austin Terrace, Toronto, ON M5R 1X8
Tel: 416-923-1171; *Fax:* 416-923-5734
info@casaloma.org; kiwanis@casaloma.org
www.casaloma.org
Founded: 1937 Owned by the City of Toronto & operated by The Kiwanis Club of Casa Loma, Casa Loma is the former home of Sir Henry Pellatt, a Canadian financier, industrialist, & military man. The decorated castle contains an 800 foot tunnel, secret passages, towers, & stables. A self-guided audio tour is available in eight languages.
Richard R. Wozenilek, Chair, Board of Trustees of Casa Loma
Lou Seiler, Director, Marketing, lseiler@casaloma.org

***Toronto:* Colborne Lodge**
c/o Museum Services, Metro Hall, 55 John St., 8th Fl., Toronto, ON M5V 3C6
Tel: 416-392-6916; *Fax:* 416-392-0375
clodge@toronto.ca
www.toronto.ca/museums; www.highpark.org/colborne.htm
Site of the 19th century home of High Park founders, John & Jemmina Howard; contains many of their original furnishings, watercolours of early Toronto, & other artifacts; coach house, tomb & restored gardens on the property; special events & programming; party room rentals; located at the south end of High Park, Colborne Lodge Dr., just north of the Queensway. Open year round.
Cheryl Hart, Museum Coordinator

***Toronto:* The Enoch Turner Schoolhouse (1848)**
106 Trinity St., Toronto, ON M5A 3C6
Tel: 416-863-0010
aleblanc@enochturnerschoolhouse.ca
www.enochturnerschoolhouse.ca
One of Toronto's oldest institutions & the city's first free school
Andrew LeBlanc, Administrator

***Toronto:* Fort York National Historic Site**
100 Garrison Rd., Toronto, ON M5V 3K9
Tel: 416-392-6907; *Fax:* 416-392-6917
fortyork@toronto.ca
www.toronto.ca/culture/museums/fort-york.htm
Founded: 1934 Built by Lieutenant-Governor John Graves Simcoe as a garrison in 1793, Fort York was purchased by the City of Toronto in 1909 and restored as a museum in 1934. Its fortified walls contain the largest collection of original War of 1812 buildings in Canada. Some of the restored interiors reflect the life of the garrison community, while others serve as exhibit space for artifacts on a military theme. The site offers seasonal guided tours as well as musket, drill, and music demonstrations.
Mr. David O'Hara, Site Administrator, 416-392-6907 ext 222, dohara@toronto.ca

***Toronto:* Gardiner Museum of Ceramic Art**
***Also known as:* Gardiner Museum**
111 Queen's Park, Toronto, ON M5S 2C7
Tel: 416-586-8080; *Fax:* 416-586-8085
mail@gardinermuseum.on.ca
www.gardinermuseum.on.ca
Containing 3,000+ historical and contemporary pieces, the Gardiner Museum is North America's premier specialized ceramic museum; gift shop; Gail Brooker Ceramic Research Library; Jamie Kennedy's Gardiner Restaurant; permanent and special exhibits; studio spaces and ceramic courses; talks, book launches, films and other programs.
Alexandra Montgomery, Executive Director

***Toronto:* Gibson House Museum**
5176 Yonge St., Toronto, ON M2N 5P6
Tel: 416-395-7432; *Fax:* 416-395-7442
gibsonhouse@toronto.ca
www.toronto.ca/museums
Gibson House, built in 1851, was the home of Scottish immigrant David Gibson and his family. Gibson, a land surveyor, played a role in the mapping of early Toronto and spent some years in exile in the U.S. for his participation in the Rebellion of 1837 in Upper Canada.
Elizabeth Nelson-Raffaele, Curator

***Toronto:* Mackenzie House**
82 Bond St., Toronto, ON M5B 1X2
Tel: 416-392-6915; *Fax:* 416-392-0114
machouse@toronto.ca
www.toronto.ca/museums
Founded: 1950 The final home of Toronto's first mayor, William Lyon Mackenzie who gained notoriety during the 1837 Upper Canada Rebellion, this 1858 Georgian rowhouse has been refurnished in period style and also showcases a print shop.
Ms Janet Schwartz, Site Coordinator

***Toronto:* Montgomery's Inn**
4709 Dundas St. West, Toronto, ON M9A 1A8
Tel: 416-394-8113; *Fax:* 416-394-6027
montinn@toronto.ca
www.montgomerysinn.com
Founded: 1975 Built in 1830, the restored inn reflects life in 1847. Its library holds photographs, artifacts, and archival materials documenting the history of Etobicoke; tearoom; gift shop; seasonal programs; community theatre and music; workshops
Mike Lipowski, Curator, 416/394-8112

***Toronto:* Museum of Childhood (MOC)**
121 Brunswick Ave., Toronto, ON M5S 2M3
Tel: 416-368-2866; *Fax:* 416-504-0316
Extensive collection of childhood toys, clothes, furniture, books; opening date before year 2005; educational presentations & traveling exhibits available
Loet Vos, President

***Toronto:* The Queen's Own Rifles of Canada Regimental Museum**
Casa Loma, 1 Austin Terrace, Toronto, ON M5R 1X8
Tel: 905-407-3675
Display artifacts pertinent to the history of the regiment from 1860-present

***Toronto:* Queen's York Rangers Regimental Museum**
660 Fleet St., Toronto, ON M5V 1A9
Tel: 416-203-4200
Traces the history of the Queen's York Rangers, an active reconnaissance unit of the Army Reserve; displays begin wth the Seven Year's War, through the American Revolution & settlement of Upper Canada & through the campaigns of 19th century & two world wars

***Toronto:* Redpath Sugar Museum**
95 Queen's Quay East, Toronto, ON M5E 1A3
Tel: 416-933-8341; *Fax:* 416-366-7550
Toll-Free: 800-267-1517
Consumer-Canada@redpathsugar.com
www.redpathsugars.com
Founded: 1979 The Redpath Sugar Museum displays the history of sugar production & refining, models of transportation that bring sugar to the refinery, as well as the story of the Redpath family. The museum offers a program for schools.
Scott Brownrigg, Contact, Media Inquiries, 416-644-4927

***Toronto:* Royal Canadian Military Institute Museum**
426 University Ave., Toronto, ON M5G 1S9
Tel: 416-597-0286; *Fax:* 416-597-6919
info@rcmi.org
www.rcmi.org
Artifacts related to Canadians' participation in the military; library open to researchers & members; open year round
Gregory Loughton, Curator, gregory.loughton@rcmi.org

***Toronto:* The Royal Regiment of Canada Museum**
***Also known as:* The Royals' Museum**
Fort York Armoury, 660 Fleet St., Toronto, ON M5V 1A9
Tel: 416-755-1727
rregtc.gmail.com
www.army.dnd.ca/rregtc/coy/museum.html
Founded: 1996 Military artifacts, dating from 1862, of the The Royal Regiment of Canada, & predecessors: the 10th Royal Grenadiers (Toronto Regiment), & the 3rd, 123rd, 124th, 204th & 58th Battalions; archives; school tours by appointment. Located next to the Royals' WO's & Sergeants' Mess on the 2nd floor, at the east end of Fort York Armoury.
Capt. Bruce Barbeau, Curator

***Toronto:* The Salvation Army Museum**
2 Overlea Blvd., Toronto, ON M4H 1P4
Tel: 416-425-2111
heritage_centre@can.salvationarmy.org
heritage.salvationarmy.ca
Open to public & gives a pictorial outline of Salvation Army history, particularly as it pertains to Canada & Bermuda, through the use of artifacts, photographs & special techniques; no fee; wheelchair accessible; open Mon.-Fri., closed all statutory holidays
Col. John E. Carew, Director

***Toronto:* Scadding Cabin**
c/o York Pioneers & Historical Society, PO Box 45026, 2482 Yonge St., Toronto, ON M4P 3E3
Tel: 416-494-0503
yorkpioneers@gmail.com; information@explace.on.ca
www.yorkpioneers.org; www.explace.on.ca
Built for John Scadding, clerk to Lieutenant-Governor John Graves Simcoe, the cabin is Toronto's oldest dwelling. Located at Exhibition Place, southeast of 25 British Columbia Rd.; wooden house, built in late 1700s, contains furniture which belonged to John Graves Simcoe; open late Aug.-Labour Day (during CNE)

***Toronto:* Scarborough Historical Museum**
1007 Brimley Rd., Toronto, ON M1P 3E8
Tel: 416-338-8807; *Fax:* 416-338-8805
shm@toronto.ca
www.toronto.ca/museums
Includes Cornell House, McCowan Log Cabin & Hough Carriage Works; picnic area; parking
Madeleine Callaghan, Manager/Curator

***Toronto:* Sesquicentennial Museum & Archives**
Toronto District School Board, 155 College St., Toronto, ON M5T 1P6
Tel: 416-397-3680; *Fax:* 416-397-3685
smachin@planeteer.com
Preserves the history of the TDSB & its schools; collects, documents, researches, exhibits, & historical artifacts, fine art, & archival, & published material for its educational community - students, parents, staff & trustees & its citizens
Greg McKinnon, Manager & Board Archivist
David Sowerbatts, Conservator

***Toronto:* Spadina Museum: Historic House & Gardens**
285 Spadina Rd., Toronto, ON M5R 2V5
Tel: 416-392-6910; *Fax:* 416-392-0382
spadina@toronto.ca
www.toronto.ca/culture/museums/spadina.htm
1866 mansion contains four generations of décor, reflecting art movements such as Art Nouveau
Nancy Reynolds, Site Coordinator
Karen Edwards, Curator

***Toronto:* Taras H. Shevchenko Museum**
1614 Bloor St. West, Toronto, ON M6P 1A7
Tel: 416-534-8662; *Fax:* 416-535-1063
shevchenkomuseum@bellnet.ca
www.infoukes.com/shevchenkomuseum
The museum is dedicated to the art, life and literary legacy of Ukraine's renowned poet, Taras Schevchenko; the Toronto site is the only Shevchenko museum in the Americas; library; art exhibits; Ukrainian folk art and handicrafts. Open year round.
Wm. Harasym, President

***Toronto:* Textile Museum of Canada**
55 Centre Ave., Toronto, ON M5G 2H5
Tel: 416-599-5321; *Fax:* 416-599-2911
info@textilemuseum.ca
www.textilemuseum.ca
Unique exhibitions & programming; focus on the traditions & aesthetics of historic & contemporary textiles
Patricia Bentley, Sr. Curator

***Toronto:* Todmorden Mills Heritage Museum & Art Centre**
67 Pottery Rd., Toronto, ON M4K 2B8
Tel: 416-396-2819
todmorden@toronto.ca
www.toronto.ca/culture/museums/todmorden.htm
Depicts early industry in Toronto; new papermill galleries & theatre feature frequent exhibitions & is available for rental
Ulana Baluk, Administrator

***Toronto:* Toronto Police Museum & Discovery Centre**
40 College St., Toronto, ON M5G 2J3
Tel: 416-808-7020; *Fax:* 416-808-7023
museum@torontopolice.on.ca
www.torontopolice.on.ca
Interactive displays; collection includes uniforms, badges, communication & transportation equipment; high profile crimes; open year round
Norina D'Agostini
Gabi Voigt

***Toronto:* Toronto's First Post Office (TFPO)**
260 Adelaide St. East, Toronto, ON M5A 1N1
Tel: 416-865-1833; *Fax:* 416-865-9414
tfpo@total.net
www.townofyork.com
Canada's only surviving pre-1851 Post Office; restored as a museum & full postal service operation; gift shop
Danielle Pesneau, Curator

***Toronto:* Ukrainian Museum of Canada**
Ukrainian Women's Association of Canada, Ontario Branch, 620 Spadina Ave., Toronto, ON M5S 2H4
Tel: 416-923-3318; *Fax:* 416-923-8266
svi@stvladimir.on.ca
Open Mon.-Fri., Sat.-Sun. by appt. only
Halya Kluchko, Curator

***Toronto:* York Museum**
Centennial Recreation Centre, 2694 Eglinton Ave. West, Toronto, ON M6M 1T9
Tel: 416-394-2759
yorkmuseum@toronto.ca
www.toronto.ca/culture/york_museum.htm
York Museum tells the story of the former City of York. Artifacts range from a 3,000 year old stone axe as a reminder of the First Nations history in the area, to a telephone switchboard. Phone 416-338-0492 to arrange a visit.

***Tweed:* Tweed & Area Heritage Centre**
***Also known as:* Houston House 1897**
PO Box 665, 40 Victoria St. North, Tweed, ON K0K 3J0
Tel: 613-478-3989; *Fax:* 613-478-6457
tweedheritageinfo@on.aibn.com
www.ruralroutes.com/tweedheritage
Founded: 1988 An information centre, art gallery, museum, archives & genealogical research centre; local arts & crafts promotional centre
E. Morton, Curator

***Uxbridge:* Thomas Foster Memorial Temple**
PO Box 190, 51 Toronto St. South, Uxbridge, ON L9P 1T1
Tel: 905-852-9181; *Fax:* 905-852-9164
Toll-Free: 888-559-9022
www.town.uxbridge.on.ca
Built by former mayor of Toronto, Thomas Foster, in 1935/36 as a memorial to his wife, unique in the design of Byzantine architecture; holds tours on the 1st & 2nd Sun., June-Sept.; special concerts throughout the year, with special program in Oct.
Bev Northeast, Contact, bnortheast@powergate.ca

***Uxbridge:* Uxbridge Historical Centre**
***Also known as:* Uxbridge-Scott Museum & Archives**
PO Box 1301, 7239 Conc. 6, Uxbridge, ON L9P 1N5
Tel: 905-852-5854; *Fax:* 905-852-5854
museum@town.uxbridge.on.ca
uxlib.com/museum
Displays of artifacts & photos to help tell the story of the Uxbridge area; special display on The Oak Ridges Moraine; 10 heritage buildings on site; picnic grounds
Allan McGillivray, Curator

***Vernon:* Osgoode Township Historical Society & Museum**
PO Box 74, 7814 Lawrence St., Vernon, ON K0A 3J0
Tel: 613-821-4062
oths@magma.ca
www.magma.ca/~oths
The Osgoode Township Historical Society & Museum preserves the development of the Township of Osgoode, situated south of Ottawa, Ontario. Artifacts include indigenous Native & pioneer articles & documents, such as historic furniture & clothing, & agricultural tools & equipment. The Museum is open Tuesdays to Saturdays.
Jenn Hume, Contact

***Wasaga Beach:* Nancy Island Historic Site**
c/o Wasaga Beach Provincial Park, 11 - 22nd St. North, Wasaga Beach, ON L9Z 2V9
Tel: 705-429-2516; *Fax:* 705-429-7983
nancyisland@wasagabeachpark.com
www.wasagabeachpark.com
Remains of the British schooner "Nancy"; replica of Upper Lakes lighthouse; artifacts related to marine aspects of War of 1812

***Waterford:* Spruce Row Museum**
PO Box 457, Waterford, ON N0E 1Y0
Tel: 519-443-4211; *Fax:* 519-443-5640
sprucerow.museum@norfolkcounty.on.ca
www.norfolkcounty.on.ca; www.sprucerowmuseum.ca
History of the Waterford & Townsend area; includes unique collection of agricultural equipment representative of southern Ontario
Jennifer Hunt-Beauchamp, Curator

***Waterloo:* Brubacher House Museum**
c/o University of Waterloo, North Campus, Waterloo, ON N2L 3G6
Tel: 519-886-3855
bhouse@watserv1.uwaterloo.ca
www.grebel.uwaterloo.ca/bhouse
Built in 1850, the Brubacher House was later purchased by the University of Waterloo. The home's interior was rebuilt to reflect a Pennsylvania German Mennonite home from the 1850 to 1890 era. Many of the furnishings in the Brubacher House, collected from local Mennonite families, also reflect the time period. Operated by Conrad Grebel University College & the Mennonite Historical Society of Ontario, the House is open from the beginning of May to the end of October.

***Waterloo:* Earth Sciences Museum**
***Also known as:* Biology-Earth Sciences Museum**
Centre for Environmental & Information Technology, University of Waterloo, Waterloo, ON N2L 3G1
Tel: 519-888-4567; *Fax:* 519-746-7484
esmuseum@uwaterloo.ca
www.earth.uwaterloo.ca/outreach/museum
Dinosaurs, gems, minerals & a 60-tonne rock garden
Peter Russell, Director

***Waterloo:* Museum & Archive of Games**
Burt Matthews Hall, University of Waterloo, 200 University Avenue West, Waterloo, ON N2L 3G1
Tel: 519-888-4424; *Fax:* 519-886-2440
musinfo@healthy.uwaterloo.ca
www.gamesmuseum.uwaterloo.ca/
Specializes in the collection, presentation & display of games, both Canadian & international collections; researchers act as a resource for archiving related materials related to games & also provide research facilities & expertise to persons interested in pursuing the study of Games
Prof. Rhonda Ryman, Asst. Curator
Dr. Ronald Johnson, Curator

***Waterloo:* Museum of Visual Science & Optometry**
Optometry Bldg., University of Waterloo, Waterloo, ON N2L 3G1
Tel: 519-885-1211; *Fax:* 519-725-0784
www.optometry.uwaterloo.ca/museum/index.htm
Antique spectacles; eye examining equipment; historical documents & books; open; year round

***Wawa:* Lake Superior Provincial Park Visitor Centre**
PO Box 267, Wawa, ON P0S 1K0
Tel: 705-856-2284; *Fax:* 705-856-1333
www.ontarioparks.com
Open in July & Aug., this interpretive centre includes information on the Lake Superior Provincial Park's natural & cultural features & the area's recreational opportunities

***Welland:* Ball's Falls Centre for Conservation**
c/o Niagara Peninsula Conservation Authority, 250 Thorold Rd. West, 3rd Fl., Welland, ON L3C 3W2
Tel: 905-788-3135; *Fax:* 905-788-1121
www.npca.ca
The Ball's Falls Centre for Conservation offers information about the Niagara Peninsula's history, the natural history of the Twenty Valley & its watershed, & the Niagara Escarpment Biosphere Reserve. Historical homes, a mill, & a church are available for touring.
Christine Hayward, Curator
Diane L. Bois, Administrative Assistant, Operations, dbois@conservation-niagara.on.ca

***Welland:* Welland Historical Museum**
65 Hooker St., Welland, ON L3C 5G9
Tel: 905-732-2215
whmchin@niagara.com
History of Welland including the Welland Canal & its industries; open Tue.-Sat.; kids summer camps in July & Aug.; children's museum
Susan Noakes, Curator/Director

***Wellington:* Wellington Heritage Museum**
290 Main St., Wellington, ON K0K 3L0
Tel: 613-399-5015; *Fax:* 613-476-9835
wellmuseum@pecounty.on.ca (May - September)
Other contact information: E-mail, October - April: museums@pecounty.on.ca

The local history collection of the Wellington Heritage Museum is housed within a Quaker Meeting House, which was built in 1885. The museum features a tribute to the Society of Friends, who helped develop the county. A special collection is the Douglas A. Crawford Canning Industry Collection. Wellington Heritage Museum is open from May to mid October.
Jennifer Lyons, Head Curator, 613-476-2148
Janice Hubbs, Site Curator, 613-399-5015

Westport: **Rideau District Museum**
PO Box 305, Westport, ON K0G 1X0
Tel: 613-273-2502; *Fax:* 613-273-3222
bwlaird@rideau.net
Founded: 1961 Housed in 1850s blacksmith & carriage shop with forges & bellows intact & showing many artifacts from the local district, including a 9-foot tall 19th-century statue of Sally Grant, the Blind Lady of Justice
Wendy Briggs-Jude, Chair, 613-273-5449

White Lake: **Waba Cottage Museum & Gardens**
PO Box 167, Museum Rd., White Lake, ON K0A 3L0
Tel: 613-623-4341
Situated in an 8-acre park amongst heritage buildings, boat launch & flower gardens
B. Stewart, Chair

Whitney: **Algonquin Visitor Centre & Algonquin Logging Museum**
PO Box 219, Whitney, ON K0J 2M0
Tel: 613-637-2828; *Fax:* 613-637-2138
info@algonquinpark.on.ca
www.algonquinpark.on.ca
Other contact information: Park Information: 705/633-5572
Visitor Centre contains exhibits on the Park's natural & human history, restaurant, & bookstore; wheelchair accessible; Logging Museum presents the history of logging from 1830's to current times; exhibits include a recreated Camboose camp & a steam powered amphibious tug. Visitor Centre open year round. Logging Museum open daily 9:00-5:00 from late June until Thanksgiving.
Rick Stronks, Chief Park Naturalist

Williamstown: **The Nor'Westers & Loyalist Museum**
PO Box 69, Williamstown, ON K0C 2J0
Tel: 613-347-3547
museum@bellnet.ca
Housed in a Georgian-style building; stories of loyalist pioneers & partners of the Northwest Fur Trade Company
Joan P. MacDonald, Chair

Windsor: **Ojibway Nature Centre**
5200 Matchette Rd., Windsor, ON N9C 4E8
Tel: 519-966-5852; *Fax:* 519-966-9658
www.ojibway.ca
The Ojibway Nature Centre presents displays about the natural history & ecology of the Ojibway Prairie Complex. Visitors will also discover a live exhibit area, featuring the Eastern Fox Snake & the Eastern Massasauga Rattlesnake. The Centre is staffed by naturalists, who provide lessons & conducted tours. Events & programs are available for all ages.

Windsor: **Serbian Heritage Museum of Windsor (SHM)**
6770 Tecumseh Rd. East, Windsor, ON N8T 1E6
Tel: 519-944-4884; *Fax:* 519-974-3963
members.tripod.com/swo_heritage/serbian.htm
Founded: 1987 Artifacts & archival material of Serbian people in Windsor dating back to 1920s; tours, educational programming & lectures; gift shop; open year round

Windsor: **Willistead Manor**
1899 Niagara St., Windsor, ON N8Y 1K3
Tel: 519-253-2365; *Fax:* 519-253-5101
willisteadmanor@city.windsor.on.ca
36-room mansion, built 1904-1906; viewing by appt. Available for special events.

Windsor: **Windsor's Community Museum**
Also known as: **François Baby House**
254 Pitt St. West, Windsor, ON N9A 5L5
Tel: 519-253-1812; *Fax:* 519-253-0919
wmuseum@city.windsor.on.ca
www.citywindsor.ca
Founded: 1958 The Museum includes the François Baby House on Pitt St. W., and the Duff-Baby Interpretation Centre, located at 221 Mill St.; changing exhibits on the history of the Windsor region; houses over 15,000 artifacts, paintings, drawings, prints and photos, maps, newspapers and books, and a large archival collection. Open year round.
Madelyn Della Valle, Curator

Wingham: **North Huron District Museum**
PO Box 1522, 273 Josephine St., Wingham, ON N0G 2W0
Tel: 519-357-1096; *Fax:* 519-357-1110
nhdmuseum@wightman.ca
Special events & bi-monthly exhibits featuring the history of North Huron's writers, painters, businesses, farmers & people; Special exhibit & garden dedicated to Alice Munro

Woodstock: **Woodstock Museum National Historic Site**
Museum Square, 466 Dundas St., Woodstock, ON N4S 1C4
Tel: 519-537-8411; *Fax:* 519-537-7235
museum@city.woodstock.on.ca
www.woodstockmuseum.ca
Other contact information: E-mail, Registrar: apollard@city.woodstock.on.ca
The Woodstock Museum National Historic Site exhibits the local history of Woodstock from 10,000 B.C. to 2001. At the former Town Hall & Market House, which was built in 1853, visitors can see the 1879 Council Chambers & the 1889 Grand Hall. The museum contains a research room, with books & vertical files. It is open to the public by appointment only. School education programs are available, by phoning 519-539-2382, extension 2903, or e-mailing the Education Officer at the following address: kgill@city.woodstock.on.ca. The museum is open year-round.
Karen Houston, Curator, khouston@city.woodstock.on.ca

Prince Edward Island

Provincial Museums

Prince Edward Island Museum & Heritage Foundation / Le Musée et la Fondation du patrimoine de l'Ile-du-Prince-É
2 Kent St., Charlottetown, PE C1A 1M6
Tel: 902-368-6600; *Fax:* 902-368-6608
mhpei@gov.pe.ca
www.peimuseum.com
The organization is the operator of seven provincial museums & heritage sites across Prince Edward Island. Sites include the Elmira Railway Museum, Basin Head Fisheries Museum, Orwell Corner Historic Village & Agricultural Museum, Beaconsfield Historic House, Eptek Art & Culture Centre, The Acadian Museum of Prince Edward Island, & Green Park Shipbuilding Museum & Yeo House. Open year-round are the Beaconsfield Historic House, the Eptek Art & Culture Centre, & the The Acadian Museum of Prince Edward Island. The others are open during the summer months. The Prince Edward Island Museum & Heritage Foundation also has the responsibility for the provincial collection of over 85,000 artifacts.
Dr. David L. Keenlyside, Executive Director, 902-368-6601, Fax: 902-368-6608, dlkeenlyside@gov.pe.ca
Nora Young, Executive Assistant, njyoung@edu.pe.ca

Local Museums in Prince Edward Island

Alberton: **Alberton Museum**
PO Box 515, Alberton, PE C0B 1B0
Tel: 902-853-4048; *Fax:* 902-853-4066
www.townofalberton.ca/history/museum.htm
Founded: 1964 Genealogy resources on area families; old photo collection; history of the fox industry; Micmac Indian displays; displays of antique furniture, glassware, textiles & toys. Open June - Sept. Located at 457 Church St. in Alberton.
Dr. Allan J. MacRae, Curator

Belle River PO: **Ripley's Believe It or Not! Museum**
PO Belle River, Belle River PO, PEI C0A 1B0
Tel: 902-963-2242; *Fax:* 902-962-2017
Other contact information: Off season Tel: 902/962-2022
Ripley's presents displays of unual events and things. Located on RR#6 in Cavendish; Robert Ripley's collection of the unusual; open June - Sept.
Tom McMillan

Charlottetown: **Car Life Museum Inc.**
45 Oak Dr., Charlottetown, PE C1A 6T6
Tel: 902-892-1754
Located on Highway 1 in Bonshaw, Prince Edward Island, the Car Life Museum features restored cars which date back to 1898. The museum also houses farm machinery from the early 1800s & the early 1900s. The Car Life Museum is open from June to September.
Doris MacKay, Contact, 902-675-3555

Charlottetown: **Green Gables House**
2 Palmers Lane, Charlottetown, PE C1A 5V6
Tel: 902-963-7874
peinp-pnipe@pc.gc.ca
www.pc.gc.ca/lhn-nhs/pe/greengables/visit/index_E.asp
Dedicated to Anne of Green Gables, a fictional but nonetheless, famous character created by Lucy Maud Montgomery for her book series "Anne of Green Gables". Open May 1 - Oct. 31

Charlottetown: **Port-la-Joye-Fort Amherst National Historic Site of Canada**
c/o Parks Canada, 2 Palmer's Lane, Charlottetown, PE C1A 5V8
Tel: 902-566-7626; *Fax:* 902-566-8295
information@pc.gc.ca
www.pc.gc.ca/lhn-nhs/pe/amherst/activ.aspx
Visitors to the Port-la-Joye-Fort Amherst National Historic Site of Canada learn the history of the Mi'kmaq of Prince Edward Island. Interpretive services are available in July & August. Guided tours are offered in both English & French. The grounds are open from June to October.

Charlottetown: **Province House National Historic Site of Canada**
2 Palmer's Lane, Charlottetown, PE C1A 5V6
Tel: 902-566-7626; *Fax:* 902-566-8295
information@pc.gc.ca
www.pc.gc.ca/lhn-nhs/pe/provincehouse/index_e.asp
Includes Confederation Chamber, site of historic discussions regarding union of the BNA colonies; remains of the Legislative Bldg. for PEI; open year round

Charlottetown: **Spoke Wheel Car Museum**
RR#3, Charlottetown, PE C1A 7J7
Antique automobiles

Cornwall: **Royal Atlantic Wax Museum**
PO Box 762, Cornwall, PE C0A 1H0
Tel: 902-963-2350
119 life-sized wax figures; open daily early June - late Sept.

Ellerslie: **Ellerslie Shellfish Museum**
Ellerslie, PE C0B 1J0
Tel: 902-853-2181
Aquariums of live fish & shellfish; history of oyster cultivation
Joanne Wallace, Director

Kensington: **Anne of Green Gables Museum at Silver Bush**
PO Box 491, Kensington, PE C0B 1M0
www.annesociety.org/anne/
Artifacts, books & photographs related to the life & times of Lucy Maud Montgomery

Kensington: **The Keir Memorial Museum**
RR#1, Kensington, PE C0B 1M0
Tel: 902-836-3054; *Fax:* 902-836-4801
ygillespie@auracom.com
Open July - Sept.
Yvonne Gillespie, Treasurer

Kensington: **Lucy Maud Montgomery Birthplace**
6461 Route 20, Kensington, PE C0B 1M0
Tel: 902-886-2596
Open May - Thanksgiving

Kensington: **Veterans' Memorial Military Museum**
PO Box 182, Kensington, PE C0B 1M0
Tel: 902-836-3600; *Fax:* 902-836-7488
Military memorabilia mostly from WWI & WWII; Boer War items

Montague: **Garden of the Gulf Museum**
PO Box 1237, 564 Main St., Montague, PE C0A 1R0
Tel: 902-838-2467
ggmuseum@eastlink.ca
www.montaguemuseum.com
Other contact information: Off-season Phone: 902/838-2820
Founded: 1958 Early island history; open June - Sept. PEI's oldest Museum.

Murray Harbour: **Log Cabin Museum**
Route 18 A, Murray Harbour, PE C0A 1V0
Tel: 902-962-2201
Local history

O'Leary: **Prince Edward Island Potato Museum**
PO Box 602, O'Leary, PE C0B 1V0
Tel: 902-859-2039; *Toll-Free:* 800-565-3457
info@peipotatomuseum.com
www.peipotatomuseum.com
The history of the potato industry is depicted at the Prince Edward Island Potato Museum. Visitors will see a collection of machinery & farm implements related to growing & harvesting potatoes. The museum also includes the Potato Hall of Fame. It is open from mid May to mid October.
Donna Rowley, Manager, 902-853-2312

Richmond: **The Bottle Houses / Les Maisons de Bouteilles**
PO Box 72, Richmond, PE C0B 2E0
Tel: 902-854-2987
www.teleco.org/SitesWebs/bouteilles/index.html
Other contact information: Off season: 902/854-2254
Three fantasy-like buildings made of over 25,000 vari-coloured bottles, creating a symphony of light & colour within; located in Cape Egmont; flower gardens; giftshop; bilingual service
Réjeanne Arsenault, Owner/Operator

Rustico: **Farmers' Bank of Rustico**
Hunter River, RR#3, Rustico, PE C0A 1N0
Tel: 902-963-3168
info@farmersbank.ca
www.farmersbank.ca
Other contact information: (off season): 902/963-2304
Banking artifacts; precursor to the Credit Union movement in North America
J.D. MacDonald, President

Summerside: **International Fox Museum & Hall of Fame Inc.**
286 Fitzroy St., Summerside, PE C1N 1J2
Tel: 902-436-2400
email@address.com
www.isn.net/~cmapei/ifox/
Located at historic Holman Homestead & Gardens; museum tells the story of the PEI silver fox industry heyday between 1894 & WWII

Tignish: **Tignish Cultural Centre**
PO Box 398, Maple St., Tignish, PE C0B 2B0
Tel: 902-882-1999; *Fax:* 902-882-3144
culturalcentre@tignish.com
www.tignish.com
Local history

West Point: **West Point Lighthouse**
Lot 8, 364 Cedar Dunes Park Rd., West Point, PE C0B 1V0
Tel: 902-859-3605; *Fax:* 902-859-1510
Toll-Free: 800-764-6854
westpointlighthouse@gmail.com
www.westpointlighthouse. com
Founded: 1983 The West Point Development Corporation restored the historic West Point Lighthouse, which was built in 1875 & had a keeper until 1963. The lighthouse is one of the tallest on Prince Edward Island. Today, the lighthouse continues to operate as a navigational aid.

Quebec

Provincial Museums

Canadian Centre for Architecture (CCA) / Centre Canadien d'Architecture
1920, rue Baile, Montréal, QC H3H 2S6
Tel: 514-939-7026; *Fax:* 514-939-7020
info@cca.qc.ca; press@cca.qc.ca (Press Relations)
www.cca.qc.ca
Other contact information: Phone, Administration: 514-939-7000; E-mail, Tours: schools@cca.qc.ca
Founded: 1979 The Canadian Centre for Architecture is a museum & an international research centre. The Centre raises awareness of the role of architecture, stimulates design innovation, & promotes scholarly research.
Phyllis Lambert, Founding Director & Chair
Mirko Zardini, Director & Chief Curator
Louise Désy, Curator, Photography
Isabelle Huiban, Head, Media Relations, ihuiban@cca.qc.ca

McCord Museum of Canadian History / Musée McCord d'histoire canadienne
690, rue Sherbrooke ouest, Montréal, QC H3A 1E9
Tel: 514-398-7100; *Fax:* 514-398-5045
info@mccord.mcgill.ca
www.mccord-museum.qc.ca
Founded: 1921 The museum started with the collections of David Ross McCord and a building from McGill University. It conserves a variety of objects reflecting the social history and material culture of Montreal, Quebec and Canada. Exhibits include over 1,440,000 pieces and range from paintings, costumes & decorative arts, to archives of texts and photographs. Open year round with summer/winter hrs.
Ms Suzanne Sauvage, President/CEO, suzanne.sauvage@mccord.mcgill.ca
Nicole Vallières, Director Ph.D., Collection, Research & Programmes, nicole.vallières@mccord.mcgill.ca
Philip Leduc, Director, Operations, philip.leduc@mccord.mcgill.ca

Musée de l'Amerique française (MAF)
2, côte de la Fabrique, Québec, QC G1R 3V6
Tél: 418-692-2843; *Téléc:* 418-646-9705
Ligne sans frais: 866-710-8031
mcq@mcq.org
www.mcq.org
Le plus ancien musée au Canada; la collection regroupe des instruments d'enseignement des sciences, monnaies anciennes, médailles, collections de minéralogie, de géologie, de numismatique, de zoologie, de botanique, de fossiles, livres anciens, et de peinture; expositions et activités; centre de référence; boutique; café.
Danielle Poiré, Directrice-générale (intérim)

Musée de la civilisation
CP 155 B, 85, rue Dalhousie, Québec, QC G1K 7A6
Tél: 418-643-2158; *Téléc:* 418-646-9705
Ligne sans frais: 866-710-8031
mcq@mcq.org
www.mcq.org
Founded: 1988 Le musée est doté de la plus importante collection ethnographique et historique du Québec et se distingue par sa muséologie innovatrice; programmation thématique; activités éducatives et culturelles; ateliers, visites commentées; boutique; café.
Danielle Poiré, Directrice générale (intérim)

Pointe-à-Callière, Montréal Museum of Archaeology & History
Angle de la Commune, 350, place Royale, Montréal, QC H2Y 3Y5
Tel: 514-872-9150
info@pacmusee.qc.ca; rhumaines@pacmusee.qc.ca (HR)
www.pacmusee.qc.ca
Other contact information: E-mail, Public Services Department: glemay@pacmusee.qc.ca
Founded: 1992 The Montréal Museum of Archaeology & History is situated on the site where, in 1642, a mass celebrated the founding of Montréal. Pointe-à-Callière was also the location of a home built in 1688 by the third governor of Montréal, Chevalier Louis Hector de Callière. The site features architectural remains, & the museum houses hundreds of artifacts.
Sophie Brochu, President & CEO
Francine Lelièvre, Executive Director
John LeBoutillier, Secretary-Treasurer
Raymond Montpetit, Coordinator, Historical Research

Local Museums in Quebec

Alma: **L'Odyssée des Bâtisseurs**
1671, av du Pont Nord, Alma, QC G8B 5G2
Tél: 418-668-2606; *Téléc:* 418-668-5851
Ligne sans frais: 866-668-2606
info@odysseedesbatisseurs.com
www.odysseedesbatisseurs.com
Axé sur l'importance de l'eau au coeur du développement, le parc thématique L'Odyssée des Bâtisseurs vous invite à visiter des expositions vivantes, admirer un panorama naturel et industriel extraordinaire et vivre une expérience multimédia 360 saisissante à l'intérieur d'un ancien château d'eau.
Danielle Larouche, Directrice générale

Alouette: **Bagotville Air Defence Museum / Musée de la Défense aérienne de Bagotville**
PO Box 567 Main, Alouette, QC G0V 1A0
Tel: 418-677-7159; *Fax:* 418-677-4104
museebagotville@forces.qc.ca
www.bagotville.net
Founded: 1997 Canadian Military Aviation Museum
Claude Chamberland, Director
Captain Mauril Dufort, 3 Wing Heritage Officer

Angliers: **Site historique T.E Draper/Chantier de Gédéon**
CP 82, 11, rue du T.E. Draper, Angliers, QC J0Z 1A0
Tél: 819-949-4431; *Téléc:* 819-949-4431
tedraper@tlb.sympatico.ca
www3.telebecinternet.com/tedraper
Montez à bord du remorqueur de bois T.E. Draper; visitez le chantier de Gédéon, la reconstitution d'un camp de bûcherons des années 1930-1940.
Cathy Fraser, Contact

Anse-au-Griffon: **Manoir Leboutillier, lieu historique national du Canada**
578, boul Griffon, Anse-au-Griffon, QC G4X 6A4
Tél: 418-892-5150; *Téléc:* 418-892-5189
manoir.leboutillier@globetrotter.net
Built in 1850s by John Le Boutillier; open June - mid-Oct.

Asbestos: **Musée minéralogique d'Asbestos / Asbestos Mineralogical Museum**
341, boul St-Luc, Asbestos, QC J1T 2W4
Tél: 819-879-6444
Minerals from the Jeffrey Mine; local mining history; exploration & survey instruments; workshops for schools; seasonal opening
A.J. Millen, Directeur

Authier: **École du Rang II d'Authier**
CP 74, 269 Rang II, Authier, QC J0Z 1C0
Tél: 819-782-3289; *Ligne sans frais:* 866-336-3289
ecolrgll@tlb.sympatico.ca
pwp.lino.com/ecolrgll
Représente les écoles de rang qui ont meublé le paysage rural du Québec dans les années quarantes
Sasha Lambert, Responsable

Batiscan: **Vieux presbytère de Batiscan**
340, rue Principale, Batiscan, QC G0X 1A0
Tél: 418-362-2051; *Téléc:* 418-362-1373
direction@presbytere-batiscan.com
www.presbytere-batiscan.com
Datant de 1816, propose une reconstitution fidèle de l'intérieur de la maison au milieu du 19e siècle; aperçu du quotidien du curé Fréchette et de sa ménagère Adéline, les deux habitants du presbytère à cette époque; exposition temporaire à chaque année; sentier ornithologique; aire de repos et de pique-nique; boutique souvenir.

Beauharnois: **Parc archéologique de la Pointe-du-Buisson**
333, rue Émond, Beauharnois, QC J0S 1J0
Tel: 450-429-7857; *Fax:* 450-429-5921
pointe@ville.melocheville.qc.ca
www.pointedubuisson.com/
Archaeology site; prehistoric objects which form a collection that is recognized in the scientific world as one of the most important in the NE of the continent; research, outreach education; over two million objects and fragments of artifacts and ecofacts that mark SW Quebec.
Maurice Binette

Beaumont: **Moulin de Beaumont**
2, rte du Fleuve, Beaumont, QC G0R 1C0
Tél: 418-833-1867
mbeaumont@bellnet.ca
1821 flour mill; open May 15 - June 24, Sept. & Oct., Sat & Sun., Tues. - Fri by appt.; June 24 - Aug., Tues. - Sat.
Gilles Sheedy, Directeur

Bergeronnes: **Centre Archéo Topo**
498, rue de la Mer, Bergeronnes, QC G0T 1G0
Tél: 418-232-6286; *Téléc:* 418-232-6695
Ligne sans frais: 866-832-6286
archeo95@bellnet.ca
www.archeotopo.qc.ca
L'histoire de la région de La Haute-Côte-Nord; exposition interactive retrace la vie des tribus amérindiennes dans la région; jeux didactiques; ateliers pour les enfants et les jeunes; excursions; spectacle multimédia; boutique.

Les Bergeronnes: **Centre d'interprétation et d'observation de Cap-de-Bon-Désir**
13, ch du Cap-de-Bon-Désir, Les Bergeronnes, QC G0T 1G0
Tél: 418-232-6751; *Téléc:* 418-235-6468
Ligne sans frais: 888-773-8888
parcscanada-que.pc.qc.ca
www.quebecmaritime.ca
Promontoire naturel pour l'observation des mammifères marins; guides-interprètes; salle d'exposition, phare. Ouvert mi-juin-mi-octobre.

Berthierville: **Chapelle des Cuthbert de Berthier**
461, rue de Bienville, Berthierville, QC J0K 1A0
Tél: 450-836-7336; *Téléc:* 450-836-8158
www.patrimoineberthier.org
La plus ancien temple protestant au Québec; expositions, visites commentées; pique-nique sur place; ouverte tous les jours, du juin au fête du Travil, 10h-18h

Berthierville: **Musée Gilles-Villeneuve**
960, av Gilles-Villeneuve, Berthierville, QC J0K 1A0
Tél: 450-836-2714; *Téléc:* 450-836-3067
Ligne sans frais: 800-639-0103
museegillesvilleneuve@bellnet.ca
www.museegillesvilleneuve.com
Founded: 1995 Le musée a pour mandat perpétuer le souvenir de Gilles Villeneuve, le grand coureur automobile du F1; voitures, photographies, Galerie M. Trudel.
Alain Bellehumeur, Superviseur

Bonaventure: **Musée acadien du Québec à Bonaventure**
95, av Port Royal, Bonaventure, QC G0C 1E0
Tél: 418-534-4000; *Téléc:* 418-534-4105
reception@museeacadien.com
www.museeacadien.com
Jean-Claude Cyr, Directeur

Boucherville: **Maison Louis-Hippolyte Lafontaine**
314, boul Marie-Victorin, Boucherville, QC J4B 1X1
Tél: 514-449-8328; *Téléc:* 514-449-4709

Cascapédia-Saint-Jules: **Musée de la rivière Cascapédia / The Cascapedia River Museum**
275, rte 299, Cascapédia-Saint-Jules, QC G0C 1T0
Tél: 418-392-5079; *Téléc:* 418-392-5070
info@cascapedia.org
www.cascapedia.org
Le musée raconte l'histoire de la région autour de la rivière Cascapédia, la pêche au saumon, et le patrimoine gaspésien; boutique.

Causapscal: **Maison Dr. Joseph-Frenette**
3, rue Frenette, Causapscal, QC G0J 1J0
Tél: 418-756-5999; *Téléc:* 418-756-3344
www.maisondrjosephfrenette.com
Joseph Frenette exerçait la profession, aujourd'hui disparue, de médecin de campagne. Il consacra sa vie à soigner des malades et des blessés, à faire naître des enfants, à sauver des vies. Tel un livre ouvert, cette exposition fait découvrir son univers familial et professionnnel et à comprendre le rôle primordial du médecin de campagne dans l'histoire du Québec.

***Causapscal:* Site historique Matamajaw**
53C, rue Saint-Jacques sud, Causapscal, QC G0J 1J0
Tél: 418-756-5999; *Téléc:* 418-756-3344
faucuscar@globetrotter.net
www.causapscal.net
Ancien lieu de villégiature de Sir John A. McDonald et de Lord Mount Stephen, le Matamajaw Salmon Club a attiré les membres de la haute société anglaise, américaine et canadienne durant la fin du 19e et au début du 20e siècle. Le Site Matamajaw est le seul ancien établissement privé accessible au public en Amérique du Nord.

***Chambly:* Lieu historique du Fort-Chambly**
2, rue Richelieu, Chambly, QC J3L 2B9
Tél: 514-658-1585; *Téléc:* 514-658-7216
Ligne sans frais: 888-773-8888
parcscanada-que@pc.gc.ca
www.pc.gc.ca/lhn-nhs/qc/fortchambly
Présente l'histoire et les coutumes de la Nouvelle-France de 1665-1760; expositions; activités.

***Chambord:* Village Historique de Val-Jalbert**
95, rue St-Georges, Chambord, QC G0W 1G0
Tel: 418-275-3132; *Fax:* 418-275-5875
valjalbert@valjalbert.com
www.sepaq.com/ct/val/fr/
Partially restored ghost town; created by the 1901 opening of a pulp & paper mill; as the years went by the town flourished & several services & buildings were added including a train station, convent, hotel & general store; on Aug. 13, 1927 the plant shut down forcing workers to leave Val-Jalbert; today it's a rich historical, industrial & religious patrimony; fall height of 72 m.
André Turgeon, Directeur

***Château-Richer:* Centre d'interpretation de la Côte-de-Beaupré**
CP 40, 7976, av Royale, Château-Richer, QC G0A 1N0
Tél: 418-824-3677; *Téléc:* 418-824-5907
info@histoire-cotedebeaupre.org
www.histoire-cotedebeaupre.org
Présente les aspects culturels, géographiques, historiques et patrimoniaux qui témoignent de la beauté de la région; activités pédagogiques complémentaires au programme d'enseignement; ouvert tous les jours, 9h30-16h30
Luc Trépanier, Directeur général

***Château-Richer:* Musée de l'Abeille**
***Also known as:* Economusée du miel**
8862, boul Sainte-Anne, Château-Richer, QC G0A 1N0
Tél: 418-824-4411; *Téléc:* 418-824-4422
info@musee-abeille.com
www.musee-abeille.com
Centre d'interprétation; l'exposition Des Abeilles et Des Hommes; visites guidées; informations sur le miel; boutique.
Redmond Hayes, President

***Chicoutimi:* Centre historique des Soeurs de Notre-Dame du Bon-Conseil de Chicoutimi**
700, rue Racine est (porte 688), Chicoutimi, QC G7H 1V2
Tél: 418-543-4861; *Téléc:* 418-543-7194
centrehistorique@sndbc.qc.ca
www.sndbc.qc.ca; www.reseaumuseal.com;
www.museevirtuel.ca

***Chicoutimi:* La Pulperie de Chicoutimi**
300, rue Dubuc, Chicoutimi, QC G7J 4M1
Tél: 418-698-3100; *Téléc:* 418-698-3158
Ligne sans frais: 877-998-3100
info@pulperie.com
www.pulperie.com
Collection de plus de 26 000 ojets et oeuvres; maison Arthur-Villeneuve; expositions d'art et d'ethnologie; vestiges restaurés des anciennes installations de la Compagnie de pulpe de Chicoutimi; parc.
Jacques Fortin, Directeur général

***Coaticook:* Beaulne Museum / Musée Beaulne**
96, rue Union, Coaticook, QC J1A 1Y9
Tel: 819-849-6560; *Fax:* 819-849-9519
info@museebeaulne.qc.ca
www.museebeaulne.qc.ca
Other contact information: Alternative E-mail:
bonjour@museebeaulne.qc.ca
Founded: 1964 Beaulne Museum depicts the history & achievements of the local Norton family, who were known for manufacturing railway jacks & their philanthropy. The museum is located in Château Arthur Osmore Norton, a Victorian-style mansion which was built in 1912. Beaulne Museum is open year round from Tuesday to Sunday.

***Cookshire:* Compton County Historical Museum Society / Societé d'histoire du musée du comté Compton**
PO Box 967, 374 Route 253, Cookshire, QC J0B 1M0
Tel: 819-875-5256; *Fax:* 819-875-3182
mus.eatoncorner@gmail.com
mus.eatoncorner.com
Housed in a former Congregationalist Church built in 1842. Address is 374 Route 253, Eaton Corner, Quebec.
Pat Boychuck, President

***Coteau-du-Lac:* Lieu historique national du Canada de Coteau-du-Lac**
***Also known as:* Coteau-du-Lac National Historic Site of Canada**
308A, ch du Fleuve, Coteau-du-Lac, QC J0P 1B0
Tél: 450-763-5631; *Téléc:* 450-763-1654
Ligne sans frais: 888-773-8888
parcscanada-que@pch.gc.ca
www.pc.gc.ca/fra/lhn-nhs/qc/coteaudulac
Exposition et activités: le site stratégique de Coteau-du-Lac, le Blockhaus, coin de famille, circuit nature, jardin archéologique, reconstitution militaire, marché champêtre.

***Desbiens:* Centre d'histoire et d'archéologie de la Métabetchouane**
243, rue Hébert, Desbiens, QC G0W 1N0
Tél: 418-346-5341; *Téléc:* 418-346-5341
cham@digicom.ca
www.chamans.com
Founded: 1995 Site historique et archéologique; histoire d'il y a 5,000 ans; poste de traite; salle de découverte; animation; exposition thématique; 20 juin - sept. ou par réservation

***La Doré:* Le Moulin des Pionniers de La Doré**
4201, rue des Peupliers, La Doré, QC G8J 1E4
Tél: 418-256-8242; *Téléc:* 418-256-3799
Ligne sans frais: 866-272-2842
info@moulindespionniers.qc.ca
www.moulindespionniers.qc.ca
Moulin à scie à pouvoir hydraulique, toujours à l'oeuvre depuis 1889; Maison de Marie, une des plus anciennes maisons de La Doré, avec un potager et une grange-étable; petite ferme avec des animaux; camp qui abrite un restaurant et un bar; auberge "La Nuit Boréale"; sentiers pédestres; tour d'observation; expositions; programmation.
Guylaine Lapointe, Contact, info@moulindespionniers.qc.ca

***Drummondville:* Le Village Québecois d'Antan inc.**
1425, rue Montplaisir, Drummondville, QC J2B 7T5
Tél: 819-478-1441; *Téléc:* 819-478-8155
Ligne sans frais: 877-710-0267
renseignements@villagequebecois.com
www.villagequebecois.com
Founded: 1977 Reconstitution d'un village canadien-français du siècle dernier (1810-1910)
Pierre Derouin, Directeur général, pierre@villagequebecois.com
France Lemoine, Trésorière, france@villagequebecois.com
Simon Bourgault, Directeur, Communications, simon@villagequebecois.com

***Duhamel-Ouest:* Lieu historique national du Canada du Fort-Témiscamingue / Fort Témiscamingue National Historic Site of Canada**
834, ch Vieux-Fort, Duhamel-Ouest, QC J9V 1N7
Tél: 819-629-3222; *Téléc:* 819-629-2977
Ligne sans frais: 888-773-8888
fort.temiscamingue@pc.gc.ca
www.pc.gc.ca/fra/lhn-nhs/qc/temiscamingue
Rappelle la présence millénaire des algonquins et l'histoire de ce poste de traite situé au détroit du Lac Témiscamingue.

***Forestville:* Petite Anglicane**
2, 2e rue, Forestville, QC G0T 1E0
Tél: 418-587-6148
Archéologie locale, les gardes-feu, les remèdes d'autrefois, la vie domestique, nos pionniers, l'histoire de Forestville en photos; expositions temporaires; visites guidées

***Gaspé:* Magasin générale Hyman & Sons et l'entrepôt**
Parc national du Canada Forillon, 122, boul Gaspé, Gaspé, QC G4X 1A9
Tél: 418-368-5505; *Téléc:* 418-368-6837
parcscanada-que@pc.qc.ca
www.pc.gc.ca/Forillon
Magasin au centre du village, de l'époque 1920, autrefois la propriété de la compagnie de pêche "William Hyman and Sons", au Parc national du Canada Forillon; animation en costumes; programmation; visites guidées.

***Gaspé:* Musée de la Gaspésie**
80, boul Gaspé, Gaspé, QC G4X 1A9
Tél: 418-368-1534; *Téléc:* 418-368-1535
info@museedelagaspesie.ca
www.museedelagaspesie.ca
Le musée favoriser la connaissance et l'appréciation de l'histoire et du patrimoine gaspésiens; activités de conservation et de recherche; collections y compris les disciplines de l'ethnologie, l'histoire, les beaux-arts, les sciences naturelles, l'archéologie; archives; boutique; programmation.
Sébastien Lévesque, Directeur général, direction@museedelagaspesie.ca

***Gaspé:* Parc national du Canada Forillon / Forillon National Park of Canada**
122 boul Gaspé, Gaspé, QC G4X 1A9
Tél: 418-368-5505; *Téléc:* 418-368-6837
parcscanada-quebec@pc.gc.ca
www.pc.gc.ca/forillon

***Gatineau:* Musée de l'Auberge Symmes**
***Also known as:* Musée d'Aylmer Museum Inc.**
PO Box 311, 1, rue Front, Gatineau, QC J9H 5E6
Tel: 819-682-0291; *Fax:* 819-682-6594
Symmes@ca.inter.net

***Godbout:* Musée amérindien et inuit de Godbout**
134, ch Pascal-Comeau, Godbout, QC G0H 1G0
Tél: 418-568-7306
Cécile Grenier, Directrice
Claude Grenier, Directeur

***Granby:* Centre d'interpretation de la Nature du Lac Boivin**
700, rue Drummond, Granby, QC J2G 8C7
Tél: 450-375-3861; *Téléc:* 450-375-3736
marco.lemay@cscantons.qc.ca
www.darwin.cyberscol.qc.ca/centre/cinlb/
Founded: 1980 A pour mission de conserver le territoire, les habitats, la faune et la flore de la région
Mario Fortin, Directeur général

***Guérin:* Musée de Guérin**
CP 1110, 913, rue Principale, Guérin, QC J0Z 2E0
Tél: 819-784-7014; *Téléc:* 819-784-7014
musee-guerin@sympatico.ca
Le Musée de Guérin offre deux expositions permanentes: "Autour du clocher" et "Le Réveil rural" qui retracent la vie religieuse et agricole des années 1940-50. Situé sur la "Terre de la Fabrique", concédée au début de la paroisse, le site du musée comprend encore un lieu du culte et la ferme de Monsieur le Curé

***Havre-Aubert:* Aquarium des Iles-de-la-Madeleine / Island Aquarium**
982 route 199, Havre-Aubert, QC G0B 1J0
Tél: 418-937-2277; *Téléc:* 418-937-2277
info@aquariumdesiles.ca
www.ilesdelamadeleine.com/aquarium

***Hâvre-Aubert:* Musée de la Mer Inc.**
1023, Rte. 199, Hâvre-Aubert, QC G4T 9C8
Tél: 418-937-5711; *Téléc:* 418-937-2449
info@museedelamer-im.com
www.ilesdelamadeleine-guidetouristique.com/Ile-du-Havre/Musee-de-la-Mer
L'histoire des Iles-de-la-Madeleine, l'évolution de la navigation, l'histoire de la pêche; collections de roches, de minéraux, de coquillages; photos et objets marins. Ouvert à l'année.
Michelle Joannette, Directrice générale

***Inukjuak:* Musée commémoratif et Centre de transmission de la culture Daniel Weetaluktuk / Daniel Weetaluktuk Commemorative Museum & Cultural Transmis**
General Delivery, Inukjuak, QC J0M 1M0
Tél: 819-254-8919; *Téléc:* 819-254-8148
Ligne sans frais: 866-897-2287
avataq-inukjuak@avataq.qc.ca
www.avataq.qc.ca
Le centre contribue à la protection et à la diffusion de la culture des Inuits d'Inukjuak et du Nunavik; collection de plus de 400 objets anciens et contemporains présentés dans leur contexte culturel d'origine; oeuvres d'art, vêtements traditionnels, artefacts; exposition permanente; expositions temporaires.
Louis Gagnon, Conservateur, louisgagnon@avataq.qc.ca

***Inverness:* Musée du Bronze d'Inverness**
1760, ch Dublin, Inverness, QC G0S 1K0
Tél: 418-453-2101; *Téléc:* 418-453-7711
info@museedubronze.com
www.museedubronze.com
Voué à la recherche, la mise en valeur, la diffusion, la fabrication, l'interprétation et l'éducation relative à l'art du bronze; fonderie; ateliers; visites guidées; jardin; programmation.
Michelle Joannette, Directrice générale

***L'Islet-sur-Mer:* Musée maritime du Québec**
***Also known as:* Musée maritime Bernier**
55, ch des Pionniers est, L'Islet-sur-Mer, QC G0R 2B0
Tél: 418-247-5001; *Téléc:* 418-247-5002
info@mmq.qc.ca
www.mmq.qc.ca
Founded: 1968 Le musée a pour mission la sauvegarde, l'étude, et la mise en valeur du patrimoine maritime se rattrachant au fleuve Saint-Laurent, et de la porte des Grands Lacs; la conservation des navires historiques; expositions permanentes: "Gens du pays, gens du fleuve", "Capt. Joseph-Elzéar Bernier", "Ilitita...Bernier, ses hommes et les Inuits", et "Pirates ou corsaires?"; boutique; visites guidées; accessible aux personnes à mobilité réduite.
Amélia Lemay, Adjointe à la direction

Kahnawake: **Musée Kateri Tekakwitha**
PO Box 70, Kahnawake, QC J0L 1B0
Tel: 450-632-6030; *Fax:* 450-632-6031
kateritekakwithasanctuary@yahoo.ca
Religious & ethnic artifacts dating back to the 17th century; historical mission buildings (rectory 1717, church 1845) contain Blessed Kateri's tomb (1656-1680) & precious works of art including the Deerfield Bell (17th - 19th cent.); open all year 10-5; Kahnawake is a native Mohawk reservation
Alvaro Salazar, Pastor F.M.M.

Kamouraska: **Musée régional de Kamouraska**
69, av Morel, Kamouraska, QC G0L 1M0
Tél: 418-492-9783; *Téléc:* 418-492-3144
museekam@videotron.ca
www.museekamouraska.com
Founded: 1977 Il assume fidèlement sa mission de protection, conservation et diffusion du riche patrimoine historique et culturel de tout Kamouraska
Yvette Raymond, Directrice générale

Knowlton: **Brome County Historical Museum (BCHS)**
PO Box 690, 130 Lakeside, Knowlton, QC J0E 1V0
Tel: 450-243-6782
bchs@endirect.qc.ca
Managed by the Brome County Historical Society, the Brome County Museum presents the history of Brome County & the surrounding region. The museum's grounds feature an old fire hall from 1904, an academy building from 1854, & the Brome County Court House from 1858-1859. The court house contains the archives of the Brome County Historical Society. The museum is open from mid May to mid September. The archives are open year round.

Lac-Drolet: **Maison du Granit**
301, rte du Morne, Lac-Drolet, QC G0Y 1C0
Tél: 819-549-2566
info@maisondugranit.ca
www.maisondugranit.ca
Founded: 1989 A pour mission de collecter et de diffuser l'histoire de l'industrie du granit et de ses artisans les tailleurs de pierre; exposition permanente; expositions thématiques; visites guidées; jardin panoramique.

Lachine: **Lieu historique national du Canada du Commerce-de-la-fourrure-à-Lachine / The Fur Trade at Lachine National Historic Site of Canada**
1255, boul St-Joseph, Lachine, QC H8S 2M2
Tél: 514-637-7433; *Téléc:* 514-637-5325
parcscanada-que@pc.qc.ca
www.pc.gc.ca/lhn-nhs/qc/lachine.aspx
A bord d'un canot, découvrez le point de départ des grands explorateurs du continent nord-américain; programmes et activités; exposition sur l'apogée du commerce des fourrures; visites thématiques.

Lachine: **Musée de Lachine**
1, ch du Musée, Lachine, QC H8S 4L9
Tél: 514-634-3478; *Téléc:* 514-637-6784
museedelachine@lachine.ca
lachine.ville.montreal.qc.ca/musee
Includes Maison leBer-LeMoyne & the Dépendance, the oldest complete buildings on the Island of Montreal as well as the Benoît-Verdickt Pavillion, a contemporary art exhibition centre; the Pavillion de l'Entrepôt presents multidisciplinary & multicultural exhibitions; educational program available for school-aged visitors as well as others; open Wed. - Sun.; guided tours Thurs. & Fri. by appt.
Marc Pitre, Directeur

Lachine: **Musée des Soeurs de Sainte-Anne**
1300, boul Saint-Joseph, Lachine, QC H8S 2M8
Tél: 514-637-4616; *Téléc:* 514-637-2746
msainteanne@ca.inter.net
Musée communautaire de la Congrégation des Soeurs de Sainte-Anne. Le musée a pour mission de faire découvrir la vie des Soeurs de Sainte-Anne marquée par les lieux et les époques où elles ont évolué; open year-round, winter by appt. only
Murielle Gagnon, Responsable du musée

Lac-Mégantic: **Musée Namesokanjic**
#200, 5527, rue Frontenac, Lac-Mégantic, QC G6B 1H6
Tél: 819-583-2441; *Téléc:* 819-583-5920
greffier@ville.lac-megantic.qc.ca
www.lac-megantic.qc.ca
Outils forestiers, objets domestiques, photographies, costumes; programmation et activités.
Jean-François Grandmont, Personne ressource

Lasalle: **Moulin Fleming**
9675, boul LaSalle, Lasalle, QC H8R 2W8
Tél: 514-367-6439
Open May - Sept.

Laval: **Musée Armand-Frappier, Centre d'interprétation des biosciences / Armand-Frappier Museum**
531, boul des Prairies, Laval, QC H7V 1B7
Tél: 450-686-5641; *Téléc:* 450-686-5391
musee-afrappier@iaf.inrs.ca
www.musee-afrappier.qc.ca
Founded: 1992 Le musée offre des activités pour favoriser la compréhension d'enjeux scientifiques reliés à la santé humaine, animale & environnementale; il fait connaître l'oeuvre du Dr Armand Frappier, microbiologiste.
Guylaine Archambault, Directrice générale, guylaine.archambault@iaf.inrs.ca
Caroline Labelle, Agente de réservation, caroline.labelle@iaf.inrs.ca

Laval: **Musée écologique - (C.J.N.) Vanier**
3995, boul Lévesque Saint-Vincent-de-Paul, Laval, QC H7E 2R3

Lévis: **Musée du College de Lévis**
9, rue Mgr Gosselin, Lévis, QC G6V 5K1
Tél: 418-837-8600
Fermé au public, ouvert sur demande
Loic Bernard, Directeur/Conservateur

Lévis: **Société historique Alphonse-Desjardins (SHAD)**
Also known as: **Maison Alphonse-Desjardins**
6, rue du Mont-Marie, Lévis, QC G6V 1V9
Tél: 418-835-2090; *Téléc:* 418-835-9173
Ligne sans frais: 866-835-8444
info@maisonalphonsedesjardins.com
www.desjardins.com
La maison de style néo-gothique fut construite en 1883 pour Alphonse Desjardins, fondateur des caisses populaires. C'est là que Desjardins a conçu son grand projet coopératif et qu'ont débuté, en 1901, les activités de la Caisse populaire de Lévis
Esther Normand, Conservation & Administration Agent

Longueuil: **Musée Marie-Rose Durocher**
a/s 80, rue St-Charles est, Longueuil, QC J4H 1A9
Tél: 450-651-8104; *Téléc:* 450-651-8636
centremarierose@yahoo.ca
www.snjm.org
Le Centre Marie-Rose est ouvert au public; le musée présente des expositions à caractère religieux et historique de la vie de Marie-Rose Durocher, fondatrice de la Congrégation des Soeurs des Saints Noms de Jésus et de Marie; collection de tableaux et d'artefacts.
Thérèse Laplante, Directrice

Malartic: **Musée Régional des Mines et des arts de Malartic**
CP 4227, 650, rue de la Paix, Malartic, QC J0Y 1Z0
Tél: 819-757-4677; *Téléc:* 819-757-4140
museum@lino.com
Open year round.
Jean Massiscotte, Directeur

La Malbaie: **Musée de Charlevoix**
10, ch du Hâvre, La Malbaie, QC G5A 2Y8
Tél: 418-665-4411; *Téléc:* 418-665-4560
info@museedecharlevoix.qc.ca
museedecharlevoix.qc.ca
Main fields of interest: ethno-history and folk art; textual art; decroative arts; fine arts; history
Patrice Giroux, Directeur général

Maniwaki: **Le centre d'interprétation de l'historique de la protection de la forêt contre le feu**
8, rue Comeau, Maniwaki, QC J9E 2R8
Tél: 819-449-7999; *Téléc:* 819-449-5102
info@ci-chateaulogue.qc.ca
www.ci-chateaulogue.qc.ca
Le Château Logue; centre d'interprétation; expositions y compris l'histoire des grands feux de forêts au Québec, la forêt exploitée, et la forêt protégée; visites et randonnées gratuites; tour d'observation.
François Ledoux, Directeur

La Martre: **Corporation du Centre d'interprétation archéologique de la Gaspésie**
6, rue des Fermières, La Martre, QC G0E 2H0
Tél: 418-288-1318
ci_archeologie_gaspesie@hotmail.com
Interprète sur la préhistoire gaspésienne dont l'accent est mis sur la période paléoindienne récente; exposition et sentier d'interprétation
Carlos Suich, Administrateur

Mashteuiatsh: **Musée amérindien de Mashteuiatsh**
1787, rue Amishk, Mashteuiatsh, QC G0W 2H0
Tél: 418-275-4842; *Téléc:* 418-275-7494
Ligne sans frais: 888-875-4042
nadyabegin.adm.museeilnu@cgocable.ca
www.museeilnu.ca
Sauvegarde l'héritage ilnu et permet aux autochtones, la population et les touristes d'en prendre connaissance; expositions permanentes et temporaires; programmes éducatifs.
Bibiane Courtois, Directrice générale

Matane: **Musée du Vieux-Phare**
968 ave. du Phare ouest, Matane, QC G4W 1V7
Tél: 418-562-9766; *Téléc:* 418-562-1917

Melbourne: **Richmond County Historical Society Museum**
1296 Rte. 243, Melbourne, QC J0B 2B0
Tel: 819-845-2303; *Téléc:* 819-826-1332
pages.globetrotter.net/e-dhealy/
To research & preserve historical facts in the Richmond County area; museum refurbished as a typical home of the late 1800s; archives centre

Métabetchouan-Lac-à-la-Croix: **Centre d'interprétation de l'agriculture et de la ruralité**
281, rue St-Louis, Métabetchouan-Lac-à-la-Croix, QC G8G 2C8
Tél: 418-349-3633; *Téléc:* 418-349-5013
Ligne sans frais: 877-611-3633
ciar@cgocable.ca
www.ciar-lacalacroix.com
Founded: 1976 Situé au coeur d'une plaine agricole, le CIAR est un site désigné pour découvrir la richesse du patrimoine agricole du Saguenay-Lac-Saint-Jean. A travers l'exposition Gens de la terre, découvrez 150 ans d'histoire, us et coutumes des ancêtres, qui ont bâti le paysage actuel. Labyrinthe dans un Champ de Maïs; ferme pédagogique; camp d'étabissement (1868); programmes éducatifs.
France Lemoine, Directrice générale

Mont Saint-Hilaire: **Centre de la nature Mont Saint-Hilaire**
422, ch des Moulins, Mont Saint-Hilaire, QC J3G 4S6
Tél: 450-467-1755; *Téléc:* 450-467-8015
info@centrenature.qc.ca
www.centrenature.qc.ca
A pour mission d'assurer l'intégrité du patrimoine naturel de la montagne, offrir un contact avec la nature et une gamme d'activités éducatives et culturelles, et promouvoir la conservation des milieux naturels de la région; ouvert 365 jours par année; offre un réseau de 24 km de sentiers, et un trottoir de bois accessible aux personnes à mobilité restreinte
Kees Vanderheyden, Directeur

Montebello: **Lieu historique national du Canada du Manoir-Papineau / Manoir-Papineau National Historic Site of Canada**
500, rue Notre-Dame, Montebello, QC J0V 1L0
Tél: 819-423-6965; *Téléc:* 819-423-6455
Ligne sans frais: 888-773-8888
parcscanada-que@pc.gc.ca
www.pc.gc.ca/fra/lhn-nhs/qc/papineau
La maison de la famille Papineau, 1848-1850; plus de 800 objets, meubles, vêtements, oeuvres d'art, livres et documents; fresques de Napoléon Bourassa; Concerts d'Amédée; jardin.

Montmagny: **Manoir de l'accordéon**
301, boul Taché est, Montmagny, QC G5V 1C5
Tél: 418-248-7927; *Téléc:* 418-248-1596
accordeon@montmagny.com
accordeon.montmagny.com
Research centre & collection of accordians

Montréal: **Atelier d'histoire Hochelaga-Maisonneuve**
2929, av Jeanne-D'Arc, Montréal, QC H1W 3W2
Tél: 514-899-9979; *Téléc:* 514-259-6466
atelier.hhm@gmail.com
www.ulaval.ca/vvap/PAGES/pagesprojets/hochelaga.ht ml
Mise en valeur les quatre églises historiques d'Hochelaga-Maisonneuve; expositions en patrimoine; visites guidées d'églises et de bâtiments patrimoniaux à Montréal.

Montréal: **Basilique Notre-Dame de Montréal**
110, rue Notre-Dame ouest, Montréal, QC H2Y 1T2
Tél: 514-842-2925; *Téléc:* 514-842-3370
info@basiliquenddm.org
www.basiliquenddm.org
Construite entre 1824 & 1829, la basilique accueille des centaines de milliers de visiteurs chaque année; réputée pour la richesse de sa décoration intérieure: les vitraux, les éléments d'architecture, et les oeuvres d'art; visites guidées (individuels/groupes); visites scolaires; services religieux; événements; concerts; location de salles; boutique.
Yoland Tremblay, Directeur général

Montréal: **Biodôme de Montréal**
4777, av Pierre-De Coubertin, Montréal, QC H1V 1B3
Tél: 514-868-3000; *Téléc:* 514-868-3065
biodome@ville.montreal.qc.ca
www2.ville.montreal.qc.ca/biodome/; www.biodome.qc.ca
Le Biodôme recrée des Écosystèmes des Amériques: forêt tropicale, forêt laurentienne, Saint-Laurent marin, monde polaire. Notez que le Biodôme est fermé pour une durée indéterminée en raison d'un conflit de travail à la Ville de Montréal.

Rachel Léger, Directrice

***Montréal:* The Black Watch of Canada (RHR) Regimental Memorial Museum**
2067, rue Bleury, Montréal, QC H3A 2K2
Tel: 514-496-1686; *Fax:* 514-496-2758
info@blackwatchcanada.com
www.blackwatchcanada.com
Uniforms, photographs & artifacts from early 1860s to present; open Tue. evenings, 7-9 pm & by appt.
Bruce D. Bolton, Director
Anne B. Stewart, Curator

***Montréal:* Canadian Jewish Virtual Museum & Archives / Archives et Musée virtuels juifs canadiens**
c/o Canadian Jewish Congress Charities Committee, National Archives, 1590 Docteur Penfield Ave., Montréal, QC H3G 1C5
Tel: 514-931-7531; *Fax:* 514-931-0548
curator@cjvma.org
www.cjvma.org
Founded: 2001 Initiated by Congregation Shaar Hashomayim, Canada's oldest Ashkenazi synagogue, the Canadian Jewish Virtual Museum & Archives is an online museum of Canadian Jewish history. The virtual museum & archives allows users to discover information about Jewish culture & Jewish life in Canada. Categories include museum, vignettes, & archives.
Dr. Norma Joseph, Co-Chair, Site Advisory
Carole Rocklin, Co-Chair, Site Advisory
Janice Rosen, Site Coordinator, Cdn Jewish Congress Charities Committee, National Archives, curator@cjvma.org

***Montréal:* Centre d'exposition de l'Université de Montréal**
Pavillon de la Faculté d'aménagement, CP 6128 Centre-ville, Montréal, QC H3C 3J7
Tél: 514-343-6111; *Téléc:* 514-343-2183
www.expo.umontreal.ca
Comment s'y rendre: Pavillon de la faculté de l'Aménagement, 2940, ch d la Côte-Sainte-Catherine, local 0056, Montréal. Centre d'exposition multidisciplinaire. Comprend: collection herbier Marie-Victorin; collection du département d'anthropologie; collection du Laboratoire de recherche sur les musiques du monde; oeuvres d'art; design industriel
Louise Grenier, Directrice, l.grenier@umontreal.ca

***Montréal:* Chapelle Notre-Dame-de-Bon-Secours/Musée Marguerite Bourgeoys**
400, rue Saint-Paul est, Montréal, QC H2Y 1H4
Tél: 514-282-8670; *Téléc:* 514-282-8672
info@marguerite-bourgeoys.com
www.marguerite-bourgeoys.com
Chapelle, musée d'histoire, et site archéologique; programmation diversifiée, visites guidées, boutique, location des salles.
Danielle Dubois, Director General

***Montréal:* Écomusée du fier monde**
2050, rue Amherst, Montréal, QC H2L 3L8
Tél: 514-528-8444; *Téléc:* 514-528-8686
ecomusee@globetrotter.net
www.ecomusee.qc.ca
Highlights the history of the Centre-Sud heritage since 1980 which is a mircososm of the industrial revoltuion which took place in Canada during the latter half of the 19th century.

***Montréal:* Insectarium de Montréal / Montreal Insectarium**
4581, rue Sherbrooke est, Montréal, QC H1X 2B2
Tél: 514-872-1400; *Téléc:* 514-872-0662
insectarium@ville.montreal.qc.ca
www.ville.montreal.qc.ca/insectarium
Largest insectarium in North America; 140,000 scientific specimens collection; 20,000 exhibition collection (including 4,000 on public display); about 100 species of arthropods live collection

***Montréal:* Lieu historique national de Sir George-Etienne Cartier**
***Also known as:* Maison Cartier**
458, Notre-Dame est, Montréal, QC H2Y 1C8
Tel: 514-283-2282; *Fax:* 514-283-5560
Toll-Free: 888-773-8888
parkscanada-que@pc.qc.ca
Other contact information: TDD:1-866-558-2950
Commemorates the life and accomplishments of Sir George-Étienne Cartier; Cartier family homes; performances and re-enactments that vary depending on season; Open March - December
Thomas Piché, Régisseur

***Montréal:* Maison de la poste/Post Office House**
1250, rue Université, Montréal, QC H3B 3B0
Tel: 514-846-5401

***Montréal:* Maison de Mère d'Youville**
138, rue Saint-Pierre, Montréal, QC H2Y 2L7
Tél: 514-842-9411; *Téléc:* 514-842-7855
asscong@sgm.qc.ca
www.sgm.qc.ca/sqm
Founded: 1981 Ancien couvent des Soeurs Grises; l'hospice et le couvent restauré en 1981; la chapelle mise en valeur en 1991; les anciens magasins-entrepôts rénovés; par rendez-vous.
Sr. Jacqueline St-Yves

***Montréal:* Maison Saint-Gabriel**
2146, Place Dublin, Montréal, QC H3K 2A2
Tél: 514-935-8136; *Téléc:* 514-935-5692
msgrcip@globetrotter.qc.ca
www.maisonsaint-gabriel.qc.ca
Founded: 1966 La Maison est la maison d'accueil des Filles du Roy et pendant 300 ans, la maison de ferme de la Congrégation de Notre-Dame; un exemple de l'architecture du Régime français; expositions qui expliquent le rôle de Marguerite Bourgeoys et la vie à la colonie de l'Ile de Montréal pendant le 17e siècle; jardin; visites guidées.
Madeleine Juneau, Directrice générale

***Montréal:* Montréal History Centre / Centre d'histoire de Montréal**
***Also known as:* Fire Station**
335, Place d'Youville, Montréal, QC H2Y 3T1
Tel: 514-872-3207; *Fax:* 514-872-9645
chm@ville.montreal.qc.ca
www2.ville.montreal.qc.ca/chm/engl/centre-doca. shtm
Founded: 1983 This city museum is located in an old firehall. Here Montreal's story is told through exhibits, models, sets, videos and 8,000 photographs from 1642 until today.

***Montréal:* The Montréal Holocaust Memorial Centre / Le Centre commémoratif de l'Holocauste à Montréal**
Maison Cummings, 5151, ch. de la Côte-Sainte-Catherine, Montréal, QC H3W 1M6
Tel: 514-345-2605; *Fax:* 514-344-2651
info@mhmc.ca
www.mhmc.ca
To collect, research & preserve historical, cultural & ethnographic material related to Jewish communities in Europe & North Africa which fell under Nazi rule
Alice Herscovitch, Executive Director

***Montréal:* Musée de BMO Banque de Montréal / BMO Bank of Montreal Museum**
129, rue St-Jacques, Montréal, QC H2Y 1L6
Tél: 514-877-6810; *Téléc:* 514-877-7341
yolaine.toussaint@bmo.com
The office of the Cashier of Canada's oldest banking institution is recreated; open year round (closed on non-banking days); free, self-guided tour
Yolaine Toussaint, Archivist

***Montréal:* Musée de L'Oratoire Saint-Joseph du Mont-Royal / Museum of Saint Joseph Oratory of Mount-Royal**
3800, ch Queen Mary, Montréal, QC H3V 1H6
Tél: 514-733-8211; *Téléc:* 514-733-9735
Ligne sans frais: 877-672-8647
pelerinage@osj.qc.ca
www.saint-joseph.org
Founded: 1955 Le musée se consacre à l'art chrétien et à l'histoire et le patrimoine québécoise; expositions thématiques. L'Oratoire mise en valeur la vie et l'oeuvre de frère André; visites commentées; boutique; bibliothèque/archives/centre de recherche.
André Bergeron, Directeur

***Montréal:* Musée des Hospitalières de l'Hôtel-Dieu de Montréal**
201, av des Pins ouest, Montréal, QC H2W 1R5
Tél: 514-849-2919; *Téléc:* 514-849-4199
museehospitalieres@bellnet.ca
www.museedeshospitalieres.qc.ca
Founded: 1992 Le musée introduit l'histoire des Hospitalières de Saint-Joseph et des Hospitalières de l'Hôtel-Dieu; exposition permanent; programmation et activités; boutique; salles de conférence à louer; 20 000 objets; archives.
Louise Verdant, Directrice générale

***Montréal:* Musée des ondes Émile Berliner**
1050, rue Lacasse, local C-220, Montréal, QC H4C 2Z3
Tél: 514-932-9663
info@berliner.montreal.museum
www.berliner.montreal.museum
Founded: 1996 Émile Berliner a inventé le gramophone, le disque horizontal, et la matrice pour imprimer les disques. Le musée possède plus de 30 000 objets et se consacre à l'histoire de l'industrie des ondes; archives; activités.

***Montréal:* Musée du Château Ramezay / Château Ramezay Museum**
280, rue Notre-Dame est, Montréal, QC H2Y 1C5
Tél: 514-861-3708; *Téléc:* 514-861-8317
info@chateauramezay.qc.ca
www.chateauramezay.qc.ca
Founded: 1895 Le musée est consacré à la conservation, et la mise en valeur d'une collection axée sur l'histoire de Montréal et du Québec; plus de 25 000 objets, oeuvres d'art, artefacts ethnologiques et archéologiques, objets numismatiques; photographies; meubles; costumes; bibliothèque; jardin; boutique; café.
André J. Delisle, Directeur général/Conservateur

***Montréal:* Musée du Château-Dufresne**
2929, av Jeanne-d'Arc, Montréal, QC H1W 3W2
Tél: 514-259-9201; *Téléc:* 514-259-6466
spoirier@chateaudufresne.com
www.chateaudufresne.com
Le Château, construit entre 1915 et 1918 pour servir de résidence aux frères Oscar et Marius Dufresne, met en pratique les principes du style Beaux-Arts. Programmation culturelle; visites guidées; expositions; salles à louer pour réceptions.
Mr. Paul Labonne, Directeur général, plabonne@chateaudufresne.com

***Montréal:* Musée du Cinéma/Cinémathèque québécoise**
335, boul de la Maisonneuve est, Montréal, QC H2X 1K1
Tél: 514-842-9763; *Téléc:* 514-842-1816
info@cinematheque.qc.ca
www.cinematheque.qc.ca
Founded: 1963 La Cinémathèque a le mandat de conserver, documenter et mettre en valeur le patrimoine cinématographique et télévisuel national et international.
Yolande Racine, Directrice générale

***Montréal:* Musée Édouard-Dubeau**
Université de Montréal, #D-129, 2900, rue Édouard-Montpetit, Montréal, QC H3C 3J7
Tél: 514-343-6750; *Téléc:* 514-343-2233
rueld@medent.umontreal.ca
History of dentistry in Québec

***Montréal:* Musée Juste pour rire**
2111, boul Saint-Laurent, Montréal, QC H2X 2T5
Tél: 514-845-4000; *Téléc:* 514-849-5462
probitaille@hahaha.com
musee.hahaha.com
Founded: 1993 Le musée est consacré à la reconnaissance du rire et de l'humeur comme phénomènes culturels de civilisation; centre d'expositions thématiques; espace multifonctionnel pour des événements publics, corporatifs, ou privés; activités et spectacles pour enfants.
Stéphanie Lirette, Directrice

***Montréal:* Musée Marc-Aurèle Fortin**
118, rue St-Pierre, Montréal, QC H2Y 2L7
Tel: 514-845-6108; *Fax:* 514-845-6100
mafortin@museemafortin.org
www.museemafortin.org
Founded: 1984 L'oeuvre prodigieuse de Marc-Aurèle Fortin, grand peinture québécois.
Jacqueline Sabourin, Directrice

***Montréal:* Le Musée Stewart au Fort de l'Ile Sainte-Hélène / The Stewart Museum at the Fort Ile Sainte-Hélène**
CP 1200 A, Montréal, QC H3C 2Y9
Tél: 514-861-6701; *Téléc:* 514-284-0123
info@stewart-museum.org
stewart-museum.org
Fermeture temporaire; l'exposition permanente renouvelée du musée sera accessible au public dès l'automne 2010; activités scolaires et culturelles.
Bruce D. Bolton, Directeur
Guy Vadeboncoeur, Conservateur

***Montréal:* Phonothèque québécoise, Musée du son**
335, boul de Maisonneuve est, Montréal, QC H2X 1K1
Tél: 514-282-0703; *Téléc:* 514-282-0019
phono@bellnet.ca
www.phonotheque.org
histoire des archives sonores, de l'industrie du disque, etc. History of sound archives, sound recording and radio industry.
Alcée Penet, Secrétaire de la Phonothèque québécoise

***Montréal:* Redpath Museum**
McGill University, 859, rue Sherbrooke ouest, Montréal, QC H3A 2K6
Tel: 514-398-4086; *Fax:* 514-398-3185
redpath.museum@mcgill.ca
www.mcgill.ca/redpath
Extensive collections in paleontology, mineralogy, zoology & ethnology; family workshop series "Discovery Workshop"
Dr. David M. Green, Director

***Montréal:* Royal Canadian Ordnance Corps Museum**
***Also known as:* RCOC Museum**
Longue-Pointe Garrison, CP 4000 K, 6560, rue Hochlega, Montréal, QC H1N 3R9
Tél: 514-252-2777
www.rcocmuseum.com/RCOCMuseum.html
Founded: 1962 An accredited military museum of the Department of National Defence, the Royal Canadian Ordnance Corps Museum depicts the historical mission of the Royal Canadian Ordnance Corps, & other pre-unification support elements of the Canadian Army, the RCAF, & the RCN. These service elements united in 1968 to create the Logistics Branch of the Canadian Forces. The collection of the RCOC Museum is housed in a 1943 building, which originally served as Longue-Pointe Garrison's St-Barbara Catholic & Protestant chapels.
LCol (ret'd) Al Truelove, Director & President, Royal Canadian Ordnance Corps Museum Committee
Andrew Gregory, Curator PhD, agregory17@cogeco.ca
Jacques Monast, Technical Advisor

***Montréal:* Univers Maurice Rocket Richard Universe**
2800, rue Viau, Montréal, QC H1V 3J3
Tél: 514-872-6666; *Téléc:* 514-872-6928

***Mont-Saint-Grégoire:* Centre d'interprétation du milieu écologique du Haut-Richelieu**
16, ch du Sous-Bois, Mont-Saint-Grégoire, QC J3B 6Z5
Tél: 450-346-0406
services@cimehautrichelieu.qc.ca
www.cimehautrichelieu.qc.ca
A pour mission la conservation du Mont-Saint-Grégoire, et d'autres sites naturels dans la région du Haut-Richelieu
Renée Gagnon, Directice générale

***Mont-Saint-Hilaire:* Maison amérindienne**
510, Montée des Trente, Mont-Saint-Hilaire, QC J3H 2R8
Tél: 450-464-2500; *Téléc:* 450-464-0071
info@maisonamerindienne.com
www.maisonamerindienne.com
Founded: 2000 Un lieu d'échanges, de partage et de rapprochement des peuples à travers des activités culturelles (expositions, contes et légendes, conférences), environnementales et gastronomiques; seul site multinations, situé dans une érablière.
André Michel, Fondateur

***New Richmond:* Gaspesian British Heritage Village**
351, boul Perron ouest, New Richmond, QC G0C 2B0
Tel: 418-392-4487; *Fax:* 418-392-5907
heritagevillage@globetrotter.net
www.gaspesianvillage.com
British heritage in Gaspé from 1760 to 1900s; June 24th - Aug. 22nd
Mike Geraghty, President

***Nicolet:* Musée des religions du monde**
900, boul Louis-Fréchette, Nicolet, QC J3T 1V5
Tél: 819-293-6148; *Téléc:* 819-293-4161
musee@museedesreligions.qc.ca
www.museedesreligions.qc.ca
Le musée se consacre à l'histoire des rites religieux du bouddhisme, de l'hindouisme, de l'islam, du judaïsme, et du christianisme; location de salle; boutique; programmation et activités; les installations du musée sont adaptées pour les personnes à mobilité réduite.
Jean-François Royal, Directeur

***Nicolet:* Musée historique des Soeurs de l'Assomption de la Sainte Vierge**
Pavillon Leduc, 251, rue St-Jean-Baptiste, Nicolet, QC J3T 1X9
Tél: 819-293-2011; *Téléc:* 819-293-8315
musee@sasv.ca
www.musee-soeurs-assomption.net
Founded: 1979 Collection permanente du patrimoine des fondatrices et des fondateurs de la Congrégation; costume religieux; tableaux; meubles; instruments de musique; sculptures; objets liturgiques.
Sr. Gisèle Saint-Louis, Directrice

***Notre-Dame-de-l'Ile-Perrot:* Parc historique Pointe-du-Moulin**
2500, boul Don-Quichotte, Notre-Dame-de-l'Ile-Perrot, QC J7V 7P2
Tél: 514-453-5936; *Téléc:* 514-453-1473
moulin@netrevolution.com
www.pointedumoulin.com

***Notre-Dame-du-Nord:* Centre thématique fossilifère du lac Témiscamingue / Lake Timiskaming Fossil Centre**
CP 296, 5, rue Principale, Notre-Dame-du-Nord, QC J0Z 3B0
Tél: 819-723-2500; *Téléc:* 819-723-2369
musee@fossiles.qc.ca
www.fossiles.qc.ca
A pour mission de mettre en valeur la période Orodovicien-Silurien dans la région; recherche; expositions; boutique.
Andrée Nault, Directrice

***Nouvelle:* Musée d'histoire naturelle du parc de Miguasha**
231, rte Miguasha ouest, Nouvelle, QC G0C 2E0
Tél: 418-794-2475; *Téléc:* 418-794-2033
parc.miguasha@sepaq.com

***Odanak:* Musée des Abénakis**
Société historique d'Odanak, 108, Waban-Aki, Odanak, QC J0G 1H0
Tél: 450-568-2600; *Téléc:* 450-568-5959
info@museedesabenakis.ca
www.museedesabenakis.ca
Ouvert en 1962 et complètement rénové en 2005, le premier musée amérindien au Québec vous souhaite la bienvenue. Au coeur d'un site historique, un ensemble d'activité est offert pour plaire à toute la famille. Spectacle multimédia, expositions, belvédère, église catholique, chapelle et aire de pique-nique rendront la visite inoubliable.
Michelle Bélanger, Directrice générale

***Otterburn Park:* Muséobus - Le Musée des enfants**
760, ch des Patriotes, Otterburn Park, QC J3H 1Z5
Tél: 450-464-0201; *Téléc:* 450-446-4644
info@museobus.qc.ca
www.museobus.qc.ca
Musée mobile aménagé dans des autobus scolaires; propose des expositions scientifiques interactives et des sentiers d'interprétation; piste d'hébertisme et aire de pique-nique; programmation; Camp Éco Nature.

***Pabos Mills:* Centre d'interprétation du Parc du Bourg de Pabos**
75, rue de la Plage, Pabos Mills, QC G0C 2J0
Tél: 418-689-6043; *Téléc:* 418-689-4240
bourg@globetrotter.net
www.lebourgdepabos.com
Promouvoir l'histoire de la seule seigneurie de la Nouvelle-France à exploiter commercialement la pêche; ouvert tous le jours, juin-septembre.

***Paspébiac:* Site historique du Banc-de-Pêche-de-Paspébiac**
CP 430, 3e rue, rte du Banc, Paspébiac, QC G0C 2K0
Tél: 418-752-6229; *Téléc:* 418-752-6408
shbp@globetrotter.net
www.shbp.ca
Sea heritage & traditional trades; tours; gift shop; restaurant; open June - Oct.

***Percé:* Centre d'interprétation du Parc national de l'Ile-Bonaventure et du Rocher-Percé**
4, rue du Quai, Percé, QC G0C 2L0
Tél: 418-782-2240; *Téléc:* 418-782-2241
parc.ibrperce@sepaq.com
www.sepaq.com
A pour mission de protéger un refuge d'oiseaux migrateurs, et le patrimoine historique de la région
Rémi Plourde, Directeur

***Percé:* Musée Le Chafaud**
145, rte 132, Percé, QC G0C 2L0
Tél: 418-782-5100; *Téléc:* 418-782-5565
lebjl@globetrotter.net

***Péribonka:* Musée Louis-Hémon**
700, rte Maria-Chapdelaine, Péribonka, QC G0W 2G0
Tél: 418-374-2177; *Téléc:* 418-374-2516
museelh@destination.ca
museelh.destination.ca/
Chantale Simard, Directrice

***La Pocatière:* Musée François-Pilote**
100, 4e av, La Pocatière, QC G0R 1Z0
Tél: 418-856-3145; *Téléc:* 418-856-5611
museefpilote@leadercsa.com
www.leadercsa.com/museefrancoispilote
Founded: 1973 Voir la paroisse rurale d'autrefois sous tous ses aspects, des salles reconstituées d'habitations, de bureaux de professionnels et d'artisans, une collection de sciences naturelles, agriculture et sciences pures, enseignement agricole; expositions; programmes scolaires; rampe d'acces et ascenseur disponible.
Paul-André Leclerc, Directeur général

***Pointe-à-la-Croix:* Battle of the Restigouche National Historic Site of Canada**
PO Box 359, rte 132, Pointe-à-la-Croix, QC G0C 1L0
Tel: 418-788-5676; *Fax:* 418-788-5895
Toll-Free: 888-773-8888
parkscanada-que @pc.gc.ca
www.pc.gc.ca/eng/lhn-nhs/qc/ristigouche/index.aspx
Other contact information: TDD: 1-866-787-6221
Located at the mouth of the Restigouche River, the Battle of the Restigouche National Historic Site is the scene of the last naval battle between France & England for possession of North America in 1760. Visitors to the site can see the vestiges of the vessel, The Machault, as well as several artifacts from the wreck. The national historic site is open daily from June to mid-October.

***La Prairie:* Société d'histoire de la Prairie de la Magdeleine**
249, rue Sainte-Marie, La Prairie, QC J5R 1G1
Tél: 450-659-1393
histoire@laprairie-shlm.com
Historical society active in the areas of genealogy, historical research & guided tours
René Jolicoeur, Président

***Québec:* Centre d'interprétation de Place-Royale**
27, rue Notre-Dame, Québec, QC G1K 4E9
Tél: 418-646-3167; *Téléc:* 418-646-9705
Ligne sans frais: 866-710-8031
mcqweb@mcq.org
www.mcq.org/fr/cipr/
Founded: 1999 Site historique; le Centre est situé au premier établissement français permanent en Amérique; expositions, visites commentées, animations historiques, espace découverte, activités éducatives, ateliers.

***Québec:* Centre d'interprétation du Vieux-Port-de-Québec / Old Port of Québec Interpretation Centre**
CP 2474, 100, Quai Saint-André, Québec, QC G1K 7R3
Tél: 418-648-3300; *Téléc:* 418-648-3678
Ligne sans frais: 888-773-8888
parkscanada-que@pc.gc.ca
www.pc.gc.ca/vieuxport
Histoire du Vieux-Port-de-Québec au 19e siècle; expositions; ateliers interactifs; présentations audio-visuelles; visites guidées extérieures et intérieures
Nicole Ouellet, Responsable

***Québec:* La Citadelle de Québec & Le Musée du Royal 22e Régiment**
La Citadelle, 1, côte de la Citadelle, Québec, QC G1R 4V7
Tél: 418-694-2815; *Téléc:* 418-694-2853
information@lacitadelle.qc.ca
www.lacitadelle.qc.ca
Founded: 1980 Située sur le Cap Diamant, La Citadelle est un site du patrimoine mondial de l'UNESCO, et la résidence officielle du Royal 22e Régiment. Le musée offre des visites guidées, activités, et collections d'artefacts militaires (médailles, insignes, uniformes et textiles, armes).
Jocelyne Milot, Directrice

***Québec:* Lieu historique national du Canada Cartier-Brébeuf / Cartier-Brébeuf National Historic Site of Canada**
CP 10 B, 175, rue de l'Espinay, Québec, QC G1K 7A1
Tél: 418-648-4038; *Téléc:* 418-948-9181
Ligne sans frais: 888-773-8888
parcscanada-que@pc.gc.ca
www.pc.gc.ca/fra/lhn-nhs/qc/cartierbrebeuf
Commémore l'hivernage de Jacques Cartier et de ses compagnons en 1535-1536, à proximité du village iroquoïen de Stadaconé; activités.
Linda Bernier, Contact

***Québec:* Lieu historique national du Canada de la Grosse-Ile-et-le-Mémorial-des-Irlandais / Grosse-Ile & the Irish Memorial National Historic Site of C**
CP 10 B, 2, rue d'Auteuil, Québec, QC G1K 7R3
Tél: 418-248-8841; *Téléc:* 866-790-8991
Ligne sans frais: 888-773-8888
parcscanada-que@pc.gc.ca
www.pc.gc.ca/fra/lhn-nhs/qc/grosseile
Commémore l'importance de l'immigration au Canada, plus particulièrement via la porte d'entrée de Québec, et les événements tragiques vécus par les immigrants irlandais en ce lieu, notamment l'épidémie de typhus de 1847.

***Québec:* Lieu historique national du Canada des Fortifications-de-Québec / Fortifications of Québec National Historic Site of Canada**
CP 10 B, 2, rue d'Auteuil, Québec, QC G1K 7A1
Tél: 418-648-7016; *Téléc:* 418-648-2506
Ligne sans frais: 888-773-8888
www.pc.gc.ca/fra/lhn-nhs/qc/fortifications
Trésor de l'UNESCO; la Citadelle et ses environs, terrasse Dufferin, Château Frontnac; visites guidées.
Nicole Ouellet, Régisseure

***Québec:* Lieu historique national du Canada des Forts-de-Lévis**
***Also known as:* Fort Numéro-Un/Fort No.1**
CP 2474 Terminus, 41, ch du Gouvernement, Québec, QC G1K 7R3
Tél: 418-835-5182; *Téléc:* 418-835-5443
Ligne sans frais: 800-463-6769

***Québec:* Maison Henry-Stuart**
82, Grande Allée ouest, Québec, QC G1R 2G6
Tél: 418-647-4347; *Téléc:* 418-647-6483
Ligne sans frais: 800-494-4347
cmsq@cmsq.qc.ca
www.cmsq.qc.ca/mhs
Construite en 1849, la maison représente un exemple d'un type d'habitation courant aux 19e siècle à Québec; collection d'objets, meubles; visites thématiques; jardin.

***Québec:* Musée Bon-Pasteur**
14, rue Couillard, Québec, QC G1R 3S9
Tél: 418-694-0243; *Téléc:* 418-694-6233
info@museebonpasteur.com
www.museebonpasteur.com
Founded: 1992 L'histoire de la Congrégation des Servantes du Coeur Immaculé de Marie (Soeurs du Bon-Pasteur de Québec); condition féminine au XIXe siècle; meubles et peintures d'époque; visites personnalisées en français et en anglais (portugais sur demande)
Claudette Ledet, Directrice

***Québec:* Musée de géologie René-Bureau**
Pavillon Adrien Pouliot, Université Laval, Québec, QC G1K 7P4
Tél: 418-656-2131; *Téléc:* 418-656-7339
alevesqu@ggl.ulaval.ca
40,000 geological specimens
André Lévesque, Conservateur du musée

***Québec:* Musée des Augustines de l'Hôtel-Dieu de Québec**
32, rue Charlevoix, Québec, QC G1R 5C4
Tél: 418-692-2492; *Téléc:* 418-692-2668
mahdq@augustines.ca
www.augustines.ca
Founded: 1958 Tableaux canadiens et européens, meubles, vaisselle, broderies, instruments médicaux. Le musée est en réaménagement et est fermée jusqu'en 2011.
S. Nicole Perron, Directrice du Musée AMJ

***Québec:* Musée des Ursulines de Québec**
12, rue Donnacona, Québec, QC G1R 3Y7
Tél: 418-694-0694; *Téléc:* 418-694-2136
murq@vmuq.com
www.ursulines-uc.com
Le musée met en valeur la collection pédagogique des Ursulines de Québec; documents; instruments de musique; objets scientifiques; spécimens d'histoire naturelle; photographies; broderies; tableaux.
Christine Turgeon, Directrice

***Québec:* Musée Naval de Québec / Naval Museum of Québec**
***Also known as:* Musée naval Stanislas-Déry**
170, rue Dalhousie, Québec, QC G1K 8M7
Tél: 418-694-5387; *Téléc:* 418-694-5550
info@museenavaldequebec.com
www.museenavaldequebec.com
Le musée a pour mission de conserver et communiquer l'histoire navale du Saint-Laurent, et de la Réserve navale du Canada.

***Québec:* Parc des Champs-de-Bataille nationaux / National Battlefields Park**
390, av de Bernières, Québec, QC G1R 2L7
Tél: 418-648-4071; *Téléc:* 418-648-3809
information@ccbn-nbc.gc.ca
www.ccbn-nbc.gc.ca
Les Plaines d'Abraham; Parc des Braves; Maison de la découverte des plaines d'Abraham; Exposition multimédia Odyssée Canada; Tours Martello; Souper mystère de 1814 à la tour Martello 2; Bus d'Abraham: tour guidé des plaines d'Abraham, Maison patrimoniale Louis S.-St-Laurent, Kiosque Edwin-Bélanger, Jardin Jeanne d'Arc
Michel Leullier, Directeur

***Québec:* Site patrimonial du Parc-de-L'Artillerie**
***Also known as:* Parc-de-L'Artillerie**
CP 10 B, 2, rue d'Auteuil, Québec, QC G1K 7A1
Tél: 418-648-7016; *Téléc:* 418-648-2506
Ligne sans frais: 888-773-8888
parcscanada-que@pc.gc.ca
www.pc.gc.ca/fra/lhn-nhs/qc/artiller/index.aspx

***Richmond:* Centre d'interprétation de l'ardoise**
5, rue Belmont, Richmond, QC J0B 2H0
Tél: 819-826-3313; *Téléc:* 819-826-5757
ardoise@globetrotter.net
www.centreardoise.ca; www.townshipsheritage.com
Founded: 1992 A pour mission de promouvoir le patrimoine de l'ardoise dans la vallée du Saint-Françcois; le centre est logé dans une église presbytérienne construite en 1889, ayant une toiture en ardoise; métiers, techniques et divers usages de cette pierre; histoires de l'industrie sont racontées
Denise Lupien

***Rimouski:* Musée régional de Rimouski**
35, rue Saint-Germain ouest, Rimouski, QC G5L 4B4
Tél: 418-724-2272; *Téléc:* 418-725-4433
mrdr@globetrotter.net
www.museerimouski.qc.ca
Le musée, qui loge dans la plus ancienne église de pierre de la région, présente des collections thématiques sur l'art contemporain, histoire et sciences; oeuvres et artefacts; guides interprétifs; activités.
Franck Michel, Directeur général

***Rimouski:* Site historique maritime de la Pointe-au-Père**
1000, rue du Phare, Rimouski, QC G5M 1L8
Tél: 418-724-6214; *Téléc:* 418-721-0815
www.shmp.qc.ca
Founded: 1980 Le musée regroupe les artefacts du navire l'Empress of Ireland, et met en valeur le Phare-de-Pointe-au-Père et le sous-marin ONONDAGA, désarmé par la Défense nationale en 2000.

***Rimouski-Est:* Site historique de la Maison Lamontagne**
707, boul du Rivage, Rimouski-Est, QC G5L 1E9
Tél: 418-722-4038; *Téléc:* 418-722-4038
maisonlamontagne@globetrotter.net
www.maisonlamontagne.com
Open - 24 juin - 5 sept.
Fanny Côté, Directrice

***Rivière-du-Loup:* Musée des bateaux miniatures et de légendes du Bas-Saint-Laurent**
80, boul Cartier, Rivière-du-Loup, QC G5R 2M9
Tél: 418-868-0800; *Téléc:* 418-856-1815
Ligne sans frais: 866-868-0800
info@museedebateauxminiatures.com
www.museedebateauxminiatures.com
Exposition de 160 bateaux miniatures faits par 20 artistes de la région; boutique souvenir; petite galerie d'art; visites guidées.

***Rivière-du-Loup:* Musée du Bas-St-Laurent**
300, rue St-Pierre, Rivière-du-Loup, QC G5R 3V3
Tél: 418-862-7547; *Téléc:* 418-862-3019
musee@mbsl.qc.ca
www.mbsl.qc.ca
Founded: 1975 Consacré à la photographie ethnologique, art moderne, et à l'éducation; conservation, recherche, et diffusion; plus de 2 000 objets ethnologiques, et plus de 300 objets d'art; plus de 125 000 photographies anciennes; expositions itinérantes; publication; boutique; location de salles.
Pierre Landry, Directeur général

***Rivière-Éternite:* Centre de découverte et de services Le Béluga (secteur Baie Sainte-Marguerite)**
Parc National du Saguenay, 91, rue Notre-Dame, Rivière-Éternite, QC G0V 1P0
Tél: 418-272-1556; *Téléc:* 418-272-1516
Ligne sans frais: 800-665-6527
parc.saguenay@sepaq.com
www.sepaq.com/pq/sag/fr/interpretation.html
Exposition permanente "Baie comme bélugas"; l'histoire et l'importance de protéger le béluga dans son milieu naturel; activités de découverte.

***Rivière-Éternite:* Centre de découverte et de services le Fjord du Saguenay (secteur de la Baie-Éternité)**
Parc National du Saguenay, 91, rue Notre-Dame, Rivière-Éternite, QC G0P 1P0
Tél: 418-272-1556; *Téléc:* 418-272-3438
parc.saguenay@sepaq.com
www.sepaq.com/pq/sag/fr/interpretation.html
Découvrez les secrets du fjord; exposition permanente

***Rouyn-Noranda:* La Maison Dumulon**
CP 242, 191, av du Lac, Rouyn-Noranda, QC J9X 5C3
Tél: 819-797-7125; *Téléc:* 819-797-7109
maison.dumulon@rouyn-noranda.ca
www.maison-dumulon.ca
Founded: 1980 La maison de la famille Dumulon est une reconstitution fidèle du bâtiment d'origine; visites guidées; animation; activités spéciales; location de salles; boutique. L'église orthodoxe russe Saint-Georges est administrée par la Corporation de La maison Dumulon.
Geneviève C. Gauthier, Directrice

***Saguenay:* Musée du Fjord**
3346, boul de la Grande-Baie sud, Saguenay, QC G7G 1B2
Tél: 418-697-5077; *Téléc:* 418-697-5079
Ligne sans frais: 866-697-5077
info@museedufjord.com
www.museedufjord.com
Founded: 1960 Consacré à la préservation et la mise en valeur du patrimoine historique, naturel et artistique du territoire du fjord du Saguenay; exposition permanente; expositions temporaires thématiques; programmation; artefacts historiques; photographies; documents.
Guylaine Simard, Directrice

***Saint-André-Avellin:* Musée des Pionniers de Saint-André-Avellin**
20, rue Bourgeois, Saint-André-Avellin, QC J0V 1W0
Tél: 819-983-2624; *Téléc:* 819-983-3702
www.petite-nation.qc.ca/patrimoine/musee.html
Relate la vie rurale des 19e et 20e siècles; meubles, objets, outils et machines en expositions; livres du XIXe siècle; photographies.
Raymond Whissell, Sec.-Très.

***Saint-André-d'Argenteuil:* Musée régional d'Argenteuil / Caserne-de-Carillon - Lieu historique national du Canada**
44, rte du Long-Sault, Saint-André-d'Argenteuil, QC J0V 1X0
Tél: 450-537-1893
info@museearg.com
Historical exhibitions: 8 exhibition rooms
Noreen Lowe, Registrar
Jean-Claude de Guire, Curator

***Saint-Constant:* Exporail: Musée ferroviaire canadien / Exporail: Canadian Railway Museum**
110, rue St-Pierre, Saint-Constant, QC J5A 1G7
Tel: 450-638-1522; *Fax:* 450-638-1563
info@exporail.org
www.exporail.org
Canada's largest collection of railway equipment (150 vehicles, a turntable, 2 train stations, a new exhibit pavilion)
Marie-Claude Reid, Director

***Sainte-Anne-de-Beaupré:* Musée de Sainte-Anne-de-Beaupré**
9803, boul Sainte-Anne, Sainte-Anne-de-Beaupré, QC G0A 3C0
Tél: 418-827-6873; *Téléc:* 418-827-6870
musee@ssadb.qc.ca
www.sanctuairesainteanne.org
Le musée retrace l'histoire d'un pèlerinage et rend hommage à la Vierge Marie; expositions permanentes et temporaires; visites guidées; jardins; magasin du Sanctuaire.

***Sainte-Foy:* Maison Hamel-Bruneau**
CP 218, 2608, ch Saint-Louis, Sainte-Foy, QC G1V 1N2
Tél: 418-641-6280; *Téléc:* 418-654-4151
patrimoinestefoysillery@ville.quebec.qc.ca
www.ville.quebec.qc.ca; www.paricilavisite.qc.ca
Construit vers 1857; maison historique abrite un centre de diffusion culturelle; programmation thématique variée; concerts; activités; jardins, aire de pique-nique.

***Sainte-Foy:* Musée de géologie**
Université Laval, Département de géologie, Pavillon Adrien-Pouliot, Cité Universitaire, Sainte-Foy, QC G1K 7P4
Tel: 418-656-2131; *Fax:* 418-656-7339
alevesqu@ggl.ulaval.ca
André Lévesque, Conservateur

***Sainte-Marie:* Maison J.A. Vachon**
383, rue de la Coopérative, Sainte-Marie, QC G6E 3X5
Tél: 418-387-4052; *Téléc:* 418-387-2454
Ligne sans frais: 866-387-4052
ville.sainte-marie.qc.ca; vachon.com
Canada's largest snack cake factory; open Apr. 1-Oct. 31, Mon.-Fri.; weekends (June 24-Sept. 3)
Bernard Thibault

***Saint-Eustache:* Moulin Légaré / Légaré Mill**
232, rue St-Eustache, Saint-Eustache, QC J7R 2L7
Tél: 450-974-5400; *Téléc:* 450-974-5219
info@corporationdumoulinlegare.com
www.corporationdumoulinlegare.com
Founded: 1975 This 1762 flour mill has never once stopped working since its completion. The miller produces wheat and buckwheat flour with the original millstones and flour is sold on site. Activities are available for students.
Ms Mélanie Séguin, Director, 450-974-5001 X-5203, mseguin@corporationdumoulinlegare.com

***Saint-Eustache:* Musée de Saint-Eustache et de ses Patriotes**
235, rue Saint-Eustache, Saint-Eustache, QC J7R 2L8
Tél: 450-974-5170; *Téléc:* 450-974-5174
musee@ville.saint-eustache.qc.ca
ville.saint-eustache.qc.ca/tourisme2003 /musee_patriotes.htm

***Saint-Hyacinthe:* Musée du Centre Élisabeth-Bergeron**
805, av Raymond, Saint-Hyacinthe, QC J2S 5T9
Tél: 450-773-6067; *Téléc:* 450-773-8044
ceb@sjsh.org
www.sjsh.org
Présente la vie et l'oeuvre de la fondatrice des Soeurs de Saint-Joseph-de-Saint-Hyacinthe; l'histoire d'une communauté de religieuses enseignantes, fondée en terre Maskoutaine; quatre salles d'exposition, visite commentée comprenant une présentation audiovisuelle, un arrêt au tombeau de la vénérable Élisabeth Bergeron ainsi qu'à la chapelle; ouvert tous les jours.

***Saint-Hyacinthe:* Musée du séminaire de Saint-Hyacinthe**
650, rue Girouard est, Saint-Hyacinthe, QC J2S 7B7
Tél: 450-774-0203; *Téléc:* 450-774-7101
Cash_ntic.qc.ca
Museum of natural sciences, archeology, ethnology, religious heritage & works of art

***Saint-Jean-Port-Joli:* Musée de sculpture sur bois des Anciens Canadiens**
CP 66, 332, av de Gaspé ouest, Saint-Jean-Port-Joli, QC G0R 3G0
Tél: 418-598-3392; *Téléc:* 418-598-3329
info@museedesancienscanadiens.com
www.museedesancienscanadiens.com
Collection de plus de 250 sculptures originales, et un vidéo sur la sculpture sur bois et sur neige. Le musée est ouvert du mai jusqu'au novembre.
Camile Michaud
Jean-Guy Desjardins
Denis Michaud

***Saint-Jean-sur-Richelieu:* Musée du Haut-Richelieu**
***Also known as:* Musée d'histoire et de la céramique québécoise**
182, Jacques-Cartier nord, Saint-Jean-sur-Richelieu, QC J3B 7W3
Tél: 450-347-0649; *Téléc:* 450-347-9994
info@museeduhaut-richelieu.com
www.museeduhaut-richelieu.com
L'histoire du Haut-Richelieu.

***Saint-Joseph-de-Beauce:* Musée Marius Barbeau**
139, rue Sainte-Christine, Saint-Joseph-de-Beauce, QC G0S 2V0
Tél: 418-397-4039; *Téléc:* 418-397-6151
info@museemariusbarbeau.com
www.museemariusbarbeau.com
Le musée a pour mission la conservation, la recherche et la mise en valeur le patrimoine de la Beauce, tant du point de vue historique, ethnologique et artistique.
Lucie Duval, Personne ressource

***Saint-Joseph-de-la-Rive:* Musée maritime de Charlevoix**
CP 1, 305, rue de l'Église, Saint-Joseph-de-la-Rive, QC G0A 3Y0
Tél: 418-635-1131; *Téléc:* 418-635-2600
expom@charlevoix.net
www.musee-maritime-charlevoix.com
Conserve et communique le patrimoine maritime à travers l'histoire des goélettes qui ont naviguées sur le Saint-Laurent; bâtiment central thématique, scierie, atelier et magasin de l'époque; exposition sur l'astroblème; archives; boutique.

***Saint-Joseph-de-la-Rive:* Papeterie Saint-Gilles**
***Also known as:* Economusee(R) du papier**
CP 40, 304, rue Félix Antoine-Savard, Saint-Joseph-de-la-Rive, QC G0A 3Y0
Tél: 418-635-2430; *Téléc:* 418-635-2613
Ligne sans frais: 866-635-2430
papier@papeteriesaintgilles.com
www.papeteriesaintgilles.com
Papier fait à la main, 100% coton, sans acide et chiné de pétales de fleurs de la région, selon des techniques traditionnelles datant du XVIIe siècle

***Saint-Lambert:* Musée du costume et du textile du Québec**
349, Riverside, Saint-Lambert, QC J4P 1A8
Tél: 450-923-6601; *Téléc:* 450-923-6600
info@mctq.org
www.mctq.org
Founded: 1979 Le musée se consacre à la recherche, la conservation, l'éducation, et la diffusion; expositions de costume, textiles, et de la fibre; boutique.
Mme Suzanne Chabot, Directrice générale

***Saint-Prime:* Musée du fromage cheddar**
148, av Albert-Perron, Saint-Prime, QC G8J 1L4
Tél: 418-251-4922; *Téléc:* 418-251-1172
Ligne sans frais: 888-251-4922
cheddar@bellnet.ca
www.museecheddar.org
La vieille Fromagerie Perron est la seule survivante de sa catégorie au Québec. Aujourd'hui transformée en lieu d'interprétation elle vous raconte la fabrication traditionnelle du cheddar; visites guidées; boutique souvenir, vente de fromage; casiers verrouillés pour vélos; ouverte au public juin - sept. et sur réservation pour le reste de l'année.
Mme Diane Hudon, Directrice générale

***Sept-Iles:* Musée Shaputuan / Shaputuan Museum**
290, boul des Montagnais, Sept-Iles, QC G4R 5R2
Tél: 418-962-4000; *Téléc:* 418-962-3131
shaputuan@bbsi.net
www.ville.sept-iles.qc.ca
A pour mission de perpétuer la culture des Innus; le musée s'engage a acquérir, étudier et interpréter la culture; expositions; activités.

***Shawinigan:* Cité de l'Énergie**
CP 156, 1000, av Melville, Shawinigan, QC G9N 6T9
Tél: 819-536-8516; *Téléc:* 819-536-2982
Ligne sans frais: 866-900-2483
infocite@qc.aira.com
www.citedelenergie.com
Centre de sciences, expositions, spectacle multimédia, tour d'observation Hydro-Québec
Robert Trudel

***Shawinigan-Sud:* Église Notre-Dame-de-la-Présentation**
825, av 2e, Shawinigan-Sud, QC G9P 1E1
Tél: 819-536-3652; *Téléc:* 819-536-4170
eglisendp@cgocable.ca
www.eglisendp.qc.ca
Lieu historique national du Canada; protection et mise en valeur des oeuvres de Leduc dans l'église
France St-Amant, Coordonnatrice

***Sherbrooke:* Centre d'interprétation de l'histoire de Sherbrooke**
275, rue Dufferin, Sherbrooke, QC J1H 4M5
Tél: 819-821-5406; *Téléc:* 819-821-5417
info@societehistoire.com
shs.ville.sherbrooke.qc.ca
Founded: 1992 A pour mission de préserver le patrimoine local, et promouvoir l'histoire de Sherbrooke et les Cantons-de-l'Est
Josée Delage, Directrice

***Sherbrooke:* Musée de la nature et des sciences de Sherbrooke**
225, rue Frontenac, Sherbrooke, QC J1H 1K1
Tél: 819-564-3200; *Téléc:* 819-564-7388
Ligne sans frais: 877-434-3200
info@naturesciences.qc.ca
www.naturesciences.qc.ca
Situé dans une ancienne usine de textile, le Musée renferme une collection de près de 100 000 objets dont 65 000 en sciences naturelles; expositions; théâtre d'objets intéractifs sur la fonction du cerveau; services d'animation et d'éducation et une salle multifonctionnelle disponible en location.
Mme Marie-Claude Bibeau, Directrice générale

***Sherbrooke:* Musée Régimentaire les Fusiliers de Sherbrooke**
64, rue Belvédère sud, Sherbrooke, QC J1H 4B4
Tél: 819-564-5940; *Téléc:* 819-564-5641
fusdesherbrooke@videotron.ca
membres.lycos.fr/fusiliers/
Capt. Beaudoin, Conservatrice

***Sillery:* Villa Bagatelle**
1563 ch St-Louis, Sillery, QC G1S 1G1
Tel: 418-681-3010; *Fax:* 418-681-3865
cataraqui@globetrotter.net
www.museocapitale.qc.ca/050a.htm
Exhibition Centre & garden

***Sorel-Tracy:* Biophare**
6, rue St-Pierre, Sorel-Tracy, QC J3P 3S2
Tél: 450-780-5740; *Téléc:* 450-780-5734
Ligne sans frais: 877-780-5740
info@biophare.com
www.biophare.com
Founded: 1994 Dédiée à la réserve de la biosphère du lac Saint-Pierre; présente une exposition permanente "l'observatoire du lac Saint-Pierre"; musée, groupes scolaires, boutique, location de salles.
Marc Mineau, Directeur général

***Stanbridge East:* Missisquoi Museum / Musée Missisquoi**
2 River St., Stanbridge East, QC J0J 2H0
Tel: 450-248-3153; *Fax:* 450-248-0420
info@missisquoimuseum.ca
www.museemissisquoi.ca
Founded: 1964 Museum is house in the 1830 three-story, red brick, Cornell Mill. Exhibitions include Missisquoi County Archives, and explore the historic development of the county. Other buildings on site are the Walbridge Barn and Hodge's General Store.
Pamela Realffe, Executive Secretary
Heather Darch, Curator
Judy Antle, Archivist

***Stanstead:* Stanstead Historical Society / Société Historique de Stanstead**
***Also known as:* Colby-Curtis Museum**
535, rue Dufferin, Stanstead, QC J0B 3E0
Tel: 819-876-7322; *Fax:* 819-876-7936
info@colbycurtis.ca
www.colbycurtis.ca
Founded: 1929 Operates the Colby Curtis Museum & Carrollcroft Property
Pierre Rastoul, Director/Curator

***St-Denis:* Maison Chapais**
CP 70, 2, rte 132 est, St-Denis, QC G0L 2R0
Tél: 418-498-2353; *Téléc:* 418-498-4070
www.maisonchapais.com
Founded: 1990 Monument historique daté de 1834; trois étages et diverses dépendances; réservations préférables pour les groupes; visites guidées de la maison et ses jardins oubliés; galerie-boutique offre cadeaux et souvenirs, livres.
Sylviane Pilote, Directrice générale

***St-Lin-Laurentides:* Lieu historique national du Canada de Sir-Wilfrid-Laurier / Sir Wilfrid Laurier National Historic Site of Canada**
945, 12e av, St-Lin-Laurentides, QC J5M 2W4
Tél: 450-439-3702; *Téléc:* 450-439-5721
Ligne sans frais: 888-787-8888
parcscanada-que@pc.gc.ca
www.pc.gc.ca/fra/lhn-nhs/qc/wilfridlaurier
Centre d'interprétation; exposition présente la vie et l'oeuvre de Sir Wilfrid Laurier.
Thomas Piché, Régisseur

***St-Paul-de-l'Ile-aux-Noix:* Lieu historique national du Canada du Fort-Lennox / Fort Lennox National Historic Site of Canada**
1 - 61st Ave., St-Paul-de-l'Ile-aux-Noix, QC J0J 1G0
Tél: 450-291-5700; *Téléc:* 450-291-4389
Ligne sans frais: 888-773-8888
parcscanada-que @pc.gc.ca
www.pc.gc.ca/fra/lhn-nhs/qc/lennox
Visites guidées; activités; caserne, poudrière, corps de garde, et prison; expositions: "Ces messieurs les officiers", et "Le fort Lennox, Oeuvre des ingénieurs royaux".

***Sutton:* Eberdt Museum of Communications**
30A, rue Principale, Sutton, QC J0E 2K0
Tél: 514-538-2649
mchs@aide-internet.org
Special collection for TV and radio

***Sutton:* Musée des communications et d'histoire de Sutton**
CP 430, 30A, rue Principale, Sutton, QC J0E 2K0
Tél: 450-538-3222
mchs@aide-internet.org
History of communication

***Tadoussac:* Centre d'interprétation des mammifères marins**
***Also known as:* CIMM**
108, de la Cale-Sèche, Tadoussac, QC G0T 2A0
Tél: 418-235-4701; *Téléc:* 418-235-4325
info@gremm.org
www.gremm.org
Founded: 2005 A pour mission la conservation du milieu marin & la recherche scientifique sur les mammifères marins du Saint-Laurent

***Tadoussac:* La maison des Dunes**
Rte du Moulin Baude, Tadoussac, QC G0T 2A0
Tél: 418-235-4238; *Téléc:* 418-235-1203
Maison faisant partie du patrimoine local, transformée en centre d'interprétation; exposition permanente; présentations, par des naturalistes, sur le phénomène des dunes de sable

***Tadoussac:* La Petite chapelle de Tadoussac**
***Also known as:* La Chapelle des Indiens**
CP 69, rue Bord de l'Eau, Tadoussac, QC G0T 2A0
Tél: 418-235-4657; *Téléc:* 418-235-4433
www.tadoussac.com

***Tadoussac:* Poste de Traite Chauvin Trading Post**
157, rue du Bord-de-l'Eau, Tadoussac, QC G0T 2A0
Tél: 418-235-4657; *Téléc:* 418-235-4433
tourisme@bellnet.ca
Réplique du premier poste de traite des fourrures du 17e siècle; présente des objets se rapportant à la vie des autochtones et les produits d'échange; dégustation de phoque tous les dimanches
Gaby Villeneuve

***Thetford Mines:* Musée minéralogique et minier de Thetford Mines**
711, boul Frontenac ouest, Thetford Mines, QC G6E 7Y8
Tél: 418-335-2123; *Téléc:* 418-335-5605
service.client@museemineralogique.com
www.museemineralogique.com
Founded: 1976 Présente l'histoire géologique, minière & social de la région de L'Amiante; expositions; activités educatives; excursions
François Cinq-Mars, Directeur,
f.cinq-mars@museemineralogique.com

***Trois-Rivières:* Centre d'exposition sur l'industrie des pâtes et papiers**
CP 368, 800, Parc portuaire, Trois-Rivières, QC G9A 5H3
Tél: 819-372-4633; *Téléc:* 819-374-1900
ceipp@v3r.net
www.ceipp.net

Le Centre d'exposition s'engage à vous faire découvrir l'histoire de la région papetière du Québec; activités; groupes scolaires et adultes; ouvert tous les jours 10h-18h, du 30 mai au 27 septembre (2009) et sur réservation pour les groupes

Trois-Rivières: **Lieu historique national du Canada des Forges-du-Saint-Maurice / Forges du Saint-Maurice National Historic Site of Canada**
10 000, boul des Forges, Trois-Rivières, QC G9C 1B1
Tél: 819-378-5116; *Téléc:* 819-378-0887
Ligne sans frais: 888-773-8888
parcscanada-que@pc.gc.ca
www.pc.gc.ca/fra/lhn-nhs/qc/saintmaurice
A 20 minutes de Trois-Rivières, commémore l'établissement de la première communauté industrielle au Canada; ouvert de mi-mai à mi-oct.; groupes sur réservation.

Trois-Rivières: **Musée des Ursulines de Trois-Rivières**
734, rue des Ursulines, Trois-Rivières, QC G9A 5B5
Tél: 819-375-7922; *Téléc:* 819-375-0238
mutr@cgocable.ca
www.musee-ursulines.qc.ca; www.ursulines-uc.com
Conserve et met en valeur l'histoire des Ursulines dès 1697; expositions thématiques, visites guidées, galerie d'art.
Josée Grandmont

Trois-Rivières: **Musée militaire de Trois-Rivières**
Also known as: **Musée du 12e Régiment blindé du Canada**
574, rue St-François-Xavier, Trois-Rivières, QC G9A 1R6
Tél: 819-371-5290; *Téléc:* 819-371-5292
museemilitaire@cgocable.ca
www.mediat-muse.qc.ca/web_12e.html; www.12rbc.ca
Musée et manège militaire; exposition retraçant l'histoire du régiment; salles d'armes; collections d'uniformes, pièces d'équipements, armes blanches et armes à feu en usage dans les Forces canadiennes.

Trois-Rivières: **Musée Pierre Boucher**
Séminaire Saint-Joseph, 858, rue Laviolette, Trois-Rivières, QC G9A 5S3
Tél: 819-376-4459; *Téléc:* 819-378-0607
museepierre-boucher@ssj.qc.ca
Musée fondé en 1920 par Mgr Albert Tessier pour protéger et sauvegarder le patrimoine local et régional; art contemporain (québecois et canadien); un programme d'animation adapté pour les groupes scolaires et les groupes d'adultes est centré sur les expositions temporaires, consacrées aux artistes contemporains et aux collections du musée; le musée est ouvert gratuitement du mardi au dimanche
Françoise Chainé, Directrice

Trois-Rivières: **Musée québécois de culture populaire**
200, rue Laviolette, Trois-Rivières, QC G9A 6L5
Tél: 819-372-0406; *Téléc:* 819-372-9907
info@culturepop.qc.ca
www.culturepop.qc.ca
Founded: 2001 Le Musée propose six expositions audacieuses, non conventionnelles et empreintes de plaisir à la manière des Québécois; reliée au Musée, la Vieille prison de Trois-Rivières, offre une visite-expérience, guidée par des ex-détenus.
Benoît Gauthier, Directeur

Ulverton: **Moulin à laine d'Ulverton / Ulverton Woolen Mills**
210, ch Porter, Ulverton, QC J0B 2B0
Tél: 819-826-3157; *Téléc:* 819-826-6266
info@moulin.ca
www.moulin.ca
Founded: 1982 Initie aux méthodes artisanales et industrielles de production et de traitement de la laine

Valcourt: **Musée J. Armand Bombardier**
1001, av J.A. Bombardier, Valcourt, QC J0E 2L0
Tél: 450-532-5300; *Téléc:* 450-532-2260
info@museebombardier.com
www.museebombardier.com
Le musée présente la vie et l'oeuvre de Joseph-Armand Bombardier, mécanicien, inventeur et entrepreneur; retrace l'évolution de l'industrie de la motoneige; expositions; activités.
Louise Lemay, Directrice des communications
Richard Codère, Conservateur

Val-d'Or: **La Cité de l'Or**
CP 212, 90, av Perreault, Val-d'Or, QC J9P 4P3
Tél: 819-825-7616; *Téléc:* 819-825-9853
Ligne sans frais: 877-582-5367
courrier@citedelor.qc.ca
www.citedelor.com
Site historique du patrimoine minier en Abitibi-Témiscamingue; visites guidées à la seule mine d'or du Québec accessible à 91 mètre sous terre; expositions; boutique; par réservation.
Ghislaine Brousseau, Responsable des réservations

Valleyfield: **Écomusée des Deux-Rives**
75, rue St-Jean-Baptiste, Valleyfield, QC J6T 1Z6
Tel: 450-370-4855; *Fax:* 450-370-4861
ecomusee@rocler.qc.ca

Vaudreuil-Dorion: **Musée régional de Vaudreuil-Soulanges (MRVS)**
431, av St-Charles, Vaudreuil-Dorion, QC J7V 2N3
Tel: 450-455-2092; *Fax:* 450-455-6782
Toll-Free: 877-455-2092
info@mrvs.qc.ca
www.mrvs.qc.ca
Exposition permanente et expositions temporaires; collections spécialisées; ethnologie et histoire; collection beaux-arts; circuits patrimoniaux; centre de documentation en généaologie et histoire régionale; visities guidées, activités, ateliers, programmation; location de salles; boutique; café.
Daniel Bissonnette, Directeur générale

Victoriaville: **Musée Laurier**
16, rue Laurier ouest, Victoriaville, QC G6P 6P3
Tél: 819-357-8655; *Téléc:* 819-357-8655
info@museelaurier.com
museelaurier.com
Founded: 1929 Résidence de Sir Wilfrid Laurier, ancien premier ministre du Canada, et sa femme Lady Laurier, maintenant la propriété de la Société du Musée Laurier; collection d'objets d'art et de meubles, sculpture, et oeuvres en art contemporain.
Richard Pedneault, Directeur/Conservateur

Windsor: **Parc histoique de la Poudrière de Windsor / Windsor Powder Mill Historical Park**
342, rue St-Georges, Windsor, QC J1S 2Z5
Tél: 819-845-5284; *Téléc:* 819-845-5615
poudriere@bellnet.ca
www.lapoudriere.qc.ca
Fondée en 1864, dans la foulée de la guerre de session, la Poudrière de Windsor s'est investie dans la fabrication de poudre noire, un composé essentiel des explosifs. Jusqu'en 1922, la ville de Windsor a vécu au rythme de cette industrie dangereuse. On peut maintenant découvir les secrets, le comment et le pourquoi de cette industrie via une toute nouvelle exposition permanente et la visite guidé
Thomas Dandurand, Directeur général

Saskatchewan

Provincial Museums

Royal Saskatchewan Museum
2445 Albert St., Regina, SK S4P 4W7
Tel: 306-787-2815; *Fax:* 306-787-2820
rsminfo@royalsaskmuseum.ca
www.royalsaskmuseum.ca
Saskatchewan's natural & human history; archaeology; entomology; botany; natural history; paleontology; geology. Life Sciences Gallery; Earth Sciences Gallery; First Nations Gallery; Paleo Pit interactive gallery for children ; Megamunch, a half-size robotic Tyrannosaurus rex. Publication of informational booklets & nature notes, giftshop, research library.
Harold Bryant, Curator, Earth Sciences
David Baron, Director
Keith Roney, Curator, Life Sciences
Margaret Hanna, Curator, Aboriginal History
Ron Tillie, Supervisor, Exhibits
Paula Hill, Public Programs, Education
Ferne Johnston, Administrator

Western Development Museum (WDM)
2935 Melville St., Saskatoon, SK S7J 5A6
Tel: 306-934-1400; *Fax:* 306-934-4467
Toll-Free: 800-363-6345
info@wdm.ca
www.wdm.ca
The Western Development Museum preserves Saskatchewan's collective heritage, in order to raise awareness of & interest in the cultural & economic development of western Canada. The Curatorial Centre in Saskatoon coordinates services for the museum's branches in Moose Jaw, North Battleford, Saskatoon, & Yorkton. Tours of the Curatorial Centre may be arranged through the education & extension staff.
David Klatt, Executive Director
Cal Glasman, Director, Administration, cglasman@wdm.ca
Ruth Bitner, Curator, Collections, rbitner@wdm.ca
Warren Clubb, Curator, Exhibits, wclubb@wdm.ca
Dianne Craig, Manager, Corporate Development, dcraig@wdm.ca
Terry Thompson, Manager, Facilities, tthompson@wdm.ca
Brian Newman, Coordinator, Exhibits, bnewman@wdm.ca
Leslee Newman, Coordinator, Education & Extension, lnewman@wdm.ca
Jan Olsen, Coordinator, Marketing, jolsen@wdm.ca
Juanelle Finlay, Library Technician, jfinlay@wdm.ca

Local Museums in Saskatchewan

Abernethy: **Abernethy Nature-Heritage Museum**
PO Box 158, Abernethy, SK S0A 0A0
Tel: 306-333-2202
anhm@sasktel.net
www.saskmuseums.org
Heritage & antique artifacts with a core exhibit of more than 300 wildlife specimens mounted by the late Ralph Stueck (1897-1979); video presentation of Stueck's "talking goose" & other folklore; activities/hands-on displays for children; small art gallery; 1930's classroom. Open daily May - Sept. Wheelchair accessible.
Eileen Gaye, President

Abernethy: **Motherwell Homestead Natural Historic Site**
PO Box 247, Abernethy, SK S0A 0A0
Tel: 306-333-2116; *Fax:* 306-333-2210
motherwell-homestead@pc.gc.ca
www.pc.gc.ca/motherwell
Founded: 1983 The site includes Lanark Place, the farmstead estate of pioneer farmer and politician, W.R. Motherwell, who had a significant influence on the development of scientific agriculture in Western Canada. The homestead depicts the lifestyles, costumes, and architecture of the early 20th century, with costumed guides. Open Victoria Day - Labour Day.
Flo Miller, Site Coordinator, flo.miller@pc.gc.ca

Alida: **Gervais Wheels Museum**
PO Box 40, Alida, SK S0C 0B0
Tel: 306-443-2303
Pioneer artifacts, music boxes, gramophones, North American automobiles

Arcola: **Arcola Museum**
PO Box 354, Arcola, SK S0C 0G0
Tel: 306-455-2462
Open May-Sept.
Margaret Olsen, Contact
Ruth Gardner, Contact

Assiniboia: **Assiniboia & District Museum**
PO Box 1211, 506 - 3rd Ave. West, Assiniboia, SK S0H 0B0
Tel: 306-642-5353; *Fax:* 306-642-4216
assini.museum@sasktel.net
southcentralmuseums.ca/assiniboia.html
Other contact information: Phone, appointments: 306-642-4790
The Assiniboia & District Museum features vintage cars from 1916 to 1964, a grain elevator, a Pole Shed with agricultural machinery, a school room & a military display. The museum is open seven days a week during July & August, & Monday to Friday from September to June.

Avonlea: **Avonlea & District Museum - Heritage House**
PO Box 401, Main St., Avonlea, SK S0H 0C0
Tel: 306-868-2101; *Fax:* 306-868-2221
jeankincaid@sasktel.net
Founded: 1980 The Avonlea & District Museum displays artifacts which depict the geological age, plus the history of native people, pioneers, & ranchers in the area. The Truax Anglican Church is situated on the grounds. The museum is open from June to September. At other times of the year, appointments can be arranged.
Jean Kincaid, President

Battleford: **Fort Battleford National Historic Site of Canada**
PO Box 70, Battleford, SK S0M 0E0
Tel: 306-937-2621; *Fax:* 306-937-3370
battleford.info@pc.gc.ca
www.parkscanada.gc.ca/battleford
Other contact information: TDD: 306/937-3199
NWMP post, c. 1886; open May long weekend - Sept. long weekend
Glenn Ebert, Site Coordinator

Battleford: **Fred Light Museum**
PO Box 40, Battleford, SK S0M 0E0
Tel: 306-937-7111; *Fax:* 306-937-2450
Pioneer artifacts, gun collection, military artifacts; open May - Sept.
Bernadette Leslie, Supervisor

Battleford: **Saskatchewan Baseball Hall of Fame & Museum**
PO Box 1388, 292 - 22nd St., Battleford, SK S0M 0E0
Tel: 306-446-1983; *Fax:* 306-446-0509
saskbaseballmuseum@sasktel.net
Founded: 1983 Has over 3,000 artifacts dealing with baseball plus 6,000 items of archival nature such as pictures, books & magazines
Jane Shury, Executive Director

Beauval: **Frazer's Museum**
PO Box 64, Beauval, SK S0M 0G0
Aboriginal & pioneer artifacts, including articles from Hudson's Bay Company, missionaries & Métis people

Big River: **Big River Memorial Museum**
PO Box 220, 205 Third Ave. North, Big River, SK S0J 0E0
Tel: 306-469-2112
The Big River Memorial Museum contains items from fishing & logging in the area.

Biggar: **Biggar Museum & Gallery**
PO Box 1598, 105 - 3rd Ave. West, Biggar, SK S0K 0M0
Tel: 306-948-3451; *Fax:* 306-948-3478
biggarmuseum@sasktel.net
www.biggarmuseum.com
Founded: 1972 The museum collects historical artifacts from the settlement of the town of Biggar & the surrounding district. Among it collections are a general store display & a reconstruction of the Biggar train station. Biggar Museum & Gallery is open year round.
Anne Livingston, Executive Director

Biggar: **Homestead Museum**
PO Box 542, Biggar, SK S0K 0M0
Tel: 306-948-3427
Prairie pioneer village including sod house, school, church, barn, general store, 1913 house, 1920 house & bunk house & cook car; collection of Historical Character dolls; open daily Victoria Day - Oct.
Roger Martin, Director

Blaine Lake: **Blaine Lake Museum**
PO Box 10, Blaine Lake, SK S0J 0J0
Tel: 306-497-2531
The Blaine Lake Museum is situated in the CNR station, which was built in 1912. The museum depicts the local history of the area.

Briercrest: **Briercrest & District Museum**
PO Box 216, Briercrest, SK S0H 0K0
Tel: 306-799-2103; *Fax:* 306-799-2115
The Briercrest & District Museum houses collections from the Briercrest area's earliest settlers & their descendants. Examples of the museum's artifacts include household items & small farm equipment. The museum is open from May to September.

Broadview: **Broadview Historical Museum**
PO Box 556, Broadview, SK S0G 0K0
Tel: 306-696-3244
www.broadview.ca/museum
Founded: 1972 Articles related to Broadview's history are collected & displayed. Visitors can see the Highland School, a blacksmith shop, a post office, a sod house, a log home, & a Canadian Pacific Railway station & caboose. Broadview Historical Museum is open from the beginning of June to the end of August.

Bulyea: **Lakeside Museum**
PO Box 101, Bulyea, SK S0G 0L0
Tel: 306-725-4558
Native & pioneer artifacts; Boer War, World War I & II exhibits; display of dinosaur bones; open by appointment
Robert Swanston, Director

Cabri: **Cabri & District Museum**
PO Box 230, 202 - 1st St. South, Cabri, SK S0N 0J0
Tel: 306-587-2339
Displays include artifacts from World War I & World War II, First Nations, & household & farm items. The museum is open from May to September.

Cadillac: **Cadillac Museum**
PO Box 118, Centre St., Cadillac, SK S0N 0K0
Tel: 306-785-2128; *Fax:* 306-785-2042
Household articles & early 20th century tools; clothing; fire-fighting equipment; quilt exhibit; demonstrations. Open upon request
Luanne Hancock, Contact

Canwood: **Canwood Museum**
PO Box 269, 635 - 3rd Ave. East, Canwood, SK S0J 0K0
Founded: 1971 Canwood Museum is a community museum located in an old schoolhouse. Displays include farm artifacts, clothing, & pictures.

Carlyle: **Rusty Relics Museum Inc.**
PO Box 840, 115 Railway Ave. W., Carlyle, SK S0C 0R0
Tel: 306-453-2266; *Fax:* 306-453-2812
rustyrelicsmuseum@gmail.com
www.virtualmuseum.ca
A museum of pioneer life in Saskatchewan; artifacts relating to Carlyle area displayed in room settings in a 1910 CN railway station; includes a 1943 CPR caboose, a CN Motor car, CN tool shed with railway tools, furnished 1905 one-room country school, agricultural machinery & old church
Wilbert Hume, President

Climax: **Climax Community Museum Inc.**
PO Box 246, Climax, SK S0N 0N0
Tel: 306-293-2124; *Fax:* 306-293-2051
www.virtualmuseum.ca
Pioneer collection - domestic, tools, farm machinery, military, hospital & sports, community archives
Victor Van Allen, President/Curator

Coronach: **Coronach District Museum**
PO Box 449, Coronach, SK S0H 0Z0
Tel: 306-267-4923
Features historical displays, records, photos & artifacts representing the lives of pioneers of the area
Judy Greenwood, Chair

Craik: **Prairie Pioneer Museum**
PO Box 157, 541 Parks Rd., Craik, SK S0G 0V0
Tel: 306-734-2480
www.craik.ca/pioneer.html
Founded: 1966 The pioneer way of life in Craik & rural Saskatchewan is portrayed at the Prairie Pioneer Museum. Buildings include two rural schools & a heritage house, which was built in 1906. Artifacts, such as household furnishings & medical & veterinary instruments, are on display. The museum is open during the summer, & is accessible year-round by request.
Mary Eva, Contact

Cupar: **Cupar & District Heritage Museum**
PO Box 164, Cupar, SK S0G 0Y0
Tel: 306-723-4324
Founded: 1955 Open May - Sept. or by appt.
Wes Bailey, Chair

Cut Knife: **Clayton McLain Memorial Museum**
PO Box 8, 111A Hill Ave., Cut Knife, SK S0M 0N0
Tel: 306-398-2920; *Fax:* 306-398-2951
cmmmcutknife@gmail.com
www.cmmmcutknife.ca; cmmmcutknife.blogspot.com; www.virtualmuseum.ca
Located in Tomahawk Park; local history, including First Nations artifacts from early life & Battle of Cutknife Hill, and McLain family collection; archives include personal papers, photgraphs, and a complete collection of the local newspaper; educational programming; research services; open June-Sept.

Denare Beach: **Northern Gateway Museum**
PO Box 70, Beaver Dr., Denare Beach, SK S0P 0B0
Tel: 306-362-2141; *Fax:* 306-362-2257
ngmuseum@sasktel.net
Founded: 1957 The Northern Gateway Museum houses artifacts from fur trade excavations, First Nations life, gold rush activities, & mining operations. Archives include architectural records, photographs, & films.

Dinsmore: **Yester-Years Community Museum**
PO Box 216, Dinsmore, SK S0L 0T0
Features the main museum, blacksmith shop, butter & post office buildings; open July & Aug. upon request
Helyn Tryyki, President

Dodsland: **Dodsland Museum**
125, Dodsland, SK S0L 0V0
Tel: 306-356-2178
Old grocery store on lower floor represents a village of the past; top floor represents living quarters of the past
Weldon Bacon, Director

Duck Lake: **Duck Lake Regional Interpretive Centre**
PO Box 328, Duck Lake, SK S0K 1J0
Tel: 306-467-2057; *Fax:* 306-467-2257
Toll-Free: 866-467-2057
duckmuf@sasktel.net
www.dlric.org
Founded: 1959 Frontier of First Nation, Métis & Pioneer Society, 1870-1905; artifact & art galleries, theatre, gift shop, 24m viewing tower, conference facilities
Celine Perillat, Executive Director

Duff: **Duff Community Heritage Museum**
PO Box 57, Duff, SK S0A 0S0
Tel: 306-728-3275
www.spreda.sk.ca/community_Duff.htm
Open by appointment only, this tourist attraction has been built out of an old church and features a recreational pioneer-era kitchen and old rural schoolhouse, along with various other historical items and photos from the village's history.

Eastend: **Eastend Museum & Cultural Centre**
PO Box 214, Eastend, SK S0N 0T0
Tel: 306-295-3564
Tie Rail Ranch House, blacksmith shop, operating 1903 Cae Steam Engine, 1927 Federal Truck, & a stage coach; LaRose Building contains 1500 items; Open daily May - Labour Day
Shelly Parker, President
Glen Duke, Treasurer
Doreen Stewart, Secretary

Edam: **Harry S. Washbrook Museum**
PO Box 182, Edam, SK S0M 0V0
Tel: 306-397-2260
Local pioneer & First Nations artifacts

Elbow: **Elbow Museum & Historical Society**
PO Box 207, Elbow, SK S0H 1J0
Tel: 306-854-2277; *Fax:* 306-854-2229
elbow@sasktel.net
www.elbowsask.com
Housed in an old schoolhouse; sodhouse built in 1965 & July 1999; artifacts represent era of late 1800s & early 1900s
Joan Soggie, Chair

Elrose: **Elrose Heritage Society**
PO Box 556, 4th Ave.E., Elrose, SK S0L 0Z0
Tel: 306-378-2213
Directors collect, restore & catalogue artifacts & antiques; museum open Sun., Wed., & Fri. May - Sept.; guided tours conducted; gift shop
Florence Rowley, Secretary
Betty Rudd, President

Esterhazy: **Esterhazy Community Museum**
PO Box 371, Esterhazy, SK S0A 0X0
Tel: 306-745-2988
Pioneer artifacts, taxidermy & music rooms, old store, model of potash mine; fashion show; antique doll and toy show

Esterhazy: **Kaposvar Historic Site**
PO Box 13, Esterhazy, SK S0A 0X0
Tel: 306-745-2715
1907 church & rectory; Annual Pilgrimage on the fourth Sun. in Aug.
Rose Kacsmar, Secretary

Estevan: **Estevan Art Gallery & Museum**
118 - 4th St., Estevan, SK S4A 0T4
Tel: 306-634-7644; *Fax:* 306-634-2490
eagm@sasktel.net
www.eagm.ca
NWMP Museum, local artifacts; open summer season; plus art with 2 contemporary exhibiting galleries, with travelling exhibitions, giftshop; open year round
Griffith Aaron Baker, Director/Curator

Eston: **Prairie West Historical Centre & Society**
PO Box 910, Eston, SK S0L 1A0
Tel: 306-962-3772
Local history museum & art gallery; wildflower garden
Betty James, Programme Coordinator/Curator

Foam Lake: **Foam Lake Museum**
PO Box 1041, 113 Bray Ave., Foam Lake, SK S0A 1A0
Tel: 306-272-4292
Local pioneer museum documenting the settlement of the area. Open June 1st - Aug. 31st and by appointment.
Ruth Gushulak, President
Fina Anderson, Secretary

Fort Qu'appelle: **Fort Qu'Appelle Museum**
PO Box 1093, Fort Qu'appelle, SK S0G 1S0
Tel: 306-332-6033
valleycalls@sasktel.net
www.fortquappelle.com/history.html
1864 Hudson Bay Co. post; open June-Sept.
J. Norman, Vice-President
L. Anderson, President

Frenchman Butte: **Frenchman Butte Museum**
PO Box 10, Frenchman Butte, SK S0M 0W0
Tel: 306-344-4478; *Fax:* 306-344-4566
info@frenchmanbuttemuseum.ca
www.frenchmanbuttemuseum.ca
Pioneer & CNR artifacts; arrowhead & gun collections, mounted birds

Frobisher: **Frobisher Threshermen's Museum**
PO Box 194, Frobisher, SK S0C 0Y0
Tel: 306-486-4513
Steam engines, wooden threshing separators, gas & diesel tractors, ploughshares

Glen Ewen: **Glen Ewen Community Antique Centre**
Glen Ewen, SK S0C 1C0
Tel: 306-925-2221
Features a collection of antique cars that includes a 1910 Ford & a 1937 Packard; also showcases guns, dishes & household articles from the early 1900s; open seasonally or by request
Arne Hansen, Director

Glentworth: **Glentworth Museum**
PO Box 174, Glentworth, SK S0H 1V0
Tel: 306-266-4320
Local history artifacts

Goodsoil: **Goodsoil Historical Museum**
PO Box 370, Goodsoil, SK S0M 1A0
Tel: 306-238-4565; *Fax:* 306-238-4991
schamber@sasktel.net
www.saskmuseums.org
Founded: 1977 Natural stone school building built in 1945; first teacherage built in 1934 of logs; miniature church with original

steeple from church destroyed by tornado; over 2,500 artifacts, many dating from 1800s; old machinery; doll house with hundreds of dolls from around the world. Open June 30 - Aug. 31
Alex Schamber, President, schamber@sasktel.net
Rudy Leiter, Secretary

***Gravelbourg:* Gravelbourg & District Museum**
PO Box 862, 300 Main St., Gravelbourg, SK S0H 1X0
Tel: 306-648-2332
Open July & Aug.
Louis Stringer, Manager

***Grenfell:* Grenfell Museum Assoc.**
PO Box 1156, 711 Wolseley Ave., Grenfell, SK S0G 2B0
Tel: 306-697-2930; *Fax:* 306-697-2500
Restored 1904 Queen Anne turreted house; added attraction is the annex with furniture & tools of bygone days as well as an outstanding military display
Lloyd Arthur, President
Mary Christie, Secretary

***Hague:* Saskatchewan River Valley Museum**
PO Box 630, Hague, SK S0K 1X0
Tel: 306-225-2112; *Fax:* 306-225-4642
rivervalleymuseum@sasktel.net
www.saskmuseums.org; www.townofhague.com; www.virtualmuseum.ca
Approx. 6,000 artifacts, including First Nations & Mennonite; original European house/barn; country school; Mennonite church; horse-drawn farming machinery, blacksmith tools, pre-1950 furniture & appliances; open May long weekend - Thanksgiving
Len Wudrich, Vice-President
Gerry Kuehn, President

***Harris:* Harris Museum**
PO Box 131, 204 Railway Ave., Harris, SK S0L 1K0
Tel: 306-656-2002; *Fax:* 306-656-2172
Founded: 1989 The volunteer operated Harris Museum features local history & archives, plus a C.N. Water Tower & a gas engine water pump. The museum is open from May to September, or by appointment.
Harvey Neil, President
RoseAnn Mireau, Past President, 306-656-4449
Betty McFarlane, Contact, 306-656-4725
Dolores Neil, Contact, 306-656-2172

***Hazenmore:* Heritage Hazenmore Museum**
PO Box 103, Hazenmore, SK S0N 1C0
Tel: 306-264-5149
Local history; open on request

***Hodgeville:* Hodgeville Community Museum**
***Also known as:* Country Craft Shoppe & Homestead Museum**
PO Box 264, 102 - 1st St. West, Hodgeville, SK S0H 2B0
Tel: 306-677-2693; *Fax:* 306-677-2707
Eight rooms depicting an early homestead; crafts, gifts & tearoom
Linda Straub, President

***Hudson Bay:* Hudson Bay Museum**
PO Box 931, Hudson Bay, SK S0E 0Y0
Tel: 306-865-2170
Preserving artifacts of the area; open May 15 - Sept. 10
Jean Geddes, President
Emily Lundeen, Secretary

***Humboldt:* Humboldt & District Museum & Gallery**
PO Box 2349, Humboldt, SK S0K 2A0
Tel: 306-682-5226; *Fax:* 306-682-1430
humboldt.museum@sasktel.net
www.humboldtmuseum.ca
Focus on the Humboldt Telegraph Station of 1878, as well as the settlement of Humboldt & district, & the spiritual influence of St. Peter's Abbey; housed in a 1912 post office building
J. Hoesgen, Curator

***Imperial:* Imperial & District Museum**
PO Box 269, Imperial, SK S0G 2J0
Tel: 306-963-2280
Local history; open by appt.
Marilyn Koza, Co-Chair
Fred Grigg, Co-Chair

***Imperial:* Nels Berggren Museum**
PO Box 125, Royal St., Imperial, SK S0G 2J0
Tel: 306-963-2033
Lamps, clocks, sewing machines, musical instruments, art

***Indian Head:* Indian Head Museum**
PO Box 566, Indian Head, SK S0G 2K0
Tel: 306-695-3800
1907 two-storey fire hall displaying artifacts of local pioneer days; also 1926 one-room school, 1883 Bell Farm Cottage; replica of 1930s one-bay village garage; farm implements
Arnold Dales, President

***Ituna:* Ituna Cultural & Historical Museum**
Old Ituna & District Recreation Centre, 3rd St., Ituna, SK S0A 1N0
Tel: 306-795-3348
Local history including Ukrainian & aboriginal artifacts; open July-Aug.

***Kamsack:* Kamsack & District Museum**
PO Box 991, Queen Elizabeth Boulevard, Kamsack, SK S0A 1S0
Tel: 306-542-4415
Exhibits focus on both First Nations and European history; Housed in a former power plant, the museum contains one of the original diesel engines which generated the town's electricity until 1958; rooms furnished in the style of a typical 1920s pioneer dwelling. Open May - Sept.; car show & shine mid-June
Fr. John Morarity, President
Nick Trofimenkoff, Secretary/Treasurer

***Kelliher:* Kelliher & District Heritage Museum Inc.**
PO Box 111, Kelliher, SK S0A 1V0
Tel: 306-675-2183
Walter Oleksyn

***Kenosee Lake:* Cannington Manor Provincial Park**
PO Box 220, Kenosee Lake, SK S0C 2S0
Tel: 306-739-5251; *Fax:* 306-577-2622
manor.cannington@gov.sk.ca
www.tpcs.gov.sk.ca/CanningtonManor
Other contact information: Phone, Off Season: 306-577-2600
In the late 1800s, partners in the Moose Mountain Trading Company established the village of Cannington Manor. Buildings from this village have been reconstructed or restored for visitors. Buildings at the site include a Land Titles Office, a bachelor's cabin, a Moose Mountain Trading Company store, a carpenter's shop, a blacksmith shop, a flour mill, & the Mitre Hotel. Cannington Manor is open from Victoria Day to Labour Day.

***Kerrobert:* Kerrobert & District Museum**
PO Box 463, 15 Saskatchewan Ave., Kerrobert, SK S0L 1R0
Tel: 306-834-5277
Replica of the first tent store and pioneer furniture; Open May-Sept.
Mary Andrews, Secretary

***Kincaid:* Kincaid Museum**
PO Box 177, Kincaid, SK S0H 2J0
Tel: 306-264-3910
Local historical material

***Kindersley:* Kindersley & District Plains Museum**
PO Box 599, 903 - 11th Ave. East, Kindersley, SK S0L 1S0
Tel: 306-463-6620
Wide collection of early farm machinery and tools, household items, education items and items from school and churches; fire hall and fire truck; miliary display, a general store, post office & print shop; an archaeological display; Open May to mid-Sept.

***Kinistino:* Kinistino & District Pioneer Museum Inc.**
PO Box 10, Kinistino, SK S0J 1H0
Tel: 306-864-2838
Displays of artifacts from fur trade & pioneer times; oldest purely agricultural settlement in Saskatchewan; open July - Aug. or by appt.
Shelley Holmes, Sec.-Treas.

***Kipling:* Kipling & District Historical Society**
PO Box 414, Kipling, SK S0G 2S0
Tel: 306-736-8254
e.hamelin@sasktel.net
Elaine Hamelin, Secretary

***Kisbey:* Kisbey Museum**
PO Box 5, 291 Ross St., Kisbey, SK S0C 1L0
Tel: 306-462-2162
Detailed history & pictures of Kisbey's namesake, R. Claude Kisbey; 1,000+ objects; open Thu. through July & Aug. & by request
Velma Hale, President

***Lancer:* Lancer Centennial Museum**
PO Box 3, Lancer, SK S0N 1G0
Tel: 306-689-2925; *Fax:* 306-689-2890
Open June-Sept.
Cliff Murch

***Langham:* Langham & District Heritage Village & Museum**
PO Box 516, 302 Railway St., Langham, SK S0K 2L0
Tel: 306-283-4342; *Fax:* 306-283-4772
www.langham.ca
Preserves & exhibits artifacts illustrating the history & culture of Langham & area; special events & programming. Open May long weekend to Sept. 30, Wed. 9-12 & Sat. 9-3, or by appointment.
Doreen Nickel, President

***Lanigan:* Lanigan & District Heritage Centre**
PO Box 424, Lanigan, SK S0K 2M0
Tel: 306-365-2569; *Fax:* 306-365-2960
lanigan.dist.heritage@sasktel.net
www.sasktelwebsite.natildha/
Founded: 1994 The Lanigan & District Heritage Association's mission is to preserve the Lanigan CPR Station, where the Centre is currently housed; includes a museum, tourism information, agricultural interpretive display, potash exposition, caboose, recreation & coffee area & storage. Located at 75 Railway Ave., Lanigan.
Ruth Wildeman, Secretary
Andrew Cebryk, Chair

***Lashburn:* Lashburn Centennial Museum**
PO Box 275, Corner of Main Street and 1st Ave., Lashburn, SK S0M 1H0
Tel: 306-285-4145
www.saskmuseums.org/museums/museum_search.php?id=107
Vetern's Gallery with artifacts from the Boer War to Korean War; 1908 Gully School; Artifacts of the Barr Colony settlers; log cabin and blacksmith shop.

***Leross:* Kellross Heritage Museum**
PO Box 215, 2nd Ave., Leross, SK S0A 1V0
Tel: 306-675-6144
Open by appt. from June 15
Louise Tereposky

***Leroy:* Leroy & District Heritage Museum**
PO Box 47, Leroy, SK S0K 2P0
Tel: 306-286-3288
Open July & Aug.

***Lumsden:* Lumsden Heritage Museum**
c/o Lumsden Historical Society, PO Box 91, 50 Qu'Appelle Dr. West, Lumsden, SK S0G 3C0
Tel: 306-731-2905

***Luseland:* Luseland & Districts Museum**
Grand Ave., Luseland, SK S0L 2A0
Tel: 306-372-4692
valfin@sasktel.net
Open Sat. or by request
Donna Ruhohr, Chair
Isabell Kasas, Vice-Chair

***Macklin:* Macklin & District Museum**
***Also known as:* Eid House**
PO Box 423, 5002 Herald St., Macklin, SK S0L 2C0
Tel: 306-753-2610
town.macklin@sasktel.net
www.macklin.ca/museum.htm
Founded: 1990 Built in 1919 by Frank Shaw, the town's first bank manager, the house later became a hospital during the 1920s. Open Tu, Th, F, summer.

***Macrorie:* Macrorie Museum**
PO Box 177, Macrorie, SK S0L 2E0
Tel: 306-243-4327; *Fax:* 306-243-4507
Consists of 3 sites: an old post office, insurance office, & living quarters which depict the local farming area; an old brick school, heritage site; a caboose & jigger; open Mon. in July & Aug. 2-4, or by appt.
Geraldine Torvik, Treasurer
Lynne Cooper, President
Jean Delparte, Secretary

***Maidstone:* Maidstone & District Historical & Cultural Society**
PO Box 250, Maidstone, SK S0M 1M0
Tel: 306-893-2890
May - Sept.
Bill McGilvery, President

***Main Centre:* Main Centre Heritage Museum**
PO Box 42, Main Centre, SK S0H 2V0
Tel: 306-784-2953
Local history & early pioneering artifacts; school & church history; Herbert Ferry Crossing display; open by appt. May - Sept.
Iris Siemens, Secretary
Dora Wall, Chair

***Maple Creek:* Fort Walsh National Historic Site**
PO Box 278, Maple Creek, SK S0N 1N0
Tel: 306-662-2645; *Fax:* 306-662-2711
fort.walsh@pc.gc.ca
www.pc.gc.ca/lhn-nhs/sk/walsh/index_e.asp
Other contact information: TTD: 306/662-3124
NWMP fort & Cypress Hills Massacre site; open mid May - last weekend in Sept.
David Rohatensky, Site Manager

***Maple Creek:* Jasper Cultural & Historical Centre**
PO Box 1504, Maple Creek, SK S0N 1N0
Tel: 306-662-2434; *Fax:* 306-662-4359
admin@jaspercentre.ca
www.jaspercentre.ca/0000pg.asp/ID/3344/SID/120
Open Mon.-Fri. in winter; daily in summer
Sally Douglas, Manager

***Maple Creek:* Southwest Saskatchewan Oldtimers Museum**
PO Box 1540, 218 Jasper St., Maple Creek, SK S0N 1N0
Tel: 306-662-2474
oldtimers@sasktel.net
Ranching, First Nations, NWMP, firearms; open May 20 to Sept. 30

***Maryfield:* Maryfield Museum**
PO Box 262, Maryfield, SK S0G 3K0
Tel: 306-646-2201
Clocks, tools, record players, telephones

***McCord:* McCord & District Museum**
PO Box 82, McCord, SK S0H 2T0
Tel: 306-478-2522
ba.wilson@xplornet.com
www.southcentralmuseums.ca/mccord.html
Founded: 1973 Museum is housed in a 1928 CPR railway station and exibits includehistorical items from households and businesses in the area. Of note is an actual caboose on tracks beside the museum. A companion museum is the 1913 church at the opposite end of the street which displays religious articles from various churches in the region.

***Meadow Lake:* Meadow Lake Museum**
PO Box 610, 120 - 1st St. East, Meadow Lake, SK S9X 1Y5
Tel: 306-236-3622; *Fax:* 306-236-4299
meadowlake_townml@sasktel.net
www.meadowlake.ca
Exhibits are related to pioneers, farming, lumbering, & birds. The museum is open from Victoria Day to Labour Day.
Cecil Midgett, Contact

***Melfort:* Melfort & District Museum**
PO Box 3222, 401 Melfort St. West, Melfort, SK S0E 1A0
Tel: 306-752-5870; *Fax:* 306-752-5556
melfort.museum@sasktel.net
www.cityofmelfort.ca
Founded: 1971 Community museum, archives, pioneer village; agricultural machinery displays; located adjacent to the Melfort fairgrounds.
Gailmarie Anderson, Curator

***Melville:* Melville Heritage Museum Inc.**
PO Box 2528, Melville, SK S0A 2P0
Tel: 306-728-2070; *Fax:* 306-728-2070
Regional museum, located in the former Luther Academy (1913-1926); artifacts & histories of local, provincial & national interest; includes chapel, library, Grand Trunk Pacific/CNR & Military; over 100 original B & W framed photographs depict Melville's first quarter century; gift shop; murals; limited wheelchair access
Marj Redenbach, Curator

***Melville:* Melville Railway Museum**
PO Box 1240, Melville, SK S0A 2P0
Tel: 306-728-6840; *Fax:* 306-728-5911
city.clrk@city.melville.sk.ca
www.city.melville.sk.ca/siteengine/activep age.asp?PageID=188
Former CNR steam locomotive #5114; a J-4-5 class 4-6-2 built in 1919; also former Grand Trunk Pacific station from Duff, Saskatchewan containing artifacts including exhibits of communications equipment, from telegraphs, and telephones. There are also records from the Grand Trunk Railway and CNR, including employee records
Mr. Michael Hotsko, City Manager, mhotsko@melville.ca

***Middle Lake:* Middle Lake Museum**
PO Box 157, Middle Lake, SK S0K 2X0

***Milden:* Milden Community Museum**
PO Box 218, Milden, SK S0L 2L0
Tel: 306-935-2199
A community museum holding local artifacts including those of an old-time school, hospital & bedroom
Margaret Herd, Secretary
Brenda Latsay, President

***Moose Jaw:* Moose Jaw Museum & Art Gallery**
Crescent Park, Moose Jaw, SK S6H 0X6
Tel: 306-692-4471; *Fax:* 306-694-8016
mjamchin@sasktel.net
www.mjmag.ca
Founded: 1966 The building houses art, history & science exhibits, with a wide range of human history artifacts with strong representation of First Nations beadwork, women's clothing, and clothing-related artifacts from 1880 onward. There is a gift shop. The Learning Centre offers programs for school children and art classes for all ages. Open year round; admission by donation.
Heather Smith, Curator

***Moose Jaw:* Sukanen Ship Pioneer Village & Museum of Saskatchewan**
PO Box 2071, Moose Jaw, SK S6H 7T2
Tel: 306-693-7315
pmjohnson@Sasktel.net
www.sukanenmuseum.ca
38 acres of land; pioneer village of 20 buildings; antique farm with machinery; 100 collector tractors; 40 cars & trucks
Abe Giesbretch, Secretary
R. Jones, President

***Moose Jaw:* Western Development Museum**
***Also known as:* Moose Jaw Western Development Museum**
50 Diefenbaker Dr., Moose Jaw, SK S6J 1L9
Tel: 306-693-5989; *Fax:* 306-691-0511
moosejaw@wdm.ca
www.wdm.ca
Moose Jaw is one of four exhibit branches of Saskatchewan's Western Development Museum. The other branches are located in North Battleford, Saskatoon, & Yorkton. The Moose Jaw Western Development Museum displays the history of transportation, from the canoe to the railway. The museum also features the Snowbirds Gallery, which presents Canadian military aerobatic flight history.
Katherine Fitton, Manager, Moose Jaw, kfitton@wdm.ca
David Samson, Museum Technician, dsamson@wdm.ca
Jackie Hall, Officer, Programs & Education, jhall@wdm.ca
Shirley Stenko, Officer, Visitor Services, sstenko@wdm.ca

***Moosomin:* Jamieson Museum**
PO Box 236, 306 Gertie St., Moosomin, SK S0G 3N0
Tel: 306-435-3156
Pre-1900 house, church, military collection; open May - Oct.

***Morse:* Morse Museum & Cultural Centre**
PO Box 308, Morse, SK S0H 3C0
Tel: 306-629-3230; *Fax:* 306-629-3230
morsemuseum@sasktel.net
former school, built in 1912; open year round

***Mossbank:* Mossbank & District Museum Inc.**
PO Box 278, Mossbank, SK S0H 3G0
Tel: 306-354-2889
A community history museum dedicated to the history of No. 2 Bombing & Gunnery School which was located three miles east of Mossbank during WWII; blacksmith shop & blacksmith's house are now classified as provincial heritage property
Roy Tollefson, President

***Naicam:* Naicam Museum**
PO Box 238, Naicam, SK S0K 2Z0
Tel: 306-874-2280; *Fax:* 306-874-5444
www.townofnaicam.ca/museum.htm
History & archives of Naicam & District in Heritage building (pioneer school)
Ruby J. Lindsay, Secretary
Joan Gerguson, Chair
Doris Poole, Director

***Nipawin:* Nipawin & District Living Forestry Museum**
PO Box 1917, Hwy. 35 West, Nipawin, SK S0E 1E0
Tel: 306-862-9299
Situated on 14 acres; open May - Aug.
James Grandfield

***Nokomis:* Nokomis District Museum & Heritage Co-op**
PO Box 417, Nokomis, SK S0G 3R0
Tel: 306-528-2979
Displays & artifacts of early days & local history; open June 1 - Labour Day daily 10-5
Karen Lee, Director

***North Battleford:* Western Development Museum**
***Also known as:* North Battleford Western Development Museum**
PO Box 183, North Battleford, SK S9A 2Y1
Tel: 306-445-8033; *Fax:* 306-445-7211
nbattleford@wdm.ca
www.wdm.ca
North Battleford is one of four exhibit branches of Saskatchewan's Western Development Museum. The other branches are located in Moose Jaw, Saskatoon, & Yorkton. The North Battleford Western Development Museum provides visitors with the opportunity to explore a Heritage Farm & Village. Sights include a Wheat Pool grain elevator, a 1910 Case 110 tractor, A Co-op store, homes, & churches.
Wayne Fennig, Manager, North Battleford, wfennig@wdm.ca
Joyce Smith, Manager, Operations, jsmith@wdm.ca
Cheryl Stewart, Coordinator, Education & Volunteers, cstewart@wdm.ca
Daniel Stewart, Museum Technician, dstewart@wdm.ca

***Outlook:* Outlook & District Heritage Museum & Gallery**
PO Box 1095, 100 Railway Ave., Outlook, SK S0L 2N0
Tel: 306-867-8285
outlookmuseum@sasktel.net
Located in a former railway station, the Outlook & District Heritage Museum & Gallery is open from June to August. Exhibits include a caboose & an old jail cell. The Museum also keeps copies of the local newspaper, entitled "The Outlook", dating back to 1910.

***Oxbow:* Ralph Allen Memorial Museum**
PO Box 361, Oxbow, SK S0C 2B0
Tel: 306-483-5082
mbartolf@sasktel.net
Open May - Sept.
Michael Bartolf, 2nd Vice-President
Otto Neuman, President

***Paynton:* Bresaylor Heritage Museum**
PO Box 33, Main St., Paynton, SK S0M 2J0
Tel: 306-895-4813
The Bresaylor Heritage Museum collects artifacts from the Bresaylor & Paynton area. Items date back to 1882, when the earliest residents settled in Bresaylor. The museum is open in July & August, & at other times of the year by appointment.

***Pelly:* Fort Pelly Livingston Museum**
PO Box 24, 306- 1st Ave. S, Pelly, SK S0A 2Z0
Tel: 306-595-2030
www.pelly.ca/museum.html
Brian Clough

***Plenty:* Plenty & District Museum**
PO Box 99, Main St., Plenty, SK S0L 2R0
Tel: 306-932-4727
Situated in a 1911 building, which once served as Plenty's post office & hardware store, the Plenty & District Museum depicts pioneer life in the community & surrounding area. Farming equipment is featured in a separate building.

***Porcupine Plain:* Porcupine Plain & District Museum**
PO Box 171, Elm St., Porcupine Plain, SK S0E 1H0
Tel: 306-278-2317; *Fax:* 306-278-2073
www.porcupineplain.com
Other contact information: Phone, Appointments: 306-278-2834; 306-278-2073
Founded: 1968 The Porcupine Plain & District Museum features local pioneer artifacts, such as antique machinery & clothing. The museum also houses a bird displat, with birds from the Porcupine Plain & Somme area. The soldier settlement consists of a log home, a schoolhouse, & a church. The Porcupine Plain & District Museum is open from the beginning of July to the Labour Day weekend in September. At other times, tours may be arranged.

***Prairie River:* Prairie River Museum**
***Also known as:* Prairie River Heritage Society**
PO Box 9, Prairie River, SK S0E 1J0
Tel: 306-889-4248
prhs.fl.waskowic@sasktel.net
Railway, agriculture, lumbering, trapping, First Nations artifacts

***Prelate:* St. Angela's Museum & Archives**
PO Box 220, Prelate, SK S0N 2B0
Tel: 306-673-2200; *Fax:* 306-673-2635
To preserve valuable history of pioneer Saskatchewan & of the pioneer Ursulines of St. Angela's Convent Academy at Prelate Saskatchewan; collection tells story of Ursuline life & apostolate that were used in chapel, classroom & other departments
Sister Hermana Blatz, Director

***Prince Albert:* Diefenbaker House**
246 19th Street W., Prince Albert, SK S6V 8A9
Tel: 306-764-2992
historypa@citypa.com
historypa.com
Residence of John G. Diefenbaker immediately prior to his becoming Prime Minister of Canada; museum furnished as it was in Mr. Diefenbaker's day & also includes phtographic displays of his life & associations in Prince Albert
James Benson, Manager

***Prince Albert:* Evolution of Education Museum**
10 River St. East, Prince Albert, SK S6V 8A9
Tel: 306-764-2992
historypa@citypa.com
historypa.com
Founded: 1963 Housed in the original Claytonville one-room rural school & features a class-room setting, plus displays of many early educational materials & artefacts
James Benson, Manager

***Prince Albert:* Prince Albert Historical Museum**
10 River St. East, Prince Albert, SK S6V 8A9
Tel: 306-764-2992
historypa@citypa.com
historypa.com

History, life-styles & people of Prince Albert & area; souvenir shop & tea room
James Benson, Manager

Prince Albert: Rotary Museum of Police & Corrections
c/o Prince Albert Historical Society, 10 River St. East, Prince Albert, SK S6V 8A9
Tel: 306-764-2992
historypa@citypa.com
historypa.com
Housed in the guardhouse of the Prince Albert division of the NorthWest Mounted Police & Royal Northwest Mounted police; features artifacts, equipment & uniforms from the RCMP, Prince Albert City Police, the Provincial Correctional Service & the Correctional Service of Canada, as well as from the Saskatchewan Provincial Police
James Benson, Manager

Raymore: Raymore Pioneer Museum Inc.
PO Box 453, Raymore, SK S0A 3J0
Tel: 306-476-2180; *Fax:* 306-746-4314
Collection of local pioneer artifacts
Wayne Focht, Sec.-Treas.

Regina: Alex Youck School Museum
1600 - 4th Ave., Regina, SK S4R 8C8
Tel: 306-352-8200
Open by appt. only
Alex Youck, Director

Regina: Cumberland House Provincial Historic Park
#530, 3211 Albert St., Regina, SK S4S 5W6
Tel: 306-787-9572; *Fax:* 306-787-7000
Toll-Free: 800-205-7070
inquiry@serm.gov.sk.ca

Regina: Government House Museum & Heritage Property (GH)
4607 Dewdney Ave., Regina, SK S4T 1B7
Tel: 306-787-0846; *Fax:* 306-787-5714
ckuyek@gr.gov.sk.ca
www.gr.gov.sk.ca/govhouse
Former residence of the Lieutenant Governor of the Northwest Territories & the Province of Saskatchewan
Charlotte Kuyek, Community Relations Co-ordinator

Regina: Regina Plains Museum
1835 Scarth St., 2nd Fl., Regina, SK S4P 2G9
Tel: 306-780-9435; *Fax:* 306-565-2979
rp.museum@sasktel.net
www.reginaplainsmuseum.com
Founded: 1960 Regina Plains Museum is the civic history museum of the city. It is open year-round.
Christa Donaldson, Executive Director
Jan Morier, Coordinator, Communications

Regina: Saskatchewan Military Museum
The Armouries, 1600 Elphinstone St., Regina, SK S4T 3N1
Tel: 306-585-3771
www.saskmuseums.org
Collects & preserves Saskatchewan's military history from 1885 to the present; artifacts, uniforms, badges & medals, vehicles, ammunition; photos, archival material & paintings
Maj. (Ret'd) C. Keith Inches, Curator, keithinches@sasktel.net

Regina: Saskatchewan Pharmacy Museum
#700, 4010 Pasqua St., Regina, SK S4S 6S4
Tel: 306-584-2292; *Fax:* 306-584-9695
saskpharm@sk.sympatico.ca
www.skpharmacists.ca
Collection & preservation of pharmacy artifacts, documentation of pharmacy history
Bill Paterson, President

Regina: Saskatchewan Sports Hall of Fame & Museum
2205 Victoria Ave., Regina, SK S4P 0S4
Tel: 306-780-9232; *Fax:* 306-780-9427
sshfm@sasktel.net
www.sshfm.com
Founded: 1966 3,000 sq. ft. of exhibit space celebrating the sport heritage of Saskatchewan; open year round with extended summer hours
Sheila Kelly, Executive Director

Riverhurst: F.T. Hill Museum
PO Box 201, Riverhurst, SK S0H 3P0
Tel: 306-353-2112; *Fax:* 306-353-2220
Gun collection, aboriginal artifacts, pioneer items; open June 15 - Aug. 31 & by appt.
Betty Peterson

Rocanville: Rocanville & District Museum
PO Box 490, Rocanville, SK S0A 3L0
Tel: 306-645-2113; *Fax:* 306-645-2087
roc.cap@sasktel.net
Other contact information: Phone, Appointments: 306-645-2164
Located at the corner of Qu'appelle Avenue & St. Albert Street, the Rocanville & District Museum showcases a CPR station, a church, a schoolhouse, a blacksmith shop, & a Masonic Lodge. The museum is open during July & August, & by appointment at other times of the year.

La Ronge: Mistasinihk Place Interpretive Centre
c/o Saskatchewan Culture, Youth & Recreation, PO Box 5000, La Ronge, SK S0J 1L0
Tel: 306-425-4350; *Fax:* 306-425-4336
Aboriginal artifacts, artwork by northern artists, displays about northern industries & activites

Rose Valley: Rose Valley & District Heritage Museum
PO Box 248, Rose Valley, SK S0E 1M0
Tel: 306-322-4545; *Fax:* 306-322-5822
jrustad@sask.tel.net
Museum with artifacts from area 1900 to present; open July & Aug., Mon.- Fri.; off season viewing available by request
Judy Rustad, President, 306/322-4474
Irene Martinson, Sec.-Treas., 306/322-4642

Rosetown: Rosetown & District Museum
PO Box 37, Rosetown, SK S0L 2V0
Tel: 306-882-3106
Natural history specimens, photographs, handicrafts

Rosthern: Mennonite Heritage Museum
PO Box 116, Rosthern, SK S0K 3R0
Tel: 306-232-4415
Museum housed in school, artifacts from 1800 to present, collection of World Wheat champion; open May to Sept.

Rouleau: Rouleau & District Museum
PO Box 132, Rouleau, SK S0G 4H0
Tel: 306-776-2363
www.virtualmuseum.ca
A rural town street setting with houses, barn, blacksmith shop, school & other buildings; archives; special events, such as the annual threshing bee in Aug., & other programming. Open by appt., May - Sept.
Gareth Argue, President

St Brieux: Musée St. Brieux Museum
CP 224, 300 Barbier Dr., St Brieux, SK S0K 3V0
Tél: 306-275-2123
Documentation au sujet de la vie des pionniers, de leurs origines, des missions environnantes et de l'église catholique pré-Vatican II; des tournées en français ou en anglais sont offertes
Chantel Schur, Curator

St Victor: McGillis House
St Victor, SK S0H 3T0
Tel: 306-642-3171
www.willowbunch.ca
Located in St. Victor's regional park, McGillis House was built in 1890. Artifacts in the home include Métis items, kerosene lanterns, early saddles & bridles, & a feathered buffalo skull.

St Walburg: St. Walburg & District Museum
PO Box 87, St Walburg, SK S0M 2T0
Tel: 306-248-3631
Local exhibits from pioneer days to 1945

Saskatoon: Diefenbaker Canada Centre
University of Saskatchewan, 101 Diefenbaker Pl., Saskatoon, SK S7N 5B8
Tel: 306-966-8384; *Fax:* 306-966-6207
dief.centre@usask.ca
artsandscience.usask.ca/diefenbaker
The Diefenbaker Canada Centre includes a museum, archives, & research centre. The centre houses artifacts, such as a personal library, papers, & memorabilia, that were bequeathed to the University of Saskatchewan by former prime minister of Canada, John G. Diefenbaker. The archives features collections of press clippings, photographs, & documents related to Diefenbaker's life & Canadian history.
Teresa Carlson, Acting Director, 306-966-8383, teresa.carlson@usask.ca
Trent Evanisky, Coordinator, Special Exhibits, 306-966-8386
Rob Paul, Coordinator, Archives, 306-966-8387, rob.paul@usask.ca

Saskatoon: Fort Carlton Provincial Historic Park
#102, 112 Research Dr., Saskatoon, SK S7K 2H6
Tel: 306-467-5205; *Fax:* 306-933-5215
fortcarlton@gov.sk.ca
www.saskparks.net
Located 26 km. west of Duck Lake on Hwy. 212; a reconstructed Hudson's Bay Company fur trade post; open May - Sept.
Janice Crawford, Contact

Saskatoon: Meewasin Valley Authority (MVA)
402 - 3rd Ave. South, Saskatoon, SK S7K 3G5
Tel: 306-665-6888; *Fax:* 306-665-6117
meewasin@meewasin.com
www.meewasin.com
Founded: 1979 Conservation agency for the South Saskatchewan River
Susan Lamb, CEO, 306-665-6887

Saskatoon: Museum of Antiquities
#116, College Bldg., University of Saskatchewan, 107 Administration Pl., Saskatoon, SK S7N 5A2
Tel: 306-966-7818; *Fax:* 306-966-1954
museum_antiquities.usask.ca
www.usask.ca/antiquities/
Founded: 1974 A collection of Near Eastern, Egyptian, Greek, Roman & Medieval sculpture in full scale replica as well as original works & coinage
Tracene Harvey, Acting Director

Saskatoon: Natural Sciences Museum
Dept. of Biology & Geological Sciences, University of Saskatchewan, 112 Science Pl., Saskatoon, SK S7N 5E2
Tel: 306-966-4399; *Fax:* 306-966-4461
peta.bonhams@usask.ca
www.usask.ca
Designed to show evolution through time beginning with marine invertebrates & ending with evolution of animals; displays of living plants & animals correspond to fossils & create an integrated learning experience; free self-guided tours year-round; brochures downloaded from website
Dr. P. Bonham-Smith, Head, Biology, peta.bonhams@usask.ca
Dr. B. Pratt, Geology, brian.pratt@usask.ca

Saskatoon: Ukrainian Museum of Canada (UMC)
910 Spadina Cres. East, Saskatoon, SK S7K 3H5
Tel: 306-244-3800; *Fax:* 306-652-7620
ukrmuse@sasktel.net
www.umc.sk.ca
The Ukrainian Museum preserves & encourages Ukrainian folk arts in Canada. The permanent gallery tells the story of Ukrainian immigration to Canada with displays of folk arts, including costumes, embroideries, weaving, ceramics, & Easter eggs. The museum's collection of textiles is one of the largest of its kind in North America.
Janet C.P. Danyliuk, Director

Saskatoon: Wanuskewin Heritage Park
Penner Rd., RR#4, Saskatoon, SK S7K 3J7
Tel: 306-931-6767; *Fax:* 306-931-4522
Toll-Free: 877-547-6546
wanuskewin@wanuskewin.com
www.wanuskewin.com
Founded: 1992 The Wanuskewin Heritage Park represents the life of the Northern Plains First Nations people. Visitors will find tipi rings, bison kill sites, a medicine wheel, & pottery fragments. The 116 hectare park operates under the leadership & guidance of First Nations people. It is open year-round.

Saskatoon: Western Development Museum
***Also known as:* Saskatoon Western Development Museum**
2610 Lorne Ave. South, Saskatoon, SK S7J 0S6
Tel: 306-931-1910; *Fax:* 306-934-0525
saskatoon@wdm.ca
www.wdm.ca
Saskatoon is one of four exhibit branches of Saskatchewan's Western Development Museum. The other branches are located in Moose Jaw, North Battleford, & Yorkton. The Saskatoon Western Development Museum presents a 1910 Boomtown. Visitors can explore more than thirty buildings, including a blacksmith shop & a general store. The museum is also home to the Saskatchewan Agricultural Hall of Fame.
Tom Waiser, Manager, Saskatoon, twaiser@wdm.ca
Corinne Daelick, Coordinator, Education & Volunteers, cdaelick@wdm.ca
Julie Jackson, Museum Technician, jjackson@wdm.ca

Sceptre: Great Sandhills Museum
PO Box 29, Sceptre, SK S0N 2H0
Tel: 306-623-4345; *Fax:* 306-623-4612
gshs@sasktel.net
www.greatsandhillsmuseum.com
Dedicated to collect, portray & preserve the heritage of the "Great Sandhills" District in SW Saskatchewan through natural history specimens
Gertrude Hale, President

Scout Lake: St. Mary's Historical Society of Maxstone
PO Box 33, Scout Lake, SK S0H 3V0
Tel: 306-642-3150
lornesfarm@sasktel.net
Heritage site includes old church (1917) & graveyard, oldschool; open year round, by appt. only
Lorne Kwasnicki, Director

Shaunavon: Grand Coteau Heritage & Cultural Centre
PO Box 966, Centre St., Shaunavon, SK S0N 2M0
Tel: 306-297-3882; *Fax:* 306-297-3668
gchcc@sasktel.net
www.shaunavonmuseum.ca
Natural history museum, heritage museum, art gallery, public library; open year round
Ingrid Cazakoff, Director

Shell Lake: **Shell Lake Museum**
c/o Shell Lake Village Office, PO Box 280, Shell Lake, SK S0J 2G0
Tel: 306-427-2272
The Shell Lake Museum is located in the historic station house. The site also features a log house. It is open on weekends during the summer.

Sintaluta: **Sintaluta Community Museum**
PO Box 186, Sintaluta, SK S0G 4N0
Tel: 306-727-4421
Pioneer & regional artifacts, farm implements housed in former bank, Anglican Church & cottage, c. 1899 & 1907

Spalding: **Reynold Rapp Museum**
PO Box 308, Spalding, SK S0K 4C0
Tel: 306-872-2276; *Fax:* 306-287-4030
Housed in Reynold Rapp M.P.'s family home
Blanche Franko, President
Garth Ulrich, Secretary

Spy Hill: **Wolverine Hobby & Historical Society Inc.**
PO Box 268, Spy Hill, SK S0A 3W0
Tel: 306-534-2200
Three buildings, former country school, former retail outlet & Lutheran church; touring/visiting on request
Glenn Walz, President

Star City: **Star City Heritage Museum**
PO Box 38, 217 - 5th St., Star City, SK S0E 1P0
Tel: 306-863-2309
Star City's Heritage Museum presents World War I & World War II memorabilia, personal & household items, & farm equipment. The museum is open from June to August & by appointment during the off season.

Stoughton: **Stoughton & District Museum**
PO Box 492, 327 Main St., Stoughton, SK S0G 4T0
Tel: 306-457-2413; *Fax:* 306-457-3162
stoughtontown@sasktel.net
Pioneer items; open June to Sept.
Betty Wright, Contact

Strasbourg: **Strasbourg & District Museum**
PO Box 369, Strasbourg, SK S0G 4VO
Tel: 306-725-3293
Pioneer & First Nations artifacts, mounted animals & birds

Sturgis: **Sturgis Station House Museum**
PO Box 255, 306 Railway Ave. SE, Sturgis, SK S0A 4A0
Tel: 306-548-2108; *Fax:* 306-548-2089
Aboriginal & early settlers artifacts; open June to Aug.

Unity: **Unity & District Heritage Museum**
Unity Regional Park, General Delivery, Unity, SK S0K 4L0
Tel: 306-228-4464; *Fax:* 306-228-2149
www.townofunity.com/recreation/museum.php
The Unity & District Heritage Museum includes the following attractions: a 1909 CP Rail Station, the 1908 St. Thomas Anglican Church, the 1926 St.zwarthmore United Church, restored schools, an original home of Unity, a blacksmith shop, & a harness shop. The museum is open from mid May to October.

Val Marie: **Perrault's Museum**
PO Box 216, Val Marie, SK S0N 2T0
Tel: 306-298-2241
Extensive collection on Will James, artist & author of westerns in the 30s; buffalo collection as the last buffalo hunt & hunter in Canada was in Val Marie; approx. 40 oil paintings of sceneries of the Grasslands National Park by Lise Perrault
Lise Perrault, Directrice

Vanguard: **Vanguard Centennial Museum**
General Delivery, Vanguard, SK S0N 2V0
Tel: 306-582-2244
vanguard@chinook.lib.sk.ca
Pioneer articles
Iris Minifie, Curator, 306/582-6010, harry.minifie@sasktel.net

Verigin: **National Doukhobour Heritage Village**
PO Box 99, Verigin, SK S0A 4H0
Tel: 306-542-4441; *Fax:* 306-542-2017
Doukhobour artifacts, photos, handicrafts, clothing, hand tools; barns, a blacksmith shop & agricultural equipment; model of early Doukhobour village
Philip Perepelkin, Manager

Verwood: **Verwood Community Museum**
PO Box 213, Verwood, SK S0H 4G0
Tel: 306-642-5767
Pioneer articles housed in former church built in 1916

Wadena: **Wadena & District Museum & Gallery**
PO Box 1208, Wadena, SK S0A 4J0
Tel: 306-338-3454; *Fax:* 306-338-3804
wadena.museum@sasktel.net
Early settlers; 1904 CNR station house; 1907 Sunderland School No.1; blacksmith shop; furnishings; artifacts; open June - Aug., Tue.-Sun.
Barb Peace

Wakaw: **Batoche National Historic Site of Canada (BNHS)**
PO Box 1040, RR#1, Wakaw, SK S0K 4P0
Tel: 306-423-6227; *Fax:* 306-423-5400
batoche@pc.gc.ca
www.pc.gc.ca/eng/lhn-nhs/sk/batoche/index.aspx
Other contact information: TTD: 306-423-5540
The Batoche National Historic Site of Canada, on the banks of the South Saskatchewan River, is the scene of the last battlefield in the Northwest Rebellion of 1885. The site displays the remains & several restored buildings of the village of Batoche. The life of the Métis at Batoche between 1860 & 1900 is depicted. The site is open from May to September.

Wakaw: **Diefenbaker Law Office**
PO Box 760, Wakaw, SK S0K 4P0
Tel: 306-233-5157
Replica of the former prime minister's law office, located in Wakaw from 1918-1925

Wakaw: **Wakaw Heritage Society Museum**
PO Box 475, 300 1st St.S., Wakaw, SK S0K 4P0
Tel: 306-233-4257
Collections associated with pioneer life

Waskesiu Lake: **Prince Albert National Park of Canada Northern Prairies Field Unit, PO Box 100, Waskesiu Lake, SK S0J 2Y0**
Tel: 306-663-4522
panp.info@pc.gc.ca
www.pc.gc.ca/eng/pn-np/sk/princealbert/index.aspx
Protecting part of the boreal forest, Prince Albert National Park features the cabin of conservationist Grey Owl, a white pelican nesting colony, & a free-ranging herd of plains bison. Visitors to the park can participate in interpretive programs & special events. The park is open year-round, & the Interpretive Centre is open from the end of June to September.
Alan Fehr, Field Unit Superintendent, Northern Prairies

Wawota: **Wawota & District Museum**
PO Box 179, 101 Main St., Wawota, SK S0G 5A0
Tel: 306-739-2110
www.wawota.com/museum.htm
Founded: 1980 The Wawota & District Museum consists of the following buildings: the main building which was built in the early 1900s & used as a municipal office, a 1909 fire hall, the Bethany Schoolhouse, & a farm equipment shed. The museum is open during July & August, & by appointment at other times.

Weekes: **Dunwell & Community Museum**
PO Box 120, Weekes, SK S0E 1V0
Tel: 306-278-2906
Restored CNR station, pioneer artifacts & Ukrainian clothes

Weyburn: **Soo Line Historical Museum**
PO Box 1016, 411 Industrial Lane, Weyburn, SK S4H 2L2
Tel: 306-842-2922; *Fax:* 306-842-2922
slhm@sasktel.net
www.silver.sasktelwebsite.net
Largest private collection of silver in the world; collection of artifacts that were used by Weyburn & District pioneers
Jacquie Mallory, Curator

Weyburn: **Turner Curling Museum**
PO Box 370, 157 3rd St. NE, Weyburn, SK S4H 2K6
Tel: 306-848-3218; *Fax:* 306-842-2001
wneiszner@weyburn.ca
www.weyburn.ca
The museum was established by the late Don Turner & his wife Elva Turner; collection includes curling stones, brooms, clothing, pins, crests & books from around the world; tours available; open by appointment.
Elva Turner, Contact

White Fox: **White Fox Museum**
PO Box 68, White Fox, SK S0J 3B0
Tel: 306-276-2106
Trapper's cabin, tool & harness shop, pioneer items

Whitewood: **Whitewood Historical Museum**
PO Box 752, 607 North Railway, Whitewood, SK S0G 5C0
Tel: 306-735-4388
Pioneer school room & home, military display, Hungarian, French, Finnish & Swedish collections; open July - Aug.

Wilcox: **Athol Murray College of Notre Dame Archives & Museum**
Archives / Museum Bldg., Athol Murray College of Notre Dame Campus, PO Box 100, Wilcox, SK S0G 5E0
Tel: 306-732-2080; *Fax:* 306-732-2008
nd.archives@notredame.sk.ca
www.notredame.sk.ca
The Athol Murray College of Notre Dame Archives & Museum collects & preserves items that tell the story of Père Athol Murray & the history of the Athol Murray College of Notre Dame. The archives & museum features Père Athol Murray's collection of Rare Books, the Rex Beach Repository, the Parthenon Frieze, the Nicholas de Grandmaison Art Portrait collection, sculptures, & stained glass windows. The archives & museum is open seven days a week in July & August, & Monday to Friday from September to June.
Terry McGarry, Curator

Wilkie: **Wilkie & District Museum**
PO Box 26, Wilkie, SK S0K 4W0
Tel: 306-843-2717
love@sk.sympatico.ca
Open summer; by appt. the rest of the year
Frances Love, Sec.-Treas.

Willow Bunch: **Willow Bunch Museum**
PO Box 157, 16 Édouard Beaupré St., Willow Bunch, SK S0H 4K0
Tel: 306-473-2806; *Fax:* 306-473-2789
www.willowbunch.ca
Other contact information: Phone, Mid Sept. - Mid May: 306-473-2762 or 306-473-2279
Founded: 1972 The Willow Bunch Museum is located in a Convent school which was built in 1914 by the Sisters of the Cross. One attraction is the display about Edouard Beaupré, an eight foot, three inch tall circus performer who was born in Willow Bunch in 1881. The museum is open from mid May to mid September. Tours may be arranged during the off-season.
Doris O'Reilly, Director

Wolseley: **Wolseley & District Museum**
PO Box 218, Wolseley, SK S0G 5H0
Tel: 306-698-2360; *Fax:* 306-698-2360
Local history of the Wolseley including decorative arts, furnishings, household objects, and maps.
Robert Campbell, Contact

Wood Mountain: **Wood Mountain Rodeo Ranch Museum**
PO Box 53, Wood Mountain, SK S0H 4L0
Tel: 306-266-4953
www.woodmountain.ca/RodRanc.html
Other contact information: Phone, Tour Bookings: 306-266-2000
Located in the Wood Mountain Regional Park, Wood Mountain Rodeo Ranch Museum offers a glimpse into the life of ranchers & cowboys who arrived in the area in the 1880s. Exhibits include the history of the Wood Mountain Stampede, which is the oldest continuous rodeo in Canada. An extensive archival collection is also housed at the museum. The museum is open from May to September.
Lois Todd, Museum Contact

Wynyard: **Wynyard & District Museum**
PO Box 743, Wynyard, SK S0A 4T0
CPR hand car, household accesories, farm implements, WWI materials

Yorkton: **Western Development Museum**
Also known as: **Yorkton Western Development Museum**
PO Box 98, Hwy. 16 West, Yorkton, SK S3N 2V6
Tel: 306-783-8361; *Fax:* 306-782-1027
yorkton@wdm.ca
www.wdm.ca
Yorkton is one of four exhibit branches of Saskatchewan's Western Development Museum. The other branches are located in Moose Jaw, North Battleford, & Saskatoon. The Yorkton Western Development Museum presents the times when immigrants settled in western Canada, including the English, Ukrainians, Doukhobors, Germans, Swedes, & Icelanders.
Susan Mandziuk, Manager, Yorkton, smandziuk@wdm.ca
Carla Madsen, Programmer, Education & Special Events, cmadsen@wdm.ca
Phil Lane, Supervisor, Building, plane@wdm.ca

Yukon Territory

Territorial Museums

MacBride Museum
1124 First Ave., Whitehorse, YT Y1A 1A4
Tel: 867-667-2709; *Fax:* 867-633-6607
info@macbridemuseum.com
www.macbridemuseum.com
Founded: 1951 The Yukon Historical Society acquired the unoccupied Government Telegraph Office built in 1900, and in the 1960s opened it to the public as a museum to house the growing collection of cultural & natural history: Yukon heritage from pre-history to present. Exhibits include archeological & paleontological specimens; ethnographic artifacts, historic artifacts, photographs & archival materials; large industrial & transportation artifacts. Also there are outdoor displays, two heritage buildings.
Ms Patricia Cunning, Executive Director, MacBride Museum Society, pcunning@macbridemuseum.com
Patricia Cunning, Executive Director

Local Museums in Yukon Territory

***Burwash Landing:* Kluane Museum of Natural History**
PO Box 45, Historic Mile 1093, Alaska Hwy., Burwash Landing, YT Y0B 1V0
Tel: 867-841-5561; *Fax:* 867-841-5605
klvanemus@yknet.yk.ca
Workclass wildlife display, native handicrafts; open Victoria Day - Labour Day

***Dawson City:* Dawson City Museum**
PO Box 303, Dawson City, YT Y0B 1G0
Tel: 867-993-5291; *Fax:* 867-993-5839
dcmuseum@yknet.yk.ca
users.yknet.yk.ca/dcpages/Museum.html
Three main galleries include objects and photographs which tells of the story of the Klondike era through the Godl Rush; native history; open mid-May to mid- Sept.; other times by appt.
Cheryl Thompson, Director/Administrator
Julia D. Pike, Director/Curator

***Dawson City:* Klondike National Historic Sites**
PO Box 390, Dawson City, YT Y0B 1G0
Tel: 867-993-5462; *Fax:* 867-993-7203
dawson.info@pc.gc.ca
www.pch.gc.ca
Historic buildings; artifacts; documents; related to Klondike history, Yukon Consolidated Gold Corp. & the Dawson Daily News
G. MacMillan, Supt.

***Haines Junction:* Kluane National Park**
PO Box 5495, Haines Junction, YT Y0B 1L0
Tel: 867-634-7250; *Fax:* 867-634-7208
kluane.info@pc.gc.ca
www.pc.gc.ca/kluane
Natural & cultural history of Kluane National Park & Reserve of Canada; information on park services, hiking & other activities

***Keno City:* Keno City Mining Museum**
PO Box 17, Keno City, YT Y0B 1M0
Tel: 867-995-2792; *Fax:* 867-995-3103
www.kenocity.info/museum.htm
Other contact information: Winter phone: 867/995-2411
History of mining of gold & silver in the early 1900s (tools, equipment artifacts); open June-Sept.

***Teslin:* George Johnston Tlingit Indian Museum**
***Also known as:* Teslin Historical & Museum Society**
PO Box 146, Km 1294 Mile 804, Alaska Hwy., Teslin, YT Y0A 1B0
Tel: 867-390-2550
gjmuseum@hotmail.com
www.gjmuseum.yk.net
Inland Tlingit ethnographic & 20th centrury artifacts; open May 22-Sept. 4

***Whitehorse:* Fort Selkirk**
c/o Tourism & Culture, Cultural Services Branch, PO Box 2703, Whitehorse, YT Y1A 2C6
Tel: 867-667-5386; *Fax:* 867-667-8023
Toll-Free: 800-661-0408
doug.olynyk@gov.yk.ca
Accessible only by boat or plane; contact Selkirk First Nation, Pelly Crossing, YK Y0B 1P0; 867/537-3331; Fax: 867/537-3902; Attn: Emma Alfred; open mid-May - mid-Sept. URL is a portal to the virtual museum.
Doug Olynyk, Historic Sites Coordinator, Yukon Cultural Services Branch

***Whitehorse:* LePage Park**
c/o Yukon Historical & Museums Association, 3126 Third Ave., Whitehorse, YT Y1A 1E7
Tel: 867-667-4704; *Fax:* 867-667-4506
yhma@yknet.yk.ca
heritageyukon.ca/
Walking tours by interpreters in period costume, June - Aug.; open year round
Brent Slobodin, President

***Whitehorse:* Old Log Church Museum**
PO Box 31461, 3rd Ave. & Elliot St., Whitehorse, YT Y1A 6K8
Tel: 867-668-2555; *Fax:* 867-667-6258
logchurch@klondiker.com
Open May - Labour Day
Taryn Parker, Curator

***Whitehorse:* Yukon Beringia Interpretive Centre**
PO Box 2703, Mile 914, Alaska Hwy., Whitehorse, YT Y1A 2C6
Tel: 867-667-8855; *Fax:* 867-667-8854
beringia@gov.yk.ca
www.beringia.com
Beringia was an ancient place, situated between two continents on the edge of the Arctic. The land connection between Siberia & Alaska was part of the larger area known as Beringia. The land of ice was home to huge mammals, such as woolly mammoths & scimitar cats, & the first people of North America. The Yukon Beringia Interpretive Centre is open from May to September. During the winter, it is open on Sundays, or by appointment.

***Whitehorse:* Yukon Transportation Museum**
30 Electra Cres., Whitehorse, YT Y1A 6E6
Tel: 867-668-4792; *Fax:* 867-633-5547
info@goytim.ca
www.yukontransportationmuseum.ca
Transportation displays depicting the first commercial aircraft in the Yukon; construction of the Alaska Highway, the White Pass & Yukon Route Railway. Open daily 10-6, mid-May - end of August.
Casey Mclaughlin, Executive Director/Curator, casey@goytm.ca
Cathy Ritchie, Assistant Director/Curator, cathy@goytm.ca

National Parks & Outdoor Education Centres

Alberta

Local National Parks & Outdoor Education Centres in Alberta

***Banff:* Banff National Park**
PO Box 900, Banff, AB T1L 1K2
Tel: 403-762-1550; *Fax:* 403-762-3380
banff.vrc@pc.gc.ca
www.pc.gc.ca/pn-np/ab/banff/index_e.asp
In the fall of 1883, three Canadian Pacific Railway construction workers stumbled across a cave containing hot springs on the eastern slopes of Alberta's Rocky Mountains. From that humble beginning was born Banff National Park, Canada's first national park and the world's third. Spanning 6,641 square kilometres (2,564 square miles) of valleys, mountains, glaciers, forests, meadows and rivers, Banff National Park is one of the world's premier destination spots. Hours of Operation: Winter, 9:00-5:00; Spring, 9:00-7:00; Summer, 8:00-8:00; Fall, 9:00-7:00

***Fort Saskatchewan:* Elk Island National Park**
Site 4, R.R.#1, Fort Saskatchewan, AB T8L 2N7 Canada
Tel: 780-922-5790; *Fax:* 780-992-2983
elk.island@pc.gc.ca
www.pc.gc.ca/pn-np/ab/elkisland/index_E.asp
Located less than an hour away from Edmonton, Elk Island National Park of Canada protects the wilderness of the aspen parkland, one of the most endangered habitats in Canada. This beautiful oasis is home to herds of free roaming plains bison, wood bison, moose, deer, and elk. Also boasting over 250 species of birds, the park is a bird watcher's paradise. Be it for wildlife viewing, hiking, cross-country skiing, picnicking or overnight camping, there is something for everyone at Elk Island National Park. Hours: Campground Reservations, Administration Building and Wardern Operations Building open year round, 8:00-4:00; Sandy Beach Campground, Golf Course open May-Oct weather permitting; winter campground open Oct-April weather permitting.

***Jasper:* Jasper National Park of Canada**
PO Box 10, Jasper, AB T0E 1E0
Tel: 780-852-6176; *Fax:* 780-852-6177
pnj.jnp@pc.gc.ca
www.pc.gc.ca/pn-np/ab/jasper/index_E.asp
Jasper is the largest and most northerly Canadian rocky mountain national park, part of a spectacular World Heritage Site. Comprised of delicate and carefully protected ecosystems, Jasper's scenery is none-the-less rugged and mountainous. In this special corner of Canada you can thrill to the thunder of Sunwapta Falls, enjoy the serene beauty of Mount Edith Cavell, connect with nature along 1,000-plus kilometres of trails, experience Athabasca Glacier up close or just resign yourself to a relaxing soak in Miette Hotsprings. Hours of Operation: Winter 9:00-4:00; Spring 9:00-5:00; Summer 8:30-7:00; Fall 9:00-5:00

***Waterton Park:* Waterton Lakes National Park of Canada**
PO Box 200, Waterton Park, AB T0K 2M0
Tel: 403-859-2224; *Fax:* 403-859-5152
waterton.info @pc.gc.ca
www.pc.gc.ca/pn-np/ab/waterton/index_E.asp
Rugged, windswept mountains rise abruptly out of gentle prairie grassland in spectacular Waterton Lakes National Park. Here, several different ecological regions meet and interact in a landscape shaped by wind, fire, flooding, and abundant plants and wildlife. The park helps protect the unique and unusually diverse physical, biological and cultural resources found in the Crown of the Continent: one of the narrowest places in the Rocky Mountains. The highlight of Waterton's sparkling chain of lakes is the international Upper Waterton Lake, the deepest lake in the Canadian Rockies. In 1932, the park was joined with Montana's Glacier National Park to form the Waterton-Glacier International Peace Park - a world first. Hours of Operation: Park Receptionist year round, M-F 8:00-4:00; Campsites and Parkways May-Oct.

British Columbia

Local National Parks & Outdoor Education Centres in British Columbia

***Field:* Yoho National Park of Canada**
PO Box 99, Field, BC V0A 1G0
Tel: 250-343-6783; *Fax:* 250-343-6012
yoho.info@pc.gc.ca
www.pc.gc.ca/pn-np/bc/yoho/index_E.asp
Established in 1886, Yoho National Park is one of 41 national parks in Canada. Our nation's parks celebrate and help protect the diversity of Canada's landscapes and the life within. Yoho represents the western slopes of the Rocky Mountains region, and is also a Cree expression of awe and wonder for this place of rock walls, spectacular waterfalls and soaring peaks. In the shadow of the Great Divide, Yoho holds the secrets of ancient ocean life, the power of ice and water, and unique plant and animal communities that continue to evolve today. Hours of Operation: Parklands are open year round; Visitor Centre open in Winter 9:00-4:00, Spring 9:00-5:00, Summer 9:00-7:00, Fall 9:00-5:00; campgrounds open Spring-Fall.

***Queen Charlotte:* Gwaii Haanas National Park Reserve and Haida Heritage Site**
PO Box 37, Queen Charlotte, BC V0T 1S0
Tel: 250-559-8818; *Fax:* 250-559-8366
gwaii. haanas@pc.gc.ca
www.pc.gc.ca/pn-np/bc/gwaiihaanas/index_E.asp
Together, the Government of Canada and the Council of the Haida Nation manage the special place called Gwaii Haanas through a unique agreement signed in 1993. The two parties strongly agree on the need to protect Gwaii Haanas, even though the question of ownership is unresolved. Gwaii Haanas embodies the essence of the rugged beauty and rich ecology of the Pacific coast. It is a celebration of more than ten thousand years of Haida connection with the land and sea. For some visitors, this opportunity to witness a living culture, and immerse themselves in nature is a spiritual experience. Hours of Operation: M-F 8:00-12:00, 1:00-4:30.

***Radium Hot Springs:* Kootenay National Park of Canada**
PO Box 220, Radium Hot Springs, BC V0A 1M0
Tel: 250-347-9505; *Fax:* 250-347-9980
kootenay.info@pc.gc.ca
www.pc.gc.ca/pn-np/bc/kootenay/index_E.asp
Established in 1920, Kootenay National Park is one of 41 national parks in Canada. Together, they celebrate and protect the diversity of the nation's great landscapes. Kootenay National Park represents the south-western region of the Canadian Rocky Mountains. From glacier-clad peaks along the Continental Divide to semi-arid grasslands of the Rocky Mountain Trench, where cactus grows, this is a park rich in diversity of landscapes and ecology. Hours of Operation: Parklands are open year round. Parks Canada administration office in Radium Hot Springs is open year round, M-F 8:00-12:00, 12:30-4:00.

***Revelstoke:* Glacier National Park of Canada**
PO Box 350, Revelstoke, BC V0E 2S0
Tel: 250-837-7500; *Fax:* 250-837-7536
revglacier. reception@pc.gc.ca
www.pc.gc.ca/pn-np/bc/glacier/index_E.asp
Glacier National Park of Canada protects, for all time, a portion of the Columbia Mountains Natural Region, in the interior wet belt of British Columbia. The steep, rugged mountains, warm, moist climate and wide variety of plant and animal life are typical of this natural region. The park protects unique stands of old-growth cedar and hemlock and critical habitat for threatened and endangered wildlife species such as the mountain caribou, mountain goat and grizzly bear. The Rogers Pass National Historic Site is located in Glacier National Park. Rogers Pass was so designated for its importance in the construction and development of the country's first major national transportation route. Hours of Operation: Winter 7:00-5:00; Spring 8:30-4:30; Summer 7:30 am-8:00 pm; Fall (November) M, Th-Su 8:30-4:30.

***Revelstoke:* Mount Revelstoke National Park of Canada**
PO Box 350, Revelstoke, BC V0E 2S0
Tel: 250-837-7500; *Fax:* 250-837-7536
revglacier. reception@pc.gc.ca
www.pc.gc.ca/pn-np/bc/revelstoke/index_E.asp
Mount Revelstoke National Park is a place of contrasts. Take a drive along the summit parkway through a variety of geographical zones. From dense old-growth rainforest of giant cedar and pine, travel up through subalpine forest, and finally alpine meadows and tundra. Marvel at the spectacular view of the ice-clad peaks of the Monashee Mountains and, to the east, the Selkirk Mountains. The Giant Cedars hiking trail takes you through a stand of ancient Western Red Cedars, and the Skunk Cabbage trail introduces you to jungle-like wetland, a birder's paradise. Hours of Operation: Welcome Station Kiosk, June-Aug

7:00 am-8:30 pm. Parkway, Spring & Fall 9:00-5:00, Summer 7:00 am-8:30 pm.

***Sidney:* Gulf Islands National Park Reserve of Canada**
2220 Harbour Rd., Sidney, BC V8L 2P6
Tel: 250-654-4000; *Fax:* 250-654-4014
gulf.islands@pc.gc.ca
www.pc.gc.ca/pn-np/bc/gulf/index_E.asp
Established in 2003, Gulf Islands National Park Reserve safeguards a portion of British Columbia's beautiful southern Gulf Islands archipelago. These islands are representative of the Strait of Georgia Lowlands, one of the most ecologically at risk natural regions in southern Canada. The first new national park reserve of the twenty-first century includes thirty-five square kilometres of land and intertidal area on fifteen islands, numerous islets and reefs, and approximately twenty-six square kilometres of marine areas. We encourage you to experience this exceptional coastal island landscape and the cultures of the people who live here so that the memories you take home are those that last a lifetime in your heart but leave no lasting trace on park ecosystems. Hours of Operation: Most parklands have full services and charge fees from May-Oct, but parklands are open year round.

***Ucluelet:* Pacific Rim National Park Reserve of Canada**
PO Box 280, 2185 Ocean Terrace Rd., Ucluelet, BC V0R 3A0
Tel: 250-726-7721; *Fax:* 250-726-4720
pacrim.info@pc.gc.ca
www.pc.gc.ca/pn-np/bc/pacificrim/index_E.asp
Welcome to Pacific Rim National Park Reserve of Canada. Backed by the Insular Mountains Range of Vancouver Island and facing the open Pacific Ocean, Pacific Rim presents the rich natural and cultural heritage of Canada's west coast. Its cool and wet maritime climate produces an abundance of life in the water and on land. Lush coastal temperate rainforest gives way to bountiful and diverse intertidal and subtidal areas. These natural wonders are interwoven with the long and dynamic history of the Nuu-chah-nulth First Nations and European explorers and settlers. Hours of Operation: year round.

Manitoba

Local National Parks & Outdoor Education Centres in Manitoba

***Churchill:* Wapusk National Park of Canada**
PO Box 127, Churchill, MB R0B 0E0
Tel: 204-675-8863; *Fax:* 204-675-2026
Toll-Free: 888-773-8888
wapusk.np@pc.gc.ca
www.pc.gc.ca/pn-np/mb/wapusk/index_ E.asp
Wapusk means "White Bear" in Cree. The park earns its name because it protects one of the world's largest known polar bear maternity denning areas. It represents the Hudson James Lowlands natural region bordering on Hudson Bay. The park lies on the transition between boreal forest and Arctic tundra. The geology, biodiversity, and cultural history of the area all contribute to the unique wilderness character of Wapusk National Park of Canada. Hours of Operation: Access to Wapusk is via authorized commercial tour operators in Churchill. Wapusk National Park has limited visitor capacity at present. Unescorted visits to the park are not recommended.For the most current list of operators, please contact the park office (1-888-773-8888, 1-204-675-8863).

***Wasagaming:* Riding Mountain National Park of Canada**
Wasagaming, MB R0J 2H0
Tel: 204-848-7275; *Fax:* 204-848-2596
rmnp.info@pc.gc.ca
www.pc.gc.ca/pn-np/mb/riding/index_E.asp
Situated amidst a sea of agricultural land, Riding Mountain rises dramatically from the prairie landscape. Forming part of the Manitoba Escarpment, this "island" reserve protects a wide variety of wildlife and vegetation areas. The park has numerous hiking trails, and Agassiz Tower overlooks a panoramic view of prairies stretching out to the north. Wasagaming, the park's townsite, offers a full range of visitor services including accommodation, restaurants and shopping. Hours of Operation: Administration Office M-F 8:00-12:00, 12:30-4:00; Visitor Centre, Spring & Fall M-Su 9:30-5:30, Summer 9:30-8:00.

New Brunswick

Local National Parks & Outdoor Education Centres in New Brunswick

***Alma:* Fundy National Park of Canada**
PO Box 1001, Alma, NB E4H 1B4
Tel: 506-887-6000; *Fax:* 506-887-6008
fundy.info@pc.gc.ca
www.pc.gc.ca/pn-np/nb/fundy/index_E.asp
Fundy National Park of Canada encompasses some of the last remaining wilderness in southern New Brunswick. Here, the conifer dominated Caledonia Highlands roll down to meet the fog-generating Bay of Fundy. The tidal fluctuation of the Bay of Fundy is the highest in the world. Watch fishing boats come and go to the rhythm of the bay. Inland, explore lush forests and deep stream valleys. Hours of Operation: Headquarters Vistory Reception Centre, Spring & Fall 8:00-4:30; Summer 8:00 am-10:00 pm.

***Kouchibouguac National Park:* Kouchibouguac National Park of Canada**
186 Rte. 117, Kouchibouguac National Park, NB E4X 2P1
Tel: 506-876-2443; *Fax:* 506-876-4802
kouch.info@pc.gc.ca
www.pc.gc.ca/eng/pn-np/nb/kouchibouguac/index.aspx
Founded: 1969 Kouchibouguac National Park of Canada is a Canadian Heritage protected area. One of two wilderness Canadian national parks in New Brunswick, Kouchibouguac is a mosaic of bogs, salt marshes, tidal rivers, freshwater systems, sheltered lagoons, abandoned fields, & tall forests, which characterize the Maritime Plain Natural Region. The name Kouchibouguac is of Mi'kmaq origin & means "river of the long tides". This 238 square kilometre national park provides many family activities. There are 60 kilometres of cycling paths for both hikers & cyclists. Canoeing, kayaking, swimming, camping, bird watching, as well as cross country skiing, snowshoeing. & tobogganing in winter, are also available in this area, located on New Brunswick's eastern coast line.

Newfoundland & Labrador

Local National Parks & Outdoor Education Centres in Newfoundland & Labrador

***Glovertown:* Terra Nova National Park of Canada**
Glovertown, NL A0G 2L0
Tel: 709-533-2801; *Fax:* 709-533-2706
info.tnnp@pc.gc.ca
www.pc.gc.ca/pn-np/nl/terranova/index_E.asp
Terra Nova National Park of Canada is a place where long fingers of the North Atlantic Ocean touch the island boreal forest of Eastern Newfoundland. Rocky headlands provide shelter from the awesome power of the open ocean. The landscape of the park varies from the rugged cliffs and sheltered inlets of the coastal region to the rolling forested hills, bogs and ponds of the inland. Cultural history abounds in the remnants of sawmills and past human cultures. Hours of Operation: Administration Building, M-F 8:00-4:00; Visitor Centre, Jan 10-May 17 Th-M 9:00-4:00, May 18-June 21 Sa-Su 10:00-5:00, June 22-Sept 2 Sa-Su 9:00-7:00, Sept 3-Oct 8 Th-M 10:00-5:00.

***Nain:* Torngat Mountains National Park of Canada**
PO Box 471, 2 Service Rd., Nain, NL A0P 1L0
Tel: 709-922-1290; *Fax:* 709-922-1294
Toll-Free: 888-922-1290
torngats.info@pc.qc.ca
The Torngat Mountains National Park of Canada is located in northern Labrador and encompasses roughly 10,000 km2. It extends from Saglek Fjord in the south, to the very northern tip of Labrador; and from the provincial boundary with Quebec in the west, to the waters of the Labrador Sea in the east. The national park will protect an area of spectacular Arctic wilderness, with towering mountains, breathtaking fjords, gentle river valleys and rugged coastal landscapes - a wilderness that has been home to the Inuit and their ancestors for thousands of years. Dramatic Nachvak Fjord, which lies near the centre of the park, was formed by a glacier cutting through the Torngat Mountains as it flowed to the sea during the last ice age. Today, the Torngat Mountains include the highest peaks in continental eastern North America, and are dotted by many small glaciers.

***Rocky Harbour:* Gros Morne National Park of Canada**
PO Box 130, Rocky Harbour, NL A0K 4N0
Tel: 709-458-2417; *Fax:* 709-458-2059
grosmorne.info @pc.gc.ca
www.pc.gc.ca/pn-np/nl/grosmorne/index_E.asp
Gros Morne National Park of Canada was designated a UNESCO World Heritage Site in 1987. It is an area of great natural beauty with a rich variety of scenery, wildlife, and recreational activities. Visitors can hike through wild, uninhabited mountains and camp by the sea. Boat tours bring visitors under the towering cliffs of a freshwater fjord carved out by glaciers. Waterfalls, marine inlets, sea stacks, sandy beaches, and colourful nearby fishing villages complete the phenomenal natural and cultural surroundings of Gros Morne National Park of Canada. Hours of Operation: Park Headquaters, M-F 8:00-12:00, 1:00-4:30; Visitor Centre, April 30-May 18 M-F 9:00-4:00, May 19-June 22 9:00-5:00, June 23-Sept 3 9:00 am-9:00 pm, Sept 4-Oct 8 9:00-5:00, Oct 9-Oct 26 M-F 9:00-4:00.

Northwest Territories

Local National Parks & Outdoor Education Centres in Northwest Territories

***Fort Simpson:* Nahanni National Park Reserve of Canada**
PO Box 348, Fort Simpson, NT X0E 0N0
Tel: 867-695-3151; *Fax:* 867-695-2446
nahanni.info@pc.gc.ca
www.pc.gc.ca/pn-np/nt/nahanni/index_E.asp
Nahanni National Park Reserve of Canada protects a portion of the Mackenzie Mountains Natural Region offering the adventurous visitor a wilderness experience. A key feature of the park is the Naha Dehé (South Nahanni River). Four great canyons line this spectacular whitewater river. At Nailicho (Virginia Falls) the river plunges in a thunderous plume. The park's sulphur hotsprings, alpine tundra, mountain ranges, and forests of spruce and aspen are home to many species of birds, fish and mammals. A visitor centre in Fort Simpson features displays on the history, culture and geography of the area. The park was inscribed on UNESCO's World Heritage List in 1978. Hours of Operation: Winter, M-F 8:30-12:00, 1:00-5:00; Summer, daily 8:00-12:00, 1:00-5:00.

***Fort Smith:* Wood Buffalo National Park of Canada**
149 McDougal Rd., Fort Smith, NT X0E 0P0
Tel: 867-872-7960; *Fax:* 867-872-3910
Toll-Free: - - 0
wbnp.info@pc.gc.ca
www.pc.gc.ca/buffalo
As part of Canada's system of national parks and national historic sites, Wood Buffalo National Park of Canada is our country's largest national park and one of the largest in the world. It was established in 1922 to protect the last remaining herds of bison in northern Canada. Today, it protects an outstanding and representative example of Canada's Northern Boreal Plains. Hours of Operation: Park is open year round; Fort Smith Visitor Reception Centre open 9:00 AM- noon and 1 PM - 5 PM, Monday to Friday; 1 PM - 5 PM on summer weekends (3rd weekend in May until Labour Day)

***Fort Smith:* Wood Buffalo National Park of Canada**
750, Fort Smith, NT X0E 0P0
Tel: 867-872-7900; *Fax:* 867-872-3910
wbnp.info@pc.gc.ca
www.pc.gc.ca/pn-np/nt/woodbuffalo/index_E.asp
As part of Canada's system of national parks and national historic sites, Wood Buffalo National Park of Canada is our country's largest national park and one of the largest in the world. It was established in 1922 to protect the last remaining herds of bison in northern Canada. Today, it protects an outstanding and representative example of Canada's Northern Boreal Plains. Hours of Operation: Fort Smith Visitor Reception Centre, Oct-Apr M-F 9:00-12:00, 1:00-5:00; May-Sept M-F 9:00-12:00, 1:00-5:00, Sa-Su 1:00-5:00, park is open year round.

***Inuvik:* Ivvavik National Park of Canada**
PO Box 1840, Inuvik, NT X0E 0T0
Tel: 867-777-8800; *Fax:* 867-777-8820
Inuvik.info@pc.gc.ca
www.pc.gc.ca/pn-np/yt/ivvavik/index_E.asp
Ivvavik, meaning 'a place for giving birth, a nursery', in Inuvialuktun, the language of the Inuvialuit, is the first national park in Canada to be created as a result of an aboriginal land claim agreement. The park protects a portion of the calving grounds of the Porcupine caribou herd and represents the Northern Yukon and Mackenzie Delta natural regions. Hours of Operation: Park is open year round, with no available services.

***Paulatuk:* Tuktut Nogait National Park of Canada**
PO Box 91, Paulatuk, NT X0E 1N0
Tel: 867-580-3233; *Fax:* 867-580-3234
inuvik.info@pc.gc.ca
www.pc.gc.ca/pn-np/nt/tuktutnogait/index_E.asp
With rolling tundra, wild rivers, precipitous canyons, and a variety of unique wildlife and vegetation, Tuktut Nogait ('young caribou') is one of Canada's undiscovered gems. This remote park is located 170 kilometres north of the arctic circle and is home to the Bluenose West caribou herd, wolves, grizzly bears, muskoxen, arctic char, and a high density of raptors. The wildlife and land have supported aboriginal peoples for thousands of years, from the Copper and Thule cultures to contemporary Inuvialuit. Hours of Operation: open year round.

***Sachs Harbour:* Aulavik National Park of Canada**
PO Box 29, Sachs Harbour, NT X0E 0Z0
Tel: 867-690-3904; *Fax:* 867-690-4808
Inuvik.info@pc.gc.ca
www.pc.gc.ca/pn-np/nt/aulavik/index_E.asp
Aulavik, meaning "place where people travel" in Inuvialuktun, protects more than 12,000 square kilometres of arctic lowlands on the north end of Banks Island. The park encompasses a variety of landscapes from fertile river valleys to polar deserts, buttes and badlands, rolling hills, and bold seacoasts. At the

heart of Aulavik is the Thomsen River, which offers visitors a chance to paddle one of the continent's most northerly navigable waterways. This pristine arctic environment is home to both the endangered Peary caribou and to the highest density of muskoxen in the world. The wildlife and land have supported aboriginal peoples for more than 3,400 years, from Pre-Dorset cultures to contemporary Inuvialuit. Hours of Operation: Open year round.

Nova Scotia

Local National Parks & Outdoor Education Centres in Nova Scotia

***Ingonish Beach:* Cape Breton Highlands National Park of Canada**
Ingonish Beach, NS B0C 1L0
Tel: 902-224-2306; *Fax:* 902-285-2866
information@pc.gc.ca
www.pc.gc.ca/pn-np/ns/cbreton/index_E.asp
The headlands and cliffs of Cape Breton Highland tower over the rich, natural heritage that is all around. Home to the famous Cabot Trail, the land is blessed with spectacular scenery, abundant wildlife and a human history that stretches back to the last Ice Age. The park offers many accessible treasures and experiences remarkable in their diversity, beauty, and wonder. Hours of Operation: park is open year round; Visitor Centre May 5-June 27 9:00-5:00, June 28-Aug 22 8:00 am-8:00 pm, Aug 23-Sept 26 9:00-6:00, Sept 27-Oct 28 9:00-5:00.

***Maitland Bridge:* Kejimkujik National Park and National Historic Site of Canada**
PO Box 236, Maitland Bridge, NS B0T 1B0
Tel: 902-682-2772; *Fax:* 902-682-3367
kejimkujik. info@pc.gc.ca
www.pc.gc.ca/pn-np/ns/kejimkujik/index_E.asp
Kejimkujik, the only inland national park of Canada in the Maritimes, features abundant lakes and rivers ideal for canoeing. The lush woodlands and gently rolling landscapes are home to a variety of wildlife. Visitors will find historic canoe routes, portages and many beautiful hiking trails in the park. Hours of Operation: Visitor Reception Centre, Labour day-Mid June 8:30-4:30, midJune-Labour day 8:30am-9:00 pm; Campground Kiosk Mid June-Labour day 9:00am-9:00 pm.

Nunavut

Local National Parks & Outdoor Education Centres in Nunavut

***Iqaluit:* Quttinirpaaq National Park of Canada**
PO Box 278, Iqaluit, NU X0A 0H0
Tel: 867-975-4673; *Fax:* 867-975-4674
nunavut.info@pc.gc.ca
www.pc.gc.ca/pn-np/nu/quttinirpaaq/index_E.asp
Welcome ... to the top of the world! During the brief arctic summer on Quttinirpaaq, the sun remains high in the sky bathing the land in continuous daylight. There is no darkness to mark the passage of time telling you when to sleep and when to wake. There are no trees to remind you of lands further south. The scale of the land is both immense and intimate at the same time. Intricate patterns of rock, frost-cracked ground, willows and wildflowers at your feet extend out from where you stand into endless vistas in the clear, dry air. Glaciers on a mountainside 15 km away seem to be details in a landscape within reach. Hours of Operation: Warden station only staffed furing the summer field season. Parks Canada Office in Iqaluit is open M-F 8:30-12:00, 1:00-5:00 year round.

***Pangnirtung:* Auyuittuq National Park of Canada**
PO Box 353, Pangnirtung, NU X0A 0R0
Tel: 867-473-2500; *Fax:* 867-473-8612
nunavut.info@pc.gc.ca
www.pc.gc.ca/pn-np/nu/auyuittuq/index_E.asp
Sweeping glaciers and polar sea ice meet jagged granite mountains in Auyuittuq National Park of Canada. Established in 1976, Auyuittuq - an Inuktitut word meaning "land that never melts" - protects 19,089 km 2 of glacier-scoured terrain. Located in the eastern Arctic, on southern Baffin Island, the park includes the highest peaks of the Canadian Shield, the Penny Ice Cap, marine shorelines along coastal fiords, and Akshayuk Pass, a traditional travel corridor used by the Inuit for thousands of years. Whether you wish to climb Auyuittuq's rugged peaks, ski on its pristine icefields, or hike the scenic Akshayuk Pass, this park offers unique opportunities to experience the beauty and majesty of the Arctic. Hours of Operation: Winter M-F 8:30-12:00, 1:00-5:00, Summer hours are posted in June.

***Pond Inlet:* Sirmilik National Park of Canada**
PO Box 300, Pond Inlet, NU X0A 0S0
Tel: 867-899-8092; *Fax:* 867-899-8104
sirmilik.info@pc.gc.ca
www.pc.gc.ca/sirmilik
Founded: 2001 As part of Canada's national parks system, Sirmilik National Park represents the Northern Eastern Arctic Lowlands Natural Region and portions of the Lancaster Sound Marine Region. The park will comprise four separate land areas. Bylot Island is a spectacular area of rugged mountains, icefields and glaciers, coastal lowlands and seabird colonies. Oliver Sound is a long, narrow fiord with excellent opportunities for boating, hiking and camping. Borden Peninsula is an extensive plateau dissected by broad river valleys. The park features landforms and superb wilderness hiking and camping, and a major seabird colony in the vicinity of Baillarge Bay. Hours of Operation: Administration and Visitor Centre, M-F 8:30-12:00, 1:00-5:00.

Ontario

Local National Parks & Outdoor Education Centres in Ontario

***Heron Bay:* Pukaskwa National Park of Canada**
PO Box 212, Heron Bay, ON P0T 1R0
Tel: 807-229-0801; *Fax:* 807-229-2097
ont-pukaskwa @pc.gc.ca
www.pc.gc.ca/pn-np/on/pukaskwa/index_E.asp
Pukaskwa National Park's exceptional beauty is revealed in its vistas of Lake Superior and in the rugged, ancient landscape of the Canadian Shield and northern forest. The spirit of the wilderness envelopes those who explore this special place. The only wilderness national park in Ontario, Pukaskwa protects 1878 square km of an ecosystem that features boreal forest and Lake Superior shoreline. Hours of Operation: Administration Building M-F 8:30-4:30 year round.

***Leamington:* Point Pelee National Park of Canada**
407 Monarch Lane, RR 1, Leamington, ON N8H 3V4
Tel: 519-322-2365; *Fax:* 519-322-1277
pelee.info@pc.gc.ca
www.pc.gc.ca/pn-np/on/pelee/index_E.asp
A lush Carolinian forest oasis at the southern tip of Canada, Point Pelee National Park resounds with migrating song birds in the spring, hums with cicadas in the summer, flutters with Monarch butterflies in the fall and is a peaceful place of reflection in the winter. Located 50 km (30 miles) south-east of Windsor, Ontario, Point Pelee National Park of Canada is one of Canada's smallest national parks, and yet this tiny green oasis attracts approximately 300 000 visitors each year. Our goal is to bring people and the environment together. From picnic areas to the Visitor Centre, to famous vistas like the Tip and the Marsh Boardwalk, all facilities and services are designed to ensure a memorable experience and to preserve the Park's natural environment. Hours of Operation: Oct-March 7:00am-7:00pm; April 6:00am-10:00pm; May 1-May 21 5:00am-10:00pm; May 22-Oct 8 6:00am-10:00pm.

***Mallorytown:* St. Lawrence Islands National Park of Canada**
2 County Road 5, RR 3, Mallorytown, ON K0E 1R0
Tel: 613-923-5261; *Fax:* 613-923-1021
ont-sli@pc.gc.ca
www.pc.gc.ca/pn-np/on/lawren/index_E.asp
Conceived in the 1870s, St. Lawrence Islands is a tiny jewel with a rich and complex natural and human history. The park is located in the heart of the Thousand Islands tourist area. Make St. Lawrence Islands National Park a leisurely and scenic stop on your way through Eastern Ontario. Hours of Operation: Administration Office, M-F 8:00-4:30 year round; Islands, May 18-Oct 8; Mallourytown Landing Visitor Centre, May 18-June 10 & Sept 7-Oct 8, F-Su 10:00-4:00, June 15-Sept 3 Su-Th 10:00-4:00, Fr-Sa 10:00-6:00.

***Midland:* Georgian Bay Islands National Park of Canada**
PO Box 9, 911 Wye Valley Rd., Midland, ON L4R 4K6
Tel: 705-526-9804; *Fax:* 705-526-5939
info.gbi@pc.gc.ca
www.pc.gc.ca/pn-np/on/georg/index_E.asp
Protecting one of Canada's national treasures for your enjoyment: from the Honey Harbour area to Twelve Mile Bay in southern Georgian Bay, you will discover spectacular landscapes, time-worn rock faces, diverse habitats and the rugged beauty of the Canadian Shield. These magnificent islands are accessible by boat only. The largest island, Beausoleil offers island tent camping, overnight and day docking, heritage education programs and hiking trails. Wheelchair accessible sites and reserved campsites are also available at the Cedar Spring campground on Beausoleil Island. Hours of Operation: Parks Canada Welcome Centre, Spring & Fall Sa-Su 9:00-5:00, Summer daily 10:00-6:00.

***Tobermory:* Bruce Peninsula National Park of Canada**
PO Box 189, Tobermory, ON N0H 2R0
Tel: 519-596-2233; *Fax:* 519-596-2298
bruce-fathomfive @pc.gc.ca
www.pc.gc.ca/pn-np/on/bruce/index_E.asp
In the heart of a World Biosphere Reserve, the 'Bruce' is a place of global significance. The massive, rugged cliffs of the park are inhabited by thousand year old cedar trees, overhanging the crystal clear waters of Georgian Bay. The park is comprised of an incredible array of habitats from rare alvars to dense forests and clean lakes. Together these form a greater ecosystem - the largest remaining chunk of natural habitat in southern Ontario. Hours of Operation: Administration Office, M-F 8:00-4:30; Cyprus Lake Campground Office, daily from May-Oct.

Prince Edward Island

Local National Parks & Outdoor Education Centres in Prince Edward Island

***Charlottetown:* Prince Edward Island National Park of Canada**
2 Palmers Lane, Charlottetown, PE C1A 5V6
Tel: 902-672-6350; *Fax:* 902-672-6370
pnipe.peinp@pc.gc.ca
www.pc.gc.ca/pn-np/pe/pei-ipe/index_E.asp
Prince Edward Island National Park of Canada is home to sand dunes, barrier islands and sand pits, beaches, sandstone cliffs, wetlands and forests. These diverse habitats provide a home for a variety of plants and animals, including the endangered Piping Plover. The National Park also features unique cultural resources, notably Green Gables and Dalvay-by-the-Sea National Historic Site. In 1998, six kilometres of the Greenwich Peninsula were added to the Park to protect unique dune formations, rare plants and animals, as well as archaeological findings dating back 10,000 years. Hours of Operation: Greenwich Interpretation Centre, May 20-June 26 & Aug 22-Oct 9 9:00-4:30, June 27-Aug 21 9:00-6:00; Rntrance Kiosks, early June-late August; Cavendish Visitor Centre, late May-mid Oct.

Quebec

Local National Parks & Outdoor Education Centres in Quebec

***Gaspé:* Forillon National Park of Canada**
122 Gaspé Boulevard, Gaspé, QC G4X 1A9
Tel: 418-368-5505; *Fax:* 418-368-6837
Toll-Free: 888-773-8888
parkscanada-que @pc.gc.ca
www.pc.gc.ca/pn-np/qc/forillon/index_E.asp
Forillon, a national park created in 1970, is located at the farthest reach of the Gaspé Peninsula. Its majestic landscapes cover a 244 km2 area that is carved out of the sea, cliffs and mountains. Forillon protects a representative sample of the Notre-Dame and Mégantic mountain regions and certain elements of the Gulf of St. Lawrence marine region. The presence of ten different rock formations, colonies of seabirds and enigmatic artic-alpine plants give this park its unique character. Within this seaside park, the Grande-Grave National Heritage Site attests to the way of life of fishing families. Hours of Operation: Park is open all year round, with services mostly offered between June and October.

***Havre-Saint-Pierre:* Mingan Archipelago National Park Reserve of Canada**
1340 de la Digue St., Havre-Saint-Pierre, QC G0G 1P0
Tel: 418-538-3331; *Fax:* 418-538-3595
parkscanada-que @pc.gc.ca
www.pc.gc.ca/pn-np/qc/mingan/index_E.asp
Beyond the 50th parallel, along the North Shore of the Gulf of St. Lawrence, lies a remarkably beautiful scattering of some forty limestone islands and more than 1000 granitic islets and reefs. The territory, the "Mingan Archipelago", became a national park reserve in 1984. This necklace of land carved out of the limestone bedrock is the site of spectacular natural monuments which bear witness to the never-ending wear of the sea and of the centuries. And there is an abundance of life in this strange half-world: plants of variegated hues and shapes, seabirds gathered in colonies, seals, dolphins and whales, swarming the blue vastness in which the islands bathe. Hours of Operation: Havre-Saint-Pierre Reception and Interpretation Center & Longue-Pointe-de-Mingan Reception and Interpretation Centre open June-September.

***Shawinigan:* La Mauricie National Park of Canada**
PO Box 160 Bureau-chef, 702 5th Street, Shawinigan, QC G9N 6T9
Tel: 819-538-3232; *Fax:* 819-536-3661
parkscanada-que @pc.gc.ca
www.pc.gc.ca/pn-np/qc/mauricie/index_E.asp
Covering an area of 536 km2, the park gives off an air of serenity throughout its gently contoured terrain. On this vast plateau of rolling hills intersected by valleys and dotted with myriads of lakes, life moves in perfect unison with nature. Here only the changes of the seasons mark the passage of time, retouching the landscape with subtle strokes and calling visitors with a promise of both activity and relaxation. Since its creation in 1970, the park has safeguarded the continuing integrity of this richly endowed land, protecting it as a representative sample of

the southernmost part of the Canadian Shield. Welcome to this haven of peace! La Mauricie National Park, a conservation area that relies on your involvement! Hours of Operation: Reception Centre, May 11-24 & Sept 4-Oct 14 Sa-Th 9:00-4:30, F 9:00 am-10:00 pm, May 25-Sept 3 daily 7:00 am-10:00 pm.

Saskatchewan

Local National Parks & Outdoor Education Centres in Saskatchewan

***Val Marie:* Grasslands National Park of Canada**
PO Box 150, Val Marie, SK S0N 2T0
Tel: 306-298-2257; *Fax:* 306-298-2042
grasslands.info @pc.gc.ca
www.pc.gc.ca/pn-np/sk/grasslands/index_E.asp
Grasslands is the first national park of Canada to preserve a portion of the mixed prairie grasslands. Eavesdrop on a prairie dog town or learn about how Sitting Bull took refuge here after the battle of the Little Bighorn in 1876. Guided hikes, interpretive trails, bird watching, and nature photography are popular activities in Grasslands. Hours of Operation: Parklands are open year round; Visitor Reception Centre is open daily from mid-May to Labour Day, 8:00-5:00, and from Sept-May, the Centre is open M-F, 8:00-4:30.

***Waskesiu Lake:* Prince Albert National Park of Canada**
PO Box 100, Waskesiu Lake, SK S0J 2Y0
Tel: 306-663-4522
panp.info@pc.gc.ca
www.pc.gc.ca/pn-np/sk/princealbert/index_E.asp
Prince Albert National Park protects a slice of the 'boreal' forest. It is also a meeting place or transition zone between the parkland and the northern forest. The park features many outstanding natural wonders and cultural treasures, including the only fully protected white pelican nesting colony in Canada, the isolated, lakeside cabin of conservationist Grey Owl and a free-ranging herd of plains bison. During a visit, enjoy special events and interpretive programs that help you make more connections with the patterns and processes of this ecosystem. The townsite of Waskesiu, located in the park, provides extensive services for visitors. Hours of Operation: Parklands are open year round; Information Centre is open daily 8:00am-8:00 pm from mid-May-early Sept, and on weekends during peak cross country ski season.

Yukon Territory

Local National Parks & Outdoor Education Centres in Yukon Territory

***Haines Junction:* Kluane National Park and Reserve of Canada**
PO Box 5495, Haines Junction, YT Y0B 1L0
Tel: 867-634-7250; *Fax:* 867-634-7208
kluane.info@pc.gc.ca
www.pc.gc.ca/pn-np/yt/kluane/index_E.asp
A gem in the family of Parks Canada's national treasures, Kluane National Park and Reserve of Canada covers an area of 21,980 square kilometres. It is a land of precipitous, high mountains, immense icefields and lush valleys that yield a diverse array of plant and wildlife species and provides for a host of outdoor activities. Kluane National Park and Reserve is also home to Mount Logan (5959 m/19,545 ft), Canada's highest peak. As part of a larger system of national parks and historic sites found throughout Canada, Kluane National Park and Reserve protects and presents a nationally significant example of Canada's North Coast Mountains natural region and the associated regional cultural heritage. Fostering public understanding, appreciation and enjoyment of Kluane National Park and Reserve while ensuring ecological and commemorative integrity for present and future generations is Parks Canada's goal. Hours of Operation: Visitor Centre, mid-May-mid Sept, daily 9:00-5:00.

***Old Crow:* Vuntut National Park of Canada**
Old Crow, YT Y0B 1N0
Tel: 867-667-3910; *Fax:* 867-966-3432
brenda.frost-charlie @pc.gc.ca
www.pc.gc.ca/pn-np/yt/vuntut/index_E.asp
Vuntut National Park was established in 1995 after extensive negotiations through the Vuntut Gwitchin First Nation's Final Land Claims Agreement between the Vuntut Gwitchin of Old Crow and the Government of Canada and the Yukon. Vuntut, which means "among the lakes" in the Gwitchin language, encompasses 4,345. sq. km of wilderness in the northwestern corner of the Yukon Territory. The park is bounded by the height of land and Ivvavik National Park of the north, the international boundary and the Arctic National Wildlife Refuge to the west, Black Fox Creek to its confluence with the Old Crow River to the east and the Old Crow River to the south. Hours of Operation: Park is open year round, with no services available.

Observatories

Alberta

Local Observatories in Alberta

***Calgary:* Rothney Astrophysical Observatory (RAO)**
Physics & Astronomy Dept., University of Calgary, Calgary, AB T2N 1N4
Tel: 403-220-5385; *Fax:* 403-289-3331
rao@phas.ucalgary.ca
phas.ucalgary.ca/rao
Other contact information: Open House Info: 403/220-7977
The RAO is the University of Calgary's astronomical facility which is home to the following amazing telescopes: the 0.4-m Clarke-Milone Telescope (which is controlable via the internet), the 0.5-m Baker Nunn Telescope (used to search for asteroids), & the 1.8-m A.R. Cross Telescope (one of the 3 largest in Canada). The RAO boasts a fabulous Interpretive Centre which is open for drop-in visits M, Tu, W, 12-4.
Dr. P. Langill, Director
Dr. R. Plume, Associate Director

***Edmonton:* Devon & Campus Observatories**
Dept. of Physics, University of Alberta, Edmonton, AB T6G 2J1
Tel: 780-492-5410; *Fax:* 780-492-0714
Dhube@phys.ualberta.ca
www.phys.ualberta.ca
Consists of a 0.5m-diameter telescope equipped with a prime focus CCD camera; research programs are directed toward stellar photometry & the detection of faint, extended sources such as HII regions & supernova remnants; Campus Observatory has permanently mounted 12 & 14 inch telescopes & an exhibit area; facility used for undergraduate instruction & public observing during academic year
Dr. Douglas P. Hube
Dr. Sharon Morsink, morsink@phys.ualberta.ca

British Columbia

Local Observatories in British Columbia

***Kamuela:* Canada-France-Hawaii Telescope**
65-1238 Mamalahoa Hwy., Kamuela, HI 96743 USA
Tel: 808-885-7944; *Fax:* 808-885-7288
veillet@cfht.hawaii.edu
www.cfht.hawaii.edu/
The CFH observatory hosts a world-class, 3.6 meter optical/infrared telescope. The observatory is located atop the summit of Mauna Kea, a 4200 meter, dormant volcano located on the island of Hawaii. By appointment only.

***Penticton:* Dominion Radio Astrophysical Observatory c/o NRC Herzberg Institute of Astrophysics, PO Box 248, Penticton, BC V2A 6J9**
Tel: 250-493-2277; *Fax:* 250-493-7767
hia-www@nrc-cnrc.gc.ca
www.nrc-cnrc.gc.ca
Founded: 1960 A world-class radio astronomy facility with several telescopes on site; guided tours Sundays during July and August, 2-5 p.m.; visitor centre open weekdays from Thanksgiving to Easter; open 7 days per week from Easter to Thanksgiving.
Dr. Sean Dougherty, Group Leader Ph.D., sean.dougherty@nrc-cnrc.gc.ca

***Vancouver:* Gordon MacMillan Southam Observatory (GSO)**
1100 Chestnut St., Vancouver, BC V6J 3J9
Tel: 604-738-7827; *Fax:* 604-736-5665
info@spacecentre.ca
www.hrmacmillanspacecentre.com/observatory.htm
Part of the Pacific Space Centre
Ms Donna Livingstone, Executive Director

***Vancouver:* University of British Columbia Observatory**
***Also known as:* Wreck Beach Observatory**
2219 Main Mall, Vancouver, BC V6T 1Z4
Tel: 604-822-3853; *Fax:* 604-822-5324
matthews@astro.ubc.ca
www.astro.ubc.ca/
Telescope open for free public viewing on clear Sat. evenings, year round; free tours by appt.
Dr. Jaymie Matthews
Dr. Harvey Richer

***Victoria:* Climenhaga Observatory**
Dept. of Physics & Astronomy, University of Victoria, PO Box 3055 MS-7700, Victoria, BC V8W 3P6
Tel: 250-721-7750; *Fax:* 250-721-7715
robb@uvic.ca
www.astro.uvic.ca
Russell Robb

***Victoria:* Dominion Astrophysical Observatory (DAO) / Observatoire fédéral d'astrophysique**
Herzberg Inst. of Astrophysics, National Research Council of Canada, 5071 West Saanich Rd., Victoria, BC V9E 2E7
Tel: 250-363-0001; *Fax:* 250-363-0045
hia-www@nrc-cnrc.gc.ca
www.hia-iha.nrc-cnrc.gc.ca
Open year round; see website for hours
James Hesser, Director

Manitoba

Local Observatories in Manitoba

***Winnipeg:* The Lockhart Planetarium**
University of Manitoba, 380 University College, 500 Dysart Rd., Winnipeg, MB R3T 2M8
Tel: 204-474-9785; *Fax:* 204-261-0021
www.umanitoba.ca/faculties/science/astronomy/lockhart/lockhart.html
Planetarium theatre; display area; astronomy reference library

***Winnipeg:* Manitoba Planetarium**
190 Rupert Ave., Winnipeg, MB R3B 0N2
Tel: 204-956-2830; *Fax:* 204-942-3679
info@manitobamuseum.mb.ca
www.manitobamuseum.mb.ca
A 287 seat space theatre equipped with Zeiss MkV star projector, which is capable of reproducing the night sky as seen from any location on Earth; complimented with advanced video project & multmedia projectors; shows & programs change throughout the year
Javier Schwersensky, Director, Programs
Scott Young, Manager, Planetarium & Science Gallery, Planetary & Science Gallery Programs, scyoung@ManitobaMuseum.mb.ca

Nova Scotia

Local Observatories in Nova Scotia

***Halifax:* Burke-Gaffney Observatory (BGO)**
Loyola Bldg., Saint Mary's University, 923 Robie St., Halifax, NS B3H 3C3
Tel: 902-420-5633; *Fax:* 902-420-5141
apwww.stmarys.ca/bgo/
40 cm reflecting telescope; public tours held on the 1st & 3rd Sat. of each month at 7 pm (Nov.-Mar.) or 9 pm (Apr.-Oct.), weather permitting; call 902/496-8257 on Sat. afternoon for the status of that evening's tour; Mon. evenings or daytime groups by arrangement
Dr. G.A. Welch, Director

Ontario

Local Observatories in Ontario

***Hamilton:* W.J. McCallion Planetarium**
Dept. of Physics & Astronomy, McMaster University, 1280 Main St. West, Hamilton, ON L8S 4M1
Tel: 905-525-9140; *Fax:* 905-546-1252
planetarium@physics.mcmaster.ca
www.physics.mcmaster.ca/planetarium/

***London:* Hume Cronyn Memorial Observatory**
Astronomy, University of Western Ontario, London, ON N6A 3K7
Tel: 519-661-2111; *Fax:* 519-661-2033
dfgray@uwo.ca
www.astro.uwo.ca/~dfgray/cronyn.html
Built in 1939, observatory houses a 25 cm refactor currently used for teaching & visitor programs
David F. Gray, Observatory Director

***London:* University of Western Ontario Astronomical Observatory**
***Also known as:* Elginfield Observatory**
Dept. of Physics & Astronomy, University of Western Ontario, 1151 Richmond St., London, ON N6A 3K7
Tel: 519-661-3283; *Fax:* 519-661-2033
chair@physics.uwo.ca
phobos.astro.uwo.ca/~dfgray/
David F. Gray, Observatory Director

***Richmond Hill:* David Dunlap Observatory**
PO Box 360, Richmond Hill, ON L4C 4Y6
Tel: 905-884-9562; *Fax:* 905-884-2672
info@astro.utoronto.ca
www.astro.utoronto.ca/DDO/
Wed. mornings: 10 am; Fri. & Sat. evenings Apr.-Oct. by reservation; call the information number or visit the website for the schedule & description of tours
P.G. Martin, Director

Sudbury: **Doran Planetarium**
Fraser Bldg., Laurentian University, 935 Ramsey Lake Rd., Sudbury, ON P3E 2C6
Tel: 705-675-1151; *Fax:* 705-675-4868
plegault@laurentian.ca
www.oldwebsite.laurentian.ca/physics/planetarium/Planetarium.html
Astronomical presentation, show & lecture in both French & English
Paul-Émile Legault, Director

Quebec

Local Observatories in Quebec

Notre-Dame-des-Bois: **Astrolab du Parc du Mont Mégantic**
CP 24, 189, rte du Parc, Notre-Dame-des-Bois, QC J0B 2E0
Tél: 819-888-2941; *Téléc:* 819-888-2943
Ligne sans frais: 800-665-6527
astronomie@astrolab.qc.ca
www.astrolab.qc.ca
Summer programs

Saskatchewan

Local Observatories in Saskatchewan

Saskatoon: **University of Saskatchewan Observatory**
Dept. of Physics & Engineering Physics, University of Saskatchewan, 116 Science Pl., Saskatoon, SK S7N 5E2
Tel: 306-966-6429; *Fax:* 306-966-6400
physics.usask.ca/observatory/
Open every Saturday evening after dark for public viewing through the telescope
Stan Shadick

Performing Arts - Dance

International

The Royal Scottish Country Dance Society (RSCDS)
12 Coates Cres., Edinburgh EH3 7AF United Kingdom
info@rscds.org
www.rscds.org
To preserve & further the practice of traditional Scottish Country Dancing; to provide or assist in providing special education or instruction in the practice of Scottish Country Dances
Elspeth Gray, Secretary

Alberta

Alberta Ballet
Nat Christie Centre, 141 - 18 Ave. SW, Calgary AB T2S 0B8 Canada
Tel: 403-245-4222; *Fax:* 403-245-6573
info@albertaballet.com
www.albertaballet.com
To enrich & bring beauty to people's lives through creating, performing & teaching ballet

Alberta Dance Alliance (ADA)
Percy Page Centre, 11759 Groat Rd., 2nd Fl., Edmonton AB T5M 3K6 Canada
Tel: 780-422-8107; *Fax:* 780-422-2663
Toll-Free: 888-422-8107
info@abdancealliance.ab.ca
www.abdancealliance.ab.ca
To foster & promote the appreciation & practice of dance in Alberta, through administrative, technical, & informative services, programs, advocacy, & special events
Bobbi Westman, Executive Director

Brian Webb Dance Co.
PO Box 53092, Edmonton AB T5N 48A Canada
Tel: 780-452-3282; *Fax:* 780-497-4330
webbcdf@shaw.ca
www.bwdc.ca
The Brian Webb Dance Company is a producer and presenter of contemporary dance. The BWDC is a community-minded, dynamic, artistic builder: a team builder; we build our work through collaboration - the democratic exchange of ideas to create something new.
Brian Webb, Artistic Director

Catalyst Theatre Society of Alberta
8529 Gateway Blvd., Edmonton AB T6E 6P3 Canada
Tel: 780-431-1750; *Fax:* 780-433-3060
info@catalysttheatre.ca
www.catalysttheatre.ca
To create & present original Canadian work that explores new possibilities for theatre

Decidedly Jazz Danceworks
1514 - 4th St. SW, Calgary AB T2R 0Y4 Canada
Tel: 403-245-3533; *Fax:* 403-245-3584
djd@decidedlyjazz.com
www.decidedlyjazz.com
Creates concert jazz dance that sustains the spirit and traditions of jazz. Mixes groove, African roots, rhythm, improvisation, interplay with musicians, and deeply human soul, has distinguished DJD on the international jazz dance stage. Offers a season of performances, touring, and jazz classes.
Vicki Adams Willis, Artistic Director
Kathi Sundstrom, General Manager

Springboard Dance
205 - 8th Ave. SE, 2nd Fl., Calgary AB T2G 0K9 Canada
Tel: 403-265-3230; *Fax:* 403-294-7457
www.springboardperformance.com
Social Media: www.facebook.com/group.php?gid=87776623119
To produce, create & perform intellectually & sensually stimulating modern dance
Trina Rasmuson
Shelly Tegnazzini
Nicole Mion

Sun Ergos, A Company of Theatre & Dance
Priddis Greens, 130 Sunset Way, Priddis AB T0L 1W0 Canada
Tel: 403-931-1527; *Fax:* 403-931-1534
Toll-Free: 800-743-3351
waltermoke@sunergos.com
www.sunergos.com
Social Media: www.facebook.com/pages/SunErgos/189482516084
To witness, maintain & develop the ethnocultural roots of theatre & dance, without prejudice of race, creed, sex, or cultural background, to celebrate the differences & recognize the similarities among all peoples; to provide the best possible theatre & dance within the urban & rural communities, nationally & internationally
Robert Greenwood, Artistic & Managing Director
Dana Luebke, Artistic & Production Director

Vinok Worldance
PO Box 4867, Edmonton AB T6E 5G7 Canada
Tel: 780-454-3739; *Fax:* 780-454-3436
vinok@vinok.ca
www.vinok.ca
To present music & dances of the world to audiences all across Canada; to reflect world dance as a way of celebrating life, involving dance, music, song, improvisation & the expression of a people
Doyle Marko, Artistic Director
Leanne Koziak, Executive Director

British Columbia

Ballet British Columbia
677 Davie St., 6th Fl., Vancouver BC V6G 2B6 Canada
Tel: 604-732-5003; *Fax:* 604-732-4417
info@balletbc.com
www.balletbc.com
To commission & perform a balanced repertoire rooted in classical technique, which encompasses the best new ballets & late 20th century classics
Emily Molnar, Interim Artistic Director

Dance Centre
Scotiabank Dance Centre, 677 Davie St., Level 6, Vancouver BC V6B 2G6 Canada
Tel: 604-606-6400; *Fax:* 604-606-6401
info@thedancecentre.ca
www.thedancecentre.ca
To raise the profile of dance in BC; to serve as a focal point & advocate for issues & concerns affecting the entire dance community; to coordinate the resources & activities of this wide ranging community
Heather Bray, Marketing Manager
Mirna Zagar, Executive Director

DanceArts Vancouver
Scotiabank Dance Centre, 677 Davie St., 7th Fl., Vancouver BC V6B 2G6 Canada
Tel: 604-606-6425; *Fax:* 604-606-6432
info@dancearts.bc.ca
To increase the exposure of performing arts through the presentation of interdisciplinary performances & workshops; to present contemporary dance work & interdisciplinary dance/theatre/music performances of the highest quality; to act as a catalyst & animator for dance & associated arts in the community & to offer infrastructure & presentation support of that activity
Judith Marcuse, Artistic Director

EDAM Performing Arts Society (EDAM)
303 - 8th Ave. East, Vancouver BC V5T 1S1 Canada
Tel: 604-876-9559; *Fax:* 604-876-9525
info@edamdance.org
www.edamdance.org
To explore new directions in dance & the performing arts
Peter Bingham, Artistic Director
Mona Hamill, Administrative Director

Goh Ballet Society
2345 Main St., Vancouver BC V5T 3C9 Canada
Tel: 604-872-4014; *Fax:* 604-872-4011
admin@gohballet.com
www.gohballet.com
Social Media: www.twitter.com/GohBallet
The Goh Ballet Academy was established in 1978 with the mission to prepare aspiring dancers for professional careers by providing rigorous training in the vocabulary and artistry of classical ballet.
Fei Wong, President
Chan Hon Goh, Artistic Director

Kinesis Dance Society
Scotia Bank Dance Centre, Level 7, 677 Davie St., Vancouver BC V6B 2G6 Canada
Tel: 604-684-7844; *Fax:* 604-684-7834
info@kinesisdance.org
www.kinesisdance.org
To contribute new & provocative works of contemporary dance to the local, national & international dance scene; to educate through workshops & cultural exchanges & to collaborate with other media, such as film, video & theatre
Paras Terezakis, Artistic Director

Lola Dance
#104, 336 - 1st Ave. East, Vancouver BC V5T 4R6 Canada
Tel: 604-683-6552; *Fax:* 604-681-1431
info@loladance.org
www.loladance.org
To create an inspired creative dance environment for choreography & performance; Participating in educational initiatives, by offering instruction in dance, youth outreach programming, residencies, teaching while on tour, choreographic workshops, & special youth presentations; To enhance the growth of the arts community & the cultural heritage of Vancouver, British Columbia & Canada
Lola MacLaughlin, Artistic Director & Founder

Mascall Dance
1130 Jervis St., Vancouver BC V6E 2C7 Canada
Tel: 604-689-9339; *Fax:* 604-689-9399
admin@mascalldance.ca
www.mascalldance.ca
To provide a forum for research, creation, performance, education, documentation & dissemination of contemporary dance & related disciplines
Jennifer Mascall, Artistic Director

Vancouver Moving Theatre (VMT)
PO Box 88270, Stn. Chinatown, Vancouver BC V6A 4A4 Canada
Tel: 604-628-5672
savannahandterry@axion.net
www.vancouvermovingtheatre.com
To develop a new form of interdisciplinary art influenced by the Pacific Rim culture of Vancouver; to present services & products to affirm the importance of art in questions of healing, humanity & the soul
Savannah Walling, Artistic Director
Terry Hunter, Executive Director

Manitoba

Canadian Square & Round Dance Society (CSRDS)
115 Holly Dr., Oakbank MB R0E 1J2 Canada
Tel: 204-444-3115; *Fax:* 204-444-5768
Toll-Free: 866-206-6696
info@squaredance.ca
www.csrds.ca
To link information about Canadian square & round dancing associations together in order to promote awareness, inspire activity, & to offer information
Lorraine Kozera, Secretary
John Kozera, Secretary
Alan Clay, President
Doreen Clay, President

Dance Manitoba Inc.
Pantages Playhouse Theatre, #204, 180 Market Ave. East, Winnipeg MB R3B 0P7 Canada
Tel: 204-989-5260; *Fax:* 204-989-5268
info@dancemanitoba.org
www.dancemanitoba.org
To promote the development of dance through festivals, workshops, & showcases

Royal Winnipeg Ballet (RWB)
380 Graham Ave., Winnipeg MB R3C 4K2 Canada
Tel: 204-956-0183; *Fax:* 204-943-1994
Toll-Free: 800-667-4792
ballet@rwb.org
www.rwb.org
To enrich the human experience by teaching, creating & performing outstanding dance

Ruth Cansfield Dance
806 Osborne St., Winnipeg MB R3L 2C7 Canada
Tel: 204-284-5810; *Fax:* 204-284-1131
Toll-Free: 866-405-5810
info@ruthcansfield.com
To create & perform the choreography of Ruth Cansfield; to use our collective talent & energy to create an educational experience that will benefit the community as a whole, dancers & non-dancers alike; to pursue tours that will enable the company to carry our dance message to provincial, national, & international dance audiences
Ken Manson, Vice-President
Jon McPhail, Administration Director
Ruth Cansfield, Artistic Director
Ellie Cansfield, President

Winnipeg's Contemporary Dancers
#204, 211 Bannatyne Ave., Winnipeg MB R3B 3P2 Canada
Tel: 204-452-0229; *Fax:* 204-287-8618
info@winnipegscontemporarydancers.ca
www.winnipegscontemporarydancers.ca
Winnipeg 's Contemporary Dancers' goal is to create a place on the local, national and international arts landscape that enables vital intersections, linkages and exchange among dance creators, dance interpreters, spectators and communities. Our values, programs, and activities are based on respect for our history, the ongoing development of our artists, and to our place in the community.

New Brunswick

Les Productions DansEncorps Inc.
#12A, 140, rue Botsford, Moncton NB E1C 4X5 Canada
Tél: 506-855-0998; *Téléc:* 506-852-3401
dencorps@nb.aibn.com
www.dansencorps.ca
Création, production, formation et diffusion de spectacles de danse; contribution au développement des arts au Nouveau-Brunswick
Chantal Cadieux, Directrice artistique

Nova Scotia

Dance Nova Scotia
1113 Marginal Rd., Halifax NS B3H 4P7 Canada
Tel: 902-422-1749; *Fax:* 902-422-0881
office@dancens.ca
www.dancens.ca
To promote, stimulate & encourage the development of dance as a cultural, educational & social activity

Two Planks & a Passion Theatre Association (TP&aP)
PO Box 190, 555 Ross Creek Rd., Canning NS B0P 1H0 Canada
Tel: 902-582-3073; *Fax:* 902-582-7943
mail@twoplanks.ca
www.twoplanks.ca; www.twoplanksandpassion.blogspot.com
Social Media: www.facebook.com/group.php?gid=2337674729
To develop & present high quality, professional theatre both regionally & nationally which reflects Canadian life, with strong roles for women; to develop & build an artistic centre in Canning, NS, accessible to both the local community & to artists of all disciplines & residencies
Ken Schwartz, Artistic Director

Ontario

Ballet Creole
375 Dovercourt Rd., Toronto ON M6J 3E5 Canada
Tel: 416-960-0350; *Fax:* 416-960-2067
info@balletcreole.org
www.balletcreole.org
Preserves and perpetuates traditional and contemporary African culture and increases awareness of the rich African culture that exists in Canada. Establishes a dynamic new Canadian artistic tradition based on a fusion of diverse dance and music traditions. Promotes multicultural understanding through education and quality entertainment to national and international audiences.
Patrick Parson, Artistic Director

Ballet Jörgen
c/o George Brown College, Casa Loma Campus, Room 126, Building C, 160 Kendal Ave., Toronto ON M5R 1M3 Canada
Tel: 416-961-4725; *Fax:* 416-415-2865
info@balletjorgen.ca
www.balletjorgen.ca
To operate exclusively as a charitable organization to administer & employ its property, assets & rights for the purpose of raising the public's awareness of ballet as an art form by establishing, maintaining & operating a ballet company; to advance knowledge & increase public recognition of ballet by developing a repertoire of original dance productions for performance, film & video for the benefit of the community at large; to advance artistic appreciation & education of the general public of choreography as a distinctive art form by commissioning & making available to the public presentations by a variety of choreographers
Bengt Jörgen, Artistic Director & CEO

Canada Dance Festival Society
PO Box 1376, Stn. B, 53 Elgin St., Ottawa ON K1P 5R4 Canada
Tel: 613-947-7000; *Fax:* 613-943-1399
cdffdc@nac-cna.ca
www.canadadance.ca
Social Media: www.facebook.com/group.php?gid=13144509823
To hold a festival of dance every two years
Brian H. Webb, Artistic Director
Pamela Fralick, Chair

Canadian Children's Dance Theatre (CCDT)
509 Parliament St., Toronto ON M4X 1P3 Canada
Tel: 416-924-5657; *Fax:* 416-924-4141
info@ccdt.org
www.ccdt.org
The Canadian Children's Dance Theatre is a modern dance repertory company of 13 to 19-year old dancers based in Toronto, Canada. Founded in 1980 by Deborah Lundmark and Michael deConinck Smith to present gifted young artists in professional productions, the Company has staged more than one thousand performances from Barrie to Beijing.
Elizabeth Varty, Marketing, Development & Arts Education
Deborah Lundmark, Artistic Director & Resident Choreographer
Michael de Coninck Smith, Co-Artistic Director & Production Manager

Canadian Dance Teachers Association (CDTA) / Association canadienne des professeurs de danse
c/o President, 178 Barrick Rd., Port Colbourne ON L3K 4B4 Canada
Tel: 905-834-0077
donna.moreau@sympatico.ca
www.cdtanational.ca
To advance education in the field of dance & maintain throughout Canada an organization of qualified dance teachers; to promote friendship & the exchange of ideas & information among the dance teachers of Canada, to provide an organization to represent Canadian dance teachers internationally

Dance Ontario Association / Association Ontario Danse
Case Goods Bldg. 74, The Distillery District, #304, 55 Mill St., Toronto ON M5A 3C4
Tel: 416-204-1083; *Fax:* 416-204-1085
contact@danceontario.ca
www.danceontario.ca
To support the advancement of all forms of dance; To offer a unified voice on dance issues

Dance Oremus Danse (DOD)
240 Dovercourt Rd., Toronto ON M6J 3E1 Canada
Tel: 416-536-9002; *Fax:* 416-536-9002
pauljamesdwyer@yahoo.ca
www.danceoremusdanse.org
To increase the public's appreciation of the aesthetic arts by promoting & encouraging the philosophy, movement practices & dance forms of Isadora Duncan (1877-1927) & European neo-classical dance, via seminars, workshops, courses on dance, performance, publishing & other media
Paul James Dwyer, Founder/Artistic Director

Dance Umbrella of Ontario (DUO)
#201, 490 Adelaide St. West, Toronto ON M5V 1T2 Canada
Tel: 416-504-6429; *Fax:* 416-504-8702
Toll-Free: 800-919-5019
duo@danceumbrella.net
www.danceumbrella.net
To assist & support professional dance creators in Ontario dance centres
Christine Moynihan, Executive Director

Dancemakers
The Case Goods Warehouse, Bldg. #74, #306, 55 Mill St., Toronto ON M5A 3C4 Canada
Tel: 416-367-1800; *Fax:* 416-367-1870
info@dancemakers.org
www.dancemakers.org
To bring dance of challenging physicality & emotional impact to audiences by drawing on the diverse talents & individual strengths of its artists; to develop & support works which both provoke & entertain

Dancer Transition Resource Centre (DTRC) / Centre de ressources et transition pour danseurs (CRTD)
The Lynda Hamilton Centre, #500, 250 The Esplanade, Toronto ON M5A 1J2 Canada
Tel: 416-595-5655; *Fax:* 416-595-0009
Toll-Free: 800-667-0851
nationaloffice@dtrc.ca
www.dtrc.ca
The Centre helps dancers make necessary transitions into, within & from professional performing, as well as operating a resource centre for the dance community & the public, offering seminars, education materials & information. It is a registered charity, BN: 101258077RR0001.

Danny Grossman Dance Company
#202, 157 Carlton St., Toronto ON M5A 2K3 Canada
Tel: 416-408-4543; *Fax:* 416-408-2518
info@dannygrossman.com
www.dannygrossman.com
To strive to build a dance legacy in Canada by preserving important dance works & undertaking residencies & workshops to educate & inspire the next generation of dancers & dance audiences
Helen Chapman, Managing Director
Danny Grossman, Artistic Director

Fringe Festival of Independent Dance Artists (FFIDA)
Toronto ON Canada
Tel: 416-214-5854
info@ffida.org
Michael Menegon, Artistic Director

Fujiwara Dance Inventions
#201, 490 Adelaide St. West, Toronto ON M5V 1T2 Canada
Tel: 416-593-4710; *Fax:* 416-504-8702
info@fujiwaradance.com
www.fujiwaradance.com
To dance into insight, through the creation, performance, & teaching of dance; To encounter & express the mysteries of human nature as they are manifest in the body, before words
Denise Fujiwara, Artistic Director

Gina Lori Riley Dance Enterprises
401 Sunset Ave., Windsor ON N9B 3P4 Canada
Tel: 519-253-3000
riley2@uwindsor.ca
www.ginaloririleydanceenterprises.com
To advance the art of dance through the development of new work, performance & through community education in an exemplary manner as a contemporary modern professional Canadian dance company
Gina Lori Riley, Artistic Director

Le Groupe Dance Lab / Le Groupe lab de danse
#2, 2 Daly St., Ottawa ON K1N 6E2 Canada
Tel: 613-235-1492; *Fax:* 613-235-1651
info@legroupe.org
www.legroupe.org
Social Media: www.facebook.com/group.php?gid=21206927029
To nurture artists & audiences, while proving a haven where choreographers can make challenging choices & venture down new roads in their working methods; to devote full-time resources to choreographers who immerse themselves in the creative process
Tony Chong, Associate Artistic Director
Peter Boneham, Artistic Director
Anthony Pan, General Manager

National Ballet of Canada
Walter Carsen Centre, 470 Queens Quay West, Toronto ON M5V 3K4 Canada
Tel: 416-345-9686; *Fax:* 416-345-8323
info@national.ballet.ca
www.national.ballet.ca
The National Ballet of Canada, a company with more than 60 dancers & its own full symphony orchestra, & ranking as one of the world's top international dance organizations, is Canada's premiere dance company. The Four Seasons Centre for the Performing Arts is the performance venue while the company is in Toronto.

Ontario Ballet Theatre
1133 St. Clair Ave. West, Toronto ON M6E 1B1 Canada
Tel: 416-656-9568; *Fax:* 416-651-4803
tara@ontarioballettheatre.com
www.ontarioballettheatre.com
To nurture & develop an appreciation of contemporary & classical ballet by reaching new audiences through artistic excellence

Ontario Folk Dance Association (OFDA)
35 Touraine Ave., Toronto ON M3H 1R3 Canada
ontariofolkdancers@gmail.com
www.ofda.ca
To promote the practice of international folk arts & dance; to prepare, collect & disseminate information & material relating to folk arts & dance

Opéra Atelier (OA)
St. Lawrence Hall, 157 King St. East, 4th Fl., Toronto ON M5C 1G9 Canada
Tel: 416-703-3767; *Fax:* 416-703-4895
opera.atelier@operaatelier.com
www.operaatelier.com
To produce opera, ballet, & drama from the 17th & 18th centuries
Jane Hargraft, General Manager

Royal Academy of Dance / Canada
#500, 1200 Sheppard Ave. East, Toronto ON M2K 2S5 Canada
Tel: 416-489-2813; *Fax:* 416-489-3222
Toll-Free: 888-709-0895
info@radcanada.org
www.radcanada.org
To provide dance education & training

Toronto & District Square & Round Dance Association
8 Seven Oaks Circle, St Catharines ON L2P 3N6 Canada
Tel: 905-641-1872
www3.sympatico.ca/jerry.callen/td/
To promote, encourage & foster wider knowledge of square & round dancing; to provide for mutual exchange of philosophy & material pertaining to square & round dancing between callers, teachers, & leaders; to improve quality of square & round dancing; to encourage use of standards of uniformity relating to square & round dancing

Toronto Dance Theatre (TDT)
80 Winchester St., Toronto ON M4X 1B2 Canada
Tel: 416-967-1365; *Fax:* 416-963-4379
info@tdt.org
www.tdt.org
To develop Canadian dance works of art; to perform nationally & internationally; to explore new ideas in choreographic expression while embracing the fresh & vital aspects of inherited traditions

Québec

Ballet Ouest / Ballet West
#218, 269 boul. St. Jean, Pointe-Claire QC H9R 3J1 Canada
Tel: 514-783-1245; *Fax:* 514-939-1469
centredanse@balletouest.com
www.balletouest.com
To provide a milieu that encourages young dancers to express themselves through dance & to move from amateur to professional status; educate & develop audiences; present an alternative view to counteract the mass culture that is being fed to our youth
Susan Altschul, Company Manager
Marie St-Amour, President
Margaret Mehuys, Artistic Director

BJM DANSE (BJM)
1210, rue Sherbrooke est, Montréal QC H2L 1L9 Canada
Tél: 514-982-6771; *Téléc:* 514-982-9145
info@bjmdanse.ca
www.bjmdanse.ca
Mèdia social: www.facebook.com/group.php?gid=4068138492
Crée, produit et diffuse à l'échelle nationale et internationale des spectacles de danse contemporaine; offre à ses danseurs un entraînement professionnel; permet aux chorégraphes invités et aux danseurs de développer leur propre recherche; génère un répertoire exclusif et conserve l'esprit novateur qui anime la compagnie de puis sa création

Le Carré des Lombes
#401, 2022, rue Sherbrooke Est, Montréal QC H2K 1B9 Canada
Tél: 514-287-9339; *Téléc:* 514-287-9415
info@lecarredeslombes.com
www.lecarredeslombes.com
Mèdia social:
www.facebook.com/pages/Le-Carre-des-Lombes/161816823394
Diffuser des spectacles de danse; promouvoir la danse comme discipline artistique
Suzanne Beaucaire, Coordonatrice Génerale

Cercle d'expression artistique Nyata Nyata
4374, boul St-Laurent, 3e étage, Montréal QC H2W 1Z5 Canada
Tél: 514-849-9781; *Téléc:* 514-849-7199
info@nyata-nyata.org
www.nyata-nyata.org
Compagnie Danse Nyata Nyata is an enterprise of contemporary artistic expression, which defines its activities in the field of African dance, with the specific objective to explore and develop the particular aesthetics of this art form as it relates to music, poetry, mythology, ritual and the related arts, bringing forth essential aspects which link the ancestral with the contemporary. This process includes choreographic creation, dance performance, musical composition, writings, conferences, the teaching and promotion thereof in a local, national and international context.
Zab Maboungou, Directrice artistique

Compagnie de danse Migrations
880, av Pére-Marquette, Québec QC G1S 24A Canada
Tél: 418-684-3132; *Téléc:* 418-684-3134
migrations@qc.aira.com
www.migrationsdanse.com
Création, formation, production et diffusion de la danse et musique traditionnelle québécoise et des cultures du monde
Richard Turcotte, Directeur artistique
Blandin Garnier, Adjointe administrative

Compagnie Marie Chouinard
#715, 3981, boul St-Laurent, Montréal QC H2W 1Y5 Canada
Tél: 514-843-9036; *Téléc:* 514-843-7616
info@mariechouinard.com
www.mariechouinard.com
Mèdia social:
www.facebook.com/pages/Compagnie-Marie-Chouinard/90299878696
To be dedicated to modern & unique interpretations of dance, new artistic choreography, & expression through the movements of the human body
Marie Chouinard, Directrice artistique
Pierre Des Marais, Directeur général

Danse-Cite inc
#426, 3680, rue Jeanne-Mance, Montréal QC H2X 2K5 Canada
Tél: 514-525-3595; *Téléc:* 514-525-3536
info@danse-cite.org
www.danse-cite.org
Création et production de spectacles de danse contemporain
Daniel Soulières, Directeur artistique

Fédération des loisirs-danse du Québec
CP 1000, Succ. M, 4545, av Pierre-de Coubertin, Montréal QC H1V 3R2 Canada
Tél: 514-252-3029; *Téléc:* 514-251-8038

Fortier Danse-Création
Succ. C, #301, 2022, rue Sherbrooke Est, Montréal QC H2K 1B9 Canada
Tél: 514-529-8158; *Téléc:* 514-529-1222
admin@fortier-danse.com
www.fortier-danse.com
Mèdia social: www.facebook.com/profile.php?id=1331329089
Création et diffusion des oeuvres du chorégraphe Paul-André Fortier
Paul-André Fortier, Directeur artistique
Gilles Savary, Directeur général

Les Grands Ballets Canadiens de Montréal (GBCM)
Maison de la Danse, 4816, rue Rivard, Montréal QC H2J 2N6 Canada
Tél: 514-849-8681; *Téléc:* 514-849-0098
info@grandsballets.com
www.grandsballets.com
Maintenir la tradition du ballet classique et élargir le champ d'expression de cette forme artistique par la création; faire connaître et apprécier la danse à tous les publics grâce à la qualité de nos présentations et de nos productions

La La La Human Steps
#206, 5655, av du Parc, Montréal QC H2V 4H2 Canada
Tél: 514-277-9090; *Téléc:* 514-277-0862
info@lalalahumansteps.com
www.lalalahumansteps.com
Mèdia social:
www.facebook.com/pages/LA-LA-LA-HUMAN-STEPS/54786888171
Présenter les spectacles crées par Édouard Lock sur les plus grandes scènes du monde; compagnie de danse contemporaine
Édouard Lock, Directeur artistique

Louise Bédard Danse
#300, 2022, rue Sherbrooke Est, Montréal QC H2K 1B9 Canada
Tél: 514-982-4580; *Téléc:* 514-982-0613
infos@lbdanse.org
www.lbdanse.org
Mèdia social: www.facebook.com/lbdanse; www.twitter.com/lbdanse
Louise bédard danse is a non-profit organization founded in 1990 with the aim of pursuing modern dance creation, awareness and education activities, and offering original choreographic creations to the general public.
Louise Bédard, Directrice artistique

Lucie Grégoire Danse
#405,1030, rue Cherrier, Montréal QC H2L 1H9 Canada
Tél: 514-524-7665; *Téléc:* 514-524-7584
luciegregoire3@sympatico.ca
www.luciegregoire.ca
Lucie Grégoire, Directrice artistique

Margie Gillis Dance Foundation / Fondation de danse Margie Gillis
3519, rue St-Urbain, Montréal QC H2X 2N6 Canada
Tel: 514-845-3115; *Fax:* 514-845-4526
info@margiegillis.org
www.margiegillis.org
Social Media:
www.facebook.com/pages/Margie-Gillis/63111821500
The objective of the Margie Gillis Dance Foundation is to reach as large a public as possible with a dance program of physical and emotional integrity, directed at making the audience aware of the potential and magic of their own lives.
Margie Gillis, Artistic Director
Manon Laflamme, Administrative Director

Montréal Danse
#109, 372, rue Sainte-Catherine ouest, Montréal QC H3B 1A2 Canada
Tél: 514-871-4005; *Téléc:* 514-871-4007
info@montrealdanse.com
www.montrealdanse.com
Mèdia social:
www.facebook.com/pages/Montreal-Danse/100944976616149
Se voue à la création de vibrantes oeuvres chorégraphiques avec le concours de plusieurs chorégraphes nationaux et internationaux
Kathy Casey, Directrice artistique

O Vertigo Danse
175, rue Sainte-Catherine ouest, Montréal QC H1V 1H1 Canada
Tél: 514-251-9177; *Téléc:* 514-251-7358
info@overtigo.com
www.overtigo.com
Se consacre à la création en nouvelle danse et la diffusion des oeuvres de la fondatrice et directrice artistique de la compagnie
Diane Boucher, Directrice générale
Ginette Laurin, Directrice générale

Regroupement québécois de la danse (RQD)
#440, 3680 rue Jeanne-Mance, Montréal QC H2X 2K5 Canada
Tél: 514-849-4003; *Téléc:* 514-849-3288
info@quebecdanse.org
www.quebecdanse.org
Promouvoir, encourager et soutenir le développement artistique, social et économique des danseurs, chorégraphes et de tout

intervenant professionnel de la communauté de la danse au Québec

Saskatchewan

Dance Saskatchewan Inc.
PO Box 8789, 205A Pacific Ave., Saskatoon SK S7K 1N9 Canada
Tel: 306-931-8480; *Fax:* 306-244-1520
Toll-Free: 800-667-8480
dancesask@sasktel.net
www.dancesask.com
To support & enhance the development of all dance forms; to preserve & promote dance in Saskatchewan; to represent & educate about dance; to encourage a passion for dance; to create a viable, unified organization which represents & advocates dance interests; to foster a respect & acceptance of dance which encourages free expression of cultural identity; to establish an active, vibrant environment which focuses on job creation, performance & cultural diversity within a central dance facility
Linda Coe-Kirkham, Executive Director

Performing Arts - Music

Alberta

Alberta Band Association (ABA)
#206, 10612 - 124 St., Edmonton AB T5M 1S4 Canada
Tel: 780-488-2263; *Fax:* 780-488-4132
Toll-Free: 877-687-4239
www.albertabandassociation.com
To promote & develop the musical, educational & cultural values of bands & band music in Alberta

Alberta Choral Federation (ACF)
#103, 10612 - 124 St., Edmonton AB T5N 1S4 Canada
Tel: 780-488-7464; *Fax:* 780-488-6403
info@albertachoralfederation.ca
www.albertachoralfederation.ca
To promote choral music within the communities of Alberta; to gain support for choral music through public policy

Alberta Recording Industries Association (ARIA)
Energy Square, #1205, 10109 - 106 St. NW, Edmonton AB T5J 3L7 Canada
Tel: 780-428-3372; *Fax:* 780-426-0188
Toll-Free: 800-465-3117
To assist & advance the development of the Canadian recorded music industry; to foster the excellence, diversity & vitality of Alberta artists & the Alberta sound recording industry

Calgary Opera Association
Arrata Opera Centre, 1315 - 7 St. SW, Calgary AB T2R 1A5 Canada
Tel: 403-262-7286; *Fax:* 403-263-5428
info@calgaryopera.com
www.calgaryopera.com
Social Media: www.facebook.com/pages/Calgary-Opera/18782898651
To enrich the cultural life of the community by celebrating musical art through the performance of professional opera

Calgary Philharmonic Society (CPO)
205 - 8 Ave. SE, Calgary AB T2G 0K9 Canada
Tel: 403-571-0270; *Fax:* 403-294-7424
info@cpo-live.com
www.cpo-live.com
Social Media: www.twitter.com/calgaryphil
To provide our audience with a rich, diverse & unequalled symphonic musical experience which earns broad community support

Calgary Youth Orchestra
c/o Mount Royal College Conservatory, 4825 Mount Royal Gate SW, Calgary AB T3E 6K6 Canada
Tel: 403-240-5978; *Fax:* 403-240-6594
cyo@mtroyal.ca
www.cyo.ab.ca
To provide the best possible musical experience for the talented young musicians of the Calgary region, in an art form that is considered one of the highest forms of expression

Canadian Federation of Music Teachers' Associations (CFMTA) / Fédération canadienne des associations des professeurs de musique
13407 - 14A Ave., Surrey AB V4A 7P9 Canada
Tel: 604-531-8840; *Fax:* 604-531-8747
dbrigs@telus.net
www.cfmta.org
To promote high musical & academic qualifications among members

Canadian Society for Traditional Music (CSTM) / Société canadienne pour les traditions musicales (SCTM)
c/o 3-47 Arts Building, University of Alberta, Edmonton AB T6G 2E6 Canada
cstmsctm@ualberta.ca
www.yorku.ca/cstm
Study & promotion of musical traditions of all cultures & communities in all their aspects
Sherry Johnson, Secretary
Anna Hoefnagels, President
Chris McDonald, Treasurer

Country Music Foundation of Canada Inc.
8607 - 128 Ave., Edmonton AB T5E 0G3 Canada
Tel: 780-476-8230; *Fax:* 780-472-2584
To preserve & present Canadian country music; to maintain country music museum & Canadian Country Music Association's Hall of Honour

Edmonton Jazz Society (EJS)
11 Tommy Banks Way, Edmonton AB T6E 2M2 Canada
Tel: 780-432-0428; *Fax:* 780-433-3773
jasiek@yardbirdsuite.com
www.yardbirdsuite.com
Social Media: www.facebook.com/YardbirdSuite
To present, promote & develop the performance of live Jazz music in the City of Edmonton

Edmonton Opera Association
Winspear Centre, 9720 - 102 Ave., Edmonton AB T5J 4B2 Canada
Tel: 780-424-4040; *Fax:* 780-429-0600
edmopera@edmontonopera.com
www.edmontonopera.com
To develop & promote opera as a dynamic & progressive art form; to attract & challenge audiences & artists through a creative program of opera production & education

Edmonton Symphony Orchestra (ESO)
9720 - 102 Ave., Edmonton AB T5J 4B2 Canada
Tel: 780-428-1108; *Fax:* 780-425-0167
Toll-Free: 800-563-5081
info@winspearcentre.com
www.edmontonsymphony.com
Social Media: www.facebook.com/edmontonsymphony
To foster appreciation & enjoyment of live, professional orchestral music through presenting concert performances, educational & community programs

Edmonton Youth Orchestra Association (EYO)
PO Box 66041, Stn. Heritage Post Office, Edmonton AB T6J 6T4 Canada
Tel: 780-436-7932; *Fax:* 780-436-7932
eyo@shaw.ca
www.eyso.com
To provide young musicians with the opportunity to develop their orchestral skills & increase their knowledge & appreciation of music, while enriching the cultural life of the community through concerts & benefit performances

Festival Chorus of Calgary
EPCOR Centre for Performing Arts, 205 - 8 Ave. SE, Calgary AB T2G 0K9 Canada
Tel: 403-294-7400
lgneufeld@shaw.ca
www.festivalchorus.ca
To present two concerts per year for the Marblehead community

Lethbridge Symphony Orchestra
PO Box 1101, Lethbridge AB T1J 4A2 Canada
Tel: 403-328-6808; *Fax:* 403-380-4418
info@lethbridgesymphony.org
www.lethbridgesymphony.org

Red Deer Symphony Orchestra
Cultural Services Building, PO Box 1116, 3827, 39th St., Red Deer AB T4N 6S5 Canada
Tel: 403-340-2948; *Fax:* 403-309-4612
reddeersymphony@telus.net
www.rdso.ca
Melody McKnight, Executive Director
Claude Lapalme, Music Director

British Columbia

Delta Youth Orchestra
PO Box 131, Delta BC V4K 3N6 Canada
Tel: 604-878-4655; *Fax:* 604-943-9603
info@dyo.bc.ca
www.dyo.bc.ca
To provide an educationally oriented experience for young musicians from the lower mainland of British Columbia
Stephen Robb, Music Director

Early Music Vancouver (EMV)
1254 - 7 Ave. West, Vancouver BC V6H 1B6 Canada
Tel: 604-732-1610; *Fax:* 604-732-1602
staff@earlymusic.bc.ca
www.earlymusic.bc.ca
Social Media: www.facebook.com/earlymusicvancouver
To foster increased understanding & appreciation of early music by providing educational programs, high quality concerts at reasonable prices featuring both local & internationally acclaimed musicians & by providing informative publications

Fraser Valley Symphony Society
PO Box 122, Abbotsford BC V2S 4N8 Canada
Tel: 604-859-3877
fvssorchestra@hotmail.com
www.fraservalleysymphony.ca

Friends of Chamber Music
PO Box 38046, Stn. King Edward Mall, Vancouver BC V5Z 4L9 Canada
Tel: 604-437-5747; *Fax:* 604-437-4769
fcmtickets@yahoo.com
www.friendsofchambermusic.ca
To present the best in chamber music

Greater Victoria Youth Orchestra (GVYO)
1611 Quadra St., Victoria BC V8W 2L5 Canada
Tel: 250-360-1121; *Fax:* 250-381-3573
gvyo@telus.net
www.gvyo.org
To affirm & nourish the love of music in young people; to foster musical development of orchestra members; to serve as musical resource to the community at large

Kamloops Intermediate Orchestra
PO Box 1387, Kamloops BC V2C 6L7 Canada
Tel: 250-554-3693
To provide training & playing opportunities for regional youth
Mark Betuzzi, Music Director

Kamloops Symphony (KSO)
PO Box 57, Kamloops BC V2C 5K3 Canada
Tel: 250-372-5000; *Fax:* 250-372-5089
info@kamloopssymphony.com
www.kamloopssymphony.com
To operate & promote a symphony orchestra for the Kamloops region

Okanagan Symphony Society
PO Box 20238, #239, 1899 Springfield Rd., Kelowna BC V1Y 9H2 Canada
Tel: 250-763-7544; *Fax:* 250-763-3553
admin@okanagansymphony.com
www.okanagansymphony.com
To provide the communities of the Okanagan Valley with an orchestra that is committed to excellence in the performance of classical music

Pacific Opera Victoria (POV)
#500, 1815 Blanshard St., Victoria BC V8T 5A1 Canada
Tel: 250-382-1641; *Fax:* 250-382-4944
dshefsiek@pov.bc.ca
www.pov.bc.ca
To provide professional quality opera to the residents of Greater Victoria & Vancouver Island; to provide career-oriented Canadian artists with the opportunity to expand their repertoire & gain professional experience; to train community artists & technicians in the discipline of opera production; to enhance the understanding & enjoyment of opera as an art form

Prince George Symphony Orchestra Society (PGSO)
2880 - 15 Ave., Prince George BC V2M 1T1 Canada
Tel: 250-562-0800; *Fax:* 250-562-0844
admin@pgso.com
www.pgso.com
To provide symphonic music for Prince George & region consistent with Prince George Symphony Orchestra artistic policy that facilitates artistic development of its players; to foster & facilitate positive community image & financial responsiblity so that a wide spectrum of musical experiences is offered to players & audiences alike

Richmond Community Orchestra & Chorus
#130, 10691 Shellbridge Way, Richmond BC V6X 2W8 Canada
Tel: 604-276-2747; *Fax:* 604-270-3644
roca.office@gmail.com
www.roca.ca
Sue Tench, Administrator

Surrey Symphony Society (SSS)
#181, 6832 King George Hwy., Surrey BC V3W 4Z9 Canada
Tel: 604-572-9225
inquiries@surreyyouthorchestra.org
www.surreyyouthorchestra.org
To expand an appreciation of orchestral music among young musicians & to share this with the community through public performance

Vancouver Island Symphony
PO Box 661, 150 Commercial St., Nanaimo BC V9R 5L9 Canada
Tel: 250-754-0177; *Fax:* 250-754-0165
info@vancouverislandsymphony.com
www.viso.bc.ca
To promote & present orchestra music in the Central Vancouver Island Region
Margot Holmes, Executive Director
David W. Covey, President

Vancouver New Music (VNM)
837 Davie St., Vancouver BC V6Z 1B7 Canada
Tel: 604-633-0861; *Fax:* 604-633-0871
info@newmusic.org
www.newmusic.org
Regarded as Western Canada's major producer of contemporary music & sonic art, dedicated to the outstanding performance of the music of our time; fostering connections within the community to bring new music to a wider audience; commissions & premieres new works by Canadian composers; produces music-theatre, leading electroacoustic music, international composers & performers; produces an annual Vancouver New Music Festival; explores the interaction of contemporary music with other disciplines

Vancouver Opera (VOA) / Association de l'opéra de vancouver
835 Cambie St., Vancouver BC V6B 2P4 Canada
Tel: 604-682-2871; *Fax:* 604-682-3981
tickets@vancouveropera.ca
www.vancouveropera.ca
Social Media: www.facebook.com/vancouveropera
To share the power of opera with all who are open to receiving it, through superior performances & meaningful education programs for all ages

Vancouver Philharmonic Orchestra (VPO)
PO Box 27503, Stn. Oakridge, Vancouver BC V5Z 4M4 Canada
Tel: 604-878-9989
vpo@vcn.bc.ca
www.vanphil.ca
Cathy McCashin, President
Maura Gauditis, Vice-President
Katherine Bailey, Treasurer

Vancouver Symphony Society
601 Smithe St., Vancouver BC V6B 5G1 Canada
Tel: 604-684-9100; *Fax:* 604-684-9264
customerservice@vancouversymphony.ca
www.vancouversymphony.ca
Provides stewardship for the Vancouver Symphony Orchestra to achieve recognition as one of Canada's highest quality symphony orchestras; to perform at all times with artistic distinction & thereby enrich BC's quality of life; to expand the enjoyment & appreciation of the finest orchestral music of the past & present

Vancouver Youth Symphony Orchestra Society (VYSO)
3214 - 10 Ave. West, Vancouver BC V6K 2L2 Canada
Tel: 604-737-0714; *Fax:* 604-737-0739
vyso@telus.net
www.vyso.com
To provide orchestral training & experience to music students in Greater Vancouver & the Lower Mainland from beginner to advanced level career student

Victoria Symphony
#610, 620 View St., Victoria BC V8W 1J6 Canada
Tel: 250-385-9771; *Fax:* 250-385-7767
administration@victoriasymphony.ca
www.victoriasymphony.ca
To advance musical culture; to advance musical education among younger members of community; to encourage, foster, & promote performance of Canadian & other contemporary musicians

Manitoba

Alliance Chorale Manitoba
#212, 340 Provencher Blvd., Winnipeg MB R2H 0G7 Canada
Tél: 204-233-7423; *Téléc:* 204-233-3324
Fédération provinciale sans but lucratif qui a pour mandat de promouvoir le chant choral en français et de favoriser ainsi l'épanouissement de la culture francophone du Manitoba.

Brandon University Orchestra
Queen Elizabeth II Building, School of Music, Brandon University, 270 - 18th St., Brandon MB R7A 6A9 Canada
Tel: 204-728-9631; *Fax:* 204-728-6839
music@brandonu.ca
www.brandonu.ca/music/
Social Media: www.facebook.com/group.php?gid=31991706716

Canadian Band Association (CBA) / Association canadienne des harmonies
15 Pinecrest Bay, Winnipeg MB R2G 1W2 Canada
Tel: 204-663-1226; *Fax:* 204-663-1226
cbaband@shaw.ca
cba.usask.ca
To promote & develop the musical educational & cultural values of band & band music in Canada

Carl Orff Canada Music for Children (COC)
c/o Joan Linklater, 88 Tunis Bay, Winnipeg MB R3T 2X1 Canada
Tel: 204-261-1893
www.orffcanada.ca
To encourage the development of a wholistic music education evolved from the pedagogical philosophy & approach of Carl Orff
Joan Linklater, President

Manitoba Band Association
15 Pinecrest Bay, Winnipeg MB R2G 1W2 Canada
Tel: 204-663-1226; *Fax:* 204-663-1226
mbband@shaw.ca
www.mbband.org
To promote growth & development of bands in Manitoba

Manitoba Chamber Orchestra (MCO)
Portage Place, 393 Portage Ave., #Y300, Winnipeg MB R3B 3H6 Canada
Tel: 204-783-7377; *Fax:* 204-783-7383
mco@mts.net
www.manitobachamberorchestra.org
To perform chamber orchestra repertoire with emphasis on premiering new Canadian works & Canadian soloists

Manitoba Opera Association Inc.
Lower Level, Centennial Concert Hall, #105, 555 Main St., Winnipeg MB R3B 1C3 Canada
Tel: 204-942-7479; *Fax:* 204-949-0377
mbopera@manitobaopera.mb.ca
www.manitobaopera.mb.ca
Social Media: www.twitter.com/ManitobaOpera
To present & develop appreciation for art of opera in Manitoba; to assist in development of Canadian talent, with emphasis on Manitobans

Western Canadian Music Alliance (WCMA)
#637, 776 Corydon Ave., Winnipeg MB R3M 0Y1 Canada
Tel: 204-943-8485; *Fax:* 204-453-1594
info@wcmw.ca
www.wcmw.ca
The music industry associations of Manitoba, Alberta, and Saskatchewan work in tandem towards the shared vision of developing the infrastructure of the independent music industry in Western Canada.
Bob D'Eith, President

Winnipeg Symphony Orchestra Inc. (WSO)
#101, 555 Main St., Winnipeg MB R3B 1C3 Canada
Tel: 204-949-3950; *Fax:* 204-956-4271
lmarks@wso.mb.ca
www.wso.mb.ca
To perform a wide variety of orchestral music including classical, contemporary, pop & children's music in Manitoba & Northwestern Ontario

New Brunswick

Symphony New Brunswick / Symphonie Nouveau-Brunswick
Brunswick Square, 39 King St., Level III, Saint John NB E2L 4W3 Canada
Tel: 506-634-8379; *Fax:* 506-634-0843
symphony@nbnet.nb.ca
www.symphonynb.com
To present high-quality, live orchestral & chamber music from all periods & to promote the appreciation of music through educational activities in New Brunswick

Newfoundland and Labrador

Newfoundland Symphony Orchestra Association (NSO)
Arts & Culture Centre, PO Box 1854, St. John's NL A1C 5P9 Canada
Tel: 709-722-4441; *Fax:* 709-753-0561
nso.orchestra@nso.nfld.net
www.nso-music.com
To foster & promote in all age groups of the general public of the province an interest in & an appreciation of music; to provide the province with a symphony orchestra of the highest possible standard; to provide professional musicians, highly skilled amateur players & talented students with the opportunity of performing

Newfoundland Symphony Youth Orchestra (NSYO)
PO Box 1854, St. John's NL A1C 5P9 Canada
Tel: 709-722-4441; *Fax:* 709-753-0561
Youth Orchestra in Newfoundland
Peter Gardner, Director

Nova Scotia

African Nova Scotian Music Association (ANSMA)
PO Box 931, 1149 Main St., Dartmouth NS B2Z 1A8 Canada
Tel: 902-404-3036; *Fax:* 902-434-0462
ansma@eastlink.ca
www.ansma.com
The African Nova Scotian Music Association (ANSMA) is a not for profit organization dedicated to the development, promotion and enhancement of African Nova Scotia Music locally, nationally and internationally.
Louis (Lou) Gannon Jr., President

Association of Canadian Choral Conductors (ACCC) / Association des chefs de choeur canadiens
6303 Duncan St., Halifax NS B3L 1K4 Canada
Tel: 902-442-7054; *Fax:* 902-442-7050
accc@ca.inter.net
www.choralcanada.org
To promote choral music, particularly Canadian works, in schools, post-secondary institutions, churches & communities throughout Canada

Deep Roots Music Cooperative
PO Box 2360, Wolfville NS B4P 2G9 Canada
Tel: 902-542-7668
info@deeprootsmusic.ca
www.deeprootsmusic.ca/cooperative
To develop year-round musical programs culminating in an annual festival, and to encourage meaningful connections between cultures, community groups, artists and audiences.
Peter Mowat, Chair

Music Nova Scotia
#302, 5516 Spring Garden Rd., Halifax NS B3J 1G6 Canada
Tel: 902-423-6271; *Fax:* 902-423-8841
Toll-Free: 888-343-6426
info@musicnovascotia.ca
www.musicnovascotia.ca
To encourage the creation, development, growth and promotion of Nova Scotia's music industry.
Brian Doherty, President
Scott Long, Executive Director

Music NWT
Roman Empire Bldg., 5103 51st St., 2nd Fl., Yellowknife NT X1A 1S8 Canada
Tel: 867-873-5577; *Fax:* 867-873-5575
info@musicnwt.ca
www.musicnwt.ca
The association brings together musicians, offers workshops & other resources, & provides networking opportunities

Nova Scotia Band Association
355 Branch St, New Glasgow NS B2H 3A5 Canada
Tel: 902-751-5996; *Fax:* 902-755-8490
admin@novascotiabandassociation.com
www.novascotiabandassociation.com
To support and promote the development of bands throughout the province of Nova Scotia through communication, coordination, program development, advocacy and lobbying at the provincial level.
Barbara Stetter, President

Nova Scotia Youth Orchestra
6199 Chebucto Rd., Halifax NS B3L 1K7 Canada
Tel: 902-423-5984
nsyo@ns.sympatico.ca
www.novascotiayouthorchestra.com
To provide young musicians with the finest orchestral training; to provide live orchestral music to audiences in Nova Scotia

Scotia Chamber Players
6181 Lady Hammond Rd., Halifax NS B3K 2R9 Canada
Tel: 902-429-9467; *Fax:* 902-425-6785
admin@scotiafestival.ns.ca
www.scotiafestival.ns.ca
To enhance the quality of music by producing an annual festival of world-class chamber music in study & performance for the benefit of musicians, students & audiences

Symphony Nova Scotia (SNS)
Park Lane Mall, PO Box 218, #301, 5657 Spring Garden Rd., Halifax NS B3J 3R4 Canada
Tel: 902-421-1300; *Fax:* 902-422-1209
info@symns.cohn.dal.ca
www.symphonynovascotia.ca
To enhance the quality of life of the citizens of Nova Scotia through high quality, professionally performed orchestral music

Ontario

Alliance for Canadian New Music Projects (ACNMP) / Alliance pour des projets de musique canadienne nouvelle
Canadian Music Centre, 20 St. Joseph St., Toronto ON M4Y 1J9 Canada
Tel: 416-963-5937; *Fax:* 416-961-7198
acnmp@rogers.com
www.acnmp.ca
To provide young musicians with an opportunity to celebrate & enjoy the music of their own time & country through the organization's syllabus & its festival, Contemporary Showcase

Bach Elgar Choral Society
86 Homewood St., Hamilton ON L8P 2M4 Canada
Tel: 905-527-5995; *Fax:* 905-527-0555
bachelgar@bellnet.ca
www.bachelgar.com
To provide choral music of excellent quality & broad-based appeal to the community; to act as a cultural & educational resource

Bluegrass Music Association of Central Canada (BMACC)
c/o Secretary, 339 Wellington St. N, Woodstock ON N4S 6S6 Canada
Tel: 519-539-8967
weslowe@bmacc.ca
www.bmacc.ca
The Bluegrass Music Association of Central Canada is dedicated to the preservation and promotion of Bluegrass and Old-time music throughout Central Canada. The BMACC works to support individuals, groups and organizations involved in bluegrass and old-time music and provide leadership and promote education among fans, clubs, bands and artists.
Denis Chadbourn, President

Brampton Symphony Orchestra
PO Box 93091, Stn. Brampton South, 499 Main St. South, Brampton ON L6Y 4V8 Canada
Tel: 905-459-0853
info@bramptonsymphony.com
www.bramptonsymphony.com

Brantford Symphony Orchestra Association Inc.
PO Box 24012, 185 King George Rd., Brantford ON N3R 7X3 Canada
Tel: 519-759-8781; *Fax:* 519-759-0842
administrator@brantfordsymphony.ca
www.brantfordsymphony.com
To provide musical performances of the highest standard while encouraging area musicians & pursuing programmes of innovative outreach

Canadian Academy of Recording Arts & Sciences (CARAS) / Académie canadienne des arts et des sciences de l'enregistrement (ACASE)
345 Adelaide St. West, 2nd fl., Toronto ON M5V 1J6
Tel: 416-485-3135; *Fax:* 416-485-4978
Toll-Free: 888-440-5866
membership@carasonline.ca
www.carasonline.ca
To promote Canadian artists and music; To identify & rewardthe achievements of Canadian artists

Canadian Association for Music Therapy (CAMT) / Association de musicothérapie du Canada (AMC)
#230, 110 Cumberland St., Toronto ON M5R 3V5 Canada
Tel: 416-944-0421; *Fax:* 416-944-0431
Toll-Free: 800-996-2268
camt@musictherapy.ca
www.musictherapy.ca
To promote excellence in music therapy practice & education in Canadian clinical, educational, & community settings

Canadian Bureau for the Advancement of Music (CBAM)
Exhibition Place, Toronto ON M6K 3C3 Canada
Tel: 416-260-6451
moreinfo@thecbam.ca
www.thecbam.ca
To promote music (piano) education program for elementary school students

Canadian Children's Opera Chorus (CCOC)
Opera Centre, #215, 227 Front St. East, Toronto ON M5A 1E8 Canada
Tel: 416-366-0467; *Fax:* 416-366-9204
info@canadianchildrensopera.com
www.canadianchildrensopera.com
To be the foremost children's operatic chorus in Canada & to achieve international recognition

Canadian Country Music Association (CCMA) / Association de la musique country canadienne
30B Commercial Rd., Toronto ON M4G 1Z4 Canada
Tel: 416-947-1331; *Fax:* 416-947-5924
country@ccma.org
www.ccma.org
The federally chartered non-profit professional organization protects the heritage, & advocates the development of Canadian country music both in Canada & worldwide.

Canadian Disc Jockey Association (CDJA)
PO Box 92, Arva ON N0M 1C0 Canada
Fax: 519-472-0242
Toll-Free: 877-472-0653
pres@cdja.ca
www.cdja.org
To provide a forum for professional disc jockeys to meet & discuss mutual trade concerns, benefits, etc.; to improve the DJ service industry by establishing & promoting standards, procedures & benefits for disc jockey operations & operators across Canada; to promote the disc jockey to the consumer as an alternative & economical form of entertainment for a wide variety of applications; to assist & train the member in any way possible to professionally develop skills, knowledge, experience & business acumen in the disc jockey service sector; to represent the disc jockey service industry as a lobby & special interest group; to provide special service, advice & common benefit to disc jockeys across Canada

Canadian Independent Music Association (CIMA)
30 St. Patrick St., 2nd Fl., Toronto ON M5T 3A3 Canada
Tel: 416-485-3152; *Fax:* 416-485-4373
cima@cimamusic.ca
www.cimamusic.ca
CIMA concentrates on lobbying governments for support & copyright reform. It maintains watch on Cancon regulations & other broadcast regulatory matters, and to raise the profile of Canadian music abroad, the association also promotes the industry at international events, particularly MIDEM, held annually in Cannes, France.

Canadian League of Composers / La Ligue canadienne de compositeurs
c/o Canadian Music Centre, 20 St. Joseph St., Toronto ON M4Y 1J9 Canada
Tel: 416-964-1364; *Toll-Free:* 877-964-1364
info@composition.org
www.composition.org
The oldest organization that speaks for professional composers in a professional capacity. It endeavours to represent the best interests of composers and to monitor and influence the conditions that affect their livlihood and public image.

Canadian Music Centre (CMC) / Centre de musique canadienne
Chalmers House, 20 St. Joseph St., Toronto ON M4Y 1J9 Canada
Tel: 416-961-6601; *Fax:* 416-961-7198
info@musiccentre.ca
www.musiccentre.ca; www.centremusique.ca
To stimulate the awareness, appreciation & performance of Canadian music

Canadian Music Educators' Association (CMEA) / Association canadienne des éducateurs de musique
#A-430A, Wilfrid Laurier University, Waterloo ON N2L 3C5 Canada
Tel: 519-884-0710
edwin.wasiak@uleth.ca
www.musiceducationonline.org
To provide leadership in establishing & maintaining high standards of school music in Canada

Canadian Music Festival Adjudicators' Association (CMFAA)
c/o School of Music, Queen's University, Kingston ON K7L 3N6 Canada
Tel: 613-533-6000; *Fax:* 613-533-6808
zuki@queensu.ca
www.cmfaa.ca

Canadian Musical Heritage Society (CMHS) / Société pour le patrimoine musical canadien (SPMC)
#15, 120 Walnut Ct., Ottawa ON K1R 7W2 Canada
Tel: 613-237-0550
enquiries@cliffordfordpublications.ca
To provide research & publication of early Canadian music in a multi-volume anthology

Canadian Opera Company (COC) / Compagnie d'opéra canadienne
145 Queen St. West, Toronto ON M5A 1E8 Canada
Tel: 416-363-8231; *Fax:* 416-363-5584
Toll-Free: 800-250-4653
info@coc.ca
www.coc.ca
To produce opera of the highest international standard while attracting growing public support & participation in opera through increased accessibility & education; to attract, develop & promote young Canadian singers, musicians, stage directors, conductors, designers, technical personnel & administrators; to encourage Canadian librettists & composers to compose new works

Canadian Recording Industry Association (CRIA) / Association de l'industrie canadienne de l'enregistrement
85 Mowat Ave., Toronto ON M6K 3E3 Canada
Tel: 416-967-7272; *Fax:* 416-967-9415
info@cria.ca
www.cria.ca
CRIA develops and promotes high ethical standards in the creation, manufacture and marketing of sound recordings.

Canadian University Music Society (CUMS) / Société de musique des universités canadiennes (SMUC)
c/o Secretariat, #202, 10 Morrow Ave., Toronto ON M6R 2J1 Canada
Tel: 416-538-1650; *Fax:* 416-489-1713
journals@interlog.com
www.cums-smuc.ca/
To stimulate research, musical performance & composition; to improve instructional methods in university teaching; to provide a forum to exchange views on common problems, scholarly research in music & other matters of professional concern; to advise on new university programs & monitor existing programs

Cathedral Bluffs Symphony Orchestra (CBSO)
PO Box 51074, 18 Eglinton Sq., Toronto ON M1L 2K2 Canada
Tel: 416-879-5566
info@cathedralbluffs.com
www.cathedralbluffs.com
To provide residents of Scarborough with an opportunity to hear classical symphonic music performed by a live orchestra; to provide skilled amateur musicians & young soloists with an opportunity to perform

Choirs Ontario
1442A Bayview Ave., Toronto ON M4G 3A7 Canada
Tel: 416-923-1144; *Fax:* 416-929-0415
Toll-Free: 866-935-1144
info@choirsontario.org
www.choirsontario.org

To promote choral singing in communities, schools & universities, places of worship, etc. throughout Ontario.

Conservatory Canada
#M-2, 130 King St., London ON N6A 1C5 Canada
Tel: 519-433-3147; *Fax:* 519-433-7404
Toll-Free: 800-461-5367
mail@conservatorycanada.ca
www.conservatorycanada.ca
To promote achievement in music through a comprehensive program of study, evaluation & recognition for teachers & students; to foster the development of musical talent & potential

Counterpoint Community Orchestra
PO Box 41, 552 Church St., Toronto ON M4Y 2E3 Canada
Tel: 416-654-9806
info@ccorchestra.org
www.ccorchestra.org
Terry Kowalczuk, Music Director

Deep River Symphony Orchestra (DRSO)
PO Box 1496, Deep River ON K0J 1P0 Canada
Tel: 613-586-9385
symphony@drso.ca
www.drso.ca
To promote the development & enjoyment of music in the Upper Ottawa Valley

Edward Johnson Music Foundation (EJMF)
PO Box 1718, 50 Cork St. East, 2nd Fl., Guelph ON N1H 6Z9 Canada
Tel: 519-821-7570; *Fax:* 519-821-4403
info@edwardjohnsonmusicfoundation.org
www.edwardjohnsonmusicfoundation.org
To recognize the vital role of music in the fabric of our lives & communities; To create opportunities for children & adults to learn about, create, & enjoy music in schools & throughout the community

Etobicoke Philharmonic Orchestra (EPO)
PO Box 66, Stn. D, Toronto ON M9A 4X1 Canada
Tel: 416-239-5665; *Fax:* 416-239-5665
info@eporchestra.ca
www.eporchestra.ca
To provide an opportunity for trained amateur musicians to perform together & become acquainted with an orchestral repertoire; to provide the community with symphonic music, competently performed in a local setting; to assist serious music students in their studies through performance experience & a scholarship program

Foundation Assisting Canadian Talent on Recordings (FACTOR)
30 Commercial Rd., Toronto ON M5V 1Z4 Canada
Tel: 416-696-2215; *Fax:* 416-351-7311
general.info@factor.ca
www.factor.ca
To provide financial assistance for production of sound recordings, videos, syndicated radio programs & international tour support; English-language counterpart of Musicaction
Heather Ostertag, C.M., President/CEO
Phil Gumbley, Director of Operations
Julia Train, Communications Manager

Georgian Bay Symphony (GBS)
PO Box 133, 994 - 3rd Ave. East, Owen Sound ON N4K 5P1 Canada
Tel: 519-372-0212; *Fax:* 519-372-9023
gbs@bmts.com
www.georgianbaysymphony.ca
Social Media: www.facebook.com/pages/Georgian-Bay-Symphony/41551049364
To enhance appreciation of music which includes growth & development of regional orchestra

Guild of Canadian Film Composers (GCFC) / Guilde des compositeurs canadiens de musique de film
PO Box 22059, 45 Overlea Blvd., Toronto ON M4H 1N9 Canada
Tel: 416-410-5076; *Fax:* 416-410-4516
Toll-Free: 866-657-1117
gcfc@gcfc.ca
www.gcfc.ca
To improve the status & quality of music as it applies to film/tv/new media through education & the professional development of its members & the producing community; to represent & communicate the interests of its members to the music & film/tv/new media industries as well as other institutions; to collaborate with trade & industry associations with common interests; to represent all Canadian composers within the certified territories & producer entities detailed in our certification under the Canadian Status of the Artist Act, as the exclusive organization for collective negotiations

Halton Youth Symphony (HYS)
PO Box 494, Oakville ON L6J 5A8 Canada
Tel: 905-616-2760
manager@haltonyouthsymphony.com
www.haltonyouthsymphony.com
To inspire, encourage & challenge young musicians to build their musical skills through the experience of various forms of orchestral music; to create an enjoyable environment that promotes teamwork, leadership & community involvement

Hamilton Philharmonic Orchestra
#1002, 105 Main St. East, Hamilton ON L8N 1G6 Canada
Tel: 905-526-1677; *Fax:* 905-526-0616
communications@hpo.org
www.hpo.org
To provide artistically excellent music to patrons

Hamilton Philharmonic Youth Orchestra (HPYO)
299 Fennell Ave. West, Hamilton ON L9C 1G3 Canada
Tel: 905-573-9094
info@hpyo.com
www.hpyo.com

Hart House Orchestra
University of Toronto, 7 Hart House Circle, Toronto ON M5S 3H3 Canada
Tel: 416-978-5362
webmaestro@harthouseorchestra.ca
www.harthouseorchestra.ca

Huronia Symphony Orchestra (HSO)
PO Box 904, Barrie ON L4M 4Y6 Canada
Tel: 705-721-4752; *Fax:* 705-737-0679
office@huroniasymphony.ca
www.huroniasymphony.ca
To operate & support a symphony orchestra in Simcoe County; to provide symphonic music for people of the area as well as an opportunity for children & youth to receive instruction in orchestral music

International Symphony Orchestra of Sarnia, Ontario & Port Huron, Michigan
225 Davis St., Sarnia ON N7T 1B2 Canada
Tel: 519-337-7775; *Fax:* 519-337-1822
iso@rivernet.net
www.theiso.org
To provide cultural enrichment within the community by providing high calibre choral & symphonic performances

International Youth Symphony Orchestra
118 North Victoria St., Sarnia ON N7T 5W9 Canada
Tel: 519-337-7775; *Fax:* 519-337-1822

Kingston Symphony Association (KSA)
PO Box 1616, #206, 11 Princess St., Kingston ON K7L 5C8 Canada
Tel: 613-546-9729; *Fax:* 613-546-8580
info@kingstonsymphony.on.ca
www.kingstonsymphony.on.ca
To maintain & produce professional orchestral & symphonic music in the Kingston area

Kingston Youth Orchestra
PO Box 1616, #206, 11 Princess St., Kingston ON K7L 5C8 Canada
Tel: 613-546-9729; *Fax:* 613-546-8580

Kitchener-Waterloo Chamber Orchestra (KWCO)
197 Weber St. East, Kitchener ON N2H 1E5 Canada
Tel: 519-744-3828; *Fax:* 519-749-0832
kwchamberorchestra@gmail.com
www.kwchamberorchestra.ca
Joanna Armbruster, President
Graham Coles, Music Director

Kitchener-Waterloo Symphony Orchestra Association Inc. (KWSOA)
36 King St. West, Kitchener ON N2G 1A3 Canada
Tel: 519-745-4711; *Fax:* 519-745-4474
Toll-Free: 888-745-4717
info@kwsymphony.on.ca
www.kwsymphony.on.ca
To cultivate the tradition of live performance through the presentation of classical orchestral & popular music for the edification, enrichment, education & excitement of our community & beyond

Kitchener-Waterloo Symphony Youth Orchestra (KWSYO)
36 King St. West, Kitchener ON N2G 1A3 Canada
Tel: 519-745-4711; *Toll-Free:* 888-745-4717
info@kwsymphony.on.ca
www.kwsymphony.on.ca
Social Media: www.facebook.com/group.php?gid=2208830153

Kiwanis Music Festival Association of Greater Toronto
1422A Bayview Ave., Toronto ON M4G 3A7 Canada
Tel: 416-487-5885; *Fax:* 416-487-5784
kiwanismusic@bellnet.ca
kiwanismusictoronto.org/index.html
To bring together various choirs in music competitions

Korean-Canadian Symphony Orchestra (KGSO)
#203, 703 Bloor St. West, Toronto ON M6G 1L5 Canada
Tel: 416-534-3760
info@kcso.ca
www.kcso.ca
Myung Sook Kim, President
Richard Lee, Music Director

London Community Orchestra (LCO)
c/o 838 Wellington St. North, London ON N6A 3S7 Canada
Tel: 519-433-2074
sally.vernon@odyssey.on.ca
www.ontera.net/~lco/
To give concerts & to sponsor local young artists as soloists

London Youth Symphony (LYS)
PO Box 553, Stn. B, London ON N6A 4W8 Canada
Tel: 519-686-8070
info@londonyouthsymphony.org
www.londonyouthsymphony.org
To provide the region's most talented young musicians with the opportunity to build self-discipline, confidence & team spirit within an outstanding symphonic environment that offers professional directorship & coaching

Mariposa Folk Foundation
PO Box 383, Orillia ON L3V 6J8 Canada
Tel: 705-326-3655; *Fax:* 705-329-4099
info@mariposafolk.com
www.mariposafolk.com
The promotion & preservation of folk arts in Canada through song, story, dance, & craft. Office is located at 27 Mississaga St. West in Orillia.

Mississauga Youth Orchestra
159 Cavendish Ct., Mississauga ON L6J 5S3 Canada
Tel: 905-815-8125; *Fax:* 905-815-8516
email@myomusic.ca
www.myomusic.ca
Kathy Grell, Manager

Music for Young Children (MYC) / Musique pour jeunes enfants
39 Leacock Way, Kanata ON K2K 1T1 Canada
Tel: 613-592-7565; *Fax:* 613-592-9353
Toll-Free: 800-561-1692
myc@myc.com
www.myc.com
To develop, deliver & support comprehensive entry level music education programs of the finest quality

Music Industries Association of Canada (MIAC) / Association canadienne des industries de la musique
#807, 505 Consumers Rd., Toronto ON M2J 4V8 Canada
Tel: 416-490-1871; *Fax:* 416-490-0369
Toll-Free: 877-480-6422
info@miac.net
www.miac.net
To represent Canadian manufacturers, distributors, retailers & wholesalers of musical instruments & accessories, sound reinforcement/lighting products, published music & computer music software

National Arts Centre Orchestra of Canada (NACO) / Orchestre du Centre national des Arts (OCNA)
PO Box 1534, Stn. B, 53 Elgin St., Ottawa ON K1P 5W1 Canada
Tel: 613-947-7000; *Toll-Free:* 866-850-2787
info@nac-cna.ca
www.nac-cna.ca
Social Media: www.facebook.com/CanadasNAC;
www.twitter.com/canadasnac

National Shevchenko Musical Ensemble Guild of Canada
626 Bathurst St., Toronto ON M5S 2R1 Canada
Tel: 416-533-2725; *Fax:* 416-533-6348
info_sme@bellnet.ca
www.shevchenkomusic.com
To provide instruction in vocal, instrumental & dance for youth & adults by maintaining the Shevchenko Musical Ensemble & Shevchenko School of Dance & Music; to perpetuate Ukrainian cultural traditions

National Youth Orchestra Association of Canada
#500, 59 Adelaide St. East, Toronto ON M5C 1K6 Canada
Tel: 416-532-4470; *Fax:* 416-532-6879
Toll-Free: 888-532-4470
info@nyoc.org
www.nyoc.org
Social Media: www.twitter.com/nyoc_onjc

Niagara Youth Orchestra Association
#148, 12 - 111 Fourth Ave., St Catharines ON L2S 3P5 Canada
Tel: 905-704-0559; *Fax:* 905-704-0558
nyo@vaxxine.com
www.niagarayouthorchestra.ca
To foster among youth of Niagara Region an interest in & understanding of orchestral music of high quality

Northumberland Orchestra Society (NOC)
PO Box 1012, Cobourg ON K9A 4W4 Canada
Tel: 905-377-1477
norchestra@norchestra.org
www.norchestra.org

Oakville Chamber Orchestra
PO Box 76036, 1500 Upper Middle Rd. West, Oakville ON L6M 3H5 Canada
Tel: 905-483-6787
mail@oakvillechamber.org
www.oakvillechamber.org

Oakville Symphony Orchestra (OSO)
#114, 99 Bronte Rd., Oakville ON L6L 3B7 Canada
Tel: 905-338-1462; *Fax:* 905-338-7954
oakville.symphony@cogeco.ca
www.oakvillesymphony.com
To bring audiences a variety of music for all ages & to contribute to the cultural growth of the community

Ontario Band Association
c/o Membership Co-ordinator, 459 Concord Ave., Toronto ON M6H 2P9 Canada
membership@onband.ca
www.onband.ca
To promote & develop musical, educational & cultural values of bands in Ontario by sponsoring annual band & solo instrument competition, composition competition, original works

Opera Lyra Ottawa
#110, 2 Daly Ave., Ottawa ON K1N 6E2 Canada
Tel: 613-233-9200; *Fax:* 613-233-5431
Toll-Free: 877-233-5972
marketing@operalyra.com
www.operalyra.ca
To provide employment & training opportunities for musicians, singers, stage hands, directors, & young artists of the highest calibre from across Canada & abroad; To present fully staged operas & various small-scale operas & concerts each season
Elizabeth Howarth, General Director

Opera Ontario
Opera Hamilton, #905, 105 Main St. East, Hamilton ON L8N 1G6 Canada
Tel: 905-527-7627; *Fax:* 905-527-0014
Toll-Free: 800-575-1381
info@operaontario.com
www.operaontario.com
To provide a consistently improving quality of operatic experience that compares favorably with opera produced anywhere in the world, which will enrich the audience & encourage the widest possible participation; to produce quality professional opera that will contribute to the cultural, economic & educational quality of our unique multi-city community
Alice Willems, President
David Speers, General Director

Opera.ca
#410, 174 Spadina Ave., Toronto ON M5T 2C2 Canada
Tel: 416-591-7222
info@opera.ca
www.opera.ca
Opera.ca works with members across the country to advance the interests of Canada's opera community and create greater opportunity for opera audiences and professionals alike.
Christina Loewen, Executive Director
Sandra Cina, Coordinator, Membership & Communications

Orchestra London Canada Inc.
609 Wellington St., London ON N6A 3R6 Canada
Tel: 519-679-8558; *Fax:* 519-679-8914
rgloor@orchestralondon.ca
www.orchestralondon.ca
To enrich the quality of life in the London area by maintaining a professional orchestra, serving the community through a wide variety of musical activities

Orchestra Toronto (OT)
#402, 131 Beecroft Rd., Toronto ON M2N 6G9 Canada
Tel: 416-467-7142
otoronto@on.aibn.com
www.orchestratoronto.ca
Social Media: www.facebook.com/pages/Orchestra-Toronto/172229189138
To provide affordable family entertainment, music education, & full repertoire in all its programs

Orchestras Canada (OC) / Orchestres Canada
230-460 College St., Toronto ON M6G 1A1 Canada
Tel: 416-366-8834; *Fax:* 416-366-1780
info@oc.ca
orchestrascanada.org
Social Media: www.facebook.com/orchestrascanada?ref=ts
Strengthening Canada's orchestral community through leadership in advocacy, education & professional development

Orchestras Mississauga
4141 Living Arts Dr., Mississauga ON L5B 4B8 Canada
Tel: 905-615-4405; *Fax:* 905-615-4402
symphony.info@livingarts.on.ca
www.mississaugasymphony.ca
Social Media: www.facebook.com/group.php?v=wall&gid=14456410182
To provide & promote orchestral music; to ensure its accessibility to all segments of the community

Orillia Youth Symphony Orchestra (OYSO)
168 Parkview Ave., Orillia ON L3V 4M3 Canada
Tel: 705-326-7548
www.oyso.ca
To offer opportunity to participate in symphonic orchestra for young people 8-18 years of age

Oshawa-Durham Symphony Orchestra (ODSO)
PO Box 444, Oshawa ON L1H 7L5 Canada
Tel: 905-579-6711; *Fax:* 905-987-3083
contact@odso.ca
www.odso.ca
To bring fine orchestral music to residents of the area by operating a high-quality orchestra

Ottawa Symphony Orchestra Inc. (OSO) / Orchestre symphonique d'Ottawa
#250, 2 Daly Ave., Ottawa ON K1N 6E2 Canada
Tel: 613-231-7802; *Fax:* 613-231-3610
oso@on.aibn.com
www.ottawasymphony.com
To develop the highest possible artistic level of performance of symphonic repertoire among local musicians, local & Canadian soloists, Canadian music, partnership opportunities for performance with other local performing arts organizations, educational outreach opportunities for young audiences & young performers

Ottawa Youth Orchestra Academy (OYO) / L'Orchestre des jeunes d'Ottawa
#1, 54 Beech St., Ottawa ON K1S 3J6 Canada
Tel: 613-233-9318; *Fax:* 613-233-5038
info@oyoa-aojo.ca
www.oyoa-aojo.ca

Pembroke Symphony Orchestra
PO Box 374, Pembroke ON K8A 6X6 Canada
Tel: 613-687-2660
info@pembrokesymphony.org
pembrokesymphony.org
Angus Armstrong, Concertmaster
Gail Marion, President

Peterborough Symphony Orchestra (PSO)
PO Box 1135, Peterborough ON K9J 7H4 Canada
Tel: 705-742-1992; *Fax:* 705-742-2077
Toll-Free: 877-742-1992
info@thepso.org
www.thepso.org
To perform & develop excellence in symphonic music that will enrich, stimulate & attract the widest possible audience by presenting & perpetuating quality orchestral music to the people of Peterborough & beyond

The Queen of Puddings Music Theatre Company
The Case Good Warehouse, Bldg. 74, Studio 206, 55 Mill St., Toronto ON M5A 3C4 Canada
Tel: 416-203-4149; *Fax:* 416-203-8027
queenofpuddings@bellnet.ca
www.queenofpuddingsmusictheatre.com
Queen of Puddings has consistently produced provocative, dramatic presentations that have challenged the parameters of the opera genre. The company works solely with Canadian artists.
Dairine Ni Mheadhra, Artistic Director
John Hess, Artistic Director

Quinte Symphony
PO Box 23087, Belleville ON K8P 5J3 Canada
Tel: 613-395-3756
info@quintesymphony.com
www.quintesymphony.com
Committed to enriching the Quinte community by actively promoting an appreciation of Classical & Canadian orchestral music

Royal Canadian College of Organists (RCCO) / Collège royal canadien des organistes (CRCO)
#202, 204 St. George St., Toronto ON M5R 2N5 Canada
Tel: 416-929-6400; *Fax:* 416-929-2265
manager@rcco.ca
www.rcco.ca
To promote a high standard of organ playing, choral directing, church music & composition; to hold examinations in organ playing, choir directing, theory & general knowledge of music; to encourage recitals; to increase the understanding among church musicisans, authorities & the public of matters relating to church music

Royal Conservatory Orchestra
273 Bloor St. West, Toronto ON M5S 1W2 Canada
Tel: 416-408-2824; *Fax:* 416-408-3096
glenngouldschool@rcmusic.ca
www.rcmusic.ca
Social Media: www.twitter.com/the_rcm

Sault Symphony Association / Orchestre symphonique de Sault Ste-Marie
#2, 121 Brock St., Sault Ste Marie ON P6A 3B6 Canada
Tel: 705-945-5337; *Fax:* 705-945-8865
symphony@soonet.ca
www.saultsymphony.com
To promote symphonic music in Sault Ste Marie, the Algoma region, & the upper peninsula of Michigan

Scarborough Philharmonic Orchestra
#209, 3007 Kingston Rd., Toronto ON M1M 1P1 Canada
Tel: 416-429-0007
spo@spo.ca
www.spo.ca
To enrich the cultural life of Scarborough, through the promotion & presentation of high calibre musical performances; To develop a strong & financially viable organization

Songwriters Association of Canada (SAC) / Association des auteurs-compositeurs canadiens
129 John St., Toronto ON M5V 2E2 Canada
Tel: 416-961-1588; *Fax:* 416-961-2040
Toll-Free: 866-456-7664
sacadmin@songwriters.ca
www.songwriters.ca
To protect & develop the creative & business environments for songwriters in Canada & around the world

Soundstreams Canada
#200, 57 Spadina Ave., Toronto ON M5V 2J2 Canada
Tel: 416-504-1282; *Fax:* 416-504-1285
info@soundstreams.ca
www.soundstreams.ca
To foster & promote the development of 20th century music & music by Canadian composers, through the sponsorship of concerts, musical theatre works for young audiences, festivals & special events, recording projects, the commissioning of new works by Canadian composers & touring of Canadian artists

Sudbury Symphony Orchestra Association Inc. (SSO) / Orchestre symphonique de Sudbury inc
#266, 303 York St., Sudbury ON P3E 2A5 Canada
Tel: 705-673-1280; *Fax:* 705-673-1434
symphon1@bellnet.ca
www.sudburysymphony.com
To provide the opportunity for a broad spectrum of the public in the Sudbury Region & surrounding area to attend a stimulating program of concerts; to maintain an environment & organization which encourages artistic responsibility & commitment; to attract & maintain private & public funding in order to achieve accessibility & continuity through financial stability; to increase the awareness & appreciation of music in the community; to provide a vehicle for the participation in & ongoing development of the performance of orchestral music; to increase the awareness, appreciation & performance of Canadian music in the community

Sudbury Youth Orchestra Inc.
PO Box 2241, Stn. A, Sudbury ON P3A 4S1 Canada
Tel: 705-566-8101
info@sudburyyouthorchestra.ca
www.sudburyyouthorchestra.ca
To foster an appreciation of orchestral music; to create opportunities for orchestral performance; to provide access to education & training in an orchestral setting for the youth of Sudbury & area

Symphony Hamilton
PO Box 89007, 991 King St. West, Hamilton ON L8S 4R5 Canada
Tel: 905-526-6690
info@symphonyhamilton.ca
www.symphonyhamilton.ca
To enrich the cultural life of the Hamilton & surrounding area by maintaining a full-size community symphony orchestra; to perform a wide repertoire of symphonic music, including works by Canadian composers; to make great symphonic music accessible to a larger public by offering attractive concert programs at affordable prices

Tafelmusik Baroque Orchestra & Chamber Choir
PO Box 14, 427 Bloor St. West, Toronto ON M5S 1X7 Canada
Tel: 416-964-9562; *Fax:* 416-964-2782
info@tafelmusik.org
www.tafelmusik.org
Bringing baroque music to Toronto & the world, through concerts, recordings, & a music education programme

Tapestry New Opera Works
The Cannery, Studio 316, #58, 55 Mill St., Toronto ON M5A 3C4 Canada
Tel: 416-537-6066; *Fax:* 416-537-7841
information@tapestrynewopera.com
www.tapestrynewopera.com
To develop & produce original works of Canadian opera & music theatre
Wayne Strongman, Artistic Director

Thunder Bay Symphony Orchestra Association (TBSO)
PO Box 29192, Thunder Bay ON P7B 6P9 Canada
Tel: 807-345-4331; *Fax:* 807-622-1927
info@tbso.ca
www.tbso.ca
To maintain & nurture a professional, regional orchestra of artistic integrity & excellence; to offer a variety of programs to enrich & encourage the widest possible audience; to support the development of local young musicians

Timmins Symphony Orchestra
PO Box 1365, Timmins ON P4N 7N2 Canada
Tel: 705-267-1006; *Fax:* 705-267-1006
tsoffice@ntl.sympatico.ca
www.timsym.com

Toronto Chinese Youth Orchestra
21 Holmesdale Dr., Markham ON L6C 1S9 Canada
Tel: 905-887-7828
tcyo@rogers.com
www.tcyo.ca
Tak-Ng Lai, Music Director

Toronto Downtown Jazz Society
82 Bleecker St., Toronto ON M4X 1L8 Canada
Tel: 416-928-2033; *Fax:* 416-928-0533
tdjs@tojazz.com
www.torontojazz.com
Social Media: www.facebook.com/group.php?gid=8698568268
To produce the Toronto Downtown Jazz Festival, as well as many other events & programs to further develop jazz talent & audience appreciation; To operate as a registered charity (No. 12969 0269 RR0001); To promote community involvement, artistic excellence, & outstanding production standards
Patrick Taylor, CEO/Executive Producer
Josh Grossman, Artistic Director

The Toronto Mendelssohn Choir
60 Simcoe St., Toronto ON M5J 2H5 Canada
Tel: 416-598-0422; *Fax:* 416-598-2992
manager@tmchoir.org
www.tmchoir.org
Canada's world-renowned large vocal ensemble. It has maintained a tradition of performing the finest choral repertoire, and includes the Youth Choir.

Toronto Philharmonia
#109, 1210 Sheppard Ave. East, Toronto ON M2K 1E3 Canada
Tel: 416-499-2204; *Fax:* 416-490-9739
office@torontophil.on.ca
www.torontophil.on.ca
To provide quality, affordable classical music to City of Toronto & to Ontario communities on tour

Toronto Philharmonia Youth Orchestra
PO Box 134, Port Hope ON L1W 3W3 Canada
Tel: 416-797-2138; *Toll-Free:* 866-460-5596
info@ljyo.ca
www.ljyo.ca
Michael Lyons, Music Director

Toronto Sinfonietta
400 St. Clair Avenue E, Toronto ON M4T 1P5 Canada
Tel: 416-410-4379; *Fax:* 416-233-1054
info@torontosinfonietta.com
www.torontosinfonietta.com
Krzysztof Liebert, President
Matthew Jaskiewicz, Music Director

Toronto Symphony Orchestra (TSO)
212 King St. West, 6th Fl., Toronto ON M5H 1K5 Canada
Tel: 416-593-7769; *Fax:* 416-977-2912
www.tso.ca
Social Media: www.facebook.com/group.php?gid=52219459772
To present concerts of both established & new music at the highest artistic standard possible, while recognizing audiences' needs; to play a role in the development of future musicians & audiences

Toronto Symphony Youth Orchestra (TSYO)
212 King St. West, 6th Fl., Toronto ON M5H 1K5 Canada
Tel: 416-593-7769; *Fax:* 416-977-2912
cmatt@tso.ca
www.tso.on.ca

University of Toronto Symphony Orchestra
Faculty of Music, University of Toronto, 80 Queen's Park Cres., Toronto ON M5S 2C5 Canada
Tel: 416-978-3733; *Fax:* 416-946-3353
performance.music@utoronto.ca
www.music.utoronto.ca

University of Western Ontario Symphony Orchestra (UWOSO)
Faculty of Music, University of Western Ontario, 1151 Richmond St. North, London ON N6A 3K7 Canada
Tel: 519-661-2043; *Fax:* 519-661-3531
music@uwo.ca
www.music.uwo.ca

Wilfrid Laurier University Symphony Orchestra
Faculty of Music, 75 University Ave. West, Waterloo ON N2L 3C5 Canada
Tel: 519-884-0710; *Fax:* 519-747-9129
jdupuis@wlu.ca
To train music students to be musicians who have solid knowledge of music theory & history, & are competent performers

Windsor Symphony Orchestra (WSO)
487 Ouellette Ave., Windsor ON N9A 4J2 Canada
Tel: 519-973-1238; *Fax:* 519-973-0764
Toll-Free: 888-327-8327
jgalli@windsorsymphony.com
www.windsorsymphony.com
To enrich community life & serve as an educational resource through high quality live performance of orchestral music

York Symphony Orchestra Inc.
PO Box 355, Richmond Hill ON L4C 4Y6 Canada
Tel: 416-410-0860
yorksymphonyorchestra@hotmail.com
www.yorksymphony.ca
To provide musical enjoyment for audiences & musicians, with the goal of being recognized & supported throughout the region

Prince Edward Island

East Coast Music Association (ECMA) / Association de la musique de la côte est
#70, 90 University Ave., Charlottetown PE C1A 4K9 Canada
Tel: 902-892-9040; *Fax:* 902-892-9041
ecma@ecma.ca
www.ecma.ca
To develop, foster, promote & celebrate East Coast music locally & globally

Music PEI
#70, 90 University Ave., Charlottetown PE C1A 4K9 Canada
Tel: 902-894-6734
music@musicpei.com
www.musicpei.com
To promote, foster and develop artists and the music industry on PEI.
Shannon Pratt, President
Rob Oakie, Executive Director

Prince Edward Island Symphony Society (PEISO)
PO Box 185, 146 Richmond St., Charlottetown PE C1A 7K4 Canada
Tel: 902-892-4333
peiso@peisymphony.com
www.peisymphony.com
To establish & promote symphonic music; to further & foster appreciation of musical education; to promote the welfare of musicians; to give & arrange performances, entertainments & concerts; to employ teachers & instructors to inform the public & awaken interest

Québec

Académie de musique du Québec (AMQ)
CP 818, Succ. C, 1231, rue Panet, Montréal QC H2L 4L6 Canada
Tél: 514-528-1961; *Téléc:* 514-528-7572
prixdeurope@videotron.ca
Promouvoir le goût et l'avancement de la musique au Québec, aux professeurs oeuvrant dans le secteur privé et soucieux à la fois d'autonomie et d'encadrement, aux élèves qui désirent une reconnaissance officielle de leur travail
Jean Marchand, Président

Alliance des chorales du Québec (ACQ)
CP 1000, Succ. M, 4545, av Pierre-de-Coubertin, Montréal QC H1V 3R2 Canada
Tél: 514-252-3020; *Téléc:* 514-252-3222
information@chorale.qc.ca
www.chorale.qc.ca
Regrouper des chorales de tous styles et de tous niveaux; donner des moyens de mieux chanter; promouvoir et développer le chant choral au Québec

Association québécoise de l'industrie du disque, du spectacle et de la vidéo (ADISQ)
6420, rue Saint-Denis, Montréal QC H2S 2R7 Canada
Tél: 514-842-5147; *Téléc:* 514-842-7762
info@adisq.com
www.adisq.com
Promouvoir les intérêts des producteurs de disques, spectacles et vidéos

Canadian Amateur Musicians (CAMMAC) / Musiciens amateurs du Canada
85 Cammac Rd., Harrington QC J8G 2T2
Tel: 819-687-3938; *Fax:* 819-687-3323
Toll-Free: 888-622-8755
national@cammac.ca
www.cammac.ca
To create opportunities for musicians of all levels & ages to play music in a non-competitive environment

Canadian Music Competitions Inc. / Concours de musique du Canada inc.
#220, 1450, rue City Councillors, Montréal QC H3A 2E6 Canada
Tel: 514-284-5398; *Fax:* 514-284-6828
Toll-Free: 877-879-1959
info@cmcnational.com
www.cmcnational.com

Faire participer a une véritable expérience nationale de musique, en étroite collaboration avec les institutions et les professeurs de musique du pays, les plus doués de nos jeunes musiciennes et musiciens canadiens.

Chants Libres, compagnie lyrique de création
#303, 1908, rue Panet, Montréal QC H2L 3A2 Canada
Tél: 514-841-2642; *Téléc:* 514-841-2640
creation@chantslibres.org
www.chantslibres.org
Réunir des créateurs de toutes les disciplines (musique, théâtre, arts plastiques, arts électroniques, vidéo etc.) autour d'un point commun: la voix
Pauline Vaillancourt, Directrice générale

Concerts symphoniques de Sherbrooke inc. (CSS) / Sherbrooke Symphony Orchestra
Domain Howard, Pavillon 1, CP 610, 1300, boul de Portland, Sherbrooke QC J1H 5H9 Canada
Tél: 819-821-0227; *Téléc:* 819-821-1959
oss@abacom.com
www.css-oss.com
Faire connaître la musique symphonique dans la région et permettre aux musiciens de la région de jouer dans un orchestre professionnel

Ensemble contemporain de Montréal (ECM+)
3890 rue Clark, Montréal QC H2W 1W6 Canada
Tél: 514-524-0173; *Téléc:* 514-524-0179
info@ecm.qc.ca
www.ecm.qc.ca
Natalie Watanabe, Directrice générale

Ensemble vocal Ganymède
CP 476, Succ. C, Montréal QC H2L 4K4 Canada
Tél: 514-528-6302
contacter@evganymede.com
www.evganymede.com
Choeur d'hommes
Yvan Sabourin, Directeur

Fédération des harmonies et des orchestres symphonies du Québec (FHOSQ)
CP 1000, Succ. M, 4545, av Pierre-de-Coubertin, Montréal QC H1V 3R2 Canada
Tél: 514-252-3026; *Téléc:* 514-252-3115
info@fhosq.org
www.fhosq.org
Contribuer au développement et à l'amélioration des harmonies en tant que loisir éducatif et culturel

Jeunesses Musicales of Canada (JMC) / Jeunesses musicales du Canada
305, av du Mont-Royal est, Montréal QC H2T 1P8 Canada
Tel: 514-845-4108; *Fax:* 514-845-8241
info@jeunessesmusicales.com
www.jeunessesmusicales.ca
To promote Canadian musical artists & develop audiences

Musicaction
#2, 4385, rue Saint-Hubert, Montréal QC H2J 2X1 Canada
Tél: 514-861-8444; *Téléc:* 514-861-4423
Ligne sans frais: 800-861-5561
info@musicaction.ca
www.musicaction.ca
Développement de la musique vocale francophone au Canada
Andrée Ménard, Directrice générale

L'Opéra de Montréal (ODM) / Montréal Opera
260, boul de Maisonneuve ouest, Montréal QC H2X 1Y9 Canada
Tel: 514-985-2222; *Fax:* 514-985-2219
info@operademontreal.com
www.operademontreal.com
Social Media:
www.facebook.com/pages/Opera-de-Montreal/23275515418
To present opera productions of comparable quality & originality to those seen in the world's great opera houses; seeks the contribution of creative personnel from local & national levels, as well as inviting the best artists from abroad; supports the emergence of new Canadian opera talent

Opéra de Québec
1220, av Taché, Québec QC G1R 3B4 Canada
Tél: 418-529-4142; *Téléc:* 418-529-3735
operaqc@mediom.qc.ca
www.operadequebec.qc.ca
Produire des spectacles d'opéra professionnels à Québec
Gaston Déry, Président

Orchestre de chambre de Montréal (OCM) / Montréal Chamber Orchestra (MCO)
5476 Côte St-Antoine, Montréal QC H4A 1R2 Canada
Tél: 514-871-1224; *Téléc:* 514-871-8967
info@mco-ocm.qc.ca
www.mco-ocm.qc.ca
Se consacre au répertoire pour ensemble de chambre & oeuvres canadiennes

Orchestre symphonique de Montréal
260, boul de Maisonneuve ouest, 2e étage, Montréal QC H2X 1Y9 Canada
Tél: 514-842-3402; *Téléc:* 514-842-0728
www.osm.ca
Média social: www.twitter.com/OSM_official
L'Orchestre doit diffuser, au plus large public possible, le répertoire mondial de la musique symphonique, & les artistes de niveau international; doit assumer son rôle social & institutionnel

Orchestre symphonique de Québec
401, av Grande Allée est, Québec QC G1R 2J5 Canada
Tél: 418-643-8486; *Téléc:* 418-646-9665
billetterie@osq.qc.ca
www.osq.qc.ca
Interpréter le répertoire symphonique; être le principal moteur de l'activité musicale de la région. L'OSM est reconnu comme un organisme de grande qualité, dynamique, accessible, et financièrement sain

Orchestre symphonique de Trois-Rivières (OSTR)
CP 1281, Trois-Rivières QC G9A 5K8 Canada
Tél: 819-373-5340; *Téléc:* 819-373-6693
administration@ostr.ca
www.ostr.ca
Poursuivre l'atteinte des objectifs inhérents à ses axes de développement: éducation, implication dans son milieu, diffusion de musique symphonique, création musicale et diffusion de nouveaux produits

Orchestre symphonique des jeunes de la Montérégie
31, rue Lorne, Saint-Lambert QC J4P 2G7 Canada
Tél: 450-923-3733
courrier@aojm.org
www.aojm.org
Jean-Claude Paré, Président

Orchestre symphonique des jeunes de Montréal (OSJM)
CP 83566, Succ. Succursale Garnier, Montréal QC H2J 4E9 Canada
Tél: 514-645-0311; *Téléc:* 514-524-9894
osjmontreal@gmail.ca
www.osjm.org
Présenter le jeune musicien de talent à un auditoire et lui fournir une expérience formative sous la supervision d'artistes reconnus; encourager et soutenir le choix d'une carrière musicale qui peut mener à un grand orchestre; promouvoir un intérêt dans les concerts et développer un soutien plus diversifié dans les activités de l'orchestre; fournir à l'entreprise privée l'occasion de participer plus activement dans une activité culturelle d'envergure et l'aider à faire apprécier son rôle dans la communauté

Orchestre symphonique des jeunes du West Island (OSJWI) / West Island Youth Symphony Orchestra (WIYSO)
CP 1028, Succ. Pointe-Claire, Pointe-Claire QC H9S 4H9 Canada
Tél: 514-633-1128; *Téléc:* 514-633-1129
info@osjwi.qc.ca
www.osjwi.qc.ca
Permettre aux jeunes de 8-25 ans de jouer dans un orchestre regroupant tous les instruments sous la direction d'un chef professionel

Orchestre symphonique des jeunes Philippe-Filion
2100, boul des Hêtres, Shawinigan QC G9N 8R8 Canada
Tél: 819-539-6000; *Téléc:* 819-539-2400
morind03@cgocable.ca
Monique Gagnon Carbonneau, Directrice Musicale

Orchestre symphonique du Saguenay-Lac-St-Jean (OSSLSJ)
202, rue Jacques-Cartier est, Chicoutimi QC G7H 6R8 Canada
Tél: 418-545-3409; *Téléc:* 418-545-8287
info@lorchestre.org
www.lorchestre.org
Produire et diffuser des concerts professionnels à travers tout le Saguenay-Lac-Saint-Jean en regard des enjeux financiers et des structures d'accueil existantes. Ses qualités artistiques et administratives en constante évolution lui permettent d'exercer un leadership au sein des organismes musicaux régionaux, basé sur un partenariat serré avec le milieu, au service du développement de sa discipline et de sa communauté
Jacques Clément, Directeur artisique

Orchestre symphonique régional Abitibi-Témiscamingue
CP 2305, Rouyn-Noranda QC J9X 5A9 Canada
Tél: 819-762-0043; *Téléc:* 819-762-0274
osr@tlb.sympatico.ca
culture-at.org/osr
Média social: www.facebook.com/group.php?gid=359183264101
Diffusion de la musique classique et integration de la relève
Réginald Grenier, Président

Organization of Canadian Symphony Musicians (OCSM) / Organisation des musiciens d'orchestres symphoniques du Canada (OMOSC)
#6, 445, rue Gerard-Morrisset, Québec QC G1S 4V5 Canada
Tel: 418-688-0801
www.ocsm-omosc.org
To address issues confronting professional symphony musicians

Société chorale de Saint-Lambert / St. Lambert Choral Society
CP 36546, Succ. CSP Victoria, Saint-Lambert QC J4P 3S8
www.chorale-stlambert.qc.ca
To offer several concerts of choral music each year
Nancy Kirkwood, President
David Christiani, Music Director
Kimberley Bartczak, Accompanist

Société Pro Musica Inc. / Pro Musica Society Inc.
#201, 3505, rue rue Ste-Famille, Montréal QC H2X 2L3 Canada
Tél: 514-845-0532; *Téléc:* 514-845-1500
Ligne sans frais: 877-445-0532
info@promusica.qc.ca
www.promusica.qc.ca
Promouvoir et présenter à Montréal la plus belle musique de chambre par les meilleurs interprètes d'ici et d'ailleurs; dans la série TOPAZE, promouvoir et offrir aux jeunes familles de meilleures conditions pour assister aux concerts avec un atelier d'animation musicale pour les enfants

Saskatchewan

Regina Symphony Orchestra (RSO)
2424 College Ave., Regina SK S4P 1C8 Canada
Tel: 306-586-9555; *Fax:* 306-586-2133
Toll-Free: 800-667-8497
info@reginasymphony.com
www.reginasymphony.com
To promote & enhance the performance & enjoyment of live orchestral music in Regina & southern Saskatchewan & contribute to the cultural life of the city, province & nation

Saskatchewan Band Association (SBA)
34 Sunset Dr. North, Yorkton SK S3N 3K9
Tel: 306-783-2263; *Fax:* 306-783-2060
Toll-Free: 877-475-2263
sask.band@sasktel.net
www.saskband.org
To promote & support instrumental music in Saskatchewan; To act as a voice on issues that affect bands in Saskatchewan

Saskatchewan Orchestral Association (SOA)
PO Box 87, Hanley SK S0G 2E0 Canada
Tel: 306-544-2230; *Fax:* 306-544-2718
soa1@sasktel.net
www.saskorchestras.com
To serve as resource base & coordinating body for orchestral & string programs in Saskatchewan; to procure funds to make achievement of goals & objectives of SOA possible

Saskatoon Symphony Society (SSO)
Standard Life Bldg., #120, 128 Fourth Ave. South, Saskatoon SK S7K 1M8 Canada
Tel: 306-665-6414; *Fax:* 306-652-3364
saskatoon.symphony@sasktel.net
www.saskatoonsymphony.org
To promote, encourage & support symphonic & classical music in Saskatoon & elsewhere in Saskatchewan

Saskatoon Youth Orchestra
1610 Morgan Ave., Saskatoon SK S7H 2S1 Canada
Tel: 306-373-6408; *Fax:* 306-955-6336
syo@sasktel.net
toeww.sasktelwebsite.net/SYO.html
Wayne Toews, Music Director

South Saskatchewan Youth Orchestra (SSYO)
101 Leopold Cres., Regina SK S4T 6N5 Canada
Tel: 306-586-3007; *Fax:* 306-586-2133
ssyo.ca@gmail.com
www.ssyo.ca
To provide orchestral training to young musicians in Southern Saskatchewan
Alan Denike, Music Director

Yukon Territory

Jazz Yukon
PO Box 31307, Whitehorse YT Y1A 5P7 Canada
Tel: 867-633-3300
info@jazzyukon.ca
www.jazzyukon.ca
To promote & present jazz in the Yukon through an annual integrated program of live jazz presentations & jazz education outreach

Performing Arts - Theatre

Alberta

Alberta Playwrights' Network (APN)
2633 Hochwald Ave. SW, Calgary AB T3E 7K2 Canada
Tel: 403-269-8564; *Fax:* 403-265-6773
Toll-Free: 800-268-8564
admin@albertaplaywrights.com
www.albertaplaywrights.com
APN is a non-profit, provincial arts service organization and registered charity dedicated to fostering playwriting in Alberta.
Johanne Deleeuw, Executive Director
Brian Dooley, Edmonton Liaison

Evergreen Theatre Society
2633 Hochwald Ave. SW, Calgary AB T3E 7K2 Canada
Tel: 403-228-1384; *Fax:* 403-229-1385
Toll-Free: 877-840-9746
info@evergreentheatre.com
www.evergreentheatre.com
Social Media: www.facebook.com/group.php?gid=102554315596
To create innovative, entertaining, accessible education-tangible choices for a healthy & sustainable future
Lisa Ryan, Director, Residency
Sean Fraser, Executive Director

New West Theatre Society
#111, 210A - 12A St. North, Lethbridge AB T1J 0P5 Canada
Tel: 403-381-9378
info@newwesttheatre.com
www.newwesttheatre.com
To provide Lethbridge & surrounding region with a broad-based & diverse program of professional quality theatrical, musical & dramatic performances
Nicholas Hanson, Artistic Director
Jeremy Mason, General Manager

Theatre Alberta Society
11759 Groat Rd., 3rd Fl., Edmonton AB T5M 3K6 Canada
Tel: 780-422-8162; *Fax:* 780-422-2663
Toll-Free: 888-422-8160
theatreab@theatrealberta.com
www.theatrealberta.com
To encourage the growth of theatre in Alberta through high quality support & training opportunities to theatre professionals, educators & community theatre practitioners
Marie Gynane-Willis, Executive Director

Theatre Calgary
220 - 9 Ave. SE, Calgary AB T2G 5C4 Canada
Tel: 403-294-7440; *Fax:* 403-294-7493
info@theatrecalgary.com
www.theatrecalgary.com
Produces classical and modern theatre.
Tom McCabe, President
Dennis Garnhum, Artistic Director

Theatre Network (1975) Society
10708 - 124 St., Edmonton AB T5M 0H1 Canada
Tel: 780-453-2440; *Fax:* 780-453-2596
info@theartnetwork.ca
www.attheroxy.com
To promote original regional drama
Jill Roszell, General Manager
Bradley Moss, Artistic Director

British Columbia

Bard on the Beach Theatre Society
#301, 601 Cambie St., Vancouver BC V6B 2P1 Canada
Tel: 604-737-0625; *Fax:* 604-737-0425
Toll-Free: 877-739-0559
info@bardonthebeach.org
www.bardonthebeach.org
Social Media: www.facebook.com/bardonthebeach
To provide Vancouver residents & visitors with affordable, accessible Shakespearean productions of the finest quality
Christopher Gaze, Artistic Director
Robert Barr, Managing Director

British Columbia Drama Association
PO Box 2031, #7, 10 Commercial St., Nanaimo BC V9R 6X6 Canada
Tel: 250-591-0018; *Fax:* 250-591-0027
info@theatrebc.org
www.theatrebc.org
To promote the development of theatre in BC & Canada through a wide range of programs, services, activities, competitions, festivals & events

First Pacific Theatre Society
1440 - 12 Ave. West, Vancouver BC V6H 1M8 Canada
Tel: 604-731-5483; *Fax:* 604-733-3880
info@pacifictheatre.org
www.pacifictheatre.org
To produce high quality theatre; to operate with artistic, spiritual, relational & financial integrity
Ron Reed, Artistic Director
Alison Chisholm, Theatre Administrator
Frank Nickel, Production Manager
Andrea Loewen, Director, Public Relations
Cindy McPherson, Business Manager

First Vancouver Theatre Space Society (FVTS)
c/o Vancouver Fringe Festival, 1398 Cartwright St., Vancouver BC V6H 3R8 Canada
Tel: 604-257-0350; *Fax:* 604-253-1924
info@vancouverfringe.com
www.vancouverfringe.com
To promoting interest in the arts in Vancouver; to nurture & support artists
Eduardo Ottoni, Production Manager
David Jordan, Executive Director

Greater Vancouver Professional Theatre Alliance (GVPTA)
1405 Anderson St., 3rd Fl., Vancouver BC V6H 3R5 Canada
Tel: 604-608-6799; *Fax:* 604-608-6923
info@gvpta.ca
www.gvpta.ca
To promote live theatre & foster a thriving environment for the continued growth & development of theatre in Greater Vancouver
Sue Porter, Executive Director

Intrepid Theatre Co. Society
#2, 1609 Blanshard St., Victoria BC V8S 4P6 Canada
Tel: 250-383-2663; *Fax:* 250-380-1999
info@intrepidtheatre.com
www.intrepidtheatre.com
To educate & enhance the public's awareness & aesthetic appreciation of contemporary & progressive styles of modern theatre by encouraging, developing & producing new or experimental works for public performance; by coordinating & producing the annual Fringe Theatre Festival in Victoria
Janet Munsil, Producer
Ian Case, General Manager

Playwrights Theatre Centre
#201, 1398 Cartwright St., Vancouver BC V6H 3R8 Canada
Tel: 604-685-6228; *Fax:* 604-685-7451
plays@playwrightstheatre.com
www.playwrightstheatre.com
Playwrights Theatre Centre is committed to developing new Canadian plays. Through dramaturgy, workshops, writers' groups and other programs, we provide support to experienced, emerging, and aspiring playwrights from across the country.
Ray Wallis, President
Martin Kinch, Executive Director/Literary Manager
Linda Gorrie, Administrator

Théâtre la Seizième
#266, 1555 - 7e av ouest, Vancouver BC V6J 1S1 Canada
Tel: 604-736-2616; *Fax:* 604-736-9151
info@seizieme.ca
www.seizieme.ca/
Social Media: www.facebook.com/group.php?gid=7629935063
Promouvoir le théâtre professionnel francophone en Colombie-Britannique
Craig Holzschuh, Directeur général et artistique

Theatre Terrific Society
4397 - 2nd Ave. West, Vancouver BC V6R 1K4 Canada
Tel: 604-222-4020; *Fax:* 604-222-4020
info@theatreterrific.ca
www.theatreterrific.ca
Social Media: www.facebook.com/group.php?gid=2394111093
To provide theatrical opportunities to people with disabilities
Susanna Uchatius, Artistic Director
Nina Hirlaender Hinton, General Manager

The Vancouver Summer Festival Society
#400, 873 Beatty St., Vancouver BC V6B 2M6 Canada
Tel: 604-688-1152; *Fax:* 604-688-8441
music@festivalvancouver.bc.ca
www.festivalvancouver.bc.ca
Presents a summer music celebration that explores the connections between cultures, centuries & people; internationally acclaimed artists from around the globe join forces with some of Canada's best performers in over 40 concerts featuring classical music, world music & jazz
George Laverock, Program Director
Morna Edmundson, Administrative Director

Vancouver TheatreSports League (VTSL)
#104, 1177 West Broadway, Vancouver BC V6H 1G3 Canada
Tel: 604-738-7013; *Fax:* 604-738-8013
info@vtsl.com
www.vtsl.com
Social Media: www.twitter.com/VanTheatreSport
To challenge & inspire the community by growing & exploring exceptional improv-based work
Jay Ono, Executive Director

Western Canada Theatre Company Society (WCT)
PO Box 329, Kamloops BC V2C 5K9 Canada
Tel: 250-372-3216; *Fax:* 250-374-7099
info@westerncanadatheatre.bc.ca
www.westerncanadatheatre.bc.ca
To provide the regional community with challenging professional theatre; to entertain, educate, enrich & interact with the cultural mosaic of its community; to promote & assist the performing arts through the provision of educational, theatrical & artistic opportunities & services & through the management & operation of facilities
Lorid Marchand, General Manager

Manitoba

Le Cercle Molière
340, boul Provencher, Saint-Boniface MB R2H 0G7 Canada
Tél: 204-233-8053; *Téléc:* 204-233-2373
reception@cerclemoliere.com
www.cerclemoliere.com
Présenter des spectacles de théâtre en français au Manitoba
Roland Mahé, Directeur artistique

Manitoba Association of Playwrights (MAP)
#503, 100 Arthur St., Winnipeg MB R3B 1H3 Canada
Tel: 204-942-8941; *Fax:* 204-942-1555
mbplay@mts.net
www.mbplays.ca
Social Media: www.facebook.com/group.php?gid=5729134541
To provide support for playwrights in Manitoba through the operation of programs for emerging & established playwrights
Rory Runnells, Coordinator

Manitoba Theatre Centre (MTC)
174 Market Ave., Winnipeg MB R3B 0P8 Canada
Tel: 204-942-6537; *Fax:* 204-947-3741
Toll-Free: 877-446-4500
patronservices@mtc.mb.ca
www.mtc.mb.ca
Canada's first English-language regional theatre, with a mandate to study, practise & promote all aspects of the dramatic arts, with particular emphasis on professional production
Steven Schipper, Artistic Director
Zaz Bajon, General Manager

Prairie Theatre Exchange (PTE)
Portage Place, #Y300, 393 Portage Ave., 3rd Fl., Winnipeg MB R3B 3H6 Canada
Tel: 204-942-7291; *Fax:* 204-942-1774
pte@pte.mb.ca
www.pte.mb.ca
To operate a professional theatre of high calibre for the entertainment & edification of a broad spectrum of people; to operate a school to encourage appreciation of theatre & to provide accessible, high quality, innovative drama education; to

support the development of new plays; to foster theatre arts-related endeavours of others through use of our facilities & expertise; to manage one or more community theatre arts centres

New Brunswick

Théâtre l'Escaouette
170, rue Botsford, Moncton NB E1C 4X6 Canada
Tél: 506-855-0001; *Téléc:* 506-855-0010
gilleslosier@nb.aibn.com
www.escaouette.com
Média social:
www.facebook.com/#!/group.php?gid=24643326073
Le théâtre l'Escaouette est un lieu privilégié de création. Avec ses 25 ans d'existence, les artistes ont porté à la scène 38 textes originaux, plus de la moitié de l'ensemble de la production dramaturgique acadienne créée au Nouveau-Brunswick.
Marcia Babineau, Direction artistique & codirection générale

Theatre New Brunswick (TNB)
#31, 55 Whitting Rd., Fredericton NB E3B 5Y5 Canada
Tel: 506-460-1381; *Fax:* 506-453-9315
Toll-Free: 800-442-9779
general@tnb.nb.ca
www.tnb.nb.ca
To provide live professional theatre to the people of New Brunswick by touring & performing in nine centres throughout the province; to entertain by providing quality theatre & acting as a theatrical resource for playwrights, actors & young people interested in the field
Heather VanIderstine, Administrative Assistant

Théâtre populaire d'Acadie (TPA)
#302, 220, boul. St-Pierre ouest, Caraquet NB E1W 1A5 Canada
Tél: 506-727-0920; *Téléc:* 506-727-0923
Ligne sans frais: 800-872-0920
tpa@pacadie.ca
www.tpacadie.ca
Créer, produire, diffuser et faire rayonner le théâtre d'ici et d'ailleurs
Maurice Arsenault, Directeur artistique et général

Newfoundland and Labrador

Theatre Newfoundland Labrador
PO Box 655, Corner Brook NL A2H 6G1 Canada
Tel: 709-639-7238; *Fax:* 709-639-1006
www.theatrenewfoundland.com
Theatre Newfoundland and Labrador (TNL) is a not-for-profit organization dedicated to creating and producing professional theatre which reflects the lives and dirversity of our audiences on the provinces's west coast, extending to labrador and across the island of Newfoundland.
Jeff Pitcher, Artistic Director

Nova Scotia

Neptune Theatre Foundation
1593 Argyle St., Halifax NS B3J 2B2 Canada
Tel: 902-429-7300; *Fax:* 902-429-1211
Toll-Free: 800-565-7345
info@neptunetheatre.com
www.neptunetheatre.com
Social Media: www.facebook.com/neptunetheatre
To pursue theatrical excellence with artistic vision; to develop local & Canadian artistic talent; to encourage the youth of our community to develop a life-long interest in live theatre
Doreen E. Malone, General Manager
George Pothitos, Artistic Director

Theatre Nova Scotia (TNS)
1113 Marginal Rd., Halifax NS B3H 4P7 Canada
Tel: 902-425-3876; *Fax:* 902-422-0881
theatrens@theatrens.ca
www.theatrens.ca
To provide services, training & resources to professional & amateur theatre community throughout Nova Scotia

Ontario

The Actors' Fund of Canada / La Caisse des acteurs du Canada inc.
#301, 1000 Yonge St., Toronto ON M4W 2K2 Canada
Tel: 416-975-0304; *Fax:* 416-975-0306
Toll-Free: 877-399-8392
contact@actorsfund.ca
www.actorsfund.ca
The Actors' Fund of Canada promotes artistic excellence for performers, creators, technicians and other members of creative and production teams in all entertainment industry sectors. The Fund carries out this mission by providing encouragement and short-term financial aid to help entertainment industry workers maintain their health, housing and ability to work after an illness, injury or sudden unemployment.

Association of Summer Theatres 'Round Ontario (ASTRO)
c/o Theatre Ontario, #210, 215 Spadina Ave., Toronto ON M5T 2C7 Canada
Tel: 416-408-4556; *Fax:* 416-408-3402
tim@theatreontario.org
www.summertheatre.org
To act as an information & resource network for its members; to support the professional development of its members; to act as a liaison for its membership with arts & business organizations, the media & the community; to advocate for its membership with government, government agencies & other organizations; to undertake projects to increase awareness of the activities of its membership among the general public
Steven Thomas, President

Buddies in Bad Times Theatre
12 Alexander St., Toronto ON M4Y 1B4 Canada
Tel: 416-975-9130; *Fax:* 416-975-9293
chy@artsexy.ca
www.artsexy.ca
To promote gay, lesbian, & queer theatrical expression
Brendan Healy, Artistic Director

Canadian Association for Theatre Research (CATR) / Association canadienne de la recherche théâtrale (ACRT)
#2, 40 River St., Toronto ON M5A 3N9 Canada
nicholsg@umoncton.ca
www.catr-acrt.ca
To focus on theatre, drama, & performance in a Canadian context, including acting, directing, practical matters of theatre, historiography, & the teaching, reception, theory, & literary criticism of drama

The Canadian Stage Company
26 Berkeley St., Toronto ON M5A 2W3 Canada
Tel: 416-367-8243; *Fax:* 416-367-1768
general@canstage.com
www.canstage.com
To develop, produce & export the best in Canadian & international contemporary theatre
Louise Plunkett, Customer Service Manager
Matthew Jocelyn, Artistic & General Director

Canadian Theatre Critics Association (CTCA) / Association des critiques de théâtre du Canada
#724, 2121 Bathurst St., Toronto ON M5N 2P3 Canada
Tel: 416-782-0966; *Fax:* 416-782-0366
scenechanges@rogers.com
www.canadiantheatrecritics.ca
To promote excellence in theatre criticism; to encourage the dissemination of information on theatre on a national level; to encourage the awareness & development of Canadian theatre nationally & internationally through theatre criticism in all the media; to promote & encourage excellence in Canadian theatre through national awards; to improve the status & working conditions of theatre critics

Compagnie vox théâtre
333 King Edward Ave., Ottawa ON K1N 7M5 Canada
Tél: 613-241-1090; *Téléc:* 613-241-0250
info@voxtheatre.ca
www.voxtheatre.ca
Avec son travail de création, ses productions de théâtre chanté, ses accueils de spectacle pluridisciplinaires et ses tournées, la compagnie Vox Théâtre présente une programation complète pour les enfants et leur propose aussi des activités de formation

Gryphon Theatre Foundation
PO Box 454, Barrie ON L4M 4T7 Canada
Tel: 705-728-4613; *Fax:* 705-728-4623
boxoffice@gryphontheatre.com
www.gryphontheatre.com
Social Media: www.facebook.com/group.php?gid=34543726924
To promote interest, & provide opportunities for education in the performing arts in the Georgian Bay area; to encourage & support the development of a regional theatre in the Georgian Bay area; to provide opportunities for Canadian artistic talent; to operate a theatre company
Donna Kenwell, Chair

Harbourfront Centre
235 Queens Quay West, Toronto ON M5J 2G8 Canada
Tel: 416-973-4600; *Fax:* 416-973-6055
info@harbourfrontcentre.com
www.harbourfrontcentre.com
To nurture the growth of new cultural expression; to stimulte Canadian & international interchange; to provide a dynamic, accessible environment for the public to experience the marvels of the creative imagination
Bruce Hutchinson, Director, Marketing & Media Relations
William J.S. Boyle, CEO
Gregory Burke, Director, The Power Plant
Melanie Fernandez, Director, Community & Education
Tina Rasmussen, Director, Performing Arts
Geoffrey Taylor, Director, Harbourfront Reading Series

Native Earth Performing Arts Inc. (NEPA)
Bldg. 74, #300/305, 55 Mill St., Toronto ON M5A 3C4 Canada
Tel: 416-531-1402; *Fax:* 416-531-6377
Toll-Free: 877-854-9708
office@nativeearth.ca
www.nativeearth.ca
To enable Native actors, writers, designers, directors & technicians to work together to produce quality theatre that is vital to their development as artists & their identity as Native people; to encourage the use of theatre as form of communication within the Native community, including the use of the Native languages
Yvette Nolan, Artistic Director
Donna-Michelle St. Bernard, General Manager

Ontario Puppetry Association
714 Hedgerow Pl., London ON K7M 4G9 Canada
Tel: 613-389-2996; *Toll-Free:* 800-379-0446
dsmith@kos.net
www.onpuppet.org
Social Media: www.facebook.com/group.php?gid=7360606673
To promote recognition of puppetry as art; to distribute information on all aspects; to assist in eventual formation of national puppet theatre

Playwrights Guild of Canada (PGC)
#210, 215 Spadina Ave., Toronto ON M5T 2C7 Canada
Tel: 416-703-0201; *Fax:* 416-703-0059
Toll-Free: 800-561-3318
info@playwrightsguild.ca
www.playwrightsguild.ca
To encourage Canadian playwriting; to publish, promote & distribute Canadian plays; to provide current information of Canadian plays & their authors; to offer copyright protection; to promote the study & appreciation of Canadian plays; to safeguard freedom of expression on the stage

Professional Association of Canadian Theatres (PACT)
#555, 215 Spadina Ave., Toronto ON M5T 2C7 Canada
Tel: 416-595-6455; *Fax:* 416-595-6450
Toll-Free: 800-263-7228
marlaf@pact.ca
www.pact.ca
Social Media:
www.facebook.com/group.php?gid=189415132023
To gain recognition & support for professional theatre in Canada; to support the development of Canadian theatre companies by sharing resources & knowledge; to develop working standards & relationships with theatre professionals through their associations; to inform & connect theatres across Canada through a communications network; to act as a major force in influencing cultural policy at all levels of government

Resurgence Theatre Company (RTC)
211 Main St. South, Newmarket ON L3Y 5Y9 Canada
Tel: 905-953-2838; *Fax:* 905-895-0070
info@resurgence.on.ca
www.resurgence.on.ca
Social Media: www.facebook.com/group.php?gid=2388084182
To present the classics & ignite contemporary & new works of theatre, utilizing the energy of young & established professionals
Anthony Leo, General Manager

Shaw Festival
PO Box 774, 10 Queen's Parade, Niagara-on-the-Lake ON L0S 1J0 Canada
Tel: 905-468-2153; *Fax:* 905-468-5438
Toll-Free: 800-657-1106
dlg@shawfest.com
www.shawfest.com
Social Media:
www.facebook.com/shawfestival#!/shawfestival?v=wall
To create intellectually challenging & entertaining theatre at an affordable price
Jackie Maxwell, Artistic Director
Colleen Blake, Executive Director

Tarragon Theatre
30 Bridgman Ave, Toronto ON M5R 1X3 Canada
Tel: 416-536-5018; *Fax:* 416-533-6372
info@tarragontheatre.com
www.tarragontheatre.com
Social Media:
www.facebook.com/pages/Tarragon-Theatre/77224001635
To develop & produce new Canadian plays
Camilla Holland, General Manager
Richard Rose, Artistic Director

Théâtre de la Vieille 17
119, rue York, Ottawa ON K1N 5T4 Canada
Tél: 613-241-8562; *Téléc:* 613-241-9507
communications@vieille17.ca
www.vieille17.ca
Mèdia social: www.facebook.com/group.php?gid=116511446364
Créer et diffuser des spectacles pour la jeunesse et pour les adultes à l'échelle régionale, nationale et internationale
Esther Beauchemin, Directrice artistique et générale

Théâtre du Nouvel-Ontario (TNO)
21 Lasalle Blvd., Sudbury ON P3A 6B1 Canada
Tél: 705-525-5606; *Téléc:* 705-525-1129
tno@letno.ca
www.letno.ca
Mèdia social:
www.facebook.com/pages/Theatre-du-Nouvel-Ontario/139137429438733
Dédié à la création, à la dramaturgie franco-ontarienne et à l'accueil d'oeuvres principalement canadiennes
Geneviève Pineault, Directrice artistique et générale

Théâtre du Trillium
333 av King Edward, Ottawa ON K1N 7M5 Canada
Tél: 613-789-7643; *Téléc:* 613-789-7641
comm@theatre-trillium.com
www.theatre-trillium.com
Mèdia social: www.facebook.com/theatredutrillium
Anne-Marie White, Directrice artistique et générale

Théâtre français de Toronto
#610, 21, rue College, Toronto ON M5G 2B3 Canada
Tél: 416-534-7303; *Téléc:* 416-534-9087
Ligne sans frais: 800-819-4981
info@theatrefrancais.com
www.theatrefrancais.com
Mèdia social: twitter.com/theatrefrancais
Le Théâtre français de Toronto est un théâtre professionnel de langue française, de répertoire et de création. Il s'adresse à tous les amateurs de théâtre en français, tant les francophones que les francophiles : ce faisant, il contribue au développement culturel et pédagogique de la communauté de Toronto. Théâtre français de Toronto is a professional French-language theatre presenting repertoire as well as new work. While appealing to all lovers of French-language theatre, it contributes to the cultural and educational development of Toronto's francophone community.
Guy Mignault, Directeur artistique
Ghislain Caron, Directeur administratif

Théâtre la Catapulte
333, av King-Edward, Ottawa ON K1N 7M5 Canada
Tél: 613-562-0851; *Téléc:* 613-562-0631
communications@catapulte.ca
catapulte.ca
Mèdia social:
www.facebook.com/pages/Ottawa-ON/Theatre-la-Catapulte/221011962255
Créer et diffuser sur une échelle provinciale et nationale des productions pour adultes et adolescents; développer des nouvelles oeuvres; offir une formation continue des artistes de la relève; accueillir des productions
Jean Stéphane Roy, Directeur artistique
Maurice Demers, Président

Theatre Ontario
#210, 215 Spadina Ave., Toronto ON M5T 2C7 Canada
Tel: 416-408-4556; *Fax:* 416-408-3402
info@theatreontario.org
www.theatreontario.org
To promote the continued development of theatre arts & artists in Ontario; to support the continued development of vital & broadly accessible theatre training of the highest quality to all sectors of Ontario's theatre community; to encourage the continued development of high quality theatre & drama programs within the educational system of Ontario; to ensure that Ontario's community theatres & educators obtain access to the resources of professional theatre; to facilitate interaction & communication between community, educational & professional theatre

Toronto Alliance for the Performing Arts (TAPA)
#210, 215 Spadina Ave., Toronto ON M5T 2C7 Canada
Tel: 416-536-6468; *Fax:* 416-536-3463
Toll-Free: 800-541-0499
jacobak@tapa.ca
www.tapa.ca
To foster greater respect & support for the arts by advocating on behalf of Canadian theatre & dance, representing all cultural backgrounds, to government, supporters, & the general public; to provide services which enhance the artistic, technical, & administrative development of members

Young People's Theatre (YPT)
165 Front St. East, Toronto ON M5A 3Z4
Tel: 416-862-2222
boxoffice@youngpeoplestheatre.ca;
online@youngpeoplestheatre.ca
www.youngpeoplestheatre.ca
Social Media: www.facebook.com/LKTYPYoungPeoplesTheatre;
www.twitter.com/YPTToronto
To make a positive impact on the intellectual, social, & emotional development of young people; To produce plays for young audiences; To operate a year-round drama school for youth
Hughy Neilson, Managing Director
Alexis Buset, Technical Director
Allen MacInnis, Artistic Director
Craig Morash, Director, Finance & Operations
Jeff Cummings, Manager, Production
Jill Ward, Manager, Education & Participation
Megan Brady, Administrator, Ticketing Operations
Jan Borkowski, Coordinator, Marketing, & Graphic Designer
Isaac Thomas, Coordinator, Drama School
Aaron Carveth, Development Officer, Donor Acquisition & Retention

Prince Edward Island

Theatre PEI
PO Box 1573, Charlottetown PE C1A 7N3 Canada
Tel: 902-894-3558; *Fax:* 902-894-3558
theatre@isn.net
To make challenging, stimulating & entertaining theatre accessible to Island audiences, including schools
Daphne Harker, Administrator
Ron Irving, Artistic Director
Rob MacLean, Associate Artistic Director

Québec

Association québécoise des marionnettistes (AQM)
Centre UNIMA-CANADA (section Québec), CP 7, Succ. de Lorimier, #300, 7755, boul Saint-Laurent, Montréal QC H2H 2N6 Canada
Tél: 514-522-1919; *Téléc:* 514-521-3737
aqm@aei.ca
www.aqm.ca
Représenter ses membres et créer un terrain propice aux échanges, aux actions communes et à la réflexion sur la pratique de l'art de la marionnette

Black Theatre Workshop (BTW)
#432, 3680, Jeanne-Mance, Montréal QC H2X 2K5
Tel: 514-932-1104; *Fax:* 514-932-6311
www.blacktheatreworkshop.ca
To encourage & promote the development of a Black & Canadian theatre, rooted in a literature that reflects the creative will of Black Canadian writers & artists, & the creative collaborations between Black & other artists; To strive to create a greater cross-cultural understanding by its presence & the intrinsic value of its work
Tyrone Benskin, Artistic Director
Jacklin Webb, President

Canadian Institute for Theatre Technology (CITT) / L'Institut Canadien des Technologies Scénographiques (ICTS)
PO Box 85041, 345 Laurier Blvd., Mont-Saint-Hilaire QC J3H 5W1
Tel: 613-482-1165; *Fax:* 613-482-1212
Toll-Free: 888-271-3383
info@citt.org
www.citt.org
Social Media: www.facebook.com/group.php?gid=24629289772
To work for the betterment of the Canadian live performance community; To promote safe & ethical work practices
Adam Mitchell, President
Gerry van Hezewyk, Vice-President
Mike Dickinson, Secretary
Eric Mongerson, Treasurer
Monique Corbeil, National Coordinator

Centre des auteurs dramatiques (CEAD)
#200, 261, rue du Saint-Sacrement, Montréal QC H2Y 3V2 Canada
Tél: 514-288-3384; *Téléc:* 514-288-7043
cead@cead.qc.ca
www.cead.qc.ca
Promotion et diffusion ici et à l'étranger des textes d'auteurs québécois et d'auteurs franco-canadiens; développement dramaturgique

Conseil québécois du théâtre (CQT)
#808, 460, rue Ste-Catherine ouest, Montréal QC H3B 1A7 Canada
Tél: 514-954-0270; *Téléc:* 514-954-0165
Ligne sans frais: 866-954-0270
cqt@cqt.qc.ca
www.cqt.ca
Promouvoir et défendre les intérêts du milieu théâtral et le représenter auprès des diverses instances; concerter, animer et informer la communauté théâtrale sur toutes les questions qui touchent la pratique théâtrale; promouvoir et développer le théâtre
Martine Lévesque, Directrice générale

Fédération québécoise du théâtre amateur (FQTA)
CP 211, Succ. Saint-Élie-d'Orford, Sherbrooke QC J1R 1A1 Canada
Tél: 819-752-2501; *Téléc:* 819-758-4466
Ligne sans frais: 877-752-2501
info@fqta.ca
www.fqta.ca
Promouvoir le théâtre amateur en réunissant tous les individus et les groupes de théâtre pour contribuer à l'éducation artistique, esthétique et sociale de la population; établir un contact permanent entre les individus; fournir des occasions d'échange, de travaux, de recherches, de méthodes, de matériel et d'information ayant trait au théâtre

Théâtre des épinettes
255, rue Laframboise, Chibougamau QC G8P 2S5 Canada
Tél: 418-748-4682
Guy Lalancette

Théâtres associés inc. (TAI)
#405, 1908, rue Panet, Montréal QC H2L 3A2 Canada
Tél: 514-842-6361; *Téléc:* 514-842-9730
info@theatresassocies.ca
www.theatresassocies.ca
Théâtres associés (T.A.I.) inc. est une association qui se fait la voix d'institutions théâtrales francophones québécoises.

Théâtres unis enfance jeunesse (TUEJ)
#217, 911, rue Jean-Talon Est, Montréal QC H2R 1V5 Canada
Tél: 514-380-2337
tuej.org
Défendre les intérêts des producteurs dans le domaine du théâtre pour la jeunesse
Isabelle Boisclair, Présidente

Saskatchewan

Globe Theatre Society
Globe Theatre, Prince Edward Bldg., 1801 Scarth St., Regina SK S4P 2G9 Canada
Tel: 306-525-9553; *Fax:* 306-352-4194
Toll-Free: 866-954-5623
onstage@globetheatrelive.com
www.globetheatrelive.com
To create & produce professional theatre & make it accessible with a view to entertain, educate & challenge
Ruth Smillie, Artistic Director

Saskatchewan Playwrights Centre (SPC)
PO Box 3092, Saskatoon SK S7K 3S9 Canada
Tel: 306-665-7707; *Fax:* 306-244-0255
sk.playwrights@sasktel.net
www.saskplaywrights.ca
Social Media:
www.facebook.com/pages/Saskatchewan-Playwrights-Centre/114748828547948
Independently incorporated and governed centre devoted to developing playwrights.
Mansel Robinson, President

Theatre Saskatchewan
1077 Angus St., Regina SK S4T 1Y4 Canada
Tel: 306-352-0797; *Fax:* 306-569-7888
info@theatresaskatchewan.com
www.theatresaskatchewan.com
Strives to build a strong foundation for theatre which allows all people in Saskatchewan accessibility to live drama

La Troupe du Jour
CP 339, 914 - 20th St. West, Saskatoon SK S7K 3L3 Canada
Tél: 306-244-1040; *Téléc:* 306-652-1725
communication@latroupedujour.ca
www.latroupedujour.ca
La Troupe du Jour Inc. develops professional and community French-language theatre through the creation of new works, training, performance, and outreach. La Troupe du Jour is dedicated to the development of French-language theatre in Saskatchewan.
Denis Rouleau, General Manager/Artistic Director

Science Centres

Alberta

***Calgary:* TELUS World of Science - Calgary (TWOSC)**
***Also known as:* Calgary Science Centre**
PO Box 2100 M, #73, 701 - 11 St. SW, Calgary, AB T2P 2M5
403-268-8300, Fax: 403-237-0186,
discover@calgaryscience.ca
www.calgaryscience.ca
Multimedia Discovery Dome presentations & exhibits; open year round
William T. Peters, Executive Director

***Edmonton:* TELUS World of Science - Edmonton**
c/o Edmonton Space & Science Foundation, 11211 - 142 St. NW, Edmonton, AB T5M 4A1
780-451-3344, Fax: 780-455-5882,
info@telusworldofscienceedmonton.com
www.telusworldofscienceedmonton.com
IMAX theatre; planetarium; exhibit galleries; observatory; giftshop; café; Ham Radio Station; science & computer lab
Andrea Kuhlmann, Director, Marketing & Communications
George Smith, President & CEO

British Columbia

***Vancouver:* H.R. MacMillan Space Centre (HRMSC)**
***Also known as:* The Planetarium**
1100 Chestnut St., Vancouver, BC V6J 3J9
604-738-7827, Fax: 604-736-5665,
ddodge@hrmacmillanspacecentre.com
www.hrmacmillanspacecentre.com
Western Canada's premier earth, space science & astronomy attraction & educational resource
Donna Livingstone, Executive Director

***Vancouver:* Science World British Columbia**
1455 Quebec St., Vancouver, BC V6A 3Z7
604-443-7443, Fax: 604-443-7430,
mcotic@scienceworld.ca
www.scienceworld.ca
Hands-on exhibits; demonstrations; Omnimax theatre
Bryan Tisdall, President/CEO

Ontario

Provincial Science Centres

Ontario Science Centre / Centre des sciences de l'Ontario
770 Don Mills Rd., Toronto, ON M3C 1T3
416-696-1000, Fax: 416-696-3124,
www.ontariosciencecentre.ca
Over 800 interactive exhibits on the environment, technology, food, chemistry, communications, sport & space; exhibits, programs, demonstrations, workshops & films for the public; special programs for school groups, children, adults & senior citizens; gift shops & restaurant; Ontario's only OMNIMAX Theatre featuring a 24-metre dome screen with wrap-around sound; open year round
Lesley Lewis, Director General & CEO

Local Science Centres in Ontario

***Sudbury:* Science North**
100 Ramsey Lake Rd., Sudbury, ON P3E 5S9
705-522-3701, Fax: 705-522-4954,
www.sciencenorth.ca
Founded: 1984 Science centre, IMAX Theatre, planetarium, living butterfly gallery & special exhibits hall; exhibit design & consulting services.
Jim Marchbank, CEO
Alan Nursall, Science Director

***Toronto:* The Roberta Bondar Earth & Space Centre**
Seneca College, Newnham Campus, 1750 Finch Ave. East, Toronto, ON M2J 2X5
416-491-5050,
stars@senecac.on.ca
60-seat star theatre featuring 2000 visible stars, 5 planets, sun & moon; accessory projectors provide simulations of aurorae, meteor showers, bolides & solar & lunar eclipses

Quebec

Provincial Science Centres

The Montréal Science Centre
King-Edward Pier, Old Port of Montréal, 333 Commune St. West, Montréal, QC H2Y 2E2
514-496-4724, Fax: 514-496-0667, 877-496-4724
www.montrealsciencecentre.com
Visitors acquire an understanding of science & technology & how it affects daily living; three interactive science exhibition halls; IMAX 3D, IMMERSION STUDIOS theatres
Claude Benoit, President & CEO

Local Science Centres in Quebec

***Laval:* Cosmodôme - Centre des sciences de l'espace et Camp spatial Canada / Cosmodôme - Space Science Centre & Space Camp**
2150, rte des Laurentides, Laval, QC H7T 2T8
450-978-3600, Fax: 450-978-3624, 800-565-2267
info@cosmodome.org
www.cosmodome.org
Host to the Space Science Centre & to the Space Camp, the Cosmodôme leads its visitors on a journey through the conquest of space.
Nicole Dalpé, Director
Anne-Josée Dionne, Coordinator, Sales & Marketing, marketing@cosmodome.org

***Montréal:* Biosphère**
160, ch Tour-de-L'Isle, Montréal, QC H3G 4G8
514-496-8300, Fax: 514-283-5021,
info.biosphere@ec.gc.ca
www.biosphere.ec.gc.ca
Museum of environment
Susanne Blais, Public Relations

***Montréal:* Planétarium de Montréal / Montréal Planétarium**
1000, rue Saint-Jacques ouest, Montréal, QC H3C 1G7
514-872-4530, Fax: 514-872-8102,
info@planetarium.montreal.qc.ca
www.planetarium.montreal.qc.ca
Multimedia productions about astronomy on a giant hemispheric dome 20 metres across
Pierre Lacombe, Directeur

***Saint-Louis-du-Ha-Ha:* Aster, La Station scientifique du BSL**
59, ch Bellevue, Saint-Louis-du-Ha-Ha, QC G0L 3S0
418-854-2172, Fax: 418-854-1898, 877-775-2172
asterbsl@globetrotter.net
www.asterbsl.ca
Scientific & technical culture; activities include: "Hélios", "Léonard, Ingénieur Créateur" & "Starlab"; educational workshops for schools
Maurice Fallu-Landry, Directeur
Chantale Tardif, Directrice-adjointe

Saskatchewan

***Regina:* Saskatchewan Science Centre**
2903 Powerhouse Dr., Regina, SK S4N 0A1
306-791-7900, Fax: 306-525-0194, 800-667-6300
www.sasksciencecentre.com
Interactive science museum featuring hands-on exhibits, Kramer Imax theatre; open year-round
Scott Langen, Executive Director

Zoos

Alberta

***Calgary:* Bow Habitat Station**
1440 - 17A St. SE, Calgary, AB T2G 4T9
403-297-6561, Fax: 403-297-2839,
bowhabitat.info@gov.ab.ca
www.bowhabitat.gov.ab.ca
Includes: a Visitor Centre, which is an interpretive centre about fresh water, fish, and aquatic habitats; the Sam Livingston Fish Hatchery, a large trout hatchery; and the Pearce Estate Park Interpretive Wetland, a unique collection of constructed wetlands, self-guided trails and interpretive signs.
D. DePape, Superintendent

***Calgary:* Calgary Zoo, Botanical Garden & Prehistoric Park**
1300 Zoo Rd. NE, Calgary, AB T2E 7V6
403-232-9300, Fax: 403-237-7582, 800-588-9993
www.calgaryzoo.org
136 acres + 320 acre off-site breeding & conservation facility; educational programs; gift shop; open year round
Alex Graham, President/CEO

***Calgary:* Inglewood Bird Sanctuary**
PO Box 2100 M, Location 59, 2425 - 9 Ave. SE, Calgary, AB T2P 2M5
403-221-4500, Fax: 403-221-3775,
InglewoodBirdSanctuary@calgary.ca
Offers more than two km. of level trails; more than 250 species of birds & 300 species of plants plus several kinds of mammals have been observed in area; visitor centre; two classrooms where nature-related programs are presented by the Sanctuary's professional naturalists
Did Andrews
Tanya Noseworthy

***Edmonton:* Valley Zoo**
PO Box 2359, Edmonton, AB T5J 2R7
780-496-8787, Fax: 780-944-7529,
attractions@edmonton.ca
www.edmonton.ca/valleyzoo
Features more than 350 endangered & exotic animals; main zoo & children's zoo; minature train, merry-go-round & camel rides available; open daily except Christmas Day
Bryan Monaghan, Director

***Lacombe:* Ellis Bird Farm**
PO Box 5090, Lacombe, AB T4L 1W7
403-346-2211, Fax: 403-346-2211,
myrnap@ellisbirdfarm.ab.ca
www.ellisbirdfarm.ab.ca
Other contact information: summer phone 403/885-4477
Nestboxes; wildlife gardens; tea house; open May - Aug.
Myrna Pearman, Manager

***Patricia:* Dinosaur Provincial Park**
PO Box 60, Patricia, AB T0J 2K0
403-378-4342, Fax: 403-378-4247,
www.dinosaurpark.ca
Some of the most extensive dinosaur fossil fields in the world are found here; the area's badlands & cottonwood river habitat are the other significant features that resulted in the park's designation as a UNESCO World Heritage Site in 1979; also includes the Royal Tyrrell Museum of Palaeontology Field Station, located within the park.

British Columbia

***Aldergrove:* Greater Vancouver Zoo**
5048 - 264th St., Aldergrove, BC V4W 1N7
604-856-6825, Fax: 604-857-9008,
info@gvzoo.com
www.gvzoo.com
Over 960 animals representing 176 species; world's only albino black bear; one of North America's largest grizzly bear habitats.
Malcolm Weatherston, General Manager

***Coombs:* Butterfly World & Gardens**
PO Box 36, 1080 Winchester Rd., Coombs, BC V0R 1M0
250-248-7026, Fax: 250-752-1091,
www.nature-world.com
The Butterfly World & Gardens is a nature park with tropical gardens, orchids, ponds, birds, & butterflies. The park is open from March to October.

***Creston:* Creston Valley Wildlife Management Area (CVWMA)**
PO Box 640, 1874 Wildlife Rd., Creston, BC V0B 1G0
250-402-6900, Fax: 250-402-6910,
askus@crestonwildlife.ca
www.crestonwildlife.ca
17,000-acre wetland habitat. This diverse wildlife resource provides many recreational and educational opportunities. Hiking, cycling, canoeing, picnicking, wildlife viewing, hunting, fishing, and many other outdoor activities can be experienced here. Open May-September.
Marc-André Beaucher, Area Manager
Jim Collins, General Manager

***Duncan:* Cowichan & Chemainus Valleys Ecomuseum**
PO Box 491, Duncan, BC V9L 4T8
250-746-1611
Located at 160 Jubilee St.

***Kamloops:* British Columbia Wildlife Park**
9077 Dallas Dr., Kamloops, BC V2C 6V1
250-573-3242, Fax: 250-573-2406, 866-872-2066
info@bczoo.org
www.bczoo.org
As a non-profit organization we continually dedicate our efforts to the conservation of BC wildlife through display, interpretation, education, wildlife rehabilitation, endangered species and direct action.
Rob Purdy, General Manager

***Lake Country:* Speedwell Bird Sanctuary**
13724 Lakepine Rd., Lake Country, BC V4V 1A3
250-766-2081, Fax: 250-766-0617,
cabalerro@shaw.ca

Founded: 1985 Breeding facility for amazon parrots, pheasants; botanic garden — trees, shrubs & roses; by appt.
Dan Bruce

***Richmond:* Richmond Nature Park**
11851 Westminster Hwy., Richmond, BC V6X 1B4
604-718-6188, Fax: 604-718-6189,
nature@richmond.ca
www.richmond.ca
Features 5 km. of well-groomed trails through bog & forest; more than 100 species of birds, mammals, reptiles & amphibians may be sighted; seasonal programs & events
Kristine Bauder, Nature Park Coordinator
Petra Murphy, Recreation Facility Clerk
Lori Bartley, Coordinator, School Program

***Vancouver:* Stanley Park Ecology Society**
PO Box 5167, Vancouver, BC V6B 4B2
604-257-6908, Fax: 604-257-8378,
info@stanleyparkecology.ca
www.stanleyparkecology.ca
Encourages stewardship of the natural world through education & action & by fostering awareness; provides public programs for adults & families, school programs, wildlife information & resources promoting coexistence between people & its wild neighbours
Patricia Thomson, Executive Director

***Victoria:* Swan Lake Christmas Hill Nature Sanctuary**
3873 Swan Lake Rd., Victoria, BC V8X 3W1
250-479-0211, Fax: 250-479-0132,
info@swanlake.bc.ca
www.swanlake.bc.ca
Nature education centre; 125 acres including marshy lowlands surrounding Swan Lake and rocky, oak-forested highlands of Christmas Hill.
Terry Morrison, Executive Director

***Victoria:* Victoria Butterfly Gardens**
PO Box 190, 1461 Benvenuto Ave., Victoria, BC V8M 1R3
250-652-3822, Fax: 250-652-4683, 877-722-0272
info@butterflygardens.com
www.butterflygardens.com
Indoor tropical gardens, fish, birds, and butterflies. Open Mar 1-Oct. 31

Manitoba

***Rennie:* Alfred Hole Goose Sanctuary (AHGS)**
***Also known as:* Alf's Hole**
Whiteshell Provincial Park, PO Box 130, Rennie, MB R0E 1R0
204-369-5470, Fax: 204-369-5341,
mschneider@gov.mb.ca
www.manitobaparks.com
Wheelchair accessible Visitor Centre interprets the history of the site as well as the biology of geese; spring, summer & fall program features hands-on activities, guided hikes, school programming & special events
Larry Teetaert, Park Manager
Morgan Schneider, Park Interpreter

***Thompson:* Thompson Zoo**
226 Mystery Lake Rd., Thompson, MB R8N 1S6
204-677-7982, Fax: 204-778-4186,
thompzoo@escape.ca
thompsonzoo.ca
Over 100 animals and birds. The Thompson Zoo is the only northern Wildlife Rehab Cetnre in Manitoba. Open year round.
Erin Wilcox, Director

***Winnipeg:* Assiniboine Park Zoo**
460 Assiniboine Park Dr., Winnipeg, MB R3P 2N7
204-986-2327, Fax: 204-832-5420,
apzoo@winnipeg.ca
www.winnipeg.ca/assiniboinepark
Open daily & currently has 1,700 animals of 300 different species
Douglas Ross, Director

New Brunswick

***Lamèque:* Lamèque Zoo**
Lamèque, NB E0B 1V0
506-344-7214

***Moncton:* Magnetic Hill Zoo**
c/o City of Moncton, Community Services Dept., 655 Main St., Moncton, NB E1C 1E8
506-877-7718,
info.zoo@moncton.ca
www.moncton.org/zoo/
The Magnetic Hill Zoo is committed to safeguarding animal species and raising public awareness of endangered species. The zoo is designed with the well-being of the animals, as well as the safety of the public, in mind.
Bruce Dougan, Manager

***Saint John:* Cherry Brook Zoo Inc.**
901 Foster Thurston Dr., Saint John, NB E2K 5H9
506-634-1440, Fax: 506-634-0717,
noahsark@rogers.com
www.cherrybrookzoo.com
A non-for profit zoo situated in a 35-acre woodland that is located in the northern section of the city's 2200-acre Rockwood Park. Utilizing the unusual natural terrain of Rockwood Park, the animals are surrounded by a natural setting.
Lynda & Leonard Collrin

Newfoundland & Labrador

***Glovertown:* Terra Nova National Park (TNNP) / Parc national Terra-Nova**
Glovertown, NL A0G 2L0
709-533-2801, Fax: 709-533-2706,
info.tnnp@pc.gc.ca
www.pc.gc.ca/pn-np/nl/terranova/index_E.asp
Represents the unique character of the eastern Newfoundland Atlantic Terrestrial Natural Region; characterized by low relief & a series of rounded hills from sea level to 200 metres; home to 12 of 14 native terrestrial mammals, 8 fish species & more than 200 bird species recorded in the park; artifacts of native & European settlement

***Holyrood:* Salmonier Nature Park**
PO Box 190, Holyrood, NL A0A 2R0
709-229-7888, Fax: 709-229-7078,
brenda.pike@mail.gov.nl.ca
www.env.gov.nl.ca/snp
Open June to Thanksgiving
Tammy Keats, Manager

Nova Scotia

***Shubenacadie:* Provincial Wildlife Park**
PO Box 299, Shubenacadie, NS B0N 2H0
902-758-2040, Fax: 902-758-7011,
wildlifepark@gov.ns.ca
wildlifepark.gov.ns.ca
45 exhibits featuring native & exotic species in natural enclosures along a 2.3 km walking trail; picnic area & playground; open daily May 15-Oct. 15 & weekends only during winter season; fee
Bert J. Vissers, Director

Ontario

***Bowmanville:* Bowmanville Zoological Park**
340 King St. East, Bowmanville, ON L1C 3K5
905-623-5655, Fax: 905-623-0957,
bzpzoo@aol.com
www.bowmanvillezoo.com
Since 1919, Canada's oldest private zoo, featuring Animal Kingdom shows, elephant rides, restaurant & gift shop; CAZA accredited; open May - Sept.
Caroline Yli-Luoma, Vice-President, Sales
Alex Nagy, CEO
Michael Hackenberger, Director

***Cambridge:* African Lion Safari & Game Farm**
RR#1, Cambridge, ON N1R 5S2
519-623-2620, Fax: 519-623-9542, 800-461-9453
admin@lionsafari.com
www.lionsafari.com
African Lion Safari is a Canadian owned family business created in the name of conservation. Our manner of exhibiting animals is completely different from the traditional approach; that is, the visitor is caged in the car, and the animals roam in 2 to 20 hectare (5 to 50 acre) reserves. Our Mission is to provide an entertaining and educational environment in which to display and propagate animals in a safe manner that gives a unique viewing opportunity to all of our visitors. Open May-October.
Mike Takacs, General Manager

***Cambridge:* Wings of Paradise**
2500 Kossuth Rd., Cambridge, ON N3H 4R7
519-653-1234, Fax: 519-650-2582,
info@wingsofparadise.com
www.wingsofparadise.com
Live butterfly conservatory & tropical garden; open daily 10-5

***Earlton:* Temiskaming Wildlife Centre**
***Also known as:* Temiskaming Historical & Zoological Society of Northern Ontario**
PO Box 691, Earlton, ON P0J 1E0
705-563-8300, Fax: 705-563-2200,
info@temiskamingwildlifecentre.org
A wildlife rehabilitation facility that houses & treats local wildlife &, when possible releases them back into the wild; live animal exhibits, guided tours, workshops & special programming to educate visitors about the north & conservation issues; open June-Sept. daily 10-5, Sept.-June call in advance for bookings
Amanda Godden, Wildlife Rehab
Amanda Mongeon, Project Manager

***Kingsville:* Jack Miner Bird Sanctuary**
PO Box 39, Kingsville, ON N9Y 2E8
519-733-4034, 877-289-8328
info@jackminer.com
www.jackminer.com
Centre for the conservation of migrating Canada geese and wild ducks, originating from the waterfowl refuge management system. Open year-round, free admission; closed Sundays. Located at 322 Road 3 West, off Division Road in Kingsville.

***Midland:* Wye Marsh Wildlife Centre**
PO Box 100, 16160 Hwy. 12 E, Midland, ON L4R 4K6
705-526-7809, Fax: 705-526-3294,
info@wyemarsh.com
www.wyemarsh.com
Founded: 1984 Indoor & outdoor natural history exhibits; environmental education & recreation programs; fully accessible nature centre & trails; assistive equipment available
Laurie Schutt, Executive Director

***Morrisburg:* Upper Canada Migratory Bird Sanctuary (UCMBS) / Sanctuaire des oiseaux migrateurs Upper Canada**
Parks of the St. Lawrence, RR#1, Morrisburg, ON K0C 1X0
613-543-3704, Fax: 613-543-2847, 800-437-2233
www.uppercanadabirdsanctuary.com
A natural area with over 8 km. of nature trails, visitor centre & gift shop, campground & group camping area; offers a duck banding program, fall goose feeding program, outdoor education topics & special events such as the Annual Waterfowl Day
Sheila Lefebvre, Bird Sanctuary Programming Officer

***Orono:* Jungle Cat World Inc. (JCW)**
***Also known as:* Orono Exotic Cat World**
3667 Conc. 6, RR#1, Orono, ON L0B 1M0
905-983-5016, Fax: 905-983-9858,
info@junglecatworld.com
www.junglecatworld.com
Jungle Cat World is a wildlife park located on 15 picturesque acres. Though Jungle Cat World is home to a variety of threatened and endangered species such as lemurs, gibbons, cotton-top tamarins and spider monkeys, the park specializes in wild felines. They include the world's largest, the Siberian tiger, to the rarest, the Amur leopard, to some of the smallest like the sand cats from the African deserts.

***St Catharines:* Happy Rolph Bird Sanctuary & Children's Petting Farm**
c/o St Catharines Parks & Recreation Dept., PO Box 3012, St Catharines, ON L2N 2G6
905-937-7210, Fax: 905-646-9262
A 15-acre municipal park on the shores of Lake Ontario boasts beautiful gardens and pathways, petting farm (open Victoria Day to Thanksgiving weekend), picnic area and playground facilities.
Jim Benson

***Thunder Bay:* Chippewa Wildlife Park**
Victoriaville Civic Centre, 111 Syndicate Ave. South, Thunder Bay, ON P7E 6S4
807-625-2351, Fax: 807-625-3258,
www.thunderbay.ca
The municipally operated zoological park contains bird & mammal species, which are indigenous to northwestern Ontario. The Chippewa Wildlife Park features an elevated walkway (pedestrian boardwalk) for viewing the animals.
Paul Fayrick, Manager, Parks, 807-625-2806,
pfayrick@thunderbay.ca

***Toronto:* High Park Animal Paddocks**
c/o Parks & Recreation, City Hall, 100 Queen St. West, Toronto, ON M5H 2N2
416-392-6599,
www.toronto.ca/parks/highpark.htm
Located on Deer Pen Road, the animal paddocks have always been one of the most popular attractions, dating back to 1890 when deer were kept in High Park. Today, you will find domestic and exotic species including bison, llamas, peacocks, deer, highland cattle and sheep.
Carol Guy, Supervisor

***Toronto:* Kortright Centre for Conservation**
c/o Toronto & Region Conservation, 5 Shoreham Dr., Toronto, ON M3N 1S4
416-661-6600, Fax: 416-661-6898,
info@trca.on.ca
www.kortright.org
Largest environmental education centre in Canada. Located on 325 hectares of pristine woodlands, Kortright Centre combines a natural oasis with some of the most leading edge sustainable education programs and events in Canada.

Toronto: **Riverdale Farm, Riverdale Park**
c/o Dept. of Parks & Recreation, City Hall, 201 Winchester St., Toronto, ON M4X 1B8
416-392-6794, Fax: 416-392-0329,
farm@toronto.ca
www.friendsofriverdalefarm.com
Riverdale Farm is a Toronto Parks, Forestry and Recreation Division facility located in a park setting in the heart of the downtown community, Cabbagetown. Admission is free. Parking on neighbouring city streets only. Tour the Farm's scenic 7.5 acres along pathways through wooded areas, around ponds, and into butterfly-herb-flower-vegetable gardens.

Toronto: **Toronto Zoo**
361A Old Finch Ave., Toronto, ON M1B 5K7
416-392-5929, Fax: 416-392-5934,
www.torontozoo.com
The Toronto Zoo is Canada's premier Zoo, known for its interactive education and conservation activities. As a unique wildlife experience, we inspire people to live in ways that promote the well being of the natural world. The Zoo has over 5,000 animals representing over 460 species. Open year round.
Calvin J. White, CEO

Quebec

Bonaventure: **Bioparc de la Gaspésie**
CP 578, 123, des Vieux Ponts, Bonaventure, QC G0C 1E0
418-534-1997, Fax: 418-534-1998, 866-534-1997
info@bioparc.ca
www.bioparc.ca
Gaspesian wildlife observation centre; through a one mile walk path, visitors discover a collection of fauna & flora indigenous to the region presented in their five respective ecosystems: the Bay, the Lagoon, the River, the Forest & the Tundra
Marie-Josse Bernard, Directrice

Charlesbourg: **Jardin Zoologique du Québec**
9300, rue de la Faune, Charlesbourg, QC G1G 5H9
418-622-0313, Fax: 418-646-9239, 888-622-0312
spsnq@spsnq.qc.ca
Open year round

Granby: **Zoo de Granby / Granby Zoo**
525, rue St-Hubert, Granby, QC J2G 5P3
450-372-9113, Fax: 450-372-5531, 877-472-6299
info@zoodegranby.com
www.zoodegranby.com
The Granby Zoological Society is committed to promoting a responsible attitude towards our natural environment by dedicating its efforts to the understanding, appreciation and conservation of living beings and their habitats. Open June - Oct. (Thanksgiving Day).
Joanne Lalumière, Directrice-générale

Hemmingford: **Parc Safari Africain (Québec) Inc.**
850, route 202, Hemmingford, QC J0L 1H0
450-247-2727, Fax: 450-247-3563, 800-465-8724
info@parcsafari.com
www.parcsafari.com
In the summer, our zoological park transforms into an African landscape thanks to our large group of African animal species. Come and admire a spectacular wildlife including 800 animals from the five continents, many of which you can approach and feed. Observe and pet elephants, rhinos, giraffes, zebras, lions, macaques, chimpanzees, white tigers and many others. ALso includes a water park.

Sainte-Anne-de-Bellevue: **Ecomuseum / Écomuséum**
21125, ch Sainte-Marie, Sainte-Anne-de-Bellevue, QC H9X 3Y7
514-457-9449, Fax: 514-457-0769,
info@ecomuseum.ca
www.ecomuseum.ca
Open year round; wildlife interpretation centre; animals of the St. Lawrence Valley

Saint-Eustache: **Ferme de Reptiles Exotarium inc.**
846, ch Fresniere, Saint-Eustache, QC J7R 4K3
450-472-1827,
info@exotarium.net
www.exotarium.net
Rare & endangered reptiles, amphibians & invertebrates
Hervé Maranda, Owner

Saint-Félicien: **Centre de Conservation de la biodiversité boréale (CCBB) inc.- Zoo Sauvage de Saint-Félicien (CCBB)**
2230, boul du Jardin, Saint-Félicien, QC G8K 2P8
418-679-0543, Fax: 418-679-3647,
ccbb@borealie.org
www.borealie.org
Displays North American wildlife in an innovative context; no cages or bars; open daily May 15 - Oct. 14., 9-5
Dominique Chartier, Directrice générale

Saint-Félicien: **Zoo sauvage de Saint-Felicien**
2230, boul du Jardin, Saint-Félicien, QC G8K 2P8
418-697-0543, Fax: 418-679-3647, 800-667-5687
CCBB@borealie.org
www.borealie.org
To provide our visitors with a Zoo unlike any other, a Zoo that blends harmoniously into a yet untamed Nature, that offers a dramatic meeting place where Nature and Boreal wildlife come together, and that makes an exceptional contribution to the protection and maintenance of Boreal biodiversity through its educational, scientific and recreational activities.

Saint-Joachim: **Centre d'interprétation faunique du Cap-Tourmente**
570, ch du Cap-Tourmente, Saint-Joachim, QC G0A 3X0
418-827-4591, Fax: 418-827-6225,
cap.tourmente@ec.gc.ca

Saskatchewan

Regina: **Wascana Waterfowl Park**
Wascana Centre, PO Box 7111, Lakeshore Dr., Regina, SK S4P 3S7
306-522-3661, Fax: 306-565-2742,
wca@wascana.sk.ca
www.wascanacentre.sk.ca/waterfowlpark.html
The Wascana Waterfowl Park is a 223 hectare thriving marshland within Regina's city limits.
Van Isman, Executive Director

SECTION 3
ASSOCIATIONS

Associations in this section are listed alphabetically by subject. Directly following this page is an Entry Index arranged alphabetically by entry name, regardless of subject. Many subjects are also represented in other sections throughout the book. For example, Section 2: Arts & Culture includes Art Galleries, while this section includes Art Gallery Associations.

Association Name Index

B

D

E

J

K

L

M

N

P

V

W

Y

Z

Accounting

Canadian Academic Accounting Association (CAAA) / Association canadienne des professeurs de comptabilité (ACPC)
3997 Chesswood Dr., Toronto ON M3J 2R8 Canada
Tel: 416-486-5361; *Fax:* 416-486-6158
admin@caaa.ca
www.caaa.ca
To promote excellence in accounting education & research in Canada with particular reference to Canadian post-secondary accounting programs & Canadian issues

Canadian Bookkeepers Association
#482, 283 Danforth Ave., Toronto ON M4K 1N2 Canada
Fax: 866-804-4617
info@canadianbookkeepersassociation.com
www.c-b-a.ca
To promote, support, provide for & encourage Canadian bookkeepers; to promote & increase the awareness of Bookkeeping in Canada as a professional discipline; to support national, regional & local networking among Canadian Bookkeepers; to provide information on leading-edge procedures, education & technologies that enhance the industry, as well as, the Canadian bookkeeping professional; to support & encourage responsible & accurate bookkeeping practices throughout Canada
Norm Eady, President

Canadian Institute of Chartered Accountants (CICA) / Institut canadien des comptables agréés
277 Wellington St. West, Toronto ON M5V 3H2
Tel: 416-977-3222; *Fax:* 416-977-8585
www.cica.ca
To foster public confidence in the chartered accountant profession; To assist members to excel

Canadian Insurance Accountants Association (CIAA) / Association canadienne des comptables en assurance
c/o Taylor Enterprises Ltd., #310, 2175 Sheppard Ave. East, Toronto ON M2J 1W8
Tel: 416-971-7800; *Fax:* 416-491-1670
ciaa@ciaa.org
www.ciaa.org
To promote study, research, & development of management & insurance accounting

Certified General Accountants Association of Alberta
#100, 325 Manning Rd. NE, Calgary AB T2E 2P5
Tel: 403-299-1300; *Fax:* 403-299-1339
Toll-Free: 800-661-1078
questions@cga-alberta.org; studentservices@cga-alberta.org
www.cga-alberta.org
To represent the provincial interests of Certified General Accountants & students; To establish & enforce professional competency & ethical standards

Certified General Accountants Association of British Columbia
#300, 1867 West Broadway, Vancouver BC V6J 5L4
Tel: 604-732-1211; *Fax:* 604-732-1252
Toll-Free: 800-565-1211
info@cga-bc.org
www.cga-bc.org
Social Media: twitter.com/cgabc
To act as the governing & regulatory body responsible for Certified General Accountants in British Columbia; To train & certify British Columbia's Certified General Accountants

Certified General Accountants Association of Canada
#100, 4200 North Fraser Way, Burnaby BC V5J 5K7
Tel: 604-669-3555; *Fax:* 604-689-5845
Toll-Free: 800-663-1529
tashlie@cga-canada.org
www.cga-canada.org
To represent Certified General Accountants & students in Canada, Bermuda, the nations of the Caribbean, the People's Republic of China, & Hong Kong; To establish educational standards; To advocate for accounting professional excellence & responsible policy & practices

Certified General Accountants Association of Manitoba
4 Donald St. South, Winnipeg MB R3L 2T7
Tel: 204-477-1256; *Fax:* 204-453-7176
Toll-Free: 800-282-8001
info@cga-manitoba.org; memberservices@cga-manitoba.org
www.cga-manitoba.org
To provide professional support services for the accounting profession in Manitoba; To ensure commitment to the Code of Ethical Principles & Rules of Conduct; To empower members to excel

Certified General Accountants Association of New Brunswick / Association des comptables généraux accrédités du Nouveau-Brunswick
PO Box 1395, #10, 236 St. George St., Moncton NB E1C 8T6
Tel: 506-857-0939; *Fax:* 506-855-0887
Toll-Free: 877-462-4262
cganb@cga-nb.org
www.cga-nb.org
To advance the interests of Certified General Accountants & to inform the public in New Brunswick; To provide education & professional services to members; To uphold the Code of Ethical Principles & Rules of Conduct to protect the public

Certified General Accountants Association of Newfoundland & Labrador (CGA-NL)
#201, 294 Freshwater Rd., St. John's NL A1B 1C1
Tel: 709-579-1863; *Fax:* 709-579-0838
Toll-Free: 800-563-2426
office@cganl.org; education@cganl.org
www.cganl.org
To protect the public through commitment to The CGA Newfoundland & Labrador Code of Ethical Principles & Rules of Conduct & The CGA Newfoundland & Labrador Independence Standard; To advocate on issues to advance the interests of Certified General Accountants in Newfoundland & Labrador

Certified General Accountants Association of Nova Scotia
#230, 1801 Hollis St., Halifax NS B3J 3N4
Tel: 902-425-4923; *Fax:* 902-425-4983
office@cga-ns.org
www.cga-ns.org
To control the professional standards, conduct, & discipline of Certified General Accountants from Nova Scotia; To grant the exclusive right to the CGA designation

Certified General Accountants Association of Ontario
240 Eglinton Ave. East, Toronto ON M4P 1K8
Tel: 416-322-6520; *Fax:* 416-322-6481
Toll-Free: 800-668-1454
info@cga-ontario.org
www.cga-ontario.org
To regulate qualification, performance, & discipline standards for Certified General Accountants throughout Ontario; To grant exclusive rights to the CGA designation

Certified General Accountants Association of Prince Edward Island
PO Box 3, #105, 18 Queen St., Charlottetown PE C1A 4A1
Tel: 902-368-7237; *Fax:* 902-368-3627
contact@cga-pei.org
www.cga-pei.org
To provide professional support services to the accounting profession in Prince Edward Island

Certified General Accountants Association of Saskatchewan
#114, 3502 Taylor St. East, Saskatoon SK S7H 5H9
Tel: 306-955-4622; *Fax:* 306-373-9219
Toll-Free: 800-667-4754
info@cga-saskatchewan.org; studentservices@cga-manitoba.org
www.cga-saskatchewan.org
To ensure members' commitment to the Certified General Accountants Association of Saskatchewan Code of Ethics; To promote excellence in accounting standards & practices; To advance the interests of Saskatchewan's Certified General Accountants

Certified General Accountants Association of the Northwest Territories & Nunavut
Graham Bromley Bldg., PO Box 128, 5016 - 50th Ave., 3rd Fl., Yellowknife NT X1A 2N1
Tel: 867-873-5620; *Fax:* 867-873-4469
Toll-Free: 888-633-3221
admin@cga-nwt-nu.org
www.cga-nwt-nu.org
To provide training & professional support services to accountants in the Northwest Territories & Nunavut; To grant the exclusive rights to the CGA designation; To advance the interests of members; To protect the public; To advocate for the public interest

Certified General Accountants Association of Yukon
PO Box 31536, RPO Main St., Whitehorse YT Y1A 6K8
Tel: 867-668-4461; *Fax:* 867-668-8635
www.cga.org/canada/yukon

CGA Student Services - Maritime Region
Commerce House, PO Box 5100, #403, 236 St. George St., Moncton NB E1C 8R2 Canada
Tel: 506-857-0939; *Fax:* 506-855-0887
Toll-Free: 877-855-0887
cganb@cga-nb.org
www.cga-nb.org
The Certified General Accountants' Association of Canada gives the Association its unity and strength and ensures the portability of the CGA desgingation.

Chartered Accountants Institute of Bermuda (ICAB)
PO Box 1625, Hamilton HM GX Bermuda
Tel: 441-292-7479; *Fax:* 441-295-3121
icab@northrock.bm
www.icab.bm

CMA Canada / La Société des comptables en management accrédités
#1400, One Robert Speck Pkwy., Mississauga ON L4Z 3M3 Canada
Tel: 905-949-4200; *Fax:* 905-949-0888
Toll-Free: 800-263-7622
info@cma-canada.org
www.cma-canada.org
To drive value creation by developing professionals & resources to lead the advancement & integration of strategy, accounting & management

CMA Canada - Alberta
#300, 1210 - 8th St. SW, Calgary AB T2R 1L3 Canada
Tel: 403-269-5341; *Fax:* 403-262-5477
Toll-Free: 877-262-2000
info@cma-alberta.com
www.cma-alberta.com
Social Media: www.twitter.com/CMAAlberta
To develop & advance the competencies & market relevance of CMAs through accreditation, education, & high standards

CMA Canada - British Columbia (CMABC)
Two Bentall Centre, PO Box 269, #1055, 555 Burrard St., Vancouver BC V7X 1M8 Canada
Tel: 604-687-5891; *Fax:* 604-687-6688
Toll-Free: 800-663-9646
cmabc@cmabc.com
www.cmabc.com
To be pre-eminent in management accounting by ensuring that the body of knowledge is available, by setting & enforcing the standards of competence, ensuring availability of CMAs in the defined territory, & supporting research; to optimize the performance of enterprises by driving the continuous development of financial & strategic management professionals & shaping the strategic leadership competencies of CMAs

CMA Canada - Manitoba
#815, 240 Graham Ave., Winnipeg MB R3C 0J7 Canada
Tel: 204-943-1538; *Fax:* 204-947-3308
Toll-Free: 800-841-7148
cmamb@cma-canada.org
www.cma-manitoba.com
Social Media: www.facebook.com/cmamb
To support members in leading organizations in the application of advanced management practices

CMA Canada - Newfoundland & Labrador
PO Box 28090, Stn. Avalon Mall, #104, 31 Peet St., St. John's NL A1B 4J8 Canada
Tel: 709-726-3652; *Fax:* 709-726-5513
mbradbury@cma-nl.com
www.cma-nl.com
Mark A. Bradbury, CMA, Executive Director

CMA Canada - Northwest Territories & Nunavut
PO Box 512, Yellowknife NT X1A 2N4 Canada
Tel: 867-873-2875; *Fax:* 867-920-2503
mdemeule@cma-canada.org
www.cma-nwt.com

CMA Canada - Nova Scotia, Bermuda & PEI
Sentry Place, #300, 1559 Brunswick St., Halifax NS B3J 2G1 Canada
Tel: 902-422-5836; *Fax:* 902-423-1605
Toll-Free: 800-565-7198
nforan@cmans.com
www.cmans.com
To promote standards of excellence in management accounting

CMA Canada - Ontario
#300, 70 University Ave., Toronto ON M5J 2M4 Canada
Tel: 416-977-7741; *Fax:* 416-977-6079
Toll-Free: 800-387-2991
info@cma-ontario.org
www.cma-ontario.org

To optimize the performance of enterprises by driving the continuous development of management accounting & shaping the strategic competences of CMA's

CMA Canada - Québec
715, square Victoria, 3e étage, Montréal QC H2Y 2H7 Canada
Tél: 514-849-1155; *Téléc:* 514-849-9674
Ligne sans frais: 800-263-5390
administration@cma-quebec.org
www.cma-quebec.org
Protéger le public en contrôlant la compétence et l'intégrité de ceux et celles qui exercent la profession; favoriser la prééminence de ses membres dans le monde des affaires; assurer une formation de tout premier ordre; l'Ordre joue un rôle primordial dans l'acquisition et l'application du savoir de ses membres; il est responsable de l'émission des permis d'exercice aux candidats qui remplissent les conditions nécessaires, de la garde du tableau des membres, de la surveillance de l'exercice de la profession et du dépistage de la pratique illégale

CMA Canada - Saskatchewan
#202, 1900 Albert St., Regina SK S4P 4K8 Canada
Tel: 306-757-9428; *Fax:* 306-347-8580
Toll-Free: 800-667-3535
sask@cma-canada.org
www.cma-saskatchewan.com

CMA Canada - Yukon
PO Box 31426, Whitehorse YT Y1A 6K8 Canada
Tel: 867-668-3388; *Fax:* 867-668-2402
cmayukon@internorth.com
www.cma-canada.org/yukon.asp
To promote standards of excellence in management accounting

CMA New Brunswick (CMANB) / La Société des comptables en management du Nouveau-Brunswick
#101, 570 Queen St., Fredericton NB E3B 6Z6 Canada
Tel: 506-455-2262; *Fax:* 506-455-2266
Toll-Free: 877-676-2262
cmanb.admin@nb.aibn.com
www.cmanb.com
Represents over 400 CMAs in New Brunswick. A self-regulating association which maintains the highest standards of professional practice, in its mission to develop both professionals and resources in service to the public
Shelley Pelkey, FCMA, CEO

Guild of Industrial, Commercial & Institutional Accountants / Guilde des comptables industriels, commerciaux et institutionnels
36 Tandian Ct., Woodbridge ON L4L 8Z9
Tel: 905-264-2713; *Fax:* 905-264-1043
iciaguild@aol.com
www.guildoficia.ca
To support & promote interest in vocational accountancy; To encourage acceptance of modern accounting methods & procedures

Institute of Chartered Accountants of Alberta (ICAA)
Manulife Place, #580, 10180 - 101 St., Edmonton AB T5J 4R2 Canada
Tel: 780-424-7391; *Fax:* 780-425-8766
Toll-Free: 800-232-9406
info@icaa.ab.ca
www.icaa.ab.ca
To protect the public interest by setting & enforcing high professional & ethical standards

Institute of Chartered Accountants of British Columbia (ICABC)
One Bentall Centre, #500, 505 Burrard St., Box 22, Vancouver BC V7X 1M4 Canada
Tel: 604-681-3264; *Fax:* 604-681-1523
Toll-Free: 800-663-2677
www.ica.bc.ca
To protect & serve the public, our members & students by providing exceptional education, regulation & member services programs so that chartered accountants may provide the highest quality of professional services

Institute of Chartered Accountants of Manitoba (ICAM)
#500, 161 Portage Ave. East, Winnipeg MB R3B 0Y4 Canada
Tel: 204-942-8248; *Fax:* 204-943-7119
Toll-Free: 888-942-8248
icam@icam.mb.ca
www.icam.mb.ca
To protect the public by acting as the governing body of the profession of chartered accountancy in Manitoba; To ensure the profession observes established professional practice standards, rules of professional conduct, bylaws, & regulations

Institute of Chartered Accountants of Newfoundland (ICAN)
PO Box 21130, #501, 95 Bonaventure Ave., St. John's NL A1B 2X5 Canada
Tel: 709-753-7566; *Fax:* 709-753-3609
tbatstone@icanl.ca
www.icanl.ca
To serve the interests of society & the membership by providing leadership; To uphold the professional standards, integrity & preeminence of chartered accountants in Newfoundland & Labrador

Institute of Chartered Accountants of Nova Scotia (ICANS)
#1410, 1791 Barrington St., Halifax NS B3J 3L1 Canada
Tel: 902-425-3291; *Fax:* 902-423-4505
icans@icans.ns.ca
www.icans.ns.ca
To protect & serve the public & our members by providing exceptional services & resources within a well-regulated profession

Institute of Chartered Accountants of Ontario (ICAO) / Institut des comptables agrées de l'Ontario
69 Bloor St. East, Toronto ON M4W 1B3 Canada
Tel: 416-962-1841; *Fax:* 416-962-8900
Toll-Free: 800-387-0735
custserv@icao.on.ca
www.icao.on.ca
Mission is to foster public confidence in the Chartered Accountant profession, by acting in the public interest and helping members excel. The Institute sets and enforces the highest standards of practice, qualification and education; promotes professional excellence and ethical conduct; encourages continuous improvement of capabilities among members; promotes the profession while serving as it's primary voice in Ontario

Institute of Chartered Accountants of Prince Edward Island
PO Box 301, 129 Kent St., Charlottetown PE C1A 7K7 Canada
Tel: 902-894-4290; *Fax:* 902-894-4791
www.icapei.com
To foster public confidence in the profession of chartered accountancy in Prince Edward Island; To act in the public interest; To assist members to excel in their role as leaders in senior management, advisory, finance, tax & assurance

Institute of Chartered Accountants of Saskatchewan
3621 Pasqua St., Regina SK S4S 6W8 Canada
Tel: 306-359-1010; *Fax:* 306-569-8288
Toll-Free: 800-268-3793
inst.ca@icas.sk.ca
www.icas.sk.ca
Represents CA's and CA students in Saskatchewan; protects the public by ensuring members adhere to high professional and ethical standards of practice

Institute of Chartered Accountants of the Northwest Territories & Nunavut (ICANWT)
c/o Indian & Northern Affairs Canada, PO Box 2433, Yellowknife NT X1A 2P8 Canada
Tel: 867-873-3680; *Fax:* 867-920-4135
www.icanwt.nt.ca

Institute of Chartered Accountants of the Yukon Territory
c/o Institute of Chartered Accountants of British Columbia, Stn. 22, #500, 505 Burrard St., One Bentall Centre, Vancouver BC V7X 1M4 Canada
Tel: 604-681-3264; *Fax:* 604-681-1523
Toll-Free: 800-663-2677
www.icayk.ca

The Institute of Internal Auditors (IIA) / L'Institut des vérificateurs internes
247 Maitland Ave., Altamonte Springs FL 32701-4201 USA
Tel: 407-937-1100; *Fax:* 407-937-1101
custserv@theiia.org
www.theiia.org
To provides leadership for the global profession of internal auditing; To advocate for the profession's value

New Brunswick Institute of Chartered Accountants (NBICA) / Institut des comptables agréés du Nouveau-Brunswick
Mercantile Centre, #250, 55 Union St., Saint John NB E2L 2B2 Canada
Tel: 506-634-1588; *Fax:* 506-634-1015
nbica@nb.aibn.com
www.nbica.org
To serve members, students & the interests of the public with integrity, objectivity & a commitment to excellence; to promote & increase the knowledge, skills & proficiency of members & students; to regulate the discipline & professional conduct of members & students; to require public practitioners to carry minimum levels of professional liability insurance; to have lay representatives sit on Council; to conduct practice inspection of its public practitioners

Ordre des CGA du Québec
#1800, 500, Place d'Armes, Montréal QC H2Y 2W2 Canada
Tél: 514-861-1823; *Téléc:* 514-861-7661
Ligne sans frais: 800-463-0163
ordre@cga-quebec.org
www.cga-quebec.org
Assurer la protection du public; contrôler l'exercice de la profession par ses membres

L'Ordre des comptables agréés du Québec (OCAQ)
680, rue Sherbrooke ouest, 18e étage, Montréal QC H3A 2S3 Canada
Tél: 514-288-3256; *Téléc:* 514-843-8375
Ligne sans frais: 800-363-4688
info@ocaq.qc.ca
www.ocaq.qc.ca
Protection du public; dépister l'exercice illégal de la comptabilité publique; s'assurer de la formation adéquate des membres

Petroleum Accountants Society of Canada (PASC)
PO Box 4520, Stn. C, Calgary AB T2T 5N3 Canada
Tel: 403-262-4744; *Fax:* 403-244-2340
info@petroleumaccountants.com
www.petroleumaccountants.com
To contribute to the long term success of the Canadian petroleum industry by staying abreast of the constantly changing needs of the industry & striving to satisfy those needs
Matthew Breadner, President
Thomas Latta, Vice President
Gail Quartly, Treasurer

The Society of Professional Accountants of Canada / La Société des comptables professionnels du Canada
#1007, 250 Consumers Rd., Toronto ON M2J 4V6 Canada
Tel: 416-350-8145; *Fax:* 416-350-8146
Toll-Free: 877-515-4447
registrar@professionalaccountant.org
www.professionalaccountant.org
To provide ongoing education & to set qualifying standards, to ensure the professional competence of its members in the practice of accountancy
William O. Nichols, RPA, President

Addiction

Addictions Foundation of Manitoba (AFM) / Fondation manitobaine de lutte contre les dépendances
1031 Portage Ave., Winnipeg MB R3G 0R8 Canada
Tel: 204-944-6236; *Fax:* 204-786-7768
execoff@afm.mb.ca
afm.mb.ca
To be a sensitive, caring, learning organization dedicated to continuously improving our services related to addiction & to collaborate with community members in providing a holistic approach, resulting in an improved quality of life for Manitobans; provides prevention, education & treatment programs related to addictions to individuals & communities; conducts research into the negative effects of addictions
John Borody, CEO

Adult Children of Alcoholics (ACA)
PO Box 75061, 20 Bloor St. East, Toronto ON M5W 3T3 Canada
Tel: 416-631-3614
acatoronto@hotmail.com
acatoronto.org/Adult_Children_of_Alcoholics_Toronto
ACA is a 12-step program of adults who meet and share common experiences of living in an alcoholic or dysfunctional home. Past experiences are examined and their influence in the present is explored. By practising the 12 Steps and accepting a Higher Power, the aim is to improve lives today.

Airspace Action on Smoking & Health
Delta BC V4L 2M4 Canada
Tel: 604-943-6789; *Toll-Free:* 888-245-7722
airspace@airspace.bc.ca
airspace.bc.ca
To educate non-smokers on the effects that smoking has on them & of their legal right to smoke-free air; to help establish laws to protect the comfort, safety & health of non-smokers; to help reduce the number of future smokers

Al-Anon Family Groups (Canada), Inc. / Groupe familiaux Al-Anon
#245, 9 Antares Dr., Ottawa ON K2E 7V5 Canada
Tel: 613-723-8484; *Fax:* 613-723-0151
Toll-Free: 888-425-2666
wso@al-anon.org
www.al-anon.alateen.org

Al-Anon Groupe La Vallée de l'Espoir
CP 21, Chibougamau QC G8P 2K5 Canada
Tél: 418-748-3779
www.al-anon-quebec-est.org

Alcoholics Anonymous (GTA Intergroup) (AA)
#202, 234 Eglinton Ave. East, Toronto ON M4P 1K5 Canada
Tel: 416-487-5591; *Fax:* 416-487-5855
www.aatoronto.org
Fellowship of men & women who share their experience, strength & hope with each other so that they may solve their common problem & help others recover from alcoholism; the primary purpose is to stay sober & help other alcoholics to achieve sobriety

Alcooliques Anonymes du Québec
3920, rue Rachel est, Montréal QC H1X 1Z3 Canada
Tél: 514-376-9230; *Téléc:* 514-374-2250
region87@aa-quebec.org
aa-quebec.org/AA_Quebec/index.htm
Demeurer abstinent et aider d'autres alcooliques à le devenir
Claudette Pichette

Alcooliques Anonymes Groupe La Vallée du Cuivre
CP 21, Chibougamau QC G8P 2K5 Canada
Ligne sans frais: 866-376-6279

Canadian Assembly of Narcotics Anonymous (CANA)
PO Box 25073 RPO West Kildonan, Winnipeg MB R2V 4C7 Canada
www.canaacna.org
To help the addict who suffers from the disease of addiction

Canadian Centre on Substance Abuse (CCSA) / Centre canadien de lutte contre l'alcoolisme et les toxicomanies (CCLAT)
#300, 75 Albert St., Ottawa ON K1P 5E7 Canada
Tel: 613-235-4048; *Fax:* 613-235-8101
Toll-Free: 800-559-4514
info@ccsa.ca
www.ccsa.ca
To minimize the harm associated with addictions, including substance abuse & problem gambling
Enid Harrison, Director, Communications & Corporate Services
Michel Perron, CEO
Greg Graves, Senior Analyst, Research & Policy

Centre for Addiction & Mental Health (CAMH) / Centre de toxicomanie et de santé mentale
250 College St., Toronto ON M5T 1R8 Canada
Tel: 416-535-8501; *Toll-Free:* 800-463-6273
public_affairs@camh.net
www.camh.net
To provide treatment for & research into substance abuse & mental health issues. Clinical & research sites in Toronto & across Ontario
Paul Beeston, Chair

Council on Drug Abuse (CODA)
#505, 111 Peter St., Toronto ON M5V 2H1 Canada
Tel: 416-763-1491; *Fax:* 416-763-5343
info@drugabuse.ca
drugabuse.ca
The council is a non-profit organization that strives to prevent & reduce substance abuse, primarily among youth, by sponsoring education programs in schools. It is a registered charity, BN: 106988140RR0001.

MADD Canada / Les mères contre l'alcool au volant
#500, 2010 Winston Park Dr., Oakville ON L6H 5R7 Canada
Tel: 905-829-8805; *Toll-Free:* 800-665-6233
info@madd.ca
www.madd.ca
To stop death & injury caused by impaired driving; To support victims of this crime
Andrew Murie, CEO
Carolyn Swinson, Chair
Margaret Miller, President

Narcotiques Anonymes
1701, rue St-Luc, Chibougamau QC G8P 2N4 Canada
Tél: 418-770-5166

Parent Action on Drugs (PAD)
7 Hawksdale Rd., Rm. 121, Toronto ON M3K 1W3 Canada
Tel: 416-395-4970; *Fax:* 866-591-7685
pad@parentactionondrugs.org
www.parentactionondrugs.org
Social Media:
www.facebook.com/pages/Parent-Action-on-Drugs-PAD/390301531674
To address issues of substance use among youth through outreach, prevention, education & parent support; enhances the capacity of parents, youth & communities to promote an environment that encourages youth to make informed choices

Physicians for a Smoke-Free Canada / Médecins pour un Canada sans fumée
1226A Wellington St., Ottawa ON K1Y 3A1 Canada
Tel: 613-233-4878; *Fax:* 613-233-7797
psc@smoke-free.ca
www.smoke-free.ca

Responsible Gambling Council (Ontario) (RGC(O)) / Le Conseil ontarien pour le jeu responsable
#205, 411 Richmond St. East, Toronto ON M5A 3S5 Canada
Tel: 416-499-9800; *Fax:* 416-499-8260
Toll-Free: 888-391-1111
mail@rgco.org
www.responsiblegambling.org
RGCO is an independent, non-profit organization committed to the prevention of problem gambling. It works to increase awareness of compulsive gambling among families, community & service club leaders, & supports research into the causes & treatment. It has developed several programs to raise awareness, including high school drama tours & interactive programs for university students. And, it has created campaigns aimed at friends & spouses of those at risk. It is a registered charity, BN: 106846462RR0001.

Advertising & Marketing

The Advertising & Design Club of Canada (ADCC)
#205, 344 Bloor St. West, Toronto ON M5S 3A7 Canada
Tel: 416-423-4113; *Fax:* 416-423-3362
info@theadcc.ca
www.theadcc.ca
To recognize, support & promote creative excellence in the Canadian advertising, publishing & design community
Brian Howlett, President
Dawn Wickstrom, Executive Director

Advertising Standards Canada (ASC) / Les normes canadiennes de la publicité
South Tower, #1801, 175 Bloor St. East, Toronto ON M4W 3R8 Canada
Tel: 416-961-6311; *Fax:* 416-961-7904
Toll-Free: 888-256-8646
info@adstandards.com
www.adstandards.com
To ensure the integrity & viability of advertising through industry self-regulation.
Linda J. Nagel, President/CEO

Association canadienne des annonceurs inc.
#925, 2015, rue Peel, Montréal QC H3A 1t8 Canada
Tél: 514-842-6422; *Téléc:* 514-842-6223
Ligne sans frais: 800-883-0422
info@aca-online.com
www.aca-online.com
L'ACA est la ressource de première ligne des annonceurs à la recherche d'un leadership fiable et crédible de même que pour des conseils et un soutien en matière de communications marketing. Pour ses membres, l'ACA constitute un investissement essential au succès de leur mis en marché

Association des agences de publicité du Québec (AAPQ) / Association of Québec Advertising Agencies
#925, 2015, rue Peel, Montréal QC H3A 1T8 Canada
Tél: 514-848-1732; *Téléc:* 514-848-1950
aapq@aapq.ca
www.aapq.ca
Promouvoir et défendre les intérêts des agences membres
Yanik Deschênes, Président-directeur général

Association of Canadian Advertisers Inc. (ACA) / Association canadienne des annonceurs
#1103, 95 St. Clair Ave. West, Toronto ON M4V 1N6 Canada
Tel: 416-964-3805; *Fax:* 416-964-0771
Toll-Free: 800-565-0109
info@aca-online.com
www.aca-online.com
Promotes the common interests of advertisers & is a valuable resource to members, providing expertise, education & information

Audit Bureau of Circulation (ABC)
Canadian Member Service Office, #850, 151 Bloor St. West, Toronto ON M5S 1S4 Canada
Tel: 416-962-5840; *Fax:* 416-962-5844
service@accessabc.com
www.accessabc.com
To be the pre-eminent self-regulatory auditing organization, responsible to advertisers, advertising agencies, & the media they use, for the verification & dissemination of members' circulation data & other information for the benefit of the advertising marketplace in the United States & Canada

Canadian Advertising Research Foundation (CARF) / Fondation canadienne de recherche en publicité (FCRP)
#1005, 160 Bloor St. East, Toronto ON M4W 1B9 Canada
Tel: 416-413-3864; *Fax:* 416-413-3879
tkormann@tvb.ca
www.carf.ca
To promote greater effectiveness in advertising & marketing through completely impartial & objective research; to further, through the fostering of research, scientific practices in advertising & marketing

Canadian Automatic Merchandising Association (CAMA) / L'Association canadienne d'auto-distribution
Member Services, #100, 2233 Argentia Rd., Mississauga ON L5N 2X7 Canada
Fax: 905-826-4873
Toll-Free: 888-849-2262
info@vending-cama.com
www.vending-cama.com
CAMA represts the intersts of Vending Operators, Machine Manufacturers, and Product and Service Suppliers in Canada. It is designed to represent, support, and enhance the vending industry.

Canadian Institute of Marketing / Institut canadien du marketing
205 Miller Dr., Georgetown ON L7G 6G4 Canada
Tel: 905-877-5369; *Fax:* 905-877-5369
info@cinstmarketing.ca
www.cinstmarketing.ca
Social Media: www.facebook.com/group.php?gid=8099252591
To improve the practice of marketing in Canada by encouraging the adoption of professional standards & qualifications by practitioners & employers, & by sponsoring activities related to marketing education & training; to be a means by which those engaged in all aspects of marketing as a professional activity can represent their views & interests to governments & agencies

Canadian Marketing Association (CMA) / Association canadienne du marketing (ACM)
#607, 1 Concorde Gate, Toronto ON M3C 3N6 Canada
Tel: 416-391-2362; *Fax:* 416-441-4062
info@the-cma.org
www.the-cma.org
Social Media:
facebook.com/group.php?gid=68638569592#!/cdnmarketing
To be the pre-eminent marketing association in Canada representing the integration & convergence of all marketing disciplines, channels & technologies

Canadian Media Directors' Council (CMDC)
#1097, 1930 Yonge St., Toronto ON M4S 1Z4 Canada
Tel: 416-967-7282
bruce.claassen@genesismedia.com
www.cmdc.ca
To advance media advertising in Canada; to create more efficient processes to execute and administer media transactions by adopting industry-wide standards

Canadian Outdoor Measurement Bureau (COMB)
24 Duncan St., 2nd Fl., Toronto ON M5V 2B8 Canada
Tel: 416-968-3823; *Fax:* 416-968-9396
hthompson@comb.org
www.comb.org

Chartered Institute of Marketing Management of Ontario (CIMMO)
19 Bartley Dr., RR#3, Caledon East ON L0N 1E0 Canada
Tel: 905-880-2964
goodall@allstream.net
To provide a standard for the marketing industry & be the voice of marketing professionals in Ontario.
Nigel Goodall, Chair

Conseil des directeurs médias du Québec (CDMQ)
#925, 2015, rue Peel, Montréal QC H3A 1T8 Canada
Tél: 514-990-1899
info@cdmq.ca
www.cdmq.ca
Etre un point de convergence d'opinions et d'information, un instrument de défense des intérêts des clients/agences et un outil de promotion et de stimulation de la fonction média

Institute of Communication Agencies (ICA) / Institut des communications et de la publicité (ICP)
#3002, 2300 Yonge St., Toronto ON M4P 1E4 Canada
Tel: 416-482-1396; *Fax:* 416-482-1856
Toll-Free: 800-567-7422
ica@icacanada.ca
www.ica-ad.com
To anticipate, serve & promote the collective interests of ICA members, with regard to defining, developing & helping to maintain the highest possible standards of professional practice

Marketing Research & Intelligence Association (MRIA) / L'Association de la recherche et de l'intelligence marketing (ARIM)
Bldg. 4, #104, 2600 Skymark Ave., Mississauga ON L4W 5B2 Canada
Tel: 905-602-6854; *Fax:* 905-602-6855
Toll-Free: 888-602-6742
info@camro.org
www.mria-arim.ca
MRIA works to benefit the public & its members, by developing & delivering ethical, professional practice standards, promoting the industry, & advocating for public policy that balances the need for research with privacy & consumer rights.

National Advertising Benevolent Society (NABS) / Société nationale de bienfaisance en publicité
#903, 45 St. Clair Ave. West, Toronto ON M4V 1K9 Canada
Tel: 416-962-0446; *Fax:* 416-962-9149
Toll-Free: 800-661-6227
nabs@nabs.org
www.nabs.org
To relieve the suffering of individuals & their families who have derived the majority of their income from advertising
Mike Fenton, President & CEO
Leslie Clare, Executive Director

National Association of Major Mail Users, Inc. (NAMMU) / Association nationale des grands usagers postaux inc. (ANGUP)
#302, 517 Wellington St. West, Toronto ON M5V 1G1 Canada
Tel: 416-977-3703; *Toll-Free:* 800-453-1308
executive@nammu.org
www.nammu.org
Dedicated to working in cooperation with Canada Post to improve cost & service
Kathleen Rowe, President

Out-of-Home Marketing Association of Canada (OMAC) / Association marketing canadienne de l'affichage (AMCA)
24 Duncan St., 2nd. Fl., Toronto ON M5V 2B8 Canada
Tel: 416-968-3435; *Fax:* 416-968-6538
rcaron@omaccanada.ca
www.omaccanada.ca
To increase out-of-home's share of ad dollars by promoting the benefits & effectiveness of out-of-home media to agencies & advertisers; to develop & implement new initiatives that serve as a resource to the industry & increase understading of out-of-home media; to foster development of standards & guidelines that make out-of-home easier to plan & buy; to serve as the united voice of the industry through involvement in issues that represent the interests of its members

Print Measurement Bureau (PMB)
#1101, 77 Bloor St. West, Toronto ON M5S 1M2 Canada
Tel: 416-961-3205; *Fax:* 416-961-5052
Toll-Free: 800-762-0899
lina@pmb.ca
www.pmb.ca

Print Production Association of Ontario (PPA)
PO Box 48027, 1881 Yonge St., Toronto ON M4S 3C0 Canada
Tel: 416-410-7841
pgonsalves@interbrand.ca
To keep print buyers abreast of latest technology
Patricia Gonslaves, Executive Member
Sonya Popovich
Patricia Gonsalves
Mark Greene
Jennifer Whitfield

Promotional Product Professionals of Canada Inc. / Professionnels en produits promotionnels du Canada
#100, Côte-de-Liesse, Saint-Laurent QC H4T 2B5 Canada
Tel: 514-489-5359; *Fax:* 514-489-7760
Toll-Free: 866-450-7722
info@pppc.ca
www.promocan.com
To advance the promotional products industry; To act as the voice of the predominant advertising medium in Canada

Le Publicité Club de Montréal (PCM)
#925, 2015, rue Peel, Montréal QC H3A 1T8 Canada
Tél: 514-842-5681; *Téléc:* 514-842-8836
info@pcm.qc.ca
www.pcm.qc.ca
Promouvoir les intérêts de l'industrie publicitaire au Québec et sur les marchés extérieurs
Lyse George, Présidente
Roger Sirard, Sec.-trés.

Radio Marketing Bureau (RMB)
#316, 175 Bloor St. East, Toronto ON M4W 3R8 Canada
Tel: 416-922-5757; *Fax:* 416-922-6542
Toll-Free: 800-667-2346
info@rmb.ca
www.rmb.ca
To educate advertisers on the effective use of the radio medium to achieve & surpass their advertising objectives

Sign Association of Canada (SAC) / Association canadienne de l'enseigne (ACE)
#1519, 44 Victoria St., Toronto ON M5C 1Y2 Canada
Tel: 416-628-6608; *Fax:* 416-628-6607
Toll-Free: 877-470-9787
info@sac-ace.ca
www.sac-ace.ca
To represent & support association members

Trans-Canada Advertising Agency Network (T-CAAN)
#504, 4001 Bayview Ave., Toronto ON M2M 3Z7 Canada
Tel: 416-221-6984
marketingmonkey@sympatico.ca
www.tcaan.ca
To promote exchange of ideas, services & market intelligence among members; services areas include strategy, advertising, public relations & branding

AIDS

Action Séro Zéro
CP 246, Succ. C, Montréal QC H2L 4K1 Canada
Tél: 514-521-7778; *Téléc:* 514-521-7665
www.sero-zero.qc.ca
Services gratuits de promotion de la santé et de prévention du VIH/SIDA et des infections transmissibles sexuellement et par le sang. Bureaux: 2075, rue Plessis, local 207, Montréal.
Robert Rousseau, Directeur général

The AIDS Foundation of Canada Inc.
#302, 1224 Hamilton St., Vancouver BC V6B 2S8 Canada
Tel: 604-688-7294; *Fax:* 604-689-4888
To address the growing problem of HIV disease in Canada; to fund new & innovative ways of assisting infected/affected people with HIV; to support new ways to heighten awareness of HIV disease among the general population

AIDS Vancouver (AV)
1107 Seymour St., Vancouver BC V6B 5S8 Canada
Tel: 604-893-2201; *Fax:* 604-893-2211
TDD: 604-893-2215
Crisis Hot-Line: 604-687-2437
contact@aidsvancouver.org
www.aidsvancouver.org
Social Media: www.facebook.com/group.php?gid=48799305725
To alleviate individual & collective vulnerability to HIV & AIDS, through care, support, education, advocacy, & research

AIDS Vancouver Island (AVI)
1601 Blanshard St., Victoria BC V8W 2J5 Canada
Tel: 250-384-2366; *Fax:* 250-380-9411
Toll-Free: 800-665-2437
Crisis Hot-Line: 250-384-4554
info@avi.org
www.avi.org
Social Media:
www.facebook.com/group.php?gid=221277862889
To reduce the spread of, primarily, HIV/AIDS & also Hepatitis C &/or other co-infections; to improve the health & well-being of people infected & affected primarily by HIV/AIDS & also by Hepatitis C &/or other co-infections

Katrina Jensen, Executive Director

Black Coalition for AIDS Prevention
#207, 110 Spadina Ave., Toronto ON M5V 2K4 Canada
Tel: 416-977-9955; *Fax:* 416-977-7664
blackcap@black-cap.com
www.black-cap.com
Social Media: www.facebook.com/group.php?gid=10127593377
To reduce the spread of HIV infection in the Black communities & to enhance the quality of life for Black people living with or affected by HIV/AIDS
Shannon Thomas Ryan, Executive Director

Blood Ties Four Directions Centre
307 Strickland St., Whitehorse YT Y1A 2J9 Canada
Tel: 867-633-2437; *Fax:* 867-633-2447
Toll-Free: 877-333-2437
bloodties@klondiker.com
www.bloodties.ca
The organization acts as an information & support centre to: promote public awareness of AIDS/AIDS & hepatitis C and aid in their prevention; assist people living with HIV/AIDS & hep C.
Patricia Bacon, Executive Director

Canadian AIDS Society (CAS) / Société canadienne du sida (SCS)
#800, 190 O'Connor St., Ottawa ON K2P 2R3
Tel: 613-230-3580; *Fax:* 613-563-4998
Toll-Free: 800-499-1986
casinfo@cdnaids.ca
www.cdnaids.ca
Social Media:
www.facebook.com/group.php?gid=172950011095
To strengthen the response to HIV/AIDS across Canada; To enrich the lives of people living with HIV/AIDS

Canadian Foundation for AIDS Research (CANFAR) / Fondation canadienne de recherche sur le SIDA
#901, 165 University Ave., Toronto ON M5H 3B8 Canada
Tel: 416-361-6281; *Fax:* 416-361-5736
Toll-Free: 800-563-2873
cure@canfar.com
www.canfar.com
Social Media:
www.facebook.com/group.php?gid=147646406275
National, privately funded, charitable foundation created to raise awareness in order to fund research into all aspects of HIV infection & AIDS
Elissa Beckett, Executive Director

Canadian HIV/AIDS Legal Network / Réseau juridique canadien VIH/sida
#600, 1240 Bay St., Toronto ON M5R 2A7 Canada
Tel: 416-595-1666; *Fax:* 416-595-0094
info@aidslaw.ca
www.aidslaw.ca
To promote the human rights of people living with & vulnerable to HIV/AIDS, in Canada & internationally; through research, legal & policy analysis, education, advocacy & community mobilization
Richard Elliott, Executive Director
Richard Pearshouse, Director, Research & Policy

Coalition des organismes communautaires québécois de lutte contre le sida (COCQ-SIDA)
1, rue Sherbrooke est, Montréal QC H2X 3V8 Canada
Tél: 514-844-2477; *Téléc:* 514-844-2498
info@cocqsida.com
www.cocqsida.com
Représenter les membres afin de favoriser l'émergence et le soutien d'une action concertée dans les dossiers d'intérêt commun; faire reconnaître l'expertise et l'apport des organismes communautaires et non-gouvernementaux dans la lutte contre le sida.
Hélène Légaré, Présidente
Ken Monteith, Directeur général

Healing Our Spirit
395 Railway St., Vancouver BC V6A 1A6 Canada
Tel: 604-605-8901; *Fax:* 604-605-8902
Toll-Free: 866-605-8901
info@fnes.ca
www.healingourspirit.org
To prevent & reduce the spread of HIV infection in First Nation communities & to support those affected by HIV/AIDS.
Norma Guerin, Executive Director
Leonard George, President

Maison Plein Coeur
1611, rue Dorion, Montréal QC H2K 4A5 Canada
Tél: 514-597-0554; *Téléc:* 514-597-2788
info@maisonpleincoeur.org
www.maisonpleincoeur.org

Contribuer à prévenir le VIH-SIDA, et à promouvoir la santé chez les personnes vivant avec la maladie; offrir des services sans aucune discrimination

Toronto PWA Foundation (TPWAF)
399 Church St., 2nd Fl., Toronto ON M5B 2J6 Canada
Tel: 416-506-1400; *Fax:* 416-506-1404
info@pwatoronto.org
www.pwatoronto.org
To promote the health & well-being of all people living with HIV/AIDS by providing accessible, direct & practical services

Agriculture & Farming

Agricultural Alliance of New Brunswick (AANB) / Alliance agricole du Nouveau-Brunswick
#303, 259 Brunswick St., Fredericton NB E3B 1G8 Canada
Tel: 506-452-8101; *Fax:* 506-452-1085
alliance@fermenbfarm.ca
www.fermenbfarm.ca
To promote & advance the social & economic conditions of those engaged in agricultural pursuits; to formulate & promote agricultural policies to meet changing economic conditions

Agricultural Groups Concerned About Resources & the Environment
Ontario AgriCentre, #106, 100 Stone Rd. West, Guelph ON N1G 5L3 Canada
Tel: 519-837-1326; *Fax:* 519-837-3209
agcare@agcare.org
www.agcare.org
Lilian Schaer, Executive Director
Heather Hargrave, Coordinator, Communications

Agricultural Institute of Canada (AIC) / Institut agricole du Canada
#900, 9 Corvus Crt., Ottawa ON K2E 7Z4 Canada
Tel: 613-232-9459; *Fax:* 613-594-5190
Toll-Free: 888-277-7980
office@aic.ca
www.aic.ca
Social Media: www.facebook.com/group.php?gid=14076387524
To provide the voice for national knowledge & expertise; To promote the creation, production, & delivery of safe foods & sustainable use of related national resources in Canada & beyond

Agricultural Institute of Canada Foundation (AICF)
#900, 9 Corvus St., Ottawa ON K2E 7Z4 Canada
Tel: 613-232-9459; *Fax:* 613-594-5190
Toll-Free: 888-277-7980
office@aic.ca
www.aic.ca
To enhance agriculture & the role it plays in providing Canadians with a safe, affordable, nutritious food supply
Myles Frosst, CEO
Susan Simpson, MBA, P.Ag., President
Sandy Todd, P.Ag., Treasurer

Agricultural Producers Association of Saskatchewan (APAS)
#100, 2400 College Ave., Regina SK S4P 1C8 Canada
Tel: 306-789-7774; *Fax:* 306-789-7779
info@apas.ca
www.apas.ca
To provide farmers & ranchers with a democratically elected, grassroots, non-partisan producer organization based on rural municipal boundaries
Nial Kuyek, General Manager

Alberta Association of Agricultural Societies (AAAS)
J.G. O'Donoghue Building, #200, 7000 - 113 St., Edmonton AB T6H 5T6
Tel: 780-427-2174; *Fax:* 780-422-7755
aaas@gov.ab.ca
www.albertaagsocieties.ca
To preserve & enhance the viability of agricultural societies in Alberta
Tim Carson, Chief Executive Officer
Lisa Hardy, Executive Director
Monica Bradley, Treasurer

Alberta Canola Producers Commission (ACPC)
#170, 14315 - 118 Ave., Edmonton AB T5L 4S6 Canada
Tel: 780-454-0844; *Fax:* 780-465-5473
Toll-Free: 800-551-6652
acpc@canola.ab.ca
www.canola.ab.ca
To provide leadership in a vibrant canola industry for the benefit of Alberta canola producers; to strive to improve the long-term profitability of Alberta canola producers

Alberta Institute of Agrologists
#249, 2055 Premier Way, Sherwood Park AB T8H 0G2
Tel: 780-464-9797; *Fax:* 780-464-1171
info@aia.ab.ca
www.aia.ab.ca
AIA serves as a regulatory body within the province for matters related to agrology.

Alberta Milk
1303 - 91 St. SW, Edmonton AB T6X 1H1 Canada
Tel: 780-453-5942; *Fax:* 780-455-2196
Toll-Free: 877-361-1231
cblatz@albertamilk.com
www.albertamilk.com
To promote the sustainability of the dairy industry in Alberta

Animal Nutrition Association of Canada (ANAC) / Association de nutrition animale du Canada
#1301, 150 Metcalfe St., Ottawa ON K2P 1P1 Canada
Tel: 613-241-6421; *Fax:* 613-241-7970
info@anacan.org
www.anacan.org
ANAC advocates on behalf of the livestock & poultry feed industry with government regulators & policy-makers, & works to maintain high standards of feed & food safety.

Association des jeunes ruraux du Québec (AJRQ)
65, rang 3 est, Princeville QC G6L 4B9 Canada
Tél: 819-364-5606; *Téléc:* 819-364-5006
info@ajrq.qc.ca
www.ajrq.qc.ca
Promouvoir la formation auprès de nos membres; soutenir leur sentiment d'appartenance au milieu rural
Josiane Chabot, Présidente
Annie Chabot, Directrice générale

Association québécoise des industries de nutrition animale et céréalière (AQINAC)
#200, 4790, rue Martineau, Saint-Hyacinthe QC J2R 1V1 Canada
Tél: 450-799-2440; *Téléc:* 450-799-2445
info@aqinac.com
www.aqinac.com
Développer des relations de partenariat avec tous les paliers du Gouvernement, pour mettre en marché des aliments pour animaux de grande qualitéétablir et maintenir les meilleures relations possibles entre ses membres et les divers intervenants gouvernementaux; favoriser la mise en marché d'aliments pour animaux performants et de grande qualitédiffuser toute information pertinente en agro-alimentaire et favoriser la formation continue de ses membres; collaborer avec les autres associations organismes et établissements dans la poursuite des objectifs de l'Association; négocier des avantages tangibles pour ses membres en règle; représenter ses membres en toutes matières reliées à l'approvisionnement de biens et services dans le secteur agro-alimentaire

Atlantic Dairy Council (ADC)
PO Box 9410, Stn. A, #700, 6009 Quinpool Rd., Halifax NS B3K 5S3 Canada
Tel: 902-425-2445; *Fax:* 902-425-2441
info@adcrecycles.com
www.adrecycles.com
To maintain good relations among those engaged in dairy processing & distribution industries; to provide opportunities for industry training courses; & to enable united action on any matter concerning the welfare of the dairy trade

Beef Information Centre (BIC)
Plaza 4, #101, 2000 Argentia Rd., Mississauga ON L5N 1W1 Canada
Tel: 905-821-4900; *Fax:* 905-821-4915
Toll-Free: 888-248-2333
info@beefinfo.org
www.beefinfo.org
Social Media: facebook.com/ILoveCanadianBeef
To build consumer demand for beef

British Columbia Agriculture Council
#230, 32160 South Fraser Way, Abbotsford BC V2T 1W5 Canada
Tel: 604-854-4454; *Fax:* 604-854-4485
Toll-Free: 866-522-3477
bcac@bcagcouncil.com
www.bcac.bc.ca
To provide leadership in representing, promoting, & advocating the collective interests of all agriculture producers in the province of British Colombia; To foster cooperation & a collective response to matters affecting the future of agriculture in the province; To facilitate programs & service delivery for a number of programs that benefit the industry
Andy Dolberg, Executive Director

British Columbia Dairy Foundation
3236 Beta Ave., Burnaby BC V5G 4K4 Canada
Tel: 604-294-3775; *Fax:* 604-294-8199
Toll-Free: 800-242-6455
contactus@bcdf.ca
www.bcdairyfoundation.ca
To coordinate, plan, produce & administer dairy products promotion, education & public relations programs best suited to meet the needs of the dairy industry in British Columbia.

British Columbia Fruit Growers' Association
1473 Water St., Kelowna BC V1Y 1J6 Canada
Tel: 250-762-5226; *Fax:* 250-861-9089
info@bcfga.com
www.bcfga.com
To represent fruit growers' interests in British Columbia

British Columbia Grape Growers Association (BCGA)
PO Box 2462, Stn. R, Kelowna BC V1X 6A5 Canada
Tel: 250-442-8303; *Fax:* 250-442-4076
Toll-Free: 877-762-4652
office@grapegrowers.bc.ca
www.grapegrowers.bc.ca

British Columbia Institute of Agrologists (BCIA)
#205, 733 Johnson St., Victoria BC V8W 3C7 Canada
Tel: 250-380-9292; *Fax:* 250-380-9233
Toll-Free: 877-855-9291
p.ag@bcia.com
www.bcia.com

British Columbia Milk Producers Association (BCMPA)
3236 Beta Ave., Burnaby BC V5G 4K4 Canada
Tel: 604-294-3737; *Fax:* 604-294-8199
Toll-Free: 877-462-2672
www.bcmilkproducers.ca
The British Columbia Milk Producers Association (BCMPA) is the "voice of all dairy farmers in BC" and are advocates with governments, the media, special interest groups and environmentalists, and other industry associations. Their purpose is to advance the legitimate business interest of this province's dairy farmers and promote a vibrant, sustainable industry which supplies high quality dairy products to the consumer.
Robin Smith, Executive Director

Canada Grains Council
#1215, 220 Portage Ave., Winnipeg MB R3C 0A5 Canada
Tel: 204-925-2130; *Fax:* 204-925-2132
office@canadagrainscouncil.ca
www.canadagrainscouncil.ca
To be the primary networking group for those involved in the grain industry

Canadian 4-H Council / Conseil des 4-H du Canada
Central Experimental Farm, #26, 930 Carling Ave., Ottawa ON K1A 0C6 Canada
Tel: 613-234-4448; *Fax:* 613-234-1112
www.4-h-canada.ca
Social Media: www.facebook.com/4HCanada; twitter.com/4HCanada
To inspire youth across Canada to become contributing leaders in their communities; To support the development of Canada's rural youth

Canadian Consulting Agrologists Association (CCAA) / Association canadienne des agronomes-conseils
502 - 45 St. West, 2nd Fl., Saskatoon SK S7L 6H2 Canada
Tel: 306-933-2974; *Fax:* 306-244-4497
info@ccaa.bz
www.ccaa.bz
To provide excellence in agricultural consulting; to promote standards of competency; to maintain Standards of Ethical Conduct

Canadian Co-operative Association (CCA) / Association des coopératives du Canada (ACC)
Co-operative House, #400, 275 Bank St., Ottawa ON K2P 2L6 Canada
Tel: 613-238-6711
info@CoopsCanada.coop
www.coopscanada.coop
To develop co-operatives throughout Canada & in other countries; To promote the co-operative model; To unite co-operatives from various industry sectors & regions of Canada

Canadian Federation of Agriculture (CFA) / Fédération canadienne de l'agriculture
21 Florence St., Ottawa ON K2P 0W6 Canada
Tel: 613-236-3633; *Fax:* 613-236-5749
info@cfafca.ca
www.cfa-fca.ca
To coordinate the efforts of agricultural producer organizations throughout Canada for the purpose of promoting their common interests through collective action; to promote & advance the social & economic conditions of those engaged in agricultural pursuits; to assist in formulating & promoting national agricultural policies to meet changing national & international conditions

Canadian Feed Information Centre (CFIC)
PO Box 1251, Swift Current SK S9H 3X4 Canada
Tel: 306-773-5401; *Fax:* 306-773-3955
vknipfel@sasktel.net
To collect, classify, & provide information on the composition & nutritive value of Canadian feeds; to act as Canadian representative to INFIC & as a coordinating agency of Canadian activities.

Canadian Honey Council / Conseil canadien du miel
#236, 234 - 5149 Country Hills Blvd. NW, Calgary AB T3A 5K8 Canada
Tel: 403-208-7141; *Fax:* 403-547-4317
chc-ccm@honeycouncil.ca
www.honeycouncil.ca
To promote, develop & maintain cooperation among all persons, organizations & government personnel involved with Canadian beekeeping industry

Canadian Organic Growers Inc. (COG)
323 Chapel St., Ottawa ON K1N 7Z2
Tel: 613-216-0741; *Fax:* 613-236-0743
Toll-Free: 888-375-7383
office@cog.ca
www.cog.ca
Social Media:
www.facebook.com/pages/Canadian-Organic-Growers/2772315 16329
To conduct research into alternatives to traditional chemical & energy-intensive food growing practices; To provide a resource base & a forum open to all farmers & food growers interested in alternative agriculture; To foster the goals of a decentralized, bio-regionally-based food system; To endorse practices which promote & maintain long-term soil fertility, reduce fossil fuel uses, reduce pollution, recycle wastes & conserve non-renewable resources; To assist the farmer, grower, food processor & consumer, through education & demonstration, in understanding the value of organic foods

Canadian Pest Management Association (CPMA) / Association canadienne de la gestion parasitaire (ACGP)
PO Box 1748, Moncton NB E1C 9X5
Fax: 866-957-7378
Toll-Free: 866-630-2762
cpma@pestworld.org
www.pestworldcanada.org
To provide pest management information; To act as the voice of the pest management industry throughout Canada; Upholding the association's Code of Ethics
Bill Melville, President
Karen Furgiuele-Percy, Director, Business Development
Randy Hobbs, Director, Government Affairs
Sean Rollo, Treasurer

Canadian Plowing Organization
43 Ewen Dr., Uxbridge ON L9P 1L5 Canada
Tel: 905-852-6221
info@canadianplowing.ca
www.canadianplowing.ca
To preserve the art of match plowing in Canada; to promote the efficient operation & use of farm machinery; to promote improved farm productivity & yield efficiency through proper seed bed preparation & soil management

Canadian Seed Growers' Association (CSGA) / Association canadienne des producteurs de semences
PO Box 8455, #202, 240 Catherine St., Ottawa ON K1G 3T1 Canada
Tel: 613-236-0497; *Fax:* 613-563-7855
seeds@seedgrowers.ca
www.seedgrowers.ca

Canadian Seed Trade Association (CSTA) / Association canadienne du commerce des semences (ACCS)
#505, 39 Robertson Rd., Ottawa ON K2H 8R2 Canada
Tel: 613-829-9527; *Fax:* 613-829-3530
csta@cdnseed.org
www.cdnseed.org
The Canadian Seed Trade Association (CSTA) is committed to fostering an environment conducive to research, developing, distributing, and trading seed and associated technologies; with the goal of bettering the choices and successes of our members and their customers. Their five key goals are as follows; fostering innovation; support for a science based regulatory system; increase the use of pedigreed seed; support the understanding and use of indentity preserved systems; improve market access and understanding for the trade of seed

Canadian Society for Bioengineering (CSBE) / Société canadienne de génie agroalimentaire et de bioingénierie (SCGAB)
PO Box 23101, Stn. McGillivray, Winnipeg MB R3T 5S3 Canada
Tel: 204-233-1881; *Fax:* 204-231-8282
bioeng@shaw.ca
www.bioeng.ca
To provide expertise in the areas of farm power & machinery, structures & environment, soil & water & electrical power & processing

Canadian Society of Agronomy
S.C. Sheppard, PO Box 637, Pinawa MB R0E 1L0 Canada
Tel: 204-753-2747; *Fax:* 204-753-8478
sheppards@ecomatters.com
www.agronomycanada.com
The mission of The Canadian Society of Agronomy is dedicated to enhancing cooperation and coorindation among agronomists, to recognizing significant achievements in agronomy and to providing the oppourtunity to report and evaluate information pertinent to agronomy in Canada. The goals and objects include networking; external relations and awareness; and internal communications and coordination.

Canadian Sphagnum Peat Moss Association (CSPMA) / Association canadienne Tourbe de Sphaigne
#2208, 13 Mission Ave., St Albert AB T8N 1H6 Canada
Tel: 780-460-8280; *Fax:* 780-459-0939
cspma@peatmoss.com
www.peatmoss.com
To promote the benefits of peat moss to horticulturists and home gardeners throughout North America.

Canadian Sugar Beet Producers' Association Inc. (CSBPA)
4900 - 50 St., Taber AB T1G 1T3 Canada
Tel: 403-223-1110; *Fax:* 403-223-1022
sugarmb@telusplanet.net
To represent interests of Canadian sugar beet growers on provincial & federal government levels & on an international level through the World Association of Beet & Cane Growers; to raise public profile of the beet sugar industry.
Bruce Webster, General Manager

Canola Council of Canada
#400, 167 Lombard Ave., Winnipeg MB R3B 0T6 Canada
Tel: 204-982-2100; *Fax:* 204-942-1841
admin@canolacouncil.org
www.canolacouncil.org
To enhance the Canadian canola industry's ability to profitably produce & supply seed, oil, & meal products that offer superior value to customers throughout the world.

Certified Organic Associations of British Columbia (COABC)
#202, 3002 - 32nd Ave., Vernon BC V1T 2L7 Canada
Tel: 250-260-4429; *Fax:* 250-260-4436
office@certifiedorganic.bc.ca
www.certifiedorganic.bc.ca
To maintain a credible set of organic production & processing standards
Sarah Clark, Administrator
Kristy Wipperman, Office Manager

Christian Farmers Federation of Ontario (CFFO)
7660 Mill Rd., RR#4, Guelph ON N1H 6J1 Canada
Tel: 519-837-1620; *Fax:* 519-824-1835
cffomail@christianfarmers.org
www.christianfarmers.org
A professional organization for Christian family farm entrepreneurs; a general farm organization with an interest in a broad range of agricultural, rural & social issues that impact upon the quality of the family life & family businesses of members; as a professional organization, committed to enabling members as producers, as marketers & as citizens, developing both the entrepreneurial & community leadership of members; through involvement in public policy, promotes a family farm & stewardship perspective; as a confessional organization, committed to being upfront about the Christian value system that motivates members, in order to make the wisdom of the Christian faith available to farm practice & farm policy

Coalition of Rail Shippers (CRS)
#405, 580 Terry Fox Dr., Ottawa ON K2L 4C2 Canada
Tel: 613-599-3283; *Fax:* 613-599-1295
CRS provides input to government on matters affecting Canadian, rail freight transportation.

Conseil des industriels laitiers du Québec inc. (CILQ) / Québec Dairy Council Inc.
#200, 8585, boul St-Laurent, Montréal QC H2P 2M9 Canada
Tél: 514-381-5331; *Téléc:* 514-381-6677
info@cilq.ca
cilq.ca
Regrouper les entreprises laitières industrielles du Québec qui s'occupent des différentes phases de la transformation, distribution et commercialisation du lait et des produits laitiers; promotion, protection et développement de leurs intérêts économiques, sociaux et professionnels

Coopérative fédérée du Québec (CFQ)
#200, 9001, boul de l'Acadie, Montréal QC H4N 3H7 Canada
Tél: 514-384-6450; *Téléc:* 514-384-7176
information@lacoop.coop
www.coopfed.qc.ca
La CFQ fournit aux agriculteurs, directement ou par l'entremise de ses coopératives sociétaires, une vaste gamme de biens et de services nécessaires à l'exploitation de leur entreprise, y compris des produits pétroliers; de plus, elle transforme et commercialise sur les marchés locaux et internationaux divers produits agricoles: viande porcine, volaille, etc.
Denis Richard, Président

CropLife Canada
#627, 21 Four Seasons Pl., Toronto ON M9B 6J8
Tel: 416-622-9771
www.croplife.ca
To represent Canada's plant science industry; To foster the developmment of the industry; To build Canadians' trust & appreciation for plant science innovations

Dairy Farmers of Canada (DFC) / Les Producteurs laitiers du Canada (PLC)
21 Florence St., Ottawa ON K2P 0W6 Canada
Tel: 613-236-9997; *Fax:* 613-236-0905
info.policy@dfc-plc.ca
www.dairyfarmers.ca
To coordinate action of dairy producer organizations on all issues of national scope; to collaborate with relevant agencies in elaboration of national policies of interest to Canadian dairy industry.

Dairy Farmers of Nova Scotia (DFNS)
#100, 4060 Hwy. 236, Lower Truro NS B6L 1J9 Canada
Tel: 902-893-6455; *Fax:* 902-897-9768
hboyd@dfns.ca
www.dfns.ca
To provide a regulatory and administrative service to Nova Scotia's dairy producers.
Grian Cameron, General Manager
Barron Blois, Chair

Fédération d'agriculture biologique du Québec (FABQ)
#100, 555, boul Roland-Therrien, Longueuil QC J4H 3Y9 Canada
Tél: 450-679-0530; *Téléc:* 450-670-4867
fabq@upa.qc.ca
www.fabqbio.ca
Promouvoir l'étude, la défense et le développement des intérêts économiques, sociaux et moraux de ses membres; administrer tout le programme de la mise en marchéetudier des problèmes relatifs à la production; coopérer à la vulgarisation des techniques de production biologique; renseigner le producteur sur la production et la vente de produits biologiques certifiés
Gérard Bouchard, Président

Fédération des agricultrices du Québec (FAQ)
555, boul Roland-Therrien, Longueuil QC J4H 4E7 Canada
Tél: 450-679-0530; *Téléc:* 450-463-5228
info@agricultrices.com
www.agricultrices.com
Valoriser la profession; créer un réseau entre les femmes; avoir une force politique capable de défendre les intérêts des agricultrices; prodiguer de la formation

Fédération des producteurs de bovins du Québec (FPBQ) / Federation of Québec Beef Producers
#305, 555, boul Roland-Therrien, Longueuil QC J4H 4G2 Canada
Tél: 450-679-0530; *Téléc:* 450-442-9348
fpbq@upa.qc.ca
www.bovin.qc.ca
Regrouper et défendre les intérêts professionnels et économiques des producteurs de bovins du Québec; administrer et appliquer le plan conjoint des producteurs de bovins du Québec
Gaëtan Bélanger, Secrétaire-trésorier

Fédération des producteurs de lait du Québec (FPLQ)
555, boul Roland-Therrien, Longueuil QC J4H 3Y9 Canada
Tél: 450-679-0530
fplq@upa.qc.ca
www.lait.org
Défense et promotion des intérêts professionnels et sociaux des producteurs de lait et mise en marché du lait de la ferme.

Fédération des producteurs de porcs du Québec (FPPQ)
CP 120, 555, boul Roland-Therrien, Longueuil QC J4H 4E9 Canada
Tél: 450-679-0540; *Téléc:* 450-679-0102
Ligne sans frais: 800-363-7672
fppq@upa.qc.ca
www.leporcduquebec.qc.ca
A l'ordre du jour du Plan agroenvironnemental de la production porcine on trouve; l'application de plans de fertilisation sur toutes les fermes; la diminution des rejets de phosphore et d'azote pour éviter la surfertilisation; la réduction des odeurs; l'utilisation du lisier comme matière fertilisante; mise en place d'actions collectives.
Bernard Verret, Directeur général

Flax Council of Canada
#465, 167 Lombard Ave., Winnipeg MB R3B 0T6 Canada
Tel: 204-982-2115; *Fax:* 204-942-1841
flax@flaxcouncil.ca
www.flaxcouncil.ca
To provide a central focus for industry, producers, government, research institutions & marketing organizations; to promote flax worldwide through crop, market & product development.

Horticulture Nova Scotia (HNS)
Kentville Agricultural Centre, 32 Main St., Kentville NS B4N 1J5 Canada
Tel: 902-678-9335; *Fax:* 902-678-1280
hortns@ns.sympatico.ca
www.hortns.com
To enhance collaborative efforts among members which will strengthen & provide leadership to the horticultural industry

Keystone Agricultural Producers (KAP)
#203, 1700 Ellice Ave., Winnipeg MB R3H 0B1 Canada
Tel: 204-697-1140; *Fax:* 204-697-1109
kap@kap.mb.ca
www.kap.mb.ca
To be a democratic & effective policy organization, promoting the social, economic & physical well-being of all Manitoban agricultural producers

Manitoba Institute of Agrologists (MIA)
#201, 38 Dafoe Ave., Winnipeg MB R3T 2N2
Tel: 204-275-3721; *Fax:* 204-474-7521
mia@mts.net
www.mia.mb.ca
To act in accordance with the Agrologists Act of Manitoba; To regulate the practice of agrology in Manitoba; To ensure the knowledge, competence, & integrity of institute members, in order to protect the public interest; To act as the voice of the agrology profession

Mushrooms Canada (CMGA)
7660 Mill Rd., RR#4, Guelph ON N1H 6J1 Canada
Tel: 519-829-4125; *Fax:* 519-837-0729
info@canadianmushroom.com
www.mushrooms.ca
To encourage cooperation & communication within the Canadian industry, with various levels of government, & with related organizations internationally; To promote mushroom consumption

National Farmers Union (NFU) / Syndicat national des cultivateurs
2717 Wentz Ave., Saskatoon SK S7K 4B6 Canada
Tel: 306-652-9465; *Fax:* 306-664-6226
nfu@nfu.ca
www.nfu.ca
To improve economic & social well-being of rural people & rural communities

New Brunswick Institute of Agrologists (NBIA) / L'Institut des agronomes du Nouveau-Brunswick (IANB)
PO Box 3479, Stn. B, Fredericton NB E3B 5H2 Canada
Tel: 506-459-5536; *Fax:* 506-454-7837
nbia@nbagrologists.nb.ca
www.nbagrologists.nb.ca
To maintain high competency & professional standards for those practicing agrology in New Brunswick; to uphold the NBIA Code of Ethics; to offer advice to the public about agriculture & related areas; to formulate policies & improve the agriculture & food industry

Newfoundland & Labrador Federation of Agriculture
PO Box 1045, 308 Brookfield Rd., Bldg. 4, Mount Pearl NL A1N 3C9
Tel: 709-747-4874; *Fax:* 709-747-8827
info@nlfa.ca
www.nlfa.ca
To act as the united voice of farmers in Newfoundland & Labrador; To improve the agricultural industry in Newfoundland & Labrador; To advance the economic & social conditions of those in the agricultural industry
Paul Connors, Executive Director
Matthew Carlson, Officer, Communications
Jamie Warren, Officer, Industry Development
Gerry Sullivan, Coordinator, Agriculture Awareness & Agri-Tourism
Christa Wright, Coordinator, Agriculture in the Classroom

Newfoundland & Labrador Institute of Agrologists (NLIA)
PO Box 978, Mount Pearl NL A1N 3C9 Canada
Tel: 709-772-4170
www.aic.ca/agrology/nlia.cfm
Dedicated to the professional aspects of Canadian agriculture.
Gary Bishop, P.Ag, President/Treasurer
Samir Debnath, P.Ag., Registrar

Not Far From The Tree
90 Croatia St., Toronto ON M6H 1K9 Canada
Tel: 416-363-6441
info@notfarfromthetree.org
www.notfarfromthetree.org
The group operates a residential, fruit-picking program where teams of volunteers are dispatched to harvest fruit from trees that the owners would otherwise let go to waste. The fruit is divided equally among the owners, volunteers & a local, community food distribution organization who can make good use of it.

Nova Scotia Federation of Agriculture (NSFA)
Covington Place, 332 Willow St., 2nd Fl., Truro NS B2N 5A5 Canada
Tel: 902-893-2293; *Fax:* 902-893-7063
info@nsfa-fane.ca
www.nsfa-fane.ca
To act as the voice for the agricultural community in Nova Scotia; To ensure a competitive & sustainable future for agriculture in Nova Scotia; To build financially viable, ecologically sound, & socially responsible farm businesses in the province

Nova Scotia Fruit Growers' Association (NSFGA)
Kentville Agricultural Centre, 32 Main St., Kentville NS B4N 1J5 Canada
Tel: 902-678-1093; *Fax:* 902-679-1567
www.nsapples.com
To serve the interests of tree fruit growers in Nova Scotia

Nova Scotia Institute of Agrologists (NSIA)
PO Box 550, 35 Tower Rd., Truro NS B2N 5E3 Canada
Tel: 902-893-6520; *Fax:* 902-893-6393
nsagrologists@eastlink.ca
www.nsagrologists.ca

Ontario Agri Business Association (OABA)
#104, 160 Research Lane, Guelph ON N1G 5B2 Canada
Tel: 519-822-3004; *Fax:* 519-822-8862
info@oaba.on.ca
www.oaba.on.ca
To serve & represent firms engaged in the crop inputs, country grain elevator, & feed & farm supply industy, plus related agricultural businesses operating within Ontario

Ontario Beekeepers' Association (OBA)
#476, 8560 Tremaine Rd., Milton ON L9T 4Z1 Canada
Tel: 905-636-0661; *Fax:* 905-636-0662
info@ontariobee.com
www.ontariobee.com
To coordinate & advance the beekeeping industry in Ontario

Ontario Creamerymen's Association
26 Dominion St., Alliston ON L9R 1L5 Canada
Tel: 705-435-6751; *Fax:* 705-435-6797
allistoncreamery1@bellnet.ca

Ontario Dairy Council (ODC)
6533D Mississauga Rd., Mississauga ON L5N 1A6 Canada
Tel: 905-542-3620; *Fax:* 905-542-3624
Toll-Free: 866-542-3620
info@ontariodairies.ca
www.ontariodairies.ca
To represent interests of dairy product processors, marketers & distributors in Ontario

Ontario Federation of Agriculture (OFA)
Ontario AgriCentre, #206, 100 Stone Rd. West, London ON N1G 5L3
Tel: 519-821-8883; *Fax:* 519-821-8810
Toll-Free: 800-668-3276
info@ofa.on.ca
www.ofa.on.ca
To represent farm families throughout Ontario; To champion the interests of Ontario farmers; To work towards a sustainable future for farmers

Ontario Fruit & Vegetable Growers' Association (OFVGA) / L'Association des fruiticulteurs et des maraîchers de l'Ontario
#105, 355 Elmira Rd. North, Guelph ON N1K 1S5 Canada
Tel: 519-763-6160; *Fax:* 519-763-6604
info@ofvga.org
www.ofvga.org
Dedicated to the advancement of horticulture, working proactively through effective lobbying for the betterment of the industry & producers as a whole through advocacy, research, education, communication & marketing

Ontario Institute of Agrologists (OIA)
Ontario AgriCentre, #108, 100 Stone Rd. West, Guelph ON N1G 5L3 Canada
Tel: 519-826-4226; *Fax:* 519-826-4228
Toll-Free: 866-339-7619
info@oia.on.ca
www.oia.on.ca
OIA regulates Ontario's Professional Agrologists & ensures that competencies meet a Standard of Practice within a specific scope of agrology; ensures that business is conducted within a Code of Ethics; protects the public interest; grows the agri-life science industry; contributes to the excellence of colleagues; pursues professional development to enhance knowledge, skills & experience so they can practise science of agrology with skill, integrity & transparency.

Ontario Maple Syrup Producers' Association (OMSPA)
469 Melville Rd., Consecon ON K0K 1T0 Canada
Tel: 613-399-3300; *Fax:* 613-399-3301
Toll-Free: 866-399-3301
admin@ontariomaple.com
www.ontariomaple.com
To promote Ontario maple products through research & education

Ontario Plowmen's Association (OPA)
188 Nicklin Rd., Guelph ON N1H 7L5 Canada
Tel: 519-767-2928; *Fax:* 519-767-2101
Toll-Free: 800-661-7569
admin@plowingmatch.org
www.plowingmatch.org
Provides ledership to local plowing associations; oversees the International Plowing Match; mission is to advance interest & involvement in agriculture by promoting new technologies, environmental & safety issues; preserving the history of soil cultivation

Ordre des agronomes du Québec (OAQ)
#810, 1001, rue Sherbrooke est, Montréal QC H2L 1L3 Canada
Tél: 514-596-3833; *Téléc:* 514-596-2974
Ligne sans frais: 800-361-3833
agronome@oaq.qc.ca
www.oaq.qc.ca
Assure les utilisateurs de services agronomiques et les consommateurs de la compétence, du professionnalisme et de l'engagement des agronomes et ainsi favoriser le mieux-être de la société

Prince Edward Island Federation of Agriculture (PEIFA)
420 University Ave., Charlottetown PE C1A 7Z5 Canada
Tel: 902-368-7289; *Fax:* 902-368-7204
ianm@peifa.ca
www.peifa.ca

To provide a united voice for Island farmers

Prince Edward Island Institute of Agrologists (PEIIA)
PO Box 2712, Charlottetown PE C1A 8C3 Canada
Tel: 902-892-1943; *Fax:* 902-892-0443
peiia@pei.sympatico.ca
www.peiia.ca
To safeguard the public by ensuring its members are qualified & competent to provide knowledge & advice on agriculture & related areas

Prince Edward Island Vegetable Growers Co-op Association
PO Box 1494, 280 Sherwood Rd., Charlottetown PE C1A 7N1 Canada
Tel: 902-892-5361; *Fax:* 902-566-2383
peiveg@eastlink.ca

Québec 4-H
#224, 1040, av Belvédère, Sillery QC G1S 3G3 Canada
Tel: 418-529-4705; *Fax:* 418-529-3021
4h.bc@clubs4h.qc.ca
www.clubs4h.qc.ca
To develop life skills, such as leadership, cooperation, responsibility, & independence, for the English speaking rural youth of Québec, through achievement & skill-development

Québec Farmers' Association (QFA)
#255, 555, boul Roland-Therrien, Longueuil QC J4H 4E7 Canada
Tel: 450-679-0540; *Fax:* 450-463-5291
qfa@upa.qc.ca
www.quebecfarmers.org

Ruth's Daughters of Canada
71 Elm Grove Ave., Toronto ON M6K 2J2 Canada
Tel: 416-599-7937
www.ruthsdaughters.com
The Association offers support to women who are victims of domestic violence. Its chapters center around prayer, friendship & outreach, & also develops action plans to prevent violence against women.

Saskatchewan Association of Agricultural Societies & Exhibitions (SAASE)
PO Box 31025, Regina SK S4R 8R6 Canada
Tel: 306-565-2121; *Fax:* 306-565-2079
gduck.saase@sasktel.net
www.saase.ca
To provide the forum for exchange of ideas among Association members; to provide educational opportunities for members; to address relevant issues affecting members; to provide for district, board & provincial meetings of members; to promote fair & agricultural industry; to help promote & form new societies; to provide a liaison with the extension program of University of Saskatchewan; to assist governments & universities to reach their agricultural & educational objectives

Saskatchewan Beekeepers Association (SBA)
PO Box 55, RR#3, Yorkton SK S3N 2X5
Tel: 306-743-5469; *Fax:* 306-743-5528
whowland@accesscomm.ca
www.saskatchewanbeekeepers.ca
To support Saskatchewan's beekeeping industry; To represent the province's beekeeping industry at both the provincial & national levels

Saskatchewan Canola Growers Association (SCGA)
#210, 111 Research Dr., Saskatoon SK S7N 3R2
Tel: 306-668-2380; *Toll-Free:* 800-690-5788
www.canolagrowers.ca
To communicate the concerns of canola growers in Saskatchewan; To advance the production of canola in Saskatchewan; To increase profitability for farms; To further the marketing of canola

SeCan Association / Association SeCan
#501, 300 March Rd., Kanata ON K2K 2E2 Canada
Tel: 613-592-8600; *Fax:* 613-592-9497
Toll-Free: 800-764-5487
seed@secan.com
www.secan.com
As Canada's Seed Partner, SeCan actively seeks partnerships which promote profitability in Canadian agriculture. SeCan is the largest supplier of certified seed to Canadian farmers with more than 1,000 members from coast to coast engaged in seed production, processing and marketing. They are a private, not-for-profit, member corporation with the primary goal of accessing and promoting leading genetics.

Society of Ontario Nut Growers (SONG)
RR#3, Niagara-on-the-Lake ON L0S 1J0 Canada
Tel: 905-935-9773; *Fax:* 905-935-6887
nuttrees@grimonut.com
www.songonline.ca
To promote the interests of nut growers; to encourage scientific research in the breeding & culture of nut-bearing plants suited to Ontario conditions; to disseminate information on propagation techniques & cultural practices

Union des producteurs agricoles (UPA)
#100, 555, boul. Roland-Therrien, Longueuil QC J4H 3Y9 Canada
Tél: 450-679-0530
upa@upa.qc.ca
www.upa.qc.ca
Promouvoir, défendre et développer les intérêts professionnels, économiques, sociaux et moraux des producteurs agricoles et forestiers, sans distinction de race, de nationalité, de sexe, de langue et de croyance

Vegetable Growers' Association of Manitoba (VGAM)
PO Box 984, Portage la Prairie MB R1N 3C3 Canada
Tel: 204-428-3188; *Fax:* 204-428-3245
vgam@escape.ca
To support Manitoba's vegetable growers

Western Barley Growers Association (WBGA)
Agriculture Centre, 97 East Lake Ramp NE, Airdrie AB T4A 0C3 Canada
Tel: 403-912-3998; *Fax:* 403-948-2069
wbga@wbga.org
www.wbga.org
To provide farmers with an informed & effective voice in the agriculture industry of Western Canada

Western Canadian Shippers' Coalition (WCSC)
31 Centennial Pkwy., Delta BC V4L 2C3 Canada
Tel: 604-943-8984; *Fax:* 604-943-8936

Wild Rose Agricultural Producers
#102, 115 Portage Close, Sherwood Park AB T8H 2R5 Canada
Tel: 780-416-6530; *Fax:* 780-416-6531
Toll-Free: 888-616-6530
info@wrap.ab.ca
www.wrap.ab.ca
To represent its members at the regional, provincial & national level for the benefit of agriculture; to create an atmosphere of cooperation & communication to ensure that areas of common concern among all producers are dealt with to the benefit of agriculture as a whole

Yukon Agricultural Association
#203, 302 Steele St., Whitehorse YT Y1A 2E5 Canada
Tel: 867-668-6864; *Fax:* 867-393-9566
info@yukonag.ca
www.yukonag.ca
To provide resources and opportunities to agricultural producers in the Yukon.
Al Falle, President
Rick Tone, Executive Director

Animal Breeding

Appaloosa Horse Club of Canada (ApHCC)
PO Box 940, Claresholm AB T0L 0T0 Canada
Tel: 403-625-3326; *Fax:* 403-625-2274
aphcc@appaloosa.ca
www.appaloosa.ca
To collect records & historical data relating to origin of the Appaloosa; to file records & issue certificates of registration; to preserve, improve & standardize the breed

Ayrshire Breeders Association of Canada (ABAC) / L'Associaton des éleveurs Ayrshire du Canada
4865, boul Laurier ouest, Saint-Hyacinthe QC J2S 3V4 Canada
Tel: 450-778-3535; *Fax:* 450-778-3531
info@ayrshire-canada.com
www.ayrshire-canada.com
To bring Ayrshire breeders together for the purpose of cooperating in their efforts to further the interests of the breed; promote the breeding of purebred Ayrshire cattle in Canada; establish breeding standards; cooperate with industry partners to enhance programs; program services in English & French

Canadian Angus Association (CAA) / L'Association canadienne Angus
#142, 6715 - 8 St. NE, Calgary AB T2E 7H7 Canada
Tel: 403-571-3580; *Fax:* 403-571-3599
Toll-Free: 888-571-3580
tina1@cdnangus.ca; registry@cdnangus.ca; cacp@cdnangus.ca
www.cdnangus.ca
To offer services to enhance the growth & position of the Angus breed; to maintain breed purity

Canadian Arabian Horse Registry
#113, 37 Athabascan Ave., Sherwood Park AB T8A 4H3 Canada
Tel: 780-416-4990; *Fax:* 780-416-4860
cahr@cahr.ca
www.cahr.ca
To register purebred Arabian horses in Canada; to establish standards of breeding practices; to serve the needs of Arabian horse owners

Canadian Belgian Horse Association
17150, Conc. 10, Schomberg ON L0G 1T0 Canada
Tel: 905-939-1186; *Fax:* 905-939-7547
cbha@csolve.net
www.canadianbelgianhorse.com
Promotion & betterment of the Belgian breed of horse

Canadian Bison Association (CBA) / Association canadienne du bison
PO Box 3116, #200, 1660 Pasqua St., Regina SK S4P 3G7 Canada
Tel: 306-522-4766; *Fax:* 306-522-4768
www.canadianbison.ca
To develop the bison industry; to maintain the production of bison in a natural state (no growth hormones, chemicals, feed lots, free-range management); to be the voice for commercial breeders; to assist in the formation of regulations & guidelines in commercial production & management of Canadian Plains Bison & to promote the product & awareness of the bison industry

Canadian Blonde d'Aquitaine Association
c/o Canadian Livestock Records Corp., 2417 Holly Lane, Ottawa ON K1V 0M7 Canada
Tel: 613-731-7110; *Fax:* 613-731-0704
cbda@clrc.ca
www.canadianblondeassociation.ca

Canadian Brown Swiss & Braunvieh Association / L'association canadienne de la Suisse Brune et de la Braunvieh
RR#5, Hwy. 6 North, Guelph ON N1H 6J2 Canada
Tel: 519-821-2811; *Fax:* 519-763-6582
brownswiss@gencor.ca
www.browncow.ca
To encourage, develop & regulate breeding of Brown Swiss & Braunvieh dairy cattle.

Canadian Cattle Breeders' Association (CCBA) / Société des éleveurs de bovins canadiens (SEBC)
4865, boul Laurier ouest, Saint-Hyacinthe QC J2S 3V4 Canada
Tel: 450-774-2775; *Fax:* 450-774-9775
info@cqrl.org
www.clrc.ca/canadiancattle.shtml

Canadian Cattlemen's Association (CCA)
#310, 6715 - 8 St. NE, Calgary AB T2E 7H7
Tel: 403-275-8558; *Fax:* 403-274-5686
feedback@cattle.ca
www.cattle.ca
To act as the national voice of beef producers across Canada; To produce high-quality beef products; To maintain a profitable Canadian beef industry; To use management practices that protect the health of the animal & protect the environment

Canadian Charolais Association (CCA)
2320 - 41 Ave. NE, Calgary AB T2E 6W8 Canada
Tel: 403-250-9242; *Fax:* 403-291-9324
cca@charolais.com
www.charolais.com
To be leaders in predictable beef genetics; to register, record, transfer & promote Canadian Charolais; to provide services for membership

Canadian Co-operative Wool Growers Ltd. (CCWG)
PO Box 130, 142 Franktown Rd., Carleton Place ON K7C 3P3 Canada
Tel: 613-257-2714; *Fax:* 613-257-8896
Toll-Free: 800-488-2714
ccwghq@wool.ca
www.wool.ca
To operate as a producer-owned wool marketing cooperative; To collect, grade, & market, the majority of the Canadian wool clip

to the global market; To retail farm supplies & animal health & identification products

Canadian Cutting Horse Association (CCHA)
RR#3, Innisfail AB T4G 1T8
Tel: 403-227-4444; *Fax:* 403-227-3030
connie@ccha.ca
www.ccha.ca
To promote the cutting horse, a specially trained horse to isolate or cut an individual animal from large cattle herds

Canadian Dexter Cattle Association (CDCA) / Société canadienne des bovins Dexter
2417 Holly Lane, Ottawa ON K1V 0M7 Canada
Tel: 613-731-7110; *Fax:* 613-731-0704
ron.black@clrc.ca
www.dextercattle.ca
To preserve & promote the breeding of good quality Dexter cattle in Canada

Canadian Donkey & Mule Association (CDMA)
25766 - 48 Ave., Langley BC V4W 1J2 Canada
Tel: 604-857-4990
vallen@shaw.ca
www.donkeyandmule.com
To operate registry for donkeys & recordation for mules; to promote use, well-being & protection of donkeys & mules; to assist in training & placing donkeys for disabled riding.

Canadian Fjord Horse Association
PO Box 70, Didsbury AB T0M 0W0 Canada
www.cfha.org
To operate under the Animal Pedigree Act; To assure the success of the purebred registered Norwegian Fjord Horse in Canada

Canadian Galloway Association (CGA) / Société canadienne Galloway
c/o CLRC, 2417 Holly Lane, Ottawa ON K1V 0M7 Canada
Tel: 613-731-7110; *Fax:* 613-731-0704
galloway@clrc.ca
www.galloway.ca
To promote & regulate the breeding of Galloways, Belted Galloways & White Galloways in Canada

Canadian Gelbvieh Association (CGA)
#110, 2116 - 27 Ave. NE, Calgary AB T2E 7A6 Canada
Tel: 403-250-8640; *Fax:* 403-291-5624
gelbvieh@gelbvieh.ca
www.gelbvieh.ca
To promote Gelbvieh cattle in Canada & their registration.

Canadian Goat Society (CGS) / La Société canadienne des éléveurs de chèvres
2417 Holly Lane, Ottawa ON K1V 0M7 Canada
Tel: 613-731-9894; *Fax:* 613-731-0704
cangoatsoc@travel-net.com
www.goats.ca
The Canadian Goat Society is dedicated to maintaining the integrity of our herdbooks, providing accurate evaluation programs for performance and type and promoting the responsible and humane treatment of goats.

Canadian Guernsey Association
5653 Hwy. 6, RR#5, Guelph ON N1H 6J2 Canada
Tel: 519-836-2141; *Fax:* 519-763-6582
info@guernseycanada.ca
www.guernseycanada.ca
To provide services to breeders of Guernsey dairy cattle including records, awards, promotion, sales & shows.

Canadian Hereford Association (CHA) / Association canadienne Hereford
5160 Skyline Way NE, Calgary AB T2E 6V1 Canada
Tel: 403-275-2662; *Fax:* 403-295-1333
Toll-Free: 888-836-7242
herefords@hereford.ca
www.hereford.ca
To promote the consistent & economical production of beef; To strive to meet & exceed consumer expectations for tender, juicy, & flavourful beef products, through performance measurement, genetic selection, appropriate handling, feeding, & processing

Canadian Highland Cattle Society (CHCS) / Société canadienne des éleveurs de bovins Highland
70209 Evergreen Line, RR#3, Exeter ON N0M 1S5 Canada
Tel: 519-229-6220; *Fax:* 519-229-6220
highland@chcs.ca
www.chcs.ca
To regulate & promote breeding of Highland cattle in Canada.

Canadian Icelandic Horse Federation (CIHF)
401 Ashton Cooke Rd., Enderby BC V0E 1V5 Canada
Tel: 250-838-0234
erhard@toltaway.com
www.cihf.ca
To promote & maintain the purity of the Icelandic horse; to keep record of breeding and registration of Icelandic horse under the Canadian National Livestock Record System; to promote the awareness and secure the integrity of purebred Icelandic horses.

Canadian Limousin Association (CLA)
#13, 4101 - 19th St. NE, Calgary AB T2E 7C4 Canada
Tel: 403-253-7309; *Fax:* 403-253-1704
limousin@limousin.com
www.limousin.com
To provide collective service for Limousin breeders in Canada, record registration & produce Records of Performance on all registered animals; to promote & inform producers about Limousin cattle; to develop & implement educational agricultural programs

Canadian Livestock Records Corporation (CLRC) / Société canadienne d'enregistrement des animaux
2417 Holly Lane, Ottawa ON K1V 0M7 Canada
Tel: 613-731-7110; *Fax:* 613-731-0704
clrc@clrc.ca
www.clrc.ca
To serve the Canadian seed stock industry; to be responsible to the member breed associations & Agriculture Canada for the maintenance of records, issuance of certificates, endorsement of changes of ownership, enrolment of members, registration of individuals, identification letters, collection of fees & the deposit of same into the appropriate breed association account

Canadian Maine-Anjou Association (CMAA)
5160 Skyline Way NE, Calgary AB T2E 6V1 Canada
Tel: 403-291-7077; *Fax:* 403-291-0274
cmaa@maine-anjou.ca
www.maine-anjou.ca
To encourage, develop, & regulate the breeding of Main-Anjou cattle in Canada

Canadian Milking Shorthorn Society (CMSS)
302-400 Waterloo Ave., Guelph ON N1H 7H9 Canada
Tel: 519-824-2119; *Fax:* 519-824-2566
milking.shorthorn@gmail.com
www.cmss.on.ca
To promote & encourage the development of milking shorthorn cattle.

Canadian Morgan Horse Association (CMHA) / Association des chevaux Morgan canadien inc.
PO Box 286, Port Perry ON L9L 1A3 Canada
Tel: 905-982-0060; *Fax:* 905-982-0097
info@morganhorse.ca
www.morganhorse.ca

Canadian Murray Grey Association (CMGA)
PO Box 2093, Stettler AB T0C 2L0 Canada
Tel: 403-742-3843; *Fax:* 403-742-3857
cmga@electrotel.ca
To promote the genetics of Murray Grey Beef Cattle

Canadian Palomino Horse Association (CPHA)
c/o Lorraine Holdaway, 631 Hendershott Rd., RR#1, Hannon ON L0R 1P0 Canada
Tel: 905-692-4328
canadianpalomino@gmail.com
www.clrc.ca/palomino.shtml
To develop & promote the breeding of Palomino horses in Canada; to establish standards of breeding

Canadian Percheron Association / Association canadienne du cheval Percheron
Canada
Tel: 250-379-2855; *Fax:* 250-379-2213
canadapercheron@uniserve.com
www.canadianpercherons.com
To develop & encourage the breeding of purebred Percheron horses in Canada; to establish standards of breeding; to regulate the breeding of purebred Percheron horses

Canadian Pork Council (CPC) / Conseil canadien du porc (CCP)
#900, 200 Laurier Ave. West, Ottawa ON K1P 5Z9 Canada
Tel: 613-236-9239; *Fax:* 613-236-6658
info@cpc-ccp.com
www.cpc-ccp.com
To provide a leadership role in a concerted effort involving all levels of industry & government toward a common understanding & action plan for achieving a dynamic & prosperous pork industry in Canada.

Canadian Red Poll Cattle Association / Société Canadienne des Bovins Red Poll
2417 Holly Lane, Ottawa ON K1V 0M7 Canada
Tel: 613-731-7110; *Fax:* 613-731-0704
redpoll@clrc.ca
www.clrc.ca/redpoll.shtml
To encourage development & regulation of breeding of purebred Red Poll cattle in Canada for improvement of Canadian beef cattle industry

Canadian Sheep Breeders' Association (CSBA) / La société canadienne des éleveurs de moutons
c/o Cathy Gallivan, 1489 Route 560, Deerville NB E7K 1W7 Canada
Fax: 506-328-8165
Toll-Free: 866-956-1116
office@sheepbreeders.ca
www.sheepbreeders.ca

Canadian Sheep Federation / Fédération canadienne du mouton
130 Malcolm Rd., Guelph ON N1K 1B1 Canada
Tel: 519-824-6018; *Fax:* 866-909-5360
Toll-Free: 888-684-7739
info@cansheep.ca
www.cansheep.ca
To set national policy for the sheep industry; to endeavour to further the viability, expansion & prosperity of the Canadian sheep & wool industry.

Canadian Shorthorn Association
Canada Centre Bldg., Exhibition Park, PO Box 3771, Regina SK S4P 3N8 Canada
Tel: 306-757-2212; *Fax:* 306-525-5852
info@canadianshorthorn.com
www.canadianshorthorn.com

Canadian Simmental Association
#13, 4101 - 19 St. NE, Calgary AB T2E 7C4 Canada
Tel: 403-250-7979; *Fax:* 403-250-5121
Toll-Free: 866-860-6051
cansim@simmental.com
www.simmental.com
To encourage, develop, & regulate the breeding of Simmental cattle in Canada

Canadian Swine Breeders' Association (CSBA) / L'Association canadienne des éleveurs de porcs
Bldg 54, Central Experiemental Farm, 930 Carling Ave., Ottawa ON K1A 0C6 Canada
Tel: 613-731-5531; *Fax:* 613-233-8903
canswine@canswine.ca
www.canswine.ca
To improve & promote Canadian purebred swine; to lobby on behalf of purebred swine breeders in Canada; to direct & regulate purebred swine industry; to be involved in registration & transfer of following breeds: Berkshire, British Saddleback, Chester White, Duroc, Hampshire, Large Black, Pietrain, Poland China, Spotted, Tamworth, Welsh, Yorkshire, Landrace, Lacombe, Red Wattle (registration forms can be obtained from Canadian Livestock Records Corporation).

Canadian Tarentaise Association (CTA)
PO Box 1156, Shellbrook SK S0J 2E0 Canada
Tel: 306-773-7065; *Fax:* 306-773-7577
Toll-Free: 800-450-4181
canadiantarentaise@sasktel.net
www.canadiantarentaise.com
To develop, register & promote Tarentaise cattle in Canada.

Canadian Thoroughbred Horse Society (CTHS) / Société canadienne du cheval Thoroughbred
PO Box 172, Toronto ON M9W 5L1 Canada
Tel: 416-675-1370; *Fax:* 416-675-9525
cths@idirect.com
www.cthsnational.com
To assist & afford a means for promotion of interests of those engaged in breeding of thoroughbreds; to protect members against unbusinesslike methods; to diffuse information among members & others; to secure uniformity in usage & business conditions; to determine requirements of horses as thoroughbreds by the Society; to promote, encourage & assist in livestock & agricultural exhibitions, fairs & racing; to sponsor, assist & conduct sales of thoroughbred stock; to compile statistics of the industry; to maintain efficient supervision of breeders of thoroughbred horses; to prevent, detect & punish fraud (ie. in registration of throughbreds).

Canadian Trakehner Horse Society (CTHS)
PO Box 6009, New Hamburg ON N3A 2K6 Canada
Tel: 519-662-3209; *Fax:* 519-662-3209
cantrakhsivh@golden.net
www.cantrak.on.ca

To maintain a public registry of Trakehner horses, under the Canadian Livestock Records Corporation; to promote & preserve Trakehner horses in Canada

Canadian Welsh Black Cattle Society (CWBCS) / Société Canadienne des bovins Welsh Black
c/o Canadian Livestock Records Corporation, 2417 Holly Lane, Ottawa ON K1V 0M7 Canada
Tel: 613-731-7110
kaiser.randy@gmail.com
www.canadianwelshblack.com

GENCOR
RR#5, Guelph ON N1H 6J2 Canada
Tel: 519-821-2150; *Fax:* 519-763-6582
Toll-Free: 888-821-2150
boconnor@gencor.ca
www.gencor.ca
Gencor is farmer directed AI cooperative located in South-western Ontario

Holstein Canada
PO Box 610, 20 Corporate Pl., Brantford ON N3T 5R4 Canada
Tel: 519-756-8300; *Fax:* 519-756-3502
general@holstein.ca
www.holstein.ca
To improve the Holstein breed by ascertaining the most desirable characteristics of the breed for current & prospective conditions in Canada; to prepare, maintain & make available a genealogical record of the breed; to promote the best interests of breeders & owners of Holstein cattle

Jersey Canada (JC)
#9, 350 Speedvale Ave. West, Guelph ON N1H 7M7 Canada
Tel: 519-821-1020; *Fax:* 519-821-2723
info@jerseycanada.com
www.jerseycanada.com
To represent & promote the Jersey breed & encourage market development domestically & internationally; To provide & maintain a registration system, catalogues, & pedigree information; To update classification & milk production records

National Chinchilla Breeders of Canada (NCBC)
RR#2, Norval ON L0P 1K0 Canada
ncbc@idirect.com
www.chinnet.com/misc/ncbc.html
N.C.B.C. appoints live animal Graders in every region of Canada. These Graders will visit ranches in order to appraise and grade animals, advise ranchers and thereby ensure the high quality of breeding stock required to maintain the high standards of this Canadian Association.

Nova Scotia Mink Breeders' Association
RR#4, Weymouth NS B0W 3T0 Canada
Tel: 902-387-5100
To foster better mink breeding among the members; to help secure market advantage.

The Ontario Farm Animal Council (OFAC)
#106, 100 Stone Rd. West, Guelph ON N1G 5L3 Canada
Tel: 519-837-1326; *Fax:* 519-837-3209
info@ofac.org
www.ofac.org
To support & promote the responsible production & marketing of livestock & poultry by Ontario farmers & through a variety of initiatives, to better inform the public of the excellence of animal agriculture
John Maaskant, Chairman
Crystal Mackay, Executive Director

Salers Association of Canada (SAC) / Association salers du Canada
Stn. 879, #1, 517 - 10th Ave. South, Carstairs AB T0M 0N0
Tel: 403-337-5851; *Fax:* 403-337-3143
info@salerscanada.com; salers@telusplanet.net
www.salerscanada.com
To develop & register Salers cattle

Sask Pork
Bay 2, 502 - 45th St. West, Saskatoon SK S7L 6H2 Canada
Tel: 306-244-7752; *Fax:* 306-244-1712
info@saskpork.com
www.saskpork.com
To position the Saskatchewan pork industry as a preferred supplier of high quality, competitively priced pork products for the global market.
Neil Ketilson, General Manager

Saskatchewan Stock Growers Association (SSGA)
Main Floor, Canada Centre Building, Evraz Place, PO Box 4752, Regina SK S4P 3Y4
Tel: 306-757-8523; *Fax:* 306-569-8799
ssga@sasktel.net; ssga.admin@sasktel.net
www.skstockgrowers.com
To serve, protect, & advance the interests of the beef industry in Saskatchewan; To represent the cattle industry in Saskatchewan on the legislative front

Standardbred Canada (SC)
2150 Meadowvale Blvd., Mississauga ON L5N 6R6 Canada
Tel: 905-858-3060; *Fax:* 905-858-3111
resource@standardbredcanada.ca
www.standardbredcanada.ca
To encourage & develop the breeding of Standardbred Horses

The Western Stock Growers' Association (WSGA)
Stockmen's Centre, #101, 2116 - 27 Ave. NE, Calgary AB T2E 7A6 Canada
Tel: 403-250-9121; *Fax:* 403-250-9122
wsga@shaw.com
www.wsga.ca
To support & protect livestock growers by lobbying the government on legislation & proposed new legislation; to promote environmentally sound range management practices

Animals & Animal Science

Alberta Society for the Prevention of Cruelty to Animals
10806 - 124 St., Edmonton AB T5M 0H3 Canada
Tel: 780-447-3600; *Fax:* 780-447-4748
Toll-Free: 800-455-9003
info@albertaspca.org
www.albertaspca.org
Social Media: www.facebook.com/home.php?#!/pages/Alberta-SPCA/111468822218396
To promote education of public about welfare of domestic animals & livestock; to deal with wildlife issues; to work on improving legislation; to concentrate on enforcement & education; to have every animal in Alberta humanely treated.

Alberta Veterinary Medical Association (AVMA)
Weber Centre, #950, 5555 Calgary Trail NW, Edmonton AB T6H 5P9 Canada
Tel: 780-489-5007; *Fax:* 780-484-8311
Toll-Free: 800-404-2862
brenda.betnar@abvma.ca
www.avma.ab.ca
To represent Alberta veterinarians in small animal, large animal & mixed practice as well as those employed in government, industry or other institutions

Animal Alliance of Canada (AAC) / Alliance animale du Canada
#101, 221 Broadview Ave., Toronto ON M4M 2G3 Canada
Tel: 416-462-9541; *Fax:* 416-462-9647
info@animalalliance.ca
www.animalalliance.ca
To preserve & protect all animals; to promote harmonious relationship between people, animals & the environment; to address issues including pound seizure, cosmetic & product testing, puppy mills, pet overpopulation, exotic pet trade, the fur trade, sport hunting, factory farming, animals as "entertainment"

Animal Welfare Foundation of Canada (AWF) / Fondation du bien-être animal du Canada
#343, 300 Earl Grey Dr., Ottawa ON K2T 1C1 Canada
info@awfc.ca
www.awfc.ca
The Animal Welfare Foundation of Canada is a registered charity, supported by donors and administered by a volunteer Board of Directors. The Foundation seeks to improve the quality of life for animals in this country. Since the 1960s the Foundation, an independent watchdog organization, has been at the forefront of issues of humane care of animals in Canada.
Ian Duncan, Ph.D, President & Chair
Frances Rodenberg, Honorary Secretary

Atlantic Canadian Anti-Sealing Coalition
contact@antisealingcoalition.ca
www.antisealingcoalition.ca
The Atlantic Canadian Anti-Sealing Coalition is a collection of individuals and groups from across the Atlantic Region working to end the commercial seal hunt by peaceful and legal means.

Brandon Humane Society
2200 - 17 St. East, Brandon MB R7A 7M6 Canada
Tel: 204-728-1333
info@brandonhumanesociety.ca
www.brandonhumanesociety.ca
To provide care for & homes for abused companion animals; to educate the public about the value of humane treatment of animals.

British Columbia Society for the Prevention of Cruelty to Animals
1245 East 7th Ave., Vancouver BC V5T 1R1 Canada
Tel: 604-681-7271; *Fax:* 604-681-7022
Toll-Free: 800-665-1868
info@spca.bc.ca
www.spca.bc.ca
Social Media: www.facebook.com/home.php#!/bcspca
To protect & enhance the quality of life for domestic, farm, & wild animals in British Columbia
Craig Daniell, CEO & General Manager

Calgary Humane Society
4455 - 110 Ave. SE, Calgary AB T2C 2T7 Canada
Tel: 403-205-4455; *Fax:* 403-723-6050
admin@calgaryhumane.ca
www.calgaryhumane.ca
To foster humane treatment of animals & to promote values which demonstrate respect for animals.

Canadian Animal Health Institute (CAHI) / Institut canadien de la santé animale
#102, 160 Research Lane, Guelph ON N1G 5B2 Canada
Tel: 519-763-7777; *Fax:* 519-763-7407
cahi@cahi-icsa.ca
www.cahi-icsa.ca
To work closely with allied industry groups for the betterment of Canadian agriculture; to foster & maintain a regulatory & legislative climate which will encourage member companies to develop & market useful animal health products & services; to promote the proper use of animal health & nutrition products by livestock & poultry farmers through user education information programs; to develop a public information program which enhances appreciation of the contributions the animal health & nutrition industry makes to the economy & society

Canadian Association for Laboratory Animal Science (CALAS)
#640, 144 Front St., Toronto ON M5J 2L7
Tel: 416-593-0268; *Fax:* 416-979-1819
office@calas-acsal.org; membership@calas-acsal.org
www.calas-acsal.org
To elevate standards of laboratory animal science; To promote excellence in research; To eliminate inhumane & unnecessary use of animals in research; To enhance animal welfare

Canadian Association of Animal Health Technologists & Technicians (CAAHTT) / Association canadienne des techniciens et technologistes en santé animale (ACTTSA)
339 Booth St., Ottawa ON K1R 7K1
Tel: 800-567-2862
info@caahtt-acttsa.ca
www.caahtt-acttsa.ca
To provide coordination & resources to support members in the delivery of animal health care services
Michele Moroz, President
Chantal Cormier, Vice-President

Canadian Association of Professional Pet Dog Trainers (CAPPDT)
PO Box 85, Shelburne ON L0N 1S0 Canada
Toll-Free: 877-748-7829
info@cappdt.ca
www.cappdt.ca
To further the concept of dog-friendly & humane training techniques; to provide forum whereby professional pet dog trainers can be educated, exchange & generate ideas & network with other professionals
Pat Renshaw, Membership Secretary

Canadian Association of Zoos & Aquariums (CAZA) / Association des zoos et aquariums du Canada (AZAC)
#400, 280 Metcalfe St., Ottawa ON K2P 1R7
Tel: 613-567-0099; *Fax:* 613-233-5438
Toll-Free: 888-822-2907
info@caza.ca
www.caza.ca
To promote the welfare of animals; To provide input into legislative matters & government policy affecting the zoo & aquarium industry
Robin Hale, President
Bill Peters, National Director

Greg Tarry, Manager, Special Projects
Serge Lussier, Secretary-Treasurer

Canadian Council on Animal Care (CCAC) / Conseil canadien de protection des animaux (CCPA)
#1510, 130 Albert St., Ottawa ON K1P 5G4 Canada
Tel: 613-238-4031; *Fax:* 613-238-2837
ccac@ccac.ca
www.ccac.ca
To act on behalf of the people of Canada to ensure, through programs of education, assessment & persuasion that the use of animals in Canada, where necessary for research, teaching & testing, employs physical & psychological care according to acceptable scientific standards, & to promote an increased level of knowledge, awareness & sensitivity to the relevant ethical principles

Canadian Federation of Humane Societies (CFHS) / Fédération des sociétés canadiennes d'assistance aux animaux
#102, 30 Concourse Gate, Ottawa ON K2E 7V7 Canada
Tel: 613-224-8072; *Fax:* 613-723-0252
Toll-Free: 888-678-2347
info@cfhs.ca
www.cfhs.ca
As the national voice of societies and SPCAs, the CFHS supports its member animal welfare organizations across Canada in promoting respect & humane treatment toward all animals

Canadian Kennel Club (CKC) / Club canin canadien
#400, 200 Ronson Dr., Toronto ON M9W 5Z9 Canada
Tel: 416-675-5511; *Fax:* 416-675-6506
Toll-Free: 800-250-8040
information@ckc.ca
www.ckc.ca
To provide registry services for all officially recognized breeds of purebred dogs; To provide governance for all CKC approved events; To encourage, guide, & advance the interests of purebred dogs & their responsible owners & breeders in Canada

Canadian Society of Animal Science (CSAS) / Société canadienne de science animale
c/o Agriculture & Agri-Food Canada Research Station, CP 90, #2000, rte 108 est, Sherbrooke QC J1M 1Z3
Tél: 819-565-9171; *Téléc:* 819-564-5507
info@aic.ca
www.csas.net
To provide opportunities to discuss the problems of the Canadian animal & poultry industries, with the objective of furthering advancements in these industries; To assist in the coordination of research, teaching & technology transfer related to the animal & poultry industries; To encourage publication of scientific information; To provide an annual forum for professionals in the agricultural industry to meet & discuss the most recent technological advancements in the field of animal & poultry science

Canadian Society of Zoologists (CSZ) / Société canadienne de zoologie (SCZ)
c/o Fisheries & Oceans Canada, 531 Brandy Cove Rd., St Andrews NB E5B 2L9 Canada
Tel: 506-529-5889; *Fax:* 506-529-5862
martelldj@mar.dfo-mpo.gc.ca
www.csz-scz.ca
To promote advancement & public awareness of zoology; to facilitate sharing of knowledge & ideas among all persons interested in science & practice of zoology; to organize discussions & debates of general interest

Canadian Veterinary Medical Association (CVMA) / Association canadienne des médecins vétérinaires (ACMV)
339 Booth St., Ottawa ON K1R 7K1 Canada
Tel: 613-236-1162; *Fax:* 613-236-9681
admin@cvma-acmv.org
www.canadianveterinarians.net
To represent the interests of the veterinary profession in Canada; commits to excellence within the profession & to the well-being of animals; promotes public awareness of the contribution of animals & veterinarians to society

Canadians for Ethical Treatment of Food Animals (CETFA)
PO Box 18024, 2225 - 41 Ave. West, Vancouver BC V6M 4L3 Canada
care@cetfa.com
www.cetfa.com
Social Media: facebook.com/cetfa.news
CETFA is an investigation-based, farm animal advocacy organization that promotes the humane treatment of animals raised for food. It works to educate the public about Canada's food industry by providing information on factory farming practices.
Patricia Oswald, President
Twyla Francois, Head, Investigation

College of Veterinarians of British Columbia (CVBC)
#107, 828 Harbourside Dr., North Vancouver BC V7P 3R9 Canada
Tel: 604-929-7090; *Fax:* 604-929-7095
Toll-Free: 800-463-5399
reception@cvbc.ca
www.cvbc.ca
To serve members by promoting their professional image, providing a forum for addressing issues of importance to the profession, offering continuing education & protecting their interests & rights; to protect & serve animals & animal custodians through evaluation of veterinary competence & facility quality & by enforcing the Veterinarians Act & Bylaws

College of Veterinarians of Ontario (CVO)
2106 Gordon St., Guelph ON N1L 1G6
Tel: 519-824-5600; *Fax:* 519-824-6497
Toll-Free: 800-424-2856
inquiries@cvo.org
www.cvo.org
To protect the public by regulating & enhancing the veterinary profession in Ontario

East Coast Aquarium Society (ECAS)
c/o 91 Deerbrooke Dr., Dartmouth NS B2V 1X2 Canada
www.eastcoastaquariumsociety.ca
To further the aquarium hobby and promote the practice of keeping tropical fish.
Kathryn Purdy, President
Kelly Lively Jones, Director, Membership

Fort McMurray Society for the Prevention of Cruelty to Animals
155 MacAlpine Cres., Fort McMurray AB T9H 4A5 Canada
Tel: 780-743-8997; *Fax:* 780-791-3772
spca@altech.ab.ca
www.fortmcmurrayspca.ca
Social Media:
www.facebook.com/home.php?#!/group.php?gid=43835681529
To ensure the humane treatment of all animals in the regional municipality of Wood Buffalo.

Horse Council British Columbia (HCBC)
27336 Fraser Hwy., Aldergrove BC V4W 3N5 Canada
Tel: 604-856-4304; *Fax:* 604-856-4302
Toll-Free: 800-345-8055
reception@hcbc.ca; membership@hcbc.ca; education@hcbc.ca
www.hcbc.ca
To represent members & work on behalf of their equine interests in British Columbia; To preserve equestrian use of public lands; To foster & promote participation in equine activities; To ensure the well-being of horses

Human-Animal Bond Association of Canada (HABAC) / Association canadienne sur les relations privilégiées liant les humains et les animaux
c/o 5481 Richmond Rd., Ottawa ON K2R 1G4 Canada
Tel: 613-591-6228
colbourn@rogers.com
www.habac.ca
To promote the study of human-animal interactions & their effects; to support & advance knowledge on all aspects of animal welfare & interrelationships of skills involved in the well-being of humans & animals; to clarify the value of the human-animal bond for therapeutic purposes; to encourage & promote responsible & ethical use of animals specifically related to the human-animal bond; to sponsor the Canadian Canine Good Citizen Test; to create awareness of the value of animals in our society

Humane Society Yukon
126 Tlingit Rd., Whitehorse YT Y1A 6J2 Canada
Tel: 867-633-6019; *Fax:* 867-633-2210
shelter@northwestel.net
www.humanesocietyyukon.ca
To foster a caring, compassionate atmosphere; to promote a humane ethic & responsible pet ownership; to prevent & suppress cruelty to animals.
Corey Roussell, Administrator

Jardin zoologique du Québec (JZQ)
9300, rue de la Faune, Charlesbourg QC G1G 5H9 Canada
Tél: 418-622-0312; *Téléc:* 418-646-9239
spsnq@spsnq.qc.ca
Contribuer à l'étude, à la mise en valeur et à la conservation de la faune et de son environnement.

London Humane Society (LHS)
624 Clarke Rd., London ON N5V 3K5 Canada
Tel: 519-451-0630; *Fax:* 519-451-8995
administration@londonhumane.ca
www.londonhumanesociety.ca
To monitor animal welfare & treatment in London & Middlesex County; to afford our community's animals who have been abandoned, abused, neglected or injured with a facility dedicated to their well-being; to act as their advocate relating to animal welfare; to educate our community

Manitoba Veterinary Medical Association (MVMA)
6014 Roblin Blvd., Winnipeg MB R3R 0H4 Canada
Tel: 204-832-1276; *Fax:* 204-832-1382
Toll-Free: 866-338-6862
adowd@mvma.ca
www.mvma.ca
Veterinarians working together to enhance professional excellence for the health & welfare of animals & Manitobans.

Montréal SPCA
5215, rue Jean-Talon ouest, Montréal QC H4P 1X4 Canada
Tél: 514-735-2711; *Téléc:* 514-735-7448
admin@spcamontreal.com
www.spcamontreal.com
La Société recueille, héberge et soigne les animaux errants ou abandonnés; rend les animaux perdus à leurs propriétaires; met en adoption les animaux en santédétruit de façon humanitaire ceux qui sont indésirés ou malades; inspecte et enquête sur les plaintes de cruauté.

National Retriever Club of Canada
780 East Chestermere Dr., Chestermere AB T1X 1A6 Canada
Tel: 403-248-3347
secretary@nrcc-canada.com
www.nrcc-canada.com

New Brunswick Society for the Prevention of Cruelty to Animals / Société protectrice des animaux du Nouveau-Brunswick
PO Box 1412, Stn. A, Fredericton NB E3B 5E3 Canada
Tel: 506-458-8208; *Fax:* 506-458-8209
www.spca-nb.ca
Social Media:
www.facebook.com/group.php?gid=18023383071#!/group.php?gid=4629259647
To prevent cruelty to & encourage consideration for all animals; to pursue program of humane education.

New Brunswick Veterinary Medical Association (NBVMA) / Association des médecins vétérinaires du Nouveau-Brunswick (AMVNB)
1700 Manawagonish Rd., Saint John NB E2M 3Y5 Canada
Tel: 506-635-8100
www.nbvma-amvnb.ca
To act as the regulatory body for the practice of veterinary medicine in New Brunswick; to establish standards of practice in the profession; to promote animal health & welfare; to prevent public health problems related to animal disease

Newfoundland & Labrador Society for the Prevention of Cruelty to Animals
PO Box 1533, RCAF Rd., St. John's NL A1C 5N8 Canada
Tel: 709-726-0301; *Fax:* 709-579-8089
inquiries@spcashelter.nf.ca
www.spcashelter.nf.ca; www.cfhs.ca
To act as the voice for animal welfare in Newfoundland & Labrador; To promote humane treatment toward all animals

Newfoundland & Labrador Veterinary Medical Association (NALVMA)
PO Box 818, Mount Pearl NL A1N 3C8 Canada
Tel: 709-576-2131
nalvma@nalvma.ca
www.nalvma.ca
To promote better animal health care; to educate the general public & strive towards continued excellence in veterinary medicine.

Nova Scotia Society for the Prevention of Cruelty to Animals (NS SPCA)
PO Box 38073, #200A - 11 Akerley Blvd., Dartmouth NS B3B 1X2 Canada
Tel: 902-835-4798; *Fax:* 902-835-7885
Toll-Free: 888-703-7722
animals@spcans.ca; info@spcans.ca
www.spcans.ca
Social Media:
www.facebook.com/group.php?gid=18023383071#!/nsspca
NS SPCA strives to prevent abuse & neglect of all animals in Nova Scotia. It provides leadership in humane education through outreach activities & adoption services. It also enforces laws on

animal cruelty by issuing orders, warrants & laying charges. It is a registered charity, BN: 134704741RR0001.

Nova Scotia Veterinary Medical Association
15 Cobequid Rd., Lower Sackville NS B4C 2M9 Canada
Tel: 902-865-1876; *Fax:* 902-865-2001
info@nsvma.ca
www.nsvma.ca
To license Nova Scotia veterinarians in small animal, large animal & mixed practice as well as those employed in government, industry or other institutions

Ontario Society for the Prevention of Cruelty to Animals
16586 Woodbine Ave., RR#3, Newmarket ON L3Y 4W1 Canada
Tel: 905-898-7122
info@ospca.on.ca
ontariospca.ca
Social Media: www.facebook.com/group.php?gid=96326261647
The Society provides care & shelter for animals, especially pets. It has the legal power to enforce animal cruelty laws in the province. It investigates cruelty complaints, carries out rescues, brings perpetrators to court, & advocates for humane laws. It also promotes humane education & public awareness of the humane treatment of animals. The Society operates a Wildlife Rehabilitation Centre in Midland, ON. It is a registered charity, BN: 889691044RR0002.

Ontario Veterinary Medical Association (OVMA)
#205, 420 Bronte St. South, Milton ON L9T 0H9 Canada
Tel: 905-875-0756; *Fax:* 905-875-0958
Toll-Free: 800-670-1702
info@ovma.org
www.ovma.org
To represent Ontario veterinarians in small animal, large animal & mixed practice as well as those employed in government, industry or other institutions; programs include government & public relations, humane veterinary practice, continuing education in veterinary science & practice management & direct services to members.

Ordre des médecins vétérinaires du Québec (OMVQ)
#200, 800, av Ste-Anne, Saint-Hyacinthe QC J2S 5G7 Canada
Tél: 450-774-1427; *Téléc:* 450-774-7635
Ligne sans frais: 800-267-1427
omvq@omvq.qc.ca
www.omvq.qc.ca
Protection du public; contribuer à l'amélioration de la santé et du bien-être des animaux; formation des membres; maintien de la qualité des services vétérinaires

PIJAC Canada / Conseil consultatif mixte de l'industrie des animaux de compagnie
#202, 2495 Lancaster Rd., Ottawa ON K1B 4L5 Canada
Fax: 613-730-9111
Toll-Free: 800-667-7452
information@pijaccanada.com
www.pijaccanada.com
To ensure the highest level of pet care attainable & a guarantee of a fair & equitable representation for all facets of the Canadian pet industry.

Prince Edward Island Humane Society (PEIHS)
PO Box 20022, 309 Sherwood Rd., Charlottetown PE C1A 9E3 Canada
Tel: 902-892-1190; *Fax:* 902-892-3617
info@peihumanesociety.com
www.peihumanesociety.com
To promote & provide the human treatment of animals recognizing that each is deserving of moral concern

Prince Edward Island Veterinary Medical Association (PEIVMA)
Stn. 420 University Ave., Charlottetown PE C1A 7Z5 Canada
Tel: 902-367-3757; *Fax:* 902-838-5077
admin.peivma@gmail.com
www.peivma.com
To represent PEI veterinarians in small animal, large animal & mixed practice as well as those employed in government, industry or other institutions; to licence & regulate veterinarians in PEI

Red Deer & District SPCA
#4505, 77 St., Red Deer AB T4P 2J1 Canada
Tel: 403-342-7722; *Fax:* 403-341-3147
office@reddeerspca.com
www.reddeerspca.com
Dedicated to the care & protection of companion animals & the promotion of human treatment of animals & responsible pet ownership
Julie Crawford, Executive Director

Regina Humane Society Inc.
PO Box 3143, Regina SK S4P 3G7 Canada
Tel: 306-543-6363; *Fax:* 306-545-7661
Crisis Hot-Line: 306-543-6363
rhs.administration@sasktel.net
www.reginahumanesociety.ca
Responsible for the welfare of those animals we have domesticated & upon whose environments we encroach; we are accountable for our actions as a species; we are not opposed to the legitimate & appropriate utilization of animals in the service of man; rather, we believe that man has been endowed with moral values & does not have the right to exploit or abuse any animal in this utilization process

Responsible Dog Owners of Canada (RDOC)
160 Oakridge Blvd., Nepean ON K2G 2V2 Canada
Tel: 613-228-7764
info@responsibledogowners.ca
www.responsibledogowners.ca
To promote responsible dog ownership and public safety through education and support, cultivate respect for the rights and privileges of all members of society, both dog-owning and non-dog owning, encourage and foster recognition of the contribution that canines make in society through companionship, service/assistance and therapy and assemble a strong network of responsible dog owners to ensure the restoration and preservation of a dog-friendly society.
Candice O'Connell, Chair

Saskatchewan Society for the Prevention of Cruelty to Animals
PO Box 37, 519 - 45th St. W., Saskatoon SK S7L 5Z9 Canada
Tel: 306-382-7722; *Fax:* 306-384-3425
Toll-Free: 877-382-7722
saskspca@sasktel.netsktel.net
www.sspca.ca
Social Media: www.facebook.com/group.php?gid=18023383071#!/group.php?gid=6741122026

Société québécoise pour la défense des animaux (SQDA) / Québec Society for the Defense of Animals (QSDA)
#102, 847, rue Cherrier, Montréal QC H2L 1H6 Canada
Tél: 514-524-1970
info@sqda.org
www.sqda.org
Faire connaître et respecter le monde animal par tous les moyens possibles; obtenir une législation modifiée pour la protection de toute espèce; combattre la destruction de notre faune; exposer l'aberration de l'élevage intensif; contrôler l'expérimentation animale

Toronto Humane Society (THS)
11 River St., Toronto ON M5A 4C2 Canada
Tel: 416-392-2273; *Fax:* 416-392-9978
info@torontohumanesociety.com
www.torontohumanesociety.com
Social Media: www.facebook.com/group.php?gid=8666187799
To promote the humane care & protection of all animals & to prevent cruelty & suffering

Toronto Zoo
361A Old Finch Ave., Toronto ON M1B 5K7 Canada
Tel: 416-392-5900; *Fax:* 416-392-5863
torontozoo@torontozoo.ca
www.torontozoo.com
To support the Toronto Zoo in its efforts to conserve species diversity through conservation, education, & research

Western Federation of Individuals & Dog Organizations
8160 Railway Ave., Richmond BC V7C 3K2 Canada
Tel: 604-681-1929; *Fax:* 604-277-4285
To promote & provide education & services in matters affecting the welfare of dogs & other animals; to work in conjunction with legislative bodies on matters relating to the sale, care, custody & control of dogs & other animals; to provide information & services relating to the benefits of the human-animal bond.

World Society for the Protection of Animals (WSPA) / Société mondiale pour la protection des animaux
#960, 90 Eglinton Ave. East, Toronto ON M4P 2Y3 Canada
Tel: 416-369-0044; *Fax:* 416-369-0147
Toll-Free: 800-363-9772
wspa@wspa.ca
www.wspa.ca
Social Media: www.facebook.com/group.php?gid=143249880633
To promote effective means for the prevention of cruelty to, & relief of suffering of animals in any part of the world; 15 offices worldwide

Michelle Cliffe, Communications Manager

Yukon Schutzhund Association
32 Maple St., Whitehorse YT Y1A 4A8 Canada
Tel: 867-668-6118
mattson@northwestel.net
www.kaltersberg.com/YSAInformationPage.htm
To promote dog training for the sport of Schutzhund in the Yukon Territory.
Randy Mattson, President

ZOOCHECK Canada Inc.
788 1/2 O'Connor Dr., Toronto ON M4B 2S6 Canada
Tel: 416-285-1744; *Fax:* 416-285-4670
zoocheck@zoocheck.com
www.zoocheck.com
Zoocheck works to improve wildlife protection in Canada and to end the abuse, neglect and exploitation of individual wild animals through: investigation & research; public education & awareness campaigns; capacity building initiatives; legal programs; legislative actions.

Zoological Society of Manitoba
54 Zoo Dr., Winnipeg MB R3P 2N8 Canada
Tel: 204-982-0660; *Fax:* 204-982-0673
zooquestions@zoosociety.com
www.zoosociety.com
The Zoological Society of Manitoba functions in three roles: 1. To promote the welfare and continuation of the Society; 2. To focus on the development of Assiniboine Park Zoo, making it a collection of merit and distinction; 3. To match concern with action for the preservation of earth's wildlife and their habitat
Julie Eccles, General Manager

Zoological Society of Montréal / Société zoologique de Montréal
#525, 117, rue Ste-Catherine ouest, Montréal QC H3B 1H9 Canada
Tel: 514-845-8317
contact@zoologicalsocietymtl.org
www.zoologicalsocietymtl.org
To promote & develop interest in & knowledge of wildlife; to encourage the study of biology & nature sciences; to encourage the protection of wildlife

Antiques

Antiquarian Booksellers' Association of Canada (ABAC) / Association de la librairie ancienne du Canada (ALAC)
c/o 783 Bank St., Ottawa ON K1S 3V5 Canada
info@abac.org
www.abac.org
To maintain high standards in the antiquarian book trade; to promote interest in rare books & manuscripts

Antique Automobile Club of America (AACA)
PO Box 417, 501 West Governor Rd., Hershey PA 17033 USA
Tel: 717-534-1910; *Fax:* 717-534-9101
general@aaca.org
www.aaca.org

Historic Vehicle Society of Ontario (HVSO)
c/o Canadian Transportation Museum & Heritage Village, 6155 Arner Town Line, RR#2, Kingsville ON N9Y 2E4 Canada
Tel: 519-776-6909; *Fax:* 519-776-8321
Toll-Free: 886-776-6909
info@ctmhv.com
www.ctmhv.com/The_Museum/members_gallery.htm
To collect, restore & display vehicles, buildings & artifacts that serve to demonstrate the founding settlement of Essex County; to preserve the past to enhance the future.
Michelle Staley, Curator/Admin. Director

Manitoba Antique Association
PO Box 2881, Stn. M, Winnipeg MB R3C 4B4 Canada
manitobaantique@gmail.com
www.manitobaantiqueassociation.com
To preserve & restore antiques; To promote the admiration of all antiques

Vintage Locomotive Society Inc.
PO Box 33021, RPO Polo Park, Winnipeg MB R3G 3N4 Canada
Tel: 204-832-5259; *Fax:* 866-751-2348
info@pdcrailway.com
www.pdcrailway.com
To collect, restore for operation & maintain steam locomotives & rolling stock of early part of twentieth-century; to provide source of historical information relating to origin & past operation of acquired equipment & buildings

Archaeology

Archaeological Society of Alberta (ASA)
97 Eton Rd. West, Lethbridge AB T1K 4T9 Canada
Tel: 403-381-2655
jnermc@telus.net
www.arkyalberta.com
To promote the regulations of the Alberta Historical Act & to disseminate archaeological information by means of publications & seminars
Jim McMurchy, Executive Sec.-Treas.

Archaeological Society of British Columbia (ASBC)
PO Box 520, Stn. Bentall, Vancouver BC V6C 2N3 Canada
Tel: 604-822-2567; *Fax:* 604-822-6161
asbc.president@gmail.com
www.asbc.bc.ca
To protect the archaeological heritage of British Columbia; to promote public understanding of the scientific approach to archaeology; to encourage government to preserve archaeological & pre-historic sites

Association des archéologues du Québec (AAQ)
CP 322, Succ. Haute-Ville, Québec QC G1R 4P8 Canada
info@archeologie.qc.ca
www.archeologie.qc.ca
Définir les standards de la profession; veiller à la saine gestion et la mise en valeur du patrimoine archéologique à cause d'une éthique exemplaire et de la qualité de ses membres; agir comme interlocuteur privilégié pour tout ce qui regarde la question archéologique auprès des gouvernements et des organismes, privés ou publics, qui ont à coeur la préservation de notre patrimoine collectif
Richard Fiset, Président

Canadian Archaeological Association (CAA) / Association d'archéologie canadienne
c/o Jack Brink, Royal Alberta Museum, 12845 - 102 Ave., Edmonton AB T5N 0M6 Canada
Tel: 780-453-9151
president@canadianarchaeology.com
www.canadianarchaeology.com
To publish & disseminate archaeological knowledge in Canada; to encourage archaeological research & conservation efforts; to promote cooperation among archaeological societies & agencies
Jack Brink, President
Eric Damkjar, Vice-President
Jeff Hunston, Secretary-Treasurer

Nova Scotia Archaeology Society (NSAS)
PO Box 36090, Halifax NS B3J 3S9 Canada
Tel: 902-453-4972
dkelman@crmgroup.ca
www.novascotiaarchaeologysociety.com
To promote the preservation of Nova Scotia's archaeological sites & resources
Darryl Kelman, President
Terry J. Deveau, Vice-President
Robyn Crook, Secretary
Matt Munro, Treasurer

The Ontario Archaeological Society Inc.
#102, 1444 Queen St. East, Toronto ON M4L 1E1 Canada
Tel: 416-406-5959; *Fax:* 416-406-5959
Toll-Free: 888-733-0042
oasociety@ontarioarchaeology.on.ca
www.ontarioarchaeology.on.ca
To preserve, promote, investigate, record & publish an archaeological record of the province of Ontario

Saskatchewan Archaeological Society (SAS)
#1, 1730 Quebec Ave., Saskatoon SK S7K 1V9 Canada
Tel: 306-664-4124; *Fax:* 306-665-1928
saskarchsoc@sasktel.net
www.saskarchsoc.ca
To promote the study, preservation & appropriate utilization of the historic & pre-historic archaeological sites & artifacts of the province; to promote & carry out educational programs
Talina Cyr-Steenkamp, Executive Director
Belinda Riehl-Fitzsimmons, Administrative Assistant

Save Ontario Shipwrecks (SOS)
PO Box 2389, Blenheim ON N0P 1A0 Canada
Tel: 519-676-4110; *Fax:* 519-676-7058
rjequip@on.aibn.com
www.saveontarioshipwrecks.on.ca
Social Media: www.facebook.com/group.php?gid=68638569592
To promote & preserve Ontario's marine heritage
Michael Hill, President
Jonathan Ferguson, Secretary

Underwater Archaeological Society of British Columbia (UASBC)
c/o Vancouver Maritime Museum, 1905 Ogden Ave., Vancouver BC V6J 1A3 Canada
Tel: 604-942-9908; *Fax:* 604-980-0358
uasbc@uasbc.com
www.uasbc.com
To promote the science of underwater archaeology; to conserve, preserve & protect the maritime heritage lying beneath our coastal & inland waters

Architecture

Alberta Association of Architects (AAA)
Duggan House, 10515 Saskatchewan Dr., Edmonton AB T6E 4S1 Canada
Tel: 780-432-0224; *Fax:* 780-439-1431
info@aaa.ab.ca
www.aaa.ab.ca
To regulate the practice of architecture & interior design in Alberta for the protection of the public & the administration of the profession; to bring architects together in order to channel the energies of unique, creative individuals spiritually committed to a superior architecture

Architects Association of Prince Edward Island (AAPEI)
PO Box 1766, Charlottetown PE C1A 7N4 Canada
Tel: 902-566-3699; *Fax:* 902-566-1235
info@aapei.com
www.aapei.com

Architects' Association of New Brunswick (AANB) / Association des architectes du Nouveau-Brunswick
PO Box 5093, Sussex NB E4E 5L2
Tel: 506-433-5811; *Fax:* 506-432-1122
inquiries@aanb.org
www.aanb.org
To govern & regulate persons in New Brunswick who offer architectural services; To advance & maintain the standards of architecture in New Brunswick

The Architectural Conservancy of Ontario (ACO)
#403, 10 Adelaide St. East, Toronto ON M5C 1J3 Canada
Tel: 416-367-8075; *Fax:* 416-367-8630
Toll-Free: 877-264-8937
manager@arconserv.ca
www.arconserv.ca
To preserve buildings & structures of architectural merit & places of natural beauty or interest

Architectural Institute of British Columbia (AIBC)
#100, 440 Cambie St., Vancouver BC V6B 2N5 Canada
Tel: 604-683-8588; *Fax:* 604-683-8568
Toll-Free: 800-667-0753
info@aibc.ca
www.aibc.ca
To regulate the profession of architecture in accordance with the Architects Act; to promote & increase the knowledge, skill & proficiency of its members in all things relating to the practice of architecture; to advance & maintain high standards of qualification & professional ethics; to promote public appreciation of architecture, allied arts, sciences & the professions

Association des Architectes en pratique privée du Québec (AAPPQ) / Association of Architects in Private Practice of Québec
#425, 1980, rue Sherbrooke ouest, Montréal QC H3H 1E8 Canada
Tél: 514-937-4140; *Téléc:* 514-937-2329
aappq@aappq.qc.ca
www.aappq.qc.ca
Organiser en association et représenter les architectes en pratique privée du Québec; étudier, défendre et développer les intérêts économiques, sociaux et moraux de ses membres; promouvoir et développer l'utilisation des services de l'architecte en pratique privée au Québec ou ailleurs

Association of Architectural Technologists of Ontario (AATO)
#207, 1515 Matheson Blvd. East, Mississauga ON L4W 2P5 Canada
Tel: 905-238-7594; *Fax:* 905-238-6344
Toll-Free: 866-805-2286
aato@bellnet.ca
aato.on.ca
The Association is a government-legislated, licensing & regulatory body for Architectural Technologists & Technicians in the province. It strives to maintain the standard of professional conduct of its members, as well as advocates to all levels of government on behalf of them & the industry.

Canadian Architectural Certification Board (CACB) / Conseil canadien de certification en architecture (CCCA)
#710, 1 Nicholas St., Ottawa ON K1N 7B7 Canada
Tel: 613-241-8399; *Fax:* 613-241-7991
info@cacb.ca
www.cacb.ca
The Canadian Architectural Certification Board fulfills two seperate but related mandates: 1- Administer a program of accreditation of the Canadaian schools of architecture in accordance with "Conditions and Procedures for Accreditation" approved by the CCAC and the CCUSA and 2- Administer a program of certification of the educational qualifications of indivdual applicants in accordance withe criteria contained within the "Education Standard" approved by the CCAC.
Gordon Richards, AIBC, MRAIC, President
Myriam Blais, OAQ, Vice-President

Design Exchange (DX)
Toronto Dominion Centre, PO Box 18, 234 Bay St., Toronto ON M5K 1B2 Canada
Tel: 416-363-6121; *Fax:* 416-368-0684
info@dx.org; membership@dx.org; education@dx.org; media@dx.org
www.dx.org
To provide a design museum & centre for design research & education; To raise awareness & understanding of design
Catherine Molnar, Coordinator, Professional Programs
Daniela Bryson, Coordinator, Exhibition

Manitoba Association of Architects (MAA)
137 Bannatyne Ave. East, 2nd Fl., Winnipeg MB R3B 0R3 Canada
Tel: 204-925-4620; *Fax:* 204-925-4624
info@mbarchitects.org
www.mbarchitects.org
In fulfilling its mandate, the MAA serves to protect the public interest and advance the profession of architecture. The MAA works with its membership and other stakeholders to establish high entry standards to the profession and maintain high standards of practice.

Newfoundland Association of Architects
PO Box 5204, Stn. A, 7 Downing St., St. John's NL A1C 5V5 Canada
Tel: 709-726-8550; *Fax:* 709-726-1549
nlaa@newfoundlandarchitects.com
www.newfoundlandarchitects.com
Supporting architecture and architects in Newfoundland and Labrador.

Northwest Territories Association of Architects (NWTAA)
Administrative Office, Northern Frontier Visitors Centre, PO Box 1394, 4807 - 49th St., Yellowknife NT X1A 2P1
Tel: 867-766-4216; *Fax:* 867-920-2652
www.nwtaa.ca
To maintain the Register of Architects, in accordance with the NWT Architects Act
Deleigh Rausch, Executive Director
Darrell Vikse, Registrar
Harriet Burdett-Moulton, Chair, Registration & Licence Review
Stephen Cumming, Chair, Practice Review
Wayne Guy, Chair, Complaint Review
Kris Schlagintweit, Chair, Continuing Education

Nova Scotia Association of Architects (NSAA)
1359 Barrington St., Halifax NS B3J 1Y9 Canada
Tel: 902-423-7607; *Fax:* 902-425-7024
info@nsaa.ns.ca
www.nsaa.ns.ca
To administer the practice of architecture in Nova Scotia

Ontario Association of Architects (OAA)
111 Moatfield Dr., Toronto ON M3B 3L6
Tel: 416-449-6898; *Fax:* 416-449-5756
Toll-Free: 800-565-2724
oaamail@oaa.on.ca; practiceadvisor@oaa.on.ca (Practice Advisor)
www.oaa.on.ca
To operate in accordance with the Government of Ontario's Architects Act; To serve & protect the public interest by promoting & increasing the knowledge, skill, & proficiency of members

Ordre des architectes du Québec (OAQ)
#100, 1825, boul René-Lévesque ouest, Montréal QC H3H 1R4 Canada
Tél: 514-937-6168; *Téléc:* 514-933-0242
Ligne sans frais: 800-599-6168
info@oaq.com
www.oaq.com

Sa principale fonction est d'assurer la protection du public en régissant l'exercice de la profession d'architecte au Québec.

Royal Architectural Institute of Canada (RAIC) / Institut royal d'architecture du Canada
#330, 55 Murray St., Ottawa ON K1N 5M3 Canada
Tel: 613-241-3600; *Fax:* 613-241-5750
info@raic.org
www.raic.org
To represent Canadian architects nationally & internationally; to foster public awareness & appreciation of architecture; to engage in architectural research & education; to lobby government on architectural issues

Saskatchewan Association of Architects (SAA)
#200, 642 Broadway Ave., Saskatoon SK S7N 1A9
Tel: 306-242-0733; *Fax:* 306-664-2598
www.saskarchitects.com
To regulate the profession of architecture in Saskatchewan, in order to ensure the protection of the public interest; To advance the profession of architecture in the province; To ensure that high standards for practice & conduct are followed

Society for the Study of Architecture in Canada (SSAC) / Société pour l'étude de l'architecture au Canada (SEAC)
PO Box 2302, Stn. D, Ottawa ON K1P 5W5 Canada
info@canada-architecture.org
canada-architecture.org
To promote the study of Canadian architecture including an examination of both historical & cultural issues relating to buildings, districts, cities & the cultural landscapes; to encourage the collection & preservation of Canada's architectural records; to encourage preservation of the built environment

Arts

Alberta Foundation for the Arts (AFA)
10708 - 105 Ave., Edmonton AB T5H 0A1 Canada
Tel: 780-427-9968; *Fax:* 780-422-1162
www.affta.ab.ca
Social Media: www.facebook.com/AlbertaFoundationfortheArts
To create the best possible climate for the arts in Alberta; provides grant funding to artists, art organizations & cultural industries; manages an extensive art collection featuring Alberta artists

Alliance for Arts & Culture
#100, 938 Howe St., Vancouver BC V6Z 1N9 Canada
Tel: 604-681-3535; *Fax:* 604-681-7848
info@allianceforarts.com
www.allianceforarts.com
To project a strong voice for the local arts community; to promote the activities of the arts through a variety of programs, services & marketing strategies; & to increase public awareness of & accessibility to the arts & culture
Amir Ali Alibhai, Executive Director
Minna Schendlinger, President

Assembly of BC Arts Councils
PO Box 92, Stn. A, Nanaimo BC V9R 5G6 Canada
Tel: 250-754-3388; *Fax:* 250-754-3390
Toll-Free: 888-315-2288
info@assemblybcartscouncils.ca
www.assemblybcartscouncils.ca
To promote & advance the role of arts & culture in building community; to work with community based organizations in furthering the impact & contribution of the arts locally, regionally & province-wide

Canadian Artists' Representation (CARFAC) / Le Front des artistes canadiens
#250, 2 Daly Ave., Ottawa ON K1N 6E2
Tel: 613-233-6161; *Fax:* 613-233-6162
Toll-Free: 866-344-6161
carfac@carfac.ca
www.carfac.ca
To act as a national voice for Canada's professional visual artists; To promote a socio-economic climate that is conducive to the production of visual arts

Canadian Arts Presenting Association (CAPACOA) / Association canadienne des organismes artistiques
#200, 17 York St., Ottawa ON K1N 9J6 Canada
Tel: 613-562-3515; *Fax:* 613-562-4005
mail@capacoa.ca
www.capacoa.ca
To promote the development of the presentation of the arts in Canada; to promote & encourage greater knowledge & appreciation of the presentation of the performing arts; to encourage touring of artists & attractions throughout all regions of Canada; to provide information on artists & attractions touring regionally & nationally; to assist presenters of the arts in Canada with coordination of bookings; to provide opportunities for professional development of presenters in Canada; to promote communication & understanding between presenters of the arts in Canada; to provide forum for exchange of views concerning presentation of the performing arts generally; to provide information on regional & federal policies which relate to presentation of the arts; to provide the opportunity to make contacts nationwide

Canadian Celtic Arts Association
c/o Jean Talman, 91 Stafford St., Toronto ON M6J 3R1 Canada
jean.talman@utoronto.ca
To promote Celtic culture; to serve as a link between the diverse Celtic communities in Canada
Jean Talman, President & Membership Secretary
Donald Gillies, Treasurer

Canadian Conference of the Arts (CCA) / Conférence canadienne des arts
#406, 130 Slater St., Ottawa ON K1P 6E2 Canada
Tel: 613-238-3561; *Fax:* 613-238-4849
info@ccarts.ca
www.ccarts.ca
To ensure the lively existence & continued growth of the arts & the cultural industries in Canada; to increase the Canadian materials (works created, produced, & performed by Canadians) available to Canadians; to improve the quality of life for all artists & arts groups; to unite members to work for interests of all artists & whole cultural community; to work closely with other arts service organizations to formulate policies & advocate their adoption by governments.

Chorale Les Voix de la Vallée du Cuivre de Chibougamau inc.
CP 128, Chibougamau QC G8P 2K6 Canada
Tél: 418-748-7811
Linda Marceau

Conseil des arts et des lettres du Québec
79, boul. René Lévesque est, 3e étage, Québec QC G1R 5N5 Canada
Tél: 418-643-1707; *Téléc:* 418-643-4558
Ligne sans frais: 800-897-1707
info@calq.gouv.qc.ca
www.calq.gouv.qc.ca
Soutenir, dans toutes les régions du Québec, la création, l'expérimentation et la production dans les domaines des arts visuels, des métiers d'art, de la littérature, du théâtre, de la musique, de la danse, des arts du cirque, des arts multidisciplinaires, des arts médiatiques et de la recherche architecturale et d'en favoriser le rayonnement au Québec, au Canada et à l'étranger
Yvan Gauthier, Président/Directeur général

Council for Business & the Arts in Canada (CBAC) / Conseil pour le monde des affaires et des arts du Canada
#903, 165 University Ave., Toronto ON M5H 3B8 Canada
Tel: 416-869-3016; *Fax:* 416-869-0435
info@businessforarts.org
www.businessforarts.org
To make the partnership between business & the arts more effective in supporting the nation's creative minds.

Federation of Canadian Artists (FCA)
1241 Cartwright St., Vancouver BC V6H 4B7
Tel: 604-681-2744; *Fax:* 604-681-2740
fcaoffice@artists.ca (Education) fcaadmin@artists.ca (Membership)
www.artists.ca
To share & promote the visual arts

Governor General's Performing Arts Awards Foundation (GGPAAF) / Les Prix du Gouverneur Général pour les arts de la scène
#804, 130 Albert St., Ottawa ON K1P 5G4 Canada
Tel: 613-241-5297; *Fax:* 613-238-4849
nominations@ggpaaf.com
www.bell.ca/ggawards
To celebrate outstanding lifetime achievement in various performing arts disciplines in Canada; To raise awareness of the contributions of Canadian performing artists; To foster awareness of Francophone artists in English Canada & Anglophone artists in French Canada; To inspire future performing artists
Deborah Hennig, Executive Director
Peter Herrndorf, President/CEO
Harold Redekopp, Co-Chair
Albert Millaire, Co-Chair

Manitoba Arts Council (MAC) / Conseil des arts du Manitoba (CAM)
#525, 93 Lombard Ave., Winnipeg MB R3B 3B1 Canada
Tel: 204-945-2237; *Fax:* 204-945-5925
Toll-Free: 866-994-2787
info@artscouncil.mb.ca
www.artscouncil.mb.ca
An arms-length agency of the provincial government dedicated to artistic excellence; offers a broad based grant program for professional artists & arts organizations; promotes, preserves, supports & advocates for the arts as essential to the quality of life of all people of Manitoba.
Douglas Riske, Executive Director

Newfoundland & Labrador Arts Council (NLAC)
PO Box 98, 1 Springdale St., St. John's NL A1C 5H5 Canada
Tel: 709-726-2212; *Fax:* 709-726-0619
Toll-Free: 866-726-2212
nlacmail@nfld.net
www.nlac.nf.ca
To foster & promote the arts of the province; to carry on financial assistance programs for individual artists & arts groups; to work with the government & the community for development in the arts
Reg Winsor, Executive Director
John Doyle, Chair

Northwest Territories Arts Council
c/o NWT Education, Culture & Employment, PO Box 1320, Stn. Main, Yellowknife NT X1A 2L9 Canada
Tel: 867-920-6370; *Fax:* 867-873-0205
boris_atamanenko@gov.nt.ca
pwnhc.learnnet.nt.ca/artscouncil
To promote and encourage the arts in the Northwest Territories.

Ontario Arts Council (OAC) / Conseil des arts de l'Ontario
151 Bloor St. West, 5th Fl., Toronto ON M5S 1T6 Canada
Tel: 416-961-1660; *Fax:* 416-961-7796
Toll-Free: 800-387-0058
info@arts.on.ca
www.arts.on.ca
Social Media: www.facebook.com/group.php?gid=2408704879
Ontario's primary funding body for professional arts activity; promotes & assists the development of the arts & artists; offers 50+ funding programs
John Brotman, Executive Director

Organization of Saskatchewan Arts Councils (OSAC)
1102 - 8th Ave., Regina SK S4R 1C9 Canada
Tel: 306-586-1250; *Fax:* 306-586-1550
info@osac.sk.ca
www.osac.sk.ca
To assist the membership in their endeavors to develop, promote & present the visual arts &/or performing arts

Performing Arts NB, Inc. (PANB)
Brunswick Sq., 3rd Level, 39 King St., Saint John NB E2L 4W3 Canada
Tel: 506-635-8019; *Fax:* 506-657-7832
performingartsnb@nb.aibn.com
performingartsnb.ca
To achieve the vision of New Brunswick as a place where all residents attend a diversity of quality, live performances in their own community; all students attend performances in their own school by performing artists; artists residing in New Brunswick find a supportive arts community & the resources necessary to establish a career in the performing arts in New Brunswick & beyond; maintain a resource centre; assume an advocacy for the performing arts in the community

Prince Edward Island Council of the Arts (PEICA)
115 Richmond St., Charlottetown PE C1A 1A7 Canada
Tel: 902-368-4410; *Fax:* 902-368-4418
Toll-Free: 888-734-2784
info@peica.ca
www.peiartscouncil.com
Social Media: www.facebook.com/group.php?gid=6930656373
To make the Arts integral to the lives of all Prince Edward Islanders; through advocacy, education, distribution of funds, management of the Arts Guild & program of prizes & awards.

SaskCulture Inc.
#600, 2220 - 12th Ave., Regina SK S4P 0M8 Canada
Tel: 306-780-9284; *Fax:* 306-780-9252
saskculture.info@saskculture.sk.ca
www.saskculture.sk.ca
To bring together organizations which work to further the course of culture
Rose Gilks, General Manager
Diane Ell, Communications Manager

Scarborough Arts Council (SAC)
1859 Kingston Rd., Toronto ON M1N 1T3
Tel: 416-698-7322; *Fax:* 416-698-7972
office@scarborougharts.com
www.scarborougharts.com
To develop all arts disciplines in Scarborough, Ontario; To link artists & the community

Automotive

Alberta Motor Association (AMA)
PO Box 8180, Stn. South, 10310 - 39A G.A. MacDonald Ave., Edmonton AB T6H 5X9 Canada
Tel: 780-430-5555; *Toll-Free:* 800-642-3810
www.ama.ab.ca/cps/rde/xchg/ama

Association des propriétaires d'autobus du Québec (APAQ)
#107, 225, boul Charest est, Québec QC G1K 3G9 Canada
Tél: 418-522-7131; *Téléc:* 418-522-6455
apaq@apaq.qc.ca
www.apaq.qc.ca
Défendre les intérêts des enterprises offrant des services de transport collectif de personnes par autobus et autocars

Association des spécialistes du pneus du Québec inc. (ASPQ) / Québec Tire Specialists Association Inc.
587, ch Rhéaume, Saint-Michel QC J0L 2J0 Canada
aspq@qc.aira.com
www.aspq.ca/aspq/

Atlantic Recreation Vehicle Dealers Association (ARVDA)
PO Box 9410, Stn. A, Halifax NS B3K 5S3 Canada
Tel: 902-425-2445; *Fax:* 902-425-2441
matthew@hamblys.ca
www.arvda.ca
Wayne Hambly, President

Automobile Journalists Association of Canada (AJAC) / Association des journalistes automobile du Canada
PO Box 398, Stn. Main, Cobourg ON K9A 4L1 Canada
Toll-Free: 800-361-1516
beth@ajac.ca
www.ajac.ca
Association of professional automotive experts who report on new vehicles and new industry trends in various print and broadcast media.

Automobile Protection Association (APA) / Association pour la protection automobile
292, boul St. Joseph ouest, Montréal QC H2V 2N7 Canada
Tel: 514-272-5555; *Fax:* 514-273-0797
apamontreal@apa.ca
www.apa.ca
To inform & represent the public on major automobile-related issues

Automotive Industries Association of Canada (AIAC) / Association des industries de l'automobile du Canada
1272 Wellington St. West, Ottawa ON K1Y 3A7 Canada
Fax: 613-728-6021
Toll-Free: 800-808-2920
info.aia@aiacanada.com
www.aiacanada.com
A national trade association representing the automotive aftermarket industry in Canada & with a mandate to promote, educate & represent members

Automotive Parts Manufacturers' Association (APMA)
#801, 10 Four Seasons Pl., Toronto ON M9B 6H7 Canada
Tel: 416-620-4220; *Fax:* 416-620-9730
info@apma.ca
www.apma.ca
To promote the manufacture in Canada of automotive parts, systems, components, materials, tools, equipment & supplies, & also the provision of services used in the automotive industry & in particular for the original equipment market; to engage in activities in support of the welfare of the members of the Association

Automotive Retailers Association of British Columbia
#1, 8980 Fraserwood Ct., Burnaby BC V5J 5H7 Canada
Tel: 604-432-7987; *Fax:* 604-432-1756
info@ara.bc.ca
www.ara.bc.ca
To enhance the image & competitive status of association members throughout BC & ensure high quality service to protect the road safety of the motoring public

BCADA - The New Car Dealers of BC
#70, 10551 Shellbridge Way, Richmond BC V6X 2W9 Canada
Tel: 604-214-9964; *Fax:* 604-214-9965
info@newcardealers.ca
www.newcardealers.ca
To promote benefits & heighten awareness of issues of interest to members

British Columbia Automobile Association (BCAA)
4567 Canada Way, Burnaby BC V5G 4T1 Canada
Tel: 604-268-5500; *Fax:* 604-268-5562
Toll-Free: 800-663-1956
www.bcaa.com
BCAA is a not-for-profit organization providing motoring, travel & insurance services to members in British Columbia and the Yukon.

CAA Manitoba
PO Box 1400, 870 Empress St., Winnipeg MB R3C 2Z3 Canada
Tel: 204-262-6161
contact@caamanitoba.com
www.caamanitoba.com

CAA-Québec
444, rue Bouvier, Québec QC G2J 1E3 Canada
Tél: 418-624-2424; *Téléc:* 418-624-3297
Ligne sans frais: 800-463-7232
info@caa-quebec.qc.ca
www.caaquebec.com
Veut assurer la sécurité et paix d'esprit à chacun de ses membres ainsi qu'à ses clients en leur offrant des services et des produits de très haute qualité dans les domaines de l'automobile, du voyage, de l'habitation et des services financiers.

Canadian Automobile Association (CAA) / Association canadienne des automobilistes
National Office, #200, 1145 Hunt Club Rd., Ottawa ON K1V 0Y3 Canada
Tel: 613-247-0117; *Fax:* 613-247-0118
info@national.caa.ca
www.caa.ca
To promote, develop & implement programs & information relating to the rights, responsibilities & needs of the motorist as a consumer

Canadian Automobile Association Maritimes
378 Westmorland Rd., Saint John NB E2J 2G4 Canada
Tel: 506-634-1400; *Fax:* 506-653-9500

Canadian Automobile Association Niagara
3271 Schmon Pkwy., Thorold ON L2V 4Y6 Canada
Tel: 905-984-8585; *Fax:* 905-688-0289
www.caa.niagara.net
Robert J. Spence, President & CEO

Canadian Automobile Association North & East Ontario
c/o Administration Centre, PO Box 8350, Stn. T CSC, Ottawa ON K1G 3T2 Canada
Tel: 613-820-1890; *Fax:* 613-820-4646
Toll-Free: 800-267-8713
contactcaa@caaneo.on.ca
www.caaneo.ca
To deliver automotive, travel, insurance & related services to members & advocate on their behalf

Canadian Automobile Association North & East Ontario
PO Box 8350, Stn. T, Ottawa ON K1G 3T2 Canada
Tel: 613-820-1890; *Fax:* 613-820-4646
contactcaa@caaneo.on.ca
www.caaneo.on.ca

Canadian Automobile Association Saskatchewan
200 Albert St. North, Regina SK S4R 5E2 Canada
Tel: 306-791-4314; *Fax:* 306-949-4461
caa.admin@caasask.sk.ca
www.caasask.sk.ca
To guarantee excellent emergency road assistance, travel, & insurance services; To provide services, products, programs, & representations to government in order to meet the needs of members, clients, & employees

Canadian Automobile Association South Central Ontario
60 Commerce Valley Dr. East, Thornhill ON L3T 7P9 Canada
Tel: 905-771-3000; *Fax:* 905-771-3101
Toll-Free: 866-988-8878
info@caasco.ca
www.caasco.ca
To enrich the driving experience of members by providing travel, insurance & automotive services & information

Canadian Automobile Association South Central Ontario
60 Commerce Valley Dr. East, Thornhill ON L3T 7P6 Canada
Tel: 905-771-3000; *Fax:* 905-771-3101
Toll-Free: 866-988-8878
info@caasco.ca
www.caasco.ca

Canadian Automobile Association Windsor
1215 Ouellette Ave., Windsor ON N8X 1J3 Canada
Tel: 519-255-1212; *Fax:* 519-255-7379
windsor@caasco.ca
www.central.on.caa.ca

Canadian Automobile Dealers' Association (CADA) / Corporation des associations de détaillants d'automobiles (CADA)
85 Renfrew Dr., Markham ON L3R 0N9 Canada
Tel: 905-940-4959; *Fax:* 905-940-6870
Toll-Free: 800-463-5289
mail@cada.ca
www.cada.ca
To deal with issues of a national nature which affect the well-being of franchised automobile & truck dealers in Canada

Canadian Automobile Sport Clubs - Ontario Region Inc. (CASC-OR)
703 Petrolia Rd., Toronto ON M3J 2N6 Canada
Tel: 416-667-9500; *Fax:* 416-667-9555
Toll-Free: 877-667-9505
office@casc.on.ca
www.casc.on.ca
To provide leadership, management, advocacy & the administrative services, facilities & equipment necessary to enable members to maximize their enjoyment & participation in motorsport; to maintain controls & standards necessary for safe competition

Canadian Automotive Repair & Service Council
c/o Cars Knowledge Network, #6, 9120 Leslie St., Richmond Hill ON L4B 3J9 Canada
Tel: 905-709-1010; *Fax:* 905-709-1013
askus@cars-council.ca
www.cars-council.ca
CARS serves as a virtual gathering place to access training & education programs, to research industry issues, & to learn of new skills, technologies & trends.

Canadian Vehicle Manufacturers' Association (CVMA) / Association canadienne des constructeurs de véhicules
#400, 170 Attwell Dr., Toronto ON M9W 5Z5 Canada
Tel: 416-364-9333; *Fax:* 416-367-3221
Toll-Free: 800-758-7122
info@cvma.ca
www.cvma.ca
The CVMA creates a framework within which member companies (such as Fordand General Motors) work together to achieve shared industry objectives on a range of important issues such as consumer protection, the environment, and vehicle safety. They provide research, information, industry-government advocacy, and other services aimed at building a better understanding of the importance of a healthy automotive industry to Canada's economic well-being and prosperity.

Corporation des concessionnaires d'automobiles du Québec inc. (CCAQ)
#750, 140, Grande-Allée est, Québec QC G1R 5M8 Canada
Tél: 418-523-2991; *Téléc:* 418-523-3725
Ligne sans frais: 800-463-5189
info@ccaq.com
www.ccaq.com
Offre une multitude de services aux membres; représenter ses membres

Japan Automobile Manufacturers Association of Canada
#460, 151 Bloor St. West, Toronto ON M5S 1S4 Canada
Tel: 416-968-0150; *Fax:* 416-968-7095
jama@jama.ca
www.jama.ca

To promote increased understanding of economic & trade matters pertaining to the motor vehicle industry; To encourage closer cooperation between Canada & Japan; To represent the interests of members

Manitoba Motor Dealers Association (MMDA)
#230, 530 Century St., Winnipeg MB R3H 0Y4 Canada
Tel: 204-985-4200; *Fax:* 204-775-9125
Toll-Free: 800-949-6632
info@mmda.mb.ca
www.mmda.mb.ca
To represent franchised automobile & truck dealers in Manitoba by dealing with provincial issues which affect this membership; to advance the automotive industry in Manitoba; to uphold the code of ethics

Motor Dealers' Association of Alberta (MDA)
9249, 48 St., Edmonton AB T6B 2R9 Canada
Tel: 780-468-9552; *Fax:* 780-465-6201
info@mdaalberta.com
www.mdaalberta.com
The Motor Dealer's Association of Alberta (MDA) strives to serve the collective interest of all its members and promote positive relationships with government, industry, suppliers, consumers and media, by offering needed and effective programs and services.

Nova Scotia Automobile Dealers' Association (NSADA)
PO Box 9410, Stn. A, #700, 6009 Quinpool Rd., Halifax NS B3K 5S3 Canada
Tel: 902-425-2445; *Fax:* 902-425-2441
info@nsada.ca
www.nsada.ca
To assist & protect association members; to act as the voice of new vehicle franchised dealers in Nova Scotia

Ontario & Toronto Automobile Dealers' Association (TADA)
85 Renfrew Dr., 2nd Fl., Markham ON L3R 0N9 Canada
Tel: 905-940-6232; *Fax:* 905-940-6235
doreenr@tada.ca
www.tada.ca

Ontario Tire Dealers Association
PO Box 516, 34 Edward St., Drayton ON N0G 1P0
Tel: 888-207-9059; *Fax:* 866-375-6832
www.otda.com
To represent & promote members
Robert Bignell, Executive Director
Glenn Warnica, President
Ron Spiewak, Secretary-Treasurer
Eric Gilbert, Chair, Ontario Tire Dealers Associaton Committee

Prince Edward Island Automobile Dealers Association
PO Box 22004, 6 Jenkins Ave., Charlottetown PE C1A 9J2 Canada
Tel: 902-566-3639; *Fax:* 902-368-7116
peiada@eastlink.ca

Recreation Vehicle Dealers Association of Alberta
#305, 8657 - 51 Ave., Edmonton AB T6E 6A8 Canada
Tel: 780-455-8562; *Fax:* 780-453-3927
Toll-Free: 888-858-8787
rvda@rvda-alberta.org
www.rvda-alberta.org
To develop professionalism & customer confidence in the RV industry

Recreation Vehicle Dealers Association of British Columbia (RVDABC)
#201, 17700 - 56th Ave., Surrey BC V3S 1C7 Canada
Tel: 604-575-3868; *Fax:* 604-575-3869
info@rvda.bc.ca
www.rvda.bc.ca
To promote, protect, educate, & enhances benefits for its members

Recreation Vehicle Dealers Association of Canada (RVDA) / Association des commerçants de véhicules recréatifs du Canada
#204, 6411 Buswell St., Richmond BC V6Y 2G5 Canada
Tel: 604-718-6325; *Fax:* 604-204-0154
info@rvda.ca
www.rvda.ca
Social Media: www.facebook.com/#!/RVDAofCanada
To promote professionalism in the RV industry through educational programs & events; to present the views of the industry to government & the general public

Recreation Vehicle Dealers Association of Manitoba
69 Morin Rd., St Francois Xavier MB R4L 1A8 Canada
Tel: 204-864-2112; *Fax:* 204-864-2232
rvdamb@mts.net
www.manitobarvda.ca
To build & improve the RV industry
Kim Wozniak, Manager

Recreation Vehicle Dealers Association of Saskatchewan
342 Armstrong Way, Saskatoon SK S7N 3N1 Canada
Tel: 306-955-7832; *Fax:* 306-955-7952
info@saskatchewanrvda.ca
www.saskatchewanrvda.ca
Sheila Lardner, Manager

Saskatchewan Automobile Dealers Association (SADA)
#212, 1800 - 2nd Ave., Regina SK S4R 8T3 Canada
Tel: 306-721-2208; *Fax:* 306-721-1009
sbuckle@saskautodealers.com
www.saskautodealers.com

Used Car Dealers Association of Ontario (UCDA)
230 Norseman St., Toronto ON M8X 6A2 Canada
Tel: 416-231-2600; *Fax:* 416-232-0775
Toll-Free: 800-268-2598
info@ucda.org
www.ucda.org
To enhance the image of the industry through member education, consumer awareness of the benefits members provide, & mediation of consumer/dealer disputes
Steve Peck, President

Aviation & Aerospace

Aéro-Club des Outardes
1455, de Biencourt, Montréal QC H4E 1T1 Canada
Tél: 514-465-7806
francisco45@gmail.com
aeroclubdesoutardes.iquebec.com
Favorise la formation au pilotage, la pratique et le développement du vol à voile au Québec.

Aerospace Industries Association of Canada (AIAC) / Association des industries aérospatiales du Canada
#1200, 60 Queen St., Ottawa ON K1P 5Y7 Canada
Tel: 613-232-4297; *Fax:* 613-232-1142
info@aiac.ca
www.aiac.ca
To promote & facilitate the continued success & growth of this strategic industry; to establish & maintain a public policy environment that enables sustained aerospace industry growth; to strengthen the international competitiveness of all aerospace firms in Canada; to strengthen Canadian aerospace SME capabilities & position them as "suppliers of choice"; to represent & involve the full range of aerospace companies that operate in Canada

Air Transport Association of Canada (ATAC) / Association du transport aérien du Canada
#700, 255 Albert St., Ottawa ON K1P 6A9
Tel: 613-233-7727; *Fax:* 613-230-8648
atac@atac.ca
www.atac.ca
To advance the issues that affect members from the commercial aviation & flight training industries as well as avaiation industry suppliers
John McKenna, President & Chief Executive Officer
Bill Boucher, Vice-President, Flight Operations
Wayne Gouveia, Vice-President, Commercial General Aviation
Cedric Paillard, Vice-President, Communications & Marketing
Mike Skrobica, Vice-President, Industry Monetary Affairs
Brian Whitehead, Vice-President, Technical Operations

Airport Management Council of Ontario
10 Geddes Cres., Barrie ON L4N 7B3 Canada
Tel: 705-726-2626; *Fax:* 705-739-8520
Toll-Free: 877-636-2626
amco@amco.on.ca
www.amco.on.ca
AMCO is committed to the sustainability of airports nationally. It monitors the airport industry, lobbies, provides networking opportunities and training to airports & businesses that work to enhance airport operations.

Association québécoise du transport aérien (AQTA)
Aéroport international Jean-Lesage, 600, 6e av de l'Aéroport, Québec QC G2G 2T5 Canada
Tél: 418-871-4635; *Téléc:* 418-871-8189
aqta@aqta.ca
www.aqta.ca
Voué à la défense et la promotion des intérêts de tous les secteurs du transport aérien

British Columbia Aviation Council (BCAC)
PO Box 32366, Stn. YVR Domestic Terminal, Richmond BC V7B 1W2 Canada
Tel: 604-278-9330; *Fax:* 604-278-8210
info@bcaviationcouncil.org
www.bcaviationcouncil.org
A self-sustaining organization with the mission to "promote the safe and orderly development of aviation and aviation services to the province of British Columiba."

Canadian Aeronautics & Space Institute (CASI) / Institut aéronautique et spatial du Canada
#104, 350 Terry Fox Dr., Ottawa ON K2K 2W5 Canada
Tel: 613-591-8787; *Fax:* 613-591-7291
casi@casi.ca; membership@casi.ca
www.casi.ca
To advance the art, science, engineering, & applications of aeronautics & associated technologies in Canada; to promote Canadian competence & international competitiveness

Canadian Airports Council (CAC) / Conseil des aéroports du Canada
#706, 350 Sparks St., Ottawa ON K1R 7S8
Tel: 613-560-9302; *Fax:* 613-560-6599
sharon.redden@cacairports.ca
www.cacairports.ca
To act as the voice for Canadian airports on a great range of important issues
Jim Facette, President/CEO
Daniel-Robert Gooch, Director, Communications

Canadian Aviation Historical Society (CAHS)
PO Box 2700, Stn. D, 156 St. Pierre Rd., Ottawa ON K1P 5W7 Canada
www.cahs.com
The Society collects & disseminates information about Canada's aviation heritage. It aims to foster public interest in the field. It is a registered charity, BN: 118829589RR0001.

Canadian Aviation Maintenance Council (CAMC) / Conseil canadien de l'entretien des aéronefs (CCEA)
#155, 955 Green Valley Cres., Ottawa ON K2C 3V4 Canada
Tel: 613-727-8272; *Fax:* 613-727-7018
Toll-Free: 800-448-9715
secretariat@camc.ca
www.camc.ca
To develop occupational training standards & facilitate the implementation of a human resources strategy for the Canadian Aviation Maintenance Industry.
Raewen Borris, Leader, Communications
Robert Donald, Executive Director

Canadian Federation of AME Associations (CFAMEA)
837 Charlotte St., Fredericton NB E3B 1M7 Canada
Tel: 506-452-1809; *Fax:* 506-452-8251
www.cfamea.com

Canadian Flight Instructors Association
579 Kingston Rd., Ajax ON L1S 6M1 Canada
Tel: 905-683-8986; *Fax:* 905-683-6977
bill@jsdavidson.ca
Bill Davidson

Canadian Owners & Pilots Association (COPA)
#207, 75 Albert St., Ottawa ON K1P 5E7 Canada
Tel: 613-236-4901; *Fax:* 613-236-8646
copa@copanational.org
www.copanational.org
The recognized voice of general aviation in Canada

Canadian Seaplane Pilots Association (CSPA)
#1001, 75 Albert St., Ottawa ON K1P 5E7 Canada
Tel: 613-236-4901; *Fax:* 613-236-8646
To maintain communications among seaplane pilots; to represent them at all levels of government; to help develop regulations conducive to safe & pleasurable flying; to prepare & disseminate educational material; to advance among its members information & knowledge of seaplane flying.

International Air Transport Association / Association du transport aérien international
PO Box 113, 800, Place Victoria, Montréal QC H4Z 1M1 Canada
Tel: 514-874-0202; *Fax:* 514-874-9632
www.iata.org
To promote safe, regular & economical air transport for the benefit of the peoples of the world; to foster air commerce; to study the problems connected with air transport; to provide a means for collaboration among the air transport enterprises engaged directly or indirectly in international air transport service; to cooperate with the International Civil Aviation Organization & other international organizations; to furnish for governments a forum for developing industry working standards &, as appropriate, coordinating international fares & rates; to simplify the travelling process for the general public

International Civil Aviation Organization: Legal Affairs & External Relations Bureau
999, rue Université, Montréal QC H3C 5H7 Canada
Tel: 514-954-8219; *Fax:* 514-954-6077
icaohq@icao.int
www.icao.int
To promote the safe & orderly development of civil aviation in the world; to set international standards & regulations necessary for the safety, security, efficiency & regularity of air transport & to serve as the medium for cooperation in all fields of civil aviation.
Denys Wibaux, Director
Raymond Benjamin, Secretary General

International Industry Working Group (IIWG)
International Air Transport Association, PO Box 113, 800, Place Victoria, Montréal QC H4Z 1M1 Canada
Tel: 514-874-0202; *Fax:* 514-874-9632
obrienm@iata.org
www.iata.org
To promote & develop an open exchange of information to minimize interface problems through well-informed design, development & operation of both aircraft & airports; to study jointly solutions to major problems which impede the development of the air transport system

The Ninety-Nines Inc./International Organization of Women Pilots
4300 Amelia Earhart Rd., Oklahoma City OK 73159 USA
Tel: 405-685-7969; *Fax:* 405-685-7985
Toll-Free: 800-994-1929
99s@ninety-nines.org
www.ninety-nines.org
To promote world fellowship through flight; to provide networking & scholarship opportunities for women & aviation education in the community; to preserve the unique history of women in aviation

Northern Air Transport Association (NATA)
PO Box 2457, Yellowknife NT X1A 2P8 Canada
Tel: 867-920-2985; *Fax:* 867-920-2983
nata-yzf@theedge.ca
www.nata-yzf.ca
To promote safe & effective Northern air transportation

Recreational Aircraft Association (RAA) / Réseau aéronefs amateur
22 - 4881 Fountain St. North, Breslau ON N0B 1M0 Canada
Tel: 519-648-3030; *Toll-Free:* 800-387-1028
raa@raa.ca
www.raa.ca
To be a national leader in the development & advancement of recreational aviation; to promote recreational flying & building of amateur built aircraft, restorations of classic & antique aircraft

Ultralight Pilots Association of Canada (UPAC) / Association canadienne des pilotes d'avions ultra-légers
907289 Township Rd. 12, RR#4, Bright ON N0J 1B0 Canada
Tel: 519-684-7628
www.upac.ca
To promote ultralight aviation in Canada
K. Lubitz, President

University of Toronto Institute for Aerospace Studies
Faculty of Applied Science & Engineering, 4925 Dufferin St., Toronto ON M3H 5T6 Canada
Tel: 416-667-7700; *Fax:* 416-667-7799
info@utias.utoronto.ca
www.utias.utoronto.ca
UTIAS is a graduate studies and research institute, forming part of the faculty of Applied Science and Engineering at the University of Toronto.
D.W. Zingg, Director
H.T. Liu, Associate Director
O.L. Gülder, Associate Director

Banking

Canadian Community Reinvestment Coalition (CCRC)
PO Box 821, Stn. B, Ottawa ON K1P 241 Canada
Tel: 613-789-5753; *Fax:* 613-241-4758
cancrc@web.net
www.canrc.org
To increase the accountability of Canada's financial institutions, increase their reinvestment in the Canadian ecomony, strengthen Canada's economy, strengthen community economic development efforts across Canada, and develop leadership in the Canadian financial sevices consumer movement.

Broadcasting

The Alliance for Children & Television (ACT) / Alliance pour l'enfant et la télévision (AET)
#708, 1400, boul René-Lévesque est, Montréal QC H2L 2M2 Canada
Tel: 514-597-5417; *Fax:* 514-597-5205
alliance@act-aet.tv
www.act-aet.tv
To promote the production & carriage of quality Canadian television programming for children; to ensure the development of critical viewing skills so that families are able to use media more effectively in the home; to promote awareness of the need to help young people make the most of their experience of television & other screen-based media

Audio Engineering Society (AES)
AES Toronto Section, PO Box 292, #32E, 223 Pioneer Dr., Kitchner ON N2P 1L9 Canada
Tel: 519-894-5308
torontoaes@uex.net
www.torontoaes.org
Social Media: www.linkedin.com/groups?home=&gid=2023730&trk=anet_ug_hm
Dedicated to audio technology.
Sy Potma, Chair
Jeffery S. Bamford, Secretary
Syberen Potma, Vice Chair

BBM Canada / Sondages BBM
1500 Don Mills Rd., 3rd Fl., Toronto ON M3B 3L7 Canada
Tel: 416-445-9800; *Fax:* 416-445-8644
info@bbm.ca
www.bbm.ca
BBM is a non-profit organization that provides broadcast measurement and consumer behaviour data to broadcasters, advertisers and agencies.

Broadcast Executives Society (BES)
#100-170, 2 Bloor St. West, Toronto ON M4W 3E2 Canada
Tel: 416-413-3870; *Fax:* 416-413-3878
admin@bes.ca
www.bes.ca
To serve as forum for the broadcast industry.

Broadcast Research Council of Canada (BRC)
#1005, 160 Bloor St. East, Toronto ON M4W 1B9 Canada
Tel: 416-413-3864; *Fax:* 416-413-3879
brc@tvb.ca
www.brc.ca
To provide a forum for presentations relating to the broadcast advertising business; to provide awards to the most promising students at colleges that train people to enter the advertising business.

Canadian Association of Broadcasters (CAB) / Association canadienne des radiodiffuseurs (ACR)
PO Box 627, Stn. B, #700, 45 O'Connor St., Ottawa ON K1P 1A4 Canada
Tel: 613-233-4035; *Fax:* 613-233-6961
cab@cab-acr.ca
www.cab-acr.ca
To act as the national voice of Canada's private broadcasters; To represent the vast majority of Canadian programming services, including private radio & television stations, networks, specialty, pay, & pay-per-view services

Canadian Association of Ethnic (Radio) Broadcasters (CAEB) / Association canadienne des radiodiffuseurs ethniques
c/o CHIN Radio, #400, 622 College St., Toronto ON M6G 1B6 Canada
Tel: 416-531-9991; *Fax:* 416-531-5274
info@chinradio.com
www.chinradio.com
To foster & promote the development of multilingual / multicultural radio broadcasting in Canada

Canadian Broadcast Distribution Association (CBDA) / Association canadienne de distribution de radiodiffusion
#100, 2233 Argentia Rd., Mississauga ON L5N 2X7 Canada
Tel: 905-826-3451; *Fax:* 905-826-4873
info@cbda.ca
www.cbda.ca
The Association fosters interoperability of broadcasting services across multiple distribution platforms, facilitate the exchange of information on critical technical operational matters of interest to its members and provide education on topical issues.

Friends of Canadian Broadcasting (FCB)
#200-238, 131 Bloor St. West, Toronto ON M5S 1R8 Canada
Tel: 416-968-7496; *Fax:* 416-968-7406
friends@friends.ca
www.friends.ca
Social Media: twitter.com/friendscb
Canada-wide, non-partisan voluntary organization supported by 66,000 households whose mission is to defend and enhance the quality and quantity of Canadian programming in the Canadian audio-visual system

National Campus & Community Radio Association (NCRA) / Association nationale des radio étudiantes et communautaires (ANREC)
#230, 325 Dalhousie, Ottawa ON K1N 7G2 Canada
Tel: 613-321-1440; *Fax:* 613-321-1442
office@ncra.ca
www.ncra.ca
To encourage development of community & student radio in Canada by providing core services to community-oriented radios & representing them to government, industry & the public

Ontario Association of Broadcasters (OAB)
PO Box 54040, 5762 Hwy. 7 East, Markham ON L3P 7Y4 Canada
Tel: 905-554-2730; *Fax:* 905-554-2731
memberservices@oab.ca
www.oab.ca

Radio Advisory Board of Canada (RABC) / Conseil consultatif canadien de la radio
#811, 116 Albert St., Ottawa ON K1P 5G3 Canada
Tel: 613-230-3261; *Toll-Free:* 888-902-5768
rabc.gm@on.aibn.com
www.rabc-cccr.ca
An association of organizations which are concerned with the use of the radio spectrum; these in turn represent the users of radio communications & related service providers, manufacturers, & professional societies; its purpose is to consult & advise Industry Canada on behalf of industry on the development, management, & regulation of radio services in Canada

Radio Amateurs of Canada Inc. (RAC) / Radio Amateurs du Canada inc.
#217, 720 Belfast Rd., Ottawa ON K1G 0Z5 Canada
Tel: 613-244-4367; *Fax:* 613-244-4369
Toll-Free: 877-273-8304
rachq@rac.ca
www.rac.ca
To act as coordinating body of amateur radio organizations in Canada, liaison agency between members & other amateur organizations in Canada & other countries, coordinating & advisory agency between members & industry Canada; to promote interests of amateur radio operators through program of technical & general education in amateur matters

Radio Television News Directors' Association (Canada) (RTNDA Canada) / Association canadienne des directeurs de l'information en radio-télévision
#310, 2175 Sheppard Ave. East, Toronto ON M2J 1W8 Canada
Tel: 416-756-2213; *Fax:* 416-491-1670
Toll-Free: 877-257-8632
info@rtndacanada.com
www.rtndacanada.com
Social Media: facebook.com/group.php?gid=2366031327
RTNDA Canada is the voice of electronic journalists. It sets the standards for the field of broadcast journalism, fosters high standards of electronic news presentation, & promotes the free flow of information.

Television Bureau of Canada, Inc. (TVB) / Bureau de la télévision du Canada
#1005, 160 Bloor St. East, Toronto ON M4W 1B9 Canada
Tel: 416-923-8813; *Fax:* 416-413-3879
Toll-Free: 800-231-0051
tvb@tvb.ca
www.tvb.ca
To promote sales, marketing & research of commercial television industry in Canada

Western Association of Broadcast Engineers
#300, 8120 Beddington Blvd. NW, Calgary AB T3K 2A8 Canada
Tel: 403-630-4907; *Fax:* 403-295-3135
info@wabe.ca
www.wabe.ca
Laverne Siemens, President

Women in Film & Television - Toronto
#601, 110 Eglinton Ave. East, Toronto ON M4P 2Y1 Canada
Tel: 416-322-3430; *Fax:* 416-322-3703
wift@wift.com
www.wift.com
To provide year-round training programs, industry events, & professional awards for women & men in Canadian screen based media
Susan Ross, Chair
Sadia Zaman, Executive Director

Building & Construction

Aggregate Producers' Association of Ontario (APAO)
#2, 365 Brunel Rd., Mississauga ON L4Z 1Z5 Canada
Tel: 905-507-0711; *Fax:* 905-507-0717
mmiller@apao.com
www.apao.com

Alberta Construction Association (ACA)
18012, 107 Ave., Edmonton AB T5S 1M1 Canada
Tel: 780-455-1122; *Fax:* 780-451-2152
info@abconst.org
www.abconst.org

Alberta Ready Mixed Concrete Association (ARMCA)
9653 - 45 Ave., Edmonton AB T6E 5Z8 Canada
Tel: 780-436-5645; *Fax:* 780-436-6503
armca@telus.net
www.armca.net
To provide industry representation for the advancement of quality concrete in Alberta; to market & promote the use of concrete; to provide a consolidated industry approach to regulatory bodies; to provide networking opportunities; to provide education & training

Alberta Roadbuilders & Heavy Construction Association (ARHCA)
#201, 9333 - 45 Ave., Edmonton AB T6E 5Z7 Canada
Tel: 780-436-9860; *Fax:* 780-436-4910
Toll-Free: 866-436-9860
administration@arhca.ab.ca
www.arhca.ab.ca

Alberta Roofing Contractors Association (ARCA)
2380 Pegasus Rd. NE, Calgary AB T2E 8G8 Canada
Tel: 403-250-7055; *Fax:* 403-250-1702
Toll-Free: 800-382-8515
info@arcaonline.ca
www.arcaonline.ca
To provide continuing education for roofing contractors, their personnel & interested others; to represent the roofing contracting industry in its relationships with legislative & regulating bodies; to work closely with affiliate organizations & liaison groups in advancing professionalism of roofing contracting; to provide a forum for interaction of members; to encourage high standards of professional conduct among roofing contractors; to develop a comprehensive body of knowledge about roofing management & technology, & disseminate ideas & knowledge to members & others; to monitor new products & systems; to work for cooperation & greater understanding between contracting, inspection, manufacturing & supply segments of the roofing industry

Architectural Woodwork Manufacturers Association of British Columbia (AWMA-BC)
#160, 4664 Lougheed Hwy, Burnaby BC V5C 5T5 Canada
Tel: 604-298-3555; *Fax:* 604-298-3558
awma@awma-bc.ca
www.awma-bc.ca
To advance the highest standards of education, quality workmanship, warranties & business practices in architectural woodwork manufacturing in British Columbia

Architectural Woodwork Manufacturers Association of Canada (AWMAC)
516 - 4 St. West, High River AB T1V 1B6 Canada
Tel: 403-652-7685; *Fax:* 403-652-7384
info@awmac.com
www.awmac.com
To foster & advance the interests of those who are engaged in or who are directly or indirectly connected with or affected by the production & installation of architectural woodwork; to endeavour to achieve a closer relationship & a better understanding among the various branches of the industry

Architectural Woodwork Manufacturers Association of Canada - Manitoba
PO Box 737, 290 Burnell St., Winnipeg MB R3V 2L4 Canada
Tel: 204-222-9622; *Fax:* 204-928-7459
manitoba@awmac.com
www.awmac.com
To foster and advance the intersts of those who are engaged in or who are directly or indirectly connected with or affected by the production and installation of architectural woodwork; to endeavor to achieve a closer relationship and a better understanding among the various branches of the industry.
Harm Hazeu, President
Bill Wagar, Vice-President
Nancy Carpenter, Secretary
Ted Sherritt, Treasurer

Architectural Woodwork Manufacturers Association of Canada - Northern Alberta
c/o Beyersbergen Interiors, 15327 - 116 Ave., Edmonton AB T5M 3Z5 Canada
Tel: 780-906-9399; *Fax:* 780-456-1050
northernalberta@awmac.com
To foster and advance the interests of those who are engaged in or who are directly or indirectly connected with or affected by the production and installation of architrcutural woodwork; to endeavor to achieve a closer relationship and a better understanding among the various branches of the industry.
Joseph George, President

Architectural Woodwork Manufacturers Association of Canada - Ontario Chapter (AWMAC-ON)
70 Leek Cres., Richmond Hill ON L4B 1H1 Canada
Tel: 416-499-4000; *Fax:* 416-499-8752
info@awmacontario.com
www.awmacontario.com
To foster & advance the interests of those engaged in the production & installation of architectural woodwork in Ontario

Architectural Woodwork Manufacturers Association of Canada - Saskatchewan
PO Box 26032, Stn. Lawson Heights, Saskatoon SK S7K 8C1 Canada
Tel: 306-652-2704; *Fax:* 306-664-2552
awmac.sask@sasktel.net
To foster and advance the interests of those who are engaged in or who are directly or indirectly connected with or affected by the production and installation of architectural woodwork; to endeavor to achieve a closer relationship and a better understanding among the various branches of the lbirary.
Kerry DePape, President

Architectural Woodwork Manufacturers Association of Canada - Southern Alberta
PO Box 40124, #02A, 4803 Centre St. NW, Calgary AB T2G 5G5 Canada
Tel: 403-264-5979; *Fax:* 403-652-7384
southernalberta@awmac.com
www.awmac.com/chapters-home.php?region=sa
The Association works to advance the interests of those related to the production & installation of architectural woodwork. It endeavors to foster a closer relationship among the various branches of the industry.
Rod Roll, President
Rob Hodgins, Secretary
Larry White, AWNAC Director

Association de la construction du Québec (ACQ) / Construction Association of Québec
#205, 7400, boul les Galeries d'Anjou, Anjou QC H1M 3M2 Canada
Tél: 514-354-0609; *Téléc:* 514-354-8292
Ligne sans frais: 888-868-3424
info@prov.acq.org
www.acq.org
Promotion et défense des intérêts des entreprises de construction, de gestionnaire de plans de garantie des bâtiments résidentiels neufs (Qualité Habitation) et d'agent patronal négociateur pour tous les employeurs des secteurs institutionnel/commercial et industriel (IC/I)

Association des constructeurs de routes et grands travaux du Québec (ACRGTQ) / Québec Road Builders & Heavy Construction Association
435, av Grande-Allée est, Québec QC G1R 2J5 Canada
Tél: 418-529-2949; *Téléc:* 418-529-5139
Ligne sans frais: 800-463-4672
acrgtq@acrgtq.qc.ca
www.acrgtq.qc.ca
Défendre les intérêts des entrepreneurs en génie civil et voirie du Québec

Association des détaillants de matériaux de construction du Québec (ADMACQ) / The Building Materials Retailers Association of Québec
474, rue Trans-Canada, Longueuil QC J4G 1N8 Canada
Tél: 450-646-5842; *Téléc:* 450-646-6171
Ligne sans frais: 877-723-6220
information@admacq.qc.ca
www.admacq.qc.ca
Promouvoir l'intérêt général de ses membres-clients engagés dans la vente au détail de matériaux de construction et de quincaillerie, en leur offrant une panoplie de produits et services visant à faciliter la gestion de leurs commerces, des Québécois et la rénovation

Association des entrepreneurs en construction du Québec (AECQ) / Association of Building Contractors of Québec (ABCQ)
#101, 7905, boul Louis-H. Lafontaine, Anjou QC H1K 4E4 Canada
Tél: 514-353-5151; *Téléc:* 514-353-6689
Ligne sans frais: 800-361-4304
info@aecq.org
www.aecq.org
Étudier, promouvoir, protéger et défendre les intérêts des employeurs en matière de relations de travail; négocier les clauses du tronc commun à chacune des quatre conventions collectives sectorielles

Association des maîtres couvreurs du Québec (AMCQ) / Québec Master Roofers Association
3001, boul Tessier, Laval QC H7S 2M1 Canada
Tél: 450-973-2322; *Téléc:* 450-973-2321
Ligne sans frais: 888-973-2322
info@amcq.qc.ca
www.amcq.qc.ca
Promouvoir les intérêts généraux des entreprises de couvertures et ceux de diverses entreprises des secteurs connexes dans la province de Québec; promouvoir la hausse de la qualité des travaux de couvertures

Atlantic Building Supply Dealers Association (ABSDA)
70 Englehart St., Dieppe NB E1A 8H3 Canada
Tel: 506-858-0700; *Fax:* 506-859-0064
Toll-Free: 800-561-7114
absda@nbnet.nb.ca
www.absda.ca
To keep membership informed of new trends & developments in the industry; to provide a forum to discuss mutual problems & ideas; to provide continuing education programs for members

Atlantic Provinces Ready-Mixed Concrete Association (APRMCA) / Association des fabricants de béton préparé des provinces atlantiques
30 Damascus Rd., Bedford NS B4A 0C1 Canada
Tel: 902-443-4456; *Fax:* 902-429-6696
info@atlanticconcrete.ca
www.aprmca.com
To promote the use of ready-mixed concrete while providing leadership to the industry through the exchange of ideas & information.

British Columbia Construction Association (BCCA)
#210, 174 Wilson St., Victoria BC V9A 7N6 Canada
Tel: 250-475-1077; *Fax:* 250-475-1078
bcca@bccassn.com
www.bccassn.com
To provide excellence in the representation of & service to British Columbia's construction industry

British Columbia Construction Association - North (BCCA-N)
3851 - 18 Ave., Prince George BC V2N 1B1 Canada
Tel: 250-563-1744; *Fax:* 250-563-1107
kkrenzler@nbcca.bc.ca
www.nbcca.bc.ca
To act as a united voice on behalf of all sectors of the construction industry on concerns of the industry; To promote education, training, safety, standard practices, high standards, &

investment in the construction industry of northern British Columbia
Rosalind Thorn, President
Sue Zacharias, Chair
Bonnie Griffith, Secretary
Ken Morland, Treasurer

British Columbia Ready Mixed Concrete Association
26162 - 30A Ave., Aldergrove BC V4W 2W5 Canada
Tel: 604-626-4141; *Fax:* 604-626-4143
ccampbell@bcrmca.bc.ca
www.bcrmca.bc.ca
To work cooperatively with all levels of government to ensure the ready-mix concrete industry operates with a focus on the communities & the environment
Carolyn Campbell, Executive Director

British Columbia Road Builders & Heavy Construction Association (BCRB&HCA)
#307, 8678 Greenall Ave., Burnaby BC V5J 3M6
Tel: 604-436-0220; *Fax:* 604-436-2627
info@roadbuilders.bc.ca
www.roadbuilders.bc.ca
To represent the interests of member companies to government, media, other organizations, & the public

Building Supply Industry Association of British Columbia (BSIA of BC)
#2, 19299 - 94th Ave., Surrey BC V4N 4E6
Tel: 604-513-2205; *Fax:* 604-513-2206
Toll-Free: 888-711-5656
www.bsiabc.ca
To act as the official voice of the building supply industry in British Columbia; To provide services to members

Canadian Concrete Masonry Producers Association (CCMPA)
PO Box 54503, 1171 Avenue Rd., Toronto ON M5M 4N5 Canada
Tel: 416-495-7497; *Fax:* 416-495-8723
Toll-Free: 888-495-7497
information@ccmpa.ca
www.ccmpa.ca
Works on behalf of concrete masonry producers to build an industry as strong and as enduring as the products it manufactures

Canadian Concrete Pipe Association (CCPA) / Association canadienne des fabricants de tuyaux de béton (ACTB)
205 Miller Dr., Halton Hills ON L7G 6G4 Canada
Tel: 905-877-5369; *Fax:* 905-877-5369
info@ccpa.com
www.ccpa.com
Social Media:
www.facebook.com/group.php?gid=106265401921
To coordinate research & development, promotion, education & federal government relations programs pertaining to the marketing of high quality precast concrete waste water & storm drainage products in Canada.
John Greer, Chair

Canadian Construction Association (CCA) / Association canadienne de la construction (ACC)
#400, 75 Albert St., Ottawa ON K1P 5E7 Canada
Tel: 613-236-9455; *Fax:* 613-236-9526
cca@cca-acc.com
www.cca-acc.com
CCA, the national voice of the construction industry, serves, promotes, & enhances the construction industry by acting on behalf of its members in matters of national concern.

Canadian Masonry Contractors' Association (CMCA)
Canada Masonry Centre, 360 Superior Blvd., Mississauga ON L5T 2N7 Canada
Tel: 905-564-6622; *Fax:* 905-564-5744
www.canadamasonrycentre.com/cmca
CMCA works to advance masonry technology, skills development & the use of masonry products in construction across Canada. It provides managerial, technical, accounting & financial, promotional, marketing, & other services to organizations serving the masonry industry.

Canadian Paint & Coatings Association (CPCA) / Association canadienne de l'industrie de la peinture et du revêtement
#1200, 170 Laurier Ave. West, Ottawa ON K1P 5V5 Canada
Tel: 613-231-3604; *Fax:* 613-231-4908
cpca@cdnpaint.org
www.cdnpaint.org
To represent the paint industry among the provincial, federal & municipal governments

Canadian Precast / Prestressed Concrete Institute (CPCI) / Institut canadien du béton préfabriqué et précontraint
#100, 196 Bronson Ave., Ottawa ON K1R 6H4 Canada
Tel: 613-232-2619; *Fax:* 613-232-5139
Toll-Free: 877-937-2724
info@cpci.ca
www.cpci.ca
To stimulate & advance the common interests & general welfare of the structural precast/prestressed concrete industry, the architectural precast concrete industry & the post-tensioned concrete industry in Canada

Canadian Ready Mixed Concrete Association (CRMCA) / Association canadienne du béton préparé
#3, 365 Brunel Rd., Mississauga ON L4Z 1Z5 Canada
Tel: 905-507-1122; *Fax:* 905-890-8122
www.crmca.ca

Canadian Roofing Contractors' Association (CRCA) / Association canadienne des entrepreneurs en couverture (ACEC)
#100, 2430 Don Reid Dr., Ottawa ON K1H 1E1 Canada
Tel: 613-232-6724; *Fax:* 613-232-2893
Toll-Free: 800-461-2722
crca@on.aibn.com
www.roofingcanada.com
CRCA consists of companies actively engaged in Canada in the roofing and related sheet metal contracting business, along with companies engaged in manufactoring or supplying materials and services used in any branch of the roofing and sheet metal industry.

Canadian Welding Bureau (CWB)
8260 Parkhill Dr., Milton ON L9T 5V7 Canada
Tel: 905-542-1312; *Fax:* 905-542-1318
Toll-Free: 800-844-6790
info@cwbgroup.org
www.cwbgroup.org
CWB is a not-for-profit organization serving the welding & joining industry. It administers certification programs for CSA Standards W47.1, W47.2, W186, W178.1 & W48 series. It also provides support for welding-based programs in schools, education institutions, welding professionals & companies employing welding technology.

Cement Association of Canada (CAC) / Association canadienne du ciment
#502, 350 Sparks St., Ottawa ON K1R 7S8 Canada
Tel: 613-236-9471; *Fax:* 613-563-4498
headquarters@cement.ca
www.cement.ca
Represents all of Canada's cement producers; aims to improve & extend the uses of cement & concrete through market development, engineering, research, education, & public affairs work

Construction Association of New Brunswick Inc. (CANB)
59 Avonlea Ct., Fredericton NB E3C 1N8 Canada
Tel: 506-459-5770; *Fax:* 506-457-1913
canb1@nbnet.nb.ca
www.constructnb.ca
CANB is designed to perform a co-ordinating function for reaching consensus to effectively present the Industry's collective views to various client groups, partic-ularly to relevant departments and agencies of the provincial government.

Construction Association of Nova Scotia
Parkway Pl., City of Lakes Business Park, #3, 260 Brownlow Ave., Dartmouth NS B3B 1V9 Canada
Tel: 902-468-2267; *Fax:* 902-468-2470
cans@cans.ns.ca
www.cans.ns.ca
The Construction Association of Nova Scotia (CANS) is an industry trade association representing contractors, suppliers and service providers comprising the non-residential construction industry. CANS was founded in 1862 as the Halifax Builders' Society. Since that time, CANS membership has grown to include firms from all over Atlantic Canada as well as other regions of the country. The primary role of CANS is to represent the interests of our 600 member companies.
Carol MacCulloch, President
Donna Cruickshank, Office Manager

Construction Association of Prince Edward Island (CAPEI)
PO Box 728, #223, 40 Enman Cres., Charlottetown PE C1E 1E6 Canada
Tel: 902-368-3303; *Fax:* 902-894-9757
admin@capei.ca
www.capei.ca
To foster, promote & advance the interests & efficiency of Prince Edward Island's construction industry

Construction Specifications Canada (CSC) / Devis de construction Canada
#312, 120 Carlton St., Toronto ON M5A 4K2 Canada
Tel: 416-777-2198; *Fax:* 416-777-2197
info@csc-dcc.ca
www.csc-dcc.ca
To improve communication, contract documentation, & technical information in the construction industry

Council of Ontario Construction Associations (COCA)
#2001, 180 Dundas St. West, Toronto ON M5G 1Z8 Canada
Tel: 416-968-7200; *Fax:* 416-968-0362
info@coca.on.ca
www.coca.on.ca
To contribute to the long-term growth & profitability of the construction industry in Ontario; to speak with a unified voice to government, the industry & the public.

Glass & Architectural Metals Association (GAMA)
c/o Calgary Construction Association, 2725 - 12 St. NE, Calgary AB T2E 7J2
To advance the glass & architectural metals industry

Infrastructure Health & Safety Association (IHSA)
#400, 5110 Creekbank Rd., Mississauga ON L4W 0A1 Canada
Tel: 905-625-0100; *Fax:* 905-625-8998
Toll-Free: 800-263-5024
info@ihsa.ca
www.ihsa.ca
IHSA is part of Health & Safety Ontario. It has advisory councils that cover transportation, residential, general ICI, heavy civil & aggregates, mechanical, electrical & priority rates. IHSA cooperates with employers & workers to eliminate occupational injury & illness by offering training programs, auditing & consulting services, in addition to health & safety resources.
Al Beatie, Interim President
Donald E. Dickie, Executive Vice-President/General Manager

Lumber & Building Materials Association of Ontario (LBMAO)
#27, 5155 Spectrum Way, Mississauga ON L4W 5A1 Canada
Tel: 905-625-1084; *Fax:* 905-625-3006
Toll-Free: 888-365-2626
dwcampbell@lbmao.on.ca
www.lbmao.on.ca
To promote the welfare of members so that they are able to build a competitive advantage & remain at the leading edge of the lumber & building materials industry

Manitoba Heavy Construction Association Inc. (MHCA)
1236 Ellice Ave., Winnipeg MB R3G 0E7 Canada
Tel: 204-947-1379; *Fax:* 204-943-2279
info@mhca.mb.ca
www.mhca.mb.ca
To promote a safe workplace for employees in Manitoba's heavy construction industry; to represent the heavy construction industry in Manitoba

Manitoba Ready Mixed Concrete Association Inc. (MRMCA)
169 Kingston Row, Winnipeg MB R2M 0T1 Canada
Tel: 204-667-8539; *Fax:* 204-237-5075
info@mrmca.com
www.mrmca.com
To represent the concrete industry in Manitoba; to advance the quality of concrete in Manitoba

Master Insulators' Association of Ontario Inc.
Building 1, #101, 2600 Skymark Ave., Mississauga ON L4W 5B2 Canada
Tel: 905-279-6426; *Fax:* 905-279-6422
manager@miaontario.org
www.miaontario.org

Master Painters & Decorators Association (MPDA)
2800 Ingleton Ave., Burnaby BC V5C 6G7 Canada
Tel: 604-298-7578; *Fax:* 604-298-5183
info@mpda.net
www.paintinfo.com
To set & raise standards of industrial organizations

Mechanical Contractors Association of Alberta
#204, 2725 - 12 St. NE, Calgary AB T2E 7J2 Canada
Tel: 403-250-7237; *Fax:* 403-291-0551
Toll-Free: 800-251-0620
www.mcaalberta.com
To promote plumbing & mechanical contractors; to provide educational programs to foster improved management &

productivity in mechanical contracting; to represent mechanical contractors with their various publics - governments, design authorities, labour; to foster professional advancement & profitability of the plumbing, heating & mechanical contracting industry through its member services

Mechanical Contractors Association of British Columbia (MCABC)
#223, 3989 Henning Dr., Burnaby BC V5C 6N5 Canada
Tel: 604-205-5058; *Fax:* 604-205-5075
Toll-Free: 800-663-8473
www.mcabc.org
To encourage, support & promote the advancement of the mechanical contracting industry; to provide leadership, assistance & training to members.

Mechanical Contractors Association of Canada (MCAC) / Association des entrepreneurs en mécanique du Canada
#601, 280 Albert St., Ottawa ON K1P 5G8 Canada
Tel: 613-232-0492; *Fax:* 613-235-2793
mcac@mcac.ca
www.mcac.ca
To promote plumbing & mechanical contractors; to provide educational programs to foster improved management & productivity in mechanical contracting; to represent mechanical contractors to their various publics - governments, design authorities, labour.

Mechanical Contractors Association of Manitoba (MCAM)
#1, 860 Bradford St., Winnipeg MB R3H 0N5 Canada
Tel: 204-774-2404; *Fax:* 204-772-0233
mcam@mts.net
www.mca-mb.com
To continually improve mechanical industry standards while providing a high level of value performance & customer service for our members

Mechanical Contractors Association of New Brunswick / Association des entrepreneurs en mécanique du N.-B.
c/o Moncton Northeast Construction Association, 297 Collishaw St., Moncton NB E1C 9R2 Canada
Tel: 506-857-4128; *Fax:* 506-857-8861
info@mneca.ca
www.mneca.ca
To provide leadership & service to members; to act on behalf of members in labour relations matters, including collective bargaining; to advance & develop the industry, primarily in New Brunswick; to endeavour to improve legislation affecting the industry; to promote sound labour relations

Mechanical Contractors Association of Newfoundland & Labrador
PO Box 745, Mount Pearl NL A1N 2Y2 Canada
Tel: 709-747-5577; *Fax:* 709-368-5342
ddawe@nfld.net

Mechanical Contractors Association of Nova Scotia
c/o Construction Association of Nova Scotia, #3, 260 Brownlow Ave., Dartmouth NS B3B 1V9 Canada
Tel: 902-468-2267; *Fax:* 902-468-2470
cans@cans.ns.ca
www.cans.ns.ca

Mechanical Contractors Association of Ontario (MCAO)
#103, 10 Director Ct., Woodbridge ON L4L 7E8 Canada
Tel: 905-856-0342; *Fax:* 905-856-0385
mcao@mcao.org
www.mcao.org

Mechanical Contractors Association of Prince Edward Island
c/o Association of Commercial & Industrial Contractors of PEI, PO Box 1685, Charlottetown PE C1A 7N4 Canada
Tel: 902-566-3456; *Fax:* 902-368-2754
wmm@wmm93.pe.ca

Mechanical Contractors Association of Saskatchewan Inc. (MCAS)
Heritage Business Park, #105, 2750 Faithfull Ave., Saskatoon SK S7K 6M6 Canada
Tel: 306-664-2154; *Fax:* 306-653-7233
mca-sask@mca-sask.com
www.mca-sask.com
MCAS is a provincial non-profit, trade association that represents plumbing & heating contractors in relation to the construction industry, legislative departments of municipal & provincial government & other industry-related bodies.

National Building Envelope Council
c/o 5041 Regent St., Burnaby BC V5C 4H4 Canada
Tel: 604-473-9587
To pursue excellence in the design, construction & performance of the building envelope

National Elevator & Escalator Association (NEEA)
#708, 6299 Airport Rd., Mississauga ON L4V 1N3 Canada
Tel: 905-678-9940; *Fax:* 905-677-7634

New Brunswick Roofing Contractors Association, Inc. (NBRCA) / Association des entrepreneurs en couverture du Nouveau-Brunswick
PO Box 7242, 57 King St., 3rd Fl., Saint John NB E2L 4S6 Canada
Tel: 506-652-7003; *Fax:* 506-696-0380
info@nbrca.ca
www.nbrca.ca
To protect the public's interest in relation to roofing; to act as the voice of New Brunswick's roofing industry; to facilitate a competent & profitable roofing & sealed membrane system industry in the province; to foster excellence in roofing related activities; to ensure that members uphold the code of ethics

Newfoundland & Labrador Construction Association (NLCA)
#201, 333 Pippy Pl., St. John's NL A1B 3X2
Tel: 709-753-8920; *Fax:* 709-754-3968
info@nfld.com
www.nlca.ca
To act as the voice of the construction industry in Newfoundland & Labrador; To enhance the professionalism & productivity of members through the development of policies

Newfoundland & Labrador Road Builders / Heavy Civil Association (NLRB / HCA)
PO Box 23038, St. John's NL A1B 4J9 Canada
Tel: 709-364-8811; *Fax:* 709-364-8812
nlrbhca@nf.aibn.com; bulletin@nfld.com (Road Builders Bulletin)
www.nfld.net/roadbuilders
To act as the voice of the road construction, water & sewer, & heavy construction industries in Newfoundland & Labrador; to develop standard tendering & contractual practices & procedures

Northwest Territories Construction Association (NWTCA)
PO Box 2277, 4921 - 49th St., 3rd Fl., Yellowknife NT X1A 2P7 Canada
Tel: 867-873-3949; *Fax:* 867-873-8366
director@nwtca.ca
www.nwtca.ca
To act as a voice for construction-related business in the Northwest Territories & Nunavut

Nova Scotia Road Builders Association
#217, 11 Thornhill Dr., Dartmouth NS B3B 1R9 Canada
www.nsrba.ca
To speak for the heavy construction industry in Nova Scotia; to liaise with provincial Department of Transportation.

Ontario Concrete Pipe Association (OCPA)
5045 South Service Rd., 1st Fl., Burlington ON L7L 5Y7 Canada
Tel: 905-631-9696; *Fax:* 905-631-1905
Toll-Free: 800-435-0116
info@ocpa.com
www.ocpa.com
To represent the concrete pipe & maintenance hole industry throughout Ontario; to promote engineered concrete products of permanence

Ontario General Contractors Association (OGCA)
#703, 6299 Airport Rd., Mississauga ON L4V 1N3 Canada
Tel: 905-671-3969; *Fax:* 905-671-8212
info@ogca.ca
www.ogca.ca
Offers experience and expertise dealing with contracts, architects, engineers and owners

Ontario Industrial Roofing Contractors' Association (OIRCA)
#301, 940 The East Mall, Toronto ON M9B 6J7
Tel: 416-695-4114; *Fax:* 416-695-9920
Toll-Free: 888-336-4722
oirca@ontarioroofing.com
www.ontarioroofing.com
To act as the voice of the industrial-commercial roofing industry in Ontario; To promote excellence in roofing construction

Ontario Painting Contractors Association (OPCA)
#305, 211 Consumers Rd., Toronto ON M2J 4G8 Canada
Tel: 416-498-1897; *Fax:* 416-498-6757
Toll-Free: 800-461-3630
info@ontpca.org
www.ontpca.org
To foster, develop & maintain unity & stability among members by acting as a bargaining agent; providing services & educational opportunities; acting as a liaison between industry groups; upholding & improving the standards of the industry; promoting the use of modern specifications; advancing an attitude of ethical responsibility & pride

Ontario Pipe Trades Council
Confederation Square, #203, 45 Goderich Rd., Hamilton ON L8E 4W8 Canada
Tel: 905-573-3703; *Fax:* 905-573-0804
info@optc.org
www.optc.org
To promote the many technical, commercial & environmental benefits of the Pipe Trades & maximize their use in the construction industry; to promote the interest of the plumbing, pipe fitting, sprinkler fitting & HVAC industry in the province of Ontario
Neil McCormack, Business Manager

Pipe Line Contractors Association of Canada (PLCAC)
#201, 1075 North Service Rd. West, Oakville ON L6M 2G2 Canada
Tel: 905-847-9383; *Fax:* 905-847-7824
plcac@pipeline.ca
www.pipeline.ca

Prince Edward Island Roadbuilders & Heavy Construction Association
PO Box 1901, Charlottetown PE C1A 7N5 Canada
Tel: 902-894-9514; *Fax:* 902-894-9512
pei.roadbuilders@pei.sympatico.ca
www3.pei.sympatico.ca/pei.roadbuilders/
"Prince Edward Island Road Builders and Heavy Construction Association is comprised of companies sharing a common goal — a strong, effective voice in the Heavy Construction Industry. The Association's business is guided by a Board of Directors made up of seven representatives from the Regular Member category and two representatives from the Associate Member category who meet monthly and a Manager who maintains the day-to-day operations on behalf of the membership. We strive to encourage business with our members and promote functions where members can gather and become acquainted as well as profiling businesses in our Newsletter, The Roadrunner."

Ready Mixed Concrete Association of Ontario (RMCAO)
#3, 365 Brunel Rd., Mississauga ON L4Z 1Z5 Canada
Tel: 905-507-1122; *Fax:* 905-890-8122
dbiffis@rmcao.org
www.rmcao.org
To promote & further the business, technology & use of quality concrete through partnership between producers & the construction & specifying industries

Road Builders Association of New Brunswick (RBANB)
#5, 59 Avonlea Ct., Fredericton NB E3C 1N8 Canada
Tel: 506-454-5079; *Fax:* 506-452-7646
rbanb@nb.aibn.com
www.rbanb.com
To foster & enhance relations between the members, & between the members of other associations in construction; to acquire & disseminate information of value to the industry & to its membership; to improve & extend standards, conditions, methods & practices within the industry

Roofing Contractors Association of British Columbia (RCABC)
9734 - 201st St., Langley BC V1M 3E8 Canada
Tel: 604-882-9734; *Fax:* 604-882-1744
bporth@rcabc.org
www.rcabc.org
To provide continuing education for roofing contractors, their personnel & interested others; to represent the roofing contracting industry in its relationships with legislative & regulating bodies; to work closely with affiliate organizations & liaison groups in advancing the professionalism of roofing contracting; to provide a forum for the interaction of members; to encourage high standards of professional conduct among roofing contractors; to develop a comprehensive body of knowledge about roofing management & technology; to disseminate ideas & knowledge to members & others; to monitor new products & systems; to work for cooperation & greater

understanding between contracting, inspection, manufacturing & supply segments of the roofing industry

Roofing Contractors Association of Manitoba Inc. (RCAM)
290 Burnell St., Winnipeg MB R3G 2A7 Canada
Tel: 204-783-6365; *Fax:* 204-783-6446
info@rcam.ca
www.rcam.ca

Roofing Contractors Association of Nova Scotia (RCANS)
PO Box 141, 7 Frederick Ave., Mount Uniacke NS B0N 1Z0 Canada
Tel: 902-866-0505; *Fax:* 902-866-0506
Toll-Free: 888-278-0133
contact@rcans.ca
www.rcans.ca
RCANS is is a trade association promoting quality workmanship in the commerical, industrial & institutional roofing industry. It encourages training for roofers & was instrumental in the initiation of an apprenticeship program.

Saskatchewan Construction Safety Association Inc. (SCSA)
498 Henderson Dr., Regina SK S4N 6E3 Canada
Tel: 306-525-0175; *Fax:* 306-525-1542
Toll-Free: 800-817-2079
billj@scsaonline.ca
www.scsaonline.ca
To provide safety programs & servies to construction employers & employees in order to reduce human & financial loss associated with injuries in the construction industry

Saskatchewan Heavy Construction Association
1939 Elphinstone St., Regina SK S4T 3N3 Canada
Tel: 306-586-1805; *Fax:* 306-585-3750
slipp@saskheavy.ca
www.saskheavy.com
The Saskatchewan Heavy Construction Association is committed to the heavy construction industry by actively promoting quality, cost-effective, socially responsible services for the public and its members.

Saskatchewan Ready Mixed Concrete Association Inc. (SRMCA)
#203, 1801 McKay St., Regina SK S4N 6E7 Canada
Tel: 306-757-2788; *Fax:* 306-569-9144
www.concreteworksharder.com
SRMCA works to maintain the highest quality of concrete produced by its members. It strives to improve the industry in all aspects & represents its members in relation to governments, environmental agencies & other industry-related associations.

Sealant & Waterproofing Association (SWA)
70 Leek Cres., Richmond Hill ON L4B 1H1 Canada
Tel: 416-499-4000; *Fax:* 416-499-8752
info@swao.com
www.swao.com
To promote the exchange of ideas for the development of the highest standards & operating efficiency within the sealant & waterproofing industry

Southern Interior Construction Association (SICA)
#104, 151 Commercial Dr., Kelowna BC V1X 7W2 Canada
Tel: 250-491-7330; *Fax:* 250-491-3929
kelowna@sica.bc.ca
www.sica.bc.ca
To offer members' plans & specifications for viewing; to promote standard tendering practices
Debra Hicks, President

Structural Board Association (SBA) / Association du panneau structural
#27, 25 Valleywood Dr., Markham ON L3R 5L9 Canada
Tel: 905-475-1100; *Fax:* 905-475-1101
info@osbguide.com
www.osbguide.com
To represent manufacturers of oriented strand board; to expand market for OSB panels; to undertake & develop research programs; to monitor codes & standards; to act as liaison between governments & members
Mark P. Angelini, President/CEO

Terrazzo Tile & Marble Association of Canada (TTMAC) / Association canadienne de terrazzo, tuile et marbre
#8, 163 Buttermill Ave., Concord ON L4K 3X8
Tel: 905-660-9640; *Fax:* 905-660-0513
Toll-Free: 800-201-8599
association@ttmac.com
www.ttmac.com
To standardize terrazzo, tile, marble, & stone installation techniques, so that the industry will grow & proper; To support the hardsurface industry & its members

Toronto Construction Association
70 Leek Cres., Richmond Hill ON L4B 1H1 Canada
Tel: 416-499-4000; *Fax:* 416-499-8752
bmirsky@tcaconnect.com
www.tcaconnect.com
To develop & promote excellence within the construction industry of the Greater Toronto Area

Western Canada Roadbuilders Association
1236 Ellice Ave., Winnipeg MB R3G 0E7 Canada
Tel: 204-947-1379; *Fax:* 204-943-2279
clorenc@mhca.mb.ca
www.wcrhca.org
Represents four western provincial roadbuilders & heavy construction associations at the provincial & federal level

Western Retail Lumber Association (WRLA)
Western Retail Lumber Association Inc., #1004, 213 Notre Dame Ave., Winnipeg MB R3B 1N3
Tel: 204-957-1077; *Fax:* 204-947-5195
Toll-Free: 800-661-0253
wrla@wrla.org
www.wrla.org
To serve & promote needs & common interests of lumber, building materials & hard goods industry on the Prairies

Winnipeg Construction Association
290 Burnell St., Winnipeg MB R3G 2A7 Canada
Tel: 204-775-8664; *Fax:* 204-783-6446
wca@winnipegconstruction.ca
www.winnipegconstruction.ca

Business

Association for Corporate Growth, Toronto Chapter (ACG)
#1008, 500 Avenue Rd., Toronto ON M4V 2J6 Canada
Tel: 416-868-1881; *Fax:* 416-860-0580
acgtoronto@acg.org
www.acg.org/toronto
To foster sound corporate growth by providing its members with an opportunity to gain new ideas from speakers, seminars & discussions with people working in the field of corporate growth; to develop additional skills & techniques which will contribute to the growth of their respective organizations; to meet other corporate growth professionals who can provide counsel & valuable contacts

Better Business Bureau of Central & Northern Alberta
Capitol Place, #888, 9707 - 110 St., Edmonton AB T5K 2L9 Canada
Tel: 780-482-2341; *Fax:* 780-482-1150
Toll-Free: 800-232-7298
info@edmontonbbb.org
www.edmonton.bbb.org
To handle inquiries & complaints; To provide an ad review program; To educate the public

Better Business Bureau of Eastern & Northern Ontario & the Outaouais / Bureau d'éthique commerciale de l'Est et Nord de l'Ontario et l'Outaouais
#505, 700 Industrial Ave., Ottawa ON K1G 0Y9 Canada
Tel: 613-237-4856; *Fax:* 613-237-4878
info@ottawa.bbb.org
www.ottawa.bbb.org
To promote & foster the highest ethical relationship between business & the public through voluntary self regulation, consumer & business education, & service excellence

Better Business Bureau of Manitoba & Northwest Ontario
1030B Empress St., Winnipeg MB R3G 3H4 Canada
Tel: 204-989-9010; *Fax:* 204-989-9016
Toll-Free: 800-385-3074
bbbinquiries@mts.net
www.manitoba.bbb.org
To encourage ethical business practices through self-regulation in Manitoba.

Better Business Bureau of Mid-Western Ontario
354 Charles St., Kitchener ON N2G 4L5 Canada
Tel: 519-579-3080; *Fax:* 519-570-0072
Toll-Free: 800-459-8875
www.kitchener.bbb.org
To encourage ethical business practices through self-regulation in Mid-Western Ontario.

Better Business Bureau of Newfoundland
#301, 360 Topsail Rd., St. John's NL A1E 2B6 Canada
Tel: 709-364-2222; *Fax:* 709-364-2255
Toll-Free: 877-663-2363
info@bbbnl.org
www.nl.bbb.org
To promote and foster the highest ethical relationships between business and the public through voluntary self-regulation, consumer and business education and service excellence.

Better Business Bureau of Saskatchewan
980 Albert St., Regina SK S4R 7601 Canada
Tel: 306-352-7601; *Fax:* 306-565-6236
Toll-Free: 888-352-7601
info@bbbsask.com
www.sask.bbb.org
To be devoted to the vitality of the free enterprise system & the concerns of the consumer public; To develop, encourage, & promote an ethical marketplace

Better Business Bureau of Southern Alberta
#350, 7330 Fisher St. SE, Calgary AB T2H 2H8 Canada
Tel: 403-531-8784; *Fax:* 403-640-2514
Toll-Free: 800-661-4464
info@calgary.bbb.org
www.calgary.bbb.org
To promote & encourage ethical practices in retail market for goods & services through provision of a wide range of consultative, informative & conciliatory arbitration services for businesses & consumers.

Better Business Bureau of the Maritime Provinces
#805, 1888 Brunswick St., Halifax NS B3J 3J8 Canada
Tel: 902-422-6581; *Fax:* 902-429-6457
bbbmp@bbbmp.ca
www.maritimeprovinces.bbb.org
To provide mutually beneficial relationships between buyer & seller based on responsible business practices

Better Business Bureau of Vancouver Island
#220, 1178 Cook St., Victoria BC V8V 4A1 Canada
Tel: 250-386-6348; *Fax:* 250-386-2367
info@bbbvanisland.org
www.vi.bbb.org
Committed to the principle that fair dealing is good business for both buyer & seller & the majority of buyers & sellers are honest & responsible

Better Business Bureau of Western Ontario
PO Box 2153, #308, 200 Queens Ave., London ON N6A 4E3 Canada
Tel: 519-673-3222; *Fax:* 519-673-5966
Toll-Free: 877-283-9222
info@london.bbb.org
www.london.bbb.org
To promote the vitality of the free enterprise system & ethical business practices; To serve the concerns of business & the consuming public

Better Business Bureau of Windsor & Southwestern Ontario
#302, 880 Ouellette Ave., Windsor ON N9A 1C7 Canada
Tel: 519-258-7222; *Fax:* 519-258-1198
bbb@bbbwindsor.com
www.windsorbbb.com
Thier mission is to promote and foster the highest ethical relationship between businesses and the public through voluntary self-regulation, consumer and business education, and service education.

Better Business Bureau Serving South Central Ontario
100 James St. South, Hamilton ON L8P 2Z2 Canada
Tel: 905-526-1111; *Fax:* 905-526-1225
info@thebbb.ca, membership@thebbb.ca
www.thebbb.ca
Their mission is to develop, encourage, and promote an ethical marketplace. Their mission is to promote and foster the highest ethical relationship between businessess and the public through voluntary self-regulation, consumer and business education and service excellence.

Business Council of British Columbia
#810, 1050 Pender St. West, Vancouver BC V6E 3S7 Canada
Tel: 604-684-3384; *Fax:* 604-684-7957
info@bcbc.com
www.bcbc.com
To build a competitive & growing economy that provides opportunities for all who invest, work & live in British Columbia.

Canadian Association of Family Enterprise (CAFE) / Association canadienne des enterprises familiales
#112, 465 Morden Rd., Oakville ON L6K 3W6 Canada
Tel: 416-538-9992; *Fax:* 905-337-8260
Toll-Free: 866-849-0099
office@cafenational.org
www.cafenational.org
To improve succession statistics for family businesses across Canada where Canadian family businesses connect with peers & resources for success.

The Canadian Council for Public-Private Partnerships (CCPPP) / Le Conseil canadien pour les partenariats public-privé
1 First Canadian Place, #1600, 100 King St. West, Toronto ON M5X 1G5 Canada
Tel: 416-861-0500; *Fax:* 416-862-7661
partners@pppcouncil.ca
www.pppcouncil.ca
To act as a proponent for improvements in the quality & cost of public services provided to Canadians through innovative partnerships between the public & private sectors
Jane Peatch, Executive Director
Jane Peatch, Executive Director

Canadian Council for Small Business & Entrepreneurship (CCSBE) / Conseil canadien des PME et de l'entrepreneuriat (CCPME)
c/o Centre for Small Business & Entrepreneurship, Acadia University, 38 Crowell Dr., Willet House, Wolfville NS B4P 2R6 Canada
Tel: 902-585-1776; *Fax:* 902-585-1057
ccsbe.secretariat@acadiau.ca
www.ccsbe.org
The Canadian Council for Small Business and Entrepreneurship (CCSBE-CCPME) is a national membership-based organization promoting and advancing the developmet of small business and entreprenurship through research, education and training, networking, and dissemination of scholarly and policy-oriented information.
Jean-Marie Nkongolo-Bakenda, President
Chris Pelham, Secretary

Canadian Council of Better Business Bureaus (CCBBB) / Conseil canadien des bureaux d'éthique commerciale
#800, 2 St. Clair Ave. East, Toronto ON M4T 2T5 Canada
Tel: 416-644-4936; *Fax:* 416-644-4945
ccbbb@ccbbb.ca
www.ccbbb.ca
To protect consumers & the vitality of the free enterprise system; to foster the highest standards of responsibility & probity in business practice by advocating truth in advertising, by assuring integrity in performance of business services & by voluntary regulation & monitoring activities designed to enhance public trust & confidence in business

Canadian Council of Chief Executives (CCCE) / Conseil canadien des chefs d'entreprise
#1001, 99 Bank St., Ottawa ON K1P 6B9
Tel: 613-238-3727; *Fax:* 613-236-8679
leaders@ceocouncil.ca
www.ceocouncil.ca
To engage in policy work in Canada, North America, & the world

Canadian Federation of Independent Business (CFIB) / Fédération canadienne de l'entreprise indépendante
#401, 4141 Yonge St., Toronto ON K1P 6L7M2P 2A6
Tel: 416-222-8022; *Fax:* 416-222-6103
cfib@cfib
www.cfib-fcei.ca
To act as the voice for small businesses in Canada

Canadian Franchise Association (CFA) / Association canadienne de la franchise
#116, 5399 Eglinton Ave. West, Toronto ON M9C 5K6 Canada
Tel: 416-695-2896; *Fax:* 416-695-1950
Toll-Free: 800-665-4232
info@cfa.ca
www.cfa.ca
To promote & represent franchise excellence through a national association of businesses united by a common interest in ethical franchising.

Canadian Institute of Chartered Business Valuators (CICBV) / L'Institut canadien des experts en évaluation d'entreprises
#710, 277 Wellington St. West, Toronto ON M5V 3H2
Tel: 416-977-1117; *Fax:* 416-977-7066
admin@cicbv.ca
www.cicbv.ca
To develop high professional standards for Canadian Chartered Business Valuators; To manage the Chartered Business Valuator (CBV) designation; To govern members of the Institute with a strict Code of Ethics & Practice Standards

Canadian International Institute of Applied Negotiation (CIIAN) / L'Institut international canadien de la négociation pratique
138 Flora St., Ottawa ON K1R 5R5
Tel: 613-237-9050; *Fax:* 613-237-6951
ciian@ciian.org
www.ciian.org
Social Media: www.facebook.com/group.php?gid=48609714270; www.twitter.com/CIIAN
To build sustainable peace at local, national, & international levels
Benjamin Hoffman, President

Canadian Organization of Small Business Inc. (COSBI)
5405, 129 Ave. NW, Edmonton AB T5A 0A3 Canada
Tel: 780-423-2672
To support & promote the interests of small business & independent professionals throughout Canada; to protect the free enterprise system & the interests of independent business; to function as a lobby & service organization dealing with all levels of government or large bureaucracy; to provide members with access to information vital to business success & to present the owner/manager's point of view to decision makers in both political & private sectors
Donald Richard Eastcott, Managing Director
Roy E. Shannon, C.A., Chair

Canadian Professional Sales Association (CPSA) / Association canadienne des professionnels de la vente
#400, 655 Bay St., Toronto ON M5G 2K4
Tel: 416-408-2685; *Fax:* 416-408-2684
Toll-Free: 888-267-2772
customerservice@cpsa.com; salessuccess@cpsa.com
www.cpsa.com
Social Media: www.facebook.com/CanadianProfessionalSalesAssociation
To develop & serve sales professionals
Craig Lindsay, CSP, Chair
Rhordon Wikkramatileke, PhD, MPA, BA, Chair, Sales Institute & Secretary
Alfred Whiffen, CSP, Vice-Chair
Bob Medland, Treasurer

Canadian Society of Customs Brokers (CSCB) / Société canadienne des courtiers en douane
#320, 55 Murray St., Ottawa ON K1N 5M3 Canada
Tel: 613-562-3543; *Fax:* 613-562-3548
cscb@cscb.ca
www.cscb.ca
To act as voice of the industry to all levels of government; to provide information to members on all matters affecting customs brokerage

Canadian Youth Business Foundation (CYBF) / La Fondation canadienne des jeunes entrepreneurs
#1410, 100 Adelaide St. West, Toronto ON M5H 1S3 Canada
Tel: 416-408-2923; *Fax:* 416-408-3234
Toll-Free: 866-646-2922
info@cybf.ca
www.cybf.ca
Social Media: twitter.com/cybfcanada
CYBF helps young people who would not otherwise have the opportunity to develop their self-confidence, achieve economic independence, fulfill their ambitions, & contribute to the community through the medium of self-employment & job creation. It is a registered charity, BN: 895001261RR0001.
John Risley, O.C., Chair
Vivian Prokop, CEO

Conseil du patronat du Québec (CPQ)
#510, 1010, rue Sherbrooke ouest, Montréal QC H3A 2R7 Canada
Tél: 514-288-5161; *Téléc:* 514-288-5165
Ligne sans frais: 877-288-5161
info@cpq.qc.ca
www.cpq.qc.ca
Le CPQ intervient sur les principales tribunes où sont débattus des enjeux d'envergure pour l'ensemble de la société québécoise, dans le but de promouvoir les intérêts communs du milieu des affaires et d'assurer le mieux-être collectif, d'où sa devise Pour avoir l'assurance d'être entendu et défendu

Entrepreneurship Institute of Canada
PO Box 40043, 75 King St. South, Waterloo ON N2J 4V1 Canada
Tel: 519-885-1559; *Fax:* 519-885-0990
Toll-Free: 800-665-4497
entinst@sympatico.ca
www.entinst.ca
To distribute support & educational resources of interest to entrepreneurs to corporations, institutions, human resources departments, post-secondary educational institutions, training departments, business resource centres, libraries, & business owners across Canada & the United States

Hong Kong-Canada Business Association (HKCBA) / L'Association commerciale Hong Kong-Canada
#220, 1050 West Pender St., Vancouver BC V6E 3S7 Canada
Tel: 604-684-2410; *Fax:* 604-684-6208
nationaled@hkcba.com
www.hkcba.com
To encourage & promote trade & commercial activities across a broad range of industries between Canada & Hong Kong, & through Hong Kong to China & the Asia Pacific Region.

Italian Chamber of Commerce of Ontario (ICCO)
1502, 80 Richmond St. West, Toronto ON M5H 2A4 Canada
Tel: 416-789-7169; *Fax:* 416-789-7160
info.toronto@italchambers.ca
www.italchambers.ca
ICCO is a private, independent, not-for-profit organization whose aim is to enhance & promote business, trade & cultural relations between Canada & Italy. It acts as a liaison between the Canadian & Italian governments & their business communities.

Kelowna Chamber of Commerce
544 Harvey Ave., Kelowna BC V1Y 6C9 Canada
Tel: 250-861-3627; *Fax:* 250-861-3624
info@kelownachamber.org
www.kelownachamber.org
To improve trade & commerce & the economic, civic & social welfare of the city of Kelowna

Lloydminster Chamber of Commerce
4419 - 52 Ave., Lloydminster AB T9V 0Y8 Canada
Tel: 780-875-9013; *Fax:* 780-875-0755
contact_llc@lloydminsterchamber.com
www.lloydminsterchamber.com
To enhance private enterprise in Lloydminster & surrounding area
Pat L. Tenney, Executive Director
Peggy Bosch, President

Markham Board of Trade (MBT)
#206, 80F Centurian Dr., Markham ON L3R 8C1 Canada
Tel: 905-474-0730; *Fax:* 905-474-0685
info@markhamboard.com
www.markhamboard.com
To enhance the success of members & the Markham business community.

Meeting Professionals International (MPI)
#1700, 3030 Lyndon B. Johnson Freeway, Dallas TX 75234-2759 USA
Tel: 972-702-3000; *Fax:* 972-702-3070
feedback@mpiweb.org
www.mpiweb.org
To position meetings as a primary communications vehicle & a critical component of an organization's success; to lead the industry by serving the diverse needs of all people with a direct interest in the outcome of meetings; to educate & prepare members for their changing roles in the greater business world; to validate relevant knowledge & skills while simultaneously demonstrating a commitment to meeting excellence. Canadian office: 6519-B Mississauga Rd., Mississauga, ON L5N 1A6; phone: 905-286-4807, fax: 905-567-7191

Mission Regional Chamber of Commerce
34033 Lougheed Hwy., Mission BC V2V 5X8 Canada
Tel: 604-826-6914; *Fax:* 604-826-5916
manager@missionchamber.bc.ca
www.missionchamber.bc.ca
The Chamber fosters a network for entrepreneurial leaders to partner in education, communication & representation.

Mouvement québécois de la qualité (MQQ)
#1710, 360, rue Saint-Jacques ouest, Montréal QC H2Y 1P5 Canada
Tél: 514-874-9933; *Téléc:* 514-866-4600
mqq@qualite.qc.ca
www.qualite.qc.ca

Promouvoir et rendre accessibles aux organisations les meilleures pratiques d'affaire pour accroître leur performance et leur compétitivité
Roch Dubé, Président

The National Citizens Coalition / Coalition nationale des citoyens inc.
#501, 27 Queen St. East, Toronto ON M5C 2M6 Canada
Tel: 416-869-3838; *Fax:* 416-869-1891
Toll-Free: 888-703-5553
ncc@nationalcitizens.ca
www.nationalcitizens.ca
To promote free markets, individual freedom & responsibility under limited government & a strong defence

National Quality Institute (NQI) / Institut national de la qualité (INQ)
#307, 2275 Lakeshore West Blvd., Toronto ON M8V 3Y3 Canada
Tel: 416-251-7600; *Fax:* 416-251-9131
Toll-Free: 800-263-9648
info@nqi.ca
www.nqi.ca
To inspire & foster excellence in Canadian organizations; to enhance Canada's national well-being & global leadership through the incorporation of quality principles in business, government, education & health care; to promote, encourage & support the understanding & adoption of total quality principles & practices in all sectors of the economy across Canada; & to recognize outstanding achievement through the Canada Awards for Excellence
Allan Ebedes, President & CEO

Ontario Public Buyers Association, Inc. (OPBA)
Ridley Square, #361, 111 Fourth Ave., St Catharines ON L2S 3P5 Canada
Tel: 905-682-2644; *Fax:* 905-682-9988
info@opba.ca
www.opba.ca
To promote the ethical & effective expenditure of public funds through the principles of professional procurement

Worldwide Association of Business Coaches
c/o WABC Coaches Inc., PO Box 215, Saanichton BC V8M 2C3 Canada
Fax: 250-656-8752
info@wabccoaches.com
www.wabccoaches.com
To develop, advance & promote the emerging profession of business coaching, worldwide
Wendy Johnson, President/CEO

Centraide

Centraide Abitibi Témiscamingue et Nord-du-Québec
1009, 6e rue, Val-d'Or QC J9P 3W4 Canada
Tél: 819-825-7139; *Téléc:* 819-825-7155
courrier@centraide-atnq.qc.ca
www2.unitedway.ca
Huguette Boucher, Directrice générale

Chemical Industry

Canadian Association of Agri-Retailers (CAAR)
#107, 1090 Waverley St., Winnipeg MB R3T 0P4
Tel: 204-989-9300; *Fax:* 204-989-9306
Toll-Free: 800-463-9323
info@caar.org
www.caar.org
To represent & protect the interests of Canadian agricultural retailers

Canadian Association of Chemical Distributors (CACD) / Association canadienne des distributeurs de produits chimiques (ACDPC)
349 Davis Rd., #A, Oakville ON L6J 2X2
Tel: 905-844-9140; *Fax:* 905-844-5706
www.cacd.ca
To speak for the distribution sector of the Canadian chemical industry, reflecting the collective views of members, in dealing with governments, allied associations, & the public; To provide members of the association with services which assist them in the conduct of their business; To ensure adherence by members to a Code of Practice for Responsible Distribution

Canadian Consumer Specialty Products Association (CCSPA)
#800, 130 Albert St., Ottawa ON K1P 5G4 Canada
Tel: 613-232-6616; *Fax:* 613-233-6350
assoc@ccspa.org
www.ccspa.org
Represents the specialty chemical & formulated products industry; promotes the interests of member companies by providing a national voice, encouraging ethical practices, negotiating with government, & fostering industry cooperation

Canadian Fertilizer Institute (CFI) / Institut canadien des engrais
#802, 350 Sparks St., Ottawa ON K1R 7S8 Canada
Tel: 613-230-2600; *Fax:* 613-230-5142
fertilizer@cfi.ca
www.cfi.ca

Chemical Institute of Canada (CIC) / Institut de chimie du Canada
#550, 130 Slater St., Ottawa ON K1P 6E2 Canada
Tel: 613-232-6252; *Fax:* 613-232-5862
Toll-Free: 888-542-2242
info@cheminst.ca
www.cheminst.ca
To maintain all branches of the professions of chemical sciences & chemical engineering in their proper status among other learned & scientific professions; to encourage original research & develop & maintain high standards in profession; to enhance usefulness of profession to the public

International Plant Nutrition Institute (IPNI)
#550, 3500 Parkway Lane, Norcross GA 30092 USA
Tel: 770-447-0335; *Fax:* 770-448-0439
info@ipni.net
www.ppi-ppic.org
To assist in the design & implementation of agronomic research; to obtain scientific facts & education programs to tell those facts about balanced fertilization, particularly in relation to agricultural production systems; to conduct & provide on-site support of field experiments worldwide

Ordre des chimistes du Québec (OCQ)
#2199, 300 rue Léo-Pariseau, Montréal QC H2X 4B3 Canada
Tél: 514-844-3644; *Téléc:* 514-844-9601
information@ocq.qc.ca
www.ocq.qc.ca
L'Ordre est une corporation professionnelle dont la raison d'être est la protection du public

Society of Chemical Industry - Canadian Section (SCI)
#550, 130 Slater St., Ottawa ON K1P 6E2 Canada
scicanada@soci.org
www.soci.org
To encourage acquaintance & understanding among responsible individuals in the various fields of the industrial chemical process industries; to promote acquaintance & understanding between the chemical industry & the universities & governments; to encourage scientific education in universities by recognizing student achievements; to reward outstanding achievement in the Canadian chemical & allied industries & universities through awards & honorary lectureships; to promote communication between the members of the Canadian chemical & allied industries & those of other countries

Child & Family Services

Black Family Support Network
719, rue Des Seigneurs, Montréal QC H3J 1Y2 Canada
Tel: 514-933-1867; *Fax:* 514-933-1808
lbbfs@bell.net
Rosemary Segee, Contact

Elizabeth House / Maison Elizabeth
2131 Marlowe, Montréal QC H4A 3L4 Canada
Tel: 514-482-2488; *Fax:* 514-482-9467
info@maisonelizabethhouse.com
www.maisonelizabethhouse.com
To provide a continuum of specialized services to pregnant adolescents & women, mothers & babies, fathers, & families experiencing significant difficulty in adjusting to pregnancy & to their new roles as parents & caregivers; To support clients as they make choices & are directed to appropriate resources either in-house or in the community; To serve the anglophone community throughout the province of Quebec
Linda Schachtler, Contact

Yukon Child Care Association (YCCA)
YT
YCCA@live.com
web.mac.com/life9/YCCA
To develop a high quality, universally accessible, & affordable child care system in the Yukon; To represent caregivers & families
Cyndi Desharnais, Contact

Childbirth

Alberta Association of Midwives (AAM)
PO Box 11957, #166, 4307-130 Ave. SE, Edmonton AB T2Z 3V8 Canada
Tel: 403-214-1882
info@alberta-midwives.com
www.alberta-midwives.com
The AAM promotes awareness of the profession of midwifery, supports midwifery-centered research, participates in a provincial education program. It also represents its members in areas of remuneration, benefits and insurance.

Association of Ontario Midwives (AOM) / Association des sages-femmes de l'Ontario
#301, 365 Bloor St. E., Toronto ON M3W 3L4 Canada
Tel: 416-425-9974; *Fax:* 416-425-6905
Toll-Free: 866-418-3773
admin@aom.on.ca
www.aom.on.ca
To represent midwives & the practice of midwifery in Ontario
Kelly Stadelbauer, Executive Director

College of Midwives of British Columbia (CMBC)
#210, 1682 West 7th Ave., Vancouver BC V6J 4S6 Canada
Tel: 604-742-2230; *Fax:* 604-730-8908
information@cmbc.bc.ca
www.cmbc.bc.ca
To serve & protect the public interest by registering competent midwives who will practise safely & ethically in British Columbia

Infant Feeding Action Coalition
6 Trinity Sq., Toronto ON M5G 1B1 Canada
Tel: 416-595-9819; *Fax:* 416-591-9355
info@infactcanada.ca
www.infactcanada.ca
To protect, promote & support breastfeeding in Canada & globally; to promote better infant & maternal health; to foster appropriate mother & infant nutrition

International Society for the Study of Hypertension in Pregnancy (Canada) Inc. (ISSHP) / Société internationale pour l'étude de l'hypertension en grossesse (Canada) inc.
CHUS, Site Fleurimont, 3001, 12e av nord, Sherbrooke QC J1H 5N4 Canada
Tel: 819-346-1110; *Fax:* 819-820-6434
jean-marie.moutquin@usherbrooke.ca
To promote multidisciplinary approach to the study of hypertension in pregnancy

La Leche League Canada (LLLC) / Ligue La Leche Canada
PO Box 700, Winchester ON K0C 2K0 Canada
Tel: 613-774-4900; *Fax:* 613-774-2798
Toll-Free: 800-665-4324
ofm@LLLC.ca
www.lllc.ca
To act as a support network for breastfeeding mothers; To promote the importance of breastfeeding in Canada; To disseminate information on how to help mothers succeed in breastfeeding

Multiple Births Canada (MBC) / Naissances multiples Canada
PO Box 432, Wasaga Beach ON L0L 2P0 Canada
Tel: 705-429-0901; *Fax:* 705-429-9809
Toll-Free: 866-228-8824
office@multiplebirthscanada.org
www.multiplebirthscanada.org
To improve the quality of life for multiple birth individuals & their families through research, education, service & advocacy

Serena Canada
151 Holland Ave., Ottawa ON K1Y 0Y2 Canada
Tel: 613-728-6536; *Toll-Free:* 888-373-7362
sc@serena.ca
www.serena.ca
Serena promotes a natural family planning method based on information from a woman's body. The couple can identify the fertile, infertile & relatively infertile phases, so they themselves can choose whether or not to conceive a child. Respect for human life from conception is central to its philosophy. It is a registered charity, BN: 119145621RR0001.

Children & Youth

Alberta Associations for Bright Children (AABC)
c/o Action for Bright Children Calgary Society, PO Box 36093, Stn. Lakeview, Calgary AB T3E 7C6 Canada
Tel: 403-463-9612
www.albertaabc.org
To inform & support professionals & parents who are facing the challenge of dealing with bright, gifted, talented children; to advocate at the school board & government levels to ensure that resources & expertise are allocated in a manner that serves the children best

Alberta Child Care Association (ACCA)
#110, 10025 - 106 St., Edmonton AB T5J 1G4 Canada
Tel: 780-421-7544; *Fax:* 780-428-0080
Toll-Free: 877-421-9937
www.albertachildcare.org
ACCA is non-profit, member-based society with a mission to strengthen and advance the early learning & child care profession in Alberta.
Marg Golberg, Chair
Karen Baretta, Office Manager

Association for Bright Children (Ontario) (ABC Ontario) / Société pour enfants doués et surdoués (Ontario)
c/o 135 Brant St., Oakville ON L6K 2Z8 Canada
Tel: 416-925-6136
abcinfo@abcontario.ca
www.abcontario.ca
ABC Ontario is volunteer-based, self-support, non-profit network dedicated to providing information & support to parents of bright & gifted children. It works to increase the understanding & acceptance of bright & gifted children/youth at home, at school & in the community, & encourages society to nurture them that they may reach their full potential. It is a registered charity, BN: 118777275RR0001.

Association québécoise des centres de la petite enfance (AQCPE)
#200, 6611, rue Jarry est, Montréal QC H1P 1W5 Canada
Tél: 514-326-8008; *Téléc:* 514-326-3322
Ligne sans frais: 888-326-8008
info@aqcpe.com
www.aqcpe.com
A pour mandat la concertation des acteurs du réseau, la représentation politique de ses membres et la promotion des centres de la petite enfance, et services de soutien; représente les employeurs du secteur des CPE à l'occasion de négociations, en matière de relations du travail et de main-d'oeuvre; l'AQCPE est reconnue par le Min. de la Famille et des Aînés pour les négociations provinciales.
Jean Robitaille, Directeur général
Violaine Ouellette, Responsable des communications

B'nai Brith Youth Organization Canada (BBYO)
4700 Bathurst St., 2nd Fl., Toronto ON M2R 1W8 Canada
Tel: 416-398-2004; *Fax:* 416-398-5780
info@bbyo.on.ca
www.bbyo.on.ca
To educate young people about the richness of Jewish culture & heritage
Kevin Goodman, Program Director

Boys & Girls Clubs of Alberta
J. Percy Page Centre, 11759 Groat Rd., Edmonton AB T5M 3K6 Canada
Tel: 780-415-1734; *Fax:* 780-415-1737
www.bgccan.com/clubresults.asp?l=e&location=ab
Social Media: www.facebook.com/group.php?gid=24403790656
The Clubs offer educational, recreational & skills development programs & services to children from pre-school to young adulthood. Activities are scheduled after school, evenings & weekends, providinge a safe, supportive place where children & youth can build positive relationships, & develop confidence & skills.

Boys & Girls Clubs of Canada (BGCC) / Clubs garçons & filles du Canada
#204, 7100 Woodbine Ave., Markham ON L3R 5J2 Canada
Tel: 905-477-7272; *Fax:* 905-477-2056
info@bgccan.com
www.bgccan.com
Social Media: www.facebook.com/group.php?gid=2233316912
To provide safe, supportive place where children & youth can experience new opportunities, overcome barriers, build positive relationships & develop confidence & skills for life

Boys & Girls Clubs of Manitoba
Central Region, #204, 7100 Woodbine Ave., Markham ON L3R 5J2 Canada
Tel: 416-535-9675; *Fax:* 905-477-2056
www.bgccan.com/clubresults.asp?l=e&location=mb
The Clubs offer educational, recreational & skills development programs & services to children from pre-school to young adulthood. Activities are scheduled after school, evenings & weekends, providinge a safe, supportive place where children & youth can build positive relationships, & develop confidence & skills.
Sandra Morris, Central Region Director
Brittany Tough, Central Region Coordinator

Boys & Girls Clubs of New Brunswick
Maritime Region, c/o #204, 7100 Woodbine Ave., Markham ON L3R 5J2 Canada
Tel: 902-469-1550
www.bgccan.com/clubresults.asp?l=e&location=nb
The Clubs offer educational, recreational & skills development programs & services to children from pre-school to young adulthood. Activities are scheduled after school, evenings & weekends, providinge a safe, supportive place where children & youth can build positive relationships, & develop confidence & skills.

Boys & Girls Clubs of P.E.I.
PO Box 86, 1253 Port Hill Stn. Rd, Tyne Valley PE C0B 2C0 Canada
Tel: 902-831-3297; *Fax:* 902-831-3466
www.boysandgirlsclubsofpei.org
Their mission is to provide a safe, supportive place where children and youth can experience new oppourtunities, overcome barriers, build positive relationships and develop confidence and skills for life.

Boys & Girls Clubs of Québec / Clubs garçons et filles du Québec
Region de Québec, c/o #204, 7100 Woodbine Ave., Markham ON L3R 5J2 Canada
Tél: 905-477-7272; *Téléc:* 905-477-2056
www.bgccan.com/clubresults.asp?l=e&location=qc

Boys & Girls Clubs of Saskatchewan
J. Percy Page Centre, 11759 Groat Rd., Edmonton AB T5M 3K6 Canada
Tel: 780-415-1734; *Fax:* 780-415-1737
Toll-Free: 877-615-1734
www.bgccan.com/clubresults.asp?l=e&location=sk
The Clubs offer educational, recreational & skills development programs & services to children from pre-school to young adulthood. Activities are scheduled after school, evenings & weekends, providinge a safe, supportive place where children & youth can build positive relationships, & develop confidence & skills.

Boys & Girls Clubs of Yukon
Pacific Region, PO Box 20222, 1434 Graham St., Kelowna BC V1Y 9H2 Canada
Tel: 250-762-3914; *Fax:* 250-762-6562
www.bgccan.com/clubresults.asp?l=e&location=yt
The Clubs offer educational, recreational & skills development programs & services to children from pre-school to young adulthood. Activities are scheduled after school, evenings & weekends, providinge a safe, supportive place where children & youth can build positive relationships, & develop confidence & skills.

Canadian Association for Young Children (CAYC) / Association canadienne pour les jeunes enfants (ACJE)
#302, 1775 West 11th Ave., Vancouver BC V6J 2C1 Canada
membership@cayc.ca
www.cayc.ca
To influence policies & programs affecting critical issues related to the education & welfare of Canadian young children from birth through age nine

Canadian Child Care Federation (CCCF) / Fédération canadienne des services de garde à l'enfance (FCSGE)
#201, 383 Parkdale Ave., Ottawa ON K1Y 4R4
Tel: 613-729-5289; *Fax:* 613-729-3159
Toll-Free: 800-858-1412
info@cccf-fcsge.ca
www.cccf-fcsge.ca
To promote excellence in child care & early learning

Canadian Young Judaea
788 Marlee Ave., Toronto ON M6B 3K1 Canada
Tel: 416-781-5156; *Fax:* 416-787-3100
Toll-Free: 800-804-6661
youngjudaea@bellnet.ca
www.youngjudaea.ca
Canada Young Judaea is Canada's largest Zionist youth movement and are affiliated with six resdential summer camps across Canada; they are pluralistic and apolitical.

Child Find Alberta (CFA)
3751 - 21 St. NW, Calgary AB T2E 6T5 Canada
Tel: 403-270-3463; *Fax:* 403-270-8355
Toll-Free: 800-561-1733
info@childfind.ab.ca
www.childfind.ab.ca
Social Media: twitter.com/ChildFindAB
To aid in location of missing &/or abducted children & to reunite these children with their legal custodians; to offer relevant information & support to families who have been reunited; to prevent, through education, abduction of children & runaway children situations.

Child Find British Columbia
#208, 2722 Fifth St., Victoria BC V8T 4B2 Canada
Tel: 250-382-7311; *Fax:* 250-382-0227
Toll-Free: 888-689-3463
childvicbc@shaw.ca
childfindbc.com
To assist in the search & location of missing children, providing support to law enforcement & families; to educate & prevent the abduction & exploitation of children & provide awareness

Child Find Canada Inc. (CFC)
PO Box 237, Oakville MB R0H 0Y0 Canada
Tel: 204-870-1298
childcan@aol.com
www.childfind.ca
Supports provincial Child Find organizations in the location of & education in the prevention of missing children; increases national awareness of issues relating to missing children; advocates for the protection & rights of children.
Kathryn Anderson, National Co-Ordinator

Child Find Manitoba
#343, 800 Portage Ave., Winnipeg MB R3G 0N4 Canada
Tel: 204-945-5735; *Fax:* 204-948-2461
Toll-Free: 800-532-9135
childmb@aol.com
www.childfind.mb.ca
To assist in the location & prevention of missing children; to increase the provincial awareness of issues relating to missing children & to advocate for the protection & rights of children

Child Find Newfoundland/Labrador
#217, 31 Peet St., St. John's NL A1B 3W8 Canada
Tel: 709-738-4400; *Fax:* 709-738-0550
childnfld@aol.com
www.childfind.ca
To prevent missing children; To support the search for missing children
Jeff Sears, President

Child Find Ontario
440A Britannia Rd. East, Mississauga ON L4Z 1X9 Canada
Tel: 905-712-3463; *Fax:* 905-712-3462
Toll-Free: 800-543-8477
mail@childfindontario.ca
www.ontario.childfind.ca
Child Find Ont. assists in the search & recovery process of missing children; educates on the dangers of abduction to minimize the risk; is a registered charity, BN : 130263502RR0001.

Child Find PEI Inc.
PO Box 21008, 106C Kensington Rd., Charlottetown PE C1A 5J5 Canada
Tel: 902-368-1678; *Fax:* 902-368-1389
Toll-Free: 800-387-7962
childfind@pei.aibn.com
www.childfindpei.com
Child Find PEI is a registered, non-profit, charitable organization that assists in the location of missing children; increases awareness of the problem of missing children; teaches ways to prevent abduction; provides assistance & support to families of a missing child.

Child Find Saskatchewan Inc.
#202, 3502 Taylor St. East, Saskatoon SK S7H 5H9 Canada
Tel: 306-955-0070; *Fax:* 306-373-1311
Toll-Free: 800-513-3463
childsask@aol.com
www.childfind.sk.ca

To locate missing & abducted children & reunite them with their lawful parent or guardian; to increase public awareness of the need to protect children; to educate both parents & child on street proofing technology & to support families of missing children

Children's Creative Response to Conflict (CCRC)
211 Bronson Ave., Ottawa ON K1R 6H5 Canada
Tel: 613-234-9019
ccrccanada@gmail.com
www.ccrc-crc.ca
To help educators, parents and those who work with young people learn creative skills of non-violent conflict resolution through cooperation, communication, affirmation, problem solving, mediation and bias awareness.

Children's Wish Foundation of Canada / Fondation canadienne rêves d'enfants
#350, 1101 Kingston Rd., Pickering ON L1V 1B5 Canada
Tel: 905-839-8882; *Fax:* 905-839-3745
Toll-Free: 800-700-4437
www.childrenswish.ca
The Foundation grants wishes to children suffering from a high risk, life-threatening illnesses. It is a registered charity, BN: 124038878RR0001.

Desta Black Youth Network
Padua Centre, 1950, rue St-Antoine ouest, Montréal QC H3J 1A5 Canada
Tel: 514-932-7597; *Fax:* 514-932-9468
info@destanetwork.ca
www.destanetwork.ca
To provide an outreach initiative to young adults, from ages 18 to 25, within the Black community; To mentor marginalized youth in the areas of education, employment, & personal growth; To empower vision, strengthen authentic identity, & promote excellence

Fondation Rêves d'Enfants, div. Nord-du-Québec
423, rue Normand, Chibougamau QC G8P 1A1 Canada
Tél: 418-748-3702
Kathy Fortin

Gifted Children's Association of British Columbia (GCABC)
c/o West Coast Child Care Resource Centre, 2772 East Broadway, Vancouver BC V5M 1Y8
info@gcabc.ca
www.gcabc.ca
To support parents & others meet the needs of gifted children across British Columbia

Girl Guides of Canada (GGC) / Guides du Canada
50 Merton St., Toronto ON M4S 1A3 Canada
Tel: 416-487-5281; *Fax:* 416-487-5570
www.girlguides.ca
Social Media:
facebook.com/pages/girl-guides-of-canada/111161488925958
GGC strives to prepare girls to meet the challenges of life, & in a safe environment, teaches them such skills as bandaging wounds & coping with bullies. It encourages girls to foster friendships & develop a sense of leadership, empowering them to become responsible members of the community. It is part of a global organization of 145 countries, the largest for girls in the world. It is a registered charity, BN: 118938554RR0027.

Junior Achievement Canada (JACAN) / Jeunes Entreprises du Canada
#218, 1 Eva Rd., Toronto ON M9C 4Z5 Canada
Tel: 416-622-4602; *Fax:* 416-622-6861
Toll-Free: 800-265-0699
programs@jacan.org
www.jacan.org
International not-for-profit organization which provides practical business & economic education programs & experience for young people through partnerships with business & education communities

Junior Chamber International Canada / Jeune chambre internationale du Canada
14 Bruce Farm Dr., Toronto ON M2H 1G3 Canada
Tel: 416-886-9756; *Fax:* 416-221-9926
Toll-Free: 800-265-0484
administration@jcicanada.com
www.jcicanada.com
To contribute to the advancement of the global community by providing the opportunity for young people to develop the leadership skills, social responsibility & fellowship necessary to create positive change. Chapters across Canada.

Justice for Children & Youth (JFCY)
#1203, 415 Yonge St., Toronto ON M5B 2E7 Canada
Tel: 416-920-1633; *Fax:* 416-920-5855
Toll-Free: 866-999-5329
info@jfcy.org
www.jfcy.org
To assist & empower children & youth in obtaining fair & equal access to legal, educational, medical & social resources; to provide direct legal assistance in all areas of children's law to eligible children & youth of Metro Toronto & vicinity; to provide summary legal advice, information & assistance to young people, parents, professionals & community groups on a province-wide basis; to advocate for law & policy reform; to monitor & respond to developments & changes to the laws which affect children

Manitoba Child Care Association (MCCA)
2350 McPhillips St., 2nd Fl., Winnipeg MB R2V 4J6
Tel: 204-586-8587; *Fax:* 204-589-5613
Toll-Free: 888-323-4676
info@mccahouse.org
www.mccahouse.org
To act as the voice of child care in Manitoba; To advocate for a quality system of child care; To advance early childhood education as a profession

North America Missing Children Association Inc. (NAMCA)
Toll-Free: 800-260-0753
namca@nbnet.nb.ca
To become a liaison between parent/guardians & police to help find missing & abducted people; to help educate the public with prevention tips on runaways, abductions & kidnapping; recognized by the RCMP Missing Children Registry
Patricia Hughes, Executive Director

Ranch Ehrlo Society
PO Box 570, Pilot Butte SK S0G 3Z0 Canada
Tel: 306-781-1800; *Fax:* 306-757-0599
inquiries@ranchehrlo.ca
www.ehrlo.com
To provide a range of quality assessment, treatment, education & support services that improves the social & emotional functioning of children & youth referred to our program

Réseau Enfants Retour Canada / Missing Children's Network Canada
#420, 376, ave Victoria, Montréal QC H3Z 1C3 Canada
Tél: 514-843-4333; *Téléc:* 514-843-8211
Ligne sans frais: 888-692-4673
info@missingchildren.ca
www.missingchildren.ca
Assister les parents à la recherche de leurs enfants portés disparus; aider également les professionnels, avocats, policiers, travailleurs sociaux impliqués dans une situation de disparition d'enfant ou de prévention contre une disparition; réseau international de communication et d'aide qui oeuvre également à sensibiliser la population au problème des enfants disparus et exploités par des affiches, émissions, documents

Safe Kids Canada / Sécurijeunes Canada
#2105, 180 Dundas St. West, Toronto ON M5G 1Z8 Canada
Tel: 416-813-7288; *Fax:* 416-813-4986
Toll-Free: 888-723-3847
safekids.web@sickkids.ca
www.safekidscanada.ca
Social Media: www.twitter.com/safekidscanada
National Injury Prevention Program of the Hospital for Sick Children; promotes effective strategies to prevent unintentional injuries; builds partnerships & uses a comprehensive approach to advance safety & reduce the burden of injuries to Canada's children & youth
Pamela Fuselli, Executive Director

Scouts Canada / Scouts du Canada
1345 Baseline Rd., Ottawa ON K2C 0A7 Canada
Tel: 613-224-5131; *Fax:* 613-224-3571
Toll-Free: 888-726-8879
helpcentre@scouts.ca
www.scouts.ca
Social Media: facebook.com/group.php?gid=70367180847
The Association contributes to the education of young people through a value system based on the Scout Promise & Law. It emphasizes learning by doing, particularly in small groups, with outdoor activities as a learning resource. Scouting is based on 3 principles which are Duty to God, Others & Self. It is a registered charity, BN: 107761694RR0028.

A World of Dreams Foundation Canada / La Fondation canadienne un monde de rêves
#3575, 6900, boul déCarie, Montréal QC H3A 3L4 Canada
Tel: 514-985-3003; *Fax:* 514-985-9280
Toll-Free: 800-567-7254
info@awdreams.com
www.awdreams.com
To fulfill dreams for chronically, critically & terminally ill children
Lora Cianci, Director

Citizenship & Immigration

Canadian Association of Professional Immigration Consultants (CAPIC) / Association Canadienne des Conseillers Professionnels en Immigration (ACCPI)
#602, 245 Fairview Mall Dr., Toronto ON M2J 4T1
Tel: 416-483-7044; *Fax:* 416-309-1985
info@capic.ca
www.capic.ca
Social Media:
www.facebook.com/group.php?gid=104799452895463
To represent Certified Canadian Immigration Consultants (CCIC), or full members of the Canadian Society of Immigration Consultants (CSIC)
Katarina Onuschak, Executive Director
Monica Poon, National Coordinator
Christopher Daw, Director, Lobbying
Lynn Gaudet, Director, Communications
Deepak Kohli, Director, Membership
Tanveer Sharief, Director, Education & Training

Canadian Ukrainian Immigrant Aid Society (CUIAS)
2383 Bloor St. W., 2nd Fl., Toronto ON M6S 1P9 Canada
Tel: 416-767-4595; *Fax:* 416-767-2658
cuias@cuias.org
www.cuias.org
To sponsor & aid in settlement of Ukrainian refugees.

Centre for Information & Community Services of Ontario (CICS)
c/o Immigrant Resource Centre, 2330 Midland Ave., Toronto ON M1S 5G5 Canada
Tel: 416-292-7510; *Fax:* 416-292-7579
Crisis Hot-Line: 416-292-2832
cics@cicscanada.com
www.cicscanada.com
To provide a wide range of cost-effective, culturally-sensitive & professional services; to empower newcomers to settle & integrate into Canadian society; to promote active citizenship in the community; committed to excellence & to be a leading agency in settlement, education & social services

Eritrean Canadian Community Centre of Metropolitan Toronto (ECCC)
579 St. Clair Ave. W, Toronto ON M6C 1A3 Canada
Tel: 416-658-8580; *Fax:* 416-658-7442
info@eccctoronto.ca
www.eccctoronto.ca
The Eritrean Canadian Community Centre of Metropolitan Toronto (ECCC) is a non-profit charitable organization established in 1985. It provides immigrant and refugees settlement services and creates the environment for building capacity in the Eritrean community of Toronto.

Immigrant Centre Manitoba
100 Adelaide St., Winnipeg MB R3A 0W2 Canada
Tel: 204-943-9158; *Fax:* 204-949-0734
info@icmanitoba.com
www.international-centre.ca
To encourage pride in Canada & appreciation of Canadian citizenship; to encourage intercultural understanding in multicultural Canada; to support immigration & provide caring services to newcomers.

Jewish Immigrant Aid Services of Canada (JIAS) / Services canadiens d'assistance aux immigrants juifs
#306, 4580 Dufferin St., Toronto ON M3H 5Y2 Canada
Tel: 416-630-9051; *Fax:* 416-630-9029
national@jias.org
www.jias.org
To serve the needs of Jewish immigrants & refugees; to facilitate the legal entry of Jewish immigrants to Canada; to provide services about immigration, naturalization, resettlement & integration.

National Organization of Immigrant & Visible Minority Women of Canada (NOIVMWC) / Organisation nationale des femmes immigrantes et des femmes appartenant à une minorité visible du Canada (ONFIFAMVC)
#412, 219 Argyle St., Ottawa ON K2P 2H4 Canada
Tel: 613-232-0689; *Fax:* 613-232-0988
noivmwc@noivmwc.org
www.noivmwc.org
To ensure equality for immigrant & visible minority women within bilingual Canada by putting into place strategies that will combat sexism, racism, poverty, isolation & violence & by acting as an advocate on issues dealing with immigrant & visible minority women.

Ontario Council of Agencies Serving Immigrants (OCASI)
#200, 110 Eglinton Ave. West, Toronto ON M4R 1A3 Canada
Tel: 416-322-4950; *Fax:* 416-322-8084
generalmail@ocasi.org
www.ocasi.org; www.settlement.org
To act as a collective voice for immigrant services; to provide access for immigrants & refugees to settlement services; to provide social organizational development with community groups, policy analysis & government relations, professional development of member agency staff & research into issues facing immigrant service agencies

Ottawa Community Immigrant Services Organization (OCISO) / Organisme communautaire des services aux immigrants d'Ottawa
959 Wellington St. West, Ottawa ON K1Y 2X5 Canada
Tel: 613-725-0202; *Fax:* 613-725-9054
info@ociso.org
www.ociso.org
To enable newcomers & their families to fully participate in an open & welcoming Ottawa, through innovative services, community building & public engagement

Place Benoît Bon Courage Community Centre / Centre Communautaire Bon Courage De Place Benoît
#2, 155 Place Benoît, Ville Saint-Laurent QC H4N 2H4 Canada
Tél: 514-744-0897; *Téléc:* 514-744-6205
Provides local services for immigrants
Dayonn Vann, Contact

Conservation

Nova Scotia Federation of Anglers and Hunters (NSFAH)
PO Box 654, Halifax NS B3J 2T3 Canada
Tel: 902-477-8898
tonyrodgers@eastlink.ca
www.nsfah.ca
The Nova Scotia Federation of Anglers and Hunters is dedicated to the conservation and propagation of the wildlife in the province for those who hunt, fish, trap or otherwise wish to enjoy the wildlife resources of Nova Scotia. This will be accomplished by education, cooperation and exchange of information will all people and by uniting provincial organizations having similar objectives.
Tony Rodgers, Executive Director

Consumers

Consumers Council of Canada (CCC)
#100, 35 Madison Ave., Toronto ON M5R 2S2 Canada
Tel: 416-483-2696; *Fax:* 416-483-4128
billhuzar@consumerscouncil.com
www.consumerscouncil.com
Christina Bisanz, Executive Director
Bill Huzar, President

Consumers' Association of Canada (CAC) / Association des consommateurs du Canada
PO Box 9300, 436 Gilmour St., 3rd Fl., Ottawa ON K1G 3T9 Canada
Tel: 613-238-2533; *Fax:* 613-238-2538
info@consumer.ca
www.consumer.ca
To represent & articulate the best interests of Canadian consumers to all levels of government & to all sectors of society by continually earning recognition as the trusted voice of the consumer on a national basis; to inform & educate consumers on marketplace issues; work with government & industry to solve marketplace problems; focuses its work in the areas of food, health, trade, standards, financial services, communications industries & other marketplace issues as they emerge

Copyright

Canadian Artists Representation Copyright Collective Inc.
109A Fourth Ave., Ottawa ON K1S 2L3 Canada
Tel: 613-232-3818; *Fax:* 613-232-8384
carcc@carcc.ca
www.carcc.ca
To license and administer copyright for its affiliates, visual and media artists, in Canada.
Janice Seline, Executive Director

Culture

Albanian-Canadian Community Association
26 Six Point Rd., Toronto ON M8Z 2W9 Canada
Tel: 416-503-4704; *Fax:* 416-503-4704
info@albcan.org
www.albcan.org
Petraq Peci, Chairman

Assemblée communautaire fransaskoise (ACF)
#101, 2445 - 13 Ave., Regina SK S4P 0W1 Canada
Tél: 306-569-1912; *Téléc:* 306-781-7916
Ligne sans frais: 800-991-1912
acf@sasktel.net
www.fransaskois.sk.ca
Travaille au développement, à l'épanouissement et au rayonnement de tous ses membres; est l'entité gouvernante de la communauté fransaskoise

Assemblée parlementaire de la Francophonie (APF) Région Amérique, Assemblée nationale, 1020, rue des Parlementaires, 6e étage, Québec QC G1A 1A3 Canada
Tél: 418-643-7391; *Téléc:* 418-643-1865
alavoie@assnat.qc.ca
www.regionamerique-apf.org
Promouvoir la langue et la culture francaise; promouvoir les droits de l'homme et la démocratie
André Lavoie, Secrétaire administrative régionale

Association canadienne-française de l'Alberta (ACFA)
#303, Pav. II, 8627, rue Marie-Anne-Gaboury, Edmonton AB T6C 3N1 Canada
Tél: 780-466-1680; *Téléc:* 780-465-6773
acfa@acfa.ab.ca
www.acfa.ab.ca
Mèdia social: www.facebook.com/acfaab
Représenter la population francophone de l'Alberta; promouvoir le bien-être intellectuel, culturel et social des francophones de l'Alberta; encourager, faciliter et développer l'enseignement en français; entretenir des relations amicales avec les groupes de différentes origines ethniques et anglophones dans la province

Association canadienne-française de l'Ontario (ACFO)
3349, ch Navan, Gloucester ON K4B 1H9 Canada
Tél: 613-841-5525
dg@acfo.ca
www.acfo.ca
Appuyer le développement communautaire; rassembler les forces vives de la communauté franco-ontarienne; faire des représentations politiques

Association franco-yukonnaise (AFY)
302 rue Strickland, Whitehorse YT Y1A 2K1 Canada
Tél: 867-668-2663; *Téléc:* 867-663-3511
Ligne sans frais: 866-673-7632
afy@afy.yk.ca
www.afy.yk.ca
Le secteur culturel de l'Association franco-yukonnaise offre plusieurs activités sociales, culturelles et artistiques. La culture francophone du Yukon passe par les arts visuels, la chanson, la musique, les rires, la danse, les spectacles amateurs, la tire d'érable, les rencontres sociales et bien plus encore.

Association of Canadian Clubs / Association des cercles canadiens
#211, 2415 Holly Lane, Ottawa ON K1V 2P2 Canada
Tel: 613-236-8288; *Fax:* 613-236-8299
cdnclub@ca.inter.net
www.canadianclub.ca
To promote Canadian identity; to encourage Canadian unity; to foster throughout Canada an interest in public affairs; to cultivate attachment to Canadian institutions

Canada-Israel Cultural Foundation (CICF) / Fondation culturelle Canada-Israël
4700 Bathurst St., 2nd Fl., Toronto ON M2R 1W8 Canada
Tel: 416-932-2260; *Fax:* 416-398-5780
cicf@bellnet.ca
www.cicfweb.ca
The mission of the Canada-Israel Cultural Foundation is to act as a cultural bridge between Canada and Israel, promoting and supporting intercultural exchange with a special focus on young artists, and developing artistic life by awarding scholarships and grants.

Canadian-Scandinavian Foundation (CSF) / Fondation Canada-Scandinavie
PO Box 135, Stn. B, Montréal QC H3B 3J5 Canada
Tel: 514-398-4740; *Fax:* 514-398-7356
csf-fcs@hotmail.com
www.canada-scandinavia.ca
The Foundation raises funds to distribute to Canadian students who wish to travel to Denmark, Finland, Iceland, Norway or Sweden, to undertake studies at a Scandinavian institution. It promotes study/research projects by offering travel busaries.
Derek Yaple-Schobert, Chair
Hans Moller, President

Centre culturel franco-manitobain (CCFM)
340, boul Provencher, Saint Boniface MB R2H 0G7 Canada
Tél: 204-233-8972; *Téléc:* 204-233-3324
administration@ccfm.mb.ca
www.ccfm.mb.ca
Média social:
www.facebook.com/people/Centre-Culturel-Franco-Manitobain/1549747456
A pour objectif de maintenir, d'encourager, de favoriser et de patronner, par tous les moyens possibles, toutes les formes d'activités culturelles de langue française, et de rendre la culture canadienne-française accesible à tous les résidents de la province.

Centre francophone de Toronto (CFT)
20 Lower Spadina Ave., Toronto ON M5V 2Z1 Canada
Tél: 416-203-1220; *Téléc:* 416-203-1165
contact@centrefranco.org
www.centrefranco.org
Permettre à la population francophone du grand Toronto d'avoir accès à des services d'information, d'orientation et d'encadrement susceptibles de promouvoir la dimension humaine, culturelle et communautaire des multiples visages de la francophonie

Chateauguay Valley English-Speaking Peoples' Association (CVESPA)
1493, rte 138, CP 1357, Huntingdon QC J0S 1H0 Canada
Tel: 450-264-5386; *Fax:* 450-264-5387
Toll-Free: 800-665-9841
neilburdon@sympatico.ca
www.cvespa.org
To assure preservation, maintenance & on-going development of English-speaking population in Southwest Québec; to encourage continuous development of their institutions & cultural heritage; to assure full participation & representation of English-speaking community in all aspects of Québec society; to promote positive attitudes in English-speaking community to participate fully & harmoniously with French-speaking population; to foster activities which would bring the two communities together to improve their mutual understanding

Chinese Canadian Association of Prince Edward Island (CCAPEI)
president.ccapei@gmail.com
www.ccapei.org
Zhongyu Zhang, President

Conseil de la vie française en Amérique (CVFA)
#201, 5350, boul Henri-Bourassa, Québec QC G1H 6Y8 Canada
Tél: 418-626-5665; *Téléc:* 418-626-5663
Favoriser le développement et l'épanouissement des communautés d'origine de langue et de culture françaises en Amerique

The Council of Canadians (COC) / Le Conseil des Canadiens
#700, 170 Laurier Ave. West, Ottawa ON K1P 5V5 Canada
Tel: 613-233-2773; *Fax:* 613-233-6776
Toll-Free: 800-387-7177
inquiries@canadians.org
www.canadians.org
With chapters across the country, The Council of Canadians is Canada's largest citizens' organization, working to protect Canadian independence in areas such as energy & environment, health care & fair trade. The Council provides a critical voice on key national issues: safeguarding our social programs,

promoting economic justice, renewing Canada's democracy, asserting Canadian sovereignty, promoting alternatives to corporate-style free trade & preserving the environment

Fédération acadienne de la Nouvelle-Écosse (FANE)
La Maison acadienne, 54 Queen St., Dartmouth NS B2Y 1G3 Canada
Tél: 902-433-0065; *Téléc:* 902-433-0066
fane@federationacadienne.ca
www.federationacadienne.ca
Un regroupement d'organismes régionaux, provinciaux et institutionnels d'expression française qui s'engage à promouvoir l'épanouissement et le développement global de la communauté acadienne et francophone de la Nouvelle-Écosse.

Fédération culturelle canadienne-française (FCCF)
Place de la Francophonie, #405, 450 Rideau St., Ottawa ON K1N 5Z4 Canada
Tél: 613-241-8770; *Téléc:* 613-241-6064
Ligne sans frais: 800-267-2005
info@fccf.ca
www.fccf.ca
Défendre et promouvoir les arts et la culture de la francophonie canadienne hors-Québec.
Éric Dubeau, Directeur général

Fédération de la jeunesse canadienne-française inc. (FJCF)
#403, 450 Rideau St., Ottawa ON K1N 5Z4 Canada
Tél: 613-562-4624; *Téléc:* 613-562-3995
Ligne sans frais: 800-267-5173
fjcf@fjcf.ca
www.fjcf.ca
Etre le porte-parole national de la jeunesse canadienne-française et acadienne; assurer l'épanouissement de la jeunesse dans les secteurs de l'éducation, des arts et communications, des loisirs et de l'économie; augmenter la visibilité de la FJCF et de ses membres auprès de leurs différentes clientèles; augmenter les occasions pour les jeunes d'utiliser la langue française; renforcer le sentiment d'appartenance des jeunes, pour qu'ils soient des agents de changement dans leur communauté.

Fédération des communautés francophones et acadienne du Canada (FCFAC)
#300, 450 rue Rideau, Ottawa ON K1N 5Z4 Canada
Tél: 613-241-7600; *Téléc:* 613-241-6046
info@fcfa.ca
www.fcfa.ca
Défendre et promouvoir les droits et les intérêts des communautés francophones et acadiennes qu'elle représente.

Fondation franco-ontarienne (FFO)
#102, 559, av King Edward, Ottawa ON K1N 7N5 Canada
Tél: 613-565-4720; *Téléc:* 613-565-8539
info@fondationfranco-ontarienne.ca
www.fondationfranco-ontarienne.ca
La Fondation franco-ontarienne appuie financièrement la réalisation d'initiatives qui assurent la vitalité de la communauté franco-ontarienne
Solange Fortin, Coordonnatrice générale

Guyana Cultural Association of Montréal (GCAM)
PO Box 29640, Stn. CSP Prom du Parc, St. Hubert QC J3Y 9A9 Canada
Tel: 514-676-5771; *Fax:* 514-445-0747
gcaminfo@yahoo.com
www.gcaom.org
U. Leebert Sancho, Contact

L'Institut canadien de Québec (ICQ)
350, rue Saint-Joseph est, 4e étage, Québec QC G1K 3B2 Canada
Tél: 418-641-6788; *Téléc:* 418-641-6787
courrier@institutcanadien.qc.ca
www.icqbdq.qc.ca
Démocratiser l'accès au savoir et aux oeuvres d'imagination par un service de bibliothèque universellement accessible; sensibiliser le public aux arts et à la culture; gestion de bibliothèques publiques de la Ville de Québec.
Jean Payeur, Directeur général
Gilbert Lacasse, Président
Sylvie Fortin, Secrétaire

The Japan Foundation, Toronto / Kokosai Koryu Kikin Toronto Nihon Bunka Centre
#213, 131 Bloor St. West, Toronto ON M5S 1R1 Canada
Tel: 416-966-1600; *Fax:* 416-966-9773
info@jftor.org
www.japanfoundationcanada.org
Tokyo-based foundation established by the Government of Japan to promote Japanese culture abroad; offers a broad range of programs designed to further cultural exchange with Japan, with an emphasis on Japanese studies at the post-secondary level & Japanese language study
Masayuki Suzuki, Director
Lori Lytle, Program Officer

The Royal Commonwealth Society of Canada (RCS) / La Société royale du Commonwealth du Canada
c/o RCS Ottawa, PO Box 8023, Stn. T, Ottawa ON K1G 3H6 Canada
www.rcs.ca
A charitable, non-partisan organization which promotes knowledge of the Commonwealth & its member countries; fosters unity in diversity in matters of common concern; promotes international understanding, cooperation & peace; upholds the best traditions of the Commonwealth
Ronald Goodall, Chair
Brian Marley-Clarke, Past Chair & Treasurer

St. Vincent and the Grenadines Association of Montreal Inc. (SVGA) / L'Association St.Vincent et Grenadines de Montrèal Inc.
PO Box 396, Stn. Snowdon Station, Montréal QC H3X 3T3 Canada
Tel: 514-364-3299
www.svgamontreal.com
Thomas (Tom) Austin, President

Société de développement des entreprises culturelles (SODEC)
#800, 215, rue St-Jacques, Montréal QC H2Y 1M6 Canada
Tél: 514-841-2200; *Téléc:* 514-841-8606
Ligne sans frais: 800-363-0401
info@sodec.gouv.qc.ca
www.sodec.gouv.qc.ca
La SODEC est une société du gouvernement du Québec qui relève du ministre de la Culture, des Communications et de la Condition féminine. Elle soutient la production et la diffusion de la culture québécoise dans le champ des industries culturelles.
François Macerola, Président et chef de la direction

Société des Acadiens et Acadiennes du Nouveau-Brunswick (SAANB)
#204, 702, rue Principale, Petit-Rocher NB E8J 1V1 Canada
Tél: 506-783-4205; *Téléc:* 506-783-0629
Ligne sans frais: 888-722-2343
saanb@nb.aibn.com
www.saanb.org
La Société vise à unir tous les Acadiens et Acadiennes du Nouveau-Brunswick et les sensibiliser aux problèmes sociaux, économiques, culturels et politiques qu'ils doivent affronter; s'occuper de tout sujet ayant trait à la protection et à la promotion des droits et à l'avancement des intérêts des Acadiens et Acadiennes du Nouveau-Brunswick; entretenir des liens aussi étroits que possible avec les groupements analogues des autres provinces canadiennes et de l'étranger.

Société franco-manitobaine (SFM)
#106, 147, blvd. Provencher, Saint-boniface MB R2H 0G2 Canada
Tél: 204-233-4915; *Téléc:* 204-977-8551
Ligne sans frais: 800-665-4443
sfm@sfm-mb.ca
www.sfm-mb.ca
Porte-parole officiel de la communauté franco-manitobaine, veille à l'épanouissement de cette communauté et revendique le plein respect des droits de celle-ci; de concert avec ses partenaires, elle planifie et facilite le développement global de la collectivité et en fait la promotion

Société nationale de l'Acadie (SNA)
415, rue Notre-Dame, Dieppe NB E1A 2A8 Canada
Tél: 506-853-0404; *Téléc:* 506-853-0400
sna@nbnet.nb.ca
www.snacadie.org
Mène différentes activités sur les scènes interprovinciales et internationales afin de promouvoir et de défendre les droits et intérêts du peuple acadien
Lucie LeBouthillier, Directrice générale
Martine Aubé, Directrice adjointe
Ted Parisé, Responsable, Communications

Société Saint-Jean-Baptiste de Montréal (SSJBM)
82, rue Sherbrooke ouest, Montréal QC H2X 1X3 Canada
Tél: 514-843-8851; *Téléc:* 514-844-6369
mbeaulieu@ssjb.com
www.ssjb.com
Une société nationale qui participe de façon non partisane à l'évolution politique, sociale, économique et culturelle du Québec par ses actions, ses études, ses interventions et ses campagnes d'opinion

Townshippers' Association (TA) / Association des Townshippers
#100, 257, rue Queen, Sherbrooke QC J1M 1K7 Canada
Tel: 819-566-5717; *Fax:* 819-566-0271
Toll-Free: 866-566-5717
ta@townshippers.qc.ca
www.townshippers.qc.ca
To promote the interests of the English-speaking community in the historical Eastern Townships; to strengthen the cultural identity of this community; to encourage the full participation of the English-speaking population in the community at large

L'Union culturelle des franco-ontariennes (UCFO)
#1, 5330, ch Canotek, Ottawa ON K1J 9C1 Canada
Tél: 613-741-1334; *Téléc:* 613-741-8577
Ligne sans frais: 877-520-8226
ucfo@on.aibn.com
www.francofemmes.org/ucfo/
Améliorer les conditions et les réalités sociales des femmes francophones de l'Ontario; faciliter l'épanouissement de la femme tout en favorisant son autonomie
Diane Brissette, Présidente provinciale

Dental

Alberta Dental Assistants Association (ADAA)
#166, 14315 - 118 Ave. NW, Edmonton AB T5L 4S6 Canada
Tel: 780-486-2526; *Fax:* 780-486-2728
Toll-Free: 800-355-8940
contact@abrda.ca
www.abrda.ca
To ensure that members are valued as essential partners in the provision of high quality oral health care

Alberta Dental Association & College (ADAC)
#101, 8230 - 105 St., Edmonton AB T6E 5H9 Canada
Tel: 780-432-1012; *Fax:* 780-433-4864
Toll-Free: 800-843-3848
adaadmin@telusplanet.net
www.abda.ab.ca

Association des assistant(e)s-dentaires du Québec (CDAA/AADQ)
#203, 6705, Jean-Talon est, Saint-Léonard QC H1S 1N2 Canada
Tél: 514-722-9900; *Téléc:* 514-256-8539
info@cdaa.ca
www.cdaa.ca
Aider ses membres à parfaire leurs connaissances par des cours pratiques et théoriques; moderniser le domaine dentaire; règlementer les assistants-dentaires

Association des chirurgiens dentistes du Québec (ACDQ)
#1425, 425, boul de Maisonneuve ouest, Montréal QC H3A 3G5 Canada
Tél: 514-282-1425; *Téléc:* 514-282-0255
Ligne sans frais: 800-361-3794
info@acdq.qc.ca
www.acdq.qc.ca
L'Association a pour objet l'étude, la défense et le développement des intérêts économiques, sociaux et moraux de ses membres.
Serge Langlois, Président

Association des denturologistes du Québec (ADQ)
Complexe Raycom, #230, 8150, boul Métropolitain est, Anjour QC H1K 1A1 Canada
Tél: 514-252-0270; *Téléc:* 514-252-0392
Ligne sans frais: 800-563-6273
denturo@adq-qc.com
www.adq-qc.com
Protéger et développer les intérêts professionnels, moraux, sociaux et économiques de ses membres

British Columbia Dental Association
#400, 1765 - 8th Ave. West, Vancouver BC V6J 5C6
Tel: 604-736-7202; *Fax:* 604-736-7588
Toll-Free: 888-396-9888
post@bcdental.org
www.bcdental.org
To act as the voice of dentistry in British Columbia; To prevent oral disease

Canadian Academy of Endodontics / L'Académie canadienne d'endodontie
c/o #301, 400 St. Mary Ave., Winnipeg MB R3C 4K5 Canada
webmaster@caendo.ca
www.caendo.ca
The goal of CAE is to advance the art & science of endodontics by providing learning experiences through lectures, providing teachers of endodontics a forum for interaction, providing

information & acting as a resource to dental governing bodies, & ultimately to improving the health of the public.

Canadian Association for Dental Research (CADR) / Association canadienne de recherches dentaires (ACRD)
c/o Dr. C. Birek, Faculty of Dentistry, University of Manitoba, 780 Bannatyne Ave., Winnipeg MB R3E 0W2
Tel: 204-789-3256; *Fax:* 204-789-3913
birek@ms.umanitoba.ca
www.cadr-acrd.ca
To advance research & increase knowledge in order to improve oral health in Canada; To support & represent Canadian oral health researchers

Canadian Association of Orthodontists (CAO) / Association canadienne des orthodontists (aco)
#310, 2175 Sheppard Ave. East, Toronto ON M2J 1W8
Tel: 416-491-3186; *Fax:* 416-491-1670
Toll-Free: 877-226-8800
cao@taylorenterprises.com
www.cao-aco.org
To advance the science & art of orthodontics; To promote the highest quality of orthodontic care in Canada; To act as the official voice of Canadian orthodontic specialists

Canadian Dental Assistants Association (CDAA) / Association canadienne des assistants(es) dentaires
#203, 2255 St. Laurent Blvd., Ottawa ON K1G 4K3 Canada
Tel: 613-521-5495; *Fax:* 613-521-5572
Toll-Free: 800-345-5137
info@cdaa.ca
www.cdaa.ca
To foster opportunities for growth & to be the voice for Canadian dental assistants

Canadian Dental Association (CDA) / L'Association dentaire canadienne (ADC)
1815 Alta Vista Dr., Ottawa ON K1G 3Y6 Canada
Tel: 613-523-1770; *Fax:* 613-523-7736
reception@cda-adc.ca
www.cda-adc.ca
The authoritative national voice of dentistry, dedicated to the representation & advancement of the profession, nationally & internationally, & to the achievement of optimum oral health

Canadian Dental Hygienists Association (CDHA) / Association canadienne des hygiènistes dentaires
96 Centrepointe Dr., Ottawa ON K2G 6B1 Canada
Tel: 613-224-5515; *Fax:* 613-224-7283
Toll-Free: 800-267-5235
info@cdha.ca
www.cdha.ca
To act as the collective voice of dental hygiene in Canada; to advance the profession in support of our members; to contribute to the health & well-being of the public.

Certified Dental Assistants of BC (CDABC)
#103, 3540 West 41st Ave., Vancouver BC V6N 3E6 Canada
Tel: 604-714-1766; *Fax:* 604-714-1767
Toll-Free: 800-579-4440
info@cdabc.org
www.cdabc.org
Marlene Robinson, Executive Director
Angela Wiebe, President

College of Dental Surgeons of British Columbia (CDSBC)
#500, 1765 West 8th Ave., Vancouver BC V6J 5C6 Canada
Tel: 604-736-3621; *Fax:* 604-734-9448
Toll-Free: 800-663-9169
postmaster@cdsbc.org
www.cdsbc.org
Registers, licenses & regulates dentists & certified dental assistants. Assures British Columbians of professional standards of health care, ethics, & competence by regulating dentistry in a fair & reasonable manner; administers the Dentists Act

College of Dental Surgeons of Saskatchewan
#202, 728 Spadina Cres. East, Saskatoon SK S7K 4H7 Canada
Tel: 306-244-5072; *Fax:* 306-244-2476
cdss@dentalcollege.sk.ca
www.saskdentists.com
To operate as a provincial licensing body

College of Dental Technologists of Ontario
#300, 2100 Ellesmere Rd., Toronto ON M1H 3B7 Canada
Tel: 416-438-5003; *Fax:* 416-438-5004
info@cdto.ca
www.cdto.ca
To serve & protect the public interest by regulating & guiding the dental technology profession

Dental Association of Prince Edward Island (DAPEI)
184 Belvedere Ave., Charlottetown PE C1A 2Z1 Canada
Tel: 902-892-4022; *Fax:* 902-892-4470
dapei@pei.sympatico.ca
www.dapei.ca
DAPEI sees itself as a partner, a policy advisor, and decision maker with the public, government and its members, regarding the availability, accessibility, and affordibility of appropriate and high quality dental services for islanders.

Dental Council of Prince Edward Island
184 Belvedere Ave., Charlottetown PE C1A 2Z1 Canada
Tel: 902-892-4470; *Fax:* 902-892-4470
Council for dentists specifically in PEI.

Dentistry Canada Fund (DCF) / Fonds dentaire canadien (FDC)
c/o SciCan House, 427 Gilmour St., Ottawa ON K2P 0R5 Canada
Tel: 613-236-4763; *Fax:* 613-236-3935
information@dcf-fdc.ca
www.dcf-fdc.ca
To advance oral health in Canada through education, research, & public outreach.
Bernard Dolansky, President & Chair
Stephanie MacWhirter, Sr. Manager, Development
Donna Bierko, Manager, Operations

Denturist Association of British Columbia
#312C, 9801 King George Hwy., Surrey BC V3T 5H5 Canada
Tel: 604-582-6823; *Fax:* 604-582-0317
info@denturist.bc.ca
www.denturist.bc.ca

Denturist Association of Canada (DAC) / Association des denturologistes du Canada (ADC)
PO Box 45521, 2397 King George Hwy., Surrey BC V4A 9N3 Canada
Tel: 604-538-3123; *Fax:* 604-582-0317
Toll-Free: 877-538-3123
dacdenturist@telus.net
www.denturist.org
To promote oral health in Canada through the profession of denturism.

Denturist Association of Manitoba
PO Box 70006, #1, 1660 Kenaston Blvd., Winnipeg MB R3P 0X6 Canada
Tel: 204-897-1087; *Fax:* 204-488-2872
Toll-Free: 866-897-1087
administrator@denturistmb.org
www.denturistmb.org
To represent Manitoba denturists & ensure high quality, low cost delivery of dentures direct to the public

Denturist Association of Newfoundland & Labrador
6 Commonwealth Ave., Mount Pearl NL A1N 1W2 Canada
Tel: 709-364-3355; *Fax:* 709-364-3355

Denturist Association of Northwest Territories
PO Box 1506, Yellowknife NT X1A 2P2 Canada
Tel: 867-766-3666; *Fax:* 867-669-0103

Denturist Association of Ontario (DAO)
#106, 5780 Timberlea Blvd., Mississauga ON L4W 4W8 Canada
Tel: 905-238-6090; *Fax:* 905-238-7090
Toll-Free: 800-284-7311
info@denturistassociation.ca
www.dao.on.ca
The Association is a member-oriented, diversified & innovative centre of information for denturists & the public. They develop services that address current needs & future concerns & are the primary providers of dental prosthetics & related services.

Denturist Society of Nova Scotia
c/o Chedabucto Denture Clinic, 3951 South River Rd., Antigonish NS B2G 2H6 Canada
Tel: 902-863-3131; *Fax:* 902-863-3131

Denturist Society of Prince Edward Island
Rhyno Denture Clinic, 222 University Ave., Charlottetown PE C1A 4S7 Canada
Tel: 902-892-3253
rhynopat@hotmail.com

Manitoba Dental Assistants Association
#17, 595 Clifton Street, Winnipeg MB R3G 2X5 Canada
Tel: 204-586-7378; *Fax:* 204-783-9631
mdaa@mts.net
www.cdaa.ca/mdaa
Karen Ritchie, President

Manitoba Dental Association (MDA)
#103, 698 Corydon Ave., Winnipeg MB R3M 0X9 Canada
Tel: 204-988-5300; *Fax:* 204-988-5310
office@manitobadentist.ca
www.manitobadentist.ca
To act as the governing body for dentists and dental assistants in Manitoba; To ensure that that the oral health of Manitobans is met

National Dental Examining Board of Canada / Le bureau national d'examen dentaire du Canada
#203, 100 Bronson Ave., Ottawa ON K1R 6G8 Canada
Tel: 613-236-5912; *Fax:* 613-236-8386
director@ndeb.ca
www.ndeb.ca
According to the Act of Parliament, the NDEB is responsible for the establishment of qualifying conditions for a national standard of dental competence for general practitioners, for establishing and maintaining an examination facility to test for this national standard of dental competence and for issuing certificates to dentists who successfully meet this national standard.

New Brunswick Dental Assistants Association (NBDAA) / Association des Assistantes Dentaires du Nouveau-Brunswick
PO Box 8997, Shediac NB E4P 8W5 Canada
Tel: 506-532-9189; *Fax:* 506-532-3635
Toll-Free: 866-530-9189
bernioff@nb.sympatico.ca
www.cdaa.ca/nbdaa
Supporting Dental Assistants in New Brunswick.
Amber Caissie, President
Bernice Léger, Office Coordinator

New Brunswick Dental Society / Société dentaire du Nouveau-Brunswick
Carleton Place, PO Box 488, Stn. A, #820, 520 King St., Fredericton NB E3B 4Z9 Canada
Tel: 506-452-8575; *Fax:* 506-452-1872
nbds@nb.aibn.com
www.nbdental.com
To regulate & promote the dentistry profession in New Brunswick. To promote professional growth, high ethical standards and quality care giving through communication, education, and regulation of denistry in New Brunswick.

New Brunswick Denturists Society / Société des denturologistes du Nouveau-Brunswick
PO Box 5566, 288 West St. Pierre Blvd., Caraquet NB E1W 1B7 Canada
Tel: 506-727-7411; *Fax:* 506-727-6728
claudetteboudreau@aibn.com
www.nbdenturistsociety.ca

Newfoundland & Labrador Dental Association
The Fortis Bldg., #401, 139 Water St., St. John's NL A1C 1B2 Canada
Tel: 709-579-2362; *Fax:* 709-579-1250
nfdental@nfld.net
www.nlda.net
To promote & advance dentistry or dental surgery & related arts & sciences in all their branches; to increase the knowledge, skill, standard & proficiency of its members in the practice of dentistry or dental surgery; to maintain the honour & integrity of the dental profession; to aid in the furtherance of measures designed to improve dental health & prevent disease & disability; to cooperate with & to assist public & private dental associations, agencies & commissions in the task of providing or financing dental care; to promote measures designed to improve standards of dental care & the practice of dentistry or dental surgery; to improve the welfare & social standards of its members & encourage the cooperation of its members in the protection of their rights.

Newfoundland & Labrador Dental Board
139 Water St., 6th Fl., St. John's NL A1C 1B2 Canada
Tel: 709-579-2391; *Fax:* 709-579-1250
nfdental@nfld.net
According to the Act of Parliament, the NDEB is responsible for the establishment of qualifying conditions for a national standard of dental competence for general practitioners, for establishing and maintaining an examination facility to test for this national standard of dental competence and for issuing certificates to dentists who successfully meet this national standard.

Newfoundland Dental Assistants Association
#274, 38 Pearson St., St. John's NL A1A 3R1 Canada
To advance the career of dental assisting in Newfoundland
Vera Walsh, President

Northwest Territories & Nunavut Dental Association
PO Box 24, 4916 - 49 St., Yellowknife NT X1A 2N1 Canada
Tel: 867-873-6416; *Fax:* 867-920-7798
nwtnudentalassoc@theedge.ca

Nova Scotia Dental Assistants' Association (NSDAA)
PO Box 9142, Stn. A, Halifax NS B3K 5M8 Canada
Tel: 902-826-1922; *Fax:* 902-820-3015
nsdaa@ns.sympatico.ca
www.nsdaa.ca
To affiliate at local, provincial & national levels for the betterment of the dental assistant profession & patient care
Michelle Fowler, President
Lynda Foran, Executive Director

Nova Scotia Dental Association (NSDA)
#101, 1559 Brunswick St., Halifax NS B3J 2G1 Canada
Tel: 902-420-0088; *Fax:* 902-423-6537
nsda@eastlink.ca
www.nsdental.org

Ontario Dental Assistants Association (ODAA)
869 Dundas St., London ON N5W 2Z8
Tel: 519-679-2566; *Fax:* 519-679-8494
odaainfo@ody.ca
www.odnaa.org
To act as the certifying body for dental assistants in Ontario

Ontario Dental Association (ODA)
4 New St., Toronto ON M5R 1P6 Canada
Tel: 416-922-3900; *Fax:* 416-922-9005
Toll-Free: 800-387-1393
info@oda.on.ca
www.oda.on.ca
To represent the dentists of Ontario; to provide exemplary oral health care & promote the attainment of optimal health for the people of Ontario

Ordre des dentistes du Québec (ODQ)
625, boul René-Lévesque ouest, 15e étage, Montréal QC H3B 1R2 Canada
Tél: 514-875-8511; *Téléc:* 514-393-9248
Ligne sans frais: 800-361-4887
dirgen@odq.qc.ca
www.ordredesdentistesduquebec.qc.ca
Assurer la qualité des services en médecine dentaire par le respect de normes élevées de pratique et d'éthique et de promouvoir la santé bucco-dentaire auprès de la population du Québec

Ordre des denturologistes du Québec (ODQ)
#106, 45, Place Charles Lemoyne, Longueuil QC J4K 5G5 Canada
Tél: 450-646-7922; *Téléc:* 450-646-2509
Ligne sans frais: 800-567-2251
info@odq.com
www.odq.com

Prince Edward Island Dental Assistants Association
PO Box 404, Cornwall PE C1A 1H0 Canada
Tel: 902-566-9553; *Fax:* 902-367-2207
info@peidaa.com
Julie Ready, President

Provincial Dental Board of Nova Scotia
#102, 1559 Brunswick St., Halifax NS B3J 2G1 Canada
Tel: 902-420-0083; *Fax:* 902-492-0301
admin@pdbns.ca
www.pdbns.ca
To protect the public in the delivery of dental care by licensure & regulation

Royal College of Dental Surgeons of Ontario
6 Crescent Rd., 5th Fl., Toronto ON M4W 1T1 Canada
Tel: 416-961-6555; *Fax:* 416-961-5814
Toll-Free: 800-565-4591
info@rcdso.org
www.rcdso.org
The Royal College of Dental Surgeons of Ontario (RCDSO) is the governing body for dentists in Ontario. Their mission is to protect the public's right to quality dental services by providing leadership to the dental profession in self-regulation.

Royal College of Dentists of Canada (RCDC) / Collège Royal des Chirurgiens Dentistes du Canada
#2003, 180 Dundas St. West, Toronto ON M3G 1Z8
Tel: 416-512-6571
office@rcdc.ca
www.rcdc.ca
To provide examinations for dental sciences & for nationally recognized dental specialties in Canada
J. Richard Emery, President
Garnet Packota, Vice-President
Ernest W.N. Lam, Secretary-Treasurer
Patricia A. Main, Registrar
Paul Jackson, Examiner-in-Chief

Saskatchewan Dental Assistants' Association (SDAA)
PO Box 294, 603 - 3rd St., Kenaston SK S0G 2N0 Canada
Tel: 306-252-2769; *Fax:* 306-252-2089
sdaa@sasktel.net
www.sdaa.sk.ca
To promote excellence in dental health care; to advance public protection through enforcement of regulations, education, ethical practice, & standardization
Susan Anholt, Executive Director
Calla Effa, President
Robin McKay Ganshorn, Coordinator, Professional Development

Yukon Denturist Association
#1, 106 Main St., Whitehorse YT Y1A 2A7 Canada
Tel: 867-668-6818; *Fax:* 867-668-6811
pjallen@northwestel.net

Developing Countries

Canadian Consortium for International Social Development (CCISD)
Carleton University, 1719 Dunton Tower, Ottawa ON K1S 5B6 Canada
Tel: 613-520-2600; *Fax:* 613-520-2344
ccsid@ccs.carleton.ca
www.ccisd.ca
CCISD is a consortium of scholars, activists and organizations doing and promoting applied research and advocacy on international issues of social policy and social development.
Angela Laird, Contact

Mennonite Central Committee Canada (MCCC)
134 Plaza Dr., Winnipeg MB Canada
Tel: 204-261-6381; *Fax:* 204-269-9875
Toll-Free: 888-622-6337
canada@mennonitecc.ca
www.mcc.org/canada
To operate as a relief & development service agency; To promote relief, development, & peace

Teamwork Children's Services International
5983 Ladyburn Cres., Mississauga ON L5M 4V9
Tel: 905-542-1047
jchacha@teamworkchildrenservices.com
www.teamworkchildrenservices.com
To provide orphaned & disadvantaged children in rural areas of Africa a safe & secure faith-based home environment; To provide the children with good health, education, & vocational training, enabling them to become self-supporting & productive citizens
Joel Chacha, Program Director

Disabled Persons

Abilities Foundation of Nova Scotia (AFNS)
3670 Kempt Rd., Halifax NS B3K 4X8 Canada
Tel: 902-453-6000; *Fax:* 902-454-6121
f.joudrey@abilitiesfoundation.ns.ca
www.abilitiesfoundation.ns.ca
To enable Nova Scotians with physical disabilities to enhance their quality of life by realizing their individual potential

AboutFace
#1003, 123 Edward St., Toronto ON M5G 1E2 Canada
Tel: 416-597-2229; *Fax:* 416-597-8494
Toll-Free: 800-665-3223
info@aboutfaceinternational.org
www.aboutfaceinternational.org
To provide emotional support & information to, & on behalf of, individuals who have a facial difference & their families

Active Living Alliance for Canadians with a Disability (ALACD) / Alliance de vie active pour les canadiens/canadiennes ayant un handicap
#104, 720 Belfast Rd., Ottawa ON K1G 0Z5 Canada
Tel: 613-244-0052; *Fax:* 613-244-4857
Toll-Free: 800-771-0663
TDD: 888-771-0663
info@ala.ca
www.ala.ca
To promote inclusion & active living lifestyles of Canadians with disabilities by facilitating communication & collaboration among organizations, agencies & individuals
Jane Arkell, Director

Alberta Association for Community Living (AACL)
11724 Kingsway Ave., Edmonton AB T5G 0X5
Tel: 780-451-3055; *Fax:* 780-453-5779
Toll-Free: 800-252-7556
mail@aacl.org
www.aacl.org
Social Media:
www.facebook.com/group.php?gid=165187756132&ref=ts
To advocate for fully inclusive community lives for children & adults with developmental disabilities

Alberta Association of Rehabilitation Centres (AARC)
#19, 3220 - 5 Ave. NE, Calgary AB T2A 5N1 Canada
Tel: 403-250-9495; *Fax:* 403-291-9864
acds@acds.ca
www.acds.ca
To support organizations that provide services & supports to people with disabilities; To act as a voice for the field of community rehabilitation to the political & administrative arms of government; To focus on human resource initiatives for the services sector; To provide in-service training opportunities for people employed in the field; To accredit & certify service in Alberta
Ann Nicol, CEO
Bob Greid, President
Winship Bill, Vice-President

Alberta Committee of Citizens with Disabilities (ACCD)
#106, 10423 - 178 St. NW, Edmonton AB T5S 1R5 Canada
Tel: 780-488-9088; *Fax:* 780-488-3757
Toll-Free: 800-387-2514
TDD: 780-488-9090
accd@accd.net
www.accd.net
To promote full participation in society for Albertans with disabilities

Alberta Easter Seals Society
Baker Centre, #1408, 10025 - 106 St., Edmonton AB T5J 1G4 Canada
Tel: 780-429-0137; *Fax:* 780-429-1937
Toll-Free: 877-732-7837
TDD: 780-429-2065
edmonton@easterseals.ab.ca
www.easterseals.ab.ca
To represent interests of all people with disabilities in Alberta; to promote change at all policy-making levels through public awareness campaigns, projects, seminars; to provide mobility equipment; to conduct public awareness programs; to provide recreational activities through summer camp - Camp Horizon; to provide a residential home program - Easter Seals McQueen Residence

ARCH Disability Law Centre
#110, 425 Bloor St. East, Toronto ON M4W 3R5 Canada
Tel: 416-482-8255; *Fax:* 416-482-2981
Toll-Free: 866-482-2724
TDD: 416-482-1254
archlib@lao.on.ca
www.archdisabilitylaw.ca
To defend & advance the equality rights of persons with disabilities; assisting individuals with disabilities to understand their rights & how to enforce them; working with groups representing people with disabilities throughout Ontario; representing in precedent setting cases where client cannot be represented appropriately by other legal services; summary advice & referral - lawyers who specialize in areas of law as they relate to disability provide free, confidential, basic legal advice & referral to other sources of assistance
Ivana Petricone, Executive Director

Association du Québec pour enfants avec problèmes auditifs (AQEPA)
#A446, 3700, rue Berri, Montréal QC H2L 4G9 Canada
Tél: 514-842-8706; *Téléc:* 514-842-4006
Ligne sans frais: 877-842-4006
aqepa@aqepa.org
www.aqepa.surdite.org
Regrouper les parents d'enfants sourds et malentendants; informer et sensibiliser les parents et le public

Association du Québec pour l'intégration sociale (AQIS) / Québec Association for Community Living
3958, rue Dandurand, Montréal QC H1X 1P7 Canada
Tél: 514-725-7245; *Téléc:* 514-725-2796
Ligne sans frais: 866-725-7245
direction_generale@aqis-iqdi.qc.ca
www.aqis-iqdi.qc.ca
Défendre les droits et promouvoir les intérêts des personnes ayant une déficience intellectuelle

Association for Community Living - Manitoba
#6, 120 Maryland St., Winnipeg MB R3G 1L1 Canada
Tel: 204-786-1607; *Fax:* 204-789-9850
aclmb@mts.net
www.aclmb.ca
To promote the welfare of people with handicaps & their families; to speak on behalf of people with developmental disabilities in Manitoba; to ensure that every person in Manitoba has access to supports necessary to live with dignity & to participate fully in the community of his/her choice

Association for the Neurologically Disabled of Canada (AND) / Association canadienne pour les handicapés neurologiques
56 Centre St., Thornhill ON L4J 1E9 Canada
Tel: 416-244-1992; *Fax:* 416-244-4099
Toll-Free: 800-561-1497
info@and.ca
www.and.ca
To help the neurologically disabled achieve their full potential

Association for Vaccine Damaged Children
c/o Mary James, 67 Shier Dr., Winnipeg MB R3R 2H2
To inform parents of the risks of immunization; To support parents in any challenging situation with public health authorities

Association québécoise pour le loisir des personnes handicapées (AQLPH)
CP 1000, Succ. M, 4545, av Pierre-de-Coubertin, Montréal QC H1V 3R2 Canada
Tél: 514-252-3144; *Téléc:* 514-252-8360
info@aqlph.qc.ca
www.aqlph.qc.ca
Promouvoir le droit à un loisir de qualité (éducatif, sécuritaire, valorisant et de détente); promouvoir la participation et la libre expression de la personne face à son loisir; promouvoir l'accès à tous les champs d'application du loisir (tourisme, plein air, sport et activité physique, loisir scientifique, socio-éducatif et socioculturel) pour toutes les personnes handicapées du Québec sans restriction d'âge, de sexe, ni de type d'handicap
Guylaine Laforest, Directrice générale

BALANCE
#302, 4920 Dundas St. West, Toronto ON M9A 1B7 Canada
Tel: 416-236-1796; *Fax:* 416-236-4280
info@balancefba.org
www.balancefba.org
To provide instruction & support to individuals with visual impairment to enable them to live independently & confidently in their community; to promote independence, decision making & self-fulfillment

The Bob Rumball Centre for the Deaf (BRCD)
2395 Bayview Ave., Toronto ON M2L 1A2 Canada
Tel: 416-449-9651; *Fax:* 416-449-8881
TDD: 416-449-2728
info@bobrumball.org
www.bobrumball.org
To provide opportunities for a higher quality of life for deaf people while preserving & promoting their language & culture; to foster & develop good relations with the community at large & actively promote the Centre; to work closely with the various ministries of the provincial government & related agencies.
Alistair M. Fraser, Chairman
Robert L. Rumball, Interim Executive Director
Karen Chambers, Manager of Finance
Shirley Cassel, Supervisor of Centre Programs

British Columbia Association for Community Living (BCACL)
227 - 6th St., New Westminster BC V3L 3A5
Tel: 604-777-9100; *Toll-Free:* 800-618-1119
info@bcacl.org
www.bcacl.org
Social Media: www.facebook.com/group.php?gid=112557852110381
To enhance the lives of persons with developmental disabilities & their families; To promote the participation of people with developmental disabilities in all aspects of community life; To support activities dedicated to building inclusive communities that value the diverse abilities of all people

Canadian Abilities Foundation
#270, 340 College St., Toronto ON M5T 3A9 Canada
Tel: 416-923-1885; *Fax:* 416-923-9829
Toll-Free: 888-700-4476
able@abilities.ca
www.abilities.ca
Social Media: www.facebook.com/group.php?gid=2384460966
To provide information, inspiration & opportunity to Canadians with disabilities
Raymond D. Cohen, President & Publisher
Jennifer Rivkin, Managing Editor
Christine Staddon, Coordinator, Special Projects

Canadian Association for Community Living (CACL) / Association canadienne pour l'intégration communautaire
Kinsmen Building, York University, 4700 Keele St., Toronto ON M3J 1P3
Tel: 416-661-9611; *Fax:* 416-661-5701
inform@cacl.ca
www.cacl.ca
To ensure the following for people with intellectual disabilities: the same rights, & access to choice, services, & supports as others; the same opportunities to live in freedom & dignity with the necessary supports to do so; & the ability to articulate & realize their rights & aspirations

Canadian Association of the Deaf (CAD) / Association des sourds du Canada
#203, 251 Bank St., Ottawa ON K2P 1X3 Canada
Tel: 613-565-2882; *Fax:* 613-565-1207
TDD: 613-565-8882
info@cad.ca
www.cad.ca
Social Media: www.facebook.com/group.php?gid=57872523519
To protect & promote the rights, needs, & concerns of deaf Canadians

The Canadian Council of the Blind (CCB) / Le Conseil canadien des aveugles
#401, 396 Cooper St., Ottawa ON K2P 2H7 Canada
Tel: 613-567-0311; *Fax:* 613-567-2728
Toll-Free: 877-304-0968
ccb@ccbnational.net
www.ccbnational.net
To promote the well-being of individuals who are blind or vision-impaired through higher education, profitable employment & social association, & to create a closer relationship between blind & sighted friends; to organize a nation-wide organization of people who are blind & vision-impaired & groups of blind persons throughout Canada; to promote measures for the conservation of sight & the prevention of blindness

Canadian Council on Rehabilitation & Work (CCRW) / Le Conseil canadien de la réadaptation et du travail (CCRT)
#1202, 1 Yonge St., Toronto ON M5E 1E5 Canada
Tel: 416-260-3060; *Toll-Free:* 800-664-0925
TDD: 416-260-9223
info@ccrw.org
www.ccrw.org
To improve employment opportunities for persons with disabilities in Canada; to promote the equitable & meaningful employment of persons with disabilities

Canadian Cultural Society of The Deaf, Inc. (CCSD) / Société culturelle canadienne des Sourds
The Stone Distillery, The Distillery Historic District, #101, 55 Mill St., Toronto ON M5A 3C4 Canada
Tel: 416-203-1086
info@deafculturecentre.ca
www.ccsdeaf.com
To ensure that the cultural needs of deaf & hard-of-hearing people are being met; organization concentrates its efforts in the area of the performing arts, sign language, deaf literature, the visual arts & heritage resources

Canadian Foundation for Physically Disabled Persons (CFPDP)
731 Runnymede Rd., Toronto ON M6N 3V7 Canada
Tel: 416-760-7351; *Fax:* 416-760-9405
whynot@sympatico.ca
www.cfpdp.com
To provide financial assistance to organizations sharing concern for physically disabled adults; to help create awareness in the public & business communities, & in government of the needs of physically disabled adults in the areas of housing, employment, education, accessibility, sports & recreation, & research.

Canadian Guide Dogs for the Blind (CGDB)
PO Box 280, 4120 Rideau Valley Dr. North, Manotick ON K4M 1A3 Canada
Tel: 613-692-7777; *Fax:* 613-692-0650
cgdb@sympatico.ca
www.guidedogs.ca
To assist visually-impaired Canadians with their mobility by providing & training them in the use of professionally trained guide dogs.

Canadian Hard of Hearing Association (CHHA) / Association des malentendants canadiens (AMEC)
#205, 2415 Holly Lane, Ottawa ON K1V 7P2
Tel: 613-526-1584; *Fax:* 613-526-4718
Toll-Free: 800-263-8068
TDD: 613-526-2692
chhanational@chha.ca
www.chha.ca
To act as the voice of all hard of hearing Canadians; To promote the integration of hard of hearing people into society

Canadian Hearing Society (CHS) / Société canadienne de l'ouïe
271 Spadina Rd., Toronto ON M5R 2V3 Canada
Tel: 416-928-2500; *Fax:* 416-928-2525
Toll-Free: 877-347-3427
TDD: 877-347-3429
info@chs.ca
www.chs.ca
To provide services that enhance the independence of deaf, deafened & hard of hearing people, & that encourage prevention of hearing loss

Centre de réadaptation Constance-Lethbridge (CRCL) / Constance Lethbridge Rehabilitation Centre
7005, boul de Maisonneuve ouest, Montréal QC H4B 1T3 Canada
Tél: 514-487-1770; *Téléc:* 514-487-0284
lharvey@ssss.gouv.qc.ca
www.constance-lethbridge.qc.ca
Offre des services spécialisés et ultraspécialisés à des adultes ayant une déficience motrice, en externe ou à domicile, de réadaptation, d'adaptation, de préparation et de support à l'intégration sociale ou professionnelle aux clientèles ayant des problèmes orthopédiques, neurologiques et rhumatologiques; offre aussi une expertise d'évaluation de la conduite automobile, d'évaluation et d'orientation des capacités de travail de la personne handicapée; un atelier de travail est accessible pour les personnes handicapées qui ne peuvent intégrer les centres de travail adapté de la communauté

Christian Record Services Inc.
PO Box 31119, #119, 1300 King St. East, Oshawa ON L1H 8N9 Canada
Tel: 905-436-6938; *Fax:* 905-436-7102
Toll-Free: 888-899-0006
crs-ncb@hotmail.com
www.crsblindservices.ca
To enrich the lives of blind, deaf, visually, physically & hearing impaired persons regardless of race, creed, economic status or sex.

CNIB (CNIB) / INCA (INCA)
1929 Bayview Ave., Toronto ON M4G 3E8 Canada
Fax: 416-480-7700
Toll-Free: 800-563-2642
info@cnib.ca
www.cnib.ca
Social Media: www.facebook.com/myCNIB
A private, voluntary, not-for-profit organization providing rehabilitation & library services to persons with vision loss, including deaf-blind persons across Canada. The mission is to ameliorate the condition of persons with vision loss in Canada; to prevent blindness; to promote sight enhancement services; to direct services to more than 100,000 Canadians with vision loss, provided through a network of more than 57 service centres, within 13 provincial & territorial operating divisions. Employing more than 1,000 professionals across Canada, CNIB's focus is on service & support, including library services, research, advocacy, public education, accessible design consulting, fundraising & administration. CNIB is Canada's largest producer of materials in alternative formats, including braille & DAISY talking books, & a supplier of assistive technologies for persons with vision loss

Community Living Ontario (CLO) / Intégration communautaire Ontario
#403, 240 Duncan Mill Rd., Toronto ON M3B 3S6 Canada
Tel: 416-447-4348; *Fax:* 416-447-8974
Toll-Free: 800-278-8025
info@communitylivingontario.ca
www.communitylivingontario.ca
Social Media: www.twitter.com/CLOntario
To lobby on behalf of people with intellectual disabilities in Ontario; to ensure that every person in Ontario has access to supports to live with dignity & to participate in the community of his/her choice

Council of Canadians with Disabilities (CCD) / Conseil des Canadiens avec déficiences
#926, 294 Portage Ave., Winnipeg MB R3C 0B9 Canada
Tel: 204-947-0303
TDD: 204-947-4757
ccd@ccdonline.ca
www.ccdonline.ca
To improve the status of disabled citizens in Canadian society; to promote self-help for persons with disabilities; to provide a democratic structure for disabled citizens to voice concerns; to monitor federal legislation; to share information & cooperate with disabled persons' organizations in Canada & in other countries; to establish a positive image of disabled Canadians

DisAbled Women's Network of Canada / Réseau d'Action des Femmes Handicapées du Canada
#505, 110, rue Ste. Thérèse, Montréal QC H2Y 1E6 Canada
Tel: 514-396-0009; *Fax:* 514-396-6585
Toll-Free: 866-396-0074
admin@dawncanada.net
www.dawncanada.net
DAWN Canada's mission is to end the poverty, isolation, discrimination & violence experienced by women with disabilities; to ensure that they get the services & support needed, as well as the access to opportunities granted non-disabled people.
Carmela Sebastiana Hutchison, President
Bonnie L. Brayton, National Executive Director

The Easter Seal Society (Ontario) (TESS) / Société du timbre de Pâques de l'Ontario
#700, One Concorde Gate, Toronto ON M3C 3C6 Canada
Tel: 416-421-8377; *Fax:* 416-696-1035
Toll-Free: 800-668-6252
info@easterseals.org
www.easterseals.org
To help children with physical disabilities achieve their full individual potential & future independence

Easter Seals Canada / Timbres de Pâques Canada
#208, 90 Eglinton Ave. East, Toronto ON M4P 2Y3 Canada
Tel: 416-932-8382; *Fax:* 416-932-9844
TDD: 416-932-8151
info@easterseals.ca
www.easterseals.ca
To enhance the quality of life, self-esteem, & self-determination of Canadians with physical disabilities; To support the social & economic integration of people with disabilities

Easter Seals Newfoundland & Labrador
Southcott Hall, #712, 100 Forest Rd., St. John's NL A1A 1E5 Canada
Tel: 709-754-1399; *Fax:* 709-754-1398
Toll-Free: 888-601-6767
info@easterseals.nf.ca
www.easterseals.nf.ca
A charitable organization dedicated to maximizing the abilities & enhancing the lives of children & youth with physical disabilities through recreational, social & other therapeutic programs, direct assistance, education & advocacy.

Independent Living Canada / Vie autonome Canada
#402, 214 Montréal Rd., Ottawa ON K1L 8L8
Tel: 613-563-2581; *Fax:* 613-563-3861
TDD: 613-563-4215
info@cailc.ca
www.cailc.ca
To represent & coordinate the network of independent living centres; To guide & support independent living centres in the delivery of programs & services

Kinsmen Foundation of British Columbia & Yukon (KRF)
PO Box 34005, Stn. D, Vancouver BC V6J 4M1 Canada
Tel: 604-233-1993; *Fax:* 604-233-1992
Toll-Free: 866-335-1234
on-track@shaw.ca
www.kinclubofvancouver.com
Committed to providing funding for services & technologies empowering British Columbians with physical disabilities to live more independently

Nanaimo Association for Community Living (NACL)
83 Victoria Cres., Nanaimo BC V9R 5B9 Canada
Tel: 250-741-0224; *Fax:* 250-741-0227
nacl.office@nanaimoacl.com
www.nanaimoacl.com
To support all people with disabilities to achieve the highest quality of life through participation, independence, inclusion & education

National Institute of Disability Management & Research (NIDMAR) / Institut national de recherche et de gestion de l'incapacité au travail
#202, 830 Shamrock St., Victoria BC V8X 2V1 Canada
Tel: 250-386-4388; *Fax:* 250-386-4398
nidmar@nidmar.ca
www.nidmar.ca
Committed to reducing the human, social, & economic cost of disability to workers, employers, & society by providing education, research, policy development, & implementation resources to promote workplace-based integration programs.
Wolfgang Zimmermann, Executive Director

New Brunswick Association for Community Living / Association du Nouveau-Brunswick pour l'intégration communautaire
#209, 440 Wilsey Rd., Fredericton NB E3B 7G5 Canada
Tel: 506-453-4400; *Fax:* 506-453-4422
Toll-Free: 866-622-2548
nbacl@nbnet.nb.ca
www.nbacl.nb.ca
To promote the welfare of people with handicaps & their families; to lobby for developmentally disabled people in New Brunswick; to ensure that every person in New Brunswick has access to supports to live with dignity & participate in the community of his/her choice

Newfoundland & Labrador Association for Community Living (NLACL)
PO Box 8414, 31 Peet St., St. John's NL A1B 3N7 Canada
Tel: 709-722-0790; *Fax:* 709-722-1325
Toll-Free: 800-701-8511
nlacl@nf.aibn.com
www.nlacl.ca
To develop communities in Newfoundland & Labrador that welcome individuals with developmental disabilities

Nova Scotia Association for Community Living (NSACL)
#2, 22-24 Dundas St., Dartmouth NS B2Y 4L2 Canada
Tel: 902-469-1174; *Fax:* 902-461-0196
nsacl@accesswave.ca
To work for the benefit of persons of all ages who have an intellectual disability in Nova Scotia; To ensure those with an intellectual disability have the same rights & access as all other persons
Mary Rothman, Executive Director
Roger Isnor, President

Nova Scotia Hearing & Speech Foundation
#5, 1350 Bedford Hwy., Bedford NS B4A 1E1 Canada
Tel: 902-423-1947; *Fax:* 902-423-3765
Toll-Free: 866-278-5678
info@hearingandspeech.ca
www.hearingandspeech.ca
To provide hearing services to all Nova Scotians & speech-language services to preschool children & adults; To work with community volunteer leaders, the families & friends of those who are hearing or speech impaired, our partners in government, & the medical & academic communities; To raise funds to support critical Centres' needs
Cheryl MacLeod, Office Manager
Phil Otto, Chair

Ontario Federation for Cerebral Palsy (OFCP)
#104, 1630 Lawrence Ave. West, Toronto ON M6A 1C8 Canada
Tel: 416-244-9686; *Fax:* 416-244-6543
Toll-Free: 877-244-9686
TDD: 866-246-9122
info@ofcp.on.ca
www.ofcp.on.ca
OFCP strives improve the quality of life of persons with cerebral palsy through a broad range of programs, education, support of research & the delivery of needed services to people with cerebral palsy, & other physical disabilities, & their families.

Ontario March of Dimes (OMOD) / Marche des dix sous de l'Ontario
10 Overlea Blvd., Toronto ON M4H 1A4 Canada
Tel: 416-425-3463; *Fax:* 416-425-1920
Toll-Free: 800-263-3463
info@marchofdimes.ca
www.marchofdimes.ca/dimes
To maximize the independence, personal empowerment & community participation of people with physical disabilities

Pamiqsaiji Association for Community Living
PO Box 708, Rankin Inlet NU X0C 0G0 Canada
Tel: 867-645-2542; *Fax:* 867-645-2543
pamiqacl@qiniq.com
Yvonne Cooper, Manager

Prince Edward Island Association for Community Living (PEIACL)
161 St. Peters Rd., Charlottetown PE C1A 5P7 Canada
Tel: 902-566-4844; *Fax:* 902-368-8057
info@peiacl.ca
www.peiacl.ca
Working on behalf of individuals with an intellectual disability & their families; empowering families to increase options available to Islanders with an intellectual disability

Prince Edward Island Council of People with Disabilities (PEICOD)
Landmark Plaza, #2, 5 Lower Malpeque Rd., Charlottetown PE C1E 1R4 Canada
Tel: 902-892-9149; *Fax:* 902-566-1919
Toll-Free: 888-473-4263
peicod@peicod.pe.ca
www.peicod.pe.ca
To improve the quality of life of people with disabilities on PEI
Marcia Carroll, Executive Director

Québec Easter Seal Society / Société des timbres de Pâques du Québec
#810, 1155 University St., Montréal QC H3B 3A7 Canada
Tel: 514-866-1969; *Fax:* 514-866-6124
Toll-Free: 800-263-1969
info@easterseal.qc.ca
Funding agency which provides financial assistance to handicapped children with purchase of specialized equipment; contributes towards programs for children's camps

R.C.L. (Québec) for the Disabled / R.C.L. (Québec) pour les Handicapés
#410, 1000, rue Saint-Antoine ouest, Montréal QC H3C 3R7 Canada
Tel: 514-866-3689; *Fax:* 514-866-6303
rclqc_handicapes@lycos.com
To provide assistance to adults with physical disabilities; to assist such adults to be more independent in their lives; to provide specialized equipment for severely disabled persons; to offer loans of wheelchairs, hospital beds, walking aids; to provide transportation from rural regions to treatment centres

The Roeher Institute / L'Institut Roeher
Kinsmen Bldg., York University, 4700 Keele St., Toronto ON M3J 1P3 Canada
Tel: 416-661-9611; *Fax:* 416-661-5701
Toll-Free: 800-856-2207
info@roeher.ca
www.roeher.ca
To promote the equality, participation & self-determination of people with intellectual & other disabilities, by examining the causes of marginalization & by providing research, information & social development opportunities

Saskatchewan Abilities Council
2310 Louise Ave., Saskatoon SK S7J 2C7 Canada
Tel: 306-374-4448; *Fax:* 306-373-2665
provincialservices@abilitiescouncil.sk.ca
www.abilitiescouncil.sk.ca
To enhance the independence & community participation of people of varying abilities in Saskatchewan

Saskatchewan Association for Community Living (SACL)
3031 Louise St., Saskatoon SK S7J 3L1
Tel: 306-955-3344
sacl@sacl.org
www.sacl.org
To enhance the lives of individuals with intellectual disabilities throughout Saskatchewan; To develop programs & services to meet the needs of people with intellectual disabilities

Silent Voice Canada Inc.
#300, 50 St. Clair Ave. East, Toronto ON M4T 1M9 Canada
Tel: 416-463-1104; *Fax:* 416-778-1876
TDD: 416-463-3928
silent.voice@silentvoice.ca
www.silentvoice.ca
To serve deaf children, deaf youth & adults & their families in the GTA; to improve communication & relationships between the deaf & hearing in families & in our community; to provide services in a sign language environment

Société pour les enfants handicapés du Québec (SEHQ) / Québec Society for Disabled Children
2300, boul René-Lévesque ouest, Montréal QC H3H 2R5 Canada
Tél: 514-937-6171; *Téléc:* 514-937-0082
Ligne sans frais: 877-937-6171
sehq@enfantshandicapes.com
www.enfantshandicapes.com
Média social: www.twitter.com/SEHQ

Voué au bien-être des enfants handicapés et de leur famille; grâce aux contributions publiques qui lui sont versées et aux efforts conjugués de bénévoles et des permanents, la société offre des services directs et professionnels qui favorisent le développement personnel des enfants et leur intégration dans la communauté.

Society for Manitobans with Disabilities Inc. (SMD)
825 Sherbrook St., Winnipeg MB R3A 1M5 Canada
Tel: 204-975-3010; *Fax:* 204-975-3073
Toll-Free: 866-282-8041
TDD: 204-784-3012
info@smd.mb.ca
smd.mb.ca

To promote the full participation & equality of people with disabilities by providing a full range of rehabilitation services & by facilitating the development of a receptive & supportive environment.

Special Needs Planning Group
70 Ivy Cres., Stouffville ON L4A 5A9 Canada
Tel: 905-640-8285; *Fax:* 905-640-8285
graemetreeby@sympatico.ca
www.specialneedsplanning.ca

The "Special Needs" Planning Group is an organization that is made up entirely of parents of people with disabilities. They use a team approach to planning using Planners, Lawyers and Accountants, all of whom are specialists in planning for people with disabilities.
Graeme S. Treeby, Contact

The Speech and Stuttering Institute
#2 - 150 Duncan Mill Rd., Toronto ON M3B 3M4 Canada
Tel: 416-491-7771; *Fax:* 416-491-7215
sfotcc@speechfoundation.org
www.speechfoundation.org

To provide treatment of & foster the development of innovative speech/language therapy programs; to support education & research in communication disorders

Vision Institute of Canada (VIC)
York Mills Centre, #110, 16 York Mills Rd., Toronto ON M2P 2E5 Canada
Tel: 416-224-2273; *Fax:* 416-224-9234
visioninstitute@globalserve.net
visioninstitute.optometry.net

To improve the quality of vision care in the community; to provide eye & vision care to persons with special needs
Paul Chris, Executive Director
Catherine Chiarelli, Chief of Clinical Services

Vocational & Rehabilitation Research Institute (VRRI)
3304 - 33 St. NW, Calgary AB T2L 2A6 Canada
Tel: 403-284-1121; *Fax:* 403-284-1146
info@vrri.org
www.vrri.org

To be leaders in innovative services & research that support persons with disabilities to live as contributing & valued members of the community
Leslie Tamagi, Executive Director
Bob Sainsbury, Chair

Yellowknife Association for Community Living
PO Box 981, 4912 - 53 St., Yellowknife NT X1A 2N7 Canada
Tel: 867-920-2644; *Fax:* 867-920-2348
info@ykacl.ca
www.ykacl.ca

To promote the welfare of people with handicaps & their families; to lobby on behalf of people with developmental disabilities in the Northwest Territories; to ensure that every person in Northwest Territories has access to supports to live with dignity & to participate in the community of his/her choice

Yukon Association for Community Living (YACL)
PO Box 31478, Whitehorse YT Y1A 6K8 Canada
Tel: 867-667-4606; *Fax:* 867-668-8169
yaclwhse@northwestel.net

To promote the welfare of people with intellectual disabilities & their families; to ensure that every person in the Yukon has access to supports necessary to live with dignity & to participate fully in the community of his/her choice

Disarmament

Coalition to Oppose the Arms Trade (COAT)
541 McLeod St., Ottawa ON K1R 5R2 Canada
Tel: 613-231-3076
overcoat@rogers.com
coat.ncf.ca
Social Media: www.facebook.com/group.php?gid=2337208773

To actively oppose the arms trade and support the anti-war movement.
Richard Sanders, Coordinator

Drilling

Alberta Water Well Drilling Association (AWWDA)
PO Box 130, Lougheed AB T0B 2V0 Canada
Tel: 780-386-2335; *Fax:* 780-386-2344
awwda@telusplanet.net
www.awwda.com

The AWWDA is a non-profit, non-sectarian organization with certain objectives including: assisting, promoting, encouraging, and supporting the interest and welfare of the water well industry in all of its phases; fostering aid and promote scientific education, standard research, and technique in order to improve methods of well construction and development and advance the science of groundwater in the province of Alberta.

Association des enterprises spécialiseés en eau du Québec
5930, boul Louis-H. Lafontaine, MontréAl QC H1M 1S7 Canada
Tél: 514-353-9960; *Téléc:* 514-353-3393
Ligne sans frais: 800-468-8160
contact@aeseq.com
www.aeseq.com

L'AESEQ est la seule association qui regroupe les entrepreneurs de construction oeuvrant dans tous les secteurs du cycle de l'eau décentralisé au Québec

British Columbia Ground Water Association (BCGWA)
c/o Office Of The Secretary, 1708 - 197A St., Langley BC V2Z 1K2 Canada
Tel: 604-530-8934; *Fax:* 604-530-8934
secretary@bcgwa.org
www.bcgwa.org

To advance the ground water industry, through professional & technical leadership; to promote the responsible development & use of ground water resources in British Columbia; to protect the underground water supply
Remi Allard, President
Tim Oster, Vice-President
Dave Mellis, Treasurer
Joan Perry, Secretary

Canadian Association of Drilling Engineers (CADE)
#800, 540 - 5 Ave. SW, Calgary AB T2P 0M2 Canada
Tel: 403-264-4311; *Fax:* 403-263-3796
info@cade.ca
www.cade.ca

To provide a forum for the exchange of technical drilling knowledge & expertise

Canadian Association of Oilwell Drilling Contractors (CAODC)
#800, 540 - 5 Ave. SW, Calgary AB T2P 0M2 Canada
Tel: 403-264-4311; *Fax:* 403-263-3796
info@caodc.ca
www.caodc.ca

To represent drilling rig contractors; to provide ongoing means of communication between drilling & well servicing contractors, governments, other industry sector participants, & the general public; to improve standards for safety & training, equipment & technical procedures; to coordinate programs between government bodies & contractors; oversees the Rig Technician Trade & Apprenticeship Program in Alberta, British Columbia & Saskatchewan

Canadian Diamond Drilling Association (CDDA)
City Centre Building, 101 Worthington St. East, North Bay ON P1B 1G5 Canada
Tel: 705-476-6992; *Fax:* 705-476-9494
office@cdda.ca
www.canadiandrilling.com

To foster the commercial interests of members; to promote the simplifications, standardization & interchangeability of diamond drilling equipment; to recognize the safety & health of employees; to foster the protection of the natural environment; to secure the elimination of unfair or uneconomic practices within the industry & freedom from unjust or unlawful exactions; to establish & maintain uniformity & equity in the customs & commercial usages of the diamond drilling business; to acquire & disseminate valuable business information; to promote communication among those engaged in the industry.

Canadian Ground Water Association (CGWA) / Association canadienne des eaux souterraines
#100-409, 1600 Bedford Hwy., Bedford NS B4A 1E8
Tel: 902-845-1885; *Fax:* 902-845-1886
info@cgwa.org
www.cgwa.org

To act as the national voice of the ground water industry in Canada; To encourage the management & protection of ground water
Wayne C. MacRae, Executive Officer
John Freisen, President

Manitoba Water Well Association (MWWA)
PO Box 1648, Winnipeg MB R3C 2Z6
Tel: 204-479-3777
info@mwwa.ca
www.mwwa.ca

To promote & support the water well industry in Manitoba
Jeff Bell, President
Lynn Giersch, Business Manager
Marilyn Schneider, Secretary-Treasurer

New Brunswick Ground Water Association
31 Gray Rd., Penobsquis NB E4E 5S7 Canada
Tel: 506-433-6767; *Fax:* 506-432-6888
nbgwa@nb.sympatico.ca
www.nbgwa.ca

Mission statement is based around preserving and protecting New Brunswick's "most precious and natural resource": water. They aim to promote education of its members and the public and to promote the development of ground water guidelines and strategies.
Roger Roy, President
Terry Burpee, Sec.-Treas.

Newfoundland/Labrador Ground Water Association
PO Box 160, Doyles NL A0N 1J0 Canada
Tel: 709-955-2561; *Fax:* 709-955-3402
gwater@nf.sympatico.ca

To promote the protection & management of ground water in Newfoundland & Labrador

Nova Scotia Ground Water Association (NSGWA)
#417, 3 - 644 Portland St., Dartmouth NS B2W 2M3 Canada
Fax: 902-435-0089
Toll-Free: 888-242-4440
nsgwa@ns.aliantzinc.ca
www.nsgwa.ca

To act as the voice of the industry to all levels of government; To encourage the management & protection of ground water

Ontario Ground Water Association (OGWA)
48 Front St. East, Strathroy ON N7G 1Y6
Tel: 519-245-7194; *Fax:* 519-245-7196
www.ogwa.ca

To protect & promote Ontario's ground water; To provide guidance to members, government representatives, & the public
Greg Bullock, President
Rob MacKinnon, Secretary-Treasurer
Anne Gammage, Office Manager

Prince Edward Island Ground Water Association
PO Box 857, RR#2, Cornwall PE C0A 1H0
Tel: 902-675-2360; *Fax:* 902-675-2360

To promote the protection of ground water in Prince Edward Island

Saskatchewan Ground Water Association (SGWA)
PO Box 9434, Saskatoon SK S7K 7E9
Tel: 306-244-7551; *Fax:* 306-343-0001

To act as the voice of the ground water industy throughout Saskatchewan; To promote the management of ground water throughout the province

Economics

Association des économistes québécois (ASDÉQ)
CP 6128, Succ. Centre-ville, Montréal QC H3C 3J7 Canada
Tél: 514-342-7537; *Téléc:* 514-342-3967
Ligne sans frais: 866-342-7537
national@asdeq.org
www.asdeq.org

Assurer la promotion professionnelle des économistes

Association des professionnels en développement économique du Québec (APDEQ) / Economic Development Professionals Association of Québec
CP 297, #203-B, 189, rue Tupper, Magog QC J1X 3W8 Canada
Tél: 819-868-9778; *Téléc:* 819-868-9907
Ligne sans frais: 800-361-8470
info@apdeq.qc.ca
www.apdeq.qc.ca
L'APDEQ a son siège social à Magog, en Estrie. Elle compte sur deux employés permanents qui assurent le développement de l'organisme, la gestion des dossiers, le suivi des décisions du conseil d'administration, la gestion générale et les services aux membres. Son personnel soutient également le travail des administrateurs et des autres personnes qui siègent sur les divers comités.
Patrice Gagnon, Directeur général

Atlantic Association of Applied Economists (AAAE)
c/o 1583 Hollis St., 5th Fl., Halifax NS B3J 1V4 Canada
Tel: 902-420-4601; *Fax:* 902-420-4644
www.chebucto.ns.ca/Commerce/AAAE/
To provide forums for current economic & public policy issues

Atlantic Provinces Economic Council (APEC) / Conseil économique des provinces de l'Atlantique
#500, 5121 Sackville St., Halifax NS B3J 1K1 Canada
Tel: 902-422-6516; *Fax:* 902-429-6803
info@apec-econ.ca
www.apec-econ.ca
To be the leading advocate for the economic development of the Atlantic region and accomplishes this by: monitoring and analysing current and emerging economic trends and policies; communicating the results of this analysis to its mbmers on a regular basis; consulting with a wide audience; dissminating its research and policy analysis to business, gov't, and the community at large; advocating the appropriate public and private sector policy responses.
Elizabeth Beale, President & CEO

Canada West Foundation (CWF)
#900, 1202 Centre St. SE, Calgary AB T2G 5A5 Canada
Tel: 403-264-9535; *Fax:* 403-269-4776
cwf@cwf.ca
www.cwf.ca
To operate as a public policy research institute; To introduce western perspectives into current Canadian policy debates; To produce & disseminate objective research to serve as a catalyst for informed public debate & initiatives for active citizen education & engagement in the Canadian public policy process

Canadian Agricultural Economics Society (CAES) / Société canadienne d'agroéconomie (SCAE)
University Of Victoria, PO Box 1700, Stn. CSC, Rm. 360, Business & Economics Bldg., Victoria BC V8W 2Y2 Canada
caes@aganalysis.com
www.caes.ca
To address problems related to the economics of food production & marketing & the quality of rural life through extension, research, teaching, & policy making in government & private industry

Canadian Association for Business Economics, Inc. (CABE) / Association canadienne de science économique des affaires, inc.
PO Box 828, Stn. B, Ottawa ON K1P 5P9
Tel: 613-238-4831; *Fax:* 613-238-7698
info@cabe.ca
www.cabe.ca
To represent the interests of business economists in Canada; To enhance the professionalism of business economists

Canadian Economics Association (CEA) / Association canadienne d'économique
Département des Sciences Économiques, Université du Québec à Montréal, PO Box 8888, Stn. Centre-Ville, Montréal QC H3C 3P8
Tel: 514-987-3000
www.economics.ca
To represent academic economists; To advance economic knowledge

Canadian Law & Economics Association
Faculty of Law, University of Toronto, 78 Queen's Park Cres., Toronto ON M5S 2C5
Tel: 416-978-6767; *Fax:* 416-978-7899
kristin.demuth@utoronto.ca
www.canlecon.org
Nadia Gulezko, Contact
Margaret F. Brinig, President

C.D. Howe Institute / Institut C.D. Howe
#300, 67 Yonge St., Toronto ON M5E 1J8 Canada
Tel: 416-865-1904; *Fax:* 416-865-1866
cdhowe@cdhowe.org
www.cdhowe.org
Research & educational institute identifying current & emerging economic & social policy issues facing Canadians; to recommend particular policy options; to communicate conclusions of research to domestic & international audiences.

Centre interuniversitaire de recherche en économie quantitative (CIREQ)
Pavillon Lionel-Groulx, Université de Montréal, CP 6128, Succ. Centre-Ville, 3150, rue Jean-Brillant, local C-6088, Montréal QC H3C 3J7 Canada
Tél: 514-343-6557; *Téléc:* 514-343-5831
cireq@umontreal.ca
www.cireq.umontreal.ca
Recherches dans les domaines de l'économétrie théorique et appliquée, de l'économie financière et de la théorie économique

The Conference Board of Canada / Le Conference Board du Canada
255 Smyth Rd., Ottawa ON K1H 8M7 Canada
Tel: 613-526-3280; *Fax:* 613-526-4857
Toll-Free: 866-711-2262
contactcboc@conferenceboard.ca
www.conferenceboard.ca
To be dedicated to applied research, notably in public policy, economic trends, & organizational performance

Economic Developers Association of Canada (EDAC) / Association canadienne de développement économique
#200, 7 Innovation Dr., Flamborough ON L9H 7H9 Canada
Tel: 905-689-8771; *Fax:* 905-689-5925
admin@edac.ca
www.edac.ca
EDAC works to contribute to Canada's economic, social. & environmental well-being by advancing economic development as a distinct, recognized profession, & enhancing professional competence & ethical service.

Economic Developers Council of Ontario Inc. (EDCO)
PO Box 8030, Cornwall ON K6H 7H9 Canada
Tel: 613-931-9827; *Fax:* 613-931-9828
Toll-Free: 877-818-7666
edco@sympatico.ca
www.edco.on.ca
To provide a forum for economic development related educational activities; to increase the profile of EDCO & the profession; to encourage & create an awareness of economic development issues with relevant government agencies; to promote & develop Ontario as a premier location for economic activity by increasing employment & prosperity, & enhancing the quality of life within the Ontario municipalities.

The Fraser Institute
1770 Burrard St., 4th Fl., Vancouver BC V6J 3G7 Canada
Tel: 604-688-0221; *Fax:* 604-688-8539
Toll-Free: 800-665-3558
info@fraserinstitute.ca
www.fraserinstitute.ca
Social Media: www.twitter.com/FraserInstitute
To redirect public attention to the role competitive markets play in the economic well-being of all Canadians

The North-South Institute (NSI) / L'Institut Nord-Sud
#200, 55 Murray St., Ottawa ON K1N 5M3 Canada
Tel: 613-241-3535; *Fax:* 613-241-7435
nsi@nsi-ins.ca
www.nsi-ins.ca
To analyze, for Canadians & others, the economic, social, & political implications of global change & to propose policy alternatives to promote global development & justice

Public Policy Forum / Forum des politiques publiques
#1405, 130 Albert St., Ottawa ON K1P 5G4 Canada
Tel: 613-238-7160; *Fax:* 613-238-7990
mail@ppforum.ca
www.ppforum.com
To promote better public policy & better public management through dialogue among leaders from the public, private, labour & voluntary sectors
David J. Mitchell, President
Yves Poisson, Vice-President
Ted Williamson, Director, Finance & Administration

Rotman Institute for International Business
University of Toronto, 105 St. George St., Toronto ON M5S 3E6 Canada
Tel: 416-978-5781
riib@utoronto.ca
www.rotman.utoronto.ca
RIIB merges the former Institute for Policy Analysis and the Institute for International Business, and focusses on research on the global business environment, enterprise decision making in the global economy, and the urban service economy.
Wendy Dobson, B.Sc.N., MPA, S, Co-Director
Ignatius J. (Ig) Horstmann, B.A., Ph.D., Co-Director, ihorstmann@rotman.utoronto.ca

Education

Agence universitaire de la Francophonie (AUF)
CP 49714, Succ. Musée, 3034, boul Edouard-Montpetit, Montréal QC H3T 1J7 Canada
Tél: 514-343-6630; *Téléc:* 514-343-5783
recorat@auf.org
www.auf.org
Le but principal est le développement, au sein de l'espace francophone, d'une coopération internationale pour assurer à la fois le dialogue permanent des cultures et la circulation des personnes, des idées, des expériences entre institutions universitaires, dans l'intérêt de l'éducation et du progrès de la science.

Alberta Catholic School Trustees Association
#325, 9940 - 106 St., Edmonton AB T5K 2N2 Canada
Tel: 780-484-6209; *Fax:* 780-484-6248
admin@acsta.ab.ca
www.acsta.ab.ca

Alberta Home & School Councils' Association (AHSCA)
#1200, 9925 - 109 St., Edmonton AB T5K 2J8 Canada
Tel: 780-454-9867; *Fax:* 780-455-0167
Toll-Free: 800-661-3470
parents@albertaschoolcouncils.ca
www.ahsca.ab.ca
To be the voice of parents/families committed to the best possible education for Alberta children, so that they may reach their potential to participate in society in a meaningful & responsible way
Michele Mulder, Executive Director
Marilyn Sheptycki, President
Brad Vonkeman, Vice-President

Alberta School Boards Association (ASBA)
#1200, 9925 - 109 St., Edmonton AB T5K 2J8 Canada
Tel: 780-482-7311; *Fax:* 780-482-5659
kayers@asba.ab.ca
www.asba.ab.ca
ASBA promotes the availability of high quality schooling for all & assists member boards in fulfilling their mission of achieving excellence in education.

Alberta Teachers' Association (ATA)
Barnett House, 11010 - 142 St., Edmonton AB T5N 2R1 Canada
Tel: 780-447-9400; *Fax:* 780-455-6481
Toll-Free: 800-232-7208
government@teachers.ab.ca
www.teachers.ab.ca
Social Media: www.facebook.com/ABteachers
To advance the cause of education in Alberta; to improve the teaching profession; to increase public interest in & support for education; to cooperate with other bodies having similar objectives

Alliance canadienne des responsables et enseignants en français (langue maternelle) (ACREF) / Canadian Association for the Teachers of French as a First Language
Place de la Francophonie, Succ. A, #401, 450, rue Reideau, Ottawa ON K1N 5Z4 Canada
Tél: 613-744-3192; *Téléc:* 613-744-0154
acref@franco.ca
www.franco.ca/acref
Développer un réseau d'identification nationale des professeurs de français langue maternelle; favoriser le développement et l'épanouissement des associations provinciales vouées à l'enseignement du français langue maternelle; promouvoir la diffusion de l'information en matière de théories pédagogiques, de formation à l'approche communicative, et de pratiques scolaires et d'idéologie visant l'identité des francophones, l'égalité en tant que groupe national et le contrôle des structures éducatives; appuyer les organismes provinciaux lors de leur rencontre annuelle; développer des instruments de diffusion de

l'information à l'intention de ses membres; favoriser le développement d'une politique nationale en ce qui a trait à la gestion des institutions d'enseignement et voir à ce qu'elle respecte l'autonomie des francophones

Association canadienne d'éducation de langue française (ACELF)
268, rue Marie-de-l'Incarnation, Québec QC G1N 3G4 Canada
Tél: 418-681-4661; *Téléc:* 418-681-3389
info@acelf.ca
www.acelf.ca

L'ACELF inspire et soutient le développement et l'action des institutions éducatives francophones du Canada

Association canadienne des professeurs d'immersion (ACPI) / Canadian Association of Immersion Teachers (CAIT)
#201, 57 Auriga Dr., Nepean ON K2E 8B2 Canada
Tél: 613-228-0333; *Téléc:* 613-727-3831
acpi@sevec.ca
acpi.scedu.umontreal.ca

Association des cadres scolaires du Québec
#170, 1195, av Lavigerie, Québec QC G1V 4N3 Canada
Tél: 418-654-0014; *Téléc:* 418-654-1719
acsq@acsq.qc.ca
www.acsq.qc.ca

Valoriser le statut professionnel de ses membres et promouvoir leurs intérêts professionnels et éconimiques; Collaborer avec les autorités gouvernementales et les organismes intéressés, au développement ordonné du système scolaire, par une participation constante et adéquate à l'élaboration et à la mise en oeuvre des politiques relatives à l'éducation

Association des collèges privés du Québec (ACPQ)
1940, boul Henri-Bourassa est, Montréal QC H2B 1S2 Canada
Tél: 514-381-8891; *Téléc:* 514-381-4086
acpq@cadre.qc.ca
www.acpq.net

Défendre les intérêts de ses collèges membres et contribuer au développement de l'enseignement collégial privé au Québec

Association des directeurs généraux des commissions scolaires du Québec (ADIGECS)
a/s Directeur exécutif, #200, 195 ch de Chambly, Longueuil QC J4H 3L3 Canada
Tél: 450-674-6700; *Téléc:* 450-674-7337
www.adigecs.qc.ca

Contribuer à l'avancement de l'éducation au Québec; protéger les intérêts de ses membres notamment au chapitre des conditions de travail

Association des enseignantes et des enseignants franco-ontariens (AEFO) / Franco-Ontarian Teachers' Association
681 ch. Belfast, Ottawa ON K1G 0Z4 Canada
Tél: 613-244-2336; *Téléc:* 613-563-7718
Ligne sans frais: 888-609-7718
aefo@aefo.on.ca
www.aefo.on.ca

L'Association des enseignantes et des enseignants franco-ontariens (AEFO) est un syndicat francophone regroupant les travailleuses et les travailleurs au service des établissements publics et privés francophones en Ontario. Elle défend les intérêts individuels et collectifs de ses membres et fait la promotion de leur profession et du fait français.

Association des enseignantes et des enseignants francophones du Nouveau-Brunswick (AEFNB)
CP 712, 650, rue Montgomery, Fredericton NB E3B 5B4 Canada
Tél: 506-452-8921; *Téléc:* 506-453-9795
aefnb@nbnet.nb.ca
www.aefnb.nb.ca

Représenter les intérêts des enseignantes et des enseignants francophones de la province; favoriser et maintenir au Nouveau-Brunswick des services éducatifs de langue française de première qualité

Association for Baha'i Studies (ABS) / Association d'études Baha'is
34 Copernicus St., Ottawa ON K1N 7K4 Canada
Tel: 613-233-1903; *Fax:* 613-233-3644
abs-na@bahai-studies.ca
www.bahai-studies.ca

To foster Baha'i scholarship & to demonstrate the value of this scholarly approach; to promote courses of study on the Baha'i faith; to foster relationships with various leaders of thought & persons of capacity; to publish scholarly materials examining the Baha'i faith, especially on its application to the concerns & needs of humanity; to organize annual meetings & develop chapters of the Association around the world

Association for Canadian Studies (ACS) / Association d'études canadiennes (AEC)
1822A, rue Sherbooke ouest, Montréal QC H3H 1E4 Canada
Tel: 514-925-3094; *Fax:* 514-925-3095
general@acs-aec.ca
www.acs-aec.ca

To initiate & supports activities in the areas of research, teaching, communications, & the training of students in the field of Canadian studies, especially in interdisciplinary & multidisciplinary perspectives; To strive to raise public awareness of Canadian issues; To provide the Canadian Studies community, principally within Canada, with a wide range of activities & programs

Association francophone internationale des directeurs d'établissements scolaires (AFIDES)
500, boul Crémazie est, Montréal QC H2P 1E7 Canada
Tél: 514-383-7335; *Téléc:* 514-384-2139
Ligne sans frais: 877-783-7335
afides@afides.org
www.afides.org

Promouvoir les échanges entre les responsables francophones d'établissements scolaires pour répondre à des besoins de perfectionnement international par la coopération et les échanges

Association francophone pour le savoir (ACFAS)
425, rue de la Gauchetière est, Montréal QC H2L 2M7 Canada
Tél: 514-849-0045; *Téléc:* 514-849-5558
acfas@acfas.ca
www.acfas.ca

Promouvoir et soutenir la science et la technologie pour encourager le développement culturel et économique de la société

Association of Atlantic Universities (AAU) / Association des universités de l'Atlantique
#403, 5657 Spring Garden Rd., Halifax NS B3J 3R4 Canada
Tel: 902-425-4230; *Fax:* 902-425-4233
info@atlanticuniversities.ca
www.atlanticuniversities.ca

To assist in assuring the quality & coordination of higher education in Atlantic Provinces; to provide a forum for university administrators to discuss & coordinate their views, interests & concerns in support of higher education in the Atlantic provinces

Association of British Columbia Teachers of English as an Additional Language (B.C. TEAL)
#206, 640 West Broadway, Vancouver BC V5Z 1G4 Canada
Tel: 604-736-6330; *Fax:* 604-736-6306
admin@bcteal.org
www.bcteal.org

To foster & promote effective instruction in English as a second language in BC; to raise the professional status of BC ESL teachers; to promote communication among BC ESL professionals

Association of Canadian Community Colleges (ACCC) / Association des collèges communautaires du Canada
#200, 1223 Michael St. North, Ottawa ON K1J 7T2 Canada
Tel: 613-746-2222; *Fax:* 613-746-6721
info@accc.ca
www.accc.ca

To provide leadership in supporting member institutions in their provision of learning opportunities which promote both individual development & that of the society & economy

Association of Canadian Faculties of Dentistry (ACFD) / Association des facultés dentaires du Canada (AFDC)
#204, 100 Bronson Ave., Ottawa ON K1R 6G8 Canada
Tel: 613-237-6505; *Fax:* 613-236-8386
director@acfd.ca
www.acfd.ca

To assure the quality of dental education & research in Canada. It also strives to keep its members informed of issues regarding University-based dental education and promote communication between its members.

Association of Canadian Universities for Northern Studies (ACUNS) / Association universitaire canadienne d'études nordiques
#405, 17 York St., Ottawa ON K1N 9J6 Canada
Tel: 613-562-0515; *Fax:* 613-562-0533
office@acuns.ca
www.acuns.ca
Social Media: twitter.com/acunsaucen

The Association encourages the government & private sector to support polar scholarship, fostering programs to increase public awareness of polar sciences & research. It represents its member universities & colleges, encouraging the establishment of funds & resources to ensure a network of trained researchers, regional managers & educators.

Association of Colleges of Applied Arts & Technology of Ontario (ACAATO) / Association des collèges d'arts appliqués et de technologie de l'Ontario
#1010, 655 Bay St., Toronto ON M5G 2K4 Canada
Tel: 416-596-0744; *Fax:* 416-596-2364
www.collegesontario.org

To advance a strong college system for Ontario

Association of Deans of Pharmacy of Canada (ADPC) / Association des doyens de pharmacie du Canada (ADPC)
3919 - 13th Ave. West, Vancouver BC V6R 2T1 Canada
Tel: 604-222-0221; *Fax:* 604-222-2574
fabbott@telus.net

Association of Early Childhood Educators Ontario (AECEO)
#211, 40 Orchard View Blvd., Toronto ON M4R 1B9
Tel: 416-487-3157; *Fax:* 416-487-3758
Toll-Free: 866-932-3236
info@aeceo.ca
www.aeceo.ca

To support early childhood educators throughout Ontario

Association of Educational Researchers of Ontario (AERO) / Association ontarienne des chercheurs et chercheuse en éducation
c/o Dufferin-Peel Catholic District School Board, 40 Matheson Blvd. West, Mississauga ON L5R 1C5 Canada
Tel: 905-890-0708
susan.palijan@dpcdsb.org
www.aero-ontario.org

To promote & improve research, education, planning & development pertaining to education in the Ontario school system

Association of Faculties of Medicine of Canada (AFMC) / L'Association des facultés de médecine du Canada (AFMC)
#800, 265 Carling Ave., Ottawa ON K1S 2E1 Canada
Tel: 613-730-0687; *Fax:* 613-730-1196
nbusing@afmc.ca
www.afmc.ca

To represent the interests of members in medical research policy formulation; to promote & advance academic medicine through the review & development of standards for medical education, through the development of national policies appropriate to the aims & purposes of Canadian faculties of medicine, through the fostering of research, & through representation of Canadian faculties of medicine to professional associations & governments

Association of Independent Schools & Colleges in Alberta (AISCA)
#201, 11830 - 111 Ave., Edmonton AB T5G 0E1 Canada
Tel: 780-469-9868; *Fax:* 780-469-9880
office@aisca.ab.ca
www.aisca.ab.ca

To defend & promote the right of parents to determine the context for their children's education; to create a positive social, fiscal & political environment in which independent schools are free to maintain their identity as they serve the public interest; to support & encourage independent schools in providing significant educational choices for parents & their children; to foster public understanding & appreciation of independent schools & their services

Association of Registrars of the Universities & Colleges of Canada (ARUCC) / Association des registraires des universités et collèges du Canada
c/o University of Calgary, 2500 University Dr. NW, Calgary AB T2N 1N4 Canada
Tel: 403-220-3832; *Fax:* 403-289-1253
sekulic@ucalgary.ca
www.arucc.ca

ARUCC was developed in response to the professional needs of student administrative services personnel in universities.

Association of Universities & Colleges of Canada (AUCC) / Association des universités et collèges du Canada
#600, 350 Albert St., Ottawa ON K1R 1B1 Canada
Tel: 613-563-1236; *Fax:* 613-563-9745
info@aucc.ca
www.aucc.ca
To foster & promote the interests of higher education

Association of University Forestry Schools of Canada (AUFSC) / Association des écoles forestières universitaires du Canada
c/o School of Forestry, Lakehead University, 955 Oliver Rd., Thunder Bay ON P7B 5E1 Canada
Tel: 807-343-8511

Association provinciale des enseignantes et enseignants du Québec (APEQ) / Québec Provincial Association of Teachers (QPAT)
#1, 17035, boul Brunswick, Kirkland QC H9H 5G6 Canada
Tél: 514-694-9777; *Téléc:* 514-694-0189
Ligne sans frais: 800-361-9870
reception@qpat-apeq.qc.ca
www.qpat-apeq.qc.ca
Alan Lombard, Executive Director

Association québécoise des professeurs de français (AQPF)
#222, 2095, Frank-Carrel, Sainte-Foy QC G1N 4L8 Canada
Tél: 418-683-0947; *Téléc:* 418-527-4765
Ligne sans frais: 800-267-0947
apqf@bellnet.ca
www.aqpf.qc.ca
Les principaux champs d'intervention sont - la didactique et l'enseignement du français langue maternelle du préscolaire à l'universitél'enseignement du français aux adultes; l'alphabétisation; l'enseignement du français langue seconde; promotion de la langue française, de la culture québécoise et de la francophonie

Association québécoise des troubles d'apprentissage (AQETA) / Learning Disabilities Association of Québec (LDAQ)
#300, 284, rue Notre-Dame ouest, Montréal QC H2Y 1T7 Canada
Tél: 514-847-1324; *Téléc:* 514-281-5187
info@aqeta.qc.ca
www.aqeta.qc.ca
Faire connaître les troubles d'apprentissage; faire la promotion des besoins et des droits collectifs des enfants et des adultes qui en sont atteints

Association québécoise du personnel de direction des écoles (AQPDE)
#308, 2700, Jean-Perriny, Québec QC G2C 1S9 Canada
Tél: 418-845-5088; *Téléc:* 418-845-9699
info@aqpde.ca
www.aqpde.ca
Défendre et promouvoir les intérêts professionnels, sociaux et économiques des membres, favoriser leur participation et établir une concertation avec les autres organismes du réseau de l'éducation pour assurer les meilleures conditions de ses membres
Serge Rodrigue, Président

Black Educators Association of Nova Scotia (BEA)
2136 Gottingen St., Halifax NS B3K 3B3 Canada
Tel: 902-424-7036; *Fax:* 902-424-0636
Toll-Free: 800-565-3398
beaadulted@eastlink.ca
www.thebea.ns.ca
To monitor and ensure the development of an equitable education system, so that African Nova Scotians are able to achieve their maximum potential.

British Columbia Confederation of Parent Advisory Councils (BCCPAC)
#350, 5172 Kingsway, Burnaby BC V5H 2E8 Canada
Tel: 604-687-4433; *Fax:* 604-687-4488
Toll-Free: 866-529-4397
info@bccpac.bc.ca
www.bccpac.bc.ca
To advance the public school education & well-being of children in British Columbia

British Columbia School Trustees Association (BCSTA) / Association des commissaires d'écoles de Colombie-Britannique
1580 West Broadway, 4th Fl., Vancouver BC V6J 5K9 Canada
Tel: 604-734-2721; *Fax:* 604-732-4559
bcsta@bcsta.org
www.bcsta.org
To promote effective boards of public school trustees working together for BC students. It is a non-profit, voluntary organization dedicated to assisting school boards in their key work; improving student achievement through community engagement.

British Columbia Teachers' Federation (BCTF) / Fédération des enseignants de la Colombie-Britannique
#100, 550 - 6th Ave. West, Vancouver BC V5Z 4P2
Tel: 604-871-2283; *Fax:* 604-871-2293
Toll-Free: 800-663-9163
benefits@bctf.ca; rovergaard@bctf.ca (Media Relations)
www.bctf.ca
To represent 41,000 public school teachers in the province of British Columbia; To support 33 provincial specialist associations, such as the British Columbia Teacher-Librarians' Association & the British Columbia Music Educators' Association; To advocate for the professional, economic, & social goals of teachers

Canadian Alliance of Student Associations (CASA) / Alliance canadienne des associations étudiantes (ACAE)
PO Box 3408, Stn. D, Ottawa ON K1P 6H8 Canada
Tel: 613-236-3457; *Fax:* 613-236-2386
casacomm@casa.ca
www.casa.ca
Zach Churchill, National Director
Rick Theis, Government Relations Coordinator
Jillian Flake, Officer, Public Relations & Communications
Lisa Fry, Research & Policy

Canadian Asian Studies Association (CASA) / Association canadienne des études asiatiques (ACEA)
c/o Concordia University, #SB115, 1455, rue de Maisonneuve ouest, Montréal QC H3G 1M8
Tel: 514-848-2280; *Fax:* 514-848-4514
casa_acea@bellnet.ca
canadianasianstudies.concordia.ca
To expand & disseminate knowledge about Asia in Canada

Canadian Association for American Studies (CAAS) / Association d'études américaines au Canada
c/o Dana Medoro, Associate Professor, University of Manitoba, 636 Fletcher Argue, Winnipeg MB R3T 5V5
webmaster@american-studies.ca
www.american-studies.ca
Social Media: www.facebook.com/group.php?gid=75085833950
To encourage study & research concerning the United States; To examine the implications of American studies for Canada & the world

Canadian Association for Co-operative Education (CAFCE) / Association canadienne de l'enseignement coopératif
#205, 834 Yonge St., Toronto ON M4W 2H1
Tel: 416-483-3311; *Fax:* 416-483-3365
cafce@cafce.ca
www.cafce.ca
To act as the voice for post-secondary co-operative education in Canada; To advance post-secondary co-operative education throughout the country; To establish national standards

Canadian Association for Graduate Studies (CAGS) / Association canadienne pour les études supérieures (ACES)
#205, 260 Dalhousie St., Ottawa ON K1N 7E4 Canada
Tel: 613-562-0949; *Fax:* 613-562-9009
cags@uottawa.ca
www.cags.ca
To promote excellence in graduate education; to foster research, scholarship, & creative activity; to provide a nationwide link for the exchange of information between graduate schools & granting councils, research, business, & industrial sectors, & all levels of government; to hold meetings & conferences; to publish materials to advance graduate education; to develop & maintain national standards for graduate degree programs; to support the regular external evaluation of these standards; to deal with other matters of concern to Deans & Associate Deans of graduate studies

Canadian Association for Pastoral Practice & Education (CAPPE) / Association canadienne pour la pratique et l'éducation pastorales (ACPEP)
660 Francklyn St., Halifax NS B3H 3B5
Tel: 902-820-3085; *Fax:* 902-820-3087
Toll-Free: 866-442-2773
office@cappe.org
www.cappe.org
To support persons involved in pastoral care & pastoral counselling in Canada; To set standards & monitor professional practice; To accredit educational centres in a range of settings

Canadian Association for Scottish Studies (CASS)
Dept. of History, Centre for Scottish Studies, University of Guelph, 1008 MacKinnon Ext., Guelph ON N1G 2W1 Canada
Tel: 519-824-4120; *Fax:* 519-766-9516
scottish@uoguelph.ca
www.uoguelph.ca/scottish
To promote interest in Scottish history, literature, & culture

Canadian Association for Teacher Education (CATE) / Association canadienne pour la formation des enseignants (ACFE)
#204, 260 Dalhousie St., Ottawa ON K1N 7E4 Canada
Tel: 613-241-0018; *Fax:* 613-241-0019
www.csse.ca/CATE/home.htm
To encourage scholarly study & research in education, with special emphasis on teacher education; to provide for the membership a national forum for the presentation & discussion of significant studies in education, with special emphasis on teacher education

Canadian Association for the Advancement of Netherlandic Studies (CAANS) / Association canadienne pour l'avancement des études néerlandaises (ACAEN)
c/o Secretary-Treasurer, 613 Huyck's Point Rd., Wellington ON K0K 3L0 Canada
www.caans-acaen.ca
With chapters across Canada, CAANS aims to stimulate awareness & interest in, & to promote the study of Netherlandic languages (Dutch, Flemish, Afrikaans), as well as Netherlandic literature, history & culture. The association provides a forum for discussion in these areas, holds an annual conference, publishes research, & sponsors relevant cultural & scholarly activities such as meetings, presentations, lectures & discussions

Canadian Association for the Study of Discourse & Writing (CASDW) / Association canadienne de rédactologie (ACR)
c/o W. Brock MacDonald, Woodsworth College, University of Toronto, 119 St. George St., Toronto ON M5S 1A9 Canada
wb.macdonald@utoronto.ca
cattw-acprts.mcgill.ca
To advance the study & teaching of discourse, writing, & communication in both academic & nonacademic settings
Doreen Starke-Meyerring, President
Anne Parker, Secretary

Canadian Association for University Continuing Education (CAUCE) / Association pour l'éducation permanente dans les universités du Canada (AEPUC)
c/o Centre for Continuing & Distance Education, U. of Saskatchewan, #464, 221 Cumberland Ave. North, Saskatoon SK S7N 1M3
Tel: 306-966-5604; *Fax:* 306-966-5590
cauce.secretariat@usask.ca
www.cauce-aepuc.ca
To enlarge the quality & scope of educational opportunities for adults at the university level

Canadian Association of College & University Student Services (CACUSS) / Association des services aux étudiants des universités et collèges du Canada (ASEUCC)
c/o Events Management Plus Inc., #310, 4 Cataraqui St., Kingston ON K7L 1Z7 Canada
Tel: 613-531-9210; *Fax:* 613-531-0626
contact@cacuss.ca
www.cacuss.ca
CACUSS represents & serves persons who work in Canadian post-secondary institutions in student affairs & services. The association offers advocacy & assistance on issues that affect the quality of student life on Canadian university & college campuses.

Canadian Association of Foundations of Education (CAFE) / Association canadienne des fondements de l'éducation (ACFE)
Univ. of Manitoba, Faculty Of Education, 256 St John's College, Winnipeg MB R3T 2M5 Canada
Tel: 204-474-8741; *Fax:* 204-474-7551
mandzukd@ms.umanitoba.ca
www.csse.ca/CAFE/home.htm
To provide a forum for discussing the contribution of the social sciences & humanities (eg. history of education, philosophy of education, sociology of education) to educational theory, research & practice

Canadian Association of Geographers (CAG) / Association canadienne des géographes
Department of Geography, McGill University, #425, 805, rue Sherbrooke ouest, Montréal QC H3A 2K6
Tel: 514-398-4946; *Fax:* 514-398-7437
valerie.shoffey@cag-acg.ca (Executive Secretary)
www.cag-acg.ca
To promote the discipline of geography in Canada & internationally

Canadian Association of Independent Schools (CAIS)
12 Bannockburn Ave., Toronto ON M5M 2M8 Canada
Tel: 416-780-1779
director@cais.ca
www.cais.ca

Canadian Association of Principals (CAP) / Association canadienne des directeurs d'école
#220, 300 Earl Grey Dr., Kanata ON K2T 1C1 Canada
Tel: 613-622-0346; *Fax:* 613-622-0258
cap@bellnet.ca
www.cdnprincipals.org
To represent the professional perspectives of principals & vice-principals at the national level & to provide the leadership necessary to ensure quality educational opportunities for Canadian students.

Canadian Association of School Social Workers & Attendance Counsellors (CASSWAC)
c/o Portage la Prairie School Div., 36 - 13th St. NW, Portage la Prairie MB R1N 2T5 Canada
Tel: 204-857-7687
jmurray@plpsd.mb.ca
www.casswac.ca

Canadian Association of Schools of Nursing (CASN) / Association canadienne des écoles de sciences infirmières (ACESI)
#15, 99 Fifth Ave., Ottawa ON K1S 5K4 Canada
Tel: 613-235-3150; *Fax:* 613-235-4476
inquire@casn.ca
www.casn.ca
CASN/ACESI represents Canadian nursing programs. The association is the national voice for nursing education & nursing research.

Canadian Association of Second Language Teachers (CASLT) / Association canadienne des professeurs de langues secondes (ACPLS)
#300, 950 Gladstone Ave., Ottawa ON K1Y 3E6 Canada
Tel: 613-727-0994; *Fax:* 613-727-3831
Toll-Free: 877-727-0994
admin@caslt.org
www.caslt.org
To promote & advance nationally learning of second languages; to encourage activities & research in field of second language

Canadian Association of Slavists (CAS) / Association canadienne des slavistes
Alumni Hall, Dept. of Slavic Languages & Literatures, Univ. of Toronto, #403, 121 St. Joseph St., Toronto ON M5S 1J4 Canada
Tel: 416-926-1300; *Fax:* 416-333-8243
www.ualberta.ca/~csp/cas/contact.html
The learned society comprises scholars & professionals with interests in the social, economic, & political life of Slavic people, in addition to their languages, cultures, & histories. Understanding of Slavic societies & dialogue are promoted by CAS, by disseminating information about the past & present of the Slavic world.

Canadian Association of University Business Officers (CAUBO) / Association canadienne du personnel administratif universitaire (ACPAU)
#320, 350 Albert St., Ottawa ON K1R 1B1 Canada
Tel: 613-230-6760; *Fax:* 613-563-7739
cworkman@caubo.ca
www.caubo.ca
To promote the professional & effective management of the administrative, financial & business affairs of higher education; to have the professional standards of its members & to strengthen the contribution of higher education to the well being of Canada

Canadian Association of University Research Administrators (CAURA) / Association canadienne d'administrateurs de recherche universitaire (ACARU)
#600, 350 Albert St., Ottawa ON K1R 1B1 Canada
admin@caura-acaru.ca
www.caura-acaru.ca
CAURA is a national voice for research administrators, & is committed to improving the profession at educational institutions, hospitals & research facilties. It provides a forum for discussion & exchange of information on current issues & policies.

Canadian Association of University Teachers (CAUT) / Association canadienne des professeures et professeurs d'université (ACPPU)
2705 Queensview Dr., Ottawa ON K2B 8K2
Tel: 613-820-2270; *Fax:* 613-820-7244
acppu@caut.ca
www.caut.ca
To act as the national voice for academic staff; To promote academic freedom; To improve the quality & accessibility of post-secondary education in Canada

Canadian Bureau for International Education (CBIE) / Bureau canadien de l'éducation internationale (BCEI)
#1550, 220 Laurier Ave. West, Ottawa ON K1P 5Z9 Canada
Tel: 613-237-4820; *Fax:* 613-237-1073
info@cbie.ca
www.cbie.ca
To promote international understanding & development through the free movement of people & active exchange of ideas, information & technologies across national borders.

Canadian Catholic School Trustees' Association (CCSTA) / Association canadienne des commissaires d'écoles catholique
Catholic Education Centre, 570 West Hunt Club Rd., Nepean ON K2G 3R4 Canada
Tel: 613-224-4455; *Fax:* 613-224-3187
ccsta@ottawacatholicschools.ca
www.ccsta.ca
To protect the right to Catholic education in Canada; to promote excellence in Catholic education across Canada

Canadian College of Teachers (CCT) / Collège canadien des enseignants et des enseignantes
2490 Don Reid Dr., Ottawa ON K1H 1E1 Canada
Tel: 613-558-4705
allan@winnipeg.com
www.cct-cce.com
To serve the certified teachers in all regions of Canada through the promotion of teaching as a scholarly profession

Canadian Council for the Advancement of Education Inc. (CCAE) / Le Conseil canadien pour l'avancement de l'éducation
PO Box 41161, Stn. Elmvale, Ottawa ON K1G 5K9 Canada
Tel: 613-421-7950; *Fax:* 613-421-7960
admin@ccaecanada.org
www.ccaecanada.org
Excellence in educational advancement is promoted through networking opportunities, professional development, & mutual support.
Catherine MacNeill, Executive Director
Ray Satterthwaite, President

Canadian Council of Teachers of English Language Arts (CCTELA)
#10, 730 River Rd., Winnipeg MB R2M 5A4 Canada
Tel: 204-255-1676; *Fax:* 204-253-2562
cctela@mts.net
www.cctela.ca
To provide a national voice in education relating to English Language Arts; to serve as a forum for communication among provincial councils concerning English Language Arts; to provide a system of communication & cooperation for teachers of English Language Arts at all levels in Canada; to encourage research, experimentation & investigation in English Language Arts teaching; to sponsor, promote & lobby for programs of benefit to Canadian students.

Canadian Council of University Physical Education & Kinesiology Administrators (CCUPEKA) / Conseil canadien des administrateurs universitaires en éducation physique et kinésiologie (CCAUEPK)
c/o Dr. J. Starkes, Department of Kinesiology, McMaster University, Hamilton ON L8S 4K1 Canada
www.ccupeka.ca
To serve as an accrediting body for physical education & kinesiology programs at universities in Canada; to offer a voice for academics, through lobbying initiatives

Canadian Education Association (CEA) / Association canadienne d'éducation (ACE)
#300, 317 Adelaide St. West, Toronto ON M5V 1P9 Canada
Tel: 416-591-6300; *Fax:* 416-591-5345
info@cea-ace.ca
www.cea-ace.ca
To promote the improvement of education & assist the educational community by providing opportunities to study & stimulate dialogue on issues of common interest; to share ideas, experiences & information; to establish & maintain linkages with government bodies, non-government agencies & individuals; to analyze trends & directions through research; to participate in learning activities.

Canadian Ethnic Studies Association (CESA) / Société canadienne d'études ethniques (SCEE)
Dept. of Geography, Univ. of Winnipeg, 515 Portage Ave., Winnipeg MB R3B 2E9 Canada
cesa@uwinnipeg.ca
cesa.uwinnipeg.ca
To encourage scholarly debate about theoretical & practical issues in Canadian ethnic studies

Canadian Faculties of Agriculture & Veterinary Medicine (CFAVM) / Facultés d'agriculture et de médecine vétérinaire du Canada
77 Townsend Dr., Nepean ON K2J 2V3 Canada
Tel: 613-825-6873
dhedley000@sympatico.ca
www.cfavm.ca

Canadian Federation for Humanities & Social Sciences (CFHSS) / Fédération canadienne des sciences humaines (FCSH)
#415, 151 Slater St., Ottawa ON K1P 5H3 Canada
Tel: 613-238-6112; *Fax:* 613-238-6114
fedcan@fedcan.ca
www.fedcan.ca
The Federation represents the Canadian research community by working to support & advance research in the humanities & social sciences in Canada.

Canadian Federation of Business School Deans (CFBSD) / Fédération canadienne des doyens des écoles d'administration
3000, ch de la Côte-Sainte-Catherine, Montréal QC H3T 2A7
Tel: 514-340-7116; *Fax:* 514-340-7275
info@cfbsd.ca; conferences@cfbsd.ca; surveys@cfbsd.ca
www.cfbsd.ca
To encourage the professional development of business school administrators; To promote excellence in management education; To represent management education to the government, the business community, & the media

Canadian Federation of Students (CFS) / Fédération canadienne des étudiantes et étudiants (FCEE)
338C Somerset St. West, Ottawa ON K2P 0J9
Tel: 613-232-7394; *Fax:* 613-232-0276
web@cfs-fcee.ca
www.cfs-fcee.ca
To represent the collective interests of college & university students across Canada; To act as a unified voice for Canadian university & college students

Canadian Federation of University Women (CFUW) / Fédération canadienne des femmes diplômées des universités (FCFDU)
Head Office, #305, 251 Bank St., Ottawa ON K2P 1X3 Canada
Tel: 613-234-8252; *Fax:* 613-234-8221
cfuwgen@rogers.com
www.cfuw.org
To pursue knowledge; to promote education; to improve the status of women & human rights; to participate actively in public affairs in a spirit of cooperation & friendship

Canadian Foundation for Economic Education (CFEE) / Fondation d'éducation économique
#201, 110 Eglinton Ave. West, Toronto ON M4R 1A3
Tel: 416-968-2236; *Fax:* 416-968-0488
Toll-Free: 888-570-7610
mail@cfee.org
www.cfee.org
To enhance the economic capabilities of Canadians
Jean Olier Caron, Chair
Lori Cranson, Chair
Steve Petherbridge, Advisor

Canadian Home & School Federation (CHSF) / Fédération canadienne des associations foyer-école (FCAFE)
c/o Fisher Park School, 250 Holland Ave., Ottawa ON K1Y 0Y6 Canada
Tel: 613-798-2837; *Fax:* 613-798-2838
chsf@bellnet.ca
www.canadianhomeandschool.com
To improve the quality of Canadian public education available to children & youth; To act as the national voice of parents with children in public schools

Canadian Interuniversity Sport (CIS) / Sport interuniversitaire canadien (SIC)
#N205, 801 King Edward, Ottawa ON K1N 6N5 Canada
Tel: 613-562-5670; *Fax:* 613-562-5669
cisoffice@universitysport.ca
www.cis-sic.ca
Social Media: www.twitter.com/CIS_SIC
To act as the national governing body for men's & women's university sport in Canada

Canadian Network for Innovation in Education (CNIE)
#204, 260 Dalhousie St., Ottawa ON K1N 7E4 Canada
Tel: 613-241-0018; *Fax:* 613-241-0019
cnie-rcie@cnie-rcie.ca
www.cade-aced.ca
To develop & promote the use of technologies, practices, & policies that foster access to learning for students

Canadian School Boards Association (CSBA) / Association canadienne des commissions/conseils scolaires
PO Box 2095, Stn. D, Ottawa ON K1P 5W3 Canada
Tel: 613-235-3724; *Fax:* 613-238-8434
admin@cdnsba.org
www.cdnsba.org
To provide leadership for school boards throughout Canada by supporting the efforts of the provincial/territorial school board/trustee associations; to promote educational excellence at the elementary/secondary levels as a national imperative; to foster & promote the maintenance of the principles of local autonomy in education in Canada through elected representation; to provide for & maintain liaison with the Cabinet & all branches of the federal government & members of Parliament & to make representation on behalf of school boards in Canada; to maintain a national profile for school boards & to make representation on their behalf to other national organizations; to provide for interprovincial communication on issues & developments in public education that take place on a provincial/territorial, national or international level

Canadian Society for Education through Art (CSEA) / Société canadienne d'éducation par l'art (SCEA)
Faculty of Education, Department of Curriculum and Instruction, PO Box 3010, Stn. CSC, University of Victoria, Victoria BC V8W 3N4 Canada
Tel: 250-721-7896; *Fax:* 250-721-7598
info@csea-scea.ca
www.csea-scea.ca
The Canadian Society for Education through Art, is a voluntary association and is the only Canadian national organization that brings together art educators, gallery educators, and others wtih simialr intersts and concerns.

Canadian Society for the Study of Education (CSSE) / Société canadienne pour l'étude de l'éducation (SCEE)
#204, 260 Dalhousie St., Ottawa ON K1N 7E4 Canada
Tel: 613-241-0018; *Fax:* 613-241-0019
csse-scee@csse.ca
www.csse.ca
To advance knowledge & inform practice in educational settings; to promote the advancement of Canadian research & scholarship in education; to provide for the discussion of studies, issues & trends in education, & for the dissemination of research findings; to promote exchange among members & other educational researchers in Canada & internationally; to foster partnerships &, through educational research, influence public policy & help determine the nature, structure & funding of the research agenda

Canadian Society for the Study of Higher Education (CSSHE) / La Société canadienne pour l'étude de l'enseignement supérieur (SCEES)
PO Box 34091, Stn. Fort Richmond, Winnipeg MB R3T 5T5 Canada
Tel: 204-474-6404; *Fax:* 204-474-7561
www.ss.ucalgary.ca/csshe/
To advance the knowledge of post-secondary education through the promotion of research & its dissemination through publications & learned meetings

Canadian Society of Biblical Studies (CSBS) / Société canadienne des études bibliques (SCEB)
c/o Prof. Robert A. Derrenbacker, Jr., Regent College, 5800 University Blvd., Vancouver BC V6T 2E4 Canada
rderrenbacker@regent-college.edu
www.ccsr.ca/csbs
To stimulate the critical investigation of the classical biblical literature & related literature

Canadian Teachers' Federation (CTF) / Fédération canadienne des enseignantes et des enseignants (FCE)
2490 Don Reid Dr., Ottawa ON K1H 1E1 Canada
Tel: 613-232-1505; *Fax:* 613-232-1886
Toll-Free: 866-283-1505
info@ctf-fce.ca
www.ctf-fce.ca
Promotes a strong publicly funded education system for Canada, one that enhances the country's competitiveness in a knowledge based global economy & gives children the opportunity to become active, engaged citizens

Canadian Test Centre Inc. (CTC) / Services d'évaluation pédagogique
#7-8, 85 Citizen Ct., Markham ON L6G 1A8 Canada
Tel: 905-513-6636; *Fax:* 905-513-6639
Toll-Free: 800-668-1006
info@canadiantestcentre.com
www.canadiantestcentre.com
To publish & distribute test products; to support teachers to make their testing programs work; to invest in research & development projects which aim to improve the measurement & evaluation of student ability & achievement.
Ernest W. Cheng, Managing Director

Canadian University & College Conference Organizers Association (CUCCOA) / Association des coordonnateurs de congrès des universités et des collèges du Canada (ACCUCC)
312 Oakwood Ct., Newmarket ON L3Y 3C8 Canada
Tel: 905-954-0102; *Fax:* 905-895-1630
inquiries@cuccoa.org
www.cuccoa.org
Exists for the purpose of information sharing, professional development & group marketing
Carol Ford, Manager

Canadian University & College Counselling Association (CUCCA) / Association canadienne de counseling universitaire et collégial
c/o Canadian Association of College & University Student Services, #310, 4 Cataraqui St., Kingston ON K7K 1Z7 Canada
Tel: 613-531-9210; *Fax:* 613-531-0626
www.cacuss.ca/en/divisions/CUCCA/overview.htm

Centre d'animation de développement et de recherche en éducation (CADRÉ)
1940, boul Henri-Bourassa est, Montréal QC H2B 1S2 Canada
Tél: 514-381-8891; *Téléc:* 514-381-4086
Ligne sans frais: 888-381-8891
info@cadre.qc.ca
www.cadre.qc.ca

Centre franco-ontarien de ressources pédagogiques (CFORP)
435 Donald St., Ottawa ON K1K 4X5 Canada
Tél: 613-747-8000; *Téléc:* 613-747-2808
Ligne sans frais: 877-742-3677
cforp@cforp.on.ca
www.cforp.on.ca
Le Centre franco-ontarien est un organisme à but non lucratif qui publie du matériel pédagogique et qui le distribue aux écoles de langue française depuis 1974

The Commonwealth of Learning (COL)
#1200, 1055 Hastings St. West, Vancouver BC V6E 2E9 Canada
Tel: 604-775-8200; *Fax:* 604-775-8210
info@col.org
www.col.org
To create & widen access to education & to improve its quality, utilising distance education techniques & associated communications technologies to meet the particular requirements of member countries
John Daniel, President & CEO
Dave Wilson, CAE, Communications Manager

Comparative & International Education Society of Canada (CIESC) / Société canadienne d'éducation comparée et internationale (SCECI)
University of Western Ontario, #2, 1151 Richmond St., London ON N6A 5B8 Canada
www.edu.uwo.ca/ciesc/
To promote international knowledge & understanding in education; To examine educational systems in international & comparative framework

Confederation of Alberta Faculty Associations (CAFA)
Univ. of Alberta, 11043 - 90 Ave., Edmonton AB T6G 2E1 Canada
Tel: 780-492-5630; *Fax:* 780-436-0516
lori.morinville@ualberta.ca
www.ualberta.ca/~cafa/
CAFA is a professional organization of faculty and faculty association in Alberta Universities and is comprised of three associations; The Association of Academic Staff; University of Alberta, Athabasca University Faculty Association; and The University of Lethbridge Faculty Association. The objects of the Conferdation are to promote the quality of education in the province and to promote the well-being of Alberta Universities and their academic staff.

Confederation of University Faculty Associations of British Columbia (CUFA BC)
#315, 207 West Hastings St., Vancouver BC V6B 1H7 Canada
Tel: 604-646-4677; *Fax:* 604-646-4676
cufabc@sfu.ca
www.cufa.bc.ca

Conférence des recteurs et des principaux des universités du Québec (CREPUQ) / Conference of Rectors & Principals of Quebec Universities
c/o Conférence des recteurs et des principaux, #200, 500, rue Sherbrooke ouest, Montréal QC H3A 3C6 Canada
Tél: 514-288-8524; *Téléc:* 514-288-0554
info@crepuq.qc.ca
www.crepuq.qc.ca
Est un organisme privé qui regroupe, sur une base volontaire, tous les établissements universitaires québécois; sert de forum permanent d'échanges et de concertation qui permet aux gestionnaires de partager leurs expériences en vue d'améliorer l'efficacité générale du système universitaire québécois.

Conference of Independent Schools (Ontario) (CIS)
PO Box 27, Whitby ON L1N 5R7 Canada
Tel: 905-665-8622; *Fax:* 905-665-8635
admin@cisontario.ca
www.cisontario.ca
To provide a collegial forum to promote excellence in education among its member schools

Council of Atlantic Ministers of Education & Training (CAMET) / Conseil atlantique des ministres de l'Éducation et de la Formation (CAMEF)
PO Box 2044, Halifax NS B3J 2Z1 Canada
Tel: 902-424-5352; *Fax:* 902-424-8976
camet-camef@cap-cpma.ca
www.camet-camef.ca
To allow the ministers responsible for education & training in New Brunswick, Nova Scotia, Newfoundland & Labrador, & Prince Edward Island to collaborate & respond to needs identified in public & post-secondary education; To enhance cooperation in public & post-secondary education to improve learning for Atlantic Canadians
Rhéal Poirier, Secretary

Council of Canadian Law Deans (CCLD) / Conseil des doyens et des doyennes des facultés de droit du Canada (CDFDC)
57 Louis Pasteur, Ottawa ON K1N 6N5 Canada
Tel: 613-824-9233; *Fax:* 613-824-9233
brigitteccld@rogers.com
www.ccld-cdfdc.ca

Council of Catholic School Superintendents of Alberta
AB Canada
superintendents@ccssa.ab.ca
www.ccssa.ab.ca
Provides a forum for discussion regarding the direction & development of Catholic Education in Alberta

Council of Ontario Universities (COU) / Conseil des universités de l'Ontario
#1100, 180 Dundas St. West, Toronto ON M5G 1Z8 Canada
Tel: 416-979-2165; *Fax:* 416-979-8635
cou@cou.on.ca
www.cou.on.ca
To work with & on behalf of members to meet public policy expectations related to accountability, diversity of educational opportunity, financial self-reliance, & responsiveness to educational & marketplace needs

Elementary Teachers' Federation of Ontario (ETFO) / Fédération des enseignantes et des enseignants de l'élémentaire de l'Ontario (FEEO)
#1000, 480 University Ave., Toronto ON M5G 1V2 Canada
Tel: 416-962-3836; *Fax:* 416-642-2424
Toll-Free: 888-838-3836
glewis@etfo.org
www.etfo.ca

To regulate relations between employees & employer, including but not limited to securing & maintaining, through collective bargaining, the best possible terms & conditions of employment; to advance the cause of education & the status of teachers & educational workers; to promote a high standard of professional ethics & a high standard of professional competence; to foster a climate of social justice in Ontario & continue a leadership role in such areas as anti-poverty, non-violence & equity; to promote & protect the interests of all members of the Federation & the students in their care; to cooperate with other organizations in Ontario, Canada & elsewhere, having the same or like objects.
Louise Ewing, Office Manager
Gene Lewis, General Secretary
Ruth Alam, Office Manager
Emily Noble, President

Fédération des cégeps
500, boul Crémazie est, Montréal QC H2P 1E7 Canada
Tél: 514-381-8631; *Téléc:* 514-381-2263
comm@fedecegeps.qc.ca
www.fedecegeps.qc.ca

De promouvoir le développement de l'enseignement collégial; au nom de ses membres, la Fédération établit des contacts et étudie des dossiers communs avec différents partenaires gouvernementaux et privés, notamment en ce qui concerne les affaires pédagogiques, étudiantes, matérielles et financières, et les ressources humaines du réseau

Fédération des comités de parents du Québec inc. (FCPQ)
2263, boul Louis-XIV, Québec QC G1C 1A4 Canada
Tél: 418-667-2432; *Téléc:* 418-667-6713
Ligne sans frais: 800-463-7268
courrier@fcpq.qc.ca
www.fcpq.qc.ca

La Fédération des comités de parents du Québec (FCPQ) tire sa raison d'être de l'existence, dans chacune des commissions scolaires, d'un comité de parents représentant les parents des élèves des écoles publiques primaires et secondaires. La mission ultime de la FCPQ est de défendre et de promouvoir les droits et les intérêts des parents des élèves des écoles publiques primaires et secondaires de façon à assurer la qualité de l'éducation offerte aux enfants.

La Fédération des commissions scolaires du Québec (FCSQ)
CP 10490, Succ. Sainte-Foy, 1001, av Bégon, Québec QC G1V 4C7 Canada
Tél: 418-651-3220; *Téléc:* 418-651-2574
info@fcsq.qc.ca
www.fcsq.qc.ca

Tout en conservant ses tâches premières de coordination et d'unification, la mission de la Fédération s'est élargie, au fil des ans, pour rencontrer deux objectifs principaux : contribuer à promouvoir l'éducation ainsi que représenter et défendre avec détermination les intérêts des commissions scolaires.

Fédération des établissements d'enseignement privés (FEEP)
1940, boul Henri-Bourassa est, Montréal QC H2B 1S2 Canada
Tél: 514-381-8891; *Téléc:* 514-381-4086
Ligne sans frais: 888-381-8891
info@feep.qc.ca
www.cadre.qc.ca

Soutien des établissements membres sur les plans administratifs, pédagogiques et de la vie scolaire; représentation auprès du gouvernement

Fédération nationale des enseignants et des enseignantes du Québec (FNEEQ) / National Federation of Québec Teachers
1601, av de Lorimier, Montréal QC H2K 4M5 Canada
Tél: 514-598-2241; *Téléc:* 514-598-2190
fneeq.reception@csn.qc.ca
www.fneeq.qc.ca

La Fédération nationale des enseignants et des enseignants du Québec (FNEEQ) est une fédération de la CSN qui regroupe les syndicats de l'enseignement. La mission première de la FNEEQ est l'amélioration des conditions de travail par l'entremise de la négociation et de l'application d'une convention collective entre un employeur et le personnel enseignant et salarié

Federation of Independent School Associations of BC (FISA)
150 Robson St., Vancouver BC V6B 2A7 Canada
Tel: 604-684-6023; *Fax:* 604-684-3163
fisabc@telus.net
www.fisabc.ca

To assist independent schools in maintaining their independence while seeking fair treatment for them in legislative & financial terms.

Federation of New Brunswick Faculty Associations (FNBFA) / Fédération des associations de professeures et professeurs d'université du Nouveau-Brunswick (FAPPUNB)
#204, 361 Victoria St., Fredericton NB E3B 1W5 Canada
Tel: 506-458-8977; *Fax:* 506-458-5620
fnbfa@nb.aibn.com
www.fnbfa.ca

To promote interests of teachers, librarians & researchers in universities & colleges of New Brunswick; to advance standards of professions & to seek to improve quality of higher education in the Province.

Fédération provinciale des comités de parents du Manitoba (FPCP)
1075, promenade Autumnwood, Saint-Boniface MB R2J 1C6 Canada
Tél: 204-237-9666; *Téléc:* 204-231-1436
Ligne sans frais: 866-666-8108
fpcp@fpcp.mb.ca
www.entreparents.mb.ca

Appuyer les membres dans le développement des milieux, familial, éducatif (préscolaire et scolaire) et communautaire, propices à l'épanouissement des familles francophones

Fédération québécoise des directeurs et directrices d'établissements d'enseignement (FQDE)
#100, 7855, boul Louis-H-Lafontaine, Anjou QC H1K 4E4 Canada
Tél: 514-353-7511; *Téléc:* 514-353-2064
Ligne sans frais: 800-361-4258
info@fqde.qc.ca
www.fqde.qc.ca

Défendre les droits des directeurs, directrices, directeurs adjoints, directrices adjointes d'établissements d'enseignement, sans oublier de promouvoir l'excellence dans la direction des établissements d'enseignement au Québec: en supportant des associations de directions d'établissement d'enseignement; en faisant en sorte que les directions d'établissement d'enseignement aient un environnement de travail favorisant la réalisation du projet éducatif; en s'assurant que les directions d'établissement d'enseignement maintiennent une compétence de gestionnaire de haute qualité.

Fédération québécoise des professeures et professeurs d'université (FQPPU) / Québec Federation of University Professors
#405, 4446, boul St-Laurent, Montréal QC H2W 1Z5 Canada
Tél: 514-843-5953; *Téléc:* 514-843-6928
Ligne sans frais: 888-843-5953
federation@fqppu.or
www.fqppu.org

La Fédération québécoise des professeures et professeurs d'université (FQPPU) est un organisme à vocation politique dont la mission globale est d'ouvrer au maintien, à la défense, à la promotion et au développement de l'université comme service public et de défendre une université accessible et de qualité.

First Nations SchoolNet (FNS)
Indian & Northern Affairs Canada, Education Program Directorate, 255 Albert St., Ottawa QC K1A 0H4
Tel: 613-995-9146; *Fax:* 819-997-0632
Toll-Free: 800-567-9604
pnr-fns@ainc-inac.gc.ca
www.ainc-inac.gc.ca/edu/ep/index1-eng.asp

Established by the federal government, FNS provides internet access, computer equipment & technical support to First Nations schools on reserves across the country. Students can connect with each other, develop new skills, & participate in national & international events. Six non-profit, regional management organizations deliver the program in their respective region, working with Indian & Northern Affairs Canada.
Elinor Bradley, Director

Foundation for Educational Exchange Between Canada & the United States of America
#2015, 350 Albert St., Ottawa ON K1R 1A4 Canada
Tel: 613-688-5540; *Fax:* 613-237-2029
info@fulbright.ca
www.fulbright.ca

To support outstanding graduate students, faculty, professionals, & independent researchers in order to enhance understanding between the people of Canada & the United States
Michael K. Hawes, Executive Director
Sandy Hanna, Sr. Program Officer

Halifax Education Foundation
19 Medway Court, Dartmouth NS B2W 4G4 Canada
Tel: 902-434-2322; *Fax:* 902-434-2053

To support and enhance quality public education in all areas of the Halifax Regional Municipality.

Independent Schools Canada (ISC) / Fédération canadienne des écoles privées (FCEP)
4114 Belanger Dr., Abbotsford BC V3G 1K3 Canada
Toll-Free: 888-227-8421
fisc@shaw.ca
www.independentschools.ca

To represent interests & concerns of independent schools; to support & encourage members in the promotion & enhancement of the rightful place & responsibility of independent schools.

Institut de coopération pour l'éducation des adultes (ICEA)
#300, 5225, rue Berri, Montréal QC H2J 2S4 Canada
Tél: 514-948-2044; *Téléc:* 514-948-2046
Ligne sans frais: 877-948-2044
icea@icea.qc.ca
www.icea.qc.ca

Promouvoir l'exercice du droit des adultes à l'éducation tout au long de la vie

Learning Disabilities Association of Alberta (LDAA) / Troubles d'apprentissage - Association de l'Alberta
PO Box 29011, Stn. Lendrum, Edmonton AB T6H 5Z6 Canada
Tel: 780-448-0360; *Fax:* 780-438-0665
info@ldaa.ca
www.ldaa.ca

Supporting people with learning disabilities so that they develop to their full potential. Chapters in Calgary, Red Deer & Edmonton.

Learning Disabilities Association of Canada (LDAC) / Troubles d'apprentissage - Association canadienne (TAAC)
#616, 250 City Centre Ave., Ottawa ON K1R 6K7 Canada
Tel: 613-238-5721; *Fax:* 613-235-5391
Toll-Free: 877-238-5322
info@ldac-taac.ca
www.ldac-taac.ca

To advance the education, employment, social development, legal rights & general well-being of people with learning disabilities; to create a greater public awareness & understanding of learning disabilities; to promote & develop early recognition, diagnosis, treatment & appropriate educational, social, recreational & career-oriented programs for people with learning disabilities; to promote legislation, research & training of personnel in the field of learning disabilities

Learning Disabilities Association of Manitoba (LDAM) / Troubles d'apprentissage - Association de Manitoba
617 Erin St., Winnipeg MB R3G 2W1 Canada
Tel: 204-774-1821; *Fax:* 204-788-4090
ldamb@mts.net
www.ldamanitoba.org

To provide support to all those who are concerned with learning disabilities; To represent individuals & families with learning disabilities

Learning Disabilities Association of New Brunswick (LDANB) / Troubles d'apprentissage - Association du Nouveau-Brunswick (TA-ANB)
#203, 403 Regent St., Fredericton NB E3B 3X6 Canada
Tel: 506-459-7852; *Fax:* 506-455-9300
Toll-Free: 877-544-7852
ldanb_taanb@nb.aibn.com
www.nald.ca/ldanb

Promotes the understanding & acceptance of the ability of persons with learning disabilities to lead meaningful & successful lives. Satellite office in Saint John.

Learning Disabilities Association of Newfoundland & Labrador Inc. (LDANL)
The Board of Trade Bldg., #204, 66 Kenmount Rd., St. John's NL A1B 3V7 Canada
Tel: 709-753-1445; *Fax:* 709-753-4747
ldanl@nl.rogers.com
www.nald.ca/ldanl

To work towards to the advancement of legal rights, social development, education, employment, & the general well-being of people with learning disabilities

Learning Disabilities Association of Nova Scotia (LDANS) / Troubles d'apprentissage - Association de la Nouvelle-Écosse
#601, 46 Portland St., Dartmouth NS B2Y 1H4 Canada
Tel: 902-423-2850; *Fax:* 902-423-2834
Toll-Free: 877-238-5322
info@ldans.ca
www.ldans.ca
To advance the education, employment, social development, legal rights & general well-being of people with learning disabilities.

Learning Disabilities Association of Ontario (LDAO) / Troubles d'apprentissage - Association de l'Ontario
Box 39, #1004, 365 Bloor St. East, Toronto ON M4W 3L4 Canada
Tel: 416-929-4311; *Fax:* 416-929-3905
Toll-Free: 877-238-5322
resource@ldao.ca
www.ldao.ca
To provide leadership in learning disabilities advocacy, research, education & services; to advance the full participation of children, youth & adults with learning disabilites in today's society.

Learning Disabilities Association of Prince Edward Island (LADPEI)
#149, 40 Enman Cres., Charlottetown PE C1E 1E6 Canada
Tel: 902-894-5032
ldapei@eastlink.ca
www.ldapei.ca
To advance the interests of people with learning disabilities; To act as a voice for learning disabled people of Prince Edward Island

Learning Disabilities Association of Saskatchewan (LDAS) / Troubles d'apprentissage - Association de la Saskatchewan
3 - 701 2nd Ave. N, Saskatoon SK S7K 2C9 Canada
Tel: 306-652-4114; *Fax:* 306-652-3220
reception@ldas.org
www.ldas.org
To advance the education, employment, social development, legal rights & general well-being of people with learning disabilities. Branches in Regina & Prince Albert.

Learning Disabilities Association of The Northwest Territories (LDA-NWT)
PO Box 242, 4901 - 48th St., Yellowknife NT X1A 2N2 Canada
Tel: 867-873-6378; *Fax:* 867-873-6378
lda-nwt@arcticdata.ca
www.nald.ca/ldanwt.htm
To help people with learning disabilities achieve their potential in school, the workplace, & in society

Learning Disabilities Association of Yukon Territory (LDAY)
1154C - 1 Ave., Whitehorse YT Y1A 1A7 Canada
Tel: 867-668-5167; *Fax:* 867-668-6504
joel.macht@klondiker.com
www.nald.ca/lday.htm
To provide services & programs for Yukoners with learning disabilities so that they reach their potential & become productive members of society

Learning Enrichment Foundation (LEF)
116 Industry St., Toronto ON M6M 4L8 Canada
Tel: 416-769-0830; *Fax:* 416-769-9912
info@lefca.org
www.lefca.org
To provide programs & services to help individuals become contributors to their community's social & economic development

Manitoba Association of Parent Councils (MAPC)
#1005, 401 York Ave., Winnipeg MB R3C 0P8 Canada
Tel: 204-956-1770; *Fax:* 204-948-2855
Toll-Free: 877-290-4702
mapc1@mts.net
www.mapc.mb.ca

Manitoba Association of School Business Officials (MASBO)
375 Jefferson Ave., Winnipeg MB R2V 0N3 Canada
Tel: 204-254-7570; *Fax:* 204-254-3606
masbo@mts.net
www.masbo.ca
To provide leadership in the areas of finance, maintenance & transportation

Manitoba Association of School Superintendents (MASS)
375 Jefferson Ave., Winnipeg MB R2V 0N3 Canada
Tel: 204-487-7972; *Fax:* 204-487-7974
coralie.bryant@7oaks.org
www.mass.mb.ca
Provides leadership for public education by advocating in the best interest of learners, & supports its members through professional services.
Coralie Bryant, Executive Director

Manitoba Association of School Trustees (MAST)
191 Provencher Blvd., Winnipeg MB R2H 0G4 Canada
Tel: 204-233-1595; *Fax:* 204-231-1356
Toll-Free: 800-262-8836
www.mast.mb.ca
To provide services to school boards in Manitoba; To advocate for public education

Manitoba Federation of Independent Schools Inc. (MFIS)
630 Westminster Ave., Winnipeg MB R3C 3S1 Canada
Tel: 204-783-4481; *Fax:* 204-774-5534
www.mfis.ca
To support & encourage high educational standards & values unique to our various school communities; to represent interests & concerns of member independent schools in Manitoba

Manitoba Teachers' Society (MTS)
McMaster House, 191 Harcourt St., Winnipeg MB R3J 3H2 Canada
Tel: 204-888-7961; *Fax:* 204-831-0877
Toll-Free: 800-262-8803
www.mbteach.org
Envisions a public education system that provides equal accessibility & equal opportunity for all children, that optimizes the potential of all students as individuals & citizens, that fosters lifelong learning & that ensures a safe learning environment respectful of diversity & human dignity

Mensa Canada Society / La Société Mensa Canada
PO Box 1570, Kingston ON K7L 5C8 Canada
Tel: 613-547-0824; *Fax:* 613-531-0626
mensa@eventsmgt.com
www.canada.mensa.org
To identify & foster human intelligence for the benefit of humanity; To encourage research; To provide an intellectual & social environment for members

National Christian School Association
PO Box 26005, Saskatoon SK S7K 8C1 Canada
Tel: 306-280-9991
lbrunelle@aceministries.com
www.aisca.ab.ca/associations.htm
To continue to assure Canadians of the freedom to choose alternative Christian education
Lou Brunelle, President

National Educational Association of Disabled Students (NEADS) / Association nationale des étudiant(e)s handicapé(e)s au niveau postsecondaire
Carleton University, Rm. 426, Unicentre, 1125 Colonel By Dr., Ottawa ON K1S 5B6 Canada
Tel: 613-380-8065; *Fax:* 613-369-4391
Toll-Free: 877-670-1256
info@neads.ca
www.neads.ca
To encourage the self-empowerment of post-secondary students with disabilities; to advocate for increased accessibility at all levels so that disabled students may gain equal access to a college or university education; to provide an information resource base on services for disabled students nationwide according to a file of material from post-secondary institutions

New Brunswick Federation of Home & School Associations, Inc. (NBFHSA)
#4, 618 Queen St., Fredericton NB E3B 1C2 Canada
Tel: 506-451-6247
homeandschool.nb.aibn.com
www.nbhomeandschool.org
To ensure a quality education, enhanced by parental involvement, & a safe environment for all children.

New Brunswick Teachers' Federation (Ind.) (NBTF) / Fédération des enseignants du Nouveau-Brunswick (FENB)
PO Box 1535, 650 Montgomery St., Fredericton NB E3B 5G2 Canada
Tel: 506-452-8921; *Fax:* 506-453-9795
www.nbta.ca
To represent the interests of the Association

Newfoundland & Labrador School Boards' Association (NLSBA)
40 Strawberry Marsh Rd., St. John's NL A1B 2V5 Canada
Tel: 709-722-7171; *Fax:* 709-722-8214
brendapinto@schoolboardsnl.ca
www.schoolboardsnl.ca
To promote the interests of education in Newfoundland & Labrador

Newfoundland & Labrador Teachers' Association (NLTA) / Association des enseignants de Terre-Neuve
3 Kenmount Rd., St. John's NL A1B 1W1 Canada
Tel: 709-726-3223; *Fax:* 709-726-4302
Toll-Free: 800-563-3599
mail@nlta.nl.ca
www.nlta.nl.ca
To strive towards the professional excellence & personal well-being of teachers

Northwest Territories Teachers' Association (NWTTA)
PO Box 2340, 5018 - 48 St., Yellowknife NT X1A 2P7 Canada
Tel: 867-873-8501; *Fax:* 867-873-2366
nwtta@nwtta.nt.ca
www.nwtta.nt.ca
The Northwest Territories Teachers' Association is the professional voice of educators as they provide quality education to Northwest Territories students. With commitment to growth, respect & security for its membership, the Association represents all regions equally, advocates for public education & promotes the teaching profession

Nova Scotia Federation of Home & School Associations (NSFHSA)
6067 Quinpool Rd., Halifax NS B3L 1A2 Canada
Tel: 902-421-2663; *Fax:* 902-660-3771
Toll-Free: 800-214-8373
vanda@staff.ednet.ns.ca
www.nsfhsa.org
Social Media: www.facebook.com/group.php?gid=3295519755
To provide a forum for discussion between the home & school beyond the parent-teacher interview; to promote & secure legislation for the care & protection of & equality of educational opportunities for children; to give parents an understanding of the school & its work, assisting in interpreting the school to the public; to confer & cooperate with organizations other than the schools which concern themselves with the training & development of children & youth

Nova Scotia School Boards Association (NSSBA) / Association des conseils scolaires de la Nouvelle-Écosse
95 Victoria Rd., Dartmouth NS B3A 1V2 Canada
Tel: 902-491-2888; *Fax:* 902-429-7405
cnass@nssba.ednet.ns.ca
www.nssba.ednet.ns.ca
To act as the voice for school boards in Nova Scotia; To strive towards excellence in public education for students in the province

Nova Scotia Teachers Union (NSTU) / Syndicat des enseignants de la Nouvelle-Écosse
Dr. Tom Parker Bldg., 3106 Joseph Howe Dr., Halifax NS B3L 4L7 Canada
Tel: 902-477-5621; *Fax:* 902-477-3517
Toll-Free: 800-565-6788
nstu@nstu.ca; library@nstu.ca
www.nstu.ca
To unify the teaching profession in Nova Scotia; To improve the quality of education

Nunavut Teachers Association (NTA)
PO Box 2458, Iqaluit NU X0A 0H0 Canada
Tel: 867-979-0750; *Fax:* 867-979-0780
piadmin@ntanu.ca
www.ntanu.ca
The Nunavut Teachers Association, or NTA, is the negotiating and representative organization for teachers, vice-principals, principals, and RSO and TLC coordinators in Nunavut.
Robin Langill, President
Emile Hatch, Executive Director

Ontario Alliance of Christian Schools (OACS)
790 Shaver Rd., Ancaster ON L9G 3K9 Canada
Tel: 905-648-2100; *Fax:* 905-648-2110
oacs@oacs.org
www.oacs.org
To promote independent schools in Ontario; to promote Christian education in Canada; to provide educational services for member schools; to lobby government for educational choice. Canada's largest & oldest independent school organization, representing 79 schools with approximately 14,000 students.

Ontario Association of Career Colleges (OACC)
PO Box 340, #2, 155 Lynden Rd., Brantford ON N3T 5N3
Tel: 519-752-2124; *Fax:* 519-752-3649
www.oacc.on.ca
Social Media:
www.facebook.com/group.php?gid=148743424929
To act as the voice for the private career college sector in Ontario
Paul Kitchin, Executive Director
Lorna Mills, Manager, Office & Financial Aid
Laura Bailey, Coordinator, Media Communications

Ontario Association of Deans of Education (OADE)
#1100, 180 Dundas St. West, Toronto ON M5G 1Z8 Canada
Tel: 416-979-2165; *Fax:* 416-979-8635
oade.cou.on.ca
Josée Martel, Contact

Ontario Association of School Business Officials (OASBO)
#207, 144 Main St. North, Markham ON L3P 5T3 Canada
Tel: 905-209-9704; *Fax:* 905-209-9705
office@oasbo.org
www.oasbo.org
Dedicated to the pursuit & support of quality education for all students. OASBO is the professional organization for school business officials in Ontario. Our purpose is to improve the quality of school business management and the status, competency, leadership qualities and ethical standards of school business officials at all levels; focus is on information sharing, the promotion of learning at all opportunities, the optimization of operational processes, & the development of partnerships to promote & recognize business practices excellence.

Ontario Catholic School Trustees' Association (OCSTA)
PO Box 2064, #1804, 20 Eglinton Ave. West, Toronto ON M4R 1K8 Canada
Tel: 416-932-9460; *Fax:* 416-932-9459
ocsta@ocsta.on.ca
www.ocsta.on.ca

Ontario Confederation of University Faculty Associations (OCUFA) / Union des associations des professeurs des universités de l'Ontario
#300, 83 Yonge St., Toronto ON M5C 1S8
Tel: 416-979-2117; *Fax:* 416-593-5607
ocufa@ocufa.on.ca
www.ocufa.on.ca
To act as the voice of Ontario's approximately 15,000 university faculty & academic librarians; To advance the professional & economic interests of university faculty & academic librarians; To enhance the quality of Ontario's higher education system

Ontario Council for University Lifelong Learning
c/o Lakehead University, Thunder Bay ON P7B 5E1 Canada
Tel: 807-343-8210; *Fax:* 807-343-8008
www.ocull.ca
OCULL is a professional association for administrators and practitioners who develop and deliver degree and on-degree continuing education programs in Ontario universities. OCULL is an advocate for adult learners at Ontario universities, a collegial network, and a vehicle for professional development for its members.

Ontario Council on Graduate Studies (OCGS) / Conseil ontarien des études supérieures
#1100, 180 Dundas St. West, Toronto ON M5G 1Z8 Canada
Tel: 416-979-2165; *Fax:* 416-979-8635
ocgs@cou.on.ca
ocgs.cou.on.ca/
Strives to ensure quality graduate education & research across Ontario

Ontario English Catholic Teachers' Association (CLC) (OECTA)
#400, 65 St. Clair Ave. East, Toronto ON M4T 2Y8 Canada
Tel: 416-925-2493; *Fax:* 416-925-7764
Toll-Free: 800-268-7230
m.despault@oecta.on.ca
www.oecta.on.ca
Committed to the advancement of Catholic education; to provide professional services, support, protection & leadership
James Ryan, President
Marshall Jarvis, General Secretary

Ontario Federation of Home & School Associations Inc. (OFHSA)
51 Stuart St., Hamilton ON L8L 1B5 Canada
Tel: 905-308-9563; *Fax:* 905-308-7935
info@ofhsa.on.ca
www.ofhsa.on.ca
To provide facilities for the bringing together of members of Home & School Associations for discussion of matters of general interest & to stimulate cooperative effort; to assist in forming public opinion favorable to reform & advancement of the education of the child; to develop between educators & the general public such united effort as shall secure for every child the highest advantage in physical, mental, moral & spiritual education; to raise the standard of home & national life; to maintain a non-partisan, non-commercial, non-racial & non-sectarian organization

Ontario Federation of Independent Schools (OFIS)
2199 Regency Terrace, Ottawa ON K2C 1H2 Canada
Tel: 613-596-4013; *Fax:* 613-596-4971
info@ofis.ca
www.ofis.ca
To secure guarantees from Ontario government for independent schools' right to exist, curricular freedom, self-governance & acceptance by government of its responsibility to let education grants follow a child to any bona fide school that meets acceptable social & educational criteria

Ontario Principals' Council (OPC)
180 Dundas St. West, 25th Fl., Toronto ON M5G 1Z8
Tel: 416-322-6600; *Fax:* 416-322-6618
Toll-Free: 800-701-2362
admin@principals.on.ca
www.principals.on.ca
To support the work of Ontario's principals & vice-principals to provide excellent leadership in the public education system

Ontario Public School Boards Association (OPSBA)
439 University Ave., Toronto ON M5G 1Y8
Tel: 416-340-2540; *Fax:* 416-340-7571
webmaster@opsba.org
www.opsba.org
To represent Ontario's public school authorities & public district school boards; To advocate on behalf of the public school system in Ontario; To promote & enhance public education
Colleen Schenk, President
Gail Anderson, Executive Director
Florenda Tingle, Executive Coordinator

Ontario Secondary School Teachers' Federation (OSSTF) / Fédération des enseignants des écoles secondaires de l'Ontario (FEESO)
60 Mobile Dr., Toronto ON M4A 2P3
Tel: 416-751-8300; *Toll-Free:* 800-267-7867
www.osstf.on.ca
To protect & enhance Ontario's public education system; To establish working conditions for members
Ken Coran, President
Paul Elliott, Vice-President
Sandra Sahli, Vice-President
Wendy Bolt, General Secretary
Earl Burt, Treasurer

Ontario Society for Education Through Art (OSEA)
c/o Membership Secretary, 37 Hopewell Ave., Toronto ON M4K 3M8 Canada
www.osea.on.ca
To promote & advocate learning through the visual arts

Ontario Teachers' Federation (OTF) / Fédération des enseignantes et des enseignants de l'Ontario (FEO)
#200, 1300 Yonge St., Toronto ON M4T 1X3 Canada
Tel: 416-966-3424; *Fax:* 416-966-5450
Toll-Free: 800-268-7061
www.otffeo.on.ca
To represent the interests of all registered teachers in Ontario's publicly funded schools

ORT Canada
#200, 530 Wilson Ave., Toronto ON M3H 5Y9 Canada
Tel: 416-787-0339; *Fax:* 416-787-9420
Toll-Free: 866-991-3045
info@ort-toronto.org
www.ort-toronto.com
To fundraise in support of the worldwide vocational-training-school network of ORT.

Parent Co-operative Preschools International (PCPI)
8725 Westport Dr., Niagara Falls ON L2H 0A2 Canada
Tel: 905-374-6605; *Fax:* 905-374-0473
www.preschools.coop
To promote the family & community; to strengthen & expand the parent cooperative movement & community appreciation of parent education for adults & preschool education for children; to promote desirable standards for program, practices & conditions in parent cooperative preschools & encourage continuing education for parents, teachers & directors; to promote interchange of information among parent cooperative nursery schools, kindergartens & other parent-sponsored preschool programs; to cooperate with family living, adult education & early childhood educational organizations in the interest of more effective service relationships with parents of young children; to study & promote legislation designed to further the health & well-being of children & families

Parents partenaires en éducation (PPE)
#B-150, 2445, boul St-Laurent, Ottawa ON K1G 6C3 Canada
Tél: 613-741-8846; *Téléc:* 613-741-7322
Ligne sans frais: 800-342-0663
info@reseauppe.ca
www.reseauppe.ca
Travailler en étroite collaboration avec ses partenaires en éducation, outiller les parents dans leur rôle de partenaires en éducation et agir comme porte-parole provincial des parents; promouvoir l'excellence de l'éducation de langue française et l'épanouissement global des enfants francophones

Prince Edward Island Home & School Federation Inc. (PEIHSF)
PO Box 1012, 40 Enman Cres., Charlottetown PE C1A 7M4 Canada
Tel: 902-620-3186; *Fax:* 902-620-3187
Toll-Free: 800-916-0664
peihsf@edu.pe.ca
www.edu.pe.ca/peihsf/

Prince Edward Island School Trustees Association (PEISTA)
trusteespei@yahoo.ca
trusteespei.blogspot.com
To act as umbrella organization in coordinating & supporting efforts of school trustees in furthering education & education needs for all children in PEI

Prince Edward Island Teachers' Federation (PEITF) / Fédération des enseignants de l'Ile-du-Prince-Édouard
PO Box 6000, 24 Glen Stewart Dr., Charlottetown PE C1A 8B4 Canada
Tel: 902-569-4157; *Fax:* 902-569-3682
Toll-Free: 800-903-4157
rmacrae@peitf.com
www.peitf.com
To promote & support education as well as the professional & economic well-being of PEI teachers

Québec Association for Adult Learning Inc. (QAAL) / Association Québécoise pour l'éducation des adultes
#LB568-3, 1455 boul Maisonneuve ouest, Montréal QC H3G 1M8 Canada
Tel: 514-848-2424; *Fax:* 514-848-4520
qaal@alcor.concordia.ca
doe.concordia.ca/qaal
QAAL is a not-for-profit, English-language association that supports those who support adult learners. It promotes equality of access to information & services, & it raises public awareness of adult learning issues, notably from an English-speaker's perspective in Québec.
Michael Canuel, President
Mario Pasteris, Executive Director

Québec Association of Independent Schools (QAIS) / Association des écoles privées du Québec
PO Box 398, Stn. Snowdon, Montréal QC H3X 3T6 Canada
Tel: 514-483-6111; *Fax:* 514-483-0865
Toll-Free: 866-909-6111
qais@qc.aibn.com
www.qais.qc.ca
The Quebec Association of Independent Schools (QAIS) is an organization consisting of English elementary and secondary independent schools licensed in the public interest and located in Quebec. QAIS promotes collaboration, provides services that further educational leadership and advocates independent English language education in Quebec on behalf of its member schools.

Québec English School Boards Association (QESBA) / Association des commissions scolaires anglophones du Québec (ACSAQ)
#515, 1410, rue Stanley, Montréal QC H3A 1P8 Canada
Tel: 514-849-5900; *Fax:* 514-849-9228
Toll-Free: 877-512-7522
qesba@qesba.qc.ca
www.qesba.qc.ca
To represent English school boards in Québec

Québec Federation of Home & School Associations Inc. (QFHSA) / Fédération des associations foyer-école du Québec Inc.
#560, 3285, boul Cavendish, Montréal QC H4B 2L9 Canada
Tel: 514-481-5619; *Fax:* 514-481-5610
Toll-Free: 888-808-5619
info@qfhsa.org
www.qfhsa.org
To provide facilities for the bringing together of members of Home & School Associations for discussion of matters of general interest & to stimulate cooperative effort; to assist in forming public opinion favorable to reform & advancement of the education of the child; to develop between educators & the general public such a united effort as shall secure for every child the highest advantage in physical, mental, moral & spiritual education; to raise the standard of home & national life; to maintain non-partisan, non-commercial, non-racial & non-sectarian organization

Le Réseau d'enseignement francophone à distance du Canada (REFAD)
CP 47542, Succ. Plateau Mont-Royal, Montréal QC H2H 2S8 Canada
Tél: 514-284-9109; *Téléc:* 514-284-9363
refad@sympatico.ca
www.refad.ca
Favoriser la collaboration entre les personnes et les organisations intéressées par l'enseignement à distance en français; rassembler en réseau les établissements qui ont recours à la formation à distance en français; appuyer et compléter d'autres réseaux d'enseignement à distance existant déjà à travers le Canada; promouvoir et accroître la qualité et la quantité des programmes et des cours offerts dans la francophonie canadienne.

The Retired Teachers of Ontario (RTO) / Les Enseignants et enseignantes retraités de l'Ontario (ERO)
#300, 18 Spadina Rd., Toronto ON M5R 2S7 Canada
Tel: 416-962-9463; *Fax:* 416-962-1061
Toll-Free: 800-361-9888
info@rto-ero.org
www.rto-ero.org
To promote the interests of persons in receipt of a pension under the Ontario Teachers' Pension Act

Saskatchewan Association for Multicultural Education (SAME)
144 Marsh Cres., Regina SK S4S 5J7
Tel: 306-780-9428
same@sasktel.net
www.same.ca
To promote multicultural & anti-racist education throughout Saskatchewan; To raise awareness & acceptance of cultural diversity in the province; To respond to changes in multicultural policies & demographics; To address social justice issues
Rhonda Rosenberg, Executive Director

Saskatchewan Association of Historical High Schools (SAHHS)
c/o Luther College High School, 1500 Royal St., Regina SK S4T 6G3 Canada
Tel: 306-791-9150; *Fax:* 306-359-6962
www.luthercollege.edu

Saskatchewan Association of School Councils (SASC)
#301, 221 Cumberland Ave. North, Saskatoon SK S7N 1M3 Canada
Tel: 306-955-5723; *Fax:* 306-445-7707
www.schoolcouncils.com
To enhance the education & general well-being of children & youth; to promote the involvement of parents, students, educators & the community at large in the advancement of learning & to act as a voice for parents; to promote effective communication between the home & the school; to encourage parents to participate in educational activities & decision making

Saskatchewan School Boards Association (SSBA)
#400, 2222 - 13th Ave., Regina SK S4P 3M7 Canada
Tel: 306-569-0750; *Fax:* 306-352-9633
admin@saskschoolboards.ca
www.saskschoolboards.ca
Represents boards of education, including school division boards, conseils scolaires, & local or district boards; ensures advocacy, leadership & support for member boards of education by speaking as the voice for quality public education for all children; offers opportunities for trustee development; provides information & services

Saskatchewan Teachers' Federation (STF) / Fédération des enseignants et des enseignantes de la Saskatchewan
2317 Arlington Ave., Saskatoon SK S7J 2H8 Canada
Tel: 306-373-1660; *Fax:* 306-374-1122
Toll-Free: 800-667-7762
stf@stf.sk.ca
www.stf.sk.ca

Skills/Compétences Canada
#205, 260, boul Saint Raymond, Gatineau QC J9A 3G7 Canada
Tel: 819-771-7545; *Fax:* 819-771-5575
Toll-Free: 877-754-5226
skillscanada@skillscanada.com
www.skillscanada.com
Social Media: facebook.com/pages/Skills-Canada-Competences-Canada/117361178298289
To create dynamic synergies between industry, government, youth, educators & labour; to raise awareness of the value of a technical or skilled trade career; to champion & stimulate the development of technological & employability skills in Canadian youth to strengthen our competitive edge in the global marketplace
Donavon Elliott, President
Shaun Thorson, Executive Director
Natalee Lewis, Communications/Marketing Coordinator

Society for Educational Visits & Exchanges in Canada (SEVEC) / Société éducative de visites et d'échanges au Canada
300-950 Gladstone Ave., Ottawa ON K1Y 3E6 Canada
Tel: 613-727-3832; *Fax:* 613-727-3831
Toll-Free: 800-387-3832
info@sevec.ca
www.sevec.ca
To create, facilitate & promote enriching educational opportunities within Canada for the development of mutual respect & understanding through programs of exploration in language & culture

Society for Quality Education (SQE)
57 Twyford Rd., Toronto ON M9A 1W5 Canada
Tel: 416-231-7247; *Fax:* 416-237-0108
Toll-Free: 888-856-5535
info@societyforqualityeducation.org
www.societyforqualityeducation.org
To advance public & private education in Canada by disseminating authoritative information on educational governance & methodology.
Doretta Wilson, Executive Director
Malkin Dare, President

Society for the Promotion of the Teaching of English as a Second Language in Quebec (SPEAQ) / Société pour la promotion de l'enseignement de l'anglais, langue seconde, au Québec
#309, 7400, boul Saint-Laurent, Montréal QC H2R 2Y1 Canada
Tel: 514-271-3700; *Fax:* 514-271-4587
speaq@speaq.qc.ca
www.speaq.qc.ca
To bring together persons engaged or interested in the teaching of English as a second language in Quebec, & to promote & develop the professional & economic interests of its members; to create a favourable climate for the development of teaching English as a second language in Quebec//Promouvoir l'enseignement de l'anglais, langue seconde au Québec

TESL Canada Federation (TESL Canada)
#408, 4370 Dominion St., Burnaby BC V5G 4L7 Canada
Tel: 604-298-0312; *Fax:* 604-298-0372
Toll-Free: 800-393-9199
admin@tesl.ca
www.tesl.ca
To support the sharing of knowledge & experiences across Canada; To represents diverse interests in TESL nationally & internationally

United World Colleges
Lester B. Pearson College of the Pacific, 650 Pearson College Dr., Victoria BC V9C 4H7 Canada
Tel: 250-391-2411; *Fax:* 250-391-2412
admin@pearsoncollege.ca
www.pearsoncollege.ca
Through international education, shared experience & community service, the United World Colleges encourage young people to become responsible citizens, politically & environmentally aware, committed to the ideals of peace, justice, understanding & cooperation, & to the implementation of these ideals through action & personal example

Yukon Teachers' Association (YTA) / Association des enseignantes et des enseignants du Yukon
2064 - 2 Ave., Whitehorse YT Y1A 1A9 Canada
Tel: 867-668-6777; *Fax:* 867-667-4324
admin@yta.yk.ca
www.yta.yk.ca
YTA promotes & supports public education & represents the professional & economic needs of Yukon educators.

Electronics & Electricity

Canadian Electrical Contractors Association (CECA) / Association canadienne des entrepreneurs électriciens (ACEE)
#460, 170 Attwell Dr., Toronto ON M9W 5Z5 Canada
Tel: 416-675-3226; *Fax:* 416-675-7736
Toll-Free: 800-387-3226
ceca@ceca.org
www.ceca.org/

Canadian Electrical Manufacturers Representatives Association (CEMRA)
#300, 180 Attwell Dr., Toronto ON M9W 6A9 Canada
Tel: 905-602-8877; *Fax:* 416-679-9234
info@electrofed.com
www.electrofed.com
To represent over 300 member companies that manufacture, distribute, & service electrical, electronics, & telecommunications products

Canadian Electronic & Appliance Service Association (CEASA) / Organisation canadienne de service d'appareils domestiques
#200, 5800 Explorer Dr., Mississauga ON L4W 5K9 Canada
Tel: 905-602-8877; *Fax:* 905-602-5686
Toll-Free: 866-602-8877
info@electrofed.com
www.electrofed.com/councils/CEASA/
To enhance & improve standards of customer service for home entertainment electronic products & major appliances; to act as coordinator for member companies in dealings with governments; to provide, where possible, standard operational methods across the industry in interest of economies & easier operation

Conseil Canadien des Électrotechnologies (CCE) / Canadian Council on Electrotechnologies (CCE)
600, av de la Montagne, Shawinigan QC G9N 7N5 Canada
Tél: 819-539-1560; *Téléc:* 819-539-1558
Transfert technologique en vue de l'utilisation rationnelle et optimale de l'électricité

Consumer Electronics Marketers of Canada: A Division of Electro-Federation Canada (CEMC)
#200, 5800 Explorer Dr., Mississauga ON L4W 5K9 Canada
Tel: 905-602-8877; *Fax:* 905-602-5686
www.electrofed.com/councils/CEMC/
To represent the consumer electronic marketing industry; to provide information for CEMC members to help them make good business decisions; to report on the status of the consumer electronics market

Corporation des maîtres électriciens du Québec (CMEQ) / Corporation of Master Electricians of Québec
5925, boul Décarie, Montréal QC H3W 3C9 Canada
Tél: 514-738-2184; *Téléc:* 514-738-2192
Ligne sans frais: 800-361-9061
webmestre@cmeq.org
www.cmeq.org
Augmenter la compétence des membres; règlementer la conduite des membres et de la profession; faciliter et encourager les membres à se familiariser avec des nouvelles techniques; chercher des solutions pratiques aux problèmes communs de l'industrie électrique

Electrical Contractors Association of Alberta (ECAA)
11235 - 120 St., Edmonton AB T5G 2X9 Canada
Tel: 780-451-2412; *Fax:* 780-455-9815
Toll-Free: 800-252-9375
ecaa@ecaa.ab.ca
www.ecaa.ab.ca
To work towards increased contractors knowledge & efficiency; improved communication between industry sections; government liaison for training qualifications & regulations; overall improvement of the electrical industry

Electrical Contractors Association of BC (ECA-BC)
#201, 3989 Henning Dr., Burnaby BC V5C 6N5 Canada
Tel: 604-294-4123; *Fax:* 604-294-4120
eca@eca.bc.ca
www.eca.bc.ca
To promote use of electricity; to strengthen, encourage & promote electrical contracting industry; to promote functions assisting businessmen to become more efficient & profitable.

Electrical Contractors Association of New Brunswick Inc. (ECANB)
PO Box 322, Fredericton NB E3B 4Y9 Canada
Tel: 506-452-7627; *Fax:* 506-452-1786
dwe@eca.nb.ca
www.eca.nb.ca

Electrical Contractors Association of Ontario (ECAO)
#460, 170 Attwell Dr., Toronto ON M9W 5Z5 Canada
Tel: 416-675-3226; *Fax:* 416-675-7736
Toll-Free: 800-387-3226
ecao@ecao.org
www.ecao.org
To serve & represent the interests of the electrical contracting industry

Electrical Contractors Association of Saskatchewan
Construction house, 1939 Elphinstone St., Regina SK S4T 3N3 Canada
Tel: 306-525-0171; *Fax:* 306-347-8595
michaelf@scaonline.ca
www.ecas.ca
To voice the concerns of electrical contractors in Saskatchewan; To improvethe electrical industry

Electro-Federation Canada Inc. (EFC)
#200, 5800 Explorer Dr., Mississauga ON L4W 5K9 Canada
Tel: 905-602-8877; *Fax:* 905-602-5686
Toll-Free: 866-602-8877
info@electrofed.com
www.electrofed.com
To represent members provincially, federally, & internationally on issues affecting the electro-technical business
Milos Jancik, President/CEO
Ken Frankum, Chair
Harald Henze, Treasurer
Larry Moore, Vice-President, Consumer Councils
Joseph Neu, Vice-President, Engineering, Codes & Standards

Institute of Electrical & Electronics Engineers Inc. - Canada
PO Box 63005, Stn. Uuniversity PO, Shoppers Drug Mart #742, 102 Plaza Dr., Dundas ON L9H 4H0 Canada
Tel: 905-628-9554; *Fax:* 905-628-9554
admin@ieee.ca
www.ieee.ca
IEEE Canada advances the theory & practice of electrical, electronics & computer engineering & computer science.

Manitoba Electrical League Inc.
#104, 1780 Wellington Ave., Winnipeg MB R3H 1B3 Canada
Tel: 204-783-4125; *Fax:* 204-783-4216
office@meleague.net
www.meleague.net
To advise & inform all people of Manitoba on effective use of electricity toward maintenance & betterment of standards of living; to encourage cooperation of various branches of electrical industry in developing programs in support of common marketing objectives.

Ontario Electrical League (OEL)
#300, 180 Attwell Dr., Toronto ON M9W 6A9
Tel: 905-238-1382; *Fax:* 905-238-1420
communications@oel.org
www.oel.org
To represent & strengthen the electrical industry in Ontario

Emergency Response

Canadian Avalanche Association (CAA)
PO Box 2759, 110 MacKenzie Ave., Revelstoke BC V0E 2S0
Tel: 250-837-2435; *Fax:* 250-837-4624
Toll-Free: 800-667-1105
info@avalanche.ca
www.avalanche.ca
To foster & support a professional environment for avalanche safety operations in Canada; To represent the avalanche community to stakeholders
Ian Tomm, Executive Director
Mary Clayton, Director, Communications
Kristin Anthony-Malone, Manager, Operations
Emily Grady, Manager, Industry Training Program

Canadian Fallen Firefighters Foundation / Fondation canadienne des pompiers morts en service
#200, 440 Laurier Ave. W., Ottawa ON K1R 7X6 Canada
Tel: 613-786-3024; *Fax:* 613-782-2228
info@cfff.ca
www.cfff.ca
To serve all firefighters & their families in time of need. This registered, non-profit, charitable organization is made up of members of the Canadian Fire Service and other interested citizens dedicated to honouring Canada's fallen firefighters.
Robert Kirkpatrick, President
Douglas Wylie, 1st Vice-President
Mike McKenna, 2nd Vice-President
Doug Lock, Treasurer

The Canadian Red Cross Society (CRCS) / La Société canadienne de la Croix-Rouge
#300, 170 Metcalfe, Ottawa ON K2P 2P2 Canada
Tel: 613-740-1900; *Fax:* 613-740-1911
feedback@redcross.ca
www.redcross.ca
To help people deal with situations that threaten: their survival & safety, their security & well-being, their human dignity, in Canada & around the world; to improve the lives of vulnerable people by mobilizing the power of humanity

Civil Air Search & Rescue Association (CASARA)
National Office, PO Box 183, Stn. Westwin, Winnipeg MB R3J 3Y5 Canada
jkelly@casaranational.ca
www.casara.ca
To promote aviation safety; to provide air search resource to the military & the RCMP. Works closely with the Canadian Coast Guard & Coast Guard Auxiliary, National Search and Rescue Secretariat, & COSPAS/SARSAT

Corporation des services d'ambulance du Québec
#205, 455, rue Marais, Vanier QC G1M 3A2 Canada
Tél: 418-681-4448; *Téléc:* 418-681-4667
A l'origine, la mission de la Corporation des services d'ambulance du Québec visait exclusivement à offrir une gamme de services et d'avantages à ses membres et à défendre les intérêts de ces derniers auprès des différentes instances gouvernementales, auprès de ses membres au Québec.

Lifesaving Society / Société de sauvetage
287 McArthur Ave., Ottawa ON K1L 6P3 Canada
Tel: 613-746-5694; *Fax:* 613-746-9929
experts@lifesaving.ca
www.lifesaving.ca
The Society is a volunteer organization that works to prevent drowning & water-related incidents by providing lifesaving, lifeguarding & leadership education. It is a registered charity, BN: 119129088RR0001.

Occupational First Aid Attendants Association of British Columbia (OFAAA)
#108, 2323 Boundary Rd., Vancouver BC V5M 4V8 Canada
Tel: 604-294-0244; *Fax:* 604-294-0289
Toll-Free: 800-667-4566
ofaaa@ofaaa.bc.ca
www.ofaaa.bc.ca
To enhance the professional status of first aid attendants & to promote accessibility to high standards of first aid for the workers of the province of British Columbia

REACT Canada Inc.
32 The Queensway North, Keswick ON L4P 1E3 Canada
Tel: 905-476-5231
react@react-canada.org
www.react-canada.org
To provide skilled volunteer two-way radio communications for safety; to provide volunteer emergency radio communications for travellers; to provide safety communications for walkathons, parades, etc.; to offer speakers to community groups on correct use of radio in emergencies

St. John Ambulance / Ambulance Saint-Jean
#400, 1900 City Park Dr., Ottawa ON K1J 1A3 Canada
Tel: 613-236-7461; *Fax:* 613-236-2425
nhq@sja.ca
www.sja.ca
To enable Canadians to improve their health, safety & quality of life by providing training & community service. Courses in CPR, emergency first aid, & safety training are offered, as well as community service programs (medical first response, therapy dog services, emergency preparedness, youth programs), & first aid kits

Employment & Human Resources

Association of Canadian Search, Employment & Staffing Services (ACSESS) / Association nationale des entreprises en recrutement et placement de personnel
#100, 2233 Argentia Rd., Mississauga ON L5N 2X7 Canada
Tel: 905-826-6869; *Fax:* 905-826-4873
Toll-Free: 888-232-4962
acsess@acsess.org
www.acsess.org
To promote the advancement & growth of the employment & staffing services industry in Canada

Association of Professional Recruiters of Canada
#2210, 1081 Ambleside Dr., Ottawa ON K2B 8C8 Canada
Tel: 613-721-5957; *Fax:* 613-721-5850
info@workplace.ca
www.workplace.ca/resources/aprc_assoc.html
To establish standards & practices for the recruitment & selection of human resources in Canada & to provide members with the tools to practice at the highest professional levels
Nathaly Pinchuk, Executive Director
Brian Pascal, President

Canadian Association of Career Educators & Employers (CACEE) / Association canadienne des spécialistes en emploi et des employeurs (ACSEE)
#202, 720 Spadina Ave., Toronto ON M5S 2T9 Canada
Tel: 416-929-5156; *Fax:* 416-929-5256
Toll-Free: 866-922-3303
www.cacee.com
To facilitate the process of matching graduates with employment; a partnership of employer recruiters & career educators providing information, advice & services to students, employers & career centre personnel in the areas of career planning & student recruitment.

Canadian Career Information Association (CCIA) / Association canadienne de documentation professionnelle (ACADOP)
205 Humber College Blvd., Toronto ON M9W 5L7 Canada
Tel: 416-675-5030
karen.fast@humber.ca
www.ccia-acadop.ca
To promote the development and effective delivery of Canadian career information
Anna De Grauwe, Chair
Angella Nunes, Treasurer

Canadian Council of Human Resources Associations (CCHRA) / Conseil canadien des associations en ressources humaines (CCARH)
#603, 150 Metcalfe St., Ottawa ON K2P 1P1 Canada
Tel: 613-567-2477; *Fax:* 613-567-2478
Toll-Free: 866-560-1288
info@cchra-ccarh.ca
www.cchra-ccarh.ca
To establish national core standards for the human resources profession; to foster communications among participating associations; to be the recognized resource on equivalency for human resources qualifications across Canada; & to provide a national & international collective voice on human resources issues
Merrill Brinton, CHRP, President

Human Resources Professionals Association (HRPA)
#1902, 2 Bloor St. West, Toronto ON M4W 3E2 Canada
Tel: 416-923-2324; *Fax:* 416-923-7264
Toll-Free: 800-387-1311
info@hrpa.org
www.hrpa.ca
HRPA empowers human resources professionals by providing management & leadership support, through information resources, events, professional development, & networking opportunities.
Antoinette Blunt, Chair
William (Bill) Greenhalgh, CEO
Louise Tagliacozzo, Manager, Board Relations & Administration

International Association for Human Resource Information Management (IHRIM)
PO Box 1086, Burlington MA 01803 USA
Toll-Free: 800-804-3983
information@ihrim.org
www.ihrim.org
The world's leading clearinghouse for the HRIM industry; members are human resource information management practitioners, vendors, consultants, students and faculty; the leading association enabling members to achieve strategic

objectives through the integration of information technology & human resource management

International Maritime Organization (IMO) / Organisation maritime internationale
4 Albert Embankment, London SE1 7SR United Kingdom
info@imo.org
www.imo.org
To encourage the adoption of high standards in matters concerning maritime safety, security, efficiency of navigation & control of marine pollution from ships
Lee Adamson, Manager, Public Information
Efthimios E. Mitropoulos, Secretary General

Ordre des conseillers en ressources humaines et en relations industrielles agréés du Québec (ORHRI)
#1400, 1200, av McGill Collège, Montréal QC H3B 4G7 Canada
Tél: 514-879-1636; *Téléc:* 514-879-1722
Ligne sans frais: 800-214-1609
info@portailrh.org
www.portailrh.org
La promotion de l'importance stratégique de la gestion des ressources humaines dans la gestion des organisations ainsi que la promotion des nouveaux concepts et champs de développement qui caractérisent son évolution; la promotion des principes de gestion des ressources humaines dans les organisations en tenant compte des tendances sociales et économiques et en accord avec les valeurs de l'association; le développement des membres par le biais de programmes stratégiques de formation et de perfectionnement, des activités d'échanges et d'information et la mise en commun d'expertise professionnelle; la prise de position publique sur des sujets d'intérêt en ressources humaines; le maillage de ses membres à l'intérieur de diverses activités professionnelles et sociales

Energy

Association of Major Power Consumers in Ontario (AMPCO)
Sterling Tower, 372 Bay St., Toronto ON M5H 2W9 Canada
Tel: 416-260-0280; *Fax:* 416-260-0442
info@ampco.org
www.ampco.org
To represent Ontario's electricity-intensive companies; to ensure reliability of power supply to support the economy of Ontario & to advocate a fair & equitable pricing system for electricity; to present views on energy matters to such groups as the Ontario Energy Board, the Ontario Government, Ontario Hydro, the news media, & the general public; to provide decision makers with recommendations on resolving issues

Canadian Coalition for Nuclear Responsibility (CCNR) / Regroupement pour la surveillance du nucléaire (RSN)
PO Box 236, Stn. Snowdon, Montréal QC H3X 3T4 Canada
Fax: 514-489-5118
ccnr@web.ca
www.ccnr.org
Dedicated to education and research on all issues related to nuclear energy, whether civilian or military — including non-nuclear alternatives — especially those pertaining to Canada.

Canadian Energy Research Institute (CERI)
#150, 3512 - 33 St. NW, Calgary AB T2L 2A6 Canada
Tel: 403-282-1231; *Fax:* 403-284-4181
ceri@ceri.ca
www.ceri.ca
To provide the public, industry & the government with information concerning all aspects of energy

Canadian Fluid Power Association (CFPA) / Association canadienne d'énergie fluide
#310, 2175 Sheppard Ave. East, Toronto ON M2J 1W8 Canada
Tel: 416-499-1416; *Fax:* 416-491-1670
info@cfpa.ca
www.cfpa.ca
To build public awareness of fluid power technology; to provide a forum for the exchange of information & opinion; to represent the Canadian fluid power industry to government, educational institutions & other organizations; to ensure that members' concerns are known to those in government; to ensure that students are able to be properly prepared for careers in the fluid power industry; to ensure that members are kept abreast of the latest developments in the fluid power industry

Canadian Institute of Energy (CIE)
987 Devon Rd., North Vancouver BC V7R 1V8 Canada
Tel: 604-904-5777; *Fax:* 604-987-3073
info@cienergy.org
www.cienergy.org
To provide a Canadian perspective on energy technology, business & policy, nationally & internationally, for those affected professionally or personally by energy issues; to encourage energy research, education & dissemination of topical information; to provide an unbiased forum for discussion & debate

Canadian Nuclear Association (CNA) / Association nucléaire canadienne
#1610, 130 Albert St., Ottawa ON K1P 5G4 Canada
Tel: 613-237-4262; *Fax:* 613-237-0989
lindsayj@cna.ca
www.cna.ca
To promote the orderly & sound development of nuclear energy for peaceful purposes in Canada & abroad; to promote & foster an environment favourable to the healthy growth of the uses of nuclear energy & radioisotopes; to encourage cooperation between various industries, utilities, educational institutions, government departments & agencies, which may have a common interest in the development of economic nuclear power & the uses of radioisotopes; to provide a forum for the discussion & resolution of problems which are of concern to the members, the industry, or the Canadian public; to stimulate cooperation with other associations with similar objectives & purposes

Canadian Nuclear Society (CNS) / Société nucléaire canadienne (SNC)
655 Bay St., 17th Fl., Toronto ON M5G 2K4
Tel: 416-977-7620; *Fax:* 416-977-8131
cns-snc@on.aibn.com
www.cns-snc.ca
To promote the exchange of information about nuclear science & technology & its applications; To foster the beneficial utilization of nuclear science

Canadian Renewable Fuels Association (CRFA) / Association canadienne des carburants renouvelables
#605, 350 Sparks St., Ottawa ON K1R 7S8
Tel: 613-594-5528; *Fax:* 613-594-3076
l.ehman@greenfuels.org
www.greenfuels.org
To promote renewable fuel development & usage

Canadian Solar Industries Association Inc. (CanSIA) / Association des industries solaires du Canada inc.
#208, 2378 Holly Lane, Ottawa ON K1V 7P1 Canada
Tel: 613-736-9077; *Fax:* 613-736-8938
Toll-Free: 866-522-6742
info@cansia.ca
www.cansia.ca
To establish programs & activities to develop greater understanding of & acceleration of the use of solar energy; to enhance the growth & effectiveness of the industry & its individual members; to advance the contributions of the members; to ensure government has an understanding of the contribution a viable solar equipment industry base can make to Canada; to coordinate activities with regard to product standards, with emphasis on safety, performance, & economic impact; to collect statistics, to carry on research, experiments, conferences & publications that advance the membership; to develop working relationship with other national & international associations; to aid those engaged in or having an interest in the furthering any objectives; to promote the welfare of the Canadian solar industry to the public & governments

Canadian Wind Energy Association Inc. (CanWEA) / Association canadienne d'énergie éolienne
#810, 170 Laurier Ave. West, Ottawa ON K1P 5V5
Tel: 613-234-8716; *Fax:* 613-234-5642
Toll-Free: 800-922-6932
info@canwea.ca
www.canwea.ca
Social Media: twitter.com/canwindenergy
To promote the social, economic, & environmental benefits of wind energy in Canada; To encourage the appropriate development & application of wind energy; To create suitable environmental policy

Energy Council of Canada / Conseil canadien de l'énergie
#608, 350 Sparks St., Ottawa ON K1R 7S8 Canada
Tel: 613-232-8239; *Fax:* 613-232-1079
krystal.piamonte@energy.ca
www.energy.ca
To foster a greater understanding of energy issues; To enhance the effectiveness of the Canadian energy strategy
Murray J. Stewart, President
Brigitte Svarich, Director, Operations

Energy Probe Research Foundation (EPRF)
225 Brunswick Ave., Toronto ON M5S 2M6 Canada
Tel: 416-964-9223; *Fax:* 416-964-8239
webadmin@eprf.ca
www.eprf.ca
To educate Canadians about the benefits of conservation & renewable energy; to help Canada secure long-term energy self-sufficiency in the shortest possible time with the fewest disruptive effects & with the greatest societal, environmental & economic benefits; to provide business, government & the public with information on energy & energy-related issues; to help Canada contribute to global harmony & prosperity; recipient of the 1990 Lieutenant Governor's Conservation Award, the first time that an environmental organization has been so honoured; divisions include Energy Probe, Probe International, Environment Probe, Margaret Laurence Fund, Consumer Policy Institute, Environmental Bureau of Investigations, Urban Renaissance Institute

Planetary Association for Clean Energy, Inc. (PACE) / Société planétaire pour l'assainissement de l'énergie
#1001, 100 Bronson Ave., Ottawa ON K1R 6G8 Canada
Tel: 613-236-6265; *Fax:* 613-235-5876
pacenet@canada.com
pacenet.homestead.com
To steward & facilitate the implementation of clean energy systems worldwide

Solar & Sustainable Energy Society of Canada Inc. (SESCI) / Societé des énergie solaire et durable du Canada Inc.
c/o Frederic Pouyot, #173, 207 Bank St., Ottawa ON k2P 2N2
Tel: 613-686-4474; *Fax:* 613-533-6550
bruce@techonfoot.com
www.sesci.ca
To act as a voice for renewable energy in Canada; To increase the use of solar & sustainable energy in Canada; To support energy conservation

Wood Energy Technology Transfer Inc. (WETT)
#7, 296 Jarvis St., Toronto ON M5B 2C5 Canada
Tel: 416-968-7718; *Fax:* 416-968-6818
Toll-Free: 888-358-9388
WETT@funnel.ca
www.wettinc.ca
To promote the safe & effective use of wood burning systems, WETT maintains a training program designed to confirm & recognize the knowledge & skills of practising wood energy professionals; to provide training to new people entering the industry; to provide training to non-industry professionals such as inspectors; to provide training to specialty audiences such as volunteer firefighters & carpenters in remote communities
Anthony Laycock, Executive Director

Engineering & Technology

American Society of Mechanical Engineers (ASME)
3 Park Ave., New York NY 10016-5990 USA
Tel: 800-843-2763
infocentral@asme.org
www.asme.org
To promote the art, science, & practice of multidisciplinary engineering; To focus on the technical, educational, & research issues of the engineering & technology community; To help the engineering community develop solutions to improve the quality of life

Applied Science Technologists & Technicians of British Columbia (ASTTBC)
10767 - 148 St., Surrey BC V3R 0S4 Canada
Tel: 604-585-2788; *Fax:* 604-585-2790
techinfo@asttbc.org
www.asttbc.org
To advance the profession of applied science technology & the professional recognition of applied science technologists, certified technicians & other members in a manner that serves & protects the public interest

Association des ingénieurs municipaux du Québec (AIMQ) / Association of Québec Municipal Engineers
CP 792, Succ. B, Montréal QC H3B 3K5 Canada
Tél: 514-845-5303
aimg.rlamarche@videotron.ca
www.aimq.net
Améliorer les connaissances et le statut de l'ingénieur municipal par l'échange d'information, la coopération entre ingénieurs

municipaux et avec d'autres associations professionnelles et la promotion des intérêts communs des membres de l'Association

Association des ingénieurs-conseils du Québec (AICQ) / Consulting Engineers of Québec
#930, 1440, rue Ste-Catherine ouest, Montréal QC H3G 1R8 Canada
Tél: 514-871-2229; *Téléc:* 514-871-9903
info@aicq.qc.ca
www.aicq.qc.ca
Promouvoir et développer l'industrie du génie-conseil en regroupant des membres qui offrent des services de qualité

Association of Certified Engineering Technicians & Technologists of Prince Edward Island (ACETTPEI)
PO Box 1436, 92 Queen St., Charlottetown PE C1A 7N1 Canada
Tel: 902-892-8324
info@acettpei.ca
www.acettpei.ca
To benefit society by advancing the professions of applied science & engineering technology in Prince Edward Island

Association of Consulting Engineering Companies - Canada (ACEC)
#420, 130 Albert St., Ottawa ON K1P 5G4 Canada
Fax: 613-236-6193
Toll-Free: 800-565-0569
info@acec.ca
www.acec.ca
To assist in promoting satisfactory business relations between its Member Firms & their clients; To promote cordial relations among the various consulting engineering firms in Canada & to foster the interchange of professional, management & business experience & information among them; To safeguard the interest of the consulting engineer; To further the maintenance of high professional standards in the consulting engineering profession

Association of Consulting Engineering Companies - New Brunswick (ACEC-NB)
183 Hanwell Rd., Fredericton NB E3B 2R2
Tel: 506-470-9211; *Fax:* 506-451-9629
info@acec-nb.ca
www.cenb.nb.ca
To develop & support member firms; To improve the business environment for member firms & their clients; To further the professional standards of the consulting engineering profession
John Fudge, P.Eng, Executive Director
David McAllister, P.Eng, President
Christy Cunningham, Secretary
Karen Robichaud, Treasurer

Association of Engineering Technicians & Technologists of Newfoundland & Labrador (AETTNL)
Donovan's Industrial Park, PO Box 790, 22 Sagona Ave., Mount Pearl NL A1N 2Y2 Canada
Tel: 709-747-2868; *Fax:* 709-747-2869
Toll-Free: 888-238-8600
aettnl@aettnl.com
www.aettnl.com
AETTNL's mission is to advance the profession of Applied Science/Engineering Technology & the professional recognition of Certified Technicians & Technologists. It regulates the standards of training & practice, & protects the interests of its members & the public.

Association of Professional Engineers & Geoscientists of British Columbia (APEGBC)
#200, 4010 Regent St., Burnaby BC V5C 6N2
Tel: 604-430-8035; *Fax:* 604-430-8085
Toll-Free: 888-430-8035
apeginfo@apeg.bc.ca; communication@apeg.bc.ca
www.apeg.bc.ca
To protect the public interest in matters related to geoscience & engineering; To regulate & govern the professions of professional engineers & geoscientists in British Columbia, according to the Engineers & Geoscientists Act; To strive for professional excellence, by establishing academic, experience, & professional practice standards

Association of Professional Engineers & Geoscientists of Manitoba (APEGM)
850A Pembina Hwy., Winnipeg MB R3M 2M7 Canada
Tel: 204-474-2736; *Fax:* 204-474-5960
Toll-Free: 866-227-9600
apegm@apegm.mb.ca
www.apegm.mb.ca
To serve & protect the public interest by governing & advancing the practice of engineering in accordance with the Engineering Profession Act of Manitoba

Association of Professional Engineers & Geoscientists of New Brunswick (APEGNB) / Association des ingénieurs et géoscientifiques du Nouveau-Brunswick (AINB)
183 Hanwell Rd., Fredericton NB E3B 2R2 Canada
Tel: 506-458-8083; *Fax:* 506-451-9629
info@apegnb.com
www.apegnb.com
To establish, maintain & develop standards of knowledge & skill, qualification & practice, & professional ethics; to promote public awareness of the role of the association

Association of Professional Engineers & Geoscientists of Saskatchewan (APEGS)
#104, 2255 - 13 Ave., Regina SK S4P 0V6 Canada
Tel: 306-525-9547; *Fax:* 306-525-0851
Toll-Free: 800-500-9547
apegs@apegs.sk.ca
www.apegs.sk.ca
To achieve a safe & prosperous future through engineering & geoscience

Association of Professional Engineers of Nova Scotia (APENS)
PO Box 129, 1355 Barrington St., Halifax NS B3J 2M4 Canada
Tel: 902-429-2250; *Fax:* 902-423-9769
Toll-Free: 888-802-7367
info@apens.ns.ca
www.apens.ns.ca
To establish, maintain & develop standards of knowledge & skill, standards of qualification & practice, standards of professional ethics; to promote public awareness of the role of the association

Association of Professional Engineers of Prince Edward Island (APEPEI)
549 North River Rd., Charlottetown PE C1E 1J6 Canada
Tel: 902-566-1268; *Fax:* 902-566-5551
info@engineerspei.com
www.engineerspei.com
Engineers PEI regulates the practice of professional engineering in the province, with authority over members, licensees, engineers-in-training, & holders of certificates of authorization.

Association of Professional Engineers of the Yukon Territory (APEY)
312B Hanson St., Whitehorse YT Y1A 1Y6 Canada
Tel: 867-667-6727; *Fax:* 867-668-2142
staff@apey.yk.ca
www.apey.yk.ca
To establish, maintain & develop standards of knowledge & skill, standards of qualification & practice & standards of professional ethics; to promote public awareness of the role of the association

Association of Professional Engineers, Geologists & Geophysicists of Alberta (APEGGA)
Scotia One, #1500, 10060 Jasper Ave. NW, Edmonton AB T5J 4A2
Tel: 780-426-3990; *Fax:* 780-426-1877
Toll-Free: 800-661-7020
email@apegga.org
www.apegga.org
To register & set practice standards & coes of professional conduct & ethics for professional engineers, geologists, & geophysicists in Alberta, according to The Engineering, Geological and Geophysical Professions Act

Association of Professional Engineers, Geologists & Geophysicists of the Northwest Territories & Nunavut (NAPEGG)
#201, 4817 - 49 St., Yellowknife NT X1A 3S7 Canada
Tel: 867-920-4055; *Fax:* 867-873-4058
napegg@tamarack.nt.ca
www.napegg.nt.ca
To regulate the practices of our professions; to establish & maintain standards in order to serve & protect the public

The Association of Science and Engineering Technology Professionals of Alberta (ASET)
Phipps-McKinnon Building, #1630, 10020 - 101A Ave., Edmonton AB T5J 3G2 Canada
Tel: 780-425-0626; *Fax:* 780-424-5053
Toll-Free: 800-272-5619
asetadmin@aset.ab.ca
www.aset.ab.ca
To benefit the public & the profession by regulating & promoting safe, high quality professional technology practice; focus is on the engineering technology, applied science & information technology fields; issues credentials to qualified individuals & accredits training programs

Canadian Acoustical Association / Association canadienne d'acoustique
c/o National Research Council of Canada, Institute for Research in Construction, Ottawa ON K1A 0R6 Canada
Tel: 613-993-7985; *Fax:* 613-954-1495
secretary@caa-aca.ca
www.caa-aca.ca
To foster communication among people working in all areas of acoustics in Canada; to promote the growth & practical application of knowledge in acoustics; to encourage education, research & employment in acoustics

Canadian Advanced Technology Alliance (CATA Alliance) / Association canadienne de technologie de pointe
#416, 207 Bank St., Ottawa ON K2P 2N2
Tel: 613-236-6550
info@cata.ca; cmalette@cata.ca (Membership)
www.cata.ca
Social Media: facebook.com/group.php?gid=5391503953; http://twitter.com/CATAAlliance
CATA Alliance provides its members with a network to establish partnerships, to match up with global business opportunities. It offers communication & advocacy services, notably in dealing with the government, working to ensure that policies are favourable to Cdn. technology companies. It maintains a research repository where members can access information to advance their agendas. The ultimate goal is to give members a competitive edge.

Canadian Air Cushion Technology Society (CACTS)
c/o Canadian Aeronautics & Space Institute, #104, 350 Terry Fox Dr., Kanata ON K2K 2W5
www.casi.ca/canadianaircushiontechnologysociety.aspx
To serve the air cushion technology (hovercraft) community throughout Canada; To advance the science, technologies, & applications of air cushion technology
Jacques Laframboise, FCASI, Society Chair

Canadian Association for Composite Structures & Materials (CACSMA) / Association canadienne pour les structures et matériaux composites (ACSMAC)
c/o J. Denault, Industrial Materials Institute, Ntl. Research Council, Montréal QC H3G 1M6
Tel: 450-641-5105; *Fax:* 450-848-4596
Johanne.Denault@imi.cnrc-nrc.gc.ca
www.cacsma.ca
To support composites companies in Canada; To promote Canadian composites capabilities; To encourage the application of composites in all sectors

Canadian Council of Technicians & Technologists (CCTT) / Conseil canadien des techniciens et technologues
#295, 1101 Prince Of Wales Dr., Ottawa ON K2C 3W7
Tel: 613-238-8123; *Fax:* 613-238-8822
Toll-Free: 800-891-1140
ccttadm@cctt.ca; fq@cctt.ca (foreign qualification assessment)
www.cctt.ca
Social Media: www.twitter.com/#!/CCTTCanada
To advocate on behalf of Canada's certified technicians & technologists; To establish & maintain national competency standards
Isidore J. LeBlond, Director, Program Development
Rick Tachuk, Director, Communications
Darlene Pilon, Manager, Finance & Events Management
Valery Vidershpan, Manager, Database Development

Canadian Hydrogen & Fuel Cell Association (CHFCA)
4250 Wesbrook Mall, Vancouver BC V6T 1W5
Tel: 604-822-9178; *Fax:* 604-822-8106
info@chfca.ca
www.chfca.ca
To act as the collective voice of the hydrogen & fuel cell technologies & products sector; To support Canadian corporations, educational institutions, & governments which develop & deploy hydrogen & fuel cell products & services in Canada
John W. Tak, President & Chief Executive Officer
Terry Kimmel, Vice-President
Michael Dujardin, Controller
Javis Lui, Manager, Communications & Member Relations
Sarah Richards, Manager, Conferences & Workshops

Canadian Remote Sensing Society (CRSS) / Société canadienne de télédétection
1750 Courtlant Cres., Ottawa ON K2C 2B5 Canada
Tel: 613-234-0191; *Fax:* 613-234-9039
casi@casi.ca
www.casi.ca/canadianremotesensingsociety.aspx

To advance the art, science, engineering, & application of remote sensing in Canada; to uphold the Society's Code of Ethics
Derek R. Peddle, Chair
Monique Bernier, Vice-Chair
Anne Smith, Secretary-Treasurer

Canadian Society for Civil Engineering (CSCE) / Société canadienne de génie civil
4877, rue Sherbrooke ouest, Montréal QC H3Z 1G9
Tel: 514-933-2634; *Fax:* 514-933-3504
info@csce.ca; membership@csce.ca
www.csce.ca
To develop & maintain high standard of civil engineering practice in Canada; To enhance the public image of the civil engineering profession
Doug Salloum, Executive Director
Mahmoud Lardjane, Manager, Programs
Louise Newman, Manager, Communications
Andrea Grimaud, Officer, Membership Liaison

Canadian Society for Engineering Management (CSEM) / Société canadienne de gestion en ingénierie
1295 Hwy. 2 East, Kingston ON K7L 4V1 Canada
louisem@cogeco.ca
www.csem-scgi.org
To represent the interests & enhance the capabilities of engineers in management in order to promote & advance efficient management of commerce, industry & public affairs.
John Wood, P.Eng, President
Dominique Janssens, P.Eng, Sec.-Treas.

Canadian Society for Mechanical Engineering (CSME) / Société canadienne de génie mécanique (SCGM)
1295 Hwy. 2 East, Kingston ON K7L 4V1
Tel: 613-547-5989; *Fax:* 613-547-0195
csme@cogeco.ca
www.csme-scgm.ca
To benefit Canada & the world by fostering excellence in the practice of mechanical engineering; To support members
Rama B. Bhat, Ph.D, FCSME, President

Canadian Technical Asphalt Association (CTAA) / Association technique canadienne du bitume
#300, 895 Fort St., Victoria BC V8W 1H7 Canada
Tel: 250-361-9187; *Fax:* 250-361-9187
admin@ctaa.ca
www.ctaa.ca
To organize efforts of membership on a non-profit, public service basis; to assemble, correlate & disseminate technical information on characteristics & uses of bituminous materials; to conduct conferences at which characteristics & uses of asphaltic materials are discussed; to stimulate & encourage research on uses of asphaltic materials; to encourage colleges to teach students to study asphalt technology

Certified Technicians & Technologists Association of Manitoba (CTTAM)
#602, 1661 Portage Ave., Winnipeg MB R3J 3T7 Canada
Tel: 204-784-1088; *Fax:* 204-784-1084
admin@cttam.com
www.cttam.com
To advance the professional recognition & development of certified applied science technicians & technologists in a manner that serves the public interest

Community Energy Association
#308, 402 West Pender St., Vancouver BC V6B 1T6 Canada
Tel: 604-628-7076; *Fax:* 778-786-1613
www.communityenergy.bc.ca
To support local governments throughout British Columbia in accelerating the application of energy efficiency and renewable energy in all aspects of community design, infrastructure and community engagement for sustainability.
Norm Connolly, Executive Director

Consulting Engineers of Alberta (CEA)
Phipps-McKinnon Building, #870, 10020 - 101A Ave., Edmonton AB T5J 3G2
Tel: 780-421-1852; *Fax:* 780-424-5225
info@cea.ca
www.cea.ca
To provide leadership to foster a positive business environment for the consulting engineering firms in Alberta; To promote the engineering industry; To enhance interests & opportunities of CEA members; To provide society with high standards of engineering design & safety
Gord Johnston, P.Eng., President
Ken Pilip, Registrar
Sharon Moroskat, Manager, Finance & Administration
Hiju Song, Manager, Events & Communications

Consulting Engineers of British Columbia (CEBC)
#1258, 409 Granville St., Vancouver BC V6C 1T2
Tel: 604-687-2811; *Fax:* 604-688-7110
info@cebc.org
www.cebc.org
To improve the commercial environment for consulting engineering firms
Glenn Martin, Executive Director
Jack Lee, President
Alla Samusevich, Coordinator, Accounting & Events

Consulting Engineers of Manitoba Inc. (CEM)
PO Box 1547, Stn. Main, Winnipeg MB R3C 2Z4 Canada
Tel: 204-774-5258; *Fax:* 204-779-0788
cemca@shaw.ca
www.cemanitoba.com
To promote & enhance the business interests of the consulting engineers of Manitoba; to lead in the application of technology for the benefit of society.

Consulting Engineers of Nova Scotia (CENS)
PO Box 613, Stn. M, Halifax NS B3J 2R7
Tel: 902-461-1325; *Fax:* 902-461-1321
cens@eastlink.ca
www.cens.org
To enable the consulting engineering industry in Nova Scotia to capitalize on opportunities to grow; To promote employment of member firms

Consulting Engineers of Ontario (CEO)
#405, 10 Four Seasons Pl., Toronto ON M9B 6H7 Canada
Tel: 416-620-1400; *Fax:* 416-620-5803
staff@ceo.on.ca
www.ceo.on.ca
To further the maintenance of high professional standards in consulting engineering profession; to promote cordial relations among various consulting firms in Ontario; to foster interchange of professional management & business experience & information among consulting engineers; to develop regional representation & participation in affairs of the association.

Consulting Engineers of Saskatchewan (CES)
#12, 2010 - 7 Ave., Regina SK S4R 1C2 Canada
Tel: 306-359-3338; *Fax:* 306-522-5325
ces@sasktel.net
www.ces.sk.ca
To further the maintenance of high professional standards in consulting engineering profession; to promote cordial relations among various consulting firms in Saskatchewan; to foster interchange of professional management & business experience & information among consulting engineers; to develop regional representation & participation in affairs of the association

Consulting Engineers of Yukon (CEY)
c/o EBA Engineering Consultants Ltd., #6, 151 Industrial Rd., Whitehorse YT Y1A 2V3 Canada
Tel: 867-668-3068; *Fax:* 867-668-4349
cey@eba.ca
www.cey.ca
To maintain high professional standards in the consulting engineering profession; to promote cordial relations among various consulting firms in the Yukon; to foster interchange of professional management & business experience & information among consulting engineers; to develop regional representation & participation in affairs of the association

Continental Automated Buildings Association (CABA) / Association continentale pour l'automatisation des bâtiments
#210, 1173 Cyrville Rd., Ottawa ON K1J 7S6 Canada
Tel: 613-686-1814; *Fax:* 613-744-7833
Toll-Free: 888-798-2222
caba@caba.org
www.caba.org
Social Media: twitter.com/caba_news
To promote advanced technologies for the automation of homes & buildings in North America; to create opportunities for members

The Engineering Institute of Canada (EIC) / L'Institut canadien des ingénieurs (ICI)
1295 Hwy. 2 East, Kingston ON K7L 4V1 Canada
Tel: 613-547-5989; *Fax:* 613-547-0195
jplant1@cogeco.ca
www.eic-ici.ca
To further the development of engineering in Canada; to stimulate the advancement of the quality & scope of Canadian engineering; to meet regularly with other engineering organizations & industries to promote understanding & improvement of the profession, the diffusion of engineering information & to provide Canadian representation in specialized engineering fields; to interact with government agencies & departments for the purpose of influencing decision making on matters relating to engineering & technology; to cooperate with the provincial engineering licensing bodies, The Canadian Council of Professional Engineering, The Association of Consulting Engineers of Canada, The Canadian Academy of Engineering & other engineering organizations in matters of common interest; to promote interaction with specific interest groups; to collaborate with universities & educational institutions

Engineers Canada / Ingénieurs Canada
#1100, 180 Elgin St., Ottawa ON K2P 2K3 Canada
Tel: 613-232-2474; *Fax:* 613-230-5759
info@ccpe.ca
www.ccpe.ca
To establish & maintain a common bond between constituent associations & assist them to meet their common needs & those of their members by coordinating standards, procedures & programs across Canada, by representing the engineering profession with respect to national & international affairs & generally by increasing the profile & prestige of the engineering profession

INO / Institut national d'optique
2740, rue Einstein, Sainte-Foy QC G1P 4S4 Canada
Tel: 418-657-7006; *Fax:* 418-657-7009
info@ino.ca
www.ino.ca
To be an international leader in optics & photonics R&D, promoting economic expansion in the country by providing assistance to companies seeking to be more competitive
Jean-Guy Paquet, President & CEO

Institute of Power Engineers (IPE)
PO Box 878, Burlington ON L7R 3Y7 Canada
Tel: 905-333-3348; *Fax:* 905-333-9328
ipenat@nipe.ca
www.nipe.ca
To promote business relations, social activities & mutual understanding among power engineers.
Lorne Shewfelt, National President
Jude Rankin, 1st National Vice President
Don Purser, National Secretary

ISIS Canada Research Network (ISIS)
A250 Agricultural & Civil Engineering Bldg., 96 Dafoe Rd., Winnipeg MB R3T 2N2 Canada
Tel: 204-474-8506; *Fax:* 204-474-7519
central@isiscanada.com
www.isiscanada.com
To advance civil engineering in Canada to a world leadership position through the development & application of fibre-reinforced polymers & integrated intelligent fibre optic sensing technologies, for the benefit of all Canadians, through innovative & intelligent infrastructure. The network is comprised of 14 Canadian universities
Aftab Mufti, P.Eng., Ph.D., President

Municipal Engineers Association (MEA)
#2, 6355 Kennedy Rd., Mississauga ON L5T 2L5
Tel: 905-795-2555; *Fax:* 905-795-2660
info@municipalengineers.on.ca
www.municipalengineers.on.ca
To provide focus & unity for licensed engineers employed by municipalities in Ontario; To address issues of common concern to members; To facilitate the dissemination of information
Rick A. Kester, P.Eng, President
J. David Shantz, Executive Director

NACE International (NACE)
1440 South Creek Dr., Houston TX 77084-4906 USA
Tel: 281-228-6200; *Fax:* 281-228-6300
Toll-Free: 800-797-6223
firstservice@nace.org
www.nace.org
To protect people, assets & the environment from the effects of corrosion. Northern Area sections include: Atlantic Canada, B.C., Calgary, Canadian National Capital Section, Edmonton, Montreal, Saskatchewan & Toronto

New Brunswick Society of Certified Engineering Technicians & Technologists (NBSCETT) / Société des techniciens et des technologues agréés du génie du Nouveau-Brunswick (STTAGN-B)
#2, 385 Wilsey Rd., Fredericton NB E3B 5N6 Canada
Tel: 506-454-6124; *Fax:* 506-452-7076
Toll-Free: 800-665-8324
nbscett@nbscett.nb.ca
www.nbscett.nb.ca
To grant certification to applied science & engineering technology technicians & technologists; to protect titles & powers of discipline for its members

Ontario Association of Certified Engineering Technicians & Technologists (OACETT)
#404, 10 Four Seasons Pl., Toronto ON M9B 6H7 Canada
Tel: 416-621-9621; *Fax:* 416-621-8694
info@oacett.org
www.oacett.org
To advance the profession of applied science & engineering technology through standards for society's benefit.

Ordre des ingénieurs du Québec (OIQ)
#350, 1100, rue De La Gauchetière ouest, Montréal QC H3B 2S2 Canada
Tél: 514-845-6141; *Téléc:* 514-845-1833
Ligne sans frais: 800-461-6141
dirgen@oiq.qc.ca
www.oiq.qc.ca
Faire de la promotion et s'assurer de la qualité des services rendus à la société par les ingénieurs, individuellement et collectivement, en tant que membres d'un corps professionnel; favoriser leur épanouissement professionnel et personnel; contribuer au développement socio-économique de la société

Ordre des technologues professionnels du Québec (OTPQ)
#720, 1265, rue Berri, Montréal QC H2L 4X4 Canada
Tél: 514-845-3247; *Téléc:* 514-845-3643
Ligne sans frais: 800-561-3459
info@otpq.qc.ca
www.otpq.qc.ca
Promouvoir et assurer la compétence des technologues professionnels dans l'intérêt public

Plant Engineering & Maintenance Association of Canada (PEMAC)
#402, 6 - 2400 Dundas St. West, Mississauga ON L5K 2R8 Canada
Tel: 905-823-7255; *Fax:* 905-823-8001
mail@pemac.org
www.pemac.org
To be recognized as a nationwide centre of excellence in plant engineering & maintenance; to form positive & constructive links with industry & service sectors, in support of local & nationwide developments & productivity; to deliver strongly identifiable services & commitments across the range of disciplines embraced by the association; to educate & introduce new concepts; to provide representation at all government levels; to provide career enhancement & networking opportunities; to promote research in the field of plant engineering & maintenance

Positive Power Co-op (PPC)
#422, 2000 Appleby Line, Burlington ON L7L 7H7 Canada
Tel: 519-846-8130
www.positivepowerco-op.com
Positive Power Co-op is a not-for-profit co-operative dedicated to promoting and building community-based renewable energy projects in the Hamilton, Halton and Haldimand regions.
Stacey Hare, General Manager
Curt Hammond, Chair

Professional Engineers & Geoscientists Newfoundland & Labrador (PEG-NL)
PO Box 21207, St. John's NL A1A 5B2 Canada
Tel: 709-753-7714; *Fax:* 709-753-6131
main@pegnl.ca
www.pegnl.ca
To provide competent & ethical practice of engineering & geoscience in Newfoundland & Labrador; to ensure public confidence, sustainability, & stewardship of the professions; to provide leadership to enhance quality of life through the application & management of engineering & geoscience

Professional Engineers Ontario (PEO)
#1000, 25 Sheppard Ave. West, Toronto ON M2N 6S9 Canada
Tel: 416-224-1100; *Fax:* 416-224-8168
Toll-Free: 800-339-3716
webmaster@peo.on.ca
www.peo.on.ca
To meet the needs of Ontario society by licensing & regulating the entire practice of professional engineering in an open, transparent, inclusive manner

Saskatchewan Applied Science Technologists & Technicians (SASTT)
363 Park St., Regina SK S4N 5B2
Tel: 306-721-6633; *Fax:* 306-721-0112
info@sastt.ca
www.sastt.ca
To regulate the professional conduct of applied science technologists & certified technicians in Saskatchewan, in order to protect the public

SHAD Valley International
8 Young St. East, Waterloo ON N2J 2L3 Canada
Tel: 519-884-8844; *Fax:* 519-884-8191
info@shad.ca
www.shad.ca
To advance the scientific & technological capabilities of youth, integrated with the development of their entrepreneurial spirit; to collaborate with education, business & other communities, both domestic & international, to provide exceptional development opportunities

Society of Motion Picture & Television Engineers (SMPTE)
3 Barker Ave, 5th Fl., White Plains NY 10601 USA
Tel: 914-761-1100; *Fax:* 914-761-3115
membership@smpte.org
www.smpte.org

Society of Tribologists & Lubrication Engineers / Société des tribologistes et ingénieurs en lubrification
840 Busse Hwy., Park Ridge IL 60068-2302 USA
Tel: 847-825-5536; *Fax:* 847-825-1456
information@stle.org
www.stle.org
To promote study of tribology, friction, wear & lubrication; to function as resource for distribution of new information & techniques

TechNova
#A308, Cambridge 1, 202 Brownlow Ave., Dartmouth NS B3B 1T5 Canada
Tel: 902-463-3236; *Fax:* 902-465-7567
Toll-Free: 866-723-8867
info@technova.ca
www.technova.ca
Certifying engineering & applied science technicians & technologists for the betterment of the public & the welfare of the environment

Environmental

Action Nord Terre
535, 4e Rue, Chibougamau QC G8P 1S4 Canada
Tél: 418-748-7056
André Naud, Président

Air & Waste Management Association (A&WMA) / Association pour la prévention de la contamination de l'air et du sol
One Gateway Center, 420 Fort Duquesne Blvd., 3rd Fl., Pittsburgh PA 15222-1435 USA
Tel: 412-232-3444; *Fax:* 412-232-3450
Toll-Free: 800-270-3444
info@awma.org
www.awma.org
Social Media: www.facebook.com/group.php?gid=33499462923
To improve environmental knowledge & decisions; To assist members in critical environmental decision making & professional development; To provide a neutral forum for exchanging information & developing networking opportunities; To increase public education & outreach

Alberta Environmental Network (AEN)
#2, 6328A - 104 St. NW, Edmonton AB T6H 2K9 Canada
Tel: 780-439-1916; *Fax:* 780-433-3792
aen@web.ca
www.aenweb.ca
To facilitate communication & cooperation among environmental groups in Alberta in order to contribute to the enhancement & protection of the environment

Alberta Fish & Game Association (AFGA)
6924 - 104 St., Edmonton AB T6H 2L7
Tel: 780-437-2342; *Fax:* 780-438-6872
office@afga.org
www.afga.org
To ensure fish & wildlife habitat & resources in Alberta
Conrad Fennema, President
Martin Sharren, Executive Vice-President
Sandie Buwalda, Coordinator, Programs
Brad Fenson, Coordinator, Habitats
Kerry Grisley, Co-Manager, Operation Grassland Community
Susan Skinner, Co-Manager, Operation Grassland Community

Alberta Water Council
Petroleum Plaza, South Tower, #1400, 9915 - 108 St., Edmonton AB T5K 2G8 Canada
Tel: 780-644-7380
www.albertawatercouncil.ca
The Alberta Water Council is a stakeholder partnership that provides leadership, expertise and advocacy, to engage and empower individuals, organizations, business and governments to achieve the outcomes of the Water for Life strategy.
Gord Edwards, Executive Director

Alberta Wilderness Association (AWA)
455 - 12 St. NW, Calgary AB T2N 1Y9 Canada
Tel: 403-283-2025; *Fax:* 403-270-2743
Toll-Free: 866-313-0713
awa@shaw.ca
albertawilderness.ca
AWA is a non-profit, federally registered, charitable society that: promotes the protection of Alberta's rivers & wildlands areas; works to restore the natural ecosystems of Alberta; educates Albertans on wilderness conservation & sustainable use of natural lands & waters.

Association for Literature, Environment, and Culture in Canada (ALECC) / Association pour la littérature, l'environnement et la culture au Canada
c/o Department of English, University of Calgary, 2500 University Dr. NW, 11th Fl., Calgary AB T2N 1N4 Canada
contactus@alecc.ca
www.alecc.ca
To promote and support artistic, critical and cultural studies work on a wide range of environmental issues.
Pamela Banting, President

Bedeque Bay Environmental Management Association (BBEMA)
PO Box 8310, Emerald PE C0B 1M0 Canada
Tel: 902-886-3211
www.bbema.ca
To provide a framework for citizen-based education and action that reduced soil erosion, maintained water quality and improved the ecosystem.

Big Rideau Lake Association (BRLA)
PO Box 93, Hwy. 15, Portland ON K0G 1V0 Canada
Tel: 613-272-3629
brla@brla.on.ca
www.brla.on.ca
The Big Rideau Lake Association (BRLA) is a non-profit organization committed to long-term environmental protection and service to all who use Big Rideau Lake and share its resources.
Peter Copestake, President

BIOQuébec / Québec Bio-Industries Business Network
#300, 381, rue Notre-Dame ouest, Montréal QC H2Y 1V2 Canada
Tél: 514-733-8411; *Téléc:* 514-733-8272
reception@bioquebec.com
www.bioquebec.com
Ôtre le porte-parole des entreprises biotechnologiques du Québec; favoriser le développement et la mise en valeur des biotechnologies et des bioindustries québécoises, et ce au bénéfice de ses membres; To promote the development & the upgrading of biotechnologies; to supply strategic information of technical & economical content as well as carry out projects, events & activities; to stimulate collaboration between private industry, governments & universities; to stimulate the growth of structuring economical activities in this field; to act as a spokesman for the bio-industry in Québec
Bertrand Bolduc, Président
Perry Niro, M.Sc., Directeur général et chef de la dir

British Columbia Environment Industry Association (BCEIA)
#400, 602 West Hastings St., Vancouver BC V6B 1P2
Tel: 604-683-2751; *Fax:* 604-677-5960
info@bceia.com
www.bceia.com
To develop the environmental industry in British Columbia; To promote technological development
Bob Symington, President
Frank Came, Vice-President
Jeff Eltom, Executive Director
Michael Lyons, Secretary-Treasurer

British Columbia Environmental Network (BCEN)
#461, 1755 Robson St., Vancouver BC V6G 3B7 Canada
Tel: 604-515-1969
editor@ecobc.ca
www.ecobc.org
To facilitate communication among environmental groups & individuals so that ecological sustainability & economic stability prevail, & biological diversity & human health remain viable

British Columbia Water & Waste Association (BCWWA)
#221, 8678 Greenall Ave., Burnaby BC V5J 3M6
Tel: 604-433-4389; *Fax:* 604-433-9859
Toll-Free: 877-433-4389
contact@bcwwa.org
www.bcwwa.org
Social Media: www.facebook.com/group.php?gid=21435804125
Safeguarding public health & the environment by sharing skills, knowledge, & experience with water & wastewater industry workers in British Columbia & the Yukon; To act a voice for the water & waste community in British Columbia & the Yukon

BurlingtonGreen Environmental Association
3281 Myers Lane, Burlington ON L7N 1K6
Tel: 905-466-2171
www.burlingtongreen.org
Social Media: www.facebook.com/burlington.green.environment
To advocate for local environmental issues
Amy Schnurr, Executive Director

Campaign for Nuclear Phaseout (CNP)
#412, 1 Nicholas St., Ottawa ON K1N 7B7 Canada
www.cnp.ca
The Campaign for Nuclear Phaseout (CNP) represents a coalition of Canadian public interest organizations concerned with the environmental consequences of nuclear power generation.

Canadian Arctic Resources Committee
488 Gladstone Ave., Ottawa ON K1N 8V4 Canada
Tel: 613-759-4284; *Fax:* 613-237-3845
Toll-Free: 866-949-9006
davidg@carc.org
www.carc.org
The Canadian Arctic Resources Committee (CARC) is a citizens' organization dedicated to the long-term environmental and social well being of northern Canada and its peoples.
Chuck Birchall, Chair

Canadian Association for Laboratory Accreditation Inc. (CALA)
#310, 1565 Carling Ave., Ottawa ON K1Z 8R1
Tel: 613-233-5300; *Fax:* 613-233-5501
ecummins@cala.ca
www.cala.ca
To provide internationally-recognized accreditation services; To assist laboratories in the achievement of high levels of scientific & management excellence; To improve environmental quality & public health & safety

Canadian Association of Recycling Industries (CARI) / Association canadienne des industries du recyclage (ACIR)
#1, 682 Monarch Ave., Ajax ON L1S 4S2
Tel: 905-426-9313; *Fax:* 905-426-9314
www.cari-acir.org
To address issues facing the recycling industry in Canada & internationally; To promote commercial recycling activities

Canadian Association on Water Quality (CAWQ) / Association canadienne sur la qualité de l'eau (ACQE)
PO Box 5050, 867 Lakeshore Rd., Burlington ON L7R 4A6 Canada
Tel: 905-336-6291; *Fax:* 905-336-4877
www.cawq.ca
To promote research on scientific, technological, legal & administrative aspects of water pollution research & control; To further the exchange of information & the practical application of such research for public benefit

Canadian Centre for Pollution Prevention (C2P2) / Centre canadien pour la prévention de la pollution
#134, 215 Spadina Ave., Toronto ON M5T 2C7
Tel: 905-822-4133; *Fax:* 416-979-3936
Toll-Free: 800-667-9790
info@c2p2online.com
www.c2p2online.com
To shape the future of production & consumption; To catalyze behavioural change in order to increase sustainable practices, a healthier environment, & competitiveness
Fred Granek, Chief Operating Officer
Leah Nielsen, Coordinator, Projects
Shari Russell, Coordinator, Projects

Canadian Environment Industry Association (CEIA)
119, Concession 6 Rd., Fisherville ON NOA 1G0 Canada
Tel: 416-410-0432; *Fax:* 416-362-5231
www.grn.com/assn/can_envi.html
To promote the interests and development of Canadian companies supplying environmental technologies, products and services.

Christopher Henderson, Chair

Canadian Environmental Certification Approvals Board (CECAB) / Bureau canadien de reconnaissance professionnelle des spécialistes de l'environnement
#200, 308 - 11th Ave. SE, Calgary AB T2G 0Y2 Canada
Tel: 403-233-7484; *Fax:* 403-264-6240
certification@eco.ca
www.cecab.org
CECAB is a professional autonomous body providing national certification for Canadian environmental practitioners.
Lou Locatelli, Vice Chair

Canadian Environmental Law Association (CELA) / Association canadienne du droit de l'environnement
#301, 130 Spadina Ave., Toronto ON M5V 2L4 Canada
Tel: 416-960-2284; *Fax:* 416-960-9392
millers@cela.ca
www.cela.ca
To advocate for environmental law reform; To act in court or during hearings on behalf of citizens' groups & individuals who would otherwise be unable to afford legal assistance

Canadian Environmental Network (RCEN) / Réseau canadien de l'environnement
39 McArthur Ave., Level 1-1, Ottawa ON K1L 8L7
Tel: 613-728-9810; *Fax:* 613-728-2963
info@cen-rce.org
www.cen-rce.org
Social Media:
www.facebook.com/CanadianEnvironmentalNetwork;
www.twitter.com/#!/RCEN
To promote ecologically sound ways of life; To enhance members' work to restore, protect, & promote a clean & sustainable environment

Canadian Environmental Technology Advancement Corporation - West (CETAC)
Research Park, Univ. of Calgary, 3608 - 33rd St. NW, Calgary AB T2L 2A6 Canada
Tel: 403-777-9595; *Fax:* 403-777-9599
cetac@cetacwest.com
www.cetacwest.com
Established by Environment Canada, CETAC-West is a private sector, not-for-profit corporation committed to helping small & medium-sized enterprises that are engaged in the development & commercialization of new environmental technologies. To this end, it has created a network of technology producers, industry experts, & investment sources.
Joe Lukacs, President/CEO
Margaret Kelly, Vice-President, Alberta

Canadian Institute for Environmental Law & Policy (CIELAP) / Institut canadien du droit et de la politique de l'environnement
#305, 130 Spadina Ave., Toronto ON M5V 2L4 Canada
Tel: 416-923-3529; *Fax:* 416-923-5949
cielap@cielap.org
www.cielap.org
To provide leadership in the research & development of environmental law & policy which promotes the public interest & sustainability

Canadian Institute of Resources Law (CIRL) / Institut canadien du droit des ressources
Murray Fraser Hall, University of Calgary, #3353, 2500 University Dr. NW, Calgary AB T2N 1N4 Canada
Tel: 403-220-3200; *Fax:* 403-282-6182
cirl@ucalgary.ca
www.cirl.ca
To conduct legal & policy research for Canadian federal, provincial, & territorial departments, as well as domestic & international organizations

Canadian Land Reclamation Association (CLRA) / Association canadienne de réhabilitation des sites dégradés (ACRSD)
PO Box 61047, RPO Kensington, Calgary AB T2N 4S6
Tel: 403-289-9435; *Fax:* 403-289-9435
clra@telusplanet.net; aquila7@telusplanet.net (Magazine)
www.clra.ca
To rehabilitate disturbed lands & waterways

The Canadian Network for Environmental Education & Communication (EECOM) / Réseau canadien d'éducation et de communication relatives à l'environnement
c/o 336 Rosedale Ave., Winnipeg MB R3L 1L8 Canada
nswayze@eecom.org
www.eecom.org
To advance environmental learning in Canada; to promote environmental literacy & environmental stewardship; to contribute to a sustainable future
Natalie Swayzer, Executive Director
Grant Gardner, Chair
Rick Wishart, Treasurer

Canadian Parks Partnership (CPP) / Partenaires des parcs canadiens
#360, 1414 - 8th St. SW, Calgary AB T2R 1J6 Canada
Tel: 613-567-0099
nature@canadianparkspartnership.com
To support the overall enhancement of Canada's parks, historic sites & canals system & to foster public awareness, appreciation, understanding of & involvement in the system
Bruce Livingston, Chair

Canadian Peregrine Foundation (CPF)
#214, 1450 O'Connor Dr., Toronto ON M4B 2T8 Canada
Tel: 416-481-1233; *Toll-Free:* 888-709-3944
info@peregrine-foundation.ca
www.peregrine-foundation.ca
The Canadian Peregrine Foundation is a registered charity dedicated to assisting the recovery of the peregrine falcon and other raptors at risk.

Canadian Polystyrene Recycling Alliance (CPRA)
260 Peter St., Port Hope ON L1A 3V6
www.cpracanada.ca
To operate a vertically integrated polystyrene recycling facility to recycle polystyrene into picture frames & mouldings
Sam Alavy, President & Chief Executive Officer

Canadian Society of Environmental Biologists (CSEB) / Société canadienne des biologistes de l'environnement
PO Box 962, Stn. F, Toronto ON M4Y 2N9 Canada
cseb_on@hotmail.com
www.cseb-scbe.org
To further the conservation of natural resources of Canada & to promote the prudent management of these resources so as to minimize adverse environmental effects; to ensure high professional standards in education, research & management related to resources & environment; to advance the education of the public & to protect public interest on matters pertaining to the use of natural resources & the protection & management of the environment; to undertake environmental research & education programs; to assess & evaluate administrative & legislative policies having ecological significance in terms of conservation of resources & quality of the environment; to develop & promote policies that seek to achieve balance among resource management & utilization, protection of the environment & quality of life; to foster liaison among environmental biologists working within governmental, industrial & educational frameworks across Canada

Canadian Water & Wastewater Association (CWWA) / Association canadienne des eaux potables et usées (ACEPU)
#11, 1010 Polytek Rd., Ottawa ON K1J 9H9
Tel: 613-747-0524; *Fax:* 613-747-0523
tdellison@cwwa.ca
www.cwwa.ca
To represent the common interests of Canadian municipal water & wastewater systems to federal & interprovincial bodies

Canadian Water Resources Association (CWRA) / Association canadienne des ressources hydriques (ACRH)
c/o Membership Office, 9 Covus Crt., Ottawa ON K2E 7Z4
Tel: 613-237-9363; *Fax:* 613-594-5190
services@aic.ca
www.cwra.org
To encourage recognition of the high priority & value of water

Canadian Wildlife Federation (CWF) / Fédération canadienne de la faune
350 Michael Cowpland Dr., Kanata ON K2M 2W1 Canada
Tel: 613-599-9594; *Fax:* 613-599-4428
Toll-Free: 800-563-9453
info@cwf-fcf.org
www.cwf-fcf.org
To promote the conservation of fish & wildlife, wildlife habitat & quality aquatic environments; to foster an understanding of natural processes; to ensure adequate stocks of wildlife for the use & enjoyment of all Canadians; to sponsor research; to cooperate with legislators, government & non-government agencies in achieving conservation objectives

Carleton Sustainable Campus Network (CSCN)
Carleton University, #326 UC, 1125 Colonel By Dr., Ottawa ON K1S 5B6 Canada
Tel: 613-520-2757; *Fax:* 613-520-3989
cscn@carleton.ca
www.carleton.ca/cscn
To engage the Carleton University campus as a living laboratory and learning tool in creating a sustainable society.

Carolinian Canada Coalition
Grosvenor Lodge, 1017 Western Rd., London ON N6G 1G5 Canada
Tel: 519-433-7077; *Fax:* 519-913-2449
info@carolinian.org
www.carolinian.org
To promote the protection and conservation of the Carolinian Life Zone of Southwestern Ontario.
Gordon Nelson, Chair

Citizens for a Safe Environment (CSE)
Tel: 416-461-1092
info@csetoronto.org
www.csetoronto.org
To promomote waste management practices that protect the health of Toronto citizens, their communities and the environment.

Citizens' Clearinghouse on Waste Management (CCWM)
17 Major St., Kitchener ON N2H 4R1 Canada
www.citizenswasteinfo.org
To help citizens gain access to information that will help them solve waste management problems in their communities and across Ontario.
John Jackson, Coordinator

Citizens' Environment Watch (CEW)
#204, 147 Spadina Ave., Toronto ON M5V 2L7 Canada
Tel: 647-258-3280; *Fax:* 416-637-2717
info@citizensenvironmentwatch.org
www.citizensenvironmentwatch.org
To provide communities the tools for education, monitoring and influencing positive change and to encourage people to take an active role in restoring and sustaining nature.
Meredith Cochrane, Executive Director

Citizens' Opposed to Paving the Escarpment (COPE)
PO Box 40548, Stn. Upper Brant, Burlington ON L7P 4W1 Canada
mail@cope-nomph.org
www.cope-nomph.org
To preserve the Niagara Escarpment, by ensuring that no new highway corridors are paved across the Niagara Escarpment & that all viable alternatives to the proposed Mid-Peninsula Highway are fully considered

Clean Nova Scotia (CNS)
126 Portland St., Dartmouth NS B2Y 1H8
Tel: 902-420-3474; *Fax:* 902-424-5334
cns@clean.ns.ca
www.clean.ns.ca
Social Media: www.facebook.com/group.php?gid=8509319491
To inspire positive environmental change in Nova Scotia

Coalition on the Niagara Escarpment (CONE)
193 James St. South, Hamilton ON L8P 3A8 Canada
Tel: 905-529-4955; *Fax:* 905-529-9503
cone@niagaraescarpment.org
www.niagaraescarpment.org
CONE is a non-profit alliance of environmental groups, conservation organizations, and concerned citizens and businesses dedicated to the protection of Ontario's Niagara Escarpment.
Robert Patrick, President

Compost Council of Canada / Conseil canadien du compost
16 Northumberland St., Toronto ON M6H 1P7
Tel: 416-535-0240; *Fax:* 416-536-9892
Toll-Free: 877-571-4769
info@compost.org
www.compost.org
Social Media:
www.facebook.com/people/Compost-Council/100001137258465
To advance organics residuals recycling & compost use; To contribute to environmental sustainability
Susan Antler, Executive Director

Conservation Council of New Brunswick (CCNB) / Conseil de la conservation du Nouveau-Brunswick
180 St. John St., Fredericton NB E3B 4A9 Canada
Tel: 506-458-8747; *Fax:* 506-458-1047
info@conservationcouncil.ca
www.conservationcouncil.ca
To generate awareness of the ecological foundations of our quality of life; to promote public policies with respect to the integrity of natural systems & to contribute to a sustainable society; to advocate appropriate remedies to pressing environmental problems such as ground water contamination & hazardous wastes.

Conservation Council of Ontario (CCO) / Conseil de conservation de l'Ontario
215 Spadina Ave., Toronto ON M5T 2C7 Canada
Tel: 416-533-1635
cco@web.ca
www.greenontario.org/cco/index.html
To build a strong province-wide conservation movement

Conservation Ontario
Box 11, 120 Bayview Pkwy., Newmarket ON L3R 4W3
Tel: 905-895-0716; *Fax:* 905-895-0751
info@conservationontario.ca
www.conservation-ontario.on.ca
Social Media:
www.facebook.com/home.php?sk=group_33621230329
To represent & support a network of community-based environmental organizations; To ensure conservation, restoration, & responsible management of Ontario's wetlands, woodlands, & natural habitat

Cumulative Environmental Management Association (CEMA)
Morrison Center, #214, 9914 Morrison St., Fort McMurray AB T9H 4A4 Canada
Tel: 780-799-3947; *Fax:* 780-714-3081
info@cemaonline.ca
www.cemaonline.ca
To study the cumulative environmental effects of industrial development in the region and produce guidelines and management frameworks.
Glen Semenchuk, Executive Director

Ducks Unlimited Canada (DUC) / Canards Illimités Canada
PO Box 1160, Stonewall MB R0C 2Z0
Fax: 204-467-9028
Toll-Free: 800-665-3825
webfoot@ducks.ca; volunteer@ducks.ca; member@ducks.ca
www.ducks.ca
To conserve, restore, & manage wetlands & associated habitats, for the benefit of waterfowl, which in turn provide healthy environments for wildlife & people

Earth Day Canada (EDC) / Jour de la terre Canada
#503, 111 Peter St., Toronto ON M5V 2H1 Canada
Tel: 416-599-1991; *Fax:* 416-599-3100
Toll-Free: 888-283-2784
info@earthday.ca; donate@earthday.ca;
communications@earthday.ca
www.earthday.ca
To improve the state of the environment by motivating & helping Canadians to achieve local solutions
Jed Goldberg, President
Keith Treffry, Director, Communications
Paul Bubelis, Chair

Earth Energy Society of Canada (EESC) / Société canadienne de l'énergie du sol
Fax: 613-822-4987
info@earthenergy.ca
www.earthenergy.ca
To represent the domestic earth energy industry; To promote installations & earth energy technology as an economic & environmental option

Ecology Action Centre (EAC)
2705 Fern Lane, Halifax NS B3K 4L3 Canada
Tel: 902-429-2202; *Fax:* 902-405-3716
info@ecologyaction.ca
www.ecologyaction.ca
Social Media: www.facebook.com/EcologyActionCentre
To act as a voice for Nova Scotia's environment; to build a healthier, more sustainable Nova Scotia.

EcoPerth
2196 Old Brooke Rd., RR#2, Maberry ON K0H 2B0 Canada
Tel: 613-267-6463; *Fax:* 613-268-2907
info@ecoperth.on.ca
www.ecoperth.on.ca
To promote local projects that are environmentally sustainable and economically efficient in the Perth, Ontario area.
Bob Argue, Executive Director

Elsa Wild Animal Appeal of Canada
PO Box 45051, 2482 Yonge St., Toronto ON M4P 3E3 Canada
Tel: 416-489-8862; *Fax:* 416-489-4769
info@elsacanada.com
www.elsacanada.com
To help save endangered wildlife species in Canada

Enviro-Accès Inc.
Place Andrew-Paton, #150, 85, rue Belvédère nord, Sherbrooke QC J1H 4A7 Canada
Tél: 819-823-2230; *Téléc:* 819-823-6632
enviro@enviroaccess.ca
www.enviroaccess.ca
Supporter les petites et moyennes entreprises qui oeuvrent dans le domaine de l'environnement en leur offrant les services professionnels nécessaires au développement de leurs projets et de leurs affaires.
Manon Laporte, Présidente-directrice générale

EnviroLink
PO Box 8102, Pittsburgh PA 15217 USA
www.envirolink.org
To promote a sustainable society by connecting individuals and organizations through communication technologies.

Environmental Careers Organization of Canada / L'Organisation pour les carrières en environnement du Canada
#200, 308 - 11th Ave. SE, Calgary AB T2G 0Y2 Canada
Tel: 403-233-0748; *Fax:* 403-269-9544
info@eco.ca; techsupport@eco.ca
www.eco.ca
To provide services to all participants in the environmental sector, including educators, students, practitioners, & employers
Jon Ogryzlo, Sec.-Treas.
Grant S. Trump, President/CEO
Michael Kerford, Vice-President
Janelle Thomlinson, Director, Marketing & Communications

The Environmental Coalition of PEI
126 Richmond St., Charlottetown PE C1A 1H9 Canada
Tel: 902-566-4696; *Fax:* 902-566-4037
energy@ecopei.ca
www.ecopei.ca
To preserve & enhance the environment for all living things
Kate McDonald, Energy Coordinator

Environmental Education Association of the Yukon (EEAY)
Whitehorse YT Canada
eeyukon@gmail.com
taiga.net/YukonEE
To promote environmental education in the Yukon and foster communication between individuals and groups with and interest in environmental education.

Environmental Health Association of British Columbia (EHABC)
PO Box 30033, Stn. Saanich Centre, Victoria BC V8X 5E1 Canada
Tel: 250-658-2027
www.ehabc.org
To raise awareness within the medical community, educational institutions, and the general public to prevent further cases of environmental sensitivity from occurring.

The Environmental Law Centre (Alberta) Society (ELC)
#800, 10025 - 106 Street, Edmonton AB T5J 1G4 Canada
Tel: 780-424-5099; *Fax:* 780-424-5133
Toll-Free: 800-661-4238
elc@elc.ab.ca
www.elc.ab.ca
To conduct research in environmental & natural resources law, policy & procedure; to educate the public on environmental law; to operate an environmental law information & referral service for the benefit of the public; to monitor relevant municipal, provincial & federal environmental laws, policies & procedures, & make recommendations for reform
Cindy Chiasson, Executive Director

Environmental Managers Association of British Columbia (EMABC)
PO Box 3741, Vancouver BC V6B 3Z8 Canada
Tel: 604-998-2226; *Fax:* 604-998-2226
info@emaofbc.com
www.emaofbc.com
To encourage education, share knowledge among members and create a forum for environmental management issues in the

industrial, commercial and institutional sectors, serve as a key resource of environmental information for members and explore existing and emerging environmental issues.
Patrick Novak, President
Krista Hennebury, Executive Director

Environmental Services Association of Alberta (ESAA)
#102, 2528 Ellwood Dr. SW, Edmonton AB T6X 0A9
Tel: 780-429-6363; *Fax:* 780-429-4249
Toll-Free: 800-661-9278
info@esaa.org
www.esaa.org
To act as the voice of Alberta's environment industry
Craig Robertson, President
Randy Neumann, Secretary
Skip Kerr, Treasurer
Joe Barraclough, Director, Industry & Government Relations
Joe Chowaniec, Director, Program & Event Development

Environmental Services Association of Nova Scotia (ESANS)
Woodside Industrial Park, #211-2, 1 Research Dr., Dartmouth NS B2Y 4M9 Canada
Tel: 902-463-3538; *Fax:* 902-466-6889
contact@esans.ca
www.esans.ca
ESANS is a province-wide business organization dedicated to the promotion of environmental products, services & organizations within the environmental industry.
Adam Cooney, P.Eng., President

Environmental Youth Alliance (EYA)
PO Box 3601, Stn. Terminal, #517, 119 Pender St. West, Vancouver BC V6B 1S5 Canada
Tel: 604-689-4446; *Fax:* 604-689-4242
info@eya.ca
www.eya.ca
To save the earth through non-violent means; to promote change by educating people on our interconnectedness with Nature & involving youth in action projects; to create a youth movement that is activist-oriented & works towards environmental respect & protection.

Environnement jeunesse
454, rue Laurier est, Montréal QC H2J 1E7 Canada
Tél: 514-252-3016; *Téléc:* 514-254-5873
Ligne sans frais: 866-377-3016
infoenjeu@enjeu.qc.ca
www.enjeu.qc.ca
Promouvoir la conservation et l'amélioration de la qualité de l'environnement; développer chez les jeunes les qualités favorisant leur implication sociale.
Jérôme Normand, Directeur général

Evergreen
355 Adelaide St. West, 5th Fl., Toronto ON M5V 1S2 Canada
Tel: 416-596-1495; *Fax:* 416-596-1443
Toll-Free: 888-426-3138
info@evergreen.ca; donate@evergreen.ca
www.evergreen.ca
To bring communities & nature together for the benefit of both; To create sustaining, healthy, dynamic outdoor spaces by engaging people & encouraging local stewardship
Geoff Cape, Executive Director
Matthew Church, Director, Marketing & Communications

FaunENord
313, 3e Rue, 2e étage, Chibougamau QC G8P 1N4 Canada
Tél: 418-748-4441; *Téléc:* 418-748-1110
www.faunenord.icr.qc.ca
Une entreprise vouée à la promotion & à l'aménagement durable des ressources fauniques & des écosystèmes
Justine Desmeules

Fédération des associations pour la protection de l'environnement des lacs inc. (FAPEL)
CP 51128, Succ. Centre, Montréal QC H1N 3T8 Canada
Tél: 514-254-5361
fapel@fapel.org
fapel.org

Fédération québécoise des chasseurs et pêcheurs
#109, 6780, 1re av, Québec QC G1H 2W8 Canada
Tél: 418-626-6858; *Téléc:* 418-622-6168
Ligne sans frais: 888-523-2863
info@fedecp.qc.ca
www.fqf.qc.ca
Contribuer, dans le respect de la faune et de ses habitats, à la gestion du développement et à la perpétuation de la chasse et de la pêche comme activités traditionnelles et sportives

First Nations Environmental Network
PO Box 394, Tofino BC V0R 2Z0 Canada
Tel: 250-726-5265; *Fax:* 250-725-2357
councilfire@hotmail.com
www.fnen.org
The First Nations Environmental Network is a circle of First Nations people committed to protecting, defending, and restoring the balance of all life by honouring traditional Indigenous values and the path of our ancestors. We encourage the work of protecting, defending and healing Mother Earth. We desire and need to link grassroots Indigenous people nationally and internationally to support each other on environmental struggles and concerns. We are obligated to leave footprints for our children to follow by striving to live our life with traditional values.
Steve Lawson, Coordinator

Fondation de la faune du Québec (FFQ)
#420, 1175, av Lavigerie, Québec QC G1V 4P1 Canada
Tél: 418-644-7926; *Téléc:* 418-643-7655
Ligne sans frais: 877-639-0742
ffq@fondationdelafaune.qc.ca
www.fondationdelafaune.qc.ca
Promouvoir la conservation et la mise en valeur de la faune et de son habitat
André Martin, Président-directeur général

FortWhyte Alive
1961 McCreary Rd., Winnipeg MB R3P 2K9 Canada
Tel: 204-989-8355; *Fax:* 204-895-4700
info@fortwhyte.org
www.fortwhyte.org
Social Media:
www.facebook.com/pages/FortWhyte-Alive/471614835647?ref=ts
FortWhyte Alive is dedicated to providing programming, natural settings and facilities for environmental education and outdoor recreation. In so doing, FortWhyte promotes awareness and understanding of the natural world and actions leading to sustainable living.
Bill Elliott, President/CEO

Friends of Red Hill Valley
PO Box 61536, Hamilton ON L8T 5A1 Canada
Tel: 905-381-0240; *Fax:* 905-548-6317
redhill@hwcn.org
www.hwcn.org/forhv
To protect & enhance the Red Hill Valley in Hamilton, Ontario

Friends of the Earth Canada (FoE) / Les Ami(e)s de la Terre Canada
#300, 260 St. Patrick St., Ottawa ON K1N 5K5 Canada
Tel: 613-241-0085; *Fax:* 613-241-7998
Toll-Free: 888-385-4444
foe@foecanada.org
www.foecanada.org
To serve as a national voice for the environment, working with others to inspire the renewal of our communities & the earth, through research, education, advocacy & cooperation

Friends of the Greenbelt Foundation
#201, 69 Scollard St., Toronto ON M5R 1G2 Canada
Tel: 416-960-0001; *Fax:* 416-960-0030
info@greenbelt.ca
www.greenbelt.ca/the-foundation
The Foundation was created to help foster the Greenbelt's living countryside by nurturing and supporting activities that preserve its environmental and agricultural integrity.
Burkhard Mausberg, President

Green Action Centre (RCM)
303 Portage Ave., 3rd Fl., Winnipeg MB R3B 2B4 Canada
Tel: 204-925-3777; *Fax:* 204-942-4207
Toll-Free: 866-394-8880
info@resourceconservation.mb.ca
www.resourceconservation.mb.ca
Social Media:
www.facebook.com/group.php?gid=134760813229244
To promote ecological sustainability by developing alternatives to currently unsustainable practices; our principal activity is environmental education; our partners & clients include businesses, schools, non-profit groups, governments, recyclers, home gardeners & general public
Randall McQuaker, Executive Director

Greenpeace Canada
33 Cecil St., Toronto ON M5T 1N1 Canada
Tel: 416-597-8408; *Fax:* 416-597-8422
Toll-Free: 800-320-7183
supporter.ca@greenpeace.org
www.greenpeacecanada.org
Social Media: facebook.com/greenpeace.canada
Greenpeace is an independent, non-profit organization best known for non-violent direct actions to raise awareness on issues such as biodiversity, pollution of the Earth, nuclear threats & disarmament; it brings public opinion to bear on decisions makers. Public protest is only one of many Greenpeace strategies; it conducts scientific, economic & political research, publicizes environmental problems, recommends environmentally sound solutions & lobbies for change.

Greenspace Alliance of Canada's Capital
PO Box 55085, 240 Sparks St., Ottawa ON K1P 1A1 Canada
greenspace@greenspace-alliance.ca
www.greenspace-alliance.ca
To preserve green spaces in the National Capital area.
Cheryl Doran, Chair

Hamilton Industrial Environmental Association (HIEA)
PO Box 35545, Hamilton ON L8H 7S6 Canada
Tel: 905-561-4432
info@hiea.org
www.hiea.org
To improve the local environment - air, land and water - through joint and individual activities, and by partnering with the community to enhance future understanding of environmental issues and help establish priorities for action.
Jim Stirling, Chair

Harmony Foundation of Canada / Fondation Harmonie du Canada
PO Box 50022, #15, 1594 Fairfield Rd., Victoria BC V8S 1G1 Canada
Tel: 250-380-3001; *Fax:* 250-380-0887
harmony@islandnet.com
www.harmonyfdn.ca
To encourage development which is socially & environmentally sustainable; To strive towards ecological stability, long-term prosperity, & social harmony

Hope for Wildlife Society
PO Box 1, 5909 Hwy. 207, #14 R.R.#2, Head of Chezzetcook NS B0J 1N0 Canada
Tel: 902-452-3339
info@hopeforwildlife.net
www.hopeforwildlife.net
Specializing in the care, treatment and rehabilitation of injured or orphaned native fur bearing mammals, sea birds and songbirds both indigenous to the Nova Scotia area as well as non-indigenous species and pets.
Hope Swinimer, CVPM, Founder & Director

Institut de recherche en biologie végétale (IRBV) / Plant Biology Research Institute (PBRI)
4101, rue Sherbrooke est, Montréal QC H1X 2B2 Canada
Tél: 514-343-2121
irbv@irbv.umontreal.ca
www.irbv.umontreal.ca
To develop a centre of excellence in plant biology; both in fundamental research and its applicaitons; train students in plant biology at the master, doctoral, and post-doctoral levels; further training and knowledge of its researchers and technical personnel; promote the technological transfer of its scientific research results to users; provide complementary services to the community in fields relevant to plant biology, where expertise in the field is lacking.
Anne Bruneau, Directrice

Institute for Sustainable Energy, Economy and Environment Student's Association (ISEEESA)
Scrubfield Hall, #199B, 2500 University Dr., Calgary AB T2N 1N4 Canada
info@iseeesa.ca
www.iseeesa.ca
To promote and create initiatives that reflect the growing movement to obtain a cleaner energy supply, healthy environment, and efficient economy.
Mark Blackwell, President

International Council for the Exploration of the Sea (ICES)
H.C. Andersens Blvd. 44-46, Copenhagen VDK-1553 Denmark
info@ices.dk
www.ices.dk
To coordinate research & monitor activities to understand the marine environment & resources & man's impact upon them, including the identification of priority marine contaminants, their distribution, transport & effects; to provide advice regarding marine resources & pollution to member governments & international regulatory commissions; to publish & disseminate the results of research
Gerd Hubold, General Secretary
Sylvain Paradis, ICES Delegate, Canada
Michael M. Sinclair, ICES Delegate, Canada

International Institute for Sustainable Development (IISD) / Institut international du développement durable (IIDD)
161 Portage Ave. East, 6th Fl., Winnipeg MB R3B 0Y4 Canada
Tel: 204-958-7700; *Fax:* 204-958-7710
info@iisd.ca
www.iisd.org
To promote sustainable development in decision-making in Canada & abroad by undertaking sustainable development research, advising government, business & organizations, analyzing & reporting on issues & events, & publishing & disseminating sustainable development information. Offices in Winnipeg, Ottawa, New York, & Geneva.
David Runnalls, President/CEO
William H. Glanville, Vice-President & COO

Jasper Environmental Association (JEA)
PO Box 2198, Jasper AB T0E 1E0 Canada
Tel: 780-852-4152; *Fax:* 780-852-4152
jea2@telus.net
www.jasperenvironmental.org
To support Parks Canada in administering Jasper National Park in accordance with Canadian legislation, Parks Canada principles and policies and the wishes of the Canadian public.

Manitoba Eco-Network Inc. (MEN) / Réseau écologique du Manitoba inc.
#3, 303 Portage Ave., Winnipeg MB R3B 2B4 Canada
Tel: 204-947-6511; *Fax:* 204-989-8476
info@mbeconetwork.org
www.mbeconetwork.org
To educate the public on environmental issues; to conduct research on environmental issues; to facilitate communications between environmental groups & the general public

Manitoba Environment Officers Association Inc. (MEOA)
147 Norcross Cres., Winnipeg MB R3X 1J2 Canada
meoa@mts.net
www.meoa.ca
To enhance the public health and safety of Manitobans and to protect, maintain and rehabilitate Manitoba's environment ecosystems through the diligent duties of educated Environment Officers and to obtain for Environment Officers continued education and recognition of their efforts.
Bill Barr, President

Manitoba Environmental Industries Association Inc. (MEIA)
#100, 62 Albert St., Winnipeg MB R3B 1E9
Tel: 204-783-7090; *Fax:* 204-783-6501
admin@meia.mb.ca
www.meia.mb.ca
To assist members in the business of the environment; To connect business, government, & stakeholders with environmental issues
John Fjeldsted, Executive Director
Vaughn Bullough, President
Rosemary Deans, Coordinator, Education & Training
Deb Tardiff, Coordinator, Education & Training
Sheldon McLeod, Secretary
John Pikel, Treasurer

Manitoba Wildlife Federation (MWF)
70 Stevenson Rd., Winnipeg MB R3H 0W7
Tel: 204-633-5967; *Fax:* 204-632-5200
info@mwf.mb.ca; vpHunting@mwf.mb.ca; vpPrograms@mwf.mb.ca
www.mwf.mb.ca
To devote members to the causes of conservation & the participation in the wise use of natural resources; To encourage the propagation of game & fish; To promote the enforcement of game laws; To cooperate with government departments
Reid Woods, President
Lori Thomas, Director, Administration
Rachelle Aime, Vice-President, Education
Ken MacMaster, Vice-President, Membership
Larry Millan, Vice-President, Environment & Habitat
Reg Wiebe, Coordinator, Hunter Education

Municipal Waste Association (MWA)
#100, 127 Wyndham St. North, Guelph ON N1H 4E9 Canada
Tel: 519-823-1990; *Fax:* 519-823-0084
carrie@municipalwaste.ca
www.municipalwaste.ca
To expedite the flow of information regarding 3R programs to municipalities & other community & government groups; to act as an information forum for municipal recycling coordinators; allows member municipalities to act as a unified voice in promoting progressive waste reduction & recycling alternatives
Vivian De Giovanni, Executive Director
Sherry Arcaro, Chair

National Energy Conservation Association Inc. (NECA) / Association nationale pour la conservation de l'énergie
250 McDermot Ave., Winnipeg MB R3B 0S5
Tel: 204-956-5888; *Fax:* 204-956-5819
Toll-Free: 800-263-5974
neca@neca.ca
www.neca.ca
To promote energy efficiency in the building sector; To work towards a sustainable future
Ryan Dalgleish, Contact, Business Development

The Nature Conservancy of Canada (NCC) / Société canadienne pour la conservation de la nature
#400, 36 Eglinton Ave. West, Toronto ON M4R 1A1
Tel: 416-932-3202; *Fax:* 416-932-3208
Toll-Free: 800-465-0029
nature@natureconservancy.ca
www.natureconservancy.ca
Social Media: www.twitter.com/NatureConsCDA
To protect Canada's biodiversity through long-term stewardship & property securement

New Brunswick Environment Industry Association (NBEIA) / L'Association des industries de l'environnement du Nouveau-Brunswick (AIENB)
PO Box 637, Stn. A, Fredericton NB E3B 5B3 Canada
Tel: 506-455-0212; *Fax:* 506-452-0213
nbeia@nbnet.nb.ca
www.nbeia.nb.ca
To promote the growth of environmental business in New Brunswick
Pierre Landry, President
Eric Cook, Secretary-Treasurer

New Brunswick Environmental Network (NBEN) / Réseau environnemental du Nouveau-Brunswick (RENB)
167 Creek Rd., Waterford NB E4E 4L7
Tel: 506-433-6101; *Fax:* 506-433-6111
nben@nben.ca
www.nben.ca
Social Media: www.facebook.com/pages/NBEN-RENB/134259049952351
To strengthen the environmental movement throughout New Brunswick; To promote ecologically sound ways of life
Mary Ann Coleman, Executive Director
Joanna Brown, Coordinator, Yourth Outreach & Events
Raissa Marks, Coordinator, Education & Outreach Programs

New Brunswick Wildlife Federation (NBWF) / Fédération de la faune du Nouveau-Brunswick
576, rue Principale, St. Leonard NB E7E 2H5 Canada
www.nbwildlifefederation.org
To foster sound management & wise use of the renewable & non-renewable natural resources of New Brunswick; to assist & encourage the enforcement of those game laws which are in keeping with the objectives of the Federation & to strive for better management & game laws where & when necessary; to educate membership & the public, with particular emphasis upon conservation & safety; to represent the interests & concerns of New Brunswick sportsmen; to cooperate with government departments & all related groups, where interests are mutual.

Newfoundland & Labrador Environmental Industry Association (NEIA)
Parsons Bldg., #101, 90 O'Leary Ave., St. John's NL A1B 2C7 Canada
Tel: 709-772-3333; *Fax:* 709-772-3213
info@neia.org
www.neia.org
To promote the growth & development of the environmental industry of Newfoundland & Labrador; to promote ethical behavior & high standards for environmental products & services; to provide a strong, unified voice toward all private sector, government & non-profit entities involved in the Newfoundland environmental industry.
Linda Bartlett, Executive Director
Bill Scott, President

Newfoundland & Labrador Wildlife Federation (NWLF)
15 Conran St., St. John's NL A1E 5L8
Tel: 709-368-6180
ward.sampson@nf.sympatico.ca
www.nlwf.ca
To foster awareness & enjoyment of the natural world; To promote the sustainable use of natural resources; To protect wildlife & its habitat through conservation & effective wildlife management

North American Recycled Rubber Association (NARRA)
#24, 1621 McEwen Dr., Whitby ON L1N 9A5 Canada
Tel: 905-433-7769; *Fax:* 905-433-0905
narra@oix.com
www.recycle.net/recycle/assn/narra
The Association provides a unified voice, as well as a communication network & research facility, for issues of concern to those involved in rubber recycling across North America.
Diane Sarracini, Office Manager

Nova Scotia Environmental Network (NSEN)
3115 Veith St., Halifax NS B3K 3G9
Tel: 902-454-6846; *Fax:* 902-453-3633
nsen@cen-rce.org; board_nsen@cen-rce.org
www.nsen.ca
To conserve & enhance the natural environment; To achieve a sustainable future for Nova Scotia; To connect environmental & health organizations

Nova Scotia Nature Trust (NSNT)
PO Box 2202, 2085 Maitland St., Halifax NS B3J 3C4 Canada
Tel: 902-425-5263; *Fax:* 902-429-5263
Toll-Free: 877-434-5263
nature@nsnt.ca
www.nsnt.ca
To protect Nova Scotia's outstanding natural legacy through land conservation.
Nil d'Entremont, President
Bonnie Sutherland, Executive Director

Oak Ridges Moraine Foundation (ORMF)
The Gate House, 13990 Dufferin St. North, King City ON L7B 1B3 Canada
Tel: 905-833-5733; *Fax:* 905-833-8379
support@ormf.com
www.ormf.com
To provide support and encouragement for activities that preserve, protect, and restore the environmental integrity of the Oak Ridges Moraine and support a trail along it.
Kim Gavine, Executive Director

Offshore Energy Environmental Research Association (OEER)
Bank of Montreal Building, PO Box 2664, #400, 5151 George St., Halifax NS B3J 3P7 Canada
Tel: 902-424-8479; *Fax:* 902-424-0528
Toll-Free: 888-257-8688
oeer@offshoreenergyresearch.ca
www.offshoreenergyresearch.ca
To build research capacity in Nova Scotia and to assess the potential impacts of: petroleum exploration, development and production and renewable energy technologies (ocean currents, wind, tides and waves) on the marine environment.
Wayne St-Amour, Executive Director

ONEIA - Ontario Environment Industry Association
2395 Speakman Drive, Mississauga ON L5K 1B3 Canada
Tel: 416-531-7884; *Fax:* 905-855-0406
info@oneia.ca
www.oneia.ca
To promote the growth of environment business in Ontario
Shai Spetgang, Manager, Membership Recruitment and Sponsor Relations
Alex Gill, Executive Director

Ontario Environment Industry Association (ONEIA)
#218, 330 Adelaide St. West, Toronto ON M5V 1R4 Canada
Tel: 416-531-7884
info@oneia.ca
www.oneia.ca
To represent the interests of the environmental industry in Ontario; To promote environmental business to industry & government in Ontario
Alex Gill, Executive Director

Ontario Environmental Network (OEN)
PO Box 1412, Stn. Main, North Bay ON P1B 8K6
Tel: 705-840-2888; *Fax:* 705-840-5862
oen@oen.ca
www.oen.ca
To encourage discussions of ways to protect the environment; To increase environmental awareness throughout Ontario; To serve the environmental non-profit, non-governmental community in Ontario

Ontario Federation of Anglers & Hunters (OFAH)
PO Box 2800, 4601 Gutheir Drive, Peterborough ON K9J 8L5 Canada
Tel: 705-748-6324; *Fax:* 705-748-9577
ofah@ofah.org
www.ofah.org

To save & defend from waste the natural resources of Ontario, its soils, minerals, air, water, forests & wildlife

Ontario Pollution Control Equipment Association (OPCEA)
PO Box 137, Midhurst ON L0L 1X0
Tel: 705-725-0917; *Fax:* 705-725-1068
opcea@opcea.com
www.opcea.com
To assist members in the promotion of their services & equipment in Ontario

Ontario Steelheaders
PO Box 604, Brantford ON N3T 5T3 Canada
president@ontariosteelheaders.ca
www.ontariosteelheaders.ca
To improve access and habitat for migratory rainbow trout, provide young rainbow trout with suitable nursery habitat, provide relevent and appropriate input to government, agencies and other organizations, and to educate members and the public on relevent issues, conservation practises and proper angling techniques.

Ontario Streams
50 Bloomington Rd. West, Aurora ON L4G 3G8 Canada
Tel: 905-713-7399; *Fax:* 905-713-7361
www.ontariostreams.on.ca
To promote the conservation & rehabilitation of streams & wetlands, through education & community involvement
Doug Forder, M.Sc, Field Supervisor

Ontario Waste Management Association (OWMA) / Société ontarienne de gestion des déchets
#3, 2005 Clark Blvd., Brampton ON L6T 5P8
Tel: 905-791-9500; *Fax:* 905-791-9514
contact@owma.org
www.owma.org
To act as the voice of the private sector waste industry in Ontario; To protect the enviroment by properly managing waste & recyclable materials

Ottawa Duck Club (ODC)
841 Kingsmere Ave., Ottawa ON K2A 3J8 Canada
www.ottawaduckclub.com
To actively improve the nesting habitat for waterfowl and other birds along the Ottawa River.
Bill Bower, President

Ottawa Riverkeeper
#2, 379 Danforth Ave., Ottawa ON K2A 0E1 Canada
Tel: 613-321-1120; *Fax:* 613-822-5258
Toll-Free: 888-953-3737
www.ottawariverkeeper.ca
To protect and promote the ecological health and diversity of the Ottawa River and its tributaries.
Meredith Brown, Executive Director

Peace Valley Environment Association (PVEA)
PO Box 6062, Fort St John BC V1J 4H6 Canada
pvea@shaw.ca
www.peacevalley.ca
To protect and defend the natural environment of the Peace Valley area of British Columbia

The Pembina Institute
219 - 19 St. NW, Calgary AB T2N 2H9 Canada
Tel: 403-269-3344; *Fax:* 403-269-3377
www.pembina.org
To develop & promote public policy & educational programs which protect the environment & encourage environmentally sound resource management strategies; to implement a conserver society
Ed Whittingham, Executive Director

Pitch-In Canada (PIC) / Passons à l'action Canada
PO Box 45011, Stn. Ocean Park RPO, White Rock BC V4A 9L1
Fax: 604-535-4653
Toll-Free: 877-474-8244
pitch-in@pitch-in.ca
www.pitch-in.ca
To improve communities & the envionment by providing programs to reduce, re-use, recycle, & properly manage & dispose waste
Misha Cook, BA, Executive Director
Lisa Davis, Project Coordinator

The Pollution Probe Foundation (PPF)
#402, 625 Church St., Toronto ON M4Y 2G1 Canada
Tel: 416-926-1907; *Fax:* 416-926-1601
pprobe@pollutionprobe.org
www.pollutionprobe.org
A registered Canadian charity which seeks to define environmental problems through research; to promote understanding through education & to press for practical solutions through advocacy. The organization is non-partison & works collaboratively with government agencies, other non-profit organizations, & private business to engage key issues & find solutions. Offices in Toronto & Ottawa

Prince Edward Island Eco-Net (PEIEN)
126 Richmond St., Charlottetown PE C1A 1H9 Canada
Tel: 902-566-4170; *Fax:* 902-566-4037
peien@isn.net
www.peieconet.org
Social Media: www.facebook.com/peieconet?ref=ts
To promote communication & cooperation among ENGO's (Environmental NGO's) & between ENGO's & governments; to provide referral services; to coordinate workshops & conferences; to provide consultations; to publish & distribute information
Susan Hawkins, Executive Director

Prince Edward Island Wildlife Federation
#103B, 420 University Ave., Charlottetown PE C1A 7Z5 Canada
Tel: 902-892-3332; *Fax:* 902-892-3334
peiwfft@pei.aibn.com
To foster sound management & wise use of the renewable resources of PEI; to assist & encourage the enforcement of those game laws which are in keeping with the objectives of the Federation & to strive for better management & game laws where & when necessary; to cooperate with government departments & related groups where interests are mutual; to educate membership & the public, with particular emphasis upon conservation & safety; to represent the interests & concerns of PEI sportsmen

Recycling Council of Alberta (RCA)
PO Box 23, Bluffton AB T0C 0M0 Canada
Tel: 403-843-6563; *Fax:* 403-843-4156
info@recycle.ab.ca
www.recycle.ab.ca
To promote & facilitate waste reduction, recycling, & resource conservation in Alberta
Philippa Wagner, President
Olena Juzkiw, Secretary
Paula Kuryk, Treasurer

Recycling Council of British Columbia (RCBC)
#10, 119 West Pender St., Vancouver BC V6B 1S5
Tel: 604-683-6009; *Fax:* 604-683-7255
Toll-Free: 800-667-4321
rcbc@rcbc.bc.ca; hotline@rcbc.bc.ca
www.rcbc.bc.ca
Social Media:
www.facebook.com/home.php?sk=group_10340005498
To promote the principles of zero waste; To decrease British Columbia's environmental footprint
Brock Macdonald, Executive Director
Anna Rochelle, Director, Finance
Harvinder Gill, Manager, Information Services
Ben Ramos, Manager, Member & Technology Services

Recycling Council of Ontario (RCO) / Conseil du recyclage de l'Ontario
#225, 215 Spadina Ave., Toronto ON M5T 2C7
Tel: 416-657-2797; *Toll-Free:* 888-501-9637
rco@rco.on.ca
www.rco.on.ca
Social Media: www.twitter.com/#!/RCOntario
To minimize impact on the environment by eliminating waste
Jo-Anne St. Godard, Executive Director
Diane Blackburn, Manager, Events
David Hanson, Program Manager, Waste Diversion Certification Program
Sarah Mills, Manager, Special Projects & Take Back the Light
Lucy Robinson, Manager, Member Relations
Catherine Leighton, Coordinator, Special Projects
Andrew Reeves, Coordinator, Outreach & Communications

Réseau environnement
#220, 911, rue Jean Talon est, Montréal QC H2R 1V5 Canada
Tél: 514-270-7110; *Téléc:* 514-270-7154
info@reseau-environnement.com
www.reseau-environnement.com
Regrouper des entreprises spécialisées dans la gestion des déchets commerciaux, industriels et des services municipaux reliés à l'environnement; assurer l'avancement des technologies et de la science, la promotion des expertises et le soutien des activités en environnement
Josée Méthot, Directrice générale

Réseau québécois des groupes écologistes (RQGE)
1557-A, avenue Papineau, Montréal QC H2K 4H7 Canada
Tél: 514-392-0096
info@rqge.qc.ca
www.rqge.qc.ca
Réseau de services et d'information pour les groupes écologiques du Québec; aider les groupes à communiquer entre eux

Resource Efficient Agricultural Production (REAP Canada)
Glenaladale House, PO Box 125, 21111, ch Lakeshore, Sainte-Anne-de-Bellevue QC H9X 3V9 Canada
Tel: 514-398-7743; *Fax:* 514-398-7972
info@reap-canada.com
www.reap-canada.com
To improve farm profits & productivity while minimizing adverse health & environmental effects

Rideau Environmental Action League (REAL)
PO Box 1061, Smiths Falls ON K7A 5A5 Canada
Tel: 613-283-9500; *Fax:* 613-283-9500
info@realaction.ca
www.realaction.ca
To conduct community-wide environmental projects and promote environmental improvements within the Town of Smiths Falls and Lanark, Leeds and Grenville Counties.
Barb Hicks, President

Rideau Valley Conservation Authority (RVCA)
PO Box 599, 3889 Rideau Valley Dr., Manotick ON K4M 1A5 Canada
Tel: 613-692-3571; *Fax:* 613-692-0831
Toll-Free: 800-267-3504
postmaster@rvca.ca
www.rvca.ca
To advocate for clean water, natural shorelines and sustainable land use throughout the Rideau Valley watershed.
Mary A. Bryden, Chair
Charles Billington, Executive Director

Sackville Rivers Association (SRA)
PO Box 45071, Sackville NS B4E 2Z6 Canada
Tel: 902-865-9238
sackvillerivers@ns.sympatico.ca
www.sackvillerivers.ns.ca
To promote the preservation, restoration and enhancement of the Sackville River Watershed.
Walter N. Regan, President

Sarnia-Lambton Environmental Association (SLEA)
1489 London Rd., Sarnia ON N7S 1P6 Canada
Tel: 519-332-2010; *Fax:* 519-332-2015
www.sarniaenvironment.com
To monitor ambient environmental conditions to assess the impact of its members on the local environment's air, water and soil.
Dean Edwardson, General Manager

Saskatchewan Eco-Network (SEN)
#203, 115 - 2 Ave. North, Saskatoon SK S7K 2B1
Tel: 306-652-1275; *Fax:* 306-665-2128
sen@link.ca
www.econet.sk.ca
To provide educational activities to develop an awareness of conservation & enhancement of the environment

Saskatchewan Environmental Industry & Managers' Association (SEIMA)
#113, 2505 - 11th Ave., Regina SK S4P 0K6
Tel: 306-543-1567; *Fax:* 306-543-1568
info@seima.sk.ca
www.seima.sk.ca
To act as the voice of practitioners in Saskatchewan's environmental industry on environmental matters; To promote responsible environmental management in the province; To develop the environmental industry in Saskatchewan
Lloyd Saul, President
Greg Kuntz, Vice-President
Kathleen Livingston, Executive Director & COO
Jackie Presnell, Secretary
Fred Antunes, Treasurer
Kevin Marpole, Manager, Environmental Innovations
Robbi Humble, Coordinator, Green Team

Saskatchewan Environmental Society (SES)
PO Box 1372, #203, 115 - 2nd Ave. North, Saskatoon SK S7K 3N9
Tel: 306-665-1915; *Fax:* 306-665-2128
info@environmentalsociety.ca
www.environmentalsociety.ca
The Society works to maintain the integrity of Saskatchewan's forests, farmlands and natural prairie landscapes; protect the

atmosphere, and promote energy conservation and the development of renewable energy resources; and build sustainable communities, responsible waste management, and enhanced water quality in the province's lakes and rivers.

Saskatchewan Soil Conservation Association (SSCA)
PO Box 1360, Indian Head SK S0G 2K0
Tel: 306-695-4233; *Fax:* 306-695-4236
Toll-Free: 800-213-4287
info@ssca.ca
www.ssca.ca
To improve the land & environment; To increase public awareness of soil conservation; To promote conservation production systems to Saskatchewan producers
Blair McClinton, P.Ag., Executive Manager
Marilyn Martens, Office Manager

Saskatchewan Waste Reduction Council (SWRC)
203 Idylwyld Dr. South, Saskatoon SK S7M 1L6 Canada
Tel: 306-931-3242; *Fax:* 306-665-2128
info@saskwastereduction.ca
www.saskwastereduction.ca
To help Saskatchewan & its people attain the environmental, economic & cultural benefits that come from reducing waste; to establish an information & education network for all groups interested in waste reduction; to provide accurate, balanced information on waste reduction, with particular emphasis on municipal solid waste & dangerous waste goods; to encourage all sectors to begin reducing waste in all areas of their lives; to encourage policy development, legislation & research on reducing waste in Saskatchewan

Saskatchewan Wildlife Federation (SWF)
9 Lancaster Rd., Moose Jaw SK S6J 1M8
Tel: 306-692-8812; *Fax:* 306-692-4370
Toll-Free: 877-793-9453
sask.wildlife@sasktel.net
www.swf.sk.ca
Social Media:
www.facebook.com/pages/Saskatchewan-Wildlife-Federation/17 8255362147
To promote the wise use & management of natural resources in Saskatchewan
Darrell Crabbe, Executive Director
Marilee Herone, Manager, Office
Maureen Horrocks, Coordinator, Communications
Jim Kroshus, Coordinator, Habitat Trust Land
Adam Matichuk, Coordinator, Fisheries Project
JeanAnne Prysliak, Coordinator, Education Program

Sea Shepherd Conservation Society (SSCS)
PO Box 48446, Vancouver BC V7X 1A2 Canada
Tel: 604-688-7325
canada@seashepherd.org
www.seashepherd.org
Social Media:
www.facebook.com/seashepherdconservationsociety
Investigates & documents violations of international laws, regulations & treaties protecting marine wildlife species; involved with the enforcement of these laws when there is no enforcement by national governments or international regulatory organizations

SEEDS Foundation
#400, 144 - 4th Ave. SW., Calgary AB T2P 3N4 Canada
Tel: 403-221-0835; *Fax:* 403-221-0876
Toll-Free: 800-661-8751
seeds@telusplanet.net
www.seedsfoundation.ca
Social Media:
www.facebook.com/pages/SEEDS-Foundation/11702119164813 3
To provide educational support materials & professional assistance to teachers in the area of energy, environment & sustainable development; to work toward the development of a society which understands & is committed to actions leading to wise stewardship of resources, resource use & the environment

Seventh Generation Community Projects
c/o Trucker House Renewal Centre, #155, 99 Fifth Ave., Ottawa ON K1S 5P5 Canada
Tel: 613-446-2117
seventhgeneration@tuckerhouse.ca
www.seventhgeneration.ca
Seventh Generation Community Projects promotes integrated sustainable living practices in the greater Ottawa area by hosting events, creating resources, networking, and supporting green businesses.
Scott McKenzie, Contact

Severn Sound Environmental Association (SSEA)
67 Fourth St., Midland ON L4R 3S9 Canada
Tel: 705-527-5166; *Fax:* 705-527-5167
www.severnsound.ca
To forge cooperative initiatives to address environmental issues by planning, designing, arranging funding and implementing environmental projects and promoting a sustainable Severn Sound community.
Keith Sherman, Executive Director

Sierra Club of British Columbia (SCBC)
#302, 733 Johnson St., Victoria BC V8W 3L7 Canada
Tel: 250-386-5255; *Fax:* 250-386-4453
info@sierraclub.bc.ca
www.sierraclub.bc.ca
Social Media:
www.facebook.com/pages/Sierra-Club-BC/136350861428
To explore, enjoy & protect the country's forests, waters, wildlife & wilderness

Sierra Club of Canada (SCC) / Sierre club du Canada
#412, 1 Nicholas St., Ottawa ON K1N 7B7
Tel: 613-241-4611; *Fax:* 613-241-2292
Toll-Free: 888-810-4204
info@sierraclub.ca
www.sierraclub.ca
Social Media: www.facebook.com/sierraclubcanada
To develop a diverse, well-trained grassroots network, working to protect the integrity of our global ecosystems; To focus on five overriding threats: loss of animal & plant species, deterioration of the planet's oceans & atmosphere, the ever-growing presence of toxic chemicals in all living things, destruction of our remaining wilderness, spiralling population growth & overconsumption
John Bennett, Executive Director
Anowara Baqi, CFO
Tania Beriau, Development Director
Daniel Spence, Director, Communications

Sierra Club of Canada - Ontario Chapter
#102, 24 Mercer St., Toronto ON M5V 1H3 Canada
Tel: 416-960-9606; *Fax:* 416-960-0020
info@sierraclub.on.ca
www.sierraclub.on.ca

Sierra Club of Canada - Prairie Chapter
6328 - 104 St., Edmonton AB T6H 2K9 Canada
Tel: 780-439-1160; *Fax:* 780-437-3932
prairie.chapter@sierraclub.ca
www.sierraclub.ca/prairie/
Program areas: energy; health communities; protecting biodiversity; training & support
Lindsay Telfer, Chapter Director

Small Water Users Association of BC
4167 Highway 3A, Nelson BC V1L 6N1 Canada
Tel: 250-825-4308
smallwaterusers@shaw.ca
www.smallwaterusers.com
The Small Water Users Association of BC is a new non-profit society dedicated to serving the interests of small water systems (1 to 300 connections) throughout British Columbia.
Denny Ross-Smith, Executive Director

Society Promoting Environmental Conservation (SPEC)
2150 Maple St., Vancouver BC V6J 3T3
Tel: 604-736-7732; *Fax:* 604-736-7115
admin@spec.bc.ca
www.spec.bc.ca
To address environmental issues in British Columbia, with a focus on urban communities in the Lower Mainland & the Georgia Basin; To encourage policies that lead to urban sustainability

Solid Waste Association of North America (SWANA)
PO Box 7219, #700, 1100 Wayne Ave., Silver Spring MD 20907-7219 USA
Tel: 301-467-9262; *Fax:* 301-589-7068
info@swana.org
www.swana.org
To serve individuals & communities responsible for the operation & management of solid waste management systems; To advance professional standards in the field through training programs, technical assistance, & education

Southeast Environmental Association (SEA)
PO Box 1500, 41 Woods Islands Hill, Montague PE C0A 1R0 Canada
Tel: 902-838-3351; *Fax:* 902-838-0610
sea@pei.aibn.com
www.seapei.ca
To protect, maintain, and enhance the ecology of south eastern Prince Edward Island for the environmental, social, and economic well being of area residents.
Sarah Jane Bell, Coordinator
Edgar Dewar, Chair

Sustainable Urban Development Association (SUDA)
2637 Council Ring Rd., Mississauga ON L5L 1S6 Canada
Tel: 416-400-0553
mail@suda.ca
www.suda.ca
To foster a healthy natural environment by providing information about ways in which cities can become more efficient in the land, material, water and energy resources, and highly supportive of sustainable transportation.

TD Friends of the Environment Foundation / Fondation des amis de l'environnement TD
#1100, 45 O'Connor St., Ottawa ON K1P 1A4 Canada
Tel: 613-782-1196; *Fax:* 613-783-6319
Toll-Free: 800-361-5333
tdfef@td.com
www.td.com/fef/
To protect & preserve the Canadian environment
Matthew Fortier, Regional Manager, ON North & East, National Programs

Thousand Islands Watershed Land Trust (TIWLT)
19 Reynolds Rd., Landsdowne ON K0E 1L0 Canada
www.tiwlt.ca
To permanently protect land in the Thousand Islands watershed region through acquisition or conservation agreements, and to achieve good land management through stewardship agreements and education.
Dann Michols, President

United Nations Environment Programme (UNEP) / Programme des nations unies pour l'environnement
Regional Office for North America, #506, 900 - 17th St. NW, Washington DC 20006 USA
Tel: 202-785-0465; *Fax:* 202-785-2096
info@rona.unep.org
www.rona.unep.org
To provide leadership & encourage partnership in caring for the environment by inspiring, informing & enabling nations & peoples to improve their quality of life without compromising that of future generations
Amy Fraenkel, Regional Director
Robin Burgess, Finance/Administration

Water Environment Association of Ontario (WEAO)
PO Box 176, Milton ON L9T 4N9
Tel: 416-410-6933; *Fax:* 416-410-1626
julie.vincent@weao.org
www.weao.org
To advance the water environment industry. To promote sound public policy

Western Canada Water (WCWWA)
PO Box 1708, 126 - 3rd Ave. West, Cochrane AB T4C 1B6
Tel: 403-709-0064; *Fax:* 403-709-0068
Toll-Free: 877-283-2003
member@wcwwa.ca
www.wcwwa.ca
To advance support for water professionals throughout western Canada
Audrey Arisman, Executive Director

Western Canada Wilderness Committee (WCWC)
227 Abbott St., Vancouver BC V6B 2K7 Canada
Tel: 604-683-8220; *Fax:* 604-683-8229
Toll-Free: 800-661-9453
info@wildernesscommittee.org
www.wildernesscommittee.org
To work for the protection of Canadian & the Earth's wilderness through research & education; to promote the principles which achieve ecologically sustainable communities

Wild Bird Care Centre (WBCC)
PO Box 11159, Nepean ON K2H 7T9 Canada
Tel: 613-828-2849
mojo@wildbirdcarecentre.org
www.wildbirdcarecentre.org
To assess, treat, and rehabilitate sick, orphaned, or injured wild birds before releasing them back to the wild.
Kathy Nihei, Founder

Wildlife Habitat Canada (WHC) / Habitat faunique Canada (HFC)
#310, 1740 Courtwood Cres., Ottawa ON K2C 2B5 Canada
Tel: 613-722-2090; *Fax:* 613-722-3318
Toll-Free: 800-669-7919
reception@whc.org
www.whc.org
Social Media:
www.facebook.com/pages/Wildlife-Habitat-Canada/124492716000
To promote the conservation, restoration & enhancement of wildlife habitat to retain diversity, distribution & abundance of wildlife; to provide a funding mechanism for the conservation, restoration & enhancement of wildlife habitat in Canada; to foster coordination & leadership in the conservation, restoration & enhancement of wildlife habitat in Canada

Wildlife Preservation Canada (WPC) / Conservation de la faune au Canada
RR#5, 5420 Hwy. 6 North, Guelph ON N1H 6J2
Tel: 519-836-9314; *Fax:* 519-836-8840
Toll-Free: 800-956-6608
admin@wildlifepreservation.ca
www.wildlifepreservation.ca
Social Media:
www.facebook.com/group.php?gid=141989432535249
To save endangered animal species from extinction in Canada & internationally
Elaine Williams, Executive Director
H. Alec B. Monro, President
Jessica Steiner, Recovery Biologist
Ellen Reinhart, Contact, Member & Donor Relations

Wood Buffalo Environmental Association (WBEA)
#100, 330 Thickwood Blvd., Fort McMurray AB T9K 1Y1 Canada
Tel: 780-799-4420
info@wbea.org
www.wbea.org
To provide state of the art air monitoring system that meets the needs of residents and stakeholders in the Wood Buffalo Region.
Carna MacEachern, Executive Director
Ann Dort-MacLean, President

World Wildlife Fund - Canada (WWF-Canada) / Fonds mondial pour la nature
#410, 245 Eglinton Ave. East, Toronto ON M4P 3J1 Canada
Tel: 416-489-8800; *Fax:* 416-489-3611
Toll-Free: 800-267-2632
ca-panda@wwfcanada.org
www.wwf.ca
Social Media: www.facebook.com/WWFCanada
To conserve wild animals, plants & habitats for their own sake & the long-term benefit of people; to protect the diversity of life on earth; to stop, & eventually reverse, the accelerating degradation of our planet's natural environment, & to help build a future in which humans live in harmony with nature
Patricia Koval, Chair
Gerald Butts, President & CEO
Arlin Hackman, Vice-President, Conservation
Mary Deacon, Vice-President, Conservation Advancement
Grahame Cliff, Vice-President, Finance & Administration
Christina Topp, Vice-President, Marketing & Communications
Robert Rangeley, Vice-President, Atlantic Region

Yukon Conservation Society (YCS)
302 Hawkins St., Whitehorse YT Y1A 1X6 Canada
Tel: 867-668-5678; *Fax:* 867-668-6637
ycs@ycs.yk.ca
www.yukonconservation.org
To pursue ecosystem well-being throughout the Yukon & beyond
Karen Baltgailis, Executive Director
Georgia Greetham, Coordinator, Office
Sue Kemmett, Coordinator, Forestry
Anne Middler, Coordinator, Energy
Lewis Rifkind, Coordinator, Mining

Yukon Environmental Network
PO Box 30097, Whitehorse YT Y1A 5M2 Canada
Tel: 867-668-5678; *Fax:* 867-668-6637
yukonenvironet@gmail.com
Susan Davis, Coordinator

Yukon Fish & Game Association (YFGA)
509 Strickland St., Whitehorse YT Y1A 2K5
Tel: 867-667-4263; *Fax:* 867-667-4237
www.yukonfga.ca
To ensure the long-term management of fish, wildlife, & outdoor recreational resources in the Yukon; To improve wildlife habitat
Gord Zealand, Executive Director
Jillian Mclellan, Office Administrator

Equipment & Machinery

AMC - Agricultural Manufacturers of Canada
PO Box 636, Stn. Main, Regina SK S4P 3A3 Canada
Tel: 306-522-2710; *Fax:* 306-781-7293
Toll-Free: 800-959-7462
amc@a-m-c.ca
www.a-m-c.ca
To foster & promote the growth & development of the agricultural equipment manufacturing industry; to identify industry problems & take remedial action; to encourage governments to enact legislation & offer programs that enhance the growth potential of industry; to provide a forum for members to exchange ideas & discuss their industry as it relates to the national & international economy

Association des marchands de machines aratoires de la province de Québec (AMMAQ)
7, rue Bernier, Bedford QC J0J 1A0 Canada
Tél: 450-248-7946; *Téléc:* 450-248-3264
info@ammaq.ca
www.ammaq.ca
Aider et regrouper tous les concessionnaires de machineries agricoles de toute la province; compiler des statistiques et des renseignements sur la vente de machines aratoires dans la province du Québec; obtenir une plus grande coopération entre les marchands de machines aratoires des diverses régions de la province; promouvoir la vente et l'utilisation des machines aratoires

Association des propriétaires de machinerie lourde du Québec inc. (APMLQ)
#259, 2750, ch Ste-Foy, Sainte-Foy QC G1V 1V6 Canada
Tél: 418-650-1877; *Téléc:* 418-650-3361
Ligne sans frais: 800-268-7318
apmlq@videotron.ca
www.apmlq.com/
Informer et instruire ses membres au moyen de publications; maintenir un secrétariat permanent dans un but de liaison entre les membres et de contact avec différentes autorités; négocier avec les autorités publiques toutes ententes susceptibles de promouvoir les buts de l'Association et ceux de ses membres

Association of Equipment Manufacturers - Canada (AEM-Canada)
World Exchange Plaza, PO Box 81067, #880, 111 Albert St., Ottawa ON K1P 1B1 Canada
Tel: 613-566-4568; *Fax:* 613-566-2026
www.aem.org
The Association acts as a voice for its members to the public & on a governmental level. It is also a regulatory body setting standars for safety, offering a variety of educational programs & seminars. AEM also serves as a disseminating body providing it members with current information & news on the industry.

Canada East Equipment Dealers' Association (CEEDA)
64 Temperance St., Aurora ON L4G 2P8
Tel: 905-841-6888; *Fax:* 905-841-1214
info@orfeda.com
www.orfeda.com
To promote the welfare of equipment trade retailers in the Maritimes & Ontario; To represent dealer interests in government legislation & regulation; To foster cooperation among manufacturers & distributors; To promote high standards for the retail equipment industry

Canadian Association of Defence & Security Industries (CADSI) / Association des industries canadiennes de défense et de sécurité (AICDS)
#1250, 130 Slater St., Ottawa ON K1P 6E2
Tel: 613-235-5337; *Fax:* 613-235-0784
cadsi@defenceandsecurity.ca
www.defenceandsecurity.ca
To represent Canadian defence & security industries domestically & internationally
Tim Page, President
Janet Thorsteinson, Vice-President, Government Relations
Andrea Walton, Manager, Operations & Administration
Steven Hillier, Manager, Marketing & Membership
Martine Proulx, Director, Events
Stefanie van Duynhoven, Assistant, Communications

Canadian Association of Equipment Distributors (CAED)
4531 Southclark Pl., Ottawa ON K1T 3V2 Canada
Tel: 613-822-8861; *Fax:* 613-822-8862
mswan@caed.org
www.caed.org
To represent the equipment industry in Canada; to promote cooperation between distributors & manufacturers; to encourage environmentally sound business practices

Canadian Process Control Association (CPCA)
2100 Banbury Cres., Oakville ON L6H 5P6 Canada
Tel: 905-844-6822; *Fax:* 905-901-9913
cpca@cpca-assoc.com
www.cpca-assoc.com
To promote the industry & its members to customers, academia, & public bodies; To provide a forum to exchange technical, industry, & regulatory information; To develop industry statistics; To encourage professional & ethical behaviour & quality standards among members

Municipal Equipment & Operations Association (Ontario) Inc.
38 Summit Ave., Kitchener ON N2M 4W5 Canada
Tel: 519-741-2780; *Fax:* 519-741-2750
admin@meoa.org
www.meoa.org
A network of individuals working directly with equipment & operations, to exchange information, promote high standards in the field & cost effective public service in Ontario.

Ethnic Groups

Jamaica Association of Montréal Inc.
4065, Jean-Talon ouest, Montréal QC H4P 1W6 Canada
Tel: 514-737-8229; *Fax:* 514-737-4861
jamaica_inc@yahoo.ca
www.jam-montreal.com
Educational, cultural & social activities for the Jamaican community; after-school & evening classes & programs for youth & adults; Saturday morning program for children; restaurant on site
Noel Alexander, Contact

New Brunswick African Association Inc.
www.nbafricans.com
The New Brunswick African Association Inc. is a community based organization focused on supporting the African community in New Brunswick to sustain, grow and thrive.
Donath Mrawira, Ph.D., P.Eng, President

Events

Alberta Music Festival Association
PO Box 416, Blairmore AB T0K 0E0 Canada
Tel: 403-562-2434; *Fax:* 403-562-7501
president@albertamusicfestival.org
www.albertamusicfestival.org
To coordinate, regulate & assist activities of local Alberta festivals of music & speech arts; to encourage formation of additional local festivals

Associated Manitoba Arts Festivals, Inc. (AMAF)
#202, 1151 Pembina Hwy., Winnipeg MB R3T 2A3 Canada
Tel: 204-945-4578; *Fax:* 204-948-2073
amaf@mts.net
www.amaf.mb.ca
To promote & encourage participation in growth & development of & appreciation for creative & performing arts in partnership with local festivals

Association des professionnels en exposition du Québec (APEQ)
868, rue Brisette, Sainte-Julie QC J3E 2B1 Canada
Tél: 514-990-0224; *Téléc:* 450-922-7238
info@apeq.org
www.apeq.org
Faire reconnaître le rôle vital de l'industrie des expositions dans la vie économique, industrielle, culturelle et sociale au Québec; promouvoir, auprès du monde des affaires, l'efficacité des expositions comme moyen de promotion, de commercialisation et de communication; favoriser l'éducation de ses membres
Jacques Perreault, Directeur général

Canadian Association of Exposition Management (CAEM) / Association canadienne des directeurs d'expositions
PO Box 218, #2219, 160 Tycos Dr., Toronto ON M6B 1W8
Tel: 416-787-9377; *Fax:* 416-596-1808
Toll-Free: 866-441-9377
info@caem.ca
www.caem.ca
To represent & improve the exposition & trade show industry in Canada

Canadian Association of Fairs & Exhibitions (CAFE) / Association canadienne des foires et expositions
43 Eccles St., Ottawa ON K1R 6S3 Canada
Tel: 613-233-0012; *Fax:* 613-233-1154
Toll-Free: 800-663-1714
info@canadian-fairs.ca
www.canadian-fairs.ca
To provide leadership in the development of the Canadian Fair Industry; to represent the Canadian fairs & exhibitions sector at the national level

Carnaval de Québec / Québec Winter Carnival
290, rue Joly, Québec QC G1L 1N8 Canada
Tél: 418-626-3716; *Téléc:* 418-626-7252
Ligne sans frais: 866-422-7628
comm@carnaval.qc.ca
www.carnaval.qc.ca
Depuis 50 ans, le Carnaval de Québec s'est donné la mission d'organiser annuellement une fête populaire hivernale dans le but de faire bénéficier à Québec une activité économique, touristique et sociale de première qualité dont les gens de la région seront fiers.
André Roy, Président
Jean-François Côté, Directeur général

Exhibitions Association of Nova Scotia (EANS)
40 Gateway Rd., Halifax NS B3M 1M9 Canada
Tel: 902-443-2039; *Fax:* 902-443-6721
www.eans.ca
EANS is a non-profit organization promoting such events as fairs & exhibitions across the province.

Federation of Canadian Music Festivals (FCMF) / La Fédération canadienne des festivals de musique
C/O Executive Director, 113 Elm Park Rd., Winnipeg MB R2M 0W3 Canada
Tel: 204-231-2401; *Fax:* 204-231-5735
Toll-Free: 800-961-5162
fcmf@mts.net
www.fcmf.org
Umbrella organization for 230+ local & provincial festivals; to develop & encourage Canadian talent in the performance & knowledge of classical music; to encourage the study & practice of the art of music alone or in conjunction with related arts; to organize the National Music Festival in which winners from each province participate
Cindy Rublee, Executive Director
Dianne Johnstone, President

Federation of Music Festivals of Nova Scotia
82 High St., New Glasgow NS B2H 2W9 Canada
Tel: 902-752-9590
jessie@novaanalytics.ca

Festivals & Events Ontario (FEO)
#301, 5 Graham St., Woodstock ON N4S 6J5 Canada
Tel: 519-537-2226; *Fax:* 519-537-2226
info@festivalsandeventsontario.ca
www.festivalsandeventsontario.ca
Festivals & Events Ontario (FEO) was established in 1987 as an association devoted to the growth and stability of the festival and event industry in Ontario. FEO provides festival and event organizers across the province with a networking forum offering professional development opportunities and resources aimed to encourage professionalism and excellence in the delivery of festivals and special events. The association also serves industry members whose goods and services are of use and benefit to Ontario's festivals and special events.
Gary Masters, Executive Director
Debbie Mann, Sales and Technical Coordinator

Festivals et Événements Québec (FEQ)
CP 1000, Succ. M, 4545, av Pierre-de-Coubertin, Montréal QC H1V 3R2 Canada
Tél: 514-252-3037; *Téléc:* 514-254-1617
Ligne sans frais: 800-361-7688
info@satqfeq.com
www.festivals.qc.ca/accueil.aspx
Regrouper les fêtes, festivals et événements, de les promouvoir et de leur offrir des services qui favorisent leur développement

Greater Vancouver International Film Festival Society (VIFF)
1181 Seymour St., Vancouver BC V6B 3M7 Canada
Tel: 604-685-0260; *Fax:* 604-688-8221
viff@viff.org
viff.org
To operate the Annual Vancouver International Film Festival, bringing to British Columbia the best in current art cinema from around the world as well as buried treasures from past international cinema

International Special Events Society - Toronto Chapter (ISES)
312 Oakwood Court, Newmarket ON L3Y 3C8 Canada
Tel: 905-898-7434; *Fax:* 905-895-1630
Toll-Free: 866-729-4737
info@isestoronto.com
www.isestoronto.com
Social Media: www.facebook.com/group.php?gid=7607457535
To educate, advance & promote the special events industry & its network of professionals along with related industries; to uphold the integrity of the special events profession to the public through "Principles of Professional Conduct & Ethics"; to acquire & disseminate useful business information; to foster a spirit of cooperation among members & other special events professionals
Carol Ford, Executive Director

New Brunswick Competitive Festival of Music Inc.
PO Box 2022, Saint John NB E2L 3T5 Canada
Tel: 506-847-7228
info@nbcfm.ca
www.nbcfm.ca
To hold a competitive & non-competitive music festival where students of all ages & music disciplines, including piano, vocal, strings, & band may meet, compete on a friendly basis & learn from expert adjudication

New Brunswick Federation of Music Festivals Inc. (NBFMF) / La Fédération des festivals de musique du Nouveau-Brunswick inc. (FFMNB)
14640 Rte. 2, Somerville NB E7P 2S4 Canada
Tel: 506-375-6752
waybar@nbnet.nb.ca

Newfoundland Federation of Music Festivals
c/o 1 Marigold Place, St. John's NL A1E 5N7 Canada
Tel: 709-722-9376
www.fcmf.org/province.htm
To coordinate activities of local music festivals & conduct a provincial music festival annually; to participate in the CIBC National Music Festival.

Ontario Music Festivals Association (OMFA)
c/o Pam Allen, 1422 Bayview Ave., #A, Toronto ON M4G 3A7
Toll-Free: 888-307-6632
mail@omfa.info
www.omfa.info
To promote the performance of classical music by Ontario's youth; To encourage knowledge of classical music

Performing Arts BC
PO Box 22042, Penticton BC V2A 8L1 Canada
Tel: 250-493-7279; *Fax:* 250-493-7279
festival@bcprovincials.com
www.bcprovincials.com

Prince Edward Island Kiwanis Music Festival Association
c/o 227 Keppoch Rd., Stratford PE C1B 2J5 Canada
Tel: 902-569-2885; *Fax:* 902-569-2885
ddcampbell@eastlink.ca
To make possible performances of young & older musicians in a semi-professional atmosphere; to adjudicate using professionals; & to encourage performance & study in music
Diane Campbell, Provincial Administrator

Provincial Exhibition of Manitoba
115 - 10th St., Brandon MB R7A 4E7 Canada
Tel: 204-726-3590; *Fax:* 204-725-0202
Toll-Free: 877-729-0001
info@brandonfairs.com
www.brandonfairs.com
To showcase agriculture; to link urban & rural regions through education & awareness while providing entertainment, community pride & economic enhancement to the region
Karen Oliver, General Manager
Neil Thomson, President

Québec Competitive Festival of Music / Festival de concours du Québec
136 Duke of Kent St., Pointe Cliare QC H9R 1X9 Canada
Tél: 514-398-4535; *Téléc:* 514-398-8061
davidson@music.mcgill.ca

Royal Agricultural Winter Fair Association (RAWF) / Foire agricole royale d'hiver
The Ricoh Coliseum, 100 Princes' Blvd., Toronto ON M6K 3C3 Canada
Tel: 416-263-3400; *Fax:* 416-263-3488
info@royalfair.org
www.royalfair.org
To promote excellence in agricultural & equestrian activities through world class competition, exhibitions & education

Saskatchewan Music Festival Association Inc.
#14, 62 Westfield Dr., Regina SK S4S 2S4 Canada
Tel: 306-757-1722; *Fax:* 306-347-7789
Toll-Free: 888-892-9929
sask.music.festival@sasktel.net
www.smfa.ca
Oldest organized cultural organization in Saskatchewan; to provide a classical competitive music festival system of the highest standard at the local, provincial & national levels

Tangofest
c/o #1801, 2350 Dundas St. West, Toronto ON M6P 4B1 Canada
Tel: 416-536-8446
info@tangofest.ca
www.tangofest.ca
Musharraf Farooqi, Executive Director

Toronto International Film Festival Inc.
#1600, 2 Carlton St., Toronto ON M5B 1J3
Tel: 416-967-7371; *Toll-Free:* 877-968-3456
customerrelations@tiff.net; humanresources@tiff.net
www.tiffg.ca
To lead in creative & cultural discovery through the moving image

Vancouver International Children's Festival
402 - 873 Beatty St., Vancouver BC V6B 2M6 Canada
Tel: 604-708-5655; *Fax:* 604-708-5661
info@childrensfestival.ca
www.childrensfestival.ca
To provide performing arts programs to young people in a festival environment; to encourage critical thinking & a lifelong interest in learning, the arts & cultural development

Western Association of Exhibition Management (WAEM)
1475 East Georgia St., Vancouver BC V5L 2A9 Canada
Tel: 604-205-3955; *Fax:* 604-205-5490
info@waem.org
www.waem.org
Nick Szrejter, Secretary

Farming

Friends of the Central Experimental Farm (FCEF)
Building 72, Central Experimental Farm, Ottawa ON K1A 0C6 Canada
Tel: 613-230-3276; *Fax:* 613-230-1238
info@friendsofthefarm.ca
www.friendsofthefarm.ca
To preserve, maintain, protect and enhance the Arboretum, the Ornamental Gardens and other public areas of the Central Experimental Farm in Ottawa, Ontario, Canada.
Polly McColl, President

Prince Edward Island Certified Organic Producers Co-op
PO Box 1776, Charlottetown PE C1A 7N4 Canada
Tel: 902-894-9999
www.organicpei.com
To increase organic production, research and market development; invite growers into the organic industry and promote and educate Islanders about organic food.
Mark Bernard, President

Fashion & Textiles

Alberta Men's Wear Agents Association
PO Box 66037, Stn. Heritage, Edmonton AB T6J 6T4 Canada
Tel: 780-455-1881; *Fax:* 780-455-3969
amwa@shaw.ca
www.trendsapparel.com

Allied Beauty Association (ABA)
#26-27, 145 Traders Blvd. East, Mississauga ON L4Z 3L3 Canada
Tel: 905-568-0158; *Fax:* 905-568-1581
Toll-Free: 800-268-6644
abacan@idirect.com
www.abacanada.com
To encourage & create a greater understanding & knowledge of the professional beauty industry to the salons, the public, the federal & provincial governments, & to members

Apparel Manufacturers Association of Ontario
#504, 124 O'Connor St., Ottawa ON K1P 5M9 Canada
Tel: 613-231-3220; *Fax:* 613-231-2305
www.ontarioapparel.com

BeautyCouncil (BC)
899 West 8th Ave., Vancouver BC V5Z 1E3 Canada
Tel: 604-871-0222; *Fax:* 604-871-0299
Toll-Free: 800-663-9283
info@ciabc.net
www.ciabc.net
To strive for the highest standards of excellence in professional cosmetology services through its member enhancement programs & to service the public through education & knowledge.

Canadian Apparel Federation (CAF) / Fédération canadienne du vêtement
#708, 151 Slater St., Ottawa ON K1P 5H3 Canada
Tel: 613-231-3220; *Fax:* 613-231-2305
info@apparel.ca
www.apparel.ca
To provide a forum for provincial apparel associations representing the vast majority of the country's manufacturers; to exercise leadership in relations with government, suppliers & the general public

Canadian Association of Wholesale Sales Representatives (CAWS) / Association canadienne des représentants de ventes en gros
PO Box 54546, 1771 Avenue Rd., Toronto ON M5M 4N5 Canada
Tel: 416-782-8961; *Fax:* 416-782-5876
caws@bellnet.ca
www.caws.ca
To represent comission sales agents on a national level. Serves as an umbrella organization for affiliate markets across Canada which are responsible for the coordination of trade shows directed towards the retail buyer.

Canadian Textile Association (CTA) / La Fédération canadienne du textile
4505 Paddock Trail, Niagara Falls ON L2H 3E6 Canada
Tel: 905-371-8985; *Fax:* 905-371-9238
Toll-Free: 877-897-1474
info@cdntexassoc.com
www.cdntexassoc.com
To advance & disseminate knowledge of textiles; to promote sound procedures of textile processing; to encourage & sponsor textile research & investigation; to assist in the establishment of standards in the textile industry; to promote & encourage schools, classes & libraries for the study of textile technology; to collaborate with international groups in advancing the foregoing objectives

Canadian Textiles Institute (CTI) / Institut canadien des textiles
#500, 222 Somerset St. West, Ottawa ON K2P 2G3 Canada
Tel: 613-232-7195; *Fax:* 613-232-8722
cti@textiles.ca
www.textiles.ca

Cosmetology Association of Nova Scotia
126 Chain Link Dr., Halifax NS B3S 1A2 Canada
Tel: 902-468-6477; *Fax:* 902-468-7147
Toll-Free: 800-765-8757
www.nscosmetology.ca
The Cosmetology Act and By-Laws ensures that all persons practicing cosmetology (i.e. hairdressing facial/make-up and manicure-pedicure services) possess the requisite skill and knowledge to properly perform all duties pertaining to these occupations.

Groupe CTT Group (CTT) / CTT Group Centre for Textile & Geosynthetic Technologies
3000, rue Boullé, Saint-Hyacinthe QC J2S 1H9 Canada
Tél: 450-778-1870; *Téléc:* 450-778-3901
Ligne sans frais: 877-288-8398
info@gcttg.com
www.groupecttgroup.com; www.gcttg.com
Favoriser le développement des matériaux textiles et de stimuler l'avancement technologique de l'industrie textile et géosynthétique par des activités telles que la recherche et le développement, l'assistance technique, la formation sur mesure, l'information spécialisé et l'animation du milieu

Institut des manufacturiers du vêtement du Québec (IMVQ) / Apparel Manufacturers Institute of Québec (AMIQ)
#801, 555, rue Chabanel ouest, Montréal QC H2N 2H8 Canada
Tél: 514-382-3846; *Téléc:* 514-383-1689
info@vetementquebec.com
www.vetementquebec.com
Vêtement Québec (IMVQ) joue des rôles multiples - elle est une source, notamment, d'information, de formation, d'inspiration et de motivation. Toutefois, d'abord et avant tout, c'est une association. Vêtement Québec est le regroupement professionnel des hommes et des femmes qui dirigent un grand nombre des entreprises de vêtements les plus progressives du pays, ainsi que d'entreprises qui offrent des produits et des services essentiels au secteur.

Luggage, Leathergoods, Handbags & Accessories Association of Canada (LLHA)
PO Box 144, Stn. A, Toronto ON M9C 4V2 Canada
Fax: 519-624-6408
Toll-Free: 866-872-2420
info@llha.ca
www.llha.ca
To promote the growth of the industry in Canada; To foster the interchange of ideas

Manitoba Fashion Institute (MFI)
c/o Sterling Glove, 165 Selkirk Ave. East, Winnipeg MB R2W 2L3 Canada
Tel: 204-586-8189; *Fax:* 204-582-2992
To increase awareness & to promote a positive image of the apparel industry in Manitoba; to ensure that the industry continues to remain an integral component of the Manitoba economy.

Men's Clothing Manufacturers Association Inc. (MCMA) / Association des manufacturiers de vêtements pour hommes inc.
#801, 555, rue Chabanel ouest, Montréal QC H2N 2H8 Canada
Tel: 514-382-3846; *Fax:* 514-383-1689
david.mcma@macten.net

Ontario Fashion Exhibitors (OFE)
PO Box 218, #2219, 160 Tycos Dr., Toronto ON M6B 1W8
Tel: 416-596-2401; *Fax:* 416-596-1808
Toll-Free: 800-765-7508
www.ofeshows.ca
To produce fashion marketplace events

Prairie/Saskatoon Apparel Market
601 - 331 Smith St., Winnipeg MB R3C 2G9 Canada
Tel: 204-942-2060; *Fax:* 204-947-0561
pammarkt@mts.net

Shoe Manufacturers' Association of Canada (SMAC) / Association des manufacturiers de chaussures du Canada
#203, 90, rue Morgan, Baie d'Urfe QC H9X 3A8
Tel: 514-457-3436; *Fax:* 514-457-8004
hanna@shoecanada.com
To represent & serve Canadian footwear manufacturers; To protect the Canadian domestic shoe industry

Western Apparel Market
910 Mainland St., Vancouver BC V6B 1A9 Canada
Tel: 604-682-5719; *Fax:* 604-682-3892
wambc@telus.net

Western Canada Children's Wear Markets (WCCWM)
#264, 1951 Glen Dr., Vancouver BC V6A 4J6 Canada
Tel: 604-681-1719; *Fax:* 604-681-1730
jeffswartz@telus.net

Film & Video

Academy of Canadian Cinema & Television (ACCT) / Académie canadienne du cinéma et de la télévision
49 Ontario St., Toronto ON M5A 2V1 Canada
Tel: 416-366-2227; *Fax:* 416-366-8454
Toll-Free: 800-644-5194
info@academy.ca
www.academy.ca
The Academy promotes & celebrates exceptional creative achievement in the Canadian film & television industries. Its mandate is to heighten public awareness & increase audience appreciation of Canadian film & television productions through its national Award programs: Genie Awards, Gemini Awards, & Prix Gémeaux. It is a registered charity, BN :106681471RR0001.

Alberta Motion Picture Industries Association (AMPIA)
#318, 8944 - 182 St. NW, Edmonton AB T5T 2E3 Canada
Tel: 780-944-0707; *Fax:* 780-426-3057
Toll-Free: 800-814-7779
abrooks@ampia.org
www.ampia.org
To develop & sustain the motion picture industry indigenous to Alberta

Association des producteurs de films et de télévision du Québec (APFTQ)
Edifice City Centre, #1030, 1450, rue City Councillors, Montréal QC H3A 2E6 Canada
Tél: 514-397-8600; *Téléc:* 514-392-0232
info@apftq.qc.ca
www.apftq.qc.ca
Représente ses membres auprès des gouvernements et organismes et encourage la coopération étroite entre tous les intervenants de l'industrie cinématographique et télévisuelle

Association des réalisateurs et réalisatrices du Québec (ARRQ)
Maison de la Réalisation, 5154, rue St-Hubert, Montréal QC H2J 2Y3 Canada
Tél: 514-842-7373; *Téléc:* 514-842-6789
secretariat@arrq.qc.ca
www.arrq.qc.ca
Défendre les intérêts et les droits professionnels, économiques, culturels, sociaux et moraux des réalisateurs pigistes membres, travaillant principalement dans les domaines du cinéma et de la télévision

Atlantic Filmmakers Cooperative (AFCOOP)
PO Box 2043, Halifax NS B3J 2Z1 Canada
Tel: 902-420-4572; *Fax:* 902-420-4573
membership@afcoop.ca
www.afcoop.ca
Social Media:
www.facebook.com/group.php?gid=2270148397&ref=ts
An accessible member-run centre for the production & presentation of creative films in a collaborative, learning environment

Canadian Association of Film Distributors & Exporters (CAFDE) / Association canadienne des distributeurs et exportateurs de films (ACDEF)
#1001, 2 Bloor St. West, Toronto ON M4W 3E2 Canada
Tel: 416-415-7217; *Fax:* 416-944-2212
teast@cafde.ca
To foster & promote the health of the Canadian motion picture industry by strengthening the Canadian owned & controlled distribution/export sector
Ted East, President & CEO

Canadian Film & Television Production Association (CFTPA) / Association canadienne de production de film et télévision
#902, 151 Slater St., Ottawa ON K1P 5H3 Canada
Tel: 613-233-1444; *Fax:* 613-233-0073
Toll-Free: 800-656-7440
ottawa@cftpa.ca
www.cftpa.ca
To promote & support development, growth & stabilization of Canadian film & television industry

Canadian Film Centre (CFC) / Centre canadien du film
2489 Bayview Ave., Toronto ON M2L 1A8 Canada
Tel: 416-445-1446; *Fax:* 416-445-9481
info@cdnfilmcentre.com
www.cfccreates.com
To operate as Canada's foremost film, televion, & new media institution; To advance Canadian creative talent, content, & values worldwide, through training, production, promotion & investment

Canadian Film Institute (CFI) / Institut canadien du film (ICF)
#120, 2 Daly Ave., Ottawa ON K1N 6E2 Canada
Tel: 613-232-6727; *Fax:* 613-232-6315
info@cfi-ifc.ca
www.cfi-icf.ca
To promote Canadian cinema; to assist in locating sources for rental or purchase of individual films/videos; to give subject & content information on theatrical & non-theatrical films & videos from both private & public sources; to give general information on Canadian & international film, video & television production, distribution, exhibition, & related subjects

Canadian Filmmakers Distribution Centre (CFMDC)
#119, 401 Richmond St. West, Toronto ON M5V 3A8 Canada
Tel: 416-588-0725; *Fax:* 416-588-7956
cfmdc@cfmdc.org
www.cfmdc.org
To promote & distribute the work of independent Canadian filmmakers.

Canadian Motion Picture Distributors Association (CMPDA) / Association canadienne des distributeurs de film
#1603, 22 St. Clair Ave. East, Toronto ON M4T 2S4 Canada
Tel: 416-961-1888; *Fax:* 416-968-1016
info@cmpda.ca
www.cmpda.org
To act as the voice of U.S.A. studios who market feature films, prime time entertainment programming for television & pay TV, & pre-recorded videos & DVDs in Canada; to coordinate recommendations on matters affecting national distributors of feature films, pre-recorded videocassettes, & television programs; to protect the rights of copyright owners

Canadian Picture Pioneers (CPP)
#1762, 250 The East Mall, Toronto ON M9B 6L3 Canada
Tel: 416-368-1139
cdnpicturepioneers@rogers.com
www.canadianpicturepioneers.ca
To provide assistance for the welfare of those in the motion picture industry in Canada

Canadian Society of Cinematographers (CSC)
#131, 3007 Kingston Rd., Toronto ON M1M 1P1 Canada
Tel: 416-266-0591; *Fax:* 416-266-3996
admin@csc.ca; editor@csc.ca (Communications & Publications)
www.csc.ca
To promote the art and craft of cinematography

La Cinémathèque québécoise
335, boul de Maisonneuve est, Montréal QC H2X 1K1 Canada
Tél: 514-842-9763; *Téléc:* 514-842-1816
info@cinematheque.qc.ca
www.cinematheque.qc.ca
Conservation et mise en valeur du patrimoine cinématographique et télévisuel; promouvoir la culture cinématographique; créer des archives de cinéma; acquérir et conserver des films ainsi que toute la documentation qui s'y rattache; projeter ces films et exposer ces documents de facon non commerciale à des fins historique, pédagogique et artistique.
Pierre Jutras, Directeur, Conservation et programmation
Suzanne Hénault, Présidente
Yolande Racine, Directrice générale

Directors Guild of Canada (DGC) / La Guilde canadienne des réalisateurs
#402, 111 Peter St., Toronto ON M5V 2H1 Canada
Tel: 416-482-6640; *Fax:* 416-482-6639
Toll-Free: 888-972-0098
mail@dgc.ca
www.dgc.ca
DGC is a national labour organization representing key creative & logistical personnel in the film & television industry. The Guild began as an association of creative film directors & expanded into all areas of the production, design & editing of film & television in Canada. A primary mandate is to promote & advance the quality & vitality of Canadian feature film & television production.

The Harold Greenberg Fund
Astral Media, BCE Place, #100, 181 Bay St., Toronto ON M5J 2T3 Canada
Tel: 416-956-5431; *Fax:* 416-363-9005
hgfund@tv.astral.com
www.astralmedia.com
To foster the development & production of feature-length movies written by Canadians & the production of family television series
John Galway, President

Independent Media Arts Alliance (IMAA) / Alliance des arts médiatiques indépendants (AAMI)
3995, rue Berri, Montréal QC H2L 4H2 Canada
Tel: 514-522-8240; *Fax:* 514-987-1862
info@imaa.ca
www.imaa.ca
To promote discussion among media art centres; to coordinate independent film & video centres

The Motion Picture Theatre Associations of Canada (MPTAC) / Les associations des propriétaires des cinémas du Canada
#304, 1240 Bay St., Toronto ON M5R 2A5 Canada
Tel: 416-969-7057; *Fax:* 416-922-5667
mptac.ca@ca.inter.net
www.mptac.ca
To maintain a national trade association of motion picture theatre exhibitors, consisting of owners, operators, executives & managers; to forward & promote the general welfare & prosperity of motion picture exhibitors; to gather, receive & disseminate such information as may seem helpful to members & associatedorganizations; to interchange ideas in rendering mutual assistance & to provide helpful vocational advice & guidance, & to act as a group representing national interests.

The Moving Pictures Travelling Canadian Film Festival Society
#300, 856 Homer Street, Vancouver BC V6B 2W5 Canada
Tel: 604-681-4549; *Fax:* 604-687-4937
Toll-Free: 877-858-3456
info@movingpictures.ca
To make Canadian films available in regions of the country that have limited access to them; to develop an audience for & awareness of Canadian films in Canada by exhibiting Canada's best films
Sauching Ng, Festival Director

National Screen Institute - Canada (NSI)
#400, 141 Bannatyne Ave., Winnipeg MB R3B 0R3 Canada
Tel: 204-956-7800; *Fax:* 204-956-5811
Toll-Free: 800-952-9307
info@nsi-canada.ca
www.nsi-canada.ca
To supply innovative, focused, applied professional training, leading participants to successful careers as writers, directors & producers in Canada's film & television industry

North of Superior Film Association (NOSFA)
#352, 1100 Memorial Ave., Thunder Bay ON P7B 4A3 Canada
Tel: 807-625-5450
info@nosfa.ca
www.nosfa.ca
To promote film and appreciation of film in the Thunder Bay area.
Marty Mascarin, President
Catherine Powell, Festival Coordinator

Northern Film & Video Industry Association (NFVIA)
PO Box 31340, Whitehorse YT Y1A 5P7 Canada
Tel: 867-456-2978
info@nfvia.com
www.nfvia.com
Supports the film & video sector in the Yukon by focussing on areas such as human resource development in the industry, development of infrastructure & production support, marketing, strategic alliances & partnerships, & membership services
Andy Crowther, President

On Screen Manitoba
#100, 62 Albert St., Winnipeg MB R3B 1E9 Canada
Tel: 204-927-5898; *Fax:* 204-943-4007
info@onscreenmanitoba.com
www.onscreenmanitoba.com
To build & represent the motion picture industry in Manitoba; to foster excellence & innovation in the industry
Tara Walker, Executive Director
Angie Lamirande, Manager, Marketing & Membership

Saskatchewan Motion Picture Industry Association (SMPIA)
1831 College Ave., 3rd Fl., Regina SK S4P 4V5 Canada
Tel: 306-525-9899; *Fax:* 306-569-1818
Toll-Free: 877-247-6742
info@smpia.sk.ca
www.smpia.sk.ca
Social Media: www.facebook.com/group.php?gid=43556252872
Committed to the intrinsic cultural & economic value of motion pictures;to work toward the creation & advancement of opportunities for the production, promotion & appreciation of motion pictures in Saskatchewan

Yukon Film Society (YFS)
4137C, 4th Ave., Whitehorse YT Y1A 1H8 Canada
Tel: 867-393-3456
yukonfilmsociety@yknet.ca
www.yukonfilmsociety.com
To present independent and alternative media art works to Yukon audiences and to support the production and distribution of works by Yukon media artists.
Mitch Miyagawa, President
Ross Burnet, General Manager

Finance

L'Alliance des Caisses populaires de l'Ontario limitée (ACPOL)
CP 3500, 1870 Bond St., North Bay ON P1B 4V6 Canada
Tél: 705-474-5634; *Téléc:* 705-474-5326
support@acpol.com
www.caissealliance.com

Association de planification fiscale et financière (APFF) / Fiscal & Financial Planning Association
#660, 1100, boul. René-Lévesque ouest, Montréal QC H3B 4N4 Canada
Tél: 514-866-2733; *Téléc:* 514-866-0113
Ligne sans frais: 877-866-0113
apff@apff.org
www.apff.org
Regrouper les personnes intéressées à la planification fiscale successorale et financière; publier et diffuser l'information dans ces domaines; favoriser la recherche
Jean Groleau, Président
Renée Gallant, 1re Vice-présidente/Trésorière

Association des cadres municipaux de Montréal (ACMM)
2e étage, 281, rue St-Paul, Montréal QC H2Y 1H1 Canada
Tél: 514-499-1130; *Téléc:* 514-499-1737
admin@acmm.qc.ca
www.acmm.qc.ca
A pour objet l'établissement de relations ordonnées entre l'employeur et les membres ainsi que l'étude, la défense et le développement des intérêts économiques sociaux, moraux et professionnels de ces derniers

Association of Canadian Financial Corporations (ACFC) / Association des compagnies financières canadiennes
Sussex Centre, #401, 50 Burnhamthorpe Rd. West, Mississauga ON L5B 3C2 Canada
Tel: 905-949-4920; *Fax:* 905-896-9380
To represent financial industry

Association of Canadian Pension Management (ACPM) / Association canadienne des administrateurs de régimes de retraite
#304, 1255 Bay St., Toronto ON M5R 2A9
Tel: 416-964-1260; *Fax:* 416-964-0567
info@acpm.com
www.acpm.com
To act as the voice of Canada's pension industry; To foster the growth of the the national retirement income system

Canada's Venture Capital & Private Equity Association (CVCA) / Association canadienne du capital de risque et d'investissement (ACCR)
Heritage Bldg., MaRS Centre, #120J, 101 College St., Toronto ON M5G 1L7 Canada
Tel: 416-487-0519; *Fax:* 416-487-5899
cvca@cvca.ca
www.cvca.ca
The CVCA provides advocacy, networking, information, & professional development for venture capital & private equity professionals.

Canadian Association of Insolvency & Restructuring Professionals (CAIRP) / Association canadienne des professionnels de l'insolvabilité et de la réorganisation (ACPIR)
277 Wellington St. West, Toronto ON M5V 3H2 Canada
Tel: 416-204-3242; *Fax:* 416-204-3410
info@cairp.ca
www.cairp.ca
To develop, educate, support & give value to members; to foster the provision of insolvency, business recovery service with integrity, objectivity & competence, in a manner that instils the highest degree of public trust; & advocate for a fair, transparent & effective system of insolvency/business recovery administration throughout Canada

Canadian Association of Pension Supervisory Authorities (CAPSA) / Association canadienne des organismes de contrôle des régimes de retraite (ACOR)
c/o CAPSA Secretariat, PO Box 85, 5160 Yonge St., 17th Fl., Toronto ON M2N 6L9
Tel: 416-590-7081; *Fax:* 416-590-7070
capsa-acor@fsco.gov.on.ca
www.capsa-acor.org
To facilitate an efficient & effective pension regulatory system in Canada

Canadian Association of Student Financial Aid Administrators
PO Box 2875, Stony Plain AB T7Z 1Y3 Canada
gpreston@can-reg.com
www.casfaa.ca
Represents financial aid administrators & awards officers in universities & colleges across Canada
Ken McLellan, Treasurer

Canadian Bankers Association (CBA) / Association des banquiers canadiens
PO Box 348, Stn. Commerce Court West, 199 Bay St., 30th Fl., Toronto ON M5L 1G2
Tel: 416-362-6092; *Fax:* 416-362-7705
Toll-Free: 800-263-0231
inform@cba.ca
www.cba.ca
To advocate for policies that contribute to a beneficial banking system

Canadian Finance & Leasing Association (CFLA) / Association canadienne de financement et de location (ACFL)
#301, 15 Toronto St., Toronto ON M5C 2E3 Canada
Tel: 416-860-1133; *Fax:* 416-860-1140
Toll-Free: 877-213-7373
info@cfla-acfl.ca
www.cfla-acfl.ca
To ensure an environment in Canada where asset-based financing, equipment & vehicle-leasing industry can be profitable
David Powell, President/CEO
Sherry Xinhua Jia-Hatheway, Director, Finance & Administration
Vanessa Foran, CAE, Director, Policy

Canadian Institute of Financial Planning (CIFPs)
#600, 3660 Hurontario St., Mississauga ON L5B 3C4
Tel: 647-723-6450; *Fax:* 647-723-6457
Toll-Free: 866-933-0233
cifps@cifps.ca
www.cifps.ca
To train & qualify advisors to become Certified Financial Planners; To represent members on matters of common interest
Keith Costello, President & Chief Executive Officer
Shirley Myers, Vice-President, Member Services & Business Development
Anthony Williams, CFP, Director, Academic Affairs
Andrew Cunningham, Manager, Information Services
Odele Burton, Corporate Secretary

Canadian Investor Relations Institute (CIRI) / Institut canadien de relations avec les investisseurs
#201, 1470 Hurontario St., Mississauga ON L5G 3H4
Tel: 905-274-1639
enquiries@ciri.org
www.ciri.org
To advance the practice of investor relations; To raise the stature of the profession in Canada; To act as the voice of investor relations professionals throughout Canada
Tom Enright, President & Chief Executive Officer
Yvette Lokker, Director, Communications & Professional Development
Karen Clutsam, Coordinator, Membership
Jennifer McInnis, Coordinator, Programming
Lisa Williams, Coordinator, Publications
Brenda McCutcheon, Bookkeeper

Canadian Payments Association (CPA) / Association canadienne des paiements (ACP)
180 Elgin St., 12th Fl., Ottawa ON K2P 2K3
Tel: 613-238-4173; *Fax:* 613-233-3385
info@cdnpay.ca
www.cdnpay.ca
To establish & operate safe & efficient national clearing & settlements systems; To facilitate the interaction of its systems with others involved in the exchange, clearing & settlement of payments; To facilitate the development of new payment methods & technologies

The Canadian Payroll Association (CPA) / L'Association canadienne de la paie (ACP)
#1600, 250 Bloor St. East, Toronto ON M4W 1E6 Canada
Tel: 416-487-3380; *Fax:* 416-487-3384
Toll-Free: 800-387-4693
infoline@payroll.ca
www.payroll.ca
To provide payroll leadership, through advocacy & education

Canadian Pension & Benefits Institute (CPBI) / Institut canadien de la retraite et des avantages sociaux (ICRA)
CPBI National Office, #305, 465, rue St-Jean, Montréal QC H2Y 2R6
Tel: 514-288-1222; *Fax:* 514-288-1225
info@cpbi-icra.ca; members@cpbi-icra.ca
www.cpbi-icra.ca
To provide continuing education & networking forums related to pensions, employee benefits, & investments

The Canadian Securities Institute (CSI) / L'Institut canadien des valeurs mobilières
200 Wellington St., 15th Fl., Toronto ON M5V 3C7 Canada
Tel: 416-364-9130; *Fax:* 416-359-0486
Toll-Free: 866-866-2601
customer_support@csi.ca
www.csi.ca
To enhance the knowledge of securities & financial industry professionals & promote knowledge & understanding of investing among the public

Credit Counselling Canada (CCC) / Conseil de Credit du Canada
Columbia Sky Train Station Bldg., #330, 435 Columbia St., New Westminster BC V3L 5N8 Canada
Tel: 604-527-8999; *Fax:* 604-527-8008
Toll-Free: 888-527-8999
www.creditcounsellingcanada.ca
To ensure all Canadians have access to not-for-profit credit counselling; to ensure a quality of service is provided to Canadians by member agencies; to advocate on issues relevant to money management & the wise use of credit along with public policy & legislative issues around these; to promote awareness of the existence & availability of non-profit credit counselling; to cultivate positive working relationships with stakeholders
Scott Hannah, Contact

Credit Institute of Canada (CIC) / L'Institut canadien du crédit
#216C, 219 Dufferin St., Toronto ON M6K 3J1
Tel: 416-572-2615; *Fax:* 416-572-2619
Toll-Free: 888-447-3324
geninfo@creditedu.org
www.creditedu.org
Social Media: www.ncfef.com
To provide credit education for credit & financial professionals in Canada

Credit Union Central of Canada (CUCC) / La Centrale des caisses de crédit du Canada
Corporate Office, #500, 300 The East Mall, Toronto ON M9B 6B7
Tel: 416-232-1262; *Fax:* 416-232-9196
Toll-Free: 800-649-0222
inquiries@cucentral.com; help@cucentral.com
www.cucentral.ca
Social Media: www.facebook.com/group.php?gid=132090159243
To act as the national voice for the Canadian credit union system; To facilitate the national cooperative movement; To provide services to ensure best practices are met at all credit unions; To develop opportunities for cooperative growth

Fédération des caisses populaires acadiennes
Place de l'Acadie, CP 5554, 295, boul St-Pierre ouest, Caraquet NB E1W 1B7 Canada
Tél: 506-726-4000; *Téléc:* 506-726-4001
info@acadie.net
www.acadie.com
Améliorer la qualité de vie de ceux et celles qui y adhèrent tout en contribuant à l'autosuffisance socio-économique de la collectivité acadienne du Nouveau-Brunswick, dans le respect de son identité linguistique et ses valeurs coopératives

Fédération des caisses populaires du Manitoba
#200, 605 rue Des Meurons, Winnipeg MB R2H 2R1 Canada
Tél: 204-237-8988; *Téléc:* 204-233-6405
federation@ciasse.biz
www.caisse.biz
Contribuer à l'essor économique et socio-culturel des manitobains en poursuivant le développement des services et du réseau financiers dont les avoirs sont gérés, administrés et contrôlés par des francophones

Financial Executives International Canada (FEIC)
#1201, 170 University Ave., Toronto ON M5H 3B3
Tel: 416-366-3007; *Fax:* 416-366-3008
Toll-Free: 866-677-3007
www.feicanada.org
To promote ethical conduct in the practice of financial management; To contribute to the legal & policy making process in Canada

Financial Planning Standards Council (FPSC)
#902, 375 University Ave., Toronto ON M5G 2J5
Tel: 416-593-8587; *Fax:* 416-593-6903
Toll-Free: 800-305-9886
inform@fpsc.ca; communications@fpsc.ca
www.fpsc.ca
Social Media: twitter.com/FPSC_Canada
To develop, enforce, & promote competency & ethical standards in financial planning by those who have earned the designation of Certified Financial Planner (CFP)
Debbie Ammeter, L.L.B., CFP, Chair
James W. Kraft, CA, CFP, CLU, T, Vice-Chair
Cary List, CA, CFP, President & Chief Executive Officer
John Wickett, PhD, Senior Vice-President, Standards & Certification
Stephen Rotstein, B.A. LL.B., General Counsel & Vice-President, Policy & Enforcement
Tamara Smith, MBA, Vice-President, Marketing & Consumer Affairs

Institute of Canadian Bankers (ICB) / Institut des banquiers canadiens
#400, 625, boul René-Lévesque ouest, Montréal QC H3B 1R2 Canada
Tel: 514-282-9480; *Fax:* 514-878-4260
Toll-Free: 800-361-7339
icb.info@csi.ca
www.csi.ca/icb
To provide financial services training & education, in areas such as banking, wealth management, insurance, investment, trust & management studies; To award professional designations, such as a Bachelor of Commerce degree (in partnership with Nipissing University) & a Master of Business Administration in Financial Services degree (in partnership with the University of Québec & Dalhousie University)

Investment Counsel Association of Canada (ICAC) / Association des conseillers en gestion de portefeuille du Canada
#1602, 110 Yonge St., Toronto ON M5C 1T4 Canada
Tel: 416-504-1118; *Fax:* 416-504-1117
icacinfo@investmentcounsel.org
www.investmentcounsel.org
To represent the Investment Counsel and portfolio managers in Canada; To advocate high standards of unbiased portfolio management in the interest of investors
Katie Walmsley, President
Bob Hill, Chair

Investment Funds Institute of Canada (IFIC) / L'Institut des fonds d'investissement du Canada
11 King St. West, 4th Fl., Toronto ON M5H 4C7 Canada
Tel: 416-363-2150; *Fax:* 416-861-9937
Toll-Free: 866-347-1961
WebAdmin@ific.ca
www.ific.ca
To act as the voice of the investment funds industry in Canada; To enhance the integrity & growth of the Canadian mutual fund industry

Investment Industry Regulatory Organization of Canada (IIROC) / Organisme canadien de réglementation du commerce des valeurs mobilières (OCRCVM)
#1600, 121 King St. West, Toronto ON M5H 3T9 Canada
Tel: 416-364-6133; *Fax:* 416-364-0753
publicaffairs@iiroc.ca
www.iiroc.ca
To oversee investment dealers & trading activity on debt & equity marketplaces in Canada; To focus on regulatory & investment industry standards, protecting investors & strengthening market integrity

Investors Association of Canada (IAC)
PO Box 84, #2500, 1 Dundas St. West, Toronto ON M5G 1Z3 Canada
contact@iac.ca
www.iac.ca
To be a source of investor education

Municipal Finance Officers' Association of Ontario (MFOA)
2169 Queen St. East. 2nd Fl., Toronto ON M4L 1J1 Canada
Tel: 416-362-9001; *Fax:* 416-362-9226
dan@mfoa.on.ca
www.mfoa.on.ca
To represent the interests of municipal finance officers throughout Ontario; To promote the interests of members

Mutual Fund Dealers Association of Canada (MFDA) / Association canadienne des courtiers de fonds mutuels
#1000, 121 King St. West, Toronto ON M5H 3T9 Canada
Tel: 416-361-6332; *Toll-Free:* 888-466-6332
mfda@mfda.ca
www.mfda.ca
The Mutual Fund Dealers Association of Canada (MFDA) is the national self-regulatory organization (SRO) for the distribution side of the Canadian mutual fund industry. The MFDA is structured as a not-for-profit corporation and its Members are mutual fund dealers that are licensed with provincial securities commissions
Larry M. Waite, President & CEO

Mark T. Gordon, Executive Vice-President

Ontario Association of Credit Counselling Services (OACCS)
PO Box 189, Grimsby ON L3M 4G3 Canada
Tel: 905-945-5644; *Fax:* 905-945-4680
Toll-Free: 888-746-3328
oaccs@indebt.org
www.indebt.org
To represent member agencies & provide them with a forum for the pursuit of common interests in order to support, strengthen & enhance not-for-profit credit counselling services; to enhance the quality & availability of not-for-profit credit counselling

Pension Investment Association of Canada (PIAC) / Association canadienne des gestionnaires de fonds de retraite
39 River St., Toronto ON M5A 3P1 Canada
Tel: 416-640-0264; *Fax:* 416-646-9460
info@piacweb.org
www.piacweb.org
To promote the financial security of pension fund beneficiaries through sound investment policy & practices
Peter Waite, CAE, Executive Director

Registered Deposit Brokers Association (RDBA)
#308A, 49 High St., Barrie ON L4N 5J4 Canada
Tel: 705-730-7599; *Fax:* 705-730-0477
Toll-Free: 866-261-6263
www.rdba.ca
To represent interests of deposit clients & independent deposit brokers
Vacant, Vice-President
Brenda Molnar, Executive Director
Brian L. Smith, President

Social Investment Organization (SIO)
184 Pearl St., 2nd Fl., Toronto ON M5H 1L5 Canada
Tel: 416-461-6042; *Fax:* 416-461-2481
info@socialinvestment.ca
www.socialinvestment.ca
To take a leadership role in coordinating the SRI agenda in Canada; to raise public awareness of SRI in Canada; to reach out to other groups interested in SRI; to provide information on SRI to our members & the public
Eugene Ellmen, Executive Director
Andrika Boshyk, Assistant Director

Women in Capital Markets (WCM) / Les femmes sur les marchés financiers
#301, 250 Consumers Rd., Toronto ON M2J 4V6 Canada
Tel: 416-502-3614; *Fax:* 416-495-8723
info@wcm.ca
www.wcm.ca
To enable capital markets professionals to reach their greatest potential for success; to advance woment within Canadian financial services
Caroline Dabau, Chair
Martha Fell, Chief Executive Officer
Cindy Gareau, Executive Director

World Lottery Association (WLA)
Montréal Office, #2000, 500, rue Sherbrooke ouest, Montréal QC H3A 3G6 Canada
Tel: 514-282-0273; *Fax:* 514-873-8999
lr@world-lotteries.org
www.world-lotteries.org
To control runaway gambling; to protect territorial integrity & promote the role of state-licensed lotteries as generators of funds for good causes

Fisheries & Fishing Industry

Association québécoise de l'industrie de la pêche (AQIP) / Québec Fish Processor Association
#843, 2600, boul Laurier, Sainte-Foy QC G1V 4W2 Canada
Tél: 418-654-1831; *Téléc:* 418-654-1376
aqip@quebectel.com
www.quebecweb.com/aqip/
Défendre les intérêts professionnels des industries québécoises de la transformation des produits marins; travailler au développement des services; aider à l'amélioration de la productivité en usines

Atlantic Fishing Industry Alliance
38B John St., Yarmouth NS B5A 3H5 Canada
Tel: 902-446-4477
To represent organizations in the harvesting, processing and marketing sectors of the commercial fishing industry in the Maritime Provinces.

Atlantic Salmon Federation (ASF) / Fédération du saumon atlantique
PO Box 5200, St Andrews NB E5B 3S8 Canada
Tel: 506-529-4581; *Fax:* 506-529-4438
savesalmon@asf.ca
www.asf.ca
To protect, conserve, & restore wild Atlantic salmon & their ecosystems

British Columbia Salmon Farmers Association (BCSFA)
#302, 871 Island Hwy., Campbell River BC V9W 2C2 Canada
Tel: 250-286-1636; *Fax:* 250-286-1574
Toll-Free: 800-661-7256
info@salmonfarmers.org
www.salmonfarmers.org
To promote the interests of persons, firms & corporations growing & selling farmed salmon in BC
Mary Ellen Walling, Executive Director

British Columbia Seafood Alliance (BCSA)
#1100, 1200 West 73rd Ave., Vancouver BC V6P 6G5 Canada
Tel: 604-377-9213; *Fax:* 604-683-4510
cburridge@telus.net
www.bcseafoodalliance.com
To represent the interests & values of a majority of BC's seafood industries to the federal & provincial governments & to the general public; to promote the conservation & environmentally sustainable use & production of seafood resources in BC; to foster an economically viable & internationally competitive seafood industry
Christina Burridge, Executive Director
Gina Johansen, Safety and Assistance

British Columbia Shellfish Growers Association (BCSGA)
2002 Comox Ave., Unit F, Comox BC V9M 3M6 Canada
Tel: 250-890-7561; *Fax:* 250-890-7563
roberta@bcsga.ca
www.bcsga.ca
Advancing the sustainable growth & prosperity of the BC shellfish industry in a global economy by providing leadership & advocacy to members & stakeholders while maintaining the integrity of the marine environment

Canadian Aquaculture Industry Alliance (CAIA) / Alliance de l'industrie canadienne de l'aquiculture
PO Box 81100, Stn. World Exchange Plaza, #705, 116 Albert St., Ottawa ON K1P 1B1
Tel: 613-239-0612; *Fax:* 613-239-0619
info@aquaculture.ca
www.aquaculture.ca
Social Media: @CDNaquaculture
To represent the interests of aquaculture operators, feed companies, suppliers, & provincial finfish & shellfish aquaculture associations on both the national & international scenes; To ensure the international competitiveness of the Canadian aquaculture industry
Ruth Salmon, Executive Director
Sherry Sadler, Coordinator, Projects

Canadian Centre for Fisheries Innovation (CCFI) / Centre canadien d'innovations des pêches
PO Box 4920, Stn. C, Ridge Rd., St. John's NL A1C 5R3 Canada
Tel: 709-778-0517; *Fax:* 709-778-0516
ccfi@mi.mun.ca
www.ccfi.ca
To work with the fishing industry to improve productivity & profitability of fishery through science & technology

Canadian Council of Professional Fish Harvesters (CCPFH) / Conseil canadien des pêcheurs professionnels (CCPP)
#712, 1 Nicholas St., Ottawa ON K1N 7B7 Canada
Tel: 613-235-3474; *Fax:* 613-231-4313
fish@ccpfh-ccpp.org
www.ccpfh-ccpp.org
To represent the interests of professional fish harvesters across Canada in their dealings with the federal, provincial & territorial governments on national issues of common concern; to provide organizational structure & leadership for the development of a program of professionalization for fish harvesters in collaboration with the organizations representing professional fishers across Canada; to act as a national industry sector council to plan & implement training & adjustment programs for the fish harvesting industry in Canada
John Sutcliffe, Executive Director
Earle McCurdy, President
Ronnie Heighton, Vice-President
Daniel Landry, Secretary
O'Neil Cloutier, Treasurer

Environment Resources Managament Association
PO Box 857, Grand Falls-Windsor NL A2A 2P7 Canada
Tel: 709-489-7350
www.exploitsriver.ca/association.php
To promote the development of the Exploits River as a major Atlantic Salmon producing river.

Fisheries Council of Canada (FCC)
#900, 170 Laurier Ave. West, Ottawa ON K1P 5V5
Tel: 613-727-7450; *Fax:* 613-727-7453
info@fisheriescouncil.org
www.fisheriescouncil.ca
To represent Canada's fish & seafood industry

Fisheries Council of Canada - British Columbia Representative
4214 - 199A St., Langley BC V3A 4V6 Canada
Tel: 604-530-7258; *Fax:* 604-530-2015
gjconsult@telus.net

Fishermen and Scientists Research Society (FSRS)
PO Box 25125, Halifax NS B3M 4H4 Canada
Tel: 902-876-1160; *Fax:* 902-876-1320
www.fsrs.ns.ca
To establish and maintain a network of fishermen and scientific personnel that are concerned with the long-term sustainability of the marine fishing industry in the Atlantic Region.
Patricia King, General Manager

Guysborough County Inshore Fishermen's Association (GCIFA)
PO Box 98, 990 Union St., Canso NS B0H 1H0 Canada
Tel: 902-366-2266; *Fax:* 902-366-2679
gcifa@gcifa.ns.ca
www.gcifa.ns.ca
To provide community based management of the fishing resource and to ensure a sustainable resource fishery and habitat, healthy fish stocks and act as an information liaison between inshore fishermen and the Dept. of Fisheries, as well as provide effective representation within the industry and other associations.
Eugene O'Leary, President

International Pacific Halibut Commission (IPHC)
PO Box 95009, Seattle WA 98145-2009 USA
Tel: 206-634-1838; *Fax:* 206-632-2983
info@iphc.washington.edu
www.iphc.washington.edu
Mandated to research and manage Pacific halibut stocks, within the Convention waters of the U.S. and Canada.
Bruce M. Leaman, Executive Director
Larry Johnson, Canadian Commissioner
Laura Richards, Canadian Commissioner
Gary Robinson, Canadian Commissioner
James Balsiger, US Commissioner
Ralph Hoard, US Commissioner
Phillip Lestenkof, US Commissioner

New Brunswick Salmon Growers Association (NBSGA)
226 Limekiln Rd., Letang NB E5C 2A8
Tel: 506-755-3526; *Fax:* 506-755-6237
info@nbsga.com
www.nbsga.com
To act as the voice of New Brunswick's salmon farming industry; To implement fish health initiatives to produce high-quality finfish
Pamela Parker, Executive Director
Sybil Smith, Director, Operations
Betty House, Coordinator, Research & Development
Jim Hanley, Manager, Wharf

North Atlantic Salmon Conservation Organization (NASCO)
11 Rutland Sq., Edinburgh EH1 2AS United Kingdom
hq@nasco.int
www.nasco.int
To promote the conservation, restoration, enhancement & rational management of salmon stocks in North Atlantic
A. Isaksson, President, (NASCO Council, Iceland)
Malcolm Windsor, OBE, Secretary
Peter Hutchinson, Assistant Secretary

North Pacific Anadromous Fish Commission (NPAFC)
#502, 889 West Pender St., Vancouver BC V6C 3B2 Canada
Tel: 604-775-5550; *Fax:* 604-775-5577
secretariat@npafc.org
www.npafc.org
To promote the conservation of anadromous stocks in the North Pacific Ocean
Vladimir Fedorenko, Executive Director
Suam Kim, President, (Korea)
Guy Beaupré, Canadian Representative

Nova Scotia Salmon Association (NSSA)
PO Box 396, Chester NS B0J 1J0 Canada
nssalmo@yahoo.ca
www.novascotiasalmon.ns.ca
To further the conservation & wise management of wild Atlantic salmon & trout
Carl Purcell, President

Prince Edward Island Fishermen's Association (PEIFA)
#102, 420 University Ave., Charlottetown PE C1A 7Z5
Tel: 902-566-4050; *Fax:* 902-368-3748
adminpeifa@pei.eastlink.ca; researchpeifa@pei.eastlink.ca
www.peifa.org
To represent fishermen across Prince Edward Island; To act as a single, united voice on behalf of Island fishers on industry issues

Seafood Producers Association of Nova Scotia
Queen Square, PO Box 991, #1801, 45 Alderney Dr., Dartmouth NS B2Y 3Z6 Canada
Tel: 902-463-7790; *Fax:* 902-469-8294
spans@ns.sympatico.ca

Food & Beverage Industry

Association des brasseurs du Québec (ABQ) / Québec Brewers Association
#888, 2000, rue Peel, Montréal QC H3A 2W5 Canada
Tél: 514-284-9199; *Téléc:* 514-284-0817
Ligne sans frais: 800-854-9199
asbq@brasseurs.qc.ca
brasseurs.qc.ca

Association of Canadian Biscuit Manufacturers (ACBM) / Association canadienne des manufacturiers de biscuits
#301, 885 Don Mills Rd., Toronto ON M3C 1V9 Canada
Tel: 416-510-8036; *Fax:* 416-510-8043
paigee@fspmc.com
To effectively represent common interests & concerns of member companies who manufacture biscuits in Canada by providing a forum to exchange information & resolve issues; to establish & maintain systems sufficient to ensure early consultation & effective representation in areas of government policy & regulation which affect members' interests; to promote a balanced view of the industry's role, performance & motives; to act as a credible source of information & assistance to the biscuit industry, as a forum for developing consensus positions on issues where an industry position may usefully & legally be established; to develop an effective organization plan including structure, staff membership & finances

Association of Canadian Distillers (ACD) / Association des distillateurs canadiens
#1203, 275 Slater St., Ottawa ON K1P 5H9 Canada
Tel: 613-238-8444; *Fax:* 613-238-3411
info@acd.ca
www.canadiandistillers.com
To protect & advance the interests of its members, & to promote & protect, both nationally & internationally, the well-being & viability of the Canadian distilling industry; committed to fostering responsible attitudes toward the consumption of distilled spirits (gin, vodka, rum, Canadian Whisky) in Canada; to aggressively pursuing & enhancing the recognition of the name & positive reputation of Canadian Whisky as Canada's unique appellation distilled spirits product; & to preserving & protecting the integrity & standards of all distilled products

Atlantic Food & Beverage Processors Association
500 St. George St., Moncton NB E1C 1Y3 Canada
Tel: 506-389-7892; *Fax:* 506-854-5850
info@atlanticfood.ca
www.atlanticfood.ca
To actively support the food processors in the region in their efforts to operate efficiently and profitably.
Don Newman, Executive Director

Breakfast Cereal Manufacturers of Canada (BCMC)
#301, 885 Don Mills Rd., Toronto ON M3C 1V9 Canada
Tel: 416-510-8036; *Fax:* 416-510-8044
ileanal@fcpmc.com
To provide a forum for members to review issues of significance to the breakfast industry; to represent industry with government
Kathleen Kennedy, Manager

Brewers Association of Canada / L'Association des brasseurs du Canada
#650, 100 Queen St., Ottawa ON K1P 1J9 Canada
Tel: 613-232-9601; *Fax:* 613-232-2283
info@brewers.ca
www.brewers.ca
To represent brewing companies operating in Canada; to collect information & statistics about the brewing industry; to provide information about the industry to the public

Brewing & Malting Barley Research Institute (BMBRI) / Institut de recherche - brassage et orge de maltage
#1510, One Lombard Pl., Winnipeg MB R3B 0X3 Canada
Tel: 204-927-1407; *Fax:* 204-947-5960
info@bmbri.ca
www.bmbri.ca
Supporting the development & evaluation of new malting barley varieties in Canada

Canadian Association of Foodservice Professionals (CAFP)
#130, 10691 Shellbridge Way, Richmond BC V6X 2W8 Canada
Tel: 604-248-0215; *Fax:* 604-270-3644
Toll-Free: 877-599-2237
national@cafp.com
www.cafp.com
To enhance the prestige of the food service profession through improving standards of service; to promote education in the industry & to provide increased opportunity for youth to train for the food service profession; to promote research in food service & nutrition; to work for food service regulation & legislation in the public interest; to promote through good fellowship & personal association new opportunities for increased management efficiency & exchange of professional information

Canadian Association of Sales & Marketing Agencies (CASMA)
#301, 885 Don Mills Rd., Toronto ON M3C 1V9 Canada
Tel: 416-385-2322; *Fax:* 416-510-8043
btordoff@casmaonline.ca
www.casmaonline.ca

Canadian Bottled Water Association (CBWA) / Association canadienne des embouteilleurs d'eau
#337-24, 155 East Beaver Creek Rd., Richmond Hill ON L4B 2N1 Canada
Tel: 905-886-6928; *Fax:* 905-886-9531
info@cbwa.ca
www.cbwa.ca
Committed to environmentally responsible practices, CBWA supports & promotes bottled water as a healthy, safe & convenient food product. Dialogue is encourage between industry, government, consumers, & other stakeholders.
Elizabeth Griswold, Executive Director

Canadian College & University Food Service Association (CCUFSA)
National Office, Drew Hall, University of Guelph, Guelph ON N1G 2W1 Canada
Tel: 519-824-4120; *Fax:* 519-837-9302
boeckner@uoguelph.ca
www.ccufsa.on.ca
To enhance the quality of campus life through the growth & development of food service operations in colleges & universities

Canadian Council of Grocery Distributors (CCGD) / Conseil canadien de la distribution alimentaire (CCDA)
#402, 6455, rue Jean-Talon est, Montréal QC H1S 3E8
Tel: 514-982-0267
www.ccgd.ca
To advance & promote the Canadian grocery & foodservice distribution industry at regional & national levels; To act as the voice for the grocery industry in Canada, on policies such as labour laws, & environment initiatives

Canadian Federation of Independent Grocers (CFIG) / Fédération canadienne des épiciers indépendants
#902, 2235 Sheppard Ave. East, Toronto ON M2J 5B5
Tel: 416-492-2311; *Fax:* 416-492-2347
Toll-Free: 800-661-2344
info@cfig.ca
www.cfig.ca
To equip & enable independent, franchised, & specialty grocers for sustainable success; To act as a united voice for independent grocers across Canada

Canadian Health Food Association (CHFA) / Association canadienne des aliments de santé
#302, 235 Yorkland Blvd., Toronto ON M2J 4Y8
Tel: 416-497-6939; *Fax:* 905-479-3214
Toll-Free: 800-661-4510
info@chfa.ca
www.chfa.ca
Social Media: www.facebook.com/group.php?gid=12940324924
To act as the voice of the natural products industry; To promote natural & organic products as an integral part of health & well-being; To ensure the growth of the natural & organic industry
Deborah Callbreath, Chair
Natalie Cajic, Specialist, Communications

Canadian Meat Council (CMC) / Conseil des viandes du Canada
#305, 955 Green Valley Cres., Ottawa ON K2C 3V4 Canada
Tel: 613-729-3911; *Fax:* 613-729-4997
info@cmc-cvc.com
www.cmc-cvc.com
The Council expresses the views of the membership with government, all elements of the food industry, consumer organizations, the research & academic community, & the media. High standards of industry integrity, & a vast range of wholesome, nutritional meat products are fostered by the Council.

Canadian Meat Science Association (CMSA) / Association scientifique canadienne de la viande (ASCB)
Dept. of Agricultural, Food & Nutritional Science, Univ. of Alberta, #4-10, Agriculture / Forestry Centre, Edmonton AB T6G 2P5 Canada
Tel: 780-492-3239; *Fax:* 780-492-4265
cindy.rowles@ualberta.ca
cmsa-ascv.ca/default.htm
CMSA promotes the application of science & technology to the production, processing, packaging, distribution, preparation, evaluation, & utilization of all meat & meat products. Useful, coordinated research, educational techniques, & service activities are developed & promoted.
Frances Nattress, President
Cindy Delaloye, Sec.-Treas.

Canadian National Millers Association (CNMA)
#103, 408 Queen St., Ottawa ON K1R 5A7 Canada
Tel: 613-238-2293; *Fax:* 613-235-5866
dwiggins@canadianmillers.ca
www.canadianmillers.ca
To serve as a vehicle for consultation between the milling industry, government departments & agencies; to promote regulatory & public policy environment that enhances international competitiveness; to provide international trade development to the industry; to disseminate information about the industry & Canadian wheat flour quality; to work directly & in cooperation with the trade offices abroad

Canadian Produce Marketing Association (CPMA) / Association canadienne de la distribution de fruits et légumes
162 Cleopatra Dr., Ottawa ON K2G 5X2 Canada
Tel: 613-226-4187; *Fax:* 613-226-2984
question@cpma.ca
www.cpma.ca
To increase the market for fresh fruits & vegetables in Canada, by encouraging cooperation & information exchange in all segments, at the domestic & international level

Canadian Snack Food Association (CSFA) / Association canadienne des fabricants des grignotines
#301, 885 Don Mills Rd., Toronto ON M3C 1V9 Canada
Tel: 416-510-8036; *Fax:* 416-510-8044
ileanal@4reflections.com
To provide the leadership required for sustained growth & competitiveness of the industry; to influence policy formulation, legislation & regulations at all levels of government in the best interests of the industry

Canadian Sugar Institute (CSI) / Institut canadien du sucre
Water Park Pl., #620, 10 Bay St., Toronto ON M5J 2R8 Canada
Tel: 416-368-8091; *Fax:* 416-368-6426
info@sugar.ca
www.sugar.ca

Canadian Vintners Association (CVA) / L'Association des vignerons du Canada
#200, 440 Laurier Ave. West, Ottawa ON K1R 7X6 Canada
Tel: 613-782-2283; *Fax:* 613-782-2239
info@canadianvintners.com
www.canadianvintners.com
To formulate & promote policies that will advance the interests & goals of the Canadian wine sector.

Coffee Association of Canada (CAC) / Association du café du Canada
#301, 885 Don Mills Rd., Toronto ON M3C 1V9 Canada
Tel: 416-510-8032; *Fax:* 416-510-8044
info@coffeeassoc.com
www.coffeeassoc.com
Dedicated to addressing industry-wide issues on behalf of our members, keeping them fully informed, & allowing them to focus on the proprietary concerns of building their businesses

Confectionery Manufacturers Association of Canada (CMAC) / Association canadienne des fabricants de confiseries
#301, 885 Don Mills Rd., Toronto ON M3C 1V9 Canada
Tel: 416-510-8034; *Fax:* 416-510-8043
info@cmaconline.ca
www.confectioncanada.com
To increase confectionery consumption & production; to achieve global competitiveness; to grow confectionery consumption in a responsible manner as an enjoyable food that is part of a healthy, active lifestyle.

Conseil de la transformation agroalimentaire et des produits de consommation (CTAC) / Council of Food Processing & Consumer Products
#102, 200, rue MacDonald, Saint-Jean-sur-Richelieu QC J3B 8J6 Canada
Tél: 450-349-1521; *Téléc:* 450-349-6923
info@conseiltac.com
www.conseiltac.com
Le porte-parole officiel des manufacturiers de produits alimentaires du Québec qui s'y regroupent à titre de membres fabricants; canalise les représentations des manufacturiers, en particulier auprès des gouvernements; coordonne l'action des membres en vue de promouvoir leurs intérêts économiques, sociaux et professionnels; suscite l'éducation des consommateurs sur les valeurs d'une bonne alimentation; favorise la promotion des produits fabriqués par les membres; établit des liaisons entre les manufacturiers, les producteurs, les fournisseurs, les distributeurs, les consommateurs et les autres maillons de la chaîne alimentaire; encourage la recherche dans les domaines de l'agriculture, de l'alimentation et du marketing

Flavour Manufacturers Association of Canada (FMAC) / Association canadienne de fabricants des arômes
#301, 885 Don Mills Rd., Toronto ON M3C 1V9 Canada
Tel: 416-510-8036; *Fax:* 416-510-8044
ileanal@fcpmc.com
To serve the needs of the Canadian flavour industry by providing a forum for the examination of industry problems, assisting in the implementation of solutions, & fostering a global perspective for creativity, innovation & competition.

Food & Consumer Products of Canada (FCPC) / Produits alimentaires et de consommation du Canada (PACC)
#301, 885 Don Mills Rd., Toronto ON M3C 1V9
Tel: 416-510-8024; *Fax:* 416-510-8043
info@fcpc.ca
www.fcpc.ca
To represent the food & consumer products industry, from small privately-owned companies to big glboal multinationals
Nancy Croitoru, President & Chief Executive Officer
Lesley McKeever, Senior Vice-President, Industry Affairs & Membership
Errol Cerit, Senior Director, Industry Affairs
Rachel Kagan, Senior Director, Environment & Sustainability Policy
Janice Emery-Carter, Manager, Education Centre
Linda Saunby, Coordinator, Public Affairs
Heather Spencer, Coordinator, Member Services
Jami Nirenberg, Coordinator, Events

Food Processors of Canada (FPC) / Fabricants de produits alimentaires du Canada
350 Sparks St., Ottawa ON K1R 7S8 Canada
Tel: 613-722-1000; *Fax:* 613-722-1404
fpc@foodprocessors.ca; conferences@foodprocessors.ca
www.foodprocessors.ca
To provide professional services & advice to members on matters such as manufacturing, trade, & commerce

New Brunswick Maple Syrup Association (NBMSA)
#223, 1350 Regent St., Fredericton NB E3C 2G6 Canada
Tel: 506-458-8889; *Fax:* 506-454-0652
yrp@nb.aibn.com
www.maple.infor.ca
The New Brunswick Maple Syrup Association (NBMSA) is a non-profit organization, dedicated to representing the interests of its members, and facilitating the industry through advertisement and the constant improvement of quality and standards by collaborating with various organizations towards the enrichment of the ever-growing maple industry.
Yvon Poitras, General Manager

Ontario Coffee & Vending Service Association (OCVSA)
#301, 885 Don Mills Rd., Toronto ON M3C 1V9 Canada
Tel: 416-510-8032; *Fax:* 416-510-8044
info@coffeeassoc.com
www.coffeeassoc.com/ocvsa.htm

Ontario Food Processors Association (OFPA)
7660 Mill Rd., RR#4, Guelph ON N1S 6J1 Canada
Tel: 519-767-5599; *Fax:* 519-763-4164
ofpa@sentex.net
Represents fruit and vegetable processors in Ontario

Ontario Independent Meat Processors (OIMP)
7660 Mill Rd., Guelph ON N1H 6J1 Canada
Tel: 519-763-4558; *Fax:* 519-763-4164
Toll-Free: 800-263-3797
info@oimp.ca
www.oimp.ca
To support & foster a safe & wholesome meat & poultry industry, maintaining viability & high quality through ongoing education, research & representation at all levels of government

Pet Food Association of Canada (PFAC) / Association des fabricants d'aliments pour animaux familiers du Canada
PO Box 35570, 2528 Bayview Ave., Toronto ON M2L 2Y4
Tel: 416-447-9970; *Fax:* 416-443-9137
info@pfac.com
www.pfac.com
To provide association members with a unified voice on issues that affect the pet food industry in Canada

Refreshments Canada / Association canadienne de l'industrie des boissons gazeuses
20 Bay St., 12th Fl., Toronto ON M5J 2N8 Canada
Tel: 416-362-2424; *Fax:* 416-362-3229
info@refreshments.ca
www.refreshments.ca
To represent soft drink bottlers, distributors, franchise houses & industry suppliers on a variety of issues

Tea Association of Canada (TAC) / Association du thé du Canada
#602, 133 Richmond St. West, Toronto ON M5H 2L3 Canada
Tel: 416-510-8647; *Fax:* 416-510-8044
info@tea.ca
www.tea.ca
To represent & advance the interests of Canada's tea industry to all levels of government in an effort to improve the conditions under which the industry operates & to promote better business relations between the industry's players
Louise Roberge, CAE, President

Wine Council of Ontario
#B205, 110 Hannover Dr., St Catharines ON L2W 1A4 Canada
Tel: 905-684-8070; *Fax:* 905-684-2993
info@winesofontario.org
www.winesofontario.org
A non-profit trade association which plays a leadership role in the marketing, promotion, and future directions of the Ontario wine industry
Sherri Haigh, Contact

Yukon Food Processors Association (YFPA)
PO Box 20437, Whitehorse YT Y1A 7A2 Canada
Tel: 867-393-3189
processors.yukonfood.com
To represent the food processing industry in the Yukon Territory.
Michell Spittal, President

Forestry & Forest Products

Alberta Forest Products Association (AFPA)
#500, 10709 Jasper Ave., Edmonton AB T5J 3N3
Tel: 780-452-2841; *Fax:* 780-455-0505
info@albertforestproducts.ca
www.albertaforestproducts.ca
To represent companies that manufacture forest products throughout Alberta
Brady Whittaker, President & Chief Executive Officer
Norm Dupuis, Director, Grade Bureau
Brock Mulligan, Director, Communications
Keith Murray, Director, Policy & Regulation
Carola von Sass, Director, Health & Safety

Alberta Forestry Association
4331 - 114B St., Edmonton AB T6J 1N8 Canada
Tel: 780-432-3683; *Fax:* 780-430-8349
jimrmefc@telusplanet.net
To maintain Alberta's forests as a productive & renewable resource; to increase public awareness, school education & natural appreciation of forests; to bring about better understanding of forests to people of all ages & backgrounds

Association of British Columbia Forest Professionals (ABCFP)
#1030, 1188 Georgia St. West, Vancouver BC V6E 4A2 Canada
Tel: 604-687-8027; *Fax:* 604-687-3264
info@abcfp.ca
www.abcfp.ca
To protect the public interest in the practice of professional forestry by ensuring the competence, independence & integrity of its members; to ensure that every person practising professional forestry is accountable to the association & to the public

Association of Registered Professional Foresters of New Brunswick (ARPFNB) / Association des forestiers agréés du Nouveau-Brunswick (AFANB)
#221, 1350 Regent St., Fredericton NB E3C 2G6 Canada
Tel: 506-452-6933; *Fax:* 506-450-3128
info@arpfnb.ca
www.arpfnb.ca
To manage the forest resources of New Brunswick for the sustained development of these resources; to assure the proficiency & competency of Registered Professional Foresters in New Brunswick

Canadian Forestry Association (CFA) / Association forestière canadienne
#200, 1027 Pembroke St., Pembroke ON K8A 3M4
Tel: 613-732-2917; *Fax:* 613-732-3386
Toll-Free: 866-441-4006
dlemkay@bell.net (GM); teachingkits@canadianforestry.com
www.canadianforestry.com
To advocate for the wise use & protection of Canada's forest, water, & wildlife resources; To nurture economic & environmental health, through the management & conservation of forest resources; To provide a national voice for provincial forestry agencies

Canadian Forestry Association of New Brunswick (CFANB) / Association forestière canadienne du Nouveau-Brunswick (AFCNB)
Maritime College of Forest Technology, #248, 1350 Regent St., Fredericton NB E3C 2G6 Canada
Tel: 506-452-1339; *Fax:* 506-452-7950
Toll-Free: 866-405-7000
info@cfanb.ca
www.cfanb.ca
Champions trees & forests of NB; explains their importance in people's lives; promotes environmental, commercial, recreational & inspirational benefits; underlying principle is stewardship & understanding that an inter-dependency exists among all parts of the environment; encourages conservation & wise use of natural resources

Canadian Hardwood Plywood & Veneer Association (CHPVA) / Association canadienne du Contreplaqué et de Placages de bois dur (ACCPBD)
47, rue de Richelieu, Chambly QC J3L 2C3 Canada
Tel: 514-733-2777; *Fax:* 514-733-2777
michel.tremblay2@bellnet.ca
www.chpva.ca
To protect the interests & conserve the rights of those involved in the manufacture & distribution of hardwood veneer & plywood & their suppliers in Canada.

Canadian Institute of Forestry / Institut forestier du Canada
c/o The Canadian Ecology Centre, PO Box 430, 6905 Hwy. 17 West, Mattawa ON P0H 1V0
Tel: 705-744-1715; *Fax:* 705-744-1716
admin@cif-ifc.org; questions@cif-ifc.org
www.cif-ifc.org
To act as the national voice of forest practitioners

Canadian Lumber Standards Accreditation Board (CLSAB)
#406, 960 Quayside Dr., New Westminster BC V3M 6G2 Canada
Tel: 604-524-2338; *Fax:* 604-524-6932
info@clsab.ca
www.clsab.ca

Canadian Lumbermen's Association (CLA) / Association canadienne de l'industrie du bois (ACIB)
#200, 30 Concourse Gate, Ottawa ON K2E 7V7 Canada
Tel: 613-233-6205; *Fax:* 613-233-1929
info@cla-ca.ca
www.canadianlumbermen.com
To promote the interests & conserve the rights of those engaged in lumbering operations or in the manufacture, sale or distribution of lumber & other related products

Canadian Pallet Council (CPC) / Conseil des palettes du Canada
239 Division St., Cobourg ON K9A 3P9 Canada
Tel: 905-372-1871; *Fax:* 905-373-0230
info@cpcpallet.com
www.cpcpallet.com

Canadian Plywood Association
735 - 15 St. West, North Vancouver BC V7M 1T2 Canada
Tel: 604-981-4190; *Fax:* 604-985-0342
info@canply.org
www.canply.org
Canadian plywood organization.
Judy White, Office Manager
James F. Shaw, President

Canadian Pulp & Paper Network for Innovation in Education & Research / Réseau canadien de pâtes et papiers pour l'innovation en éducation et en recherche
570, boul St-Jean, Pointe-Claire QC H9R 3J9 Canada
Tel: 514-630-4100; *Fax:* 514-630-4107
papier@paprican.ca
www.papiernet.ca
To act as the voice of Canadian university faculty involved in teaching & research for the pulp & paper industry
Patrice Mangin, Chair
Richard Kerekes, Director

Canadian Well Logging Society (CWLS)
Scotia Centre, #2200, 700 - 2nd St. SW, Calgary AB T2P 2W1 Canada
Tel: 403-269-9366; *Fax:* 403-269-2787
roy_benteau@eogresources.com
www.cwls.org

Canadian Wood Council (CWC) / Conseil canadien du bois (CCB)
#400, 99 Bank St., Ottawa ON K1P 6B9 Canada
Tel: 613-747-5544; *Fax:* 613-747-6264
Toll-Free: 800-463-5091
admin@cwc.ca
www.cwc.ca
To represent Canadian manufacturers of wood products use in construction, the council role of insuring market access for wood products accomplished through codes standards, the production & communication of technical information & in educational programs for students & construction professionals

Canadian Wood Pallet & Container Association (CWPCA) / Association canadienne des manufacturiers de palettes et contenants
#201, 2141 Thurston Dr., Ottawa ON K1G 6C9 Canada
Tel: 613-521-6468; *Fax:* 613-521-1835
Toll-Free: 877-224-3555
info@canadianpallets.com
www.canadianpallets.com
To promote the general welfare of the wooden pallet & container manufacturing industry; to improve services directly or otherwise; to cooperate with officers of government & business in any program considered essential to the national welfare or economy; to engage in any other lawful activities & enjoy powers, rights & privileges granted or conferred upon associations of a similar nature.

Canadian Wood Preservers Bureau (WPC) / Préservation du bois Canada
#202, 2141 Thurston Dr., Ottawa ON K1G 6C9 Canada
Tel: 613-737-4337; *Fax:* 613-247-0540
info@woodpreservation.ca
www.woodpreservation.ca
To provide a quality assurance program for the treated wood industry

Christmas Tree Farmers of Ontario (CFTO)
#1, 9251 County Rd., Palgrave ON L0N 1P0 Canada
Fax: 905-729-0548
Toll-Free: 800-661-3530
ctfo@christmastrees.on.ca
www.christmastrees.on.ca
CFTO is an association devoted to farmers who specialize in Christmas tree growing.

College of Alberta Professional Foresters
#209, 10544 - 106 St., Edmonton AB T5H 2X6 Canada
Tel: 780-432-1177; *Fax:* 780-432-7046
office@capf.ca
www.capf.ca
To maintain an accurate register of registered professional foresters in Alberta; To set standards of professional conduct & competence for members; To administer the title, Registered Professional Forester (RPF)
Ted Gooding, President

Conseil de l'industrie forestière du Québec (CIFQ) / Québec Forestry Industry Council (QFIC)
#200, 1175, av Lavigerie, Sainte-Foy QC G1V 4P1 Canada
Tél: 418-657-7916; *Téléc:* 418-657-7971
info@cifq.qc.ca
www.cifq.qc.ca
Représente la très grande majorité des entreprises de sciage résineux, de pâtes, papiers, cartons et panneaux oeuvrant au Québec; se consacre à la défense des intérêts de ces entreprsies, à la promotion de leur contribution au développement socio-économique, à la gestion intégrée et à l'aménagement durable des forêts, de même qu'à l'utilisation optimale des ressources naturelles; oeuvre auprès des instances gouvernementales, des organismes publics et parapublics, des associations et de la population; encourage un comportement responsable de ses membres en regard des dimensions environnementales, économiques et sociales de leurs activités.

Consulting Foresters of British Columbia
PO Box 98, Pender Island BC V0N 2M0 Canada
Tel: 250-656-8818
info@cfbc.bc.ca
www.cfbc.bc.ca
To maintain high professional standards in forestry consulting; To advance contact between its members, client groups, & the public at large

Council of Forest Industries (COFI)
Pender Place I Business Building, #1501, 700 Pender St. West, Vancouver BC V6C 1G8
Tel: 604-684-0211; *Fax:* 604-687-4930
info@cofi.org
www.cofi.org
To be the voice of the British Columbia interior forest industry; To offer member companies services in areas such as international market & trade development, community relations, public affairs, quality control, & forest policy

La Fédération des producteurs de bois du Québec (FPBQ)
#565, 555, boul Roland-Therrien, Longueuil QC J4H 4E7 Canada
Tél: 450-679-0530; *Téléc:* 450-679-4300
bois@upa.qc.ca
www.fpbq.qc.ca
Défendre les intérêts de l'ensemble des propriétaires de boisés du Québec ainsi que l'élaboration et la promotion des politiques souhaitables et nécessaires pour atteindre cet objectif; représenter les propriétaires de boisés privés auprès des pouvoirs publics et des autres groupes de la société au niveau provincial et national; coordonner l'ensemble des activités des Syndicats et Offices de producteurs de bois ainsi que l'établissement, le maintien et le développement entre eux d'une étroite collaboration
Jean-Pierre Dansereau, Directeur

Fored BC
#213, 4438 - 10th Ave. West, Vancouver BC V6R 4R8 Canada
Tel: 604-737-8555; *Fax:* 604-737-8598
Toll-Free: 888-288-7337
info@foredbc.org; education@foredbc.org; admin@foredbc.org
www.landscapesmag.com
To provide education to lifelong learners in all segments of society about the environment & its resources to achieve better environmental decisions & health outcomes; To engage citizens, communities, & volunteers to rehabilitate, protect, & enhance the environment

Forest Products Association of Canada (FPAC) / Association des produits forestiers du Canada
#410, 99 Bank St., Ottawa ON K1P 6B9
Tel: 613-563-1441; *Fax:* 613-563-4720
ottawa@fpac.ca; customercentre@fpac.ca
www.fpac.ca
To be the voice of Canada's wood, pulp & paper producers nationally & internationally in the areas of government, trade, & environmental affairs; To advance the Canadian forest products industry's global competitiveness & sustainable stewardship; To operate in a mannner which is economically viable, environmentally responsible, & socially desirable
Avrim Lazar, President & Chief Executive Officer
Andrew Casey, Vice-President, Public Affairs & International Trade
Catherine Cobden, Vice-President, Economics & Regulatory Affairs
Isabelle Des Chênes, Vice-President, Market Relations & Communications
Mark Hubert, Vice-President, Climate Change Leadership
Susan Murray, Executive Director, Public Relations
David Church, Director, Transportation & Recycling
Roger Cook, Director, Environment
Andrew DeVries, Director, Conservation Biology & Aboriginal Affairs
Jon Flemming, Director, Ecomonics & Trade Policy
Paul Lansbergen, Director, Energy, Economics, & Climate Change
Joel Neuheimer, Director, Market Affairs
Étienne Bélanger, Manager, Forestry Issues
George Wamala, Manager, Government Relations & Policy

Forest Products Association of Nova Scotia (FPANS)
PO Box 696, Truro NS B2N 5E5
Tel: 902-895-1179; *Fax:* 902-893-1197
www.fpans.ca
To act as the voice of the forest industry in Nova Scotia; To cooperate with industry, federal, provincial, & municipal governments, & other stakeholders to ensure adherence to forest management & stewardship policies; To promote sustainable management & viability of the forest industry
Steve Talbot, Executive Director
Jeff Bishop, Coordinator, Communications

Manitoba Forestry Association Inc.
900 Corydon Ave., Winnipeg MB R3M 0Y4 Canada
Tel: 204-453-3182; *Fax:* 204-477-5765
mfainc@mts.net
www.mbforestryassoc.ca
To promote the wise use & management of all natural renewable resources, with emphasis on forests; to promote the planting of trees; to promote private land forestry (woodlots); to act as liaison among government, industry & the general public.

Maritime Lumber Bureau (MLB) / Bureau de bois de sciage des Maritimes
PO Box 459, Amherst NS B4H 4A1 Canada
Tel: 902-667-3889; *Fax:* 902-667-0401
Toll-Free: 800-667-9192
mlb@ns.sympatico.ca
www.mlb.ca
An accredited quality control agency for the lumber industry in the region.
Diana L. Blenkhorn, President & CEO

National Aboriginal Forestry Association (NAFA)
#300, 396 Cooper St., Ottawa ON K2P 2H7 Canada
Tel: 613-233-5563; *Fax:* 613-233-4329
hbombay@nafaforestry.org
www.nafaforestry.org
To promote & support increased Aboriginal involvement in forest management & related commercial opportunities; to assist Aboriginal communities in their quest to achieve a standard of land care which is balanced, sustainable & reflective of the traditional knowledge & forest values of Aboriginal peoples; to facilitate capacity-building in forest management through the development of human resource strategies & models for increased participation in natural resource decision making; to address the need for Aboriginal forest land rehabilitation & increased Aboriginal control over forest resources through the development of appropriate policy & programming
Harry M. Bombay, Executive Director
Peggy Smith, RPF, Senior Advisor
Janet Pronovost, Office Manager

New Brunswick Forest Products Association Inc. (NBFPA) / L'Association des produits forestiers du Nouveau-Brunswick (APFNB)
Hugh John Flemming Forestry Centre, 1350 Regent St., Fredericton NB E3C 2G6 Canada
Tel: 506-452-6930; *Fax:* 506-450-3128
info@nbforestry.com
www.nbforestry.com
The New Brunswick Forest Products Association is a non-government, non-profit organization that represents its forest industry members by serving as a common voice in relations with the government and the public, promoting a healthy New Brunswick forest, raising public awareness of sustainable forest management practices, and providing a forum for the exchange of information, ideas, and concerns.

Newfoundland & Labrador Forest Protection Association
PO Box 728, Mount Pearl NL A1N 2C2 Canada
Tel: 709-729-1012; *Fax:* 709-368-2740
nlfpa@nfld.com
www.nlfpa.nfol.ca
To maintain Newfoundland's forests as a productive & renewable resource;to increase public awareness, school education & natural appreciation of forests; to bring about better understanding of forests to people of all ages & backgrounds.

Nova Scotia Forestry Association (NSFA)
PO Box 6901, Port Hawkesbury NS B9A 2W2 Canada
Tel: 902-625-2935
dwaycott@nsfa.ca
www.nsfa.ca
To conserve Nova Scotia's forests; To promote the wise use & management of forest resources

Ontario Forest Industries Association (OFIA) / l'Industrie forestière de l'Ontario
#950, 20 Toronto St., Toronto ON M5C 2B8
Tel: 416-368-6188; *Fax:* 416-368-5445
info@ofia.com
www.ofia.com
To act as a unified voice on behalf of member companies to ensure industry positions are considered; To respond to industry issues, such as economic, environmental, & technological developments

Ontario Forestry Association (OFA) / Association forestière de l'Ontario
#701, 200 Consumers Rd., Toronto ON M2J 4R4 Canada
Tel: 416-493-4565; *Fax:* 416-493-4608
Toll-Free: 800-387-0790
forestry@oforest.on.ca
www.oforest.on.ca
To promote sound land use & full development protection & utilization of Ontario's forest resources for maximum public advantage; to increase public awareness, school education & natural appreciation of forests; to bring about better understanding of forests to people of all ages & backgrounds

Ontario Lumber Manufacturers' Association (OLMA) / Association des manufacturiers de bois de sciage de l'Ontario
PO Box 97530, #1202, 55 York St., Toronto ON M1C 4Z1
Tel: 416-367-9717; *Fax:* 416-367-3415
info@olma.ca
www.olma.ca
To ensure a sound & renewable forest economy; To oversee lumber grading licenses & quality control at member sawmills in Ontario; To ensure market access within Northern America, Europe, & Japan

Ontario Professional Foresters Association (OPFA)
PO Box 91523, #201, 5 Wesleyan St., Georgetown ON L7G 2E2 Canada
Tel: 905-877-3679; *Fax:* 905-877-6766
opfa@opfa.ca
www.opfa.ca
To serve the public interest by actively contributing to the sustainability of Ontario's forests through the establishment of professional standards, encouraging the adoption & use of best practices, & ensuring the competency of those who practice professional forestry

Ontario Urban Forest Council (OUFC)
#23/25, 1523 Warden Ave., Toronto ON M1R 4Z8 Canada
Tel: 416-936-6735; *Fax:* 416-291-9584
jradec@mountpleasantgroup.com
www.oufc.org
To promote & assist in the protection & preservation of shade trees; to cooperate with all associations, government agencies, industry & individuals with a mutual interest in preserving & developing Ontario's shade tree heritage & landscape; to promote management of urban forest in Ontario

Ordre des ingénieurs forestiers du Québec (OIFQ)
#110, 2750, rue Einstein, Québec QC G1P 4R1 Canada
Tél: 418-650-2411; *Téléc:* 418-650-2168
oifq@oifq.com
www.oifq.com
Assurer la protection du public; assurer la qualité des services rendus au public québécois; favoriser l'amélioration continue de l'expertise et de la compétence des ingénieurs forestiers; mettre en place des actions favorisant la durabilité de l'aménagement forestier pour le bénéfice de l'ensemble de la société

Prince Edward Island Forest Improvement Association (PEIFIA)
c/o Richard Gill, RR#5, Mount Stewart PE C0A 1T0 Canada
Tel: 902-651-2059

Registered Professional Foresters Association of Nova Scotia (RPFANS)
PO Box 1031, Truro NS B2N 5G9
Tel: 902-893-0099
contact@rpfans.ca
www.rpfans.ca
To improve the holistic management of forest resources in Nova Scotia
Roger Aggas, Registrar
Mike Brown, Treasurer

Regroupement des associations forestières régionales du Québec
#100, 138, rue Wellington nord, Sherbrooke QC J1H 5C5 Canada
Tél: 819-562-3388; *Téléc:* 819-562-2433
info@afce.qc.ca
www.afvsm.qc.ca/region.htm
Daniel Archambault

Saskatchewan Forestry Association (SFA)
#139, 1061 Central Ave., Prince Albert SK S6V 4V4
Tel: 306-763-2189; *Fax:* 306-763-6456
info@whitebirch.ca
www.whitebirch.ca
To promote the wise use, protection, & management of forests, water, & wildlife in Saskatchewan

Sustainable Forestry Initiative
#700, 900 - 17th St. NW, Washington DC 20006 USA
info@sfiprogram.org
www.sfiprogram.org
Social Media: www.twitter.com/#!/sfiprogram
To promote sustainable forest management; To maintain & improve the sustainable forestry certification program
Kathy Abusow, President & Chief Executive Officer
Rick Cantrell, Vice-President & Chief Operating Officer
Danny Karch, Director, Green Building
Allison Welde, Director, Conservation Partnerships & Communications

Wood Preservation Canada (WPC) / Préservation du bois Canada
#202, 2141 Thurston Dr., Ottawa ON K1G 6C9
Tel: 613-737-4337; *Fax:* 613-247-0540
info@woodpreservation.ca
www.woodpreservation.ca
To represent, support & promote the treated wood industry in Canada

Fraternal

Benevolent & Protective Order of Elks of Canada
#100, 2629 - 29 Ave., Regina SK S4S 2N9 Canada
Tel: 306-359-9010; *Fax:* 306-565-2860
Toll-Free: 888-843-3557
ger@elks-canada.org
www.elks-canada.org
To promote & support community needs, through volunteer efforts of local lodges

Les Chevaliers de Colomb du Québec / Knights of Columbus of Québec
670, av Chambly, Saint-Hyacinthe QC J2S 6V4 Canada
Tél: 450-768-0616; *Téléc:* 450-768-1660
Ligne sans frais: 866-893-3681
info@chevaliersdecolomb.com
www.chevaliersdecolomb.com
Un groupe d'entraide et une société fraternelle, qui unit des hommes de foi; l'ordre n'est pas rattaché à la structure juridique de l'Église catholique mais c'est un ordre de laïcs catholiques et exclusivement masculin

Les Chevaliers de Colomb du Québec, District No 37, Conseil 5198
CP 141, 124, rue des Forces Armées, Chibougamau QC G8P 2L5 Canada
Tél: 418-748-2411
www.chevaliersdecolomb.com
Jacques Fortin, Député de district
Reynald Bouchard, Grand Chevalier

Empire Club of Canada
Fairmont Royal York Hotel, 100 Front St. West, Level H, Toronto ON M5J 1E3 Canada
Tel: 416-364-2878; *Fax:* 416-364-7271
empireclub@bellnet.ca
www.empireclubfoundation.com

Foresters
Forester House, 789 Don Mills Rd., Toronto ON M3C 1T9 Canada
Tel: 416-429-3000; *Fax:* 416-467-2518
Toll-Free: 800-828-1540
service@foresters.com
www.foresters.com
A fraternal benefit society which provides life insurance & other financial products to its members

Grand Orange Lodge of Canada
94 Sheppard Ave. West, Toronto ON M2N 1M5 Canada
Tel: 416-223-1690; *Fax:* 416-223-1324
Toll-Free: 800-565-6248
secretary@grandorangelodge.ca
www.grandorangelodge.ca
To encourage its members to actively participate in the Protestant church of their choice; to actively support the Canadian system of government; to anticipate legislation & its impact on the civil & religious liberties of all Canadians; to provide social activities which will enrich the lives of its members; to participate in benevolent activities which will enrich our communities & our country

International Association of Rebekah Assemblies
c/o The Sovereign Grand Lodge IOOF, 422 Trade St., Winston-Salem NC 27101 USA
Tel: 336-725-6037; *Fax:* 336-773-1066
Toll-Free: 800-766-1838
iarasec@aol.com
www.ioof.org/rebekahs.html
The Rebekah lodges are the female auxiliary of the Independent Order of Odd Fellows, but are open to both women and men.

IODE Canada (IODE)
#254, 40 Orchard View Blvd., Toronto ON M4R 1B9 Canada
Tel: 416-487-4416; *Fax:* 416-487-4417
Toll-Free: 866-827-7428
iodecanada@bellnet.ca
www.iode.ca
To improve the quality of life for children, youth & those in need through education, social service & citizenship programs

Knights Hospitallers, Sovereign Order of St. John of Jerusalem, Knights of Malta, Grand Priory of Canada (OSJ)
Grand Chancery Canada, 52 Kingswood Dr., Bowmanville ON L1E 1Z3 Canada
Tel: 905-579-0326; *Fax:* 905-579-3773
To propagate the principles of chivalry; care for the sick, aged, invalid, poor & children in need; protect & defend Christianity throughout the world; combat errors; champion the truth; promote & encourage the spirit of Brotherhood & charity within the order; members are expected to be united in brotherhood & charity
Joseph Frendo Cumbo, Grand Master
M. Sillato, Secretary General
Violet Sillato, Treasurer General

Knights of Pythias - Domain of British Columbia
#B7, 7155 ETC Hwy., Kamloops BC V2C 4T1 Canada
Tel: 250-573-3056
www.members.shaw.ca/veng/
Edward J. Eagles, Grand Secretary

Ladies' Orange Benevolent Association of Canada
c/o Grand Orange Lodge of Canada, 94 Sheppard Ave. West, Toronto ON M2N 1M5 Canada
Fax: 416-223-1324
Toll-Free: 800-565-6248
www.grandorangelodge.ca/loba; www.orangenet.org/loba.htm

Order of Sons of Italy in Canada
34 Lincoln St., Welland ON L3C 5J1 Canada
Tel: 905-892-3352
www.ordersonsofitalycanada.com
A fraternal organization of Canadians of Italian heritage, they work together to achieve the following purposes; SERVICE & CHARITY: To assist the needy, the ill, and disabled through financial support, the provision of housing, and other support programs; COMMUNITY INVOLVEMENT: To encourage the active participation of our members in the political, social and economic life of our community; to participate in programs combating discrimination, racism, and social injustice; HERITAGE: To promote and preserve the Italian language, culture, and traditions in our country.

The Order of United Commercial Travelers of America (UCT)
#300, 901 Centre St. North, Calgary AB T2E 2P6 Canada
Tel: 403-277-0745; *Fax:* 403-277-6662
Toll-Free: 800-267-2371
lmaxwell@uct.org
www.uct.org
Provide members with affordable insurance and support through fraternal benefit and discount programs.
Lindsay Maxwell, Chief Agent

Réseau Hommes Québec (RHQ)
#134, 911, rue Jean-Talon est, Montréal QC H2R 1V5 Canada
Tél: 514-276-4545; *Ligne sans frais:* 877-908-4545
info@rhq.ca
www.rhq.ca
Organisme sans but lucratif; a pour mission d'entretenir un réseau de groupes autogérés d'écoute, de parole & d'entraide aux hommes
Guy Corneau, Fondateur

Royal Arch Masons of Canada
361 King St. West, Hamilton ON L8P 1B4 Canada
Tel: 905-522-5775; *Fax:* 905-522-5099
Melvyn J. Duke, Grand Scribe E.

Society of Kabalarians of Canada
1160 West 10th Ave., Vancouver BC V6H 1J1 Canada
Tel: 604-263-9551; *Fax:* 604-263-5514
Toll-Free: 866-489-1188
info1@kabalarians.com
www.kabalarians.com
The Society promotes Kabalarian philosophy, which teaches a constructive way of life through the understanding of the Mathematical Principle, encouraging people to live a more progressive, constructive life.

Sons of Scotland Benevolent Association
#202, 40 Eglinton Ave. East, Toronto ON M4P 3A2 Canada
Tel: 416-482-1250; *Fax:* 416-482-9576
Toll-Free: 800-387-3382
info@sonsofscotland.com
www.sonsofscotland.com
Undertake & support activities which promote the elements of Scottish culture in Canada; honour the history & heritage of Scots in Canada; support & raise funds for charitable organizations; provide fraternal & insurance benefits for members

Yukon Order of Pioneers (YOOP)
Tel: 867-667-2564
h_rwilcox@hotmail.com
www.yukon-seniors-and-elders.org/yukonorder.home.htm
The Yukon Order of Pioneers is decicated to the advancement of the Yukon Territory, the mutual protection of its members, and to uniting those members in the strong tie of Brotherhood and to preserving the names of all Yukon Pioneers on its rolls and the collecting and preservation of the literature and incidents of the Orders history.
Rob Wilcox, President

Funeral Services

Alberta Funeral Service Association (AFSA)
#5, 5431 - 43 St., Calgary AB T2X 3C9 Canada
Tel: 403-342-2460; *Fax:* 403-342-2495
Toll-Free: 800-803-8809
inquiry@afsa.ca
www.afsa.ab.ca
To promote & improve funeral service in Alberta

Cemetery & Crematorium Association of British Columbia (CCABC)
#211, 2187 Oak Bay Ave., Victoria BC V8R 1G1 Canada
Tel: 866-587-3213
info@ccabc.org
www.ccabc.org
To promote high standards of ethics & service in the cemetery & crematorium profession in British Columbia; to act as a collective voice to regulators

Corporation des thanatologues du Québec (CTQ)
#115, 4600, boul Henri-Bourassa, Québec QC G1H 3A5 Canada
Tél: 418-622-1717; *Téléc:* 418-622-5557
Ligne sans frais: 800-463-4935
info@corpothanato.com
www.corpothanato.com
Marc Porier, Président

Funeral & Cremation Services Council of Saskatchewan
3847C Albert St., Regina SK S4S 3R4 Canada
Tel: 306-584-1575; *Fax:* 306-584-1576
Toll-Free: 800-892-0116
sask.funeral@sasktel.net
www.fcscs.ca
Terry Zip, Chair
R.G. (Bob) Carter, Registrar

Funeral Advisory & Memorial Society (FAMS)
55 St. Phillips Rd., Toronto ON M9P 2N8 Canada
Tel: 416-241-6274
info@fams.ca
www.fams.ca
To provide unbiased consumer advice on funeral planning

Funeral Service Association of British Columbia (FSABC)
#211, 2187 Oak Bay Ave., Victoria BC V8R 1G1 Canada
Tel: 250-592-3213; *Fax:* 250-592-4362
Toll-Free: 800-665-3899
info@bcfunerals.com
www.bcfunerals.com
To promote, through education, communication, & leadership, the highest standards of ethics & service in the funeral profession

Funeral Service Association of Canada (FSAC) / L'Association des services funéraires du Canada
#6, 14845 Yonge St., Suite 192, Aurora ON L4G 6H8 Canada
Tel: 905-841-7779; *Toll-Free:* 866-841-7779
info@fsac.ca
www.fsac.ca
To provide a collective voice for the Canadian funeral professional; To provide high quality professional services with dignity & competence; To ensure compliance with all provisions of the law; To provide information about services

Manitoba Funeral Service Association (MFSA)
PO Box 48067, Stn. RPO Lakewood, Winnipeg MB R2J 4A3
Tel: 204-947-0927; *Fax:* 204-269-7148
info@mfsa.mb.ca
www.mfsa.mb.ca
To serve funeral directors & funeral homes throughout Manitoba; To advance funeral service; To uphold a code of ethics
Jody Nicholson, President
Thorunn Petursdottir, Executive Director
Janice Dryden, Secretary-Treasurer

Newfoundland & Labrador Funeral Services Association (NLFSA)
PO Box 138, Winterton NL A0G 3M0 Canada
Tel: 709-586-2721; *Fax:* 709-586-2888
contact@nlfuneralboard.ca
www.nlfuneralboard.ca/nlfuneralservices.html
The Association offers funeral service support for the province of NFLD & Labrador.
Milton Peach, President
Wayne Bennett, Vice-President

Ontario Association of Cemetery & Funeral Professionals (OACFP)
PO Box 10173, 27 Legend Ct., Ancaster ON L9K 1P3 Canada
Tel: 905-383-6528; *Toll-Free:* 888-558-3335
info@oacfp.com
www.oacfp.com
To promote high standards of service & the professional operation of cemeteries, funeral homes, crematoria, & related bereavement services

Ontario Funeral Service Association (OFSA)
#203, 3425 Harvester Rd., Burlington ON L7N 3N1
Tel: 905-637-3371; *Fax:* 905-637-3583
Toll-Free: 800-268-2727
info@ofsa.org
www.ofsa.org
To maintain high standards of services & ethical business practices among Ontario's funeral homes for the welfare of the public; To represent & support Ontario's independently owned funeral establishments
Myles O'Riordan, President
Cathie Turner, Vice-President
Kerri Douglas, Executive Coordinator
Lesley Bingley, Secretary-Treasurer

Prince Edward Island Funeral Directors & Embalmers Association
PO Box 540, Kensington PE C0B 1M0
Tel: 902-836-3313; *Fax:* 902-836-4461
To ensure professional services of the highest standards
Faye Doucette, President

Fur Trade

Canadian Association for Humane Trapping (CAHT)
PO Box 7115, Stn. Maplehurst, Burlington ON L7T 4J8 Canada
Tel: 905-637-9623; *Fax:* 905-637-3912
caht1@cogeco.ca
www.caht.ca
To reduce & eliminate suffering of animals trapped for whatever reason; to work with governments, trappers, the commercial fur industry, animal welfare organizations & the public-at-large to bring about actual trapping improvements

The Fur Council of Canada (FCC) / Conseil canadien de la fourrure
#1270, 1435, rue Saint-Alexandre, Montréal QC H3A 2G4 Canada
Tel: 514-844-1945; *Fax:* 514-844-8593
info@furcouncil.com
www.furcouncil.com
To promote all aspects of the fur trade

Fur Institute of Canada (FIC) / Institut de la fourrure du Canada (IFC)
#701, 331 Cooper St., Ottawa ON K2P 0G5 Canada
Tel: 613-231-7099; *Fax:* 613-231-7940
info@fur.ca
www.fur.ca
To promote the sustainable & wise use of Canadian fur resources
Robert B. Cahill, Executive Director
Bruce Williams, Chair
Mary Baskin, Manager, Corporate & Communications

Fur-Bearer Defenders (FBD)
#101, 225 - 17th Ave. East, Vancouver BC V5V 1A6 Canada
Tel: 604-435-1850; *Fax:* 604-435-1840
fbd@banlegholdtraps.com
www.banlegholdtraps.com; www.dogcatfur.com
To stop trapping cruelty & protect fur-bearing animals

Furriers Guild of Canada
#211, 4174 Dundas St. West, Toronto ON M8X 1X3 Canada
Tel: 416-234-9494; *Fax:* 416-234-2244
furriersguildca@ica.net
To promote Canadian fur retailers

Galleries & Museums

Alberta Museums Association
Rossdale House, 9829 - 103 St., Edmonton AB T5K 0X9 Canada
Tel: 780-424-2626; *Fax:* 780-425-1679
info@museums.ab.ca
www.museums.ab.ca
To promote understanding, access & excellence within Alberta's museums for the benefit of society

Association Museums New Brunswick (AMNB) / Association des musées du Nouveau-Brunswick
668 Brunswick St., Fredericton NB E3B 1H6 Canada
Tel: 506-452-2908; *Fax:* 506-459-0481
amnb@nb.aibn.com
www.amnb.ca
To preserve New Brunswick's heritage by uniting, promoting & advancing our heritage workers, supporters & organizations

Association of Manitoba Museums (AMM)
#1040, 555 Main St., Winnipeg MB R3B 1C3 Canada
Tel: 204-947-1782; *Fax:* 204-942-3749
Toll-Free: 866-747-9323
info@museumsmanitoba.com
www.museumsmanitoba.com
To strengthen the museum community by promoting excellence in preserving & presenting Manitoba's heritage; To improve the AMM's ability to communicate with its members; To continue a training program

Atlantic Provinces Art Gallery Association (APAGA)
c/o MSVU Art Gallery, 166 Bedford Hwy., Halifax NS B3M 2J6 Canada
Tel: 902-457-6160; *Fax:* 902-457-2447
info@apaga.com
www.apaga.ca
To pursue & promote high standards of excellence in care & presentation of works of art in public art galleries in the Atlantic region; to encourage the closest possible cooperation between art galleries, museums & artists; to serve as an advisory body in matters of professional interest

British Columbia Museums Association (BCMA)
#204, 26 Bastion Sq., Victoria BC V8W 1H9 Canada
Tel: 250-356-5700; *Fax:* 250-387-1251
Toll-Free: 800-663-7867
bcma@museumsassn.bc.ca
www.museumsassn.bc.ca
To promote the protection & preservation of the objects, specimens, records & sites significant to the natural, creative & human history of British Columbia; to aid in the improvement of museums & galleries as educational institutions; to assist in the development of the museum profession.

Canadian Federation of Friends of Museums (CFFM) / Fédération canadienne des amis de musées (FCAM)
c/o Art Gallery of Ontario, 317 Dundas St. West, Toronto ON M5T 1G4 Canada
Tel: 416-979-6650; *Fax:* 416-979-6674
cffm_fcam@ago.net
www.cffm-fcam.ca
To serve as source of information & expertise for friends of museums, interests, experiences & concerns, & by linking such groups together; to serve as communications network & national voice for those who are dedicated to support & promotion of museums for the benefit of all Canadians

Canadian Museums Association (CMA) / Association des musées canadiens
#400, 280 Metcalfe St., Ottawa ON K2P 1R7 Canada
Tel: 613-567-0099; *Fax:* 613-233-5438
Toll-Free: 888-822-2907
info@museums.ca
www.museums.ca
The CMA works for the advancement of a strong, vital, & valued Canadian museum sector.

Community Museums Association of Prince Edward Island
PO Box 22002, 161 St. Peter's Rd., Charlottetown PE C1A 9J2 Canada
Tel: 902-892-8837; *Fax:* 902-892-1459
info@museumspei.ca
www.museumspei.ca
To foster & support museums, historical societies & other non-profit organizations concerned with heritage of PEI.
Barbara Boys MacCormac, President
Barry King, Ph.D., Executive Director

ICOM Museums Canada / ICOM Musées Canada
#400, 280 Metcalfe St., Ottawa ON K2P 1R7 Canada
Tel: 613-567-0099; *Fax:* 613-233-5438
icom@museums.ca
To advance the cause of museums throughout the world & in Canada; to provide liaison with International Council of Museums in Paris; to hold annual meeting in conjunction with Canadian Museums Association.

Museum Association of Newfoundland & Labrador (MANL)
The Colonial Building, PO Box 5785, Military Rd., St. John's NL A1C 5X3 Canada
Tel: 709-722-9034; *Fax:* 709-722-9035
manl@nf.aibn.com
www.manl.nf.ca
To protect & preserve the cultural & natural heritage of Newfoundland & Labrador; To unite, support & promote members; To improve & promote museums

Museums Association of Saskatchewan (MAS)
422 McDonald St., Regina SK S4N 6E1 Canada
Tel: 306-780-9279; *Fax:* 306-780-9463
mas@saskmuseums.org
www.saskmuseums.org
To work for the advancement of strong & vibrant museums in Saskatchewan; To encourage the preservation & understanding of the province's cultural & natural heritage; To serve Saskatchewan museums

Ontario Association of Art Galleries (OAAG)
#617, 111 Peter St., Toronto ON M5V 2H1 Canada
Tel: 416-598-0714; *Fax:* 416-598-4128
oaag@oaag.com
www.oaag.org
To encourage the highest standards for the exhibition, interpretation, & conservation of the visual arts; to develop tools to assist gallery professionals in achieving institutional goals; to advance positive, responsive relations with government, its agencies, & the citizens of Ontario.

Ontario Museum Association (OMA) / Association des musées de l'Ontario
George Brown House, 50 Baldwin St., Toronto ON M5T 1L4 Canada
Tel: 416-348-8672; *Fax:* 416-348-0438
communications@museumsontario.com
www.museumsontario.com
To enhance the mission of museums as significant cultural resources in the service of Ontario society & its development

Organization of Military Museums of Canada, Inc. (OMMC) / L'Organisation des musées militaires du Canada inc.
PO Box 213, Gatineau QC J9H 5E5 Canada
Tel: 819-682-5192; *Fax:* 819-682-8348
ommc@storm.ca
www.ommc.ca
To preserve the military heritage of Canada by encouraging the establishment & operation of military museums; to educate museum staffs through lectures, discussions, workshops, visits, publications & exhibits; to cooperate with others having the same or similar purposes.

La Société des musées québécois (SMQ)
CP 8888, Succ. Centre-Ville - UQAM, Montréal QC H3C 3P8 Canada
Tél: 514-987-3264; *Téléc:* 514-987-3379
info@smq.uqam.ca
www.musees.qc.ca
Au service du développement de la muséologie au Québec

Yukon Historical & Museums Association (YHMA)
3126 - 3 Ave., Whitehorse YT Y1A 1E7 Canada
Tel: 867-667-4704; *Fax:* 867-667-4506
yhma@northwestel.net
www.heritageyukon.ca
To preserve & foster an appreciation of the Yukon's history & culture; to act as forum for other museum & heritage organizations in the region
Tracey Anderson, Executive Director

Gas & Oil

Canadian Association of Petroleum Producers (CAPP) / Association canadienne des producteurs pétroliers
#2100, 350 - 7 Ave. SW, Calgary AB T2P 3N9 Canada
Tel: 403-267-1100; *Fax:* 403-261-4622
communication@capp.ca; membership@capp.ca; publications@capp.ca
www.capp.ca
To represent companies that produce Canada's natural gas & crude oil; To enhance the economic sustainability of the Canadian upstream petroleum industry; To ensure work is conducted in a safe & environmentally & socially responsible manner; To work with government to develop regulatory requirements

Canadian Energy Pipeline Association (CEPA)
#1860, 205 - 5th Ave. SW, Calgary AB T2P 2V7 Canada
Tel: 403-221-8777; *Fax:* 403-221-8760
info@cepa.com
www.cepa.com
The Canadian Energy Pipeline Association (CEPA) represents Canada's trasmissions pipeline companie. Their members transport 97% of Canada's daily crude oil and natural gas production from producing regions to markets throughout Canada and the United States.
Brenda Kenny, President
Myra Paul, Administrative Assistant

Canadian Gas Association (CGA) / Association canadienne du gaz
#809, 350 Sparks St., Ottawa ON K1R 7S8
Tel: 613-748-0057; *Fax:* 613-748-9078
info@cga.ca
www.cga.ca
To act as the voice of the natural gas distribution industry in Canada
Timothy M. Egan, President & Chief Executive Officer
Paula Dunlop, Director, Public Affairs & Strategy
Bryan Gormely, Director, Policy, Economics, & Information
Jim Tweedie, Director, Operations, Safety, & Integrity Management
Valerie Prokop, Manager, Finance & Corporate Services

Canadian Society of Petroleum Geologists (CSPG)
#600, 640 - 8th Ave. SW, Calgary AB T2P 1G7 Canada
Tel: 403-264-5610; *Fax:* 403-264-5898
cspg@cspg.org
www.cspg.org
To advance the science of geology, especially as it relates to petroleum, natural gas & other fossil fuels; to promote the technology of exploration for finding & producing these resources; to foster the spirit of scientific research; to develop a sense of pride & community among Canadian Petroleum Geologists; to provide the means to ensure that the Canadian Petroleum Geologist is the best trained, best supported & most skillful practitioner in the world

Gas Processing Association Canada (GPAC)
#505, 900 - 6th Ave. SW, Calgary AB T2P 3K2 Canada
Tel: 403-705-0223; *Fax:* 403-263-6886
info@gpacanada.com
www.gpacanada.com
To promote interaction & exchange of ideas & technology that will add value to those who are involved with or affected by the hydrocarbon processing industry

Industrial Gas Users Association Inc. (IGUA) / Association des consommateurs industriels de gaz (ACIG)
#1201, 99 Metcalfe St., Ottawa ON K1P 6L7 Canada
Tel: 613-236-8021; *Fax:* 613-230-9531
www.igua.ca
To provide a coordinated & effective voice for industrial firms depending on natural gas as fuel or feedstock; to represent industrial users of natural gas before regulatory boards & governments

NOIA
Atlantic Place, #602, 215 Water St., St. John's NL A1C 6C9 Canada
Tel: 709-758-6610; *Fax:* 709-758-6611
www.noianet.com
To assist, promote & facilitate the participation of members in ocean industries, with particular emphasis on oil & gas, to enhance their growth & development; to promote the growth of ocean industry; to act as a focal point for representations to government bodies & agencies; to act as a source of information & education for members
Robert Cadigan, President & CEO

Offshore/Onshore Technologies Association of Nova Scotia (OTANS)
#400, 1718 Argyle St., Halifax NS B3J 3N6 Canada
Tel: 902-425-4774; *Fax:* 902-422-2332
otans@otans.com
www.otans.com
To identify, promote & support the development of opportunities both offshore & onshore in the oil & gas industry

Ontario Petroleum Institute Inc. (OPI)
#104, 555 Southdale Rd. East, London ON N6E 1A2 Canada
Tel: 519-680-1620; *Fax:* 519-680-1621
opi@ontpet.com
www.ontpet.com
To promote responsible exploration & development by Ontario's oil, gas, hydrocarbon storage, & solution-mining industries

Petroleum Research Atlantic Canada (PRAC)
1321 Edward St., Halifax NS B3H 3H5 Canada
Tel: 902-494-2960; *Fax:* 902-494-2489
info@pr-ac.ca
www.pr-ac.ca
To build petroleum-related research & development capability & capacity throughout Atlantic Canada; to establish research priorities, coordinate research proposals, provide seed funding for research & development, identify opportunities & provide support in the administration of research programs
David Finn, President

Petroleum Services Association of Canada (PSAC)
#1150, 800 - 6 Ave. SW, Calgary AB T2P 3G3
Tel: 403-264-4195; *Fax:* 403-263-7174
info@psac.ca
www.psac.ca
To represent the supply, manufacturing, & service sectors of the upstream petroleum industry
Mark Salkeld, President & Chief Executive Officer
Elizabeth Aquin, Senior Vice-President
Patrick J. Delaney, Vice-President, Health & Safety
Kelly Morrison, Director, Communications & Stakeholder Relations
Heather Doyle, Manager, Meetings & Events
Holly Kerr, Manager, Communications & Member Relations

Petroleum Society of CIM
#425, 500 - 5th Ave. SW, Calgary AB T2P 3L5 Canada
Tel: 403-237-5112; *Fax:* 403-262-4792
info@petsoc.org
www.petsoc.org
To promote the advancement & sharing of technology in petroleum exploration, production, transportation & marketing

through publications, meetings, courses, networking & the recognition of individuals who have contributed to the society & the petroleum industry
Anthony Au, Treasurer

Propane Gas Association of Canada Inc. (PGAC) / Association canadienne du gaz propane inc.
#800, 717 - 7th Ave. SW, Calgary AB T2P 3C4
Tel: 403-543-6500; *Fax:* 403-543-6508
Toll-Free: 877-784-4636
info@propanegas.ca
www.propanegas.ca
To act as the national voice of the Canadian propane industry; To supports its members in the development of a safe, environmentally responsible Canadian propane industry

Gems & Jewellery

Alberta Federation of Rock Clubs (AFRC)
14827 - 45 Ave., Edmonton AB T6H 5R4 Canada
Tel: 780-430-6694
paulinez@telus.net
www.afrc.ca
To assist member clubs by providing information & expertise; to promote the study of the Earth Sciences
Alice Watts, President
Pauline Zeschuk, Secretary

Canadian Gemmological Association (CGA)
1767 Avenue Rd., Toronto ON M5M 3Y8 Canada
Tel: 416-785-0962; *Fax:* 416-785-9043
Toll-Free: 877-244-3090
info@canadiangemmological.com
www.canadiangemmological.com
To set a standard for excellence in the practice of gemmology

Canadian Institute of Gemmology (CIG) / Institut canadien de gemmologie
c/o School of Jewellery Arts, PO Box 57010, Vancouver BC V5K 5G6 Canada
Tel: 604-530-8569
wolf@cigem.ca
www.cigem.ca
To serve the jewellery industry & the general public
Wolf Kuehn, Executive Director

Canadian Jewellers Association (CJA)
#600, 27 Queen St. East, Toronto ON M5C 2M6 Canada
Tel: 416-368-7616; *Fax:* 416-368-1986
Toll-Free: 800-580-0942
cja@canadianjewellers.com
www.canadianjewellers.com
The members of CJA are entrusted with the responsibility of sale and service of jewellery, watches and related products and agree to the following: maintaining the highest level of personal integrity, honesty, and business ethics; comply with all government laws and regulations relating to the jewellery and watch industry; supoort and abide by the regulations, constitution, and objectives of the CJA and Code of Ethics; provide high standards; provide knowledge and expertise; to clearly establish the guarnatee and/or service policy regarding all merch; to adhere to sound business practices; to refrain from all forms of copyright and trademark infringement.

Corporation des bijoutiers du Québec (CBQ) / Québec Jewellers' Corporation
868, rue Brisette, Sainte-Julie QC J3E 2B1 Canada
Tél: 514-485-3333; *Téléc:* 450-649-8984
info@cbq.qc.ca
www.cbq.qc.ca
La promotion des membres, la défence de leurs intérêts économiques et sociaux et le développement du professionnalisme chez les membres; garantir au public un meilleur service et l'intégrité des bijoutiers membres; accroître la compétence des gens du métier; favoriser l'exercise du métier selon l'art et la science

Gem & Mineral Federation of Canada (GMFC) / Fédération canadienne des gemmes et des minéraux
PO Box 42015, Stn. North, Winfield BC V4V 1Z8 Canada
Tel: 250-376-4878
president@gmfc.ca
www.gmfc.ca
To promote earth sciences; to protect collecting sites; to educate collectors; to foster good will, friendship & rapport among all
Winifred Robertson, President

Jewellers Vigilance Canada Inc. (JVC)
#600, 27 Queen St. East, Toronto ON M5C 2M6 Canada
Tel: 416-368-4840; *Fax:* 416-368-5552
Toll-Free: 800-636-9536
info@jewellersvigilance.ca
www.jewellersvigilance.ca
Jewellers Vigilance Canada (JVC) was established in 1987 as an independent non-profit association with a mandate to advance ethical practices, establish a level playing field for the Canadian jewellery industry and provide crime prevention education for the trade.

Government & Public Administration

Alberta Association of Municipal Districts & Counties (AAMD&C)
2510 Sparrow Dr., Nisku AB T9E 8N5
Tel: 780-955-3639; *Fax:* 780-955-3615
aamdc@aamdc.com
www.aamdc.com

Alberta Municipal Clerks Association (AMCA)
c/o City of Spruce Grove, 315 Jespersen Dr., Spruce Grove AB T7X 3E8 Canada
Tel: 780-962-7634
communications@albertamunicipalclerks.com
www.albertamunicipalclerks.com
To provide a forum for exchange of ideas among the municipal clerks of the municipalities of Alberta; to provide a means for presentation of suggested amendments in legislation to senior government; to work in conjunction with any other organization, having as its objective the betterment of administration of local government

Alberta Rural Municipal Administrators Association
6027 - 4 St. NE, Calgary AB T2K 4Z5 Canada
Tel: 403-275-0622; *Fax:* 403-275-8179
d_vschmaltz@shaw.ca
www.armaa.ca

Alberta Urban Municipalities Association (AUMA)
10507 Saskatchewan Dr. NW, Edmonton AB T6E 4S1 Canada
Tel: 780-433-4431; *Fax:* 780-433-4454
Toll-Free: 800-310-2862
main@auma.ca
www.auma.ca
To provide leadership in advocating local government interests to the provincial government & other organizations, & to provide services that address the needs of its membership

Association des directeurs généraux des municipalités du Québec
#129, 10, rue Hugues-Pommier, Beauport QC G1E 4T9 Canada
Tél: 418-660-7591; *Téléc:* 418-660-0848
adgmq@adgmq.qc.ca
www.adgmq.qc.ca/
Permettre l'amélioration des connaissances et du statut de ses membres et la promotion de la formule de gestion conseil/directeur général

Association des directeurs municipaux du Québec (ADMQ)
#500, 580, av Grande-Allée est, Québec QC G1R 2K2 Canada
Tél: 418-647-4518; *Téléc:* 418-647-4115
admq@admq.qc.ca
admq.qc.ca/
De voir à la promotion et à la défense des membres en plus d'offrir un soutien professionnel constant au niveau des outils de formation et de communication

Association francophone des municipalités du Nouveau-Brunswick inc. (AFMNB)
#322, 702, rue Principale, Petit-Rocher NB E8J 1V1 Canada
Tél: 506-542-2622; *Téléc:* 506-542-2618
Ligne sans frais: 888-236-2622
afmnb@afmnb.org
www.afmnb.org
Promouvoir le développement des municipalités francophones du Nouveau-Brunswick
Lise Ouellette, Directrice générale
Jean Lanteigne, Président

Association internationale des maires francophones - Bureau à Québec (AIMF)
CP 700, Succ. Haute-Ville, #312, 2, rue des Jardins, Québec QC G1R 4S9 Canada
Tél: 418-641-6434; *Téléc:* 418-641-6318
Favoriser les échanges et la coopérations entre les villes membres
Jean-Paul L'Allier

Association of Manitoba Municipalities (AMM)
1910 Saskatchewan Ave. West, Portage la Prairie MB R1N 0P1 Canada
Tel: 204-857-8666; *Fax:* 204-856-2370
amm@amm.mb.ca
www.amm.mb.ca
To provide communications link between municipalities; to lobby for municipal governments with senior levels of government
Joe Masi, Executive Director
Ron Bell, President

Association of Municipal Administrators of New Brunswick (AMANB) / Association des administrateurs municipaux du Nouveau-Brunswick (AAMNB)
PO Box 30044, Stn. Prospect Plaza RPO, Fredericton NB E3B 0H8 Canada
Tel: 506-453-4229; *Fax:* 506-444-5452
amanb@nb.aibn.com
www.amanb-aamnb.ca
To promote & advance status of persons employed in field of municipal administration; to advance quality of administration of municipal services; to encourage closer official & personal relationship among members to facilitate interchange of ideas & experience; to establish & maintain standards of performance for members; to assist in provision of formal training & educational facilities

Association of Municipal Administrators, Nova Scotia (AMANS)
#1106, 1809 Barrington St., Halifax NS B3J 3K8 Canada
Tel: 902-423-2215; *Fax:* 902-425-5592
amans@eastlink.ca
www.amans.ca
To improve the quality of local government in Nova Scotia through the development of educational programs; to provide a forum for the exchange of ideas; to provide a resource to municipal officials; to provide service to members to improve their professional capabilities

Association of Municipal Managers, Clerks & Treasurers of Ontario (AMCTO) / Association des directeurs généraux, secrétaires et trésoriers municipaux de l'Ontario (ASTMO)
#910, 2680 Skymark Ave., Mississauga ON L4W 5L6 Canada
Tel: 905-602-4294; *Fax:* 905-602-4295
amcto@amcto.com
www.amcto.com
To foster administrative excellence in local government; to identify & meet training & education needs in local government; to be an influential voice for local government; to provide an effective communication forum for local government; to promote public awareness of & confidence in local government; to facilitate change within AMCTO

Association of Municipalities of Ontario (AMO)
#801, 200 University Ave., Toronto ON M5H 3C6
Tel: 416-971-9856; *Fax:* 416-971-6191
Toll-Free: 877-426-6527
amo@amo.on.ca; municom@amo.on.ca; policy@amo.on.ca
www.amo.on.ca
To support & enhance strong & effective municipal government in Ontario; To represent almost all of Ontario's 444 municipal governments

Association of Yukon Communities (AYC)
#15, 1114 - 1st Ave., Whitehorse YT Y1A 1A3 Canada
Tel: 867-668-4388; *Fax:* 867-668-7574
ayc@northwestel.net
www.ayc.yk.ca
To further the establishment of responsible government at the community level; to provide a united approach to issues affecting local governments; to advance ambitions & goals of member communities by developing a shared common vision of the future; to represent members in matters affecting them & the welfare of their communities; to provide programs & services of common interest & benefit to members

Association québécoise du loisir municipal (AQLM)
CP 1000, Succ. M, 4545, av Pierre-de-Coubertin, Montréal QC H1V 3R2 Canada
Tél: 514-252-3142; *Téléc:* 514-252-3150
infoaqlm@loisirmunicipal.qc.ca
www.loisirmunicipal.qc.ca
Intégrer le domaine de vie communautaire au mandat de loisir; affirmer la maîtrise d'oeuvre de la municipalité en loisir; faire valoir le service municipal de loisir comme partenaire du réseau des organisations locales (institutionnelles et associatives); promouvoir l'expertise des professionnels du loisir; démontrer l'utilité et les bénéfices du loisir; développer des pratiques professionnelles en loisir

Canadian Association of Municipal Administrators (CAMA)
PO Box 128, Stn. A, Fredericton NB E3B 4Y2
Tel: 866-771-2262
admin@camacam.ca
www.camacam.ca
To advance excellence in municipal management throughout Canada
Jacques Des Ormeaux, President
Ron Shaw, Treasurer

Canadian Council on Social Development (CCSD) / Conseil canadien de développement social (CCDS)
#100, 190 O'Connor St., Ottawa ON K2P 2R3
Tel: 613-236-8977; *Fax:* 613-236-2750
council@ccsd.ca; research@ccsd.ca; media@ccsd.ca; work@ccsd.ca
www.ccsd.ca
To develop & promote prgressive social policies, on issues such as child well-being, poverty, housing, employment. cultural diversity, & social inclusion

Cities of New Brunswick Association
PO Box 1421, Stn. A, 95 Duffie Dr., Fredericton NB E3B 5E3 Canada
Tel: 506-693-0008; *Fax:* 506-693-0009
cnbacnb@nbnet.nb.ca
Sandra Mark, Executive Director

Corporation des officiers municipaux agréés du Québec (COMAQ) / Corporation of Chartered Municipal Officers of Québec
Édifice Lomer-Gouin, #R02, 575, rue Saint-Amable, Québec QC G1R 2G4 Canada
Tél: 418-527-1231; *Téléc:* 418-527-4462
Ligne sans frais: 800-305-1031
info@comaq.qc.ca
www.comaq.qc.ca
Regrouper les cadres municipaux des cités et villes du Québec; promouvoir la formation professionnelle par l'organisation de cours; protéger les intérêts sociaux-économiques des membres.

Council of Maritime Premiers/Council of Atlantic Premiers (CMP/CAP) / Conseil des premiers ministres des Maritimes/Conseil des premiers ministres de l'Alantique
PO Box 2044, #1006, 5161 George St., Halifax NS B3J 2Z1 Canada
Tel: 902-424-7590; *Fax:* 902-424-8976
info@cap-cpma.ca
www.cap-cpma.ca
Don Osmond, Secretary

Democracy Watch
PO Box 821, Stn. B, #1210, 1 Nicholas St., Ottawa ON K1P 5P9 Canada
Tel: 613-241-5179; *Fax:* 613-241-4758
dwatch@web.net
www.dwatch.ca
To advocate for democratic reform, government accountability, and corporate responsibility.
Duff Conacher, Coordinator

Federation of Canadian Municipalities (FCM) / Fédération canadienne des municipalités
24 Clarence St., Ottawa ON K1N 5P3 Canada
Tel: 613-241-5221; *Fax:* 613-241-7440
federation@fcm.ca
www.fcm.ca
FCM is the national voice of municipal government that represents the interests of municipalities on policy & program matters that fall within federal jurisdiction. Its goal in serving elected municipal officials is the improvement of the quality of life in all communities.

Federation of Northern Ontario Municipalities (FONOM)
PO Box 2175, Stn. A, Sudbury ON P3A 4S1
Tel: 705-586-9120; *Fax:* 705-586-9195
fonom@eastlink.ca
www.fonom.org
To act as the voice for the people of northeastern Ontario communities; To work for the betterment of municipal government by striving for improved legislation respecting local government in northern Ontario

Federation of Prince Edward Island Municipalities Inc. (FPEIM)
1 Kirkdale Rd., Charlottetown PE C1E 1R3 Canada
Tel: 902-566-1493; *Fax:* 902-566-2880
info@fpeim.ca
www.fpeim.ca
To represent the interests of the cities, towns & communities within PEI; to secure united action for the protection of individual municipalities & municipal interests as a whole; to act as a clearing house for the collection, exchange & dissemination of information of concern & interest to member municipalities; to provide training, education & development opportunities for elected & appointed municipal officials

Fédération Québécoise des Municipalités (FQM)
#560, 2954, boul Laurier, Sainte-Foy QC G1V 4T2 Canada
Tél: 418-651-3343; *Téléc:* 418-651-1127
fqm@fqm.ca
www.fqm.ca
Etre la porte-parole des régions; défendre les intérêts de ses membres
Bernard Généreux, Président

Foreign Service Community Association (FSCA) / Association de la communauté du service extérieur (ACSE)
L.B. Pearson Building, 125 Sussex Dr., Ottawa ON K1A 0G2 Canada
Tel: 613-944-5729; *Fax:* 613-995-9335
fsca.acse@international.gc.ca
www.fsca-acse.org
To support the employees, spouses, & dependants of Canadian foreign service departments; To act as a liaison between families of the Canadian Foreign Service & Foreign Affairs Canada (FAC), the Canadian International Development Agency (CIDA), International Trade Canada (ITCan), Citizenship & Immigration Canada (CIC), & the Department National Defence (DND)

Government Finance Officers Association (GFOA)
#2700, 203 North LaSalle St., Chicago IL 60601-1210 USA
Tel: 312-977-9700; *Fax:* 312-977-4806
inquiry@gfoa.org
www.gfoa.org
To serve the public finance profession in the the United States & Canada

Institute of Public Administration of Canada (IPAC) / Institut d'administration publique du Canada (IAPC)
#401, 1075 Bay St., Toronto ON M5S 2B1
Tel: 416-924-8787; *Fax:* 416-924-4992
www.ipac.ca
To advance public service excellence, by sharing effective practices & policy in public administration; To lead public administration research in Canada; To further professional, non-artisan public service

Institute On Governance (IOG) / Institut sur la gouvernance
122 Clarence St., Ottawa ON K1N 5P6 Canada
Tel: 613-562-0090; *Fax:* 613-562-0097
info@iog.ca
www.iog.ca
To explore, share & promote responsible & responsive governance in Canada & abroad; to help governments, the voluntary sector & communities put it into practice.
Maryantonett Flumian, President
Laura Edgar, Vice President
John Graham, Senior Associate
Scott Serson, Chair

Local Government Management Association of British Columbia (LGMA)
Central Building, 620 View St., 7th Fl., Victoria BC V8W 1J6
Tel: 250-383-7032; *Fax:* 250-384-4879
office@lgma.ca; editor@lgma.ca (magazine); ads@lgma.ca
www.lgma.ca
To promote professional management & leadership excellence in local government; To create awareness of local government officers' roles in the community

Manitoba Municipal Administrators' Association Inc.
533 Buckingham Rd., Winnipeg MB R3R 1B9 Canada
Tel: 204-255-4883; *Fax:* 204-255-2623
mmaa@mts.net
www.mmaa.mb.ca
The Manitoba Municipal Administrators' Association (MMAA) is a dynamic, action-orientated organization for Municipal Employees. The MMAA focusses on the needs of our membership and are committed to their professional development.

Municipalities Newfoundland & Labrador
460 Torbay Rd., St. John's NL A1A 5J3 Canada
Tel: 709-753-6820; *Fax:* 709-738-0071
Toll-Free: 800-440-6536
mnl@municipalitiesnl.com
www.municipalitiesnl.com
To assist communities in their endeavour to achieve & sustain strong & effective local government thereby improving the quality of life for all the people of this province.

National Association of Federal Retirees (FSNA) / L'Association nationale des retraités fédéraux (ANRF)
1052 St. Laurent Blvd., Ottawa ON K1K 3B4 Canada
Tel: 613-745-2559; *Fax:* 613-745-5457
info@fsna.com
www.fsna.com
To protect & enhance the rights & benefits of retired federal employees, & seniors in general, & to cooperate with other seniors'/pensioners' organizations on objectives of mutual interest

Northwest Territories Association of Communities (NWTAC)
Finn Hansen Bldg., #200, 5105 - 50th St., Yellowknife NT X1A 1S1 Canada
Tel: 867-873-8359; *Fax:* 867-873-3042
Toll-Free: 866-973-8359
www.nwtac.com
To promote the exchange of information amongst the community governments of the Northwest Territories and to provide a united front for the realization of goals.
Yvette Gonzalez, CEO

Northwestern Ontario Municipal Association (NOMA)
PO Box 10308, Thunder Bay ON P7B 6T8
Tel: 807-683-6662
admin@noma.on.ca
www.noma.on.ca
To consider matters of interest to municipalities in northwestern Ontario; To procure enactment of legislation which may be advantageous to northwestern Ontario's municipalities

Ontario Municipal Human Resources Association (OMHRA)
#307, 1235 Fairview St., Burlington ON L7S 2K9
Tel: 905-525-4000; *Fax:* 905-525-9833
admin@omhra.ca
www.omhra.ca
To provide direction on issues of human resources management; To represent the interests of the association, related to legislation & policies

Ontario Municipal Management Institute (OMMI)
618 Balmoral Dr., Oshawa ON L1J 3A7 Canada
Tel: 905-434-8885; *Fax:* 905-434-7381
www.ommi.on.ca
To enhance management skills, in order to strengthen local government administration

Ontario Small Urban Municipalities (OSUM)
c/o Association of Municipalities of Ontario, #801, 200 University Ave., Toronto ON M5H 3C6
Tel: 416-971-9856; *Fax:* 416-971-6191
Toll-Free: 877-426-6527
amo@amo.on.ca
www.amo.on.ca//AM/Template.cfm?Section=What_s_New7
To take matters which affect Ontario's small urban communities to the attention of the provincial & federal governments

The Public Affairs Association of Canada (PAAC) / Association des affaires publiques du Canada
#301, 250 Consumers Rd., Toronto ON M2J 4V6 Canada
Tel: 416-367-2223; *Fax:* 416-495-8723
info@publicaffairs.ca
www.publicaffairs.ca
To improve the professionalism of members to enhance the relations of members' organizations with their publics

Rural Municipal Administrators' Association of Saskatchewan (RMAA)
PO Box 130, Wilcox SK S0G 5E0
Tel: 306-732-2030; *Fax:* 306-732-4495
rmaa@sasktel.net
www.rmaa.ca
To address the needs of rural administrators in Saskatchewan

Saskatchewan Association of Rural Municipalities (SARM)
2075 Hamilton St., Regina SK S4P 2E1 Canada
Tel: 306-757-3577; *Fax:* 306-565-2141
Toll-Free: 800-667-3604
sarm@sarm.ca
www.sarm.ca
To represent & advocate for rural municipal government in Saskatchewan

Saskatchewan Urban Municipalities Association (SUMA)
#200, 2222 - 13th Ave., Regina SK S4P 3M7 Canada
Tel: 306-525-3727; *Fax:* 306-525-4373
suma@suma.org
www.suma.org
To work to enhance urban life in Saskatchewan, by providing administrative & consultative services to members, a forum for the discussion & resolution of current issues, & a negotiating vehicle for improvements in legislation, financing & programs. SUMA provides information & training for aldermen & mayors, and group benefits for its members

Society of Local Government Managers of Alberta
PO Box 308, 4629 - 54 Ave., Bruderheim AB T0B 0S0 Canada
Tel: 780-796-3836; *Fax:* 780-796-2081
linda.davies@shaw.ca
www.clgm.net
Linda M. Davies, Executive Director/Registrar

Union des municipalités du Québec (UMQ)
#680, 680, rue Sherbrooke ouest, Montréal QC H3A 2M7 Canada
Tél: 514-282-7700; *Téléc:* 514-282-8893
info@umq.qc.ca
www.umq.qc.ca
Au bénéfice des citoyens, représenter les municipalités auprès du gouvernement et contribuer à l'efficience de gestion des municipalités.
Pierre Prévost, Directeur général par intérim
Robert Coulombe, Président

Union of British Columbia Municipalities
#60, 10551 Shellbridge Way, Richmond BC V6X 2W9 Canada
Tel: 604-270-8226; *Fax:* 604-270-9116
ubcm@civicnet.bc.ca
www.civicnet.bc.ca
To provide a common voice for local government
Richard Taylor, Executive Director
Brenda Binnie, President

Union of Municipalities of New Brunswick (UMNB) / Union des municipalités du Nouveau-Brunswick
#4, 79 Main St., Rexton NB E4W 1Z9 Canada
Tel: 506-523-4522; *Fax:* 506-523-4523
umnb@nb.aibn.com
To unite the municipalities of New Brunswick through their respective councils into a body whose common efforts shall be devoted solely to the achievement of that which is the common good of all
Raymond Murphy, Executive Director

Union of Nova Scotia Municipalities (UNSM)
#1106, 1809 Barrington St., Halifax NS B3J 3K8 Canada
Tel: 902-423-8331; *Fax:* 902-425-5592
mainunsm@eastlink.ca
www.unsm.ca
To research, promote & represent provincial interests of local government
Kenneth Simpson, Executive Director
Judy Webber, Event Planner/Financal Officer

Urban Municipal Administrators' Association of Saskatchewan (UMAAS)
PO Box 603, Hudson Bay SK S0E 0Y0 Canada
Tel: 306-865-2825; *Fax:* 306-865-2800
umaas@sasktel.net
www.umaas.ca
Richard Dolezsar, Executive Director

Health & Medical

Acoustic Neuroma Association of Canada (ANAC) / Association pour les neurinomes acoustiques du Canada
#163, 171A Rink St., Peterborough ON K0J 2J6 Canada
Tel: 705-750-1550; *Toll-Free:* 800-561-2622
info@anac.ca
www.anac.ca
To provide support & information for those who have experienced acoustic neuromas or other tumors affecting the cranial nerves; to furnish information on patient rehabilitation to physicians & health care personnel; to promote & support research; to educate the public regarding symptoms suggestive of acoustic neuromas, thus promoting early diagnosis & consequent successful treatment

Acupuncture Foundation of Canada Institute (AFCI) / Institut de la fondation d'acupuncture du Canada
#204, 2131 Lawrence Ave. East, Toronto ON M1R 5G4 Canada
Tel: 416-752-3988; *Fax:* 416-752-4398
info@afcinstitute.com
www.afcinstitute.com
To define & maintain the highest professional standards for the use of acupuncture; to gain recognition of acupuncture's legitimate place in western medicine as a safe, efficient complement to conventional medical treatment; to design educational training programs for physicians, physiotherapists, RNs, dentists, chiropractors & naturopaths in the methodology & practice of acupuncture

African Medical & Research Foundation Canada (AMREF Canada)
#407, 489 College St., Toronto ON M5G 1A5 Canada
Tel: 416-961-6981; *Fax:* 416-961-6984
info@amrefcanada.org
www.amrefcanada.org
Development agency working to enhance community health in East & Southern Africa; headquartered in Nairobi, Kenya; eleven national offices in both Europe & America; acts as support office in raising private & public funds for overseas health programs & also plays active role in maintaining working relations with Canadian International Development Agency (CIDA)

Alberta & Northwest Territories Lung Association
PO Box 4500, Stn. South, #208, 17420 Stony Plain Rd., Edmonton AB T5E 6K2
Tel: 780-488-6819; *Fax:* 780-488-7195
Toll-Free: 888-566-5864
info@ab.lung.ca
www.ab.lung.ca
Social Media: www.facebook.com/group.php?gid=192015860715
To educate the public & medical professionals about lung health

Alberta Association of Naturopathic Practitioners (AANP)
PO Box 21142, 665 - 8th St. SW, Calgary AB T2P 4H5 Canada
Tel: 403-266-2446
aanb_ab@telusplanet.net
www.naturopathic-alberta.com

Alberta Association of Optometrists (AAO)
#100, 8407 Argyll Rd., Edmonton AB T6C 4B2 Canada
Tel: 780-451-6824; *Fax:* 780-452-9918
Toll-Free: 800-272-8843
alberta.association@optometrists.ab.ca
www.optometrists.ab.ca
To promote excellence in the practice of Optometry, to enhance public recognition of Optometry as the primary vision care provider in Alberta, and to advance the interests of the profession.

Alberta Heritage Foundation for Medical Research (AHFMR)
#1500, 10104 - 103 Ave., Edmonton AB T5J 4A7 Canada
Tel: 780-423-5727; *Fax:* 780-429-3509
Toll-Free: 877-423-5727
info@ahfmr.ab.ca
www.ahfmr.ab.ca
To support basic biomedical, clinical & health research in Alberta; contributes funds to scientific community to carry out research
Jacques Magnan, Interim President & CEO
Kathleen Thurber, Director, Communications & Education

Alberta Medical Association
12230 - 106 Ave. NW, Edmonton AB T5N 3Z1 Canada
Tel: 780-482-2626; *Fax:* 780-482-5445
Toll-Free: 800-272-9680
amamail@albertadoctors.org
www.albertadoctors.org/home
To advocate on behalf of its physician members; to provide leadership & support for their role in the provision of quality health care

Alberta Public Health Association (APHA)
c/o ACICR, 4075 RTF, 8308 - 114th St., Edmonton AB T6G 2E1 Canada
Tel: 780-492-6014; *Fax:* 780-492-7154
info@apha.ab.ca
www.apha.ab.ca
To promote & protect the health of the public through advocacy, partnerships, & education

Allergy Asthma Information Association (AAIA) / Allergie Asthme association d'information
#118, 295 The West Mall, Toronto ON M9C 4Z4
Tel: 416-621-4571; *Fax:* 416-621-5034
Toll-Free: 800-611-7011
admin@aaia.ca
www.aaia.ca
To create a safer environment for Canadians with allergies, asthma, & anaphylaxis; To assist persons coping with allergies; To act as a national voice for individuals affected by allergy, asthma, & anaphylaxis
Mary Allen, Chief Executive Officer
Louis Isabella, Treasurer

ALS Society of Canada (ALS) / La Société canadienne de la SLA (SLA)
#200, 3000 Steeles Ave. East, Markham ON L3R 4T9 Canada
Tel: 905-248-2052; *Fax:* 905-248-2019
Toll-Free: 800-267-4257
bg@als.ca
www.als.ca
Social Media: www.facebook.com/group.php?gid=7533609459
To support research towards a cure for ALS; to support ALS partners in their provision of quality care for persons affected by ALS

Alzheimer Manitoba
#10, 120 Donald St., Winnipeg MB R3C 4G2 Canada
Tel: 204-943-6622; *Fax:* 204-942-5408
Toll-Free: 800-378-6699
alzmb@alzheimer.mb.ca
www.alzheimer.mb.ca
To alleviate the individual, family & social consequences of Alzheimer type dementia while supporting the search for a cure

Alzheimer Society Canada (ASC) / Société Alzheimer Canada
#1600, 20 Eglinton Ave. West, Toronto ON M4R 1K8 Canada
Tel: 416-488-8772; *Fax:* 416-322-6656
Toll-Free: 800-616-8816
info@alzheimer.ca
www.alzheimer.ca
Social Media: www.facebook.com/group.php?gid=31592784821
Identifies, develops & facilitates national priorities that enable members to alleviate personal & social consequences of Alzheimer's disease & related disorders; promotes research & leads the search for a cure

Alzheimer Society of Alberta & Northwest Territories
10531 Kingsway Ave., Edmonton AB T5H 4K1 Canada
Tel: 780-488-2266; *Fax:* 780-488-3055
Toll-Free: 866-950-5465
info@alzheimer.ab.ca
www.alzheimer.ab.ca
The Society strives to alleviate the personal & social consequences of Alzheimer disease through the development, support & coordination of local societies & chapters. It also promotes the search for a cure through education & research. It is a registered charity, BN: 129690343RR0001.

Alzheimer Society of BC
#300, 828 West 8th Ave., Vancouver BC V5Z 1E2 Canada
Tel: 604-681-6530; *Fax:* 604-669-6907
Toll-Free: 800-667-3742
info@alzheimerbc.org
www.alzheimerbc.org
To alleviate the personal & social consequences of Alzheimer disease & related dementias; to promote public awareness & to search for the causes & the cures

Alzheimer Society of New Brunswick / Société alzheimer du nouveau brunswick
33 Main St., Fredericton NB E3A 1B7 Canada
Tel: 506-459-4280; *Fax:* 506-452-0313
Toll-Free: 800-664-8411
info@alzheimernb.ca
www.alzheimernb.ca
To alleviate the personal & social consequences of Alzheimer disease; to promote the search for a cause & cure

Alzheimer Society of Newfoundland & Labrador
PO Box 37013, 687 Water St., St. John's NL A1E 1C2 Canada
Tel: 709-576-0608; *Fax:* 709-576-0798
Toll-Free: 877-776-0608
alzheimersociety@nf.aibn.com
www.alzheimernl.org
To support the search for the cause & cure of Alzheimer Disease; to raise public awareness of the personal & social impact of the disease; to promote the provision of support to families & caregivers in Newfoundland

Alzheimer Society of Nova Scotia
#300, 6009 Quinpool Rd., Halifax NS B3K 5J7 Canada
Tel: 902-422-7961; *Fax:* 902-422-7971
Toll-Free: 800-611-6345
info@alzheimer.ns.ca
www.alzheimer.ns.ca
To enhance the quality of life of people with Alzheimer disease through providing & promoting public education & family support; to engage in advocacy on behalf of people with Alzheimer disease & their families; to promote research at the provincial & national levels
Menna MacIsaac, Executive Director

Alzheimer Society of PEI
166 Fitzroy St., Charlottetown PE C1A 1S1 Canada
Tel: 902-628-2257; *Fax:* 902-368-2715
Toll-Free: 866-628-2257
society@alzpei.ca
www.alzpei.ca
To support & assist Islanders affected by Alzheimer Disease; to raise the level of awareness & educate the public at large about the disease

Alzheimer Society Of Saskatchewan Inc. (ASOS)
#301, 2550 - 12 Ave., Regina SK S4P 3X1 Canada
Tel: 306-949-4141; *Fax:* 306-949-3069
Toll-Free: 800-263-3367
info@alzheimer.sk.ca
www.alzheimer.sk.ca
To alleviate the personal & social consequences of Alzheimer's disease & related disorders & to promote the search for a cause & a cure
Joanne Bracken, Executive Director
Kathleen Defoe, Coordinator, Finance & Administration

Alzheimer Society Ontario / Société Alzheimer Ontario
#1600, 20 Eglinton Ave. West, Toronto ON M4R 1K8 Canada
Tel: 416-967-5900; *Fax:* 416-967-3826
Toll-Free: 800-879-4226
staff@alzheimeront.org
www.alzheimerontario.org
Social Media: www.facebook.com/group.php?gid=45861243971
To improve the quality of life for persons with Alzheimer disease & their families; to inform & educate the public & health care professionals about Alzheimer disease; to coordinate a chapter network & liaison in order to present a united voice to the Government of Ontario & other provincial groups on matters relating to legal concerns, health care, research, & community needs; to raise funds for research

Aplastic Anemia & Myelodysplasia Association of Canada (AAMAC)
#321, 11181 Yonge St., Richmond Hill ON L4S 1L2 Canada
Tel: 905-780-0698; *Fax:* 905-780-1648
Toll-Free: 888-840-0039
info@aamac.ca
www.aamac.ca
To disseminate information concerning the disease; to form a nation-wide support network for patients, families & medical professionals; to support Canadian Blood Services & their programs; to raise funds for research

Arthritis Society / Société de l'arthrite
#1700, 393 University Ave., Toronto ON M5G 1E6 Canada
Tel: 416-979-7228; *Fax:* 416-979-8366
Toll-Free: 800-321-1433
info@arthritis.ca
www.arthritis.ca
Social Media: facebook.com/arthritissociety
The Society is a not-for-profit organization devoted solely to funding & promoting arthritis research, programs & patient care. There are division offices in each province & nearly 1,000 community branches throughout Canada. It is a registered charity, BN: 108071671RR0003.

Association canadienne des ataxies familiales (ACAF) / Canadian Association of Friedreich's Ataxia
#110, 3800, rue Radisson, Montréal QC H1M 1X6 Canada
Tél: 514-321-8684; *Téléc:* 514-899-9158
ataxie@lacaf.org
www.lacaf.org
Recueillir des dons du public pour financer les recherches médicales qui se font sur l'Ataxie de Friedreich ainsi que d'améliorer la condition de vie des personnes ataxiques; (personne qui est affligée par la maladie de l'Ataxie de Friedreich)

Association d'orthopédie du Québec
CP 216, #3000, 2, Complexe Desjardins, Montréal QC H5B 1G8 Canada
Tél: 514-844-0803; *Téléc:* 514-844-6786
aoq@fmsq.org
www.orthoquebec.ca/
Valoriser le statut professionnel de ses membres; promouvoir leurs intérêts économiques; contribuer au développement de la chirurgie orthopédique et de la traumatologie par le biais d'activités de formation médicale continue

Association d'oto-rhino-laryngologie et de chirurgie cervico-faciale du Québec
#3000, 2, Complexe Desjardins, Montréal QC H5B 1G8 Canada
Tél: 514-350-5125; *Téléc:* 514-350-5165
assorl@fmsq.org
www.orlquebec.org
Valoriser le statut professionnel de ses membres, promouvoir leurs intérêts scientifiques, économiques et professionnels, et contribuer au développement de l'oto-rhino-laryngologie

Association de neurochirurgie du Québec (ANCQ)
#3000, 2, Complexe Desjardins, Montréal QC H5B 1G8 Canada
Tél: 514-350-5120; *Téléc:* 514-350-5100
ancq@fmsq.org
www.ancq.net
La neurochirurgie est la spécialité qui s'occupe du traitement médico-chirurgical des pathologies du système nerveux central et de ses enveloppes (cerveau, moelle épinière, crâne et rachis) ainsi que du système nerveux périphérique (nerfs). L'ANCQ a pour mission le développement des intérêts économiques, sociaux, moraux et scientifiques de ses membres

L'Association de spina-bifida et d'hydrocéphalie du Québec (ASBHQ)
#542, 3333, ch. Queen-Mary, Montréal QC H3V 1A2 Canada
Tél: 514-340-9019; *Téléc:* 514-340-9109
Ligne sans frais: 800-567-1788
info@spina.qc.ca
www.spina.qc.ca
Promouvoir et défendre les droits, les intérêts et le bien-être des personnes ayant le spina-bifida et l'hydrocéphalie; sensibiliser le public à la nature du spina-bifida et de l'hydrocéphalie ainsi qu'aux besoins des personnes ayant ces malformations; favoriser et soutenir la recherche sur les causes, les nouveaux traitements et les techniques de prévention du spina-bifida et de l'hydrocéphalie

Association des Allergologues et Immunologues du Québec
CP 216, Succ. Desjardins, #3000, 2, Complexe Desjardins, Montréal QC H5B 1G8 Canada
Tél: 514-350-5101; *Téléc:* 514-350-5146
jdelisle@fmsq.org
www.allerg.qc.ca

Association des cardiologues du Québec
#3000, 2, Complexe Desjardins, Montréal QC H5B 1G8 Canada
Tél: 514-350-5106; *Téléc:* 514-350-5156
acq@fmsq.org
Gaëtan Houde, Président
Louise Girard, Directrice

Association des chiropraticiens du Québec
7960, boul Métropolitain est, Anjou QC H1K 1A1 Canada
Tél: 514-355-0557; *Téléc:* 514-355-0070
Ligne sans frais: 866-292-4476
acq@chiropratique.com
www.chiropratique.com
Défendre les intérêts professionnels, sociaux et économiques de ses membres

Association des chirurgiens cardio-vasculaires et thoraciques du Québec / Association of Cardiovascular & Thoracic Surgeons of Québec
Hôpital Général Juif, Bureau A-520, 3755 Chemin de la Côte Ste-Catherine, Montréal QC H3T 1E2 Canada
Tél: 514-340-8222; *Téléc:* 514-340-7561

Association des chirurgiens généraux du Québec / Québec Association of General Surgeons
#3000, 2, Complexe Desjardins, Montréal QC H5B 1G8 Canada
Tél: 514-350-5107; *Téléc:* 514-350-5157
www.chirurgiequebec.ca
Objectifs sont la protection et défense des intérêts professionnels collectifs des chirurgiens et l'enseignement chirurgical continu

Association des conseils des médecins, dentistes et pharmaciens du Québec (ACMDP) / Association of Councils of Physicians, Dentists & Pharmacists of Québec
#212, 560, boul Henri-Bourassa ouest, Montréal QC H3L 1P4 Canada
Tél: 514-858-5885; *Téléc:* 514-858-6767
acmdp@acmdp.qc.ca
www.acmdp.qc.ca
Offrir l'information, la motivation, et la formation médico-administrative nécessaire aux Conseils des médecins, dentistes, et pharmaciens membres afin qu'ils accomplissent adéquatement leurs tâches

Association des dermatologistes du Québec (ADQ) / Association of Dermatologists of Québec
#3000, 2, Complexe Desjardins, Montréal QC H5B 1G8 Canada
Tél: 514-350-5111; *Téléc:* 514-350-5161
dermato@fmsq.org
www.adq.org
Syndicat professionnel: assure la défense des intérêts économiques, professionnels et scientifiques de ses membres

Association des gastro-entérologues du Québec (AGEQ)
CP 216, Succ. Desjardins, 2, Complexe Desjardins, Montréal QC H5B 1G8 Canada
Tél: 514-350-5112; *Téléc:* 514-350-5146
sbergeron@FMSQ.ORG
www.ageq.qc.ca
Notre site a une mission d'information et de formation aux membres, une mission d'information et de formations aux médecins de première ligne, aux patients souffrant de pathologies gastro-intestinales et aux autres médecins intéressés par la gastro-entérologie. Enfin, notre site a la mission de créer des liens avec la communauté médicale internationale.

Association des médecins biochimistes du Québec
#3000, 2, Complexe Desjardins, Montréal QC H5B 1G8 Canada
Tél: 514-350-5105; *Téléc:* 514-350-5151
ambq@fmsq.org
www.ambq.med.usherbrooke.ca
Promouvoir l'utilisation optimale des tests de laboratoire au Québec en offrant, au professionnel de la santé et au patient, les meilleurs services de diagnostic et de dépistage de maladies grâce à des techniques biochimiques et immunologiques

Association des médecins de langue française du Canada (AMLFC)
8355, boul Saint-Laurent, Montréal QC H2P 2Z6 Canada
Tél: 514-388-2228; *Téléc:* 514-388-5335
Ligne sans frais: 800-387-2228
info@amlfc.org
www.amlfc.org

Association des médecins endocrinologues du Québec
CP 216, Succ. Desjardins, #3000, 2, Complexe Desjardins, Montréal QC H5B 1G8 Canada
Tél: 514-350-5135; *Téléc:* 514-350-5049
Ligne sans frais: 800-561-0703
ameq@fmsq.org
www.ameq.qc.ca
L'Association est un porte-parole des endocrinologues; elle favorise les intérêts scientifiques de ses membres et organise plusieurs réunions afin de permettre une formation médicale continue des endocrinologues
Jean-Hugues Brossard, Président

Association des médecins généticiens du Québec
#300, 2, Complexe Desjardins, Montréal QC H5B 1G8 Canada
Tél: 514-350-5141; *Téléc:* 514-350-5151
mfcaron@fmsq.org
Emmanuelle Lemyre, Présidente
Sandrine Guillot, Directrice

Association des médecins gériatres du Québec
CP 216, Succ. Desjardins, #3000, 2, Complexe Desjardins, Montréal QC H5B 1G8 Canada
Tél: 514-350-5145; *Téléc:* 514-350-5151
amgq@fmsq.org; clavoie@fmsq.org
www.fmsq.org/amgq

Association des médecins hématologistes-oncologistes du Québec (AMHOQ)
#3000, 2, Complexe Desjardins, Montréal QC H5B 1G8 Canada
Tél: 514-350-5121; *Téléc:* 514-350-5126
Ligne sans frais: 800-561-0703
amhoq@fmsq.org
Daniel Bélanger, Président

Association des médecins microbiologistes-infectiologues du Québec (AMMIQ)
#3000, 2, Complexe Desjardins, Montréal QC H5B 1G8 Canada
Tél: 514-350-5104; *Téléc:* 514-350-5144
info@ammiq.org
www.ammiq.org
L'Association regroupe des médecins (de laboratoire et dans le diagnostic clinique) spécialisés dans l'épidémiologie, le traitement et la prévention des maladies infectieuses
Charlotte Lavoie, Directrice

Association des médecins ophtalmologistes du Québec (AMOQ)
CP 216, Succ. Desjardins, 2, Complexe Desjardins, Montréal QC H5B 1G8 Canada
Tél: 514-350-5124; *Téléc:* 514-350-5174
amoq@fmsq.org
www.amoq.org
Promouvoit les intérêts professionnels et économiques de ses membres; se préoccupe du maintien de la compétence; suscite et appuie des activités scientifiques susceptibles de favoriser l'avancement de l'ophtalmologie; se préoccupe de l'accessibilité aux soins ophtalmologiques

Association des médecins rhumatologues du Québec (AMRQ)
#3000, 2, Complexe Desjardins, Montréal QC H5B 1G8 Canada
Tél: 514-350-5136; *Téléc:* 514-350-5029
amrq@fmsq.org
www.fmsq.org
La rhumatologie se consacre au diagnostic et au traitement des pathologies qui touchent les articulations, les os, les muscles et tendons et parfois tout organe dans le cadre de maladies systémiques. Ceci regroupe au-delà de 100 conditions pouvant aller de l'arthrite rhumatoïde au lupus érythémateux disséminé en passant par l'arthrose, les vasculites et l'ostéoporose.
Denis Choquette, Président

Association des médecins spécialistes en médecine nucléaire du Québec (AMSMNQ)
#3000, 2, Complexe Desjardins, Montréal QC H5B 1G8 Canada
Tél: 514-350-5133; *Téléc:* 514-350-5151
Ligne sans frais: 800-561-0703
amsmnq@fmsq.org
www.medecinenucleaire.com/

Association des médecins spécialistes en santé communautaire du Québec (AMSSCQ)
#3000, 2, Complexe Desjardins, Montréal QC H5B 1G8 Canada
Tél: 514-350-5138; *Téléc:* 514-350-5151
amsscq@fmsq.org
www.amsscq.org
L'association a pour rôle de promouvoir les intérêts professionnels et économiques de ses membres

Association des néphrologues du Québec
#3000, 2, Complexe Desjardins, Montréal QC H5B 1G8 Canada
Tél: 514-350-5134; *Téléc:* 514-350-5151
mfcaron@fmsq.org

Association des neurologues du Québec (ANQ)
CP 216, Succ. Desjardins, #3000, 2, Complexe Desjardins, Montréal QC H5B 1G8 Canada
Tél: 514-350-5122; *Téléc:* 514-350-5172
anq@fmsq.org
www.anq.qc.ca
Représente des médecins spécialistes qui diagnostique et traite les maladies affectant le système nerveux central ainsi que le système nerveux périphérique

Association des obstétriciens et gynécologues du Québec (AOGQ)
#3000, 2, Complexe Desjardins, Montréal QC H5B 1G8 Canada
Tél: 514-849-4969; *Téléc:* 514-849-5011
info@gynecoquebec.com
www.gynecoquebec.com
Promouvoir l'intérêt professionnel scientifique et économique de ses membres

Association des optométristes du Québec (AOQ) / Québec Optometric Association
#740, 1265, rue Berri, Montréal QC H2L 4X4 Canada
Tél: 514-288-6272; *Téléc:* 514-288-7071
aoq@aoqnet.qc.ca
www.aoqnet.qc.ca
Syndicat professionnel voué au développement des meilleures conditions de pratique économiques et professionnelles pour les optométristes du Québec

Association des pathologistes du Québec (APQ)
CP 216, #3000, 2, Complexe Desjardins, Montréal QC H5B 1G8 Canada
Tél: 514-350-5102; *Téléc:* 514-350-5152
Ligne sans frais: 800-561-0703
patho@fmsq.org
www.apq.qc.ca

Association des pédiatres du Québec
#3000, 2, Complexe Desjardins, Montréal QC H5B 1G8 Canada
Tél: 514-350-5127; *Téléc:* 514-350-5177
pediatrie@fmsq.org
www.fmsq.org

Association des pharmaciens des établissements de santé du Québec (APES)
#320, 4050, rue Molson, Montréal QC H1Y 3N1 Canada
Tél: 514-286-0776; *Téléc:* 514-286-1081
info@apesquebec.org
www.apesquebec.org
Linda Vaillant, Directrice générale
France Boucher, Directrice générale adjointe

Association des physiatres du Québec (APQ)
#3000, 2, Complexe Desjardins, Montréal QC H5B 1G8 Canada
Tél: 514-350-5119; *Téléc:* 514-350-5147
apq@fmsq.org
www.fmsq.org
La physiatrie est la spécialité médicale vouée à la prévention, au diagnostic et au traitement médical des douleurs et des troubles de l'appareil locomoteur (la colonne vertébrale, les os, les muscles, les tendons, les articulations, les vaisseaux et le cerveau)

Association des pneumologues de la province de Québec (APPQ)
#3000, 2, Complexe Desjardins, Montréal QC H5B 1G8 Canada
Tél: 514-350-5117; *Téléc:* 514-350-5153
appq@fmsq.org
www.fmsq.org; www.pneumologue.ca
Promouvoir les intérêts professionnels et économiques de ses membres; se préoccuper du maintien de leur compétence; se prononcer sur les problématiques de la pneumologie dans les meilleurs intérêts de la population

Association des radiologistes du Québec
CP 216, Complexe Desjardins, Montréal QC H5B 1G8 Canada
Tél: 514-350-5129; *Téléc:* 514-350-5179
bureau@arq.qc.ca
www.arq.qc.ca
Regrouper les médecins spécialisés en radiologie; défendre leurs intérêts et promouvoir leur spécialité

Association des radio-oncologues du Québec (AROQ)
#3000, 2, Complexe Desjardins, Montréal QC H5B 1G8 Canada
Tél: 514-350-5130; *Téléc:* 514-350-5126
aroq@fmsq.org
www.aroq.ca; www.fmsq.org

Association des sexologues du Québec (ASQ)
#404, 7400, boul Saint-Laurent, Montréal QC H2R 2V1 Canada
Tél: 514-270-9289; *Téléc:* 514-270-6351
www.associationdessexologues.com
Susciter auprès du public une meilleure connaissance de la sexologie et du rôle du sexologue, en favorisant et en maintenant les normes scientifiques et professionnelles les plus élevées dans l'exercice de la sexologie et dans la formation des sexologues

Association des spécialistes en chirurgie plastique et esthétique du Québec (ASCPEQ)
CP 216, Succ. Desjardins, 2, Complexe Desjardins, Montréal QC H5B 1G8 Canada
Tél: 514-350-5109; *Téléc:* 514-350-5246
www.ascpeq.org
L'Association entend se consacrer essentiellement au développement continu de l'art et de la science de la chirurgie plastique et esthétique, entre autres par la diffusion de renseignements pertinents auprès du public, par la promotion d'une relation médecin-patient fondée sur la communication, la compréhension et le respect mutuel, ainsi que par une contribution active aux programmes d'éducation et de formation continue et par une participation critique aux débats relatifs au rôle et à la place des professionnels de la santé au sein de la société québécoise
André Chollet, Président

Association des spécialistes en médecine d'urgence du Québec
#3000, 2, Complexe Desjardins, Montréal QC H5B 1G8 Canada
Tél: 514-350-5115; *Téléc:* 514-350-5116
asmuq@fmsq.org
www.asmuq.org/
Stephen Rosenthal, Président

Association des spécialistes en médecine interne du Québec
#3000, 2, Complexe Desjardins, Montréal QC H5B 1G8 Canada
Tél: 514-350-5118; *Téléc:* 514-350-5168
med.interne@fmsq.org
Marc Giasson, Président

Association des urologues du Québec (AUQ) / Quebec Urological Association (QUA)
#3000, 2, Complexe Desjardins, Montréal QC H5B 1G8 Canada
Tél: 514-350-5131; *Téléc:* 514-350-5181
auq@fmsq.org
www.auq.org

Association diabète Québec (ADQ) / Québec Diabetes Association
#300, 8550, boul Pie-IX, Montréal QC H1Z 4G2 Canada
Tél: 514-259-3422; *Téléc:* 514-259-9286
Ligne sans frais: 800-361-3504
info@diabete.qc.ca
www.diabete.qc.ca
Regrouper les diabétiques et favoriser l'entraide; les renseigner sur les façons de faire face à la maladie; informer le grand public et le sensibiliser à la condition de personnes souffrant du diabète; ouvrir de nouvelles voies dans le domaine de la recherche pour en venir à triompher du diabète

Association médicale du Québec (AMQ) / Québec Medical Association (QMA)
#3200, 380, rue Saint-Antoine ouest, Montréal QC H2Y 3X7 Canada
Tel: 514-866-0660; *Fax:* 514-866-0670
Toll-Free: 800-363-3932
admin@amq.ca
www.amq.ca
Rassembler et soutenir les médecins du Québec afin de garantir à la population québécoise des conditions et des soins de santé de qualité

Association of Local Public Health Agencies (ALPHA)
#1306, 2 Carlton St., Toronto ON M5G 1T6
Tel: 416-595-0006; *Fax:* 416-595-0030
info@alphaweb.org
www.alphaweb.org
To provide leadership in public health management to health units in Ontario; To assist local public health units in the provision of efficient & effective services

Association of Medical Microbiology & Infectious Disease Canada (AMMI Canada) / Association pour la microbiologie médicale et l'infectiologie Canada
#101, 298 Elgin St., Ottawa ON K2P 1M3
Tel: 613-260-3233; *Fax:* 613-260-3235
info@ammi.ca; communications@ammi.ca; manager@ammi.ca
www.ammi.ca
To represent the broad interests of researchers & physicians who specialize in the fields of infectious diseases & medical microbiology in Canada; To contribute to the health of people at risk of, or affected by, infectious diseases; To promote & facilitate research; To develop policies for the prevention, diagnosis, & management of infectious diseases

Association pour la santé publique du Québec (ASPQ) / Québec Public Health Association
#200, 4126, rue St-Denis, Montréal QC H2W 2M5 Canada
Tél: 514-528-5811; *Téléc:* 514-528-5590
info@aspq.org
www.aspq.org

Préserver, améliorer et maintenir la santé publique: en identifiant les problèmes de santé publique; en initiant, participant et promouvant la recherche en santé publique; en vulgarisant les pratiques et principes tendant à préserver, améliorer et maintenir la santé publique; en participant à l'élaboration de politiques opérationnelles; en incitant et aidant au perfectionnement des membres; en publiant pour les membres des travaux scientifiques ou autres destinés à améliorer leur compétence; en informant les membres des derniers développements et découvertes en santé publique
Lucie Granger, Directrice Générale
Martine Deschênes, Adjointe administrative

Association québécoise de l'épilepsie
#111, 1015, côte du Beaver Hall, Montréal QC H2Z 1S1 Canada
Tél: 514-875-5595; *Téléc:* 514-875-0077
aqe@cam.org
www.cam.org/~aqe/
Veiller au mieux-être des personnes épileptiques et à leurs familles; promouvoir les droits des personnes épileptiques; sensibiliser le public à l'épilepsie; promouvoir l'intégration scolaire et au travail

Association québécoise de la fibrose kystique (AQFK) / Québec Cystic Fibrosis Association
#510, 425, rue Viger ouest, Montréal QC H2Z 1X2 Canada
Tél: 514-877-6161; *Téléc:* 514-877-6116
Ligne sans frais: 800-363-7711
www.aqfk.qc.ca
Sensibiliser la population sur la fibrose kystique; amasser des fonds pour la recherche médicale; améliorer la qualité de vie des personnes atteintes de FK; découvrir un remède ou un moyen de contrôler la fibrose kystique.

Asthma Society of Canada (ASC) / Société canadienne de l'asthme
#2306, 4680 Yonge St., Toronto ON M2N 6K1 Canada
Tel: 416-787-4050; *Fax:* 416-787-5807
Toll-Free: 866-787-4050
info@asthma.ca
www.asthma.ca
To optimize the health of people with asthma through education and asthma awareness.

Autism Northwest Territories
4904 Matonabee St., Yellowknife NT X1A 1X8 Canada
Tel: 867-920-4206; *Fax:* 867-873-0235
autism@hotmail.com

Autism Ontario
#004, 1179A King St. West, Toronto ON M6K 3C5 Canada
Tel: 416-246-9592; *Fax:* 416-246-9417
www.autismontario.com
To ensure that each individual with autism spectrum disorders is provided the means to achieve quality of life as a respected member of society

Autism Society Alberta (ASA)
#101, 11720 Kingsway Ave., Edmonton AB T5G 0X5 Canada
Tel: 780-453-3971; *Fax:* 780-447-4948
autism@austismedmonton.org
www.autismedmonton.org
To improve the understanding of autism throughout Alberta by the dissemination of information to parents, health care workers, educators, government, private agencies & the public

Autism Society Canada (ASC) / Société canadienne d'autisme
PO Box 22017, 1670 Heron Rd., Ottawa ON K1V 0C2 Canada
Tel: 613-789-8943; *Fax:* 613-789-6985
info@autismsocietycanada.ca
www.autismsocietycanada.ca
To provide support on a national basis to people affected by autism & related conditions through the collective efforts of Canadian provincial & territorial autism societies; to provide information & general referrals to the public regarding autism & related conditions; to promote public awareness of autism & related conditions; to encourage research in fields related or relevant to autism & related conditions; to communicate with government, agencies, & other organizations on behalf of persons affected by autism & related conditions; to promote actions to ensure people with autism & related conditions live in an environment that supports their well-being & enables them to reach their full potential; to promote & encourage the convening of conferences focused on autism & related conditions

Autism Society Manitoba
825 Sherbrook St., 2nd Fl., Winnipeg MB R3A 1M5 Canada
Tel: 204-783-9563; *Fax:* 204-975-3027
Toll-Free: 800-225-9108
info@autismmanitoba.com
www.autismmanitoba.com
To promote the quality of life for people with Pervasive Developmental Disorder/Autism & their families; to promote full inclusion, dignity & development of personal skills & abilities for our members

Autism Society New Brunswick
PO Box 1493, Stn. A, Fredericton NB E3B 5G2 Canada
Toll-Free: 888-773-1916
autism_nb@yahoo.com
www.autismnb.org
Social Media:
www.facebook.com/group.php?gid=120942775566
To promote public awareness, understanding & acceptance of persons with autism while providing support to families for the realization of services & programs within their community

Autism Society Newfoundland & Labrador (ASNL)
PO Box 14078, 70 Clinch Cres., St. John's NL A1B 4G8 Canada
Tel: 709-722-2803; *Fax:* 709-722-4926
Toll-Free: 866-722-2803
info@autism.nf.net
www.autism.nf.net
Social Media: wwww.twitter.com/AutismSocietyNL
To promote the diagnosis, treatment, education & integration into the community of all autistic persons; to provide information about autism; to promote research; to promote integrated care for autistic persons; to encourage the formation of parent support groups around the province

Autism Society of British Columbia
#301, 3701 East Hastings St., Burnaby BC V5C 2H6 Canada
Tel: 604-434-0880; *Fax:* 604-434-0801
Toll-Free: 888-437-0880
info@autismbc.ca
www.autismbc.ca
To promote awareness of autism & the needs of families with a child or adult with autism; to provide advocacy, resources, & referrals to families of people with autism in BC

Autism Society of Nova Scotia (ASNS)
PO Box 195, Dartmouth NS B2Y 3Y3 Canada
Tel: 902-429-5529
autismns@ns.aliantzinc.ca
www.autismsocietynovascotia.ca
To advocate for, educate the public about, & provide support to, persons with autism/pervasive developmental disorders & their families

Autism Society of PEI
PO Box 3243, 135 Kent St., Charlottetown PE C1A 8W5 Canada
Tel: 902-566-4844; *Toll-Free:* 888-360-8681
Nathalie@autismsociety.pe.ca
www.autismsociety.pe.ca
Austim resources available in PEI

Autism Treatment Services of Canada (ATSC) / Association canadienne pour l'obtention des services aux personnes autistiques
404 - 94 Ave. SE, Calgary AB T2J 0E8 Canada
Tel: 403-253-2291; *Fax:* 403-253-6974
Toll-Free: 888-301-2872
atsc@autism.ca
www.autism.ca
The Society is an Alberta-based organization working to ensure that a comprehensive range of services exists across Canada to meet the needs of individuals with autism & their families, & that autistic people are given the opportunity to achieve maximum independence & productivity within the community. It is a registered charity, BN: 132329541RR0001.

Autism Yukon
508F Main St., Whitehorse YT Y1A 2B9 Canada
Tel: 867-667-6406; *Fax:* 867-667-6408
info@autismyukon.org
www.autismyukon.org

Breast Cancer Action (BCA) / Sensibilisation au cancer du sein
Riverside Mall, 739A Ridgewood Ave., Ottawa ON K1V 6M8 Canada
Tel: 613-736-5921; *Fax:* 613-736-8422
info@bcaott.ca
www.bcaott.ca
To advocate establishment of a national resource office, directed by women affected by breast cancer, to serve as clearinghouse for information about treatment, legislative action, access to treatments & support services; to advocate for a designated centre for excellence to accelerate research; to advocate greater emphasis on developing earlier detection; to promote increased survivor participation in cancer care planning & policy making; to promote better education of family physicians & women in early detection & follow-up
Diane Ryan, President

Breast Cancer Society of Canada / Société du cancer du sein du Canada
420 East St. North, Sarnia ON N7T 6Y5
Tel: 519-336-0746; *Fax:* 519-336-5725
Toll-Free: 800-567-8767
bcsc@bcsc.ca
www.bcsc.ca
Social Media: www.facebook.com/breastcancersocietyofcanada
To support research into the prevention, detection, & treatment of breast cancer
Marsha Davidson, Executive Director
Dawn Hamilton, Coordinator, Fund Development
Bunny Caughlin, Officer, Operations
Johanne Deschamps, Officer, Communications

The British Columbia Association of Optometrists (BCAO)
#502, 1755 West Broadway, Vancouver BC V6J 4S5 Canada
Tel: 604-737-9907; *Fax:* 604-737-9967
Toll-Free: 888-393-2226
info@optometrists.bc.ca
www.optometrists.bc.ca
To maintain standards; to represent membership to government & other health care professions; to raise public levels of awareness about optometry, good vision & eye care.

British Columbia Cancer Foundation (BCCF)
#200, 601 Broadway St. West, Vancouver BC V5Z 4C2 Canada
Tel: 604-877-6040; *Fax:* 604-877-6161
Toll-Free: 888-906-2873
info@bccancer.bc.ca
www.bccancer.bc.ca
To reduce the incidence of cancer, reduce the mortality rate from cancer, & improve the quality of life for those living with cancer, through the acquisition, development, & stewardship of resources

British Columbia Centre for Ability Association (BCCFA)
2805 Kingsway, Vancouver BC V5R 5H9 Canada
Tel: 604-451-5511; *Fax:* 604-451-5651
home@centreforability.bc.ca
www.centreforability.bc.ca
To provide community-based services that enhance the quality of life for children, youth & adults with disabilities & their families in ways that facilitate & build competencies & foster inclusion in all aspects of life

British Columbia Chiropractic Association (BCCA)
#125, 3751 Shell Rd., Richmond BC V6X 2W2 Canada
Tel: 604-270-1332; *Fax:* 604-278-0093
Toll-Free: 866-256-1474
info@bcchiro.com
www.bcchiro.com

British Columbia Lung Association (BCLA)
2675 Oak St., Vancouver BC V6H 2K2
Tel: 604-731-5864; *Fax:* 604-731-5810
Toll-Free: 800-665-5864
info@bc.lung.ca
www.bc.lung.ca
Social Media:
www.facebook.com/home.php?#!/BCLungAssociation
To support lung health research, education, prevention, & advocacy; To help people manage respiratory diseases, including asthma, COPD (chronic bronchitis and emphysema), lung cancer, sleep apnea, & tuberculosis

British Columbia Lupus Society (BCLS)
#200, 1645 - 7 Ave. West, Vancouver BC V6J 1S4 Canada
Tel: 604-714-5564; *Toll-Free:* 866-585-8787
info@bclupus.org
www.bclupus.org
To provide education & support to Lupus patients & their friends & families; to increase public awareness of lupus

British Columbia Medical Association (BCMA)
#115, 1665 West Broadway, Vancouver BC V6J 5A4 Canada
Tel: 604-736-5551; *Fax:* 604-736-4566
Toll-Free: 800-665-2262
communications@bcma.bc.ca
www.bcma.org
To promote a social, economic & political climate in which members can provide the citizens of British Columbia with the highest standard of health care while achieving maximum professional satisfaction & fair economic reward.

British Columbia Naturopathic Association (BCNA)
2238 Pine St., Vancouver BC V6J 5G4 Canada
Tel: 604-736-6646; *Fax:* 604-736-6048
Toll-Free: 800-277-1128
bcna@bcna.ca
www.bcna.ca
To act on behalf of the naturopathic profession in British Columbia; to advance the welfare of members of the profession

British Columbia Transplant Society (BCTS)
555 West 12th Ave., 3rd Fl., Vancouver BC V5Z 3X7 Canada
Tel: 604-877-2240; *Fax:* 604-877-2111
Toll-Free: 800-663-6189
BCTS_Webmaster@bcts.hnet.bc.ca
www.transplant.bc.ca
To lead & coordinate all activities related to organ transplantation & donation, ensuring high standards of quality & efficient management.

Canada Health Infoway / Inforoute Santé du Canada
#1200, 1000, rue Sherbrooke ouest, Montréal QC H3A 3G4 Canada
Tel: 514-868-0550; *Fax:* 514-868-1120
Toll-Free: 866-868-0550
info@infoway-inforoute.ca
www.infoway-inforoute.ca
To accelerate the development of compatible electronic health information systems, which provide healthcare professionals with rapid access to complete & accurate patient information, enabling better decisions about diagnosis & treatment.
Richard C. Alvarez, President & CEO

Canadian Agency for Drugs & Technologies in Health (CADTH) / Agence canadienne des médicaments et des technologies de la santé (ACMTS)
#600, 865 Carling Ave., Ottawa ON K1S 5S8
Tel: 613-226-2553; *Fax:* 613-226-5392
info@cadth.ca; publications@cadth.ca
www.cadth.ca
To offer evidence-based information & impartial advice to health care decision makers about the effectiveness of drugs & other health technologies
Brian O'Rourke, President & CEO

Canadian Alliance of Physiotherapy Regulators / Alliance canadienne des organismes de réglementation de la physiothérapie
#501, 1243 Islington Ave., Toronto ON M8X 1Y9 Canada
Tel: 416-234-8800; *Fax:* 416-234-8820
email@alliancept.org
www.alliancept.org
To facilitate the sharing of information & build consensus on national regulatory issues in order to assist member regulators in fulfilling their mandate of protecting the public interest

Canadian Anesthesiologists' Society (CAS) / Société canadienne des anesthésiologistes (SCA)
#208, One Eglinton Ave. East, Toronto ON M4P 3A1 Canada
Tel: 416-480-0602; *Fax:* 416-480-0320
anesthesia@cas.ca; adminservices@cas.ca
www.cas.ca
To advance the medical practice of anesthesia throughout Canada

Canadian Association for Clinical Microbiology & Infectious Diseases (CACMID) / Association canadienne de microbiologie clinique et des maladies contagieuses
c/o Dr. A. Petrich, St. Luke's Wing, St. Joseph's Healthcare, #424L, 50 Charlton Ave. East, Hamilton ON L8N 4A6 Canada
Tel: 905-522-1155; *Fax:* 905-521-6083
www.cacmid.ca
To enhance the cooperation of professionals specializing in clinical microbiology & infectious disease; to act as the voice for clinical microbiology & infectious disease professionals; to develop standards in the field of clinical microbiology

Canadian Association for Health Services & Policy Research (CAHSPR) / Association canadienne pour la recherche sur les services et les politiques de la santé (ACRSPS)
292 Somerset St. West, Ottawa ON K2P 0J6 Canada
Tel: 613-235-7180; *Fax:* 613-235-5451
cahspr@cahspr.ca
www.cahspr.ca
To improve the quality, relevance, & application of health services & policy research
Kevin Barclay, Executive Director
Renaldo Battista, President
Marcel Saulnier, Secretary
Eric Latimer, Treasurer

Canadian Association of Cardio-Pulmonary Technologists (CACPT)
PO Box 848, Stn. A, Toronto ON M5W 1G3 Canada
contactus@cacpt.ca
www.cacpt.ca
To establish maintain high standards for Registered Cardio-Pulmonary Technologists

Canadian Association of Centres for the Management of Hereditary Metabolic Diseases
c/o Dept. of Genetics, Childrens' Hospital of E. Ontario, 401 Smyth Rd., Ottawa ON K1H 8L1 Canada
www.garrod.ca
The GARROD Association is a national body for the coordination of the management of inherited metabolic disorders. It provides a forum for the exchange of information & develops guidelines for the investigation & treatment of the diseases.
Murray Potter, President
Pranesh Chakraborty, Sec.-Treas.

Canadian Association of Child Neurology (CACN) / L'Association canadienne de neurologie pédiatrique (ACNP)
#709, 7015 Macleod Trail SW, Calgary AB T2H 2K6
Tel: 403-229-9544; *Fax:* 403-229-1661
www.ccns.org/society_CACN.html
To advance knowledge about the development of the nervous system from conception, as well as the diseases of the nervous system in children; To improve treatment of young people with neurological handicaps
Joseph Dooley, President
Jerome Yager, Sec.-Treas.
Sally Gregg, Managing Director

Canadian Association of Emergency Physicians (CAEP) / Association canadienne des médecins d'urgence (ACMU)
#104, 1785 Alta Vista Dr., Ottawa ON K1G 3Y6
Tel: 613-523-3343; *Fax:* 613-523-0190
Toll-Free: 800-463-1158
admin@caep.ca; board@caep.ca; committees@caep.ca
www.caep.ca
To act as the national voice of emergency medicine; To empower physicians to provide excellent emergency care, through leadership, continuing education, & advocacy

Canadian Association of Gastroenterology / Association canadienne de gastroentérologie
#224, 1540 Cornwall Rd., Oakville ON L6J 7W5 Canada
Tel: 905-829-2504; *Fax:* 905-829-0242
Toll-Free: 888-780-0007
www.cag-acg.org
The CAG supports and engages in the study of gastroenterology; promotes patient care, research, teaching and professional development in the field; and promotes and maintains the highest ethical standards of practice.

Canadian Association of General Surgeons (CAGS) / Association canadienne des chirurgiens généraux (ACCG)
774 Echo Dr., Ottawa ON K1S 5N8 Canada
Tel: 613-730-6280; *Fax:* 613-730-1116
cags@rcpsc.edu
www.cags-accg.ca
To assist all general surgeons with continuing education; facilitate & promote surgical research; develop policies & new ideas in the areas of clinical care, education & research

Canadian Association of Medical Biochemists (CAMB) / Association des médecins biochimistes du Canada (AMBC)
774 Echo Dr., Ottawa ON K1S 5N8 Canada
Tel: 613-730-8177; *Fax:* 613-730-1116
Toll-Free: 800-668-3740
camb@rcpsc.edu
www.camb-ambc.ca

Canadian Association of Medical Oncologists (CAMO) / Association canadienne des oncologues médicaux (ACOM)
c/o CAMO Secretariat Office, 774 Echo Dr., Ottawa ON K1S 5N8 Canada
Tel: 613-730-6284; *Fax:* 613-730-1116
camo@rcpsc.edu
www.cos.ca/camo/default.asp
Charles Butts, President
Kara Laing, Secretary-Treasurer

Canadian Association of Medical Radiation Technologists (CAMRT) / Association canadienne des technologues en radiation médicale (ACTRM)
#1000, 85 Albert St., Ottawa ON K1P 6A4
Tel: 613-234-0012; *Fax:* 613-234-1097
Toll-Free: 800-463-9729
editorialoffice@camrt.ca
www.camrt.ca
To act as the certifying body for medical radiation technologists & therapists throughout Canada

The Canadian Association of Naturopathic Doctors (CAND) / Association canadienne des docteurs en naturopathie
1255 Sheppard Ave. East, Toronto ON M2K 1E2 Canada
Tel: 416-496-8633; *Fax:* 416-496-8634
Toll-Free: 800-551-4381
info@cand.ca
www.cand.ca
CAND is a not-for-profit professional organization that promotes naturopathic medicine to the public, insurance companies & corporations. CAND encourages professional, educational & networking activities among its members, & standardization of educational requirements for practitioners
Shawn O'Reilly, Executive Director
Alex McKenna, Marketing Director

Canadian Association of Neuropathologists (CANP) / Association canadienne de neuropathologistes
QE2 Health Sciences Centre, Rm 738, Mackenzie Bldg., 5788 University Ave., Halifax NS B3H 1V8 Canada
Tel: 902-473-3156; *Fax:* 902-473-1049
robert.macaulay@cdha.nshealth.ca
canp.medical.org
To organize the annual scientific meeting; to promote the professional & educational objectives of neuropathologists.

Canadian Association of Occupational Therapists (CAOT) / Association canadienne des ergothérapeutes (ACE)
CTTC Building, #3400, 1125 Colonel By Dr., Ottawa ON K1S 5R1
Tel: 613-523-2268; *Fax:* 613-523-2552
Toll-Free: 800-434-2268
insurance@caot.ca
www.caot.ca
Social Media: www.facebook.com/CAOT.ca
To develop & promote the profession of occupational therapy in Canada & abroad; To assist occupational therapists achieve excellence in their professional practice by offering services, products, events, & networking opportunities

Canadian Association of Optometrists (CAO) / Association canadienne des optométristes
234 Argyle Ave., Ottawa ON K2P 1B9
Tel: 613-235-7924; *Fax:* 613-235-2025
Toll-Free: 888-263-4676
info@opto.ca
www.opto.ca
To represent & assist the profession of optometry in Canada; To improve the quality, availability, & accessibility of vision & eye care

Canadian Association of Oral & Maxillofacial Surgeons (CAOMS) / Association canadienne de spécialistes en chirurgie buccale et maxillo-faciale (ACSCBMF)
#100, 32 Colonnade Rd., Ottawa ON K2E 7J6
Tel: 613-721-1816; *Fax:* 613-721-3581
Toll-Free: 888-369-5641
caoms@caoms.com; (Secretariat);
executivedirector@caoms.com
www.caoms.com

Canadian Association of Paediatric Surgeons (CAPS) / Association de la chirurgie infantile canadienne
c/o Children's Hospital Of Eastern Ontario, 401 Smyth Rd., Ottawa ON K1H 8L1 Canada
Tel: 613-737-7600; *Fax:* 613-738-4849
bass.caps@gmail.com
www.caps.ca
The aim of CAPS is to improve the surgical care of infants and children in Canada.

Canadian Association of Pathologists (CAP) / Association canadienne des pathologistes
774 Echo Dr., Ottawa ON K1S 5N8 Canada
Tel: 613-730-6230; *Fax:* 613-730-1116
Toll-Free: 800-668-3740
cap@rcpsc.edu
www.cap.medical.org

Canadian Association of Physical Medicine & Rehabilitation (CAPM&R) / Association canadienne de médecine physique et de réadaptation
774 Echo Dr., Ottawa ON K1S 5N8 Canada
Tel: 613-730-6245; *Fax:* 613-730-1116
capmr@rcpsc.edu
www.capmr.ca
The CAPM&R represents and promotes the interests of the speciality of physiatry in Canada by providing and maintaing a national forum and network. It advances and increases awareness of the specialty through strategic alliances and partnerships, public policy, and professional and practice development.

Canadian Association of Prosthetics & Orthotics (CAPO) / Association canadienne en prothéses et orthéses
#605, 294 Portage Ave., Winnipeg MB R3C 0B9 Canada
Tel: 204-949-4970; *Fax:* 204-947-3627
capo@mts.net
www.pando.ca
To promote the prosthetic/orthotic profession in Canada & abroad

Canadian Association of Radiologists (CAR) / L'Association canadienne des radiologistes
#310, 377 Dalhousie St., Ottawa ON K1N 9N8 Canada
Tel: 613-860-3111; *Fax:* 613-860-3112
info@car.ca
www.car.ca
Voluntary organization representing the goals & the interests of imaging specialists; to promote the clinical, educational, research & political goals of Canadian radiology to members, organized radiology, medical associations, government & the public

Canadian Association of Speech-Language Pathologists & Audiologists (CASLPA) / Association canadienne des orthophonistes et audiologistes
#1000, 1 Nicholas St., Ottawa ON K1N 7B7 Canada
Tel: 613-567-9968; *Fax:* 613-567-2859
Toll-Free: 800-259-8519
caslpa@caslpa.ca
www.caslpa.ca
The Association supports & represents the professional needs & development of speech-language pathologists & audiologists. Through this support, the needs of people with communication disorders are championed.

Canadian Association of Thoracic Surgeons (CATS) / Association canadienne des chirurgiens thoraciques
c/o J. Clifton, Department of Surgery, University of British Columbia, 910 West 10th Ave., Vancouver BC V5Z 4E3
Tel: 604-875-5355
www.canats.org
To represent thoracic surgeons across Canada
Joanne Clifton, Secretariat
Donna Maziak, President
Drew Bethune, Secretary-Treasurer & Chair, Programs
Andrew Seely, Chair, Research
Rosaire Vaillancourt, Chair, Continuing Professional Development

Canadian Association of Transplantation
10207 - 107 St., Fort Saskatchewan AB T8L 2H9 Canada
Toll-Free: 800-263-2833
transplantcanada@yahoo.ca
www.transplant.ca
Health professionals committed to facilitating & enhancing the transplant process
Ingrid Larsen, President

Canadian Athletic Therapists Association (CATA) / Association canadienne des thérapeutes du sport
#402, 1040 - 7th Ave. SW, Calgary AB T2P 3G9 Canada
Tel: 403-509-2282; *Fax:* 403-509-2280
info@athletictherapy.org
www.athletictherapy.org
CATA is dedicated to delivery of quality care through injury prevention, emergency services & rehabilitative techniques.

Canadian Blood Services (CBS) / Societé canadienne du sang
1800 Alta Vista Dr., Ottawa ON K1G 4J5 Canada
Tel: 613-739-2300; *Fax:* 613-731-1411
Toll-Free: 888-236-6283
feedback@blood.ca; fundraising@blood.ca
www.bloodservices.ca
Social Media:
www.facebook.com/home.php?#!/CanadianBloodServices
To manage the blood supply for Canadians; to ensure blood safety in every branch of its structure & in every decision
Leah Hollins, Chair
Graham D. Sher, Chief Executive Officer

Canadian Brain Tumour Tissue Bank
#301, 620 Colborne St.,, London ON N6B 3R9 Canada
Tel: 519-642-7755; *Fax:* 519-642-7192
Toll-Free: 800-265-5106
braintumor@braintumor.ca
www.braintumor.ca
To supply optimally collected brain tumour tissue to researchers all over the country, internationally & locally in the hopes that some day the cause of & the cure for brain tumours will be found.

Canadian Cancer Society (CCS) / Société canadienne du cancer
National Office, #200, 10 Alcorn Ave., Toronto ON M4V 3B1 Canada
Tel: 416-961-7223; *Fax:* 416-961-4189
Toll-Free: 888-939-3333
ccs@cancer.ca; info@cis.cancer.ca
www.cancer.ca
Social Media: www.facebook.com/canadiancancersociety
The Society collects donations to fund cancer research in Canada. It disseminates information on cancer prevention & treatments, advocating for healthy environment & lifestyle to reduce the incidence of cancer, and also offers individual & group support programs for caregivers, family & friends of cancer patients. It is a registered charity, BN: 118829803RR0001.

Canadian Cancer Society Research Institute
#200, 10 Alcorn Ave., Toronto ON M4V 3B1
Tel: 416-961-7223; *Fax:* 416-961-4189
ccsri@cancer.ca; research@cancer.ca; agiorgi@cancer.ca (Media)
www.cancer.ca/research
To act as a strong voice in the cancer research community; To support a broad range of projects that involve Canadian investigators across the spectrum of cancer research

Canadian Cardiovascular Society (CCS) / Société canadienne de cardiologie
#1403, 222 Queen St., Ottawa ON K1P 5V9 Canada
Tel: 613-569-3407; *Fax:* 613-569-6574
Toll-Free: 877-569-3407
info@ccs.ca
www.ccs.ca
To promote cardiovascular health & care through knowledge translation, dissemination of research & encouragement of best practices, professional development & leadership in health policy

Canadian Celiac Association (CCA) / L'Association canadienne de la maladie coeliaque
#400, 5025 Orbitor Dr., Bldg. 1, Mississauga ON L4W 4Y5 Canada
Tel: 905-507-6208; *Fax:* 905-507-4673
Toll-Free: 800-363-7296
info@celiac.ca
www.celiac.ca
CCA works to increase awareness of celiac & dermatitis herpetiformis among government institutions, health care professionals & the public. It provides information about the disease & a gluten-free diet, & encourges research through the establishment of the J.A. Campbell Research Fund. It is a registered charity, BN: 106844244RR0001.

Canadian Chiropractic Association (CCA) / Association chiropratique canadienne (ACC)
#600, 30 St. Patrick St., Toronto ON M5T 3A3
Tel: 416-585-7902; *Fax:* 416-585-2970
Toll-Free: 877-222-9303
www.chiropracticcanada.ca
To see every Canadian have full & equitable access to chiropractic care; To promote the integration of chiropractic into the Canadian health care system

Canadian Coalition for Immunization Awareness & Promotion (CCIAP) / La Coalition canadienne pour la sensibilisation et la promotion de la vaccination (CCSPV)
c/o Canadian Public Health Association, #400, 1565 Carling Ave., Ottawa ON K1Z 8R1 Canada
Tel: 613-725-3769; *Fax:* 613-725-9826
immunize@cpha.ca
www.immunize.cpha.ca
To contribute to the control/elimination/eradication of vaccine preventable diseases in Canada by increasing awareness of the benefits & risks of immunization for all ages.
Bonnie Henry, Chair
Susan Bowles, Vice-Chair

Canadian College of Health Leaders (CCHL) / Collège canadien des leaders en santé
292 Somerset St. West, Ottawa ON K2P 0J6
Tel: 613-235-7218; *Fax:* 613-235-5451
Toll-Free: 800-363-9056
info@cchl-ccls.ca; communications@cchse.org
www.cchl-ccls.ca
Social Media:
www.facebook.com/group.php?gid=154324094612698;
twitter.com/CCHL_CCLS
To advance excellence in health leadership; To act as a collective voice for the profession

Canadian College of Medical Geneticists (CCMG) / Collège canadien de généticiens médicaux
774 Echo Dr., Ottawa ON K1S 5N8 Canada
Tel: 613-730-6250; *Fax:* 613-730-1116
ccmg@rcpsc.edu
www.ccmg.medical.org
To establish & maintain professional & ethical standards for medical genetics services in Canada; to certify individuals who provide medical genetics services; to encourage research activities

Canadian Council of Food & Nutrition (CCFN) / Conseil canadien des aliments et de la nutrition
2810 Matheson Blvd. East, 1st Fl., Mississauga ON L4W 4X7 Canada
Tel: 905-625-5746; *Fax:* 905-265-9372
info@ccfn.ca
www.ccfn.ca
The multi-sectoral trusted voice for science-based food & nutrition policy & information in Canada.
Francey Pillo-Blocka, President & CEO

Canadian Critical Care Society (CCCS) / Société canadienne de soins intensifs
c/o Toronto General Hospital, 10 Eaton North, Room 220, 200 Elizabeth St., Toronto ON M5G 2C4 Canada
Tel: 416-340-4800; *Fax:* 416-340-4211
info@canadiancriticalcare.org
www.canadiancriticalcare.org
To develop training & educational guidelines

Canadian Cystic Fibrosis Foundation (CCFF) / Fondation canadienne de la fibrose kystique (FCFK)
#601, 2221 Yonge St., Toronto ON M4S 2B4 Canada
Tel: 416-485-9149; *Fax:* 416-485-0960
Toll-Free: 800-378-2233
info@cysticfibrosis.ca
www.cysticfibrosis.ca; www.fibrosekystique.ca
To help people with Cystic Fibrosis through funding research towards a cure or control; supports high quality care; promotes public awareness; raises & allocates funds for these purposes

Canadian Deafblind & Rubella Association (CDBRA) / Association canadienne de la surdicécité et de la rubéole
2652 Morien Hwy., Port Morien NS B1B 1C6 Canada
Tel: 902-737-1453; *Fax:* 902-737-1095
Toll-Free: 866-229-5832
cdbra@seaside.ns.ca
www.cdbra.ca
To provide services to deafblind Canadians & advocacy for deafblindness

Canadian Dermatology Association (CDA) / Association canadienne de dermatologie (ACD)
#425, 1385 Bank St., Ottawa ON K1H 8N4
Tel: 613-738-1748; *Fax:* 613-738-4695
Toll-Free: 800-267-3376
contact.cda@dermatology.ca;
member.services@dermatology.ca
www.dermatology.ca
To advance the science of medicine & surgery related to the health of the skin; To support & advance patient care; To represent dermatologists in Canada

Canadian Diabetes Association (CDA) / Association canadienne du diabète
#1400, 522 University Ave, Toronto ON M5G 2R5 Canada
Tel: 416-363-0177; *Fax:* 416-408-7117
Toll-Free: 800-226-8464
info@diabetes.ca
www.diabetes.ca
Social Media:
www.facebook.com/group.php?gid=129834841137
To advance the welfare of Canadians with diabetes; to support research into the causes, complications, treatment, & cure of diabetes; to promote & strengthen services for people affected by diabetes & their families; to work with health professionals to improve standards in care the & treatment of diabetes; to develop guidelines for diabetes education in Canada; to promote the rights of Canadians affected by diabetes in an effort to bring about positive change in the areas of public awareness, government policy, health policy issues & employment

Canadian Down Syndrome Society (CDSS) / Société canadienne du syndrome de Down
811 - 14 St. NW, Calgary AB T2N 2A4 Canada
Tel: 403-270-8500; *Fax:* 403-270-8291
Toll-Free: 800-883-5608
info@cdss.ca
www.cdss.ca
To ensure equitable opportunities for all Canadians with Down syndrome; to make sure all Canadians with Down syndrome have the right supports to give them the same opportunities that everyone else has

Canadian Dyslexia Association (CDA) / Association canadienne de la dyslexie
207 Bayswater Ave., Ottawa ON K1Y 2G5 Canada
Tel: 613-722-2699; *Fax:* 613-722-4799
info@dyslexiaassociation.ca
www.dyslexiaassociation.ca

Canadian Epilepsy Alliance (CAE) / L'Alliance canadienne de l'épilepsie (ACE)
#224, 510 King St. East, Toronto ON M5C 1E5 Canada
Tel: 416-964-9095; *Fax:* 416-964-2492
www.epilepsymatters.com
To promote independence & quality of life for people with epilepsy & their families, through support services, information, advocacy, & public awareness
Catherine Sauerwein, President

Canadian Foundation for the Study of Infant Deaths (CFSID) / Fondation canadienne pour l'étude de la mortalité infantile
#403, 60 James St., St Catharines ON L2R 7E7 Canada
Tel: 905-688-8884; *Fax:* 905-688-3300
Toll-Free: 800-363-7437
sidsinfo@sidscanada.org
www.sidscanada.org
To provide information & emotional support to families of infants who have died due to Sudden Infant Death Syndrome (SIDS); to carry out programs of public education & awareness; to promote & support research activities into the cause(s) of SIDS & its effects on families

Canadian Health Coalition (CHC) / Coalition canadienne de la santé
2841 Riverside Dr., Ottawa ON K1V 8X7 Canada
Tel: 613-521-3400; *Fax:* 613-521-9638
info@medicare.ca
www.healthcoalition.ca
To create good health; to preserve & strengthen the Canada Health Act, the foundation of Medicare; to make the health care system democratic, accountable & representative; to provide a continuum of care from large institutions to the home; to protect our investment in the skills & abilities of our health care workers; to ensure fair wages for all health care providers; to eliminate profit-making from illness; to reduce over-prescribing & make drugs affordable; to stop fee-for-service payments; to expand methods of health care & the role of non-physician health providers

Canadian Hematology Society (CHS) / Société canadienne d'hématologie
#199, 435 St. Laurent Blvd., Ottawa ON K1K 2Z8 Canada
Tel: 613-748-9613; *Fax:* 613-748-6392
cag@ca.inter.net
www.canadianhematologysociety.org
To represent members of the Society & provide information about hematology

Canadian Hemochromatosis Society (CHS) / Société canadienne de l'hémochromatose
#272, 7000 Minoru Blvd., Richmond BC V6Y 3Z5 Canada
Tel: 604-279-7135; *Fax:* 604-279-7138
Toll-Free: 877-223-4766
office@toomuchiron.ca
www.toomuchiron.ca
To increase awareness among the public & medical community with regards to the importance of family screening, early diagnosis & treatment of Hemochromatosis
Elizabeth Minish, National President
Ross Gilley, National Vice-President

Canadian Hemophilia Society (CHS) / Société canadienne de l'hémophilie
#400, 1255 rue University, Montréal QC H3B 3B6 Canada
Tel: 514-848-0503; *Fax:* 514-848-9661
Toll-Free: 800-668-2686
chs@hemophilia.ca
www.hemophilia.ca
To find a cure & to provide services to people with hemophilia or other inherited bleeding disorders; to serve persons infected with HIV or hepatitis through blood & blood products

Canadian Hospice Palliative Care Association (CHPCA) / Association canadienne de soins palliatifs (ACSP)
Annex B, Saint-Vincent Hospital, 60 Cambridge St. North, Ottawa ON K1R 7A5 Canada
Tel: 613-241-3663; *Fax:* 613-241-3986
Toll-Free: 800-668-2785
info@chpca.net
www.chpca.net
CHPCA provides leadership in the pursuit of excellence in the care of people approaching death in Canada, in order to lessen suffering, loneliness, & grief. The national association works to develop national standards of practice for hospice palliative care.
Sharon Baxter, Executive Director
Wendy Wainwright, President
Andrea Taylor, Secretary-Treasurer

Canadian Institute of Child Health (CICH) / Institut canadien de la santé infantile
#300, 384 Bank St., Ottawa ON K2P 1Y4 Canada
Tel: 613-230-8838; *Fax:* 613-230-6654
cich@cich.ca
www.cich.ca
To promote the health & well-being of Canadian children through consultation, collaboration, research & advocacy by building alliances & coalitions & by creating resources on health promotion, disease & injury prevention relevant to child & family health in Canada; to identify issues of concern by monitoring the health & well-being of children in Canada; to promote & improve the health & well-being of mothers & infants in all settings; to promote the healthy physical development of children in a safe environment & reduce childhood injuries; to promote the healthy psycho-social development of children in supportive & nurturing environments; to facilitate empowerment of individuals & communities to achieve the above goals for Canadian children & their families; to facilitate collaborative work between consumers, professional, non-professional & government agencies that results in appropriate actions for identified needs

Canadian Institute of Public Health Inspectors (CIPHI) / Institut Canadien des inspecteurs en santé publique (ICISP)
#720, 999 West Broadway Ave., Vancouver BC V5Z 1K5
Tel: 604-739-8180; *Fax:* 604-738-4080
Toll-Free: 888-245-8180
questions@ciphi.ca; office@ciphi.ca
www.ciphi.ca
To protect the health of all Canadians; To advance the environmental & health sciences; To enhance the field of public health inspection through certification, information, & advocacy

Canadian Liver Foundation (CLF) / Fondation canadienne du foie (FCF)
#1500, 2235 Sheppard Ave. East, Toronto ON M2J 5B5 Canada
Tel: 416-491-3353; *Fax:* 416-491-4952
Toll-Free: 800-563-5483
clf@liver.ca
www.liver.ca
Social Media:
facebook.com/home.php?#!/pages/Canadian-Liver-Foundation/6584473365
To reduce the incidence & impact of all liver disease by funding liver research & education; promote liver health through programs & publications

Canadian Lung Association (CLA) / Association pulmonaire du Canada
#300, 1750 Courtwood Cres., Ottawa ON K2C 2B5
Tel: 613-569-6411; *Fax:* 613-569-8860
Toll-Free: 800-566-5864
info@lung.ca
www.lung.ca
To improve & promote lung health across Canada

Canadian Marfan Association / Association du syndrome de Marfan
PO Box 42257, Stn. Centre Plaza, 128 Queen St. S, Mississauga ON L5M 4Z0 Canada
Tel: 905-826-3223; *Fax:* 905-826-2125
Toll-Free: 866-722-1722
info@marfan.ca
www.marfan.ca
To increase public awareness of Marfan Syndrome in Canada; to provide accurate, timely information about this condition to affected patients, their families & health care personnel; to encourage the establishment of Marfan self-help groups in communities across Canada; to support & foster research
Shirley Otway, Contact, Southern Alberta
Roy Braunberger, Contact, Lacombe, Alberta
Lisa McDonald, Contact, British Columbia
Jan Landsiedel, Contact, Manitoba & N.W. Ontario
Robert French, Contact, Newfoundland
Michelle Reid, Contact, Nova Scotia
Michael Stern, Contact, Montréal
Arleta Taylor, Contact, Saskatchewan
Eva Theofilopoulos, Executive Manager, GTA Chapter

Canadian Massage Therapist Alliance (CMTA) / Alliance canadienne de massothérapeutes
c/o Massage Therapists' Association of British Columbia, #180, 1200 - 73rd Ave., Vancouver BC V6P 6G5 Canada
Tel: 604-873-4467; *Fax:* 604-873-6211
locke@massagetherapy.bc.ca
www.cmta.ca
To foster & advance the art, science & philosophy of massage therapy through nationwide cooperation in a professional, ethical & practical manner for the betterment of health care in Canada
Brenda Locke, Executive Director

Canadian Medical Association (CMA) / Association médicale canadienne (AMC)
1867 Alta Vista Dr., Ottawa ON K1G 5W8
Tel: 613-731-8610; *Fax:* 613-236-8864
Toll-Free: 888-855-2555
cmamsc@cma.ca; cmatechsupport@cma.ca (technical support)
www.cma.ca
Social Media: www.twitter.com/CMA_Docs
To act as the national voice of physicians in Canada; To serve the Canadian medical community; To promote the highest standards of health & health care

The Canadian Medical Protective Association / Association canadienne de protection médicale
PO Box 8225, Stn. T, 875 Carling Ave., Ottawa ON K1G 3H7 Canada
Tel: 613-725-2000; *Fax:* 613-725-1300
Toll-Free: 800-267-6522
mediainquiries@cmpa.org
www.cmpa-acpm.ca
Founded by a group of Canadian doctors for their mutual protection against legal actions based on allegations of malpractice or negligence
John E. Gray, MD, CCFP, FCFP, Executive Director & CEO
William S. Tucker, President
Michael R. Lawrence, MB, BS, 1st Vice-President
Lawrence E. Groves, MD, MCFP, 2nd Vice-President

Canadian MedicAlert Foundation / Fondation canadienne MedicAlert
#800, 2005 Sheppard Ave. East, Toronto ON M2J 5B4 Canada
Tel: 416-696-0267; *Fax:* 416-696-0156
Toll-Free: 800-668-1507
medinfo@medicalert.ca
www.medicalert.ca
Social Media:
facebook.com/pages/Canadian-MedicAlert-Foundation/26463546528?v=info
To provide lifelong access to personal & medical information in order to protect & save the lives of its members; MedicAlert is a non-profit organization that provides all Canadians with medical protection in an emergency situation.

Canadian Memorial Chiropractic College (CMCC)
6100 Leslie St., Toronto ON M2H 3J1 Canada
Tel: 416-482-2340; *Fax:* 416-646-1114
Toll-Free: 800-463-2923
communications@cmcc.ca
www.cmcc.ca
To advance the art, science & philosophy of chiropractic; to educate chiropractors; to further the development of the chiropractic profession; to improve the health of society
Ron Brady, Chair of the Board
J.A. Moss, President

Canadian Natural Health Association (CNHA)
#105, 5 Wakunda Pl., Toronto ON M4A 1A2 Canada
Tel: 416-686-7056; *Toll-Free:* 866-686-7056
mark.ansara@3web.net
To establish leadership in healthy, natural lifestyle education & support services; to assist by providing resources to help make people healthier

Canadian Network of Toxicology Centres (CNTC) / Réseau canadien des centres de toxicologie
Bovey Bldg., 2nd Fl., Gordon St., Guelph ON N1G 2W1 Canada
Tel: 519-824-4120; *Fax:* 519-837-3861
dwarner@uoguelph.ca
www.uoguelph.ca/cntc/
To be recognized & respected for excellence in research, training, analysis & communication of information focused on critical toxicology issues for ecosystem & human health; to achieve this through innovative, multi-disciplinary teamwork & partnerships between the public & private sector

Canadian Neurological Sciences Federation (CCNS) / Fédération des sciences neurologiques du Canada
#709, 7015 Macleod Trail SW, Calgary AB T2H 2K6
Tel: 403-229-9544; *Fax:* 403-229-1661
info@cnsfederation.org
www.cnsfederation.org
To enhance the care of patients with diseases of the nervous system; To act as the umbrella organization for the following societies: Canadian Neurological Society, Canadian Neurosurgical Society, Canadian Society of Clinical Neurophysiologists, & Canadian Association of Child Neurologists
Dan Morin, Chief Executive Officer
Marika Fitzgerald, Manager, Finance & Administration
Donna Irvin, Administrator, Membership Services
Lisa Bicek, Coordinator, Professional Development
Cindy Leschyshyn, Editorial Coordinator, Journal

Canadian Neurological Society (CNS) / Société canadienne de neurologie
#709, 7015 Macleod Trail SW, Calgary AB T2H 2K1 Canada
Tel: 403-229-9544; *Fax:* 403-229-1661
brains@ccns.org
www.cnsfederation.org/
To promote & encourage all aspects of neurology, including research, education, assessment & accreditation; provide for annual scientific sessions to promote the knowledge & practice of neurology

Canadian Occupational Therapy Foundation (COTF) / La Fondation canadienne d'ergothérapie (FCE)
CTTC Bldg., #3401, 1125 Colonel By Dr., Ottawa ON K1S 5R1 Canada
Tel: 613-523-2268; *Fax:* 613-523-2552
Toll-Free: 800-434-2268
skamble@cotfcanada.org
www.cotfcanada.org
To fund & promote research & scholarship in occupational therapy in Canada
Sangita Kamblé, CAE, Executive Director
Sandra Wittenberg, Executive Assistant

Canadian Oncology Societies
c/o 82-84 Barrie St., Kingston ON K7L 3N6 Canada
Tel: 613-533-6000; *Fax:* 613-533-2941
bvancersluis@ctg.queensu.ca
www.cos.ca
COS strives to increase and exchange knowledge in the field of oncology; to promote the application of such knowledge in the prevention and diagnosis of cancer and the care of cancer patients and their families; to promote interdisciplinary approaches to patient care and research in cancer; to provide a forum for the presentation and discussion of scientific knowledge and advances in oncology; to further continuing education for groups and indivduals involved in the care of patients who require special attention; support public cancer education programs; to support and assist the Canadian Cancer Society and the National Cancer Insitute; to advise government and other agencies on the provision of health services relevent to oncology.

Canadian Ophthalmological Society (COS) / Société canadienne d'opthalmologie (SCO)
#610, 1525 Carling Ave., Ottawa ON K1Z 8R9 Canada
Tel: 613-729-6779; *Fax:* 613-729-7209
cos@eyesite.ca
www.eyesite.ca
To assure the provision of optimal eye care to all Canadians by promoting excellence in ophthalmology & providing services to support its members in practice

Canadian Organization for Rare Disorders (CORD)
#600, 151 Bloor St. West, Toronto ON M5S 1S4 Canada
Tel: 416-969-7464; *Toll-Free:* 877-302-7273
office@cord.ca
www.cord.ca
To advocate for health policy that works for people with rare disorders; to promote research & services for all rare disorders in Canada; to increase access to genetic screening & genetic counselling for rare disorders
Durhane Wong-Rieger, President
Ed Koning, Vice-President
John Adams, Treasurer

Canadian Orthopaedic Association (COA) / Association canadienne d'orthopédie
#360, 4150, rue Ste-Catherine ouest, Montréal QC H3Z 2Y5 Canada
Tel: 514-874-9003; *Fax:* 514-874-0464
cynthia@canorth.org
www.coa-aco.org
To provide continuing medical education for orthopaedic surgeons
Douglas C. Thomson, CEO

Canadian Orthopaedic Foundation (COF) / Fondation orthopédique du Canada (FOC)
PO Box 7029, Innisfil ON L9S 1A8 Canada
Tel: 416-410-2341; *Toll-Free:* 800-461-3639
mailbox@canorth.org
www.canorth.org
To foster excellence in the provision of health care to patients with musculoskeletal disease or injury, in a cost effective manner, based on significant outcome studies, by supporting research, educating its members & securing funding from government & other health care funding agencies

Canadian Orthoptic Council / Conseil canadien d'orthoptique
CHUL, 2705 Boul, Laurier, Ste. Foy QC G1V 4G2 Canada
Fax: 418-654-2188
info@orthopticscanada.org
www.orthopticscanada.org
To establish standards in the training of orthoptic students; to establish standards for orthoptic training centres; to provide examinations of orthoptic students in order to determine their proficiency in orthopotics & to award a certificate of competency to qualified students who pass the examinations; to require evidence of continuing education of certified orthoptists; to establish standards for the professional ethical conduct of certified orthoptists.

Canadian Paediatric Society (CPS) / Société canadienne de pédiatrie
2305 St. Laurent Blvd., Ottawa ON K1G 4J8 Canada
Tel: 613-526-9397; *Fax:* 613-526-3332
info@cps.ca
www.cps.ca
To advocate for the health needs of children & youth; to provide continuing education to paediatricians; to establish national guidelines for paediatric care & practice

Canadian Pain Society / Société canadienne pour le traitement de la douleur
#202, 1143 Wentworth St. West, Oshawa ON L1J 8P7
Tel: 905-404-9545; *Fax:* 905-404-3727
office@canadianpainsociety.ca
www.canadianpainsociety.ca
To foster research on pain; To improve the management of patients with acute & chronic pain

Canadian Paraplegic Association (CPA) / Association canadienne des paraplégiques
#230, 1101 Prince of Wales Dr., Ottawa ON K2C 3W7 Canada
Tel: 613-723-1033; *Fax:* 613-723-1060
Toll-Free: 800-720-4933
info@canparaplegic.org; cpanational@canparaplegic.org
www.canparaplegic.org
To assist persons with spinal cord injuries & other physical disabilitieto to cope with the changes caused by their injury, to become independent & self-reliant, & to lead productive lives

Canadian Pediatric Foundation (CPF) / La fondation canadienne de pédiatrie
2305 St. Laurent Blvd., Ottawa ON K1G 4J8 Canada
Tel: 613-526-9397; *Fax:* 613-526-3332
cpf@cps.ca
www.cps.ca
To promote improved health care & social well-being for the children of Canada, particularly for disadvantaged groups; to promote better standards of health care for children throughout the world, particularly where Canadian aid is active.
Marie Adèle Davis, Executive Director

Canadian Physiotherapy Association (CPA) / L'Association canadienne de physiothérapie
#410, 2345 Yonge St., Toronto ON M4P 2E5 Canada
Tel: 416-932-1888; *Fax:* 416-932-9708
Toll-Free: 800-387-8679
information@physiotherapy.ca
www.physiotherapy.ca
To provide leadership & direction to the profession; to foster excellence in practice, education & research; to promote high standards of health in Canada

Canadian Podiatric Medical Association (CPMA) / Association médicale podiatrique canadienne
#2063, 61 Broadway Blvd., Sherwood Park AB T8H 2C1 Canada
Toll-Free: 888-220-3338
askus@podiatrycanada.org
www.podiatrycanada.org
To effectively serve & provide guidance to its members & the podiatry profession in Canada; to serve the public; to provide the authoritative national voice for podiatrists in Canada; to recognize a particular responsibility to contribute to the development of national positions & standards related to the podiatric medical profession through education, research, materials & personnel
Mario Turanovic, President

Canadian Porphyria Foundation Inc. (CPF) / La Fondation canadienne de la porphyrie
PO Box 1206, Neepawa MB R0J 1H0 Canada
Tel: 204-476-2800; *Fax:* 204-476-2800
Toll-Free: 866-476-2801
porphyria@cpf-inc.ca
www.cpf-inc.ca
Dedicated to improving the quality of life for Canadians affected by the porphyrias through programs of awareness, education, service, advocacy & research; committed to promoting public & medical professional awareness; assembling, printing & distributing up-to-date educational information to physicians, health care personnel, diagnosed patients & others affected by porphyria; offering support programs to affected individuals & their families; promoting the family social welfare of affected individuals; educating & informing physicians & others in health care about the porphyrias so that early diagnosis & proper treatment will be realized; promoting & providing financial assistance for research; committed to encouraging, supporting & serving physicians & researchers in their efforts to find more effective treatments & to increasing physician, patient & community awareness & thereby cultivating support for research
Lois J. Aitken, President/Executive Director

Canadian Post-MD Education Registry (CAPER) / Système informatisé sur les stagiaires post-MD en formation clinique
#800, 265 Carling Ave., Ottawa ON K1S 2E1 Canada
Tel: 613-730-1204; *Fax:* 613-730-1196
caper@afmc.ca
www.caper.ca
To provide accurate & timely data pertaining to Post-MD training & physician resources in Canada to assist medical schools, governments & other work longitudinal research pertaining to physicians training & supply
Yannick Fortin, Project Manager
Hélène LeBlanc, Executive Assistant

Canadian Public Health Association (CPHA) / Association canadienne de santé publique (ACSP)
#400, 1565 Carling Ave., Ottawa ON K1Z 8R1
Tel: 613-725-3769; *Fax:* 613-725-9826
info@cpha.ca
www.cpha.ca
Social Media:
www.facebook.com/group.php?gid=159289860285?ref
To represent public health in Canada; To support universal & equitable access to the necessary conditions to achieve health for all Canadians; To provide links to the international public health community

Canadian Public Health Association - NB/PEI Branch
#34, 2865 Rothesay Rd., Rothesay NB E3B 4P2 Canada
Tel: 506-847-0311; *Fax:* 506-847-0311
Cristin Muecke, President
Ann Harling, Secretary-Treasurer

Canadian Public Health Association - NWT/Nunavut Branch
PO Box 1000, Stn. 1000, Iqaluit NU X0A 0H0 Canada
Tel: 867-975-5774; *Fax:* 867-975-5755
isobol@gov.nu.ca
Isaac Sobol, President

Canadian Rheumatology Association (CRA) / Société canadienne de rhumatologie
912 Tegal Pl., Newmarket ON L3X 1L3 Canada
Tel: 905-952-0698; *Fax:* 905-952-0708
cra@rogers.com
www.rheum.ca; www.rhumato.ca
To represent Canadian rheumatologists & promote their pursuit of excellence in arthritis care & research in Canada through leadership, education & communication

Canadian Sickle Cell Society / La société de l'anémie falciforme du Canada
#33, 6999, Côte des Neiges, Montréal QC H3S 2B8 Canada
Tel: 514-735-5100; *Fax:* 514-735-5109
cslaf@total.net
To educate the public at large & at risk; to recruit & train volunteers; to provide effective lobbying for the improvement of services to the families & individuals affected by sickle cell anemia; to identify sickle disease or traits; to provide individual & family counselling.

Canadian Society for Clinical Investigation (CSCI) / Société canadienne de recherches cliniques (SCRC)
774 Echo Dr., Ottawa ON K1S 5N8 Canada
Tel: 613-730-6240; *Fax:* 613-730-1116
csci@rcpsc.edu
www.csci-scrc.org
To promote research in the field of human health throughout Canada; to lobby for research funding; to support Canadian researchers in their endeavours & at all stages of their careers by supporting knowledge translation & fostering communities of health science researchers

Canadian Society for International Health (CSIH) / Société canadienne de la santé internationale
#1105, 1 Nicholas St., Ottawa ON K1N 7B7
Tel: 613-241-5785; *Fax:* 613-241-3845
csih@csih.org
www.csih.org
To promote international health & development through mobilization of Canadian resources; To advocate & facilitate research, education, & service activities in international health; To further Canadian strengths of progressive health policy & programming in all fields where global & domestic health concerns meet; To contribute to the evolving global understanding of health & development

Canadian Society for Medical Laboratory Science (CSMLS) / Société canadienne de science de laboratoire médical
PO Box 2830, Stn. LCD 1, 33 Wellington Ave. North, Hamilton ON L8N 3N8
Tel: 905-528-8642; *Fax:* 905-528-4968
www.csmls.org
To promote & maintain a nationally accepted standard of medical laboratory technology; to promote, maintain, & protect professional identity & interests of medical laboratory technologists

Canadian Society for Surgical Oncology (CSSO) / Société canadienne d'oncologie chirurgicale
c/o J. Hanes, Surgical Oncology, Princess Margaret Hospital, #3-130, 610 University Ave., Toronto ON M5G 2M9 Canada
Tel: 416-946-6583; *Fax:* 416-946-6590
jane.hanes@uhn.on.ca
www.cos.ca/csso
To encourage optimum patient care through a multi-disciplinary treatment approach; to promote surgical oncology training programs in Canadian universities
Jane Hanes, CSSO Coordinator
Richard Nason, President
Carmen Giacomantonio, Secretary-Treasurer

Canadian Society for the History of Medicine (CSHM) / Société canadienne d'histoire de la médecine (SCHM)
c/o McMaster Univ., History of Medicine, #3NIO Health Sciences Ctr, Hamilton ON L8N 3Z5 Canada
Tel: 905-525-9140; *Fax:* 905-522-9509
www.cshm-schm.ca
To promote the study & communication of the history of health & medicine
Patricia Prestwich, President
C. Peter Warren, Vice-President
Peter Twohig, Secretary-Treasurer

Canadian Society for Transfusion Medicine (CSTM) / Société canadienne de médecine transfusionnelle
774 Echo Dr., Ottawa ON K1S 5N8 Canada
Tel: 613-260-6198; *Fax:* 613-730-1116
office@transfusion.ca
www.transfusion.ca
To promulgate throughout Canada a high level of ethics & professional standards; to create national & regional opportunities for the presentation & discussion of research & developments in this & allied fields; to initiate & maintain a program of continuing education; to promote good laboratory & good manufacturing practices; to establish mutually beneficial working relationships with relevant national & international societies & organizations & to be the primary voice for transfusion medicine in Canada

Canadian Society for Vascular Surgery (CSVS) / Société canadienne de chirurgie vasculaire
c/o Christiane Dowsing, Society Manager, 774 Echo Dr., Ottawa ON K1S 5N8
Tel: 613-730-6263; *Fax:* 613-730-1116
csvs@royalcollege.ca
www.canadianvascular.ca
To promote vascular health for Canadians

Canadian Society of Allergy & Clinical Immunology (CSACI) / Société canadienne d'allergie et d'immunologie clinique
774 Echo Dr., Ottawa ON K1S 5N8
Tel: 613-730-6272; *Fax:* 613-730-1116
csaci@rcpsc.edu
www.csaci.ca
To ensure optimal patient care by advancing the knowledge & practice of allergy, clinical immunology, & asthma
Charles Frankish, President
Richard Warrington, Vice-President
Stuart Carr, Secretary-Treasurer

Canadian Society of Cardiac Surgeons / Société des chirurgiens cardiaques
#1403, 222 Queen St., ottawa ON K1P 5V9 Canada
Toll-Free: 877-569-3407
cscs@ccs.ca
www.ccs.ca/cscs

Canadian Society of Clinical Neurophysiologists (CSCN) / Société canadienne de neurophysiologistes cliniques
PO Box 5456, Stn. A, #709, 7015 Macleod Trail SW, Calgary AB T2H 1X8 Canada
Tel: 403-229-9544; *Fax:* 403-229-1661
brains@ccns.org
www.ccns.org
CSCN promotes & encourages all aspects of neurophysiology, including research & education, in addition to assessment & accreditation in the field.

Canadian Society of Cytology (CSC) / Société canadienne de cytologie
c/o Dr. Dirk van Niekirk, BC Cancer Agency, 600 West 10th Ave., Vancouver BC V5Z 4E6 Canada
dvanniek@bccancer.bc.ca
www.cap.medical.org/cytology.htm
To promote & support education in cytology; to maintain a high standard of practice within the discipline of cytopathology; to foster the development of cytopathology in Canada

Canadian Society of Diagnostic Medical Sonographers (CSDMS)
PO Box 1220, Kemptville ON K0G 1J0 Canada
Tel: 613-258-0855; *Fax:* 613-258-0899
Toll-Free: 888-273-6746
info@csdms.com
www.csdms.com
To enhance patient care by promoting the science of diagnostic medical ultrasound
Kathleen Foran, Executive Director

Canadian Society of Endocrinology & Metabolism (CSEM) / Société canadienne d'endocrinologie et métabolisme (SCEM)
774 Echo Dr., Ottawa ON K1S 5N8
Tel: 613-730-6224; *Fax:* 613-730-1116
CSEM@rcpsc.edu
www.endo-metab.ca
To advance the discipline of endocrinology & metabolism in Canada
Cheri L. Deal, PhD, MD, FRCPC, President
Ivy Fettes, Secretary-Treasurer

Canadian Society of Gastroenterology Nurses & Associates (CSGNA)
#224 - 1540 Cornwall Rd., Oakville ON L6J 7W5 Canada
Tel: 905-829-8794; *Fax:* 905-829-0242
Toll-Free: 866-544-8794
csgnaexecutiveassistant@csgna.com
www.csgna.com
To enhance the educational & professional growth of the membership within the resources available.
Joanne Glen, President
Cindy James, Treasurer

Canadian Society of Internal Medicine (CSIM) / Société canadienne de médecine interne
774 Echo Dr., Ottawa ON K1S 5N8 Canada
Tel: 613-730-6244; *Fax:* 613-730-1116
www.csimonline.com

The Canadian Society of Intestinal Research
855 - 12th Ave., Vancouver BC V5Z 1M9 Canada
Tel: 604-875-4875; *Fax:* 604-875-4429
Toll-Free: 866-600-4875
info@badgut.com
www.badgut.com
To increase public awareness; to provide patient educational materials; to fund medical research regarding a broad range of gastrointestinal diseases & disorders
Gail Attara, Executive Director
Kwynn Vodnak, Associate Director

Canadian Society of Nephrology (CSN) / Société canadienne de néphrologie (SCN)
c/o Dr. A. Garg, Kidney Clinical Research, London Health Sciences Ctr., #ELL-101, 800 Commissioners Rd. East, London ON N6A 4G5
Tel: 519-685-8502; *Fax:* 519-685-8269
smkelly@mun.ca (CSN Secretariat)
www.csnscn.ca
To advance the practice of Nephrology; To promote the highest quality of care for patients with renal diseases, by setting high standards for medical training & education; To encourage research in biomedical sciences related to the kidney, kidney disorders & renal replacement therapies

Canadian Society of Nuclear Medicine (CSNM) / La Société canadienne de médecine nucléaire (SCMN)
774 Echo Dr., Ottawa ON K1S 5N8 Canada
Tel: 613-730-6254; *Fax:* 613-730-1116
csnm@rcpsc.edu
www.csnm-scmn.ca
The Society is concerned with public policy & aspects of nuclear medicine practice pertaining to standards of clinical practice & training for specialists. Safety & research are also concerns of the Society.

Canadian Society of Nutrition Management / Société canadienne de gestion de la nutrition
#300, 1370 Don Mills Rd., Toronto ON M3B 3N7 Canada
Fax: 416-441-0591
Toll-Free: 866-355-2766
csnm@csnm.ca
www.csnm.ca
CSNM fosters an environment in which members can achieve success in their chosen field.

Canadian Society of Orthopaedic Technologists (CSOT) / Société canadienne des technologistes en orthopédie
#715A, 18 Wynford Dr., Toronto ON M3C 3S2 Canada
Tel: 416-445-4516; *Fax:* 416-489-7356
csot@look.ca
www.pappin.com/csot
To promote & develop training programmes, professional standards; encourage uniform training programs & examinatios; promote & facilitate cooperation between Orthopaedic Technologists & the medical profession.

Canadian Society of Otolaryngology - Head & Neck Surgery (CSO-HNS) / Société canadienne d'otolaryngologie et de chirurgie cervico-faciale
Administrative Office, 221 Millford Cres., Elora ON N0B 1S0
Tel: 519-846-0630; *Fax:* 519-846-9529
Toll-Free: 800-655-9533
cso.hns@sympatico.ca
www.entcanada.org
To improve patient care in otolaryngology - head & neck surgery; To maintain high professional & ethical standards

Canadian Society of Plastic Surgeons (CSPS) / Société canadienne des chirurgiens plasticiens
#4, 1469, boul St-Joseph est, Montréal QC H2K 1M6 Canada
Tel: 514-843-5415; *Fax:* 514-843-7005
Toll-Free: 800-665-5415
csps_sccp@bellnet.ca
www.plasticsurgery.ca
The Society advances the art & science of plastic surgery.

Canadian Society of Respiratory Therapists (CSRT) / La Société canadienne des thérapeutes respiratoires (SCTR)
#102, 1785 Alta Vista Dr., Ottawa ON K1G 3Y6 Canada
Tel: 613-731-3164; *Fax:* 613-521-4314
Toll-Free: 800-267-3422
info@csrt.com
www.csrt.com
To provide leadership toward the advancement of cardiorespiratory care; To achieve excellence through the definition of roles, standards, & scope of clinical practice

Canadian Spinal Research Organization (CSRO)
#2, 120 Newkirk Rd., Richmond Hill ON L4C 9S7 Canada
Tel: 905-508-4000; *Fax:* 905-508-4002
Toll-Free: 800-361-4004
csro@globalserve.net
www.csro.com
To improve the physical quality of life for people with spinal injuries; to reduce the incidence of spinal cord injuries through awareness programs for the public & prevention programs with targeted groups
Wayne Archibald, Director, Research
Barry Munro, President

Canadian Sport Massage Therapists Association (CSMTA) / Association canadienne des massothérapeutes du sport
#306, 50 Eccleston Dr., Toronto ON M4A 1K8 Canada
Tel: 416-285-1745; *Fax:* 416-285-1914
natoffice@csmta.ca
www.csmta.ca
To provide leadership in the field of sport massage therapy & education in Canada through the establishment of professional standards & qualifications of its members, as a certifying body
Trish Scheidel, President
Joanne Baker, National Office Coordinator
Aurel Hamran, President, Alberta Chapter
Kim Mark-Goldsworthy, President, BC Chapter
Johanna Thackwray, President, Ontario Chapter
Al Bodnarchuk, President, Saskatchewan Chapter

Canadian Thoracic Society (CTS) / Société canadienne de thoracologie (SCT)
c/o National Office, The Lung Association, #300, 1750 Courtwood Cres., Ottawa ON K2C 2B5
Tel: 613-569-6411; *Fax:* 613-569-8860
Toll-Free: 888-566-5864
ctsinfo@lung.ca
www.lung.ca/cts
To enhance the prevention & treatment of respiratory diseases

Canadian Transplant Association (CTA) / Association canadienne des greffes
c/o Neil Folkins, 11649 St. Albert Trail NW, Edmonton AB T5M 3L6
Toll-Free: 877-779-5991
www.organ-donation-works.org
To promote a healthy lifestyle for transplant recipients
Dave Smith, President
Neil Folkins, Director, Membership
Kathy Tachynski, Secretary
Debbie Lanktree, Treasurer

Canadian Urological Association (CUA) / Association des urologues du Canada
#1155, 1155, rue University, Montréal QC H3B 3A7 Canada
Tel: 514-395-0376; *Fax:* 514-875-0205
cua@cua.org
www.cua.org

Canadians for Health Research (CHR) / Les Canadiens pour la recherche médicale
PO Box 126, Westmount QC H3Z 2T1 Canada
Tel: 514-398-7478; *Fax:* 514-398-8361
info@chrcrm.org
www.chrcrm.org
To further understanding & communication among the public, the scientific community & government; to promote stability & quality in Canadian health research; to meet goals through the direct provision of information on request, & development & circulation of literature & special programming; to sponsor periodic conferences, workshops, a journalism award, & a student essay competition.

CancerCare Manitoba (CCMB)
675 McDermot Ave., Winnipeg MB R3E 0V9 Canada
Tel: 204-787-2197; *Toll-Free:* 866-561-1026
donate@cancercare.mb.ca
www.cancercare.mb.ca
To provide exceptional care for patients & their families
Annitta L. Stenning, Executive Director
Sandra Tym, Director, Finance & Administration
Roberta Koscielny, Director, Communications & Public Affairs

Catholic Health Association of British Columbia (CHABC)
9387 Holmes St., Burnaby BC V3N 4C3 Canada
Tel: 604-524-3427; *Fax:* 604-524-3428
smhouse@shawlink.ca
chabc.bc.ca
To witness to the healing ministry and abiding presence of Jesus. Inspired by the Gospel, this Association strives to have a universal concern for health as a condition for full human development.

Catholic Health Association of Canada (CHAC) / Association catholique canadienne de la santé (ACCS)
1247 Kilborn Pl., Ottawa ON K1H 6K9 Canada
Tel: 613-731-7148; *Fax:* 613-731-7797
info@chac.ca
www.chac.ca
The Association strengthens & supports the ministry of Catholic health care organizations & providers through advocacy & governance.

Catholic Health Association of Manitoba (CHAM) / Association catholique manitobaine de la santé (ACMS)
SBGH Education Bldg., #N5067, 409 Taché Ave., Winnipeg MB R2H 2A6 Canada
Tel: 204-235-3136; *Fax:* 204-235-3811
executivedirector@cham.mb.ca
www.cham.mb.ca
To carry out the healing ministry of the Catholic Church in the delivery of both health & social services in Manitoba; to treat the people of Manitoba with compassion & respect for all; to recognize the spiritual dimension integral to health & healing

Catholic Health Association of Saskatchewan (CHAS)
1702 - 20 St. West, Saskatoon SK S7M 0Z9 Canada
Tel: 306-655-5330; *Fax:* 306-655-5333
cath.health@sasktel.net
www.chassk.ca
To provide leadership in mission, ethics, spiritual care, & social justice in Saskatchewan; to promote the sanctity of life & the dignity of all

Catholic Health Corporation of Ontario (CHCO)
PO Box 1879, 712 College Ave. West, Guelph ON N1H 7A1 Canada
Tel: 519-767-5600; *Fax:* 519-767-5602
chco@chco.ca
www.chco.ca
Sponsors member institutions and thereby continues and strengthens Catholic health care in Ontario

Childhood Cancer Foundation Candlelighters Canada (CCCFC) / Fondation pour le Cancer chez l'enfant
#801, 21 St. Clair Ave. East, Toronto ON M4T 1L9 Canada
Tel: 416-489-6440; *Fax:* 416-489-9812
Toll-Free: 800-363-1062
info@childhoodcancer.ca
www.childhoodcancer.ca
Candlelighters Canada is a national volunteer charitable organization dedicated to improving the quality of life for families experiencing the effects of childhood cancer, through the provision of resources, parent support & the promotion of research. It is a registered charity, BN# 131897654RR0001.

Chiropractic Awareness Council (CAC)
595 Woolwich St., Guelph ON N1H 3Y5 Canada
Tel: 519-822-1879; *Fax:* 519-822-1239
Toll-Free: 877-997-9927
totalhealth@chiropracticawarenesscouncil.org
www.chiropracticawarenesscouncil.org
To promote public awareness of chiropractic life principles by promoting an awareness of the devastating effects of vertebral subluxation complex on the expression of human health potential; to educate the public with the conviction that chiropractic care is a integral aspect of health for people of all ages & to society in general
Steven Silk, Chair

Christian Health Association of Alberta (CHAA)
132 Warwick Rd., Edmonton AB T5X 4P8 Canada
Tel: 780-488-8074; *Fax:* 780-475-7968
chaaa@compusmart.ab.ca
www.chaaa.ab.ca
Represents the shared vision & values of those seeking to make visible Jesus the Healer; provides support & leadership to members & the community through education, advocacy & collaboration

Chronic Pain Association of Canada (CPAC)
PO Box 66017, Stn. Heritage, #130, 2323 - 111 St., Edmonton AB T6J 6T4 Canada
Tel: 780-482-6727; *Fax:* 780-433-3128
cpac@chronicpaincanada.com
www.chronicpaincanada.com
To advance the treatment & management of chronic intractable pain; to develop research projects to promote the discovery of a cure for this disease; to educate both the health care community & the public

Collège des médecins du Québec (CMQ)
2170, boul René-Lévesque ouest, Montréal QC H3H 2T8 Canada
Tél: 514-933-4441; *Téléc:* 514-933-3112
Ligne sans frais: 888-633-3246
info@cmq.org
www.collegedesmedecins.qc.ca
Promouvoir une médecine de qualité pour protéger le public et contribuer à l'amélioration de la santé des Québécois

College of Chiropractors of Alberta (CCOA)
Manulife Place, 11203 - 70 St. NW, Edmonton AB T5B 1T1 Canada
Tel: 780-420-0932; *Fax:* 780-425-6583
office@albertachiro.com
www.albertachiro.com
To ensure quality chiropractic care that enhances the well-being & protects the rights of the people of Alberta; to promote the art, science & philosophy of chiropractic & its value in the health care community

College of Dietitians of Alberta
#740, 10707 - 100 Ave., Edmonton AB T5J 3M1 Canada
Tel: 780-448-0059; *Fax:* 780-489-7759
Toll-Free: 866-493-4348
office@collegeofdietitians.ab.ca
www.collegeofdietitians.ab.ca
The College is the regulatory body of registered dieticians/nutritionists in Alberta, setting entry requirements, standards of practice. It is accountable to both the government & the public.
Doug Cook, Executive Director & Registrar

College of Dietitians of British Columbia (CDBC)
#103, 1765 West 8th Ave., Vancouver BC V6J 5C6 Canada
Tel: 604-736-2016; *Fax:* 604-736-2018
Toll-Free: 877-736-2016
info@collegeofdietitiansbc.org
www.collegeofdietitiansbc.org
To serve & protect the nutritional health of the public through quality dietetic practice

College of Dietitians of Manitoba
#36, 1313 Border St., Winnipeg MB R3H 0X4 Canada
Tel: 204-694-0532; *Fax:* 204-889-1755
Toll-Free: 866-283-2823
office.cdm@mts.net
www.manitobadietitians.ca
The College is the regulating body within the province for dietitians & the profession of dietetics, setting education standards, ensuring competency of members.

College of Dietitians of Ontario (CDO) / L'Ordre des diététistes de l'Ontario
PO Box 30, #1810, 5775 Yonge St., Toronto ON M2M 4J1 Canada
Tel: 416-598-1725; *Fax:* 416-598-0274
Toll-Free: 800-668-4990
information@cdo.on.ca
www.cdo.on.ca
To promote awareness of & access to competent, high quality nutritional care for Ontarians.
Mary Lou Gignac, Registrar

College of Family Physicians of Canada (CFPC) / Collège des médecins de famille du Canada
2630 Skymark Ave., Mississauga ON L4W 5A4 Canada
Tel: 905-629-0900; *Fax:* 905-629-0893
Toll-Free: 800-387-6197
info@cfpc.ca
www.cfpc.ca
To improve the health of Canadians by promoting high standards of medical education & care in family practice, by contributing to public understanding of healthful living, by supporting ready access to family physician services, & by encouraging research & disseminating knowledge about family medicine

College of Physicians & Surgeons of Alberta (CPSA)
Telus Plaza South, #2700, 10020 - 100 St. NW, Edmonton AB T5J 0N3 Canada
Tel: 780-423-4764; *Fax:* 780-420-0651
Toll-Free: 800-561-3899
info@cpsa.ab.ca
www.cpsa.ab.ca
To serve the public & guide the medical profession; to identify factors affecting competent medical practice; to promote quality improvement in medical practice; to ensure practitioners meet our registration standards; to resolve complaints involving practitioners fairly & effectively.

College of Physicians & Surgeons of British Columbia (CPSBC)
#400, 858 Beatty St., Vancouver BC V6B 1C1 Canada
Tel: 604-733-7758; *Fax:* 604-733-3503
Toll-Free: 800-461-3008
www.cpsbc.ca

College of Physicians & Surgeons of Manitoba (CPSM)
#1000, 1661 Portage Ave., Winnipeg MB R3J 3T7 Canada
Tel: 204-774-4344; *Fax:* 204-774-0750
Toll-Free: 877-774-4344
cpsm@cpsm.mb.ca
www.cpsm.mb.ca

College of Physicians & Surgeons of New Brunswick / Collège des médecins et chirurgiens du Nouveau-Brunswick
#300, One Hampton Rd., Rothesay NB E2E 5K8 Canada
Tel: 506-849-5050; *Fax:* 506-849-5069
Toll-Free: 800-667-4641
info@cpsnb.org
www.cpsnb.org

College of Physicians & Surgeons of Newfoundland & Labrador
#603, 139 Water St., St. John's NL A1C 1B2 Canada
Tel: 709-726-8546; *Fax:* 709-726-4725
cpsnl@cpsnl.ca
www.cpsnl.ca
To protect the public; to regulate the practice of medicine & medical practitioners

College of Physicians & Surgeons of Nova Scotia (CPSNS)
#5005, 7071 Bayers Rd., Halifax NS B3L 2C2 Canada
Tel: 902-422-5823; *Fax:* 902-422-5035
Toll-Free: 877-282-7767
mmchugh@cpsns.ns.ca
www.cpsns.ns.ca
To govern the practice of medicine in the public interest

College of Physicians & Surgeons of Ontario (CPSO)
80 College St., Toronto ON M5G 2E2 Canada
Tel: 416-967-2603; *Fax:* 416-961-3330
Toll-Free: 800-268-7096
feedback@cpso.on.ca
www.cpso.on.ca
The best quality care for the people of Ontario by the doctors of Ontario

College of Physicians & Surgeons of Prince Edward Island
199 Grafton St., Charlottetown PE C1A 1L2 Canada
Tel: 902-566-3861; *Fax:* 902-566-3861
mmacdonald@collegeofphysicians.pe.ca
www.cpspei.ca
The College is the regulatory body for physicians in the province, responsible for licensing all medical doctors, maintaining medical standards, handling complaints from the public, & delivering disciplinary action.

College of Physicians & Surgeons of Saskatchewan (CPSS)
#500, 321A - 21st St. East, Saskatoon SK S7K 0C1 Canada
Tel: 306-244-7355; *Fax:* 306-244-0090
cpss@quadrant.net
www.quadrant.net/cpss/
The College of Physicians and Surgeons is a statutory, self-regulating body established by legislation of the Government of Saskatchewan and charged with the responsibility of: Licencing properly qualified medical practitioners; developing and ensuring the standards of practice in all fields of medicine; investigating and disciplining of all doctors whose standards of medical care, ethical or professional conduct are questioned.

Community & Hospital Infection Control Association Canada / Association pour la prévention des infections à l'hôpital et dans la communauté - Canada
PO Box 46125, RPO Westdale, Winnipeg MB R3R 3S3 Canada
Tel: 204-897-5990; *Fax:* 204-895-9595
Toll-Free: 866-999-7111
chicacda@mts.net
www.chica.org
To promote excellence in the practice of infection prevention & control; to employ evidence based practice & application of epidemiological principles to improve the health of Canadians
Marion Yetman, President

Consumer Health Organization of Canada (CHOC)
#1901, 355 St. Clair Ave. West, Toronto ON M5P 1N5 Canada
Tel: 416-924-9800; *Fax:* 416-924-6404
info@consumerhealth.org
www.consumerhealth.org
To encourage the prevention of all kinds of illness through knowledge; to help the individual, the family & the community to enjoy the benefits of a more wholesome lifestyle; to promote harmony & cooperation between like-minded groups.

Crohn's & Colitis Foundation of Canada (CCFC) / Fondation canadienne des maladies inflammatoires de l'intestin
#600, 60 St. Clair Ave. East, Toronto ON M4T 1N5 Canada
Tel: 416-920-5035; *Fax:* 416-929-0364
Toll-Free: 800-387-1479
ccfc@ccfc.ca
www.ccfc.ca; www.thegutsygeneration.ca
To find a cure for Crohn's disease & ulcerative colitis; To raise funds for medical research; To educate individuals with inflammatory bowel disease, their families, health professionals, & the public

Dietitians of Canada (DC) / Les diététistes du Canada
#604, 480 University Ave., Toronto ON M5G 1V2
Tel: 416-596-0857; *Fax:* 416-596-0603
centralinfo@dietitians.ca
www.dietitians.ca
To advance health, through food & nutrition; To act as the voice of the profession in Canada

Doctors Manitoba
20 Desjardins Dr., Winnipeg MB R3X 0E8 Canada
Tel: 204-985-5888; *Fax:* 204-985-5844
Toll-Free: 888-322-4242
www.docsmb.org
To advocate for Manitoba physicians, representing their professional & economic interests.

Doctors Nova Scotia
25 Spectacle Lake Dr., Dartmouth NS B3B 1X7 Canada
Tel: 902-468-1866; *Fax:* 902-468-6578
webmaster@doctorsns.com
www.doctorsns.com
To maintain the integrity of the medical profession; To represent members; To promote high quality health care & disease prevention in Nova Scotia

Dystonia Medical Research Foundation Canada / Fondation de recherches médicales sur la dystonie
#909, 100 Adelaide St. West, Toronto ON M5H 1S3 Canada
Tel: 416-488-6974; *Fax:* 416-488-5878
Toll-Free: 800-361-8061
info@dystoniacanada.org
www.dystoniacanada.org
DMRF Canada aims to advance & support research relating to dystonia; to build awareness about the illness in order to educate both medical & lay communities; and to sponsor patient & family support groups & programs. It is a registered charity, BN: 126616598RR0001.

Epilepsy & Seizure Association of Manitoba
#4, 1805 Main St., Winnipeg MB R2V 2A2 Canada
Tel: 204-783-0466; *Fax:* 204-784-9689
Toll-Free: 866-374-5377
epilepsy.seizures.mb@mts.net
www.manitobaepilepsy.org
The Association aims to improve the quality of life of persons with epilepsy through a broad range of programs, education, support of research & services. It is a registered charity, BN: 108087826RR0001.

Epilepsy Canada (EC) / Épilepsie Canada
#336, 2255B Queen St. East, Toronto ON M4E 1G3 Canada
Fax: 905-764-1231
Toll-Free: 877-734-0873
epilepsy@epilepsy.ca
www.epilepsy.ca
To enhance the quality of life for persons affected by epilepsy; To promote & support research into all aspects of epilepsy; To facilitate educational initiatives; To increase public & professional awareness of epilepsy; To fund research; To encourage governments to address the needs of people with epilepsy

Epilepsy Ontario / Épilepsie Ontario
#308, 1 Promenade Circle, Thornhill ON L4J 4P8 Canada
Tel: 905-764-5099; *Fax:* 905-764-1231
Toll-Free: 800-463-1119
info@epilepsyontario.org
epilepsyontario.org
EO is a non-profit, non-governmental health organization promoting optimal quality of life for people living with seizure disorders. It advocates for awareness, support services, and research into these disorders and maintains a network of local agencies, contacts & associates to provide services, counselling & referrals. It is a registered charity, BN: 118900844RR0001.

Ethiopiaid
#600, 325 Dalhousie St., Ottawa ON K1N 7G2
Tel: 613-697-4843
info@ethiopiaid.ca
www.ethiopiaid.ca
Ethiopiaid aims to create lasting and positive change in Ethiopia by tackling the problems of poverty, ill health and poor education.
As a fundraising organisation, we donate directly to local community projects in Ethiopia. These partners already hold the answers, they simply need a helping hand from people like you to carry out their work.

Eye Bank of BC (EBBC)
Eye Care Centre, 2550 Willow St., Vancouver BC V5Z 3N9 Canada
Tel: 604-875-4567; *Fax:* 604-875-5316
Toll-Free: 800-667-2060
eyebankofbc@vch.ca
www.eyebankofbc.ca
To acquire human donor eye tissue for the purposes of corneal transplant, scelra grafts & medical research.

Eye Bank of Canada - Ontario Division
One Spadina Cres., Toronto ON M5S 2J5 Canada
Tel: 416-497-8735; *Fax:* 416-978-1522
eye.bank@utoronto.ca
eyebank.med.utoronto.ca
To provide donated eye tissue for surgical use in those whose vision can be restored or improved through corneal transplantation or other eye surgery

Fédération des médecins omnipraticiens du Québec (FMOQ) / Québec Federation of General Practitioners
#1000, 1440, rue Ste-Catherine ouest, Montréal QC H3G 1R8 Canada
Tél: 514-878-1911; *Téléc:* 514-878-4455
Ligne sans frais: 800-361-8499
info@fmoq.org
www.fmoq.org
Étude et défense des intérêts économiques, sociaux, moraux et scientifiques des associations et de leurs membres; promouvoir et développer le rôle de l'omnipraticien dans les sphères de la

vie économique, sociale, scientifique et culturelle en définissant d'une façon objective le statut propre à l'omnipraticien

Fédération des médecins spécialistes du Québec (FMSQ) / Federation of Medical Specialists of Québec
CP 216, Succ. Desjardins, #3000, 2, Complexe Desjardins, Montréal QC H5B 1G8 Canada
Tél: 514-350-5000; *Téléc:* 514-350-5100
Ligne sans frais: 800-561-0703
president@fmsq.org
www.fmsq.org
Défendre et promouvoir les intérêts économiques, professionnels et scientifiques des médecins spécialistes

Federation of Canadian Naturists (FCN)
PO Box 186, Stn. D, Toronto ON M9A 4X2 Canada
Tel: 416-410-6833; *Fax:* 416-410-6833
Toll-Free: 888-512-6833
information@fcn.ca
www.fcn.ca
To promote naturism (social nudism) as a healthy, wholesome & completely natural lifestyle

Federation of Regulatory Authorities of Canada (FMRAC) / Fédération des ordres des médecins du Canada
#103, 2283 St. Laurent Blvd., Ottawa ON K1G 5A2 Canada
Tel: 613-738-0372; *Fax:* 613-738-9169
info@fmrac.ca
www.fmrac.ca
To provide a national structure for the provincial & territorial medical regulatory authorities; To present & pursue issues of common concern & interest; To share, consider, & develop positions on such matters

Fédération québécoise de l'autisme et des autres troubles envahissants du développement (FQATED) / Québec Federation for Autism & Other Pervasive Developmental Disorders
#104, 65, rue de Castelnau ouest, Montréal QC H2R 2W3 Canada
Tél: 514-270-7386; *Téléc:* 514-270-9261
Ligne sans frais: 888-830-2833
secretariatfqa@contact.net
www.autisme.qc.ca
Promouvoir et défendre les droits et les intérêts de la personne autiste ou ayant un trouble envahissant du développement afin qu'elle accède à une vie digne et à une meilleure autonomie sociale possible.

Fédération québécoise des massothérapeutes (FQM)
1265, av Mont-Royal est, Montréal QC H2J 1Y4 Canada
Tél: 514-597-0505; *Téléc:* 514-597-0141
Ligne sans frais: 800-363-9609
administration@fqm.qc.ca
www.fqm.qc.ca
Regrouper les massothérapeutes afin de promouvoir la massothérapie sous l'intérêt public et de valoriser la profession de la massothérapie
Sylvie Bédard, Directrice générale

Fédération québécoise des sociétés Alzheimer (FQSA) / Federation of Québec Alzheimer Societies
#211, 5165, rue Sherbrooke ouest, Montréal QC H4A 1T6 Canada
Tél: 514-369-7891; *Téléc:* 514-369-7900
Ligne sans frais: 888-636-6473
info@alzheimerquebec.ca
www.alzheimerquebec.ca
Alléger les conséquences personnelles et sociales de la maladie d'Alzheimer; diffuser l'information auprès du public sur la maladie d'Alzheimer et sur les services offerts par notre réseau; soutenir les sociétés qui offrent aide et formation; promouvoir et encourager la recherche sur la maladie d'Alzheimer entre autres par la gestion d'un fonds provincial de la recherche; établir des relations et faire des représentations auprès des autorités concernées

A fleur de sein & Objectif Santé Mammaire
CP 518, 492, 2e Rue, Chibougamau QC G8P 2X9 Canada
Tél: 418-748-7914; *Téléc:* 418-748-4422
afleurdesein@tlb.sympatico.ca
www.cbcn.ca/afleurdesein/
Offrir solidarité, présence, écoute & entraide à ceux & celles qui sont atteints d'un cancer, quel qu'il soit
Marie Lefrançois, Présidente, A fleur de sein
Nicole Pagé, Coordonnatrice, Objectif Santé Mammaire

La Fondation canadienne du rein, section Chibougamau
CP 462, Chibougamau QC G8P 2Y8 Canada
Tél: 418-748-4730
Hélène Ross-Arseneault

Fondation de la banque d'yeux du Québec inc. / Québec Eye Bank Foundation
5415, boul de l'Assomption, Montréal QC H1T 2M4 Canada
Tél: 514-252-3886; *Téléc:* 514-252-3821
fondby@ssss.gouv.qc.ca
Financement de la recherche sur les maladies de l'oeil et plus particulièment de la cornée (greffe)

Fondation des maladies du coeur du Québec (FMCQ) / Heart & Stroke Foundation of Québec
#500, 1434, rue Sainte-Catherine ouest, Montréal QC H3G 1R4 Canada
Tél: 514-871-1551; *Téléc:* 514-871-9385
Ligne sans frais: 800-567-8563
www.fmcoeur.qc.ca
Forte de l'engagement de ses donateurs, de ses bénévoles et de ses employés, a pour mission de contribuer à l'avancement de la recherche et de promouvoir la santé du coeur, afin de réduire les invalidités et les décès dus aux maladies cardiovasculaires et aux accidents vasculaires cérébraux

Fondation québécoise du cancer
2075, rue de Champlain, Montréal QC H2L 2T1 Canada
Tél: 514-527-2194; *Téléc:* 514-527-1943
Ligne sans frais: 877-336-4443
cancerquebec.mtl@fqc.qc.ca
www.fqc.qc.ca
Vouée à l'amélioration de la condition de la personne atteinte de cancer et de ses proches; offrir des services d'hôtellerie, d'écoute et d'information pour gens atteints du cancer; améliorer la qualité de vie des patients et celle de leurs proches.
Michel Gélinas, Président-fondateur

The Foundation Fighting Blindness (FFB)
890 Yonge St., 12th Fl., Toronto ON M4W 3P4 Canada
Tel: 416-360-4200; *Fax:* 416-360-0060
Toll-Free: 800-461-3331
info@ffb.ca
www.ffb.ca
To support & promote research directed to finding the causes, treatments & ultimately the cures for retinitis pigmentosa, macular degeneration & related retinal diseases

Health Action Network Society (HANS)
#202, 5262 Rumble St., Burnaby BC V5J 2B6 Canada
Tel: 604-435-0512; *Fax:* 604-435-1561
info@hans.org; membership@hans.org; events@hans.org
www.hans.org
To support complementary & alternative health care; To provide resources about preventive medicine & natural therapeutics; To facilitate delivery of integrated health care; To act as a voice for natural health consumers in Canada

Health Association of African Canadians (HAAC)
1149 Main St., Dartmouth NS B2Z 1A8 Canada
Tel: 902-405-4222
haac@chebucto.ns.ca
www.haac.ca
To promote and improve the health of African Canadians in Nova Scotia through community engagement, education, policy recommendations, partnerships, and research participation.
Phyllis Marsh-Jarvis, President

Health Care Public Relations Association of Canada (HCPRA) / Association des relations publiques des organismes de la santé, Canada (ARPOS)
PO Box 36029, 1106 Wellington St., Ottawa ON K1Y 4V3 Canada
Tel: 613-729-2102; *Fax:* 613-729-7708
info@hcpra.org
www.hcpra.org
To address the concerns of the public relations professionals in Canadian health care settings
Jane Petricic, National Coordinator
Pat Stephens, HCPRA President

Health Sciences Centre Foundation (HSCF)
Thorlakson Building, 820 Sherbrook St., #MS1, Winnipeg MB R3A 1R9 Canada
Tel: 204-787-2022; *Fax:* 204-787-2804
Toll-Free: 800-679-8493
hsc_foundation@hsc.mb.ca
www.hscfoundation.mb.ca
To promote health care excellence by funding medical research & clinical projects to the benefit of diverse communities served by the Health Sciences Centre
F.L. (Lynn) Bishop, Chair
Dawne Smithson, CFRE, Vice-President/COO

Heart & Stroke Foundation of Alberta, NWT & Nunavut (HSFA)
#100, 119 - 14 St. NW, Calgary AB T2N 1Z6 Canada
Tel: 403-264-5549; *Fax:* 403-237-0803
Toll-Free: 888-473-4636
www.hsf.ab.ca
The Association disseminates information about heart disease & stroke, & also promotes research into new drugs, therapies, treatments in disorders leading to heart disease & stroke. It conducts several events to campaign for funds. It is a registered charity, BN: 118780840RR0001.
Roderick J. McKay, Chair
Diana Krecsy, CEO

Heart & Stroke Foundation of British Columbia & Yukon (HSFBCY)
1212 West Broadway, Vancouver BC V6H 3V2 Canada
Tel: 604-736-4404; *Fax:* 604-736-8732
Toll-Free: 888-473-4636
info@hsf.bc.ca
www.heartandstroke.bc.ca
To further the study, prevention & relief of cardiovascular disease

Heart & Stroke Foundation of Canada (HSFC) / Fondation des maladies du coeur du Canada
#1402, 222 Queen St., Ottawa ON K1P 5V9 Canada
Tel: 613-569-4361; *Fax:* 613-569-3278
www.heartandstroke.ca
To further the study, prevention & reduction of disability & death from heart disease & stroke through research, education & the promotion of healthy lifestyles

Heart & Stroke Foundation of Manitoba (HSFM)
The Heart & Stroke Bldg., 6 Donald St., Winnipeg MB R3L 0K6 Canada
Tel: 204-949-2000; *Fax:* 204-957-1365
www.heartandstroke.mb.ca
To eliminate heart disease & stroke through education, advocacy, & research

Heart & Stroke Foundation of New Brunswick / Fondation des maladies du coeur du Nouveau-Brunswick
#606, 133 Prince William St., Saint John NB E2L 2B5 Canada
Tel: 506-634-1620; *Fax:* 506-648-0098
Toll-Free: 800-663-3600
heart.stroke@hsf.nb.ca
www.heartandstroke.nb.ca
To improve the health of residents of New Brunswick by preventing & reducing disability & death from heart disease & stroke, through research, health promotion & advocacy

Heart & Stroke Foundation of Newfoundland & Labrador
PO Box 5819, Stn. C, 1037 Topsail Rd., St. John's NL A1C 5X3 Canada
Tel: 709-753-8521; *Fax:* 709-753-3117
www.heartandstroke.nf.ca
To work in Newfoundland & Labrador to advance research, advocate, & promote healthy lifestyles so that heart disease & stroke will be eliminated & their impact reduced

Heart & Stroke Foundation of Nova Scotia (HSFNS)
5161 George St., 7th Fl., Halifax NS B3J 1M7 Canada
Tel: 902-423-7530; *Fax:* 902-492-1464
Toll-Free: 800-423-4432
contactus@heartandstroke.ns.ca
www.heartandstroke.ns.ca
To eliminate heart disease & stroke; To advance research; To promote healthy living; To engage in advocacy activities

Heart & Stroke Foundation of Ontario (HSFO)
PO Box 2414, #1300, 2300 Yonge St., Toronto ON M4P 1E4 Canada
Tel: 416-489-7111; *Fax:* 416-489-6885
Toll-Free: 888-473-4636
www.heartandstroke.on.ca
To eliminate heart disease & stroke by advancing research & promoting healthy living; To advocate in areas such as a smoke-free world, equal access to quality stroke care, obesity targeting, elimination of trans-fat, & resuscitation/CPR

Heart & Stroke Foundation of Prince Edward Island Inc.
PO Box 279, 180 Kent St., Charlottetown PE C1A 7K4 Canada
Tel: 902-892-7441; *Fax:* 902-368-7068
Toll-Free: 888-473-4636
info@hsfpei.ca
www.heartandstroke.pe.ca

To improve the health of Islanders through the funding of heart disease & stroke research & the provision of heart & stroke education & programs

Heart & Stroke Foundation of Saskatchewan (HSFS) / Fondation des maladies du coeur de la Saskatchewan
279 - 3 Ave. North, Saskatoon SK S7K 2H8 Canada
Tel: 306-244-2124; *Fax:* 306-664-4016
Toll-Free: 888-473-4636
heart.stroke@hsf.sk.ca
www.heartandstroke.sk.ca
Social Media: facebook.com/heartandstroke
The Foundation is a volunteer-driven, non-profit organization with the ultimate goal to eliminate & reduce the impact of heart disease & stroke. It aims to advance research, promote healthy living, & advocates a healthy public policy. It is a registered charity, BN: 107955817RR0001.

Hepatitis Outreach Society
Halifax Shopping Centre, PO Box 29120, 2973 Oxford St., Halifax NS B3J 4T8 Canada
Tel: 902-420-1767; *Fax:* 902-463-6725
Toll-Free: 800-521-0572
info@hepatitisoutreach.com
www.hepatitisoutreach.com
To educate Nova Scotians about Hepatitis and its prevention, reduce social stigmatization and isolation; and prevent the spread of Hepatitis.
Angus Campbell, Contact

Huntington Society of Canada / Société Huntington du Canada
#400, 151 Frederick St., Kitchener ON N2H 2M2 Canada
Tel: 519-749-7063; *Fax:* 519-749-8965
Toll-Free: 800-998-7398
info@huntingtonsociety.ca
www.huntingtonsociety.org
To aspire for a world free of Huntington disease; To maximize the quality of life of people living with HD

Hypertension Canada
c/o Judi Farrell, #211, 3780 - 14th Ave., Markham ON L3R 9Y5
Tel: 905-943-9400; *Fax:* 905-943-9401
admin@hypertension.ca
www.hypertension.ca
To advance health by preventing & controlling high blood presseure
Ross Feldman, President
Judi Farrell, Executive Director
Pierre Larochelle, Vice-President
John Blair, Secretary
Robert Brooks, Treasurer

International Association for Medical Assistance to Travellers (IAMAT)
2162 Gordon St., Guelph ON N1L 1G6 Canada
Tel: 519-836-0102; *Fax:* 519-836-3412
info@iamat.org
www.iamat.org
To make competent care available to the traveller around the world; to make direct grants to medical institutions
Mike Marcolongo, B.A., Director

Juvenile Diabetes Research Foundation Canada (JDRF)
#311, 7100 Woodbine Ave., Markham ON L3R 5J2 Canada
Tel: 905-944-8700; *Fax:* 905-944-0800
Toll-Free: 877-287-3533
general@jdrf.ca; communications@jdrf.ca
www.jdrf.ca
To support research to find a cure for diabetes & its complications; To increase awareness of diabetes, particularly Juvenile (Type 1) diabetes

The Kidney Foundation of Canada (KFOC) / La Fondation canadienne du rein
#300, 5165, rue Sherbrooke ouest, Montréal QC H4A 1T6 Canada
Tel: 514-369-4806; *Fax:* 514-369-2472
Toll-Free: 800-361-7494
webmaster@kidney.ca
www.kidney.ca
To improve the health & quality of life of people living with kidney disease; to fund research & related clinical education; to provide services for the special needs of individuals living with kidney disease; to advocate for access to high quality health care; to actively promote awareness of & commitment to organ donation

L.E. Society of Saskatchewan (LESS)
c/o Royal University Hospital, PO Box 88, 103 Hospital Dr., Saskatoon SK S7N 0W0 Canada
Tel: 306-781-6123; *Toll-Free:* 877-566-6123
less@sasklupus.com
www.sasklupus.com
To provide support for those affected by lupus through understanding, education, public awareness & research

Leprosy Mission Canada / La Mission évangélique contre la lèpre (Canada)
#100, 100 Mural St., Richmond Hill ON L4B 1J3 Canada
Tel: 905-886-2885
info@leprosy.ca
www.leprosy.ca
TLM Canada provides care and support to leprosy patients in many parts of the world including India, Bangladesh, and Nigeria.

The Leukemia & Lymphoma Society of Canada (LLSC) / Société de leucémie et lymphome du Canada
#804, 2 Lansing Square, Toronto ON M2J 4P8 Canada
Tel: 416-661-9541; *Fax:* 416-661-7799
Toll-Free: 877-668-8326
PutnsR@lls.org
www.lls.org/canada
To cure leukemia, lymphoma, Hodgkin's disease & myeloma, & to improve the quality of life of patients & their families
Bob Rae, OC, PC, QC, National Spokesperson
Rudy Putns, CEO

Lupus Canada
#3, 3555 14th Avenue, Markham ON L3R 0H5 Canada
Tel: 905-513-0004; *Fax:* 905-513-9516
Toll-Free: 800-661-1468
info@lupuscanada.org
www.lupuscanada.org
Social Media:
www.facebook.com/group.php?gid=69263929055&ref=ts
To improve the lives of people living with lupus; To encourage cooperation among the lupus organizations in Canada

Lupus Foundation of Ontario (LFO)
PO Box 687, 294 Ridge Rd. North, Ridgeway ON L0S 1N0 Canada
Tel: 905-894-4611; *Fax:* 905-894-4616
Toll-Free: 800-368-8377
lupusont@vaxxine.com
www.vaxxine.com/lupus
To serve the lupus patient community as a charitable organization

Lupus New Brunswick
#17, 55 Grant St., Moncton NB E1A 3R3 Canada
Tel: 506-384-6227; *Toll-Free:* 877-303-8080
lupins@rogers.com
www.lupusnb.ca
Social Media: facebook.com/group.php?gid=113746565332566
The group promotes eduction & public awarness of lupus. It brings together lupus patients, friends, family, & other interested persons for a network of support.

Lupus Newfoundland & Labrador
PO Box 8121, Stn. A, Kenmount Rd., St. John's NL A1B 3M9 Canada
Tel: 709-368-8130
lupusnfld@nl.rogers.com
www.envision.ca/webs/lupusnfldlab
Dale Williams, President

Lupus Nova Scotia
PO Box 38038, Dartmouth NS B3B 1X2 Canada
Tel: 902-425-0358; *Fax:* 902-798-0772
Toll-Free: 800-394-0125
lubpussocietyns@ns.sympatico.ca
www.lupuscanada.org/novascotia
The Society informs, educates & supports all those afflicted with lupus. It promotes public & professional awareness of the disease as a prevalent & controllable one, as well as funding research for its cure. It is a registered charity, BN: 133533158RR0001.

Lupus Ontario (OLA)
#230, 2900 John St., Markham ON L3R 5G3 Canada
Tel: 905-415-1099; *Fax:* 905-415-9874
Toll-Free: 877-240-1099
info@lupusontario.org
www.lupusontario.org
To serve the needs of Lupus sufferers in Ontario

Lupus PEI
PO Box 23002, Charlottetown PE C1E 1Z6 Canada
Tel: 902-892-3875; *Fax:* 902-626-3585
Toll-Free: 800-661-1468
bargri@pei.sympatico.ca
www.lupuscanada.org/pei
The organization promotes public awareness of lupus on PEI, while offering support & educational materials to lupus patients, their families & friends.

Lupus Society of Alberta (LESA)
#200, 1301 - 8 St. SW, Calgary AB T2R 1B7 Canada
Tel: 403-228-7956; *Fax:* 403-228-7853
Toll-Free: 888-242-9182
lupuslsa@shaw.ca
www.lupus.ab.ca
To provide education & support on lupus issues & enable research to find a cure.

Lupus Society of Manitoba Inc.
#105, 386 Broadway Ave., Winnipeg MB R3C 3R6 Canada
Tel: 204-942-6825; *Fax:* 204-942-4894
Toll-Free: 888-942-6825
lupus@mts.net
To provide support, encouragement & education to lupus patients & their families

Manitoba Association of Optometrists (MAO)
#200B, 392 Academy Rd., Winnipeg MB R3N 0B8 Canada
Tel: 204-943-9811; *Fax:* 204-943-1208
mao@optometrists.mb.ca
www.optometrists.mb.ca
To regulate the practice of optometry in Manitoba, in accordance with The Optometry Act & Regulation; To represent optometrists in Manitoba; To protect & promote the vision care needs & eye health of Manitobans

Manitoba Chiropractors' Association (MCA)
#610, 1445 Portage Ave., Winnipeg MB R3G 3P4 Canada
Tel: 204-942-3000; *Fax:* 204-942-3010
info@mbchiro.org
www.mbchiro.org
To act as both a regulatory body & a professional association to serve the public & the chiropractors of Manitoba; To foster high standards of chiropractic health care for Manitobans; To ensure that safe, ethical, & competent servicew are provided by Manitoba chiropractors

Manitoba Lung Association
629 McDermot Ave., Winnipeg MB R3A 1P6
Tel: 204-774-5501; *Fax:* 204-772-5083
Toll-Free: 888-566-5864
info@mb.lung.ca
www.mb.lung.ca
To improve lung health

Manitoba Medical Service Foundation Inc. (MMSF)
599 Empress St., Winnipeg MB R3G 3P3 Canada
Tel: 204-788-6801; *Fax:* 204-774-1761
info@mmsf.ca
www.mmsf.ca
To consider the provision of funds for the advancement of scientific, educational, & other activities to maintain & improve the health & welfare of the citizens of Manitoba
John McKenzie, Executive Director
Allen Rouse, Chair

Manitoba Naturopathic Association (MNA)
PO Box 2339, Stn. Main, #2, 161 Stafford St., Winnipeg MB R3C 4A6 Canada
Tel: 204-947-0381; *Fax:* 204-452-7044
To act as a regulatory body for the profession of naturopathy, in accordance with The Naturopathic Act of Manitoba

Manitoba Paraplegia Foundation Inc.
825 Sherbrook St., Winnipeg MB R3A 1M5 Canada
Tel: 204-786-4753; *Fax:* 204-786-1140
winnipeg@canparaplegic.org
www.cpamanitoba.ca/mpf
To provide support for research & prevention activities; to provide direct aid to paraplegics & quadriplegics for home modifications, vocational aid & other items to assist spinal cord injured Manitobans to lead independent lives within the community; to provide support for special projects undertaken on behalf of spinal cord injured persons in Manitoba

Manitoba Public Health Association (MPHA)
c/o Klinic Community Health Centre, 870 Portage Ave., Winnipeg MB R3G 0P1 Canada
manitobapha@mts.net
www.manitobapha.ca
To influence health, social, environmental, & economic policy decisions, in order to improve the well-being of people in

Manitoba; to ensure that health promotion, health protection, & disease protection are part of services
Barb Wasilewski, President

Medical Council of Canada (MCC) / Le Conseil médical du Canada
PO Box 8234, Stn. T, #100, 2283 St. Laurent Blvd., Ottawa ON K1G 3H7 Canada
Tel: 613-521-6012; *Fax:* 613-521-9509
MCC_Admin@mcc.ca
www.mcc.ca
To establish & promote a qualification in medicine, known as the Licentiate of the Medical Council of Canada, such that the holders thereof are acceptable to medical licensing authorities for the issuance of a licence to practise medicine

Medical Devices Canada
#900, 405 The West Mall, Toronto ON M9C 5J1 Canada
Tel: 416-620-1915; *Fax:* 416-620-1595
Toll-Free: 866-586-3332
info@medec.org
www.medec.org
To achieve a business & regulatory environment favourable to the growth of the industry & ensuring the availability of new cost-effective medical technologies that benefit Canadians.

Medical Society of Prince Edward Island (MSPEI)
2 Myrtle St., Stratford PE C1B 2W2 Canada
Tel: 902-368-7303; *Fax:* 902-566-3934
Toll-Free: 888-368-7303
www.mspei.org
To promote health & improvement of medical services; to prevent disease; to represent members at national bodies & government; to consider all matters concerning the professional welfare of members.

The Michener Institute for Applied Health Sciences
222 St. Patrick St., Toronto ON M5T 1V4 Canada
Tel: 416-596-3101; *Fax:* 416-596-3180
Toll-Free: 800-387-9066
info@michener.ca
www.michener.on.ca
To design, develop & deliver the best educational programs, products & services in applied health sciences
Cathy Fooks, Chair
Paul Gamble, Secretary/President & CEO

Multiple Sclerosis Society of Canada (MS) / Société canadienne de la sclérose en plaques
#700, 175 Bloor St. East, Toronto ON M4W 3R8 Canada
Tel: 416-922-6065; *Fax:* 416-922-7538
Toll-Free: 800-268-7582
info@mssociety.ca
www.mssociety.ca
To be a leader in finding a cure for multiple sclerosis & enabling people affected by MS to enhance their quality of life

Muscular Dystrophy Association of Canada (MDAC) / Association canadienne de la dystrophie musculaire (ACDM)
#900, 2345 Yonge St., Toronto ON M4P 2E5 Canada
Tel: 416-488-0030; *Fax:* 416-488-7523
Toll-Free: 866-687-2538
info@muscle.ca
www.muscle.ca
To improve the quality of life of persons who have muscular dystrophy through a broad range of programs, education, support of research & the delivery of needed services to people with muscular dystrophy & their families

Myasthenia Gravis Association of British Columbia (MGABC)
2805 Kingsway Ave., Vancouver BC V5R 5H9 Canada
Tel: 604-451-5511; *Fax:* 604-451-5651
mgabc@centreforability.bc.ca
www.myastheniagravis.ca
To provide information & support to British Columbians who suffer from Myasthenia Gravis (Grave Muscular Disease) & to their caregivers; to increase public awareness of the disease; to gather & disseminate specific information on Myasthenia Gravis to healthcare providers in British Columbia; to foster & support research into the causes & treatment of Myasthenia Gravis

National Eating Disorder Information Centre (NEDIC)
ES 7-421, 200 Elizabeth St., Toronto ON M5G 2C4 Canada
Tel: 416-340-4156; *Fax:* 416-340-4736
Toll-Free: 866-633-4220
nedic@uhn.on.ca
www.nedic.ca
The National Eating Disorder Information Centre (NEDIC) is a non-profit organization founded in 1985 to provide information and resources on eating disorders and food and weight preoccupation. One of their main goals is to inform the public about eating disorders and related issues.

National ME/FM Action Network / Réseau national d'action EM/FM encéphalomyélite myalgique/fibromyalgie
#512, 33 Banner Rd., Nepean ON K2H 8V7 Canada
Tel: 613-829-6667; *Fax:* 613-829-8518
ag922@ncf.ca
www.mefmaction.net
To offer support, advocacy, education & research into the many, varied, anomalies connected with Myalgic Encephalomyelitis/Chronic Fatigue Syndrome & Fibromyalgia (ME/FM)

New Brunswick Association of Dietitians (NBAD) / Association des diététistes du Nouveau-Brunswick (ADNB)
#101, 333 Champlain St., Dieppe NB E1A 1P2 Canada
Tel: 506-856-6881; *Fax:* 506-856-6855
registrar@adnb-nbad.com; info@adnb-nbad.com
www.adnb-nbad.com
To regulate the practice of dietetics within New Brunswick.

New Brunswick Association of Naturopathic Doctors
2278 King George Hwy., Miramichi NB E1V 6N6 Canada
Tel: 506-773-3700; *Fax:* 506-773-3704
www.nband.ca
To educate the public on the philosophies and values of Naturopathic Medicine and to promote the profession within the province.
Crystal Charest, Contact

New Brunswick Association of Optometrists (NBAO) / Association des optométristes du Nouveau-Brunswick
#1, 490 Gibson St., Fredericton NB E3A 4E9 Canada
Tel: 506-458-8759; *Fax:* 506-450-1271
nbao@nbnet.nb.ca
www.nbao.ca

New Brunswick Catholic Health Association (NBCHA)
1773 Water St., Miramichi NB E1N 1B2 Canada
Tel: 506-778-5302; *Fax:* 506-778-5303
nbcha@nb.aibn.com
www.chanb.com/chanb/
The New Brunswick Catholic Health Association is a provincial Christian organization promoting health care in the tradition of the Catholic Church. The Association fosters healing in all its aspects: Physical, psychological, social and spiritual

New Brunswick Chiropractors' Association (NBCA) / Association des chiropraticiens du Nouveau-Brunswick
#200, 125 Whiting Rd., Fredericton NB E3B 5Y5 Canada
Tel: 506-445-6800; *Fax:* 506-457-1114
comments@nbchiropractic.ca
www.nbchiropractic.ca
To regulate the practice of chiropractic & govern its members in accordance with the Act & the by-laws, in order to serve & protect the public interests; to establish, maintain, develop & enforce standards of qualification for the practice of chiropractic, including the required knowledge, skill & efficiency; to establish, maintain, develop & enforce standards of professional ethics; to promote public awareness of the role of the Association & the work of chiropractic, & to communicate & cooperate with other professional organizations for the advancement of the best interests of the Association, including the publication of books, papers & journals; & to encourage studies in chiropractic & provide assistance & facilities for special studies & research

New Brunswick Lung Association / Association pulmonaire du Nouveau-Brunswick
65 Brunswick St., Fredericton NB E3B 1G5
Tel: 506-455-8961; *Fax:* 506-462-0939
Toll-Free: 800-565-5864
nblung@nbnet.nb.ca
www.nb.lung.ca
To promote wellness throughout New Brunswick & prevent lung disease

New Brunswick Medical Society (NBMS) / Société médicale du Nouveau-Brunswick
176 York St., Fredericton NB E3B 3N7 Canada
Tel: 506-458-8860; *Fax:* 506-458-9853
nbms@nbnet.nb.ca
www.nbms.nb.ca
To advance medical science in all its branches; to promote improvement of medical services; to prevent disease in cooperation with health officers & all others engaged in such work; to maintain high scientific & professional status for its members; to promote medical science & related arts & sciences

Newfoundland & Labrador Association of Optometrists (NLAO)
PO Box 8042, Stn. C, St. John's NL A1B 3M7 Canada
Tel: 709-739-8284; *Fax:* 709-739-8378
nlao@nl.rogers.com
www.nao.opto.ca
The Association provides an online resource for Doctors of Optometry & other healthcare providers in Newfoundland & Labrador. It owns & operates Newfoundland Vision Services Inc., a not for profit corporation providing safety eyewear to industrial employers in the province

Newfoundland & Labrador Chiropractic Association
25 Allandale Rd., Upper Level, St. John's NL A1B 2Z6 Canada
Tel: 709-739-7762; *Fax:* 709-739-7703
nlca@nf.aibn.com
www.nlchiropractic.ca

Newfoundland & Labrador College of Dietitians (NLCD)
PO Box 1756, Stn. C, St. John's NL A1C 5P5 Canada
Tel: 709-753-4040; *Toll-Free:* 877-753-4040
www.nlcd.ca; www.dietitians.ca
To regulate Registered Dietitians & to ensure competency in the dietetic profession, in the interest of the people in Newfoundland.

Newfoundland & Labrador Lung Association (NLLA)
Carnell Building, PO Box 13457, Stn. A, 15 Pippy Pl., 2nd Fl., St. John's NL A1B 4B8 Canada
Tel: 709-726-4664; *Fax:* 709-726-2550
Toll-Free: 888-566-5864
info@nf.lung.ca; health@nf.lung.ca
www.nf.lung.ca
To achieve healthy breathing for the people of Newfoundland & Labrador
Greg Noel, Acting Executive Director

Newfoundland & Labrador Medical Association (NLMA)
164 MacDonald Dr., St. John's NL A1A 4B3 Canada
Tel: 709-726-7424; *Fax:* 709-726-7525
Toll-Free: 800-563-2003
nlma@nlma.nf.ca
www.nlma.nf.ca
To represent & support physicians in Newfoundland & Labrador; provide leadership in the promotion of good health & the provision of quality health care to the people of the province

Newfoundland & Labrador Public Health Association (NLPHA)
PO Box 8172, St. John's NL A1B 3M9 Canada
To advocate for the physical, emotional, social, & environmental well-being of Newfoundland & Labrador's people & communities
Fay Matthews, President
Elizabeth Wright, Secretary
Pat Murray, Treasurer

Northwest Territories Medical Association (NWTMA)
PO Box 1732, Yellowknife NT X1A 2P3 Canada
Tel: 867-920-4575; *Fax:* 867-920-4575
nwtmedassoc@ssimicro.com
www.nwtma.ca
The voice of physicians in the Territory, the Northwest Territories Medical Association (NWTMA) advocates on behalf of its members and the citizens of the North for access to high quality health care, and provides leadership and guidance to its members.
Anna Reid, President
Marlena Guzowski, Executive Director

Nova Scotia Association of Naturopathic Doctors
#16, 3514 Joseph Howe Dr., Halifax NS B3L 4H7 Canada
Tel: 902-431-8001; *Fax:* 902-542-4554
www.nsand.ca
The NSAND is the professional association representing licensed NDs in Nova Scotia.
Sarah Baille, ND, Co-President
Jyl Bishop Veale, ND, Co-President

Nova Scotia Association of Optometrists (NSAO)
PO Box 9410, Stn. A, #700, 6009 Quinpool Rd., Halifax NS B3K 5S3 Canada
Tel: 902-435-2845; *Fax:* 902-425-2441
nsao@accesswave.ca
www.nsoptometrists.ca
To foster excellence in the delivery of vision & eye health services in Nova Scotia; To act as the voice of optometry in Nova Scotia

Nova Scotia College of Chiropractors (NSCC)
PO Box 9410, Stn. A, 6009 Quinpool Road, Halifax NS B3K 5S3 Canada
Tel: 902-425-2445; *Fax:* 902-425-2441
inquiries@chiropractors.ns.ca
www.chiropractors.ns.ca
To promote & improve the proficiency of chiropractors in all matters relating to the practice of chiropractic; to protect the public from untrained & unqualified persons acting as chiropractors; to advance the chiropractic profession

Nova Scotia Dietetic Association (NSDA)
#212, 1496 Bedford Hwy., Bedford NS B4A 1E5 Canada
Tel: 902-835-0253; *Fax:* 902-835-0523
info@nsdassoc.ca
www.nsdassoc.ca
The Association is the regulatory body for dietitions & nutritionists in the province, & has a mandate to register & discipline (when necessary) practitioners to ensure safe, ethical & competent dietetic practice.

Nova Scotia Lung Association (LANS)
6331 Lady Hammond Rd., Halifax NS B3K 2S2
Tel: 902-443-8141; *Fax:* 902-445-2573
Toll-Free: 888-566-5864
info@ns.lung.ca
www.ns.lung.ca
To control & prevent lung disease in Nova Scotia; To help people who live with lung disease

Occupational & Environmental Medical Association of Canada (OEMAC) / Association canadienne de la médecine du travail et de l'environnement (ACMTE)
#1430, 1101 Upper Middle Rd. East, Oakville ON L6H 5Z9
Tel: 905-849-9925; *Fax:* 905-338-8523
oemac@oemac.org
www.oemac.org
To act as the voice of the Canadian occupational & environmental medicine sector

Ontario Association of Naturopathic Doctors (OAND)
#603, 789 Don Mills Rd., Toronto ON M3C 1T5 Canada
Tel: 416-233-2001; *Fax:* 416-233-2924
Toll-Free: 877-628-7284
info@oand.org
www.oand.org
To act as a voice for naturopathic doctors in Ontario

Ontario Association of Optometrists (OAO)
Plaza 3, #300, 2000 Argentia Rd., Mississauga ON L5N 1V9 Canada
Tel: 905-826-3522; *Toll-Free:* 800-540-3837
wbishop@optom.on.ca
www.optom.on.ca
To advance the profession of optometry at the government, regulatory, & public levels

Ontario Chiropractic Association (OCA) / Association chiropratique de l'Ontario
#30, 5160 Explorer Dr., Mississauga ON L4W 4T7 Canada
Tel: 905-629-8211; *Fax:* 905-629-8214
Toll-Free: 877-327-2273
lirwin@chiropractic.on.ca
www.chiropractic.on.ca
To serve its members by promoting the philosophy, art & science of chiropractic & thereby enhance the health & well-being of the citizens of Ontario

Ontario Lung Association (OLA)
573 King St. East, Toronto ON M5A 4L3
Tel: 416-864-9911; *Fax:* 416-864-9916
Toll-Free: 888-344-5864
olalung@on.lung.ca; airquality@on.lung.ca; tobacco@on.lung.ca
www.on.lung.ca
To provide lung health information & support to people affected by lung disease; To prevent & control chronic lung disease

Ontario Medical Association (OMA)
#900, 150 Bloor St. West, Toronto ON M5S 3C1
Tel: 416-599-2580; *Fax:* 416-340-2944
Toll-Free: 800-268-7215
info@oma.org; membership@oma.org
www.oma.org
To represent the clinical, political, & economic interests of Ontario physicians; To promote an accessible, quality health-care system

Ontario Public Health Association (OPHA) / Association pour la santé publique de l'Ontario
Lawrence Square, #310, 700 Lawrence Ave. West, Toronto ON M6B 3B4
Tel: 416-367-3313; *Fax:* 416-367-2844
Toll-Free: 800-267-6817
info@opha.on.ca
www.opha.on.ca
To provide leadership on issues affecting public health in Ontario; To strengthen the influence of persons involved in public & community health across Ontario
Carol Timmings, President
Liz Haugh, Vice-President

Opticians Association of Canada (OAC)
#2706, 83 Garry St., Winnipeg MB R3C 4J9 Canada
Tel: 204-982-6060; *Fax:* 204-947-2519
Toll-Free: 800-842-3155
canada@opticians.ca
www.opticians.ca
Lorne Kashin, President

Ordre des ergothérapeutes du Québec (OEQ)
#920, 2021, av Union, Montréal QC H3A 2S9 Canada
Tél: 514-844-5778; *Téléc:* 514-844-0478
Ligne sans frais: 800-265-5778
ergo@oeq.org
www.oeq.org
Protéger le public; assurer la qualité d'ergothérapie; promouvoir l'accessibilité aux services d'ergothérapie; soutenir la pratique professionnelle et son évolution; favoriser le rayonnement de la profession

Ordre des orthophonistes et audiologistes du Québec (OOAQ)
#601, 235, boul René-Levesque est, Montréal QC H2X 1N8 Canada
Tél: 514-282-9123; *Téléc:* 514-282-9541
Ligne sans frais: 888-232-9123
info@ooaq.qc.ca
www.ooaq.qc.ca
L'Ordre des orthophonistes et audiologistes du Québec, un organisme régi par le code des professions, a pour mission d'assurer la protection du public en regard du domaine d'exercice de ses membres, soit les troubles de la communication humaine; surveille l'exercice professionnel des orthophonistes et des audiologistes et voit à favoriser l'accessibilité du public à des services de qualitécontribue à l'intégration sociale des individus et à l'amélioration de la qualité de vie de la population québécoise

Ordre professionnel des diététistes du Québec (OPDQ)
#1220, 2155, rue Guy, Montréal QC H3H 2R9 Canada
Tél: 514-393-3733; *Téléc:* 514-393-3582
Ligne sans frais: 888-393-8528
opdq@opdq.org
www.opdq.org
Assurer la protection du public en contrôlant notamment l'exercice de la profession par ses membres.

Ordre professionnel des physiothérapeutes du Québec (OPPQ)
#1000, 7151, Jean Talon est, Anjou QC H1M 3N8 Canada
Tél: 514-351-2770; *Téléc:* 514-351-2658
Ligne sans frais: 800-361-2001
physio@oppq.qc.ca
www.oppq.qc.ca
Assurer la protection du public en surveillant l'exercice de la physiothérapie par ses membres et en contribuant à leur développement professionnel
Lucie Forget, Présidente/directrice générale

Organ Donors Canada / Donneurs d'organes du Canada
5326 Ada Blvd. NW, Edmonton AB T5W 4N7 Canada
Tel: 780-474-9363
Information service dedicated to assisting the process of anatomical gift giving in Canada & increasing public awareness of the need for, & the human & economic advantages of all types of human organ & tissue donations for transplant, teaching & research.

Osteoporosis Canada / Ostéoporose Canada
#301, 1090 Don Mills Rd., Toronto ON M3C 3R6 Canada
Tel: 416-696-2663; *Fax:* 416-696-2673
Toll-Free: 800-463-6842
info@osteoporosis.ca
www.osteoporosis.ca
To encourage research into the prevention, diagnosis, & treatment of osteoporosis; to improve access to osteoporosis care & support

Ovarian Cancer Canada (OCC) / Cancer de l'ovaire Canada (COC)
#101, 145 Front St. East, Toronto ON M5A 1E3 Canada
Tel: 416-962-2700; *Fax:* 416-962-2701
Toll-Free: 877-413-7970
info@ovariancanada.org
www.ovariancanada.org
To support women & their families living with the disease; to raise awareness in the general public & with health care professionals; to fund research to develop reliable early detection techniques, improved treatments & ultimately, a cure.
Elisabeth Ross, Executive Director
Moira Lambertus, Information Coordinator

Parkinson Society - Maritime Region
#830, 5991 Spring Garden Rd., Halifax NS B3H 1Y6 Canada
Tel: 902-422-3656; *Fax:* 902-422-3797
Toll-Free: 800-663-2468
info@parkinsonmaritimes.ca
www.parkinsonmaritimes.ca
Mary Hatcher, Executive Director

Parkinson Society British Columbia (PSBC)
#600, 890 West Pender St., Vancouver BC V6C 1J9 Canada
Tel: 604-662-3240; *Fax:* 604-687-1327
Toll-Free: 800-668-3330
info@parkinson.bc.ca
www.parkinson.bc.ca
Diane Robinson, Executive Director

Parkinson Society Canada / Société Parkinson Canada
#316, 4211 Yonge St., Toronto ON M2P 2A9 Canada
Tel: 416-227-9700; *Fax:* 416-227-9600
Toll-Free: 800-565-3000
general.info@parkinson.ca
www.parkinson.ca
To raise funds for research into the causes & treatment of Parkinsons; to provide services which support Parkinsonians & their families; to disseminate information about the condition to individuals & organizations across Canada

Parkinson Society Canada - Central & Northern Ontario Region
#321, 4211 Yonge St., Toronto ON M2P 2A9 Canada
Tel: 416-227-1200; *Fax:* 416-227-1520
Toll-Free: 800-565-3000
info.cno@parkinson.ca
www.cno.parkinson.ca
Debbie Davis, CEO

Parkinson Society Canada - Manitoba Region
7 - 414 Westmount Dr., Winnipeg MB R2J 1P2 Canada
Tel: 204-786-2637; *Fax:* 204-786-2327
Toll-Free: 866-999-5558
laura.asher@parkinson.ca
www.parkinson.ca
Howard Koks, Executive Director

Parkinson Society Canada - Southwestern Ontario Region
Meadowbrook Business Park, #117, 4500 Blaikie Rd., London ON N6L 1G5 Canada
Tel: 519-652-9437; *Fax:* 519-652-9267
Toll-Free: 888-851-7376
info@parkinsonsociety.ca
www.parkinsonsociety.ca
Carolyn Conners, CEO

Parkinson Society Newfoundland & Labrador
#305, 136 Crosbie Rd., St. John's NL A1B 3K3 Canada
Tel: 709-574-4428; *Fax:* 709-754-5868
Toll-Free: 800-567-7020
parkinson@nf.aibn.com
Patricia Morrissey, Executive Director

Parkinson Society of Canada - Toronto Chapter
#321, 4211 Yonge St., Toronto ON M2P 2A9 Canada
Tel: 416-227-1200; *Fax:* 416-227-1520
Toll-Free: 800-565-3000
communications@parkinson.ca
www.parkinson.ca
Parkinson Society Canada is the national voice of Canadians living with Parkinson's whose purpose is to ease the burden and find a cure through research, education, advocacy, and support services. Their vision revolves around wanting people with Parkinson's to have access to more uniform services across the country; to work to ensure greater consistency and equitable access; to address gaps in the isolated and disadvantages regions; to maximize the funds available to support people living w/ Parkinson's by adopting best practices; and by spending donor money in the most effective way.
Debbie Davis, CEO (Central & Northern Ontario)

Sarah Rooje, CNO Admin./Client Services

Parkinson Society of Ottawa
1053 Carling Ave., Ottawa ON K1Y 4E9 Canada
Tel: 613-722-9238; *Fax:* 613-722-3241
psoc@lri.ca
www.parkinsons.ca
Dennise Taylor-Gilhen, Executive Director

The Parkinson's Society of Southern Alberta (PSSA)
#102, 5636 Burbank Cres. SE, Calgary AB T2H 1Z6 Canada
Tel: 403-243-9901; *Fax:* 403-243-8283
Toll-Free: 800-561-1911
pssa@parkinsons-society.org
www.parkinsons-society.org
PSSA is dedicated to helping people and families of Southern Alberta who live with Parkinson's and related disorders
John Petryshen, CEO

Post-Polio Awareness & Support Society of BC (PPASS/BC)
102 - 9775 - 4th St., Sidney BC V8L 2Z8 Canada
Tel: 250-655-8849; *Fax:* 250-655-8859
ppass@ppassbc.com
www.ppassbc.com
To develop awareness, communication & education between society & community; to disseminate information concerning research & treatment about Post-Polio Syndrome; to support polio survivors other than through direct financial aid

Post-Polio Network Manitoba Inc. (PPN-MB)
#204, 825 Sherbrook St., Winnipeg MB R3A 1M5 Canada
Tel: 204-975-3037; *Fax:* 204-975-3027
www.smd.mb.ca/post_polio_network_manitoba_inc.aspx
To serve as a support group & information centre for polio survivors throughout Manitoba, especially those suffering from post-polio syndrome; to acquaint the medical community & those responsible for government services as to the nature & extent of the problems associated with the late effects of polio

Prince Edward Island Association of Optometrists (PEIAO)
PO Box 1812, Charlottetown PE C1A 7N5
Tel: 902-626-3937; *Fax:* 902-626-3973
info@peioptometrists.ca
www.peioptometrists.ca
To promote the professional interests of optometrists in Prince Edward Island Association; To improve optometrists' proficiency

Prince Edward Island Chiropractic Association (PEICA)
228 Grafton St., Charlottetown PE C1A 1L5
Tel: 902-894-4400; *Fax:* 902-894-3762
chiro.whitty@pei.aibn.com
To represent the chiropractic profession in Prince Edward Island; To advance the chiropractic profession in the province; To encourage high standards of service; To protect the residents of Prince Edward Island from unqualified individuals acting as chiropractors

Prince Edward Island Dietetic Association
153 Spring St., Summerside PE C1N 3G2 Canada
Tel: 902-436-2438
peidrb@pei.sympatico.ca
To promote, encourage & improve the status of dietitians & nutritionists in the province of PEI; to promote & increase the knowledge & proficiency of its members in all matters relating to nutrition & dietetics; to promote public awareness

Prince Edward Island Lung Association
#2, 1 Rochford St., Charlottetown PE C1A 9L2
Tel: 902-892-5957; *Fax:* 902-566-9901
Toll-Free: 888-566-5864
info@pei.lung.ca
www.pei.lung.ca
To improve the respiratory health of Islanders through education, advocacy & research; To raise funds to support medical research

Psoriasis Society of Canada / Société psoriasis du Canada
National Office, PO Box 25015, Halifax NS B3M 4H4 Canada
Tel: 902-443-8680; *Fax:* 902-443-2073
Toll-Free: 800-656-4494
www.psoriasissociety.org
To provide programs & services to people who suffer from psoriasis in Canada; to encourage formation of support groups where individual sufferers may share experiences & exchange information; to provide facts about psoriasis to medical community, general public & teaching profession; to promote & encourage research directed towards treatment & cure for psoriasis
Judy Misner, President

Charmaine Fader, Vice-President
Diana Stevens, Secretary
Diane Drake, Director

Public Health Association of British Columbia (PHABC)
#219, 2187 Oak Bay Ave., Vancouver BC V8R 1G1 Canada
Tel: 250-595-8422; *Fax:* 250-595-8622
admin@phabc.org
www.phabc.org
To constitute a special resource in BC for the betterment & maintenance of the population's health at the community & personal level
Shannon Turner, President

Public Health Association of Nova Scotia (PHANS)
PO Box 33074, Halifax NS B3L 4T6 Canada
Tel: 902-477-2960; *Fax:* 902-477-4584
phans@cpha.ca
www.phans.ca
Marie McCully Collier, President

Québec Black Medical Association
#101, Sherbrooke St. W, Montréal QC H3H 1E4 Canada
Tel: 514-937-8432; *Fax:* 514-933-5929
The Québec Black Medical Association aims to enable young people from the Black community to pursue careers as health professionals and to advance medical practice and research in Quebec.
E.C. Tucker, Contact

Québec Lung Association (QLA) / Association pulmonaire du Québec (APQ)
5790, av Pierre-de-Coubertin, Montréal QC H1N 1R4
Tel: 514-287-7400; *Fax:* 514-287-1978
Toll-Free: 888-768-6669
info@pq.lung.ca; info@pq.poumon.ca
www.pq.poumon.ca
To provide resources in Québec about lung cancer, chronic obstructive pulmonary disease, sarcoidosis, tuberculosis, asthma, chronic bronchitis, sleep apnea, pneumonia, & emphysema

The Royal College of Physicians & Surgeons of Canada (RCPSC) / Le Collège royal des médecins et chirurgiens du Canada (CRMCC)
774 Echo Dr., Ottawa ON K1S 5N8 Canada
Tel: 613-730-8177; *Fax:* 613-730-8830
Toll-Free: 800-668-3740
info@royalcollege.ca
rcpsc.medical.org
The Royal College of Physicians and Surgeons of Canada is the national professional association that oversees the medical education of specialists in Canada. The Royal College is dedicated to setting the highest standards in postgraduate medical education - through national certification examinations and lifelong learning programs - and to promoting sound health policy.

Saint Elizabeth Health Care (SEHC) / Les soins de santé Sainte-Elizabeth
#300, 90 Allstate Pkwy., Markham ON L3R 6H3 Canada
Tel: 905-940-9655; *Fax:* 905-940-9934
communications@saintelizabeth.com;
www.saintelizabeth.com
To serve the physical, emotional, & spiritual needs of people in their homes & communities
Shirlee M. Sharkey, President & CEO
Noreen Taylor, Chair
Theodore Freedman, Vice-Chair
Heather Gomes, Treasurer
Ron Yamada, Secretary

Saskatchewan Association of Naturopathic Practitioners (SANP)
1814 Lorne Ave., Saskatoon SK S7H 1Y4 Canada
Tel: 306-955-2633; *Fax:* 306-955-2638
naturdoctor@sasktel.net
www.sanp.ca
To act as the governing body for naturopathic doctors in Saskatchewan; To license & regulate naturopathic physicians in the province; To ensure members are educated & trained according to strict standards

Saskatchewan Association of Optometrists (SAO)
#108, 2366 Ave. C North, Saskatoon SK S7L 5X5
Tel: 306-652-2069; *Fax:* 306-652-2642
Toll-Free: 877-660-3937
sao@sasktel.net
www.optometrists.sk.ca
To license the delivery of optometric care in Saskatchewan; To regulate doctors of optometry throughout the province; To ensure excellence in the delivery of vision & eye health services across Saskatchewan; To enforce high standards of optometric eye care, in order to protect the public; To act as the voice of optometry in Saskatchewan

Saskatchewan Dietitians Association (SDA)
PO Box 3894, #17, 2010 - 7th Ave., Regina SK S4R 1C2
Tel: 306-359-3040; *Fax:* 306-359-3046
registrar@saskdietitians.org
www.saskdietitians.org
To protect the public by registering competent dietitians; To set standards of practice; To uphold codes of conduct; To provide a framework for continuing competence, consisting of a self-assessment tool, a learning plan, & a quality assurance audit

Saskatchewan Families for Effective Autism Treatment (SASKFEAT)
PO Box 2150, Tisdale SK S0E 1T0
Tel: 306-862-4768
saskfeat@hotmail.com
www.saskfeat.com
To act as a voice for the concerns & needs of parents & families of autistic children & individuals in Saskatchewan; To find the most effective treatment for autistic children & individuals

Saskatchewan Lung Association
1231 - 8 St. East, Saskatoon SK S7H 0S5
Tel: 306-343-9511; *Fax:* 306-343-7007
Toll-Free: 888-566-5864
info@sk.lung.ca
www.sk.lung.ca
To improve respiratory health & overall quality of life; To advocate for support of education & research

Saskatchewan Medical Association (SMA)
#402, 321A - 21st St. East, Saskatoon SK S7K 0C1
Tel: 306-244-2196; *Fax:* 306-653-1631
Toll-Free: 800-667-3781
sma@sma.sk.ca
www.sma.sk.ca
To represent physicians in Saskatchewan; To advance the professional, educational, & economic welfare of physicians in the province

Saskatchewan Parkinson's Disease Foundation (SPDF)
Royal University Hospital, PO Box 102, 103 Hospital Dr., Saskatoon SK S7N 0W8 Canada
Tel: 306-966-1348; *Fax:* 306-966-8030
spdf@sasktel.net
www.parkinson.ca/en/9.5.saskatchewan%20L1.html
To provide education & support services in Saskatchewan to ease the burdens of people living with Parkinson's disease & their families; To support research to find a cure for Parkinson's disease
Linda Beatty, Contact

Saskatchewan Public Health Association Inc.
PO Box 845, Regina SK S4P 3B1 Canada
terry.gibson@saskatoonhealthregion.ca
To constitute a resource in Saskatchewan for the improvement & maintenance of health
Saqib Shahab, President

Société canadienne de la sclérose en plaques (Division du Québec) (SCSP) / Multiple Sclerosis Society of Canada (Québec Division)
Tour Est, #1010, 550, rue Sherbrooke ouest, Montréal QC H3A 1E7 Canada
Tél: 514-849-7591; *Téléc:* 514-849-8914
Ligne sans frais: 800-268-7582
info.qc@scleroseenplaques.ca
www.scleroseenplaques.ca/qc
Soutenir la recherche sur la SP; offrir des services aux personnes atteintes de la maladie et à leurs familles; sensibiliser le public à la sclérose en plaques et maintenir les relations avec les gouvernements.
François Coupal, Chair

Société Huntington du Québec (SHQ) / Huntington Society of Québec (HSQ)
2300, boul René-Lévesque ouest, Montréal QC H3H 2R5 Canada
Tél: 514-282-4272; *Téléc:* 514-937-0082
Ligne sans frais: 877-282-4272
shq@huntingtonqc.org
www.hsc-ca.org

Société Parkinson du Québec / Parkinson Society Québec
#1470, 550 rue Sherbrooke ouest, Montréal QC H3A 1B9 Canada
Tél: 514-861-4422; *Téléc:* 514-861-4510
Ligne sans frais: 800-720-1307
infos@parkinsonquebec.ca
www.parkinsonquebec.ca
Nathalie Ross, Directrice générale

Society of Obstetricians & Gynaecologists of Canada (SOGC) / Société des obstétriciens et gynécologues du Canada
780 Echo Dr., Ottawa ON K1S 5R7
Tel: 613-730-4192; *Fax:* 613-730-4314
Toll-Free: 800-561-2416
helpdesk@sogc.com
www.sogc.org
To promote excellence in the practice of obstetrics & gynaecology; To produce national clinical guidelines for medical education on women's health issues; To promote optimal, comprehensive women's health care

Society of Rural Physicians of Canada (SRPC) / Société de la médecine rurale du Canada
PO Box 893, 269 Main St., Shawville QC J0X 2Y0 Canada
Tel: 819-647-7054; *Fax:* 819-647-2485
Toll-Free: 877-276-1949
admin@srpc.ca
www.srpc.ca
To provide equitable medical care for rural communities; to provide sustainable working conditions for rural physicians
Karl Stobbe, President
Lee Teperman, Administrative Officer

Spina Bifida & Hydrocephalus Association of Canada (SBHAC) / Association de spina-bifida et d'hydrocephalie du Canada
#428, 167 Lombard Ave., Winnipeg MB R3B 0V3 Canada
Tel: 204-925-3650; *Fax:* 204-925-3654
Toll-Free: 800-565-9488
info@sbhac.ca
www.sbhac.ca
To improve the quality of life of all individuals with spina bifida &/or hydrocephalus & their families through awareness, education, advocacy & research; to reduce the incidence of neural tube defects

The Terry Fox Foundation / La Fondation Terry Fox
#303, 46165 Yale Rd., Chilliwack BC V2P 2P2 Canada
Tel: 604-701-0246; *Fax:* 604-701-0247
Toll-Free: 888-836-9786
national@terryfoxrun.org
www.terryfoxrun.org
Social Media: www.facebook.com/TheTerryFoxFoundation
To maintain the vision & principles of Terry Fox while raising money for cancer research through the annual Terry Fox Run, memoriam donations & planned gifts. All money raised by the Foundation is distributed through the National Cancer Institute of Canada
Darrell Fox, National Director
Judith Fox-Alder, International Director

Thalidomide Victims Association of Canada (TVAC) / Association canadienne des victimes de la thalidomide (ACVT)
Centre commercial Joseph Renaud, #211, 6830, boul Joseph Renaud, Montréal QC H1K 3V4 Canada
Tel: 514-355-0811; *Fax:* 514-355-0860
mercedes.acvt@sympatico.ca
www.thalidomide.ca
To monitor the drug thalidomide & to meet the needs of thalidomide survivors; to empower & enhance the quality of life of Canadian thalidomidors

Thyroid Foundation of Canada / La Fondation canadienne de la Thyroïde
#304, 797 Princess St., Kingston ON K7L 1G1 Canada
Tel: 613-544-8364; *Fax:* 613-544-9731
Toll-Free: 800-267-8822
www.thyroid.ca
To provide leadership to the fight against thyroid disease

Toronto Children's Care Inc. (TCC)
26 Gerrard St. East, Toronto ON M5B 1G3 Canada
Tel: 416-977-0458; *Fax:* 416-977-8807
info@rmhtoronto.org
www.rmhtoronto.org
To provide a home away from home for out-of-town families whose children are receiving treatment in Toronto hospitals for serious illness; we strongly believe that when a child is seriously ill, the love & support of family can be as important as any course of treatment

Tourette Syndrome Foundation of Canada (TSFC) / La Fondation canadienne du syndrome de Tourette
#206, 194 Jarvis St., Toronto ON M5B 2B7 Canada
Tel: 416-861-8398; *Fax:* 416-861-2472
Toll-Free: 800-361-3120
tsfc@tourette.ca
www.tourette.ca
Through education, advocacy, self-help, & the promotion of research, the TSFC assists individuals affected by Tourette Syndrome & its associated disorders.
Rosie Wartecker, Executive Director
Lorne Perrin, President
Ray Robertson, Secretary
Sybil Berenstein, Treasurer

Trillium Gift of Life Network
#900, 522 University Ave., Toronto ON M5G 1W7 Canada
Tel: 416-363-4001; *Fax:* 416-363-4002
Toll-Free: 800-263-2833
info@giftoflife.on.ca
www.giftoflife.on.ca
To enable every Ontario resident to make an informed decision to donate organs & tissue; to support healthcare professionals in implementing their wishes; maximize organ & tissue donation in Ontario in a respectful & equitable manner through education, research, services & support
Frank Markel, PhD, President & CEO

Turner's Syndrome Society (TSS) / Société du syndrome de Turner
323 Chapel St., Ottawa ON K1N 7Z2 Canada
Tel: 613-321-2267; *Fax:* 613-321-2268
Toll-Free: 800-465-6744
tssincan@web.net
www.turnersyndrome.ca
To improve the quality of life for individuals & families affected by Turner's Syndrome; to strive to accomplish this through providing public & professional awareness about the needs & concerns of individuals with Turner's Syndrome & their families through the development of communication networks to provide mutual support

United Ostomy Association of Canada Inc. (UOAC)
PO Box 825, 50 Charles St. East, Toronto ON M4Y 2N7 Canada
Tel: 416-595-5452; *Fax:* 416-595-9924
Toll-Free: 888-969-9698
info@ostomycanada.ca
www.ostomycanada.ca
To assist all persons with gastrointestinal or urinary diversions, & their families & caregivers, by providing emotional & practical support & help, information & instruction

Vocational Rehabilitation Association of Canada (VRA Canada)
#310, 310 Cataraqui St., Kingston ON K7K 1Z7 Canada
Tel: 613-507-5530; *Fax:* 888-441-8002
Toll-Free: 888-876-9992
info@vracanada.com
www.vracanada.com
To support members in promoting & providing the professional delivery of rehabilitation services

Yukon Medical Association
5 Hospital Rd., Whitehorse YT Y1A 3H7 Canada
Tel: 867-393-8949; *Fax:* 867-393-8869
yma@yukondoctors.ca
www.yukondoctors.ca
A voluntary association of Yukon doctors; advocates on behalf of members; promotes professionalism in medical practice & accessibility to quality health care for Yukoners
Rao Tadepalli, President
Stephanie Buchanan, Vice-President
Isabelle Gagnon, Secretary-Treasurer

Yukon Public Health Association (YPHA)
Tel: 867-393-8784
Established to strengthen the impact of people who are active in public and community health throughout the Yukon through education, awareness, public participation and building of partnerships and networks
Ron Pearson, Contact
Val Pike, President

Heating, Air Conditioning, Plumbing

Canadian Institute of Plumbing & Heating (CIPH) / Institut canadien de plomberie et de chauffage
#330, 295 The West Mall, Toronto ON M9C 4Z4
Tel: 416-695-0447; *Fax:* 416-695-0450
Toll-Free: 800-639-2474
info@ciph.com
ww.ciph.com
To act as a unified voice for plumbing, heating, hydronic, PVF, & waterworks across Canada

Heating, Refrigeration & Air Conditioning Contractors Association Atlantic
Tel: 902-425-0475
John Sutherland, Contact
Dallas McDonald, Contact

Heating, Refrigeration & Air Conditioning Institute of Canada (HRAI) / Institut canadien du chauffage, de la climatisation et de la réfrigération (ICCCR)
Bldg. 1, #201, 2800 Skymark Ave., Mississauga ON L4W 5A6 Canada
Tel: 905-602-4700; *Fax:* 905-602-1197
Toll-Free: 800-267-2231
hraimail@hrai.ca
www.hrai.ca
To serve the HRAI membership & HVACR industry in Canada by facilitating industry solutions, coordinating a strong national membership, representing the industry to their publics, conducting accountable association activities, providing quality member/customer services, & educating & training industry members

Ontario Plumbing Inspectors Association (OPIA)
129 Dumble Ave., Peterborough ON K9H 5A9 Canada
Tel: 705-742-7777; *Fax:* 705-742-5218
sgould@city.peterborough.on.ca
www.opia.info
To promote uniform enforcement of plumbing regulations; close liaison & interchange of ideas & knowledge between members of the OPIA & members of other associations; provide education & training to members & the industry

Ontario Refrigeration & Air Conditioning Contractors Association (ORAC)
#43, 6770 Davand Dr., Mississauga ON L5T 2G3
Tel: 905-670-0010; *Fax:* 905-670-0474
info@orac.ca
www.orac.ca
To represent Ontario's contractor practitioners in the refrigeration & air conditioning trade; To enhance quality & efficiency in the industry to benefit customers

Refrigeration Service Engineers Society (Canada) (RSES Canada)
PO Box 3, Stn. B, Toronto ON M9W 5K9 Canada
Tel: 905-842-9199; *Toll-Free:* 877-955-6255
www.rsescanada.com
To lead all segments of the HVAC industry by providing superior educational & training programs; to create an environment that encourages maximum member participation in the development & decision process of the Society

Thermal Environmental Comfort Association (TECA)
PO Box 73105, Stn. Evergreen RO, Surrey BC V3R 0J2 Canada
Tel: 604-594-5956; *Fax:* 604-594-5091
Toll-Free: 888-577-3818
training@teca.ca
www.teca.ca
To offer the residential heating, cooling and ventilation industry up-to-date training courses and a collective voice in local and provincial issues.
Terry Regier, President

History, Heritage, Genealogy

Alberta Family History Society (AFHS)
712 - 16 Ave. NW, Calgary AB T2M 0J8 Canada
Tel: 403-214-1447
afhs@afhs.ab.ca
www.afhs.ab.ca
To encourage accuracy & thoroughness in family histories & genealogical research; to establish relations with related societies to promote common interests
Irene Oickle, Membership
Kay Clarke, President

Alberta Historical Resources Foundation (AHRF)
8820 - 112 St., Edmonton AB T6G 2P8 Canada
Tel: 780-431-2300; *Fax:* 780-427-5598
culture.alberta.ca/ahrf/default.aspx
To assist in the preservation of Alberta's historic sites, buildings & objects; to encourage & promote public awareness of the province's past; grants are awarded in the spring & fall at each year to a wide variety of community-based heritage initiatives
David Link, Director

Alberta Pioneer Railway Association
PO Box 70014, Stn. Londonderry, Edmonton AB T5C 3R6 Canada
Tel: 780-472-6229; *Fax:* 780-968-0167
hdixon@incentre.net
www.railwaymuseum.ab.ca
To collect, preserve, restore, exhibit & interpret artifacts which represent the history & social impact of the railways in Western Canada, with emphasis on Canadian National Railways & Northern Alberta Railways & their predecessors in northern & central Alberta

Architectural Heritage Society of Saskatchewan (AHSS)
202 - 1275 Broad St., Regina SK S4R 1Y2 Canada
Tel: 306-359-0933; *Fax:* 306-359-3899
sahs@sasktel.net
www.ahsk.ca
To promote, support & facilitate the preservation, conservation, restoration & reuse of distinct architectural & historical heritage properties (designated or potential) throughout the province, ensuring that our built heritage is maintained for present & future citizens to appreciate the contributions & craftsmanship of past generations; to enhance the current social, economic & environmental quality of life

Association québécoise d'interprétation du patrimoine (AQIP)
CP 48048, Québec QC G1R 5R5 Canada
Tél: 418-525-0888
aqip@aqip.ca
www.aqip.ca
Stimuler la communication entre les individus et les organismes intéressés à l'interprétation du patrimoine naturel, culturel, historique et industriel; promouvoir l'interprétation du patrimoine québécois auprès des gouvernements, des organismes, des médias et du public en général; stimuler l'acquisition de connaissances et la recherche liée à l'interprétation du patrimoine
René Charest, Président

British Columbia Genealogical Society (BCGS)
PO Box 88054, Stn. Lansdowne Mall, Richmond BC V6X 3T6 Canada
Tel: 604-502-9119; *Fax:* 604-502-9119
bcgs@bcgs.ca
www.bcgs.ca
To perpetuate the heritage of BC; to collect, preserve & publish material relevant to promotion of ethical principles, scientific methods & effective techniques in genealogical & historical research.

British Columbia Historical Federation (BCHF)
PO Box 5254, Stn. B, Victoria BC V8R 6N4 Canada
Tel: 604-277-2627; *Fax:* 604-277-2657
info@bchistory.ca
www.bchistory.ca
To offer assistance to writers of BC history; to disburse loans for publishing to members only; to offer a scholarship for undergraduate history major; to sponsor an annual competition for writers of BC history; to stimulate public interest & to encourage historical research in BC history

British Columbia Railway Historical Association (BCRHA)
1148 Balmoral Rd., Victoria BC V8T 1B1 Canada
Tel: 250-383-7063
bcrha@shaw.ca
www.trainweb.org/bcrha
To preserve railway exhibits, manuscripts & film of BC railways

Bus History Association, Inc. (BHA)
965 McEwan Ave., Windsor ON N9B 2G1 Canada
Tel: 519-977-0664
bdrouillard3@cogeco.ca
www.bus-history.org
To preserve & record data, information & other related materials of the bus industry, both within North America & worldwide

Canada's National History Society (CNHS) / Société d'histoire nationale du Canada
Bryce Hall, 515 Portage Ave., Main Fl., Winnipeg MB R3B 2E9 Canada
Tel: 204-988-9300; *Fax:* 204-988-9309
Toll-Free: 866-952-3444
memberservices@canadashistory.ca
www.historysociety.ca
To promote greater popular interest in Canadian history
Deborah Morrison, President & CEO

Canadian Association for Conservation (CAC) / Association canadienne pour la conservation et la restauration (ACCR)
c/o Danielle Allard, #419, 207 Bank St., Ottawa ON K2P 2N2
Tel: 613-231-3977; *Fax:* 613-231-4406
coordinator@cac-accr.com
www.cac-accr.ca
To promote conservation of Canadian cultural property

Canadian Association of Professional Heritage Consultants (CAPHC) / Association canadienne d'experts-conseils en patrimoine (ACECP)
George Brown House, #211, 50 Baldwin St., Toronto ON M5T 1L4 Canada
Tel: 416-515-7450; *Fax:* 416-515-0961
admin@caphc.ca
www.caphc.ca
To represent & further the professional interests of heritage consultants active in both the private & public sectors; to establish & maintain principles & standards of practice for heritage consultants; to enhance awareness & appreciation of heritage resources, & the contribution of heritage consultants; to foster communication among private practitioners, public agencies, & the public at large in matters related to heritage conservation

Canadian Catholic Historical Association - English Section (CCHA) / Société canadienne d'histoire de l'église catholique - Section anglaise
c/o St. Michael's College, 81 St. Mary St., Toronto ON M5S 1J4 Canada
Tel: 905-893-9754; *Fax:* 416-934-3444
www.umanitoba.ca/colleges/st_pauls/ccha/ccha.html
The Association promotes interest & research in the history of the Canadian Catholic Church, its dioceses, religious communities, institutions, parishes, buildings, sites, & personalities. It is divided into English & French sections.

Canadian Heritage Information Network (CHIN) / Réseau canadien d'information sur le patrimoine (RCIP)
#2F1, 15 rue Eddy, Gatineau QC K1A 0M5 Canada
Tel: 819-994-1200; *Fax:* 819-994-9555
Toll-Free: 800-520-2446
service@chin.gc.ca
www.chin.gc.ca; www.virtualmuseum.ca
To engage national & international audiences in Canadian heritage, through leadership & innovation in digital content, partnerships, & lifelong learning opportunities

Canadian Historical Association (CHA) / Société historique du Canada (SHC)
395 Wellington St., Ottawa ON K1A 0N4 Canada
Tel: 613-233-7885; *Fax:* 613-567-3110
cha-shc@lac-bac.gc.ca
www.cha-shc.ca
To encourage historical research, stimulate public interest in history, promote the preservation of Canadian heritage & to publish their area of specialization or venues of work

Canadian Oral History Association (COHA) / Société canadienne d'histoire orale (SCHO)
c/o University of Winnipeg, 515 Portage Ave., Winnipeg MB R3B 2E9 Canada
janisthiessen@shaw.ca
www.canoha.ca
To encourage & support the creation & preservation of sound recordings which document the history & culture of Canada; to develop standards of excellence & increase competence in the field of oral history through study, education & research.

Canadian Railroad Historical Association (CRHA) / Association canadienne d'histoire ferroviaire
110, rue St-Pierre, Saint-Constant QC J5A 1G7 Canada
Tel: 450-632-2410; *Fax:* 450-638-1563
info@exporail.org
www.exporail.org
To collect, preserve & disseminate information/items relating to the history of railways in Canada

Canadian Society for the Study of Names (CSSN) / Société canadienne d'onomastique (SCO)
c/o GNBC Secretariat, Centre for Topographic Information, #634, 615 Booth St., Ottawa ON K1A 0E9 Canada
Tel: 613-992-3892; *Fax:* 613-943-8282
TDD: 613-996-4397
geonames@NRCan.gc.ca
geonames.rncan.gc.ca/info/cssn_e.php
CSSN promotes the study of all aspects of names & naming in Canada & elsewhere.
Wolfgang Ahrens, President
Léo LaBrie, Sec.-Treas.

Canadian Society of Church History (CSCH) / Société canadienne d'histoire de l'Église
c/o Robynne R. Healey, Dept. of History, Trinity Western University, 7600 Glover Rd., Langley BC V2Y 1Y1 Canada
robynne.healey@twu.ca
www.augustana.ab.ca/csch/
To encourage research in the history of Christianity, especially the history of Christianity in Canada

Canadian Society of Mayflower Descendants
deb121clarke@rogers.com
www.rootsweb.com/~canms/canada.html

Canadian Warplane Heritage (CWH)
9280 Airport Rd., Mount Hope ON L0R 1W0 Canada
Tel: 905-679-4183; *Fax:* 905-679-4186
Toll-Free: 877-347-3359
museum@warplane.com
www.warplane.com
To acquire documents; perserve & maintain a complete collection of aircraft that were flown by Canadians & the Canadian military services from the beginning of World War II to the present, including other related aviation artifacts & memorabilia of significant historic importance to this period; to instruct, educate & entertain the general public through the maintenance & rotation of displays, flight demonstrations, special events & activities, & to encourage Canadians of all ages to become actively involved in the preservation of these aircraft & artifacts; to provide facilities for the restoration & protection, interpretation & exhibits of the collection; to maintain supportive exhibits in tribute to the thousands of men & women who built, serviced & flew these aircraft & in memory of those who did not return
Pamela Rickards, Deputy Director
Robin Hill, Manager, Marketing

Canadiana.org
#468, 395 Wellington St., Ottawa ON K1A 0N4 Canada
Tel: 613-235-2628; *Fax:* 613-235-9752
info@canadiana.org
www.canadiana.org/eco.php?doc=cihm
To ensure preservation of & foster access to print Canadiana by microfilming & scanning a comprehensive collection of pre-1920 materials written by Canadians, about Canada, or published in Canada

Conseil des monuments et sites du Québec (CMSQ)
82, Grande-Allée ouest, Québec QC G1R 2G6 Canada
Tél: 418-647-4347; *Téléc:* 418-647-6483
Ligne sans frais: 800-494-4347
cmsq@cmsq.qc.ca
www.cmsq.qc.ca
Oeuvrer à valoriser et faire connaître les monuments et les sites aux autorités et à la population du Québec; rassembler les individus, organismes et groupes partageant sa mission; entreprendre les actions appropriées à la mise en valeur et à la sauvegarde des éléments patrimoniaux

The CRB Foundation (CRBF) / La Fondation CRB
1170, rue Peel, 8e étage, Montréal QC H3B 4P2 Canada
Tel: 514-878-5250; *Fax:* 514-878-5299
To encourage young people to strengthen their knowledge & appreciation of their history, heritage & cultural identity
Charles R. Bronfman, Chair
Johanne McDonald, Director of Operations

Family History Society of Newfoundland & Labrador
Waterford Valley Plaza, 657 Topsail Rd., St. John's NL A1E 2E3 Canada
Tel: 709-754-9525; *Fax:* 709-754-6430
fhs@fhsnl.ca
www.fhsnl.ca
To encourage & promote the study of family history in Newfoundland & Labrador; To collect & preserve local genealogical & historical records & materials; to foster education in genealogical research

Fédération des sociétés d'histoire du Québec
CP 1000, Succ. M, 4545, av Pierre-De Coubertin, Montréal QC H1V 3R2 Canada
Tél: 514-252-3031; *Téléc:* 514-251-8038
Ligne sans frais: 866-691-7207
fshq@histoirequebec.qc.ca
www.histoirequebec.qc.ca
Regrouper les organisations historiques de Québec.
Richard M. Bégin, Président

Federation of Nova Scotian Heritage (FNSH)
1113 Marginal Rd., Halifax NS B3H 4P7 Canada
Tel: 902-423-4677; *Fax:* 902-422-0881
Toll-Free: 800-355-6873
fnsh@hfx.andara.com
To support, promote & link NS heritage groups; to be a leader in heritage issues; to promote heritage awareness in Nova Scotia; to coordinate professional & volunteer development.

Fédération québécoise des sociétés de généalogie (FQSG)
CP 9454, Succ. Sainte-Foy, Québec QC G1V 4B8 Canada
Tél: 418-653-3940; *Téléc:* 418-653-3940
federationgenealogie@bellnet.ca
www.federationgenealogie.qc.ca
Représenter les sociétés de généalogie locales et régionales; la promotion et l'épanouissement de la généalogie au Québec et son rayonnement à l'étranger sont les buts visés

Genealogical Association of Nova Scotia (GANS) / Association généalogique de la Nouvelle-Écosse
#222, 3045 Robie St., Halifax NS B3K 4P6 Canada
Tel: 902-454-0322
gans@chebucto.ns.ca
www.chebucto.ns.ca/Recreation/GANS
To encourage interest in & to raise standards of research in genealogy through workshops & publications; to acquaint members with research materials & methods to serve as medium of exchange for genealogical information; to support the collection & preservation of documents & other genealogical materials; to foster recognition of the value of genealogy to a proper study of the social sciences.

Genealogical Institute of The Maritimes (GIM) / Institut généalogique des Provinces Maritimes
PO Box 36022, 5675 Spring Garden Rd., Halifax NS B3J 1G0 Canada
don.clark@ns.sympatico.ca
nsgna.ednet.ns.ca/gim/
The Genealogical Institute of the Maritimes, a non-profit organization, was established in 1983 under the auspices of the Council of Maritime Premiers. As well as pursuing geneaology, the play an educational role in upgrading the quality of professional family history research in the Maritimes and strive for excellence in research and encourage others to do the same.

Halifax Citadel Regimental Association (HCRA)
PO Box 9080, Stn. A, Halifax NS B3M 5K7 Canada
Tel: 902-426-1990
info@regimental.com
www.regimental.com
To assist Parks Canada in the administration and delivery of the historical interpretive program and associated activities at the Halifax Citadel National Historic Site of Canada and raise funds in support of that program.
Brian Andrecyk, President
Roderick MacLean, Administrative Officer

Heritage Canada Foundation (HCF) / Fondation Héritage Canada
5 Blackburn Ave., Ottawa ON K1N 8A2 Canada
Tel: 613-237-1066; *Fax:* 613-237-5987
Toll-Free: 866-964-1066
heritagecanada@heritagecanada.org
www.heritagecanada.org
To foster & ensure the understanding, protection & sustainable evolution of Canada's heritage buildings & historic places

L'Héritage canadien du Québec (HCQ) / The Canadian Heritage of Québec (CHQ)
1181, rue de la Montagne, Montréal QC H3G 1Z2 Canada
Tél: 514-393-1417; *Téléc:* 514-393-9444
chq@total.net
www.hcq-chq.org/french/
Organisme qui se consacre à la préservation des terrains & des constructions revêtant une valeur historique/architecturale dans la province du Québec

Heritage Foundation of Newfoundland & Labrador
PO Box 5171, 1 Springdale St., St. John's NL A1C 5V5 Canada
Tel: 709-739-1892; *Fax:* 709-739-5413
Toll-Free: 888-739-1892
info@heritagefoundation.ca
www.heritagefoundation.ca
To stimulate an understanding of & appreciation for the architectural heritage of Newfoundland & Labrador; to support & contribute to the preservation, maintenance & restoration of buildings of architectural or historical significance; to designate buildings & structures as Registered Heritage Structures; may make grants for purpose of preservation, maintenance, or restoration (Deadline for submitting grant application is Mar. 1 & Sept. 1 of each year)

Heritage Society of British Columbia
914 Garthland Pl. West, Victoria BC V9A 4J5 Canada
Tel: 250-384-4840
hsbc@islandnet.com
www.heritagebc.ca
To represent groups involved with heritage projects & issues
Rick Goodacre, Executive Director
Jonathan Yardley, President
Leslie Gilbert, Sec.-Treas.

Historic Sites Association of Newfoundland & Labrador (HSANL)
PO Box 5542, St. John's NL A1C 5W4 Canada
Tel: 709-753-9262; *Fax:* 709-753-0879
Toll-Free: 877-753-9262
info@historicsites.ca
www.historicsites.ca
To preserve, promote, & interpret the history & heritage of Newfoundland & Labrador, in partnership with Parks Canada
Catherine Dempsey, Executive Director

Historic Theatres' Trust (HTT) / Société des salles historiques
PO Box 539, Stn. Westmount, Montréal QC H3Y 3H9 Canada
Tel: 514-933-8077
theatres1@sympatico.ca
To develop an increased appreciation within the Canadian public concerning the preservation of historic Canadian theatres; to provide technical documentation & expertise to encourage improved methods of preserving, restoring, maintaining, operating & researching historic theatres
Claude Fortin, Sec.-Treas.
Dane Lanken, Vice-President
Janet MacKinnon, President

Historical Society of Alberta (HSA)
Lancaster Building, PO Box 4035, Stn. C, #622, 304 - 8th Ave. SW, Calgary AB T2P 1C5 Canada
Tel: 403-261-3662; *Fax:* 403-269-6029
albertahistory@telus.net
www.albertahistory.org
To preserve & promote the history of Alberta; to encourage the study & preservation of Canadian & Albertan history; to rescue from oblivion the memories, experiences & knowledge of early inhabitants.

Huguenot Society of Canada / Société Huguenote du Canada
#105 - 4936 Yonge St., Toronto ON M2N 6S3 Canada
To perpetuate the memory of the Huguenots; to keep in touch with Huguenot descendants & Huguenots worldwide

ICOMOS Canada
PO Box 737, Stn. B, Ottawa ON K1P 5P8 Canada
Tel: 613-749-0971
canada@icomos.org
www.canada.icomos.org
To further the conservation, protection, rehabilitation, & enhancement of monuments, groups of buildings & sites; To encourage primary research in many important fields

J. Douglas Ferguson Historical Research Foundation
PO Box 5079, Shediac NB E4P 8T8 Canada
Tel: 506-532-6025; *Fax:* 506-532-6025
www.nunet.ca/jdfhrf/main.php
The Foundation is a non-profit, educational organization that gives financial support to a broad range of activities aimed at preserving the heritage of early historical currency, banks & other issuers of money, coins, tokens & paper money issued throughout Canada since the 18th century. It is a registered charity, BN: 118973437RR0001.
Geoffrey G. Bell, Chair
Cliff Beattie, President
Len Buth, Treasurer

Jewish Genealogical Society of Canada (JGSC)
PO Box 91006, 2901 Bayview Ave., Toronto ON M2K 2Y6 Canada
info@jgstoronto.ca
www.jgstoronto.ca
To foster interest in Jewish genealogical research; To facilitate the pursuit of Jewish genealogical research domestically & internationally; To provide a forum for the exchange of knowledge & information among people interested in Jewish genealogy
Shelley Stillman, President
Lucy Sadowski, Secretary
Steve Gora, Treasurer

Literary & Historical Society of Québec (LHSQ) / Société littéraire et historique de Québec
44, chaussée des Écossais, Québec QC G1R 4H3 Canada
Tel: 418-694-9147; *Fax:* 418-694-0754
info@morrin.org
www.morrin.org
To preserve, develop & share the diverse cultural life of the Québec City region's English-speaking community through innovative, responsive & effective services

Manitoba Genealogical Society Inc. (MGS)
1045 St. James St., #E, Winnipeg MB R3H 1B1 Canada
Tel: 204-783-9139; *Fax:* 204-783-0190
contact@mbgenealogy.com
www.mbgenealogy.com
To collect & preserve local genealogical & historical records & materials; to foster education in genealogical research through society workshops & seminars; to encourage production of genealogical publications relating especially to Manitoba

Manitoba Historical Society (MHS)
61 Carlton St., Winnipeg MB R3C 1N7 Canada
Tel: 204-947-0559; *Fax:* 204-943-1093
info@mhs.mb.ca; questions@mhs.mb.ca; journal@mhs.mb.ca
www.mhs.mb.ca
To promote public interest in, and preservation of Manitoba's historical resources; To encourage research relating to the history of Manitoba

Monarchist League of Canada (MLC) / Ligue Monarchiste du Canada
Tel: 905-912-0916
chairman@monarchist.ca
www.monarchist.ca
To promote loyalty to the Sovereign & a broader understanding of constitutional monarchy as part of Canada's parliament, history, social fabric, culture & traditions

New Brunswick Genealogical Society Inc. (NBGS, Inc.) / Société Généalogique du Nouveau-Brunswick Inc.
PO Box 3235, Stn. B, Fredericton NB E3A 5G9 Canada
sbalch@nbnet.nb.ca
www.nbgs.ca
To promote & facilitate family historical research in New Brunswick

New Brunswick Historical Society
Loyalist House, 120 Union St., Saint John NB E2L 1A3 Canada
Tel: 506-652-3590
www.loyalisthouse.com
To promote the study, research & discussion of New Brunswick history; to collect & preserve New Brunswick history; to publish & educate. The Society owns & operates Loyalist House.

New Westminster Hyack Festival Association
204, 6th St., New Westminster BC V3L 3A1 Canada
Tel: 604-522-6894; *Fax:* 604-522-6094
info@hyack.bc.ca
www.hyack.bc.ca
The New Westminster Hyack Festival Association organizes and facilitates events in the City of New Westminster while preserving history and tradition, in order to promote the City, stimulate the local economy, and entertain and involve people in a fun-filled atmosphere. Its events are recognized both locally and internationally, fostering a positive image for the City of New Westminster and its surrounding areas.
Melanie Vogel, Executive Director

Newfoundland Historical Society (NHS)
Office: #15, 90 Military Rd., PO Box 23154 Churchill Sq., St. John's NL A1B 4J9 Canada
Tel: 709-722-3191; *Fax:* 709-729-7989
nhs@nf.aibn.com
www.infonet.st-johns.nf.ca/providers/nfldhist
To promote study, research & public discussion of Newfoundland & Labrador's history; to record the history of the province; to promote preservation of historic sites

Ontario Black History Society (OBHS) / Société historique des Noirs de l'Ontario
Ontario Heritage Centre, #402, 10 Adelaide St. East, Toronto ON M5C 1J3 Canada
Tel: 416-867-9420; *Fax:* 416-867-8691
admin@blackhistorysociety.ca
www.blackhistorysociety.ca
To study Black history in Canada; to recognize, preserve & promote the contribution of Black peoples & their collective histories through education, research & cooperation; to promote the inclusion of material on Black history in school curricula; to sponsor & support educational conferences & exhibits in this field.

Ontario Electric Railway Historical Association
PO Box 578, 13629 Guelph Line Rd., Milton ON L9T 5A2 Canada
Tel: 519-856-9802; *Fax:* 519-856-1399
streetcar@hcry.org
www.hcry.org
To collect & return to operating capacity, electric railway equipment representing North American city & interurban systems

Ontario Genealogical Society (OGS) / Société de généalogie de l'Ontario
#102, 40 Orchard View Blvd., Toronto ON M4R 1B9 Canada
Tel: 416-489-0734; *Fax:* 416-489-9803
provoffice@ogs.on.ca
www.ogs.on.ca
To encourage, bring together & assist all those interested in the pursuit of family history; to promote genealogical research; to set standards for genealogical excellence; to make available the knowledge, availability, diversity & comprehensiveness of the genealogical resources of Ontario; to share expertise in other geographic areas

Ontario Historical Society (OHS) / La Société historique de l'Ontario
34 Parkview Ave., Toronto ON M2N 3Y2 Canada
Tel: 416-226-9011; *Fax:* 416-226-2740
ohs@ontariohistoricalsociety.ca
www.ontariohistoricalsociety.ca
To bring people together who are interested in preserving some aspect of Ontario's history; to encourage & assist museums, historical societies & other heritage groups to research, preserve & interpret artifacts, architecture, archaeological sites & archival resources of local communities; to provide a forum to exchange ideas, research & experiences related to the history of Ontario; to sponsor programs & projects with a wide general appeal that help discover Ontario history

Pier 21 Society
1055 Marginal Rd., Halifax NS B3H 4P6
Tel: 902-425-7770; *Fax:* 902-423-4045
info@pier21.ca
www.pier21.ca
To preserve & share information about the Canadian immigration experience through history
John E. Oliver, Chair
Robert Moody, Chief Executive Officer
Kristine Kovacevic, Manager, Museum Visitor Services
Carrie-Ann Smith, Manager, Research
Peter Malloy, Treasurer

Postal History Society of Canada (PHSC)
PO Box 82055, 1400 - 12th Ave. SW, Calgary AB T3C 3W5 Canada
www.postalhistorycanada.org
To promote the study of postal history of Canada

Prince Edward Island Genealogical Society Inc. (PEIGS)
PO Box 2744, Charlottetown PE C1A 8C4 Canada
peigs_queries@yahoo.ca
www.peigs.ca
To encourage & promote the study of family history in PEI; to collect & preserve local genealogical & historical records & materials; to foster education in genealogical research

Prince Edward Island Museum & Heritage Foundation (PEIMHF) / Le Musée et la fondation du patrimoine de l'Île-du-Prince-Édouard
2 Kent St., Charlottetown PE C1A 1M6 Canada
Tel: 902-368-6600; *Fax:* 902-368-6608
mhpei@gov.pe.ca
www.peimuseum.com
To study, preserve, interpret & protect the human & natural heritage of PEI

Québec Family History Society (QFHS) / Société de l'histoire des familles du Québec
PO Box 1026, Pointe-Claire QC H9S 4H9 Canada
Tel: 514-695-1502; *Fax:* 514-695-3508
admin@qfhs.ca
www.qfhs.ca
To promote genealogy & genealogical research in Québec (particularly English & Protestant records) to collect & preserve books, manuscripts & other related material; to conduct workshops & seminars & discuss topics of interest to members

Regroupement des organismes du patrimoine franco-ontarien (ROPFO)
CP 74205, #B151, 2445, boul. Saint-Laurent, Ottawa ON K1G 6C3 Canada
Tél: 613-567-6363; *Téléc:* 613-567-6563
info@ropfo.ca
www.ropfo.ca
Promouvoir la conservation du patrimoine franco-ontarien
Linda Lauzon, Directrice générale

Richard III Society of Canada
c/o 156 Drayton Ave., Toronto ON M4C 3M2 Canada
richardiii@cogeco.ca
home.cogeco.ca/~richardiii/
In the belief that traditional accounts of the character & career of Richard III are neither supported by sufficient evidence nor reasonably tenable, the Society aims to promote research into his life & times to secure a re-assessment of the material relating to this period & this monarch's role in English history.

Royal Heraldry Society of Canada / Société royale héraldique du Canada
PO Box 8128, Stn. T, Ottawa ON K1G 3H9 Canada
Tel: 613-998-1976
secretary@heraldry.ca
www.heraldry.ca
Social Media: www.facebook.com/group.php?gid=35284796074
To maintain, foster & develop the heraldic traditions of Canadians by: increasing public awareness of heraldry & the society; advocating with governments for the protection & proper use of heraldry in Canada; advising the Canadian Heraldic Authority on matters of mutual concern

The Royal Nova Scotia Historical Society (RNSHS)
PO Box 2622, Halifax NS B3J 3P7 Canada
david.sutherland@dal.ca
nsgna.ednet.ns.ca/rnshs
To promote an understanding & appreciation of Nova Scotia's history & cultural development; to encourage the preservation of published & archival materials & artifacts; to read papers pertaining to Nova Scotia's history at meetings of the society; to publish selected papers in the society's periodical

Saskatchewan Cultural Exchange Society (SCES)
2431 - 8 Ave., Regina SK S4R 5J7 Canada
Tel: 306-780-9494; *Fax:* 306-780-9487
sces@sasktel.net
www.sces.ca
To support & facilitate cultural exchange & communication by providing a base for sharing community cultural experiences; to attract & involve practising artists in a cultural exchange in Saskatchewan; to enhance the opportunities for residents of smaller communities in Saskatchewan to experience & learn about contemporary cultural production; to provide an alternative for artists to interact with the public

Saskatchewan Genealogical Society (SGS)
PO Box 1894, #110, 1514 - 11th Ave., Regina SK S4P 3E1 Canada
Tel: 306-780-9207
saskgenealogy@sasktel.net
www.saskgenealogy.com
To provide assistance in researching family history throughout the world; to preserve heritage documents; to collect materials for study

Société canadienne d'histoire de l'Église Catholique - Section française (SCHEC) / Canadian Catholic Historical Association - French Section
SCHEC, Université du Québec à Trois-Rivières, 3351, boul des Forges, Trois-Rivières QC G9A 5H7 Canada
Tél: 819-376-5011; *Téléc:* 819-376-5179
www.cieq.ca/schec
Grouper les personnes intéressées à l'histoire de l'Église catholique au Canada; stimuler l'intérêt pour cette histoire dans le grand public; tenir des congrès annuels dans diverses régions du Canada afin de susciter un dialogue entre chercheurs participants et de promouvoir les travaux d'histoire régionale
René Hardy, Président

Société d'histoire régionale de Chibougamau
646, 3e Rue, Chibougamau QC G8P 1P1 Canada
Tél: 418-748-3124
Christian Claveau, Président

Société franco-ontarienne d'histoire et de généalogie (SFOHG)
#B151, 2445 boul St-Laurent, Ottawa ON K1G 6C3 Canada
Tél: 613-729-5769; *Téléc:* 613-729-2209
Ligne sans frais: 866-307-9995
info@sfohg.com
www.sfohg.com
Permettre à ses membres de découvrir le patrimoine franco-ontarien par l'entremise de l'histoire et de la généalogie
Linda Lauzon, Directrice générale
Michel Duquet, Chargé de projets
Richard St-Georges, Président
Juliette Denis, Vice-présidente

Société généalogique canadienne-française (SGCF)
3440, rue Davidson, Montréal QC H1W 2Z5 Canada
Tél: 514-527-1010; *Téléc:* 514-527-0265
info@sgcf.com
www.sgcf.com
Regrouper toutes les personnes désireuses de partager des connaissances généalogiques et leur histoire de famille par les conférences et la publication de travaux de recherche
Gisèle Monarque, Présidente

La Société historique de Québec
1070, De La Chevrotière, Québec QC G1R 3J4 Canada
Tél: 418-692-0556; *Téléc:* 418-692-0614
shq1@bellnet.ca
www.societehistoriquedequebec.qc.ca
Étudier et diffuser l'histoire de la ville de Québec et de sa région; relever et mettre en valeur le patrimoine de la même région
Jean Dorval, Président
Jean-François Caron, Trésorier
Doris Drolet, Secrétaire

United Empire Loyalists' Association of Canada (UELAC)
Dominion Office, The George Brown House, #202, 50 Baldwin St., Toronto ON M5T 1L4 Canada
Tel: 416-591-1783; *Fax:* 416-591-7506
uela@becon.org
www.uelac.org
To unite together descendants of those families who, as a result of the American revolutionary war, sacrificed their homes in retaining their loyalty to the British Crown; to keep alive the knowledge of the early contributions of hundreds of thousands of Loyalists of many cultures, creeds & colours
Fredrick H. Hayward, UE, President
Carl Stymiest, UE, Sr. Vice-President

West Coast Railway Association (WCRA)
PO Box 2790, Vancouver BC V6B 3X2 Canada
Tel: 604-524-1011; *Fax:* 604-876-4104
Toll-Free: 800-722-1233
info@wcra.org
www.wcra.org
Collects, preserves, restores, operates & exhibits artifacts relating to the history of railways, especially those of BC; the West Coast Railway Heritage Park in Squamish BC develops educational exhibits on railway heritage for all age groups; the tour program encourages the public to travel today's railways to see Canada

Homosexuality

Alliance des gais et lesbiennes Laval-Laurentides (AGLLL Inc.)
CP 98030, 95, boul Labelle, Sainte-Thérèse QC J7E 5R4 Canada
aglll@hotmail.com
www.algi.qc.ca/asso/aglll/
Groupe de discussion; activités

AlterHéros
CP 476, Succ. C, Montréal QC H2L 4K4 Canada
Tél: 514-846-1398
info@alterheros.com
www.alterheros.com
Organisme communautaire bénévole à but non lucratif qui favorise l'insertion sociale des personnes d'orientation homosexuelle, bisexuelle et d'identité transsexuelle
Marc-Olivier Ouellet, Fondateur

Amazones des grands espaces
Montréal QC Canada
Tél: 514-525-3663
info@plein-air-amazones.org
www.plein-air-amazones.org
Club de plein air pour lesbiennes

ARC: Aînés et retraités de la communauté
Montréal QC Canada
Tél: 514-529-7471
arcmontreal@hotmail.com
www.algi.qc.ca/asso/retraitesgais
Groupement de personnes gaies aînées ou retraitées; activités sociales, culturelles ou sportives. Contactez Raymond B. au 514-529-7471 ou Nicholas au 514-343-1117

Archives gais du Québec
#202, 4067, boul St-Laurent, Montréal QC H2W 1Y7 Canada
Tél: 514-287-9987
www.agq.qc.ca
Organisme communautaire à but non lucratif qui a le mandat de recevoir, conserver et préserver tout document de l'histoire des gais et lesbiennes du Québec - revues, journaux, coupures de presse, livres et vidéos, photos
Ian Blair, Président

Association des Gais et Lesbiennes du Bas-St-Laurent
info_aglbsl@yahoo.ca
www.algi.qc.ca/asso/aglbsl/
Activités sociales et sportives; contact: Jean-François, administrateur.

Association des lesbiennes et des gais sur Internet (ALGI)
CP 476, Succ. C, Montréal QC H2L 4K4 Canada
Tél: 514-528-8424; *Téléc:* 514-528-9708
info@algi.qc.ca
www.algi.qc.ca
Favoriser l'expression des lesbiennes et des gais au moyen de l'Internet; favoriser l'échange entre les individus et les organismes de la communauté gaie et lesbienne dans un esprit d'entraide

Association des pères gais de Montréal inc. (APGM) / Gay Fathers of Montréal Inc.
4245, rue Laval, Montréal QC H2W 2J6 Canada
Tél: 514-528-8424; *Téléc:* 514-528-9708
peresgais@yahoo.ca
www.algi.qc.ca/asso/apgm/
Regrouper les hommes qui sont à la fois pères et gais; offrir support et aide aux hommes gais soucieux d'éduquer leurs enfants; permettre au père gai de se situer face à la condition de vie au moyen d'échanges, de discussion et d'information; promouvoir la condition des pères gais et la défense de leurs intérêts communs

Bi Unité Montréal (BUM)
CP 476, Succ. C, Montréal QC H2L 4K4 Canada
webmaster@biunitemontreal.org
www.algi.qc.ca/asso/bum/
Association à but non lucratif; a pour mission de fair connaître la bisexualité et de rassembler les bisexuel(le)s dans un lieu commun pour qu'ils/qu'elles puissent s'informer, se divertir, et se supporter.

Les Bolides
Montréal QC Canada
info@lesbolides.org
www.lesbolides.org
Ligue de quilles
Fernand

Canadian Lesbian & Gay Archives (CLGA)
PO Box 699, Stn. F, 34 Isabella St., Toronto ON M4Y 1N1 Canada
Tel: 416-777-2755
queeries@clga.ca
www.clga.ca
To acquire, preserve & make available to the public information in any medium about lesbians & gays, with an emphasis on Canada.
Martin Lanigan, President

Centre communautaire des gais et lesbiennes de Montréal
CP 476, Succ. C, Montréal QC H2L 4K4 Canada
Tél: 514-528-8424; *Téléc:* 514-528-9708
info@ccglm.org
www.ccglm.org
Organisme sans but lucratif qui agit pour améliorer la condition des membres de nos communautés - lesbiennes, gais, bisexuel(les), transexuel(les), transgenres, et allosexuel(les); bibliothèque

Centre d'orientation sexuelle de l'université McGill (COSUM) / McGill University Sexual Identity Centre (MUSIC)
Dép. de psychiatrie, Hôpital général de Montréal, #A2-160, 1650, av Cedar, Montréal QC H3G 1A4 Canada
Tél: 514-934-1934; *Téléc:* 514-934-8471
music-cosum@mcgill.ca
www.mcgill.ca/cosum; www.algi.qc.ca/asso/cosum
Offre des psychothérapies individuelles à court terme, psychothérapies de groupe & de couple ou familiales
Karine J. Igartua, MDCM, FRCPC, CM, Psychiatre

Centre de solidarité lesbienne
#301, 4126, rue St-Denis, Montréal QC H2W 2M5 Canada
Tél: 514-526-2452; *Téléc:* 514-526-3570
info@solidaritelesbienne.qc.ca
www.solidaritelesbienne.qc.ca
Le Centre est accessible aux personnes à mobilité réduite; organisme sans but lucratif qui a pour mission d'améliorer les conditions de vie des lesbiennes en leur offrant des services et des interventions adaptés à leur réalité et ce, dans les domaines de la violence conjugales, du bien-être et de la santé.

Coalition des familles homoparentales
Montréal QC Canada
Tél: 514-846-1543
info@familleshomoparentales.org
www.familleshomoparentales.org
Milite pour la reconnaissance légale et sociale des familles homoparentales; groupe bilingue de parents lesbiens, gais, bisexuels et transgenres. Québec: 418-523-5572
Mona Greenbaum, Directrice

Coalition for Lesbian & Gay Rights in Ontario (CLGRO) / Coalition pour les droits des lesbiennes et personnes gaies en Ontario
PO Box 822, Stn. A, Toronto ON M5W 1G3 Canada
Tel: 416-405-8253
query@clgro.org
www.clgro.org
To work towards feminism, lesbian, gay & bisexual liberation by engaging in public struggle for full human rights, by promoting access & diversity within our communities, & by strengthening cooperative networks for lesbian, gay & bisexual activism

Comité des gais et lesbiennes du conseil central du Montréal métropolitain (CSN) (CGLCCMM-CSN)
Montréal QC Canada
Tél: 514-598-2012
www.algi.qc.ca/asso/cglccmm
Jacques Tricot

Community One Foundation
PO Box 760, Stn. F, Toronto ON M4Y 2N6 Canada
Tel: 416-920-5422
info@communityone.ca
www.communityone.ca
To raise & disburse funds for the advancement of lesbian, gay, bisexual & transgender projects, artists & organizations; to fund projects in the areas of health & social services, arts & culture, research & education, political & legal
Philip Wong, Executive Director
Lenore MacAdam, Board Co-Chair
Larry Hughsam, Board Co-Chair/Treasurer

Conseil québécois des gais et lesbiennes du Québec (CQGL)
CP 182, Succ. C, Montréal QC H2L 4K1 Canada
Tél: 514-759-6844
info@cqgl.ca
www.cqgl.ca
A pour mission concrétiser notre leitmotive 'S'engager pour l'égalité sociale'. Adresse civique: #105, 4360, rue d'Iberville, Montréal, QC.
Steve Foster, Président

Council on Homosexuality & Religion (CHR) / Conseil de l'homosexualité et la religion
PO Box 1912, Winnipeg MB R3C 3R2 Canada
Tel: 204-772-8215; *Fax:* 204-478-1160
Toll-Free: 888-399-0005
cvogel@mts.net
To foster the welfare of homosexually-oriented persons & promote the understanding & acceptance of homosexuality within religious institutions; to provide counselling & referral services; to conduct workshops, seminars & lectures; to provide a library & a range of publications on homosexuality & religion; to assist others in the same activities

Dignity Canada Dignité
PO Box 2102, Stn. D, Ottawa ON K1P 5W3 Canada
Tel: 613-746-7279
info@dignitycanada.org
www.dignitycanada.org
To voice the concerns of Roman Catholic sexual minorities; To promote the development of sexual theology, justice, & acceptance of the lesbian & gay community; To reinforce a sense of dignity & to encourage gay men & lesbian women to become more active members in the Church & society
Dennis Benoit, President
Frank Testin, Sec.-Treas.

Egale Canada
#430, 1 Nicholas St., Ottawa ON K1N 7B7 Canada
Tel: 613-230-1043; *Fax:* 613-230-9395
Toll-Free: 888-204-7777
egale.canada@egale.ca
www.egale.ca
To advance equality & justice for lesbian, gay, bisexual & transgendered persons, & their families in Canada

Fondation Mario-Racine / Mario Racine Foundation
2075, rue Plessis, Local 110, Montréal QC H2L 2Y4 Canada
Tél: 514-528-5940
info@fondation-mario-racine.qc.ca
www.fondation-mario-racine.qc.ca
A pour mission de favoriser le développement communautaire et culturel des gais et lesbiennes à Montréal; est engagée dans la réalisation du Centre communautaire des gais et lesbiennes de Montréal.
Michel Durocher, MBA, Président

Gai-Côte-Sud
#100, 708, 4e Av, La Pocatière QC G0R 1Z0 Canada
gaicotesud@hotmail.com
www.algi.qc.ca/asso/gcs/
Favoriser le bien-être des gais, lesbiennes, bisexuel(les) et transgenres de la région.
Magella Dionne, Président

GRIS-Centre-du-Québec
Tél: 819-477-3953
risennev@cgocable.ca
Richard Senneville, Président

Groupe de discussion au masculin (GDM)
CP 476, Succ. C, Montréal QC H2L 4K4 Canada
Tél: 514-528-8424
gdminfo@gmail.com
www.gai-gdm.org

Groupe de recherche et d'intervention sociale (GRIS-Montréal)
CP 476, Succ. C, Montréal QC H2L 4K4 Canada
Tél: 514-590-0016; *Téléc:* 514-590-0764
info@gris.ca
www.gris.ca
Favoriser un meilleure connaissance des réalités homosexuelles et de faciliter l'intégration des gais, lesbiennes et bisexuel(les) dans la société
Robert Pilon, Président

Groupe gai de l'Outaouais
Gatineau QC Canada
Tél: 819-776-2727
marlan@videotron.ca
www.algi.qc.ca/asso/gdhgfo/
Discussions, rencontres, activités sociales; les rencontres ont lieu les mercredis soir à 19h30, au Bureau régional d'action sida, 109, rue Wright, local 003 (Gatineau, secteur Hull).

Groupe gai de l'Université Laval
Pavillon Mauice-Pollack, 2305, rue de l'Université, Québec QC G1V 0A6 Canada
Tél: 418-656-2131
ggul@public.ulaval.ca
www.algi.qc.ca/asso/ggul/

Groupe régional d'intervention social - Québec (GRIS-Québec)
363, rue de la Couronne, local 202, Québec QC G1K 6E9 Canada
Tél: 418-523-5572; *Téléc:* 418-523-9758
gris@grisquebec.org
www.grisquebec.org
Guy Lefebvre, Coordonnateur

Hors sentiers
5828, rue de Normanville, Montréal QC H2S 2B4 Canada
Tél: 450-963-9710
hors_sentiers@yahoo.ca
www.algi.qc.ca/asso/horssentiers/
Groupe de plein air

Jeunesse Lambda
a/s Centre communautaire des gais et lesbiennes de Montréal, 2075, rue Plessis, 3e étage, Montréal QC H2L 2Y4 Canada
Tél: 514-528-7535
info@jeunesselambda.org
www.algi.qc.ca/asso/jlambda/
Groupe d'accueil francophone de discussion et d'activités par et pour les jeunes gais, lesbiennes, bisexuel(les). Adresse postale: CP 32125, CSP Saint-André, Montréal QC H2L 4Y5
Gabriel Boisvert, Président

Projet 10 / Project 10
#218, 2000, Northcliffe, Montréal QC H4A 3K5 Canada
Tél: 514-989-4585; *Téléc:* 514-989-0001
questions@p10.qc.ca
www.p10.qc.ca; www.myspace.com/p10montreal
Ligne d'entraide anonyme et confidentielle; services pour les jeunes lesbiennes, gais, bisexuel(le)s, intersexuel(le)s, allosexuel(le)s, trans, et bispirituel(le)s
Carly Boyce, Co-coordinatrice
Shauna Thomas, Co-coordinatrice

Réseau des lesbiennes du Québec (RLQ) / Québec Lesbian Network
#110, 2075, rue Plessis, Montréal QC H2L 2Y4 Canada
Tél: 514-528-8424
rlqln.info@gmail.com
rlq-qln.algi.qc.ca
Diane Heffernan, Coordonnatrice

TimeOut / TempsLibre
PO Box 1087, Stn. B, Ottawa ON K1P 5R1 Canada
timeout@gayottawa.com
www.gayottawa.com
Sporting, social and recreational events for the gay community in Ottawa and area.

La Trame
CP 845, Succ. Desjardins, Montréal QC H5B 1B9 Canada
Tél: 514-374-0227
la.trame@hotmail.com
www.latrame.blogspot.com
Regroupement pour lesbiennes dans le domaine des arts, de la culture et du loisir
Mireille Robillard, Contact

Horticulture & Gardening

Les Amis du Jardin botanique de Montréal / Friends of the Montréal Botanical Garden
#A-206, 4101, rue Sherbrooke est, Montréal QC H1X 2B2 Canada
Tél: 514-872-1493; *Téléc:* 514-872-3765
www.amisjardin.qc.ca
Promouvoir une culture scientifique et une culture générale concernant la nature, l'environnement et la botanique; supporter, par des actions concrètes, le Jardin botanique dans sa mission afin d'assurer son développement; informer les membres, de façon privilégiée, des plus récents progrès scientifiques; présenter au public les différentes composantes du Jardin botanique et en vulgariser le rôle, les actions et le contenu; valoriser la flore mondiale, particulièrement celle du Québec et promouvoir la conservation de la nature; représenter le grand public auprès des instances du Jardin
Michèle-E. Hogue, Directrice générale
Paule Lamontagne, Présidente

British Columbia Landscape & Nursery Association (BCLNA)
#102, 5783 - 176A St., Surrey BC V3S 6S6 Canada
Tel: 604-574-7772; *Fax:* 604-574-7773
Toll-Free: 800-421-7963
info@bclna.com
www.bclna.com
To work together to improve quality & standards of the industry

Canadian Horticultural Council (CHC) / Conseil canadien de l'horticulture
9 Corvus Ct., Ottawa ON K2E 7Z4 Canada
Tel: 613-226-4880; *Fax:* 613-226-4497
webmaster@hortcouncil.ca
www.hortcouncil.ca
To improve horticultural & allied industries including production, grading, packing, transportation, storage & marketing

Canadian Iris Society (CIS)
c/o Ed Jowett, 1960 Sideroad 15, RR#2, Tottenham ON L0G 1W0 Canada
Tel: 905-936-9941
cdn-iris@rogers.com
www.cdn-iris.ca
To encourage, improve & extend the cultivation of the Iris & to collaborate with other societies for this purpose, as well as to regulate the nomenclature & colour classification of this flower.
Ed Jowett, President
Ann Granatier, Secretary

Canadian Nursery Landscape Association (CNLA)
7856 Fifth Line South, Milton ON L9T 2X8 Canada
Tel: 905-875-1399; *Fax:* 905-875-1840
Toll-Free: 888-446-3499
info@canadanursery.com
www.canadanursery.com
To coordinate provincial member groups in the Canadian horticultural industry; to set national standards; to work with government; to develop national priorities

Canadian Ornamental Plant Foundation (COPF) / Fondation canadienne des plantes ornementales
5A - #218, 975 McKeown Ave., North Bay ON P1B 9P2 Canada
Tel: 705-495-2563; *Fax:* 705-495-1449
Toll-Free: 800-265-1629
info@copf.org
www.copf.org
To encourage new plant development by strengthening relations between growers & breeders for the benefit of the horticulture industry

Canadian Rose Society (CRS)
c/o #504, 334 Queen Mary Rd., Kingston ON K7M 7E7
info@canadianrosesociety.org
www.canadianrosesociety.org
To provide information about rose growing, speakers, judges, nurseries & suppliers, & rose shows; To correspond with people with similar interests throughout Canada & around the world

Canadian Society for Horticultural Science (CSHS) / Société canadienne de science horticole
#1112, 141 Laurier Ave. West, Ottawa ON K1P 5J3 Canada
Tel: 613-232-9459; *Fax:* 613-594-5190
services@aic.ca
www.cshs.ca
To advance research, teaching, information, & technology related to all horticultural crops

City Farmer - Canada's Office of Urban Agriculture
PO Box 74567, Stn. Kitsilano, Vancouver BC V6K 4P4 Canada
Tel: 604-685-5832
cityfarm@interchange.ubc.ca
www.cityfarmer.org
Social Media: cityfarmer.info
City Farmer encourages gardening in an urban environment. The website carries information for communities & schools about organic farming, composting, pest control.

Fédération des sociétés d'horticulture et d'écologie du Québec (FSHÉQ)
CP 1000, Succ. M, 4545, av Pierre-de-Coubertin, Montréal QC H1V 3R2 Canada
Tél: 514-252-3010; *Téléc:* 514-251-8038
fsheq@fsheq.com
www.fsheq.com
Regrouper tous les organismes voués à l'horticulture; faire la promotion de l'horticulture.
Thérèse Tourigny, Directrice générale

Fédération interdisciplinaire de l'horticulture ornementale du Québec (FIHOQ)
#300E, 3230, rue Sicotte ouest, Saint-Hyacinthe QC J2S 7B3 Canada
Tél: 450-774-2228; *Téléc:* 450-774-3556
fihoq@fihoq.qc.ca
www.fihoq.qc.ca
Grouper en fédération les associations professionnelles qui s'occupent d'horticulture ornementale au Québec; étudier, promouvoir, protéger et développer de toutes manières les intérêts économiques, sociaux et professionnels de ses membres; imprimer, éditer des revues, journaux, périodiques et plus généralement, toutes publications du domaine de l'horticulture ornementale aux fins d'information, de culture professionnelle et de propagande; organiser et tenir des cours, conférences, congrès, assemblées, expositions et autres réunions pour la promotion, le développement et la vulgarisation de l'horticulture ornementale; promouvoir la protection du consommateur dans le domaine de l'horticulture ornementale; assurer une représentation tant sur le plan local et national, que sur le plan international des personnes oeuvrant dans le domaine de l'horticulture ornementale au Québec.

Flowers Canada (FC) / Fleurs Canada
Retail & Distribution Sector, #305, 99 Fifth Ave., Ottawa ON K1S 5P5 Canada
Fax: 866-671-8091
Toll-Free: 800-447-5147
flowers@flowerscanada.org
www.flowerscanada.org
To act as the voice of the Canadian floriculture industry; To improve the Canadian floriculture industry
Arman Patel, Executive Director

Landscape Alberta Nursery Trades Association (LANTA)
#200, 10331 - 178 St., Edmonton AB T5S 1R5 Canada
Tel: 780-489-1991; *Fax:* 780-444-2152
Toll-Free: 800-378-3198
info@landscape-alberta.com
www.landscape-alberta.com
To advance the Alberta ornamental horticulture industry through unity, education & professionalism

Landscape New Brunswick Horticultural Trades Association (LNBHTA)
PO Box 742, Saint John NB E2L 4B3 Canada
Fax: 506-633-1621
Toll-Free: 866-752-6862
nbhta@nbnet.nb.ca
www.nbhta.ca
The mission of LNB is to further the development of the ornamental horticulture industry by focusing on the environment, education, promotion and professionalism. LNB is here to represent our members and to help them achieve their goals what so ever those goals may be.
John Evans, President

Landscape Newfoundland & Labrador (LNL)
PO Box 8062, St. John's NL A1B 3M9 Canada
Tel: 709-726-5651; *Fax:* 709-726-8441
davek@nl.rogers.com
www.landscapenf.org
Our vision is one that promotes professionalism at all levels of the Industry, and achieves the highest standards of excellence in delivery of services and products across all sectors of our industry.
David Kiell, Executive Director

Landscape Nova Scotia
Executive Plus Business Centre, #44, 201 Brownlow Ave., Dartmouth NS B3B 1W2 Canada
Tel: 902-463-0519; *Fax:* 902-463-6308
Toll-Free: 877-567-4769
info@landscapenovascotia.ca
www.landscapenovascotia.ca
Landscape Nova Scotia's mission is to promote high standards in product quality, professional service and conduct in the landscape and horticulture industry. We have been a voice for the landscape and horticultural industry for more than 20 years in Nova Scotia, and are committed to providing consumers with options to make informed decisions.
Scott Mosher, President

Landscape Ontario Horticultural Trades Association (LOHTA)
7856 Fifth Line South, RR#4, Milton ON L9T 2X8 Canada
Tel: 905-875-1805; *Fax:* 905-875-3942
Toll-Free: 800-265-5656
www.horttrades.com
To be a leader in representing, promoting & fostering a favourable environment for the advancement of the horticultural industry in Ontario

North American Native Plant Society (NANPS)
PO Box 84, Stn. D, Toronto ON M9A 4X1 Canada
Tel: 416-631-4438
nanps@nanps.org
www.nanps.org
Dedicated to the study, conservation & cultivation of North America's wild flora.

Ontario Horticultural Association (OHA)
312 Simcoe St., Tilsonburg ON N4G 2J6 Canada
Tel: 519-842-9829; *Fax:* 519-648-9716
president@gardenontario.org
www.gardenontario.org
To promote civic beautification, preservation of the environment, youth work & education of many aspects of horticulture
Jim Mabee, President

Prince Edward Island Horticultural Association
404 Mount Edward Rd, Charlottetown PE C1E 2A1 Canada
Tel: 902-566-2733; *Fax:* 902-566-5637
peihort@pei.aibn.com

Rhododendron Society of Canada (RSC)
RR#2, St George Brant ON N0E 1N0 Canada
Tel: 519-448-1537
To share information on rhododendrons
H.G. Hedges, Contact

Royal Botanical Gardens (RBG) / Les jardins botaniques royaux
680 Plains Rd. West, Hamilton ON L7T 4H4 Canada
Tel: 905-527-1158; *Fax:* 905-577-0375
Toll-Free: 800-694-4769
info@rbg.ca
www.rbg.ca
To be recognized in Canada & throughout the world for its unique contribution to the collection, research, exhibition, & interpretation of the plant world & for the development of public understanding & appreciation of the relationship between the plant world, humanity, & the rest of nature
Mark C. Runciman, Executive Director

Saskatchewan Nursery Landscape Association (SNLA)
c/o Landscape Alberta Nursery Trades Association, #200, 10331 - 178 St., Edmonton AB T5S 1R5 Canada
Tel: 780-489-1991; *Fax:* 780-444-2152
Toll-Free: 866-383-4711
rebecca@canadanursery.com
www.snla.ca

Seeds of Diversity Canada (SoDC) / Semences du patrimoine Canada
PO Box 36, Stn. Q, Toronto ON M4T 2L7 Canada
Toll-Free: 866-509-7333
mail@seeds.ca
www.seeds.ca
To search out & preserve rare & endangered varieties of vegetables, fruits, flowers, herbs & grains
Bob Wildfong, Executive Director
Judy Newman, Office Manager
Valérie Girard, Communication Coordinator

Société d'Horticulture et d'Écologie de Prévost
CP 611, Prévost QC J0R 1T0 Canada
Tél: 450-224-9252
Florence Frigon, Présidente

Hospitals

Accreditation Canada / Agrément Canada
#100, 1730 St. Laurent Blvd., Ottawa ON K1G 5L1
Tel: 613-738-3800; *Fax:* 613-738-7755
Toll-Free: 800-814-7769
LearnMore@accreditation.ca;
Communications@accreditation.ca
www.accreditation.ca
To improve quality in health services through accreditation; To provide health care organizations with a voluntary, external peer review to assess the quality of their services

Alberta Long Term Care Association (ALTCA)
Centre 104, #509, 5241 Calgary Trail South, Edmonton AB T6H 5G8 Canada
Tel: 780-435-0699; *Fax:* 780-436-9785
Toll-Free: 888-212-4581
info@ab-cca.ca
www.longtermcare.ab.ca

Association des établissements privés conventionnés - santé services sociaux (AEPC)
#200, 204, rue Notre-Dame ouest, Montréal QC H2Y 1T3 Canada
Tél: 514-499-3630; *Téléc:* 514-873-7063
info@aepc.qc.ca
www.aepc.qc.ca
Promouvoir l'amélioration continue de la qualité des soins et des services donnés au sein des entreprises membres; protéger et promouvoir l'entreprise privée dans le domaine de la santé et du bien-être

Association of Canadian Academic Healthcare Organizations (ACAHO)
780 Echo Dr., Ottawa ON K1S 5R7 Canada
Tel: 613-730-5818; *Fax:* 613-730-4314
brimacombe@acaho.org
www.acaho.org
To lobby for health care research & teaching hospitals

Association of Ontario Health Centres (AOHC) / Association des centres de santé de l'Ontario (ACSO)
#500, 907 Lawrence Ave. West, Toronto ON M6A 3B6 Canada
Tel: 416-236-2539; *Fax:* 416-236-0431
mail@aohc.org
www.aohc.org
To promote community based primary care, health promotion & illness prevention services, focusing on the broader determinants of health such as education, employment, poverty, isolation & housing

Association québécoise d'établissements de santé et de services sociaux (AQESSS) (AQESS) / Québec Hospital Association
#400, 505, boul de Maisonneuve ouest, Montréal QC H3A 3C2 Canada
Tél: 514-842-4861; *Téléc:* 514-282-4271
Ligne sans frais: 800-361-4661
www.aqesss.qc.ca
Représenter et promouvoir les intérêts de ses membres et leur fournir des services qui répondent à leurs besoins

Auxiliaires bénévoles de l'Hôpital de Chibougamau
51, 3e Rue, Chibougamau QC G8P 1N1 Canada
Tél: 418-748-2676
Marie-Ange Fréchette, Présidente

Canadian Association of Healthcare Auxiliaries (CAHA) / L'association des auxiliaires bénévoles des soins de santé du Canada
c/o Canadian Healthcare Assn., #100, 17 York St., Ottawa ON K1N 9J6 Canada
Tel: 613-236-9364; *Fax:* 613-236-9350
caha.office@rogers.com
www.caha.freeservers.com
To assist provincial members in providing support to local auxiliaries through leadership, education, advocacy, communication & representation

Canadian Association of Paediatric Health Centres (CAPHC) / Association canadienne des centres de santé pédiatriques
c/o Canadian Association of Paediatric Health Centres, #104, 2141 Thurston Dr., Ottawa ON K1G 6C9 Canada
Tel: 613-738-4164; *Fax:* 613-738-3247
eoorbine@caphc.org
www.caphc.org
To improve the health of children within Canada through research activities & through advocacy with governments & health care organizations; to provide information exchange amongst members.

Canadian Healthcare Association (CHA) / Association canadienne des soins de santé
#100, 17 York St., Ottawa ON K1N 9J6 Canada
Tel: 613-241-8005; *Fax:* 613-241-5055
info@cha.ca
www.cha.ca
To improve the delivery of health services in Canada through policy development, advocacy & leadership

Canadian Home Care Association (CHCA) / Association canadienne de soins et services à domicile
#401, 17 York St., Ottawa ON K1N 9J6 Canada
Tel: 613-569-1585; *Fax:* 613-569-1604
www.cdnhomecare.ca
To promote the development, integration, delivery, public awareness & evaluation of quality home care services in Canada; to provide national leadership to strengthen & unify the home care sector; to collect & disseminate information about home care; to encourage or commission research; to influence policy & legislation; to establish a code of ethics
Alice Mah Wren, President

Continuing Care Association of Nova Scotia (CCANS)
c/o Sunshine Personal Home Care, 38A Withrod Dr., Halifax NS B3N 1B1
Tel: 902-956-0090
ccans@eastlink.ca
www.nsnet.org/ccans
To represent continuing care facilities throughout Nova Scotia

Health Association of PEI (HAPEI)
10 Pownal St., Charlottetown PE C1A 3V6 Canada
Tel: 902-368-3901; *Fax:* 902-368-3231
emholmes@ihis.org
To influence the change & development of the health delivery system; to provide services which assist members in managing their human, financial & physical resources.

Health Employers Association of British Columbia (HEABC)
#200, 1333 West Broadway, Vancouver BC V6H 4C6 Canada
Tel: 604-736-5909; *Fax:* 604-736-2715
contact@heabc.bc.ca
www.heabc.bc.ca
To serve a diverse group of over 300 publicly funded healthcare employers; To represent the entire spectrum of healthcare employers

Hospital Auxiliaries Association of Ontario (HAAO)
#2800, 200 Front St. West, Toronto ON M5V 3L1 Canada
Tel: 416-205-1407; *Fax:* 416-205-1337
Toll-Free: 800-598-8002
ebarbeau@haao.com
www.haao.com
To advocate for community partnerships to support health care in Ontario; To promote volunteer services
Joan Babij, President
Joan Farlinger, Vice-President
Janet Simms-Baldwin, Secretary
Margaret Anne Robertson, Treasurer

New Brunswick Association of Healthcare Auxiliaries
220 Driftwood Loop, Fredericton NB E3B 7P2 Canada
Tel: 506-452-5432
r3jbooker@health.nb.ca
R. John Booker, President

New Brunswick Association of Nursing Homes, Inc. (NBANH) / Association des foyers de soins du Nouveau-Brunswick, inc. (AFSNB)
#302, 1113 Regent St., Fredericton NB E3B 3Z2 Canada
Tel: 506-460-6262; *Fax:* 506-460-6253
www.nbanh.com
The Association assists members in the provision of quality & efficient care to their residents.

New Brunswick Healthcare Association (NBHA) / L'Association des soins de santé du Nouveau-Brunswick (ASSNB)
861 Woodstock Rd., Fredericton NB E3B 7R7 Canada
Tel: 506-451-0750; *Fax:* 506-451-0760
nbha@nbhealthcare.com
www.nbhealthcare.com
To improve health services delivery in New Brunswick by influencing health policy; to strive to be a well respected and influential leader in healthcare in New Brunswick, and a major driver for change.

Newfoundland & Labrador Health Boards Association (NLHBA)
2nd Fl. Beothuck Bldg., 20 Crosbie Pl., St. John's NL A1B 3Y8 Canada
Tel: 709-364-7701; *Fax:* 709-364-6460
nlhba@nlhba.nf.ca
www.nlhba.nl.ca
To work collaboratively with the province's publicly-funded health system through dynamic leadership in advocacy, the creation & exchange of ideas, & development of consistent policies, standards, & guidelines. The Association also provides collective bargaining & labour relations services to provincial Residential Boards, & facilitates physician recruitment & group purchasing

Northwest Territories Health Care Association (NWTHCA)
c/o Hay River Community Health Board, 3 Gaetz Dr., Hay River NT X0E 0R0 Canada
Tel: 867-874-7110; *Fax:* 867-874-7109
Working together for wellness

Nova Scotia Association of Health Organizations (NSAHO)
Bedford Professional Centre, 2 Dartmouth Rd., Halifax NS B4A 2K7 Canada
Tel: 902-832-8500; *Fax:* 902-832-8505
sandi@nsaho.ns.ca
www.nsaho.ns.ca
To promote an effective, efficient & integrated quality health system for all Nova Scotians through leadership in influencing the development of public policy, representing & advocating members' interests & providing services to assist its members meet the health care needs of their communities

Ontario Association of Medical Laboratories (OAML)
#710, 5160 Yonge St., Toronto ON M2N 6L9 Canada
Tel: 416-250-8555; *Fax:* 416-250-8464
oaml@oaml.com
www.oaml.com
To act as the voice of Ontario's community laboratory sector; To promote professionalism, technical excellence, & accountability in the delivery of laboratory services throughout Ontario

Ontario Association of Non-Profit Homes & Services for Seniors (OANHSS)
#700, 7050 Weston Rd., Woodbridge ON L4L 8G7 Canada
Tel: 905-851-8821; *Fax:* 905-851-0744
drubin@oanhss.org
www.oanhss.org
To support members in the provision of quality non-profit long term care, seniors' community services, & housing

Ontario Hospital Association (OHA)
#2800, 200 Front St. West, Toronto ON M5V 3L1
Tel: 416-205-1300; *Fax:* 416-205-1301
Toll-Free: 800-598-8002
info@oha.com
www.oha.com
To build a strong, innovative, & sustainable health care system that meets patient care needs throughout Ontario; To promote an efficent & effective health care system

Ontario Long Term Care Association (OLTCA)
345 Renfrew Dr., 3rd Fl., Markham ON L3R 9S9 Canada
Tel: 905-470-8995; *Fax:* 905-470-9595
Info@oltca.com
www.oltca.com
Provides professional leadership to the long-term care sector; to empower long-term care facilities to provide high quality & cost-effective health care & accommodation services

The Regional Health Authorities of Manitoba (RHAM)
#2, 203 Duffield St., Winnipeg MB R3J 0H6 Canada
Tel: 204-833-1721; *Fax:* 204-940-2042
mebbitt@rham.mb.ca
www.rham.mb.ca

Saskatchewan Association of Health Organizations (SAHO)
#600, 2002 Victoria Ave., Regina SK S4P 0R7 Canada
Tel: 306-347-5500; *Fax:* 306-525-1960
info@saho.org
www.saho.org
To serve members through advocacy, support, & programs
Susan Antosh, President/CEO
Alex Taylor, Chair

Housing

Association of Condominium Managers of Ontario (ACMO)
#100, 2233 Argentia Rd., Mississauga ON L5N 2X7 Canada
Tel: 905-826-6890; *Fax:* 905-826-4873
Toll-Free: 800-265-3263
rcm@acmo.org
www.acmo.org
To enhance the quality performance of condominium property managers & management companies in Ontario

Association provinciale des constructeurs d'habitations du Québec inc. (APCHQ) / Provincial Association of Home Builders of Québec
5930, boul Louis-H.-Lafontaine, Anjou QC H1M 1S7 Canada
Tél: 514-353-9960; *Téléc:* 514-353-4825
Ligne sans frais: 800-468-8160
www.apchq.com
Depuis 1997, l'APCHQ est la plus importante gestionnaire de mutuelles de prévention du domaine de la construction. Étant le seul agent négociateur patronal des relations de travail dans le secteur résidentiel, elle défend les intérêts de quelque 12 000 employeurs et 25 000 travailleurs
Marc Savard, Directeur général
Frédéric Birtz, Directeur des opérations

Canadian Association of Home & Property Inspectors (CAHPI) / Association canadienne des inspecteurs de biens immobiliers
PO Box 13715, Ottawa ON K2K 1X6 Canada
Tel: 613-839-5344; *Fax:* 613-839-2554
Toll-Free: 888-748-2244
info@cahpi.ca
www.cahpi.ca
To promote & enhance the professionalism & competency of professional home & property inspectors
Bill Sutherland, President
Sharry Featherston, Administrator/Registrar
Blaine Swan, Treasurer

Canadian Condominium Institute (CCI)
#310, 2175 Sheppard Ave. East, Toronto ON M2J 1W8 Canada
Tel: 416-491-6216; *Fax:* 416-491-1670
cci.national@taylorenterprises.com
www.cci.ca
To serve as a central clearinghouse & research centre on condominium issues & activities across the country; to provide objective research for practitioners & government agencies regarding all aspects of condominium operations; to offer professional assistance; to improve legislation & represent condominiums; to develop standards

Canadian Federation of Apartment Associations (CFAA) / Fédération canadienne des Associations de propriétaires immobiliers
#640, 1600 Carling Ave., Ottawa ON K1Z 1G3 Canada
Tel: 613-235-0101; *Fax:* 613-238-0101
admin@cfaa-fcapi.org
www.cfaa-fcapi.org
To represent members on political & economic issues at the national level & to facilitate the exchange of information & materials amongst members while maintaining the highest professional & ethical standards in all activities
John Dickie, President
David Benes, Administrator

Canadian Home Builders' Association (CHBA) / Association canadienne des constructeurs d'habitations
#500, 150 Laurier Ave. West, Ottawa ON K1P 5J4 Canada
Tel: 613-230-3060; *Fax:* 613-232-8214
chba@chba.ca
www.chba.ca
To assist its members in serving the needs & meeting the aspirations of Canadians for housing; to be the voice of the residential construction industry in Canada; to achieve an environment in which members can operate profitably; to promote affordability & choice in housing for all Canadians; to support the professionalism of members

Canadian Housing & Renewal Association (CHRA) / Association canadienne d'habitation et de rénovation urbaine (ACHRU)
#310, 130 Slater St., Ottawa ON K1P 6E2 Canada
Tel: 613-594-3007; *Fax:* 613-594-9596
info@chra-achru.ca
www.chra-achru.ca
To provide access to adequate & affordable housing

Canadian Manufactured Housing Institute (CMHI)
#500, 150 Laurier Ave. West, Ottawa ON K1P 5J4 Canada
Tel: 613-563-3520; *Fax:* 613-232-8600
cmhi@cmhi.ca
www.cmhi.ca
To be the voice of the manufactured housing industry in Canada; to seek, identify & solidify the development of new, profitable market opportunities for manufactured housing, both domestically & internationally; to promote housing affordability for all Canadians.

Confederation of Resident & Ratepayer Associations (CORRA)
231 Dunvegan Rd., Toronto ON M5P 2P3 Canada
Fax: 416-483-0122
The association coordinates the activities of & lobbies for member associations to promote better urban life & beneficial legislation. It acts as watchdog to protect city neighbourhoods, parks & waterfront.

Cooperative Housing Association of Newfoundland & Labrador
PO Box 453, #206, 75 Barbour Dr., Mount Pearl NL A1N 2C4 Canada
Tel: 709-747-5615; *Fax:* 709-747-5606
chanal@nl.rogers.com
chanal.no-ip.org
Bill Vardy, President

Cooperative Housing Federation of British Columbia (CHF BC)
#200, 5550 Fraser St., Vancouver BC V5W 2Z4 Canada
Tel: 604-879-5111; *Fax:* 604-879-4611
Toll-Free: 866-879-5111
info@chf.bc.ca
www.chf.bc.ca
To expand non-profit co-operative housing; to promote better housing conditions in BC; to share skills & information with the co-operative housing community; represent housing co-ops to governments & the general public
Thom Armstrong, Executive Director

Cooperative Housing Federation of Canada (CHF Canada) / Fédération de l'habitation coopérative du Canada (FHCC)
#311, 225 Metcalfe St., Ottawa ON K2P 1P9 Canada
Tel: 613-230-2201; *Fax:* 613-230-2231
Toll-Free: 800-465-2752
info@chfcanada.coop
www.chfc.ca
To unite, represent, & serve the co-op housing community across Canada

Federation of Metro Toronto Tenants' Associations (FMTA)
#500, 27 Carlton St., Toronto ON M5B 1L2 Canada
Tel: 416-646-1772; *Fax:* 416-921-4177
Crisis Hot-Line: 416-921-9494
hotline@torontotenants.org; membership@torontotenants.org
www.torontotenants.org
To inform & educate tenants; To encourage the organization of tenants; To lobby for tenant protection laws; To promote affordable housing

Ontario Association of Property Standards Officers Inc.
#1000, 1 Municipal Dr., Aurora ON L4G 6J1 Canada
www.oapso.org

Ontario Non-Profit Housing Association (ONPHA)
#400, 489 College St., Toronto ON M6G 1A5
Tel: 416-927-9144; *Fax:* 416-927-8401
Toll-Free: 800-297-6660
mail@onpha.org; communications@onpha.org
municipal@onpha.org
www.onpha.on.ca
To build a strong non-profit housing sector in Ontario; To strive for excellence in non-profit housing management; To represent non-profit housing
Keith Ward, President
Sharad Kerur, Executive Director
Jo Ferris-Davies, Director, Member Development & Education
Alice Radley, Treasurer
Diana Summers, Manager, Policy, Research, & Government Relations
Rhona Duncan, Coordinator, Communications & Marketing

ShareOwner Education Inc.
#806, 4 King St. West, Toronto ON M5H 1B6
Tel: 416-595-9600; *Fax:* 416-595-0400
Toll-Free: 800-268-6881
customercare@shareowner.com
www.shareowner.com
To offer practical education & portfolio training to individual investors & investment clubs, so that they may invest successfully in quality growth stocks; Increasing stock market literacy
John Bart, Chief Mentor

Human Rights & Civil Liberties

Alberta Civil Liberties Research Centre (ACLRC)
c/o Faculty of Law, University of Calgary, 2500 University Dr. NW, Calgary AB T2N 1N4 Canada
Tel: 403-220-2505; *Fax:* 403-284-0945
aclrc@ucalgary.ca
www.aclrc.com
To promote awareness among Albertans about civil liberties & human rights through research & education

Amnesty International - Canadian Section (English Speaking)
312 Laurier Ave. East, Ottawa ON K1N 1H9 Canada
Tel: 613-744-7667; *Fax:* 613-746-2411
Toll-Free: 800-266-3789
info@amnesty.ca
www.amnesty.ca
AI Canada is part of a worldwide movement which is independent of any government, political grouping, ideology, economic interest or religious creed. It's primary aim is to bring public attention to abuses of human rights standards, particularly cases where people are imprisoned for their beliefs, or "prisoners of conscience." It holds that mass public pressure, expressed through effective forms of action, is critical to preventing & ending human rights violations. It also works to abolish the death penalty, torture, & other cruel treatment of prisoners, to end political killings & "disappearances." It is a registered charity, BN: 118785914RR0001.

Amnistie internationale, Section canadienne (Francophone) / Amnesty International, Canadian Section (Francophone)
6250, boul Monk, Montréal QC H4E 3H7 Canada
Tél: 514-766-9766; *Téléc:* 514-766-2088
Ligne sans frais: 800-565-9766
info@amnistie.ca
www.amnistie.ca
Mouvement d'intervention directe formé de bénévoles qui visent à la libération des prisonniers d'opinion, la tenue de procès équitables pour les prisonniers politiques, l'abolition de la torture et la cessation des "disparitions" et assassinats politiques

Black Coalition of Québec / La Ligue des Noirs du Québec
5201, boul Decarie, Montréal QC H3W 3C2 Canada
Tel: 514-489-3830; *Fax:* 514-489-2843
info@liguedesnoirs.org
www.liguedesnoirs.org
The Coalition speaks for the Black community in the defence of individual human rights and against all forms of discrimination
Dan Philip, Founding Director

British Columbia Civil Liberties Association (BCCLA)
#550, 1188 West Georgia St., Vancouver BC V6E 4A2 Canada
Tel: 604-687-2919; *Fax:* 604-687-3045
info@bccla.org
www.bccla.org
To protect & enhance civil liberties & human rights in British Columbia

Canada Tibet Committee (CTC)
#2250, 300 Léo-Pariseau, Montréal QC H2X 4B3 Canada
Tel: 514-487-0665
ctcoffice@tibet.ca
www.tibet.ca
To create a structure where concerned Canadians can work together with their Tibetan friends to develop increased awareness in Canada.

The Canadian Centre/International P.E.N. (PEN)
#301, 24 Ryerson Ave., Toronto ON M5T 2P3 Canada
Tel: 416-703-8448; *Fax:* 416-703-3870
info@pencanada.ca
www.pencanada.ca
To foster understanding among writers of all nations; to fight for freedom of expression wherever it is endangered; to work for preservation of world's literature
Ellen Seligman, President
Isobel Harry, Executive Director
Kendra Ward, Office Manager

Canadian Civil Liberties Association (CCLA) / Association canadienne des libertés civiles
#506, 360 Bloor St. West, Toronto ON M5S 1X1 Canada
Tel: 416-363-0321; *Fax:* 416-861-1291
mail@ccla.org
www.ccla.org

Canadian Tribute to Human Rights (CTHR) / Monument canadien pour les droits de la personne (MCDP)
#170, 99 - 5th Ave., Ottawa ON K1P 5P5 Canada
Tel: 613-828-5492; *Fax:* 613-828-3647
info@cthr-mcdp.com
www.cthr-mcdp.com
To ensure public awareness of the presence in Ottawa of the Tribute monument as a symbol of Canadians' committment to preserving & fostering human rights; to promote use of the site as a focal point for all groups working for human rights in Canada & internationally; to spread the concept of public places dedicated to human rights in other capital cities of countries that have affirmed the UN Universal Declaration of Human Rights.

Citizens for Public Justice (CPJ)
#501, 309 Cooper St., Ottawa ON K2P 0G5 Canada
Fax: 613-232-1275
Toll-Free: 800-667-8046
cpj@cpj.ca
www.cpj.ca
To promote public justice in Canada by shaping key public policy debates through research and analysis, publishing and public dialogue. CPJ encourages citizens, leaders in society and governments to support policies and practices which reflect God's call for love, justice and stewardship.
Joe Gunn, Executive Director

CPJ Corp. (CPJ)
#501, 309 Cooper St., Ottawa ON K2P 0G5 Canada
Fax: 613-232-1275
Toll-Free: 800-867-8046
cpj@cpj.ca
www.cpj.ca
To promote public justice in Canada byshaping key public policy debates through research & analysis, publishing & public dialogue; CPJ encourages citizens, leaders in society & governments to support policies & practices which reflect God's call for love, justice & stewardship

Equitas - International Centre for Human Rights Education / Equitas - Centre international d'éducation aux droits humains
#1100, 666, rue Sherbrooke ouest, Montréal QC H3A 1E7 Canada
Tel: 514-954-0382; *Fax:* 514-954-0659
info@equitas.org
www.equitas.org
To provide human rights education in Canada & abroad, based on the principles elaborated in the Universal Declaration of Human Rights

Human Rights Institute of Canada (HRIC) / Institut canadien des droits humains
#905, 280 Albert St., Ottawa ON K1P 5G8 Canada
Tel: 613-232-2920; *Fax:* 613-232-3735
hric@humanrightsinstitute.com
www.humanrightsinstitute.com
To advance the Canadian quest for freedom, justice & equality in a democratic society; to do so by cooperation with other groups & individuals, public meetings & conferences, submissions to parliamentary & other bodies, publicity, complaint to United Nations; to use independent, non-partisan professional research as a basis for all positions that may be taken; based on universal declaration of human rights, applies in-depth legal techniques to determine & recommend solutions.

International Centre for Human Rights & Democratic Development (ICHRDD) / Centre international des droits de la personne et du développement démocratique
#1100, 1001, boul de Maisonneuve est, Montréal QC H2L 4P9 Canada
Tel: 514-283-6073; *Fax:* 514-283-3792
dd-rd@dd-rd.ca
www.dd-rd.ca
To work with civil society organizations & governments, in Canada & abroad, for the benefit of developing countries; to act as a mediator, to facilitate dialogue & to work on projects where consensus between civil society & governments has not yet been built; to promote human rights & strengthen democratic institutions around the world through partnerships with human rights, indigenous peoples' & women's rights groups, as well as democratic movements & governments.
Rémy M. Beauregard, President

League for Human Rights of B'nai Brith Canada / Ligue des droits de la personne de B'nai Brith Canada
15 Hove St., Toronto ON M3H 4Y8 Canada
Tel: 416-633-6224; *Fax:* 416-630-2159
Toll-Free: 800-892-2624
league@bnaibrith.ca
www.bnaibrith.ca/league/league.htm
To strive for human rights for all Canadians; to improve inter-community relations; to combat racism & racial discrimination; to prevent bigotry & anti-Semitism.
Frank Dimant, CEO

Macedonian Human Rights Movement of Canada (MHRMC) / Mouvement canadien de défense des droits de la personne dans la communauté macédonienne
#434, 157 Adelaide St., Toronto ON M5H 4E7 Canada
Tel: 416-850-7125; *Fax:* 416-850-7127
info@mhrmi.org
www.mhrmi.org
To secure & maintain the human rights of all Macedonians wherever they live through advocacy & education
Andy Plukov, Treasurer
Luby Vidinovski, Vice-President
Bill Nicholov, President
Mark Opashinov, Secretary

Minority Rights Association of Greater Châteauguay
#310, 155 boul. St.-Jean Baptiste, Châteauguay QC J6K 3B1 Canada
Tel: 450-699-5910
Margaret Wilheim, Contact

Industry

Canadian Mechanical Contracting Education Foundation (CMCEF)
#601, 280 Albert St., Ottawa ON K1P 5G8 Canada
Tel: 613-232-5169; *Fax:* 613-235-2793
cmef@cmcef.org
www.cmcef.org
To ensure a stronger Mechanical Contracting Industry by initiating and conducting essential educational and research programs which enhance this industry's ability to operate efficiently and economically for the benefit of those served by the industry.
Tania Johnston, Executive Director

Information Technology

Association for Image & Information Management International - 1st Canadian Chapter (AIIM Canada)
c/o Teranet Inc., #600, 1 Adelaide St. East, Toronto ON M5C 2V9 Canada
winnie.tsang@teranet.ca
www.aiim.org/chapters/firstcanadian
To connect users & suppliers of e-business technologies & services

Association of Professional Computer Consultants - Canada (APCC)
#400, 2323 Yonge St., Toronto ON M4P 2C9 Canada
Tel: 416-545-5275; *Toll-Free:* 800-487-2722
info@apcconline.com
www.apcconline.com
To promote the interests of independent computer consultants; to provide cost-saving services to members; to provide members with a forum for interaction & exchange

Canadian Association of Internet Providers (CAIP) / Association canadienne des fournisseurs internet (ACFI)
#416, 207 Bank St., Ottawa ON K2P 2N2 Canada
Tel: 613-236-6550; *Fax:* 613-236-8189
info@cata.ca
www.caip.ca
To foster the growth of a healthy & competitive Internet service industry in Canada through collective & cooperative action on issues of mutual interest.
Tom Copeland, Chair

Canadian Association of SAS Users (CASU) / Association canadienne des utilisateurs SAS (ACUS)
#500, 280 King St. East, Toronto ON M5A 1K7 Canada
Tel: 416-363-4424; *Fax:* 416-363-5399
To provide support to all Canadian SAS user groups; to assist them in the most efficient & effective use of the SAS system for information delivery; to provide updates on research & development of institute software & services.

Canadian Community of Computer Educators (CCCE)
15 Lone Oak Ave., Brampton ON L6S 5V4 Canada
info@ccce.on.ca
www.ccce.on.ca
To ensure excellence in education & training to support information technology

Canadian Image Processing & Pattern Recognition Society (CIPPRS) / Association canadienne de traitement d'images et de reconnaissance des formes (ACTIRF)
Dept. of Computer Sciences, Univ. of Western Ontario, Middlesex College 383, London ON N6A 5B7 Canada
Tel: 519-661-2111; *Fax:* 519-661-3515
barron@csd.uwo.ca
www.cipprs.org
To promote research & development activities in image & signal processing for solving pattern recognition problems.

Canadian Information Processing Society (CIPS) / L'Association canadienne de l'informatique (ACI)
#801, 5090 Explorer Dr., Mississauga ON L4W 4T9 Canada
Tel: 905-602-1370; *Fax:* 905-602-7884
Toll-Free: 877-275-2477
info@cips.ca
www.cips.ca
Social Media: www.facebook.com/group.php?gid=2459351719
To define & foster the IT profession; to encourage & support the IT practitioner & to advance the theory & practice of IT, while safeguarding the public interest

CANARIE
#500, 45 O'Connor St., Ottawa ON K1P 1A4 Canada
Tel: 613-943-5454; *Fax:* 613-943-5443
info@canarie.ca
www.canarie.ca
Canada's advanced internet development organization; to facilitate & promote the development of Canada's communications infrastructure; to stimulate next-generation products, applications & services; to communicate the benefits of an information-based society. CANARIE also intends to act as a catalyst and partner with governments, industry and the research community to increase overall IT awareness, ensure continuing promotion of Canadian technological excellence and ultimately, foster long-term productivity and improvement of living standards.
Guy Bujold, President & CEO

Centre international pour le développement de l'inforoute en français (CIDIF)
165, Blvd. Hébert, Edmundston NB E3V 2S8 Canada
Tél: 506-737-5280; *Téléc:* 506-737-5281
info@cidif.org
www.cidif.org
Fournir des outils et des services spécialisés afin de contribuer à rendre l'utilisation de logiciels et l'internet transparente aux usagers de différentes cultures et de différentes langues
Roger Gervais, Directeur général

Chinese Canadian Information Processing Professionals (CIPro)
PO Box 316, 7305 Woodbine Ave., Markham ON L3R 3V7 Canada
info@cipro.ca
www.cipro.ca

COACH - Canada's Health Informatics Association (COACH)
#301, 250 Consumers Rd., Toronto ON M2J 4V6 Canada
Tel: 416-494-9324; *Fax:* 416-495-8723
Toll-Free: 888-253-8554
info@coachorg.com
www.coachorg.com
To improve the health of Canadians & enhance the management of Canada's health system by advancing the practice of health information management & effective utilization of associated technologies

Communications & Information Technology Ontario (CITO)
#200, 2625 Queensview Dr., Ottawa ON K2B 8K2 Canada
Tel: 613-726-3420; *Fax:* 613-726-3424
Toll-Free: 566-759-6014
To be a catalyst for innovation & entrepreneurship in Ontario's communications & information technology industry; to promote the interchange of people, ideas & technologies between industry & universities by advancing university-based research & supporting universities in graduating students in communications & information technology

Electronic Frontier Canada Inc. (EFC) / Frontière électronique du Canada
20 Richmond Ave., Kitchener ON N2G 1Y9 Canada
Tel: 905-525-9140; *Fax:* 905-546-9995
damien@efc.ca
www.efc.ca
EFC works to ensure that the principals embodied in the Canadian Charter of Rights & Freedoms are protected as new computing, communications & information technologies emerge.
David Jones, President
Jeffrey Shallit, Vice-President/Treasurer
Richard Rosenberg, Vice-President

GS1 Canada
#800, 1500 Don Mills Rd., Toronto ON M3B 3L1 Canada
Tel: 416-510-8039; *Fax:* 416-510-1916
Toll-Free: 800-567-7084
info@gs1ca.org
www.gs1ca.org
To act as a facilitator for the use of electronic information transactions in support of Canadian users.

Information & Communications Technology Council of Canada (ICTC) / Conseil des technologies de l'information et des communications du Canada (CTIC)
#300, 116 Lisgar St., Ottawa ON K2P 0C2 Canada
Tel: 613-237-8551; *Fax:* 613-230-3490
info@ictc-ctic.ca
www.ictc-ctic.ca
To serve the software development profession by developing joint ventures in courseware design & delivery, by integrating training & education processes, by helping to ensure sufficient supply & quality of new entrants to the profession & by promoting an attractive image & definition of software workers
Faye West, Chair

Information Resource Management Association of Canada (IRMAC)
PO Box 5639, Stn. A, Toronto ON M5W 1N8 Canada
Tel: 403-329-2672; *Fax:* 403-329-2038
info@irmac.ca
www.irmac.ca
To provide a forum for members to exchange information about data administration & information resource management

Information Technology Association of Canada (ITAC) / Association canadienne de la technologie de l'information
#801, 5090 Explorer Dr., Mississauga ON L4W 4T9 Canada
Tel: 905-602-8345; *Fax:* 905-602-8346
info@itac.ca
www.itac.ca
Represents 1,300 companies in the computing & telecommunications hardware, software, services & electronic content sectors; identifies & leads on issues that affect the industry; advocates initiatives to enable continued growth & development.
Alberta Fraccaro, Accounting Coordinator
Bill Munson, Vice President
Brendan Seaton, President, ITAC Health
Carlo Viola, Director, Finance

Information Technology Industry Alliance of Nova Scotia (ITANS)
PO Box 9410, Stn. A, Halifax NS B3K 5S3 Canada
Tel: 902-423-5332; *Fax:* 902-484-5094
info@itans.ns.ca
www.itans.ns.ca
ITANS mission is to promote the growth and development of the IT Industry in Nova Scotia through the sharing of experiences, internal and external collaborations, and disseminating IT oppourtunities and information.
Michael McConnell, CEO

The Instrumentation, Systems & Automation Society of America (ISA)
PO Box 12277, 67 Alexander Dr., Research Triangle Park NC 27709 USA
Tel: 919-549-8411; *Fax:* 919-549-8288
info@isa.org
www.isa.org
To be the foremost worldwide society involved with the science & application of measurement & control technologies; to advance members' competence, professionalism & recognition

National Capital FreeNet (NCF) / Libertel de la Capitale Nationale
Trailhead Building, #302, 1960 Scott St., Ottawa ON K1Z 8L8 Canada
Tel: 613-520-9001; *Fax:* 613-520-3524
ncf@ncf.ca
www.ncf.ca
Free, computer-based information sharing network; links the people & organization of the National Capital region; provides useful information & enables an open exchange of ideas with the world; prepares people for full participation in a rapidly changing communications environment

Newfoundland & Labrador Association of Technology Companies (NLATC)
#5, 391 Empire Ave., St. John's NL A1E 1W6 Canada
Tel: 709-772-8324; *Fax:* 709-757-6284
info@nati.net
www.nati.net
To act collectively for technical organizations in Newfoundland industry in cooperation with educational & public sectors to promote the growth of innovative technical industries in Newfoundland & Labrador & the rest of Canada
Paul Dubé, Chief Executive Officer

reBOOT Canada
#110, 136 Geary Ave., Toronto ON M6H 4H1 Canada
Tel: 416-534-6017; *Fax:* 416-534-6083
rose@rebootcanada.ca
www.rebootcanada.ca
Refurbishes old computers received from individual & corporate donors & distributes them, free of charge, to other charitable organizations
Nicholas Brinckman, Executive Director

Insurance Industry

Advocis
#209, 390 Queens Quay West, Toronto ON M5V 3A2 Canada
Tel: 416-444-5251; *Fax:* 416-444-8031
Toll-Free: 800-563-5822
info@advocis.ca
www.advocis.ca
To represent what our members do best - Advice & Advocacy; to carry on the tradition of effectively representing our members' interests with all levels of government, regulators, & industry, always with the intention of putting the interests of consumers first

Canadian Association of Blue Cross Plans (CABCP) / Association Canadienne des Croix Bleue (ACCB)
Stn. 2000, Toronto ON M9C 5P1 Canada
Toll-Free: 888-261-4033
www.bluecross.ca
To maintain & monitor standards of performance by association members; to ensure members manage effectively supplementary health, dental, life insurance, & disability income products on an individual and group basis

Canadian Association of Mutual Insurance Companies (CAMIC) / Association canadienne des compagnies d'assurance mutuelles (ACCAM)
#205, 311 McArthur Ave., Ottawa ON K1L 6P1 Canada
Tel: 613-789-6851; *Fax:* 613-789-7665
nlafreniere@camic.ca
www.camic.ca
To provide information, research, advocacy to its members in areas of general concerns & to negotiate supply agreements for goods & services of common needs. Objectives: to promote a strong, health and competitive insurance market; to support regulatory efficiency and legislative change; to inform member companies on matters affecting the industry and to build consensus on action plans; to promote self-regulation for the property and casualty insurance industry

Canadian Board of Marine Underwriters (CBMU)
#100, 2233 Argentia Rd., Mississauga ON L5N 2X7 Canada
Tel: 905-826-4768; *Fax:* 905-826-4873
info@cbmu.com
www.cbmu.com
To procure & disseminate information of interest to marine underwriters & others; to facilitate the exchange of views & ideas which work to improve the marine underwriting industry & marine insurance; to promote & protect the interest of the underwriting community

Canadian Independent Adjusters' Association (CIAA) / Association canadienne des experts indépendants (ACEI)
Centennial Centre, #100, 5401 Eglinton Ave. West, Toronto ON M9C 5K6
Tel: 416-621-6222; *Fax:* 416-621-7776
Toll-Free: 877-255-5589
info@ciaa-adjusters.ca
www.ciaa-adjusters.ca
To provide leadership for independent adjusters in Canada; To develop & maintain high standards of professionalism; To represent the interests of independent adjusters at the regional, provincial, & national levels

Canadian Institute of Actuaries (CIA) / Institut canadien des actuaires (ICA)
#800, 150 Metcalfe St., Ottawa ON K2P 1P1
Tel: 613-236-8196; *Fax:* 613-233-4552
secretariat@actuaries.ca
www.actuaries.ca
To set & ensure educational & professional standards for members; To operate a review & disciplinary system; To maintain liaison with government authorities & other professions & organizations; To promote research

Canadian Life & Health Insurance Association Inc. (CLHIA) / Association canadienne des compagnies d'assurances de personnes inc.
#1700, 1 Queen St. East, Toronto ON M5C 2X9
Tel: 416-777-2221; *Fax:* 416-777-1895
Toll-Free: 800-268-8099
info@clhia.ca
www.clhia.ca
To represent the interests of member life & health insurance companies

Centre for Study of Insurance Operations (CSIO) / Centre d'étude de la pratique d'assurance (CEPA)
#500, 110 Yonge St., Toronto ON M5C 1T4
Tel: 416-360-1773; *Fax:* 416-364-1482
Toll-Free: 800-463-2746
helpdesk@csio.com
www.csio.com
To act as the national standards association for property & casualty insurance by representing property & casualty industry initiatives; To provide a competitive advantage for the independent broker distribution channel
Robert Fitzgerald, Chair
Steven Kaukinen, President
Francine Davis, Manager, EDI & Forms Standards
Sebastian Penalosa, Manager, Network & Membership Services
Connie Strange, Manager, XML Standards

Chambre de l'assurance de dommages (CHAD)
#1200, 999, boul de Maisonneuve ouest, Montréal QC H3A 3L4 Canada
Tél: 514-842-2591; *Téléc:* 514-842-3138
Ligne sans frais: 800-361-7288
info@chad.qc.ca
www.chad.ca
Assurer la protection du public en matière d'assurance de dommages et d'expertise en règlement de sinistres; encadrer de façon préventive et disciplinaire la pratique professionnelle des individus et des organisations oeuvrant dans ces domaines

Chambre de la sécurité financière (CSF)
300, rue Léo-Pariseau, 26e étage, Montréal QC H3A 3C6 Canada
Tél: 514-282-5777; *Téléc:* 514-282-2225
Ligne sans frais: 800-361-9989
renseignements@chambresf.com
www.chambresf.com
Assurer la protection du public en maintenant la discipline et en veillant à la formation et à la déontologie de ses membres
Luc Labelle, Président

Facility Association
PO Box 121, #2400, 777 Bay St., Toronto ON M5G 2C8 Canada
Tel: 416-863-1750; *Fax:* 416-868-0894
Toll-Free: 800-268-9572
mail@facilityassociation.com
www.facilityassociation.com
To ensure the availability of automobile insurance for owners & licensed drivers of motor vehicles who may otherwise have difficulty obtaining such insurance.

Financial Services Commission of Ontario (FSCO) / Commission des services financiers de l'Ontario (CSFO)
PO Box 85, 5160 Yonge St., 17th Fl., Toronto ON M2N 6L9 Canada
Tel: 416-250-7250; *Fax:* 416-590-7070
Toll-Free: 800-668-0128
contactcentre@fsco.gov.on.ca
www.fsco.gov.on.ca
To provide regulatory services that protect the public interest; to make recommendations to the Min. of Finance about the regulared sectors; to provide resources for the proper functioning of the Tribunal

GAMA International Canada / GAMA International du Canada
#209, 390 Queens Quay West, Toronto ON M4V 3A2 Canada
Tel: 416-444-5252; *Fax:* 416-444-8031
Toll-Free: 800-563-5822
info@gamacanada.com
www.gamacanada.com
To focus on professional development for leaders involved in the distribution of financial services

Groupement des assureurs automobiles (GAA)
Tour de la Bourse, CP 336, #2410, 800 Place-Victoria, Montréal QC H3A 3C6 Canada
Tél: 514-288-4321; *Ligne sans frais:* 877-288-4321
cinfo@gaa.qc.ca
www.gaa.qc.ca
Administrer, de façon efficace et selon les décisions du conseil d'administration, tous les mandats certifiés au Groupement des assureurs automobiles par la Loi sur l'assurance automobile du Québec
Brigitte Corbeil, Directeur général

L'Institut d'assurance de dommages du Québec (IADQ)
#2230, 1200, av McGill College, Montréal QC H3B 4G7 Canada
Tél: 514-393-8156; *Téléc:* 514-393-9222
iadqmontreal@iadq.qc.ca
montrealcourriel@institutdassurance.ca
Organiser des cours, des séminaires et des conférences; promouvoir le rayonnement des titres professionnels PAA et FPAA d'assurance du Canada (AIAC & FIAC). Organisme sans but lucratif, qui a été mis sur pied par l'industrie de l'assurance de dommages pour donner la formation professionnelle à tous ceux qui oeuvrent dans ce secteur au Québec

Insurance Brokers Association of Alberta (IBAA)
3010 Calgary Trail, Edmonton AB T6J 6V4 Canada
Tel: 780-424-3320; *Fax:* 780-424-7418
Toll-Free: 800-318-0197
ibaa@ibaa.ca; education@ibaa.ca; convention@ibaa.ca
www.ibaa.ca
To preserve & strengthen insurance brokers

Insurance Brokers Association of British Columbia (IBABC)
#1300, 1095 West Pender St., Vancouver BC V6E 2M6 Canada
Tel: 604-606-8000; *Fax:* 604-683-7831
www.ibabc.org
To promote the member insurance broker as the premiere distributor of general insurance products & services in British Columbia

Insurance Brokers Association of Manitoba (IBAM)
#205, 530 Kenaston Blvd., Winnipeg MB R3N 1Z4 Canada
Tel: 204-488-1857; *Fax:* 204-489-0316
Toll-Free: 800-204-5649
info@ibam.mb.ca
www.ibam.mb.ca
To promote insurance brokers as the primary providers of insurance products & services in Manitoba

Insurance Brokers Association of New Brunswick (IBANB) / Association des courtiers d'assurances du Nouveau-Brunswick
PO Box 1523, #201, 590 Brunswick St., Fredericton NB E3B 5G2 Canada
Tel: 506-450-2898; *Fax:* 506-450-1494
ibanb@nbinsurancebrokers.ca
www.ibanb.org
To champion the professional, independent insurance broker system in New Brunswick

Insurance Brokers Association of Newfoundland (IBAN)
Chimo Bldg., 151 Crosbie Rd., 3rd Floor, St. John's NL A1B 4B4 Canada
Tel: 709-726-4450; *Fax:* 709-754-4399
iban@nfld.net
www.iban.ca
Association of insurance brokers in Newfoundland. Insurance brokers work on behalf of clients to secure the best coverage in the market from federally regulated insurance companies
Mary Geralyn Rahal, Office Administrator

Insurance Brokers Association of Nova Scotia (IBANS)
380 Bedford Hwy, Halifax NS B3M 2L4 Canada
Tel: 902-876-0526; *Fax:* 902-876-0527
info@ibans.com
www.ibans.com
To promote the independent insurance broker as the premier distributor of property & casualty insurance products & other related insurance services in Nova Scotia
Stephen Greene, Executive Director

Insurance Brokers Association of Ontario (IBAO)
#700, 1 Eglinton Ave. East, Toronto ON M4P 3A1 Canada
Tel: 416-488-7422; *Fax:* 416-488-7526
Toll-Free: 800-268-8845
contact@ibao.com
www.ibao.org
To act as the authoritative voice of independent brokers in Ontario; To serve the interests of member brokers; To preserve & enhance the value & integrity of the independent broker insurance distribution system

Insurance Brokers Association of Prince Edward Island
c/o Hyndman & Co. Limited, PO Box 790, 57 Queen St., Charlottetown PE C1A 4A5 Canada
Tel: 902-566-4244; *Fax:* 902-566-5990
hyndmaninsurance@anchorgroup.com
Helen Hyndman, Contact

Insurance Brokers Association of Saskatchewan (IBAS)
#310, 2631 - 28 Ave., Regina SK S4S 6X3 Canada
Tel: 306-525-5900; *Fax:* 306-569-3018
IBASinfo@ibas.sk.ca
www.ibas.sk.ca
To promote & preserve the independent insurance brokerage system as a secure, knowledgeable, cost-effective, customer-oriented, professional method of insurance delivery

Insurance Institute of British Columbia (IIBC)
#1110, 800 West Pender St., Vancouver BC V6C 2V6 Canada
Tel: 604-681-5491; *Fax:* 604-681-5479
Toll-Free: 888-681-5491
IIBCmail@insuranceinstitute.ca
www.iibc.org

Insurance Institute of Canada (IIC) / Institut d'assurance du Canada (IAC)
18 King St. East, 6th Fl., Toronto ON M5C 1C4 Canada
Tel: 416-362-8586; *Fax:* 416-362-4239
Toll-Free: 866-362-8585
IICmail@insuranceinstitute.ca
www.insuranceinstitute.ca
To design, develop, & delivers insurance educational programs & texts; To prepare examinations & awards diplomas; To provide a graduate society; To develop career information on behalf of the property/casualty insurance industry

Insurance Institute of Manitoba (IIM)
#533, 167 Lombard Ave., Winnipeg MB R3B 0V3 Canada
Tel: 204-956-1702; *Fax:* 204-956-0758
iimmail@insuranceinstitute.ca
www.insuranceinstitute.ca
To provide educational services in the general insurance industry in both English and French, such as the Chartered Insurance Professional (CIP), & Fellow Chartered Insurance Professional (FCIP) programs

Insurance Institute of New Brunswick (IINB)
25 Hedgewood Dr., Moncton NB E1E 2W4 Canada
Tel: 506-386-5896; *Fax:* 506-386-1130
IINBmail@insuranceinstitute.ca
www.insuranceinstitute.ca

Insurance Institute of Newfoundland & Labrador Inc. (IINL)
Chimo Bldg., 151 Crosbie Rd., St. John's NL A1B 4B4 Canada
Tel: 709-754-4398; *Fax:* 709-754-4399
IINLmail@insuranceinstitute.ca
www.insuranceinstitute.ca

Insurance Institute of Northern Alberta (IINA)
202 Solar Court, 10350 - 124 St., Edmonton AB T5N 3V9 Canada
Tel: 780-424-1268; *Fax:* 780-420-1940
IINAmail@insuranceinstitute.ca
www.insuranceinstitute.ca
The Insurance Institute of Northern Alberta provides products and services to the general insurance industry, and ensures the maintenance of a uniform standard of education for the general Insurance Business throughout Canada

Insurance Institute of Nova Scotia (IINS)
#503, 73 Tacoma Dr., Dartmouth NS B2W 3Y6 Canada
Tel: 902-433-0070; *Fax:* 902-433-0072
IINSmail@insuranceinstitute.ca
www.insuranceinstitute.ca
To provide educational products & services to the general insurance industry, such as the Chartered Insurance Professional (CIP) & the Fellow Chartered Insurance Professional (FCIP) designation programs

Insurance Institute of Ontario (IIO)
18 King St. East, 16th Fl., Toronto ON M5C 1C4 Canada
Tel: 416-362-8586; *Fax:* 416-362-8081
agervasio@insuranceinstitute.ca
www.insuranceinstitute.ca
To deliver general insurance educational services in English & French, which are consistent with the standardized curriculum offered throughout Canada, such as the Fellow Chartered Insurance Professional (FCIP) & the Fellow Chartered Insurance Professional (FCIP) designation programs

Insurance Institute of Prince Edward Island (IIPEI)
PO Box 811, 51 University Ave., Charlottetown PE C1A 4K8 Canada
Tel: 902-892-1692; *Fax:* 902-368-7305
IIPEImail@insuranceinstitute.ca
www.insuranceinstitute.ca

Insurance Institute of Saskatchewan (IIS)
#310, 2631 - 28 Ave., Regina SK S4S 6X3 Canada
Tel: 306-525-9799; *Fax:* 306-569-3018
IISmail@insuranceinstitute.ca
www.insuranceinstitute.ca
To offer educational products & services to the general insurance industry in both English & French, such as the Fellow Chartered Insurance Professional (FCIP) & the Chartered Insurance Professional (CIP) designation programs
Jennifer Meshka, CIP, President
Lisa Todd, FCIP, CRM, Secretary
Joanne Duke, Manager

Insurance Institute of Southern Alberta (IISA)
#1110, 833 - 4 Ave. SW, Calgary AB T2P 3T5 Canada
Tel: 403-266-3427; *Fax:* 403-269-3199
IISAmail@insuranceinstitute.ca
www.insuranceinstitute.ca
To advance the efficiency, expertise & ability of people employed in the insurance & financial services industry

LOMA Canada
675 Cochrane Dr., East Tower, 6th Floor, Markham ON L3R 0B8 Canada
Tel: 905-530-2302; *Fax:* 905-530-2001
lomacanada@loma.org
www.lomacanada.org
To serve its member companies by encouraging & assisting individuals to acquire knowledge & understanding of business of life & health insurance & related financial services.

Marine Insurance Association of British Columbia (MIABC)
c/o Coast Underwriters Ltd., #1610, 200 Granville St., Vancouver BC V6C 1S4 Canada
Tel: 604-629-3820; *Fax:* 604-629-8561
www.m-i-a-b-c.org
To represent the goals & interests of the marine insurance industry in British Columbia

Nuclear Insurance Association of Canada (NIAC) / Association canadienne d'assurance nucléaire
c/o CGI, 150 Commerce Valley Dr. West, Lock Box 200, Markham ON L3T 7Z3 Canada
Tel: 905-695-6657; *Fax:* 905-771-5312
NIAC is a voluntary, non-profit association of insurers. Members may provide insurance protection by participation in property and liability pools; the association underwrites and accepts nuclear risks located within Canadian territorial limits for Nuclear Liability and Physical Damage (liability &/or property insurance)

Ontario Insurance Adjusters Association (OIAA)
29 De Jong Dr., Mississauga ON L5M 1B9 Canada
Tel: 905-542-0576; *Fax:* 905-542-1301
Toll-Free: 888-259-1555
manager@oiaa.com
www.oiaa.com
To promote & maintain a high standard of ethics in the business of insurance claims adjusting

Ontario Mutual Insurance Association (OMIA)
PO Box 3187, 350 Pinebush Rd., Cambridge ON N3H 4S6 Canada
Tel: 519-622-9220; *Fax:* 519-622-9227
information@omia.com
www.omia.com
To assist mutual insurance companies to achieve excellence in service provision

Regroupement des cabinets de courtage d'assurance du Québec (RCCAQ) / Insurance Brokers Association of Québec - Assembly
#139, 955, rue D'Assigny, Longueuil QC J4K 5C3 Canada
Tél: 450-674-6258; *Téléc:* 450-674-3609
Ligne sans frais: 800-516-6258
info@rccaq.com
www.rccaq.com
Promouvoir les intérêts socio-économiques des membres
Mario Lanouette, Président
Johanne Lamanque, Directrice générale

Reinsurance Research Council (RRC) / Conseil de recherche en réassurance (CRR)
#7, 296 Jarvis St., Toronto ON M5B 2C5 Canada
Tel: 416-968-0183; *Fax:* 416-968-6818
mail@rrccanada.org
www.rrccanada.org
Represents the majority of professional reinsurers registered in Canada; conducts research into all lines of property/casualty reinsurance, presents the views of its members where appropriate, and provides liaison with governments, the primary insurance market, & other interested parties; promotes high standards of service and ethical business practices; develops and maintains cordial relations among members and with kindred associations and the public

Risk & Insurance Management Society Inc. (RIMS)
c/o Thomas Oystrick, RIMS Canada Council, Mount Royal University, 4825 Mount Royal Gate SW, Calgary AB T3E 6K6
canada@rims.org; membership@rims.org
www.rimscanada.ca
To advance the practice of risk management in Canada

Saskatchewan Municipal Hail Insurance Association (SMHI)
2100 Cornwall St., Regina SK S4P 2K7 Canada
Tel: 306-569-1852; *Fax:* 306-522-3717
Toll-Free: 877-414-7644
smhi@smhi.ca
www.smhi.ca
To provide spot-loss hail insurance coverage to Saskatchewan grain farmers at cost

Society of Public Insurance Administrators of Ontario (SPIAO)
c/o The Municipality Of Clarington, 40 Temperance St., Bowmanville ON L1C 3A6 Canada
info@spiao.ca
www.spiao.ca
To exchange knowledge & pursue matters dealing with risk & insurance management; to promote cooperation among all local government bodies which have interests in the field of risk & insurance management; to encourage development of educational training programs; to collect & disperse information

Underwriters' Laboratories of Canada (ULC) / Laboratoires des assureurs du Canada
7 Underwriters Rd., Toronto ON M1R 3A9 Canada
Tel: 416-757-3611; *Fax:* 416-757-8727
Toll-Free: 866-937-3852
ulcinfo@ulc.ca
www.ulc.ca
ULC is an independent product safety testing, certification & inspection organization. It supports domestic governmental product safety regulations, & works with international safety systems to help further trade with adherence to local safety requirements. It develops & publishes standards, classifications & specifications for products as they relate to fire, accident or property hazards, electrical safety.

Interior Design

Associated Designers of Canada (ADC)
#201, 192 Spadina Ave., Toronto ON M5T 2C2 Canada
Tel: 416-410-4209; *Fax:* 416-703-6601
Toll-Free: 800-361-2721
adc@designers.ca
www.designers.ca
To promote, pursue & protect the interests & needs of set, costume, lighting & sound designers working in Canada

Association des designers industriels du Québec (ADIQ)
CP 182, Succ. Rosemont, Montréal QC H1X 3B7 Canada
Tél: 514-287-6531; *Téléc:* 514-278-3049
info@adiq.ca (Noémi Marquis)
www.adiq.ca
Mission est du soutenir, représenter et promourvoir les membres professionels et mettre en valeur la profession.
Mario Gagnon, Président
Assam Michel Daoud, Vice-président

Association of Canadian Industrial Designers (ACID) / Association des designers industriels du Canada
157 Adelaide St. West, Toronto ON M5H 4E7 Canada
info@designcanada.org
www.designcanada.org
To represent Canadian industrial designers throughout world. The ACID represents the collective interests of designers and is dedicated to increasing the knowledge, skill and proficiency of its members through networking, discussion forums, seminars and trade events.

Association of Interior Designers of Nova Scotia (IDNS)
PO Box 2042, Halifax NS B3J 3B4 Canada
Tel: 902-425-4367
info@idns.ca
www.idns.ca
Interior Designers of Nova Scotia (IDNS) is a professional association of registered Interior Designers. IDNA promotes the profession and its mandate acts to serve both the interests of public and the interior design industry. IDNS: protects the health, safety, and well-being of the general public, develops and maintains standards of practice of interior design; encourages the continuing education of practicing interior designers; upholds the Code of Ethics for the professional practice of interior design; promotes and extends the profession of interior design by providing a liaison between the profession and the public.

Association of Registered Interior Designers of New Brunswick (ARIDNB) / Association des designers d'intérieur immatriculés du Nouveau-Brunswick (ADIINB)
PO Box 1541, Fredericton NB E3B 5G2 Canada
Tel: 506-459-3014
info@aridnb.ca
www.aridnb.ca
To establish & maintain standards of knowledge, skill, & professional ethics among association members; to serve the public interest by governing the practice of interior design in New Brunswick

Association of Registered Interior Designers of Ontario (ARIDO)
#220, 6 Adelaide St. East, Toronto ON M5C 1H6 Canada
Tel: 416-921-2127; *Fax:* 416-921-3660
Toll-Free: 800-334-1180
adminoffice@arido.ca
www.arido.ca
To govern the conduct & professional standards of members; To increase awareness of the profession & ensure rights of interior designers & the public they serve

Association professionnelle des designers d'intérieur du Québec (APDIQ)
#306, 19, Cours Le Royer Ouest, Montréal QC H2Y 1W4 Canada
Tél: 514-284-6263; *Téléc:* 514-284-6112
Ligne sans frais: 888-247-2790
apdiq@videotron.ca
www.apdiq.com
Promouvoir la reconnaissance des designers d'intérieur comme ordre professionnel; assurer la qualité de leurs services; les regrouper pour faire évoluer leur profession; veiller aux intérêts du public; édicter et assurer le respect des règles d'éthique professionnelle

British Columbia Industrial Designer Association (BCID)
PO Box 33943, Vancouver BC V6J 4L7 Canada
Tel: 604-608-3204; *Fax:* 604-608-3204
email@bcid.com
www.bcid.com
The Association is the public voice for its members, representing their interests nationally. It maintains a set of standards to preserve the integrity of the profession, and keeps a register of professional industrial designers in the province.

Interior Designers Association of Saskatchewan (IDAS)
PO Box 32005, Stn. Erindale, Saskatoon SK S7S 1N8 Canada
Tel: 306-343-3311; *Fax:* 306-249-3011
char.vaughn@sasktel.net
www.idas.ca
To promote an understanding of the profession to the public & to support members in their profession through continuing education & networking

Interior Designers Institute of British Columbia (IDIBC)
#400, 601 West Broadway, Vancouver BC V5Z 4C2 Canada
Tel: 604-298-5211; *Fax:* 604-421-5211
info@idibc.org
www.idibc.org
To act as the single representative voice of the Interior Design profession in British Columbia; to advance the profession through public recognition & provide leadership & services to members through programs, communication & education; to benefit public health, safety & welfare, contribute to the enhancement of the environment & increase the perception, appreciation & value of design in the community.
Robert Ledingham, RID/IDC, President
Paul Zanette, RID/IDC, Vice President, National

Interior Designers of Alberta (IDA)
PO Box 21171, Edmonton AB T6R 2V4 Canada
Tel: 780-413-0013; *Fax:* 780-413-0076
info@interiordesignalberta.com
www.interiordesignalberta.com

Interior Designers of Canada (IDC) / Designers d'intérieur du Canada
#220, 6 Adelaide St. East, Toronto ON M5C 1H6 Canada
Tel: 416-594-9310; *Fax:* 416-921-3660
info@interiordesigncanada.org
www.interiordesigncanada.org
To advance the interior design industry in Canada through high standards of education for the profession, professional responsibility, professional development, & communication

Professional Interior Designers Institute of Manitoba
137 Bannatyne Ave. East, 2nd Fl., Winnipeg MB R3B 0R3 Canada
Tel: 204-925-4625; *Fax:* 204-925-4624
pidim@shaw.ca
www.pidim.ca

International Cooperation/International Relations

AFS Interculture Canada (AFSIC)
1425, boul René-Lévesque ouest, Montréal QC H3G 1T7 Canada
Tel: 514-288-3282; *Fax:* 514-843-9119
Toll-Free: 800-361-7248
info-canada@afs.org
www.afscanada.org
Social Media: www.facebook.com/group.php?gid=20406511761
To promote global education & international development through intercultural exchange programs for both young people & adults; offers international internships; forms part of the largest network of international exchange programs in the world

Aga Khan Foundation Canada
The Delegation of the Ismaili Imamat, 199 Sussex Dr., Ottawa ON K1N 1K6 Canada
Tel: 613-237-2532; *Fax:* 613-567-2532
Toll-Free: 800-267-2532
info@akfc.ca
www.akfc.ca
To support cost-effective development projects in Asia & Africa in the fields of primary health care, education & rural development, with special attention paid to the needs of women. Major initiatives include: The Pakistan-Canada Social Institutions Development Program; the Tajikistan Institutional Support Program and the Non-Formal Education Program of the Bangladesh Rural Advancement Committee.
Khalil Z. Shariff, CEO

Atlantic Council of Canada (ACC) / Conseil atlantique du Canada (CAC)
Stn. 701, 165 University Ave., Toronto ON M5H 3B8 Canada
Tel: 416-979-1875; *Fax:* 416-979-0825
info@atlantic-council.ca
www.atlantic-council.ca
To inform Canadians of the purpose & benefits of Canada's membership in the Atlantic Alliance & NATO.

Canada World Youth (CWY) / Jeunesse Canada Monde (JCM)
2330, rue Notre-Dame ouest, 3e étage, Montréal QC H3J 1N4 Canada
Tel: 514-931-3526; *Fax:* 514-939-2621
Toll-Free: 800-605-3526
recruitment@cwy-jcm.org
www.canadaworldyouth.org
Social Media: www.facebook.com/group.php?gid=6244934985
To increase people's ability to participate actively in the development of just, harmonious & sustainable societies; to create exceptional learning opportunities for communities, groups & individuals wishing to acquire skills & explore new ideas.

Canadian Association for Latin American & Caribbean Studies (CALACS) / Association canadienne des études latino-américaines et caraïbes (ACELAC)
CCASLS SB-115, Corcordia Univ., 1455 de Maisonneuve ouest, Montréal QC H3G 1M8 Canada
Tel: 514-848-2280; *Fax:* 514-848-4514
calacs_acelac@bellnet.ca
calacs.concordia.ca
To facilitate networking & the exchange of information among those engaged in teaching & research on Latin America & the Caribbean in Canada & abroad; to foster throughout Canada, especially within the universities, colleges, & other centres of higher education, the expansion of information on & interest in Latin America & the Caribbean; to represent the academic & professional interest of Canadian Latin Americanists
Annamaria Piccioni, Executive Director
Stuart McCook, President

Canadian Association for the Study of International Development (CASID) / L'Association canadienne d'études du développement international (ACEDI)
c/o The North-South Institute, #200, 55 Murray St., Ottawa ON K1N 5M3 Canada
Tel: 613-241-3535; *Fax:* 613-241-7435
casid@nsi-ins.ca
www.casid-acedi.ca
National, bilingual, interdisciplinary & pluralistic association devoted to the study of international development in all parts of the world
Diane Pichette, Secretary

Canadian Commission for UNESCO / Commission canadienne pour l'UNESCO
PO Box 1047, 350 Albert St., Ottawa ON K1P 5V8 Canada
Tel: 613-566-4414; *Fax:* 613-566-4405
Toll-Free: 800-263-5588
info@unesco.ca
www.unesco.ca
An arm's length agency of the Government of Canada; to promote Canadian participation in the programmes & activities of UNESCO; to advise the government of Canada on its policies toward UNESCO; to act as a forum for Canadian civil society & government to discuss matters relating to UNESCO
David A. Walden, Secretary-General

Canadian Council for International Co-operation (CCIC) / Conseil canadien pour la coopération internationale
#300, 1 Nicholas St., Ottawa ON K1N 7B7 Canada
Tel: 613-241-7007; *Fax:* 613-241-5302
info@ccic.ca
www.ccic.ca
A coalition of Canadian voluntary sector organizations working globally to achieve sustainable human development; CCIC seeks to end global poverty, & to promote social justice & human dignity for all

Canadian Foundation for the Americas (FOCAL) / Fondation canadienne pour les Amériques
#720, 1 Nicholas St., Ottawa ON K1N 7B7 Canada
Tel: 613-562-0005; *Fax:* 613-562-2525
focal@focal.ca
www.focal.ca
To foster informed & timely debate & dialogue on issues of importance to decision-makers throughout Canada & the Americas; to develop a greater understanding of important hemispheric issues & to help build a stronger community of the Americas
Carlo Dade, Executive Director
Madeleine Bélanger, Director, Communications

Canadian Friends of Burma (CFOB) / Les Amis canadiens de la Birmanie
#206, 145 Spruce St., Ottawa ON K1R 6P1 Canada
Tel: 613-237-8056; *Fax:* 613-563-0017
cfob@cfob.org
www.cfob.org
To promote democracy & human rights in Burma by working within the global movement, & educating & activating Canadian involvement in the struggle for peace in Burma
Tin Maung Htoo, Executive Director

Canadian Friends of Ukraine (CFU)
South Bldg., 620 Spadina Ave., 2nd Fl., Toronto ON M5S 2H4
Tel: 416-964-6644; *Fax:* 416-964-6085
canfun@interlog.com
www.canadianfriendsofukraine.com
To strengthen Canadian-Ukrainian relations; To promote democracy & reform in Ukraine

Canadian Institute for Conflict Resolution (CICR) / Institut canadien pour la résolution des conflits
c/c St. Paul University, 223 Main St., Ottawa ON K1S 1C4 Canada
Tel: 613-235-5800; *Fax:* 613-235-5801
Toll-Free: 866-684-2427
info@cicr-icrc.ca
www.cicr-icrc.ca
To foster, develop & communicate resolution processes for individuals, organizations & communities in Canada & internationally; to embody, within the conflict resolution process, the positive attributes of common sense, sensitivity, compassion & spirituality.

Canadian Institute of Cultural Affairs / Institut canadien des affaires culturelles
655 Queen St. East, Toronto ON M4M 1G4
Tel: 416-691-2316; *Fax:* 416-691-2491
Toll-Free: 877-691-1422
ica@icacan.ca
www.icacan.ca
To empower people to develop leadership capacity; To contribute to positive social change

Canadian International Council (CIC) / Conseil international du Canada
PO Box 210, 45 Willcocks St., Toronto ON M5S 1C7 Canada
Tel: 416-977-9000; *Fax:* 416-946-7319
Toll-Free: 800-668-2442
mailbox@canadianinternationalcouncil.org
www.canadianinternationalcouncil.org
To strengthen Canada's role in international affairs; To advance research & dialogue on international affairs

Canadian Peace Alliance (CPA) / Alliance canadienne pour la paix
#13, 427 Bloor St. West, Toronto ON M5S 1X7 Canada
Tel: 416-588-5555; *Fax:* 416-588-5556
cpa@web.ca
www.acp-cpa.ca
To involve Canadians in the worldwide movement to stop the arms race, ensure the non-violent settlement of disputes & guarantee the security & well-being of all peoples.

Canadian Physicians for Aid & Relief (CPAR)
1425 Bloor St. West, Toronto ON M6P 3L6 Canada
Tel: 416-369-0865; *Fax:* 416-369-0294
Toll-Free: 800-263-2727
info@cpar.ca
www.cpar.ca
Social Media: twitter.com/cpar
To help impoverished communities in developing nations become prosperous while maintaining harmony with the environment; projects tackle all aspects of poverty & emphasize healthy community empowerment & integrated community based development.

CARE Canada
#200, 9 Gurdwara Rd., Ottawa ON K2E 7X6 Canada
Tel: 613-228-5600; *Fax:* 613-226-5777
Toll-Free: 800-267-5232
info@care.ca
www.care.ca
To serve individuals & families in the poorest communities of the world; to promote innovative solutions & to advocate for global responsibility

Carrefour de solidarité internationale inc.
165, rue Moore, Sherbrooke QC J1H 1B8 Canada
Tél: 819-566-8595; *Téléc:* 819-566-8076
info@csisher.com
www.csisher.com
Susciter la solidarité de la population de l'Estrie pour la justice sociale au plan international.

Centre canadien d'étude et de coopération internationale (CECI) / Canadian Centre for International Studies & Cooperation
3000, rue Omer-Lavallée, Montréal QC H1Y 3R8 Canada
Tél: 514-875-9911; *Téléc:* 514-875-6469
Ligne sans frais: 877-875-2324
info@ceci.ca
www.ceci.ca
Le CECI combat la pauvreté et l'exclusion; renforce les capacités de développment des communautés défavorisées; appuie des initiatives de paix, de droits humains et d'équitémobilise des ressources et favorise l'échange de savoir-faire.

CHF
323 Chapel St., Ottawa ON K1N 7Z2 Canada
Tel: 613-237-0180; *Fax:* 613-237-5969
Toll-Free: 866-242-4243
info@chf-partners.ca
www.chf-partners.ca
To assist local NGOs in developing countries involved in community development, with particular emphasis on food production, water supply security, energy & income generation

Child Haven International / Accueil international pour l'enfance
19014 - 7th Conc., RR#1, Maxville ON K0C 1T0 Canada
Tel: 613-527-2829; *Fax:* 613-527-1118
fred@childhaven.ca
www.childhaven.ca
To assist any child of any nationality who needs in-country care or a private family home; to provide institutions & cottage or

village industries for giving training in handcrafts, music, agricultural methods; to promote the integrity of the family by providing help for adolescents or adults who have special needs & by community development & medical aid projects

Children's International Summer Villages (Canada) Inc. (CISV) / Villages internationaux d'enfants
PO Box 1384, Stn. B, Ottawa ON K1P 5R4 Canada
Tel: 613-230-2949
canada@cisv.org
www.cisv.ca
To promote cross-cultural friendship, through educational programs for youth & adults in 60 countries; To prepare indivduals to become active & contributing members of a peaceful society; To stimulate the life-long development of amicable relationships & effective & appropriate leadership towards a fair & just world

Christian Blind Mission International (CBMI)
PO Box 800, 3844 Stoufville Rd., Stouffville ON L4A 7Z9 Canada
Tel: 905-640-6464; *Fax:* 905-640-4332
Toll-Free: 800-567-2264
cbm@cbmcanada.org
www.cbmcanada.org
With core values based on Christian faith, CBMI serves the blind & disabled in the developing world, irrespective of nationality, race, sex, or religion; prevents & treats blindness & other disabilities through medical care, rehabilitation training & integration programs; helps people to help themselves.

CNEC - Partners International
#56, 8500 Torbram Rd., Brampton ON L6T 5C6 Canada
Tel: 905-458-1202; *Fax:* 905-458-4339
Toll-Free: 800-883-7697
info@partnersinternational.ca
www.partnersinternational.ca

CODE
321 Chapel St., Ottawa ON K1N 7Z2 Canada
Tel: 613-232-3569; *Fax:* 613-232-7435
Toll-Free: 800-661-2633
codehq@codecan.org
www.codecan.org
To enable people to learn by developing partnerships that provide resources for learning, to promote awareness & understanding & to encourage self-reliance; to support training for teachers & librarians; to coordinate books donations from North American publishers to schools & libraries in the developing world

CoDevelopment Canada (CODEV)
#260, 2747 East Hastings St., Vancouver BC V5K 1Z8 Canada
Tel: 604-708-1495; *Fax:* 604-708-1497
codev@codev.org
www.codev.org
CoDev is a BC-based, non-profit agency that works for social change in Latin American, facilitating relationships between Northern & Southern organizations that share a commitment to workers' rights, community development & women's rights. It helps organizations involve disenfranchised groups in local decision-making processes, develop policy, & lobby both the public & private sectors. It is a registered charity, BN: 130153463RR0001.

Compassion Canada
PO Box 5591, London ON N6A 5G8 Canada
Tel: 519-668-0224; *Fax:* 519-685-1107
Toll-Free: 800-563-5437
info@compassion.ca
www.compassion.ca
To provide sponsors for children in Third World countries; to aid community development projects in cooperation with Canadian International Development Agency; to be an advocate for children, to release them from their spiritual, economic, social & physical poverty & to enable them to become responsible & fulfilled Christian adults

Conseil canadien de la coopération et de la mutualité (CCCM)
275, rue Bank, 4e étage, Ottawa ON K2P 2L6 Canada
Tél: 613-789-5492; *Téléc:* 613-789-0743
info@cccm.coop
www.cccm.coop
Le Conseil vise à promouvoir la coopération en vue du développement socio-économique des communautés francophones du Canada.
Brigitte Gagné, Directrice générale

Conseil de coopération de l'Ontario (CCO)
#201, 435, boul St-Laurent, Ottawa ON K1K 2Z8 Canada
Tél: 613-745-8619; *Téléc:* 613-745-4649
Ligne sans frais: 866-290-1168
info@cco.coop
www.cco.coop
Favoriser la prise en charge socio-économique de la communauté francophone de l'Ontario par le biais de la coopération

Conseil québécois de la coopération et de la mutualité (CCQ)
#204, 5955, rue Saint-Laurent, Lévis QC G6V 3P5 Canada
Tél: 418-835-3710; *Téléc:* 418-835-6322
info@coopquebec.coop
www.coopquebec.qc.ca
Organisme de regroupement, sur une base volontaire, des organisations coopératives du Québec pour favoriser l'action concertée de ses membres, promouvoir l'authenticité coopérative, défendre les intérêts de ses membres

CUSO-VSO
44 Eccles St., Ottawa ON K1R 6S4 Canada
Tel: 613-829-7445; *Fax:* 613-829-7996
Toll-Free: 888-434-2876
questions@cuso-vso.org
www.cuso-vso.org
Social Media: www.facebook.com/cusovso
CUSO-VSO is a non-profit development agency that works through skilled volunteers to aid global social justice; to address poverty, human rights violations, HIV/AIDS, inequity & environmental degradation; to give Canadians information, the experiences & the tools they need to become active global citizens.

Forum for International Trade Training (FITT) / Forum pour la formation en commerce international
#300, 116 Lisgar St., Ottawa ON K2P 0C2 Canada
Tel: 613-230-3553; *Fax:* 613-230-6808
Toll-Free: 800-561-3488
info@fitt.ca
www.fitt.ca
Committed to providing quality programs' training & certification in international trade designed to prepare businesses & individuals to compete successfully in world markets.
Caroline Tompkins, CAE, President

Group of 78 / Groupe des 78
#206, 145 Spruce St., Ottawa ON K1R 6P1 Canada
Tel: 613-230-0860; *Fax:* 613-563-0017
group78@web.net
www.web.net/~group78
The association advocates peace, disarmament, sustainable development & strengthening of the United Nations. It is a registered charity, BN : 130562085RR0001.

HOPE International Development Agency
214 - 6 St., New Westminster BC V3L 3A2 Canada
Tel: 604-525-5481; *Fax:* 604-525-3471
Toll-Free: 866-525-4673
hope@hope-international.com
www.hope-international.com
To help the poverty-stricken section of Third World people to attain the basic necessities of life; to inform Canadians regarding issues related to the developing world & HOPE's activities; their mandate is to provide alternative technological and educational support to people in developing countires where enviornmental countries where economic, and/or social circumstances have interfered with the ability of local communities to sustain themselves by using traditional methods. Other offices in Afghanistan, Australia, Cambodia, Ethiopia, Japan, Myanmar, New Zealand, the U.K., and the U.S.

Horizons of Friendship (HOF)
PO Box 402, Stn. Main, 50 Covert St., Cobourg ON K9A 4L1 Canada
Tel: 905-372-5483; *Fax:* 905-372-7095
Toll-Free: 888-729-9928
info@horizons.ca
www.horizons.ca
To address the root causes of poverty & injustice through the cooperation of people from the south & north; To support Central American & Mexican partner organizations which undertake local initiatives; To raise awareness in Canada of global issues; To work with Canadian organizations at the local & national levels

Inter Pares / Among Equals
221 Laurier Ave. East, Ottawa ON K1N 6P1 Canada
Tel: 613-563-4801; *Fax:* 613-594-4704
Toll-Free: 866-563-4801
info@interpares.ca
www.interpares.ca
To build equality of people, North & South, by collaborating with & supporting justice for people around the world; Inter Pares applies 4 principles: Leadership by Women, Participation, Sustainability & Respect for Cultural Values

International Relief Agency Inc. (IRA)
#84, 95 Wood St., Toronto ON M4Y 2Z3 Canada
Tel: 416-928-0901
ira@ica.net
To promote free enterprise, national freedoms & democracy

Mahatma Gandhi Canadian Foundation for World Peace
PO Box 60002, RPO University of Alberta, Edmonton AB T6G 2S4 Canada
Tel: 780-492-5504; *Fax:* 780-492-0113
yhong@ualberta.ca
www.gandhi.ca
To conduct programs & activities that promote the teachings & philosophy of Mahatma Gandhi in order to advance peace & understanding amongst peoples of the world
Prem Kalia, Chair

Manitoba Council for International Cooperation (MCIC) / Conseil du Manitoba pour la coopération internationale
#302, 280 Smith St., Winnipeg MB R3C 1K2 Canada
Tel: 204-987-6420; *Fax:* 204-956-0031
info@mcic.ca; mcic@web.ca
www.mcic.ca
To promote international development that protects the environment; To coordinate the development work of member agencies

The Marquis Project, Inc.
912 Rosser Ave., Brandon MB R7A 0L4 Canada
Tel: 204-727-5675; *Fax:* 204-727-5683
marquisp@mts.net
www.marquisproject.com
To inform rural Manitobans of global issues; to link concerns to those of Third World peoples; to encourage concrete positive action in response to global concerns

Ontario Council for International Cooperation (OCIC) / Conseil de l'Ontario pour la coopération internationale
#405, 344 Bloor St. West, Toronto ON M6S 5A2 Canada
Tel: 416-972-6303; *Fax:* 416-972-6996
info@ocic.on.ca
www.ocic.on.ca
Community of Ontario-based international development and global education organizations and individual associate members working globally for social justice

Operation Eyesight Universal
4 Parkdale Cres. NW, Calgary AB T2N 3T8 Canada
Tel: 403-283-6323; *Fax:* 403-270-1899
info@operationeyesight.ca
www.operationeyesight.ca
To eliminate avoidable blindness through the development & support of permanent, self-sustaining, quality blindness prevention & sight restoration programs for those people in greatest need

Oxfam Canada
#400, 250 City Centre Ave., Ottawa ON K1R 6K7 Canada
Tel: 613-237-5236; *Fax:* 613-237-0524
Toll-Free: 800-466-9326
info@oxfam.ca; donor_relations@oxfam.ca
www.oxfam.ca
To build solutions for the creation of a fair world, without poverty & injustice

Peace Brigades International (Canada) (PBI)
145 Spruce St., Ottawa ON K1R 6P1 Canada
Tel: 613-237-6968
info@pbicanada.org
www.pbicanada.org/home
To explore & implement non-violent approaches to peacekeeping & support for basic human rights; to provide protective accompaniment & peace education training in Colombia, Indonesia, & Mexico
Christine Jones, National Coordinator

Physicians for Global Survival (Canada) (PGS) / Médecins pour la survie mondiale (Canada)
#208, 145 Spruce St., Ottawa ON K1R 6P1 Canada
Tel: 613-233-1982; *Fax:* 613-233-9028
pgsadmin@web.ca
www.pgs.ca
Committed to the abolition of nuclear weapons, the prevention of war, the promotion of non-violent means of conflict resolution & social justice in a sustainable world

Project Peacemakers
745 Westminster Ave., Winnipeg MB R3G 1A5 Canada
Tel: 204-775-8178; *Fax:* 204-784-1339
info@projectpeacemakers.org
www.projectpeacemakers.org
Social Media:
facebook.com/pages/project-peacemakers/108617822532248
Project Peacemakers is a group of people working for peace from a faith perspective. Its activities are varied, from peace delegations in war zones to educational forums on such issues as child soldiers & violent video games.

Project Ploughshares
57 Erb St. West, Waterloo ON N2L 6C2 Canada
Tel: 519-888-6541; *Fax:* 519-888-0018
plough@ploughshares.ca
www.ploughshares.ca
Ecumenical peace agency of the Canadian Council of Churches that identifies, develops & advances approaches that build peace & prevent war

Saskatchewan Council for International Co-operation (SCIC) / Conseil de la Saskatchewan pour la co-opération internationale
2138 McIntyre St., Regina SK S4P 2R7 Canada
Tel: 306-757-4669; *Fax:* 306-757-3226
scic@web.net
www.earthbeat.sk.ca
To act as the umbrella organization for international development agencies in Saskatchewan; to distribute international development funds provided by the Government of Saskatchewan; to facilitate communications among member agencies in Saskatchewan and across Canada; to support cooperative government relations, public education, & fundraising

Save a Family Plan (SAFP)
PO Box 3622, London ON N6A 4L4 Canada
Tel: 519-672-1115; *Fax:* 519-672-6379
safpinfo@safp.org
www.safp.org
Implements sustainable family & community development programs in 5 states in India, with 41 social service societies, 26 homes of health, approximately 10,550 grass roots community organiziations & 15,000 poor families; programs are developed through needs assessments; within all aspects of programming, environmental & gender impact assessments are undertaken. Offices in Canada, the U.S. & India

Save the Children - Canada (SCC) / Aide à l'enfance - Canada
#300, 4141 Yonge St., Toronto ON M2P 2A8 Canada
Tel: 416-221-5501; *Fax:* 416-221-8214
Toll-Free: 800-668-5036
sccan@savethechildren.ca
www.savethechildren.ca
Fights for children's rights; delivers immediate & lasting improvements to children's lives worldwide in Canada & 10 countries overseas

Science for Peace (SfP) / Science et paix
c/o University College, #306A, 15 King's College Circle, Toronto ON M5S 3H7
Tel: 416-978-3606; *Fax:* 416-978-3606
sfp@physics.utoronto.ca
www.scienceforpeace.ca
To understand & act against forces of militarism, social injustice, & environmental destruction

United Nations Association in Canada (UNAC) / Association canadienne pour les Nations-Unies (ACNU)
#300, 309 Cooper St., Ottawa ON K2P 0G5 Canada
Tel: 613-232-5751; *Fax:* 613-563-2455
info@unac.org
www.unac.org
To study international problems & Canada's relationship to them as a member of the UN & its related agencies; to foster mutual understanding, goodwill & cooperation between the people of Canada & those of other countries, with the object of promoting peace & justice; to study possible courses of action in the field of international affairs; to work for support by the government & the people of Canada for desirable policies; to furnish information about & stimulate public interest in the UN & its various agencies which have been established for direct or indirect promotion of international order, justice & security; to foster national commitment to principles of multilateralism & international cooperation

World Federalist Movement - Canada (WFMC)
#207, 145 Spruce St., Ottawa ON K1R 6P1 Canada
Tel: 613-232-0647; *Fax:* 613-563-0017
wfcnat@web.ca
www.worldfederalistscanada.org
Education, research, political support for strengthening the United Nations & rule of law in world affairs
Warren Allmand, PC, OC, QC, President
Fergus Watt, Executive Director
Simon Rosenblum, Chair

World University Service of Canada (WUSC) / Entraide universitaire mondiale du Canada (EUMC)
1404 Scott St., Ottawa ON K1Y 2N2 Canada
Tel: 613-798-7477; *Fax:* 613-798-0990
Toll-Free: 800-267-8699
wusc@wusc.ca
www.wusc.ca
We believe that all peoples are entitled to the knowledge & skills necessary to contribute to a more equitable world; to foster human development & global understanding through education & training
Paul Davidson, Executive Director
Ravi Gupta, Associate Executive Director

World Vision Canada (WVC) / Vision Mondiale
1 World Dr., Mississauga ON L5T 2Y4 Canada
Tel: 905-565-6100; *Fax:* 905-696-2162
Toll-Free: 866-595-5550
info@worldvision.ca
www.worldvision.ca
An international partnership of Christians committed to the poor; a Christian relief organization dedicated to children, families and communities, with a mission to overcome poverty and injustice, and serve all people regardless of religion, race, ethnicity or gender; active in 90+ countries around the world.
Dave Toycen, President & CEO

Labour Relations

ADR Institute of Canada (ADRIC) / Institut d'arbitrage et de médiation du Canada
#405, 234 Eglinton Ave. East, Toronto ON M4P 1K5 Canada
Tel: 416-487-4733; *Fax:* 416-487-4429
Toll-Free: 877-475-4353
admin@adrcanada.ca
www.adrcanada.ca
To promote the use of arbitration & mediation (ADR - alternative dispute resolution) to settle disputes; to provide information & education on ADR to practitioners, parties, the public, & the business, professional & government communities; to assist those wishing to use ADR through the provision of Arbitration & Mediation Rules, administrative services, & information about the process & member arbitrators & mediators

Association canadienne des relations industrielles (ACRI) / Canadian Industrial Relations Association
Département des relations industrielles, Université Laval, Pavillon J.-A.-deSève, Sainte-Foy QC G1K 7P4 Canada
Tél: 418-656-2468; *Téléc:* 418-656-3175
acri-cira@rlt.ulaval.ca
www.cira-acri.ca
Promouvoir la discussion, la recherche, et la formation dans le domaine des relations industrielles

Association of Workers' Compensation Boards of Canada (AWCBC) / Association des commissions des accidents du travail du Canada
6551B Mississauga Rd., Mississauga ON L5N 1A6 Canada
Tel: 905-542-3633; *Fax:* 905-542-0039
contact@awcbc.org
www.awcbc.org
To facilitate cooperation among Canadian Boards & Commissions; to foster greater public understanding or dialogue about workplace health & safety & workers' compensation

Canadian Association of Administrators of Labour Legislation (CAALL) / Association canadienne des administrateurs de la législation ouvrière (ACALO)
CAALL Secretariat, Phase II, Place du Portage, 165, rue Hôtel-de-Ville, 8e étage, Gatineau QC K1A 0J2 Canada
Tel: 819-953-0969; *Fax:* 819-953-9779
CAALL-secretariat@hrsdc-rhdsc.gc.ca
www.caall-acalo.org/home_e.shtml
To provide a forum for federal, provincial, & territorial senior officials; to develop agenda, background papers. & logistics for meetings of Ministers responsible for Labour; to follow-up on issues as directed by Ministers

Canadian Association of Labour Media (CALM) / Association canadienne de la presse syndicale (ACPS)
76 Westmount Ave., Toronto ON M6H 3K1
Tel: 416-656-2256; *Fax:* 416-656-7649
Toll-Free: 888-290-2256
editor@calm.ca
www.calm.ca
To provide training, labour-friendly news, & graphics for labour communicators

Canadian Committee on Labour History (CCLH) / Comité canadien sur l'histoire du travail
c/o Canadian Committee on Labour History, Athabasca University, #1200, 10011 - 109 St., Edmonton AB T5J 3S8 Canada
cclh@athabascau.ca
www.cclh.ca
To promote & publish scholarly research in the area of Canadian labour history & related topics
G.S. Kealey, Treasurer

Canadian Injured Workers Alliance (CIWA) / L'Alliance canadienne des victimes d'accidents et de maladies du travail (ACVAMT)
PO Box 10098, 1201 Jasper Dr., Thunder Bay ON P7B 6T6 Canada
Tel: 807-345-3429; *Fax:* 807-344-8683
Toll-Free: 877-787-7010
ciwa@vianet.ca
www.ciwa.ca
To support & strengthen the work of local & provincial groups by providing a forum for exchanging information & experiences; To provide training & educational resources in partnership with these groups to ensure that injured workers maintain control over their destinies & that the groups themselves be democratically controlled by the workers
Phil Brake, National Coordinator

Cape Breton Injured Workers Association (CBIWA)
714 Alexandra St., Sydney NS B1S 2H4 Canada
Tel: 902-539-4650; *Fax:* 902-539-4171
cbiaw@ns.aliantzinc.ca
www.cbiwa.com
The Cape Breton Injured Workers Association is a volunteer group, located in Sydney, Nova Scotia working on behalf of injured workers by providing information, assisting with claims and appeals, and continuing a dialogue with the Workers' Compensation Board of Nova Scotia.

Centre canadien d'arbitrage commercial (CCAC) / Canadian Commercial Arbitration Centre (CCAC)
#06, 215, rue Caron, Québec QC G1K 5V6 Canada
Tél: 418-649-1374; *Téléc:* 418-649-0845
Ligne sans frais: 877-909-3794
info@ccac-adr.org
www.ccac-adr.org
Fournir des services de conciliation, de médiation et d'arbitrage pour les activités commerciales et de consommation; offrir des activités de formation aux arbitres et médiateurs; analyse de dossiers litigieux et études pour des organismes privés et publics

Construction Labour Relations - An Alberta Association (CLRA)
#207, 2725 - 12 St. NE, Calgary AB T2E 7J2 Canada
Tel: 403-250-7390; *Fax:* 403-250-5516
Toll-Free: 800-308-9466
www.clra.org
To represent construction employers in collective bargaining, collective agreement administration, administrative labour law, lobbying.
R. Neil Tidsbury, President

Construction Labour Relations Association of British Columbia
PO Box 820, 97 - 6 St., New Westminster BC V3L 4Z8 Canada
Tel: 604-524-4911; *Fax:* 604-524-3925
wendym@clra-bc.com
www.clra-bc.com

Construction Labour Relations Association of Newfoundland & Labrador Inc. (CLRA)
Ultramar Bldg., Main Floor, PO Box 8144, Stn. A, 39 Pippy Pl., St. John's NL A1B 3M9 Canada
Tel: 709-753-5770; *Fax:* 709-753-5771
nchaplin@clra.nf.net

Institut de médiation et d'arbitrage du Québec (IMAQ)
CP 874, Succ. B, Montréal QC H3B 3k5 Canada
Tél: 514-282-3327; *Téléc:* 514-282-2214
info@imaq.org
www.imaq.org
Promouvoir les méthodes alternatives de résolution de conflits (médiation, arbitrage); donner accès par internet à la population et aux entreprises à une banque de médiateurs et d'arbitres accrédités selon leur: spécialité (médiateur ou arbitre), région, langue de communication, catégorie de membre, profession, domaine d'expertise

Inter-American Commercial Arbitration Commission (IACAC)
OAS Administrative Bldg., Rm. 211, 19th & Constitution Ave. NW, Washington DC 20006 USA
Tel: 202-458-3249; *Fax:* 202-458-3293
sice@sice.oas.org
To promote conciliation, amicable composition & arbitration in the international commercial settling of disputes in the Western hemisphere

Provincial Building & Construction Trades Council of Ontario
35 International Blvd., Toronto ON M9W 6H3 Canada
Tel: 416-679-8887; *Fax:* 416-679-8882
info@ontariobuildingtrades.com
www.ontariobuildingtrades.com

Pulp & Paper Employee Relations Forum
6035 - 237 A Place, Langley BC V2Z 1A7 Canada
Tel: 604-532-0642; *Fax:* 604-532-0639
smaclean@paperforum.com
paperforum.com
To act primarily as a research & information service for the industry; to service the pulp & paper industry in job evaluation, benefit & pension plan administration & trusteeship, contract interpretation & any other matters relating to labour relations

Union of Injured Workers of Ontario, Inc.
2888 Dufferin St., Toronto ON M6B 3S6 Canada
Tel: 416-785-8787; *Fax:* 416-785-6390
uiw@web.net
Serving injured workers & their families; advocacy, counselling, information & referral
Philip Biggin, Executive Director

Western Employers Labour Relations Association
#203, 27126 Fraser Hwy., Langley BC V4W 3P6 Canada
Tel: 604-857-5540; *Fax:* 604-857-5547
westernemployers@welra.com
www.welra.com

World at Work
PO Box 4520, Stn. A, Toronto ON M5W 4M4 Canada
Toll-Free: 877-951-9191
customerrelations@worldatwork.com
www.worldatwork.org
To promote the education of compensation & benefits professionals
Anne Ruddy, Executive Director

Labour Unions

Agriculture Union
#1000, 233 Gilmour St., Ottawa ON K2P 0P2 Canada
Tel: 613-560-4306; *Fax:* 613-235-0517
www.agrunion.com
To advance the workplace interests of its membership; To fight for a society that recognizes the value of the important public services provided by Agriculture Union members
Bob Kingston, National President

Air Canada Pilots Association (ACPA) / L'Association des pilotes d'Air Canada
#205, 6299 Airport Rd., Mississauga ON L4V 1N3 Canada
Tel: 905-678-9008; *Fax:* 905-678-9016
Toll-Free: 800-634-0944
info@acpa.ca
acpa.ca
Andy Wilson, President
Ron Pellatt, Secretary-Treasurer
Paul Strachan, Chair, Master Executive Council

Air Line Pilots Association, International - Canada (ALPA)
#1301, 155 Queen St., Ottawa ON K1P 6L1 Canada
Tel: 613-569-5668; *Fax:* 613-569-5681
www.alpa.org
Social Media:
www.facebook.com/pages/We-Are-ALPA/200676905671
To promote & represent the interests of the airline pilot profession & to safeguard the rights of individual members; to promote & maintain the highest standards of flight safety; to function as trade union & professional association
John Prater, President
W. Randolph Helling, Sec.-Treas.

Alberta Federation of Labour (AFL) / Fédération du travail de l'Alberta
10654 - 101 St., Edmonton AB T5H 2S1
Tel: 780-483-3021; *Fax:* 780-484-5928
Toll-Free: 800-661-3995
afl@afl.org
www.afl.org
Social Media:
www.facebook.com/group.php?gid=14904202843997O
To act as a central labour body, representing Alberta's organized workers & their families; To improve conditions for Alberta's workers, their families, & communities
Gil McGowan, President
Nancy Furlong, Secretary-Treasurer
Linda Robinson, Financial Administrator
Jerry Toews, Community Organizer
Terry Inigo-Jones, Senior Staff Contact, Communications

Alberta Union of Provincial Employees / Syndicat de la fonction publique de l'Alberta
10451 - 170 St., Edmonton AB T5P 4S7 Canada
Tel: 780-930-3300; *Fax:* 780-930-3392
Toll-Free: 800-232-7284
www.aupe.org
Carl Soderstrom, Director, Labour Relations
Ron Hodgins, Executive Director

Alliance des professeures et professeurs de Montréal (APPM)
8225, boul Saint-Laurent, Montréal QC H2P 2M1 Canada
Tél: 514-384-5756; *Téléc:* 514-383-4880
presidence@alliancedesprofs.qc.ca
www.alliancedesprofs.qc.ca
Salvadora Garcia, Directrice générale

Alliance du personnel professionnel et technique de la santé et des services sociaux (APTS)
#1050, 1111 rue Saint-Charles Ouest, Longueuil QC J4K 5G4 Canada
Tél: 450-670-2411; *Téléc:* 450-679-0107
Ligne sans frais: 866-521-2411
info@aptsq.com
www.aptsq.com
Regrouper les organisations syndicales représentant toutes les catégories des personnes salariées professionnelles ou paramédicales travaillant dans le domaine de la santédéfendre, promouvoir et sauvegarder les intérêts collectifs des membres
Dominique Verreault, Présidente
Thérèse Sainte-Marie, Directrice administrative

Alliance of Canadian Cinema, Television & Radio Artists (ACTRA) / Alliance des artistes canadiens du cinéma, de la télévision et de la radio
#300, 625 Church St., Toronto ON M4Y 2G1 Canada
Tel: 416-489-1311; *Fax:* 416-489-8076
Toll-Free: 800-387-3516
national@actra.ca
www.actra.ca
Social Media: twitter.com/ACTRAnat
To represent performers in recorded media; to negotiate & administer collective agreements which set minimum rates & basic conditions governing work; to advocate public policies designed to create strong Canadian broadcasting & film industries in order to provide work opportunities for members in their own country
Raymond Guardia, Regional Executive Director
Ferne Downey, National President
Anna Falsetta, National Director, Finance & Administration

Amalgamated Transit Union (AFL-CIO/CLC) / Syndicat uni du transport (FAT-COI/CTC)
5025 Wisconsin Ave. NW, Washington DC 20016 USA
Tel: 202-537-1645; *Fax:* 202-244-7824
www.atu.org

American Federation of Musicians of the United States & Canada (AFL-CIO/CLC) (AFM) / Fédération des musiciens des États-Unis et du Canada (FAT-COI/CTC)
#600, 1501 Broadway, New York NY 10036 United States
Tel: 212-869-1330; *Fax:* 212-764-6134
www.afm.org
The largest organization in the world which represens of professional musicians in both Canada and the US. Helps in negotiating fair agreements, protectingownership of recorded music, securing benefits such as health care and pension or lobbying our legislators. AFM is committed to raising industry standards and placing the professional musician in the foreground of the cultural landscape.

Association canadienne des métiers de la truelle, section locale 100 (CTC) / Trowel Trades Canadian Association, Local 100 (CLC)
a/s FTQ-Construction, #2900, 565, rue Crémazie est, Montréal QC H2M 2V6 Canada
Tél: 514-381-7300; *Téléc:* 514-381-5173
Ligne sans frais: 877-666-4060
www.ftqconstruction.org
La FTQ-Construction a, bien entendu, de manière très précise le mandat de négocier les conventions collectives applicables dans les sous secteurs d'activités (industriel, commercial et institutionnel, génie civil et voirie, résidentiel) et de voir à leur application. Mais bien au-delà de ce mandat traditionnel, la FTQ-Construction veut s'assurer d'être présent dans l'ensemble des débats représentant un intérêt pour les travailleurs et les travailleuses qu'il représente.
Yves Mercure, Président

Association nationale des peintres et métiers connexes, section locale 99 (CTC) (ANPMC) / National Association of Painters & Allied Trades, Local 99 (CLC)
#200, 5275, rue Jean-Talon est, Saint-Léonard QC H1S 1L2 Canada
Tél: 514-593-5413; *Téléc:* 514-727-8331
Ligne sans frais: 877-593-5413
info@local99.org
local99.org/index.asp
Aider nos membres dans leur métier; faire respecter les conventions collectives sur les chantiers
Georges Lannéval, Directeur général

Association of Allied Health Professionals: Newfoundland & Labrador (Ind.) (AAHP) / Association des professionnels unis de la santé: Terre-Neuve et Labrador (ind.)
6 Mount Carson Ave., Mount Pearl NL A1N 3W9 Canada
Tel: 709-722-3353; *Fax:* 709-722-0987
Toll-Free: 800-728-2247
info@aahp.nf.ca
www.aahp.nf.ca
Patti O'Keefe, President

Association of Canadian Film Craftspeople
Local 2020 Communications, Energy & Paperworkers Union of Canada, #108, 3993 Henning Dr., Burnaby BC V5C 6P7 Canada
Tel: 604-299-2232; *Fax:* 604-299-2243
info@acfcwest.com
www.acfcwest.com
Wendy Subity, President
Richard Chilton, Ssecretary/Treasurer
Greg Chambers, Business Manager

Association of Canadian Financial Officers (ACFO) / Association canadienne des agents financiers
#400, 2725 Queensview Dr., Ottawa ON K2B 0A1 Canada
Tel: 613-728-0695; *Fax:* 613-761-9568
Toll-Free: 877-728-0695
general@acfo-acaf.com
www.acfo-acaf.com
To unite in a democratic organization all public service financial administrators for which the association becomes or applies to become a bargaining agent; to serve the welfare of its members through effective collective bargaining with their employers; to obtain for members the best levels of compensation for services rendered to their employers & the best terms & conditions of employment; to protect the rights & interests of all members in all matters upon their employment or upon their relationship with their employers; to seek to maintain high professional standards & promote their professional development; to affiliate as appropriate with other associations, unions or labour organizations for the purpose of enhancing the interests of members in the attainment of their professional & bargaining goals
Milt Isaacs, CMA, President & Chair
Robert Loiselle, CGA, Executive Vice-President
Raoul Andersen, MBA, Vice-President
Tony Bourque, CGA, Vice-President
Karen Hall, CGA, Vice-President
Nicole Bishop-Tempke, CGA, Vice-President
John Leduc, CGA, MBA, Vice-President
Daniel J. Larose, Executive Director

Association of New Brunswick Professional Educators (ANBPE) / Association des éducateurs professionnels du Nouveau-Brunswick
c/o Wayne Milner, Counselling Services, NBCC Moncton, #1101A, 1234 Mountain Rd., Moncton NB E1C 8H9 Canada
To operate as a bargaining unit of the New Brunswick Union of Public & Private Employees (NBUPPE / NUPGE)

Association professionnelle des ingénieurs du gouvernement du Québec (ind.) (APIGQ) / Association of Professional Engineers of the Government of Québec (Ind.)
Complexe Iberville, #600, 2954, boul Laurier, Sainte-Foy QC G1V 4T2 Canada
Tél: 418-683-3633; *Téléc:* 418-683-6878
lepont@apigq.qc.ca
www.apigq.qc.ca
Association professionnelle des ingénieurs du Gouvernement de Québec.
Michel Gagnon, ing., Président

Association professionnelle des inhalothérapeutes du Québec (ind.) / Professional Association of Inhalation Therapists of Québec (Ind.)
#201, 4101, rue Molson, Montréal QC H1Y 3L1 Canada
Tél: 514-251-8050; *Téléc:* 514-259-8084
Ligne sans frais: 800-361-3498
accueil@apiq.ca
www.apiq.ca
négocier une convention collective adaptée aux besions des membres; voir à l'application de la convention collective; défendre et promouvoir les intérêts sociaux économiques des membres; améliorer les conditions de travail des membres; faciliter des relations de travail harmonieuses au niveau local grâce à la tenue de comités de relations professionnelles (CRP); adapter les conditions de travail des membres au vécu et aux impératifs du milieu; promourvoir une vie syndicale active.

Association professionnelle des technologistes médicaux du Québec (ind.) / Québec Professional Association of Medical Technologists (Ind.)
1595, rue St-Hubert, 3e étage, Montréal QC H2L 3Z2 Canada
Tél: 514-524-3734; *Téléc:* 514-524-7863
Ligne sans frais: 800-361-4306
info@aptmq.qc.ca
L'étude, la sauvegarde et le développement des intérêts économiques, sociaux, moraux, éducatifs et professionnels de ses membres et particulièrement la négotiation et l'application de la convention collective
Francine Genest, Présidente

Atlantic Communication & Technical Workers' Union (Ind.) (AC&TWU) / Syndicat des travailleurs en communication et des techniciens de l'Atlantique (ind.)
#7, 50 Akerley Blvd., Dartmouth NS B3B 1R8 Canada
Tel: 902-453-2058; *Fax:* 902-422-4647
Toll-Free: 800-565-2289
Bruce W. Lambert, Business Manager & Financial Secret

Atlantic Federation of Musicians (AFM)
221 Herring Cove Rd., Halifax NS B3P 1L3 Canada
Tel: 902-479-3200; *Fax:* 902-479-1312
Toll-Free: 866-240-4809
afm571@eastlink.ca
www.afm571.ca

Bricklayers, Masons Independent Union of Canada (CLC) / Syndicat indépendant des briqueteurs et des maçons du Canada (CTC)
#200, 1263 Wilson Ave., Toronto ON M3M 3G3 Canada
Tel: 416-241-1183; *Fax:* 416-241-9845
Giuseppe Bellotto, President
John Meiorin, Secretary

British Columbia Carpenters Union (BCPCC)
#305, 2806 Kingsway, Vancouver BC V5R 5T5 Canada
Tel: 604-437-0471; *Fax:* 604-437-1110
info@bccarpentersunion.com
www.bccarpentersunion.com
The objects of the Council are to organize workers; encourage an apprenticeship system & higher standard of skill; to develop, improve & enforce the program & standards of occupational safety & health; to cultivate friendship; to develop good public relations with the community; to assist each other to secure employment & to reduce the hours of daily labour
Jan Noster, President
Pat Haggarty, Sec.-Treas.

British Columbia Federation of Labour (BCFL) / Fédération du travail de la Colombie-Britannique
#200, 5118 Joyce St., Vancouver BC V5R 4H1
Tel: 604-430-1421; *Fax:* 604-430-5917
bcfed@bcfed.com; admin@bcfed.ca; media@bcfed.ca; educate@bcfed.ca
www.bcfed.com
To promote the interests of affiliated unions & their members; To advance the economic & social welfare of the workers of British Columbia; To act as the single voice for workers' rights in British Columbia
Jim Sinclair, President
Angela Schira, Secretary-Treasurer
Gord Lechner, Director, Occupational Health & Safety Education Centre
Summer McFadyen, Director, Political Action
Sheila Moir, Director, Occupational Health & Safety
Jane Staschuk, Director, Women's Rights, Education, & Training
Evan Stewart, Director, Communications, Transportation, & First Nations
Carole Sundin, Director, Administration
Dayna Sykes, Director, Young Workers & Human Rights
Jessie Uppal, Director, Campaigns, Community, & Social Action

British Columbia Ferry & Marine Workers' Union (CLC) (BCFMWU) / Syndicat des travailleurs marins et de bacs de la Colombie-Britannique (CTC)
1511 Stewart Ave., Nanaimo BC V9S 4E3 Canada
Tel: 250-716-3454; *Fax:* 250-716-3455
Toll-Free: 800-663-7009
mailroom@bcfmwu.com
www.bcfmwu.com
To unite in the Union all workers eligible for membership; to seek the best possible wage standards & improvements in the conditions of employment for these workers & to represent members in protecting & maintaining their rights; to act as the representative of the membership; to establish free child day care for all individuals; to engage in educational, legislative, political, civic, social, welfare, community & other activities to safeguard & promote economic & social benefits & justice for all workers, unionized & non-unionized.
Kelly Carson, Sec.-Treas.
Richard Goode, President

British Columbia Government & Service Employees' Union (BCGEU) / Syndicat des fonctionnaires provinciaux et de service de la Colombie-Britannique
4911 Canada Way, Burnaby BC V5G 3W3 Canada
Tel: 604-291-9611; *Fax:* 604-291-6030
Toll-Free: 800-663-1674
www.bcgeu.ca
Judi Filion, Treasurer
Darryl Walker, President

Canada Employment & Immigration Union (CEIU) / Syndicat de l'emploi et de l'immigration du Canada (SEIC)
#1004, 233 Gilmour St., Ottawa ON K2P 0P2 Canada
Tel: 613-236-9634; *Fax:* 613-236-7871
courchs@ceiu-seic.ca
www.ceiu-seic.ca
To unite all the union members in the Canada Employment & Immigration Commission, the Department of Employment & Immigration & the Immigration Appeal Board, & anyone who wishes to join in a single union acting on their behalf by processing appeals & grievances; to unite all members by fostering an understanding of the fundamental differences between the interests of the members & those of the employer; to assure a union presence at the workplace through collective strength of membership
Jeannette Meunier-McKay, National President
Steve McCuaig, National Executive Vice-President

Canadian Actors' Equity Association (CLC) (CAEA)
44 Victoria St., 12th Fl., Toronto ON M5C 3C4 Canada
Tel: 416-867-9165; *Fax:* 416-867-9246
info@caea.com; membership@caea.com; reception@caea.com
www.caea.com
CAEA negotiates & administers collective agreements, provides benefit plans, information & support, & acts as an advocate for its membership.
Allan Teichman, President
Arden R. Ryshpan, Executive Director
Lynn McQueen, Director, Communications

Canadian Association of Professional Employees (CAPE)
World Exchange Plaza, 100 Queen St., 4th Fl., Ottawa ON K1P 1J9 Canada
Tel: 613-236-9181; *Fax:* 613-236-6017
Toll-Free: 800-265-9181
general@acep-cape.ca
www.acep-cape.ca
To negotiate & monitor collective agreement for all federal government economists, sociologists & statisticians.
Claude Poirier, President

Canadian Federal Pilots Association (CFPA) / Association des pilotes fédéraux du Canada (APFC)
#509, 350 Sparks St., Ottawa ON K1R 7S8 Canada
Tel: 613-230-5476; *Fax:* 613-230-2668
cfpa@cfpa-apfc.ca
www.cfpa-apfc.ca
Greg Holbrook, Chair
Denis Brunelle, Vice-Chair
Greg McConnell, Sec.-Treas.

Canadian Federation of Nurses Unions (CFNU) / La Fédération canadienne des syndicats d'infirmières/infirmiers
2841 Riverside Dr., Ottawa ON K1V 8X7 Canada
Tel: 613-526-4661; *Fax:* 613-526-1023
Toll-Free: 800-321-9821
cfnu@nursesunions.ca
www.nursesunions.ca
To advance the social, economic & general welfare of its members; To act on national matters of significant concern to the Federation; To promote unity among nurses' unions & other allied health care workers who share the objectives of the CFNU; To provide a national forum to promote desirable legislation on matters of national significance; To preserve free democratic unionism & collective bargaining in Canada; To support other organizations sharing the Union's objectives

Canadian Football League Players' Association (CFLPA) / Association des joueurs de la ligue de football canadienne
#207, 603 Argus Rd., Oakville ON L6J 6G6 Canada
Tel: 905-844-7852; *Fax:* 905-844-5127
Toll-Free: 800-616-6865
admin@cflpa.com
www.cflpa.com
The Canadian Football League Players' Association ("C.F.L.P.A.") was established in 1965 and has since that time represented the professional football players in the Canadian Football League ("C.F.L.") with the objective of establishing fair and reasonable working conditions for the players.
Stu Laird, President
Mike O'Shea, 1st Vice-President
Jay McNeil, 2nd Vice-President
Sean Fleming, Member-at-Large
Edward Molstad, Legal Counsel
Fred James, Benefits Chairman
Deanne Mitchell, Executive Assistant

Canadian Iron, Steel & Industrial Workers' Union (Ind.)
17 East Broadway, Vancouver BC V5T 1V4 Canada
Tel: 604-681-6002; *Fax:* 604-873-9112

Canadian Labour Congress (CLC) / Congrès du travail du Canada (CTC)
National Headquarters, 2841 Riverside Dr., Ottawa ON K1V 8X7
Tel: 613-521-3400; *Fax:* 613-521-4655
www.canadianlabour.ca
Social Media: www.facebook.com/clc.ctc
To represent the interests of affiliated workers across Canada; To act as an umbrella organization for affiliated regional labour councils, provincial federations, Canadian unions, & international unions
Ken Georgetti, President
Barbara Byers, Executive Vice-President
Marie Clarke Walker, Executive Vice-President
Hassan Yussuff, Secretary-Treasurer
Karl Flecker, Director, Anti-Racism & Human Rights
Andrew Jackson, Director, Social & Economic Policy
Daniel Mallett, Director, Political Action
Lucien Royer, Director, International
Colleen Kilty, Manager, Human Resources
Dennis Gruending, Contact, Communications, Media Calls

Canadian Marine Officers' Union (AFL-CIO/CLC) / Syndicat canadien des officiers de la marine marchande (FAT-COI/CTC)
17 Front St. North, Thorold ON L2V 1X3 Canada
Tel: 905-227-6226; *Fax:* 905-227-9164
cmou@cogeco.net
www.cmou.ca
Richard Vezina, President

Canadian Marine Pilots' Association (CMPA) / Association des pilotes de la marine canadienne
#1302, 155 Queen St., Ottawa ON K1P 6L1
Tel: 613-232-7777; *Fax:* 613-232-7667
cmpa@tnpa.ca
www.marinepilots.ca
To represent Canadian marine pilots; To raise awareness of marine pilots' role to protect public safety; To ensure a healthy Canadian marine sector
Simon Pelletier, President
Bernard Boissonneault, Vice-President
Mike Burgess, Vice-President
Fred Denning, Vice-President
Andrew Rae, Vice-President

Canadian Media Guild (CMG) / La Guilde canadienne des médias
#810, 310 Front St. West, Toronto ON M5V 3B5 Canada
Tel: 416-591-5333; *Fax:* 416-591-7278
Toll-Free: 800-465-4149
info@cmg.ca
www.cmg.ca
To advance the interests of Guild members through collective bargaining

Canadian Merchant Service Guild (CLC) (CMSG) / Guilde de la marine marchande du Canada (CTC) (GMMC)
#150, 1150 Morrison Dr., Ottawa ON K2H 8S9 Canada
Tel: 613-829-9531; *Fax:* 613-596-6079
cmsgott@on.aibn.com
www.cmsg-gmmc.ca
To promote the social, economic, cultural, educational & material interests of ships' masters, chief engineers, officers, pilots & of other persons whose employment is directly related to maritime operations
Lawrence Dempsey, National President
Mark Boucher, National Sec.-Treas.

Canadian National Federation of Independent Unions (CNFIU) / Fédération canadienne nationale des syndicats indépendants (FCNSI)
#200, 526 Winona Rd. North, Stoney Creek ON L8E 5E9 Canada
Tel: 905-735-0531; *Fax:* 905-643-8319
Toll-Free: 800-638-9438
info@cnfiu.com
www.cnfiu.com
To encourage & promote the formation of independent unions
Ann Waller, President
Brenda Lowes, Sec.-Treas.

Canadian Postmasters & Assistants Association (CPAA) / Association canadienne des maîtres de poste et adjoints (ACMPA)
281 Queen Mary St., Ottawa ON K1K 1X1 Canada
Tel: 613-745-2095; *Fax:* 613-745-5559
mail@cpaa-acmpa.ca
www.cpaa-acmpa.ca
Leslie A. Schous, National President
Pierre Charbonneau, National Vice-President
Shirley L. Dressler, National Sec.-Treas.
Pat E. Fagan, National Vice-President

Canadian Telephone Employees' Association (Ind.) / Association canadienne des employés de téléphone (ind.)
PO Box 103, #1903, 777 Bay St., Toronto ON M5G 2C8 Canada
Tel: 416-977-2251; *Fax:* 416-977-9738
Toll-Free: 800-595-2696
CTEA Mission is to be the best union for our members. Their strategy is to depend on responsible elected Representatives and District Committees to develop and reflect membership opinion; to provide membership control of their union through the General Council; to remain independent in the labour movement.
Brenda Knight, President

Canadian Union of Postal Workers (CUPW) / Syndicat des travailleurs et travailleuses des postes (STTP)
377 Bank St., Ottawa ON K2P 1Y3 Canada
Tel: 613-236-7238; *Fax:* 613-563-7861
www.cupw-sttp.org
CUPW is a democratic union. They are involved with various campaigns and activities which help support their members.
Denis Lemelin, National President
George Kuehnbaum, National Sec.-Treas.

Canadian Union of Public Employees (CUPE) / Syndicat canadien de la fonction publique (SCFP)
1375 St. Laurent Blvd., Ottawa ON K1G 0Z7
Tel: 613-237-1590; *Fax:* 613-237-5508
cupemail@cupe.ca
www.cupe.ca
To advance the social, economic, & general welfare of both active & retired employees; To promote required legislation
Paul Moist, National President
Claude Généreux, National Secretary-Treasurer
Daniel Légère, General Vice-President
Lucie Levasseur, General Vice-President
Barry O'Neill, General Vice-President
Barry Graham, General Vice-President, Saskatchewan
Fred Hahn, General Vice-President, Ontario
Stephen Howard, Director, Communications

Centrale des syndicats démocratiques (CSD)
#300, 801, 4e rue, Québec QC G1J 2T7 Canada
Tél: 418-529-2956; *Téléc:* 418-529-6323
info@csd.qc.ca
www.csd.qc.ca
CSD est composée des associations de salariés constituées ou non en vertu de la Loi des syndicats professionnels qui y adhèrent et souscrivent aux objectifs de la CSD; CSD a comme première croyance la liberté de la personne humaine, tant dans son intelligence que dans la recherche de la satisfaction de ses besoins matériels; elle est donc libre de toute attache politique et se reconnaît comme un mouvement de fraternité et de solidarité dédié entièrement à la formation, à l'information, à la défense et à la promotion collective des travailleuses et des travailleurs.
François Vaudreuil, Président

Centrale des syndicats du Québec (CSQ)
9405, rue Sherbrooke est, Montréal QC H1L 6P3 Canada
Tél: 514-356-8888; *Téléc:* 514-356-9999
Ligne sans frais: 800-465-0897
communications.montreal@csq.qc.net
www.csq.qc.net
Média social: twitter.com/CSQ_centrale
De regrouper dans un même mouvement des personnels salariés ayant des aspirations et des intérêts communs et de promouvoir leurs intérêts professionnels, sociaux, et économiques; dans cette perspective, elle travaille à établir un environnement syndical et professionnel exempt de harcèlement sexuel et favorise la vie syndicale par le partage des ressources; elle intervient au soutien direct de ses affiliés et assure différents services liés aux relations de travail et à la vie professionnelle (recherche dans le domaine de l'éducation, etc.)

CEP Local 2003
#105, 2065 Dundas St. East, Mississauga ON L4X 2W1 Canada
Tel: 905-238-0877; *Fax:* 905-238-9567
Toll-Free: 800-263-0855
cuoe@cuoe.org
www.ceplocal2003.org
Paul Sauve, National President
George Reid, National Vice-President
Kenneth B. Spiece, National Treasurer
Larry Lynch, National Recording Secretary

Christian Labour Association of Canada (CLAC) / Association chrétienne du travail du Canada
2335 Argentia Rd., Mississauga ON L5N 5N3 Canada
Tel: 905-812-2855; *Fax:* 905-812-5556
Toll-Free: 800-268-5281
headoffice@clac.ca
www.clac.ca
CLAC is a certified, independent Canadian labour union that promotes labour relations based on the principles of Christian social action, a cooperative style, organizing workers in all sectors to involve them in the affairs of the enterprise.
Dick Heinen, Executive Director

Communications, Energy & Paperworkers Union of Canada (CEP) / Syndicat canadien des communications, de l'énergie et du papier (SCEP)
301 Laurier Ave. West, Ottawa ON K1P 6M6 Canada
Tel: 613-230-5200; *Fax:* 613-230-5801
Toll-Free: 877-230-5201
info@cep.ca
www.cep.ca
To improve pay & working conditions through collective bargaining & to represent members at grievance hearings; to present a common front with other unions & community groups to governments on issues that affect all workers, from minimum wage to medicare
Gaétan Ménard, Sec.-Treas.
Dave Coles, President

Compensation Employees' Union (Ind.) (CEU) / Syndicat des employés d'indemnisation (ind.)
#200, 8120 Granville Ave., Richmond BC V6Y 1P3 Canada
Tel: 604-278-4050; *Fax:* 604-278-5002
www.ceu.bc.ca
The Compensation Employees' Union was certified in 1974. The CEU is an all inclusive bargaining unit representing all workers at the Workers' Compensation Board that are not excluded by law. The membership ranges from cleaners, support positions, technicial positions, officer level positions, physiologists, and lawyers.
Sandra Wright, President
Carol Velon, Secretary

Confédération des syndicats nationaux (CSN) / Confederation of National Trade Unions
1601, av De Lorimier, Montréal QC H2K 4M5 Canada
Tél: 514-598-2121; *Téléc:* 514-598-2052
csncommunications@csn.qc.ca
www.csn.qc.ca
La Confédération limite ses activités principalement au Québec, quoique certains locaux soient établis hors de la province; comprend 9 fédérations, 13 conseils centraux et 2 800 syndicats
Pierre Patry, Trésorier
Claudette Carbonneau, Présidente
Lise Poulin, Secrétaire générale

Congress of Union Retirees Canada (CURC) / Association des syndicalistes retraités du Canada (ASRC)
2841 Riverside Dr., Ottawa ON K1V 8X7
Tel: 613-526-7422; *Fax:* 613-521-4655
curc@clc-ctc.ca
curc.clc-ctc.ca
To ensure that the concerns of senior citizens & union retirees are heard across Canada
Pat Kerwin, President
Len Hope, First Vice-President
Doug MacPherson, Second Vice-President
Bob McGarry, Secretary
Betty Ann Bushell, Treasurer

Customs Excise Union Douanes Accise (CEUDA)
1741 Woodward Dr., Ottawa ON K2C 0P9 Canada
Tel: 613-723-8008; *Fax:* 613-723-7895
web@ceuda.ca; magazine@ceuda.ca
www.ceuda.psac.com
To address CEUDA members' concerns on a timely basis
Ron Moran, National President
Michelle Tranchemontagne, Legal Counsel & Director, Office
Jonathan Choquette, Officer, Communications & Political Coordination

Employees' Association, St. Mary's of the Lake Hospital (CNFIU) / Association des employés, l'Hôpital Saint Mary's of the Lake (FCNSI)
PO Box 207, Kingston ON K7L 4V8 Canada
Tel: 613-544-5220

Fédération autonome du collégial (ind.) (FAC) / Autonomous Federation of Collegial Staff (Ind.)
#400, 1259, rue Berri, Montréal QC H2L 4C7 Canada
Tél: 514-848-9977; *Téléc:* 514-848-0166
Ligne sans frais: 800-701-1369
fac@lafac.qc.ca
www.lafac.qc.ca
Défendre et développer les intérêts économiques, sociaux, pédagogiques et professionnels du personnel enseignant des cégeps; défendre le droit d'association, la libre négociation et la liberté d'action syndicale; négocier et s'assurer de l'application des conventions collectives; de représenter ses syndicats affiliés partout où leurs intérêts sont débattus.

Fédération CSN - Construction (CSN) / CNTU Federation - Construction (CNTU)
2100B, boul de Maisonneuve est, 4e étage, Montréal QC H2K 4S1 Canada
Tél: 514-598-2421; *Téléc:* 514-598-2425
sec-montreal@csnconstruction.qc.ca
www.csnconstruction.qc.ca
Alain Mailhot, Président
François Trépanier, Secrétaire général
Yves Coté, Coordonateur

Fédération de la métallurgie (CSN) / Federation of Metal Trades (CNTU)
#204, 2100, boul de Maisonneuve est, Montréal QC H2K 4S1 Canada
Tél: 514-529-4937; *Téléc:* 514-529-4935
metallurgie@csn.qc.ca
www.metallurgie.csn.qc.ca
Alain Lampron, Président
Jean-Pierre Tremblay, Secrétaire
Yvan Gamelin, Trésorier

Fédération de la santé et des services sociaux
1601, av de Lorimier, Montréal QC H2K 4M5 Canada
Tél: 514-598-2210; *Téléc:* 514-598-2223
fsss@fsss.qc.ca
www.fsss.qc.ca
De promouvoir et sauvegarder la santé, la sécurité et les intérêts des personnes employées des établissements affiliés ou en voie d'affiliation; de représenter ses membres auprès de la Confédération des syndicats nationaux en lui soumettant toutes questions d'intérêt général; de représenter ses membres, de concert avec le CSN, partout où les intérêts généraux des travailleuses et travailleurs le justifient; d'aider à conclure, en faveur des syndicats affiliés, des conventions collectives de travail et en favoriser l'application; de collaborer à l'éducation des travailleuses et travailleurs et à la formation de responsables et militantes et militants syndicaux; d'assurer les services à ses syndicats affiliés; de favoriser et d'établir des liens inter-syndicaux avec les autres travailleuses et travailleurs dans le secteur public et para-public et dans le secteur privé du Québec et du Canada

Fédération des employées et employés de services publics inc. (CSN) (FEESP) / Federation of Public Service Employees Inc. (CNTU)
1601, av de Lorimier, Montréal QC H2K 4M5 Canada
Tél: 514-598-2231
feesp.courrier@csn.qc.ca
www.feesp.csn.qc.ca
Il est composé de quatre personnes élues, du coordonnateur ou coordonnatrice des services et de la personne déléguée syndicale.
Danielle Beaulieu, Présidente

Fédération des enseignants de cégeps
9405, rue Sherbrooke est, Montréal QC H1L 6P3 Canada
Tél: 514-356-8888; *Téléc:* 514-354-8535
fec@csq.qc.net
www.fec.csq.qc.net
Elle reste donc, encore aujourd'hui, une organisation qui jouit, à l'intérieur de la CSQ, d'une autonomie totale pour tout ce qui touche la négociation et l'application de la convention collective, les orientations concernant les dossiers professionnels et les politiques collégiales de même que pour ce qui touche la gestion de son personnel et de son budget. Plus encore aujourd'hui qu'hier, la FEC et ses syndicats participent aux décisions de la Centrale puisque celle-ci a multiplié, au cours des années, ses instances décisionnelles et consultatives auxquelles participent directement la FEC et ses syndicats.

Fédération des intervenantes en petite enfance du Québec (FIPEQ)
9405, rue Sherbrooke est, Montréal QC H1L 6P3 Canada
Tél: 514-356-8888; *Téléc:* 514-356-9999
Ligne sans frais: 800-465-0897
fipeq@csq.qc.net
www.petitmonde.com
La Fédération des intervenantes en petite enfance du Québec (FIPEQ) est vouée à la promotion de la profession, à la défense des droits et des intérêts ainsi qu'à l'amélioration des conditions de vie de toutes les intervenantes, tant travailleuses autonomes que salariées, oeuvrant au service des centres de la petite enfance.
Sylvie Tonnelier, Présidente

Fédération des médecins résidents du Québec inc. (ind.) (FMRQ) / Québec Federation of Residents (Ind.)
#510, 630, rue Sherbrooke ouest, Montréal QC H3A 1E4 Canada
Tél: 514-282-0256; *Téléc:* 514-282-0471
Ligne sans frais: 800-465-0215
fmrq@fmrq.qc.ca
www.fmrq.qc.ca
L'étude, la défense et le développement des intérêts économiques, sociaux, moraux et scientifiques des syndicats et des leurs membres.
Jean Gouin, Executive Director
Patrick Labelle, Administrative Director

Fédération des policiers et policières municipaux du Québec (ind.) (FPMQ) / Québec Federation of Policemen (Ind.)
7955, boul Louis-Hippolyte-La Fontaine, Anjou QC H1K 4E4 Canada
Tél: 514-356-3321; *Téléc:* 514-356-1158
Ligne sans frais: 800-361-0321
info@fpmq.org
www.fpmq.org
L'étude et la défense des intérêts économiques, professionnels, sociaux et moraux de ses associations-membres et de tous les policiers que celles-ci regroupent.
Denis Côté, Président
Christine Beaulieu, Directrice, Communications

Fédération des professionnèles (FPCSN) / Quebec Federation of Managers & Professional Salaried Workers (CNTU)
1601, av de Lorimier, Montréal QC H2K 4M5 Canada
Tél: 514-598-2143; *Téléc:* 514-598-2491
Ligne sans frais: 888-633-2143
fp@csn.qc.ca
www.fpcsn.qc.ca
Regroupe plus de 7000 professionnèles oeuvrant dans différents secteurs d'activités: santé et services sociaux, organismes gouvernementaux, éducation, secteur municipal, médecines alternatives, secteur juridique, intégration à l'emploi, professionnèles autonomes, organismes communautaires, etc
Michel Tremblay, Président
Lucie Dufour, Secrétaire générale

Fédération des professionnelles et professionnels de l'éducation du Québec (FPPE) / Québec Federation of Professional Employees in Education
9405, rue Sherbrooke est, Montréal QC H1L 6P3 Canada
Tél: 514-356-0505; *Téléc:* 514-356-1324
infos@fppe.qc.ca
www.fppe.qc.ca
De promouvoir et de développer les intérêts professionnels, sociaux et économiques des professionnelles et professionnels de l'éducation du Québec ainsi que de défendre les droits fondamentaux compris à l'intérieur des chartes, le droit d'association, le droit à la libre négociation et le droit à la liberté d'action syndicale; de représenter ses syndicats affiliés à un niveau national; d'orienter et de coordonner la représentation de ses syndicats affiliés auprès des instances de la Centrale; de diriger et de coordonner la négociation des conventions collectives; de concilier les conflits qui peuvent naître entre les syndicats affiliés; de mettre à la disposition des syndicats affiliés et de leurs membres des services de qualité en matière de négociation et d'application des conditions de travail et des droits sociaux, d'information et de formation syndicale.
Jean Falardeau, Président
Johanne Pomerleau, Vice-présidente
Patrice Lemay, Vice-président, Affaires administratives

Fédération des Syndicats de l'Enseignement (FSE)
CP 100, 320, rue Saint-Joseph est, Québec QC G1K 9E7 Canada
Tél: 418-649-8888; *Téléc:* 418-649-1914
fse@csq.qc.net
www.fse.qc.net
Promouvoir les intérêts professionnels, sociaux et économiques du personnel enseignant des commissions scolaires; orienter et coordonner la représentation des syndicats affiliés auprès des instances de la Centrale et de représenter les syndicats affiliés là où leurs intérêts et leurs droits sont débattus; assumer prioritairement la responsabilité des négociations, les aspects sectoriels des relations du travail et de l'action juridique ainsi que les questions professionnelles à caractère sectoriel; favoriser la concertation entre les syndicats affiliés et concilier les divergences qui pourraient naître entre eux.

Fédération des syndicats de la santé et des services sociaux (F4S-CSQ)
9405, rue Sherbrooke est, Montréal QC H1L 6P3 Canada
Tél: 514-356-8888; *Téléc:* 514-356-2845
f4s@csq.qc.net
www.sante.csq.qc.net/index.cfm/2,0,1672,9553,2883,0,html
Réunis en congrès les 7 et 8 juin 2007, les déléguées et délégués de la Fédération du personnel de la santé et des services sociaux (FPSSS-CSQ) et de la Fédération des syndicats de professionnelles et professionnels de la santé et des services sociaux (FSPPSSS-CSQ) ont décidé à l'unanimité d'unir leurs forces et de fonder une nouvelle fédération : la Fédération des syndicats de la santé et des services sociaux (F4S-CSQ), affiliée à la Centrale des syndicats du Québec (CSQ).
René Beauséjour, Président

Fédération des travailleurs et travailleuses du Québec - Construction
#2900, 565, boul Crémazie est, Montréal QC H2M 2V6 Canada
Tél: 514-381-7300; *Téléc:* 514-381-5173
Ligne sans frais: 877-666-4060
www.ftqconstruction.org
On peut facilement affirmer que la mission d'une association syndicale est quasi sans limite. La FTQ-Construction a, bien entendu, de manière très précise le mandat de négocier les conventions collectives applicables dans les sous secteurs d'activités (industriel, commercial et institutionnel, génie civil et voirie, résidentiel) et de voir à leur application. Mais bien au-delà de ce mandat traditionnel, la FTQ-Construction veut s'assurer d'être présent dans l'ensemble des débats représentant un intérêt pour les travailleurs et les travailleuses qu'il représente.
Richard Goyette, Directeur général

Fédération des travailleuses et travailleurs du papier et de la forêt (CSN) (FTPF) / Federation of Paper & Forest Workers (CNTU)
#350, 155, boul Charest est, Québec QC G1K 3G6 Canada
Tél: 418-647-5775; *Téléc:* 418-647-5884
direction.ftpf@videotron.net
www.ftpf.csn.qc.ca
Groupe CNW exploite sept bureaux au Canada, dont deux bureaux CNW Telbec au Québec. De ses bureaux de Vancouver, de Calgary, de Toronto, d'Ottawa, de Montréal, de Québec et de Halifax, CNW répond avec efficacité aux besoins du marché canadien, et ce, 24 heures par jour, 365 jours par année, tout en assurant un service en anglais et en français.
Suzanne Lareau, Présidente-directrice générale
Claire Chouinard, Directrice, Communications & marketing

Fédération du personnel de l'enseignement privé (FPEP)
9405, rue Sherbrooke est, Montréal QC H1L 6P3 Canada
Tél: 514-356-8888; *Téléc:* 514-356-1866
fpep@csq.qc.net
www.fpep.csq.qc.net
Promouvoir les intérêts professionnels, sociaux et économiques de ses membres; défendre le droit d'association, de libre négociation et la liberté d'action syndicale; représenter ses syndicats membres

Fédération du personnel de soutien scolaire (CSQ) (FPSS) / Federation of Support Staff
9405, rue Sherbrooke est, 4e étage, Montréal QC H1L 6P3 Canada
Tél: 514-356-8888; *Téléc:* 514-493-3697
webfpss@csq.qc.net
www.fpss.csq.qc.net
Le seul regroupement au Québec représentant exclusivement du personnel de soutien scolaire des écoles et des centres. Elle est affiliée à la Centrale des syndicats du Québec (CSQ)

Fédération du personnel du loisir, de la culture et du communautaire (CEQ) (FPLCC)
9405, rue Sherbrooke est, Montréal QC H1L 6P3 Canada
Tél: 514-356-8888; *Téléc:* 514-356-9999
fplcc@csq.qc.net
www.csq.qc.net/fede/fplcc.htm
Regroupe les syndicats qui représentent le personnel oeuvrant dans les secteurs du loisir, du sport, de la culture du tourisme et du communautaire

Fédération du personnel professionnel des collèges (FPPC)
9405, rue Sherbrooke est, Montréal QC H1L 6P3 Canada
Tél: 514-356-8888; *Téléc:* 514-356-3377
fppc@csq.qc.net
www.fppc.csq.qc.net
Défendre et promouvoir la fonction professionnelle dans les collèges
Bernard Bérubé, Président

Fédération du personnel professionnel des universités et de la recherche (FPPU)
CP 500, Trois-Rivières QC G9A 5H7 Canada
Tél: 819-376-5043; *Téléc:* 819-376-5234
fppu@uqtr.ca
www.fppu.qc.ca
La FPPU est la seule organisation syndicale regroupant exclusivement le personnel professionnel des universités et de la recherche

Fédération indépendante des syndicats autonomes (FISA) / Independent Federation of Autonomous Unions
#201, 1778, boul Wilfrid-Hamel, Québec QC G1N 3Y8 Canada
Tél: 418-529-4571; *Téléc:* 418-529-4695
Ligne sans frais: 800-407-3472
info@fisa.ca
www.fisa.ca
Fournir des services d'organisation, de conseils, de représentation et d'aide financière aux associations membres.
Jean Gagnon, Président

Fédération nationale des communications (CSN) (FNC) / National Federation of Communication Workers (CNTU)
1601, av de Lorimier, Montréal QC H2K 4M5 Canada
Tél: 514-598-2132; *Téléc:* 514-598-2431
fnc@fncom.org
www.fncom.org
La défense des intérêts économiques, sociaux, politiques et professionnels des membres.

Fraternité interprovinciale des ouvriers en électricité (CTC) (FIPOE) / Interprovincial Brotherhood of Electrical Workers (CLC)
#11100, 565, boul Crémazie est, Montréal QC H2M 2W2 Canada
Tél: 514-385-3476; *Téléc:* 514-385-9298
fratip@fipoe.org
www.fipoe.org
Regrouper des électriciens de construction, des installateurs de systèmes d'alarmes et des monteurs de ligne.
Gérald Castilloux, Président
Jean Lavallée, Directeur général

Fraternité nationale des forestiers et travailleurs d'usine (CTC) / National Brotherhood of Foresters & Industrial Workers (CLC)
Locale 299, #101, 2, boul Desaulniers, Saint-Lambert QC J4P 1L2 Canada
Tél: 450-465-2218; *Téléc:* 450-465-1301
Ligne sans frais: 800-317-1818
fnftu@qc.aira.com
www.scep299.ca
L'étude, la sauvegarde et le développement des intérêts économiques, et l'application de conventions collectives
Sylvie Labelle, Adjointe au président
Yves Guérette, Président

Government Services Union (GSU) / Syndicat des services gouvernementaux
#100, 1770 Woodward Dr., Ottawa ON K2C 0P8 Canada
Tel: 613-226-5983; *Fax:* 613-226-8241
gsu-ssg@psac.com
www.gsu-ssg.ca
Their members provide compensation, audit, procurement, disposal telecommunications and informatics, translation, real property and reciever general services to some 100 federal government departments and agencies. They also provide information about government programmes and research the opinions of Canadians.
Mark Brunell, President

Grain Services Union (CLC) (GSU) / Syndicat des services du grain (CTC)
2334 McIntyre St., Regina SK S4P 2S2 Canada
Tel: 306-522-6686; *Fax:* 306-565-3430
Toll-Free: 866-522-6686
gsu.regina@sasktel.net
www.gsu.ca
They represent Saskatchewan Wheat Pool Workers and represent members working for a variety of companies within Canada.
Carolyn Illerbrun, President
Hugh J. Wagner, Secretary/Manager

Health Sciences Association of Alberta (HSAA) / Association des sciences de la santé de l'Alberta (ind.)
10212 - 112 St., Edmonton AB T5K 1M4
Tel: 780-488-0168; *Fax:* 780-488-0534
Toll-Free: 800-252-7904
www.hsaa.ca
To conduct activities as a labour union to enhance the quality of life for HSAA members & society
Elisabeth Ballermann, President
Patricia Heffel, Director, Administrative Services
Lynette McAvoy, Director, Labour Relations
Roni Hermanutz, Manager, Human Resources
Joanne Monro, Officer, Occupational Health & Safety
Scott Pattison, Officer, Communications

Health Sciences Association of Saskatchewan (HSAS) / Association des sciences de la santé de la Saskatchewan (ind.)
#42, 1736 Quebec Ave., Saskatoon SK S7K 1V9 Canada
Tel: 306-955-3399; *Fax:* 306-955-3396
Toll-Free: 888-565-3399
hsasstoon@sasktel.net; hsasregina@sasktel.net
www.hsa-sk.com
To conduct activities as an independent union representing its members who are health sciences professionals in Saskatchewan
Bill Craik, Executive Director
Chris Driol, President
Cathy Dickson, Vice-President
Mary Spurr, Secretary
Karen Wasylenko, Treasurer

Hospital Employees' Union (HEU) / Syndicat des employés d'hôpitaux
5000 North Fraser Way, Burnaby BC V5J 5M3 Canada
Tel: 604-438-5000; *Fax:* 604-739-1510
Toll-Free: 800-663-5813
heu@heu.org
www.heu.org
To unite & associate together all employees employed in hospital, medical or related work for the purpose of securing concerted action in whatever may be regarded as conducive to their best interests; to embrace the concept of equality of treatment for all in hospital, medical or related employment, with respect to wages & job opportunities, recognizing their obligation to provide high-quality care; to defend & preserve the right of all persons to high standards of medical & hospital treatment
Ken Robinson, President
Judy Darcy, Secretary & Business Manager

International Alliance of Theatrical Stage Employees, Moving Picture Technicians, Artists & Allied Crafts of the U.S., Its Territories & Canada (IATSE)
1430 Broadway, 20th Fl., New York NY 10018 USA
Tel: 212-730-1770; *Fax:* 212-921-7699
webmaster@iatse-intl.org
www.iatse-intl.org
Matthew D. Loeb, International President
John M. Lewis, Director, Canadian Affairs

International Association of Bridge, Structural, Ornamental & Reinforcing Iron Workers (AFL-CIO) / Association internationale des travailleurs de ponts, de fer structural et ornemental (FAT-COI)
#400, 1750 New York Ave. NW, Washington DC 20006 USA
Tel: 202-383-4800; *Fax:* 202-638-4856
www.ironworkers.org
This union represents ironworkers and works for employment oppourtunties, fair pay, health and welfare benefits, continuing education, and other workers' rights since 1896.
Joseph J. Hunt, President
Fred Marr, Director, Canadian Operations

International Association of Fire Fighters (AFL-CIO/CLC) (IAFF) / Association internationale des pompiers (FAT-COI/CTC)
#300, 1750 New York Ave. NW, Washington DC 20006-5395 USA
Tel: 202-737-8484; *Fax:* 202-737-8418
www.iaff.org
IAFF has established professional standards for the North American fire service with active political & legislative programs, & with experts in the fields of occupational health & safety, fire-based emergency medical services & hazardous materials training. It provides a voice in the development & implementation of new training & equipment, & has worked to ensure the staffing of fire & EMS departments.
Harold A. Schaitberger, General President

International Association of Machinists & Aerospace Workers (IAMAW) / Association internationale des machinistes et des travailleurs de l'aérospatiale
Machinists Bldg., 9000 Machinists Pl., Upper Marlboro MD 20772-2687 USA
Tel: 301-967-4500
websteward@iamaw.org
www.goiam.org
Social Media: facebook.com/machinistsunion; twitter.com/machinistsunion
IAMAW is an industrial trade union that is the negotiating body for its members.
R. Thomas Buffenbarger, President

International Brotherhood of Boilermakers, Iron Ship Builders, Blacksmiths, Forgers & Helpers (AFL-CIO) (IBB) / Fraternité internationale des chaudronniers, constructeurs de navires en fer, forgerons, forgeurs et aides (FAT-COI)
New Brotherhood Bldg., #570, 753 State Ave., Kansas City MO 66101 USA
Tel: 913-371-2640; *Fax:* 913-281-8101
www.boilermakers.org
The Brotherhood is a diverse union representing boilermakers and other workers in the U.S. and Canada in construction, repair, maintenance, manufacturing, professional emergency medical services, and related industries. The Western Canadian Section serves the territory from Thunder Bay west, including Manitoba, Saskatchewan, Alberta, British Columbia, Yukon & NWT. The Eastern Canadian Section serves territory east of Thunder Bay, including Ontario, Quebec, New Brunswick, Nova Scotia, PEI, & Newfoundland & Labrador
Newton B. Jones, International President
Joseph Maloney, International Vice President, Western Canada
Edward Power, International Vice President, Eastern Canada

International Brotherhood of Electrical Workers (AFL-CIO/CFL) (IBEW) / Fraternité internationale des ouvriers en électricité (FAT-COI/FCT)
900 Seventh St. NW, Washington DC 20001 USA
Tel: 202-833-7000; *Fax:* 202-728-7676
www.ibew.org
The International Brotherhood of Electrical Workers (IBEW) represents approximately 725,000 members who work in a wide variety of fields, including utilities, construction, telecommunications, broadcasting, manufacturing, railroads and government.

International Federation of Professional & Technical Engineers (AFL-CIO/CLC) (IFPTE) / Fédération internationale des ingénieurs et techniciens (FAT-COI/CTC)
#701, 501 3rd St. NW, Washington DC 20001 USA
Tel: 202-239-4880
www.ifpte.org
To represent employees in a wide variety of occupations in the technical, administrative & professional fields
Gregory J. Junemann, President

International Longshore & Warehouse Union (CLC) / Syndicat international des débardeurs et magasiniers (CTC)
1188 Franklin St., 4th Fl., San Francisco CA 94109 USA
Tel: 415-775-0533; *Fax:* 415-775-1302
info@ilwu.org
www.ilwu.org
ILWU is an international warehouse union representing the rights of their members.
Robert McEllrath, President

International Longshoremen's Association (AFL-CIO/CLC) (ILA) / Association internationale des débardeurs (FAT-COI/CTC)
#930, 17 Battery Pl., New York NY 10004 USA
Tel: 212-425-1200; *Fax:* 212-425-2928
jmcnamara@ilaunion.org
ilaunion.org
Richard P. Hughes, President
Robert E. Gleason, Sec.-Treas.

International Union of Bricklayers & Allied Craftworkers (AFL-CIO/CFL) (BAC) / Union internationale des briqueteurs et métiers connexes (FAT-COI/FCT)
620 F St. NW, Washington DC 20004 USA
Tel: 202-783-3788; *Toll-Free:* 888-880-8222
askbac@bacweb.org
www.bacweb.org
John J. Flynn, President

International Union of Elevator Constructors (AFL-CIO/CFL) (IUEC) / Union internationale des constructeurs d'ascenseurs (FAT-COI/FCT)
7154 Columbia Gateway Dr., Columbia MD 21046 USA
Tel: 410-953-6150; *Fax:* 410-953-6169
contact@iuec.org
www.iuec.org

International Union of Operating Engineers (AFL-CIO/CFL) / Union internationale des opérateurs de machines lourdes (FAT-COI/FCT)
1125 - 17 St. NW, Washington DC 20036 USA
Tel: 202-429-9100; *Fax:* 202-778-2613
www.iuoe.org
Vincent J. Giblin, President

International Union of Painters & Allied Trades (AFL-CIO/CFL) / Syndicat international des peintres et métiers connexes (FAT-COI/FCT)
1750 New York Ave. NW, Washington DC 20006 USA
Tel: 202-637-0700
mail@iupat.org
www.iupat.org

International Union, United Automobile, Aerospace & Agricultural Implement Workers of America, Local 251 (CLC) (UAW) / Syndicat international des travailleurs unis de l'automobile, de l'aérospatiale et de l'outillage agricole d'Amérique (C
8000 East Jefferson Ave., Detroit MI 48214 USA
Tel: 313-926-5000; *Toll-Free:* 800-243-8829
www.uaw.org
UAW is one of the largest & most diverse unions in North America, with members in virtually every sector of the economy. It is the collective bargaining body for its members, negotiating for wages & benefits.
Bob King, President
Dennis Williams, Sec.-Treas.

Laborers' International Union of North America (AFL-CIO/CLC) (LiUNA) / Union internationale des journaliers d'Amérique (FAT-COI/CTC)
905 - 16 St. NW, Washington DC 20006 USA
Tel: 202-737-8320; *Fax:* 202-737-2754
communications@liuna.org
www.liuna.org
Union fighting for better wages and benefits, safer jobsites, more successful employers, and a strong voice for the people.
Armand Sabitoni, General Sec.-Treas.
Terence M. O'Sullivan, President

Major League Baseball Players' Association (Ind.) / Association des joueurs de la Ligue majeure de baseball (ind.)
12 East 49th St., 24th Fl., New York NY 10017 USA
Tel: 212-826-0808; *Fax:* 212-752-4378
feedback@mlbpa.org
www.majorleaguebaseball.com/
To represent and protect the interests of professional baseball players in the United States.
Donald M. Fehr, Executive Director
Gene Orza, Chief Operating Officer

Management & Professional Employees Society of BC Hydro (Ind.) (MAPES) / Société des employés professionnels et administratifs (ind.)
12388 - 88 Ave., Surrey BC V3W 7R7 Canada
Tel: 604-590-7454; *Fax:* 604-597-6656
john.vandermaar@powertech.bc.ca
To bargain collectively with Powertech Labs Inc. & its subsidiaries or successors on behalf of the members of the society with respect to all matters concerning terms & conditions of employment; to encourage & promote innovative concepts & procedures in the field of industrial relations; to adopt such procedures to the resolution of disputes between the society & the companies
Livio Gambone, President

Manitoba Association of Health Care Professionals (MAHCP) / Association des professionnels de la santé du Manitoba
#101, 1500 Notre Dame Ave., Winnipeg MB R3E 0P9 Canada
Tel: 204-772-0425; *Fax:* 204-775-6829
Toll-Free: 800-315-3331
info@mahcp.ca
www.mahcp.com
MAHCP is a union of health care professionals dedicated to protecting, advocating for, and advancing the rights of its members through labour relations activities.
Wendy Despins, President

Manitoba Federation of Labour / Fédération du travail du Manitoba
#303, 275 Broadway, Winnipeg MB R3C 4M6 Canada
Tel: 204-947-1400; *Fax:* 204-943-4276
www.mfl.mb.ca
To advance economic & social welfare of working people in Manitoba; to encourage workers to vote & exercise full rights & responsibilities.
Darlene Dziewit, President

Maritime Fishermen's Union (CLC) (MFU) / Union des pêcheurs des Maritimes (CTC) (UPM)
408 Main St., Shediac NB E4P 2G1 Canada
Tel: 506-532-2485; *Fax:* 506-532-2487
shediac@mfu-upm.com
www.mfu-upm.com
The Maritime Fishermen's Union (MFU) represents over 1,800 fishermen/owner-operators, in New Brunswick and Nova Scotia. The MFU works to maintain a sustainable inshore fishery and defends the principal of the fishermen/owner-operator. Most MFU fishers practice a multi-species fishery with vessels under 15 meters.
Christian Brun, Executive Secretary

Mechanical Service Contractors of Canada (MSCC)
#601, 280 Albert St., Ottawa ON K1P 5G8 Canada
Tel: 613-232-0017; *Fax:* 613-235-2793
daryl@mcac.ca
www.servicecontractor.ca
The Mechanical Service Contractors of Canada (MSCC), a division of the Mechanical Contractors Association of Canada, is dedicated to mechanical service, repair and retrofit contractors.
Daryl Sharkey, Chief Operating Officer

National Automobile, Aerospace, Transportation & General Workers Union of Canada (CLC) (CAW-Canada) / Syndicat national de l'automobile, de l'aérospatiale, du transport et des autres travailleurs et travailleuses du Canada
205 Placer Ct., Toronto ON M2H 3H9 Canada
Tel: 416-497-4110; *Fax:* 416-495-6559
caw@caw.ca
www.caw.ca
To improve the working conditions & general economic & social conditions of Canadian workers
Basil "Buzz" Hargrove, National President
Jim O'Neil, National Sec.-Treas.
Luc Desnoyers, Québec Director

Native Brotherhood of British Columbia (NBBC) / Fraternité des Indiens de la Colombie-Britannique
#710, 100 Park Royal South, Vancouver BC V7T 1A2 Canada
Tel: 604-913-3372; *Fax:* 604-913-3374
nbbc@nativevoice.bc.ca
www.nativevoice.bc.ca
To advance the social, spiritual, economic & physical conditions of its members, including higher standards of education, health & living conditions; to cooperate with other organizations which concern themselves with the advancement of Indian welfare; focus is on capacity building, including fisheries, marine resources, tourism & eco-tourism, forestry & other resources with economic potential & opportunities

Natural Resources Union (NRU)
#600, 233 Gilmour St., Ottawa ON K2P 0P2 Canada
Tel: 613-560-4378; *Fax:* 613-233-7012
info@nru-srn.com
www.nru-srn.com
Claudia Thompson, National President

New Brunswick Federation of Labour (NBFL) / Fédération des travailleurs et travailleuses du Nouveau-Brunswick
#314, 96 Norwood Ave., Moncton NB E1C 6L9
Tel: 506-857-2125; *Fax:* 506-383-1597
nbfl@nbnet.nb.ca; fttnb@nbnet.nb.ca
www.nbfl-fttnb.ca
To act as the central voice of labour in New Brunswick; To build solidarity & support between unions; To advance the economic & social welfare of New Brunswick's workers
Michel Boudreau, President
Ron Oldfield, First Vice-President
Thérèse Tremblay, Second Vice-President
Alex Bailey, Vice-President, Youth
Sandy Harding, Vice-President, Women's Issues
Danny King, Secretary-Treasurer

Newfoundland & Labrador Association of Public & Private Employees (NAPE)
PO Box 8100, 330 Portugal Cove Pl., St. John's NL A1B 3M9 Canada
Tel: 709-754-0700; *Fax:* 709-754-0726
Toll-Free: 800-563-4442
inquiries@nape.nf.ca
www.nape.nf.ca
The largest union in Newfoundland & Labrador.
Bert Blundon, Sec.-Treas.
Carol Furlong, President
Arlene Sedlickas, Vice President

Newfoundland & Labrador Federation of Labour (NLFL) / Fédération du travail de Terre-Neuve et du Labrador
NAPE Bldg., PO Box 8597, Stn. A, 330 Portugal Cove Pl., 2nd Fl., St. John's NL A1B 3P2 Canada
Tel: 709-754-1660; *Fax:* 709-754-1220
fed@nlfl.nf.ca
www.nlfl.nf.ca
The voice of labour in the province, with 30 affiliated unions, & over 500 locals in 6 district labour councils
Lana Payne, President
Linda Rideout, Executive Secretary

Northern Territories Federation of Labour / Fédération du travail des Territoires du Nord
PO Box 2787, Yellowknife NT X1A 2R1 Canada
Tel: 867-873-3695; *Fax:* 867-873-6979
ntfl@yk.com
www.ntfl.yk.com
An umbrella labour organization serving workers in the NWT & Nunavut, & the voice of all unions & workers in Canada's northern region; office located at 9 Stanton Plaza, 100 Borden Dr. in Yellowknife.
Mary Lou Cherwaty, President

Nova Scotia Federation of Labour / Fédération du travail de la Nouvelle-Écosse
#225, 3700 Kempt Rd., Halifax NS B3K 4X8 Canada
Tel: 902-454-6735; *Fax:* 902-454-7671
info@nsfl.ns.ca
www.nsfl.ns.ca
The Federation speaks on behalf of and represents the interests of organized and unorganized workers. It promotes decent wages and working conditions, improved health and safety laws and lobbies for fair taxes and strong social programs. It works for social equality, and to end racism and discrimination.
Rick Clarke, President
Ivy Shaw, Sec.-Treas.

Nova Scotia Government & General Employees Union (NSGEU) / Syndicat de la fonction publique de la Nouvelle-Écosse
100 Eileen Stubbs Ave., Dartmouth NS B3B 1Y6 Canada
Tel: 902-424-4063; *Fax:* 902-424-2111
Toll-Free: 877-556-7438
inquiry@nsgeu.ns.ca
www.nsgeu.ns.ca
The Nova Scotia Government & General Employees Union (NSGEU) is the largest union in the province of Nova Scotia and is the recognized bargaining agent for 26,000 public and private sector employees. Our members work in the civil service, school boards, universities, hospitals, liquor stores, correctional facilities, Regional Health Boards, municipalities, and other establishments across the Province.
Joan Jessome, President

Nova Scotia Union of Public & Private Employees (CCU) (NSUPE) / Syndicat des employés du secteur public de la Nouvelle-Écosse (CCU)
6309 Chebucto Rd., Halifax NS B3L 1K9 Canada
Tel: 902-422-9495; *Fax:* 902-429-7655
nsupe@ns.sympatico.ca
www.nsupe.ca
NSUPE is a trade union dedicated to bettering and protecting the livelihood and the social and economic well-being of its members, their families and fellow citizens.
John Hanrahan, President
Nancy Travis, Vice-President

Nunavut Employees Union (NEU)
PO Box 869, Iqaluit NU X0A 0H0 Canada
Tel: 867-979-4209; *Fax:* 867-979-4522
Toll-Free: 877-243-4424
info@neu.ca
www.neu.ca
The Nunavut Employees Union represents the interests of the employees of the Government of Nunavut, the Northwest Territories Power Corporation who live in Nunavut, Workers Compensation Board in Nunavut, Nunavut Housing Corporation,

and the unionized employees of Nunavut municipalities and Housing Associations. Most of our members work for the Government of Nunavut and live all across the territory. Others belong to Canada Labour Code bargaining units representing Housing Associations and Authorities, Hamlet and town employees, and support staff in schools. NEU members are social workers and nurses, health care professionals, power plant workers, security guards, hamlet bylaw officers, renewable resource officers, engineers, and many more.
Doug Workman, President
Brian Boutilier, Executive Director

Office & Professional Employees International Union (AFL-CIO/CLC) / Union internationale des employés professionnels et de bureau (FAT-COI/CTC)
1660 L St. NW, Washington DC 20036 USA
Tel: 202-393-4464
opeiu@opeiu.org
www.opeiu.org
Michael Goodwin, President

Ontario Federation of Labour (OFL) / Fédération du travail de l'Ontario
#202, 15 Gervais Dr., Toronto ON M3C 1Y8 Canada
Tel: 416-441-2731; *Fax:* 416-441-0722
Toll-Free: 800-668-9138
TDD: 416-443-6305
info@ofl.ca
www.ofl.ca
To represent the interests of organized workers in Ontario; to provide support services to its affiliated local unions & labour councils.
Flora Clegg, President
Judy Chow, Sec.-Treas.

Ontario Professional Fire Fighters Association (OPFFA) / Association des pompiers professionnels de l'Ontario (ind.)
292 Plains Rd. East, Burlington ON L7T 2C6
Tel: 905-681-7111; *Fax:* 905-681-1489
www.opffa.org
Fred LeBlanc, President
Mark McKinnon, Executive Vice-President
Barry Quinn, Secretary-Treasurer
Jeff Braun-Jackson, Office Manager & Researcher

Ontario Public Service Employees Union (OPSEU) / Syndicat des employées et employés de la fonction publique de l'Ontario
100 Lesmill Rd., Toronto ON M3B 3P8 Canada
Tel: 416-443-8888; *Fax:* 416-443-9670
Toll-Free: 800-268-7376
opseu@opseu.org
www.opseu.org
To negotiate collective agreements; to conduct membership education; to lobby governments to maintain & improve public services; to defend the principle of social unionism by speaking out on public policy issues such as taxes, free trade, privatization, health care, social services, occupational health & safety, & employment equity.
Smokey Thomas, President

Operative Plasterers' & Cement Masons' International Association of the US & Canada (AFL-CIO/CFL) - Canadian Office
Varette Bldg., #1902, 130 Albert St., Ottawa ON K1P 5G4 Canada
Tel: 613-236-0653; *Fax:* 613-230-5138
cdnoffice@buildingtrades.ca
www.buildingtrades.ca
We represent over 400,000 construction workers who belong to the 15 affiliated international Building Trades unions in Canada.
Robert Blakely, Director, Canadian Affairs

Prince Edward Island Federation of Labour / Fédération du travail de l'Ile-du-Prince-Édouard
22 Enman Cres., Charlottetown PE C1A 1E6 Canada
Tel: 902-368-3068; *Fax:* 902-368-3192
peifed@pei.aibn.com
www.peifl.ca
Carl Pursey, President

Prince Edward Island Union of Public Sector Employees / Syndicat de la fonction publique de l'Ile-du-Prince-Édouard
PO Box 1116, 4 Enman Cres. South, Charlottetown PE C1A 7M8 Canada
Tel: 902-892-5335; *Fax:* 902-569-8186
Toll-Free: 800-897-8773
peiupse@peiupse.ca
www.peiupse.ca

Shelly Ward, President

Professional Association of Foreign Service Officers (Ind.) (PAFSO) / L'Association professionnelle des agents du service extérieur (ind.) (APASE)
#412, 47 Clarence St., Ottawa ON K1N 9K1 Canada
Tel: 613-241-1391; *Fax:* 613-241-5911
info@pafso.com
www.pafso.com
Ron Cochrane, Executive Director

Professional Association of Internes & Residents of Newfoundland (PAIRN) / Association professionnelle des internes et résidents de Terre-Neuve
c/o Student Affairs, Health Sciences Complex, Memorial University, #2867, 300 Prince Philip Dr., St. John's NL A1B 3V6
Tel: 709-777-7118; *Fax:* 709-777-6968
pairn@mun.ca
www.pairn.nl.ca
To collaborate with local & national health care organizations to advocate on behalf of internes, resident physicians, & fellows of Newfoundland & Labrador; To advocate for the acknowledgement of the resident's role in medical education
Chris Smith, President
Pamela Hebbard, Vice-President
Deanna Murphy, Secretary
Sohaib Al-Asaaed, Treasurer

Professional Association of Interns & Residents of Saskatchewan (PAIRS) / Association professionnelle des internes et résidents de la Saskatchewan (ind.)
C Wing, Royal University Hospital, PO Box 23, #5687, 103 Hospital Dr., 5th Fl., Saskatoon SK S7N 0W8
Tel: 306-655-2134; *Fax:* 306-655-2134
pairs.sk@usask.ca
www.usask.ca/pairs
To represent resident physicians of Saskatchewan at the university & hospital levels, as well as provincially & nationally; To improve education, salaries, & other benefits for resident physicians
Gavin Beck, President
Sue Sidhu, Vice-President
Nove Kalia, Secretary-Treasurer
Joan Cheyne, Executive Director

Professional Association of Residents & Interns of Manitoba (PARIM) / Association professionnelle des résidents et internes du Manitoba
#AD107, 720 McDermot Ave., Winnipeg MB R3E 0T3
Tel: 204-787-3673; *Fax:* 204-787-2692
parim@mts.net
www.parim.org
To represent the concerns of all residents & interns in Manitoba; To advocate for the well-being of residents & interns; To promote quality medical education & excellent patient care
Marc Fournier, Co-President
Paul Wawryko, Co-President
Jay Hingwala, Vice-President, Internal Affairs & Finance
Fatemeh Kojori, Vice-President, Social & Well-being
Kanwal Kumar, Vice-President, Communications

Professional Association of Residents in the Maritime Provinces (PARI-MP) / Association professionnelle des résidents des provinces maritimes
Halifax Professional Centre, #460, 5991 Spring Garden Rd., Halifax NS B3H 1Y6
Tel: 902-404-3595; *Fax:* 902-404-3599
Toll-Free: 877-972-7467
sandi@parimp.ca
www.parimp.ca
To represent the interests of resident physicians who train at Dalhousie University; To improve the well-being & working conditions of residents in the Maritimes; To advocate on the behalf of residents
Laine Green, President
Matt Smith, Vice-President
Bryan Chung, Secretary
Kerri Purdy, Treasurer
Sandi Carew Flemming, Executive Director
Leanne Bryan, Coordinator, Benefits & Events

Professional Association of Residents of Alberta (PARA) / Association professionnelle des résidents de l'Alberta
Garneau Professional Center, #340, 11044 - 82 Ave., Edmonton AB T6G 0J2
Tel: 780-432-1749; *Fax:* 780-432-1778
para-ab@shawbiz.ca
www.para-ab.ca
To represent physicians completing further training in residency programs; To promote excellence in education & patient care; To advocate for health care issues & for improvement in working conditions, salary, & benefits for resident physicians of Alberta
Michelle Carle, President
Henry Conter, Vice-President, Internal Affairs
Kenman Gan, Vice-President, Operations & Finance
Jillian Schwartz, Vice-President, External Affairs
Sarah Thomas, Executive Director
Tana Findlay, Executive Director, Operations

Professional Association of Residents of British Columbia (PAR-BC) / Association professionnelle des résidents de la Colombie-Britannique
#2010, 401 West Georgia St., Vancouver BC V6B 5A1
Tel: 604-876-7636; *Fax:* 604-876-7690
Toll-Free: 888-877-2722
par@par-bc.org
www.par-bc.org
To bargain collectively on behalf of residents in British Columbia; To foster the personal well-being of members
Mark Masterson, President
Sam Gharbi, Vice-President
Sana Ahmed, Director, Communications
May Tee, Director, Finance

Professional Employees Association (Ind.) (PEA) / Association des employés professionnels (ind.)
#201, 1001 Wharf St., Victoria BC V8W 1T6 Canada
Tel: 250-385-8791; *Fax:* 250-385-6629
jjensen@pea.org
www.pea.org
To provide collective bargaining representation to professionals employed in the provincial public service & elsewhere in the BC public sector
Jodi Jensen, Executive Director

Professional Engineers Government of Ontario
#206, 3199 Bathurst St., Toronto ON M6A 2B2 Canada
Tel: 416-784-1284; *Fax:* 416-784-1366
pego@pego.on.ca
www.pego.on.ca
The Professional Engineers Government of Ontario (PEGO) is a certified bargaining association representing Professional Engineers and Ontario Land Surveyors working directly for the Government of the Province of Ontario.
John Gasbarri, President

The Professional Institute of the Public Service of Canada (PIPSC) / Institut professionnel de la fonction publique du Canada
250 Tremblay Rd., Ottawa ON K1G 3J8 Canada
Tel: 613-228-6310; *Fax:* 613-228-9048
Toll-Free: 800-267-0446
www.pipsc.ca
To serve members by serving as their collective bargaining agent & by providing representational services
Gary Corbett, President
Edward Gillis, COO/Executive Secretary

Public Service Alliance of Canada (CLC) (PSAC) / Alliance de la Fonction publique du Canada (CTC) (AFPC)
233 Gilmour St., Ottawa ON K2P 0P1 Canada
Tel: 613-560-4200; *Fax:* 613-567-0385
Toll-Free: 888-604-7722
www.psac.com
To unite all workers in a single democratic organization; to obtain for all public service employees the best standards of compensation & other conditions of employment & to protect the rights & interests of all public service employees; to maintain & defend the right to strike
John Gordon, National President
Jeannie Baldwin, Regional Executive Vice-President, Atlantic
Kay Sinclair, Regional Executive Vice-President, B.C.
Robyn Benson, Regional Executive Vice-President, Prairies
Patty Ducharme, National Vice-President
Gerry Halabecki, Regional Executive Vice-President, Ontario
Jérôme Turcq, Vice-président exécutif régional, Québec
Jean-François Des Lauriers, Regional Executive Vice-President, North
Maria Fitzpatrick, Regional Executive Vice-President, National Capital Region

Pulp, Paper & Woodworkers of Canada (CCU) (PPWC)
#201, 1184 - 6 Ave. West, Vancouver BC V6H 1A4 Canada
Tel: 604-731-1909; *Fax:* 604-731-6448
Toll-Free: 888-992-7792
louise@web.net
www.ppwc.ca
Chris Elias, President

Research Council Employees' Association (Ind.) (RCEA) / Association des employés du conseil de recherches (ind.) (AECR)
PO Box 8256, Ottawa ON K1G 3H7 Canada
Tel: 613-746-9341; *Fax:* 613-745-7868
office@rcea.ca
www.rcea.ca
The RCEA is the certified bargaining agent for six groups and categories and represents the majority of NRC employees. These groups and categories are: AD (Administrative Support) Group, AS (Administrative Services) Group, CS (Computer Systems Administration) Group, OP (Operational) Category, PG (Purchasing and Supply) Group, and TO(Technical) Category.
Serge Croteau, President
Laurette T. Ernst, Office Manager

Royal Newfoundland Constabulary Association (RNCA) / Fraternité des policiers de la gendarmerie royale de Terre-Neuve
125 East White Hills Rd., St. John's NL A1A 5R7 Canada
Tel: 709-739-5946; *Fax:* 709-739-6276
office@rnca.ca
www.rnca.ca
The goals and objectives of the RNCA are to improve benefits and working conditions for police officers, improve public safety and strive to create a positive relationship between the police and the community they protect.
Todd Barron, President

Saskatchewan Government & General Employees' Union (SGEU) / Syndicat de la fonction publique de la Saskatchewan
1440 Broadway Ave., Regina SK S4P 1E2 Canada
Tel: 306-522-8571; *Fax:* 306-352-1969
Toll-Free: 800-667-5221
general@sgeu.org
www.sgeu.org
Bob Bymoen, President

Saskatchewan Joint Board, Retail, Wholesale & Department Store Union (CLC) / Conseil mixte du syndicat des employés de gros, de détail et de magasins à rayons de la Saskatchewan (CTC)
1233 Winnipeg St., Regina SK S4R 1K1 Canada
Tel: 306-569-9311; *Fax:* 306-569-9521
Toll-Free: 877-747-9378
rwdsu.regina@sasktel.net
www.rwdsu.sk.ca
Chris Banting, Secretary Treasurer

Schneider Employees' Association (Ind.) / Association des employés de Schneider (ind.)
321 Courtland Ave. East, Kitchener ON N2G 3X8 Canada
Tel: 519-741-5000; *Fax:* 519-744-5099
sea321@execulink.com
Dennis Lesperance, National President

Seafarers' International Union of Canada (AFL-CIO/CLC) / Syndicat international des marins canadiens (FAT-COI/CTC)
1333, rue Saint-Jacques, Montréal QC H3C 4K2 Canada
Tel: 514-931-7859; *Fax:* 514-931-3667
siuofcanada@seafarers.ca
www.seafarers.ca
Michel Desjardins, President

Service Employees International Union (AFL-CIO/CLC) / Union internationale des employés des services (FAT-COI/CTC)
1800 Massachusetts Ave. NW, Washington DC 20036 USA
Tel: 202-730-7000; *Fax:* 202-898-3402
Toll-Free: 800-424-8592
TDD: 202-730-7481
www.seiu.org
Social Media: facebook.com/seiu?via=sidebar
SEIU is focused on uniting workers in 3 sectors: healthcare, property services, & public services. The union aims to improve the lives of its members, their families, & the services they provide.

Sheet Metal Workers' International Association (AFL-CIO/CFL) (SMWIA) / Association internationale des travailleurs du métal en feuilles (FAT-COI/FCT)
1750 New York Ave. NW, 6th Fl., Washington DC 20006 USA
Tel: 202-783-5880
info@smwia.org
www.smwia.org
SMWIA aims to establish & maintain desirable working conditions for its members, & is their collective bargaining agent.
Mike Sullivan, General President

Shipyard General Workers' Federation of British Columbia (CLC) / Fédération des ouvriers des chantiers navals de la Colombie-Britannique (CTC)
#130, 111 Victoria Dr., Vancouver BC V5L 4C4 Canada
Tel: 604-254-8204; *Fax:* 604-254-7447
office@bcshipyardworkers.com
www.bcshipyardworkers.com
George MacPherson, President
Quentin Del Vecchio, General Secretary

Société des Auteurs de Radio, Télévision et Cinéma (SARTEC) / Society of Writers in Radio, Television & Cinema
1229, rue Panet, Montréal QC H2L 2Y6 Canada
Tél: 514-526-9196; *Téléc:* 514-526-4124
information@sartec.qc.ca
www.sartec.qc.ca
Regroupe les auteurs de langue française oeuvrant au Canada dans les domaines de la radio, de la télévision, du cinéma ou de l'audiovisuel; a pour objet l'étude, la défense et le développement des intérêts économiques, sociaux et moraux de ses membres
Yves Légaré, Directeur général
Marc Grégoire, Président

Société des technologues en nutrition (STN)
895, boul Charest ouest, Québec QC G1N 2C9 Canada
Tél: 418-990-0309
stn@stnq.ca
www.stnq.ca
Signer des contrats collectifs de travail; surveiller la mise en application des conditions de travail des membres; promouvoir la défense et les intérêts économiques et professionnels des membres

The Society of Energy Professionals
#300, 425 Bloor St. East., Toronto ON M4W 3R4 Canada
Tel: 416-979-2709; *Fax:* 416-979-5794
Toll-Free: 866-288-1788
society@society.on.ca
www.thesociety.ca
To represent the interests of the professional, administrative, & associated employees in all aspects of their employment with Ontario Hydro
Rodney Sheppard, President

Society of Professional Engineers & Associates (SPEA) / Société des ingénieurs professionnels et associés
#2, 2275 Speakman Dr., Mississauga ON L5K 1B1
Tel: 905-823-3606; *Fax:* 905-823-9602
www.spea.ca
To represent scientists, engineers, technologists, & tradespeople who work for Atomic Energy of Canada Limited (AECL) in Mississauga, Ontario & abroad
Peter White, President
Val Aleyaseen, Chair, Membership
Vincent Tume, Secretary
Brian Girard, Treasurer

Space Systems Engineers & Scientists Association (SSESA) / Association des ingénieurs et des scientifiques des systèmes spatiaux (AISSS)
1073, rue Saint-Denis, Montréal QC H2X 3J3 Canada
Tel: 514-844-1347; *Fax:* 514-844-8037
lauzon.d@ems-t.ca
www.aisss-ssesa.org
Dominick Lauzon, President

Syndicat de la fonction publique du Québec inc. (ind.) (SFPQ) / Québec Government Employees' Union (Ind.)
5100, boul des Gradins, Québec QC G2J 1N4 Canada
Tél: 418-623-2424; *Téléc:* 418-623-6109
communication@sfpq.qc.ca
www.sfpq.qc.ca
Assurer la défense des intérêts économiques, politiques et sociaux des membres et le développement de leurs conditions de vie; faire la promotion des services publics comme moyen démocratique de répondre aux besoins de la population
Lucie Martineau, Présidente général

Syndicat de professionnelles et professionnels du gouvernement du Québec (SPGQ) / Union of Professional Employees of the Québec Government
7, rue Vallière, Québec QC G1K 6S9 Canada
Tél: 418-692-0022; *Téléc:* 418-692-1338
Ligne sans frais: 800-463-5079
courrier@spgq.qc.ca
www.spgq.qc.ca
Gilles Dussault, Président
Michael Isaacs, Secrétaire

Syndicat des agents de la paix en services correctionnels du Québec (ind.) (SAPSCQ) / Union of Prison Guards of Québec (Ind.)
4906, boul Gouin est, Montréal QC H1G 1A4 Canada
Tél: 514-328-7774; *Téléc:* 514-328-0889
Ligne sans frais: 800-361-3559
s.lemaire@sapscq.com
www.sapscq.com
Service syndical pour les agents de la paix en services correctionnels du Québec
Stéphane Lemaire, Président national
Arthur Kassombola, Vice-président
Sylvain Maltais, Secrétaire général

Syndicat des agents de maîtrise de TELUS (ind.) (SAMT) / TELUS Professional Employees Union (Ind.) (TPEU)
#605, 2, St-Germain est, Rimouski QC G5L 8T7 Canada
Tél: 418-722-6144; *Téléc:* 418-724-0765
samt2@globetrotter.net
La sauvegarde et la promotion des intérêts professionnels, scientifiques, économiques, sociaux, culturels et politiques de ses membres; faire bénéficier les membres et les travailleurs en général des avantages de l'entraide et des négociations collectives; obtenir pour ses membres un meilleur niveau de vie et de meilleures conditions de travail; représenter les membres auprès de l'employeur
Harold Morrissey, Président
Lynda Fortin, Secrétaire

Syndicat des employé(e)s de magasins et de bureau de la Société des alcools du Québec (ind.) / Québec Liquor Board Store & Office Employees Union (Ind.)
1065, rue St-Denis, Montréal QC H2X 3J3 Canada
Tél: 514-849-7754; *Téléc:* 514-849-7914
Ligne sans frais: 800-361-8427
info@semb-saq.com
www.semb-saq.com/index.html
Katia Lelièvre, Présidente

Syndicat des employés en radio-télédiffusion de Télé-Québec (CSQ) / Télé-Québec Television Broadcast Employees' Union
1000, rue Fullum, Montréal QC H2K 3L7 Canada
Tél: 514-529-2805; *Téléc:* 514-873-0826
sert@colba.net
sert.csq.qc.net/

Syndicat des intervenants professionnels de la santé du Québec (SIPSQ)
#850, 1001, rue Sherbrooke est, Montréal QC H2L 1L3 Canada
Tél: 514-521-4469; *Téléc:* 514-521-0086
Ligne sans frais: 866-480-0086
infocps@cpsq.qc.ca
Organisation syndicale
Maria Piazza, Présidente

Syndicat des physiothérapeutes et des thérapeutes en réadaptation physique du Québec (SPTRPQ)
#850, 1001, rue Sherbrooke est, Montréal QC H2L 1L3 Canada
Tél: 514-521-4469; *Téléc:* 514-521-0086
Défendre et promouvoir les intérêts sociaux, économiques et éducatifs de ses membres
Pauline Caux, Présidente

Syndicat des pompiers et pompières du Québec (CTC) (SPQ) / Québec Union of Firefighters (CLC)
#3900, 565, boul Crémazie est, Montréal QC H2M 2V6 Canada
Tél: 514-383-4698; *Téléc:* 514-383-6782
Ligne sans frais: 800-461-4698
spq@spq-ftq.com
www.spq-ftq.com
Gilles Raymond, Président

Syndicat des professeures et professeurs de l'Université de Sherbrooke (SPPUS)
2500, boul Université, Sherbrooke QC J1K 2R1 Canada
Tél: 819-821-7656; *Téléc:* 819-821-7995
sppus@usherbrooke.ca
www.usherbrooke.ca/sppus
Voir à l'application de la convention collective; défendre les intérêts des membres

Syndicat des professeurs de l'État du Québec (ind.) (SPEQ) / Union of Professors for the Government of Québec (Ind.)
#1003, 2120, rue Sherbrooke est, Montréal QC H2K 1C3 Canada
Tél: 514-525-7979; *Téléc:* 514-525-4655
Ligne sans frais: 877-525-7979
info@speq.org
www.speq.org
Le Syndicat des professeurs de l'État du Québec (SPEQ) a été accrédité le 8 septembre 1965 pour représenter les fonctionnaires enseignants salariés.
Claude Tanguay, Président

Syndicat des professionnels et des techniciens de la santé du Québec (SPTSQ) / Québec Union of Health Professionals & Technicians
#850, 1001, rue Sherbrooke est, Montréal QC H2L 1L3 Canada
Tél: 514-521-4469; *Téléc:* 514-521-0086
Défense des intérêts socio-économiques de ses membres

Syndicat des technicien(ne)s et artisan(e)s du réseau français de Radio-Canada (ind.) (STARF) / CBC French Network Technicians' Union (Ind.)
1250, rue de la Visitation, 1er étage, Montréal QC H2L 3B4 Canada
Tél: 514-524-1100; *Téléc:* 514-524-6023
Ligne sans frais: 888-838-1100
secretariat@starf.qc.ca
www.starf.qc.ca
Benoît Celestino, Président
Marie-France Clément, Secrétaire-trésorier

Syndicat des technologues en radiologie du Québec (ind.) (STRQ) / Union of Radiology Technicians of Québec
#850, 1001, rue Sherbrooke est, Montréal QC H2L 1L3 Canada
Tél: 514-521-4469; *Téléc:* 514-521-0086
Étude, développement et la défense des intérêts professionnels, économiques, sociaux et éducatifs de ses membres et particulièrement la négociation et l'application de conventions collectives.
Robert Carrier, Président

Syndicat des travailleurs de la construction du Québec (CSD)
#300, 801, 4e rue, Québec QC G1J 2T7 Canada
Tél: 418-522-3918; *Téléc:* 418-529-6323
www.csdconstruction.qc.ca
Défendre et promouvoir les intérêts sociaux et économiques de ses membres
Patrick Daigneault, Président
Guy Terrault, Vice-président
Gilles C. Coulombe, Secrétaire

Syndicat du personnel technique et professionnel de la Société des alcools du Québec (ind.) (SPTPSAQ) / Québec Liquor Board's Union of Technical & Professional Employees (Ind.)
905, rue de Lorimier, Montréal QC H2K 3V9 Canada
Tél: 514-873-5878; *Téléc:* 514-873-5896
sptp@bellnet.ca
Yves St-Georges, Président

Syndicat général du cinéma et de la télévision - Section Office national du film (ind.) (SGCT)
#25A, 2340, ch Lucerne, Mont-Royal QC H3R 2J8 Canada
Tél: 514-344-9399; *Téléc:* 514-344-9509
Représenter les cinéastes et techniciens employés par l'Office National du Film du Canada

Syndicat interprovincial des ferblantiers et couvreurs, la section locale 2016 à la FTQ-Construction
#400, 8550, boul Pie IX, Montréal QC H1Z 4G2 Canada
Tél: 514-374-1515; *Téléc:* 514-374-2282
Ligne sans frais: 866-374-1515
administration@ftq2016.org
www.ftq2016.org
Voir à la promotion et à la défense des intérêts économiques et sociaux des membres; assurer l'intégrité du métier de ferblantier et couvreur en défendant sa juridiction professionnelle et en assurant sa sécurité d'emploi; représenter les travailleurs, que leur travail soit effectué à l'intérieur du chantier de construction ou non; cultiver des sentiments de solidarité parmis les travailleurs; obtenir des améliorations dans les conditions de travail de ses membres
Dorima Aubut, Directeur provincial

Syndicat professionnel des diététistes et nutritionnistes du Québec (SPDNQ) / Québec Professional Union of Dieticians (Ind.)
2665, rue Beaubien est, Montréal QC H1Y 1G8 Canada
Tél: 514-725-5535; *Téléc:* 514-725-4433
executif@spdnq.qc.ca
www.spdnq.qc.ca
Claudette Péloquin-Antoun, Présidente

Syndicat professionnel des ingénieurs d'Hydro-Québec (ind.) (SPIHQ) / Hydro-Québec Professional Engineers Union (Ind.)
#1400, rue University, Montréal QC H3B 3X1 Canada
Tél: 514-845-4239; *Téléc:* 514-845-0082
Ligne sans frais: 800-567-1260
spihq@spihq.qc.ca
www.spihq.qc.ca
Le Syndicat travaille pour la défense & le développement des intérêts économiques, sociaux, & professionnels des membres
Ramzi Chahine, Président
Michel Touchette, Secrétaire

Syndicat professionnel des médecins du gouvernement du Québec (ind.) (SPMGQ) / Professional Union of Government of Québec Physicians (Ind.)
1390, rue du Père-Jamet, Sainte-Foy QC G1W 3G5 Canada
Tél: 418-266-4670; *Téléc:* 418-266-4672
christine.gagne@csst.qc.ca
Représenter les médecins à l'emploi du gouvernement du Québec
Christine Gagné, Présidente

Syndicat québécois de la construction (SQC) / North Shore Construction Inc. (Ind.)
2121, av Sainte-Anne, Saint-Hyacinthe QC J2S 5H5 Canada
Tél: 450-773-8833; *Téléc:* 450-773-2232
Ligne sans frais: 888-773-8834
info@sqc.ca
www.sqc.ca
Sylvain Gendron, Président

Teaching Support Staff Union (TSSU)
Simon Fraser University, AQ 5129/5130, 8888 University Dr., Burnaby BC V5A 1S6 Canada
Tel: 604-291-4735; *Fax:* 604-291-5369
tssu@tssu.ca
www.tssu.ca
Social Media: www.twitter.com/TSSU
Scott Drake, Organizer

Teamsters Canada (CLC)
#804, 2540, boul Daniel Johnson, Laval QC H7T 2S3 Canada
Tél: 450-682-5521; *Téléc:* 450-681-2244
Ligne sans frais: 866-888-6466
info@teamsters-canada.org
www.teamsters.ca
Média social: www.facebook.com/group.php?gid=5512214518
Robert Bouvier, Président
Tom Fraser, Vice-président
Don McGill, Vice-président

Teamsters Canada Rail Conference (TCRC) / Conference ferroviaire de Teamsters Canada (CFTC)
#1710, 130 Albert St., Ottawa ON K1P 5G4 Canada
Tel: 613-235-1828; *Fax:* 613-235-1069
info@teamstersrail.ca
www.teamstersrail.ca
Dan Shewchuk, President

Telecommunications Employees Association of Manitoba (Ind.) (TEAM) / Association des employés en télécommunications du Manitoba (ind.)
#200, 1 Wesley Ave., Winnipeg MB R2H 1K1 Canada
Tel: 204-984-9470; *Fax:* 204-231-2809
Toll-Free: 877-984-9470
team@teamunion.mb.ca
www.teamunion.mb.ca
Misty Hughes-Newman, President

Telecommunications Workers' Union (CLC) (TWU) / Syndicat des travailleurs en télécommunications (CTC) (STT)
5261 Lane St., Burnaby BC V5H 4A6 Canada
Tel: 604-437-8601; *Fax:* 604-435-7760
Toll-Free: 888-986-3971
twu@twu-stt.ca
www.twu-stt.ca
John Carpenter, Vice-President
Betty Carrasco, Vice-President
George Doubt, President
Sherryl Anderson, Sec.-Treas.

Union canadienne des travailleurs en communication (ind.) / Canadian Union of Communication Workers (Ind.)
502, 90e av, Lasalle QC H8R 2Z7 Canada
Tél: 514-595-9095; *Téléc:* 514-595-8911
uctcpresident@bellnet.ca
www.unionuctc.com
Pierre Lebrun, Président

Union des artistes (UDA) / Artists' Union
#400, 1441, boul. René-Lévesque ouest, Montréal QC H3G 1T7 Canada
Tél: 514-288-6682; *Téléc:* 514-285-6789
info@uniondesartistes.com
www.uniondesartistes.com
Identification, étude, défense et développement des intérêts économiques, sociaux et moraux de ses membres
Raymond Legault, Président
François Ferland, Directeur général

Union of Canadian Transportation Employees (UCTE) / Union canadienne des employés des transports (UCET)
#702, 233 Gilmour St., Ottawa ON K2P 0P2 Canada
Tel: 613-238-4003; *Fax:* 613-236-0379
ucte_webmaster@psac.com
www.ucte.com
The Union represents members working in the public & private sectors of the Canadian transportation industry (ports, airports, NAV Canada, pilotage authorities, transportation companies, canals, the Dept. of Transport, lighthouses, ships and Canadian Coast Guard bases)
Michael Wing, National President

Union of National Defence Employees (UNDE) / Union des employés de la Défense nationale (UEDN)
#700, 116 Albert St., Ottawa ON K1P 5G3 Canada
Tel: 613-594-4505; *Fax:* 613-594-8233
Toll-Free: 866-594-4505
www.unde-uedn.com
John MacLennan, National President

Union of Northern Workers / Syndicat des travailleurs du Nord
#200, 5112 - 52 St., Yellowknife NT X1A 3Z5 Canada
Tel: 867-873-5668; *Fax:* 867-920-4448
Toll-Free: 877-906-4447
www.unw.ca
Todd Parsons, President

Union of Postal Communications Employees (UPCE) / Syndicat des employés des postes et des communications (SEPC)
#701, 233 Gilmour St., Ottawa ON K2P 0P2 Canada
Tel: 613-560-4342; *Fax:* 613-594-3849
sepc-upce@psac.com
www.upce.ca
Represents Canada Post members employed in administrative, clerical, technical & professional capacities
Richard L. Des Lauriers, National President

Union of Solicitor General Employees (USGE) / Syndicat des employés du Solliciteur général (SESG)
#603, 233 Gilmour St., Ottawa ON K2P 0P2 Canada
Tel: 613-232-4821; *Fax:* 613-232-3311
info@usge-sesg.com
www.usge-sesg.com
Mireille Laniel, Operations Manager

Union of Taxation Employees (UTE) / Syndicat des employé(e)s de l'impôt (SEI)
#602, 233 Gilmour St., Ottawa ON K2P 0P2 Canada
Tel: 613-235-6704; *Fax:* 613-234-7290
www.ute-sei.org
Betty Bannon, National President

Union of Veterans' Affairs Employees (UVAE) / Syndicat des employé(e)s des affaires des anciens combattants (SEAC)
#703, 233 Gilmour St., Ottawa ON K2P 0P2 Canada
Tel: 613-560-5460; *Fax:* 613-237-8282
thauvey@psac.com
uvae-seac.ca
Yvan Thauvette, National President

UNITE HERE Canada
460 Richmond St. West, 2nd Fl., Toronto ON M5V 1Y1 Canada
Tel: 416-510-0887; *Fax:* 416-510-0891
Toll-Free: 800-268-4046
info@unitehere.ca
www.unitehere.ca
Alexandra Dagg, National Co-Director
Nick Worhaug, National Co-Director

United Association of Journeymen & Apprentices of the Plumbing & Pipe Fitting Industry of the U.S. & Canada (AFL-CIO/CFL) / Association unie des compagnons & apprentis de l'industrie de la plomberie & de la tuyauterie des Etats-Unis & du Canada
3 Park Place, Annapolis MD 21401 USA
Tel: 410-269-2000; *Fax:* 410-267-0262
ua.org

United Brotherhood of Carpenters & Joiners of America (AFL-CIO/CLC) / Fraternité unie des charpentiers et menuisiers d'Amérique (FAT-COI/CTC)
101 Constitution Ave. NW, Washington DC 20001 USA
Tel: 202-546-6206; *Fax:* 202-543-5724
www.carpenters.org
Douglas J. McCarron, General President

United Food & Commercial Workers Canada (UFCW CANADA)
#300, 61 International Blvd., Toronto ON M9W 6K4 Canada
Tel: 416-675-1104; *Fax:* 416-675-6919
ufcw@ufcw.ca
www.ufcw.ca
One of Canada's largest private sector union.
Wayne Hanley, National President

United Food & Commercial Workers' International Union (UFCW) / Union internationale des travailleurs et travailleuses unis de l'alimentation et du commerce
1775 K St. NW, Washington DC 20006 USA
Tel: 202-223-3111; *Fax:* 202-466-1562
ufcw@ufcw.ca
www.ufcw.org
Social Media: www.facebook.com/group.php?gid=19812849944
Joseph T. Hansen, International President
Anthony M. Perrone, International Sec.-Treas.

United Mine Workers of America (CLC) / Mineurs unis d'Amérique (CTC)
8315 Lee Hwy., Fairfax VA 22031 USA
Tel: 703-208-7200
www.umwa.org
Cecil Roberts, President

United Steelworkers of America (AFL-CIO/CLC) / Métallurgistes unis d'Amérique (FAT-COI/CTC)
5 Gateway Center, Pittsburgh PA 15222 USA
Tel: 412-562-2400
webmaster@uswa.org
www.uswa.org
Leo W. Gerard, International President

United Transportation Union (AFL-CIO/CLC) - Canada
71 Bank St., 7th Fl., Ottawa ON K1P 5N2 Canada
Tel: 613-747-7979; *Fax:* 613-747-2815

Yukon Employees Union (YEU) / Syndicat des employés du Yukon
#201, 2285 Second Ave., Whitehorse YT Y1A 1C9 Canada
Tel: 867-667-2331; *Fax:* 867-667-6521
admint@yeu.ca
www.yeu.ca
To unite all members of the Alliance over which this Union has jurisdiction into a single union capable of acting on their behalf; to obtain through democratic means for all members the best possible standards of wages, salaries & other conditions of employment, & to protect the interests, rights & privileges of all such employees
Laurie Butterworth, President

Denise L. Norman, Executive Director

Yukon Federation of Labour (YFL) / Fédération du travail du Yukon
#102, 106 Strickland St., Whitehorse YT Y1A 2J5 Canada
Tel: 867-667-6676; *Fax:* 867-633-5558
yfl@yukonfed.com
www.yukonfed.com
Doug Rody, Director, Policy & Legislative Affairs

Landscape Architecture

Alberta Association of Landscape Architects (AALA)
PO Box 21052, Edmonton AB T6R 2V4
Tel: 780-435-9902; *Fax:* 780-413-0076
aala@aala.ab.ca
www.aala.ab.ca
To advance the quality of the professional practice of landscape architecture in Alberta
Mark Nolan, Registrar
Brian Charanduk, Treasurer

Association des architectes paysagistes du Québec (AAPQ)
4655, De Lorimier, Montréal QC H2H 2B4 Canada
Tél: 514-990-7731; *Téléc:* 877-990-7731
info@aapq.org
www.aapq.org
Promouvoir la création et la valorisation du paysage en milieu naturel et construit dans le but de constituer un cadre de vie sain, fonctionnel, esthétique, axé sur les besoins de la population et répondant aux exigences écologiques

Atlantic Provinces Association of Landscape Architects (APALA)
PO Box 653, Stn. Halifax CRO, Halifax NS B3J 2Z1 Canada
info@apala.ca
www.apala.ca
To promote, improve & advance the profession; to maintain standards of professional practice & conduct consistent with the need to serve & to protect the public interest; to support improvement &/or conservation of the natural, cultural, social & built environment

British Columbia Society of Landscape Architects (BCSLA)
#110, 355 Burrard St., Vancouver BC V6C 2G8 Canada
Tel: 604-682-5610; *Fax:* 604-681-3394
admin@bcsla.org
www.bcsla.org
To promote, improve & advance the profession; to maintain standards of professional practice & conduct consistent with the need to serve & protect the public interest; to support the improvement &/or conservation of the natural, cultural, social & built environment.

Canadian Society of Landscape Architects (CSLA) / Association des architectes paysagistes du Canada (AAPC)
PO Box 13594, Ottawa ON K2K 1X6 Canada
Tel: 866-781-9799; *Fax:* 866-871-1419
info@csla.ca
www.csla.ca
To support the improvement &/or conservation of the natural, cultural, social & built environment; to promote visibility, recognition, acceptance & understanding of the profession by communicating its value in relation to that of the public good

Manitoba Association of Landscape Architects (MALA)
131 Callum Cres., Winnipeg MB R2G 2C7 Canada
Tel: 204-663-4863; *Fax:* 204-668-5662
malaoffice@shaw.ca
www.mala.net
To promote, improve & advance the profession; to maintain standards of professional practice & conduct consistent with the need to serve & protect public interest; to support improvement &/or conservation of the natural, cultural, social & built environment

Newfoundland & Labrador Association of Landscape Architects (NLALA)
PO Box 5262, Stn. C, St. John's NL A1C 5W1 Canada
Tel: 709-579-5855; *Fax:* 709-579-5844
info@tract.nf.net
www.nlala.com

Northwest Territories Association of Landscape Architects (NWTALA)
PO Box 1394, Yellowknife NT X1A 2P1 Canada
Tel: 867-920-2986; *Fax:* 867-920-2986
atborow@internorth.com
To represent landscape architects in the Northwest Territories

Ontario Association of Landscape Architects (OALA)
#407, 3 Church St., Toronto ON M5E 1M2 Canada
Tel: 416-231-4181; *Fax:* 416-231-2679
oala@oala.ca
www.oala.ca
To promote, improve & advance the profession; to maintain standards of professional practice & conduct consistent with the need to serve & to protect the public interest; to support improvement &/or conservation of the natural, cultural, social & built environment

Saskatchewan Association of Landscape Architects (SALA)
#200, 642 Broadway Ave., Saskatoon SK S7N 1A9 Canada
www.sala.sk.ca
To promote, improve, & advance the profession of landscape architecture; to maintain standards of professional practice & conduct

Language, Linguistics, Literature

ABC CANADA Literacy Foundation / Fondation pour l'alphabétisation ABC CANADA
#235, 4211 Yonge St., Toronto ON M4P 2A9 Canada
Tel: 416-218-0010; *Fax:* 416-218-0457
Toll-Free: 800-303-1004
info@abc-canada.org
www.abc-canada.org
A joint initiative of business & labour, supporting the development of an educated & adaptable workforce through the fostering of a lifelong learning culture; ABC CANADA supports the development of a fully literate Canadian population
Margaret Eaton, President
Kathy St. John, Director, Development

Association canadienne de traductologie (ACT) / Canadian Association for Translation Studies (CATS)
a/s École de traduction et d'interprétation, Université d'Ottawa, 70, av Laurier est, Ottawa ON K1N 6N5 Canada
www.uottawa.ca/associations/act-cats/
Société savante qui regroupe des chercheurs, des professeurs et des praticiens qui se consacrent ou s'intéressent à l'étude ou à l'enseignement de la traduction et des disciplines apparentées

Association of Canadian Corporations in Translation & Interpretation (ACCTI) / Association canadienne de compagnies de traductions et d'interpretation
#306, 421 Bloor St. East, Toronto ON M4W 3T1 Canada
Tel: 416-975-5000; *Fax:* 416-975-0505
english_info@accti.org; info_francais@accti.org
www.accti.org
To unite the Canadian translation industry, providing a quality standard to protect the public & service providers alike; to arrange for arbitration in the event of a dispute; to operate in the best interest of members
Paul Penzo, President
Maryse M. Benhoff, Vice-President

Association of Translators & Interpreters of Alberta (ATIA) / Association des traducteurs et interprètes de l'Alberta
PO Box 546, Stn. Main, Edmonton AB T5J 2K8 Canada
Tel: 780-434-8384; *Toll-Free:* 888-434-2842
bernadette.david@shaw.ca
www.atia.ab.ca

Association of Translators & Interpreters of Nova Scotia (ATINS) / Association des traducteurs et interprètes de la nouvelle-écosse
PO Box 372, Halifax NS B3J 2P8 Canada
Tel: 902-443-0350
info@atins.org
www.atins.org
To ensure that clients have access to a body of qualified professionals; to promote the profession & the development of its members
Bruce Knowlden, President

Association of Translators & Interpreters of Ontario (ATIO) / Association des traducteurs et interprètes de l'Ontario
#1202, 1 Nicholas St., Ottawa ON K1N 7B7 Canada
Tel: 613-241-2846; *Fax:* 613-241-4098
Toll-Free: 800-234-5030
info@atio.on.ca
www.atio.on.ca

To promote a high degree of professionalism & to protect the interest of those who use the language services provided by its members; to organize professional development activities & to encourage exchanges among its members

Association of Translators & Interpreters of Saskatchewan (ATIS) / Association des traducteurs et interprètes de la Saskatchewan
2341 Broad St., Regina SK S4P 1Y9 Canada
Tel: 306-522-2847
www.atis-sk.ca
To provide a collective voice for members; to ensure that members exercise the profession in accordance with their code of ethics; to administer admission procedures of national certification examination; to provide a list of current certified members

Association of Translators, Terminologists & Interpreters of Manitoba (ATIM) / Association des traducteurs, terminologues et des interprètes du Manitoba
PO Box 83, 200, av de la Cathédrale, Winnipeg MB R2H 0H7 Canada
Tel: 204-797-3247
info@atim.mb.ca
www.atim.mb.ca
ATIM is a non-profit association whose objectives are to provide a collective voice for its members, ensure that members exercise their profession in accordance with its Code of Ethics, & protect the public interest by ensuring the quality of the services rendered by its members.

Association of Visual Language Interpreters of Canada (AVLIC) / Association des interprètes en langage visuel du Canada
PO Box 56025, Valley Centre RPO, Langley BC V3A 8B3 Canada
Tel: 604-308-0197; *Fax:* 604-530-0867
avlic@avlic.ca
www.avlic.ca
To represent interpreters whose working languages are English & American Sign Language (ASL); to promote high standards & uniformity within the profession of interpreting

The Brontë Society - Canada
142 Glenforest Rd., Toronto ON M4N 1Z9 Canada
Tel: 416-488-0888
judith_watkins@rogers.com
To bring closer together all who honour the Brontë sisters; to act as the guardian of such letters, writings & personal belongings as could be acquired for the Museum; to dispel legend & false sentiments regarding the Brontë story
Judith Watkins, Canadian Representative

Canadian Association for Commonwealth Literature & Language Studies (CACLALS) / Association canadienne pour l'étude des langues et de la littérature du Commonwealth
c/o Kristina Fagan, Department of English, University of Saskatchewan, 9 Campus Dr., Saskatoon SK S7N 5A5
ww.caclals.ca
To promote the study of Commonwealth literature in Canada; To encourage the reading of Canadian literature abroad
Susan Gingell, President
Kristina Fagan, Secretary-Treasurer
Neil ten Kortenaar, Editor, Chimo

Canadian Comparative Literature Association (CCLA) / Association canadienne de littérature comparée (ACLC)
c/o Markus Reisenleitner, Department of Humanities, York University, 217 Vanier College, Toronto ON M3H 1P3
www.complit.ca
Karin Beeler, President
Susan Ingram, Vice-President
Pascal Gin, Secretary
Markus Reisenleitner, Treasurer

Canadian Linguistic Association (CLA) / Association canadienne de linguistique (ACL)
c/o University of Toronto Press, Journals Division, 5201 Dufferin Ave., Toronto ON M3H 5T8 Canada
Tel: 416-667-7810; *Fax:* 416-667-7881
daniel.hall@utoronto.ca
www.chass.utoronto.ca/~cla-acl/
To advance scientific study of linguistics & language in Canada

Canadian Literary & Artistic Association / Association littéraire et artistique canadienne inc.
PO Box 61534, Stn. Tétreault-Ville, Montréal QC H1L 6R1 Canada
Tel: 514-993-1556
alaican@aei.ca
www.alai.ca
Promoting and protecting copyright as well as to study questions regarding the protection and the applicability of these rights.

Canadian Parents for French (CPF)
#310, 176 Gloucester St., Ottawa ON K2P 0A6 Canada
Tel: 613-235-1481; *Fax:* 613-230-5940
cpf@cpf.ca
www.cpf.ca
CPF provides educational opportunities for young Canadians to learn & use the French language; recognizes & supports English & French as Canada's two official languages & believes that young Canadians should have opportunities to become bilingual in these languages; primary focus is to create & promote opportunities for young Canadians to learn & use French as a second language

Canadian Translators, Terminologists & Interpreters Council (CTTIC) / Conseil des traducteurs, terminologues et interprètes du Canada (CTTIC)
#1202, One Nicholas St., Ottawa ON K1N 7B7 Canada
Tel: 613-562-0379; *Fax:* 613-241-4098
info@cttic.org
www.cttic.org
To ensure uniform standards for the practice of the profession; to make available to the public a body of reliable professionals in translation, terminology & interpretation

Centre interdisciplinaire de recherches sur les activités langagières (CIRAL)
Pavillon Charles-de-Koninck, Université Laval, #2260-A, Faculté des lettres, Québec QC G1V 0A6 Canada
Tél: 418-656-3040; *Téléc:* 418-656-7144
ciral@ciral.ulaval.ca
www.ciral.ulaval.ca
Le Centre interdisciplinaire de recherches sur la activités langagières (CIRAL) regroupe cinq équipes régulières, une vingtaine de chercheurs et quelque soixante-dix étudiants de deuxième et troisième cycles. Tous partagent la même conception des questions linguistiques : la langue est indissociable de l'histoire et de la culture des groupes qui la parlent, et elle évolue en fonction des contacts interethniques et des pressions socioculturelles qui s'exercent sur elle.

Corporation des traducteurs, traductrices, terminologues et interprètes du Nouveau-Brunswick (CTINB) / Corporation of Translators, Terminologists & Interpreters of New Brunswick
CP 427, Fredericton NB E3B 4Z9 Canada
Tél: 506-458-1519
ctinb@nbnet.nb.ca
www.ctinb.nb.ca
Donner à ses membres une voix collective; promouvoir le perfectionnement professionnel de ses membres; veiller à ce que ses membres respectent son Code de déontologie; faire connaître le rôle professionnel de ses membres dans la sociétéprotéger l'intérêt public en faisant subir des examens d'admission à la CTINB et d'agrément des membres ainsi qu'en examinant les plaintes reçues à l'égard des membres; entretenir des liens avec les organismes semblables et avec les établissements de formation universitaire dans les domaines de la traduction, de la terminologie et de l'interprétation

Esperanto Association of Canada (KEA) / Association canadienne d'esperanto
6358-A, rue de Bordeaux, Montréal QC H2G 2R8 Canada
www.esperanto.ca/en/kea
To promote & teach the neutral international language of Esperanto

Fédération canadienne pour l'alphabétisation en français (FCAF)
#205, 235 ch Montréal, 2e étage, Ottawa ON K1L 6C7 Canada
Tél: 613-749-5333; *Téléc:* 613-749-2252
Ligne sans frais: 888-906-5666
info@fcaf.net
www.fcaf.net
Promouvoir l'alphabétisation en français au Canada; assurer une concertation des intervenantes en alphabétisation en français au Canada.
Normand Lévesque, Directeur général
Colette Arseneault, Présidente
Isabelle Salesse, Vice-présidente

Internatial Unio For Kanadio (sic) (IUK)
92 Glenholm Av., Toronto ON M6H 3B1 Canada
Tu tranzform el deifektik ingglish langweij intu el rasional kanadio [sic]
Jonathan Keitz, Prezzident

Jane Austen Society of North America (JASNA)
#105, 195 Wynford Dr., Toronto ON M3C 3P3 Canada
Tel: 416-425-2195; *Toll-Free:* 800-836-3911
info@jasna.org
www.jasna.org
Dedicated to the appreciation of Jane Austen & her writings

L. M. Montgomery Institute (LMMI)
University of Prince Edward Island, 550 University Ave., Charlottetown PE C1A 4P3 Canada
Tel: 902-628-4346; *Fax:* 902-628-4345
lmmi@upei.ca
www.lmmontgomery.ca
With a focus on scholarship & teaching, the Institute provides resources & educational opportunities to students & scholars researching the life, works & influence of L.M. Montgomery
Mark Leggott, Chair

Literary Translators' Association of Canada (LTAC) / Association des traducteurs et traductrices littéraires du Canada (ATTLC)
Concordia University LB 601, 1455, boul de Maisonneuve ouest, Montréal QC H3G 1M8 Canada
Tel: 514-848-2424; *Fax:* 514-848-4514
info@attlc-ltac.org
www.attlc-ltac.org
To promote literary translation & interests of literary translators.

Movement for Canadian Literacy (MCL) / Rassemblement canadien pour l'alphabétisation (RCA)
#300, 180 Metcalfe St., Ottawa ON K2P 1P5 Canada
Tel: 613-563-2464; *Fax:* 613-563-2504
mcl@literacy.ca
www.literacy.ca
To act as a national voice for literacy for Canadians

National Adult Literacy Database (NALD) / Base de données en alphabétisation des adultes (BDAA)
Sterling House, 767 Brunswick St., Fredericton NB E3B 1H8 Canada
Tel: 506-457-6900; *Fax:* 506-457-6910
Toll-Free: 800-720-6253
contactnald@nald.ca
www.nald.ca
To provide an information network, in both official languages; to support the Canadian literacy community: adult learners, practitioners, organizations & governments
Katherine d'Entremont, Executive Director

Ordre des traducteurs, terminologues et interprètes agréés du Québec (OTTIAQ)
#1108, 2021, rue Union, Montréal QC H3A 2S9 Canada
Tél: 514-845-4411; *Téléc:* 514-845-9903
Ligne sans frais: 800-265-4815
info@ottiaq.org
www.ottiaq.org
Promouvoir la qualité et l'efficacité de la communication en s'assurant de la compétence de ses membres dans les domaines de la traduction, de la terminologie et de l'interprétation. L'Ordre remplit ainsi son mandat de protection du public

Quebec English Literacy Alliance (QELA)
PO Box 3542, Knowlton QC J0E 1V0 Canada
Tel: 450-242-2360; *Fax:* 450-242-2543
Toll-Free: 866-242-7352
qelamail@gmail.com
www.qela.qc.ca
To be the unified voice of Quebec English literacy providers nationally & provincially
Louise Quinn, Executive Director

Saskatchewan Elocution & Debate Association (SEDA) / Association d'élocution et des débats de la Saskatchewan
1860 Lorne St., Regina SK S4P 2L7 Canada
Tel: 306-780-9243; *Fax:* 306-781-6021
info@saskdebate.com
www.saskdebate.com
To foster debate & public speaking

Saskatchewan Organization for Heritage Languages Inc. (SOHL)
2144 Cornwall St., Regina SK S4P 2K7 Canada
Tel: 306-780-9275; *Fax:* 306-780-9407
sohl@sasktel.net
www.heritagelanguages.sk.ca
To promote & develop teaching of heritage languages in Saskatchewan; to act in advocacy capacity to make representation to government, institutions & boards regarding matters pertaining to heritage languages; to promote cooperation with & mutual support of provincial organizations with similar aims & objectives; to encourage inter-provincial & national liaison

Société québécoise d'espéranto (SQE) / Québec Esperanto Society (QES)
6358A, rue de Bordeaux, Montréal QC H2G 2R8 Canada
informo@esperanto.qc.ca
www.esperanto.qc.ca
Faire connaître et aider à l'apprentissage de l'espéranto; organiser des rencontres et favoriser l'utilisation de la langue; présenter les avantages de la langue et le mouvement mondial

Society of Translators & Interpreters of British Columbia (STIBC)
#511, 850 West Hastings St., Box 33, Vancouver BC V6C 1E1 Canada
Tel: 604-684-2940; *Fax:* 604-684-2947
stibc@stibc.org
www.stibc.org
To promote the interests of translators & interpreters in BC; to serve the public by applying a Code of Ethics members must comply with; by setting & maintaining high professional standards through education & certification

Sweetgrass First Nations Language Council
PO Box 1506, 184 Mohawk St., Brantford ON N3T 5V6 Canada
Tel: 519-759-2650; *Fax:* 519-759-8912
amos@woodland-centre.on.ca
www.woodland-centre.on.ca
To provide overall leadership in the retention & revitalization of First Nations languages; to identify resources, both human & material, for the maintenance of Anishinaabeg (Algonkian) & Ogwehowe (Iroquoian) cultural values, traits & institutions of these First Nations: Delaware, Cree, Odawa, Potawotomi, Ojibwe/Chippewa, Cayuga, Mohawk, Onondaga, Seneca & Tuscarora

Universala Esperanto Asocio
PO Box 2159, Sidney BC V8L 3S6 Canada
esperanto@shaw.ca
www.uea.org
To promote the use of the international language Esperanto; to work toward the solution to the language problem within international relations; to help improve human relations by making every effort to diminish national, racial, religious, & political tensions; to promote solidarity among all Esperantists & respect for all people

World Literacy of Canada (WLC) / Alphabétisation mondiale Canada
#236, 401 Richmond St. West, Toronto ON M5V 3A8 Canada
Tel: 416-977-0008; *Fax:* 416-977-1112
info@worldlit.ca
www.worldlit.ca
To promote international development & social justice through support of community-based programs that emphasize adult literacy & non-formal education
Sandra Onufryk, President
Marguerite Pigott, Vice-President
Jamie Zeppa, Secretary
Mamta Mishra, Executive Director

Law

The Advocates' Society
#1700, 480 University Ave., Toronto ON M5G 1V2 Canada
Tel: 416-597-0243; *Fax:* 416-597-1588
mail@advocates.ca
www.advocates.ca
To teach the skills & ethics of advocacy through information sharing, educational programs, seminars, conferences, workshops, etc.; to speak out on behalf of advocates; to protect the right to representation by an independent bar; to initiate appropriate reforms to the legal system

Alberta Civil Trial Lawyers' Association (ACTLA)
#550, 10055 - 106 St., Edmonton AB T5J 2Y2 Canada
Tel: 780-429-1133; *Fax:* 780-429-1199
Toll-Free: 800-665-7248
admin@actla.com
www.actla.com
To advocate for a strong civil justice system that protects the rights of all Albertans

Alberta Federation of Police Associations (AFPA)
Energy Square, #100, 7024 - 101 Ave., Edmonton AB T6A 0H7 Canada
Fax: 403-795-7173
information@albertapolice.ca
www.albertapolice.ca
To address local, provincial, & national police association issues

Alberta Government Civil Lawyers Association (AGCLA)
Bowker Building, Civil Law Division, Alberta Justice, 9833 - 109 St., 5th Fl., Edmonton AB T5K 2E8 Canada
Tel: 780-422-0500; *Fax:* 780-425-0307
To promote & provide continuing education to members in all spheres of civil law

Alberta Law Foundation (ALF)
#300, 407 - 8 Ave. SW, Calgary AB T2P 1E5 Canada
Tel: 403-264-4701; *Fax:* 403-294-9238
contact@albertalawfoundation.org
www.albertalawfoundation.org
To conduct research into & recommend reform of law & administration of justice; to establish, maintain & operate law libraries; to contribute to legal education & knowledge of people of Alberta; to provide assistance to Native people's legal & student programs
David Aucoin, Executive Director
Diana M. Porter, Administrative Assistant

Association des juristes d'expression française de l'Ontario (AJEFO)
#201, 214 ch Montréal, Ottawa ON K1L 8L8 Canada
Tél: 613-842-7462; *Téléc:* 613-842-8389
bureau@ajefo.ca
www.ajefo.ca
Représenter les intérêts des avocates, des avocats, des juges, des fonctionnaires de la justice, des professeures, des professeurs, des étudiantes et des étudiants en droit, et des autres participants et participantes du monde juridique, qui travaillent à la promotion des services juridiques en français sur le territoire de l'Ontario; viser à assurer un accès égal à la justice, sans pénalité, délai, obstacle ou hésitation à l'utilisation du français par l'appareil judiciaire, les membres du Barreau ou la population francophone de notre province

Association des juristes d'expression française de la Saskatchewan (AJEFS) / French Jurists Association of Saskatchewan
#6, 4625, rue Albert, Regina SK S4S 6B6 Canada
Tél: 306-924-8543; *Téléc:* 306-569-2609
Ligne sans frais: 800-991-1912
ajefs@sasktel.net
www.ajefs.ca
Développer et promouvoir les droits et services en français auprès des instances juridiques et gouvernementales; informer et sensibiliser la population fransaskoise sur la vulgarisation des lois et l'utilisation des services juridiques en français

Association des policières et policiers provinciaux du Québec (ind.) (APPQ) / Québec Provincial Police Association (Ind.)
1981, rue Léonard-De Vinci, Sainte-Julie QC J3E 1Y9 Canada
Tél: 450-922-5414; *Téléc:* 450-922-5417
dagenais@appq-sq.qc.ca
www.appq-sq.qc.ca
Promouvoir le bien-être de ses membres et voir à leurs intérêts sociaux, moraux et culturels
Jean-Guy Dagenais, Président
Jocelyn Boucher, Vice-président, Ressources humaines
Luc Fournier, Vice-président, Finances
Jacques Painchaud, Vice-président, Discipline et déontologie
Pierre Veilleux, Vice-président, Griefs et formation
Daniel Rolland, Vice-président, Ress. matérielles et santé et sécurité du travail

Association of Black Lawyers & Notaries
#10, 10, rue Notre-Dame est, Montréal QC H2Y 1B7 Canada
Tel: 514-878-9112
Provides referrals to Black lawyers & notaries in the Montréal area
Sharon Sandiford, Contact

Association of Canadian Court Administrators (ACCA) / Association des administrateurs judiciaires du Canada
#518B, 45 Main St. East, Hamilton ON L8P 1H4 Canada
Tel: 905-645-5333; *Fax:* 905-645-5375
www.acca-aajc.ca
To improve the administration of justice through the application of modern management techniques; to promote coordination of research activities relating to court administration & furnish a forum for the interchange of practical information relating to court administration; to aid in the improvement of court administration in general, with particular emphasis on the study, development, & use of scientific & technological methods; to increase the proficiency of court managers
Debbie Baker, President
Christine Mosher, Secretary
Anne Roland, Treasurer
Linda Bogard, Vice-President

Association of Legal Court Interpreters & Translators (ALCIT) / Association des traducteurs et interprètes judiciares (ATIJ)
483, rue Saint-Antoine est, Montréal QC H2Y 1A5 Canada
Tel: 514-845-3113; *Fax:* 514-845-3006
admin@atij.ca
www.atij.ca; www.alcit.ca
The members of the Association work for numerous organizations and Law Courts, although most commonly for the Municipal Court of Montréal and the City of Montréal Police Department. The members currently translate and interpret in 102 languages.

Barreau de Montréal / Bar of Montréal
Palais de Justice, #980, 1, rue Notre Dame est, Montréal QC H2Y 1B6 Canada
Tél: 514-866-9392; *Téléc:* 514-866-1488
info@barreaudemontreal.qc.ca
www.barreaudemontreal.qc.ca
Administrer une corporation professionnelle

British Columbia Federation of Police Officers (Ind.)
PO Box 42601, #105, 1005 Columbia St., New Westminster BC V3M 6H5 Canada
Tel: 604-650-1510; *Fax:* 604-850-1303
www.bcfedpolice.com
Daryl Tottenhan, Director

Canadian Association of Black Lawyers (CABL) / L'Association des Avocats Noirs du Canada
#300, 20 Toronto St., Toronto ON M5C 2B8 Canada
www.cabl.ca
Frank Walwyn, President

Canadian Association of Chiefs of Police (CACP) / Association canadienne des chefs de police (ACCP)
582 Somerset St. West, Ottawa ON K1R 5K2 Canada
Tel: 613-233-1106; *Fax:* 613-233-6960
cacp@cacp.ca
www.cacp.ca
To encourage & develop cooperation among all Canadian police organizations & members in pursuit & attainment of common objects to create & develop the highest standards of efficiency in law enforcement through the fostering & encouragement of police training, education & research; to promote & maintain a high standard of ethics, integrity, honour & conduct in profession of law enforcement; to encourage & advance the study of modern & progressive practices in prevention & detection of crime; to foster uniformity of police practices & cooperation for the protection & security of the people of Canada

Canadian Association of Legal Translators / Association canadienne des juristes-traducteurs
PO Box 919, Stn. B, Ottawa ON K1P 5P9 Canada
To promote double qualification as lawyer (or jurist) & as translator for the translation of legal documents.

Canadian Association of Police Boards (CAPB) / Association canadienne des commissions de police
PO Box 4670, Stn. E, Ottawa ON K1S 5H8 Canada
Tel: 819-682-1440; *Fax:* 819-682-4569
jlanzon.capb.ca
www.capb.ca
To express views & positions of municipal governing authorities; To provide means for collection & sharing of information & discussion of matters relating to policing services; To consider matters of national interest; To comment on social, economic, cultural, & legislative questions which may affect the quality, efficiency, & costs of policing services; To promote the quality & uniformity of policing services; To educate the public on matters relating to the governance of policing services; To act as a lobbying group to liaise between federal, provincial & municipal governmental authorities, & the federal & provincial solicitors general; To provide a forum for participation by civilian governors

of municipal policing services & other agencies; To promote & encourage greater cooperation to serve the interest of the public; To advance criminal justice

Canadian Association of Provincial Court Judges (CAPCJ) / L'Association canadienne des juges de cours provinciales
c/o Judge Alan T. Tufts, Nova Scotia Provincial Court, 87 Cornwallis St., Kentville NS B4N 2E5
Tel: 902-679-6070; *Fax:* 902-679-6190
atufts@judicom.ca (Judge Alan T. Tufts)
www.judges-juges.ca
To ensure the soundness of provincial & territorial courts across Canada

Canadian Bar Association (CBA) / Association du barreau canadien
#500, 865 Carling Ave., Ottawa ON K1S 5S8 Canada
Tel: 613-237-2925; *Fax:* 613-237-0185
Toll-Free: 800-267-8860
info@cba.org
www.cba.org
To promote improvements in the law; to promote improvements in the administration of justice; to promote individual lawyer training; to advocate in the public interest; to represent the profession on a national & international level; to promote the interests of the CBA; to promote equality in the profession

The Canadian Corporate Counsel Association (CCCA) / L'Association canadienne des conseillers juridiques d'entreprises
#410, 20 Toronto St., Toronto ON M5C 2B8 Canada
Tel: 416-869-0522; *Fax:* 416-869-0946
ccca@ccca-cba.org
www.cancorpcounsel.org
To provide quality education, information & other services & resources of specific interest to corporate counsel in Canada, & to facilitate communication & networking among such counsel
Derek Edward Patterson, President
Kari F. Horn, Treasurer

Canadian Council on International Law (CCIL) / Conseil canadien de droit international (CCDI)
275 Bay St., Ottawa ON K1R 5Z5 Canada
Tel: 613-235-0442; *Fax:* 613-232-8228
info@ccil-ccdi.ca
www.ccil-ccdi.ca
To bring together scholars of international law & organizations engaged in teaching & research at Canadian universities; to encourage & conduct studies in international law with a view to its progressive development & codification; to foster the study of legal aspects of Canada's international problems & to advocate their solution in accordance with existing or developing principles of international law.

Canadian Criminal Justice Association (CCJA) / Association canadienne de justice pénale (ACJP)
#308, 1750 Courtwood Cres., Ottawa ON K2C 2B5 Canada
Tel: 613-725-3715; *Fax:* 613-725-3720
ccja@bellnet.ca
www.ccja-acjp.ca
To promote good criminal justice policies & services

Canadian Institute for the Administration of Justice (CIAJ) / Institut canadien d'administration de la justice (ICAJ)
Faculté de droit, Univ. de Montréal, PO Box 6128, Stn. Centre-Ville, #3421, 3101, chemin de la Tour, Montréal QC H3C 3J7 Canada
Tel: 514-343-6157; *Fax:* 514-343-6296
ciaj@ciaj-icaj.ca
www.ciaj-icaj.ca
To improve the quality of justice for all Canadians

Canadian Law & Society Association (CLSA) / Association canadienne de droit et société (ACDS)
c/o Journals Division, University of Toronto Press, 5201 Dufferin St., Toronto ON M3H 5T8 Canada
Tel: 416-667-7810; *Fax:* 416-667-7881
Toll-Free: 800-221-9985
www.acds-clsa.org
To encourage socio-legal inquiry both domestically & internationally

Canadian Maritime Law Association / Association canadienne de droit maritime
#4600, 800, place Victoria, Montréal QC H4Z 1H6 Canada
Tel: 514-849-4161; *Fax:* 514-849-4167
cmla@cmla.org
www.cmla.org
To represent all Canadian commercial maritime interests for the uniform development of Canadian & international maritime law affecting marine transportation & related aspects

Canadian Petroleum Law Foundation
PO Box 4143, Stn. C, Calgary AB T2T 5M9 Canada
Tel: 403-237-2423
lara.h.pella@esso.ca
www.cplf.org
To study oil & gas laws
Ben Rogers, President
Miles Pittman, Treasurer

Canadian Police Association (CPPA) / L'Association canadienne des policiers (ACPP)
#100, 141 Catherine St., Ottawa ON K2P 1C3 Canada
Tel: 613-231-4168; *Fax:* 613-231-3254
cpa-acp@cpa-acp.ca
www.cpa-acp.ca

Chambre des notaires du Québec
#600, 1801, av McGill College, Montréal QC H3B 3L2 Canada
Tél: 514-879-1793; *Téléc:* 514-879-1923
Ligne sans frais: 800-668-2473
information@cdnq.org
www.cdnq.org
La Chambre des notaires doit, conformément à la loi et sous la surveillance de l'Office des professions du Québec, assurer principalement la protection du public utilisateur des services professionnels de notaire.
Pierre Cléroux, Directeur général

Church Council on Justice & Corrections (CCJC) / Conseil des églises pour la justice et la criminologie
#303, 200 Isabella St., Ottawa ON K1S 1V7 Canada
Tel: 613-563-1688; *Fax:* 613-237-6129
info@ccjc.ca
www.ccjc.ca
To strengthen churches' ministry in fields of crime prevention, justice & corrections; to initiate, encourage & support programs which sensitize congregations & educate volunteer groups to participate in development of community responses to crime, justice & corrections; to promote a healing justice; to examine & respond to policy concerns with assistance of churches; to call on churches to address issues; to provide resources to churches & other related organizations.

Community Legal Education Association (Manitoba) Inc. (CLEA) / Association d'éducation juridique communautaire (Manitoba) inc.
#205, 414 Graham Ave., Winnipeg MB R3C 0L8 Canada
Tel: 204-943-2382; *Fax:* 204-943-3600
info@communitylegal.mb.ca
www.communitylegal.mb.ca
To provide legal education & information programs to Manitobans

Community Legal Education Ontario (CLEO)
#600, 119 Spadina Ave., Toronto ON M5V 2L1 Canada
Tel: 416-408-4420; *Fax:* 416-408-4424
cleo@cleo.on.ca
www.cleo.on.ca; www.cleonet.ca
To provide public legal education services & programs that benefit the low income community, disadvantaged persons, such as immigrants & refugees, seniors, women, & injured workers in Ontario

Community Legal Information Association of Prince Edward Island (CLIA)
Sullivan Bldg., 1st Fl., PO Box 1207, Charlottetown PE C1A 7M8 Canada
Tel: 902-892-0853; *Fax:* 902-368-4096
Toll-Free: 800-240-9798
clia@cliapei.ca
www.cliapei.ca
To provide Islanders with understandable, useful information about the Canadian laws & the justice system.

Congress of Black Lawyers and Jurists of Québec
#500, 445, boul St-Laurent, Montréal QC H2Y 3T8 Canada
Tel: 514-954-3471; *Fax:* 514-954-3451
Please call prior to visit

Continuing Legal Education Society of BC
#300, 845 Cambie St., Vancouver BC V6B 5T2 Canada
Tel: 604-669-3544; *Fax:* 604-669-9260
Toll-Free: 800-663-0437
custserv@cle.bc.ca
www.cle.bc.ca
To meet the present & future educational needs of the legal profession in British Columbia

Criminal Lawyers' Association (CLA)
#7, 296 Jarvis St., Toronto ON M5B 2C5 Canada
Tel: 416-214-9875; *Fax:* 416-968-6818
anthony@criminallawyers.ca
www.criminallawyers.ca
To be the voice for criminal justice & civil liberties in Canada

Federation of Law Reform Agencies of Canada
c/o Manitoba Law Reform Commission, 405 Broadway, 12th Fl., Winnipeg MB R3C 3L6 Canada
Tel: 604-822-0142; *Fax:* 604-822-0144
Collection of 8 law reform agencies, from various provinces, who meet yearly to exchange information.
Jeffrey A. Schnoor, President

Federation of Law Societies of Canada (FLSC) / Fédération des ordres professionnels de juristes du Canada
World Exchange Plaza, #1810, 45 O'Connor St., Ottawa ON K1P 1A4
Tel: 613-236-7272; *Fax:* 613-236-7233
info@flsc.ca
www.flsc.ca
To coordinate the law societies of Canada; To act as a voice for Canadian law societies

Fondation du barreau du Québec
Maison du Barreau, #404, 445, boul Saint-Laurent, Montréal QC H2Y 3T8 Canada
Tél: 514-954-3400; *Téléc:* 514-954-3449
Ligne sans frais: 800-361-8495
fondation@barreau.qc.ca
www.barreau.qc.ca
Média social: www.facebook.com/barreauduquebec
Subventionner, primer et supporter des travaux axés vers l'intérêt public et utiles à la pratique du droit.
Gilles Ouimet, Président

Foundation for Legal Research / La foundation pour la recherche juridique
c/o Law Foundation of British Columbia, #1340, 605 Robsen St., Vancouver BC V6B 5J3 Canada
Toll-Free: 800-267-8860
www.cba.org
To support & maintain scholarships, bursaries & prizes in the field of legal research
John R.R. Jennings, Chair
Francois Letourneaux, Secretary
Stephen Bresolin, Treasurer

Institute of Law Clerks of Ontario (ILCO)
#502, 20 Adelaide St. East, Toronto ON M5C 2T6 Canada
Tel: 416-214-6252; *Fax:* 416-214-6255
receiption@ilco.on.ca
www.ilco.on.ca
To provide an organized network for promoting unity, cooperation & mutual assistance among Law Clerks in Ontario; to advance & protect their status & interests; to promote their education for the purpose of increasing their knowledge, efficiency & professional ability.

International Centre for Criminal Law Reform & Criminal Justice Policy (ICCLR)
1822 East Mall, Vancouver BC V6T 1Z1 Canada
Tel: 604-822-9875; *Fax:* 604-822-9317
icclr@law.ubc.ca
www.icclr.law.ubc.ca
To improve the quality of justice through reform of criminal law, policy & practice; to provide advice, information, research & proposals for policy development & legislation
Kathleen Macdonald, Executive Director

International Commission of Jurists (Canadian Section) (ICJ) / La Commission internationale de juristes (section canadienne) (CIJ)
#500, 865 Carling Ave., Ottawa ON K1S 5S8 Canada
Tel: 613-237-2925; *Fax:* 613-237-0185
patw@cba.org
www.icjcanada.org
To works internationally with the parent organization to monitor & promote the rule of law & the impartiality & independence of the judiciary in countries where these are threatened or non-existent; to act nationally & locally to promote awareness of these issues & human rights generally

Law Foundation of British Columbia
#1340, 605 Robson St., Vancouver BC V6B 5J3 Canada
Tel: 604-688-2337; *Fax:* 604-688-4586
lfbc@tlfbc.org
www.lawfoundationbc.org
To allocate funds to programs that will benefit the general public of British Columbia; To act in accordance with The Legal Profession Act & distribute income in areas that promote & advance a just society & the rule of law, such as legal aid, law libraries, legal education, legal research, & law reform; To conduct operations with recognition of the diverse population of British Columbia
Wayne Robertson, Executive Director

Dev Dley, Chair
Jo-Anne Kaulius, Director, Finance

Law Foundation of Newfoundland & Labrador
Murray Premises, 2nd Fl., PO Box 5907, #49, 55 Elizabeth Ave., St. John's NL A1C 5X4 Canada
Tel: 709-754-4424; *Fax:* 709-754-4320
www.atyp.com/lawfoundationnl/
To provide grants for the following services in Newfoundland & Labrador that advance public understanding of the law & access to legal services: the Legal Aid Commission as established under the Legal Aid Act; law libraries; legal research; legal education; scholarships for studies relevant to law; law reform; & legal referral services

Law Foundation of Nova Scotia
PO Box 325, Halifax NS B3J 2N7 Canada
Tel: 902-422-8335; *Fax:* 902-492-0424
nslawfd@nslawfd.ca
www.nslawfd.ca
To establish & maintain a fund to be used for the examination, research, revision & reform of & public access to the law, legal education, the administration of justice in the province & any other purposes incidental or conducive to or consequential upon the attainment of any such objects
Kerry L. Oliver, Executive Director

Law Foundation of Ontario / La fondation du droit de l'Ontario
PO Box 19, #3002, 20 Queen St. West, Toronto ON M5H 3R3 Canada
Tel: 416-598-1550; *Fax:* 416-598-1526
general@lawfoundation.on.org
www.lawfoundation-on.org
Mark J. Sandler, Chair
Elizabeth Goldberg, Chief Executive Officer

Law Foundation of Prince Edward Island
49 Water St., Charlottetown PE C1A 7K2 Canada
Tel: 902-566-1666
To establish & maintain a fund & use the proceeds thereof for the purposes of: legal education & research on law reform; the editing & printing of decisions of the Supreme Court & the Provincial Court of PEI; the promotion of legal aid; aid in the establishment, operation & maintenance of law libraries in PEI
M. Jane Ralling, Chair

Law Foundation of Saskatchewan
#200, 2208 Scarth St., Regina SK S4P 2J6 Canada
Tel: 306-352-1121; *Fax:* 306-522-6222
lfsk@virtusgroup.ca
www.lawfoundation.sk.ca
To maintain a fund to support legal aid, law reform, law libraries, legal education, & legal research
Robert Arscott, F.C.A., Secretary
Karen Prisciak, Q.C., Chair
J. Gordon Wicijowski, LL.D., F.C.A., Treasurer

Law Society of Alberta (LSA)
#500, 919 - 11th Ave. SW, Calgary AB T2R 1P3 Canada
Tel: 403-229-4700; *Fax:* 403-228-1728
Toll-Free: 800-661-9003
www.lawsocietyalberta.com
To serve the public by promoting a high standard of legal services & professional conduct through the governance & regulation of an independent legal profession; to govern all lawyers who practise law in Alberta; responsible for admitting lawyers to the Bar, professional conduct & discipline of lawyers
Don Thompson, Executive Director
Sheila Serup, Manager
Rodney A. Jerke, Q.C., President

Law Society of British Columbia
845 Cambie St., 8th Fl., Vancouver BC V6B 4Z9 Canada
Tel: 604-669-2533; *Fax:* 604-669-5232
communications@lsbc.org
www.lawsociety.bc.ca
To ensure that the public is well served by a competent, honourable & independent legal profession
Timothy E. McGee, CEO & Executive Director
Gordon Turriff, QC, President

Law Society of Manitoba (LSM) / La Société du Barreau du Manitoba
219 Kennedy St., Winnipeg MB R3C 1S8 Canada
Tel: 204-942-5571; *Fax:* 204-956-0624
admin@lawsociety.mb.ca
www.lawsociety.mb.ca
To ensure the public in Manitoba is well served by the legal profession

Law Society of New Brunswick / Barreau du Nouveau-Brunswick
#206, 1133 Regent St., Fredericton NB E3B 3Z2 Canada
Tel: 506-458-8540; *Fax:* 506-451-1421
general@lawsociety-barreau.nb.ca
www.lawsociety-barreau.nb.ca
The Law Society was officially created in 1846. The Provincial Legislative Assembly adopted Chapter 48 of the Provincial Statutes which in effect incorporated what was then called the "Barristers' Society" for the "purpose of securing in the Province a learned and honourable legal profession, for establishing order and good conduct among its members and for promoting knowledgeable development and reform of the law".
Marc L. Richard, Q.C., Executive Director
David R. Ames, Q.C., President

Law Society of Newfoundland & Labrador
PO Box 1028, St. John's NL A1C 5M3 Canada
Tel: 709-722-4740; *Fax:* 709-722-8902
CLE@lawsociety.nf.ca
www.lawsociety.nf.ca
The Law Society is the regulatory body for the legal profession in the province. It ensures that law students are appropriately educated and trained through articling and Bar Admission programs and exams, and provides continuing legal education to practitioners. Office is located at 196-198 Water St., St. John's.
Peter G. Ringrose, Executive Director

Law Society of Nunavut (LSNU)
PO Box 149, Iqaluit NU X0A 0H0 Canada
Tel: 867-979-2330; *Fax:* 867-979-2333
lawsociety@qiniq.com
www.lawsociety.nu.ca
To govern our membership & protect the public. Office is located at Bldg. 812, Unit 4, Iqualuit.
Craig Goebel, CEO

Law Society of Prince Edward Island
PO Box 128, 49 Water St., Charlottetown PE C1A 7K2 Canada
Tel: 902-566-1666; *Fax:* 902-368-7557
lawsociety@lspei.pe.ca
www.lspei.pe.ca
To uphold & protect the public interest in the administration of justice; to establish standards for the education, professional responsibility & competence of members & applicants for membership; to ensure the independence, integrity & honour of the society & its members; to regulate the practice of law; to uphold & protect the interests of members.
Susan M. Robinson, Executive Director & Sec.-Treas.

Law Society of Saskatchewan
#1100, 2002 Victoria Ave., Regina SK S4P 0R7 Canada
Tel: 306-569-8242; *Fax:* 306-352-2989
reception@lawsociety.sk.ca
www.lawsociety.sk.ca
To govern the legal profession by upholding high standards of competence & integrity; ensuring the independence of the profession; advancing the administration of justice, the profession & the rule of law, all in the public interest
A. Kirsten Logan, Q.C., Secretary & Co-Director, Administration
Allan T. Snell, Q.C., General Counsel & Co-Director, Administration

Law Society of the Northwest Territories / Le Barreau des Territoires du Nord-Ouest
Diamond Plaza, PO Box 1298, Stn. Main, 5204 - 50th Ave., 4th Fl., Yellowknife NT X1A 2N9 Canada
Tel: 867-873-3828; *Fax:* 867-873-6344
info@lawsociety.nt.ca
www.lawsociety.nt.ca
To serve the public by an independent, responsible & responsive legal profession.
Linda Whitford, Executive Director

Law Society of Upper Canada / Barreau du Haut-Canada
Osgoode Hall, 130 Queen St. West, Toronto ON M5H 2N6 Canada
Tel: 416-947-3300; *Fax:* 416-947-3924
Toll-Free: 800-668-7380
lawsociety@lsuc.on.ca
www.lsuc.on.ca
To govern the legal profession in the public interest by ensuring that the people of Ontario are served by lawyers who meet high standards of learning, competence & professional conduct.
Malcolm L. Heins, CEO
Diana Miles, Director, Professional Development & Competence

Law Society of Yukon (LSY)
#202, 302 Steele St., Whitehorse YT Y1A 2C5 Canada
Tel: 867-668-4231; *Fax:* 867-667-7556
info@lawsocietyyukon.com
www.lawsocietyyukon.com
To govern legal profession in the Yukon.
Lynn Daffe, Executive Director

Legal Education Society of Alberta (LESA)
#2610, 10104 - 103 Ave., Edmonton AB T5J 0H8 Canada
Tel: 780-420-1987; *Fax:* 780-425-0885
Toll-Free: 800-282-3900
lesa@lesa.org
www.lesa.org
To educate providers of legal services in Alberta; To increase awareness of issues affecting the legal profession; To maintain & increase professional responsibility & competence; To develop & provide education in law, skills, & ethics

Legal Information Society of Nova Scotia (LISNS)
5523B Young St., Halifax NS B3K 1Z7 Canada
Tel: 902-454-2198; *Fax:* 902-455-3105
Toll-Free: 800-665-9779
lisns@legalinfo.org
www.legalinfo.org
To provide Nova Scotians easy access to information & resources about the law

The Manitoba Law Foundation / La Fondation manitobaine du droit
412 McDermot Ave., Winnipeg MB R3C 0A9 Canada
bpalace@gatewest.net
To provide funds for legal education, legal research, legal aid, law reform & the establishment, operation & maintenance of law libraries

Municipal Law Enforcement Officers' Association (Ontario) Inc.
c/o City Of Barrie, PO Box 400, Barrie ON L4M 4T5 Canada
Tel: 705-739-4241; *Fax:* 705-739-4279
mleo@mleoa.ca
www.mleoa.ca
To bring members into helpful association with each other to maintain professional standards; to encourage & assist in the education & training programs for Municipal Law Enforcement Officers

New Brunswick Law Foundation / Fondation pour l'avancement du droit au Nouveau-Brunswick
#206, 1133 Regent St., Fredericton NB E3B 3Z2 Canada
Tel: 506-458-8540; *Fax:* 506-451-1421
general@lawsociety-barreau.nb.ca
www.lawsociety.nb.ca
To receive the interest earned on lawyers' mixed trust accounts & to use these funds to support law-related projects to benefit residents of New Brunswick
David R. Ames, President

New Brunswick Police Association / Association policière du Nouveau-Brunswick
284 Main St., Sackville NB E4L 3H5 Canada
Tel: 506-536-3445; *Fax:* 506-536-2745
Toll-Free: 800-561-4422
www.policenb.ca
Dean Secord, President

Northwest Territories Association of Provincial Court Judges
c/o Territorial Court of Northwest Territories, PO Box 550, 4093 - 49th St., Yellowknife NT X1A 2N4 Canada
Tel: 867-873-7604; *Fax:* 867-873-0203

Northwest Territories Law Foundation
PO Box 2594, 5212 - 55th St., Yellowknife NT X1A 2P9 Canada
Tel: 867-873-8275; *Fax:* 867-873-6383
action@theedge.ca
www.lawsociety.nt.ca/NWTLawFoundation/tabid/212/Default.aspx
To provide funding in the Northwest Territories in the following areas: the establishment & operation of law libraries; the provision of legal education; research in law & the administration of justice; recommendations for law reform; legal aid programs & similar programs; & the Assurance Fund
Wendy Carter, Executive Manager
Glenn Tait, Chair
Gerard Phillips, Vice-Chair

Nova Scotia Barristers' Society (NSBS)
#1101, 1645 Granville St., Halifax NS B3J 1X3 Canada
Tel: 902-422-1491; *Fax:* 902-429-4869
info@nsbs.org
www.nsbs.org

To set & enforce standards of professional responsibility & ethics for lawyers; To license & discipline members of the profession, in accordance with the Legal Profession Act
Darrel I. Pink, Executive Director
Joel E. Pink, Q.C., President
Jacqueline L. Mullenger, Director, Admissions & Professional Development
Victoria Rees, Director, Professional Responsibility

Ontario Association of Corrections & Criminology
PO Box 949, Stn. K, Toronto ON M4P 2V3 Canada
Tel: 416-304-1974; *Fax:* 416-304-1977
info@oacconline.org
www.oacconline.org
The Association effects co-operation among individuals, groups & governmental organizations interested & active in the field of correctional & criminal justice. It works to further the study of correctional, criminological & criminal justice issues.

Ontario Association of Police Services Boards (OAPSB)
10 Peel Centre Dr., Brampton ON L6T 4B9 Canada
Tel: 905-458-1488; *Fax:* 905-458-2260
Toll-Free: 800-831-7727
admin@oapsb.ca
www.oapsb.ca
To act as the voice of police services boards to government; To provide services to assist police services boards in Ontario

Ontario Crown Attorneys Association (OCAA)
PO Box 30, #1015, 180 Dundas St. West, Toronto ON M5G 1Z8
Tel: 416-977-4517; *Fax:* 416-977-1460
reception@ocaa.ca
www.ocaa.ca
To promote & protect the professional interests of crown counsels, assistant crown attorneys, & articling students

People's Law School
#150, 900 Howe St., Vancouver BC V6Z 2M4 Canada
Tel: 604-331-5400; *Fax:* 604-331-5401
staff@publiclegaled.bc.ca
www.publiclegaled.bc.ca
To make law & legal system understandable & accessible to people of British Columbia

Police Association of Nova Scotia (PANS) / Association des policiers de la Nouvelle-Écosse
#22, 1000 Windmill Rd., Dartmouth NS B3B 1L7 Canada
Tel: 902-468-7555; *Fax:* 902-468-2202
Toll-Free: 888-468-2798
David W. Fisher, CEO

Police Association of Ontario (PAO) / Association des policiers de l'Ontario
#1-3, 6730 Davand Dr., Mississauga ON L5T 2K8 Canada
Tel: 905-670-9770; *Fax:* 905-670-9755
pao@pao.on.ca
www.pao.on.ca
Preserving safe communities

Probation Officers Association of Ontario (POAO)
#6245, 2100 Bloor St. West, Toronto ON M6S 5A5 Canada
Tel: 905-329-3219
info@poao.org
www.poao.org
POAO is a voluntary, non-profit organization representing the professional interests of the probation & parole Officers across the province. It is not a union, but it provides representation on legislative issues to policy makers. It is also a forum for exchange of experience & information.

The Public Interest Advocacy Centre (PIAC) / Centre pour la défense de l'intérêt public
#1204, One Nicholas St., Ottawa ON K1N 7B7 Canada
Tel: 613-562-4002
piac@piac.ca
www.piac.ca
To provide legal services on a non-profit basis to groups & individuals addressing public interest issues of broad concern who would not otherwise have access to such services; the centre's special interests are telecommunications, energy, transportation, broadcasting, privacy, technical services & consumer protection

Public Legal Education Association of Saskatchewan, Inc. (PLEA Sask.)
#300, 201 - 21st East, Saskatoon SK S7K 0B8 Canada
Tel: 306-653-1868; *Fax:* 306-653-1869
plea@plea.org
www.plea.org
To educate & inform the people of Saskatchewan about the law & the legal system

Public Legal Information Association of Newfoundland (PLIAN)
Tara Place, #227, 31 Peet St., St. John's NL A1B 3W8 Canada
Tel: 709-722-2643; *Fax:* 709-722-0054
Toll-Free: 888-660-7788
info@publiclegalinfo.com
www.publiclegalinfo.com
To provide plain language legal information to the general public of Newfoundland, in both official languages, through a telephone enquiry line, public speaking engagements, publications, & a lawyer referral service

Saskatchewan Federation of Police Officers (SFPO)
26 Chase Cres., Regina SK S4R 7Y4 Canada
Tel: 306-539-0960
www.saskpolice.com
To advance police work as a profession; To support members in their police careers
Bernie Eiswirth, Executive Officer
Haye Dave, President

Société de criminologie du Québec (SCQ)
#201, 2000, boul Saint-Joseph est, Montréal QC H2H 1E4 Canada
Tél: 514-529-4391; *Téléc:* 514-529-6936
crimino@societecrimino.qc.ca
www.societecrimino.qc.ca
Mission: de contribuer à l'évolution du système de justice pénale, de favoriser les échanges & les débats entre tous les intéressés à l'avancement de la justice pénale, & de favoriser & encourager la recherche

The Society of Notaries Public of British Columbia
PO Box 44, #1220, 625 Howe St., Vancouver BC V6C 2T6 Canada
Tel: 604-681-4516; *Fax:* 604-681-7258
Toll-Free: 800-663-0343
society@notaries.bc.ca
www.notaries.bc.ca

Toronto Lawyers Association
361 University Ave., Toronto ON M5G 1T3 Canada
Tel: 416-327-5700; *Fax:* 416-947-9148
aliu@tlaonline.ca
www.tlaonline.ca
Provides lawyers with key services; timely & relevant information; education about issues & opportunities affecting members; advocacy on behalf of the profession

Yukon Law Foundation
PO Box 31789, Whitehorse YT Y1A 6L3 Canada
Tel: 867-667-7500; *Fax:* 867-393-3904
execdir@yukonlawfoundation.com
www.yukonlawfoundation.com
The objects of the Foundation are to maintain and manage a fund accumulated primarily from the interest on lawyers' trust accounts
Deana Lemke, Executive Director
Malcolm Campbell, Chair

Yukon Public Legal Education Association (YPLEA)
PO Box 2799, Yukon College, Whitehorse YT Y1A 5K4 Canada
Tel: 867-668-5297; *Fax:* 867-668-5541
Toll-Free: 866-667-4305
yplea@yukoncollege.yk.ca
www.yplea.com
To provide free legal information to Yukoners & promote greater accessibility to the legal system
Robert Pritchard, Contact

Libraries & Archives

Administrators of Small Public Libraries of Ontario (ASPLO)
c/o Brant County Public Library, 12 William St., Paris ON N3L 1K7 Canada
Tel: 519-442-2433; *Fax:* 519-442-7582
gay.kozakselby@county.brant.on.ca

Alberta Association of College Librarians (AACL)
c/o Red Deer College, PO Box 5005, Red Deer AB T4N 5H5 Canada
Tel: 403-342-3306
alice.mcnair@rdc.ab.ca
www.aacl.engineseven.com

Alberta Association of Library Technicians (AALT)
PO Box 700, Edmonton AB T5J 2L4
Toll-Free: 866-350-2258
marketing@aalt.org; membership@aalt.org; journal@aalt.org
www.aalt.org
Social Media: www.facebook.com/group.php?gid=96867929556
To foster & enhance the professional image of library technicians in Alberta; To support library technicians throughout the province
Allison Stewart, President
Melanie Belliveau, Director, Marketing
Sarah Stephens, Director, Membership
Becky Deobald, Secretary
Lilla Lesko, Treasurer

Alberta Library Trustees Association (ALTA)
#6-24, 7 Sir Winston Churchill Sq., Edmonton AB T5J 2V5
Tel: 780-481-1725; *Fax:* 780-572-4447
admin@librarytrustees.ab.ca; president@librarytrustees.ab.ca
www.librarytrustees.ab.ca
Social Media: www.facebook.com/group.php?gid=89423578711
To act as the collective voice for library trustees in Alberta; To develop effective trustees

Archives Association of British Columbia (AABC)
#249, 34A-2755 Lougheed Hwy., Port Coquitlam BC V3B 5Y9 Canada
aabc@aabc.bc.ca
www.aabc.bc.ca
AABC is the voice of archivists & archival institutions in British Columbia. It undertakes projects that strengthen the archival network in the province, through preservation & promotion of access to British Columbia's documentary heritage
Lara Wilson, President
Lisa Glandt, Secretary
Sharon Walz, Treasurer

Archives Association of Ontario (AAO) / L'Association des archives de l'Ontario
#202, 10 Morrow Ave., Toronto ON M6R 2J1 Canada
Tel: 416-538-1650; *Fax:* 416-489-1713
aao@aao.fis.utoronto.ca
aao.fis.utoronto.ca
To encourage, through the establishment of networks, the public knowledge & appreciation of archives & their function; to promote the advancement of general education in the preservation of the cultural heritage & identity of the various regions of the province; to represent the interests of the archival community before the government of Ontario, local government & other provincial institutions of a public or private nature; to provide professional guidance & leadership through communication & cooperation with all persons, groups & associations interested in the preservation & use of records of the human experience in Ontario
Heather McCafferty-Leger, President
Marianne Henskens, Executive Director
Mary Gladwin, Secretary

Archives Council of Prince Edward Island
Public Archives, George Coles Bldg., PO Box 1000, Charlottetown PE C1A 7M4 Canada
Tel: 902-368-4290; *Fax:* 902-368-6327
acpei@gov.pe.ca
www.archives.pe.ca
To facilitate the development of the archival system in PEI; to make recommendations about the system's operation & financing; to develop & facilitate the implementation & management of programs to assist the archival community; to communicate archival needs & concerns to decision-makers, researchers & the general public

Archives Society of Alberta (ASA)
PO Box 4067, Stn. South Edmonton, Edmonton AB T6E 4S8 Canada
Tel: 780-424-2697; *Fax:* 780-425-1679
jahsena@shaw.ca
www.archivesalberta.org
To provide professional leadership among persons engaged in practice of archival science; to promote development of archives & archivists in Alberta; to encourage cooperation of archivists & archives with all those interested in preservation & use of documents of human experience
Debby Shoctor, President

Art Libraries Society of North America (ARLIS/NA)
Technical Enterprises, Inc., 7044 S. 13th St., Oak Creek WI 53154 USA
Tel: 414-768-8000; *Fax:* 414-768-8001
Toll-Free: 800-817-0621
info@arlisna.org
www.arlisna.org
The Society's mission is to foster excellence in art & design librarianship & image management.

Elizabeth Clarke, Executive Director
Amy Lucker, President
Marilyn Russell, Vice-President
Edward (Ted) Goodman, Treasurer

Association des archivistes du Québec (AAQ)
CP 9768, Succ. Sainte-Foy, Québec QC G1V 4C3 Canada
Tél: 418-652-2357; *Téléc:* 418-646-0868
infoaaq@archivistes.qc.ca
www.archivistes.qc.ca
Regrouper les personnes qui offrent aux organisations et à leurs clientèles des services liés à la gestion de leur information organique et consignée; offrir à ses membres des services en français et propres à assurer le développement, l'enrichissement et la promotion de leur profession et de leur discipline; assurer aux membres les services susceptibles de favoriser et d'accroître les échanges et la communication internes et externes des idées et des connaissances; promouvoir le développement professionnel des membres en s'impliquant activement au plan de la formation et du perfectionnement, en favorisant la recherche et le développement et en assurant une représentation adéquate de la profession au sein de la société et auprès des corps politiques
Andrée Gingras, Directrice générale

Association des bibliothécaires du Québec (ABQ) / Québec Library Association (QLA)
CP 1095, Pointe-Claire QC H9S 4H9 Canada
Tél: 514-697-0146; *Téléc:* 514-697-0146
abqla@abqla.qc.ca
www.abqla.qc.ca
Média social: www.facebook.com/group.php?gid=52867661827

Association des bibliothécaires professionnel(le)s du Nouveau-Brunswick (ABPNB) / Association of Professional Librarians of New Brunswick (APLNB)
CP 423, Succ. A, Fredericton NB E3B 4Z9 Canada
Tél: 506-458-7058; *Téléc:* 506-453-4831
info@abpnb-aplnb.ca
www.abpnb-aplnb.ca
Promouvoir les bibliothécaires et les services de bibliothèques au Nouveau-Brunswick; to promote librarians & library services in New Brunswick.
Victoria Volkanova, Présidente
Hector Alvarez, Secrétaire
Robin Sexton-Mayes, Trésorier

Association des bibliothèques de droit de Montréal (ABDM) / Montréal Association of Law Libraries (MALL)
Tour de la Bourse, CP 482, 800, Square Victoria, Montréal QC H4Z 1J7 Canada
www.abdm-mall.org
Vise à permettre aux gens qui travaillent dans les bibliothèques de droit et qui exercent des fonctions connexes de communiquer et d'échanger des idées; d'encourager l'avancement de la profession; de maintenir et d'accroître l'utilité des bibliothèques de droit; promouvoir la coopération
Nathalie Bélanger, Présidente

Association des bibliothèques publiques de l'Estrie (ABIPE)
5086, rue Frontenac, Lac-Mégantic QC G6B 1H3 Canada
Tél: 819-845-7115; *Téléc:* 819-845-5516
mpmorin@abacom.com
www.bpq-estrie.qc.ca
Regrouper les bibliothèques publiques d'Estrie pour en favoriser le développement; informer les membres et échanger sur toute question pertinente au dossier des bibliothèques; représenter les intérêts des bibliothèques membres de la région 05 en étant leur porte-parole officiel auprès des instances gouvernementales et autres; organiser et réaliser des activités d'animation culturelle; sensibiliser le milieu au rôle et à l'importance de la bibliothèque publique dans la communauté
Marie-Pascale Morin, Présidente
Karine Corbeil, Vice-présidente

Association for Manitoba Archives (AMA)
PO Box 26005, Stn. Maryland, Winnipeg MB R3G 3R3 Canada
Tel: 204-942-3491; *Fax:* 204-942-3492
ama1@mts.net
www.mbarchives.mb.ca
To promote understanding & awareness of the role & use of archives; to promote standards, procedures & practices in the management of archives; to provide assistance & education to persons seeking to improve their skills in the development, management or operation of archives

Association of Canadian Archivists (ACA)
PO Box 2596, Stn. D, Ottawa ON K1P 5W6
Tel: 613-234-6977; *Fax:* 613-234-8500
aca@archivists.ca
www.archivists.ca
To ensure the preservation & accessibility of Canada's documentary heritage; To provide professional leadership among persons engaged in the discipline & practice of archival science; To promote the development of archives & archivists in Canada; To encourage cooperation of archivists with all those interested in the preservation & use of documents of human experience

Association of Canadian Map Libraries & Archives (ACMLA) / Association des cartothèques et archives cartographiques du Canada (ACACC)
c/o Legal Deposit, Maps, Published Heritage, Library & Archives Canada, 550, boul de la Cité, Gatineau ON K1N ON4
membership@acmla.org; president@acmla.org;
secretary@acmla.org
www.acmla.org
To represent Canadian map librarians & cartographic archivists, as well as others who are interested in geographic information; To develop professional standards & international cataloguing rules for the management & access to geographic information; To promote the contributions of map libraries & cartographic archives

Association of Newfoundland & Labrador Archives (ANLA)
PO Box 23155, RPO Churchill Sq., St. John's NL A1B 4J9 Canada
Tel: 709-726-2867; *Fax:* 709-729-7989
anla@nf.aibn.com
www.anla.nf.ca
To provide professional leadership among persons engaged in practice of archival science; to promote development of archives & archivists in Newfoundland & Labrador; to encourage cooperation of archivists with all those interested in preservation & use of documents of human experience
Stephanie Harlick, President

Association of Parliamentary Libraries in Canada (APLIC) / Association des bibliothèques parlementaires au Canada (ABPAC)
c/o Melissa Bennett, Librarian, Saskatchewan Legislative Library, #234, 2405 Legislative Dr., Regina SK S4S 0B3
mbennett@legassembly.sk.ca (President)
www.aplic-abpac.ca
To improve parliamentary library service in Canada; To encourage cooperation with related officials & organizations

Association pour l'avancement des sciences et des techniques de la documentation (ASTED)
#202, 3414, av du Parc, Montréal QC H2X 2H5 Canada
Tél: 514-281-5012; *Téléc:* 514-281-8219
info@asted.org
www.asted.org
Promouvoir l'excellence des services documentaires et de leur personnel; inspirer la législation et promouvoir les intérêts des services documentaires et d'information; exercer au sein de la francophonie nord-américaine le leadership documentaire

Atlantic Provinces Library Association (APLA)
c/o School of Information Management, Kenneth C. Rowe Management Bldg., 6100 University Ave., Halifax NS B3H 3J5
executive@yahoo.ca
www.apla.ca
Social Media: www.facebook.com/group.php?gid=10792140537
To promote library & information service & workers throughout the Atlantic region; To represent & support the interests of persons who work in libraries in the Atlantic provinces; To cooperate with other library associations & similar organizations; To develop & offer effective continuing education programs
Jocelyne Thompson, President
Lou Duggan, Vice-President
Ann Smith, Vice-President, Membership
Debbie Costelo, Secretary
Bill Slauenwhite, Treasurer

Bibliographical Society of Canada (BSC) / Société bibliographique du Canada (SBC)
PO Box 575, Stn. P, Toronto ON M5S 2T1 Canada
gretagolick@rogers.com
www.library.utoronto.ca/bsc
To promote the scholarly study of history, description & transmission of texts in all media & formats; emphasis on Canada; promote the study & practice of bibliography; further the study, research & publication of book hisory & print culture; promote preservation & conservation of manuscript, archival & published materials in various formats; encourage utilization & analysis of relevant manuscript & archival sources as a foundation of bibliographical scholarship & book history

Les bibliothèques publiques des régions de Québec et Chaudière-Appalaches
4705, rue de la Promenade-des-Soeurs, Cap-Rouge QC G1Y 2W2 Canada
Tél: 418-641-6143; *Téléc:* 418-650-7795
info@bibliotheques.qc.ca
www.bibliotheques.qc.ca
Regrouper les responsables des bibliothèques publiques de ces régions; promouvoir et défendre les intérêts de ces bibliothèques; représenter le secteur des bibliothèques publiques des ces régions au sein des organismes à caractères culturel et social.
Suzanne Rochefort, Présidente

Les bibliothèques publiques du Québec (BPQ)
7855, av San-Francisco, Brossard QC J4X 2A4 Canada
Tél: 514-886-7779; *Téléc:* 450-923-7042
lucie.lachapelle@bibliothequespubliquesduquebec.ca
www.bibliothequespubliquesduquebec.ca
Agit à titre de représentant officiel des bibliothèques publiques du Québec

British Columbia Courthouse Library Society
800 Smithe St., Vancouver BC V6Z 2E1 Canada
Tel: 604-660-2910; *Fax:* 604-660-9418
Toll-Free: 800-665-2570
bccls@bccls.bc.ca
www.bccls.bc.ca
Johanne Blenkin, Executive Director

British Columbia Library Association (BCLA)
#150, 900 Howe St., Vancouver BC V6Z 2M4
Tel: 604-683-5354; *Fax:* 604-609-0707
Toll-Free: 888-683-5354
office@bcla.bc.ca
www.bcla.bc.ca
To encourage library development throughout British Columbia; To coordinate library services to various parts of the province; To promote cooperation between libraries; To advance the mutual interests of libraries & library personnel

British Columbia Library Trustees' Association (BCLTA)
PO Box 4334, Stn. Terminal, Vancouver BC V6B 3Z7
Tel: 604-913-1424; *Fax:* 604-913-1413
admin@bclta.org
www.bclta.org
To develop & support library trustees who govern local public libraries in British Columbia; To advance public library service in the province

Canadian Association for Information Science (CAIS) / Association canadienne des sciences de l'information (ACSI)
c/o Nadia Caidi, Faculty of Information, #335, 45 Willcocks St., Toronto ON M5S 1C7
Tel: 416-978-4664
nadia.caidi@utoronto.ca
www.cais-acsi.ca
To advance information science in Canada by encouraging & facilitating the exchange of information on the use, access, retrieval, organization, management, & dissemination of information

Canadian Association for School Libraries (CASL)
c/o Canadian Library Association, 328 Frank St., Ottawa ON K2P 0X8
Tel: 613-232-9625; *Fax:* 613-563-9895
info@cla.ca; membership@cla.ca; cpd@cla.ca (Continuing Education)
www.cla.ca/AM/Template.cfm?Section=CASL2
To promote school library programs throughout Canada as an important element in the educational process; To encourage excellence in every aspect of school libraries
Linda Shantz-Keresztes, President
Diana Gauthier, Secretary-Treasurer
Derrick Grose, Editor, School Libraries in Canada: A Journal of the CASL
Victoria Pennell, Editor, Impact

Canadian Association of Children's Librarians (CACL)
c/o Canadian Library Association, 328 Frank St., Ottawa ON K2P 0X8
Tel: 613-232-9625
www.cla.ca/AM/Template.cfm?Section=CAPL2
To address issues of interest to librarians who work with & for children

Canadian Association of College & University Libraries (CACUL)
c/o Canadian Library Association, 328 Frank St., Ottawa ON K2P 0X8
Tel: 613-232-9625; *Fax:* 613-563-9895
info@cla.ca; membership@cla.ca; cpd@cla.ca (Continuing Education)
www.cla.ca/AM/Template.cfm?Section=CACUL
To develop & promote high standards of librarianship & of library & information services in post-secondary education institutions
Pam Ryan, President
Gillian Byrne, Vice-President & Director, Membership
Wendy Rodgers, Director, Awards
Carol Shepstone, Director, Grants
Christine E. Sammon, Secretary-Treasurer

Canadian Association of Family Resource Programs / Association canadienne des programmes de ressources pour la famille
#707, 331 Cooper St., Ottawa ON K2P 0G5
Tel: 613-237-7667; *Fax:* 613-237-8515
Toll-Free: 866-637-7226
info@frp.ca
www.frp.ca
To promote the well-being of families, through provision of leadership, consultation, & resources to organizations which care for children & support families; To act as the national voice for family resource programs; To advance social policy, research, resource development, & training for those who support the capacity of families to raise their children

Canadian Association of Law Libraries (CALL) / Association canadienne des bibliothèques de droit (ACBD)
PO Box 1570, #310, 4 Cataraqui St., Kingston ON K7L 5C8 Canada
Tel: 613-531-9338; *Fax:* 613-531-0626
office@callacbd.ca
www.callacbd.ca
To promote law librarianship; To develop Canadian law libraries; To promote access to legal information

Canadian Association of Music Libraries, Archives & Documentation Centres (CAML) / Association canadienne des bibliothèques, archives et centres de documentation musicaux inc. (ACBM)
c/o Music Section, Library & Archives Canada, 395 Wellington St., Ottawa ON K1A 0N4
kirsten.walsh@ubc.ca (President); sacassin@yorku.ca (Webmaster)
www.yorku.ca/caml
To represent librarians, researchers, & archivists in the field of music

Canadian Association of Public Libraries (CAPL)
c/o Canadian Library Association, 328 Frank St., Ottawa ON K2P 0X8
Tel: 613-232-9625; *Fax:* 613-563-9895
info@cla.ca
www.cla.ca/AM/Template.cfm?Section=CAPL2
Social Media: www.facebook.com/group.php?gid=7514940812
To further & improve public library service throughout Canada
Andre Gagnon, President
Nancy Mackenzie, Vice-President
Maureen Sawa, Secretary-Treasurer

Canadian Association of Research Libraries (CARL) / Association des bibliothèques de recherche du Canada (ABRC)
Morisset Library, University of Ottawa, #239, 65 University St., Ottawa ON K1N 9A5
Tel: 613-562-5385; *Fax:* 613-562-5297
carladm@uottawa.ca
www.carl-abrc.ca
To provide leadership to the Canadian research library community; To address issues affecting research libraries, such as federal research policy, copyright, open access publication, & preservation; To encourage broad access to scholarly information; To seek public policy encouraging of research

Canadian Association of Special Libraries & Information Services (CASLIS)
c/o Canadian Library Association, 328 Frank St., Ottawa ON K2P 0X8
Tel: 613-232-9625; *Fax:* 613-563-9895
info@cla.ca; membership@cla.ca; cpd@cla.ca (Continuing Education)
www.cla.ca/caslis
Social Media: www.facebook.com/group.php?gid=27554915813
To support information professionals across Canada who work in special libraries & information services; To strengthen the special library community
Robyn Stockand, President
Juanita Richardson, Vice-President
Melissa Fraser, Secretary
Laura Lemmens, Treasurer

Canadian Council of Archives (CCA) / Conseil canadien des archives
#501, 130 Albert St., Ottawa ON K1P 5G4 Canada
Tel: 613-565-1222; *Fax:* 613-565-5445
Toll-Free: 866-254-1403
cca@archivescanada.ca
www.cdncouncilarchives.ca
To facilitate development of Canadian archival system & its coordination; to make recommendations to system's operation & financing; to develop & facilitate implementation & management of programs to assist archival community; to communicate archival needs & concerns to decision-makers, researchers & the general public.

Canadian Health Information Management Association (CHIMA)
#1404, 148 Fullarton St., London ON N6A 5P3 Canada
Tel: 519-438-6700; *Fax:* 519-438-7001
Toll-Free: 877-332-4462
gail.crook@echima.ca
www.echima.ca
To contribute to the promotion of wellness & the provision of quality healthcare through excellence in health information management; to assure competency of practice through credentialling, standards & continuing education; to promote value of health record professionals within the relevant publics

Canadian Health Libraries Association (CHLA) / Association des bibliothèques de la santé du Canada (ABSC)
39 River St., Toronto ON M5A 3P1
Tel: 416-646-1600; *Fax:* 416-646-9460
info@chla-absc.ca; pr@chla-absc.ca (Public Relations)
www.chla-absc.ca
To lead health librarians towards excellence

Canadian Library Association (CLA) / Association canadienne des bibliothèques (ACB)
#400, 1150 Morrison Dr., Ottawa ON K2H 8S9
Tel: 613-232-9625; *Fax:* 613-563-9895
info@cla.ca; membership@cla.ca; publishing@cla.ca; orders@cla.ca
www.cla.ca
Social Media: www.facebook.com/group.php?gid=2229890224
To develop high standards of librarianship & of library & information services across Canada
Karen Adams, President
Kelly Moore, Executive Director
Judy Green, Manager, Marketing & Communications
Penny Warne, Manager, Web & IT Infrastructure
Wendy Walton, Manager, Conference & Events
Ingrid Langhammer, Treasurer
Carla Chami, Coordinator, Conference Registration

Canadian Library Trustees Association (CLTA)
c/o Canadian Library Association, 328 Frank St., Ottawa ON K2P 0X8
Tel: 613-232-9625; *Fax:* 613-563-9895
info@cla.ca; membership@cla.ca; cpd@cla.ca (Continuing Education)
www.cla.ca/AM/Template.cfm?Section=CLTA
To represent the interests of public library trustees in Canada; To foster excellence in public library service & public library trusteeship; To support communication among library trustee associations in Canada & abroad
Jan Harder, President
Betty Thomas, Vice-President
Elaine Kivisto, Secretary-Treasurer

Canadian Urban Libraries Council (CULC)
c/o Brampton Public Library, 65 Queen St. East, Brampton ON L6W 3L6 Canada
Tel: 905-793-4636; *Fax:* 905-453-0810
info@culc.ca
www.culc.ca
To identify the issues & choices available in developing urban public library services; to explore the philosophy & principles that govern public library service in urban areas; to comment on the state of public library service in Canada; to facilitate the exchange of ideas & information between member libraries; to influence legislation & financing of urban public libraries; to promote & work in conjunction with other library organizations in Canada to achieve an urban public library service which is comprehensive, economic & efficient; to provide the means for communication & information sharing between members of the public library community; to promote formal & informal cooperation with organizations & institutions in Canada & outside Canada whose goals & objectives are relevant to large urban public library service

Church Library Association of Ontario (CLAO)
c/o Margaret Godefroy, CLAO Membership Secretary, #603, 155 Navy St., Oakville ON L6J 2Z7
Tel: 905-845-0222
agodefroy@cogeco.ca (Membership Secretary)
www.churchlibraries.ca
Social Media:
www.facebook.com/group.php?gid=117754255215
To help church libraries in Ontario make the most of their resources
Arthur McClelland, President & Archivist
Marcella Haanstra, Coordinator, Outreach
Jane Rocoski, Coordinator, Resources
Mary Ryan, Coordinator, Conferences
Thelma Campbell, Secretary
Margaret Godefroy, Secretary, Membership
Michelle Rickard, Editor, Newsletter

Corporation des bibliothécaires professionnels du Québec (CBPQ) / Corporation of Professional Librarians of Québec
#103, 353, rue St. Nicolas, Montréal QC H2Y 2P1 Canada
Tél: 514-845-3327; *Téléc:* 514-845-1618
info@cbpq.qc.ca
www.cbpq.qc.ca
Développer les services de bibliothèques; établir des normes de compétence; encourager et stimuler la recherche en bibliothéconomie; promouvoir et développer les intérêts professionnels de ses membres

Council of Archives New Brunswick (CANB) / Conseil des archives du Nouveau-Brunswick
PO Box 1204, Stn. A, 23 Dineen Dr., Fredericton NB E3B 5C8 Canada
Tel: 506-453-4327; *Fax:* 506-453-3288
archives.advisor@gnb.ca
www.canbarchives.ca/canb
To address the needs of the archival institutions in New Brunswick; to provide training & information on developments in the profession; to encourage information sharing & cooperation in educational opportunities with Maritime sister provinces & national associations

Council of Nova Scotia Archives (CNSA)
6016 University Ave., Halifax NS B3H 1W4 Canada
Tel: 902-424-7093; *Fax:* 902-424-0628
advisor@councilofnsarchives.ca
www.councilofnsarchives.ca
To foster education of archival standards & practices to preserve Nova Scotia's documentary heritage; To promote archival standards, procedures, & practices

Council of Prairie & Pacific University Libraries (COPPUL)
2005 Sooke Rd., Victoria BC V9B 5Y4 Canada
Tel: 250-391-2554; *Fax:* 250-391-2556
coppul@royalroads.ca
www.coppul.ca
To coordinate the activities of the Prairie & Pacific university libraries in promoting enhanced information services by means of cooperative collection development, resource sharing, rapid document delivery, & other such methods of transmitting or sharing resources; to act as an information sharing body

Federal Libraries Coordination Secretariat
chives Canada, 395 Wellington St., Ottawa ON K1A 0N4 Canada
Tel: 819-934-7427; *Fax:* 819-934-7534
FLCS-SCBGF@lac-bac.gc.ca
www.collectionscanada.ca/cfl-cbgf
To coordinate federal libraries service reports to the Recordkeeping & Library Coordination Office of the Government Records Branch

Golden Horseshoe Health Libraries Association
c/o BCHS Resource Library, 200 Terrace Hill St., Brantford ON N3R 1G9 Canada
Tel: 905-519-5544
www.chla-absc.ca/?q=en/node/71
The Association's mission is to improve health and health care by promoting excellence in access to information.
Barbara Gray, President

Halifax Library Association
c/o 5940 South St., Halifax NS B3H 1S6 Canada
www.smu.ca/administration/archives/hla
Social Media: www.facebook.com/group.php?gid=20160077946
To promote libraries and their services, and to encourage more extensive cooperation and interdependence among libraries in the geographic area of Halifax Regional Municipality.

Collette Saunders, President

Health Libraries Association of British Columbia (HLABC)
c/o Devon Greyson, UBC Centre for Health Services & Policy Research, #201, 2206 East Mall, Vancouver BC V6T 1Z3
Tel: 604-822-7353; *Fax:* 604-822-5690
devon-at-chspr.ubc.ca (President)
www.hlabc.bc.ca
Social Media: www.facebook.com/group.php?gid=2347253553
To support the work of health librarians throughout British Columbia
Devon Greyson, President
Brooke Ballantyne-Scott, Vice-President
Elisheba Muturi, Secretary
Anne Allgaier, Treasurer & Contact, Membership

Indexing Society of Canada / Société canadienne d'indexation
PO Box 664, Stn. P, Toronto ON M5S 2Y4 Canada
www.indexers.ca
To encourage the production & use of indexes & abstracts; to promote the recognition of indexers & abstractors; to improve indexing & abstracting techniques; to improve communication among individual indexers & abstractors.

Library Association of Alberta (LAA)
80 Baker Cres. NW, Calgary AB T2L 1R4
Tel: 403-284-5818; *Fax:* 403-282-6646
Toll-Free: 877-522-5550
info@laa.ca; info@albertalibraryconference.com
www.laa.ca
To facilitate the improvement of library services in Alberta; To promote library service throughout Alberta; To encourage cooperation among libraries & information centres across the province; To promote intellectual freedom in Alberta

Library Boards Association of Nova Scotia (LBANS)
c/o Janet Ness, Secretary, Library Boards Association of Nova Scotia, 53 Sherwood Dr., Wolfville NS B4P 2K5
Tel: 902-542-7386
janet_ness@hotmail.com
www.standupforlibraries.ca
To preserve & support quality public library service throughout Nova Scotia
Gary Archibald, Executive Director
Mary MacLellan, President
Shirley McNamara, Vice-President
Janet Ness, Secretary
Marie Hogan Loker, Treasurer

London Area Health Libraries Association (LAHLA)
c/o South Huron Hospital, Shared Library Services, 24 Huron St. West, Exeter ON N0M 1S2 Canada
Tel: 519-235-5168; *Fax:* 519-235-4476
linda.wilcox@shha.on.ca
Linda Wilcox, President

Manitoba Association of Health Information Providers (MAHIP)
c/o J.W. Crane Memorial Library, University of Manitoba, 2109 Portage Ave., Winnipeg MB R3J 0L3 Canada
Tel: 204-831-2107
angela_osterreicher@umanitoba.ca
www.chla-absc.ca/?q=en/node/75
To promote the provision of quality library service to the health community in Manitoba by communication & mutual assistance.
Angela Osterreicher, President

Manitoba Association of Library Technicians (MALT)
PO Box 1872, Winnipeg MB R3C 4R1
malt_info@yahoo.com
www.malt.mb.ca
Social Media: www.facebook.com/group.php?gid=47603963419
To promote & advance the role of library technicians throughout Manitoba; To respond to issues that relate to the library & information services community
Catherine Taylor, President
Marge Dyck, Secretary
Elizabeth Stregger, Treasurer
Jodi Turner, Coordinator, Membership
Eric Wesselius, Editor, Newsletter

Manitoba Library Association (MLA)
#606, 100 Arthur St., Winnipeg MB R3B 1H3
Tel: 204-943-4567; *Fax:* 866-202-4567
manitobalibrary@gmail.com
www.mla.mb.ca
Social Media: www.facebook.com/group.php?gid=6003904478
To develop, support, & promote library & information services in Manitoba for the benefit of the library community & Manitoba residents
Emma Hill Kepron, President
Alex Homanchuk, Vice-President
Katherine Penner, Secretary
Kathy Rusnak, Treasurer
Dawn Bassett, Director, Professional Development
Evelyn Bruneau, Director, Fund Development
Stephen Carney, Director, Communications
Ian Fraser, Director, Advocacy
Vera Keown, Director, Conferences
Alison Pattern, Director, Membership

Manitoba School Library Association (MSLA)
c/o Claudia Klausen, Emerson Elementary School, 323 Emerson Ave., Winnipeg MB R2G 1V3
www.manitobaschoollibraries.com
To advocate for school library programs in Manitoba; To provide professional development opportunities for members
Vivianne Fogarty, President
Heather Eby, Secretary
Claudia Klausen, Treasurer
Jeff Anderson, Co-Chair, Conferences
Lorie Battershill, Chair, Publications
Jo-Anne Gibson, Chair, Awards
Kim Marr, Chair, Membership
Christine Robinson, Co-Chair, Conferences

Maritimes Health Libraries Association (MHLA) / Association des bibliothèques de la santé des Maritimes (ABSM)
c/o W.K. Kellogg Health Sciences Library, Tupper Medical Building, PO Box 2100, 5850 College St., Halifax NS B3H 1X5 Canada
Tel: 902-494-2483
www.chla-absc.ca/mhla/
To support members in the provision of quality information services for the health care community in the maritime provinces

New Brunswick Library Trustees' Association (NBLTA) / Association des commissaires de bibliothèque du Nouveau-Brunswick, inc.
c/o Doug Goss, 209 Saunders Rd., McAdam NB E6J 1M3 Canada
gossdj@nbed.nb.ca
To promote the public libraries of New Brunswick & to develop greater understanding of library trustees' responsibilities.
Doug Goss, Chair

Newfoundland & Labrador Health Libraries Association (NLHLA)
c/o Health Sciences Library, Memorial Univ. of Newfoundland, St. John's NL A1B 3V6 Canada
Tel: 709-737-6676; *Fax:* 709-737-6866
lbarnett@mun.ca
www.infonet.st-johns.nf.ca/nlhla/
To promote the provision of a high quality library service to the health community in Newfoundland & Labrador through mutual assistance & communication; to provide professional support to the membership by offering continuing education opportunities
Linda Barnett, Secretary
Alison Reid, President

Northern Alberta Health Libraries Association
c/o J.W. Scott Health Sciences Library, University of Alberta, 2K3.28 Walter MacKenzie Ctr., Edmonton AB T6G 2R7 Canada
nahla@nahla.ca
www.chla-absc.ca/nahla
This chapter of NAHLA exists to provide a forum for networking among libararians, library technicians and other interested in health libraries and health information.
Thane Chambers, President

Northern Lights Health Library Association
c/o Sault Area Hospital, 969 Queen Street East, Sault Ste Marie ON P6A 2C4 Canada
Tel: 705-759-3434; *Fax:* 705-759-3847
aslettk@sah.on.ca
Kim Aslett, President

Northwest Territories Archives Council (NWTAC)
c/o Northwest Territories Archives, Gov't of Northwest Territories, PO Box 1320, Yellowknife NT X1A 2L9 Canada
Tel: 867-873-7698; *Fax:* 867-873-0205
peter_harding@gov.nt.ca
www.pwnhc.ca/nwtac
To facilitate development of the archival system in the Northwest Territories; to make recommendations about the system's operation & financing; to develop & facilitate implementation & management of programs to assist the archival community; to communicate archival needs & concerns to decision-makers, researchers & the general public.

Northwestern Ontario Health Libraries Association (NOHLA)
c/o S. Regalado, Librarian, SJCG Library Svs., St. Joseph's Care Group, PO Box 2930, 580 Algoma St. North, Thunder Bay ON P7B 5G4 Canada
Tel: 807-343-4362; *Fax:* 807-343-4306
regalads@tbh.net; cmackenzie@hscn.on.ca
Sophie M. Regalado, MISt, MA, Chair

Nova Scotia Government Libraries Council (NSGLC)
c/o Dept. of Justice Library
Tel: 902-424-7699; *Fax:* 902-424-0546
lamietm@gov.ns.ca
www.nsglc.ednet.ns.ca
To provide a forum for government libraries to discuss common problems & share information

Nova Scotia Library Association (NSLA)
c/o Kelli WooShue, Halifax Public Libraries, 60 Alderney Dr., Dartmouth NS B2Y 4P8
Tel: 902-490-5710
wooshuk@halifax.ca; nslanewsletter@gmail.com (Newsletter)
www.nsla.ns.ca
To promote the value of libraries; To facilitate the exchange of ideas & information among library workers in Nova Scotia
Faye MacDougall, President
Denise Corey, Secretary
Carin Cress, Treasurer
Jeremy Henderson, Convenor, Newsletter
Debbie Kaleva, Convenor, Continuing Education
Theresa MacDonald, Convenor, Conferences
Jeff Mercer, Convenor, Membership
Kelli Wooshue, Convenor, Public Relations & Promotions

Ontario Association of Library Technicians (OALT) / Association des bibliotechniciens de l'Ontario (ABO)
Abbey Market, PO Box 76010, 1500 Upper Middle Rd. West, Oakville ON L6M 3H5
info@oaltabo.on.ca
www.oaltabo.on.ca
To promote the interests of library & information technician graduates & students throughout Ontario; To advance library & information technician graduates & students
Michael David Reansbury, President
Daisy Collins, Treasurer
Donna Brown, Coordinator, External Communications
Amna Hussain, Coordinator, Internal Communications
Amy Dwyer, Coordinator, Membership
Millie Yip, Coordinator, Chapters
Kathi Vandenheuvel, Archivist

Ontario College & University Library Association (OCULA)
135 Fennell Ave. W., Hamilton ON L9C 1E9 Canada
Tel: 905-575-1212; *Fax:* 416-941-9581
info@accessola.com
www.accessola.com
To support librarians & to improve Library Science in Ontario's college & university libraries

Ontario Council of University Libraries (OCUL)
c/o Library, University of Toronto, 130 St. George Street, Toronto ON M5S 1A5 Canada
Tel: 416-978-4211; *Fax:* 416-978-6755
www.ocul.on.ca
Faye Abrams, Projects Officer

Ontario Library & Information Technology Association (OLITA)
c/o OLA, 100 Lombard, Toronto ON M5C 1M3 Canada
Tel: 416-363-3380; *Fax:* 416-941-9581
info@accessola.com
www.accessola.com/olita/
Planning, development, design, application & integration of technology in the library & information environment with the impact of emerging technologies on library service, & with the effect of automated technologies on people
Michael Vandenburg, President

Ontario Library Association (OLA)
#201, 50 Wellington St. East, Toronto ON M5E 1C8
Tel: 416-363-3388; *Fax:* 416-941-9581
Toll-Free: 866-873-9867
info@accessola.com
www.accessola.com
Social Media: www.facebook.com/group.php?gid=2233680329
To provide opportunities for people in the library & information field to share experience & expertise, & to create innovative solutions
Shelagh Paterson, Executive Director
Tanis Fink, President
Paul Takala, Treasurer

Helios He, Manager, Operations
Beckie MacDonald, Manager, Member Services
Liz Kerr, Director, Education
Michelle Fortier, Coordinator, Programs & Registration
Meredith Tutching, Coordinator, Programs & Registration

Ontario Library Boards' Association (OLBA)
c/o Ontario Library Association, #201, 50 Wellington St. East, Toronto ON M5E 1C8
Tel: 416-363-3388; *Fax:* 416-941-9581
Toll-Free: 866-873-9867
info@accessola.com; membership@accessola.com
www.accessola.com/olba
To represent Ontario public library board members on issues that affect library board leadership; To advance public library board development & improve the management & services of libraries throughout Ontario; To enhance the visibility of library boards
Joyce Cunningham, President
Frances Ryan, Vice-President

Ontario Public Library Association (OPLA)
#201, 50 Wellington St. East, Toronto ON M5E 1C8
Tel: 416-363-3388; *Fax:* 416-941-9581
Toll-Free: 866-873-9867
info@accessola.com
www.accessola.com/opla/bins/index.asp
To foster the expansion & improvement of public library service in Ontario; To support public librarians throughout Ontario; To encourage standards & certification for public library workers
Tammy Robinson, President
Lila Saab, Vice-President
Joanna Aegard, Secretary
Laura Carter, Treasurer
Rudi Denham, Editor, HoOPLA

Ontario School Library Association (OSLA)
c/o Ontario Library Association, #201, 50 Wellington St. East, Toronto ON M5E 1C8
Tel: 416-363-3388; *Fax:* 416-941-9581
Toll-Free: 866-873-9867
www.accessola.com/osla
To act as the voice of elementary & secondary school teacher-librarians in Ontario; To promote teacher-librarians as curriculum leaders; To support student success

Ottawa Valley Health Libraries Association (OVHLA) / Association des bibliothèques de santé de la Vallée d'Outaouais
c/o Children's Hospital of Eastern Ontario, 401 Smyth Rd., Ottawa ON K1H 8L1 Canada
Tel: 613-737-7600
msampson@cheo.on.ca
www.chla-absc.ca/ovhla
The Ottawa Valley Health Libraries Association / l'Association des Bibliothèques de la Santé de la Vallée de l'Outaouais is an association of over twenty health-related libraries whose purpose is to promote the provision of quality library services in the health sciences throughout the Ottawa Valley and the Outaouais. It was formed in 1994 through the amalgamation of the Ottawa-Hull Health Libraries Association and the OHA Region 9 chapter of the Ontario Health Libraries Association and is a chapter of the Ontario Health Libraries Association (OHLA) and the Canadian Health Libraries Association (CHLA).
Margaret Sampson, President
Amanda Hodgson, Secretary

Prince Edward Island Professional Librarians Association (PEIPLA)
c/o Holland College Library Services, Manager Library Services, Charlottetown PE Canada
Tel: 902-566-9350; *Fax:* 902-566-9522
pmdoucette@hollandcollege.com
peipla.wordpress.com
Patricia Doucette, President
Liam O'Hare, Sec.-Treas.

Regroupement des bibliothèques publiques de l'Abitibi-Témiscamingue (RBPAT)
201, ave. Dallaire, Rouyn-Noranda QC J9X 4T5 Canada
Tél: 819-762-4305; *Téléc:* 819-762-5903
info@crsbpat.qc.ca
www.biblrn.qc.ca/rbpat/
Promotion du livre et de la lecture en Abitibi-Témiscamingue; promotion des bibliothèques

Regroupement des bibliothèques publiques de la Côte-Nord
Bibliothèque centrale de prêt de la Côte-Nord, 59, rue Napoléon, Sept-Iles QC G4R 5C5 Canada
Tél: 418-962-1020
info@rbpcn.com
Yvon Grondin, Président

Regroupement Les bibliothèques publiques du Saguenay-Lac-Saint-Jean (RABLES)
100, rue Price ouest, Alma QC G8B 4S1 Canada
Tél: 418-662-6425; *Téléc:* 418-662-7593
Ligne sans frais: 800-563-6425
sbolduc@reseaubiblioslsj.qc.ca
catweb.crsbpslsj.biblio.qc.ca
Promouvoir les bibliothèques publiques; concertation dans des dossiers concernant les bibliothèques publiques; faire connaître nos services
Sophie Bolduc, Directrice générale (par intérim)

Réseau des archives du Québec (RAQ)
a/s Archives nationales du Québec à Montréal, 535 av Viger est, local 5.27.1, Montréal QC H2L 2P3 Canada
Tél: 514-864-9213
raq@bellnet.ca
www.raq.qc.ca
Promouvoir le développement et la mise en valeur des archives historiques; favoriser l'échange et la mise en commun d'information, d'expérience et de ressources; devenir un instrument de consultation et un groupe de pression reconnu des divers intervenants des milieux archivistiques

Saskatchewan Association of Library Technicians, Inc. (SALT)
PO Box 24019, Saskatoon SK S7K 8B4
Fax: 306-543-4487
salt@lib.sk.ca
www.lib.sk.ca/salt
To promote the value of library technicians in Saskatchewan
Dorothy Richard, President
Carole-Anne Wilson-Hough, Secretary

Saskatchewan Council for Archives & Archivists (SCAA)
#202, 2080 Broad St., Regina SK S4P 1Y3 Canada
Tel: 306-780-9414
scaa@sasktel.net
www.scaa.sk.ca
To facilitate the development of the archival system in Saskatchewan; to develop standard archival policies & practices; to promote public awareness of the use of archives

Saskatchewan Health Libraries Association (SHLA)
c/o Regina-Qu'Appelle Health Region, Health Sciences Library, 1440 - 14th Ave., Regina SK S4P 0W5 Canada
Tel: 306-766-3833; *Fax:* 306-766-3839
kelly.mcivor@usask.ca
www.lib.sk.ca/shla/
To promote access to health care literature for physicians & allied health care staff
Kelly McIvor, President

Saskatchewan Library Association (SLA)
#15, 2010 - 7th Ave., Regina SK S4R 1C2
Tel: 306-780-9413; *Fax:* 306-780-9447
slaexdir@sasktel.net; slaprograms@sasktel.net
www.saskla.ca
Social Media:
www.facebook.com/group.php?gid=106445391816
To further the development of library services in Saskatchewan

Saskatchewan Library Trustees Association (SLTA)
c/o Wendy Thienes, PO Box 573, Shaunavon SK S0N 2M0
Tel: 306-297-6368; *Fax:* 306-297-3668
wendy.thienes@gmail.com
www.libraries.gov.sk.ca/slta
To foster the development of libraries & library services throughout Saskatchewan
Wendy Thienes, Executive Director
Bev Dubois, President
Dennis Taylor, Vice-President
Kae Campbell, Treasurer

Southern Alberta Health Libraries Association (SAHLA)
c/o Health Sciences Library, University of Calgary, 3330 University Dr. NW, Calgary AB T2N 4N1 Canada
Tel: 403-220-6858; *Fax:* 403-282-7992
sahla@sahla.org
www.sahla.org
Taryn Lenders, President

Southwestern Ontario Health Library Information Network
c/o Hotel Dieu Grace Hospital Medical Library, 1030 Ouellette Ave., Windsor ON N9A 1E1 Canada
Tel: 519-973-4411
linda.wilcox@shha.on.ca
www.chla-absc.ca/sohlin
Linda Wilcox, President

Special Libraries Association (SLA)
331 South Patrick St., Alexandria VA 22314-3501 USA
Tel: 703-647-4900; *Fax:* 703-647-4901
cschatz@sla.org (Public Relations); membership@sla.org
www.sla.org
To promote & strengthen information professionals from around the globe
Janice R. Lachance, Chief Executive Officer
Linda Broussard, Chief Community Officer
Quan O. Logan, Chief Technology Officer
Doug Newcomb, Chief Policy Officer

Toronto Health Libraries Association (THLA)
PO Box 94056, 3409 Yonge St., Toronto ON M4N 2L0 Canada
Tel: 416-485-0377; *Fax:* 416-485-6877
president@thla.ca
www.thla.ca
To promote the provision of quality library service to the health community; to encourage communication & cooperation among members & to foster their professional development; to consult & collaborate with other professional, technical & scientific organizations in matters of mutual interest
Weina Wang, President

Yukon Council of Archives (YCA)
PO Box 31089, Whitehorse YT Y1A 5P7 Canada
Tel: 867-667-5321; *Fax:* 867-393-6253
yukoncouncilofarchives@yahoo.ca
www.yukoncouncilofarchives.ca
To facilitate the development of the archival system in the Yukon; to make recommendations about the system's operation & financing; to develop & facilitate implementation & management of programs to assist the archival community; to communicate archival needs & concerns to decision-makers, researchers & the general public

Yukon Teacher-Librarians' Association (YTLA)
2064 - 2nd Ave., Whitehorse YT Y1A 1A9 Canada
Tel: 867-668-6777; *Fax:* 867-667-4324
admin@yta.yk.ca
www.yta.yk.ca
A committee of Yukon Teachers' Association
Sandra Henderson, President

Literacy

Regroupement de Bouches à Oreilles (RBO)
265, rue Lanctôt, Chibougamau QC G8P 1C1 Canada
Tél: 418-748-2239; *Téléc:* 418-748-2735
www.abc02.org/chibougamau/
Formation de base: compter, lire, écrire
Céline Laliberté, Coordonnatrice

Literary Arts

L'arc-en-ciel littéraire
CP 180, Succ. C, Montréal QC H2L 4K1 Canada
arcenciellitteraire@yahoo.ca
arcenciellitteraire.site.voila.fr
Le seul regroupement d'écrivains GLBT au Québec; promouvoit la littérature gaie et des auteurs gais
Réjean Roy, Président fondateur

Long-Term Care

New Brunswick Special Care Home Association Inc.
c/o Seely Lodge Inc., 2443 Westfield Rd., Saint John NB E2M 6L4 Canada
Tel: 506-738-8514; *Fax:* 506-738-0892
janseely@rogers.com
www.nbscha.com
To assist licensed members of the New Brunswick Special Care Home Association Inc. in providing quality, cost effective long term care for seniors and special needs adults in cooperation with the Department of Social Development.
Jan Seely, President

Management & Administration

Administrative Sciences Association of Canada (ASAC) / Association des sciences administratives du Canada
c/o Sobey School of Business, Saint Mary's University, Halifax NS B3H 3C3 Canada
Tel: 902-496-8139
jean.mills@smu.ca
www.asac.ca

To develop teaching & research in management studies at Canadian universities

Alberta Institute Purchasing Management Association of Canada (AIPMAC)
Centre 104, #612, 5241 Calgary Trail, Edmonton AB T6H 5G8 Canada
Tel: 780-944-0355; *Fax:* 780-944-0356
Toll-Free: 866-610-4089
info@aipmac.ab.ca
www.aipmac.ab.ca
To develop the profession by ensuring that professional status is accessible to all purchasing practitioners in the province; high standards of eligibility & professional conduct will be developed, maintained & enforced to enhance the profession & protect public interest in the province of Alberta
Jacki Richards, Chief Operating Officer
Jean Loitz, President
Bernie Dauvin, Treasurer

ARMA Canada (ARMA)
PO Box 6000, Fredericton NB E3B 5H1 Canada
Tel: 506-453-5618; *Fax:* 506-462-2046
www.armacanada.org
Social Media: www.facebook.com/group.php?gid=14876329775
ARMA is a not-for-profit, professional association focussed on managing records & information - both paper & electronic. It works to advance records & information management as a discipline & a profession, & organizes programs of research, education, training & networking.

Association des MBA du Québec (AMBAQ)
#900, 500, rue Sherbrooke ouest, Montréal QC H3A 3C6 Canada
Tél: 514-282-3810; *Téléc:* 514-844-7556
mba@affaires.com
www.ambaq.com
Òtre le porte-parole des MBA du Québec; constituer un réseau actif de diplômés et étudiants MBA; favoriser le développement personnel et professionnel des membres; valoriser et promouvoir le diplôme MBA

Association of Administrative Assistants (AAA) / Association des adjoints administratifs
c/o 11110 - 108 St., Edmonton AB T5G 2T2 Canada
Tel: 780-423-2929; *Fax:* 780-407-3340
info@aaa.ca
www.aaa.ca
To establish a national standard of qualifications for an administrative assistant; to help assistants to reach this standard by providing opportunities for advanced education; to make management aware of the value of the fully-qualified administrative assistant

Association of Cultural Executives (ACE) / Association des cadres d'institutions culturelles (ACIC)
PO Box 22044, Stn. Westmount, Waterloo ON N2L 6J7 Canada
Tel: 519-579-8564; *Fax:* 519-743-6773
Toll-Free: 888-363-3591
info@acecontact.org
www.acecontact.org
To develop professional cultural executives; to manage Canada's cultural resources with priorities on training, recognition & improved working conditions for cultural managers in Canada

Association of Fundraising Professionals (AFP)
#412, 260 King St. East, Toronto ON M5A 4L5 Canada
Tel: 416-941-9212; *Fax:* 416-941-9013
Toll-Free: 800-796-7373
info@afptoronto.org
www.afptoronto.org
To advance philanthropy by enabling people & organizations to practice effective & ethical fundraising

Association of Professional Executives of the Public Service of Canada (APEX) / L'Association professionnelle des cadres de la fonction publique du Canada
#508, 75 Albert St., Ottawa ON K1P 5E7 Canada
Tel: 613-995-6252; *Fax:* 613-943-8919
info@apex.gc.ca
www.apex.gc.ca
Denise Amyot, President
Hanny Toxopeus, Chief Executive Officer

British Columbia Institute of the Purchasing Management Association of Canada
#300, 435 Columbia St., New Westminster BC V3L 5N8 Canada
Tel: 604-540-4494; *Fax:* 604-540-4023
Toll-Free: 800-411-7622
accreditation@bcipmac.ca
www.bcipmac.ca
BC Institute PMAC is an incorporated, not-for-profit association that maintains a code of ethics for the profession to regulate quality & integrity.
Chris Duggan, President
Geraldine Kennedy, Executive Director

Canadian Association of Management Consultants (CMC - Canada) / Association canadienne des conseillers en management
#815, 4 King St. West, Toronto ON M5H 1B6
Tel: 416-860-1515; *Fax:* 416-860-1535
Toll-Free: 800-268-1148
consulting@cmc-canada.ca
www.cmc-canada.ca
To foster excellence & integrity in the management consulting profession; To administer the Certified Management Consultant (CMC) designation in Canada; To advance the practice & profile of the profession of management consulting in Canada; To promote ethical standards

Canadian Association of School Administrators (CASA) / Association canadienne des administrateurs et des administratrices scolaires (ACAS)
1123 Glenashton Dr., Oakville ON L6H 5M1 Canada
Tel: 905-845-2345; *Fax:* 905-845-2044
leslea@opsoa.org
www.casa-acas.ca
To promote & enhance effective administration & leadership in provision of quality education in Canada; to provide a national voice on educational matters; to promote & provide opportunity for professional development to the membership; to promote communication & liaison with national & international organizations having an interest in education; to provide a variety of services to the membership; to recognize outstanding contributions to education in Canada

Canadian Executive Service Organization (CESO) / Service d'assistance canadienne aux organismes (SACO)
PO Box 328, #700, 700 Bay St., Toronto ON M5G 1Z6 Canada
Tel: 416-961-2376; *Fax:* 416-961-1096
Toll-Free: 800-268-9052
toronto@ceso-saco.com
www.ceso-saco.com
Social Media: www.facebook.com/pages/CESO-SACO/102471409807904
To enhance the socio-economic well-being of the peoples & the communities of Canada, developing nations & emerging market economies

Canadian Institute of Certified Administrative Managers (CICAM)
#800, 2 St. Clair Ave. East, Toronto ON M4T 2T5 Canada
Tel: 416-921-7962; *Fax:* 416-921-3959
Toll-Free: 800-233-5864
mailbox@cicam.org
www.cicam.org
To advance science of management & administration; to develop & recognize competent professional managers & to gain recognition for members.

Canadian Institute of Management (CIM) / Institut canadien de gestion
National Office, 15 Collier St., Lower Level, Barrie ON L4M 1G5 Canada
Tel: 705-725-8926; *Fax:* 705-725-8196
Toll-Free: 800-387-5774
office@cim.ca
www.cim.ca
CIM promotes the senior management profession by offering a series of educational programs from single courses to professional certification. Programs are available through universities & colleges across Canada.

Canadian Management Centre
150 York St., 5th Fl., Toronto ON M5H 3S5 Canada
Fax: 416-313-4985
Toll-Free: 877-262-2519
cmcinfo@cmctraining.org
www.cmctraining.org
To play a key role in strengthening the ability of Canada's business leaders, managers & organizations to compete & succeed in today's challenging & changing business environment. A not-for-profit organization, the CMC provides a full range of professional development & management education services to companies, government agencies & individuals

Canadian Public Relations Society Inc. (CPRS) / La Société canadienne des relations publiques
#346, 4195 Dundas St. West, Toronto ON M8X 1Y4
Tel: 416-239-7034; *Fax:* 416-239-1076
admin@cprs.ca
www.cprs.ca
Social Media: twitter.com/CPRSNational
To oversee the practice of public relations practitioners in Canada, to ensure the protection of the public interest; To advance the professional stature of public relations practitioners; To promote the ethical practice of public relations & communications management

Canadian Society of Association Executives (CSAE) / Société canadienne des directeurs d'association (SCDA)
#1100, 10 King St. East, Toronto ON M5C 1C3 Canada
Tel: 416-363-3555; *Fax:* 416-363-3630
Toll-Free: 800-461-3608
csae@csae.com
www.csae.com
CSAE provides members with the environment, knowledge & resources to develop excellence in not-for-profit leadership, through networking, education, advocacy, information & research

Canadian Society of Corporate Secretaries (CSCS)
#255, 55 St. Clair Ave. West, Toronto ON M4V 2Y7 Canada
Tel: 416-921-5449; *Fax:* 416-967-6320
Toll-Free: 800-774-2850
info@cscs.org
www.cscs.org
To provide members with the tools necessary to become expert in corporate secretarial practice & to strengthen the corporate secretary's profile in the company.
Pamela Smith, Administrative Director
Lynn Beauregard, President

Canadian Society of Physician Executives (CSPE) / Société canadienne des médecins gestionnaires
PO Box 59005, 1559 Alta Vista Dr., Ottawa ON K1G 5T7 Canada
Tel: 613-731-9331; *Fax:* 613-731-1779
carol.rochefort@cma.ca
www.cspexecs.com
To develop physician leaders to be successful in health care leadership & management roles
Carol Rochefort, Director

Confédération nationale des cadres du Québec (CNCQ)
a/s Association des cadres des collèges du Québec, 2430, ch Ste-Foy, Sainte-Foy QC G1V 1TZ Canada
Tél: 418-877-1500; *Téléc:* 418-877-4469
info@cncq.qc.ca
www.cncq.qc.ca/
Venir en aide et supporter les associations affiliées de cadres.
Gilles Lachance, Président

Corporation des approvisionneurs du Québec (CAQ)
Complexe Tassé, #302, 895, boul Séminaire nord, Saint-Jean-sur-Richelieu QC J3A 1J2 Canada
Tél: 450-357-0033; *Téléc:* 450-357-0044
Ligne sans frais: 800-977-1877
info@caq.qc.ca
www.caq.qc.ca
La Corporation des approvisionneurs du Québec assure le développement professionnel de ses membres et veille à promouvoir et favoriser l'implantation des meilleures pratiques en matière de gestion de la chaîne d'approvisionnement au sein des entreprises québécoises afin que la valeur stratégique de l'approvisionnement puisse contribuer pleinement à l'essor des entreprises et à la société québécoise.
Bernard Côté, a.p.a., MBA, Président

Couchiching Institute on Public Affairs (CIPA)
#301, 250 Consumers Rd., Toronto ON M2J 4V6 Canada
Tel: 416-642-6374; *Fax:* 416-495-8723
Toll-Free: 866-647-6374
couch@couch.ca
www.couch.ca
To bring together interested Canadians to discuss important public policy issues with experts & other members of the general public

Fédération des secrétaires professionnelles du Québec (FSPQ)
#300-11, 1173, boul Charest ouest, Québec QC G1N 2C9 Canada
Tél: 418-527-5041
info@fspq.qc.ca
www.fspq.qc.ca
Travail à la valorisation de la profession.
Line Ross, Présidente

Institute of Certified Management Consultants of Alberta (CMC-Alberta)
c/o CMC-Canada National Office, #815, 4 King St. West, Toronto ON M5H 1B6 Canada
Tel: 416-860-1515; *Fax:* 416-860-1535
Toll-Free: 800-268-1148
consulting@cmc-canada.ca
www.cmc-canada.ca/provincial_institutes.cfm?Portal_ID=1; www.icmc
To act under the regulations of the Professional & Occupational Associations Registration Act; To work as the regulatory authority for provisional registrants, certified management consultants, & fellow certified management consultants in Alberta; To ensure that members abide by professional & ethical standards

Institute of Certified Management Consultants of Atlantic Canada
c/o CMC-Canada National Office, #815, 4 King St. West, Toronto ON M5H 1B6 Canada
Tel: 416-860-1515; *Fax:* 416-860-1535
Toll-Free: 800-268-1148
consulting@cmc-canada.ca
www.cmc-canada.ca/provincial_institutes.cfm?Portal_ID=2
CMC-Atlantic Canada is a provincial institute which fosters excellence & integrity in the management consulting profession.

Institute of Certified Management Consultants of British Columbia (CMC-BC)
c/o CMC-Canada National Office, #815, 4 King St. West, Toronto ON M5H 1B6 Canada
Tel: 416-860-1515; *Fax:* 416-860-1535
Toll-Free: 800-268-1148
consulting@camc.com; cmc-bc@shaw.ca
www.cmc-canada.ca/provincial_institutes.cfm?Portal_ID=3
To protect the general public & clients by ensuring that the Institute's Code of Professional Conduct is followed by the certified management consultant profession; To ensure that certified members comply with all applicable legislation & laws
Simon Wong, CMC, President
Mary Colak, CMC, Vice-President
Ken Lee, CMC, Treasurer

Institute of Certified Management Consultants of Manitoba (CMC-Manitoba) / Institut manitobain des conseillers en administration agréés
c/o CMC-Canada National Office, #815, 4 King St. West, Toronto ON M5H 1B6 Canada
Tel: 416-860-1515; *Fax:* 416-860-1535
Toll-Free: 800-268-1148
consulting@cmc-canada.ca
www.cmc-canada.ca/provincial_institutes.cfm?Portal_ID=4
To foster & promote the development & acceptance of the profession of management consulting; to promote excellence in the practice of the profession for the benefit of members, clients & the community at large.

Institute of Certified Management Consultants of Saskatchewan
c/o CMC-Canada National Office, #815, 4 King St. West, Toronto ON M5H 1B6 Canada
Tel: 416-860-1515; *Fax:* 416-860-1535
Toll-Free: 800-662-2972
consulting@cmc-canada.ca
www.cmc-canada.ca/provincial_institutes.cfm?Portal_ID=7
Frank Hart, President
Peggie Koenig, B.Comm., MBA, C, Registrar

Institute of Chartered Secretaries & Administrators - Canadian Division (ICSA Canada) / Institut des secrétaires et administrateurs agréés au Canada
#310, 2175 Sheppard Ave. E., Toronto ON M2J 1W8 Canada
Tel: 416-944-9727; *Fax:* 416-491-1670
Toll-Free: 800-501-3440
info@icsacanada.org
www.icsacanada.org
The organization represents and serves Chartered Secretaries & Administrators, professionals who are hired by organizations to administer key areas such as corporate governance, director/officer/shareholder matters, compliance & regulatory matters, & financial matters.

Institute of Corporate Directors (ICD) / Institut des administrateurs de sociétés
#602, 40 University Ave., Toronto ON M5J 1T1 Canada
Tel: 416-593-7741; *Fax:* 416-593-0630
admin@icd.ca
www.icd.ca
To enhance the quality of corporate governance in Canada

Institute of Professional Management (IPM)
#2210, 1081 Ambleside Dr., Ottawa ON K2B 8C8 Canada
Tel: 613-721-5957; *Fax:* 613-721-5850
info@workplace.ca
www.workplace.ca
Nathaly Pinchuk, Executive Director
Brian Pascal, President

International Personnel Management Association - Canada (IPMA-Canada)
National Office, #74, 21 Midland Cres., Ottawa ON K2H 8P6 Canada
Tel: 613-226-2297; *Fax:* 613-226-2298
Toll-Free: 866-226-5002
info@ipma-aigp.ca
www.ipma-aigp.ca
To promote excellence in the practice of human resource management; to promote & enhance the HR profession in Canada & globally; to provide professional development & training for the HR community; to maintain a code of ethics & standards of practice; to recognize excellence through national & local awards programs

Manitoba Institute of the Purchasing Management Association of Canada (MIPMAC)
#200, 5 Donald St., Winnipeg MB R3L 2T4 Canada
Tel: 204-231-0965; *Fax:* 204-233-1250
Toll-Free: 877-231-0965
mbpmac@mts.net
www.mb.pmac.ca
MIPMAC is committed to offering a professional development program coupled with networking opportunities to advance supply chain management.
Peter Buscemi, President
Jocelyn Wilson, Office Representative

New Brunswick Purchasing Management Institute (NBPMI)
PO Box 8977, Shediac NB E4P 8W5 Canada
Tel: 506-533-9418; *Fax:* 506-532-3635
www.pmacnb.com
NBPMI is dedicated to being the leading source of education, training, & development in the field of purchasing & supply chain management. It provides members with networking opportunities & offers them training for a Supply Chain Management Professional (SCMP) designation.
Sylvia Janssen, President
Bernice Léger, Admin. Assistant

Newfoundland & Labradour Institute of the Purchasing Management Association of Canada (NLIPMAC)
PO Box 29011, Stn. Torbay Road, St. John's NL A1A 5B5 Canada
Tel: 709-778-4033; *Fax:* 709-724-5625
info@pmacnl.org
www.pmacnl.org
The Institute delivers education, training, & professional development programs in the province, so members may earn a Supply Chain Management Professional (SCMP) designation.
Nancy Harte, Seminar Contact

Northwest Territories Institute of the Purchasing Management Association of Canada
PO Box 2736, Yellowknife NT X1A 3T1 Canada
Tel: 867-873-9324; *Fax:* 867-920-4112
lee_mcgreish@gov.nt.ca
www.nt.pmac.ca
A non profit organization registered with the Societies Act in the Northwest Territories. We provide information and Education leading to a professional designation as a C.P.P. (Certified Professional Purchaser) the only accredited and legally recognized designation in the fields of Purchasing and Supply Management in Canada.
Lee McGreish, President

Nova Scotia Institute of the Purchasing Management Association of Canada (NSIPMAC)
PO Box 21, Stn. CRO, Halifax NS B3J 2L4 Canada
Tel: 902-425-4029; *Fax:* 902-431-7220
info@nsipmac.com
www.nsipmac.com
NSIPMAC delivers education, training & professional development programs in the province, so members may earn a Supply Chain Management Professional (SCMP) designation.
Peter Chaffey, President
Nancy Christian, Program Coordinator

Ontario Institute of the Purchasing Management Association of Canada
PO Box 64, #2704, 1 Dundas St. West, Toronto ON M5G 1Z3 Canada
Tel: 416-977-7566; *Fax:* 416-977-4135
Toll-Free: 877-726-6968
info@oipmac.ca
www.ontarioinstitute.com
The preeminent supply chain managemen organisation in Ontario, supporting a growing global SCM community of over 20,00 active members and program participants in meeting their professional and lifelong learning goals. Their programs taught by leading North American academics and professional trainers, are designed to build/enhance the professional competence and strategic perspective of practitioners at all levels of career progression, from entry-, to mid-, to senior/executive levels of functional responsibility.
R. David Fletcher, President/CEO

Ordre des administrateurs agréés du Québec (OAAQ)
#100, 910, rue Sherbrooke ouest, Montréal QC H3A 1G3 Canada
Tél: 514-499-0880; *Téléc:* 514-499-0892
Ligne sans frais: 800-465-0880
info@adma.qc.ca
www.adma.qc.ca
Favorise auprès des professionnels de l'administration, l'innovation et l'atteinte d'un niveau de compétence supérieur pour qu'ils contribuent de façon proactive et dynamique au développement des entreprises et des organisations; assure la protection du public en garantissant le respect des normes et standards professionnels en administration, en conformité avec le code de déontologie et par le biais des mécanismes prévus au code des professions; contribue à l'avancement de l'administration, discipline essentielle au développement social et économique du Québec.
Denise Brosseau, Directrice générale et Secrétaire

Purchasing Management Association of Canada (PMAC) / Association canadienne de gestion des achats (ACGA)
PO Box 112, #2701, 777 Bay St., Toronto ON M5G 2C8 Canada
Tel: 416-977-7111; *Fax:* 416-977-8886
Toll-Free: 888-799-0877
info@pmac.ca
www.pmac.ca
PMAC advances strategic supply chain management by providing training, education, & professional development for supply chain management professionals in Canada.

Saskatchewan Institute of the Purchasing Management Association of Canada (SIPMAC)
#221A, 3521 - 8th Street E, Saskatoon SK S7H 0W5 Canada
Tel: 306-653-8899; *Fax:* 306-653-8870
Toll-Free: 866-665-6167
sipmac@sasktel.net
www.si.pmac.ca
To promote & improve supply management practices in the profession through education & raising the awareness of the supply management profession within Saskatchewan
Nicole Burgess, Executive Director

Strategic Leadership Forum, The Toronto Society for Strategic Management (SLF)
75 Dunkirk Rd., Toronto ON M4C 2M5 Canada
Tel: 416-574-1832; *Fax:* 647-436-3599
membership@slftoronto.com
strategicleadershipforum.camp9.org
To provide our community of members with an independent & intellectually challenging forum that delivers practical insights & interactions on strategic management & leadership

Manufacturing & Industry

APICS Association for Operations Management
#300, 1370 Don Mills Rd., Toronto ON M3B 3N7 Canada
Tel: 416-366-5388; *Fax:* 416-381-4054
info@apics.ca
www.apics.ca
The Canadian region of APICS, an international organization offering programs & materials on business management techniques; promotes education in resource management

Association de la recherche industrielle du Québec (ADRIQ)
#901, 1155, rue University, Montréal QC H3B 3A7 Canada
Tél: 514-337-3001; *Téléc:* 514-337-2229
adriq@adriq.com
www.adriq.com
Claude Demers, Président

Association of Independent Corrugated Converters
PO Box 73063, Stn. White Shields, 2300 Lawrence Ave. East, Toronto ON M1P 4Z5 Canada
Tel: 905-727-9405; *Fax:* 905-727-1061
info@aicc11.com
www.aiccbox.org
To provide a forum for the independent corrugated converter on legitimate matters of mutual interest; to enhance the level of professionalism of the independent converter in the operation of his/her business; to implement democratically determined goals on matters civil & governmental which have a positive effect on all independent corrugated converters

British Columbia Paint Manufacturers' Association (BCPMA)
c/o Cloverdale Paint Inc., 6950 King George Hwy., Surrey BC V3W 4Z1 Canada
Tel: 604-596-6261; *Fax:* 604-597-2677
www.bcpma.bc.ca
To act as the voice of paint manufacturers in British Columbia; to promote the welfare of association members

Canadian Appliance Manufacturers Association (CAMA)
c/o Electro-Federation Canada, #200, 5800 Explorer Dr., Mississauga ON L4W 5K9 Canada
Tel: 905-602-8877; *Fax:* 905-602-5686
Toll-Free: 866-602-8877
info@electrofed.com
www.electrofed.com/councils/CAMA/
To represent member interests in the establishment of product standards & in environmental legislation; to advocate the safe removal of mercury & other ozone depleting substances from older appliances; to support the development of energy efficient products

Canadian Association of Mould Makers (CAMM)
c/o St. Clair College (FCEM), PO Box 16, 2000 Talbot Rd. West, Windsor ON N9A 6S4 Canada
Tel: 519-255-7863; *Fax:* 519-255-9446
info@camm.ca
www.camm.ca
To address the concerns of Canadian mould making companies & to present a united voice on legislative issues to provincial & federal governments
Dan Moynahan, President
Giancarlo DiMaio, Treasurer
Diane Deslippe, Manager, Office

Canadian Brush Manufacturers Association (CBMA) / Association canadienne des fabricants de brosses
#310, 2175 Sheppard Ave. East, Toronto ON M2J 1W8 Canada
Tel: 416-971-7800; *Fax:* 416-491-1670
cbma@cbma.org
www.cbma.org

Canadian Carpet Institute / Institut canadien du tapis
1064 Carboro Rd., Ottawa ON K1K 1H8 Canada
Tel: 819-684-8444; *Fax:* 819-684-5444
info@canadiancarpet.org
www.canadiancarpet.org
To serve as a forum in developing industry consensus for action on common problems & opportunities; to enhance the well-being of the Canadian carpet industry by any & all means consistent with the members, & the public interest

Canadian Cosmetic, Toiletry & Fragrance Association (CCTFA) / Association canadienne des cosmétiques, produit de toilette et parfums
#102, 420 Britannia Rd. East, Mississauga ON L4Z 3L5 Canada
Tel: 905-890-5161; *Fax:* 905-890-2607
cctfa@cctfa.ca
www.cctfa.ca
To encourage trust & confidence in the Canadian cosmetic, toiletry & fragrance industry & in the safety, efficacy & quality of its products; To be the princiapal voice of the personal care industry, including cosmetic-like drug products & cosmetic-like natural health products (NHP), interfacing on a timely basis with governemtn & elected representatives, to ensure development & effective representationof industry positions on a ll regulatory issues; to have the personal care industyr perceived by consumers at large as being socially concerned, responsible & involved with Canadian society; this will be primarily achieved through the CCTFA Foundation &;the Look Good Feel Better program.

Canadian Council of Furniture Manufacturers (CCFM) / Conseil canadien des fabricants de meubles
c/o Accro Furniture Industries, 305 McKay Ave., Winnipeg MB R2G 0N5 Canada
Tel: 204-654-1114; *Fax:* 204-654-2792
info@accro-acmechrome.com

Canadian Hardware & Housewares Manufacturers' Association (CHHMA) / Association canadienne des fabricants de produits de quincaillerie et d'articles ménagers
#101, 1335 Morningside Ave., Toronto ON M1B 5M4 Canada
Tel: 416-282-0022; *Fax:* 416-282-0027
chhma@chhma.ca
www.chhma.ca
To assist members to sell more & do it more profitably

Canadian Innovation Centre (CIC)
c/o Waterloo Research & Technology Park, #15, 295 Hagey Blvd., Waterloo ON N2L 6R5 Canada
Tel: 519-885-5870; *Fax:* 519-513-2421
Toll-Free: 800-265-4559
info@innovationcentre.ca
www.innovationcentre.ca
To advance innovation by helping our clients make better business decisions through information, education & commercialization.
Ted Cross, Chair & CEO

Canadian Kitchen Cabinet Association (CKCA) / Association canadienne de fabricants d'armoires de cuisine (ACAC)
130 Albert St., Ottawa ON K1P 5G4 Canada
Tel: 613-567-9171; *Fax:* 613-567-4664
info@ckca.ca
www.ckca.ca
To promote the interests & conserve the rights of those engaged in the manufacture of kitchen cabinets, bathroom vanities & related millwork as well as their suppliers & dealers.

Canadian Laboratory Suppliers Association (CLSA) / Association canadienne de fournisseurs de laboratoire
#131, 525 Highland Rd. West, Kitchener ON N3M 5P4 Canada
Tel: 519-579-7598; *Fax:* 519-579-8134
jhowes@clsassoc.com
www.clsassoc.com
The Canadian Labratory Suppliers Association is a group of scientific companies committed to promoting and serving the Canadian laboratory marketplace. It provides a non-competitive environment for executives of Canada's leading scientific suppliers to share ideas and concepts. The CLSA's objective is to provide market analysis on the scientific industry, and to understand and discuss issues that influence the Canadian laboratory scientific market.

Canadian Manufacturers & Exporters (CME) / Manufacturiers et Exportateurs Canada
#1500, 1 Nicholas St., Ottawa ON K1N 7B7 Canada
Tel: 613-238-8888; *Fax:* 613-563-9218
national@cme-mec.ca
www.cme-mec.ca
Canada's leading business network; to continuously improve the competitiveness of Canadian industry & to expand export business by: aggressive, effective advocacy to government at all levels; delivering timely, relevant information, programs & support of superior quality & value; providing opportunities for education, learning & professional growth; & promoting the development & implementation of advanced technology

Canadian Office Products Association
#402, 2800 Skymark Ave., Mississauga ON L4W 5A6
Tel: 905-624-9462; *Fax:* 905-624-0830
Toll-Free: 800-267-7524
info@copa.ca
www.copa.ca

Canadian Plastics Industry Association (CPIA) / Association canadienne de l'industrie des plastiques
#712, 5915 Airport Rd., Mississauga ON L4V 1T1 Canada
Tel: 905-678-7748; *Fax:* 905-678-0774
national@cpia.ca
www.cpia.ca
To advance the prosperity & international competitiveness of the Canadian plastics industry in an environmentally & socially responsible manner

Canadian Sanitation Supply Association (CSSA) / Association canadienne des fournisseurs de produits sanitaires
PO Box 10009, 910 Dundas St. West, Whitby ON L1P 1P7 Canada
Tel: 905-665-8001; *Fax:* 905-430-6418
Toll-Free: 866-684-8273
info@cssa.com
www.cssa.com
To provide a high degree of professionalism, technical knowledge & business ethics within the membership; to promote greater public awareness, appreciation & understanding of the sanitation industry

Canadian Tooling & Machining Association (CTMA)
#3, 140 McGovern Dr., Cambridge ON N3H 4R7 Canada
Tel: 519-653-7265; *Fax:* 519-653-6764
Toll-Free: 888-437-3661
info@ctma.com
www.ctma.com
To be an effective, broad-based, respected organization, representing the Canadian tooling & machining industry, nationally & internationally

Canadian Toy Association / Canadian Toy & Hobby Fair (CTA) / L'Association canadienne du Jouet
#212, 7777 Keele St., Concord ON L4K 1Y7 Canada
Tel: 905-660-5690; *Fax:* 905-660-6103
info@cdntoyassn.com
www.cdntoyassn.com

Canadian Urethane Manufacturers Association (CUMA)
151 Briarcliffe Cres., Waterloo ON N2L 5T6 Canada
Tel: 519-884-2855; *Fax:* 519-884-0653
www.cumahome.org

Canadian Window & Door Manufacturers Association (CWDMA) / Association canadienne des manufacturiers de portes et fenêtres (ACMPF)
#1208, 130 Albert St., Ottawa ON K1P 5G4 Canada
Tel: 613-235-5511; *Fax:* 613-235-4664
info@cwdma.ca
www.cwdma.ca
The CWDMA represents its members in all aspects of the window & door manufacturing industry, including formulating & promoting high standards of quality in manufacturing, design, marketing, distribution, sales & application of all types of window & door products.

Door & Hardware Institute in Canada
#310, 2175 Sheppard Ave. East, Toronto ON M2J 1W8 Canada
Tel: 416-492-6502; *Fax:* 416-491-1670
maryloum@taylorenterprises.com
www.dhicanada.ca
A professional organization that serves the Canadian member as the professional development, information, advocate & certification resource for the total distribution process in the architectural openings industry.

National Floor Covering Association (NFCA) / Association nationale des revêtements de sol
987 Clarkson Rd. South, Mississauga ON L5J 2V8 Canada
Tel: 905-822-2280; *Fax:* 905-822-2494
www.nfcaonline.ca
To unite the Canadian regional & provincial associations in a spirit of cooperation; to improve & enhance the floorcovering industry; to share information & ideas; to undertake & support programs which will improve communications at all levels of the industry

Organization of CANDU Industries (OCI) / Association des industries CANDU
#102, 345 Kingston Rd., Pickering ON L1V 1A1 Canada
Tel: 905-509-0073
mrwash@eagle.ca
www.oci-aic.org
To represent companies in the Canadian private sector engaged in the supply of goods & services for CANDU power plants in export markets; to provide a focal point for industrial collaboration between the private sector of Canada's nuclear industry & foreign purchasers of a CANDU plant; functions separately from AECL, but participates with it in the design, manufacture, construction & commissioning of CANDU facilities in foreign countries

Paint & Decorating Retailers Association Canada (PDRA)
403 Axminister Dr., Fenton MO 63026-2941 USA
Tel: 636-326-2636; *Fax:* 636-326-1823
Toll-Free: 800-737-0107
info@pdra.org
www.pdra.org
To educate, promote & represent the interests of decorating products dealers in Canada

The Rubber Association of Canada (RAC) / Association canadienne de l'industrie du caoutchouc
Plaza 4, #250, 2000 Argentia Rd., Mississauga ON L5N 1W1 Canada
Tel: 905-814-1714; *Fax:* 905-814-1085
info@rubberassociation.ca
www.rubberassociation.ca
To upgrade & maintain good industry/government working relations; to explore ways of improving industry competitiveness & efficiency; to promote safety in members' products, in their use & in the workplace; to promote expansion & profitability of Canadian rubber manufacturing units; to enhance standing of Canadian rubber industry worldwide; to provide members with industry marketing statistics

Saskatchewan Trade & Export Partnership Inc. (STEP)
PO Box 1787, #320, 1801 Hamilton St., Regina SK S4P 3C6
Tel: 306-787-9210; *Fax:* 306-787-6666
Toll-Free: 877-313-7244
inquire@sasktrade.com
www.sasktrade.com
To work in partnership with Saskatchewan exporters & emerging exporters to maximize commercial success in global ventures; To deliver custom export solutions & market intelligence to member companies; To coordinate international development projects
Lionel LaBelle, President & CEO
Nicole Grande, Administrative Coordinator
Heather Swan, Manager, Corporate Services
Janice Lawless, Membership Coordinator
Stephanie Pappas, Technology & Communications
Brad Michnik, Executive Director, Trade Development

Marine Trades

Association of Canadian Port Authorities (ACPA)
#1502, 85 Albert St., Ottawa ON K1P 6A4 Canada
Tel: 613-232-2036; *Fax:* 613-232-9554
leroux@acpa-ports.net
www.acpa-ports.net
To encourage, mentor & stimulate the development of excellence within Canadian ports

British Columbia Marine Trades Association (BCMTA)
#300, 1275 West 6th Ave., Vancouver BC V6H 1A6 Canada
Tel: 604-683-5191; *Fax:* 604-893-8808
mta@bcmta.com
www.bcmta.com
The voice of the BC recreational marine industry

British Columbia Maritime Employers Association (BCMEA)
#500, 349 Railway St., Vancouver BC V6A 1A4 Canada
Tel: 604-688-1155; *Fax:* 604-684-2397
www.bcmea.com

Canadian Centre for Marine Communications (CCMC)
PO Box 8454, 155 Ridge Rd., St. John's NL A1B 3N9 Canada
Tel: 709-579-4872; *Fax:* 709-579-0495
ccmc@ccmc.nf.ca
www.ccmc.nf.ca
CCMC's mission is to develop the Canadian marine information and communications technology (ICT) industry in cooperation with industry, government, and academia.

Canadian Navigation Society (CNS)
c/o Canadian Aeronautics & Space Institute, #104, 350 Terry Fox Dr., Kanata ON K2K 2W5
www.casi.ca/canadiannavigationsociety.aspx
To advance the science, technologies, & applications of navigation
Susan Skone, Society Chair

Chamber of Maritime Commerce (CMC) / Chambre du commerce maritime (CCM)
#700, 350 Sparks St., Ottawa ON K1R 7S8 Canada
Tel: 613-233-8779; *Fax:* 613-233-3743
email@cmc-ccm.com
www.cmc-ccm.com
To bring together all sectors of the economy that rely on a cost efficient & safe marine transportation system

The Great Lakes Marine Heritage Foundation
55 Ontario St., Kingston ON K7L 2Y2 Canada
Tel: 613-542-2261; *Fax:* 613-542-0043
marmus@marmuseum.ca
www.marmuseum.ca
Mark Siemons, Chair

National Marine Manufacturers Association (NMMA)
#5100, 200 E. Randolph Dr., Chicago IL 60601 USA
Tel: 312-946-6200
www.nmma.org
NMMA is dedicated to creating, promoting and protecting an environment where members can achieve financial success through excellence in manufacturing, in selling, and in servicing their customers.
Thomas Dammrich, President
Linda Waddell, Vice President, Northern Shows

National Marine Manufacturers Association Canada (NMMA)
#8, 14 McEwan Dr., Bolton ON L7E 1H1 Canada
Tel: 905-951-0009; *Fax:* 905-951-0018
sanghel@nmma.org
www.cmma.ca
The CMMA is committed to being a leader; in promoting boating, advocacy with government and providing value added services to foster the financial success of the marine industry.
Rick Layzell, Chair

Shipbuilding Association of Canada / Association de la construction navale du Canada
#1502, 222 Queen St., Ottawa ON K1P 5V9 Canada
Tel: 613-232-7127; *Fax:* 613-238-5519
pcairns@cfncon.com
www.shipbuilding.ca
Represents the interests of the Canadian shipbuilding, ship repair & associated marine equipment & services industries

Mental Health

Association des médecins-psychiatres du Québec (AMPQ) / Québec Psychiatrists' Association
CP 216, Succ. Desjardins, 2, complexe Desjardins, Tour de l'Est, 30e étage, Montréal QC H5B 1G8 Canada
Tél: 514-350-5128; *Téléc:* 514-350-5198
sbresse@fmsq.org; ampq@fmsq.org
www.ampq.org
Promouvoir les intérêts professionnels et économiques de ses membres

Canadian Art Therapy Association (CATA) / L'association canadienne d'art thérapie
26 Earl Grey Rd., Toronto ON M4J 3L2
www.catainfo.ca
To promote the development & maintenance of professional standards of art therapy training, registration, research, & practice in Canada; To heighten awareness of art therapy as an important mental health discipline

Canadian Association for Suicide Prevention (CASP) / L'Association canadienne pour la prévention du suicide (ACPS)
870 Portage Ave., Winnipeg MB R3G 0P1
Tel: 204-784-4073; *Fax:* 204-772-7998
casp@casp-acps.ca; admin@casp-acps.ca
www.casp-acps.ca
To reduce the suicide rate; To minimize the harmful consequences of suicide

Canadian Centre for Stress & Well-Being
#1801, 1 Yonge St., Toronto ON M5E 1W7 Canada
Tel: 416-363-6204; *Fax:* 416-658-9536
smcen@yahoo.com
To provide education about stress management; to increase health & wellness

Canadian Group Psychotherapy Association (CGPA)
Tel: 416-736-5225; *Fax:* 416-736-5782
tsimonik@rogers.com
www.cgpa.ca
To promote excellence in standards of training, practice, & research; to encourage & provide for the education of mental health professionals in group psychotherapy
Terry Simonik, RN, MEd, FCGPA, President
Linda McFadyen, Secretary
Alina Isaac, Treasurer

Canadian Institute of Stress (CIS)
PO Box 665, Stn. U, Toronto ON M8Z 5Y9
info@stresscanada.org
www.stresscanada.org
To provide programs & tools for individuals & workplaces to handle stress

Canadian Mental Health Association (CMHA) / Association canadienne pour la santé mentale
Phenix Professional Building, #303, 595 Montreal Rd., Ottawa ON K1K 4L2 Canada
Tel: 613-745-7750; *Fax:* 613-745-5522
info@cmha.ca
www.cmha.ca
To promote mental health as well as support the resilience & recovery of people experiencing mental illness, through advocacy, education, research & service

Canadian Psychiatric Association (CPA) / Association des psychiatres du Canada
#701, 141 Laurier Ave. West, Ottawa ON K1P 5J3 Canada
Tel: 613-234-2815; *Fax:* 613-234-9857
Toll-Free: 800-267-1555
cpa@cpa-apc.org
www.cpa-apc.org
To forge a strong, collective voice for Canadian psychiatrists & to promote an environment that fosters excellence in the provision of clinical care, education & research

Canadian Psychiatric Research Foundation (CPRF) / Fondation canadienne de recherche en psychiatrie (FCRP)
#200, 133 Richmond St., Toronto ON M5H 2L3 Canada
Tel: 416-351-7757; *Fax:* 416-351-7765
Toll-Free: 800-915-2773
admin@cprf.ca
www.cprf.ca
To discover better treatments & cures for mental illness & addiction, by funding mental health & addiction research to improve the health of Canadians
Jean Milligan, Executive Director
Andrea Swinton, Director, Fund Development & Marketing

Canadian Psychoanalytic Society (CPS) / Société canadienne de psychanalyse (SCP)
7000, ch Côte-des-Neiges, Montréal QC H3S 2C1 Canada
Tel: 514-738-6105; *Fax:* 514-738-6393
psyanal@qc.aira.com
www.psychoanalysis.ca
The Canadian Umbrella organization for Psychoanalysts.

Canadian Psychological Association (CPA) / Société canadienne de psychologie
#702, 141 Laurier Ave. West, Ottawa ON K1P 5J3 Canada
Tel: 613-237-2144; *Fax:* 613-237-1674
Toll-Free: 888-472-0657
cpa@cpa.ca
www.cpa.ca
CPA works to improve the health & welfare of Canadians by promoting psychological research, education, & practice.

Centre de ressources et d'intervention pour hommes abusés sexuellement dans leur enfance (CRIPHASE) / Resource and Intervention Center for Men Sexually Abused during their Childhood
#100, 8105, rue de Gaspé, Montréal QC H2P 2J9 Canada
Tél: 514-529-5567; *Téléc:* 514-529-0571
info@criphase.org
www.criphase.org
Services et ressources pour hommes abusés sexuellement dans leur enfance; groupes, activités/ateliers
Benoit St-Jean, Directeur général

Child & Parent Resource Institute (CPRI)
600 Sanatorium Rd., London ON N6H 3W7 Canada
Tel: 519-858-2774; *Fax:* 519-858-3913
www.cpri.thehealthline.ca
To enhance the quality of life of children & youth with complex mental health or developmental challenges; to assist their families so these children & youth can reach their full potential
Anne Stark, Administrator

Children's Mental Health Ontario (CMHO) / Santé Mentale pour Enfants Ontario (SMEO)
#309, 40 St. Clair Ave. East, Toronto ON M4T 1M9 Canada
Tel: 416-921-2109; *Fax:* 416-921-7600
Toll-Free: 888-234-7054
info@cmho.org
www.kidsmentalhealth.ca

To promote, support & strengthen a sustainable system of mental health services for children, youth & their families

Fédération des familles et amis de la personne atteinte de maladie mentale (FFAPAMM) / Federation of Families & Friends of Persons with a Mental Illness
#203, 1990, rue Jean-Talon nord, Sainte-Foy QC G1N 4K8 Canada
Tél: 418-687-0474; *Téléc:* 418-687-0123
Ligne sans frais: 800-323-0474
info@ffapamm.qc.ca
www.ffapamm.qc.ca
La FFAPAMM se veut le porte-parole provincial des associations de familles et amis de la personne atteinte de maladie mentale. Tout en ayant à coeur de défendre et promouvoir les intérêts de ses membres, elle a également le mandat de les soutenir dans leur développement, de sensibiliser l'opinion publique aux problèmes reliés à la maladie mentale et de créer des programmes de communication et d'éducation.
Hélène Fradet, Directrice générale

International Schizophrenia Foundation
16 Florence Ave., Toronto ON M2N 1E9 Canada
Tel: 416-733-2117; *Fax:* 416-733-2352
centre@orthomed.org
www.orthomed.org
To raise the levels of diagnosis, treatment & prevention of the schizophrenias & related disorders; to reduce the fear & stigma; to provide the best possible treatment & rehabilitation services.

Mood Disorders Association of Ontario (MDAO)
#602, 36 Eglinton Ave., Toronto ON M4R 1A1 Canada
Tel: 416-486-8046; *Fax:* 416-486-8127
Toll-Free: 888-486-8236
info@mooddisorders.on.ca
www.mooddisorders.on.ca
To provide information, education & support to those affected by depression & manic depression, their families & friends; to develop & maintain a network of supportive self-help groups; to improve the quality of life of people who experience mood disorders, their families & friends; to advocate for a flexible & responsive system of care

Mood Disorders Society of Canada (MDSC) / La Société pour les troubles de l'humeur du Canada
#736, 3-304 Stone Rd. West, Guelph ON N1G 4W4 Canada
Tel: 519-824-5565; *Fax:* 519-824-9569
info@mooddisorderscanada.ca
www.mooddisorderscanada.ca
The MDSC works nationally to ensure that issues related to mood disorders are understood and considered in the setting of research priorities, the development of treatment strategies, and the creation of government programs and policies. The Mood Disorders Society of Canada is one of the leading national, voluntary health organizations in the fields of depression, bipolar illness, and associated mood disorders
Phil Upshall, National Executive Director
John Starzynski, President

Ontario Psychological Association (OPA)
#221, 730 Yonge St., Toronto ON M4Y 2B7
Tel: 416-961-5552; *Toll-Free:* 800-268-0069
info@psych.on.ca; opa@psych.on.ca
www.psych.on.ca
To advance the practice & science of psychology in Ontario communities; To promote the highest ethical standards in the profession

L'Ordre des psychologues du Québec (OPQ)
#510, 1100, av Beaumont, Montréal QC H3P 3H5 Canada
Tél: 514-738-1881; *Téléc:* 514-738-8838
Ligne sans frais: 800-363-2644
www.ordrepsy.qc.ca
Assurer la protection du public; contrôler l'exercice de la profession par ses membres; veiller à la qualité des services dispensés par ses membres; favoriser le développement de la compétence professionnelle, le respect des normes déontologiques et l'accessibilité aux services psychologiques
Rose-Marie Charest, Présidente

The Organization for Bipolar Affective Disorders Society (OBAD)
1019 - 7th Ave. SW, Calgary AB T2P 1A8 Canada
Tel: 403-263-7408; *Toll-Free:* 866-263-7408
obad@obad.ca
www.obad.ca
Their mission is to help people affected directly or indirectly by Bipolar Disorder, Depression, and Anxiety live better lives
Kaj Korvela, Executive Director

Saskatchewan Psychiatric Association
c/o Dhanapal Natarajan, Regina Qu'Appelle Health Region, 2180 - 23rd Ave., Regina SK S4S 0A5
kidsdoctor@accesscomm.ca
To increase psychiatric knowledge in Saskatchewan

Schizophrenia Society of Canada (SSC) / Société canadienne de schizophrénie
#100, 4 Fort St., Winnipeg MB R3C 1C4
Tel: 204-786-1616; *Fax:* 204-783-4898
Toll-Free: 800-263-5545
info@schizophrenia.ca
www.schizophrenia.ca
To improve the quality of life for those affected by schizophrenia & psychosis; To advocate on behalf of individuals & families affected by schizophrenia for improved treatment & services

Survivors of Suicide Support Program
10 Trinity Sq., Toronto ON M5G 1B1 Canada
Tel: 416-595-1716
karen@torontodistresscentre.com
To ensure the best possible mental health services & resources in Peterborough & area; to ensure best possible care, support & community reintegration of mentally ill & emotionally distressed; to encourage growth of community mental health services; to increase public awareness & understanding of mental health illness; to act in an advocacy capacity on issues related to mental health
Karen Lefotsky, Contact

Mentally Challenged Persons

Autism Resolution Ontario
Tel: 416-352-8813
info@autismresolutionontario.com
www.autismresolutionontario.com
Sharon Aschaiek, Founder

Military & Veterans

Air Cadet League of Canada / Ligue des cadets de l'air du Canada
66 Lisgar St., Ottawa ON K2P 0C1 Canada
Tel: 613-991-4349; *Fax:* 613-991-4347
Toll-Free: 877-422-6359
webadmin@aircadetleague.com
www.aircadetleague.com
Social Media: www.facebook.com/group.php?gid=19248248746
To promote & encourage a practical interest in aeronautics among young people; to assist those intending to pursue a career in aviation

Air Force Association of Canada (AFAC) / L'Association des forces aériennes du Canada
PO Box 2460, Stn. D, Ottawa ON K1P 5W6 Canada
Tel: 613-232-2303; *Fax:* 613-232-2156
Toll-Free: 866-351-2322
director@airforce.ca
www.airforce.ca
To promote a viable well-equipped air force & a strong Canadian aerospace industry

Army Cadet League of Canada (ACLC) / Ligue des cadets de l'armée du Canada
66 Lisgar St., Ottawa ON K2P 0C1 Canada
Tel: 613-991-4348; *Fax:* 613-990-8701
Toll-Free: 877-276-9223
national@armycadetleague.ca
www.armycadetleague.ca
The League is a civilian, non-profit organization working in partnership with local communities & Canadian Forces to support the Royal Canadian Army Cadets. Together with the Dept. of National Defense, it is a supervisory sponsor for 450 cadet corps across Canada, providing accommodation, transportation, & financial support for the 21,000 army cadets. It promotes the corps & assists in recruitment. The League is a registered charity, BN: 108071564RR0001.

Army, Navy & Air Force Veterans in Canada (ANAVETS) / Les Anciens combattants de l'armée, de la marine et des forces aériennes au Canada
#2, 6 Beechwood Ave., Ottawa ON K1L 8B4 Canada
Tel: 613-744-0222; *Fax:* 613-744-0208
anavets@storm.ca
www.anavets.ca
The Association unites veterans & their supporters to maintain entitlements & benefits. It provides a fraternal milieu for its members by acquiring & operating clubs & homes. It also strives to promote patriotism in Canada, & nurture cooperation & unity within the British Commonwealth.

Canadian Association of Veterans in United Nations Peacekeeping
PO Box 46026, 2339 Ogilvie Rd., Gloucester ON K1J 9M7 Canada
Tel: 902-538-3399
griffisgrove@xcountry.tv
www.cavunp.org
To perpetuate the memories of fallen comrades; to provide assistance to serving & retired Canadian peacekeepers & their families; to provide education about peacekeeping & peacekeepers
Ronald R. Griffis, National President
J. Robert O'Brien, CD, Chair
Paul Greensides, CD, National Secretary-Treasurer

Canadian Battlefields Foundation
c/o Canadian War Museum, 1 Vimy Pl., Ottawa ON K1R 1C2 Canada
Tel: 613-731-7767
gruchy@canadianbattlefieldsfoundation.ca
www.canadianbattlefieldsfoundation.ca
To act with Le Mémorial to educate the international public with respect to Canada's role in the Second World War & to educate Canadians through providing scholarships, bursaries & prizes to carry on research into military history; to raise & disburse funds to support these activities.
H.G. Needham, CD (Ret'd), Treasurer
Charles Belzile, CMM, CM, CD, President
Antonio Lamer, CP, CC, CD, Honorary Patron

Canadian Corps Association
201 Niagara St., Toronto ON M5V 1C9 Canada
Tel: 416-504-6694

The Canadian Corps of Commissionaires / Le Corps Canadien des Commissionnaires
#201, 100 Gloucester St., Ottawa ON K2P 0A4 Canada
Tel: 613-688-0710; *Fax:* 613-688-0719
Toll-Free: 888-688-0715
info@commissionaires.ca
www.commissionaires.ca
To promote the cause of Commissionaires by the creation of meaningful employment opportunities for former members of the Canadian Forces, the Royal Canadian Mounted Police & others who wish to contribute to the security & well-being of Canadians

Canadian Merchant Navy Veterans Association Inc. (CMNVA) / L'Association des Anciens Combattants de la marine marchande canadienne Inc.
PO Box 496, Annapolis Royal NS B0S 1A0 Canada
sailorjail@ns.sympatico.ca
www3.ns.sympatico.ca/sailorjail/
To renew old friendships & bring together ex-Canadian merchant seamen; to promote increased recognition of the role of the merchant navy during wartime; to liaise with government to obtain full benefits & pension as recognized veterans

Canadian Peacekeeping Veterans Association (CPVA)
PO Box 905, Kingston ON K7L 4X8 Canada
Tel: 506-627-6437
info@cpva.ca
www.cpva.ca
To assist Canadians who have served on peacekeeping missions
Ray Kokkonen, CD, President

Commission canadienne d'histoire militaire (CCHM) / Canadian Commission of Military History (CCMH)
Quartier général de la Défense nationale, 101 Colonel By Dr., Ottawa ON K1A 0K2 Canada
Téléc: 613-990-8579
La CCHM est une organisation bénévole, ne comptant qu'un Conseil de direction, sans membres, collaborant à la Commission internationale d'histoire militaire (CIHM) du Comité international des Sciences historiques (CISH) de Genève, Suisse; La Commission canadienne cherche à servir de lien entre les historiens militaires canadiens et la communauté internationale des chercheurs et écrivains en histoire militaire; La Commission canadienne travaille aussi à mieux faire connaître l'histoire militaire canadienne au Canada et à l'étranger

Commonwealth War Graves Commission - Canadian Agency (CWGC) / Commission des sépultures de guerre du Commonwealth
#1707, 66 Slater St., Ottawa ON K1A 0P4 Canada
Tel: 613-992-3224; *Fax:* 613-995-0431
cwgc-canada@vac-acc.gc.ca
www.cwgc.org
To ensure Commonwealth War Burials in Canada & the USA are marked & maintained; to ensure maintenance of memorials to the missing; to keep records & registers; the Canadian Agency is

responsible to discharge Commission duties for Commonwealth war graves in North America (this comprises some 3,200 cemeteries & over 19,000 commemorations).

Conference of Defence Associations (CDA) / Conférence des associations de la défense
#400B, 222 Somerset St. West, Ottawa ON K2P 2G3 Canada
Tel: 613-236-1252; *Fax:* 613-236-8191
cda@cda-cdai.ca
cda-cdai.ca
To place before people of Canada problems of defence & the well-being of Canada's Armed Forces

Federation of Military & United Services Institutes of Canada (FMUSIC) / Fédération des instituts militaires et des instituts des services unis du Canada (FIMIC)
PO Box 1700, Stn. Forces, Kingston ON K7K 7B4 Canada
To support development & maintenance of effective Canadian military & non-military defence & security policies & capabilities; to further the aims of individual member institutes in a collective manner; to promote a better understanding by the general public in Canada of the need to meet the defence commitments of Canada

Jewish War Veterans of Canada / Les Anciens Combattants Juifs du Canada
#353, 1111 Finch Ave., Toronto ON M3J 2E5 Canada
Tel: 905-669-5989; *Fax:* 416-736-6744
drlevy@rogers.com
www.cjwv.org
To maintain the spirit of comradeship by helping comrades & their families; To preserve memories & records of patriotic service; To honour the memory of Jewish war veterans of Canada; To uphold Jewish honour & encourage doctrines of liberty & equal rights

Korea Veterans Association of Canada Inc. (KVA) / Association canadienne des vétérans de la Corée (ACVC)
#21, 160 Conway Dr., London ON N6E 3M6
Tel: 519-668-5999
rochonp@execulink.com
www.kvacanada.com
To promote awareness of Canada's role in the Korean War; To represent veterans & their families

Military Collectors Club of Canada (MCC of Canada)
c/o John Zabarylo, Secretary-treasurer, PO Box 64009, 525 London St., Winnipeg MB R2K 3Y4 Canada
Tel: 204-669-0871
militarycollectorsclubofcanada@yahoo.ca
www.mccofc.org
John Zabarylo, Sec.-Treas.

National Council of Veteran Associations (NCVA)
c/o The War Amps Of Canada, 2827 Riverside Dr., Ottawa ON K1V 0C4 Canada
Tel: 613-731-3821; *Fax:* 613-731-3234
Toll-Free: 800-465-2677
communications@waramps.ca
www.waramps.ca/cliff/ncva.html
The NCVA was formed following the end of the Second World War. In this way, presentations to the Government of Canada would be considerably enhanced. Submissions to Parliamentary Committees have included issues such as opposition to the CBC-TV series The Valour and The Horror; the Canadian War Museum, and compensation for Merchant Seamen and Canadian Far East PoWs. This joint action has resulted in compensation being granted to the latter two groups as well as increased benefits to members of the Canadian Armed Forces.
H. Clifford Chadderton, Chair

The Naval Officers' Association of Canada (NOAC) / L'Association des officiers de la marine du Canada
12 Zokol Cres., Kanata ON K2K 2K5 Canada
Tel: 613-270-9597
noacexdir@msn.com
www.noac-national.ca/noac
To maintain active interest in the Maritime affairs of Canada; To oversee 15 member branches in major cities from coast to coast & a member branch in Brussels, Belgium

Navy League of Canada / Ligue navale du Canada
66 Lisgar St., Ottawa ON K2P 0C1 Canada
Tel: 613-302-1744; *Fax:* 613-990-8701
Toll-Free: 800-375-6289
national@navyleague.ca
www.navyleague.ca
Social Media: twitter.com/NavyLeagueCA
To promote an interest in maritime affairs generally throughout Canada; to prepare, publish & disseminate information & encourage debate relating to the role & importance of maritime matters in the interests of Canada; to promote, organize, sponsor, support & encourage the education & training of the youth of the country through Cadet movements & other youth groups with a maritime orientation; to hold conferences, symposia & meetings for the discussion & exchange of views in matters relating to the objects of The League; to raise funds as may be deemed necessary, for the welfare & benefit of seamen, for their dependents & for Seamen's Homes, Hostels & other institutions in Canada, including the establishment, operation & maintenance thereof; to co-operate with any kindred society having either in whole or in part comparable objects to The League

New Brunswick Signallers Association (NB Sigs)
c/o Fred LeBlanc, 17 Dewitt Acres, Fredericton NB E3A 6S3 Canada
Tel: 506-472-3215
fredleb@nbnet.nb.ca
www.nbsigs.ca
Claude Jodouin, President

Princess Patricia's Canadian Light Infantry Association
Canadian Forces Base Edmonton, PO Box 10500, Stn. Forces, Edmonton AB T5J 4J5 Canada
Tel: 780-973-4011; *Fax:* 780-973-1613
scott.br@forces.gc.ca
assoc.ppcli.com

Royal Canadian Air Force Benevolent Fund (RCAF BF) / Caisse de bienfaisance de l'Aviation royale du Canada
Legion House, #202, 359 Kent St., Ottawa ON K2P 0R6 Canada
Tel: 613-992-6082; *Fax:* 613-992-3426
rcafbf@magma.ca
To relieve distress & promote the well-being of members & former members of the RCAF & their dependents
Marion Blair, Secretary-Manager

The Royal Canadian Legion (RCL) / La Légion royale canadienne
Dominion Command, 86 Aird Place, Ottawa ON K2L 0A1 Canada
Tel: 613-591-3335; *Fax:* 613-591-9335
info@legion.ca
www.legion.ca
To serve veterans, ex-military & military members, their families, communities & Canada

Royal Canadian Military Institute (RCMI)
426 University Ave., Toronto ON M5G 1S9 Canada
Tel: 416-597-0286; *Fax:* 416-597-6919
Toll-Free: 800-585-1072
info@rcmi.org
www.rcmi.org
Promotion of navy, army & air force art, science, literature & interests; promotion of good fellowship & esprit de corps amongst the officers of the various branches of the services; maintenance of a clubhouse for the accommodation, recreation, enlightenment, convenience & entertainment of its members.
Chris Corrigan, Executive Director

Royal Canadian Mounted Police Veterans' Association / Association des anciens de la Gendarmerie royale du Canada
1200 Vanier Pkwy., Ottawa ON K1A 0R2 Canada
Tel: 613-993-8633; *Fax:* 613-993-4353
Toll-Free: 877-251-1771
rcmp.vets@rcmp-grc.gc.ca
www.rcmpvetsnational.ca

Royal Canadian Naval Benevolent Fund (RCNBF)
PO Box 505, Stn. B, Ottawa ON K1P 5P6 Canada
Tel: 613-996-5087; *Fax:* 613-236-8830
Toll-Free: 888-557-8777
rcnbf@sympatico.ca
www.rcnbf.ca
To relieve distress & promote the well-being of members & former members of the naval forces of Canada & Canadian merchant navy war veterans & of their dependants

Ste. Anne's Association of War Veterans Inc. / Association Ste-Anne des anciens combattants inc.
305, boul des Anciens Combattants, Sainte-Anne-de-Bellevue QC H9X 1Y9 Canada
Tel: 514-457-3440; *Fax:* 514-457-8412
Toll-Free: 800-361-9287
steanne@vac-acc.gc.ca
To provide qualified veterans, civilians & their families with benefits & services to which they are entitled; to promote their well-being & self-sufficiency as participating members of their communities; to keep the memory of their acheivements & sacrifice alive for all Canadians

Mines & Mineral Resources

Association de l'exploration minière de Québec (AEMQ)
#203, 132, avenue du Lac, Rouyn-Noranda QC J9X 4N5 Canada
Tél: 819-762-1599; *Téléc:* 819-762-1522
aemq@aemq.org
www.aemq.org
Développer, défendre et promouvoir l'exploration minière au Québec
Ghislain Poirier, Président
Mélissa Desrochers, Vice-présidente, Communications

Association for Mineral Exploration British Columbia (AMEBC)
#800, 889 Pender St. West, Vancouver BC V6C 3B2 Canada
Tel: 604-689-5271; *Fax:* 604-681-2363
info@amebc.ca
www.amebc.ca
To promote & assist development & growth of mining of mineral exploration in BC

Association minière du Québec (AMQ) / Québec Mining Association
Place de la Cité - Tour Belle Cour, #720, 2590, boul Laurier, Québec QC G1V 4M6 Canada
Tél: 418-657-2016; *Téléc:* 418-657-2154
mines@amq-inc.com
www.amq-inc.com
Promouvoir le développement de l'industrie des mines, de la métallurgie et des industries connexes; défendre les intérêts généraux de ses membres; soutenir les efforts de ses membres quant au bien-être, à la sécurité et à la prévention des accidents au travail

Association of Applied Geochemists (AEG)
PO Box 26099, 72 Robertson Rd., Nepean ON K2H 9R0 Canada
Tel: 613-828-0199; *Fax:* 613-828-9288
office@appliedgeochemists.org
www.appliedgeochemists.org
To promote interest in the applications of geochemistry to mineral & petroleum exploration, resource evaluation & related fields

Canadian Copper & Brass Development Association
#415, 49 The Donway West, Toronto ON M3C 3M9 Canada
Tel: 416-391-5599; *Fax:* 416-391-3823
Toll-Free: 877-640-0946
coppercanada@onramp.ca
www.coppercanada.ca
To promote, foster & stimulate use of products of Canadian copper & brass industry. To represent and support the primary producers fabricators, manufacturers, and consumers of copper and copper alloys in Canada, by increasing industry and public awareness of copper's capabilites and advantages compared to other metals and materials, and by providing technical services related to copper's use.

Canadian Institute of Mining, Metallurgy & Petroleum (CIM) / Institut canadien des mines, de la métallurgie et du pétrole
CIM National Office, #1250, 3500, boul de Maisonneuve ouest, Westmount QC H3Z 3C1
Tel: 514-939-2710; *Fax:* 514-939-2714
cim@cim.org
www.cim.org
To act as a source of leadership for its members, by offering conferences & courses, liaising with government departments, commissioning special volumes & reports, & publishing technical papers

Canadian Mineral Analysts (CMA) / Analystes des minéraux canadiens
444 Harold Ave. West, Winnipeg MB R2C 2E2 Canada
Tel: 204-224-1443
jgregorchuk@shaw.ca
www.canadianmineralanalysts.com
To promote communication among analysts in the mining industry & persons engaged in analytical procedures & the development of methods
John Gregorchuk, Managing Secretary
Sean Murry, Treasurer
Eric Arseneault, Executive Secretary

Chamber of Mineral Resources of Nova Scotia (CMRNS)
PO Box 2171, Windsor NS B0N 2T0 Canada
Tel: 902-798-0187; *Fax:* 902-798-2141
terry.daniels@ns.sympatico.ca
To ensure Nova Scotia is recognized internationally as having mineral resources worthy of investment; to develop mineral deposits; to work for government policies that provide a framework for a competitive mining industry within the global marketplace; to promote mining as a corporate industry creating wealth & long-term stable employment, with responsible environmental & social attitudes

Chamber of Mines of Eastern British Columbia
215 Hall St., Nelson BC V1L 5X4 Canada
Tel: 250-352-5242; *Fax:* 250-352-7227
chamberofminesebc@netidea.com
www.cmebc.com
To act as advocate for the mining industry in British Columbia; to provide a collective voice on behalf of prospectors & miners; to provide information on exploration & mining; to educate the public through accessibility to mineral museum & library.
Jack Denny, President
Dennis Llewellyn, Chamber Manager

Chrysotile Institute
#1640, 1200, av McGill College, Montréal QC H3B 4G7 Canada
Tel: 514-877-9797; *Fax:* 514-877-9717
info@chrysotile.com
www.chrysotile.com/
To promote the implementation & enforcement of effective regulations, standards, work practices & techniques for the safe use of asbestos.

Coal Association of Canada
#150, 205 - 9th Ave. SE, Calgary AB T2G 0R3 Canada
Tel: 403-262-1544; *Fax:* 403-265-7604
Toll-Free: 800-910-2625
info@coal.ca
www.coal.ca
To promote coal as a vital energy source that is abundant, safe, reliable, environmentally and economically acceptable.
Allen Wright, President & CEO
George White, Chair

East Kootenay Chamber of Mines
#201, 12 - 11th Avenue South, Cranbrook BC V1C 2P1 Canada
Tel: 250-489-2255; *Fax:* 250-426-8755
www.ekcm.org/chamber2
Ross Stanfield, President

Mineralogical Association of Canada (MAC) / Association minéralogique du Canada
490, rue de la Couronne, Québec QC G1K 9A9
Tel: 418-653-0333; *Fax:* 418-653-0777
office@mineralogicalassociation.ca
www.mineralogicalassociation.ca
To promote & advance knowledge of mineralogy & the allied disciplines of petrology, crystallography, mineral deposits, & geochemistry

Mining Association of British Columbia (MABC)
#900, 808 West Hastings St., Vancouver BC V6C 2X4 Canada
Tel: 604-681-4321; *Fax:* 604-681-5305
mabcinfo@mining.bc.ca
www.mining.bc.ca
To speak on behalf of mineral producers; To represent the interests of British Columbia's mining industry; To communicate with senior government decision-makers, communities, NGOs, First Nations, & the media; To act as the industry's voice regarding issues such as environmental regulations, taxation, infrastructure demands, labour issues, health & safety, & international trade

Mining Association of Canada (MAC) / Association minière du Canada
#1105, 350 Sparks St., Ottawa ON K1R 7S8 Canada
Tel: 613-233-9391; *Fax:* 613-233-8897
info@mining.ca
www.mining.ca
To represent the interests of member companies engaged in mineral exploration, extraction & refining; to work with governments on public policy pertaining to minerals

Mining Association of Manitoba Inc. (MAMI)
#700, 305 Broadway Ave., Winnipeg MB R3C 3J7 Canada
Tel: 204-989-1890
pmarsden@mines.ca
www.mines.ca
To represent mining & exploration companies in Manitoba.

Mining Society of Nova Scotia
88 Leeside Dr., Sydney NS B1R 1S6 Canada
Tel: 902-567-2147; *Fax:* 902-567-2147
florence@ns.sympatico.ca

New Brunswick Mining Association / L'Association minière du Nouveau-Brunswick
#312, 236 St. George Blvd., Moncton NB E1C 1W1 Canada
Tel: 506-857-3056; *Fax:* 506-857-3059

NWT & Nunavut Chamber of Mines
PO Box 2818, Yellowknife NT X1A 2R1 Canada
Tel: 867-873-5281; *Fax:* 867-920-2145
nwtmines@ssimicro.com
www.miningnorth.com
To promote & assist the development & growth of mining & mineral exploration in NWT & Nunavut

Ontario Mining Association (OMA)
#520, 5775 Yonge St., Toronto ON M2M 4J1 Canada
Tel: 416-364-9301; *Fax:* 416-364-5986
pmcbride@oma.on.ca
www.oma.on.ca
To help improve the competitiveness of the Ontario mineral industry

Prospectors & Developers Association of Canada (PDAC) / Association canadienne des prospecteurs & entrepreneurs
135 King St. East, Toronto ON M5C 1G6
Tel: 416-362-1969; *Fax:* 416-362-0101
info@pdac.ca
www.pdac.ca
To protect & promote the interests of the Canadian mineral exploration & development sector

Saskatchewan Mining Association (SMA)
#1500, 2002 Victoria Ave., Regina SK S4P 0R7
Tel: 306-757-9505; *Fax:* 306-569-1085
saskmining@sasktel.net
www.saskmining.ca
To ensure the safe & profitable development of mineral resources in Saskatchewan; To act as the voice of the mining industry throughout the province; To promote understanding of the development of mineral resources in Saskatchewan

Yukon Chamber of Mines (YCM)
3151B - 3rd Ave., Whitehorse YT Y1A 1G1 Canada
Tel: 867-667-2090; *Fax:* 867-668-7127
info@ycmines.ca
www.ycmines.ca
Provides services to members, with a focus on the mining industry; promotes responsible exploration and sustainable mining practices

Yukon Mine Training Association (YMTA)
#120, 205 Black St., Whitehorse YT Y1A 2M8 Canada
Tel: 867-633-6463; *Fax:* 867-633-2605
info@ymta.org
www.yukonminetraining.com
To maximize employment opportunities emerging from the growth of the mining and related resource sectors in the North for First Nations and other Yukoners.
Al Doherty, Chair
Tracy Thomas, Executive Director

Yukon Prospectors' Association (YPA)
3151B - 3rd Ave., Whitehorse YT Y1A 1G1 Canada
north-land.com/ypa
To promote and advocate for the mining industry and miners of the Yukon Territory
Jim McFaull, President

Multiculturalism

Affiliation of Multicultural Societies & Service Agencies of BC (AMSSA)
#205, 2929 Commercial Dr., Vancouver BC V5N 4C8 Canada
Tel: 604-718-2777; *Fax:* 604-298-0747
Toll-Free: 888-355-5560
amssa@amssa.org
www.amssa.org
To provide leadership in advocacy & education in British Columbia for anti-racism, human rights & social justice; to support members in serving immigrants, refugees & culturally diverse communities

Australia-New Zealand Association (ANZA)
3 - 8 Ave. West, Vancouver BC V5Y 1M8 Canada
Tel: 604-876-7128
info@anzaclub.org
www.anzaclub.org
To foster friendly relations between British Columbia, Canada, Australia & New Zealand

B'nai Brith Canada (BBC)
15 Hove St., Toronto ON M3H 4Y8 Canada
Tel: 416-633-6224; *Fax:* 416-630-2159
bnb@bnaibrith.ca
www.bnaibrith.ca
To bring men & women of the Jewish faith together in fellowship to serve the Jewish community through combating anti-Semitism, bigotry & racism in Canada & abroad; carrying out & supporting activities which ensure the security & survival of the State of Israel & Jewish communities worldwide; community service through various volunteer activities, cultivation of leadership, charitable work, advocacy & government relations

B'nai Brith Canada Institute for International Affairs
15 Hove St., Toronto ON M3H 4Y8 Canada
Tel: 416-633-6224; *Fax:* 416-630-2159
institute@bnaibrith.ca
www.bnaibrith.ca/institute.html
To identify & fight human rights abuses throughout the world, with special emphasis on Jewish communities worldwide
Frank Dimant, CEO
Ruth Klein, National Director

Baltic Federation in Canada
1590 Stewart Cres., Milton ON L9T 6P9 Canada
Tel: 905-693-8780
www.balticfederation.ca
To provide political representation for its member organizations of Estonian, Latvian & Lithuanian Canadians

Belgo-Canadian Association (BCA)
121 Chillery Ave., Toronto ON M1K 4T5 Canada
Tel: 416-261-4603
www.belgo-canadian.com

Black Cultural Society for Nova Scotia
1149 Main St., Dartmouth NS B2Z 1A8 Canada
Tel: 902-434-6223; *Fax:* 902-434-2306
Toll-Free: 800-465-0767
contact@bccns.com
www.bccns.com
To create among members of the Black community an awareness of their past, their heritage & identity; to provide programs & activities to explore, learn about, understand & appreciate Black history, achievements & experiences in Canadian life.
Henry V. Bishop, Director & Chief Curator
Leslie Oliver, President

Canadian Arab Federation (CAF) / La Fédération Canado-Arabe
1057 McNicoll Ave., Toronto ON M1W 3W6
Tel: 416-493-8635; *Fax:* 416-493-9239
Toll-Free: 866-886-4675
info@caf.ca
www.caf.ca
To represent Canadian Arabs on issues related to public policy; To protect civil liberties & the equality of human rights

The Canadian Doukhobor Society (CDS)
#27, Comp 4, R.R.#1, South Slocan BC V0G 2G0 Canada
Tel: 250-428-9634; *Fax:* 250-428-3519
awishlow@kootenay.com
To promote brotherhood, universal peace & the spiritual growth of our members
Marion Verigin, Secretary
Anne Stormes, Treasurer
Alex Wishlow, Chair

Canadian Ethnocultural Council (CEC) / Conseil ethnoculturel du Canada
#400, 176 Gloucester St., Ottawa ON K2P 0A6 Canada
Tel: 613-230-3867; *Fax:* 613-230-8051
cec@web.net
www.ethnocultural.ca
The Canadian Ethnocultural Council (CEC) is a non-profit, non-partisan coalition of national ethnocultural umbrella organizations which, in turn, represent a cross-section of ethnocultural groups across Canada.

Canadian Institute for Jewish Research (CIJR) / Institut canadien de recherche sur le Judaïsme
PO Box 175, Stn. H, Montréal QC H3G 2K7
Tel: 514-486-5544; *Fax:* 514-486-8284
cijr@isranet.org
www.isranet.org
To increase public understanding of Jewish Israel & general Jewish world issues

Canadian Jewish Congress (CJC) / Congrès juif canadien
#650, 100 Sparks St., Ottawa ON K1P 5B7 Canada
Tel: 613-233-8703; *Fax:* 613-233-8748
canadianjewishcongress@cjc.ca
www.cjc.ca
To act as decision-making body of the Jewish community in Canada; to act on behalf of Canadian Jewish community on issues & concerns affecting Jews in Canada & around the world; to foster interaction between interests & needs of Jewish community in Canada & Canadian society at large on a broad range of political, charitable & social justice issues

Canadian Latvian Business & Professional Association (CLBPA)
123 Overland Dr., Toronto ON M3C 2C7 Canada
Tel: 416-444-5201; *Fax:* 416-444-5208
alex@budrevics.com

Canadian Polish Congress (CPC) / Congrès canadien polonais
288 Roncesvalles Ave., Toronto ON M6R 2M4 Canada
Tel: 416-532-2876; *Fax:* 416-532-5730
kongres@kpk.org
www.kpk.org
To represent Polish-Canadians & to defend their interests; to coordinate & support the work of Polish-Canadian organizations in Canada; to foster Polish culture & assist Polish immigrants; to inform Canadians about Poland's contribution to culture & to maintain liaisons with Poland

Canadian Slovak League
#6, 259 Traders Blvd. East, Mississauga ON L4Z 2E5 Canada
Tel: 905-507-8004
info@ksliga.com
www.ksliga.com

Canadian Tibetan Association of Ontario (CTAO)
#201, 160 Springhurst Ave., Toronto ON M6K 1C2
Tel: 416-410-5606; *Fax:* 416-410-5606
info@ctao.org
www.ctao.org
To represent Tibetans in Ontario; To serve the needs of the Tibetan community in the province; To promote cross-cultural understanding
Norbu Tsering, President
Lhakpa Tsering, Manager, Administration
Tashi Dhondup, Coordinator, Culture & Education
Woeser Jongdong, Coordinator, Education & Public Relations
Tenzin Ngodupng, Coordinator, Youth & Sports
Jampa Nyendak, Coordinator, Spiritual
Lobsang Mentuh, Treasurer

Canadian Zionist Federation (CZF) / La fédération sioniste canadienne
#206, 1, carré Cummings, Montréal QC H3W 1M6 Canada
Tel: 514-739-7300; *Fax:* 514-739-9412
czfnational@fedcjamtl.org
www.doingzionism.org/federations/fed_home.asp?fed=czf
To promote the Zionist ideal among the Jewish population in Canada; to assist in strengthening the Jewish State of Israel; to enrich Canadian Jewish life through the provision of Jewish education & information on Israel & Zionism, through the promotion of Aliyah & activities among Jewish youth in Canada.

Canadian-Croatian Congress / Kanadsko-Hrvatski Kongres
3550 Commercial St., Vancouver BC V5A 4E9 Canada
Tel: 604-871-7190; *Fax:* 604-879-2256
www.canada.crocc.org
To represent the Croatian Canadian community before the people & Government of Canada
Ivan Curman, President

Chinese Canadian National Council (CCNC) / Conseil national des canadiens chinois
#507, 302 Spadina Ave., Toronto ON M5T 2E7 Canada
Tel: 416-977-9871; *Fax:* 416-977-1630
national@ccnc.ca
www.ccnc.ca
To promote the rights of all individuals, in particular, those of Chinese Canadians & to encourage their full & equal participation in Canadian society; to create an environment in Canada in which the rights of all individuals are fully recognized & protected; to promote understanding & cooperation between Chinese Canadians & all other ethnic, cultural, & racial groups in Canada; to encourage & develop in persons of Chinese descent, a desire to know & respect their historical & cultural heritage, & to educate them in adopting a creative & positive attitude towards the Chinese Canadian contribution to society & the Chinese Canadian heritage

Clans & Scottish Societies of Canada (CASSOC)
#78, 24 Fundy Bay Blvd., Newmarket ON L3Y 6T6 Canada
Tel: 905-898-6381; *Fax:* 905-773-0991
Toll-Free: 800-593-0518
editor@cassoc.ca
www.cassoc.ca
To foster the organization of & cooperation between Scottish associations, federations, clans, societies & groups through initiation & coordination of projects & undertakings; to advance Scottish cultural heritage in Canada

Cypriot Federation of Canada / Fédération chypriote du Canada
6 Thorncliff Park Dr., Toronto ON M4H 1H1 Canada
Tel: 416-696-7400; *Fax:* 416-696-9465
cypriotfederation@rogers.com

Czech & Slovak Association of Canada
PO Box 564, 3044 Bloor St. West, Toronto ON M8X 2Y8 Canada
Tel: 416-925-2241; *Fax:* 416-925-1940
ustredi@cssk.ca
www.cssk.ca
To develop the highest standards of citizenship in Canadians of Czech or Slovak origin by encouraging, carrying on & participating in activities of national, patriotic, cultural & humanitarian nature; to act in matters affecting status rights & welfare of Canadians of Czech or Slovak origin; to cultivate in members appreciation of their mother tongue, cultural heritage & historical traditions; to promote growth of spirit in toleration, understanding & goodwill between all ethnic elements in Canada; to conduct research & encourage studies.

Federation of Canada-China Friendship Associations
#705, 175, rue Laurier, Gatineau QC J8X 4G3 Canada
Tel: 819-777-8434
lolan.merklinger@sympatico.ca
www.fccfa.ca
To work with students from the Peoples' Republic of China studying in Canada; to take groups to China; to welcome delegations coming from China; to promote cultural exchanges

Federation of Canadian Turkish Associations (FCTA)
#15, 1170 Sheppard Ave. West, Toronto ON M3K 2A3 Canada
Tel: 647-230-9397
info@canturkfed.net
www.canturkfed.net
To support & encourage activities of member associations aimed at making Turkish culture & Turks better known; to promote closer relations with Canadians & other ethnic communities

Federation of Chinese Canadian Professionals (Ontario) (FCCP)
Coral Place, 55 Glenn Hawthorne Blvd., Mississauga ON L5R 3S6 Canada
Tel: 905-890-3235; *Fax:* 905-568-5293
webmaster@fccpontario.com
www.fccpontario.com

Federation of Chinese Canadian Professionals (Québec) (FCCP Québec) / Fédération des professionnels chinois canadiens (Québec)
PO Box 1004, Stn. B, Montréal QC H3B 3K5 Canada
Tel: 514-747-2488
htan222@yahoo.ca
www.fccp.ca
To promote the well-being of Chinese Canadian professionals in Québec; To liaise & cooperate with Chinese Canadian professionals in other parts of Canada & throughout the world; To provide a strong voice for the group
Howard Tan, President
John Chen, Vice-President
Renee Chin, Treasurer

Federation of Danish Associations in Canada / Fédération des associations danoises du Canada
679 Eastvale Ct., Gloucester ON K1J 6Z7 Canada
home.ca.inter.net/~robuch/dan-fed.htm
To promote cooperation among Danish Canadian organizations; To promote preservation & understanding of Danish tradition & heritage

Federation of Korean Canadian Associations
1133 Leslie St., Toronto ON M3L 2J6 Canada
Tel: 416-383-0777; *Fax:* 416-383-1113
koreancanadian@canada.org
www.koreancanadian.org

Federation of Scottish Clans in Nova Scotia (FSCNS)
PO Box 477, Lower Sackville NS B4C 3K3 Canada
info@scotsns.ca
www.scotsns.ca
To act as the voice for Nova Scotia's clans, Scottish-cultural communities, & cultural associations; To create appreciation for the Scottish culture, traditions, & heritage
Thomas (Tom) E.S. Wallace, President
Frank L. Logan, 1st Vice-President
Carol Terry, Secretary
Jean Watson, Treasurer

Finnish Canadian Cultural Federation / Fédération culturelle finno-canadienne
128 Quartz Ave., Timmins ON P4N 4L6 Canada
margaretk@personainternet.com
www.finnishcanadian.com
To act as non-political coordinator between associations, congregations, clubs & other groups of Finnish ethnic background; to promote Finland & Canadians of Finnish origin; to promote Canada & its Finnish ethnic community in Finland; to support Annual Finnish Canadian Grand Festival

Finnish Organization of Canada
PO Box 65070, Toronto ON M4K 3Z2 Canada
Tel: 416-651-0317; *Fax:* 416-651-0236

German-Canadian Congress (GCC) / Congrès germano-canadien
#58, 81 Garry St., Winnipeg MB R3C 4J9 Canada
Tel: 204-989-8300; *Fax:* 204-989-8304
gccmb@hotmail.com
gccongressmb.tripod.com
To serve as official voice for 2.7 million Canadians of German-speaking background

Goethe-Institut (Montréal)
418, rue Sherbrooke est, Montréal QC H2L 1J6 Canada
Tel: 514-499-0159; *Fax:* 514-499-0905
info@montreal.goethe.org
www.goethe.de/montreal
The Goethe-Institur is the cultural institue of the Federal Republic of Germany with a global reach. They promote knowledge of the German language abroad and foster international cultural cooperation. They convey a comprehensive picture of Germany by providing information on Germany's cultural, social, and political life. They perform the principle talks of cultural and educational policy, they work in partnership with public and private cultural bodies, the German federal states and municipalities, and the corporate sector.

Goethe-Institut (Toronto)
PO Box 136, #201, 100 University Ave., Toronto ON M5J 1V6 Canada
Tel: 416-593-5257; *Fax:* 416-593-5145
info@toronto.goethe.org
www.goethe.de/toronto
To provide cultural programs, international cultural cooperation, German language teaching, & library & information services

Greater Vancouver Japanese Canadian Citizens' Association
Nikkei Heritage Centre, #200, 6688 Southoaks Cres., Burnaby BC V5E 4M7 Canada
Tel: 604-777-5222; *Fax:* 604-777-5223
gvjcca@shaw.ca

Hellenic Canadian Congress / Congrès hellénique du Québec
846 Pape Ave., 2nd Fl., Toronto ON M4K 3T6 Canada
Tel: 416-461-0824; *Fax:* 416-463-9514
To collect as many names of individuals & businesses as possible in order to get an accurate & up-to-date census of Canadians of Hellenic heritage & their activities
Jimmy Sidiropoulos, President

Holocaust Education Centre
Lipa Green Centre, Sherman Campus, 4600 Bathurst St., 4th Fl., Toronto ON M2R 3V2 Canada
Tel: 416-635-2883; *Fax:* 416-635-0925
neuberger@ujafed.org
www.holocaustcentre.com
The Centre provides regular educational & remembrance activities, including workshops for teachers, students, community commemorations & survivor testimony to fulfill its mandate of preserving the past & educating future generations on the lessons of the Holocaust.

Hungarian Canadian Cultural Centre
840 St. Clair Ave. West, Toronto ON M6C 1C1 Canada
Tel: 416-654-4926; *Fax:* 416-654-4927
office@hccc.org
www.hccc-e.org
The Centre preserves & showcases Hungarian heritage in the Canadian mosaic.

Icelandic National League of North America (INL/NA)
#103, 94 - 1st Ave., Gimli MB R0C 1B1 Canada
Tel: 204-642-5897; *Fax:* 204-642-9382
inl@mts.net
www.inlofna.org
To foster & promote good citizenship among people of Icelandic descent; to foster & strengthen a mutual understanding of kinship, language, literature & cultural bonds among people of Icelandic origin & descent in North America & the people of Iceland; to cooperate with organizations which have similar purposes & objectives; to actively support various cultural & ethnic developments including education, history, publishing & the arts

Irish Canadian Cultural Association of New Brunswick (ICCA NB)
c/o 189 Carlisle Rd., Douglas NB E3A 7M8 Canada
info@newirelandnb.ca
www.newirelandnb.ca
To recognize & honour the contributions made by our ancestors to Canada by holding an annual Irish Festival, promoting an Irish Studies program at universities & sponsoring Irish cultural & social programs & events

Islamic Foundation of Toronto
441 Nugget Ave., Toronto ON M1S 5E1 Canada
Tel: 416-321-0909; *Fax:* 416-321-1995
info@islamicfoundation.ca
www.islamicfoundation.ca

Islamic Information Foundation (IIF)
8 Laurel Lane, Halifax NS B3M 2P6 Canada
Tel: 902-445-2494; *Fax:* 902-445-2494
To promote better understanding of Islam among Muslims & Christians through information provided in print, audio & video forms & through lecture, seminars & interfaith dialogues

Italian Cultural Institute / Istituto Italiano di Cultura
496 Huron St., Toronto ON M5R 2R3 Canada
Tel: 416-921-3802; *Fax:* 416-962-2503
www.iictoronto.esteri.it
To promote Italian culture & language in its many expressions in a spirit of vital interaction with the host country; to provide information on Italy's cultural heritage & contemporary cultural production; classrooms & library; offices in Toronto & Woodbridge.

Jamaican Canadian Association (JCA)
995 Arrow Rd., Toronto ON M9M 2Z5 Canada
Tel: 416-746-5772; *Fax:* 416-746-7035
info@jcassoc.com
www.jcassoc.org
To provide social interaction among members & to facilitate desirable relations with Canadian society; to represent the Caribbean community on public matters; to respond to the diverse social service needs of members; to facilitate economic, social & cultural integration of Caribbean people within Canadian society

Japanese Canadian Association of Yukon (JCAY)
531 Grove St., Whitehorse YT Y1A 5J9 Canada
Tel: 867-393-2588
Fumi Torigai, Contact

Kashmiri Canadian Council (KCC)
#44516, 2376 Eglinton Ave. East, Toronto ON M1K 5K3 Canada
Tel: 416-282-6933; *Fax:* 416-282-7488
kcc@kashmiri-cc.ca
www.kashmiri-cc.ca

Latvian National Federation in Canada / Fédération nationale lettone au Canada
4 Credit Union Dr., Toronto ON M4A 2N8 Canada
Tel: 416-755-2353; *Fax:* 416-913-1631
inak@inak.org
www.lnak.org
LNFC is the unifying central organization for all Latvians across Canada, representing their interests at the city, provincial & federal levels. It maintains contacts with other Canadian non-governmental organizations, & expedites projects both in Canada & in Latvia.

League of Ukrainian Canadians
83-85 Christie St., Toronto ON M6G 3B1 Canada
Tel: 416-516-8223; *Fax:* 416-516-4033
Toll-Free: 866-714-4132
luc@lucorg.com
www.lucorg.com
The League is a cultural & political organization to aid Ukrainian people living in Canada & in Ukraine; dedicated to the continued growth & development of a prosperous Ukrainian community in Canada.

The Lithuanian Canadian Community / La Communauté lithuanienne du Canada
1 Resurrection Rd., Toronto ON M9A 5G1 Canada
Tel: 416-533-3292; *Fax:* 416-533-2282
info@klb.org
www.klb.org
To promote, maintain, & encourage the survival of the Lithuanian culture & language in Canada & abroad

Lithuanian Canadian R.C. Cultural Society
Anapilis Christian Community Centre, 2185 Stavebank Rd., Mississauga ON L5C 1T3 Canada
Tel: 905-275-4672; *Fax:* 905-275-4364
tevzib@rogers.com
www.tevzib.com
The Society provides news & information for Canadians of Lithuanian origin or descent.

Maltese-Canadian Society of Toronto, Inc. (MCST)
235 Medland St., Toronto ON M6P 2N6 Canada
Tel: 416-767-3645; *Fax:* 416-767-5707
mcst@intiss.com
The organization strives for the betterment of the Maltese community in Toronto. It also preserves & promotes the Maltese language & culture in Canada.

Manitoba Multicultural Resources Centre Inc. (MMRC)
#101, 1555 St. James St., Winnipeg MB R3H 1B5 Canada
Tel: 204-831-6672
Helps Canadians express their cultural identity through research & documentation of our common heritage, thereby creating a positive intercultural relationship among Canadian groups.

Mizrachi Organization of Canada
296 Wilson Ave., Toronto ON M3H 1S8 Canada
Tel: 416-630-9266; *Fax:* 416-630-2305
mizrachi@rogers.com
www.mizrachi.ca
A religious Zionist organization which coordinates Zionist-oriented programming for the Orthodox Jewish communities in Canada; fundraising for educational & social welfare institutions in Israel; offices in Toronto & Montréal

Multicultural Association of Northwestern Ontario (MANWO)
511 Victoria Ave. East, Thunder Bay ON P7C 1B1 Canada
Tel: 807-622-4666; *Fax:* 807-622-7271
Toll-Free: 800-692-7692
manwoyc@tbaytel.net
my.tbaytel.net/manwoyc/manwo.html
MANWO is a regional umbrella organization for multicultural organizations, cultural groups, & ethno-cultural communities working together to promote the concept of multiculturalism. It serves as the region's resource centre for information, training & resources on citizenship, multiculturalism & race relations. It delivers settlement services to newcomers, & is also the parent organization of the Regional Multicultural Youth Centre, an inclusive group linking youths in small & isolated communities. The Youth Centre develops proactive programs to enhance the quality of life & improve social conditions of children & young adults.

Multicultural Association of Nova Scotia (MANS) / Association multiculturelle de la Nouvelle-Écosse
1113 Marginal Rd., Halifax NS B3H 4P7 Canada
Tel: 902-423-6534; *Fax:* 902-422-0881
admin@mans.ns.ca; communications@mans.ns.ca
www.mans.ns.ca
To develop & influence multicultural policy & to promote equality; to create a sense of belonging & respect for all cultures

Multicultural History Society of Ontario (MHSO)
c/o Oral History Museum, #307, 901 Lawrence Ave. West, Toronto ON M5S 1C3 Canada
Tel: 416-979-2973; *Fax:* 416-979-7947
mhso.mail@utoronto.ca
www.mhso.ca
Working with communities, schools, cultural agencies and institutions to preserve, record and make accessible archival and other material which demonstrate the role of immigration and ethnicity in shaping the culture and economic growth of Ontario and Canada. Library is located at St. Michael's College, University of Toronto.

Muslim Association of Canada (MAC)
#332, 1568 Merivale Rd., Ottawa ON K2G 5Y7 Canada
Tel: 613-321-5000; *Fax:* 613-321-5001
mac@macnet.ca
www.macnet.ca
Seeks to promote a balanced, constructive & integrated Islamic presence in Canada; operates in 11 Canadian cities

Muslim Education & Welfare Foundation of Canada (MEWFC)
2580 McGill St., Vancouver BC V5K 1H1 Canada
Tel: 604-255-9941; *Fax:* 604-255-9941
To provide for the educational, religious & welfare needs of the Muslim community

Muslim World League - Canada
#3, 6680 Campobello Rd., Mississauga ON L5N 2L8 Canada
Tel: 905-542-1050; *Fax:* 905-542-1054
mwl@mwlcanada.org
www.mwlcanada.org
The League is a non-profit, non-governmental organization that serves the religious needs of Muslims in Canada. It promotes Islam & Islamic teachings among Canadian Muslims & helps non-Muslims grasp an accurate understanding of the religion. It also serves as a resource centre, publishing booklets & flyers on current issues.

National Association of Canadians of Origin in India (NACOI) / Association nationale des Canadiens d'origine indienne
PO Box 2308, Stn. D, Ottawa ON K1P 5W5 Canada
dbdavis@web.net
www.web.net/~dbdavis
To encourage Canadians of origins in India to fully participate in Canadian society; to provide a national voice to Canadian of origins in India; to provide a forum for exchanges of ideas, issues, & common concerns; to facilitate communication within & with other organizations; to assure & protect rights of Canadians of origins in India

National Association of Japanese Canadians (NAJC)
#1, 222 Osborne St., Winnipeg MB R3L 1Z3 Canada
Tel: 204-943-2910; *Fax:* 204-947-3145
national@najc.ca
www.najc.ca
To promote & develop a strong Japanese Canadian identity, thereby strengthening local communities & the national organization; to strive for equal rights & liberties for all persons & racial & ethnic minorities in particular.

National Congress of Italian Canadians (NCIC) / Congrès national des italo-canadiens
PO Box 8144, Stn. Terminal, Ottawa ON K1G 3H6 Canada
www.ncf.ca/italcongress/

National Council of Trinidad & Tobago Organizations in Canada (NCTTOC)
#1, 66 Oakmeadow Blvd., Toronto ON M1E 4G5 Canada
Tel: 416-283-9672; *Fax:* 416-283-9672
manniedick@hotmail.com
To provide a national focus for representing the concerns of Trinidad & Tobago Nationals; to advocate on behalf of Trinidad & Tobago Nationals & their families in Canada; to develop & maintain a system of communication, information sharing & networking among Trinidad & Tobago organizations; to provide information, referrals, advocacy, & support to new arrivals from Trinidad & Tobago
Emmanuel J. Dick, President

National Federation of Pakistani Canadians Inc. (NFPC)
#1100, 251 Laurier Ave. W, Ottawa ON K1P 5J6 Canada
Tel: 613-741-8881; *Fax:* 613-745-4696
tanveer_ottawa@hotmail.com
To preserve & promote the heritage, culture & language of Pakistani Canadians; to generate goodwill & understanding among ethnic & mainstream communities; to provide support to new immigrants; to create awareness of Canadian issues in the Pakistani community

New Brunswick Multicultural Council (NBMC) / Conseil multiculturel du Nouveau-Brunswick (CMNB)
#301, 390 King St., Fredericton NB E3B 1E3 Canada
Tel: 506-453-1091; *Fax:* 506-474-8095
nbmc@nb-mc.ca
www.nb-mc.ca
To represent multicultural & multi-racial interests of all member associations; to encourage development & formation of new

associations; to encourage member associations in their multicultural, inter-cultural & inter-racial progarams & activities

Pacific Peoples Partnership (PPP)
#407, 620 View St., Victoria BC V8W 1J6 Canada
Tel: 250-381-4131; *Fax:* 250-388-5258
info@pacificpeoplespartnership.org
www.pacificpeoplespartnership.org
To promote increased understanding of social justice, environment, development, health & other issues of importance to the people of the Pacific Islands; to support equitable, environmentally sustainable development & social justice in the region

Polish Alliance of Canada
1015 Barton St. East, Hamilton ON L8L 3C8 Canada
Tel: 905-545-0799

Scotiabank Caribana Festival
263 Davenport Rd., Toronto ON M5R 1J9 Canada
Tel: 416-391-5608; *Fax:* 416-391-5693
info@caribanafestival.com
www.caribanafestival.com
Social Media: facebook.com/scotiabankcaribana
Organized by the Festival Management Committee, the event is a weeks-long, city-wide celebration of everything Caribbean, from food to arts & crafts, culminating with a parade of costumed dancers from regional dance schools & clubs, mas bands & a kaleidoscope of music genres, including calypso, soca, reggae, hip hop, chutney, steel pan.

Serbian National Shield Society of Canada
#303, 1900 Sheppard Ave. East, Toronto ON M2J 4T4 Canada
Tel: 416-496-7881; *Fax:* 416-493-0335
diddra@sympatico.ca
To promote & inform about interests & heritage of Canadian Serbs
Bora Dragasevich, President

UIA Federations Canada
#315, 4600 Bathurst St., Toronto ON M2R 3V3 Canada
Tel: 416-636-7655; *Fax:* 416-636-9897
info@uiafed.org
www.jewishcanada.org
To manage funds destined for Israel & to ensure that these funds are managed in Israel in accordance with terms set by Revenue Canada

UJA Federation of Greater Toronto
4600 Bathurst St., Toronto ON M2R 3V2 Canada
Tel: 416-635-2883; *Fax:* 416-635-9565
info@ujafed.org
www.jewishtoronto.net
To preserve & strengthen Jewish life in Toronto, Canada & Israel, through philanthropic, volunteer & professional leadership. The UJA is committed to social justice on behalf of the Jewish poor & vulnerable locally & internationally, to strengthening ties with Israel & its people, to supporting Israel's struggle to meet its social welfare needs, to combatting antisemitism in all its forms around the world, to nurturing shared values with Canadians of all faiths, to promoting Jewish education, to building a vibrant Jewish communal life. The following Pillars identify main areas of focus for UJA: Jewish Education & Identity; Strategic Planning & Community Engagement; Integrated Development; Operations & Corporate Relations; Business & Finance
Ted Sokolsky, President & CEO
David Engel, Chair

Ukrainian Canadian Congress (UCC) / Congrès des ukrainiens canadiens
#647, 167 Lombard Ave., Winnipeg MB R3B 0V3 Canada
Tel: 204-942-4627; *Fax:* 204-947-3882
Toll-Free: 866-942-4627
ucc@ucc.ca
www.ucc.ca
To protect, promote & enhance cultural identity of Ukrainians throughout Canada & beyond; to maintain, develop & enhance Ukrainian culture & language as integral elements of Canada's multicultural mosaic; to encourage participation of Ukrainian Canadians in cultural, social, economic, & political life in Canada; to actively advance better communication, understanding & mutual respect between Ukrainian Canadians & other ethnocultural communities; to foster sense of unity, cohesiveness & cooperation among member organizations
Paul Grod, President

Ukrainian Canadian Research & Documentation Centre (UCRDC) / Centre canadien-ukrainien de recherches et de documentation
#200, 620 Spadina Ave., Toronto ON M5S 2H4 Canada
Tel: 416-966-1819; *Fax:* 416-966-1820
info@ucrdc.org
www.ucrdc.org
To collect, store & promote information pertaining to Ukrainian historical events & Ukrainian Canadian experiences
Wsevolod Isajiw, Chair

Urban Alliance on Race Relations (UARR)
#507, 302 Spadina Ave., Toronto ON M5T 2E7 Canada
Tel: 416-703-6607; *Fax:* 416-703-4415
info@urbanalliance.ca
www.urbanalliance.ca
To promote a stable & healthy multiracial environment in the community, by creating awareness of current issues, assisting institutions to develop solid policies & practices, & promoting full participation by the community to dismantle barriers to equal opportunity
Sri-Guggan Sri-Skanda Rajah, President
Yumei Lin, Administrative Assistant

Vietnamese Canadian Federation / Fédération vietnamienne du Canada
249 Rochester St., Ottawa ON K1R 7M9 Canada
Tel: 613-230-8282; *Fax:* 613-230-8281
vietfederation@yahoo.ca
www.vietfederation.ca
To provide focal point for activities of the Vietnamese community in the National Capital Region & across Canada; to serve as resource centre on Vietnamese culture & issues related to resettlement & integration of Vietnamese refugees & immigrants in Canada; to maintain solidarity among the Vietnamese associations across Canada; to harmonize their activities for a better achievement of their common objectives; to work for the preservation & development of Vietnamese culture & for the enrichment of Canadian culture; to foster the spirit of mutual help & community responsibility
Diep Trinh, Executive Director
Ut V. Ngo, President
Duc Q. Duong, Treasurer

Museums

Museum London
421 Ridout St. North, London ON N6A 5H4 Canada
Tel: 519-661-0333; *Fax:* 519-661-2559
info@museumlondon.ca
www.museumlondon.ca
To enrich public knowledge & enjoyment of the art & history of the London region & Canada
Brian Meehan, Executive Director

Native Peoples

Aboriginal Friendship Centres of Saskatchewan
1615, 29th St., Saskatoon SK S7L 0N6 Canada
Tel: 306-955-0762; *Fax:* 306-955-0972
afcs.pa@sasktel.net
www.afcs.ca
The objectives of the Aboriginal Friendship Centres (AFC) of Sask. are: the promotion of the goals and objectives of its member Friendship Centres; the facilitation of communication and cooperation amongst all Centres w/in SK,.; the providing of information regarding the operation and dvlp. of AFCs to the public; negotiation with all tiers of gov't on matters of concern to the member Centres; assistance in Program Dvlp.; and assistance to all members in terms of funding information, debt recovery plans, financial negotiation, and networking.
Lennard Young, Provincial Director
Glen Lafleur, President

Aboriginal Nurses Association of Canada (ANAC) / Association des infirmières et infirmiers autochtones du Canada
#502, 56 Sparks St., Ottawa ON K1P 5A9 Canada
Tel: 613-724-4677; *Fax:* 613-724-4718
Toll-Free: 866-724-3049
info@anac.on.ca
www.anac.on.ca
Social Media: www.facebook.com/group.php?gid=8896466083
ANAC works with & on behalf of Aboriginal nurses to promote the development & practice of Aboriginal nursing in order to improve the health of Aboriginal people.

Aboriginal Women's Association of Prince Edward Island
PO Box 145, Lennox Island PE C0B 1P0 Canada
Tel: 902-831-3059; *Fax:* 902-831-3468
awapei@pei.aibn.com
The purpose of the project is to address issues of concern to off-reserve Aboriginal women and to improve the educational, social and economic environments in which they live. The resource centre offers culturally sensitive programs and services to off-reserve Aboriginal families and children from birth to age 6.

Alberta Aboriginal Women's Society
PO Box 5168, Stn. Main, Peace River AB T8S 1R8 Canada
Tel: 780-624-3416; *Fax:* 780-624-3409
aaws@telusplanet.net
Ruth Kidder, President

Alberta Native Friendship Centres Association (ANFCA)
10336 - 121 St., Edmonton AB T5N 1K8 Canada
Tel: 780-423-3138; *Fax:* 780-425-6277
info@anfca.com
www.anfca.com
To assist friendship centres in communication, funding & training

Alliance autochtone du Québec inc. / Native Alliance of Québec Inc.
21, rue Brodeur, Gatineau QC J8Y 2P6 Canada
Tél: 819-770-7763; *Téléc:* 819-770-6070
info@aaqnaq.com
www.aaqnaq.com

Assembly of First Nations (AFN) / Assemblée des Premières Nations (APN)
Trebla Building, 473 Albert St., Ottawa ON K1R 5B4 Canada
Tel: 613-241-6789; *Fax:* 613-241-5808
Toll-Free: 866-869-6789
imcleod@afn.ca
www.afn.ca
The AFN Secretariat acts as an advocate for First Nations on many issues, including Aboriginal & Treaty Rights, economic development, education, languages & literacy, health, housing, social development, justice, land claims & the environment
Shawn Atleo, National Chief

Assembly of Manitoba Chiefs
#200, 260 St. Mary Ave., Winnipeg MB R3C 0M6 Canada
Tel: 204-956-0610; *Fax:* 204-956-2109
Toll-Free: 888-324-5483
assembly@manitobachiefs.com
www.manitobachiefs.com/
The AMC Chiefs work to promote and preserve our inherent Aboriginal and treaty rights while striving to improve the quality of life of the First Nation citizens in Manitoba.
Irene Linklater, Executive Director

Association for Native Development in the Performing & Visual Arts (ANDPVA)
#171, 601 Christie St., Toronto ON M6G 4C7 Canada
Tel: 416-535-4567; *Fax:* 416-535-9331
info@andpva.com
www.andpva.com
To coordinate & develop programs that will encourage Indigenous peoples & communities to become more actively involved in the arts; to act as liaison for Native groups & individuals who are seeking funds for specific arts projects

Association of Iroquois & Allied Indians
387 Princess Ave., London ON N6B 2A7 Canada
Tel: 519-434-2761; *Fax:* 519-679-1653
general@aiai.on.ca
www.aiai.on.ca

British Columbia Association of Aboriginal Friendship Centres (BCAAFC)
#200, 506 Fort St., Victoria BC V8W 1E6 Canada
Tel: 250-388-5522; *Fax:* 250-388-5502
admin@bcaafc.com
www.bcaafc.com
The BCAAFC promotes the betterment of Aboriginal Friendship Centres in British Columbia by acting as a unifying body for the Centres. It establishes & maintains communications between Aboriginal Friendship Centres, other associations, & government.

British Columbia Native Women's Society
4213 Alexis Park Dr., Vernon BC V1T 7T8 Canada
Tel: 250-542-5029
mbono@sd22.bc.ca
www.bcnativewomen.com
Mollie Bono

Canadian Aboriginal & Minority Supplier Council (CAMSC)
95 Berkeley St., Toronto ON M5A 2W8 Canada
Tel: 416-941-0004; *Fax:* 416-941-9282
info@camsc.ca
www.camsc.ca
Dedicated to the economic empowerment of Aboriginal & visible minority communities through business development & employment; to identify & certify Aboriginal & minority-owned businesses, & to integrate them into the supply chain of major corporations in Canada.
Garth Scully, Chair
Orrin O. Benn, President

Canadian Association for the Study of Indigenous Education (CASIE) / Association canadienne pour l'etude de l'education des autochtones (ACÉFÉ)
c/o Canadian Society for the Study of Education, #204, 260 Dalhousie St., Ottawa ON K1N 7E4 Canada

Canadian Council for Aboriginal Business (CCAB) / Conseil canadien pour le commerce autochtone
#204, 250 The Esplanade, Toronto ON M5A 1J2 Canada
Tel: 416-961-8663; *Fax:* 416-961-3995
info@caab.com
www.ccab.com
To promote full participation of Aboriginal communities in the Canadian economy

Canadian Native Friendship Centre (CNFC)
11205 - 101 St. NW, Edmonton AB T5G 2A4 Canada
Tel: 780-479-1999; *Fax:* 780-479-0043
cnfc@shawbiz.ca
www.cnfc.ca
To improve the quality of life of Aboriginal Peoples in an urban environment by supporting self-determined activities encouraging equal access to & participation in Canadian society while respecting Aboriginal cultural distinctiveness
Barb Maytwayashing, Management Director

Centre indien cri de Chibougamau
95, rue Jaculet, Chibougamau QC G8P 2G1 Canada
Tél: 418-748-7667
Centre social pour les Autochtones de la région; centre d'exposition pour les artisans cri
Jo-Ann Toulouse, Directice générale

Chiefs of Ontario
#804, 111 Peter St., Toronto ON M5V 2H1 Canada
Tel: 416-597-1266; *Fax:* 416-597-8365
Toll-Free: 877-517-6527
margaret@coo.org
www.chiefs-of-ontario.org
Chiefs of Ontario is a coordinating body for 134 First Nation communities located within the boundaries of the province of Ontario. The purpose of the Chiefs of Ontario office is to enable the political leadership to discuss regional, provincial and national priorities affecting First Nation people in Ontario and to provide a unified voice on these issues.
Lori Jacobs, Executive Director

Confederacy of Mainland Mi'kmaq (CMM)
PO Box 1590, 57 Martin Cresc., Truro NS B2N 6N7 Canada
Tel: 902-895-6385; *Fax:* 902-893-1520
Toll-Free: 877-892-2424
www.cmmns.com
To proactively promote and assist Mi'kmaw communities' initiatives toward self determination and enhancement of community.
Donald M. Julien, Executive Director

Congress of Aboriginal Peoples (CAP) / Congrès des Peuples Autochtones
867 St. Laurent Blvd., Ottawa ON K1K 3B1 Canada
Tel: 613-747-6022; *Fax:* 613-747-8834
info@abo-peoples.org
www.abo-peoples.org
Represents approximately 3/4 million Aboriginal people living off-reserve in Canada

Council of Yukon First Nations (CYFN)
11 Nisutlin Dr., Whitehorse YT Y1A 3S4 Canada
Tel: 867-393-9200
www.cyfn.ca
The Council of Yukon First Nations is the central political organization for the First Nation people of the Yukon. It's mission is to serve the needs of First Nations within the Yukon and the MacKenzie delta.
Andy Carvill, Grand Chief

Federation of Newfoundland Indians
CIBC Bldg., PO Box 956, #7, 9 Main St., 3rd Fl., Corner Brook NL A2H 6J3 Canada
Tel: 709-634-0996; *Fax:* 709-634-3477
Toll-Free: 800-563-2549
adminasst@fni.nf.ca
www.fni.nf.ca

Federation of Saskatchewan Indian Nations
Asimakaniseekan Askiy Reserve, #100, 103A Packham Ave., Saskatoon SK S7N 4K4 Canada
Tel: 306-665-1215; *Fax:* 306-244-4413
www.fsin.com
The Federation represents 74 First Nations in Saskatchewan & honours the spirit & intent of the Treaties & their rights. It is committed to fostering the economic, educational & social endeavours of the First Nation people, & adhernece to democratic procedure & civil law.

Femmes autochtones du Québec inc. (FAQ) / Québec Native Women's Association Inc.
CP 1989, Kahnawake QC J0L 1B0 Canada
Tél: 450-632-0088; *Téléc:* 450-632-9280
Ligne sans frais: 800-363-0322
info@faq-qnw.org
www.faq-qnw.org
Appuyer les efforts des femmes autochtones pour l'amélioration de leurs conditions de vie par la promotion de la non-violence, de la justice et de l'égalité des droits et de les soutenir dans leur engagement au sein de leur communauté.

First Nations Confederacy of Cultural Education Centres
#302, 666 Kirkwood Ave., Ottawa ON K1Z 5X9 Canada
Tel: 613-728-5999; *Fax:* 613-728-2247
info@fnccec.com; cecp@fnccec.com
www.fnccec.com
To advocate for the recovery, maintenance, enhancement & preservation of First Nations languages, cultures, & traditions

Grand Council of the Crees / Grand Conseil des Cris
2, rue Lakeshore, Némiscau QC J0Y 3B0 Canada
Tel: 819-673-2600; *Fax:* 819-673-2606
cra@lino.ca
www.gcc.ca
Social Media: www.facebook.com/gcccra
The Council is the political body representing the Cree people. It also fosters, promotes, protects & assists in preserving the way of life, values & traditions of the Cree people of Quebec.
Mathew Coon Come, Grand Chief
Bill Namagoose, Executive Director

Indian Council of First Nations of Manitoba, Inc. (ICFNM)
PO Box 10299, Opaskwayak MB R0B 2J0 Canada
Tel: 204-623-7227; *Fax:* 204-623-4041
jhead@mts.net
To organize non-status & off-reserve Indians of Manitoba; to represent to all levels of Canadian government the constitutional position of non-status Indians in Manitoba; to ensure access for non-status & off-reserve Indians in all programs & services of federal, provincial & municipal governments of Canada; to promote democratic participation in constitutional processes for members; leadership development within non-status & off-reserve Indian community; to provide historical & pertinent information on non-status & off-reserve Indians to membership; to organize community groups throughout Manitoba; to develop constitutional position paper for non-status & off-reserve Indians in Manitoba; to organize & conduct annual assemblies; to attend constitutional workshops & first Ministers' meetings.
Andrew Kirkness, Grand Chief

Indigenous Bar Association
#9, 9785 - 152B St., Surrey BC V3R 9W2 Canada
Tel: 604-951-8807; *Fax:* 604-951-8806
glangan@indigenousbar.ca
www.indigenousbar.ca
To recognize & respect the spiritual basis of our Indigenous laws, customs & traditions; to promote the advancement of legal & social justice for Indigenous peoples in Canada; to promote reform of policies & laws affecting Indigenous peoples in Canada; to foster public awareness within the legal community, the Indigenous community & the general public in respect of legal & social issues of concern to Indigenous peoples in Canada; to provide a forum & network amongst Indigenous lawyers
Germaine Langan, Administrative Support

Inuit Art Foundation (IAF) / Fondation d'art Inuit
2081 Merivale Rd., Ottawa ON K2G 1G9 Canada
Tel: 613-224-8189
iaf@inuitart.org; projects@inuitart.org
www.inuitart.org
To facilitate the creative expression of Inuit artists; To foster an increased understanding of this expression in a local & global context; To assist in the marketing of Inuit art; To promote Inuit art through exhibits, publications & public events

Inuit Tapiriit Kanatami
#1101, 75 Albert St., Ottawa ON K1P 5E7 Canada
Tel: 613-238-8181; *Fax:* 613-234-1991
Toll-Free: 866-262-8181
info@itk.ca
www.itk.ca
To ensure the survival of Inuit culture in Canada.

Labrador Native Women's Association
PO Box 542, Stn. B, Happy Valley-Goose Bay NL A0P 1S0 Canada
Tel: 709-896-5071; *Fax:* 709-896-5071
mnha@nf.aibn.com

Makivik Corporation / Société Makivik
PO Box 179, Kuujjuaq QC J0M 1C0 Canada
Tel: 819-964-2925; *Fax:* 819-929-3982
Toll-Free: 877-625-4825
info@makivik.org
www.makivik.org
A non-profit organization owned by the Inuit of Nunavik, the Corporation promotes the social & economic interests of the Inuit people; receives, administers & invests Inuit compensation funds received under the James Bay & Northern Québec Agreement, & promotes the political, social & economic development of the Nunavik region. Offices in Kuujjuaq, Montreal, Ottawa, Quebec City
Pita Aatami, President
Anthony Ittoshat, Treasurer
Andy Moorhouse, Corporate Secretary

Manitoba Association of Friendship Centres (MAC)
#200, 388 Donald St., Winnipeg MB R3B 2J4 Canada
Tel: 204-942-6299; *Fax:* 204-942-6308
info@mac.mb.ca
www.mac.mb.ca
To assist friendship centres in communication, funding & training.

Manitoba Indian Cultural Education Centre (MICEC)
119 Sutherland Ave., Winnipeg MB R2W 3C9 Canada
Tel: 204-942-0228; *Fax:* 204-947-6564
micec@shawcable.com
www.micec.com
To stimulate, reidentify, maintain, expand & promote the cultural interests, lives & identity of Manitoba First Nations in every manner & respect whatsoever, & to promote an awareness of the traditional history of the First Nation Peoples of Manitoba; to advance the interests of First Nation Peoples who are registered members of the reserves within Manitoba, whether residing on or outside them; to cooperate with other organizations concerned with the interests of First Nation Peoples; to establish & promote research services; to assist in the development of accurate curriculum for use in schools within Manitoba; to produce audio, visual, & written materials relevant to cultural education development
Dennis Daniels, Executive Director

Manitoba Métis Federation / Fédération des Métis du Manitoba
Head Office, #300, 150 Henry Ave., Winnipeg MB R3B 0J7 Canada
Tel: 204-586-8474; *Fax:* 204-947-1816
mmf@mmf.mb.ca
www.mmf.mb.ca
Objectives include: promoting and instilling pride in the history and culture of the Métis people; educating members with respect to their legal, political, social and other rights; promoting the participation and represention of the Métis people in key political and economic bodies and organizations; promoting the political, legal, social and economic interests and rights of its members.

Maritime Aboriginal Peoples Council (MAPC)
172 Truro Heights Rd., Truro NS B6L 1X1 Canada
Tel: 902-895-2982; *Fax:* 902-895-3844

Métis Nation - Saskatchewan
406 Jessop Ave., Saskatoon SK S7N 2S5 Canada
Tel: 306-343-8285; *Fax:* 306-343-0171
Toll-Free: 888-343-6667
reception@mnsask.ca
www.mn-s.ca

Métis Nation Northwest Territories
PO Box 1375, 5125 - 50 St., Yellowknife NT X1A 2P1 Canada
Tel: 867-873-3505; *Fax:* 867-873-3395
metisnwt@internorth.com
Gary Bohnet, President

Métis Nation of Alberta
Delia Gray Bldg., #100, 41738 Kingsway Ave., Edmonton AB T5G 0X5 Canada
Tel: 780-455-2200; *Fax:* 780-452-8948
Toll-Free: 800-252-7553
apoitras@metis.org
www.albertametis.ca
To represent the interests of the Métis people of Alberta & ensure the advancement of their culture & well-being.

Métis Nation of Ontario
#3, 500 Old St. Patrick St., Ottawa ON K1N 9G4 Canada
Tel: 613-798-1488; *Fax:* 613-722-4225
Toll-Free: 800-263-4889
ottawareception@metisnation.org
www.metisnation.org
The Métis Nation of Ontario (MNO) brings Métis people together to celebrate and share their rich culture and heritage and to forward the aspirations of the Métis people in Ontario as a collective.
Gary Lipinski, President

Métis National Council (MNC) / Ralliement national des Métis
#201, 350 Sparks St., Ottawa ON K1R 7S8 Canada
Tel: 613-232-3216; *Fax:* 613-232-4262
Toll-Free: 800-928-6330
info@metisnation.ca
www.metisnation.ca
To represent the Métis both nationally & internationally; To secure a healthy space for the Métis Nation's existence within Canada

Métis National Council of Women (MNCW) / Conseil national des femmes métisses, inc. (CNFM)
PO Box 293, Woodlawn ON K0A 3M0 Canada
Tel: 613-567-4287; *Fax:* 613-567-9644
Toll-Free: 888-867-2635
info@metiswomen.ca
www.metiswomen.ca
To unite & organize Métis women in Canada; to maintain & promote respect for the individual rights, freedoms & gender equality of Métis women; to foster & promote the image of Métis women; to promote the preservation & enhancement of Métis culture; to facilitate & promote the development of services generally for the Métis & specifically for Métis women; to influence policy & to be actively involved in policy development in all organizations & at all levels that impact upon Métis women & their children; to establish & maintain cooperative & productive working relationships with the federal & provincial governments & all their related organizations as well as with other Aboriginal organizations; to actively seek funding for the Organization & its projects & activities; to represent the cultural, legal, political, social & economic issues of Métis women& their families & address their issues & concerns.
Sheila D. Genaille, LL.D. honoris c, President

Métis Provincial Council of British Columbia
#905, 1130 West Pender St., Vancouver BC V6E 4A4 Canada
Tel: 604-801-5853; *Fax:* 604-801-5097
Toll-Free: 800-940-1150
traceyt@mnbc.ca
www.mpcbc.bc.ca
Supporting the Métis population in British Columbia.
Bruce Dumont, President

Métis Settlements General Council
#200, 10335 - 172 St., Edmonton AB T5S 1K9 Canada
Tel: 780-822-4096; *Fax:* 780-489-9558
Toll-Free: 888-213-4400
reception@msgc.ca
www.msgc.ca
The Council represents 8 settlements, addresses socio-economic issues on their behalf, & promotes good governance & community involvement
Gerald Cunningham, President

Mi'Kmaq Association for Cultural Studies (MACS)
47 Maillard St., Membertou NS B1S 2P5 Canada
Tel: 902-567-1752; *Fax:* 902-567-0776
macs@mikmaq-assoc.ca
www.mikmaq-assoc.ca
To promote, maintain & protect the customs, language, history, tradition & culture of the Mi'Kmaq people; to facilitate & promote understanding & awareness of our culture among the public; to teach the culture, language & history of the Mi'Kmaq people to others

Mi'kmaq Native Friendship Centre
2158 Gottingen St., Halifax NS B3K 3B4 Canada
Tel: 902-420-0686; *Fax:* 902-423-6130
Social Media: facebook.com/group.php?gid=8114695398
The Centre promotes the educational & cultural advancement of native people in & about the Halifax/Dartmouth area. It assists people of native descent who have newly arrived in the area to settle in. Also, it strives to create & improve mutual understanding between people of native descent & others.
Gordon V. King, Executive Director

Mother of Red Nations Women's Council of Manitoba (MORN)
#300, 141 Bannatyne Ave., Winnipeg MB R3B 0R3 Canada
Tel: 204-942-6676; *Fax:* 204-942-7639
Toll-Free: 866-258-6726
morn@morn.ca
morn.cimnet.ca
MORN represents the voice of Aboriginal women in Manitoba. It serves as their primary political & advocacy organization. The association strives to promote, protect & support the spiritual, emotional, physical & mental well-being of all Aboriginal women & children in the province.

National Aboriginal Achievement Foundation
#759, 2160 Fourth Line Rd., Oshweken ON N0A 1M0 Canada
Tel: 416-926-0775; *Fax:* 416-926-7554
Toll-Free: 800-329-9780
info@naaf.ca
www.naaf.ca
Roberta Jamieson, CEO
John Kim Bell, Founder

National Aboriginal Circle Against Family Violence
Kahnawake Business Complex, PO Box 2169, Kahnawake QC J0L 1B0 Canada
Tel: 450-638-2968; *Fax:* 450-638-9415
www.nacafv.ca
To reduce & eliminate family violence in our Aboriginal communities; programs are culturally appropriate, & support shelters & family violence prevention centres
Brenda Combs, Chair

National Association of Friendship Centres (NAFC) / Association nationale des centres d'amitié
275 MacLaren St., Ottawa ON K2P 0L9 Canada
Tel: 613-563-4844; *Fax:* 613-594-3428
nafcgen@nafc.ca
www.nafc-aboriginal.com
To assist friendship centres in communication, funding & training

Native Addictions Council of Manitoba (NACM)
160 Salter St., Winnipeg MB R2W 4K1 Canada
Tel: 204-586-8395; *Fax:* 204-589-3921
nacm@escape.ca
www.mts.net/~nacm/
To provide traditional holistic healing services to First Peoples through treatment of addictions; each member of First Peoples has the right to wellness.

Native Council of Nova Scotia (NCNS)
129 Truro Heights Rd., Truro NS B6L 1X2 Canada
Tel: 902-895-1523; *Fax:* 902-895-0024
Toll-Free: 800-565-4372
info@ncns.ca
www.ncns.ca
To aid & assist people of Aboriginal ancestry in Nova Scotia; to work with all levels of government, public & private agencies, & industry to improve social, educational & employment opportunities for Aboriginal people; to foster & strengthen cultural identity & pride; to inform the public of the special needs of Native People; to cooperate with other Native organizations

Native Council of Prince Edward Island
6 F.J. McAuley Ct., Charlottetown PE C1A 9M7 Canada
Tel: 902-892-5314; *Fax:* 902-368-7464
Toll-Free: 877-591-3003
admin@ncpei.com
www.ncpei.com
Welcome to the Native Council of Prince Edward Island (NCPEI) The Native Council of Prince Edward Island is a Community of Aboriginal People residing off reserve in traditional Mi'kmaq territory. NCPEI is the self governing authority for all off reserve Aboriginal people living on Epekwitk (PEI).

Native Counselling Services of Alberta (NCSA)
10975 - 124 St., Edmonton AB T5M 0H9 Canada
Tel: 780-451-4002; *Fax:* 780-428-0187
www.ncsa.ca
A non-profit organization with a mandate to promote wellness for Aboriginal individuals, families and communities. The services provided include restorative justice, social programming, community development and wellness initiatives.

Native Friendship Centre of Montréal Inc. (NFCM) / Centre d'amitié autochtone de Montréal Inc.
2001, boul St-Laurent, Montréal QC H2X 2T3 Canada
Tel: 514-499-1854; *Fax:* 514-499-9436
info@nfcm.org
www.nfcm.org
To promote, develop & enhance the quality of life of the urban Aboriginal community of Montréal
Leandro Tolentino, Interim Executive Director

Native Investment & Trade Association (NITA)
6520 Salish Dr., Vancouver BC V6N 2C7 Canada
Tel: 604-275-6670; *Fax:* 604-275-0307
Toll-Free: 800-337-7743
nita@express.ca
www.native-invest-trade.com
To promote, establish & maintain trade/investment opportunities in Native communities; encourages free enterprise solutions to economic & social problems confronting Native communities, but remains sensitive to their special cultural heritage, needs, requirements; views non-governmental business involvement with First Nations as a vital step towards greater self-reliance; fosters business ventures with high employment potential; promotes projects with potential for sustainable economic growth; conducts research into innovative approaches to economic development of Native communities
Calvin Helin, President

Native Women's Association of Canada (NWAC) / L'Association des femmes autochtones du Canada (AFAC)
Six Nations of the Grand River, PO Box 331, 1721 Chiefswood Rd., Ohsweken ON N0A 1M0 Canada
Tel: 519-445-0990; *Fax:* 519-445-0924
www.nwac-hq.org
To enhance, promote & foster the social, economic, cultural & political well-being of First Nations & Métis women with First Nations & Canadian societies; to help empower women by being involved in developing & changing legislation which affects them, & by involving them in the development & delivery of programs promoting equal opportunity for Aboriginal women. Satellite office located at 1292 Wellington St. West, Ottawa, 613-722-3033.

New Brunswick Aboriginal Peoples Council (NBAPC)
320 St. Mary's St., Fredericton NB E3A 2S4 Canada
Tel: 506-458-8422; *Fax:* 506-451-6130
www.nbapc.org
The off-reserve Aboriginal voice for 28,255 Status & Non-status First Nations who reside in New Brunswick

New Brunswick Aboriginal Women's Council
120 Paul St., Fredericton NB E3A 2V8 Canada
Tel: 506-458-1114; *Fax:* 506-451-9386
nbawci@nb.aibn.com

Newfoundland Native Women's Association
PO Box 22, Benoits Cove NL A0L 1A0 Canada
Tel: 709-789-3430; *Fax:* 709-789-2207
nf.nativewomen@nf.aibn.com
The Native Womens Association of Canada (NWAC) is founded on the collective goal to enhance, promote, and foster the social, economic, cultural and political well-being of First Nations and Métis women within First Nation, Métis and Canadian societies.

Northwest Territories Council of Friendship Centres
c/o Soaring Eagle Friendship Centre, #2, 8 Gagnier St., Hay River NT X0E 1G1 Canada
Tel: 867-874-2792; *Fax:* 867-874-2894
To assist friendship centres in the Northwest Territories

Nova Scotia Native Women's Society
PO Box 805, Truro NS B2N 5E8 Canada
Tel: 902-893-7402; *Fax:* 902-897-7162
gracefrancis@eastlink.ca

Ontario Coalition of Aboriginal Peoples (OCAP)
PO Box 189, Wabigoon ON P0V 2W0 Canada
Tel: 807-938-1321
www.o-cap.ca
A not-for-profit advocacy organization representing the rights & interests of Métis, Status & Non-Status Aboriginal peoples living off-reserve in urban, rural or remote areas. Focus is on training programs & employment services

Ontario Federation of Indian Friendship Centres (OFIFC)
219 Front St. East, Toronto ON M5A 1E8
Tel: 416-956-7575; *Fax:* 416-956-7577
Toll-Free: 800-772-9291
ofifc@ofifc.org; oahai@ofifc.org (health advocacy initiative)
www.ofifc.org

To represent the collective interests of Ontario's friendship centres; To administer programs delivered by friendship centres, such as justice, health, employment, & family support; To improve the quality of life for Aboriginal people for equal access & participation in Canadian society

Ontario Native Women's Association (ONWA)
212 Miles St. East, Thunder Bay ON P7C 1J6
Tel: 807-623-3442; *Fax:* 807-623-1104
Toll-Free: 800-667-0816
www.nwac-hq.org
To foster & promote the economic, social, cultural, & political well-being of First Nations & Métis women in Ontario; To represent Native women on issues that affect their lives

Quaker Aboriginal Affairs Committee (QAAC)
60 Lowther Ave., Toronto ON M5R 1C7 Canada
Tel: 416-920-5213; *Fax:* 416-920-5214
qaac@quaker.ca
cfsc.quaker.ca/pages/contact_abor.html
Support for Aboriginal fights & justice, public education & campaigns
Jennifer Preston, Program Coordinator

Regroupement des centres d'amitié autochtone du Québec (RCAAQ)
#250, 225, rue Max-Gros-Louis, Wendake QC G0A 4V0 Canada
Tél: 418-842-6354; *Téléc:* 418-842-9795
Ligne sans frais: 877-842-6354
infos@rcaaq.info
www.rcaaq.info
Etre la voix provinciale des centres existants ou en voie de développement et de leurs communautés; appuyer ses membres dans l'atteinte de leurs objectifs; favoriser leur concertation et les représenter collectivement pour qu'ils remplissent au mieux leur mandat

Saskatchewan Aboriginal Women's Circle Corporation
PO Box 1174, 89 Broadway St. East, Yorkton SK S3N 2X3 Canada
Tel: 306-783-1228; *Fax:* 306-783-1771
sawcc@hotmail.com
www.sawcc.sk.ca
To walk in balance with guidance by the creator; to unite people together as healthy nations to ensure a better life for future generations

Society of Yukon Artists of Native Ancestry (SYANA)
#205, 302 Steele St., Whitehorse YT Y1A 2C5 Canada
Tel: 867-668-2695
To promote greater knowledge & appreciation of Native art & artists; To develop Native arts; To encourage Native & public participation in the arts
Linda Polyck, Contact

2-Spirited People of the First Nations (TPFN)
#202, 593 Yonge St., Toronto ON M4Y 1Z4 Canada
Tel: 416-944-9300; *Fax:* 416-944-8381
info@2spirits.com
www.2spirits.com
To create a place where Aboriginal 2-Spirited people can grow & learn together as a community, fostering a positive, self-sufficient image, honouring our past & building a future; to work together toward bridging the gap between the 2-Spirited, Lesbian, Gay, Bisexual & Transgendered community & our Aboriginal identity
Art Zoccole, Executive Director

Union of British Columbia Indian Chiefs
#500, 342 Water St., Vancouver BC V6B 1B6 Canada
Tel: 604-684-0231; *Fax:* 604-684-5726
ubcic@ubcic.bc.ca
www.ubcic.bc.ca
To settle land claims & aboriginal rights in BC; to improve the social, economic, health, education of Aboriginal people in BC; to provide a political voice for Aboriginal people in BC
Stewart Phillip, President

Union of Nova Scotia Indians (UNSI)
PO Box 961, 47 Maillard St., Membertou NS B1S 2P5 Canada
Tel: 902-539-4107; *Fax:* 902-564-2137
rec@unsi.ns.ca
www.unsi.ns.ca
To promote welfare & progress of Native people in Nova Scotia; to liaise with all Native people on relevant issues; to defend & advise on Native rights; to cooperate with Native & non-Native agencies & organizations to the benefit of Nova Scotia Native people
Joe B. Marshall, Executive Director

Union of Ontario Indians (UOI)
Nipissing First Nation, PO Box 711, North Bay ON P1B 8J8 Canada
Tel: 705-497-9127; *Fax:* 705-497-9135
Toll-Free: 877-702-5200
recnip@anishinabek.ca
www.anishinabek.ca
The UOI represents 42 First Nations throughout the province of Ontario from Golden Lake in the east, Sarnia in the south, Thunder Bay and Lake Nipigon in the north. The 42 First Nations have an approximate combined population of 42,000 citizens, one third of the province of Ontario's aboriginal population.
John Beaucage, Grand Council Chief

United Native Nations Society
#341, 1979 Marine Dr., North Vancouver BC V7G 3G2 Canada
Tel: 604-688-1821; *Fax:* 604-980-0324
Toll-Free: 800-555-9756
unn@unns.bc.ca
www.unns.bc.ca

Woodland Cultural Centre (WCC)
PO Box 1506, 184 Mohawk St., Brantford ON N3T 5V6 Canada
Tel: 519-759-2650; *Fax:* 519-759-8912
woodlandcentre@execulink.com
www.woodland-centre.on.ca
To preserve the values & practices of First Nation cultures through the storage & exhibits of First Nation National Treasures; to bring about acceptable positive change in our communities & in the interaction with western Euro-society; to provide a place where people can receive teachings & guidance from our First Nation existence; to instill pride in self, children & our existence as Nations in the world community
Amos Key Jr., Executive Director

Yukon Aboriginal Women's Council
#102, 307 Jarvis St., Whitehorse YT Y1A 2H3 Canada
Tel: 867-667-6162; *Fax:* 867-668-7539
Toll-Free: 866-667-6162
yawc@northwestel.net

Naturalists

Avicultural Advancement Council of Canada (AACC)
PO Box 123, Chemainus BC V0R 1K0 Canada
Tel: 250-246-4803; *Fax:* 250-246-4912
exec@aacc.ca
www.aacc.ca
To establish & maintain a national association of interested societies & individuals to promote the advancement of aviculture in Canada; to represent the Canadian avicultural community internationally; to disseminate information; to support recognized expert aviculturalists; to assist all levels of government in preparing informed legislation & policy relating to aviculture; to establish standards for the exhibition of birds in Canada; to provide a national identification leg band registry; to establish an avian species preservation program in Canada

British Columbia Nature (Federation of British Columbia Naturalists) (FBCN)
c/o Parks Heritage Centre, 1620 Mount Seymour Rd., North Vancouver BC V7G 2R9
Tel: 604-985-3057
manager@bcnature.ca
www.bcnature.ca
To protect biodiversity, species at risk, & natural areas throughout British Columbia; To present a unified voice on conservation & environmental issues
Betty Davison, Office Manager
Rosemary Fox, Chair, Conservation
Joan Snyder, Chair, Education
Pat Westheuser, Chair, Awards

British Columbia Waterfowl Society
5191 Robertson Rd., RR#1, Delta BC V4K 3N2 Canada
Tel: 604-946-6980; *Fax:* 604-946-6980
www.reifelbirdsanctuary.com
To encourage conservation of wetlands; to spur public awareness on importance of conservation of estuaries; to operate George C. Reifel Migratory Bird Sanctuary.

Federation of Alberta Naturalists (FAN)
11759 Groat Rd., Edmonton AB T5M 3K6 Canada
Tel: 780-427-8124; *Fax:* 780-422-2663
info@fanweb.ca
www.fanweb.ca
To encourage Albertans to increase knowledge & understanding of natural history & ecological processes; to provide a unified voice for naturalists on conservation issues; to organize field meetings, conferences, nature camps, research symposia, & other activities.

Jack Miner Migratory Bird Foundation, Inc.
PO Box 39, Kingsville ON N9Y 2E8 Canada
Tel: 519-733-4034; *Toll-Free:* 877-289-8328
info@jackminer.com
www.jackminer.com
The sanctuary provides food, shelter & protection to migratory water fowl, tags birds & tracks migration patterns

Natural History Society of Newfoundland & Labrador
c/o The Osprey, PO Box 1013, Stn. C, St. John's NL A1C 5M3 Canada
Tel: 709-754-0455
nhs@nhs.nf.ca
www.nhs.nf.ca
The Natural History Society is a province-wide organization with a primary interest in promoting the enjoyment and protection of all wildlife and natural history resources in the Province of Newfoundland and Labrador and surrounding waters.
Allan Stein, Acting Vice-President
Don Steele, Secretary

Nature Canada / Canada Nature
#300, 75 Albert St., Ottawa ON K1P 5E7
Tel: 613-562-3447; *Fax:* 613-562-3371
Toll-Free: 800-267-4088
info@naturecanada.ca
www.naturecanada.ca
Social Media: www.facebook.com/NatureCanada;
www.twitter.com/#!/NatureCanada
To protect & conserve wildlife & habitats throughout Canada

Nature Manitoba (MNS)
Hammond Building, #401, 63 Albert St., Winnipeg MB R3B 1G4
Tel: 204-943-9029; *Fax:* 204-943-9029
info@naturemanitoba.ca; editor@naturemanitoba.ca (Newsletter)
www.naturemanitoba.ca
Social Media:
www.facebook.com/pages/Nature-Manitoba/67945358869
To foster the popular & scientific study of nature; To preserve the natural environment; To act as a voice for people interested in the outdoors & natural history

Nature NB
#110, 924 Prospect St., Fredericton NB E3B 2T9 Canada
Tel: 506-459-4209; *Fax:* 506-459-4209
nbfn@nb.aibn.com
www.naturenb.ca
To preserve wildlife & protect its natural habitat; to promote a public interest in & a knowledge of natural history; to promote, encourage & cooperate with organizations & individuals who have similar interests & objectives; to consider matters of environmental concern.

Nature Nova Scotia (Federation of Nova Scotia Naturalists)
c/o Nova Scotia Museum of Natural History, 1747 Summer St., Halifax NS B3H 3A6
Tel: 902-582-7176
doug@fundymud.com
www.naturens.ca
To support the interests of naturalists clubs; To represent naturalists clubs throughout Nova Scotia
Bob Bancroft, President
Sue Abbot, Vice-President
Doug Linzey, Secretary
Jean Gibson, Treasurer

Nature Québec
#207, 870, av de Salaberry, Québec QC G1R 2T9 Canada
Tél: 418-648-2104; *Téléc:* 418-648-0991
conservons@naturequebec.org
www.naturequebec.org
Regrouper les individus et les sociétés oeuvrant en sciences naturelles et en environnement; maintenir des processus écologiques essentiels; préserver la diversité génétique; utiliser soutenablement des espèces et des écosystèmes
Christian Simard, Directeur général

Nature Saskatchewan
#206, 1860 Lorne St., Regina SK S4P 2L7
Tel: 306-780-9273; *Fax:* 306-780-9263
Toll-Free: 800-667-4668
info@naturesask.ca
www.naturesask.ca
To foster appreciation & understanding for the natural environment; To document & protect the biological diversity of Saskatchewan; To preserve the natural eco-systems of the province

Ontario Nature
#201, 366 Adelaide St. West, Toronto ON M5V 1R9 Canada
Tel: 416-444-8419; *Fax:* 416-444-9866
Toll-Free: 800-440-2366
info@ontarionature.org
www.ontarionature.org
To promote knowledge, understanding & respect for Ontario's natural heritage & commitment to its conservation & protection on the part of the FON membership, landowners, decision makers & the general public; to seek legislation, policies, practices & institutions which permanently protect Ontario's natural ecosystem & indigenous biodiversity, including the establishment of a comprehensive natural heritage system for Ontario with an enlarged system of parks & other protected areas linked by a network of existing & rehabilitated natural corridors.

Society of Canadian Ornithologists (SCO) / Société des ornithologistes du Canada (SOC)
a/s Thérèse Beaudet, SCO Membership Secretary, 1281, ch des Lièges, St-Jean de l'Ile d'Orléans QC G0A 3W0
beaudet.lamothe@sympatico.ca
www.sco-soc.ca
To support research to understand & conserve Canadian birds; To represent Canadian ornithologists

Nursing

Academy of Canadian Executive Nurses (ACEN)
c/o Association Strategy Group, #1, 136 Lewis St., Ottawa ON K2P 0S7 Canada
Tel: 613-235-3033; *Fax:* 613-233-6158
info@acen.ca
www.acen.ca
To advance nursing practice, education, research, & leadership; To work in partnership with other national organizations to influence health policy & set direction of healthcare in Canada to assure quality of care to Canadians
Noreen Linton, President
Marcia James, Admininistrative Coordinator

Association of Registered Nurses of Newfoundland & Labrador (ARNNL)
55 Military Rd., St. John's NL A1C 2C5 Canada
Tel: 709-753-6040; *Fax:* 709-753-4940
Toll-Free: 800-563-3200
info@arnnl.nf.ca
www.arnnl.nf.ca
To maintain & improve ethical & professional standards of nursing education & practice; to encourage members to participate & promote public welfare; to promote & maintain unity & the best interests of nurses of the province; to encourage an attitude of mutual understanding with nurses of other countries

Association of Registered Nurses of Prince Edward Island (ARNPEI)
53 Grafton St., Charlottetown PE C1A 1K8 Canada
Tel: 902-368-3764; *Fax:* 902-628-1430
info@arnpei.ca
www.arnpei.ca
Professional Association for Registered Nurses in P.E.I.

British Columbia Nurses' Union (BCNU) / Syndicat des infirmières de la Colombie-Britannique
4060 Regent St., Burnaby BC V5C 6P5 Canada
Tel: 604-433-2268; *Fax:* 604-433-7945
Toll-Free: 800-663-9991
contactbcnu@bcnu.org
www.bcnu.org

Canadian Association for Nursing Research (CANR) / Association canadienne pour la recherche infirmière
c/o P. Petrucka, College of Nursing, University of Saskatchewan, 107 Wiggins Rd., Saskatoon SK S7N 5E5
Tel: 306-337-2228; *Fax:* 306-966-6221
pammla.petrucka@usask.ca
www.canr.ca
To foster practice-based nursing research & research-based nursing practice across Canada
Pamela Hawranik, RN,PhD
Pammla Petrucka, Secretary
Riek van den Berg, Treasurer

Canadian Association for the History of Nursing (CAHN) / Association canadienne pour l'histoire du nursing
723 Colborne St., New Westminster BC V3L 5V6 Canada
www.cahn-achn.ca
To promote interest in the history of nursing; To develop scholarship in the field
Geertje Boschma, President
Sandra Bassendowski, Secretary
Carol Helmstadter, Treasurer

Canadian Association of Burn Nurses (CABN) / Association canadienne des infirmières et infirmiers en soins aux brûlés
c/o Shannon Bonn, IWK Health Centre, PO Box 9700, 5850-5980 University Ave., Halifax NS B3K 6R8 Canada
shannon.bonn@iwk.nshealth.ca
www.cabn.ca
To provide education related to burn care; To research & develop national burn standards; Promoting & supporting nurses & other care providers
Shannon Bonn, President
Amelia Potter, Vice-President
Judy Sleith, Treasurer

Canadian Association of Critical Care Nurses (CACCN) / Association canadienne des infirmières et infirmiers en soins de phase aiguë
PO Box 25322, London ON N6A 1X6 Canada
Tel: 519-649-5284; *Fax:* 519-649-1458
Toll-Free: 866-477-9077
caccn@caccn.ca
www.caccn.ca
To maintain & enhance the quality of patient & family centered care throughout Canada; To develop standards of critical care nursing practice

Canadian Association of Nephrology Nurses & Technologists (CANNT) / Association canadienne des infirmières et infirmiers et technologues de néphrologie (ACITN)
#322, 336 Yonge St., Barrie ON L4N 4C8 Canada
Tel: 705-720-2819; *Fax:* 705-720-1451
Toll-Free: 877-720-2819
cannt@cannt.ca
www.cannt.ca
To improve the care of renal patients through support of educational opportunities for association members; to evaluate the performance & competence of nephrology nurses & technologists against the CANNT Standards of Practice
Alison Thomas, President
Susan Placko, Treasurer & Coordinator, Website

Canadian Association of Neuroscience Nurses (CANN) / Association canadienne des infirmiers et infirmières en sciences neurologiques (ACIISN)
c/o Aline Mayer, Membership Chairperson, CANN, 30 Chantilly Gate, Stittsville ON K2S 2B1
canninfo@cann.ca; cjnn@cann.ca (Journal)
www.cann.ca
To prevent illness & to improve health outcomes for people with, or at risk for, neurological disorders; To establish standards of practice for neuroscience nurses

Canadian Association of Nurses in AIDS Care (CANAC) / Association canadienne des infirmières et infirmiers en sidologie
PO Box 93, Pontypool ON L0A 1K0 Canada
info@canac.org
www.canac.org
The Canadian Association of Nurses in AIDS Care (CANAC) is a national professional nursing organization committed to fostering excellence in HIV/AIDS nursing, promoting the health, rights and dignity of persons affected by HIV/AIDS and to preventing the spread of HIV infection.
Jennifer Shaw, Executive Assistant

Canadian Association of Nurses in Oncology (CANO) / Association canadienne des infirmières en oncologie (ACIO)
#201, 375 West 5th Ave., Vancouver BC V5Y 1J6 Canada
Tel: 604-874-4322; *Fax:* 604-874-4378
cano@malachite-mgmt.com
www.cano-acio.ca
The organization advocates for improved cancer care for all Canadians.

Canadian Association of Pediatric Nurses (CAPN) / Association canadienne des infirmières et infirmiers en pédiatrie (ACIIP)
c/o The Hospital for Sick Children, Room 7763, 555 University Ave., Toronto ON M5G 1X8 Canada
Tel: 416-813-6998; *Fax:* 416-813-8082
karen.breen-reid@sickkids.ca
To advocate for the health care needs of children & their families; to promote education in prediatric nursing; to facilitate opportunities for Canadian nurses to unite & address issues related to pediatric nursing; to promote a high standard of pediatric nursing practice in Canada in developing national standards of care & advocating for the certification of pediatric nurses in Canada; to promote the professional growth & fulfilment of pediatric nurses in Canada; to promote research in pediatric nursing
Barbara Bearivage, Sec.-Treas.
Karen Breen-Reid, Interim President

Canadian Council of Cardiovascular Nurses (CCCN) / Conseil canadien des infirmières et infirmiers en nursing cardiovasculaire (CCINC)
#1402, 222 Queen St., Ottawa ON K1P 5V9 Canada
Tel: 613-569-4361; *Fax:* 613-569-3278
info@cccn.ca
www.cccn.ca
The national professional association promotes & maintains high standards of cardiovascular nursing through education, research, health promotion, strategic alliances & advocacy.

Canadian Council of Practical Nurse Regulators (CCPNR)
c/o College Of LPN's of Alberta (CLPNA), #13163, 143 St., Edmonton AB T5L 4S8 Canada
Tel: 780-484-8886; *Fax:* 780-484-9069
chair@ccpnr.ca
www.ccpnr.ca
Responsible for the safety of the public through the regulation of Licensed/Registered Practical Nurses.
Linda Stranger, RN, MSA, Chair

Canadian Federation of Mental Health Nurses (CFMHN) / Fédération canadienne des infirmières et infirmiers en santé mentale
#109, 1 Concorde Gate, Toronto ON M3C 3N6 Canada
Tel: 416-426-7029; *Fax:* 416-426-7280
info@cfmhn.ca
www.cfmhn.ca
The CFMHN is a national voice for psychiatric and mental health (PMH) nursing. They wish to assure leadership in the development and application of nursing standards that inform and affect psychiatric and mental health nursing practice; examine and influence government policy, and address national issues related to mental health and mental illness; communicate and collaborate with national and international groups that share our professional interests; faciliate excellence in psychiatric and mental health nursing by providing members with educational and networking resources.
Chris Davis, President

Canadian Gerontological Nursing Association (CGNA) / Association canadienne des infirmières et infirmiers en gérontologie
c/o Membership, #370, 101-1001 West Broadway, Vancouver BC V6H 4E4 Canada
cgna@cgna.net
www.cgna.net
To promote high standards of gerontological nursing practice; to promote educational programs in gerontological nursing; to participate in affairs which promote the health of elderly persons; to promote networking opportunities for nurses; to promote & disseminate gerontological nursing research; to present the views of the Association to government, education, professional & other appropriate bodies.

Canadian Holistic Nurses Association (CHNA) / Association canadienne des infirmières en soins holistiques
c/o Marie Knapp, RR#7, Owen Sound ON N4K 6V5 Canada
Tel: 519-371-1255
info@chna.ca
www.chna.ca
To further the development of holistic nursing practice; to promote CHNA standards of practice
Marie Knapp, President
Michele Bourgeois, Secretary

Canadian Nurses Association (CNA) / Association des infirmières et infirmiers du Canada
50 Driveway, Ottawa ON K2P 1E2 Canada
Tel: 613-237-2133; *Fax:* 613-237-3520
Toll-Free: 800-361-8404
info@cna-aiic.ca; executiveoffice@cna-aiic.ca;
media@cna-aiic.ca
www.cna-aiic.ca
To advance the discipline of nursing; to advocate for public policy that incorporates the principles of primary health care & respects the principles, conditions & spirit of the Canada Health Act; to advance the regulation of Registered Nurses in the interest of the public; to advance international health policy & development in Canada

Canadian Nurses Foundation (CNF) / Fondation des infirmières et infirmiers du Canada
50 Driveway, Ottawa ON K2P 1E2 Canada
Tel: 613-237-2133; *Fax:* 613-237-3520
Toll-Free: 800-361-8404
info@cnf-fiic.ca
www.cnf-fiic.ca
CNF promotes the health of Canadians by enhancing nursing education & research.
Hélène Sabourin, Executive Director
Jonelle Istead, Director, Fundraising

Canadian Nurses Protective Society (CNPS) / Société de protection des infirmières et infirmiers du Canada (SPIIC)
50 Driveway, Ottawa ON K2P 1E2 Canada
Tel: 613-237-2092; *Fax:* 613-237-6300
Toll-Free: 800-267-3390
info@cnps.ca
www.cnps.ca
To offer legal liability protection related to nursing practice to eligible Registered Nurses

Canadian Occupational Health Nurses Association (COHNA) / Association canadienne des infirmières et infirmiers en santé du travail (ACIIST)
c/o Health Canada, #412, 101 - 22nd St. E, Saskatoon SK S7K 0E1 Canada
valerie_adrian@hc-sc.gc.ca
www.cohna-aciist.ca
To promote national standards for occupational health nursing practice; to advance the profession by providing a national forum for the exchange of ideas & concerns; to enhance the profile of occupational health nurses; to improve the health & safety of workers; to contribute to the health of the community by providing quality health services to workers; to encourage continuing education
Valerie Adrian, President
Marg Creen, Secretary/Treasurer
Ellen Coe, Vice President

Canadian Orthopaedic Nurses Association (CONA) / Association canadienne des infirmières et infirmiers en orthopédie
2890 Gosnell Rd., Kelowna BC V1Y 3K2 Canada
judy.macaulay@ubc.ca
www.cona-nurse.org
To foster professional growth of the membership in the assessment, treatment & rehabilitation of individuals with neuromuscular & skeletal alterations; to promote nursing research related to orthopaedics

Canadian Vascular Access Association (CVAA) / Association canadienne d'Accès Vasculaire
PO Box 66572, 685 McCowan Rd., Toronto ON M1J 3N8 Canada
Tel: 416-696-7761; *Fax:* 416-696-8437
www.cvaa.info
To establish & promote standards of intravenous therapy to enhance patient care & safety

The College & Association of Registered Nurses of Alberta (CARNA)
11620 - 168 St., Edmonton AB T5M 4A6 Canada
Tel: 780-451-0043; *Fax:* 780-452-3276
Toll-Free: 800-252-9392
carna@nurses.ab.ca
www.nurses.ab.ca
To set nursing practice standards & to ensure Albertans receive safe, competent, & ethical nursing services

College of Licensed Practical Nurses of Alberta (CLPNA)
13163 - 146 St., Edmonton AB T5L 4S8 Canada
Tel: 780-484-8886; *Fax:* 780-484-9069
Toll-Free: 800-661-5877
info@clpna.com
www.clpna.com
To regulate & lead the profession in a manner that protects & serves the public through excellence in Practical Nursing.

College of Licensed Practical Nurses of BC (CLPNBC)
#260, 3480 Gilmore Way, Burnaby BC V5G 4Y1 Canada
Tel: 604-660-5750; *Fax:* 604-660-2899
Toll-Free: 888-440-6900
info@clpnbc.org
www.clpnbc.org
To regulate practical nursing in the public interest
Gordon MacDonald, Executive Director-Registrar

College of Licensed Practical Nurses of Manitoba (CLPNM)
463 St. Anne's Rd., Winnipeg MB R2M 3C9 Canada
Tel: 204-663-1212; *Fax:* 204-663-1207
Toll-Free: 877-663-1212
info@clpnm.ca
www.clpnm.ca
The governing body for the Licensed Practical Nurses in Manitoba. The College's duty is to carry out its activities and govern its members in a manner that serves and protects the public interest. The College establishes requirements to enter the profession and assures the quality of the practice of LPNs through the development and enforcement of standards and practice and continuing competence programs.
Verna Holgate, Executive Director

College of Licensed Practical Nurses of Newfoundland & Labrador
9 Paton St., St. John's NL A1B 4S8 Canada
Tel: 709-579-3843; *Fax:* 709-579-8268
Toll-Free: 888-579-2576
info@clpnnl.ca
www.clpnnl.ca
The College for Licensed Practical Nurses of Newfoundland and Labrador (CLPNNL), in accordance with the Licensed Practical Nurses' Act, has the legislative responsibility for regulating the practice of Licensed Practical Nurses in NFLD. The mission of CLPNNL is to promote safety and protection of the general public through the provision of safe, competent and ethical nursing care.
Paul D. Fisher, LPN, Executive Director/Registrar

College of Licensed Practical Nurses of Nova Scotia (CLPNNS)
Cogswell Tower, #1212, 2000 Barrington St., Halifax NS B3J 3K1 Canada
Tel: 902-423-8517; *Fax:* 902-425-6811
info@clpnns.ca
www.clpnns.ca
To represent licensed practical nurses within the health care system; to protect the public by providing safe, competent nursing care.

College of Nurses of Ontario (CNO) / Ordre des infirmières et infirmiers de l'Ontario
101 Davenport Rd., Toronto ON M5R 3P1 Canada
Tel: 416-928-0900; *Fax:* 416-928-6507
Toll-Free: 800-387-5526
cno@cnomail.org
www.cno.org
To protect the public's right to quality nursing services by providing leadership to the nursing profession in self-regulation.

College of Registered Nurses of British Columbia (CRNBC)
2855 Arbutus St., Vancouver BC V6J 3Y8 Canada
Tel: 604-736-7331; *Fax:* 604-738-2272
Toll-Free: 800-565-6505
info@crnbc.bc.ca
www.crnbc.bc.ca
To provide safe & appropriate nursing practice regulated by nurses in the public interest; to promote good practice, prevent poor practice & intervene when practice is unacceptable.

College of Registered Nurses of Manitoba (CRNM)
890 Pembina Hwy., Winnipeg MB R3M 2M8 Canada
Tel: 204-774-3477; *Fax:* 204-775-6052
Toll-Free: 800-665-2027
info@crnm.mb.ca
www.crnm.mb.ca
To regulate the practice of registered nurses & to advance the quality of nursing to protect the public interest

College of Registered Nurses of Nova Scotia (CRNNS)
#4005, 7071 Bayers Rd., Halifax NS B3L 2C2 Canada
Tel: 902-491-9744; *Fax:* 902-491-9510
Toll-Free: 800-565-9744
info@crnns.ca
www.crnns.ca
Registered nurses regulating their profession to promote excellence in nursing practice.

College of Registered Psychiatric Nurses of Alberta
#201, 9711 - 45 Ave., Edmonton AB T6E 5V8 Canada
Tel: 780-434-7666; *Fax:* 780-436-4165
Toll-Free: 877-234-7666
crpna@crpna.ab.ca
www.crpna.ab.ca
The mission of CRPNA is to; protect and servce the public interest by ensuring members provide safe, competent and ethical practice; address the needs of members and the public through education, regulation, advocacy.

College of Registered Psychiatric Nurses of British Columbia
#307, 2502 St. Johns St., Port Moody BC V3H 2B4 Canada
Tel: 604-931-5200; *Fax:* 604-931-5277
Toll-Free: 800-565-2505
donna_higenbottam@crpnbc.ca
www.crpnbc.ca
To serve & protect the public; to assure a safe, accountable & ethical level of psychiatric nursing practice

College of Registered Psychiatric Nurses of Manitoba (CRPNM)
1854 Portage Ave., Winnipeg MB R3J 0G9 Canada
Tel: 204-888-4841; *Fax:* 204-888-8638
crpnm@crpnm.mb.ca
www.crpnm.mb.ca
To ensure that members of the profession provide safe & effective psychiatric nursing services to the public of Manitoba, in accordance with the Registered Psychiatric Nurses Act

Community Health Nurses of Canada (CHNC) / Infirmières et infirmiers en santé communautaire au Canada
182 Clendenan Ave., Toronto ON M6P 2X2
Tel: 647-239-9554; *Fax:* 416-426-7280
info@chnc.ca
www.chnc.ca
To act as the voice of community health nurses across Canada; To respond to issues which affect community health nurses
Kate Thompson, BScN, MSc, CCHN, President
Evelyn Butler, RN, BN, MPA, Administrative Manager
Ruth Schofield, RN, MSc(T), Secretary
Anne Clarotto, RN, BN, MHS, Treasurer
Yvette Laforet-Fliesser, RN, BScN, MScN,, Officer, Communications

Fédération interprofessionnelle de la santé du Québec (FIQ)
1234, av Papineau, Montréal QC H2K 0A4 Canada
Tél: 514-987-1141; *Téléc:* 514-987-7273
Ligne sans frais: 800-363-6541
info@fiqsante.qc.ca
www.fiqsante.qc.ca
Améliorer les conditions de travail des infirmières, infirmiers & cardiorespiratoires; s'associer aux luttes des femmes et être présente dans les débats concernant les orientations du système de santé

Gerontological Nursing Association of Ontario (GNA)
PO Box 368, Stn. K, Toronto ON M4P 2G7 Canada
info@gnaontario.org
www.gnaontario.org
To promote a high standard of nursing care & related health services for older adults; To enhance professionalism in the practice of gerontological nursing

Licensed Practical Nurses Association & Regulatory Board of PEI
PO Box 20058, 161 St. Peter's Rd., Charlottetown PE C1A 9E1 Canada
Tel: 902-566-1512; *Fax:* 902-892-6315
info@lpna.ca
www.lpna.ca
To represent practical nurses within the health care system

Manitoba Nurses' Union (MNU) / Syndicat des infirmières du Manitoba
#301, 275 Broadway, Winnipeg MB R3C 4M6 Canada
Tel: 204-942-1320; *Fax:* 204-942-0958
Toll-Free: 800-665-0043
www.nursesunion.mb.ca
To represent & support all categories of licensed nurses in Manitoba; To safeguard the role of nurses in the health care system of Manitoba

National Emergency Nurses Affiliation (NENA) / Affiliation des infirmières et infirmiers d'urgence
112 Old River Rd., RR#2, Mallorytown ON K0E 1R0 Canada
www.nena.ca
To represent the Canadian emergency nursing specialty.
Landon James, President

New Brunswick Nurses Union (NBNU) / Syndicat des infirmières et infirmiers du Nouveau-Brunswick (SIINB)
103 Woodside Lane, Fredericton NB E3C 2R9 Canada
Tel: 506-453-0820; *Fax:* 506-453-0828
Toll-Free: 800-442-4914
www.nbnu-siinb.nb.ca
The New Brunswick Nurses Union is a labour organization for nurses employed in the province. It is an open and democratic organization which promotes the participation of the maximum

number of members in decision-making. Their mission is to enhance the social, economic, and general worklife of nurses and their vision is NBNU as a professional, credible, and respected voice advocating for nurses and quality health care.

Newfoundland & Labrador Nurses' Union (NLNU) / Syndicat des infirmières de Terre-Neuve et du Labrador
PO Box 416, Stn. C, 229 Major's Path, St. John's NL A1C 5J9 Canada
Tel: 709-753-9961; *Fax:* 709-753-1210
Toll-Free: 800-563-5100
nlnu@nlnu.nf.net
www.nlnu.nf.ca

Nova Scotia Nurses' Union (NSNU)
30 Frazee Ave., Dartmouth NS B3B 1X4 Canada
Tel: 902-469-1474; *Fax:* 902-466-6935
Toll-Free: 800-469-1474
www.nsnu.ns.ca
The NSNU represents Registered Nurses and Licensed Practical Nurses working in acute and long term care, with the VON and Canadian Blood Services

Nurses Association of New Brunswick (NANB) / Association des infirmières et infirmiers du Nouveau-Brunswick (AIINB)
165 Regent St., Fredericton NB E3B 7B4 Canada
Tel: 506-458-8731; *Fax:* 506-459-2838
Toll-Free: 800-442-4417
aiinb@aiinb.nb.ca; nanb@nanb.nb.ca
www.aiinb.nb.ca; www.nanb.nb.ca
To act as the professional voice & regulatory body of nursing in New Brunswick; To protect the public by maintaining standards for nursing education & practice

Ontario Nurses' Association (ONA) / Association des infirmières et infirmiers de l'Ontario
#400, 85 Grenville St., Toronto ON M5S 3A2 Canada
Tel: 416-964-8833; *Fax:* 416-964-8864
Toll-Free: 800-387-5580
onamail@ona.org
www.ona.org
Social Media: twitter.com/ontarionurses
To improve the socio-economic welfare of members.

Operating Room Nurses Association of Canada (ORNAC) / Association des infirmières et infirmiers de salles d'opération du Canada
Tel: 604-466-7965
info@ornac.ca
www.ornac.ca
To promote operating nursing for the betterment of surgical patient care

Ordre des infirmières et infirmiers auxiliaires du Québec (OIIAQ)
531, rue Sherbrooke est, Montréal QC H2L 1K2 Canada
Tél: 514-282-9511; *Téléc:* 514-282-0631
Ligne sans frais: 800-283-9511
oiiaq@oiiaq.org
www.oiiaq.org
Favoriser le développement professionnel des infirmières et infirmiers auxiliaires du Québec pour viser l'excellence dans l'exercice professionnel et tendre à une plus grande humanisation des soins
Jacques Gaulin, Président

Ordre des infirmières et infirmiers du Québec (OIIQ)
4200, boul Dorchester ouest, Westmount QC H3Z 1V4 Canada
Tél: 514-935-2501; *Téléc:* 514-935-1799
Ligne sans frais: 800-363-6048
inf@oiiq.org
www.oiiq.org
Média social: www.facebook.com/Ordre.infirmieres.infirmiers.Quebec
Assurer la protection du public; contrôler l'exercice de la profession par ses membres

Practical Nurses Canada
#255, 55 St. Clair Ave. West, Toronto ON M1E 4X9
Tel: 416-922-5968; *Fax:* 416-967-6320
Toll-Free: 866-454-5968
info@pncanada.ca
www.pncanada.ca
To promote competent, safe, holistic practical nursing care throughout Canada

Practical Nurses Federation of Ontario (PFNO)
Building 4, #200, 5025 Orbitor Dr., Mississauga ON L4W 4Y5
Tel: 905-602-6705; *Fax:* 905-602-4666
To conduct the business of a trade union, representing registered practical nurses in Ontario; To improve the working conditions of registered practical nurses throughout the province

Prince Edward Island Nurses' Union (PEINU) / Syndicat des infirmières de l'Ile-du-Prince-Édouard
326 Patterson Dr., Charlottetown PE C1A 8K4 Canada
Tel: 902-892-7152; *Fax:* 902-368-2974
Toll-Free: 866-368-2974
office@peinu.com
www.peinu.com
To regulate employment relations between nurses & employers through collective bargaining & negotiation of written contracts with employers implementing progressively better conditions of employment

Registered Nurses Association of Ontario (RNAO) / L'Association des infirmières et infirmiers autorisés de l'Ontario
158 Pearl St., Toronto ON M5H 1L3 Canada
Tel: 416-599-1925; *Fax:* 416-599-1926
Toll-Free: 800-268-7199
info@rnao.org
www.rnao.org
Social Media: www.facebook.com/group.php?gid=30442334943
To promote excellence in nursing practice; to advocate the role of nursing in empowering the people of Ontario to achieve & maintain their optimal health; to provide membership-centred services

The Registered Nurses Association of the Northwest Territories & Nunavut (RNANT/NU)
PO Box 2757, Yellowknife NT X1A 2R1 Canada
Tel: 867-873-2745; *Fax:* 867-873-2336
admin@rnantnu.ca
www.rnantnu.ca
To promote & ensure competent nursing practice for the people of the NWT

Registered Practical Nurses Association of Ontario (RPNAO)
Bldg. 4, #200, 5025 Orbitor Dr., Mississauga ON L4W 4Y5 Canada
Tel: 905-602-4664; *Fax:* 905-602-4666
info@rpnao.org
www.rpnao.org
Social Media: www.facebook.com/group.php?gid=15186044118
Dedicated to decisions that enhance professional practical nursing

Registered Psychiatric Nurses Association of Saskatchewan (RPNAS)
2055 Lorne St., Regina SK S4P 2M4 Canada
Tel: 306-586-4617; *Fax:* 306-586-6000
rpnas@rpnas.com
www.rpnas.com
The Registered Psychiatric Nurses Association of Saskatchewan regulates psychiatric nursing as a distinct profession.

Saskatchewan Association of Licensed Practical Nurses (SALPN)
#100, 2216 Lorne St., Regina SK S4P 2M7
Tel: 306-525-1436; *Fax:* 306-347-7784
Toll-Free: 888-257-2576
lpnadmin@salpn.com (general); praccon@salpn.com (practice)
www.salpn.com
To regulate Licensed Practical Nurses (LPNs) in Saskatchewan, in order to ensure public safety; To ensure that Saskatchewan's Licensed Practical Nurses provide professional nursing care; To maintain an efficient investigation & disciplinary process

Saskatchewan Registered Nurses' Association (SRNA)
2066 Retallack St., Regina SK S4T 7X5
Tel: 306-359-4200; *Fax:* 306-525-0849
Toll-Free: 800-667-9945
info@srna.org; SRNAnewsbulletin@srna.org; register@srna.org
www.srna.org
To ensure competent, knowledge-based, & ethical nursing in Saskatchewan, for the protection of the public; To establish registration & licensure requirements

Saskatchewan Union of Nurses (SUN) / Syndicat des infirmières de la Saskatchewan
2330 - 2nd Ave., Regina SK S4R 1A6 Canada
Tel: 306-525-1666; *Fax:* 306-522-4612
Toll-Free: 800-667-7060
regina@sun-nurses.sk.ca
www.sun-nurses.sk.ca
To advocate to protect the rights of members; to enhance the socio-economic & general welfare of members through collective bargaining, research, & education

Union of Psychiatric Nurses / Syndicat des infirmières psychiatriques
#200, 508 Clarke Rd., Coquitlam BC V3J 3X2 Canada
Tel: 604-931-2471; *Fax:* 604-931-1070
Toll-Free: 877-931-2471
dmclaren@telus.net
www.upnbc.org
Sherry Moller, President
Philip Oosterman, Director, Operations & Membership Services

Union québécoise des infirmières et infirmiers (UQII) / Québec Union of Nurses
9405, rue Sherbrooke est, Montréal QC H1L 6P3 Canada
Tél: 514-356-8888; *Téléc:* 514-356-9999
uqii@csq.qc.net
L'UQII assure la représentation de ses membres, donne aux syndicats une structure politique et fournit, en collaboration avec la CSQ, des services aux membres en matière de relations de travail, de professionnel, de négociation et de formation
Monique Bélanger, Présidente

United Nurses of Alberta (UNA) / Infirmières unies de l'Alberta
Park Plaza, 10611 - 98 Ave., 9th Fl., Edmonton AB T5K 2P7 Canada
Tel: 780-425-1025; *Fax:* 780-426-2093
Toll-Free: 800-252-9394
provincialoffice@una.ab.ca
www.una.ab.ca
Social Media: twitter.com/unitednurses
To advance the social, economic & general welfare of nurses & other allied personnel

Victorian Order of Nurses for Canada (VON Canada) / Infirmières de l'Ordre de Victoria du Canada
110 Argyle Ave., Ottawa ON K2P 1B4 Canada
Tel: 613-233-5694; *Fax:* 613-230-4376
Toll-Free: 888-866-2273
national@von.ca
www.von.ca
VON is dedicated to being a leader in the delivery of innovative comprehensive health & social services & to influencing the development of health & social policy in Canada; to meet rapidly changing social & external challenges; VON is accredited by Canadian Council on Health Services Accreditation

Yukon Registered Nurses Association (YRNA)
#204, 4133 - 4th Ave., Whitehorse YT Y1A 1H8 Canada
Tel: 867-667-4062; *Fax:* 867-668-5123
yrna@yknet.ca
www.yrna.ca
YRNA is the regulatory body and professional association for registered nurses in the Yukon. YRNA is responsible for establishing and promoting standards of practice for registered nurses, for regulating nursing practice and for advancing professional excellence. YRNA speaks out on health care issues, advocating for the development of healthy public policy in the interest of the public.

Packaging

North American Packaging Association - Canada
#400, 701 Evans Ave., Toronto ON M9C 1A3 Canada
Tel: 416-626-7056; *Fax:* 416-626-7054
info@paperbox.org
www.paperbox.org
The Canadian Paperboard Packaging Association merged with the North American Packaging Association in September, 2006. NAPA is an international trade association representing paperboard packaging converters & industry suppliers

Packaging Association of Canada (PAC) / Association canadienne de l'emballage
#E420, 2255 Sheppard Ave. East, Toronto ON M2J 4Y1 Canada
Tel: 416-490-7860; *Fax:* 416-490-7844
info@pac.ca
www.pac.ca
To represent both users & suppliers on the strength of environmental & economic policy

Paper Packaging Canada
#3, 1995 Clark Blvd., Brampton ON L6T 4W1 Canada
Tel: 905-458-1247; *Fax:* 905-458-2052
info@paperpackaging.ca
www.paperpackaging.ca
The association represents containerboard mill sites, corrugator plants, sheet plants and related industries; works together with other players in the paper industry to develop an agenda of common concerns and issues.

Patents & Copyright

Access Copyright
#800, One Yonge St., Toronto ON M5E 1E5 Canada
Tel: 416-868-1620; *Fax:* 416-868-1621
Toll-Free: 800-893-5777
info@accesscopyright.ca
www.accesscopyright.ca
To licence copyright users who wish to reproduce copyright-protected works; to collect a fee for this service & to distribute royalties to the copyright owners whose works have been copied; to provide protection for copyright owners as well as legal access to published works for copyright users

Canadian Copyright Institute (CCI)
#107, 192 Spadina Ave., Toronto ON M5T 2C2 Canada
Tel: 416-975-1756; *Fax:* 416-975-1839
info@thecci.ca
www.canadiancopyrightinstitute.ca
To encourage a better understanding of the law of copyright on the part of members, public & users of copyright material; to engage in & foster research in copyright law

Canadian Musical Reproduction Rights Agency (CMRRA) / Agence canadienne des droits de production musicaux limitée
#320, 56 Wellesley St. West, Toronto ON M5S 2S3 Canada
Tel: 416-926-1966; *Fax:* 416-926-7521
inquiries@cmrra.ca
www.cmrra.ca
Represents the majority of music publishers & copyright owners doing business in Canada; on their behalf, issues licences & collects royalties for the reproduction of copyrighted musical works on CDs, cassettes & other sound carriers, & in films, TV programs & advertising; owned by the Canadian Music Publishers Association
David A. Basskin, President
Fred Merritt, Vice-President, Finance & Administration

Copyright Collective of Canada (CCC) / Société de perception de droit d'auteur du Canada (SPDAC)
#1603, 22 St. Clair Ave. East, Toronto ON M4T 2S3 Canada
Tel: 416-961-1888; *Fax:* 416-968-1016
speacock@ccofcan.org
The Copyright Collective of Canada represents owners (producers and distributors) of the U.S. independent motion picture and television production industry for all drama and comedy programming (such as companies represented by the Motion Picture Association of America), except for that carried on the PBS network stations.

Intellectual Property Institute of Canada (IPIC) / Institut de la Propriété Intellectuelle du Canada (IPIC)
#606, 60 Queen St., Ottawa ON K1P 5Y7 Canada
Tel: 613-234-0516; *Fax:* 613-234-0671
info@ipic.ca
www.ipic.ca
To promote the protection of intellectual property in Canada & abroad in order to enhance Canada's economic prospects as a sovereign nation & to foster cooperation between Canada & its trading partners around the world.

Society of Composers, Authors & Music Publishers of Canada (SOCAN) / Société canadienne des auteurs, compositeurs et éditeurs de musique
41 Valleybrook Dr., Toronto ON M3B 2S6 Canada
Tel: 416-445-8700; *Fax:* 416-445-7108
Toll-Free: 800-557-6226
socan@socan.ca
www.socan.ca
SOCAN is the Canadian copyright collective that administers the performing rights of members & of affiliated international organizations by licensing the use of music in Canada

Pharmaceutical

Alberta College of Pharmacists (ACP)
#1200, 10303 Jasper Ave., Edmonton AB T5J 3N6 Canada
Tel: 780-990-0321; *Fax:* 780-990-0328
Toll-Free: 877-227-3838
acpinfo@pharmacists.ab.ca
www.pharmacists.ab.ca
Greg Eberhart, CAE, Registrar

Association of Faculties of Pharmacy of Canada (AFPC) / Association des facultés de pharmacie du Canada
3919 - 13th Ave. West, Vancouver BC V6R 2T1 Canada
Tel: 604-222-0221; *Fax:* 604-222-2574
fabbott@telus.net
www.afpc.info
To develop & implement policies & programs which will provide a forum for exchange of ideas, ensure a liaison with other organizations; to foster & promote excellence in pharmaceutical education & research in Canada

Association professionnelle des pharmaciens salariés du Québec (APPSQ)
3560, rue la Verendrye, Sherbrooke QC J1L 1Z6 Canada
Tél: 819-563-6464; *Téléc:* 819-563-6464
appsq@hotmail.com
Syndicat professionnel voué à la défense des intérêts des pharmaciens salariés du Québec

Association québécoise des pharmaciens propriétaires (AQPP) / Québec Association of Pharmacy Owners
4378, av Pierre-de Coubertin, Montréal QC H1V 1A6 Canada
Tél: 514-254-0676; *Téléc:* 514-254-1288
Ligne sans frais: 800-361-7765
info@aqpp.qc.ca
www.aqpp.qc.ca
Assure l'étude, la défense et le développement des intérêts économiques, sociaux et professionnels de ses membres.

British Columbia Pharmacy Association (BCPhA)
#1530, 1200 West 73rd Ave., Vancouver BC V6P 6G5
Tel: 604-261-2092; *Fax:* 604-261-2097
Toll-Free: 800-663-2840
info@bcpharmacy.ca
www.bcpharmacy.ca
To support & advance the economic & professional well-being of members, with the goal that they will provide improved health care in British Columbia

Canada's Research-Based Pharmaceutical Companies (Rx&D) / Les companies de recherche pharmaceutique du Canada
#1220, 55 Metcalfe St., Ottawa ON K1P 6L5 Canada
Tel: 613-236-0455; *Fax:* 613-236-6861
info@canadapharma.org
www.canadapharma.org
To discover new medicines that improve the quality of health care available for every Canadian

Canadian Association for Pharmacy Distribution Management (CAPDM) / Association canadienne de la gestion de l'approvisionnement pharmaceutique (ACGAP)
#301A, 3800 Steeles Ave. West, Woodbridge ON L4L 4G9 Canada
Tel: 905-265-1706; *Fax:* 905-265-9372
david@capdm.ca
www.capdm.ca
The association acts as a resource & an advocacy voice for its members to advance the pharmacy distribution system as an effective, efficient, & safe delivery system for patient health care in Canada.

Canadian Association of Pharmacy Students & Interns (CAPSI) / Association canadienne des étudiants et internes en pharmacie (ACEIP)
PO Box 68552, 360A Bloor St. West, Toronto ON M5S 1X0 Canada
president@capsi.ca
www.capsi.ca
To prepare members for moral, social, ethical obligations to be upheld in the profession of pharmacy; to promote high standards of pharmacy education throughout Canada; to promote means by which members may enhance their professional knowledge & skills; to promote mutual interests & liaison with international pharmacy students, interns & society at large

Canadian Association of Pharmacy Technicians (CAPT)
#164, 9-6975 Meadowvale Town Centre Circle, Mississauga ON L5N 2V7
Tel: 416-410-1142
info@capt.ca; members@capt.ca
www.capt.ca
To act as the voice of pharmacy assistants

The Canadian Council for Accreditation of Pharmacy Programs (CCAPP) / Le Conseil canadien de l'agrément des programmes de pharmacie
#200, 1765 West 8th Ave., Vancouver BC V6J 5C6 Canada
Tel: 604-676-4230; *Fax:* 604-676-4231
www.ccapp-accredit.ca
To assess the quality of professional pharmacy degree programs in Canadian universities; to promote the continued improvement of such programs
David Hill, Executive Director

The Canadian Council on Continuing Education in Pharmacy (CCCEP) / Le conseil canadien de l'éducation permanente en pharmacie
#102, 4010 Pasqua St., Regina SK S4S 7B9 Canada
Tel: 306-545-7790; *Fax:* 306-545-7795
info@cccep.ca; admin.assistant@cccep.ca
www.cccep.ca
To act as the national coordinating & accrediting body for continuing education in pharmacy in Canada; to enhance the quality of continuing pharmacy education; to advance pharmacy practice
Arthur Whetstone, Executive Director
Anick Minville, President
Bev Zwicker, Vice-President

Canadian Foundation for Pharmacy (CFP) / Fondation canadienne pour la pharmacie
5809 Fieldon Rd., Mississauga ON L5M 5K1 Canada
Tel: 905-997-3238; *Fax:* 905-997-4264
dacorn@cfpnet.ca
www.cfpnet.ca
To provide programs for the advancement of the pharmacy profession in Canada
Fred Smith, President
Dayle Acorn, Executive Director

Canadian Generic Pharmaceutical Association (CGPA) / L'Association canadienne du médicament générique (ACMG)
#409, 4120 Yonge St., Toronto ON M2P 2B8 Canada
Tel: 416-223-2333; *Fax:* 416-223-2425
info@canadiangenerics.ca
www.canadiangenerics.ca
To promote an environment which supports & enhances the provision of affordable generic & innovative medications to Canadians & patients around the world through research, development & manufacturing of pharmaceuticals & fine chemicals in Canada

Canadian Pharmacists Association (CPhA) / Association des pharmaciens du Canada
1785 Alta Vista Dr., Ottawa ON K1G 3Y6
Tel: 613-523-7877; *Fax:* 613-523-0445
Toll-Free: 800-917-9489
info@pharmacists.ca; members@pharmacists.ca
www.pharmacists.ca
Social Media: www.twitter.com/CPhAAPhC
To advance the profession of pharmacy to contribute to the health of Canadians; To represent & support pharmacists across Canada

Canadian Society of Hospital Pharmacists (CSHP) / Société canadienne des pharmaciens d'hôpitaux
#3, 30 Concourse Gate, Ottawa ON K2E 7V7
Tel: 613-736-9733; *Fax:* 613-736-5660
info@cshp.ca
www.cshp.ca
To advance safe, effective medication use & patient care in hospitals & related health care settings throughout Canada; To act as an influential voice for hospital pharmacy; To encourge professional growth & practice excellence

College of Pharmacists of British Columbia
#200, 1765 - 8 Ave. West, Vancouver BC V6J 5C6 Canada
Tel: 604-733-2440; *Fax:* 604-733-2493
Toll-Free: 800-663-1940
info@bcpharmacist.org
www.bcpharmacists.org
Safe & effective pharmacy practice outcomes for the people of British Columbia.

Council for Continuing Pharmaceutical Education (CCPE) / Conseil de formation pharmaceutique continue (CFPC)
3489, rue Ashby, Saint-Laurent QC H4R 2K3 Canada
Tel: 514-333-8362; *Fax:* 514-333-1119
Toll-Free: 888-333-8362
info@ccpe-cfpc.com
www.ccpe-cfpc.com
To provide educational programs to establish improved professional standards within the Canadian pharmaceutical

industry; to better meet the needs & expectations of our internal & external stakeholders in the healthcare industry

Manitoba Pharmaceutical Association
200 Tache Ave., Winnipeg MB R2H 1A7 Canada
Tel: 204-233-1411; *Fax:* 204-237-3468
info@mpha.mb.ca
napra.ca/pages/manitoba
The Association administers the Manitoba Pharmaceutical Act. It gives license to & monitors pharmacists in the province, setingt standards of practice & investigating complaints.

Manitoba Society of Pharmacists Inc. (MSP)
#202, 90 Garry St., Winnipeg MB R3C 4H1 Canada
Tel: 204-956-6680; *Fax:* 204-956-6686
Toll-Free: 800-677-7170
info@msp.mb.ca
www.msp.mb.ca
To act as the voice of pharmacists in Manitoba on economic & professional issuess

National Association of Pharmacy Regulatory Authorities (NAPRA) / Association nationale des organismes de réglementation de la pharmacie
#750, 220 Laurier Ave. West, Ottawa ON K1P 5Z9 Canada
Tel: 613-569-9658; *Fax:* 613-569-9659
info@napra.ca
www.napra.ca
To facilitate the activities of provincial pharmacy regulatory authorities in their service of public interest
Carole Bouchard, Executive Director

NDMAC, Advancing Canadian Self-Care
#406, 1111 Prince of Wales Dr., Ottawa ON K2C 3T2 Canada
Tel: 613-723-0777; *Fax:* 613-723-0779
ndmac@ndmac.ca
www.ndmac.ca
To contribute to quality of life & cost-effective health care for Canadians by creating & maintaining an environment for the growth of responsible self-medication.

New Brunswick Pharmaceutical Society (NBPhS) / Ordre des pharmaciens du N.-B.
#8, 1224 Mountain Rd., Moncton NB E1C 2T6 Canada
Tel: 506-857-8957; *Fax:* 506-857-8838
Toll-Free: 800-463-4434
info@nbpharmacists.ca
www.nbpharmacists.ca
To protect the public by regulating the profession of pharmacy in New Brunswick.

New Brunswick Pharmacists' Association (NBPA) / Association des pharmaciens du Nouveau-Brunswick (APNB)
#410, 212 Queen St., Fredericton NB E3B 1A8
Tel: 506-459-6008; *Fax:* 506-453-0736
Toll-Free: 888-358-2345
nbpa@nbnet.nb.ca; newsroom@nbpharma.ca
www.nbpharma.ca
To advance the profession of pharmacy in New Brunswick; To represent the interests of members & the profession of pharmacy
Paul Blanchard, Executive Director

Nova Scotia College of Pharmacists (NSCP)
1464 Dresden Row, Halifax NS B3J 3T5 Canada
Tel: 902-422-8528; *Fax:* 902-422-0885
info@nspharmacists.ca
www.nspharmacists.ca
To govern the practice of pharmacy in Nova Scotia to benefit the health & well being of the public

Ontario College of Pharmacists (OCP)
483 Huron St., Toronto ON M5R 2R4
Tel: 416-962-4861; *Fax:* 416-847-8200
Toll-Free: 800-220-1921
ocpclientservices@ocpinfo.com
www.ocpinfo.com
To administer the Regulated Health Professions Act; To regulate the practice of pharmacy, in accordance with standards of practice; To ensure that members provide quality pharmaceutical service & care to the public

Ontario Pharmacists' Association (OPA)
#800, 375 University Ave., Toronto ON M5G 2J5
Tel: 416-441-0788; *Fax:* 416-441-0791
mail@opatoday.com
www.opatoday.com
To promote excellence in the practice of pharmacy & the wellness of patients; To act as the voice of pharmacists throughout Ontario

Ordre des pharmaciens du Québec (OPQ)
#301, 266, rue Notre Dame ouest, Montréal QC H2Y 1T6 Canada
Tél: 514-284-9588; *Téléc:* 514-284-3420
Ligne sans frais: 800-363-0324
ordrepharm@opq.org
www.opq.org
Protection du public en matières de services pharmaceutiques.

Pharmacy Association of Nova Scotia (PANS)
#225, 170 Cromarty Dr., Dartmouth NS B3B 0G1
Tel: 902-422-9583; *Fax:* 902-422-2619
pans@pans.ns.ca
www.pans.ns.ca
To advance the professional, academic, & commercial aspects of pharmacy & pharmacists throughout Nova Scotia; To represent the interests of Nova Scotia's pharmacists; To improve public health in Nova Scotia

The Pharmacy Examining Board of Canada (PEBC) / Le Bureau des examinateurs en pharmacie du Canada (BEPC)
717 Chursh St., Toronto ON M4W 2M4 Canada
Tel: 416-979-2431; *Fax:* 416-599-9244
pebcinfo@pebc.ca
www.pebc.ca
To establish qualifications for pharmacists; to provide for examinations of those qualifications

Prince Edward Island Pharmacy Board
PO Box 89, Trans Canada Hwy., Crapaud PE C0A 1J0 Canada
Tel: 902-658-2780; *Fax:* 902-658-2198
peipharm@pei.aibn.com
To prescribe qualifications, grant authorization & monitor adherence to established standards, so as to promote high standards & safeguard the public with regard to pharmaceutical service

Saskatchewan College of Pharmacists (SCP)
#700, 4010 Pasqua St., Regina SK S4S 7B9
Tel: 306-584-2292; *Fax:* 306-584-9695
info@saskpharm.ca
www.napra.ca/pages/Saskatchewan
To regulate pharmacists, pharmacies, & drugs in Saskatchewan; To register pharmacists who meet the education & training qualifications specified in "The Pharmacy Act, 1996"; To issue permits to operate pharmacies

Photography

Alberta Professional Photographers Association (APPA)
9404 - 129A Ave., Edmonton AB T5E 0N7 Canada
Tel: 780-483-4275; *Fax:* 780-472-7720
es@ppoc-alberta.ca
www.ppoc-alberta.ca
The organization has been formed to establish a strong national identity for all those involved in the photographic industry and includes provincial factions which abide by a specific code of ethics.

Canadian Association for Photographic Art (CAPA) / L'Association canadienne d'art photographique
PO Box 357, Logan Lake BC V0K 1W0 Canada
Tel: 604-824-9490; *Fax:* 604-824-9496
capa@capacanada.ca
www.capacanada.ca
To promote the advancement of photography as an art form in Canada

Canadian Association of Photographers & Illustrators in Communications (CAPIC) / Association canadienne de photographes et illustrateurs de publicité
Case Goods Bldg. 74, #302, 55 Mill St., Toronto ON M5A 3C4 Canada
Tel: 416-462-3677; *Fax:* 416-462-9570
Toll-Free: 888-252-2742
info@capic.org; administrator@capic.org
www.capic.org
Social Media: www.facebook.com/group.php?gid=33315648062
To safeguard & promote the rights of photographers, illustrators, & digital artists who work in the Canadian communications industry

Canadian Imaging Trade Association (CITA) / Association canadienne de l'industrie de l'imagerie
PO Box 71058, 570 Mulock Dr., Newmarket ON L3X 1Y8 Canada
Tel: 416-226-2750; *Fax:* 416-226-3347
cita2@sympatico.ca
www.citacanada.ca
To promote traditional & emerging imaging technologies (manufacturers/importers & distributors of photographic & electronic imaging equipment & sensitized materials)

Corporation des maîtres photographes du Québec inc. (CMPQ) / Québec Corporation of Master Photographers Inc.
358, rue Brock, Drummondville QC J2B 1C8 Canada
Tél: 514-990-7313; *Téléc:* 819-663-7850
information@cmpq.qc.ca
www.cmpq.qc.ca
La Corporation des Maîtres Photographes du Québec inc. est un organisme sans but lucratif qui s'est donné comme objectif l'avancement de la photographieprofessionnelle tout en assurant aux consommateurs la protection et un haut niveau de qualité.

Paved Arts New Media Inc.
424 - 20th St. West, Saskatoon SK S7M 0X4 Canada
Tel: 306-652-5502
www.pavedarts.ca
To develop photography & photo-based art

Photo Marketing Association International - Canada (PMAI)
PO Box 81191, Ancaster ON L9G 4X2 Canada
Tel: 905-304-8800; *Fax:* 905-304-7700
Toll-Free: 800-461-4350
bmoggach@pmai.org
www.pmai.org/content.aspx?id=110
To disseminate timely information while providing market research & business improvement products & services that contribute to increased profitability & business growth for its membership

Photographic Historical Society of Canada (PHSC)
PO Box 239, 6021 Yonge St., Toronto ON M2M 3W2 Canada
Tel: 416-691-1555; *Fax:* 416-693-0018
info@phsc.ca
www.phsc.ca
To facilitate the sharing of photographic knowledge & to help research & preserve Canada's photographic heritage

Professional Photographers Association of British Columbia (PPABC)
PO Box 1329, Aldergrove BC V4W 2V1 Canada
Tel: 604-857-1569; *Fax:* 604-857-1570
Toll-Free: 877-857-1569
sandyg@uniserve.com
www.ppabc.com
To promote & foster the personal ethics & professional development of the working photographer &/or specialist through education, fellowship & public awareness

Professional Photographers Association of Canada - Atlantic / Atlantique (PPAC Atlantic)
136 Russell Lake Dr., Dartmouth NS B2W 6J5 Canada
Tel: 902-462-1502; *Fax:* 902-468-7818
beth@tenwoldephoto.com
www.mppaphoto.com
To uphold the association's code of ethics
Sib Pye, CPA, President
Peter Tenwolde, Treasurer
Beth Tenwolde, Executive Secretary

Professional Photographers of Canada 1970 Incorporated (PPOC) / Photographes Professionnels du Canada
209 Light St., Woodstock ON N4S 6H6
Tel: 519-537-2555; *Fax:* 519-537-5573
Toll-Free: 888-643-7762
www.ppoc.ca
To promote excellence in professional imaging; To elevate professional standards & ethics; To act as a voice for the photographic profession on legal matters & legislative issues

Professional Photographers of Ontario Inc. (PPO)
209 Light St., Woodstock ON N4S 6H6 Canada
Tel: 519-537-2555; *Fax:* 519-537-5573
Toll-Free: 888-643-7762
info@ppontario.com
www.ppontario.com
To provide an educational, business & creative environment for professional photographers & with the purpose of promoting the highest standard of personal & creative excellence within the craft

Saskatchewan Professional Photographers Association Inc.
2057 Athol St., Regina SK S4T 3E6 Canada
Tel: 306-757-1470; *Toll-Free:* 888-643-7762
admin@sppa.org
www.sppa.org
To advance professional photography through educational seminars, fellowship & competitions

Planning & Development

Alberta Association, Canadian Institute of Planners (AACIP)
PO Box 596, Edmonton AB T5J 2K8 Canada
Tel: 780-435-8716; *Fax:* 780-452-7718
Toll-Free: 888-286-8716
aacip@aacip.com
www.aacip.com
To expand the depth & enhance the credibility of the association; To promote professional growth of practicing planners throughout Alberta, the Northwest Territories, & Nunavut; To maximize membership potential; To provide an effective level of service to the membership

Association of Professional Community Planners of Saskatchewan
3803 Lakeview Ave., Regina SK S4S 1H3 Canada
president@apcps.ca
www.apcps.ca
To promote & maintain professionalism in planning field

Atlantic Planners Institute (API) / Institut des Urbanistes de l'atlantique (IVA)
57 Parkside Dr., Charlottetown PE C1E 1N1 Canada
Tel: 902-892-3684; *Toll-Free:* 800-207-2138
krlewis@pei.eastlink.ca
www.atlanticplanners.org
Represents professional planners in New Brunswick, Prince Edward Island, Nova Scotia, Newfoundland & Labrador. They provide the processing of membership applications, maintenance of the membership roster, production of a regularly-scheduled newsletter, funding guarantess for the annual conference organizing committee.

Canadian Association of Certified Planning Technicians (CACPT)
PO Box 3844, Stn. C, Hamilton ON L8H 7R6 Canada
Tel: 905-578-4681; *Fax:* 905-578-9581
director@cacpt.org
www.cacpt.org
To maintain high standards for Planning Technicians & other related planning professionals
Diane LeBreton, CPT, BES, Executive Director
Julie Owens, President
Norman Pearson, PhD, CPT, MCIP, Registrar

Canadian Institute of Planners (CIP) / Institut canadien des urbanistes (ICU)
#1112, 141 Laurier Ave. West, Ottawa ON K1P 5J3 Canada
Tel: 613-237-7526; *Fax:* 613-237-7045
Toll-Free: 800-207-2138
general@cip-icu.ca
www.cip-icu.ca
To advance professional planning excellence, through the delivery of membership & public services in Canada & abroad

Intergovernmental Committee on Urban & Regional Research (ICURR) / Comité intergouvernemental de recherches urbaines et régionales (CIRUR)
#206, 40 Wynford Dr., Toronto ON M3C 1J5 Canada
Tel: 416-973-5629; *Fax:* 416-973-1375
www.muniscope.ca
ICURR supports local and regional governments, as well as private and non-profit companies through subsidized information and networking services. Muniscope is Canada's national resource on municipal issues, with subscription-based research and library services available on economic development, finance and taxation, housing and infrastructure, transportation, planning, and sustainability.

Manitoba Professional Planners Institute (MPPI)
137 Bannatyne Ave., 2nd Fl., Winnipeg MB R3B 0R3 Canada
Tel: 204-943-3637; *Fax:* 204-925-4624
mjohnson@mts.net
www.mppi.mb.ca
MPPI is responsible for handling membership applications and services, and for the enforcement of the Code of Professional Conduct. MPPI, along with the Association of Community Planners of Saskatchewan, jointly publishes the membership newsletter SCENARIO and sponsors workshops and seminars for the purpose of informing the membership of relevant developments and issues in the planning field.

Ontario Professional Planners Institute (OPPI) / Institut des planificateurs professionnels de l'Ontario
#201, 234 Eglinton Ave. East, Toronto ON M4P 1K5
Tel: 416-483-1873; *Fax:* 416-483-7830
Toll-Free: 800-668-1448
info@ontarioplanners.on.ca
www.ontarioplanners.on.ca
To act as the voice of Ontario's planning profession; To provide leadership on policies related to planning & development

Ordre des urbanistes du Québec (OUQ)
#410, 85, rue St-Paul ouest, Montréal QC H2Y 3V4 Canada
Tél: 514-849-1177; *Téléc:* 514-849-7176
info@ouq.qc.ca
www.ouq.qc.ca
Assurer la protection du public dans l'exercice de la profession par ses membres et la promotion de la pratique de l'urbanisme au Québec

Planning Institute of British Columbia (PIBC)
#110, 355 Burrard St., Vancouver BC V6C 2G8 Canada
Tel: 604-696-5031; *Fax:* 604-696-5032
Toll-Free: 866-696-5031
info@pibc.bc.ca
www.pibc.bc.ca
To promote orderly use of land, buildings & natural resources; to maintain high standard of professional competence; to protect rights & interests of those engaged in planning profession

Urban Development Institute of Canada (UDI) / Institut de développement urbain du Canada
200-602 West Hastings St., Vancouver BC V6B 1P2 Canada
Tel: 604-669-9585; *Fax:* 604-689-8691
info@udi.org
www.udi.bc.ca
To promote wise, efficient & productive urban growth; to be an effective voice of the land development & property management industry at all levels of government; to serve as a forum for the exchange of knowledge, experience & research on land use planning & development
Maureen Enser, Executive Director
Jeff Fisher, Deputy Executive Director

Police

Ontario Association of Chiefs of Police (OACP)
#605, 40 College St., Toronto ON M5G 2J3 Canada
Tel: 416-926-0424; *Fax:* 416-926-0436
Toll-Free: 800-816-1767
oacpadmin@oacp.ca
www.oacp.on.ca
The Association coordinates police training & education. It advocates on behalf of its membership, expressing concerns & priorities to the government, public & to any other bodies.

Politics

Alberta Greens
PO Box 61251, Stn. Brentwood, Calgary AB T2L 2K6 Canada
Tel: 403-282-4788; *Fax:* 403-289-6658
secretary@albertagreens.ca
albertagreens.ca
To encourage the development of an attitude that everyone is part of the land; to encourage strict control of all forms of pollution; to promote programs teaching consensus & facilitation; to facilitate the process of all interested community members becoming involved in education, both learning & teaching, guided by the long-term sustainability of the Earth community; to create the opportunity for Albertans to become involved in the strategic planning process

Alberta Liberal Party
10247 - 124 St., Edmonton AB T5N 1P8 Canada
Tel: 780-414-1124; *Fax:* 780-414-1125
Toll-Free: 800-661-9201
office@albertaliberal.com
www.albertaliberal.com
To elect Liberals to the Legislative Assembly of Alberta; to enunciate & promote liberal principles & policies; to initiate & maintain effective electoral constituencies

Bloc québécois (BQ)
3750, boul Crémazie est, 4e étage, Montréal QC H2A 1B4 Canada
Tél: 514-526-3000; *Téléc:* 514-526-2868
www.blocquebecois.org
Gilles Duceppe, Chef

Canadian Political Science Association (CPSA) / Association canadienne de science politique (ACSP)
#204, 260 Dalhousie St., Ottawa ON K1N 7E4 Canada
Tel: 613-562-1202; *Fax:* 613-241-0019
cpsa@csse.ca
www.cpsa-acsp.ca
CPSA encourages & develops political science & its relationship with other disciplines.

Christian Heritage Party of Canada (CHP) / Parti de l'héritage du Canada
PO Box 4958, Stn. E, Ottawa ON K1S 5J1 Canada
Tel: 819-281-6686; *Fax:* 819-281-7174
Toll-Free: 888-868-3247
nationaloffice@chp.ca
www.chp.ca
To provide true Christian leadership & uphold biblical principles in federal legislation; to attain the leadership of the federal government of Canada through the existing democratic process
Jim Hnatiuk, National Leader
Tom Kroesbergen, Interim President

Communist Party of Canada (CPC) / Parti Communiste du Canada
Central Committee, 290A Danforth Ave., Toronto ON M4K 1N6 Canada
Tel: 416-469-2446; *Fax:* 416-469-4063
info@cpc-pcc.ca
www.communist-party.ca
The Party aims to establish a socialist society in Canada, in which the principal means of producing & distributing wealth will be the common property of society as a whole.
Miguel Figueroa, Party Leader

Communist Party of Canada (Marxist-Leninist) (CPC(ML)) / Parti communiste du Canada (marxiste-léniniste)
National Headquarters, 1876, rue Amherst, Montréal QC H2L 3L7 Canada
Tel: 514-522-1373; *Fax:* 514-522-1373
Toll-Free: 800-263-4203
office@cpcml.ca
www.cpcml.ca
The Party holds that the attainment of communism will bring the complete emancipation of the working class. It holds that all people have claims on the society by virtue of being human and that this is the overriding principle of society, along with gender equality and freedom of conscience & lifestyle.
Anna Di Carlo, Party Leader
Hélène Héroux, Chief Agent

Conservative Party of Canada / Parti conservateur du Canada
#1204, 130 Albert St., Ottawa ON K1P 5G4 Canada
Tel: 613-755-2000; *Fax:* 613-755-2001
Toll-Free: 866-808-8407
www.conservative.ca
Social Media: www.facebook.com/pmharper; www.twitter.com/PMHarper
The Conservative Party provided Canadians with an alternative to the Liberal government. It developed innovative and practical new policy ideas such as the Federal Accountability Act, the Public Transit Tax Credit and the Apprenticeship Incentive Grant- ideas Conservatives would later implement in government.
Stephen Harper, PC, MP, Leader

Green Party of British Columbia (GPBC)
Dominion Bldg., PO Box 2827, Stn. Terminal, #610, 207 West Hastings St., Vancouver BC V6B 3X2 Canada
Tel: 604-687-1199; *Fax:* 604-909-4722
Toll-Free: 888-473-3686
info@greenparty.bc.ca
www.greenparty.bc.ca
To form healthy communities with diverse economies by involving the citizens of British Columbia in the political process; To offer voters in British Columbia fiscal responsibility, socially progressive policies, & environmental sustainability

Green Party of Canada (GPC) / Parti vert du Canada
PO Box 997, Stn. B, #204, 396 Cooper St., Ottawa ON K1P 5R1 Canada
Tel: 613-562-4916; *Fax:* 613-482-4632
Toll-Free: 888-868-3447
info@greenparty.ca
www.greenparty.ca
Social Media: www.twitter.com/canadiangreens
To promote a platform that includes debt reduction, eco-jobs, saving Canada's forests, supporting small business, use of soft energies, sovereignty for First Nations, & a guarantee of full rights for women

The Green Party of Manitoba
PO Box 26023, Stn. Maryland, Winnipeg MB R3C 3R3 Canada
Tel: 204-488-2831; *Fax:* 204-992-2712
Toll-Free: 866-742-4292
info@greenparty.mb.ca
www.greenparty.mb.ca

James Beddome, President

Green Party of New Brunswick
PO Box 3723, Stn. B, Fredericton NB E3A 5L8 Canada
Tel: 506-447-8499; *Fax:* 506-447-8489
Toll-Free: 888-662-8683
info@greenpartynb.ca
www.greenpartynb.ca

Jack MacDougall, Leader

The Green Party of Ontario (GPO) / Parti Vert d'Ontario
PO Box 1132, Stn. F, Toronto ON M4Y 2T8 Canada
Tel: 416-977-7476; *Fax:* 416-977-5476
Toll-Free: 888-647-3366
admin@gpo.ca
www.gpo.ca

International Political Science Association (IPSA) / Association internationale de science politique (AISP)
#331, 1590, av Docteur-Penfield, Montréal QC H3G 1C5 Canada
Tel: 514-848-8717; *Fax:* 514-848-4095
info@ipsa.ca
www.ipsa.ca

To promote the advancement of political science through the collaboration of scholars in different parts of the world; IPSA has consultative status with the Economic & Social Council of the United Nations & with UNESCO
Guy Lachapelle, Secretary General
Mathieu St-Laurent, Coordinator, Membership & External Relations

The Liberal Party of Canada (LPC) / Le Parti Libéral du Canada (PLC)
#400, 81 Metcalfe St., Ottawa ON K1P 6M8 Canada
Tel: 613-237-0740; *Fax:* 613-235-7208
info@liberal.ca
www.liberal.ca
Social Media: www.facebook.com/LiberalCA; www.twitter.com/Liberal_party

To seek a common ground of understanding among the people of the provinces & territories of Canada; to advocate liberal philosophies, principles & policies; to promote the election of candidates of the Liberal Party to the Parliament of Canada

The Liberal Party of Canada (British Columbia) (LPC(BC)) / Parti libéral du Canada (Colombie-Britannique)
#460, 580 Hornby St., Vancouver BC V6C 3B6 Canada
Tel: 604-664-3777; *Fax:* 604-874-8966
Toll-Free: 888-411-6511
info@lpcbc.com
www.lpcbc.com; www.teambc.ca

Diane Rabbani, Executive Director

The Liberal Party of Canada (Manitoba) / Parti libéral au Manitoba
635 Broadway, Winnipeg MB R3C 0X1 Canada
Tel: 204-988-9540; *Fax:* 204-988-9549
lpcmb@liberalpartyofcanada-mb.ca
www.liberalpartyofcanada-mb.ca

Liberal Party of Canada (Ontario) (LPC(O)) / Parti libéral du Canada (Ontario)
#205, 10 St. Mary St., Toronto ON M4Y 1P9 Canada
Tel: 416-921-2844; *Fax:* 416-921-3880
Toll-Free: 800-361-3881
admin@lpco.ca
www.lpco.ca

The Liberal Party of Canada (Ontario) represents the Federal Liberal Party and its 106 Electoral District Associations in Ontario. LPC(O) works with the thousands of members and volunteers in Ontario to ensure that it is a healthy and vibrant political organization.

The Liberal Party of Canada in Alberta (LPC(A))
Guardian Bldg., #50, 10240 - 124 St. NW, Edmonton AB T5N 3W6 Canada
Tel: 780-424-1984; *Fax:* 780-424-1966
Toll-Free: 800-879-8294
office@liberalalberta.ca
www.liberalalberta.ca

Carole Halko, Administrator

Liberal Party of Newfoundland & Labrador / Parti libéral de Terre-Neuve et du Labrador
Beothuk Bldg., #205, 20 Crosbie Place, St. John's NL A1B 3Y8 Canada
Tel: 709-754-1813; *Fax:* 709-754-0820
Toll-Free: 866-726-7116
libcan@nf.aibn.com
www.nlliberals.ca.perfectdaycanada.com
Social Media: www.twitter.com/nlliberals

The Liberal Party in Newfoundland and Labrador has been the dominant political party since confederation in 1949 and are responsible for many of the major social transformations that has occurred in this province in the last half century. Those developments, which include Memorial University, countless new schools across the province and an greatly improved standard of living, have made the Liberal Party the voice of social development in Newfoundland and Labrador.

Liberal Party of Nova Scotia
PO Box 723, #304, 1660 Hollis St., Halifax NS B3J 2T3 Canada
Tel: 902-429-1993; *Fax:* 902-423-1624
TDD: 902-429-1772
office@liberal.ns.ca
www.liberal.ns.ca
Social Media: www.twitter.com/StephenMcNeil

Stephen McNeil, Leader
Derek M. Wells, President

Liberal Party of Prince Edward Island / Parti libéral de l'Ile du Prince Édouard
PO Box 2559, #205, 129 Kent St., Charlottetown PE C1A 8C2 Canada
Tel: 902-368-3449; *Fax:* 902-368-3687
Toll-Free: 877-740-3449
office@liberal.pe.ca
www.liberal.pe.ca
Social Media: www.facebook.com/group.php?gid=38261891616

Representing the Liberal Party of PEI.

The Libertarian Party of Canada
2938E More Cres., Regina SK S4V 0T7 Canada
Tel: 416-443-5423
info@libertarian.ca
www.libertarian.ca

New Brunswick Liberal Association
715 Brunswick St., Fredericton NB E3B 1H8 Canada
Tel: 506-453-3950; *Fax:* 506-453-2476
Toll-Free: 800-453-2476
info@liberal.ca
www.nbliberal.ca

New Democratic Party (NDP) / Nouveau Parti Démocratique
Federal Office, #300, 279 Laurier West, Ottawa ON K1P 5J9 Canada
Tel: 613-236-3613; *Fax:* 613-230-9950
Toll-Free: 866-525-2555
TDD: 866-776-7742
jack@fed.ndp.ca
www.ndp.ca
Social Media: www.facebook.com/JackLayton; twitter.com/jacklayton

Offers Canadians an alternative political vision based on the principles of democratic socialism; as the political movement that initiated Medicare, the Old Age Pension & other vital programs for people, we seek to protect & expand these programs which we believe can be accomplished through prudent & effective government & through a truly fair tax system; NDP is affiliated with the Socialist International, a world wide association of social democratic & labour parties that seek social justice & world peace & that reject all forms of totalitarian rule

Nunavut Liberal Party
PO Box 1059, Iqaluit NU X0A 0H0 Canada
Tel: 867-979-1488; *Fax:* 867-979-1478

Representing the Liberal Party in Nunavut.
Alain Carrière, Riding President
Willie Adams, Provinvial Senator (Nunavut)

Parti communiste du Québec
CP 482, Succ. Place d'Armes, Montréal QC H2Y 3H3 Canada
Tél: 514-528-6142
info@pcq.qc.ca
www.pcq.qc.ca

Unifier avec la classe ouvrière et les couches populaires pour que s'installe le pouvoir populaire dans le but de construire le socialisme

Parti libéral du Québec (PLQ) / Québec Liberal Party (QLP)
7240, rue Waverly, Montréal QC H2R 2Y8 Canada
Tél: 514-288-4364; *Téléc:* 514-288-4364
Ligne sans frais: 800-361-1047
reception@lpcq.ca
www.plq.org

Jean Charest, Chef du Parti
Marc Tanguay, Président

Parti québécois (PQ)
#150, 1200 ave. Papineau, Montréal QC H2K 4R5 Canada
Tél: 514-526-0020; *Téléc:* 514-526-0272
Ligne sans frais: 800-363-9531
info@pq.org
www.pq.org
Média social: www.facebook.com/group.php?gid=9067252699

Réaliser démocratiquement la souveraineté du Québec pour s'épanouir comme peuple francophone, pour ne plus être minoritaire, pour mettre fin au gaspillage, pour se doter d'une politique économique qui répond aux intérêts du Québec; donner au Québec une place dans le monde

Parti Vert du Québec (PVQ) / Green Party of Québec
#220, 10000 rue Lajeunesse, Montréal QC H3L 2E1 Canada
Tél: 514-303-7750; *Ligne sans frais:* 888-998-8378
info@partivertquebec.org
www.partivertquebec.org

Guy Rainville, Chef

Saskatchewan Liberal Association / Association libérale de la Saskatchewan
845A McDonald St., Regina SK S4N 2X5 Canada
Tel: 306-522-8507; *Fax:* 306-569-9271
contact@saskliberals.ca
www.saskliberal.ca
Social Media: www.facebook.com/group.php?gid=2399956913

Socialist Party of Canada (SPC) / Parti Socialiste du Canada
PO Box 4280, Victoria BC V8X 3X8 Canada
spc@iname.com
www.worldsocialism.org/canada/

To promote the establishment of socialism - a system of society based upon the common ownership & democratic control of the means & instruments for producing & distributing wealth by & in the interest of society as a whole
John Ayers, Contact

Western Arctic Liberal Party
PO Box 965, Yellowknife NT XIA 2N7 Canada
Tel: 867-445-2377; *Fax:* 867-766-4915
lroeland@iandd.ca

Lana Roeland, President

Yukon Liberal Party
PO Box 183, #108 Elliot St., Whitehorse YT Y1A 2C6 Canada
Tel: 867-667-4748; *Fax:* 867-667-4720
info@ylp.ca
www.ylp.ca

Poultry & Eggs

Alberta Egg Producers' Board (AEPB)
#101, 90 Freeport Blvd. NE, Calgary AB T3J 5J9 Canada
Tel: 403-250-1197; *Fax:* 403-291-9216
Toll-Free: 877-302-2344
info@eggs.ab.ca
www.eggs.ab.ca

To be the best producers & marketers of eggs

Atlantic Provinces Hatchery Federation
PO Box 550, Truro NS B2N 5E3 Canada
Tel: 902-893-6532; *Fax:* 902-893-6035
aoderkirk@gov.ns.ca

British Columbia Broiler Hatching Egg Producers' Association (BCBHEC)
#180, 32160 South Fraser Way, Abbotsford BC V2T 1W5 Canada
Tel: 604-850-1854; *Fax:* 604-850-1683
info@bcbhec.com
www.bcbhec.com

The Association has the following responsibilities: to establish a better understanding & appreciation with the public & other interested parties regarding the industry; to stimulate & encourage improvements related to sales & scientific development in the field; to promote the exchange of ideas in an effort to find solutions to problems in the broiler hatching egg industry; to encourage economical plans to assists producers; & to provide better contact with hatcheries, feed suppliers, processors, & broiler growers.

Canadian Broiler Hatching Egg Marketing Agency (CBHEMA) / Office canadien de commercialisation des oeufs d'incubation de poulet à chair (OCCOIPC)
#1101, 75 Albert St., Ottawa ON K1P 5E7 Canada
Tel: 613-232-3023; *Fax:* 613-232-5241
info@chep-poic.ca
www.chep-poic.ca
To ensure that our members produce enough hatching eggs to meet the needs of the broiler industry
Gyslain Loyer, Chair
Errol Halkai, General Manager

Canadian Turkey Marketing Agency (CTMA) / Office canadien de commercialisation du dindon
Bldg. One, #202, 7145 West Credit Ave., Mississauga ON L5N 6J7 Canada
Tel: 905-812-3140; *Fax:* 905-812-9326
ctma@canadianturkey.ca
www.canadianturkey.ca
To develop & strengthen the Canadian Turkey market through an effective supply management systems that stimulates growth & profitability for stakeholders
Philip J. Boyd, Executive Director

Chicken Farmers of Canada (CFC) / Les Producteurs de poulet du Canada
#1007, 350 Sparks St., Ottawa ON K1R 7S8 Canada
Tel: 613-241-2800; *Fax:* 613-241-5999
cfc@chicken.ca
www.chicken.ca
To build an evidence-based, consumer driven Canadian chicken industry that provides opportunities for profitable growth for all stakeholders
David Fuller, Chair

Éleveurs de volailles du Québec
#250, 555, boul Roland-Therrien, Longueuil QC J4H 4G1 Canada
Tél: 450-679-0530; *Téléc:* 450-679-5375
evq@upa.qc.ca
www.volaillesduquebec.qc.ca
A pour mission l'étude, la défense et le développement des intérêts économiques, sociaux et moraux de ses membres; favorise et stimule la mobilisation et la participation de ses membres tout en les consultant et en les informant; développe et renforce la mise en marché collective des poulets et des dindons produits au Québec, en mettant en place des services garantissant le fonctionnement optimal du plan conjoint et des autres outils de mise en marché
Martin Dufresne, Président

Fédération des producteurs d'oeufs de consommation du Québec (FPOCQ)
#320, 555, boul Roland-Therrien, Longueuil QC J4H 4E7 Canada
Tél: 450-679-0530; *Téléc:* 450-679-0855
info@oeuf.ca
www.oeuf.ca
Favoriser le développement durable de l'industrie québécoise des oeufs et ce par: le respect de l'environnement et le bien-être des animaux; en procurant un revenu équitable aux intervenants du secteur; en répondant aux attentes des consommateurs avec des oeufs et produits de haute qualité

Printing Industry & Graphic Arts

British Columbia Printing & Imaging Association (BCPIA)
PO Box 75218, Stn. WRPO, White Rock BC V4B 5L4 Canada
Tel: 604-542-0902; *Fax:* 604-538-8581
mknoch@bcpia.org
www.bcpia.org
To be the voice of the BC printing industry & its employees; to provide services & benefits which encourage fellowship, education, community involvement & high standards in business conduct.
Marilynn Knoch, Executive Director

Canadian Printing Industries Association (CPIA) / Association canadienne de l'imprimerie (ACI)
#1110, 151 Slater St., Ottawa ON K1P 5H3 Canada
Tel: 613-236-7208; *Fax:* 613-232-1334
info@cpia-aci.ca
www.cpia-aci.ca
To advance the quality of management in the printing & allied trades; to offer services through a network of local & related organizations including representations to various sectors; to enhance the image & profile of the industry

Canadian Printing Ink Manufacturers Association (CPIMA)
52 Palmer Rd., Grimsby L3M 5L4 Canada
Tel: 905-309-5883; *Fax:* 905-309-5838
cpima@sympatico.ca
www.cpima.org
To exchange information that will be of benefit to members, the ink industry, & the printing industry
Shiona Finlayson, President

New Brunswick Printing Industries Association (NBPIA) / Association des industries d'imprimerie du Nouveau-Brunswick (AIINB)
c/o Quebecor World Atlantic, PO Box 6250, Stn. A, Saint John NB E2L 4S3 Canada
Tel: 506-633-3600; *Fax:* 506-633-3607
laureen.douglas@quebecorworld.com
Jacques Bourgeois, President
Stuart Taylor, Sec.-Treas.

Ontario Printing & Imaging Association (OPIA)
#14, 2601 Matheson Blvd. East, Mississauga ON L4W 5A8
Tel: 905-602-4441; *Fax:* 905-602-9798
info@opia.on.ca
www.opia.on.ca
To provide leadership for a successful printing & imaging industry in Ontario
Mike McInnes, Chair
Kim Stewart, Vice-Chair
Tracey Preston, President
Ryan Anderson, Treasurer

Printing & Graphics Industries Association of Alberta (PGIA)
PO Box 61229, RPO Kensington, Calgary AB T2N 4S6 Canada
Tel: 403-281-1421; *Fax:* 403-225-1421
info@pgia.ca
www.pgia.ca
Committed to the advancement of a healthy, effective & ethical graphic arts industry by providing leadership in the development of imaged communications; by enabling members to work to strengthen the industry

Printing Equipment & Supply Dealers' Association of Canada (PESDA)
11 Alderbrook Place, Bolton ON L7E 1V3 Canada
Tel: 416-524-1954; *Fax:* 905-951-6374
bkirk@pesda.com
www.pesda.com
To promote & advance the interests of the printing equipment, consumables & related services industries in Canada

Saskatchewan Graphic Arts Industries Association (SGAIA)
PO Box 7152, Saskatoon SK S7K 4J1
Tel: 306-373-3202; *Fax:* 306-373-3246
sgaia@sasktel.net
www.sgaia.org
To promote the interests of Saskatchewan's printing & allied industries; To increase the influence of graphic arts industry to the government & the general business community; To promote programs for the graphic arts industry at universities & technical institutions
Daryl Schaffer, President
Don Breher, Executive Director
Daryl Breckner, Secretary-Treasurer

Society of Graphic Designers of Canada (GDC) / Société des designers graphiques du Canada
Arts Court, 2 Daly Ave., Ottawa ON K1N 6E2 Canada
Tel: 613-567-5400; *Fax:* 613-564-4428
Toll-Free: 877-496-4453
info@gdc.net
www.gdc.net
Social Media: twitter.com/gdcntl
To maintain a defined, recognized & competent body of graphic designers; to promote high standards of graphic design for benefit of Canadian industry, commerce, public service & education

Prisoners & Ex-Offenders

Canadian Association of Elizabeth Fry Societies (CAEFS) / Association canadienne des sociétés Elizabeth Fry (ACSEF)
#701, 151 Slater St., Ottawa ON K1P 5H3 Canada
Tel: 613-238-2422; *Fax:* 613-232-7130
caefs@web.net
www.elizabethfry.ca
A federation of autonomous societies which work with & on behalf of women & girls involved with the justice system, in particular criminalized women; dedicated to offering services & programs to women in need, advocating for reforms & offering fora within which the public may be informed about & participate in all aspects of the justice system as it affects women

Canadian Coalition Against the Death Penalty (CCADP) / Coalition canadien contre la peine de mort
80 Lillington Ave., Toronto ON M1N 3K7 Canada
Tel: 416-693-9112; *Fax:* 416-693-9112
info@ccadp.org
www.ccadp.org
To provide information about abuses of the death penalty internationally; to ensure Canada does not return to the death penalty
Tracy Lamourie, Director & Founder
Dave Parkinson, Director & Founder

The John Howard Society of Canada / Société John Howard du Canada
809 Blackburn Mews, Kingston ON K7P 2N6 Canada
Tel: 613-384-6272; *Fax:* 613-384-1847
national@johnhoward.ca
www.johnhoward.ca
To promote effective, just, & humane responses to the causes & consequences of crime

Operation Springboard
#800, 2 Carlton St., Toronto ON M5B 1J3 Canada
Tel: 416-977-0089; *Fax:* 416-977-2840
tterranova@operationspringboard.on.ca
www.operationspringboard.on.ca
To design & provide services & programs that effectively reintegrate offenders into the community as responsible individuals; to develop crime prevention strategies; to promote community involvement in design & provision of services along with continuous effort to encourage understanding & support; to bring forward recommendations that will improve effectiveness of the criminal justice system.

Quakers Fostering Justice (QFJ)
PO Box 20057, Stn. RPO Mission Hills, Mission BC V2V 7P8 Canada
Tel: 604-832-0954
qfj@quaker.ca
To build caring community without need for prisons; to explore alternatives to prison based on economic, social justice & fulfillment of human needs; to foster awareness within & outside Quaker community of roots of crime & violence in society; to reach & support prisoners, guards, victims & families

St. Leonard's Society of Canada (SLSC) / Société St-Léonard du Canada
Bronson Centre, #208, 211 Bronson Ave., Ottawa ON K1R 6H5 Canada
Tel: 613-233-5170; *Fax:* 613-233-5122
Toll-Free: 888-560-9760
www.stleonards.ca
Committed to the prevention of crime through programs which promote responsible community living & safer communities

Seventh Step Society of Canada
PO Box 85040, Stn. Albert Park, Calgary AB T2A 7R7 Canada
Tel: 403-995-4029
seventh@7thstep.ca
www.7thstep.ca
Self-help organization dedicated to help adult & young offenders to become useful & productive members of society; to provide follow-up to those who wish to use organization as means to maintain freedom
Patrick Graham, Executive Director

Public Utilities

Canadian Association of Members of Public Utility Tribunals (CAMPUT) / Association canadienne des membres des tribunaux d'utilité publique
#646, 200 North Service Rd. West, Oakville ON L6M 2Y1 Canada
Tel: 905-827-5139; *Fax:* 905-827-3260
info@camput.org
www.camput.org
To improve public utility regulation in Canada

Canadian Public Works Association (CPWA) / Association Canadienne des Travaux Publics
#191, 253 College St., Toronto ON M5T 1R5 Canada
Tel: 202-408-9541; *Fax:* 202-408-9542
cpwa@cpwa.net
www.cpwa.net
Their mission statement is to be recognized as the "voice of public works" in Canada; to create a forum for public works professionals in Canada to exchange inforamation, develop ideas, and share skills, knowledge, and technologies on issues unique to Canada; to increase membership and participation.

Electricity Distributors Association (EDA)
#1100, 3700 Steeles Ave. West, Vaughan ON L4L 8K8 Canada
Tel: 905-265-5300; *Fax:* 905-265-5301
Toll-Free: 800-668-9979
email@eda-on.ca
www.eda-on.ca
To be the voice of Ontario's electricity distributors, the publicly & privately owned companies that deliver electricity to Ontario homes, businesses & public institutions. Focus is on advocacy & representation to government, analysis of legislation & market regulations, communication & networking among members & industry colleagues

Ontario Municipal Water Association (OMWA)
c/o Doug Parker, 43 Chelsea Cres., Belleville ON K8N 4Z5
Tel: 613-966-1100; *Fax:* 613-966-3024
Toll-Free: 888-231-1115
dparker@omwa.org
www.omwa.org
To act as the voice of municipal water supply in Ontario; To ensure the safety, quality, reliability, & sustainability of drinking water in Ontario

Utility Contractors' Association of Ontario Inc. (UCA)
#201, 1075 North Service Rd. West, Oakville ON L6M 2G2 Canada
Tel: 905-847-7305; *Fax:* 905-847-7824
info@pipeline.ca
www.uca.on.ca
Barry L. Brown, General Manager

Publishing

Alberta Weekly Newspapers Association (AWNA)
3228 Parsons Rd., Edmonton AB T6H 5R7
Tel: 780-434-8746; *Fax:* 780-438-8356
Toll-Free: 800-282-6903
info@awna.com; display@awna.com (ad material); releases@awna.com
www.awna.com
To assist members to publish high quality community newspapers; To serve advertisers by providing information about the markets of community newspapers in Alberta

Alcuin Society
PO Box 3216, Vancouver BC V6B 3X8 Canada
info@alcuinsociety.com
www.alcuinsociety.com
To sponsor educational programs; to publish journal; to offer awards & citations for excellence in book arts

Association des libraires du Québec (ALQ)
#580, 1001, boul de Maisonneuve est, Montréal QC H2L 4P9 Canada
Tél: 514-526-3349; *Téléc:* 514-526-3340
info@alq.qc.ca
www.alq.qc.ca
Regrouper, pour leur bénéfice mutuel, les libraires engagées dans la vente au détail au Québec et celles engagées dans la vente du livre en langue française au Canada; fournir des services, faire des études, fournir de l'information, tenir des réunions et des rencontres et contribuer à des programmes pour le bénéfice et l'amélioration de ses membres; encourager la vente au détail du livre au Québec; encourager la communication et la collaboration entre les éditeurs, les distributeurs et les autres participants de l'industrie du livre; aider les libraires à encourager la lecture; lutter contre toute forme de censure

Association nationale des éditeurs de livres (ANEL)
2514, boul Rosemont, Montréal QC H1Y 1K4 Canada
Tél: 514-273-8130; *Téléc:* 514-273-9657
Ligne sans frais: 866-900-2635
info@anel.qc.ca
www.anel.qc.ca
Soutenir le développement d'une industrie nationale de l'édition québécoise et canadienne de langue française; établir entre ses membres des rapports de bonne confraternitéétudier et défendre les intérêts tant généraux que politiques et économiques de ses membres; étudier toute question relative à la profession et diffuser l'information auprès de ses membres; constituer une représentation réelle et efficace de la profession à toute les instances pertinentes

Association of Book Publishers of British Columbia (ABPBC)
#600, 402 West Pender St., Vancouver BC V6B 1T6 Canada
Tel: 604-684-0228; *Fax:* 604-684-5788
e.admin@books.bc.ca
www.books.bc.ca
To encourage writing, publishing, distribution & promotion of books written by BC & Canadian authors; to cooperate with other associations & organizations to further the reading & studying of books; to work for the development & maintenance of strong competitive book publishing houses owned & controlled in BC & Canada; to further professional training for individuals engaged in book publishing

Association of Canadian Publishers (ACP) / Association des éditeurs canadiens
#306, 174 Spadina Ave., Toronto ON M5T 2C2 Canada
Tel: 416-487-6116; *Fax:* 416-487-8815
admin@canbook.org
www.publishers.ca
To encourage writing, publishing, distribution & promotion of books written by Canadian authors in particular, & reading & study of books in general; to represent the members at international book fairs; to facilitate the exchange of information & professional expertise among members

Association of Canadian University Presses (ACUP) / Association des presses universitaires canadiennes (APUC)
#700, 10 St. Mary St., Toronto ON M4Y 2W8 Canada
Tel: 416-978-2239; *Fax:* 416-978-4738
clarose@utpress.utoronto.ca
To support scholarly publishing by university presses in Canada.

Association of English Language Publishers of Québec (AELAQ) / Association des éditeurs de langue anglaise du Québec
#3, 1200, av Atwater, Montréal QC H3Z 1X4 Canada
Tel: 514-932-5633; *Fax:* 514-932-5456
info@aelaq.org
www.aelaq.org
To raise the profile of English-language books published in Québec

Association of Manitoba Book Publishers (AMBP)
#404, 100 Arthur St., Winnipeg MB R3B 1H3 Canada
Tel: 204-947-3335; *Fax:* 204-956-4689
ambp@mts.net
www.bookpublishers.mb.ca
To promote Manitoba publishing industry

Association québécoise des salons du livre (AQSL)
CP 353, #105, 110 rue de l'Évêche est, Rimouski QC G5L 7C3 Canada
Tél: 418-723-7456; *Téléc:* 418-725-4543
Ligne sans frais: 888-542-2075
info@aqsl.ca
www.aqsl.org
Association sans but lucratif, qui a pour mission la promotion du livre, du périodique et de la lecture; elle défend les intérêts des Salons membres et favorise la recherche, la documentation, les contacts professionnels, la création et la diffusion du livre

Atlantic Community Newspapers Association (ACNA)
#216, 7075 Bayers Rd., Halifax NS B3L 2C2
Tel: 902-832-4480; *Fax:* 902-832-4484
Toll-Free: 877-842-4480
info@acna.com
www.acna.com
To promote excellence, credibility, & the economic well-being of member community newspapers throughout Atlantic Canada

Atlantic Publishers Marketing Association (APMA)
1484 Carlton St., Halifax NS B3H 3B7 Canada
Tel: 902-420-0711; *Fax:* 902-423-4302
apma.admin@atlanticpublishers.ca
www.atlanticpublishers.ca
To promote the growth & development of Canadian-owned publishing houses based in Atlantic Canada

Book & Periodical Council (BPC)
#107, 192 Spadina Ave., Toronto ON M5T 2C2 Canada
Tel: 416-975-9366; *Fax:* 416-975-1839
info@thebpc.ca
www.bookandperiodicalcouncil.ca
To increase the level of awareness & the use of Canadian materials by the general public & in educational systems at all levels; to ensure the public has an adequate & representative range of Canadian books & periodicals in sales outlets, library systems & educational institutions; to strengthen book & periodical distribution systems; to support the development of new & existing Canadian-owned companies & encourage their growth & expansion; to improve market conditions & contractual arrangements as well as promotion & publicity given to Canadian writers & their work; to encourage the development of writing & publishing projects of social & cultural importance; to improve the cultural & economic climate in which the Canadian book & periodical industries exist; to discourage expansion of foreign ownership in all sectors of the book & periodical publishing industries

Book Promoters Association of Canada (BPAC)
PO Box 75115, Stn. Hudson Bay Postal Outlet, "The Wicket", 20 Bloor St. East, Toronto ON M4W 3T3
Tel: 905-430-5134
bookpromoters@gmail.com
bookpromotersassociationofcanada.blogspot.com
To enhance the professional skills of members; To foster professional attitudes & business practices within its membership; To raise the public & industry profile of book promotion as an integral part of the book publishing & selling process; To reward & encourage BPAC members & potential members, & those connected to the publishing industry, through the regular endowment of various awards

Book Publishers Association of Alberta (BPAA)
10523 - 100 Ave., Edmonton AB T5J 0A8 Canada
Tel: 780-424-5060; *Fax:* 780-424-7943
info@bookpublishers.ab.ca
www.bookpublishers.ab.ca
To work for maintenance & growth of strong book publishing houses owned & controlled in Alberta; to speak for common interests of constituent members; to liaise & cooperate with other associations for the good of the Canadian publishing industry

British Columbia & Yukon Community Newspapers Association (BCYCNA)
#122, 1020 Mainland St., Vancouver BC V6B 2T4 Canada
Tel: 604-669-9222; *Fax:* 604-684-4713
Toll-Free: 866-669-9222
info@bccommunitynews.com
www.bccommunitynews.com
To encourage excellence in the publishing of community newspapers

Canadian Book Manufacturers' Association (CBMA)
#906, 75 Albert St., Ottawa ON K1P 5E7 Canada
Tel: 613-236-7208; *Fax:* 613-236-8169
neilfitz@istar.ca
Jeff Wilkins, Chair

Canadian Bookbinders & Book Artists Guild (CBBAG) / Guilde canadienne des relieurs et des artisans du livre
#112, 60 Atlantic Ave., Toronto ON M6K 1X9 Canada
Tel: 416-581-1071; *Fax:* 416-581-1053
cbbag@cbbag.ca
www.cbbag.ca
Social Media: www.facebook.com/group.php?gid=77394956232
To create a spirit of community among hand workers in the book arts & those who love books; to promote greater awareness of the book arts; to increase educational opportunities, & foster excellence through exhibitions, workshops, lectures, & publications.

Canadian Booksellers Association (CBA)
#700, 789 Don Mills Rd., Toronto ON M3C 1T5 Canada
Tel: 416-467-7883; *Fax:* 416-467-7886
Toll-Free: 866-788-0790
enquiries@cbabook.org
www.cbabook.org
To promote a high standard of business methods & ethics among members; to define & expand the role of booksellers within the Canadian publishing process; to provide professional advice to prospective & practising booksellers
Susan Dayus, Executive Director
Paul McNally, President
Steve Budnarchuk, Vice-President
Tim Pearce, Treasurer

Canadian Children's Book Centre (CCBC)
#101, 40 Orchard View Blvd., Toronto ON M4R 1B9 Canada
Tel: 416-975-0010; *Fax:* 416-975-8970
info@bookcentre.ca
www.bookcentre.ca
Social Media: facebook.com/pages/the-canadian-childrens-book-centre/169843829712033

The Centre promotes the reading, writing, & illustrating of Canadian books for young readers, providing programs, publications & resources for teachers, librarians, authors, illustrators, publishers, booksellers & parents. It is a registered charity, BN: 124389164RR0001.

Canadian Circulations Audit Board Inc. (CCAB) / Office canadien de vérification de la diffusion
Div. of BPA International, #800, 1 Concorde Gate, Toronto ON M3C 3N6 Canada
Tel: 416-487-2418; *Fax:* 416-487-6405
www.bpaww.com
To issue standardized statements of data reported by a member; to verify the figures shown in these statements by auditors' examination of any & all records considered by the corporation to be necessary; to disseminate these data for the benefit of any individual or company requiring such information

Canadian Community Newspapers Association (CCNA)
#200, 890 Yonge St., Toronto ON M4W 3P4 Canada
Tel: 416-482-1090; *Fax:* 416-482-1908
Toll-Free: 877-305-2262
info@ccna.ca
www.communitynews.ca
The Canadian Community Newspapers Association (CCNA) is the national voice of the community press in Canada.

Canadian Newspaper Association (CNA) / Association canadienne des journaux (ACJ)
c/o Newspapers Canada, #200, 890 Yonge St., Toronto ON M4W 3P4
Tel: 416-923-3567; *Fax:* 416-923-7206
Toll-Free: 877-305-2262
info@newspaperscanada.ca; publisher@newspaperscanada.ca
www.newspaperscanada.ca
To ensure the continuance of a free press to serve readers effectively, by combining the experience, expertise, & dedication of members; To increase the profile & effectiveness of Canada's newspaper industry

The Canadian Press (CP) / La presse canadienne
36 King St. East, Toronto ON M5C 2L9 Canada
Tel: 416-364-0321; *Fax:* 416-364-0207
sales@thecanadianpress.com
www.thecanadianpress.com
Social Media: twitter.com/CdnPress_News
National news cooperative owned & financed by Canada's daily newspapers

Canadian Publishers' Council (CPC)
#203, 250 Merton St., Toronto ON M4S 1B1 Canada
Tel: 416-322-7011; *Fax:* 416-322-6999
bpellas@pubcouncil.ca
www.pubcouncil.ca
Canada's main English-language book publishing trade association, representing the interests of 21 companies who publish books & other media for elementary & secondary schools, colleges & universities, professional & reference, retail, & library markets

Canadian Telebook Agency
#401, 110 Eglinton Ave. West, Toronto ON M4R 1A3 Canada
Tel: 416-545-1595; *Fax:* 416-545-1590
admin@cta.geis.com
To simplify the complex task of sourcing books that are published &/or distributed in Canada; to provide an automated vehicle for ordering these books.

Canadian University Press (CUP) / Presse universitaire canadienne
#503, 920 Yonge St., Toronto ON M4W 3C7 Canada
Tel: 416-962-2287; *Toll-Free:* 866-250-5595
president@cup.ca
www.cup.ca
To elevate the standard of post-secondary student journalism; to foster communication among post-secondary student newspapers; to provide a national press service for post-secondary student newspapers; to provide facilities for the dissemination of news of importance to post-secondary students

Circulation Management Association of Canada (CMC) / Association canadienne des chefs de tirage
PO Box 349, #6, 50 Main St. East, Beeton ON L0G 1A0 Canada
Tel: 905-729-1046; *Fax:* 905-729-4432
cmc@tamicirc.ca
www.circ.org
CMC provides professional development, promotes fellowship within the circulation profession, & raises the profile of circulation professionals by rewarding outstanding achievement.

Connexions Information Sharing Services
#305, 489 College St., Toronto ON M6G 1A5 Canada
Tel: 416-964-1511
www.connexions.org
To link people striving to create positive solutions to social, environmental, economic & international problems; to encourage development of a more just & democratic society; to disseminate information & ideas that contribute to this goal

Conseil de presse du Québec (CPQ) / Québec Press Council
#A208, 1000, rue Fullum, Montréal QC H2K 3L7 Canada
Tél: 514-529-2818; *Téléc:* 514-873-4434
Ligne sans frais: 877-250-3060
info@conseildepresse.qc.ca
www.conseildepresse.qc.ca
Défendre la liberté de la presse, le droit du public à l'information; recevoir les plaintes du public concernant l'information journaux, télé, radio, internet.
Guy Amyot, Secrétaire général

Hebdos Québec
538, place Saint-Henri, Montréal QC H4C 2R9 Canada
Tél: 514-861-2088; *Téléc:* 514-861-1966
Ligne sans frais: 866-861-2088
communications@hebdos.com
www.hebdos.com
Favoriser et stimuler le développement du secteur des hebdomadaires en offrant à ses membres divers services en matière de recherche, de marketing et de formation; projeter une image crédible de la presse hebdomadaire, de la défendre, et de la rendre plus visible et plus accessible

International Board on Books for Young People - Canadian Section (IBBY - Canada) / Union internationale pour les livres de jeunesse
c/o Canadian Children's Book Centre, #101, 40 Orchard View Blvd., Toronto ON M4R 1B9 Canada
Tel: 416-975-0010; *Fax:* 416-975-8970
info@ibby-canada.org
www.ibby-canada.org
To promote the belief that all children everywhere should have the ability to read a wide & rich selection of books at the level of their needs & interests; To build bridges of understanding & tolerance through children's books

The Literary Press Group of Canada (LPG)
#501, 192 Spadina Ave., Toronto ON M5T 2C2 Canada
Tel: 416-483-1321; *Fax:* 416-483-2510
info@lpg.ca
www.lpg.ca
A not-for-profit association of Canadian literary book publishers, with a mandate to advocate on behalf of its members, & to foster the survival, growth & maintenance of strong Canadian-owned & controlled literary book publishing houses

Livres Canada Books
#504, 1 Nicholas St., Ottawa ON K1N 7B7 Canada
Tel: 613-562-2324; *Fax:* 613-562-2329
info@livrescanadabooks.com
www.livrescanadabooks.com
The association defends the interests of Canadian book publishers by providing market intelligence products and services, information and resources on digital publishing, as well as financial, promotion and logisitical support; the association administers the Foreign Rights Marketing Assistance Program, a component of the Canada Book Fund, as well as mentoring programs and other funding initiatives

Magazines Canada
#700, 425 Adelaide St. West, Toronto ON M5V 3C1 Canada
Tel: 416-504-0274; *Fax:* 416-504-0437
info@magazinescanada.ca
www.magazinescanada.ca; www.cmpa.ca
To promote the value of Canadian magazine publishing industry; To serve Canadian magazines through advocacy & special initiatives; To foster an environment where new magazines are nurtured; To support established magazines; To protect the Canadian consumer magazine industry

Manitoba Community Newspapers Association (MCNA)
#600, 275 Portage Ave., Winnipeg MB R3B 2B3 Canada
Tel: 204-947-1691; *Fax:* 204-947-1919
Toll-Free: 800-782-0051
tanis@mcna.com; kimb@mcna.com
www.mcna.com
To serve community newspaper publishers in Manitoba; To act as the industry voice for the issues of community newspaper publishers; To encourage high standards in publishing

Manitoba Press Council Inc.
#101, 2033 Portage Ave., Winnipeg MB R3J 0K8 Canada
Tel: 204-888-5189; *Fax:* 204-831-6359
query@mbpress.org
www.mbpress.org
To promote professional & ethical standards of journalism; to consider complaints against member newspapers; to make findings of complaints public; to assist in the preservation of the freedom of the press

National Magazine Awards Foundation (NMAF) / Fondation nationale des prix du magazine canadien
#700, 425 Adelaide St. West, Toronto ON M5V 3C1 Canada
Tel: 416-422-1358; *Fax:* 416-504-0437
staff@magazine-awards.com
www.magazine-awards.com
Social Media: twitter.com/natmagawards
To promote excellence in the communication arts industry in Canada through an awards program for Canadian magazine writers, editors, photographers, illustrators & art directors
Patrick Walsh, President

Ontario Community Newspapers Association (OCNA)
#103, 3050 Harvester Rd., Burlington ON L7N 3J1
Tel: 905-639-8720; *Fax:* 905-639-6962
www.ocna.org
Social Media: www.facebook.com/group.php?gid=171125688577
To support members with information about the Ontario community newspaper industry & market; To improve the competitive position of the industry

Ontario Press Council / Conseil de presse de l'Ontario
#1706, 2 Carlton St., Toronto ON M5B 1J3 Canada
Tel: 416-340-1981; *Fax:* 416-340-8724
info@ontpress.com
www.ontpress.com
To receive & adjudicate complaints from the public against Ontario newspapers; to defend freedom of expression on behalf of the public & press

Periodical Marketers of Canada (PMC)
South Tower, #1007, 175 Bloor St. East, Toronto ON M4W 3R8 Canada
Tel: 416-968-7311; *Fax:* 416-968-6281
To represent Canadian wholesalers; To promote Canadian magazines

Québec Community Newspaper Association (QCNA) / Association des journaux régionaux du Québec (AJRQ)
#5, 400, boul Grand, L'Ile-Perrot QC J7V 4X2 Canada
Tel: 514-453-6300; *Fax:* 514-453-6330
info@qcna.qc.ca
www.qcna.org
To promote Québec community English media; to serve as clearinghouse for information; to promote good journalism among members; to enhance the role of the media as social catalysts; to represent its members to pertinent government departments; to interact with other provincial & national newspaper associations in Canada; to help members better their financial condition

Saskatchewan Publishers Group (SPG)
2405 - 11th Ave., Regina SK S4P 0K4 Canada
Tel: 306-780-9808; *Fax:* 306-780-9810
spg@saskpublishers.sk.ca
www.saskpublishers.sk.ca
To promote the Saskatchewan book publishing industry; to provide a forum for sharing information & ideas; to speak for the common interests of its members; to undertake specific projects, programs & studies; to work closely with other publishing & cultural organizations across Canada
Brenda Niskala, Co-Executive Director
Jillian Bell, Co-Executive Director

Saskatchewan Weekly Newspapers Association (SWNA)
#14, 401 - 45th St. West, Saskatoon SK S7L 5Z9
Tel: 306-382-9683; *Fax:* 306-382-9421
Toll-Free: 800-661-7962
www.swna.com
To assist persons to issue press releases, buy advertising, & place classifieds in member newspapers in central Saskatchewan & the Northwest Territories

Société de développement des périodiques culturels québécois (SODEP)
#716, 460, rue Ste-Catherine ouest, Montréal QC H3B 1A7 Canada
Tél: 514-397-8669; *Téléc:* 514-397-6887
info@sodep.qc.ca
www.sodep.qc.ca
Travailler à l'essor et au rayonnement des revues culturelles; établir et entretenir des liens avec le milieu de l'enseignement, les bibliothèques, les médias et les maisons de distribution; représenter et promouvoir les intérêts professionnels, éthiques et économiques des éditeurs; favoriser les échanges internationaux

Toronto Press Club (TPC)
PO Box 262, Stn. Commerce Court South, Toronto ON M4L 1E8 Canada
Tel: 416-363-0651; *Fax:* 416-363-9717
www.torontopressclub.net
Bill Somerville, President

Radio Broadcasting

Halifax Amateur Radio Club (HARC)
PO Box 663, Halifax NS B3J 2T3 Canada
Tel: 902-490-6421
www.halifax-arc.org
To promote amateur radio and Ham radio and provide a forum for the exchange of ideas and information related to radio communications and technical experimentation in Nova Scotia.
Murray MacDonald, President

Real Estate

Alberta Association of the Appraisal Institute of Canada (AA-AIC)
#245, 495 - 36 St. NE, Calgary AB T2A 6K3 Canada
Tel: 403-207-7892; *Fax:* 403-207-7857
info@appraisal.ab.ca
www.appraisal.ab.ca
To maintain professional ethics & standards in real estate valuation; to qualify real estate appraisers

Alberta Building Officials Association
PO Box 27058, City Centre RPO, Red Deer AB T4N 6X8
www.aboa.ab.ca
Goals of the organization are to improve standards of building inspection; to be a discussion forum for shared issues and concerns; to assit in the education of building inspector in the areas of administration, technical, and other branches of the profession; to promote the importance of the building official's role.

Alberta Real Estate Association (AREA)
#300, 4954 Richard Rd. SW, Calgary AB T3E 6L1 Canada
Tel: 403-228-6845; *Fax:* 403-228-4360
Toll-Free: 800-661-0231
info@abrea.ab.ca
www.abrea.ab.ca

Annapolis Valley Real Estate Board
PO Box 117, 2110 Hwy. 1, Auburn NS B0P 1A0 Canada
Tel: 902-847-9336; *Fax:* 902-847-9869

Appraisal Institute of Canada (AIC) / Institut canadien des évaluateurs
#403, 200 Catherine St., Ottawa ON K2P 2K9 Canada
Tel: 613-234-6533; *Fax:* 613-234-7197
info@aicanada.ca
www.aicanada.ca
Social Media: twitter.com/AIC_Canada
The self-regulating body is a real estate appraisal association in Canada that grants professional designations in real estate appraisal. It strives to maintain high standards in real estate appraisal to protect the public interest

Association des courtiers et agents immobiliers du Québec (ACAIQ) / Québec Real Estate Association
#300, 6300, rue Auteuil, Brossard QC J4Z 3P2 Canada
Tél: 450-676-4800; *Téléc:* 450-676-7801
Ligne sans frais: 800-440-5110
info@acaiq.com
www.acaiq.com
Protéger le public par l'encadrement des activités professionnelles de tous les courtiers et agents immobiliers exerçant au Québec
Robert Nadeau, Président et chef de la direction

Association des propriétaires du Québec inc. (APQ) / Quebec Landlords Association (QLA)
8350, boul St-Laurent, Montréal QC H2P 2M3 Canada
Tél: 514-382-9670; *Téléc:* 514-382-9676
Ligne sans frais: 888-382-9670
info@apq.org
www.apq.org
Défendre les droits et les intérêts des propriétaires de logements locatifs du Québec

L'Association du Québec de l'Institut canadien des évaluateurs (AQICE) / Québec Association of the Appraisal Institute of Canada
587, ch Rhéaume, Saint-Michel QC J0L 2J0 Canada
Tél: 450-454-0377; *Téléc:* 450-454-1166
Ligne sans frais: 877-454-0377
aqice@qc.aira.com
www.aqice.ca
La mission de l'Institut canadien des évaluateurs est de protéger l'intérêt du public en s'assurant que ses membres offrent des services d'expert-conseil selon des normes élevées de pratique professionnelle
Ginette St-Jean, Executive Director

Association of Battlefords Realtors
PO Box 611, North Battleford SK S9A 2Y7 Canada
Tel: 306-445-6300; *Fax:* 306-445-9020
bfords.realestate@sasktel.net
To advance & promote interest of those engaged in real estate as brokers, agents, valuators, examiners, & experts; to increase public confidence in & respect for those engaged in real estate

Association of Regina Realtors Inc.
1854 McIntyre St., Regina SK S4P 2P9 Canada
Tel: 306-791-2700; *Fax:* 306-781-7940
arr@reginarealtors.com
www.reginarealtors.com
Ian Johnston, President

Association of Saskatchewan Realtors (ASR)
2811 Estey Dr., Saskatoon SK S7J 2V8 Canada
Tel: 306-373-3350; *Fax:* 306-373-5377
Toll-Free: 877-306-7732
info@saskatchewanrealestate.com
www.saskatchewanrealestate.com
Represents real estate boards & their realtor members on government affairs & provincial issues; develops standards of professional practice; administers training; provides information to members, governments & the public; provides support services to members; registers brokers & salespeople; develops special projects for the educational benefit of all registrants in Saskatchewan

Bancroft District Real Estate Board
PO Box 1522, 69 Hastings St. North, Bancroft ON K0L 1C0 Canada
Tel: 613-332-3842
bdreb@bancroftrealestate.on.ca
www.bancroftrealestate.on.ca

Barrie & District Real Estate Board Inc.
30 Mary St., Barrie ON L4N 1S8 Canada
Tel: 705-739-4650; *Fax:* 705-721-9101
info@barrie.mls.ca
www.barrie.mls.ca
Provides continuing education, Multiple Listing Service (MLS), statistical information and many other services to its members. The geographical area served by the Association includes the City of Barrie and part or all of the surrounding townships including Springwater, Oro-Medonte, Innisil, Essa, Bradford-West Gwillimbury, and Clearview.

Brampton Real Estate Board (BREB)
#10, 35 Van Kirk Dr., Brampton ON L7A 1A5 Canada
Tel: 905-791-9913; *Fax:* 905-791-9430
info@breb.org
www.breb.org
Social Media: twitter.com/thebreb
The Brampton Real Estate Board is dedicated to helping members achieve their real estate related goals.

Brandon Real Estate Board (BREB)
907 Princess Ave., Brandon MB R7A 6E3 Canada
Tel: 204-727-4672; *Fax:* 204-727-8331
info@breb.mb.ca
www.breb.mb.ca
Real estate support for Realtors in Brandon.

Brantford Regional Real Estate Association Inc. (BRREA)
106 George St., Brantford ON N3T 2Y4 Canada
Tel: 519-753-0308; *Fax:* 519-753-8638
brantfordreb@rogers.com
www.brrea.com
Real estate support for Realtors working in Brantford.

British Columbia Association of the Appraisal Institute of Canada (BCAAIC)
#845, 1200 West 73rd Ave., Vancouver BC V6P 6G5 Canada
Tel: 604-266-8287; *Fax:* 604-266-3034
Toll-Free: 888-707-8287
info@appraisal.bc.ca
www.appraisal.bc.ca
To represent, promote & support our members as leaders in the counselling, analysis & evaluation of real property. Chapters: Fraser Valley, Nanaimo, Okanagan, Vancouver, Kamloops, Northwest, Prince George, Victoria, and Kootenay

British Columbia Northern Real Estate Board
2609 Queensway, Prince George BC V2L 1N3 Canada
Tel: 250-563-1236; *Fax:* 250-563-3637
inquiries@bcnreb.bc.ca
boards.mls.ca/bcnreb/
Dorothy Friesen, President

British Columbia Real Estate Association (BCREA)
#1420, 701 Georgia St. W., Vancouver BC V7Y 1C6 Canada
Tel: 604-683-7702; *Fax:* 604-683-8601
bcrea@bcrea.bc.ca
www.bcrea.bc.ca
Promotes the interests of & advocates for the real estate profession on behalf of its members; secures public support & trust in the profession; promotes property rights & real estate related issues; ensures high standards of ethics & professionalism through ongoing education of realtors

Brooks Real Estate Board
PO Box 997, Brooks AB T1R 1B8 Canada
Tel: 403-362-4643; *Fax:* 403-362-3276
brecoop@telusplanet.net

Building Owners & Managers Association - Canada
#850, 36 Toronto St., Toronto ON M5C 2C5 Canada
Tel: 416-214-1912; *Fax:* 416-260-3838
info@bomacanada.ca
www.bomacanada.ca
To represent the Canadian commerical real estate industry on matters of national concern; To develop a strong communications network between local associations; To promote professionalism of members through education programs & effective public relations activity
Deb Cross, CAE, Executive Vice-President
Diana Osler-Zortega, President

Calgary Real Estate Board Cooperative Limited (CREB)
300 Manning Rd. NE, Calgary AB T2E 8K4 Canada
Tel: 403-263-0530; *Fax:* 403-218-3688
ron.esch@creb.ca
www.creb.com

Canadian Institute of Professional Home Inspectors Inc.
#720, 999 West Broadway, Vancouver BC V5Z 1K5 Canada
Tel: 604-732-0617
info@edwitzke.com
www.edwitzke.com
To inspect all components of building for structural soundness, damage assessment, dry rot, pest problems, energy efficiency, compliance with grading, zoning, legal requirements & safety laws; to inspect all manner of the buildings, including new or existing residential or commercial buildings to determine the condition of a building, for contractors in recommending procedures for compliance with legal requirements, or for insurance companies in assessing damages & general public

The Canadian Real Estate Association (CREA) / Association canadienne de l'immeuble
200 Catherine St., 6th Fl., Ottawa ON K2P 2K9 Canada
Tel: 613-237-7111; *Fax:* 613-234-2567
Toll-Free: 800-842-2732
info@crea.ca
www.crea.ca
To enhance member professionalism, competency & profitability; to advocate government policies which improve the industry's market environment & enhance individual rights with respect to the ownership of real property

Cariboo Real Estate Association
2609 Queensway, Prince George BC V2L 1N3 Canada
Tel: 250-563-1236; *Fax:* 250-563-3637

Supporting Real Estate Agents and buyers in Cariboo, B.C.

Central Alberta Realtors Association
4922 - 45 St., Red Deer AB T4N 1K6 Canada
Tel: 403-343-0881; *Fax:* 403-347-9080
office@CARAssociation.ca
www.rdreb.ca

Chambre immobilière Centre du Québec Inc.
139C, rue Hériot, Drummondville QC J2C 2B1 Canada
Tél: 819-477-1033; *Téléc:* 819-474-7913
chambre@cgocable.ca

Chambre immobilière de l'Abitibi-Témiscamingue Inc. (CIAT)
#203, 33, av Horne, Rouyn-Noranda QC J9X 4S1 Canada
Tél: 819-762-1777; *Téléc:* 819-762-4030
ciat@cablevision.qc.ca
www.ciat.qc.ca

Chambre immobilière de l'Estrie inc.
19, rue King ouest, Sherbrooke QC J1H 1N4 Canada
Tél: 819-566-7616; *Téléc:* 819-566-7688
info@mon-toit.net
www.mon-toit.net
Promouvoir et protéger les intérêts de l'industrie immobilière du Québec afin que les Chambres et les membres accomplissent avec succès leurs objectifs d'affaires.

Chambre immobilière de l'Outaouais
106, boul Sacré-Coeur, Gatineau QC J8X 1E1 Canada
Tél: 819-771-5221; *Téléc:* 819-771-8715
info@avecunagent.com
www.avecunagent.com

Chambre immobilière de la Haute Yamaska Inc. (CIHY) / Haute Yamaska Real Estate Board
#3, 45, rue Centre, Granby QC J2G 5B4 Canada
Tél: 450-378-6702; *Téléc:* 450-375-5268
administration.cihy@videotron.ca
Offrir des services de formation et d'information pour les agents immobiliers.

Chambre immobilière de la Mauricie Inc. / Trois-Rivières Real Estate Board
#102, 1640 - 6e rue, Trois-Rivières QC G8Y 5B8 Canada
Tél: 819-379-9081; *Téléc:* 819-379-9262
cimauricie@cgocable.ca
www.cimauricie.com

Chambre immobilière de Lanaudière Inc.
765, boul Manseau, Joliette QC J6E 3E8 Canada
Tél: 450-759-8511; *Téléc:* 450-759-6557
www.immobilierlanaudiere.com

Chambre immobilière de Québec
990, av Holland, Québec QC G1S 3T1 Canada
Tél: 418-688-3362; *Téléc:* 418-688-3577
Ligne sans frais: 866-688-3362
info@ciq.qc.ca
www.fciq.ca
Promouvoir et protéger les intérêts de l'industrie immobilière du Québec afin que les Chambres et les membres accomplissent avec succès leurs objectifs d'affaires.

Chambre immobilière de Saint-Hyacinthe Inc.
CP 667, Saint-Hyacinthe QC J2S 7P5 Canada
Tél: 450-799-2210; *Téléc:* 450-799-2230
chimmob@cgocable.ca
Promouvoir et protéger les intérêts de l'industrie immobilière du Québec afin que les Chambres et les membres accomplissent avec succès leurs objectifs d'affaires.

Chambre immobilière des Laurentides (CIL)
570, boul. des Laurentides, Piedmont QC J0R 1K0 Canada
Tél: 450-240-0006; *Téléc:* 450-240-0096
optionlaurentides@cgocable.ca
www.chambreimmobilieredeslaurentides.ca
Sa mission est la promotion, la représentation et le développement des intérêts professionnels, économiques et sociaux de ses membres

Chambre immobilière du Grand Montréal / Greater Montréal Real Estate Board
600, ch du Golf, Ile-des-Soeurs QC H3E 1A8 Canada
Tél: 514-762-2440; *Téléc:* 514-762-1490
Ligne sans frais: 888-762-2440
cigm@cigm.qc.ca
www.cigm.qc.ca

Chambre immobilière du Saguenay-Lac St-Jean Inc. (CISL)
#140, 2655, boul du Royaume, Jonquière QC G7S 4S9 Canada
Tél: 418-548-8808; *Téléc:* 418-548-2588
chambre@immobiliersaguenay.com
www.immobiliersaguenay.com
Regrouper les membres afin de leur fournir des services, assurer la qualité de leur travail, défendre et promouvoir leurs intérêts; protéger et promouvoir le commerce de l'immobilier et encourager l'accès à la propriétéoffrir de la formation et du perfectionnement dans le domaine immobilier afin d'assurer et de garantir le professionnalisme de l'industrie; faciliter au public en général l'accès à l'information dans le domaine immobilier

Chatham-Kent Real Estate Board
PO Box 384, 252 Wellington St. W., Chatham ON N7M 5K5 Canada
Tel: 519-352-4351; *Fax:* 519-351-1498
ckreb@mnsi.net
boards.mls.ca/chatham

Chilliwack & District Real Estate Board
#1, 8433 Harvard Pl., Chilliwack BC V2P 7Z5 Canada
Tel: 604-792-0912; *Fax:* 604-792-6795
cadreb@telus.net
cadreb.com
Real estate board serving Chilliwack, Agassiz, Hope, Boston Bar and Harrison.

Cornwall & District Real Estate Board
407B Pitt St., Cornwall ON K6J 3R3 Canada
Tel: 613-932-6457; *Fax:* 613-932-1687
cdreb@cogeco.net
boards.mls.ca/cornwall
Real estate board for Cornwall and area.

Durham Region Real Estate Board (DRREB)
#14, 50 Richmond St. East, Oshawa ON L1G 7C7 Canada
Tel: 905-723-8184; *Fax:* 905-723-7531
drar@durhamrealestate.org
www.durhamrealestate.org
To pursue excellence & professionalism in real estate through commitment & service

Edmonton Real Estate Board Co-operative Listing Bureau Ltd.
14220 - 112 Ave., Edmonton AB T5M 2T8 Canada
Tel: 780-451-6666; *Fax:* 780-452-1135
connection@ereb.com
www.ereb.com

Estevan Real Estate Board
PO Box 445, 403 - 9th Ave., Estevan SK S4A 2A4 Canada
Tel: 306-634-7885; *Fax:* 306-634-8610
boards.mls.ca/estevan
The Estevan Real Estate Board is a participant in the on-line Multiple Listing Service for the province of Saskatchewan, which provides marketing services for members. This includes postings on the residential properties web site mls.ca and the similar site for commercial and agribusiness listings, CLS.CA.

Fédération des Chambres immobilières du Québec (FCIQ)
600, ch du Golf, Verdun QC H3E 1A8 Canada
Tél: 514-762-0212; *Téléc:* 514-762-0365
fciq@fciq.ca
www.fciq.ca
Promouvoir et protéger les intérêts de l'industrie immobilière du Québec afin que les Chambres et les membres accomplissent avec succès leurs objectifs d'affaires

Fort McMurray Realtors Association
9909 Sutherland St., Fort McMurray AB T9H 1V3 Canada
Tel: 780-791-1124; *Fax:* 780-743-4724
moskalykc@shaw.ca
boards.mls.ca/fortmcmurray

Fraser Valley Real Estate Board
PO Box 99, 15463 - 104 Ave., Surrey BC V3T 4W4 Canada
Tel: 604-930-7600; *Fax:* 604-588-0325
Toll-Free: 800-906-0258
mls@fvreb.bc.ca
www.fvreb.bc.ca
To provide the most efficient real estate marketing service.

Georgian Triangle Real Estate Board
54 Third St., Collingwood ON L9Y 1K3 Canada
Tel: 705-445-7295; *Fax:* 705-445-7253
realestate@gtreb.com
www.gtreb.com
The Georgian Triangle Real Estate Board is dedicated to embracing new technologies, advancing quality education and high ethical standards in support of their membership while delivering MLS and real estate services consistant with the chaning regulations and market dynamics of our profession.

Greater Moncton Real Estate Board Inc.
541 St. George Blvd., Moncton NB E1E 2B6 Canada
Tel: 506-857-8200; *Fax:* 506-857-1760
gmreb@nb.aibn.com
www.monctonrealestateboard.com
The Greater Moncton Real Estate Board provides its members with the strcuture and services to enhance REALTOR professionalism, standards of business practice and ethics in meeting the real estate needs of the community.

Guelph & District Real Estate Board
400 Woolwich St., Guelph ON N1H 3X1 Canada
Tel: 519-824-7270; *Fax:* 519-824-6730
info@gdar.ca
www.gdreb.ca
A real estate board representing Guelph, Elora, and Fergus.

Hamilton-Burlington & District Real Estate Board (HBDREB)
505 York Blvd., Hamilton ON L8R 3K4 Canada
Tel: 905-529-8101; *Fax:* 905-529-4349
info@rahb.ca
www.rahb.ca
To pursue excellence & professionalism in real estate through commitment & service

Highland Real Estate Board
c/o The Prudential Highland Properties, #104, 219 Main St., Antigonish NS B2G 2C1 Canada
Tel: 902-863-1878; *Fax:* 902-863-1933

Huron Perth Real Estate Board
#6, 55 Lorne Ave. East, Stratford ON N5A 6S4 Canada
Tel: 519-271-6870; *Fax:* 519-271-3040
hpreb@wightman.ca
boards.mls.ca/huron
"The Board enforces a strict Code of Ethics and Standards of Business Practice to it's members to maintain the integrity of organized real estate; to promote interest in the marketing of real estate; and to promote, encourage and protect the ownership of real property to the public."

Institute of Municipal Assessors
#206, 10720 Yonge St., Richmond Hill ON L4C 3C9 Canada
Tel: 905-884-1959; *Fax:* 905-884-9263
info@assessorsinstitute.ca
www.assessorsinstitute.ca
The IMA is the largest Canadian professional association representing members that practice in the field of Property Assessment and related Property Taxation functions.

Kamloops & District Real Estate Association (KADREA)
#101, 418 St. Paul St., Kamloops BC V2C 2J6 Canada
Tel: 250-372-9411; *Fax:* 250-828-1986
cboer@kadrea.com
www.boards.mls.ca/kamloops

Kawartha Lakes Real Estate Association
31 Kent St. East, Lindsay ON K9V 2C3 Canada
Tel: 705-324-4515; *Fax:* 705-324-3916
sschell@kawarthalakes-mls.ca
www.kawarthalakes-mls.ca
Members are actively involved in a variety of community projects through the association's sponsorship and other local organizations as they promote the wonderful lifestyle that the Kawartha Lakes area affords them.

Kingston & Area Real Estate Association
720 Arlington Park Pl., Kingston ON K7M 8H9 Canada
Tel: 613-384-0880; *Fax:* 613-384-0863
info@karea.ca
www.karea.ca
A not-for-profit organization that represents 494 real estate professionals who are also members of the Canadian Real Estate Association (CREA) and the Ontario Real Estate Association (OREA).

Kootenay Real Estate Board (KREB)
#208, 402 Baker St., Nelson BC V1L 4H8 Canada
Tel: 250-352-5477; *Fax:* 250-352-7184
kreb@netidea.com; kreb@telus.net
The Association promotes interest in real estate markets in all aspects through service to members & the public.

Lethbridge & District Association of Realtors
522 - 6 St. South, Lethbridge AB T1J 2E2 Canada
Tel: 403-328-8838; *Fax:* 403-328-8906
lreb2@telus.net
www.ldar.ca

LDAR is a member service organization providing real estate information on the Lethbridge area. It serves as a forum to network & build connections within the real estate community.

London & St. Thomas Real Estate Board
342 Commissioners Rd. West, London ON N6J 1Y3 Canada
Tel: 519-641-1400; *Fax:* 519-641-4613
mls@lstreb.com
www.lstreb.com

Manitoba Association of the Appraisal Institute of Canada (MB AIC)
#193, 162 - 2025 Corydon Ave., Winnipeg MB R3P 0N5 Canada
Tel: 204-934-1177; *Fax:* 204-947-1332
mbaic@mts.net
www.aimanitoba.ca

Manitoba Building Officials Association
PO Box 2063, Winnipeg MB R3C 3R4 Canada
Tel: 204-832-1512; *Fax:* 204-897-8094
info@mboa.mb.ca
www.mboa.mb.ca

Manitoba Real Estate Association (MREA)
1240 Portage Ave., 2nd Fl., Winnipeg MB R3G 0T6 Canada
Tel: 204-772-0405; *Fax:* 204-775-3781
Toll-Free: 800-267-6019
cduheme@mrea.mb.ca; rfinch@mrea.mb.ca (education)
www.realestatemanitoba.com
To represent the interest of Manitoba's licensed realtors

Medicine Hat Real Estate Board Co-operative Ltd.
403 - 4 St. SE, Medicine Hat AB T1A 0K5 Canada
Tel: 403-526-2879; *Fax:* 403-526-0307
mhreb@telus.net
boards.mls.ca/medicinehat/

Melfort Real Estate Board
c/o Royal Lepage Hodgins Realty, PO Box 3070, 101 Burrows Ave. West, Melfort SK S0E 1A0 Canada
Tel: 306-752-5751; *Fax:* 306-752-5754

Midland-Penetang District Real Estate Board Inc.
PO Box 805, 578 King St., Midland ON L4R 4P4 Canada
Tel: 705-526-8706; *Fax:* 705-526-0701
info@midland-penetang-mls.ca

Mississauga Real Estate Board
#29, 3355 The Collegeway, Mississauga ON L5L 5T3 Canada
Tel: 905-608-6732; *Fax:* 905-608-9988
administration@mreb.ca
www.mreb.ca
Organization of Realtors, it is dedicated to the beneficial visibility of the industry.

Moose Jaw Real Estate Board
79 Hochelaga St. West, Moose Jaw SK S6H 2E9 Canada
Tel: 306-693-9544; *Fax:* 306-692-4463
mjreb@sasktel.net
www.moosejawrealestateboard.com
The Board promotes the real estate sector in the area & provides a forum for local realtors to exchange information.

Muskoka & Haliburton Association of Realtors (MHAR)
34 Cairns Cres., Huntsville ON P1H 1Y3 Canada
Tel: 705-788-1504; *Fax:* 705-788-2040
spond@mhar.on.ca
www.mhar.on.ca
Within the boundaries of the Muskoka & Haliburton Association of REALTORSr, there are seven major geographical areas: Gravenhurst in the south, Bracebridge, Muskoka Lakes in the western part of the area, Huntsville & Almaguin Highlands in the north and Lake of Bays and Haliburton in the eastern part of the area. Each of the areas contains a unique blend of both prestigious year-round recreational properties on large lakes, and lower and mid-range prized cottage properties on the smaller serene lakes.

New Brunswick Association of Real Estate Appraisers (NBAREA) / Association des évaluateurs immobiliers du Nouveau-Brunswick (AEIN-B)
#204, 403 Regent St., Fredericton NB E3B 3X6 Canada
Tel: 506-450-2016; *Fax:* 506-450-3010
nbarea@nb.aibn.com
www.nbarea.org
To enhance the profession & to protect the public

New Brunswick Building Officials Association (NBBOA) / L'Association des officiels de la construction du Nouveau-Brunswick
PO Box 3193, Stn. B, Fredericton NB E3A 5G9 Canada
Tel: 506-658-2911; *Fax:* 506-632-6199
secretary@nbboa.ca
www.nbboa.ca
To achieve & maintain the highest levels of professionalism in membership, education & qualifications; legislative interpretation; building inspection service; building & construction safety.

New Brunswick Real Estate Association (NBREA) / Association des agents des immeubles du Nouveau-Brunswick
#1, 22 Durelle St., Fredericton NB E3C 1N8 Canada
Tel: 506-459-8055; *Fax:* 506-459-8057
Toll-Free: 800-762-1677
info@nbrea.ca
www.nbrea.ca
To strengthen & promote standards of professionalism in the real estate industry

Newfoundland & Labrador Association of Realtors
28 Logy Bay Rd., St. John's NL A1A 1J4 Canada
Tel: 709-726-5110
boards.mls.ca/nl/index.htm

Newfoundland & Labrador Association of the Appraisal Institute of Canada
PO Box 1571, Stn. C, St. John's NL A1C 5P3 Canada
Tel: 709-753-7644; *Fax:* 709-753-7627
naaic@nf.aibn.com
To promote the appraisal profession throughout Newfoundland & Labrador
Sherry House, Executive Director
Neil Tedstone, AACI,P.App, President

Niagara Association of REALTORS (NAR)
116 Niagara St., St Catharines ON L2R 4L4 Canada
Tel: 905-684-9459; *Fax:* 905-687-7010
admin@mls-niagara.com
www.mls-niagara.com
To provide members with the structure & services to facilitate the marketing of real estate; to ensure a high standard of business practices & ethics; to effectively serve the real estate needs of the members

North Bay Real Estate Board
926 Cassells St., North Bay ON P1B 4A8 Canada
Tel: 705-472-6812; *Fax:* 705-472-0529
nbreb@nbreb.com
www.nbreb.com
Represents real estate agents and member offices in North Bay.

Northern Lights Real Estate Board
1101 - 103 Ave., Dawson Creek BC V1G 2G8 Canada
Tel: 250-782-4876; *Fax:* 250-782-8574
nlreb@shawcable.com

Northern New Brunswick Real Estate Board Inc. / Chambre immobilière du nord du Nouveau-Brunswick
PO Box 185, #5, 360 Parkside Dr., Bathurst NB E2A 3Z2 Canada
Tel: 506-548-3045; *Fax:* 506-548-4002
nnbreb@nb.sympatico.ca
boards.mls.ca/n-newbrunswick/index.htm
Covers a large and diverse geographic area that includes the cities of Bathurst, Miramichi, Campbellton, and Dalhousie.

Northumberland Hills Association of Realtors
#23, 1011 Elgin St. West, Cobourg ON K9A 5J4 Canada
Tel: 905-372-8630; *Fax:* 905-372-1443
districtrealestate@bellnet.ca
boards.mls.ca/northumberland
The real estate board covers the municipalities of Cobourg & Port Hope, from Lake Ontario to Rice Lake, & as far east as the Township of Cramahe & Hwy. 115.

Nova Scotia Association of REALTORS (NSAR)
#100, 7 Scarfe Ct., Dartmouth NS B3B 1W4 Canada
Tel: 902-468-2515; *Fax:* 902-468-2533
Toll-Free: 800-344-2001
info@nsar.ns.ca
www.nsar-mls.ca
Provides Realtors with services & representation to enable them to best serve the public in real estate transactions

Nova Scotia Real Estate Appraisers Association (NSREAA)
#602, 5670 Spring Garden Rd., Halifax NS B3J 1H6 Canada
Tel: 902-422-4077; *Fax:* 902-422-3717
nsreaa@nsappraisal.ns.ca
www.nsappraisal.ns.ca
The Association regulates the practice of real estate appraisal in Nova Scotia, establishes and promotes the interests of appraisers, develops and maintains high standards of knowledge and best practices in the field, develops and enforces professional ethics, promotes public awareness of the profession, and encourages studies in real estate appraisal

The Oakville, Milton & District Real Estate Board
125 Navy St., Oakville ON L6J 2Z5 Canada
Tel: 905-844-6491; *Fax:* 905-844-6699
info@omdreb.on.ca
www.omdreb.on.ca

Okanagan Mainline Real Estate Board (OMREB)
#112, 140 Commercial Dr., Kelowna BC V1X 7X6 Canada
Tel: 250-491-4560; *Fax:* 250-491-4580
admin@omreb.com
www.omreb.com
To provide a forum for the exchange of property-related information between members so that they may provide the public with outstanding service; to establish & maintain optimum standards of business practices; to provide continuing education for the betterment of the members' knowledge; to monitor proposed & legislated laws which inhibit or restrict the right of Canadians or British Columbians to own or use real property

Ontario Association of the Appraisal Institute of Canada (OA-AIC)
#108, 16 Four Seasons Place, Toronto ON M9B 6E5 Canada
Tel: 416-695-9333; *Fax:* 416-695-9321
Toll-Free: 800-771-8087
info@oaaic.on.ca
www.oaaic.on.ca
To serve the public interest by advancing high standards in the analysis & valuation of real property matters by enhancing the professional competence of its members.

Ontario Building Officials Association Inc. (OBOA) / Association de l'Ontario des officers en bâtiment inc.
#8, 200 Marycroft Ave., Woodbridge ON L4L 5X4 Canada
Tel: 905-264-1662; *Fax:* 905-264-8696
admin@oboa.on.ca
www.oboa.on.ca
To foster & cooperate in the establishment of uniform regulations relating to the fire protection & structural adequacy of buildings & the safety & health of the occupants; to promote the understanding & uniform interpretation & enforcement of these regulations & their companion documents; to provide assistance in the development & improvement of these regulations & their companion documents; to promote a close liaison & interchange of ideas on these regulations with related associations, the building industry, government & the consumer public

Ontario Real Estate Association (OREA)
99 Duncan Mill Rd., Toronto ON M3B 1Z2 Canada
Tel: 416-445-9910; *Fax:* 416-445-2644
Toll-Free: 800-265-6732
info@orea.com
www.orea.com
To represent the vocational interests of members; to advocate for a better working environment; to communicate with members & the public; to develop educational opportunities for the betterment of the real estate profession; to develop programs to assist members in providing quality services to the public; to develop & administer the educational courses required for registration to trade in real estate on behalf of The Real Estate Council of Ontario

Orangeville & District Real Estate Board
228 Broadway Ave., Orangeville ON L9W 1K5 Canada
Tel: 519-941-4547; *Fax:* 519-941-8482
odreb@bellnet.ca
www.odreb.com

Orillia & District Real Estate Board
PO Box 551, #7, 3 Progress Dr. S., Orillia ON L3V 6H1 Canada
Tel: 705-325-9958; *Fax:* 705-325-0605
realtor.mls.ca/boards/orillia
To provide a governing body for professional standards & business practices; to provide multiple listing services.

Ottawa Real Estate Board (OREB) / Chambre d'immeuble d'Ottawa
1826 Woodward Dr., Ottawa ON K2C 0P7 Canada
Tel: 613-225-2240; *Fax:* 613-225-6420
orebadmin@ottawarealestate.org
www.ottawarealestate.org

Parry Sound Real Estate Board
47A James St., Parry Sound ON P2A 1T6 Canada
Tel: 705-746-4020; *Fax:* 705-746-2955
psreb@vianet.on.ca
www.parrysoundrealestateboard.ca

Peterborough & the Kawarthas Association of Realtors Inc. (PKAR)
PO Box 1330, 273 Charlotte St., Peterborough ON K9J 7H5 Canada
Tel: 705-745-5724; *Fax:* 705-745-9377
info@peterbororealestate.com
www.peterbororealestate.com

Portage La Prairie Real Estate Board
39 Royla Rd. North, Portage la Prairie MB R1N 1T9 Canada
Tel: 204-857-4111
preb@escape.ca

Powell River Sunshine Coast Real Estate Board
PO Box 307, 4699 Marine Avenue, Powell River BC V8A 5C2 Canada
Tel: 604-485-6944; *Fax:* 604-485-6944
prscreb@shaw.ca
Geri Powell, Board Administrator

Prince Albert & District Association of Realtors
615 Branion Dr., Prince Albert SK S6V 2R9 Canada
Tel: 306-764-8755; *Fax:* 306-763-0555
pareb@sasktel.net
www.princealbertrealtors.ca
Supporting Realtors in the Prince Albert Real Estate community.

Prince Edward Island Association of the Appraisal Institute of Canada
PO Box 1796, Charlottetown PE C1A 7N4 Canada
Tel: 902-368-3355; *Fax:* 902-368-3582
peiaic@xplornet.com
Scott Wilson, AACI, P.App., President
Suzanne Pater, Executive Director

Prince Edward Island Real Estate Association
75 St. Peter's Rd., Charlottetown PE C1A 5N7 Canada
Tel: 902-368-8451; *Fax:* 902-894-9487
office@peirea.com
www.peirea.com

Quinte & District Real Estate Board
PO Box 128, 51 Cannifton Rd. North, Cannifton ON K0K 1K0 Canada
Tel: 613-969-7873; *Fax:* 613-962-1851
quinte.MLS@reach.net
www.quinterealestate.ca

Real Estate Board of Cambridge
75 Ainslie St. North, Cambridge ON N1R 3J7 Canada
Tel: 519-623-3660; *Fax:* 519-623-8253
cambridge-admin@rogers.com
www.realestateboardcambridge.com

Real Estate Board of Greater Vancouver
2433 Spruce St., Vancouver BC V6H 4C8 Canada
Tel: 604-730-3000; *Fax:* 604-730-3100
www.rebgv.org
Robert K. Wallace, CEO

Real Estate Board of the Fredericton Area Inc. (FREB)
544 Brunswick St., Fredericton NB E3B 1H5 Canada
Tel: 506-458-8163; *Fax:* 506-459-8922
freb01@rogers.com
www.frederictonrealestateboard.com
To address member education, motivation & appreciation

Real Estate Institute of Canada (REIC) / Institut canadien de l'immeuble (ICI)
#208, 5407 Eglinton Ave. West, Toronto ON M9C 5K6 Canada
Tel: 416-695-9000; *Fax:* 416-695-7230
Toll-Free: 800-542-7342
infocentral@reic.com
www.reic.ca
To advance opportunities for persons involved in real estate

Real Property Association of Canada
#1410, One University Ave., Toronto ON M5J 2P1 Canada
Tel: 416-642-2700; *Fax:* 416-642-2727
info@realpac.ca
www.realpac.ca
To represent the real estate industries point of view to government at all levels on legislative & regulatory matters

REALTORS Association of Grey Bruce Owen Sound (RAGBOS)
517 - 10 St., Hanover ON N4N 1R4 Canada
Tel: 519-364-3827; *Fax:* 519-364-6800
info@ragbos.com
www.ragbos.ca
To provide a web-based multiple listing service for its members

Realtors Association of Lloydminster & District
#203, 5009 - 48 St., Lloydminster AB T9V 0H7 Canada
Tel: 780-875-6939; *Fax:* 780-875-5560
lloydreb@telus.net
boards.mls.ca/lloydminster

Renfrew County Real Estate Board
197 Pembroke St. East, Pembroke ON K8A 3J6 Canada
Tel: 613-735-5840; *Fax:* 613-735-0405
orebadmin@ottawarealestate.org
www.ottawarealestate.org/about_rcreb.shtml

Rideau-St. Lawrence Real Estate Board
#12, 1275 Kensington Pkwy., Brockville ON K6V 6C3 Canada
Tel: 613-342-3103; *Fax:* 613-342-1637
rideau@bellnet.ca
boards.mls.ca/rideau

Saint John Real Estate Board Inc.
Hilyard Place, #120, 600 Main St., Saint John NB E2K 1J5 Canada
Tel: 506-634-8772; *Fax:* 506-634-8775
www.sjrealestateboard.ca
To provide services to & set standards for members; to preserve & promote the MLS marketing system to benefit buyers & sellers of real property

Sarnia-Lambton Real Estate Board (SLREB)
555 Exmouth St., Sarnia ON N7T 5P6 Canada
Tel: 519-336-6871; *Fax:* 519-344-1928
slreb@fonenet.ca
www.mls-sarnia.com

Saskatchewan Association of the Appraisal Institute of Canada
3803 Lakeview Ave., Regina SK S4S 1H3 Canada
Tel: 306-352-4195; *Fax:* 306-352-6913
skaic@sasktel.net
www.skaic.org

Saskatchewan Building Officials Association Inc. (SBOA)
PO Box 460, North Battleford SK S9A 2Y6 Canada
Tel: 306-445-1733; *Fax:* 306-445-1739
membership@sboa.sk.ca; conference@sboa.sk.ca
www.sboa.sk.ca

Saskatoon Region Association of REALTORS (SRAR)
1149 - 8 St. East., Saskatoon SK S7H 0S3 Canada
Tel: 306-244-4453; *Fax:* 306-343-1420
info@srar.ca
www.srar.ca
To represent the real estate interests of its members & the public; to provide services & programs to enhance the professionalism, competency & effectiveness of its members; to advocate public policy towards improving the real estate market environment

Sault Ste Marie Real Estate Board (SSMREB)
#206, 477 Queen St. East, Sault Ste Marie ON P6A 1Z5 Canada
Tel: 705-949-4560; *Fax:* 705-949-5935
www.saultstemarierealestate.ca

Simcoe & District Real Estate Board
191 Queensway West, Simcoe ON N3Y 2M8 Canada
Tel: 519-426-4454; *Fax:* 519-426-9330
realsim@kwic.com
www.norfolk-mls.ca

South Okanagan Real Estate Board (SOREB)
365 Van Horne St., Penticton BC V2A 8S4 Canada
Tel: 250-492-0626; *Fax:* 250-493-0832
soreb@vip.net
www.soreb.org

To pursue excellence & professionalism in real estate, through quality education & high ethical standards; To protect the interest of the membership & the public

Sudbury Real Estate Board
190 Elm St., Sudbury ON P3C 1V3 Canada
Tel: 705-673-3388; *Fax:* 705-673-3197
sreb@vianet.on.ca
www.sudburyrealestateboard.on.ca

Swift Current Real Estate Association
#211, 12 Cheadle St. West, Swift Current SK S9H 0A9 Canada
Tel: 306-773-4326; *Fax:* 306-773-3917
screa@sasktel.net

Thompson Real Estate Board
55 Selkirk Ave., Thompson MB R8N 0M5 Canada
Tel: 204-778-6303; *Fax:* 204-778-5652
brealt@norcom.mb.ca

Thunder Bay Real Estate Board
1135 Barton St., Thunder Bay ON P7B 5N3 Canada
Tel: 807-623-8422; *Fax:* 807-623-0375
info@thunderbay-MLS.on.ca
www.thunderbay-mls.on.ca

Tillsonburg District Real Estate Board
PO Box 35, 1 Library Lane, Tillsonburg ON N4G 4H3 Canada
Tel: 519-842-9361; *Fax:* 519-688-6850
tburgreb@bellnet.ca
www.tburgreb.ca

Timmins Real Estate Board
225 Algonquin Blvd. East, Timmins ON P4N 1B4 Canada
Tel: 705-268-5451; *Fax:* 705-264-6420
treb@ntl.sympatico.ca

Toronto Real Estate Board (TREB)
1400 Don Mills Rd., Toronto ON M3B 3N1 Canada
Tel: 416-443-8100; *Fax:* 416-443-0797
www.torontorealestateboard.com

Valley Real Estate Board Inc. / Association Immobilière de la Vallée Ltée
PO Box 192, 72 Daigle St., Edmundston NB E3V 1M1 Canada
Tel: 506-737-8083; *Fax:* 506-737-8145
valleyboard@nb.aibn.com

Vancouver Island Real Estate Board (VIREB)
6374 Metral Dr., Nanaimo BC V9T 2L8 Canada
Tel: 250-390-4212; *Fax:* 250-390-5014
bbenoit@vireb.com
www.vireb.com
To provide cost-effective tools, services & information necessary to foster professionalism & maintain the realtor's position as the primary focus in the real estate industry

Victoria Real Estate Board (VREB)
3035 Nanaimo St., Victoria BC V8T 4W2 Canada
Tel: 250-385-7766; *Fax:* 250-385-8773
vreb@vreb.org
www.vreb.org
To promote & enhance the use of the real estate services that its members provide to the public

West Central Alberta Real Estate Board
162 Athabasca Ave., Hinton AB T7V 2A5 Canada
Tel: 780-865-7511; *Fax:* 780-865-7517
wcareb@shaw.ca
Sandy Atfield, Executive Officer
Marcel Dery, President

Weyburn Real Estate Board
110 Souris Ave., Weyburn SK S4H 2Z8 Canada
Tel: 306-848-1000; *Fax:* 306-842-3989
remax.weyburn@sasktel.net

Windsor-Essex County Real Estate Board
3020 Deziel Dr., Windsor ON N8W 5H8 Canada
Tel: 519-966-6432; *Fax:* 519-966-4469
info@windsorrealestate.com
www.windsorrealestate.com

Winnipeg Real Estate Board (WREB)
1240 Portage Ave., Winnipeg MB R3G 0T6 Canada
Tel: 204-786-8854; *Fax:* 204-784-2343
jwood@winnipegrealtors.ca
www.winnipegrealtors.ca
To serve members & to promote the benefits of organized real estate

Woodstock-Ingersoll & District Real Estate Board
#6, 65 Springbank Ave., Woodstock ON N4S 8V8 Canada
Tel: 519-539-3616; *Fax:* 519-539-1975
widreb@bellnet.ca
boards.mls.ca/woodstock

Yellowknife Real Estate Board
#201, 5204 - 50 Ave., Yellowknife NT X1A 1E2 Canada
Tel: 867-920-4624; *Fax:* 867-873-6387
officecomp@ssimicro.com
boards.mls.ca/yellowknife
Nicole Chernish, Secretary/Treasurer & Executive Off

York Region Real Estate Board (YRREB)
28 Main St. North, Newmarket ON L3Y 3Z7 Canada
Tel: 905-895-7624; *Fax:* 905-895-9216
To serve the best interests of members through education, products & services, & ethical standards

Yorkton Real Estate Association Inc. (YREA)
#040, 41 Broadway West, Yorkton SK S3N 0L6 Canada
Tel: 306-783-3067; *Fax:* 306-782-3231
yrea@sasktel.net
To promote a high level of professionalism among members by providing leadership in the real estate industry & in the community

Yukon Real Estate Association
49 Waterfront Pl., Whitehorse YT Y1A 6V1 Canada
Tel: 867-633-4290; *Fax:* 867-667-2299
colleen@yrea.ca; president@yrea.ca
www.yrea.yk.ca
To promote interest in marketing of real estate in all its aspects & to advance & improve relations of members of society with public

Recreation, Hobbies & Games

Alberta Camping Association (ACA)
Percy Page Centre, 11759 Groat Rd., Edmonton AB T5M 3K6 Canada
Tel: 780-427-6605; *Fax:* 780-427-6695
info@albertacamping.com
www.albertacamping.com
To promote & coordinate organized camping in Alberta by providing camp information & leadership direction as well as promoting high standards of camp programs & activities for all populations; to take a leading role in the recognition & promotion of professional standards for organized camps in Alberta
Laureen Wray, President
Scott Lister, Treasurer

Alberta Recreation & Parks Association (ARPA)
11759 Groat Rd., Edmonton AB T5M 3K6 Canada
Tel: 780-415-1745; *Fax:* 780-451-7915
Toll-Free: 877-544-1747
arpa@arpaonline.ca
www.arpaonline.ca
Social Media: www.facebook.com/arpaonline; www.twitter.com/#!/arpaonline
To promote accessibility to recreation & parks & their benefits to Albertans; To work toward economic sustainability, natural resource protection, & conservation within provincial parks & natural environments
Rick Curtis, Executive Director
Steve Allan, Manager, Finance & Operations
Carol Petersen, Manager, Recreation & Community Development
Lisa Tink, Manager, Children & Youth Programs
Mandi Wise, Coordinator, Communications

Alberta Snowmobile Association (ASA)
11759 Groat Rd., Edmonton AB T5M 3K6 Canada
Tel: 780-427-2695; *Fax:* 780-415-1779
info@altasnowmobile.ab.ca
www.altasnowmobile.ab.ca
To promote safe recreational snowmobiling in the province of Alberta

Alberta Sport Parachuting Association (ASPA)
#63, 2505 - 42 St., Edmonton AB T6L 7G8 Canada
admin@aspa.ca
www.aspa.ca
To promote & facilitate the development of the sport of skydiving in Alberta
Henry Komant, Acting President
Tina Connolly, Program Coordinator

Alberta Sprint Racing Canoe Association
11759 Groat Rd., Edmonton AB T5M 3K6 Canada
Tel: 780-203-3987
arsca@shaw.ca
www.albertasprintcanoe.com

Alberta Whitewater Association (AWA)
Percy Page Centre, 11759 Groat Rd., Edmonton AB T5M 3K6 Canada
Tel: 780-427-6717; *Fax:* 780-427-0524
kayakawa@telusplanet.net
www.albertawhitewater.ca
To encourage whitewater paddlesport activities

All Terrain Vehicle Association of Nova Scotia (ATVANS)
PO Box 46020, Stn. Novalea, Halifax NS B3K 5V8 Canada
Tel: 902-241-3200; *Toll-Free:* 877-288-4244
admin@atvans.org
www.atvans.org
To represent the interest of ATV'ers to Government, Land owners, other recreation user groups and the general public and educate, inform and organize ATV'ers to preserve and expand ATV recreational opportunities to promote safe family activities.
Mike Marriott, President
Ray Gouthro, Executive Director

Association des camps du Québec inc. (ACQ) / Québec Camping Association
CP 1000, Succ. M, 4545, av Pierre-de-Coubertin, Montréal QC H1V 3R2 Canada
Tél: 514-252-3113; *Téléc:* 514-252-1650
Ligne sans frais: 800-361-3586
info@camps.qc.ca
www.camps.qc.ca
Assurer le développement, la promotion et la qualité des camps de vacances; s'assurer de la formation du personnel des camps
Louis Jean, Directeur général
François Vézina, Président

Association of Canadian Mountain Guides (ACMG) / Association des guides de montagne canadiens
PO Box 8341, Canmore AB T1W 2V1 Canada
Tel: 403-678-2885; *Fax:* 403-609-0070
acmg@acmg.ca
www.acmg.ca
The Association represents mountain guides in dealing with both public & private official bodies. It is the regulatory body, maintaining standards of guiding, & acts as a public relations body to promote the sport in a safe & educational manner.

Association québécoise de canoë-kayak de vitesse (AQCKV)
CP 1000, Succ. M, 4545, av Pierre-de Coubertin, Montréal QC H1V 3R2 Canada
Tél: 514-252-3086; *Téléc:* 514-252-3094
directeur.technique@aqckv.qc.ca
www.aqckv.qc.ca
Promouvoir les activités de canoë-kayak de vitesse au Québec

British Columbia Camping Association
c/o Sasamat Outdoor Centre, 3302 Senkler Rd., Belcarra BC V3H 4S3 Canada
Tel: 604-931-6449; *Fax:* 604-939-8522
info@bccamping.org
www.bccamping.org
To facilitate the development of organized camping in order to provide educational, character-building & constructive recreational experiences for all people; to develop awareness & appreciation of the natural environment
Hart Banack, President

British Columbia Fishing Resorts & Outfitters Association (BCFROA)
PO Box 3301, Kamloops BC V2C 6B9 Canada
Tel: 250-374-6836; *Fax:* 250-374-6640
Toll-Free: 800-374-6836
bcfroa@bcfroa.ca
www.bcfroa.ca
Works with the public & private sector to protect areas currently in use; to preserve the wildlife experience in BC for the enjoyment of future generations; a lobby group whose members are dedicated to providing a quality outdoor experience

British Columbia Hang Gliding & Paragliding Association (BCHPA)
www.bchpa.ca
The focus of BCHPA is the protection, maintenance & improvement of flying sites throughout the province.

British Columbia Recreation & Parks Association (BCRPA)
#101, 4664 Lougheed Hwy., Burnaby BC V5C 5T5
Tel: 604-629-0965; *Fax:* 604-629-2651
Toll-Free: 866-929-0965
bcrpa@bcrpa.bc.ca; registration@bcrpa.bc.ca
www.bcrpa.bc.ca
To establish & sustain healthy lifestyles & communities in British Columbia
Dean Gibson, President
Suzanne Allard Strutt, Chief Executive Officer
Holly-Ann Burrows, Manager, Communication
Sandra Couto, Manager, Finance
Kara Misra, Manager, Parks & Recreation
Misty Thomas, Manager, Fitness Program

British Columbia Sailing Association
#223, 3820 Cessna Dr., Richmond BC V7B 0A2 Canada
Tel: 604-333-3628; *Fax:* 604-333-3626
crew@bcsailing.bc.ca
www.bcsailing.bc.ca
The provincial sport authority for sailing.

British Columbia Snowmobile Federation (BCSF)
Stn. 400, 2439 Poulton Ave., Houston BC V0Y 1Z0 Canada
Tel: 250-845-7705; *Fax:* 250-845-7715
Toll-Free: 877-537-8716
office@bcsf.org
www.bcsf.org
To encourage & promote the sport of operating snowmobiles in BC by enhancing cooperation & communication between & among snowmobile clubs, recreation industry & racing divisions, the provincial government, other motorized recreational organizations & groups supportive of snowmobiling

The Bruce Trail Conservancy
PO Box 857, Hamilton ON L8N 3N9 Canada
Tel: 905-529-6821; *Fax:* 905-529-6823
Toll-Free: 800-665-4453
info@brucetrail.org
www.brucetrail.org
Social Media: www.facebook.com/group.php?gid=111645892194726
To secure, develop & manage the Bruce Trail as a public footpath along the Niagara Escarpment from Queenston to Tobermory, thereby promoting preservation of the escarpment's ecological & cultural integrity & fostering an appreciation of its natural beauty. The Bruce Trail, designated as a UNESCO World Biosphere Reserve, is Canada's oldest and longest footpath.

Campground Owners Association of Nova Scotia (COANS)
c/o Arm of Gold Campground, 24 Church Rd., Little Bras d'Or, Cape Breton NS B1Y 2Y2 Canada
Tel: 902-736-6671
info@campingnovascotia.com
www.campingnovascotia.com
To provide the best camping experience possible throughout our diverse province; to improve standards at all the province's campgrounds; to provide leadership to this important segment of the provincial economy.
John Brennick, President
Chris Miller, Vice-President

Canadian Aerophilatelic Society (CAS) / La société canadienne d'aérophilatélie (SCA)
203A Woodfield Dr., Nepean ON K2G 4P2
www.aerophilately.ca
To represent Canadian aerophilatelists nationally & internationally

The Canadian Association of Fitness Professionals / Association canadienne des professionnels en conditionnement physique
#110, 255 Consumers Rd., Toronto ON M2J 1R4 Canada
Tel: 416-493-3515; *Fax:* 416-493-1756
Toll-Free: 800-667-5622
info@canfitpro.com
www.canfitpro.com
Social Media: www.facebook.com/group.php?gid=2524100816
Can-Fit-Pro takes today's fitness professionals' challenges & creates tomorrow's solutions through ongoing relative knowledge & personal enrichment
Maureen Hagan, Executive Director
Kathy Ash, Contact, Administration

Canadian Association of Numismatic Dealers (CAND) / Association canadienne des marchands numismatiques
c/o Jo-Anne Simpson, Executive Secretary, PO Box 10272, Stn. Winona, Stoney Creek ON L8E 5R1
Tel: 905-643-4988; *Fax:* 905-643-6329
email@cand.org
www.cand.org
To ensure professionalism by members of the association
Michael Findlay, President
Paul Koolhaas, Vice-President
Wendy Hoare, Secretary-Treasurer

Canadian Association of Wooden Money Collectors (CAWMC)
c/o Norm Belsten, 86 Hamilton Dr., Newmarket ON L3Y 3E8 Canada
nbelsten@sympatico.ca
Norm Belsten, Contact

Canadian Baton Twirling Federation (CBTF) / Fédération baton canadienne
35 Traynor Bay, Winnipeg MB R2M 4H7 Canada
Tel: 204-257-2206; *Fax:* 204-257-2206
info_cbtf@canada.com
www.cbtf.ca

Canadian Boating Federation / Fédération nautique du Canada
410, rue Victoria, Valleyfield QC J6K 4M3
Tel: 450-377-4122; *Fax:* 450-377-5282
cbfnc@bellnet.ca
www.cbfnc.ca

Canadian BodyBuilding Federation (CBBF) / Fédération canadienne de culturisme
info@cbbf.ca
www.cbbf.ca
To act as the governing body for amateur bodybuilding, fitness, & body fitness (figure) competition
Mark Smishek, President
Karen MacLean, Vice-President
John MacLellan, Secretary-Treasurer

Canadian Bridge Federation (CFB) / La Fédération canadienne incorporée de bridge
2719 East Jolly Pl., Regina SK S4V 0X8 Canada
Tel: 306-761-1677; *Fax:* 306-789-4919
jan@cbf.ca
www.cbf.ca
To conduct grassroot bridge events in Canada; to select & subsidize teams to World Championships.

Canadian Camping Association (CCA) / Association des camps du Canada (ACC)
2494, rte 125 sud, St-Donat QC J0T 2C0
Tel: 819-424-2662; *Fax:* 819-424-2662
Toll-Free: 877-427-6958
info@ccamping.org
www.ccamping.org
To develop & promote organized camping for all populations across Canada; To further the interests & welfare of children, youth, & adults through camping; To encourage high standards in camping
Jeff Bradshaw, President

Canadian Casting Federation
c/o Toronto Sportsmen's Association, 17 Mill St., Toronto ON M2P 1B3 Canada
Tel: 416-487-4477; *Fax:* 416-487-4478
www.torontosportsmens.ca/Casting.html
To teach casting skills, covering fly, bait, & spinning

Canadian Correspondence Chess Association (CCCA) / L'Association canadienne des échecs par correspondance (ACEC)
#4, 1669 Country Rd., L'Orignal QC K0B 1K0 Canada
Tel: 613-632-3166
ccca@cogeco.ca
correspondencechess.com/ccca/index.htm

Canadian Council of Snowmobile Organizations (CCSO) / Conseil canadien des organismes de motoneige (CCOM)
PO Box 21059, Thunder Bay ON P7A 8A7
Tel: 807-345-5299
ccso.ccom@tbaytel.net
www.ccso-ccom.ca
To provide leadership & support to organized snowmobiling in Canada

Canadian Fitness & Lifestyle Research Institute (CFLRI) / Institut canadien de la recherche sur la condition physique et le mode de vie
#201, 185 Somerset St. West, Ottawa ON K2P 0J2 Canada
Tel: 613-233-5528; *Fax:* 613-233-5536
info@cflri.ca
www.cflri.ca
To conduct research, monitor trends, & make recommendations to increase physical activity & improve health in Canada

Canadian Flag Association (CFA) / Association canadienne de vexillologie (ACV)
50 Heathfield Dr., Toronto ON M1M 3B1 Canada
Tel: 416-267-9618; *Fax:* 416-267-9618
kevin.harrington@sympatico.ca
www.crwflags.com/fotw/flags/vex-cfa.html
To gather, organize & disseminate flag information with particular emphasis on flags having some association with Canada; to promote vexillology; to encourage & facilitate exchange of ideas between flag scholars, flag makers, flag collectors, flag designers & flag historians

Canadian International DX Club (CIDX)
PO Box 67063, Stn. Lemoyne, Saint-Lambert QC J4R 2T8
cidxclub@yahoo.com
www.anarc.org/cidx
To serve radio enthusiasts throughout the world

Canadian Motorcycle Association (CMA) / Association motocycliste canadienne
PO Box 448, Hamilton ON L8L 8C4 Canada
Tel: 905-522-5705; *Fax:* 905-522-5716
registration@canmocycle.ca
www.canmocycle.ca
To encourage & develop motorcycling for the benefit & enjoyment of its members

Canadian Orienteering Federation (COF) / Fédération canadienne de course d'orientation
1239 Colgrove Ave. NE, Calgary AB T2C 5C3 Canada
Tel: 403-283-0807; *Fax:* 403-451-1681
info@orienteering.ca
www.orienteering.ca
Social Media: www.facebook.com/group.php?gid=64406548384

Canadian Paper Money Society (CPMS)
Attn: Dick Dunn, PO Box 562, Pickering ON L1V 2R7 Canada
Tel: 905-509-1146
info@cpmsonline.ca
www.nunetcan.net/cpms.htm
The aims and ojectives of the Society are to encourage and support historical studies of banks and other paper money issuing authorities in Canada, to preserve their history and statistical records, and through research and publishing the results thereof, ensure that information, documents, and other evidence of Canada's financial development will be preserved.

Canadian Parks & Recreation Association (CPRA) / Association canadienne des parcs et loisirs
PO Box 83069, 1180 Walkley Rd., Ottawa ON K1V 2M5
Tel: 613-523-5315
info@cpra.ca
www.cpra.ca
To advocate on the benefits of parks & recreation services

Canadian Parks & Wilderness Society (CPAWS) / Société pour la nature et les parcs du Canada (SNAP)
#506, 250 City Centre Ave., Ottawa ON K1R 6K7
Tel: 613-569-7226; *Fax:* 613-569-7098
Toll-Free: 800-333-9453
info@cpaws.org
www.cpaws.org
Social Media: www.facebook.com/cpaws; www.twitter.com/#!/cpaws
To act as the Canadian voice for public wilderness protection

Canadian Power & Sail Squadrons (Canadian Headquarters) (CPS) / Escadrilles canadiennes de plaisance (ECP)
26 Golden Gate Ct., Toronto ON M1P 3A5 Canada
Tel: 416-293-2438; *Fax:* 416-293-2445
Toll-Free: 888-277-2628
hgg@cps-ecp.ca
www.cps-ecp.ca
To increase awareness & knowledge of safe boating by educating & training members & the general public, by fostering fellowship among members, & establishing partnerships & alliances with organizations & agencies interested in boating

Canadian Racing Pigeon Union Inc.
#C, 261 Tillson Ave., Tillsonburg ON N4G 5X2 Canada
Tel: 519-842-9771; *Fax:* 519-842-8809
Toll-Free: 866-652-5704
crpu@execulink.com
www.canadianracingpigeonunion.com
To promote the sport of pigeon racing in Canada

Canadian Sport Parachuting Association (CSPA) / Association canadienne du parachutisme sportif (ACPS)
300 Forced Rd., Russell ON K4R 1A1 Canada
Tel: 613-445-1881; *Fax:* 613-445-2698
office@cspa.ca
www.cspa.ca

Canadian Stamp Dealers' Association (CSDA) / Association canadienne des négociants en timbres-poste (ACNTP)
PO Box 81, Stn. Lambeth, London ON N6P 1P9 Canada
director@csdaonline.com
www.csdaonline.com

Canadian Table Soccer Federation
8311, rue Ouimet, Brossard QC J4Y 3B3 Canada
Tel: 514-668-2326
secretary@canadafoos.com
To oversee & monitor the growth of foosball in Canada.

Canadian Table Tennis Association (CTTA) / Association canadienne de tennis de table
#400, 2211 Riverside Dr., Ottawa ON K1H 7X5 Canada
Tel: 613-733-6272; *Fax:* 613-733-7279
ctta@ctta.ca
www.ctta.ca
To increase the popularity of the sport of table tennis through programs & activities; to increase participation in table tennis at all levels

Canadian Toy Collectors' Society Inc. (CTCS)
#245, 91 Rylander Blvd., Unit 7, Toronto ON M1B 5M5 Canada
ctcsweb@hotmail.com
www.ctcs.org
To promote interest in the collection & display of all types of toys, childhood memorabilia & literature; to acquire, maintain & house a collection of toys & to restore & preserve Canadian toys of historic significance.
Ron Blair, President

Canadian Trapshooting Association (CTA)
RR#1, Penhold AB T0M 1R0 Canada
Tel: 403-886-2600; *Fax:* 403-886-2600
To promote clay target shooting as a recreational sport among shooters of every age, both sexes, & at every level of ability, the ultimate objective being to compete in the world championships held each year in Ohio
Bob Brown, President

Canadian Yachting Association (CYA) / Association canadienne de yachting
Portsmith Olympic Harbour, 53 Yonge St., Kingston ON K7M 6G4 Canada
Tel: 613-545-3044; *Fax:* 613-545-3045
Toll-Free: 877-416-4720
sailcanada@sailing.ca
www.sailing.ca
To promote the sport of sailing in Canada

Canoe Kayak New Brunswick
c/o Doug Forbes, 42 Third St., Rothesay NB E2H 1M9 Canada
Tel: 506-849-0793
communications@canoekayaknb.org
www.canoekayaknb.org
Canoe-Kayak New Brunswick is a non-profit volunteer organization dedicated to the promotion of safe recreational paddling in the province of New Brunswick.
Tim Humes, President

Canoe Kayak Nova Scotia (CKNS)
5516 Spring Garden Rd., 4th Fl., Halifax NS B3J 1G6 Canada
Tel: 902-425-5454; *Fax:* 902-425-5606
canoens@sportnovascotia.ca
www.ckns.ca

Canoe Kayak Saskatchewan (CKS)
1870 Lorne St., Regina SK S4P 2L7 Canada
Tel: 306-729-4220; *Fax:* 306-729-4216
cks@accesscomm.ca
www.saskcanoe.ca
To operate as the provincial sport governing body for canoe & kayak in Saskatchewan

Bibliothèque et Archives nationales Québec

Audiovisuel à retourner au traitement

Réparation requise

- ☐ Antivol
- ☐ Boîtier brisé
- ☐ Plages défectueuses (nº de plages : ____________________)
- ☐ Problèmes son ou image (Temps : ____________________)
- ☐ Cote ou identification visuelle
- ☐ Pages du livret déchirées ou détachées (p. ____________________)
- ☐ Ruban brisé
- ☐ Codes à barres

Traitement requis

- ☐ Document non inscrit **ou** nº de document non valide
- ☐ Manque accompagnement. SVP corriger la notice d'exemplaire
- ☐ En transit local
- ☐ Erreur de catégorie documentaire

- ☐ **Urgent – Réservation en attente**
- ☐ Autres (préciser) :

____

____

____

Date : ______ / ______ / ______ Nom : ____________________
(jour) (mois) (année)

Canoe Newfoundland & Labrador
PO Box 23072, Stn. Churchill Sq., St. John's NL A1B 4J9 Canada
Tel: 709-364-1601; *Fax:* 709-368-8357
tumblehome.nfld@gmail.com
www.canoenfld.ca
Tumblehome Canoe Club is a local canoeing club that welcomes members from all parts of the province. It is a non-profit group of canoeing enthusiasts who get together regularly to enjoy the sport of canoeing and socialize with other canoeing lovers.
Corey Locke, President

Canoe Ontario
c/o OCSRA, 570 Blenheim Cres., Oakville ON L6J 6P6 Canada
Tel: 905-337-8314
jorlando1@cogeco.ca
www.canoeontario.ca
John Orlando, Treasurer

CanoeKayak BC
20585 - 124A Ave., Maple Ridge BC V2X 0M6 Canada
Tel: 604-465-5268; *Fax:* 604-460-0587
info@canoekayakbc.ca
www.canoekayakbc.ca
Mary Jane Abbot, Executive Director

CanoeKayak Canada (CKC)
#705, 2197 Riverside Dr., Ottawa ON K1H 7X3 Canada
Tel: 613-260-1818; *Fax:* 613-260-5137
christine@canoekayak.ca
www.canoekayak.ca
To increase the number of Canadians participating in canoeing & kayaking; to enable participants to realize excellence by providing sound athlete development programs & membership support systems

CanoeKayak Canada - Atlantic Division
c/o Sport NS, 5516 Spring Garden Rd., 4th Fl., Halifax NS B3J 3G6 Canada
Tel: 902-425-5450; *Fax:* 902-425-5606
ccaatlantic@sportnovascotia.ca
www.ccaatlantic.ca
Liz Orton, Program Coordinator

Charlottetown Duplicate Bridge Club
500 Queen St., Charlottetown PE C1A 8K9 Canada
Tel: 902-894-3067

Chess Federation of Canada / Fédération canadienne des échecs
#E1, 2212 Gladwin Cres., Ottawa ON K1B 5N1 Canada
Tel: 613-733-2844; *Fax:* 613-733-5209
Toll-Free: 800-563-4476
info@chess.ca
www.chess.ca
To coordinate chess play across Canada

Citizens for Safe Cycling (CfSC)
PO Box 248, Stn. B, Ottawa ON K1P 6C4 Canada
Tel: 613-722-4454; *Fax:* 613-722-4454
info@safecycling.ca
www.safecycling.ca
To promote cycling as fun, healthy, safe, economical, and environmentally-friendly transportation and recreation.
Zlatko Krstulich, President

Classical & Medieval Numismatic Society (CMNS)
PO Box 956, Stn. B, Toronto ON M2K 2T6 Canada
Tel: 416-490-8659; *Fax:* 416-490-6452
billmcdo@idirect.com
www.cmns.ca
To promote & encourage study & research in the field of numismatics & history as they relate to ancient & medieval coinage & related subjects; to publish the writings that are the result of such activity.
W.H. McDonald, Executive Sec.-Treas.

Climb Yukon Association
climbyukon@gmail.com
www.climbyukon.net
To develop to the climbing community in the Yukon as a recreational opportunity for adults and youth, to raise awareness of, and address access and safety concerns.
Ryan Agar, President

Dominion of Canada Rifle Association (DCRA) / L'Association de tir dominion du canada
45 Shirley Blvd., Ottawa ON K2K 2W6 Canada
Tel: 613-829-8281; *Fax:* 613-829-0099
office@dcra.ca
www.dcra.ca

Fédération de saut de barils du Canada / Canadian Barrel Jumping Federation
1465, Place Louis-Fréchette, Saint-Bruno QC J3V 2T8 Canada
Tél: 450-653-9460
Promotion du sport du saut de barils; tenir le championnat canadien annuellement; reconnaître nos champions et les records

Fédération des clubs de motoneigistes du Québec (FCMQ)
CP 1000, Succ. M, 4545, av Pierre-de Coubertin, Montréal QC H1V 3R2 Canada
Tél: 514-252-3076; *Téléc:* 514-254-2066
info@fcmq.qc.ca
www.fcmq.qc.ca
La Fédération des clubs de motoneigistes du Québec est un organisme à but non lucratif, voué au développement et à la promotion de la pratique de la motoneige dans tout le Québec
Mario Côté, Président

Federation of Mountain Clubs of British Columbia
PO Box 19673, 130 West Broadway, Vancouver BC V5T 4E7 Canada
Tel: 604-873-6096; *Fax:* 604-873-6086
fmcbc@mountainclubs.bc.ca
www.mountainclubs.bc.ca
To promote hiking & mountaineering

Federation of Ontario Cottagers' Associations (FOCA)
#201, 159 King St., Peterborough ON K9J 2R8
Tel: 705-749-3622; *Fax:* 705-749-6522
info@foca.on.ca
www.foca.on.ca
To ensure a healthy future for waterfront Ontario; To support the interests of Ontario's cottagers

Fédération québécoise de camping et de caravaning inc. (FQCC)
CP 100, 1560, rue Eiffel, Boucherville QC J4B 5Y1 Canada
Tél: 450-650-3722; *Téléc:* 450-650-3721
Ligne sans frais: 877-650-3722
info@fqcc.ca
www.fqcc.ca
Unir les adepts du camping et du caravaning; entreprendre et coordonner des actions relatives au camping et au caravaning.
Louise Saindon, Présidente
Claude Cournoyer, Trésorier

Fédération québécoise de canoë-kayak d'eau vive
CP 1000, Succ. M, 4545, av Pierre-de Coubertin, Montréal QC H1V 3R2 Canada
Tél: 514-252-3099; *Téléc:* 514-252-3094
fqckev@kayak.qc.ca
www.kayak.qc.ca
Promouvoir le sport et la pratique d'activités en eau vive au Québec

Fédération québécoise de la marche
CP 1000, Succ. M, 4545, av Pierre-de Coubertin, Montréal QC H1V 3R2 Canada
Tél: 514-252-3157; *Téléc:* 514-252-5137
Ligne sans frais: 866-252-2065
infomarche@fqmarche.qc.ca
www.fqmarche.qc.ca
Promotion de la marche et de la randonnée pedestre; support au développement de lieux de marche

Fédération québécoise des échecs (FQE) / Québec Chess Federation
CP 1000, Succ. M, Montréal QC H1V 3R2 Canada
Tél: 514-252-3034; *Téléc:* 514-251-8038
info@fqechecs.qc.ca
www.fqechecs.qc.ca
Promouvoir l'étude, l'enseignement et la pratique du jeu d'échecs au Québec

Fédération québécoise des jeux récréatifs (FQJR)
CP 1000, Succ. M, 4545, av Pierre-de Coubertin, Montréal QC H1V 3R2 Canada
Tél: 514-252-3032
jeuxrecr@fqjr.qc.ca
www.fqjr.qc.ca
La Fédération oeuvre activement à l'avènement d'une école autonome et responsable où l'élève est le centre de toutes les préoccupations et de toutes les décisions. Cette école rend possible, en véritable partenariat, le travail de tous ses intervenants : directeur, enseignants, parents et administrateurs, concertés dans l'élaboration, la mise en oeuvre et la réussite d'un projet éducatif correspondant aux besoins de son milieu. Le rôle de chacun y est reconnu à la valeur de sa contribution.
André Leclerc, Directeur général

Fédération québécoise du canot et du kayak (FQCK)
CP 1000, Succ. M, 4545, av Pierre-de Coubertin, Montréal QC H1V 3R2 Canada
Tél: 514-252-3001; *Téléc:* 514-252-3091
info@canot-kayak.qc.ca
www.canot-kayak.qc.ca
Regrouper les organismes et individus intéressés à la pratique du canotage récréatif et du canot-camping et de promouvoir la pratique de ces activités en utilisant le canot ouvert de type amérindien autrement appelé Canot Canadien

Guide Outfitters Association of British Columbia (GOABC)
PO Box 94675, Richmond BC V6Y 4A4 Canada
Tel: 604-278-2688; *Fax:* 604-278-3440
info@goabc.org
www.goabc.org
Dale Drown, General Manager

Halifax North West Trails Association (HNWTA)
c/o 27 Warwick Lane, Halifax NS B3M 4J3 Canada
Tel: 902-443-5051
info@halifaxnorthwesttrails.ca
www.halifaxnorthwesttrails.ca
To promote the creation, protection and maintenance of trails within the Halifax Mainland North area.
Todd Beal, Chair

Hang Gliding & Paragliding Association of Atlantic Canada (HPAAC)
General Delivery, Diligent River NS B0M 1H0 Canada
Tel: 902-254-2972
jnewman@eastlink.ca
www.hpaac.ca
To develop & promote the sports of hang glinding & paragliding in Atlantic Canada
Judith Newman, Contact

Hang Gliding & Paragliding Association of Canada (HPAC) / Association canadienne de vol libre (ACVL)
5 Millennium Dr., Stratford PE C1B 2H2 Canada
Fax: 902-367-3358
Toll-Free: 877-370-2078
admin@hpac.ca
www.hpac.ca
To promote unpowered foot-launched flight in hang gliders & paragliders.
Domagoj Juretic, President
Sam Jeyes, Business Manager

Hike Ontario
#400, 165 Dundas St. West, Mississauga ON L5B 2N6 Canada
Tel: 905-277-4453; *Toll-Free:* 800-894-7249
info@hikeontario.com
www.hikeontario.com
To act as the voice for hikers & walkers in Ontario; To encourage hiking, walking & trail development in Ontario; To promote trail maintenance. best practices, & safe hiking; To enhance environmental awareness, conservation & sustainable trails

Ikaluktutiak Paddling Association
PO Box 125, Cambridge Bay NU X0B 0C0 Canada
Tel: 867-983-2068
ipanorth69@gmail.com
Rob Harmer, President

International Computer Games Association (ICGA)
c/o David N.L. Levy, 34 Courthope Rd., Hampstead, London NW3 2LD England
info@icga.org; board@icga.org; journal@icga.org
To promote computer games; To share technical knowledge; To foster developments in the man-machine area

Manitoba Camping Association (MCA)
#302, 960 Portage Ave., Winnipeg MB R3G 0R4 Canada
Tel: 204-784-1134; *Fax:* 204-784-4177
info@mbcamping.ca; sunshinefund@mbcamping.ca
www.mbcamping.ca
To act as a coordinating body for organized camping in Manitoba; To promote organized camping as an educational and recreational experience
Bryan Ezako, Executive Director
Laura-Ann Peterson, Coordinator, General Office Administration & Sunshine Fund Program

Manitoba Paddling Association Inc. (MPA)
200 Main St., Winnipeg MB R3C 4M2 Canada
Tel: 204-925-5678; *Fax:* 204-925-5703
mpa@sport.mb.ca; dragonboat@sport.mb.ca
www.mpa.mb.ca

To act as the governing body for all competitive paddling sports in Manitoba, including kayak, canoe, & dragon boat; To develop high performance athletes to compete for Manitoba nationally & to qualify for the national team; To develop coaches to coach from the grassroots to the high performance levels; To service paddlers from beginners to elite athletes; To ensure the existence of paddling clubs in Manitoba

Manitoba Sport Parachute Association (MSPA)
#309, 200 Main St., Winnipeg MB R3C 4M2 Canada
Tel: 204-925-5682; *Fax:* 204-925-5703
president@mspa.mb.ca
www.mspa.mb.ca
To promote awareness & participation in skydiving in Manitoba
Jill Forbes, President

Model Aeronautics Association of Canada Inc. (MAAC) / Modélistes Aéronautiques Associés du Canada
#9, 5100 South Service Rd., Burlington ON L7L 6A5 Canada
Tel: 905-632-9808; *Fax:* 905-632-3304
maachq@on.aibn.com
www.maac.ca
To foster, enhance, assist, aid & engage in scientific development; to provide central organization to record & disseminate information relating to model aeronautics; to guide & direct national model aviation activities; to direct technical organization of national & international model aircraft contests

National Association of Watch & Clock Collectors (NAWCC)
514 Poplar St., Columbia PA 17512 USA
Tel: 717-684-8261; *Fax:* 717-684-0878
www.nawcc.org
To stimulate interest in timepieces; to collect & preserve horological materials & information; to work with others in exhibiting timepieces; to encourage timepiece collection; to disseminate information on timepieces; to facilitate timepiece markets.
J. Steven Humphrey, Executive Director
Chuck Auman, Controller

National Darts Federation of Canada (NDFC) / Fédération nationale de dards du Canada
2417, rue Montante, Ascot QC J1H 6M3 Canada
Tel: 819-823-1392; *Fax:* 819-821-3539
secretary@ndfc.ca
www.ndfc.ca
To promote & organize Darts events & promote the betterment of the game

National Firearms Association (NFA)
PO Box 52183, Edmonton AB T6G 2T5 Canada
Tel: 780-439-1394; *Fax:* 780-439-4091
info@nfa.ca
www.nfa.ca

New Brunswick Competitive Canoe Association
c/o Sport New Brunswick, 181 Kennebecasis River Rd., Hampton NB E5N 6L1 Canada
nbcca_m@hotmail.com
J. Timothy Flood, President

Newfoundland & Labrador Camping Association
PO Box 50846, SS#3, St. John's NL A1B 4M2 Canada
Tel: 709-576-6198; *Fax:* 709-576-8146
malcolmcturner@gmail.com
To facilitate the development of organized camping in order to provide educational, character-building & constructive recreational experiences for all people; to develop awareness & appreciation of the natural environment
Malcolm C. Turner

Newfoundland & Labrador Paddling Association (NLPA)
103« Forest Rd., St. John's NL A1A 1E4 Canada
To promote recreational canoeing & kayaking in Newfoundland & Labrador; to represent the interests of the canoeing & kayaking public
Allan Goodridge, President
Brian Hemeon, Vice-President, Canoeing
Darren MacDonald, Vice-President, Kayaking
Neil Burgess, Secretary
Alex Mcgruer, Treasurer

Northwest Territories Recreation & Parks Association (NWTRPA)
PO Box 841, Yellowknife NT X1A 2N6 Canada
Tel: 867-873-5340; *Fax:* 867-669-6791
admin@nwtrpa.org
www.nwtrpa.org
To increase public awareness of recreation & parks; to enhance the quality of life of residents of the NWT through fostering the development of recreation & parks services
Robin Langille, President
Geoff Ray, Executive Director

Nova Scotia Trails Federation (NSTF)
5516 Spring Garden Rd., 4th Fl., Halifax NS B3J 1G6 Canada
Tel: 902-425-5450; *Fax:* 902-425-5606
nstrails@sportnovascotia.ca
www.novascotiatrails.com
Social Media: www.twitter.com/NSTrails
To promote the development and responsible use of recreational trails for the benefit and enjoyment of all Nova Scotians and visitors to our province.
Ted Scrutton, President

Ontario Camps Association (OCA)
#403, 250 Merton St., Toronto ON M4S 1B1
Tel: 416-485-0425; *Fax:* 416-485-0422
info@ontariocamps.ca
www.ontariocamps.ca
To promote youth camping throughout Ontario; To maintain high standards for organized camping; To advocate on issues which impact members
Rick Howard, President
Aruna Ogale, Executive Director

Ontario Federation of Snowmobile Clubs (OFSC)
#9, 501 Welham Rd., Barrie ON L4N 8Z6
Tel: 705-739-7669; *Fax:* 705-739-5005
www.ofsc.on.ca
To support member snowmobile clubs & volunteers; To establish & maintain quality snowmobile trails; To further the enjoyment of organized snowmobiling

Ontario Marine Operators Association (OMOA)
15 Laurier Rd., Penetanguishene ON L9M 1G8
Tel: 705-549-1667; *Fax:* 705-549-1670
Toll-Free: 888-547-6662
omoa@marinasontario.com
www.marinasontario.com
To promote recreational boating throughout Ontario

Ontario Numismatic Association (ONA)
c/o Bruce Raszmann, PO Box 40033, Stn. Waterloo Square, 75 King St. South, Waterloo ON N2J 4V1
www.ontario-numismatic.org

Ontario Parks Association (OPA)
7856 - 5th Line South, RR#4, Milton ON L9T 2X8
Tel: 905-864-6182; *Fax:* 905-864-6184
Toll-Free: 866-560-7783
opa@ontarioparksassociation.ca
www.ontarioparksassociation.ca
To develop & protect parks & green spaces in Ontario
Paul Ronan, Executive Director
Shelley May, Coordinator, Operations & Administration

Ontario Recreation Facilities Association Inc. (ORFA)
#102, 1 Concorde Gate, Toronto ON M3C 3N6
Tel: 416-426-7062; *Fax:* 416-426-7385
Toll-Free: 800-661-6732
info@orfa.com; admin@orfa.com
www.orfa.com
To provide leadership for the recreation facility profession in Ontario; To promote the professional operation of recreation facilities throughout the province

Ontario Recreational Canoeing and Kayaking Association (ORCKA)
#411, 1185 Eglinton Ave. East, Toronto ON M3C 3C6 Canada
Tel: 416-426-7016; *Fax:* 416-426-7363
info@orca.on.ca
www.orca.on.ca
To promote development of safe, competent & knowledgeable recreational canoeists

Ontario Research Council on Leisure (ORCOL) / Conseil Ontarien de Recherche en Loisir
c/o Recreation & Leisure Studies, Faculty of Applied Health Sciences, University of Waterloo, Waterloo ON N2L 3G1
smale@healthy.uwaterloo.ca
www.orcol.uwaterloo.ca
To disseminate research about leisure & recreation, including culture, tourism, fitness, & sports

Ontario Sportfishing Guides' Association (OSGA)
c/o Fish 'n' Fun, 4504 Trent Trail, RR2, Washago ON L0K 2B0 Canada
info@ontariofishcharters.ca
www.ontariofishcharters.ca
The Association monitors & participates in any regulation reform regarding sportfishing in the province. It lobbies as a unified voice on behalf of its members, & serves as a network where members can promote & learn from each other.

Ontario Trails Council
#130, 556 O'Connor Dr., Kingston ON K7P 1N3 Canada
Tel: 613-389-7678; *Fax:* 613-389-6329
Toll-Free: 877-668-7245
admin@ontariotrails.on.ca
www.ontariotrails.on.ca
To promote the creation, development, preservation, management & use of an integrated, recreational, multi-seasonal trail network in Ontario; interested in all types of trails for non-motorized & motorized (where applicable) use in all seasons; acquisition & conversion of Ontario's abandoned railway rights-of-way to linear greenways for year-round recreational activities for the people of Ontario

Ontario Vintage Radio Association (OVRA)
197 Humberside Ave., Toronto ON M6P 1K7 Canada
Tel: 416-769-9627
www.ovra.ca
The Association acts to preserve Canada's radio history, literature & equipment. It serves as a forum for members to exchange information & continue the legacy of the original club.

Orienteering Association of British Columbia (OABC)
4337 San Cristo Pl., Victoria BC V8N 5G5 Canada
www.orienteeringbc.ca

Outdoor Recreation Council of British Columbia (ORC)
47 West Broadway, Vancouver BC V5Y 1P1 Canada
Tel: 604-873-5546
outdoorrec@orcbc.ca
www.orcbc.ca
To advise industry & government in the development & implementation of outdoor recreation & conservation plans for BC; to contribute to the coordination of regional outdoor recreation by assisting in the establishment of a provincial network of outdoor recreationists to address recreational use conflicts & to advise government & industry on local & regional needs for noncompetitive outdoor recreation; to encourage active participation by the residents of BC in outdoor recreation activities; to promote the quality & diversity of outdoor recreation opportunities in BC by working cooperatively with government, industry, business & the public.

Outward Bound Canada
996 Chetwynd Rd., RR #2, Burks Falls ON P0A 1C0 Canada
Fax: 705-382-5959
Toll-Free: 888-688-9273
www.outwardbound.ca
To promote self-reliance, care & respect for others, responsibility to community & concern for the environment
Dave Wolfenden, Executive Director

Paddle Canada (PC) / Pagaie Canada
PO Box 20069, Stn. RPO Taylor-Kidd, Kingston ON K7P 2T6 Canada
Tel: 613-547-3196; *Fax:* 613-547-4880
Toll-Free: 888-252-6292
info@paddlingcanada.com
www.paddlingcanada.com
To promote all forms of recreational paddling to Canadians of diverse abilities, culture or age; to advocate for a healthy natural environment; to develop an appreciation for the canoe & the kayak in our Canadian heritage

Paddle Manitoba
PO Box 2663, Winnipeg MB R3C 4B3 Canada
Tel: 204-338-6722
info@paddle.mb.ca
www.paddle.mb.ca
Paddle Manitoba is a non-profit association, the advocate & instructional organization promoting safe canoeing & kayaking in the province. It encourages new entrants into paddling by supporting activities necessary to develop skills.

Parks & Recreation Ontario (PRO) / Parcs et loisirs de l'Ontario
#302, 1 Concorde Gate, Toronto ON M3C 3N6 Canada
Tel: 416-426-7142; *Fax:* 416-426-7371
pro@prontario.org
www.prontario.org
Strives to enhance the quality of life, health & well-being of people, their communities & their environments; to advocate provincially for parks & recreation issues; to provide networking as well as multi-discipline professional development opportunities

Prince Edward Island Canoe Kayak Association
RR#4, Alliston, Montague PE C0A 1R0 Canada
Tel: 902-962-3883; *Fax:* 902-962-3883
justin.heidi@windsinc.com
www.windsinc.com/canoekayak/canoekayak.htm
Justin Richard Batten, President

Prince Edward Island Recreational Canoeing Association
PO Box 5604, RR#5, Charlottetown PE C1A 7J8 Canada
Tel: 902-368-6355; *Fax:* 902-368-6186

Prince Edward Island Underwater Council
c/o Sport PEI, 3 Queen St., Charlottetown PE C1A 7K7 Canada
Tel: 902-368-4110
a.cannon@pei.sympatico.ca
The PEI Underwater Council's mission is to help support and promote the sport of scuba diving in Prince Edward Island through safety, advocacy, cultural & environmental awareness, self-governance and education.

Recreation and Parks Association of the Yukon (RPAY)
4061, 4th Ave., Whitehorse YT Y1A 1H1 Canada
Tel: 867-668-3010; *Fax:* 867-668-2455
rpay@klondiker.com
www.rpay.org
To promote, encourage and foster the growth and development of all areas of recreation throughout the Yukon Territory.
Ian Spencer, President
Anne Morgan, Executive Director

Recreation Facilities Association of British Columbia (RFABC)
PO Box 320, #110, 174 Wilson St., Victoria BC V9A 7N7
Fax: 604-414-0068
Toll-Free: 877-285-3421
info@rfabc.com
www.rfabc.com
To promote safe & successful operating standards for community centres, swimming pools, arenas, stadiums, & parks in British Columbia; Encouraging professionalism among recreation facility operators

Recreation New Brunswick
#34, 55 Whiting Rd., Fredericton NB E3B 5Y5 Canada
Tel: 506-459-1929; *Fax:* 506-450-6066
info@recreationnb.ca
www.recreationnb.ca
To develop a professional organization for members; to enhance the image of recreation to government & the general public; to develop liaisons with other recreation groups; to affect legislation in the field of recreation & parks; to expand the NB Skills Program for Management Volunteers; to promote the need for education for leisure
Jamie Shanks, Executive Director

Recreation Newfoundland & Labrador
Bldg. 810, Pleasantville, PO Box 8700, Stn. A, St. John's NL A1B 4J6 Canada
Tel: 709-729-3892; *Fax:* 709-729-3814
www.recreationnl.com
To promote, foster & develop recreation; to provide a full range of services to enrich the concept of leisure throughout Newfoundland & Labrador; to enable individual citizens to improve their quality of life.
Wanda Wight, President
Gary Milley, Executive Director

Recreation Nova Scotia (RNS)
#309, 5516 Spring Garden Rd., Halifax NS B3J 1G6 Canada
Tel: 902-425-1128; *Fax:* 902-422-8201
info@recreationns.ns.ca
www.recreationns.ns.ca
To build healthier futures through programs & services that promote the benefits of recreation
Rhonda Lemire, Executive Director
Laurene Rehman, President
Bev Mahon, Coordinator, Communications & Fund Development

Recreational Canoeing Association BC (RCABC)
1755 East 7th Ave., Vancouver BC V5N 1S1 Canada
Tel: 604-253-5410; *Fax:* 604-253-5490
sec@bccanoe.com
www.bccanoe.com
Alan Thomson, President
Jean Chandler, Secretary

Roller Sports Canada / Sports à roulettes du Canada
c/o Roller Sports Manitoba, #312, 200 Main St., Winnipeg MB R3C 4M2 Canada
Tel: 204-925-5699; *Fax:* 204-925-5703
rollersportsmb@shawbiz.ca
www.rollersport.mb.ca

Royal Canadian Numismatic Association (RCNA)
#432, 5694 Hwy. 7 East, Markham ON L3P 1B4
Tel: 647-401-4014; *Fax:* 905-472-9645
info@rcna.ca
www.canadian-numismatic.org
To encourage & promote education in the science of numismatics, through the study of coins, paper money, medals, tokens, & all other numismatic items, with special emphasis on material pertaining to Canada

The Royal Philatelic Society of Canada (RPSC) / La Société royale de philatélie du Canada (SRPC)
PO Box 929, Stn. Q, Toronto ON M4T 2P1 Canada
Tel: 416-921-2077; *Fax:* 416-921-1282
Toll-Free: 888-285-4143
info@rpsc.org
www.rpsc.org
To promote the hobby of stamp collecting; to use stamps & postal history in education for youths & adults

S.A.L.T.S. Sail & Life Training Society (SALTS)
PO Box 5014, Stn. B, Victoria BC V8R 6N3 Canada
Tel: 250-383-6811; *Fax:* 250-383-7781
Toll-Free: 888-383-6811
info@salts.ca
www.salts.ca
Social Media: www.facebook.com/saltsvictoria?ref=ts
Christian organization that believes through the medium of sail training both spiritual & physical development is encouraged in each individual

Saskatchewan Association of Recreation Professionals (SARP)
2205 Victoria Ave., Regina SK S4P 0S4
Tel: 306-780-9267; *Fax:* 306-525-4009
Toll-Free: 800-667-7780
sarp.sk@sasktel.net
www.sarp-online.ca
To represent & support present & future recreation professionals; To promote the pursuit of excellence in the profession; To advocate for the profession
Warren Poncsak, Executive Director
Chantelle Erdman, Chantelle

Saskatchewan Camping Association (SCA)
3950 Castle Rd., Regina SK S4S 6A4
Tel: 306-586-4026; *Fax:* 306-790-8634
info@saskcamping.ca
www.saskcamping.ca
To promote the development of quality organized camping in Saskatchewan; To act as the voice for leaders of organized camps throughout Saskatchewan
Donna Wilkinson, Executive Director

Saskatchewan Parks & Recreation Association (SPRA)
#100, 1445 Park St., Regina SK S4N 4C5 Canada
Tel: 306-780-9231; *Fax:* 306-780-9257
Toll-Free: 800-563-2555
office@spra.sk.ca
www.spra.sk.ca
To stimulate & advance parks, recreation & leisure activities, facilities & programs in Saskatchewan
Norm Campbell, CEO
Randy Durovick, Manager, Corporate Services
John Firnesz, Program Manager

Saskatchewan Snowmobile Association Inc. (SSA)
PO Box 533, 221 Centre St., Regina Beach SK S0G 4C0 Canada
Tel: 306-729-3500; *Fax:* 306-729-3505
Toll-Free: 800-499-7533
sasksnow@sasktel.net
www.sasksnowmobiling.sk.ca
To promote the benefits of snowmobiling & increase access & participation; to provide leadership & support to members; to establish & maintain safe, high quality trails; to provide support to club development. Annual events include the AGM, trade show, awards banquet, & provincial snowmobilie festival

Shooting Federation of Canada (SFC) / Fédération de tir du Canada (FTC)
45 Shirley Blvd., Nepean ON K2K 2W6 Canada
Tel: 613-727-7483; *Fax:* 613-727-7487
info@sfc-ftc.ca
www.sfc-ftc.ca
National governing body of recreational & Olympic shooting sports, representing firearms users in matters of legislation, shooting sports promotion, & program activities

Snowmobilers Association of Nova Scotia (SANS)
5516 Spring Garden Rd., 4th Fl., Halifax NS B3J 3G6 Canada
Tel: 902-425-5450; *Fax:* 902-425-5606
info@snowmobilersNS.com
www.snowmobilersns.com
To provide leadership & support to member snowmobile clubs so that they may enjoy quality recreational snowmobiling opportunities on a province-wide network of safe & well-developed snowmobile trails

Snowmobilers of Manitoba Inc.
2121 Henderson Hwy., Winnipeg MB R2G 1P8 Canada
Tel: 204-940-7533; *Fax:* 204-940-7531
info@snoman.mb.ca
www.snoman.mb.ca
To provide strong leadership & support to member clubs; to develop & maintain safe & environmentally responsible snowmobile trails; to further the enjoyment of organized snowmobiling throughout Manitoba

Soaring Association of Canada (SAC) / Association canadienne de vol à voile (ACVV)
#107, 1025 Richmond Rd., Ottawa ON K2B 8G8 Canada
Tel: 613-829-0536; *Fax:* 613-829-9497
sac@sac.ca
www.sac.ca
To promote, enhance & protect the sport of soaring in Canada; to provide information & services to the soaring community: licensing, medical requirements for glider pilots, aircraft certification, technical issues, courses & training, insurance plan, services to clubs

Sport Parachute Association of Saskatchewan
PO Box 37056, Regina SK S4S 7K3 Canada
Tel: 306-934-8528
www.skydive.sk.ca
Craig Skihar, President
Burk Reiman, Vice-President

Taoist Tai Chi Society of Canada
134 Darcy St., Toronto ON M5T 1K3 Canada
Tel: 416-656-2110; *Fax:* 416-654-3937
headoffice@taoist.org
www.taoist.org
To make Taoist Tai Chi available to all &, through its teaching & practice, promote health improvement, cultural exchange & helping others

Trail Riders of the Canadian Rockies
PO Box 6742, Stn. D, Calgary AB T2P 2E6 Canada
Tel: 403-652-8672; *Fax:* 403-261-2813
admin@trail-rides.ca
www.trail-rides.ca
To encourage travel on horseback through the Canadian Rockies; to foster the maintenance & improvement of old trails & the building of new trails; to promote good fellowship among those who visit & live in the Canadian Rockies; to encourage the appreciation of outdoor life & the study & conservation of mountain ecology; to assist in every way possible to ensure the preservation of the National Parks of Canada for the use & enjoyment of the public; to cooperate with other organizations with similar aims
Terry Stowell, Executive Director
Penny Egeland, Secretary

Trans Canada Trail Foundation (TCTF) / Fondation du sentier transcanadien
43, av Westminster nord, Montréal QC H4X 1Y8 Canada
Tel: 514-485-3959; *Fax:* 514-485-4541
Toll-Free: 800-465-3636
info@tctrail.ca
www.tctrail.ca
To promote & coordinate the planning, designing & building of a continuous, shared-use recreation trail that winds its way through every Province & Territory
Deborah Apps, President & CEO

Tunnelling Association of Canada (TAC) / Association canadienne des tunnels
c/o Earthtech, 105 Commerce Valley Dr. West, 7th Fl., Markham ON L3T 7W3 Canada
Tel: 905-886-7022
info@tunnelcanada.ca
www.tunnelcanada.ca
To promote Canadian tunnelling & underground excavation technologies, & safe design, construction & maintenance; to facilitate information exchange; to represent the tunnelling community in matters of public & technical concern; to publish a

Canadian registry of tunnels, underground excavations & similar works
Derek Zoldy, Treasurer
Garry Stevenson, President

Velo Halifax Bicycle Club
PO Box 125, Dartmouth NS B2Y 3Y2 Canada
www.velohalifax.ca
Walton Watt, Registrar

Whitewater Kayaking Association of British Columbia (WKABC)
PO Box 91549, Stn. West Vancouver, Vancouver BC V7V 3P2 Canada
Tel: 604-515-6376
admin@whitewater.org
www.whitewater.org
To encourage & expand the safety & enjoyment of river kayaking

Whitewater Ontario
411 Carnegie Beach Rd., Port Perry ON L9L 1B6 Canada
Tel: 905-985-4585; *Fax:* 905-985-5256
Toll-Free: 888-322-2849
info@whitewaterontario.ca
www.whitewaterontario.ca
Whitewater Ontario is the sport governing body in the province, and represents provincial interests within the national body Whitewater Canada and the Canadian Canoe Association
Claudia Kerkoff, Vice-President

Wilderness Canoe Association (WCA)
PO Box 91068, 2901 Bayview Ave., Toronto ON M2K 2Y6 Canada
Tel: 416-223-4646
info@wildernesscanoe.ca
www.wildernesscanoe.ca
Organization of individuals interested in wilderness travel, mainly by canoe, kayak, and backpacking and, in winter, by skis and snowshoes
Aleks Gusev, Chair

YMCA Canada
42 Charles St. East, 6th Fl., Toronto ON M4Y 1T4 Canada
Tel: 416-967-9622; *Fax:* 416-967-9618
www.ymca.ca
Social Media: www.facebook.com/YMCACanada
Dedicated to the growth of all persons in spirit, mind & body, & in a sense of responsibility to each other & the global community; fosters & stimulates the development of strong member associations & advocates on their behalf regionally, nationally & internationally
Scott Haldane, President/CEO
Marty Reynolds, Chair

Yukon Canoe & Kayak Club
PO Box 40080, 3 Sitka Cres., Whitehorse YT Y1A 6M6 Canada
Tel: 867-456-4827
current@yckc.ca
www.yckc.ca

Yukon Outdoors Club
4061, 4th Ave., Whitehorse YT Y1A 1H1 Canada
yukonoutdoorsclub@gmail.com
www.yukonoutdoorsclub.ca
The Yukon Outdoors Club is a non-profit society whose activities include co-ordinating trips to promote the enjoyment of the outdoors.
Tony Gonda, President

YWCA Canada / Association des jeunes femmes chrétiennes du Canada
#422, 75 Sherbourne St., Toronto ON M5A 2P9 Canada
Tel: 416-962-8881; *Fax:* 416-962-8084
national@ywcacanada.ca
www.ywcacanada.ca
Social Media: www.facebook.com/ywcacanada
A charitable, voluntary organization which coordinates the YWCA movement in Canada, and has a mission to advocate for the equity and equality rights and needs of women. The YWCA works actively to raise awareness on the prevention of violence against women, and the need for universal, accessible and quality child care.
Elizabeth Bourns, President
Michelle Bullas, Vice President

Recycling

New Brunswick Solid Waste Association (NBSWA) / l'Association des déchets solides du Nouveau-Brunswick (ADSNB)
32 Wedgewood Dr., Rothesay NB E2E 3P7 Canada
Tel: 506-849-4218; *Fax:* 506-847-1369
Toll-Free: 877-777-4218
nbswa@nbnet.nb.ca
www.recyclenb.ca
The New Brunswick Solid Waste Association is a non-profit group dedicated to promoting and furthering the principles of solid waste management in New Brunswick. Made up of volunteer members of the regional Solid Waste Commissions and Corporations in the province, the NBSWA is actively involved in numerous environmental issues surrounding solid waste and waste diversion
Don Shea, Executive Director

Reproductive Issues

Birthright International / Accueil Grossesse
777 Coxwell Ave., Toronto ON M4C 3C6 Canada
Tel: 416-469-1111; *Fax:* 416-469-1772
Toll-Free: 800-550-4900
info@birthright.org
www.birthright.org
A tax-exempt, charitable, interdenominational organization, Birthright provides non-judgmental support to women facing an unplanned pregnancy, helping them carry their baby to term. It is unaffliated with any religous, political or public agency.

Canadian Federation for Sexual Health (CFSH) / Fédération canadienne pour la santé sexuelle
#430, One Nicholas St., Ottawa ON K1N 7B7 Canada
Tel: 613-241-4474; *Fax:* 613-241-7550
Toll-Free: 888-270-7444
admin@cfsh.ca
www.cfsh.ca
CFSH envisions a global society that celebrates healthy sexuality, its diversity of expression & reproductive choice as fundamental human rights for individuals throughout life. CFSH is a national network that takes leadership in advancing sexual & reproductive health & rights in Canada & abroad through: Public education & awareness; Support for the delivery of programs & services in Canada; Advocacy; International projects & liaison with the International Planned Parenthood Federation

Canadian Fertility & Andrology Society (CFAS) / Société canadienne de fertilité et d'andrologie
#1107, 1255, rue University, Montréal QC H3B 3W7
Tel: 514-524-9009; *Fax:* 514-524-2163
info@cfas.ca
www.cfas.ca
To speak on behalf of interested parties in the field of assisted reproductive technologies & research in reproductive sciences

Canadians for Choice (CFC) / Canadien(ne)s pour la liberté de choix
PO Box 539, Stn. B, Ottawa ON K1N 7E4 Canada
Tel: 613-789-9958; *Fax:* 613-789-9960
Toll-Free: 888-642-2725
info@canadiansforchoice.ca
www.canadiansforchoice.ca
Dedicated to ensuring reproductive choice for all Canadians through education, research, training & public policy
Norman Barwin, President
Barbara Legowski, Vice-President
Patricia LaRue, Executive Director

Fédération du Québec pour le planning des naissances (FQPN)
#405, 110, rue Ste-Thérèse, Montréal QC H2Y 1E6 Canada
Tél: 514-866-3721; *Téléc:* 514-866-1100
info@fqpn.qc.ca
www.fqpn.qc.ca
Promouvoir les droits des femmes dans le domaine de la santé, particulièrement la reproduction et la sexualitépromouvoir l'accès à une information critique et fiable, la liberté de choix et le consentement des femmes face à leur propre corps.

Infertility Awareness Association of Canada (IAAC) / Association canadienne de sensibilisation à l'infertilité (ACSI)
#342, 2100, av Marlowe, Montréal QC H4A 3L5 Canada
Tel: 514-484-2891; *Fax:* 514-484-0454
Toll-Free: 800-263-2929
info@iaac.ca
www.iaac.ca
To offer assistance, support & education to individuals with infertility concerns; to increase the awareness & understanding of the causes, treatments & the emotional impact of infertility through the development of educational programs.
Jocelyn Smith, President

League for Life in Manitoba / Ligue pour la vie au Manitoba
Winnipeg MB Canada
Tel: 204-233-8047; *Fax:* 204-233-0523
l4l@mts.net
www.leagueforlife.mb.ca
To engage in non-sectarian educational activities in order to encourage & promote among the general public an understanding & awareness of the dignity & worth of each individual human life, whatever its state & circumstances; to foster respect for all human life. The League provides information & referral services dealing with pregnancy & end of life issues, such as abortion, euthanasia & assisted suicide, & provides a voice for those opposed to abortion.
Marie-Jo Laroche, Executive Director

Natural Family Planning Association
#205, 3050 Yonge St., Toronto ON M4N 2K4 Canada
Tel: 416-481-5465
nfptoronto@primus.ca
www.naturalfamilyplanning.ca
The Association promotes the Billings Ovulation Method of natural family planning which is based on an awareness of a woman's physical systems to gauge optimum fertility state. It is a registered charity, BN: 129904280RR0001.
Merrilyn Currie, Executive Director

Newfoundland & Labradour Right to Life Association
PO Box 5427, St. John's NL A1C 5W2 Canada
Tel: 709-579-1500; *Fax:* 709-579-1600
nffriendsforlife@nl.rogers.com
www.nlprolife.org; www.nlfriendsofrighttolife.net
The Association upholds the sacredness & inviolability of human life from conception to natural death. It disseminates information on such to authorities & the public, supporting mothers during & after pregnancy. It networks with similar organizations, & promotes medical research to support its beliefs.
Linda Holden, President

Ontario Coalition for Abortion Clinics (OCAC)
PO Box 495, Stn. P, 427 Bloor St. West, Toronto ON M5S 2Z1
Tel: 416-969-8463; *Fax:* 416-789-0762
ocac@sympatico.ca
To work for reproductive rights & access to abortions

Options for Sexual Health (OPT)
3550 East Hastings St., Vancouver BC V5K 2A7 Canada
Tel: 604-731-4252; *Fax:* 604-731-4698
Toll-Free: 800-739-7367
admin@optbc.org
www.optionsforsexualhealth.org
To promote optimal sexual health for all British Columbians by supporting reproductive choice, reducing unplanned pregnancy, & providing quality education, information & clinical services

Planned Parenthood - Newfoundland & Labrador Sexual Health Centre (NLSHC)
203 Merrymeeting Rd., St. John's NL A1C 2W6 Canada
Tel: 709-579-1009; *Fax:* 709-726-2308
Toll-Free: 877-666-9847
info@nlsexualhealthcentre.org
www.nlsexualhealthcentre.org
To promote positive sexual health attitudes & practices throughout Newfoundland & Labrador; to support & respect individual choice

Planned Parenthood Alberta (PPA)
#102, 1212 1st St. SE, Calgary AB T2G 2H8 Canada
Tel: 403-283-8591; *Fax:* 403-283-8563
ppalberta@plannedparenthoodalta.com
www.plannedparenthoodalta.com
To support reproductive choice & promote sexual health for all Albertans

Planned Parenthood Saskatoon Centre (PPSC)
Macro Bldg., #301, 115 2nd Ave. North, Saskatoon SK S7K 1M1 Canada
Tel: 306-244-7989; *Fax:* 306-652-4034
info@sexualhealthcentresaskatoon.ca
www.sexualhealthcentresaskatoon.ca
To ensure that information, resources & support services of the highest quality regarding sexuality, contraception & reproduction are available & accessible to all in our community who need them; to encourage responsible decision-making & behaviour which is respectful of the needs & of the choices available to each individual

Evelyn Reisner, Executive Director

Pro-Life BC (PLBC)
#112, 32868 Ventura Ave., Abbotsford BC V2S 6J3 Canada
Tel: 604-853-3425; *Fax:* 604-853-3413
Toll-Free: 877-774-4625
life@prolifebc.ca
www.prolifebc.ca
To educate the people of British Columbia regarding the sanctity & value of all human life from conception to natural death
Yvonne Douma, Executive Director
Michelle Doherty, President
Monique Van Berkel, Assistant to Executive Director

Right to Life Association of Toronto
#302, 120 Eglinton Ave., Toronto ON M4P 1E2 Canada
Tel: 416-483-7869; *Fax:* 416-483-7052
office@righttolife.to
www.rtl-toronto.org
Social Media: www.facebook.com/righttolifeto
To uphold the right to life as the basic human right on which all others depend; to provide information & services to that end

Sexuality Education Resource Centre Manitoba (SERC)
555 Broadway, 2nd Fl., Winnipeg MB R3C 0W4 Canada
Tel: 204-982-7800; *Fax:* 204-982-7819
Toll-Free: 800-432-1957
info@serc.mb.ca
www.serc.mb.ca
To promote universal access to comprehensive, reliable information & services on sexuality & related health issues by fostering awareness, understanding, & support through education

World Organization Ovulation Method Billings Inc.
1506 Dansey Ave., Coquitlam BC V3K 3J1 Canada
Tel: 604-936-4472; *Fax:* 604-936-5690
info@woomb.ca
www.woomb.ca
To teach fertility awareness & natural family planning
Lou Specken, President

Research & Scholarship

Advanced Foods & Materials Network / Réseau des aliments et des matériaux d'avant-garde
#215, 150 Research Lane, Guelph ON N1G 4T2 Canada
Tel: 519-822-6253; *Fax:* 519-824-8453
www.afmnet.ca
Ron Woznow, Executive Director
Rickey Yada, Ph.D., Scientific Director

AllerGen NCE Inc.
Michael DeGroote Centre for Learning & Discovery, McMaster University, #3120, 1200 Main St. West, Hamilton ON L8N 2A5
Tel: 905-525-9140; *Fax:* 905-524-0611
info@allergen-nce.ca
www.allergen-nce.ca
To support research, capacity building activities, & networking regarding allergic disease in Canada; To reduce the morbidity, mortality & socio-economic impacts of allergy, asthma, & related immune diseases
Judah Denburg, CEO & Scientific Director
Diana Royce, Chief Operating Officer & Managing Director
Mark Mitchell, Manager, Research & Partnerships
Marta Rudyk, Manager, Communications & Coordinator, Knowledge Mobilization
Allison Brown, Coordinator, Research
Michelle Harkness, Coordinator, Highly Qualified Personnel & Events

AquaNet - Network in Aquaculture
Ocean Sciences Centre, Memorial University of Newfoundland, St. John's NL A1C 5S7 Canada
Tel: 709-737-3245; *Fax:* 709-737-3500
info@aquanet.ca
www.aquanet.ca
To foster a sustainable aquaculture sector in Canada through high quality research & education
Scott McKinley, Executive Scientific Director

ArcticNet Inc.
Pavillon Alexandre-Vachon, Université Laval, #4081, 1045, av de la Médecine, Québec QC G1V 0A6
Tel: 418-656-5830; *Fax:* 418-656-2334
arcticnet@arcticnet.ulaval.ca
www.arcticnet-ulaval.ca
To study the impacts of climate change in the coastal Canadian Arctic; To engage Inuit organizations, northern communities, universities, research institutes, industry, government, & international agencies as partners in the scientific process
Martin Fortier, Executive Director
Louis Fortier, Scientific Director
Réal Choquette, Administrative Director
Jean-Luc Bernier, Officer, Communications
Keith Levesque, Coordinator, Ship-based Research
Josée Michaud, Coordinator, Data

AUTO21 - The Automobile of the 21st Century
754 California Ave., Windsor ON N9B 2Z2 Canada
Tel: 519-253-3000; *Fax:* 519-971-3626
info@auto21.ca
www.auto21.ca
Sandra Bortolotti, Operations Manager
Stephanie Campeau, Communications Manager

Canadian Arthritis Network (CAN) / Le Réseau canadien de l'arthrite
#1002, 522 University Ave., Toronto ON M5T 1W7
Tel: 416-586-4770; *Fax:* 416-586-8395
can@arthritisnetwork.ca
www.arthritisnetwork.ca
To improve the quality of life for people with arthritis; To support integrated, trans-disciplinary research & development, with a focus upon inflammatory joint diseases, osteoarthritis, & bioengineering for restoration of joint function
Robin Armstrong, Chair
John Riley, MHA, Managing Director
Claire Bombardier, MD, FRCPC, Co-Scientific Director
Monique Gignac, PhD, Co-Scientific Director
Brian Bobechko, Director, Research & Development
Stacey Johnson, MSc, Director, Communications
Joanner Wright, Manager, Training & International Programs

Canadian Association for Research in Nondestructive Evaluation (CARNDE) / Association canadienne de recherches en évaluation non-destructive (ACREND)
75, boul de Montagne, Boucherville QC J4B 6Y4 Canada
Tel: 450-641-5252; *Fax:* 450-641-5106
jean.bussiere@nrc.ca
www.nrc.ca
To foster, coordinate & disseminate results of research, development & application of new or advanced NDE techniques in Canada; to promote technology transfer by encouraging collaboration between universities, research organizations & industrial or governmental users; to raise the profile of NDE research in Canada by publicizing the need for & economic benefits arising from advances in NDE
Jean Bussière, Research Editor

Canadian Carbonization Research Association (CCRA)
PO Box 2460, Burlington ON L8N 3J5 Canada
Tel: 905-548-4796
www.cancarb.ca
To fund coke & coal research in Canada for benefit of member companies

Canadian Centre for Policy Alternatives (CCPA) / Centre canadien de politique alternative
#205, 75 Albert St., Ottawa ON K1P 5E7 Canada
Tel: 613-563-1341; *Fax:* 613-233-1458
ccpa@policyalternatives.ca
www.policyalternatives.ca
To promote research on economic & social issues facing Canada; to monitor current developments in economy & study important trends that affect Canadians; to demonstrate thoughtful alternatives to the limited perspectives of business, research institutes & government agencies; to put forward research that reflects concerns of women & men, labour & business, churches, cooperatives & voluntary agencies, governments, minorities, disadvantaged & fortunate individuals

Canadian Committee of Byzantinists
Talbot College, Univ. of Western Ontario, London ON N6A 3K7 Canada
Tel: 519-661-3045; *Fax:* 519-850-2388
splinter@uwo.ca
To network among Canadian Byzantinists; to promote communications & exchange of information; to promote Byzantine Studies in Canada

Canadian Federation for Robotics
c/o Precarn Inc., #510, 1525 Carling Ave., Ottawa ON K1Z 8R9 Canada
Tel: 613-727-9576; *Fax:* 613-727-5672
johnston@precarn.ca
www.precarn.ca
To promote interest in the use of & the application of robotics technologies by Canadian firms by planning & supporting
Paul Johnston, President

Canadian Genetic Diseases Network (CGDN) / Réseau canadien sur les maladies génétiques (RCMG)
#201, 2150 Western Pkwy., Vancouver BC V6T 1Z4 Canada
Tel: 604-221-7300; *Fax:* 604-221-0778
info@cgdn.ca
www.cgdn.ca
A nation-wide consortium of Canada's top investigators & core-technology facilities in human genetics, partnered with colleagues from industry to conduct leading-edge research within an "Institute without Walls"; to achieve international competitiveness in scientific research with social & economic benefits
Rob Abbott, CEO

Canadian Institute for Advanced Research (CIFAR) / Institut canadien de recherches avancées (ICRA)
#1400, 180 Dundas St. West, Toronto ON M5G 1Z8 Canada
Tel: 416-971-4251; *Fax:* 416-971-6169
info@cifar.ca
www.ciar.ca
To stimulate leading-edge research projects vital to Canada's future prosperity.
Richard W. Ivey, Chair
Chaviva Hosek, President/CEO

Canadian Institute for Mediterranean Studies (CIMS) / Institut canadien d'études méditerranéennes
c/o Carr Hall, Department of Italian Studies, University of Toronto, 100 St. Joseph St., Toronto ON M5S 1J4
www.utoronto.ca/cims
To study all aspects of Mediterranean culture & civilization, past & present

Canadian Institute for Photonics Innovations (CIPI)
Université Laval, Pavillion d'optique-photonique, #2111, 2375 rue de la Terrasse, Québec QC G1V 0A6 Canada
Tel: 418-656-3013; *Fax:* 418-656-2995
cipi@cipi.ulaval.ca
www.cipi.ulaval.ca
Photonics - science of generating, manipulating, transmitting & detecting light
Robert Corriveau, President

Canadian Institute of Strategic Studies (CISS) / Institut canadien d'études stratégiques
#702, 165 University Ave., Toronto ON M5H 3B8 Canada
Tel: 416-322-8128; *Fax:* 416-322-8129
Toll-Free: 800-831-5695
info@ciss.ca
www.ciss.ca
To stimulate research, study, analysis & discussion of the strategic implications of major national & international issues, events & trends as they affect Canada & Canadians; to enhance the national security of Canada, that is, the preservation of a way of life acceptable to the Canadian people & compatible with needs & legitimate aspirations of others.

Canadian Institute of Ukrainian Studies (CIUS) / Institut canadien d'études ukrainiennes
#4-30, Pembina Hall, University of Alberta, Edmonton AB T6G 2H8
Tel: 780-492-2972; *Fax:* 780-492-4967
cius@ualberta.ca
www.cius.ca
To develop Ukrainian scholarship in Canada; To organize research in Ukrainian & Ukrainian-Canadian studies

Canadian Language & Literacy Research Network
Elborn College, University of Western Ontario, 1201 Western Rd., London ON N6G 1H1 Canada
Tel: 519-661-3619; *Fax:* 519-661-4223
info@cllrnet.ca
www.cllrnet.ca
The Canadian Language and Literacy Research Network will improve language and literacy skills in Canadian children, enabling them to contribute more effectively to the social and economic lfie of their communities.
Donald G. Jamieson, CEO/Scientific Director

Canadian Mathematical Society (CMS) / Société mathématique du Canada
#105, 1785 Alta Vista Dr., Ottawa ON K1G 3Y6 Canada
Tel: 613-733-2662; *Fax:* 613-733-8994
office@cms.math.ca
www.cms.math.ca
To promote & advance the discovery, learning & application of mathematics.

Canadian Mining Industry Research Organization (CAMIRO)
935 Ramsey Lake Rd., Sudbury ON P3E 2C6 Canada
Tel: 705-673-6595; *Fax:* 705-671-6606
info@camiro.org
www.camiro.org
To manage collaborative mining research in the divisions of exploration, mining, & metallurgical processing; to contribute to the safety, growth, & competitiveness of the Canadian mineral industry

Canadian Nautical Research Society (CNRS) / Société canadienne pour la recherche nautique
PO Box 511, Kingston ON K7L 4W5 Canada
www.cnrs-scrn.org
To stimulate & promote nautical research in Canada; to enhance Canada's understanding of its maritime heritage; to foster communication in nautical affairs, to organize meetings, & to cooperate with other agencies promoting nautical research

Canadian Network for Vaccines & Immunotherapeutics
#790, 5160, boul Décarie, Montréal QC H3X 2H9 Canada
Tel: 514-343-6111; *Fax:* 514-343-7854
michel.klein@canvac.ca
www.canvac.ca
Michel Klein, Executive Director

Canadian Numismatic Research Society (CNRS)
PO Box 1351, Victoria BC V8W 2W7 Canada
Fax: 250-598-5539
ragreene@telus.net
www.nunetcan.net/cnrs/cnrs.htm
To promote reseach & study of numismatics

Canadian Operational Research Society (CORS) / Société canadienne de recherche opérationelle (SCRO)
PO Box 2225, Stn. D, Ottawa ON K1P 5W4 Canada
cors@uwindsor.ca
www.cors.ca
To advance the theory & practice of O.R. in Canada; to stimulate & promote contacts between people interested in the subject

Canadian Philosophical Association (CPA) / Association canadienne de philosophie
C/O University of Ottawa, #241, 70 Laurier Ave. East, Ottawa ON K1N 6N5 Canada
Tel: 613-562-5367; *Fax:* 613-562-5370
acpa@uottawa.ca
www.acpcpa.ca
To advance the discipline of philosophy in Canada

Canadian Quaternary Association / Association canadienne pour l'étude du Quaternaire
c/o Joshua Kurek, Department of Biology, Queen's University, 116 Barrie St., Kingston ON K7L 3N6
www.canqua.com
To study & advance knowledge of the quaternary period

Canadian Research Institute for the Advancement of Women (CRIAW) / Institut canadien de recherches sur les femmes (ICREF)
#408, 151 Slater St., Ottawa ON K1P 5H3 Canada
Tel: 613-563-0681; *Fax:* 613-563-0682
info@criaw-icref.ca
www.criaw-icref.ca
To advance the position of women in society through feminist & women-centred research; to encourage, coordinate & communicate research about the reality of women's lives & ensure an equal place for women & their experiences in the body of knowledge about Canada; to recognize & affirm the diversity of women's experiences; to demystify the research process & promote connections between research, social action & social change; to facilitate communication among feminist researchers & research organizations world-wide

Canadian Society for Aesthetics (CSA) / Société canadienne d'esthétique (SCE)
c/o Dawson College, 4729, av de Maisonneuve, Westmount QC H3Z 1M3 Canada
info@csa-sce.ca
www.csa-sce.ca
To keep aesthetic theorists in close touch with the creative & critical practices that are the basis of their discipline; to increase awareness of aesthetic issues among Canadian citizens & develop the intellectual & conceptual resources for dealing with them.

Canadian Society for Eighteenth-Century Studies (CSECS) / Société canadienne d'étude du dix-huitième siècle (SCEDS)
c/o CSECS Secretary, Department of English, University of Victoria, PO Box 3070, Stn. CSC, Victoria BC V8W 3W1 Canada
gdfulton@uvic.ca
c18.net/scedhs-csecs/
To sustain, in Canada, interest in eighteenth-century civilization in Europe & the New World; to encourage, from a wide interdisciplinary base, research on the eighteenth-century; to make known to eighteenth-century specialists the work done in this area in Canada.
Betty A. Schellenberg, President
Gordon Fulton, Secretary
Gefen Bar-On, Treasurer

The Canadian Society for Mesopotamian Studies (CSMS) / La Société canadienne des études mésopotamiennes
c/o Dept. of Near & Middle Eastern Civilizations, 4 Bancroft Ave., 4th Fl., Toronto ON M5S 1C1 Canada
Tel: 416-978-4531; *Fax:* 416-978-3305
gframe@chass.utoronto.ca
To stimulate interest among the general public in the culture, history & archaeology of Mesopotamia, in particular the civilizations of Sumer, Babylon & Assyria, as well as neighbouring ancient civilizations

Canadian Society for the Study of Religion (CSSR) / Société canadienne pour l'étude de la religion (SCER)
c/o Dr. Mark D. Chapman, #100, 30 Carrier Dr., Toronto ON M9W 5T7 Canada
mchapman@alumni.uwaterloo.ca
www.ccsr.ca/cssr
To promote research in the study of religion, with particular reference to Canada; to encourage a critical examination of the teaching of the discipline
Michel Desjardins, President
Mark Chapman, Membership Secretary
Richard Mann, Treasurer

Canadian Society of Patristic Studies (CSPS) / Association canadienne des études patristiques
c/o Dr. S. Muir, Religious Studies, Concordia University College of AB, 7128 Ada Blvd., Edmonton AB T5B 4E4
www.ccsr.ca/csps
To encourage the academic study of the Church Fathers
Tim Hegedus, President
Lorraine Buck, Vice-President
George Bevan, Secretary
Steven Muir, Treasurer

Canadian Sociological Association (CSA)
#SB-323, 1455, boul de Maisonneuve ouest, Montréal QC H3G 1M8 Canada
Tel: 514-848-8780; *Fax:* 514-848-8780
info@csaa.ca
www.csaa.ca
To promote research, publication & teaching in sociology in Canada

Canadian Stroke Network (CSN) / Réseau canadien contre les accidents cérébrovasculaires
#301, 600 Peter Morand Cres., Ottawa ON K1G 5Z3 Canada
Tel: 613-562-5696; *Fax:* 613-521-9215
info@canadianstrokenetwork.ca
www.canadianstrokenetwork.ca
To reduce the physical, social, & economic consequences of stroke on individuals & society through leadership in research; To develop & implement national strategies in stroke research; To maximize health & economic benefits; To build a consensus across Canada on stroke policy
Michael Cloutier, Chair
Antoine Hakim, MD, CEO & Scientific Director
Katie Lafferty, Executive Director
Mike Sharma, Deputy Director

Canadian Technion Society
#206, 970 Lawrence Ave. West, Toronto ON M6A 3B6 Canada
Tel: 416-789-4545; *Fax:* 416-789-0255
Toll-Free: 800-935-8864
info@cdntech.org
www.cdntech.org
Social Media: www.facebook.com/pages/Canadian-Technion-Society/120072721377514
To support Technion Israel Institute of Technology; to promote exchange of scientific information between Israel & Canada, scholarships, research, etc.

Canadian Theosophical Society Inc. / Association théosophique canadienne inc.
27 Northmount Cr. NW, Calgary AB T2K 2V6 Canada
Tel: 403-275-7817
office@theosophical.ca
www.theosophical.ca
To form a nucleus of the Universal Brotherhood of Humanity, without distinction of race, creed, sex, caste, or colour; to encourage the study of comparative religion, philosophy, & science; to investigate unexplained laws of nature & the powers latent in man

Canadian Water Network (CWN) / Réseau canadien de l'eau
University of Waterloo, 200 University Ave. West, Waterloo ON N2L 3G1 Canada
Tel: 519-888-4567; *Fax:* 519-883-7574
info@cwn-rce.ca
www.cwn-rce.ca
To create a national partnership in innovation that promotes environmentally responsible stewardship & opportunities with respect to Canada's water resources resulting in sustained prosperity & improved quality of life for Canadians.
Bernadette Conant, Director of Programs
Mark Servos, Scientific Director
David Cotter, Director of Communications

Cancer Research Society (CRS) / Société de recherche sur le cancer
#402, 625, av Président-Kennedy, Montréal QC H3A 3S5 Canada
Tel: 514-861-9227; *Fax:* 514-861-9220
Toll-Free: 866-343-2262
info@src-crs.ca
src-crs.ca
CRS is a not-for-profit organization that supports basic cancer research through funding & seed money. Grants & fellowships are allocated to universities & hospitals involved in research across Canada. It is a registered charity, BN: 119153229RR0001.
Mario Chevrette, President
Andy Chabot, Executive Director

Centre for Research on Latin America & The Caribbean (CERLAC)
8th Fl., York Research Tower, 4700 Keele St., Toronto ON M3J 1P3 Canada
Tel: 416-736-5237; *Fax:* 416-736-5688
cerlac@yorku.ca
www.yorku.ca/cerlac
To offer an interdisciplinary research unit concerned with economic development, political & social organization & cultural contributions of Latin America & the Caribbean; to build academic & cultural links between these regions & Canada; informs researchers, policy advisors & public on matters concerning the regions; to assist in development of research & teaching institutions that directly benefit people of the regions

Classical Association of Canada (CAC) / Société canadienne des études classiques (SCEC)
Vari Hall, Department of History, York University, #2178, 4700 Keele St., Toronto ON M3J 1P3 Canada
Tel: 416-736-2100
www.cac-scec.ca
John Serrati, Secretary
Jonathan Edmundson, President
Annabel Robinson, Treasurer

Commission canadienne pour la théorie des machines et des mécanismes (CCToMM) / Canadian Committee for the Theory of Machines & Mechanisms
Faculté d'ingénierie, Univ. de Moncton, Moncton NB E1A 3E9 Canada
me.queensu.ca/people/notash/CCToMM/
Promouvoir le développement dans le domaine des machines et des mécanismes par la recherche théorique et expérimentale et leurs applications pratiques.
Roger Boudreau, Secrétaire général
Leila Notash, Responsable des communications

FPInnovations
580, boul Saint-Jean, Pointe-Claire QC H9R 3J9 Canada
Tel: 514-694-1140; *Fax:* 514-694-4351
admin@fpinnovations.ca
www.feric.ca
To develop & assist with the implementation of innovative & safe forest operational solutions, which encompass areas such as the engineering, environmental, & human aspects of forestry & wildland fire operations; To improve sustainable forest operations in Canada; To provide members with knowledge &

technology, based on research, to conduct cost-competitive, quality forest operations

Geomatics for Informed Decisions Network
#3732, Pavillon Casault, Université Laval, Québec QC G1V 0A6 Canada
Tel: 418-656-7758; *Fax:* 418-656-2611
info@geoide.ulaval.ca
www.geoide.ulaval.ca
Réal Choquette, Network Manager
Mark Zacharias, Executive Director

Great Lakes Institute for Environmental Research (GLIER)
University of Windsor, 401 Sunset Ave., Windsor ON N9B 3P4 Canada
Tel: 519-253-3000; *Fax:* 519-971-3616
glier@uwindsor.ca
cronus.uwindsor.ca/glier

Humanist Association of Canada (HAC) / Association humaniste du Canada
401B Weber St. North, Waterloo ON N2J 3J2 Canada
Fax: 613-739-5969
Toll-Free: 877-486-2671
hac_memberships@yahoo.ca
www.humanistcanada.com
To bring together people who share a non-theistic view of the world; to educate the public about humanism & its ethics & values.

Innovation Management Association of Canada (IMAC) / Association canadienne de la gestion de l'innovation (ACGI)
c/o CATAAlliance, #416, 207 Bank St., Ottawa ON K2P 2N2 Canada
Tel: 613-236-6550; *Fax:* 613-236-8189
info@cata.ca
www.cata.ca/imac/
To enhance the productivity & effectiveness of Canadian research development & technology-based innovations

Institute for Research on Public Policy / Institut de recherche en politiques publiques
#200, 1470, rue Peel, Montréal QC H3A 1T1 Canada
Tel: 514-985-2461; *Fax:* 514-985-2559
irpp@irpp.org
www.irpp.org
Independent, nonprofit research institution seeking to improve public policy in Canada by generating research, providing insight and sparking debate that will contribute to the public policy decision-making process and strengthen the quality of public policy decisions made by Canadian governments, citizens, institutions and organizations.

Institute for Robotics & Intelligent Systems (IRIS) / Institut de robotique et d'intelligence des systèmes
Precarn Incorporated, #510, 1525 Carling Ave., Ottawa ON K1Z 8R9 Canada
Tel: 613-727-9576; *Fax:* 613-727-5672
info@precarn.ca
www.precarn.ca
To promote collaborative applied research in intelligent systems of importance to Canadian industry; to strengthen the research & development interaction between universities & industry.
Henri Rothschild, B.Sc., M.Sc., P, President & CEO, Precarn Incorporated
Rick Schwartzburg, Senior Manager, Academic Partnerships
Derek Best, Director, Research Programs

Institute for Stuttering Treatment & Research (ISTAR)
College Plaza, #1500, 8215 - 112 St., Edmonton AB T6G 2C8 Canada
Tel: 780-492-2619; *Fax:* 780-492-8457
istar@ualberta.ca
www.istar.ualberta.ca
To provide the best possible treatment for stuttering children & adults; to conduct research into the nature & treatment of stuttering; to provide advanced professional training for speech pathologists; to increase public awareness & understanding of stuttering. Calgary satellite office: c/o The Hearing Loss Clinic, #122 - 40 Sunpark Plaza SE, Calgary, AB T2X 3X7; phone 403-201-7285

Institute of Urban Studies (IUS)
University of Winnipeg, #103, 520 Portage Ave., Winnipeg MB R3C 0G2 Canada
Tel: 204-982-1140; *Fax:* 204-943-4695
ius@uwinnipeg.ca
ius.uwinnipeg.ca
To undertake policy-oriented research in the field of Urban Studies; to serve as a resource centre for the community; to provide educational services to the University community & the community-at-large.
Jino Distasio, Director

International Council for Canadian Studies (ICCS) / Conseil international d'études canadiennes (CIEC)
#303, 250 City Centre Ave., Ottawa ON K1R 6K7 Canada
Tel: 613-789-7834; *Fax:* 613-789-7830
lise.nichol@iccs-ciec.ca
www.iccs-ciec.ca
To promote scholarly study, research, teaching & publication about Canada in all disciplines & all countries; to enhance communications among its members to facilitate & develop such scholarly activities; to disseminate research results & to publicize researchers' activities in the area of Canadian Studies; to encourage the development of an international community of Canadianists.

International Council for Central & East European Studies (Canada) (ICCEES) / Conseil international d'études de l'Europe centrale et orientale (Canada)
Intl. Studies Program, Glendon College, York University, 2275 Bayview Ave., Toronto ON M4N 3M6 Canada
Tel: 416-736-2100; *Fax:* 416-487-6852
stankosk@glendon.yorku.ca
www.rusin.fi/ICCEES
To foster study of East European affairs & to encourage dissemination of this knowledge among specialists; to create an international community of scholars.

International Geographical Union - Canadian Committee
Simon Fraser Univ., Dept. of Geography, 8888 University Dr., Burnaby BC V5A 1S6 Canada
Tel: 604-291-3321; *Fax:* 604-291-5841
agill@sfu.ca
www.igu-net.org/uk/what_is_igu/nationalcommittees.html
To promote international programs in geography within Canada; to promote activities within IGU programs relevant to Canada & to coordinate Canadian participation; to formulate Canadian position & advise the National Research Council on Canadian participation in IGU activities

International Society for Research in Palmistry Inc. / Société internationale de recherches en chirologie inc.
576, rte 315, ChéNéVille QC J0V 1E0 Canada
Tel: 819-428-4298; *Fax:* 819-428-4495
Toll-Free: 866-428-3799
info@birlacenter.com
www.birlacenter.com/palmistry
The Society offers individual & group counselling through palmistry & astrology based on Eastern Vedic System.

Lakehead Social History Institute (LSHI)
c/o Lakehead University, 955 Oliver Rd., Thunder Bay ON P7B 5E1 Canada
Tel: 807-767-0934; *Fax:* 807-767-0934
epp@swedesincanada.ca
www.swedesincanada.ca
To encourage & promote research in the social history of Thunder Bay specifically & Northwestern Ontario generally
Ernie Epp, Chief Officer
Donald W. Sjöberg, Chief Officer

Mathematics of Information Technology & Complex Systems (MITACS)
Technology Enterprise Facility, University of British Columbia, #301, 6190 Agronomy Rd., Vancouver BC V6T 1Z3 Canada
Tel: 604-822-9189; *Fax:* 604-822-3689
mitacs@mitacs.ca
www.mitacs.math.ca
MITACS leads Canada's effort in the generation, application and commercialization of new mathematical tools and methodologies within a world-class research program. The network initiates and fosters linkages with industrial, governmental, and not-for-profit organizations that require mathematical technologies to deal with problems of strategic importance to Canada. MITACS is driving the recruiting, training, and placement of a new generation of highly mathematically skilled personnel that is vital to Canada's future social and economic wellbeing. Offices in Vancouver, Toronto, Montréal, St. John's & Fredericton.
Arvind Gupta, CEO & Scientific Director

The M.S.I. Foundation
#12230, 106 Avenue NW, Edmonton AB T5N 3Z1 Canada
Tel: 780-421-7532; *Fax:* 780-425-4467
info@msifoundation.ca
www.msifoundation.ca
To foster & support research into any aspect of the provision of medical & allied health services to the people of Alberta
M. Yates, Associate Secretary
L.H. Le Riche, Chairperson

Ontario Centres of Excellence - Centre for Earth & Environmental Technologies (OCE-ETech)
#200, 156 Front St. West, Toronto ON M5J 2L6 Canada
Tel: 416-861-1092; *Fax:* 416-971-7164
Toll-Free: 866-759-6014
anne.wettlaufer@oce-ontario.org
www.oce-ontario.org
ETech engages firms, clients & academic partners in the following areas: clean water technologies, resource management, sustainable agricultue & agri-food, sustainable infrastructure, clean air technologies, waste management & sustainable infrastrucutre; organizations & academics are encouraged to contact ETech to find out how to access the broad range of services available
Tom Corr, President & CEO
Tanya Dunn, Executive Assistant, Office of President

Ontario Public Interest Research Group (OPIRG) / Groupe de recherche d'intérêt public de l'Ontario
North Borden Building, #101, 563 Spadina Ave., Toronto ON M5S 2J7 Canada
Tel: 416-978-7770; *Fax:* 416-971-2292
opirg.toronto@utoronto.ca
www.opirguoft.org
To make information available to the general public that enables them to make informed decisions on issues & understand & possibly influence decisions made by others on their behalf; to provide an alternative to the information provided by the academic community, government & business; to offer an analysis of environmental & social issues aimed at motivating change & placing issues in the broader social, economic & political perspective in which they need to be understood

Pearson Peacekeeping Centre (PPC) / Centre pour le maintien de la paix Pearson
HCI Bldg., #5110, 1125 Colonel By Dr., Ottawa ON K1S 5B6 Canada
Tel: 613-520-5617; *Fax:* 613-520-3787
info@peaceoperations.org
www.peaceoperations.org
To enhance the Canadian contribution to international peace & security through education, training & research in in all aspects of peace operations
Suzanne Monaghan, President

Pulp & Paper Technical Association of Canada (PAPTAC) / Association technique des pâtes et papiers du Canada
#1070, 740, rue Notre-Dame ouest, Montréal QC H3C 3X6 Canada
Tel: 514-392-0265; *Fax:* 514-392-0369
ccrotogino@paptac.ca
www.paptac.ca
To provide means for the interchange of knowledge & expertise among its members; to improve the skill levels & effectiveness of present & future employees through training & education; to provide technical & practical information on pulp & paper manufacture & use
Greg Hay, Executive Director
André Bernier, Chair

The Royal Canadian Geographical Society (RCGS) / La Société géographique royale du Canada
39 McArthur Ave., Ottawa ON K1L 8L7
Tel: 613-745-4629; *Fax:* 613-744-0947
Toll-Free: 800-267-0824
rcgs@rcgs.org
www.rcgs.org
To impart a broader knowledge of Canada, including its environmental, economic, & social challenges, as well as it natural & cultural heritage

Royal Canadian Institute (RCI)
#H7D, 700 University Ave., Toronto ON M5G 1X6 Canada
Tel: 416-977-2983; *Fax:* 416-962-7314
royalcanadianinstitute@sympatico.ca
www.royalcanadianinstitute.org
To increase public understanding of science; to create an environment in which science can flourish & be appreciated

The Royal Society for the Encouragement of Arts, Manufactures & Commerce (RSA)
8 John Adam St., London WC2N 6EZ United Kingdom
general@rsa.org.uk
www.rsa.org.uk
Social Media: www.facebook.com/theRSAorg; www.twitter.com/theRSAorg
To encourage the development of a principled, prosperous society & the release of human potential

The Royal Society of Canada (RSC) / La Société royale du Canada
170 Waller St., Ottawa ON K1N 9B9 Canada
Tel: 613-991-6990; *Fax:* 613-991-6996
theacademies@rsc.ca
www.rsc.ca
To promote learning & research in the arts, humanities & sciences in Canada; in its role as a National Academy, to draw on the breadth of knowledge & expertise of its members to recognize & honour distinguished accomplishments; to advise on the state of scholarship & culture across Canada; to inform the public on noteworthy social, scientific & ethical questions of the day; it is organized into three academies covering the arts & humanities, the social sciences, & the natural & applied sciences

Society for the Study of Egyptian Antiquities (SSEA) / Société pour l'Étude de l'Égypte Ancienne
PO Box 578, Stn. P, Toronto ON M5S 2T1 Canada
Tel: 416-906-0180; *Fax:* 416-978-3305
info@thessea.org
www.thessea.org
To stimulate interest in Egyptology; to assist with research & training in the field; to sponsor & promote archaeological expeditions to Egypt

Stem Cell Network (SCN) / Réseau de cellules souches
#501 Smyth Rd., Room CCW-6189, Ottawa ON K1H 8L6 Canada
Tel: 613-739-6675
info@stemcellnetwork.ca
www.stemcellnetwork.ca
To investigate the immense therapeutic potential of stem cells for the treatment of diseases currently incurable by conventional approaches
Drew Lyall, Executive Director
Lisa Willemse, Director of Communications

Traffic Injury Research Foundation (TIRF) / Fondation de recherches sur les blessures de la route
#200, 171 Nepean St., Ottawa ON K2P 0B4 Canada
Tel: 613-238-5235; *Fax:* 613-238-5292
Toll-Free: 877-238-5235
deanm@trafficinjuryresearch.com
www.trafficinjuryresearch.com
To reduce traffic related deaths & injuries, through the design, promotion, & implementation of prevention programs & policies based on sound research
Robyn D. Robertson, President & CEO
Dean Morin, Manager, Marketing & Communications

Restaurants & Food Services

Association des fournisseurs d'hôtels et restaurants inc. (AFHR) / Hotel & Restaurant Suppliers Association Inc. (HRSA)
#230, 9300, boul Henri-Bourassa ouest, Saint-Laurent QC H4S 1L5 Canada
Tel: 514-334-5161; *Fax:* 514-334-1279
Toll-Free: 888-766-0601
info@afhr.com
www.afhr.com
Informer et parfaire les connaissances des professionnels de l'industrie; offrir une vitrine aux fournisseurs par le biais du site web de l'association; centre d'information pour les hôtels, restaurants et institutions à la recherche de fournisseurs; programme d'escomptes pour les membres sur divers services; l'AFHR organise le Salon Rendez-vous HRI
Victor Francoeur, President & CEO
Isabelle Julien, Operation Manager
Hughes Moisan, Vice-President, Business Development

Association des restaurateurs du Québec (ARQ) / Québec Restaurant Association
6880, Louis-H.-La Fontaine, Montréal QC H1M 2T2 Canada
Tél: 514-527-9801; *Téléc:* 514-527-3066
Ligne sans frais: 800-463-4237
arqc@arqc.qc.ca
www.restaurateurs.ca
Fournir à l'ensemble des restaurateurs du Québec des services complets d'information, de formation, d'escomptes, d'assurances et de représentation gouvernementale

British Columbia Restaurant & Foodservices Association (BCRFA)
439 Helmcken St., Vancouver BC V6B 2E6 Canada
Tel: 604-669-2239; *Fax:* 604-669-6175
Toll-Free: 800-663-4482
info@bcrfa.com
www.bcrfa.com
To be the voice of the hospitality industry in British Columbia; the advocat of the restaurant industry.

Canadian Culinary Federation (CCFCC) / Fédération Culinaire Canadienne
c/o Roy Butterworth, 30 Hamilton Ct., Riverview NB E1B 3C3
admin@ccfcc.ca
www.ccfcc.ca
To promote a Canadian food culture both nationally & internationally; To encourage professional excellence among chefs & cooks throughout Canada

Canadian Restaurant & Foodservices Association (CRFA) / Association canadienne des restaurateurs et des services alimentaires
316 Bloor St. West, Toronto ON M5S 1W5 Canada
Tel: 416-923-8416; *Fax:* 416-923-1450
Toll-Free: 800-387-5649
sjones@crfa.ca
www.crfa.ca
To create a favourable business environment & deliver tangible value to members in all sectors of Canada's foodservice industry

Manitoba Restaurant & Food Services Association (MRFA)
103-D Scurfield Blvd., Winnipeg MB R3Y 1M6 Canada
Tel: 204-783-9955; *Fax:* 204-783-9909
Toll-Free: 877-296-2909
info@mrfa.mb.ca
www.mrfa.mb.ca
The MRFA has four primary objectives; to lobby government and other regulatory bodies on issues affecting you and your business; to present educational seminars and social programs; to provide member services such as insurance programs and credit card savings; to represent the restaurant and foodservice industry effectively through a large membership.

Société des chefs, cuisiniers et pâtissiers du Québec (SCCPQ)
3577, rue Sainte-Catherine est, Montréal QC H1W 2E6 Canada
Tél: 514-528-1083; *Téléc:* 514-528-1037
www.sccpq.ca
Mise en valeur et émulation de la profession; reconnaissance professionnelle au niveau national

Retail Trade

Association des détaillants en alimentation du Québec (ADA) / Québec Food Retailers' Association
#1100, 300 rue Léo-Pariseau, Montréal QC H2X 4C1 Canada
Tél: 514-982-0104; *Téléc:* 514-849-3021
Ligne sans frais: 800-363-3923
info@adaq.qc.ca
www.adaq.qc.ca
Représenter et défendre les intérêts professionnels, socio-politiques et économiques de tous les détaillants du Québec, et ce, quels que soient leur bannière et le type de surface qu'ils opèrent

Association nationale des distributeurs aux petites surfaces alimentaires (ANDPSA) / National Convenience Stores Distributors Association (NACDA)
#410, 1695, boul Laval, Laval QC H7S 2M2 Canada
Tel: 450-967-3858; *Fax:* 450-967-8839
Toll-Free: 800-686-2823
nacda@nacda.ca
www.nacda.ca
Promouvoir le bien-être et les intérêts de nos membres distributeurs-grossistes ainsi que de l'industrie

Canadian Association of Chain Drug Stores (CACDS) / Association canadienne des chaînes de pharmacies
#301, 45 Sheppard Ave. East, Toronto ON M2N 5W9 Canada
Tel: 416-226-9100; *Fax:* 416-226-9185
cacds@cacds.com
www.cacds.com
CACDS strives to ensure a strong chain drug store sector access to high quality products & health care services to Canadians.
Nadine Saby, President/CEO
Russell Cohen, Chair
Reza Farmand, Treasurer
Nancy Bagworth, Director, Communications

Canadian Gift & Tableware Association (CGTA) / Association canadienne de cadeaux et d'accessoires de table
42 Voyager Ct. South, Toronto ON M9W 5M7 Canada
Tel: 416-679-0170; *Fax:* 416-679-0175
Toll-Free: 800-611-6100
info@cgta.org
www.cgta.org
To create & manage sales opportunities for the gift industry

Canadian Sporting Goods Association (CSGA) / Association canadienne d'articles de sport (ACAS)
#420, 300, rue du Saint-Sacrement, Montréal QC H2Y 1X4 Canada
Tel: 514-393-1132; *Fax:* 514-393-9513
Toll-Free: 888-393-3002
csga@csga.ca
www.csga.ca
To conduct quality trade shows & to provide forum responsive to the professional needs of its members; to initiate programs designed to stimulate sports activity participation as considered feasible

Conseil québécois du commerce de détail (CQCD) / Retail Council of Québec
#910, 630, rue Sherbrooke ouest, Montréal QC H3A 1E4 Canada
Tél: 514-842-6681; *Téléc:* 514-842-7627
Ligne sans frais: 800-364-6766
cqcd@cqcd.org
www.cqcd.org
Promouvoir, représenter et valoriser le secteur du commerce de détail au Québec et les détaillants qui en font partie afin d'assurer le sain développement et la prospérité du secteur

Direct Sellers Association of Canada (DSA) / Association de ventes directes du Canada
#250, 180 Attwell Dr., Toronto ON M9W 6A9 Canada
Tel: 416-679-8555; *Fax:* 416-679-1568
info@dsa.ca
www.dsa.ca
The Association represents companies that manufacture & distribute goods & services through independent sales contractors, away from a fixed retail location; encourages strong consumer protection, through Codes of Ethics & Business Practices; engages in discussion with government & industry; acts as the voice of the direct selling industry to government in pursuit of better business opportunities for Canadian entrepreneurs.

Gift Packaging & Greeting Card Association of Canada (GPGCA) / Association canadienne du papier cadeau et de la carte de voeux
1407 Military Trail, Toronto ON M1C 1A7 Canada
Tel: 416-281-8147; *Fax:* 416-286-4868
greetingcardoffice@rogers.com
To foster the well-being of manufacturers & distributors of gift packaging products, greeting cards & related paper products in Canada.

Pool & Hot Tub Council of Canada / Conseil canadien des piscines et spas
5 MacDougall Dr., Brampton ON L6S 3P3 Canada
Tel: 905-458-7242; *Fax:* 905-458-7037
Toll-Free: 800-879-7066
office@poolcouncil.ca
www.poolcouncil.ca
To promote the image & sales of the pool, spa & hot tub industry throughout Canada; to promote & enhance consumer awareness of the industry's products; to encourage & promote increased health & safety standards within the industry; to support efforts to improve pool, hot tub & spa equipment facilities, services & products; &, generally, to promote & advance the common interests of members

Retail Council of Canada (RCC) / Conseil canadien du commerce de détail
#800, 1255 Bay St., Toronto ON M5R 2A9 Canada
Tel: 416-922-6678; *Fax:* 416-922-8011
Toll-Free: 888-373-8245
mboydbonsu@retailcouncil.org
www.retailcouncil.org
To be the best at delivering the services our retail members value most; to serve, promote & represent the diverse needs of Canada's retailing industry to the highest standards of quality

Shelfspace, the Association for Retail Entrepreneurs
#208 - 1730 - West 2nd Ave., Vancouver BC V6J 1H6 Canada
Tel: 604-736-0368; *Fax:* 604-736-3154
Toll-Free: 800-663-5135
inquiry@shelfspace.ca
www.shelfspace.ca
Social Media:
www.facebook.com/pages/Shelfspace/149758123522
To enhance the professionalism & profitability of our members
Mark Startup, CAE, President & CEO

Retirees

McMaster University Retirees Association (MURA)
c/o McMaster University, Gilmour Hall, #B108, 1280 Main St. W, Hamilton ON L8S 4L8 Canada
Tel: 905-525-9140
mura@mcmaster.ca
mura.mcmaster.ca
The McMaster University Retirees Association seeks to contribute in as many ways as possible to the welfare, prestige, and excellence of the University and to encourage and promote a spirit of fraternity and unity among the members of the Association, and to provide means for continuing the associations which retirees enjoyed as employees of the University.

Safety & Accident Prevention

Alberta Safety Council
4831 - 93 Ave. NW, Edmonton AB T6B 3A2 Canada
Tel: 780-462-7300; *Fax:* 780-462-7318
Toll-Free: 800-301-6407
www.safetycouncil.ab.ca
To create awareness & provide educational & training programs to citizens of Alberta on how to maintain a safe environment at home, in traffic, at work & at play

Association de la santé et de la sécurité des pâtes et papiers et des industries de la forêt du Québec (ASSIFQ-ASSPPQ)
Place Iberville II, #210, 1175, av Lavigerie, Sainte-Foy QC G1V 4P1 Canada
Tél: 418-657-2267; *Téléc:* 418-651-4622
Ligne sans frais: 888-632-9326
info@santesecurite.org
www.santesecurite.org
A pour mission de soutenir et d'accompagner les entreprises dans l'amélioration continue de la santé et de la sécurité du travail

Association des chefs en sécurité incendie du Québec (ACSIQ) / Québec Association of Fire Chiefs
5, rue Dupré, Beloeil QC J3G 3J7 Canada
Tél: 450-464-6413; *Téléc:* 450-467-6297
Ligne sans frais: 888-464-6413
www.acsiq.qc.ca
Regroupe les personnes détanant un poste de commande dans le domaine de la prévention et de la lutte contre les incendies

Association paritaire pour la santé et la sécurité du travail - Administration provinciale
#10, 1220, boul Lebourgneuf, Québec QC G2K 2G4 Canada
Tél: 418-624-4801; *Téléc:* 418-624-4858
apssap@apssap.qc.ca
www.apssap.qc.ca
L'Association a pour mission de supporter la prise en charge paritaire de la prévention en matière de santé, de sécurité et d'intégrité physique des personnes du secteur de l'Administration provinciale.

Association paritaire pour la santé et la sécurité du travail - Affaires municipales (APSAM)
#710, 715, carré Victoria, Montréal QC H2Y 2H7 Canada
Tél: 514-849-8373; *Téléc:* 514-849-8873
Ligne sans frais: 800-465-1754
info@apsam.com
www.apsam.com
Développer et promouvoir les moyens nécessaires pour protéger la santé et la sécurité des personnes à l'emploi des municipalités et des organismes qui y sont reliés, dans l'ensemble du Québec; fournir aux employeurs et travailleurs des municipalités du Québec des services de formation, d'information, de recherche et de conseil

Association paritaire pour la santé et la sécurité du travail - Affaires sociales
#950, 5100, rue Sherbrooke est, Montréal QC H1V 3R9 Canada
Tél: 514-253-6871; *Téléc:* 514-253-1443
Ligne sans frais: 800-361-4528
info@asstsas.qc.ca
www.asstsas.qc.ca
Une association sectorielle paritaire vouée exclusivement à la prévention en santé et en sécurité du travail dans le secteur de la santé et des services sociaux

Association paritaire pour la santé et la sécurité du travail - Habillement
#301, 2271, boul Fernand-Lafontaine, Longueuil QC J4G 2R7 Canada
Tél: 450-651-4348; *Téléc:* 450-442-2332
info@aspme.org
www.asp-habillement.org/
Specializes in the prevention of work-related injuries in the apparel sector.
Alain Plourde, Directeur général

Association paritaire pour la santé et la sécurité du travail - Imprimerie et activités connexes
#450, 7450, boul Galeries d'Anjou, Anjou QC H1M 3M3 Canada
Tél: 514-355-8282; *Téléc:* 514-355-6818
www.aspimprimerie.qc.ca
Fournir aux employeurs et aux travailleurs du secteur imprimerie et activités connexes des services d'information, de formation, de conseil et de recherche pour favoriser la prise en charge de la prévention dans les entreprises

Association paritaire pour la santé et la sécurité du travail - Mines et services miniers (APSM)
#570, 979, av de Bourgogne, Sainte-Foy QC G1W 2L4 Canada
Tél: 418-653-1933; *Téléc:* 418-653-7726
info@apsam.com
www.apsam.com

Association paritaire pour la santé et la sécurité du travail - Produits en métal et électriques
#301, 2271, boul Fernand-Lafontaine, Longueuil QC J4G 2R7 Canada
Tél: 450-442-7763; *Téléc:* 450-442-2332
jarsenault@aspme.org
www.aspme.org

Association paritaire pour la santé et la sécurité du travail - Services automobiles
#150, 8, rue de la Place-Du-Commerce, Brossard QC J4W 3H2 Canada
Tél: 450-672-9330; *Téléc:* 450-672-4835
Ligne sans frais: 800-363-2344
info@autoprevention.qc.ca
www.autoprevention.qc.ca
Depuis 1983, Auto Prévention aide les travailleurs et les employeurs du secteur des services automobiles à prendre en charge la santé et la sécurité au travail, afin d'éliminer les risques d'accidents et de maladies professionnelles.

Association québécoise des pompiers volontaires et permanents
#460, 9401, des Saints Côte, Mirabel QC J7N 2X4 Canada
Tél: 514-990-1338
Média social: www.facebook.com/group.php?gid=27982231370
Aider à promouvoir la prévention des incendies; aider, soutenir et susciter des efforts en vue de réduire les pertes de vie; favoriser le perfectionnement en vue de combattre plus efficacement les incendies; promouvoir l'éducation populaire en général sur la protection et la prévention des incendies; faire des recommandations auprès des corps politiques et gouvernementaux

Association sectorielle - Fabrication d'équipement de transport et de machines (ASFETM) / Sectorial Association - Transportation Equipment & Machinery Manufacturing (SATEMM)
#202, 3565, rue Jarry est, Montréal QC H1Z 4K6 Canada
Tél: 514-729-6961; *Téléc:* 514-729-8628
Ligne sans frais: 888-527-3386
info@asfetm.com
www.asfetm.com
Aider les employeurs et les travailleurs à prévenir les accidents du travail et les maladies professionnelles, en faisant pour eux de la recherche, en leur dispensant de l'information, de la formation et de l'assistance technique qui visent essentiellement à rendre impossibles les accidents et les maladies au travail, et en privilégiant, à cette fin, l'élimination de cette possibilité à sa source même selon un processus de participation paritaire
Arnold Dugas, Directeur général
Suzanne Ready, Chargée de l'information

Association Sectorielle Transport Entreposage (ASTE)
#301, 6455, boul Jean-Talon est, Montréal QC H1S 3E8 Canada
Tél: 514-955-0454; *Téléc:* 514-955-0449
Ligne sans frais: 800-361-8906
info@aste.qc.ca
www.aste.qc.ca
L'Association Sectorielle Transport Entreposage est une organisme en prèvention, autonome et paritaire, sans but lucratif, fondé et administré par des reprétants des employeurs et des syndicats.
Alain Lajoie, Directeur général

Board of Canadian Registered Safety Professionals (BCRSP) / Conseil canadien des professionnels en securité agréés
6519B Mississauga Rd., Mississauga ON L5N 1A6 Canada
Tel: 905-567-7198; *Fax:* 905-567-7191
Toll-Free: 888-279-2777
bcrsp@sympatico.ca
www.bcrsp.ca
To protect & promote occupational health & safety, environmental safety, & public safety, through the registration of qualified health & safety professionals committed to a code of ethics

Canada Safety Council (CSC) / Conseil canadien de la sécurité (CCS)
1020 Thomas Spratt Pl., Ottawa ON K1G 5L5 Canada
Tel: 613-739-1535; *Fax:* 613-739-1566
canadasafetycouncil@safety-council.org
www.safety-council.org
Social Media: www.facebook.com/canada.safety
To exercise leadership in a national effort to prevent death, injury & economic loss caused by accidents in the traffic, occupational & public environments; focus is on safety education & support of safety legislation

Canadian Association of Fire Chiefs (CAFC) / Association canadienne des chefs de pompiers (ACCP)
#702, 280 Albert St., Ottawa ON K1P 5G8 Canada
Tel: 613-270-9138; *Fax:* 613-233-9138
info@cafc.ca
www.cafc.ca
To lead & represent the Canadian Fire Service on public safety issues with the vision of being nationally recognized as the fire service voice of authority

Canadian Association of Road Safety Professionals (CARSP) / Association canadienne des professionnels de la sécurité routière (ACPSER)
c/o Joseph Chan, Transportation Centre, University of Saskatchewan, 57 Campus Dr., Saskatoon SK S7N 5A9 Canada
Tel: 306-966-7010; *Fax:* 306-966-7014
askcarsp@magma.ca
www.carsp.ca
The association preserves & shares professional experience regarding road safety. It promotes research & professional development & facilitates communication & cooperation among road safety groups & agencies.
Joseph Chan, Membership Sec. and Treasurer
Paul Boase, President

Canadian Automatic Sprinkler Association (CASA)
#302, 335 Renfrew Dr., Markham ON L3R 9S9 Canada
Tel: 905-477-2270; *Fax:* 905-477-3611
info@casa-firesprinkler.org
www.casa-firesprinkler.org
To advance the fire sprinkler art as applied to the conservation of life & property from fire.

Canadian Centre for Occupational Health & Safety (CCOHS) / Centre canadien d'hygiène et de sécurité au travail (CCHST)
135 Hunter St. East, Hamilton ON L8N 1M5 Canada
Tel: 905-572-2981; *Fax:* 905-572-2206
Toll-Free: 800-668-4284
clientservices@ccohs.ca
www.ccohs.ca
Social Media: www.facebook.com/CCOHS
To promote health & safety in the workplace, & the physical & mental health of working people in Canada

Canadian Fire Safety Association (CFSA)
#310, 2175 Sheppard Ave. East, Toronto ON M2J 1W8 Canada
Tel: 416-492-9417; *Fax:* 416-491-1670
cfsa@taylorenterprises.com
www.canadianfiresafety.com
To promote fire safety through seminars, safety training courses, scholarships & regular meetings.

Canadian Radiation Protection Association (CRPA) / Association canadienne de radioprotection (ACRP)
PO Box 83, Carleton Place ON K7C 3P3 Canada
Tel: 613-253-3779; *Fax:* 888-551-0712
secretariat2007@crpa-acrp.ca
www.crpa-acrp.ca
To develop scientific knowledge for protection from the harmful effects of radiation; to encourage research; to assist in the development of professional standards in the discipline

Canadian Security Association (CANASA) / L'Association canadienne de la sécurité
#201, 50 Acadia Ave., Markham ON L3R 0B3 Canada
Tel: 905-513-0622; *Fax:* 905-513-0624
Toll-Free: 800-538-9919
staff@canasa.org
www.canasa.org
Social Media: twitter.com/CANASA_News
To act as the national voice of the security industry; To promote & protect the interests of members; To increase public awareness of the security industry's effectiveness in reducing risk; To develop & promote programs consistent with the needs of members; To develop & promote programs which will lead to the reduction of false dispatches & improved response; To influence regulations affecting the members

Canadian Society of Air Safety Investigators (CSASI)
139 West 13th Ave., Vancouver BC V5Y 1V8 Canada
avsafe@rogers.com
To ensure air safety through investigation

Canadian Society of Safety Engineering, Inc. (CSSE) / Société canadienne de la santé et de la sécurité, inc.
39 River St., Toronto ON M5A 3P1 Canada
Tel: 416-646-1600; *Fax:* 416-646-9460
wglover@associationsfirst.com
www.csse.org
To be the voice of safety in Canada

Centre patronal de santé et sécurité du travail du Québec (CPSSTQ) / Employers Center for Occupational Health & Safety of Quebec
#1000, 500, rue Sherbrooke ouest, Montréal QC H3A 3C6 Canada
Tél: 514-842-8401; *Téléc:* 514-842-9375
reception@centrepatronalsst.qc.ca
www.centrepatronalsst.qc.ca
Fournir de l'information et de la formation en SST aux entreprises regroupées par les associations patronales membres du Centre patronal
Germaine Archambault, Président
Denise Turenne, pdg, Présidente-directrice générale

Council of Canadian Fire Marshals & Fire Commissioners (CCFMFC) / Conseil canadien des directeurs provinciaux et des commissaires des incendies
c/o 491 McLeod Hill Rd., Fredericton NB E3A 6H6
Tel: 506-453-1208; *Fax:* 506-457-0793
philippag@rogers.com
www.ccfmfc.ca
To contribute to a reduction in the number of fire deaths
Ben Laroche, President
Christopher Jones, Vice-President
Philippa Gourley, Secretary-Treasurer

Council of Private Investigators - Ontario (CPIO)
#200, 148 York St., London ON N6A 1A9 Canada
Tel: 416-955-9450
director@cpi-ontario.com
www.cpi-ontario.com
To represent the interests of private investigators in Ontario

Federal Association of Security Officials (FASO) / Association fédérale des représentants de la sécurité
PO Box 2384, Stn. D, Ottawa ON K1P 5W5 Canada
Tel: 613-990-2615; *Fax:* 613-990-8297
Toll-Free: 888-330-3276
info@faso-afrs.ca
www.faso-afrs.ca
To enhance the performance & career development of federal security officers through enhancing the security function in government & improving the professionalism of security officers.
Claude J.G. Levesque, President

Fire Prevention Canada (FPC)
PO Box 47037, Ottawa ON K1B 5P9 Canada
Tel: 613-749-3844; *Fax:* 613-749-0109
Toll-Free: 877-906-6651
info@fiprecan.ca
www.fiprecan.ca
Working with the public & private sectors to achieve fire safety through education.

Industrial Accident Victims Group of Ontario (IAVGO)
#203, 489 College St., Toronto ON M6G 1A5 Canada
Tel: 416-924-6477; *Toll-Free:* 877-230-6311
www.iavgo.org
Our community legal clinic provides free services to injured workers in Ontario including legal advice, legal representation, public legal education, advocacy training and community development.

Institut de recherche Robert-Sauvé en santé et en sécurité du travail (IRSST) / Robert Sauvé Occupational Health & Safety Research Institute
505, boul de Maisonneuve ouest, 15e étage, Montréal QC H3A 3C2 Canada
Tél: 514-288-1551; *Téléc:* 514-288-7636
communications@irsst.qc.ca
www.irsst.qc.ca
Contribuer par la recherche et le développement à l'amélioration de la santé et de la sécurité des travailleurs et plus spécifiquement, à l'élimination à la source des dangers pour leur santé, leur sécurité et leur intégrité physique ainsi qu'à la réadaptation des travailleurs victimes d'accidents ou de maladies professionnelles; fournir au Réseau public québécois de la prévention en santé et en sécurité du travail - composé de CSST, des Centres locaux de services communautaires, des Régies de la santé et des services sociaux et des associations sectorielles paritaires - les services et l'expertise nécessaires à leur action; diffuser les connaissances issues de ces recherches et de ces expertises auprès des milieux de travail et en favoriser le transfert; accorder des bourses d'études supérieures en santé et en sécurité du travail; agir comme laboratoire de référence au Québec, dans le domaine de l'hygiene industrielle.

Newfoundland & Labrador Safety Council
Regatta Plaza II, #84, 86 Elizabeth Ave., 2nd Fl., St. John's NL A1A 1W7 Canada
Tel: 709-754-0210; *Fax:* 709-754-0010
info@safetycouncil.net
The Newfoundland and Labrador Safety Council is dedicated to the prevention of injuries and fatalities; represents all the major sectors of the province's industry, business, government departments, volunteer organizations and many individuals who have a personal interest in safety, both on and off the job.

Nova Scotia Safety Council
Vantage Point 3, #3F, 110 Chain Lake Dr., Halifax NS B3S 1A9 Canada
Tel: 902-454-9621; *Fax:* 902-454-6027
www.nssafety.ns.ca
The Safety Council develops & provides quality safety & health services, education & training programs to improve the quality of life of Nova Scotians.

Ontario Association of Fire Chiefs (OAFC)
#206, 335 Bayly St. West, Ajax ON L1S 6M2 Canada
Tel: 905-426-9865; *Fax:* 905-426-3032
Toll-Free: 800-774-6651
administration@oafc.on.ca
www.oafc.on.ca
To ensure that Ontario has a well trained & well equipped fire service

Ontario Industrial Fire Protection Association (OIFPA)
193 James St. South, Hamilton ON L8P 3A8
Tel: 905-527-0700; *Fax:* 905-527-6254
oifpa@interlynx.net
www.oifpa.org
To unite individuals with a concern for fire protection within Ontario's industrial community

Ontario Safety League (OSL) / Ligue de sécurité de l'Ontario
Bldg. 11, #100, 5045 Orbitor Dr., Mississauga ON L4W 4Y4 Canada
Tel: 905-625-0556; *Fax:* 905-625-0677
info@osl.org
www.osl.org
Safety through education with an emphasis on traffic & child safety

Opération Nez rouge / Operation Red Nose
Maison Couillard, Université Laval, 2539, rue Marie-Fitzbach, Québec QC G1V 0A6 Canada
Tél: 418-653-1492; *Téléc:* 418-653-3315
Ligne sans frais: 800-463-7222
www.operationnezrouge.com
Service de chauffeur privé gratuit & bénévole offert pendant la période des Fêtes à tout automobiliste qui a consommé de l'alcool, our qui ne se sent pas en état de conduire son véhicule.
Étienne Talbot, Directeur général

Préventex - Association paritaire du textile
1936, rue Rossignol, Brossard QC J4X 2C6 Canada
Tél: 450-671-6925; *Téléc:* 450-671-9267
info@preventex.qc.ca
www.preventex.qc.ca
Amener les employeurs et les travailleurs du secteur à prendre charge activement de la prévention des accidents du travail et des maladies professionnelles

Radiation Safety Institute of Canada / Institut de radioprotection du Canada
Head Office & National Education Centre, #300, 165 Avenue Rd., Toronto ON M5R 3S4
Tel: 416-650-9090; *Fax:* 416-650-9920
Toll-Free: 800-263-5803
info@radiationsafety.ca
www.radiationsafety.ca
Social Media:
www.facebook.com/group.php?gid=143472245714096
To be an independent source for knowledge about radiation safety in the environment, the community, & the workplace
Fergal Nolan, MA, DPhil, President & Chief Executive Officer
Bruce Sylvester, Vice-President, Finance & Administration
Mike Haynes, Scientific Director
Natalia Mozayani, Program Manager
Tara Hargreaves, Scientist & Coordinator, Training

Safe Communities Foundation (SCF)
#201, 64 Charles St. East, Toronto ON M4Y 1T1 Canada
Tel: 416-964-0008; *Fax:* 416-964-0089
info@safecommunities.ca
www.safecommunities.ca
To help people come together in the community to create a sense of awareness, understanding, support & leadership to implement effective local programs to eliminate injuries & suffering; to improve the health & safety of workers & people of all ages throughout the community
Paul Kells, Founder & President
Jocelyne Achat, Vice-Chair

Safe Workplace Promotion Services Ontario (SWPSO)
Centre for Health & Safety Innovation, #300, 5110 Creekbank Rd., Mississauga ON L4W 0A1 Canada
Tel: 905-614-1400; *Fax:* 905-614-1414
Toll-Free: 877-494-9777
customercare@wsps.ca
www.wsps.ca
WSPS is a not-for-profit organization with a mandate to meet the health & safety needs of businesses in the agricultural, manufacturing & service industries. It provides programs, products, & services for the prevention of injury & illness.

Safety Services Manitoba (SSM)
#3, 1680 Notre Dame Ave., Winnipeg MB R3H 1H6 Canada
Tel: 204-949-1085; *Fax:* 204-949-2897
Toll-Free: 800-661-3321
registrar@safetyservicesmanitoba.ca
www.safetyservicesmanitoba.ca
To prevent accidental injury or occupational illness in Manitoba by providing effective safety & health programs.

Safety Services New Brunswick (SSNB) / Services de Sécurité Nouveau-Brunswick
#204, 440 Wilsey Rd., Fredericton NB E3B 7G5 Canada
Tel: 506-458-8034; *Fax:* 506-444-0177
Toll-Free: 877-762-7233
info@safetyservicesnb.ca
www.safetyservicesnb.ca
To promote traffic, occupational & public safety issues & practices through safety training courses & programs, educational material, public information, safety campaigns & conferences.
Bill Walker, President & CEO
Jim Arsenault, Director of OSH & Traffic Training

Saskatchewan Safety Council
445 Hoffer Dr., Regina SK S4N 6E2 Canada
Tel: 306-757-3197; *Fax:* 306-569-1907
ssc@sasksafety.org
sasksafety.org

Scholarly

Canadian Association for the Study of Humanities and the Environment
c/o Institute for Governance Studies, Simon Fraser University, Burnaby BC V5A 1S6 Canada
Tel: 778-782-4293; *Fax:* 778-782-4786
igs@sfu.ca
www.sfu.ca/igs/cashe.html
Rebecca Raglon, Secretary

Scientific

Alberta Society of Professional Biologists (ASPB)
PO Box 21104, Edmonton AB T6R 2V4
Tel: 780-434-5765; *Fax:* 780-413-0076
pbiol@aspb.ab.ca
www.aspb.ab.ca
To promote excellence in the practice of biology; To provide a voice for professional biologists in Alberta
P. Ross Bradford, Executive Director
Bette Beswick, Registrar
Monika Burak, Coordinator, Finance
Shauna Prokopchuk, Coordinator, Membership & Communications
Joy Sager, Coordinator, Association & Events

Arctic Institute of North America (AINA)
University of Calgary, 2500 University Dr. NW, Calgary AB T2N 1N4 Canada
Tel: 403-220-7515; *Fax:* 403-282-4609
arctic@ucalgary.ca
www.arctic.ucalgary.ca
To encourage & support scientific research pertaining to the polar regions

Association des microbiologistes du Québec (AMQ)
5094A, av. Charlemagne, Montréal QC H1X 3P3 Canada
Tél: 514-728-1087; *Téléc:* 514-374-3988
amq@microbiologistes.ca
www.microbiologistes.ca
L'association regroupe les microbiologistes du Québec oeuvrant principalemtn en environnement, en alimentaire et en pharmaceutique. Elle a pour but d'étudier, de protéger et de développer les intérêts économiques, sociaux et professionnels des microbiologistes et de promouvoir l'essor de la microbiologie en général; est impliquée au niveau de l'accréditation des laboratoires d'analyses microbiologiques et elle est représentée au sein de plusieurs comités ou associations.

Association of Canadian Ergonomists (ACE) / L'Association canadienne d'ergonomie
#1003, 105-150 Crowfoot Cres. NW, Calgary AB T3G 3T2 Canada
Tel: 403-219-4001; *Fax:* 403-451-1503
Toll-Free: 888-432-2223
info@ace-ergocanada.ca
www.ace-ergocanada.ca
To advance human factors/ergonomics through encouraging a high quality of practice, education & research; to facilitate communication among members; to represent the discipline; to increase awareness of human factors/ergonomics; to identify resources

Association of Professional Biology (APB)
#300, 1095 McKenzie Ave., Victoria BC V8P 2L5
Tel: 250-483-4283; *Fax:* 250-483-3439
apbbc@apbbc.bc.ca
www.apbbc.bc.ca
To promote & assist professional practitioners of applied biology
Megan Hanacek, Managing Director & Registrar

Atlantic Provinces Council on the Sciences (APCS) / Conseil des provinces atlantiques pour les sciences (CPAS)
1390 Le Marchant St., Halifax NS B3H 3P9 Canada
Tel: 902-494-3421; *Fax:* 902-494-6643
apics@dal.ca
www.apics.dal.ca
To advance science & technology through education & public awareness & the promotion of scientific literacy education & research throughout the region

Biophysical Society of Canada (BSC) / La société de biophysique du Canada
a/s Dept. de chimie-biologie, Univ. du Québec à Trois-Rivières, CP 500, Trois-Rivières QC G9A 5H7 Canada
Tel: 819-376-5011; *Fax:* 819-376-5057
fragata@uqtr.ca
www.uqtr.ca/sbc/
To promote biophysical research & education; to encourage cross-feeding of ideas between the physical & biological sciences; to foster & support scientific meetings, workshops & discussions in biophysics; to represent Canadian biophysics & biophysicists

BIOTECanada
#420, 130 Albert St., Ottawa ON K1P 5G4 Canada
Tel: 613-230-5585; *Fax:* 613-563-8850
info@biotech.ca
www.biotech.ca
To provide a unified voice fostering an environment that responds to the needs of the biotechnology industry & research community, both nationally & internationally
Peter Brenders, President & CEO

Canadian Association for Anatomy, Neurobiology, & Cell Biology (CAANCB) / Association canadienne d'anatomie, de neurobiologie et de biologie cellulaire (ACANBC)
Dr. W.H. Baldridge, Department of Anatomy, Faculty of Medicine, Dalhousie University, Halifax BC B3H 4H7
Tel: 613-533-2864; *Fax:* 613-533-2566
www.caancb.blogspot.com
To advance knowledge of anatomy; To represent anatomical sciences throughout Canada

Canadian Association of Palynologists (CAP) / Association canadienne des palynologues
c/o Dr. Mary A. Vetter, Luther College, University of Regina, Regina SK S4S 0A2
www.scirpus.ca/cap/cap.shtml
To advance all aspects of palynology in Canada
Matthew Peros, President
Mary A. Vetter, Secretary-Treasurer
Terri Lacourse, Editor, CAP Newsletter

Canadian Association of Physicists (CAP) / Association canadienne des physiciens et physiciennes (ACP)
MacDonald Bldg., #112, 150 Louis Pasteur Priv., Ottawa ON K1N 6N5 Canada
Tel: 613-562-5614; *Fax:* 613-562-5615
cap@uottawa.ca
www.cap.ca
CAP is a broadly-based national network of physicists working in Canadian educational, industrial, and research settings. They are a strong advocacy group for support of, and excellence in, physics research and education.

Canadian Astronomical Society (CASCA) / Société canadienne d'astronomie
Business Office, Dept. of Physics, Queens Univ., Kingston ON K7L 3N6 Canada
Tel: 613-533-6439; *Fax:* 613-533-6463
casca@astro.queensu.ca
www.casca.ca

Canadian Botanical Association (CBA) / Association botanique du Canada (ABC)
PO Box 160, Aberdeen SK S0K 0A0
Tel: 613-364-4074; *Fax:* 613-364-4027
lconsaul@mus-nature.ca
www.cba-abc.ca
Representing Canadian Botany & botanists nationally & internationally, the Association responds quickly & professionally on matters that are of concern to Canadian botanists.

Canadian College of Physicists in Medicine (CCPM) / Collège canadien des physiciens en médecine
PO Box 72024, Kanata North RPO, Kanata ON K2K 2P4 Canada
Tel: 613-599-1948; *Fax:* 613-599-1949
www.ccpm.ca
To identify, through certification, individuals who have acquired & maintained a standard of knowledge & skill essential to the practice of medical physics, in order to serve the public

Canadian Federation of Earth Sciences (CFES) / Fédération canadienne des sciences de la Terre
c/o Managing Director, 210 Main St., Wolfville NS B4P 1C4 Canada
Tel: 902-542-6125
cfes@magma.ca
www.geoscience.ca
To promote coordination & cooperation in activities in Canadian geoscientific education; to advise on science policy involving the earth sciences; to provide an informed opinion to the public of Canada on matters of public concern.

Canadian Hydrographic Association (CHA) / Association canadienne d'hydrographie
867 Lakeshore Rd., Burlington ON L7R 4A6 Canada
Tel: 905-336-4491
www.hydrography.ca
The scientific & technical group has the following objectives: to advance the development of hydrography & associated activities in Canada; to further the knowledge & professional development of members; to enhance & demonstrate the public need for hydrography; & to help the development of hydrographic sciences in developing countries; & to embrace the desciplines of marine cartography, hydrographic surveying, offshore exploration, marine geodesy, & tidal studies.

Canadian Institute of Food Science & Technology (CIFST) / Institut canadien de science et technologie alimentaires (ICSTA)
#1311, 3-1750 The Queensway, Toronto ON M9C 5H5
Tel: 905-271-8338; *Fax:* 905-271-8344
cifst@cifst.ca
www.cifst.ca
To advance food science & technology; To act as a voice for scientific issues related to the Canadian food industry

Canadian Medical & Biological Engineering Society (CMBES) / Société canadienne de génie biomédical inc. (SCGB)
1485 Laperrière Ave., Ottawa ON K1Z 7S8
Tel: 613-728-1759
secretariat@cmbes.ca
www.cmbes.ca
To advance the theory & practice of medical device technology; To advance individuals who are engaged in interdisciplinary work involving medicine, engineering, & the life sciences; To represent the interests of biomedical & clinical engineering to government agencies
Murat Firat, MSc., President
Mike Capuano, Chair, Professional Affairs
Tim J. Zakutney, MHSc, PEng, CCE, Chair, Awards
Martin Poulin, M.Eng., P.Eng., Treasurer
Melanie Chayra, Secretariat

Canadian Meteorological & Oceanographic Society (CMOS) / Société canadienne de météorologie et d'océanographie (SCMO)
PO Box 3211, Stn. D, Ottawa ON K1P 6H7 Canada
Tel: 613-990-0300; *Fax:* 613-990-1617
communications@cmos.ca; accounts@cmos.ca;
publications@cmos.ca
www.cmos.ca
To advance meteorology & oceanography in Canada

Canadian Physiological Society (CPS) / Société canadienne de physiologie
c/o Dr. Melanie Woodin, Dept. of Cell & Systems Biology, U. of Toronto, 25 Harbord St., Toronto ON M5S 3G5
www.cpsscp.ca
To disseminate & discuss scientific information of interest to researchers in physiology & biological sciences
Melanie Woodin, Secretary

Canadian Phytopathological Society (CPS) / Société Canadienne de Phytopathologie (SCP)
c/o Crop Protection & Food Research Ctr Agriculture & Agri-Food Canada, 1391 Sandford St., London ON N5V 4T3
connk@agr.gc.ca
www.cps-scp.ca
To encourage & support research, education, & dissemination of knowledge on the nature, cause, & control of plant diseases; To promote communication among plant pathologists; To broaden educational opportunities for members

Canadian Science & Technology Historical Association (CSTHA) / Association pour l'histoire de la science et de la technologie au Canada (AHSTC)
PO Box 9724, Stn. T, Ottawa ON K1G 3H9 Canada
secretary@cstha-ahstc.ca
www.cstha-ahstc.ca
To foster the study of Canada's scientific & technological heritage through research, publication, teaching & preservation of artifacts & records

Canadian Society for Analytical Sciences & Spectroscopy
PO Box 46122, 2339 Ogilvie Rd., Ottawa ON K1J 9M7 Canada
Fax: 204-954-5984
www.csass.org

To organize programs of scientific & general interest for the educational benefit of members & the public; to organize annual scientific conferences & workshops on various aspects of pure & applied spectroscopy in the chemical, biological, geochemical & metallurgical sciences

Canadian Society for the History & Philosophy of Science (CSHPS) / Société Canadienne d'Histoire et Philosophie des Sciences (SCHPS)
c/o Dr. Andrew Reynolds, Department of Philosphy & Religious Studies, Cape Breton University, Sydney NS B1P 6L2
andrew_reynolds@cbu.ca
www.cshps.ca; www.schps.ca
To explore all aspects of science, past & present

The Canadian Society for the Weizmann Institute of Science (CSWIS)
4700 Bathurst St., 2nd Fl., Toronto ON M2R 1W8 Canada
Tel: 416-733-9220; *Fax:* 416-733-9430
Toll-Free: 800-387-3894
weizmann@ca.inter.net
www.weizmann.ac.il; www.weizmann.ca
To marshal Canadian support for the Weizmann Institute of Science in Rehovot, Israel; to help build & maintain scientific facilities; to acquire costly up-to-date research equipment & instrumentation; to set up endowments for research centres; to establish professional chairs & scholarships

The Canadian Society of Biochemistry, Molecular & Cellular Biology / Société canadienne de biochimie et de biologie moléculaire et cellulaire
c/o Department of Biochemistry, University of Toronto, Medical Sciences Bldg., 1 King's College Circle, Toronto ON M5S 1A8 Canada
Tel: 416-978-0774
rob.reedijk@utoronto.ca
www.csbmcb.ca

Canadian Society of Exploration Geophysicists (CSEG)
#600, 640 - 8th Ave. SW, Calgary AB T2P 1G7
Tel: 403-262-0015
cseg.office@shaw.ca
www.cseg.ca
To promote the science of geophysics

Canadian Society of Forensic Science (CSFS)
PO Box 37040, 3332 McCarthy Rd., Ottawa ON K1V 0W0 Canada
csfs@bellnet.ca
www.csfs.ca
To promote the study of forensic science; to maintain professional standards in the discipline of forensic science

Canadian Society of Microbiologists (CSM) / Société canadienne des microbiologistes
CSM-SCM Secretariat, #305, 1750 Courtwood Cres., Ottawa ON K2C 2B5 Canada
Tel: 613-225-8889; *Fax:* 613-225-9621
info@csm-scm.org
www.csm-scm.org
To advance microbiology in all its aspects; to facilitate interchange of ideas between microbiologists

Canadian Society of Pharmacology & Therapeutics (CSPT) / Société de pharmacologie du Canada
Dept. of Physiology & Pharmacology, University of Western Ontario, M216 Medical Services Bldg., London ON N6A 5C1
Tel: 519-661-3312
www.pharmacologycanada.org
To promote research & education in the disciplines of pharmacology & experimental therapeutics

Canadian Society of Plant Physiologists (CSPP) / Société canadienne de physiologie végétale (SCPV)
c/o Dr. Harold Weger, Department of Biology, University of Regina, 3737 Wascana Pkwy., Regina SK S4S 0A2 Canada
treasurer@cspp-scpvca.ca
www.cspp-scpv.ca
To promote the teaching & public awareness of plant physiology in Canada

Canadian Society of Soil Science (CSSS) / Société canadienne de la science du sol
Business Office, PO Box 637, Pinawa MB R0E 1L0
Tel: 204-753-2747; *Fax:* 204-753-8478
sheppards@ecomatters.com
www.csss.ca
To be actively engaged in land use, soils research, & classification

Canadian Space Society (CSS) / La société canadienne de l'espace
Parc Downsview Park, 65 Carl Hall Rd., Toronto ON M3K 2E1 Canada
www.css.ca
To conduct technical & outreach projects; to promote the involvement of Canadians in space development
Kevin Shortt, President
Vivian Lee, Coordinator, Membership

Citizen Scientists
c/o Rouge Valley Conservation Centre, 1749 Meadowvale Rd., Toronto ON M1B 5W8 Canada
info@citizenscientists.ca
www.citizenscientists.ca
Social Media: www.facebook.com/group.php?gid=2259994028
To monitor local watersheds, foster local environmental stewardship, and educate volunteers and the public.

Club d'astronomie Quasar de Chibougamau
783, 6e Rue, Chibougamau QC G8P 2W4 Canada
Tél: 418-748-4642
www.faaq.org/clubs/quasar/
Pierre Bureau, Président

Genetics Society of Canada (GSC) / Société de génétique du Canada
c/o The Snider's Web, 59 Aulac Rd., Aulac NB E4L 2V6 Canada
Tel: 506-536-1768; *Fax:* 902-484-5694
gsc@thesnidersweb.com
life.biology.mcmaster.ca/GSC/
To provide means of liaison between geneticists for coordination & development of genetics & science policy in Canada; to promote facilities for reporting, exchanging & disseminating knowledge related to genetics & to make known theSociety's views on genetic knowledge which is of direct concern to the Canadianpublic.

Geological Association of Canada (GAC) / Association géologique du Canada (AGC)
Department of Earth Sciences, Memorial University of Newfoundland, #ER4063, Alexander Murray Bldg., St. John's NL A1B 3X5
Tel: 709-737-7660; *Fax:* 709-737-2532
gac@mun.ca; gacpublications@mun.ca (GEOLOG newsmagazine)
www.gac.ca
To advance the wise use of geoscience in academic, professional, & public circles

Innovation and Technology Association of Prince Edward Island (ITAP)
PO Box 241, Charlottetown PE C1A 7K4 Canada
Tel: 902-894-4827; *Fax:* 902-894-4867
itap@itap.ca
www.itap.ca
To provide advocacy and support to our members, through projects in the key areas of export development, communication and leadership development.
Kelly Dawson, President

Institute of Textile Science (ITS) / Institut des sciences textiles
c/o Jerry Bauerle, BodyCote Ortech Inc., 2395 Speakman Dr., Mississauga ON L5K 1B3 Canada
Tel: 905-822-4111; *Fax:* 905-823-1446
info@textilescience.ca
www.textilescience.ca
To promote the dissemination & interchange of knowledge concerning textile science; to encourage research & development related to textile science & technology, including the establishment & granting of awards

International Association of Hydrogeologists - Canadian National Chapter (IAH-CNC)
c/o WESA, 3108 Carp Rd., Carp ON K0A 1L0 Canada
Tel: 613-839-3053
www.iah.ca
To advance the science of hydrogeology & exchange hydrogeologic information internationally
Nell van Walsum, Secretary

International Association of Science & Technology for Development (IASTED)
Bldg B6, #101, 2509 Dieppe Ave. SW, Calgary AB T3E 7J9 Canada
Tel: 403-288-1195; *Fax:* 403-247-6851
calgary@iasted.com
www.iasted.org
To further economic development by promoting science & technology.

International Oceans Institute of Canada (IOIC)
c/o Dalhousie Univ., 1226 LeMarchant St., Halifax NS B3H 3P7 Canada
Tel: 902-494-6918; *Fax:* 902-494-1334
ioi@dal.ca
internationaloceaninstitute.dal.ca
To promote responsible management of the world's oceans & sustainable development of marine resources; to protect the integrity of the ocean environment; to promote sustainable resource development; to improve the quality of ocean-dependent human life, including health & safety of maritime communities; to further these objectives, all aspects of the ocean environment are pursued - resource management & development, marine environmental quality, ocean law & policy, high seas management, coastal zone management, marine transportation, ocean science & technology, tourism & recreation, ocean industries & maritime boundary delimitation

Life Science Association of Manitoba (LSAM)
1000 Waverley St., Winnipeg MB R3T 0P3 Canada
Tel: 204-272-5095; *Fax:* 204-272-2961
info@lsam.ca
www.lsam.ca
Association representing the life science industry in Manitoba; provides services for companies in the industry; promotes economic development
Dawson Reimer, President

Microscopical Society of Canada (MSC) / Société de Microscopie du Canada
c/o Occupational & Environmental Health Laboratory, McMaster Univ., #3H50, 1200 Main St. West, Hamilton ON L8N 3Z5 Canada
Tel: 905-525-9140; *Fax:* 905-528-8860
clarkn@mcmaster.ca
msc.rsvs.ulaval.ca

North Pacific Marine Science Organization (PICES)
c/o Institute of Ocean Sciences, PO Box 6000, Sidney BC V8L 4B2 Canada
Tel: 250-363-6366; *Fax:* 250-363-6827
secretariat@pices.int
www.pices.int
To promote & coordinate marine research in the northern North Pacific & adjacent seas especially northward of 30 degrees North; to advance scientific knowledge about the ocean environment, global weather & climate change, living resources & their ecosystems & the impacts of human activities; to promote the collection & rapid exchange of scientific information on these issues
Alexander Bychkov, Executive Secretary

Nova Scotian Institute of Science (NSIS)
Science Services, Killam Library, Dalhousie Univ., 6225 University Ave., Halifax NS B3H 4H8 Canada
Tel: 902-494-3621; *Fax:* 902-494-2062
nsis@chebucto.ns.ca
www.chebucto.ns.ca/Science/NSIS
To provide a forum for scientists & those interested in science

Ontario Kinesiology Association (OKA)
6519B Mississauga Rd., Mississauga ON L5N 1A6 Canada
Tel: 905-567-7194; *Fax:* 905-567-7191
info@oka.on.ca
www.oka.on.ca
To promote the application of the science of human movement to other professionals & to the community; to uphold the standards of the profession of kinesiology; to assist kinesiologists in the performance of their duties & responsibilities

Royal Astronomical Society of Canada (RASC) / Société royale d'astronomie du Canada
203 - 4920 Dundas St. West, Toronto ON M9A 1B7 Canada
Tel: 416-924-7973; *Fax:* 416-924-2911
Toll-Free: 888-924-7272
nationaloffice10000@rasc.ca
www.rasc.ca
Social Media:
www.facebook.com/home.php?#!/group.php?gid=2393127970
To promote the advancement of astronomy across Canada

Science Alberta Foundation
#260, 3512 - 33 St. NW, Calgary AB T2L 2A6 Canada
Tel: 403-220-0077; *Fax:* 403-284-4132
info@sciencealberta.org
www.sciencealberta.org
To increase science literacy by creating innovative programs for all Albertans

Society of Toxicology of Canada (STC) / Société de toxicologie du Canada
PO Box 55094, Montréal QC H3G 2W5 Canada
Tel: 514-697-9219; *Fax:* 514-697-9309
stcsecretariat@mcgill.ca
www.stcweb.ca
To promote acquisition, facilitate dissemination & encourage utilization of knowledge in the science of toxicology

Southern Ontario Seismic Network (SOSN)
c/o University of Western Ontario, London ON N6A 5B7 Canada
Tel: 519-661-3605; *Fax:* 519-661-3198
www.gp.uwo.ca
To obtain information on the seismicity and seismic hazards of a region of southern Ontario in which a number of nuclear power facilities are located.
R.F. Mereu, Administrator

Statistical Society of Canada (SSC) / Société statistique du Canada
#105, 1785 Alta Vista Dr., Ottawa ON K1G 3Y6 Canada
Tel: 613-733-2662; *Fax:* 613-733-1386
info@ssc.ca; admin@ssc.ca
www.ssc.ca
To promote the development & use of statistics & probability; to ensure that decisions that affect society are based upon valid & appropriate statistics & interpretation; to encourage high standards for statistical education & practice

Youth Science Foundation Canada (YSF) / Fondation sciences jeunesse Canada (FSJ)
PO Box 523, Stn. R, Toronto ON M4G 4E1 Canada
Tel: 416-341-0040; *Fax:* 416-341-0040
Toll-Free: 866-341-0040
info@ysf-fsj.ca
www.ysf-fsj.ca
YSF assists Canadian youth to develop skills & knowledge for excellence in science & technology.
Reni Barlow, Executive Director
Lorne Heslop, Chair
Thomas C. Lee, Sec.-Treas.

Search & Rescue

New Brunswick Ground Search and Rescue Association (NBGSARA)
c/o President
Tel: 506-850-3461; *Fax:* 506-462-2105
www.nbgsara.nb.ca
The New Brunswick Ground Search and Rescue Association (NBGSARA) represents the Province of New Brunswick's 11 regional ground search and rescue teams. Comprised entirely of volunteers, these teams provide assistance to the RCMP and local police departments in locating and extracting missing persons in wilderness locations.
Joseph LaBelle, President

Senior Citizens

Active Living Coalition for Older Adults (ALCOA) / Coalition d'une vie active pour les aîné(e)s
PO Box 143, Shelburne ON L0N 1S0 Canada
Tel: 519-925-1676; *Fax:* 905-925-3955
Toll-Free: 800-549-9799
alcoa@ca.inter.net
www.alcoa.ca
To encourage older Canadians to maintain & enhance their well-being & independence through a lifestyle that embraces daily physical activities
Don Fletcher, Chair
Patricia Clark, Executive Director

Advocacy Centre for the Elderly (ACE)
#701, 2 Carlton St., Toronto ON M5B 1J3
Tel: 416-598-2656; *Fax:* 416-598-7924
www.advocacycentreelderly.org
To provide legal services to low income senior citizens

Alberta Council on Aging
#210, 14964 - 121A Ave., Edmonton AB T5V 1A3 Canada
Tel: 780-423-7781; *Fax:* 780-425-9246
Toll-Free: 888-423-9666
info@acaging.ca
www.acaging.ca
To define the needs of aging & the aged & to bring the current needs to the attention of government or voluntary agencies & to take action where appropriate; to identify & encourage relevant areas of research & systematic compilation of information affecting aging; to encourage & develop discussion on all problems affecting aging; to inform government at any level on the potential impact of policies & legislation on the aging; to print, publish, distribute & sell publications related to aging; to foster interagency liaison & cooperation
Gary Pool, President
Paul Lemay, Vice-President

Alberta Provincial Pensioners & Senior Citizens Organization (APSCO)
#334, 1237 - 4 Ave. South, Lethbridge AB T1J 0P9 Canada
Tel: 403-327-3264
gwaldern@uleth.ca
Working to improve & maintain the well being of all pensioners & senior citizens; present & represent needs to all levels of governments
Violet Segouin, Treasurer
Betty Waldern, President

Alberta Senior Citizens Sport & Recreation Association (ASCSRA)
#101, 525 - 11 Ave. SW, Calgary AB T2R 0C9 Canada
Tel: 403-297-2703; *Fax:* 403-297-6669
ascsra@telus.net
www.alberta55plus.ca
To promote sport & recreation development for seniors (55+) across Alberta; to act as a provincial voice to ensure input by age categories for seniors in Alberta Winter & Summer Games; to promote future Alberta Seniors' Games

Association des personnes en perte d'autonomie de Chibougamau inc. & Jardin des aînés
101, av du Parc, Chibougamau QC G8P 3A5 Canada
Tél: 418-748-4411
Chantal Lessard, Directrice générale

Canadian Association on Gerontology (CAG) / Association canadienne de gérontologie
#106, 222 College St., Toronto ON M5T 3J1 Canada
Tel: 613-271-1083; *Fax:* 613-599-7027
cagacg@igs.net
www.cagacg.ca
To develop the theoretical & practical understanding of individual & population aging through multidisciplinary research, practice, education & policy analysis in gerontology; to seek the improvement of the conditions of life of elderly people in Canada

Canadian Pensioners Concerned Inc. (CPC) / Retraités canadiens en action (RCA)
6 Trinity Sq., Toronto ON M5G 1B1 Canada
Tel: 416-368-5222; *Fax:* 416-368-0443
Toll-Free: 888-822-6750
info@canpension.ca
www.canpension.ca
To provide joint action on seniors issues; to collect authoritative factual material & distribute it in usable form to relevant persons & authorities

CARP
#1304, 27 Queen St. East, Toronto ON M5C 2M6 Canada
Tel: 416-363-8748; *Fax:* 416-363-8747
Toll-Free: 888-363-2279
support@carp.ca
www.carp.ca
The Association is a national, non-partisan organization that promotes the rights & quality of life of older Canadians through advocacy, education, information & CARP-recommended services & programs.

Club de l'âge d'or Les intrépides de Chibougamau
126, rue des Forces-Armées, Chibougamau QC G8P 3A1 Canada
Tél: 418-748-7541
Henriette Roy, Présidente

Council for Black Aging
3007 Delisle, Montréal QC H4C 1M8 Canada
Tel: 514-935-4951; *Fax:* 514-935-8466
The Council for Black Aging works as an advocate for the needs of Black seniors, undertaking activities designed to advance the interests of Black elders, keeping Black seniors better informed of issues relating to the availability of health and social services, and developing a unique day centre and a nursing home for Black elders.
Elisee Faure, Contact

Elder Active Recreation Association (ERA)
4061, 4th Ave., Whitehorse YT Y1A 1H1 Canada
Tel: 867-633-5010
www.yukon-seniors-and-elders.org/era.home.htm
To enhance the quality of life of Yukon seniors and elders by supporting them in living healthy lives with independence and dignity; to support seniors and elders in helping other seniors and elders to live full, active and healthy lives, and to develop active communities throughout the Yukon where seniors and elders can make positive lifestyle choices, exchange wisdom and connect with others in friendship, recreation and creativity.
Bill Simpson, President

FADOQ - Mouvement des aînés du Québec / Québec Federation of Senior Citizens
CP 1000, Succ. M, 4545, av Pierre-de Couberin, Montréal QC H1V 3R2 Canada
Tél: 514-252-3017; *Téléc:* 514-252-3154
Ligne sans frais: 800-828-3344
info@fadoq.ca
www.fadoq.ca
Promouvoir un concept positif du vieillissement; encourager le maintien et l'amélioration de la qualité de vie et de l'autonomie des aînés; initier et soutenir l'organisation d'activités physiques et de loisirs; redonner aux aînés une nouvelle fierté en les revalorisant à leurs propres yeux comme à ceux de la sociétéremettre entre les mains des aînés la gestion de leurs affaires

Fédération des aînées et aînés francophones du Canada (FAAFC)
#300, 450 rue Rideau, Ottawa ON K1N 5Z4 Canada
Tél: 613-564-0212; *Téléc:* 613-564-0212
info@faafc.ca
www.faafc.ca/fr
Défendre les droits des personnes à la retraite; défendre les droits des préretraités; programmes intergénérationnels; protection de la langue et la culture française
Roger Doiron, Président
Jean-Luc Racine, Directeur général
Michel Vézina, Premier vice-président, Saskatchewan
André Faubert, Deuxième vice-présidente, Québec
Richard Martin, Trésorier, Terre-Neuve & Labrador
Mélina Gallant, Secrétaire, Ile-du-Prince-Édouard
Marie-Christine Aubrey, Administratrice, Territoire du Nord-Ouest
Louis Bernardin, Administrateur, Manitoba
Roland Gallant, Administrateur, Nouveau-Brunswick
Charles Gaudet, Administrateur, Nouvelle-Écosse
Claire Grisé, Administratrice, Colombie-Britannique
Germaine Lehodey, Administratrice, Alberta
Francine Poirier, Administratrice, Ontario
Roxanne Thibaudeau, Administratrice, Yukon

Help the Aged (Canada) (HTA) / Aide aux aînés (Canada)
#205, 1300 Carling Ave., Ottawa ON K1Z 7L2 Canada
Tel: 613-232-0727; *Fax:* 613-232-7625
Toll-Free: 800-648-1111
info@helptheaged.ca; adoptagran@helptheaged.ca
www.helptheaged.ca; www.aideauxainescanada.ca
To meet the needs of poor or destitute elderly people in Canada & the developing world

Manitoba Association on Gerontology (MAG)
884 William Ave., Winnipeg MB R3E 0Z6 Canada
Tel: 204-783-8389
To sustain the social values & philosophy which strengthen & advance human dignity & personal fulfillment during the course of aging; to cooperate with a variety of service providers to address common issues in the field of gerontology

Manitoba Society of Seniors (MSOS)
#202, 323 Portage Ave., Winnipeg MB R3B 2C1 Canada
Tel: 204-942-3147; *Fax:* 204-943-1290
Toll-Free: 800-561-6767
membership@msos.mb.ca
www.msos.mb.ca
To represent Manitobans age 50+ by advocating for their needs & concerns & by promoting a positive image of aging in the community.

National Pensioners & Senior Citizens Federation (NPSCF) / Fédération nationale des retraités et citoyens âgés
c/o Fern Haight, PO Box 393, Hanley SK S0G 2E0 Canada
Tel: 306-544-2737; *Fax:* 306-544-2757
fern.h@sasktel.net
www.npscf.org
To act as an advisory body providing central contacts, facilities for research, surveys, uniform objectives & a national expansion of the pensioners movement; to stimulate public interest in the welfare of senior citizens by means of adequate pensions & social security that will provide comfortable housing & decent living; to protect the rights & interests of pensioners & prospective pensioners; to prevent discrimination & undue delay in granting pensions; to project a social friendly fellowship among the pensioners of Canada

New Brunswick Senior Citizens Federation Inc. (NBSCF) / Fédération des citoyens aînés du Nouveau-Brunswick inc. (FCANB)
36 Albert St., Moncton NB E1C 1W1 Canada
Tel: 506-857-8242; *Fax:* 506-857-0315
Toll-Free: 800-453-4333
horizons@nbnet.nb.ca
www.nbscf.ca
To promote the general welfare & leadership of NB's senior citizens regardless of language, race, colour, sex, or creed; to elevate the social, moral, & intellectual standing of NB's senior citizens; to provide information, coordination, communication, & advocating services to members
Isabelle Thériault-Arseneault, Administration Officer

Older Adult Centres' Association of Ontario (OACAO) / Association des centres pour aînés de l'Ontario
43 North Riverdale Dr., Inglewood ON L7C 3K3 Canada
Tel: 905-838-0240; *Fax:* 905-838-1053
Toll-Free: 866-835-7693
lbloom@oacao.org
www.oacao.org
To ensure that seniors in Ontario have opportunities & choices that lead to healthy, active lifestyles

Ontario Coalition of Senior Citizens' Organizations (OCSCO) / Coalition des organismes d'aînés et d'aînées de l'Ontario (COAAO)
#207, 660 Briar Hill Ave., Toronto ON M6B 4B7 Canada
Tel: 416-785-8570; *Fax:* 416-785-7361
Toll-Free: 800-265-0779
ocsco@web.net
www.ocsco.ca
To improve the quality of life for Ontario's seniors by encouraging seniors' involvement in all aspects of society, by keeping them informed of current issues, and by focusing on programs to benefit an aging population.

Prince Edward Island Senior Citizens Federation Inc. (PEISCF)
#117, 40 Enman Cres., Charlottetown PE C1E 1E6 Canada
Tel: 902-368-9008; *Fax:* 902-368-9006
Toll-Free: 877-368-9008
peiscf@pei.aibn.com
www.peiscf.com
To advance the education opportunities for seniors on PEI; to improve the quality of life for seniors by advising government & other decision making bodies regarding seniors' concerns; to improve the quality of life for seniors; to increase societal understanding of seniors & the aging process through positive role modelling

Routes to Learning Canada (RLC)
4 Cataraqui St., Kingston ON K7K 1Z7 Canada
Fax: 613-530-2096
Toll-Free: 866-745-1690
information@routestolearning.ca
www.routestolearning.ca
To develop, manage & facilitate educational experiences for older adults through cooperative partnership with educational agents; to balance education & travel in an environment of comradeship & respect; to continue to experiment with pilot projects to reach broader populations of older adults; to be a "learner-centered" organization that responds to the learning needs of older adults; to work towards a better understanding of our relationship with our current populations; to use new methods of reaching out to an ever more diverse multicultural Canada; to promote cost-effective educational opportunities to an ever widening group of older adults
Victoria Pearson, President/CEO

SAGE - Seniors Association of Greater Edmonton
15 Sir Winston Churchill Sq., Edmonton AB T5J 2E5 Canada
Tel: 780-423-5510; *Fax:* 780-426-5175
info@mysage.ca
www.mysage.ca
To enhance the quality of life of older persons through service, innovation, advocacy & voluntarism

United Senior Citizens of Ontario Inc. (USCO)
3033 Lakeshore Blvd. West, Toronto ON M8V 1K5 Canada
Tel: 416-252-2021; *Fax:* 416-252-5770
Toll-Free: 888-320-2222
office@uscont.ca
www.uscont.ca
To further the interests & promote the welfare of the senior population in Ontario; to provide for an exchange of ideas for member groups; to assist in the formation of senior citizens clubs
Ken Cunningham, President

Service Clubs

Association des Grands Frères/Grandes Soeurs du Québec (GFGS) / Big Brothers/Big Sisters of Québec
#206, 4030, rue St-Ambroise, Montréal QC H4C 2C7 Canada
Tél: 514-286-9531; *Téléc:* 514-286-1131
Ligne sans frais: 888-286-9531
info@gfgsq.ca
www.gfgs.qc.ca
Favoriser l'épanouissement de jeunes âgés de 6 à 16 ans privés de la presence d'un de leurs parents en les jumelant avec un adulte mature, qui s'engage à le rencontrer 3-4 heures par semaine pour échanger et faire des activités, selon leurs goûts réciproques

Big Brothers Big Sisters of Canada (BBBSC) / Les Grands Frères Grandes Soeurs du Canada
#113E, 3228 South Service Rd., Burlington ON L7N 3H8 Canada
Tel: 905-639-0461; *Fax:* 905-639-0124
Toll-Free: 800-263-9133
www.bbbsc.ca
To provide leadership to member agencies as they develop programs to meet the changing needs of young people

British Columbia Lions Society for Children with Disabilities (BCLS)
3981 Oak St., Vancouver BC V6H 4H5 Canada
Tel: 604-873-1865; *Fax:* 604-873-0166
Toll-Free: 800-818-4483
info@lionsbc.ca
www.lionsbc.ca
To provide as many services as possible to children with disabilities; to enhance the lives of children with special needs; to continue building, not only specialized services & facilities, but challenging young hearts & minds as well; giving children with disabilities self-esteem, self-confidence & a sense of independence

Canadian Federation of Junior Leagues / Fédération canadienne des jeunes ligues
4 Steeplehill Cres., Carlisle ON L0R 1H3 Canada
Tel: 905-659-9339
info@cfjl.org
www.cfjl.org
The Canadian Federation of Junior Leagues has served as the link amoung Junior Leagues within Canada for the purpose networking and sharing best practices amoungst Canadian Leagues. The Principle purpose of the Federation is to promote a strong national presence in Canada and to increase the international input to the Association of Junior Intertional, Inc.

Canadian Progress Club / Club progrès du Canada
#143, 75 Lavinia St., New Glasgow NS B2H 1N5 Canada
Fax: 888-337-9826
Toll-Free: 877-944-4726
info@progressclub.ca
www.progressclub.ca
To assist those in need as well as creating & preserving a spirit of friendship that is sincere; to advance the best interests of the community in which that club is located.

Club Kiwanis Chibougamau
CP 61, Chibougamau QC G8P 2K5 Canada
Tél: 418-748-2231
Roy Lavoie, Président

Club Lions de Chibougamau
CP 11, Chibougamau QC G8P 2K5 Canada
lionschibougamau@hotmail.com
lionschibougamau.icr.qc.ca
Robin Pearson

Club Optimiste Chibougamau
1614, rue St-Jacques, Chibougamau QC G8P 2L7 Canada
Tél: 418-748-7272
Sylvie Cayouette, Présidente

Club Optimiste de Rivière-du-Loup inc.
CP 1344, Rivière-du-Loup QC G5R 4L9 Canada
Tél: 418-862-8454; *Téléc:* 418-862-3366
service@optimiste.org
www.optimiste.org
Les clubs Optimistes ® Inspirent le meilleur chez les jeunes depuis 1919 en rencontrant les besoins des jeunes de toutes les collectivités du monde. Ils organisent des projets de service communautaire positifs qui visent à tendre la main à la jeunesse.
Denise Desbiens, Présidente

Kin Canada
PO Box KIN, 1920 Hal Rogers Dr., Cambridge ON N3H 5C6 Canada
Tel: 519-653-1920; *Fax:* 519-650-1091
Toll-Free: 800-742-5546
kinhq@kincanada.ca
www.kincanada.ca
A volunteer organization enriching our communities through service,while embracing national pride, positive values, personal development & lasting friendships. Kin Canada is one of the largest supporters of Cystic Fibrosis research & care in Canada.

Kiwanis International/Eastern Canada & the Caribbean District
PO Box 26040, 260 St. Paul Ave., Brantford ON N3R 7X4 Canada
Tel: 519-304-0745; *Fax:* 519-756-3183
Toll-Free: 888-921-9054
district@kiwanisecc.org
www.kiwanisecc.org

Kiwanis International/Western Canada District
c/o 14622, 95 Ave., Edmonton AB T5N 0B3 Canada
Tel: 780-452-9735; *Fax:* 780-452-9735
www.kiwaniswesterncanada.org

Last Post Fund (LPF) / Fonds du Souvenir
#401, 505, boul René-Lévesque ouest, Montréal QC H2Z 1Y7 Canada
Tel: 514-866-2727; *Fax:* 514-866-2147
Toll-Free: 800-465-7113
lpfnoqc@lastpostfund.ca
www.lastpostfund.ca
To ensure that no war veterans, or certain other persons who meet the wartime service eligibility criteria, are denied a funeral & burial due to lack of funds

Soroptimist Foundation of Canada
c/o #104, 13311 Yonge Street, Richmond Hill ON L4E 3L6 Canada
corinne@cmrlaw.ca
www.soroptimistfoundation.ca
To provide bursaries, scholarships & fellowships to Canadian students & Canadian schools, colleges & universities for the advancement of education & in particular to further the appreciation of social needs, & the study of community, national & international problems

Variety - The Children's Charity (Ontario)
3701 Danforth Ave., Toronto ON M1N 2G2 Canada
Tel: 416-367-2828; *Fax:* 416-367-0028
info@varietyontario.ca
www.varietyontario.ca
Variety will be the leading charity for children with special needs & their families; remain committed to improving their quality of life & integration into society
Maureen Burgess, Executive Director

Variety - The Children's Charity of BC
4300 Still Creek Dr., Burnaby BC V5C 6C6 Canada
Tel: 604-320-0505; *Fax:* 604-320-0535
Toll-Free: 800-381-2040
info@variety.bc.ca
www.variety.bc.ca
To raise funds throughout the province of B.C. for the benefit of B.C.'s children with special needs; to provide funds for capital costs; to create new centres or improve existing facilities & purchase specialized equipment
Barbara Hislop, Executive Director

Variety - The Children's Charity of Manitoba, Tent 58 Inc.
#2 - 1313 Border St., Winnipeg MB R3H 0X4 Canada
Tel: 204-982-1058; *Fax:* 204-475-3198
office@varietymanitoba.com
www.varietymanitoba.com
To raise funds for the immediate, tangible needs of the disabled & disadvantaged children of Manitoba, by mobilizing volunteer initiatives
Wayne Rogers, Executive Director

Variety Club of Northern Alberta, Tent 63
#1205 Energy Square, 10109 - 106th St., Edmonton AB T5J 3L7 Canada
Tel: 780-448-9544; *Fax:* 780-448-9289
Raises funds for the children of Northern Alberta who have disabilities or are disadvantaged
Sue McEachern, Executive Director

Variety Club of Southern Alberta
#201 - 1740B, 11A St. NE, Calgary AB T2E 6M6 Canada
Tel: 403-228-6168; *Fax:* 403-245-9282
info@varietyalberta.ca
www.varietyclub61.ab.ca
To provide disabled & disadvantaged children with the means to enjoy quality life experiences; to support research for below the knee amputee children; to provide assistance & bursaries to children in special situations
Audrey Garratt, Chief
Graham Kuntz, Executive Director

Social Clubs

Brunch-rencontre pour personnes seules
#102, 161, rue du Parc, Chibougamau QC G8P 2H3 Canada
Tél: 418-748-4951
Réjeanne Lalancette

Canadian Black Community Association
#30, 6999, Côte-des-Neiges, Montréal QC H3S 2B6 Canada
Tel: 514-737-8321; *Fax:* 514-737-6893
Cultural, recreational & social activities for youth & adults; after-school tutorials; summer camp; Teen Leadership Program; adult classes & sports activities
Michael Gittens, Contact

Social Response/Social Services

Agincourt Community Services Association (ACSA)
#100, 4155 Sheppart Ave. East, Toronto ON M1S 1T4 Canada
Tel: 416-321-6912; *Fax:* 416-321-6922
info@agincourtcommunityservices.com
www.agincourtcommunityservices.com
To address a variety of issues including systemic poverty, hunger, housing, homelessness, unemployment, accessibility and social isolation in the Scarborough community.
Gael Gilbert, Executive Director
Paul Rook, Chair

Alberta Association of Marriage & Family Therapy (AAMFT)
420 Norway Cres., Sherwood Park AB T8A 5Z4 Canada
Tel: 403-524-0873; *Fax:* 780-434-7511
Toll-Free: 877-435-5070
info@aamft.ab.ca
www.aamft.ab.ca
To provide individual marriage & family therapy; to provide educational seminars for therapists

Alberta Association of Services for Children & Families (AASCF)
Bonnie Doon Mall, #945, 10020 - 101A Ave., Edmonton AB T6C 4E3 Canada
Tel: 780-428-3660; *Fax:* 780-428-3844
aascf@aascf.com
www.aascf.com
To provide opportunities for deliverers of services to meet with each other to exchange views & develop quality service in Alberta; to establish a structure which can provide information to membership & the public in support of social policy on behalf of Alberta children & families; to create a mechanism for action in social policy & public attitudes relating to the welfare of children & families; to support ongoing development & implementation of standards of service for human service providers & maintain accountability to these standards through an accreditation process; to advocate on behalf of the membership; to promote professional development of member agencies; to support research into child & family welfare issues relevant to member agencies; to advise government on social policy

Alberta Block Parent Association
#1501, 820 - 5nd Ave. SW, Calgary AB T2P 0N4 Canada
Tel: 403-262-2864; *Fax:* 403-262-5221
Toll-Free: 866-586-7666
albertabpa@shaw.ca
www.albertablockparent.ca/
Their responsibilites include: assisting with start-up of new programs; ongoing support and resources for established programs; ensuring that faltering programs are properly closed down.

Alberta College of Social Workers (ACSW) / Association des travailleurs sociaux de l'Alberta
#550, 10707 - 100 Ave. NW, Edmonton AB T5J 3M1 Canada
Tel: 780-421-1167; *Fax:* 780-421-1168
Toll-Free: 800-661-3089
acsw@acsw.ab.ca
www.acsw.ab.ca
To promote, regulate & govern the profession of social work in the Province of Alberta; to advocate for skilled & ethical social work practices & for policies, programs & services that promote the profession & protect the best interests of the public

Applegrove Community Complex
60 Woodfield Rd., Toronto ON M4L 2W6 Canada
Tel: 416-461-8143
applegrove@applegrovecc.ca
www.applegrovecc.ca
To provide social service programs for infants, children, teens, adults and seniors living in the Queen-Greenwood area of Toronto.
Susan Fletcher, Executive Director
Pierre Trudel, Chair

Association des services de réhabilitation sociale du Québec inc. (ASRSQ) / Association of Social Rehabilitation Agencies of Québec Inc.
2000, boul St-Joseph est, Montréal QC H2H 1E4 Canada
Tél: 514-521-3733; *Téléc:* 514-521-3753
webmaster@asrsq.ca
www.asrsq.ca
Promouvoir la participation des citoyens dans l'administration de la justice, la prévention du crime et la réhabilitation des délinquants adultes

The Association of Social Workers of Northern Canada (ASWNC) / L'Association des travailleurs sociaux du Nord canadien (ATSNC)
PO Box 2963, Yellowknife NT X1A 2R2 Canada
Tel: 867-699-7964
geried@socialworknorth.com
www.socialworknorth.com
Dana Jennejohn, President

Association québécoise des personnes de petite taille (AQPPT) / Association of Little People of Quebec
#308, 6300, av du Parc, Montréal QC H2V 4H8 Canada
Tél: 514-521-9671; *Téléc:* 514-521-3369
info@aqppt.org
www.aqppt.org
Promouvoir des intérêts et défendre les droits des personnes de petite taille et faciliter leur intégration scolaire, sociale et professionnelle.

Association québécoise Plaidoyer-Victimes (AQPV)
#201, 4305, rue d'Iberville, Montréal QC H2H 2L5 Canada
Tél: 514-526-9037; *Téléc:* 514-526-9951
aqpv@aqpv.ca
www.aqpv.ca
Défense des droits et des intérêts des victimes d'actes criminels par la discussion, la sensibilisation, la formation, la concertation et la recherche
Marie-Hélène Blanc, Directrice générale

Battlefords United Way Inc.
PO Box 904, #93, 891 - 99th St., North Battleford SK S9A 2Z3 Canada
Tel: 306-445-1717; *Fax:* 306-445-1720
office@battlefords.unitedway.ca
www.battlefords.unitedway.ca
To improve lives & build community by engaging individuals & mobilizing collective action
Treena Rathwell, Executive Director
Michael Brokop, Treasurer

Bereaved Families of Ontario (BFO)
PO Box 10015, Stn. Watline, Mississauga ON L4Z 4G5 Canada
Tel: 416-440-0290; *Fax:* 416-440-0304
Toll-Free: 800-236-6364
info@bereavedfamilies.net
www.bereavedfamilies.net
To create programs, services & resources to support bereaved families; committed to self-help & mutual aid; focus is on families who have experienced the death of a child
Bill Allan, Chair
Melissa Mould, President

Birchmount Bluffs Neighbourhood Centre (BBNC)
93 Birchmount Rd., Toronto ON M1N 3J7 Canada
Tel: 416-396-4310; *Fax:* 416-396-4314
info@bbnc.ca
www.bbnc.ca
The mission of the Birchmount Bluffs Neighbourhood Centre (BBNC) is to provide programs and supports and foster social inclusion within the community, with a focus on individuals that face a barrier to service.
Enrique Robert, Executive Director

Block Parent Program of Canada Inc. (BPPCI) / Programme Parents-Secours du Canada inc.
50 Dunlop St. East, Lower Level, Barrie ON L4N 6S7 Canada
Tel: 705-792-4245; *Fax:* 705-792-4245
Toll-Free: 800-663-1134
info@blockparent.ca
www.blockparent.ca
To provide immediate assistance through a safety network & to offer supporting community education programs

Block Watch Society of British Columbia (BCBPS)
#120, 12414 - 82nd Ave., Surrey BC V3W 3E9 Canada
Tel: 604-418-3827; *Fax:* 604-501-2509
Toll-Free: 877-602-3358
blockwatch@blockwatch.com
www.blockwatch.com
To build safe neighbourhoods across British Columbia; to encourage bonds among local residents & businesses to create a crime free area through community participation; to assist in the reduction of crime; to improve relations between police & communities

Brant United Way (BUW)
30 Brant Ave., Brantford ON N3T 3C6 Canada
Tel: 519-752-7848; *Fax:* 519-752-7913
info@brantunitedway.org
www.brantunitedway.org
To help people in their time of need
Dianne Austin, Executive Director

British Columbia Association of Social Workers (BCASW) / Association des travailleurs sociaux de la Colombie-Britannique
#402, 1755 West Broadway, Vancouver BC V6J 4S5 Canada
Tel: 604-730-9111; *Fax:* 604-730-9112
Toll-Free: 800-665-4747
bcasw@bcasw.org
www.bcasw.org
Represents member concerns regarding the practice of social work in BC, professional education & regulation.

British Columbia Council for Families (BCCF)
#204, 2590 Granville St., Vancouver BC V6H 3H1 Canada
Tel: 604-660-0675; *Fax:* 604-732-4813
Toll-Free: 800-663-5638
bccf@bccf.bc.ca
www.bccf.bc.ca
To strengthen, encourage & support families through information, education, research & advocacy

British Columbia Federation of Foster Parent Associations (BCFFPA)
#207, 22561 Dewdney Trunk Rd., Maple Ridge BC V2X 3K1 Canada
Tel: 604-466-7487; *Fax:* 604-466-7490
Toll-Free: 800-663-9999
bcffpa@istar.ca
www.bcfosterparents.ca
To be the collective voice for all foster parents & to promote fostering; to act as a channel of communication between authorized child welfare agencies & foster parents concerning children & foster children in particular

Campbell River & District United Way
PO Box 135, Campbell River BC V9W 5A7 Canada
Tel: 250-702-2911
A non-profit organization that raises and distributes funds to member agencies that are providing support and services to residents in the Campbell River area. They are committed to building a strong and healthy community for all. The role of the United Way is to match the resources (and fundraising campaign) to those areas of greatest need.
Brad Bayly, Community Development Coordinator

Canada Without Poverty / Canada Sans Pauvreté
#1210, 1 Nicholas St., Ottawa ON K1N 7B7 Canada
Tel: 613-789-0096; *Fax:* 613-244-5777
Toll-Free: 800-810-1076
www.cwp-csp.ca
To eradicate poverty in Canada by promoting income and social security for all Canadians, and by promoting poverty eradication as a human rights obligation.

Canadian Association for the Prevention of Discrimination & Harassment in Higher Education (CAPDHHE) / Association canadienne pour la prévention de la discrimination et ou harcèlement en milieu d'enseignement supérieur (ACPDHMES)
c/o University of British Columbia, Vancouver BC V6T 1Z2 Canada
Tel: 604-822-4859; *Fax:* 604-822-3260
amlong@equity.ubc.ca
www.capdhhe.org

To provide professional development for individuals employed at colleges & universities in the area of discrimination & harassment, including harassment as identified under human rights law
Anne-Marie Long, President

Canadian Association of Sexual Assault Centres (CASAC) / Association canadienne des centres contre les agressions à caractère sexuel (ACCCACS)
77 East 20th Ave., Vancouver BC V5V 1L7 Canada
Tel: 604-876-2622; *Fax:* 604-876-8450
casac01@shaw.ca
www.casac.ca
To work for an end to violence against women & toward women's equality; to provide a national voice for anti-rape workers.

Canadian Association of Social Workers (CASW) / Association canadienne des travailleurs sociaux (ACTS)
#402, 383 Parkdale Ave., Ottawa ON K1Y 4R4
Tel: 613-729-6668; *Fax:* 613-729-9608
casw@casw-acts.ca
www.casw-acts.ca
To represent Canadian professional social workers; To strengthen & advances the social work profession in Canada; To preserve excellence within the profession

Canadian Career Development Foundation (CCDF) / Fondation canadienne pour le développement de carrière (FCDC)
#202, 119 Ross Ave., Ottawa ON K1Y 0N6 Canada
Tel: 613-729-6164; *Fax:* 613-729-3515
Toll-Free: 877-729-6164
information@ccdf.ca
www.ccdf.ca
To advance the understanding & practice of career development.

Canadian Centre for Victims of Torture (CCVT)
194 Jarvis St., 2nd Fl., Toronto ON M5B 2B7 Canada
Tel: 416-363-1066; *Fax:* 416-363-2122
mabai@ccvt.org
www.ccvt.org
To offer support & arrange medical, legal & social care for torture victims & their families; to increase public awareness in Canada & abroad of torture & its effects upon survivors & their families

Canadian Council for Refugees (CCR) / Conseil canadien pour les réfugiés
#302, 6839, rue Drolet, Montréal QC H2S 2T1 Canada
Tel: 514-277-7223; *Fax:* 514-277-1447
info@ccrweb.ca
www.ccrweb.ca
Committed to the rights & protection of refugees in Canada & around the world & to the settlement of refugees & immigrants in Canada.

Canadian Counselling & Psychotherapy Association (CCPA) / L'Association canadienne de counseling et de psychothérapie (ACCP)
#114, 223 Colonnade Rd. South, Ottawa ON K2E 7K3 Canada
Tel: 613-237-1099; *Fax:* 613-237-9786
Toll-Free: 877-765-5565
info@ccpa-accp.ca
www.ccpa-accp.ca
CCPA is a national, bilingual organization dedicated to the enhancement of the counselling profession in Canada. It promotes policies & practices which support the provision of accessible, competent, & accountable counselling services throughout the human lifespan, & in a manner sensitive to the pluralistic nature of society.

Canadian Crossroads International (CCI) / Carrefour canadien international
#201, 49 Bathurst St., Toronto ON M5V 2P2 Canada
Tel: 416-967-1611; *Fax:* 416-967-9078
Toll-Free: 877-967-1611
info@cciorg.ca
bbnc.cciorg.ca
Social Media: twitter.com/Crossroads_CCI
CCI is a development organization that is reducing poverty & increasing women's rights around the world. It works with local organizations in West Africa, Southern Africa & South America. Organizations in developing countries select Canadian, partner organizations working on similar issues, so that they can help develop programs & meet their development goals. CCI supports the exchange of skilled volunteers. It is a registered charity, BN: 129814570RR0001.

Canadian Feed The Children (CFTC)
174 Bartley Dr., Toronto ON M4A 1E1 Canada
Tel: 416-757-1220; *Fax:* 416-757-3318
Toll-Free: 800-387-1221
contact@canadianfeedthechildren.ca
www.canadianfeedthechildren.ca
To alleviate the impact of poverty on children; we work with local partners overseas & in Canada to enhance the well-being of children & the self-sufficiency of their families & communities.
Jim Dahl, Executive Director

Canadian Grandparents' Rights Association (CGRA)
#207, 14980 - 104 Ave., Surrey BC V3R 1M9 Canada
Tel: 604-585-8242; *Fax:* 604-585-8241
Toll-Free: 866-585-8242
cgra222@vcn.bc.ca
www.vcn.bc.ca/cgra222/
Promotes, supports, and assists Grandparents and their families in maintaining or re-establishing family ties and family stability where the family has been disrupted; especially those ties between grandparents and grandchildren.
Nancy Wooldridge, National President
Florence Knight, National Director

Canadian Social Work Foundation (CSWF) / Fondation canadienne du service social
PO Box 64177, 1620 Scott St., Ottawa ON K1Y 4V2 Canada
Tel: 613-729-6668; *Fax:* 613-729-9608
casw@casw-acts.ca
www.casw-acts.ca
To edit & publish books, papers, journals & other forms of literature respecting social work in order to disseminate information to the public; to encourage studies; to promote, develop & sponsor activities strengthening social work

Canadian Society for the Prevention of Cruelty to Children (CSPCC)
PO Box 700, 362 Midland Ave., Midland ON L4R 4P4 Canada
Tel: 705-526-5647; *Fax:* 705-526-0214
cspcc@bellnet.ca
www.empathicparenting.org
To increase public awareness of the long-term consequences of child abuse & neglect; to encourage primary prevention initiatives for improved nurturing of children in their earliest years of life

Canadian Urban Institute (CUI)
PO Box 612, #402, 555 Richmond St. West, Toronto ON M5V 3B1 Canada
Tel: 416-365-0816; *Fax:* 416-365-0650
cui@canurb.com
www.canurb.com
The Canadian Urban Institute (CUI) is a non-profit organization dedicated to providing solutions to important issues that have an impact on the quality of life in urban areas and communicating those solutions to a wide audience through a variety of media.
Glen Murray, President & CEO

Canadians Addressing Sexual Exploitation (CASE) / Canadiens opposés à l'exploitation sexuelle (COES)
360 County Rd. 31, Belle River ON N0R 1A0 Canada
Tel: 519-728-3432
case@4case.ca
www.4case.ca
C.A.S.E believes that pornography has a negative impact on men, children, women, and communities and therefore their mission is to exist to protect all children from sexual explotation and their vision is to education, influence, and partner.

Canadians Concerned About Violence in Entertainment (C-CAVE)
167 Glen Rd., Toronto ON M4W 2W8 Canada
Tel: 416-961-0853; *Fax:* 416-929-2720
info@c-cave.com
www.c-cave.com
To provide public education on research findings related to media violence through popular culture, commodities marketed primarily to children, adolescents & adults.

Carrefour communautaire de Chibougamau
CP 163, 512, rte 167, Chibougamau QC G8P 2K6 Canada
Tél: 418-748-7266
Brigitte Rosa, Coordonnatrice
Huguette Fradet, Présidente

Castlegar United Way
1995 - 6 Ave., Castlegar BC V1N 4B7 Canada
Tel: 250-365-7331; *Fax:* 250-365-5778
office@castlegar.unitedway.ca
www.castlegar.unitedway.ca
To build & help sustain a quality of community life that is good for families & business.
Steve Martin, President

Catholic Charities of The Archdiocese of Toronto
#400, 1155 Yonge St., Toronto ON M4T 1W2 Canada
Tel: 416-934-3401; *Fax:* 416-934-3402
info@catholiccharitiestor.org
www.catholiccharitiestor.org
Catholic Charities of the Archidiocese of Toronto is dedicated to ensuring the provision of health and social sciences and to provide leadership and advocacy on behalf of the member agencies and those in need. The people served live and work throughout the Greater Toronto Area, as well as, in Simcoe, Durham, Peel, and York.

Centraide Bas St-Laurent
#303, 1555, boul. Jacques Cartier, Mont-Joli QC G5H 2W1 Canada
Tél: 418-775-5555; *Téléc:* 418-775-5525
direction@centraidebsl.org
www.centraidebsl.org
Organisme sans but lucratif de lutte à la pauvreté et de soutien aux personnes démunies.
Michel Daigle, Directeur général

Centraide Centre du Québec
#200, 154, rue Dunkin, Drummondville QC J2B 5V1 Canada
Tél: 819-477-0505; *Téléc:* 819-477-6719
bureau@centraide-cdq.ca
www.centraide-cdq.ca
Rassembler les personnes et les ressources du Centre-du-Québec afin de contribuer au développement social de la communauté et d'améliorer la qualité de vie de ses membres les plus vulnérables et ce, en lien avec les organismes communautaires.
Annie Jean, Directrice générale

Centraide du Grand Montréal / Centraide of Greater Montréal
493, rue Sherbrooke ouest, Montréal QC H3A 1B6 Canada
Tél: 514-288-1261; *Téléc:* 514-350-7282
communications@centraide-mtl.org
centraide-mtl.org
Their mission is to maximize financial & volunteer resources in order to promote mutual aid, social commitment & self-reliance as effective means of improving the quality of life of our community, & especially of its needeiest members.
Michèle Thibodeau-DeGuire, Présidente et Directrice générale

Centraide Duplessis
#217, 456, rue Arnaud, Sept-Iles QC G4R 3B1 Canada
Tel: 418-962-2011; *Fax:* 418-968-4694
administration@centraideduplessis.org
Denis Miousse, Directeur général

Centraide Estrie
1150, rue Belvédère sud, Sherbrooke QC J1H 4C7 Canada
Tél: 819-569-9281; *Téléc:* 819-569-5195
centraide_estrie@qc.aibn.com, bureau@estrie.centraide.ca
www.estrie.centraide.ca
Vise à soutenir les organismes bénévoles et communautaires engagés directement auprès des clientèles les plus démunies et vulnérables.
Claude Forgues, Directeur général

Centraide Gaspésie Iles-de-la-Madeleine
#E216, 230, rte du Parc, Sainte-Anne-des-Monts QC G4V 2C4 Canada
Tél: 418-763-2171; *Téléc:* 418-763-7677
centraidegim@globetrotter.net
www.gim.centraide.ca
Soulager la misère et la souffrance humaine.
Yvon Lemieux, Directeur général

Centraide Gatineau-Labelle-Hautes-Laurentides
671, rue de la Madone, Mont-Laurier QC J9L 1T2 Canada
Tél: 819-623-4090; *Téléc:* 819-623-7646
bureau@glhl.centraide.ca
www.gatineaulabellehlaurentides.centraide.ca
Annie Lajoie, Directrice générale

Centraide Haute-Côte-Nord/Manicouagan
#301, 858, rue de Puyjalon, Baie-Comeau QC G5C 1N1 Canada
Tél: 418-589-5567; *Téléc:* 418-295-2567
info@centraidehcnmanicouagan.ca
www.centraidehcnmanicouagan.ca
Christine Brisson, Directrice générale

Centraide KRTB-Côte-du-Sud
100, 4e av, La Pocatière QC G0R 1Z0 Canada
Tél: 418-856-5105; *Téléc:* 418-856-4385
centraideportage@bellnet.ca
centraidekrtbcotedusud.org
Notre mission est d'aider les gens, d'affecter les ressources en fonction des besoins, d'améliorer la qualité de vie de chacun et de renforcer le soutien communautaire. Donnez un coup de

main au destin et participez aux efforts déployés par le Mouvement Centraide Portage-Taché.
Sylvain Roy, Directeur général

Centraide Lanaudière
1446, rue de Lanaudière, Joliette QC J6E 3P2 Canada
Tél: 450-752-1999; *Téléc:* 450-752-2603
cent.lanaudiere@qc.aira.com
www.joliette.centraide.ca
Promouvoir l'entraide, le partage et l'engagement bénévole et communautaire
Louise Guilbault, Directrice générale

Centraide Laurentides
CP 335, 281, rue Brière, Saint-Jérôme QC J7Z 5T9 Canada
Tél: 450-436-1584; *Téléc:* 450-436-3025
bureau@laurentides.centraide.ca
www.centraidelaurentides.org
Contribuer, par la promotion du partage et de l'engagement bénévole et communautaire, à la construction d'une société d'entraide vouée à l'amélioration de la qualité de vie des personnes en difficulté
Suzanne M. Piché, Directrice générale
Monique Richer, Présidente
Violette Gingras, Directrice de communications

Centraide Mauricie
880, Place Boland, Trois-Rivières QC G8Z 4H2 Canada
Tél: 819-374-6207; *Téléc:* 819-374-6857
centraide.mauricie@bellnet.ca
www.centraidemauricie.ca
Travailler à un changement social pour une société plus juste, plus humaine et plus démocratique à travers la promotion de l'entraide, la solidarité et l'engagement bénévole afin de répondre aux besoins socio-économiques de notre communauté.
Lise Beaulieu, Directrice générale

Centraide Outaouais
74, boul. Montclair, Gatineau QC J8Y 2E7 Canada
Tél: 819-771-7751; *Téléc:* 819-771-0301
information@centraide-outaouais.qc.ca
www.centraide-outaouais.qc.ca
Mobiliser le gens et rassembler les ressources pour améliorer la qualité de vie de personnes plus vulnérables et contribuer au développement de collectivités solidaires.
Guylaine Beaulieu, Directrice générale

Centraide Québec
#101, 3100, av Bourg-Royal, Québec QC G1C 5S7 Canada
Tél: 418-660-2100; *Téléc:* 418-660-2111
centraide@centraide-quebec.com
www.centraide-quebec.com
Levées de fonds et attribution de subventions à 166 organismes communautaires pour aider les personnes les plus démunies
Pierre Métivier, Président/Directeur général

Centraide Richelieu-Yamaska
320, ave. de la Concorde nord, Saint-Hyacinthe QC J2S 4N7 Canada
Tél: 450-773-6679; *Téléc:* 450-773-4734
bureau@centraidery.org
www.richelieuyamaska.centraide.ca
Centraide Portage-Taché, c'est une organisation charitable, qui repose sur l'engagement bénévole et qui se donne comme mission d'améliorer les conditions de vie des plus démuni(e)s de son territoire.
Manon Bouthot, Directrice générale

Centraide Saguenay-Lac St-Jean
#107, 475, boul. Talbot, Chicoutimi QC G7H 4A3 Canada
Tél: 418-543-3131; *Téléc:* 418-543-0665
centraideslsj@bellnet.ca
www.centraidesaglac.ca
Rassembler et développer des ressources financières et bénévoles afin d'aider les diverses communautés du Saguenay-Lac-St-Jean à organiser et à promouvoir l'entreaide, l'engagement social et la prise en charge afin d'améliorer la qualité de vie de sa collectivité et de ses membres les plus démunis et les plus vulnérables.
Martin St-Pierre, Directeur général

Centraide sud-ouest du Québec
#200, 100, rue Ste-Cécile, Salaberry-de-Valleyfield QC J6T 1M1 Canada
Tél: 450-371-2061; *Téléc:* 450-377-2309
centraid@rocler.qc.ca
www.centraidesudouest.org
Grâce à votre don, il y a du changement possible. En effet, la misère qu'elle soit physique, morale, psychologique ou matérielle peut toucher tout le monde, peu importe la classe sociale. Donner à Centraide Sud-Ouest, c'est susciter un changement positif dans notre communauté

Steve Hickey, Directeur général

Centre for Suicide Prevention
#320, 1202 Centre St. SE, Calgary AB T2G 5A5 Canada
Tel: 403-245-3900; *Fax:* 403-245-0299
csp@suicideinfo.ca
www.suicideinfo.ca
To acquire & distribute suicide prevention information.

The Child Abuse Survivor Monument Project (CASMP)
274 Rhodes Ave., Toronto ON M4L 3A3 Canada
Tel: 416-469-4764; *Fax:* 416-963-8892
mci@irvingstudios.com
www.childabusemonument.org
To build a memorial monument for & by survivors of child abuse to assist with the personal & social healing of the ravages of child abuse
Michael C. Irving, Artistic Director

Child Care Advocacy Association of Canada (CCAAC) / Association canadienne pour la promotion des services de garde à l'enfance (ACPSGE)
#714, 151 Slater St., Ottawa ON K1N 7Z2 Canada
Tel: 613-594-3196; *Fax:* 613-594-9375
info@ccaac.ca
www.ccaac.ca
To work toward expanding the child care system & improving its quality; advocates the development of an affordable, comprehensive, high-quality, not-for-profit child care system that is supported by public funds & accessible to every Canadian family who wishes to use it

Child Welfare League of Canada (CWLC) / Ligue pour le bien-être de l'enfance du Canada (LBEC)
226 Argyle Ave., Ottawa ON K2P 1B9 Canada
Tel: 613-235-4412; *Fax:* 613-235-7616
info@cwlc.ca
www.cwlc.ca
To provide public education on the needs of all children, youth & their families through research, information & other services directed toward enhancing & improving public awareness; to facilitate the development of standards in services to children, youth & their families; to encourage excellence in the delivery of these services
Peter M. Dudding, M.M., M.S.W., R, Executive Director

Christie-Ossington Neighbourhood Centre (CONC)
854 Bloor St. West, Toronto ON M6G 1M2 Canada
Tel: 416-534-8941; *Fax:* 416-534-8704
www.conccommunity.org
The Christie Ossington Neighbourhood Centre is dedicated to improving the quality of life in the Christie Ossington community by working in collaboration with residents, community institutions, agencies, local businesses and stakeholders to create a safe and healthy community.
Lynn Daly, Executive Director
Danny Anckle, Chair

Community Action Resource Centre (CARC)
1652 Keele St., Toronto ON M6M 3W3 Canada
Tel: 416-652-2273; *Fax:* 416-652-8992
info@communityarc.ca
www.communityarc.ca
The Community Action Resource Centre works to build the capacity of communities by mobilizing resources and providing supportive social services, for the empowerment of individuals and groups with a focus on serving the most vulnerable and disadvantaged. Services are offered in English, Portugese and Spanish.

Community Social Planning Council of Toronto (CSPC)
#1001, 2 Carlton St., Toronto ON M5B 1J3 Canada
Tel: 416-351-0095; *Fax:* 416-351-0107
info@socialplanningtoronto.org
www.socialplanningtoronto.org
Social Media: twitter.com/planningtoronto
The Council is an independent body that promotes community-based, social policy, planning & civic participation at both the local & city-wide levels through analysis & action-oriented research on social issues.

Comox Valley United Way
PO Box 3097, Courtenay BC V9N 5N3 Canada
Tel: 250-338-1151; *Fax:* 250-897-1099
June Munro, Executive Director

Confédération des organismes familiaux du Québec inc. (COFAQ)
#205, 4360 rue D'Iberville, Montréal QC H2H 2L8 Canada
Tél: 514-521-4777; *Téléc:* 514-521-6272
famille@cofaq.qc.ca
www.cofaq.qc.ca
Représenter les familles et revendiquer leurs droits auprès des diverses instances publiques et privées; promouvoir des projets innovateurs et le développement d'expertises satisfaisant aux besoins des familles et leurs organisations; réaliser des activités de soutien auprès des membres

Cooper Institute / L'Institut Cooper
81 Prince St., Charlottetown PE C1A 4R3 Canada
Tel: 902-894-4573; *Fax:* 902-368-7180
www.cooperinstitute.ca
Cooper Institute is an education and community development centre in the province of Prince Edward Island, Canada. The main program areas of our organization are focussed on livable income for all, food sovereignty and cultural diversity and inclusion. Within these programs, we conduct research and popular education projects on provincial, national, and international level.
Joe Byrne, President

COSTI Immigrant Services
Education Centre, 1710 Dufferin St., Toronto ON M6E 3P2 Canada
Tel: 416-658-1600; *Fax:* 416-658-8537
info@costi.org
www.costi.org
COSTI provides educational, social & employment support to help immigrants in the greater Toronto area attain self-sufficiency in Canadian society. Services are provided in over 60 languages.
Bruno M. Suppa, President
Mario J. Calla, Executive Director

Cowichan United Way
#102, 435 Trunk Rd., Duncan BC V9L 2P5 Canada
Tel: 250-748-1312; *Fax:* 250-748-7652
office@cowichan.unitedway.ca
www.cowichan.unitedway.ca
To fundraise for charities; to provide guidance & counsel to charitable organization; to take leadership role in raising awareness of community needs
Jackie Scott, Secretary
Carol Stenberg, Executive Secretary

Deep River District United Way
PO Box 188, Deep River ON K0J 1P0 Canada
Tel: 613-584-3985
office@deepriver.unitedway.ca
www.deepriver.unitedway.ca
To unite the major fund-raising campaigns of benevolent, charitable, health & community welfare agencies in the Deep River district by means of an annual campaign & other fundraising activities
Bob French, President
Nancy Bourgoin, Treasurer
Sue Deon, Secretary

Delta Family Resource Centre
Jane & Sheppard Mall, #14, 2721 Jane St., Toronto ON M3L 1S3 Canada
Tel: 416-747-1172; *Fax:* 416-747-7415
contactus@dfrc.ca
www.dfrc.ca
To support the needs of families & children within the community; Offering services in English, Spanish, Italian, Hindi, Punjabi, Laotian, Gujarati, Somali, Cantonese, Tamil, Mandarin, Thi, Ewe, Twi, Urdu, Dari, & Ga
Rosalyn Miller, Executive Director

Distress Centres Ontario (DCO)
#475A, 700 Lawrence Ave. West, Toronto ON M6A 3B4
Tel: 416-486-2242; *Fax:* 416-486-8405
info@dcontario.org
www.dcontario.org
To transfer best practices between member centres; To promote, support & sustain member agencies

Doorsteps Neighbourhood Services
PO Box 95, #211, 1700 Wilson Ave., Toronto ON M3L 1B2 Canada
Tel: 416-243-5480; *Fax:* 416-243-7406
mbeckford@doorsteps.ca
www.doorsteps.ca
To focus on community education, prevention, & the enhancement of resiliency of individuals & communities
Morris Beckford, Executive Director

Dying with Dignity (DWD) / Mourir dans la dignité
#802, 55 Eglinton Ave. East, Toronto ON M4P 1G8 Canada
Tel: 416-486-3998; *Fax:* 416-486-5562
Toll-Free: 800-495-6156
info@dyingwithdignity.ca
www.dyingwithdignity.ca
To improve the quality of dying for all Canadians in accordance with their own wishes, values & beliefs

Edmonton Social Planning Council (ESPC)
#37, 9912 - 106 St., Edmonton AB T5K 1C6 Canada
Tel: 780-423-2031; *Fax:* 780-425-6244
info@edmontonsocialplanning.ca
www.edmontonsocialplanning.ca
To provide leadership to the community & its organizations in addressing social issues & effecting change to social policy

Elgin-St.Thomas United Way Services
300 South Edgeware Rd., St Thomas ON N5P 4L1 Canada
Tel: 519-631-3171; *Fax:* 519-631-9253
office@stthomasunitedway.ca
www.stthomasunitedway.ca
To be a leader in improving the quality of life for all people in Elgin County.
Sharon Lechner, CEO

Eston United Way
PO Box 23, Eston SK S0L 1A0 Canada
Tel: 306-962-3612
Raising money in order to create positive and lasting changes in communities.
Brenda Myer, President

Family & Community Support Services Association of Alberta (FCSSAA)
Belmead Professional Bldg., #106, 8944 - 182 St., Edmonton AB T5T 2E3 Canada
Tel: 780-415-4791; *Fax:* 780-415-4793
fcssaa@telus.net
www.fcssaa.ab.ca
To advocate on behalf of local communities & programs to the general public, municipal governments, regional services, provincial & national agencies, & authorities; To educate individuals, communities, boards, & staff

Family Mediation Canada (FMC) / Médiation Familiale Canada
#180, 55 Northfield Dr. East, Waterloo ON N2K 3T6 Canada
Tel: 519-585-3118; *Fax:* 416-849-0643
Toll-Free: 877-362-2005
fmc@fmc.ca; carrie@fmc.ca
www.fmc.ca
To improve the provision for cooperative conflict resolution in areas such as separation & divorce, child welfare, adoption, parent & teen counselling, age-related issues, & wills & estates

Family Service Canada (FSC) / Services à la famille - Canada
c/o 312 Parkdale Ave., Ottawa ON K1Y 4X45 Canada
Tel: 613-722-9006; *Fax:* 613-722-8610
Toll-Free: 800-668-7808
info@familyservicecanada.org
www.familyservicecanada.org
To promote families as the primary source of nurturing & development of individuals, their relationship in families & communities, through promoting & ensuring the best policies & services for families in Canada.

Family Service Toronto (FST)
355 Church St., Toronto ON M5B 1Z8 Canada
Tel: 416-595-9230; *Fax:* 416-595-0242
sau@familyservicetoronto.org
www.fsatoronto.com
FST is a social service agency that helps low-income individuals & families in need. It is a registered charity, BN: 107376063RR0001.

Fédération des associations de familles monoparentales et recomposées du Québec (FAFMRQ) / Federation of Single-Parent Family Associations of Québec
584, rue Guizot est, Montréal QC H2P 1N3 Canada
Tél: 514-729-6666; *Téléc:* 514-729-6746
fafmrq.info@videotron.ca
www.fafmrq.org
Travailler à améliorer les conditions socio-économiques des familles monoparentales et recomposées du Québec.

Fédération des centres d'action bénévole du Québec (FCABQ)
1557, av Papineau, Montréal QC H2K 4H7 Canada
Tél: 514-843-6312; *Téléc:* 514-843-6485
Ligne sans frais: 800-715-7515
info@fcabq.org
www.fcabq.org
Promouvoir l'action bénévole au Québec; former un centre d'action bénévole; organiser la semaine de l'action bénévole.

Flemingdon Neighbourhood Services
#104, 10 Gateway Blvd., Toronto ON M3C 3A1 Canada
Tel: 416-424-2900; *Fax:* 416-424-3455
info@fnservices.org
www.fnservices.org
Committed to enhancing the over-all quality of life for residents of Flemingdon Park and the City of Toronto by increasing access to information and community resources for our clients through advocacy, empowerment and education.
John Carey, Executive Director

Food Banks Canada / Banques alimentaires Canada
#303, 2968 Dundas St. West, Toronto ON M6P 1Y8
Tel: 416-203-9241; *Fax:* 416-203-9244
info@cafb-acba.ca
www.foodbankscanada.ca
To act as the voice for the hungry in Canada; To find short term & long term solutions for Canadians who are assisted by food banks

Foster Parent Support Services Society (FPSS)
145 - 735 Goldstream Ave., Victoria BC V9B 2X4 Canada
Tel: 778-430-5459; *Fax:* 778-430-5463
admin@fpsss.com
www.fpsss.com
The FPSS Foster Parent Support Services Society is a Grass Roots organization committed to providing meaningful and accessible support, education and networking services which will continually enhance the skills and abilities of foster parents to deliver the best care possible to the children in their homes.

Fred Victor Centre
59 Adelaide St. East, Toronto ON M5C 1K6 Canada
Tel: 416-364-8228; *Fax:* 416-364-4728
www.fredvictor.org
To offer a continuum of community services, housing options and advocacy for adults who are experiencing homelessness, marginalization and poverty. Over 150 beds and spaces are available across 6 sites and programs.
Mark Aston, Executive Director

Frontiers Foundation (FF/OB) / Fondation Frontière
419 Coxwell Ave., Toronto ON M4L 3B9 Canada
Tel: 416-690-3930; *Fax:* 416-690-3934
Toll-Free: 800-668-4130
marcoguzman@frontiersfoundation.ca
www.frontiersfoundation.ca
Social Media:
www.facebook.com/pages/Frontiers-Foundation/66661443145
To implement the enduring relief of human poverty throughout Canada & also abroad in tangible advancement projects.

Good Jobs Coalition
407 Gervais Dr., Toronto ON M3C 1Y8 Canada
Tel: 416-441-3663
info@goodjobscoalition.ca
www.goodjobscoalition.ca
The Good Jobs for All Coalition is an alliance of community, labour, social justice, youth and environmental organizations in the Toronto region. It was formed in 2008 to start a focused dialogue on how to improve living and working conditions in Canada's largest urban centre.

Goodwill Industries of Alberta
8761 - 51 Ave., Edmonton AB T6E 5H1 Canada
Tel: 780-944-1414; *Fax:* 780-463-7396
goodwill@goodwill.ab.ca
www.goodwill.ab.ca
Social Media: www.twitter.com/goodwillab
To help persons with disabilities & disadvantages; To build a strong future through rehabilitation & training
Wendy Doughty, Chair
Heather Rennebohm, President & CEO

Goodwill Industries of Toronto
#1400, 365 Bloor St. East, Toronto ON M4W 3L4 Canada
Tel: 416-362-4711; *Fax:* 416-362-0720
TDD: 416-815-4791
info@goodwill.on.ca
www.goodwill.on.ca
To provide effective vocational programs & services to people who face employment barriers to enable them to become as independent as possible.

GRAND Society
c/o #509, 14 Spadina Rd., Toronto ON M5R 3M4 Canada
Tel: 416-513-9404
To provide emotional support to grandparents who have been denied access to their grandchildren; to make the public & professionals aware of this problem; to influence provincial family law to recognize the rights of grandparents

Grande Prairie & Region United Way
#213, 11330 - 106 St., Grande Prairie AB T8V 7X9 Canada
Tel: 780-532-1105; *Fax:* 780-532-3532
info@gpunitedway.org
www.gpunitedway.org
United Ways brings people together to strenghten our community- nuturing health and well being, building self-sufficiency, reducing barriers to independence, creating oppourtunities for children and youth, promoting understanding, dignity and respect. All dollars are raised locally are allotted to local and regional agencies.
Gladys Blackmore, President/Executive Director

Groupe d'entraide des personnes séparées/divorcées
#106, 161, av du Parc, Chibougamau QC G8P 2H3 Canada
Tél: 418-748-2777
Rita Tremblay

Huron United Way
PO Box 211, #207, 35A East St., Goderich ON N7A 3Z2 Canada
Tel: 519-524-7900; *Fax:* 519-524-1121
huronunitedway@tcc.on.ca
www.huronunitedway.ca
United Way is a registered charitable organization. They are a community of people with a common goal of caring. By heling people in their community, they are changing lives. Fundraising is an essential part of the United Way's mission.
Jerry McDonnell, Chair

Imagine Canada
#600, 2 Carlton St., Toronto ON M5B 1J3 Canada
Tel: 416-597-2293; *Fax:* 416-597-2294
Toll-Free: 800-263-1178
info@imaginecanada.ca
www.imaginecanada.ca
To support Canada's charities, non-profit organizations & socially conscious businesses & champion the work they do in our communities. Offices in Toronto, Ottawa & Calgary.

InformOntario (IO)
3010 Forest Glade Dr., Windsor ON N8R 1L5 Canada
info@informontario.on.ca
www.informontario.on.ca
Represents 65 community information centres around the province; assists the Centres by developing subject & name authorities for database management, standards for statistical data gathering & standards for management of information centres; encourages professional development through annual conferences & workshops; supports local fundraising efforts; community information centres (CICs) provide information about human services & make referrals appropriate to the needs of the individual; the service blends resources & expertise in information technology with a committment to the individual; some CIC's also provide a social reporting service by analyzing inquiry data, trends & gaps in human services & reporting these findings to appropriate agencies & governments

International Social Service Canada (ISSC) / Service Social International Canada (SSIC)
#506, 1580 Merivale Rd., Ottawa ON K2G 4B5 Canada
Tel: 613-236-6161; *Fax:* 613-233-7306
issc@issc-ssic.ca
www.issc-ssic.ca
To provide linkages to social service organizations worldwide; to help resolve individual & family problems resulting from the movement of people across national borders

Kids First Parent Association of Canada
3916 32nd St. NW, Edmonton AB T6T 1J9 Canada
Tel: 604-291-0088
info@kidsfirstcanada.org
www.kidsfirstcanada.org
Concerned with the care & well-being of children; parents lobbying to protect their right & choice to raise children in a family setting; to provide support to anyone wanting to further this cause in other communities.

Kids Help Phone (KHP) / Jeunesse j'écoute
#300, 439 University Ave., Toronto ON M5G 1Y8 Canada
Tel: 416-586-5437; *Fax:* 416-586-0651
Toll-Free: 800-668-6868
info@kidshelp.sympatico.ca
www.kidshelpphone.ca

To provide a national, bilingual, 24-hours a day, 365 days of the year, toll-free, professionally staffed, confidential counselling service to young people; To offer counselling online through the Kids Help Phone website; To contribute to awareness of childrens's issues & the development of policies & practices to help Canadian children

Lakeland United Way
PO Box 8369, #204, 1301 - 8th Ave., Cold Lake AB T9M 1N3 Canada
Tel: 780-826-0045; *Fax:* 780-639-2699
luw2699@telus.net
www.lakelandunitedway.com
Umbrella fundraising organization for a variety of local charities & social services.
Ajaz Quraishi, President

Lawyers for Social Responsibility (LSR) / Avocats en faveur d'une conscience sociale (AFCS)
c/o 5120 Carney Rd. NW, Calgary AB T2L 1G2 Canada
Tel: 403-282-8260
bevdelong@shaw.ca
www.peacelawyers.ca
To advise the public, politicians, & government officials on the application of the law to foreign & defence policies; To call for use of law, not use of force, to resolve conflicts

Lloydminster & District United Way
4419 - 52nd Ave., Lloydminster AB T9V 0Y8 Canada
Tel: 780-875-3743; *Fax:* 780-875-3793
luw@telusplanet.net
www.lloydminster.unitedway.ca
Eric Rounce, President

Manitoba Association of Social Workers (MASW) / Association des travailleurs sociaux du Manitoba
#101, 2033 Portage Ave., Winnipeg MB R3J 0K6 Canada
Tel: 204-888-9477; *Fax:* 204-831-6359
www.maswmirsw.ca
To act as the voice of the social work profession; To develop professional standards of social work practice; To ensure the accountability of the social work profession

Manitoba Association of Women's Shelters (MAWS)
c/o Genesis House, PO Box 389, Winkler MB R6W 4A6 Canada
Tel: 204-325-9957; *Fax:* 204-325-5889
Crisis Hot-Line: 877-977-0007
www.maws.mb.ca
MAWS is dedicated to the elimination of violence against women. It was created to provide support to member shelters for abused women & their children. It works to share information & resources with its member shelters, increase training of staff & increase services for clients. By acting as a unified voice for its members, the association also aims to enhance negotiations with funders. It is a registered charity, BN: 880786892RR0001.

Manitoba Block Parent Program
466 Gertrude Ave., Winnipeg MB R3L 0M8 Canada
Tel: 204-284-7562
bppw@mts.net
www.winnipegblockparents.mb.ca
It is the mission of the Block Parent Program to provide a network of police-screened easily recognizable, safe places for the members of the community, primarily children.
George Jarvis, President

Manitoba Institute of Registered Social Workers (MIRSW)
#101, 2033 Portage Ave., Winnipeg MB R3J 0K6 Canada
Tel: 204-888-9477; *Fax:* 204-831-6359
masw@mts.net
www.maswmirsw.ca
To certify members; To act as the regulatory arm of the social work profession; To encourage ethical standards of practice to protect the public

La Mine d'Or, entreprise d'insertion sociale
449, 3e Rue, Chibougamau QC G8P 1N6 Canada
Tél: 418-748-4183; *Téléc:* 418-748-2837
informations@laminedor.org
www.laminedor.org
Organisme sans but lucratif, qui a pour mission l'insertion sociale & professionnelle des personnes en situation d'exclusion; offre une passerelle aux participants vers le marché du travail, la formation ou d'autres alternatives
Suzan Amyot, Présidente

Mouvement ATD Quart Monde Canada / ATD Fourth World Movement Canada
6747, rue Drolet, Montréal QC H2S 2T1 Canada
Tél: 514-279-0468; *Téléc:* 514-279-7759
www.atdquartmonde.ca
Développer un courant de refus de la misère en donnant la priorité aux plus pauvres, dans le respect des droits et de la dignité de la personne; contribuer à l'action du Mouvement dans le monde

Neepawa & District United Way
PO Box 1545, Neepawa MB R0J 1H0 Canada
Tel: 204-476-5803
office@neepawa.unitedway.ca
www.neepawa.unitedway.ca
Local United Way Chapter raising funds to help community organization.
Angela Pearen-Burnside, President

Nelson & District United Way
PO Box 89, Nelson BC V1L 5P7 Canada
Tel: 250-352-6012
united_way@netidea.com
www.uw.kics.bc.ca
Local chapter of the United Way raising funds for community organizations.
Carol-Joy Kaill, President

New Brunswick Association of Food Banks
c/o Grand Falls Regional Food Bank Inc., 363 Portage Rd., Grand Falls NB E3Z 1M2 Canada
Tel: 506-473-2001; *Fax:* 506-473-6883
To support member agencies in their efforts to alleviate hunger; to serve as a provincial voice for same.

New Brunswick Association of Social Workers (NBASW) / Association des travailleurs sociaux du Nouveau-Brunswick
PO Box 1533, Stn. A, Fredericton NB E3B 5G2 Canada
Tel: 506-459-5595; *Fax:* 506-457-1421
Toll-Free: 877-495-5595
nbasw@nbasw-atsnb.ca
www.nbasw-atsnb.ca
To regulate the profession of social work; to protect the public; to set standards; to promote the profession

New Brunswick Block Parent Association (NBBPAI)
#47, 100 Howe Crt., Oromocto NB E2V 2R3
Fax: 506-446-5992
Toll-Free: 800-665-4900
info@blockparent.ca
www.blockparent.ca
To provide immediate assistance to community members, especially children & seniors, through a safety network; To serve 35 communities & 500 homes throughout New Brunswick
Linda Patterson, President

Newfoundland & Labrador Association of Social Workers (NLASW) / Association des travailleurs sociaux de Terre-Neuve et Labrador
PO Box 39039, St. John's NL A1E 5Y7 Canada
Tel: 709-753-0200; *Fax:* 709-753-0120
info@nlasw.ca
www.nlasw.ca
To ensure excellence in social work in Newfoundland & Labrador; to speak out & take appropriate action on issues of social concern; to disseminate information & provide opportunities for continuing education; to provide consultation to agencies involved in training for or delivering human services; to promote the development & the enhancement of social service delivery system suited to the needs of Newfoundlanders. Office located at 177 Hamlyn Rd., St. John's.

Non-Smokers' Rights Association (NSRA) / Association pour les droits des non-fumeurs
#221, 720 Spadina Ave., Toronto ON M5S 2T9 Canada
Tel: 416-928-2900; *Fax:* 416-928-1860
toronto@nsra-adnf.ca
www.nsra-adnf.ca
To promote public health by stopping illness & death due to tobacco, including second-hand smoke

Northumberland United Way
#203, 1005 Elgin St. West, Cobourg ON K9A 5J4 Canada
Tel: 905-372-6955; *Fax:* 905-372-4417
office@northumberland.unitedway.ca
www.northumberland.unitedway.ca
To raise & allocate funds in an efficient manner & to promote the effective delivery of services in response to current & emerging social needs in Northumberland County.
Lynda Kay, Executive Director
Cathy Cavanagh, Manager, Finance & Operations

Nova Scotia Association of Social Workers (NSASW) / Association des travailleurs sociaux de la Nouvelle-Écosse
Plaza 1881, #106, 1891 Brunswick St., Halifax NS B3J 2G8 Canada
Tel: 902-429-7799; *Fax:* 902-429-7650
nsasw@nsasw.org
www.nsasw.org
Promotes & regulates the practice of social work so the members can provide a high standard of service that respects diversity, promotes social justice & enhances the worth, self-determination & potential of individuals, families & communities

Nova Scotia Block Parent Advisory Board
Tel: 902-849-3525
michael.byrne@novascotiablockparent.com
www.novascotiablockparent.com
Jean Hiltz, Chairman

One Parent Families Association of Canada / Association des familles uniparentales du Canada
PO Box 111, Pickering ON L1V 2R2 Canada
Tel: 905-831-7098; *Fax:* 905-831-2580
Toll-Free: 877-773-7714
opfa222@aol.com
www.opfa.net
To develop & provide a broad comprehensive program for the enlightenment & guidance of single parents & their children on the special problems they encounter & for assistance on the various readjustments involved.

Ontario Association for Marriage & Family Therapy (OAMFT)
PO Box 693, Tottenham ON L0G 1W0
Toll-Free: 800-267-2638
admin@oamft.on.ca
www.oamft.on.ca
To serve members of the association, the profession of marriage & family therapy, & the public; To uphold the Code of Ethics of the American Association for Marriage & Family Therapy

Ontario Association of Children's Aid Societies (OACAS) / Association ontarienne des sociétés de l'aide à l'enfance
75 Front St. East, 2nd Fl., Toronto ON M5E 1V9 Canada
Tel: 416-987-7725; *Fax:* 416-366-8317
info@oacas.org
www.oacas.org
The voice of child welfare in Ontario, dedicated to providing leadership for the achievement of excellence in the protection of children & in the promotion of their well-being within their families & communities

Ontario Association of Interval & Transition Houses (OAITH)
#1404, 2 Carleton St., Toronto ON M5B 1J3
Tel: 416-977-6619
oaith2@web.ca
www.oaith.ca
To work towards social change by ensuring that the voices of abused women are heard; To remove barriers to equality for women & children

Ontario Association of Social Workers (OASW) / Association des travailleuses et travailleurs sociaux de l'Ontario (ATTSO)
410 Jarvis St., Toronto ON M4Y 2G6 Canada
Tel: 416-923-4848; *Fax:* 416-923-5279
info@oasw.org
www.oasw.org; www.findasocialworker.ca; www.socialworkjobs.ca
To act as the voice of social workers in Ontario

Ontario Block Parent Program Inc. (OBPPI)
902 Maitland St., London ON N5Y 2X1 Canada
Tel: 519-438-2016; *Toll-Free:* 800-563-2771
mrooke902@rogers.com
www.blockparent.on.ca
To provide immediate assistance through a safety network & to offer supportive community education programs; to provide a network of police screened, easily recognizable safe homes for members of the community, especially children, to turn to in times of distress; to educate children about the program, safety on the streets & safety within the home; to develop promotions & materials to educate the community about the program, latch key children & streetproofing; to work together with the police, educators & other community groups toward safer communities
Marg Rooke, Chair

Ontario Coalition for Better Child Care (OCBCC)
#206, 489 College St., Toronto ON M6G 1A5 Canada
Tel: 416-538-0628; *Fax:* 416-538-6737
Toll-Free: 800-594-7514
info@childcareontario.org
www.childcareontario.org
Advocates on behalf of Ontario's non-profit, licensed child care programs

Ontario Coalition of Rape Crisis Centres (OCRCC) / Coalition des centres anti-viol de l'Ontario
c/o TRCC, PO Box 6597, Stn. A, Toronto ON M5W 1X4 Canada
Tel: 416-597-1171; *Fax:* 416-597-9648
ocrcc_pres@hotmail.com
www.ocrcc.ca
To work for prevention & eradication of sexual assault; to implement legal, social & attitudinal changes regarding sexual assault; to provide mechanism for communication, education & mobilization to alleviate political & geographical isolation of rape crisis centres in Ontario; to encourage, direct & generate research into sexual violence; to work with Canadian Association of Sexual Assault Centres (see listing) on developing national policies; to liaise with other provincial organizations addressing similar issues

Ontario Community Support Association (OCSA) / Association ontarienne de soutien communautaire
#104, 970 Lawrence Ave. West, Toronto ON M6A 3B6 Canada
Tel: 416-256-3010; *Fax:* 416-256-3021
Toll-Free: 800-267-6272
ocsainfo@ocsa.on.ca
www.ocsa.on.ca
To support & represent the common goals of community-based, not-for-profit health & social service organizations which assist individuals to live at home in their own community

Ontario Municipal Social Services Association (OMSSA) / Association des services sociaux des municipalités de l'Ontario
#100, 5720 Timberlea Blvd., Mississauga ON L4W 4W2 Canada
Tel: 905-629-3115; *Fax:* 905-629-1633
info@omssa.com
www.omssa.com
To promote high standards of competency within the profession to ensure quality delivery of human services in communities; to improve social policies & programs in the areas of affordable housing, homelessness prevention, children's services, & social assistance; to act as the voice for Consolidated Municipal Service Managers in Ontario

The Ontario Trillium Foundation / La Fondation Trillium de l'Ontario
45 Charles St. East, 5th Fl., Toronto ON M4Y 1S2 Canada
Tel: 416-963-4927; *Fax:* 416-963-8781
Toll-Free: 800-263-2887
TDD: 416-963-7905
trillium@trilliumfoundation.org
www.trilliumfoundation.org
To work with others to make strategic investments to build healthy, sustainable & caring communities in Ontario
L. Robin Cardozo, CEO

Ordre professionnel des travailleurs sociaux du Québec (OPTSQ)
#520, 255, boul. Crémazie est, Montréal QC H2M 1M2 Canada
Tél: 514-731-3925; *Téléc:* 514-731-6785
Ligne sans frais: 888-731-9420
info.general@optsq.org
www.optsq.org
Assurer la protection du public par le contrôle de l'exercice de la profession, par la formation continue, et le développement professionnel.

Parcelles de tendresse
CP 582, Chibougamau QC G8P 2Y8 Canada
Tél: 418-748-3644
Pierette Boulay

Parent Finders of Canada
19 English Bluff Rd., Delta BC V4M 2M4 Canada
Tel: 604-948-1069; *Fax:* 604-948-2036
www.parentfinders.org
To assist adult adoptees/foster persons & birth relatives to obtain background information from adoption files kept in social services departments; to assist in search & reunion; to promote a feeling of openness about the adoption experience & a better understanding about the longing for a reunion between adult adoptees & birth relatives

Parent Support Services Society of BC (PSSS)
#204, 5623 Imperial St., Burnaby BC V5J 1G1 Canada
Tel: 604-669-1616; *Fax:* 604-669-1636
Toll-Free: 877-345-9777
office@parentsupportbc.ca
www.parentsupportbc.ca
The Society promotes parent support circles to help parents & guardians learn positive parenting skills & receive emotional support. The circles are anonymous, confidential self-help groups that meet weekly to learn effective, non-abusive ways to discipline their children. It is a registered charity, BN: 106778780RR0001.

Parents-secours du Québec inc. (PSQI)
#203, 17, rue Fusey, Trois-Rivières QC G8T 2T3 Canada
Ligne sans frais: 800-588-8173
info@parentssecours.ca
www.parentssecours.ca
Parents-Secours du Québec inc. (PSQI) est un organisme à but non lucratif qui assure la sécurité et la protection des enfants et des aînés-es en offrant un réseau de foyers-refuges sécuritaires tout en contribuant à promouvoir la prévention par l'information et l'éducation.

People, Words & Change (PWC) / Monde des mots
Heartwood House, 153 Chapel St., Ottawa ON K1N 1H5 Canada
Tel: 613-234-2494; *Fax:* 613-234-4223
info@pwc-ottawa.ca
www.nald.ca/pwc
To teach adults to read & write in English

Petites-Mains
7595 St.-Laurent Boul., Montréal QC H2R 1W9 Canada
Tél: 514-738-8989; *Téléc:* 514-738-6193
info@petitesmains.com
www.petitesmains.com
Petites-Mains a pour mission de venir en aide aux gens, surtout les femmes immigrantes, monoparentales, sans revenu et prestataires de l'Assistance-Emploi. Il aide ces femmes à sortir de leur isolement, à échanger avec d'autres, à apprendre un métier, à intégrer le marché du travail et à vivre en dignité dans la société.
Nahid Aboumansour, Contact

PFLAG Canada Inc.
PO Box 29211, 1633 Mountain Rd., Moncton NB E1G 4R3 Canada
Tel: 506-869-8191; *Fax:* 506-387-8349
Toll-Free: 888-530-6777
pflagcanada@nb.aibn.com
www.pflagcanada.ca
To support individuals with questions & concerns about sexual orientation or gender identity; to make Canada a more accepting place for persons of all gender identities & sexual orientations
Cherie MacLeod, Executive Director
Stacy Green, President
Jayme Harper, Vice-President
Ryan Walkinshaw, Treasurer

Plan Canada
#1001, 95 St. Clair Ave. West, Toronto ON M4V 3B5 Canada
Tel: 416-920-1654; *Fax:* 416-920-9942
Toll-Free: 800-387-1418
info@plancanada.ca
plancanada.ca
Social Media: www.facebook.com/PlanCanada
International child-focused development agency to help children, their families & communities in developing countries; to raise funds through sponsorship program & implement programs in health, education & community development overseas

Porcupine United Way
PO Box 984, #312, 60 Wilson Ave., Timmins ON P4N 7H6 Canada
Tel: 705-268-9696; *Fax:* 705-268-9700
puw@ntl.sympatico.ca
porcupineunitedway.com
To promote the organized capacity of people to care for one another
Jean Warren, Executive Director

Portage Plains United Way
224 Saskatchewan Ave. East, Portage la Prairie MB R1N 0K9 Canada
Tel: 204-857-4440; *Fax:* 204-239-1740
ppuw@mts.net
www.portageplainsuw.ca
To unite our community to enhance the quality of life for those in need
Darrell Lee, President
Tara Pettinger, Executive Director

Powell River & District United Way
PO Box 379, Powell River BC V8A 5C2 Canada
Tel: 604-485-2791
bennobabe@shaw.ca
www.unitedwayofpowellriver.ca
Pat Hull, President

Prince Edward Island Association of Social Workers / Association des travailleurs sociaux de l'Ile-du-Prince-Édouard
81 Prince St., Charlottetown PE C1A 4R3
Tel: 902-368-7337; *Fax:* 902-368-7080
vrc@eastlink.cat
To acknowledge & promote the work of social workers in Prince Edward Island; To advance the social work profession throughout the province, to ensure well-being for residents

Prince Edward Island Block Parent Advisory Board
RR#3 Middleton, Summerside PE C1N 4J9 Canada
Tel: 902-887-2480; *Fax:* 902-887-2874
kjoffer@eastlink.ca
www.blockparent.ca
To create safer environment for children & others by designating & creating awareness of safe Block Parent homes in the community.

Prince George United Way
1600 - 3rd Ave., Prince George BC V2L 3G6 Canada
Tel: 250-561-1040; *Fax:* 250-562-8102
trevorw@pguw.bc.ca
www.pguw.bc.ca
To promote the organized capacity of persons to care for one another through voluntarism, leadership & education; to ensure the effective raising & allocation of charitable funds for community-based social services & to foster the effective provision of services that are in the best interest of the community
Trevor Williams, Executive Director
Scotty Raitt, President

Project Genesis
4735 Côte-Ste.-Catherine, Montréal QC H3W 1M1 Canada
Tel: 514-738-2036; *Fax:* 514-738-6385
Community group that provides community organization, advocacy, and education, as well as legal advice involving tenant rights, debt & bankruptcy, family law, and immigration
Michael Chervin, Contact

Québec Association of Marriage & Family Therapy (QAMFT) / Association québécoise pour la thérapie conjugale et familiale
#300, 360 Victoria Avenue, Westmount QC H3H 2N4 Canada
Tel: 514-315-6111
info@qamft.org
www.qamft.org
To promote understanding, research & education in the field of couple & family therapy & to ensure that public needs are met by practitioners of the highest quality
Andrew Sofin, President

Reena
927 Clark Ave. West, Thornhill ON L4J 8G6 Canada
Tel: 905-889-6484; *Fax:* 905-889-3827
Toll-Free: 877-324-4114
info@reena.org
www.reena.org
To integrate developmentally disabled people towards independent living within community, with emphasis on Judaic programming
Sandy Keshen, President & CEO
Minnie Ross, Manager, Communications

Regroupement des Auberges du Coeur
#32, 2000, boul Saint-Joseph est, Montréal QC H2H 1E4 Canada
Tél: 514-523-8559; *Téléc:* 514-523-5148
regroupement@aubergesducoeur.com
www.aubergesducoeur.com
Défendre l'existence & l'autonomie des ressources communautaires d'hébergement pour jeunes adolescents & jeunes adultes en difficulté ou sans abri; agir comme porte-parole des jeunes sans abri; favoriser entre les maisons, les jeunes & les partenaires des communautés d'appartenance de chacune des Auberges des échanges sur les besoins des jeunes
Pierre Audette, Directeur général

The Right to Die Society of Canada (RTDSC) / Société Canadienne pour le Droit de Mourir (SCDM)
145 Macdonell Ave., Toronto ON M6R 2A4 Canada
Tel: 416-535-0690; *Toll-Free:* 866-535-0690
contact-rtd@righttodie.ca
www.righttodie.ca

To work with legislators, policy makers & the public to expand the range of humane options for people who are suffering intolerably from incurable conditions & who want a self-directed dying; to work with sufferers to expand their awareness of the options that are legal & may be appropriate for them
Ruth von Fuchs, President & Secretary

Ronald McDonald House Charities of Canada (RMHC) / Oeuvres pour enfants Ronald McDonald du Canada
McDonald's Place, Toronto ON M3C 3L4 Canada
Tel: 416-443-1000; *Fax:* 416-446-3762
Toll-Free: 800-387-8808
www.rmhc.ca
To help children in need by improving the physical & emotional quality of life for children with serious illnesses, disabilities &/or chronic conditions, allowing them to lead happier, healthier & more productive lives

Samaritan's Purse Canada
20 Hopewell Way NE, Calgary AB T3J 5H5 Canada
Tel: 403-250-6565; *Fax:* 403-250-6567
Toll-Free: 800-663-6500
canada@samaritan.org
www.samaritanspurse.ca
A nondenominational evangelical Christian international relief organization with projects around the globe, meeting both physical & spiritual needs of people who are victims of war, poverty, natural disasters, disease & famine. Focus is on emergency relief & development programs, medical projects. International offices in Canada, Australia, Germany, Ireland, the Netherlands, the U.S. & the U.K.

Saskatchewan Association of Social Workers (SASW) / Association des travailleurs sociaux de la Saskatchewan
Edna Osborne House, 2110 Lorne St., Regina SK S4P 2M5
Tel: 306-545-1922; *Fax:* 306-545-1895
Toll-Free: 877-517-7279
sasw@accesscomm.ca
www.sasw.ca
To conduct the work of a professional regulator; To act as the voice of social workers in Saskatchewan; To develop & maintain standards of knowledge, skill, conduct, & competence among members to serve & protect the public interest

Secours aux lépreux (Canada) inc. (SLC) / Leprosy Relief (Canada) Inc.
#305, 1805, rue Sauvé ouest, Montréal QC H4N 3H4 Canada
Tél: 514-744-3199; *Téléc:* 514-744-9095
Ligne sans frais: 866-744-3199
info@slc-lr.ca
www.slc-lr.ca
Venir en aide médicalement et soulager les victimes de la lèpre et de la tuberculose

Sex Information & Education Council of Canada (SIECCAN) / Conseil d'information et éducation sexuelles du Canada
850 Coxwell Ave., Toronto ON M4C 5R1 Canada
Tel: 416-466-5304; *Fax:* 416-778-0785
sieccan@web.ca
www.sieccan.org
To inform & educate public & professionals about all aspects of human sexuality in order to support the positive integration of sexuality into people's lives

ShareLife
1155 Yonge St., Toronto ON M4T 1W2 Canada
Tel: 416-934-3400; *Fax:* 416-934-3412
Toll-Free: 800-263-2595
slife@archtoronto.org
www.sharelife.org
ShareLife is the Catholic Community's response to helping the whole community through Catholic agencies by effectively raising & allocating funds

Social Planning & Research Council of BC (SPARC)
4445 Norfolk St., Burnaby BC V5G 0A7 Canada
Tel: 604-718-7733; *Fax:* 604-736-8697
info@sparc.bc.ca
www.sparc.bc.ca
Social Media: www.twitter.com/SPARC_BC
To promote the social, economic & environmental well-being of citizens & communities; to advocate the principles of social justice, equality & the dignity & worth of all people in our multicultural society; to conduct research & planning for public information, education & citizen participation in developing social policies & programs

Social Planning Council of Ottawa-Carleton / Conseil de planification sociale d'Ottawa-Carleton
#501, 280 Metcalfe St., Ottawa ON K2P 1R7 Canada
Tel: 613-236-9300; *Fax:* 613-236-7060
office@spcottawa.on.ca
www.spcottawa.on.ca
To provide the residents of Ottawa-Carleton with the means to exercise informed leadership on issues affecting their social & economic well-being

Social Planning Council of Winnipeg
412 McDermot Ave., Winnipeg MB R3A 0A9 Canada
Tel: 204-943-2561; *Fax:* 204-942-3221
info@spcw.mb.ca
www.spcw.mb.ca
Social Media: www.facebook.com/group.php?gid=54256670713
To identify & define social planning issues, needs & resources in the community; to develop & promote policy & program options to policy-makers; to support community groups & the voluntary human service sector; to raise community awareness of social issues & human service needs, social policy options & service delivery alternatives; to serve as a link between the three levels of government & community neighbourhoods

Society of Transition Houses - BC & Yukon
#325, 119 West Pender St., Vancouver BC V6B 1S5 Canada
Tel: 604-669-6943; *Fax:* 604-682-6962
Toll-Free: 800-661-1040
admin@bcysth.ca
www.bcysth.ca
To educate, promote & advocate on issues of violence against women; to support an organization that provides or seeks to provide shelter &/or services to women & their children who experience violence

SOS Children's Villages Canada / SOS Villages d'Enfants Canada
#200, 244 Rideau St., Ottawa ON K1N 5Y3 Canada
Tel: 613-232-3309; *Fax:* 613-232-6764
Toll-Free: 800-767-5111
info@soschildrensvillages.ca
www.soschildrensvillages.ca
To assist SOS-Children's Villages in Canada & abroad through financial & operating support; to care for orphaned, abandoned & other children in need of long-term placement; to create opportunities for children to become happy, stable, responsible members of society

Springtide Resources
PO Box 7, #220, 215 Spadina Ave., Toronto ON M5T 2C7 Canada
Tel: 416-968-3422; *Fax:* 416-968-2026
TDD: 416-968-7335
info@womanabuseprevention.com
www.springtideresources.org
Social Media: facebook.com/springtide.resources
The non-profit organization aims to increase public awareness of the many aspects of violence against women & its effect on children. It works to change the social conditions that subject women to abuse by providing training & resources proactively. It is a registered charity, BN: 108053653RR0001.

Streetkids' Foundation (SKF)
First Global Place, #201, 7 Concorde Pl., Toronto ON M3C 3N4 Canada
Tel: 416-391-1801; *Fax:* 416-391-2616
To assist street kids to become self-sufficient; to reduce the number of teens who take to the streets both in Canada & abroad

Swift Current United Way
PO Box 485, #203B Professional Bldg. - 12 Cheadle St. West, Swift Current SK S9H 0A9 Canada
Tel: 306-773-4828; *Fax:* 306-773-4870
unitedway@sasktel.net
Jennifer Olfert, Executive Director

Thompson Crisis Centre
PO Box 1226, Thompson MB R8N 1P1 Canada
Tel: 204-677-9668; *Fax:* 204-677-9042
Toll-Free: 800-442-0613
To provide immediate assistance through a walk-in facility & a 24-hour emergency telephone service; to provide a safe place for the women & their children who are victims of physical/emotional abuse; to provide services to women & their children needing longer term support

Thompson, Nicola, Cariboo United Way
#203, 239 Victoria St., Kamloops BC V2C 2A1 Canada
Tel: 250-372-9933; *Fax:* 250-372-5926
office@unitedwaytnc.ca
www.unitedwaytnc.ca

To enable all citizens to join in a community wide effort to fund & provide in consort with others, effective delivery of health & social services & programs in response to the needs of the community
Brenda Aynsley, Executive Director

Toronto Community Foundation (TCF)
#1603, 2 Bloor St. West, Toronto ON M4W 3H1 Canada
Tel: 416-921-2035; *Fax:* 416-921-1026
info@tcf.ca
www.tcf.ca
To connect philanthropic individuals and families to charitable organizations in Toronto. TCF invests charitable gifts from donors into income-earning endowment funds, and makes grants from the earnings to support a range of charities
Rahul K. Bhardwaj, President & CEO
Rosalyn Morrison, VP, Community Initiatives
Carole Boivin, VP, Communications & Marketing, Communications
Anne Brayley, VP, Professional Advisory Services
Susan Hartnett, VP, Finance

211 Toronto
c/o Findhelp Information Services, #125, 543 Richmond St. W., Toronto ON M5V 1Y6 Canada
Tel: 416-392-4605; *Fax:* 416-392-4404
www.211toronto.ca
211 Toronto is a service of Findhelp Information Services (formerly Community Information Toronto). Comprehensive information & referral services provided in English, French & other languages; resources for information & referral professionals; call centre; newcomer services; Possibilities online employment resource centre; training & outreach

United Generations Ontario (UGO) / Générations Unies Ontario
1185 Eglinton Ave. East, Toronto ON M3C 3C6 Canada
Tel: 416-426-7115; *Fax:* 416-426-7421
info@unitedgenerations.ca
www.unitedgenerations.ca
Coalition of human service organizations & individuals who are dedicated to promoting programs that bring young & old together in a spirit of cooperation, mutual support, shared affection & regard; to empower people to take a constructive part in the life of their own communities & to create a vital volunteer exchange in caring & sharing
Russ De Cou, Executive Director
Richard Cox, Chief Operating Officer

United Way Central & Northern Vancouver Island
3156 Barons Rd., Nanaimo BC V9T 4B5 Canada
Tel: 250-729-7400; *Fax:* 250-729-8084
info@uwcnvi.ca
www.uwcnvi.ca
To improve lives by engaging individuals & mobilizing collective action
Lynne Brown, COO

United Way Community Services of Guelph & Wellington
85 Westmount Rd., Guelph ON N1H 5J2 Canada
Tel: 519-821-0571; *Fax:* 519-821-7847
info@unitedwayguelph.com
www.unitedwayguelph.com
Steve Allen, President
Ken Dardano, Executive Director

United Way for the City of Kawartha Lakes (UWVC)
50 Mary St. West, Lindsay ON K9V 2N6 Canada
Tel: 705-878-5081; *Fax:* 705-878-0475
office@ckl.unitedway.ca
www.ckl.unitedway.ca
To promote the organized capacity of people & groups in Victoria County to care for each other
Penny Barton Dyke, Executive Director

United Way of Ajax-Pickering-Uxbridge
#303, 230 Westney Rd. West, Ajax ON L1S 7J5 Canada
Tel: 905-686-0606; *Fax:* 905-686-0609
office@uwayapu.org
www.uwayapu.org
To increase the ability of the people of Ajax & Pickering to care for one another through leadership in community problem solving including generation & allocation of financial & other resources
Edna Klazek, Executive Director

United Way of Brandon & District Inc.
Scotia Towers, 201-1011 Rosser Ave., Brandon MB R7A 0L5 Canada
Tel: 204-571-8929; *Fax:* 204-727-8939
office@brandonuw.ca
www.brandonuw.ca

Debbie Arsenault, CEO

United Way of Burlington & Greater Hamilton
177 Rebecca St., Hamilton ON L8R 1B9 Canada
Tel: 905-527-4543; *Fax:* 905-527-5152
uway@uwaybh.ca
www.uwaybh.ca
To empower a diverse community to achieve positive social development
Len Lifchus, CEO

United Way of Calgary & Area
#600, 1202 Centre St. SE, Calgary AB T2G 5A5 Canada
Tel: 403-231-6265; *Fax:* 403-355-3135
uway@calgaryunitedway.org
www.calgaryunitedway.org
To invest in 250 programs offered by 130 agencies in Calgary, Airdrie, Cochrane, High River, Okotoks & Strathmore
Linda Hohol, Chair
Ruth Ramsden-Wood, President

United Way of Cambridge & North Dumfries
150 Main St., Cambridge ON N1R 6P9 Canada
Tel: 519-621-1030; *Fax:* 519-621-6220
ron@uwcambridge.on.ca
www.uwcambridge.on.ca
To enhance the quality of life in Cambridge & North Dumfries by caring for & contributing to community needs
Heidi Duarte, Manager, Development & Marketing
Brad Park, Director, Development
Ron Dowhaniuk, Executive Director

United Way of Canada - Centraide Canada
#404, 56 Sparks St., Ottawa ON K1P 5A9 Canada
Tel: 613-236-7041; *Fax:* 613-236-3087
Toll-Free: 800-267-8221
info@unitedway.ca
www.unitedway.ca; www.centraide.ca
To increase the organized capacity of people to care for one another
Patricia McDermott, Chair
Al Hatton, President/CEO

United Way of Cape Breton
Cabot House, PO Box 1929, 500 Kings Rd., 2nd Fl., Sydney NS B1P 6W4 Canada
Tel: 902-562-5226; *Fax:* 902-562-5721
unitedway@ns.aliantzinc.ca
www.sydney.unitedway.ca
Allister Taylor, Executive Director

United Way of Central Alberta
4811 - 48th St., Red Deer AB T4N 1S6 Canada
Tel: 403-343-3900; *Fax:* 403-309-3820
info@caunitedway.ca
www.caunitedway.ca
To improve lives & build community by engaging individuals & mobilizing collective action
Heather Gardiner, CEO

United Way of Chatham-Kent County
PO Box 606, 425 McNaughton Ave. West, Chatham ON N7M 5K8 Canada
Tel: 519-354-0430; *Fax:* 519-354-9511
united.way@united-kent.on.ca
unitedway.chatham-kent.on.ca
To build the organized capacity of people to care for one another
Karen S. Kirkwood-Whyte, Executive Director
Patrick Weaver, President

United Way of Cranbrook & Kimberley
PO Box 657, 930 Baker St., Cranbrook BC V1C 4J2 Canada
Tel: 250-426-8833; *Fax:* 250-426-5455
cranunitedway@shaw.ca; office@cranbrook.unitedway.ca
www.cranbrook.unitedway.ca
To ensure the effective raising & allocation of charitable funds for community based social services that are in the best interest of the community
Donna Brady, Executive Director

United Way of Cumberland County
PO Box 535, 43 Prince Arthur St., Amherst NS B4H 4A1 Canada
Tel: 902-667-2203; *Fax:* 902-667-3819
unitedway.cumberland@ns.aliantzinc.ca
Jeff Brennan, Chair
Cathy Skinner, Executive Director

United Way of Elrose & District Corp.
PO Box 123, Elrose SK S0L 0Z0 Canada
Tel: 306-378-2532
Jack Elliott, Chair

United Way of Estevan
PO Box 611, Estevan SK S4A 2A5 Canada
Tel: 306-634-7348; *Fax:* 306-634-2197
secretary@unitedwayofestevan.com
James Lainton, Chair

United Way of Fort McMurray
#207, 9912A Franklin Ave., Fort McMurray AB T9H 2K5 Canada
Tel: 780-791-0077; *Fax:* 780-791-0088
office@fortmcmurray.unitedway.ca
fmunitedway.com
To provide effective support for social health & welfare services in the community of Fort McMurray
Diane Shannon, Executive Director

United Way of Greater Moncton & Southeastern NB Region Inc. / Centraide de la région du Grand Moncton et du Sud-Est du NB Inc.
PO Box 768, 123 Halifax St., Moncton NB E1C 8M9 Canada
Tel: 506-858-8600; *Fax:* 506-858-0584
office@moncton.unitedway.ca
www.gmsenbunitedway.ca
Social Media: www.facebook.com/group.php?gid=76467525679
To raise funds to increase the organized capacity of people to care for one another
Debbie McInnis, Executive Director

United Way of Greater Saint John Inc.
61 Union St., 2nd Fl., Saint John NB E2L 1A2 Canada
Tel: 506-658-1212; *Fax:* 506-633-7724
office@saintjohn.unitedway.ca
www.saintjohn.unitedway.ca
Elizabeth Jadoo, Executive Director

United Way of Greater Simcoe County
#100, 136 Bayfield St., Barrie ON L4M 3B1 Canada
Tel: 705-726-2301; *Fax:* 705-726-4897
info@unitedwaysimcoecounty.on.ca
www.unitedwaysimcoecounty.on.ca
United Way of Greater Simcoe County has been making a difference in our community for over 47 years by assessing local needs and distributing resources to help those most in need.
Seija Suutari, CEO
Bethany Obermayer, Director, Finance & Administration

United Way of Haldimand-Norfolk
PO Box 472, #3, 39 Kent St. North, Simcoe ON N3Y 3L5 Canada
Tel: 519-426-5660; *Fax:* 519-426-0017
Toll-Free: 866-792-7394
uw@unitedwayhn.on.ca
www.unitedwayhn.on.ca
To improve people's lives & to strengthen the community
Evelyn Nobbs, Executive Director
Mark Liota, President

United Way of Halifax Region
Royal Bank Bldg., 46 Portland St., 7th Fl., Halifax NS B2Y 1H4 Canada
Tel: 902-422-1501; *Fax:* 902-423-6837
info@unitedwayhalifax.ca
www.unitedwayhalifax.ca
To strengthen neighbourhoods & communities by providing programs & services that link people & resources, encourage participation & increase giving
Catherine J. Woodman, President/CEO

United Way of Halton Hills
PO Box 286, Georgetown ON L7G 4Y5 Canada
Tel: 905-877-3066; *Fax:* 905-877-3067
office@haltonhills.unitedway.ca
www.haltonhills.unitedway.ca
To provide leadership in the raising & responsible allocation of funds to meet human needs & to improve social conditions in a caring community
Janet Foster, Executive Director

United Way of Kingston, Frontenac, Lennox & Addington
417 Bagot St., Kingston ON K7K 3C1 Canada
Tel: 613-542-2674; *Fax:* 613-542-1379
uway@unitedwaykfla.ca
www.unitedwaykfla.ca
To strengthen & support the organized capacity of our diverse community to care for one another
Bhavana Varma, President
Clara Lambert, Director, Finance
Maura Doyle, Campaign Manager

United Way of Kitchener-Waterloo & Area
20 Erb St. West, 11th Fl., Waterloo ON N2L 1T2 Canada
Tel: 519-888-6100; *Fax:* 519-888-7737
info@united-way-kw.org
www.uwaykw.org
Through collaboration, build on our community's resources & strengthen our capacity to improve the quality of life for all
Dave Fitzpatrick, Board Chair
Jan Varner, CEO

United Way of Lanark County
15 Bates Dr., Carleton Place ON K7C 4J8 Canada
Tel: 613-253-9074; *Fax:* 613-235-9075
unitedway@trytel.com
www.lanarkunitedway.com
Sarah Bridson, Executive Director

United Way of Leeds & Grenville
PO Box 576, 42 George St., Brockville ON K6V 5V7 Canada
Tel: 613-342-8889; *Fax:* 613-342-8850
unitedway@ripnet.com
www.uwlg.org
Judi Baril, Executive Director

United Way of Lethbridge & South Western Alberta
1277 - 3 Ave. South, Lethbridge AB T1J 0K3 Canada
Tel: 403-327-1700; *Fax:* 403-317-7940
uwaysw@telusplanet.net
www.lethbridgeunitedway.ca
To build a better community by organizing the capacity of people to care for one another

United Way of London & Middlesex
409 King St., London ON N6B 1S5 Canada
Tel: 519-438-1721; *Fax:* 519-438-9938
uwl@uwlondon.on.ca
www.uwlondon.on.ca
To exercise leadership in coordinating people & organizations to assist those in need in our community
Andrew Lockie, CEO

United Way of Milton
PO Box 212, 1 Chris Hadfield Way, Milton ON L9T 4N9 Canada
Tel: 905-875-2550; *Fax:* 905-875-2402
office@milton.unitedway.ca
www.miltonunitedway.ca
To act as a voluntary fundraising organization to serve the people of the Milton area, reaching out for & with the recognized charitable agencies to ensure human services that enhance the quality of life in our community
Anne Eadie, Executive Director

United Way of Morden & District Inc.
114 Nelson St., Morden MB R6M 1S2 Canada
Tel: 204-822-6992
mordendistrictuw@gmail.com
To serve as an umbrella group representing 17 charitable agencies in Morden & perform only one community-wide canvassing campaign on their behalf
Cindy Kolwalski, Chair

United Way of Niagara Falls & Greater Fort Erie
MacBain Community Ctr., 7150 Montrose Rd., Niagara Falls ON L2H 3N3 Canada
Tel: 905-354-9342; *Fax:* 905-354-2717
unitedway@mail.caninet.com
www.unitedwayniagara.org
Carol Stewart-Kirkby, Executive Director

United Way of North Okanagan Columbia Shuswap
3107 - 32 Ave., Vernon BC V1T 2M2 Canada
Tel: 250-549-1346; *Fax:* 250-549-1357
office@vernon.unitedway.ca
www.vernon.unitedway.ca
To promote a healthy, caring inclusive community; To strenghten our community's capacity to address social issues
Linda Yule, Executive Director

United Way of Oakville (UWO)
#200, 466 Speers Rd., Oakville ON L6K 3W9 Canada
Tel: 905-845-5571; *Fax:* 905-845-0166
info@uwoakville.org
www.uwoakville.org
Bringing people & resources together to strengthen our community
Barbara Burton, CEO
Tim Johnston, Chair

United Way of Oshawa-Whitby-Clarington-Brock & Scugog
345 Simcoe St. South, Oshawa ON L1H 4J2 Canada
Tel: 905-436-7377; *Fax:* 905-436-6414
mail@unitedwayowc.com
www.unitedwayowc.com
Cindy J. Murray, Executive Director
Robert Howard, Campaign Director

United Way of Oxford
#2, 65 Springbank Ave. North, Woodstock ON N4S 8V8 Canada
Tel: 519-539-3851; *Fax:* 519-539-3209
Toll-Free: 877-280-1391
info@unitedwayoxford.ca
www.unitedwayoxford.ca
To build the organized capacity of the community to care for one another
Kelly Gilson, Executive Director

United Way of Peel Region
#300, 5170 Dixie Rd., Mississauga ON L4W 1E3 Canada
Tel: 905-602-3650; *Fax:* 905-602-3651
TDD: 905-602-3653
jpereira@unitedwaypeel.org
www.unitedwaypeel.org
Social Media: twitter.com/Unitedwaypeel
United Way of Peel Region was established in 1967 and serves the communities of Mississauga, Brampton and Caledon, improving social conditions so that everyone can thrive. United Way provides a strong voice for social change that strengthens communities and improves lives.
Shelley White, Executive Director
Shirley Crocker, Director, Finance & Administration
Ted Fauteux, Director, Resource Development
Liz Leake, Director, Communications & Marketing
Anita Stellinga, Director, Community Investment

United Way of Perth County
32 Erie St., Stratford ON N5A 2M4 Canada
Tel: 519-271-7730; *Fax:* 519-273-9350
Toll-Free: 877-818-8867
info@unitedwayperth.on.ca
www.unitedwayperth.on.ca
To strengthen & support the ability of the people of our community to care for one another
Ellen Balmain, Executive Director
Shelley Groenestege, President

United Way of Peterborough & District
277 Stewart St., Peterborough ON K9J 3M8 Canada
Tel: 705-742-8839; *Fax:* 705-742-9186
office@uwpeterborough.ca
www.uwpeterborough.ca
To improve lives & build community by engaging individuals & mobilizing collective action; to provide resources, services & programs for community leadership
Len Lifchus, Executive Director

United Way of Pictou County
Victoria Plaza, PO Box 75, #1, 342 Stewart St., New Glasgow NS B2H 5E1 Canada
Tel: 902-755-1754; *Fax:* 902-755-0853
info@pictoucountyunitedway.ca
www.pictoucountyunitedway.ca
Social Media: www.facebook.com/group.php?gid=81512980650
To strengthen communities by facilitating programs & services that link people & resources; encourage participation; increase giving
Dodie Goodwin, Executive Director

United Way of Prince Edward Island / Centraide PEI
PO Box 247, 180 Kent St., Charlottetown PE C1A 7K4 Canada
Tel: 902-894-8202; *Fax:* 902-894-9643
Toll-Free: 877-902-4438
inquiries@peiunitedway.com
www.peiunitedway.com
To provide funds needed to meet community needs & build stronger communities
Clair F. Smith, Executive Director
Paul Chaulk, President

United Way of Quinte
Sears Unity Place, PO Box 815, 249 William St., Belleville ON K8N 5B5 Canada
Tel: 613-962-9531; *Fax:* 613-962-4165
office@belleville.unitedway.ca
www.unitedwayofquinte.ca
Social Media: www.facebook.com/group.php?gid=75482448853
To provide leadership in a collaborative endeavor with our member agencies & others to increase the capacity of our community to respond to human service needs

Julia Gosson, Executive Director

United Way of Regina
1440 Scarth St., Regina SK S4R 2E9 Canada
Tel: 306-757-5671; *Fax:* 306-522-7199
office@unitedwayregina.ca
www.unitedwayregina.ca
To improve lives & to build the community by engaging individuals & mobilizing collective action
Joanne Grant, CEO
Tracey Mann, Vice-President, Community Impact & Investments
Kristin Gushuliak, Campaign Manager

United Way of St Catharines & District
#3, 80 King St., Ground Fl., St Catharines ON L2R 7G1 Canada
Tel: 905-688-5050; *Fax:* 905-688-2997
office@stcatharines.unitedway.ca
www.unitedwaysc.ca
To increase the organized capacity of people to care for one another
Frances Hallworth, Executive Director

United Way of Sarnia-Lambton
PO Box 548, 420 East St. North, Sarnia ON N7T 6Y5 Canada
Tel: 519-336-5452; *Fax:* 519-383-6032
info@theunitedway.on.ca
www.theunitedway.on.ca
To generate resources enabling the community to respond to human care priorities in Sarnia-Lambton
Dave Brown, Executive Director
Paddy Roach, Manager, Resource Development
Pamela Bodkin, Director, Community Investment & Finance

United Way of Saskatoon & Area
100, 506 - 25 St. East, Saskatoon SK S7K 4A7 Canada
Tel: 306-975-7700; *Fax:* 306-244-0583
office@unitedwaysaskatoon.ca
www.unitedwaysaskatoon.ca
Sheri Benson, Executive Director

United Way of Sault Ste Marie
7A Oxford St., Sault Ste Marie ON P6B 1R7 Canada
Tel: 705-256-7476; *Fax:* 705-759-5899
uwssm@ssmunitedway.ca
www.saultstemarie.unitedway.ca
To improve lives & build community by engaging individuals & mobilizing collective action
Gary Vipond, Executive Director

United Way of Slave Lake Society
PO Box 1985, Slave Lake AB T0G 2A0 Canada
Tel: 780-849-3820

United Way of South Eastern Alberta
PO Box 783, Stn. M, #101, 928 Allowance Ave., Medicine Hat AB T1A 7G7 Canada
Tel: 403-526-5544; *Fax:* 403-526-5244
utdway@telus.net
www.utdway.ca
Cam Jacques, President of the Board
Holly Beauchamp-Stadnicki, Director, Fund Development

United Way of South Georgian Bay
PO Box 284, #9, 275 First St., Collingwood ON L9Y 3Z5 Canada
Tel: 705-444-1141; *Fax:* 705-444-0981
dkunitedwaysgb@gmail.com
www.unitedwaysgb.ca
To serve the south Georgian Bay area by promoting, supporting & facilitating the organized capacity of people to help one another
Debbie Kesheshian, Executive Director

United Way of Stormont, Dundas & Glengarry / Centraide de Stormont, Dundas & Glengarry
331 Water St. East, Cornwall ON K6H 1A5 Canada
Tel: 613-932-2051; *Fax:* 613-932-7534
info@unitedwaysdg.com
www.unitedwaysdg.com
To improve lives & build our community by working together
Claudette Blanchard, Campaign Clerk
Kevin Wilson, President
Karen Turchetto, Executive Director

United Way of the Alberta Capital Region
15132 Stony Plain Rd., Edmonton AB T5P 3Y3 Canada
Tel: 780-990-1000; *Fax:* 780-990-0203
united@myunitedway.ca
www.unitedthisistheway.ca
We bring people & resources together to build caring, vibrant communities
Dale Mulek, Chair

Robert Ascah, Vice-President, Government Relations, Research & Analysis
Anne Smith, Secretary/Treasurer

United Way of the Central Okanagan & South Okanagan/Similkameen
249 Lawrence Ave., Kelowna BC V1Y 6L2 Canada
Tel: 250-860-2356; *Fax:* 250-868-3206
Toll-Free: 888-636-2356
office@kelowna.unitedway.ca
www.kelownaunitedway.com
To increase the organized capacity of people in our community to care for one another
Harry Grossmith, CEO
Judy Doucette, Office Manager

United Way of the Fraser Valley (UWFV)
#201, 31667 South Fraser Way, Abbotsford BC V2T 1T8 Canada
Fax: 604-852-2316
Toll-Free: 888-251-7777
wayne@uwfv.bc.ca
www.uwfv.bc.ca
To promote the organized capacity of people to care for one another
Wayne Green, Executive Director

United Way of the Lower Mainland
4543 Canada Way, Burnaby BC V5G 4T4 Canada
Tel: 604-294-8929
info@uwlm.ca
www.uwlm.ca
Michael McKnight, President & CEO

United Way of Thompson Inc.
PO Box 202, Thompson MB R8N 1N1 Canada
Tel: 204-778-5564; *Fax:* 204-778-5564
uway@mts.net
To promote the organized capacity of people to care for one another
Bobbie Montean, Executive Director

United Way of Trail
792 Rossland Ave., Trail BC V1R 3T3 Canada
Tel: 250-364-0999; *Fax:* 250-364-1564
unitedw@telus.net
To raise funds which are allocated to 26 affiliated non-profit organizations
Trish Milne, Executive Director

United Way of Windsor-Essex County
#A1, 300 Giles Blvd. East, Windsor ON N9A 4C4 Canada
Tel: 519-258-0000; *Fax:* 519-258-2346
united@weareunited.com
www.weareunited.com
To promote & strengthen the organized capacity of people to care for one another
Sheila Wisdom, Executive Director

United Way of Winnipeg / Winnipeg Centraide
5 Donald St., 3rd Fl., Winnipeg MB R3L 2T4 Canada
Tel: 204-477-5360; *Fax:* 204-453-6198
uway@unitedwaywinnipeg.mb.ca
www.unitedwaywinnipeg.mb.ca
To support & strengthen the organized capacity of people to care for one another
Susan Lewis, President

United Way of York Region (UWYR)
#200, 80F Centurian Dr., Markham ON L3R 8C1 Canada
Tel: 905-474-9974; *Fax:* 905-474-0051
Toll-Free: 877-241-4516
vnorman@uwyr.on.ca
www.uwyr.on.ca
To improve the quality of life in the communities of York Region; to ascertain & address critical human needs by fostering innovative, responsible & inclusive partnerships of financial & other resources
Daniele Zanotti, CEO

United Way South Niagara (UWSN) / Centraide de Niagara Sud
Seaway Mall, 800 Niagara St., Welland ON L3C 5Z4 Canada
Tel: 905-735-0490; *Fax:* 905-735-5432
office@southniagara.unitedway.ca
www.unitedway.websweet.ca
To promote, develop & support the organized capacity of our community members to care for one another; to mobilize volunteer & financial resources in a common cause of caring
Bill Auchterlonie, Executive Director

United Way Toronto
26 Wellington St. East, 2nd Fl., Toronto ON M5E 1W9 Canada
Tel: 416-777-2001; *Fax:* 416-777-0962
TDD: 416-359-2083
www.unitedwaytoronto.com; www.uwgt.org
Social Media: www.facebook.com/group.php?gid=108587420188
To meet urgent human needs & improve social conditions by mobilizing the community's volunteer & financial resources in a common cause of caring
Frances Lankin, President & CEO
Alnasir Samji, Chair

United Way/Centraide (Central NB) Inc.
#400, 1133 Regent St., Fredericton NB E3B 3Z2 Canada
Tel: 506-459-7773; *Fax:* 506-451-1104
unitedwy@nbnet.nb.ca
www.unitedwaycentral.com
To be a leader in helping to create & sustain a caring & healthy community
Frank Russell, Executive Director

United Way/Centraide of the Upper Ottawa Valley Inc.
PO Box 727, 214 Church St., Pembroke ON K8A 6X9 Canada
Tel: 613-735-0436; *Fax:* 613-735-8362
Toll-Free: 888-592-2213
unitedw@nrtco.net; office@pembroke.unitedway.ca
www.pembroke.unitedway.ca
To identify & address the needs of our community by organizing the resources of community members to care for one another
Etienne Lantos, Chair
Sheila Bucholtz, Executive Director

United Way/Centraide Ottawa (UW/CO)
363 Coventry Rd., Ottawa ON K1K 2C5 Canada
Tel: 613-228-6700; *Fax:* 613-228-6730
info@unitedwayottawa.ca
www.unitedwayottawa.ca
Social Media: www.facebook.com/group.php?gid=35673670196
To bring people & resources together to build a strong, healthy, safe community for all; to build & support a network of high priority, results-oriented community services; to offer leadership in bringing the community together; to excel in fundraising; to invest resources & charitable funds in partnership with the community; to inform & engage community stakeholders
Michael Allen, President/CEO

United Way/Centraide Sudbury & District
#6E, 105 Elm St., Sudbury ON P3C 1T3 Canada
Tel: 705-560-3330; *Fax:* 705-560-3337
office@sudbury.unitedway.ca
www.unitedwaysudbury.com
To increase the organized capacity of people to care for one another through effective fundraising & allocation of these funds
Vicky Lafond, Executive Director

Vanier Institute of The Family (VIF) / Institut Vanier de la famille
94 Centrepointe Dr., Ottawa ON K2G 6B1 Canada
Tel: 613-228-8500; *Fax:* 613-228-8007
Toll-Free: 800-331-4937
webmaster@vifamily.ca
www.vifamily.ca
To create awareness of, & to provide leadership on the importance & strengths of families in Canada, & the challenges families face in all their diverse structures; information from the institute's research, consultation & policy development is conveyed through advocacy, education & communications vehicles to elected officials, policymakers, educators, the media, the public & Canadian families themselves
Clarence Lochhead, Executive Director
Verna Bruce, President

Victims of Violence Canadian Centre for Missing Children (VOV)
211 Pretoria Ave., Ottawa ON K1S 1X1 Canada
Tel: 613-233-0052; *Fax:* 613-233-2712
Toll-Free: 888-606-0000
vofv@victimsofviolence.on.ca
www.victimsofviolence.on.ca
To help crime victims regain control of their lives by reducing fear & trauma; to prevent future victimization through crime prevention information; to strengthen local efforts to assist crime victims & witnesses
Gary Rosenfeldt, Executive Director

Volunteer Canada / Bénévoles Canada
353 Dalhousie St., Ottawa ON K1N 7G1 Canada
Tel: 613-231-4371; *Fax:* 613-231-6725
Toll-Free: 800-670-0401
info@volunteer.ca
www.volunteer.ca
To support volunteerism & civic participation through special projects & programs
Ruth MacKenzie, President

Volunteer Grandparents (VIP)
#203, 2101 Holdom Ave., Burnaby BC V5B 0A4 Canada
Tel: 604-736-8271; *Fax:* 604-294-6814
info@volunteergrandparents.ca
www.volunteergrandparents.ca
To support & encourage multigenerational relationships & the concept of extended family by matching screened volunteers (50+) with families with children between the age of 3-14
Stephen Sjoberg, President

The War Amputations of Canada / Les Amputés de guerre du Canada
2827 Riverside Dr., Ottawa ON K1V 0C4 Canada
Tel: 613-731-3821; *Fax:* 613-731-3234
Toll-Free: 800-465-2677
communications@waramps.ca
www.waramps.ca
To provide a wide range of assistance to all Canadian war amputees & child amputees; promotes the advancement of prosthetics & prosthetic research through grants to facilities undertaking research in field of prosthetics
H. Clifford Chadderton, CEO
Laurie Rasberry, National President
Claire Roy, Director of Administration

Weyburn & District United Way
PO Box 608, Weyburn SK S4H 2K7 Canada
Tel: 306-842-7880
weyburn.unitedway@accesscomm.ca
www.weyburnunitedway.com
Gary Erickson, President

Winkler & District United Way
PO Box 1528, Winkler MB R6W 4B4 Canada
Tel: 204-829-3843
ron@wiband.ca
Karen Schellenberg, President

Yorkton & District United Way Inc.
PO Box 44, Yorkton SK S3N 2V6 Canada
Tel: 306-783-2582; *Fax:* 306-783-2502
bandgofyorkton@sasktel.net
To unite & facilitate community fundraising on behalf of our membership of local, charitable organizations
Brian Pohorelic, Chair
Lisa Washington, Secretary

Sports

Abbotsford Female Hockey Association (AFHA)
2167 Essex Dr., Abbotsford BC V2S 7R8 Canada
info@abbotsfordfemalehockey.com
www.abbotsfordfemalehockey.com
The Abbotsford Female Hockey Association seeks to provide an opportunity for females of all ages and all skill levels to play hockey in Abbotsford in an all female league.
Jerry Ward, President

Alberta 5 Pin Bowlers' Association (A5-PBA)
432 - 14 St. South, Lethbridge AB T1J 2X7 Canada
Tel: 403-320-2695; *Fax:* 403-320-2676
Toll-Free: 800-762-3075
a5pba@telusplanet.net
www.alberta5pin.com

Alberta Amateur Speed Skating Association (AASSA)
2500 University Dr. NW, Calgary AB T2N 1N4 Canada
Tel: 403-220-7911; *Fax:* 403-220-9226
aassa@ucalgary.ca
www.albertaspeedskating.ca
Wendy Walker, Office Administrator

Alberta Bicycle Association (ABA)
Percy Page Centre, 11759 Groat Rd., Edmonton AB T5M 3K6 Canada
Tel: 780-427-6352; *Fax:* 780-427-6438
Toll-Free: 877-646-2453
info@albertabicycle.ab.ca
www.albertabicycle.ab.ca
To promote all aspects of cycling in Alberta

Alberta Bobsleigh Association
Bob Niven Training Centre, #205, 88 Canada Olympic Rd. SW, Calgary AB T3B 5R5 Canada
Tel: 403-297-2721; *Fax:* 403-286-7213
slide@albertabobsleigh.com
www.albertabobsleigh.com
Social Media: facebook.com/group.php?gid=68082934483&ref=search
To develop a broad interest in bobsleigh in Alberta; to provide opportunities for all Albertans to participate in bobsleigh; to provide opportunities for Albertans to progress to national & international levels
Tim Dyrgas, President

Alberta Broomball Association
Percy Page Centre, 11759 Groat Rd., Edmonton AB T5M 3K6 Canada
Tel: 780-459-7668; *Fax:* 780-460-0527
neigel@telus.net
Greg Mastervick, President

Alberta Curling Federation (ACF)
11759 Groat Rd., Edmonton AB T5M 3K6 Canada
Tel: 780-643-0809; *Fax:* 780-427-8103
jim@albertacurling.ab.ca
www.albertacurling.ab.ca

Alberta Deaf Sports Association (ADSA)
11404 - 142 St., Edmonton AB T5M 1V1 Canada
adsa@shaw.ca
adsa.deafalberta.org
To coordinate sport & recreation activities for the deaf in Alberta; to promote competition at the local, provincial, regional & national levels; to select Alberta athletes to compete in national championships for the World Games of the Deaf

Alberta Diving
426 Reeves Cres., Edmonton AB T6R 2A4 Canada
Tel: 780-988-5571; *Fax:* 780-988-7753
www.albertadiving.ca
To act as the governing body in Alberta for the Olympic sport of amateur diving; to strive for personal & organizational excellence in all areas of diving

Alberta Equestrian Federation (AEF)
#100, 251 Midpark Blvd. SE, Calgary AB T2X 1S3 Canada
Tel: 403-253-4411; *Fax:* 403-252-5260
Toll-Free: 877-463-6233
www.albertaequestrian.com
Dixie Crowson, President
Sonia Dantu, Executive Director

Alberta Golf Association (AGA)
#22, 11410 - 27 St. SE, Calgary AB T2Z 3R6 Canada
Tel: 403-236-4616; *Fax:* 403-236-2915
Toll-Free: 888-414-4849
info@albertagolf.org
www.albertagolf.org
To fulfill the needs of members

Alberta Luge Association (ALA)
Rm 201, BNTC, 88 Canada Olympic Rd. SW, Calgary AB T3B 5R5 Canada
Tel: 403-202-6570; *Fax:* 403-247-5497
admin@albertaluge.com
www.albertaluge.com
To ensure the continued successful growth of the sport of luge in Alberta through the development of its athletes, coaches & volunteers at the recreational & elite levels
Darryl Gunn, President

Alberta Northern Lights Wheelchair Basketball Society
6788 - 99th St., Edmonton AB T6E 5B8 Canada
Tel: 780-433-4310; *Fax:* 780-431-1764
Toll-Free: 800-465-2992
info@albertanorthernlights.com
www.albertanorthernlights.com
To develop health, fitness, & sport for men, women, & children with physical disabilities

Alberta Rugby Football Union
Percy Page Centre, 11759 Groat Rd., Edmonton AB T5M 3K6 Canada
Tel: 780-415-1773; *Fax:* 780-422-5558
Toll-Free: 866-784-2922
rugbyab@telus.net
www.rugbyalberta.com

Alberta Schools' Athletic Association (ASAA)
Percy Page Centre, 11759 Groat Rd., Edmonton AB T5M 3K6 Canada
Tel: 780-427-8182; *Fax:* 780-415-1833
info@asaa.ca
www.asaa.ca
To provide leadership in the promotion of high school sport; to regulate sports competition & promote the belief that education includes development of the whole person
John F. Paton, Executive Director
Dave M. Jones, President

Alberta Soaring Council
PO Box 13, Black Diamond AB T0L 0H0 Canada
Tel: 403-933-4968
asc@platinum.ca
www.soaring.ab.ca
To promote soaring sports provincially in all aspects, & plan & support local & provincial events & national competitions

Alberta Soccer Association
Commonwealth Stadium, 1100 Stadium Rd., Edmonton AB T5H 4E2 Canada
Tel: 780-474-2200; *Fax:* 780-474-6300
Toll-Free: 866-250-2200
www.albertasoccer.com
To govern & promote the sport of soccer in Alberta

Alberta Sports & Recreation Association for the Blind (ASRAB)
#007, 15 Colonel Baker Pl. NE, Calgary AB T2E 4Z3 Canada
Tel: 403-262-5332; *Fax:* 403-265-7221
Toll-Free: 888-882-7722
marilyn@asrab.ab.ca
www.asrab.ab.ca
To provide recreation & sports opportunities for Albertans who are blind & partially sighted

Alberta Tennis Association (ATA)
11759 Groat Rd., Edmonton AB T5M 3K6 Canada
Tel: 780-415-1661; *Fax:* 780-415-1693
info@tennisalberta.com
www.tennisalberta.com
To facilitate participation, development & visibility of tennis throughout Alberta

Alberta Volleyball Association (AVA)
Percy Page Centre, 11759 Groat Rd., Edmonton AB T5M 3K6 Canada
Tel: 780-415-1703; *Fax:* 780-415-1700
info@albertavolleyball.com
www.albertavolleyball.com
To promote volleyball in Alberta; to provide competitive opportunities for members

Alberta Water Polo Association (AWPA)
PO Box 54, 2225 Macleod Trail South, Edmonton AB T2G 5B6 Canada
Tel: 403-475-6747; *Fax:* 403-475-6748
office@albertawaterpolo.ca
www.albertawaterpolo.ca
To provide a safe and positive environment for the on-going development and growth of water polo in Alberta for the recreational to the elite athlete.

Alpine Canada ALPIN
#153, 401 - 9th Ave. SW, Calgary AB T2P 3C5 Canada
Tel: 403-777-3200; *Fax:* 403-777-3213
info@canski.org
www.canski.org
The ACA is the governing body for ski racing in Canada. Founded in 1920 and accounting for close to 200,000 supporting members, ACA represents coaches, officials, supporters and athletes, including elite racers of the Canadian Alpine Ski Team and the Canadian Disabled Alpine Ski Team.
Gary Allan, President
Jennifer Duggan, Manager, National Services

The Alpine Club of Canada (ACC) / Club alpin du Canada
PO Box 8040, Indian Flats Rd., Canmore AB T1W 2T8 Canada
Tel: 403-678-3200; *Fax:* 403-678-3224
info@alpineclubofcanada.ca
www.alpineclubofcanada.ca
To encourage & promote mountaineering & mountain crafts; to educate Canadians in the appreciation of mountain heritage; to explore alpine & glacial regions primarily in Canada; to preserve the natural beauty of mountains & their fauna & flora; to promote mountain art & literature; to disseminate scientific & educational knowledge concerning mountains & mountaineering through meetings & publications; to conduct summer & ski mountaineering camps

American & Canadian Underwater Certification Inc.
379 West St., Brantford ON N3R 3V9 Canada
Tel: 519-750-5767; *Fax:* 519-750-5769
acuchq@acuc.ca
www.acuc.es/
To supply quality training for sport scuba divers & instructors; to teach the highest standards in safety, sport & marine conservation

Aquatic Federation of Canada / Fédération canadienne des sports aquatiques
4 Calgary St., St. John's NL A1A 3W2 Canada
Tel: 709-753-2398; *Fax:* 709-753-2398
whogan@nl.rogers.com
www.swimming.ca/AFC.aspx

Arctic Winter Games International Committee (AWGIC)
#400, 5201 - 50 Ave., Yellowknife NT X1A 3S9 Canada
Tel: 867-873-7245; *Fax:* 867-920-6467
www.awg.ca
To provide common ground for developing Northern athletes; to promote cultural & social exchanges among Northern regions of the continent

Association chasse & pêche de Chibougamau
CP 171, Chibougamau QC G8P 2K6 Canada
Tél: 418-748-2021
info@acpcchibougamau.com
www.acpcchibougamau.com
Favoriser et développer parmi les membres l'esprit sportif en préservant la conservation des richesses naturelles
Serge Picard, Président

Association des plongeurs de Chibougamau
535, 4e Rue, Chibougamau QC G8P 1S4 Canada
Tél: 418-748-7056
André Naud

Association sportive des aveugles du Québec inc. (ASAQ)
CP 1000, Succ. M, 4545, av Pierre-de Coubertin, Montréal QC H1V 3R2 Canada
Tél: 514-252-3178; *Téléc:* 514-254-1303
infoasaq@sportsaveugles.qc.ca
www.sportsaveugles.qc.ca
Promouvoir la pratique du sport amateur auprès des personnes handicapées de la vue et de favoriser ainsi leur intégration

Association sportive des sourds du Québec inc. (ASSQ)
CP 1000, Succ. M, 4545, av Pierre-de Coubertin, Montréal QC H1V 3R2 Canada
Tél: 514-252-3069; *Téléc:* 514-252-3049
info@assq.org
www.assq.org
Promouvoir le sport, les loisirs et l'activité physique chez les personnes sourdes et malentendantes du Québec

Athabasca Landing Pool Association (ALPA)
4705 - 48th Ave., Athabasca AB T9S 1R3 Canada
Tel: 780-675-5656; *Fax:* 780-675-4700
athpool@telusplanet.net
To provide the facilities & services, for all members of the community, to promote the education, enjoyment, health, safety, fitness & quality of aquatics
Jaymie Mullin, Manager
Alan Fisher, President

Athletics Canada / Athlétisme Canada
#B1-110, 2445 St-Laurent Blvd, Ottawa ON K1G 6C3 Canada
Tel: 613-260-5580; *Fax:* 613-260-0341
athcan@athletics.ca
www.athletics.ca
Social Media: twitter.com/athleticscanada
To promote & encourage participation via competitions from the grass roots level through to the very highest level of proficiency; to assist coaches, officials & executives in fulfilling their goals through courses, conferences & clinics; to provide regular communication lines with members; to continually review & update technical programs; to assist in the research & investigation of potential new facilities; to engender more public awareness, interest & acceptance of the sport of track & field

Atlantic Canada Trail Riding Association
Sylvia Gillies, #344 Route 875, Belleisle Creek NB E5P 1C8 Canada
To promote safe horsemanship & friendly competition in the long distance trail competition
Roy Drinnan, Chair

Badminton Alberta
c/o Alberta Badminton Centre, 60 Patterson Blvd. SW, Calgary AB T3H 2E1 Canada
Tel: 403-297-2722; *Fax:* 403-297-2706
Toll-Free: 888-397-2722
info@badmintonalberta.ca
www.badmintonalberta.ca
To promote the sport of badminton

Badminton BC
#252, 3820 Cessna Dr., Richmond BC V7B 0A2 Canada
Tel: 604-333-3595; *Fax:* 604-333-3594
Toll-Free: 800-483-2473
info@badmintonbc.com
www.badmintonbc.com
To provide leadership to develop & promote badminton in BC by increasing the membership base, facilitating a higher standard of participation through competitive & development opportunities for players, coaches, officials & volunteers
Brock Turner, Executive Director
Ken Thiesen, Operations & Programs Manager

Badminton Canada
#99, 2201 Riverside Dr., Ottawa ON K1H 8K9 Canada
Tel: 613-569-2424; *Fax:* 613-569-3232
badminton@badminton.ca
www.badminton.ca
To provide centralized support, &/or leadership in furthering member association objectives, act as custodian of the laws of badminton & to foster outstanding player development; to act for its members in helping to assure national & international class competition for Canada's outstanding badminton players, & to establish Canada as a leading participant in international badminton

Badminton New Nouveau Brunswick
PO Box 355, Stn. Main, Bathurst NB E2A 3Z3 Canada
Tel: 506-783-4654
badminton@bnnb.ca
www.bnnb.ca
Badminton NB is a registered, non-profit organization which organizes junior and senior badminton tournaments.

Badminton Newfoundland & Labrador Inc.
PO Box 21248, #213, 810 East White Hills Rd., St. John's NL A1A 5B2 Canada
Tel: 709-576-7606; *Fax:* 709-576-7493
badminton@sportnl.ca
www.sportnl.ca/badminton/index.html
Social Media: facebook.com/group.php?gid=3468211930
BNL is the non-profit, volunteer, sports governing body for badminton in Newfoundland and Labrador.

Badminton Québec
4940, rue Hochelaga est, Montréal QC H1V 1E7 Canada
Tél: 514-252-3066; *Téléc:* 514-252-3175
badmintonquebec@videotron.ca
www.badmintonquebec.com
Promouvoir et développer le sport sur tout le territoire québécois en regroupant tous ses membres, les personnes et associations intéressées au rayonnement de notre discipline

Baseball Alberta (BA)
Percy Page Centre, 11759 Groat Rd., Edmonton AB T5M 3K6 Canada
Tel: 780-427-8943; *Fax:* 780-427-9032
bradwolansky@baseballalberta.com
www.baseballalberta.com
Social Media:
www.facebook.com/pages/Baseball-Alberta/130042917037092?ref=ts
To offer the opportunity for youth from 6-60 to participate in the great game of baseball, both recreational & competitive, in all areas of the province, large or small & by so doing, make baseball the premier sport in the Province of Alberta

Baseball BC
#310, 15225 - 104th Ave., Surrey BC V3R 6Y8 Canada
Tel: 604-586-3310; *Fax:* 604-586-3311
info@baseball.bc.ca
www.baseball.bc.ca
Through its programs and leadership, Baseball B.C. in cooperation with its affiliates, supports the development of baseball and aspirations of its members, by offering oppourtunities and setting procedures, standards and policies.

Baseball Canada / Fédération canadienne de baseball amateur
2212 Gladwin Cres., #A7, Ottawa ON K1B 5N1 Canada
Tel: 613-748-5606; *Fax:* 613-748-5767
info@baseball.ca
www.baseball.ca

To promote the development of baseball across Canada through support of provincial organizations & design of programs, including athletes, coaches, events, umpires & partner groups
Jim Baba, Director General
Ray Carter, President

Baseball New Brunswick (BNB) / Baseball Nouveau-Brunswick
#13, 900 Hanwell Rd., Fredericton NB E3B 6A2 Canada
Tel: 506-451-1329; *Fax:* 506-451-1325
baseballnb2003@nb.aibn.com
www.baseballnb.ca

Baseball Nova Scotia (BNS)
5516 Spring Garden Rd., 4th Fl., Halifax NS B3J 1J Canada
Tel: 902-425-5450; *Fax:* 902-425-5606
www.baseballnovascotia.com
To represent baseball teams & leagues under the jurisdiction of BaseballCanada.
Brad Lawlor, Executive Director

Baseball Ontario
#3, 131 Sheldon Dr., Cambridge ON N1R 6S2 Canada
Tel: 519-740-3900; *Fax:* 519-740-6311
baseball@baseballontario.com
www.baseballontario.com

Basketball Alberta
Percy Page Centre, 11759 Groat Rd., Edmonton AB T5M 3K6 Canada
Tel: 780-427-9044; *Fax:* 780-427-9124
bballab@basketballalbert.ab.ca
www.basketballalberta.ca
Vision: "To be premier facilitators of participation, development, and excellence in basketball". Mission: "To champion the sport of basketball as a game for life by inspiring unity facilitating development and delivering superior value".

Basketball BC
#310, 7155 Kingsway, Burnaby BC V5E 2V1 Canada
Tel: 604-718-7852; *Fax:* 604-525-7762
hoopsbc@basketball.bc.ca
www.basketball.bc.ca
To be British Columbia's leading resource for basketball; To build the game of basketball

Basketball Manitoba
200 Main St., Winnipeg MB R3C 4M2 Canada
Tel: 204-925-5775; *Fax:* 204-925-5929
Toll-Free: 800-282-8069
info@basketball.mb.ca
www.basketball.mb.ca
To operate as the provincial sport governing body for basketball in Manitoba; To ensure all Manitobians have access to the programs run by the association & that the game of basketball is enjoyed by as many people as possible

Basketball New Brunswick (BNB) / Basketball Nouveau-Brunswick
#13, 900 Hanwell Rd., Fredericton NB E2E 6A2 Canada
Tel: 506-849-4667; *Fax:* 506-451-1325
info@basketball.nb.ca
www.basketball.nb.ca
To promote, develop & encourage sport & recreation aspects of basketball in New Brunswick; to assist in establishment of basketball clubs throughout New Brunswick; to liaise with government & private agencies interested in promoting & supporting basketball

Basketball Nova Scotia
5516 Spring Garden Rd., 4th Fl., Halifax NS B3J 1G6 Canada
Tel: 902-425-5450; *Fax:* 902-425-5606
bnsadmin@basketball.ns.ca
www.basketball.ns.ca
To promote & encourage the game of basketball throughout the province

Basketball NWT
info@bnwt.ca
www.bnwt.ca
The Association encourages maximum participation in basketball, develops athletes, & provides opportunities for cultural & social interchange among all involved in the sport. Website is under development, please check back regularly for updates!

Basketball PEI
PO Box 302, 40 Enman Cres., Charlottetown PE C1A 7K7 Canada
Tel: 902-368-4208; *Fax:* 902-368-4208
Toll-Free: 800-247-6712
info@basketballpei.ca
www.basketballpei.ca
To develop basketball in the province of Prince Edward Island in a fun environment

Basketball Saskatchewan Inc. (BSI)
2205 Victoria Ave., Regina SK S4P 0S4 Canada
Tel: 306-780-9264; *Fax:* 306-525-4009
mbarr@basketballsask.com
www.basketballsask.com
To support & improve basketball opportunities in Saskatchewan

Basketball Yukon
4061, 4th Ave., Whitehorse YT Y1A 1H1 Canada
Tel: 867-668-3802
bballyukon@klondiker.com
www.basketballyukon.ca
To be leading a unified basketball community in the territory that is delivering quality programs and services from entry level to national competitions.
Tim Brady, President
Linda Sutherland, Administrative Assistant

Biathlon Alberta
Bob Niven Training Centre, #100, 88 Canada Olympic Rd., Calgary AB T3B 5R5
Tel: 403-202-6548; *Fax:* 403-297-2702
info@biathlon.ca
www.biathlon.ca
To promote, develop & maintain biathlon in Alberta
Ken Davies, President
Andy Holmwood, Executive Director

Biathlon Canada
#111, 2197 Riverside Dr., Ottawa ON K1H 7X3 Canada
Tel: 613-748-5608; *Fax:* 613-748-5762
jthomson@biathloncanada.ca
www.biathloncanada.ca
To achieve consistent international podium performance by leading, promoting, developing & governing biathlon in Canada to the highest standard of excellence

Biathlon Yukon
PO Box 31673, Whitehorse YT Y1A 6L3 Canada
www.sportyukon.com/membership/?member=11
To enhance opportunities for all Yukon persons in their pursuit of excellence & in their enjoyment of participation in biathlon
Keith Clarke, President
Katrina Brogden, Secretary

Bicycle Newfoundland & Labrador
PO Box 2127, Stn. C, St. John's NL A1C 5R6 Canada
Tel: 709-738-2597
admin@bnl.nf.ca
www.bnl.nf.ca
Social Media:
facebook.com/pages/Bicycle-NL/144379652267580
Leon Organ, President

Bicycle Nova Scotia (BNS)
5516 Spring Garden Rd., 4th Fl., Halifax NS B3J 1G6 Canada
Tel: 902-425-5454; *Fax:* 902-425-5606
staff@bicycle.ns.ca
www.bicycle.ns.ca
The coordinating body for sport, recreational & transportation cycling in Nova Scotia

Bicycle Trade Association of Canada (BTAC) / Association canadienne de l'industrie du vélo (ACIV)
17 Main St. North, Newmarket ON L3Y 3Z6 Canada
Tel: 905-853-5031; *Fax:* 905-853-7632
Toll-Free: 866-528-2822
info@btac.org
www.btac.org
Janet O'Connell, Executive Director

Blind Sports Nova Scotia
c/o CNIB, 6136 Almon St., Halifax NS B3K 1T8 Canada
Tel: 902-453-1480; *Fax:* 902-454-6570
info@blindsportsnovascotia.ca
www.blindsportsnovascotia.ca
Blind Sports Nova Scotia is an organization that presents sport and recreational activities for visually impaired athletes in Nova Scotia.

Bobsleigh Canada Skeleton
140 Canada Olympic Rd. SW, Calgary AB T3B 5R5 Canada
Tel: 403-247-5950; *Fax:* 403-247-5951
ddreher@bobsleigh.ca
www.bobsleigh.ca/
To strive to create Olympic & world champions

Bowling Federation of Canada / Fédération des quilles du Canada
c/o Administrator, #206, 720 Belfast Rd., Ottawa ON K1G 0Z5 Canada
Tel: 613-744-5090; *Fax:* 613-744-2217
info@canadabowls.ca
www.canadabowls.ca
To promote & foster the sport of bowling in Canada; To promote among the recognized national organizations in Canada, sportmanship, good fellowhsip, & the continued interest in the future development of bowling throughout Canada

Bowling Federation of Saskatchewan
#101, 1805 - 8th Ave., Regina SK S4R 1E8 Canada
Tel: 306-780-9412; *Fax:* 306-780-9455
bowling@sasktel.net
saskbowl.com
Working together through cooperation & harmonization to access & allocate funding for our members programs & services in order to enhance the sport of bowling
Rhonda Sereda, Executive Director

Bowling Proprietors' Association of BC
#209, 332 Columbia St., New Westminster BC V3L 1A6 Canada
Tel: 604-522-2990; *Fax:* 604-522-2055
bowl4fun@bowlbc.com
www.bowlbc.com
Ken Clarke, President

Bowling Proprietors' Association of Canada (BPAC)
#10A, 250 Shields Ct., Markham ON L3R 9W7 Canada
Tel: 905-479-1560; *Fax:* 905-479-8613
info@bowlcanada.ca
www.bowlcanada.ca
The aim of this association is to improve general conditions in the bowling industry, to promote to the general public the benefits of bowling, to create a better relationship between the many bowling establishments across Canada and to encourage any and all practices which are in the best interests of the game.

Bowling Proprietors' Association of Ontario (BPAO)
#202, 500 Alden Rd., Markham ON L3R 5H5 Canada
Tel: 905-940-8200
bpao@bpao.ca
www.bpao.ca
To improve conditions in bowling industry; to protect members from unreasonable legislation; to bring attention to the pleasures of bowling

Bowls BC (BBC)
#148, 5525 West Blvd., Vancouver BC V6M 3W6 Canada
www.bowlsbc.ca
To foster & promote the game of Lawn Bowls; to make the game available to all in accordance within the Canadian Human Rights Code within the Province of British Columbia
Keith Terlson, President
Pat Cutt, Vice-President
Marjorie Mitchell, Treasurer
Juanita Tucker, Secretary

Bowls Canada Boulingrin (BCB)
#207, 720 Belfast Rd., Ottawa ON K1G 0Z5 Canada
Tel: 613-244-0021; *Fax:* 613-244-0041
Toll-Free: 800-567-2695
office@bowlscanada.com
www.bowlscanada.com
To promote, foster & safeguard the sport of indoor & outdoor lawn bowling in all its forms in Canada, through events & programs

Bowls Manitoba
200 Main St., Winnipeg MB R3C 4M2 Canada
Tel: 204-925-5694; *Fax:* 204-925-5703
bowls@shawbiz.ca
www.bowls.mb.ca
To promote lawnbowling in the province of Manitoba; To host various lawnbowling events
Cathy Derewianchuk, Executive Director

Bowls Saskatchewan Inc.
#102, 1860 Lorne St., Regina SK S4P 2L7 Canada
Tel: 306-780-9426; *Fax:* 306-781-6021
bowlsask@sasktel.net
www.bowls.sk.ca
To promote & expand the sport of bowls, which contains programs that accommodate/challenge all those interested, with the result that bowls becomes a high profile sport
Karen Swanson, Executive Director
Jean Roney, President

Boxing Alberta
Percy Page Centre, 11759 Groat Rd., Edmonton AB T5M 3K6 Canada
Tel: 780-427-6515; *Fax:* 780-427-1205
www.boxingalberta.com
Jim Titley, President
Dennis Belair, Executive Director

Boxing BC Association
250 Willingdon Ave., Burnaby BC V5C 5E9 Canada
Tel: 604-291-7921; *Fax:* 604-291-7927
boxingbc@telus.net
www.boxing.bc.ca
To provide all citizens of British Columbia access to & participation in the opportunities, programs & activities
Scotty Jackson, President

Boxing Ontario
#202, 3 Concorde Gate, Toronto ON M3C 3N7 Canada
Tel: 416-426-7250; *Fax:* 416-426-7367
info@boxingontario.com
www.boxingontario.com
This is the only governing body for amateur boxing in Ontario. It aims to organize, promote, develop interest and participation in the sport in the province.
Tom Hennessey, President
Matt Kennedy, Executive Director

Boxing Saskatchewan
PO Box 4711, Regina SK S4P 3Y3 Canada
Tel: 306-525-6678; *Fax:* 306-569-3454
skboxing@accesscomm.ca
www.boxingsask.com
This is a non-profit society that enforces rules and regulations governing amateur boxing in the province. It also promotes the formation of new clubs.
Frank Fiacco, President
Graham Craig, Executive Director

British Columbia Amateur Hockey Association (BCAHA) / Association de hockey amateur de la Colombie-Britannique
6671 Oldfield Rd., Saanichton BC V8M 2A1 Canada
Tel: 250-652-2978; *Fax:* 250-652-4536
info@bchockey.net
www.bchockey.net
To foster, improve & perpetuate amateur hockey in BC.

British Columbia Ball Hockey Association (BCBHA)
1302 Cliveden Ave., Delta BC V3M 6G4 Canada
Tel: 604-812-6720; *Fax:* 604-588-7760
www.bcbha.com
To govern the sport of ball hockey in British Columbia; to establish bylaws & regulations, in order to ensure a safe & fun activity; to uphold the rules& regulations of ball hockey
Wade Traversy, President
Kris Little, Vice-President
Rob Moxness, Secretary
Roger Sidhu, Treasurer

British Columbia Blind Sports & Recreation Association (BCBSRA)
#330, 5055 Joyce St., Vancouver BC V5R 6B2 Canada
Tel: 604-325-8638; *Fax:* 604-325-1638
info@bcblindsports.bc.ca
www.bcblindsports.bc.ca
To provide sports, physical recreation & fitness activities & programs for persons of all ages who are blind/visually impaired; to alleviate isolating & inhibiting effects of blindness/visual impairment; to improve physical capabilities & self-image of blind/visually impaired individuals by providing opportunities for them to learn; to encourage, promote & maintain interest in & cooperation with all such amateur sports & recreation organizations. Toll free number 0-604-325-8638, after the tone enter 7617.

British Columbia Broomball Society
c/o 5356 Lochside Dr., Victoria BC V8Y 2G7 Canada
www.bcbroomball.ca
Rick Przybysz, President
Bruce MacRae, Sec.-Treas.

British Columbia Competitive Trail Riders Association (BCCTRA)
c/o 2980 Giovando Road, Nanaimo BC V9X 1K5 Canada
Tel: 250-245-4405
nicole.vaugeois@viu.ca
www.bcctra.ca
To promote & improve the rapidly growing sport of competitive trail riding in BC
Nicole Vagueois, Sec.-Treas.

British Columbia Deaf Sports Federation (BCDSF)
#254, 3820 Cessna Dr., Richmond BC V7B 0A2 Canada
Fax: 604-738-7175
TDD: 604-333-3606
bcdeafsports@telus.net
www.bcdeafsports.bc.ca
To provide & support the development of competitive sporting events in BC among deaf & hard of hearing athletes; to encourage training for deaf coaches; to provide financial assistance to deaf athletes to participate in local, provincial & national competitions

British Columbia Diving
2630 Dogwood Dr., Surrey BC V4A 3K5 Canada
Tel: 604-541-9332; *Fax:* 604-541-9303
info@bcdiving.ca
www.bcdiving.ca

British Columbia Golf Association (BCGA)
#2105, 21000 Westminster Hwy., Richmond BC V6V 2S9 Canada
Tel: 604-279-2580; *Fax:* 604-207-9535
Toll-Free: 888-833-2242
info@bcga.org
www.bcga.org
To promote interest in golf in BC; to protect the mutual interests of member clubs & their members; to establish & enforce uniformity in the rules of the game; to establish, control, & conduct amateur championships, matches & competitions; to interest & develop junior golfers; to select all teams to represent BC in national & international matches.

British Columbia Ringette Association (BCRA) / Association de ringuette de Colombie-Britannique
#319, 789 West Pender St., Vancouver BC V6C 1H2 Canada
Fax: 604-629-0876
www.bcringette.org

British Columbia Rugby Union
#203, 210 West Broadway, Vancouver BC V5Y 3W2 Canada
Tel: 604-737-3065; *Fax:* 604-737-3916
bcrugby@telus.net
www.bcrugby.com
To promote, sustain & manage the game of rugby in BC in a manner that will ensure wide participation & the continuous development in a safe & responsible manner

British Columbia School Sports (BCSS)
#100, 4585 Canada Way, Burnaby BC V5G 4L6 Canada
Tel: 604-737-3066; *Fax:* 604-737-9844
info@bcschoolsports.ca
www.bcschoolsports.ca
To encourage student participation in extra-curricular athletics, assist schools in the development & delivery of their programs & provide governance for interschool competition
Sue Keenan, Executive Director
Raj Puri, President

British Columbia Soccer Association
#510, 375 Water St., Vancouver BC V6B 5C6 Canada
Tel: 604-299-6401; *Fax:* 604-299-9610
bcsoccer@gmail.com
www.bcsoccer.net

British Columbia Speed Skating Association
PO Box 2023, Stn. A, Abbotsford BC V2T 3T8 Canada
Tel: 604-746-4349; *Fax:* 604-746-4549
lorna@speed-skating.bc.ca
www.speed-skating.bc.ca
The organization wishes to foster the growth and development of Speed Skating in B.C. by providing quality services and support programs to all members in their pursuit of a healthy lifestyle while encouraging challenges and promoting excellence.
Ted Houghton, Executive Director

British Columbia Water Polo Association (BCWPA)
#227, 3820 Cessna Dr., Richmond BC V7B 0A2 Canada
Tel: 604-333-3480; *Fax:* 604-333-3450
bcwaterpolo@telus.net
www.bcwaterpolo.com
To develop water polo in BC; to train provincal team & national team athletes

British Columbia Wrestling Association (BCWA)
#335, 2416 Main St., Vancouver BC V5T 3E2 Canada
Tel: 604-737-3092; *Fax:* 604-737-6043
info@bcwrestling.com
www.bcwrestling.com
To promote & enhance the well-being of young people through their participation in wrestling

Broomball Newfoundland & Labrador
734 Birch St., Labrador City NL A2V 1C8 Canada
Tel: 709-944-5780; *Fax:* 709-944-5780
clarkep@nf.sympatico.ca
Harold Clarke, President

Calgary Boxing & Wrestling Commission (CBWC)
PO Box 2100, Stn. M #63, Calgary AB T2P 2M5 Canada
Tel: 403-268-5367
The CBWC acts as a regulation body for professional boxing & wrestling within the City of Calgary.

Canada Basketball
#11, 1 Westside Dr., Toronto ON M9C 1B2 Canada
Tel: 416-614-8037; *Fax:* 416-614-9570
info@basketball.ca
www.basketball.ca
Basketball Canada is the national sport governing body for amateur basketball in Canada; to develop the sport of basketball domestically & to contribute to the development of basketball internationally
Wayne Parrish, Executive Director & CEO

Canada Games Council (CGC) / Conseil des jeux du Canada
#701, 2197 Riverside Dr., Ottawa ON K1H 7X3 Canada
Tel: 613-526-2320; *Fax:* 613-526-4068
canada.games@canadagames.ca
www.canadagames.ca
To govern as well as to promote the Canada Games - a major national multi-sport event for prospective high performance athletes in all provinces & territories of Canada.

Canada's Sports Hall of Fame / Temple de la renommée des sports du Canada
Exhibition Place, 115 Princes' Blvd., Toronto ON M6K 3C3 Canada
Tel: 416-260-6789; *Fax:* 416-260-9347
info@cshof.ca
www.cshof.ca
To inspire Canadian identity and national pride by telling the compelling stories of those outstanding achievements that make up Canada's sports history.
Sheryn Posen, COO
J. Trevor Eyton, Chair

Canadian 5 Pin Bowlers' Association (C5PBA) / Association canadienne des cinq quilles (AC5Q)
#206, 720 Belfast Rd., Ottawa ON K1G 0Z5 Canada
Tel: 613-744-5090; *Fax:* 613-744-2217
c5pba@c5pba.ca
www.c5pba.ca
The sports organization of male & female 5 pin bowlers provides programs & services to its members for their participation in organized 5-pin bowling. It also regulates bowling systems to standardize the sport.

Canadian Academy of Sport Medicine (CASM) / Académie canadienne de médecine du sport (ACMS)
#4, 5330 Canotek Rd., Ottawa ON K1J 9C1
Tel: 613-748-5851; *Fax:* 613-748-5792
Toll-Free: 877-585-2394
bfalardeau@casm-acms.org
www.casm-acms.org
To promote excellence in the practice of medicine, as it applies to physical activity; To advance the art & science of sport medicine

Canadian Adult Recreational Hockey Association (CARHA)
#610, 1420 Blair Pl., Ottawa ON K1J 9L8 Canada
Tel: 613-244-1989; *Fax:* 613-244-0451
Toll-Free: 800-267-1854
hockey@carhahockey.ca
www.carhahockey.ca
To develop & provide a wide range of innovative hockey benefits & solutions of the highest standards to our customers that respond to their various needs in an effort to build & retain relationships among the adult recreational hockey community across Canada

Canadian Amateur Boxing Association (CABA) / Association canadienne de boxe amateur (ACBA)
888 Belfast Rd., Ottawa ON K1G 0Z6
Tel: 613-238-7700; *Fax:* 613-238-1600
caba@boxing.ca
www.boxing.ca
To develop & maintain uniform rules & regulations to govern amateur boxing competitions in Canada; To develop coaches & officials; To organize national team programs, including development, training, & competition

Canadian Amateur Wrestling Association (CAWA) / Association canadienne de lutte amateur
#7, 5370 Canotek Rd., Gloucester ON K1J 9E6
Tel: 613-748-5686; *Fax:* 613-748-5756
info@wrestling.ca
www.wrestling.ca
To operate as the national sport governing body for Olympic style wrestling in Canada; To implement a long term athlete development model; To develop coaches, officials, & administrators; To achieve podium finishes for Canadian wrestlers at World Championships & Olympic Games

Canadian Amputee Sports Association (CASA) / Association canadienne des sports pour amputés
1399 Weslemkoon Lake Rd., Gilmour ON K0L 1W0 Canada
Tel: 613-474-1397
bobfox1@hotmail.com
www.canadianamputeesports.ca
To promote & organize amateur sport competitions in Canada for persons who are without a limb or part of a limb; to promote research in prosthetic devices for sport activities; to select a Canadian national team for participation in international sports events for amputees

Canadian Aquafitness Leaders Alliance Inc. (CALA)
125 Lilian Dr., Toronto ON M1R 3W6 Canada
Tel: 416-751-9823; *Fax:* 416-755-1832
Toll-Free: 888-751-9823
cala_aqua@mac.com
www.calainc.org
Social Media:
www.facebook.com/profile.php?id=100001107894346
To provide high quality training, certification & communication network for aquafitness leaders & aquatic rehabilitation specialists; to promote professionalism & excellence through careful integration of the mind, body & spirit
Charlene Kopansky, President

Canadian Association for Disabled Skiing (CADS) / Association canadienne pour les skieurs handicapés (ACSH)
91 Nelson St., Barrie ON L4M 4K4
Tel: 705-725-4845; *Fax:* 705-725-4804
michelle.bavington@sympatico.ca
www.disabledskiing.ca
To assist individuals with a disability to participate in recreational & competitive snow skiing & snowboarding

Canadian Association for Disabled Skiing - Alberta (CADS Alberta)
11759 Groat Rd., Edmonton AB T5M 3K6 Canada
Tel: 780-427-8104; *Fax:* 780-427-0524
info@cadsalberta.ca
www.cadsalberta.ca
CADS Alberta is a volunteer-based organization assisting individuals with a disability to lead fuller lives through active participation in recreational & competitive snow skiing & snowboarding. It is a registered charity, BN: 133967406RR0001.
Mike Low, President
Allyson Szafranski, Executive Coordinator

Canadian Association for Disabled Skiing - Newfoundland & Labrador Division
6 Albany Pl., St. John's NL A1E 1Y2 Canada
Tel: 709-753-3625; *Fax:* 709-777-4884
margaret.tibbo@easternhealth.ca
Marg Tibbo, Secretary

Canadian Association for Disabled Skiing Nova Scotia
c/o Alpine Ski Nova Scotia, 5516 Spring Garden Rd., Halifax NS B3J 1G6 Canada
Tel: 902-425-5450; *Fax:* 902-425-5606
alpinens@sportnovascotia.ca
Lorraine Burch

Canadian Association of Nordic Ski Instructors (CANSI)
c/o Secrétariat, 8 Douglas Rd., Chelsea QC J9B 1K4
Tel: 819-360-6700; *Fax:* 819-827-0017
office@cansi.ca; membership@cansi.ca
www.cansi.ca
CANSI promotes & advances cross-country & Telemark skiing in Canada, establishing standards, & offering levels of certification in technique & training. Its primary focus is certifying instructors to teach the general public.

Canadian Association of Snowboard Instructors (CASI) / Association canadienne des moniteurs de surf des neiges (ACMS)
#220, 4900, Jean-Talon ouest, Montréal QC H4P 1W9 Canada
Tel: 514-748-2648; *Fax:* 514-748-2476
Toll-Free: 800-811-6428
national@casi-acms.com
www.casi-acms.com
To promote the sport of snowboarding, snowboard instruction & coaching & the professions of snowboard teaching & coaching in Canada by training & certifying snowboard instructors & coaches; to ensure that a standard of safe & efficient snowboard instruction is maintained.
Dan Genge, Executive Director

Canadian Ball Hockey Association / Association canadienne de hockey-balle
#5, 56 Pennsylvania Ave., Concord ON L4K 3V9 Canada
Tel: 905-832-6200; *Fax:* 905-856-1331
info@cbha.com
www.cbha.com
Social Media: www.facebook.com/group.php?gid=20107004444
Registered, non-profit organization recognized by the International Street & Ball Hockey Federation, Canadian Hockey Association & Sport Canada; promotes the sport of ball hockey; arranges championships

Canadian Blind Sports Association Inc. / Association canadienne des sports pour aveugles inc.
#325, 5055 Joyce St., Vancouver BC V5R 6B2 Canada
Tel: 604-419-0480; *Fax:* 604-419-0481
Toll-Free: 866-604-0480
jane@canadianblindsports.ca
www.canadianblindsports.ca
To facilitate opportunities for Canadians who are legally blind to participate in amateur sport at the national/international level, & to thereby enhance a healthy lifestyle & individual well-being.

Canadian Broomball Federation / Fédération canadienne de ballon sur glace
#302, 200 Main St., Winnipeg MB R3C 4M2 Canada
Tel: 204-925-5656; *Fax:* 204-925-5703
cbfbroomball@shaw.ca
www.broomball.ca

Canadian Centre for Ethics in Sport (CCES) / Centre canadien pour l'éthique dans le sport
#350, 955 Green Valley Cr., Ottawa ON K2C 3V4 Canada
Tel: 613-521-3340; *Fax:* 613-521-3134
info@cces.ca
www.cces.ca
Foster ethical sport for all Canadians
Roger Jackson, Chair
Paul Melia, CEO

Canadian Cerebral Palsy Sports Association (CCPSA) / Association canadienne de sport pour paralytiques cérébraux (ACPSA)
PO Box 41009, 1910 St. Laurent Blvd., Ottawa ON K1G 5K9 Canada
Tel: 613-748-1430; *Fax:* 613-748-1355
Toll-Free: 866-247-9934
ccpsa@bellnet.ca
www.ccpsa.ca
To act as umbrella group for all provincial cerebral palsy sport organizations; to design programs that are designed for athletes with cerebral palsy & non-progressive head injuries.

Canadian Colleges Athletic Association / Association canadienne du sport collégial
c/o St. Lawrence College, 2 Belmont St., Cornwall ON K6H 4Z1 Canada
Tel: 613-937-1508; *Fax:* 613-937-1530
sandra@ccaa.ca
www.ccaa.ca
To operate as the national governing body for men's & women's college sport in Canada

Canadian Curling Association (CCA) / Association canadienne de curling
1660 Vimont Ct., Cumberland ON K4A 4J4 Canada
Tel: 613-834-2076; *Fax:* 613-834-0716
Toll-Free: 800-550-2875
cca@curling.ca
www.curling.ca
To attract, retain & advance participants to grow the sport of curling

Canadian Cycling Association (CCA) / Association cycliste canadienne
#203, 2197 Riverside Dr., Ottawa ON K1H 7X3 Canada
Tel: 613-248-1353; *Fax:* 613-248-9311
general@canadian-cycling.com
www.canadian-cycling.com/
To organize & promote cycling in Canada, including road racing, track, & mountain biking, for sport & fitness

Canadian Deaf Ice Hockey Federation (CDIHF)
c/o C. Cooper, #137, 201 Queen Victoria Dr., Hamilton ON L8W 1W7
cdihf@rogers.com
www.cdihf.deafhockey.com
Social Media:
www.facebook.com/group.php?gid=152070790142
To offer ice hockey programs for deaf & hard of hearing participants; To administer a hockey team to represent Canada internationally

Canadian Deaf Sports Association (CDSA) / Association des sports des sourds du Canada (ASSC)
#202A, 10217, boul Pie IX, Montréal QC H1H 3Z5 Canada
Tel: 514-321-4520; *Fax:* 514-321-2937
Toll-Free: 800-855-0511
office@assc-cdsa.com
www.assc-cdsa.com
To promote & facilitate the practice of fitness, amateur sports & recreation among deaf people of all ages in Canada from the local recreational level to Olympics calibre.

Canadian Fencing Federation (CFF) / Fédération canadienne d'escrime
10 Masterson Dr., St Catharines ON L2T 3P1 Canada
Tel: 647-476-2401; *Fax:* 647-476-2402
cff@fencing.ca
www.fencing.ca
To promote & develop the sport of fencing in Canada.

Canadian Football League (CFL) / Ligue canadienne de football (LCF)
50 Wellington St. East, 3rd Fl., Toronto ON M5E 1C8 Canada
Tel: 416-322-9650; *Fax:* 416-322-9651
info@cfl.ca
www.cfl.ca
Social Media: www.facebook.com/CFL; twitter.com/CFL

Canadian Freestyle Ski Association / Association canadienne de ski acrobatique
808 Pacific St., Vancouver BC V6Z 1C2 Canada
Tel: 604-714-2233; *Fax:* 604-714-2232
info@freestyleski.com
www.freestyleski.ca
The national governing body of the sport of freestyle skiing with a mandate to develop the sport within Canada; to represent our country internationally; to promote the safe development of the sport; to promote excellence in national & international competitions
Peter Judge, CEO

Canadian Golf Industry Association / Association canadienne de l'industrie du golf
7 Aspendale Dr., Toronto ON M1P 4J5 Canada
Tel: 416-289-1305; *Fax:* 416-289-1412
cgiacgi@bellnet.ca

Canadian Golf Superintendents Association (CGSA) / Association canadienne des surintendants de golf
#205, 5520 Explorer Dr., Mississauga ON L4W 5L1
Tel: 905-602-8873; *Fax:* 905-602-1958
Toll-Free: 800-387-1056
cgsa@golfsupers.com
www.golfsupers.com
Social Media:
www.facebook.com/group.php?gid=151227228150
To promote excellence in golf course management & environmental responsibility; To uphold the Canadian Golf Superintendents Association Principles Of Professional Practice & Code of Ethics & Conduct

Canadian Handball Association (CHA) / Fédération de balle au mur du Canada
30 Melwood Ave., Halifax NS B3N 1E3 Canada
Tel: 902-477-2902; *Fax:* 902-431-3145
handball@cdnhandball.ca
www.cdnhandball.ca
To promote handball in Canada

Canadian Jiu-jitsu Association Inc. / Association canadienne du jiu-jitsu inc.
c/o Pro Spar Martial Arts Centre, #10, 4 Alliance Blvd., Barrie ON L4M 5J1 Canada
Tel: 705-725-9186; *Toll-Free:* 800-352-1338
info@canadianjiujitsu.com
www.canadianjiujitsu.com
To promote & develop the martial arts & the sport of jiu-jitsu in Canada.

Canadian Kendo Federation (CKF) / Fédération canadienne de kendo
8013 Hunter St., Burnaby BC V5A 2B8
Tel: 604-420-0438; *Fax:* 604-420-1971
hokusa@kendo-canada.com
www.kendo-canada.com

Canadian Lacrosse Association (CLA) / Association canadienne de crosse (ACC)
#B4, 2211 Riverside Dr., Ottawa ON K1H 7X5 Canada
Tel: 613-260-2028; *Fax:* 613-260-2029
info@lacrosse.ca
www.lacrosse.ca
Social Media: www.twitter.com/LacrosseCanada
To promote, develop & preserve the sport of Lacrosse & its heritage as Canada's national summer sport.

Canadian Luge Association / Association canadienne de luge
88 Canada Olympic Rd. SW, Calgary AB T3B 5R5 Canada
Tel: 403-202-6581; *Fax:* 403-247-8820
tfarstad@coda.ca
www.luge.ca
To provide leadership & pursue success in promotion & development of all aspects of luge.

Canadian Masters Athletic Association (CMAA)
426 Valermo Dr., Toronto ON M8W 2L9 Canada
Tel: 416-252-7047
masters@sympatico.ca
www.canadianmastersathletics.com
Brian Keaveney, President
Joan Christiensen, Membership

Canadian Masters Cross-Country Ski Association (CMCSA) / Association canadienne des maîtres en ski de fond
c/o 2 MacNeil Cres., Stephenville NL A2N 3E3 Canada
www.canadian-masters-xc-ski.ca/en_index.htm
Th Association promotes Masters cross-country skiing across Canada, establishing rules & regulations for activities, & representing members at meetings at the WMA.

Canadian Modern Pentathlon Association (CAMPA) / Association canadienne du pentathlon moderne
70 Como Gardens, Hudson QC J0P 1H0 Canada
Tel: 450-458-7974; *Fax:* 450-458-1746
president@pentathloncanada.ca
www.pentathloncanada.ca
To promote multi-discipline Olympic sport (ie. fencing, swimming, shooting, running & riding)

Canadian Olympic Committee (COC) / Comité olympique canadien
#900, 21 St Clair Ave. East, Toronto ON M4T 1L9 Canada
Tel: 416-962-0262; *Fax:* 416-967-4902
www.olympic.ca
Social Media: www.twitter.com/CDNOlympicTeam
To develop & advance sports & the Olympic Movement for all Canadians from coast-to-coast
Chris Rudge, CEO

Canadian Paralympic Committee (CPC) / Comité paralympique canadien
#1401, 85 Albert St., Ottawa ON K1P 6A4 Canada
Tel: 613-569-4333; *Fax:* 613-569-2777
reachus@paralympic.ca
www.paralympic.ca
To develop & grow the Paralympic Movement in Canada and who envisions a strong and vibrant Paralympic Movement in Canada.

Canadian Polo Association (CPA)
#301, 250 Consumers Rd., Toronto ON M2J 4V6
Tel: 416-494-0724; *Fax:* 416-495-8723
Toll-Free: 888-494-0724
info@polocanada.ca
www.polocanada.ca
To develop & maintain standards of excellence for the sport of polo in Canada; To promote polo across the nation

Canadian Pony Club (CPC)
PO Box 127, Baldur MB R0K 0B0 Canada
Tel: 204-535-2368; *Fax:* 204-535-2289
Toll-Free: 888-286-7669
info@canadianponyclub.org
www.canadianponyclub.org
The Club encourages & instructs young people to ride & care for their horses, while promoting loyalty, character & sportsmanship.

Canadian Powerlifting Organization (CPO)
PO Box 51180 RPO Beddington, Calgary AB T3K EV9 Canada
Fax: 403-698-2434
powerlifting@gmail.com; info@wpc-canada.com
www.worldpowerlifting.com/cpo
Promoting powerlifting in Canada

Canadian Powerlifting Union (CPU)
#17, 1063 Coteau St. West, Moose Jaw SK S6H 5G3 Canada
Tel: 306-694-6116; *Fax:* 306-693-3301
jbutt@sasktel.net
www.powerlifting.ca
To oversee & regulate all IPF style powerlifting in Canada

Canadian Professional Golfers' Association (CPGA) / Association canadienne des golfeurs professionnels
13450 Dublin Line, RR#1, Acton ON L7J 2W7 Canada
Tel: 519-853-5450; *Fax:* 519-853-5449
Toll-Free: 800-782-5764
cpga@cpga.com
www.cpga.com
The Canadian Professional Golfer's Association is a member based non-profit organization representing golf professionals across Canada.

Canadian Racquetball Association (CRA) / Association canadienne de racquetball
25 Golflinks Dr., Ottawa ON K2J 4Y1 Canada
Tel: 613-692-5394
emlane@rogers.com
www.racquetball.ca
To promote racquetball as a sport & physical activity; to provide leadership by developing & coordinating services & programs designed to meet the needs of the racquetball community

Canadian Rhythmic Sportive Gymnastic Federation (CRSGF) / Fédération canadienne de gymnastique rythmique sportive
c/o 2288 Covington Pl., Victoria BC V8N 5N6 Canada
Tel: 250-472-3322; *Fax:* 250-472-2659
dfrattaroli@shaw.ca
To promote Rhythmic Gymnastics for lifetime growth, fitness & the pursuit of excellence.

Canadian Ski Coaches Federation (CSCF) / Fédération des entraîneurs de ski du Canada
#220, 4900 Jean Talon ouest, Montréal QC H4P 1W9 Canada
Tel: 514-748-2648; *Fax:* 514-748-2476
Toll-Free: 800-811-6428
national@snowpro.com
www.snowpro.com/csia/e
To help produce the best skiers in the world for Canada
Michel Lamothe, Chief Executive Officer

Canadian Ski Council (CSC) / Conseil canadien du ski
21 Fourth St. East, Collingwood ON L9Y 1T2 Canada
Tel: 705-445-9140; *Fax:* 705-445-0525
info@skicanada.org
www.skicanada.org
To encourage participation in recreational skiing & snowboarding.

Canadian Ski Instructors' Alliance (CSIA) / Alliance des moniteurs de ski du Canada
#220, 4900, Jean Talon ouest, Montréal QC H4P 1W9 Canada
Tel: 514-748-2648; *Fax:* 514-748-2476
Toll-Free: 800-811-6428
national@snowpro.com
www.snowpro.com/csia/e
To promote professionalism & high standards for the profession of ski instruction; certifies ski instructors across Canada

Canadian Ski Marathon (CSM) / Marathon canadien de ski
#200, 81 Jean-Proulx, Gatineau QC J8Z 1W2 Canada
Tel: 819-770-6556; *Fax:* 819-770-7428
Toll-Free: 877-770-6556
ski@csm-mcs.com
www.csm-mcs.com
The Canadian Ski Marathon is an historic cross-county ski tour for people of all ages in celebration of Canadian winter. Their mission is to organize an annual and fully supported weekend in the wilderness, the Canadian Ski Marathon provides a uniquely Canadian cross-country skiing event with a broad appeal.

Canadian Ski Patrol System (CSPS) / Patrouille canadienne de ski (OPCS)
4531 Southclark Pl., Ottawa ON K1T 3V2 Canada
Tel: 613-822-2245; *Fax:* 613-822-1088
Toll-Free: 900-565-2777
info@skipatrol.ca
www.csps.ca
To provide first aid & safety programs throughout Canada

Canadian Snowsports Association (CSA) / L'Association canadienne des sports d'hiver (ACSH)
#202, 1451 West Broadway, Vancouver BC V6H 1H6 Canada
Tel: 604-734-6800; *Fax:* 604-669-7954
lillianalderton@hotmail.com
www.canadaskiandsnowboard.net
Federation for nine ski & snowboard disciplines: alpine, cross-country, freestyle, jumping, nordic combined, snowboard, telemark, speed skiing & disabled skiing; to develop elite amateur athletes & to pursue excellence at national & international level competition

Canadian Soccer Association (CSA) / Association canadienne de soccer
237 Metcalfe St., Ottawa ON K2P 1R2 Canada
Tel: 613-237-7678; *Fax:* 613-237-1516
info@soccercan.ca
www.canadasoccer.com
To promote the growth & development of soccer for all Canadians at all levels; to provide leadership & good governance for the sport

Canadian Society for Exercise Physiology (CSEP) / Société canadienne de physiologie de l'exercice (SCPE)
#370, 18 Louisa St., Ottawa ON K1R 6Y6
Tel: 613-234-3755; *Fax:* 613-234-3565
Toll-Free: 877-651-3755
info@csep.cap; support@csep.ca (member directory inquiries)
www.csep.ca
Social Media: www.facebook.com/group.php?gid=291577755198; www.twitter.com/CSEPdotCA
To promote the generation, synthesis, transfer, & application of knowledge & research related to exercise physiology, encompassing physical activity, fitness, health, nutrition, epidemiology, & human performance; To act as the voice for exercise physiology in Canada

Canadian Society for Psychomotor Learning & Sport Psychology (CSPLSP) / Société canadienne d'apprentissage psychomoteur et de psychologie du sport (SCAPPS)
c/o Dr. N. Holt, Faculty of Physical Ed. & Rec., University of Alberta, Van Vliet Centre, Edmonton AB T6G 2H9
nick.holt@ualberta.ca
www.scapps.org
To promote the study of motor development, motor learning, motor control, & sport psychology

Canadian Sport Horse Association (CSHA)
PO Box 970, 7904 Franktown Rd., Richmond ON K0A 2Z0 Canada
Tel: 613-686-6161; *Fax:* 613-686-6170
csha@canadian-sport-horse.org
www.c-s-h-a.org
Social Media: www.facebook.com/group.php?gid=10649610317
To ensure the production and promotion of a sound, solid horse, with a good disposition, capable of competing successfully in the Olympic Disciplines at all levels of competition.
Paul Morgan, President
David Lancaster, Treasurer

Canadian Team Handball Federation (CTHF) / Fédération canadienne de handball olympique (FCHO)
453, rue Jacob-Nicol, Sherbrooke QC J1J 4E5 Canada
Tel: 819-563-7937; *Fax:* 819-563-5352
f.lebeau@videotron.ca
www.handballcanada.ca

Canadian Tenpin Federation, Inc. (CTF) / Fédération canadienne des dix-quilles, inc.
916 3 Ave. N., Lethbridge AB T1H 0H3 Canada
Tel: 403-381-2830; *Fax:* 403-381-6247
www.gotenpinbowling.ca
To promote & foster the sport of tenpin bowling in Canada by maintaining active membership in the world's appropriate affiliated tenpin organizations, providing competitive opportunities for all skill levels, culminating in the selection of a

National Team; to encourage the development of skills through a national coaching certification program

Canadian Therapeutic Riding Association / Association canadienne d'équitation thérapeutique
#11, 5420 Hwy. 6 North, RR#5, Guelph ON N1H 6J2 Canada
Tel: 519-767-0700; *Fax:* 519-767-0435
ctra@golden.net
www.cantra.ca
To foster therapeutic riding for persons with disabilities by establishing riding standards in collaboration with the medical profession; to accredit programs, certify instructors & promote research; to promote equestian sport & competition for persons with disabilities

Canadian University Football Coaches Association (CUFCA)
c/o Huskies Football, St. Mary's University, Halifax NS B3H 3C3 Canada
Tel: 902-420-5550
To improve the coaching of Canadian Interuniversity Athletic Union (CIAU) football teams; to improve the technical aspects of play in CIAU football
Blake Nill, President

Canadian Wheelchair Basketball Association (CWBA) / Association canadienne de basketball en fauteuil roulant (ACBFR)
#B2, 2211 Riverside Dr., Ottawa ON K1H 7X5 Canada
Tel: 613-260-1296; *Fax:* 613-260-1456
Toll-Free: 877-843-2922
info@wheelchairbasketball.ca
www.wheelchairbasketball.ca
To promote & develop opportunities in the game of wheelchair basketball
Wendy Gittens, Executive Director
Steven Bach, President

Canadian Wheelchair Sports Association (CWSA) / Association canadienne des sports en fauteuil roulant (ACSFR)
#108, 2255 St. Laurent Blvd., Ottawa ON K1G 4K3 Canada
Tel: 613-523-0004; *Fax:* 613-523-0149
info@cwsa.ca
www.cwsa.ca
To promote excellence & develop opportunities for Canadians in wheelchair sport; CWSA is the leader of wheelchair sport development in the capacity of advisor, resource & advocate for athletes with a disability

Cape Breton County Minor Hockey Association (CBCMHA)
PO Box 6003, 95 Keltic Dr., Coxheath NS B1S 3V9 Canada
Tel: 902-562-1767; *Fax:* 902-562-1833
info@cbchma.org
www.cbcmha.ca
The Cape Breton County Minor Hockey Association is dedicated to the advancement of minor hockey and promoting the development and personal growth of all participants through progressive leadership, by ensuring meaningful and equal opportunities, and providing enjoyable experiences in a safe and respectful environment.

Centre de plein air du Mont Chalco
CP 55, Chibougamau QC G8P 2K5 Canada
Tél: 418-748-7162
Adresse: 264, rte 167, Chibougamau, QC.
Serge Boutin, Directeur des opérations

Cerebral Palsy Sports Association of British Columbia (CPSABC)
6235A - 136th St., Surrey BC V3X 1H3 Canada
Tel: 604-599-5240; *Fax:* 604-599-5241
Toll-Free: 877-711-3111
sportinfo@telus.net
www.cpsports.com
To provide sports & recreational opportunities for people with cerebral palsy, head injury, stroke & similar disabilities at the local, regional, provincial & national level; to provide access to appropriate programming for members including segregated & integrated opportunities
Terri Moore, Executive Director

Charlottetown Minor Baseball Association
c/o 42 Trafalgar St., Charlottetown PE C1A 3Z1 Canada
Tel: 902-628-4028
daleclair@pei.eastlink.ca
David LeClair, President

Club 'Les Pongistes d'Ungava'
109, rue Obalski, Chibougamau QC G8P 2E8 Canada
Tél: 418-748-4903
Lynn Labbé

Club d'auto-neige Chibougamau inc.
CP 43, Chibougamau QC G8P 2K5 Canada
Tél: 418-748-3065
Mario Simard

Club de boxe Chibougamau
224, rue Mgr Houe, Chibougamau QC G8P 2Y5 Canada
Tél: 418-748-2592
David Pelletier, Président

Club de football Troilus de Chibougamau-Chapais
CP 622, Chibougamau QC G8P 2Y8 Canada
Tél: 418-748-3554
footballchibougamau.com
Serge Bouchard, Président

Club de golf de Chibougamau inc.
CP 81, Chibougamau QC G8P 2K5 Canada
Tél: 418-748-3249
Adresse: 130, rue des Forces Armées, Chibougamau, QC; Club: 418-748-4709
Richard Simard

Club de karaté Shotokan
417, rue Demers, Chibougamau QC G8P 1E8 Canada
Tél: 418-748-3639
France Bélanger, Présidente

Club de nage synchronisée Synchrogamau de Chibougamau
CP 181, Chibougamau QC G8P 2K6 Canada
Tél: 418-748-3198
Maureen Tanguay

Club de natation Natchib inc.
CP 213, Chibougamau QC G8P 2K7 Canada
Tél: 418-748-3214
Denise Caron

Club de patinage artistique Les lames givrées inc.
CP 453, Chibougamau QC G8P 2X9 Canada
Tél: 418-748-2339
Joline Bélanger

Club nautique de Chibougamau inc.
CP 395, Chibougamau QC G8P 2X8 Canada
Tél: 418-748-6628
Marcel Steinmetzer

Club Vélogamik
CP 594, Chibougamau QC G8P 2Y8 Canada
Tél: 418-748-6406
Fabien Laprise, Président

Coaches Association of British Columbia (CABC)
#200, 3820 Cessna Drive, Richmond BC V7B 0A2 Canada
Tel: 604-333-3600; *Fax:* 604-333-3450
info@coaches.bc.ca
www.coaches.bc.ca
To ensure the development, certification & ongoing education of all BC coaches through the provision of the best possible programs & services
Gordon May, CAE, Executive Director

Coaches Association of PEI (CAPEI)
PO Box 302, Charlottetown PE C1A 7K7 Canada
Tel: 902-569-0583; *Fax:* 902-368-4548
Toll-Free: 800-247-6712
cgcrozier@sportpei.pe.ca
www.coachespei.ca
To educate, develop & promote coaching & coaches for the benefit of athletes, sport & the community in general; to encourage fair play, integrity & the pursuit of excellence
Cheryl G. Crozier, Executive Director

Coaching Association of Canada (CAC) / Association canadienne des entraîneurs
#300, 141 Laurier Ave. West, Ottawa ON K1P 5J3 Canada
Tel: 613-235-5000; *Fax:* 613-235-9500
coach@coach.ca
www.coach.ca
To improve implementation & delivery of National Coaching Certification Program; to establish coaching as viable career within the Canadian sports system & to increase the number of qualified full-time & part-time remunerated coaches at various levels within the sport system

Commission de Ski pour Personnes Handicapées du Québec (CSPHQ)
165 Place Lilas, Pincourt QC J7V 5B6 Canada
Tél: 514-425-8894; *Téléc:* 514-425-8894
hwohler@yahoo.com
Promouvoir et pratiquer le ski alpin
Henry Wohler, President

The Commonwealth Games Association of Canada Inc. (CGAC) / Association canadienne des jeux du Commonwealth inc.
#120, 2255 St. Laurent Blvd., Ottawa ON K1G 4K3 Canada
Tel: 613-244-6868; *Fax:* 613-244-6826
info@commonwealthgames.ca
www.commonwealthgames.ca

Cricket Canada
Sport Alliance Centre, #306, 1185 Eglinton Ave. East, Toronto ON M3C 3C3 Canada
Tel: 416-426-7209
canada@cricamericas.com
www.canadiancricket.org
To foster growth & development of cricket in Canada

Cross Country Canada (CCC) / Ski de fond Canada (SFC)
c/o Bill Warren Training Centre, #100, 1995 Olympic Way, Canmore AB T1W 2T6 Canada
Tel: 403-678-6791; *Fax:* 403-678-3644
Toll-Free: 877-609-3215
info@cccski.com
www.cccski.com
To develop & deliver programs designed to achieve international excellence in cross-country skiing; to provide national programs for continuous development of cross-country skiing from introductory experience to international excellence, for participants of all ages & abilities, fostering the principles of ethical conduct & fair play
Jim McCarthy, President
Davin MacIntosh, Executive Director
Cathy Sturgeon, Director, Administration & Communication

Curl BC
#320, 1367 West Broadway, Vancouver BC V6H 4A9 Canada
Tel: 604-737-3040; *Fax:* 604-737-1476
Toll-Free: 800-667-2875
curling@curlbc.ca
www.curlbc.ca
To deliver all curling programs & services in British Columbia
Scott Braley, Executive Director & CEO
Terry Vandale, President

Curling Chibougamau
733, boul Campbell, Chibougamau QC G8P 1L2 Canada
Tél: 418-748-2671
Serge Boutin, Directeur

Curling Québec
CP 1000, Succ. M, 4545, av Pierre-de Coubertin, Montréal QC H1V 3R2 Canada
Tél: 514-252-3088; *Téléc:* 514-252-3342
Ligne sans frais: 888-292-2875
info@curling-quebec.qc.ca
www.curling-quebec.qc.ca
Offrir aux amateurs de curling, et à tous ceux désirant le devenir, la possibilité de jouer au curling à l'intérieur d'une structure organisée appuyée par divers services

Cycling Association of the Yukon
4061, 4th Avenue, Whitehorse YT Y1A 1H1 Canada
Tel: 867-668-4990; *Fax:* 867-668-8212
sue.richards@gov.yk.ca

Cycling British Columbia (CBC)
#201, 210 West Broadway, Vancouver BC V5Y 3W2 Canada
Tel: 604-737-3034; *Fax:* 604-737-3141
assist@cycling.bc.ca
www.cycling.bc.ca
To enable, enhance & encourage cycling in British Columbia
Ryan Keith, Chief Executive Officer

Cycling PEI (CPEI)
Sport PEI, PO Box 302, 40 Enman Cresent, Charlottetown PE C1A 7K7 Canada
Tel: 902-368-4985; *Fax:* 902-368-4548
mconnolly@sportpei.pe.ca
www.cpei.ca
To develop cycling in PEI
Mike Connolly, Executive Director

Disabled Skiers Association of BC (DSABC)
#220, 3820 Cessna Dr., Richmond BC V7B 0A2 Canada
Tel: 604-333-3630; *Fax:* 604-333-3450
disabledskiers@telus.net
www.disabledskiingbc.com
To contribute to the quality of life by promoting the sport of skiing for disabled persons
Brian Forrester, Executive Director
Kevin ter Kuile, President

Distance Riders of Manitoba Association (DRMA)
PO Box 47, Gr 36, RR#2, Dugald MB R0E 0K0 Canada
Tel: 204-444-2314
www.kucera.mb.ca/drma
DRMA promotes endurance riding in the province of Manitoba & brings together equestrians interested in the sport.
Myna Cryderman, President
Linda Cruden, Membership Director

Dive Ontario
216 Gilwood Park Dr., Penetanguishene ON L9M 1Z6 Canada
Tel: 705-355-3483; *Fax:* 705-355-4663
info@diveontario.com
www.diveontario.com
Social Media: facebook.com/group.php?gid=7005127562
Janice Moore, President

Diving Plongeon Canada (DPC) / Association canadienne du plongeon amateur Inc.
#703, 2197 Riverside Dr., Ottawa ON K1H 7X3 Canada
Tel: 613-736-5238; *Fax:* 613-736-0409
cada@diving.ca
www.diving.ca
To promote the growth & awareness of diving in Canada; To contribute to the development of globally accepted standards of diving; To support the rules & regulations of international competition

Dr. James Naismith Basketball Foundation / La fondation de basketball Dr James Naismith
PO Box 1030, 14 Bridge St., Almonte ON K0A 1A0 Canada
Tel: 613-256-0492; *Fax:* 613-256-7883
naismith@trytel.com
To establish & operate the Naismith International Basketball Centre which will reflect the remarkable heritage & development of Naismith's game in Canada & around the world.
John Gosset, Executive Director
Allen G. Rae, President

Drive Canada
PO Box 2062, Vancouver BC V6B 3S3 Canada
Tel: 604-875-1905; *Fax:* 604-857-9582
drivecanada@shaw.ca
www.drivecanada.org
Simon Rosenman, President

Edmonton Bicycle & Touring Club (EBTC)
PO Box 52017, Stn. Garneau, Edmonton AB T6G 2T5 Canada
Tel: 780-424-2453
info@bikeclub.ca
www.bikeclub.ca
Social Media: facebook.com/group.php?gid=21002145481
Sid Bennett, President

Edmonton Combative Sports Commission (ECSC)
10250 - 101 St. NW, 13th Fl., Edmonton AB T6J 3P4 Canada
Tel: 780-495-0382; *Fax:* 780-429-6976
ecsc.ca
The ECSC regulates, governs & controls boxing, wrestling & full-contact karate bouts & contests within Edmonton; enforces the CPBF safety code.

Endurance Riders Association of British Columbia (ERABC)
c/o 1624 Duncan Dr., Delta BC V4L 1S2 Canada
info@erabc.com
www.erabc.com
ERABC fosters interest in the equestrian sport of endurance riding & promotes training & competition opportunities for beginning & advanced riders. It also assists in the development & preservation of courses or terrain suitable for endurance competitions.
Terre O'Brennan, Ride Manager

Endurance Riders of Alberta (ERA)
c/o President, PO Box 418, Seba Beach AB T0E 2B0 Canada
Tel: 780-797-5404
www.enduranceridersofalberta.com
Carol Wadey, Treasurer
Owen Fulcher, President

Equestrian Association for the Disabled
8360 Leeming Rd., RR#3, Mount Hope ON L0R 1W0
Tel: 905-679-8323; *Fax:* 905-679-1705
www.tead.on.ca
To enhance the life of children & adults with physical, mental, & emotional handicaps, through equestrian therapy

Equine Canada (EC) / Canada Hippique
#100, 2685 Queensview Dr., Ottawa ON K2B 8K2 Canada
Tel: 613-248-3433; *Fax:* 613-248-3484
Toll-Free: 866-282-8395
inquiries@equinecanada.ca
www.equestrian.ca
To promote & develop a unified Canadian Equine Community, an economically viable horse industry, & access to the use of horses for leisure, sport & commerce

Fédération de basketball du Québec (FBBQ) / Québec Basketball Federation
CP 1000, Succ. M, 4545, av Pierre-De Coubertin, Montréal QC H1V 3R2 Canada
Tél: 514-252-3057; *Téléc:* 514-252-3357
Ligne sans frais: 866-557-3057
basket@basketball.qc.ca
www.basketball.qc.ca
Développement et promotion de la discipline; formation de joueurs, entraîneurs et arbitres; organisation de compétitions provinciales; programme Poursuite de l'Excellence (Équipes et Espoirs du Québec)

Fédération de patinage artistique du Québec (FPAQ)
CP 1000, Succ. M, 4545, av Pierre-de-Coubertin, Montréal QC H1V 3R2 Canada
Tél: 514-252-3073; *Téléc:* 514-252-3170
patinage@patinage.qc.ca
www.patinage.qc.ca
Rendre accessible à tous, les programmes de Patinage Canada, que ce soit par amour, par plaisir ou pour atteindre l'excellence; a l'unisson, nous contribuons ainsi à l'avancement de notre sport.
Josée Beauséjour, Directeur exécutif

Fédération de Patinage de Vitesse du Québec
930, av Roland Beaudin, Sainte-Foy QC G1V 4H8 Canada
Tél: 418-651-1973; *Téléc:* 418-651-1977
fpvq@fpvq.org
www.fpvq.org
Depuis un peu plus d'un mois déjà, les athlètes du Centre national courte piste sont en entraînement hors glace sous la surveillance des entraîneurs et avec la grande collaboration du groupe Actiforme.
Robert Dubreuil, Directeur général

Fédération de pétanque du Québec
CP 1000, Succ. M, 4545, av Pierre-de Coubertin, Montréal QC H1V 3R2 Canada
Tél: 514-252-3077
petanque@loisirquebec.qc.ca
www.petanque.qc.ca
Développement du sport de pétanque

Fédération de rugby du Québec (FRQ) / Quebec Rugby Union
CP 1000, Succ. M, 4545, av Pierre-de Coubertin, Montréal QC H1V 3R2 Canada
Tél: 514-252-3189; *Téléc:* 514-252-3159
rugbyquebec@rugbyquebec.qc.ca
www.rugbyquebec.qc.ca
Promouvoir le sport et la santé physique en général, et sans limiter ce qui précède le sport du rugby; organiser des tournois de Rugby dans la province de Québec; regrouper les associations régionales et les clubs de Rugby du Québec

Fédération de soccer du Québec
955, av Bois-de-Boulogne, Laval QC H7N 4G1 Canada
Tél: 450-975-3355; *Téléc:* 450-975-1001
courriel@federation-soccer.qc.ca
www.federation-soccer.qc.ca

Fédération de volleyball du Québec (FVBQ)
CP 1000, Succ. M, 4545, av Pierre-de Coubertin, Montréal QC H1V 3R2 Canada
Tél: 514-252-3065; *Téléc:* 514-252-3176
info-fvbq@volleyball.qc.ca
www.volleyball.qc.ca
Régir le volleyball à l'intérieur et à l'extérieur du Québec; promouvoir le volleyball; former les intervenants impliqués dans l'encadrement du participant; offrir des services aux membres

Fédération du baseball amateur du Québec
CP 1000, Succ. M, 4545, av Pierre-de Coubertin, Montréal QC H1V 3R2 Canada
Tél: 514-252-3075; *Téléc:* 514-252-3134
info@baseballquebec.qc.ca
www.baseballquebec.qc.ca
La mission de la Fédération du baseball amateur du Québec inc. est de : Donner un cadre général d'ordre et de discipline à tous les intervenants du baseball québécois; Reconnaître le droit pour tous les joueurs d'évoluer au baseball selon des normes et critères précis; Donner un cadre pour l'application d'une réglementation uniforme dans tout le Québec; Fournir les moyens à chacun de s'amuser, de participer et de se perfectionner afin de donner un idéal à ceux qui aspirent à une carrière.

Fédération du plongeon amateur du Québec (FPAQ)
CP 1000, Succ. M, 4545, av Pierre-de-Coubertin, Montréal QC H1V 3R2 Canada
Tél: 514-252-3096; *Téléc:* 514-252-3094
fpaq@plongeon.qc.ca
www.plongeon.qc.ca
Régir le plongeon sur l'ensemble du territoire québécois; promouvoir le plongeon et sa pratique; tenir et organiser des stages de formation et des compétitions de plongeon; regrouper les associations de plongeon

Fédération équestre du Québec inc. (FEQ)
CP 1000, Succ. M, 4545, av Pierre-de Coubertin, Montréal QC H1V 3R2 Canada
Tél: 514-252-3053; *Téléc:* 514-252-3165
infocheval@feq.qc.ca
www.feq.qc.ca
Promotion et développement de l'activité équestre au Québec
Richard Mongeau, Directeur général

Fédération internationale de bobsleigh et de tobogganing
Via Piranesi, 44/B, Milan 120137 Italy
egarde@tin.it
www.fibt.com

Fédération Internationale de Luge de Course (FIL) / International Luge Federation
Rathausplatz 9, Berchtesgaden 83471 Germany
office@fil-luge.org
www.fil-luge.org
Promotion et participation aux compétitions de la luge dans le monde; organise des championnats du monde, des coupes du monde, des championnats régionaux; organise des cours et séminaires pour des arbitres et des entraîneurs

Federation of Broomball Associations of Ontario
515 Gascon St., Russell ON K4R 1C6 Canada
Tel: 613-445-0904; *Fax:* 613-445-9844
gerry.wever@ontariobroomball.ca
www.ontariobroomball.ca
To serve broomball players, coaches, & leagues in Ontario
Gerry Wever, President

Federation of Canadian Archers Inc. (FCA) / Fédération canadienne des archers inc.
#108, 2255 St. Laurent Blvd., Ottawa ON K1G 4K3 Canada
Tel: 613-260-2113; *Fax:* 613-260-2114
information@fca.ca
www.fca.ca
To promote & develop the sport of archery in a safe & ethical manner; To act as the official representative for archery to the federal government, & national & international sport organizations

Fédération québécoise de ballon sur glace
CP 1000, Succ. M, 4545, av Pierre-de Coubertin, Montréal QC H1V 3R2 Canada
Tél: 514-252-3078; *Téléc:* 514-252-3051
info@fqbg.net
www.fqbg.net
La Fédération Québecoise de Ballon sur Glace a pour but de promouvoir le sport du ballon sur glace dans la province de Québec
Richard Mimeau, Président

Fédération québécoise de boxe olympique (FQBO)
CP 1000, Succ. M, 4545, av Pierre-de Coubertin, Montréal QC H1V 3R2 Canada
Tél: 514-252-3047; *Téléc:* 514-254-2144
Ligne sans frais: 866-241-3779
info@fqbo.qc.ca
www.fqbo.qc.ca
Kenneth Piché, Directeur général
Victoria Sullivan-Smith, Adjointe administrative

Fédération québécoise des activités subaquatiques (FQAS)
CP 1000, Succ. M, 4545, av Pierre-de Coubertin, Montréal QC H1V 3R2 Canada
Tél: 514-252-3009; *Téléc:* 514-254-1363
Ligne sans frais: 866-391-8835
info@fqas.qc.ca
www.fqas.qc.ca
Regrouper les adeptes de la plongée et des activités subaquatiques; promouvoir la sécurite dans la pratique des activités subaquatiques; informer et renseigner ses membres et

la population sur les bienfaits de la pratique; promouvoir ces activités comme moyen de formation et comme loisir
Jean-Sébastien Naud, Directeur général

Fédération québécoise des sports cyclistes (FQSC) / Québec Cycling Sports Federation
4545, av Pierre-de-Coubertin, Montréal QC H1V 3R2 Canada
Tél: 514-252-3071; *Téléc:* 514-252-3165
reception@fqsc.net
www.fqsc.net
Régie et promotion des sports cyclistes au Québec

Fédération québécoise du sport étudiant (FQSE)
CP 1000, Succ. M, 4545, av Pierre-De Coubertin, Montréal QC H1V 3R2 Canada
Tél: 514-252-3300; *Téléc:* 514-254-3292
www.fqse.qc.ca; www.sportetudiant.com
Favoriser les actions éducatives dans le domaine de l'activité physique et sportive que se donne le milieu de l'éducation dans le but de contribuer, et cela dans les trois ordres d'enseignement, au développement intégral des élèves, des étudiantes et des étudiants du Québec.

Fédération sportive de ringuette du Québec
CP 1000, Succ. M, 4545, av Pierre-de-Coubertin, Montréal QC H1V 3R2 Canada
Tél: 514-252-3085; *Téléc:* 514-254-1069
ringuette@ringuette-quebec.qc.ca
www.ringuette-quebec.qc.ca
Promouvoir le sport de la ringuette au Québec

Field Hockey Canada (FHC) / Hockey sur gazon Canada
#240, 1101 Prince of Wales Dr., Ottawa ON K2C 3W7 Canada
Tel: 613-521-8774; *Fax:* 613-521-0261
fhc@fieldhockey.ca
www.fieldhockey.ca
Social Media: www.facebook.com/group.php?gid=151599479507
To promote the development & growth of field hockey in Canada; To provide coaching, training, & competitive opportunities to prepare Canada's national teams

Football Canada
#100, 2255 St. Laurent Blvd., Ottawa ON K1G 4K3 Canada
Tel: 613-564-0003; *Fax:* 613-564-6309
info@footballcanada.com
footballcanada.com
Through its members, to initate, regulate, & manage the programs, services & activities that promote participation & excellence in Canadian Amateur Football.

Football PEI
40 Enman Cres., Charlottetown PE C1E 1E6 Canada
Tel: 902-368-4262; *Fax:* 902-368-4548
admin@footballcanada.com
www.footballpei.com
To operate as the provincial sport governing body for amateur football in Prince Edward Island; To promote & further the development of the sport in its three forms - flag, tackle, & touch
Glen Flood, Executive Director
Carl Adams, President

Golf Association of Ontario (GAO)
PO Box 970, Uxbridge ON L9P 1N3 Canada
Tel: 905-852-1101; *Fax:* 905-852-8893
Toll-Free: 800-668-2949
administration@gao.ca
www.gao.ca
Social Media: twitter.com/GAOGolf
To develop & promote golf in the province

Golf Manitoba Inc.
420 - 145 Pacific Ave., Winnipeg MB R3B 2Z6 Canada
Tel: 204-925-5730; *Fax:* 204-925-5731
golfmb@golfmanitoba.mb.ca
golfmanitoba.mb.ca
The Association determines policies & standards relating to the development & promotion of golf in the province.

Golf Newfoundland & Labrador (GNL)
77 Morgan Dr., Gander NL A1V 2K3 Canada
Tel: 709-722-2470; *Fax:* 709-722-8104
golf@hnl.ca
www.golfnewfoundland.ca
Greg Hillier, President

Golf Québec
#110, 415, rue Bourke, Dorval QC H9S 3W9 Canada
Tél: 514-633-1088; *Téléc:* 514-633-1074
golfquebec@golfquebec.org
www.golfquebec.org
Assurer le leadership; favoriser la croissance et le développement du golf amateur dans toute la province tout en préservant l'intégrité et les traditions du jeu

Gymnastics Canada Gymnastique (GCG)
#120, 1900 City Park Dr., Ottawa ON K1J 1A3 Canada
Tel: 613-748-5637; *Fax:* 613-748-5691
info@gymcan.org
www.gymcan.org
To lead, promote, facilitate & guide gymnastics in Canada as a sport for the pursuit of excellence & world prominence, & as an activity for lifelong participation; to act as the national umbrella organization for provincial & territorial associations which are members; to publish & enforce a standard set of rules & regulations to serve as guidelines for all members; to represent Canadian gymnastics as a member of national & international agencies & federations, & to coordinate application of their regulations in Canada; to promote, develop & direct high performance gymnastics programs; to promote, facilitate & guide development of national gymnastics programs; to promote, guide & encourage general gymnastics activities; to promote gymnastics as a healthy & safe sport/activity

Halifax County United Soccer Club
#7, 102 Chain Lake Dr., Halifax NS B3S 1A7 Canada
Tel: 902-876-8784; *Fax:* 902-446-3620
info@hcusoccer.ca
www.hcusoccer.ca
To foster a love of soccer and help individuals of all ages achieve their full potential.
Mike Maddalena, President
Laura Yost, Administrator

Halifax Sport and Social Club (HSSC)
PO Box 8821, Halifax NS B3K 5M5 Canada
Tel: 902-431-8326
info@halifaxsport.ca
www.halifaxsport.ca
To offer co-ed recreational sport leagues, tournaments and social events for adults.
Lael Morgan, General Manager

Hockey Alberta / Hockey l'Alberta
#1, 7875 - 48 Ave., Red Deer AB T4P 2K1 Canada
Tel: 403-342-6777; *Fax:* 403-346-4277
operations@hockeyalberta.ca
www.hockey-alberta.ca
Social Media: www.facebook.com/group.php?gid=43831380491
To serve those who serve the athletes by providing good governance, quality services, programs & education

Hockey Canada
#N204, 801 King Edward Ave., Ottawa ON K1N 6N5 Canada
Tel: 613-562-5677; *Fax:* 613-562-5676
Toll-Free: 800-667-2242
nsouliere@hockeycanada.ca
www.hockeycanada.ca
Social Media: www.facebook.com/HockeyCanada
Dedicated to the advancement of amateur hockey for all individuals through progressive leadership, ensuring meaningful opportunities & enjoyable experiences in a safe, sustainable environment

Hockey Manitoba
508 - 145 Pacific Ave., Winnipeg MB R3B 2Z6 Canada
Tel: 204-925-5755; *Fax:* 204-925-5761
info@hockeymanitoba.mb.ca
www.hockeymanitoba.mb.ca
Social Media: www.facebook.com/pages/Hockey-Manitoba/296995075852?
To foster, develop, & promote amateur hockey throughout Manitoba; To encourage fair play; To secure the enforcement of rules as adopted by by the assosciation; To conduct games between member clubs to determine provincial champions
Brian Franklin, President
Peter Woods, Executive Director
Bernie Reichardt, Director, Hockey Development

Hockey New Brunswick (HNB) / Hockey Nouveau-Brunswick
PO Box 456, 861 Woodstock Rd., Fredericton NB E3B 4Z9 Canada
Tel: 506-453-0089; *Fax:* 506-453-0868
www.hnb.ca

Hockey Newfoundland & Labrador (NLHA) / Association de hockey de Terre-Neuve et Labrador
PO Box 176, 13B High St., Grand Falls-Windsor NL A2A 2J4 Canada
Tel: 709-489-5512; *Fax:* 709-489-2273
office@hockeynl.ca
www.hockeynl.ca
Support for hockey in Canada including minor, junior, senior, female and development.

Hockey North
3506 McDonald Dr., Yellowknife NT X1A 2H1 Canada
Tel: 867-874-6903; *Fax:* 867-874-4603
ccarriere@northwestel.net
www.hockeynorth.ca
Cheryl Carriere, Executive Director

Hockey Northwestern Ontario (HNO)
#100, 216 Red River Rd., Thunder Bay ON P7B 1A6 Canada
Tel: 807-623-1542; *Fax:* 807-623-0037
info@hockeyhno.com
www.hockeyhno.com

Hockey Nova Scotia
#200, 6300 Lady Hammond Rd., Halifax NS B3K 2R6 Canada
Tel: 902-454-9400; *Fax:* 902-454-3883
www.hockeynovascotia.ca
Social Media: www.facebook.com/group.php?gid=2222858784

Hockey PEI
PO Box 302, 40 Enman Cres., Charlottetown PE C1A 7K7 Canada
Tel: 902-368-4334; *Fax:* 902-368-4337
info@hockeypei.com
www.hockeypei.com

Hockey Québec (FQHG)
#210, 7450, boul. les Galeries d'Anjou, Montréal QC H1M 3M3 Canada
Tél: 514-252-3079; *Téléc:* 514-252-3158
info@hockey.qc.ca
www.hockey.qc.ca
Média social: www.facebook.com/group.php?gid=66611750398
Assurer l'encadrement du hockey sur glace; favoriser la promotion et le développement de la personne qui pratique le hockey

Horse Trials New Brunswick
c/o Donna Lee Cole, 7515 Rte.102, Browns Flat NB E5M 2N8 Canada
Tel: 506-468-2098
www.htnb.org
Donna Lee Cole, President
Louise McSheffrey, Secretary

Horse Trials Nova Scotia (HTNS)
60 Rockwell Drive, Mount Uniacke NS B0N 1Z0 Canada
Tel: 902-866-3889
www.htns.org
To foster & encourage safe & fun enjoyment of the sport of Horse Trials (eventing) through regular training & education of riders, coaches, horses & officials
Kim Elliott-Foster, President

International Badminton Federation (IBF)
Stadium Badminton Kuala Lumpur, Batu 3 «, Jalan Cheras, Kuala Lumpur 56000 Malaysia
bwf@internationalbadminton.org
www.internationalbadminton.org
To control the game of badminton, from an international aspect, in all countries; to uphold the Laws of Badminton as at present adopted
Kang Young Joong, President

International Curling Information Network Group (ICING)
73 Appleford Rd., Hamilton ON L9C 6B5 Canada
Tel: 905-389-7781
psmith@icing.org
www.icing.org
To provide information about the sport of curling worldwide
Peter M. Smith, Contact

International Masterathlete Federation (IMAF)
PO Box 185, Richmond Hill ON L4B 4R5 Canada
Tel: 905-473-9714; *Fax:* 905-473-9715
Toll-Free: 888-883-3315
To promote health, fitness, & longevity through participation in sport
Liz Roach, President
Iain Douglas, Vice-President

Island Horse Council (IHC)
PO Box 1887, Charlottetown PE C1A 7N5 Canada
islandhorsecouncil@yahoo.ca
www.islandhorsecouncil.ca
To act as a voice for the horse industry on Prince Edward Island; to promote the development of all aspects of horsemanship

Japan Karate Association of Yukon
4061, 4th Ave., Whitehorse YT Y1A 1H1 Canada
Tel: 867-334-9009
www.sportyukon.com/membership/?member=80
To promote and facilitate Karate in the Yukon Territory.
Mike Tribes, President

Jeux Olympiques Spéciaux du Québec Inc. (JOSQ) / Québec Special Olympics
5311, de Maisonneuve ouest, 2e étage, Montréal QC H7A 1Z5 Canada
Tél: 514-843-8778; *Téléc:* 514-843-8223
Ligne sans frais: 877-743-8778
info@olympiquesspeciaux.qc.ca
www.specialolympicsquebec.qc.ca
Mèdia social:
www.facebook.com/olympiquesspeciauxquebec?ref=mf
Les Olympiques spéciaux, actifs dans plus de 150 pays, ont pour mission d'enrichir, par le sport, la vie des personnes présentant une déficience intellectuelle. Plus de 2.25 millions d'athlètes spéciaux, de tous âges, sont inscrits dans le monde dont plus de 31 000 au Canada et 3 600 aux programmes récréatifs ou compétitifs offerts dans toutes les régions du Québec. Les 14 sports officiels sont pratiqués à l'intérieur d'un réseau de compétitions annuelles, comptant plus de 80 événements conçus pour tous les niveaux d'habiletés.
Pierre Bélanger, Directeur général

Jockey Club of Canada / Jockey Club du Canada
PO Box 66, Stn. B, Toronto ON M9W 5K9 Canada
Tel: 416-675-7756; *Fax:* 416-675-6378
jockeyclub@bellnet.ca
www.jockeyclubcanada.com

Judo Canada
#212, 1725 St. Laurent, Ottawa ON K1G 3V4 Canada
Tel: 613-738-1200; *Fax:* 613-738-1299
info@judocanada.org
www.judocanada.org
To promote the principles & teachings of the sport of Kodokan Judo; to work towards the advancement of Judo throughout Canada

Judo-Québec inc
CP 1000, Succ. M, 4545, av Pierre-de-Coubertin, Montréal QC H1V 3R2 Canada
Tél: 514-252-3040; *Téléc:* 514-254-5184
info@judo-quebec.qc.ca
www.judo-quebec.qc.ca
Assurer la promotion et le développement du judo au Québec; éduquer, développer et servir nos membres
Daniel De Angelis, Président
Patrick Esparbès, Directeur général
Patrick Vesin, Coordonnateur technique

Karate Ontario
#160, 2 County Ct. Blvd., Brampton ON L6W 4V1 Canada
Tel: 905-455-2170
info@karateontario.org
www.karateontario.org
To promote & perpetuate karate as a martial art & lifetime activity; to promote karate for physical fitness, mental fitness, & as a way of life; to develop provincial standards & programs; to encourage all participants in safely achieving their maximum at the recreational or competitive level; to provide safe competitive opportunities for karate-ka wishing to participate in the sport aspect of karate; to govern the amateur sport of karate & the conduct of all karate-ka under its jurisdiction
Joshua Drury, Secretary

Lawn Bowls Association of Alberta
Percy Page Centre, 11759 Groat Rd., 3rd Fl., Edmonton AB T5M 3K6 Canada
Tel: 780-427-8119; *Fax:* 780-452-5932
lawnbowl@telusplanet.net
www.bowls.ab.ca
David Simpson, President
Mary Ward, Secretary
Margaret Bruce, Treasurer

Ligue de dards Ungava
712, 6e Rue ouest, Chibougamau QC G8P 2V1 Canada
Tél: 418-748-6732
Claire Patoine

Little League Canada / Petite ligue Canada
235 Dale Ave., Ottawa ON K1G 0H6 Canada
Tel: 613-731-3301; *Fax:* 613-731-2829
canada@littleleague.org
www.littleleague.ca
To provide baseball & softball programs to every boy or girl wishing to participate
Roy Bergerman, President & Chair

Marthe Dubroy, Secretary
Bruce Campbell, Treasurer

Lloydminster & District Fish & Game Association
PO Box 116, Lloydminster AB T9V 0X9 Canada
Tel: 780-875-3641
admin@lloydfishandgame.org
www.lloydfishandgame.org
To advocate for and assist in the conservation & management of fish, wildlife & habitat for the continuing benefit of association members and the general public

Lutte NB Wrestling
gdouc5110@rogers.com
www.luttenbwrestling.ca

Manitoba Amateur Boxing Association
#302, 200 Main St., Winnipeg MB R3C 4M2 Canada
Tel: 204-925-5658
Rosemary Broadbent

Manitoba Amateur Broomball Association (MABA)
#305, 200 Main St., Winnipeg MB R3C 4M2 Canada
Tel: 204-925-5668; *Fax:* 204-925-5703
Toll-Free: 866-792-7666
info@mbbroomball.com
www.mbbroomball.com
To promote the sport of broomball in Manitoba; to offer opportunities to members in competing in provincial & national championships
Alan Park, President
Scott Marohn, Vice President

Manitoba Badminton Association
200 Main St., Winnipeg MB R3C 4M2 Canada
Tel: 204-925-5679; *Fax:* 204-925-5703
Toll-Free: 888-243-0890
badminton@shawbiz.ca
www.badminton.mb.ca
To provide the leadership that promotes the growth of badminton throughout Manitoba as a lifelong sport

Manitoba Ball Hockey Association
200 Main St., Winnipeg MB R3C 4M2 Canada
Tel: 204-925-5602
mbha1@hotmail.com
www.manitobaballhockey.com
Social Media: www.facebook.com/group.php?gid=50027852199
Jeff Dzikowcz, President

Manitoba Baseball Association
200 Main St., Winnipeg MB R3C 4M2 Canada
Tel: 204-925-5763; *Fax:* 204-925-5928
info.baseball@sport.mb.ca
www.baseballmanitoba.ca
To foster the participation, development & competition of amateur baseball in Manitoba

Manitoba Blind Sport Association
#311, 200 Main St., Winnipeg MB R3C 4M2 Canada
Tel: 204-925-5694; *Fax:* 204-925-5703
blindsport@shawbiz.ca
www.blindsport.mb.ca
Since 1976, the Manitoba Blind Sports Association has been the recognized not-for-profit sport governing body for blind and visually impaired athletes in the province. Our mission is to encourage participation in sport at all levels of skill and ability by blind and visually impaired Manitobans, and to develop athletes of a national and international calibre.

Manitoba Boxing Commission
#420, 213 Notre Dame Ave., Winnipeg MB R3B 1N3 Canada
Tel: 204-945-8954; *Fax:* 204-945-1675
mansport@sport.mb.ca
To supervise & control all matters pertaining to professional boxing exhibitions in Manitoba; to license & regulate professional boxing; to conduct training seminars for officials of professional boxing

Manitoba Curling Association (MCA)
#309, 145 Pacific Ave., Winnipeg MB R3B 2Z6 Canada
Tel: 204-925-5723; *Fax:* 204-925-5720
mca@curlmanitoba.org
www.curlmanitoba.org
To promote the sport of curling in Manitoba.

Manitoba Diving Association
Sport Manitoba Building, 200 Main St., Winnipeg MB R3C 1A8 Canada
Tel: 204-925-5654; *Fax:* 204-925-5703
headcoach@panamdiving.com
www.manitobadiving.com
Provides strong ethical and values driven foundation for diving throughout Manitoba and Canada, and supports athletic development, personal growth and community awareness through excellence in leadership

Manitoba Five Pin Bowling Federation, Inc.
#219, 200 Main St., Winnipeg MB R3C 4M2 Canada
Tel: 204-925-5766; *Fax:* 204-925-5767
Toll-Free: 800-282-8069
www.mfpbf.org
To provide services & resources to its members which enable them to increase membership & promote bowling as a lifetime sport through effective programs at all levels of participation
Deanne Zilinsky, Executive Director

Manitoba Freestyle Wrestling Association
200 Main St., Winnipeg MB R3C 4M2 Canada
Tel: 204-925-5670; *Fax:* 204-925-5703
mbfreewr@mb.sympatico.ca

Manitoba High Schools Athletic Association (MHSAA)
#405, 200 Main St., Winnipeg MB R3C 4M2 Canada
Tel: 204-925-5640; *Fax:* 204-925-5624
info@mhsaa.ca
www.mhsaa.mb.ca
To promote the value of sports in Manitoba secondary schools; To provide athletic & educational opportunities so that students reach their full potential
Morris Glimcher, Executive Director
Don Hurton, President

Manitoba Horse Council Inc.
#207, 200 Main St., Winnipeg MB R3C 4M2 Canada
Tel: 204-925-5718; *Fax:* 204-925-5792
admin@manitobahorsecouncil.ca
www.manitobahorsecouncil.ca
Dave Myers, President
Sheilagh Antoniuk, Executive Director

Manitoba Ringette Association (MRA) / Association de ringuette du Manitoba
Sport Manitoba, #309, 200 Main St., Winnipeg MB R3C 4M2 Canada
Tel: 204-925-5710; *Fax:* 204-925-5925
ringette@sport.mb.ca
www.manitobaringette.ca
To promote ringette throughout the province

Manitoba Soaring Council
200 Main St., Winnipeg MB R3C 4M2 Canada
Tel: 204-925-5682; *Fax:* 204-925-5703
www.wgc.mb.ca/msc/Manitoba_Soaring_Council_Home_Page.htm
To foster the art of soaring as an environmentally friendly safe & competitive life sport accessible to all Manitobans

Manitoba Speed Skating Association
145 Pacific Ave., Winnipeg MB R3B 2Z6 Canada
Tel: 204-925-5657; *Fax:* 204-925-5792
Toll-Free: 888-628-9921
mssa@shawbiz.ca
www.mbspeedskating.org
The MSSA is dedicated to the development, growth and effective administration of the sport of speed skating in Manitoba through the provision of leadership, support and promotion of its members and clubs.
Paul Daeninck, President

Manitoba Trail Riding Club Inc.
838 Alfred Ave., Winnipeg MB R2X 0T6 Canada
Kelli.Hayhurst@pwgsc.gc.ca
www.mbtrailridingclub.ca
Was formed to meet the needs of a growing number of horse people who wanted a type of riding other than in the show ring which could demonstrate good horsemanship and promote sound, sensible trail horses.
Kelli Hayhurst, President
Mary Anne Kirk, Treasurer

Manitoba Underwater Council (MUC)
PO Box 711, Winnipeg MB R3C 2K3 Canada
Tel: 204-632-8508
info@manunderwater.com
www.manunderwater.com
To coordinate, preserve, support & promote sport diving clubs & associations; to promote safety in diving; to exchange & disseminate information concerning the sport of skin & scuba diving & to foster conservation

Manitoba Volleyball Association (MVA)
200 Main St., Winnipeg MB R3C 4M2 Canada
Tel: 204-925-5783; *Fax:* 204-925-5786
mbvolley@sport.mb.ca
www.manitobavolleyball.com

To govern the sport of volleyball in Manitoba; to promote the development & growth of volleyball in the province

Minor Hockey Alliance of Ontario
71 Albert St., Stratford ON N5A 3K2 Canada
Tel: 519-273-7209; *Fax:* 519-273-2114
alliance@alliancehockey.com
www.alliancehockey.com
Tony Martindale, Executive Director

National Snow Industries Association (NSIA) / Association nationale des industries de la neige
#810, 245, av Victoria, Montréal QC H3Z 2M6 Canada
Tel: 514-939-7370; *Fax:* 514-939-7371
Toll-Free: 800-263-6742
central.station@nsia.ca
www.nsia.ca
To promote the sport of skiing, snowboarding & outdoor winter-related products

New Brunswick Ball Hockey Association (NBBHA)
16 Reflection Lane, Quispamsis NB E2E 6E7 Canada
Tel: 506-333-7772; *Fax:* 506-847-8585
sheila@committedtoyourgoals.com
Sheila Elliott, Contact

New Brunswick Broomball Association
c/o Daniel Savoie
Tel: 506-381-0919
Daniel Savoie, Contact

New Brunswick Candlepin Bowlers Association
PO Box 4315, 11 Sawyer Rd., Woodstock NB E7M 6B7 Canada
Tel: 506-328-8418
To promote candlepin bowling, a sport unique to the Maritimes & New England
Bill Hamilton, Contact

New Brunswick Curling Association (NBCA) / Association de Curling du Nouveau-Brunswick (ACNB)
PO Box 812, Moncton NB E1C 8N6 Canada
Tel: 506-854-9143; *Fax:* 506-388-5708
Toll-Free: 800-592-2875
nbca@nb.sympatico.ca
www.nbcurling.nb.ca
To promote curling in New Brunswick; to establish & govern rules for curling competitions in New Brunswick

New Brunswick Equestrian Association (NBEA)
c/o Sport NB, #13, 900 Hanwell Rd., Fredericton NB E3B 6A3 Canada
Tel: 506-454-2353; *Fax:* 506-454-2363
generalinfo@equestrian.nb.ca
www.equestrian.nb.ca
Jeremy Hoyt, President
Jennifer Everett, Secretary

New Brunswick Golf Association (NBGA) / Association de golf du nouveau brunswick
PO Box 1555, Stn. A, Fredericton NB E3B 1G2 Canada
Tel: 506-451-1324; *Fax:* 506-451-1348
nbgolf@nbnet.nb.ca
www.nbga.nb.ca
To determine policies & standards relating to the development & promotion of amateur golf in New Brunswick
Pierre Arsenault, Executive Director

New Brunswick Lawn Bowling Association
929A Cloverdale Rd., Riverview NB E1B 5E6 Canada
rkhm118@aol.com
Dugald Richford, Executive Secretary

New Brunswick Sailing Association (NBSA)
c/o Executive Director, 105 Bird Ave., Fredericton NB E2A 2H8 Canada
Tel: 506-472-2117
www.nbsailing.nb.ca
The New Brunswick Sailing Association (NBSA) is the provincial governing body for boating and the sport of sailing in the province and is the Canadian Yachting Association's representative in New Brunswick. NBSA is a non-profit volunteer association with a mission to provide leadership, coordination and training to meet the needs of all New Brunswick boaters.
Sharon Mills, Executive Director

Newfoundland & Labrador Amateur Wrestling Association (NLAWA)
1 Wade's Ln., Flatrock NL A1K 1C3 Canada
Fax: 709-643-5103
contact@nlawa.com
www.nlawa.com
The NLAWA is a small organization comprised of coaches, officials, parents and athletes who are dedicated to advancing the sport of wrestling in Newfoundland and Labrador

Newfoundland & Labrador Ball Hockey Association (NLBHA)
PO Box 2579, Stn. C, St. John's NL A1C 6K1 Canada
Tel: 709-729-0689
paulbarron@gov.nl.ca
To promote the sport of ball hockey in Newfoundland & Labrador; to maintain rules & regulations of the sport
Paul Barron, President

Newfoundland & Labrador Basketball Association
PO Box 21029, St. John's NL A1A 5B2 Canada
Tel: 709-576-0247; *Fax:* 709-576-8787
nlba@sportnf.com
www.nlba.nf.ca
To develop & promote the sport of basketball across Newfoundland; to assest in the establishment of basketball clubs throughout Newfoundland & Labrador.

Newfoundland & Labrador Curling Association
c/o Bob Osborne, 54 Hoyles Ave., St. John's NL A1B 1E3
Tel: 709-738-3640
www.curlingnl.ca

Newfoundland & Labrador Soccer Association
PO Box 21029, St. John's NL A1A 5B2 Canada
Tel: 709-576-0601; *Fax:* 709-576-0588
nlsa@sportnl.ca
www.nlsa.ca
To provide opportunities for the general public to engage in the game of soccer while having fun & competition

Newfoundland & Labrador Speed Skating Association (NLSSA)
81 Birchy Cove Dr., Corner Brook NL A2H 6W8 Canada
Tel: 709-785-1403
rzrenos@gmail.com

Newfoundland & Labrador Volleyball Association (NLVA)
PO Box 21248, St. John's NL A1A 5B2 Canada
Tel: 709-576-0817; *Fax:* 709-576-7493
nlvaruss@sportnl.ca
www.nlva.net
To promote volleyball in Newfoundland & Labrador; to provide competitive opportunities for its members

Newfoundland Baseball
83 Ashford Dr., Mount Pearl NL A1N 3N7 Canada
Tel: 709-368-2819; *Fax:* 709-368-6080
nlbaseball@nl.rogers.com
www.sport.ca/nlbaseball
Supports amatuer baseball in Newfoundland.

Newfoundland Equestrian Association (NEA)
PO Box 372, Stn. C, St. John's NL A1C 5J9 Canada
www.horsenewfoundland.com
Katrina Butler, President
Sheila Anstey, Vice-President & Director, Competitions
Katie Murray, Secretary
Cathy Favre, Treasurer

North American Riding for the Handicapped Association (NARHA)
PO Box 33150, Denver CO 80233 USA
Tel: 303-452-1212; *Fax:* 303-252-4610
Toll-Free: 800-369-7433
narha@narha.org
www.narha.org
Promotes the benefit of the horse riding for individuals with physical, emotional & learning disabilities
Carol Nickell, CEO

Northern Alberta Curling Association (NACA)
#110, 9440 - 49 St., Edmonton AB T6B 2M9 Canada
Tel: 780-440-4270; *Fax:* 780-463-4519
naca@planet.eon.net
northernalbertacurling.com

Northern Ontario Curling Association
PO Box 940, Unit #4, 214 Main St. West, Atikokan ON P0T 1C0 Canada
Tel: 807-597-8730; *Fax:* 807-597-4241
Toll-Free: 888-597-8730
info@curlnoca.ca
www.curlnoca.ca

Northern Ontario Hockey Association (NOHA)
108 Lakeshore Dr., North Bay ON P1A 2A8 Canada
Tel: 705-474-8851; *Fax:* 705-474-6019
noha@noha.on.ca
www.noha.on.ca
To foster the sport of amateur hockey in northern Ontario
Bryce Kulik, President
Chris May, Executive Director

Northwest Territories 5 Pin Bowlers' Association (NWT5PBA)
PO Box 2643, Yellowknife NT X1A 2P9 Canada
Tel: 867-873-8189; *Fax:* 867-873-8237
gary@nwt5pba.ca
www.nwt5pba.ca
To promote 5 pin bowling
Gary Black, President

Northwest Territories Broomball Association
Stn. 529 Range Lake Road, Yellowknife NT X1A 3Y1 Canada
nwtbroomball@yahoo.ca
www.nwtbroomball.com
Jan Vallillee, President

Northwest Territories Curling Association
c/o PO Box 11089, Yellowknife NT X1A 3X7 Canada
nwtca@auroranet.nt.ca
www.curlingnwt.ssimicro.com

Northwest Territories Ringette / Association de ringuette des Territoires Nord-Ouest
#2, 496 Range Lake Rd., Yellowknife NT X1A 3R5 Canada
Tel: 867-920-7419; *Fax:* 867-920-2843
nwt_ringette@yahoo.com

Northwest Territories Soccer Association (NWTSA)
PO Box 11089, Yellowknife NT X1A 3X7 Canada
Tel: 867-669-8326; *Fax:* 867-669-8327
Toll-Free: 800-661-0797
www.nwtkicks.ca
The NWT Soccer Association is a volunteer-run organization and the governing body for all soccer activities in the NWT; focus is on the grassroots development of our game, as well as the promotion of high performance
Melanie Kornacki, Sport Consultant
Ryan Fequet, President

Northwest Territories Volleyball Association (NWTVA)
Tel: 867-920-2712
terrel_hobbs@nwtvolleyball.ca
www.nwtvolleyball.ca
To develop athletes & coaches to compete as Team NWT in the Arctic Winter Games & the Canada Games

Northwestern Ontario Curling Association (NWOCA)
433 Catherine St., Thunder Bay ON P7E 1K9 Canada
Tel: 807-622-8254; *Fax:* 807-626-9622
www.norontcurl.tripod.com

Northwestern Québec Curling Association (NWQCA) / Association de curling du Nord-Ouest québécois
281, 3e rue est, Amos QC J9T 2A7 Canada
Tel: 819-732-2089; *Fax:* 819-732-1617

Nova Scotia Badminton Association
5516 Spring Garden Rd., Halifax NS B3J 1G6 Canada
Tel: 902-425-5450; *Fax:* 902-425-5606
nsbadminton@sportnovascotia.ca
www.nsba.ca

Nova Scotia Ball Hockey Association
100 Auburn Drive, Dartmouth NS B2W 3S6 Canada
Tel: 902-462-5433; *Fax:* 902-477-0243
To promote ball hockey in Nova Scotia & to host provincial tournaments
Bill Davidson, Contact

Nova Scotia Boxing Authority (NSBA)
c/o Amanda Noonan, PO Box 864, 5516 Spring Garden Rd., 2nd Fl., Halifax NS B3J 2V2 Canada
Tel: 902-457-0413; *Fax:* 902-484-6937
anoonan@micco.ca
The Nova Scotia Boxing Authority (NSBA) was established in 1975 to regulate professional boxing. In 1981 the authority superseded local boxing commissions. The object and purpose of the authority are to supervise and regulate boxing, establish and enforce uniform rules for the conduct of boxing, and train officials in accordance with nationally established standards. The NSBA, which answers to the minister of health promotion and protection, is now responsible for regulating all combat sports.
Michael MacDonald, Chairman
Hubert Earle, Director, Combat Sports

Nova Scotia Broomball Association (NSBA)
c/o Rob McKellar, PO Box 3010, Stn. South, Halifax NS Canada
Tel: 902-548-2600

Nova Scotia Curling Association (NSCA)
5516 Spring Garden Rd., 4th Fl., Halifax NS B3J 1G6 Canada
Tel: 902-421-2875; *Fax:* 902-425-5606
nsca@sportnovascotia.ca
www.nscurl.com

Nova Scotia Distance Riding Association (NSDRA)
RR#3, Site 802, Newport NS B0N 2A0 Canada

Nova Scotia Equestrian Federation
5516 Spring Garden Rd., 4th Fl., Halifax NS B3J 1G6 Canada
Tel: 902-425-5450; *Fax:* 902-425-5606
nsef@sportnovascotia.ca
www.horsenovascotia.ca
Heather Myrer, Executive Director

Nova Scotia Golf Association (NSGA)
#4, 24 Simmonds Dr., Dartmouth NS B3B 1R3 Canada
Tel: 902-468-8844; *Fax:* 902-484-5327
adminexec@ns.aliantzinc.ca
www.nsga.ns.ca
To promote, foster & develop golf at all levels in Nova Scotia; to provide a liaison between member clubs & the Royal Canadian Golf Association; to consult & assist with member clubs on turf maintenance, handicap procedures, slope ratings, rule interpretations & junior development; to organize tournaments, in cooperation with member clubs, that determine provincial champions.
David Campbell, Executive Director
Shelley Pineault, Executive Assistant

Nova Scotia Powerlifting Association
Sydney NS B1P 3W7 Canada
Tel: 902-567-0893
president@nspowerlifting.org
www.nspowerlifting.org
To provide opportunities for lifters to learn the sport of powerlifting through seminars, gyms & clubs; to participate in meets locally, nationally & internationally

Nova Scotia Rugby Football Union
5516 Spring Garden Rd., Halifax NS B3J 1G6 Canada
Tel: 902-425-5450; *Fax:* 902-425-5606
rugby@sportnovascotia.ca
www.rugbyns.ns.ca
To promote, control, encourage & develop the game of rugby union football throughout Nova Scotia

Nova Scotia School Athletic Federation
5516 Spring Garden Rd., Halifax NS B3J 3G6 Canada
Tel: 902-425-8662; *Fax:* 902-425-5606
dweston@sportnovascotia.ca
nssaf.ednet.ns.ca
Motto: "Education Through Sport" which thus emphasises the value of sport in relation to the multitude of benefits that participation gives to their students.
Darrell Dempster, Executive Director
Dianne Weston, Secretary

Nova Scotia Table Tennis Association (NSTTA)
9 Londra Ct., Dartmouth NS B2W 5A5 Canada
Tel: 902-406-6286
www.freewebs.com/nstta
Erica Ans, President

Nova Scotia Tennis Association
5516 Spring Garden Rd., Halifax NS B3J 1G6 Canada
Tel: 902-425-5450; *Fax:* 902-425-5606
tennisns@sportnovascotia.ca
www.tennisnovascotia.ca

Nunavut Speed Skating Association
PO Box 761, Iqaluit NU X0A 0H0 Canada
Tel: 867-979-1226; *Fax:* 867-975-3384
jtmaurice@northwestel.net
www.nunavutspeedskating.ca
John Maurice, President

NWT Badminton Association
4407 School Draw Ave., Yellowknife NT X1A 2K2 Canada
Tel: 867-669-2606
jimu@ssimicro.com
www.nwtbadminton.yk.com

NWT Speed Skating Association
PO Box 2664, Yellowknife NT X1A 2P9 Canada
pamela@ssimicro.com
www.nwtspeedskating.ca
To promote the sport of speed skating in the NWT
Pam Dunbar, President

Ontario 5 Pin Bowlers' Association (O5PBA)
#302, 3 Concorde Gate, Toronto ON M3C 3N7 Canada
Tel: 416-426-7167; *Fax:* 416-426-7364
o5pba@o5pba.ca
www.o5pba.ca

Ontario Amateur Wrestling Association (OAWA)
#213, 3 Concorde Gate, Toronto ON M3C 3N7 Canada
Tel: 416-426-7274; *Fax:* 416-426-7343
admin@oawa.ca
www.oawa.ca
To provide essential services & programs dedicated to developing amateur wrestling at all age levels within Ontario

Ontario Badminton Association (OBA)
#209, 3 Concorde Gate, Toronto ON M3C 3N7 Canada
Tel: 416-426-7192; *Fax:* 416-426-7346
info@ontariobadminton.on.ca
www.ontariobadminton.on.ca
To provide an organized, structured environment for the activity of badminton

Ontario Ball Hockey Association (OBHA)
#5, 56 Pennsylvania Ave., Concord ON L4K 3V9 Canada
Tel: 905-738-3320; *Fax:* 905-738-3321
www.ontarioballhockey.ca
Social Media: www.facebook.com/group.php?gid=2374843443
To promote & increase participation in the sport of ball hockey in Ontario; to improve opportunities for competition at all levels of participation; to create & implement leadership opportunities for officials, coaches & administrators; to establish standards of play & for quality of equipment to ensure good sport & safety for all participants
Mauro Cugini, Executive Director

Ontario Basketball
#311, 3 Concorde Gate, Toronto ON M3C 3N7 Canada
Tel: 416-426-7200; *Fax:* 416-426-7360
info@basketball.on.ca
www.basketball.on.ca
To promote & develop basketball on an amateur basis in the province of Ontario.

Ontario Blind Sport Association (OBSA)
#104, 3 Concorde Gate, Toronto ON M3C 3N6 Canada
Tel: 416-426-7191; *Fax:* 416-426-7361
Toll-Free: 888-711-1112
matt@osrc.com
www.blindsports.on.ca

Ontario Competitive Trail Riding Association Inc. (OCTRA)
R.R.#4, Tottenham ON L0G 1W0 Canada
Tel: 905-936-3362
webmaster@octra.on.ca
www.octra.on.ca
To encourage the growth & popularity of competitive trail, endurance riding & Ride'n'Tie; to establish a set of rules & quality for managing & judging same; to encourage & maintain a high standard of horsemanship & sportsmanship amongst competitors; to encourage the selection, care, training & conditioning of horses for long distance riding; to provide guidance & help to clubs & groups in establishing & running competitive rides; to ensure that all rides are run humanely so as to avoid cruelty & suffering to competing animals; to formulate promotional & educational programs; to foster goodwill & understanding between horse owners, land owners & conservation authorities with a view to opening up more land for riding trails
Mark Ford, President
Joe Mezenberg, Vice-President
Marg Murray, Secretary
Kelly Corbyn, Treasurer

Ontario Curling Association (OCA)
Office Mall 2, #2B, 1400 Bayly St., Pickering ON L1W 3R2 Canada
Tel: 905-831-1757; *Fax:* 905-831-1083
Toll-Free: 877-668-2875
doug@ontcurl.com
www.ontcurl.com
The Ontario Curling Association is an association of curling clubs covering the southern part of Ontario. Services and programs, including a variety of competitions are supplied to the clubs and their members

Ontario Cycling Association (OCA) / Association cycliste ontarienne
#307, 3 Concorde Gate, Toronto ON M3C 3N7
Tel: 416-426-7416; *Fax:* 416-426-7349
info@ontariocycling.org; ocamagazine@ontariocycling.org
www.ontariocycling.org
To act as the provincial governing body for road, track & cyclocross, mountain biking, & BMX racing in Ontario; To develop & deliver quality programs & services for the sport of cycling in Ontario
Duncan Vipond, President
Malcolm Eade, Vice-President, Administration & Finance
Glenn Meeuwisse, Vice-President, High Performance
Matthias Schmidt, Vice-President, Development
Jim Crosscombe, Executive Director
Denise Kelly, Director, Provincial Coaching
Chris Baskys, Coordinator, Membership
Nicky Pearson, Coordinator, BMX Growth & Development

Ontario Deaf Sports Association
#303, 3 Concorde Gate, Toronto ON M3C 3N7 Canada
Tel: 416-413-0299
office@ontariodeafsports.on.ca
www.ontariodeafsports.on.ca

Ontario Equestrian Federation (OEF)
#203, 9120 Leslie St., Richmond Hill ON L4B 3J9 Canada
Tel: 905-709-6545; *Fax:* 905-709-1867
Toll-Free: 877-441-7112
horse@horse.on.ca
www.horse.on.ca
Committed to equine welfare & to providing leadership & support to the individuals, associations & industries in Ontario's horse community
Deborah Thompson, Executive Director
Gary Yaghdjian, President
Kathy Fremes, Secretary

Ontario Federation of School Athletic Associations (OFSAA) / Fédération des associations du sport scolaire de l'Ontario
#204, 3 Concorde Gate, Toronto ON M3C 3N7
Tel: 416-426-7391; *Fax:* 416-426-7317
lindsey@ofsaa.on.ca (Newsletter)
www.ofsaa.on.ca
Social Media: www.facebook.com/group.php?gid=57198022397
To enhance school sport in Ontario; To handle issues that affect students, coaches, schools, & communities; To work with volunteer teacher-coaches to offer provincial championships & festivals for student-athletes across Ontario

Ontario Hockey Federation (OHF)
Sport Alliance of Ontario Bldg., #212, 3 Concorde Gate, Toronto ON M3C 3N7
Tel: 416-426-7249; *Fax:* 416-426-7347
info@ohf.on.ca
www.ohf.on.ca
Joe Drago, Executive Director
Bill Bowman, 1st Vice-President
Frank Pindar, 2nd Vice-President
Phil McKee, Executive Director
Wayne Tod, Secretary-Treasurer
Ryan Berg, Coordinator, Hockey Development
Cheryl Boston, Coordinator, Communications, Marketing, & Events

Ontario Horse Trials Association (OHTA)
#186, 3-304 Stone Rd. West, Guelph ON N1G 4W4 Canada
ohta@hotmail.ca
www.horsetrials.on.ca
OHTA is a volunteer, not-for-profit organization whose main functions are to support, develop & promote events in Ontario.

Ontario Lawn Bowls Association
c/o Elaine Stevenson, 23018 Lakeridge Rd., RR#2, Sunderland ON L0C 1H0
Tel: 705-228-8058
olba@olba.ca
www.olba.ca
Arja Nesbitt, President
Elaine Houtby, Vice-President
Alan Dean, 2nd Vice-President
Bob O'Neil, Executive Director
Edith Pedden, Secretary
Richard Peart, Treasurer

Ontario Minor Hockey Association (OMHA)
#3, 25 Brodie Dr., Richmond Hill ON L4B 3K7
Tel: 905-780-6642; *Fax:* 905-780-0344
omha@omha.net
www.omha.net
Social Media: twitter.com/HometownHockey
To provide community-based minor hockey programming for men, women, & children; To monitor the safety of the game, from equipment to rules

Ontario Ringette Association (ORA) / Association de ringuette de l'Ontario
#207, 3 Concorde Gate, Toronto ON M3C 3N7 Canada
Tel: 416-426-7204; *Fax:* 416-426-7359
info@ontario-ringette.com
www.ontario-ringette.com
To promote fun, fitness & friendship in a safe play environment; dedicated to quality performance & fair play opportunity for all ages

Ontario Rugby Union (ORU)
#702A, 1185 Eglinton Ave. East, Toronto ON M3C 3C6 Canada
Tel: 416-426-7050; *Fax:* 416-426-7369
rugbyregistration@osrc.com
www.rugbyontario.com

Ontario Soaring Association
10 Courtwood Pl., Toronto ON M2K 1Z9 Canada
Tel: 416-223-6487

Ontario Soccer Association (OSA)
7601 Martin Grove Rd., Vaughan ON L4L 9E4 Canada
Tel: 905-264-9390; *Fax:* 905-264-9445
TheOSA@soccer.on.ca
www.soccer.on.ca
Provides leadership and support for the advancement of soccer in collaboration and cooperation with their membership partners and other stakeholders by providing programs and services

Ontario Speed Skating Association (OSSA)
Memorial Hall, PO Box 1179, 2 Queen St., 2nd Fl., Lakefield ON K0L 2H0 Canada
Tel: 705-652-0653; *Fax:* 705-652-1227
jdeschenes@speedskatingontario.org
www.speedskatingontario.org
To promote & develop the sport of speed skating in Ontario.
Jackie Deschenes, Executive Director
Bill Allen, Director of Sport

Ontario Tennis Association (OTA)
#200, 1 Shoreham Dr., Toronto ON M3N 3A7
Tel: 416-514-1100; *Fax:* 416-514-1112
Toll-Free: 800-387-5066
ota@tennisontario.com
www.tennisontario.com
To act as the provincial governing body for tennis in Ontario; To promote participation in tennis in Ontario; To create tennis opportunities for players of every level, from grassroots to national calibre athlete; To encourage the quest for excellence for all players

Ontario Trail Riders Association (OTRA)
PO Box 3038, Elmvale ON L0L 1P0 Canada
www.otra.ca
To identify, develop, & preserve multi-use trails throughout Ontario

Ontario Underwater Council (OUC)
#104, 1185 Eglinton Ave. East, Toronto ON M3C 3C6 Canada
Tel: 416-426-7033; *Fax:* 416-426-7280
ouc@underwatercouncil.com
www.underwatercouncil.com
To represent all divers in Ontario; to promote the sport of scuba diving
Raimund Krob, President

Ontario Volleyball Association (OVA)
#304, 3 Concorde Gate, Toronto ON M3C 3N7 Canada
Tel: 416-426-7316; *Fax:* 416-426-7109
Toll-Free: 800-563-5938
ova@ontariovolleyball.org
www.ontariovolleyball.org
Social Media: twitter.com/ova_updates
To lead in the promotion & development of volleyball in Ontario.

Ontario Water Polo Association (OWPA) / L'Association de water polo d'Ontario
#206, 3 Concorde Gate, Toronto ON M3C 3N7 Canada
Tel: 416-426-7028; *Fax:* 416-426-7356
info@ontariowaterpolo.ca
www.ontariowaterpolo.ca

Ontario Women's Hockey Association (OWHA) / Association de hockey féminin de l'Ontario
#3, 5155 Spectrum Way, Mississauga ON L4W 5A1 Canada
Tel: 905-282-9980; *Fax:* 905-282-9982
info@owha.on.ca
owha.on.ca
To provide & develop opportunities for girls & women to play female hockey in all aspects of female hockey; to foster & encourage leadership programs in all areas related to the development of female hockey in Ontario & to promote hockey as a game played primarily for enjoyment while also fostering sportsmanship
Fran Rider, President

Ottawa District Minor Hockey Association (ODMHA)
#300, 1247 Kilborn Place, Ottawa ON K1H 6K9 Canada
Tel: 613-224-3589; *Fax:* 613-224-4625
www.odmha.on.ca
Social Media: www.facebook.com/group.php?gid=2228819818
The Ottawa & District Minor Hockey Association is dedicated to promoting and fosyering minor hockey through fair play and maintaining and increasing interest in the game of hockey by ensuring that all organized minor hockey is developed within the Branch in accordance to prescribed standards.
Mike Depratto, President

Ottawa Valley Curling Association (OVCA)
PO Box 40129, Ottawa ON K1V 0W8 Canada
Tel: 613-521-5822; *Fax:* 613-521-5344
Toll-Free: 800-385-6621
events@ovca.com
www.ovca.com
To foster curling in the Ottawa & St. Lawrence Valleys & Outaouais
Perry Anderson, President
Lily Ooi, Coordinator, Events

Paralympic Sports Association (Alberta) (PSA)
10024 - 79 Ave., Edmonton AB T6E 1R5 Canada
Tel: 780-439-8687; *Fax:* 780-432-0486
info@parasports.net
www.parasports.net
To provide sports & recreation programs for people with a physical disability
Kim McDonald, Executive Director

Paralympics PEI
c/o Royalty Center House Of Sport, PO Box 841, 40 Enman Cres., Charlottetown PE C1A 7L9 Canada
Tel: 902-368-4540; *Fax:* 902-368-4548
info@website.paralympicspei.pe.ca
www.paralympicspei.pe.ca
To ensure the ample provision of sport & recreation opportunities for persons who are physically challenged
Tracy Stevenson, Executive Director

ParaSport Ontario
#104, 3 Concorde Gate, Toronto ON M3C 3N7 Canada
Tel: 416-426-7187; *Fax:* 416-426-7361
Toll-Free: 800-265-1539
info@parasportontario.ca
www.parasportontario.ca
To provide leadership, resources, & opportunities to ensure a strong community for persons with a disability in the Ontario sport & recreation community

Patrouille de ski St-Jean
651, 6e Rue ouest, Chibougamau QC G8P 2T8 Canada
Tél: 418-748-6914
Patrice Bolduc

Peace Curling Association (PCA)
PO Box 265, Grande Prairie AB T8V 3A4 Canada
Tel: 780-532-4782; *Fax:* 780-538-2485
peaccurl@telusplanet.net
www.peacecurl.org
Bob Cooper, President

Pemberton Soaring Centre
Pemberton BC V0N 2L1 Canada
Tel: 604-894-5727; *Fax:* 604-894-5776
Toll-Free: 800-831-2611
info@pembertonsoaring.com
www.pembertonsoaring.com
To coordinate soaring activities in BC; to encourage formation of new clubs & training of new instructors

Physical & Health Education Canada / Éducation physique et santé Canada
#301, 2197 Riverside Dr., Ottawa ON K1H 7X3
Tel: 613-523-1348; *Fax:* 613-523-1206
Toll-Free: 800-663-8708
info@phecanada.ca
www.phecanada.ca
To promote quality school health progams & the healthy development of Canadian children & youth

Prince Edward Island Alpine Ski Association
PO Box 2026, Charlottetown PE CIA 7N7 Canada
Tel: 902-368-4110; *Fax:* 902-368-4548
Toll-Free: 800-247-6712
sports@sportpei.pe.ca
www.sportpei.pe.ca
Fred Horrelt, President

Prince Edward Island Amateur Baseball Association
PO Box 302, Charlottetown PE C1A 7K7 Canada
Tel: 902-368-4208; *Fax:* 902-368-4548
Toll-Free: 800-235-5687
kmcintosh@sportpei.pe.ca
www.baseballpei.ca
To promote & develop minor & amateur baseball in PEI.

Prince Edward Island Amateur Boxing Association
2595 Horne Cross Rd., Wilsloe PE C1E 1Z3 Canada
Tel: 902-394-1574; *Fax:* 902-628-3865
Holly Morrison, President

Prince Edward Island Badminton Association
c/o Sport PEI, PO Box 302, Charlottetown PE C1A 7K7 Canada
Tel: 902-368-4262; *Fax:* 902-368-4548

Prince Edward Island Curling Association (PEICA)
PO Box 302, 40 Enman Cres., Charlottetown PE C1A 7K7 Canada
Tel: 902-368-4986; *Fax:* 902-368-4548
glucas@sportpei.pe.ca
www.peicurling.com
To advance & promote curling as a competitive & recreational sport in Prince Edward Island
Ray McCourt, President

Prince Edward Island Five Pin Bowlers Association Inc.
c/o Sport PEI, PO Box 302, Charlottetown PE C1A 7K7 Canada
Tel: 902-368-4110; *Fax:* 902-368-4548
Toll-Free: 800-247-6712
sports@sportpei.pe.ca
www.pei5pba.com
Sue MacPherson, President

Prince Edward Island Golf Association
PO Box 51, Charlottetown PE C1A 7K2 Canada
Tel: 902-393-3293; *Fax:* 902-628-2260
peiga@peiga.ca
www.peiga.ca
The total improvement of golf on PEI
Don Chandler, Executive Director
Jean Kelly, President

Prince Edward Island Hockey Referees Association
c/o Hockey PEI, 40 Enman Cres., Charlottetown PE C1A 7K7 Canada
Tel: 902-367-8373
troyhowatt@eastlink.ca
www.peihra.com
Troy Howatt, Chair

Prince Edward Island Lawn Bowling Association
Sport PEI, PO Box 302, Charlottetown PE C1A 7K7 Canada
Tel: 902-368-4110
sharonrenner@eastlink.ca
To provide guidance to bowlers and all people interested in the sport. They wish to assit in the growth and development of Lawn Bowling on PEI Island, they wish to promote and encourage fair play in the sport at club level and at National lvel, they wish to develop leadership and to provide oppourtunities for development in the field of coaching, umpiring, and administration. They also provide interesting tournaments and events throughout the playing season.
Sharon Renner, President

Prince Edward Island Roadrunners Club
40 Villa Ave., Charlottetown PE C1A 2B1 Canada
runners@peiroadrunners.ca
www.peiroadrunners.ca
The PEI RoadRunners Club is an organization whose objective is to promote and encourage running as a sport and healthful exercise. The Club welcomes all runners, regardless of ability and attempts to meet the needs of the competitive, as well as, the recreational runner.
Kim Bailey, President

Prince Edward Island Sailing Association (PEISA)
PO Box 6708, York Point PE C0A 1H0 Canada
www.peisailing.com
The PEI Sailing Association is a volunteer organization that promotes sailing in the province of Prince Edward Island, Canada. As the provincial chapter of the Canadian Sailing Association the PEI Sailing Association provides support and training to anybody interested in learning to sail or expanding their sailing.
Ellen McPhail, Executive Director

Prince Edward Island School Athletic Association (PEISAA)
109 Water St., Summerside PE C1N 1A8 Canada
Tel: 902-888-8037; *Fax:* 902-432-2659
grturtle@gov.pe.ca
www.edu.pe.ca/peisaa
Supporting sports including but not exclusive to, badminton, softball, wrestling, golf, cross country, curling, and volleyball, in PEI.
Garth Turtle, Executive Director
Lona Ryan, Game Reporting
Gerald MacCormack, Secretary-Treasurer

Prince Edward Island Soccer Association (PEISA)
PO Box 1863, 40 Enman Cres., Charlottetown PE C1A 7N5 Canada
Tel: 902-368-6251; *Fax:* 902-569-7693
admin@peisoccer.com
www.peisoccer.com
To promote & regulate soccer in PEI; to provide competitive opportunities for members.

Prince Edward Island Tennis Association
PO Box 302, 40 Enman Cres., Charlottetown PE C1A 7K7 Canada
Tel: 902-368-4985; *Fax:* 902-368-4548
mconnolly@sportpei.pe.ca
www.tennispei.ca
To promote the sport of tennis on PEI.

Prince Edward Island Track & Field Association
c/o Sport PEI, 3 Queen St., Charlottetown PE C1A 7K7 Canada
Tel: 902-368-4110

Prince Edward Island Water Ski Association
c/o Regional President, 8 Falconwood Rd., Charlottetown PE C1A 6B5 Canada
Tel: 902-894-5740
Stuart Smith, President

Provincial Water Polo Association (PWPA)
c/o Sport Nova Scotia, 5516 Spring Garden Rd., Halifax NS B3J 1G6 Canada
lavoie.ghg@forces.gc.ca
www.hfxh2o.ca
The Provincial Water Polo Association (PWPA) was created in late 2006, and its prime mission is to promote the sport of water polo in Nova Scotia.
Guy Lavoie, Contact

Québec Ball Hockey Association
#203, 5960 Jean-Talon E, St. Leonard QC H1S 1M2 Canada
Tel: 514-251-9346; *Fax:* 514-251-8285
info@ballhockeynews.ca
www.ballhockeynews.ca
Tony Iannitto

Québec Lawn Bowling Federation / Fédération de Boulingrin du Québec
#662 Oak Ave., Saint-Lambert QC J4P 2R6 Canada
www.qlbf.org
Debbie Smits, Contact

Rhythmic Gymnastics Alberta (RGA)
c/o Percy Page Centre, 11759 Groat Rd., 3rd Fl., Edmonton AB T5M 3K6 Canada
Tel: 780-427-8152; *Fax:* 780-427-8153
Toll-Free: 800-881-2504
rga@rgalberta.com
www.rgalberta.com
Social Media: www.facebook.com/pages/Rhythmic-Gymnastics-Alberta/298160665303?ref=ts
To foster & encourage participation & the development of excellence in rhythmic gymnastics
Joan Jack, President
Odette Lindstrom, Treasurer
Helen Marchak, Vice-President

Rhythmic Gymnastics Manitoba Inc. (RGM)
Sport Manitoba Bldg., 200 Main St., Winnipeg MB R3C 4M2 Canada
rhythmic@sport.mb.ca
www.rgmanitoba.com
To support & promote rhythmic gymnastic programs

Ringette Association of Saskatchewan (RAS) / Association de ringuette de Saskatchewan
#204, 1860 Lorne St., Regina SK S4P 2L7 Canada
Tel: 306-780-9432; *Fax:* 306-780-9460
executivedirector@ringettesask.com
www.ringettesask.com
To develop, promote, communicate & administer programs, policies & procedures which will enhance the development & participation of coaches, players, officals, volunteers & administrators from all levels throughout Saskatchewan

Ringette Canada (RC) / Ringuette Canada
#201, 5510 Canotek Rd., Ottawa ON K1J 9J4 Canada
Tel: 613-748-5655; *Fax:* 613-748-5860
ringette@ringette.ca
www.ringette.ca
To formulate, publish & administer national policies beneficial to the sport & to enforce laws & regulations governing ringette; to encourage ringette participants to strive for excellence in teamwork, team spirit & team discipline

Ringette New Brunswick (RNB) / Ringuette Nouveau-Brunswick
c/o Marise Aufrey, Administrative Assistant, 940 Centrale St., Memramcook NB E4K 3T4 Canada
Tel: 506-758-2546
MariseA@rrsb.nb.ca
www.sport.nb.ca/ringette/
To ensure the well-being & development of ringette athletes in New Brunswick

Ringette Nova Scotia
5516 Spring Garden Rd., 4th Fl., Halifax NS B3J 1G6 Canada
Tel: 902-425-5450; *Fax:* 902-425-5606
ringette@sportnovascotia.ca
www.ringette.ns.ca
To promote, develop & administer the sport of ringette within Nova Scotia

Rowing Canada Aviron (RCA) / Association canadienne d'aviron amateur
100 - 4636 Elk Lake Dr., Victoria BC V8Z 5M1 Canada
Fax: 250-361-4211
Toll-Free: 877-722-4769
rca@rowingcanada.org
www.rowingcanada.org
To encourage the formation of rowing clubs & provincial associations; to encourage the organization of national regattas; to define & to maintain the principles of amateurism in all competitions; to organize, develop & select national rowing teams to represent Canada internationally

Royal Canadian Golf Association (RCGA) / Association royale de golf du Canada
Golf House, #1, 1333 Dorval Dr., Oakville ON L6M 4X7 Canada
Tel: 905-849-9700; *Fax:* 905-845-7040
cboag@rcga.org
www.rcga.org
Social Media: www.facebook.com/group.php?gid=61328126412
To work with the provincial golf associations & our member clubs to foster the growth & development of golf

Royal Canadian Golf Association Foundation
#1, 1333 Dorval Dr., Oakville ON L6M 4X7 Canada
Tel: 905-849-9700; *Fax:* 905-845-7040
Toll-Free: 800-263-0009
khewson@rcga.org
www.rcga.org
To raise & grant funds for the betterment of golf in Canada
Karen Hewson, Executive Director

Sask Sport Inc.
1870 Lorne St., Regina SK S4P 2L7 Canada
Tel: 306-780-9300; *Fax:* 306-781-6021
sasksport@sasksport.sk.ca
www.sasksport.sk.ca
To ensure the total development of amateur sport through the provincial sport governing bodies; to promote extensive participation towards excellence

Saskatchewan 5 Pin Bowlers' Association
#100, 1805 - 8th Ave., Regina SK S4R 1E8 Canada
Tel: 306-780-9412; *Fax:* 306-780-9455
bowling@sasktel.net
saskbowl.com
To develop trust & harmony among member organizations; to assist in the development & promotion of the sport of bowling through the provision of stable funding
Rhonda Sereda, Executive Director

Saskatchewan Amateur Speed Skating Association (SASSA)
2205 Victoria Ave., Regina SK S4P 0S4 Canada
Tel: 306-780-9400; *Fax:* 306-525-4009
sassa@sasktel.net
www.saskspeedskating.ca
Working together to develop & promote the sport of speed skating at all levels as a fun, competitive, healthy, family activity
Shawn MacLennan, Executive Director

Saskatchewan Amateur Wrestling Association (SAWA)
510 Cynthia St., Saskatoon SK S7L 7K7 Canada
Tel: 306-975-0822; *Fax:* 306-242-8007
sk.wrestling@shaw.ca
www.saskwrestling.com
To govern and promote the sport of wrestling in Saskatchewan.

Saskatchewan Badminton Association (SBA)
3615 Pasqua St., Regina SK S4S 6W8 Canada
Tel: 306-780-9368; *Fax:* 306-780-9369
saskbadminton@sasktel.net
www.saskbadminton.ca
Dedicated to the development of badminton in Saskatchewan.

Saskatchewan Baseball Association (SBA)
1870 Lorne St., Regina SK S4P 2L7 Canada
Tel: 306-780-9237; *Fax:* 306-352-3669
mramage@sasktel.net
www.saskbaseball.ca
To provide quality baseball programs to interested participants at whatever level they may choose

Saskatchewan Blind Sports Association Inc.
510 Cynthia St., Saskatoon SK S7L 7K7 Canada
Tel: 306-975-0888; *Toll-Free:* 877-772-7798
sbsa.sk@shaw.ca
www.saskblindsports.ca
To assist persons who are blind or with visual impairment to achieve excellence in sport, satisfaction in recreation, independence, self-reliance & full community participation

Saskatchewan Broomball Association (SBA)
2205 Victoria Ave., Regina SK S4P 0S4 Canada
Tel: 306-780-9215; *Fax:* 306-525-4009
saskbroomball@sasktel.net
www.saskbroomball.ca
To promote multi-level programs to members & non-member groups in both competitive & recreational settings; to promote broomball within the province of Saskatchewan
Greg Perreaux, Executive Director

Saskatchewan Curling Association (SCA)
613 Park St., Regina SK S4N 5N1 Canada
Tel: 306-780-9202; *Fax:* 306-780-9404
Toll-Free: 877-722-2875
saskcurling@sasktel.net
www.saskcurl.com/sca/scahome.htm
To govern and promote the sport of curling in Saskatchewan.

Saskatchewan Cycling Association
2205 Victoria Ave., Regina SK S4P 0S4 Canada
Tel: 306-780-9299; *Fax:* 306-525-4009
cycling@accesscomm.ca
www.saskcycling.ca
To promote and enhance the Saskatchewan cycling experience while recognizing its benefits to the individual and society.
Wayne Walker, President

Saskatchewan Deaf Sports Association
1860 Lorne St., Regina SK S4P 2L7 Canada
Toll-Free: 800-855-0511
www.saskdeafsports.ca
SDSA is a provincial organization that fosters sporting opportunities to members of the deaf & hard-of-hearing communities. With the aid of local clubs, it selects & trains deaf & hard-of-hearing athletes for international competitions.

Saskatchewan Diving
1870 Lorne St., Regina SK S4P 2L7 Canada
Tel: 306-780-9405; *Fax:* 306-781-6021
skdiving@accesscomm.ca
www.saskdiving.ca
To develop & promote safe diving; To ensure that diving clubs operate with safety & integrity; to provide opportunities for self fulfillment & the pursuit of excellence

Saskatchewan Golf Association
510 Cynthia St., Saskatoon SK S7L 7K7 Canada
Tel: 306-975-0850; *Fax:* 306-975-0840
info@saskgolf.ca
www.saskgolf.ca
To promote & maintain amateur golf in Saskatchewan by providing access to information/clinics on golf skills development, rules, handicapping & etiquette

Saskatchewan Hockey Association (SHA) / Association de hockey de la Saskatchewan
#2, 575 Park St., Regina SK S4N 5B2 Canada
Tel: 306-789-5101; *Fax:* 306-789-6112
carissal@sha.sk.ca
www.sha.sk.ca

To administer the operation of amateur hockey in the Province of Saskatchewan; to foster & promote amateur hockey within the province & to assist in the promotion of amateur hockey outside the province; to promote, supervise & administer all competitions for amateur hockey within the jurisdiction of the SAHA

Saskatchewan Horse Federation (SHF)
2205 Victoria Ave., Regina SK S4P 0S4 Canada
Tel: 306-780-9244; *Fax:* 306-525-4009
sk.horse@sasktel.net
www.saskhorse.ca
Mae Smith, Executive Director

Saskatchewan Long Riders
C/O Diane Trundle, Stn. 429, Balgonie SK S0G 0E0 Canada
Tel: 306-978-1225; *Fax:* 306-230-1224
bsutherland@shaw.ca
www.sasklongriders.com
To govern and promote the sport of Long Distance Riding in Saskatchewan.
Rachel Croskery, President

Saskatchewan Rugby Union (SRU)
510 Cynthia St., Saskatoon SK S7L 7K7 Canada
Tel: 306-975-0895; *Fax:* 306-242-8007
sru@sasktel.net
www.saskrugby.com
To encourage, promote, organize, administer & otherwise regulate the sport of Rugby Union Football in the province of Saskatchewan in accordance with the laws of the game in a safe & proper manner

Saskatchewan Ski Association - Skiing for Disabled (SASKI)
17 Clark Cres., Saskatoon SK S7H 3L8 Canada
Tel: 306-374-7745; *Fax:* 306-955-5979
sask.ski@sasktel.net
www.saski.ca
To promote all aspects of winter skiing in Saskatchewan, including alpine, biathlon, cross country & skiing for disabled, & to provide assistance to clubs & individual athletes, instruction & training, adaptive equipment, & a resource library
Alana Ottenbreit, Executive Director
Pat Prokopchuk, Contact, Skiing for Disabled
Doug Sylvester, Contact, Biathlon

Saskatchewan Soccer Association Inc. (SSA)
1870 Lorne St., Regina SK S4P 2L7 Canada
Tel: 306-780-9225; *Fax:* 306-780-9480
k.sumner@sasksoccer.com
www.sasksoccer.com
Social Media:
www.facebook.com/pages/Saskatchewan-Soccer-Association/83226704916

Saskatchewan Volleyball Association
1750 McAra St., Regina SK S4N 6L4 Canada
Tel: 306-780-9250; *Fax:* 306-780-9288
officemanager@saskvolleyball.ca
www.saskvolleyball.ca
Social Media:
www.facebook.com/group.php?gid=121947301797
To develop interest, participation & excellence in volleyball through the promotion & provision of quality services for all

School Sports Newfoundland & Labrador (SSNL)
PO Box 8700, Bldg. 810, Pleasantville NL A1B 4J6 Canada
Tel: 709-729-2795; *Fax:* 709-729-2705
ssnl@sportnl.ca
www.schoolsportsnl.ca
To organize, promote & govern all high school sports within the province; to assist student athletes in reaching their full physical, educational & social potential through participation & sportsmanship in interscholastic sports
Karen Richard, Executive Director

Skate Canada / Patinage Canada
865 Shefford Rd., Ottawa ON K1J 1H9 Canada
Tel: 613-747-1007; *Fax:* 613-748-5718
Toll-Free: 888-747-2372
skatecanada@skatecanada.ca
www.skatecanada.ca
Social Media:
www.facebook.com/group.php?gid=129815677038
Dedicated to the principles of enabling every Canadian to participate in skating throughout their lifetime for fun, fitness &/or achievement

Snowboard Yukon
72 Teslin Rd., Whitehorse YT Y1A 3M6 Canada
Tel: 867-456-2174
info@snowboardyukon.com
www.snowboardyukon.com
To organize and sanction events, train athletes and coaches, form and administer teams for out of territory competitions, and represent Yukon riders in the Canadian Snowboard Federation.
Chris McNutt, President

Soccer New Brunswick
#2, 125 Russ Howard Dr., Moncton NB E1C 0L7 Canada
Tel: 506-382-7529; *Fax:* 506-382-5621
office@soccernb.org
www.soccernb.org
Social Media:
www.facebook.com/group.php?gid=183461681180
To foster & promote the development & growth of the sport of soccer in New Brunswick & to assure equitable accessibility through quality programs

Soccer Nova Scotia
210 Thomas Raddall Dr., Halifax NS B3S 1K3 Canada
Tel: 902-445-0265; *Fax:* 902-445-0258
soccerns@ns.sympatico.ca
www.soccerns.ns.ca
To promote the sport of soccer in Nova Scotia, by providing information & resources to aid player training, coaching education, referee programs

Softball Canada
#212, 223 Colonnade Rd., Ottawa ON K1H 7X3 Canada
Tel: 613-523-3386; *Fax:* 613-523-5761
info@softball.ca
www.softball.ca
Social Media:
www.facebook.com/pages/Softball-Canada/203017655217
To develop & promote softball in Canada

Southern Alberta Curling Association (SACA)
#720, 3 St. NW, Calgary AB T2N 1N9 Canada
Tel: 403-246-9300; *Fax:* 403-246-9349
curling@saca.ca
www.saca.ca
To encourage active participation for residents of all ages in our communities by helping member curling clubs offer a wide variety of programs. To assist in providing opportunities to participate in curling.

Special Olympics Alberta (SOA)
Percy Page Centre, 11759 Groat Rd., Edmonton AB T5M 3K6 Canada
Tel: 780-415-0719; *Fax:* 780-422-2663
Toll-Free: 800-444-2883
info@specialolympics.ab.ca
www.specialolympics.ab.ca
To enrich the lives of Albertans with an intellectual disability, through sport

Special Olympics BC (SOBC)
#210, 3701 East Hastings St., Burnaby BC V5C 2H6 Canada
Tel: 604-737-3078; *Fax:* 604-737-3080
Toll-Free: 888-854-2276
info@specialolympics.bc.ca
www.specialolympics.bc.ca
The Association provides individuals with intellectual disability the opportunity to enhance their lives & celebrate personal achievement through positive sport experiences.

Special Olympics Canada (SOC) / Jeux olympiques spéciaux
#700, 60 St. Clair Ave. East, Toronto ON M4T 1N5 Canada
Tel: 416-927-9050; *Fax:* 416-927-8475
info@specialolympics.ca
www.specialolympics.ca
To provide sport training & competition for people with a mental disability, at local, regional, provincial, national & international levels, year round

Special Olympics Manitoba (SOM)
#402, 200 Main St., Winnipeg MB R3C 4M2 Canada
Tel: 204-925-5628; *Fax:* 204-925-5624
som@specialolympics.mb.ca
www.specialolympics.mb.ca
To enrich the lives of Manitobans with an intellectual disability, through sport

Special Olympics New Brunswick
#107, 146 Main St., Fredericton NB E3A 1C8 Canada
Tel: 506-459-3999; *Fax:* 506-451-1325
Toll-Free: 888-362-5926
info@sonb.ca
nb.specialolympics.ca

Special Olympics Newfoundland & Labrador
#426, 354 Water St., St. John's NL A1C 1C4 Canada
Tel: 709-738-1923; *Fax:* 709-738-0119
Toll-Free: 877-738-1913
sonl@sonl.ca
www.sonl.ca
To provide sport, fitness & recreation programs for individuals with a mental handicap

Special Olympics Northwest Territories
PO Box 1691, Yellowknife NT X1A 2N1 Canada
Tel: 867-873-6906; *Fax:* 867-669-0225
braden@internorth.com
www.sonwt.ca
Valery Braden, President

Special Olympics Nova Scotia (SONS)
PO Box 3010, #305, 5516 Spring Garden Rd., Halifax NS B3J 1G6 Canada
Tel: 902-429-2266; *Fax:* 902-425-5606
Toll-Free: 866-299-2019
greekmr@sportnovascotia.ca
www.sons.ca

Special Olympics Ontario (SOO)
#300, 18 Wynford Dr., Toronto ON M3C 3S2 Canada
Tel: 416-447-8326; *Fax:* 416-447-6336
Toll-Free: 888-333-5515
www.osoinc.com
To provide sports training & competition for people with an intellectual disability through community-based programs

Special Olympics Prince Edward Island (SOPEI)
PO Box 822, #240, 40 Enman Cres., Charlottetown PE C1A 7L9 Canada
Tel: 902-368-8919; *Fax:* 902-892-4553
Toll-Free: 800-287-1196
sopei@sopei.com
www.sopei.com
To provide sport, recreation & fitness for the mentally disabled in PEI; to provide competitive opportunities for its members

Special Olympics Saskatchewan
353 Broad St., Regina SK S4R 1X2 Canada
Tel: 306-780-9247; *Fax:* 306-780-9441
Toll-Free: 888-307-6226
sos@specialolympics.sk.ca
www.specialolympics.sk.ca

Special Olympics Yukon (SOY) / Les Jeux Olympiques Spéciaux du Yukon
4061 - 4 Ave., Whitehorse YT Y1A 1H1 Canada
Tel: 867-668-6511; *Fax:* 867-667-4237
specialolympics@sportyukon.com
To provide a full continuum of sport apportunities for Yukoners with a mental disability

Speed Skate New Brunswick
246 St. Pierre East Blvd., Caraquet NB E1E 1B1 Canada
Tel: 506-727-6334; *Fax:* 506-727-6334
speedskatenb@gmail.com
ssnb.homestead.com
The association provides members with access to coaching & chances to compete. It serves as a hub for information on the sport & for members to network.
Ray Harris, President
Peter Steele, Provincial Coach

Speed Skate Nova Scotia
10 Thistle Dr., North Sydney NS B2A 3R1 Canada
Tel: 902-794-8954
laurolea@ns.sympatico.ca
Terri Dixon, President

Speed Skate PEI
PO Box 383, Charlottetown PE C1A 7K7 Canada
Tel: 902-628-6606
info@speedskatepei.ca
www.speedskatepei.com
Supporting the sport of speedskating in PEI.
Wendy A. Francis, President
Alban Moran, Secretary

Speed Skating Canada (SSC) / Patinage de vitesse Canada
#402, 2781 Lancaster Rd., Ottawa ON K1B 1A7 Canada
Tel: 613-260-3669; *Fax:* 613-260-3660
ssc@speedskating.ca
www.speedskating.ca
To develop & promote long & short track speed skating in Canada; to prepare athletes, coaches, officials & volunteers to make contributions to speed skating & to Canada's image abroad through development & international programs

Sport Alliance of Ontario
3 Concorde Gate, Toronto ON M3C 3N7 Canada
Tel: 416-426-7000; *Fax:* 416-426-7381
jjoseph@sportalliance.com
www.sportalliance.com
To provide facilities, services & business expertise to enable provincial sport, recreation & fitness organizations to serve the people of Ontario
Jim Bradley, CEO
Larry Rudner, Interim CFO

Sport BC
#260, 3820 Cessna Dr., Richmond BC V7B 0A2 Canada
Tel: 604-333-3400; *Fax:* 604-333-3401
info@sport.bc.ca
www.sport.bc.ca
Social Media: www.facebook.com/pages/Sport-BC/86675020979
To provide leadership, direction, & support to member organizations in their delivery of sport opportunities to all British Columbians

Sport Manitoba
200 Main St., Winnipeg MB R3C 4M2 Canada
Tel: 204-925-5600; *Fax:* 204-925-5916
Toll-Free: 866-774-2220
info@sport.mb.ca
www.sportmanitoba.ca
To create the best sport community in Canada through provision of resources to recognized sport organizations, enabling them to encourage participation in sport at all levels of skill & ability & to develop athletes of national & international calibre

Sport New Brunswick / Sport Nouveau-Brunswick
#13, 900 Hanwell Rd., Fredericton NB E3B 6A2 Canada
Tel: 506-451-1320; *Fax:* 506-451-1325
director@sportnb.com
www.sportnb.com
To promote the development of amateur sport in New Brunswick through services, programs, advocacy

Sport Newfoundland & Labrador
PO Box 8700, St. John's NL A1B 4J6 Canada
Tel: 709-576-4932; *Fax:* 709-576-7493
sportnl@sportnl.ca
www.sportnl.ca
To promote & advance amateur sport throughout Newfoundland & Labrador; to represent collective interests & goals of members; to provide various programs & services; to liaise & lobby with government, communities, media & other representative organizations; to provide direction & leadership on issues which affect members

Sport North Federation
Don Cooper Building, PO Box 11089, 4908 - 49 St., Yellowknife NT X1A 3X7 Canada
Tel: 867-669-8326; *Fax:* 867-669-8327
Toll-Free: 800-661-0797
www.sportnorth.com

Sport Nova Scotia (SNS)
PO Box 3010, Stn. South, 5516 Spring Garden Rd., Halifax NS B3J 1G6 Canada
Tel: 902-425-5450; *Fax:* 902-425-5606
sportns@sportnovascotia.ca
www.sportnovascotia.ca
To promote the development of amateur sport in Nova Scotia through services, programs, advocacy & technical consultation

Sport PEI Inc.
PO Box 302, Charlottetown PE C1A 7K7 Canada
Tel: 902-368-4110; *Fax:* 902-368-4548
Toll-Free: 800-247-6712
sports@sportpei.pe.ca
www.sportpei.pe.ca
To assist in the development & promotion of amateur sport in the province of Prince Edward Island; To offer services & programs to meet the needs of the membership

Sport Physiotherapy Canada (SPC)
#416, 11411A Carling Ave., Ottawa ON K1Z 1A7 Canada
Tel: 613-748-5794; *Fax:* 613-748-5792
info@sportphysio.ca
www.sportphysio.ca
To promote professional development of members; To ensure high-quality health care for Canada's athletes

Sport Yukon
4061 - 4 Ave., Whitehorse YT Y1A 1H1 Canada
Tel: 867-668-4236; *Fax:* 867-667-4237
news@sportyukon.com
www.sportyukon.com
To promote the development of amateur sport in the Yukon through services, programs, advocacy

Sports-Québec
CP 1000, Succ. M, 4545, av Pierre-De Coubertin, Montréal QC H1V 3R2 Canada
Tél: 514-252-3114; *Téléc:* 514-254-9621
sports@sportsquebec.com
www.sportsquebec.com
Assurer la synergie de ses membres et de ses partenaires du système sportif québécois et du système sportif canadien pour favoriser le développement et l'épanouissement de l'athlète et la promotion de la pratique sportive

Squash Canada
#401, 2197 Riverside Dr., Ottawa ON K1H 7X3 Canada
Tel: 613-731-7385; *Fax:* 613-731-6291
squash.canada@squash.ca
www.squash.ca

STARS Sports Association
PO Box 15, Okotoks AB T1S 1A4 Canada
Tel: 403-938-3475; *Fax:* 403-938-3625
info@starsvolleyball.ca; info@starsbasketball.com
To offer positive, educational sport experiences for young people throughout Canada; to build self-esteem, self-respect, & respect for others through sport; to benefit youth by developing both technical & personal skills

Summerside & Area Minor Hockey Association (SAMHA)
PO Box 1454, Summerside PE C1N 4K4 Canada
info@summersideminorhockey.com
www.summersideminorhockey.com
Bruce Cameron, President

Swim Yukon
4061, 4th Ave., Whitehorse YT Y1A 1H1 Canada
www.swimyukon.ca
Swim Yukon is the Sport Governing Body for competitive swimming in the Yukon.
Ron Sumanik, President

Swimming/Natation Canada
#700, 2197 Riverside Dr., Ottawa ON K1H 7X3 Canada
Tel: 613-260-1348; *Fax:* 613-260-0804
natoffice@swimming.ca
www.swimming.ca
Social Media: www.facebook.com/group.php?gid=56320144853
To direct & develop competitive swimming in Canada; to represent Canada in international organizations & events

Synchro Canada / Association canadienne de nage synchronisée amateur
#200, 1010 Polytek St., Unit 14, Gloucester ON K1J 9H9 Canada
Tel: 613-748-5674; *Fax:* 613-748-5724
catherine@synchro.ca
www.synchro.ca
To develop and operate the sport of synchronized swimming in Canada, through a variety of programs designed to develop athletes, coaches & officials
Catherine Gosselin-Després, Chief Operations Officer
Diane Oligny, Chief Technical Officer

Synchro Yukon Association
4061, 4th Ave., Whitehorse YT Y1A 1H1 Canada
Tel: 867-668-7441
specialk@northwestel.net
www.sportyukon.com/membership/?member=34
To promote the sport of Synchronized Swimming in the Yukon.
Sandra Duncan, President

Table Tennis Yukon
4061, 4th Ave, Whitehorse YT Y1A 1H1 Canada
Tel: 867-668-3358
stockdale@yknet.ca
www.sportyukon.com/membership/?member=72
To promote the sport of Table Tennis in the Yukon.
David Stockdale, President

Temiskaming & Northern Ontario Curling Association
c/o Stephen Chenier, PO Box 735, Englehart ON P0J 1H0 Canada
Tel: 705-647-2589; *Fax:* 705-544-8525
jcdhh@ntl.sympatico.ca
www.tnoca.curlingclub.ca

Tennis BC
#204, 210 West Broadway, Vancouver BC V5Y 3W2 Canada
Tel: 604-737-3086; *Fax:* 604-737-3124
tbc@tennisbc.org
tennisbc.org

Tennis Canada
Rexall Centre, #100, 1 Shoreham Dr., Toronto ON M3N 3A6 Canada
Tel: 416-665-9777; *Fax:* 416-665-9017
Toll-Free: 877-283-6647
info@tenniscanada.com
www.tenniscanada.com
To stimulate participation & excellence in the sport at the local, provincial, national & international levels; to provide encouragement, support, leadership & example to organizations & individuals who seek to enhance the enjoyment, quality & image of Canadian tennis. Offices in Toronto & Montreal

Tennis Manitoba
#303, 200 Main St., Winnipeg MB R3C 4M2 Canada
Tel: 204-925-5660; *Fax:* 204-925-5703
tennismb@shawbiz.ca
www.tennismanitoba.com
To stimulate participation & advancement in tennis by all Manitobans

Tennis New Brunswick
PO Box 604, Fredericton NB E3B 5A6 Canada
Tel: 506-444-0885
tnb@tennisnb.net
www.tennisnb.net

Tennis Newfoundland & Labrador
Bldg. 810, PO Box 8700, Stn. Pleasantville, St. John's NL A1B 4J6 Canada
Tel: 709-765-0426; *Fax:* 709-722-1670
tennis@sportnl.ca
www.tennisnl.ca
Tennis Newfoundland & Labrador is committed to growing and promoting the sport of tennis throughout Newfoundland and Labrador and to increase participation at levels consistent with the personal goals and aspirations of competitors in all age groups

Tennis Northwest Territories
PO Box 671, Yellowknife NT X1A 2N5 Canada
Tel: 867-873-2018
eastarm@ssimicro.com
www.tennisnwt.ca
Fran Hurcomb, President

Tennis Québec (TQ)
285, rue Faillon ouest, Montréal QC H2R 2W1 Canada
Tél: 514-270-6060; *Téléc:* 514-270-2700
courrier@tennis.qc.ca
www.tennis.qc.ca
Promotion et développement du tennis au Québec auprès de toutes les catégories d'âge et de tous les calibres

Tennis Saskatchewan
2205 Victoria Ave., Regina SK S4P 0S4 Canada
Tel: 306-780-9410; *Fax:* 306-525-4009
tennissask@sasktel.net
www.tennissask.com
To advance tennis throughout Saskatchewan by stimulating participation & excellence in the sport; to provide players throughout Saskatchewan with systematic opportunities to participate in tennis & to achieve a level of competence consistent with their abilities & aspirations, with particular emphasis on youth; to stage tennis events; to produce teams & athletes capable of winning national championships

Tennis Yukon Association
4 Kluhini Cres., Whitehorse YT Y1A 3P3 Canada
Tel: 867-393-2621; *Fax:* 867-393-2621
tennisyukon@mac.com
www.tennisyukon.com
To promote the sport of Tennis in the Yukon.
Stacy Lewis, President

Toronto Bicycling Network
PO Box 279, #200, 131 Bloor St. West, Toronto ON M5S 1R8 Canada
Tel: 416-760-4191
info@tbn.ca
www.tbn.ca
Brian Mclean, President

Toronto Cycling Committee (TCC)
850 Coxwell Ave., 2nd Fl., Toronto ON M4C 5R1 Canada
Tel: 416-392-7592
btww@toronto.ca
www.toronto.ca/cycling
Adrian A. Heaps, Chair

Trail Riding Alberta Conference (TRAC)
738 Wheeler Road, Edmonton AB T6M 2E8 Canada
Tel: 403-486-0957
shanharms@shaw.ca
www.trailriding.ab.ca
To finish is to win
Brent Seufert, President

Triathlon Canada
#106, 3 Concorde Gate, Toronto ON M3C 3N7 Canada
Tel: 416-426-7180; *Fax:* 416-426-7294
info@triathloncanada.com
www.triathloncanada.com
To function as the National Federation for triathlon & duathlon in Canada, & to represent Canada internationally; to promote the triathlon & duathlon, both competitive & non-competitive in Canada; to encourage support of Triathlon Canada programmes by the public generally; to provide guidance, information & assistance to the provincial triathlon associations, zones & clubs in respect to these objects & in the development of programmes for competitive & non-competitive triathletes & duathletes; to affiliate all provincial associations to Triathlon Canada who are the Provincial Sports Governing Bodies, or who are in the process of becoming the Provincial Sports Governing Bodies in their province; to organize training courses for triathletes, duathletes, coaches & administrators to national & international standards; to promote other multi-disciplined endurance events & excluding the traditional decathlon, pentathlon, heptathlon, modern pentathlon & biathlon, which are part of existing National Federations
Alan Trivett, Executive Director

Vélo New Brunswick
536 McAllister Rd., Riverview NB E1B 4G1 Canada
Tel: 506-474-0214
Christine.Martin@velo.nb.ca
www.velo.nb.ca
To promote all aspects of the activity of bicycling, competitive & recreational, both on & off the road

Vélo Québec
1251, rue Rachel est, Montréal QC H2J 2J9 Canada
Tél: 514-521-8356; *Téléc:* 514-521-5711
Ligne sans frais: 800-567-8356
velo_quebec@velo.qc.ca
www.velo.qc.ca
Mèdia social: www.facebook.com/VeloQuebec
Jean-François Pronovost, Directeur général

Volleyball BC
Harry Jerome Sports Centre, 7564 Barnet Hwy., Burnaby BC V5A 1E7 Canada
Tel: 604-291-2007; *Fax:* 604-291-2602
contact@volleyballbc.ca
www.volleyballbc.ca
To promote volleyball in BC; to provide competitive opportunities for members

Volleyball Canada (VC)
#202, 5510 Canotek Rd., Gloucester ON K1J 9J5 Canada
Tel: 613-748-5681; *Fax:* 613-748-5727
info@volleyball.ca
www.volleyball.ca
To lead the growth of & excellence in the sport of volleyball for all Canadians

Volleyball New Brunswick
#13, 900 Hanwell Rd., Fredericton NB E3B 6A3 Canada
Tel: 506-451-1346; *Fax:* 506-451-1325
vnb@nb.aibn.com
www.vnb.nb.ca
To promote volleyball in New Brunswick; to provide competitive opportunities for its members

Volleyball Nova Scotia
5516 Spring Garden Rd., 4th Floor, Halifax NS B3J 1G6 Canada
Tel: 902-425-5450; *Fax:* 902-425-5606
vns@sportnovascotia.ca
www.volleyballnovascotia.ca
To promote volleyball in Nova Scotia; to provide competitive opportunities for its members

Volleyball Prince Edward Island
PO Box 302, Charlottetown PE C1N 7K7 Canada
Tel: 902-569-0583; *Fax:* 902-368-4548
Toll-Free: 800-247-6712
cgcrozier@sportpei.pe.ca
www.volleyballpei.com
To promote volleyball in PEI; to provide competitive opportunities for members

Volleyball Yukon
4061 - 4th Ave., Whitehorse YT Y1A 1H1 Canada
Tel: 867-334-4592; *Fax:* 867-667-4237
bunpalamar@whtvcable.com
www.volleyballyukon.com
To promote volleyball in the Yukon; to provide competitive opportunities for its members

Water Polo Canada (WPC)
#12, 1010 Polytek St., Gloucester ON K1G 9H9 Canada
Tel: 613-748-5682; *Fax:* 613-748-5777
dvilleneuve@waterpolo.ca
www.waterpolo.ca
To promote growth in sport of water polo in Canada; to administer Canada's high performance programs (Olympics, Pan Am Games, etc.) in water polo

Water Polo Saskatchewan Inc.
1860 Lorne St., Regina SK S4P 2L7 Canada
Tel: 306-780-9260; *Fax:* 306-780-9467
admin@wpsask.ca
www.wpsask.ca

Water Ski & Wakeboard Canada / Ski nautique et planche Canada
#210, 223 Colonnade Rd. South, Ottawa ON K2E 7K3 Canada
Tel: 613-526-0685; *Fax:* 613-526-4380
wswc@waterski-wakeboard.ca
www.waterski-wakeboard.ca
To promote & organize water skiing in Canada

Whitehorse Cross Country Ski Club
#200, 1 Sumanik Dr., Whitehorse YT Y1A 6J6 Canada
Tel: 867-668-4477
info@xcskiwhitehorse.ca
www.xcskiwhitehorse.ca
To maintain high quality ski trails and facilities, maintain a safe environment, ensure the long-term viability of the club and secure land tenure for the Yukon's trail system.
Mike Gladish, Manager
Tom Ullyett, President

Whitehorse Minor Hockey Association
4061, 4th Ave., Whitehorse YT Y1A 1H1 Canada
Tel: 867-393-4698
www.whitehorseminorhockey.ca
Promotes and coordinates minor hockey leagues in Whitehorse.
John Grant, President

Whitehorse Minor Soccer Association (WMS)
4061, 4th Ave., Whitehorse YT Y1A 1H1 Canada
Tel: 867-667-2445
wms@sportyukon.com
www.yukonsoccer.yk.ca/minor
Provides low-cost, easily accessible indoor and outdoor soccer opportunities to the youth of Whitehorse.
Gerald Haase, President

Wild Rose Ball Hockey Association
7604 - 182 St., Edmonton AB T5T 1Y9 Canada
Tel: 780-970-0637; *Fax:* 780-484-9957
info@wrbha.com
www.wrbha.com
Craig Thiessen, Contact

World Curling Federation (WCF)
74 Tay St., Perth PH2 8N Scotland
wcf@dial.pipex.com
www.worldcurling.net
To represent curling internationally & to facilitate the growth of the sport through a network of member nations
Lester Harrison, President
Kate Caithness, Vice-President
Mike Thomson, Secretary General

Wrestling Nova Scotia
General Delivery, Bear River NS B0S 1B0 Canada
Tel: 902-857-1761
wrestlingns@canada.com
www.wrestlingnovascotia.ca

Youth Bowling Canada (YBC)
c/o Bowl Canada, #10A, 250 Shields Ct., Markham ON L3R 9W7 Canada
Tel: 905-479-1560; *Fax:* 905-479-8613
info@bowlcanada.ca
www.youthbowling.ca; www.bowlcanada.ca
Social Media:
facebook.com/pages/youth-bowling-canada/103402153046873
YBC is a program operating under the auspices of the Bowling Proprietors' Association of Canada (Bowl Canada), a not-for-profit organization comprised of 500 member centres across the country. The YBC league is divided in 5-pin & 10-pin, & further broken down in 3 age groups: bantam, junior & senior.

Yukon Aboriginal Sport Circle (YASC)
4061, 4th Ave., Whitehorse YT Y1A 1H1 Canada
Tel: 867-668-2840; *Fax:* 867-667-4237
aboriginalsport@sportyukon.com
www.yasc.ca
The Yukon Aboriginal Sport Circle is a non-profit society dedicated to the advancement of Aboriginal recreation and sport in the Yukon through a variety of programs to increase participation and skill levels and to increase awareness.
Greg Edgelow, Executive Director
Brian MacDonald, President

Yukon Amateur Hockey Association
4061, 4th Ave., Whitehorse YT Y1A 1H1 Canada
Tel: 867-393-4501
yaha@sportyukon.com
www.yukonhockey.ca
The Yukon Amateur Hockey Association is the sports governing body for amateur hockey in the Yukon.
Walter Brennan, President

Yukon Badminton Association
4061 - 4th Ave., Whitehorse YT Y1A 1H1 Canada
Tel: 867-668-4821
bluestone@northwestel.net

Yukon Broomball League
4061, 4th Ave., Whitehorse YT Y1A 1H1 Canada
Tel: 867-668-3589
biz@yukonbroomball.com
www.yukonbroomball.com
To promote and facilitate Broomball in the Yukon Territory.
Allan Milford, President

Yukon Curling Association (YCA)
4061 - 4th Ave., Whitehorse YT Y1A 1H1 Canada
Tel: 867-668-7121; *Fax:* 867-667-4237
yca@sportyukon.com
yukoncurling.inthehack.com

Yukon Freestyle Ski Association
4061, 4th Ave., Whitehorse YT Y1A 1H1 Canada
Tel: 867-633-5615; *Fax:* 867-393-8779
www.sportyukon.com/membership/?member=71
To promote and facilitate freestyle skiing in the Yukon Territory.
Laura Wilson, Registrar

Yukon Golf Association
4061, 4th Ave., Whitehorse YT Y1A 1H1 Canada
Tel: 867-633-3364
zealandg@northwestel.net
www.sportyukon.com/membership/?member=57
The Yukon Golf Association is an organization that enhances opportunities for all Yukonners in their pursuit of excellence and in their enjoyment of participation.
Gordon Zealand, President

Yukon Horse and Rider Association (YHRA)
PO Box 31482, Whitehorse YT Y1A 6K8 Canada
Tel: 867-456-2030
info@yhra.ca
www.yhra.ca
The YHRA is dedicated to the sport of horseback riding in the Yukon Territory, Canada. The Association aims to encourage good horsemanship and help promote interest in the light horse industry.
Paul Choquette, President

Yukon Indian Hockey Association (YIHA)
PO Box 31769, Whitehorse YT Y1A 6L3 Canada
Tel: 867-456-7294; *Fax:* 867-456-7290
info@yiha.ca
www.yiha.ca
Social Media:
www.facebook.com/group.php?gid=169614299786
The Yukon Indian Hockey Association is a non-profit organization created to establish a hockey league in the Yukon to enable Native athletes to compete with other Canadian Provinces and Territories in the sport.
Karee Vallevand, President

Yukon Schools' Athletic Association (YSAA)
c/o Porter Creek Secondary School, 1405 Hickory St., Whitehorse YT V1A 4M4 Canada
paul.macdonald@yesnet.yk.ca
www.yesnet.yk.ca/ysaa/ysaainside.html
To encourage participation of students in inter school athletics, emphasize interschool athletics as an integral part of the total educational process and plan, promote, supervise and administer a program of inter-school athletics in all approved competitions.

Paul MacDonald, President

Yukon Shooting Federation
4061, 4th Ave., Whitehorse YT Y1A 1H1 Canada
Tel: 867-668-6776
www.sportyukon.com/membership/?member=64
To promote and facilitate air rifle and air pistol shooting in the Yukon Territory.
Jim Sias, President

Yukon Soccer Association
4061 - 4th Ave., Whitehorse YT Y1A 1H1 Canada
Tel: 867-633-4625; *Fax:* 867-667-4237
yukonsoccer@sportyukon.com
www.yukonsoccer.yk.ca
The Yukon Soccer Association is the sport governing body for the sport of soccer in the Yukon Territory. It is a volunteer based organization that coordinates and administers various programs devoted to the promotion and development of soccer.
Kim King, Administrator

Yukon Speed Skating Association
11 Buttercup Pl., Whitehorse YT Y1A 5V1 Canada
Tel: 867-668-4591; *Fax:* 867-393-8101
Bruce Henry, Branch President

Yukon Underwater Diving Association (YUDA)
alyon@yukon.net
www.yukonweb.com/community/yuda/
The Yukon Underwater Diving Association (YUDA) is a non-profit organization created by sport divers to promote the sport of underwater diving in the Yukon, Northern British Columbia and South East Alaska.
Allyn Lyon, President

Yukon Weightlifting Association
4061, 4th Ave., Whitehorse YT Y1A 1H1 Canada
www.sportyukon.com/membership/?member=79
To promote and facilitate competitive weightlifting in the Yukon Territory.
Moira Lassen, President

Standards & Testing

Cable Television Standards Foundation / Fondation des normes de télévision par câble
#515, 350 Albert St., Ottawa ON K1P 5G4 Canada
Tel: 613-230-5442; *Fax:* 613-230-5679
To provide basic structure & facilitate cable industry membership for purpose of self-regulation & adjudicative role of its second body (Cable Television Standards Council)

Canadian Educational Standards Institute (CESI) / Institut canadien des normes d'enseignement
PO Box 3013, 2 Ridley Rd., St Catharines ON L2R 7C3 Canada
Tel: 905-684-5658; *Fax:* 905-684-5057
execdir@cesi.edu
www.cesi.edu
To develop & promote educational standards & to foster compliance with those standards related to independent elementary & secondary school education.

Canadian Evaluation Society (CES) / Société canadienne d'évaluation
1485 Laperriere Ave., Ottawa ON K1Z 7S8 Canada
Tel: 613-725-2526; *Fax:* 613-729-6206
secretariat@evaluationcanada.ca
www.evaluationcanada.ca
To advance evaluation for its members & the public; To establish & maintain CES as the recognized national organization which represents the evaluation community; To provide a forum for the advancement of theory & practice of evaluation; To develop competencies, ethics, & standards to improve the practice of evaluation; To advocate for high-quality evaluation with practitioners, local chapters, nationally & internationally; To promote the use of evaluation in society

Canadian General Standards Board (CGSB) / Office des normes générales du Canada (ONGC)
CGSB, #6B1, Place Du Portage III, Gatineau QC K1A 1G6 Canada
Tel: 819-956-0425; *Fax:* 819-956-1634
Toll-Free: 800-665-2472
ncr.cqsb-onqc@pwqsc.qc.ca
www.ongc-cgsb.gc.ca
To develop standards, through accreditation with the Standards Council of Canada; To offer conformity assessment services, including product certification & registration of quality & environmental management systems, conforming to ISO standards
Terrence Davies, Acting Director

Canadian Institute for NDE
135 Fennell Ave. West, Hamilton ON L8N 3T2 Canada
Tel: 905-387-1655; *Fax:* 905-574-6080
Toll-Free: 800-964-9488
info@cinde.ca
www.cinde.ca
To advance scientific, engineering, technical knowledge in the field of nondestructive testing; to gather & disseminate information relating to nondestructive testing useful to individuals & beneficial to the general public; to promote nondestructive testing through courses of instruction, lectures, meetings, publications, conferences, etc.

Canadian Metric Association (CMA) / Association métrique canadienne
PO Box 35, Fonthill ON L0S 1E0 Canada
Tel: 905-892-3800
albertjmettler@gmail.com
To promote nationwide adoption of metric system & its modern expanded version; to contribute to better understanding of metric system; to provide guidance in correct use of metric units & symbols; to support introduction of international metric standards; to encourage implementation of other international standards & practices; to advocate rational choice of numerical values for sizes of food package & other consumer products

Steel & Metal Industries

Canadian Die Casters Association (CDCA) / Association canadienne des mouleurs sous pression
#3, 247 Barr St., Renfrew ON K7V 1J6 Canada
Fax: 613-432-6840
Toll-Free: 866-809-7032
info@diecasters.ca
www.diecasters.ca
To assist die casters in dealing with governments & other organizations on industry issues; to provide a united voice for members

Canadian Foundry Association (CFA) / Association des fonderies canadiennes
#1500, 1 Nicholas St., Ottawa ON K1N 7B7 Canada
Tel: 613-789-4894; *Fax:* 613-789-5957
judy@foundryassociation.ca
www.foundryassociation.ca
To assist & represent the membership in dealing with government on industry specific issues; to communicate information to the industry, which will assist its members in strengthening their own competitive position & ensuring a strong Canadian foundry industry

Canadian Institute of Steel Construction (CISC) / Institut canadien de la construction en acier (ICCA)
#200, 3760 - 14th Ave., Markham ON L3R 3T7 Canada
Tel: 905-946-0864; *Fax:* 905-946-8574
info@cisc-icca.ca
www.cisc-icca.ca
To promote good design & safety, together with efficient & economical use of steel as a means of expanding the construction markets for structural steel, joists & platework

Canadian Sheet Steel Building Institute (CSSBI) / Institut canadien de la tôle d'acier pour le bâtiment (ICTAB)
#2A, 652 Bishop St. North, Cambridge ON N3H 4V6 Canada
Tel: 519-650-1285; *Fax:* 519-650-8081
info@cssbi.ca
www.cssbi.ca
The CSSBI's vision statement is to make steel the material of choice for building construction in Canada.

Canadian Steel Construction Council (CSCC) / Conseil canadien de la construction en acier
#300, 201 Consumers Rd., Toronto ON M2J 4G8 Canada
Tel: 416-491-9898; *Fax:* 416-491-6461
hakrentz@telus.net
To represent the manufacturers of steel products, including: open-web steel joists, steel platework, corrugated steel pipe, sheet steel, & steel fasteners; to promote the use of steel in construction through research & engineering

Canadian Steel Producers Association (CSPA) / Association canadienne des producteurs d'acier (ACPA)
#906, 350 Sparks St., Ottawa ON K1R 7S8 Canada
Tel: 613-238-6049; *Fax:* 613-238-1832
info@canadiansteel.ca
www.canadiansteel.ca
To represent the steel producers that melt & pour steel in Canada

Canadian Steel Trade & Employment Congress
#501, 234 Eglinton Ave. East, Toronto ON M4P 1K7 Canada
Tel: 416-480-1797; *Fax:* 416-480-2986
general@cstec.ca
www.cstec.ca
To provide a forum for communication among steel companies, steelworkers, & governments to work for the betterment of the industry & its workforce

Corrugated Steel Pipe Institute (CSPI) / Institut pour tuyaux de tôle ondulée
#2A, 652 Bishop St. North, Cambridge ON N3H 4V6 Canada
Tel: 519-650-8080; *Fax:* 519-650-8081
info@cspi.ca
www.cspi.ca
To promote & encourage general & wider use of corrugated steel pipe for drainage & other uses across Canada; to initiate & support research, marketing, promotion, public relations & advertising programs designed to broaden the markets for CSP products; to cooperate with public & private agencies engaged in the formulation of specifications & designs for drainage & other underground structures; to provide the industry & the public with documented experience & up-to-date technical information on CSP products & their proper use & application; to enhance, through responsible public relations practices, the reputation & image of the Canadian CSP industry; to cooperate with allied industry & government authorities; to encourage & participate in educational endeavours in colleges & universities.

Nickel Institute
#1801, 55 University Ave., Toronto ON M5J 2H7 Canada
Tel: 416-591-7999; *Fax:* 416-591-7987
ni_toronto@nickelinstitute.org
www.nickelinstitute.org
Market development & applications oriented non-profit research organization of international nickel industry; to provide information for nickel users, designers, specifiers, educators & others interested in nickel-containing materials & their applications

Ontario Sheet Metal Contractors Association (OSM)
#26, 30 Wertheim Ct., Richmond Hill ON L4B 1B9 Canada
Tel: 905-886-9627; *Fax:* 905-886-9959
shtmetal@bellnet.ca
www.osmca.org
OSM is a not-for-profit association & the accredited, employer bargaining agency responsible for the negotiation & administration of all provincial collective agreements between OSM, the Ontario Sheet Metal Workers' & Roofers' Conference & the Sheet Metal Workers International Association. It is the lobbying voice for all national, provincial & corporate issues which directly affect its membership.

Reinforcing Steel Institute of Ontario (RSIO)
PO Box 40620, Stn. RPO Six Points Plaza, Toronto ON M9B 6K8 Canada
Tel: 416-239-7746; *Fax:* 416-239-7745
administrator@rebar.org
www.rebar.org

Surveying & Mapping

Alberta Land Surveyors' Association (ALSA)
#1000, 10020 - 101A Ave., Edmonton AB T5J 3G2 Canada
Tel: 780-429-8805; *Fax:* 780-429-3374
Toll-Free: 800-665-2572
info@alsa.ab.ca
www.alsa.ab.ca
The ALSA is a self-governing professional association which regulates the practice of land surveying.

Association of British Columbia Land Surveyors (ABCLS)
#301, 2400 Bevan Ave., Sidney BC V8L 1W1
Tel: 250-655-7222; *Fax:* 250-655-7223
office@abcls.ca
www.abcls.ca
To set educational requirements for land surveyors; To regulate professional land surveyors in British Columbia

Association of Canada Lands Surveyors / Association des arpenteurs des terres du Canada
100E, 900 Dynes Rd., Ottawa ON K2C 3L6 Canada
Tel: 613-723-9200; *Fax:* 613-723-5558
admin@acls-aatc.ca
www.acls-aatc.ca
To establish & maintain standards of qualification for Canada Lands Surveyors; to regulate Canada Lands Surveyors; to establish & maintain standards of conduct, knowledge & skill among members of the Association & permit holders; to govern the activities of members of the Association & permit holders; to cooperate with other organizations for the advancement of

surveying; & to perform the duties & exercise the powers that are imposed or conferred on the Association by the Act
Jean-Claude Tétreault, Executive Director

Association of Manitoba Land Surveyors
#202, 83 Gary St., Winnipeg MB R3C 4J9 Canada
Tel: 204-943-6972; *Fax:* 204-957-7602
amls@mts.net
www.amls.ca
To license qualified persons becoming commissioned land surveyors; to protect public interests concerning land boundary matters

Association of New Brunswick Land Surveyors (ANBLS) / Association des arpenteurs-géomètres du Nouveau-Brunswick (AA-GN-B)
#312, 212, Queen St., Fredericton NB E3B 1A8
Tel: 506-458-8266; *Fax:* 506-458-8267
anbls@nbnet.nb.ca
www.anbls.nb.ca
To regulate & govern the practice of land surveying in New Brunswick; To develop & maintain standards of knowledge, skill, & professional ethics

Association of Newfoundland Land Surveyors
#203, 62-64 Pippy Pl., St. John's NL A1B 4H7 Canada
Tel: 709-722-2031; *Fax:* 709-722-4104
anls@nf.aibn.com
www.surveyors.nf.ca
To establish & maintain standards of knowledge, skill, & professional conduct in the practice of land surveying, in order to serve & protect the public interest in Newfoundland; to regulate & govern the practice of land surveying in the province

Association of Nova Scotia Land Surveyors (ANSLS)
325A Prince Albert Rd., Dartmouth NS B2Y 1N5 Canada
Tel: 902-469-7962; *Fax:* 902-469-7963
ansls@accesswave.ca
www.ansls.ca
To establish & maintain standards of professional ethics among its members, student members & holders of a certificate of authorization, in order that the public interest may be served & protected; & knowledge & skills among its members, student members & holders of a certificate of authorization; to regulate the practice of professional land surveying & govern the profession in accordance with the Act, the regulations & the by-laws; & to communicate & cooperate with other professional organizations for the advancement of the best interests of the surveying profession

Association of Ontario Land Economists
PO Box 97510, 364 Old Kingston Rd., Toronto ON M1C 4Z1 Canada
Tel: 416-283-0440; *Fax:* 416-283-1399
aole.org
To continue attracting membership-quality professionals engaged in land economics pursuits; to broaden & enrich the professional development of members; to promote & maintain high ethical work standards throughout our membership; to make submissions to government for improvements in law & public administration bearing on land economics

Association of Ontario Land Surveyors (AOLS)
1043 McNicoll Ave., Toronto ON M1W 3W6 Canada
Tel: 416-491-9020; *Fax:* 416-491-2576
Toll-Free: 800-268-0718
blain@aols.org
www.aols.org
AOLS is responsible for the licensing and governance of professional land surveyors, in accordance with the Surveyors Act. The self-governing association ensures that public interest is paramount.

Association of Prince Edward Island Land Surveyors (APEILS)
PO Box 20100, Charlottetown PE C1A 9E3 Canada
Tel: 902-566-9966

Canadian Cartographic Association (CCA) / Association canadienne de cartographie
c/o Department of Geography, University of Victoria, PO Box 3050, Stn. CSC, Victoria BC V8W 3P5 Canada
awood@mun.ca
www.cca-acc.org
To promote interest in cartographic materials; To encourage research in the field of cartography; To advance education in cartography

Canadian Council of Land Surveyors (CCLS) / Conseil Canadien des arpenteurs-géomètres
#100E, 900 Dynes Rd., Ottawa ON K2C 3N6 Canada
Tel: 613-226-5110; *Fax:* 613-723-5558
Toll-Free: 800-241-7200
admin@ccls-ccag.ca
www.ccls-ccag.ca
To represent the disciplines of cadastral, geodetic, hydrographic, & photogrametric surveying & land information management; To provide proactive leadership to its member associations; To provide national strategies, & national & international representation for land surveyors within the geomatics profession

Canadian Geophysical Union (CGU) / Union géophysique canadienne (UGC)
c/o Dept. of Geology & Geophysics, University of Calgary, ES #278, 2500 University Dr. NW, Calgary AB T2N 1N4 Canada
Tel: 403-220-2794; *Fax:* 403-284-0074
cgu@ucalgary.ca
www.cgu-ugc.ca
To bring together & promote the geophysical sciences; To provide a focus for geophysicists at Canadian universities, government agencies, & industry in fields of study encompassing the composition & processes of the whole earth, including hydrology, space studies, & geology

Canadian Institute of Quantity Surveyors (CIQS)
#19, 90 Nolan Ct., Markham ON L3R 4L9 Canada
Tel: 905-477-0008; *Fax:* 905-477-6774
Toll-Free: 866-345-1168
info@ciqs.org
www.ciqs.org
To represent the quantity surveying & construction estimating profession in Canada

Geomatics Industry Association of Canada (GIAC) / Association canadienne des entreprises de géomatique
Covent Glen, PO Box 62009, 6491 Jeanne D'Arc Blvd., Ottawa ON K1C 2S0 Canada
Fax: 613-851-1256
dhtessier@giac.ca
www.giac.ca
To strengthen business climate; to maintain cooperative relations with government; to promote expanded role for members in provision of geomatics products & services; to encourage adoption by governments of improved policies & practices for procurement of geomatics products & services; to promote member firms as source of high quality, professional services; to promote Canadian geomatics industry abroad.

Ordre des arpenteurs-géomètres du Québec (OAGQ) / Québec Land Surveyors Association
#350, 2954, boul Laurier, Sainte-Foy QC G1V 4T2 Canada
Tél: 418-656-0730; *Téléc:* 418-656-6352
oagq@oagq.qc.ca
www.oagq.qc.ca
La protection du public et le contrôle de la profession

Saskatchewan Land Surveyors' Association (SLSA)
#230, 408 Broad St., Regina SK S4R 1X3
Tel: 306-352-8999; *Fax:* 306-352-8366
info@slsa.sk.ca
www.slsa.sk.ca
To uphold the stewardship & standards of the legal survey profession in Saskatchewan; To regulate & govern members in the practice of professional land surveying & professional surveying; To ensure the competency of members; To administer the profession to protect the public

Taxation

Association of Municipal Tax Collectors of Ontario
#119, 14845 - 6 Yonge St., Aurora ON L4G 6H8 Canada
Tel: 905-725-0019
amtco@sympatico.ca
www.amtco.on.ca
To bring those persons in the Municipal field of tax collecting into helpful association with each other so that through improved relations, united effort, participation and involvement promote their professional knowledge and general interests; to promote improved standards of ethics and efficiency in tax collection methods, procedures and to consider, resolve and recommend amendments to Provincial Acts which may improve the tax billing and collection administration; to encourage submissions and disseminate information of interest to its members; to encourage and assist in the development of educational training programs for collection personnel; to cooperate with other municipal associations; to foster good public relations

Canadian Property Tax Association, Inc. (CPTA) / Association canadienne de taxe foncière, inc
#225, 6 Lansing Sq., Toronto ON M2J 1T5
Tel: 416-493-3276; *Fax:* 416-493-3905
cpta@on.aibn.com
www.cpta.org
To facilitate the exchange of information about industrial & commercial property tax issues throughout Canada

Canadian Tax Foundation (CTF) / L'Association canadienne d'études fiscales (ACEF)
#1200, 595 Bay St., Toronto ON M5G 2N5
Tel: 416-599-0283; *Fax:* 416-599-9283
Toll-Free: 877-733-0283
lchapman@ctf.ca
www.ctf.ca
To create a greater understanding of the Canadian tax system; To improve the Canadian tax system
Charles J.R. Taylor, CA, Chair
Scott Wilkie, Vice-Chair
Larry Chapman, FCA, Director & Chief Executive Officer
Jane Meagher, Director, Québec Office
Debbie Selley, CGA, Treasurer
Judy Singh, Librarian

Canadian Taxpayers Federation (CTF)
#105, 438 Victoria Ave. East, Regina SK S4N 0N7
Tel: 306-352-7199; *Fax:* 306-352-7203
admin@taxpayer.com
www.taxpayer.com
Social Media: www.facebook.com/group.php?gid=6095483909
To advocate for the common interest of taxpayers; To effect public policy change
Michael Binnion, Chair
Troy Lanigan, President & Chief Executive Officer
Derek Fildebrandt, Director, National Research
Lee Harding, Director, New Development
Melanie Harvie, Manager, Finance
Shannon Morrison, Manager, Administration

Canadian Taxpayers Federation - Alberta (CTF)
#202, 10621 - 100th Ave., Edmonton AB T5J 0B3
Tel: 800-661-0187; *Fax:* 877-482-1744
ab.director@taxpayer.com
www.taxpayer.com
Social Media: twitter.com/scotthennig
To advocate on behalf of taxpayers across Alberta
Scott Hennig, Director, Alberta

Canadian Taxpayers Federation - British Columbia (CTF)
PO Box 20539, Stn. Howe St. RPO, Vancouver BC V6Z 2N8
Tel: 800-699-2282; *Fax:* 604-608-6773
bc.director@taxpayer.com
www.taxpayer.com
To advocate lower taxes, less waste & accountable government
Maureen Bader, Director, British Columbia

Canadian Taxpayers Federation - Ontario (CTF)
Varette Bldg., #512, 130 Albert St., Ottawa ON K1P 5G4
Tel: 800-265-0442; *Fax:* 613-234-7748
federal.director@taxpayer.com
www.taxpayer.com
Social Media: twitter.com/KevinGaudet
To engage in advocacy activities specific to Ontario
Kevin Gaudet, Director, Federal & Ontario

Canadian Taxpayers Federation - Saskatchewan & Manitoba (CTF)
#212, 428 Portage Ave., Winnipeg MB R3C 0E2
Tel: 204-982-2150; *Fax:* 204-982-2154
Toll-Free: 800-772-9955
ccraig@taxpayer.com
www.taxpayer.com
Social Media: twitter.com/colincraig1
To advocate on behalf of taxpayers in the prairie provinces
Colin Craig, Director, Prairies

Teaching

Québec Board of Black Educators (QBBE)
#310, Cavendish Blvd., Montréal QC H4B 2M5 Canada
Tel: 514-481-9400; *Fax:* 514-481-0611
qbbe@videotron.ca
www.qbbe.org
The Quebec Board of Black Educators mission is to promote the development of educational services for Black Youth and other youth between the ages of 5 to 25 who reside in the Greater Montreal area.
Phylicia Burke, Contact
Clarence Bayne, President

Telecommunications

Bell Aliant Pioneers
PO Box 1430, Saint John NB E2L 4K2 Canada
Toll-Free: 800-565-1436
candace.salkey@aliant.ca
The Bell Aliant Pioneer Volunteers is the largest corporate based volunteer organization in Atlantic Canada and is comprised of current and former Bell Aliant employees and its predecessor companies.
Candace Salkey, Manager

Canadian Association of Telecom Dealers (CATD)
39 Parisian Rd., Brampton ON L6P 2T2 Canada
Tel: 416-273-8797
The Canadian Association of Telecom Dealers is a national association of independent telecommunication service providers, dealers and manufacturers.

Canadian Call Management Association (CAM-X)
#10, 24 Olive St., Grimsby ON L3M 2B6 Canada
Tel: 905-309-0224; *Fax:* 905-309-0225
Toll-Free: 800-896-1054
info@camx.ca
www.camx.ca
To promote the welfare of the message-handling industry & related services through the encouragement & maintenance of high standards of ethics & services; the exchange of information & the rendering of mutual aid & assistance between member organizations.
Linda Osip, Executive Director

Canadian Independent Telephone Association (CITA) / Association canadienne du téléphone indépendant
1402 Queen St. West, Alton ON L7K 0C3 Canada
Tel: 519-940-0460; *Fax:* 519-940-1137
mhtaylor@allstream.net
www.cita.ca
To promote the increase & improvement of telephone service in Canada; to promote & protect the common business interest of members; to produce & distribute literature; to represent the industry before regulatory bodies, either federal or provincial.

Canadian Internet Registration Authority (CIRA)
#306, 350 Sparks St., Ottawa ON K1R 7S8 Canada
Tel: 613-237-5335; *Fax:* 800-285-0517
www.cira.ca
CIRA is a not for profit Canadian corporation responsible for operating the dot-ca internet country code.
Byron Holland, President & CEO

Canadian Telecommunications Consultants Association (CTCA)
#179, 160-2 County Court Blvd., Brampton ON L6J 4V1 Canada
Tel: 416-233-7946; *Fax:* 905-451-9410
Toll-Free: 800-463-2569
admin@ctca.ca; membership@ctca.ca
www.ctca.ca
CTCA advocates high standards of professionalism & expertise in the provision of telecommunications solutions. Towards this vision, the association encourages the dissemination & exchange of information among telecommunications consultants & organizations.

Canadian Wireless Telecommunications Association (CWTA) / Association canadienne des télécommunications sans fil (ACTS)
#1110, 130 Albert St., Ottawa ON K1P 5G4 Canada
Tel: 613-233-4888; *Fax:* 613-233-2032
info@cwta.ca
www.cwta.ca
The authority on wireless issures, trends & developments in Canada; represents cellular, PCS, messaging, mobile radio, fixed wireless & movile satellite service providers as well as companies that develop & produce products & services for the industry.

Frequency Co-ordination System Association (FCSA) / Association pour la coordination des fréquences
#700, 1 Nicholas St., Ottawa ON K1N 7B7 Canada
Tel: 613-241-3080; *Fax:* 613-241-9632
amoreno.fcsa@sympatico.ca
www.fcsa.ca
To operate & administer computerized Microwave Information & Coordination System (MICS); to provide cost-effective, timely & high quality centralized administrative & technical services to allow members to be able to effectively plan & coordinate frequencies for microwave communication systems on national basis.

Halifax Regional CAP Association (HRCAP)
c/o 1673 Barrington St., 2nd Fl., Halifax NS B3J 1Z9 Canada
Tel: 902-482-4729; *Fax:* 902-482-5014
admin@hrca.ns.ca
www.halifaxcap.ca
Social Media: www.twitter.com/hrcap
To deliver quality service to communities through their locally operated Community Access Program (CAP) sites.
Ryan Deschamps, Chair

Ontario Pioneers
21 Meadowland Dr., Brampton ON L6W 2R5 Canada
Tel: 905-451-5607; *Fax:* 905-453-3996
she.rob@sympatico.ca
Sheila O'Donoghue, Manager

SaskTel Pioneers
2121 Saskatchewan Dr., 12th Fl., Regina SK S4P 3Y2 Canada
Tel: 306-777-2515; *Toll-Free:* 866-944-4442
sasktel.pioneers@sasktel.sk.ca
www.sasktelpioneers.com
Darrell Liebrecht, Manager

Telecommunities Canada Inc.
c/o President, #220, 4252 Commerce Circle, Victoria BC V8Z 4M2 Canada
Tel: 250-479-2851; *Fax:* 250-727-6418
shearman@victoria.tc.ca
www.tc.ca
To ensure that all Canadians are able to participate in community-based communications & electronic information services by promoting and supporting local community network initiatives; to represent & promote Canadian community networking movement at the national & international level
Gareth Shearman, President

TelecomPioneers
950 - 15th St., 12th Fl., Denver CO 80202 USA
Tel: 303-571-1200; *Fax:* 303-572-0520
Toll-Free: 800-872-5995
info@pioneersvolunteer.org
www.telecompioneers.org
TelecomPioneers is the largest industry-related volunteer organizationin the world, comprising of over 600,000 current and retired telecommunications employees who have joined together to make their communities better places to live and work.
Marty Lee, President

TelecomPioneers of Alberta
9 Munro Cresc., Red Deer AB T4N 0H8 Canada
Tel: 403-343-1201
chap46@telus.net
Ken Davies, Manager

TelecomPioneers of Canada
PO Box 880, 1505 Barrington St., Halifax NS B3J 2W3 Canada
Fax: 902-484-5189
Toll-Free: 888-994-3232
www.telecompioneers.ca
The TelecomPioneers of Canada is a network of current and former telecom industry employees, their partners and their families and are commited to improving the quality of life in Canada's communities.
J. Michael Sears, President

Tenants & Landlords

Action Dignité de Saint-Léonard
9089A, boul Viau, Saint-Léonard QC H1R 2V6 Canada
Tél: 514-251-2874; *Téléc:* 514-251-2874
actdigsl@cooptel.qc.ca
Groupe de défense des droits des locataires

Association des locataires de l'×le-des-Soeurs (ALIS/NITA) / Nuns' Island Tenants Association
CP 63008, 40, Place du Commerce, Verdun QC H3E 1V6 Canada
Tél: 514-667-0914; *Téléc:* 514-995-2773
alis_nita@yahoo.com
Défense des droits des locataires

Comité d'action des citoyennes et citoyens de Verdun
3972, rue de Verdun, Verdun QC H4G 1K9 Canada
Tél: 514-769-2228; *Téléc:* 514-769-0825
cacv@videotron.ca
www.cacv-verdun.org
Le CACV soutien les personnes les plus démunies afin qu'elles améliorent leurs conditions de vie dans une optique de prise en charge
Chantal Lamarre, Directrice

Comité d'action Parc Extension (CAPE)
#9, 419, St-Roch, Montréal QC H3N 1R8 Canada
Tél: 514-278-6028; *Téléc:* 514-278-0900
cape@cooptel.qc.ca
www.comitelogement.org
A pour mission d'améliorer les conditions de vie de tous les citoyens/citoyennes du quartier Parc Extension

Comité des citoyens et citoyennes du quartier Saint-Sauveur
301, rue Carillon, Québec QC G1K 5B3 Canada
Tél: 418-529-6158
cccqss@bellnet.ca
www.cccqss.org

Comité logement de Lacine-Lasalle
426, rue St-Jacques, Lachine QC H8R 1E8 Canada
Tél: 514-544-4294; *Téléc:* 514-366-0505
logement.lachine-lasalle@videotron.ca

Comité logement du Plateau Mont-Royal
4450, St-Hubert, local 328, Montréal QC H2J 2W9 Canada
Tél: 514-527-3495; *Téléc:* 514-527-6653
clplateau@yahoo.ca

Comité logement Rosemont
5350, rue Lafond, local R-145, Montréal QC H1X 2X2 Canada
Tél: 514-597-2581; *Téléc:* 514-524-9813
info@comitelogement.org
www.comitelogement.org
Défendre et promouvoir les droits des locataires du quartier Rosemont
Martine Poitras, Coordonnatrice

Conseil communautaire Notre-Dame-de-Grâce / Notre-Dame-de-Grâce Community Council
5964, av Notre-Dame-de-Grâce, Montréal QC H4A 1N1 Canada
Tél: 514-484-1471; *Téléc:* 514-484-1687
ndgcc@ndg.ca
www.ndg.ca
Gillian Keefe, Directrice

POPIR-Comité logement (St-Henri, Petite Bourgogne, Ville Émard, Côte St-Paul)
4017, rue Notre-Dame ouest, Montréal QC H4C 1R3 Canada
Tél: 514-935-4649; *Téléc:* 514-935-4067
popir@videotron.ca

Tourism & Travel

Alberta Hotel & Lodging Association
#401, 5241 Calgary Trail South, Edmonton AB T6H 5G8 Canada
Tel: 780-436-6112; *Fax:* 780-436-5404
Toll-Free: 888-436-6112
info@ahla.ca
www.ahla.ca
To enhance the image, the quality & efficiency of the hotel industry in Alberta
Dave Kaiser, President & CEO

Algoma Kinniwabi Travel Association (AKTA)
#204, 485 Queen St. East, Sault Ste Marie ON P6A 1Z9 Canada
Tel: 705-254-4293; *Fax:* 705-254-4892
Toll-Free: 800-263-2546
info@algomacountry.com
www.algomacountry.com
To promote the Algoma Country region to the travelling public
Lori Johnson, President

Almaguin-Nipissing Travel Association
PO Box 351, 1375 Seymour St., North Bay ON P1B 8H5 Canada
Tel: 705-474-6634; *Fax:* 705-474-9271
Toll-Free: 800-387-0516
info@ontariosnearnorth.on.ca
www.ontariosnearnorth.on.ca
To market Ontario's Near North as a four-seasons family-oriented outdoor vacation destination on behalf of the organized tourist industry

Association des hôteliers du Québec (AHQ) / Québec Hoteliers' Association
#1004, 425, boul De Maisonneuve ouest, Montréal QC H3A 3G5 Canada
Tél: 514-448-6215; *Téléc:* 514-849-1157
Ligne sans frais: 877-769-9776
info@hoteliersquebec.org
www.hoteliersquebec.org

Regrouper les établissements hôteliers pour les représenter, défendre leurs intérêts et leurs fournir des services et ce, tout en collaborant au développement de la qualité de la profession hôtelière et de l'industrie touristique en général
Micheline de Gongre, Présidente-directrice générale

Association moto-tourisme Chibougamau
CP 580, Chibougamau QC G8P 2Y8 Canada
Tél: 418-745-3765
Jean-Paul Mercier

Association of Canadian Travel Agencies (ACTA) / Association canadienne des agences de voyages
#328, 2560 Matheson Blvd. East, Mississauga ON L4W 4Y9 Canada
Tel: 905-282-9294; *Fax:* 905-282-9826
Toll-Free: 866-725-2282
actacan@acta.travel
www.acta.ca
To provide leadership for the retail travel professional
Heather Craig-Peddie, Director, Operations
David McCaig, President/COO

Association of Canadian Travel Agencies - Atlantic (ACTA)
PO Box 21007, Quispamsis NB E2E 4Z4 Canada
Tel: 506-847-4030; *Fax:* 506-847-4048
Toll-Free: 866-725-2282
actaatlantic@acta.travel
www.acta.ca
To represent & defend the interests of the retail travel services industry; To serve as the focal point for the retail travel services industry, where ideas & resources are pooled into initiatives designed to create & maintain a healthly business & legislative environment
Lorie Cohen Hackett, Regional Manager

Association of Canadian Travel Agents - Alberta/NWT
PO Box 73034, 6290 - 199 St., Edmonton AB T5T 3X1 Canada
Tel: 780-756-6606; *Fax:* 780-756-6639
Toll-Free: 800-667-8314
cgannon@acta.ca
To represent the retail travel sector of Canada's tourism industry, with a focus on Albertan travel agents
Allan Ronneseth, Regional, Chair
Colleen Gannon, Regional Manager

Association of Canadian Travel Agents - British Columbia/Yukon
#213, 5760 Minoru Blvd., Richmond BC V6X 2A9 Canada
Tel: 604-231-0544; *Fax:* 604-231-6020
actabcyu@telus.net
David McCaig, Regional Manager

Association of Canadian Travel Agents - Manitoba
#700, 177 Lombard Ave., Winnipeg MB R3B 0W5 Canada
Tel: 204-831-0831; *Fax:* 204-925-8000
smmorris@mts.net
Shelley Morris, Regional Manager

Association of Canadian Travel Agents - Ontario
#328, 2560 Matheson Blvd. East, Mississauga ON L4W 4Y5 Canada
Tel: 905-282-9294; *Fax:* 905-282-9826
Toll-Free: 888-257-2282
actaon@on.aibn.com
www.acta.ca
To represent the retail travel sector of Canada's tourism industry, with a focus on Ontario travel agents
Heather Craig-Peddie, Director of Operations
Mike Foster, Regional Chair

Association of Canadian Travel Agents - Québec / Association des agents de voyages du Québec
#401, 152, rue Notre-Dame est, Montréal QC H2Y 3P6 Canada
Tél: 514-397-9977; *Téléc:* 514-397-1581
actaquebec@acta.travel
Défense des droits et intérêts de l'industrie du voyage
Henri Castillo, Directeur général

Association touristique des Laurentides (ATL) / Laurentian Tourist Association
14 142, rue de la Chapelle, Mirabel QC J7J 2C8 Canada
Tél: 450-436-8532; *Ligne sans frais:* 800-561-6673
info-tourisme@laurentides.com
www.laurentides.com
Unir tous les agents, corporations, corps publics et municipaux, associations et organismes, entreprises, oeuvrant dans le domaine touristique dans la région nord de Montréal; orienter et favoriser le développement et l'activité touristique régionale dans le meilleur intérêt régional; obtenir au nom de toute la région des interventions gouvernementales ou autres propres à favoriser son développement touristique

Association touristique régionale de Charlevoix
495, boul de Comporté, La Malbaie QC G5A 3G3 Canada
Tél: 418-665-4454; *Téléc:* 418-665-3811
Ligne sans frais: 800-667-2276
info@tourisme-charlevoix.com
www.tourisme-charlevoix.com/fr/accueil/index.asp
Acceuil, promotion, développement de Charlevoix en tourisme

Association touristique régionale de Duplessis (ATRD)
312, av Brochu, Sept-Iles QC G4R 2W6 Canada
Tél: 418-962-0808; *Téléc:* 418-962-6518
Ligne sans frais: 888-463-0808
info@tourismeduplessis.com
www.tourismeduplessis.com
Regrouper efficacement, sur une base géographique et sectorielle, les diverses entreprises touristiques de la région; proposer un plan d'action annuel dans lequel sont déterminés les priorités, les programmes et les services offerts à ses membres
Marie-Soleil Vigneault, Directrice générale
Danys Jomphe, Président

Association touristique régionale du Saguenay-Lac-Saint-Jean
#100, 412, boul. Saguenay Est, Chicoutimi QC G7H 7Y8 Canada
Tél: 418-543-9778; *Téléc:* 418-543-1805
Ligne sans frais: 800-463-9651
info@tourismesaglac.net
www.saguenaylacsaintjean.net
Au service et à l'écoute de ses membres et de l'industrie touristique régionale dans son ensemble, elle est une organisation de concertation dont les principales activités visent à promouvoir à développer la qualité de l'expérience touristique, à assurer l'accueil et l'information et la mise en marché
Carol Martel, Directeur général
Robert Bilodeau, Président

Association touristique régionale Manicouagan
#304, 337, boul LaSalle, Baie-Comeau QC G4Z 2Z1 Canada
Tél: 418-294-2876; *Téléc:* 418-294-2345
Ligne sans frais: 888-463-5319
atrmanic@globetrotter.net
www.tourismemanicouagan.com/fr/
Promouvoir la région comme destination touristique et mettre en valeur ses attraits
Denis Cardinal, Directeur général

Associations touristiques régionales associées du Québec (ATRAQ) / Québec Regional Tourist Associations Inc.
#330, 1575, boul de l'Avenir, Laval QC H7S 2N5 Canada
Tél: 450-686-8358; *Téléc:* 450-686-9630
Ligne sans frais: 877-686-8358
information@atrassociees.com
www.atrassociees.com
Regroupe l'ensemble des associations touristiques régionales oeuvrant au Québec en vue de les représenter et défendre leurs intérêts collectifs; les promouvoir et leur offrir des services; entend contribuer ainsi au développement de l'industrie touristique québécoise
Louis Rome, Directeur général

British Columbia Lodging & Campgrounds Association (BCLCA)
#209, 3003 St. John's St., Port Moody BC V3H 2C4 Canada
Tel: 604-945-7676; *Fax:* 604-945-7606
Toll-Free: 888-923-4678
info@bclca.com
www.bclca.com
To promote the public's utilization of member lodging & campground businesses; to monitor & make representation to governments on legislation affecting the interests of British Columbia's lodging & campground businesses; to speak for the membership on matters of general or specific interest; to encourage members to strive for excellence in accommodation & service
Joss Penny, Executive Director

Cambridge Tourism
750 Hespeler Rd., Cambridge ON N3H 5L8 Canada
Tel: 519-622-2336; *Fax:* 519-622-0177
Toll-Free: 800-749-7560
visit@cambridgetourism.com
www.cambridgetourism.com
To develop tourism initiatives & build partnerships that pool ideas & resources to promote Cambridge as a viable travel destination, generating greater economic impact for the city & other tourism stakeholders.
Greg Durocher, President, Chamber of Commerce
Jeanette Mahoney, Visitor Services Coordinator, Chamber of Commerce

Camping Québec
#700, 2001, rue de la Metropole, Longueuil QC J4G 1S9 Canada
Tél: 450-651-7396; *Téléc:* 450-651-7397
Ligne sans frais: 800-363-0457
www.destinationcamping.ca
Défendre les intérêts de nos membres; offrir des services de publications et promotion, des activitées, des escomptes sur achats et programmes divers.
Marysè Catellier, Vice-président exécutif

Canadian Hotel Marketing & Sales Executives (CHMSE)
26 Avonhurst Rd., Toronto ON M9A 2G8 Canada
Tel: 416-252-9800; *Fax:* 416-252-7071
info@chmse.com
www.chmse.com
To be the leading association in providing professional development opportunities to sales & marketing executives within the Canadian hospitality industry
Shelley Macdonald, Executive Director
Julie Wiggins, Vice-President
Susan Aguilo, Vice-President
Monika Nowak, Vice-President
Linda Stott, President

Canadian Institute of Travel Counsellors (CITC) / Institut canadien des conseillers en voyages
#406, 505 Consumers Rd., Toronto ON M2J 4V8 Canada
Tel: 416-484-4450; *Fax:* 416-484-4140
Toll-Free: 800-589-5776
info@citc.ca
www.citc.ca
To lead the Canadian travel industry to be the most skilled & professional work force in the industry, & to ensure that the CTC/CTM designations are recognized, accepted & valued by the travel industry & consumers as the ultimate achievement in professionalism.
Steve Gillick, President/COO

Canadian Recreational Vehicle Association (CRVA) / Association canadienne du véhicule récréatif
#310, 2175 Sheppard Ave. East, Toronto ON M2J 1W8 Canada
Tel: 416-971-7800; *Fax:* 416-491-1670
crva@crva.ca
www.crva.ca
To promote recreational vehicle lifestyle
Don Mockford, Executive Vice-President

Canadian Resort Development Association (CRDA)
147 Liberty St., Toronto ON M6K 3G3 Canada
Tel: 416-960-4930; *Fax:* 416-533-0591
Toll-Free: 800-646-9205
crda@rogers.com
www.crda.com
To engender a better understanding of the value of the vacation ownership product; to ensure fair & ethical treatment by all industry participants, through legislation or industry self-management; to educate & inform within the membership & outwardly to the public.
Ross Perlmutter, Executive Director

Canadian Tourism Research Institute
255 Smyth Rd., Ottawa ON K1H 8M7 Canada
Tel: 613-526-3280; *Fax:* 613-526-4857
Toll-Free: 866-711-2262
ctri@conferenceboard.ca
www.conferenceboard.ca/ctri/

Cariboo Chilcotin Coast Tourism Association
#204, 350 Barnard St., Williams Lake BC V2G 4T9 Canada
Tel: 250-392-2226; *Fax:* 250-392-2838
Toll-Free: 800-663-5885
info@landwithoutlimits.com
www.landwithoutlimits.com
The Association promotes tourism products of the Cariboo Chilcotin Coast region of BC. Products & services include, access to an extensive image bank, travel guide & DVD, familiarization tour assistance, itinerary planning assistance, property inspection/recommendations, regional knowledge.
Wylie Bystedt, Chair
Amy Thacker, CEO

Central Nova Tourist Association (CNTA)
65 Treaty Trail, Millbrook NS B6L 1W3 Canada
Tel: 902-893-8782; *Fax:* 902-893-2269
Toll-Free: 800-895-1177
info@centralnovascotia.com
www.centralnovascotia.com
To contribute to the Central Nova area becoming the most important tourist destination in Nova Scotia, resulting in new tourism initiatives & strengthened businesses; we will accomplish this by working as a team dedicated to effective communication & production of our community
Joyce Mingo, Executive Director

Convention & Visitors Bureau of Windsor, Essex County & Pelee Island
City Centre, #103, 333 Riverside Dr. West, Windsor ON N9A 5K4 Canada
Tel: 519-255-6530; *Fax:* 519-255-6192
Toll-Free: 800-265-3633
cvb@city.windsor.on.ca
www.visitwindsor.com
The Convention and Visitors Bureau is to help make the most of your visit to Windsor, Essex County & Pelee Island.
Gordon Orr, Managing Director

Cornwall & Seaway Valley Tourism
11 Water St. West, Cornwall ON K6J 1A1 Canada
Tel: 613-938-4748; *Fax:* 613-938-4751
Toll-Free: 800-937-4748
info@cornwalltourism.com
www.cornwalltourism.com
To promote Cornwall & Seaway Valley as a viable visitor & convention destination
Michael Lalonde, Executive Manager

Council of Tourism Associations of British Columbia (COTA)
#1208, 409 Granville St., Vancouver BC V6C 1T2 Canada
Tel: 604-685-5956; *Fax:* 604-685-5915
cotabc@telus.net
www.cotabc.com
To advocate the interests of members to provincial & federal governments, businesses & media, in order to inform them of the opportunities & concerns of the tourism industry; To promote tourism in British Columbia
Jim Storie, Chair
Stephen Regan, President/CEO
Peter Larose, Director, Policy & Planning

Destination Winnipeg Inc. (DW)
#300, 259 Portage Ave., Winnipeg MB R3B 2A9 Canada
Tel: 204-943-1970; *Fax:* 204-942-4043
Toll-Free: 800-665-0204
wpginfo@destinationwinnipeg.ca
www.destinationwinnipeg.ca
To act as Winnipeg's economic development & tourism services agency, by marketing the city & providing related economic development & tourism services
Nick Logan, Chair
Stuart Duncan, President

Evangeline Trail Tourism Association (ETTA)
5518 Prospect Rd., New Minas NS B4N 3K8 Canada
Tel: 902-861-1645
To represent the private sector of tourism industry; to promote tourism in the Nova Scotia area of Evangeline Trail; to publish articles, pamphlets & books about the area; to administer & operate local tourist bureaus in cooperation with various Boards of Trade & local tourism committees
Beth Caldwell, Executive Director

Fondation Tourisme Jeunesse
3514, ave. Lacombe, Montréal QC H3T 1M1 Canada
Tél: 514-252-3208; *Téléc:* 514-252-3024
fondationtourismejeunesse@gmail.com
www.tourismejeunesse.org
Rendre accessible le tourisme aux jeunes, en développant divers outils et services, notamment par le biais des bureaux d'information voyages et des auberges de jeunesse du Québec

Fredericton Tourism
PO Box 130, 11 Carleton St., Fredericton NB E3B 4Y7 Canada
Tel: 506-460-2041; *Fax:* 506-460-2474
Toll-Free: 888-888-4768
www.tourismfredericton.ca
The organization is a division of the Dept. of Development Services of the City of Fredericton, & it is responsible for marketing the city & surrounding area as a tourism destination. It develops & runs a variety of cultural programs largely focused in the Historic Garrison District. Also, it operates 2 municipal Visitor Information Centres, Lighthouse on the Green, & River Valley Crafts retail shop.
David Seabrook, Tourism Manager
Frank Flanagan, Director, Development Services

The Georgian Triangle Tourist Association & Tourist Information Centre
30 Mountain Rd., Collingwood ON L9Y 5H7 Canada
Tel: 705-445-7722; *Toll-Free:* 888-227-8667
info@georgiantriangle.com
www.georgiantriangle.com
Social Media: www.facebook.com/group.php?gid=99129054579
To promote tourism & convention industries in the Georgian Triangle
Nancy Kindler, Executive Director

Halifax Tourism, Culture & Heritage
PO Box 1749, Halifax NS B3J 3A5 Canada
Tel: 902-490-5948; *Fax:* 902-490-5950
ivc@region.halifax.ns.ca
www.halifaxinfo.com
The entire Halifax region delights with its impressive array of entertainment, museums, galleries, historic sites, fine restaurants, colourful gardens and lively nightlife. Through our 188 communities, explore charming seaside towns, sun-drenched beaches, sparkling coves and miles of rugged shoreline guarded by graceful lighthouses. Imagine the vivacity of city living, the charms of small town life and the pristine beauty of nature - all in one place.
Lewis M. Rogers, Director

HomeLink International Home Exchange (HLCA)
1707 Platt Cres., North Vancouver BC V7J 1X9 Canada
Tel: 604-987-3262
info@homelink.ca
www.homelink.ca
To produce directories listing homes for vacation exchange worldwide
Jack Graber, Director

Hospitality Newfoundland & Labrador (HNL)
ICON Bldg., 187 Kenmonunt Rd., 2nd Fl., St. John's NL A1B 3P9 Canada
Tel: 709-722-2000; *Fax:* 709-722-8104
Toll-Free: 800-563-0700
hnl@hnl.ca
www.hnl.ca
To develop & promote tourism & hospitality industry throughout Newfoundland & Labrador.
Carol-Ann Gilliard, Chief Executive Officer

Hostelling International - Canada (HI-C)
#400, 205 Catherine St., Ottawa ON K2P 1C3 Canada
Tel: 613-237-7884; *Fax:* 613-237-7868
info@hostellingintl.ca
www.hostellingintl.ca
To help all people, especially young people, to a greater knowledge, care & love of the countryside by providing recreational activity programs, hostels or other simple accommodations for them on their travels.

Hotel Association of Canada Inc. (HAC) / Association des hôtels du Canada
#1206, 130 Albert St., Ottawa ON K1P 5G4 Canada
Tel: 613-237-7149; *Fax:* 613-237-8928
info@hotelassociation.ca
www.hotelassociation.ca
To represent members both nationally & internationally; to provide cost-effective services which stimulate & encourage a free market accommodation industry
Andrea Myers, Director, Marketing & Member Services
Anthony P. Pollard, President
Walter Willett, Director, Business Development

Hotel Association of Nova Scotia (HANS)
PO Box 473, Stn. M, Halifax NS B3J 2P8 Canada
Tel: 902-425-4890
www.novascotiahotels.ca
To make Nova Scotia a year-round travel destination; To act as the official voice of the collective member hotels; To provide support for appropriate advisory boards & committees; To develop & encourage a coordinated joint marketing effort
Jeff Ransome, President

Hotel Association of Prince Edward Island
c/o 129 Queen St., Charlottetown PE C1A 4B3 Canada
Tel: 902-368-3688; *Fax:* 902-368-3108
Elaine Thompson, President

Institut de tourisme et d'hôtellerie du Québec (ITHQ)
3535, rue Saint-Denis, Montréal QC H2X 3P1 Canada
Tél: 514-282-5108; *Téléc:* 514-873-4529
Ligne sans frais: 800-361-5111
webmestre@ithq.qc.ca
www.ithq.qc.ca
Formation professionnelle en hôtellerie, restauration et tourisme.
Lucille Daoust, Directrice générale
Robert Gagnon, Président

Klondike Visitors Association (KVA)
PO Box 389C, Dawson City YT Y0B 1G0 Canada
Tel: 867-993-5575; *Fax:* 867-993-6415
kva@dawson.net
www.dawsoncity.ca
Social Media:
facebook.com/pages/dawson-city-yukon/182559814930
The Association responds to visitor information requests & liaises with municipal & territorial governments to encourage Tourism-related initiatives. It promotes Dawson City, Yukon & the Klondike Region as a year-round tourist destination.
Gary Parker, Executive Director

Kootenay Rockies Tourism
PO Box 10, 1905 Warren Ave., Kimberley BC V1A 2Y5 Canada
Tel: 250-427-4838; *Fax:* 250-427-3344
Toll-Free: 800-661-6603
info@kootenayrockies.com
www.kootenayrockies.com
To coordinate & execute tourism marketing initiatives of private sector partners.
Chris Dadson, President

Muskoka Tourism
1342 Hwy. 11 North, RR#2, Kilworthy ON P0E 1G0 Canada
Tel: 705-689-0660; *Fax:* 705-689-9118
Toll-Free: 800-267-9700
info@muskokatourism.ca
www.discovermuskoka.ca
To market the region's tourism resources to the public, media & group tour travel markets

Niagara Falls Tourism
5400 Robinson St, Niagara Falls ON L2G 2A6 Canada
Tel: 905-356-6061; *Fax:* 905-356-5567
Toll-Free: 800-563-2557
office@niagarafallstourism.com
www.niagarafallstourism.com
Niagara Falls Tourism (Visitor and Convention Bureau) is the official tourism marketing organization of the Community, responsible for developing public and private sector programs that produce incremental visitor business and resulting economic development returns for the City, its residents and the business community

North of Superior Tourism Association (NOSTA)
119 South May St., Thunder Bay ON P7E 1A9 Canada
Tel: 807-346-1130; *Fax:* 807-346-1135
Toll-Free: 800-265-3951
info@nosta.on.ca
www.nosta.on.ca
Social Media: www.facebook.com/group.php?gid=55057890985
To market the tourism opportunities for vacationing in Northwestern Ontario.
Done Pearl, Executive Director

Northern British Columbia Tourism Association (NBCTA)
PO Box 2373, 1274 - 5th Ave., Prince George BC V2N 2S6 Canada
Tel: 250-561-0432; *Fax:* 250-561-0450
Toll-Free: 800-663-8843
info@nbctourism.com
www.nbctourism.com
To promote & develop the tourism industry of northern British Columbia
Anthony Everett, CEO

Northern Frontier Visitors Association (NFVA)
#4, 4807 - 49 St., Yellowknife NT X1A 3T5 Canada
Tel: 867-873-4262; *Fax:* 867-873-3654
Toll-Free: 877-881-4262
info@northernfrontier.com
www.northernfrontier.com
To promote the Northern Frontier Region as an attractive area for tourism; to foster, encourage & assist in any way the growth of tourism into & within the Northern Frontier Region; to increase awareness within the Northern Frontier Region of the potential tourism holds as a viable, clean, labour intensive industry.
Denie Olmstead, Executive Director

Northern Rockies Alaska Highway Tourism Association (NRAHTA)
PO Box 6850, Stn. Main, #300, 9523 - 100 St., Fort St John BC V1J 4J3 Canada
Tel: 250-785-2544; *Fax:* 250-785-4424
Toll-Free: 888-785-2544
info@hellonorth.com
www.hellonorth.com

To coordinate opportunites for sustainable tourism growth & development by fostering memorable year round visitor experiences; promoting social & economic benefits to members & wider community.
April Moi, Executive Director

Northwest Ontario Sunset Country Travel Association
PO Box 647W, Kenora ON P9N 3X6 Canada
Tel: 807-468-5853; *Fax:* 807-468-5484
Toll-Free: 800-665-7567
info@ontariossunsetcountry.ca
www.ontariossunsetcountry.ca
To develop, promote & advertise through cooperation, coordination & communication with clients & organizations for the betterment of tourism in Sunset Country & the province.
Gerry Cariou, Executive Director

Northwest Territories Tourism (NWTT)
PO Box 610, Yellowknife NT X1A 2N5 Canada
Tel: 867-873-5007; *Fax:* 867-873-4059
Toll-Free: 800-661-0788
info@spectacularnwt.com;
communications@spectacularnwt.com
www.spectacularnwt.com
To support the development of a strong tourism sector in the Northwest Territories for the benefit of tourists, residents, & communities; To promote pan-territorial tourism; To act as a voice for the tourism industry; To preserve the integrity of the cultural & natural heritage of the Northwest Territories
Gerard (Gerry) LePrieur, Executive Director

Nunavut Tourism
PO Box 1450, Iqaluit NU X0A 0H0 Canada
Tel: 867-979-6551; *Fax:* 867-979-1261
Toll-Free: 866-686-2888
info@nunavuttourism.com
www.nunavuttourism.com
To represent the tourism industry for the private sector in Nunavut; to promote & market Nunavut tourism products
Bill Lyall, Chair
Paul Lewis, CEO
Betty Ann Eaton, Vice-Chair

NWC, the Business Travellers' Association (NWC)
PO Box 336, 28 Queen Elizabeth Way, Winnipeg MB R3C 2H6 Canada
Tel: 204-284-8900; *Fax:* 204-284-8909
Toll-Free: 800-665-6928
nwcta@nwcta.com
www.nwcta.com
To protect & introduce benefits for individual business travellers
Diane McDonald, Membership Services Coordinator

Office du tourisme et des congrès de Québec (OTCQ) / Québec City & Area Tourism & Convention Board
399, rue St-Joseph est, Québec QC G1K 8E2 Canada
Tél: 418-641-6654; *Téléc:* 418-641-6578
Ligne sans frais: 877-783-1608
danielle.doyon@quebecregion.com
www.quebecregion.com
Organisme responsable de la mise en marché de la région touristique de Québec
Pierre Labrie, Directeur général
Daniel Gagnon, Directeur, Communication et publicité
Gilles Proulx, Directeur, Administration, accueil et services aux membres
Hélène Pomerleau, Directrice, Promotion, ventes et services

Ontario Accommodation Association (OAA)
#2, 347 Pido Rd., RR#6, Peterborough ON K9J 6X7 Canada
Tel: 705-745-4982; *Fax:* 705-745-4983
Toll-Free: 800-461-1972
info@ontarioaccommodation.com
www.ontarioaccommodation.com
To serve Ontario's independent accommodation industry
Bruce M. Gravel, President

Ontario East Tourism Association (OETA)
PO Box 730, #200, 104 St. Lawrence St., Merrickville ON K0G 1N0 Canada
Tel: 613-269-4113; *Fax:* 613-659-4306
Toll-Free: 800-567-3278
info@realontario.ca
www.realontario.ca
To encourage visitation to Eastern Ontario by means of cooperative tourism marketing
Rose Bertoia, Executive Director
John Bonser, President

Ontario Private Campground Association (OPCA)
#8, 220 Royal Crest Ct., Markham ON L3R 9Y2 Canada
Tel: 905-947-9500; *Fax:* 905-947-9501
Toll-Free: 877-672-2226
opca@campingontario.ca
www.campingontario.ca
To support & improve the operation of private campgrounds in Ontario by establishing standards, disseminating information & by representation in the tourist industry & at all levels of government
Beth Potter, Executive Director

Ontario Restaurant, Hotel & Motel Association (ORHMA)
#8-201, 2600 Skymark Ave., Mississauga ON L4W 5B2 Canada
Tel: 905-361-0268; *Fax:* 905-361-0288
Toll-Free: 800-668-8906
info@orhma.com
www.orhma.com
To foster a positive business climate for the hospitality industry in Ontario; To represent members before municipal & provincial governments
David Blades, Chair
Tony Elenis, President & CEO
Al Richards, Secretary-Treasurer
Michelle Saunders, Manager, Government Relations
Alice Tjan, Manager, Membership Services

Ontario's Wilderness Region
PO Box 920, 76 McIntyre Rd., Schumacher ON P0N 1G0 Canada
Tel: 705-360-1989; *Fax:* 705-268-5526
Toll-Free: 800-461-3766
info@ontarioswildernessregion.com
www.ontarioswildernessregion.com
To increase awareness in target markets of tourism possibilities in our geographic region.
Jennifer Rowe, Executive Director
Sean Mackey, President

Ottawa Tourism / Tourisme Ottawa
#1800, 130 Albert St., Ottawa ON K1P 5G4 Canada
Tel: 613-237-5150; *Fax:* 613-237-7339
Toll-Free: 800-363-4465
info@ottawatourism.ca
www.ottawatourism.ca
To maximize the number of visits to Ottawa & Canada's Capital Region through effective marketing & communication programs; to help develop & promote awareness of the contribution of tourism in the community; to facilitate the development & promotion of the products, services & needs of members
Noel Buckley, President & CEO

Ottawa Valley Tourist Association (OVTA)
9 International Dr., Pembroke ON K8A 6W5 Canada
Tel: 613-732-4364; *Fax:* 613-735-2492
Toll-Free: 800-757-6580
adventureplayground@ottawavalley.org
info@ottawavalley.travel
The Ottawa Valley Tourist Association (OVTA) is a non-profit organization designed to stimulate and promote tourism in Renfrew County. Our goal is to create a presence in the tourism marketplace. In order to position the Ottawa Valley as an interesting and popular travel destination in the minds of travelers, a joint effort among tourism suppliers and OVTA's dedicated tourism staff is required.
Mitchell Wilkie, Manager
Charlotte Gebhart, President

Peterborough & the Kawarthas Tourism
1400 Crawford Dr., RR#5, Peterborough ON K9J 6X6 Canada
Tel: 705-742-2201; *Fax:* 705-742-2494
Toll-Free: 800-461-6424
info@thekawarthas.net
www.thekawarthas.net
Barbara van Vierzen, Manager, Customer Service

Pictou County Tourist Association
980 East River Rd., New Glasgow NS B2H 3S8 Canada
Tel: 902-752-6383; *Fax:* 902-752-6503
Toll-Free: 877-816-2326
admin@tourismpictoucounty.com
www.tourismpictoucounty.com
To promote the county to residents & visitors

Rainbow Country Travel Association (RCTA)
2726 Whippoorwill Ave., Sudbury ON P3G 1E9 Canada
Tel: 705-522-0104; *Fax:* 705-522-3132
Toll-Free: 800-465-6655
info@rainbowcountry.com
www.rainbowcountry.com
Social Media:
www.facebook.com/group.php?gid=100931223286939
Donna MacLeod, Executive Director

Resorts Ontario
29 Albert St. North, Orillia ON L3V 5J9 Canada
Tel: 705-325-9115; *Fax:* 705-325-7999
Toll-Free: 800-363-7227
escapes@resorts-ontario.com
www.resorts-ontario.com
To serve & promote the collective interests of resorts, lodges & inns of Ontario

Saskatchewan Hotel & Hospitality Association (SHHA)
#302, 2080 Broad St., Regina SK S4P 1Y3 Canada
Tel: 306-522-1664; *Fax:* 306-525-1944
Toll-Free: 800-667-1118
lorane.has@sasktel.net
www.hotelsofsask.com
Bill Nelson, Executive Director

Stratford Tourism Alliance
47 Downie St., Stratford ON N5A 1W7 Canada
Tel: 519-271-5140; *Fax:* 519-273-1818
Toll-Free: 800-561-7926
info@welcometostratford.com
www.welcometostratford.com
A marketing organization promoting Stratford as a destination for leisure travelers & others; provides services to members, assistance, information & guidance to visitors, convention planners, & media contacts about the advantages of Stratford & surrounding area as a destination
Eugene Zakreski, Executive Director
Christina Phillips, Membership &Advertising Coordinator
Cathy Rehberg, Marketing Coordinator

Sudbury Visitor & Convention Services
PO Box 5000, Stn. A, 200 Brady St., Sudbury ON P3A 5P3 Canada
Tel: 705-674-4455; *Fax:* 705-671-6767
Toll-Free: 877-304-8222
renee.germain@sudbury.ca
www.grandsudbury.ca
Renee Germain, Coordinator

Thompson Okanagan Tourism Association (TOTA)
2280-D Leckie Rd., Kelowna BC V1X 6G6 Canada
Tel: 250-860-5999; *Fax:* 250-860-9993
Toll-Free: 800-567-2275
info@totabc.com
www.totabc.com
To increase members' revenue & sustainability through cooperative marketing, ongoing education & government liaison
Deanna Rainey, CEO
Carolyn Carr, Director of Marketing

Tourism Brantford
399 Wayne Gretzky Pkwy., Brantford ON N3R 8B4 Canada
Tel: 519-751-9900; *Fax:* 519-751-2617
Toll-Free: 800-265-6299
tourism@brantford.ca
www.visitbrantford.ca
To ensure quality visitor services through awareness, education, marketing & communications; to enhance the development of the tourism industry as an economic generator & to enhance the quality of life in our community
Susan Sager, Manager, Tourism & Marketing

Tourism Burlington
414 Locust St., Burlington ON L7S 1T7 Canada
Tel: 905-634-5594; *Fax:* 905-634-7220
Toll-Free: 877-499-9989
info@tourismburlington.com
www.tourismburlington.com
To increase tourism, resulting in economic benefits through utilization of recreational, cultural, commercial & personal resources
Pam Belgrade, Executive Director

Tourism Calgary
#200, 238 - 11 Ave. SE, Calgary AB T2G 0X8 Canada
Tel: 403-263-8510; *Fax:* 403-262-3809
Toll-Free: 800-661-1678
www.tourismcalgary.com
A non-profit destination marketing organization, providing services to members to promote Calgary as a destination for

travel industry professionals, as well as leisure & business travelers
Aldon Wells, Acting CEO

Tourism Cape Breton
PO Box 1448, Sydney NS B1P 6R7 Canada
Tel: 902-563-4636; *Fax:* 902-564-5422
Toll-Free: 800-565-0000
info@cbisland.com
www.cbisland.com
Sandra MacDonald, General Manager

Tourism Hamilton
34 James St. South, Hamilton ON L8P 2X8 Canada
Tel: 905-546-2666; *Fax:* 905-546-2667
Toll-Free: 800-263-8590
tourism@hamilton.ca
www.tourismhamilton.com
To promote & increase the tourism & convention industries in Greater Hamilton
David Adames, Executive Director

Tourism Industry Association of Canada (TIAC) / Association de l'industrie touristique du Canada (AITC)
#803, 130 Albert St., Ottawa ON K1P 5G4 Canada
Tel: 613-238-3883; *Fax:* 613-238-3878
swong@tiac.travel
www.tiac-aitc.ca
To enhance Canada's tourism industry by removing regulatory & legislative barriers to growth
Randall Williams, President/CEO
Ken Lambert, Chair
Christopher Jones, Vice President, Public Affairs

Tourism Industry Association of New Brunswick Inc. (TIANB) / Association de l'industrie touristique du Nouveau-Brunswick inc.
PO Box 23001, #440, 500 Beaverbrook Ct., Fredericton NB E3B 7B3 Canada
Tel: 506-458-5646; *Fax:* 506-459-3634
Toll-Free: 800-668-5313
info@tianb.com
www.tianb.com
To act as the provincial tourism & hospitality organization of New Brunswick, existing to fulfill the needs of its membership, in cooperation with both private & public sector partners; committed to be a representative, industry driven organization which provides leadership & direction, making tourism & hospitality the leading & most viably sustainable industry in New Brunswick
Joanne Bérubé-Gagné, President

Tourism Industry Association of Nova Scotia (TIANS)
2089 Maitland St., Halifax NS B3K 2Z8 Canada
Tel: 902-423-4480; *Fax:* 902-422-0184
Toll-Free: 800-948-4267
information_central@tians.org
www.tians.org
To lead, support, represent & enhance the Nova Scotia tourism industry
Darlene Grant Fiander, President
Danny Morton, Chair
Bill Walsh, Sec.-Treas.

Tourism Industry Association of PEI (TIAPEI)
PO Box 2050, 25 Queen St., 3rd Fl., Charlottetown PE C1A 7N7 Canada
Tel: 902-566-5008; *Fax:* 902-368-3605
Toll-Free: 866-566-5008
tiapei@tiapei.pe.ca
www.tiapei.pe.ca
To represent tourism related businesses, associations, institutions, & individuals; to encourage tourism to & within PEI
Thom MacMillan, President

Tourism Industry Association of the Yukon
#3, 1109 - 1st Ave., Whitehorse YT Y1A 5G4 Canada
Tel: 867-668-3331; *Fax:* 867-667-7379
tiayukon@klondiker.com
www.tiayukon.com
To represent all sectors & businesses of the tourism industry; to foster & promote travel in Yukon; to encourage increase & improvement of visitor facilities, services & attractions; to enhance & stimulate business climate in industry; to enhance awareness of importance of tourism; to design & deliver marketing programs
Patti Balsillie, CEO

Tourism London
696 Wellington Rd. South, London ON N6C 4R2 Canada
Tel: 519-661-5000; *Fax:* 519-661-6160
Toll-Free: 800-265-2602
tourism@londontourism.ca
www.londontourism.ca
To promote London through co-operative partnerships as the tourism, sports tourism & meeting destination of choice resulting in positive economic impact on the city of London
John Winston, General Manager

Tourism Regina Convention & Visitor Bureau
PO Box 3355, Hwy. 1 East, Regina SK S4P 3H1 Canada
Tel: 306-789-5099; *Fax:* 306-789-3171
Toll-Free: 800-661-5099
www.tourismregina.com
Providing information & services to visitors & meeting planners, Tourism Regina is a non-profit organization dedicated to promoting tourism in Regina, & business opportunities for its members
Loni Kaufmann, Executive Director
Alison Fraser, Dir., Sales, Conventions & Events
Cindy Wright, Membership Services Manager

Tourism Saint John / Bureau de tourisme et de congrés de Saint John
PO Box 1971, 15 Market Sq., 11th Fl., Saint John NB E2L 4L1 Canada
Tel: 506-658-2990; *Fax:* 506-632-6118
Toll-Free: 866-463-8639
visitsj@saintjohn.ca
www.tourismsaintjohn.com; www.venuesaintjohn.com
To position Saint John as the premier all-season, visitor, meeting & event destination on New Brunswick's Bay of Fundy; to generate revenues & publicity for the city of Saint John & its tourism operators & businesses through increased visitation, service excellence & the provision of advice & partnering opportunities
Margaret Totten, Manager

Tourism Sarnia Lambton (TSL)
556 North Christina St., Sarnia ON N7T 5W6 Canada
Tel: 519-336-3232; *Fax:* 519-336-3278
Toll-Free: 800-265-0316
info@tourismsarnialambton.com
www.tourismsarnialambton.com
To promote tourism to Lambton County, creating economic value for the entire community
Leona Allen, Office Administrator
John Dickson, General Manager/Executive Director

Tourism Saskatoon
#101, 202 Fourth Ave. North, Saskatoon SK S7K 0K1 Canada
Tel: 306-242-1206; *Fax:* 306-242-1955
Toll-Free: 800-567-2444
info@tourismsaskatoon.com
www.tourismsaskatoon.com
To operate as Saskatoon's destination management organization, maximizing the economic benefit for Saskatoon through tourism
Todd Brandt, CEO

Tourism Simcoe County
Simcoe County Museum, 1151 Hwy. 26 West, Minesing ON L0L 1Y2 Canada
Tel: 705-726-8502; *Fax:* 705-728-9130
Toll-Free: 800-487-6642
tourism@simcoe.ca
discover.simcoe.ca
The association promotes & develops the tourism industry of Simcoe County & area.
Bryan MacKell, Director, Planning, Development & Tourism, Simcoe County
Tori Martin, Administrator

Tourism Thunder Bay
500 Donald St. East, Thunder Bay ON P7E 5V3 Canada
Tel: 807-625-2149; *Fax:* 807-623-5468
Toll-Free: 800-667-8386
visit@thunderbay.com
www.visitthunderbay.com
To market Thunder Bay as a destination for individuals & groups
Paul Pepe, Tourism Manager
Rose Marie Tarnowski, Coord., Convention & Visitor Svcs.

Tourism Toronto (TCVA)
Queen's Quay Terminal at Harbourfront, PO Box 126, 207 Queen's Quay West, Toronto ON M5J 1A7 Canada
Tel: 416-203-2600; *Fax:* 416-203-6753
Toll-Free: 800-499-2514
toronto@torcvb.com
www.torontotourism.com
Social Media: www.facebook.com/visittoronto
To promote Toronto as a convention & visitor destination; to position Toronto as one of the world's great cities & a year-round destination for leisure & business
David Whitaker, President/CEO
Andrew Weir, Vice-President, Communications

Tourism Vancouver/Greater Vancouver Convention & Visitors Bureau
#210, 200 Burrard St., Vancouver BC V6C 3L6 Canada
Tel: 604-682-2222; *Fax:* 604-682-1717
www.tourismvancouver.com
Social Media: www.facebook.com/insidevancouver
To lead the cooperative effort of positioning Greater Vancouver as a preferred travel destination in all targeted markets worldwide, thereby creating opportunities for member & community sharing of the resulting economic, environmental, social & cultural benefits
Rick Antonson, President/CEO
Paul Vallee, Exec. Vice-President
Ted Lee, CFO

Tourism Victoria/Greater Victoria Visitors & Convention Bureau
Administration Office, 31 Bastion Sq., 4th Fl., Victoria BC V8W 1J1 Canada
Tel: 250-414-6999; *Fax:* 250-361-9733
Toll-Free: 800-663-3883
info@tourismvictoria.com
www.tourismvictoria.com
To oversee the development & promotion of the tourism industry in Greater Victoria
Robert Gialloreto, CEO
Helen Welch, Vice-President, Marketing

Tourisme Abitibi-Témiscamingue
#100, 155 av Dallaire, Rouyn-Noranda QC J9X 4T3 Canada
Tél: 819-762-8181; *Téléc:* 819-762-5212
Ligne sans frais: 800-808-0706
info@tourisme-abitibi-temiscamingue.org
www.abitibi-temiscamingue-tourism.org
Promotion du tourisme en Abitibi-Témiscamingue
Randa Napky, Directeur général
Jocelyn Carrier, Présidente

Tourisme Baie-James (TBJ) / James Bay Tourism
CP 134, 1252, rte 167 sud, Chibougamau QC G8P 2K6 Canada
Tél: 418-748-8140; *Téléc:* 418-748-8150
Ligne sans frais: 888-748-8140
info@tourismebaiejames.com
www.tourismebaiejames.com
Assure dans le cadre de ses responsabilités corporatives, des mandats en matière de concertation régionale, d'accueil, d'information, de signalisation, de promotion et de développement touristique
Christian Claveau, Président

Tourisme Bas-Saint-Laurent
148, rue Fraser, 2e étage, Rivière-du-Loup QC G5R 1C8 Canada
Tél: 418-867-1272; *Téléc:* 418-867-3245
Ligne sans frais: 800-563-5268
info@bassaintlaurent.ca
www.tourismebas-st-laurent.com
Accueil, développement et promotion touristique
Pierre Laplante, Directeur général
Gaston Gendreau, Président

Tourisme Cantons-de-l'Est
20, rue Don-Bosco sud, Sherbrooke QC J1L 1W4 Canada
Tél: 819-820-2020; *Téléc:* 819-566-4445
Ligne sans frais: 800-355-5755
www.cantonsdelest.com
A pour mission de faire de la région des Cantons-de-l'Est une des meilleures destinations touristique du Québec en toutes saisons
Alain Larouche, Directeur général
Francine Patenaude, Directrice, Marketing & développement

Tourisme Centre-du-Québec
20, boul Carignan ouest, Princeville QC G6L 4M4 Canada
Tél: 819-364-7177; *Téléc:* 819-364-2120
Ligne sans frais: 888-816-4007
gturcotte@tcdq.com
www.tourismecentreduquebec.com

Guylaine Turcotte, Adjointe administrative

Tourisme Chaudière-Appalaches (ATCA)
800, autoroute Jean-Lesage, Saint-Nicolas QC G7A 1E3 Canada
Tél: 418-831-4411; *Téléc:* 418-831-8442
Ligne sans frais: 888-831-4411
info@chaudiereappalaches.com
www.chaudiereappalaches.com
Favoriser le développement et la promotion de l'industrie touristique de son territoire tout en contribuant à la réussite des entreprises qui en sont members
Richard Moreau, Director général

Tourisme Gaspésie
357, route de la Mer, Sainte-Flavie QC G0J 2L0 Canada
Tél: 418-775-2223; *Téléc:* 418-775-2234
Ligne sans frais: 800-463-0323
info@tourisme-gaspesie.com
www.tourisme-gaspesie.com
Orienter et favoriser la promotion, le développement et l'activité touristique dans le meilleur intérêt de la Gaspésie; promouvoir, organiser et coordonner divers programmes de promotion et de développement touristique ayant comme conséquence d'accroître la clientèle touristique et prolongation des séjours dans la Gaspésie
Sylvain Tanguay, Directeur général
Joëlle Ross, Directrice adjointe

Tourisme Iles de la Madeleine
128, ch Principal, Cap-aux-Meules QC G4T 1C5 Canada
Tél: 418-986-2245; *Téléc:* 418-986-2327
Ligne sans frais: 877-624-4437
info@tourismeilesdelamadeleine.com
www.tourismeilesdelamadeleine.com/magdalen-islands/index.cfm
Regrouper les entreprises de l'industrie touristique de l'archipel afin d'accroître les efforts de développement et de promotion
Nancy Vézina, Directrice générale par intérim

Tourisme Lanaudière
3568, rue Church, Rawdon QC J0K 1S0 Canada
Tél: 450-834-2535; *Téléc:* 450-834-8100
Ligne sans frais: 800-363-2788
info@lanaudiere.ca
www.lanaudiere.ca/fr/
Faire la promotion, développement, commercialisation de l'offre touristiques de la région auprès des clienteles des différents marchés; améliorer l'accueil & l'information touristique
Évangéline Richard, Présidente

Tourisme Laval
2900, boul Saint-Martin ouest, Laval QC H7T 2J2 Canada
Tél: 450-682-5522; *Téléc:* 450-682-7304
Ligne sans frais: 877-465-2825
info@tourismelaval.com
www.tourismelaval.com
Andrée Courteau, Directeur général
Jean-Louis Bédard, Président

Tourisme Mauricie
1882, rue Cascade, Shawinigan QC G9N 8S1 Canada
Tél: 819-536-3334; *Téléc:* 819-536-3373
Ligne sans frais: 800-567-7603
info@tourismemauricie.com
www.tourismemauricie.com
M. André Nollet, Directeur général

Tourisme Montérégie
2001, Boul. De Rome, 3e étage, Brossard QC J4W 3K5 Canada
Tél: 450-466-4666; *Téléc:* 450-466-7999
Ligne sans frais: 866-469-0069
info@tourisme-monteregie.qc.ca
www.tourisme-monteregie.qc.ca
Éric Fournier, Directeur général
Brigitte Marcotte, Coordonnatrice, Communications

Tourisme Montréal/Office des congrès et du tourisme du Grand Montréal / Greater Montréal Convention & Tourism Bureau
CP 979, #100, 1255 Peel St., Montréal QC H3C 2W3 Canada
Tél: 514-873-2015; *Téléc:* 514-864-3838
Ligne sans frais: 877-266-5687
info@tourisme-montreal.org
www.tourism-montreal.org; www.tourisme-montreal.org
François Goulet, Vice-président exécutif

Tourisme Outaouais
103, rue Laurier, Gatineau QC J8X 3V8 Canada
Tél: 819-778-2222; *Téléc:* 819-778-7758
Ligne sans frais: 800-265-7822
info@tourisme-outaouais.ca
www.tourisme-outaouais.ca
Prospérité économique de la région par le développement et la promotion du produit touristique; structurer, organiser, orchestrer tout projet susceptible de générer des activités touristiques à retombées économiques importantes; assumer un accueil de qualité et une diffusion de l'information

Travellers' Aid Society of Toronto (TAS)
#B19-23, Union Station, 65 Front St. West, Toronto ON M5J 1E6 Canada
Tel: 416-366-7788; *Fax:* 416-366-0829
exec.director@travellersaid.ca
www.travellersaid.ca
To provide a base of needed information for travellers as well as shelter & other help in crisis situations
I.A.J. Sloan, President

Vancouver Coast & Mountains Tourism Region
#600, 210 West Broadway St., Vancouver BC V5Y 3W2 Canada
Tel: 604-638-6927; *Fax:* 604-739-0153
Toll-Free: 800-667-3306
info@vcmbc.com
www.vcmbc.com
Social Media: www.twitter.com/vcmbc
Kevan Ridgway, Executive Director
Doleen Dean, Coordinator

Wilderness Tourism Association of the Yukon (WTAY)
#4, 1114 First Ave., Whitehorse YT Y1A 1A3 Canada
Tel: 867-668-3369; *Fax:* 867-668-3370
www.wtay.com
The Wilderness Tourism Association of the Yukon represents the wilderness and adventure tourism industry in the Yukon Territory, Canada. The organization provides marketing, advocacy, research, consultation, referral and education resources.
Neil Hartling, President

Trade

Asia Pacific Foundation of Canada (APFC) / Fondation Asie Pacifique du Canada
#220, 890 West Pender St., Vancouver BC V6C 1J9 Canada
Tel: 604-684-5986; *Fax:* 604-681-1370
info@asiapacific.ca
www.asiapacific.ca
Independent think tank on Canada's relations with Asia; to bring together people & knowledge to provide the most current & comprehensive research, analysis & information on Canada's transpacific relations; to promote dialogue on economic, security, political & social issues, helping to influence public policy & foster informed decision-making in the Canadian public, private & non-governmental sectors
Yuen Pau Woo, President & Co-CEO
Paul Evans, Co-CEO & Chair
Melinda Czerwinski, Coordinator, Communications

Association of International Automobile Manufacturers of Canada (AIAMC) / Association des fabricants internationaux d'automobiles du Canada
PO Box 5, #1804, 2 Bloor St. West, Toronto ON M4W 3E2 Canada
Tel: 416-595-8251; *Fax:* 416-595-2864
auto@aiamc.com
www.aiamc.com
To represent before federal, provincial & territorial governments the interests of members engaged in the manufacturing, importation, distribution & servicing of light-duty vehicles

British Canadian Chamber of Trade & Commerce
PO Box 1358, Stn. K, Toronto ON M4P 3J4 Canada
Tel: 416-502-0847; *Fax:* 416-502-9319
central@bcctc.ca
www.bcctc.ca
To foster reciprocal trading between Canada & the U.K.
Philip Gorlick, Executive Director, Eastern
Liam J. Hopkins, Executive Director, Western
Ann Mulvale, Executive Director, Central

Canada Beef Export Federation
#235, 6715 - 8th St. NE, Calgary AB T2E 7H7 Canada
Tel: 403-274-0005; *Fax:* 403-274-7275
canada@cbef.com
www.cbef.com
The Canada Beef Export Federation facilitates the expansion of strategic global markets for Canadian beef products and identifies and develops key export markets to increase the sale of Canadian beef products. Their objective revolves around securing and increasing markets outside the USA for Canadian beef products in order to decrease export dependence on the United States.
Ted Haney, President
Gib Drury, Chairman

Canada China Business Council (CCBC) / Conseil commercial Canada Chine
#1501, 330 Bay St., Toronto ON M5H 2S8 Canada
Tel: 416-954-3800; *Fax:* 416-954-3806
ccbc@ccbc.com
www.ccbc.com
CCBC is a private, not-for-profit business association dedicated to building business success in China & Canada by offering service & support, from direct operational support in China, to trade & investment advocacy on its members' behalf. Specifically, it aims to stimulate investment, trade in goods & services, & technology transfer.

Canadian Association of Footwear Importers (CAFI)
c/o Canadian Association of Importers & Exporters, #300, 160 Eglinton Ave. East, Toronto ON M4P 3B5
Tel: 416-595-5333; *Fax:* 416-595-8226
info@iecanada.com
www.importers.ca/about_us/cafi.html
To represent the interests of the footwear importing community across Canada
Amesika Baeta, Director, Committee

Canadian Association of Importers & Exporters / Association canadienne des importateurs & exportateurs
#300, 160 Eglinton Ave. East, Toronto ON M4P 3B5
Tel: 416-595-5333; *Fax:* 416-595-8226
info@iecanada.com
www.importers.ca
To act as the voice of Canadian importers & exporters; To support Canadian importers & exporters so that they remain profitable & competitive in a global market

Canadian Association of Regulated Importers (CARI) / Association canadienne des importateurs règlementés
#203, 2525 St. Laurent Blvd., Ottawa ON K1H 8P5 Canada
Tel: 613-738-1729; *Fax:* 613-733-9501
devalk@magma.ca
www.cariimport.org
The CARI ensures the right and ability for importers to do business like other businesses, and to create one voice for commodities on the import control list or otherwise controlled by regulations.

Canadian Council for the Americas (CCA) / Conseil Canadien pour les Amériques
#2300, 1066 West Hastings St., Vancouver BC V6E 3X2 Canada
Tel: 778-388-5206; *Fax:* 604-806-6112
info@cca-bc.com
www.cca-bc.com
Principal private sector link between Canada & the countries of Latin America & the Caribbean.
André Nudelman, Chair
Leon Teicher, Secretary

Canadian Courier & Logistics Association (CCLA)
#119-660 Eglinton Ave. East, Box 333, Toronto ON M4G 2K2 Canada
Tel: 416-696-9995; *Fax:* 416-696-9993
Toll-Free: 877-766-6604
info@canadiancourier.org
www.canadiancourier.org
To serve the needs, promote the interests & concerns, & enhance the reputation of the courier industry in Canada regardless of size or type of operation
David Turnbull, President & CEO

Canadian Meat Importers & Exporters Committee (CMIC) / Comité canadien des importeurs de viande
#300, 160 Eglinton Ave. East, Toronto ON M4P 3B5 Canada
Tel: 416-595-5333; *Fax:* 416-595-8226
info@iecanada.com
www.caie.ca/about_us/cmiec.html
To act as the representative voice of Canadian meat importers with respect to the activities of the federal & provincial governments & agencies & other bodies affecting the commercial interests of meat importers in Canada.
Amesika Baeta, Contact

Citizens Concerned About Free Trade (CCAFT)
PO Box 1983, Saskatoon SK S7K 3S5 Canada
Tel: 306-664-8443; *Fax:* 306-244-3790
Toll-Free: 877-937-8263
davidorchard@sasktel.net
www.davidorchard.com
To provide information & mobilize those opposed to the Free Trade Agreements & the loss of Canadian sovereignty; to have

Canada exercise the termination clauses of both the FTA & NAFTA so that we can protect our resources & play an independent role in world affairs.

Electronics Import Committee (EIC)
#300, 160 Eglinton Ave. East, Toronto ON M4P 3B5 Canada
Tel: 416-595-5333; *Fax:* 416-595-8226
info@iecanada.com
www.iecanada.com

The Electronic Import Committee (EIC) focuses on the needs of members who import electronic goods. The EIC represents members' interests before government and regulatory bodies.
Joy Nott, President
Amesika Baeta, Director

Groupe export agroalimentaire Québec - Canada (GEAQC) / Agri-Food Export Group Québec - Canada
668, montée Montarville, Saint-Bruno QC J3V 6B1 Canada
Tél: 450-461-6266; *Téléc:* 450-461-6255
Ligne sans frais: 800-563-9767
info@groupexport.ca
www.clubexport.ca

Développer des services adaptés aux besoins réels de nos membres afin d'augmenter leurs ventes sur les marchés internationaux; faciliter l'accès aux programmes gouvernementaux dont nous avons la gestion.
André A. Coutu, Président-directeur général

Hong Kong Trade Development Council
Office Tower, Convention Plaza, 1 Harbour Rd., 38th Fl., Wanchai Hong Kong
hktdc@tdc.org.hk
www.tdctrade.com

to promote external trade in goods & services; to create & facilitate opportunities in international trade for Hong Kong companies; to strengthen Hong Kong as the global trade platform of Asia; to assist manufacturers, traders & service providers through marketing opportunities, trade contacts, market knowledge & competitive skills; network of over 40 offices worldwide

International Cheese Council of Canada (ICCC)
c/o CAIE, #300, 160 Eglinton Ave. East, Toronto ON M4P 3B5 Canada
Tel: 416-595-5333; *Fax:* 416-595-8226
info@iecanada.com
www.caie.ca

To act as the representative voice of Canadian importers of cheese, with respect to the activities of the federal & provincial governments & agencies & all other bodies affecting the commercial interests of cheese importers in Canada; to monitor & analyze all developments relating to the importation of cheese into Canada; to contribute to the formulation, revision & amendment of government policy relating to the commercial regulatory framework within which Canadian cheese importers operate their businesses; to promote the commercial interests of members in a public relations capacity; to liaise with other industry & trade associations working in cheese-related sectors
Amesika Baeta, Committee Director
Jane Carter, Administrative Assistant

Ontario Association of Trading Houses (OATH)
PO Box 43086, 4841 Yonge St., Toronto ON M2N 6N1 Canada
Tel: 416-223-2028; *Fax:* 416-223-5707
info@oath.on.ca
www.oath.on.ca

To develop & expand international trade; To help Canadian companies to increase their international trade & investment
Karel Urban, President
David Archer, Vice-President
Saeed Omar, Vice-President
Louis Papp, Vice-President

The Parliamentary Centre / Le Centre parlementaire
#802, 255 Albert St., Ottawa ON K1P 6A9 Canada
Tel: 613-237-0143; *Fax:* 613-235-8237
parlcent@parl.gc.ca
www.parlcent.ca

To strengthen legislatures through continuous learning & innovation in parliamentary development, mutual sharing & practical parliamentary experience, & the provision of advisory services

Trade Facilitation Office Canada (TFOC) / Bureau de promotion du commerce Canada
#300, 56 Sparks St., Ottawa ON K1P 5A9 Canada
Tel: 613-233-3925; *Fax:* 613-233-7860
Toll-Free: 800-267-9674
info@tfocanada.ca
www.tfocanada.ca

To help improve the economic well-being of developing countries through increased integration into the global economy
Dwayne Wright, Executive Director

World Trade Centre Montréal (WTCM)
#6000, 380, rue St-Antoine ouest, Montréal QC H2Y 3X7 Canada
Tél: 514-871-4002; *Téléc:* 514-849-3813
Ligne sans frais: 877-590-4040
wtcmontreal@ccmm.qc.ca
www.ccmm.qc.ca/fr/lachambre-World_Trade_Centre_Montreal

Appuyer, former et conseiller les entreprises, associations, institutions et organismes de développement économiques dans leurs démarches sur les marchés internationaux
Michel Leblanc, Président et chef de la direction
Lise Aubin, Vice-présidente, Exploitation & Administration

Transportation & Shipping

Alberta Construction Trucking Association (ACTA)
PO Box 4520, Stn. C, Calgary AB T2T 5N3 Canada
Tel: 403-244-4487; *Fax:* 403-244-2340

To develop & promote the business of transporting construction & construction-related material

Alberta Motor Transport Association (AMTA)
3660 Blackfoot Trail SE, Calgary AB T2G 4E6 Canada
Tel: 403-243-4161; *Fax:* 403-243-4610
Toll-Free: 800-267-1003
amtamsc@amta.ca
www.amta.ca

To take a leadership role in fostering a healthy, vibrant industry. PUBLICATIONS: Quaterly Newsletter; Annual Source Book; Western Canada Highway News Magazine.
Mayne Root, Executive Director
Richard Warnock, President

Association du camionnage du Québec inc. (ACQ) / Québec Trucking Association Inc.
#200, 6450, rue Notre Dame ouest, Montréal QC H4C 1C4 Canada
Tél: 514-932-0377; *Téléc:* 514-932-1358
Ligne sans frais: 800-361-5813
info@carrefour-acq.org
www.carrefour-acq.org

Favoriser l'amélioration des normes de sécurité, d'efficacité et d'éthique dans l'industrie du camionnage; maintenir un contact avec l'autorité gouvernementale, les usagers des services de camionnage et le public en général; soutenir le perfectionnement professionnel; soutenir les entreprises dans la défense de leurs intérêts.

Association du transport écolier du Québec (ATEQ)
#300, 5300, boul des Galeries, Québec QC G2K 2A2 Canada
Tél: 418-622-6544; *Téléc:* 418-622-6595
Ligne sans frais: 877-622-6544
courrier@ateq.qc.ca
www.ateq.qc.ca

Association du transport urbain du Québec (ATUQ)
#8090, 800, rue de la Gauchetière, Montréal QC H5A 1J6 Canada
Tél: 514-280-4640; *Téléc:* 514-280-7053
info@atuq.com
www.atuq.com

Organisme de concertation et de représentation politique qui a pour mandat d'assurer la promotion du transport en commun et la défense des intérêts de ses membres auprès des partenaires de l'industrie et des différentes instances gouvernementales
Jean-Jacques Beldié, Président
Monique Léveillé, Secrétaire générale
Roxane Fafard, Responsable, Communications et relations publiques
Martine Diotte, Responsable, Bureau d'études et de recherche

Association nationale des camionneurs artisans inc. (ANCAI)
#235, 670, rue Bouvier, Québec QC G2J 1A7 Canada
Tél: 418-623-7923; *Téléc:* 418-623-0448
infos@ancai.com
www.ancai.com

Défendre les intérêts des transporteurs en vrac (gravier et forêts) auprès des gouvernements, organismes patronaux et entreprises privées

Association québécoise du transport et des routes inc. (AQTR)
#200, 1255, rue University, Montréal QC H3B 3B2 Canada
Tél: 514-523-6444; *Téléc:* 514-523-2666
info@aqtr.qc.ca
www.aqtr.qc.ca

Assumer un leadership technique; définir des règles en matière de sécurité et d'environnement; favoriser l'échange international des expertises; promouvoir la recherche et le développement des expertises et des produits en transport; promouvoir la formation dans le domaine des transports; assumer la représentativité de l'AQTR par la participation aux principaux forums sur les transports; contribuer à servir la société par l'éducation et l'information du grand public.

Atlantic Provinces Trucking Association (APTA)
#400, 725 Champlain St., Dieppe NB E1A 1P6 Canada
Tel: 506-855-2782; *Fax:* 506-853-7424
Toll-Free: 866-866-1679
apta@apta.ca
www.apta.ca

To promote an efficient, safe & environmentally sound trucking industry in Atlantic Canada. PUBLICATIONS: Atlantic Trucking Magazine (quaterly); Atlantic Report Newsletter (monthly) (only to members).

British Columbia Supercargoes' Association
#206, 3711 Delbrook Ave., North Vancouver BC V7N 3Z4 Canada
Tel: 604-878-1258; *Fax:* 604-904-6545
admin@supercargoes.bc.ca; president@supercargoes.bc.ca
www.supercargoes.bc.ca

To provide expert marine cargo planning & onsite management & supervision of shiploading & discharge of all types of cargoes & vessels on the west coast of North America
Terry Stuart, President
David Hood, Director
Magnus Fjortoft, Director

British Columbia Trucking Association (BCTA)
#100, 20111 - 93A Ave., Langley BC V1M 4A9 Canada
Tel: 604-888-5319; *Fax:* 604-888-2941
Toll-Free: 800-565-2282
bcta@bctrucking.com
www.bctrucking.com

To act as the recognised voice of the commercial road transportation industry in British Columbia, by consulting & communicating with the industry, government & the public; to promote a prosperous, safe, efficient & responsible road transportation industry; to provide programs & services to members

Bytown Railway Society (BRS)
PO Box 47076, Ottawa ON K1B 5P9 Canada
Tel: 613-745-1201; *Fax:* 613-745-1201
info@bytownrailwaysociety.ca
www.bytownrailwaysociety.ca

To promote an interest in railways & railway history, with particular emphasis on Canadian railways. PUBLICATIONS: Canadian Trackside Guide, The Quebec Railway Light and Power Company, Montreal Streetcars- Vol.2. People and Places, Montreal and Southern Counties Railway Co., The Ottawa Streetcar Company, Hamilton's Other Railway.

Canadian Association of Movers (CAM) / Association canadienne des déménageurs (ACD)
#404, 2200 Sherobee Rd., Mississauga ON L5A 3Y3 Canada
Tel: 905-848-6579; *Fax:* 905-848-8499
Toll-Free: 866-860-0065
admin@mover.net
www.mover.net

To further the interests of the owner-managed moving & storage companies by providing for its members leadership, motivation, research, education, programs of mutual benefit, consultation & technical advice

Canadian Association of Railway Suppliers / Association canadienne des fournisseurs de chemins de fer
#901, 99 Bank St., Ottawa ON K1P 6B9 Canada
Tel: 613-237-3888; *Fax:* 613-237-4888
info@railwaysuppliers.ca
www.railwaysuppliers.ca

Canadian Bus Association (CBA) / Association canadienne de l'autobus
c/o #2001, 45 O'Connor St., Ottawa ON K1P 1A4 Canada
Tel: 613-238-1800; *Fax:* 613-241-4936
mresnick@rothwellgroup.ca

To act as the national voice of the Canadian bus industry; to act as a national forum for the discussion of bus-related issues & the establishment of positions in relation to industry-wide areas of concern; to function as a technical & operational information gathering & exchange mechanism; to further the objectives of safety, convenience & quality of the motor coach industry.

Canadian Business Aviation Association (CBAA) / Association canadienne de l'aviation d'affaires (ACAA)
#430, 55 Metcalfe St., Ottawa ON K1P 6L5 Canada
Tel: 613-236-5611; *Fax:* 613-236-2361
info@cbaa.ca
www.cbaa.ca
CBAA acts as a collective voice for the business aviation community in Canada, assisting its members in all aviation related matters, & promoting the Canadian business community globally.

Canadian Council of Motor Transport Administrators (CCMTA) / Conseil canadien des administrateurs en transport motorisé (CCATM)
2323 St. Laurent Blvd., Ottawa ON K1G 4J8 Canada
Tel: 613-736-1003; *Fax:* 613-736-1395
ccmta-secretariat@ccmta.ca
www.ccmta.ca
CCMTA coordinates operational matters dealing with the administration, regulation, & control of motor vehicle transportation & highway safety.

Canadian Ferry Operators Association (CFOA) / Association canadienne des opérateurs de traversiers
c/o Anthonie A. de Hoog, CFOA Executive Director, 21 Meredith Dr., Sussex Corner NB E4E 2T8 Canada
Tel: 506-433-4810; *Fax:* 506-432-9505
adehoog@cfoa.ca
www.cfoa.ca
To establish & maintain a standard of professional & technical excellence in the operation of Canadian ferries; to promote & protect the interests of members of the association

Canadian Heartland Training Railway
PO Box 1174, Camrose AB T4V 1X2 Canada
Tel: 780-679-4008; *Fax:* 780-672-4032
www.chtr.ca
To support the practical training needs of the railway industry in Canada & around the world
Joe Bracken, President

Canadian Industrial Transportation Association (CITA) / Association canadienne de transport industriel (ACTI)
#405, 580 Terry Fox Dr., Ottawa ON K2L 4C2 Canada
Tel: 613-599-3283; *Fax:* 613-599-1295
info@cita-acti.ca
www.cita-acti.ca
CITA-ACTI actively promotes a competitive and cost effective North American transportation system serving Canada and its NAFTA allies. Their vision is to be recognized as the "National Voice" of industrial transportation in Canada through increased membership and member representation in all regions of the county.

Canadian Institute of Traffic & Transportation (CITT) / Institut canadien du trafic et du transport
#400, 10 King St. East, Toronto ON M5C 1C3 Canada
Tel: 416-363-5696; *Fax:* 416-363-5698
info@citt.ca
www.citt.ca
Social Media:
www.facebook.com/group.php?gid=148552441716
Designation granting body in logistics management.

Canadian International Freight Forwarders Association, Inc. (CIFFA) / Association des transitaires internationaux canadiens, inc. (ATIC)
#480, 170 Attwell Dr., Toronto ON M9W 5Z5 Canada
Tel: 416-234-5100; *Fax:* 416-234-5152
Toll-Free: 866-282-4332
ciffa@ciffa.com
www.ciffa.com
To represent & support members of the Canadian international freight forwarding industry in providing the highest level of quality & professional services to their clients.

Canadian National Railways Police Association (Ind.) (CNRPA) / Association des policiers des chemins de fer nationaux du Canada (ind.)
6479 Miller's Grove, Mississauga ON L5N 3E5 Canada
Tel: 905-824-0856; *Fax:* 905-824-4584
fjmorgan@ica.net
www.cnrpa.ca
Frank Morgan, National President

Canadian Northern Society (CNoS)
PO Box 1174, Camrose AB T4V 1X2 Canada
Tel: 780-672-3099
canadiannorthern@telus.net
www.canadiannorthern.ca
To preserve prairie heritage
Leslie S. Kozma, President
Lorrie R. Tiegs, Vice-President
Shawn I. Smith, Treasurer

Canadian Parking Association (CPA)
#350, 2255 St. Laurent Blvd., Ottawa ON K1G 4K3 Canada
Tel: 613-727-0700; *Fax:* 613-727-3183
info@canadianparking.ca
www.canadianparking.ca
The Association is the national organization that represents the parking industry & provides a dynamic forum for learning & sharing to enhance member's ability to serve the public & improve the economic vitality of communities.
Carole Whitehorne, Executive Director

Canadian Ports Clearance Association
#500, 101 Syndicate Ave. North, Thunder Bay ON P7C 3V4 Canada
Tel: 807-623-8491; *Fax:* 807-623-2676
Shipping agent

Canadian Professional Logistics Institute / Institut canadien des professionnels de la logistique
#200, 160 John St., Toronto ON M5V 2E5 Canada
Tel: 416-363-3005; *Fax:* 416-363-5598
Toll-Free: 877-363-3005
loginfo@loginstitute.ca
www.loginstitute.ca
To establish professional standards, certification & a program of professional development for the Logistics community.

Canadian Shipowners Association (CSA) / Association des armateurs canadiens (AAC)
#705, 350 Sparks St., Ottawa ON K1R 7S8 Canada
Tel: 613-232-3539; *Fax:* 613-232-6211
csa@shipowners.ca
www.shipowners.ca
To promote an economic & competitive Canadian marine transportation industry; to support a national policy conducive to the development & maintenance of the Canadian flag merchant fleet in the inland, coastal & Arctic waters of Canada & foster the growth of a Canadian flag deep sea merchant fleet.

Canadian Transport Lawyers Association
c/o S.S.T. Thibault, Heenan Blaikie LLP, #600, 900, rue René-Lévesque ouest, Québec QC G1R 2B5 Canada
www.ctla.ca
Geoffrey L. Spencer, President
Louis A. Amato-Gauci, Vice-President & Secretary
Douglas I. Evanchuk, Treasurer
Stephanie S.T. Thibault, Director, Communications

Canadian Transport Workers Union (Ind.) (CTWU) / Syndicat canadien des travailleurs du transport (ind.)
c/o Local #213, 73 Misty St., Kitchener ON N2B 3V6 Canada
Tel: 519-896-2671
Don White, President

Canadian Transportation Equipment Association (CTEA) / Association d'équipement de transport du canada (AETC)
#3B, 16 Barrie Blvd., St Thomas ON N5P 4B9 Canada
Tel: 519-631-0414; *Fax:* 519-631-1333
transportation@ctea.on.ca
www.ctea.ca
To promote excellence in commercial vehicle manufacturing; to develop standard practices
Don Moore, P.Eng., Executive Director
John Michel, President
Stan Delaney, Administrator, Communications

Canadian Transportation Research Forum (CTRF) / Groupe de recherches sur les transports au Canada
PO Box 23033, Woodstock ON N4T 1R0 Canada
Tel: 519-421-9701; *Fax:* 519-421-9319
feedback@ctrf.ca, cawoudsma@ctrf.ca
www.ctrf.ca
To promote the development of research in transportation & related fields; to publish research papers through media & through national & regional forum meetings.

Canadian Trucking Alliance (CTA) / L'Alliance canadienne du camionnage (ACC)
324 Somerset St. West, Ottawa ON K2P 0J9 Canada
Tel: 613-236-9426; *Fax:* 866-823-4076
info@cantruck.ca
www.cantruck.com
To promote business excellence in trucking; to participate in the development of public policy which supports the economic growth, safety & prosperity of the industry; to provide services, including research, development, products & information to meet the needs of the industry. PUBLICATIONS: Dangerous Goods: A Trucker's Guide; Crossing International Borders:A Trucker's Guide; National Safety Code: A Trucker's Guide.

Canadian Trucking Human Resources Council (CTHRC) / Conseil canadien des ressources humaines en camionnage
#203, 720 Belfast Rd., Ottawa ON K1G 0Z5 Canada
Tel: 613-244-4800; *Fax:* 613-244-4535
info@cthrc.com
www.cthrc.com
To respond to the human resource needs of the trucking industry

Canadian Urban Transit Association (CUTA) / Association canadienne du transport urbain (ACTU)
#1401, 55 York St., Toronto ON M5J 1R7
Tel: 416-365-9800; *Fax:* 416-365-1295
transit@cutaactu.ca
www.cutaactu.ca
To represent the public transit community throughout Canada; To strengthen the industry

Canadians for Responsible & Safe Highways (CRASH)
PO Box 1042, Stn. B, Ottawa ON K1P 5R1 Canada
Tel: 613-860-0529; *Fax:* 613-567-6204
Toll-Free: 800-530-9945
CRASH strives to ensure that safety, environmental & economic concerns are fully considered by governments when the latter establish & administer regulations pertaining to trucking operations on public highways.
Harry Gow, President

Carefree Society Transportation Service
2832 Queensway St., Prince George BC V2L 4M5 Canada
Tel: 250-562-1394; *Fax:* 250-562-1393
carefree_society@telus.net
To provide transportation services for the disabled in our community
Cathy Hickman, Executive Director
Lynnelle Sutherland, President

Central British Columbia Railway & Forest Industry Museum Society
850 River Rd., Prince George BC V2L 5S8 Canada
Tel: 250-563-7351; *Fax:* 250-563-3697
trains@pgrfm.bc.ca
www.pgrfm.bc.ca
Administers Prince George Railway & Forest Industry Museum
Laura Williams, General Manager

Chartered Institute of Logistics & Transport (CILT)
Earlstrees Court, Earlstrees Rd., Corbyn NN17 4Ax United Kingdom
enquiry@ciltuk.org.uk
www.cilt-international.com
To promote, encourage & coordinate the study & advancement of the science & art of transportation in all its branches
Bernard Auton, Director General

Chartered Institute of Logistics and Transport in North America (CILT) / Institut agréé de la logistique et des transports Amérique du Nord
#900, 275 Slater St., Ottawa ON K1P 5H9 Canada
Tel: 613-688-1438; *Fax:* 613-688-0966
ghonima@ciltna.com
www.ciltna.com
To promote, encourage, coordinate study & advancement of science & art of transportation.
Gilles Legault, FCILT, Chair
Hazem Ghonima, FCILT, CEO
Donald McKnight, FCILT Executive Director
Sam Barone, FCILT Treasurer
Mike Paré, FCILT Secretary

Chatham Railroad Museum Society
PO Box 434, 2 McLean St., Chatham ON N7M 5K5 Canada
Tel: 519-352-3097
To present history from a retired CN baggage car

Club de trafic de Québec
CP 72, Saint-Jean-Chrysostome QC G6Z 2L3 Canada
Tél: 418-654-5446; *Téléc:* 418-619-1044
jcoulombe@videotron.ca
www.clubtraficqc.org
Regrouper les représentants oeuvrant dans le domaine du transport de la grande région de Québec
Allain Gagnon, Président
Julie Coulombe, Secrétaire-trésorière

Company of Master Mariners of Canada
c/o R. Wallace, 305 Michigan St., Victoria BC V8V 1R6 Canada
www.mastermariners.ca
The Company is a central body of command-level mariners that represents senior officers of the Canadian Merchant Service. It maintains the standard of ability & professional conduct of the officers, & also develops education, training & qualifications for young cadets. It helps liaison between Canada's commercial, governmental & military fleets.

Dewdney-Alouette Railway Society (DARS)
22520 - 116 Ave., Maple Ridge BC V2X 0S4 Canada
Tel: 604-463-5311; *Fax:* 604-463-5317
mrmuseum@telus.net
The Society preserves the railway history of Maple Ridge, promotes the craft of model railroading, & offers advice to the public who are engaged in the building & operating of model railroads.

Edmonton Radial Railway Society (ERRS)
PO Box 76057, Stn. Southgate, Edmonton AB T6H 5Y7 Canada
Tel: 780-437-7721; *Fax:* 780-437-3095
info@edmonton-radial-railway.ab.ca
www.edmonton-radial-railway.ab.ca
The Society collects, preserves & restores vintage streetcars, primarily those from 1908-1951.
Hans Ryffel, President

Electric Vehicle Council of Ottawa Inc. (EVCO)
PO Box 4044, Stn. E, Ottawa ON K1S 5B1 Canada
info@evco.ca
www.evco.ca
To provide information about electric road vehicles, in Canada & worldwide

Electric Vehicle Society of Canada (EVS)
21 Burritt Rd., Toronto ON M1R 3S5
Tel: 416-755-4324; *Fax:* 416-755-4324
info@evsociety.ca
www.evsociety.ca
To investigate & promote clean transportation technologies
Howard W. Hutt, President
Joel Clemens, Treasurer
Emile Stevens, Contact, Membership
Robert Weekley, Editor, EVSurge

Freight Carriers Association of Canada (FCA)
#3-4, 427 Garrison Rd., Fort Erie ON L2A 6E6 Canada
Tel: 905-994-0560; *Fax:* 905-994-0117
Toll-Free: 800-559-7421
info@fca-natc.org
www.fca-natc.org
To provide quality information, products & services to users, providers & third parties involved in motor carrier transportation. PUBLICATIONS: Fuel Price and Surcharge Information Bulletin (weekly); Currency Exchange Bulletin (2X/month -14th and last day of the month).

Hope Air / Vols d'espoir
Procter & Gamble Bldg., #703, 4711 Yonge St., Toronto ON M2N 6K8 Canada
Tel: 416-222-6335; *Fax:* 416-222-6930
Toll-Free: 877-346-4673
mail@hopeair.org
www.hopeair.org
To provide free air transportation to Canadians in financial need who must travel between their own communities & recognized facilities for medical care
Doug Keller-Hobson, Executive Director
Wayne Twaits, Chair
Robert Reeves, Vice-Chair

Huntsville & Lake of Bays Railway Society
26 Centre St. North, Huntsville ON P1H 1X4 Canada
Tel: 705-635-2227; *Fax:* 705-635-2227
nicholls@vianet.ca
www.portageflyer.org
Maintains & displays original artifacts of the old Huntsville & Lake of Bays Railway, plus vintage railway equipment of the turn of the century
Russell A.F. Nicholls, President

Industrial Truck Association (ITA)
#460, 1750 K St. NW, Washington DC 20006 USA
Tel: 202-296-9880; *Fax:* 202-296-9884
www.indtrk.org
Represents the manufacturers of lift trucks & their suppliers who do business in Canada, the United States or Mexico

INFORM Inc.
5 Hanover Sq., 19th Fl., New York NY 10004 USA
Tel: 212-361-2400; *Fax:* 212-361-2412
inform@informinc.org
www.informinc.org
To examine the effects of business practices on the environment & human health
Virginia Ramsey, President
Julia J. Mair, Director, Foundation & Corporate Relations
Sophie Cardona, Manager, Communications & Operations

Intermodal Association of North America (IANA)
#1100, 11785 Beltsville Dr., Calverton MD 20705 USA
Tel: 301-982-3400; *Fax:* 301-982-4815
iana@intermodal.org
www.intermodal.org
IANA is the leading industry trade association representing the combined interests of intermodal freight transportation companies & their suppliers
Joanne F. Casey, President/CEO
Greg P. Steffire, Chair

International Association of Ports & Harbours (IAPH)
7F South Tower, New Pier Takeshiba, 1-16-1 Kaigan, Minato-Ku, Tokyo 105-0022 Japan
info@iaphworldports.org
www.iaphworldports.org
To promote the development of the international port & maritime industry by fostering cooperation among members in order to build a more cohesive partnership among the world's ports & harbors, thereby promoting peace in the world & the welfare of mankind; to ensure that the industry's interests & views are represented before international organizations involved n the regulation of international trade & transportation & incorporated in the regulatory initiatives of these organizations; & to collect, analyse, exchange & distribute information on developing trends in international trade, transportation, ports & the regulations of these industries
Satoshi Inoue, Secretary General
H. Thomas Kornegay, Executive Director

Locomotive & Railway Historical Society of Western Canada
#4104, 2120 Southland Dr. SW, Calgary AB T2V 4W3 Canada
Tel: 403-265-9229; *Fax:* 403-261-1057
laniganj@telus.net
To promote the preservation of railway equipment integral to the history of Western Canada; to act in a consultative capacity on heritage rail projects
James E. Lanigan, President

Manitoba Trucking Association
25 Bunting St., Winnipeg MB R2X 2P5 Canada
Tel: 204-632-6600; *Fax:* 204-694-7134
info@trucking.mb.ca
www.trucking.mb.ca
Serves the needs of the trucking industry & its interested parties by promoting a healthy business environment & advocating safety, education, & responsibility.

Motorcycle & Moped Industry Council (MMIC) / Le Conseil de l'industrie de la motocyclette et du cyclomoteur (CIMC)
#201, 3000 Steeles Ave. East, Markham ON L3R 4T9 Canada
Tel: 416-491-4449; *Fax:* 416-493-1985
Toll-Free: 877-470-6642
info@mmic.ca
www.mmic.ca
The Motorcycle and Moped Industry Council (MMIC) is a national, non-profit trade association that represents the manufacturers and distributors of street legal motorcycles and related products and services in Canada.

National Association of Railroad Passengers (NARP)
#308, 900 - 2 St. NE, Washington DC 20002-3557 USA
Tel: 202-408-8362; *Fax:* 202-408-8287
narp@narprail.org
www.narprail.org
To encourage & promote a more balanced US transporation system including promotion of federal & state policies beneficial to all forms of rail service, urban rail transit, rural public transporation & intermodal terminals
Ross Capon, President

National Transportation Brokers Association
PO Box 238, Markham ON L3P 3J7 Canada
Tel: 416-798-7211
info@ntba-brokers.com
www.ntba-brokers.com
Promotes and continually improves business relationships among shippers, carriers, government and freight brokers

New Brunswick Potato Shippers Association
8824 Route 2, Grand Falls NB E3Z 1P8 Canada
Tel: 506-473-5520; *Fax:* 506-473-6701
tatered@nbnet.nb.ca
The shippers association monitors industry growth
Ed Kavanaugh, President

North America Railway Hall of Fame
RPO Centre, PO Box 20040, St Thomas ON N5P 4H4 Canada
Tel: 519-633-2535; *Fax:* 519-633-3087
info@narhf.org
www.narhf.org
To establish a tribute to those who have made significant contributions relating to the railway industry in North America; honour railway organizations, related innovations & technical accomplishments; preserve & display a collection of library materials & railway heritage artifacts related to the Hall of Fame inductees; to educate the public about the impact of railway transportation on history & the development of communities, nations & international relations
Paul Corriveau, President

Northwestern Ontario Air Carriers Association (NOACA)
PO Box 4075, 143 Cedar Point Dr., Sioux Lookout ON P8T 1J9 Canada
Tel: 807-737-7470; *Fax:* 807-583-2812
Jennifer Chwastyk, Vice-Chair

Ontario Community Transit Association (OCTA)
#306, 4141 Yonge St., Toronto ON M2P 2A8
Tel: 416-229-6222; *Fax:* 416-229-6281
www.octa.on.ca
To strengthen & improve public transit services in Ontario; To ensure excellence & sustainability in public transit

Ontario Good Roads Association (OGRA)
#2, 6355 Kennedy Rd., Mississauga ON L5T 2L5
Tel: 905-795-2555; *Fax:* 905-795-2660
info@ogra.org
www.ogra.org
Social Media: www.twitter.com/Ont_Good_Roads
To represent the transportation & public works-related interests of Ontario's municipalities & First Nation communities; To deliver programs & services that meet the needs of members; To support municipalities in the provision of effective & efficient transportation systems throughout Ontario

Ontario Milk Transport Association (OMTA)
#301, 660 Speedvale Ave. West, Guelph ON N1K 1E5 Canada

Ontario Traffic Conference (OTC)
#2, 6355 Kennedy Rd., Mississauga ON L5T 2L5 Canada
Tel: 647-346-4050; *Fax:* 647-346-4060
info@otc.org
www.otc.org
Social Media: twitter.com/ontariotraffic
To improve traffic conditions & traffic safety in municipalities of Ontario

Ontario Trucking Association (OTA)
555 Dixon Rd., Toronto ON M9W 1H8 Canada
Tel: 416-249-7401; *Fax:* 416-245-6152
info@ontruck.org
www.ontruck.org
Canada's largest trade association representing companies & industry suppliers; provides political advocacy, education & information services to North American freight transport companies with operations in Ontario.

Ontario Trucking Association Education Foundation Inc.
555 Dixon Rd., Toronto ON M9W 1H8 Canada
Tel: 416-249-7401; *Fax:* 416-245-6152
education.foundation@ontruck.org

Operation Lifesaver (OL) / Opération Gareautrain
#1401, 99 Bank St., Ottawa ON K1P 6B9 Canada
Tel: 613-564-8100; *Fax:* 613-567-6726
admin@operationlifesaver.ca
www.operationlifesaver.ca
To create an awareness by the general public of the potential hazards of rail/highway crossings; to improve drivers' & pedestrians' behaviour at these intersections; to inform the public of the dangers associated with trespassing on railway property; & to reduce the number of accidents resulting in fatalities, injuries & monetary losses
Dan Di Tota, National Director

Pharmaceutical & Personal Care Logistics Association (PPCLA) / Association de logistique des soins personnels et pharmaceutiques
PO Box 40598, Stn. Six Points Plaza, Toronto ON M9B 6K8 Canada
Tel: 416-232-6817; *Fax:* 416-232-6818
Toll-Free: 866-293-1238
ppcla@ppcla.org
www.ppcla.org
To develop & promote the interchange of ideas & information concerning traffic & transportation matters of the pharmaceutical & toilet preparations industry; to foster fair dealings & cordial relationships among members & between representatives of the various modes of transportation employed by members
Scott Gibson, Executive Director

Private Motor Truck Council of Canada (PMTC) / Association canadienne du camionnage d'entreprise (ACCE)
#115, 1660 North Service Rd. East, Oakville ON L6H 7G3 Canada
Tel: 905-827-0587; *Fax:* 905-827-8212
Toll-Free: 877-501-7682
info@pmtc.ca
www.pmtc.ca
Recognized as the leader of the private trucking community in Canada; represents the varied interests of private fleet operators with integrity & sound business practices.

The Railway Association of Canada (RAC) / L'Association des chemins de fer du Canada (ACFC)
#901, 99 Bank St., Ottawa ON K1P 6B9 Canada
Tel: 613-567-8591; *Fax:* 613-567-6726
rac@railcan.ca
www.railcan.ca
To promote the commercial viability & the safe & efficient operation of the Canadian railway industry; to act on behalf of, or work jointly with, member companies to promote public policy & regulation that provides equitable treatment between shipping modes; to provide factual information on the railway industry for the public, government & industry, & to provide the views of the industry on public policy issues. PUBLICATIONS: Interchange; Canadian Railway Medical Rules Handbook; Locomotive Emissions Monitoring Program 2009; Canada's Railway Lead North America.

Saskatchewan Trucking Association (STA)
1335 Wallace St., Regina SK S4N 3Z5 Canada
Tel: 306-569-9696; *Fax:* 306-569-1008
Toll-Free: 800-563-7623
ttoope@sasktrucking.com
www.sasktrucking.com
Helps the industry fight its battles in everything from deregulation to weights and measures. Represents the industry in discussions with government

The Shipping Federation of Canada / La Fédération maritime du Canada
#326, 300, rue St-Sacrement, Montréal QC H2Y 1X4 Canada
Tel: 514-849-2325; *Fax:* 514-849-8774
Toll-Free: 877-534-7367
info@shipfed.ca
www.shipfed.ca

Société des traversiers du Québec (STQ)
250, rue Saint-Paul, Québec QC G1K 9K9 Canada
Tél: 418-643-2019; *Téléc:* 418-643-7308
Ligne sans frais: 877-787-7483
stq@traversiers.gouv.qc.ca
www.traversiers.gouv.qc.ca
Contribuer à la mobilité des personnes et des marchandises en assurant des services de transport maritime de qualité, sécuritaires et fiables, favorisant ainsi l'essor social, économique et touristique du Québec
Georges Farrah, Président/directeur général

Sydney & Louisburg Railway Historical Society / Le Musée de chemin de fer de Sydney à Louisburg
7330 Main St., Louisbourg NS B1C 1P5 Canada
To commemorate the history of the S&L Railway by preserving & displaying the artifacts & documents which survive; to commemorate the people who worked for the S&L Railway; to explain the local & commercial history of the area which relates to the S&L Railway; to explain & commemorate the general themes of railway & transportation history & technology

Toronto Transportation Society (TTS)
PO Box 5187, Stn. A, Toronto ON M5W 1N5 Canada
ttswebmaster@torontotransportationsociety.org
www.torontotransportationsociety.org
To afford persons interested in transportation by land, facilities for discussion & exchange of information
Kevin Nichol, President

Transport Action Canada
Bronson Centre, PO Box 858, Stn. B, #303, 211 Bronson Ave., Ottawa ON K1P 5P9 Canada
Tel: 613-594-3290; *Fax:* 613-594-3271
info@transport-action.ca
www.transport-action.ca
National federation of environmental & consumer groups concerned about the importance of transportation on our environment & quality of life; to inform Canadians of the need for a coherent national transport policy which recognizes that conservation of resources must be a priority & that access to good public transportation is a right of all Canadians; to work for the improvement & greater use of bus & rail transportation in the interests of public safety, social equity & the protection of the environment; to press for the coordination of all transport services for the benefit of users; to demand more attention to the needs of pedestrians, cyclists & public transport users; to maximize the use of the energy-efficient rail & marine modes for the shipment of freight. PUBLICATIONS: National Transport Newsletter.
David Jeanes, President
Justin Bur, VP East
Peter Lacey, VP West
Tony Turrittin, Secretary
Klaus Beltzner, Treasurer
Bert Titcomb, Manager

Transportation Association of Canada (TAC) / Association des transports du Canada (ATC)
2323 St. Laurent Blvd., Ottawa ON K1G 4J8 Canada
Tel: 613-736-1350; *Fax:* 613-736-1395
secretariat@tac-atc.ca
www.tac-atc.ca
To promote the provision of safe, efficient, effective & environmentally sustainable transportation services in support of Canada's social & economic goals; to act as a neutral forum for the discussion of transportation issues & matters; to act as a technical focus in the highway transportation area. PUBLICATIONS: TAC News.

Truck Training Schools Association of Ontario Inc. (TTSAO)
Fax: 519-858-0920
Toll-Free: 866-475-9436
training@ttsao.com
www.ttsao.com
To provide the trucking industry with the highest quality driver training programs for entry level individuals that earn & maintain public confidence, adhering to sound & ethical business practices
Gus Rahim, President

Truckers Association of Nova Scotia
PO Box 1527, 184 Arthur St., Truro NS B2N 5V2 Canada
Tel: 902-895-7447; *Fax:* 902-897-0487
Toll-Free: 800-232-6631
contact@tans.ca
www.tans.ca
Promotes all matters aiding the development and improvement of the trucking industry and the allied trades in Nova Scotia, including social, recreational, benevolent, educational and charitable activities. In addition, the Truckers Association of Nova Scotia makes presentations to government and other regulatory bodies in relation to the economic welfare of the trucking industry and is the main proponent in gaining access to the provincial haul rates and beneficial changes to the contract specifications used by the contractors
Dave Roberts, Contact

Upper Canada Railway Society
PO Box 122, Stn. A, Toronto ON M5W 1A2 Canada
Tel: 416-921-4023
ucrs@btinternet.com
To work to preserve history & railways of Canada
Scott Haskill, President

The Van Horne Institute for International Transportation & Regulatory Affairs
#620 Earth Sciences Bldg., 2500 University Dr. NW, Calgary AB T2N 1N4 Canada
Tel: 403-220-8455; *Fax:* 403-282-4663
vanhorne@ucalgary.ca
www.vanhorne.info/
To contribute to public policy development & education in the areas of transportation & regulated industries. PUBLICATIONS: On-Trac.
Peter C. Wallis, President & CEO
Sarah Ingram, Programs Manager
Carla Frede, Webmaster
Mel Belich, Chairman

Western Transportation Advisory Council (WESTAC)
#1140, 800 Pender St. West, Vancouver BC V6C 2V6 Canada
Tel: 604-687-8691; *Fax:* 604-687-8751
infoservices@westac.com
www.westac.com
To advance Western Canadian economy through the improvement of the region's transportation system.
Lisa Baratta, Director, Strategy
Ruth Sol, President
Marcella Szel, Chairman (Executive Committee)
Lois Jackson, Chairman of the Board

Universities

African Students Association of Concordia (ASAC)
Concordia Hall Building, Concordia University, #1031-7, 1455 boul de Maisonneuve ouest, Montréal QC H4A 1M8 Canada
Tel: 514-848-2424
asacextcomm@gmail.com
asac.concordia.ca
To represent the students of African descent at Concordia University; To facilitate the social networking of African students; To promote African culture & awareness at Concordia University & in the greater Montreal community
Yves F. Nimbona, President

Visual Art, Crafts, Folk Arts

AICA Canada Inc.
172 Roselawn Ave., Toronto ON M4R 1E6 Canada
www.artfocus.com/aicacanada.com/index.html
To broaden communication about the visual arts; To promote the values of art criticism as a discipline; To act on behalf of the physical & moral defense of works of art

Alberta Craft Council (ACC)
10186 - 106 St., Edmonton AB T5J 1H4 Canada
Tel: 780-488-6611; *Fax:* 780-488-8855
Toll-Free: 800-362-7238
acc@albertacraft.ab.ca
www.albertacraft.ab.ca
To stimulate, develop & support craft in Alberta through communication, education, exhibition, & participation
Tom McFall, Executive Director
James Lavoie, Chair

Art Dealers Association of Canada Inc. (ADAC) / Association des marchands d'art du Canada
#302, 511 King St. West, Toronto ON M5V 1K4 Canada
Tel: 416-934-1583; *Fax:* 416-934-1584
Toll-Free: 866-435-2322
info@ad-ac.ca
www.ad-ac.ca
To promote & encourage public awareness of visual arts in Canada & abroad

Artists in Stained Glass (AISG)
www.aisg.on.ca
Artists in Stained Glass (AISG) is a not-for-profit association established to encourage the development of stained glass as a contemporary art form, in Ontario & throughout Canada. It exists only online, & has no contact address other than its url.

Association des collections d'entreprises / Corporate Art Collectors Association
Secrétariat: Banque Nationale du Canada, 600, rue de la Gauchetière ouest, 8e étage, Montréal QC H3C 4L2 Canada
Tél: 514-394-8533; *Téléc:* 514-394-6258
Ligne sans frais: 800-361-6266
joann.kane@bnc.ca
Réunir les conservateurs et les propriétaires de collections corporatives; favoriser l'échange d'information, d'idées, d'expériences, d'expertise, de systèmes ou de services; représenter de façon générale les intérêts de ses membres; favoriser la diffusion de l'art au Québec

The Canadian Art Foundation
#320, 215 Spadina Ave., Toronto ON M5T 2C7 Canada
Tel: 416-368-8854; *Fax:* 416-368-6135
Toll-Free: 800-222-4762
info@canadianart.ca
www.canadianart.ca
The Foundation is a charitable organization established to foster & support the visual arts in Canada and to celebrate artists & their creativity with a program of events, lectures, competitions, publications & educational initiatives. Programs include: Room with a View; International Art Tours; Anne Lind International Program; RBC Canadian Painting Competition; the Canadian Art

Editorial Residency; the Canadian Art School Hop; and the Youth Arts Bursary
Ann Webb, Executive Director
Sara Graham, Development & Administrative Coord
Melony Ward, Publisher, Canadian Art
Richard Rhodes, Editor, Canadian Art

Canadian Association of Professional Conservators (CAPC) / Association canadienne des restaurateurs professionnels (ACRP)
c/o Canadian Museums Association, #400, 280 Metcalfe St., Ottawa ON K2P 1R7 Canada
Fax: 613-233-5438
swarren@technomuses.ca (Applications)
www.capc-acrp.ca
To foster high standards within the conservation profession through accreditation; to facilitate public access to professional conservators

Canadian Craft & Hobby Association (CCHA)
55 Macewan Park Rd. NW, Calgary AB T3K 3G1 Canada
Tel: 403-770-1023; *Fax:* 403-668-9166
ccha@cdncraft.org
www.cdncraft.org
To further the success of every business engaged in Canada's craft & hobby industry by providing an arena for the discussion of goals & plans; to foster industry expansion through development & implementation of dynamic programs & activities; to provide a forum for meeting new people, learning new ideas & profiting from benefits of working together

Canadian Crafts Federation (CCF) / Fédération canadienne des métiers d'art (FCMA)
PO Box 6000, 457 Queen St., Fredericton NB E3B 5H1 Canada
Tel: 506-444-3315; *Fax:* 506-457-7352
info@canadiancraftsfederation.ca
www.canadiancraftsfederation.ca
To represent provincial & territorial crafts councils & the Canadian crafts sector; to advance & promote the vitality & excellence of Canadian crafts nationally & internationally to the benefit of Canadian craftspeople & the community at large

Canadian Guild of Crafts / Guilde canadienne des métiers d'art
1460, rue Sherbrooke ouest, #B, Montréal QC H3G 1K4 Canada
Tel: 514-849-6091; *Fax:* 514-849-7351
Toll-Free: 866-477-6091
info@canadianguild.com
www.canadianguildofcrafts.com
To preserve, encourage & promote Canadian crafts; to organize & sponsor exhibitions of the work of recognized & promising artists in the fields of arts & crafts; to educate interested groups about Canadian & native crafts through tours & lectures

Canadian Quilters Association (CQA) / Association canadienne de la courtepointe (ACC)
c/o 6 Spruce St., Pasadena NL A0L 1K0 Canada
Tel: 709-686-5882; *Fax:* 709-686-5883
Toll-Free: 877-672-8777
administration@canadianquilter.com
www.canadianquilter.com
The promotion of a greater understanding, appreciation & knowledge of the art, techniques & heritage of patchwork, appliqué & quilting; the promotion of the highest standards of workmanship & design in both traditional & innovative work the fostering of a climate of cooperation amongst quiltmakers across the country.

Canadian Society of Painters in Water Colour (CSPWC) / Société canadienne de peintres en aquarelle (SCPA)
#102, 258 Wallace Ave., Toronto ON M6P 3M9 Canada
Tel: 416-533-5100
info@cspwc.com
www.cspwc.com
To promote the use of experimentation with water-based media; to encourage new artists

Conseil des arts de Montréal (CAM)
1210, rue Sherbrooke est, Montréal QC H2L 1L9 Canada
Tél: 514-280-3580; *Téléc:* 514-280-3784
info-cam@cum.qc.ca
www.artsmontreal.org
Média social: www.twitter.com/ConseilArtsMtl
Soutenir, encourager et harmoniser les initiatives d'ordre artistique et culturel sur le territoire de la ville de Montréal.

Conseil des arts textiles du Québec (CATQ)
811A, rue Ontario est, Montréal QC H2L 2T2 Canada
Tél: 514-524-6645; *Ligne sans frais:* 800-524-6645
info@catq.qc.ca
www.catq.qc.ca
Regrouper les artistes en arts textiles et encourager la collaboration entre eux; favoriser le développement des arts textiles par la promotion, la diffusion, documentation et l'information; fournir des services aux membres en rapport avec les buts de la corporation; organiser des activités dans le but d'atteindre les objectifs de la corporation.
Isabel Moreau, Coordanatrice Administrative

Conseil des métiers d'art du Québec (ind.) (CMA) / Québec Crafts Council (Ind.)
#400, 350, rue St-Paul est, Montréal QC H2Y 1H2 Canada
Tél: 514-861-2787; *Téléc:* 514-861-9191
cmaq@metiers-d-art.qc.ca
www.metiers-d-art.qc.ca
Pour distribuer les créations métiers d'art auprès des grossistes canadiens et étrangers.
Serge Demers, Directeur général

Craft Council of Newfoundland & Labrador
Devon House, 59 Duckworth St., St. John's NL A1C 1E6 Canada
Tel: 709-753-2749; *Fax:* 709-753-2766
info@craftcouncil.nf.ca
www.craftcouncil.nf.ca
To produce high quality work; to assist & advise members in wide variety of craft-related areas

Crafts Association of British Columbia (CABC) / Conseil de l'artisanat de la Colombie-Britannique
Granville Island, 1386 Cartwright St., Vancouver BC V6H 3R8 Canada
Tel: 604-687-6511; *Fax:* 604-687-6711
Toll-Free: 888-687-6511
info@cabc.net
www.cabc.net
To develop excellence in crafts

Embroiderers' Association of Canada, Inc. (EAC)
c/o EAC President, PO Box 341, Lakefield ON K0L 2H0 Canada
www.eac.ca
The Association is a national, non-profit organization that aims to preserve traditional techniques & promote new challenges in embroidery through education & networking. It offers course in embroidery & certifies teachers. It is a registered charity, BN: 136380672RR0001.
Sue Thomas, President
Marilyn Marshall, Treasurer

Folklore Canada International (FCI)
2040, rue Alexandre-de-Sève, Montréal QC H2L 2W4 Canada
Tel: 514-524-8552; *Fax:* 514-524-0262
patrimoine@qc.aira.com
www.folklore-canada.org
Social Media:
facebook.com/group.php?gid=84023872908&v=wall
The Association is a non-profit organization committed to showcasing Canadian cultural pluralism. It promotes folk arts; organizes cultural exhanges between groups at national & international levels; organizes international folk arts festivals.

Manitoba Crafts Council (MCC)
c/o Arts & Cultural Industries Assn of Manitoba, #501, 62 Albert St., Winnipeg MB R3B 1E9 Canada
Tel: 204-927-2787
mcc@mts.net
www.manitobacrafts.ca
To promote the development & appreciation of fine craft; to facilitate a supportive environment in which fine, contemporary craft may flourish.

The Metal Arts Guild of Canada (MAGC)
88 Elm Grove Ave., Toronto ON M6K 2J3 Canada
Tel: 416-252-6242
maguild@interlog.com
www.metalartsguild.ca
Social Media: www.twitter.com/MAGcanada
To be committed to the exchange of information & ideas encouraging appreciation for the metal arts; To promote & develop the metal arts; To further education in the metal arts; To encourage members to experiment with all the forms that metal takes
Sarah Dougal-Hamel, President
Kathryn Dieroff, Treasurer

New Brunswick Crafts Council / Conseil d'artisanat du Nouveau-Brunswick
PO Box 1231, Stn. A, Fredericton NB E3B 5C8 Canada
Tel: 506-450-8989; *Fax:* 506-457-6010
Toll-Free: 866-622-7238
nbcrafts@nb.aibn.com
www.nbcraftscouncil.ca
Social Media:
www.facebook.com/#!/group.php?gid=2411474486
To provide opportunities & support to members by developing, promoting & fostering an appreciation of excellence in craft.
Beth Biggs, Executive Director
Kitty Bourne, Administrator

Nova Scotia Designer Crafts Council (NSDCC)
1113 Marginal Rd., Halifax NS B3H 4P7 Canada
Tel: 902-423-3837; *Fax:* 902-422-0881
office@nsdcc.ns.ca
www.nsdcc.ns.ca
To encourage & promote the craft movement in Nova Scotia; to increase public awareness & appreciation of craft products & activities

Ontario Crafts Council (OCC)
990 Queen St. West, Toronto ON M6J 1H1 Canada
Tel: 416-925-4222; *Fax:* 416-925-4223
info@craft.on.ca
www.craft.on.ca
To have craft recognized as a valuable part of life and the excellence of Ontario craft and craftspeople acknowledged across Canada and around the world.

Prince Edward Island Crafts Council (PEICC)
PO Box 20071, Stn. Sherwood, Charlottetown PE C1A PE3 Canada
Tel: 902-892-5152; *Fax:* 902-628-8740
info@peicraftscouncil.com
www.peicraftscouncil.com
To promote the making & acceptance of quality handcrafted items through the provision of programs & services
Darrin White, President
Barb Boss, Executive Director

Royal Canadian Academy of Arts (RCA) / Académie royale des arts du Canada
#375, 401 Richmond St. West, Toronto ON M5V 3A8 Canada
Tel: 416-408-2718; *Fax:* 416-408-2286
rcaarts@interlog.com
www.rca-arc.ca
To celebrate the achievement of excellence & innovation by visual artists across Canada; to encourage the new generation of artists; to facilitate the exchange of ideas about visual culture for the benefit of all Canadians

Saskatchewan Craft Council (SCC)
813 Broadway Ave., Saskatoon SK S7N 1B5 Canada
Tel: 306-653-3616; *Fax:* 306-244-2711
Toll-Free: 866-653-3616
saskcraftcouncil@sasktel.net
www.saskcraftcouncil.org
To promote, support & develop excellence in craft
Ken Wilkinson, Chair
Mark Stobbe, Executive Director

Sculptors Society of Canada (SSC) / Société des sculpteurs du Canada
c/o J.M. Young, #204, 60 Atlantic Ave., Toronto ON M6K 1X9 Canada
Tel: 416-533-0126
gallery@cansculpt.org
www.cansculpt.org
Social Media:
www.facebook.com/#!/pages/Sculptors-Society-of-Canada/116512211729231
To promote Canadian sculpture; to provide encouragement to sculptors through public exhibitions & discussions in Canada & other countries

Society of Canadian Artists (SCA) / Société des artistes canadiens (SAC)
Lawrence Plaza, PO Box 54029, 500 Lawrence Ave. West, Toronto ON M6A 3B7 Canada
Tel: 416-584-9823
info@societyofcanadianartists.com
www.societyofcanadianartists.com
To promote recognition of its member-artists through exhibitions, seminars, workshops, travelling shows

Visual Arts Nova Scotia (VANS)
1113 Marginal Rd., Halifax NS B3H 4P7 Canada
Tel: 902-423-4694; *Fax:* 902-422-0881
Toll-Free: 866-225-8267
vans@visualarts.ns.ca
vans.ednet.ns.ca
To promote a better understanding of arts & artists in Nova Scotia; to provide practical assistance to artists; to act in an advisory capacity to public & private interests

Visual Arts Ontario (VAO)
PO Box 1159, Stn. TDC, 77 King St. West, Toronto ON M5K 1P2 Canada
Tel: 416-591-8883; *Fax:* 416-591-2432
info@vao.org
www.vao.org
To assist working artists & to provide information on art to the general public; to facilitate municipal/community involvement in the visual arts; to forge links between the visual arts & the informal & formal education systems; to provide access to groups traditionally underserviced for the reasons of geography, gender, race or linguistic distinctions

Wildlife

Club d'ornithologie de Mirabel (COMIR)
CP 3418, 9009, Rte Arthur-Sauvé, Mirabel QC J7N 2T8 Canada
Tél: 450-258-4924
info@comirabel.org
comirabel.org
Le territoire couvert part le COMIR s'étend de la rivière des Mille-Iles au Sud, Prévost au Nord, la rivière des Outaouais (Rivière Rouge) à l'Ouest et la route 117 à l'Est.
Normande Lapensée, Présidente
Denis Lauzon, Vice-président

Spruce City Wildlife Association (SCWA)
Stn. 1384 River Rd., Prince George BC V2L 5S8 Canada
Tel: 250-563-5437; *Fax:* 250-563-5438
info@scwa.bc.ca
www.scwa.bc.ca
The Spruce City Wildlife Association is a non-profit organization made up of families, individuals and corporations in Prince George concerned about public involvement in local environmental and conservation matters.
Denise Collett, President/Treasurer

Women

Alberta Women's Institutes (AWI)
5405 - 36 Ave., Wetaskiwin AB T9A 3C7 Canada
Tel: 780-312-2440; *Fax:* 780-312-2482
altawi@telusplanet.net
An organization of women of all ages who achieve change through personal growth, communication & education
Fern Killeen, Executive Director

Alliance des femmes de la francophonie canadienne (AFFC)
Place de la francophonie, #302, 450, rue Rideau, Ottawa ON K1N 5Z4 Canada
Tél: 613-241-3500; *Téléc:* 613-241-6679
Ligne sans frais: 866-535-9422
info@affc.ca
www.affc.ca
Favorise l'autonomie des femmes canadiennes-françaises sur tous les plans; assure le respect des droits des femmes francophones vivant en milieu minoritaire; soutien le développement de l'action collective et politique des femmes au Canada français; souligne la spécificité des femmes francophones auprès des instances gouvernementales, des diverses associations et du grand public

Association féminine d'éducation et d'action sociale (AFEAS) / Feminine Association for Education & Social Action
5999, rue de Marseille, Montréal QC H1N 1K6 Canada
Tél: 514-251-1636; *Téléc:* 514-251-9023
info@afeas.qc.ca
www.afeas.qc.ca
Avec ses Activités femmes d'ici organisées sur tout le territoire québécois, l'Afeas informe ses membres, suscite des échanges et des débats et les incite à participer davantage aux différentes structures de la société. Les membres de l'Afeas réalisent, dans leur milieu, des actions concrètes, en vue d'un changement social.

Association féminine d'éducation et d'action sociale - Chibougamau
CP 293, Chibougamau QC G8P 2K7 Canada
Tél: 418-748-2031
Martine Savard

Association Marie-Reine de Chibougamau
CP 295, Chibougamau QC G8P 2K7 Canada
Tél: 418-748-4289
Aider les femmes & les enfants victimes de violence
Fernande Fiset

Association of Canadian Women Composers (ACWC) / L'Association des femmes compositeurs canadiennes (AFCC)
20 St. Joseph St., Toronto ON M4Y 1J9 Canada
Tel: 416-239-5195
info@acwc.ca
www.acwc.ca
To promote the music of Canadian women composers through concerts, commissions, publications, recordings, etc.

British Columbia Women's Institutes (BCWI)
#203B, 750 Cottonwood Ave., Kamloops BC V2B 3X2 Canada
Tel: 250-554-5406; *Fax:* 250-554-5406
info@bcwi.org
www.bcwi.org
To help discover, stimulate & develop leadership among women; to assist, encourage & support women to become knowledgeable & responsible citizens; to ensure basic human rights for women & to work towards their equality; to be a strong voice through which matters of utmost concern can reach the decision makers; to network with organizations sharing similar objectives; to promote the improvement of agricultural & other rural communities & to safeguard the environment

Canadian Association for the Advancement of Women & Sport & Physical Activity (CAAWS) / Association canadienne pour l'avancement des femmes du sport et de l'activité physique (ACAFS)
#202N, 801 King Edward Ave., Ottawa ON K1N 6N5
Tel: 613-562-5667; *Fax:* 613-562-5668
caaws@caaws.ca
www.caaws.ca
To promote an equitable sport & physical activity system, in which girls & women are participants & leaders; To foster equitable support & diverse opportunities, in sport & physical activity for females across Canada

Canadian Association of Women Executives & Entrepreneurs (CAWEE) / Association canadienne des femmes cadres et entrepreneurs
#202, 720 Spadina Ave., Toronto ON M5S 2T9 Canada
Tel: 416-756-0000; *Fax:* 416-862-0315
contact@cawee.net
www.cawee.net
To provide an environment for successful businesswomen to grow & develop, both professionally & personally, through business & community involvement

Canadian Federation of Business & Professional Women's Clubs (CFBPWC) / Fédération canadienne des clubs des femmes de carrières commerciales et professionnelles (FCCFCCP)
45 Brixham Rd., London ON N6K 1P5 Canada
Tel: 519-473-3505
bpw@bpwcanada.com
www.bpwcanada.com
To develop & encourage women to pursue business, the professions & industry; to work toward the improvement of economic, employment & social conditions for women; to work for high standards of service in business, the professions, industry & public life; to stimulate interest in federal, provincial & municipal affairs, & to encourage women to participate in the business of government at all levels; to encourage & assist women & girls to acquire further education & training

Canadian Hadassah WIZO
#900, 1310, av Greene, Montréal QC H3Z 2B8 Canada
Tel: 514-937-9431; *Fax:* 514-933-6483
info@chw.ca
www.chw.ca
Canada's leading Jewish women's philanthropic organization extends material & moral support of Jewish women of Canada to needy individuals in Hadassah-WIZO welfare institutions in Israel; encourages Jewish & Hebrew culture in Canada; cooperates with other organizations; promotes Canadian ideals of democracy. Forty locations across Canada

Canadian Women in Communications (CWC) / Association canadienne des femmes en communication (AFC)
#804, 67 Yonge St., Toronto ON M5E 1J8 Canada
Tel: 416-363-1880; *Fax:* 416-363-1882
Toll-Free: 800-361-2978
cwcafc@cwc-afc.com
www.cwc-afc.com
To advance the role of women in the communications sector
Nicole Lang, Chair, Calgary Chapter
Lisa Woznica, Co-Chair, GTA Chapter
Angela J. Wheldon, Co-Chair, NCR Chapter
Judith Campbell, Vice-President
Diane Johnson, Chair, BC Chapter
Sue Timanson, Chair, Edmonton Chapter
Claire A. Cockell, Co-Chair, GTA Chapter
Marye Menaard-Bos, Co-Chair, NCR Chapter
Christianne Vaillancourt, Chair, NB Chapter
Loraine Dumas, Chair, Québec
Nathalie Noël, Chair, SW Ontario Chapter
Stephanie MacKendrick, President
Robin Hildebrandt, Chair, Manitoba Chapter

Canadian Women's Foundation (CWF) / Fondation canadienne des femmes
#504, 133 Richmond St. West, Toronto ON M5H 2L3 Canada
Tel: 416-365-1444; *Fax:* 416-365-1745
Toll-Free: 866-293-4483
TDD: 416-365-1732
info@canadianwomen.org
www.cdnwomen.org
Social Media:
www.facebook.com/#!/CanadianWomensFoundation
To improve the lives of women & girls through economic & social change; to raise funds & make grants to charitable projects that help women & girls achieve greater self-reliance & economic independence

Caribbean Pioneer Women of Canada
PO Box 51, Stn. Snowdon, Montréal QC H3X 3T3 Canada
Tel: 514-488-3716
jntsmith@yahoo.com
Social & cultural events & activities
Janet Smith, Contact

Centre Afrique au Féminin
419, rue St-Roch, Montréal QC H3N 1K2 Canada
Tél: 514-272-3274; *Téléc:* 514-272-8617
www.familis.org
Offre un lieu de recontres pour toutes les femmes, ces familles & ce dans une ambiance conviviale; classes, activités, halte-garderie, dépannage alimentaire
Valerie Balton

Centre de Femmes Les Elles du Nord
#2, 570, 3e Rue, Chibougamau QC G8P 1N9 Canada
Tél: 418-748-7171
Ghyslaine Bergeron, Présidente
Linda Boulanger, Coordonnatrice

Cercle des Fermières - Chibougamau
CP 123, Chibougamau QC G8P 2K6 Canada
Tél: 418-748-2126
www.cfq.qc.ca
Keri Dallaire

Comité condition féminine Baie-James
#203, 552, 3e Rue, Chibougamau QC G8P 1N9 Canada
Tél: 418-748-4408; *Téléc:* 418-748-2486
ccfbj@tlb.sympatico.ca
ccfbj.com
A pour mission l'amélioration des conditions de vie des Jamésiennes
Mamon Fortier, Présidente

Coverdale Centre for Women Inc.
10 Culloden Court, Saint John NB E2L 3B9 Canada
Tel: 506-634-1649; *Fax:* 506-634-1647
coverdalesj@yahoo.ca
Coverdale Center for Women Inc. provides programs and services for women including self-development programs in groups and individual counseling. It is a drop-in center where women can find support, referrals to community services, general counseling, addiction counselling, positive recreation, and self-improvement courses.
Lynda Hanson, Acting Executive Director

Les EssentiElles
Centre de la francophonie, 302, rue Strickland, Whitehorse YT Y1A 2K1 Canada
Tél: 867-668-2636; *Téléc:* 867-668-3511
elles@yknet.ca
www.lesessentielles.org

Organisme à but non lucratif qui représente les intérêts des femmes francophones du Yukon.
Julie Ménard, Coordonnatrice

Federated Women's Institutes of Canada (FWIC) / Fédération des instituts féminins du Canada
PO Box 209, 359 Blue Lake Rd., St George ON N0E 1N0 Canada
Tel: 519-448-3873; *Fax:* 519-448-3506
fwic@bellnet.ca
www.nald.ca/fwic.htm
To act as a united voice for Women's Institutes of Canada; To promote Canadian agriculture & community living

Federated Women's Institutes of Ontario (FWIO)
7382 Wellington Rd. 30, RR#5, Guelph ON N1H 6J2 Canada
Tel: 519-836-3078; *Fax:* 519-836-9456
lynnr@fwio.on.ca
www.fwio.on.ca
To assist & encourage women to become more knowledgeable & responsible citizens; to promote & develop good family life skills; to help discover, stimulate & develop leadership; to help identify & resolve need in the community

Fédération des femmes du Québec (FFQ)
#309, 110, rue St-Thérèse, Montréal QC H2Y 1E6 Canada
Tél: 514-876-0166; *Téléc:* 514-876-0162
info@ffq.qc.ca
www.ffq.qc.ca

Federation of Medical Women of Canada (FMWC) / Fédération des femmes médecins du Canada
780 Echo Dr., Ottawa ON K1S 5R7 Canada
Tel: 613-569-5881; *Fax:* 613-569-4432
Toll-Free: 877-771-3777
fmwcmain@fmwc.ca
www.fmwc.ca
Committed to the professional, social, & personal advancement of women physicians & to the promotion of the well-being of women in the medical profession & in society at large

Halifax Women's Network
PO Box 48030, Bedford NS B4A 3Z2 Canada
info@halifaxwomensnetwork.com
www.halifaxwomensnetwork.com
To provide opportunities for professional women to enhance their careers, increase their contacts, create a positive image, and strengthen their links to the community.
Lee Ross, President

Immigrant Women Services Ottawa (IWSO) / Services pour femmes immigrantes d'Ottawa
#400, 219 Argyle St., Ottawa ON K2P 2H4 Canada
Tel: 613-729-3145; *Fax:* 613-729-9308
infomail@immigrantwomenservices.com
www.immigrantwomenservices.com
To empower & enable immigrant women in the Ottawa region to participate in the elimination of all forms of abuse against women; to raise awareness among immigrant women who are abused, in order to break down their isolation & enable them to advocate on their own behalf; to develop a crisis service for immigrant women who are abused to give them full access to mainstream resources; to develop cross-cultural training for shelters & mainstream agencies regarding the special needs of immigrant women in order to ensure that existing services are accessible & appropriate to them & their families; to educate immigrant communities to work toward ending violence against women.

Interval House
#200, 131 Bloor St., Toronto ON M5S 1R8 Canada
Tel: 416-924-1411; *Fax:* 416-928-9020
info@intervalhouse.ca
www.intervalhouse.ca
To provide a continuum of services that enable abused women & children to have access to safe shelter & responsive services that help them establish lives free from violence; To provide integrated & specialized services related to counselling, advocacy, outreach, legal & housing support, as well as programs to help build economic self-sufficiency

Jewish Women International of Canada (JWIC)
#210, 638A Sheppard Ave. West, Toronto ON M3H 2S1 Canada
Tel: 416-630-9313; *Fax:* 416-630-9319
Toll-Free: 866-333-5942
jwic@jwicanada.com
www.jwicanada.com
Works locally, nationally & internationally to strengthen the effectiveness of women in the Jewish community & society; to foster the emotional well-being of children; to perpetuate Jewish values & secure world Jewry. Programs include ending violence towards women, sexual assault awareness, emergency housing for women & children, & advocacy to end child poverty in Canada. Offices in Toronto & Montréal, & chapters in Toronto, Montréal, B.C., Windsor & Winnipeg.
Jill Lieberman, President
Penny Krowitz, CAE, Executive Director

Korean Canadian Women's Association (KCWA)
27 Madison Ave., Toronto ON M5R 2S2 Canada
Tel: 416-340-1234; *Fax:* 416-340-8114
kcwa@kcwa.net
www.kcwa.net
To empower Korean Canadian families and other vulnerable members of the community-at-large to live free from violence, poverty and inequity through the provision of culturally sensitive and linguistically appropriate services for the purpose of enhancing the well-being of immigrant families and promoting their successful integration into Canadian society.

Manitoba Women's Institutes (MWI)
1129 Queens Ave., Brandon MB R7A 1L9 Canada
Tel: 204-945-8976; *Fax:* 204-328-5294
mbwi@mts.net
www.gov.mb.ca/agriculture/organizations/wi/
Focuses on personal development, the family, agriculture, rural development & community action, locally & globally

MATCH International Centre / Centre international Match
#310, 411 Roosevelt Ave., Ottawa ON K2A 3X9 Canada
Tel: 613-238-1312; *Fax:* 613-238-6867
Toll-Free: 888-414-8717
info@matchinternational.org
www.matchinternational.org
Social Media:
facebook.com/pages/Match-International/149004639694?v=info
Guided by a feminist vision of sustainable development which recognizes the diversity of women & respects their efforts toward self-determination; works in partnership with women's groups in Africa, Asia, the Caribbean, & South America toward the empowerment of women through political, economic, social, & cultural justice.

Mouvement des Femmes Chrétiennes
3013, ch des Trois-Cantons, Nicholas Denys NB E3K 3C1 Canada
Tél: 506-783-4745; *Téléc:* 506-783-4745
secretariat@mfcnational.net
www.mfcnational.net
A pour mission former des femmes efficaces & dynamiques sur le plan familial, paroissial, social & chrétien; développer une mentalité chrétienne en faisant l'union de la vie & de la foi; transformer le milieu de vie par des projets concrets

Na'amat Canada Inc.
National Office, #6, 7005 Kildare Rd., Montréal QC H4W 1C1 Canada
Tel: 514-488-0792; *Fax:* 514-487-6727
Toll-Free: 888-278-0792
naamat@total.net
www.naamat.com
To enhance the status of women, children & families in Israel & Canada; as part of a world-wide progressive Jewish women's organization in partnership with Na'amat Israel, we believe that every person is entitled to self-respect & equal opportunity within a just society. Councils across Canada, including Calgary (Susan Inhaber, President; naamatcalgary@yahoo.ca), & Hamilton (Deena Sacks & Tory Metzger, Co-Presidents; naamathamilton@gmail.com)

National Action Committee on the Status of Women (NAC) / Comité canadien d'action sur le statut de la femme (CCA)
#203, 234 Eglinton Ave. East, Toronto ON M4P 1K5 Canada
Tel: 416-932-1718; *Fax:* 416-932-0646
nac@web.ca
www.nac-cca.ca
To shape public opinion, influence decision makers & mobilize membership & the Canadian public to work for equality & justice for all women
Sandra Carnegie Douglas, Executive Coordinator
Denise Andrea Campbell, President

National Association of Women & the Law (NAWL) / Association nationale de la femme et du droit (ANFD)
#305, 251 Bank St., Ottawa ON K1Y 4T3 Canada
Tel: 613-241-7570; *Fax:* 613-241-4657
info@nawl.ca
www.nawl.ca
To promote the equality rights of women through legal education, research & law reform advocacy; to improve the legal status of women in Canada through law reform; to dismantle barriers to all women's equality

National Council of Jewish Women of Canada
#118, 1588 Main St., Winnipeg MB R2V 1Y3 Canada
Tel: 204-339-9700; *Fax:* 204-334-3779
info@ncjwc.org
www.ncjwc.org
To further human welfare in the Jewish & general communities; to help fulfill unmet needs & to serve the individual & the community.

The National Council of Women of Canada (NCWC) / Le Conseil national des femmes du Canada
#205, 251 Bank St., Ottawa ON K2P 1X3 Canada
Tel: 613-232-5025; *Fax:* 613-232-8419
Toll-Free: 877-319-0993
ncwc@magma.ca
www.ncwc.ca
To empower all women to work together towards improving the quality of life for women, families & society through a forum of member organizations & individuals

Native Women's Association of the N.W.T.
PO Box 2321, 5017 49th St., Yellowknife NT Canada
Tel: 867-873-5509; *Fax:* 867-873-3152
www.nativewomens.com
Provides training & education programs for native women in the Western Arctic
Nancy Peel, Executive Director

New Brunswick Women's Institute (NBWI)
Victoria Health Centre, #279, 65 Brunswick St., Fredericton NB E3B 1G5 Canada
Tel: 506-454-0798; *Fax:* 506-451-8949
nbwi@nb.aibn.com
www.nbwi.ca
To help discover, stimulate & develop leadership among women; to assist, encourage & support women to become knowledgeable & responsible citizens; to ensure basic human rights for women & work towards their equality; to network with other organizations sharing similar objectives; to promote the improvement of agricultural & other rural communities & to safeguard the environment

Newfoundland & Labrador Women's Institutes
PO Box 1854, St. John's NL A1C 5P9 Canada
Tel: 709-753-8780; *Fax:* 709-753-8780
nlwi@nfld.com
www.nlwi.ca
The present day Newfoundland and Labrador Women's Institutes is an informal, educational organization for women to work together to expand their skills, broaden their interests, plan meetings, workshops and conferences, and strengthen the quality of life for themselves, their families and their communities. The NLWI is a non-partisan, non-sectarian, non-racial organization
Barbara Taylor, President

NSERC/Petro-Canada Chair for Women in Science & Engineering
c/o Faculty of Engineering & Applied Sciences, Memorial University, St. John's NL A1B 3X5 Canada
Tel: 709-737-7960; *Fax:* 709-737-7658
cwse@morgan.ucs.mun.ca
www.mun.ca/cwse/
To encourage women in Canada to enter careers in science, engineering, mathematics & computer sciences; to encourage women in Canada to attain high levels of professional achievement in these fields; to serve as an information centre for & about women in these fields; to make people aware of Canadian women scientists & engineers & of career opportunities available to them; to provide a forum for discussion of subjects of interest to members
Carolyn J. Emerson, Chair, Atlantic Region

The Older Women's Network (OWN) / Réseau des femmes aînées
115 The Esplanade, Toronto ON M5E 1Y7 Canada
Tel: 416-214-1518; *Fax:* 416-214-1541
info@olderwomensnetwork.org
www.olderwomensnetwork.org
To initiate & support discussion on issues relevant to the well-being of older women; To develop & support legislation to expand opportunities for housing, economic security, & optimum health; To monitor the media in order to encourage a more realistic & positive portrayal of older women; To support the efforts of young women to achieve equal opportunity, freedom from discrimination, abuse & exploitation, & the right to reproductive choice; To support the needs of children; To liaise with movements for social justice in Canada & abroad

Prince Edward Island Business Women's Association (PEIBWA)
161 St. Peter's Rd., Charlottetown PE C1A 5P7 Canada
Tel: 902-892-6040; *Fax:* 902-892-6050
Toll-Free: 866-892-6040
office@peibwa.org
www.peibwa.org
To assist women in business to succeed by providing services and programs to meet their objectives.
Michelle Ryder-MacEwen, President

Prince Edward Island Women's Institute (PEIWI)
40 Enman Cres., Charlottetown PE C1E 1E6 Canada
Tel: 902-368-4860; *Fax:* 902-368-4439
wi@gov.pe.ca
www.womensinstitute.pe.ca
To help discover, stimulate & develop leadership among women; to assist, encourage & support women to become knowledgeable & responsible citizens; to ensure basic human rights for women & to work towards their equality; to be a strong voice through which matters of utmost concern can reach the decision makers; to network with organizations sharing similar objectives; to promote the improvement of agricultural & other rural communities & to safeguard the environment

Québec Women's Institutes (QWI)
Macdonald Campus, McGill University, Raymond Bldg., PO Box 58, 21111, ch Lakeshore, Montréal QC H9X 3V9 Canada
Tel: 514-398-7844; *Fax:* 514-398-7972
lhoy@sympatico.ca
To help discover, stimulate & develop leadership among women; to assist, encourage & support women to become knowledgeable & responsible citizens; to ensure basic human rights for women & to work toward their equality; to be a strong voice through which matters of utmost concern can reach the decision makers; to promote the improvement of agricultural & other rural communities & to safeguard the environment

Réseau des femmes d'affaires du Québec inc. (RFAQ)
#100, 10794, rue Lajeunesse, Montréal QC H3L 2E8 Canada
Tél: 514-521-2441; *Téléc:* 514-521-1410
Ligne sans frais: 800-332-2683
info@rfaq.ca
www.rfaq.ca
Ce réseau de plus de 2 000 membres est le seul réseau d'affaires qui s'est donné comme mission de faire reconnaître l'importance et les mérites des femmes dans le milieu des affaires ici comme sur les quatre autres continents afin de contribuer à leur succès et au développement de leur rôle et de leur influence dans toutes les sphères de l'activité économique.

Réseau Femmes Québec (RFQ)
#134, 911, rue Jean-Talon est, Montréal QC H2R 1V5 Canada
Tél: 514-484-2375
reseau.femmes.quebec@gmail.com
www.reseau-femmes-quebec.qc.ca
Nadia Nadège, Présidente

Réseau national d'action-éducation des femmes (RNAEF)
#302, 450, rue Rideau, Ottawa ON K1N 5Z4 Canada
Tél: 613-241-3500; *Téléc:* 613-241-6679
affc@franco.ca
www.affc.ca/rnaef
Obtenir des changements sociaux et économiques qui apporteront une société égalitaire et équitable en privilégiant, chez les femmes francophones du Canada, l'éducation en français sous toutes ses formes pour ainsi améliorer leurs conditions de vie

Saskatchewan Women's Institutes (SWI)
117 Science Pl., Rm. 10.2, Kirk Hall, Saskatoon SK S7N 5C8 Canada
Tel: 306-272-4191
sask.wi@usask.ca
To help discover, stimulate & develop leadership among women; to assist, encourage & support women to become knowledgeable & responsible citizens; to ensure basic human rights for women & to work towards their equality; to be a strong voice through which matters of the utmost concern can reach the decision makers; to promote the improvement of agricultural & other rural communities & to safeguard the environment

Society for Canadian Women in Science & Technology (SCWIST) / Société des canadiennes dans la science et la technologie
#471, 411 Dunsmuir St., Vancouver BC V6B 1X4 Canada
Tel: 604-893-8657; *Fax:* 604-893-8692
scwist@sfu.ca
www.harbour.sfu.ca/scwist/
To promote equal opportunities for women in scientific, technical & engineering careers; to educate public about careers in science & technology particularly to improve social attitudes on the stereotyping of careers in science; to assist educators by providing current information on careers & career training in sciences & scientific policies

South Asian Women's Centre (SAWC)
8163 Main St., Vancouver BC V5X 3L2 Canada
Tel: 604-325-6637; *Fax:* 604-325-4462
sawc@asia.com
www.sawc.8m.com
The South Asian Women's Centre is a space for South Asian women to work actively for social change. The centre strongly believes that women can change their own lives and the lives of others in our communities, in our society, and even globally. The centre supports the development of non-oppressive attitudes and behaviours by critiquing and combating sexism, racism, homophobia, caste/classism, ageism and ableism.

Transition House Association of Nova Scotia (THANS)
#319, 1657 Barrington St., Halifax NS B3J 2A1 Canada
Tel: 902-429-7287; *Fax:* 902-429-0561
coordinator@thans.ca
www.thans.ca
The Transition House Association of Nova Scotia (THANS) member organizations provide transitional services to women (and their children) who are experiencing violence and abuse, including culturally relevant services to Mi'kmaw people. THANS eleven member organizations work with women and their children in thirteen locations across Nova Scotia.
Pamela Harrison, Provincial Coordinator

Western Businesswomen's Association (WBA)
#302, 1107 Homer St., Vancouver BC V6B 2Y1 Canada
Tel: 604-688-0951; *Fax:* 604-681-4545
Teena Keizer, Administrator

Women Business Owners of Manitoba (WBOM)
PO Box 2748, Winnipeg MB R3C 4B3 Canada
Tel: 204-775-7981; *Fax:* 204-897-8094
info@wbom.ca
www.wbom.ca
Supports & inspires excellence, learning & growth in business
Yvonne Thompson, President
Christine Dubyts, Vice-President
Charlene Hiebert, Treasurer

Women Entrepreneurs of Canada (WEC) / Les Femmes chefs d'entreprises du Canada
Toronto Chapter & Head Office, 202, 720 Spadina Ave., Toronto ON M5S 2T9 Canada
Tel: 416-921-5150; *Fax:* 416-929-5256
Toll-Free: 866-207-4439
wec@wec.ca
www.wec.ca
Social Media: www.facebook.com/group.php?gid=5398494151
To bring together all women who own or control an industry, company, retail trade or service entreprise, who have been in business a minimum of four years; to foster communication & trade among members; to represent women entrepreneurs to government & the media; to encourage professional growth & continuing education; to provide networking, social support, advocacy & business opportunities for members
Carissa Reiniger, President

Women on the Rise
5775 rue Saint-Jacques, Montréal QC H4A 2E8 Canada
Tel: 514-485-7418; *Fax:* 514-485-7418
womenontherise@bellnet.cs
To promote the well-being of women and their children, especially in the Black anglophone community, by offering them self-help activities and encouraging them to develop their potential.
Grace Campbell, Director

Women's Art Association of Canada (WAAC)
23 Prince Arthur Ave., Toronto ON M5R 1B2 Canada
Tel: 416-922-2060; *Fax:* 416-922-4657
womensart@bellnet.ca
www.womensartofcanada.ca
To provide scholarships for the arts through the following schools & colleges: The Royal Conservatory of Music of Toronto; The Ontario College of Art; The Faculty of Music, University of Toronto; The National Ballet School; Sheridan College

Women's Art Resource Centre (WARC)
#122, 401 Richmond St. West, Toronto ON M5V 3A8 Canada
Tel: 416-977-0097; *Fax:* 416-977-7425
warc@warc.net
www.warc.net

Women's Centre of Montreal / Centre des femmes de Montréal
3585, rue Saint-Urbain, Montréal QC H2X 2N6 Canada
Tél: 514-842-1066; *Téléc:* 514-842-6376
cfmwcm@centredesfemmesdemtl.org
www.centredesfemmesdemtl.org
The mission of the Women's Centre of Montréal is to provide services to help women help themselves. To accomplish its mission, the Centre offers educational and vocational training, information, counselling and referral services. The Centre communicates women's concerns to the public and acts as a catalyst for change regarding women's issues.
Johanne Bélisle, Directrice générale

Women's Counselling & Referral & Education Centre (WCREC)
#303B, 489 College St., Toronto ON M6G 1A5
Tel: 416-534-7501
generalmail@wcrec.org; phoneline@wcrec.org; resources@wcrec.org
www.wcrec.org
To promote the mental & emotional well-being of women; To provide free community-based, alternative, non-medical mental health services in Toronto & in other areas through contact by phone & e-mail

Women's Healthy Environments Network
#400, 215 Spadina Ave., Toronto ON M5T 2C7 Canada
Tel: 416-928-0880; *Fax:* 416-644-0116
office@womenshealthyenvironments.ca
www.womenshealthyenvironments.ca
To provide a forum for communication; to conduct research on issues relating to women in their environments of planning, health, ecology, workplace design, community development & urban & rural sociology & economy

Women's Institutes of Nova Scotia (WINS)
NSAC, PO Box 550, 35 Rock Garden Rd., Truro NS B2N 5E3 Canada
Tel: 902-893-6520; *Fax:* 902-893-6393
wins@gov.ns.ca
www.gov.ns.ca/agri/wi/
To provide women with opportunities to enhance their lives through community service & involvement, education & leadership development

Women's Inter-Church Council of Canada (WICC) / Conseil oecuménique des chrétiennes du Canada
47 Queen's Park Cres. East, Toronto ON M5S 2C3
Tel: 416-929-5184; *Fax:* 416-929-4064
wicc@wicc.org
www.wicc.org
To focus on national & international issues affecting women, growth in ecumenism, action for social justice, & the sharing of spirituality & prayer

Women's International League for Peace & Freedom (WILPF)
#901, 6659 Southoak Cres., Burnaby BC V5E 4M9 Canada
Tel: 604-517-0581
joangord@shaw.ca
www.wilpf.int.ch/world/canada.htm
To unite women throughout the world into a force working to put an end to war; to work for social, economic & political equality for all people in all nations.
Ellen Woodsworth, President
Bruna Nota, Vice-President

Women's Legal Education & Action Fund (LEAF) / Fonds d'action et d'éducation juridiques pour les femmes (FAEJ)
#703, 60 St. Clair Ave. East, Toronto ON M4T 1N5 Canada
Tel: 416-595-7170; *Fax:* 416-595-7191
Toll-Free: 888-824-5323
info@leaf.ca
www.leaf.ca
The Fund promotes equality for women, primarily by using the gender equality provisions of the Canadian Charter of Rights & Freedoms. It sponsors test cases before the Canadian courts, human rights commissions & government agencies on behalf of women, & provides public education on the issue of gender equality. It is a registered charity, BN: 108219916RR0001.

Women's Network PEI
PO Box 233, 40 Enman Cres., Charlottetown PE C1A 7K4 Canada
Tel: 902-368-5040; *Fax:* 902-368-5039
Toll-Free: 888-362-7373
wnpei@wnpei.org
www.wnpei.org
To strengthen & support the efforts of PEI women to improve their status in society

Writers & Editors

Association de la presse francophone (APF) / Association of Francophone Newspapers
267 Dalhousie St., Ottawa ON K1N 7E3 Canada
Tél: 613-241-1017; *Téléc:* 613-241-6313
apf@apf.ca
www.apf.ca
Promouvoir l'existence d'une presse communautaire écrite en langue française aussi vigoureuse et aussi répandue que possible dans les communautés de langue française à l'extérieur du Québec; contribuer à l'amélioration de sa qualité et de son rayonnement; défendre énergiquement les principes de la liberté de parole et de la presse écrite
Gilles Haché, Président
Francis Potié, Directeur

Canadian Association of Journalists (CAJ) / L'Association canadienne des journalistes
c/o Algonquin College, #B224, 1385 Woodroffe Ave., Ottawa ON K2G 1V8 Canada
Tel: 613-526-8061; *Fax:* 613-521-3904
caj@caj.ca
www.caj.ca
To promote excellence in journalism; to encourage & promote investigative journalism

Canadian Authors Association (CAA)
74 Mississaga St. East, Orillia ON L3V 1V5
Tel: 705-653-0323; *Toll-Free:* 866-216-6222
admin@canauthors.org
www.canauthors.org
To promote & protect Canadian authors & their works; To act as a voice for writers

Canadian Ethnic Media Association (CEMA)
24 Tarlton Rd., Toronto ON M5P 2M4 Canada
Tel: 416-260-3625; *Fax:* 416-260-3810
madeline.ziniak@rci.rogers.com
www.canadianethnicmedia.com
To promote & preserve the value of the ethnic media in Canada; to advance understanding of Canada's cultural diversity
Ace Alvarez, President
Madaine Ziniak, Chair
Doreen Vanini, Secretary
Irene Chu, Treasurer

Canadian Farm Writers' Federation (CFWF)
PO Box 250, Ormstown QC J0S 1K0 Canada
Fax: 450-829-2226
Toll-Free: 877-782-6456
hugh@quanglo.ca
www.cfwf.ca
To serve the interests of agricultual journalists
John Greig, President
Myrna Stark Leader, Vice-President
Hugh Maynard, Secretary-Treasurer

Canadian Journalism Foundation (CJF) / La Fondation pour le journalisme canadien
117 Peter St., 3rd Fl., Toronto ON M5V 2G9 Canada
Tel: 416-955-0394; *Fax:* 416-955-0395
info@cijf-fjc.ca
www.cjf-fjc.ca
To honour outstanding achievements in the field of journalism in Canada through grants, awards & scholarships; to promote & support programs & seminars at or in conjunction with qualified educational institutions in journalism.
Jody Jacobson, Executive Director
Heather McCall, Program Manager

Canadian Science Writers' Association (CSWA) / Association canadienne des rédacteurs scientifiques
PO Box 75, Stn. A, Toronto ON M5W 1A2 Canada
Toll-Free: 800-796-8595
office@sciencewriters.ca
www.sciencewriters.ca
To foster excellence in science communication; to increase public awareness of Canadian science & technology

Canadian Society of Children's Authors, Illustrators & Performers (CANSCAIP) / La société canadienne des auteurs, illustrateurs et artistes pour enfants
#104, 40 Orchard View Blvd., Toronto ON M4R 1B9 Canada
Tel: 416-515-1559
office@canscaip.org
www.canscaip.org
To promote the growth of children's literature by establishing the rapport with teachers, librarians & children; to establish communication between publishers & society; to encourage the development of new writers, illustrators & performers

The Crime Writers of Canada (CWC)
PO Box 113, 3007 Kingston Rd., Toronto ON M1M 1P1 Canada
Tel: 416-597-9938
info@crimewriterscanada.com
www.crimewriterscanada.com
To promote Canadian crime writing
Cheryl Freedman, Sec.-Treas.

Editors' Association of Canada (EAC) / Association canadienne des réviseurs (ACR)
#505, 27 Carlton St., Toronto ON M5B 1L2 Canada
Tel: 416-975-1379; *Fax:* 416-975-1637
Toll-Free: 866-226-3348
info@editors.ca; webmaster@editors.ca
www.editors.ca; www.reviseurs.ca
Social Media: twitter.com/eac_acr
EAC is a federally incorporated, not-for-profit association that promotes & maintains standards of professional editing & publishing. It sets guidelines to help editors secure fair pay & good working conditions, fosters networking among editors, & cooperates with other publishing associations in areas of common concern.

Federation of British Columbia Writers (FBCW)
PO Box 3887, Stn. Terminal, Vancouver BC V6B 2Z3 Canada
Tel: 604-683-2057; *Fax:* 604-608-5522
bcwriters@shaw.ca
www.bcwriters.com
To develop, support, inform, & promote writers in British Columbia; To foster a community for writing in British Columbia

Fédération québécoise du loisir littéraire (FQLL)
CP 1000, Succ. M, 4545, av Pierre-de Coubertin, Montréal QC H1V 3R2 Canada
Tél: 514-252-3033; *Téléc:* 514-251-8038
Ligne sans frais: 866-533-3755
info@litteraire.ca
www.litteraire.ca
Offre au grand public l'accès à toutes les formes de l'expression littéraire et artistique dans un contexte de loisir, d'éducation et de perfectionnement

The League of Canadian Poets (LCP)
#608, 920 Yonge St., Toronto ON M4W 3C7 Canada
Tel: 416-504-1657; *Fax:* 416-504-0096
info@poets.ca
www.poets.ca
To develop the art of poetry; to enhance the status of poets & nurture a professional poetic community; to facilitate the teaching of Canadian poetry at all levels of education; to enlarge the audience for poetry by encouraging publication, performance & recognition of poetry nationally & internationally; to uphold freedom of expression

Manitoba Writers' Guild Inc. (MWG)
#206, 100 Arthur St., Winnipeg MB R3B 1H3 Canada
Tel: 204-942-6134; *Fax:* 204-942-5754
Toll-Free: 888-637-5802
www.mbwriter.mb.ca
To provide services & support writers in Manitoba

The Ontario Poetry Society (TOPS)
c/o I.B. Iskov, 31 Marisa Ct., Thornhill ON L4J 6H9 Canada
Tel: 905-738-0309
ibiskov_tops2000@yahoo.ca
www.theontariopoetrysociety.ca
To establish a democratic organization for members to unite in friendship for emotional support & encouragement in all aspects of poetry, including writing, editing, performing & publishing
Kate Marshall Flaherty, Secretary
Shirley A. McCormick, President
Debbie Okun Hill, Vice-President
Bunny Iskov, Treasurer

Professional Writers Association of Canada (PWAC)
#123, 215 Spadina Ave., Toronto ON M5T 2C7 Canada
Tel: 416-504-1645; *Fax:* 416-913-2327
info@pwac.ca
www.pwac.ca
To protect & promote interests of periodical writers in Canada; to develop & maintain professional standards in editor/writer relationships by instituting use of standard publication agreement in all freelance assignments; to improve quality of periodical writing in Canada; to work actively for survival of periodical writing in a highly competitive communications market; to lobby for higher standard fees for freelance magazine & newspaper writing; to mediate grievances between writers & editors; to provide professional development workshops; to lobby for freedom of press & expression; to offset isolation of freelance writers by circulating news, information on market

Québec Writers' Federation (QWF) / Fédération des Écrivaines et Écrivains du Québec
1200, av Atwater, Montréal QC H3Z 1X4 Canada
Tel: 514-933-0878
admin@qwf.org
www.qwf.org
The Federation encourages & supports English-language writing in Québec to ensure a lasting place for English literature in the province's cultural scene. It sponsors events, writing programs, & it honours literary excellence through annual awards. The organization is a registered charity, BN: 140319518RR0001.

Saskatchewan Writers Guild (SWG)
PO Box 3986, Regina SK S4P 3R9 Canada
Tel: 306-757-6310; *Fax:* 306-565-8554
Toll-Free: 800-667-6788
swg@sasktel.net
www.skwriter.com
To promote excellence in writing by Saskatchewan writers; to advocate for Saskatchewan writers; to promote the teaching of Saskatchewan & Canadian literature & instruction in the art of writing at all levels of education; to improve public access to writers & their work; to develop professionalism in the business of writing; to improve the economic status of Saskatchewan writers

Société des écrivains canadiens (SEC)
#105, 870, av Salaberry, Québec QC G1R 2T9 Canada
Tél: 418-843-9816; *Téléc:* 418-843-9816
www.culture-quebec.qc.ca/sec/
Grouper en association les écrivains de langue française, de nationalité canadienne, domiciliés ou non au Canada, auteurs d'un ou de plusieurs livres publiés au Canada ou ailleurs par des éditeurs homologués; servir et défendre les intérêts de la littérature canadienne; prendre toutes les mesures nécessaires ou opportunes pour assurer le respect de la propriété littéraire de ses membres.
Georges Hélal, Président général
Louis Lasnier, Secrétaire général

Société professionnelle des auteurs et des compositeurs du Québec (SPACQ)
#115, 4030, rue St-Ambroise, Montréal QC H4C 2C7 Canada
Tél: 514-845-3739; *Téléc:* 514-845-1903
Ligne sans frais: 866-445-3739
info@spacq.qc.ca
www.spacq.qc.ca
Défendre les droits et les intérêts moraux, professionnels et économiques des auteurs et des compositeurs, ainsi que les droits qui se rapportent aux oeuvres, auprès des autorités gouvernementales.

Society of American Travel Writers - Canadian Chapter (SATW)
24 Louisa St., Toronto ON M8V 2K6 Canada
Tel: 416-521-7462; *Fax:* 416-521-7467
bea@bcpictures.com
www.satw.ca

Union des écrivaines et écrivains québécois (UNEQ)
La Maison des écrivains, 3492, av Laval, Montréal QC H2X 3C8 Canada
Tél: 514-849-8540; *Téléc:* 514-849-6239
Ligne sans frais: 888-849-8540
ecrivez@uneq.qc.ca
www.uneq.qc.ca
Élaborer des politiques et administrer des programmes en vue de favoriser le développement de la littérature québécoise et sa diffusion au Québec comme à l'étranger, en vue également de faire reconnaître la profession d'écrivain de telle sorte que les intérêts moraux, sociaux et économiques des auteurs soient respectés
Stanley Péan, Président
Pierre Lavoie, Directeur général

Writers Association for Resourceful Minds (WARM)
614, rue Martel, Longueuil QC J4J 1C5 Canada
Tel: 450-651-7044
warmwriters@yahoo.com
geocities.com/warmwriters
To provide both established authors & aspiring writers in the Montréal area with conferences, seminars & workshops on all aspects of writing both fiction & non-fiction
Jeanette Paul, President
Alex MacLeod, Vice-President
Harry Ghosh, Treasurer

Writers Guild of Alberta (WGA)
Percy Page Centre, 11759 Groat Rd., Edmonton AB T5M 3K6 Canada
Tel: 780-422-8174; *Fax:* 780-422-2663
Toll-Free: 800-665-5354
mail@writersguild.ab.ca
www.writersguild.ab.ca
To provide a meeting ground & collective voice for the writers of Alberta; to promote excellence in writing in Alberta
Carol Holmes, Executive Director
Blaine Newton, President
Audrey Seehagen, Vice-President

Writers Guild of Canada (WGC)
#401, 366 Adelaide St. West, Toronto ON M5V 1R9 Canada
Tel: 416-979-7907; *Fax:* 416-979-9273
Toll-Free: 800-567-9974
info@wgc.ca
www.wgc.ca
Voice of professional Canadian screenwriters; to lobby on their behalf; to protect their interests; to raise the profile of screenwriters & screenwriting
Maureen Parker, Executive Director

Writers' Alliance of Newfoundland & Labrador (WANL)
PO Box 2681, Stn. C, #102, 155 Water St., St. John's NL A1C 6K1 Canada
Tel: 709-739-5215; *Fax:* 709-739-5931
wanl@nfld.com
www.writersalliance.nf.ca
Social Media: www.twitter.com/WANL
To enhance the quality of writing in Newfoundland & Labrador through such programmes as workshops, meetings, readings; to encourage & develop public awareness & appreciation for the work of writers in Newfoundland & Labrador
Théa Morash, Executive Director

Writers' Federation of New Brunswick (WFNB)
PO Box 37, Stn. A, Fredericton NB E3B 4Y2 Canada
Tel: 506-459-7228; *Fax:* 506-459-7228
wfnb@nb.aibn.com
www.umce.ca/wfnb
To promote New Brunswick writing; to assist writers of New Brunswick at all stages of their development by providing services; to uphold the right to free artistic expression; to provide additional educational services to schools & libraries; to contribute to the enhancement of literary arts
Grace Morris, Secretary
Marilyn Lerch, President
Laurie Glenn Norris, Treasurer
Lee Thompson, Executive Director

Writers' Federation of Nova Scotia (WFNS)
1113 Marginal Rd., Halifax NS B3H 4P7 Canada
Tel: 902-423-8116; *Fax:* 902-422-0881
talk@writers.ns.ca
www.writers.ns.ca
To foster creative & professional writing; to provide advice & assistance to writers; to encourage greater public recognition of Nova Scotia writers
Jane Buss, Executive Director
Susan Mersereau, Program Officer

The Writers' Trust of Canada
#200, 90 Richmond St. East, Toronto ON M5C 1P1 Canada
Tel: 416-504-8222; *Fax:* 416-504-9090
info@writerstrust.com
www.writerstrust.com
Is a national charitable organization providing support to writers through various programs & awards; celebrates the talents & achievements of our country's writers; is committed to exploring & introducing to future generations the traditions that will enrich our common literary heritage & strengthen Canada's cultural foundations
Peter Kahnert, Chair
Don Oravec, Executive Director
Amanda Hopkins, Program Coordinator

The Writers' Union of Canada (TWUC)
#200, 90 Richmond St. East, Toronto ON M5C 1P1 Canada
Tel: 416-703-8982; *Fax:* 416-504-9090
info@writersunion.ca
www.writersunion.ca
To unite writers for the advancement of their common interests; to foster writing in Canada; to maintain relations with publishers; to exchange information among members; to safeguard the freedom to write & to publish; to advance good relations with other writers & their organizations in Canada & all parts of the world
Erna Paris, Chair
Deborah Windsor, Executive Director

Youth

Black Community Resource Centre (BCRC)
#497, 6767, ch de la Côte-des-Neiges, Montréal QC H3S 2T6 Canada
Tel: 514-342-2247; *Fax:* 514-342-2283
bcrc@qc.aira.com
www.bcrcmontreal.com/bcrc/; www.blackyouthproject.org/bcrc/
BCRC is a resource-based organization committed to helping English-speaking visible minority youth rekindle their dreams and achieve their full potential. The Centre takes a comprehensive approach, with a strategy that is progressive, multi-interventionist and holistic; emphasis is on infrastructure support and training, prevention and empowerment, community-building, collaboration, and an inclusive perspective. BCRC has a mandate to provide support services to individuals, communities, para-public and public organizations, and develops and implements health, education, socio-cultural and economic development programs.

Centre Afrika
1644, rue St-Hubert, Montréal QC H2L 3Z3 Canada
Tél: 514-843-4019
centreafrika@centreafrika.com
www.centreafrika.com
Activités sociales & culturelles et activités spirituelles/religieuses
Jean-François Bégin

Club Richelieu Boréal de Chibougamau
CP 522, Chibougamau QC G8P 2X9 Canada
Tél: 418-748-3008
portail.richelieu.org
Josée Bélanger

Force Jeunesse
#322, 1000, rue Saint-Antoine ouest, Montréal QC H3C 3R7 Canada
Tél: 514-384-8666; *Téléc:* 514-384-6442
info@forcejeunesse.qc.ca
www.forcejeunesse.qc.ca
Force Jeunesse est un regroupement de jeunes travailleurs issus de différents milieux dont le principe fondateur est l'équité intergénérationnelle; agit concrètement en revendiquant des mesures qui améliorent la situation économique et sociale des jeunes.
Jonathan Plamondon, Président

Head and Hands / A deux mains
5833, rue Sherbrooke ouest, Montréal QC H4A 1X4 Canada
Tel: 514-481-0277; *Fax:* 514-481-2336
info@headandhands.ca
www.headandhands.ca
Medical, social & legal services for youth; Young Parents Program; information & referral
Marlo Turner-Ritchie, Contact

Jeunes en partage
Succ. 204, 2e Avenue, Chibougamau QC G8P 2Z5 Canada
Tél: 418-748-2935
Dany Larouche

Richelieu International (RI)
#25, 1010 rue Polytek, Ottawa ON K1J 9J1 Canada
Tél: 613-742-6911; *Téléc:* 613-742-6916
Ligne sans frais: 800-267-6525
international@richelieu.org
www.richelieu.org
A pour mission l'épanouissement de la personalité de ses membres & au développement de leurs aptitudes personnelles & collectives; la promotion de la langue française; aider la jeunesse
Laurier Thériault, Directeur général
Denis Daigle, Directeur administratif

SECTION 4
BROADCASTING

The listings in this section are arranged by province, then city within province, except the Major Broadcasting Companies, which are arranged alphabetically by company name.

Major Broadcasting Companies

Arctic Radio
316 Green Street, Flin Flon, MB R8A 0H2
Tel: 204-687-3469
cfar@arcticradio.ca
www.arcticradio.ca

Operates 3 AM Radio stations in Northern Manitoba.
Maureen Kozar, Manager, mkozar@arcticradio.ca

Astral Media Inc.
PO Box 2700, 1800, av McGill College, Montréal, QC H3A 3J6
Tel: 514-939-5000; *Fax:* 514-939-1515
www.astral.com

Canada's largest broadcaster of English-and French-language pay and specialty television services and is currently involved, on its own or with partners, in 20 television services. Astral Media and its television networks also play a vital role as the largest private sector investor in Canadian feature films. Astral Media owns 82 radio stations. Astral Media employs more than 8,000 people at its facilities in Montréal, Toronto, and a number of cities throughout Québec and the Atlantic provinces
André Bureau, Chairman of the Board
Ian Greenberg, President/CEO
Sidney Greenberg, Vice-President

Astral Media Radio
1717, boul. René-Lévesque Est, Montréal, QB H2L 4T9
Tel: 514-529-3229; *Fax:* 614-529-9308
www.astralmediaradio.com

Owns 29 radio stations, including 21 French-language FM stations in Québec
Ian Greenberg, President/CEO
André Bureau, Chairman of the Board
Sidney Greenberg, Vice-President

Astral Media Radio Atlantic
206 Rockwood Avenue, Fredericton, NB E3B 2M2
Tel: 506-455-1069; *Fax:* 506-452-2345
www.astralmedia.com

Owns 8 radio stations located in Fredericton, Bathurst, Woodstock and Grand Falls in New Brunswick, and Truro, Nova Scotia. These stations are focused on serving the local communities in which they are based.
André Bureau, Chairman of the Board
Ian Greenberg, President/CEO

Atlantic Television Network (ATV)
2885 Robie St., Halifax, NS B3K 5Z4
Tel: 902-453-4000; *Fax:* 902-454-3302
admin@atlantistv.eu
atlantictv.net
Social Media: twitter.com/AtlantisATV

The ATV (Atlantic Television Network) launched September 13, 1972. It is an online television network providing 24/7 output

Bayshore Broadcasting Corporation
270 Ninth St. East, Owen Sound, ON N4K 5P5
Tel: 519-376-2030; *Fax:* 519-371-4242
bayshore@radioowensound.com
www.radioowensound.com

Bayshore Broadcasting Corporation is an independent broadcaster. It operates radio stations in Grey, Bruce, Simcoe, & Huron counties in southern Ontario. The following stations are operated by Bayshore Broadcasting: 560 CFOS, Mix 106 (CIXK-FM), Country 93 (CKYC-FM), 98 the Beach (CFPS-FM), 97.7 the Beach (CHGB-FM), 104.9 the Beach (CHWC-FM), & Sunshine 89 (89.1 FM).
Doug Caldwell, President

Blackburn Radio Inc.
#204, 700 Richmond St., London, ON N6A 5C7
Tel: 519-679-8680; *Fax:* 519-679-5321
info@630cfco.com
www.blackburnradio.com
Social Media: twitter.com/BLACKBURNRADIO

Blackburn Radio is an AM-FM radio broadcaster which operates stations in Chatham, Leamington, London, Sarnia, Windsor, and Wingham. Facebook link is: www.facebook.com/pages/Country-929-FM630-AM-CFCO/206597195084
Richard Costley-White, President/CEO
Ron Dann, General Manager, Sarnia, rdann@blackburnradio.com

Camosun College - Village 900
3100 Foul Bay Road, Victoria, BC V8P 5J2
Tel: 250-370-3658; *Fax:* 250-370-3679
feedback@village900.ca
www.village900.ca

Village 900 is a non-profit campus/instructional radio station located at Camosun College in Victoria, British Columbia.
Colin Easton, President Board of Directors
Kim O'Hare, VP Board of Directors

Canadian Broadcasting Corporation - Canadian Broadcasting Centre
Société Radio-Canada
PO Box 500 A, 250 Front St. West, Toronto, ON M5W 1E6
Tel: 416-205-3311
Toll-Free: 866-306-4636
cbcinput@cbc.ca
www.cbc.ca
Other information: TDD: 416/205-6688

The CBC is a Canadian crown corporation & serves as Canada's national public radio & television broadcaster; in French, the CBC is called la Société Radio-Canada (SRC), & the corporation also operates Radio Canada International (RCI); offers programming in English, French & 8 Aboriginal languages on radio, & in 9 languages on RCI; provides regional & local television programming in both official languages; broadcasts locally produced programs in English & native languages for people living in the far north; primarily funded by federal statutory grants.
Timothy W. Casgrain, Chair, Board of Directors

Canadian Broadcasting Corporation - Head Office (CBC)
Société Radio-Canada
PO Box 3220 C, 181 Queen St., Ottawa, ON K1Y 1E4
Tel: 613-288-6000
liaison@cbc.ca
www.cbc.radio-canada.ca
Social Media: www.facebook.com/CBCRadioCanada

CBC/Radio-Canada is Canada's national public broadcaster & one of its largest cultural institutions. Services are offered on radio, television, the Internet, satellite radio, digital audio, as well as through its record & music distribution service & wireless WAP & SMS messaging services.
Timothy W. Casgrain, Chair, Board of Directors
Hubert T. Lacroix, President/CEO, CBC/Radio-Canada

Canwest Global Communications Corp.
CanWest Global Pl., 201 Portage Ave., 31st Fl., Winnipeg, MB R3B 3L7
Tel: 204-956-2025; *Fax:* 204-947-9841
www.canwestglobal.com

CanWest Global Communications Corp. is Canada's leading international media company. The Company's diversified holdings include CanWest MediaWorks, which in turn owns Global Television, a coast-to-coast Canadian broadcasting network that reaches more than 94% of English - speaking Canada; CH, a second station group that broadcasts in Montreal, Hamilton and Victoria; eight specialty channels that offer niche programming including Prime TV; radio stations in Winnipeg, Kitchener, and Halifax in 2006, and the National Post newspaper
Derek H. Burney, Chairman
Leonard Asper, President/CEO
David A. Asper, Exec. Vice-President

Cariboo Central Interior Radio Inc.
1940 Third Ave., Prince George, BC V2M 1G7
Tel: 250-564-2524; *Fax:* 250-564-6611

Operates AM & FM radio stations in British Columbia
Terry Shepherd, President & Managing Director

Cariboo Central Interior Radio Inc.
150 West Columbia Street, PO Box 1370, Vanderhoof, BC V0J 3A0
Tel: 250-567-4914; *Fax:* 250-567-4982
ciradio@hwy16.com

Owns and operates several radio stations serving the British Columbia Interior.

Cégep De Rimouski
60, rue de lévêché Quest, Rimouski, QC G5L 4H6
Tel: 418-723-1880; *Fax:* 418-724-4961
infoscol@cegep-rimouski.qc.ca
www.cegep-rimouski.qc.ca

CHUM Radio Kingston
#10, 993 Princess St., Kingston, ON K7L 1H3
Tel: 613-544-1380; *Fax:* 613-546-9751
www.chumkingston.com

Operates 3 radio stations in the Kingston area: 103.7 BOB FM, 98.3 FLY FM, and 98.9 The Drive.
Greg Hinton, Vice President/General Manager, greg.hinton@chumkingston.com
Brian Johnston, Sales Manager, brian.johnston@chumkingston.com
Jennifer Yascheshyn, Program Director, jennifer.yascheshyn@chumkingston.com

CJMR
284 Church Street, Oakville, ON L6J 7N2
Tel: 905-845-2821; *Fax:* 905-842-1250
contact@cjmr1320.ca
www.cjmr.ca

An ethnic radio station serving the Greater Toronto Area in 15 different languages.

CKPR Inc.
87 Hill Street North, Thunder Bay, ON P7A 5V6
Tel: 807-346-2600; *Fax:* 807-345-9923
radio@ckpr.com
www.ckpr.com

A community radio station serving Thunder Bay, Ontario.

CKUA Radio Network
10526 Jasper Ave., Edmonton, AB T5J 1Z7
Tel: 403-428-7595; *Fax:* 403-428-7624
Toll-Free: 800-494-2582
radio@ckua.org
www.ckua.com

The CKUA Radio Network was founded in 1927 on the University of Alberta campus in Edmonton. CKUA is Canada's first educational broadcaster and Canada's first public broadcaster. CKUA's radio signal is carried province-wide on AM and FM through a network of 17 transmitters, strategically located throughout Alberta. CKUA also broadcasts in western Canada on select satellite providers and around the world through ckua.com. Recognized as the voice of Alberta artists, musicians and cultural enthusiasts
Ken Regan, General Manager
Wanda Bornn, Sales Manager

Coast Radio
909 Ironwood Street, Campbell River, BC V9W 3E5
Tel: 250-287-7106; *Fax:* 250-287-7170
coastradio@coastradio.com
www.coastradio.com

COGECO inc.
#100, 612 rue Saint-Jacques, Montréal, QC H3C 5R1
Tel: 514-390-6035; *Fax:* 514-390-0773
www.cogeco.ca

COGECO is a diversified telecommunication company which strives to meet the communication needs of consumers and advertisers through broadcasting, in Québec and cable distribution in Canada and Portugal. Second largest cable system operator in Ontario, Québec and Portugal, in terms of the number of basic cable service customers served. COGECO is the controlling shareholder of the TQS network serving Québec's major markets in the French language through the operation of nine television stations
Louis Audet, President/CEO
Pierre Gagné, Vice-President/CFO, Finances

Concordia University
1455 de Maisonneuve Boulevard W, Montreal, QC H3G 1M8
Tel: 514-848-2424
www.concordia.ca

Operates CJLO, a not-for-profit instructional radio station operating out of the Loyola Campus of Concordia University.

Corus Entertainment Inc.
BCE Place, #1630, 181 Bay St., Toronto, ON M5J 2T3
Tel: 416-642-3770; *Fax:* 416-642-3779
www.corusent.com

Corus Entertainment is one of Canada's most successful integrated media and entertainment companies. Television services include: YTV, Treehouse, W Network, CMT, The Documentary Channel, SCREAM, Discovery Kids, Telelatino and TELETOON (50%); Western Canada's exclusive pay-TV movie service on six thematic channels under the Movie Central brand; three local over-the-air television stations; Corus Custom Networks advertising services for television and Max Trax, a residential subscription digital music service. They also operate 52 radio stations throughout Canada
John Cassaday, CEO
John Hayes, President, Corus Radio

CPAM Radio Union.com Inc.
3733, Jarry Est, 2e Étage, Montreal, QC H1Z 2G1
Tel: 514-287-1288; *Fax:* 514-287-3299
info@cpam-radiounion.com
www.cpam-radiounion.com

Station de radio AM ethnique de langue française à Montréal, CPAM offre une programmation axée sur les besoins et la culture des communautés ethnoculturelles francophones d'origine haïtienne, latino-américaine et africaine de la région métropolitaine de Montréal

† French language station

CTVglobemedia Inc.
299 Queen St. West, Toronto, ON M5V 2Z5
Tel: 416-384-8000
ctvglobemediacommunications@ctvglobemedia.com
www.ctvglobemedia.com
CTVglobemedia, Canada's largest private broadcaster, offers a wide range of news, sports, information, and entertainment programming, via radio and television; CTVglobemedia's main broadcast media asset is CTV Television Inc.; it also owns CHUM, now called CTV Limited, and operates Toronto radio stations CP24 Radio 1050 (formerly 1050 CHUM), and CHUM-FM; the CHUM Radio Network is a subsidiary of CTVglobemedia, as is The Globe and Mail newspaper.
Ivan Fecan, President/CEO

Dauphin Broadcasting Co. Ltd.
27-3 Avenue NE, Dauphin, MB R7N 0Y5
Tel: 204-638-3230; *Fax:* 204-638-8257
730ckdm@mb.sympatico.ca
730ckdm.com
Operates 730 CKDM, a community radio station serving Dauphin, Manitoba for over 50 years.
Rene Maillard, President

Diffusion Laval inc.
2040, Autoroute Laval, Laval, QC H7S 2M9
Tél: 450-680-1570; *Téléc:* 450-680-1598
info@laval1570am.com
www.boomer1570.ca
CFAV/Radio Boomer 1570 AM; Laval 1570 AM (septembre, 2010).
Michel Mathieu, Président/Directeur général

Fairchild Radio
135 East Beaver Creek Road, Unit 7-8, Richmond Hill, ON L4B 1E2
Tel: 905-763-3350; *Fax:* 905-889-9828
operation@am1430.com
www.fairchildradio.com
Chinese Canadian multicultural radio network with stations in Toronto, Vancouver, and Calgary. Provides program schedules and internet simulcasting
Thomas Fung, Chairman

Fairchild Television Ltd. (FTV)
Aberdeen Centre, #3300, 4151 Hazelbridge Way, Vancouver, BC V6X 4J7
Tel: 604-295-1313; *Fax:* 604-295-1300
info@fairchildtv.com
www.fairchildtv.com
Provides programming mainly in Cantonese and Mandarin, broadcast through cable and satellite across Canada and part of the U.S.
Joe Chan, President

Fawcett Broadcasting Ltd.
PO Box 777, Fort Frances, ON P9A 3N1
Tel: 807-274-7580; *Fax:* 807-274-8746
Operates AM & FM radio stations in north-western Ontario
Lois Fawcett, President

Golden West Broadcasting Ltd.
#201, 125 Centre Ave., Altona, MB R0G 0B0
Tel: 204-324-6464; *Fax:* 204-324-8918
www.gwm.ca
Headquartered in Altona, Manitoba. Golden West has 28 radio stations scattered across Manitoba, Saskatchewan, and Alberta
Elmer Hildebrand, President & CEO
David Wiebe, General Manager

Groupe Radio Antenne 6
568, boul St-Joseph, Roberval, QC G8H 2K6
Tel: 418-275-1831
Operates 5 stations in Lac-Saint-Jean region; also has a presence in Abitibi, Outaouais, and Montreal
Marc-André Levesque, President

Groupe TVA inc.
1600, boul de Maisonneuve est, Montréal, QC H2L 4P6
Tél: 514-526-9251; *Téléc:* 514-598-0673
www.tva.canoe.com
Groupe TVA fondée en 1960 sous le nom de Corporation Télé-Métropole inc., est une entreprise de communication intégrée active dans les secteurs de la diffusion, de la production de produits audiovisuels, de la publication de magazines, de l'édition ainsi que de la distribution de films.
Pierre Dion, Président/Chef de la direction
Yves Beaupré, Vice-président, Exploitation

Harvard Broadcasting Inc.
2060 Halifax St., Regina, SK S4P 1T7
Tel: 306-546-6200; *Fax:* 306-781-7338
rpettigrew@harvardbroadcasting.com
www.harvardbroadcasting.com
Harvard Broadcasting came into being in 1977, when The Hill Companies purchased CKCK-TV, the Regina-based CTV affiliate station. In 1981, Harvard expanded into radio with the purchase of CKRM and CFMQ, also both local stations. Today, Harvard Broadcasting Inc. includes 620 CKRM, Lite 92 FM, and 104.9 The Wolf in Regina and CFEX-FM, X92.9, in Calgary and CFVR-FM in Fort McMurray
Bruce Cowie, Vice-President

Hector Broadcasting Co. Ltd.
84 Provost Street, PO Box 519, New Glasgow, NS B2H 5E7
Tel: 902-752-4200; *Fax:* 902-755-2468
ckec@ckec.com
www.ckec.com
Operates 1320 CKEC, a community radio station serving Pictou County, NS

Hildebrand Group
366 - 3rd Ave. S, Saskatoon, SK S7K 1M5
Tel: 306-244-1975; *Fax:* 306-665-5501
cjww.radio@sasktel.net
www.cjwwradio.com
Operates 600 CJWW out of Saskatoon.
Vic Dubois, General Manager
Ken McFarlane, General Sales Manager
Myles Myrol, Retail Sales Manager

Inuit Broadcasting Corporation (IBC)
#301, 331 Cooper St., Ottawa, ON K2P 0G5
Tel: 613-235-1892; *Fax:* 613-230-8824
www.inuitbroadcasting.ca
The Inuit Broadcasting Corporation provides a window to the Arctic by producing television programming by Inuit, for Inuit. IBC has 5 production centres scattered across Nunavut, with 34 Inuit staff at every level of the production chain, from director of network programming to technical producer to administrative assistant. IBC is a founding member of Television Northern Canada & the Aboriginal Peoples Television Network.
Debbie Brisebois, Executive Director

Island Radio Ltd.
4550 Willingdon Rd., Nanaimo, BC V9T 2H3
Tel: 250-758-1131; *Fax:* 250-758-4644
info@islandradio.bc.ca
www.islandradio.bc.ca
Island Radio consists of six radio stations on Vancouver Island, British Columbia
Paul Larsen, President

James Bay Broadcasting Corp. Inc.
PO Box 400, Moosonee, ON P0L 1Y0
Tel: 705-336-2466; *Fax:* 705-336-2186
Operates CHMO, a community radio station that serves Moosonee and Moose Factory, Ontario.

The Jim Pattison Broadcast Group
460 Pemberton Terrace, Kamloops, BC V2C 1T5
Tel: 250-372-3322; *Fax:* 250-374-0445
info@jpbroadcast.com
www.jpbroadcast.com
The Jim Pattison Broadcast Group is Canada's largest private western-based broadcasting company
Rick Arnish, President
Joel Simmons, Technical Director
Bruce Davis, VP Sales

Klondike Broadcasting Ltd.
203-4103 4th Avenue, Whitehorse, YK Y1A 1H6
Tel: 867-668-6100; *Fax:* 867-668-4209
ckrwcopy@ckrw.com
www.ckrw.com
Operates CKRW-FM in Whitehorse, YK.
Jennifer Johnstone, General Manager, ckrwcopy@ckrw.com
Eva Birdman, Sales & Ad Copy, marketing@ckrw.com

Learning Skills Television of Alberta
Also known as: ACCESS - The Education Station
3720 - 76 Ave., Edmonton, AB T6B 2N9
Tel: 780-440-7777; *Fax:* 780-440-8899
Toll-Free: 888-440-4640
access@incentre.net
www.accesslearning.com
Television broadcasting and multimedia learning company based in Edmonton, AB. Established in 1994 to privatize Alberta's provincial educational television service. LTA is the designated educational broadcasting Authority for Alberta as defined in the Broadcasting Act

Ron Keast, President
Peter Palframan, Vice-President, Finance & Administration

Lethbridge Community College
Student Service Centre, 3000 College Drive South, Lethbridge, AB T1K 1L6
Tel: 403-329-7237; *Fax:* 403-320-1461
Operates CRLC The Kodiak, a college radio station.

Mainstream Broadcasting Corporation
#100-1200 West 73rd Avenue, Vancouver, BC V6P 6G5
Tel: 604-263-1320; *Fax:* 604-261-0310
www.am1320.com
Mainstream Broadcasting Corporation is a British Columbia media company owned and operated by local Vancouver resident and businessman, James Ho. In 1993, OCV programming was incorporated into the multicultural AM radio station of CHMB AM 1320, serving the needs of Vancouver's multicultural community.
James Ho, President
Teresa Wat, CEO/COO
George Feng, VP Business Development

Maritime Broadcasting System
5121 Sackville St., Halifax, NS B3J 1K1
Tel: 902-425-1225; *Fax:* 902-423-2093
mail@mbsradio.com
www.mbsradio.com
Originally established in 1969 as Eastern Broadcasting Limited, MBS Radio is a 100% maritime owned, private broadcasting company, with 25 radio stations and 410 employees serving communities in the three Maritime Provinces of Nova Scotia, New Brunswick and Prince Edward Island
Merv Russell, President

MCTV-TV
699 Frood Rd., Sudbury, ON P3C 5A3
Tel: 705-674-8301; *Fax:* 705-671-2789
Scott Lund, Vice-President

Merritt Broadcasting
#201, 2196 Quilchena Avenue, PO Box 1630, Merritt, BC V1K 1B8
Tel: 250-378-4288; *Fax:* 250-378-6979
news@cjnl.com
Devoted to local community service

NewCap Inc.
745 Windmill Rd., Dartmouth, NS B3B 1C2
Tel: 902-468-7557; *Fax:* 902-468-7558
ncc@ncc.ca
www.ncc.ca
NewCap is one of Canada's leading radio broadcasters with 76 licences across Canada
Robert G. Steele, President & CEO
David J. Murray, COO
Scott Weatherby, CFO & Corporate Secretary

Newcap Radio
745 Windmill Road, Dartmouth, NS B3B 1C2
Tel: 902-468-7557; *Fax:* 902-468-7558
ncc@newcapradio.com
www.ncc.ca.ca
Newcap Radio is one of Canada's leading radio broadcasters with 76 licences across Canada. The Company reaches millions of listeners each week through a variety of formats and is a recognized industry leader in radio programming, sales and networking.
Harry R Steele, Chairman
Robert G Steele, President/CEO
David J Murray, COO

Newfoundland Broadcasting Co. Ltd.
PO Box 2020, 446 Logy Bay Rd., St. John's, NL A1C 5S2
Tel: 709-722-5015; *Fax:* 709-726-5017
ntv@ntv.ca
www.ntv.ca
Reaches 8 million households across Canada via digital cable & satellite

Okalakatiget Society
PO Box 160, Nain, NL A0P 1L0
Tel: 709-922-2955; *Fax:* 709-922-2293
okradio@oksociety.com
www.oksociety.com
The OKalaKatiget Society was incorporated in 1982. Stationed in Nain, Labrador the Society provides a regional, native communication service for the people on the North Coast and the Lake Melville region of Labrador. People have come to rely on the Society for information and entertainment via radio and television. Their mandate is to preserve and promote the language and culture of the Inuit within the region
Fran Williams, Exec. Director

† French language station

Radio Canada International
1400, boul René-Lévesque est, Montréal, QC H2L 2M2
Tel: 514-597-7500; *Fax:* 514-597-6607
www.rcinet.ca
Social Media: www.facebook.com/CBCRadioCanada
Radio Canada International has been broadcasting around the World since 1945, with live radio in English, French, Spanish, Portuguese, Arabic, Mandarin, and Russian. RCI's mandate is to increase awareness of Canadian values, as well as its social, economic and cultural activities to specific geographic areas as determined in consultation with the government of Canada. RCI also has the complementary mandate of addressing these same topics to new immigrants to Canada.
Jean Larin, Executive Director

RAWLCO Radio Ltd.
715 Saskatchewan Cres. West, Saskatoon, SK S7M 5V7
Tel: 306-934-2222; *Fax:* 306-477-0002
Rawlco Radio Ltd. is a Saskatchewan company with radio stations in Saskatoon, Regina, Prince Albert, North Battleford, and Meadow Lake. Operates 12 radio stations
Michael Zaplitny, Vice-President

Red River College
2055 Notre Dame Avenue, Winnipeg, MB R3H 0J9
Tel: 204-632-3960
www.rrc.mb.ca
Home of 92.9 KICK-FM, a non-profit instructional radio station based at Red River College in Winnipeg, Manitoba.

RNC MEDIA
#1523, 1, Place Ville Marie, Montréal, QC H3B 2B5
Tél: 514-866-8686; *Téléc:* 514-866-8056
www.rncmedia.ca
Radiodiffusion (Planète Radio, Radio X); télédiffusion (TVA Gatineau-Ottawa et Abitibi-Témiscamingue; TQS Gatineau-Ottawa et Abitibi-Témiscamingue; SRC Abitibi-Témiscamingue); programmation de haute qualité et services de publicité.
Raynald Brière, Président/Chef de la direction, rbriere@rncmedia.ca
Pierre R. Brosseau, Président exécutif du conseil, pbrosseau@rncmedia.ca

Rogers Broadcasting Ltd.
777 Jarvis St., Toronto, ON M4Y 3B7
Tel: 416-935-8200; *Fax:* 416-935-8202
Rogers Broadcasting has 46 AM and FM radio stations across Canada. Television properties include Toronto multicultural television broadcasters OMNI.1 (CFMT) and OMNI.2, televised and electronic shopping service, The Shopping Channel, Rogers Sportsnet and manages two digital television services
Anthony P. Viner, President/CEO
Chuck McCoy, Exec. Vice-President, Programming

SCN
#E-313, 2440 Broad St., Regina, SK S4P 0A5
Tel: 306-787-0490; *Fax:* 306-787-0496
Toll-Free: 800-667-5055
inquiries@scn.ca
www.scn.ca
SCN operates as an agency of the Government of Saskatchewan, in accordance with The Communications Network Corporation Act (1989). The Minister of Culture Youth and Recreation serves as the Minister Responsible for SCN
Jim Johns, Manager, Information Systems
David Stanchuk, Manager, Technology
Ken Alecxe, President & CEO
Richard Gustin, Executive Director, Programming
Twyla MacDougall, Executive Director, Finance & Human Resources & Strategic Plannin
Maureen MacDonald, Manager, Communications

Seneca College
1750 Finch Avenue East, Toronto, ON M2J 2X5
Tel: 604-263-1320; *Fax:* 604-261-0310
www.senecac.on.ca
Home of Radio CS, a not-for-profit instructional radio station.
Dr. Rick Miner, President
Jean Anne McLeod BA, Chair of the Board of Governors

Shaw Communications Inc.
Also known as: Shaw Cable
#900, 630 - 3rd Ave. SW, Calgary, AB T2P 4L4
Tel: 403-750-4500; *Fax:* 403-750-4501
Toll-Free: 888-750-7429
www.shaw.ca
Shaw Communications Inc. is a diversified communications company. Its core business is the provision of broadband cable television, high-speed Internet, digital phone, telecommunications services, & satellite direct-to-home services to more than 3 million customers throughout Canada.
J.R. Shaw, Executive Chair
Peter Bissonnette, President & CEO

Société Radio-Canada
Canadian Broadcasting Corporation
1400, boul René-Lévesque est, Montréal, QC H2L 2M2
Tél: 514-597-6000; *Téléc:* 514-597-5545
Ligne san frais: 866-306-4636
auditoire@radio-canada.ca
www.radio-canada.ca
Social Media: www.facebook.com/CBCRadioCanada
Radio-Canada est le radiodiffuseur public national du Canada et l'une des plus grandes institutions culturelles du pays. Avec ses 28 services offerts sur des plateformes comme la radio, la télévision, Internet, la radio par satellite, l'audio numérique, sans compter son service de distribution de disques et de musique et ses services de messagerie sans fil WAP et SMS, CBC/Radio-Canada est maintenant accessible aux Canadiens à leur convenance.
Hubert T. Lacroix, Président/Chef de la direction, CBC/Radio-Canada

Standard Broadcasting Corp. Ltd.
2 St. Clair Ave. West, 2nd Fl., Toronto, ON M4V 1L6
Tel: 416-960-9911; *Fax:* 416-323-6828
www.standardradio.com
Launched in 1927; 51 stations provide music and information to 29 markets across Canada
Gary Slaight, President/CEO
Ian Lurie, Vice-President/CFO
Bill Herz, Vice-President, Sales
Dave Simon, Vice-President, Engineering

Standard Radio Office
2 St. Clair Avenue West, 2nd Floor, Toronto, ON M4V 1L6
Tel: 416-960-9911; *Fax:* 416-323-6828
www.standardradio.com
Standard Radio is the largest privately owned broadcast company in Canada
Gary Slaight, President/CEO
Ian Lurie, VP/CFO
Dave Simon, VP Engineering

Steele Communications
PO Box 8-590, 391 Kenmount Rd., St. Johns, NL A1B 3P5
Tel: 709-726-5590; *Fax:* 709-726-4633
www.vocm.com
Steele Communications is the broadcast leader in Newfoundland and Labrador, with a network of 26 radio licenses across the province. Providing both AM and FM networks in a variety of formats, delivering to listeners, consistent quality programming with a local focus
Greg Hinton, VP/General Manager

Taqramiut Nipingat Inc. (TNI)
Also known as: Voice of the North
#200, 1985 - 55 Ave., Dorval, QC H9P 1G9
Tel: 514-683-2330; *Fax:* 514-683-1078
tnigeneral@taqramiut.qc.ca
www.taqramiut.qc.ca
Taqramiut Nipingat Inc. is a non-profit organization incorporated on September 8, 1975 under Part II of the Canada Business Corporation Act. Offers video production and a variety of broadband telecommunications services to institutional and individual clients on a profit generating basis. TNI's 15 hours of weekly radio programs are broadcast via the Northern Service of the Canadian Broadcast Corporation
George Kakayuk, President
Sammy Duncan, Vice-President

Télé Inter-Rives ltée
Inter-Riverbank Television
15, rue de la Chute, Rivière-du-Loup, QC G5R 5B7
Tél: 418-867-8080; *Téléc:* 418-867-4710
Tele Inter-Rives Ltd. dirige 4 stations de télévision régionales dans l'est du Québec; CKRT-TV (SRC), CIMT-TV, CHAU (TVA), et CFTF (V).

Télé-Québec
Also known as: Société de télédiffusion du Québec
1000, rue Fullum, Montréal, QC H2K 3L7
Tél: 514-521-2424; *Téléc:* 514-873-2601
info@telequebec.tv
www.telequebec.qc.ca
La Société a pour objet d'exploiter une entreprise de télédiffusion éducative et culturelle afin d'assurer, par tout mode de diffusion, l'accessibilité de ses produits au public.
Télé-Québec est une société publique de production et de diffusion, desservant plus de 92 % de la population québécoise à travers son réseau riche de 17 émetteurs, alimenté par un lien satellite portant sa programmation de Montréal.
Michèle Fortin, Présidente/Directrice générale

TQS inc.
#100, 612, rue St-Jacques, Montréal, QC H3C 5R1
Tel: 514-390-6035; *Fax:* 514-390-0773
tvpublic@tqs.ca
www.tqs.ca
Established in September 1986; covers all Quebec regions
René Guimond, President/CEO
Monique Lacharité, Exec. Vice-President, Finance & Administration

TVOntario (OECA)
Also known as: Ontario Educational Communications Authority
PO Box 200 Q, 2180 Yonge St., Toronto, ON M4T 2T1
Tel: 416-484-2600; *Fax:* 416-484-6285
Toll-Free: 800-613-0513
asktvo@tvontario.org
www.tvontario.org
In 1970, TVOntario was established as the Ontario Educational Communications Authority (OECA) by the government of Ontario, for the purpose of using technology to support the province's education priorities. TVO, TVOntario's English-language service, is Canada's oldest educational broadcaster, and is available to over 98% of Ontario homes. TVO provides educational programming and online resources that enhance and extend learning at home and in the classroom, as well as promoting Ontario's rich cultural identity
Lisa de Wilde, CEO

VOWR
PO Box 7430, Patrick St., St. Johns, NF A1E 3Y5
Tel: 709-579-9233
vowr@vowr.org
www.vowr.org
Radio station VOWR broadcasts from studios located in Wesley United Church in St. John's, Newfoundland, Canada. The station's first broadcast occurred on July 24, 1924
JG Joyce, Founder of VOWR

Wawatay Native Communications Society
PO Box 1180, Sioux Lookout, ON P8T 1B7
Tel: 807-737-2951; *Fax:* 807-737-3224
Toll-Free: 800-243-9059
christinec@wawatay.on.ca
www.wawatay.on.ca
Wawatay Native Communications Society is a self-governing, independent community-driven entrepreneurial native organization dedicated to using appropriate technologies to meet the communication needs of people of Aboriginal ancestry in Northern Ontario
Christine Chisel, Executive Director

AM Radio Stations

Alberta

***Athabasca:* CKBA** (Freq: 850)
Owned by: **NewCap Inc.***
#2, 4907 - 51 St., Athabasca, AB T9S 1E7
Tel: 780-675-5301; *Fax:* 780-675-4938
jpeckham@ab.ncc.ca
Mark Maheau, Vice-President

***Banff:* CJMT** (Freq: 1340)
Owned by: **CHMN-FM**
Banff, AB

***Blairmore:* CJEV** (Freq: 1340)
Owned by: **NewCap Inc.***
PO Box 840, 13213 - 20 Ave., Blairmore, AB T0K 2E2
Tel: 403-562-2806; *Fax:* 403-562-8114

***Brooks:* CIBQ** (Freq: 1340)
Owned by: **NewCap Inc.***
PO Box 180, #8, 403 - 2nd Ave. West, Brooks, AB T1R 0S3
Tel: 403-362-3418; *Fax:* 403-362-8168
John Petrie, Station Manager

***Calgary:* CBR** (Freq: 1010)
Owned by: **Canadian Broadcasting Corporation***
PO Box 2640 D, 1724 Westmount Blvd. NW, Calgary, AB T2P 2M7
Tel: 403-521-6000
www.calgary.cbc.ca

***Calgary:* CFAC** (Freq: 960)
Owned by: **Rogers Broadcasting Ltd.***
2723 - 37 Ave. NE, Calgary, AB T1Y 5R8
Tel: 403-246-9696
www.fan960.com
Kelly Kirch, Program Director

** For details on this company see listing in Major Broadcasting Companies section; † French language station*

***Calgary:* CFFR** (Freq: 660)
Owned by: **Rogers Broadcasting Ltd.***
2723 - 37 Ave. NE, Calgary, AB T1Y 5R8
Tel: 403-291-0000; *Fax:* 403-291-4368
www.660news.com

***Calgary:* CHQR** (Freq: 770)
Owned by: **Corus Entertainment Inc.***
#105, 630 - 3 Ave. SW, Calgary, AB T2P 4L4
Tel: 403-716-6500; *Fax:* 403-716-2111
Toll-Free: 800-563-7770
www.am770chqr.com
John Vos, Program Director

***Calgary:* CKMX** (Freq: 1060)
Owned by: **Standard Radio Office***
1110 Centre St. NE, 3rd Fl., Calgary, AB T2E 2R2
Tel: 403-240-5800; *Fax:* 403-240-5801
www.classiccountryam1060.com

***Camrose:* CFCW** (Freq: 790)
Owned by: **CFCW**
Camrose, AB

***Drumheller:* CKDQ** (Freq: 910)
Owned by: **NewCap Inc.***
PO Box 1480, 515 Hwy. 10 East, Drumheller, AB T0J 0Y0
Tel: 403-823-3384; *Fax:* 403-823-7241
ckdq@ab.ncc.ca
Hugh MacDonald, General Manager

***Edmonton:* AM 930 The Light** (Freq: 930)
5316 Calgary Trail, Edmonton, AB T6H 4J8
Tel: 780-466-4930; *Fax:* 780-469-5335
www.cjca.ca/cms
Malcolm Hunt, Program Director
Carlo Bruno, Business Manager

***Edmonton:* CBX** (Freq: 740)
Owned by: **Canadian Broadcasting Corporation***
#123, Edmonton City Centre, Edmonton, AB T5J 2Y8
Tel: 780-468-7500
www.cbc.ca/edmonton

***Edmonton:* CFCW** (Freq: 790)
Owned by: **NewCap Inc.***
#600, 5241 Calgary Trail NW, Edmonton, AB T6H 5G8
Tel: 780-468-3939; *Fax:* 780-435-0844
www.cfcw.com

***Edmonton:* CFRN** (Freq: 1260)
Owned by: **Standard Radio Office***
#100, 18520 Stony Plain Rd., Edmonton, AB T5S 2E2
Tel: 780-486-2800; *Fax:* 780-489-6927
team1260@cfrn.com
www.cfrn.com

***Edmonton:* CHED** (Freq: 630)
Owned by: **Corus Entertainment Inc.***
5204 - 84 St., Edmonton, AB T6E 5N8
Tel: 780-440-6300; *Fax:* 780-469-5937
info@630ched.com
www.630ched.com

***†Edmonton:* CHFA** (Freq: 680)
Owned by: **Canadian Broadcasting Corporation***
CP 555, 123, 10062 - 102 Ave., Edmonton, AB T5J 2P4
Tél: 780-468-7800; *Téléc:* 780-468-7812
lecarnet@radio-canada.ca
François Pageau, Chef, Émissions radio & télévision françaises (AB)

***Edmonton:* CHQT** (Freq: 880)
Owned by: **Corus Entertainment Inc.***
5204 - 84 St., Edmonton, AB T6E 5N8
Tel: 780-424-8800; *Fax:* 780-469-5937
www.cool880.com

***Edson:* CJYR** (Freq: 970)
Owned by: **NewCap Inc.***
PO Box 7800, 4813 - 4th Ave., Edson, AB T7E 1V8
Tel: 780-723-4461; *Fax:* 780-723-3765

***High Prairie:* CKVH** (Freq: 1020)
Owned by: **NewCap Inc.***
PO Box 2219, High Prairie, AB T0G 1E0
Tel: 780-523-5111; *Fax:* 780-523-3360
ckvh@ab.ncc.ca

***High River:* CHRB** (Freq: 1140)
Owned by: **Golden West Broadcasting Ltd.***
11 - 5th Ave. SE, High River, AB T1V 1G2
Tel: 403-652-2472; *Fax:* 403-652-7861
Toll-Free: 866-652-2472
am1140@am1140.com
www.am1140radio.com
J. Young, Station Manager

***Lethbridge:* CLCC** (Freq: closed circuit)
Owned by: **Lethbridge College***
Student Service Centre, 3000 College Dr. South, Lethbridge, AB T1K 1L6
Tel: 403-329-7237; *Fax:* 403-320-1461

***Medicine Hat:* CHAT** (Freq: 1270)
Owned by: **The Jim Pattison Broadcast Group***
PO Box 1270, Medicine Hat, AB T1A 7H5
Tel: 403-548-8282; *Fax:* 403-548-8270
www.1270chat.com
Dwaine Dietrich, General Manager

***Peace River:* CKYL** (Freq: 610)
PO Box 300, Peace River, AB T8S 1T5
Tel: 780-624-2535; *Fax:* 780-624-5424
www.ylcountry.com
Terry Babiy, General Manager

***St Paul:* CHLW** (Freq: 1310)
#201, 4341 - 50 Ave., St Paul, AB T0A 3A3
Tel: 780-645-4425; *Fax:* 780-645-2383
dwhite@newcap.ca
www.angelfire.com/ca/chlw
Danny White, Station Manager

***Stettler:* CKSQ** (Freq: 1400)
Owned by: **NewCap Inc.***
PO Box 2050, 4812A - 50th St., Stettler, AB T0C 2L0
Tel: 403-742-2930; *Fax:* 403-742-0660

***Wainwright:* CKKY** (Freq: 830)
Owned by: **NewCap Inc.***
1037 - 2nd Ave.. 2nd Fl., Wainwright, AB T9W 1K7
Tel: 780-842-4311; *Fax:* 780-842-4636
Ron Prochner, Station Manager

***Westlock:* CFOK** (Freq: 1370)
Owned by: **NewCap Inc.***
#17, 10030 - 106 St., Westlock, AB T7P 2K4
Tel: 780-349-4421; *Fax:* 780-349-6259
wbetts@newcap.ca
Wray Betts, Station Manager

***Wetaskiwin:* CKJR** (Freq: 1440)
Owned by: **NewCap Inc.***
5214A - 50 Ave., Wetaskiwin, AB T9A 0S8
Tel: 780-352-0144; *Fax:* 780-352-5656
www.catcountry.ca

British Columbia

***100 Mile House:* CKBX** (Freq: 840)
Owned by: **Cariboo Central Interior Radio Inc.***
260 - 3rd St., 100 Mile House, BC V0K 2E0
Tel: 250-395-3848; *Fax:* 250-395-4147
trard@vistaradio.ca
www.thewolfonline.ca
Tracey Gard, Director

***Burns Lake:* CFLD** (Freq: 760)
Owned by: **CFBV**
PO Box 600, Burns Lake, BC V0J 1E0
Tel: 250-692-3414
Bill Waugh

***Campbell River:* CFWB** (Freq: 1490)
Owned by: **Coast Radio***
909 Ironwood St., Campbell River, BC V9W 3E5
Tel: 250-287-7106; *Fax:* 250-287-7170
coastradio@coastradio.com
www.coastradio.com
N.E. Browne, President
Greg Phelps, Operations Manager

***Creston:* CFKC** (Freq: 1340)
Owned by: **Standard Radio Office***
PO Box 310, 1013 Canyon St., Creston, BC V0B 1G0
Tel: 250-428-5312; *Fax:* 250-428-5015
kbs@sri.ca
www.kbsradio.ca

***Dawson Creek:* CJDC** (Freq: 890)
Owned by: **Standard Radio Office***
901 - 102 Ave., Dawson Creek, BC V1G 2B6
Tel: 250-782-3341; *Fax:* 250-782-3154
peacereception@sri.ca
www.cjdcam.com
Tracy Gard

***Golden:* CKGR** (Freq: 1400)
Owned by: **Standard Radio Office***
PO Box 1403, 825 - 10th Ave. South, Golden, BC V0A 1H0
Tel: 250-344-7177; *Fax:* 250-344-8138
myezrock.com
Harvey Davidson, President

***Granisle:* CHLD** (Freq: 1480)
Owned by: **Vista Broadcast Group**
Granisle, BC

***Invermere:* CKIR** (Freq: 870)
742 - 13th St., Invermere, BC V0A 1K4
Tel: 250-342-4434

***Kamloops:* CHNL** (Freq: 610)
611 Lansdowne St., Kamloops, BC V2C 1Y6
Tel: 250-372-2292; *Fax:* 250-372-2293
info@radionl.com
www.radionl.com
Robbie Dunn, General Manager, rdunn@radionl.com
Jim Reynolds, Manager, Operations, programming@radionl.com
Peter Angle, Manager, Sales, advertising@radionl.com

***Kelowna:* CKFR** (Freq: 1150)
Owned by: **Standard Radio Office***
#300, 435 Bernard Ave., Kelowna, BC V1Y 6N8
Tel: 250-860-8600; *Fax:* 250-880-8856
Paul Mann, General Manager

***Kelowna:* CKOV** (Freq: 630)
Owned by: **The Jim Pattison Broadcast Group***
3805 Lakeshore Rd., Kelowna, BC V1W 3K6
Tel: 250-762-3331; *Fax:* 250-762-2141
Toll-Free: 888-763-4212
info@ckov63.com
www.ckov63.com
Rick Arnish, President
Bruce Davis, General Manager & VP

***Merritt:* CJNL** (Freq: 1230)
Owned by: **Merritt Broadcasting***
PO Box 1630, #201, 2196 Quilchena Ave., Merritt, BC V1K 1B8
Tel: 250-378-4288; *Fax:* 250-378-6979
news@cjnl.com

***Oliver:* CJOR-1** (Freq: 1490)
Owned by: **CJOR**
Oliver, BC

***Osoyoos:* CIOR** (Freq: 1400)
PO Box 539, Osoyoos, BC V0H 1V0
Tel: 250-295-6991; *Fax:* 250-495-7228
Osr@tvcablelan.com
Hawse Ross, General Manager

***Penticton:* CJOR** (Freq: 1240)
33 Carmi Ave., Penticton, BC V2A 3G4
Tel: 250-492-2800; *Fax:* 250-493-0370

***Penticton:* CKOR** (Freq: 800)
Owned by: **Standard Radio Office***
33 Carmi Ave., Penticton, BC V2A 3G4
Tel: 250-492-2800; *Fax:* 250-493-0370

***Port Hardy:* CFNI** (Freq: 1240)
Owned by: **Coast Radio***
Magic 1240, PO Box 1240, 5050 Beaver Harbour Rd., Port Hardy, BC V0N 2P0
Tel: 250-949-6500; *Fax:* 250-949-6580
cfni@cablerocket.com
www.coastradio.com
N.E. Browne, President
Greg Phelps, Operations Manager

***Prince Rupert:* CFPR** (Freq: 860)
Owned by: **Canadian Broadcasting Corporation***
#1, 222 - 3 Ave. West, Prince Rupert, BC V8J 1L1
Tel: 250-624-2161; *Fax:* 250-627-8594
daybreaknorth@cbc.ca
www.cbc.ca/bc
Laura Chapin, Sr. Announcer/Operator

** For details on this company see listing in Major Broadcasting Companies section; † French language station*

Quesnel: **CKCQ** (Freq: Broadcasts at 920 AM in Quesnel, and at 570 AM in Williams Lake)
#502, 410 Kinchant St., Quesnel, BC V2J 7K5
Tel: 250-992-7046; *Fax:* 250-992-2354
www.vistaradio.ca
Brian Edwards, President

Revelstoke: **CKCR** (Freq: 1340)
Owned by: **Standard Radio Office***
PO Box 1420, Revelstoke, BC V0E 2F0
Tel: 250-837-2149; *Fax:* 250-837-5577
www.revelstoke.myezrock.com

Richmond: **CISL** (Freq: 650)
Owned by: **Standard Radio Office***
#20, 11151 Horseshoe Way, Richmond, BC V7A 4S5
Tel: 604-272-6500; *Fax:* 604-272-0917
oldies@650cisl.com
www.650cisl.com
Gary Slaight, President

Richmond: **CJVB** (Freq: 1470; Fairchild Radio Group)
Owned by: **Fairchild Radio***
#2090, 4151 Hazelbridge Way, Richmond, BC V6X 4J7
Tel: 604-295-1234; *Fax:* 604-295-1201
general@am1470.com
www.am1470.com
George Lee, Sr. Vice-President & General Manage

Smithers: **CFBV** (Freq: 870)
PO Box 335, Smithers, BC V0J 2N0
Tel: 250-847-2277; *Fax:* 250-847-9411
thepeak@bulkley.net
Gareth Reid, General & Sales Manager

Summerland: **CHOR** (Freq: 1450)
Owned by: **Standard Radio Office***
PO Box 1170, #200, 901 Main St., Summerland, BC V0H 1Z0
Tel: 250-494-0333; *Fax:* 250-493-0370

Terrace: **CFTK** (Freq: 590)
Owned by: **Standard Radio Office***
4625 Lazelle Ave., Terrace, BC V8G 1S4
Tel: 250-638-6316; *Fax:* 250-638-6320
www.standardradio.com
Bryan Edwards, President
Tim MacLean, Vice-President

Vancouver: **CBU** (Freq: 690)
Owned by: **Canadian Broadcasting Corporation***
PO Box 4600, 775 Cambie St., Vancouver, BC V6B 4A2
Tel: 604-662-6920; *Fax:* 604-662-6088
www.cbc.ca/bc

Vancouver: **CFTE** (Freq: 1410)
#300, 380 West 2nd Ave., Vancouver, BC V5Y 1C8
Tel: 604-871-9000; *Fax:* 604-871-2901
www.teamradio.ca
James Stuart, Vice President/General Manager, CHUM Radio Vancouver

Vancouver: **CHMB** (Freq: 1320)
#100, 1200 West 73 Ave., Vancouver, BC V6P 6G7
Tel: 604-263-1320; *Fax:* 604-263-0320
info@am1320.com
www.am1320.com
Wayne Lee, General Manager

Vancouver: **CHMJ** (Freq: 730)
Owned by: **Corus Entertainment Inc.***
#2000, 700 West Georgia St., Vancouver, BC V7Y 1K9
Tel: 604-681-7511; *Fax:* 604-331-2722
www.am730traffic.com

Vancouver: **CISL** (Freq: 650)
Owned by: **CISL**
Vancouver, BC

Vancouver: **CKBD** (Freq: 600)
Owned by: **The Jim Pattison Broadcast Group***
#300, 1401 - 8th Ave. West, Vancouver, BC V6H 1C9
Tel: 604-731-6111; *Fax:* 604-731-0493
600am@600am.com
www.600am.com

Vancouver: **CKNW** (Freq: 980)
Owned by: **Corus Entertainment Inc.***
#2000, 700 West Georgia St., Vancouver, BC V7Y 1K9
Tel: 604-331-2711; *Fax:* 604-331-2722
info@cknw.com
www.cknw.com
J.J. Johnston, General Manager

Vancouver: **CKST** (Freq: 1040)
#300, 380 West 2nd Ave., Vancouver, BC V5Y 1C8
Tel: 604-871-9000; *Fax:* 604-871-2901
www.teamradio.ca
James Stuart, Vice President/General Manager, CHUM Radio Vancouver

Vancouver: **CKWX** (Freq: 1130)
Owned by: **Rogers Broadcasting Ltd.***
2440 Ash St., Vancouver, BC V5Z 4J6
Tel: 604-873-2599; *Fax:* 604-873-0877
news1130@news1130.rogers.com
www.news1130.com

Vanderhoof: **CIVH** (Freq: 1340)
Owned by: **Central Interior Radio Inc.***
PO Box 1370, 150 West Columbia St., Vanderhoof, BC V0J 3A0
Tel: 250-567-4914; *Fax:* 250-567-4982
ciradio@hwy16.com
Tom Bulmer, Station Manager

Victoria: **C-FAX** (Freq: 1070)
1420 Broad St., Victoria, BC V8W 2B1
Tel: 250-386-1070; *Fax:* 250-920-4603
cfax.reception@chumradio.com
www.cfax1070.com
Adam Salvisburg, Production Manager
Alan Brown, Senior Account Manager

Victoria: **CKMO** (Freq: 900)
Owned by: **Camosun College***
3100 Foul Bay Rd., Victoria, BC V8P 5J2
Tel: 250-370-3658; *Fax:* 250-370-3679
feedback@village900.ca
www.village900.ca
Doug Ozeroff, General Manager

White Rock: **KARI** (Freq: 550)
PO Box 75150, White Rock, BC V4B 5L3
Tel: 604-536-7733
info@kari55.com
www.kari55.com

Williams Lake: **CKWL** (Freq: 570)
Owned by: **Cariboo Central Interior Radio Inc.***
83 South First Ave., Williams Lake, BC V2G 1H4
Tel: 250-392-6551; *Fax:* 250-392-4142
tgard@vistaradio.ca
www.thewolfonline.ca
Tracey Gard, Manager, 250-392-6551 ex

Manitoba

Altona: **CFAM** (Freq: 950)
Owned by: **Golden West Broadcasting Ltd.***
PO Box 950, 125 Centre Ave. East, Altona, MB R0G 0B0
Tel: 204-324-6464; *Fax:* 204-324-8918
arlindueck@goldenwestradio.com
Elmer Hildebrand, President & CEO

Boissevain: **CJRB** (Freq: 1220)
Owned by: **Golden West Broadcasting Ltd.***
Boissevain, MB
Elmer Hildebrand, President & CEO

Brandon: **CKLQ** (Freq: 880)
624 - 14 St. East, Brandon, MB R7A 7E1
Tel: 204-725-0515; *Fax:* 204-726-1270
qcountry@cklq.mb.ca
www.cklq.mb.ca
David Baxter, President
Don Kille, General Manager

Dauphin: **CKDM** (Freq: Broadcasting classic rock, adult contemporary & new country music at 730 AM in Dauphin)
Owned by: **Dauphin Broadcasting Co. Ltd.***
27 - 3rd Ave., Dauphin, MB R7N 0Y5
Tel: 204-638-3230; *Fax:* 204-638-8257
Toll-Free: 866-997-2536
730ckdm@mts.net
www.730ckdm.com
Allan Truman, General Manager

Flin Flon: **CFAR** (Freq: 590)
Owned by: **Arctic Radio (1982) Ltd.***
316 Green St., Flin Flon, MB R8A 0H2
Tel: 204-687-3469; *Fax:* 204-687-6786
cfar@arcticradio.ca
www.arcticradio.ca
Maureen Kozar, Office Manager

Tom O'Brien

Portage la Prairie: **CFRY** (Freq: 920)
Owned by: **Golden West Broadcasting Ltd.***
PO Box 920, 350 River Rd., Portage la Prairie, MB R1N 0N6
Tel: 204-239-5111; *Fax:* 204-857-3456
info@goldenwestradio.com
www.cfryradio.ca

Steinbach: **CHSM** (Freq: 1250)
Owned by: **Golden West Broadcasting Ltd.***
#105, 32 Brandt St., Steinbach, MB R5G 2J7
Tel: 204-326-3737; *Fax:* 204-326-2299
info@goldenwestradio.com
www.am1250online.com

The Pas: **CJAR** (Freq: 1240)
Owned by: **Arctic Radio (1982) Ltd.***
PO Box 2980, 130 - 3rd St. West, The Pas, MB R9A 1R7
Tel: 204-623-5307; *Fax:* 204-623-5337
cjar@arcticradio.ca
www.arcticradio.ca

Thompson: **CHTM** (Freq: 610)
Owned by: **Arctic Radio (1982) Ltd.***
103 Cree Rd., Thompson, MB R8N 0B9
Tel: 204-778-7361; *Fax:* 204-778-5252
chtm@arcticradio.ca
www.arcticradio.ca
Tom O'Brien

Winkler: **CKMW** (Freq: 1570)
Owned by: **Golden West Broadcasting Ltd.***
PO Box 399, #201, 295 Main St., Winkler, MB R6W 4A6
Tel: 204-325-7602; *Fax:* 204-325-2206
info@goldenwestradio.com
www.ckmwradio.com
Elmer Hildebrand

Winnipeg: **CBW** (Freq: 990)
Owned by: **Canadian Broadcasting Corporation***
PO Box 160, 541 Portage Ave., Winnipeg, MB R3C 2H1
Tel: 204-788-3222; *Fax:* 204-788-3227
John Bertrand, Regional Director

Winnipeg: **CFRW** (Freq: 1290)
1445 Pembina Hwy., Winnipeg, MB R3T 5C2
Tel: 204-477-5120; *Fax:* 204-453-0815
info@cfrw.ca
www.cfrw.ca
Chris Brooke, Program Director
Lorne Anderson, Technical Director

Winnipeg: **CHFC** (Freq: 1230)
Owned by: **Canadian Broadcasting Corporation***
c/o CBC Winnipeg, PO Box 160, 541 Portage Ave., Winnipeg, MB R3C 2H1
Tel: 204-788-3222; *Fax:* 204-788-3225
John Bertrand, General Manager

Winnipeg: **CJOB** (Freq: 680)
Owned by: **Corus Entertainment Inc.***
930 Portage Ave., Winnipeg, MB R3G 0P8
Tel: 204-786-2471; *Fax:* 204-783-4512
www.cjob.com

Winnipeg: **CKJS** (Freq: 810)
Owned by: **NewCap Inc.***
520 Corydon Ave., Winnipeg, MB R3L 0P1
Tel: 204-477-1221; *Fax:* 204-453-8244
info@ckjs.com
www.ckjs.com
Tony Carta, President, carta@ckjs.com

†*Winnipeg:* **CKSB** (Freq: 1050)
Owned by: **Canadian Broadcasting Corporation***
607, rue Langevin, Winnipeg, MB R2H 2W2
Tél: 204-788-3236; *Téléc:* 204-788-3245
rene_fontaine@radio-canada.ca
www.radio-canada.ca/regions/manitoba
Gilles Fréchette, Chef des Émissions

Winnipeg: **CMOR** (Freq: closed circuit)
Owned by: **Red River College***
#CM20, 2055 Notre Dame Ave., Winnipeg, MB R3H 0J9
Tel: 204-632-2475; *Fax:* 204-632-7896
cmor@rrc.mb.ca
www.rrcsa.com/index.php?content=cmor
Guy Lissier, Advertising Director

** For details on this company see listing in Major Broadcasting Companies section; † French language station*

New Brunswick

***Campbellton:* CKNB** (Freq: 950)
Owned by: **Maritime Broadcasting System***
100 Water St., Campbellton, NB E3N 3G7
Tel: 506-753-4415; *Fax:* 506-789-9505
cknb@nb.sympatico.ca
www.mbsradio.com/www/cknb/index.html
Claude Arseneault, Manager
Mark Firth, Program Director

†*Caraquet:* CJVA (Freq: 810)
Owned by: **CKLE-FM**
Caraquet, NB

***Fredericton:* CBZ** (Freq: 970)
Owned by: **Canadian Broadcasting Corporation***
PO Box 2200 A, 1160 Regent St., Fredericton, NB E3B 5G4
Tel: 506-451-4000
www.cbc.ca/nb
Susan Mitton, Regional Director - Radio

***Fredericton:* CKHJ** (Freq: 1260)
Owned by: **Astral Media Radio Atlantic***
206 Rookwood Ave., Fredericton, NB E3B 2M2
Tel: 506-454-2444; *Fax:* 506-452-4345
Bob Coy, President

***Moncton:* CBA** (Freq: 1070)
Owned by: **Canadian Broadcasting Corporation***
PO Box 950, 250 University Ave., Moncton, NB E1C 8N8
Tel: 506-853-6666; *Fax:* 506-853-6400
www.cbc.ca/nb
Social Media: twitter.com/cbcnb
Dan Goodyear, Executive Producer, CBC, New Brunsw
Mary-Pat Schutta, Program Manager, CBC, New Brunswick
John Channing, Sales Manager, CBC, New Brunswick

***Saint John:* CFBC** (Freq: Broadcasting oldies of the 50's, 60's and 70's at 930 AM in Saint John. Sister stations: CIOK FM & CJYC FM)
Owned by: **Maritime Broadcasting System***
226 Union St., Saint John, NB E2L 1B1
Tel: 506-658-5100; *Fax:* 506-658-5116
mail@mbsradio.com
www.mbsradio.com

***Sussex:* CJCW** (Freq: 590)
Owned by: **Maritime Broadcasting System***
PO Box 5900, Sussex, NB E4E 5M2
Tel: 506-432-2529; *Fax:* 506-433-4900
cjcw@nbnet.nb.ca
Roger White

Newfoundland & Labrador

***Carbonear:* CHVO** (Freq: 560)
1 CHVO Dr., Carbonear, NL A1Y 1A2
Tel: 709-596-1560; *Fax:* 709-596-8626
Toll-Free: 800-595-1560
www.vocm.com
Aiden Hibbs, Manager

***Corner Brook:* CBY** (Freq: 990)
Owned by: **Canadian Broadcasting Corporation***
PO Box 610, 162 Premier Dr., Corner Brook, NL A2H 6G1
Tel: 709-637-1151; *Fax:* 709-634-8506
www.cbc.ca/nl

***Corner Brook:* CFCB** (Freq: 570)
Owned by: **NewCap Inc.***
PO Box 570, 345 O'Connell Dr., Corner Brook, NL A2H 6H5
Tel: 709-634-4570; *Fax:* 709-634-4081
cfcb@vocm.com
Daryl Stevens, Operation Manager
Darlene Myers, Sales Manager
Mike Murphy, General Manager

***Corner Brook:* CFLW** (Freq: 1340)
Owned by: **Steele Communications***
PO Box 570, 345 O'Connel Dr., Corner Brook, NL A2H 6H5
Tel: 709-282-3601

***Gander:* CBG-AM** (Freq: 1400)
Owned by: **Canadian Broadcasting Corporation (CBC)***
PO Box 369, Gander, NL A1V 1W7
Tel: 709-256-4311; *Fax:* 709-651-2021
Toll-Free: 800-563-7933
www.cbc.ca/nl; www.cbc.ca/radio
Social Media: www.facebook.com/radiocbc; www.twitter.com/cbcradio
Other information: Phone, Transmission Information: 1-888-353-7006; TDD: 1-866-220-6045
Maureen Anonsen, Manager, Partnership & Communications
Debbie Hynes, Senior Officer, Communications, 709-576-5150
Wayne Tilley, Manager, Accounts, 709-576-5019

***Gander:* CKGA** (Freq: 650)
Owned by: **NewCap Inc.***
PO Box 650, Gander, NL A1V 1X2
Tel: 709-651-3650; *Fax:* 709-651-2542
ckga.newsroom@nf.sympatico.ca

***Grand Falls-Windsor:* CBT-AM** (Freq: 540)
Owned by: **Canadian Broadcasting Corporation (CBC)***
PO Box 218, 2 Harris Ave., Grand Falls-Windsor, NL A2A 2Y2
Tel: 709-489-2102; *Fax:* 709-489-1055
Toll-Free: 800-563-7933
www.cbc.ca/nl; www.cbc.ca/radio
Social Media: www.facebook.com/radiocbc; www.twitter.com/cbcradio
Other information: Phone, Transmission Information: 1-888-353-7006
Denise Wilson, Managing Director, Newfoundland & Labrador
Kathy Porter, Executive Producer, English Radio
Debbie Hynes, Senior Officer, Communications, 709-576-5150

***Grand Falls-Windsor:* CKCM** (Freq: 620)
Owned by: **NewCap Inc.***
PO Box 620, 35A Grenfell Heights, Grand Falls-Windsor, NL A2A 2K2
Tel: 709-489-2192; *Fax:* 709-489-8626
ckcm@vocm.com
John Steele
John Murphy

***Grand Falls-Windsor:* CKIM** (Freq: 1240)
VOCM Radio Newfoundland Ltd., PO Box 620, 35 Grenfell Heights, Grand Falls-Windsor, NL A2A 2K2
Tel: 709-489-2192; *Fax:* 709-489-8626

***Happy Valley-Goose Bay:* CFLN** (Freq: 1230)
Owned by: **NewCap Inc.***
PO Box 160 C, 176 Hamilton River Rd., Happy Valley-Goose Bay, NL A0P 1C0
Tel: 709-896-2968; *Fax:* 709-896-8708

***Marystown:* CHCM** (Freq: 740)
Owned by: **NewCap Inc.***
PO Box 560, Ville Marie Dr., Marystown, NL A0E 2M0
Tel: 709-279-2560; *Fax:* 709-279-3538
Russell Murphy, General Manager

***Mount Pearl:* VOAR** (Freq: 1210)
1041 Topsail Rd., Mount Pearl, NL A1N 5E9
Tel: 709-745-8627; *Fax:* 709-745-1600
Toll-Free: 800-563-1991
voar@voar.org
www.voar.org
Sherry Griffin, Station Manager

***Port au Choix:* CFNW** (Freq: 790)
Owned by: **CFCB**
Port au Choix, NL

***St. John's:* CBN-AM** (Freq: 640)
Owned by: **Canadian Broadcasting Corporation (CBC)***
PO Box 12010 A, St. John's, NL A1B 3T8
Tel: 709-576-5000; *Fax:* 709-576-5234
Toll-Free: 800-563-7933
www.cbc.ca/nl; www.cbc.ca/radio
Social Media: www.facebook.com/radiocbc; www.twitter.com/cbcradio
Other information: Phone, CBC Radio One Newsroom: 709-576-5225
Denise Wilson, Managing Director, Newfoundland & Labrador
Kathy Porter, Executive Producer, English Radio
Maureen Anonsen, Manager, Partnership & Communications, 709-576-5013
Debbie Hynes, Senior Officer, Communications, 709-576-5150

***St. John's:* CJYQ** (Freq: 930)
Owned by: **NewCap Inc.***
PO Box 8590 A, 391 Kenmount Rd., St. John's, NL A1B 3P5
Tel: 709-726-5590; *Fax:* 709-726-4633
www.radionewfoundland.net
John Murphy, General Manager
Bob Templeton, President
Hilary Montbourquette, Operations Manager

***St. John's:* CKVO** (Freq: 710)
Owned by: **NewCap Inc.***
VOCM(AM), PO Box 8590 A, 391 Kenmount Rd., St. John's, NL A1B 3P5
Tel: 709-466-2710; *Fax:* 709-726-8626
feedback@vocm.com
www.vocm.com
John Murphy, General Manager

***St. John's:* VOCM** (Freq: 590)
Owned by: **NewCap Inc.***
PO Box 8590, 391 Kenmount Rd., St. John's, NL A1B 3P5
Tel: 709-726-5590; *Fax:* 709-726-4633
feedback@vocm.com
www.vocm.com

***St. Johns':* VOWR** (Freq: 800)
Owned by: **VOWR Radio Board***
PO Box 7430, Patrick St., St. Johns', NL A1E 3Y5
Tel: 709-579-9233; *Fax:* 709-579-9232
vowr@vowr.org
www.vowr.org
Marvin Barnes, Chair
John Tessier, Station Manager
Brian Wentzell, Treasurer

***Stephenville:* CFGN** (Freq: 1230)
Owned by: **NewCap Inc.***
60 West St., Stephenville, NL A2N 1C6
Tel: 709-643-2191; *Fax:* 709-643-5025
cfsx@vocm.com

***Stephenville:* CFSX** (Freq: 870)
Owned by: **NewCap Inc.***
60 West St., Stephenville, NL A2N 1C6
Tel: 709-643-2191; *Fax:* 709-643-5025
cfsx@vocm.com
Gerry Murphy, Manager

Northwest Territories

***Inuvik:* CFCT** (Freq: 600)
Owned by: **Canadian Broadcasting Corporation***
Radio Station CHAK, Bag 8, Bag # 8, Inuvik, NT X0E 0T0
Tel: 867-777-7600; *Fax:* 867-777-7640
Peter Skinner, General Manager

***Inuvik:* CHAK** (Freq: 860)
Owned by: **Canadian Broadcasting Corporation***
155 MacKenzie Rd., Bag Service No. 8, Inuvik, NT X0E 0T0
Tel: 867-920-5400; *Fax:* 867-777-7640
www.cbc.ca/north

***Yellowknife:* CFYK** (Freq: 1340)
Owned by: **Canadian Broadcasting Corporation***
PO Box 160, 5002 Forest Dr., Yellowknife, NT X1A 2N2
Tel: 867-920-5400; *Fax:* 867-920-5440
www.cbc.ca/north

Nova Scotia

***Amherst:* CKDH** (Freq: 900)
Owned by: **Maritime Broadcasting System***
32 Church St., Amherst, NS B4H 4B8
Tel: 902-667-3875; *Fax:* 902-667-4490
ckdh@ckdh.net
www.ckdh.net
Gary Crowell, General Manager

***Digby:* CKDY** (Freq: 1420)
Owned by: **Maritime Broadcasting System***
53 Sydney St., Digby, NS
Tel: 902-245-2111; *Fax:* 902-245-9720
avr@avrnetwork.com
www.avrnetwork.com

***Halifax:* CFDR** (Freq: 780)
Owned by: **NewCap Inc.***
PO Box 9316 A, Halifax, NS B3K 6B2
Tel: 902-453-2530; *Fax:* 902-453-3132
www.780kixx.ca
Ted Hyland, General Manager

** For details on this company see listing in Major Broadcasting Companies section; † French language station*

***Halifax:* CFSM** (Freq: 550)
Student Union Bldg., 5th Fl., St. Mary's University, Halifax, NS B3H 3C3
Tel: 902-496-8776; *Fax:* 902-425-4636
cfsm@squid.stmarys.ca
Kevin Smith, Station Manager
Mark Lee, Program Director

***Halifax:* CJCH** (Freq: 920)
PO Box 9316, RPO, CSC, Halifax, NS B3K 6A7
Tel: 902-453-2524; *Fax:* 902-453-3132
Scott Bodnarchuck, General Manager

***Middleton:* CKAD** (Freq: 1350)
Owned by: **Maritime Broadcasting System***
PO Box 550, 10 Bridge St., Middleton, NS B0S 1P0
Tel: 902-825-3429; *Fax:* 902-825-6009
avr@avrnetwork.com
www.avrnetwork.com
Dianne Best, General Manager

***New Glasgow:* CKEC** (Freq: 1320)
Owned by: **Hector Broadcasting Co. Ltd.***
PO Box 519, 84 Provost St., New Glasgow, NS B2H 5E7
Tel: 902-752-4200; *Fax:* 902-755-2468
ckec@ckec.com
www.ckec.com
Michael Freeman, Vice-President
D.B. Freeman, CEO

***Sydney:* CBI** (Freq: CBC Radio One; 1140AM)
Owned by: **Canadian Broadcasting Corporation***
285 Alexandra St., Sydney, NS B1S 2E8
Tel: 902-539-5050; *Fax:* 902-563-1562
www.cbc.ca
Andrew Cochran, Managing Director for the Maritimes

***Sydney:* CHER** (Freq: 950)
Owned by: **Maritime Broadcasting System***
318 Charlotte St., Sydney, NS B1P 1C8
Tel: 902-564-5596; *Fax:* 902-562-1873
www.capebretonradio.com

***Sydney:* CJCB** (Freq: 1270)
Owned by: **Maritime Broadcasting System***
318 Charlotte St., Sydney, NS B1P 1C8
Tel: 902-564-5596; *Fax:* 902-564-1873
www.cjcbradio.com

***Windsor:* CFAB** (Freq: 1450)
Owned by: **Maritime Broadcasting System***
169A Water St., Windsor, NS B0N 2T0
Tel: 902-798-2111; *Fax:* 902-798-8140
avr@avrnetwork.com
www.avrnetwork.com

Nunavut

***Iqaluit:* CFFB** (Freq: 1230)
Owned by: **Canadian Broadcasting Corporation***
PO Box 490, Iqaluit, NU X0A 0H0
Tel: 867-979-6100; *Fax:* 867-979-6147
patrick_nagle@cbc.ca
cbc.ca/north
Patrick Nagle, Area Manager

Ontario

***Atikokan:* CKDR-6** (Freq: 1240)
Owned by: **CKDR-FM**
Atikokan, ON

***Belleville:* CJBQ** (Freq: 800)
PO Box 488, 10 Front St. South, Belleville, ON K8N 5B2
Tel: 613-969-5555; *Fax:* 613-969-8122
info@cjbq.com
www.cjbq.com
Bill Morton

***Brampton:* CIAO** (Freq: 530)
Owned by: **CKMW Radio Ltd.**
5302 Dundas St. West, Brampton, ON M9B 1B2
Tel: 416-213-1035; *Fax:* 416-233-8617
www.am530.ca
Bill Evanov, President

***Brantford:* CKPC** (Freq: 1380)
571 West St., Brantford, ON N3T 5P8
Tel: 519-759-1000; *Fax:* 519-753-1470
am1380@ckpc.on.ca
www.ckpc.on.ca

Richard Buchanan, President/General Manager

***Chatham:* CFCO** (Freq: 630)
Owned by: **Blackburn Radio Inc.***
PO Box 100, 117 Keil Dr. South, Chatham, ON N7M 5K1
Tel: 519-352-3000; *Fax:* 519-354-2880
info@630cfco.com
www.630cfco.com

***Cobourg:* CHUC** (Freq: 1450)
PO Box 520, Cobourg, ON K9A 4L3
Tel: 905-372-5401; *Fax:* 905-372-6280
chuc@chuc1450.com
www.chuc1450.com
Don Conway, President

***Cornwall:* CJUL** (Freq: 1220)
Owned by: **Corus Entertainment Inc.***
709 Cotton Mill St., Cornwall, ON K6H 7K7
Tel: 613-932-5180; *Fax:* 613-938-0355
Toll-Free: 888-678-8122
www.am1220.ca
Scott Armstrong, General Manager, scott@seawayvalley.com

***Ear Falls:* CKDR-4** (Freq: 1450)
Owned by: **CKDR-FM**
Ear Falls, ON

***Guelph:* CJOY** (Freq: 1460)
Owned by: **Corus Entertainment Inc.***
75 Speedvale Ave. East, Guelph, ON N1E 6M3
Tel: 519-824-7000; *Fax:* 519-824-4118
cjoy@cjoy.com
www.cjoy.com

***Hamilton:* CHAM** (Freq: 820)
Owned by: **Standard Radio Office***
#401, 883 Upper Wentworth St., Hamilton, ON L9A 4Y6
Tel: 905-574-1150; *Fax:* 905-575-6429
Toll-Free: 866-559-7677
www.820cham.com
Tom Cooke, Vice-President & General Manager

***Hamilton:* CHML** (Freq: 900)
Owned by: **Corus Entertainment Inc.***
#900, 875 Main St. West, Hamilton, ON L8S 4R1
Tel: 905-521-9900; *Fax:* 905-521-2306
www.900chml.com

***Hamilton:* CKOC** (Freq: 1150)
Owned by: **Standard Radio Office***
#401, 883 Upper Wentworth St., Hamilton, ON L9A 4Y6
Tel: 905-574-1150; *Fax:* 905-575-6429
ckoc@oldies1150.com
www.oldies1150.com
Tom Cooke, Manager

***Hudson:* CKDR-3** (Freq: 1450)
Owned by: **CKDR-FM**
Hudson, ON

***Ignace:* CKDR-1** (Freq: 1340)
Owned by: **CKDR-FM**
Ignace, ON

***Kingston:* CKLC** (Freq: 1380)
Owned by: **CTVglobemedia Inc./CHUM Radio Kingston***
PO Box 1380, #10, 993 Princess St., Kingston, ON K7L 1H3
Tel: 613-544-1380; *Fax:* 613-546-9751
gperrin@chumkingston.com
Gary Perrin, General Manager

***Kitchener:* CKGL** (Freq: 570)
Owned by: **Rogers Broadcasting Ltd.***
305 King St. West, 11th Fl., Kitchener, ON N2G 4E4
Tel: 519-743-2611; *Fax:* 519-743-7510
news570@rogers.com
www.570news.com

***Kitchener:* CKKW** (Freq: 1090)
Owned by: **CKKW**
Kitchener, ON

***London:* CFPL** (Freq: 980)
Owned by: **Corus Entertainment Inc.***
380 Wellington St., London, ON N6A 5B5
Tel: 519-931-6000; *Fax:* 519-679-1967
www.am980.ca
Dave Farough, General Manager

***London:* CJBK** (Freq: 1290)
Owned by: **Standard Radio Office***
743 Wellington Rd. South, London, ON N6C 4R5
Tel: 519-686-2525; *Fax:* 519-686-9067
www.cjbk.com
Braden Doerr, President & General Manager, bdoerr@sri.ca

***London:* CKSL** (Freq: 1410)
Owned by: **Standard Radio Office***
743 Wellington St. South, London, ON N6C 4R5
Tel: 519-686-2525; *Fax:* 519-686-3658
www.oldies1410.com
Braden Doerr, General Manager

***Moosonee:* CHMO** (Freq: 1450)
Owned by: **James Bay Broadcasting Corp. Inc.***
PO Box 400, 38 First St., Moosonee, ON P0L 1Y0
Tel: 705-336-2466; *Fax:* 705-336-2186
John Kirk, President

***North Bay:* CKAT** (Freq: 600)
Owned by: **Rogers Broadcasting Ltd.***
PO Box 3000, 743 Main St. East, North Bay, ON P1B 8K8
Tel: 705-474-2000; *Fax:* 705-474-7761
Peter McKeown, General Manager

***Oakville:* CJMR** (Freq: 1320)
Owned by: **CJMR 1320 Radio Ltd.***
284 Church St., Oakville, ON L6J 7N2
Tel: 905-271-1320; *Fax:* 905-842-1250
hmcdonald@whiteoaksgroup.ca
Harry H. McDonald, Vice-President & General Manager

***Oakville:* CJYE** (Freq: 1250)
Broadcast Centre, 284 Church St., Oakville, ON L6J 7N2
Tel: 905-845-2821; *Fax:* 905-842-1250
contact@joy1250.ca
www.joy1250.ca
Harry H. McDonald, General Manager
Michael H. Caine, President

***Ottawa:* CBOF-1** (Freq: 990)
Owned by: **Canadian Broadcasting Corporation***
PO Box 3220 C, 250 Lanark Ave., Ottawa, ON K1Y 1E4
Tel: 613-724-1200; *Fax:* 613-562-8447
commho@ottawa.cbc.ca
www.cbc.ca
Denis Simard, General Manager

***Ottawa:* CFGO** (Freq: 1200)
87 George St., Ottawa, ON K1N 9H7
Tel: 613-750-1200; *Fax:* 613-739-4040
dmitchell@team1200.com
www.team1200.com
Dianne Wilson

***Ottawa:* CFRA** (Freq: 580)
87 George St., Ottawa, ON K1N 9H7
Tel: 613-789-2486; *Fax:* 613-523-6423
www.cfra.com

***Ottawa:* CIWW** (Freq: 1310)
Owned by: **Rogers Broadcasting Ltd.***
2001 Thurston Dr., Ottawa, ON K1G 6C9
Tel: 613-736-2001; *Fax:* 613-736-2002
www.oldies1310.com
Scott Parsons, General Manager

***Owen Sound:* CFOS** (Freq: 560)
Owned by: **Bayshore Broadcasting Corporation***
PO Box 280, 270 - 9th St. East, Owen Sound, ON N4K 5P5
Tel: 519-376-2030; *Fax:* 519-371-4242
bayshore@bayshorebroadcasting.ca
www.bayshorebroadcasting.ca
Ross Kentner, General Manager, rkentner@bayshorebroadcasting.ca
Kevin Brown, General Sales Manager, kbrown@bayshorebroadcasting.ca
Rob Brignell, Director, Marketing & Business Development, rbrignell@bayshorebroadcasting.ca

***Peterborough:* CKPT** (Freq: 99.7)
PO Box 177, 59 George St. North, Peterborough, ON K9J 6Y8
Tel: 705-742-8844; *Fax:* 705-742-1417
energy997@chumradio.com
www.energy997.ca
Steve Fawcett, General Manager

** For details on this company see listing in Major Broadcasting Companies section; † French language station*

***Peterborough:* CKRU** (Freq: 980)
Owned by: **Corus Entertainment Inc.***
151 King St., Peterborough, ON K9J 2R8
Tel: 705-748-6101; *Fax:* 705-742-7708
www.980kruz.ca

***Red Lake:* CKDR-5** (Freq: 1340)
Owned by: **CKDR-FM**
Red Lake, ON

***Richmond Hill:* CHKT** (Freq: 1430)
Owned by: **Fairchild Radio***
#7-8, 135 East Beaver Creek Rd., Richmond Hill, ON L4B 1E2
Tel: 905-763-3360; *Fax:* 905-889-9828
www.fairchildradio.com
Cyril Lai, General Manager

***Sarnia:* CHOK** (Freq: 1070)
Owned by: **Blackburn Radio Inc.***
1415 London Rd., Sarnia, ON N7S 1P6
Tel: 519-542-5500; *Fax:* 519-542-1520
www.chok.com

***Sioux Lookout:* CKDR-2** (Freq: 1400)
Owned by: **CKDR-FM**
Sioux Lookout, ON

***St Catharines:* CHSC** (Freq: 1220)
36 Queenston St., St Catharines, ON L2R 2Y9
Tel: 905-682-6691; *Fax:* 905-682-9434
info@1220chsc.ca
www.1220chsc.ca

***St Catharines:* CKTB** (Freq: 610)
Owned by: **Standard Radio Office***
12 Yates St., St Catharines, ON L2R 6Z4
Tel: 905-684-1176; *Fax:* 905-684-4800
newsroom@610cktb.com
www.610cktb.com
Clyde Ross, clyder@610cktb.com

***Stratford:* CJCS** (Freq: 1240)
376 Romeo St. South, Stratford, ON N5A 4T9
Tel: 519-271-2450; *Fax:* 519-271-3102
info@cjcsradio.com
www.cjcsradio.com
Steve Rae, President

***Sudbury:* CIGM** (Freq: 790)
Owned by: **Rogers Broadcasting Ltd.***
880 Lasalle Blvd., Sudbury, ON P3A 1X5
Tel: 705-566-4480; *Fax:* 705-560-7232
www.790cigm.com
Claude Beaudoin, President
Jim Hamm, General Manager

***Thunder Bay:* CKPR** (Freq: 580)
Owned by: **CJSD Inc.***
87 Hill St. North, Thunder Bay, ON P7A 5V6
Tel: 807-346-2600; *Fax:* 807-345-9923
radio@ckpr.com
www.ckpr.com

***Tillsonburg:* CKOT** (Freq: 1510)
PO Box 10, 77 Broadway St., Tillsonburg, ON N4G 4H3
Tel: 519-842-4281; *Fax:* 519-842-4284
jlamers@country1510.com
John D. Lamers, President & General Manager

***Toronto:* AM 740**
#205, 550 Queen St. East, Toronto, ON M5A 1V2
Tel: 416-544-0740; *Fax:* 905-842-1250
www.am740.ca
Social Media:
www.facebook.com/pages/AM740-Zoomer-Radio/114114771541
George Grant, President/CEO, ggrant@classical963fm.com
Gene Stevens, Director, Programming & Operations, gstevens@am740radio.ca
Christopher Randall, Director, Promotions, christopher@mzmedia.com
Steven J. Shiaman, Director, Retail Sales, sshiaman@am740radio.ca

***Toronto:* CFMJ** (Freq: 640)
Owned by: **Corus Entertainment Inc.***
#1600, 1 Dundas St. West, Toronto, ON M5G 1Z3
Tel: 416-221-6400; *Fax:* 416-847-3300
www.640toronto.com

***Toronto:* CFRB** (Freq: 1010)
Owned by: **Standard Radio Office***
2 St. Clair Ave. West, 2nd Fl., Toronto, ON M4V 1L6
Tel: 416-924-5711; *Fax:* 416-872-8683
gm@cfrb.com
cfrb.com
Pat Holiday, Vice-President & General Manager

***Toronto:* CFTR** (Freq: 680)
Owned by: **Rogers Broadcasting Ltd.***
777 Jarvis St., Toronto, ON M4Y 3B7
Tel: 416-935-8468; *Fax:* 416-935-8480
680info@680news.com
www.680news.com
John Hinnen, Vice-President, Radio News Programming
Derek Berghuis, General Manager

***Toronto:* CHIN** (Freq: 1540)
622 College St., Toronto, ON M6G 1B6
Tel: 416-531-9991; *Fax:* 416-531-5274
info@chinradio.com
www.chinradio.com
Leonard Lombardi, President

***Toronto:* CHWO** (Freq: 740)
PO Box 740 A, Toronto, ON M5W 4K6
Tel: 416-544-0740; *Fax:* 905-842-1250
general@am740radio.ca
www.am740.ca

†*Toronto:* CJBC (Freq: 860)
Owned by: **Canadian Broadcasting Corporation***
CP 500 A, 205 Wellington St. West, Toronto, ON M5W 1E6
Tél: 416-205-2522; *Téléc:* 416-205-5622

***Toronto:* CJCL** (Freq: 590)
Owned by: **Rogers Broadcasting Ltd.***
The Fan, 777 Jarvis St., Toronto, ON M4Y 3B7
Tel: 416-935-0590; *Fax:* 416-413-4116
contact@fan590.com
www.fan590.com
Nelson Millmen, Station Manager

***Toronto:* CP24 Radio 1050** (Freq: 1050)
299 Queen St. West, Toronto, ON M5V 2Z5
Tel: 416-384-2700
now@cp24.com
www.cp24.com
Robert McLaughlin, Vice President/General Manager, CP24

***Toronto:* CRSC** (Freq: closed circuit)
Owned by: **Seneca College***
1750 Finch Ave. East, Toronto, ON M2J 2X5
Tel: 416-491-5050; *Fax:* 416-756-2765

***Toronto:* CSCA** (Freq: closed circuit)
Owned by: **Seneca College***
#2051, 70 The Pond Rd., Toronto, ON M3J 3M6
Tel: 416-491-5050; *Fax:* 416-739-1856
scainfo@senecac.on.ca
scainfo@senecac.on.ca

***Waterloo:* CKKW** (Freq: 1090)
#207, 255 King St. North, Waterloo, ON N2J 4V2
Tel: 519-884-4470; *Fax:* 519-884-6482
www.oldies1090.com

†*Windsor:* CBEF (Freq: 540)
Owned by: **Canadian Broadcasting Corporation (CBC)***
825 Riverside Dr. West, Windsor, ON N9A 5K9
Tél: 519-255-3411; *Ligne sans frais:* 800-551-2985
auditoire@radio-canada.ca; liaison@radio-canada.ca
www.radio-canada.ca/radio

***Windsor:* CKLW** (Freq: 800)
1640 Ouellette Ave., Windsor, ON N8X 1L1
Tel: 519-258-8888; *Fax:* 519-258-0182
www.am800cklw.com
Eric Proksch, Vice President/General Manager

***Windsor:* CKWW** (Freq: 580)
1640 Ouellette Ave., Windsor, ON N8X 1L1
Tel: 519-258-8888; *Fax:* 519-258-0182
info@am580radio.com
www.am580radio.com
Eric Proksch, Vice President/General Manager

***Wingham:* CKNX** (Freq: 920)
Owned by: **Blackburn Radio Inc.***
215 Carling Terrace, Wingham, ON N0G 2W0
Tel: 519-357-1310; *Fax:* 519-357-1897
info@am920.ca
www.am920.ca

Prince Edward Island

***Charlottetown:* CFCY** (Freq: 630)
Owned by: **Maritime Broadcasting System***
5 Prince St., Charlottetown, PE C1A 4P4
Tel: 902-892-1066; *Fax:* 902-566-1338
www.cfcy.pe.ca

Québec

†*Alma:* CFGT (Freq: 1270)
Owned by: **Groupe Radio Antenne 6***
#200, 460, rue Sacré-Coeur ouest, Alma, QC G8B 1L9
Tél: 418-662-6673; *Téléc:* 418-662-6070
Marc-André Levesque

***Baie-Comeau:* CFRP** (Freq: 620)
907, rue de Puyjalon, Baie-Comeau, QC G5C 1N3
Tel: 418-589-3771; *Fax:* 418-589-9086
www.chlc.com
Mike Minville, directeur de la programmation, programmes971-1005@globetrotter.net

†*Chibougamau:* CJMD (Freq: 1240)
Owned by: **Groupe Radio Antenne 6***
539, 3e rue, Chibougamau, QC G8P 1N8
Tél: 418-275-1831; *Téléc:* 418-275-2475
Marc-André Levesque

†*Chicoutimi:* CKRS (Freq: 590)
Owned by: **Corus Québec***
CP 1090, 121, rue Racine est, Chicoutimi, QC G7H 5G4
Tél: 418-545-2577; *Téléc:* 418-545-9186
auditoire@ckrs.ca
www.ckrs.ca
Michel Gagnon

†*Gaspé:* CHGM (Freq: 1150)
Owned by: **CHNC**
Gaspé, QC

†*Gatineau:* CJRC (Freq: 1150)
Owned by: **Corus Entertainment Inc.***
150, rue Edmonton, Gatineau, QC J8Y 3S6
Tél: 819-561-8801; *Téléc:* 819-561-3333
www.cjrc1150.com
Richard Lachance

†*La Tuque:* CFLM (Freq: 1240)
CP 850, 529, rue St-Louis, La Tuque, QC G9X 3P6
Tél: 819-523-4575; *Téléc:* 819-676-8000

***Laval:* CFAV** (Freq: 1570)
Owned by: **Diffusion Laval Inc***
2040, autoroute Laval, Laval, QC H7S 2M9
Tel: 450-680-1570; *Fax:* 450-680-1570
radio@boomer1570.ca.ca
www.boomer1570.ca
Claire Bellefeville, General Manager

***Montréal:* CFMB** (Freq: 1280)
35, rue York, Montréal, QC H3Z 2Z5
Tel: 514-483-2362; *Fax:* 514-483-1362
admin@cfmb.ca
www.cfmb.ca
Anne-Marie Stanczykowski, Vice-President
Andrew Mielewczyk

***Montréal:* CINF** (Freq: 690)
Owned by: **Corus Entertainment Inc.***
#1100, 800 rue de Gauchetière Ouest, Montréal, QC H5A 1M1
Tel: 514-787-0690; *Fax:* 514-849-0733
www.info690.com
Maurice Tietolman

***Montréal:* CINW** (Freq: 940)
Owned by: **Corus Entertainment Inc.***
#333, 215, rue St-Jacques, Montréal, QC H2Y 1M6
Tel: 514-849-0940; *Fax:* 519-849-0733
www.940news.com

** For details on this company see listing in Major Broadcasting Companies section; † French language station*

***Montréal:* CJAD** (Freq: 800)
Owned by: **Standard Radio Office***
1411, rue du Fort, Montréal, QC H3H 2R1
Tel: 514-989-2523; *Fax:* 514-989-3847
www.cjad.com
Rob Braide, Vice-President & General Manager

***Montréal:* CJLO** (Freq: closed circuit)
Owned by: **Concordia University***
#CC-430, 7141, rue Sherbrooke ouest, Montréal, QC H4B 1R6
Tel: 514-848-8663; *Fax:* 514-848-7450
manager@cjlo.com
www.cjlo.com

***Montréal:* CJWI** (Freq: 1610)
Owned by: **CPAM Radio Union.com Inc***
3733 Jarry Est, 2e étage, Montréal, QC H1Z 2G1
Tel: 514-287-1288; *Fax:* 514-287-3299
info@cpam-radiounion.com
www.cpam-radiounion.com
Jean-Ernest Pierre

†*Montréal:* CKAC (Freq: 730)
#1100, 800, rue de la Gauchetière Ouest, Montréal, QC H5A 1M1
Tél: 514-787-0730; *Téléc:* 514-787-7943
www.ckac.com
Sylvain Chamberland, Vice-président exécutif-Directeur g

***Montréal:* CKGM** (Freq: 990)
#300, 1310, av Greene, Montréal, QC H3Z 2B5
Tel: 514-931-4487; *Fax:* 514-931-4079
writetous@team990.com
www.team990.com
Jim Waters, President, CHUM Limited

†*New Carlisle:* CHNC (Freq: 610)
153, boul Gérard-D.-Levesque, New Carlisle, QC G0C 1Z0
Tél: 418-752-2215; *Téléc:* 418-752-6939
radiochnc@globetrotter.net
www.radiochnc.com
Francis Rémillard, General Manager, francis@radiochnc.com
Brigitte Paquet, Sales Director, brigitte@radiochnc.com

†*Québec:* CHRC (Freq: 800)
2136, ch Sainte-Foy, Québec, QC G1V 1R8
Tél: 418-688-8080; *Téléc:* 418-682-8429
www.chrc.com

†*Rimouski:* CJBR (Freq: 900)
Owned by: **Canadian Broadcasting Corporation***
273, rue St-Jean Baptiste ouest, Rimouski, QC G5L 4J8
Tél: 418-723-2217; *Téléc:* 418-723-6126
www.radio-canada.ca

†*Rimouski:* Radio étudiante CAJT (Freq: Radio étudiante du Cégep de Rimouski; programmation; discothèque contenant plus de 6 200 albums répertoriés sous différents supports; deux postes Internet.)
Owned by: **CEGEP de Rimouski***
Cégep de Rimouski, 60, rue de l'Évêché ouest, Rimouski, QC G5L 4H6
Tél: 418-723-1880; *Téléc:* 418-724-4961
Ligne sans frais: 800-463-0617
radio.cajt@mail.com; infoscol@cegep-rimouski.qc.ca
www.cegep-rimouski.qc.ca
Philippe Daigle, Contact

†*Roberval:* CFED (Freq: 1340)
Owned by: **Groupe Radio Antenne 6***
568, boul St-Joseph, Roberval, QC G8H 2K6
Tél: 418-275-1831; *Téléc:* 418-275-2475
Marc-André Levesque

***Saint-Constant:* CJMS** (Freq: 1040)
143, rue St-Pierre, Saint-Constant, QC J5A 2G9
Tel: 514-990-2567; *Fax:* 450-632-1052
cjms1040@citenet.net
www.cjms.ca
Jean-François Dubois

***Shawinigan:* CKSM** (Freq: 1220)
Owned by: **Astral Media Inc.***
6183, boul Royal, Shawinigan, QC G9N 8P3
Tel: 819-539-4899

†*Sherbrooke:* CHLT (Freq: 630)
Owned by: **Astral Media Inc.***
4020, boul de Portland, Sherbrooke, QC J1L 2V6
Tél: 819-563-6363; *Téléc:* 819-566-4222
Ligne sans frais: 800-842-2458
www.chlt630.com

†*Trois-Rivières:* CHLN (Freq: 550)
Owned by: **Astral Media Inc.***
#1200, 1500, rue Royale, Trois-Rivières, QC G9A 4J4
Tél: 819-376-3556; *Téléc:* 819-374-3222
nouvelles@chln550.com
www.chln550.com

Saskatchewan

***Estevan:* CJSL** (Freq: 1280)
Owned by: **Golden West Broadcasting Ltd.***
#200, 1236 - 5th St., Estevan, SK S4A 0Z6
Tel: 306-634-1280; *Fax:* 306-634-6364
info@goldenwestradio.com
Laverne Pappel, Station Manager

†*Gravelbourg:* CBKF-1 (Freq: Première Chaîne; 690AM)
Owned by: **CBKF-FM; Société Radio-Canada**
Gravelbourg, SK

***Kindersley:* CFYM** (Freq: 1210)
Owned by: **CJYM**
Kindersley, SK

***Melfort:* CKJH** (Freq: 750)
Radio CJVR Ltd., PO Box 750, 611 Main St. North, Melfort, SK S0E 1A0
Tel: 306-752-2587; *Fax:* 306-752-5932
Toll-Free: 800-668-2587
sales@cjvr.com
www.ck750.com
Ken Singer, Vice President

***Moose Jaw:* CHAB** (Freq: 800)
Owned by: **Golden West Broadcasting Ltd.***
1704 Main St. North, Moose Jaw, SK S6J 1L4
Tel: 306-694-0800; *Fax:* 306-692-8880
www.chabradio.com

***North Battleford:* CJNB** (Freq: 1050)
PO Box 1460, 1711 - 100th St., North Battleford, SK S9A 2Z5
Tel: 306-445-2477; *Fax:* 306-445-4599
cjnb@rawlco.com
David Dekker

***Prince Albert:* CKBI** (Freq: 900)
Owned by: **RAWLCO Radio Ltd.***
PO Box 900, 1316 Central Ave., Prince Albert, SK S6V 7R4
Tel: 306-763-7421; *Fax:* 306-764-1850
Toll-Free: 800-667-9000
900ckbi@rawlco.com
www.900ckbi.com
Jim Scarrow, General Manager/Vice-President

***Regina:* CBK-FM** (Freq: 96.9)
Owned by: **Canadian Broadcasting Corporation (CBC)***
PO Box 540 Main, 2440 Broad St., Regina, SK S4P 4A1
Tel: 306-347-9540
www.cbc.ca/sask; www.cbc.ca/radio2
Other information: Phone, Regina Radio: 306-347-9692
Lenora Sturge, Coordinator, Program Marketing, 306-347-9714
Justin Anders, Regional Web Developer, 306-788-3285

***Regina:* CJME** (Freq: 980)
Owned by: **RAWLCO Radio Ltd.***
#210, 2401 Saskatchewan Dr., Regina, SK S4P 4H8
Tel: 306-525-0000; *Fax:* 306-347-8557
www.cjme.com

***Regina:* CKRM** (Freq: 620)
Owned by: **Harvard Broadcasting Inc.***
1900 Rose St., Regina, SK S4P 0A9
Tel: 306-546-6200; *Fax:* 306-781-7338
Toll-Free: 866-767-0620
www.620ckrm.com
Michael Olstrom

***Rosetown:* CJYM** (Freq: 1330)
Owned by: **Dace Broadcasting Corp.**
PO Box 490, Rosetown, SK S0L 2V0
Tel: 306-882-2686; *Fax:* 306-882-3037
www.cjym.com
D.W. (Wax) Williams, President

Dennis Dyck, Vice-President/General Manager

†*Saskatoon:* CBKF-2 (Freq: Première Chaîne; 860AM)
Owned by: **CBKF-FM; Société Radio Canada***
144 - 2nd Ave., Saskatoon, SK S7K 1K5
Tél: 306-956-7400; *Téléc:* 306-956-7476
David Kyle, General Manager

***Saskatoon:* CJWW** (Freq: 600)
366 - 3 Ave. South, Saskatoon, SK S7K 1M5
Tel: 306-244-1975; *Fax:* 306-665-5501
cjwwradio@sasktel.net
www.cjwwradio.com
Vic Dubois, General Manager

***Saskatoon:* CKOM** (Freq: 650)
Owned by: **RAWLCO Radio Ltd.***
715 Saskatchewan Cres. West, Saskatoon, SK S7M 5V7
Tel: 306-934-2222; *Fax:* 306-477-0002
www.ckom.com
Ted Farr

***Shaunavon:* CJSN** (Freq: 1490)
Owned by: **Golden West Broadcasting Ltd.***
PO Box 1176, 410 Centre St., Shaunavon, SK S0N 2M0
Tel: 306-297-2671; *Fax:* 306-297-3051
info@goldenwestradio.com
www.cjsn1490.ca

***Swift Current:* CKSW** (Freq: 570)
Owned by: **Golden West Broadcasting Ltd.***
134 Central Ave. North, Swift Current, SK S9H 0L1
Tel: 306-773-4605; *Fax:* 306-773-6390
Toll-Free: 800-821-8073
cmr@goldenwestradio.com
www.ckswradio.ca
Deborah Gager, General Manager & Sales

***Weyburn:* CFSL** (Freq: 1190)
Owned by: **Golden West Broadcasting Ltd.***
PO Box 340, 305 Souris Ave., Weyburn, SK S4H 2K2
Tel: 306-848-1190; *Fax:* 306-842-2720
info@goldenwestradio.com
Laverne Pappel, Station Manager

***Yorkton:* CJGX** (Freq: 940)
120 Smith St. East, Yorkton, SK S3N 3V3
Tel: 306-782-2256; *Fax:* 306-783-4994
country@gx94radio.com
www.gx94radio.com
Lyle Walsh, President
Lyle Walsh, General Manager

Yukon Territory

***Whitehorse:* CFWH** (Freq: 570)
Owned by: **Canadian Broadcasting Corporation***
3103 - 3rd Ave., Whitehorse, YT Y1A 2A2
Tel: 867-668-8400
cbcnorth@cbc.ca
www.cbc.ca/north
Doug Caldwell, Area Manager
Mike Linder, Sr. News Editor

***Whitehorse:* CKRW** (Freq: 610)
Owned by: **Klondike Broadcasting Co.Ltd.***
#203, 4103 - 4th Ave., Whitehorse, YT Y1A 1H6
Tel: 867-668-6100; *Fax:* 867-668-4209
ckrwcopy@ckrw.com
www.ckrw.com
Jennifer Jonstone, General Manager

FM Radio Stations

Alberta

***Blairmore:* CJPR-FM** (Freq: 94.9)
Owned by: **NewCap Inc.***
PO Box 840, Blairmore, AB T0K 0E0
Tel: 403-562-2806; *Fax:* 403-562-8114

***Calgary:* CBR-FM** (Freq: 102.1)
Owned by: **Canadian Broadcasting Corporation***
PO Box 2640, 1724 Westmount Blvd. NW, Calgary, AB T2P 2M7
Tel: 403-521-6000
www.cbc.ca/calgary
Helen Henderson, Deputy Regional Director of Radion

** For details on this company see listing in Major Broadcasting Companies section; † French language station*

***Calgary:* CFGQ-FM** (Freq: 107.3)
Owned by: **Corus Entertainment Inc.***
#105, 630 - 3 Ave. SW, Calgary, AB T2P 4L4
Tel: 403-716-6500; *Fax:* 403-716-2111
www.q107fm.ca
Garth Ross, Music Director

***Calgary:* CHFM-FM** (Freq: 95.9)
Owned by: **Rogers Broadcasting Ltd.***
#240, 2723 - 37 Ave. NE, Calgary, AB T1Y 5R8
Tel: 403-246-9696; *Fax:* 403-246-4126
www.lite96.ca

***Calgary:* CHKF-FM** (Freq: 94.7)
Owned by: **Fairchild Radio***
#109, 2723 - 37 Ave. NE, Calgary, AB T1Y 5R8
Tel: 403-717-1940; *Fax:* 403-717-1945
general@fm947.com
www.fm947.com

***Calgary:* CIBK-FM** (Freq: 98.5)
Owned by: **Standard Radio Office***
1110 Centre St. NE, Calgary, AB T2E 2R2
Tel: 403-240-5800; *Fax:* 403-240-5801
feedback@vibe985.com
www.vibe985.com
Tom Peacock, General Manager

***Calgary:* CIQX-FM** (Freq: 103.1)
Owned by: **NewCap Inc.***
#100, 1110 Centre St. NE, Calgary, AB T2E 2R2
Tel: 403-271-6366; *Fax:* 403-278-6772
feedback@california103.com
www.california103.com
Stephen Peck, General Manager

***Calgary:* CJAY-FM** (Freq: 92.1)
Owned by: **Standard Radio Office***
1110 Centre St. North, Calgary, AB T2E 2R2
Tel: 403-240-5850; *Fax:* 403-240-5801
info@cjay92.com
www.cjay92.com
Tom Peacock, General Manager

***Calgary:* CJSI-FM** (Freq: 88.9)
4510 Macleod Trail South, Calgary, AB T2G 0A4
Tel: 403-276-1111; *Fax:* 403-276-1114
www.cjsi.ca

***Calgary:* CJSW-FM** (Freq: 90.9)
#127, MacEwan Hall, University of Calgary, Calgary, AB T2N 1N4
Tel: 403-220-3902; *Fax:* 403-289-8212
cjswfm@ucalgary.ca
www.cjsw.com
Chad Saunders, Station Manager

***Calgary:* CKIS-FM** (Freq: 96.9)
Owned by: **Rogers Broadcasting Ltd.***
2723 - 37 Ave. NE, Calgary, AB T1Y 5R8
Tel: 403-250-9797; *Fax:* 403-291-4368
www.jackfm.ca

***Calgary:* CKRY-FM** (Freq: 105.1)
Owned by: **Corus Entertainment Inc.***
#105, 630 - 3rd Ave. SW, Calgary, AB T2P 4L4
Tel: 403-716-6500; *Fax:* 403-716-2111
www.country105.com
Garry McKenzie, General Manager

***Calgary:* CMRC-FM** (Freq: 107.5)
4825 Richard Rd. SW, Calgary, AB T3E 6K6
Tel: 403-440-6119; *Fax:* 403-440-6563
www.cmrcradio.ca
Jillian Hunter, Station Manager

***Camrose:* CLCR-FM** (Freq: closed circuit)
4901 - 46 Ave., Camrose, AB T4V 2R3
Tel: 780-679-1541; *Fax:* 780-672-5252
aucsa@augustana.ca
www.augustana.ab.ca/sa
Matthew Gusul, Station Manager

***Canmore:* CHMN-FM** (Freq: 106.5)
Owned by: **Rogers Broadcasting Ltd.***
749 Railway Ave., Canmore, AB T1W 1P2
Tel: 403-678-2222; *Fax:* 403-678-6844

***Cold Lake:* CJXK-FM** (Freq: 95.3)
Owned by: **NewCap Inc.***
5414 - 55 St., Cold Lake, AB T9M 1R5
Tel: 780-594-2459; *Fax:* 780-594-3001
Roger Thorpe

***Drayton Valley:* CIBW-FM** (Freq: 92.9)
Owned by: **The Jim Pattison Broadcast Group***
PO Box 929, 5164 - 52 Ave., Drayton Valley, AB T7A 1V3
Tel: 780-542-9290; *Fax:* 780-542-9319
Toll-Free: 888-884-2448
bwc929@telus.net
Trevor Grinde

***Edmonton:* CBX-FM** (Freq: 90.9)
Owned by: **Canadian Broadcasting Corporation***
Edmonton, AB

***Edmonton:* CFBR-FM** (Freq: 100.3)
Owned by: **Standard Radio Office***
#100, 18520 Stony Plain Rd., Edmonton, AB T5S 2E2
Tel: 780-486-2800; *Fax:* 780-489-6927
www.thebearrocks.com
M. Forbes, General Manager, forbes@worldgate.com

***Edmonton:* CFMG-FM** (Freq: 104.9)
Owned by: **Standard Radio Office***
#100, 18520 Stony Plain Rd., Edmonton, AB T5S 2E2
Tel: 780-435-1049; *Fax:* 780-489-6927
cfmg@sri.ca
www.ezrock1049.com
Marty Forbes, Vice-President & General Manager

***Edmonton:* CFWE-FM** (Freq: 89.9)
13245 - 146th St., Edmonton, AB T5L 4S8
Tel: 780-447-2393; *Fax:* 780-454-2820
cfwe@ammsa.com
www.ammsa.com/cfwe
Bert Crowfoot, General Manager

***Edmonton:* CHBN-FM** (Freq: 91.7)
10212 Jasper Ave., Edmonton, AB T5J 5A3
Tel: 780-424-2222; *Fax:* 780-401-1600
www.thebounce.ca
Gisele Sowa, General Manager

***Edmonton:* CIRK-FM** (Freq: 97.3)
Owned by: **NewCap Inc.***
2394 West Edmonton Mall, #8882, 170 St., Edmonton, AB T5T 4M2
Tel: 780-437-4996; *Fax:* 780-435-0844
www.k-rock973.com
Randy Lemay, General Manager

***Edmonton:* CISN-FM** (Freq: 103.9)
Owned by: **Corus Entertainment Inc.***
5204 - 84 St., Edmonton, AB T6E 5N8
Tel: 780-428-1104; *Fax:* 780-469-5937
info@cisnfm.com
www.cisnfm.com
Doug Rutherford, General Manager

***Edmonton:* CJRY-FM** (Freq: 105.9)
5316 Calgary Trail, Edmonton, AB T6H 4J8
Tel: 780-466-4930; *Fax:* 780-469-5335
www.shinefm.com
Malcolm Hunt, Program Director
Carlo Bruno, Business Manager

***Edmonton:* CJSR-FM** (Freq: 88.5)
#0-09 Students Union Bldg., University of Alberta, Edmonton, AB T6G 2J7
Tel: 780-492-2477; *Fax:* 780-492-3121
www.cjsr.com
Charlotte Bourne, Administration Manager

***Edmonton:* CKER-FM** (Freq: 101.7)
5915 Gateway Blvd., Edmonton, AB T6H 2H3
Tel: 780-702-1188; *Fax:* 780-437-5129
cker@cker.ca
www.cker.ca
Roger Charest, President

***Edmonton:* CKNG-FM** (Freq: 92.5)
Owned by: **Corus Entertainment Inc.***
5204 - 84 St., Edmonton, AB T6E 5N8
Tel: 780-440-6300; *Fax:* 780-469-5937
info@joefm.ca
www.joefm.ca

***Edmonton:* CKRA-FM** (Freq: 96.3)
Owned by: **NewCap Inc.***
4752 - 99 St., Edmonton, AB T6E 5H5
Tel: 780-437-4996; *Fax:* 780-436-5719
www.96x.ca
Al Anderson, General Manager

***Edmonton:* CKUA-FM** (Freq: 94.9)
10526 Jasper Ave., 4th Fl., Edmonton, AB T5J 1Z7
Tel: 780-428-7595; *Fax:* 780-428-7624
radio@ckua.org
www.ckua.com

†*Falher:* CKRP-FM (Freq: 95.7; 102.9; 90.3)
CP 718, Falher, AB T0H 1M0
Tél: 780-837-2346; *Téléc:* 780-837-2092
akrpfm@yahoo.ca
Éric Charron
Julie Cadieux

***Fort McMurray:* CJOK-FM** (Freq: 93.3)
9912 Franklin Ave., Fort McMurray, AB T9H 2K5
Tel: 780-743-2246; *Fax:* 780-791-7250
info@cjok.fm
mymcmurray.com
Craig Picton, Program Director
Jim Schneider, Sales Manager
Kelly Boyd, General Manager

***Fort McMurray:* CKYX-FM** (Freq: 97.9)
9912 Franklin Ave., Fort McMurray, AB T9H 2K5
Tel: 780-743-2246; *Fax:* 780-791-7250
info@kyx98.fm
mymcmurray.com
Craig Picton, Program Director
Jim Schneider, Sales Manager
Kelly Boyd, General Manager

***Fort Vermilion:* CIAM-FM** (Freq: 92.7; 104.3; 95.5; 94.1; 102.9)
PO Box 609, 4709 River Rd., Fort Vermilion, AB T0H 1N0
Tel: 780-927-2426; *Fax:* 780-927-2427
Toll-Free: 866-927-2426
ciam@telus.net
www.ciamradio.com
Michael Sandstrom, General Manager

***Fox Creek:* CFFC-FM** (Freq: 92.1)
Owned by: **CKYL**
Fox Creek, AB

***Grande Prairie:* CFGP-FM** (Freq: 97.7)
#200, 9835 - 101 Ave., Grande Prairie, AB T8V 5V4
Tel: 780-539-9700; *Fax:* 780-532-1600
comments@sunfm.com
www.sunfm.com
Tom Bedore, General Manager

***Grande Prairie:* CJXX-FM** (Freq: 93.1)
Owned by: **The Jim Pattison Broadcast Group***
Big Country 93.1 FM, #202, 9817 - 101 Ave., Grande Prairie, AB T8V 0X6
Tel: 780-532-0840; *Fax:* 780-538-1266
general@bigcountryxx.com
www.bigcountryxx.com
Barbara Baxter

***High Level:* CKHL-FM** (Freq: 102.1)
PO Box 3759, High Level, AB T0H 1Z0
Tel: 780-926-4531; *Fax:* 780-926-4564
www.ylcountry.com
Terry Babiy, General Manager, tbabiy@ylcountry.com

***High River:* CFXL-FM** (Freq: 100.9)
Owned by: **Golden West Broadcasting Ltd.***
11 - 5th Ave. SE., High River, AB T1V 1G2
Tel: 403-995-9611; *Fax:* 403-938-0732
info@goldenwestradio.com
www.theeagle1009.com

***Hinton:* CFXH-FM** (Freq: Broadcasting classic hits at 97.5 FM in Hinton; a component of the Fox Radio Group)
Owned by: **NewCap Radio Inc.***
#102, 506 Carmichael Dr., Hinton, AB T7V 1S8
Tel: 780-865-8804; *Fax:* 780-865-7792
feedback@fox-radio.ca
www.thefoxradio.ca
Dave Schuk, Division General Manager

***La Crete:* CKLA-FM** (Freq: 92.1)
Owned by: **CKYL**
La Crete, AB

***Lethbridge:* CFRV-FM** (Freq: 107.7)
Owned by: **Rogers Broadcasting Ltd.***
PO Box 820, 1015 - 3rd Ave. South, Lethbridge, AB T1J 0J3
Tel: 403-328-1077; *Fax:* 403-380-1539
www.1077theriver.ca
Terry Voth, General Manager

** For details on this company see listing in Major Broadcasting Companies section; † French language station*

***Lethbridge:* CHLB-FM** (Freq: 95.5)
Owned by: **The Jim Pattison Broadcast Group***
401 Mayor Magrath Dr. South, Lethbridge, AB T1J 3L8
Tel: 403-329-0995; *Fax:* 403-329-0195
gm@country95.fm
www.country95.fm
Rob Bye, General Manager

***Lethbridge:* CJBZ-FM** (Freq: 93.3)
Owned by: **The Jim Pattison Broadcast Group***
401 Mayor Magrath Dr. South, Lethbridge, AB T1J 3L8
Tel: 403-394-9300; *Fax:* 403-329-0195
rbye@country95.fm
www.b93.fm
Rob Bye, General Manager

***Lethbridge:* CJRX-FM** (Freq: 106.7)
Owned by: **Rogers Broadcasting Ltd.***
PO Box 820, 1015 - 3rd Ave. South, Lethbridge, AB T1J 3Z9
Tel: 403-320-1220; *Fax:* 403-380-1539
www.rock106.ca
Terry Voth, General Manager, Tvoth2@rci.rogers.com

***Lethbridge:* CJTS-FM** (Freq: 97.1)
508B - 5th Ave. South, Lethbridge, AB T1J 0T9
Tel: 403-394-0971; *Fax:* 403-394-0938
97@spiritfm.ca
www.spiritfm.ca
Terry Fleming, General Manager

***Lloydminster:* CKLM-FM** (Freq: 106.1; 99.7)
Atrium Center, PO Box 21, Lloydminster, AB T9V 0K2
Tel: 780-875-5400; *Fax:* 780-875-4628
admin@borderrock.com
www.borderrock.com
Stew Dent, General Manager

***Lloydminster:* CKSA-FM** (Freq: 95.9)
Owned by: **NewCap Inc.***
5026 - 50 St., Lloydminster, AB T9V 1P3
Tel: 780-875-3321; *Fax:* 780-875-4704
Lloyd@newcap.ca
www.959lloydfm.com
Ken Ruptash, General Manager

***Nordegg:* CHBW-FM-1** (Freq: 93.9)
Owned by: **CIBW-FM**
Nordegg, AB

***Peace River:* CKKX-FM** (Freq: 106.1)
PO Box 300, 9807 - 100 Ave., Peace River, AB T8S 1T5
Tel: 780-624-2535; *Fax:* 780-624-5424
www.kix106.net

***Red Deer:* CFDV-FM** (Freq: 106.7)
Owned by: **The Jim Pattison Broadcast Group***
2840 Bremner Ave., Red Deer, AB T4R 1M9
Tel: 403-343-7105; *Fax:* 403-343-2573
news@big105.fm
www.1067thedrive.fm
Paul Mason, General Manager

***Red Deer:* CHUB-FM** (Freq: 105.5)
Owned by: **The Jim Pattison Broadcast Group***
2840 Bremner Ave., Red Deer, AB T4R 1M9
Tel: 403-343-7105; *Fax:* 403-343-2573
news@big105.fm
www.big105.fm
Paul Mason, General Manager

***Red Deer:* CIZZ-FM** (Freq: 98.9)
Owned by: **Corus Entertainment Inc.***
PO Bag 5339, Red Deer, AB T4N 6W1
Tel: 403-343-1303; *Fax:* 403-346-1230
zed99@newcap.ca
www.zedfm.com
R.C. (Ron) Thompson, General Manager
John Hayes, President

***Red Deer:* CKGY-FM** (Freq: 95.5)
Owned by: **Corus Entertainment Inc.***
PO Bag 5339, Red Deer, AB T4N 6W1
Tel: 403-348-0955; *Fax:* 403-346-1230
kgbirthdays@newcap.ca
www.ckgy.com
R.C. (Ron) Thompson, General Manager
John Hayes, President

***Redcliffe:* CFMY-FM** (Freq: 96.1)
Owned by: **The Jim Pattison Broadcast Group***
PO Box 1270, 10 Boundary Rd., Redcliffe, AB T0J 2P0
Tel: 403-548-8282; *Fax:* 403-548-8270
my96fm@jpbg.com
www.my96fm.com
Dwaine Dietrich, General Manager

***Rocky Mountain House:* CHBW-FM** (Freq: 94.5)
Owned by: **CIBW-FM**
Rocky Mountain House, AB

***Siksika:* CHDH-FM** (Freq: 97.7)
PO Box 1490, Siksika, AB T0J 3W0
Tel: 403-734-5339; *Fax:* 403-734-5497
siksikamedia@siksikanation.com

***Slave Lake:* CKWA-FM** (Freq: 92.7)
Owned by: **NewCap Inc.***
PO Box 2470, #207, 201 Main St. NE, Slave Lake, AB T0G 2A0
Tel: 780-849-2577; *Fax:* 780-849-4833

***Wainwright:* CKWY-FM** (Freq: 93.7)
Owned by: **NewCap Inc.***
#2, 1037 - 2nd Ave., Wainwright, AB T9W 1K7
Tel: 780-842-4311; *Fax:* 780-842-4636
www.waynefm.com

***Wetaskiwin:* CIHS-FM** (Freq: 93.5)
5206 - 50th Ave., Wetaskiwin, AB T9A 0S8
Tel: 780-352-2508; *Fax:* 780-352-2502
mail@cihsfm.com
www.cihsfm.com
Tony Greengrass, General Manager
Paula Osha, Station Manager

British Columbia

***100 Mile House:* CFFM-FM-2** (Freq: 99.7)
Owned by: **CFFM-FM**
100 Mile House, BC

***Abbotsford:* CKQC-FM** (Freq: 107.1)
#318, 31935 South Fraser Way, Abbotsford, BC V2T 5N7
Tel: 604-853-4756; *Fax:* 604-853-1071
country1071.com
Ken Geiger, General Manager

***Burnaby:* CFML-FM** (Freq: 104.5)
Bldg. SE-10, 3700 Willingdon Ave., Burnaby, BC V5G 3H2
Tel: 604-432-8510; *Fax:* 604-432-1792
allofus@radiocfml.com
www.radiocfml.com; www.evolution1079.com
Brian Antonson

***Burnaby:* CJSF-FM** (Freq: 90.1)
TC216, Simon Fraser University, Burnaby, BC V5A 1S6
Tel: 604-291-3727; *Fax:* 604-291-3695
cjsfmgr@sfu.ca
www.cjsf.ca
Magnus Thyrold, Station Manager
Elvira Balakshin, Program Coordinator

***Castlegar:* CKGF-FM-2** (Freq: 96.7)
525 - 11th Ave., Castlegar, BC V1N 1J6
Tel: 250-365-7600; *Fax:* 250-365-8480
Dennis Gerein, General Manager

***Castlegar:* CKQR-FM** (Freq: 99.3)
525 - 11 Ave., Castlegar, BC V1N 1J6
Tel: 250-365-7600; *Fax:* 250-365-8480
Toll-Free: 800-665-1178
dgilmore@bkradio.com
www.bkradio.com
Dennis Gerein, General Manager

***Chetwynd:* CHAD-FM** (Freq: 104.1)
PO Box 214, Chetwynd, BC V0C 1J0
Tel: 250-784-1880; *Fax:* 250-782-7566
info@chetchad.com
www.chetchad.com
Leo Sabulsky, General Manager

***Chetwynd:* CHET-FM** (Freq: 94.5)
PO Box 214, #102, 4612 North Access Rd., Chetwynd, BC V0C 1J0
Tel: 250-788-9452; *Fax:* 250-788-9402
info@peacefm.ca
www.peacefm.ca
Leo Sabulsky, General Manager

***Chilliwack:* CKSR-FM** (Freq: 98.3)
Owned by: **Rogers Broadcasting Ltd.***
#309, 46167 Yale Rd., Chilliwack, BC V2P 2N2
Tel: 604-795-5711; *Fax:* 604-702-3212
www.starfm.com
Ken Geiger, General Manager

***Courtenay:* CKLR-FM** (Freq: 97.3)
Owned by: **Island Radio Ltd.***
801B - 29th St., Courtenay, BC V9N 7Z5
Tel: 250-703-2200; *Fax:* 250-703-9611
info@973theeagle.com
www.973theeagle.com
Steve Power, Program Director

***Cranbrook:* CHBZ-FM** (Freq: 104.7)
Owned by: **The Jim Pattison Broadcast Group***
19 - 9 Ave. South, Cranbrook, BC V1C 2L9
Tel: 250-426-2224; *Fax:* 250-426-5520
info@b104.ca
www.b104.ca

***Cranbrook:* CHDR-FM** (Freq: 102.9)
Owned by: **The Jim Pattison Broadcast Group***
19 - 9 Ave. South, Cranbrook, BC V1C 2L9
Tel: 250-426-2224; *Fax:* 250-426-5520
info@thedrivefm.ca
www.thedrivefm.ca

***Cranbrook:* CJDR-FM** (Freq: 99.1)
19 - 9th Ave. South, Cranbrook, BC V1C 2L9
Tel: 250-426-2224
info@thedrivefm.ca
www.thedrivefm.ca
Rene Ross, General Manager

***Crawford Bay:* CBTE-FM** (Freq: 89.9)
Owned by: **Canadian Broadcasting Corporation (CBC)***
Crawford Bay, BC
Toll-Free: 866-306-4636
www.cbc.ca/bc; www.cbc.ca/radio
Social Media: www.facebook.com/radiocbc; www.twitter.com/cbcradio

***Duncan:* CJSU-FM** (Freq: 89.7)
130 Trans Canada Hwy., Duncan, BC V9L 2P7
Tel: 250-746-0897; *Fax:* 250-748-1517
onair@897sunfm.com
www.897sunfm.com

***Egmont:* CIEG-FM** (Freq: 104.7)
Owned by: **CISQ-FM**
Egmont, BC

***Fort Nelson:* CKRX-FM** (Freq: 102.3)
Owned by: **CKNL-FM**
Fort Nelson, BC

***Fort St John:* CHRX-FM** (Freq: 98.5)
Owned by: **Standard Radio Office***
10532 Alaska Rd., Fort St John, BC V1J 1B3
Tel: 250-785-6634; *Fax:* 250-785-4544
energyfmrequest@sri.ca
Tracey Gard

***Fort St John:* CKFU-FM** (Freq: 100.1)
10423 - 101 Ave., Fort St John, BC V1J 2B7
Tel: 250-787-7100; *Fax:* 250-263-9749
reception@moosefm.ca
www.moosefm.ca
Russ Beerling, General Manager

***Fort St John:* CKNL-FM** (Freq: 101.5)
Owned by: **Standard Radio Office***
10532 Alaska Rd., Fort St John, BC V1J 1B3
Tel: 250-785-6634; *Fax:* 250-785-4544
peacereception@sri.ca
Tracy Gard, General Manager & General Sales Man

***Gold River:* CJGR-FM** (Freq: 101.1)
Owned by: **CFWB**
Gold River, BC

***Grand Forks:* CKGF-FM** (Freq: 96.7)
7474 - 19th St., Grand Forks, BC V0H 1H0
Tel: 250-442-5844; *Fax:* 250-442-3340
www.bkradio.com

** For details on this company see listing in Major Broadcasting Companies section; † French language station*

***Kamloops:* CFBX-FM** (Freq: 92.5)
900 McGill Rd., House 8, Kamloops, BC V2C 5N3
Tel: 250-377-3988; *Fax:* 250-372-5055
radio@tru.ca
www.theX.ca
Brant Zwicker, Station Manager

***Kamloops:* CIFM-FM** (Freq: 98.3)
Owned by: **The Jim Pattison Broadcast Group***
460 Pemberton Terrace, Kamloops, BC V2C 1T5
Tel: 250-372-3322; *Fax:* 250-374-0445
info@98.3cifm.com
www.98.3cifm.com
Rick Arnish, President & General Manager

***Kamloops:* CKBZ-FM** (Freq: 100.1)
Owned by: **The Jim Pattison Broadcast Group***
460 Pemberton Terrace, Kamloops, BC V2C 1T5
Tel: 250-372-3322; *Fax:* 250-374-0445
info@b100.ca
www.b100.ca
Rick Arnish, President

***Kamloops:* CKRV-FM** (Freq: 97.5)
611 Lansdowne St., Kamloops, BC V2C 1Y6
Tel: 250-372-2197; *Fax:* 250-372-2293
river@ckrv.com
www.ckrv.com
Robbie Dunn

***Kelowna:* Astral Media Radio G.P.** (Freq: 99.9 Sun FM/CHSU-FM; 101.5 Silk FM/CILK-FM; AM 1150/CKFR-AM)
Owned by: **Standard Radio Office***
435 Bernard Ave., Kelowna, BC V1Y 6N8
Tel: 250-860-8600; *Fax:* 250-860-8856
info@thesun.net; info@silk.fm; info@am1150.ca
www.thesun.net; www.silk.fm; www.am1150.ca

***Kelowna:* CBTK-FM** (Freq: 88.9)
Owned by: **Canadian Broadcasting Corporation (CBC)***
Kelowna, BC
Toll-Free: 866-306-4636
www.cbc.ca/bc; www.cbc.ca/radio
Social Media: www.facebook.com/radiocbc; www.twitter.com/cbcradio
Jennifer Smith, Director, Sales & Marketing, Western Canada, 604-662-6616

***Kelowna:* CILK-FM** (Freq: 101.5)
1598 Pandosy St., Kelowna, BC V1Y 1P4
Tel: 250-860-1010; *Fax:* 250-860-0505
info@silk.fm
www.silk.fm

***Kelowna:* CKLZ-FM** (Freq: 104.7)
Owned by: **The Jim Pattison Broadcast Group***
3805 Lakeshore Rd., Kelowna, BC V1W 3K6
Tel: 250-763-1047; *Fax:* 250-762-2141
info@power104.fm
www.power104.fm

***Kootenay:* CJLY-FM** (Freq: 93.5; 96.5)
PO Box 767, Kootenay, BC V1L 5R4
Tel: 250-352-9600; *Fax:* 250-352-9663
www.kootenaycoopradio.com

***Lillooet:* CHLS-FM** (Freq: 100.5)
PO Box 2124, Lillooet, BC V0K 1V0
Tel: 250-256-2457; *Fax:* 250-256-7405
vivianbj@telus.net
www.lss.sd74.bc.ca/chls
Tom Willey, Station Manager

***Mackenzie:* CHMM-FM** (Freq: 103.5)
PO Box 547, 86 Centennial Ave., Mackenzie, BC V0J 2C0
Tel: 250-997-6277; *Fax:* 250-997-6222
jd@chmm.ca
www.chmm.ca
J. D. MacKenzie, Station Manager

***Nanaimo:* CHLY-FM** (Freq: 101.7)
The Radio Malaspina Society, #2, 34 Victoria Rd., Nanaimo, BC V9R 5B8
Tel: 250-716-3410; *Fax:* 250-716-1082
music@chly.ca
www.chly.ca
James Booker, Station Manager

***Nanaimo:* CHWF-FM** (Freq: 106.9)
Owned by: **Island Radio Ltd.***
4550 Wellington Rd., Nanaimo, BC V9T 2H3
Tel: 250-758-1131; *Fax:* 250-758-4644
info@1069thewolf.com
www.1069thewolf.com
Rob Bye, General Manager

***Nanaimo:* CKWV-FM** (Freq: 102.3)
Owned by: **Island Radio Ltd.***
4550 Wellington Rd., Nanaimo, BC V9T 2H3
Tel: 250-758-1131; *Fax:* 250-758-4644
info@1023thewave.com
www.1023thewave.com
Rob Bye, General Manager

***Nelson:* CKKC-FM** (Freq: 106.9)
513C Front St., Nelson, BC V1L 4B4
Tel: 250-368-5510; *Fax:* 250-368-8471
kbs@sri.ca
www.kbsradio.ca

***Parksville:* CHPQ-FM** (Freq: 99.9)
Owned by: **Island Radio Ltd.***
PO Box 1370, 141 Memorial Ave., Parksville, BC V9P 2H3
Tel: 250-248-4211; *Fax:* 250-248-4210
info@theloungefm.com
www.islandradio.bc.ca
Paul Larsen, President

***Parksville:* CIBH-FM** (Freq: 88.5)
Owned by: **Island Radio Ltd.***
141 Memorial Ave., Parksville, BC V9P 2H3
Tel: 250-248-4211; *Fax:* 250-248-4210
info@885thebeach.com
885thebeach.com
Paul Larsen, President & General Manager

***Parksville:* CKWV-FM-1** (Freq: 102.3)
Owned by: **CKWV-FM**
Parksville, BC

***Pender Harbour:* CIPN-FM** (Freq: 104.7)
Owned by: **CISQ-FM**
Pender Harbour, BC

***Penticton:* CIGV-FM** (Freq: 100.7)
125 Nanaimo Ave. West, Penticton, BC V2A 1N2
Tel: 250-493-6767; *Fax:* 250-493-0098
Toll-Free: 888-493-6767
info@giantfm.ca
www.giantfm.ca
James Robinson, General Manager

***Penticton:* CJMG-FM** (Freq: 97.1)
Owned by: **Standard Radio Office***
33 Carmi Ave., Penticton, BC V2A 3G4
Tel: 250-492-2800; *Fax:* 250-493-0370
www.thesun.net

***Port Alberni:* CJAV-FM** (Freq: 93.3)
Owned by: **Island Radio Ltd.***
3296 - 3rd Ave., Port Alberni, BC V9Y 4E1
Tel: 250-723-2455; *Fax:* 250-723-0797
info@933thepeak.com
www.933thepeak.com
Bye Rob, General Manager

***Port Alice:* CFPA-FM** (Freq: 100.3)
Owned by: **CFNI**
Port Alice, BC

***Powell River:* CJMP-FM** (Freq: 90.1)
4476 Marine Ave., Powell River, BC V8A 2K2
Tel: 604-485-2688; *Fax:* 604-485-2683
modelcommunity@prcn.org
Geraldine Braak, General Manager

***Prince George:* CBYG-FM** (Freq: 91.5)
Owned by: **Canadian Broadcasting Corporation***
#1, 890 Victoria St., Prince George, BC V2L 5P1
Tel: 250-562-6701; *Fax:* 250-562-4777
daybreaknorth@cbc.ca
www.cbc.ca/bc

***Prince George:* CFUR-FM** (Freq: 88.7)
3333 University Way, Prince George, BC V2N 4Z9
Tel: 250-960-7664; *Fax:* 250-960-5995
info@cfur.ca
www.cfur.ca
Christopher Earl, Station Manager

***Prince George:* CIRX-FM** (Freq: 94.3)
1940 - 3 Ave., Prince George, BC V2M 1G7
Tel: 250-564-2524; *Fax:* 250-562-6611
onair@94xfm.com
www.94xfm.com
Terry Shepherd, President & General Manager

***Prince George:* CJCI-FM** (Freq: 97.3)
1940 - 3 Ave., Prince George, BC V2M 1G7
Tel: 250-564-2524; *Fax:* 250-562-6611
thewolf@97fm.ca
www.97fm.ca

***Prince George:* CKDV-FM** (Freq: 99.3)
Owned by: **The Jim Pattison Broadcast Group***
1810 - 3rd Ave., 2nd Fl., Prince George, BC V2M 1G4
Tel: 250-564-8861; *Fax:* 250-562-8768
ckpgmail@ckpg.bc.ca
www.993thedrive.com
Ken Kilcullen, General Manager

***Prince George:* CKKN-FM** (Freq: 101.3)
Owned by: **The Jim Pattison Broadcast Group***
1810 3rd Ave., 2nd Fl., Prince George, BC V2M 1G4
Tel: 250-564-8861; *Fax:* 250-562-8768
ckpgmail@ckpg.bc.ca
www.1013hitsfm.com

***Prince Rupert:* CJFW-FM** (Freq: 103.1)
Owned by: **Standard Radio Office***
#212, 215 Cow Bay Rd., Prince Rupert, BC V8J 1A2
Tel: 250-624-9111; *Fax:* 250-624-3100
www.cjfw.ca
Bryan Edwards, President

***Quesnel:* CFFM-FM-2** (Freq: 94.9)
Owned by: **CFFM-FM**
Quesnel, BC

***Richmond:* CHKG-FM** (Freq: 96.1)
Owned by: **Fairchild Radio***
2090 Aberdeen Centre, 4151 Hazelbridge Way, Richmond, BC V6X 4J7
Tel: 604-708-1234; *Fax:* 604-708-1201
general@fm961.com
www.fm961.com
George Lee, Sr. Vice-President & General Manage

***Richmond:* CKZZ-FM** (Freq: 95.3)
Owned by: **Standard Radio Office***
#20, #20, 11151 Horseshoe Way, Richmond, BC V7A 4S5
Tel: 604-241-0953; *Fax:* 604-272-0917
info@z95.com
www.z95.com

***Salmon Arm:* CKXR-FM** (Freq: 91.5)
Owned by: **Standard Radio Office***
PO Box 69, 360 Ross St. NE, Salmon Arm, BC V1E 4N2
Tel: 250-832-2161; *Fax:* 250-832-2240
www.myezrock.com
Claude Beaudoin

***Sechelt:* CKKS-FM** (Freq: 104.7)
Owned by: **CISQ-FM**
Sechelt, BC

***Squamish:* CISC-FM** (Freq: A component of Mountain FM, the station broadcasts at 107.5 FM in Gibsons)
Owned by: **Rogers Communications***
#202, 40147 Glenalder Place, Squamish, BC V8B 0G2
Tel: 604-892-1021; *Fax:* 604-892-6383
mountainfm@mountainfm.com
www.mountainfm.com
Joe Polito, Manager

***Squamish:* CISP-FM** (Freq: The station is a component of Mountain FM & broadcasts at 104.5 FM in Pemberton)
Owned by: **Rogers Communications***
#202, 40147 Glenalder Place, Squamish, BC V8B 0G2
Tel: 604-892-1021; *Fax:* 604-892-6383
Toll-Free: 888-429-2724
mountainfm@mountainfm.com
www.mountainfm.com
Gary Miles, President
Joe Polito, Manager

** For details on this company see listing in Major Broadcasting Companies section; † French language station*

Squamish: **CISQ-FM** (Freq: A component of Mountain FM, the station broadcasts at 107.1 FM in Squamish, and at 102.1 FM in Whistler.)
Owned by: **Rogers Communications***
#202, 40147 Glenalder Place, Squamish, BC V8B 0G2
Tel: 604-892-1021; *Fax:* 604-892-6383
Toll-Free: 888-429-2724
moutainfm@mountainfm.com
www.mountainfm.com
Joe Polito, Manager

Terrace: **CFNR-FM** (Freq: 92.1)
4562B Queensway Dr., Terrace, BC V8G 3X6
Tel: 250-638-8137; *Fax:* 250-638-8027
cfnr.mailbag@monarch.net
www.mycfnr.com

Terrace: **CKTK-FM** (Freq: 1230)
Owned by: **Standard Radio Office***
4625 Lazelle Ave., Terrace, BC V8G 1S4
Tel: 250-635-6316; *Fax:* 250-638-6320
Doug Anderson, Station Manager

Trail: **CJAT-FM** (Freq: 95.7)
Owned by: **Standard Radio Office***
1560 Second Ave., Trail, BC V1R 1M4
Tel: 250-368-5510; *Fax:* 250-368-8471
kbs@sri.ca
www.kbsradio.ca
Karl Johnston, General Manager

Trail: **CKZX-FM** (Freq: 93.5)
Owned by: **Standard Radio Office***
1560 - 2nd Ave., Trail, BC V1R 1M4
Tel: 250-368-5510; *Fax:* 250-368-8471
www.trail.kbsradio.ca
Lee Sterry, Operations Manager

†***Vancouver:*** **CBUF-FM** (Freq: 97.7)
Owned by: **Canadian Broadcasting Corporation***
CP 4600, 700 Hamilton St., Vancouver, BC V6B 4A2
Tél: 604-662-6000
www.radio-canada.ca/regions/colombie-britannique

Vancouver: **CBU-FM** (Freq: 105.7)
Owned by: **Canadian Broadcasting Corporation***
Vancouver, BC

Vancouver: **CBUX-FM** (Freq: 90.9)
Owned by: **Canadian Broadcasting Corporation***
PO Box 4600, 775 Cambie St., Vancouver, BC V6B 4A2
Tel: 604-662-6000; *Fax:* 604-662-6335
www.radio-canada.ca/c-b

Vancouver: **CFBT-FM** (Freq: 94.5)
#300, 380 West 2nd Ave., Vancouver, BC V5Y 1C8
Tel: 604-871-9000; *Fax:* 604-871-2901
www.thebeat.com

Vancouver: **CFMI-FM** (Freq: 101.1)
Owned by: **Corus Entertainment Inc.***
#2000, 700 West Georgia St., Vancouver, BC V7Y 1K9
Tel: 604-331-2808; *Fax:* 604-331-2722
rock101@rock101.com
www.rock101.com
Lou Del Gobbo, General Manager

Vancouver: **CFOX-FM** (Freq: 99.3)
Owned by: **Corus Entertainment Inc.***
#2000, 700 West Georgia St., Vancouver, BC V7Y 1K9
Tel: 604-684-7221; *Fax:* 604-331-2722
www.cfox.com

Vancouver: **CFRO-FM** (Freq: 102.7)
#110, 360 Columbia St., Vancouver, BC V6A 4J1
Tel: 604-684-8494
www.coopradio.org
McNabb Robin, Membership & Outreach Coordinator

Vancouver: **CHQM-FM** (Freq: 103.5)
#300, 380 West 2nd Ave., Vancouver, BC V5Y 1C8
Tel: 604-871-9000; *Fax:* 604-871-2901
www.qmfm.com
Mel Kemmis, Program Director

Vancouver: **CITR-FM** (Freq: 101.9)
#233, 6138 Sub Blvd., Vancouver, BC V6T 1Z1
Tel: 604-882-1242; *Fax:* 604-882-9364
citrmgr@ams.ubc.ca
www.citr.ca
Linda Scholten, Station Manager

Vancouver: **CJJR-FM** (Freq: 93.7)
Owned by: **The Jim Pattison Broadcast Group***
#300, 1401 - 8th Ave. West, Vancouver, BC V6H 1C9
Tel: 604-731-7772; *Fax:* 604-731-0493
cjjr@jfrm.com
www.jrfm.com

Vancouver: **CKCL-FM** (Freq: 107.5)
Owned by: **Rogers Broadcasting Ltd.***
2440 Ash St., Vancouver, BC V5Z 4J6
Tel: 604-877-6357
www.1049clearfm.com
David Carsen, General Manager

Vancouver: **CKLG-FM** (Freq: 96.9)
Owned by: **Rogers Broadcasting Ltd.***
2440 Ash St., Vancouver, BC V5Z 4J6
Tel: 604-872-2557; *Fax:* 604-877-4494
www.jackfm.com
Wolfgang von Petrie

Vancouver: **CKZZ-FM** (Freq: 95.3)
Owned by: **CKZZ-FM**
Vancouver, BC

Vanderhoof: **CIRX-FM-1** (Freq: 95.9)
Owned by: **CIRX-FM**
Vanderhoof, BC

Vernon: **CICF-FM** (Freq: 105.7)
2800 - 31 St., Vernon, BC V1T 5H4
Tel: 250-545-9222; *Fax:* 250-542-2083
vernonmail@sri.ca
www.thesun.net

Vernon: **CKIZ-FM** (Freq: 107.5)
Owned by: **Rogers Broadcasting Ltd.***
3313 - 32 Ave., Vernon, BC V1T 2E1
Tel: 250-545-2141; *Fax:* 250-545-9008
www.1075kiss.com
Patrick Nicol, General Manager

Victoria: **CBCV-FM** (Freq: 90.5)
Owned by: **Canadian Broadcasting Corporation (CBC)***
1025 Pandora Ave., Victoria, BC V8V 3P6
Tel: 250-360-2227; *Fax:* 250-360-2600
Toll-Free: 866-306-4636
victoria@radio.cbc.ca
www.cbc.ca/bc; www.cbc.ca/radio
Other information: TDD: 1-866-220-6045
Jennifer Smith, Director, Sales & Marketing, Western Canda, 604-662-6616

Victoria: **CFUV-FM** (Freq: 101.9)
PO Box 3035, Victoria, BC V8W 3P3
Tel: 250-721-8702; *Fax:* 250—
director@uvic.ca
cfuv.uvic.ca

Victoria: **CHBE-FM** (Freq: 107.3)
Owned by: **CTVglobemedia Inc.**
1420 Broad St., Victoria, BC V8W 2B1
Tel: 250-382-1073
www.1073kool.fm
Robin Haggar, Program Director

Victoria: **CHTT-FM** (Freq: 103.1)
Owned by: **Rogers Broadcasting Ltd.***
817 Fort St., Victoria, BC V8W 1H6
Tel: 250-382-0900; *Fax:* 250-382-4358
www.1031jackfm.com

Victoria: **CIOC-FM** (Freq: 98.5)
Owned by: **Rogers Broadcasting Ltd.***
817 Fort St., Victoria, BC V8W 1H6
Tel: 250-382-0900; *Fax:* 250-382-4358
www.ocean985.com

Victoria: **CJZN-FM** (Freq: 91.3)
2750 Quadra St., Top Floor, Victoria, BC V8T 4E8
Tel: 250-475-6611; *Fax:* 250-475-3299
modernrock@thezone.fm
www.thezone.fm
Dan McAllister, General Manager

Victoria: **CKKQ-FM** (Freq: 100.3)
2750 Quadra St., 3rd Fl., Victoria, BC V8T 4E8
Tel: 250-475-0100; *Fax:* 250-475-3299
thecrew@theq.fm
www.theq.fm
Stu Morton, President/General Manager

Whistler: **CISW-FM** (Freq: 102.1)
PO Box 1239, 4335 Blackcomb Way, Whistler, BC V0N 1B4
Tel: 604-938-0002; *Fax:* 604-938-0015

Williams Lake: **CFFM-FM** (Freq: 97.5)
83 South First Ave., Williams Lake, BC V2G 1H4
Tel: 250-392-6551; *Fax:* 250-392-4142
www.cffmthemax.com
Tracey Gard, Manager, 250-392-6551 ex, tgard@vistaradio.ca

Manitoba

Brandon: **CINC-FM** (Freq: 91.5)
Owned by: **CINC-FM**
Brandon, MB

Brandon: **CJJJ-FM** (Freq: 106.5)
Assiniboine Community College, #223, 1430 Victoria Ave. East, Brandon, MB R7A 2A9
Tel: 204-725-8700; *Fax:* 204-726-7014
www.assiniboine.net
Bob Crighton, Station Manager

Brandon: **CKLF-FM** (Freq: 94.7)
624 - 14 St. East, Brandon, MB R7A 7E1
Tel: 204-726-8888; *Fax:* 204-726-1270
tyler@starfmradio.com
www.starfmradio.com
David Baxter, President
Don Kille, General Manager

Brandon: **CKXA-FM** (Freq: 101.1)
Owned by: **Standard Radio Office***
2940 Victoria Ave., Brandon, MB R7B 3Y3
Tel: 204-728-1150; *Fax:* 204-725-3794
staylor@hotqx.com
www.1011thefarm.com
Taylor Sharon, General Manager

Brandon: **CKX-FM** (Freq: 96.1)
Owned by: **Standard Radio Office***
2940 Victoria Ave., Brandon, MB R7B 3Y3
Tel: 204-728-1150; *Fax:* 204-725-3794
kx96@kx96online.com
www.kx96online.com
Alan Cruise, CEO & President

Cross Lake: **CFNC-FM** (Freq: 1490)
PO Box 129, Cross Lake, MB R0B 0J0
Tel: 204-676-2331; *Fax:* 204-676-2911
Joyce Halcrow, Station Manager

Portage la Prairie: **CFRY-FM** (Freq: 93.1)
Owned by: **CFRY**
Portage la Prairie, MB

Pukatawagan: **CFPX-FM** (Freq: 98.3)
General Delivery, Pukatawagan, MB R0B 1G0
Tel: 204-553-2155; *Fax:* 204-553-2158
John Colomb, General Manager

St. Boniface: **CKXL-FM** (Freq: 91.1)
340 Provencher Blvd., St. Boniface, MB R2H 0G7
Tel: 204-233-4243; *Fax:* 204-233-3646
info@envol91.mb.ca
www.envol91.mb.ca

Steinbach: **CILT-FM** (Freq: 96.7)
Owned by: **Golden West Broadcasting Ltd.***
#105, 32 Brandt St., Steinbach, MB R5G 2J7
Tel: 204-326-3737; *Fax:* 204-326-2299
info@goldenwestradio.com
www.lite967online.com

The Pas: **CINC-FM** (Freq: 92.7)
Owned by: **CINC-FM**
The Pas, MB

Thompson: **CBWK-FM** (Freq: 100.9)
Owned by: **Canadian Broadcasting Corporation***
7 Selkirk Ave., Thompson, MB R8N 0M4
Tel: 204-677-1680
north@cbc.ca
www.cbc.ca/northcountry

Thompson: **CINC-FM** (Freq: 96.3)
Owned by: **CINC-FM**
Thompson, MB

** For details on this company see listing in Major Broadcasting Companies section; † French language station*

***Winkler:* CJEL-FM** (Freq: 93.5)
Owned by: **Golden West Broadcasting Ltd.***
PO Box 399, Winkler, MB R6W 4A6
Tel: 204-325-7602; *Fax:* 204-325-2206
info@goldenwestradio.com
www.eagle935fm.com

***Winnipeg:* CBW-FM** (Freq: 98.3)
Owned by: **Canadian Broadcasting Corporation***
541 Portage Ave., Winnipeg, MB R3C 2G1
Tel: 204-788-3222
www.cbc.ca/manitoba

***Winnipeg:* CFEQ-FM** (Freq: 107.1)
738 Osborne St., Winnipeg, MB R3L 2C2
Tel: 204-944-8961; *Fax:* 204-772-5854
www.freq107.com
Tom Hiebert, General Manager

***Winnipeg:* CFQX-FM** (Freq: 104.4)
177 Lombard Ave., 3rd Fl., Winnipeg, MB R3B 0W5
Tel: 204-944-1031; *Fax:* 204-943-7687
www.qx104fm.com
Lee Sterry, General Manager

***Winnipeg:* CFWM-FM** (Freq: 99.9)
1445 Pembina Hwy., Winnipeg, MB R3T 5C2
Tel: 204-477-5120; *Fax:* 204-453-0815
bob@999bobfm.com
www.999bobfm.com
Chris Stevens, Vice President/General Manager

***Winnipeg:* CHIQ-FM** (Freq: 94.3)
1445 Pembina Hwy., Winnipeg, MB R3T 5C2
Tel: 204-477-5120; *Fax:* 204-453-0815
www.curve943.com

***Winnipeg:* CHNR-FM** (Freq: 100.7)
3586 Portage Ave., Winnipeg, MB R3K 0Z8
Tel: 204-889-2586; *Fax:* 204-831-1512
chnr@shawbiz.ca

***Winnipeg:* CHVN-FM** (Freq: 95.1)
Owned by: **Golden West Broadcasting Ltd.***
PO Box 1812, 1111 Chevrier Blvd., Winnipeg, MB R3C 3R1
Tel: 204-452-9602; *Fax:* 204-478-6735
chvn@chvnradio.com
www.chvnradio.com
Wade Kehler, General Manager

***Winnipeg:* CICY-FM** (Freq: 105.5)
1507 Inkster Blvd., Winnipeg, MB R2X 1R2
Tel: 204-772-8255; *Fax:* 204-779-5628
info@ncifm.com
www.ncifm.com
Hoa Bui, Broadcast Technical Manager

***Winnipeg:* CINC-FM** (Freq: 105.5 fm)
1507 Inkster Blvd., Winnipeg, MB R2X 1R2
Tel: 204-772-8255; *Fax:* 204-779-5628
info@ncifm.com
www.ncifm.com
David McLeod, General Manager
Marshall Lank, Director, Sales & Marketing

***Winnipeg:* CITI-FM** (Freq: 92.1)
Owned by: **Rogers Broadcasting Ltd.***
#4, 166 Osborne St., Winnipeg, MB R3L 1Y8
Tel: 204-788-3400; *Fax:* 204-788-3401
www.92citi.ca

***Winnipeg:* CJKR-FM** (Freq: 97.5)
Owned by: **Corus Entertainment Inc.***
930 Portage Ave., Winnipeg, MB R3G 0P8
Tel: 204-786-2471; *Fax:* 204-780-9750
www.power97.com
Garth Buchko, General Manager

***Winnipeg:* CJUM-FM** (Freq: 101.5)
#308, University Centre, Winnipeg, MB R3T 2N2
Tel: 204-474-7027; *Fax:* 204-269-1299
cjum@cjum.com
www.umfm.com
Jared McKetiak, Station Manager
Jared McKetiak, Program Director

***Winnipeg:* CJZZ-FM** (Freq: 99.1)
Canwest Global Pl., 201 Portage Ave., 30th Fl., Winnipeg, MB R3B 3K6
Tel: 204-253-2665; *Fax:* 204-926-1674
www.cooljazz.ca

***Winnipeg:* CKIC-FM** (Freq: 92.9)
W106, 160 Princess St., Winnipeg, MB R3B 1K9
Tel: 204-949-8473; *Fax:* 204-949-0057
www.kick.fm
Rick Everett, Station Manager

***Winnipeg:* CKMM-FM** (Freq: 103.1)
177 Lombard Ave., 3rd Fl., Winnipeg, MB R3B 0W5
Tel: 204-944-1031; *Fax:* 204-943-7687
www.hot103live.com
Russ Tyson, Vice-President, Programming & Operations

***Winnipeg:* CKUW-FM** (Freq: 95.9)
University of Winnipeg, #4CM11, 515 Portage, Winnipeg, MB R3B 2E9
Tel: 204-786-9782; *Fax:* 204-783-7080
ckuw@uwinnipeg.ca
www.ckuw.ca
Rob Schmidt, Station Manager

***Winnipeg:* CKY-FM** (Freq: 102.3)
Owned by: **Rogers Broadcasting Ltd.***
#4, 166 Osborne St., Winnipeg, MB R3L 1Y8
Tel: 204-780-3400; *Fax:* 204-788-3401
www.102clearfm.com
Geoff Poulton, General Manager

New Brunswick

***†Balmoral:* CIMS-FM** (Freq: 103.9)
CP 2561, 1991, av des Pionniers, Balmoral, NB E8E 2W7
Tél: 506-826-1040; *Téléc:* 506-826-2400
cim.traffic@restigouche.net
www.cimsfm.ca
Annie L. Levesque, General Manager

***Bathurst:* CKBC-FM** (Freq: 104.9)
Owned by: **Astral Media Radio Atlantic***
176 Main St., Bathurst, NB E2A 1A4
Tel: 506-547-1360; *Fax:* 506-547-1367
maxfm@radioatl.ca
Jamie Robichaud

***Bathurst:* CKLE-FM** (Freq: 92.9)
195 Main St., Bathurst, NB E2A 3Z1
Tel: 506-546-4600; *Fax:* 506-546-6611
superstation@ckle.fm
www.ckle.fm

***†Edmundston:* CFAI-FM** (Freq: 101.1; 105.1)
165, boul Hebert, 6e étage, Edmundston, NB E3V 2S8
Tél: 506-737-5060; *Téléc:* 506-737-5084
cfai@101rock105.com
www.101rock105.com
Serge Parent, Dir de la Station

***†Edmundston:* CJEM-FM** (Freq: 92.7)
174, rue de l'Église, Edmundston, NB E3V 1K2
Tél: 506-735-3351; *Téléc:* 506-739-5803
cjem@nbnet.nb.ca

***Edmundston:* CKMV-FM** (Freq: 95.1)
174 Church St., Edmundston, NB E3V 1K2
Tel: 506-735-3351; *Fax:* 506-739-5803
cjem@nbnet.nb.ca
Murillo Soucy, General Manager

***Fredericton:* CBZF-FM** (Freq: 99.5)
Owned by: **Canadian Broadcasting Corporation***
PO Box 2200, 1160 Regent St., Fredericton, NB E3B 5G4
Tel: 506-451-4000; *Fax:* 506-451-4170
www.cbc.ca/nb

***Fredericton:* CFXY-FM** (Freq: 105.3)
Owned by: **Astral Media Radio Atlantic***
206 Rookwood Ave., Fredericton, NB E3B 2M2
Tel: 506-454-2444; *Fax:* 506-452-2345
www.foxrocks.ca
John Eddy, Exec. Vice-President

***Fredericton:* CHSR-FM** (Freq: 97.9)
PO Box 4400, Fredericton, NB E3B 5A3
Tel: 506-453-4985
chsr@unb.ca
www.unb.ca/chsr
Tristis Ward, Station Manager
Alan Wong, Program Director

***Fredericton:* CIBX-FM** (Freq: 106.9)
Owned by: **Astral Media Radio Atlantic***
206 Rookwood Ave., Fredericton, NB E3B 2M2
Tel: 506-455-1069; *Fax:* 506-452-2345
www.capitalfm.ca
Pat Brennan, General Manager

***Fredericton:* CIXN-FM** (Freq: 96.5)
#10, 1010 Hanwell Rd., Fredericton, NB E3B 6A4
Tel: 506-454-9600; *Fax:* 506-454-0991
welcome@joyfm.ca
www.joyfm.ca
Garth McCrea, General Manager

***Fredericton:* CJPN-FM** (Freq: 90.5)
715, rue Priestman, Fredericton, NB E3B 5W7
Tel: 506-454-2576; *Fax:* 506-453-3958
cjpn@nbnet.nb.ca
www.cjpn.ca

***Fredericton:* CKTP-FM** (Freq: 95.7)
PO Box R13, 150 Cliffe St., Fredericton, NB E3A 0A1
Tel: 506-459-4487; *Fax:* 506-459-4404
info@cktpradio.com
www.cktpradio.com
Timothy Paul, General Manager

***Grand Falls:* CIKX-FM** (Freq: 93.5)
Owned by: **Astral Media Radio Atlantic***
399 Broadway Blvd., Grand Falls, NB E3Z 2K5
Tel: 506-473-9393; *Fax:* 506-473-3893
grdprod@radioatl.ca
Pat Brennan, General Manager
Rick McGuire, Program Director
Jacques LaFrance, Sales Manager

***Kedgwick:* CFJU-FM** (Freq: French language community radio at 90.1 FM in Kedgwick & in St. Quentin)
PO Box 1043, Kedgwick, NB E8B 1Z9
Tel: 506-235-9000; *Fax:* 506-235-9001
cfjufm@rogers.com
Lucille Thériault, General Manager

***Miramichi:* CFAN-FM** (Freq: 99.3)
Owned by: **Maritime Broadcasting System***
396 Pleasant St., Miramichi, NB E1V 1X5
Tel: 506-622-3311; *Fax:* 506-627-0335
cfan@nb.sympatico.ca
www.993theriver.com

***†Moncton:* CBAF-FM** (Freq: Radio-Canada Première Chaîne 88.5 MHz (FM) à Moncton; 102.3 FM à Fredericton/Saint-Jean; 105.7 FM à Bathurst; 91.5 FM à Campbellton; 100.3 FM à Edmunston; 90.3 FM à Lamèque/Caraquet; et 91.7 FM à Bon Accord.)
Owned by: **Canadian Broadcasting Corporation***
250, av Université, Moncton, NB E1C 5K3
Tél: 506-853-6666; *Téléc:* 506-853-8000
Ligne sans frais: 800-561-7010
www.radio-canada.ca/regions/acadie

***†Moncton:* CBAL-FM** (Freq: 98.3; 95.3; 101.9; 98.9)
Owned by: **Canadian Broadcasting Corporation***
CP 950, 250, av Université, Moncton, NB E1C 8N8
Tél: 506-853-6666; *Téléc:* 506-853-6739
Ligne sans frais: 800-561-7010
www.radio-canada.ca/radio
Susan Mitton, Regional Director-Radio

***Moncton:* CFQM-FM** (Freq: 103.9)
Owned by: **Maritime Broadcasting System***
1000 St. George Blvd., Moncton, NB E1E 4M7
Tel: 506-858-1220; *Fax:* 506-858-1209
magic104@radiomoncton.com
www.radiomoncton.com

***†Moncton:* CHOY-FM** (Freq: 99.9)
Owned by: **Maritime Broadcasting System***
1000, boul St-George, Moncton, NB E1E 4M7
Tél: 506-858-1220; *Téléc:* 506-858-1209
choix@radiomoncton.com
www.radiomoncton.com

***Moncton:* CITA-FM** (Freq: 105.9)
3170 Mountain Rd., Moncton, NB E1G 2W8
Tel: 506-384-1059; *Fax:* 506-854-8609
www.citafm.com

** For details on this company see listing in Major Broadcasting Companies section; † French language station*

***Moncton:* CJMO-FM** (Freq: 103.1)
Owned by: **NewCap Inc.***
27 Arsenault Ct., Moncton, NB E1E 4J8
Tel: 506-858-5525; *Fax:* 506-858-5539
c103@c103.com
www.c103.com
Dave Ostler, Sales Manager
Andrew Stewart, Program Director
Hilary Montbourquette, General Manager

***Moncton:* CJXL-FM** (Freq: 96.9)
27 Arsenault Ct., Moncton, NB E1E 4J8
Tel: 506-858-5525; *Fax:* 506-858-5539
xl96@xl96.com
www.xl96.com
Hilary Montbourquette, General Manager

***Moncton:* CKCW-FM** (Freq: 94.5)
Owned by: **CTVglobemedia Inc.***
1000 St. George Blvd., Moncton, NB E1E 4M7
Tel: 506-858-1220; *Fax:* 506-858-1209
www.radiomoncton.com
Dan Barton, General Manager

***Moncton:* CKOE-FM** (Freq: 107.3)
3030 Mountain Rd., Moncton, NB E1G 2W8
Tel: 506-388-6212; *Fax:* 506-383-9699
info@ckoefm.com
www.ckoefm.com
Kurk Parks, Station Manager

†*Moncton:* CKUM-FM (Freq: 93.5)
Université de Moncton, Centre étudiant, 2e étage, Moncton, NB E1A 3E9
Tél: 506-858-3750; *Téléc:* 506-858-4524
radioj@radioj935.com
www.radioj935.com
Michèle Routier, Directrice

***Pokemouche:* CKRO-FM** (Freq: 97.1)
142 Rte 113, Pokemouche, NB E8P 1K7
Tel: 506-336-9706; *Fax:* 506-336-9058
radio@ckro.ca
www.ckro.ca
Donald Noel, Dir de la Station

***Sackville:* CHMA-FM** (Freq: 106.9)
#303, Student Union Bldg., Mount Allison University, #303, 152A Main St., Sackville, NB E4L 1B4
Tel: 506-364-2221
chma@mta.ca
www.mta.ca/chma

***Saint John:* CBD-FM** (Freq: 91.3)
Owned by: **Canadian Broadcasting Corporation (CBC)***
PO Box 2358, 560 Main St., Saint John, NB E2L 3V6
Tel: 506-632-7750; *Fax:* 506-632-7761
Toll-Free: 866-306-4636
www.cbc.ca/nb; www.cbc.ca/radio
Social Media: www.facebook.com/radiocbc; www.twitter.com/cbcradio
Other information: TDD: 1-866-220-6045
Andrew Cochran, Managing Director, Maritimes
Dan Goodyear, Executive Producer, News, New Brunswick
Deborah Irvine, Executive Producer, Radio Saint John
Janet Irwin, Senior Regional Manager, News & Current Affairs
Nadine Antle, Regional Manager, Partnerships, Communications, Brand, & Promot, 506-451-4054
John Channing, Manager, Sales
Mary-Pat Schutta, Manager, Programs
Lori Wheeler, Senior Officer, Communications, 506-451-4080

***Saint John:* CFMH-FM** (Freq: 92.5)
Student Services, PO Box 5050, Saint John, NB E2L 4L5
Tel: 506-648-5667; *Fax:* 506-648-5541
cfmh@unbsj.ca
www.unbsj.ca/cfmh
Linda Pelletier, Station Manager

***Saint John:* CHSJ-FM** (Freq: 94.1)
PO Box 2000, Saint John, NB E2L 3T4
Tel: 506-633-3323; *Fax:* 506-644-3485
mail@country94.ca
www.country94.ca
Jim MacMullin, General Manager

***Saint John:* CHWV-FM** (Freq: 97.3)
PO Box 2000, Saint John, NB E2L 3T4
Tel: 506-633-3323; *Fax:* 506-644-3485
mail@thewave.ca
www.thewave.ca
Jim MacMillin, Genera; Manager

***Saint John:* CINB-FM** (Freq: 96.1)
PO Box 96, Saint John, NB E2L 3X1
Tel: 506-657-9600; *Fax:* 506-657-7664
www.newsongfm.com
Don Mabee, Station Manager

***Saint John:* CIOK-FM** (Freq: Broadcasts adult contemporary music of the 70's, 80's, 90's and now at 100.5 FM in Saint John. Sister stations: CFBC AM & CJYC FM)
Owned by: **Maritime Broadcasting System***
226 Union St., Saint John, NB E2L 1B1
Tel: 506-658-5100; *Fax:* 506-658-5116
mailbag@k100.ca
www.k100.ca

***Saint John:* CJEF-FM** (Freq: 103.5)
#3E, 28 King St., Saint John, NB E2L 1G3
Tel: 506-657-1035; *Fax:* 506-642-7408
onair@thepirate.ca
www.thepirate.ca
Gary Stackhouse, General Manager
Geoffrey Rnett, CEO

***Saint John:* CJYC-FM** (Freq: Broadcasting "everything that rocks" at 98.9 FM in Saint John. Sister stations: CFBC AM & CIOK FM)
Owned by: **Maritime Broadcasting System***
226 Union St., Saint John, NB E2L 1B1
Tel: 506-658-5100; *Fax:* 506-658-5116
mailbag@989bigjohnfm.com
www.989bigjohnfm.com

***Shediac:* CJSE-FM** (Freq: 89.5, 101.7, 107.5)
96, rue Providence, Shediac, NB E4P 2E9
Tel: 506-532-0080; *Fax:* 506-532-0120
Toll-Free: 800-604-0080
cjse@cjse.ca
www.cjse.ca
Gilles Arsenault

***St Stephen:* CHDT-FM** (Freq: 98.1)
112 Milltown Blvd., St Stephen, NB E3L 1G6
Tel: 506-466-1000
mail@thetide.ca
www.thetide.ca
Jim MacMillin, General Manager

***St Stephen:* WQDY-FM** (Freq: 92.7)
PO Box 305, St Stephen, NB E3L 2X2
Tel: 506-465-0989; *Fax:* 207-454-3062
Toll-Free: 888-855-2992
wqdy@wqdy.fm
www.wqdy.fm
Bill McVicar

***Woodstock:* CJCJ-FM** (Freq: 104.1)
Owned by: **Astral Media Radio Atlantic***
#1, 131 Queen St., Woodstock, NB E7M 2M8
Tel: 506-325-3030; *Fax:* 506-325-3031
Pat Brennan, General Manager
Rick McGuire, Program Director
Bev Whiteway, Sales Manager

Newfoundland & Labrador

***Corner Brook:* CFLC-FM** (Freq: 97.9)
Owned by: **NewCap Inc.***
PO Box 570, Corner Brook, NL A2H 6H5
Tel: 709-634-3111; *Fax:* 709-634-4081
Michael Murphy, Station Manager

***Corner Brook:* CKXX-FM** (Freq: 103.9)
Owned by: **NewCap Inc.***
PO Box 570, 345 O'Connell Dr., Corner Brook, NL A2H 6H5
Tel: 709-634-4570; *Fax:* 709-634-4081
www.k-rock1039.com
Mike Murphy, General Manager

***Deer Lake:* CFDL-FM** (Freq: 97.9)
Owned by: **CFCB**
Deer Lake, NL

***Gander:* CKXD-FM** (Freq: 98.7)
Owned by: **NewCap Inc.***
PO Box 650, Gander, NL A1V 1X2
Tel: 709-651-3650; *Fax:* 709-651-2542
John Murphy, General Manager

***Grand Falls-Windsor:* CKXG-FM** (Freq: 102.3; 101.3)
Owned by: **NewCap Inc.***
35A Grenfell Heights, Grand Falls-Windsor, NL A2A 2K2
Tel: 709-489-2192; *Fax:* 709-489-8626
ckxg@vocm.com
www.k-rock975.com

***Happy Valley-Goose Bay:* CFGB-FM** (Freq: 89.5)
Owned by: **Canadian Broadcasting Corporation***
PO Box 1029 C, Happy Valley-Goose Bay, NL A0P 1C0
Tel: 709-896-2911; *Fax:* 709-896-8900
www.cbc.ca/nl

***Labrador City:* CBDQ-FM** (Freq: 96.3)
Owned by: **Canadian Broadcasting Corporation (CBC)***
PO Box 576, Labrador City, NL A2V 2L3
Tel: 709-944-3616; *Fax:* 709-944-5472
Toll-Free: 800-563-7933
www.cbc.ca/nl; www.cbc.ca/radio
Social Media: www.facebook.com/radiocbc; www.twitter.com/cbcradio
Other information: Phone, Transmission Information: 1-888-353-7006; TDD: 1-866-220-6045
Denise Wilson, Managing Director, Newfoundland & Labrador
Kathy Porter, Executive Producer, English Radio
Maureen Anonsen, Manager, Partnership & Communications, 709-576-5013
Wayne Tilley, Account Manager, 709-576-5019
Debbie Hynes, Senior Officer, Communications, 709-576-5150

***Labrador City:* CJRM-FM** (Freq: 97.3)
PO Box 453, 308, rue Hudson, Labrador City, NL A2V 2K7
Tel: 709-944-7600; *Fax:* 709-944-5125
cjrm@hotmail.com

***St Andrews:* CFCV-FM** (Freq: 97.7)
Owned by: **CFSX**
St Andrews, NL

***St Anthony:* CFNN-FM** (Freq: 97.9)
Owned by: **CFCB**
St Anthony, NL

***St. John's:* CBN-FM** (Freq: 106.9)
Owned by: **Canadian Broadcasting Corporation (CBC)***
PO Box 12010 A, St. John's, NL A1B 3T8
Tel: 709-576-5000; *Toll-Free:* 800-563-7933
www.cbc.ca/nl; www.cbc.ca/radio2
Other information: Phone, Transmission: 888-353-7006
Denise Wilson, Managing Director, Newfoundland & Labrador
Kathy Porter, Executive Producer, English Radio
Maureen Anonsen, Manager, Partnership & Communications, 709-576-5013
Wayne Tilley, Manager, Accounts, 709-576-5019
Debbie Hynes, Senior Officer, Communications, 709-576-5150

***St. John's:* CFOZ-FM** (Freq: 100.3)
Owned by: **Newfoundland Broadcasting Co. Ltd.***
PO Box 2020, 446 Logy Bay Rd., St. John's, NL A1C 5S2
Tel: 709-726-2922; *Fax:* 709-726-3300
www.ozfm.com
Brian O'Connell, Station Manager

***St. John's:* CHMR-FM** (Freq: 93.5)
PO Box A-119, Memorial University, St. John's, NL A1C 5S7
Tel: 709-737-4777; *Fax:* 709-737-7688
chmr@mun.ca
www.mun.ca/chmr
Kathy Rowe, Station Manager

***St. John's:* CHOS-FM** (Freq: 95.9)
Owned by: **Newfoundland Broadcasting Co. Ltd.***
PO Box 2020, 446 Logy Bay Rd., St. John's, NL A1C 5S2
Tel: 709-726-2922; *Fax:* 709-726-3300
www.ozfm.com
Brian O'Connell, Station Manager

***St. John's:* CHOZ-FM** (Freq: 94.7)
Owned by: **Newfoundland Broadcasting Co. Ltd.***
PO Box 2020, 446 Logy Bay Rd., St. John's, NL A1C 5S2
Tel: 709-726-2922; *Fax:* 709-726-3300
requests@ozfm.com
www.ozfm.com
Doug Neal, General Manager

***St. John's:* CIOS-FM** (Freq: 98.5)
Owned by: **Newfoundland Broadcasting Co. Ltd.***
PO Box 2020, 446 Logy Bay Rd., St. John's, NL A1C 5S2
Tel: 709-726-2922; *Fax:* 709-726-3300
www.ozfm.com

** For details on this company see listing in Major Broadcasting Companies section; † French language station*

Brian O'Connell, Station Manager

St. John's: CIOZ-FM (Freq: 96.3)
Owned by: **Newfoundland Broadcasting Co. Ltd.***
PO Box 2020, 446 Logy Bay Rd., St. John's, NL A1C 5S2
Tel: 709-726-2922; *Fax:* 709-726-3300
www.ozfm.com

St. John's: CJKK-FM (Freq: 105.3)
Owned by: **Newfoundland Broadcasting Co. Ltd.***
CHOZ-FM, 446 Logy Bay Rd., St. John's, NL A1C 5R6
Tel: 709-726-2922; *Fax:* 709-726-3300
Brian O'Connell, Station Manager

St. John's: CJOZ-FM (Freq: 92.1)
Owned by: **Newfoundland Broadcasting Co. Ltd.***
PO Box 2020, 466 Logy Bay Rd., St. John's, NL A1C 5S2
Tel: 709-726-2922; *Fax:* 709-726-3300
www.ozfm.com
Brian O'Connell, Station Manager

St. John's: CKIX-FM (Freq: 99.1)
Owned by: **NewCap Inc.***
PO Box 8590, 391 Kenmount Rd., St. John's, NL A1B 3P5
Tel: 709-726-5590; *Fax:* 709-726-4633
www.991hitsfm.com
Hilary Montbourquette, Operations Manager
Bob Templeton, President
John Murphy, General Manager

St. John's: CKOZ-FM (Freq: 92.3)
Owned by: **Newfoundland Broadcasting Co. Ltd.***
CHOZ-FM, PO Box 2020, 446 Logy Bay Rd., St. John's, NL A1C 5S2
Tel: 709-726-2922; *Fax:* 709-726-3300
www.ozfm.com
Biran O'Connell, Station Manager

St. John's: CKSJ-FM (Freq: 101.1)
PO Box 28106, 48 Kenmount Rd., St. John's, NL A1B 4J8
Tel: 709-754-6748; *Fax:* 709-754-6749
onair@coast1011.com
www.coast1011.com

St. John's: CKSS-FM (Freq: 96.9)
Owned by: **Newfoundland Broadcasting Co. Ltd.***
PO Box 202, 446 Logy Bay Rd., St. John's, NL A1C 5S2
Tel: 709-726-2922; *Fax:* 709-726-3300
www.ozfm.com
Brian O'Connell, Station Manager

St. John's: VOCM-FM (Freq: 97.5)
Owned by: **NewCap Inc.***
PO Box 8590 A, 391 Kenmount Rd., St. John's, NL A1B 3P5
Tel: 709-726-5590; *Fax:* 709-726-4633
feedback@vocm.com
www.k-rock975.com

Northwest Territories

Hay River: CKHR-FM (Freq: 107.3)
PO Box 4394, Hay River, NT X0E 1G3
Tel: 403-874-2547; *Fax:* 403-874-2547
ckhr@northwestel.nt

†Yellowknife: CIVR-FM (Freq: 103.5)
CP 1586, 5106-48th St., Yellowknife, NT X1A 2P2
Tél: 867-766-3308; *Téléc:* 867-766-3314
civr@franco-nord.com
www.radiotaiga.ca
Sylvie Boisclair, General Manager

Yellowknife: CJCD-FM (Freq: 100.1)
PO Box 218, Yellowknife, NT X1A 2N2
Tel: 867-920-2523; *Fax:* 867-920-4033
info@cjcd.ca
www.cjcd.ca
Eileen Dent
Charles Dent

Yellowknife: CKLB-FM (Freq: 101.9)
4 Lessard Dr., Yellowknife, NT X1A 2G5
Tel: 867-920-2277; *Fax:* 867-920-4205
www.ncsnwt.com
Elizabeth Biscaye, Executive Director
Chris Rodgers, TV Manager

Nova Scotia

Antigonish: CFXU-FM (Freq: 92.5)
PO Box 948, St. Francis Xavier University, Antigonish, NS B2G 2X1
Tel: 902-867-3941; *Fax:* 902-867-5138
thefox@stfx.ca
radiocfxu.ca
Caitlin Can Horne, Internal Station Manager

Antigonish: CJFX-FM (Freq: 98.9)
PO Box 5800, Antigonish, NS B2G 2R9
Tel: 902-863-4580; *Fax:* 902-863-6300
cjfx@cjfx.ca
989xfm.supremeserver11.com
David MacLean, General Manager

Bridgewater: CKBW-FM (Freq: 98.1)
215 Dominion St., Bridgewater, NS B4V 2G8
Tel: 902-543-2401; *Fax:* 902-543-1208
ckbw@ckbw.com
www.ckbw.com
Michael Prud'homme, General Manager

Bridgewater: CKBW-FM-2 (Freq: 93.1)
215 Dominion St., Bridgewater, NS B4V 2G8
Tel: 902-543-2401; *Fax:* 902-543-1208
ckbw@ckbw.com
www.ckbw.com
John Wiles, General Manager

†Cheticamp: CKJM-FM (Freq: 106.1)
CP 699, Cheticamp, NS B0E 1H0
Tél: 902-224-1242; *Téléc:* 902-224-1770
info@ckjm.ca
www.ckjm.ca
Auguste LeFort, Station Manager

Digby: CJLS-FM-2 (Freq: 93.5)
Owned by: **CJLS-FM**
Digby, NS

Digby: CKDY-FM-1 (Freq: 103.3)
Owned by: **CKDY**
Digby, NS

Eastern Passage: CFEP-FM (Freq: 94.7)
PO Box 196, Eastern Passage, NS B3G 1M5
Tel: 902-469-9231; *Fax:* 902-469-0966
seasidefm@ns.sympatico.ca
www.seasidefm.com
Wayne Harrett, General Manager

Eskasoni: CICU-FM (Freq: 94.1)
PO Box 7100, 130 Anslum Rd., Eskasoni, NS B1W 1A1
Tel: 902-379-2955; *Fax:* 902-379-2966

Halifax: C100-FM (Freq: 100.1)
PO Box 9316 A, 2900 Agricola St., Halifax, NS B3K 6B2
Tel: 902-453-2524; *Fax:* 902-453-3132
chris.duggan@chumradio.com
www.c100fm.com
Trent McGrath, General Manager, trent.mcgrath@chumradio.com
Chris Duggan, Program Manager, chris.duggan@chumradio.com

†Halifax: CBAX-FM (Freq: 91.5)
CP 3000, Halifax, NS B3J 3E9
Tél: 902-420-8311; *Ligne sans frais:* 866-306-4636
www.radio-canada.ca
Andrew Cochran, Managing Director, Maritimes
Nadine Antle, Regional Manager, Partnerships, Communications, Brand, & Promot, 506-451-4054
John Channing, Manager, Nova Scotia Sales & Marketing
Kathy Large, Manager, Nova Scotia Programs
Chantal Bernard, Senior Officer, Communications, 902-420-4306

Halifax: CBHA-FM (Freq: 90.5)
Owned by: **Canadian Broadcasting Corporation (CBC)***
PO Box 3000, Halifax, NS B3J 3E9
Tel: 902-420-8311; *Fax:* 902-420-4357
Toll-Free: 866-306-4636
www.cbc.ca/ns; www.cbc.ca/radio
Social Media: www.facebook.com/radiocbc; www.twitter.com/cbcradio
Other information: Phone, CBC Radio One Newsroom, Halifax: 902-420-4350
Andrew Cochran, Managing Director, Maritimes
Janet Irwin, Senior Manager, News & Current Affairs
John Channing, Manager, Sales, Nova Scotia
Kathy Large, Manager, Programs
Chantal Bernard, Senior Officer, Communications, 902-420-4306

Halifax: CBH-FM (Freq: 102.7)
Owned by: **Canadian Broadcasting Corporation (CBC)***
PO Box 3000, Halifax, NS B3J 3E9
Tel: 902-420-8311; *Toll-Free:* 866-306-4636
www.cbc.ca/ns; www.cbc.ca/radio2
Andrew Cochran, Managing Director, Maritimes
Nancy Waugh, Executive Producer, Nova Scotia News
Chantal Bernard, Senior Officer, Communications, 902-420-4306

Halifax: CFRQ-FM (Freq: 104.3)
Owned by: **NewCap Inc.***
PO Box 9316 A, Halifax, NS B3K 6B2
Tel: 902-453-4004; *Fax:* 902-453-3132
www.q104.ca
Ted Hyland, General Manager

Halifax: CHFX-FM (Freq: Halifax's only country music station, broadcasting at 101.9 FM)
Owned by: **Maritime Broadcasting System Limited***
5121 Sackville St., 3rd Fl., Halifax, NS B3J 1K1
Tel: 902-422-1651; *Fax:* 902-422-5330
chfx@mbsradio.com
www.fx1019.ca
Robert Pace, Chairman
Ian Kent, General Sales Manager, ian.kent@mbsradio.com

Halifax: CHNS-FM (Freq: 89.9)
Owned by: **Maritime Broadcasting System***
5121 Sackville St., 3 Fl., Halifax, NS B3J 1K1
Tel: 902-425-1225; *Fax:* 902-425-5330
www.chnsradio.com

Halifax: CKDU-FM (Freq: 88.1)
Student Union Bldg., 6136 University Ave., Halifax, NS B3H 4J2
Tel: 902-494-6479; *Fax:* 902-494-1110
info@ckdu.ca
www.ckdu.ca
Michael Wile, Chair
Fiona York, Station Manager

Halifax: CKUL-FM (Freq: 96.5)
Owned by: **NewCap Inc.***
2900 Agricola St., Halifax, NS B3K 6A7
Tel: 902-453-4004; *Fax:* 902-453-3120
www.planetkool.ca
Ted Hyland, General Manager

Inverness: CJFX-FM (Freq: 102.5)
Owned by: **CJFX-FM**
Inverness, NS

Kentville: CKEN-FM (Freq: 97.7)
Owned by: **Maritime Broadcasting System***
PO Box 310, 29 Oakdene Ave., Kentville, NS B4N 1H5
Tel: 902-678-2111; *Fax:* 902-678-9894
avr@avrnetwork.com
www.avrnetwork.com

Kentville: CKWM-FM (Freq: 94.9)
Owned by: **Maritime Broadcasting System***
PO Box 310, 29 Oakdene Ave., Kentville, NS
Tel: 902-678-2111; *Fax:* 902-678-9894
avr@avrnetwork.com
www.magic949.ca
Dianne Best, General Manager

Membertou: CJIJ-FM (Freq: 99.9)
PO Box 99, 49 Tupsi Dr., Membertou, NS B1S 3K6
Tel: 902-562-0009; *Fax:* 902-539-6645
c99fm@hotmail.com
c99fm@homestead.com
Peter Christmas, Jr, General Manager

Port Hawkesbury: 101.5 The Hawk (CIGO-FM) (Freq: 101.5)
#201, 609 Church St., Port Hawkesbury, NS B9A 2X4
Tel: 902-625-1220; *Fax:* 902-625-2664
bob@1015thehawk.com
www.1015thehawk.com
Bob MacEachern, President & General Manager
Brenda MacEachern

Saulnierville: CIFA-FM (Freq: 104.1)
PO Box 8, Saulnierville, NS B0W 2Z0
Tel: 902-769-2432; *Fax:* 902-769-3101
info@cifafm.ca
www.cifa.com
Darlene Comeau, General Manager

** For details on this company see listing in Major Broadcasting Companies section; † French language station*

***Shelburne:* CJLS-FM-1** (Freq: 96.3)
Owned by: **CJLS-FM**
Shelburne, NS

†*Sydney:* CBI-FM (Freq: CBC Radio 2; 105.1)
Owned by: **Canadian Broadcasting Corporation***
Sydney, NS

***Sydney:* CKPE-FM** (Freq: 94.9)
Owned by: **Maritime Broadcasting System***
318 Charlotte St., Sydney, NS B1P 1C8
Tel: 902-564-5596; *Fax:* 902-564-1873
mail@capebretonradio.com
www.capebretonradio.com

***Truro:* CKTO-FM** (Freq: Broadcasting adult contemporary & classic rock at 100.9 FM in Truro)
Owned by: **Astral Media Radio Inc.***
187 Industrial Ave., Truro, NS B2N 6V3
Tel: 902-893-6060; *Fax:* 902-893-7771
Toll-Free: 877-891-6060
www.bigdog1009.ca
Mike Worsley, Sales Manager, mworsley@radioatl.ca

***Truro:* CKTY-FM** (Freq: Broadcasting country music at 99.5 FM in Truro)
Owned by: **Astral Media Radio Inc.***
187 Industrial Ave., Truro, NS B2N 6V3
Tel: 902-893-6060; *Fax:* 902-893-7771
Toll-Free: 877-891-6060
www.catcountry995.ca
Mike Worsley, Sales Manager, mworsley@radioatl.ca

***Yarmouth:* CJLS-FM** (Freq: 95.5)
#201, 328 Main St., Yarmouth, NS B5A 1E4
Tel: 902-742-7175; *Fax:* 902-742-3143
cjls@cjls.com
www.cjls.com
Ray Zinck, President

Nunavut

***Baker Lake:* CKQN-FM** (Freq: 99.3)
Owned by: **Canadian Broadcasting Corporation***
PO Box 13, Baker Lake, NU X0C 0A0
Tel: 867-793-2962; *Fax:* 867-793-2509

†*Iqaluit:* CFRT-FM (Freq: 107.3)
CP 880, Iqaluit, NU X0A 0H0
Tél: 867-979-4606; *Téléc:* 867-979-0800
cfrt@nunafranc.ca
www.franconunavut.ca
Daniel Cuerrier, General Manager

***Iqaluit:* CKIQ-FM** (Freq: 99.9)
PO Box 417, Iqaluit, NU X0A 0H0
Tel: 867-975-2547; *Fax:* 867-975-2598
99.9@ckiq.ca
www.ckiq.cq
Glenn Craig, Station Manager

***Rankin Inlet:* CBQR-FM** (Freq: 105.1)
Owned by: **Canadian Broadcasting Corporation***
PO Box 130, Rankin Inlet, NU X0C 0G0
Tel: 867-645-2885; *Fax:* 867-645-2820
www.cbc.ca/north

Ontario

***Aylmer:* CHPD-FM** (Freq: 107.7)
16 Talbot St., Aylmer, ON N5H 1H4
Tel: 519-773-8555; *Fax:* 519-773-8606
radio@mccayl.org
H.G. (Hein) Rempel, Manager

***Bala:* CFWP-FM** (Freq: 98.3)
PO Box 711, 2350 Muskoka Rd. 38, Bala, ON P0C 1A0
Tel: 705-762-1274; *Fax:* 705-762-2045
hawk98@wahta.com
www.wahta.com/hawkradio
Carl White, Station Manager

***Bancroft:* CHMS-FM** (Freq: 97.7)
PO Box 1240, Bancroft, ON K0L 1C0
Tel: 613-332-1423; *Fax:* 613-332-0841
moose977@hbgradio.com
www.moosefm.com

***Barrie:* CFJB-FM** (Freq: 95.7)
#205, 400 Bayfield St., Barrie, ON L4M 5A1
Tel: 705-725-7304; *Fax:* 705-721-7842
www.rock95.com

***Barrie:* CHAY-FM** (Freq: 93.1)
Owned by: **Corus Entertainment Inc.***
PO Box 937, 1125 Bayfield St. North, Barrie, ON L4M 4Y6
Tel: 705-737-3511; *Fax:* 705-737-0603
promo@thenewchay.com
www.thenewchay.com
Other information: Newsroom Phone: 705/726-1597; Fax: 705/722-5631
J. Kim Noel, General Manager

***Barrie:* CJLF-FM** (Freq: 100.3)
#111, 115 Bell Farm Rd., Barrie, ON L4M 5G1
Tel: 705-735-3370; *Fax:* 705-735-3301
www.lifeonline.fm
Scott Jackson, Station Manager, scott@lifeonline.fm
Simon Slessor, Director
Janice Baird, CFO

***Barrie:* CKMB-FM** (Freq: 107.5)
#205, 400 Bayfield St., Barrie, ON L4M 5A1
Tel: 705-725-7304; *Fax:* 705-721-7842
www.1075koolfm.com
Doug Bingley, General Manager

***Belleville:* CHCQ-FM** (Freq: 100.1)
354 Pinnacle St., Belleville, ON K8N 3B4
Tel: 613-966-0955; *Fax:* 613-967-2565
www.cool100.fm

***Belleville:* CIGL-FM** (Freq: 97.1)
PO Box 488, 10 Front St. South, Belleville, ON K8N 5B2
Tel: 613-969-5555; *Fax:* 613-969-8122
www.mix97.com

***Belleville:* CJLX-FM** (Freq: 91.3)
PO Box 4200, Belleville, ON K8N 5B9
Tel: 613-969-0923; *Fax:* 613-966-1993
contact@91x.fm; sales@91x.fm; music@91x.fm
www.91x.fm
Other information: Phone, Newsroom: 613-966-6797; Fax, News: 613-969-9382
Greg Schatzmann, General Manager

***Belleville:* CJOJ-FM** (Freq: 95.5)
354 Pinnacle St., Belleville, ON K8N 3B4
Tel: 613-966-0955; *Fax:* 613-967-2565
www.classichits955.fm
John Sherratt, President

***Bracebridge:* CFBG-FM** (Freq: 99.5)
#50, 2 Balls Dr., Bracebridge, ON P1L 1T1
Tel: 705-645-2218; *Fax:* 705-645-6957
moose995@hbgradio.com
www.moosefm.com

***Brantford:* CFWC-FM** (Freq: 93.9)
271 Greenwich St., Brantford, ON N3S 2X9
Tel: 519-759-2339; *Fax:* 519-753-1157
info@power93.ca
www.power93.ca
Vicki Schleifer, Station Manager

***Brantford:* CKPC-FM** (Freq: 92.1)
571 West St., Brantford, ON N3T 5P8
Tel: 519-759-1000; *Fax:* 519-753-1470
ops@ckpc.on.ca
www.ckpc.on.ca
Richard Buchanan, President/General Manager

***Brockville:* CFJR-FM** (Freq: 104.9)
PO Box 666, 601 Stewart Blvd., Brockville, ON K6V 5V9
Tel: 613-345-1666; *Fax:* 613-342-2438
www.1049jrfm.com
Greg Hinton, Vice President/General Manager

***Brockville:* CJPT-FM** (Freq: 103.7)
PO Box 666, 601 Stewart Blvd., Brockville, ON K6V 5V9
Tel: 613-345-1666; *Fax:* 613-342-2438
www.bob.fm
Greg Hinton, Vice President/General Manager

***Cambridge:* CJDV-FM** (Freq: 107.5)
Owned by: **Corus Entertainment Inc.***
#100, 1315 Bishop St. North, Cambridge, ON N1R 6Z2
Tel: 519-621-7510; *Fax:* 519-621-0165
www.davefm.com

***Campbellford:* CKOL-FM** (Freq: 93.7)
PO Box 551, 15 Raglan St. South, Campbellford, ON K0L 1L0
Tel: 705-653-1089
ckol-radio@excite.com
Dave Lockwood, General Manager

***Chatham:* CFCO-FM** (Freq: 92.9)
Owned by: **CFCO**
Chatham, ON

***Chatham:* CKSY-FM** (Freq: 94.3)
Owned by: **Blackburn Radio Inc.***
PO Box 100, 117 Keil Dr., Chatham, ON N7M 5K1
Tel: 519-354-2200; *Fax:* 519-354-2880
info@cksyfm.com
www.cksyfm.com

***Chatham:* CKUE-FM** (Freq: 95.1)
Owned by: **Blackburn Radio Inc.***
PO Box 100, 117 Keil Dr., Chatham, ON N7M 5K1
Tel: 519-354-2200; *Fax:* 519-354-2880
info@therock951.com
www.therock951.com
Carl Veroba

***Cobourg:* CKSG-FM** (Freq: 93.3)
PO Box 520, Cobourg, ON K9A 4L3
Tel: 905-372-5401; *Fax:* 905-372-6280
Toll-Free: 866-782-7933
info@star933.com
www.star933.com
Don Conway, President

***Cochrane:* CHPB-FM** (Freq: 98.1)
PO Box 855, 135 - 3rd St., Cochrane, ON P0L 1C0
Tel: 705-267-6467; *Fax:* 705-267-6467
moose981@hbgradio.com
www.moosefm.com

***Cochrane:* CJWL-FM** (Freq: 101.1)
PO Box 855, 153 - 3rd St., Cochrane, ON P1L 1C1
Tel: 705-272-6467; *Fax:* 705-272-6467
moose981@hbgradio.com
www.moosefm.com/cjwl/index.php

***Collingwood:* CKCB-FM** (Freq: 95.1)
Owned by: **Corus Entertainment Inc.***
1400 Hwy. 26 East, Collingwood, ON L9Y 4W2
Tel: 705-446-9510; *Fax:* 705-444-6776
www.thepeakfm.com
John Eaton, General Manager

***Cornwall:* CFLG-FM** (Freq: 104.5)
Owned by: **Corus Entertainment Inc.***
PO Box 969, 237 Water St. East, Cornwall, ON K6H 5V1
Tel: 613-932-5180; *Fax:* 613-938-0355
variety104@seawayvalley.com
www.seawayvalley.com
Paul Vincent, General Manager

†*Cornwall:* CHOD-FM (Freq: 92.1)
#202, 1111 Montreal Rd., Cornwall, ON K6H 1E1
Tél: 613-936-2463; *Téléc:* 613-936-2568
chodfm@chodfm.ca
www.chod.on.ca
François Cotê

***Cornwall:* CJSS-FM** (Freq: 101.9)
Owned by: **Corus Entertainment Inc.***
PO Box 969, 709 Cotton Mill St., Cornwall, ON K6H 7K7
Tel: 613-932-5180; *Fax:* 613-938-0355
Toll-Free: 888-678-8122
www.seawayvalley.com
Tim Wieczorek, General Manager

***Cornwall:* CKON-FM** (Freq: 97.3)
PO Box 1496, Cornwall, ON K6H 5V5
Tel: 613-575-2100; *Fax:* 613-575-2566
ckon@ckon.com
www.cnwl.igs.net/~ckon/

***Dryden:* CJIV-FM** (Freq: 97.3)
PO Box 112, Dryden, ON P8N 2Y7
Tel: 807-937-9731; *Fax:* 807-937-6490
cjiv@canada.com
www.cjiv973.net

** For details on this company see listing in Major Broadcasting Companies section; † French language station*

***Dryden:* CKDR-FM** (Freq: 92.7)
Owned by: **Fawcett Broadcasting Ltd.***
PO Box 580, 122 King St., Dryden, ON P8N 2Z3
Tel: 807-223-2355; *Fax:* 807-223-5090
mail@ckdr.net
www.ckdr.net

***Elliot Lake:* CKNR-FM** (Freq: Broadcasting adult contemporary music at 94.1 FM in Elliot Lake)
144 Ontario Ave., Elliot Lake, ON P5A 1Y3
Tel: 705-848-3608; *Fax:* 705-848-1378
Toll-Free: 800-565-7359
moose941@moosefm.com
www.moosefm.com/cknr
Erika MacLellan, Operations Manager/Sales Executive, emaclellan@moosefm.com
Bob Alexander, Promotions Director/Host, balexander@moosefm.com

***Englehart:* CJBB-FM** (Freq: 103.1)
50 Third St., Englehart, ON P0J 1H0
Tel: 705-544-1121; *Fax:* 705-544-2286
cjbb@ntl.sympatico.ca
Rick Stow, Station Manager

***Fort Frances:* CFOB-FM** (Freq: 93.1)
Owned by: **Fawcett Broadcasting Ltd.***
242 Scott St., Fort Frances, ON P9A 1G7
Tel: 807-274-5341; *Fax:* 807-274-2033
Hugh Syrja

***Guelph:* CFRU-FM** (Freq: 93.3)
University Centre, Level 2, University of Guelph, Guelph, ON N1G 2W1
Tel: 519-824-4120; *Fax:* 519-763-9603
info@cfru.ca
www.cfru.ca
Lori Guest, Music Programming Coordinator
Ignace Ntirushwamaboko, Spoken Word Coordinator
John Leacock, Music Coordinator/Advertising Coord
Richard Watson, Promotions Coordinator
Kim Iezzi, Operations Coordinator

***Guelph:* CIMJ-FM** (Freq: 106.1)
Owned by: **Corus Entertainment Inc.***
75 Speedvale Ave. East, Guelph, ON N1E 6M3
Tel: 519-824-7000; *Fax:* 519-824-4118
magic@magic106.com
www.magic106.com

***Haliburton:* CKHA-FM** (Freq: 100.9)
PO Box 1125, Haliburton, ON K0M 1S0
Tel: 705-457-9603; *Fax:* 705-457-9522
info@canoefm1009.com
www.canoefm.com
Dave Sovereign, Station Manager

***Hamilton:* CFMU-FM** (Freq: 93.3)
#B119, McMaster University Student Centre, Hamilton, ON L8S 4S4
Tel: 905-525-9140; *Fax:* 905-529-3208
bhandari@msu.mcmaster.can.ca
cfmu.mcmaster.ca
Sandeepa Bhandari, Station Manager

***Hamilton:* CING-FM** (Freq: 107.9)
Owned by: **Corus Entertainment Inc.***
875 Main St. West, Hamilton, ON L8S 4R1
Tel: 905-521-9900; *Fax:* 902-540-2453
www.country953.com

***Hamilton:* CIOI-FM** (Freq: 101.5)
PO Box 2034, 135 Fennell Ave., Hamilton, ON L8N 3T2
Tel: 905-575-2175; *Fax:* 905-575-2385
les.palango@mohawkcollege.ca
www.mohawkcollege.ca/msa/cioi
Les Palango, Station Manager
Jamie Smith, Program & Music Director
Jeff Cudahy, Chief Engineer

***Hamilton:* CIWV-FM** (Freq: 94.7)
589 Upper Wellington, Hamilton, ON L9A 3P8
Tel: 905-388-8911; *Fax:* 905-388-7947
Toll-Free: 866-388-8911
www.wave947.fm
Douglas E. Kirk, President

***Hamilton:* CJXY-FM** (Freq: 107.9)
Owned by: **Corus Entertainment Inc.***
#900, 875 Main St. West, Hamilton, ON L8S 4R1
Tel: 905-521-0953; *Fax:* 905-521-2306
www.y108.ca

***Hamilton:* CKLH-FM** (Freq: 102.9)
Owned by: **Standard Radio Office***
#401, 883 Upper Wentworth St., Hamilton, ON L9A 4Y6
Tel: 905-574-1150; *Fax:* 905-574-6429
info@k-litefm.com
www.k-lite.com
David Jones, Program Director
Tom Cooke, General Manager
Robyn Foley, News Director

***Hanover:* CFBW-FM** (Freq: 91.3 FM; Radio Station)
267 - 10th St., Hanover, ON N4N 1P1
Tel: 519-364-0200; *Fax:* 519-364-5175
bluewaterradio@on.aibn.com
www.bluewaterradio.ca
Andrew McBride, Station Manager, 519-370-9090

***†Hawkesbury:* CHPR-FM** (Freq: 102.1)
Owned by: **Radio Nord Communications Inc.***
#37, 115 Main St., Hawkesbury, ON K6A 1A1
Tél: 613-632-1000; *Téléc:* 514-632-1110
infocouleurfm@radionord.com

***†Hearst:* CINN-FM** (Freq: 91.1)
CP 2648, 1004, rue Prince, Hearst, ON P0L 1N0
Tél: 705-372-1011; *Téléc:* 705-362-7411
Ligne sans frais: 866-362-5168
cinnfm@cinnfm.com
www.cinnfm.com
Gaetane Morrissette

***Huntsville:* CFBK-FM** (Freq: 105.5)
#2, 15 Main St. East, Huntsville, ON P1H 2C6
Tel: 705-789-4461; *Fax:* 705-789-1269
105.5@morefm.ca
L. Byers, President/Owner

***Kapuskasing:* CKAP-FM** (Freq: 100.9)
Moose FM, #2A, 22 Queen St., Kapuskasing, ON P5N 1G8
Tel: 705-335-2379; *Fax:* 705-337-6391
Toll-Free: 866-505-2379
moose1009@hbgradio.com
hbgradio.com
Christopher Grossman, President

***†Kapuskasing:* CKGN-FM** (Freq: 89.7 FM Kapuskasing et 94.7 FM Smooth Rock Falls)
77, ch Brunelle nord, Kapuskasing, ON P5N 2M1
Tél: 705-335-5915; *Téléc:* 705-335-3508
Ligne sans frais: 800-385-2741
ckgn-fm@nt.net
www.ckgn.ca
Claude Chabot, Directeur général, claudechabot@ckgn.ca

***Kenora:* CJRL 89.5 Mix FM**
Owned by: **Northwoods Broadcasting Ltd.***
128 Main St. South, Kenora, ON P9N 1S9
Tel: 807-468-3181; *Fax:* 807-468-4188
cjrl@cjrl.ca
www.cjrl.ca/89fm

***Kenora:* CJRL-FM** (Freq: 89.5)
Owned by: **89.5 Mix FM***
128 Main St. South, Kenora, ON P9N 1S9
Tel: 807-468-3181; *Fax:* 807-468-4188
carolyn@89.5mix.fm
Henry Syrja, Manager

***Killaloe:* CHCR-FM** (Freq: 102.9; 104.5)
PO Box 195, 7A Lake St., 2nd Fl., Killaloe, ON K0J 2A0
Tel: 613-757-0657; *Fax:* 613-757-0818
stationmanager@chcr.org
www.chcr.org
Ambrose Mullin, Station Manager

***Kingston:* CBBK-FM** (Freq: 92.9)
Owned by: **Canadian Broadcasting Corporation (CBC)***
Kingston, ON
Toll-Free: 866-306-4636
www.cbc.ca/radio2
Social Media: www.facebook.com/CBC.Radio2.Official?ref=nf
Other information: Twitter: www.twitter.com/cbcradio2

***Kingston:* CFFX** (Freq: 104.3)
Owned by: **Corus Entertainment Inc.***
170 Queen St., Kingston, ON K7K 1B2
Tel: 613-544-2340; *Fax:* 613-544-5508
www.lite1043.ca
Mike Ferguson, General Manager
Brad Gibb, Program Director

***Kingston:* CFLY-FM** (Freq: 98.3)
#10, 993 Princess St., Kingston, ON K7L 1H3
Tel: 613-544-1380; *Fax:* 613-546-9751
flyfm@flyfmkingston.com
flyfmkingston.com
Greg Hinton, Vice President/General Manager

***Kingston:* CFMK-FM** (Freq: 96.3)
Owned by: **Corus Entertainment Inc.***
170 Queen St., Kingston, ON K7K 1B2
Tel: 613-544-2340; *Fax:* 613-544-5508
www.fm96.ca
Mike Ferguson, General Manager
Brad Gibb, Program Director

***Kingston:* CFRC-FM** (Freq: 101.9)
Carruthers Hall, Kingston, ON K7L 3N6
Tel: 613-533-2121; *Fax:* 613-533-6049
cfrc@ams.queensu.ca
www.cfrc.ca
Maureen Plunkett, Station Manager

***Kingston:* CIKR-FM** (Freq: 105.7)
#301, 863 Princess St., Kingston, ON K7L 5N4
Tel: 613-549-1057; *Fax:* 613-549-5302
feedback@krock1057.ca
www.krock1057.ca

***Kingston:* CKVI-FM** (Freq: 91.9)
#119, 235 Frontenac St., Kingston, ON K7L 3S7
Tel: 613-544-7864; *Fax:* 613-544-8795
ckvi@limestone.ca
www.thecave.ca
Max Lienhard, Station Manager

***Kirkland Lake:* CJKL-FM** (Freq: 101.5)
PO Box 430, 5 Kirkland St., Kirkland Lake, ON P2N 3J4
Tel: 705-567-3366; *Fax:* 705-567-6101
cjkl@cjklfm.com
cjklfm.com
Rob Connelly, President

***Kitchener:* CFCA-FM** (Freq: 105.3)
Owned by: **CFCA-FM**
Kitchener, ON

***Kitchener:* CHYM-FM** (Freq: 96.7)
Owned by: **Rogers Broadcasting Ltd.***
305 King St. West, Kitchener, ON N2G 4E4
Tel: 519-743-2611; *Fax:* 519-743-7510
www.chymfm.com

***Kitchener:* CJIQ-FM** (Freq: 88.3)
299 Doon Valley Dr., Kitchener, ON N2G 4M4
Tel: 519-748-5220; *Fax:* 519-748-5971
cjiqinfo@cjiq.fm
www.cjiq.fm
Paul Scott, Manager, Sales & Marketing
Mark Burley, Station Manager

***Kitchener:* CJTW-FM** (Freq: 94.3)
PO Box 1433 C, 207, 659 King St. East, Kitchener, ON N2G 4H6
Tel: 519-575-9090; *Fax:* 519-575-9119
Toll-Free: 877-741-9430
info@faithfm.org
www.faithfm.org
Dave MacDonald, General Manager

***Leamington:* CHYR-FM** (Freq: 96.7)
Owned by: **Blackburn Radio Inc.***
100 Talbot St. East, Leamington, ON N8H 1L3
Tel: 519-326-6171; *Fax:* 519-322-1110
96.7@chyr.com
www.chyr.com

***Lindsay:* CKLY-FM** (Freq: 91.9)
249 Kent St. West, Lindsay, ON K9V 2Z3
Tel: 705-324-9103; *Fax:* 705-324-4149
www.919bobfm.com
Steve Fawcett, General Manager

***Little Current:* CFRM-FM** (Freq: 101.1)
PO Box 871, 10 Campbell St. East, Little Current, ON P0P 1K0
Tel: 705-368-1419; *Fax:* 705-368-1080
radio@manitoulin.net
www.101rocks.com
Rick Nelson, Station Manager

** For details on this company see listing in Major Broadcasting Companies section; † French language station*

London: **CBBL-FM** (Freq: 100.5)
Owned by: **Canadian Broadcasting Corporation (CBC)***
#4, 208 Piccadilly St., London, ON N6A 1S1
Toll-Free: 866-306-4636
www.cbc.ca/radio2
Social Media: www.facebook.com/CBC.Radio2.Official?ref=nf
Other information: Twitter: www.twitter.com/cbcradio2

London: **CBCL-FM** (Freq: 93.5)
Owned by: **Canadian Broadcasting Corporation (CBC)***
#4, 208 Piccadilly St., London, ON N6A 1S1
Tel: 519-667-1990; *Toll-Free:* 866-306-4636
www.cbc.ca/radio
Social Media: www.facebook.com/radiocbc;
www.twitter.com/cbcradio
Other information: TDD: 1-866-220-6045

London: **CFHK-FM** (Freq: 103.1)
Owned by: **Corus Entertainment Inc.***
#222, 380 Wellington Rd., London, ON N6A 5B5
Tel: 519-931-6000; *Fax:* 519-679-1967
www.energy103.ca

London: **CFPL-FM** (Freq: 95.9)
Owned by: **Corus Entertainment Inc.***
#222, 380 Wellington St., London, ON N6A 5B5
Tel: 519-931-6000; *Fax:* 519-679-1967
www.fm96.com
Rick Moss

London: **CHJX-FM** (Freq: 105.9)
Sound of Faith Broadcasting Inc., 100 Fullarton St., London, ON N6A 1K1
Tel: 519-679-9882; *Fax:* 519-679-2459
info@gracefm.ca
www.gracefm.ca
Doug Chaplin, Station Manager

London: **CHRW-FM** (Freq: 94.9)
#250, UCC Bldg., London, ON N6A 3K7
Tel: 519-661-3601; *Fax:* 519-661-3372
chrwgm@uwo.ca
www.chrwradio.com
Grant Stein, Station Manager
Zoltan Haraszthy, Program Director
James McMillan, News & Sports Director

London: **CHST-FM** (Freq: 102.3)
1 Communications Rd., London, ON N6J 4Z1
Tel: 519-690-0102; *Fax:* 519-686-5942
www.1023bob.com
Don Mumford, General Manager, don.mumford@chumradio.com
Ann LaRocque, Sales Manager, ann.larocque@chumradio.com
Janice Pearce, Business Manager, janice.pearce@chumradio.com
Montea Sherritt, Traffic Manager, montea.sherritt@chumradio.com

London: **CIQM-FM** (Freq: 97.5)
Owned by: **Standard Radio Office***
743 Wellington Rd. South, London, ON N6C 4R5
Tel: 519-686-2525; *Fax:* 519-686-3658
www.q975.com
Braden Doerr, General Manager

London: **CIXX-FM** (Freq: 106.9)
Fanshawe College, 1460 Oxford St. East, London, ON N5V 1W2
Tel: 519-453-2810; *Fax:* 519-452-4152
www.6xnews.com
Bob Collins, Contact

London: **CJBX-FM** (Freq: 92.7)
Owned by: **Standard Radio Office***
743 Wellington Rd. South, London, ON N6C 4R5
Tel: 519-685-2525; *Fax:* 519-686-3658
bx93@bx93.com
www.bx93.com
Braden Doerr, General Manager

Marathon: **CFNO-FM** (Freq: 93.1; 100.7)
PO Box 1000, 93 Evergreen Dr., Marathon, ON P0T 2E0
Tel: 807-229-1010; *Fax:* 807-229-1686
www.cfno.fm
S. Spencer Bell, President

Midland: **CICZ-FM** (Freq: 104.1)
PO Box 609, 355 Cranston Cres., Midland, ON L4R 4L3
Tel: 705-526-2268; *Fax:* 705-526-3060
www.kicxfm.com

Mississauga: **CFRE-FM** (Freq: closed circuit)
#115, 3359 Mississauga Rd., Mississauga, ON L5L 1C6
Tel: 905-820-1640; *Fax:* 905-569-4714
www.cfreradio.com

New Liskeard: **CJTT-FM** (Freq: 104.5)
PO Box 1058, 55 Whitewood Ave., New Liskeard, ON P0J 1P0
Tel: 705-647-7334; *Fax:* 705-647-8660
cjtt@cjttfm.com
www.cjttfm.com
Other information: Phone, News & Sports: 705-647-7171; Phone, Studio: 705-647-6565

Niagara Falls: **CFLZ-FM** (Freq: 105.1)
PO Box 710, 4668 St. Clair Ave., Niagara Falls, ON L2E 6X7
Tel: 905-356-6710; *Fax:* 905-356-0644
www.river.fm
Elizabeth Lewis, General Manager

Niagara Falls: **CKEY-FM** (Freq: 101.1)
PO Box 710, 4668 St. Claire Ave., Niagara Falls, ON L2E 6X7
Tel: 905-356-6710; *Fax:* 905-356-0696
www.wild101.com
Dave Universal, Program Director, daveuniv@niagara.com

North Bay: **CHUR-FM** (Freq: 100.5)
Owned by: **Rogers Broadcasting Ltd.***
PO Box 3000, 743 Main St. East, North Bay, ON P1B 8K8
Tel: 705-479-2000; *Fax:* 705-474-7761
www.ezrocknorthbay.com
Andy Wilson, Program Director

North Bay: **CKFX-FM** (Freq: 101.9)
Owned by: **Rogers Broadcasting Ltd.***
743 Main St. East, North Bay, ON P1B 1C2
Tel: 705-474-2000; *Fax:* 705-474-7761
thefox@foxradio.ca
www.foxradio.ca
Mitch Belanger, Program Director
Mike Belanger, Program Director

North Bay: **CRFM-FM** (Freq: 89.9)
Canadore College, PO Box 5001, 100 College Dr., North Bay, ON P1B 8K9
Tel: 705-474-7600; *Fax:* 705-474-2384
info@thepanther.ca
www.ThePanther.ca

Oakville: **CORS-FM** (Freq: closed circuit)
Sheridan College, 1430 Trafalgar Rd., Oakville, ON L6H 2L1
Tel: 905-845-9430; *Fax:* 905-815-4043

Ohsweken: **CKRZ-FM** (Freq: 100.3)
PO Box 189, Ohsweken, ON N0A 1M0
Tel: 519-445-4140; *Fax:* 519-445-0177
ckrzinfo@ckrz.com
www.ckrz.com
Sandra Muse, Station Manager

Orillia: **CICX-FM** (Freq: 105.9)
Owned by: **Rogers Broadcasting Ltd.***
PO Box 550, 7 Progress Dr., Orillia, ON L3V 6K2
Tel: 705-326-3511; *Fax:* 705-326-1816
www.1059jackfm.com

Oshawa: **CJKX-FM** (Freq: 95.9; 89.9)
#207, 1200 Airport Blvd., Oshawa, ON L1J 8P5
Tel: 905-428-9600; *Fax:* 905-571-1150
kx96@kx96.fm
www.kx96.fm
Steve Kassay, Operations Manager

Oshawa: **CKDO-FM** (Freq: 107.7; 1350; 96.0)
#207, 1200 Airport Blvd., Oshawa, ON L1J 8P5
Tel: 905-571-0949; *Fax:* 905-571-1150
bfisher@accel.net
www.kx96.fm
Steve Kassay, Operations Manager

Oshawa: **CKGE-FM** (Freq: 94.9)
#207, 1200 Airport Blvd., Oshawa, ON L1J 8P5
Tel: 905-571-0949; *Fax:* 905-579-1150
Toll-Free: 866-799-7625
steve@therock.fm
www.therock.fm
Steve Kassav, Operations Manager
Stephen A. Kassay, Vice-President, Operations

Ottawa: **CBO-FM** (Freq: 91.5)
Owned by: **Canadian Broadcasting Corporation***
PO Box 3220 C, 181 Queen St., Ottawa, ON K1Y 1E4
Tel: 613-288-6000
www.cbc.ca/ottawa
Laurence Wall, Producer
Tom New, Communications Officer

Ottawa: **CBOQ-FM** (Freq: 103.3)
Owned by: **Canadian Broadcasting Corporation***
Ottawa, ON

Ottawa: **CBOX-FM** (Freq: 102.5)
Owned by: **Canadian Broadcasting Corporation***
PO Box 3220 C, 181 Queen St., Ottawa, ON K1Y 1E4
Tel: 613-288-6000
www.radio-canada.ca/regions/ontario

Ottawa: **CHEZ-FM** (Freq: 106.1)
Owned by: **Rogers Broadcasting Ltd.***
2001 Thurston Dr., Ottawa, ON K1G 6C9
Tel: 613-736-2001; *Fax:* 613-736-2002
www.chez106.com

Ottawa: **CHRI-FM** (Freq: 99.1)
#3, 1010 Thomas Spratt Pl., Ottawa, ON K1G 5L5
Tel: 613-247-1440; *Fax:* 613-247-7128
Toll-Free: 866-924-7436
chri@chri.ca
www.chri.ca
Bill Stevens, General Manager
Robert Du Broy, Director & General Manager

Ottawa: **CHUO-FM** (Freq: 89.1)
#0038, 65 University Pvt., Ottawa, ON K1N 9A5
Tel: 613-562-5965
info@chuo.fm
www.chuo.fm
Chris Jack, Interim Station Manager

Ottawa: **CIHT-FM** (Freq: 89.9)
Owned by: **NewCap Inc.***
1500 Merivale Rd., Ottawa, ON K2E 6Z5
Tel: 613-723-8990; *Fax:* 613-723-7016
www.hot899.com

Ottawa: **CISS-FM** (Freq: 105.3)
Owned by: **Rogers Broadcasting Ltd.***
2001 Thurston Dr., Ottawa, ON K1G 6C9
Tel: 613-736-2001; *Fax:* 613-736-2002
www.1053kissfm.com
Danny Kingsbury, Station Manager/Program Director

Ottawa: **CJLL-FM** (Freq: 97.9)
#100, 30 Murray St., Ottawa, ON K1N 5M4
Tel: 613-244-0979; *Fax:* 613-244-3858
chinottawa@chinradio.com
www.chinradio.com
Ed Ylanen, General Manager

Ottawa: **CJMJ-FM** (Freq: 100.3)
87 George St., Ottawa, ON K1N 9H7
Tel: 613-789-2486; *Fax:* 613-750-0100
www.majic100.fm
Al Smith, Program Director

Ottawa: **CKBY-FM** (Freq: 101.1)
Owned by: **Rogers Broadcasting Ltd.***
2001 Thurston Dr., Ottawa, ON K1G 6C9
Tel: 613-736-2001; *Fax:* 613-736-2002
www.y101.fm
Al Campagnola, General Manager, acampagn@rci.rogers.com

Ottawa: **CKCU-FM** (Freq: 93.1)
#517, University Centre, Carleton University, 1125 Colonel By Dr., Ottawa, ON K1S 5B6
Tel: 613-520-2898
info@ckcufm.com
www.ckcufm.com
Barry Rueger, Station Manager

Ottawa: **CKDJ-FM** (Freq: 107.9)
Algonquin College, 1385 Woodroffe Ave., Ottawa, ON K2G 1V8
Tel: 613-727-4723; *Fax:* 613-727-7689
crockfd@algonquincollege.com
www.ckdj.net
Kyra Kratzmann, Station Manager

Ottawa: **CKKL-FM** (Freq: 93.9)
87 George St., Ottawa, ON K1N 9H7
Tel: 613-789-2486; *Fax:* 613-739-5626
www.939bobfm.com

** For details on this company see listing in Major Broadcasting Companies section; † French language station*

Al Smith, Program Director

***Ottawa:* CKQB-FM** (Freq: 106.9)
Owned by: **Standard Radio Office***
1504 Merivale Rd., Ottawa, ON K2E 6Z5
Tel: 613-225-1069; *Fax:* 613-226-3381
Toll-Free: 800-754-1069
bearinfo@thebear.fm
www.thebear.fm

Gord Taylor, Program Director
Kath Thompson, Music, Director
Scott Broderick, General Sales Manager
Rebecca Crow, Promotion Director
Eric Stafford, General Manager

***Owen Sound:* CIXK-FM** (Freq: 106.5)
Owned by: **Bayshore Broadcasting Corporation***
PO Box 280, 270 - 9 St. East, Owen Sound, ON N4K 5P5
Tel: 519-376-2030; *Fax:* 519-371-4242
bayshore@radioowensound.com
www.radioowensound.com

Ross Kentner, General Manager, rkentner@bayshorebroadcasting.ca
Kevin Brown, General Sales Manager, kbrown@bayshorebroadcasting.ca
Rob Brignell, Director, Marketing & Business Development, rbrignell@bayshorebroadcasting.ca

***Owen Sound:* CKYC-FM** (Freq: 93.7)
Owned by: **Bayshore Broadcasting Corporation***
PO Box 280, 270 - 9 St. East, Owen Sound, ON N4K 5P5
Tel: 519-376-2030; *Fax:* 519-371-4242
bayshore@radioowensound.com
www.radioowensound.com

Ross Kentner, General Manager, rkentner@bayshorebroadcasting.ca
Kevin Brown, General Sales Manager, kbrown@bayshorebroadcasting.ca
Rob Brignell, Director, Marketing & Development, rbrignell@bayshorebroadcasting.ca

***Parry Sound:* CKLP-FM** (Freq: 103.3)
#301, 60 James St., Parry Sound, ON P2A 1T5
Tel: 705-746-2163; *Fax:* 705-746-4292
moose1033@hbgradio.com
www.hbgradio.com

Kimberley Ward-Grossman, Vice-President
Dave Keeble, Operations Manager
Christopher Grossman, President

***Pembroke:* CHVR-FM** (Freq: 96.7)
Owned by: **Standard Radio Office***
595 Pembroke St. East, Pembroke, ON K8A 3L7
Tel: 613-735-9670; *Fax:* 613-735-7748
star96@sri.ca
www.star96.ca

Al Kennedy

†*Penetanguishene:* CFRH-FM (Freq: 88.1)
CP 5099, 63, rue Main, Penetanguishene, ON L9M 2G3
Tél: 705-549-3116; *Téléc:* 705-549-6463
cfrh@lacle.ca
www.cfrh.ca

Peter Hominuk, General Manager

***Peterborough:* CFFF-FM** (Freq: 92.7)
Trent University, 715 George St. North, Peterborough, ON K9H 3T2
Tel: 705-741-4011; *Fax:* 705—
trentradio@trentradio.ca
www.trentradio.ca

***Peterborough:* CKQM-FM** (Freq: 105.1)
Country 105, PO Box 177, 59 George St. North, Peterborough, ON K9J 6Y8
Tel: 705-742-8844; *Fax:* 705-742-1417
country@chumradio.com
www.country105.fm

Steve Fawcett, General Manager
Brian Young, Program Director

***Peterborough:* CKWF-FM** (Freq: 101.5)
Owned by: **Corus Entertainment Inc.***
159 King St., Peterborough, ON K9J 2R8
Tel: 705-748-6101; *Fax:* 705-742-7708
info@thewolf.ca
www.thewolf.ca

Kathleen McNair, General Manager

***Port Elgin:* CFPS-FM** (Freq: 97.9)
Owned by: **Bayshore Broadcasting Corporation***
382 Goderich St., Port Elgin, ON N0H 2C1
Tel: 519-832-9800; *Fax:* 519-832-9808
Toll-Free: 877-652-9800
bayshore@radioowensound.com
www.radioowensound.com

Lois Reid, Business, Manager
Rob Brignell, Station Manager
Deb Shaw, Sales Manager
Don Vail, Promotion Director

***Sarnia:* CBEG-FM** (Freq: 90.3)
Owned by: **Canadian Broadcasting Corporation (CBC)***
Sarnia, ON
Toll-Free: 866-306-4636
www.cbc.ca/windsor; www.cbc.ca/radio
Social Media: www.facebook.com/radiocbc; www.twitter.com/cbcradio
Other information: TDD: 1-866-220-6045

Sandra Porteous, Managing Editor, Radio & Television, 519-255-3563
David Daigneault, Executive Producer, Radio & Television, 519-255-3410

***Sarnia:* CFGX-FM** (Freq: 99.9)
Owned by: **Blackburn Radio Inc.***
1415 London Rd., Sarnia, ON N7S 1P6
Tel: 519-542-5500; *Fax:* 519-542-1520
www.foxfm.com

***Sarnia:* CHKS-FM** (Freq: 106.3)
Owned by: **Blackburn Radio Inc.***
1415 London Rd., Sarnia, ON N7S 1P6
Tel: 519-542-5500; *Fax:* 519-542-1520
rock@k106fm.com
www.k106fm.com

***Sault Ste Marie:* CHAS-FM** (Freq: 100.5)
Owned by: **Rogers Broadcasting Ltd.***
642 Great Northern Rd., Sault Ste Marie, ON P6B 4Z9
Tel: 705-759-9200; *Fax:* 705-946-3575
www.ezrocksoo.com

Scott Sexsmith, General Manager, scott.sexsmith@ssmradio.rogers.com

***Sault Ste Marie:* CJQM-FM** (Freq: 104.3)
Owned by: **Rogers Broadcasting Ltd.***
642 Great Northern Rd., Sault Ste Marie, ON P6B 4Z9
Tel: 705-759-9200; *Fax:* 705-946-3575
www.qcountry.ca

Scott Sexsmith, General Manager, scott.sexsmith@ssmradio.rogers.com

***Simcoe:* CHCD-FM** (Freq: 98.9)
PO Box 98, 55 Park Rd., Simcoe, ON N3Y 4K8
Tel: 519-426-7700; *Fax:* 519-426-8574
www.cd989.com

Jim MacLeod, President

***Sioux Lookout:* CKWT-FM** (Freq: 89.1)
PO Box 1180, 16 - 5 Ave., Sioux Lookout, ON P8T 1B7
Tel: 807-737-2951; *Fax:* 807-737-3224
www.wrn.wawatay.on.ca

***Smiths Falls:* CJET-FM** (Freq: 92.3)
Owned by: **Rogers Broadcasting Ltd.***
PO Box 630, Smiths Falls, ON K7A 4T4
Tel: 613-283-4630; *Fax:* 613-283-7243
www.923jackfm.com

***St Catharines:* CFBU-FM** (Freq: 103.7)
500 Glenridge Ave., St Catharines, ON L2S 3A1
Tel: 905-688-2644
pd@cfbu.ca
www.cfbu.ca

Russell Gragg, Station Manager

***St Catharines:* CHRE-FM** (Freq: 105.7)
Owned by: **Standard Radio Office***
PO Box 610, 12 Yates St., St Catharines, ON L2R 6Z4
Tel: 905-688-1057; *Fax:* 905-684-4800
sgibbons@sri.ca
www.1057ezrock.com

Madelyn Hamilton, General Manager

***St Catharines:* CHTZ-FM** (Freq: 97.7)
Owned by: **Standard Radio Office***
PO Box 977, 12 Yates St., St Catharines, ON L2R 6Z4
Tel: 905-684-0977; *Fax:* 905-684-4800
www.htzfm.com

Bruce Gilbert, Program Director, pd@htzfm.com

***Stratford:* CHGK-FM** (Freq: 107.7)
376 Romeo St. South, Stratford, ON N5A 4T9
Tel: 519-271-2450; *Fax:* 519-271-3102
info@1077mixfm.com
www.1077mixfm.com

Steve Rae, General Manager

***Sturgeon Falls:* CFSF-FM** (Freq: 99.3)
#7, 12006 Hwy. 17, Sturgeon Falls, ON P2B 3K8
Tel: 705-753-6776; *Fax:* 705-753-6776
joco@bellnet.ca
www.joco.ca

Joseph Cormier, General Manager

***Sudbury:* CBBS-FM** (Freq: 90.1)
Owned by: **Canadian Broadcasting Corporation (CBC)***
15 MacKenzie St., Sudbury, ON P3C 4Y1
Tel: 705-688-3200; *Fax:* 705-688-3220
Toll-Free: 866-306-4636
www.cbc.ca/sudbury; www.cbc.ca/radio2
Social Media: www.facebook.com/CBC.Radio2.Official?ref=nf
Other information: Twitter: www.twitter.com/cbcradio2

Fiona Christensen, Managing Editor, Sudbury, 705-688-3232

†*Sudbury:* CBBX-FM (Freq: 90.9)
Owned by: **Canadian Broadcasting Corporation (CBC)***
15 Mackenzie St., Sudbury, ON P3C 4Y1
Tél: 705-688-3200; *Ligne sans frais:* 866-306-4636
www.cbc.ca/sudbury; www.radio-canada.ca

Fiona Christensen, Managing Editor, Sudbury, 705-688-3232

***Sudbury:* CBCS-FM** (Freq: 99.9)
Owned by: **Canadian Broadcasting Corporation (CBC)***
15 MacKenzie St., Sudbury, ON P3C 4Y1
Tel: 705-688-3200; *Toll-Free:* 866-306-4636
www.cbc.ca/sudbury; www.cbc.ca/radio
Social Media: www.facebook.com/radiocbc; www.twitter.com/cbcradio
Other information: Phone, Sudbury News: 705-688-3240; Toll-Free: 1-800-461-1138

Fiona Christensen, Managing Editor, 705-688-3232

†*Sudbury:* CBON-FM (Freq: 98.1)
Owned by: **Canadian Broadcasting Corporation***
15 MacKenzie St., Sudbury, ON P3C 4Y1
Tél: 705-688-3200
www.radio-canada.ca/regions/ontario

***Sudbury:* CHNO-FM** (Freq: 103.9)
493B Barrydowne Rd., Sudbury, ON P3A 3T4
Tel: 705-560-8323; *Fax:* 705-560-7765
z103@z103fm.com
www.z103fm.com

Christopher Grossman

†*Sudbury:* CHYC-FM (Freq: 98.9)
493B Barrydowne Rd., Sudbury, ON P3A 3T4
Tél: 705-560-8323; *Téléc:* 705-560-2492
chycfm@chycfm.com
www.chycfm.com

Christopher Grossman

***Sudbury:* CJMX-FM** (Freq: 105.3)
Owned by: **Rogers Broadcasting Ltd.***
880 Lasalle Blvd., Sudbury, ON P3A 1X5
Tel: 705-566-4480; *Fax:* 705-560-7232
www.ezrocksudbury.com

Gary Miles, CEO
Rick Doughty, General Manager

***Sudbury:* CJRQ-FM** (Freq: 92.7)
Owned by: **Rogers Broadcasting Ltd.***
880 Lasalle Blvd., Sudbury, ON P3A 1X5
Tel: 705-566-4480; *Fax:* 705-560-7232
www.q92rocks.com

Gary Miles, President
Rick Doughty, General Manager

***Sudbury:* CJTK-FM** (Freq: 95.5)
417 Notre Dame Ave., Sudbury, ON P3C 5K6
Tel: 705-674-2585; *Fax:* 705-688-1081
mail@cjtk.com
www.cjtk.com

Curtis L. Belcher, General Manager

** For details on this company see listing in Major Broadcasting Companies section; † French language station*

***Sudbury:* CKLU-FM** (Freq: 96.7)
935 Ramsey Rd., Sudbury, ON P3E 2C6
Tel: 705-673-6538; *Fax:* 705-675-4878
info@cklu.ca
www.cklu.ca

Sheila Bianconi, News Director
Carl Jorgensen, Operations Director
Tara Lévesque, Music Director

***Thunder Bay:* CBQ-FM** (Freq: 101.7)
Owned by: **Canadian Broadcasting Corporation***
213 Miles St. East, Thunder Bay, ON P7C 1J5
Tel: 807-625-5000; *Fax:* 807-625-5035
www.cbc.ca/thunderbay

***Thunder Bay:* CBQT-FM** (Freq: 88.3)
Owned by: **Canadian Broadcasting Corporation***
213 Miles St. East, Thunder Bay, ON P7C 1J5
Tel: 807-625-5000; *Fax:* 807-625-5035
www.cbc.ca/thunderbay/

***Thunder Bay:* CBQX-FM** (Freq: 98.7)
Owned by: **Canadian Broadcasting Corporation***
213 Miles St. East, Thunder Bay, ON P7C 1J5
Tel: 807-625-5002; *Fax:* 807-625-5035
www.cbc.radio-canada.ca

Tom Grand, General Manager

***Thunder Bay:* CFQK-FM** (Freq: 103.5; 104.5)
87 North Hill St., Thunder Bay, ON P7A 5V6
Tel: 807-346-2600; *Fax:* 807-345-9923
www.hotfm.ca

***Thunder Bay:* CJOA-FM** (Freq: 95.1)
#42, 63 Carrie St., Thunder Bay, ON
Tel: 807-344-9525; *Fax:* 807-344-9525
info@cjoa.org
www.cjoa.org

Bonnie Gauthier, Music Director

***Thunder Bay:* CJSD-FM** (Freq: 94.3)
Owned by: **CKPR Inc.***
87 Hill St. North, Thunder Bay, ON P7A 5V6
Tel: 807-346-2600; *Fax:* 807-345-9923
rock@rock94.com
www.rock94.com

Brad Hilgers, Program Director

***Thunder Bay:* CJUK-FM** (Freq: 99.9)
Owned by: **NewCap Inc.***
#200, 180 Park Ave., Thunder Bay, ON P7B 6J4
Tel: 807-345-9999; *Fax:* 807-346-5000
admin@magic999.fm
www.magic999.fm

Dennis Landriault, General Manager

***Thunder Bay:* CKTG-FM** (Freq: 105.3)
Owned by: **NewCap Inc.***
#200, 180 Park Ave., Thunder Bay, ON P7B 6J4
Tel: 807-344-2000; *Fax:* 807-346-5000
www.thegiant.fm

Darlene Palmer, General Manager

***Tillsonburg:* CKOT-FM** (Freq: 101.3)
PO Box 10, 77 Broadway St., Tillsonburg, ON N4G 4H3
Tel: 519-842-4281; *Fax:* 519-842-4284
jlamers@easy101.com

John Lamars, President & General Manager

***Timmins:* CHIM-FM** (Freq: 102.3)
226 Delnite Rd., Timmins, ON P4N 7C2
Tel: 705-264-2150
chimfm@vianet.ca
www.chimfm.com

Roger de Brabant

***Timmins:* CHMT-FM** (Freq: 93.1)
49 Cedar St. South, Timmins, ON P4N 2G5
Tel: 705-267-6070; *Fax:* 705-267-6095
moose931@hbgradio.com
www.moosefm.com

, General Manager, blecour@moosefm.com

***Timmins:* CHOH-FM** (Freq: 92.9)
#103, 32 Mountjoy St. North, Timmins, ON P4N 4V6
Tel: 705-267-6070; *Fax:* 705-267-6095
moose931@hbgradio.com
www.moosefm.com

Christopher Grossman, President

***Timmins:* CHYK-FM** (Freq: 104.1)
#103, 32 Mountjoy St. North, Timmins, ON P4N 4V6
Tel: 705-267-6070; *Fax:* 705-267-6095
chykfm@hbgroup.com
www.chykfm.com

***Timmins:* CJQQ-FM** (Freq: 92.1)
Owned by: **Rogers Broadcasting Ltd.***
260 - 2nd Ave., Timmins, ON P4N 8A4
Tel: 705-264-2351; *Fax:* 705-264-2984
www.q92timmins.com

***Timmins:* CKGB-FM** (Freq: 99.3)
Owned by: **Rogers Broadcasting Ltd.***
260 - 2nd Ave., Timmins, ON P4N 8A4
Tel: 705-264-2351; *Fax:* 705-264-2984
www.ezrocktimmins.com

Art Pultz, Operations Manager

***Toronto:* CBLA-FM** (Freq: 99.1)
Owned by: **Canadian Broadcasting Corporation (CBC)***
PO Box 500, 205 Wellington St. West, Toronto, ON M5W 1E6
Tel: 416-205-3311; *Fax:* 416-205-6336
Toll-Free: 866-306-4636
www.cbc.ca/toronto; www.cbc.ca/radio
Social Media: www.facebook.com/radiocbc;
www.twitter.com/cbcradio
Other information: Phone, Radio Newsroom: 416-205-5808;
TDD: 1-866-220-6045

Susan Marjetti, Managing Director, 416-205-5791
Don Ioi, Team Manager, Toronto Sales, 416-205-2732

***Toronto:* CBL-FM** (Freq: 94.1)
Owned by: **Canadian Broadcasting Corporation (CBC)***
PO Box 500 A, 205 Wellington St. West, Toronto, ON M5W 3G7
Tel: 416-205-3311; *Toll-Free:* 866-306-4636
www.cbc.ca/toronto; www.cbc.ca/radio2
Social Media: www.facebook.com/cbcsask;
www.twitter.com/cbcradio2

Susan Marjetti, Managing Director, 416-205-5791
Don Ioi, Team Manager, Toronto Sales

***Toronto:* CFIE-FM** (Freq: 106.5)
#323, 366 Adelaide St. East, Toronto, ON M5A 3X9
Tel: 416-703-1287; *Fax:* 416-703-4328
www.aboriginalradio.com

***Toronto:* CFMX-FM** (Freq: 96.3; 103.1)
#205, 550 Queen St. East, Toronto, ON M5A 1V2
Tel: 416-367-5353; *Fax:* 416-367-1742
info@classical963fm.com
www.classical963fm.com

John van Driel, General Manager/CEO

***Toronto:* CFNY-FM** (Freq: 102.1)
Owned by: **Corus Entertainment Inc.***
#1600, 1 Dundas St. West, Toronto, ON M5G 1Z3
Tel: 416-408-3343; *Fax:* 416-847-3333
info@edge.ca
www.edge.ca

***Toronto:* CFXJ-FM** (Freq: 93.5)
#400, 211 Yonge St., Toronto, ON M5B 1M4
Tel: 416-214-5000; *Fax:* 416-214-0660
info@flow935.com
www.flow935.com

***Toronto:* CHFI-FM** (Freq: 98.1)
Owned by: **Rogers Broadcasting Ltd.***
777 Jarvis St., Toronto, ON M4Y 3B7
Tel: 416-935-8298; *Fax:* 416-935-8288
www.chfi.com

Chuck McCoy, Toronto Market Manager
Paul Fisher, Vice-President & General Manager

***Toronto:* CHIN-FM** (Freq: 100.7)
622 College St., Toronto, ON M6G 1B6
Tel: 416-531-9991; *Fax:* 416-531-5274
info@chinradio.com
www.chinradio.com

Leonard Lombardi, President

***Toronto:* CHKT-FM** (Freq: 88.9)
Owned by: **CHKT**
Toronto, ON

***Toronto:* CHRY-FM** (Freq: 105.5)
York University, Student Centre, #413, 4700 Keele St., Toronto, ON M3J 1P3
Tel: 416-736-5293; *Fax:* 416-650-8052
chry@yorku.ca
www.yorku.ca/chry

***Toronto:* CHUM-FM** (Freq: 104.5)
250 Richmond St. West, Toronto, ON M5V 1W4
Tel: 416-925-6666; *Fax:* 416-926-4026
www.chumfm.com

David Corey, Program Director/Vice President, Programming/CTVglobmedia Inc., CHUM Radio Div
Chris Gordon, President, CTVglobemedia Inc., CHUM Radio Division

***Toronto:* CIDC-FM** (Freq: 103.5)
5302 Dundas St. West, Toronto, ON M9B 1B2
Tel: 416-213-1035; *Fax:* 416-233-8617
info@z1035.com
www.z1035.com

***Toronto:* CILQ-FM** (Freq: 107.1)
Owned by: **Corus Entertainment Inc.***
#1600, 1 Dundas St. West, Toronto, ON M5G 1Z3
Tel: 416-221-0107; *Fax:* 416-847-3300
www.q107.com

J. Hayes, President

***Toronto:* CIRV-FM** (Freq: 88.9)
1087 Dundas St. West, Toronto, ON M6J 1W9
Tel: 416-537-1088; *Fax:* 416-537-2463
info@cirvfm.com
www.cirvfm.com

Alberto Elmir, Station Manager

***Toronto:* CIUT-FM** (Freq: 89.5)
91 St. George St., Toronto, ON M5S 2E8
Tel: 416-978-0909; *Fax:* 416-946-7004
www.ciut.fm

***Toronto:* CJAQ-FM** (Freq: 92.5)
Owned by: **Rogers Broadcasting Ltd.***
777 Jarvis St., Toronto, ON M4Y 3B7
Tel: 416-935-8392; *Fax:* 416-935-8410
www.925jackfm.com

Steve Kennedy, General Manager

***Toronto:* CJBC-FM** (Freq: 90.3)
Owned by: **Canadian Broadcasting Corporation***
PO Box 500 A, Toronto, ON M5W 1E6
Tel: 416-205-3311
www.radio-canada.ca/regions/ontario

***Toronto:* CJEZ-FM** (Freq: 97.3)
Owned by: **Standard Radio Office***
2 St. Clair Ave. West, 2nd Fl., Toronto, ON M4V 1L6
Tel: 416-482-0973; *Fax:* 416-486-5696
www.ezrock.com

Mario Cecchini, Executive Vice-President

***Toronto:* CJRT-FM** (Freq: 91.1)
#100, 4 Pardee Ave., Toronto, ON M6K 3H5
Tel: 416-595-0404; *Fax:* 416-595-9413
Toll-Free: 888-595-0404
info@jazz.fm
www.jazz.fm

Bernard Webber, Chair
Ross Porter, President & CEO

***Toronto:* CKDX-FM** (Freq: 88.5)
5302 Dundas St. West, Toronto, ON M9B 1B2
Tel: 416-213-1035; *Fax:* 416-233-8617
info@foxy885.com
www.foxy885.com

***Toronto:* CKHC-FM** (Freq: 96.9)
205 Humber College Blvd., Toronto, ON M9W 5L7
Tel: 416-675-6622; *Fax:* 416-675-9730
radiohumber@humber.ca
radio.humberc.on.ca

***Toronto:* CKLN-FM** (Freq: 88.1)
55 Gould St., Toronto, ON M5B 1E9
Tel: 416-979-5251; *Fax:* 416-595-0226
ckln@ckln.fm
www.ckln.fm

David Barnard, Chair

** For details on this company see listing in Major Broadcasting Companies section; † French language station*

***Toronto:* CSCR-FM** (Freq: 90.3)
1265 Military Trail, Toronto, ON M1C 1A4
Tel: 416-287-7051
info@fustionradio.ca
www.fusionradio.ca
Liam Michell, Station Manager

***Toronto:* Virgin Radio 999 FM** (Freq: 99.9)
2 St. Clair Ave. West, Toronto, ON M4V 1L6
Tel: 416-922-9999; *Fax:* 416-872-8683
info@virginradio.com
www.virginradio999.com

***Trenton:* CJTN-FM** (Freq: 107.1)
31 Quinte St., Trenton, ON K8V 3S7
Tel: 613-771-1071
www.lite107.ca

***Waterloo:* CFCA-FM** (Freq: 105.3)
#207, 255 King St. North, Waterloo, ON N2J 4V2
Tel: 519-884-4470; *Fax:* 519-884-6482
www.koolfm.com
Paul Cugliari, Vice President/General Manager

***Waterloo:* CIKZ-FM** (Freq: 106.7)
#C2, 490 Dutton Dr., Waterloo, ON N2L 6H7
Tel: 519-746-3331; *Fax:* 519-746-3364
www.kicx106.com

***Waterloo:* CKMS-FM** (Freq: 100.3)
University of Waterloo, Bauer Warehouse, 200 University Ave. West, Waterloo, ON N2L 3G1
Tel: 519-886-2567; *Fax:* 519-884-3530
ckmsfm@web.ca
ckmsfm.uwaterloo.ca
Heather Majaury, Station Manager

***Waterloo:* CKWR-FM** (Freq: 98.5)
375 University Ave. East, Waterloo, ON N2K 3M7
Tel: 519-886-9870; *Fax:* 519-886-0090
general@ckwr.com
www.ckwr.com

***Wawa:* CJWA-FM** (Freq: 107.1)
PO Box 1447, 57 Broadway Ave., Wawa, ON P0S 1K0
Tel: 705-856-4555; *Fax:* 705-856-1520

***Welland:* CHOW-FM** (Freq: 91.7)
860 Forks Rd. West, Welland, ON L3B 5R6
Tel: 905-732-4433; *Fax:* 905-732-4780
Toll-Free: 877-342-5917
country@spirit917fm.com
Pat St John, President

***Welland:* CRNC-FM** (Freq: 90.1)
300 Woodlawn Rd., Welland, ON L3C 7L3
Tel: 905-735-2211; *Fax:* 905-736-6002
www.broadcasting.niagarac.on.ca

***Wiarton:* CHFN-FM** (Freq: 100.1)
RR#5, Wiarton, ON N0H 2T0
Tel: 519-534-1003; *Fax:* 519-534-0063
chfn@bellnet.ca
www.georgeloney.com
Jessica Nadjiwon, Station Manager

***Windsor:* CBE-FM** (Freq: 89.9)
Owned by: **Canadian Broadcasting Corporation (CBC)***
825 Riverside Dr. West, Windsor, ON N9A 5K9
Tel: 519-255-3411; *Toll-Free:* 866-306-4636
www.cbc.ca/windsor; www.cbc.ca/radio2
Social Media: www.facebook.com/cbcsask;
www.twitter.com/cbcradio2
Other information: Phone, Newsroom: 519-255-3456
Sandra Porteous, Managing Editor, Radio & Television, 519-255-3563
David Daigneault, Executive Producer, Radio & Television, 519-255-3410
Nancy Lauzon, Manager, Windsor Accounts, 519-255-3510

***Windsor:* CIDR-FM** (Freq: 93.9)
1640 Ouellette Ave., Windsor, ON N8X 1L1
Tel: 519-258-8888; *Fax:* 519-258-0182
www.939theriverradio.com
Eric Proksch, Vice President/General Manager

***Windsor:* CIMX-FM** (Freq: 88.7)
1640 Ouellette Ave., Windsor, ON N8X 1L1
Tel: 519-258-8888; *Fax:* 519-258-0182
www.89xradio.com
Social Media: www.facebook.com/89XFANS
Eric Proksch, Vice President/General Manager

***Windsor:* CJAM-FM** (Freq: 91.5)
401 Sunset Ave., Windsor, ON N9B 3P4
Tel: 519-971-3606; *Fax:* 519-971-3605
statcjam@uwindsor.ca
www.cjam.ca
Christien Gagnier

***Wingham:* CKNX-FM** (Freq: 101.7)
Owned by: **Blackburn Radio Inc.***
215 Carling Terrace, Wingham, ON N0G 2W0
Tel: 519-357-1310; *Fax:* 519-357-1897
info@1017theone.ca
www.1017theone.ca

***Woodstock:* CJFH-FM** (Freq: 94.3)
535 Mill St., Woodstock, ON N4S 7V6
Tel: 519-539-2304; *Fax:* 519-539-2100
info@hopefm.ca
www.hopefm.ca
Gary Hill, General Manager

***Woodstock:* CKDK-FM** (Freq: 103.9)
Owned by: **Corus Entertainment Inc.***
290 Dundas St., Woodstock, ON N4S 1B7
Tel: 519-539-1040; *Fax:* 519-539-7479
www.thehawk.ca
Dean Sinclair, General Manager

Prince Edward Island

***Charlottetown:* CBCT-FM** (Freq: 96.1)
Owned by: **Canadian Broadcasting Corporation (CBC)***
PO Box 2230, 430 University Ave., Charlottetown, PE C1A 8B9
Tel: 902-629-6400; *Fax:* 902-629-6518
Toll-Free: 866-306-4636
www.cbc.ca/pei; www.cbc.ca/radio
Social Media: www.facebook.com/radiocbc;
www.twitter.com/cbcradio
Other information: Phone, News: 902-629-6402; TDD: 1-866-220-6045
Andrew Cochran, Managing Director, Maritimes
Donna Allen, Executive Producer, Prince Edward Island News
Janet Irwin, Senior Regional Manager, News & Current Affairs
Lenny Jackson, Station Manager, Prince Edward Island
Nadine Antle, Regional Manager, Partnerships, Communications, Brand, & Promot, 506-451-4054
John Channing, Manager, Sales
Heather McGrath, Senior Officer, Communications, 902-629-6416

***Charlottetown:* CHLQ-FM** (Freq: 93.1)
Owned by: **Maritime Broadcasting System***
5 Prince St., Charlottetown, PE C1A 4P4
Tel: 902-892-1066; *Fax:* 902-566-1338
requests@magic93.pe.ca
www.magic93.pe.ca

***Charlottetown:* CHTN-FM** (Freq: 100.3)
Owned by: **NewCap Inc.***
90 University Ave., Charlottetown, PE C1A 4K9
Tel: 902-569-1003; *Fax:* 902-569-8693
www.ocean1003.com

***Summerside:* CJRW-FM** (Freq: 102.1)
Owned by: **Maritime Broadcasting System***
763 Water St. East, Summerside, PE C1N 4J3
Tel: 902-436-2201; *Fax:* 902-436-8573
c102@c102.com
www.c102.com
Paul M. Schurman

Québec

†*Alma:* CKYK-FM (Freq: 95.7)
#200, 460, Sacré-Coeur ouest, Alma, QC G8B 1L9
Tél: 418-662-6888
www.kykfm.com
Marc-André Levesque, Président

†*Amqui:* CFVM-FM (Freq: 99.9)
Owned by: **Astral Media Inc.***
111, rue de l'Hopital, Amqui, QC G5J 2K1
Tél: 418-629-2025; *Téléc:* 418-629-2599
nouvelle999@boomfm.astral.com
www.boomfm.com

†*Asbestos:* CJAN-FM (Freq: 99.3)
#301, 185, rue du Roi, Asbestos, QC J1T 1S4
Tél: 819-879-5439; *Téléc:* 819-879-7922
info@fm993.ca
fm993.ca

***Baie-Comeau:* CBMI-FM** (Freq: 93.7)
Owned by: **Canadian Broadcasting Corporation (CBC)***
Baie-Comeau, QC
Toll-Free: 866-306-4636
www.cbc.ca/montreal; www.cbc.ca/radio
Social Media: www.facebook.com/radiocbc;
www.twitter.com/cbcradio
Other information: TDD: 1-866-220-6045

†*Baie-Comeau:* CBSI-FM-24 (Freq: 106.1)
Owned by: **Canadian Broadcasting Corporation (CBC)***
Baie-Comeau, QC
Ligne sans frais: 866-954-1341
auditoire.quebec@radio-canada.ca
www.radio-canada.ca/regions/quebec

***Baie-Comeau:* CHLC-FM** (Freq: 97.1)
907, rue de Puyjalon, Baie-Comeau, QC G5C 1N3
Tel: 418-589-3771; *Fax:* 418-589-9086
programmes971-1005@globetrotter.net
www.chlc.com
Georges Daviault, Directeur Général

***Baie-Saint-Paul:* CHOX-1** (Freq: 94.1)
Owned by: **CHOX-FM**
Baie-Saint-Paul, QC

†*Cap-aux-Meules:* CFIM-FM (Freq: 92.7)
CP 8192, Cap-aux-Meules, QC G4T 1R3
Tél: 418-986-5233; *Téléc:* 418-986-5319
www.cfim.ca
Gisele Deraspe, Directrice générale

†*Carleton:* CIEU-FM (Freq: 94.9; 106.1)
1645, boul Perron est, Carleton, QC G0C 1J0
Tél: 418-364-7094; *Téléc:* 418-364-3150
cieufm@cieufm.com
www.cieufm.com

***Charlesbourg:* CIMI-FM** (Freq: 103.7)
#103, 4500, boul Henri-Bourassa, Charlesbourg, QC G1H 3A5
Tel: 418-624-0700; *Fax:* 418-623-2538
www.cimifm.com

***Châteauguay:* CHAI-FM** (Freq: 101.9)
25, boul St-Francis, Châteauguay, QC J6J 1Y2
Tel: 450-698-3131; *Fax:* 450-698-3339
chai@videotron.ca
chaifm.iquebec.com
Sylvain Poirier

†*Chicoutimi:* CBJ-FM (Freq: 93.7FM)
Owned by: **CBC Radio-Canada/Canadian Broadcasting Corporation***
500, rue des Sagueneens, Chicoutimi, QC G7H 6N4
Tél: 418-696-6600; *Téléc:* 418-696-6689
www.radio-canada.ca/regions/saguenay-lac

†*Chicoutimi:* CBJX-FM (Freq: Saguenay, QC; 100.9FM)
Owned by: **Société Radio-Canada; Canadian Broadcasting Corporation***
500, rue des Saguenéens, Chicoutimi, QC G7H 6N4
Tél: 418-696-6600; *Téléc:* 418-696-6689
www.radio-canada.ca/regions/saguenay-lac

***Chicoutimi:* CFIX-FM** (Freq: 96.9)
Owned by: **Astral Media Inc.***
267, rue Racine est, Chicoutimi, QC G7H 5K3
Tel: 418-543-9797; *Fax:* 418-543-7968
www.rockdetente.com

†*Chicoutimi:* CJAB-FM (Freq: 94.5)
Owned by: **Astral Media Inc.***
CP 1506, 267, rue Racine est, Chicoutimi, QC G7H 5K3
Tél: 418-545-9450; *Téléc:* 418-543-7968
www.radioenergie.com
Richard Turcotte

†*Dégelis:* CFVD-FM (Freq: 95.5)
654, 6e rue est, Dégelis, QC G5T 1Y1
Tél: 418-853-3370; *Téléc:* 418-853-3321
CFVD@FM95.ca
Gilles Caron

** For details on this company see listing in Major Broadcasting Companies section; † French language station*

†*Dolbeau-Mistassini:* CHVD-FM (Freq: 100.3)
Owned by: **Groupe Radio Antenne 6***
1975, boul Wallberg, Dolbeau-Mistassini, QC G8L 1J5
Tél: 418-276-3333; *Téléc:* 418-276-6755
chvd@antenne6.com
Marc-André Levesque, Président

***Donnacona:* CKNU-FM** (Freq: 100.9)
Owned by: **Radio Nord Communications Inc.***
274, rue Notre-Dame, Donnacona, QC G6M 1G7
Tel: 418-285-2568; *Fax:* 418-263-0286
www.tagradio.fm

†*Drummondville:* CHRD-FM (Freq: 105.3)
Owned by: **Astral Media Inc.***
2070, St-Georges, Drummondville, QC J2C 5G6
Tél: 819-475-1480; *Téléc:* 819-747-6610
receptionchrd@boomfm.com
www.boomfm.com
Joël Rioux, Directeur général

†*Drummondville:* CJDM-FM (Freq: 92.1)
Owned by: **Astral Media Inc.***
2070 rue St-Georges, Drummondville, QC J2C 5G6
Tél: 819-474-1892; *Téléc:* 819-474-6610
nouvelles@cjdm.fm
www.radioenergie.com
Pierre Gaudreau

***Fermont:* CBMR-FM** (Freq: 105.1)
Owned by: **Canadian Broadcasting Corporation (CBC)***
Fermont, QC
Toll-Free: 866-306-4636
www.cbc.ca/montreal; www.cbc.ca/radio
Social Media: www.facebook.com/radiocbc;
www.twitter.com/cbcradio
Other information: TDD: 1-866-220-6045

†*Fermont:* CFMF-FM (Freq: 103.1)
CP 280, 20, Place Daviault, Fermont, QC G0G 1J0
Tél: 418-287-5147; *Téléc:* 418-287-5776
administration@diffusionfermont.ca

†*Fort-Coulonge:* CHIP-FM (Freq: 101.7)
CP 820, 138, rue Principale, Fort-Coulonge, QC J0X 1V0
Tél: 819-683-3155; *Téléc:* 819-683-3211
Ligne sans frais: 888-775-3155
radiopontiac@chipfm.com
www.chipfm.com
Frank Doyle

***Gaspé:* CJRE-FM** (Freq: 97.9)
162, rue Jacques Cartier, Gaspé, QC G4X 1M9
Tel: 418-368-3511; *Fax:* 418-368-1663
Toll-Free: 866-360-3511
accueil@radiogaspesie.ca
www.radiogaspesie.ca
Jacques Chartier, General Manager

†*Gaspé:* CJRG-FM (Freq: 94.5)
162, rue Jacques Cartier, Gaspé, QC G4X 1M9
Tél: 418-368-3511; *Téléc:* 418-368-1663
Ligne sans frais: 866-360-3511
accueil@radiogaspesie.ca
www.radiogaspesie.ca

†*Gatineau:* CHLX-FM (Freq: 97.1)
Owned by: **Radio Nord Communications Inc.***
171A, rue Jean-Proulx, Gatineau, QC J8Z 1W5
Tél: 819-770-9710; *Téléc:* 819-770-9740
monchoix@radionord.com
www.radionord.com

†*Gatineau:* CIMF-FM (Freq: 94.9)
Owned by: **Astral Media Inc.***
15, rue Taschereau, Gatineau, QC J8Y 2V6
Tél: 819-770-2463; *Téléc:* 819-770-9338
www.rockdetente.com

***Harrington Harbour:* CFTH-FM** (Freq: French language community radio; 97.7 FM in Harrington Harbour; rebroadcasting in Baie-des-Moutons at 98.5 FM & in Kegaska at 89.9 FM.)
PO Box 88, Harrington Harbour, QC G0G 1N0
Tel: 418-795-3344; *Fax:* 418-795-3200
cfthh1@globetrotter.net
Kate Nadeau, Director
Nancy Bobbitt, Animator
Monica Anderson, Animator
Lois Jones, Secretary

***Harrington Harbour:* CFTH-FM-2** (Freq: French language community radio at 98.5 in Baie-des-Moutons)
PO Box 88, Harrington Harbour, QC G0G 1N0
Tel: 418-795-3349; *Fax:* 418-795-3200
cfthhl@globetrotter.net
Kate Nadeau, Director
Monica Anderson, Animator, 418-795-3344
Nancy Anderson, Animator, 418-795-3344, cfthonair@live.ca
Lois Jones, Animator & Secretary, 418-795-3344

†*Havre-Saint-Pierre:* CBSI-FM-7 (Freq: 92.5)
Owned by: **Canadian Broadcasting Corporation (CBC)***
Havre-Saint-Pierre, QC
Ligne sans frais: 866-954-1341
auditoire.quebec@radio-canada.ca
www.radio-canada.ca/regions/quebec

***Hâvre-Saint-Pierre:* CILE-FM** (Freq: 95.1)
992, rue du Bouleau, Hâvre-Saint-Pierre, QC G0G 1P0
Tel: 418-538-2453; *Fax:* 418-538-3870
cilemf@globetrotter.net
www.cilemf.com

***Hull:* CKTF-FM** (Freq: 104.1)
Owned by: **Astral Media Inc.***
15, rue Taschereau, Hull, QC J8Y 2V6
Tel: 819-243-5555; *Fax:* 819-243-6816
www.radioenergie.com

†*Joliette:* CJLM-FM (Freq: 103.5)
540, rue Thomas, Joliette, QC J6E 3R4
Tél: 450-756-1035; *Téléc:* 450-756-8097
radio@m1035fm.com
www.m1035fm.com
Normand Masse

†*Jonquière:* CKAJ-FM (Freq: 92.5)
CP 872, 3791, rue de la Fabrique, 4e étage, Jonquière, QC G7X 7W5
Tél: 418-546-2525; *Téléc:* 418-546-2528
www.ckaj.org

***Kahnawake:* CKRK-FM** (Freq: 103.7)
PO Box 1050, Kahnawake, QC J0L 1B0
Tel: 450-638-1313; *Fax:* 450-638-4009
programming@k103radio.com
www.k103radio.com

***Kuujjuaq:* CKUJ-FM** (Freq: 97.3)
PO Box 1082, Kuujjuaq, QC J0M 1C0
Tel: 819-964-2921; *Fax:* 819-964-2229

***L'Annonciation:* CFLO-FM** (Freq: 101.9)
Owned by: **CFLO-FM**
L'Annonciation, QC

†*La Pocatière:* CHOX-FM (Freq: 97.5)
#50, 601, 1ère av, La Pocatière, QC G0R 1Z0
Tél: 418-856-1310; *Téléc:* 418-856-3747
chox@chox97.com
www.chox97.com

***Lac-Etchemin:* CFIN-FM** (Freq: 100.5)
#11, 201, rue Claude-Bilodeau, Lac-Etchemin, QC G0R 1S0
Tel: 418-625-3737; *Fax:* 418-625-3730
cfinfm@sogetel.net
www.cfin-fm.com
Jacques Thériault

†*Lac-Mégantic:* CFJO-FM (Freq: 101.7)
Owned by: **CFJO-FM**
Lac-Mégantic, QC

†*Lac-Mégantic:* CJIT-FM (Freq: 106.7)
4766, rue Laval, Lac-Mégantic, QC G6B 1C7
Tél: 819-583-0663; *Téléc:* 819-583-0665
radiocjit@bellnet.ca
www.cjitfm.com
Ritha Breton

***Lac-Simon:* CHUT-FM** (Freq: 95.3)
1016, rue Wabanonik, Lac-Simon, QC J0Y 3M0
Tel: 819-736-4501; *Fax:* 819-736-2333
Alain Flamand, General Manager

***Lachute:* CJLA-FM** (Freq: 104.9)
Owned by: **Radio Nord Communications Inc.***
11, rue Argenteuil, Lachute, QC J8H 1X8
Tel: 450-562-8862; *Fax:* 450-562-1902
infocouleur@radionord.com
www.radionord.com

†*Laval:* CFGL-FM (Freq: 105.7)
#100, 2830, boul St-Martin est, Laval, QC H7E 5A1
Tél: 450-664-4647; *Téléc:* 450-664-4138
www.rythmefm.com
Jacques Boiteau, General Manager

***Lennoxville:* CJMQ-FM** (Freq: 88.9)
PO Box 2135, Lennoxville, QC J1M 1Z7
Tel: 819-822-9600
cjmq@ubishops.ca
www.cjmq.fm
David Teasdale

***Les Escoumins:* CHME-FM** (Freq: 94.9)
34, rue de la Reserve, Les Escoumins, QC G0T 1K0
Tel: 418-233-2700; *Fax:* 418-233-3326
chme@B2B2C.ca
Gilles Labelle

***Listuguj:* CFIC-FM** (Freq: 105.1)
PO Box 304, 44A Riverside ouest, Listuguj, QC
Tel: 418-788-5166; *Fax:* 418-788-3524
www.105hotcountry.com
Chris Dedam, General Manager

***Longueuil:* CHAA-FM** (Freq: 103.3)
91, rue St-Jean, Longueuil, QC G0T 1K0
Tel: 450-646-6800; *Fax:* 450-646-7378
general admin@fm1033.ca
www.fm1033.ca
Eric Tetreault

†*Lourdes-de-Blanc-Sablon:* CFBS-FM (Freq: 89.9)
CP 8, Lourdes-de-Blanc-Sablon, QC G0G 1W0
Tél: 418-461-2445; *Téléc:* 418-461-2425
cfbsradio@gmailcom
www.cfbsradio.com
Patrick Beurbe, Station Manager
Dominque Jones, Music Director
Vicki Driscoll, President

†*Maniwaki:* CFOR-FM (Freq: Pur rock à 99.3 FM Maniwaki)
139, rue Principal sud, Maniwaki, QC J9E 1Z8
Tél: 819-441-0993; *Téléc:* 819-441-3488
cfor993@b2b2c.ca
www.cforfm.com
Laure Voilquin, Directrice commerciale, laure@cforfm.com

†*Maniwaki:* CHGA-FM (Freq: 97.3)
163, rue Laurier, Maniwaki, QC J9E 2K6
Tél: 819-449-5590; *Téléc:* 819-449-7331
chga@bellnet.ca
www.chga.qc.ca

***Maniwaki:* CKWE-FM** (Freq: 103.9)
PO Box 309, Maniwaki, QC J9E 3C9
Tel: 819-449-5170; *Fax:* 819-449-5097
anita.tenasco@kza.qc.ca
Anita Penasco, General Manager

***Maria:* CHRG-FM** (Freq: 101.7)
PO Box 118, 120 School St., Maria, QC G0C 1Y0
Tel: 418-759-5424; *Fax:* 418-759-5424
radio@globetrotter.net
Douglas Martin, General Manager

†*Mashteuiatsh:* CHUK-FM (Freq: 107.3)
1491, rue Ouiatchouan, Mashteuiatsh, QC G0W 2H0
Tél: 418-275-4684; *Téléc:* 418-275-7964
chuk@chukfm.ca
www.chukfm.ca
Marc Gill, General Manager

***Matagami:* CHEF-FM** (Freq: 99.9)
PO Box 39, 110, boul Matagami, Matagami, QC J0Y 2A0
Tel: 819-739-9990; *Fax:* 819-739-6003
Marie-Eve C. Gallant, General Manager

†*Matane:* CBGA-FM (Freq: 102.1)
Owned by: **Canadian Broadcasting Corporation (CBC)***
Matane, QC
Tél: 514-597-6000; *Téléc:* 514-597-5545
Ligne sans frais: 800-306-4636
auditoire@radio-canada.ca
www.radio-canada.ca/radio

†*Matane:* CHOE-FM (Freq: 95.3)
800, av du Phare ouest, Matane, QC G4W 1V7
Tél: 418-562-8181; *Téléc:* 418-562-0778
choefm@globetrotter.net
www.choefm.com

** For details on this company see listing in Major Broadcasting Companies section; † French language station*

Kenneth Gagné Jr.

†*Matane:* CHRM-FM (Freq: 105.3)
800, av du Phare ouest, Matane, QC G4W 1V7
Tél: 418-562-4141; *Téléc:* 418-562-0778
Kenneth Gagné Jr.

***Mont-Laurier:* CFLO-FM** (Freq: 104.7)
332, rue de la Madone, Mont-Laurier, QC J9L 1R9
Tel: 819-623-6610; *Fax:* 819-623-7406
cflofm@cflo.ca
www.cflo.ca
Alain Desjardins

†*Montmagny:* CFEL-FM (Freq: 102.1)
Owned by: **Corus Entertainment Inc.***
191, ch des Poirier, Montmagny, QC G5V 4L2
Tél: 418-248-1122; *Téléc:* 418-248-1951
cfel@globetrotter.net
www.cfelfm.com

†*Montréal:* CBF-FM (Freq: 95.1)
Owned by: **Canadian Broadcasting Corporation (CBC)***
CP 6000 Centre-ville, 1400, boul René-Lévesque est, Montréal, QC H3C 3A8
Tél: 514-597-6000; *Ligne sans frais:* 866-306-4636
auditoire@radio-canada.ca; liaison@radio-canada.ca
www.radio-canada.ca/radio
Other information: TDD: 514-597-6013
Pia Marquard, Managing Director, Radio & Television, Québec
Sally Caudwell, Executive Producer, Montréal News, 514-597-4089, Fax: 514-597-4511
Kenny King, Senior Manager, CBC Media Sales & Marketing
Helen Evans, Program Manager, Radio Current Affairs

†*Montréal:* CBFX-FM (Freq: 100.7)
Owned by: **Canadian Broadcasting Corporation (CBC)***
CP 6000 Centre-ville, 1400, boul René-Lévesque est, Montréal, QC H3C 3A8
Tél: 514-597-6000; *Téléc:* 514-597-5545
Ligne sans frais: 866-306-4636
auditoire@radio-canada.ca
www.radio-canada.ca/espace_musique
Pia Marquard, Managing Director, Radio & Television, Québec Region
Hugh Brodie, Manager, Partnerships & Communications, Québec, 514-597-5813
Helen Evans, Program Manager, Radio Current Affairs

***Montréal:* CBJE-FM** (Freq: CBC Radio One, Chicoutimi, QC, 102.7FM)
Owned by: **Canadian Broadcasting Corporation***
PO Box 6000, 1400, boul René Lévesque est, Montréal, QC H3C 3A8
Tel: 514-597-4444; *Fax:* 514-597-4416
info@radio.cbc.ca
www.cbc.ca/radio
Patricia Pleszczynska, General Manager

***Montréal:* CBME-FM** (Freq: 88.5)
Owned by: **Canadian Broadcasting Corporation (CBC)***
PO Box 6000, Montréal, QC H3C 3A8
Tel: 514-597-6000; *Fax:* 514-597-6510
www.cbc.ca/radio
Social Media: www.facebook.com/radiocbc; www.twitter.com/cbcradio
Other information: Phone, CBC Radio One Newsroom: 514-597-6300; TDD: 1-866-220-6045
Pia Marquard, Managing Director, Radio & Television, Québec Region
Sally Caudwell, Executive Producer, News, Montréal, 514-597-4089, Fax: 514-597-4511
Mary-Jo Barr, News Director, English Services
Kenny King, Senior Manager, CBC Media Sales & Marketing
Hugh Brodie, Manager, Partnership & Communications, Québec, 514-597-5813
Helen Evans, Program Manager, Radio Current Affairs
Carolyn Warren, Regional Manager, Cultural Programming, Integrated Content

***Montréal:* CBM-FM** (Freq: 93.5)
Owned by: **Canadian Broadcasting Corporation (CBC)***
Maison Radio-Canada, PO Box 6000 Centre-ville, 1400, boul René-Lévesque est, Montréal, QC H3C 3A8
Tel: 514-597-6000; *Fax:* 514-597-5545
Toll-Free: 866-306-4636
auditoire@radio-canada.ca
www.cbc.ca/montreal; www.cbc.ca/radio2
Pia Marquard, Managing Director, Radio & Television, Québec Region
Kenny King, Senior Manager, CBC Media Sales & Marketing
Hugh Brodie, Manager, Partnership & Communications, Québec
Helen Evans, Program Manager, Radio Current Affairs

***Montréal:* CFQR-FM** (Freq: 92.5)
Owned by: **Corus Entertainment Inc.***
#100, 800, rue de la Gauchetière ouest, Montréal, QC H5A 1K6
Tel: 514-767-9250; *Fax:* 514-766-9569
reception@q92fm.com
www.q92fm.com

***Montréal:* CHOM-FM** (Freq: 97.7)
Owned by: **Standard Radio Office***
1411, rue Fort, 3e étage, Montréal, QC H3H 2R1
Tel: 514-937-2466; *Fax:* 514-846-4741
www.chom.com

†*Montréal:* CIBL-FM (Freq: 101.5)
1691, boul Pie-IX, 2e étage, Montréal, QC H1V 2C3
Tél: 514-526-2581; *Téléc:* 514-526-3583
info@cibl.cam.org
www.cibl.cam.org
Pierre Paquette, Président

***Montréal:* CINQ-FM** (Freq: 102.3)
5212, boul St-Laurent, 2e étage, Montréal, QC H2T 1S1
Tel: 514-495-2597; *Fax:* 514-495-2429
cinqfm@radiocentreville.com
www.radiocentreville.com
Magalie Pare

***Montréal:* CIRA-FM** (Freq: 91.3)
#199, 4020, St-Ambroise, Montréal, QC H4C 2C7
Tel: 514-382-3913; *Fax:* 514-858-0965
cira@radiovm.com
www.radiovm.com
Jean-Guy Roy, Dir de la Station

***Montréal:* CISM-FM** (Freq: 89.3)
#C-1509, 2332, Edouard-Montpetit, Montréal, QC H3C 3J7
Tel: 514-343-7511; *Fax:* 514-343-2418
cism@cam.org
www.cismfm.qc.ca
Dave Ouellet

***Montréal:* CITE-FM** (Freq: 107.3)
Owned by: **Astral Media Inc.***
1717, boul René-Lévesque est, Montréal, QC H2L 4T9
Tel: 514-529-3293; *Fax:* 514-288-1073
www.rockdetente.com
Sylvain Langlois, Vice-President & General Manager

***Montréal:* CJFM-FM** (Freq: 95.9)
Owned by: **Standard Radio Office***
1411, rue du Fort, Montréal, QC H3H 2R1
Tel: 514-989-2536; *Fax:* 514-989-2554
www.themix.com
Gary Slaight, President
Rob Braide, Vice-President

***Montréal:* CJPX-FM** (Freq: 99.5)
Isle Notre-Dame, Parc Jean-Drapeau, Montréal, QC H3C 1A9
Tel: 514-871-0995; *Fax:* 514-871-0990
www.cjpx.ca
Francois Pare

***Montréal:* CKDG-FM** (Freq: 105.1)
5899, av du Parc, Montréal, QC H2V 4H4
Tel: 514-273-2481; *Fax:* 514-273-3707
info@ckdgfm.ca
www.ckdgfm.ca
Marie Griffiths, Station Manager

***Montréal:* CKLX-FM** (Freq: 91.9)
Owned by: **Radio Nord Communications Inc.***
#250, 200, av Laurier ouest, Montréal, QC H2T 2N8
Tel: 514-871-0919; *Fax:* 514-871-8884
www.coleurjazz.com
Guy Banville

†*Montréal:* CKMF-FM (Freq: 94.3)
Owned by: **Astral Media Inc.***
#050, 1717, boul René-Lévesque est, Montréal, QC H2L 4T9
Tél: 514-529-3229; *Téléc:* 514-529-9308
www.radioenergie.com

†*Montréal:* CKOI-FM (Freq: 96.9)
Owned by: **Corus Entertainment Inc.***
#1100, 800, rue de la Gauchetière ouest, Montréal, QC H5A 1K6
Tél: 514-766-2311; *Téléc:* 514-766-2474
information@ckoi.com
www.ckoi.com

***Montréal:* CKUT-FM** (Freq: 90.3)
3647, rue University, Montréal, QC H3A 2B3
Tel: 514-398-6787; *Fax:* 514-398-8261
sales@ckut.ca
www.ckut.ca

†*Natashquan:* CKNA-FM (Freq: 104.1)
CP 9, 29, ch d'en Haut, Natashquan, QC G0G 2E0
Tél: 418-726-3284; *Téléc:* 418-726-3367
ckna@globetrotter.net
pages.globetrotter.net/ckna

***Pikogan:* CKAG-FM** (Freq: 100.1)
45 rue Migwan, Pikogan, QC J9T 3A3
Tel: 819-727-3237; *Fax:* 819-732-1569
ckagfm@cableamos.com

†*Pohenegamook:* CFVD-FM-2 (Freq: 92.1)
Owned by: **CFVD-FM**
Pohenegamook, QC

†*Port-Cartier:* CIPC-FM (Freq: Rock contemporain, franco/anglo, à 99.1 FM, Port-Cartier/Sept-×les)
52, rue Elie-Rochefort, Port-Cartier, QC G5B 1N2
Tél: 418-766-6868; *Téléc:* 418-766-6870
cipc991@globetrotter.net; 991@live.ca
www.laradioactive.com
Yvan Beaulieu, Directeur général, direction991@globetrotter.net
Mathieu Pineau, Directeur, Programmation, dirprog991@globetrotter.net

***Port-Menier:* CJBE-FM** (Freq: 90.1)
PO Box 15, Port-Menier, QC G0G 2Y0
Tel: 418-535-0292; *Fax:* 418-535-0292
Denis Tremblay, Dir de la Station

***Québec:* CBVE-FM** (Freq: 104.7)
Owned by: **Canadian Broadcasting Corporation***
888, rue Saint-Jean, Québec, QC G1R 5H6
Tel: 418-691-3613; *Fax:* 418-691-3610
Claude Saindon, General Manager

***Québec:* CBVE-FM** (Freq: 104.7)
Owned by: **Canadian Broadcasting Corporation***
PO Box 18800, 888, rue Saint-Jean, Québec, QC G1K 9L4
Tel: 418-691-3613; *Fax:* 418-691-3610

†*Québec:* CBV-FM (Freq: 106.3)
Owned by: **Canadian Broadcasting Corporation***
CP 18800, 888, rue St-Jean, Québec, QC G1K 9L4
Tél: 418-654-1341; *Téléc:* 418-656-8842
cbvt@radio-canada.ca
www.radio-canada.ca/regions
Louise Cordeau, Directrice de Radio-Canada, Québec

***Québec:* CBV-FM** (Freq: 106.3)
Owned by: **Canadian Broadcasting Corporation***
PO Box 18800, 888, rue Saint-Jean, Québec, QC G1K 9L4
Tel: 418-691-3620; *Fax:* 418-691-3620
www.radio-canada.ca/regions
Susan Campbell, General Manager

***Québec:* CBVX-FM** (Freq: 95.3)
Owned by: **Canadian Broadcasting Corporation***
PO Box 18800, 888, rue Saint-Jean, Québec, QC G1K 9L4
Tel: 418-691-3620; *Fax:* 418-691-3610
www.radio-canada.ca/regions/

†*Québec:* CHIK-FM (Freq: 98.9)
Owned by: **Astral Media Inc.***
900, rue d'Youville, 1er étage, Québec, QC G1R 3P7
Tél: 418-687-9900; *Téléc:* 418-687-3106
www.radioenergie.com

***Québec:* CION-FM** (Freq: 90.9; 102.5; 106.7)
3196, ch Sainte-Foy, Québec, QC G1X 1R4
Tel: 418-659-9090; *Fax:* 418-650-3306
Toll-Free: 800-447-2466
cionfm@radiogalilee.qc.ca
Denis Veilleux

** For details on this company see listing in Major Broadcasting Companies section; † French language station*

†*Québec:* CITF-FM (Freq: 107.5)
Owned by: **Astral Media Inc.***
900, rue d'Youville, 1er étage, Québec, QC G1R 3P7
Tél: 418-527-3232; *Téléc:* 418-687-3106
www.rockdetente.com

***Québec:* CJEC-FM** (Freq: 91.9)
1305, ch Ste-Foy, 4e étage, Québec, QC G1S 4Y5
Tel: 418-688-0919; *Fax:* 418-527-0919
www.rythmefm.com
Jean-Paul Lemire, General Manager

†*Québec:* CJMF-FM (Freq: 93.3)
1305, ch Ste-Foy, 4e étage, Québec, QC G1S 4Y5
Tél: 418-687-9330; *Téléc:* 418-687-0211
commentaire@le933.com
www.le933.com
Jean-Paul Lemire

†*Québec:* CKIA-FM (Freq: 88.3)
600, côte d'Abraham, Québec, QC G1R 1A1
Tél: 418-529-9026; *Téléc:* 418-529-4156
ckiafm@meduse.org
www.ckiafm.org
Andrée Pomerleau

†*Québec:* CKRL-FM (Freq: 89.1)
405, 3e av, Québec, QC G1L 2W2
Tél: 418-640-2575; *Téléc:* 418-640-1588
programmation@ckrl.qc.ca
www.ckrl.qc.ca
Jean-Pierre Bédard

†*Radisson:* CIAU-FM (Freq: 103.1)
CP 285, 143, rue Jolliet, Radisson, QC J0Y 2X0
Tél: 819-638-7033; *Téléc:* 819-638-7033
ciaufm@lino.com
www.ciaufm.com
Martin Beaucage, Station Manger

***Restigouche:* CHRQ-FM** (Freq: 106.9)
PO Box 180, 116 Riverside Dr., Restigouche, QC G0C 2R0
Tel: 418-788-2449; *Fax:* 418-788-2653
chrq1069@globetrotter.net
Sandra Bulmer, Station Manager

†*Rimouski:* CBRX-FM (Freq: 101.5)
Owned by: **Canadian Broadcasting Corporation (CBC)***
Rimouski, QC
Ligne sans frais: 866-954-1341
auditoire.quebec@radio-canada.ca
www.radio-canada.ca/espace_musique;
www.radio-canada.ca/regions/quebec

†*Rimouski:* CIKI-FM (Freq: 98.7)
Owned by: **Astral Media Inc.***
CP 3875, 875, boul St-Germain ouest, Rimouski, QC G5L 7P3
Tél: 418-724-9870; *Téléc:* 418-722-7508
www.radioenergie.com

†*Rimouski:* CJBR-FM (Freq: 101.5)
Owned by: **Canadian Broadcasting Corporation***
Rimouski, QC

†*Rimouski:* CJOI-FM (Freq: 102.9)
Owned by: **Astral Media Inc.***
CP 3875, 875, boul St-Germain ouest, Rimouski, QC G5L 7P3
Tél: 418-723-2323; *Téléc:* 418-722-7508
www.rockdetente.com

***Rimouski:* CKMN-FM** (Freq: 96.5)
323, Montée industrielle, Rimouski, QC G5M 1A7
Tel: 418-722-2566; *Fax:* 418-724-7815
ckmn-fm@cgocable.ca
www.ckmn.ca
Vic Talbot

†*Rivière-du-Loup:* CIBM-FM (Freq: 107.1)
64, rue Hôtel-de-Ville, Rivière-du-Loup, QC G5R 1L5
Tél: 418-867-1071; *Téléc:* 418-867-4940
ventes@cibm107.com
cibm107.com

†*Rivière-du-Loup:* CIEL-FM (Freq: 103.7)
64, rue Hôtel-de-Ville, Rivière-du-Loup, QC G5R 1L5
Tél: 418-862-8241; *Téléc:* 418-867-4940
info@ciel103.com
www.cibm107.com
Guy Simard

†*Roberval:* CHRL-FM (Freq: 99.5)
Owned by: **Groupe Radio Antenne 6***
568, boul St-Joseph, Roberval, QC G8H 2K6
Tél: 418-275-1831; *Téléc:* 418-275-2475
M. Levesque, General Manager

***Rouyn-Noranda:* CHIC-FM** (Freq: 88.7)
PO Box 2185, 120, 9e Rue, Rouyn-Noranda, QC J9X 5A6
Tel: 819-797-4242; *Fax:* 819-797-3803
Jocelyn Côté, General Manager, ccechic@cablevision.qc.ca

†*Rouyn-Noranda:* CHLM-FM (Freq: 90.7)
70, av Principal, Rouyn-Noranda, QC J9X 4P2
Tél: 819-762-8155; *Téléc:* 819-762-1279
www.radio-canada.ca/regions/abitibi

†*Rouyn-Noranda:* CHOA-FM (Freq: 96.5)
Owned by: **Radio Nord Communications Inc.***
380, av Murdoch, Rouyn-Noranda, QC J9X 1G5
Tél: 819-762-0741; *Téléc:* 819-762-6331
www.couleurfm.com

***Rouyn-Noranda:* CJMM-FM** (Freq: 99.1)
Owned by: **Astral Media Inc.***
33B, rue Gamble ouest, Rouyn-Noranda, QC J9X 2R3
Tel: 819-797-2566; *Fax:* 819-797-1664
www.radioenergie.com

***Saint-Gabriel-de-Brandon:* CFNJ-FM** (Freq: 99.1)
Owned by: **Radio Nord Communications Inc.***
245, rue Beauvilliers, Saint-Gabriel-de-Brandon, QC J0K 2N0
Tel: 450-835-3437; *Fax:* 450-835-3581
www.cfnj.qc.ca
Denis Roch

†*Saint-Hilarion:* CIHO-FM (Freq: 96.3)
315, ch Cartier nord, Saint-Hilarion, QC G0A 3V0
Tél: 418-457-3333; *Téléc:* 418-457-3518
ciho@charlevoix.net
www.cihofm.com

†*Saint-Hyacinthe:* CFEI-FM (Freq: 106.5)
Owned by: **Astral Media Inc.***
2596, boul Casavant ouest, Saint-Hyacinthe, QC J2S 7R8
Tél: 450-774-6486; *Téléc:* 450-774-7785
www.boomfm.com

***Saint-Jean-Port-Joli:* CHOX-4** (Freq: 100.1)
Owned by: **CHOX-FM**
Saint-Jean-Port-Joli, QC

†*Saint-Jean-sur-Richelieu:* CFZZ-FM (Freq: 104.1)
Owned by: **Astral Media Inc.***
104, rue Richelieu, Saint-Jean-sur-Richelieu, QC J3B 6X3
Tél: 450-346-0104; *Téléc:* 450-348-2274
www.boomfm.com
Pierre De Mondehare, Directeur Général par intérim

†*Saint-Jérôme:* CIME-FM (Freq: 101.3; 103.9)
Owned by: **Corus Entertainment Inc.***
120, de la Gare, Saint-Jérôme, QC J7Z 2C2
Tél: 450-431-2463; *Téléc:* 450-456-5975
www.cime.fm

***Saint-Pamphile:* CHOX-2** (Freq: 101.1)
Owned by: **CHOX-FM**
Saint-Pamphile, QC

***Saint-Pamphile:* CJDS-FM** (Freq: 94.7)
PO Box 550, 109, rue de l'église, Saint-Pamphile, QC G0R 3X0
Tel: 418-356-1303; *Fax:* 418-356-2586
cjdsradio@globetrotter.net
Jean-Claude Dignard, General Manager

***Saint-Régis:* CKON-FM** (Freq: 97.3)
Owned by: **CKON-FM**
Saint-Régis, QC

***Saint-Rémi:* CHOC-FM** (Freq: 104.9)
107, Chevrefils, Saint-Rémi, QC J0L 2L0
Tel: 450-454-5500; *Fax:* 450-454-9435
webchoc.fr.fm

†*Sainte-Anne-des-Monts:* CJMC-FM (Freq: 100.3)
170, boul Ste-Anne est, Sainte-Anne-des-Monts, QC G4V 1N1
Tél: 418-763-5522; *Téléc:* 418-763-7211

†*Sainte-Foy:* CFOM-FM (Freq: 102.9)
Owned by: **Astral Media Inc.***
2136, ch Sainte-Foy, 3e étage, Sainte-Foy, QC G1V 1R8
Tél: 418-694-1029; *Téléc:* 418-682-8430
mharvey@cfom1029.com
www.cfom1029.com
Pierre DeMondehare, General Manager

***Sainte-Foy:* CHYZ-FM** (Freq: 94.3)
#023, Pavillon Pollack, Universitaire Laval, Sainte-Foy, QC G1K 7P4
Tel: 418-656-2131; *Fax:* 450-656-3660
chyz@public.ulaval.ca
www.chyz.qc.ca
Jean-Philippe Lessard, General Manager

***Salaberry-de-Valleyfield:* CKOD-FM** (Freq: 103.1)
249, rue Victoria, Salaberry-de-Valleyfield, QC J6T 1A9
Tel: 450-373-0103; *Fax:* 450-373-4297
fm103@ckod.qc.ca
www.ckod.qc.ca
Robert Brunet, Directeur Général

†*Senneterre:* CIBO-FM (Freq: 100.5)
CP 1150, 121, 1re rue Est, Senneterre, QC J0Y 2M0
Tél: 819-737-2222; *Téléc:* 819-737-8599
cibo.fm@moncourrier.com
Guy Bilodeau, General Manager

†*Sept-Iles:* CBSI-FM (Freq: 98.1)
Owned by: **Canadian Broadcasting Corporation (CBC)***
Sept-Iles, QC
Ligne sans frais: 866-954-1341
auditoire.quebec@radio-canada.ca
www.radio-canada.ca/regions/quebec

***Sept-Iles:* CKAU-FM** (Freq: 90.1; 104.5)
PO Box 338, Sept-Iles, QC G4R 4K6
Tel: 418-927-2476; *Fax:* 418-927-2800
ckau@chau.com
www.ckau.com
Yves Rock, General Manager

†*Sept-Iles:* CKCN-FM (Freq: 94.1)
437, av Arnaud, Sept-Iles, QC G4R 3B3
Tél: 418-962-3838; *Téléc:* 418-968-6662
ckcn@globetrotter.net
www.quebec.fm/ckcn
Dominique Marquis, Directrice
Caroline Michaud, Directeur des programmes

***Sherbrooke:* CFAK-FM** (Freq: 88.3)
2500, boul de Université, Sherbrooke, QC J1K 2R1
Tel: 819-821-8000; *Fax:* 819-821-7930
info@cfak.qc.ca
www.cfak.qc.ca
Steve Bazinet, General Manager

†*Sherbrooke:* CFLX-FM (Freq: 95.5)
67, rue Wellington Nord, Sherbrooke, QC J1H 5A9
Tél: 819-566-2787; *Téléc:* 819-566-7331
cflx@cflx.qc.ca
www.cflx.qc.ca
Jose Deschenes

†*Sherbrooke:* CIMO-FM (Freq: 106.1)
Owned by: **Astral Media Inc.***
#200, 1845, rue King ouest, Sherbrooke, QC J1J 2E4
Tél: 819-347-1414; *Téléc:* 819-347-1061
www.radioenergie.com

†*Sherbrooke:* CITE-FM-1 (Freq: 102.7)
Owned by: **Astral Media Inc.***
#200, 1845, rue King ouest, Sherbrooke, QC J1L 2E4
Tél: 819-566-6655; *Téléc:* 819-566-1011
www.rockdetente.com

†*Sillery:* CHOI-FM (Freq: 98.1)
#300, 1134, ch St-Louis, Sillery, QC G1S 1E5
Tél: 418-687-9810; *Téléc:* 418-682-8427
www.choiradiox.com
Patrice Demers

†*Sorel-Tracy:* CJSO-FM (Freq: 101.7)
52, rue du Roi, Sorel-Tracy, QC J3P 4M7
Tél: 450-743-2772; *Téléc:* 450-743-0293
Ligne sans frais: 888-489-1017
cjso@cjso.qc.ca
www.cjso.qc.ca

** For details on this company see listing in Major Broadcasting Companies section; † French language station*

†*Squatec:* CFVD-FM-3 (Freq: 92.1)
Owned by: **CFVD-FM**
Squatec, QC

***St. Augustine:* CJAS-FM** (Freq: 93.5)
PO Box 100, St. Augustine, QC G0G 2R0
Tel: 418-947-2239; *Fax:* 418-947-2664
sajcr@globetrotter.net
cjasradio.pic30.com
Laurette Gallibois, General Manager

†*St-Georges-de-Beauce:* CHJM-FM (Freq: 99.7)
CP 100, 11760, 3e av, St-Georges-de-Beauce, QC G5Y 5C4
Tél: 418-227-0997; *Téléc:* 418-228-0096
adminrb@cgocable.ca
www.mix997.com

†*St-Georges-de-Beauce:* CKRB-FM (Freq: 103.3)
CP 100, 11760, 3e av, St-Georges-de-Beauce, QC G5Y 5C4
Tél: 418-228-1460; *Téléc:* 418-228-0096
admnrb@cgocable.ca
www.coolfm.biz

†*Ste-Marie-de-Beauce:* CHEQ-FM (Freq: 101.3)
#101, 1068, boul Vachon Nord, Ste-Marie-de-Beauce, QC G6E 1M6
Tél: 418-387-1013; *Téléc:* 418-387-3757
Ligne sans frais: 877-387-1013
info@cheqfm.qc.ca
www.cheqfm.qc.ca
Mario Paquin, Directeur général

†*Témiscaming:* CKVM-FM-1 (Freq: 92.1)
Owned by: **CKVM-FM**
Témiscaming, QC

†*Thetford Mines:* CFJO-FM (Freq: 97.3)
CP 69, 327, rue Labbé, Thetford Mines, QC G6G 5S3
Tél: 418-338-1009; *Téléc:* 418-338-0386
info@O973.com
www.o973.com
Annie Labbé, Directrice générale

†*Thetford Mines:* CKLD-FM (Freq: 105.5)
327, rue Labbé, Thetford Mines, QC G6G 1Z2
Tél: 418-335-7533; *Téléc:* 418-335-9009
info@passionrock.com
www.passionrock.com

***Trois-Rivières:* CFOU-FM** (Freq: 89.1)
3351, boul des Forges, Trois-Rivières, QC G9A 5H7
Tel: 819-697-2368; *Fax:* 819-697-3888
cfou@uqtr.uquebec.ca
www.cfoufm.com
Eric Leclair, General Manager

†*Trois-Rivières:* CHEY-FM (Freq: 94.7)
Owned by: **Astral Media Inc.***
#260, 1500, boul Royale, Trois-Rivières, QC G9A 6J4
Tél: 819-376-0947; *Téléc:* 819-378-1360
chey2@rock-detente.com
www.rockdetente.com

†*Trois-Rivières:* CIGB-FM (Freq: 102.3)
Owned by: **Astral Media Inc.***
#260, 1500, rue Royal, Trois-Rivières, QC G9A 6J4
Tél: 819-378-1023; *Téléc:* 819-378-1360
www.radioenergie.com

†*Val-d'Or:* CHGO-FM (Freq: 104.3)
Owned by: **Radio Nord Communications Inc.***
1729, 3e av, Val-d'Or, QC J9P 1W3
Tél: 819-825-0010; *Téléc:* 819-825-7313
www.gofm.net
André Houle, General Manager

†*Val-d'Or:* CHGO-FM (Freq: 104.3; 95.7)
Owned by: **Radio Nord Communications Inc.***
1729, 3e av, Val-d'Or, QC J9P 1W3
Tél: 819-825-9994; *Téléc:* 819-825-7313
www.gofm.net

***Val-d'Or:* CJMV-FM** (Freq: 102.7)
Owned by: **Astral Media Inc.***
173, rue Perreault, Val-d'Or, QC J9P 2H3
Tel: 819-825-2568; *Fax:* 819-825-2840
www.radioenergie.com
Marlene Trottier, General Manager

†*Verdun:* CHMP-FM (Freq: 98.5)
Owned by: **Corus Entertainment Inc.***
211, av Gordon, Verdun, QC H4G 2R2
Tél: 514-767-2435; *Téléc:* 514-761-0985
Ligne sans frais: 866-790-9850
www.985fm.ca
Jacques Papin, Directeur général
Yves Delisle, Directeur adjoint, émissions

†*Victoriaville:* CFDA-FM (Freq: 101.9)
55, rue St-Jean Baptiste, Victoriaville, QC G6P 6T3
Tél: 819-752-5545; *Téléc:* 819-752-7552
info@passionrock.com
www.passionrock.com

†*Victoriaville:* CFJO-FM (Freq: 97.3; 101.7)
CP 490, 55, rue St-Jean-Baptiste, Victoriaville, QC G6P 6T3
Tél: 819-752-2785; *Téléc:* 819-752-3182
info@o973.com
www.o973.com
Annie Labbé, Dictrice Général

†*Ville-Marie:* CKVM-FM (Freq: 93.1)
62, rue Ste-Anne, Ville-Marie, QC J9V 2B7
Tél: 819-629-2710; *Téléc:* 819-622-0716
ckvm@ckvm.qc.ca
Martin Héroux, Directeur-général

***Windsor:* CIAX-FM** (Freq: 98.3)
49 Sixth Ave., Windsor, QC J1S 1T2
Tel: 819-845-5900; *Fax:* 819-845-2692
unite@qc.aira.ca
Patrick Levesque, General Manager

Saskatchewan

***Cumberland House:* CJCF-FM** (Freq: 89.9)
PO Box 100, Cumberland House, SK S0E 0S0
Tel: 306-888-2176; *Fax:* 306-888-4444
Rachel Fiddler, General Manager

***Hudson Bay:* CFMQ-FM** (Freq: 98.1)
PO Box 1272, Hudson Bay, SK S0E 0Y0
Tel: 306-865-3065; *Fax:* 306-865-2227
cfmq@sasktel.net
www.townofhudsonbay.com
Dan Brann, General Manager

***Kenosee Lake:* CIDD-FM** (Freq: 97.7)
PO Box 121, Kenosee Lake, SK A0C 2S0
Tel: 306-577-2450
Lana Littlechief, General Manager

***La Ronge:* CBKA-FM** (Freq: CBC Radio 1; 105.9FM)
Owned by: **Canadian Broadcasting Corporation***
PO Box 959, La Ronge, SK S0J 1L0
Tel: 306-425-3324
www.cbc.ca/sk

***La Ronge:* CJLR-FM** (Freq: 89.9)
PO Box 1529, 712 Finlayson St., La Ronge, SK S0J 1L0
Tel: 306-425-4003; *Fax:* 306-425-3123
mbcradio@mbcradio.com
www.mbcradio.com

***Meadow Lake:* CFDM-FM** (Freq: 105.7)
PO Box 8168, Meadow Lake, SK S9X 1T8
Tel: 306-236-1445; *Fax:* 306-236-2821
cfdm.radio@sasktel.net
Ben Lachance, Station Manager

***Meadow Lake:* CJNS-FM** (Freq: 102.3)
PO Box 1660, 225 Centre St., Meadow Lake, SK S9X 1Z2
Tel: 306-236-6494; *Fax:* 306-236-6141

***Melfort:* CJVR-FM** (Freq: 105.1)
PO Box 750, 611 Main St. North, Melfort, SK S0E 1A0
Tel: 306-752-2587; *Fax:* 306-752-5932
Toll-Free: 800-668-2587
sales@cjvr.com
www.cjvr.com
Kevin Gemmel, Station Manager

***Moose Jaw:* CILG-FM** (Freq: 100.7)
Owned by: **CHAB**
Moose Jaw, SK

***Nipawin:* CJNE-FM** (Freq: 94.7)
PO Box 220, Nipawin, SK S0E 1E0
Tel: 306-862-9478; *Fax:* 306-862-2334
pro.cjne@sasktel.net
www.cjnefm.com
Norman Rudock, General Manager

†*North Battleford:* CBKF-FM-5 (Freq: Première Chaîne; 96.9FM)
Owned by: **CBKF-FM; Société Radio Canada***
North Battleford, SK

***North Battleford:* CJCQ-FM** (Freq: 98.1)
Owned by: **CJNB**
North Battleford, SK

***Pinehouse Lake:* CFNK-FM** (Freq: 89.9)
PO Box 370, Pinehouse Lake, SK S0J 2B0
Tel: 306-884-2011; *Fax:* 306-884-2365
Toll-Free: 306-884-2016
cfnkradio@sasktel.net
www.cfnk.radiok.sympatico.ca
Jamie Iron, General Manager

***Prince Albert:* CFMM-FM** (Freq: 99.1)
PO Box 900, 1316 Central Ave., Prince Albert, SK S6V 7R4
Tel: 306-763-7421; *Fax:* 306-764-1850
power99fm@rawlco.com
www.power99fm.com
Garth Kalin, Operations Manager

***Prince Albert:* CHQX-FM** (Freq: 101.5)
PO Box 900, 1316 Central Ave., Prince Albert, SK S6V 7R4
Tel: 306-763-7421; *Fax:* 306-764-1850
mix101@rawlco.com
www.mix101fm.com

†*Regina:* CBKF-FM (Freq: Première Chaîne; 97.7FM)
Owned by: **Société Radio Canada***
CP 540, 2440 Broad St., Regina, SK S4P 4A1
Tél: 306-347-9540; *Téléc:* 306-347-9414
Ligne sans frais: 800-413-2253
webmestre@radio-canada.ca
www.radio-canada.ca/saskatchewan
René Fontaine, Directeur des services français dan, 204-788-3236, rene.fontaine@radio-canada.ca

***Regina:* CBK-FM** (Freq: CBC Radio 2; 96.9FM)
Owned by: **Canadian Broadcasting Corporation***
2440 Broad St., Regina, SK S4P 4A1
Tel: 306-347-9540
www.cbc.ca/sask
David Kyle, News Director

***Regina:* CFWF-FM** (Freq: 104.9)
Owned by: **Harvard Broadcasting Inc.***
1900 Rose St., Regina, SK S4P 0A9
Tel: 306-546-6200; *Fax:* 306-781-7338
hurricane@thewolfrocks.com
www.thewolfrocks.com
Michael Olstrom

***Regina:* CHMX-FM** (Freq: 92.1)
Owned by: **Harvard Broadcasting Inc.***
1900 Rose St., Regina, SK S4P 0A9
Tel: 306-936-0092; *Fax:* 306-546-6200
dholien@lite92fm.com
www.lite92fm.com
Michael Olstrom

***Regina:* CIZL-FM** (Freq: 98.9)
Owned by: **RAWLCO Radio Ltd.***
#210, 2401 Saskatchewan Dr., Regina, SK S4P 4H8
Tel: 306-525-0000; *Fax:* 306-347-8557
www.z99.com
Tom Newton, Program Director

***Regina:* CJTR-FM** (Freq: 91.3)
PO Box 334 Main, Regina, SK S4P 3A1
Tel: 306-525-7274; *Fax:* 306-525-9741
radius@cjtr.ca
www.cjtr.ca
Keith Colhoun

***Regina:* CKCK-FM** (Freq: 94.5)
Owned by: **RAWLCO Radio Ltd.***
#210, 2401 Saskatchewan Dr., Regina, SK S4P 4H8
Tel: 306-525-0000; *Fax:* 306-547-8557
www.jackfmregina.com

***Saskatoon:* CFCR-FM** (Freq: 90.5)
PO Box 7544, Saskatoon, SK S7K 4L4
Tel: 306-664-6678
cfcr@cfcr.ca
www.cfcr.ca
Ron Spizziri

** For details on this company see listing in Major Broadcasting Companies section; † French language station*

Saskatoon: **CFMC-FM** (Freq: 95.1)
715 Saskatchewan Cres. West, Saskatoon, SK S7M 5V7
Tel: 306-934-2222; *Fax:* 306-477-0002
www.c95.com
Jamie Wall, General Manager

Saskatoon: **CJDJ-FM** (Freq: 102.1)
715 Saskatchewan Cres. West, Saskatoon, SK S7M 5V7
Tel: 306-934-2222; *Fax:* 306-477-0002
www.rock102rocks.com
Jamie Wall, General Manager

Saskatoon: **CJMK-FM** (Freq: 98.3)
366 - 3rd Ave. South, Saskatoon, SK S7K 1M5
Tel: 306-244-1975; *Fax:* 306-665-8484
magic@magic983.fm
www.magic983.fm

Saskatoon: **CKBL-FM** (Freq: 92.9)
366 - 3rd Ave. South, Saskatoon, SK S7K 1M5
Tel: 306-244-1975; *Fax:* 306-665-8484
thebull@929thebullrocks.com
www.929thebullrocks.com
Vic Dubois, President & General Manager

Swift Current: **CIMG-FM** (Freq: 94.1)
Owned by: **Golden West Broadcasting Ltd.***
134 Central Ave. North, Swift Current, SK S9H 0L1
Tel: 306-773-4605; *Fax:* 306-773-6390
Toll-Free: 800-821-8073
eaglecontrol@goldenwestradio.com
www.eagle94.com
Deborah Gauger, Station General Manager & Sales

Tagish: **CFET-FM** (Freq: 106.7)
Mile 234, Tagish, SK Y0B 1T0
Tel: 867-399-3012; *Fax:* 867-668-2633
info@cfetradio.ca
www.cfetradio.ca
Robert G. Hopkins, General Manager

Waskesiu: **CJVR-FM** (Freq: 106.3)
Owned by: **CJVR-FM**
Waskesiu, SK

Whitehorse: **CIAY-FM** (Freq: 100.7)
91806 Alaska Hwy., Whitehorse, SK Y1A 5B7
Tel: 867-393-2429; *Fax:* 867-393-2439
info@ciay.ca
www.ciay.ca
Rod Carby, Station Manager

Wynyard: **CJVR-FM** (Freq: 100.3)
Owned by: **CJVR-FM**
Wynyard, SK

Yorkton: **CFGW-FM** (Freq: 94.1)
Owned by: **CJGX**
Yorkton, SK

†Zenon Park: **CBKF-FM-3** (Freq: Première Chaîne; 93.5FM)
Owned by: **CBKF-FM; Société Radio Canada***
Zenon Park, SK

Yukon Territory

Whitehorse: **CHON-FM** (Freq: 98.1; 90.5)
4230A - 4 Ave., Whitehorse, YT Y1A 1K1
Tel: 867-668-6629; *Fax:* 867-668-6612
nnby@nnby.net
www.nnby.net

Television Stations

Alberta

Ashmont: **CFRN-TV-4** (Channel: 12)
Owned by: **CTVglobemedia Inc.**
Ashmont, AB

Athabasca: **CBXT-TV-1** (Channel: 8)
Owned by: **CBXT-TV**
Athabasca, AB

Athabasca: **CFRN-TV** (Channel: 13)
Owned by: **CTVglobemedia Inc.**
Athabasca, AB

Banff: **CBRT-TV-1** (Channel: 5 VHF)
Owned by: **Canadian Broadcasting Corporation (CBC)**
Banff, AB
Toll-Free: 866-306-4636
www.cbc.ca/calgary; www.cbc.ca/television
Social Media: www.twitter.com/cbccalgary
Other information: TDD: 1-866-220-6045

Banff: **CFCN-TV-2** (Channel: 7)
Owned by: **CTVglobemedia Inc.**
Banff, AB

Bassano: **CFCN-TV-7** (Channel: 10)
Owned by: **CTVglobemedia Inc.**
Bassano, AB

Battle River: **CBXAT-TV-6** (Channel: 9)
Owned by: **CBXT-TV**
Battle River, AB

Beaverlodge: **CBXT-TV** (Channel: 4)
Owned by: **Canadian Broadcasting Corporation***
Beaverlodge, AB

Bellevue: **CBRT-TV-10** (Channel: 57 UHF)
Owned by: **Canadian Broadcasting Corporation (CBC)**
Bellevue, AB
Toll-Free: 866-306-4636
www.cbc.ca/calgary; www.cbc.ca/television
Social Media: www.twitter.com/cbccalgary
Other information: TDD: 1-866-220-6045

Bonnyville: **CITL-TV4** (Channel: 7)
Owned by: **CITL-TV**
Bonnyville, AB

Bonnyville: **CKSA-TV** (Channel: 9)
Owned by: **CKSA-TV**
Bonnyville, AB

Brooks: **CFCN-TV-3** (Channel: 9)
Owned by: **CTVglobemedia Inc.**
Brooks, AB

Burmis: **CBRT-TV-8** (Channel: 47 UHF)
Owned by: **Canadian Broadcasting Corporation (CBC)**
Burmis, AB
Toll-Free: 866-306-4636
www.cbc.ca/calgary; www.cbc.ca/television
Social Media: www.twitter.com/cbccalgary
Other information: TDD: 1-866-220-6045

Burmis: **CFCN-TV-4** (Channel: 5)
Owned by: **CTVglobemedia Inc.**
Burmis, AB

Calgary: **CBRT-TV** (Channel: 9 VHF)
Owned by: **Canadian Broadcasting Corporation (CBC)***
PO Box 2640, 1724 Westmount Blvd. NW, Calgary, AB T2P 2M7
Tel: 403-521-6000; *Fax:* 403-521-6079
Toll-Free: 866-306-4636
www.cbc.ca/calgary; www.cbc.ca/television
Social Media: www.twitter.com/cbccalgary
Other information: Phone, TV Newsroom: 403-521-6055; TDD: 1-866-220-6045
Diane Humber, Director, Calgary Centre, 403-521-6252
Dave Budge, Director, News, 403-521-6016
Helen Henderson, Director, Programs, 403-521-6221
Jim Haskins, Manager, Calgary Sales Team, 403-521-6184
Shawna Kelly, Manager, Communications, 403-521-6207
Del Simon, Senior Officer, Communications, 403-521-6008

Calgary: **CFCN-TV** (Channel: 3)
Owned by: **CTVglobemedia Inc.***
80 Patina Rise SW, Calgary, AB T3H 2W4
Tel: 403-240-5600; *Fax:* 403-240-8879
calgarynews@ctv.ca
www.cfcn.ca
Patricia McDougall, Vice-President & General Manager, pmcdougall@ctv.ca

Calgary: **CICT-TV** (Channel: 7)
Owned by: **Canwest Global Communications Corp.***
222 - 23 St. NE, Calgary, AB T2E 7N2
Tel: 403-235-7777; *Fax:* 403-248-0252
www.globaltv.com/calgary

Calgary: **CKAL-TV** (Channel: 5)
535 - 7th Ave. SW, Calgary, AB T2P 0Y4
Tel: 403-508-2222; *Fax:* 403-508-2224
calgaryfeedback@a-channel.com
www.a-channel.com

Cardston: **CBRT-TV-12** (Channel: 6 VHF)
Owned by: **Canadian Broadcasting Corporation (CBC)**
Cardston, AB
Toll-Free: 866-306-4636
www.cbc.ca/calgary; www.cbc.ca/television
Social Media: www.twitter.com/cbccalgary
Other information: TDD: 1-866-220-6045

Chateh: **CBXAT-TV-7** (Channel: 5)
Owned by: **CBXT-TV**
Chateh, AB

Coleman: **CBRT-TV-11** (Channel: 17 UHF)
Owned by: **Canadian Broadcasting Corporation (CBC)**
Coleman, AB
Toll-Free: 866-306-4636
www.cbc.ca/calgary; www.cbc.ca/television
Social Media: www.twitter.com/cbccalgary
Other information: TDD: 1-866-220-6045

Coutts: **CBRT-TV-16** (Channel: 4 VHF)
Owned by: **Canadian Broadcasting Corporation (CBC)**
Coutts, AB
Toll-Free: 866-306-4636
www.cbc.ca/calgary; www.cbc.ca/television
Social Media: www.twitter.com/cbccalgary
Other information: TDD: 1-866-220-6045

Cowley: **CBRT-TV-15** (Channel: 27 UHF)
Owned by: **Canadian Broadcasting Corporation (CBC)**
Cowley, AB
Toll-Free: 866-306-4636
www.cbc.ca/calgary; www.cbc.ca/television
Social Media: www.twitter.com/cbccalgary
Other information: TDD: 1-866-220-6045

Drumheller: **CBRT-TV-2** (Channel: 6 VHF)
Owned by: **Canadian Broadcasting Corporation (CBC)**
Drumheller, AB
Toll-Free: 866-306-4636
www.cbc.ca/calgary; www.cbc.ca/television
Social Media: www.twitter.com/cbccalgary
Other information: TDD: 1-866-220-6045

Drumheller: **CFCN-TV-6** (Channel: 10)
Owned by: **CTVglobemedia Inc.**
Drumheller, AB

†Edmonton: **CBXFT-TV** (Channel: 11)
Owned by: **Canadian Broadcasting Corporation***
Edmonton City Centre, CP 555, #123, 10062 - 102 Ave., Edmonton, AB T5J 2Y8
Tél: 780-468-7500; *Téléc:* 780-468-7779
tjalberta@edmonton.radio-canada.ca
www.radio-canada.ca/regions/alberta/

Edmonton: **CBXT-TV** (Channel: 5)
Owned by: **Canadian Broadcasting Corporation***
123 Edmonton City Centre, PO Box 555, 10062 - 102nd Ave., Edmonton, AB T5J 2P4
Tel: 780-468-7500; *Fax:* 780-468-7897
kelly_walter@cbc.ca
www.cbc.ca/edmonton
Kelly Walter, Regional Sales Manager

Edmonton: **CFRN-TV** (Channel: 3)
Owned by: **CTVglobemedia Inc.***
18520 Stony Plain Rd., Edmonton, AB T5S 1A8
Tel: 780-483-3311; *Fax:* 780-484-4426
www.cfrntv.ca
Lloyd Lewis, General Manager & Vice-President

Edmonton: **CITV-TV** (Channel: 13)
Owned by: **Canwest Global Communications Corp.***
5325 Allard Way, Edmonton, AB T6H 5B8
Tel: 780-436-1250; *Fax:* 780-989-4686
globalnews.ed@globaltv.com
Tim Spelliscy, General Manager

** For details on this company see listing in Major Broadcasting Companies section; † French language station*

Edmonton: CKEM-TV (Channel: 51)
10212 Jasper Ave., Edmonton, AB T5J 5A3
Tel: 780-424-2222; *Fax:* 780-424-0357
newsnow@chumtv.com
www.a-channel.com
Jim Haskins, General Manager

Etzikom: CHAT-TV-5 (Channel: 12)
Owned by: **CHAT-TV**
Etzikom, AB

Exshaw: CBRT-TV-17 (Channel: 34 UHF)
Owned by: **Canadian Broadcasting Corporation (CBC)**
Exshaw, AB
Toll-Free: 866-306-4636
www.cbc.ca/calgary; www.cbc.ca/television
Social Media: www.twitter.com/cbccalgary
Other information: TDD: 1-866-220-6045

Exshaw: CBRT-TV-3 (Channel: 6 VHF)
Owned by: **Canadian Broadcasting Corporation (CBC)**
Exshaw, AB
Toll-Free: 866-306-4636
www.cbc.ca/calgary; www.cbc.ca/television
Social Media: www.twitter.com/cbccalgary
Other information: TDD: 1-866-220-6045

Fort McMurray: CBXT-TV-6 (Channel: 12)
Owned by: **CBXT-TV**
Fort McMurray, AB

Fort Vermilion: CBXAT-TV-5 (Channel: 11)
Owned by: **CBXT-TV**
Fort Vermilion, AB

Fox Creek: CBXT-TV-7 (Channel: 5)
Owned by: **CBXT-TV**
Fox Creek, AB

Fox Lake: CBXAT-TV-10 (Channel: 9)
Owned by: **CBXT-TV**
Fox Lake, AB

Grande Prairie: CBXAT-TV (Channel: 10)
Owned by: **CBXT-TV**
Grande Prairie, AB

Grande Prairie: CFRN-TV-1 (Channel: 13)
Owned by: **CTVglobemedia Inc.**
Grande Prairie, AB

Hand Hills: CFCN-TV-1 (Channel: 12)
Owned by: **CTVglobemedia Inc.**
Hand Hills, AB

Harvie Heights: CBRT-TV-13 (Channel: 22 UHF)
Owned by: **Canadian Broadcasting Corporation (CBC)**
Harvie Heights, AB
Toll-Free: 866-306-4636
www.cbc.ca/calgary; www.cbc.ca/television
Social Media: www.twitter.com/cbccalgary
Other information: TDD: 1-866-220-6045

High Level: CBXAT-TV-4 (Channel: 8)
Owned by: **CBXT-TV**
High Level, AB

High Prairie: CBXAT-TV-2 (Channel: 2)
Owned by: **CBXT-TV**
High Prairie, AB

High Prairie: CFRN-TV (Channel: 18)
High Prairie, AB

Hinton: CBXT-TV-3 (Channel: 8)
Owned by: **CBXT-TV**
Hinton, AB

Jasper: CBXT-TV-4 (Channel: 5)
Owned by: **CBXT-TV**
Jasper, AB

Jasper: CFRN-TV (Channel: 11)
Owned by: **CTVglobemedia Inc.**
Jasper, AB

Jean Cote: CBXAT-TV-13 (Channel: 31)
Owned by: **CBXT-TV**
Jean Cote, AB

Jean D'Or: CBXAT-TV-9 (Channel: 13)
Owned by: **CBXT-TV**
Jean D'Or, AB

Lac La Biche: CBXT-TV-5 (Channel: 10)
Owned by: **CBXT-TV**
Lac La Biche, AB

Lac La Biche: CFRN-TV-5 (Channel: 2)
Owned by: **CTVglobemedia Inc.**
Lac La Biche, AB

Lake Louise: CBRT-TV-4 (Channel: 12 VHF)
Owned by: **Canadian Broadcasting Corporation (CBC)**
Lake Louise, AB
Toll-Free: 866-306-4636
www.cbc.ca/calgary; www.cbc.ca/television
Social Media: www.twitter.com/cbccalgary
Other information: TDD: 1-866-220-6045

Lake Louise: CFLL-TV-1 (Channel: 6)
Owned by: **CFCN-TV**
Lake Louise, AB

Lethbridge: CBRT-TV-6 (Channel: 10)
Owned by: **Canadian Broadcasting Corporation (CBC)**
Lethbridge, AB
Toll-Free: 866-306-4636
www.cbc.ca/calgary; www.cbc.ca/television
Social Media: www.twitter.com/cbccalgary
Other information: TDD: 1-866-220-6045

Lethbridge: CFCN-TV (Channel: 13)
Owned by: **CTVglobemedia Inc.**
640-13 Street North, Lethbridge, AB T1H 2S8
Tel: 403-329-3644
cfcnlethbridge@ctv.ca
www.cfcn.ca

Lethbridge: CFCN-TV-5 (Channel: 13)
Owned by: **CTVglobemedia Inc.***
640 - 13 St. North, Lethbridge, AB T1H 2S8
Tel: 403-329-3644; *Fax:* 403-317-2420
cfcnlethbridge@ctv.ca
www.cfcn.ca
Dave Lelek, General & Sales Manager
Terry Vogt, News Director
Dale Munro, Chief Engineer & Operations Manager

Lethbridge: CISA-TV (Channel: 7)
Owned by: **Canwest Global Communications Corp.***
1401 - 28 St. North, Lethbridge, AB T1H 6H9
Tel: 403-327-1521; *Fax:* 403-320-2620
www.canada.com/lethbridge
Peter Deys, General Manager

Lethbridge: CJIL-TV (The Miracle Channel) (Channel: 17)
PO Box 1566, 450-31 St. N., Lethbridge, AB T1H 3Z3
Tel: 403-380-3399; *Fax:* 403-380-3322
mail@miraclechannel.ca
www.miraclechannel.ca

Lethbridge: CKAL-TV (Channel: 6)
Owned by: **CKAL-TV**
Lethbridge, AB

Lloydminster: CITL-TV (Newcap TV) (Channel: 4)
Owned by: **NewCap Inc.***
5026 - 50th St., Lloydminster, AB T9V 1P3
Tel: 780-875-3321; *Fax:* 780-875-4704
tvnews@newcap.ca
www.newcaptv.com
Mike Keller, General Manager, mkeller@newcap.ca

Lloydminster: CKSA-TV (Channel: 2)
Owned by: **NewCap Inc.***
5026 - 50 St., Lloydminster, AB T9V 1P3
Tel: 780-875-3321; *Fax:* 780-875-4704
tvnews@newcap.ca
www.newcap.ca
Mike Keller

Lougheed: CFRN-TV-7 (Channel: 7)
Owned by: **CTVglobemedia Inc.**
Lougheed, AB

Manning: CBXAT-TV-3 (Channel: 12)
Owned by: **CBXT-TV**
Manning, AB

Marten Mtn./Slave Lake: CBXAT-TV-11 (Channel: 11)
Owned by: **CBXT-TV**
Marten Mtn./Slave Lake, AB

Medicine Hat: CFCN-TV-8 (Channel: 8)
Owned by: **CTVglobemedia Inc.**
Medicine Hat, AB

Oyen: CFON-TV-1 (Channel: 2)
Owned by: **CFCN-TV**
Oyen, AB

Oyen: CHAT-TV-4 (Channel: 4, 6)
Owned by: **CHAT-TV**
Oyen, AB

Peace River: CBXAT-TV-1 (Channel: 7)
Owned by: **CBXT-TV**
Peace River, AB

Peace River: CFRN-TV-2 (Channel: 3)
Owned by: **CTVglobemedia Inc.**
Peace River, AB

Pincher Creek: CBRT-TV-9 (Channel: 15 UHF)
Owned by: **Canadian Broadcasting Corporation (CBC)**
Pincher Creek, AB
Toll-Free: 866-306-4636
www.cbc.ca/calgary; www.cbc.ca/television
Social Media: www.twitter.com/cbccalgary
Other information: TDD: 1-866-220-6045

Pincher Creek: CHPC-TV-2 (Channel: 11)
Owned by: **CFCN-TV**
Pincher Creek, AB

Provost: CITL-TV2 (Channel: 5)
Owned by: **CITL-TV**
Provost, AB

Provost: CKSA-TV (Channel: 12)
Owned by: **CKSA-TV**
Provost, AB

Rainbow Lake: CBXAT-TV-8 (Channel: 11)
Owned by: **CBXT-TV**
Rainbow Lake, AB

Red Deer: CFRN-TV-6 (Channel: 8)
Owned by: **CTVglobemedia Inc.**
Red Deer, AB

Red Deer: CHCA-TV (Channel: 6)
2840 Bremner Ave., Red Deer, AB T4R 1M9
Tel: 403-346-2573; *Fax:* 403-346-9980
info@chtv.ca
www.canada.com/chtv/reddeer
Stan Schmidt, Station Manager
Bob Bourns, Operations Manager

Red Deer: CKEM-TV (Channel: 8)
Owned by: **CKEM-TV**
Red Deer, AB

Redcliff: CHAT-TV (Channel: 6)
Owned by: **The Jim Pattison Broadcast Group***
10 Boundary Rd. S.E., Redcliff, AB T0J 2P0
Tel: 403-548-8008; *Fax:* 403-548-6766
info@chattv6-3.com
www.chattv6-3.com
Dwaine Dietrich, General Manager

Rocky Mountain House: CFMH-TV-2 (Channel: 12)
Owned by: **CFRN-TV**
Rocky Mountain House, AB

Rosemary: CBRT-TV-5 (Channel: 11 VHF)
Owned by: **Canadian Broadcasting Corporation (CBC)**
Rosemary, AB
Toll-Free: 866-306-4636
www.cbc.ca/calgary; www.cbc.ca/television
Social Media: www.twitter.com/cbccalgary
Other information: TDD: 1-866-220-6045

Slave Lake: CKHP-TV-1 (Channel: 4)
Owned by: **CFRN-TV**
Slave Lake, AB

Sundre: CFCN-TV (Channel: 7)
Owned by: **CTVglobemedia Inc.**
Sundre, AB

** For details on this company see listing in Major Broadcasting Companies section; † French language station*

Wabasca: **CBXAT-TV-12** (Channel: 7)
Owned by: **CBXT-TV**
Wabasca, AB

Wainwright: **CITL-TV1** (Channel: 6)
Owned by: **CITL-TV**
Wainwright, AB

Wainwright: **CKSA-TV** (Channel: 8)
Owned by: **CKSA-TV**
Wainwright, AB

Waterton Park: **CBRT-TV-7** (Channel: 4 VHF)
Owned by: **Canadian Broadcasting Corporation (CBC)**
Waterton Park, AB
Toll-Free: 866-306-4636
www.cbc.ca/calgary; www.cbc.ca/television
Social Media: www.twitter.com/cbccalgary
Other information: TDD: 1-866-220-6045

Waterton Park: **CJWP-TV-2** (Channel: 6)
Owned by: **CFCN-TV**
Waterton Park, AB

Whitecourt: **CBXT-TV-2** (Channel: 9)
Owned by: **CBXT-TV**
Whitecourt, AB

Whitecourt: **CFRN-TV-3** (Channel: 12)
Owned by: **CTVglobemedia Inc.**
Whitecourt, AB

British Columbia

100 Mile House: **CFJC-TV-6** (Channel: 5)
Owned by: **CFJC-TV**
100 Mile House, BC

100 Mile House: **CHAN-TV** (Channel: 3)
Owned by: **CHAN-TV**
100 Mile House, BC

16 Mile House: **CHCS-TV-1** (Channel: 7)
Owned by: **CHAN-TV**
16 Mile House, BC

Alert Bay: **CBUT-TV-16** (Channel: 11)
Owned by: **CBUT-TV**
Alert Bay, BC

Alexis Creek: **CHIL-TV-1** (Channel: 8)
Owned by: **CFJC-TV**
Alexis Creek, BC

Alexis Creek: **CIAC-TV** (Channel: 11)
Owned by: **CHAN-TV**
Alexis Creek, BC

Alice Arm: **CFTK-TV** (Channel: 7)
Owned by: **CFTK-TV**
Alice Arm, BC

Anahim Lake: **CIAL-TV-1** (Channel: 5)
Owned by: **CHAN-TV**
Anahim Lake, BC

Ashcroft: **CHAC-TV-2** (Channel: 2)
Owned by: **CHAN-TV**
Ashcroft, BC

Ashcroft: **CJAC-TV-2** (Channel: 5)
Owned by: **CFJC-TV**
Ashcroft, BC

Avola: **CFJC-TV** (Channel: 11)
Avola, BC

Avola: **CJVO-TV** (Channel: 13)
Owned by: **CHAN-TV**
Avola, BC

Barkerville: **CKPG-TV** (Channel: 9)
Owned by: **CKPG-TV**
Barkerville, BC

Barriere: **CKTV-TV-1** (Channel: 12)
Owned by: **CFJC-TV**
Barriere, BC

Barriere: **CKTV-TV-2** (Channel: 7)
Owned by: **CHAN-TV**
Barriere, BC

Beaton: **CHBC-TV** (Channel: 8)
Owned by: **CHBC-TV**
Beaton, BC

Bella Bella: **CBUT-TV** (Channel: 13)
Owned by: **CBUT-TV**
Bella Bella, BC

Bella Bella: **CFTK-TV** (Channel: 9)
Owned by: **CFTK-TV**
Bella Bella, BC

Bella Coola: **CFTK-TV** (Channel: 7)
Owned by: **CFTK-TV**
Bella Coola, BC

Blue River: **CFJC-TV** (Channel: 3)
Blue River, BC

Blue River: **CHAN-TV** (Channel: 13)
Owned by: **CHAN-TV**
Blue River, BC

Bonnington: **CBUDT-TV** (Channel: 13)
Owned by: **CBUT-TV**
Bonnington, BC

Boston Bar: **CFJC-TV-1** (Channel: 5)
Owned by: **CFJC-TV**
Boston Bar, BC

Boston Bar: **CHAN-TV** (Channel: 3)
Owned by: **CHAN-TV**
Boston Bar, BC

Bowen Island: **CBUT-TV-4** (Channel: 13)
Owned by: **CBUT-TV**
Bowen Island, BC

Bowen Island: **CHAN-TV-2** (Channel: 3)
Owned by: **CHAN-TV**
Bowen Island, BC

Brackendale: **CBUT-TV-34** (Channel: 35)
Owned by: **CBUT-TV**
Brackendale, BC

Brackendale: **CHAN-TV-5** (Channel: 9)
Owned by: **CHAN-TV**
Brackendale, BC

Bullhead Mountain: **CJDC-TV-2** (Channel: 8)
Owned by: **CJDC-TV**
Bullhead Mountain, BC

Burns Lake: **CKHS-TV** (Channel: 13)
Owned by: **CHAN-TV**
Burns Lake, BC

Cache Creek: **CHAC-TV-1** (Channel: 12)
Owned by: **CHAN-TV**
Cache Creek, BC

Cache Creek: **CJAC-TV-1** (Channel: 10)
Owned by: **CFJC-TV**
Cache Creek, BC

Campbell River: **CBUT-TV-8** (Channel: 3, 82)
Owned by: **CBUT-TV**
Campbell River, BC
Toll-Free: 866-220-6045

Canal Flats: **CBUBT-TV-1** (Channel: 12)
Owned by: **CBUT-TV**
Canal Flats, BC

Canoe: **CHBC-TV-8** (Channel: 6)
Owned by: **CHBC-TV**
Canoe, BC

Castlegar: **CBUAT-TV-2** (Channel: 3)
Owned by: **CBUT-TV**
Castlegar, BC

Castlegar: **CKTN-TV-1** (Channel: 5)
Owned by: **CHAN-TV**
Castlegar, BC

Cawston: **CHBC-TV** (Channel: 3)
Owned by: **CHBC-TV**
Cawston, BC

Celista: **CHBC-TV-6** (Channel: 3)
Owned by: **CHBC-TV**
Celista, BC

Chase: **CFJC-TV-8** (Channel: 11)
Owned by: **CFJC-TV**
Chase, BC

Chase: **CHSH-TV-1** (Channel: 7)
Owned by: **CHAN-TV**
Chase, BC

Chase: **CHSH-TV-2** (Channel: 13)
Owned by: **CHAN-TV**
Chase, BC

Cherryville: **CJCC-TV** (Channel: 13)
Owned by: **CHAN-TV**
Cherryville, BC

Cherryville: **CJWR-TV-1** (Channel: 10)
Owned by: **CHBC-TV**
Cherryville, BC

Chilliwack: **CBUT-TV-2** (Channel: 3)
Owned by: **CBUT-TV**
Chilliwack, BC

Chilliwack: **CHAN-TV-1** (Channel: 11)
Owned by: **CHAN-TV**
Chilliwack, BC

Christina Lake: **CBUAT-TV-7** (Channel: 13)
Owned by: **CBUT-TV**
Christina Lake, BC

Clearwater: **CHCW-TV-1** (Channel: 2)
Owned by: **CFJC-TV**
Clearwater, BC

Clearwater: **CHCW-TV-2** (Channel: 10)
Owned by: **CHAN-TV**
Clearwater, BC

Clinton: **CFJC-TV-4** (Channel: 9)
Owned by: **CFJC-TV**
Clinton, BC

Clinton: **CHTS-TV-1** (Channel: 13)
Owned by: **CHAN-TV**
Clinton, BC

Coal Harbour: **CBUT-TV-20** (Channel: 8)
Owned by: **CBUT-TV**
Coal Harbour, BC

Coal Harbour: **CHAN-TV** (Channel: 10)
Owned by: **CHAN-TV**
Coal Harbour, BC

Columbia Valley: **CFCN-TV** (Channel: 6)
Owned by: **CTVglobemedia Inc.**
Columbia Valley, BC

Courtenay: **CBUT-TV-1** (Channel: 9)
Owned by: **CBUT-TV**
Courtenay, BC

Courtenay: **CHAN-TV-4** (Channel: 13)
Owned by: **CHAN-TV**
Courtenay, BC

Courtenay: **CHEK-TV-5** (Channel: 13)
Owned by: **CHEK-TV**
Courtenay, BC

Cranbrook: **CBUBT-TV-7** (Channel: 65)
Owned by: **CBUT-TV**
Cranbrook, BC

Crawford Bay: **CBUCT-TV-1** (Channel: 5)
Owned by: **CBUT-TV**
Crawford Bay, BC

Crescent Valley: **CBUCT-TV-4** (Channel: 33)
Owned by: **CBUT-TV**
Crescent Valley, BC

Creston: **CBUCT-TV-2** (Channel: 3)
Owned by: **CBUT-TV**
Creston, BC

* For details on this company see listing in Major Broadcasting Companies section; † French language station

Creston: **CKTN-TV-4** (Channel: 12)
Owned by: **CHAN-TV**
Creston, BC

Dawson Creek: **CJDC-TV** (Channel: 5)
Owned by: **Standard Radio Office***
901 - 102 Ave., Dawson Creek, BC V1G 2B6
Tel: 250-782-3341; *Fax:* 250-782-3154
Toll-Free: 800-663-6634
traffic@cjdcam.com
Tracey Gard, General Manager

Donald Station: **CBUBT-TV-4** (Channel: 3)
Owned by: **CBUT-TV**
Donald Station, BC

Downie: **CHBC-TV** (Channel: 9)
Owned by: **CHBC-TV**
Downie, BC

Elks Falls Lookout: **CHAN-TV** (Channel: 49)
Owned by: **CHAN-TV**
Elks Falls Lookout, BC

Endako: **CKPG-TV** (Channel: 6)
Owned by: **CKPG-TV**
Endako, BC

Enderby: **CFEN-TV-1** (Channel: 4)
Owned by: **CHBC-TV**
Enderby, BC

Enderby: **CFEN-TV-2** (Channel: 11)
Owned by: **CHAN-TV**
Enderby, BC

Erie: **CBUAT-TV-4** (Channel: 13)
Owned by: **CBUT-TV**
Erie, BC

Falkland: **CFAW-TV** (Channel: 12)
Owned by: **CHAN-TV**
Falkland, BC

Falkland: **CFWS-TV-1** (Channel: 10)
Owned by: **CHBC-TV**
Falkland, BC

Fernie: **CBUBT-TV-9** (Channel: 8)
Owned by: **CBUT-TV**
Fernie, BC

Field: **CBUBT-TV-13** (Channel: 11)
Owned by: **CBUT-TV**
Field, BC

Fort Nelson: **CBUGT-TV** (Channel: 8)
Owned by: **CBUT-TV**
Fort Nelson, BC

Fort St James: **CFFS-TV** (Channel: 10, 3)
Owned by: **CHAN-TV**
Fort St James, BC

Fountain: **CFDF-TV-1** (Channel: 5)
Owned by: **CHAN-TV**
Fountain, BC

Fraser Lake: **CFFL-TV-1** (Channel: 9)
Owned by: **CHAN-TV**
Fraser Lake, BC

Fraser Lake: **CFFL-TV-2** (Channel: 6)
Owned by: **CKPG-TV**
Fraser Lake, BC

Fruitvale/Montrose: **CBUAT-TV-3** (Channel: 9)
Owned by: **CBUT-TV**
Fruitvale/Montrose, BC

Glacier: **CHBC-TV** (Channel: 13)
Owned by: **CHBC-TV**
Glacier, BC

Glacier Camp: **CHAN-TV** (Channel: 11)
Owned by: **CHAN-TV**
Glacier Camp, BC

Gold Bridge: **CJGB-TV-1** (Channel: 6)
Owned by: **CHAN-TV**
Gold Bridge, BC

Gold River: **CBUT-TV-12** (Channel: 7)
Owned by: **CBUT-TV**
Gold River, BC

Gold River: **CHAN-TV** (Channel: 2)
Owned by: **CHAN-TV**
Gold River, BC

Golden: **CBUBT-TV-2** (Channel: 13)
Owned by: **CBUT-TV**
Golden, BC

Grand Forks: **CBUT-TV-37** (Channel: 5)
Owned by: **CBUT-TV**
Grand Forks, BC

Grand Forks: **CKSR-TV-1** (Channel: 7)
Owned by: **CHAN-TV**
Grand Forks, BC

Granisle: **CFTK-TV** (Channel: 6)
Owned by: **CFTK-TV**
Granisle, BC

Granisle: **CIGR-TV-1** (Channel: 7)
Owned by: **CHAN-TV**
Granisle, BC

Greenwood: **CBUT-TV-31** (Channel: 13)
Owned by: **CBUT-TV**
Greenwood, BC

Grinrod: **CHBC-TV** (Channel: 72)
Owned by: **CHBC-TV**
Grinrod, BC

Hagensborg: **CBUIT-TV-4** (Channel: 11)
Owned by: **CBUT-TV**
Hagensborg, BC

Hagensborg: **CFTK-TV** (Channel: 9)
Owned by: **CFTK-TV**
Hagensborg, BC

Harrison Hot Springs: **CBUT-TV-23** (Channel: 13)
Owned by: **CBUT-TV**
Harrison Hot Springs, BC

Hazelton: **CFTK-TV** (Channel: 9)
Owned by: **CFTK-TV**
Hazelton, BC

Hendrix Lake: **CIHL-TV** (Channel: 12)
Owned by: **CHAN-TV**
Hendrix Lake, BC

Hixon: **CKPG-TV-1** (Channel: 10)
Owned by: **CKPG-TV**
Hixon, BC

Holberg: **CBUT-TV-21** (Channel: 2)
Owned by: **CBUT-TV**
Holberg, BC

Holberg: **CHAN-TV** (Channel: 4, 8)
Owned by: **CHAN-TV**
Holberg, BC

Hope: **CBUT-TV-6** (Channel: 9)
Owned by: **CBUT-TV**
Hope, BC

Houston: **CFHO-TV** (Channel: 8)
Owned by: **CHAN-TV**
Houston, BC

Hudson's Hope: **CJDC** (Channel: 11)
Owned by: **CJDC-TV**
Hudson's Hope, BC

Invermere: **CBUBT-TV-3** (Channel: 2)
Owned by: **CBUT-TV**
Invermere, BC

Jubilee Mountain: **CFCN-TV** (Channel: 8)
Owned by: **CTVglobemedia Inc.**
Jubilee Mountain, BC

Juskatla: **CFTK-TV** (Channel: 2)
Owned by: **CFTK-TV**
Juskatla, BC

Kamloops: **CFJC-TV** (Channel: 4)
Owned by: **The Jim Pattison Broadcast Group***
460 Pemberton Terrace, Kamloops, BC V2C 1T5
Tel: 250-372-3322; *Fax:* 250-374-0445
info@cfjctv.com
www.cfjctv.com
Rick Arnish, President & General Manager

Kamloops: **CHKM-TV** (Channel: 6)
Owned by: **CHAN-TV**
Kamloops, BC

Kelowna: **CHBC-TV** (Channel: 2)
Owned by: **Canwest Global Communications Corp.***
342 Leon Ave., Kelowna, BC V1Y 6J2
Tel: 250-762-4535; *Fax:* 250-868-0662
Toll-Free: 888-762-4535
comments@chbc.com
www.chbc.com

Kelowna: **CHKL-TV** (Channel: 5)
Owned by: **CHAN-TV**
Kelowna, BC

Keremeos: **CHBC-TV** (Channel: 4)
Owned by: **CHBC-TV**
Keremeos, BC

Kildala: **CFTK-TV** (Channel: 5)
Owned by: **CFTK-TV**
Kildala, BC

King Island: **CBUT-TV** (Channel: 9)
Owned by: **CBUT-TV**
King Island, BC

Kitwanga: **CFTK-TV** (Channel: 13)
Owned by: **CFTK-TV**
Kitwanga, BC

Kokish: **CHAN-TV** (Channel: 9)
Owned by: **CHAN-TV**
Kokish, BC

Kootenay Lake: **CHAN-TV** (Channel: 10)
Owned by: **CHAN-TV**
Kootenay Lake, BC

Lillooet: **CFDF-TV-2** (Channel: 13)
Owned by: **CHAN-TV**
Lillooet, BC

Lillooet: **CFMZ-TV-1** (Channel: 2)
Owned by: **CFJC-TV**
Lillooet, BC

Little Fort: **CKTV-TV-1** (Channel: 12)
Owned by: **CFJC-TV**
Little Fort, BC

Logan Lake: **CFJC-TV** (Channel: 11)
Owned by: **CFJC-TV**
Logan Lake, BC

Logan Lake: **CHLK-TV-2** (Channel: 13)
Owned by: **CHAN-TV**
Logan Lake, BC

Loos: **CBUHT-TV-2** (Channel: 6)
Owned by: **CBUT-TV**
Loos, BC

Lumby: **CHBC-TV** (Channel: 4)
Owned by: **CHBC-TV**
Lumby, BC

Lumby: **CHID-TV-2** (Channel: 9)
Owned by: **CHAN-TV**
Lumby, BC

Lytton: **CHWS-TV-1** (Channel: 11)
Owned by: **CFJC-TV**
Lytton, BC

Lytton: **CILY-TV-2** (Channel: 8)
Owned by: **CHAN-TV**
Lytton, BC

Mabel Lake: **CHPL-TV-1** (Channel: 13)
Owned by: **CHAN-TV**
Mabel Lake, BC

** For details on this company see listing in Major Broadcasting Companies section; † French language station*

Mabel Lake: **CHPP-TV-1** (Channel: 8)
Owned by: **CHBC-TV**
Mabel Lake, BC

Mackenzie: **CIMK-TV-1** (Channel: 9)
Owned by: **CHAN-TV**
Mackenzie, BC

Mackenzie: **CKPG-TV-4** (Channel: 6)
Owned by: **CKPG-TV**
Mackenzie, BC

Malakwa: **CFFI-TV-1** (Channel: 4)
Owned by: **CHBC-TV**
Malakwa, BC

Malakwa: **CFFI-TV-2** (Channel: 11)
Owned by: **CHAN-TV**
Malakwa, BC

Masset: **CHMH-TV-1** (Channel: 8)
Owned by: **CFTK-TV**
Masset, BC

McBride: **CBUHT-TV-3** (Channel: 2)
Owned by: **CBUT-TV**
McBride, BC

McBride: **CHAN-TV** (Channel: 12)
Owned by: **CHAN-TV**
McBride, BC

Merritt: **CFJC-TV-3** (Channel: 8)
Owned by: **CFJC-TV**
Merritt, BC

Mica Creek: **CHAN-TV** (Channel: 7, 4)
Owned by: **CHAN-TV**
Mica Creek, BC

Mica Creek: **CHBC-TV** (Channel: 5)
Owned by: **CHBC-TV**
Mica Creek, BC

Midway: **CBUT-TV-32** (Channel: 7)
Owned by: **CBUT-TV**
Midway, BC

Midway: **CHAN-TV** (Channel: 3)
Owned by: **CHAN-TV**
Midway, BC

Minto: **CFMT-TV-3** (Channel: 3)
Owned by: **CFJC-TV**
Minto, BC

Monte Lake: **CFJC-TV** (Channel: 8)
Monte Lake, BC

Mount Hamilton: **CFHM-TV-1** (Channel: 7)
Owned by: **CFJC-TV**
Mount Hamilton, BC

Mount Hamilton: **CHAN-TV** (Channel: 9)
Owned by: **CHAN-TV**
Mount Hamilton, BC

Mount McDonald: **CBUT-TV-27** (Channel: 59)
Owned by: **CBUT-TV**
Mount McDonald, BC

Mount Wells: **CFTK-TV** (Channel: 12)
Owned by: **CFTK-TV**
Mount Wells, BC

Moyie: **CBUBT-TV-14** (Channel: 6)
Owned by: **CBUT-TV**
Moyie, BC

Nakusp: **CJNP-TV-1** (Channel: 2)
Owned by: **CHBC-TV**
Nakusp, BC

Nakusp: **CJNP-TV-3** (Channel: 7)
Owned by: **CHAN-TV**
Nakusp, BC

Nass Valley: **CFTK-TV** (Channel: 7)
Owned by: **CFTK-TV**
Nass Valley, BC

Natal: **CBUBT-TV-10** (Channel: 11)
Owned by: **CBUT-TV**
Natal, BC

Nelson: **CBUCT-TV** (Channel: 9)
Owned by: **CBUT-TV**
Nelson, BC

Nelson: **CKTN-TV-3** (Channel: 3)
Owned by: **CHAN-TV**
Nelson, BC

New Denver: **CBUCT-TV-6** (Channel: 17)
Owned by: **CBUT-TV**
New Denver, BC

New Denver: **CHJV-TV** (Channel: 13)
Owned by: **CHAN-TV**
New Denver, BC

Newcastle Ridge: **CFKB-TV-1** (Channel: 7)
Owned by: **CHEK-TV**
Newcastle Ridge, BC

Newcastle Ridge: **CHAN-TV** (Channel: 7)
Owned by: **CHAN-TV**
Newcastle Ridge, BC

Nicola Valley: **CFJC-TV-12** (Channel: 10)
Owned by: **CFJC-TV**
Nicola Valley, BC

Nimpkish: **CBUT-TV** (Channel: 9)
Owned by: **CBUT-TV**
Nimpkish, BC

Nimpkish: **CHAN-TV** (Channel: 6)
Owned by: **CHAN-TV**
Nimpkish, BC

Noranda Mines: **CFJC-TV** (Channel: 7)
Owned by: **CFJC-TV**
Noranda Mines, BC

North Forks: **CHAN-TV** (Channel: 7)
Owned by: **CHAN-TV**
North Forks, BC

Ocean Falls: **CBUT-TV** (Channel: 11)
Owned by: **CBUT-TV**
Ocean Falls, BC

Ocean Falls: **CFTK-TV** (Channel: 2)
Owned by: **CFTK-TV**
Ocean Falls, BC

Olalla: **CHBC-TV** (Channel: 11)
Owned by: **CHBC-TV**
Olalla, BC

Olalla: **CHKC-TV-5** (Channel: 11)
Owned by: **CHAN-TV**
Olalla, BC

Oliver: **CHAN-TV** (Channel: 3)
Owned by: **CHAN-TV**
Oliver, BC

Oliver: **CHBC-TV-3** (Channel: 8)
Owned by: **CHBC-TV**
Oliver, BC

Ottertail: **CBUT-TV** (Channel: 53)
Owned by: **CBUT-TV**
Ottertail, BC

Palliser: **CBUT-TV** (Channel: 40)
Owned by: **CBUT-TV**
Palliser, BC

Peachland: **CHPT-TV-1** (Channel: 4)
Owned by: **CHBC-TV**
Peachland, BC

Peachland: **CIPL-TV** (Channel: 9)
Owned by: **CHAN-TV**
Peachland, BC

Pemberton: **CBUPT-TV** (Channel: 4)
Owned by: **CBUT-TV**
Pemberton, BC

Penticton: **CHBC-TV-1** (Channel: 13)
Owned by: **CHBC-TV**
Penticton, BC

Penticton: **CHKL-TV-1** (Channel: 10)
Owned by: **CHAN-TV**
Penticton, BC

Phoenix: **CBUT-TV-30** (Channel: 15)
Owned by: **CBUT-TV**
Phoenix, BC

Pine Valley: **CFJC-TV** (Channel: 2)
Pine Valley, BC

Port Alberni: **CBUT-TV-3** (Channel: 4)
Owned by: **CBUT-TV**
Port Alberni, BC

Port Alberni: **CHEK-TV-3** (Channel: 11)
Owned by: **CHEK-TV**
Port Alberni, BC

Port Alice: **CBUT-TV-17** (Channel: 10)
Owned by: **CBUT-TV**
Port Alice, BC

Port Alice: **CHAN-TV** (Channel: 2, 7)
Owned by: **CHAN-TV**
Port Alice, BC

Port Hardy: **CBUT-TV-19** (Channel: 6)
Owned by: **CBUT-TV**
Port Hardy, BC

Port Hardy: **CHAN-TV** (Channel: 3)
Owned by: **CHAN-TV**
Port Hardy, BC

Port McNeill: **CBUT-TV-18** (Channel: 2)
Owned by: **CBUT-TV**
Port McNeill, BC

Port Renfrew: **CJTV-TV-1** (Channel: 11)
Owned by: **CHAN-TV**
Port Renfrew, BC

Prince George: **CIFG-TV** (Channel: 12)
Owned by: **CHAN-TV**
Prince George, BC

Prince George: **CKPG-TV** (Channel: 2)
Owned by: **The Jim Pattison Broadcast Group***
1220 - 6th Ave., Prince George, BC V2L 3M8
Tel: 250-564-8861; *Fax:* 250-562-7681
ckpgmail@ckpg.bc.ca
www.993thedrive.com

Ken Kilcullen, kkilcullen@ckpg.bc.ca

Prince Rupert: **CFTK-TV** (Channel: 3)
Owned by: **Standard Broadcasting Corp. Ltd.***
#212, 215 Cow Bay Rd., Prince Rupert, BC V8J 1A2
Tel: 250-624-9111; *Fax:* 250-624-3100
smenhinick@srt.ca

Brian Langston, General Manager

Prince Rupert: **CFTK-TV-1** (Channel: 6)
Owned by: **CFTK-TV**
Prince Rupert, BC

Princeton: **CHBC-TV** (Channel: 5)
Owned by: **CHBC-TV**
Princeton, BC

Princeton: **CHNJ-TV-1** (Channel: 11)
Owned by: **CHAN-TV**
Princeton, BC

Pritchard: **CFJC-TV-19** (Channel: 5)
Owned by: **CFJC-TV**
Pritchard, BC

Pritchard: **CHKM-TV-1** (Channel: 9)
Owned by: **CHAN-TV**
Pritchard, BC

Puntzi: **CHAN-TV** (Channel: 2)
Owned by: **CHAN-TV**
Puntzi, BC

Purden: **CBUHT-TV-1** (Channel: 10)
Owned by: **CBUT-TV**
Purden, BC

Queen Charlotte: **CFTK-TV** (Channel: 4)
Owned by: **CFTK-TV**
Queen Charlotte, BC

** For details on this company see listing in Major Broadcasting Companies section; † French language station*

Quesnel: **CFJC-TV-11** (Channel: 7)
Owned by: **CFJC-TV**
Quesnel, BC

Quesnel: **CITM-TV-2** (Channel: 8)
Owned by: **CHAN-TV**
Quesnel, BC

Quesnel: **CKPG-TV-5** (Channel: 13)
Owned by: **CKPG-TV**
Quesnel, BC

Radium Hot Springs: **CBUBT-TV-5** (Channel: 77)
Owned by: **CBUT-TV**
Radium Hot Springs, BC

Revelstoke: **CHRP-TV-1** (Channel: 7)
Owned by: **CHBC-TV**
Revelstoke, BC

Revelstoke: **CHRP-TV-2** (Channel: 2)
Owned by: **CHAN-TV**
Revelstoke, BC

Rim Rock: **CFJC-TV** (Channel: 9)
Rim Rock, BC

Rimrock: **CKRR-TV-1** (Channel: 9)
Owned by: **CFJC-TV**
Rimrock, BC

Rimrock: **CKRR-TV-2** (Channel: 11)
Owned by: **CHAN-TV**
Rimrock, BC

River Jordan: **CBUT-TV** (Channel: 9)
Owned by: **CBUT-TV**
River Jordan, BC

River Jordan: **CHEK-TV** (Channel: 11)
Owned by: **CHEK-TV**
River Jordan, BC

Rock Creek: **CBUT-TV-33** (Channel: 33)
Owned by: **CBUT-TV**
Rock Creek, BC

Rock Creek: **CHAN-TV** (Channel: 3)
Owned by: **CHAN-TV**
Rock Creek, BC

Ruby Creek: **CBUT-TV-26** (Channel: 25)
Owned by: **CBUT-TV**
Ruby Creek, BC

Salmo: **CBUAT-TV-5** (Channel: 10)
Owned by: **CBUT-TV**
Salmo, BC

Salmon Arm: **CFSA-TV-1** (Channel: 13)
Owned by: **CHAN-TV**
Salmon Arm, BC

Salmon Arm: **CHBC-TV-4** (Channel: 9)
Owned by: **CHBC-TV**
Salmon Arm, BC

Santa Rosa: **CKSR-TV** (Channel: 83)
Owned by: **CHAN-TV**
Santa Rosa, BC

Savona: **CFSC-TV-1** (Channel: 8)
Owned by: **CFJC-TV**
Savona, BC

Savona: **CFSC-TV-2** (Channel: 13)
Owned by: **CHAN-TV**
Savona, BC

Sawmill: **CBUT-TV** (Channel: 7)
Owned by: **CBUT-TV**
Sawmill, BC

Sayward: **CBUT-TV-10** (Channel: 4)
Owned by: **CBUT-TV**
Sayward, BC

Shalalth: **CJBT-TV-1** (Channel: 5)
Owned by: **CFJC-TV**
Shalalth, BC

Shalalth: **CJBT-TV-2** (Channel: 11)
Owned by: **CHAN-TV**
Shalalth, BC

Shoulder Mtn.: **CFTK-TV** (Channel: 9)
Owned by: **CFTK-TV**
Shoulder Mtn., BC

Skaha Lake: **CHBC-TV-7** (Channel: 7)
Owned by: **CHBC-TV**
Skaha Lake, BC

Slocan: **CBUCT-TV-5** (Channel: 39)
Owned by: **CBUT-TV**
Slocan, BC

Smithers: **CFHO-TV-1** (Channel: 13)
Owned by: **CHAN-TV**
Smithers, BC

Smithers: **CFTK-TV** (Channel: 5)
Owned by: **CFTK-TV**
Smithers, BC
www.cftktv.com

Soda Creek: **CKSC-TV-1** (Channel: 4)
Owned by: **CFJC-TV**
Soda Creek, BC

Soda Creek: **CKSC-TV-2** (Channel: 2)
Owned by: **CHAN-TV**
Soda Creek, BC

Sointula: **CHAN-TV** (Channel: 5)
Owned by: **CHAN-TV**
Sointula, BC

Sooke: **CBUT-TV-28** (Channel: 3)
Owned by: **CBUT-TV**
Sooke, BC

Sooke: **CHEK-TV** (Channel: 13)
Owned by: **CHEK-TV**
Sooke, BC

Spences Bridge: **CJNA-TV-1** (Channel: 3)
Owned by: **CFJC-TV**
Spences Bridge, BC

Spences Bridge: **CJNA-TV-2** (Channel: 7)
Owned by: **CHAN-TV**
Spences Bridge, BC

Spillimacheen: **CBUBT-TV-6** (Channel: 69)
Owned by: **CBUT-TV**
Spillimacheen, BC

Squamish: **CBUT-TV-5** (Channel: 11)
Owned by: **CBUT-TV**
Squamish, BC

Squamish: **CHAN-TV-3** (Channel: 7)
Owned by: **CHAN-TV**
Squamish, BC

Stewart: **CFTK-TV** (Channel: 11)
Owned by: **CFTK-TV**
Stewart, BC

Surrey: **CHNU-TV** (Channel: 10)
Owned by: **Rogers Broadcasting Ltd.***
PO Box 100, 5668 192 St. Ste. 204, Surrey, BC V3S 2V7
Tel: 604-576-6880; *Fax:* 604-576-6895
info@nowtv.ca
www.nowtv.ca

Terry Mahoney, Station Manager

Tabor Mountain: **CBUHT-TV** (Channel: 78)
Owned by: **CBUT-TV**
Tabor Mountain, BC

Taghum: **CKTN-TV-2** (Channel: 23)
Owned by: **CHAN-TV**
Taghum, BC

Tahsis: **CBUT-TV-14** (Channel: 9)
Owned by: **CBUT-TV**
Tahsis, BC

Tasu: **CFTK-TV** (Channel: 11)
Owned by: **CKPG-TV**
Tasu, BC

Tatla Lake: **CIAL-TV-2** (Channel: 9)
Owned by: **CHAN-TV**
Tatla Lake, BC

Telkwa: **CFTK-TV-2** (Channel: 7)
Owned by: **CFTK-TV**
Telkwa, BC

Tête Jaune: **CBUHT-TV-4** (Channel: 10)
Owned by: **CBUT-TV**
Tête Jaune, BC

Tofino: **CBUT-TV-22** (Channel: 10)
Owned by: **CBUT-TV**
Tofino, BC

Topley Landing: **CHAN-TV** (Channel: 8)
Owned by: **CHAN-TV**
Topley Landing, BC

Trail: **CBUAT-TV-6** (Channel: 11)
Owned by: **CBUT-TV**
Trail, BC

Trail: **CKTN-TV** (Channel: 8)
Owned by: **CHAN-TV**
Trail, BC

Ucluelet: **CBUT-FM-7** (Channel: 7)
Owned by: **CBUT-TV**
Ucluelet, BC

Ucluelet: **CKUP-TV-1** (Channel: 6)
Owned by: **CHAN-TV**
Ucluelet, BC

Valemount: **CBUHT-TV-5** (Channel: 6)
Owned by: **CBUT-TV**
Valemount, BC

Valemount: **CFJC-TV** (Channel: 8)
Valemount, BC

Valemount: **CHAN-TV** (Channel: 4)
Owned by: **CHAN-TV**
Valemount, BC

†*Vancouver:* **CBUFT-TV** (Channel: 26)
Owned by: **Canadian Broadcasting Corporation***
CP 4600, 700 Hamilton St., Vancouver, BC V6B 4A2
Tél: 604-662-6000; *Téléc:* 604-662-6161

Michèle Smolkin

Vancouver: **CBUT-TV** (Channel: 2)
Owned by: **Canadian Broadcasting Corporation***
PO Box 4600, 700 Hamilton St., Vancouver, BC V6B 4A2
Tel: 604-662-6000; *Fax:* 604-662-6414
canadanow@vancouver.cbc.ca
www.vancouver.cbc.ca

Vancouver: **CHAN-TV** (Channel: 8)
Owned by: **Canwest Global Communications Corp.***
7850 Enterprise St., Vancouver, BC V6B 4A3
Tel: 604-444-9500; *Fax:* 604-444-9555
globalbc.news@globaltv.ca
www.canada.com/vancouver

Roy Gardner

Vancouver: **CIVT-TV** (Channel: 32)
Owned by: **CTVglobemedia Inc.***
#300, 750 Burrard St., Vancouver, BC V6Z 1X5
Tel: 604-608-2868; *Fax:* 604-609-5799
bccomments@ctv.ca
www.ctv9.ca

Jim Rusnak, Vice-President & General Manager

Vancouver: **CKVU-TV** (Channel: 10)
180 West 2nd St., Vancouver, BC V5Y 3T9
Tel: 604-876-1344; *Fax:* 604-874-8225
Toll-Free: 888-336-9978
contactjuliac@citytv.com
vancouver.citytv.com

Brad Phillips

Vancouver: **KVOS-TV** (Channel: 12)
#320, 1385 West 8 Ave., Vancouver, BC V6H 3V9
Tel: 604-681-1212; *Fax:* 604-736-4510
www.kvos.com

David Reid, President

Vanderhoof: **CKIN-TV-1** (Channel: 8)
Owned by: **CHAN-TV**
Vanderhoof, BC

Vavenby: **CKVA-TV-1** (Channel: 8)
Owned by: **CHAN-TV**
Vavenby, BC

** For details on this company see listing in Major Broadcasting Companies section; † French language station*

Vernon: **CHBC-TV-2** (Channel: 7)
Owned by: **CHBC-TV**
Vernon, BC

Vernon: **CHKL-TV-2** (Channel: 12)
Owned by: **CHAN-TV**
Vernon, BC

Victoria: **CHEK-TV** (Channel: 6)
Owned by: **Canwest Global Communications Corp.***
780 Kings Rd., Victoria, BC V8T 5A2
Tel: 250-383-2435; *Fax:* 250-384-7766
ch@chtv.ca
www.canada.com/chtv/vancouverisland
Ron Eberle, General Manager

Victoria: **CIVI-TV** (Channel: 17, 53)
1420 Broad St., Victoria, BC V8W 2B1
Tel: 250-381-2484; *Fax:* 250-381-2485
Toll-Free: 866-242-2484
islandcontactus@achannel.ca
www.achannel.ca/victoria
Richard Gray, Station Manager

Wells: **CKPG-TV** (Channel: 9)
Owned by: **CKPG-TV**
Wells, BC

Wells/Barkerville: **CKWB-TV** (Channel: 11)
Owned by: **CHAN-TV**
Wells/Barkerville, BC

Westwold: **CHBC-TV** (Channel: 12)
Owned by: **CHBC-TV**
Westwold, BC

Whistler: **CBUWT-TV** (Channel: 13)
Owned by: **CBUT-TV**
Whistler, BC

Williams Lake: **CFJC-TV-5** (Channel: 8)
Owned by: **CFJC-TV**
Williams Lake, BC

Williams Lake: **CITM-TV-1** (Channel: 13)
Owned by: **CHAN-TV**
Williams Lake, BC

Winlaw: **CBUCT-TV-3** (Channel: 12)
Owned by: **CBUT-TV**
Winlaw, BC

Wokas Lake: **CBUT-TV** (Channel: 60)
Owned by: **CBUT-TV**
Wokas Lake, BC

Wokas Lake: **CHAN-TV** (Channel: 11)
Owned by: **CHAN-TV**
Wokas Lake, BC

Woos Camp: **CBUT-TV** (Channel: 12)
Owned by: **CBUT-TV**
Woos Camp, BC

Manitoba

Baldy Mountain: **CBWT-TV** (Channel: 8)
Owned by: **CBWT-TV**
Baldy Mountain, MB

Brandon: **CKX-TV** (Channel: 5)
2940 Victoria Ave., Brandon, MB R7B 3Y3
Tel: 204-728-1150; *Fax:* 204-727-2505
feedbackbrandon@chumtv.com
www.ckxtv.com
Alan Cruise

Brandon: **CKYB-TV** (Channel: 4)
Owned by: **CTVglobemedia Inc.**
Brandon, MB

Cross Lake: **CBWNT-TV** (Channel: 12)
Owned by: **CBWT-TV**
Cross Lake, MB

Dauphin: **CKYD-TV** (Channel: 12)
Owned by: **CTVglobemedia Inc.**
Dauphin, MB

Easterville: **CBWHT-TV-2** (Channel: 11)
Owned by: **CBWT-TV**
Easterville, MB

Fairford: **CBWGT-TV-2** (Channel: 7)
Owned by: **CBWT-TV**
Fairford, MB

Fisher Branch: **CBWGT-TV** (Channel: 10)
Owned by: **CBWT-TV**
Fisher Branch, MB

Fisher Branch: **CKYA-TV** (Channel: 8)
Owned by: **CTVglobemedia Inc.**
Fisher Branch, MB

Flin Flon: **CBWBT-TV** (Channel: 10)
Owned by: **CBWT-TV**
Flin Flon, MB

Flin Flon: **CKYF-TV** (Channel: 13)
Owned by: **CTVglobemedia Inc.**
Flin Flon, MB

Gillam: **CBWLT-TV** (Channel: 8)
Owned by: **CBWT-TV**
Gillam, MB

Gods Lake Narrows: **CBWXT-TV** (Channel: 13)
Owned by: **CBWT-TV**
Gods Lake Narrows, MB

Grand Rapids: **CBWHT-TV** (Channel: 8)
Owned by: **CBWT-TV**
Grand Rapids, MB

Jackhead: **CBWGT-TV-1** (Channel: 5)
Owned by: **CBWT-TV**
Jackhead, MB

Lac du Bonnet: **CBWT-TV-2** (Channel: 4)
Owned by: **CBWT-TV**
Lac du Bonnet, MB

Leaf Rapids: **CBWQT-TV** (Channel: 13)
Owned by: **CBWT-TV**
Leaf Rapids, MB

Lynn Lake: **CBWRT-TV** (Channel: 6)
Owned by: **CBWT-TV**
Lynn Lake, MB

Mafeking: **CBWYT-TV** (Channel: 2)
Owned by: **CBWT-TV**
Mafeking, MB

Manigotagan: **CBWGT-TV-3** (Channel: 22)
Owned by: **CBWT-TV**
Manigotagan, MB

McCreary: **CKX-TV-3** (Channel: 11)
Owned by: **CKX-TV**
McCreary, MB

McCusker Lake: **CBWUT-TV** (Channel: 10)
Owned by: **CBWT-TV**
McCusker Lake, MB

Melita: **CKX-TV-2** (Channel: 5)
Owned by: **CKX-TV**
Melita, MB

Moose Lake: **CBWIT-TV-1** (Channel: 10)
Owned by: **CBWT-TV**
Moose Lake, MB

Nelson House: **CBWPT-TV** (Channel: 11)
Owned by: **CBWT-TV**
Nelson House, MB

Norway House: **CBWOT-TV** (Channel: 9)
Owned by: **CBWT-TV**
Norway House, MB

Oxford House: **CBWVT-TV** (Channel: 8)
Owned by: **CBWT-TV**
Oxford House, MB

Portage la Prairie: **CHMI-TV** (Channel: 13)
PO Box 13000, 350 River Rd., Portage la Prairie, MB R1N 3V3
Tel: 204-239-1113; *Fax:* 204-956-0252
www.a-channel.com
Drew Craig

Pukatawagan: **CBWBT-TV-1** (Channel: 11)
Owned by: **CBWT-TV**
Pukatawagan, MB

Snow Lake: **CBWKT-TV** (Channel: 8)
Owned by: **CBWT-TV**
Snow Lake, MB

Snow Lake: **CKYS-TV** (Channel: 11)
Owned by: **CTVglobemedia Inc.**
Snow Lake, MB

The Pas: **CBWT-TV** (Channel: 7)
Owned by: **CBWT-TV**
The Pas, MB

The Pas: **CKYP-TV** (Channel: 12)
Owned by: **CTVglobemedia Inc.**
The Pas, MB

Thompson: **CBWT-TV** (Channel: 8)
Owned by: **CBWT-TV**
Thompson, MB

Thompson: **CKYT-TV** (Channel: 9)
Owned by: **CTVglobemedia Inc.**
Thompson, MB

Waasagomach: **CBWT-TV** (Channel: 9)
Owned by: **CBWT-TV**
Waasagomach, MB

Wabowden: **CBWMT-TV** (Channel: 10)
Owned by: **CBWT-TV**
Wabowden, MB

Westman: **CKND-TV** (Channel: 2)
Owned by: **CKND-TV**
Westman, MB

†Winnipeg: **CBWFT-TV** (Channel: 3)
Owned by: **Canadian Broadcasting Corporation***
CP 160 Main, 541 Portage Ave., Winnipeg, MB R3C 2H1
Tél: 204-788-3141; *Téléc:* 204-788-3639

Winnipeg: **CBWT-TV** (Channel: 6)
Owned by: **Canadian Broadcasting Corporation***
PO Box 160, 541 Portage Ave., Winnipeg, MB R3C 2H1
Tel: 204-788-3222; *Fax:* 204-788-3167
John Bertrand, Regional Director
Dave White, TV Operation Manager

Winnipeg: **CHMI-TV** (Channel: 13)
8 Fork Markets Rd., Winnipeg, MB R3C 4Y3
Tel: 204-947-9613; *Fax:* 204-956-0811
a-channel.com

Winnipeg: **CKND-TV** (Channel: 2)
Owned by: **Canwest Global Communications Corp.***
603 St. Mary's Rd., Winnipeg, MB R2M 3L8
Tel: 204-233-3304; *Fax:* 204-233-5615
newsroom@globaltv.ca
http://globalwinnipeg.com
Tim Schellenberg

Winnipeg: **CKY-TV** (Channel: 5)
Owned by: **CTVglobemedia Inc.***
400-345 Graham Ave., Winnipeg, MB R3C 5S6
Tel: 204-788-3300; *Fax:* 204-788-3399
winnipegnews@ctv.ca
www.cky.com
Hanson Bill, Vice-President & General Manager,
whanson@ctv.ca
Tara Vosbourgh, Human Resources Manager,
tvosbourgh@ctv.ca

New Brunswick

Bathurst: **CKAM-TV** (Channel: 12)
Owned by: **CKCW-TV**
Bathurst, NB

Blackville: **CKAM-TV-3** (Channel: 9)
Owned by: **CKCW-TV**
Blackville, NB

Boiestown: **CKLT-TV-2** (Channel: 7)
Owned by: **CTVglobemedia Inc.**
Boiestown, NB

Campbellton: **CKCD-TV** (Channel: 7)
Owned by: **CKCW-TV**
Campbellton, NB

Chatham: **CKAM-TV-2** (Channel: 10)
Owned by: **CKCW-TV**
Chatham, NB

** For details on this company see listing in Major Broadcasting Companies section; † French language station*

Doaktown: **CKAM-TV-4** (Channel: 10)
Owned by: **CKCW-TV**
Doaktown, NB

†*Edmundston:* **CIMT-TV** (Channel: 4)
Owned by: **CIMT-TV**
7 Ch. Canada, Edmundston, NB E3V 1T9
Tél: 506-737-9810

Fredericton: **CBAT-TV** (Channel: 4 antenna; 3 cable)
Owned by: **Canadian Broadcasting Corporation (CBC)***
PO Box 2200, 1160 Regent St., Fredericton, NB E3B 5G4
Tel: 506-451-4000; *Toll-Free:* 866-306-4636
www.cbc.ca/nb; www.cbc.ca/television
Other information: Phone, CBC News: 506-451-4044; Fax: 506-451-4170
Andrew Cochran, Managing Director, Maritimes
Janet Irwin, Senior Regional Manager, News & Current Affairs
Nadine Antle, Regional Manager, Partnerships, Communications, Brand, & Promot, 506-451-4054
John Channing, Manager, New Brunswick Sales
Mary-Pat Schutta, Manager, New Brunswick Programs
Lori Wheeler, Senior Officer, Communications, 506-451-4080

Fredericton: **CIHF-TV** (Channel: 11)
Owned by: **CIHF-TV**
Fredericton, NB

†*Kedgwick:* **CBAFT-TV-9** (Channel: 44)
Owned by: **CBAFT-TV**
Kedgwick, NB

†*Kedgwick:* **CHAU-TV** (Channel: 3)
Owned by: **CHAU-TV**
Kedgwick, NB

Miramichi: **CIHF-TV** (Channel: 40)
Owned by: **CIHF-TV**
Miramichi, NB

†*Moncton:* **CBAFT-TV** (Channel: La chaîne 11 à Moncton; programmation régionale.)
Owned by: **Canadian Broadcasting Corporation***
250, av Université, Moncton, NB E1C 5K3
Tél: 506-853-6666; *Téléc:* 506-867-8031
Ligne sans frais: 800-561-7010
www.radio-canada.ca/regions/acadie
Social Media: www.facebook.com/CBCRadioCanada
Louise Imbeault, Director & Station Manager

†*Moncton:* **CBAFT-TV-1 - Fredericton/Saint-Jean** (Channel: La chaîne 5 à Frederiction et à Saint-Jean, N-B; programmation régionale.)
Owned by: **CBAFT-TV/Canadian Broadcasting Corporation**
a/s CBAFT-TV, 250, av Université, Moncton, NB E1C 5K3
Ligne sans frais: 800-561-7010
www.radio-canada.ca/regions/acadie
Social Media: www.facebook.com/CBCRadioCanada

†*Moncton:* **CBAFT-TV-10 - Fredericton** (Channel: La chaîne 19 à Frederiction, N-B; programmation régionale.)
Owned by: **CBAFT-TV/Canadian Broadcasting Corporation**
a/s CBAFT-TV, 250, av Université, Moncton, NB E1C 5K3
Ligne sans frais: 800-561-7010
www.radio-canada.ca/regions/acadie
Social Media: www.facebook.com/CBCRadioCanada

†*Moncton:* **CBAFT-TV-2 - Edmundston** (Channel: La chaîne 13 à Edmunston, N-B; programmation régionale.)
Owned by: **CBAFT-TV/Canadian Broadcasting Corporation**
a/s CBAFT-TV, 250, av Université, Moncton, NB E1C 5K3
Ligne sans frais: 800-561-7010
www.radio-canada.ca/regions/acadie
Social Media: www.facebook.com/CBCRadioCanada

†*Moncton:* **CBAFT-TV-4 - Grand Falls** (Channel: La chaîne 12 à Grand Falls, N-B; programmation régionale.)
Owned by: **CBAFT-TV/Canadian Broadcasting Corporation**
a/s CBAFT-TV, 250, av Université, Moncton, NB E1C 5K3
Ligne sans frais: 800-561-7010
www.radio-canada.ca/regions/acadie
Social Media: www.facebook.com/CBCRadioCanada

†*Moncton:* **CBAFT-TV-5 - Charlottetown** (Channel: La chaîne 31 à Charlottetown, I-P-É; programmation régionale.)
Owned by: **CBAFT-TV/Canadian Broadcasting Corporation**
a/s CBAFT-TV, 250, av Université, Moncton, NB E1C 5K3
Ligne sans frais: 800-561-7010
www.radio-canada.ca/regions/acadie
Social Media: www.facebook.com/CBCRadioCanada

†*Moncton:* **CBHFT-TV - Halifax** (Channel: La chaîne 13 à Halifax; programmation régionale.)
Owned by: **CBAFT-TV/Canadian Broadcasting Corporation**
a/s CBAFT-TV, 250, av Université, Moncton, NB E1C 5K3
Ligne sans frais: 800-561-7010
www.radio-canada.ca/regions/acadie
Social Media: www.facebook.com/CBCRadioCanada

†*Moncton:* **CBHFT-TV-1 - Yarmouth** (Channel: La chaîne 3 à Yarmouth, N-É; programmation régionale.)
Owned by: **CBAFT-TV/Canadian Broadcasting Corporation**
a/s CBAFT-TV, 250, av Université, Moncton, NB E1C 5K3
Ligne sans frais: 800-561-7010
www.radio-canada.ca/regions/acadie
Social Media: www.facebook.com/CBCRadioCanada

†*Moncton:* **CBHFT-TV-2 - Mulgrave** (Channel: La chaîne 7 à Mulgrave, N-É; programmation régionale.)
Owned by: **CBAFT-TV/Canadian Broadcasting Corporation**
a/s CBAFT-TV, 250, av Université, Moncton, NB E1C 5K3
Ligne sans frais: 800-561-7010
www.radio-canada.ca/regions/acadie
Social Media: www.facebook.com/CBCRadioCanada

†*Moncton:* **CBHFT-TV-3 - Sydney** (Channel: La chaîne 13 à Sydney, N-É; programmation régionale.)
Owned by: **CBAFT-TV/Canadian Broadcasting Corporation**
a/s CBAFT-TV, 250, av Université, Moncton, NB E1C 5K3
Ligne sans frais: 800-561-7010
www.radio-canada.ca/regions/acadie
Social Media: www.facebook.com/CBCRadioCanada

†*Moncton:* **CBHFT-TV-4 - Chéticamp** (Channel: La chaîne 10 à Chéticamp, N-É; programmation régionale.)
Owned by: **CBAFT-TV/Canadian Broadcasting Corporation**
a/s CBAFT-TV, 250, av Université, Moncton, NB E1C 5K3
Ligne sans frais: 800-561-7010
www.radio-canada.ca/regions/acadie
Social Media: www.facebook.com/CBCRadioCanada

†*Moncton:* **CBHFT-TV-5 - Middleton** (Channel: La chaîne 46 à Middleton, N-É; programmation régionale.)
Owned by: **CBAFT-TV/Canadian Broadcasting Corporation**
a/s CBAFT-TV, 250, av Université, Moncton, NB E1C 5K3
Ligne sans frais: 800-561-7010
www.radio-canada.ca/regions/acadie
Social Media: www.facebook.com/CBCRadioCanada

†*Moncton:* **CBHFT-TV-6 - Digby** (Channel: La chaîne 58 à Digby, N-É; programmation régionale.)
Owned by: **CBAFT-TV/Canadian Broadcasting Corporation**
a/s CBAFT-TV, 250, av Université, Moncton, NB E1C 5K3
Ligne sans frais: 800-561-7010
www.radio-canada.ca/regions/acadie
Social Media: www.facebook.com/CBCRadioCanada

†*Moncton:* **CBHFT-TV-7 - New Glasgow** (Channel: La chaîne 15 à New Glasgow, N-É; programmation régionale.)
Owned by: **CBAFT-TV/Canadian Broadcasting Corporation**
a/s CBAFT-TV, 250, av Université, Moncton, NB E1C 5K3
Ligne sans frais: 800-561-7010
www.radio-canada.ca/regions/acadie
Social Media: www.facebook.com/CBCRadioCanada

Moncton: **CIHF-TV-3** (Channel: 27)
Owned by: **CIHF-TV**
Moncton, NB

Moncton: **CKCW-TV** (Channel: 2)
Owned by: **CTVglobemedia Inc.***
191 Halifax St., Moncton, NB E1C 9R7
Tel: 506-857-2600; *Fax:* 506-857-2617
www.ctv.ca
Mike Elgie, General Manager

Newcastle: **CKAM-TV-1** (Channel: 10)
Owned by: **CKCW-TV**
Newcastle, NB

Saint John: **CIHF-TV-2** (Channel: 12)
Owned by: **CIHF-TV**
Saint John, NB

Saint John: **CKLT-TV** (Channel: 9)
Owned by: **CTVglobemedia Inc.***
#420, 75 Prince William St., Saint John, NB E2L 2B2
Tel: 506-658-1010; *Fax:* 506-658-1208
cklt@ctv.ca
www.atv.ca

†*Saint-Quentin:* **CBAFT-TV-8** (Channel: 21)
Owned by: **CBAFT-TV**
Saint-Quentin, NB

†*Saint-Quentin:* **CHAU-TV** (Channel: 31)
Owned by: **CHAU-TV**
Saint-Quentin, NB

St Stephen: **CIHF-TV** (Channel: 21)
Owned by: **CIHF-TV**
St Stephen, NB

Tignish: **CKCW-TV-2** (Channel: 5)
Owned by: **CTVglobemedia Inc.**
Tignish, NB

Woodstock: **CIHF-TV** (Channel: 38)
Owned by: **CIHF-TV**
Woodstock, NB

Woodstock: **CKLT-TV-1** (Channel: 3)
Owned by: **CTVglobemedia Inc.**
Woodstock, NB

Newfoundland & Labrador

Baie Verte: **CBNAT-TV-1** (Channel: 3, 12)
Owned by: **CBNT-TV**
Baie Verte, NL

Bay Bulls: **CJON-TV** (Channel: 10)
Owned by: **CJON-TV**
Bay Bulls, NL

Bonavista: **CJWB-TV** (Channel: 10)
Owned by: **CJON-TV**
Bonavista, NL

Brents Cove: **CBNAT-TV-18** (Channel: 10)
Owned by: **CBNT-TV**
Brents Cove, NL

Buchans: **CBNAT-TV-2** (Channel: 13)
Owned by: **CBNT-TV**
Buchans, NL

Cape Broyle: **CJBL-TV-13** (Channel: 13)
Owned by: **CJON-TV**
Cape Broyle, NL

Cartwright: **CBNT-TV-21** (Channel: 9)
Owned by: **CBNT-TV**
Cartwright, NL

Centreville-Wareham-Trinity: **CBNT-TV-16** (Channel: 2)
Owned by: **CBNT-TV**
Centreville-Wareham-Trinity, NL

Clarenville: **CBNT-TV-10** (Channel: 7)
Owned by: **CBNT-TV**
Clarenville, NL

Clarenville: **CJCN-TV-10** (Channel: 10)
Owned by: **CJON-TV**
Clarenville, NL

Coachmans Cove: **CBNAT-TV-16** (Channel: 8)
Owned by: **CBNT-TV**
Coachmans Cove, NL

* *For details on this company see listing in Major Broadcasting Companies section; † French language station*

***Conche:* CBNAT-TV-8** (Channel: 13)
Owned by: **CBNT-TV**
Conche, NL

***Corner Brook:* CBYT-TV** (Channel: 5)
Owned by: **Canadian Broadcasting Corporation***
PO Box 610, 162 Premier Dr., Corner Brook, NL A2H 6G1
Tel: 709-634-3141; *Fax:* 709-634-8506
Toll-Free: 866-220-6045
www.stjohns.cbc.ca

***Corner Brook:* CJWN-TV** (Channel: 10)
Owned by: **CJON-TV**
Corner Brook, NL

***Deer Lake:* CJLW-TV-7** (Channel: 7)
Owned by: **CJON-TV**
Deer Lake, NL

***Elliston:* CBNT-TV-7** (Channel: 4)
Owned by: **CBNT-TV**
Elliston, NL

***Fermeuse:* CBNT-TV-5** (Channel: 11)
Owned by: **CBNT-TV**
Fermeuse, NL

***Fermeuse:* CJFR-TV-12** (Channel: 12)
Owned by: **CJON-TV**
Fermeuse, NL

***Ferryland:* CBNT-TV-38** (Channel: 4)
Owned by: **CBNT-TV**
Ferryland, NL

***Fleur de Lys:* CBNAT-TV-20** (Channel: 5)
Owned by: **CBNT-TV**
Fleur de Lys, NL

***Fogo Island:* CBNAT-TV-6** (Channel: 2)
Owned by: **CBNT-TV**
Fogo Island, NL

***Fortune:* CBNT-TV-33** (Channel: 9)
Owned by: **CBNT-TV**
Fortune, NL

***Fox Harbour PB:* CBNAT-TV-10** (Channel: 7)
Owned by: **CBNT-TV**
Fox Harbour PB, NL

***Freshwater PB:* CJAP-TV** (Channel: 3)
Owned by: **CJON-TV**
Freshwater PB, NL

***Glovertown:* CBNT-TV-13** (Channel: 3)
Owned by: **CBNT-TV**
Glovertown, NL

***Grand Bank:* CJOX-TV** (Channel: 2)
Owned by: **CJON-TV**
Grand Bank, NL

***Grand Falls-Windsor:* CJCN-TV** (Channel: 4)
Owned by: **CJON-TV**
Grand Falls-Windsor, NL

***Hampden:* CBNAT-TV-23** (Channel: 13)
Owned by: **CBNT-TV**
Hampden, NL

***Harbour Breton:* CBNT-TV-22** (Channel: 13)
Owned by: **CBNT-TV**
Harbour Breton, NL

***Harbour Mille:* CBNT-TV-29** (Channel: 13)
Owned by: **CBNT-TV**
Harbour Mille, NL

***Harbour Round:* CBNAT-TV-19** (Channel: 12)
Owned by: **CBNT-TV**
Harbour Round, NL

***Hermitage:* CBNT-TV-24** (Channel: 4)
Owned by: **CBNT-TV**
Hermitage, NL

***Hickman's Harbour:* CBNT-TV-18** (Channel: 4)
Owned by: **CBNT-TV**
Hickman's Harbour, NL

***La Scie:* CBNAT-TV-21** (Channel: 9)
Owned by: **CBNT-TV**
La Scie, NL

***Lamaline:* CBNT-TV-35** (Channel: 18 UHF)
Owned by: **CBNT-TV**
Lamaline, NL

***Lawn:* CBNT-TV-36** (Channel: 6)
Owned by: **CBNT-TV**
Lawn, NL

***Lawn:* CJLN-TV** (Channel: 10)
Owned by: **CJON-TV**
Lawn, NL

***Lord's Cove:* CBNT-TV-34** (Channel: 9)
Owned by: **CBNT-TV**
Lord's Cove, NL

***Lumsden:* CBNT-TV-20** (Channel: 12)
Owned by: **CBNT-TV**
Lumsden, NL

***Marystown:* CBNT-TV-3** (Channel: 5)
Owned by: **CBNT-TV**
Marystown, NL

***Marystown:* CJMA-TV-11** (Channel: 11)
Owned by: **CJON-TV**
Marystown, NL

***Millertown:* CBNAT-TV-5** (Channel: 9)
Owned by: **CBNT-TV**
Millertown, NL

***Mings Bight:* CBNAT-TV-14** (Channel: 10)
Owned by: **CBNT-TV**
Mings Bight, NL

***Musgrave Harbour:* CBNAT-TV-11** (Channel: 9)
Owned by: **CBNT-TV**
Musgrave Harbour, NL

***Musgravetown:* CBNT-TV-17** (Channel: 9)
Owned by: **CBNT-TV**
Musgravetown, NL

***North West Brook:* CBNT-TV-11** (Channel: 4)
Owned by: **CBNT-TV**
North West Brook, NL

***Pacquet:* CBNAT-TV-17** (Channel: 6)
Owned by: **CBNT-TV**
Pacquet, NL

***Petty Harbour:* CBNT-TV-37** (Channel: 13)
Owned by: **CBNT-TV**
Petty Harbour, NL

***Placentia:* CBNT-TV-2** (Channel: 12)
Owned by: **CBNT-TV**
Placentia, NL

***Port Blandford:* CBNT-TV-32** (Channel: 2)
Owned by: **CBNT-TV**
Port Blandford, NL

***Port Hope Simpson:* CBNAT-TV-12** (Channel: 12)
Owned by: **CBNT-TV**
Port Hope Simpson, NL

***Port Rexton:* CBNT-TV-1** (Channel: 13)
Owned by: **CBNT-TV**
Port Rexton, NL

***Ramea:* CBNT-TV-25** (Channel: 13)
Owned by: **CBNT-TV**
Ramea, NL

***Random Island:* CBNT-TV-19** (Channel: 43 UHF)
Owned by: **CBNT-TV**
Random Island, NL

***Red Rock:* CJRF-TV-11** (Channel: 11)
Owned by: **CJON-TV**
Red Rock, NL

***Roddickton:* CBNAT-TV-22** (Channel: 11)
Owned by: **CBNT-TV**
Roddickton, NL

***Seal Cove:* CBNAT-TV-15** (Channel: 7)
Owned by: **CBNT-TV**
Seal Cove, NL

***Springdale:* CBNAT-TV-13** (Channel: 13)
Owned by: **CBNT-TV**
Springdale, NL

***St Alban's:* CBNT-TV-4** (Channel: 9)
Owned by: **CBNT-TV**
St Alban's, NL

***St Albans:* CJST-TV-13** (Channel: 13)
Owned by: **CJON-TV**
St Albans, NL

***St Anthony:* CBNAT-TV-4** (Channel: 6)
Owned by: **CBNT-TV**
St Anthony, NL

***St Bernard's:* CBNT-TV-30** (Channel: 6)
Owned by: **CBNT-TV**
St Bernard's, NL

***St Mary's:* CBNT-TV-6** (Channel: 10)
Owned by: **CBNT-TV**
St Mary's, NL

***St Vincent's:* CBNT-TV-26** (Channel: 7)
Owned by: **CBNT-TV**
St Vincent's, NL

***St. John's:* CBNT-TV** (Channel: 8)
Owned by: **Canadian Broadcasting Corporation***
PO Box 12010 A, 95 University Ave., St. John's, NL A1B 3T8
Tel: 709-576-5000
www.cbc.ca/nl
Social Media: www.facebook.com/cbcnl; twitter.com/cbcnl
Maureen Anonsen, Manager, Partnership & Communicatio, 709-576-5013
Debbie Hynes, Senior Communications Officer, CBC, 709-576-5050

***St. John's:* CJON-TV** (Channel: 6)
Owned by: **Newfoundland Broadcasting Co. Ltd.***
PO Box 2020, 499 Logy Bay Rd., St. John's, NL A1C 5S2
Tel: 709-722-5015; *Fax:* 709-722-0023
ntv@ntv.ca
www.ntv.ca
G. Scott Stirling, President
Douglas W. Neal, General Manager
Keith Soper, Sales Manager

***St. Lawrence:* CBNT-TV-28** (Channel: 12)
Owned by: **CBNT-TV**
St. Lawrence, NL

***Swift Current:* CBNT-TV-31** (Channel: 5)
Owned by: **CBNT-TV**
Swift Current, NL

***Swift Current:* CJSC-TV-10** (Channel: 10)
Owned by: **CJON-TV**
Swift Current, NL

***Tors Cove:* CJON-TV-5** (Channel: 2)
Owned by: **CJON-TV**
Tors Cove, NL

***Trepassey:* CJTP-TV-10** (Channel: 10)
Owned by: **CJON-TV**
Trepassey, NL

***Wesleyville:* CBNT-TV-9** (Channel: 5)
Owned by: **CBNT-TV**
Wesleyville, NL

Northwest Territories

***Yellowknife:* CFYK-TV** (Channel: 8)
Owned by: **Canadian Broadcasting Corporation***
PO Box 160, 5129 49th St., Yellowknife, NT X1A 1P8
Tel: 867-669-3500; *Fax:* 867-920-5489
Toll-Free: 866-306-4636
www.north.cbc.ca

Nova Scotia

***Annapolis Valley:* CJCH-TV-1** (Channel: 10)
Owned by: **CTVglobemedia Inc.**
Annapolis Valley, NS

***Antigonish:* CIHF-TV** (Channel: 21)
Owned by: **CIHF-TV**
Antigonish, NS

** For details on this company see listing in Major Broadcasting Companies section; † French language station*

Antigonish: CJCB-TV-2 (Channel: 9)
Owned by: CTVglobemedia Inc.
Antigonish, NS

Bay St. Lawrence: CBIT-TV-17 (Channel: 13)
Owned by: Canadian Broadcasting Corporation
Bay St. Lawrence, NS

Bay St. Lawrence: CJCB-TV-5 (Channel: 7)
Owned by: CTVglobemedia Inc.
Bay St. Lawrence, NS

Bridgetown: CJCH-TV-4 (Channel: 13)
Owned by: CTVglobemedia Inc.
Bridgetown, NS

Bridgewater: CIHF-TV-6 (Channel: 9)
Owned by: CIHF-TV
Bridgewater, NS

Cheticamp: CBIT-TV-2 (Channel: 2)
Owned by: Canadian Broadcasting Corporation
Cheticamp, NS

Dartmouth: CIHF-TV (Channel: 8)
Owned by: Canwest Global Communications Corp.*
14 Akerley Blvd., Dartmouth, NS B3B 1J3
Tel: 902-481-7400; *Fax:* 902-468-2154
Barry Saunders, General Manager

Digby: CBHT (Channel: 52)
Owned by: CBHT-TV
Digby, NS

Dingwall: CBIT-TV-16 (Channel: 12)
Owned by: Canadian Broadcasting Corporation
Dingwall, NS

Dingwall: CJCB-TV-3 (Channel: 9)
Owned by: CTVglobemedia Inc.
Dingwall, NS

Halifax: CBHT-TV (Channel: 3)
Owned by: Canadian Broadcasting Corporation*
PO Box 3000, 1840 Bell Rd., Halifax, NS B3J 3E9
Tel: 902-420-8311; *Toll-Free:* 866-306-4636
www.cbc.ca/ns
Social Media: twitter.com/cbcns
Andrew Cochran, Managing Director for the Maritimes
Kathy Large, Program Manager, CBC, Nova Scotia
Chantal Bernard, Senior Communications Officer, 902-420-4306

Halifax: CIHF-TV (Channel: 8)
Owned by: CIHF-TV
Halifax, NS

Halifax: CJCH-TV (Channel: 9)
Owned by: CTVglobemedia Inc.*
PO Box 1653, 2885 Robie St., Halifax, NS B3K 5Z4
Tel: 902-453-4000; *Fax:* 902-454-3302
Michael Elgie, General Manager

Ingonish: CBIT-TV-15 (Channel: 2)
Owned by: Canadian Broadcasting Corporation
Ingonish, NS

Inverness: CJCB-TV-1 (Channel: 6)
Owned by: CTVglobemedia Inc.
Inverness, NS

Liverpool: CBHT-TV-1
Owned by: Canadian Broadcasting Corporation
Liverpool, NS

Mabou: CBIT-TV-4 (Channel: 10)
Owned by: Canadian Broadcasting Corporation
Mabou, NS

Margaree: CBIT-TV-5 (Channel: 8)
Owned by: Canadian Broadcasting Corporation
Margaree, NS

Marinette: CJCH-TV-8 (Channel: 23)
Owned by: CTVglobemedia Inc.
Marinette, NS

Middleton: CBHT-TV-6 (Channel: 8)
Owned by: Canadian Broadcasting Corporation
Middleton, NS

Mulgrave: CBHT-TV-11 (Channel: 12)
Owned by: Canadian Broadcasting Corporation
Mulgrave, NS

Mulgrave: CIHF-TV (Channel: 28)
Owned by: CIHF-TV
Mulgrave, NS

New Glasgow: CBHT-TV-5 (Channel: 4)
Owned by: Canadian Broadcasting Corporation
New Glasgow, NS

New Glasgow: CIHF-TV (Channel: 34)
Owned by: CIHF-TV
New Glasgow, NS

New Glasgow: CJCB-TV-4 (Channel: 2)
Owned by: CTVglobemedia Inc.
New Glasgow, NS

North East Margaree: CBIT-TV-6 (Channel: 13)
Owned by: Canadian Broadcasting Corporation
North East Margaree, NS

Pleasant Bay: CBIT-TV-3 (Channel: 8)
Owned by: Canadian Broadcasting Corporation
Pleasant Bay, NS

Sheet Harbour: CBHT-TV-4 (Channel: 11)
Owned by: Canadian Broadcasting Corporation
Sheet Harbour, NS

Sheet Harbour: CJCH-TV-5 (Channel: 2)
Owned by: CTVglobemedia Inc.
Sheet Harbour, NS

Shelburne: CBHT-TV-2 (Channel: 7)
Owned by: Canadian Broadcasting Corporation
Shelburne, NS

Shelburne: CIHF-TV (Channel: 10)
Owned by: CIHF-TV
Shelburne, NS

Sherbrooke: CBHT-TV-16 (Channel: 4)
Owned by: Canadian Broadcasting Corporation
Sherbrooke, NS

Sunnybrae: CBHT-TV-17 (Channel: 6)
Owned by: Canadian Broadcasting Corporation
Sunnybrae, NS

Sydney: CBIT-TV (Channel: 5)
Owned by: Canadian Broadcasting Corporation*
285 Alexandra St., Sydney, NS B1S 2E8
Tel: 902-539-5050; *Fax:* 902-563-4170
www.cbc.ca/ns

Sydney: CIHF-TV (Channel: 11)
Owned by: CIHF-TV
Sydney, NS

Sydney: CJCB-TV (Channel: 4)
Owned by: CTVglobemedia Inc.*
PO Box 469, 1283 George St., Sydney, NS B1P 1N7
Tel: 902-562-5511; *Fax:* 902-562-9714
cjcb@ctv.ca
www.ctv.ca
Glenn McLanders, 902-562-5511

Truro: CBHT-TV-8 (Channel: 55)
Owned by: Canadian Broadcasting Corporation
Truro, NS

Truro: CIHF-TV (Channel: 18)
Owned by: CIHF-TV
Truro, NS

Truro: CJCH-TV-2 (Channel: 12)
Owned by: CTVglobemedia Inc.
Truro, NS

Wolfville: CIHF-TV (Channel: 20)
Owned by: CIHF-TV
Wolfville, NS

Yarmouth: CBHT-TV-3 (Channel: 11)
Owned by: CBHT-TV
Yarmouth, NS

Yarmouth: CIHF-TV (Channel: 45)
Owned by: CIHF-TV
Yarmouth, NS

Yarmouth: CJCH-TV-7 (Channel: 40)
Owned by: CTVglobemedia Inc.
Yarmouth, NS

Ontario

Atikokan: CBWCT-TV-1 (Channel: 7)
Owned by: CBWT-TV
Atikokan, ON

Barrie: CKVR-TV (Channel: Broadcasting on analog channel 3 (VHF) & digital channel 10 (VHF))
33 Beacon Rd., Barrie, ON L4M 4T9
Tel: 705-734-3300; *Fax:* 705-733-0302
Toll-Free: 800-461-5820
inbox@atv.ca
www.atv.ca
Peggy Hebden, Station Manager, peggy.hebden@atv.ca

Belleville: CJOH-TV (Channel: 6)
Owned by: CTVglobemedia Inc.
Belleville, ON

Big Trout Lake: CBWT-TV-1 (Channel: 13)
Owned by: CBWT-TV
Big Trout Lake, ON

†Chapeau: CBOFT-TV (Channel: 11)
Owned by: CBOFT-TV
Chapeau, ON

Chapleau: CITO-TV-4 (Channel: 9)
Owned by: CTVglobemedia Inc.
Chapleau, ON

Chatham: CKCO-TV (Channel: 42)
Owned by: CTVglobemedia Inc.
Chatham, ON

Cornwall: CJOH-TV (Channel: 8)
Owned by: CTVglobemedia Inc.
Cornwall, ON

Deseronto: CJOH-TV (Channel: 6)
Owned by: CTVglobemedia Inc.
Deseronto, ON

Dryden: CBWDT-TV (Channel: 8)
Owned by: CBWT-TV
Dryden, ON

Ear Falls: CBWJT-TV (Channel: 13)
Owned by: CBWT-TV
Ear Falls, ON

Elliot Lake: CICI-TV-1 (Channel: 3)
Owned by: CTVglobemedia Inc.
Elliot Lake, ON

Fort Frances: CBWCT-TV (Channel: 5)
Owned by: CBWT-TV
Fort Frances, ON

Hamilton: CHCH-TV (Channel: 11)
Owned by: Canwest Global Communications Corp.*
PO Box 2230 A, 163 Jackson St. West, Hamilton, ON L8N 3A6
Tel: 905-522-1101; *Fax:* 905-523-8011
www.canada.com/hamilton

Hearst: CITO-TV-3 (Channel: 4)
Owned by: CTVglobemedia Inc.
Hearst, ON

Ignace: CBWDT-TV-2 (Channel: 13)
Owned by: CBWT-TV
Ignace, ON

Kapuskasing: CFCL-TV-3 (Channel: 2)
Kapuskasing, ON

Kapuskasing: CITO-TV-1 (Channel: 10)
Owned by: CTVglobemedia Inc.
Kapuskasing, ON

Kearns: CFCL-TV-2 (Channel: 2)
Kearns, ON

Kearns: CITO-TV-2 (Channel: 11)
Owned by: CTVglobemedia Inc.
Kearns, ON

Keewatin: CJBN-TV (Channel: 13)
102 - 10th St., Keewatin, ON P0X 1C0
Tel: 807-547-2853; *Fax:* 807-547-2348
cjbn@norcomcable.ca
http://www.gokenora.com/cjbn/index.shtml
Warren Ritchie, General Manager, warren.ritchie.sjrb.ca

** For details on this company see listing in Major Broadcasting Companies section; † French language station*

Darryl Michaluk, Station Manager, darryl.michaluk@sjrb.ca

***Kenora:* CBWT-TV-7** (Channel: 8)
Owned by: **CBWT-TV**
Kenora, ON

***Kingston:* CJOH-TV** (Channel: 6)
Owned by: **CTVglobemedia Inc.**
Kingston, ON

***Kingston:* CKWS-TV** (Channel: 11)
Owned by: **Corus Entertainment Inc.***
170 Queen St., Kingston, ON K7K 1B2
Tel: 613-544-2340; *Fax:* 613-544-5508
newswatch@corusent.com (News room)
www.ckwstv.com
Other information: Phone, News Department: 613-542-9232; Fax, Sales Dept.: 613-544-3587
Mike Ferguson, General Manager
Jay Westman, News Director

***Kitchener:* CBLN-TV-1** (Channel: 56 antenna)
Owned by: **Canadian Broadcasting Corporation (CBC)**
Kitchener, ON
Toll-Free: 866-306-4636
www.cbc.ca/television
Other information: TDD: 1-866-220-6045

***Kitchener:* CKCO-TV** (Channel: 13)
Owned by: **CTVglobemedia Inc.***
PO Box 91026 C, 864 King St. West, Kitchener, ON N2G 4E9
Tel: 519-578-1313; *Fax:* 519-743-0730
viewermail@southwesternontario.ctv.ca
www.southwesternontario.ctv.ca/
Watson Dennis, VP,GM, dwatson@ctv.ca

***London:* CBLN-TV** (Channel: 40 antenna)
Owned by: **Canadian Broadcasting Corporation (CBC)**
London, ON
Toll-Free: 866-306-4636
www.cbc.ca/television
Other information: TDD: 1-866-220-6045

***London:* CFPL-TV (A-Channel-London)** (Channel: 10)
PO Box 5810, 1 Communications Rd., London, ON N6A 6E9
Tel: 519-686-8810; *Fax:* 519-668-3288
Toll-Free: 800-403-7912
newsnow@thenewpl.com
www.achannel.ca/london
Greg Mudry

***London:* CKCO-TV** (Channel: 13)
Owned by: **CTVglobemedia Inc.**
London, ON

***North Bay:* CKNY-TV (CTV North Bay)** (Channel: 10)
Owned by: **CTVglobemedia Inc.***
245 Oak St. East, North Bay, ON P1B 8P8
Tel: 705-476-3111; *Fax:* 705-495-4474
www.ctv.ca
Scott Lund, General Manager

***Oshawa:* CHEX-TV** (Channel: 22)
Owned by: **Corus Entertainment Inc.***
#7, 500 Wentworth St. East, Oshawa, ON L1H 3V9
Tel: 905-434-2421; *Fax:* 905-432-2315
www.chextv.com

***Osnaburgh:* CBWDT-TV-4** (Channel: 13)
Owned by: **CBWT-TV**
Osnaburgh, ON

†*Ottawa:* CBOFT-TV (Channel: 9)
Owned by: **Canadian Broadcasting Corporation***
CP 3220 C, Ottawa, ON K1Y 1E4
Tél: 613-724-1200; *Téléc:* 613-724-5233
standard@radio-canada.ca
www.radio-canada.ca/ottawa/

***Ottawa:* CBOT-TV** (Channel: 4)
Owned by: **Canadian Broadcasting Corporation***
PO Box 3220 C, Ottawa, ON K1Y 1E4
Tel: 613-724-1200; *Fax:* 613-724-5512
www.ottawa.cbc.ca

***Ottawa:* CHOT-TV** (Channel: 40)
Owned by: **CHOT-TV**
Ottawa, ON

***Ottawa:* CHRO-TV** (Channel: 6)
87 George St., Ottawa, ON K1N 9H7
Tel: 613-789-0606; *Fax:* 613-789-6590
ottawa.promotions@Achannel.ca
www.Achannel.ca
Don Mumford, Station Manager

***Ottawa:* CTV Ottawa** (Channel: 13)
Owned by: **CTV Inc.***
1500 Merivale Rd., Ottawa, ON K2E 6Z5
Tel: 613-224-1313; *Fax:* 613-274-4215
ctvottawa.ctv.ca
www.ottawa.ctv.ca
Louis Douville, Vice-President/General Manager

***Owen Sound:* CKCO-TV** (Channel: 2)
Owned by: **CTVglobemedia Inc.**
Owen Sound, ON

***Pembroke:* CHRO-TV (A-Channel Ottawa)** (Channel: 6)
Owned by: **CHRO-TV**
PO Box 1010, 611 TV Tower Rd., Pembroke, ON K8A 6Y6
Tel: 613-735-1036; *Fax:* 613-735-4374
www.achannel.ca/ottawa
Mike Keller, General Manager
Richard Gray, News Director

***Peterborough:* CHEX-TV** (Channel: 12)
Owned by: **Corus Entertainment Inc.***
743 Monaghan Rd., Peterborough, ON K9J 5K2
Tel: 705-742-0451; *Fax:* 705-742-7274
viewermail@chextv.com
www.chextv.com
Ron Johnston, General Manager

***Pickle Lake:* CBWDT-TV-5** (Channel: 9)
Owned by: **CBWT-TV**
Pickle Lake, ON

***Pikangikum:* CBWDT-TV-6** (Channel: 7)
Owned by: **CBWT-TV**
Pikangikum, ON

***Red Lake:* CBWET-TV** (Channel: 10)
Owned by: **CBWT-TV**
Red Lake, ON

***Sandy Lake:* CBWDT-TV-7** (Channel: 10)
Owned by: **CBWT-TV**
Sandy Lake, ON

***Sarnia:* CBLN-TV-2** (Channel: 34 antenna)
Owned by: **Canadian Broadcasting Corporation (CBC)**
Sarnia, ON
Toll-Free: 866-306-4636
www.cbc.ca/television
Other information: TDD: 1-866-220-6045

***Sarnia:* CKCO-TV** (Channel: 42)
Owned by: **CTVglobemedia Inc.**
Sarnia, ON

***Sault Ste Marie:* CHBX-TV** (Channel: 2)
Owned by: **CTVglobemedia Inc.***
PO Box 370, 119 East St., Sault Ste Marie, ON P6A 5M2
Tel: 705-759-8232; *Fax:* 705-759-7783
mctvnews@ctv.ca
http://northernontario.ctv.ca/

***Savant Lake:* CBWDT-TV-3** (Channel: 8)
Owned by: **CBWT-TV**
Savant Lake, ON

***Sioux Lookout:* CBWDT-TV-1** (Channel: 12)
Owned by: **CBWT-TV**
Sioux Lookout, ON

***Sioux Narrows:* CBWAT-TV-1** (Channel: 4)
Owned by: **CBWT-TV**
Sioux Narrows, ON

***Sudbury:* CICI-TV** (Channel: 5)
Owned by: **CTVglobemedia Inc.***
699 Frood Rd., Sudbury, ON P3C 5A3
Tel: 705-674-8301; *Fax:* 705-674-2789

***Thunder Bay:* CHFD-TV** (Channel: 4)
87 North Hill St., Thunder Bay, ON P7A 5V6
Tel: 807-346-2600; *Fax:* 807-345-9923
tbt@tbtv.com
www.tbtv.com

***Thunder Bay:* CKPR-TV** (Channel: 2)
87 North Hill St., Thunder Bay, ON P7A 5V6
Tel: 807-346-2600; *Fax:* 807-345-9923
tbt@tbtv.com
www.tbtv.com
H.F. Dougall, President

***Timmins:* CITO-TV** (Channel: 3)
Owned by: **CTVglobemedia Inc.***
PO Box 620, Timmins, ON P4N 7G3
Tel: 705-264-4211; *Fax:* 705-264-3266
www.ctv.ca
Scott Lund

†*Toronto:* CBLFT-TV (Channel: 25 UHF; 24 UHF)
Owned by: **Canadian Broadcasting Corporation (CBC)***
Société Radio-Canada, CP 500, 205 Wellington St. West, Toronto, ON M5V 3G7
Tél: 416-205-2887; *Téléc:* 416-205-2500
Ligne sans frais: 800-551-2985
auditoire@radio-canada.ca
www.radio-canada.ca/regions/ontario
Social Media: www.twitter.com/RC_TV
Other information: Phone, Television Newsroom: 416-205-2500

***Toronto:* CBLT-TV** (Channel: 5 antenna; 6 cable)
Owned by: **Canadian Broadcasting Corporation (CBC)***
PO Box 500, 205 Wellington St. West, Toronto, ON M5W 1E6
Tel: 416-205-3311; *Fax:* 416-205-2500
Toll-Free: 866-306-4636
www.cbc.ca/toronto; www.cbc.ca/television
Other information: Phone, Television Newsroom: 416-205-2500
Susan Marjetti, Managing Director, 416-205-5791
Don Ioi, Team Manager, Toronto Sales, 416-205-2732

***Toronto:* CFMT-TV** (Channel: 47)
Owned by: **Rogers Broadcasting Ltd.***
545 Lakeshore Blvd. West, Toronto, ON M5V 1A3
Tel: 416-260-0047; *Fax:* 416-260-3621
Toll-Free: 888-260-0047
info@omni1.ca
www.omnitv.ca
Leslie A. Sole, Exec. Vice-President
Madeline Ziniak, Vice-President & Exec. Producer
Jim Nelles, Vice-President, Marketing
Kelly Colasanti, Vice-President, Operations
Anthony P. Viner, President

***Toronto:* CFTO-TV** (Channel: 9)
Owned by: **CTVglobemedia Inc.***
9 Channel Nine Ct., Toronto, ON M1S 4B5
Tel: 416-332-7100; *Fax:* 416-299-2273
cftonews@ctv.ca
www.ctv.ca

***Toronto:* CHLF-TV** (Channel: 13)
PO Box 200 Q, 2180 Yonge St., Toronto, ON M4T 2T1
Tel: 416-484-2636; *Toll-Free:* 800-387-8435
tfodiffusion@tfo.org
www.tfo.org
Louise Jourdain

***Toronto:* CICA-TV (TVO)** (Channel: 19)
PO Box 200 Q, 2180 Yonge St., Toronto, ON M4T 2T1
Tel: 416-484-2600; *Fax:* 416-484-2725
askTVO@tvontario.org
www.tvo.org

***Toronto:* CIII-TV** (Channel: 41)
Owned by: **Canwest Global Communications Corp.***
81 Barber Greene Rd., Toronto, ON M3C 2A2
Tel: 416-406-5311; *Fax:* 416-446-5543
Toll-Free: 800-387-8001
globalnews.tor@globaltv.com
www.canada.com/globaltv/ontario/

***Toronto:* CITY-TV** (Channel: 57)
299 Queen St. West, Toronto, ON M5V 2Z5
Tel: 416-591-5757; *Fax:* 416-593-6397
news@citynews.ca
www.citytv.com

***Toronto:* CJMT-TV** (Channel: 44, 14)
Owned by: **Rogers Broadcasting Ltd.***
545 Lakeshore Blvd. West, Toronto, ON M5V 1A3
Tel: 416-260-0060; *Fax:* 416-260-3621
Toll-Free: 888-260-0047
info@omni2.ca
www.omnitv.ca

** For details on this company see listing in Major Broadcasting Companies section; † French language station*

***Toronto:* CKXT-TV** (Channel: 52, 15)
Owned by: **Groupe TVA***
25 Ontario St., Toronto, ON M5A 4L6
Tel: 416-601-0010; *Fax:* 416-601-0004
sendit@canoelive.ca
www.toronto1.tv, http://suntv.canoe.ca

***Wawa:* CHBX-TV-1** (Channel: 7)
Owned by: **CTVglobemedia Inc.**
Wawa, ON

***Windsor:* CBET-TV** (Channel: 9)
Owned by: **Canadian Broadcasting Corporation (CBC)***
825 Riverside Dr. West, Windsor, ON N9A 5K9
Tel: 519-255-3411; *Toll-Free:* 866-306-4636
www.cbc.ca/windsor
Other information: Phone, Windsor Newsroom: 519-255-3456
Sandra Porteous, Managing Edior, Radio & Television, 519-255-3563
David Daigneault, Executive Producer, Radio & Television, 519-255-3410
Nancy Lauzon, Manager, Windsor Accounts, 519-255-3510

***Windsor:* CHWI-TV** (Channel: 16)
75 Riverside Drive East, Windsor, ON N9A 7C4
Tel: 519-977-7432; *Fax:* 519-977-0564
http://www.windsorbusiness.com/Radio_&_TV_Stations/CHWI-TV-553-1-0-0.html
Greg Mudry

***Windsor:* CKCO-TV** (Channel: 42)
Owned by: **CTVglobemedia Inc.**
Windsor, ON

***Wingham:* CBLN-TV-4** (Channel: 45 antenna)
Owned by: **Canadian Broadcasting Corporation (CBC)**
Wingham, ON
Toll-Free: 866-306-4636
www.cbc.ca/television
Other information: TDD: 1-866-220-6045

***Wingham:* CKNX-TV** (Channel: 8)
215 Carling Terrace, Wingham, ON N0G 2W0
Tel: 519-357-4438; *Fax:* 519-357-4398
info@1017theone.ca
www.fm102.ca
Greg Mudry, Vice-President & General Manager

Prince Edward Island

***Charlottetown:* CBCT-TV** (Channel: 13 antenna)
Owned by: **Canadian Broadcasting Corporation (CBC)***
PO Box 2230, 430 University Ave., Charlottetown, PE C1A 8B9
Tel: 902-629-6400; *Toll-Free:* 866-306-4636
www.cbc.ca/pei; www.cbc.ca/television
Other information: Phone, CBC News Compass: 902-629-6403; Toll-Free: 1-800-671-2228
Andrew Cochran, Managing Director, Maritimes
Donna Allen, Executive Producer, News, Prince Edward Island
Janet Irwin, Senior Regional Manager, News & Current Affairs
Nadine Antle, Regional Manager, Partnerships, Communications, Brand, & Promot, 506-451-4054
Lenny Jackson, Station Manager, Prince Edward Island
John Channing, Manager, Sales
Heather McGrath, Senior Officer, Communications, 902-629-6416

***Charlottetown:* CIHF-TV** (Channel: 42)
Owned by: **CIHF-TV**
Charlottetown, PE

***Charlottetown:* CKCW-TV-1** (Channel: 8)
Owned by: **CTVglobemedia Inc.**
Charlottetown, PE

†*St Edward:* CBAFT-TV-6 (Channel: 9)
Owned by: **CBAFT-TV**
St Edward, PE

Québec

***Alma:* CBJET-TV-1** (Channel: 32)
Owned by: **CBMT-TV; Canadian Broadcasting Corporation**
Alma, QC

†*Anse-à-Valleau:* CHAU-TV (Channel: 12)
Owned by: **CHAU-TV**
Anse-à-Valleau, QC

***Baie-Comeau:* CBMIT-TV** (Channel: 28 UHF)
Owned by: **Canadian Broadcasting Corporation (CBC)**
Baie-Comeau, QC
Toll-Free: 866-306-4636
www.cbc.ca/television
Other information: TDD: 1-866-220-6045

†*Carleton:* CHAU-TV (Channel: 5)
Owned by: **Télé Inter-Rives ltée***
349, boul Perron, Carleton, QC G0C 1J0
Tél: 418-364-3344; *Téléc:* 418-364-7168
info@chautva.com
www.chautva.com
Thibault Octave, Directeur de l'information, othibault@chautva.com
Arseneault Chantale, Journaliste, carseneault@chautva.com

†*Carleton:* CIVK-TV (Channel: 15)
Owned by: **CIVM-TV**
Carleton, QC

†*Chandler:* CHAU-TV (Channel: 6)
Owned by: **CHAU-TV**
Chandler, QC

†*Chapais:* CBFAT-TV-1 (Channel: 12)
Owned by: **Canadian Broadcasting Corporation (CBC)**
Chapais, QC
Tél: 514-597-6000; *Téléc:* 514-597-5545
Ligne sans frais: 866-306-4636
auditoire@radio-canada.ca
www.radio-canada.ca/television
Social Media: www.twitter.com/RC_TV

†*Chibougamau:* CBFAT-TV (Channel: 5)
Owned by: **Canadian Broadcasting Corporation (CBC)**
Chibougamau, QC
Tél: 514-597-6000; *Téléc:* 514-597-5545
Ligne sans frais: 866-306-4636
auditoire@radio-canada.ca
www.radio-canada.ca/television
Social Media: www.twitter.com/RC_TV

***Chibougamau:* CBMCT-TV** (Channel: 4)
Owned by: **Canadian Broadcasting Corporation (CBC)**
Chibougamau, QC
Toll-Free: 866-306-4636
www.cbc.ca/television
Other information: TDD: 1-866-220-6045

***Chicoutimi:* CBJET-TV** (Channel: 58)
Owned by: **CBMT-TV; Canadian Broadcasting Corporation**
Chicoutimi, QC

†*Chicoutimi:* TVA - CJPM (Channel: 6)
Owned by: **Groupe TVA***
CP 600, 1, rue Mont Ste-Claire, Chicoutimi, QC G7H 5G3
Tél: 418-549-2576; *Téléc:* 418-545-1130
Ligne sans frais: 800-267-2576
cjpm@saglac.qc.ca
www.reseau.tva.ca
Roger Jobin, General & Sales Manager

†*Cloridorme:* CHAU-TV (Channel: 11)
Owned by: **CHAU-TV**
Cloridorme, QC

†*Gaspé:* CHAU-TV (Channel: 7)
Owned by: **CHAU-TV**
Gaspé, QC

***Harrington-Harbour:* CBMUT-TV** (Channel: 13 VHF)
Owned by: **Canadian Broadcasting Corporation (CBC)***
Harrington-Harbour, QC
Toll-Free: 866-306-4636
www.cbc.ca/television
Other information: TDD: 1-866-220-6045

***Hull:* CBOT-TV** (Channel: 4)
Owned by: **CBOT-TV**
Hull, QC

†*Hull:* CFGS-TV (Channel: 34)
Owned by: **Radio Nord Communications Inc.***
171A, rue Jean-Proulx, Hull, QC J8Z 1W5
Tél: 819-770-1040; *Téléc:* 819-770-0272
Robert H. Parent

†*Hull:* CHOT-TV (Channel: 40)
Owned by: **Radio Nord Communications Inc.***
171, rue Jean-Proulx, Hull, QC J8Z 1W5
Tél: 819-770-1040; *Téléc:* 819-770-1490
chot@radionord.com
www.radionord.com
Robert H. Parent

***Hull:* CIVO-TV** (Channel: 30)
Owned by: **CIVM-TV**
Hull, QC

†*Jonquière:* CFRS-TV (Channel: 4)
Owned by: **TQS inc.***
2303, rue Sir Wilfrid Laurier, Jonquière, QC G7X 5Z2
Tél: 418-542-4551; *Téléc:* 418-542-7217
cgotv-saglar@cgotv.ca
www.tqs.ca
Martin Gagnon, General Manager

†*Jonquière:* CIVO-TV
Owned by: **CIVM-TV**
Jonquière, QC

†*Jonquière:* CIVV-TV (Channel: 8)
Owned by: **Télé-Québec***
CP 23041, Jonquière, QC G7X 9Z8
Tél: 418-695-8152; *Téléc:* 418-695-8155
lgagnon@telequebec.qc.ca
telequebec.tv
Laval Gagnon

†*Jonquière:* CKTV-TV (Channel: 12)
Owned by: **TQS inc.***
2303, rue Sir Wilfrid Laurier, Jonquière, QC G7X 5Z2
Tél: 418-542-4551; *Téléc:* 418-542-7217
cgotv-saglac@cgotv.ca
www.tqs.ca

†*Kuujjuarapik:* CBFK-TV (Channel: 9)
Owned by: **Canadian Broadcasting Corporation (CBC)**
Kuujjuarapik, QC
Tél: 514-597-6000; *Téléc:* 514-597-5545
Ligne sans frais: 866-306-4636
auditoire@radio-canada.ca
www.radio-canada.ca/television
Social Media: www.twitter.com/RC_TV

***La Tabatière:* CBMLT-TV** (Channel: 10)
Owned by: **Canadian Broadcasting Corporation (CBC)**
La Tabatière, QC
Toll-Free: 866-306-4636
www.cbc.ca/television
Other information: TDD: 1-866-220-6045

***La Tuque:* CBMET-TV** (Channel: 9)
Owned by: **Canadian Broadcasting Corporation (CBC)**
La Tuque, QC
Toll-Free: 866-306-4636
www.cbc.ca/television
Other information: TDD: 1-866-220-6045

†*La Tuque:* CBVT-TV (Channel: 3)
Owned by: **Canadian Broadcasting Corporation***
La Tuque, QC

†*Lac-Mégantic:* CBVT-TV (Channel: 2)
Owned by: **Canadian Broadcasting Corporation***
Lac-Mégantic, QC

†*Matane:* CIVF-TV (Channel: 12)
Owned by: **CIVM-TV**
Matane, QC

* *For details on this company see listing in Major Broadcasting Companies section; † French language station*

†*Montréal:* CBFT-TV (Channel: 2 VHF; 19 UHF)
Owned by: **Canadian Broadcasting Corporation (CBC)***
Maison de Radio-Canada, CP 6000 Centre-ville, 1400, boul René-Lévesque est, Montréal, QC H3C 3A8
Tél: 514-597-6000; *Téléc:* 514-597-5545
Ligne sans frais: 866-306-4636
auditoire@radio-canada.ca
www.radio-canada.ca/television
Social Media: www.twitter.com/RC_TV
Other information: Phone, Montréal TV Newsroom: 514-597-6371; Fax: 514-597-6354
Pia Marquard, Managing Director, Radio & Television, Québec Region
Sally Caudwell, Executive Producer, Montréal News, 514-597-4089, Fax: 514-597-4511

***Montréal:* CBMT-TV** (Channel: 6 VHF; 20 UHF)
Owned by: **Canadian Broadcasting Corporation (CBC)***
PO Box 6000, Montréal, QC H3C 3A8
Tel: 514-597-6000; *Fax:* 514-597-6354
www.cbc.ca/montreal; www.cbc.ca/television
Other information: Phone, CBC Montréal TV Newsroom: 514-597-6371
Pia Marquard, Managing Director, Radio & Television, Québec Region
Sally Caudwell, Executive Producer, News, Montréal, 514-597-4089, Fax: 514-597-4511
Mary-Jo Barr, News Director, English Services
Laura Tarulli, Senior Manager, Production & Resources
Carolyn Warren, Regional Manager, Cultural Programming & Integrated Content
Hugh Brodie, Manager, Partnership & Communications, Québec, 514-597-5813

***Montréal:* CFCF-TV** (Channel: 12)
Owned by: **CTVglobemedia Inc.***
1205, ave. Papineau, Montréal, QC H2K 4R2
Tel: 514-273-6311; *Fax:* 514-276-9399
montrealnews@ctv.ca, mpiperni@ctv.ca
www.cfcf.ca
Donald M. Bastien, Sr V.P. and General Manager

†*Montréal:* CFJP-TV (Channel: 35)
Owned by: **TQS inc.***
#100, 612, rue St-Jacques, Montréal, QC H3C 5R1
Tél: 514-390-6035; *Téléc:* 514-390-6070
www.tqs.ca
René Guimond, Président et chef de la direction

†*Montréal:* CFTM-TV (Channel: 10)
Owned by: **Groupe TVA***
1600 Est, boul de Maisonneuve, Montréal, QC H2L 4P2
Tél: 514-526-9251; *Téléc:* 514-598-6078
relations.auditoire@tva.ca
www.tva.ca, http://tva.canoe.com

†*Montréal:* CIVM-TV (Channel: 17)
Owned by: **Télé-Québec***
1000, rue Fullum, Montréal, QC H2K 3L7
Tél: 514-521-2424; *Téléc:* 514-873-2601
Ligne sans frais: 800-361-4362
info@telequebec.tv
www.telequebec.tv
Claude Dufault, Directeur de la commandite et des v, cdufault@telequebec.tv
Desroches Gérard, Représentant, gdesroche@telequebec.tv

***Montréal:* CJNT-TV** (Channel: 62, 14)
Owned by: **Canwest Global Communications Corp.***
1600, boul de Maisonneuve est, 9e étage, Montréal, QC H2L 4P2
Tel: 514-522-4150; *Fax:* 514-522-9579
info@chmontreal.com
www.canada.com/chtv/montreal

***Montréal:* CKMI-TV (Global Quebec)** (Channel: 5)
Owned by: **Canwest Global Communications Corp.***
1600 de Maisonneuve E., Montreal, QC H2L 4P2
Tel: 514-521-4923; *Fax:* 514-590-4060
quebecprog@globaltv.ca, globalnews.que@globaltv.co
www.canada.com/globaltv/quebec/
Maureen Rogers, General Manager
Karen MacDonald, Station Manager

***Murdochville:* CBMMT-TV** (Channel: 21 UHF)
Owned by: **Canadian Broadcasting Corporation (CBC)**
Murdochville, QC
Toll-Free: 866-306-4636
www.cbc.ca/television
Other information: TDD: 1-866-220-6045

†*Notre-Dame-du-Laus:* CBOFT-TV-3 (Channel: 10)
Owned by: **CBFT-TV**
Notre-Dame-du-Laus, QC

†*Percé:* CHAU-TV (Channel: 13)
Owned by: **CHAU-TV**
Percé, QC

†*Plessisville:* CKYQ-FM (Channel: 95.7)
1646, av St-Laurent, Plessisville, QC G6L 2Y6
Tél: 819-362-3737; *Téléc:* 819-362-3414
studio@kyqfm.com
www.kyqfm.com

***Pointe-au-Père:* CFER-TV** (Channel: 5, 11)
Owned by: **Groupe TVA***
465, boul Ste-Anne, Pointe-au-Père, QC G5M 1G1
Tel: 418-722-6011; *Fax:* 418-724-7810
nouvelles@cfer.tva.ca
cfer.tva.ca

†*Port-Daniel:* CHAU-TV (Channel: 10)
Owned by: **CHAU-TV**
Port-Daniel, QC

†*Québec:* CBVT-TV (Channel: 11)
Owned by: **Canadian Broadcasting Corporation***
CP 18800, 888, rue Saint-Jean, Québec, QC G1K 9L4
Tél: 418-654-1341
www.radio-canada.ca/regions/quebec

†*Québec:* CFAP-TV (Channel: 2)
Owned by: **TQS inc.***
330, rue Saint-Vallier est, bureau 025, Québec, QC G1K 9C5
Tél: 418-624-2222; *Téléc:* 418-624-8930
regiecentraleQC@tqs.ca, tvpublic@tqs.ca
www.tqs.ca/quebec/

†*Québec:* CFER-TV-2 (Channel: 5)
Owned by: **CFER-TV**
Québec, QC

†*Québec:* CIVQ-TV (Channel: 15)
Owned by: **CIVM-TV**
Québec, QC

†*Rapides-des-Joachims:* CBOFT-TV-2 (Channel: 31)
Owned by: **CBOFT-TV**
Rapides-des-Joachims, QC

†*Rimouski:* CFER-TV (Channel: 11)
Owned by: **CFER-TV**
Rimouski, QC

†*Rimouski:* CIVB-TV (Channel: 8)
Owned by: **Télé-Québec***
79, rue de l'Évêché est, Rimouski, QC G5L 1X7
Tél: 418-727-3743; *Téléc:* 418-727-3814
bureau.rimouski@telequebec.tv
www.telequebec.tv
Diane Dube

***Rivière-Saint-Paul:* CBMPT-TV** (Channel: 11)
Owned by: **Canadian Broadcasting Corporation (CBC)**
Rivière-Saint-Paul, QC
Toll-Free: 866-306-4636
www.cbc.ca/television
Other information: TDD: 1-866-220-6045

†*Rivière-au-Rénard:* CHAU-TV (Channel: 4)
Owned by: **CHAU-TV**
Rivière-au-Rénard, QC

†*Rivière-du-Loup:* CFTF-TV (Channel: 29)
103, rue des Équipements, Rivière-du-Loup, QC G5R 5W7
Tél: 418-862-2909; *Téléc:* 418-867-4710
typublic@tqs.ca
www.tqs.ca
Nancy Fortin, Production Director
Marc Simard, Président
Ginette Dumont, Administrative Secretary
Stéphane Grégoire, Vice-President, Finances
Michel Bélanger, Vice-President, Operations

†*Rivière-du-Loup:* CIMT-TV (Channel: 9)
Owned by: **Télé Inter-Rives ltée***
15, rue de la Chute, Rivière-du-Loup, QC G5R 5B7
Tél: 418-867-1341; *Téléc:* 418-867-4710
Marc Simard, President
Ginette Dumont, Administrative Secretary
Germain Gélinas, Vice-President, Operations
Stéphane Grégoire, Vice-President, Finances

†*Rivière-du-Loup:* CKRT-TV (Channel: 7)
Owned by: **Canadian Broadcasting Corporation***
15, rue de la Chute, Rivière-du-Loup, QC G5R 5B7
Tél: 418-867-8080; *Téléc:* 418-867-4710
ckrt@icrdl.net
Marc Simard, President
Ginette Dumont, Administrative Secretary
Germain Gélinas, Vice-President, Operations
Stéphane Grégoire, Vice-President, Finances

†*Rouyn-Noranda:* CFEM-TV (Channel: 13)
Owned by: **Radio Nord Communications Inc.***
380, av Murdoch, Rouyn-Noranda, QC J9X 1G5
Tél: 819-762-0744; *Téléc:* 819-762-2280
abrosseau@radionord.com
www.radionord.com
Ghislain Beaulieu

†*Rouyn-Noranda:* CIVA-TV (Channel: 8)
Owned by: **CIVM-TV**
Rouyn-Noranda, QC

†*Rouyn-Noranda:* CKRN-TV (Channel: 4)
Owned by: **Radio Nord Communications Inc.***
380, av Murdoch, Rouyn-Noranda, QC J9X 1G5
Tél: 819-762-0744; *Téléc:* 819-762-2280
www.radionord.com
Ghislain Beaulieu

†*Saguenay:* TVA - CJPM (Channel: 6)
Owned by: **TVA - CJPM**
Saguenay, QC

***Saint-Augustin:* CBMXT-TV** (Channel: 7)
Owned by: **Canadian Broadcasting Corporation (CBC)**
Saint-Augustin, QC
Toll-Free: 866-306-4636
www.cbc.ca/television
Other information: TDD: 1-866-220-6045

†*Sainte-Foy:* CFCM-TV (Channel: 4)
Owned by: **Groupe TVA***
CP 2026, 1000, av Myrand, Sainte-Foy, QC G1V 2W3
Tél: 418-688-9330; *Téléc:* 418-681-4239
Ligne sans frais: 800-463-5608
administration@tele-4.tva.ca
www.tva.ca
Richard Renaud, Vice-President, Regional Stations &

†*Sainte-Marguerite-Marie:* CHAU-TV (Channel: 3)
Owned by: **CHAU-TV**
Sainte-Marguerite-Marie, QC

†*Sept-Iles:* CBST-TV (Channel: 3)
Owned by: **CBVT-TV**
Sept-Iles, QC

†*Sept-Iles:* CIVG-TV (Channel: 9)
Owned by: **CIVM-TV**
Sept-Iles, QC

***Sherbrooke:* CBMT-TV-3** (Channel: 50 UHF)
Owned by: **Canadian Broadcasting Corporation (CBC)**
Sherbrooke, QC
Toll-Free: 866-306-4636
www.cbc.ca/television
Other information: TDD: 1-866-220-6045

***Sherbrooke:* CFKS-TV** (Channel: 30)
Owned by: **TQS inc.***
3720, boul Industriel, Sherbrooke, QC J1L 1Z9
Tel: 819-565-9999; *Fax:* 819-565-3787
typublic@tqs.ca
www.tqs.ca

†*Sherbrooke:* CHLT-TV (Channel: 7)
Owned by: **Groupe TVA***
3330, rue King ouest, Sherbrooke, QC J1L 1C9
Tél: 819-565-7777; *Téléc:* 819-565-4650
http://tva.canoe.com/stations/chlt/

** For details on this company see listing in Major Broadcasting Companies section; † French language station*

†*Sherbrooke:* CIVS-TV (Channel: 24)
Owned by: **CIVM-TV**
Sherbrooke, QC

†*Sherbrooke:* CKSH-TV (Channel: 9)
Owned by: **TQS inc.***
3720, boul Industriel, Sherbrooke, QC J1L 1Z9
Tél: 819-565-9999; *Téléc:* 819-822-4205

†*St-Fabien-de-Panet:* CBVT-TV (Channel: 13)
Owned by: **Canadian Broadcasting Corporation***
St-Fabien-de-Panet, QC

†*St-Georges:* CBVT-TV (Channel: 6)
Owned by: **Canadian Broadcasting Corporation***
St-Georges, QC

***Thetford Mines:* CBMT-TV-4** (Channel: 32 UHF)
Owned by: **Canadian Broadcasting Corporation (CBC)**
Thetford Mines, QC
Toll-Free: 866-306-4636
www.cbc.ca/television
Other information: TDD: 1-866-220-6045

†*Tracadie:* CHAU-TV (Channel: 9)
Owned by: **CHAU-TV**
Tracadie, QC

***Trois-Rivières:* CBMT-TV-1** (Channel: 28 UHF)
Owned by: **Canadian Broadcasting Corporation (CBC)**
Trois-Rivières, QC
Toll-Free: 866-306-4636
www.cbc.ca/television
Other information: TDD: 1-866-220-6045

†*Trois-Rivières:* CFKM-TV (Channel: 16)
Owned by: **TQS inc.***
4141, boul St-Jean, Trois-Rivières, QC G9B 2M8
Tél: 819-377-6053; *Téléc:* 819-377-5442
Ligne sans frais: 800-424-1441
www.cgotv.ca
Michel Cloutier, General Manager

***Trois-Rivières:* CFKM-TV** (Channel: 29)
Owned by: **CFKM-TV**
Trois-Rivières, QC

†*Trois-Rivières:* CHEM-TV (Channel: 8)
Owned by: **Groupe TVA***
3625, boul Chanoine-Moreau, Trois-Rivières, QC G8Y 5N6
Tél: 819-376-8880; *Téléc:* 819-376-2906
tva.canoe.com/stations/chem

†*Trois-Rivières:* CIVC-TV (Channel: 45)
Trois-Rivières, QC

†*Val-d'Or:* CFVS-TV (Channel: 20)
Owned by: **Radio Nord Communications Inc.***
1729, 3e av, Val-d'Or, QC J9P 1W3
Tél: 819-762-0741; *Téléc:* 819-762-2466
Frantz Boivin

***Vieux-Fort:* CBMVT-TV** (Channel: 13)
Owned by: **Canadian Broadcasting Corporation (CBC)**
Vieux-Fort, QC
Toll-Free: 866-306-4636
www.cbc.ca/television
Other information: TDD: 1-866-220-6045

Saskatchewan

***Beauval:* CBKBT-TV** (Channel: 7)
Owned by: **CBKST-TV; Canadian Broadcasting Corporation**
Beauval, SK

***Big River:* CIPA-TV-3** (Channel: 7)
Owned by: **CTVglobemedia Inc.**
Big River, SK

***Big River:* CKBI-TV-5** (Channel: 9)
Owned by: **CKBI-TV**
Big River, SK

***Buffalo Narrows:* CBKDT-TV** (Channel: 11)
Owned by: **CBKST-TV; Canadian Broadcasting corporation**
Buffalo Narrows, SK

***Carlyle Lake:* CIEW-TV** (Channel: 7)
Owned by: **CTVglobemedia Inc.**
Carlyle Lake, SK

***Colgate:* CKCK-TV-1** (Channel: 12)
Owned by: **CTVglobemedia Inc.**
Colgate, SK

***Cumberland House:* CBWIT-TV** (Channel: 9)
Owned by: **CBWT-TV**
Cumberland House, SK

***Elrose:* CKEL-TV-1** (Channel: 7)
Elrose, SK

***Fort Qu'Appelle:* CBKT-TV-3** (Channel: 4)
Owned by: **CBKT-TV**
Fort Qu'Appelle, SK

***Fort Qu'appelle:* CKTV-TV** (Channel: 7)
Owned by: **CTVglobemedia Inc.**
Fort Qu'appelle, SK

***Golden Prairie:* CKMC-TV-1** (Channel: 10)
Owned by: **CTVglobemedia Inc.**
Golden Prairie, SK

***Greenwater Lake:* CKBI-TV-3** (Channel: 4)
Owned by: **CKBI-TV**
Greenwater Lake, SK

***Hudson Bay:* CICC-TV-3** (Channel: 11)
Owned by: **CTVglobemedia Inc.**
Hudson Bay, SK

***Humboldt:* CIWH-TV-1** (Channel: 32)
Owned by: **CTVglobemedia Inc.**
Humboldt, SK

***Ile-a-la-Crosse:* CBKCT-TV** (Channel: 9)
Owned by: **CBKST-TV; Canadian Broadcasting Corporation**
Ile-a-la-Crosse, SK

***Indian Lake:* CBWT-TV** (Channel: 10)
Owned by: **CBWT-TV**
Indian Lake, SK

***Island Falls:* CBWBT-TV-2** (Channel: 7)
Owned by: **CBWT-TV**
Island Falls, SK

***La Loche:* CBKDT-TV-2** (Channel: 13)
Owned by: **CBKST-TV; Canadian Broadcasting Corporation**
La Loche, SK

***La Ronge:* CBKST-TV-2** (Channel: 12)
Owned by: **CBKST-TV**
La Ronge, SK

***Leoville:* CBKST-TV-3** (Channel: 12)
Owned by: **CBKST-TV**
Leoville, SK

***Maple Creek:* CHAT-TV-2** (Channel: 4)
Owned by: **CHAT-TV**
Maple Creek, SK

***Meadow Lake:* CITL-TV3** (Channel: 3)
Owned by: **CITL-TV**
Meadow Lake, SK

***Meadow Lake:* CKSA-TV** (Channel: 8)
Owned by: **CKSA-TV**
Meadow Lake, SK

***Melfort:* CKBQ-TV** (Channel: 2)
Owned by: **CTVglobemedia Inc.**
Melfort, SK

***Montreal Lake:* CBKST-TV-5** (Channel: 11)
Owned by: **CBKST-TV**
Montreal Lake, SK

***Moose Jaw:* CBKT-TV-1** (Channel: 4)
Owned by: **CBKT-TV**
Moose Jaw, SK

***Moose Jaw:* CKMJ-TV** (Channel: 7)
Owned by: **CTVglobemedia Inc.**
Moose Jaw, SK

***Nipawin:* CKBQ-TV-1** (Channel: 12)
Owned by: **CTVglobemedia Inc.**
Nipawin, SK

***Norquay:* CICC-TV-2** (Channel: 7)
Owned by: **CTVglobemedia Inc.**
Norquay, SK

***North Battleford:* CFQC-TV-2** (Channel: 6)
Owned by: **CTVglobemedia Inc.**
North Battleford, SK

***North Battleford:* CKBI-TV-2** (Channel: 7)
Owned by: **CKBI-TV**
North Battleford, SK

***Palmbere Lake:* CBKDT-TV-1** (Channel: 8)
Owned by: **CBKST-TV; Canadian Broadcasting Corporation**
Palmbere Lake, SK

***Pelican Narrows:* CBWBT-TV-3** (Channel: 5)
Owned by: **CBWT-TV**
Pelican Narrows, SK

***Pinehouse Lake:* CBKST-TV-6** (Channel: 10)
Owned by: **CBKST-TV**
Pinehouse Lake, SK

***Prince Albert:* CIPA-TV** (Channel: 9)
Owned by: **CTVglobemedia Inc.***
22 - 10 St. West, Prince Albert, SK S6V 3A5
Tel: 306-922-6066; *Fax:* 306-763-3041

***Prince Albert:* CKBI-TV** (Channel: 5)
Owned by: **Canadian Broadcasting Corporation***
22 - 10 St. West, Prince Albert, SK S6V 3A5
Tel: 306-922-6066; *Fax:* 306-763-3041

†*Regina:* CBKFT-TV (Channel: 13)
Owned by: **Société Radio Canada***
CP 540, 2440 Broad St., Regina, SK S4P 4A1
Tél: 306-347-9540
rene_fountaine@radio-canada.ca
www.radio-canada.ca/regions/saskatchewan
Fontaine René, 204-788-3236, rene_fountaine@radio-canada.ca

***Regina:* CBKT-TV** (Channel: 9)
Owned by: **Canadian Broadcasting Corporation***
PO Box 540, 2440 Broad St., Regina, SK S4P 4A1
Tel: 306-347-9540; *Fax:* 306-347-9635
audienceinfo@regina.cbc.ca
www.sask.cbc.ca
Social Media: www.facebook.com/cbcsask; twitter.com/cbcsask
Lenora Sturge, Program Marketing Co-ordinator, 306-347-9714

***Regina:* CFRE-TV** (Channel: 5)
Owned by: **Canwest Global Communications Corp.***
370 Hoffer Dr., Regina, SK S4N 7A4
Tel: 306-775-4000; *Fax:* 306-721-4817
www.canada.com

***Regina:* CKCK-TV** (Channel: 2)
Owned by: **CTVglobemedia Inc.***
PO Box 2000, Regina, SK S4P 3E5
Tel: 306-569-2000; *Fax:* 306-522-0090
ckck@ctv.ca
www.ctv.ca
Dennis Dunlop, Vice-President, General Manager, Ge, CTV Saskatchewan

***Saskatoon:* CBKST-TV** (Channel: 11)
Owned by: **Canadian Broadcasting Corporation***
144 - 2nd Ave. South, Saskatoon, SK S7K 1K5
Tel: 306-956-7430; *Fax:* 306-975-7488
www.cbc.ca/sask
Social Media: www.facebook.com/cbcsask; twitter.com/cbcsask

***Saskatoon:* CFSK-TV** (Channel: 4)
Owned by: **Canwest Global Communications Corp.***
218 Robin Cres., Saskatoon, SK S7L 7C3
Tel: 306-665-6969; *Fax:* 306-665-6069
globalnews.sask@globaltv.com
www.canada.com/saskatoon
Wayne Rorke, Station Manager, wrorke@globaltv.com
Lisa Ford, News Director, lford@globaltv.com

***Saskatoon:* CTV Television Inc.** (Channel: 8)
Owned by: **CTVglobemedia Inc.***
216 - 1 Ave. North, Saskatoon, SK S7K 3W3
Tel: 306-665-8600; *Fax:* 306-665-0450
www.ctv.ca
Dennis Dunlop, General Manager

* *For details on this company see listing in Major Broadcasting Companies section; † French language station*

Southend: **CBKST-TV-8** (Channel: 13)
Owned by: **CBKST-TV**
Southend, SK

Spiritwood: **CIPA-TV-1** (Channel: 10)
Owned by: **CTVglobemedia Inc.**
Spiritwood, SK

Spiritwood: **CKBI-TV-6** (Channel: 2)
Owned by: **CKBI-TV**
Spiritwood, SK

Stanley Mission: **CBKST-TV-4** (Channel: 8)
Owned by: **CBKST-TV**
Stanley Mission, SK

Stranraer: **CBKST-TV-1** (Channel: 9)
Owned by: **CBKST-TV**
Stranraer, SK

Stranraer: **CFQC-TV-1** (Channel: 3)
Owned by: **CTVglobemedia Inc.**
Stranraer, SK

Swift Current: **CBKT-TV-4** (Channel: 5)
Owned by: **CBKT-TV**
Swift Current, SK

Swift Current: **CKMC-TV** (Channel: 12)
Owned by: **CTVglobemedia Inc.**
Swift Current, SK

Tisdale: **CKBI-TV-6** (Channel: 13)
Owned by: **CKBI-TV**
Tisdale, SK

Warmley: **CFSS-TV** (Channel: 3)
Warmley, SK

Willow Bunch: **CBKT-TV-2** (Channel: 10)
Owned by: **CBKT-TV**
Willow Bunch, SK

Willow Bunch: **CKCK-TV-2** (Channel: 6)
Owned by: **CTVglobemedia Inc.**
Willow Bunch, SK

Wynyard: **CHSS-TV** (Channel: 6)
Owned by: **CTVglobemedia Inc.**
Wynyard, SK

Wynyard: **CIWH-TV** (Channel: 12)
Owned by: **CTVglobemedia Inc.**
Wynyard, SK

Yorkton: **CTV Television Inc.** (Channel: 10, 5)
Owned by: **CTVglobemedia Inc.***
95 East Broadway, Yorkton, SK S3N 0L1
Tel: 306-786-8400; *Fax:* 306-782-7212
cciccnews@ctv.ca
www.ctv.ca
Dennis Dunlop, General Manager

Cable Companies

Alberta

Calgary: **Shaw Cable**
PO Box 90 J, 2001 - 27 Ave. NE, Calgary, AB T2A 6T9
Tel: 403-716-6070; *Fax:* 403-291-0880
www.shaw.ca
John Mlazgar, Manager, Regional System

Calgary: **Shaw Communications Inc.**
#900, 630 - 3rd Ave. SW, Calgary, AB T2P 4L4
Tel: 403-750-4500; *Fax:* 403-750-4501
Toll-Free: 888-750-7429
www.shaw.ca
Jim Shaw, CEO

Camrose: **Cable TV of Camrose**
4910 - 46 St., Camrose, AB T4V 1H1
Tel: 780-672-8839; *Fax:* 780-672-8830
www.cable-lynx.net

Edmonton: **Persona Communications**
3552 - 78th Ave., Edmonton, AB T6B 2X9
Tel: 780-440-2525; *Fax:* 780-440-2828
www.personainc.ca

Edmonton: **Regional Cablesytems - Western Division**
PO Box 4005, 3552 - 78th Ave., Edmonton, AB T6E 4S8
Tel: 780-440-2525; *Fax:* 780-440-2828
Jeff Bertram, Director, Sales & Marketing
Rick Miciak, Director, Finance
Dave Paquet, Director, Technical Services
Fred Hockerong, Vice-President & General Manager

Edmonton: **Shaw Cablesystems G.P.**
10450 - 178 St. NW, Edmonton, AB T5S 1S2
Tel: 780-665-9977; *Fax:* 780-490-3411

Fort McMurray: **Shaw Cablesystems G.P.**
#200, 208 Beaconhill Dr., Fort McMurray, AB T9H 2R1
Tel: 780-714-3717; *Fax:* 780-790-1193

Galahad: **Galahad Cablevision Society**
PO Box 31, Galahad, AB T0B 1R0
Tel: 780-583-3989; *Fax:* 780-583-3787

Gift Lake: **Gift Lake Metis Settlement**
General Delivery, Gift Lake, AB T0G 1B0
Tel: 403-767-3894

Grimshaw: **High Level Cable**
PO Box 8, Grimshaw, AB T0H 1W0
Tel: 780-332-1780

Hanna: **Prairie Cable TV Ltd.**
PO Box 520, Hanna, AB T0J 1P0
Tel: 403-854-4659; *Fax:* 403-854-4917

High Prairie: **KBS TV**
PO Box 29, 5319 - 48th St., High Prairie, AB T0G 1E0
Tel: 780-523-3223; *Fax:* 780-523-3411

Lethbridge: **Shaw Cablesystems G.P.**
1232 - 3 Ave. South, Lethbridge, AB T1J 0J9
Tel: 403-380-7352; *Fax:* 403-320-1675

Medicine Hat: **Monarch Cablesystems Ltd.**
361 - 1 St. SE, Medicine Hat, AB T1A 0A5
Tel: 403-526-4529; *Fax:* 403-504-8135
Toll-Free: 800-442-8664
info@monarchcable.net
www.monarch.net
Chad Cunningham, Sales & Marketing Manager

Oyen: **Oyen Cable**
PO Box 95, Oyen, AB T0J 2J0
Tel: 403-664-3811; *Fax:* 403-664-3811
aberg@telusplanet.net; es1016@telusplanet.net
Art Berg, Owner/Operator

Rainbow Lake: **Rainbow Lake Cable TV**
PO Box 149, Rainbow Lake, AB T0H 2Y0
Tel: 780-956-3934; *Fax:* 780-956-3570
rainbowlake@telusplanet.net
www.rainbowlake.ca

Red Deer: **Shaw Cablesystems**
4761 - 62 St., Red Deer, AB T4N 2R4
Tel: 403-340-6400; *Fax:* 403-340-6414
Toll-Free: 888-270-2433
katie.wood@sjrb.ca
www.shaw.ca
Peter Bissonnette, President

Slave Lake: **Cable TV Slave Ltd**
PO Box 1008, 800 Main St. North, Slave Lake, AB T0G 2A0
Tel: 403-849-5188; *Fax:* 403-849-6809
cable-lynx.net

Veteran: **Veteran Television Society**
PO Box 428, Veteran, AB T0C 2S0
Tel: 403-575-3892; *Fax:* 403-575-3938

British Columbia

100 Mile House: **Williams Communications**
PO Box 927, 100 Mile House, BC V0K 2E0
Tel: 250-395-3333; *Fax:* 250-397-2297

Abbotsford: **Shaw Cablesystems**
PO Box 2125 Clearbrook, 31450 Marshall Rd., Abbotsford, BC V2T 3X8
Tel: 604-856-5721; *Fax:* 604-850-2517

Ashcroft: **Copper Valley Cablevision Ltd.**
PO Box 1120, 312 - 4th St., Ashcroft, BC V0K 1A0
Tel: 250-453-2616; *Fax:* 250-453-9960
www.coppervalley.ca

Brackendale: **Britannia Cablevision**
PO Box 461, Brackendale, BC V0N 1H0
Tel: 604-898-9767
G.C. Pickard

Campbell River: **Campbell River TV Association**
500 Robron Rd., Campbell River, BC V9W 5Z2
Tel: 250-923-8899; *Fax:* 250-923-7796
jim.forsyth@crtv.net
www.crtv.net
Jim Forsyth, General Manager

Campbell River: **Sayward Valley Communications Ltd.**
#112, 1720 - 14th Ave., Campbell River, BC V9W 8B9
Tel: 250-287-4199; *Fax:* 250-287-8840
cs@saywardvalley.net
saywardvalley.net

Castlegar: **Shaw Cablesystems**
1951 Columbia Ave., Castlegar, BC V1N 2W8
Tel: 250-365-3122; *Fax:* 250-365-2676

Chilliwack: **Shaw Cablesystems**
9275 Nowell St., Chilliwack, BC V2P 7G7
Tel: 604-793-9944; *Fax:* 604-792-0966

Courtenay: **Shaw Cablesystems**
1591 McPhee Ave., Courtenay, BC V9N 3A6
Tel: 604-334-0888; *Fax:* 604-334-3640

Cranbrook: **Shaw Cablesystems G.P.**
720 Kootenay St. North, Cranbrook, BC V1C 3V2
Tel: 250-342-9415; *Fax:* 250-417-3890

Dawson Creek: **Shaw Cable**
#204, 9817 - 100 Ave., Dawson Creek, BC V1J 1Y4
Tel: 250-782-6669

Delta: **Delta Cable**
5381 Ladner Trunk Rd., Delta, BC V4K 1W7
Tel: 604-946-1144; *Fax:* 604-946-5627
admin@deltacable.com
www.deltacable.com

Duncan: **Shaw Cable**
35 Queens Rd., Duncan, BC V9L 2W1
Tel: 250-782-9113; *Fax:* —0

Fernie: **Monarch Cable**
PO Box 1769, 691 - 9 Ave., Fernie, BC V0B 1M0
Tel: 250-423-3334; *Fax:* 250-423-3855

Fort Nelson: **Northwestel Cable**
PO Box 1949, 5404 - 50th Ave., Fort Nelson, BC V0C 1R0
Tel: 250-774-3021; *Fax:* 250-774-3020
Toll-Free: 800-661-0834
cable@theedge.ca
www.tvnwt.com

Grand Forks: **Sunshine Communications**
PO Box 2618, 7474 - 19 St., Grand Forks, BC V0H 1H0
Tel: 250-442-5844; *Fax:* 250-442-2665
www.sunshinecable.com

Hope: **Hope Cable Television**
PO Box 489, 360 Wallace St., Hope, BC V0X 1L0
Tel: 604-869-2616; *Fax:* 604-869-9393
Toll-Free: 800-663-5038
www.rainbowcountry.bc.ca/archive/hopecable/

Kaslo: **Kaslo Cable Ltd.**
PO Box 637, Kaslo, BC V0G 1M0
Tel: 250-353-2547; *Fax:* 250-353-2547

Kelowna: **Shaw Cablesystems G.P.**
2350 Hunter Rd., Kelowna, BC V1X 7H6
Tel: 250-712-2307; *Fax:* 250-712-2310

Lindell Beach: **Lindell Beach Residents Association**
1946 Vera Rd., Lindell Beach, BC V2R 4X1
Tel: 604-858-4643; *Fax:* 604-858-4670
W. Woodall, TV Committee

Logan Lake: **Logan Lake TV Society**
PO Box 56, Logan Lake, BC V0K 1W0
Tel: 250-523-9339; *Fax:* 250-523-9339
ve7ffk@mail.ocis.net
Dean Neighbour, Vice President

Lower Post: **Daulu Dena Council**
PO Box 10, Lower Post, BC V0C 1W0
Tel: 250-779-3161; *Fax:* 250-779-3371
Roma Walker, Executive Director

** For details on this company see listing in Major Broadcasting Companies section; † French language station*

***Masset:* Masset Haida Television Society**
PO Box 602, 1356 Main St., Masset, BC V0T 1M0
Tel: 250-626-3994; *Fax:* 250-626-3941
cs@mhtv.ca
www.mhtv.ca
Alfred Brockley, President
Gerald Jennings, Vice-President

***Merritt:* Shaw Cablesystems (BC) Ltd.**
PO Box 908, 2 Thorpe Ave., Merritt, BC V1K 1B8
Tel: 250-378-4919

***Nanaimo:* Shaw Cable**
4316 Boban Dr., Nanaimo, BC V8A 2N5
Tel: 250-760-1966; *Fax:* 250-760-1991

***Nanaimo:* Shaw Cablesystems (BC) Ltd.**
4316 Boban Dr., Nanaimo, BC V9T 6A7
Tel: 250-760-1999; *Fax:* 250-760-1998

***Oliver:* Persona Communications Inc.**
PO Box 790, 9502 - 348th Ave., Oliver, BC V0H 1T0
Tel: 250-498-3630; *Fax:* 250-498-8810
Toll-Free: 866-737-7662
www.personainc.ca

***Penticton:* Shaw Cable**
1372 Fairview Rd., Penticton, BC V2A 5Z8
Tel: 250-492-5832; *Fax:* 250-492-3445

***Port Alberni:* Shaw Cable**
4278 - 8 Ave., Port Alberni, BC V9Y 7S8
Tel: 250-723-6295; *Fax:* 250-723-4024

***Port Hardy:* Keta Cable**
PO Box 63, 7020 Market St., Port Hardy, BC V0N 2P0
Tel: 250-949-6109; *Fax:* 250-949-6566
ketacable@cablerocket.com
www.ketacable.com

***Port Simpson:* Rose Island Ventures Inc.**
PO Box 992, Port Simpson, BC V0V 1H0
Tel: 250-625-3352; *Fax:* 250-625-3246

***Prince George:* Shaw Cablesystems G.P.**
2519 Queensway St., Prince George, BC V2L 1N1
Tel: 250-562-1345; *Fax:* 250-614-7340

***Quesnel:* Shaw Cablesystems (BC) Ltd.**
156 Front St., Quesnel, BC V2J 2K1
Tel: 250-992-7811

***Revelstoke:* Revelstoke Cable TV**
PO Box 651, 416 - 2nd St. West, Revelstoke, BC V0E 2S0
Tel: 250-837-5246; *Fax:* 250-837-2900
rctv@rctvonline.net
www.rctvonline.net
Don Gillespie

***Riondel:* Riondel Community Cable & Video Society**
PO Box 59, Riondel, BC V0B 2B0
Tel: 250-225-3433; *Fax:* 250-225-3433
www.bluebell.ca
W. Nelson, President

***Salmo:* Salmo Cabled Programmes Limited**
PO Box 402, Salmo, BC V0G 1Z0
Tel: 250-357-9553; *Fax:* 250-357-9553
L.R. Street

***Salmon Arm:* Mascon Communications Corp.**
PO Box 3386, 4901 Auto Rd. SE, Salmon Arm, BC V1E 4S2
Tel: 250-832-6000; *Fax:* 250-832-5575
mascon@mascon.bc.ca
www.mascon.bc.ca

***Salmon Arm:* Sun Country Cablevision Ltd.**
PO Box 1360, 10 Harbourfront Dr. NE, Salmon Arm, BC V1E 4P5
Tel: 250-832-9711; *Fax:* 250-832-2146
info@sunwave.net
www.sunwave.net

***Salt Spring Island:* Saltspring Cablevision (1981) Ltd.**
PO Box 300, PO Ganges, Salt Spring Island, BC V8K 2V9
Tel: 250-537-5550; *Fax:* 250-537-5550
Linda Phillips
Geoff Phillips

***Valemount:* Valemount Entertainment Society/CHVC-TV Community Television**
PO Box 922, Valemount, BC V0E 2Z0
Tel: 250-566-8288; *Fax:* 250-566-4645
tv@vctv.ca
www.vctv.ca
Andru McCracken, Station Manager
Barb Riswok, Vice-President
Penni Osadchuk, Station Manager

***Vananda:* Texada Community TV Association**
PO Box 158, Vananda, BC V0N 3K0
Tel: 604-486-7640
Jack Cawthorpe

***Vancouver:* Okanagan Skeena Group Ltd.**
1130 West Pender St., Vancouver, BC V6E 4A4
Tel: 604-685-1160; *Fax:* 604-684-3537
H. McKinnon, President

***Vernon:* Shaw Cable**
2924 - 28 Ave., Vernon, BC V1T 8W6
Tel: 250-542-4007; *Fax:* 250-542-2928
Rennie Sirianni

***Victoria:* Shaw Cablesystems G.P.**
861 Cloverdale Ave., Victoria, BC V8X 4S7
Tel: 250-475-5655; *Fax:* 250-475-7289
eservice_victoria@sjrb.ca
www.shaw.ca

***Waglisla:* Heiltsuk Cablevision Co. Ltd.**
PO Box 880, Waglisla, BC V0T 1Z0
Tel: 250-957-2381; *Fax:* 250-957-2544

***Whistler:* Whistler Cable Television Ltd.**
PO Box 630, #214, 4368 Main St., Whistler, BC V0N 1B4
Tel: 604-932-1111; *Fax:* 604-932-1852
info@whistlercable.com
www.whistlercable.com
R.J. Saperstein

***Williams Lake:* Shaw Cablesystems (BC) Ltd.**
1290 Borland Rd., Williams Lake, BC V2G 3Y1
Tel: 250-392-3911; *Fax:* 250-392-8915

***Winfield:* Wood Lake Cable**
9570 Bottom Wood Lake Rd., Winfield, BC V4V 1S7
Tel: 250-766-3123; *Fax:* 250-766-3946
Toll-Free: 800-561-3699
info@wlcweb.com
www.woodlakecable.bc.ca
Darren Muloin, General Manager

Manitoba

***Brandon:* Westman Communications Group**
1906 Park Ave., Brandon, MB R7B 0R9
Tel: 204-725-4300; *Fax:* 204-726-0853
info@westmancom.com
www.westmancom.com
David Baxter, President/CEO, Marketing & Sales
Leo Boixain, Director, Technical Operations
David Baxter, President & CEO

***La Riviere:* La Riviere TV Club Inc.**
PO Box 132, La Riviere, MB R0G 1A0
Tel: 204-242-2189
Michael Currie

***Thompson:* Shaw Cable**
50 Selkirk Ave., Thompson, MB R8N 0M7
Tel: 204-778-8949; *Fax:* 204-677-9953
shawcable11@yahoo.ca
www,shaw.ca

New Brunswick

***Bathurst:* Rogers Cable**
PO Box 880, Bathurst, NB E2A 4H7
Tel: 506-549-8877; *Fax:* 506-549-6609

***Fredericton:* Rogers Cable**
377 York St., Fredericton, NB E3B 3P6
Tel: 506-462-3642; *Fax:* 506-452-2846
sdelong@rci.rogers.com
www.rogerstelevision.com

***Miramichi:* Rogers Cable**
454 King George Hwy., Miramichi, NB E1V 1M1
Tel: 506-778-3009; *Fax:* 506-778-3035
www.rogerstelevision.com

***Moncton:* Rogers Cable**
70 Assomption Blvd., Moncton, NB E1C 1A1
Tel: 506-388-8405; *Fax:* 506-388-8622
scott.jackson@rci.rogers.com
www.rogerstelevision.com
Serge Parent, Station Manager

***Saint John:* Rogers Cable**
60 Waterloo St., Saint John, NB E2L 3P3
www.rogerstelevision.com
James A. MacMurray, Chair
C. William Stanley, President & CEO

Newfoundland & Labrador

***Burgeo:* Burgeo Broadcasting System**
147 Reach Rd., Burgeo, NL A0M 1A0
Tel: 709-886-2935; *Fax:* 709-886-1243
www.bbsict.com/bbs/bbs.html
Claude Strickland, Operations Manager, claude@bbsict.ca
Marie Rose, Program Director

***Churchill Falls:* Churchill Falls Satellite TV Association**
PO Box 252, Churchill Falls, NL A0R 1A0
Tel: 709-925-3740; *Fax:* 709-925-8220
ehillier@cancom.net
Ted Hillier, President

***Glovertown:* Glovertown Cable TV Ltd.**
PO Box 131, Glovertown, NL A0G 2L0
Tel: 709-533-2377; *Fax:* 709-533-2702

***Happy Valley-Goose Bay:* CFS Cable**
PO Box 148 A, Happy Valley-Goose Bay, NL A0P 1S0
Tel: 709-896-6900; *Fax:* 709-896-6948
Reg Wells, Chair
Jean Noseworthy, Office Manager

***Labrador City:* Community Recreation Rebroadcasting Service Association/CRRS TV**
208 Amherst Ave., Labrador City, NL A2V 2Y5
Tel: 709-944-7676; *Fax:* 709-944-7675
info@crrstv.net
www.crrstv.net

***Lewisporte:* Phoenix Cable TV**
PO Box 939, 139 Main St., Lewisporte, NL A0G 3A0
Tel: 709-535-6771; *Fax:* 709-535-0417

***Musgravetown:* BMC Cablevision Co. Ltd.**
PO Box 16, Musgravetown, NL A0C 1Z0
Tel: 709-467-5306; *Fax:* 709-467-2489

***Ramea:* Ramea Broadcasting Co.**
PO Box 23, Ramea, NL A0M 1N0
Tel: 709-625-2618; *Fax:* 709-625-2048
samuel.fiander@nf.sympatico.ca
Samuel Fiander

***Reefs Harbour:* Clearview Cable Ltd.**
PO Box 10, Reefs Harbour, NL A0K 4L0
Tel: 709-847-7441; *Fax:* 709-847-7100
clearview.harold@nf.sympatico.ca
Harold G. Tucker, President/Manager

***St. John's:* Persona Communications Inc.**
PO Box 12155 A, 17 Duffy Place, St. John's, NL A1B 4L5
Tel: 709-754-3775; *Fax:* 709-754-3883
www.personainc.ca
Dean MacDonald, EO
Brendan Paddick, President & COO

Northwest Territories

***Deline:* Great Bear Co-operative**
PO Box 159, Deline, NT X0E 0G0
Tel: 867-589-3361; *Fax:* 867-589-4517

***Fort McPherson:* Tetlit Service Co-operative**
PO Box 27, Fort McPherson, NT X0E 0J0
Tel: 867-952-2417; *Fax:* 867-952-2606

***Fort Simpson:* HR Thomson**
PO Box 313, Fort Simpson, NT X0E 0N0
Tel: 867-695-3107; *Fax:* 867-695-2144
fortsim@cancom.net
Ivan Simons, Contact

** For details on this company see listing in Major Broadcasting Companies section; † French language station*

Fort Smith: **Gardtal Holdings Ltd.**
PO Box 478, Fort Smith, NT X0E 0P0
Tel: 867-872-3456; *Fax:* 867-872-5630
gardtal@northwestel.net
www.gardtal.com
Chad Dubanow, 867/872-0080

Yellowknife: **Northwestel Cable Inc.**
PO Box 1469, 5120 - 49th St., Yellowknife, NT X1A 2P1
Tel: 867-669-5469; *Fax:* 867-920-2331
Toll-Free: 800-661-0834

Nova Scotia

Canning: **Cross Country TV Ltd.**
PO Box 310, Canning, NS B0P 1H0
Tel: 902-678-2395; *Fax:* 902-678-2455
wireless@xcountry.tv
www.xcountry.tv

Cheticamp: **Acadien Communications Ltd.**
PO Box 648, Cheticamp, NS B0E 1H0
Tel: 902-224-2226; *Fax:* 902-224-3000
www.aclnet.ca/home/default.asp

Digby: **Eastlink Cable**
PO Box 1090, 88 Warwick St., Digby, NS B0V 1A0
Tel: 902-245-2519; *Fax:* 902-245-6511

Halifax: **EastLink**
PO Box 8660 A, Halifax, NS B3K 5M3
Tel: 902-453-2800; *Fax:* 902-446-4171
Toll-Free: 888-345-1111
www.eastlink.ca
Lee Bragg
Dan McKeen

Liverpool: **Eastlink Cable**
PO Box 449, 4130 Highway #3, Liverpool, NS B0T 1K0
Tel: 902-356-3588; *Fax:* 902-354-2246
www.eastlink.ca

Lower Sackville: **Eastlink Cable**
367 Sackville Dr., Lower Sackville, NS B4C 2R7
Tel: 902-446-3588; *Fax:* 902-453-5714
www.eastlink.ca

New Minas: **Eastlink Television**
PO Box 4000, 1001 How Ave., New Minas, NS B4N 4S8
Tel: 902-681-0300; *Fax:* 902-681-6470
www.eastlink.ca

Port Hawkesbury: **Rush Communications**
PO Box 790, 23 Paint St., Port Hawkesbury, NS B0E 2V0
Tel: 902-625-3320; *Fax:* 902-625-0064
Toll-Free: 888-769-2316
info@rushcomm.ca
www.rushcomm.ca

Reserve: **Seaside Communications**
PO Box 4558, 1318 Grand Lake Rd., Reserve, NS B1E 1L2
Tel: 902-539-6250; *Fax:* 902-539-2597
Toll-Free: 866-872-2253
www.seaside.ns.ca
Roland McCaffrey, General Manager, rmccaffrey@seaside.ns.ca

Shelburne: **Seabreeze Cablevision Ltd.**
PO Box 1090, 25B King St., Shelburne, NS B0T 1W0
Tel: 902-875-1267; *Fax:* 902-875-4219
www.eastlink.ca

Sydney: **Eastlink**
61 Melody Lane, Sydney, NS B1P 3K4
Tel: 902-539-9611; *Fax:* 902-564-5428
www.eastlink.ca
Paul Power, Contact

Truro: **Eastlink**
69 Walker St., Truro, NS B2N 4A8
Tel: 902-843-3588; *Fax:* 902-843-3067
www.eastlink.ca

Nunavut

Arctic Bay: **Taqqut Co-operative** *
General Delivery, Arctic Bay, NU X0A 0A0
Tel: 867-439-9934; *Fax:* 867-439-8765
info@arcticco-op.com
inuit.pail.ca/taqqut-co-op.htm

Arviat: **Padlei Co-operative Association**
PO Box 90, Arviat, NU X0C 0E0
Tel: 867-857-2933; *Fax:* 867-857-2762
info@arcticco-op.com
arcticco-op.com/co-op_location.html

Baker Lake: **Sanavik Co-op**
PO Box 69, Baker Lake, NU X0C 0A0
Tel: 867-793-2912; *Fax:* 867-793-2594
info@arcticco-op.com
www.arcticco-op.com/acl-keewatin-baker-lake.htm

Cambridge Bay: **Ikaluktutiak Cooperative Limited**
PO Box 38, Cambridge Bay, NU X0B 0C0
Tel: 867-983-2201; *Fax:* 867-983-2085
info@arcticco-op.com
www.arcticco-op.com/acl-kitikmeot-cambridge-bay.htm

Cape Dorset: **Kingait Cablevision**
PO Box 209, Cape Dorset, NU X0A 0C0
Tel: 867-897-8080; *Fax:* 867-897-8410
mikeperry@qiniq.com
capedorset.qiniq.com
Mike Perry, Contact

Chesterfield Inlet: **Pitsiulak Co-operative**
PO Box 500, General Delivery, Chesterfield Inlet, NU X0C 0B0
Tel: 867-898-9975; *Fax:* 867-898-9056
info@arcticco-op.com
www.arcticco-op.com/acl-keewatin-chesterfield-inlet.htm

Coral Harbour: **Katudgevik Cooperative**
PO Box 201, Coral Harbour, NU X0C 0C0
Tel: 867-925-9969; *Fax:* 867-925-8308
info@arcticco-op.com
www.arcticco-op.com/acl-keewatin-coral-habour.htm

Gjoa Haven: **Kekertak Co-operative**
PO Box 120, General Delivery, Gjoa Haven, NU X0E 1J0
Tel: 867-360-7271; *Fax:* 867-360-6018

Iqaluit: **Eastern Arctic TV Ltd.**
PO Box 730, Iqaluit, NU X0A 0H0
Tel: 867-979-6707; *Fax:* 867-979-2535

Kugluktuk: **Kugluktuk Co-operative**
PO Box 279, Kugluktuk, NU X0E 0E0
Tel: 867-982-4231; *Fax:* 867-982-3070
info@arcticco-op.com
www.arcticco-op.com/acl-kitikmeot-kugluktuk.htm

Qikiqtarjuaq: **Tulugaq Co-Op**
PO Box 8, Qikiqtarjuaq, NU X0A 0B0
Tel: 867-927-8061; *Fax:* 867-927-8044
info@arcticco-op.com
www.arcticco-op.com/acl-baffin-region-qikiqtarjuaq.htm

Rankin Inlet: **Kissarvik Co-Op**
PO Box 40, Rankin Inlet, NU X0C 0G0
Tel: 867-645-2801; *Fax:* 867-645-2280
info@arcticco-op.com
www.arcticco-op.com/acl-keewatin-rankin-inlet.htm

Repulse Bay: **Naujat Co-operative**
General Delivery, Repulse Bay, NU X0C 0H0
Tel: 867-462-9943; *Fax:* 867-462-4152
info@arcticco-op.com
www.arcticco-op.com/acl-keewatin-repulse-bay.htm

Whale Cove: **Issatik Eskimo Co-op Ltd.**
PO Box 60, Whale Cove, NU X0C 0J0
Tel: 867-896-9956; *Fax:* 867-896-9087
info@arcticco-op.com
www.arcticco-op.com/acl-keewatin-whale-cove.htm

Ontario

Aurora: **Aurora Cable Internet**
350 Industrial Pkwy. South, Aurora, ON L4G 3H3
Tel: 905-727-1981; *Fax:* 905-727-7407
info.aci@rci.rogers.com
www.aci.on.ca

Barrie: **Rogers Cable**
PO Box 8500, 1 Sperling Dr., Barrie, ON L4M 6B8
Tel: 705-737-4660; *Fax:* 705-737-0778
Toll-Free: 800-461-4349
www.rogers.com

Beardmore: **Beardmore Television**
PO Box 102, Beardmore, ON P0T 1G0
Tel: 807-875-2096

Belleville: **Cablevue (Quinte) Ltd.**
PO Box 149, 10 Front St. South, Belleville, ON K8N 4Z9
Tel: 613-966-3226; *Fax:* 613-966-5329

Brampton: **Rogers Community 10**
13 Hansen Rd. South, Brampton, ON L6W 3H6
Tel: 905-457-3270; *Fax:* 905-456-1067

Brockville: **COGECO Cable Canada LP**
PO Box 806, #13A, 333 California Ave., Brockville, ON K6V 5V5
Tel: 613-342-7414; *Fax:* 613-342-6521
ron.harrison@cogeco.com

Burlington: **COGECO Cable Canada LP**
950 Syscon Rd., Burlington, ON L7R 4S1
Tel: 905-333-5343; *Fax:* 905-332-8426
Toll-Free: 800-267-9000
www.cogeco.com
Louis Audet, President & Chief Executive Officer
Louise St-Pierre, Vice-President, Customer Services & Ontario Operations
Maureen Tilson Dyment, Senior Director, Programming & Communications
Glenda Lloyd, Manager, Communications, Glenda.Lloyd@cogeco.com

Chapleau: **Superior TV System**
PO Box 669, 31 Birch St., Chapleau, ON P0M 1K0
Tel: 705-864-1462; *Fax:* 705-864-1341
supertv@vianet.ca
Sandra Roposo, Manager

Chatham: **COGECO Cable Canada LP**
491 Richmond St., Chatham, ON N7M 1R2
Tel: 519-352-8810; *Fax:* 519-352-8274
www.tvcogeco.com
Peter Martin, Manager, Programming & Community Relations

Clifford: **Maitland Cable TV**
PO Box 70, 100 Elora St. North, Clifford, ON N0G 1M0
Tel: 519-327-8012; *Fax:* 519-327-8010
mcatv@wightman.ca
www.wightman.ca

Collingwood: **Rogers Cablesystems**
4 Sandford Fleming Dr., Collingwood, ON L9Y 4V9
Tel: 705-445-3400; *Fax:* 705-445-9949
David R. Scott, System Manager

Cornwall: **COGECO Cable Canada LP**
517 Pitt St., Cornwall, ON K6J 3R4
Tel: 613-937-2507; *Fax:* 613-932-3176
viewer@cogeco.ca

Dryden: **Shaw Cable**
75 Queen St., Dryden, ON P8N 1A1
Tel: 807-223-5525; *Fax:* 807-223-4445

Dublin: **Mitchell-Seaforth Cable TV Ltd.**
123 Ontario St., Dublin, ON N0K 1E0
Tel: 519-345-2341; *Fax:* 519-345-2873
Toll-Free: 800-360-1556
cabletv@ezlink.ca
www.ezlink.ca

Eganville: **Bonnechere Cable Co. Ltd.**
PO Box 209, 179 Bonnechere St. East, Eganville, ON K0J 1T0
Tel: 613-628-2727; *Fax:* 613-628-9258
William A. MacPhee, President

Fenelon Falls: **Cable Cable Inc.**
16 Cable Rd., Fenelon Falls, ON K0M 1M0
Tel: 705-887-6433; *Fax:* 705-887-2580
www.cablecable.net
Tony Fiorini, President

Fergus: **COGECO Cable Canada LP**
475 St. Patrick St. West, Fergus, ON N1M 1M2
Tel: 519-843-3700; *Fax:* 519—
www.tvcogeco.com

Fort Frances: **Shaw Cable**
1037 First St. East, Fort Frances, ON P9A 1L8
Tel: 807-274-5522; *Fax:* 807-274-0603

Geraldton: **Astrocom Cablevision Inc.**
PO Box 910, 109 Greer Ave. West, Geraldton, ON P0T 1M0
Tel: 807-854-1569; *Fax:* 807-854-2169
jim@astrocom-on.com
www.astrocom-on.com
John S. Emmans, President

** For details on this company see listing in Major Broadcasting Companies section; † French language station*

***Goderich:* EastLink TV**
PO Box 305, 141 Huckins St., Goderich, ON N7A 4C6
Tel: 519-482-9233; *Fax:* 519-482-7098
Toll-Free: 888-345-1111
cable@cabletv.on.ca
www.cabletv.on.ca

***Gore Bay:* Gore Bay Community TV**
PO Box 371, Gore Bay, ON P0P 1H0
Tel: 705-282-1595; *Fax:* 705-282-1595

***Gravenhurst:* COGECO Cable Canada LP**
205 Jones Rd., Gravenhurst, ON P1P 1M8
Tel: 705-687-8818; *Fax:* 705-687-4789
www.tvcogeco.com

***Guelph:* Rogers Cablesystems**
130 Silvercreek Pkwy., Guelph, ON N1H 7Y5
Tel: 519-824-1900; *Fax:* 519-824-4210
Toll-Free: 888-894-1172
rogerstvweb@rogers.com
www.rogerstelevision.com
Jeremy Clark, Regional Station Manager
Al Haggith, Manager, Network Operations
Gregory K. Grimes, Station Manager

***Hamilton:* Mountain Cablevision Ltd.**
141 Hester St., Hamilton, ON L9A 2N9
Tel: 905-389-1347; *Fax:* 905-574-6330
info@mountaincable.net
www.mountaincable.net
John King

***Hamilton:* Source Cable Ltd.**
1074 Upper Wellington St., Hamilton, ON L9A 3S6
Tel: 905-574-6465; *Fax:* 905-574-4909
info@sourcecable.ca
www.sourcecable.ca

***Hamilton:* TV Hamilton**
150 Dundurn St. South, Hamilton, ON L8P 4K3
Tel: 905-523-1414; *Fax:* 905-523-8141
events@cable14.com
www.cable14.com
Brent Rickert, General Manager

***Hanover:* Saugeen Telecable Ltd.**
111 - 7th Ave., Hanover, ON N4N 2G8
Tel: 519-364-2131; *Fax:* 519-364-4380

***Hawkesbury:* COGECO Cable Canada LP - Hawkesbury Office**
1444 Aberdeen St., Hawkesbury, ON K6A 1K7
Fax: 613-632-8531
ronald.handfield@cogeco.com
www.cogeco.ca
Louis Audet, CEO

***Huntsville:* COGECO Cable Canada LP**
20 West St. South, Huntsville, ON P1H 1P2
Tel: 705-789-9801; *Fax:* 705-789-2331
www.tvcogeco.com
Michael Bradley, General Manager
Norm Bradley, President

***Keewatin:* Norcom Telecommunications Ltd.**
102 - 10th St., Keewatin, ON P0X 1C0
Tel: 807-547-2853; *Fax:* 807-547-2236
info@norcomcable.ca
www.norcomcable.ca

***Kincardine:* Kincardine Cable TV Ltd.**
223 Bruce Ave., Kincardine, ON N2Z 2P2
Tel: 519-396-8880; *Fax:* 519-396-2599
kctv@tnt21.com
www.tnt21.com

***Kingston:* COGECO Cable Systems Inc.**
PO Box 5500 Main, 170 Colborne St., Kingston, ON K7L 5M7
Tel: 613-544-6311; *Fax:* 613-545-0169
cogeco.13@cogeco.com
www.cogeco.ca

***Kitchener:* Rogers Cable**
85 Grand Crest Pl., Kitchener, ON N2G 4A8
Tel: 519-893-2101; *Fax:* 519-893-5861

***London:* Rogers Cable**
800 York St., London, ON N6A 5B1
Tel: 519-672-0030; *Fax:* 519-672-0199

***Longlac:* Longlac Indian Reserve**
PO Box 609, Longlac, ON P0T 2A0
Tel: 807-876-2292; *Fax:* 807-876-2757

***Madoc:* Hastings Cable Vision Ltd.**
31 Durham St. South, Madoc, ON K0K 2K0
Tel: 613-473-2839; *Fax:* 613-473-4853

***Markdale:* Markdale Cable TV**
20 Eliza St., Markdale, ON N0C 1H0
Tel: 519-986-2262; *Fax:* 519-986-2612
marcable@cablerocket.com
www.markdalecabletv.com
Dave Armstrong, President

***Milton:* TVCogeco**
500 Laurier Ave., Milton, ON L9T 4R3
Tel: 905-878-9306; *Fax:* 905-878-7927
sandy.french@cogeco.com
www.cogeco.ca
Mike Hancock, Producer
Sandy French, Producer

***Mississauga:* Rogers Cablesystems**
3573 Wolfedale Rd., Mississauga, ON L5C 3T6
Tel: 905-897-3906; *Fax:* 905-273-9661

***Moose Factory:* Mocreebec Development Corporation Ltd.**
PO Box 4, Moose Factory, ON P0L 1W0
Tel: 705-658-4769; *Fax:* 705-658-4487

***Newmarket:* Rogers Cable Inc.**
395A Mulock Dr., Newmarket, ON L3Y 8P3
Tel: 905-896-7199; *Fax:* 905-898-7577

***Niagara Falls:* COGECO Cable Solutions**
7170 McLeod Rd., Niagara Falls, ON L2G 3H2
Tel: 905-374-2248; *Fax:* 905-374-2398
Toll-Free: 800-706-4221
www.cogeco.com

***North Bay:* COGECO Cable Canada LP**
PO Box 3170 Main, 240 Fee St., North Bay, ON P1B 8S4
Tel: 705-472-9868; *Fax:* 705-472-7854
www.tvcogeco.com
Melanie Miller, Production Supervisor

***Norwich:* Nor-Del Cablevision Ltd.**
PO Box 340, Norwich, ON N0J 1P0
Tel: 519-879-6527; *Fax:* 519-879-6387
Toll-Free: 800-563-1954
nordel@nor-del.com
www.nor-del.com
Glenn I. Baxter, President

***Oshawa:* Rogers Cable**
301 Marwood Dr., Oshawa, ON L1H 1J4
Tel: 905-436-4141; *Fax:* 905-579-5559
Toll-Free: 800-738-7893
durham@rci.rogers.com
www.rogerstelevision.com
Steve Simic, Station Manager

***Ottawa:* Rogers Cable**
475 Richmond Rd., Ottawa, ON K2A 3Y8
Tel: 613-728-2222; *Fax:* 613-728-9793
ottawa22@rci.rogers.com
www.rogerstelevision.com

***Pembroke:* COGECO Cable Solutions**
185 Lake St., Pembroke, ON K8A 5M1
Tel: 613-735-1228; *Fax:* 613-735-6177
www.cogeco.ca

***Port Perry:* Compton Cable TV Ltd.**
PO Box 73 Main, Port Perry, ON L9L 1A2
Tel: 905-985-8171; *Fax:* 905-985-0010
community10@compton.net
www.compton.net

***Richmond Hill:* Rogers Cable**
244 Newkirk Rd., Richmond Hill, ON L4C 3S5
Tel: 905-884-8111; *Fax:* 905-884-8151

***Sault Ste Marie:* Shaw Cablesystems G.P**
23 Manitou Dr., Sault Ste Marie, ON P6B 6GN
Tel: 705-946-2234; *Fax:* 705-946-4773
www.shaw.ca
Kevin Boll, Technical Manager

***Schreiber:* Shaw Cablesystems**
224 Park St., Schreiber, ON P0T 2S0
Tel: 807-824-2619; *Fax:* 807—

***Sudbury:* Persona Communications**
PO Box 4500, #15, 500 Barrydowne Rd., Sudbury, ON P3A 5W1
Tel: 705-560-1560; *Fax:* 705-560-8385
www.personainc.ca
Brendon Paddick, President & General Manager
Irv Whipple, Director, Engineering

***Thunder Bay:* Fibre-Tel Enterprises**
1043 Gorham St., Thunder Bay, ON P7B 4A5
Tel: 807-622-0100; *Fax:* 807-626-8282

***Thunder Bay:* Shaw Cablesystems**
1635 Paquette Rd., Thunder Bay, ON P7G 2J2
Tel: 807-766-7025; *Fax:* 807-766-7022
Toll-Free: 888-472-2222

***Toronto:* Rogers Cable**
855 York Mills Rd., Toronto, ON M3B 1Z1
Tel: 416-446-6500; *Fax:* 416-446-6658

***Val Gagne:* Val Gagne Communications Association**
PO Box 1, Val Gagne, ON P0K 1W0
Tel: 705-232-6952; *Fax:* 705-232-6303
vgca@ntl.sympatico.ca
Marcel R. Fortier, President/General Manager

***Westport:* North Leeds Cablecom Inc.**
PO Box 252, 1234 - 8th Concession, Westport, ON K0G 1X0
Tel: 613-273-7000; *Fax:* 613-273-2323
cable@rideau.net
www.brockville.com

***Windsor:* COGECO Cable Canada LP**
2525 Dougall Ave., Windsor, ON N8X 5A7
Tel: 519-972-6677; *Fax:* 519-972-6688
windsorcable11@wincom.net
www.cogeco.ca
Robert Scussolin, Programming and Community Relations

***Woodstock:* Rogers Cable**
PO Box 1208, 21 Ridgeway Circle, Woodstock, ON N4S 8P6
Tel: 519-539-8103; *Fax:* 519-539-7731
Toll-Free: 866-384-4422
joe.brown@rci.rogers.com
www.rogerstelevision.com

Prince Edward Island

***Summerside:* Eastlink**
PO Box 4 Main, Summerside, PE C1N 4P6
Tel: 902-436-2249; *Fax:* 902-436-5799

Québec

†*Albanel:* Télé-câble Albanel inc.
227, rue Principale, Albanel, QC G8M 3K3
Tél: 418-279-5940; *Téléc:* 418-279-3113
info@tcalbanel.com
www.tcalbanel.com
Fernand Plourde, Fondateur

†*Betsiamites:* Télécâble Pessamit
18, rue Messek, Betsiamites, QC G0H 1B0
Tél: 418-567-8863; *Téléc:* 418-567-8868
www.pessamit.ca

†*Brossard:* Cablevision SDM-TRP inc.
8285, boul Pelletier, Brossard, QC J4X 1P6
Tél: 450-671-4251; *Téléc:* 450-923-1873
Ligne sans frais: 800-465-9215
www.totalsat.qc.ca

†*Chicoutimi:* Cablo-Saguenay
70 Pric Rue Ouest, Chicoutimi, QC G7J 1G7
Tél: 418-696-1581; *Téléc:* 418-543-7995

†*Chisasibi:* Ginwat Cable Television Inc.
CP 420, Chisasibi, QC J0M 1E0
Tél: 819-855-2191; *Téléc:* 819-855-3186

***Drummondville:* COGECO Cable Canada LP**
1970, boul Lemire, Drummondville, QC J2B 6X5
Tel: 819-477-3978; *Fax:* 819-474-5313
tvcogeco.drummondville@cgocable.ca
www.cogeco.ca
Reno Longpré, Contact

†*Eaton:* Transvision inc.
2080, rue Spring, Eaton, QC J1M 2A2
Tél: 819-346-0760; *Téléc:* 819-346-5790

** For details on this company see listing in Major Broadcasting Companies section; † French language station*

†*Fermont:* Coopérative de la télévision communautaire de Fermont
CP 1379, 20, place Daviault, Fermont, QC G0G 1J0
Tél: 418-287-5443; *Téléc:* 418-287-5776

†*Grande-Rivière-Ouest:* Briand et Moreau Câble inc.
CP 63, 205 B, rue du Parc, Grande-Rivière-Ouest, QC G0C 1W0
Tél: 418-385-2680; *Téléc:* 418-385-3705
bmcable@bmcable.ca
www.bmcable.ca

†*Havre-Saint-Pierre:* R&T Communautaire Hâvre-St-Pierre
992, rue du Bouleau, Havre-Saint-Pierre, QC G0G 1P0
Tél: 418-538-2451; *Téléc:* 418-538-3870
info@cilemf.com
www.cilemf.com

†*La Malbaie:* Coopérative de câblodistribution de St-Fidèle
8, ch St-Paul, La Malbaie, QC G5A 2G6
Tél: 418-434-2486; *Téléc:* 418-434-1076
marcel.couturier@sympatico.ca
Marcel Couturier, Secrétaire

†*Labelle:* Télécâble Nordique inc.
CP 630, 128, boul Curé-Labelle, Labelle, QC J0T 1H0
Tél: 819-686-2662; *Ligne sans frais:* 800-293-8093

†*Lennoxville:* Transvision Réseau
#105, 175 Queen St., Lennoxville, QC J1M 1K1
Tél: 819-563-1001; *Téléc:* 819-563-3116
Ligne sans frais: 877-946-3116
www.transvision.net

†*Lourdes-de-Blanc-Sablon:* Coopérative de câblodistribution de Brest
1147, boul Dr.-Camille-Marcoux, Lourdes-de-Blanc-Sablon, QC G0G 1W0
Tél: 418-461-2003; *Téléc:* 418-461-2070

†*Magog:* Cable Axion inc.
250, ch de l'Axion, Magog, QC J1X 6J2
Tél: 819-843-0611; *Téléc:* 819-868-4249
Ligne sans frais: 866-552-9466
info@axion.ca
www.axion.ca
Paul Girard, Président

†*Magog:* COGECO Cable Canada LP
15, rue St-Patrice ouest, Magog, QC J1X 1V8
Tél: 819-843-3370; *Téléc:* 819-843-0698
tvcogeco.magog@cgocable.ca
www.cogeco.ca

†*Marsoui:* GD Télévision Enrg.
CP 118, Marsoui, QC G0E 1S0
Tél: 418-288-5591; *Téléc:* 418-288-1391
ghisde@globetrotter.net

†*Matagami:* Cablevision Matagami
3, rue Vanier, Matagami, QC J0Y 2A0
Tél: 819-739-2148; *Téléc:* 819-739-2612

†*Matane:* Tele-Cable Multi-Vision inc.
655, ch de la Greve, Matane, QC G4W 7A1
Tél: 418-562-1950
Raymond Vachon, Contact

†*Montréal:* Cable VDN Inc.
#206, 2600, rue Ontario est, Montréal, QC H2K 4K4
Tél: 514-522-1590; *Téléc:* 514-522-1568
info@vdn.ca
web.vdn.ca

†*Montréal:* COGECO Cable Canada LP
#915, 5 Place Ville-Marie, Montréal, QC H3B 2G2
Tél: 514-874-2600; *Téléc:* 514-874-2625
www.cogeco.ca

†*Montréal:* Vidéotron ltée
612, rue St-Jacques, Montréal, QC H3C 4M8
Tél: 514-281-1711
www.quebecor.com
Robert Dépatie, Président/Chef de la direction

†*Percé:* Télédistribution de la Gaspésie
CP 234, 155, Place du Quai, Percé, QC G0C 2L0
Tél: 418-782-5355; *Téléc:* 418-782-5407
TDG01@bmcable.ca
www.bmcable.ca

†*Québec:* Coopérative de câblodistribution de l'arrière-pays
20860, boul Henri-Bourassa, Québec, QC G2N 1P7
Tél: 418-849-7125; *Téléc:* 418-849-7128
info@ccapcable.com
www.ccapcable.com
Jacques Perron, Directeur général
Stephane Arseneau, Directeur, Service à la clientèle

†*Rimouski:* COGECO Cable Canada LP
384, av de la Cathédrale, Rimouski, QC G5L 5L1
Tél: 418-724-6058; *Téléc:* 418-724-7167
tvcogecorimouski@cogeco.com
www.cogeco.com

†*Rivière-Saint-Jean:* Télévision communautaire Rivière-St-Jean inc.
376, St-Jean/Poste Restante, Rivière-Saint-Jean, QC G0G 2N0
Tél: 418-949-2340
Jacques Lévesque, Président

***Rivière-du-Loup:* Le Cable de Rivière-du-Loup ltée**
279A, rue Lafontaine, CP 1390, Rivière-du-Loup, QC G5R 4L9
Tel: 418-867-1479; *Fax:* 418-867-2829
riviereduloup@canalvox.com
Pierre Simon, Président

†*Saint-Gabriel-de-Valcarti:* Valcartier Cable
1743, boul Valcartier, Saint-Gabriel-de-Valcarti, QC G0A 4S0
Tél: 418-844-3666; *Téléc:* 418-844-3030
mbaker@munsgdv.ca
www.saint-gabriel-de-valcartier.ca

†*Saint-Jean-des-Piles:* Gagnon et Fils Electronique Inc.
1470, rue Principale, Saint-Jean-des-Piles, QC G0X 2V0
Tél: 819-538-8508; *Téléc:* 819—

†*Saint-Just-de-Bretenières:* Coopérative de câblodistribution de Saint-Just-de-Bretenières
11, rue du Couvent, Saint-Just-de-Bretenières, QC G0R 3H0
Tél: 418-244-3560; *Téléc:* 418-244-3560
cablo-st-just@globetrotter.net
Réjean Poulin, Président

†*Saint-Pamphile:* Guy Chouinard Cable TV
CP 216, 9, rue de L'Église, Saint-Pamphile, QC G0R 3X0
Tél: 418-356-5276; *Téléc:* 418-356-5276

***Sainte-Adèle:* COGECO Cable Canada LP**
PO Box 1375, 605, Pierre-Péladeau, Sainte-Adèle, QC J8B 1Z3
Tel: 450-229-7668; *Fax:* 450-229-7910
tvcogeco.laurentides@cgocable.ca
www.cogeco.ca
Guy Goyer, Contact

†*Sainte-Jeanne-d'Arc:* Cable FB
480, rue Principale, Sainte-Jeanne-d'Arc, QC G0W 1E0
Tél: 418-276-5309; *Téléc:* 418-276-1891
G. Gauthier

†*Sainte-Thècle:* Télécâble Groleau inc.
CP 22, 120, route 352, Sainte-Thècle, QC G0X 3G0
Tél: 418-289-2871; *Téléc:* 418-289-3871
grolo@globetrotter.net
Aurel Groleau, Contact

***Sanikiluaq:* Mitiq Co-operative**
General Delivery, Sanikiluaq, QC X0A 0W0
Tel: 867-266-8860; *Fax:* 867-266-8844
info@arcticco-op.com
www.arcticco-op.com/acl-baffin-region-sanikiluaq.htm

***Sept-Iles:* COGECO Cable Canada LP**
410, rue Evangeline, Sept-Iles, QC G4R 2N5
Tel: 418-962-3508; *Fax:* 418-962-3531

***Shannon:* Shannon Vision inc.**
50, rue St. Patrick, Shannon, QC G0A 4N0
Tel: 418-844-3849; *Fax:* 418-844-0347

***Shawinigan:* COGECO Cable Canada LP**
1222, 47e rue, Shawinigan, QC G9N 5B4
Tel: 819-539-9501; *Fax:* 819-539-6789
www.cogeco.ca

***Sillery:* Genex Communications Inc.**
#300, 1134, Grande-Allée, Sillery, QC G1S 1E5
Tel: 418-687-9810; *Fax:* 418-682-8427
patrice.demers@genexcommunications.com
www.choiradiox.com
Patrice Demers

***St-Georges-de-Beauce:* COGECO Cable Canada LP**
11197 - 2e av, St-Georges-de-Beauce, QC G5Y 1V9
Tel: 418-228-9828; *Fax:* 418-228-3015
tvcogeco.beauce@cgocable.ca
www.cogeco.ca

†*St-Zacharie:* Cablovision ACL Enr
515, 9e Avenue, St-Zacharie, QC G0M 2C0
Tél: 418-593-5262; *Téléc:* 418-593-3260

†*Ste-Catherine-de-la-Jacques-Cartier:* Coopérative de câblodistribution Ste-Catherine-Fossambault
130, rue Désiré-Juneau, Ste-Catherine-de-la-Jacques-Cartier, QC G3N 2X3
Tél: 418-875-1118; *Téléc:* 418-875-1971
gestion@coopcscf.com
www.coopcscf.com

†*Thetford Mines:* COGECO Cable Canada LP
39 - 10e Rue Sud, Thetford Mines, QC G6G 7X6
Tél: 418-338-2079; *Téléc:* 418-335-9125
tvcogeco.thetford@cgocable.ca
www.cogeco.ca

***Trois-Rivières:* COGECO Câble Québec inc.**
1630 - 6e rue, Trois-Rivières, QC G8Y 5B8
Tel: 819-693-8353; *Fax:* 819-379-2232
www.cgocable.ca
Jean-Guy Proulx, Contact

†*Val-D'Or:* Cablevision du Nord de Québec inc.
45, boul de Hôtel de Ville, Val-D'Or, QC J9P 2M5
Tél: 819-825-5133; *Ligne sans frais:* 800-567-6353
www.cablevision.qc.ca
Bernard Gauthier, Président

†*Warwick:* Cablovision Warwick inc.
CP 999, 14, boul Beaumier, Warwick, QC J0A 1M0
Tél: 819-358-5858; *Téléc:* 819-358-5592
service@cablovision.com
www.cablovision.com

†*Waswanipi:* Waswanipi Cable TV
20 Poplar St., Waswanipi, QC J0Y 3C0
Tél: 819-753-2557; *Téléc:* 819-753-2555

Saskatchewan

***Arcola:* Town of Arcola**
PO Box 359, Arcola, SK S0C 0G0
Tel: 306-455-2212; *Fax:* 306-455-2445
arcadmin@sasktel.net
www.creda.sk.ca/arcola/

***Birch Hills:* Northern Native Public Broadcasting Inc.**
PO Box 204, Birch Hills, SK S0J 0G0
Tel: 306-749-2578; *Fax:* 306—

***Craik:* Craik Cablevision**
PO Box 60, Craik, SK S0G 0V0
Tel: 306-734-2250; *Fax:* 306-734-2688
town.craik@sasktel.net
www.craik.ca
Rod Haugerud, Mayor
Jason Kemp

***Esterhazy:* Leaf Cable Inc.**
PO Box 1540, Esterhazy, SK S0A 0X0
Tel: 306-745-3592; *Fax:* 306-745-3597
Toll-Free: 866-484-0344
Mark Larsen, President
Glenda Colbourne, Manager

***Ile-a-la-Crosse:* Ile a la Crosse Communications Society Inc.**
PO Box 480, Ile-a-la-Crosse, SK S0M 1C0
Tel: 306-833-2173; *Fax:* 306-833-2042
ilexcomm@sk.sympatico.ca
Mike Bouvier, Manager

***Imperial:* Imperial Cable System**
PO Box 90, Imperial, SK S0G 2J0
Tel: 306-963-2220; *Fax:* 306-963-2445
town.imperial@sasktel.net

***Kinistino:* Kinistino Cable TV**
PO Box 10, Kinistino, SK S0J 1H0
Tel: 306-864-2461; *Fax:* 306-864-2880
townofkinistino@sasktel.net
Leonard Margolis
Shirley Jackson

* *For details on this company see listing in Major Broadcasting Companies section; † French language station*

La Ronge: **Cable Ronge Inc.**
PO Box 1397, La Ronge, SK S0J 1L0
Tel: 306-425-2276; *Fax:* 306-425-2042
marley@cableronge.sk.ca
www.cableronge.sk.ca
Marilyn Chernoff, General Manager

Limerick: **Village of Limerick**
PO Box 129, Limerick, SK S0H 2P0
Tel: 306-263-2020; *Fax:* 306-263-2013
Tammy Franks, Administrator

Moose Jaw: **Shaw Cable**
201 Manitoba St. East, Moose Jaw, SK S6H 0A4
Tel: 306-693-8585; *Fax:* 306-692-4859

Moose Jaw: **Shaw Cable Moose Jaw.**
201 Manitoba St. East, Moose Jaw, SK S6H 0A4
Tel: 306-693-8585; *Fax:* 306-692-4859
Bob Anderson, Regional Manager
Jim Shaw Jr., Chief Officer

North Battleford: **Access Communications Co-operative Ltd.**
1192 - 99 St., North Battleford, SK S9A 0P3
Tel: 306-445-4045; *Fax:* 306-445-0755
Toll-Free: 866-363-2225
help@accesscomm.ca
www.accesscomm.ca
Jim Deane, President/CEO
Trevor Derksen, Vice-President, Marketing & Sales
Carmela Haines, Vice-President, Finance & Administr

Ponteix: **Ponteix T.V. Club**
PO Box 684, Ponteix, SK S0N 1Z0
Tel: 306-625-3884; *Fax:* 306-625-3204
Dennis Ward

Prince Albert: **Shaw Cable Prince Albert**
2990 - 2nd Ave. West, Prince Albert, SK S6V 7E9
Tel: 306-922-0202; *Fax:* 306-922-7122

Regina: **Access Communications Co-operative Ltd.**
2250 Park St., Regina, SK S4N 7K7
Tel: 306-569-3510; *Fax:* 306-565-5395
Toll-Free: 866-363-2225
help@accesscomm.ca
www.accesscomm.ca
Jim Deane, President & CEO
Trevor Derksen, Vice-President, Marketing & Sales
Carmela Haines, Vice-President, Finance & Administr

Rouleau: **Rouleau Cable TV Association Inc.**
PO Box 250, Rouleau, SK S0G 4H0
Tel: 306-776-2270; *Fax:* 306-776-2482

Saskatoon: **Askivision Systems Inc.**
826 - 57th St. East, Saskatoon, SK S7K 5Z1
Tel: 519-686-0909; *Fax:* 519-686-1916
Toll-Free: 800-819-9718
cs@aski.ca
www.aski.ca
Don Wolhberg, President
Michelle Kimmett, General Manager

Saskatoon: **Shaw Cable**
2326 Hanselman Ave., Saskatoon, SK S7L 5Z3
Tel: 306-664-2121; *Fax:* 306-244-0105

Southey: **Southey Cable**
PO Box 248, Southey, SK S0G 4P0
Tel: 306-726-2202; *Fax:* 306-726-2916
www.southey.ca
C. Flaman

Swift Current: **Shaw Cable**
15 Dufferin St. West, Swift Current, SK S9H 5A1
Tel: 306-773-7218; *Fax:* 306-773-6421

Weyburn: **Access Communications Co-operative Ltd.**
120 - 10th Ave., Weyburn, SK S4H 1G9
Tel: 306-842-0320; *Fax:* 306-842-3465
Toll-Free: 866-363-2225
help@accesscomm.ca
www.accesscomm.ca
Jim Deane, President & CEO
Carmela Haines, Vice-President, Finance & Administr

Yorkton: **Image Wireless Communications - a division of YOURLINK Inc.**
PO Box 20051, 552 D Broadway Ave. East, Yorkton, SK S3N 4A9
Tel: 306-782-4388; *Fax:* 306-786-7686
Toll-Free: 888-462-4388
talk2us@imagewireless.ca
www.imagewireless.ca

Young: **Village of Young**
PO Box 359, Young, SK S0K 4Y0
Tel: 306-259-2242; *Fax:* 306-259-2247
villageofyoung2@sasktel.net
Robert Speiser, Mayor

Yukon Territory

Dawson City: **Dawson City Cable**
PO Box 308, Dawson City, YT Y0B 1G0
Tel: 867-993-7400; *Fax:* 867-993-7434
cityofdawson@yknet.ca

Whitehorse: **Northern Television Systems Ltd.**
#203, 4103 - 4th Ave., Whitehorse, YT Y1A 1H6
Tel: 867-393-2225; *Fax:* 867-393-2224
info@whtvcable.com
www.whtvcable.com

Specialty Broadcasters

Alberta

Calgary: **Max Trax**
#501, 630 - 3 Ave. SW, Calgary, AB T2P 4L4
Tel: 403-444-4233; *Fax:* 403-444-4240
www.corusmaxtrax.com

Edmonton: **CourtTV Canada**
10212 Jasper Ave., Edmonton, AB T5J 5A3
Tel: 780-440-7777; *Fax:* 780-440-8899
info@courttvcanada.ca
www.courttvcanada.ca

Edmonton: **Movie Central**
#200, 5324 Calgary Trail, Edmonton, AB T6H 4J8
Tel: 780-430-2800; *Fax:* 780-437-3188
web.moviecentral@corusent.com
www.moviecentral.ca

British Columbia

Burnaby: **Knowledge Network**
4355 Mathissi Pl., Burnaby, BC V5G 4S8
Tel: 604-431-3222; *Fax:* 604-431-3387
Toll-Free: 877-456-6988
knonline@knowledgenetwork.ca
www.knowledgenetwork.ca
Wayne Robert, General Manager

Richmond: **Talentvision TV**
3300-4151 Hazelbridge Way, Richmond, BC V6X 4J7
Tel: 604-295-1328; *Fax:* 604-295-1300
info@fairchildtv.com
www.talentvisiontv.com
Joseph Chan

Manitoba

Winnipeg: **Aboriginal Peoples Television Network**
339 Portage Ave., Winnipeg, MB R3B 2C3
Tel: 204-947-9331; *Fax:* 204-947-9307
Toll-Free: 888-330-2786
info@aptn.ca
www.aptn.ca
Social Media: www.facebook.com/pages/APTN/88781789916
Jean LaRose, CEO
Peter Strutt, Director, Programming
Vera Houle, Director, News & Current Affairs
Ken Earl, Director, Human Resources
Wayne McKenzie, Director, Operations
Sky Bridges, Director, Marketing
Jamie Veilleux, CFO

Winnipeg: **CoolTV**
#2100, One Lombard Pl., Winnipeg, MB R3B 0X3
Fax: 204-926-4853
Toll-Free: 866-729-7140
contactus@globaltv.ca
www.canada.com/topics/entertainment/tvchannels/cooltv

Winnipeg: **Dejaview**
#2100, One Lombard Pl., Winnipeg, MB R3B 0X3
Fax: 204-926-4653
Toll-Free: 866-729-7140
contactus@globaltv.ca
www.canada.com/topics/entertainment/tvchannels/dejaview

Winnipeg: **Fox Sports World Canada**
#2100, One Lombard Pl., Winnipeg, MB R3B 0X3
Fax: 204-926-4853
Toll-Free: 866-729-7140
contactus@globaltv.com
www.canada.com/topics/entertaintment/tvchannels/foxsports/

Winnipeg: **Lonestar**
#2100, One Lombard Pl., Winnipeg, MB R3B 0X3
Fax: 204-926-4853
Toll-Free: 866-729-7140
contactus@globaltv.ca
www.canada.com/topics/entertainment/tvchannels/lonestar

Winnipeg: **MenTV**
#2100, One Lombard Pl., Winnipeg, MB R3B 0X3
Fax: 204-926-4853
Toll-Free: 866-729-7140
contactus@globaltv.com
www.canada.com/topics/entertainment/tvchannels/mentv

Winnipeg: **Mystery**
#2100, One Lombard Pl., Winnipeg, MB R3B 0X3
Fax: 204-926-4853
Toll-Free: 866-729-7140
contactus@globaltv.com
www.canada.com/topics/entertainment/tvchannels/mystery

Winnipeg: **Xtreme Sports**
#2100, One Lombard Pl., Winnipeg, MB R3C 0X3
Fax: 204-926-4853
Toll-Free: 866-729-7140
contacus@globaltv.ca
www.canada.com/topics/entertainment/tvchannels/xtremesports

Nova Scotia

Halifax: **Independent Film Channel Canada**
#103, 1649 Brunswick St., Halifax, NS B3J 2G3
Tel: 902-423-2662; *Fax:* 902-423-7862
viewercomments-hfx@ifctv.ca
www.ifctv.ca
John Gill, Sr. Vice-President, Drama
Emily Morgan, Vice-President, Programming, Showcase Action, Showcase Diva

Nunavut

Yellowknife: **CBC North**
CBC Mackenzie, PO Box 160, 5002 Forrest Dr., Yellowknife, NWT X1A 2N2
Tel: 867-920-5400; *Toll-Free:* 866-306-4636
www.cbc.ca/north
Social Media:
www.facebook.com/group.php?gid=481521000412
Sue Glowach, Senior Officer, Communications, 867-669-3531, Fax: 867-669-3573
Donna Lee, Contact, CBC North News, 867-920-5448

Ontario

Burlington: **CTS - Crossroads TV System**
1295 North Service Rd., Burlington, ON L7R 4X5
Tel: 905-331-7333; *Fax:* 905-331-7222
cts@ctstv.com
www.ctstv.com
Dick Gray, President
Lorne Freed, Director, Programming & Operations

King City: **TrackPower**
765 - 15th Sideroad, King City, ON L7B 1K5
Tel: 905-773-1987; *Fax:* 905-773-1241
info@trackpower.com
www.trackpower.com

Mississauga: **BITE Television**
2196 Dunwin Dr., Mississauga, ON L5L 1C7
Tel: 905-828-2483; *Fax:* 905-828-7660
info@bite.ca
www.bitetv.ca
Jeffrey Elliot, Co-CEO/Manager, Marketing & Sales
Raja Khanna, Co-CEO, Finance
Simon Foster, Director, Sales, 905-828-2483, X, simon@glassbox.tv

** For details on this company see listing in Major Broadcasting Companies section; † French language station*

Sharon Stevens, Director, Programming, 905-828-2483, X, sharon@glassbox.tv

Mississauga: Shaw Broadcast Services
2055 Flavelle Blvd., Mississauga, ON L5K 1Z8
Tel: 905-403-2020; *Fax:* 905-403-2022
Toll-Free: 800-268-2943
www.shawbroadcast.com

Mississauga: The Shopping Channel
59 Ambassador Dr., Mississauga, ON L5T 2P9
Tel: 905-362-2020
www.theshoppingchannel.com

Newmarket: Asian Television Network
130 Pony Dr., Newmarket, ON L3Y 7B6
Tel: 905-836-6460; *Fax:* 905-853-5212
atn@asiantelevision.com
www.asiantelevision.com
Shan Chandrasekar, President/CEO/Founder
Jaya Chandrasekar, Executive Vice-President/Vice-Presi
Prakash Naidoo, Vice-President, Operations/General

North York: Telelatino Network Inc.
5125 Steeles Ave. West, North York, ON M9L 1R5
Tel: 416-744-8200; *Fax:* 416-744-0966
Toll-Free: 800-551-8401
info@tlntv.com
www.tlntv.com
Aldo DiFelice, President

Oakville: The Weather Network
2655 Bristol Circle, Oakville, ON L6H 7W1
Tel: 905-829-1159; *Fax:* 905-829-5800
www.theweathernetwork.com
Pierre L. Morrissette

Ottawa: CPAC
PO Box 81099, Ottawa, ON K1P 1B1
Tel: 613-567-2722; *Fax:* 613-567-2741
Toll-Free: 877-287-2722
comments@cpac.ca
www.cpac.ca

Ottawa: The Green Channel
342 MacLaren St., Ottawa, ON K2P 0M6
Tel: 613-238-4580; *Fax:* 613-238-5642
info@wetv.com
www.wetv.com

Toronto: Animal Planet
9 Channel Nine Ct., Toronto, ON M1S 4B5
Tel: 416-332-5000; *Fax:* 416-332-4230
comments@animalplanet.ca
www.animalplanet.ca
Social Media: twitter.com/animalplanetca

Toronto: BBC Canada
#200, 121 Bloor St. East, Toronto, ON M4W 3M5
Tel: 416-967-3249; *Fax:* 416-967-0044
Toll-Free: 866-813-3222
www.bbccanada.com

Toronto: BBC Kids
#200, 121 Bloor St. East, Toronto, ON M4W 3M5
Tel: 416-967-3250; *Toll-Free:* 866-322-2543
www.bbckids.ca

Toronto: The Biography Channel
545 Lakeshore Blvd. West, Toronto, ON M5V 1A3
Tel: 416-260-0033; *Fax:* 416-260-3810
Toll-Free: 866-260-0033
info@thebiographychannel.ca
www.thebiographychannel.ca
Malcolm Dunlop, Vice-President, Marketing & Programming
Andrea Gagliardi, Director, Consumer Marketing & Public Relations

Toronto: BookTelevision
299 Queen St. West, Toronto, ON M5V 2Z5
Tel: 416-591-7400; *Fax:* 416-591-5117
info@booktelevision.com
www.booktelevision.com
Catherine McCutcheon, Director, Specialty Sales, CTVglobe, sales@ctv.ca

Toronto: BPM: TV
105 Gordon Baker Rd., 8th Fl., Toronto, ON M2H 3P8
Tel: 416-756-2404; *Fax:* 416-756-5526
info@stornoway.com
www.stornoway.com
Martha Fusca, President/CEO, mfusca@stornoway.com
David Vowell, Director, Marketing, dvowell@stornoway.com
Cindy Boyd, Operations Manager, cboyd@stornoway.com

Toronto: Bravo! The New Style Arts Channel
299 Queen St. West, Toronto, ON M5V 2Z5
Tel: 416-591-5757; *Fax:* 416-591-7482
bravomail@bravo.ca
www.bravo.ca

Toronto: Canadian Learning Television
CHUM Ltd., 299 Queen St. West, Toronto, ON M5V 2Z5
Tel: 416-591-7400; *Fax:* 416-591-5117
info@clt.ca
www.clt.ca
Ron Keast, President & CEO
Peter Palframan, Vice-President, Finance & Operations
Ross Mayot, Vice-President, Development

Toronto: CBC News Network
PO Box 500 A, Toronto, ON M5W 1E6
Toll-Free: 866-306-4636
www.cbc.ca/news; www.cbc.ca/programguide/daily/today/cbc_news_network
Social Media: www.facebook.com/newscbc; www.twitter.com/cbcnews
Other information: TDD: 1-866-220-6045
Roger Ramalsingh, Affiliate Relations Officer

Toronto: The Christian Channel
#230, 171 East Liberty St., Toronto, ON M6K 3P6
Tel: 416-368-3194; *Fax:* 416-368-9774
info@christianchannel.ca
www.christianchannel.ca
Mark Prasuhn, President & General Manager

Toronto: The Comedy Network
9 Channel Nine Ct., Toronto, ON M1S 4B5
Tel: 416-332-5300; *Fax:* 416-332-5301
mail@thecomedynetwork.ca
www.thecomedynetwork.ca
Ed Robinson, President & General Manager

Toronto: Country Canada
PO Box 500 A, Toronto, ON M5W 1E6
Toll-Free: 866-306-4636
cbccountrycanada.ca

Toronto: Country Music Television
#18, 64 Jefferson Ave., Toronto, ON M6K 3H4
Tel: 416-534-1191; *Fax:* 416-530-5206
www.cmtcanada.com
John P. Wright

Toronto: CP24
299 Queen St. West, Toronto, ON M5V 2Z5
Tel: 416-591-5757; *Fax:* 416-593-6397
now@cp24.com
www.cp24.com

Toronto: CTV News Channel
Owned by: **CTVglobemedia Inc.***
9 Channel Nine Ct., Toronto, ON M1S 4B5
Tel: 416-384-5000
ctvcommunications@ctv.ca
www.ctv.ca/newschannel/

Toronto: The Discovery Channel
PO Box 1200, 9 Channel Nine Ct., Toronto, ON M1S 5R6
Tel: 416-332-5000
comments@discovery.ca
discoverychannel.ca

Toronto: Discovery Civilization
PO Box 1200, 9 Channel Nine Ct., Toronto, ON M1S 4R6
Tel: 416-332-5000; *Fax:* 416-332-4245
comments@discoverycivilization.ca
discoverycivilization.ca

Toronto: Discovery Health Channel
#200, 121 Bloor St. East, Toronto, ON M4W 3M5
Tel: 416-967-3248; *Toll-Free:* 866-967-3248
www.discoveryhealth.ca

Toronto: Discovery Kids Canada
#18, 64 Jefferson St., Toronto, ON M6K 3H4
Tel: 416-534-1191; *Fax:* 416-588-6987
www.discoverykids.ca

Toronto: Distribution Access
#702, 27 Queen St. East, Toronto, ON M5C 2M6
Tel: 416-363-6765; *Fax:* 416-363-7834
ontariosales@distributionaccess.com
www.distributionaccess.com/new/main.cfm
Doug Connolly, President/COO, doug.connolly@distributionaccess.com
Peter Palframan, CEO/Secretary-Treasurer

Toronto: documentary
PO Box 500 A, Toronto, ON M6W 1E6
Toll-Free: 866-306-4636
www.cbc.ca/documentarychannel/
Michael Burns, Director of Programming

Toronto: Drive-In Classics
299 Queen St. West, Toronto, ON M5V 2Z5
Tel: 416-591-7400
driveinclassics@driveinclassics.ca
www.driveinclassics.ca

Toronto: ESPN Classic Canada
9 Channel Nine Ct., Toronto, ON M1S 4B5
Tel: 416-332-5000; *Fax:* 416-332-7657
www.tsn.ca/classic

Toronto: The Family Channel Inc.
BCE Place, PO Box 787, 181 Bay St., Toronto, ON M5J 2T3
Tel: 416-956-2030; *Fax:* 416-956-2035
Toll-Free: 800-893-4862
info@family.ca
www.family.ca
Joe Tedesco, Vice-President & General Manager

Toronto: Fashion TV
299 Queen St. West, Toronto, ON M5V 2Z5
Tel: 416-591-5757; *Fax:* 416-591-3545
fashion@citytv.com
www.fashiontelevision.com

Toronto: Fine Living
#200, 121 Bloor St. East, Toronto, ON M4W 3M5
Tel: 416-967-3260; *Fax:* 416-960-0971
feedback@fineliving.ca
www.fineliving.ca

Toronto: Food Network Canada
121 Bloor St. East, Toronto, ON M4W 3M5
Tel: 416-967-1174
foodtv.ca

Toronto: G4techTV
545 Lakeshore Blvd. West, Toronto, ON M5V 1A3
Tel: 416-260-0047; *Fax:* 416-260-3810
Toll-Free: 866-260-0055
info@g4techtv.ca
www.g4techtv.ca
Andrea Gagliardi, Director, Consumer Marketing & Public Relations
Malcolm Dunlop, Vice-President, Marketing & Programming

Toronto: HGTV Canada
#200, 121 Bloor St. East, Toronto, ON M4W 3M5
Tel: 416-967-3246; *Fax:* 416-967-0971
feedback@hgtv.ca
www.hgtv.ca

Toronto: History Television Inc.
#200, 121 Bloor St. East, Toronto, ON M4W 3M5
Tel: 416-967-3252; *Fax:* 416-960-0971
feedback@historytelevision.ca
www.historytelevision.ca
Phyllis Yaffe, President/CEO
Bill Dawson, Senior Vice-President

Toronto: Home & Garden Television
#200, 121 Bloor St. East, Toronto, ON M4W 3M5
Tel: 416-967-0022; *Fax:* 416-960-0971
feedback@hgtv.ca
hgtv.ca

Toronto: HPItv
PO Box 156, 555 Rexdale Blvd., Toronto, ON M9W 5L2
Tel: 416-675-3993
www.horseplayerinteractive.com

Toronto: HPItv Canada
PO Box 156, 555 Rexdale Blcd., Toronto, ON M9W 5L2
Tel: 416-675-3993; *Fax:* 416-213-2138
www.horseplayerinteractive.com

Toronto: HPItv International
PO Box 156, 555 Rexdale Blvd., Toronto, ON M9W 5L2
Tel: 416-675-3993; *Fax:* 416-213-2138
www.horseplayerinteractive.com

Toronto: HPItv Odds
PO Box 156, 555 Rexdale Blvd., Toronto, ON M9W 5L2
Tel: 416-675-3993
www.horseplayerinteractive.com

** For details on this company see listing in Major Broadcasting Companies section; † French language station*

***Toronto:* HPItv West**
PO Box 156, 555 Rexdale Blvd., Toronto, ON M9W 5L2
Tel: 416-675-3993; *Fax:* 416-213-2138
www.horseplayerinteractive.com

***Toronto:* Ichannel**
Stornoway Communications, 115 Gordon Baker Rd., 8th Fl., Toronto, ON M2G 3R6
Tel: 416-756-2404; *Fax:* 416-756-5526
comments@ichannel.ca
www.ichannel.ca

***Toronto:* Leafs TV**
307 Lakeshore Blvd. East, Toronto, ON M5A 1C1
Tel: 416-815-2400; *Fax:* 416-681-9181
www.mapleleafs.com

***Toronto:* Movieola - The Short Film Channel**
2844 Dundas St. West, Toronto, ON M6P 1Y7
Tel: 416-492-1595; *Fax:* 416-492-9539
info@movieola.ca
www.movieola.ca

***Toronto:* MOVIEPIX**
PO Box 787, #100, 181 Bay St., Toronto, ON M5J 2T3
Tel: 416-956-2010; *Fax:* 416-956-2018
www.moviepix.ca
Karen Spierkel, Vice-President, Communications
Lisa de Wilde, President & CEO

***Toronto:* MTV Canada**
888 Yonge St., Toronto, ON M4W 2J2
Tel: 416-355-3888; *Fax:* 416-355-3993
info@mtvcanada.ca
www.mtvcanada.ca

***Toronto:* MuchLOUD**
299 Queen St. West, Toronto, ON M5V 2Z5
Tel: 416-591-7400; *Fax:* 416-591-0080
muchloud@muchmusic.com
www.muchloud.com

***Toronto:* MuchMore Music**
299 Queen St. West, Toronto, ON M5V 2Z5
Tel: 416-591-5757
muchmoremail@muchmusic.com
www.muchmoremusic.com

***Toronto:* MuchMoreRetro**
299 Queen St. West, Toronto, ON M5V 2Z5
Tel: 416-591-5757; *Fax:* 416-591-0080
request@muchmoreretro.com
www.muchmoreretro.com

***Toronto:* MuchMusic Network**
299 Queen St. West, Toronto, ON M5V 2Z5
Tel: 416-591-5757
muchmail@muchmusic.com
www.muchmusic.com
Denise Donlon, Vice-President/General Manager

***Toronto:* MuchVibe**
299 Queen St. West, Toronto, ON M5V 2Z5
Tel: 416-591-5757
muchvibe@muchmusic.com
www.muchvibe.ca

***Toronto:* National Geographic Channel**
#200, 121 Bloor St. East, Toronto, ON M4W 3M5
Tel: 416-967-3251; *Toll-Free:* 866-967-3251
www.nationalgeographic.ca

***Toronto:* NHL Network**
9 Channel Nine Ct., Toronto, ON M1S 4B5
Tel: 416-332-5000; *Fax:* 416-324-675
audiencerelations@tsn.ca
www.tsn.ca/nhl_network/

***Toronto:* Odyssey**
#300, 437 Danforth Ave., Toronto, ON M4K 1P1
Tel: 416-462-1200; *Fax:* 416-462-1818
info@odysseytv.ca
www.odysseytv.ca
Peter Maniatakos

***Toronto:* One: the Body, Mind & Spirit Channel**
Liberty Market Bldg., #230, 171 East Liberty St., Toronto, ON M6K 3P6
Tel: 416-595-6465; *Fax:* 416-368-9774
Toll-Free: 877-872-7480
www.onebodymindspirit.com
Bill Roberts, Chair/CEO
Mark Prasuhn, General Manager/COO

***Toronto:* Ontario Legislature Broadcast & Recording Service**
Legislative Bldg., Queen's Park, Toronto, ON M7A 1A2
Tel: 416-325-7900; *Fax:* 416-325-7916
www.ontla.on.ca
Bill Somerville

***Toronto:* Outdoor Life Network Canada**
9 Channel Nine Ct., Toronto, ON M1S 4B5
Tel: 416-332-7660; *Fax:* 416-332-5861
olncanada@ctv.ca
www.tsn.ca/oln

***Toronto:* OUTtv**
#200, 491 Church St., Toronto, ON M4Y 2C6
Tel: 416-979-2900; *Fax:* 416-979-1300
inquiries@pridevision.com
www.outtv.ca

***Toronto:* The Pet Network**
115 Gordon Baker Rd., 8th Fl., Toronto, ON M2H 3R6
Tel: 416-756-2404; *Fax:* 416-756-5526
www.mypetnetwork.tv

***Toronto:* Pridevision TV**
200, 491 Church St., Toronto, ON M4Y 2C6
Tel: 416-979-2900; *Fax:* 416-979-1300
inquiries@pridevisiontv.com
www.pridevisiontv.com

***Toronto:* Raptors NBA TV**
307 Lakeshore Blvd. East, Toronto, ON M5A 1C1
Tel: 416-815-2400; *Fax:* 416-681-9181
www.raptors.com

***Toronto:* Razer**
299 Queen St. West, Toronto, ON M5V 2Z5
www.razer.ca

***Toronto:* Report on Business Television**
720 King St. West, 10th Fl., Toronto, ON M5V 2T3
Tel: 416-957-8100; *Fax:* 416-657-8181
robtv.com

***Toronto:* responseTV**
#2020, 3266 Yonge St., Toronto, ON M4N 3P6
Tel: 416-737-0457; *Fax:* 416-488-0796
info@responsetv.ca
www.responsetv.ca
Beverly Milligan, President/CEO
Peter Greensmith, COO
Christie Christelis, Chief Technology Officer

***Toronto:* The Score Television Network**
PO Box 10, #435, 370 King St. West, Toronto, ON M5V 1J9
Tel: 416-977-6787; *Fax:* 416-977-0238
www.thescore.ca

***Toronto:* Scream**
#18, 64 Jefferson St., Toronto, ON M6K 3H4
Tel: 416-534-1191
scream@corusent.com
www.screamtelevision.com

***Toronto:* SexTV**
299 Queen St. West, Toronto, ON M5V 2Z5
Tel: 416-591-5757
sextvchannel@chum.com
www.sextelevision.net

***Toronto:* SHOPTV Canada**
1 Yonge St., 9th Fl., Toronto, ON M5E 1E6
Tel: 416-869-4700; *Fax:* 416-869-4566
info@tmgtv.ca
www.shoptvcanada.com
Don Shafer, Vice-President & General Manager

***Toronto:* Showcase**
#200, 121 Bloor St. East, Toronto, ON M4W 3M5
Tel: 416-967-3253; *Fax:* 416-960-0971
feedback@showcase.ca
www.showcase.ca

***Toronto:* Showcase Action**
#200, 121 Bloor St. East, Toronto, ON M4W 3M5
Tel: 416-967-3254; *Fax:* 416-967-0044
feedback@showcase.ca
www.showcase.ca/action

***Toronto:* Showcase Diva**
121 Bloor St. East, Toronto, ON M4S 3M5
Tel: 416-967-3255; *Fax:* 416-967-0044
feedback@showcase.ca
www.showcase.ca/diva

***Toronto:* Silver Screen Classics**
PO Box 6143 A, Toronto, ON M5W 1P6
Tel: 416-492-1595; *Fax:* 416-492-9539
info@silverscreenclassics.ca
www.silverscreenclassics.com

***Toronto:* Slice**
#200, 121 Bloor St. East, Toronto, ON M4W 3M5
Tel: 416-967-0022; *Fax:* 416-960-0971
Toll-Free: 886-457-4433
www.slice.ca

***Toronto:* Space - The Imagination Station**
299 Queen St. West, Toronto, ON M5V 2Z5
Tel: 416-591-5757; *Fax:* 416-591-6619
space@spacecast.com
www.spacecast.com

***Toronto:* Sports Net**
9 Channel Nine Ct., Toronto, ON M1S 4B5
Fax: 416-332-5724
feedback@sportsnet.rogers.ca
www.sportsnet.ca

***Toronto:* The Sports Network**
9 Channel Nine Ct., Toronto, ON M1S 4B5
Tel: 416-332-5000
www.tsn.ca

***Toronto:* Star! The Entertainment Information Station**
299 Queen St. West, Toronto, ON M5V 2Z5
Tel: 416-591-5290; *Fax:* 416-591-3514
info@star-tv.com
www.star-tv.com
Marcia Martin
James Wood

***Toronto:* Talk TV**
9 Channel Nine Ct., Toronto, ON M1S 4B5
Tel: 416-332-6049; *Fax:* 416-332-6041
www.talktv.ca
Ed Robinson, General Manager

***Toronto:* TELETOON Canada Inc.**
BCE Place, PO Box 787, 181 Bay St., Toronto, ON M5J 2T3
Tel: 416-956-2060; *Fax:* 416-956-2070
www.teletoon.com
Len Cochrane
Darrell Atherley
Leslie Krueger
Carole Bonneau
Trent Locke

†*Toronto:* TFO
CP 200 Q, 2180, rue Yonge, Toronto, ON M4T 2T1
Tél: 416-484-2636; *Téléc:* 416-484-2705
Ligne sans frais: 800-463-6886
asktvo@tvo.org
www.tfo.org

***Toronto:* TMN The Movie Network**
BCE Place, PO Box 787, #100, 181 Bay St., Toronto, ON M5M 3G5
Tel: 416-956-2010; *Fax:* 416-956-2018
www.themovienetwork.ca

***Toronto:* Travel + Escape**
Owned by: **CTVglobemedia Inc.***
299 Queen St. West, Toronto, ON M5V 2Z5
Tel: 416-384-5000; *Fax:* 416-384-4375
insidetravel@ctv.ca
www.travelandescape.ca

***Toronto:* Treehouse TV**
#18, 64 Jefferson Ave., Toronto, ON M6K 3H3
Tel: 416-534-1191
www.treehousetv.com

***Toronto:* TVtropolis**
#1700, 250 Yonge St., Toronto, ON M5B 2L7
Tel: 416-383-2300; *Fax:* 416-593-9844
viewerinquiries@TVtropolis.com
www.canada.com/tvtropolis/index.html

***Toronto:* Viewer's Choice Canada**
BCE Place, PO Box 787, #100, 181 Bay St., Toronto, ON M5J 2T3
Tel: 416-565-2010; *Fax:* 416-565-2018
www.viewerschoice.ca

** For details on this company see listing in Major Broadcasting Companies section; † French language station*

Toronto: Vision TV
Liberty Market Bldg., #230, 171 East Liberty St., Toronto, ON M6K 8P6
Tel: 416-368-3194; *Fax:* 416-368-9774
Toll-Free: 888-321-2567
visiontv@visiontv.ca
www.visiontv.ca
Bill Roberts, President & CEO

Toronto: W Network
#18, 64 Jefferson Ave., Toronto, ON M6K 3H4
Tel: 416-543-1191
comments@wnetwork.com
www.wnetwork.com
John Cassidy, President & CEO

Toronto: YTV Canada Inc.
#18, 64 Jefferson Ave., Toronto, ON M6K 3H3
Tel: 416-534-1191; *Fax:* 416-534-4398
info@ytv.ca
www.ytv.com
Paul Robertson, President

Québec

†*Longueuil:* Canal Evasion
992, rue Joliette, Longueuil, QC J4K 4V9
Tél: 450-677-0054; *Téléc:* 450-677-9964
info@canalevasion.com
www.canalevasion.com
Christine Hill, Directrice générale
Chantal Fortier, Directrice de la programmation
Michel Chamberland, Président et chef de la direction

†*Montréal:* ARGENT
1600, boul de Maisonneuve est, Montréal, QC H2L 4P2
Tél: 514-526-9251; *Téléc:* 514-598-6075
www.argent.canoe.com; tva.canoe.ca
Yves Daoust, Directeur général

†*Montréal:* ARTV
#A 53-1, 1400, boul René-Lévesque est, Montréal, QC H2L 2M2
Tél: 514-597-3636; *Téléc:* 514-597-3633
Ligne sans frais: 800-363-3307
www.artv.ca
Social Media: www.facebook.com/artv.ca
Marie Côté, Directrice générale

†*Montréal:* Canal D
#700, 2100, rue Sainte-Catherine ouest, Montréal, QC H3H 2T3
Tél: 514-983-3330; *Téléc:* 514-939-3151
info@chaines.astral.com
www.canald.com
Sylvain Beauregard, Director, Communications
Jean-Pierre Laurendeau, Vice-President, Programming
Judith Brosseau, Sr. Vice-President, Programming & Communications

Montréal: Canal Indigo
#900, 2100, rue Sainte-Catherine ouest, Montréal, QC H3H 2T3
Tel: 514-939-5090; *Fax:* 514-939-5098
info@canalindigo.com
www.canalindigo.com
Johanne Saint-Laurent, Vice-président et Directeur général, Astral Télé Reseaux

†*Montréal:* Le Canal Nouvelles TVA (LCN)
1600, boul de Maisonneuve est, Montréal, QC H2L 4P2
Tél: 514-526-9251; *Téléc:* 514-598-6071
lcn@tva.ca
www.lcn.canoe.com
Martin Cloutier, Dir.-gén., LCN et Argent

†*Montréal:* Canal Savoir
Canal Savoir, CP 8888 Centre-ville, Montréal, QC H3C 3P8
Tél: 514-987-6633; *Téléc:* 514-987-4337
Ligne sans frais: 888-640-2626
info@canal.qc.ca
www.canal.qc.ca
Sylvie Godbout, General Director

†*Montréal:* Canal Vie
#700, 2100, rue Ste-Catherine ouest, Montréal, QC H3H 2T3
Tél: 514-938-3330; *Téléc:* 514-939-3151
auditoire@canalvie.com
www.canalvie.com
Véronique Lussier, Director, Communications
Lyne Denault, Vice-President, Programming
Marie Collin, Sr. Vice-President, Programming & Communications

†*Montréal:* Les Chaines Télé Astral
#1600, 1800, av McGill College, Montréal, QC H3A 3J6
Tél: 514-939-3150; *Téléc:* 514-939-3151
www.astral.com
Nathalie Roy, Relationniste, Canal Vie/Historia, nroy@chaines.astral.com
Christine Marceau, Relationniste, Canal D/Séries+, cmarceau@chaines.astral.com
Ian Greenberg, Président/Chef de la direction, Astral Media inc.
André Bureau, Président du Conseil, Astral Media inc.

Montréal: Galaxie, Your Musical Universe
730, rue Wellington, Montréal, QC H3C 1T4
Fax: 514-664-1143
Toll-Free: 877-425-2943
www.galaxie.ca

†*Montréal:* Historia
2100, rue Sainte-Catherine ouest, bureau 1000, Montréal, QC H3H 2T3
Tél: 514-939-5000; *Téléc:* 514-939-1515
info@chaines.astral.com
www.astralmedia.com
Judith Brosseau, Sr. Vice-President, Programming & Communications
Fabrice Brasier, Vice-President, Programming
Sophie Dufort, Director, Communications

†*Montréal:* MétéoMédia
#251, 1755, boul René-Lévesque est, Montréal, QC H2K 4P6
Tél: 514-597-0232; *Téléc:* 514-597-1591
www.meteomedia.com

Montréal: MusiMax
355, rue Ste-Catherine ouest, Montréal, QC H3B 1A5
Tel: 514-284-7587; *Fax:* 514-284-1889
auditoire@musimax.com
www.musimax.com

†*Montréal:* MusiquePlus
355, rue Ste-Catherine ouest, Montréal, QC H3B 1A5
Tél: 514-284-7587; *Téléc:* 514-284-1889
www.musiqueplus.com; www.musimax.com; www.astral.com
Ian Greenberg, Président/Chef de la direction, Astral Media inc.

†*Montréal:* Quebecor Media inc.
612, rue St-Jacques, Montréal, QC H3C 4M8
Tél: 514-877-9777; *Téléc:* 514-877-9757
www.quebecor.com
Pierre Karl Péladeau, Président/Chef de la direction

†*Montréal:* RDI - Le réseau de l'information
CP 6000 Centre-Ville, 1400, boul René-Lévesque est, Montréal, QC H3C 3A8
Tél: 514-597-6000
rdi@montreal.radio-canada.ca
radio-canada.com/nouvelles
Martin Cloutier, Director
Gilles Desjardins, Director, Business Development

†*Montréal:* Le Reseau de l'information (RDI)
CP 6000 Centre-Ville, Montréal, QC H3C 3A8
Tél: 514-597-6000
rdi@radio-canada.ca
www.radio-canada.ca/nouvelles

Montréal: Le Réseau des Sports
#300, 1755, boul René-Lévesque est, Montréal, QC H2K 4P6
Tel: 514-599-2244; *Fax:* 514-599-2299
Toll-Free: 888-737-6363
info@rds.ca
www.rds.ca
Gerry Frappier, President & General Manager

†*Montréal:* Séries+
#1600, 1800, av McGill College, Montréal, QC H3A 3J6
Tél: 514-939-3150; *Téléc:* 514-939-3151
info@chaines.astral.com
www.astral.com
Ian Greenberg, Président/Chef de la direction, Astral Media inc.
André Bureau, Président du Conseil, Astral Media inc.

Montréal: Super Écran
#1000, 2100, rue Sainte-Catherine ouest, Montréal, QC H3H 2T3
Tel: 514-939-5090; *Fax:* 514-939-5098
www.superecran.com
Pierre Roy, Président et chef de la direction

†*Montréal:* TATV
Bureau 260, 1200, rue Papineau, Montréal, QC H2K 4R5
Téléc: 514-526-1354
Ligne sans frais: 866-877-1110
support@tc.astral.com
www.ta.tv

†*Montréal:* TV5 Québec Canada
#101, 1755, boul René-Lévesque est, Montréal, QC H2K 4P6
Tél: 514-522-5322; *Téléc:* 514-522-6572
Ligne sans frais: 877-522-6660
info@tv5.ca
www.tv5.ca
Suzanne Gouin, Présidente/Directrice générale

Montréal: Vrak.TV
2100, rue Ste-Catherine ouest, Montréal, QC H3H 2T3
Tel: 514-939-3150; *Fax:* 514-539-3151
www.vrak.tv
Véronique Lussier, Director, Communications
Marie Collin, Sr. Vice-President, Programming & Communications
Denis Dubois, Vice-President, Programming

†*Montréal:* Ztélé
a/s Astral Media, #1600, 1800, av McGill College, Montréal, QC H3A 3J6
Tél: 514-939-3150; *Téléc:* 514-939-3151
info@chaines.astral.com
www.ztele.com; www.astral.com
Social Media: www.facebook.com/ztele
Ian Greenberg, Président/Chef de la direction, Astral Media inc.
André Bureau, Président du conseil, Astral Media inc.
Sidney Greenberg, Vice-Président, Astral Media inc.

†*Québec:* Assemblée nationale du Québec - Canal de l'Assemblée
Édifice Pamphile-Le May, #211, Direction de la diffusion des débats, Québec, QC G1A 1A3
Tél: 418-643-4272; *Téléc:* 418-646-8498
diffusion.debats@assnat.qc.ca
www.assnat.qc.ca
Martin-Philippe Côté, Directeur

** For details on this company see listing in Major Broadcasting Companies section; † French language station*

SECTION 5
BUSINESS & FINANCE

The listings in this section are arranged alphabetically unless otherwise indicated below.

Accounting Firms

Major Accounting Firms

BDO Dunwoody LLP
#600, 36 Toronto St.
Toronto, ON M5C 2C5
Tel: 416-865-0111; *Fax:* 416-367-3912
national@bdo.ca
www.bdo.ca

Ownership: Private
Year Founded: 1921
Number of Employees: 1,965
Revenues: $100-500 million
Profile: Canada's sixth-largest accounting firm concentrates on the special needs of independent business & community-based organizations. The firm provides a full range of comprehensive business advisory services.
Directors:
Dianne McMullen, Chair, Policy Board
Walter Flasza, Member, Policy Board
Kenneth Grower, Member, Policy Board
Anne McArel, Member, Policy Board
Kurt Oelschlagel, Member, Policy Board
Executives:
Keith Farlinger, Chief Executive Officer
R.J. Berry, Chief Operating Officer
Offices:
Abbotsford
#100, 2890 Garden St.
Abbotsford, BC V2T 4W7 Canada
Tel: 604-853-6677; *Fax:* 604-853-4876
abbotsford@bdo.ca
Donald Gilliland, Partner
Alexandria
55 Anik St.
Alexandria, ON K0C 1A0 Canada
Tel: 613-525-1585; *Fax:* 613-525-1436
alexandria@bdo.ca
Alfred
PO Box 539
497 St-Philippe St.
Alfred, ON K0B 1A0 Canada
Tel: 613-679-1332; *Fax:* 613-679-1801
alfred@bdo.ca
Alliston
#13, 169 Dufferin St. South
Alliston, ON L9R 1E6 Canada
Tel: 705-435-5585; *Fax:* 705-435-5587
alliston@bdo.ca
Altona
26 Centre Ave. East
Altona, MB R0G 0B0 Canada
Tel: 204-324-8653; *Fax:* 204-324-1629
altona@bdo.ca
Robert Martins, Partner
Barrie
#300, 300 Lakeshore Dr.
Barrie, ON L4N 0B4 Canada
Tel: 705-726-6331; *Fax:* 705-722-6588
barrie@bdo.ca
Boissevain
372 South Railway St.
Boissevain, MB R0K 0E0 Canada
Tel: 204-534-6935
boissevain@bdo.ca
Tony DeVligere, Partner & Trustee
Bracebridge
#239, 1 Manitoba St.
Bracebridge, ON P1L 1S2 Canada
Tel: 705-645-5215; *Fax:* 705-645-8125
bracebridge@bdo.ca
Brandon
117 - 10th St.
Brandon, MB R7A 4E7 Canada
Tel: 204-727-0671; *Fax:* 204-726-4580
brandon@bdo.ca
Tony DeVliegere, Partner & Trustee
Brantford
#110B, 325 West St.
Brantford, ON N3R 3V6 Canada
Tel: 519-759-8320; *Fax:* 519-759-8421
brantford@bdo.ca
Calgary
#1900, 801 - 6 Ave. SW
Calgary, AB T2P 3W2 Canada
Tel: 403-266-5608; *Fax:* 403-233-7833
calgary@bdo.ca
Richard Edwards, Partner & Senior Vice-President
Cambridge
764 King St. East
Cambridge, ON N3H 3N9
Tel: 519-653-7126; *Fax:* 519-653-8218
cambridge@bdo.ca
Don Laird, Chartered Accountant
Cardston
259 Main St.
Cardston, AB T0K OKO Canada
Tel: 403-653-4137
cardson@bdo.ca
Charlottetown
PO Box 2158
91 Water St.
Charlottetown, PE C1A 8B9 Canada
Tel: 902-892-5365; *Fax:* 902-892-0383
Chatham
375 St. Clair St.
Chatham, ON N7L 3K3 Canada
Tel: 519-354-1560; *Fax:* 519-354-9346
chatham@bdo.ca
Cobourg
PO Box 627
204 Division St.
Cobourg, ON K9A 4L3 Canada
Tel: 905-372-6863; *Fax:* 905-372-6650
cobourg@bdo.ca
Collingwood
#202, 186 Hurontario St.
Collingwood, ON L9Y 3Z5 Canada
Tel: 705-445-4421; *Fax:* 705-445-6691
collingwood@bdo.ca
Pierre Vaillancourt, Partner
Cornwall
PO Box 644
113 Second St. East
Cornwall, ON K6H 5T3 Canada
Tel: 613-932-8691; *Fax:* 613-932-7591
cornwall@bdo.ca
Cranbrook
#200, 35 - 10 Ave. South
Cranbrook, BC V1C 2M9 Canada
Tel: 250-426-4285; *Fax:* 250-426-8886
cranbrook@bdo.ca
Harley Lee, Partner; 250-426-4285
Dryden
37 King St.
Dryden, ON P8N 3G3 Canada
Tel: 807-223-5321; *Fax:* 807-223-2978
dryden@bdo.ca
Edmonton
First Edmonton Pl.
#1000, 10665 Jasper Ave. NW
Edmonton, AB T5J 3S9 Canada
Tel: 780-423-4353; *Fax:* 780-424-2110
edmonton@bdo.ca
Embrun
PO Box 128
991 Limoges Rd.
Embrun, ON K0A 1W0 Canada
Tel: 613-443-5201; *Fax:* 613-443-2538
embrun@bdo.ca
Essex
180 Talbot St. South
Essex, ON N8M 1B6 Canada
Tel: 519-776-6488; *Fax:* 519-776-6090
essex@bdo.ca
Fort Frances
375 Scott St.
Fort Frances, ON P9A 1H1 Canada
Tel: 807-274-9848; *Fax:* 807-274-5142
fortfrances@bdo.ca
Marie Allan, Partner
Golden
PO Box 1709
#205, 421 - 9th Ave. North
Golden, BC V0A 1H0 Canada
Tel: 250-344-5845; *Fax:* 250-344-7131
golden@bdo.ca
John Wilkey, Partner
Grande Prairie
Grande Prairie Place
9909 - 102 St., 5th Fl.
Grande Prairie, AB T8V 2V4 Canada
Tel: 780-539-7075; *Fax:* 780-538-1890
grandeprairie@bdo.ca
Don Blonke, Partner
Guelph
#201, 660 Speedvale Ave. West
Guelph, ON N1K 1E5 Canada
Tel: 519-824-5410; *Fax:* 519-824-5497
Toll-Free: 877-236-4835
Hamilton
#2, 505 York Blvd.
Hamilton, ON L8R 3K4 Canada
Tel: 905-525-6800; *Fax:* 905-525-6566
Toll-Free: 888-236-2383
hamilton@bdo.ca
Hanover
485 - 10th St.
Hanover, ON N4N 1R2 Canada
Tel: 519-364-3790; *Fax:* 519-364-5334
hanover@bdo.ca
Huntsville
PO Box 5484
2 Elm St.
Huntsville, ON P1H 2K8 Canada
Tel: 705-789-4469; *Fax:* 705-789-1079
huntsville@bdo.ca
Kamloops
#300, 272 Victoria St.
Kamloops, BC V2C 1Z6 Canada
Tel: 250-372-9505; *Fax:* 250-374-6323
kamloops@bdo.ca
Kelowna
Landmark Technology Centre
#300, 1632 Dickson Ave.
Kelowna, BC V1Y 7T2 Canada
Tel: 250-763-6700; *Fax:* 250-763-4457
kelowna@bdo.ca
Kenora
#300, 301 First Ave. South
Kenora, ON P9N 4E9 Canada
Tel: 807-468-5531; *Fax:* 807-468-9774
kenora@bdo.ca
Kincardine
970 Queen St.
Kincardine, ON N2Z 2Y2 Canada
Tel: 519-396-3425; *Fax:* 519-396-9829
kincardine@bdo.ca
Kitchener
#401, 305 King St. West
Kitchener, ON N2G 1B9 Canada
Tel: 519-576-5220; *Fax:* 519-576-5471
kitchenerwaterloo@bdo.ca
Langley
#220, 19916 - 64th Ave.
Langley, BC V2Y 1A2 Canada
Tel: 604-534-8691; *Fax:* 604-534-8900
langley@bdo.ca
Lethbridge
Southland Terrace
#200, 220 - 3rd Ave. South
Lethbridge, AB T1J 0G9 Canada
Tel: 403-328-5292; *Fax:* 403-328-9534
lethbridge@bdo.ca
Lindsay
PO Box 358
165 Kent St. West
Lindsay, ON K9V 4S3 Canada
Tel: 705-324-3579; *Fax:* 705-324-0774
lindsay@bdo.ca
London
Station Park
#201, 252 Pall Mall St.
London, ON N6A 5P6 Canada
Tel: 519-672-8940; *Fax:* 519-672-5562
london@bdo.ca
MacGregor
78 Hampton St.
MacGregor, MB R0H 0R0 Canada
Tel: 204-685-2323; *Fax:* 204-685-2341
macgregor@bdo.ca
Bernard Lapchuk, Partner
Manitou
330 Main St.
Manitou, MB R0G 1G0 Canada
Tel: 204-242-2637
manitou@bdo.ca
Ron Westfall, Partner
Markham
#400, 60 Columbia Way
Markham, ON L3R 0C9 Canada
Tel: 905-946-1066; *Fax:* 905-946-9524
markham@bdo.ca
Minnedosa
39 Main St. South
Minnedosa, MB R0J 1E0 Canada
Tel: 204-867-2957
minnedosa@bdo.ca
Jeanne Mills, Partner

Mississauga
4255 Sherwoodtowne Blvd.
Mississauga, ON L4Z 1Y5 Canada
Tel: 905-270-7700; *Fax:* 905-671-7915
mississauga@bdo.ca
Mitchell
PO Box 792
11 Victoria St.
Mitchell, ON N0K 1N0 Canada
Tel: 519-348-8412; *Fax:* 519-348-4300
mitchell@bdo.ca
Montréal
Westmount Premier
#600, 4150, rue Ste-Catherine ouest
Montréal, QC H3Z 2Y5 Canada
Tel: 514-931-0841; *Fax:* 514-931-9491
montreal@bdo.ca
Morden
133 - 7th St.
Morden, MB R6M 1S3 Canada
Tel: 204-822-5486; *Fax:* 204-822-4828
morden@bdo.ca
Sam Andrew, Partner
Mount Forest
PO Box 418
191 Main St. South
Mount Forest, ON N0G 2L0 Canada
Tel: 519-323-2351; *Fax:* 519-323-3661
mountforest@bco.ca
Nakusp
PO Box 1078
220 Broadway St.
Nakusp, BC V0G 1R0 Canada
Tel: 250-265-4750; *Fax:* 250-837-7170
nakusp@bdo.ca
Ken Davidson, Partner
Newmarket
Gates of York Plaza
#2, 17310 Yonge St.
Newmarket, ON L3Y 7R8 Canada
Tel: 905-898-1221; *Fax:* 905-898-0028
Toll-Free: 866-275-8836
newmarket@bdo.ca
Michael Jones, Partner
North Bay
PO Box 20001
142 Main St. West
North Bay, ON P1B 9N1 Canada
Tel: 705-495-2000; *Fax:* 705-495-2001
Toll-Free: 800-461-6324
northbay@bdo.ca
Oakville
151 Randall St.
Oakville, ON L6J 1P5 Canada
Tel: 905-844-3206; *Fax:* 905-844-7513
oakville@bdo.ca
Orangeville
77 Broadway Ave., 2nd Fl.
Orangeville, ON L9W 1K1 Canada
Tel: 519-941-0681; *Fax:* 519-941-8272
orangeville@bdo.ca
Orillia
PO Box 670
19 Front St. North
Orillia, ON L3V 6K5 Canada
Tel: 705-325-1386; *Fax:* 705-325-6649
orillia@bdo.ca
Oshawa
Oshawa Executive Centre
#502, 419 King St. West
Oshawa, ON L1J 2K5 Canada
Tel: 905-576-3430; *Fax:* 905-436-9138
oshawa@bdo.ca
Ottawa
#204, 260 Centrum Blvd
Ottawa, ON K1E 3P4 Canada
Tel: 613-837-3300; *Fax:* 613-837-7733
Toll-Free: 800-754-1579
ottawa@bdo.ca
Owen Sound
PO Box 397
1717 - 2nd Ave. East
Owen Sound, ON N4K 5P7 Canada
Tel: 519-376-6110; *Fax:* 519-376-4741
owensound@bdo.ca
Penticton
#102, 100 Front St.
Penticton, BC V2A 1H1 Canada
Tel: 250-492-6020; *Fax:* 250-492-8110
penticton@bdo.ca
Peterborough
PO Box 1018
#202, 201 George St. North
Peterborough, ON K9J 7A5 Canada
Tel: 705-742-4271; *Fax:* 705-742-3420
Toll-Free: 888-369-6600
peterborough@bdo.ca
Petrolia
PO Box 869
4495 Petrolia Line
Petrolia, ON N0N 1R0 Canada
Tel: 519-882-3333; *Fax:* 519-882-2703
petrolia@bdo.ca
Doug Johnston, Partner
Picture Butte
339 Highway Ave.
Picture Butte, AB T0K 1V0 Canada
Tel: 403-732-4469; *Fax:* 403-732-5701
picturebutte@bdo.ca
Phillip Wever, Sr. Manager
Port Elgin
PO Box 1390
625 Mill St.
Port Elgin, ON N0H 2C0 Canada
Tel: 519-832-2049; *Fax:* 519-832-5659
portelgin@bdo.ca
Portage La Prairie
480 Saskatchewan Ave. West
Portage La Prairie, MB R1N 0M4 Canada
Tel: 204-857-2856; *Fax:* 204-239-1664
portagelaprairie@bdo.ca
John Chapman, Partner; mverwey@bdo.ca
Red Deer
4719 - 48 Ave., 3rd Fl.
Red Deer, AB T4N 3T1 Canada
Tel: 403-346-1566; *Fax:* 403-343-3070
reddeer@bdo.ca
James Scott, Partner
Red Lake
PO Box 234
207 Discovery Centre
Red Lake, ON P0V 2M0 Canada
Tel: 807-727-3227; *Fax:* 807-727-1172
redlake@bdo.ca
Revelstoke
PO Box 2100
#202, 103 - 1st St. East
Revelstoke, BC V0E 2S0 Canada
Tel: 250-837-5225; *Fax:* 250-837-7170
revelstoke@bdo.ca
Ridgetown
211 Main St. East
Ridgetown, ON N0P 2C0 Canada
Tel: 519-674-5418; *Fax:* 519-674-5410
ridgetown@bdo.ca
Rockland
#5, 2784 Laurier St.
Rockland, ON K4K 1A2 Canada
Tel: 613-446-6497; *Fax:* 613-446-7117
rockland@bdo.ca
Judith Gratton, Partner
St Pierre Jolys
Place Lavergne
#6, 467, rue Sabourin
St Pierre Jolys, MB R0A 1V0 Canada
Tel: 204-433-7508; *Fax:* 204-433-7181
saintpierrejolys@bdo.ca
Mona Marcotte, Partner
Salmon Arm
#201, 571 - 6th St. NE
Salmon Arm, BC V1E 1R6 Canada
Tel: 250-832-7171; *Fax:* 250-832-2429
salmonarm@bdo.ca
Sarnia
PO Box 730
250 Christina St. North
Sarnia, ON N7T 7V3 Canada
Tel: 519-336-9900; *Fax:* 519-332-4828
sarnia@bdo.ca
Sault Ste Marie
PO Box 1109
747 Queen St. East
Sault Ste Marie, ON P6A 5N7 Canada
Tel: 705-945-0990; *Fax:* 705-942-7979
ssm@bdo.ca
Selkirk
378 Main St.
Selkirk, MB R1A 1T8 Canada
Tel: 204-482-5626; *Fax:* 204-482-4969
selkirk@bdo.ca
Bill Findlater, Partner
Sicamous
PO Box 392
314 Finlayson St.
Sicamous, BC V0E 2V0 Canada
Tel: 250-836-4493; *Fax:* 250-837-7170
sicamous@bdo.ca
Ken Davidson, Partner
Sioux Lookout
61 King St.
Sioux Lookout, ON P8T 1A5 Canada
Tel: 807-737-1500; *Fax:* 807-737-4443
siouxlookout@bdo.ca
Slave Lake
PO Box 297
#303, Lakeland Centre
Slave Lake, AB T0G 2A0 Canada
Tel: 780-849-3622; *Fax:* 780-849-3625
slavelake@bdo.ca
Ray McComb, Partner
Sorrento
PO Box 59
#2, 1266 Trans Canada Hwy.
Sorrento, BC V0E 2W0 Canada
Tel: 250-675-3288; *Fax:* 250-832-2429
sorrento@bdo.ca
Squamish
PO Box 168
38143 - 2nd Ave.
Squamish, BC V0N 3G0 Canada
Tel: 604-892-9424; *Fax:* 604-892-9356
squamish@bdo.ca
St-Claude
76 First St.
St-Claude, MB R0G 1Z0 Canada
Tel: 204-379-2332; *Toll-Free:* 800-268-3337
stclaude@bdo.ca
Henri Magne, Partner
Stratford
134 Waterloo St. South
Stratford, ON N5A 6S8 Canada
Tel: 519-271-2491; *Fax:* 519-271-4013
stratford@bdo.ca
Montagu J. Smith, Managing Partner
Strathroy
28636 Centre Rd., RR#5
Strathroy, ON N7G 3H6 Canada
Tel: 519-245-1913; *Fax:* 519-245-5987
strathroy@bdo.ca
Sudbury
#202, 888 Regent St.
Sudbury, ON P3E 6C6 Canada
Tel: 705-671-3336; *Fax:* 705-671-9552
Toll-Free: 877-820-0404
sudbury@bdo.ca
Summerland
c/o Bell Jacoe & Co.
13211 North Victoria Rd.
Summerland, BC V0H 1Z0 Canada
Tel: 250-494-9255; *Fax:* 250-494-9755
summerland@bdo.ca
David Braumberger, Partner
Surrey
#200, 15225 - 104 Ave.
Surrey, BC V3R 6Y8 Canada
Tel: 604-584-2121; *Fax:* 604-584-3823
surrey@bdo.ca
Thunder Bay
1095 Barton St.
Thunder Bay, ON P7B 5N3 Canada
Tel: 807-625-4444; *Fax:* 807-623-8460
thunderbay@bdo.ca
Tiverton
84 Main St.
Tiverton, ON N0G 2T0 Canada
Tel: 519-368-5331
tiverton@bdo.ca
Toronto
Royal Bank Plaza, 33rd Fl.
PO Box 32
Toronto, ON M5J 2J8 Canada
Tel: 416-865-0200; *Fax:* 416-865-0887
toronto@bdo.ca
Treherne
274 Railway Ave.
Treherne, MB R0G 2V0 Canada
Tel: 204-723-2454
treherne@bdo.ca
Allan Nichol, Partner
Uxbridge
#1, 1 Brock St. East
Uxbridge, ON L9P 1P6 Canada
Tel: 905-852-9714; *Fax:* 905-852-9898
uxbridge@bdo.ca

Vancouver
#600, 925 West Georgia St.
Vancouver, BC V6L 3L2 Canada
Tel: 604-688-5421; *Fax:* 604-688-5132
vancouver@bdo.ca
Vernon
3201 - 30th Ave.
Vernon, BC V1T 2C6 Canada
Tel: 250-545-2136; *Fax:* 250-545-3364
vernon@bdo.ca
Brian Cockburn, Partner
Virden
PO Box 1900
255 Wellington St. West
Virden, MB R0M 2C0 Canada
Tel: 204-748-1200; *Fax:* 204-748-1976
virden@bdo.ca
Bob Lawrence, Partner
Vulcan
112 - 3 Ave. North
Vulcan, AB T0L 2B0 Canada
Tel: 403-485-2923; *Fax:* 403-485-6098
vulcan@bdo.ca
Walkerton
PO Box 760
121 Jackson St.
Walkerton, ON N0G 2V0 Canada
Tel: 519-881-1211; *Fax:* 519-881-3530
walkerton@bdo.ca
Welland
37 Dorothy St.
Welland, ON L3B 3V6 Canada
Tel: 905-735-6433; *Fax:* 905-735-6514
welland@bdo.ca
Whistler
#104, 1080 Millar Creek Rd.
Whistler, BC V0N 1B1 Canada
Tel: 604-932-3799; *Fax:* 604-932-3764
whistler@bdo.ca
Theresa Walterhouse, Partner
Whitehorse
#201, 3059 - 3rd Ave.
Whitehorse, YT Y1A 1E2 Canada
Tel: 867-667-7907; *Fax:* 867-668-3087
whitehorse@bdo.ca
Ben Baartman, Partner
Wiarton
PO Box 249
663 Berford St.
Wiarton, ON N0H 2T0 Canada
Tel: 519-534-1520; *Fax:* 519-534-3454
wiarton@bdo.ca
Windsor
3630 Rhodes Dr.
Windsor, ON N8W 5A4 Canada
Tel: 519-944-6900; *Fax:* 519-944-6116
windsor@bdo.ca
Wingham
PO Box 1420
152 Josephine St.
Wingham, ON N0G 2W0 Canada
Tel: 519-357-3231; *Fax:* 519-357-3230
wingham@bdo.ca
Winkler
#2, 583 Main St.
Winkler, MB R6W 1A4 Canada
Tel: 204-325-4787; *Fax:* 204-325-8040
winkler@bdo.ca
Frank Wiebe, Partner
Winnipeg
Wawanesa Bldg.
#700, 200 Graham Ave.
Winnipeg, MB R3C 4L5 Canada
Tel: 204-956-7200; *Fax:* 204-926-7201
winnipeg@bdo.ca
Woodstock
PO Box 757
94 Graham St.
Woodstock, ON N4S 8A2 Canada
Tel: 519-539-2081; *Fax:* 519-539-2571
woodstock@bdo.ca

Deloitte & Touche LLP

PO Box 8
#1200, 2 Queen St. East
Toronto, ON M5C 3G7
Tel: 416-874-3874; *Fax:* 416-874-3888
www.deloitte.ca

Ownership: Private partnership; Deloitte in Canada is a member firm of Deloitte Touche Tohmatsu.
Year Founded: 1861
Number of Employees: 5,568
Revenues: $500m-1 billion
Profile: Deloitte & Touche LLP is one of Canada's leading firms, providing a range of auditing, tax, financial advisory, & consulting services. Deloitte's offices in Québec operate under the corporate name Samson Bélair/Deloitte & Touche.
Partners:
John Bowey, Chair
Alan MacGibbon, Managing Partner & CEO
Branches:
Alma
Complexe Jacques Gagnon
#110, 100, rue St-Joseph sud
Alma, QC G8B 7A6 Canada
Tel: 418-669-6969; *Fax:* 418-668-2966
Amos
#200, 101, av 1re est
Amos, QC J9T 1H4 Canada
Tel: 819-732-8273; *Fax:* 819-732-9143
Baie-Comeau
1191, boul Laflèche, 2e étage
Baie-Comeau, QC G5C 1E1 Canada
Tel: 418-589-5761; *Fax:* 418-589-5764
Burlington
#202, 1005 Skyview Dr.
Burlington, ON L7P 5B1 Canada
Tel: 905-315-6770; *Fax:* 905-315-6700
Toll-Free: 866-836-6770
Calgary
Scotia Centre
#3000, 700 - 2nd St. SW
Calgary, AB T2P 0S7 Canada
Tel: 403-267-1700; *Fax:* 403-264-2871
Chicoutimi
#400, 901, boul Talbot
Chicoutimi, QC G7H 0A1 Canada
Tel: 418-549-6650; *Fax:* 418-549-4694
Dolbeau-Mistassini
110, 8e av
Dolbeau-Mistassini, QC G8L 1Y9 Canada
Tel: 418-276-0133; *Fax:* 418-276-8559
Edmonton
Manulife Place
#2000, 10180 - 101st St.
Edmonton, AB T5J 4E4 Canada
Tel: 780-421-3611; *Fax:* 780-421-3782
Farnham
149, rue Desjardins est
Farnham, QC J2N 2W6 Canada
Tel: 450-293-5327; *Fax:* 450-293-2817
Granby
PO Box 356
74, rue Court
Granby, QC J2G 4Y5 Canada
Tel: 450-372-3347; *Fax:* 450-372-8643
Grand-Mère
PO Box 280
1671, 6e av
Grand-Mère, QC G9T 5K8 Canada
Tel: 819-538-1721; *Fax:* 819-538-1882
Halifax
Purdy's Wharf Tower II
#1500, 1569 Upper Water St.
Halifax, NS B3J 3R7 Canada
Tel: 902-422-8541; *Fax:* 902-423-5820
Hawkesbury
300, rue McGill
Hawkesbury, ON K6A 1P8 Canada
Tel: 613-632-4178; *Fax:* 613-632-7703
Jonquière
Complexe A E Fortin
2266, boul René Lévesque
Jonquière, QC G7S 6C5 Canada
Tel: 418-542-9523; *Fax:* 418-542-8814
Kitchener
4210 King St. East
Kitchener, ON N2P 2G5 Canada
Tel: 519-650-7600; *Fax:* 519-650-7601
La Baie
365, rue Victoria
La Baie, QC G7B 3M5 Canada
Tel: 418-544-7313; *Fax:* 418-544-0275
La Sarre
226, 2e rue est
La Sarre, QC J9Z 2G9 Canada
Tel: 819-339-5764; *Fax:* 819-333-2517
Langley
#225, 20316 - 56th Ave.
Langley, BC V3A 3Y7 Canada
Tel: 604-534-7477; *Fax:* 604-534-4220
Laval
Les Tours Triomphe
#300, 2450, boul Daniel-Johnson
Laval, QC H7T 2S3 Canada
Tel: 514-978-3500; *Fax:* 514-382-4984
London
One London Place
255 Queen's Ave., 7th Fl.
London, ON N6A 5R8 Canada
Tel: 519-679-1880; *Fax:* 519-640-4625
Longueuil
Tour Est
#550, 1111, rue St-Charles ouest
Longueuil, QC J4K 5G4 Canada
Tel: 450-670-4270; *Fax:* 450-670-6420
Magog
#203, 101, rue du Moulin
Magog, QC J1X 4A1 Canada
Tel: 819-843-6596; *Fax:* 819-843-6931
Markham
#400, 15 Allstate Pkwy.
Markham, ON L3R 5B4 Canada
Tel: 905-948-6200; *Fax:* 905-948-6250
Matane
750, rue de Phare ouest
Matane, QC G42 3N2 Canada
Tel: 418-566-2637; *Fax:* 418-566-2830
Mississauga - Britannia Rd. East
#132, 425 Britannia Rd. East
Mississauga, ON L4Z 3E7 Canada
Tel: 416-601-6150; *Fax:* 416-601-6151
Mississauga - City Centre Dr.
#1100, 1 City Centre Dr.
Mississauga, ON L5B 1M2 Canada
Tel: 905-601-6150; *Fax:* 905-803-5101
Montréal
#3000, 1, Place Ville-Marie
Montréal, QC H3B 4T9 Canada
Tel: 514-393-7115; *Fax:* 514-390-4100
Ottawa
#800, 100 Queen St.
Ottawa, ON K1P 5T8 Canada
Tel: 613-236-2442; *Fax:* 613-236-2195
Prince Albert
#5, 77 - 15 St. East
Prince Albert, SK S6V 1E9 Canada
Tel: 306-763-7411; *Fax:* 306-763-0191
Prince George
#500, 299 Victoria St.
Prince George, BC V2L 5B8 Canada
Tel: 250-564-1111; *Fax:* 250-562-4950
Québec
#400, 925, ch Saint-Louis
Québec, QC G1S 4Z4 Canada
Tel: 418-624-3333; *Fax:* 418-624-0414
Regina
Bank of Montreal Bldg.
#900, 2103 - 11th Ave.
Regina, SK S4P 3Z8 Canada
Tel: 306-525-1600; *Fax:* 306-525-2244
Rimouski
287, rue Pierre-Saindon
Rimouski, QC G5L 8V5 Canada
Tel: 418-724-4136; *Fax:* 418-724-3807
Roberval
713, boul St-Joseph
Roberval, QC G8H 2L3 Canada
Tel: 418-275-2111; *Fax:* 418-275-6398
Rouyn-Noranda
155, av Dallaire
Rouyn-Noranda, QC J9X 4T3 Canada
Tel: 819-762-5764; *Fax:* 819-797-1471
Saint John
Brunswick House
PO Box 6549
44 Chipman Hill, 7th Fl.
Saint John, NB E2L 4R9 Canada
Tel: 506-632-1080; *Fax:* 506-632-1210
St Catharines
25 Corporate Park Dr., 3rd Fl.
St Catharines, ON L2S 3W2 Canada
Tel: 905-323-6000; *Fax:* 905-323-6001
Saint-Hyacinthe
2200, av Léon-Pratte
Saint-Hyacinthe, QC J2S 4B6 Canada
Tel: 450-774-4000; *Fax:* 450-774-1709
St. John's
Fort William Bldg.
10 Factory Lane
St. John's, NL A1C 6H5 Canada
Tel: 709-576-8480; *Fax:* 709-576-8460
Saskatoon
PCS Tower
#300, 122 - 1st Ave.
Saskatoon, SK S7K 7E5 Canada
Tel: 306-343-4400; *Fax:* 306-343-4480

Sept-Iles
#200, 421, av Arnaud
Sept-Iles, QC G4R 3B3 Canada
Tel: 418-962-2513; *Fax:* 418-968-6422
Sherbrooke
#300, 2727, rue King ouest
Sherbrooke, QC J1L 1C2 Canada
Tel: 819-823-1616; *Fax:* 819-564-8078
St-Félicien
1133, rue Notre-Dame
St-Félicien, QC G8K 1Z7 Canada
Tel: 418-679-4711; *Fax:* 418-679-8723
Toronto - Bay St.
BCE Place, Bay Wellington Tower
#1400, 181 Bay St.
Toronto, ON M5J 2V1 Canada
Tel: 416-601-6150; *Fax:* 416-601-6151
Toronto - King St.
#300, 121 King St.
Toronto, ON M5H 3T9 Canada
Tel: 416-601-6150; *Fax:* 416-601-5901
Toronto - Wellington St. West
30 Wellington St. West
Toronto, ON M5L 1B1 Canada
Tel: 416-601-6150; *Fax:* 416-601-5901
Toronto - Yonge St.
North York City Centre
#1700, 5140 Yonge St.
Toronto, ON M2N 6L7 Canada
Tel: 416-601-6150; *Fax:* 416-229-2524
Trois-Pistoles
546a Jean Rioux
Trois-Pistoles, QC G0L 4K0 Canada
Tel: 418-851-2232; *Fax:* 418-851-4244
Trois-Rivières
PO Box 1600
1500, rue Royale
Trois-Rivières, QC G9A 5L9 Canada
Tel: 819-691-1212; *Fax:* 819-691-1127
Val-d'Or
#240, 450 - 3e av
Val-d'Or, QC J9P 1S2 Canada
Tel: 819-825-4101; *Fax:* 819-825-1155
Vancouver
4 Bentall Centre
#2800, 1055 Dunsmuir St.
Vancouver, BC V7X 1P4 Canada
Tel: 604-669-4466; *Fax:* 604-685-0395
Windsor
#200, 150 Ouellette Place
Windsor, ON N8Y 1L9 Canada
Tel: 519-967-0388; *Fax:* 519-967-0324
Winnipeg
#2300, 360 Main St.
Winnipeg, MB R3C 3Z3 Canada
Tel: 204-942-0051; *Fax:* 204-947-9390

Ernst & Young LLP

Ernst & Young Tower, Toronto-Dominion Centre
PO Box 251
222 Bay St.
Toronto, ON M5K 1J7
Tel: 416-864-1234; *Fax:* 416-864-1174
www.ey.com

Ownership: Private
Year Founded: 1864
Number of Employees: 2,907
Profile: The following services are offered: assurance & advisory business services; corporate finance; tax; & other services. It is affiliated with Ernst & Young Orenda Corporate Finance/EGAN LLP.
Executives:
Louis P. Pagnutti, Chair/CEO
Irene David, Contact
Guy Fréchette, Contact
Murray McDonald, Contact
Fiona Macfarlane, Contact
Paul Roberts, Contact
Affiliated Companies:
Ernst & Young Orenda Corporate Finance
Offices:
Calgary
Ernst & Young Tower
1000, 440 2nd Ave. SW
Calgary, AB T2P 5E9 Canada
Tel: 403-290-4100; *Fax:* 403-290-4265
Dieppe
11 Englehart St.
Dieppe, NB E1A 7Y7 Canada
Tel: 506-853-3097; *Fax:* 506-859-7190
Note: The Dieppe office of the firm LeBlanc Nadeau Bujold merged with Ernst & Young in Sept., 2009.
Edmonton - Scotia Place
Scotia Place, 1801 Scotia 2
10060 Jasper Ave.
Edmonton, AB T5J 3R9 Canada
Tel: 780-423-5811; *Fax:* 780-428-8977
Edmonton - Stony Plain Rd.
300, 12220 Stony Plain Rd.
Edmonton, AB T5N 3Y4 Canada
Tel: 780-482-2349; *Fax:* 780-452-9060
Halifax
1959 Upper Water St., 13th Fl
Halifax, NS B3J 2Z1 Canada
Tel: 902-420-1080; *Fax:* 902-420-0503
Kitchener
515 Riverbend Dr.
Kitchener, ON N2K 3S3 Canada
Tel: 519-744-1171; *Fax:* 519-744-9604
London
One London Place, #1800
255 Queens Ave.
London, ON N6A 5S7 Canada
Tel: 519-672-6100; *Fax:* 519-438-5785
Montréal
#1900, 800, boul René-Lévesque O
Montréal, QC H3B 1X9 Canada
Tel: 514-875-6060; *Fax:* 514-879-2600
Ottawa
#1600, 100 Queen St.
Ottawa, ON K1P 1K1 Canada
Tel: 613-232-1511; *Fax:* 613-232-5324
Québec
#1200, 150, boul René-Lévesque
Québec, QC G1R 6C6 Canada
Tel: 418-524-5151; *Fax:* 418-524-0061
Saint John
#1209, 1 Germain St.
Saint John, NB E2L 4V1 Canada
Tel: 506-634-7000; *Fax:* 506-634-2129
St. John's
The Fortis Building
139 Water St., 7th Fl
St. John's, NL A1C 1B2 Canada
Tel: 709-726-2840; *Fax:* 709-726-0345
Thornhill
#600, 175 Commerce Valley Dr. West
Thornhill, ON L3T 7P6 Canada
Tel: 905-731-1500; *Fax:* 905-882-3050
Vancouver
Pacific Centre
700 West Georgia St.
Vancouver, BC V7Y 1C7 Canada
Tel: 604-891-8200; *Fax:* 604-643-5422
Winnipeg
Commodity Exchange Tower, #2700
360 Main St.
Winnipeg, MB R3C 4G9 Canada
Tel: 204-947-6519; *Fax:* 204-956-0138

Evancic Perrault Robertson

PO Box 21148, Maple Ridge Square Stn. Maple Ridge Square
Maple Ridge, BC V2X 17P
Tel: 604-476-2009; *Fax:* 604-467-1219
eprnat@epr.ca
www.epr.ca

Ownership: Private
Year Founded: 1979
Profile: Evancic Perrault Robertson is a firm of Certified General Accountants, with member offices across the country. EPR has an international reach, through its affiliations with NACPAF (a US-based national association of CPA firms) & with Morison International (a UK-based global accountancy & law office network). The firm offers an integrated approach to auditing, accounting, taxation, & management consulting.
Executives:
Paul Walker, Chair
Camille Belliveau, Executive Director
Verle Spindor, National Administrator
Branches:
Abbotsford
#201, 2669 Langdon St.
Abbotsford, BC V2T 3L3 Canada
Tel: 604-853-1538; *Fax:* 604-853-7178
eprabby@mindlink.net
Bathurst
1935, av St. Peter
Bathurst, NB E2A 7J5 Canada
Tel: 506-548-1984; *Fax:* 506-548-0904
eprbath@eprbathurst.ca
André Doucet, Partner; adoucet@eprbathurst.ca
Bradford
PO Box 753
27 John St. West
Bradford, ON L3Z 2B3 Canada
Tel: 905-778-8964; *Fax:* 905-775-9550
Toll-Free: 800-246-5591
bbcm@bellnet.ca
Michael Falcone
Calgary
#110, 7330 Fisher St. SE
Calgary, AB T2H 2H8 Canada
Tel: 403-278-5800; *Fax:* 403-253-9479
general@eprcal.com
Les Willms, Partner; les@eprtax.com
Chatham
40 Centre Sq.
Centre St.
Chatham, ON N7M 5W3 Canada
Tel: 519-436-0556; *Fax:* 519-436-1291
rieger@ciaccess.com
Lance Rieger, Partner
Coquitlam
566 Lougheed Hwy., 2nd Fl.
Coquitlam, BC V3K 3S3 Canada
Tel: 604-936-4377; *Fax:* 604-936-8376
eprcoq@eprcoq.com
www.eprcoq.com
Ken Richardson, Partner; ken@eprcoq.com
Fort Erie
PO Box 277
#8, 450 Garrison Road
Fort Erie, ON L2A 1N2 Canada
Tel: 905-871-6620; *Fax:* 905-871-2544
eprfeo@eprnia.ca
Fredericton
#205, 206 Rookwood Ave.
Fredericton, NB E3B 2M2 Canada
Tel: 506-458-8620; *Fax:* 506-450-8286
eprfred@nbnet.nb.ca
Larry Johnston, Partner; l_johnson@eprdayekelly.com
Grande Prairie
#215, 10006 - 101st Ave.
Grande Prairie, AB T8V 0Y1 Canada
Tel: 780-539-3400; *Fax:* 780-538-1544
epgrand@telusplanet.net
David Richardson, Partner
Hamilton
176 Rymal Rd. East
Hamilton, ON L9B 1C2 Canada
Tel: 905-388-7453; *Fax:* 905-388-7397
eprhamilton@iprimus.ca
Andrew Barber, Partner; andy@epr-consulting.com
Langley
20688 - 56 Ave.
Langley, BC V3A 3Z1 Canada
Tel: 604-534-1441; *Fax:* 604-534-1491
pwalker@eprcga.com
www.eprcga.com
Paul Walker, Partner
London
#804, 150 Dufferin Ave.
London, ON N6A 5N6 Canada
Tel: 519-434-5847; *Fax:* 519-645-0727
Don DiCarlo, Partner; don@eprlon.com
Maple Ridge
22377 Dewdney Trunk Rd.
Maple Ridge, BC V2X 3J4 Canada
Tel: 604-467-5561; *Fax:* 604-467-1219
eprmr@eprcga.com
www.eprcga.com
Patrick Smith, Partner; psmith@eprcga.com
Miramichi
Waterfront Place
1773 Water St.
Miramichi, NB E1N 1B2 Canada
Tel: 506-773-6990; *Fax:* 506-773-3197
eprmira@nbnet.nb.ca
Moncton
84 Brandon St.
Moncton, NB E1C 7E9 Canada
Tel: 506-857-3893; *Fax:* 506-859-4148
Paul Robichaud, Partner; probichaud@eprmoncton.com
Niagara Falls
#7, 3930 Montrose Rd.
Niagara Falls, ON L2H 3C9 Canada
Tel: 905-358-5729; *Fax:* 905-358-7188
eprnfo@eprnia.ca
Rick Forbes, Partner; rforbes@eprnia.ca
North Vancouver
#102, 1975 Lonsdale Ave.
North Vancouver, BC V7M 2K3 Canada
Tel: 604-987-8101; *Fax:* 604-987-1794
cga@eprnv.ca

Bill Perrault, Partner; wperrault@epr.ca
Saint-Hyacinthe
#200, 450 ave St-Joseph
Saint-Hyacinthe, QC J2S 8K5 Canada
Tel: 450-774-7165; *Fax:* 450-774-1589
eprsthyacinthe@cgaquebec.com
Rene Benoit, Partner; rene.benoit@eprquebec.com
St. John's
74 O'Leary Ave.
St. John's, NL A1B 2C7 Canada
Tel: 709-726-0000; *Fax:* 709-726-2200
eprstjohns@hotmail.com
Gerald Kirby, Partner
Saskatoon
259 Robin Cres.
Saskatoon, SK S7L 6M8 Canada
Tel: 306-934-3944; *Fax:* 306-934-3409
eprstoon@sasktel.net
Colin Taylor, Partner; colintaylor@sasktel.net
Slave Lake
405 - 6th Ave. SW
Slave Lake, AB T0G 2A4 Canada
Tel: 780-849-4949; *Fax:* 780-849-3401
eprslave@telusplanet.net
Gordon Ferguson, Partner
St-Jérôme
34, rue de Martigny ouest
Saint-Jérome, QC J7Y 2E9 Canada
Tel: 450-569-2641; *Fax:* 450-569-2647
François Marchand, Partner; francois.marchand@eprquebec.com
Stonewall
Westside Plaza Mall
PO Box 1038
333 Main St.
Stonewall, MB R0C 2Z0 Canada
Tel: 204-467-5566; *Fax:* 204-467-9133
eprstonewall@shawcable.com
Ryan Smith, Partner; rsmith.sprstonewall@shawcable.com
Terrebonne
3300, boul des Entreprises
Terrebonne, QC J6X 4J8 Canada
Tel: 450-477-0377; *Fax:* 450-477-4023
Christian Pimpare, Partner; christian.pimpare@eprquebec.com
Tilbury
40 Queen Sq.
Tilbury, ON N0P 2L0 Canada
Tel: 519-682-2300; *Fax:* 519-682-0705
reiger@ciaccess.com
White Rock
#104, 1656 Martin Dr.
White Rock, BC V4A 5E7 Canada
Tel: 604-536-7778; *Fax:* 604-536-7745
Glenn Parks, Partner; gparks@eprcga.com
Winnipeg
#1010, 1661 Portage Ave.
Winnipeg, MB R3J 3T7 Canada
Tel: 204-954-9690; *Fax:* 204-786-1003
bemond@mts.net
Barry Edmond, Partner

Grant Thornton LLP

50 Bay St., 12th Fl.
Toronto, ON M5J 2Z8
Tel: 416-366-4420; *Fax:* 416-360-4944
Toll-Free: 800-366-0100
national@grantthornton.ca
www.grantthornton.ca

Ownership: Private
Year Founded: 1939
Number of Employees: 1,172
Revenues: $100-500 million
Executives:
Phil Noble, CEO & Exec. Partner
John Garritsen, Partner, Administration; jgarritsen@grantthornton.ca
John Holdstock, Partner, Client & Services; jholdstock@grantthornton.ca
Dave Peneycad, Chief Operating Officer
Bill Brushett, Partner, Client Services
Sharon Healy, Director, Human Resources; shealy@grantthornton.ca
Anita Ferrari, Regional Managing Partner; aferrari@grantthornton.ca
Kevin Ladner, Regional Managing Partner; kladner@grantthornton.ca
Rick Mudie, Regional Managing Partner; rmudie@grantthornton.ca

Branches:
Antigonish
PO Box 1480
257 Main St.
Antigonish, NS B2G 2L7 Canada
Tel: 902-863-4587; *Fax:* 902-863-0917
B.M. Cullen, Partner
Barrie
#201, 85 Bayfield St.
Barrie, ON L4M 3A7 Canada
Tel: 705-730-6574; *Fax:* 705-730-6575
R.D. Woodman, Partner
Bathurst
Harbourview Pl.
PO Box 220
#500, 275 Main St.
Bathurst, NB E2A 3Z2 Canada
Tel: 506-546-6616; *Fax:* 506-548-5622
Bridgewater
PO Box 220
197 Dufferin St.
Bridgewater, NS B4V 2W8 Canada
Tel: 902-543-8115; *Fax:* 902-543-7707
R.W. Oakley, Partner
Calgary
#1000, 112 - 4th Ave. SW
Calgary, AB T3P 0H3 Canada
Tel: 403-260-2500; *Fax:* 403-260-2571
G.G. McFarlane, Partner
Charlottetown
PO Box 187
#501, 199 Grafton St.
Charlottetown, PE C1A 7K4 Canada
Tel: 902-892-6547; *Fax:* 902-566-5358
J.K. Ladner, Partner
Corner Brook
PO Box 356
#49, 51 Park St.
Corner Brook, NL A2H 6E3 Canada
Tel: 709-634-4382; *Fax:* 709-634-9158
R.G. Flynn, Partner
Digby
Basin Place
PO Box 848
68 Water St.
Digby, NS B0V 1A0 Canada
Tel: 902-245-2553; *Fax:* 902-245-6161
Digby@GrantThornton.ca
M. Rutherford, Partner
Edmonton
Scotia Place 2
#1401, 10060 Jasper Ave. NW
Edmonton, AB T5J 3R8 Canada
Tel: 780-422-7114; *Fax:* 780-426-3208
G.G. McFarlane, Partner; 403-260-2500
Fredericton
PO Box 1054
#400, 570 Queen St.
Fredericton, NB E3B 5C2 Canada
Tel: 506-458-8200; *Fax:* 506-453-7029
Bruce Lewis, Partner
Grand Falls - Windsor
PO Box 83
9 High St.
Grand Falls-Windsor, NL A2A 2J3 Canada
Tel: 709-489-6622; *Fax:* 709-489-6625
K. Simms, Principal
Halifax
Cogswell Tower
#1100, 2000 Barrington St.
Halifax, NS B3J 3K1 Canada
Tel: 902-421-1734; *Fax:* 902-420-1068
Michele Williams, Partner
Hamilton
Standard Life Centre
#1040, 120 King St. West
Hamilton, ON L8P 4V2 Canada
Tel: 905-525-1930; *Fax:* 905-527-4413
D.A. MacLean, Partner
Kelowna
#200, 1633 Ellis St.
Kelowna, BC V1Y 2A8 Canada
Tel: 250-712-6800; *Fax:* 250-661-3416
J.P. Mills, Partner
Kentville
PO Box 68
15 Webster St.
Kentville, NS B4N 3V9 Canada
Tel: 902-678-7307; *Fax:* 902-679-1870
G.B. Caldwell, Partner

Langley
#320, 8700 - 200th St.
Langley, BC V2Y 0G4 Canada
Tel: 604-532-3761; *Fax:* 604-532-8130
T.G. Davies, Partner
London
#406, 140 Fullarton St.
London, ON N6A 5P2 Canada
Tel: 519-672-2930; *Fax:* 519-672-6455
P.R. Coleman, Partner
Markham
#200, 15 Allstate Pkwy.
Markham, ON L3R 5B4 Canada
Tel: 905-475-1100; *Fax:* 905-475-8906
A.R. Byrne, Partner
Marystown
PO Box 518
2 Queen St.
Marystown, NL A0E 2M0 Canada
Tel: 709-279-2300; *Fax:* 709-279-2340
Marystown@GrantThornton.ca
Miramichi
135 Henry St.
Miramichi, NB E1V 2N5 Canada
Tel: 506-622-0637; *Fax:* 506-622-5174
H.K. Raper, Partner
Mississauga
#401, 350 Burnhamthorpe Rd. West
Mississauga, ON L5R 3J1 Canada
Tel: 905-804-0905; *Fax:* 905-804-0509
G.R. Popp, Partner
Moncton
PO Box 1005
#500, 633 Main St.
Moncton, NB E1C 8P2 Canada
Tel: 506-857-0100; *Fax:* 506-857-0105
Jean Marc Delaney, Partner
Montague
PO Box 70
1 Bailey Dr.
Montague, PE C0A 1R0 Canada
Tel: 902-838-4121; *Fax:* 902-838-4802
C. Chapman, Partner
New Glasgow
PO Box 427
610 East River Rd.
New Glasgow, NS B2H 5E5 Canada
Tel: 902-752-8393; *Fax:* 902-752-4009
B.L. Wilson, Partner
New Liskeard
PO Box 2170
17 Wellington St.
New Liskeard, ON P0J 1P0 Canada
Tel: 705-647-8100; *Fax:* 705-647-7026
R.R. Hacquard, Partner
New Westminster
628 - 6th Ave., 6th Fl.
New Westminster, BC V3M 6Z1 Canada
Tel: 604-521-3761; *Fax:* 604-521-8170
R.W. Mudie, Partner
North Bay
#200, 222 McIntyre St. West
North Bay, ON P1B 2Y8 Canada
Tel: 705-472-6500; *Fax:* 705-472-7760
G.G. Weckwerth, Partner
Orillia
#300, 6 West St. North
Orillia, ON L3V 5B8 Canada
Tel: 705-326-7605; *Fax:* 705-326-0837
R.D. Woodman, Partner
Port Colborne
PO Box 336
222 Catharine St, #B
Port Colborne, ON L3K 5W1 Canada
Tel: 905-834-3651; *Fax:* 905-834-5095
J. Brennan, Principal
Saint John
Brunswick House
44 Chipman Hill, 4th Fl.
Saint John, NB E2L 2A9 Canada
Tel: 506-634-2900; *Fax:* 506-634-4569
G. Dewar, Partner
St. John's
PO Box 8037
187 Kenmount Rd.
St. John's, NL A1B 3P9 Canada
Tel: 709-722-5960; *Fax:* 709-722-7892
Jeff Pardy, Partner
Sault Ste Marie
421 Bay St., 5th Fl.
Sault Ste Marie, ON P6A 1X3 Canada
Tel: 705-945-9700; *Fax:* 705-945-9705
B.C. Magill, Partner

Summerside
Royal Bank Bldg.
PO Box 1660
220 Water St.
Summerside, PE C1N 2V5 Canada
Tel: 902-436-9155; *Fax:* 902-436-6913
L.B. Murray, Partner
Sydney
George Place
#200, 500 George St.
Sydney, NS B1P 1K6 Canada
Tel: 902-562-5581; *Fax:* 902-562-0073
J. MacNeil, Partner
Thunder Bay
#300, 979 Alloy Dr.
Thunder Bay, ON P7B 5Z8 Canada
Tel: 807-345-6571; *Fax:* 807-345-0032
D. Vanderwey, Partner
Truro
PO Box 725
#400, 35 Commercial St.
Truro, NS B2N 5E8 Canada
Tel: 902-893-1150; *Fax:* 902-893-9757
G.D. Hutchings, Partner
Vancouver
#1600, 333 Seymour St.
Vancouver, BC V6B 0A4 Canada
Tel: 604-687-2711; *Fax:* 604-685-6569
Vancouver@GrantThornton.ca
P.B. Noble, Partner
Victoria
888 Fort St., 3rd Fl.
Victoria, BC V8W 1H8 Canada
Tel: 250-383-4191; *Fax:* 250-381-4623
S. Mehinagic, Partner
Wetaskiwin
5108 - 51st Ave.
Wetaskiwin, AB T9A 0V2 Canada
Tel: 780-352-1679; *Fax:* 780-352-2451
T.R. Bolivar, Partner
Winnipeg
94 Commerce Drive
Winnipeg, MB R3P 0Z3 Canada
Tel: 204-944-0100; *Fax:* 204-957-5442
D.H. Anthony, Partner
Yarmouth
PO Box 297
328 Main St.
Yarmouth, NS B5A 4B2 Canada
Tel: 902-742-7842; *Fax:* 902-742-0224
M. Rutherford, Partner

KPMG

Commerce Court West
PO Box 31, Commerce Court Stn. Commerce Court
199 Bay St.
Toronto, ON M5L 1B2

Tel: 416-777-8500; *Fax:* 416-777-8818
webmaster@kpmg.ca
www.kpmg.ca

Ownership: Private
Year Founded: 1860
Number of Employees: 4,500
Assets: $500m-1 billion
Revenues: $500m-1 billion
Executives:
Bill Thomas, Chief Executive Officer
John Herhalt, Managing Partner, Advisory Services
Greg Wiebe, Managing Partner, Tax
Peter Doyle, Managing Partner, Audit
Jean-Pierre Desrosiers, Managing Partner, Markets
Mary Lou Hamher, CFO
Mario Paron, Chief HR Officer
Vancouver - Burnaby
#2400, 4720 Kingsway
Burnaby, BC V5H 4N2
Branches:
Abbotsford
32575 Simon Ave.
Abbotsford, BC V2T 4W6 Canada
Tel: 604-854-2200; *Fax:* 604-853-2756
Calgary
Bow Valley Square II
#2700, 205 - 5th Ave. SW
Calgary, AB T2P 4B9 Canada
Tel: 403-691-8000; *Fax:* 403-691-8008
Jason Brown, Partner, Audit
Curtis Lester, Partner, Tax
Chilliwack
#200, 9123 Mary St.
Chilliwack, BC V2P 4H7 Canada
Tel: 604-793-4700; *Fax:* 604-793-4747
Edmonton
Commerce Pl.
10125 - 102 St.
Edmonton, AB T5J 3V8 Canada
Tel: 780-429-7300; *Fax:* 780-429-7379
Robert Borrelli, Partner, Audit
Fredericton
Frederick Sq., TD Tower
#700, 77 Westmorland St.
Fredericton, NB E3B 6Z3 Canada
Tel: 506-452-8000; *Fax:* 506-450-0072
Todd MacIntosh, Partner, Tax
Halifax
Purdy's Wharf, Tower One
#1500, 1959 Upper Water St.
Halifax, NS B3J 3N2 Canada
Tel: 902-429-6000; *Fax:* 902-423-1307
Gregory Simpson, Partner, Tax
Hamilton
Commerce Place
#700, 21 King St. West
Hamilton, ON L8P 4W7 Canada
Tel: 905-523-8200; *Fax:* 905-523-2222
Kamloops
#200, 206 Seymour St.
Kamloops, BC V2C 6P5 Canada
Tel: 250-372-5581; *Fax:* 250-828-2928
Kelowna
#300, 1674 Bertram St.
Kelowna, BC V1Y 9G4 Canada
Tel: 250-763-5522; *Fax:* 250-763-0044
Kingston
#400, 863 Princess St.
Kingston, ON K7L 5N4 Canada
Tel: 613-549-1550; *Fax:* 613-549-6349
Lethbridge
Lethbridge Centre Tower
#500, 400 - 4th Ave. South
Lethbridge, AB T1J 4E1 Canada
Tel: 403-380-5700; *Fax:* 403-380-5760
London
#1400, 140 Fullarton St.
London, ON N6A 5P2 Canada
Tel: 519-672-4880; *Fax:* 519-672-5684
Moncton
Place Marvin's
One Factory Lane
Moncton, NB E1C 9M3 Canada
Tel: 506-856-4400; *Fax:* 506-856-4499
Montréal
#1500, 600 boul de Maisonneuve Ouest
Montréal, QC H3A 0A3 Canada
Tel: 514-840-2100; *Fax:* 514-840-2187
Philippe Grubert, Partner, Audit
Brian Mustard, Partner, Tax
North Bay
PO Box 990
#300, 925 Stockdale Rd.
North Bay, ON P1B 8K3 Canada
Tel: 705-472-5110; *Fax:* 705-472-1249
Ottawa
World Exchange Plaza
#2000, 160 Elgin Street
Ottawa, ON K2P 2P8 Canada
Tel: 613-212-5764; *Fax:* 613-212-2896
Andrew Newman, Partner, Audit
Prince George
#400, 177 Victoria St.
Prince George, BC V2L 5R8 Canada
Tel: 250-563-7151; *Fax:* 250-563-5693
Regina
McCallum Hill Centre, Tower II
1881 Scarth St., 20th Fl.
Regina, SK S4P 4K9 Canada
Tel: 306-791-1200; *Fax:* 306-757-4703
Saint John
Harbour Bldg.
PO Box 2388
#306, 133 Prince William St.
Saint John, NB E2L 3V6 Canada
Tel: 506-634-1000; *Fax:* 506-633-8828
St Catharines
#901, One Saint-Paul St.
St Catharines, ON L2R 7L2 Canada
Tel: 905-685-4811; *Fax:* 905-682-2008
Saskatoon
#600, 128 - 4th Ave. South
Saskatoon, SK S7K 1M8 Canada
Tel: 306-934-6200; *Fax:* 306-934-6233
Sault Ste Marie
#200, 111 Elgin St.
Sault Ste Marie, ON P6A 6L6 Canada
Tel: 705-949-5811; *Fax:* 705-949-0911
Sudbury
Claridge Executive Centre
144 Pine St.
Sudbury, ON P3C 1X3 Canada
Tel: 705-675-8500; *Fax:* 705-675-7586
Laurie Bissonette, Partner, Audit
Toronto
Yonge Corporate Centre
#200, 4100 Yonge St.
Toronto, ON M2P 2H3 Canada
Tel: 416-228-7000; *Fax:* 416-228-7123
Vancouver
Pacific Centre
PO Box 10426
777 Dunsmuir St.
Vancouver, BC V7Y 1K3 Canada
Tel: 604-691-3000; *Fax:* 604-691-3031
Jim Bennett, Partner, Audit
Carlo De Mello, Partner, Audit
Vernon
Credit Union Bldg.
3205 - 32 St., 3rd Fl.
Vernon, BC V1T 9A2 Canada
Tel: 250-503-5300; *Fax:* 250-545-6440
Waterloo
Marsland Centre
115 King St. South
Waterloo, ON N2J 5A3 Canada
Tel: 519-747-8800; *Fax:* 519-747-8811
Shelley Wickenheiser, Partner, Tax
Windsor
Greenwood Centre
#618, 3200 Deziel Dr.
Windsor, ON N8W 5K8 Canada
Tel: 519-251-3500; *Fax:* 519-251-3530
Winnipeg
#2000, One Lombard Place
Winnipeg, MB R3B 0X3 Canada
Tel: 204-957-1770; *Fax:* 204-957-0808

MacKay LLP

#1100, 1177 West Hastings St.
Vancouver, BC V6E 4T5

Tel: 604-687-4511; *Fax:* 780-425-8780
Toll-Free: 800-351-0426
HughLivingstone@Van.MacKayLLP.ca
www.mackayllp.ca
Other Contact Information: Fax: 604/687-5805

Ownership: Private
Year Founded: 1969
Number of Employees: 220
Profile: Services provided include bookkeeping, audit & accounting, taxation, corporate financing, executive financial planning, microcomputer support, management consulting, business investigation, valuation & litigation support, solvency & restructuring, & international affiliations.
Executives:
Deborah Graystone, Partner
Peter Busch, Partner
Sean Gilbert, Partner
Russell D. Law, Partner
Hugh G. Livingstone, Partner
Craig Elliott, Partner
Matthew So, Partner
York Wong, Partner
Hugh Livingstone, Manager
Branches:
Calgary - 7 Avenue
Iveagh House
#1700, 717 - 7 Ave. SW
Calgary, AB T2P 0Z3 Canada
Tel: 403-294-9292; *Fax:* 403-294-9262
Calgary@Cal.MacKay.ca
Calgary - Macleod Trail
Southcentre Executive Tower
#400, 11012 MacLeod Trail SE
Calgary, AB T2J 6A5 Canada
Tel: 403-640-2227; *Fax:* 403-640-2505
calgary@cal.mackay.ca
Christine Heemskerk, General Manager
Edmonton
Highfield Place
#705, 10010 - 106th St.
Edmonton, AB T5J 3L8 Canada
Tel: 780-420-0626; *Fax:* 780-425-8780
Toll-Free: 800-622-5293
edmonton@edm.mackay.ca
Don Smith, General Manager
Donald J. Smith
Bob McAneeley
Brent Penner

Kelowna
#500, 1620 Dickson Ave.
Kelowna, BC V1Y 9Y2 Canada
Tel: 250-763-5021; *Fax:* 250-763-3600
Toll-Free: 866-763-5021
kelowna@kel.mackay.ca
Don Turri, General Manager
Don Turri
Ken Laloge
Chris White
Dan Basso
Angela C. Bailey

Surrey
#112, 7565 - 132nd St.
Surrey, BC V3W 1K5 Canada
Tel: 604-591-6181; *Fax:* 604-591-5676
surrey@van.mackay.ca
Keith Gagnon, Manager
Jack Arnold
Bill Gill
Keith Gagnon

Whitehorse
#200, 303 Strickland St.
Whitehorse, YT Y1A 2J8 Canada
Tel: 867-667-7651; *Fax:* 867-668-3797
markp@mackayandpartners.ca
Blaine Anderson
Norman McIntyre
Mark Pike

Yellowknife
PO Box 727
#301, 5120 - 49th St
Yellowknife, NT X1A 1P8 Canada
Tel: 867-920-4404; *Fax:* 867-920-4135
Toll-Free: 866-920-4404
yellowknife@yel.mackay.ca
John Laratta
Gillian Lee

Meyers Norris Penny (MNP)
715 - 5th Ave. SW, 7th Fl.
Calgary, AB T2P 2X6
Tel: 403-444-0150; *Fax:* 403-444-0199
www.mnp.ca

Year Founded: 1945
Number of Employees: 1300
Revenues: $100-500 million
Profile: MNP is a leading Western Canadian chartered accountancy & business advisory firm. In addition to traditional accounting services like taxation & assurance, MNP offers business services including corporate financing, human resource consulting, business & strategic planning, succession planning, valuations support, information technology consulting, self-employment training, & agricultural advisory services.
Executives:
Daryl Ritchie, FCA, Chief Executive Officer; daryl.ritchie@mnp.ca
Kelly Bernakevitch, FCA, Executive Vice-President, Operations; kelly.bernakevitch@mnp.ca
Ted Poppitt, CA, Executive Vice-President, Practice Development; ted.poppitt@mnp.ca
Laurel Wood, CMC, Executive Vice-President, Advisory Services; laurel.wood@mnp.ca
Steve Kerr, CMA, Chief Financial Officer; steve.kerr@mnp.ca
Randy Mowat, Vice-President, Marketing; randy.mowat@mnp.ca
Phil O'Brien-Moran, Vice-President, Technology; phil.obrienmoran@mnp.ca
Bob Twerdun, CA, Vice-President, Human Capital; bob.twerdun@mnp.ca
Charmaine Toms, General Counsel; charmaine.toms@mnp.ca
Affiliated Companies:
Tamarack Capital Advisors Inc.
Offices:

Abbotsford
#300, 2975 Gladwin Rd.
Abbotsford, BC V2T 5T4 Canada
Tel: 604-853-9471; *Fax:* 604-850-3672
Darrell P. Tracey, Contact; darrell.tracey@mnp.ca

Airdrie
#110A, 400 Main St. NE
Airdrie, AB T4B 2N1 Canada
Tel: 403-912-6235; *Fax:* 403-912-6332

Brandon
1401 Princess Ave.
Brandon, MB R7A 7L7 Canada
Tel: 204-727-0661; *Fax:* 204-726-1543
Toll-Free: 800-446-0890
Jeff Cristall, Contact; jeff.cristall@mnp.ca

Brooks
PO Box 1210
247 - 1st St. West
Brooks, AB T1R 1C1 Canada
Tel: 403-362-8909; *Fax:* 403-362-6869
Toll-Free: 877-500-5696

Burnaby
Metrotower II
#900, 4720 Kingsway
Burnaby, BC V5H 4N2 Canada
Tel: 604-435-4317; *Fax:* 604-435-4319

Calgary - Bantrel
#900, 700 6th Ave. SW
Calgary, AB T2P 0T8 Canada
Tel: 403-263-3385; *Fax:* 403-648-4115
Kelly Brook, Contact; kelly.brook@mnp.ca

Calgary - North
#210, 5010 - 4th St. NE
Calgary, AB T2K 5X8 Canada
Tel: 403-275-8457; *Fax:* 403-275-8416
Don Isaman, Contact; don.isaman@mnp.ca

Calgary Downtown - MNP Place
#300, 622 - 5th Ave. SW
Calgary, AB T2P 0M6 Canada
Tel: 403-263-3385; *Fax:* 403-269-8450
Durell Wiley, Contact; durell.wiley@mnp.ca

Cambridge
#600, 73 Water St. N.
Cambridge, ON N1R 7L6 Canada
Tel: 519-623-3820; *Fax:* 519-623-3144
Rhonda Lovell, CA; rhonda.lovell@mnp.ca

Campbell River
#201, 990 Cedar St.
Campbell River, BC V9W 7Z8 Canada
Tel: 250-287-2131; *Fax:* 250-287-2134
Toll-Free: 800-450-9977

Chilliwack
#1, 45780 Yale Rd.
Chilliwack, BC V2P 2N4 Canada
Tel: 604-792-1915; *Fax:* 604-795-6526
Toll-Free: 800-444-4070
Darrell P. Tracey, Contact; darrell.tracey@mnp.ca

Courtenay
467 Cumberland Rd.
Courtenay, BC V9N 2C5 Canada
Tel: 250-338-5464; *Fax:* 250-338-0609
Toll-Free: 800-445-9988
Ben Vanderhorst, Contact

Dauphin
PO Box 6000
32 - 2nd Ave. SW
Dauphin, MB R7N 2V5 Canada
Tel: 204-638-6767; *Fax:* 204-638-8634
Toll-Free: 877-500-0790
Gerry Musey, Contact; gerry.musey@mnp.ca

Deloraine
PO Box 528
130 Broadway St. North
Deloraine, MB R0M 0M0 Canada
Tel: 204-747-2842; *Fax:* 204-747-2956
Julee Galvin, CA; julee.galvin@mnp.ca

Drumheller
PO Box 789
365 - 2nd St. East
Drumheller, AB T0J 0Y0 Canada
Tel: 403-823-7800; *Fax:* 403-823-8914
Toll-Free: 877-932-3387
Jeff Hall; jeffhall@mnp.ca

Duncan
372 Coronation Ave.
Duncan, BC V9L 2T3 Canada
Tel: 250-748-3761; *Fax:* 250-746-1712
Gordon John, CA; gordon.john@mnp.ca

Edmonton - City Centre
#400, 10104 - 103 Ave. NW
Edmonton, AB T5J 0H8 Canada
Tel: 780-451-4406; *Fax:* 780-454-1908
Gordon Reid, Contact; gordon.reid@mnp.ca

Edmonton - South
#201, 9426 - 51 Ave. NW
Edmonton, AB T6E 5A6 Canada
Tel: 780-462-8626; *Fax:* 780-462-8643
Murray Gray, Contact; murray.gray@mnp.ca

Estevan
#100, 1219 - 5th St.
Estevan, SK S4A 0Z5 Canada
Tel: 306-634-2603; *Fax:* 306-634-8708
Brian Drayton; brian.drayton@mnp.ca

Fort McMurray
9707 Main St.
Fort McMurray, AB T9H 1T5 Canada
Tel: 780-791-9000; *Fax:* 780-791-9047
Pat Olivier; pat.olivier@mnp.ca

Fort St. John
#2, 10611 - 102nd St.
Fort St. John, BC V1J 5L3 Canada
Tel: 250-785-8166; *Fax:* 250-785-5660
Marvin Beaumont, Contact; marvin.beaumont@mnp.ca

Grande Prairie
214 Place
PO Box 43
9909 - 102 St.
Grande Prairie, AB T8V 2V4 Canada
Tel: 780-831-1700; *Fax:* 780-539-9600
Toll-Free: 888-831-2870
Bridget Henniger; bridget.henniger@mnp.ca

Hope
PO Box 1689
100-E Fort St.
Hope, BC V0X 1L0 Canada
Tel: 604-869-9599; *Fax:* 604-869-3044
Toll-Free: 800-969-6060
Keith Britz, Contact; keith.britz@mnp.ca

Humboldt
PO Box 2590
701 - 9th St.
Humboldt, SK S0K 2A0 Canada
Tel: 306-682-2673; *Fax:* 306-682-5910
Toll-Free: 877-500-0789
Larry Rode, Contact; larry.rode@mnp.ca

Kelowna
600 - 1628 Dickson Ave.
Kelowna, BC V1Y 9X1 Canada
Tel: 250-763-8919; *Fax:* 250-763-1121
John Orisko, Contact; john.orisko@mnp.ca

Kenora
315 Main St. South
Kenora, ON P9N 1T4 Canada
Tel: 807-468-3338; *Fax:* 807-468-1418
Joseph Fregeau; jfregeau@fregeauandtompkin.ca

Killarney
501 Broadway Ave.
Killarney, MB R0K 1G0 Canada
Tel: 204-523-4633; *Fax:* 204-523-4538
Toll-Free: 877-500-0760

Lacombe
#5, 5265 - 45th St.
Lacombe, AB T4L 2A2 Canada
Tel: 403-782-7790; *Fax:* 403-782-7703
Gerald Wasylyshen; gerald.wasylyshen@mnp.ca

Leduc
#200, 5019 - 49th Ave.
Leduc, AB T9E 6T5 Canada
Tel: 780-986-2626; *Fax:* 780-986-2621
Deborah A. Sarnecki; deborah.sarnecki@mnp.ca

Lethbridge
3425 - 2nd Ave. South
Lethbridge, AB T1J 4V1 Canada
Tel: 403-329-1552; *Fax:* 403-329-1540
Gordon Tait, Contact; gord.tait@mnp.ca

Lloydminster
2905 - 50 Ave.
Lloydminster, SK S9V 0N7 Canada
Tel: 306-825-9855; *Fax:* 306-825-9640
Ralph Cormack; ralph.cormack@mnp.ca

Maple Ridge
#201 - 11939 224th St.
Maple Ridge, BC V2X 6B2 Canada
Tel: 604-463-8831; *Fax:* 604-463-0401
Tere Stykalo, Contact; tere.stykalo@mnp.ca

Medicine Hat
PO Box 580
666 - 4 St. SE
Medicine Hat, AB T1A 7G5 Canada
Tel: 403-527-4441; *Fax:* 403-526-6218
Toll-Free: 877-500-0786
Michael Keck, Managing Partner; michael.keck@mnp.ca

Melfort
PO Box 2020
601 Main St.
Melfort, SK S0E 1A0 Canada
Tel: 306-752-5800; *Fax:* 306-752-5933
Toll-Free: 877-500-0787
John Harder, Contact; john.harder@mnp.ca

Moosomin
PO Box 670
715 Main St.
Moosomin, SK S0G 3N0 Canada
Tel: 306-435-3347; *Fax:* 306-435-2494
Toll-Free: 877-500-0784
Layne McFarlane, Contact; layne.mcfarlane@mnp.ca

Nanaimo
PO Box 514
96 Wallace St.
Nanaimo, BC V9R 5L5 Canada
Tel: 250-753-8251; *Fax:* 250-754-3999
Toll-Free: 877-340-3330
Lucie Gosselin; lucie.gosselin@mnp.ca
Neepawa
PO Box 760
251 Davidson St.
Neepawa, MB R0J 1H0 Canada
Tel: 204-476-2326; *Fax:* 204-476-3663
Toll-Free: 877-500-0795
Marvin Beaumont, Contact; marvin.beaumont@mnp.ca
Peace River
PO Box 6030
10012 - 101st St.
Peace River, AB T8S 1S1 Canada
Tel: 780-624-3252; *Fax:* 780-624-8758
Bill Hirtle, CA; william.hirtle@mnp.ca
Port Moody
#601 - 205 Newport Dr.
Port Moody, BC V3H 5C9 Canada
Tel: 604-949-2088; *Fax:* 604-949-0509
Harry Gross; harry.gross@mnp.ca
Portage La Prairie
780 Saskatchewan Ave. West
Portage La Prairie, MB R1N 0M7 Canada
Tel: 204-239-6117; *Fax:* 204-857-3972
Jerry Lupkowski, Contact; jerry.lupkowski@mnp.ca
Prince Albert
25 - 11th St. East
Prince Albert, SK S6V 0Z8 Canada
Tel: 306-764-6873; *Fax:* 306-763-0766
Garth Busch; garth.busch@mnp.ca
Red Deer
4922 - 53 St.
Red Deer, AB T4N 2E9 Canada
Tel: 403-346-8878; *Fax:* 403-341-5599
Toll-Free: 877-500-0779
Tim Dekker, Contact; tim.dekker@mnp.ca
Red Lake
179 Howey St.
Red Lake, ON P0V 2M0 Canada
Tel: 807-727-1114
Gary Porter; gary.porter@mnp.ca
Regina
Royal Bank Bldg.
#900, 2010 - 11th Ave.
Regina, SK S4P 0J3 Canada
Tel: 306-790-7900; *Fax:* 306-790-7990
Toll-Free: 877-500-0780
Don Stewart, Contact; don.stewart@mnp.ca
Richmond Hill
#4, 10 West Pearce
Richmond Hill, ON L4B 1B6 Canada
Tel: 905-763-2436; *Fax:* 905-709-9952
Kris Holbeck; kris.holbeck@mnp.ca
Rimbey
PO Box 317
4714 - 50th Ave.
Rimbey, AB T0C 2J0 Canada
Tel: 403-843-4666; *Fax:* 403-843-4616
Chris Simpson, Contact; chris.simpson@mnp.ca
Rocky Mountain House
PO Box 2138
5004 - 50th St.
Rocky Mountain House, AB T4T 1B6 Canada
Tel: 403-845-2422; *Fax:* 403-845-3794
Gary Porter; gary.porter@mnp.ca
Saskatoon
800 - 119 4th Ave. South
Saskatoon, SK S7K 5X2 Canada
Tel: 306-665-6766; *Fax:* 306-665-9910
Toll-Free: 877-500-0778
David Kunaman, Contact; david.kunaman@mnp.ca
Steinbach
#100 - 250 Main St.
Steinbach, MB R5G 1Y8 Canada
Tel: 204-326-9816; *Fax:* 204-326-9586
Alyson Kennedy; alyson.kennedy@mnp.ca
Surrey
#316, 5455 - 152 St.
Surrey, BC V3S 5A5 Canada
Tel: 604-574-7211; *Fax:* 778-571-3549
Rick Bisson; rick.bisson@mnp.ca
Swift Current
50 - 1st Ave. NE
Swift Current, SK S9H 4W4 Canada
Tel: 306-773-8375; *Fax:* 306-773-7735
Toll-Free: 877-500-0762
Thunder Bay
#210, 1205 Amber Dr.
Thunder Bay, ON P7B 6M4 Canada
Tel: 807-623-2141; *Fax:* 807-622-1282
Ed Stromsmoe; ed.stromsmoe@mnp.ca
Toronto
#1100, 2 Bloor St. E.
Toronto, ON M4W 1A8 Canada
Tel: 416-596-1711; *Fax:* 416-596-7894
Don Hornford; don.hornford@mnp.ca
Vancouver
PO Box 49148
#2300, 1055 Dunsmuir St.
Vancouver, BC V1T 1J1 Canada
Tel: 604-685-8408; *Fax:* 604-685-8594
Ronald Anderson; ronald.anderson@mnp.ca
Vernon
#100, 2903 - 35th Ave.
Vernon, BC V1T 2S7 Canada
Tel: 778-475-5678; *Fax:* 778-475-5618
Tom Plishka; tom.plishka@mnp.ca
Virden
PO Box 670
233 Queen St. West
Virden, MB R0M 2C0 Canada
Tel: 204-748-1340; *Fax:* 204-748-3294
Tom Kirkup, Contact; tom.kirkup@mnp.ca
Waterloo
554 Weber St. N.
Waterloo, ON N2L 5C6 Canada
Tel: 519-725-7700; *Fax:* 519-725-7708
Heather Farfard; heather.farfard@mnp.ca
Weyburn
#301 - 117 3rd St. NE
Weyburn, SK S4H 0W3 Canada
Tel: 306-842-8915; *Fax:* 306-842-1966
Sean Wallace, CA, CFP; sean.wallace@mnp.ca
Winnipeg
#2500, 201 Portage Ave.
Winnipeg, MB R3B 3K6 Canada
Tel: 204-775-4531; *Fax:* 204-783-8329
Dena Weiss; dena.weiss@mnp.ca
Winnipeg - Polo Park
#301, 1661 Portage Ave.
Winnipeg, MB R3J 3T7 Canada
Tel: 204-336-6167; *Fax:* 204-772-9687
Toll-Free: 877-500-0795
Wayne McWhirter, Contact; wayne.mcwhirter@mnp.ca

Welch LLP
151 Slater St., 12th Fl.
Ottawa, ON K1P 5H3
Tel: 613-236-9191; *Fax:* 613-236-8258
www.welchllp.com
Former Name: Welch & Company LLP
Ownership: Private
Year Founded: 1918
Number of Employees: 200
Profile: The firm serves business, government, & not-for-profit clients. Taxation, accounting, auditing, personal financial planning, & wealth management services are provided.
Executives:
Michel Bossé, CA, Principal, Ottawa; mbosse@welchllp.com
Micheal Burch, CA, CFP, Managing Partner, Ottawa; mburch@welchllp.com
Don Timmins, CA, Partner, Ottawa; dtimmins@welchllp.com
Branches:
Belleville
525 Dundas St. East
Belleville, ON K8N 1G4 Canada
Tel: 613-966-2844; *Fax:* 613-966-2206
Glenn Collins, CA, Partner; gcollins@welch.on.ca
Campbellford
PO Box 1209
57 Bridge St. East
Campbellford, ON K0L 1L0 Canada
Tel: 705-653-3194; *Fax:* 705-653-1703
Marie Northey, CA, Partner; mnorthey@welch.on.ca
Cornwall
36 Second St. East
Cornwall, ON K6H 1Y3 Canada
Tel: 613-932-4953; *Fax:* 613-932-1731
Ron Mulligan, CA, Partner; rmulligan@welchllp.com
Gatineau
#201, 975, boul St-Joseph
Gatineau, QC J8Z 1W8 Canada
Tel: 819-771-7381; *Fax:* 819-771-3089
Guy Coté, CA, Partner; gcote@levesquemarchand.ca
Napanee
36 Bridge St. East
Napanee, ON K7R 1J8 Canada
Tel: 613-354-2169; *Fax:* 613-354-2160
Dan Atkinson, FCA, Partner; datkinson@welch.on.ca
Pembroke
PO Box 757
270 Lake St.
Pembroke, ON K8A 6X9 Canada
Tel: 613-735-1021; *Fax:* 613-735-2071
Hal Ward, CA, Partner; hward@welchllp.com
Picton
290 Main St.
Picton, ON K0K 2T0 Canada
Tel: 613-476-3283; *Fax:* 613-476-1627
Charles Thompson, CA, Partner; cthompson@welch.on.ca
Renfrew
101 Raglan St. North
Renfrew, ON K7V 1N7 Canada
Tel: 613-432-8399; *Fax:* 613-432-9154
Dan Amyotte, CA, Partner; damyotte@welchllp.com
Trenton
#4, 290 Dundas St. West
Trenton, ON K8V 3S1 Canada
Tel: 613-392-1287; *Fax:* 613-392-5456
John Bailey, CA, Partner; jbailey@welch.on.ca
Tweed
PO Box 807
63 Victoria St. North
Tweed, ON K0K 3J0 Canada
Tel: 613-478-5051; *Fax:* 613-478-3069
Marie Northey, CA, Partner; mnorthey@welch.on.ca

Accounting Firms by Province

Alberta

***Banff:* Collins Barrow Chartered Accountants - Banff**
Cascade Plaza
PO Box 1000
#370, 317 Banff Ave.
Banff, AB T1L 1H4
Tel: 403-762-8383; *Fax:* 403-762-8384
cbbanff@cbrockies.com
www.cbrockies.com

***Banff:* Kenway Mack Slusarchuk Stewart Bow Valley LLP Chartered Accountants**
PO Box 930
201 Bear St.
Banff, AB T1L 1A9
Tel: 403-762-2271; *Fax:* 403-762-8817
info@kmss.ca
www.kmss.ca

***Calgary:* Alger & Associates Inc.**
#400, 602 - 11th Ave. SW
Calgary, AB T2R 1J8
Tel: 403-298-5800; *Fax:* 403-296-2988
Toll-Free: 310-8888
www.alger.ca

***Calgary:* Bernard Martens Professional Corp.**
38 West Springs Gate SW
Calgary, AB T3H 4P5
Tel: 403-255-1262; *Fax:* 403-640-4652

***Calgary:* Buchanan Barry LLP**
#800, 840 - 6th Ave. SW
Calgary, AB T2P 3E5
Tel: 403-262-2116; *Fax:* 403-265-0845
mailbox@buchananbarry.ca
www.buchananbarry.ca

***Calgary:* Catalyst Chartered Accountants & Consultants**
#250, 200 Quarry Park Blvd. SE
Calgary, AB T2C 5E3
Tel: 403-296-0082; *Fax:* 403-296-0088
inquire@catalystsolutions.ca
www.catalystsolutions.ca

***Calgary:* CompassTAX Chartered Accountants**
Dorchester Square
#600, 1333 - 8th St. SW
Calgary, AB T2R 1M6
Tel: 403-531-2200; *Fax:* 403-263-1826
Toll-Free: 866-531-2281
www.compasstax.ca

***Calgary:* Daunheimer Lynch Anderson LLP**
6620 Crowchild Trail SW
Calgary, AB T3E 5R8
Tel: 403-217-5925; *Fax:* 403-217-5934
Toll-Free: 888-452-5925
www.dlallp.com

Calgary: Dick Cook Whyte Schulli Chartered Accountants
#555, 999 - 8th St. SW
Calgary, AB T3K 2L2
Tel: 403-245-1717; Fax: 403-244-9306

Calgary: DNTW Chartered Accountants, LLP
5917 - 1A St. SW
Calgary, AB T2H 0G4
Tel: 403-209-2248; Fax: 403-539-2248
calgary.help@dntw.com
www.dntw.com

Calgary: D.W. Robart Professional Corporation
#1480, 540 - 5th Ave. SW
Calgary, AB T2P 0M2
Tel: 403-266-2611; Fax: 403-265-8626
don@robart.ca

Calgary: Flood & Associates Consulting Ltd.
#410, 840 - 6 Ave. SW
Calgary, AB T2P 3E5
Tel: 403-263-1523; Fax: 403-263-1524
flood_co@telusplanet.net

Calgary: Garrett Gray Chartered Accountants
Parkside Place
#920, 602 - 12 Ave. SW
Calgary, AB T2R 1J3
Tel: 403-806-2850; Fax: 403-806-2854
info@garrettgray.com
www.garrettgray.com

Calgary: Hamilton & Rosenthal Chartered Accountants
1034 - 8th Ave. SW
Calgary, AB T2P 1J2
Tel: 403-266-2175; Fax: 403-514-2211
www.hamrose.com

Calgary: Kenway Mack Slusarchuk Stewart LLP
#220, 333 - 11 Ave. SW
Calgary, AB T2R 1L9
Tel: 403-233-7750; Fax: 403-266-5267
info@kmss.ca
www.kmss.ca

Calgary: Kirk Wormley Chartered Accountant
#806, 7015 Macleod Trail SW
Calgary, AB T2H 2K6
Tel: 403-266-5607; Fax: 403-201-0248
kirkwormley@shaw.ca
www.kirkwormley.ca

Calgary: Lalani & Co.
#101, 4707 - 1 St. SW
Calgary, AB T2G 0A1
Tel: 403-693-3310; Fax: 403-214-7869

Calgary: Laurie Mounteer Professional Corp.
560 Parkridge Dr. SE
Calgary, AB T2J 4Z3
Tel: 403-249-9944
laurie@mounteer.ca
www.expatax.ca

Calgary: Lo Porter Hétu
#601, 2535 - 3 Ave. SE
Calgary, AB T2A 7W5
Tel: 403-283-1088; Fax: 403-283-1044
calgary@porterhetu.com
www.porterhetu.com

Calgary: The Matthews Group
#201, 1508 - 8th St. SW
Calgary, AB T2R 1R6
Tel: 403-229-0066; Fax: 403-229-2817
matthewsgrp@telus.net
www.matthewsgrp.com

Calgary: McKinnon & Co., Chartered Accountants
740, 10655 Southport Rd. SW
Calgary, AB T2W 4Y1
Tel: 403-262-9260

Calgary: Mitchell Kelly Jones & Associates Inc.
#1070, 340 - 12 Ave. SW
Calgary, AB T2R 1L5
Tel: 403-265-8545; Fax: 403-265-8554

Calgary: PricewaterhouseCoopers LLP, Canada - Calgary
Petro-Canada Centre
#3100, 111 - 5th Ave. SW
Calgary, AB T2P 5L3
Tel: 403-509-7500; Fax: 403-781-1825
www.pwc.com/ca

Calgary: Vertefeuille Rempel Chartered Accountants
#401, 304 - 8 Ave. SW
Calgary, AB T2P 1C2
Tel: 403-294-0733; Fax: 403-294-0734
Toll-Free: 877-794-0733
www.vertrempel.com

Canmore: Collins Barrow Chartered Accountants - Canmore
#1, 714 - 10th St.
Canmore, AB T1W 2A6
Tel: 403-678-4444; Fax: 403-678-5163
cbcanmore@cbrockies.com
www.cbrockies.com

Cochrane: W. Callaway Professional Corporation
PO Box 61
Site 5, RR#1
Cochrane, AB T4C 1A1
Tel: 403-932-5433; Fax: 403-932-5577
bill@wcallaway.com
www.wcallaway.com

Drayton Valley: Collins Barrow Chartered Accountants - Drayton Valley
PO Box 6927
5204 - 52nd Ave.
Drayton Valley, AB T7A 1S3
Tel: 780-542-4468; Fax: 780-542-5275
Toll-Free: 888-542-4468
draytonvalley@collinsbarrow.com

Edmonton: Bernhard Brinkmann Chartered Accountant
PO Box 82090, Yellowbird Stn. Yellowbird
#200, 3205 - 97 St. NW
Edmonton, AB T6N 1B7
Tel: 780-434-2756; Fax: 780-463-7605
bhbrinkmann@brinkmann.ca
www.brinkmann.ca

Edmonton: Collins Barrow Chartered Accountants - Edmonton
Commerce Place
#2380, 10155 - 102 St. NW
Edmonton, AB T5J 4G8
Tel: 780-428-1522; Fax: 780-425-8189
edmonton@collinsbarrow.com

Edmonton: DFK Canada Inc.
1923 - 151 Ave.
Edmonton, AB T5Y 1W1
Tel: 780-472-4334; Fax: 780-472-4334
exec@dfk.ca
www.dfk.ca

Edmonton: Givens LLP, Edmonton
#201, West Chambers - 12220 Stony Plain Rd.
Edmonton, AB T5N 3Y4
Tel: 780-482-7337; Fax: 780-482-7423
edmonton@porterhetu.com
www.porterhetu.com

Edmonton: Hawkings Epp Dumont Chartered Accountants
Mayfield Square I
10476 Mayfield Rd.
Edmonton, AB T5P 4P4
Tel: 780-489-9606; Fax: 780-484-9689
www.hawkings.com

Edmonton: King & Company
#1201, Energy Sq.
10109 - 106 St.
Edmonton, AB T5J 3L7
Tel: 780-423-2437; Fax: 780-426-5861

Edmonton: Koehli Wickenberg Chartered Accountants
#105, 4990 - 92nd Ave.
Edmonton, AB T6B 2V4
Tel: 780-466-6204; Fax: 780-466-6262

Edmonton: Liu Raymond C S Chartered Accountant
#410, 10665 Jasper Ave.
Edmonton, AB T5J 3S9
Tel: 780-429-1047

Edmonton: PricewaterhouseCoopers LLP, Canada - Edmonton
Toronto-Dominion Tower, Edmonton City Centre
#1501, 10088 - 102 Ave. NW
Edmonton, AB T5J 3N5
Tel: 780-441-6700; Fax: 780-441-6776
www.pwc.com/ca

Edmonton: Romanovsky & Associates, Chartered Accountants
10260 - 112 St.
Edmonton, AB T5K 1M4
Tel: 780-447-5830; Fax: 780-451-6291
Toll-Free: 800-861-5830
www.romanovsky.com

Edmonton: SVS Group LLP
#100, 17010 - 103 Ave.
Edmonton, AB T5S 1K7
Tel: 780-486-3357; Fax: 780-486-3320
dvisser@svsgroup.ca
www.svsgroup.ca

Edmonton: Watson Aberant Chartered Accountants (L.L.P.)
4212 - 98th St.
Edmonton, AB T6E 6A1
Tel: 780-438-5969; Fax: 780-437-3918
info@watsonaberant.com

Fort Saskatchewan: Givens LLP, Fort Saskatchewan
9928 - 99 Ave.
Fort Saskatchewan, AB T8L 4G8
Tel: 780-998-2110; Fax: 780-998-0276
fortsask@porterhetu.com
www.porterhetu.com

High River: Muth & Company
PO Box 5039
19 - 3 Ave. SE
High River, AB T1V 1M3
Tel: 403-652-4272; Fax: 403-652-2339
highriver@porterhetu.com
www.porterhetu.com

Lacombe: Cookson Kooyman Chartered Accountants
#220, 5001 - 52nd St.
Lacombe, AB T4L 2A6
Tel: 403-782-3361; Fax: 403-782-3070
lacombe@ckca.net

Leduc: Luchak Wright Wnuk Chartered Accountants
4716 - 51 Ave.
Leduc, AB T9E 6Y8
Tel: 780-986-8383; Fax: 780-986-4499
Toll-Free: 888-986-8383
lww@lwwca.com
www.lwwca.com

Lethbridge: John Van Dyk, Professional Corporation
#801B, 3 Ave. South
Lethbridge, AB T1J 2B9
Tel: 403-317-4500; Fax: 403-317-4501
justin.vandyk@telus.net

Lethbridge: Young Parkyn McNab LLP (YPM)
#100, 530 - 8 St. South
Lethbridge, AB T1J 2J8
Tel: 403-382-6800; Fax: 403-327-8990
Toll-Free: 800-665-5034
www.ypm.ca

Red Deer: Collins Barrow Chartered Accountants - Red Deer
#300, 5010 - 43 St.
Red Deer, AB T4N 6H2
Tel: 403-342-5541; Fax: 403-347-3766
reddeer@collinsbarrow.com
www.collinsbarrowreddeer.ab.ca

Slave Lake: Nash & Company
PO Box 129
Slave Lake, AB T0G 2A0
Tel: 780-849-3977; Fax: 780-849-3244
slavelake@porterhetu.com
www.porterhetu.com

St Paul: Desjardins & Company
PO Box 1600
4440 - 50 Ave.
St Paul, AB T0A 3A0
Tel: 780-645-5516; Fax: 780-645-6010
office@desjardins-co.com
www.desjardins-co.com

Stettler: **Gitzel Krejci Dand Peterson**
PO Box 460
4912 - 51 St.
Stettler, AB T0C 2L0
Tel: 403-742-4431; *Fax:* 403-742-1266
Toll-Free: 877-742-4431
gkdpca@gkdpca.com
www.gkdpca.com

Sundre: **Valerie L. Burrell Chartered Accountant**
#201, 101 - 6 St. SW
Sundre, AB T0M 1X0
Tel: 403-638-3116; *Fax:* 403-638-9166
valb@telusplanet.net
www.sundre-cornerbrook.com/Accountant/

Vegreville: **Wilde and Company**
PO Box 70
4902 - 50th St.
Vegreville, AB T9C 1R1
Tel: 780-632-3673; *Fax:* 780-632-6133
Toll-Free: 800-808-0998
office@wildeandco.com
www.wildeandco.com

Wainright: **Hall & Company**
291 - 10th St.
Wainright, AB T9W 1N7
Tel: 780-842-6106; *Fax:* 780-842-5540
Toll-Free: 888-842-6106
barry@hallco.ca
www.hallco.ca

British Columbia

Abbotsford: **McDonald & Co.**
#301, 2955 Gladwin Rd.
Abbotsford, BC V2T 5T4
Tel: 604-853-5225

Burnaby: **Barkman & Tanaka**
Lougheed Plaza
#225, 9600 Cameron St.
Burnaby, BC V3J 7N3
Tel: 604-421-2591; *Fax:* 604-421-1171

Burnaby: **Kanester Johal Chartered Accountants**
#208, 3993 Henning Dr.
Burnaby, BC V5C 6P7
Tel: 604-451-8300; *Fax:* 604-451-8301
info@kjca.com
www.kjca.com

Burnaby: **Kemp Harvey Goodison Inc.**
#210, 6400 Roberts St.
Burnaby, BC V5G 4C9
Tel: 604-291-1470; *Fax:* 604-291-0264
Burnaby@khgcga.com
www.khgcga.com

Burns Lake: **M. McPhail & Associates Inc.**
PO Box 597
Burns Lake, BC V0J 1E0
Tel: 250-692-7595; *Fax:* 250-692-3872
mcphail@mcphailcga.com
www.mcphailcga.com

Campbell River: **Chase Sekulich Chartered Accountants**
#101, 400 Tenth Ave.
Campbell River, BC V9W 4E3
Tel: 250-287-8331; *Fax:* 250-287-7224
Toll-Free: 866-317-8331
office@chasesekulich.com
www.chasesekulich.com; www.bcdebtsolutions.com

Campbell River: **Eidsvik & Co.**
#303, 1100 Island Hwy.
Campbell River, BC V9W 8C6
Tel: 250-286-6629; *Fax:* 250-286-6779

Castlegar: **Craig Gutwald Inc.**
880 Waterloo Rd.
Castlegar, BC V1N 4K8
Tel: 250-365-0434; *Fax:* 250-365-0469
www.gutwald.ca

Duncan: **Atchison Palmer Leslie Chartered Accountants**
#301, 394 Duncan St.
Duncan, BC V9L 3W4
Tel: 250-748-1426; *Fax:* 250-748-9724
www.aplaccountants.com

Grand Forks: **Kemp Harvey Burch Kientz Inc.**
PO Box 2020
619 Central Ave.
Grand Forks, BC V0H 1H0
Tel: 250-442-2121; *Fax:* 250-442-5825
GrandForks@khgcga.com
www.khgcga.com

Kelowna: **Chun & Company**
#202, 3320 Richter St.
Kelowna, BC V1W 4V5
Tel: 250-860-8687; *Fax:* 250-860-8413
www.chun.ca

Kelowna: **Wahl & Associates**
#103, 1441 Ellis St.
Kelowna, BC V1Y 2A3
Tel: 250-762-3362; *Fax:* 250-762-3409
info@wahlcga.com
www.wahlcga.com

Madeira Park: **Bonnie Murray Inc.**
PO Box 70
Madeira Park, BC V0N 2H0
Tel: 604-883-2857; *Fax:* 604-883-2861

Maple Ridge: **Choquette & Company Accounting Group**
10662 - 240A St.
Maple Ridge, BC V2W 2B1
Tel: 604-463-8202; *Fax:* 604-463-8210
Toll-Free: 800-667-9254
info@choquetteco.com
www.choquetteco.com
Other Contact Information: Skype: 604-463-8202

Nanaimo: **Church Pickard & Co.**
#301, 17 Church St.
Nanaimo, BC V9R 5H5
Tel: 250-754-6396; *Fax:* 250-754-8177
Toll-Free: 866-754-6396
mail@churchpickard.com
www.churchpickard.com

Nanaimo: **Gary Ruffle Ltd.**
5107 Somerset Dr., #C
Nanaimo, BC V9T 2K5
Tel: 250-758-5557; *Fax:* 250-758-5720
garyruffleltd@shaw.ca
www.garyruffleltd.com

Nanaimo: **Robert F. Fischer & Company Inc., C.G.A.**
#13, 327 Prideaux St.
Nanaimo, BC V9R 2N4
Tel: 250-753-7287; *Fax:* 250-753-7453

Nelson: **Carmichael, Toews, Irving Inc.**
247 Baker St.
Nelson, BC V1L 4H4
Tel: 250-354-4451; *Fax:* 250-354-4427
admin@cti-cga.com
www.cti-cga.com

New Denver: **Mark Adams Ltd.**
316 6th Ave.
New Denver, BC V0G 1S0
Tel: 250-358-2411

North Vancouver: **C. Topley & Company Ltd.**
#200, 260 West Esplanade
North Vancouver, BC V7M 3G7
Tel: 604-987-8688; *Fax:* 604-904-8628
Toll-Free: 877-363-3437

North Vancouver: **Gray & Associates**
#201, 1075 West 1st St.
North Vancouver, BC V7P 3T4
Tel: 604-990-0550; *Fax:* 604-990-0509
Toll-Free: 800-990-0550
info@grayandassociates.ca
grayandassociates.ca

North Vancouver: **J. Casperson & Associates Ltd.**
221 Rondoval Cres.
North Vancouver, BC V7N 2W6
Tel: 604-983-2113; *Fax:* 604-983-2114
jindra@jcasperson.com
jcaspersonassociatesltd.supersites.ca

North Vancouver: **MacDonald Tash & Associates**
#120, 889 Harbourside Dr.
North Vancouver, BC V7P 3S1
Tel: 604-987-2300; *Fax:* 604-987-2888
taxmatters@taxmatters.ca
www.taxmatters.ca

North Vancouver: **Misam Canada Consulting Ltd.**
#107, 998 Harbourside Dr.
North Vancouver, BC V7P 3T2
Tel: 604-984-3309; *Fax:* 604-984-3308
info@misamcanada.com
www.misamcanada.com
Social Media: www.twitter.com/MCS_Consulting XXÇ

Oliver: **Kemp Harvey Casorso Inc.**
PO Box 1478
34864 - 97th St.
Oliver, BC V0H 1T0
Tel: 250-498-4977; *Fax:* 250-498-4330
Oliver@khgcga.com
www.khgcga.com

Osoyoos: **Kemp Harvey Kemp - Osoyoos**
8901 Main St.
Osoyoos, BC V0H 1V0
Tel: 250-495-3223; *Fax:* 250-495-3559
Toll-Free: 888-9850-5595
Osoyoos@khgcga.com
www.khgcga.com

Osoyoos: **White Kennedy, Chartered Accountants - Osoyoos**
PO Box 260
#204, 8309 Main St.
Osoyoos, BC V0H 1V0
Tel: 250-495-2688; *Fax:* 250-495-3525
osoyoos@whitekennedy.com
www.whitekennedy.com

Penticton: **Harvey Lister & Webb Incorporated**
502 Ellis St.
Penticton, BC V2A 4M3
Tel: 250-492-8821; *Fax:* 250-492-8288
info@harveylisterwebb.com
www.harveylisterwebb.com

Penticton: **Kemp Harvey Kemp - Penticton**
445 Ellis St.
Penticton, BC V2A 4M1
Tel: 250-492-8800; *Fax:* 250-492-6921
Penticton@khgcga.com
www.khgcga.com

Penticton: **White Kennedy, Chartered Accountants - Penticton**
#201, 99 Padmore Ave. East
Penticton, BC V2A 7H7
Tel: 250-493-0600; *Fax:* 250-493-4709
penticton@whitekennedy.com
www.whitekennedy.com

Port Coquitlam: **Kemp Harvey de Roca Chan Inc.**
#2300, 2850 Shaughnessy St.
Port Coquitlam, BC V3C 6K5
Tel: 604-552-4388; *Fax:* 604-552-7709
poco@khgcga.com
www.khgcga.com

Port Moody: **Gregory & Associates**
#402, 130 Brew St.
Port Moody, BC V3H 0E3
Tel: 604-939-2929; *Fax:* 604-936-4002
info@gregorywhittle.ca
www.gregorywhittle.ca

Prince George: **Terlesky Braithwaite Janzen, Certified General Accountants**
#300, 180 Victoria St.
Prince George, BC V2L 2J2
Tel: 250-564-2014; *Fax:* 250-564-5613
Toll-Free: 888-564-2014
tbjpg@tbjcga.com
www.tbjcga.com

Richmond: **Bruce Dunn & Company Inc., Chartered Accountants**
#200, 5760 Minoru Blvd.
Richmond, BC V6X 2A9
Tel: 604-241-8824; *Fax:* 604-241-8800
info@brucedunn.ca
www.brucedunn.ca

Richmond: **Greig Sheppard Ltd.**
5090 - 8171 Ackroyd Rd.
Richmond, BC V6X 3K1
Tel: 604-270-7601; *Fax:* 604-270-3314
cga@greigsheppard.com
www.greigsheppard.com

Richmond: **Jerry's Accounting Ltd.**
#530, 130 - 8191 Westminster Hwy.
Richmond, BC V6X 1A7
Tel: 604-273-7789; *Fax:* 604-273-9449
jerryky@shaw.ca
www.jerryaccounting.com

Richmond: **Sunny Sun & Associates Inc.**
#708, 6081 No. 3 Rd.
Richmond, BC V6Y 2B2
Tel: 604-270-4610; *Fax:* 604-270-4618
info@sunnycga.com
www.sunnycga.com

Squamish: **McMillan Thorn, Certified General Accountants - Squamish**
PO Box 2120
38013 - 3rd Ave.
Squamish, BC V0N 3G0
Tel: 604-892-5281; *Fax:* 604-892-5276
squamish@mcmillanthorn.com
www.mcmillanthorn.com

Surrey: **Heming, Wyborn & Grewal**
#200, 17618 - 58 Ave.
Surrey, BC V3S 1L3
Tel: 604-576-9121; *Fax:* 604-576-2890
hwgca@hwgca.com
www.hwgca.com

Surrey: **Luckett Wenman & Associates**
#204, 10252 - 135th St.
Surrey, BC V3T 4C2
Tel: 604-584-3566; *Fax:* 604-584-0629
Toll-Free: 866-584-3566
contact@luckettwenman.com
www.luckettwenman.com

Surrey: **PricewaterhouseCoopers LLP, Canada - Surrey**
10190 - 152A St., 3rd Fl.
Surrey, BC V3R 1J7
Tel: 604-806-7000; *Fax:* 604-806-7806
www.pwc.com/ca

Surrey: **Sharma & Associates**
#205, 8388 - 128th St.
Surrey, BC V3W 4G2
Tel: 604-597-5612; *Fax:* 604-590-5808
satish@sharmacga.com; hari@sharmacga.com
www.sharmacga.com

Surrey: **Sunny Sun & Associates Inc. - Surrey**
#200, 10193 - 152A St.
Surrey, BC V3R 4H6
Tel: 604-270-4613; *Fax:* 604-270-4618
info@sunnycga.com
www.sunnycga.com

Surrey: **Van Wensem, Eakins & George**
17678 - 58A Ave.
Surrey, BC V3S 8V7
Tel: 604-576-9242; *Fax:* 604-576-9258
info@vweg-cga.com
www.vweg-cga.com

Terrace: **Demers & Associates**
#201, 4716 Lazelle Ave.
Terrace, BC V8G 1T2
Tel: 250-638-8705; *Fax:* 250-638-0600
info@demerscga.com
www.demerscga.com

Vancouver: **Bing C. Wong & Associates Ltd.**
124 East Pender St., 3rd Fl.
Vancouver, BC V6A 1T3
Tel: 604-682-7561; *Fax:* 604-682-7665

Vancouver: **Blair Crosson Voyer Chartered Accountants**
Commerce Pl.
#1650, 400, Burrard St.
Vancouver, BC V6C 3A6
Tel: 604-684-3371; *Fax:* 604-684-9832

Vancouver: **Campbell, Saunders Ltd.**
#1000, 570 Granville St.
Vancouver, BC V6C 3P1
Tel: 604-915-5550; *Fax:* 604-915-5560
info@csvan.com
www.csvan.com

Vancouver: **Cawley & Associates**
1622 - 7th Ave. West, 3rd Fl.
Vancouver, BC V6J 1S5
Tel: 604-731-1191; *Fax:* 604-731-3511
bcawley@cawley.ca
www.cawley.ca

Vancouver: **Collins Barrow Chartered Accountants - Vancouver**
Burrard Bldg.
#800, 1030 West Georgia St.
Vancouver, BC V6E 3B9
Tel: 604-685-0564; *Fax:* 604-685-2050
vancouver@collinsbarrow.com

Vancouver: **D&H Group**
1333 West Broadway St., 10th Fl.
Vancouver, BC V6H 4C1
Tel: 604-731-5881; *Fax:* 604-731-9923
info@dhgroup.ca
www.dhgroup.ca

Vancouver: **David Lin, Certified General Accountant**
5728 East Blvd.
Vancouver, BC V6M 4M4
Tel: 604-267-0381
dlin@telus.net
www3.telus.net/davidlin

Vancouver: **Davidson & Co.**
Stock Exchange Tower
PO Box 10372
#1200, 609 Granville St.
Vancouver, BC V7Y 1G6
Tel: 604-687-0947; *Fax:* 604-687-6172
davidson@davidson-co.com
www.davidson-co.com

Vancouver: **Equity Business Services Inc.**
#200, 1892 West Broadway
Vancouver, BC V6J 1Y9
Tel: 604-874-9080; *Fax:* 604-874-9080
ehoy@equityinc.ca
www.equityinc.ca

Vancouver: **Galloway Botteselle & Company**
Maple Place Professional Centre
#300, 2000 West 12th Ave.
Vancouver, BC V6J 2G2
Tel: 604-736-6581; *Fax:* 604-736-0152
vancouver@porterhetu.com
www.porterhetu.com

Vancouver: **Greenberg Associates**
North Office Tower, Oakridge Centre
#489, 650 West 41st Ave.
Vancouver, BC V5Z 2M9
Tel: 604-264-5170; *Fax:* 604-264-5101
general@cga-gb.com
www.cga-gb.com

Vancouver: **Lam Lo Nishio Chartered Accountants**
659-G Moberly Rd.
Vancouver, BC V5Z 4B2
Tel: 604-872-8883; *Fax:* 604-872-8889
info@lamlonishio.ca
www.lamlonishio.ca

Vancouver: **Lancaster & David, Chartered Accountants**
PO Box 10122, Pacific Centre Stn. Pacific Centre
#510, 701 West Georgia St.
Vancouver, BC V7Y 1C6
Tel: 604-717-5526; *Fax:* 604-717-5560
admin@lancasteranddavid.ca
www.lancasteranddavid.ca

Vancouver: **Manning Elliott**
1050 West Pender, 11th Fl.
Vancouver, BC V6J 3S7
Tel: 604-714-3600; *Fax:* 604-714-3669
info@manningelliott.com
www.manningelliott.com

Vancouver: **N.I. Cameron Inc.**
#303, 475 Howe St.
Vancouver, BC V6C 2B3
Tel: 604-669-9631; *Fax:* 604-669-1848
info@nicameroninc.com
www.nicameroninc.com

Vancouver: **PricewaterhouseCoopers LLP, Canada - Vancouver**
PricewaterhouseCoopers Place
250 Howe St., 7th Fl.
Vancouver, BC V6C 3S7
Tel: 604-806-7000; *Fax:* 604-806-7806
www.pwc.com/ca

Vancouver: **Quantum Accounting Services Inc.**
#205, 873 Beatty St.
Vancouver, BC V6B 2M6
Tel: 604-662-8985; *Fax:* 604-662-8986
www.qas.bc.ca

Vancouver: **Rolfe, Benson Chartered Accountants**
#1400, 900 West Hastings St.
Vancouver, BC V6C 1E3
Tel: 604-684-1101; *Fax:* 604-684-7937
admin@rolfebenson.com
www.rolfebenson.com

Vancouver: **Smythe Ratcliffe Chartered Accountants**
#700, 355 Burrard St.
Vancouver, BC V6C 2G8
Tel: 604-687-1231; *Fax:* 604-688-4675
reception@smytheratcliffe.com
www.smytheratcliffe.com

Vancouver: **Stan W. Lee**
North Tower
#628, 650 West 41st Ave.
Vancouver, BC V5Z 2M9
Tel: 604-291-6016; *Fax:* 604-291-2018
stan@stanwleeca.com
www.stanwleeca.com

Vancouver: **Strategex Group**
#210, 1075 West Georgia St.
Vancouver, BC V6E 3C9
Tel: 604-688-2355; *Fax:* 604-688-2315
www.strategexgroup.ca

Vancouver: **Watson Dauphinee & Masuch Chartered Accountants**
#420, 1501 West Broadway Ave.
Vancouver, BC V6J 4Z6
Tel: 604-734-3247; *Fax:* 604-734-4802
info@wdmca.com
www.wdmca.com

Vernon: **Clark Robinson**
3109 - 32nd Ave.
Vernon, BC V1T 2M2
Tel: 250-545-7264; *Fax:* 250-542-5116
info@clarkrobinson.com
www.clarkrobinson.com

Vernon: **Kemp Harvey Laidman-Betts Inc.**
#204, 3334 - 30th Ave.
Vernon, BC V1T 2C8
Tel: 250-545-1544; *Fax:* 250-260-3641
Toll-Free: 877-547-1544
Vernon@khgcga.com
www.khgcga.com

Vernon: **Willis Associates**
#100, 2903 - 35th Ave.
Vernon, BC V1T 2S7
Tel: 250-549-2922; *Fax:* 250-542-8300
Toll-Free: 888-333-2922
www.willisassociates.ca

Victoria: **Burkett & Abercrombie Chartered Accountants**
#200, 3561 Shelbourne St.
Victoria, BC V8P 4G8
Tel: 250-370-9718; *Fax:* 250-370-9179
accountants@burkett.ca
www.burkett.ca

Victoria: **Feil & Co.**
1580 Cook St.
Victoria, BC V8T 3N8
Tel: 250-382-6177; *Fax:* 250-385-0154
email@feilnco.com
www.feilnco.com

Victoria: **Ian B. Lawson & Co. Inc.**
Shamrock Professional Centre
#201, 830 Shamrock St.
Victoria, BC V8X 2V1
Tel: 250-475-0222; *Fax:* 250-475-0229
victoria@porterhetu.com
www.porterhetu.com; www.iblawson.shawbiz.ca

Westbank: **White Kennedy, Chartered Accountants - Westbank**
#1, 2429 Dobbin Rd.
Westbank, BC V4T 2L4
Tel: 250-768-3400; *Fax:* 240-768-3445
westbank@whitekennedy.com
www.whitekennedy.com

Whistler: **Gershon & Company**
#207A, 4368 Main St.
Whistler, BC V0N 1B0
Tel: 604-938-1892; *Fax:* 604-938-1870
www.gershonandco.com

Whistler: **Gordon J. Wiber & Associates Inc.**
#22, 1212 Alpha Lake Rd.
Whistler, BC V0N 1B2
Tel: 604-935-1114; *Fax:* 604-935-1154
www.whistlerca.com

Whistler: **J. Casperson & Associates Ltd. - Whistler**
2509 Whistler Road
Whistler, BC V7X 1B0
Tel: 604-932-2450
jindra@jcasperson.com
jcaspersonassociatesltd.supersites.ca

Whistler: **McMillan Thorn, Certified General Accountants - Whistler**
#204, 1085 Millar Creek Rd.
Whistler, BC V0N 1B1
Tel: 604-938-1544; *Fax:* 604-938-1577
mail@mcmillanthorn.com
www.mcmillanthorn.com

Manitoba

Carman: **Nakonechny & Power Chartered Accountants Ltd.**
PO Box 880
31 Main St. South
Carman, MB R0G 0J0
Tel: 204-745-2061; *Fax:* 204-745-6322
www.nakandpow.com

Souris: **Karen G. Duthie, CGA**
PO Box 927
Souris, MB R0K 2C0
Tel: 204-483-3903; *Fax:* 204-483-2489
kduthie@porterhetu.com
www.porterhetu.com

Swan River: **Pacak Kowal Hardie & Company, Chartered Accountants**
PO Box 1660
#100, 4th Avenue North
Swan River, MB R0L 1Z0
Tel: 204-734-9331; *Fax:* 204-734-4785
Toll-Free: 800-743-8447
pkhl@pkhl.ca
www.pacakkowalhardie.com

Swan River: **Reimer & Company Inc.**
PO Box 146
359 Kelsey Trail
Swan River, MB R0L 1Z0
Tel: 204-734-2599; *Fax:* 204-734-3184
info@reimerco.ca
www.reimerco.ca

Thompson: **Kendall Wall Pandya, Chartered Accountants**
118 Cree Rd.
Thompson, MB R8N 0C1
Tel: 204-778-7312; *Fax:* 204-778-7919

Winnipeg: **A.L. Schellenberg, Chartered Accountant**
474 Panet Rd.
Winnipeg, MB R2C 3B9
Tel: 204-669-5143; *Fax:* 204-669-5145
leon@mts.net

Winnipeg: **BCCA LLP Chartered Accountants**
#1505, 444 St. Mary Ave.
Winnipeg, MB R3C 3T1
Tel: 204-957-7000; *Fax:* 204-949-1191
mail@bccallp.com
www.bccallp.com

Winnipeg: **Booke & Partners**
#500, 5 Donald St.
Winnipeg, MB R3L 2T4
Tel: 204-284-7060; *Fax:* 204-284-7105
www.bookeandpartners.ca

Winnipeg: **Chochinov Porter Hétu**
#1250, 363 Broadway Ave.
Winnipeg, MB R3C 3N9
Tel: 204-956-1685; *Fax:* 204-957-7694
schochinov@porterhetu.com
www.porterhetu.com

Winnipeg: **Collins Barrow Chartered Accountants - Winnipeg**
Century Plaza
#401, 1 Wesley Ave.
Winnipeg, MB R3C 4C6
Tel: 204-942-0221; *Fax:* 204-944-8371
winnipeg@collinsbarrow.com

Winnipeg: **Craig & Ross Chartered Accountants**
#1515, 1 Lombard Place
Winnipeg, MB R3B 0X3
Tel: 204-956-9400; *Fax:* 204-956-9424
info@craigross.com
www.craigross.com

Winnipeg: **Craig R. Burgess, CGA**
383 McMillan Ave.
Winnipeg, MB R3L 0N3
Tel: 204-334-8972; *Fax:* 204-334-8448
cburgess@porterhetu.com
www.porterhetu.com

Winnipeg: **The Exchange Chartered Accountants LLP**
#100, 123 Bannatyne Ave.
Winnipeg, MB R3B 0R3
Tel: 204-943-4584; *Fax:* 204-957-5195
info@exg.ca
www.exg.ca

Winnipeg: **Gaudette Elvers LLP**
738 Osborne St.
Winnipeg, MB R3L 2C2
Tel: 204-489-2781; *Fax:* 204-452-5956
gelvers@porterhetu.com; egaudette@porterhetu.com
www.porterhetu.com

Winnipeg: **Knowles Warkentin & Bridges, Chartered Accountants**
#800, 125 Garry St.
Winnipeg, MB R3C 3P2
Tel: 204-982-3878; *Fax:* 204-982-3888
connor@kwb.ca
www.kwb.ca

Winnipeg: **Lazer Grant LLP Chartered Accountants & Business Advisors**
#300, 309 McDermot Ave.
Winnipeg, MB R3A 1T3
Tel: 204-942-0300; *Fax:* 204-957-5611
Toll-Free: 800-220-0005
LazerGrant@lazergrant.ca
www.lazergrant.ca

Winnipeg: **M Group Chartered Accountants**
710 Corydon Ave.
Winnipeg, MB R3M 0X9
Tel: 204-992-7200; *Fax:* 204-992-7208
info@mgroup.ca
www.mgroup.ca

Winnipeg: **Magnus & Buffie Chartered Accountants**
#1810, 444 St. Mary Ave.
Winnipeg, MB R3C 3T1
Tel: 204-942-4441; *Fax:* 204-944-0400

Winnipeg: **PKBW Group, Chartered Accountants & Business Advisors Inc.**
219 Fort St.
Winnipeg, MB R3C 1E2
Tel: 204-942-0861; *Fax:* 204-947-6834
senez@pkbwgroup.ca
www.pkbwgroup.ca

Winnipeg: **Pope & Brookes, DFK LLP, Chartered Accountants**
#300, 530 Kenaston Blvd.
Winnipeg, MB R3N 1Z4
Tel: 204-487-7957; *Fax:* 204-487-1243
advice@pb-dfk.com
www.pb-dfk.com

Winnipeg: **PPW Chartered Accountants LLP**
#209, 1661 Portage Ave.
Winnipeg, MB R3J 3T7
Tel: 204-772-4936; *Fax:* 204-774-4462
solutions@ppw.ca
www.ppw.ca

Winnipeg: **PricewaterhouseCoopers LLP, Canada - Winnipeg**
Richardson Bldg.
#2300, 1 Lombard Pl.
Winnipeg, MB R3B 0X6
Tel: 204-926-2400; *Fax:* 204-994-1020
www.pwc.com/ca

Winnipeg: **RDK Chartered Accountant Ltd.**
5 Whitkirk Place
Winnipeg, MB R3R 2A2
Tel: 204-885-5280; *Fax:* 204-831-6670
admin@rdkcharteredaccountant.com
www.rdkcharteredaccountant.com

Winnipeg: **Scarrow & Donald LLP**
#100, 5 Donald St.
Winnipeg, MB R3L 2T4
Tel: 204-982-9800; *Fax:* 204-474-2886
sd@scarrowdonald.mb.ca
www.scarrowdonald.mb.ca

New Brunswick

Campbellton: **Allen, Paquet & Arseneau LLP**
PO Box 519
207 Roseberry St.
Campbellton, NB E3N 3G9
Tel: 506-789-0820; *Fax:* 506-759-7514
apada@apa-ca.com
www.apa-ca.com

Edmundston: **LeBlanc Nadeau Bujold - Edmundston**
25 Carrier St.
Edmundston, NB E3V 4A3
Tel: 506-735-1820; *Fax:* 506-735-1821
edmundston@lnb.ca
www.lnb.ca

Florenceville: **McCain & Company Chartered Accountants**
PO Box 437
393 Main St.
Florenceville, NB E7L 1Y9
Tel: 506-392-5517; *Fax:* 506-392-5341
fhmccain@mccainandco.com
www.mccainandco.com

Fredericton: **Bringloe Feeney**
#401, 212 Queen St.
Fredericton, NB E3B 1A8
Tel: 506-458-8326; *Fax:* 506-458-9293

Fredericton: **Bringloe Feeney LLP**
#401, 212 Queen St.
Fredericton, NB E3B 1A8
Tel: 506-458-8326; *Fax:* 506-458-9293
shawn.bringloe@bringloefeeney.ca

Fredericton: **Thornton VanTassel Chartered Accountants - Fredericton**
514 Queen St.
Fredericton, NB E3B 1B9
Tel: 506-451-9261; *Fax:* 506-459-7595
edwin.corey@thorntonvantassel.com
www.thorntonvantassel.com

Grand Falls: **LeBlanc Nadeau Bujold - Grand Falls**
796, boul Éverard H. Daigle
Grand Falls, NB E3Z 3C8
Tel: 506-473-4240; *Fax:* 506-473-9450
grand-falls@lnb.ca
www.lnb.ca

Grand Falls: **Thornton VanTassel Chartered Accountants - Grand Falls**
#201, 218 Broadway Blvd.
Grand Falls, NB E3Z 2J9
Tel: 506-473-5068; *Fax:* 506-473-7077
joe.mcphail@thorntonvantassel.com
www.thorntonvantassel.com

Moncton: **Boudreau Porter Hétu**
66 Donald Ave.
Moncton, NB E1A 3B1
Tel: 506-857-0262; *Fax:* 506-857-0232
eboudreau@porterhetu.com
www.porterhetu.com

Moncton: **PricewaterhouseCoopers LLP, Canada - Moncton**
#100, 1199 Main St.
Moncton, NB E1C 0L9
Tel: 506-859-8822; *Fax:* 506-859-8829
www.pwc.com/ca

Perth-Andover: **Thornton VanTassel Chartered Accountants - Perth-Andover**
#2, 15 Station St.
Perth-Andover, NB E7H 4Y2
Tel: 506-273-2276; *Fax:* 506-273-2033
jim.vantassel@thorntonvantassel.com
www.thorntonvantassel.com

Plaster Rock: **Thornton VanTassel Chartered Accountants - Plaster Rock**
240A Main St.
Plaster Rock, NB E7G 2E1
Tel: 506-356-2641; *Fax:* 506-356-8493
theresa.wark@thorntonvantassel.com
www.thorntonvantassel.com

Riverview: **Stevenson & Partners LLP**
567 Coverdale Rd.
Riverview, NB E1B 3K7
Tel: 506-387-4044; *Fax:* 506-387-7270
sp@parternsnb.com
www.acgca.ca

Rothesay: **Steeves Porter Hétu**
Professional Centre
PO Box 4591
9 Scott Ave.
Rothesay, NB E2E 5X3
Tel: 506-847-7471; *Fax:* 506-847-3151
dsteeves@porterhetu.com
www.porterhetu.com

Saint John: **Beers Neal LLP**
#301, 53 King St.
Saint John, NB E2L 1G5
Tel: 506-632-9020; *Fax:* 506-632-9030
www.acgca.ca

Saint John: **Curry & Betts**
Admiral Beatty Building
PO Box 6789, A Stn. A
72 Charlotte St., 1st Fl.
Saint John, NB E2L 4S2
Tel: 506-635-8181; *Fax:* 506-633-5943
Toll-Free: 888-635-8181
www.curry-betts.ca

Saint John: **PricewaterhouseCoopers LLP, Canada - Saint John**
Brunswick House
PO Box 789
#300, 44 Chipman Hill
Saint John, NB E2L 4B9
Tel: 506-632-1810; *Fax:* 506-632-8997
www.pwc.com/ca

Saint John: **Ralph H. Green & Associates**
#200, 53 King St.
Saint John, NB E2L 1G5
Tel: 506-632-3000; *Fax:* 506-632-1007
igreen@rhgreenassociates.ca
www.rhgreenassociates.ca

St. Stephen: **L K Toombs Chartered Accountants**
#207, 73 Milltown Blvd.
St. Stephen, NB E3L 1G5
Tel: 506-466-3291; *Fax:* 506-466-9825
lktpc@nb.aibn.com
www.acgca.ca

Sussex: **Turnbull and Kindred**
PO Box 4608
44 Moffett Ave.
Sussex, NB E4E 5L8
Tel: 506-433-4202
aturnbull@porterhetu.com; jkindred@porterhetu.com
www.porterhetu.com

Newfoundland & Labrador

Corner Brook: **J. Pike & Company Ltd.**
A98-98 Broadway
Corner Brook, NL A2H 4C8
Tel: 709-639-7774; *Fax:* 709-639-7775

Creston: **Jody Murphy, Chartered Accountant**
PO Box 508
437 Creston Blvd.
Creston, NL A0E 1K0
Tel: 709-279-1888; *Fax:* 709-279-1895
jmurphyca@nf.sympatico.ca

Gander: **Walters Hoffe**
30 Roe Ave.
Gander, NL A1V 1X5
Tel: 709-651-4100

Mount Pearl: **Feltham Attwood**
#202, 39 Commonwealth Ave.
Mount Pearl, NL A1N 1W7
Tel: 709-364-7300; *Fax:* 709-364-7731
debra@feltham-attwood.ca
www.porterhetu.com

St. John's: **Belanger Clarke Follett & McGettigan**
53 Bond St.
St. John's, NL A1C 1S9
Tel: 709-579-2161; *Fax:* 709-738-2391

St. John's: **PricewaterhouseCoopers LLP, Canada - St. John's**
Atlantic Place
#802, 215 Water St.
St. John's, NL A1C 6C9
Tel: 709-722-3883; *Fax:* 709-722-5874
www.pwc.com/ca

Northwest Territories

Yellowknife: **Avery Cooper & Co.**
Laurentian Building
PO Box 1620
4918, 50th St.
Yellowknife, NT X1A 2P2
Tel: 867-873-3441; *Fax:* 867-873-2353
Toll-Free: 800-661-0787
avery@averyco.nt.ca
www.averyco.nt.ca

Nova Scotia

Amherst: **sj mcisaac Chartered Accountants**
PO Box 217
Amherst, NS B4H 3Z2
Tel: 902-661-1027; *Fax:* 902-667-0884
Toll-Free: 877-282-6632
www.sjmcisaac.ca

Bedford: **David B. Etter**
117 Brentwood Dr.
Bedford, NS B4A 3S3
Tel: 902-456-1031; *Fax:* 902-835-5431
detter@porterhetu.com
www.porterhetu.com

Bedford: **WBLI Chartered Accountants**
26 Union St.
Bedford, NS B4A 2B5
Tel: 902-835-7333; *Fax:* 902-835-5297
www.wbli.ca

Bridgewater: **Belliveau Veinotte Inc.**
PO Box 29
11 Dominion St.
Bridgewater, NS B4V 2W6
Tel: 902-543-4278; *Fax:* 902-543-1818
office@bvca.ca
www.acgca.ca

Cheticamp: **Harold Patrick Aucoin CGA, Inc.**
15262 Cabot Trail
Cheticamp, NS B0E 1H0
Tel: 902-224-3748; *Fax:* 902-224-2092
haroldaucoin@haroldaucoincga.ca
www.haroldaucoincga.ca; www.porterhetu.com

Dartmouth: **Hunter Tellier Belgrave Adamson**
Cambridge 1
#200, 202 Brownlow Ave.
Dartmouth, NS B3B 1T5
Tel: 902-468-1949; *Fax:* 902-468-4865
service@achba.ca

Dartmouth: **Jean-Marc Chassé Inc.**
#44, 201 Browlow Ave.
Dartmouth, NS B3B 1W2
Tel: 902-468-0282; *Fax:* 902-468-6150
jmchasse@porterhetu.com
www.porterhetu.com

Dartmouth: **McNeil Porter Hétu**
344 Prince Albert Rd.
Dartmouth, NS B2Y 1N6
Tel: 902-464-9300; *Fax:* 902-464-7246
dmcneil@porterhetu.com
www.porterhetu.com

Halifax: **Dockrill Horwich Rossiter**
#440, 36 Solutions Dr.
Halifax, NS B3S 1N2
Tel: 902-835-0232; *Fax:* 902-835-0060
www.acgca.ca

Halifax: **Lyle Tilley Davidson**
#720, 1718 Argyle St.
Halifax, NS B3J 3N6
Tel: 902-423-7225; *Fax:* 902-422-3649
info@ltdca.com; ward@ltdca.com
www.ltdca.com

Halifax: **PricewaterhouseCoopers LLP, Canada - Halifax**
#400, 1601 Lower Water St.
Halifax, NS B3J 3P6
Tel: 903-491-7400; *Fax:* 903-422-1166
www.pwc.com/ca

New Glasgow: **Williams MacDonald Inc.**
400 East River Rd.
New Glasgow, NS B2H 3P7
Tel: 902-752-0463; *Fax:* 902-755-2823
www.acgca.ca

Sydney: **MGM & Associates Chartered Accountants**
PO Box 1
Sydney, NS B1P 6G9
Tel: 902-539-3900; *Fax:* 902-564-6062
mail@mgm.ca
www.mgm.ca

Sydney: **PricewaterhouseCoopers LLP, Canada - Sydney**
#220, 500 Grange St.
Sydney, NS B1P 1K6
Tel: 902-564-0802; *Fax:* 902-564-1470
www.pwc.com/ca

Truro: **PricewaterhouseCoopers LLP, Canada - Truro**
PO Box 632, Prince Stn. Prince
710 Prince St.
Truro, NS B2N 5E5
Tel: 902-895-1641; *Fax:* 902-893-0460
www.pwc.com/ca

Wolfville: **Bishop & Company Chartered Accountants Inc.**
189 Dykeland St.
Wolfville, NS B4P 1A3
Tel: 902-542-7665; *Fax:* 902-542-4554
rbishop@bcica.ca

Ontario

Ajax: **Thomas and Chase**
#211, 50 Commercial Ave.
Ajax, ON L1S 2H5
Tel: 905-686-2407; *Fax:* 905-686-2276
thomaschase@on.aibn.com
www.thomasandchase.com; www.porterhetu.com

Ajax: **TonioloPetersTurnerMoore LLP**
#6, 676 Monarch Ave.
Ajax, ON L1S 4S2
Tel: 905-427-6768; *Fax:* 905-427-1505
www.tptmcga.com

Almonte: **Colby McGeachy PC**
PO Box 970
258 Greystone Cres.
Almonte, ON K0A 1A0
Tel: 613-259-2878; *Fax:* 613-256-7569
Toll-Free: 866-259-2878
ecolby@porterhetu.com
www.porterhetu.com

Ancaster: **Brownlow & Associates**
259 Wilson St. East
Ancaster, ON L9G 2B8
Tel: 905-648-0404; *Fax:* 905-648-0403
Toll-Free: 888-648-0404
info@brownlowcas.com
www.brownlowcas.com

Arnprior: **Dave H. Laventure Professional Corporation**
106 McGonigal St. West, #B
Arnprior, ON K7S 1M4
Tel: 613-623-3181; *Fax:* 613-623-4299
www.porterhetu.com

Aylmer: **Den Harder McNames Button CGA**
174 Sydenham St. East
Aylmer, ON N5H 1L7
Tel: 519-773-5348; *Fax:* 519-773-7409
cbutton@epraylmer.com

Bancroft: **Dale Rose, CGA and Peter Stone, CA**
PO Box 1209
294 Hastings St. North
Bancroft, ON K0L 1C0
Tel: 613-332-0834; *Fax:* 613-332-4154
Toll-Free: 800-333-0834
drose@porterhetu.com; pstone@porterhetu.com
www.porterhetu.com

Barrie: **Alan Martin Associates - Barrie**
72 Ross St.
Barrie, ON L4N 1G3
Tel: 705-727-0407; *Fax:* 705-727-7677

Barrie: **KoutroulakisTurnerMoore LLP**
204 Dunlop St. West
Barrie, ON L4N 1B3
Tel: 705-722-5519; *Fax:* 705-722-7840
pkoutroulakis@turnermoore.com
www.turnermoore.com

Barrie: **Powell, Jones**
121 Anne St. South
Barrie, ON L4N 7B6
Tel: 705-728-7461; *Fax:* 705-728-8317
info@powelljones.ca
www.powelljones.ca

Belleville: **Soden & Co.**
25 Campbell St.
Belleville, ON K8N 1S6
Tel: 613-968-3495; *Fax:* 613-968-7359

Belleville: **Wilkinson & Company LLP**
PO Box 757
139 Front St.
Belleville, ON K8N 5B5
Tel: 613-966-5105; *Fax:* 613-962-7072
Toll-Free: 888-728-3890
bellevil@wilkinson.net
www.wilkinson.net

Bobcaygeon: **Collins Barrow Chartered Accountants - Bobcaygeon**
PO Box 10
21 King St. West
Bobcaygeon, ON K0M 1A0
Tel: 705-738-4166; *Fax:* 705-738-5787
bobcaygn@collinsbarrow.com

Bobcaygeon: **TeeuwenTurnerMoore LLP**
PO Box 1065
3401 County Rd. 36
Bobcaygeon, ON
Tel: 705-738-1581; *Fax:* 705-738-0031
lteeuwen@turnermoore.com
www.turnermoore.com

Bradford: **FalconeTurnerMoore LLP**
PO Box 753
27 John St. West
Bradford, ON L3Z 2B3
Tel: 905-778-8964; *Fax:* 905-775-9550
Toll-Free: 800-246-5591
mfalcone@turnermoore.com
www.turnermoore.com

Brampton: **Buttar & Associates Inc.**
Jaipur Chrysler Centre
#1, 470 Chrysler Dr.
Brampton, ON L6S 0C1
Tel: 905-866-6543; *Fax:* 905-866-6566
www.buttar.ca

Brampton: **Kenneth Bell CA Business Advisory Group**
#34, 18 Regan Rd.
Brampton, ON L7A 1C2
Tel: 905-453-0844; *Fax:* 905-453-1530
www.kenbell.ca

Brampton: **SMCA Professional Corporation**
#201, 197 County Court Blvd.
Brampton, ON L6W 4P6
Tel: 905-451-4034; *Fax:* 905-451-7158
Toll-Free: 888-524-4844
carrollm@smca.ca
www.smca.ca

Brantford: **Millard, Rouse & Rosebrugh LLP**
PO Box 367
96 Nelson St.
Brantford, ON N3T 5N3
Tel: 519-759-3511; *Fax:* 519-759-7961
csmith@millards.com
www.millards.com

Brantford: **Susan L. Rice**
#15, 340 Henry St.
Brantford, ON N3S 7V9
Tel: 519-752-8290; *Fax:* 519-752-9784
srice@obwr.ca

Brockville: **G.A. Porter, CA**
21 Ormond St.
Brockville, ON K6V 2K2
Tel: 613-865-9664
gporter@porterhetu.com
www.porterhetu.com

Brockville: **George Caners Chartered Accountant**
#210, 9 Broad St.
Brockville, ON K6V 6Z4
Tel: 613-342-1555; *Fax:* 613-342-2845
Toll-Free: 888-829-9952
www.caners.com

Burlington: **Bateman MacKay**
PO Box 5015
4200 South Service Rd.
Burlington, ON L7R 3Y8
Tel: 905-632-6400; *Fax:* 905-639-2285
Toll-Free: 866-787-1117
info@batemanmackay.com
www.batemanmackay.com
Other Contact Information: Toronto Phone: 416-360-6400

Burlington: **Durward Jones Barkwell & Company LLP**
#103, 3430 South Service Rd.
Burlington, ON L7N 3T9
Tel: 905-681-6900; *Fax:* 905-681-6874
Toll-Free: 866-407-5318
burl@djb.com
www.djb.com

Burlington: **Prapavessis Jasek**
3410 South Service Rd., Lower Fl.
Burlington, ON L7N 3T2
Tel: 905-634-8999; *Fax:* 905-634-5057
jim@pj.on.ca
www.pj.on.ca

Burlington: **Scott & Pichelli Ltd.**
#109, 3600 Billings Ct.
Burlington, ON L7N 3N6
Tel: 905-632-5853; *Fax:* 905-632-6113
www.bankruptcy-trustees.ca/

Burlington: **Steven J. Obranovich**
650 Plains Rd. East
Burlington, ON L7T 2E9
Tel: 905-632-8400; *Fax:* 905-632-9505
sobranovich@obwr.ca

Burlington: **Stevenson & Lehocki**
310 Plains Rd. East
Burlington, ON L7T 4J2
Tel: 905-632-0640; *Fax:* 905-632-0645
joe@stevensonlehocki.com
www.stevensonlehocki.com

Burlington: **Wade & Partners LLP, Chartered Accountants**
#102, 5096 South Service Rd.
Burlington, ON L7L 5H4
Tel: 905-333-9888; *Fax:* 905-333-9583
ca@wadegroup.ca
www.wadegroup.ca

Cambridge: **Graham Mathew & Partners LLP**
PO Box 880
150 Pinebush Rd.
Cambridge, ON N1R 5X9
Tel: 519-623-1870; *Fax:* 519-623-9490
admin@gmpca.com
www.gmpca.com

Carleton Place: **Collins Barrow Chartered Accountants - Carleton Place**
143-A Bridge St.
Carleton Place, ON K7C 2V6
Tel: 613-253-0014; *Fax:* 613-253-0129
carletonplace@collinsbarrow.com

Chatham: **Collins Barrow Chartered Accountants - Chatham**
62 Keil Dr. South
Chatham, ON N7M 3G8
Tel: 519-351-2024; *Fax:* 519-351-8831
chatham@collinsbarrow.com

Chatham: **Gilhula & Grant**
PO Box 488
141 Grand Ave. East
Chatham, ON N7L 1W1
Tel: 519-352-3470; *Fax:* 519-352-7344
gilgrant@ciaccess.com

Chelmsford: **Collins Barrow Chartered Accountants - Chelmsford**
PO Box 673
48 Main St. East
Chelmsford, ON P0M 1L0
Tel: 705-855-9024; *Fax:* 705-855-3693
chelmsford@collinsbarrow.com

Churchill: **MayerhoferTurnerMoore LLP**
1027 Sloan Circle Dr.
Churchill, ON L0L 1K0
Tel: 705-456-8069; *Fax:* 705-456-8071
wmayerhofer@turnermoore.com
www.turnermoore.com

Concord: **Burghout Viola, Chartered Accountants**
#105, 7941 Jane St.
Concord, ON L4K 4L6
Tel: 905-738-6402; *Fax:* 905-738-1805
john@burghoutviola.com
www.burghoutviola.com

Concord: **Miller, Saperia & Company**
#418, 1600 Steeles Ave. West
Concord, ON L4K 4M2
Tel: 905-660-6840; *Fax:* 905-660-6729

Concord: **Starkman Salsberg & Feldberg**
#316, 1600 Steeles Ave. West
Concord, ON L4K 4M2
Tel: 905-669-9900; *Fax:* 905-669-9901

Elginburg: **Randy E. Brown CGA**
2908 Leeman Rd.
Elginburg, ON K0H 1M0
Tel: 613-542-0151; *Fax:* 613-549-1427
rbrown@porterhetu.com

Elmvale: **Alan Martin Associates**
42 Queen St.
Elmvale, ON L0L 1P0
Tel: 705-322-2440; *Fax:* 705-322-1462

Elora: **Collins Barrow Chartered Accountants - Elora**
PO Box 580
342, Gerrie Rd.
Elora, ON N0B 1S0
Tel: 519-846-5315; *Fax:* 519-846-9120
info@collinsbarrow.com

Exeter: **Collins Barrow Chartered Accountants - Exeter**
PO Box 2405
412 Main St.
Exeter, ON N0M 1S7
Tel: 519-235-0345; *Fax:* 519-235-3235
exeter@collinsbarrow.com

Fort Erie: **Durward Jones Barkwell & Company, Fort Erie**
#15, 1264 Garrison Rd.
Fort Erie, ON L2A 1P1
Tel: 905-871-3565; *Fax:* 905-871-9232
Toll-Free: 866-720-2194
forterie@djb.com
www.djb.com

Fredericton: **Nicholson & Beaumont Chartered Accountants**
328 King St.
Fredericton, ON E3B 5C2
Tel: 506-458-9815; *Fax:* 506-459-7575
jbeaumont@porterhetu.com
www.porterhetu.com

Gravenhurst: **C.R. Barclay, CA, CMA, MBA**
10 Woods Hollow
Gravenhurst, ON P1P 1Y7
Tel: 705-684-8115; *Fax:* 705-684-8227
Toll-Free: 877-644-4838
cbarclay1@cogeco.ca

Grimsby: **Durward Jones Barkwell & Company, Grimsby**
PO Box 261
8 Christie St.
Grimsby, ON L3M 4G5
Tel: 905-945-5439; *Fax:* 905-945-1103
Toll-Free: 866-830-7531
grimsby@djb.com
www.djb.com

Grimsby: **Southcott Davoli Professional Corporation**
PO Box 68
76 Main St. West
Grimsby, ON L3M 4G1
Tel: 905-945-4942; *Fax:* 905-945-0306
contactus@southdav.com

Guelph: **Bairstow, Smart & Smith LLP**
100 Gordon St.
Guelph, ON N1H 4H6
Tel: 519-822-7670; *Fax:* 519-822-6997
bss@bssllp.ca
www.bssllp.ca

Guelph: **Embree & Co. LLP**
#8, 350 Speedvale Ave. West
Guelph, ON N1H 7M7
Tel: 519-821-1555; *Fax:* 519-821-6168
Toll-Free: 866-531-1555
www.embreelp.ca

Guelph: **Robinson, Lott & Brohman LLP**
15 Lewis Rd.
Guelph, ON N1H 1E9
Tel: 519-822-9933; *Fax:* 519-822-9212
Toll-Free: 866-822-9992
guelph_inquiries@rlb.ca
www.rlb.ca

Guelph: **Weiler & Company**
#3, 512 Woolwich St.
Guelph, ON N1H 3X7
Tel: 519-837-3111; *Fax:* 519-837-1049
Toll-Free: 888-239-3111
weiler@weiler.ca
www.weiler.ca

Halton Hills: **BrightTurnerMoore LLP**
305 Mountainview Rd. South
Halton Hills, ON L7G 4K1
Tel: 905-702-1730; *Fax:* 905-702-1731
pbright@turnermoore.com
www.turnermoore.com

Hamilton: **BC&C Professional Corporation**
20 Jackson St. West
Hamilton, ON L8P 1L2
Tel: 905-570-1370; *Fax:* 905-570-1212
fred@bccpc.ca
www.bccpc.ca

Hamilton: **Durward Jones Barkwell & Company, Hamilton**
Standard Life Bldg.
#780, 120 King St. West
Hamilton, ON L8P 4V2
Tel: 905-525-9520; *Fax:* 905-522-3113
Toll-Free: 866-358-8240
hamilton@djb.com
www.djb.com

Hamilton: **Galano, Enzo & Associates**
#400, 20 Hughson St. South
Hamilton, ON L8N 2A1
Tel: 905-528-0144; *Fax:* 905-528-0144
enzo@netinc.ca

Hamilton: **Herpers Chagani Gowling Inc.**
#300, 4 Hughson St. South
Hamilton, ON L8N 3Z1
Tel: 905-529-3328; *Fax:* 905-529-3980
Toll-Free: 310-3328
www.bankruptcyanswers.com

Hamilton: **MacGillivray Partners, LLP**
33 Main St. East
Hamilton, ON L8N 4K5
Tel: 905-523-7732; *Fax:* 905-572-9333
hamilton@macgillivray.com
www.macgillivray.com

Hamilton: **PricewaterhouseCoopers LLP, Canada - Hamilton**
21 King St. West, Main Fl.
Hamilton, ON L8P 4W7
Tel: 905-777-7000; *Fax:* 905-777-7060
www.pwc.com/ca

Hamilton: **Taylor Leibow LLP, Accountants & Advisors**
#700, 105 Main St. East
Hamilton, ON L8N 1G6
Tel: 905-523-0000; *Fax:* 905-523-4681
Toll-Free: 888-287-2525
info@taylorleibow.com
www.taylorleibow.com

Hamilton: **ThomsonTurnerMoore LLP**
645 Upper James St.
Hamilton, ON L9C 2Y9
Tel: 905-388-7229; *Fax:* 905-388-3134
jrthomson@turnermoore.com
www.thomsonturnermoore.ca

Hearst: **Collins Barrow Chartered Accountants - Hearst**
PO Box 637
1021 George St.
Hearst, ON P0L 1N0
Tel: 705-362-4261; *Fax:* 705-362-4641
hearst@collinsbarrow.com

Jackson's Point: **Duncan Goodwin, CGA**
#4, 915 Lake Dr.
Jackson's Point, ON L0E 1L0
Tel: 905-722-8587; *Fax:* 904-722-6519
dgoodwin@porterhetu.com
www.porterhetu.com

Kapuskasing: **Collins Barrow Chartered Accountants - Kapuskasing**
2 Ash St.
Kapuskasing, ON P5N 3H4
Tel: 705-337-6411; *Fax:* 705-335-6563
kapuskasing@collinsbarrow.com

Kelowna: **Kemp Harvey Hunt Ward Inc.**
#101, 1593 Sutherland Ave.
Kelowna, ON V1Y 5Y7
Tel: 250-763-8029; *Fax:* 250-763-5155
Kelowna@khgcga.com
www.khgcga.com

Kenora: **Claudette M. Edie, CGA**
685 Lakeview Dr.
Kenora, ON P9N 3P6
Tel: 807-468-8899; *Fax:* 807-468-6800
cedie@porterhetu.com
www.porterhetu.com

Kingston: **Collins Barrow Chartered Accountants - Kingston**
#301, 1471 Counter St.
Kingston, ON K7M 8S8
Tel: 613-544-2903; *Fax:* 613-544-6151
kingston@collinsbarrow.com

Kingston: **Davies & Wyngaarden Chartered Accountants**
Clock Tower Plaza
819 Norwest Rd.
Kingston, ON K7P 2N4
Tel: 613-389-8177; *Fax:* 613-389-7789
Toll-Free: 888-715-3555
acctg@dwca.com
www.dwca.com

Kingston: **GibsonTurnerMoore LLP**
4 Cataraqui St.
Kingston, ON K7K 1Z7
Tel: 613-547-5099; *Fax:* 613-547-5102
sgibson@turnermoore.com
www.turnermoore.com

Kitchener: **Clarke Starke & Diegel (CSD)**
#202, 871 Victoria St. North
Kitchener, ON N2B 3S4
Tel: 519-579-5520; *Fax:* 519-570-3611
www.csdca.com

Kitchener: **YNC LLP**
650 Riverbend Dr., Suite A1
Kitchener, ON N2K 3S2
Tel: 519-772-0125; *Fax:* 519-772-0428
info@yncllp.ca
www.youngandcompany.ca

Leamington: **Collins Barrow Leamington LLP**
92 Talbot St. East
Leamington, ON N8H 1L3
Tel: 519-326-2666; *Fax:* 519-326-7008
leamington@collinsbarrow.com
www.collinsbarrow.com

Lindsay: **Collins Barrow Chartered Accountants - Lindsay**
237 Kent St. West
Lindsay, ON K9V 2Z3
Tel: 705-324-5031; *Fax:* 705-328-3121
lindsay@collinsbarrow.com

London: **Collins Barrow Chartered Accountants - London**
PO Box 5005
#700, 495 Richmond St.
London, ON N6A 5G4
Tel: 519-679-8550; *Fax:* 519-679-1812
london@collinsbarrow.com

London: **Davis Martindale LLP**
373 Commissioners Rd. West
London, ON N6J 1Y4
Tel: 519-673-3141; *Fax:* 519-645-1646
info@davismartindale.com
www.davismartindale.com

London: **GiannoulisTurnerMoore LLP**
266 Oxford St. East
London, ON N6A 1V1
Tel: 519-439-4440; *Fax:* 519-439-3888
jgiannoulis@turnermoore.com
www.turnermoore.com

London: **MacNeill Edmundson**
82 Wellington St.
London, ON N6B 2K3
Tel: 519-660-6060; *Fax:* 519-672-6416
info@meb.on.ca
www.meb.on.ca

London: **Michael A. King, Chartered Accountant**
#502, 383 Richmond St.
London, ON N6A 3C4
Tel: 519-679-8391; *Fax:* 519-679-1446
mike@michaelkingca.ca
www.michaelkingca.ca

London: **Neal, Pallett & Townsend LLP Chartered Accountants**
#300, 633 Colborne St.
London, ON N6B 2V3
Tel: 519-432-5534; *Fax:* 519-432-6544
www.nptca.com

London: **PricewaterhouseCoopers LLP, Canada - London**
#300, 465 Richmond St.
London, ON N6A 5P4
Tel: 519-640-8000; *Fax:* 519-640-8015
www.pwc.com/ca

London: **SummersTurnerMoore LLP**
857 Consortium Ct.
London, ON N6E 2S8
Tel: 519-686-4114; *Fax:* 519-686-4884
csummers@turnermoore.com
www.turnermoore.com

Manotick: **Collins Barrow Chartered Accountants - Manotick**
PO Box 291
1136 Clapp Lane
Manotick, ON K4M 1A3
Tel: 613-692-2553; *Fax:* 613-692-2995
manotick@collinsbarrow.com
www.collinsbarrowottawa.com

Manotick: **Newton & Co.**
PO Box 978
5494 Manotick Main St.
Manotick, ON K4M 1A8
Tel: 613-236-2939; *Fax:* 613-692-2874
www.newtonco.com

Markham: **Kestenberg, Rabinowicz & Partners**
2797 John St.
Markham, ON L3R 2Y8
Tel: 905-946-1300; *Fax:* 905-946-9797
rrabinowicz@krp.ca
www.krp.ca

Markham: **Sheldon & Brates Tax Consultants Ltd.**
#220, 60 Renfrew Dr.
Markham, ON L3R 0E1
Tel: 905-475-5400; *Fax:* 905-475-4246
sheldonbrates.com

Milton: **Mercer & Mercer**
245 Commercial St.
Milton, ON L9T 2J3
Tel: 905-876-1144; *Fax:* 905-876-4209
mail@mercerandmercer.com
www.mercerandmercer.com

Mississauga: **Bimal Shah**
#14, 5484 Tomken Rd.
Mississauga, ON L4W 2Z6
Tel: 905-629-2653; *Fax:* 905-629-8701
info@shah-cga.com
www.shah-cga.com

Mississauga: **Bolton & Dignan, Chartered Accountants**
6509 Mississauga Rd., Unit D
Mississauga, ON L5N 1A6
Tel: 905-858-5006

Mississauga: **Clarkson Rouble LLP**
5190 Shuttle Dr.
Mississauga, ON L4W 4J8
Tel: 905-629-4047; *Fax:* 905-629-3070
office@crllp.ca
clarksonrouble.on.ca/

Mississauga: **Clewes & Associates Life Insurance Consultancy Inc.**
#803, 251 Queen St. South
Mississauga, ON L5M 1L7
Tel: 416-493-5586; *Fax:* 416-493-5061
www.clewesconsult.com

Mississauga: **D'AnnaTurnerMoore LLP**
#3A, 3045 Southcreek Rd.
Mississauga, ON L4X 2X6
Tel: 416-410-4118; *Fax:* 416-352-7600
info@DannaTurnerMoore.com
www.dannaturnermoore.com

Mississauga: **H&A Forensic Accounting**
#400, 2680 Matheson Blvd. East
Mississauga, ON L4W 0A5
Tel: 416-233-5577; *Fax:* 416-233-5578
www.haforensics.com

Mississauga: **Kutum & Associates**
#A1, 5659 McAdam Rd.
Mississauga, ON L4Z 1N9
Tel: 905-276-1154; *Fax:* 905-276-2003
info@kutum.com
www.kutum.com

Mississauga: **Laurel L. Stultz**
#211, 1425 Dundas St. East
Mississauga, ON L4X 2W4
Tel: 905-602-0001
info@certifiedgeneralaccountant.ca
www.certifiedgeneralaccountant.ca
Other Contact Information: Cell: 416-996-3919

Mississauga: **Lemoine Hyland Group LLP**
#207, 2085 Hurontario St.
Mississauga, ON L5A 4G1
Tel: 905-275-7794; *Fax:* 905-275-5677
Toll-Free: 877-544-7687
rlemoine@lhgroup.com
lhgroup.com

Mississauga: **MDP Chartered Accountants (MDP LLP)**
#200, 4230 Sherwoodtowne Blvd.
Mississauga, ON L4Z 2G6
Tel: 905-279-7500; *Fax:* 905-279-9300
mdp@mdp.on.ca
www.mdp.on.ca

Mississauga: **PricewaterhouseCoopers LLP, Canada - Mississauga**
Mississauga Executive Centre
#1100, 1 Robert Speck Pkwy.
Mississauga, ON L4Z 3M3
Tel: 905-949-7400; *Fax:* 905-949-7415
www.pwc.com/ca

Mississauga: **Sidler & Company LLP**
#204/205, 6465 Millcreek Dr.
Mississauga, ON L5N 5R3
Tel: 905-821-9215; *Fax:* 905-821-8212
info@sidler.ca
www.sidler.ca

Montréal: **PricewaterhouseCoopers LLP, Canada - Montréal**
1250, boul. René-Lévesque ouest
Montréal, ON H3B 2G4
Tel: 514-205-5000; *Fax:* 514-938-5709
www.pwc.com/ca

Nepean: **Jack R. Bowerman, CA - Professional Corporation**
#10, 28 Concourse Gate
Nepean, ON K2E 7T7
Tel: 613-723-8202; *Fax:* 613-723-1216
Toll-Free: 800-282-1879
info@jrbowerman.com
www.jrbowerman.com

Niagara Falls: **Durward Jones Barkwell & Company, Niagara Falls**
PO Box 873
#1, 6100 Thorold Stone Rd.
Niagara Falls, ON L2E 6V6
Tel: 905-357-5711; *Fax:* 905-357-7932
Toll-Free: 866-223-8459
nfalls@djb.com
www.djb.com

Niagara Falls: **WhiteHillTurnerMoore LLP**
#10, 3483 Portage Rd.
Niagara Falls, ON L2J 2K5
Tel: 905-358-1652; *Fax:* 905-358-8759
dwhite@turnermoore.com; jhill@turnermoore.com
www.turnermoore.com

North Bay: **Collins Barrow Chartered Accountants - North Bay**
630 Cassells St.
North Bay, ON P1B 4A2
Tel: 705-494-9336; *Fax:* 705-494-8783
northbay@collinsbarrow.com
www.collinsbarrowsudburynipissing.com

Orleans: **Andrews & Company, Chartered Accountants**
540 Lacolle Way
Orleans, ON K4A 0N9
Tel: 613-837-8282; *Fax:* 613-837-7482
website@andrews.ca
www.andrews.ca; www.porterhetu.com

Orleans: **EthierTurnerMoore LLP**
352 Timbertrain Terrace
Orleans, ON K4A 5A6
Tel: 613-837-7829; *Fax:* 613-834-4741
methier@turnermoore.com
www.turnermoore.com

Orleans: **Pyndus & Associates Ltd.**
1813 Woodhaven Heights
Orleans, ON K1E 2W3
Tel: 613-834-5054; *Fax:* 613-837-1591
pyndus.associates@sympatico.ca
www3.sympatico.ca/cpyndus/

Ottawa: **Charles Ghadban Accounting**
544 Bronson Ave.
Ottawa, ON K1R 6J9
Tel: 613-234-7856
info@ghadbanaccounting.com
www.ghadbanaccounting.com

Ottawa: **Collins Barrow Chartered Accountants - Ottawa**
#400, 301 Moodie Dr.
Ottawa, ON K2H 9C4
Tel: 613-820-8010; *Fax:* 613-820-0465
ottawa@collinsbarrow.com
www.collinsbarrowottawa.com

Ottawa: **David Ingram & Associates**
329 Waverly St.
Ottawa, ON K2P 0V9
Tel: 613-234-8023; *Fax:* 613-234-8925
info@accessfp.com

Ottawa: **Gary G. Timmons, Chartered Accountant**
#105, 2442 St. Joseph Blvd.
Ottawa, ON K1C 1G1
Tel: 613-830-0200; *Fax:* 613-830-8824
gtimmons@gtimmons.com
www.gtimmons.com

Ottawa: **Ginsberg Gluzman Fage & Levitz, LLP**
287 Richmond Rd.
Ottawa, ON K1Z 6X4
Tel: 613-728-5831; *Fax:* 613-728-8085
info@ggfl.ca
www.ggfl.ca

Ottawa: **Hartel Financial Management Corporation**
540 Lacolle Way
Ottawa, ON K4A 0N9
Tel: 613-837-8282; *Fax:* 613-837-7482
jleblanc@hartel.ca; brighten@hartel.ca
www.hartel.ca; www.porterhetu.com

Ottawa: **Logan Katz LLP**
#105, 6 Gurdwara Rd.
Ottawa, ON K2E 8A3
Tel: 613-228-8282; *Fax:* 613-228-8284
office@logankatz.com
www.logankatz.com

Ottawa: **McLarty & Co.**
#110, 495 Richmond Rd.
Ottawa, ON K2A 4B2
Tel: 613-726-1010; *Fax:* 613-726-9009
www.mclartyco.ca

Ottawa: **Newton & Co.**
#1205, 150 Isabella St.
Ottawa, ON K1S 1V7
Tel: 613-236-2939; *Fax:* 613-236-1220
nco@newtonco.com
www.newtonco.com

Ottawa: **Newton & Co., Ottawa**
#1205, 150 Isabella St.
Ottawa, ON K1S 1V7
Tel: 613-236-2939; *Fax:* 613-236-1220
www.newtonco.com

Ottawa: **PricewaterhouseCoopers LLP, Canada - Ottawa**
#800, 99 Bank St.
Ottawa, ON K1P 1E4
Tel: 613-237-3702; *Fax:* 613-237-3963
www.pwc.com/ca

Ottawa: **Robertson Sharpe & Associates**
#2, 200 Colonnade Rd.
Ottawa, ON K2E 7M1
Tel: 613-727-3845; *Fax:* 613-727-7075
info@robertson-sharpe.com
www.robertson-sharpe.com

Ottawa: **Rosalind Schlessinger Certified General Accountant**
332 Gilmour St.
Ottawa, ON K2P 0R3
Tel: 613-235-1807; *Fax:* 613-235-2253

Ottawa: **Scott Rankin & Gardiner Chartered Accountants**
#207, 2650 Queensview Dr.
Ottawa, ON K2B 8H6
Tel: 613-596-2767; *Fax:* 613-596-2775

***Ottawa:* Surgeson Carson Associates Inc.**
#8, 99 Fifth Ave.
Ottawa, ON K1S 5K4
Tel: 613-567-6434; *Fax:* 613-567-0752
questions@surgesoncarson.com
www.surgesoncarson.com

***Ottawa:* Swindells & Company**
#101, 1700 Woodward Dr.
Ottawa, ON K2C 3R8
Tel: 613-230-1010; *Fax:* 613-230-1957
www.swindellsandwheatley.com

***Ottawa:* Thomas R. West CGA Professional Corporation**
21 Perrin Ave.
Ottawa, ON K2J 2Y1
Tel: 613-825-8871; *Fax:* 613-825-4089
Tom@Thomasrwestcga.com
www.thomasrwestcga.com

***Owen Sound:* Gaviller & Company LLP**
PO Box 460
#201, 945 - 3rd Ave. East
Owen Sound, ON N4K 5P7
Tel: 519-376-5850; *Fax:* 519-376-5532
Toll-Free: 800-567-7234
www.gaviller.com

***Penetanguishene:* Alan Martin Associates - Penetanguishene**
75 Main St.
Penetanguishene, ON L9M 1S8
Tel: 705-549-3146; *Fax:* 705-549-5736

***Peterborough:* Collins Barrow Chartered Accountants - Peterborough**
418 Sheridan St.
Peterborough, ON K9H 3J9
Tel: 705-742-3418; *Fax:* 705-742-9775
peterborough@collinsbarrow.com

***Peterborough:* Jon S. Thornton, Chartered Accountant**
PO Box 2402
294 Rink St.
Peterborough, ON K9J 7Y8
Tel: 705-742-2308; *Fax:* 705-748-4824
jon@thorntonca.com
www.thorntonca.com

***Peterborough:* WrightlyTurnerMoore LLP**
#203, 311 George St. North
Peterborough, ON K9J 3H3
Tel: 705-745-8643; *Fax:* 705-745-6358
robin@rewcga.com
www.rewcga.com

***Richmond Hill:* MDS LLP**
#4, 30 Wertheim Ct.
Richmond Hill, ON L4B 1B9
Tel: 905-881-2244; *Fax:* 905-881-8006
reception@mdsllp.com
www.mdsllp.com

***Richmond Hill:* Truster Zweig LLP**
#200, 66 West Beaver Creek Rd.
Richmond Hill, ON L4B 1G5
Tel: 416-222-5555; *Fax:* 905-707-1322
tzcas@trusterzweig.com
www.trusterzweig.ca

***Richmond Hill:* Willington Martin Professional Corporation**
#510. 100 York Blvd.
Richmond Hill, ON L4B 1J8
Tel: 905-770-3532; *Fax:* 905-770-4128
jwillington@porterhetu.com; tmartin@porterhetu.com
www.porterhetu.com; www.inbalance.org

***Ridgetown:* UreTurnerMoore LLP**
23 Cecil St.
Ridgetown, ON N0P 2C0
Tel: 519-674-5551; *Fax:* 519-674-0983
aure@turnermoore.com

***Sarnia:* Collins Barrow Chartered Accountants - Sarnia**
1350 L'Heritage Dr.
Sarnia, ON N7S 6H8
Tel: 519-542-7725; *Fax:* 519-542-8321
sarnia@collinsbarrow.com

***Sarnia:* Hazlitt Steeves Harris LLP**
301 Front St. North
Sarnia, ON N7T 5S6
Tel: 519-336-6133; *Fax:* 519-336-9995
www.hshca.com

***Sarnia:* TurnerMoore Group (TMG)**
PO Box 212
866 Confederation St.
Sarnia, ON N7T 7H9
Tel: 519-344-1271; *Fax:* 519-344-1268
bmoore@turnermoore.com
www.turnermoore.com

***St Catharines:* Durward Jones Barkwell & Company, St. Catharines**
PO Box 505
69 Ontario St.
St Catharines, ON L2R 6V9
Tel: 905-684-9221; *Fax:* 905-684-0566
Toll-Free: 866-219-9431
stcath@djb.com
www.djb.com

***St Catharines:* Finucci Watters LLP**
58 St. Paul St. West
St Catharines, ON L2S 2C5
Tel: 905-682-2406; *Fax:* 905-682-1466
rwatters@porterhetu.com; afinucci@porterhetu.com
www.porterhetu.com

***St Catharines:* O'BrienTurnerMoore LLP**
266 Welland Ave.
St Catharines, ON L2R 2P8
Tel: 905-682-8299; *Fax:* 905-687-9741
Toll-Free: 877-682-8299
tobrien@turnermoore.com
www.turnermoore.com

***St Thomas:* Kee, Perry & Lassam**
15 Barrie Blvd.
St Thomas, ON N5P 4B9
Tel: 519-631-6360; *Fax:* 519-631-2198
info@kpl-accountants.ca
www.kpl-accountants.ca

***Stoney Creek:* Durward Jones Barkwell & Company, Stoney Creek**
PO Box 56062
#7C, 45 Goderich Rd.
Stoney Creek, ON L8G 5C9
Tel: 905-561-2992; *Fax:* 905-561-7152
Toll-Free: 866-897-2965
screek@djb.com
www.djb.com

***Stouffville:* Joe Nemni Financial Services**
33 Katherine Cres.
Stouffville, ON L4A 1K4
Tel: 905-640-0065
jnemni@sympatico.ca
www.joenemni.com

***Stratford:* Collins Barrow Chartered Accountants - Stratford**
413 Hibernia St.
Stratford, ON N5A 5W2
Tel: 519-272-0000; *Fax:* 519-272-0030
stratford@collinsbarrow.com

***Sturgeon Falls:* Collins Barrow Chartered Accountants - Sturgeon Falls**
#7, 12006 Hwy. 17 East
Sturgeon Falls, ON P2B 3K8
Tel: 705-753-1830; *Fax:* 705-753-2496
sturgeonfalls@collinsbarrow.com
www.collinsbarrowsudburynipissing.com

***Sudbury:* Collins Barrow Chartered Accountants - Sudbury**
1174 St. Jerome St.
Sudbury, ON P3A 2V9
Tel: 705-560-5592; *Fax:* 705-560-8832
sudbury@collinsbarrow.com
www.collinsbarrowsudburynipissing.com

***Thornhill:* Brockman & Partners Forensic Accountants Inc.**
10 Maxwell Ct.
Thornhill, ON L4J 6Y3
Tel: 905-764-3851; *Fax:* 905-764-3537
jay.brockman@brockmanandpartners.ca
www.brockmanandpartners.ca

***Thornhill:* Harendorf, Lebane, Moss LLP**
#200, 8500 Leslie St.
Thornhill, ON L3T 7M8
Tel: 905-886-8812; *Fax:* 905-886-6034
Toll-Free: 888-337-9222
hsm@hsmllpcas.com
www.hsmca.ca

***Thornhill:* Herb Kokotow, Chartered Accountant**
3 German Mills Rd.
Thornhill, ON L3T 4H4
Tel: 905-764-6175
kokotow6175@rogers.com
www.charteredaccountantontario.ca

***Thornhill:* Ralph Lando Orvitz**
#300, 8500 Leslie St.
Thornhill, ON L3T 7M8
Tel: 905-889-1549; *Fax:* 905-889-2054
Ralph@ralphlandoorvitz.ca
www.ralphlandoorvitz.ca

***Thunder Bay:* Fukushima Enstrom LLP**
577 Eleventh Ave.
Thunder Bay, ON P7B 2R5
Tel: 807-345-1393; *Fax:* 807-345-4630
mail@fe-llp.com

***Toronto:* Albert L. Stal**
#301, 1370 Don Mills Rd.
Toronto, ON M3B 3N7
Tel: 416-449-0130; *Fax:* 416-449-6694

***Toronto:* Bass & Murphy Chartered Accountants LLP**
885 Progress Ave., #LPH1
Toronto, ON M1H 3G3
Tel: 416-431-3030; *Fax:* 416-431-3340
tom@bassmurphy.com
www.bassmurphy.com

***Toronto:* Beallor & Partners LLP**
28 Overlea Blvd.
Toronto, ON M4H 1B6
Tel: 416-423-0707; *Fax:* 416-423-7000
service@beallor.com
www.beallor.com

***Toronto:* Bennett Gold LLP, Chartered Accountants**
#900, 150 Ferrand Dr.
Toronto, ON M3C 3E5
Tel: 416-449-2249; *Fax:* 416-449-4133
rygold@bennettgold.ca
www.bennettgold.ca

***Toronto:* Brief Rotfarb Wynberg Cappe**
#402, 3854 Bathurst St.
Toronto, ON M3H 3N2
Tel: 416-635-9080; *Fax:* 416-635-0462
lcappe@brwc.com
www.brwc.com

***Toronto:* Cadesky & Associates LLP - King St.**
Toronto-Dominion Centre, Royal Trust Tower
PO Box 93
#2401, 77 King St. West
Toronto, ON M5K 1G8
Tel: 416-594-9500; *Fax:* 416-594-9501
taxpros@cadesky.com
www.cadesky.com

***Toronto:* Cadesky & Associates LLP - Sheppard Ave. East**
Atria III
#1001, 2225 Sheppard Ave. East
Toronto, ON M2J 5C2
Tel: 416-498-9500; *Fax:* 416-498-9501
taxpros@cadesky.com
www.cadesky.com

***Toronto:* Canham Rogers Chartered Accountants**
#500, 2 Lansing Sq.
Toronto, ON M2J 4P8
Tel: 416-494-8000; *Fax:* 416-494-8032
Info@CanhamRogers.com
www.canhamrogers.com

***Toronto:* Chaplin & Co. Chartered Accountants**
#710, 1110 Finch Ave. West
Toronto, ON M3J 2T2
Tel: 416-667-7060; *Fax:* 416-663-3746
ca@chaplinco.com
www.chaplinco.com

Toronto: **ChiShenTurnerMoore LLP**
#408, 515 Consumers Rd.
Toronto, ON M2J 4Z2
Tel: 416-410-0400; *Fax:* 416-756-0388
jchi@turnermoore.com; hshen@turnermoore.com
www.turnermoore.com

Toronto: **Cholkan & Stepczuk LLP**
#300, 1 Eva Rd.
Toronto, ON M9C 4Z5
Tel: 416-695-9500; *Fax:* 416-695-3837
Toll-Free: 800-3639500
info@c-s.ca
www.cholkan.com

Toronto: **The Clarke Henning Group**
#801, 10 Bay St.
Toronto, ON M5J 2R8
Tel: 416-364-4421; *Fax:* 416-367-8032
Toll-Free: 888-422-1241
ch@clarkehenning.com
www.clarkehenning.com

Toronto: **Cole & Partners**
#2000, 80 Richmond St. West
Toronto, ON M5H 2A4
Tel: 416-364-9700; *Fax:* 416-364-9707
www.coleandpartners.com

Toronto: **Collins Barrow Toronto LLP**
#1900, 390 Bay St.
Toronto, ON M5H 2Y2
Tel: 416-361-1622; *Fax:* 416-480-2646
www.collinsbarrowtoronto.com

Toronto: **Cooper & Company Ltd.**
#108, 1120 Finch Ave. West
Toronto, ON M3J 3H7
Tel: 416-665-3383; *Fax:* 416-665-0897
info@cooperco.ca
www.cooperco.ca

Toronto: **Cunningham LLP**
#810, 2001 Sheppard Ave. East
Toronto, ON M2J 4Z8
Tel: 416-496-1051; *Fax:* 416-496-1546
Toll-Free: 800-461-4618
info@cunninghamca.com
www.cunninghamca.com

Toronto: **Duffy, Allain & Rutten LLP**
908 The East Mall
Toronto, ON M9B 6K2
Tel: 416-620-7740

Toronto: **Emondson Ball Davies LLP, Chartered Accountants**
#501, 10 Milner Business Ct.
Toronto, ON M1B 3C6
Tel: 416-293-5560; *Fax:* 416-293-5377
www.ebdcas.com

Toronto: **Finucci Watters LLP (Toronto)**
#802, 390 Bay St.
Toronto, ON M5H 2Y2
Tel: 647-259-1766; *Fax:* 647-259-1776
afinucci@finucciwatters.com
www.porterhetu.com

Toronto: **Galloway Consulting Group Inc.**
#703, 1200 Eglinton Ave. East
Toronto, ON M3C 1H9
Tel: 416-803-5638; *Fax:* 416-449-7342
info@gallowayconsulting.ca
www.gallowayconsulting.ca

Toronto: **Gardner Zuk Dessen, Chartered Accountants**
#205, 265 Rimrock Rd.
Toronto, ON M3J 3C6
Tel: 416-631-9800; *Fax:* 416-631-9183
info@gzd.ca
www.gzd.ca

Toronto: **Hilborn Ellis Grant LLP**
PO Box 49
#3100, 401 Bay St.
Toronto, ON M5H 2Y4
Tel: 416-364-1359; *Fax:* 416-364-9503
www.heg.ca

Toronto: **Kelly Porter Hétu**
475 Queen St. East
Toronto, ON M5A 1T9
Tel: 416-955-0060; *Fax:* 416-955-0061
jkelly@porterhetu.com
www.porterhetu.com

Toronto: **Kenneth Michalak**
1576 Bloor St. West
Toronto, ON M6P 1A4
Tel: 416-588-2808; *Fax:* 416-588-3634
Toll-Free: 866-258-4788
info@kjmcga.coma
www.kjmcga.com

Toronto: **Klingbaum Barkin LLP**
The Madison Centre
#1906, 4950 Yonge St.
Toronto, ON M2N 6K1
Tel: 416-512-1221; *Fax:* 416-512-1284
mk@klingbaumbarkin.com
www.klingbaumbarkin.com

Toronto: **Koster, Spinks & Koster LLP (KSK)**
4 Glengrove Ave. West
Toronto, ON M4R 1N4
Tel: 416-489-8100; *Fax:* 416-489-9194
info@ksk.ca
www.ksk.ca

Toronto: **Kwan Chan Law Chartered Accountants Professional Corporation**
#910, 4950 Yonge St.
Toronto, ON M2N 6K1
Tel: 416-226-6862

Toronto: **M. Schwab Accounting Services Ltd.**
#606, 94 Cumberland St.
Toronto, ON M5R 1A3
Tel: 416-324-9933; *Fax:* 416-324-8733

Toronto: **McGovern, Hurley, Cunningham LLP**
#300, 2005 Sheppard Ave. East
Toronto, ON M2J 5B4
Tel: 416-496-1234; *Fax:* 416-496-0125
info@mhc-ca.com
www.mhc-ca.com

Toronto: **Mehl & Reynolds LLP**
#200, 1 Yorkdale Rd.
Toronto, ON M6A 3A1
Tel: 416-787-0681; *Fax:* 416-787-7630
webhome.idirect.com/~gmr

Toronto: **Michael Argue, Chartered Accountant, Professional Corporation**
#206, 1210 Sheppard Ave. East
Toronto, ON M2K 1E3
Tel: 416-490-8544; *Fax:* 416-490-8096
michaelargue@bellnet.ca
www.argueca.com

Toronto: **Michael I. Atlas, Chartered Accountant**
#2500, 120 Adelaide St. West
Toronto, ON M5H 1T1
Tel: 416-860-9175; *Fax:* 416-860-9189
matlas@taxca.com
www.taxca.com

Toronto: **Mintz & Partners LLP**
#200, 1 Concorde Gate
Toronto, ON M3C 4G4
Tel: 416-391-2900; *Fax:* 416-391-2748
info@mintzca.com
www.mintzca.com

Toronto: **Nevcon Accounting Services**
PO Box 43541
1531 Bayview Ave.
Toronto, ON M4G 4G8
Tel: 416-487-7996; *Fax:* 416-946-1098
Toll-Free: 888-463-8366
info@nevcon.com
www.nevcon.com

Toronto: **PKF Hill LLP**
#200, 41 Valleybrook Dr.
Toronto, ON M3B 2S6
Tel: 416-449-9171; *Fax:* 416-449-7401
info@pkfhill.com
www.pkfhill.com

Toronto: **PricewaterhouseCoopers LLP, Canada**
Royal Trust Tower, Toronto-Dominion Centre
PO Box 82
Toronto, ON M5K 1G8
Tel: 416-863-1133; *Fax:* 416-365-8178
www.pwc.com/ca

Toronto: **PricewaterhouseCoopers LLP, Canada - Toronto - King St. West**
145 King St. West
Toronto, ON M5H 1V8
Tel: 416-869-1130; *Fax:* 416-863-0926
www.pwc.com/ca

Toronto: **PricewaterhouseCoopers LLP, Canada - Toronto - Yonge St.**
North American Life Bldg.
#1900, 5700 Yonge St.
Toronto, ON M2M 4K7
Tel: 416-218-1500; *Fax:* 416-218-1499
www.pwc.com/ca

Toronto: **Renée S. Karn, CGA**
86 Acton Ave.
Toronto, ON M3H 4H1
Tel: 416-499-0012; *Fax:* 416-499-0194
rkarn@porterhetu.com
www.porterhetu.com

Toronto: **Rich Rotstein LLP**
South Tower
#303, 175 Bloor St. East
Toronto, ON M4W 3R8
Tel: 416-863-1400; *Fax:* 416-863-4881
lsr@richrotstein.com; lwr@richrotstein.com
www.richrotstein.com

Toronto: **Rosen & Associates Limited**
PO Box 101
#2200, 121 King St. West
Toronto, ON M5H 3T9
Tel: 416-363-4515; *Fax:* 416-363-4849
l.gallant@rosen-associates.com
www.rosen-associates.com

Toronto: **Rosenberg Smith & Partners LLP**
#200, 2000 Steeles Ave. West
Toronto, ON L4K 3E9
Tel: 416-798-4997; *Fax:* 905-660-3064
rsp@rsp.ca
www.rsp.ca

Toronto: **Rosenthal Consulting Group**
13 Balmoral Ave.
Toronto, ON M4V 1J5
Tel: 416-617-9966; *Fax:* 416-964-2371
hsrosenthal@alumni.uwaterloo.ca

Toronto: **Rumanek & Company Ltd.**
#714, 1280 Finch Ave. West
Toronto, ON M3J 3K6
Tel: 416-665-8326; *Fax:* 416-665-7634
info@trustee-in-bankruptcy.com
www.rumanek.com; www.trustee-in-bankruptcy.com

Toronto: **SBLR LLP Chartered Accountants**
#300, 2345 Yonge St.
Toronto, ON M4P 2E5
Tel: 416-488-2345; *Fax:* 416-488-3765
www.sblr.ca

Toronto: **Segal & Partners Inc.**
#500, 2005 Sheppard Ave. East
Toronto, ON M2J 5B4
Tel: 416-391-1460; *Fax:* 416-391-2285
Toll-Free: 800-206-7307
info@segalpartners.com
www.segalbankruptcy.com

Toronto: **Serbinski Partners PC**
183 Sheppard Ave. West
Toronto, ON M2N 1M9
Tel: 416-733-0300; *Fax:* 416-352-6004
Toll-Free: 888-878-2937
mtscpa@serbinski.com
www.serbinski.com

Toronto: **SF Partnership, LLP**
The Madison Centre
#400, 4950 Yonge St.
Toronto, ON M2N 6K1
Tel: 416-250-1212; *Fax:* 416-250-1225
general@sfgroup.ca
www.sfgroup.ca

***Toronto:* Sloan Partners LLP**
#6, 4646 Dufferin St.
Toronto, ON M3H 5S4
Tel: 416-665-7735; *Fax:* 416-649-7725
info@sloangroup.ca
www.sloangroup.ca

***Toronto:* Soberman LLP Chartered Accountants**
#1100, 2 St. Clair Ave. East
Toronto, ON M4T 2T5
Tel: 416-964-7633; *Fax:* 416-964-6454
info@soberman.com
www.soberman.com

***Toronto:* Sone & Rovet**
#406, 1200 Sheppard Ave. East
Toronto, ON M2K 2S5
Tel: 416-498-7200; *Fax:* 416-498-6877
www.sonerovet.com

***Toronto:* Spergel Inc.**
#200, 505 Consumers Rd.
Toronto, ON M2J 4V8
Tel: 416-497-1660; *Fax:* 416-494-7199
Toll-Free: 800-563-8251
aspergel@trustee.com
www.trustee.com

***Toronto:* Stewart & Kett Financial Advisors Inc.**
#911, 123 Front St. West
Toronto, ON M5J 2M2
Tel: 416-362-6322; *Fax:* 416-362-6302
www.stewartkett.com

***Toronto:* Tomlin Associates**
#445, 700 Lawrence Ave. West
Toronto, ON M6A 3B4
Tel: 416-488-6969; *Fax:* 416-783-9117
larry.tomlin@gmail.com
www.tomlin.ca
Other Contact Information: Cell: 416-302-8169

***Toronto:* V.B. Sharma Professional Corporation, Chartered Accountants**
#200, 3390 Midland Ave.
Toronto, ON M1V 5K3
Tel: 416-292-4431; *Fax:* 416-292-7247
vbsharma@vbsharma.ca
www.vbsharma.ca

***Toronto:* Zeifman & Company**
201 Bridgeland Ave.
Toronto, ON M6A 1Y7
Tel: 416-256-4000; *Fax:* 416-256-4001
info@zeifman.ca
www.zeifman.ca

***Toronto:* Zwaig Consulting Inc.**
#801, 20 Adelaide St. East
Toronto, ON M5X 2T6
Tel: 416-863-0140; *Fax:* 416-863-0428
zwaigm@zwaig.com
www.zwaig.com

***Trenton:* Wilkinson & Company LLP**
PO Box 400
71 Dundas St. West
Trenton, ON K8V 5R6
Tel: 613-392-2592; *Fax:* 613-392-8512
Toll-Free: 888-713-7283
trenton@wilkinson.net
www.wilkinson.net

***Vaughan:* Collins Barrow Chartered Accountants - Vaughan**
#600, 3300 Hwy. 7 West
Vaughan, ON L4K 4M3
Tel: 416-213-2600; *Fax:* 905-669-8705
info@collinsbarrowvaughan.com

***Vaughan:* Domenic Galati CGA**
#510, 3100 Steeles Ave. West
Vaughan, ON L4K 3R1
Tel: 416-745-0245
dgalati@porterhetu.com
www.porterhetu.com

***Vaughan:* PellegrinoTurnerMoore LLP**
#35, 100 Bass Pro Mills Dr.
Vaughan, ON L4K 5X1
Tel: 905-761-8080; *Fax:* 905-761-8190
robert@pellegrinogroup.ca
www.pellegrinogroup.ca

***Wallaceburg:* TurnerMoore LLP**
233 Nelson St.
Wallaceburg, ON N8A 4G5
Tel: 519-627-9971; *Fax:* 519-627-0400
peturner@turnermoore.com
www.turnermoore.com

***Waterloo:* PricewaterhouseCoopers LLP, Canada - Waterloo**
#201, 95 King St. South
Waterloo, ON N2J 5A2
Tel: 519-570-5700; *Fax:* 519-570-5730
www.pwc.com/ca

***Waterloo:* Transport Financial Services Ltd.**
105 Bauer Pl.
Waterloo, ON N2L 6B5
Tel: 519-886-8070; *Fax:* 519-886-5214
Toll-Free: 800-461-5970
www.tfsgroup.com/tfs

***Welland:* Durward Jones Barkwell & Company, Welland**
PO Box 9
171 Division St.
Welland, ON L3B 5N9
Tel: 905-735-2140; *Fax:* 905-735-4706
Toll-Free: 866-552-0997
welland@djb.com
www.djb.com

***Welland:* Lifestyle Financial Planning & Management Services Ltd.**
190 Division St.
Welland, ON L3B 4A2
Tel: 905-732-1640; *Fax:* 905-732-1397
stalosi@lifestylefinancial.com
www.lifestylefinancial.com

***Windsor:* BellemoreTurnerMoore LLP**
#6, 242 Lauzon Rd.
Windsor, ON N8S 3L6
Tel: 519-944-4777; *Fax:* 519-944-4011
dbellemore@turnermoore.com
www.turnermoore.com

***Windsor:* BoggsTurnerMoore LLP**
711 Kennedy Dr. West
Windsor, ON N9G 1S8
Tel: 519-972-3030; *Fax:* 519-972-4904
gboggs@turnermoore.com
www.turnermoore.com

***Windsor:* Collins Barrow Windsor LLP**
3260 Devon Dr.
Windsor, ON N8X 4L4
Tel: 519-258-5800; *Fax:* 519-256-6152
windsor@collinsbarrow.com
www.collinsbarrow.com

***Windsor:* Hyatt Lassaline LLP**
#203, 2510 Ouellette Ave.
Windsor, ON N8X 1L4
Tel: 519-966-4626; *Fax:* 519-966-9206
www.hyattlassaline.com

***Windsor:* PricewaterhouseCoopers LLP, Canada - Windsor**
245 Ouellette Ave., 3rd Fl.
Windsor, ON N9A 7J4
Tel: 519-985-8900; *Fax:* 519-258-5457
www.pwc.com/ca

***Windsor:* Roth Mosey & Partners LLP**
#300, 3100 Temple Dr.
Windsor, ON N8W 5J6
Tel: 519-977-6410; *Fax:* 519-977-7083
info@roth-mosey.com
www.roth-mosey.com

***Woodbridge:* NandanCharkoTurnerMoore LLP**
#9, 70 Silton Rd.
Woodbridge, ON L4L 8B9
Tel: 905-265-8400
rnandan@turnermoore.com
www.turnermoore.com

***Woodbridge:* Rashid & Quinney Chartered Accountants**
#401, 216 Chrislea Rd.
Woodbridge, ON L4L 8S5
Tel: 905-856-2677; *Fax:* 905-856-2679
rick@randg.ca

***Woodstock:* Thornton VanTassel Chartered Accountants - Woodstock**
318 Connell St.
Woodstock, ON E7M 6B7
Tel: 506-324-8040; *Fax:* 506-325-2262
stephen.thornton@thorntonvantassel.com
www.thorntonvantassel.com

Prince Edward Island

***Charlottetown:* Beaton Fitzpatrick Murray**
PO Box 2158
#200, 155 Belevedere Ave.
Charlottetown, PE C1A 8B9
Tel: 902-892-5365; *Fax:* 902-892-0383
bfm@bfm.pe.ca
www.bfm.pe.ca

***Summerside:* Peter M. Baglole, Chartered Accountant**
PO Box 1373
#7, 293 Water St.
Summerside, PE C1N 4K2
Tel: 902-436-1663; *Fax:* 902-436-1604
peter@baglole.ca
www.baglole.ca

***Summerside:* Schurman Sudsbury & Associates Ltd.**
189 Water St.
Summerside, PE C1N 1B2
Tel: 902-436-2171; *Fax:* 902-436-0960
schurman-sudsbury@isn.net

Quebec

***Anjou:* Brunet, Roy, Dubé, Comptables agrées**
#1200, 7100 rue Jean-Talon
Anjou, QC H1M 3S3
Tél: 514-255-1001

***Blainville:* Lévesque CA, Comptables agréés**
#204, 10, boul. de la Seigneurie est
Blainville, QC J7C 3V5
Tél: 450-437-8969; *Téléc:* 450-437-8996
infos@levesqueca.com
www.levesqueca.com

***Drummondville:* Samson Bélair/Deloitte & Touche s.e.n.c.r.l.**
212, rue Heriot
Drummondville, QC J2C 1J8
Tel: 819-477-6311; *Fax:* 819-477-9572
www.deloitte.com

***Joliette:* Martin, Boulard & Associés, sencrl**
#200, 37, Place Bourget sud
Joliette, QC J6E 5G1
Tél: 450-759-2825; *Téléc:* 450-752-1235
jvarin@mba.qc.ca

***Lachine:* Martin & Cie**
1100, rue Notre-Dame
Lachine, QC H8S 2C4
Tel: 514-637-7887; *Fax:* 514-637-3566
l.martin@martin-cie.com
www.martin-cie.com

***Longueuil:* Dubé & Tétreault, Comptables agréés, S.E.N.C.**
#200, 3065, ch. de Chambly
Longueuil, QC J4L 1N3
Tel: 450-442-0944; *Fax:* 450-442-2166
richard@dube-tetreault.com
www.dube-tetreault.com

***Montréal:* A. Bertucci, Chartered Accountant**
1445, rue Lambert Closse
Montréal, QC H3H 1Z5
Tel: 514-932-3229; *Fax:* 514-932-4634
abertucci@abertucci.com
www.abertucci.com

***Montréal:* Accountatax Inc./ Comptataxe inc.**
147, rue Spring Garden
Montréal, QC H9B 2T7
Tel: 514-685-7394; *Fax:* 514-685-7411
Toll-Free: 877-685-7394
www.accountatax.ca

***Montréal:* Aubry, Hijazi, CA - s.e.n.c.r.l.**
#215, 1331, av. Green
Montréal, QC H3Z 2A5
Tel: 514-935-7787; *Fax:* 514-935-5865

Montréal: **Beauchemin Trépanier Comptables agréés inc.**
#1102, 4200, boul. St-Laurent
Montréal, QC H2W 2R2
Tel: 514-847-0182; *Fax:* 514-849-9082
bt@btca.qc.ca
www.btca.qc.ca

Montréal: **Bessner Gallay Kreisman**
#600, 4150, rue Ste-Catherine Ouest
Montréal, QC H3Z 2Y5
Tel: 514-908-3600; *Fax:* 514-908-3630
www.bgsk.com

Montréal: **Fine et associés/ Fine & Associates**
5101, rue Buchan
Montréal, QC H4P 1S4
Tél: 514-731-0761; *Téléc:* 514-731-4639

Montréal: **Gestion Tellier St-Germain**
PO Box 324, P.A.T. Stn. P.A.T.
11536, rue de la Gauchetière
Montréal, QC H1B 5J5
Tel: 514-640-8922; *Fax:* 514-640-4801
ghislaine@gestionrg.qc.ca
www.gestionrg.qc.ca

Montréal: **Goldsmith Hersh s.e.n.c.r.l.**
#200, 1411, rue Fort
Montréal, QC H3H 2N6
Tel: 514-933-8611; *Fax:* 514-933-1142
info@ghmca.com
www.gmhca.com

Montréal: **Le Groupe Belzile Tremblay**
2675, rue Masson
Montréal, QC H1Y 1W3
Tel: 514-384-3620; *Fax:* 514-384-3710
bt@belziletremblay.ca
www.belziletremblay.ca

Montréal: **H&A eDiscovery**
#401, 360, rue Notre Dame ouest
Montréal, QC H2Y 1T9
Tel: 514-844-5577; *Fax:* 514-844-1088
www.haediscovery.com; www.haforensics.com

Montréal: **Info Comptabilité Plus**
#201, 2035, Côte de Liesse
Montréal, QC H4N 2M5
Tel: 514-337-2677; *Fax:* 514-337-1594
info@infocplus.com
www.infocplus.com

Montréal: **J. Kromida, Chartered Accountant**
750, av. Sainte-Croix
Montréal, QC H4L 3Y2
Tel: 514-747-3413; *Fax:* 514-747-0799
jamesk@kromida.com
www.kromida.com

Montréal: **Jacques Davis Lefaivre & Associés**
#1900, 1080, côte du Beaver Hall
Montréal, QC H2Z 1S8
Tél: 514-878-2600; *Téléc:* 514-878-2600
Ligne sans frais: 800-363-6800
jdl@jdl.ca

Montréal: **JDM Consultation Inc.**
#203, 759, carré Victoria
Montréal, QC H2Y 2J7
Tel: 514-844-4536; *Fax:* 514-849-8647
jimmy@menegakis.ca
www.menegakis.ca

Montréal: **Jean J. Drouin, CGA**
#201, 6455, rue Christophe-Colomb
Montréal, QC H2S 2G5
Tel: 514-274-6831; *Fax:* 514-274-8128
info@drouin-cga.com

Montréal: **Leclerc Forensic Accountants - Montréal**
#2821, 1, Place Ville-Marie
Montréal, QC H3B 4R4
Tel: 514-798-5874; *Fax:* 514-788-4837
www.leclerc-ifa.com

Montréal: **Martel Desjardins**
Édifice de la Banque Nationale de Paris
#1440, 1981, av. McGill College
Montréal, QC H3A 2Y1
Tel: 514-849-2793; *Fax:* 514-849-7104
md@marteldesjardins.com
www.marteldesjardins.com

Montréal: **Mazars Harel Drouin**
#1200, 215, rue Saint-Jacques
Montréal, QC H2Y 1M6
Tel: 514-845-9253; *Fax:* 514-845-3859
www.mazars.ca

Montréal: **MCA Consulting Group**
5240-B, rue Saint Denis
Montréal, QC H2J 2M2
Tel: 514-277-8081; *Fax:* 514-276-9150
info@groupemca.com
www.groupemca.com

Montréal: **Padgett Business Services**
88, boul. Brunswick
Montréal, QC H9B 2C5
Tel: 514-684-8086; *Fax:* 514-684-0884
www.padgettwestisland.com

Montréal: **Perreault, Wolman, Grzywacz & Co.**
#814, 5250, rue Ferrier
Montréal, QC H4P 2N7
Tél: 514-731-7987; *Téléc:* 514-731-8782
www.pwgca.com

Montréal: **Petrie Raymond Inc.**
#1000, 255, boul. Crémazie est
Montréal, QC H2M 1M2
Tél: 514-342-4740; *Téléc:* 514-737-4049
info@petrieraymond.qc.ca
www.petrieraymond.qc.ca/

Montréal: **Porter Hétu International**
5800, av. Monkland, 2ième étage
Montréal, QC H4A 1G1
Tel: 514-369-7529; *Fax:* 514-482-0036
www.porterhetu.com

Montréal: **PSB Boisjoli**
#400, 3333, boul. Graham
Montréal, QC H3R 3L5
Tel: 514-341-5511; *Fax:* 514-342-0589
www.psb.ca

Montréal: **RSM Richter**
#1820, 2, Place Alexis Nihon
Montréal, QC H3Z 3C2
Tel: 514-934-3400; *Fax:* 514-934-3408
mtlinfo@rsmrichter.com
www.richter.ca

Montréal: **Ruby Stein Wagner S.E.N.C. Chartered Accountants**
Place du Parc
#1900, 300, rue Léo-Pariseau
Montréal, QC H2X 4B5
Tel: 514-842-3911; *Fax:* 514-849-3447
Toll-Free: 866-842-3911
info@rswca.com
www.rswca.com

Montréal: **Schlesinger Newman Goldman**
#1100, 625, boul. René-Lévesque ouest
Montréal, QC H3B 1R2
Tel: 514-866-8553; *Fax:* 514-866-8469
info@sng.ca
www.sng.ca

Montréal: **Schwartz Levitsky Feldman LLP (SLF)**
1980, rue Sherbrooke ouest, 10e étage
Montréal, QC H3H 1E8
Tel: 514-937-6392; *Fax:* 514-933-9710
www.slf.ca

Montréal: **Stamos Porter Hétu**
800, av. Ste. Croix
Montréal, QC H4L 3Y2
Tel: 514-744-1100; *Fax:* 514-744-2200
jstamos@porterhetu.com
www.porterhetu.com

Montréal: **Victor & Gold Chartered Accountants**
#400, 759, carré Victoria
Montréal, QC H2Y 2J7
Tel: 514-282-1836; *Fax:* 514-282-6640
www.victorgold.com

Montréal: **WAKED**
#2825, 500, Place d'Armes
Montréal, QC H2Y 2W2
Tel: 514-875-6400; *Fax:* 514-861-6301
info@wakedcma.com
www.wakedcma.com

Québec: **Bergeron Lavigne SENC**
1780, Damiron
Québec, QC G2E 5S8
Tel: 418-877-8705; *Fax:* 418-877-0057
michelbergeronca@videotron.ca
www.guideformationquickbooks.com

Québec: **Blouin, Julien, Potvin Comptables agréés, S.E.N.C.**
#300, 2795, boul. Laurier
Québec, QC G1V 4M7
Tel: 418-651-0405; *Fax:* 418-651-0285
groupe@boulinjulienpotvin.qc.ca

Québec: **Brassard Carrier, Comptables Agréés**
#200, 1651, ch. Ste-Foy
Québec, QC G1S 2P1
Tel: 418-682-2929; *Fax:* 418-682-0282
info@groupebca.com
www.groupebca.com

Québec: **Cauchon Turcotte Thériault Latouche**
Place Iberville Un
#310, 1195, av. Lavigerie
Québec, QC G1V 4N3
Tel: 418-658-8808; *Fax:* 418-658-3136
equipe@cttlca.com
www.cttlca.com

Québec: **Choquette Corriveau, Chartered Accountants**
Place Iberville I
#300, 1195, av. Lavigerie
Québec, QC G1V 4N3
Tel: 418-658-5555; *Fax:* 418-658-1010
courrier@choquettecorriveau.com
choquettecorriveau.com

Québec: **Dallaire Forest Kirouac S.E.N.C.R.L.**
#580, 1175, av. Lavigerie
Québec, QC G1V 4P1
Tel: 418-650-2266; *Fax:* 418-650-2529
Toll-Free: 877-650-2266
comptable@dfk.qc.ca
www.dfk.qc.ca

Québec: **Gagnon, Moisan, Comptables agréés**
#227, 945, av. Newton
Québec, QC G1P 4M3
Tel: 418-871-6262; *Fax:* 418-871-9526
www.fortune1000.ca/gagnon-moisan/

Québec: **Gariépy, Gravel, Larouche comptables agréés S.E.N.C.**
601, av. du Cénacle
Québec, QC G1E 6W4
Tel: 418-666-3704; *Fax:* 418-666-6913
www.gglca.qc.ca

Québec: **Laberge Lafleur Brown S.E.N.C.R.L.**
Place de la Cité
#1060, 2590, boul. Laurier
Québec, QC G1V 4M6
Tel: 418-659-7265; *Fax:* 418-659-5937
www.llbca.com

Québec: **Leclerc Forensic Accountants - Québec**
#360, 580, Grande-Allée est
Québec, QC G1R 2K2
Tel: 418-780-5874; *Fax:* 418-780-3191
www.leclerc-ifa.com

Québec: **Legaré Porter Hétu**
#201, 3181 ch. Ste-Foy
Québec, QC G1X 1R3
Tel: 418-780-1333; *Fax:* 418-780-1339
miclegar@porterhetu.com
www.porterhetu.com

Québec: **Malenfant Dallaire Comptables Agréés**
Place de la Cité
#872, 2600, boul. Laurier
Québec, QC G1V 4W2
Tel: 418-654-0636; *Fax:* 418-654-0639
maldal@malenfantdallaire.com
www.malenfantdallaire.com

Québec: **PricewaterhouseCoopers LLP, Canada - Québec**
Place de la Cité, Tour Cominar
#1700, 2640, boul. Laurier
Québec, QC G1V 5C2
Tel: 418-522-7001; *Fax:* 418-522-5663
www.pwc.com/ca

Québec: **Roy, Labrecque, Busque, Comptables Agréés**
#160, 5055, boul. Hamel ouest
Québec, QC G2E 2G6
Tel: 418-871-0013; *Fax:* 418-871-0162
rlb@roylabrecquebusque.com
www.roylabrecquebusque.com

Québec: **Signature comptable Mc Nicoll CA inc.**
#210, 1220, boul. Lebourgneuf
Québec, QC G2K 2G4
Tel: 418-622-6666; *Fax:* 418-622-3904
mcnicollp@signaturecomptable.ca
www.signaturecomptable.ca

Saint-Hubert: **Hébert, Turgeon, CGA Inc.**
7695, ch. de Chambly
Saint-Hubert, QC J3Y 5K2
Tel: 450-676-0624; *Fax:* 450-676-7677
info@htcga.qc.ca
www.htcga.qc.ca

Saint-Rémi: **Lefaivre Labrèche Gagné, sencrl**
151, rue Perras
Saint-Rémi, QC J0L 2L0
Tél: 450-454-3974; *Téléc:* 450-454-7320
info@lefaivre-labreche.com
www.le-lab-ca.qc.ca

Shawville: **Smith Porter Hétu**
PO Box 896
389, rue Main
Shawville, QC J0X 2Y0
Tel: 819-647-2403; *Fax:* 819-647-3103
pbsmith@porterhetu.com
www.porterhetu.com; www.thetaxsmith.com

St-Laurent: **Porter Hétu International (Québec) inc.**
790, boul. Marcel-Laurin
St-Laurent, QC H4M 2M6
Tel: 514-744-1500; *Fax:* 514-744-6441
mplaliberte@porterhetu.com; esauve@porterhetu.com
www.porterhetu.com

Ste-Thérèse: **Marcil Girard Porter Hétu International**
8, rue St-Charles
Ste-Thérèse, QC J7E 2A2
Tel: 450-430-7526; *Fax:* 450-430-6809
guylaine@porterhetu.com
www.porterhetu.com

Saskatchewan

Esterhazy: **Skilnick Miller Moar Grodecki & Kreklewich, Chartered Accountants - Esterhazy**
Bank of Montreal Bldg.
420 Main St.
Esterhazy, SK S0A 1X0
Tel: 306-745-6611; *Fax:* 306-745-2899
kenmoar@sasktel.net
www.skilnick.ca

Melville: **Skilnick Miller Moar Grodecki & Kreklewich, Chartered Accountants**
PO Box 1660
#155, 3rd Ave. East
Melville, SK S0A 2P0
Tel: 306-728-4525; *Fax:* 306-728-2599
melvilleoffice@skilnick.ca
www.skilnick.ca

Saskatoon: **Byron J. Reynolds, Chartered Accountant**
PO Box 32029, Erindale Stn. Erindale
Saskatoon, SK S7S 1N8
Tel: 306-384-1130; *Fax:* 306-373-6431
br@byronjreynolds.ca
www.byronjreynolds.ca

Saskatoon: **Hergott Duval Stack LLP**
Saskatoon Square
#1200, 410 - 22nd St. East
Saskatoon, SK S7K 5T6
Tel: 306-934-8000; *Fax:* 306-653-5859
www.hergott.com

Saskatoon: **Hounjet Tastad Harpham**
1633A Quebec Ave.
Saskatoon, SK S7K 1V6
Tel: 306-653-5100; *Fax:* 306-653-5141
www.hth-accountants.ca

Saskatoon: **Lizée Gauthier Certified General Accountants**
473 - 2nd Ave. North
Saskatoon, SK S7K 2C1
Tel: 306-653-4444; *Fax:* 306-665-5662
lizee@sasktel.net

Saskatoon: **PricewaterhouseCoopers LLP, Canada - Saskatoon**
#200, 123 - 2nd Ave. South
Saskatoon, SK S7K 7E6
Tel: 306-668-5900; *Fax:* 306-652-1315
www.pwc.com/ca

Domestic Banks: Schedule I

See Index for Bank of Canada, and the Federal Business Development Bank, which are Crown Corporations, listed in the Government Section. *Chartered banks in Canada are incorporated by letters patent. They are governed by the Bank Act, which establishes the legislative framework for Canada's banking system. The Bank Act provides for the incorporation of banks. The Office of the Superintendent of Financial Institutions Canada regulates and supervises the Canadian financial system.*

Domestic banks are federally regulated Canadian banks. The subsidiaries of foreign banks are federally regulated foreign banks. Both domestic and foreign banks have the same powers, restrictions and obligations under the Bank Act.

Foreign bank representative offices are established by foreign banks in Canada. They act as a liaison between the foreign bank and its clients in Canada. These offices generally promote the services of the foreign bank, and do not accept deposits in Canada.

Foreign bank branches are federally regulated. They are permitted to establish specialized, commercially-focused branches in Canada, in accordance with the Bank Act. Full service branches generally are not permitted to accept deposits of less than $150,000.

ATB Financial exemplifies a savings bank in Canada. In Alberta, ATB Financial operates under the authority of the Alberta Treasury Branches Act Chapter A-37.9, 1997 and Treasury Branches Regulation 187/97.

Alterna Bank
400 Albert St., 3rd Fl.
Ottawa, ON K1R 5B2
Tel: 613-560-0120; *Toll-Free:* 866-560-0120
questions@alterna.ca
www.alterna.ca

Former Name: CS Alterna Bank
Ownership: Wholly-owned subsidiary of Alterna Savings & Credit Union Limited.
Year Founded: 2000

The Bank of Nova Scotia (BNS)/ La Banque de Nouvelle-Écosse
Scotia Plaza
44 King St. West
Toronto, ON M5H 1H1
Tel: 416-866-6161; *Fax:* 416-866-3750
email@scotiabank.com
www.scotiabank.com
Other Contact Information: Telex: WUI6719400

Also Known As: Scotiabank
Ownership: Public
Year Founded: 1832
Number of Employees: 42,046

Bank West
PO Box 5328
#1010, 24th St. SE
High River, AB T1V 1A7
Tel: 403-652-2107; *Fax:* 403-652-2237
Toll-Free: 888-440-2265
info@bankwest.ca
www.bankwest.ca

Ownership: Owned by Western Financial Group
Year Founded: 2002
Number of Employees: 15
Assets: $50-100 million
Revenues: Under $1 million

BMO Financial Group (BMO)
119, rue St-Jacques ouest
Montréal, QC H2Y 1L6
Tel: 514-877-7373; *Fax:* 514-877-7399
Toll-Free: 877-225-5266
feedback@bmo.com; remarque@bmo.com (French);
mutualfunds@bmo.com
www.bmo.com
Other Contact Information: 1-877-225-5266 (French);
1-800-665-8800 (Cantonese & Mandarin); 1-866 889-0889 (TTY service); mosaik@bmo.com (Credit cards)

Former Name: Bank of Montréal
Ownership: Public
Year Founded: 1817
Number of Employees: 37,000+
Assets: $412,000,000,000 Year End: 20081031

Bridgewater Bank
Also listed under: *Financing & Loan Companies*
#150, 926 - 5th Ave. SW
Calgary, AB T2P 0N7
Tel: 403-232-6556; *Fax:* 403-233-2609
Toll-Free: 888-837-2326
www.bridgewaterfinancial.ca

Former Name: Bridgewater Financial Services Ltd.
Ownership: Private. Wholly owned subsidiary of Alberta Motor Association.
Year Founded: 1997
Number of Employees: 170

Canadian Imperial Bank of Commerce (CIBC)/ Banque Canadienne Impériale de Commerce
Commerce Court
PO Box 1, Stn Commerce Court
Toronto, ON M5L 1A2
Tel: 416-980-2211; *Fax:* 416-218-9440
Toll-Free: 800-465-2422
customer.care@cibc.com; investorrelations@cibc.com
www.cibc.com
Other Contact Information: 1-800-465-2255 (Customer Care);
1-800-465-4653 (Credit Cards); 1-888-264-6843 (Mortgages);
416-980-4523 (Corporate Communications & Public Affairs)

Ownership: Public
Year Founded: 1858
Number of Employees: 40,000
Assets: 3,700,000,000 Year End: 20081031

Canadian Tire Financial Services Ltd. (CTAL)
Also listed under: *Financial Planning & Investment Management Companies*
PO Box 3000
Welland, ON L3B 5S5
Toll-Free: 866-681-2837
www.ctfs.com

Ownership: Wholly-owned subsidiary of Canadian Tire Corporation Limited
Year Founded: 1966
Number of Employees: 1,300

Canadian Western Bank (CWB)/ Banque Canadienne de l'Ouest
#3000, 10303 Jasper Ave.
Edmonton, AB T5J 3X6
Tel: 780-423-8888; *Fax:* 780-423-8897
comments@cwbank.com
www.cwbank.com

Also Known As: Canada's Western Bank
Ownership: Widely held Canadian corporation
Year Founded: 1984
Number of Employees: 1,000

Citizens Bank of Canada
#401, 815 West Hastings St.
Vancouver, BC V6C 1B4
Tel: 604-682-7171; *Fax:* 604-708-7790
Toll-Free: 888-708-7800
service@citizensbank.ca
www.citizensbank.ca

Ownership: Subsidiary of Vancouver City Savings Credit Union
Year Founded: 1997
Number of Employees: 120

Dundee Bank of Canada (DBC)
44 King St. West
Toronto, ON M5H 1H1
Fax: 416-849-1700
Toll-Free: 866-884-3434
support@dbc.ca
www.dbc.ca

Former Name: Dundee Wealth Bank
Ownership: Member of Dundee Financial Group (DFG), a division of Dundee Wealth Management Inc.
Year Founded: 2006

First Nations Bank of Canada
224 - 4th Ave. South
Saskatoon, SK S7K 5M5
Tel: 306-931-2409; *Fax:* 306-955-6811
Toll-Free: 888-454-3622
service@firstnationsbank.com
www.firstnationsbank.com
Ownership: Private
Year Founded: 1996
Number of Employees: 05
Assets: $100-500 million
Revenues: $5-10 million

General Bank of Canada(GBC)
c/o LeMarchand Mansion
#6, 11523 - 100 Ave.
Edmonton, AB T5K 0J8
Tel: 780-443-5626; *Fax:* 780-443-5628
Toll-Free: 877-443-5620
info@generalbank.ca
www.generalbank.ca
Ownership: Parent company is Firstcan Management Inc.
Year Founded: 2005

Laurentian Bank of Canada/ Banque Laurentienne du Canada
1981, av. McGill College
Montréal, QC H3A 3K3
Toll-Free: 877-522-3863
www.laurentianbank.ca
Other Contact Information: 1-866-262-2231 (TTY service); 514-284-4500, ext. 7511 or 8143 (Inverstors & analysts); 514-284-4500, ext. 7511 (Media)
Ownership: Public
Year Founded: 1846
Number of Employees: 3,393
Assets: $19,000,000,000+ Year End: 20081031
Revenues: $630,500,500 Year End: 20081031

Manulife Bank of Canada
PO Box 1602, Waterloo Stn. Waterloo
#500MA, 500 King St. North
Waterloo, ON N2J 4C6
Tel: 519-747-7000; *Toll-Free:* 877-765-2265
manulife_bank@manulife.com
www.manulifebank.ca
Ownership: Private. Wholly-owned subsidiary of Manulife Financial.
Year Founded: 1993
Number of Employees: 200+
Assets: $1-10 billion

National Bank of Canada (NBC)/ Banque Nationale du Canada(BNC)
National Bank Tower
600, rue de La Gauchetière ouest
Montréal, QC H3B 4L2
Tél: 514-394-6081; *Téléc:* 514-394-8434
www.nbc.ca
Former Name: The Provincial Bank of Canada; The Mercantile Bank of Canada
Ownership: Public
Year Founded: 1859
Number of Employees: 18,322

Pacific & Western Bank of Canada
#2002, 140 Fullarton St.
London, ON N6A 5P2
Tel: 519-645-1919; *Fax:* 519-645-2060
Toll-Free: 866-979-1919
www.pwbank.com
Ownership: Parent company is Pacific & Western Credit Corp., a public company.
Year Founded: 1979
Assets: $1-10 billion
Revenues: $5-10 million

President's Choice Bank (PC Bank)
431 King St. West
Toronto, ON M5V 1K5
Tel: 416-204-2600; *Toll-Free:* 888-723-8881
www.banking.pcfinancial.ca
Also Known As: President's Choice Financial
Ownership: PC Bank is a joint venture between Loblaw Companies & CIBC.

Royal Bank of Canada (RBC)
200 Bay St.
Toronto, ON M5J 2S5
Tél: 416-974-5151; *Téléc:* 416-955-7800
www.rbc.com
Also Known As: RBC Financial Group
Year Founded: 1869
Number of Employees: 65,045

The Toronto-Dominion Bank
TD Centre
PO Box 1
Toronto, ON M5K 1A2
Tel: 416-982-8222; *Toll-Free:* 866-222-3456
www.td.com
Also Known As: TD Bank; TD Canada Trust
Ownership: Public
Year Founded: 1855
Number of Employees: 51,163

Foreign Banks: Schedule II

Amex Bank of Canada
Also listed under: *Credit Card Companies*
101 McNabb St.
Markham, ON L3R 4H8
Tel: 905-474-0870; *Toll-Free:* 800-668-2639
www.americanexpress.com/canada
Other Contact Information: Toll-Free TTY/TTY: 1-866-549-6426; Local TTY/TTY: 905-940-7702
Ownership: Wholly-owned subsidiary of American Expess Travel Related Services Company, Inc., New York, USA.
Year Founded: 1853
Number of Employees: 3,700

Bank of China (Canada)
The Exchange Tower
PO Box 356
#2730, 130 King St. West
Toronto, ON M5X 1E1
Tel: 416-362-2991; *Fax:* 416-362-3047
Ownership: Wholly owned subsidiary of the Bank of China Limited, Beijing, China.
Year Founded: 1992
Number of Employees: 85
Assets: $100-500 million
Revenues: $10-50 million

The Bank of East Asia (Canada)
East Asia Centre
#102-103, 350 Hwy. 7 East
Richmond Hill, ON L4B 3N2
Tel: 905-882-8182; *Fax:* 905-882-5220
info@hkbea.com, OsEnquiry@hkbea.com
ca.hkbea.com
Other Contact Information: (852) 3608 0200 (Phone, Overseas Branch Operations & Development Department in Hong Kong)
Ownership: Private. Member of The Bank of East Asia Group, Hong Kong.
Year Founded: 1991

Bank of Tokyo-Mitsubishi UFJ (Canada)
#1700, South Tower, Royal Bank Plaza
PO Box 42
Toronto, ON M5J 2J1
Tel: 416-865-0220; *Fax:* 416-865-0196
www.bk.mufg.jp/english
Ownership: Foreign. Part of The Bank of Tokyo-Mitsubishi UFJ, Ltd., Tokyo,Japan.
Year Founded: 1996

BNP Paribas (Canada)
1981, av. McGill College
Montréal, QC H3A 2W8
Tél: 514-285-6000; *Téléc:* 514-285-6278
bnpp.canada@americas.bnpparibas.com
www.bnpparibas.ca
Former Name: Banque Nationale de Paris (Canada)
Ownership: Foreign. Wholly owned subsidiary of BNP Paribas, Paris, France
Year Founded: 1961
Number of Employees: 240
Assets: $1-10 billion

Citibank Canada
Citigroup Place
#1700, 123 Front St. West
Toronto, ON M5J 2M3
Tel: 416-947-5500; *Fax:* 416-947-5387
www.citibank.com/canada
Ownership: Wholly owned indirect subsidiary of Citibank, N.A.
Year Founded: 1982
Number of Employees: 5,000+

CTC Bank of Canada (CTCB)
1518 West Broadway
Vancouver, BC V6J 1W8
Tel: 604-683-3882; *Fax:* 604-683-3723
service@ctcbank.com
www.ctcbank.com
Ownership: Private. Part of Chinatrust Commercial Bank.

Habib Canadian Bank
#1B, 918 Dundas St. East
Mississauga, ON L4Y 4H9
Tel: 905-276-5300; *Fax:* 905-276-5400
info@habibcanadian.com
www.habibcanadian.com
Ownership: Private. Foreign. Wholly owned by Habib Bank of AG Zurich, Switzerland.
Year Founded: 1967
Assets: $50-100 million
Revenues: $1-5 million

HSBC Bank Canada
#300, 885 West Georgia St.
Vancouver, BC V6C 3E9
Tel: 604-525-4722; *Fax:* 604-641-1849
Toll-Free: 888-310-4722
info@hsbc.ca
www.hsbc.ca
Ownership: Subsidiary of HSBC Holdings plc, London, UK.
Year Founded: 1981
Number of Employees: 7,500

ICICI Bank Canada
PO Box 396
Toronto, ON M3C 2S7
Toll-Free: 888-424-2422
customercare.ca@icicibank.com
www.icicibank.ca
Ownership: Wholly-owned subsidiary of ICICI Bank Limited, Mumbai, India.

ING Bank of Canada
111 Gordon Baker Rd.
Toronto, ON M2H 3R1
Tel: 416-758-5344; *Fax:* 416-756-2422
Toll-Free: 800-464-3473
clientservices@ingdirect.ca
www.ingdirect.ca
Other Contact Information: 1-866-464-3473 (Toll Free, French service)
Social Media: facebook.com/superstarsaver; twitter.com/superstarsaver
Also Known As: ING DIRECT
Ownership: Wholly owned subsidiary of ING Group, Netherlands
Year Founded: 1997
Number of Employees: 850+
Assets: $10-100 billion

J.P. Morgan Bank Canada
South Tower, Royal Bank Plaza
PO Box 80
#1800, 200 Bay St.
Toronto, ON M5J 2J2
Tel: 416-981-9200; *Fax:* 416-981-9133
www.jpmorgan.com

Korea Exchange Bank of Canada (KEBOC)
Madison Centre
#103, 4950 Yonge St.
Toronto, ON M2N 6K1
Tel: 416-222-5200; *Fax:* 416-222-5822
www.kebcanada.com
Year Founded: 1981
Number of Employees: 90

MBNA Canada Bank
1600 James Naismith Dr.
Ottawa, ON K1B 5N8
Tel: 613-907-4800; *Fax:* 613-907-3501
Toll-Free: 800-404-1319
www.mbna.com/canada
Other Contact Information: 1-877-862-7759 (Toll Free for card applications); 1-800-872-5758 (TTY/TTD)
Ownership: Private. MBNA Corporation, Wilmington, Delaware, USA.
Year Founded: 1997

Mega International Commercial Bank (Canada)
Madison Centre
#1002, 4950 Yonge St.
Toronto, ON M2N 6K1
Tel: 416-947-2800; *Fax:* 416-947-9964
megato@ipoline.com
www.megabank.com.tw
Former Name: International Commercial Bank of Cathay (Canada)
Ownership: Wholly-owned subsidiary of Mega International Commercial Bank Co., Ltd., Taipei City, Taiwan.

Mizuho Corporate Bank (Canada) (MHCB)
PO Box 29
#1102, 100 Yonge St.
Toronto, ON M5C 2W1
Tel: 416-874-0222; *Fax:* 416-367-3452
Toll-Free: 800-668-5917
www.mizuhocbk.co.jp/english
Former Name: Mizuho Bank (Canada)
Ownership: Foreign. Part of Mizuho Corporate Bank, Ltd., Tokyo, Japan.
Year Founded: 2000

Société Générale (Canada)
#1800, 1501, av. McGill College
Montréal, QC H3A 3M8
Tél: 514-841-6000; *Téléc:* 514-841-6250
www.socgen.com
Ownership: Wholly-owned subsidiary of Société Générale Group, Paris, France.
Year Founded: 1974

State Bank of India (Canada)
#1600, Royal Bank Plaza, North Tower
PO Box 81, Royal Bank Stn. Royal Bank
200 Bay St.
Toronto, ON M5J 2J2
Tel: 416-865-0414; *Fax:* 416-865-1735
Toll-Free: 800-668-8947
sbican@sbicanada.com
www.sbicanada.com
Ownership: Subsidiary of State Bank of India
Year Founded: 1982
Number of Employees: 45
Assets: $100-500 million
Revenues: $1-5 million

Sumitomo Mitsui Banking Corporation of Canada
#1400, Ernst & Young Tower
PO Box 172, TD Centre Stn. TD Centre
Toronto, ON M5K 1H6
Tel: 416-368-4766; *Fax:* 416-367-3565
www.smbc.co.jp/aboutus/english
Former Name: Sakura Bank (Canada); The Sumitomo Bank of Canada
Ownership: Private. Foreign. Wholly owned subsidiary of Sumitomo Mitsui Banking Corporation, Tokyo, Japan.
Year Founded: 2001
Number of Employees: 32

UBS Bank (Canada)
Also listed under: *Financial Planning & Investment Management Companies; Investment Management*
#800, 154 University Ave.
Toronto, ON M5H 3Z4
Tel: 416-343-1800; *Fax:* 416-343-1900
Toll-Free: 800-268-9709
www.ubs.com/canada
Also Known As: UBS Canada
Ownership: Foreign. Public.
Year Founded: 1856
Number of Employees: 70,000
Assets: $100 billion +
Revenues: $10-100 billion

Foreign Banks: Schedule III

ABN AMRO Bank N.V., Canada Branch
Toronto-Dominion Centre
PO Box 114, T-D Centre Stn. T-D Centre
#1500, 79 Wellington St. West, 15th Fl.
Toronto, ON M5K 1G8
Tel: 416-367-0850; *Fax:* 416-367-7937
canada.branch@abnamro.com
www.abnamro.ca
Other Contact Information: canada.jobs@abnamro.com (Employment Enquiries); 416-367-7943 (Business & Commercial Fax); 416-367-7937 (Corporate & Institutional Fax)
Ownership: Branch of ABN AMRO Bank N.V.
Year Founded: 1824

Bank of America, National Association
#2500, 200 Front St. West
Toronto, ON M5V 3L2
Tel: 416-349-4100; *Fax:* 416-349-4278
Toll-Free: 800-387-1729
www.bankofamerica.com

Capital One Bank (Canada Branch)
Also listed under: *Credit Card Companies*
#1300, 5650 Yonge St.
Toronto, ON M2M 4G3
Fax: 416-228-5113
Toll-Free: 800-481-3239
ombudsman@capitalone.com
www.capitalone.ca
Other Contact Information: Customer Relations Address: PO Box 503, Stn. D, Toronto, ON M1R 5L1; Payment Address: PO Box 521, Stn. D, Toronto, ON M1R 5S4
Ownership: Foreign. Part of Capital One Services, Inc., McLean, VA, USA.

Comerica Bank
South Tower, Royal Bank Plaza
PO Box 61
#2210, 200 Bay St.
Toronto, ON M5J 2J2
Tel: 416-646-4797; *Fax:* 416-367-6435
www.comerica.com
Ownership: Foreign. Branch of Comerica Bank, Detroit, Michigan, USA.

Credit Suisse Securities (Canada), Inc.
PO Box 301, First Canadian Pl. Stn. First Canadian Pl.
#3000, 1 First Canadian Pl.
Toronto, ON M5X 1C9
Tel: 416-352-4500; *Fax:* 416-352-4680
www.csfb.com
Ownership: Part of Credit Suisse Group, Zurich, Switzerland.

Deutsche Bank AG
Commerce Court West
PO Box 263
#4700, 199 Bay St.
Toronto, ON M5L 1E9
Tel: 416-682-8000; *Fax:* 416-682-8383
deutsche.bank@db.com
www.db.com
Ownership: Foreign. Branch of Deutsche Bank AG, Frankfurt, Germany.

Dexia Crédit Local S.A. Canada
PO Box 201
#1620, 800, carré Victoria
Montréal, QC H4A 1E3
Tel: 514-868-1200
webmaster@dexia.com
www.dexia.com
Ownership: Branch of Dexia Crédit Local, Paris, France.

Fifth Third Bank
20 Bay St., 12th Fl.
Toronto, ON M5J 2N8
Tel: 416-216-4638
www.53.com
Ownership: Foreign. Branch of Fifth Third Bank, Cincinnati, Ohio, USA

First Commercial Bank
#100, 5611 Cooney Rd.
Richmond, BC V6X 3J6
Tel: 604-207-9600; *Fax:* 604-207-9638
www.firstbank.com
Ownership: Foreign. Branch of First Commercial Bank, Taiwan.

HSBC Bank USA, National Association
70 York St., 4th Fl.
Toronto, ON M5J 1S9
Tel: 416-868-8000
www.us.hsbc.com, www.hsbc.ca

JPMorgan Chase Bank, National Association
South Tower, Royal Bank Plaza
PO Box 80
#1800, 200 Bay St.
Toronto, ON M5J 2J2
Tel: 416-981-9200; *Fax:* 416-981-9175
Toll-Free: 888-430-9844
www.jpmorganchase.com
Former Name: The Chase Manhattan Bank; Morgan Guaranty Trust Co. of New York; Sears Bank Canada
Ownership: Branch of J.P. Morgan Chase & Co. Inc., Chicago, IL, USA.

Maple Bank GmbH
c/o Maple Financial Group Inc., Maritime Life Tower, TD Centre
PO Box 328
#3500, 79 Wellington St. West
Toronto, ON M5K 1K7
Tel: 416-350-8200; *Fax:* 416-350-8226
info@maplefinancial.com
www.maplebank.com; www.maplefinancial.com
Former Name: First Marathon Bank GmbH
Ownership: Subsidiary of Maple Financial Group Inc.

Mellon Bank, N.A., Canada Branch
PO Box 16
#1710, 95 Wellington St. West
Toronto, ON M5J 2N7
Tel: 416-860-0777
www.mellon.com
Ownership: Foreign. Branch of Mellon Financial Corp., Pittsburgh, PA, USA.
Year Founded: 1983

National City Bank - Canada Branch
The Exchange Tower
PO Box 462
#2140, 130 King St. West
Toronto, ON M5X 1E4
Tel: 416-361-1744; *Fax:* 416-361-0085
www.nationalcity.com
Ownership: owned by National City Bank, Cleveland, Ohio
Year Founded: 1845
Number of Employees: 5

Ohio Savings Bank, Canadian Branch
Centre Tower, Clarica Centre
#3110, 3300 Bloor St. West
Toronto, ON M8X 2X3
Toll-Free: 800-696-2222
www.ohiosavings.com
Ownership: Foreign. Branch of Ohio Savings Bank, Cleveland, OH, USA.

Rabobank Nederland
Royal Trust Tower
#4520, 77 King St. West
Toronto, ON M5K 1E7
Tel: 416-941-9777; *Fax:* 416-941-9750
www.rabobank.com
Former Name: Rabobank Canada
Ownership: Cooperative. Foreign. Branch of Rabobank Nederland, Netherlands
Year Founded: 2001
Number of Employees: 14
Assets: $1-10 billion

State Street Bank & Trust Company - Canada
Also listed under: *Trust Companies*
#1100, 30 Adelaide St. East
Toronto, ON M5C 3G6
Tel: 416-362-1100; *Fax:* 416-956-2525
Toll-Free: 888-287-8639
www.statestreet.com
Former Name: State Street Trust Company Canada
Ownership: State Street Corporation
Year Founded: 1990
Number of Employees: 700

Union Bank of California, N.A.
#730, 440 - 2 Ave. SW
Calgary, AB T2P 5E9
Tel: 403-264-2700; *Fax:* 403-264-2770
www.uboc.com
Ownership: Parent Union BanCal Corporation
Year Founded: 1864

United Overseas Bank Limited (UOB)
Vancouver Centre
PO Box 11616
#1680, 650 West Georgia St.
Vancouver, BC V6B 4N9
Tel: 604-662-7055; *Fax:* 604-662-3356
UOB.Vancouver@uobgroup.com
www.uobgroup.com
Ownership: Foreign. Branch of United Overseas Bank Limited, Singapore.
Year Founded: 1987

U.S. Bank National Association - Canada Branch
Adelaide Centre
#2300, 120 Adelaide St. West
Toronto, ON M5H 1T1
Toll-Free: 877-332-7461
www.usbankcanada.com
Ownership: Part of U.S. Bank, Minneapolis, MN, USA.

WestLB AG
North Tower, Royal Bank Plaza
PO Box 41
#2301, 200 Bay St.
Toronto, ON M5J 2J1
Tel: 416-216-5000; *Fax:* 416-216-5020
info@westlb.de
www.westlb.com
Ownership: Foreign. Branch of WestLB AG, Düsseldorf, Germany.

Foreign Banks Representative Offices

Allied Irish Banks, p.l.c. (AIB)
20 Bay St., 12th Fl.
Toronto, ON M5J 2N8
www.aib.ie
Ownership: Foreign. Office of Allied Irish Banks p.l.c., Dublin, Ireland.

American Express Bank Ltd.
#1350, 1090 West Georgia St.
Vancouver, BC V6E 3V7
Ownership: Foreign. Office of American Express Bank, New York, NY, USA.

Banco Comercial dos Açores
836 Dundas St. West
Toronto, ON M6J 1V5
Tel: 416-603-0802; *Fax:* 416-603-8892
www.bca.pt

Banco Espirito Santo e Comercial de Lisboa, SA
860C College St.
Toronto, ON M6H 1A2
Tel: 416-530-1700
www.bes.pt
Ownership: Private

Banco Santander Totta, SA
1110 Dundas St. West
Toronto, ON M6J 1X2
Tel: 416-538-7111
www.santandertotta.pt

Bank Hapoalim B.M.
#2105, 4950 Yonge St.
Toronto, ON M2N 6K1
Tel: 416-398-4250; *Fax:* 416-398-4246
www.bankhapoalim.com

Bank Leumi Le-Israel, B.M.
#400, 1 carré Westmount
Montréal, QC H3Z 2P9
Tel: 514-931-4457; *Fax:* 514-931-5240
english.leumi.co.il
Ownership: Office of Bank Leumi Le-Israel, B.M., Tel Aviv, Israel.
Year Founded: 1902
Assets: $10-100 billion
Revenues: $100-500 million

Bank of Cyprus, Canada Representative Office
#302, 658 Danforth Ave.
Toronto, ON M4J 5B9
Tel: 416-461-5570; *Fax:* 416-461-6062
Toll-Free: 888-529-2265
info@bankofcyprus.ca
www.bankofcyprus.ca
Ownership: Office of the Bank of Cyprus Group, Cyprus.
Year Founded: 1997

Bank of Ireland Asset Management (U.S.) Limited
#2460, 1800, av. McGill College
Montréal, QC H3A 3J6
Tel: 514-849-6868; *Fax:* 514-849-8118
canada@biam.boi.ie
www.biam.ie
Year Founded: 1987

Bank of Valletta p.l.c., Canada Representative Office
West Tower
#625, 3300 Bloor St. West, 6th Fl.
Toronto, ON M8X 2X2
Tel: 416-234-2265; *Fax:* 416-234-2281
Toll-Free: 800-567-2265
bovcanada@bov.com
www.bov.com

Bank Vontobel AG
#1760, 999 West Hastings St.
Vancouver, BC V6C 2W2
Tel: 604-688-1122; *Fax:* 604-688-1123
www.vontobel.com
Ownership: Office of Bank Vontobel AG, Zürich, Switzerland.

Banque Centrale Populaire du Maroc
#1514, 1010 rue Sherbrooke ouest
Montréal, QC H3A 2R7
Tel: 514-281-1855; *Fax:* 514-281-1974
gbpmaroc@qc.aira.com
www.bp.co.ma

Baring Asset Management Inc.
TD Canada Trust Tower, Brookfield Place
161 Bay St., 27th Fl.
Toronto, ON M5J 2S1
Tel: 416-572-2400; *Fax:* 416-572-4100
william.tsotsos@barings.com
www.baring-asset-can.com
Ownership: Private
Year Founded: 1977

Bayerische Landesbank
#2060, 1501, av. McGill College
Montréal, QC H3A 3M8
Tel: 514-985-0047; *Fax:* 514-985-3459
info.montreal@bayernlb.com
www.bayernlb.de
Ownership: Foreign. Part of Bayerische Landesbank (BayernLB), Munich, Germany.

Caixa Economica Montepio Gual
1286 Dundas St. West
Toronto, ON M6J 1X7
Tel: 416-588-7776; *Fax:* 416-588-0030
mg503@montepio.pt
www.montepio.pt

Calyon
#1900, 2000, av McGill College
Montréal, QC
Ownership: Office of Credit Agricole Group, Paris, France.
Year Founded: 2004

Centurion Bank of Punjab, Ltd.
#337, 1515 Britannia Rd. East
Mississauga, ON L4W 4K1
Tel: 905-696-0943; *Fax:* 905-696-0976
nri.services@centurionbop.co.in
www.centurionbop.co.in
Ownership: Office of Centurion Bank of Punjab, India.

Crédit Libanais S.A.L. Representative Office (Canada)
Place du Canada
#1325, 1010, rue de la Gauchetière ouest
Montréal, QC H3B 2N2
Tel: 514-866-6688; *Fax:* 514-866-6220
Toll-Free: 800-864-5512
info@creditlibanais.com
www.creditlibanais.com
Ownership: Office of Credit Libanais S.A.L., Beirut, Lebanon.

Cyprus Popular Bank Ltd.
484 Danforth Ave., 2nd Fl.
Toronto, ON M4K 1P6
Tel: 416-466-8180; *Fax:* 416-466-9609
Toll-Free: 877-524-5422
laiki.toronto@laiki.com, laikiebank@laiki.com
www.laiki.com
Also Known As: Laiki Bank
Ownership: Office of Laiki Group, Cyprus.

Jamaica National Overseas (Canada) Ltd.
1672 Eglinton Ave. West
Toronto, ON M6E 2H2
Tel: 416-784-2075; *Fax:* 416-784-2076
Toll-Free: 800-462-9003
info@jnocanada.com, rosbourne@jnocanada.com, sstamp@jnocanada.com
www.jnbs.com
Ownership: Office of Jamaica National Building Society, Kingston Jamaica.

Japan Bank for International Cooperation - Toronto Liaison Office (JBIC)
Exchange Tower
PO Box 493, 2 First Canadian Pl. Stn. 2 First Canadian Pl.
#3660, 130 King St. West
Toronto, ON M5X 1E5
Tel: 416-865-1700; *Fax:* 416-865-0124
www.jbic.go.jp
Ownership: Office of Japan Bank for International Cooperation, Tokyo, Japan.

JCB International (Canada) Ltd.
Also listed under: *Credit Card Companies*
#510, 1030 West Georgia St.
Vancouver, BC V6E 2Y3
Tel: 604-689-8110; *Fax:* 604-689-8101
www.jcbinternational.com
Ownership: Office of JCB International Co., Ltd., Tokyo, Japan
Year Founded: 1961

JS Trasta komercbanka
#800, St. Clair Ave. East
Toronto, ON M4T 2T5
Tel: 416-644-4941; *Fax:* 416-644-4946
canada@tkb.lv, info@tkb.lv
www.tkb.lv
Ownership: Office of JS Trasta komercbanka, Riga, Latvia.

Landsbanki Islands hf
George Mitchell House
5112 Prince St.
Halifax, NS B3J 1L3
Tel: 902-576-3100
info@landsbanki.is
www.landsbanki.is
Ownership: Office of Landsbanki Islands hf, Reykjavik, Iceland.

Lebanese Canadian Bank, s.a.l.
#1508, 1, Place Ville-Marie
Montréal, QC H3B 2B5
Tel: 514-871-3999; *Fax:* 514-871-2079
www.lebcanbank.com
Other Contact Information: Alternative Phone Numbers: 514-871-1905; 514-871-1913; 514-871-1926

National Bank of Pakistan
#210, 175 Commerce Valley Dr. West
Thornhill, ON L3T 7P6
Tel: 905-707-0244; *Fax:* 905-707-1040
chiefrep@nbpcanada.com, enquiries@nationalbank.com.pk
www.nbp.com.pk
Ownership: Office of National Bank of Pakistan, Karachi, Pakistan.

Schroder Investment Management North America Limited - Canadian Representative Office
Also listed under: *Financial Planning & Investment Management Companies*
Canada Trust Tower, BCE Place
#4720, 161 Bay St.
Toronto, ON M5J 2S1
Tel: 416-360-1200; *Fax:* 416-360-1202
www.schroders.com/ca
Former Name: Schroder Investment Management Canada Limited
Ownership: Office of Schroders plc, London, UK.

Stanford International Bank Ltd. (SIBL)
#3010, 1800, av. McGill College
Montréal, QC H3A 3J6
Tel: 514-985-3600
www.stanfordinternational.com
Ownership: Office of Stanford International Bank Ltd., St. Johns, Antigua, West Indies.
Year Founded: 2004

UBS AG
PO Box 3
#650, 999 West Hastings St.
Vancouver, BC V6C 2W2
Tel: 604-691-8061; *Fax:* 604-691-8098
www.ubs.com
Ownership: Office of UBS AG, Zürich, Switzerland.

Victoria Mutual Building Society - Canadian Representative Office (VMBS)
3117A Dufferin St.
Toronto, ON M6A 2S9
Tel: 416-652-8652; *Fax:* 416-652-5266
Toll-Free: 800-465-6500
manager@vmbs.com
www.vmbs.com
Ownership: Office of Victoria Mutual Building Society, Kingston, Jamaica.

Westdeutsche Landesbank Girozentrale
North Tower, Royal Bank Plaza
PO Box 41
#2301, 200 Bay St.
Toronto, ON M5J 2J1
Tel: 416-216-5000; *Fax:* 416-216-5020
info@westlb.de
www.westlb.de
Also Known As: WestLB
Ownership: Office of Westdeutsche Landesbank Girozentrale, Düsseldorf, Germany

Savings Banks

ATB Financial
ATB Place
9888 Jasper Ave. NW
Edmonton, AB T5J 1P1
Tel: 780-408-7000; *Fax:* 780-422-4178
Toll-Free: 800-332-8383
atbinfo@atb.com
www.atb.com
Former Name: Alberta Treasury Branches
Ownership: Crown. 100% owned by the Provincial Government of Alberta
Year Founded: 1938
Number of Employees: 5,000

Boards of Trade & Chambers of Commerce

International Chambers & Business Councils

British Canadian Chamber of Trade & Commerce
PO Box 1358, Stn. K, Toronto ON M4P 3J4 Canada
Tel: 416-502-0847; *Fax:* 416-502-9319
central@bcctc.ca
www.bcctc.ca
Philip Gorlick, Executive Director, Eastern
Liam J. Hopkins, Executive Director, Western
Ann Mulvale, Executive Director, Central

Canada China Business Council (CCBC) / Conseil commercial Canada Chine
#1501, 330 Bay St., Toronto ON M5H 2S8 Canada
Tel: 416-954-3800; *Fax:* 416-954-3806
ccbc@ccbc.com
www.ccbc.com

Canada Czech Republic Chamber of Commerce (CNACC)
PO Box 163, Stn. A, Toronto ON M9C 4V3 Canada
Tel: 416-559-2868; *Fax:* 289-232-1352
admin@ccrcc.net
www.ccrcc.net
Miroslav Princ, MBA, Chamber President

Canada-Arab Business Council (CABC) / Conseil de commerce canado-arabe (CCCA)
#600, 357 Bay St., Toronto ON M5M 2T7 Canada
Tel: 416-362-0050; *Fax:* 416-362-7633
info@canada-arabbusiness.org
www.canada-arabbusiness.org
Affiliation(s): Canadian Chamber of Commerce
Dwain Lingenfelter, Chairman/CEO

Canada-Finland Chamber of Commerce
c/o Finnish Credit Union, 191 Eglinton Ave. East, Toronto ON M4P 1K1 Canada
Tel: 416-486-1533; *Fax:* 416-486-1592
info@canadafinlandcc.com
www.canadafinlandcc.com

Canada-India Business Council (C-IBC) / Conseil de commerce Canada-Inde
#302, 1 St. Clair Ave. East, Toronto ON M4T 2V7 Canada
Tel: 416-214-5947; *Fax:* 416-214-9081
info@canada-indiabusiness.ca
www.canada-indiabusiness.ca

Canada-Indonesia Business Council
PO Box 11-C, #110, 260 Adelaide St. East, Toronto ON M5A 1N1 Canada
Tel: 416-366-8490; *Fax:* 416-947-1534
Peter J. Dawes, Chair

Canada-Poland Chamber of Commerce of Toronto
77 Stoneham Rd., Toronto ON M9C 4Y7 Canada
Tel: 416-621-2032; *Fax:* 416-621-2472
info@canada-poland.com
www.canada-poland.com
Wojciech Sniegowski, President

Canadian Armenian Business Council Inc. (CABC) / Conseil commercial canadien-arménien inc.
#302-2, 1805, rué Sauve ouest, Montréal QC H4N 3B8 Canada
Tel: 514-333-7655; *Fax:* 514-333-7280
info@cabc.ca
www.cabc.ca
Publications: CABC [Canadian Armenian Business Council Inc.] Business Directory

Canadian Council for the Americas (BCCC)
#300, 160 Eglington Ave. East, Toronto ON M5G 2K8 Canada
Tel: 416-364-3555; *Fax:* 416-595-8226
cca@iecanada.com
www.ccacanada.com

Canadian Council for the Americas (CCA) / Conseil Canadien pour les Amériques
#2300, 1066 West Hastings St., Vancouver BC V6E 3X2 Canada
Tel: 778-388-5206; *Fax:* 604-806-6112
info@cca-bc.com
www.cca-bc.com
André Nudelman, Chair
Leon Teicher, Secretary

Canadian German Chamber of Industry & Commerce Inc. / Deutsch-Kanadische Industrie- und Handelskammer
#1500, 480 University Ave., Toronto ON M5G 1V2 Canada
Tel: 416-598-3355; *Fax:* 416-598-1840
info@germanchamber.ca
www.germanchamber.ca
Publications: Canadian German Headlines: CGCIC Newsletter, Membership Directory of the Canadian German Chamber of Industry & Commerce

Canadian-Croatian Chamber of Commerce
630 The East Mall, Toronto ON M9B 4B1 Canada
Tel: 416-641-2829; *Fax:* 416-641-2700
contactus@croat.ca
www.croat.ca
Joh Marion, President

Chambre de commerce Canada-Pologne
PO Box 326, Stn. Ahuntsic, Montréal QC H3L 3N8 Canada
Tel: 514-278-7617; *Fax:* 514-384-6936
info@chambrecp.ca
www.chambrecp.ca
Catherine Zemelka, Executive Director

Chambre de commerce Canado-Tunisienne (CCCT) / Tunisian Canadian Chamber of Commerce
#806, 276, rue St-Jacques, Montréal QC H2Y 1N3 Canada
Tél: 514-847-1281; *Téléc:* 514-849-4910
info@cccantun.ca
www.cccantun.ca
Abdeljelil Ouanès, Président

Chambre de commerce française au canada (CCFC) / French Chamber of Commerce
#202, 1819, boul René-Lévesque ouest, Montréal QC H3H 2P5 Canada
Tél: 514-281-1246; *Téléc:* 514-289-9594
acceuil@ccfcmtl.ca
www.ccife.org/canada/montreal
Florent Belleste, Directeur

Danish Canadian Chamber of Commerce
#2110, 2 Bloor St. West, Toronto ON M4W 3E2 Canada
Tel: 416-923-1811; *Fax:* 416-962-3668
info@dccc.ca
www.dccc.ca
Anders Fisker, Chair
Knud Westergaard, Executive Director

Indo-Canada Chamber of Commerce (ICCC) / Chambre de commerce Indo-Canada
#900, 45 Sheppard Ave. East, Toronto ON M2N 5W9 Canada
Tel: 416-224-0090; *Fax:* 416-224-0089
Toll-Free: 866-873-4222
iccc@iccc.org
www.iccc.org
Asha Luthra, President
Neena Gupta, Vice-President & Corp. Secretary

International Chamber of Commerce (ICC) / Chambre de Commerce Internationale
38, cours Albert 1er, Paris 75008 France
icc@iccwbo.org
www.iccwbo.org
Affiliation(s): United Nations; World Trade Organization

Ireland-Canada Chamber of Commerce (ICCC)
121 Decarie Circle, Toronto ON M9B 3J6 Canada
Tel: 416-622-7773; *Fax:* 416-621-3433
main@iccto.com
www.iccto.com
Michael Power, President

Italian Chamber of Commerce of Ontario (ICCO)
1502, 80 Richmond St. West, Toronto ON M5H 2A4 Canada
Tel: 416-789-7169; *Fax:* 416-789-7160
info.toronto@italchambers.ca
www.italchambers.ca
Publications: Partners Magazine

Southeast Asia-Canada Business Council
5294 Imperial St., Burnaby BC V5J 1E4 Canada
Tel: 604-439-0779; *Fax:* 604-439-0284
info@asean-canadatrade.org
www.asean-canadatrade.org

The Swedish-Canadian Chamber of Commerce (SCCC)
#2120, 2 Bloor St. West, Toronto ON M4W 3E2 Canada
Tel: 416-925-8661; *Fax:* 416-929-8639
mglindmark@sccc.ca
www.sccc.ca
Monika G. Lindmark, Executive Director

Swiss Canadian Chamber of Commerce (Montréal) Inc. / Chambre de commerce Canado-Suisse (Montréal) Inc.
1572 Dr. Penfield Ave., Montréal QC H3G 1C4 Canada
Tel: 514-937-5822; *Fax:* 514-693-1032
info@cccsmtl.com
www.cccsmtl.com

World Chambers Federation (WCF)
38 cours Albert 1er, Paris 75008 France
wcf@iccwbo.org
www.iccwbo.org; www.worldchambersfederation.org
Affiliation(s): Specialized div. of International Chamber of Commerce
François-Gabriel Ceyrac, Director

Chambers of Mines

Alberta Chamber of Resources
#1940, 10180 - 101 St., Edmonton AB T5J 3S4 Canada
Tel: 780-420-1030; *Fax:* 780-425-4623
acr-mail@acr-alberta.com
www.acr-alberta.com

Chamber of Mineral Resources of Nova Scotia (CMRNS)
PO Box 2171, Windsor NS B0N 2T0 Canada
Tel: 902-798-0187; *Fax:* 902-798-2141
terry.daniels@ns.sympatico.ca
Affiliation(s): Mining Association of Canada

Chamber of Mines of Eastern British Columbia
215 Hall St., Nelson BC V1L 5X4 Canada
Tel: 250-352-5242; *Fax:* 250-352-7227
chamberofminesebc@netidea.com
www.cmebc.com
Jack Denny, President
Dennis Llewellyn, Chamber Manager

East Kootenay Chamber of Mines
#201, 12 - 11th Avenue South, Cranbrook BC V1C 2P1 Canada
Tel: 250-489-2255; *Fax:* 250-426-8755
www.ekcm.org/chamber2
Ross Stanfield, President

NWT & Nunavut Chamber of Mines
PO Box 2818, Yellowknife NT X1A 2R1 Canada
Tel: 867-873-5281; *Fax:* 867-920-2145
nwtmines@ssimicro.com
www.miningnorth.com
Affiliation(s): Mining Association of Canada; Canadian Institute of Mining, Metallurgy & Petroleum

Yukon Chamber of Mines (YCM)
3151B - 3rd Ave., Whitehorse YT Y1A 1G1 Canada
Tel: 867-667-2090; *Fax:* 867-668-7127
info@ycmines.ca
www.ycmines.ca
Affiliation(s): Mining Association of Canada

Provincial & Territorial Boards of Trade & Chambers of Commerce

Alberta Chambers of Commerce (ACC)
#1808, 10025 - 102A Ave., Edmonton AB T5J 2Z2 Canada
Tel: 780-425-4180; *Fax:* 780-429-1061
Toll-Free: 800-272-8854
info@abchamber.ca
www.abchamber.ca
Affiliation(s): Canadian Chamber of Commerce

British Columbia Chamber of Commerce
#1201, 750 West Pender St., Vancouver BC V6C 2T8 Canada
Tel: 604-683-0700; *Fax:* 604-683-0416
bccc@bcchamber.org
www.bcchamber.org
Social Media: www.facebook.com/pages/BC-Chamber-of-Commerce/141727519198122

Creston Chamber of Commerce
PO Box 268, 1607 Canyon St., Creston BC V0B 1G0 Canada
Tel: 250-428-4342; *Fax:* 250-428-9411
Toll-Free: 866-528-4342
crestonchamber@kootenay.com
www.crestonbc.com/chamber

Fédération des chambres de commerce du Québec
555, boul. René-Lévesque ouest, 19e étage, Montréal QC H2Z 1B1 Canada
Tél: 514-844-9571; *Téléc:* 514-844-0226
Ligne sans frais: 800-361-5019
info@fccq.ca
www.fccq.ca

The Manitoba Chambers of Commerce
227 Portage Ave., Winnipeg MB R3B 2A6 Canada
Tel: 204-948-0100; *Fax:* 204-948-0110
Toll-Free: 877-444-5222
mbchamber@mbchamber.mb.ca
www.mbchamber.mb.ca

New Brunswick Chamber of Commerce (NBCC)
#21, 236 St. George St., Moncton NB E1C 1W1 Canada
Tel: 506-854-9920; *Fax:* 506-854-8910
pierrev@nb.aibn.com
Pierre Michaud, Contact

Newfoundland & Labrador Chamber of Commerce
PO Box 352, 109 Trans Canada Hwy., Gander NL A1V 1W7 Canada
Tel: 709-651-6522; *Fax:* 709-256-5808
nlcc@nf.aibn.com
www.nlchamber.ca
Maureen O'Reilly, Executive Director

Northwest Territories Chamber of Commerce
NWT Commerce Place, #13, 4910 - 50th Ave., Yellowknife NT X1A 3S5 Canada
Tel: 867-920-9505; *Fax:* 867-873-4174
admin@nwtchamber.com
www.nwtchamber.com
Robin Wotherspoon, Executive Director
Don Yamkowy, President
Ann Marie Tout, Vice-President
Doreen Farrants, Secretary
Steve Meister, Treasurer

Nova Scotia Chambers of Commerce
605 Prince Street, Truro NS B2N 5B6 Canada
Tel: 902-895-6329; *Fax:* 902-897-6641
info@nschamber.ca
www.nschamber.ca
Dan Fougere, President

Ontario Chamber of Commerce (OCC)
#505, 180 Dundas St. West, Toronto ON M5G 1Z8 Canada
Tel: 416-482-5222; *Fax:* 416-482-5879
info@occ.on.ca
www.occ.on.ca
Social Media: twitter.com/OntarioCofC

Ontario Gay & Lesbian Chamber of Commerce
39 River St., Toronto ON M5A 3P1 Canada
Tel: 416-646-1600
info@oglcc.com
www.oglcc.com
John Kenyon, President

Prince Edward Island Chamber of Commerce
c/o Drake Truck Bodies, Riverview Crescent, RR#1, Vernon Bridge PE C0A 2E0 Canada
Tel: 902-651-2782; *Fax:* 902-652-2786
Allison Drake, President

Saskatchewan Chamber of Commerce
Chateau Tower, #1630, 1920 Broad St., Regina SK S4P 3V2 Canada
Tel: 306-352-2671; *Fax:* 306-781-7084
info@saskchamber.com
www.saskchamber.com

Swiss Canadian Chamber of Commerce (Ontario) Inc. (SCCC)
756 Royal York Rd., Toronto ON M8Y 2T6 Canada
Tel: 416-236-0039; *Fax:* 416-236-3634
sccc@swissbiz.ca
www.swissbiz.ca

Yukon Chamber of Commerce (YCC)
#101, 307 Jarvis St., Whitehorse YT Y1A 2H3 Canada
Tel: 867-667-2000; *Fax:* 867-667-2001
Toll-Free: 800-661-0543
president@yukonchamber.com
www.yukonchamber.com

Alberta

Airdrie Chamber of Commerce
PO Box 3661, Airdrie AB T4B 2B8 Canada
Tel: 403-948-4412; *Fax:* 403-948-3141
info@airdriechamber.ab.ca
www.airdriechamber.ab.ca

Alberta Beach & District Chamber of Commerce
PO Box 280, Alberta Beach AB T0E 0A0 Canada
Tel: 780-924-3889; *Fax:* 780-924-3425
gwte@telusplanet.net
Phyllis Stark, President

Alix Chamber of Commerce
PO Box 145, Alix AB T0C 0B0 Canada
Tel: 403-747-2405; *Fax:* 403-747-2403
cpete@oanet.com
www.villageofalix.ca

Athabasca & District Chamber of Commerce (ADCofC)
PO Box 3074, Athabasca AB T9S 2B9 Canada
Tel: 780-213-4600
Affiliation(s): Canadian Chambers of Commerce

Barrhead Chamber of Commerce
PO Box 4524, Barrhead AB T7N 1A4 Canada
Tel: 403-674-2338; *Fax:* 403-674-5648
info@barrheadchamber.ca
www.barrheadchamber.ca

Bashaw Chamber of Commerce
PO Box 645, Bashaw AB T0B 0H0 Canada
bashawcc@gmail.com
www.townofbashaw.com/chamber
Peter Graham, President

Bassano & District Chamber of Commerce
PO Box 849, General Delivery, Bassano AB T0J 0B0 Canada
Tel: 403-641-3014

Beaverlodge Chamber of Commerce
PO Box 303, Beaverlodge AB T0H 0C0 Canada
Tel: 780-354-8785; *Fax:* 780-354-2107
olsom@telusplanet.net

Beiseker & District Chamber of Commerce
PO Box 277, Beiseker AB T0M 0G0 Canada
Tel: 403-947-2356; *Fax:* 403-947-3227
Al Henuset, Contact

Blackfalds Chamber of Commerce
PO Box 249, Blackfalds AB T0M 0J0 Canada
Tel: 403-885-2386; *Fax:* 403-885-2386
Curtis Pedde, President

Bluffton Chamber of Commerce
PO Box 38, RR#2, Bluffton AB T0C 0M0 Canada
Tel: 403-843-6514; *Fax:* 403-843-3506
lawman@telusplanet.net
Lawrence Wright, President

Bonnyville & District Chamber of Commerce
PO Box 6054, Hwy. 28 West, Bonnyville AB T9N 2G7 Canada
Tel: 780-826-3252; *Fax:* 780-826-4525
manager@bonnyvillechamber.ab.ca
www.bonnyvillechamber.com
Lorne Ringuette, President
Al Arbour, Vice President

Bow Island / Burdett District Chamber of Commerce
PO Box 1001, 502 Centre St., Bow Island AB T0K 0G0 Canada
Tel: 403-545-5134; *Fax:* 403-542-2449
info@bowislandchamber.com
www.bowislandchamber.com/

Boyle & District Chamber of Commerce
PO Box 496, Boyle AB T0A 0M0 Canada
Tel: 780-689-4646; *Fax:* 780-689-2250

Bragg Creek Chamber of Commerce
PO Box 216, Bragg Creek AB T0L 0K0 Canada
Tel: 403-949-0004; *Fax:* 403-949-2748
office@braggcreekchamber.ca
www.braggcreekchamber.ca
Chris Tucker, President
Shannon Duncan, Secretary

Breton & District Chamber of Commerce
PO Box 364, Breton AB T0C 0P0 Canada
Tel: 780-696-2557; *Fax:* 780-696-2572

Brooks & District Chamber of Commerce
PO Box 400, #6, 403 - 2 Ave. West, Brooks AB T1R 1B4 Canada
Tel: 403-362-7641; *Fax:* 403-362-6893
manager@brookschamber.ab.ca
www.brookschamber.ab.ca

Calgary Chamber of Commerce
100 - 6 Ave. SW, Calgary AB T2P 0P5 Canada
Tel: 403-750-0400; *Fax:* 403-266-3413
chinfo@calgarychamber.com
www.calgarychamber.com

Camrose Chamber of Commerce
5402 - 48 Ave., Camrose AB T4V 0J7 Canada
Tel: 780-672-4217; *Fax:* 780-672-1059
camcham@telusplanet.net
www.camrosechamber.ca

Cardston & District Chamber of Commerce
PO Box 1212, 490 Main St., Cardston AB T0K 0K0 Canada
Tel: 403-795-1032
Info@CardstonChamber.com
www.cardstonchamber.com/

Caroline & District Chamber of Commerce
PO Box 90, Caroline AB T0M 0M0 Canada
Tel: 403-722-4066; *Fax:* 403-722-4002
ccoc@telus.net
www.carolinechamber.ca
Reg Dean, President
Deana Knight, Manager

Carstairs Chamber of Commerce
PO Box 370, Carstairs AB T0M 0N0 Canada
Tel: 403-337-3341
www.town.carstairs.ab.ca/chamber.html
Dennis Schmick, President
Karen Kneeland, Vice-President

Claresholm & District Chamber of Commerce
PO Box 1092, Claresholm AB T0L 0T0 Canada
Tel: 403-625-4229
info@claresholchamber.com
www.claresholmchamber.com
Russell Sawatsky, President

Coaldale & District Chamber of Commerce
PO Box 1117, 1401 - 20 Ave., Coaldale AB T1M 1M9 Canada
Tel: 403-345-2358; *Fax:* 403-345-2339
info@coaldalechamber.com
www.coaldalechamber.com

Cochrane & District Chamber of Commerce
#5, 205 - 1st St. East, Cochrane AB T4C 1X6 Canada
Tel: 403-932-6810; *Fax:* 403-932-6824
c.business@cochranechamber.ca
www.cochranechamber.ca
Adamo Cocuzzoli, President
Dawn Martin, Coordinator

Cold Lake Regional Chamber of Commerce
PO Box 454, Cold Lake AB T9M 1P1 Canada
Tel: 780-594-4747; *Fax:* 780-594-3711
clrcc@incentre.net
www.coldlakechamber.ca
Rob Brassard, President
Sherri Bohme, Executive Director

Consort Chamber of Commerce
PO Box 490, 4901 - 50 Ave., Consort AB T0C 1B0 Canada
Tel: 403-577-3623; *Fax:* 403-577-2024
webmaster@village.consort.ab.ca
www.village.consort.ab.ca/ChamberofCommerce.htm
Peter G. Ringrose, Executive Director

Coronation Chamber of Commerce
PO Box 960, Coronation AB T0C 1C0 Canada
Tel: 403-578-4220; *Fax:* 403-578-3020

Cremona Water Valley & District Chamber of Commerce
PO Box 356, 106 Railway Ave. West, Cremona AB T0M 0R0 Canada
Tel: 403-335-8398; *Fax:* 403-637-7022
vhoogenboom@aol.com
www.cremonawatervalley.com
Gabriel Grenier, President

La Crete & Area Chamber of Commerce
PO Box 1088, La Crete AB T0H 2H0 Canada
Tel: 780-928-2278; *Fax:* 780-928-2234
office@lacretechamber.com
www.lacretechamber.com
Larry Buhler, President
Barbara Peters, Office Manager

Crossfield Chamber of Commerce
PO Box 1490, Crossfield AB T0M 0S0 Canada
crossfieldchamber@shaw.ca
www.crossfieldchamber.com

Crowsnest Pass Chamber of Commerce
PO Box 706, Blairmore AB T0K 0E0 Canada
Tel: 403-562-7108; *Fax:* 403-562-7493
Toll-Free: 888-562-7108
cncpchamber@telus.net
www.crowsnest-pass.com
Affiliation(s): Alberta Chamber of Commerce

Delburne & District Chamber of Commerce
PO Box 254, Delburne AB T0M 0V0 Canada
Tel: 403-749-2808; *Fax:* 403-749-2800
delburne@telusplanet.net
www.delburne.ca
Brenda Smith, President

Devon & District Chamber of Commerce
35 Athabasca Ave., Devon AB T9G 1G5 Canada
Tel: 780-987-5177; *Fax:* 780-987-5135
devoncc@telus.net

Diamond Valley Chamber of Commerce
PO Box 61, Turner Valley AB T0L 2A0 Canada
Tel: 403-652-3700; *Fax:* 866-855-2065
info@diamondvalleychamber.com
www.diamondvalleychamber.com
R. Williamson, President

Didsbury Chamber of Commerce
PO Box 981, 1811 - 20 St., Didsbury AB T0M 0W0 Canada
Tel: 403-335-3265; *Fax:* 403-335-3265
info@didsburychamber.ca
www.didsburychamber.ca
Margo Ward, President
Joelle Fournier, Office Manager

Drayton Valley & District Chamber of Commerce (DVDCC)
PO Box 5318, Drayton Valley AB T7A 1R5 Canada
Tel: 780-542-7578; *Fax:* 780-542-9211
chambrdv@telusplanet.net
www.dvchamber.com

Drumheller & District Chamber of Commerce (DDCC)
PO Box 999, 60 First Ave. West, Drumheller AB T0J 0Y0 Canada
Tel: 403-823-8100; *Fax:* 403-823-4469
info@drumhellerchamber.com
www.drumhellerchamber.com

Eckville & District Chamber of Commerce
PO Box 609, Eckville AB T0M 0X0 Canada
Tel: 403-746-2353; *Fax:* 403-746-3470
eckville@telusplanet.net
www.eckvillechamber.com
Mitch Krescy, President

Edgerton & District Chamber of Commerce
PO Box 303, Edgerton AB T0B 1K0 Canada
Tel: 780-755-3947
Kim Kimball, President

Edmonton Chamber of Commerce
World Trade Centre, Sun Life Place, #700, 9990 Jasper Ave., Edmonton AB T5J 1P7 Canada
Tel: 780-426-4620; *Fax:* 780-424-7946
info@edmontonchamber.com
www.edmontonchamber.com

Edson & District Chamber of Commerce
5433 - 3rd Ave., Edson AB T7E 1L5 Canada
Tel: 780-723-4918; *Fax:* 780-723-5545
info@edsonchamber.com
www.edsonchamber.com

Elk Point Chamber of Commerce
PO Box 639, Elk Point AB T0A 1A0 Canada
Tel: 780-724-4087; *Fax:* 780-724-4087
vbooker@stpaul.greatwest.ca

Evansburg & Entwistle Chamber of Commerce
PO Box 598, Evansburg AB T0E 0T0 Canada
Tel: 780-727-4035; *Fax:* 780-727-4035
info@partnersonthepembina.com
www.partnersonthepembina.com

Fairview & District Chamber of Commerce
PO Box 1034, Fairview AB T0H 1L0 Canada
Tel: 780-835-5999; *Fax:* 780-835-5991
executivedirector@fairviewchamber.com
www.fairviewchamber.com

Falher Chamber of Commerce
PO Box 814, Falher AB T0H 1M0 Canada
Tel: 780-925-2708; *Fax:* 780-837-2647
patrysha@incredibleimpressions.com
Affiliation(s): Falher & Area Economic Development & Tourism

Foremost & District Chamber of Commerce
PO Box 272, Foremost AB T0K 0X0 Canada
Tel: 403-867-3077; *Fax:* 403-867-3579
cofc4mst@la.shockware.com
www.foremostalberta.com

Fort Macleod & District Chamber of Commerce
PO Box 178, Fort MacLeod AB T0L 0Z0 Canada
Tel: 403-553-3355
EDO@FortMacleod.com
www.fortmacleod.com/business/chamber_commerce.cfm
Emily McTighe, President

Fort McMurray Chamber of Commerce
#304, 9612 Franklin Ave., Fort McMurray AB T9H 2J9 Canada
Tel: 780-743-3100; *Fax:* 780-790-9757
fmcoc@telus.net
www.fortmcmurraychamber.ca

Fort Saskatchewan Chamber of Commerce
PO Box 3072, 10030 - 99 Ave., Fort Saskatchewan AB T8L 2T1 Canada
Tel: 780-998-4355; *Fax:* 780-998-1515
chamber@fortsaskchamber.com
www.fortsaskchamber.com
Affiliation(s): Alberta Chamber of Commerce; Canadian Chamber of Commerce

Fort Vermilion & Area Board of Trade
PO Box 456, Fort Vermilion AB T0H 1N0 Canada
Tel: 780-927-3505
Frank Rosenberger, President

Fox Creek Chamber of Commerce
PO Box 774, Fox Creek AB T0H 1P0 Canada
Tel: 780-622-2670; *Fax:* 780-622-2677
fcchamb@telus.net
Bernie Hornby, President
Barb Souter, Treasurer
Rose Hearn, Secretary

Glendon & District Chamber
PO Box 300, Glendon AB T0A 1P0 Canada
Tel: 780-635-2557
Ron Mack, President

Grande Cache Chamber of Commerce
PO Box 1342, Grande Cache AB T0E 0Y0 Canada
Tel: 780-827-3790; *Fax:* 780-827-5698
Affiliation(s): Alberta Chamber of Commerce; Canadian Chamber of Commerce

Grande Prairie & District Chamber of Commerce
#217, 11330 - 106 St., Grande Prairie AB T8V 7X9 Canada
Tel: 780-532-5340; *Fax:* 780-532-2926
info@gpchamber.com
www.grandeprairiechamber.com

Grimshaw Chamber of Commerce
PO Box 919, Grimshaw AB T0H 1W0 Canada
Tel: 780-332-4370; *Fax:* 780-332-4375
blossomb@telus.net
Theresa Bruce, President
Jenny Borys, Secretary

Hanna & District Chamber of Commerce
PO Box 2248, Hanna AB T0J 1P0 Canada
Tel: 403-854-4004; *Fax:* 403-854-4060
hannachamber@telus.net
www.aroundhanna.com/hannachamberofcommerce
Barb Larson, Chamber Manager

Hardisty & District Chamber of Commerce
PO Box 628, Hardisty AB T0B 1V0 Canada
Tel: 780-888-3836
ernie.ziegler@midfieldsupply.com
Rob Rondeau, President

High Level & District Chamber of Commerce
10803 - 96 St., High Level AB T0H 1Z0 Canada
Tel: 780-926-2470; *Fax:* 780-926-4017
hlchambr@incentre.net
www.highlevelchamber.com
Sylvia Kennedy, President
Daina French, Administrative contact

High River & District Chamber of Commerce
PO Box 5244, 149B Macleod Trail SW, High River AB T1V 1M4 Canada
Tel: 403-652-3336; *Fax:* 403-652-7660
hrdcc@telus.net
www.highriverchamber.com
Clair Noad, President
Lynette McCracken, Executive Director

Hinton & District Chamber of Commerce
309 Gregg Ave., Hinton AB T7V 2A7 Canada
Tel: 780-865-2777; *Fax:* 780-865-1062
Toll-Free: 877-446-8666
hintoncc@telus.net
www.hintonchamber.com

Hythe & District Chamber of Commerce
PO Box 404, Hythe AB T0C 2C0 Canada
Tel: 780-356-2168; *Fax:* 780-356-2009
chamber@hythe.ca
www.hythe.ca/chamber.html
Steve Greene, Chair

Innisfail & District Chamber of Commerce
5031 - 40th St., Innisfail AB T4G 1H8 Canada
Tel: 403-227-1177; *Fax:* 403-227-6749
ichamber@telusplanet.net
www.innisfailchamber.ca

Irma & District Chamber of Commerce
PO Box 284, Irma AB T0B 2H0 Canada
Tel: 780-754-3996
cwilli@telusplanet.net
Claudia Williams, President

Jasper Park Chamber of Commerce
PO Box 98, 632 Connaught Dr., Jasper AB T0B 1E0 Canada
Tel: 780-852-3858; *Fax:* 780-852-4932
Toll-Free: 800-473-8135
info@jaspercanadianrockies.com
www.jaspercanadianrockies.com
Social Media: www.twitter.com/jasperthabear
George Andrew, President
Krista Rodger, General Manager

Kainai Chamber of Commerce
PO Box 350, Stand Off AB T0L 1Y0 Canada
Tel: 403-737-8207
chamber@bloodtribe.org
Tony Manyfingers, President
Donald Cotton, Manager

Killam & District Chamber of Commerce
PO Box 272, Killam AB T0B 2L0 Canada
Tel: 780-385-3644

Lac La Biche & District Chamber of Commerce
PO Box 804, 10307, 100 St., Lac La Biche AB T0A 2C0 Canada
Tel: 780-623-2818; *Fax:* 780-623-7217
llbcofc@telusplanet.net
www.llbchamber.ca
Affiliation(s): Alberta Chamber of Commerce
Elaine Poulin, Executive Director
Bill Abougoush, President

Lacombe & District Chamber of Commerce
6005 - 50 Ave., Lacombe AB T4L 1K7 Canada
Tel: 403-782-4300; *Fax:* 403-782-4302
info@lacombechamber.ca
www.lacombechamber.ca

Leduc & District Chamber of Commerce
6420 - 50 St., Leduc AB T9E 7K9 Canada
Tel: 780-986-5454; *Fax:* 780-986-8108
info@leduc-chamber.com
www.leduc-chamber.com

Legal & District Chamber of Commerce
PO Box 338, General Delivery, Legal AB T0G 1L0 Canada
Tel: 780-456-3424
www.legalchamberofcommerce.com
Affiliation(s): Greater Edmonton Regional Chambers of Commerce
Frank Klassen, President
Carol Tremblay, Secretary

Lethbridge Chamber of Commerce
#200, 529 - 6 St. South, Lethbridge AB T1J 2E1 Canada
Tel: 403-327-1586; *Fax:* 403-327-1001
office@lethbridgechamber.com
www.lethbridgechamber.com

Lloydminster Chamber of Commerce
4419 - 52 Ave., Lloydminster AB T9V 0Y8 Canada
Tel: 780-875-9013; *Fax:* 780-875-0755
contact_llc@lloydminsterchamber.com
www.lloydminsterchamber.com
Pat L. Tenney, Executive Director
Peggy Bosch, President

Mallaig Chamber of Commerce
PO Box 144, Mallaig AB T0A 2K0 Canada
Tel: 780-635-3849

Mannville & District Chamber of Commerce
PO Box 54, Mannville AB T0B 2W0 Canada
Tel: 780-763-3795

Marwayne & District Chamber of Commerce
PO Box 183, Marwayne AB T0B 2X0 Canada
Tel: 780-847-3962; *Fax:* 780-847-3324
vilmar@telusplanet.net
www.village.marwayne.ab.ca

Mayerthorpe & District Chamber of Commerce
PO Box 1279, Mayerthorpe AB T0E 1N0 Canada
Tel: 780-786-2444
Arnold Lotholz, Treasurer
Cynthia Eichhorn, President

McLennan Chamber of Commerce
PO Box 90, McLennan AB T0H 2L0 Canada
Tel: 780-324-3894; *Fax:* 780-324-3932

Medicine Hat & District Chamber of Commerce
413 - 6th Ave. SE, Medicine Hat AB T1A 2S7 Canada
Tel: 403-527-5214; *Fax:* 403-527-5182
info@medicinehatchamber.com
www.medicinehatchamber.com
Affiliation(s): Alberta Chamber of Commerce; Canadian Chamber of Commerce

Millet & District Chamber of Commerce
PO Box 389, Millet AB T0C 1Z0 Canada
Tel: 780-387-4534
milletchamber@canada.com
Debbie Swanson, President

Morinville & District Chamber of Commerce
PO Box 3130, Morinville AB T8R 1S1 Canada
Tel: 780-939-9462; *Fax:* 780-939-3087
chamber@town.morinville.ab.ca
www.morinvillechamber.com

Nanton & District Chamber of Commerce
PO Box 711, Nanton AB T0L 1R0 Canada
Tel: 403-646-2029
president@nantonchamber.com
www.nantonchamber.com

Okotoks & District Chamber of Commerce
PO Box 1053, 14 McRae St., Okotoks AB T1S 1B1 Canada
Tel: 403-938-2848; *Fax:* 403-938-6649
okotokschamber@telus.net
www.okotokschamber.ca

Olds & District Chamber of Commerce
PO Box 4210, Olds AB T4H 1P8 Canada
Tel: 403-556-7070; *Fax:* 403-556-1515
oldscham@telusplanet.net
www.oldsalberta.com
Debbie Packer, President
Barb Babiak, Executive Director
Paul Hildebrand, Vice-President

Onoway & District Chamber of Commerce
PO Box 723, Onoway AB T0E 1V0 Canada
Tel: 780-967-4754
tbulletin@icrossroads.com
Lyle Robinson, President

Oyen & District Chamber of Commerce
PO Box 718, Oyen AB T0J 2J0 Canada
Tel: 403-664-0406
oyenecho@telusplanet.net

Picture Butte & District Chamber of Commerce
PO Box 540, Picture Butte AB T0K 1V0 Canada
Tel: 403-732-4302; *Fax:* 403-732-4703
chamber@picturebutte.ca

Pigeon Lake Regional Chamber of Commerce (PLRCC)
#6B Village Dr., Westerose AB T0C 2V0 Canada
Tel: 780-586-6263; *Fax:* 780-586-3667
plchambe@telusplanet.net
www.pigeonlakechamber.ca
Affiliation(s): Alberta Chambers of Commerce
Darlene Kobeluck, Manager
Sharon Will, President

Pincher Creek & District Chamber of Economic Development
PO Box 2287, Pincher Creek AB T0K 1W0 Canada
Tel: 403-627-5199; *Fax:* 403-627-5850
info@pincher-creek.com
www.pincher-creek.com

Ponoka & District Chamber of Commerce
PO Box 4188, Ponoka AB T4J 1R6 Canada
Tel: 403-783-3888; *Fax:* 403-783-3888
chamber@ponoka.org

Provost & District Chamber of Commerce
PO Box 637, Provost AB T0B 3S0 Canada
Tel: 780-753-6643
chamberofcommerce@provost.ca

Rainbow Lake Chamber of Commerce
PO Box 272, Rainbow Lake AB T0H 2Y0 Canada
Tel: 780-956-3030; *Fax:* 780-956-3882
tschulter@rainbowcable.ca
John Watt, Mayor

Raymond Chamber of Commerce
General Delivery, Raymond AB T0K 2S0 Canada
Tel: 403-752-3057
Russell Court, President

Red Deer Chamber of Commerce
3017 Gaetz Ave., Red Deer AB T4N 5Y6 Canada
Tel: 403-347-4491; *Fax:* 403-343-6188
rdchamber@reddeerchamber.com
www.reddeerchamber.com

Redwater & District Chamber of Commerce
c/o The Town Of Redwater Town Office, PO Box 322, 4924 - 47 St., Redwater AB T0A 2W0 Canada
Tel: 780-942-3519; *Fax:* 780-942-4321

Rimbey Chamber of Commerce
PO Box 87, Rimbey AB T0C 2J0 Canada
Tel: 403-843-2020; *Fax:* 403-843-2027
rimbeychamber@rimbey.com

Rocky Mountain House & District Chamber of Commerce
PO Box 1374, 5406 - 48 St., Rocky Mountain House AB T4T 1B1 Canada
Tel: 403-845-5450; *Fax:* 403-845-7764
Toll-Free: 800-565-3793
rmhcofc@rockychamber.org
www.rockychamber.org
Affiliation(s): AB Chamber of Commerce; Canadian Chamber of Commerce

St Albert Chamber of Commerce
71 St. Albert Rd., St Albert AB T8N 6L5 Canada
Tel: 780-458-2833; *Fax:* 780-458-6515
chamber@stalbertchamber.com
www.stalbertchamber.com

St Paul & District Chamber of Commerce
PO Box 887, St Paul AB T0A 3A0 Canada
Tel: 780-645-6800; *Fax:* 780-645-6059
Toll-Free: 888-733-8367
admin@stpaulchamber.ca
www.stpaulchamber.ca
Affiliation(s): Alberta Chambers of Commerce

Sedgewick Chamber of Commerce
PO Box 625, Sedgewick AB T0B 4C0 Canada
Tel: 780-384-3912; *Fax:* 780-384-3938

Sexsmith & District Chamber of Commerce
PO Box 146, Sexsmith AB T0H 3C0 Canada
Tel: 780-568-4663; *Fax:* 780-568-4115
chmbrtos@telusplanet.net

Sherwood Park & District Chamber of Commerce
100 Ordze Ave., Sherwood Park AB T8B 1M6 Canada
Tel: 780-464-0801; *Fax:* 780-449-3581
Toll-Free: 866-464-0801
admin.spchamber@shaw.ca
www.sherwoodparkchamber.com

Slave Lake & District Chamber of Commerce
PO Box 190, Slave Lake AB T0G 2A0 Canada
Tel: 780-849-3222; *Fax:* 780-849-6894
sldcc@telusplanet.net
www.slavelakechamberofcommerce.ca

Smoky Lake & District Chamber of Commerce
PO Box 635, Smoky Lake AB T0A 3C0 Canada
Tel: 780-656-3842; *Fax:* 780-451-3321
wilddeer@mcsnet.ca
Wayne Taylor, President

Spruce Grove & District Chamber of Commerce
PO Box 4210, 99 Campsite Rd., Spruce Grove AB T7X 3B4 Canada
Tel: 780-962-2561; *Fax:* 780-962-4417
info@sprucegrovechamber.com
www.sprucegrovechamber.com

Stettler Regional Board of Trade & Community Development
6606 - 50th Ave., Stettler AB T0C 2L2 Canada
Tel: 403-742-3181; *Fax:* 403-742-3123
Toll-Free: 877-742-9499
info@stettlerboardoftrade.com
www.stettlerboardoftrade.com

Stony Plain & District Chamber of Commerce
4815 - 44 Ave., Stony Plain AB T7Z 1V5 Canada
Tel: 780-963-4545; *Fax:* 780-963-4542
info@stonyplainchamber.ca
www.stonyplainchamber.ca

Strathmore & District Chamber of Commerce
PO Box 2222, Strathmore AB T1P 1K2 Canada
Tel: 403-901-3175; *Fax:* 403-901-1785
contactus@strathmoredistrictchamber.com
strathmoredistrictchamber.com
Robert Desjardins, President
Vi Giesbrecht, Administrative Assistance

Sundre Chamber of Commerce
PO Box 1085, Sundre AB T0M 1X0 Canada
Tel: 403-638-3245
info@sundrechamber.com
www.sundrechamber.com
Heidi Overgard, Secretary
James Eklund, President

Swan Hills Chamber of Commerce
PO Box 149, Swan Hills AB T0G 2C0 Canada
Tel: 780-333-4477; *Fax:* 780-333-4547
town@townofswanhills.com

Sylvan Lake Chamber of Commerce
4802, 48 St., Sylvan Lake AB T4S 1S6 Canada
Tel: 403-887-3048; *Fax:* 403-887-4944
info@sylvanlakechamber.com
www.sylvanlakechamber.com
Laurie Breeze, Administrator
Danine Weber, President

Taber & District Chamber of Commerce
4702 - 50 St., Taber AB T1G 2B6 Canada
Tel: 403-223-2265; *Fax:* 403-223-2291
admin@taberchamber.com
www.taberchamber.com

Thorhild Chamber of Commerce
PO Box 384, 638 - 6th Ave., Thorhild AB T0A 3J0 Canada
Tel: 780-398-2575; *Fax:* 780-398-2010
thorhildchamber@telus.net
John Dickey, President
Ed Cowley, Secretary

Thorsby & District Chamber of Commerce
PO Box 197, Thorsby AB T0C 2P0 Canada
Tel: 780-789-2100; *Fax:* 780-789-2155
jfhunter@netcom.ca
Clarence Kruger, President

Three Hills & District Chamber of Commerce
PO Box 277, Three Hills AB T0M 2A0 Canada
Tel: 780-662-4441; *Fax:* 780-443-7171
Timothy J. Shearlaw, President

Tofield & District Chamber of Commerce
PO Box 967, General Delivery, Tofield AB T0B 4J0 Canada
Tel: 780-661-4441; *Fax:* 780-662-3725
www.tofieldalberta.ca/chamber.htm
David Williamson, President

Trochu Chamber of Commerce
PO Box 607, Trochu AB T0M 2C0 Canada
Tel: 403-442-2785
Linda Hayes, President

Two Hills & District Chamber of Commerce
PO Box 225, Two Hills AB T0B 4K0 Canada
Tel: 780-632-3395; *Fax:* 780-657-2158
diane_zawalykut@digitalweb.net
Robert Marsh, President

Valleyview Chamber of Commerce
PO Box 270, Valleyview AB T0H 3N0 Canada
Tel: 780-524-5150; *Fax:* 780-524-2727
valvadmn@telusplanet.net
www.albertafirst.com/profiles/statspack/20479.html
Gary Peterson, Town Manager
Bob Hall, Regional Manager

Vegreville & District Chamber of Commerce
Civic Bldg., PO Box 877, 5009 - 50 Ave., Vegreville AB T9C 1R9 Canada
Tel: 780-632-2771; *Fax:* 780-632-6958
vegchamb@telusplanet.net
www.vegrevillechamber.com

Vermilion & District Chamber of Commerce
4606 - 52nd St., Vermilion AB T9X 0A1 Canada
Tel: 780-853-6593; *Fax:* 780-853-1740
vermcofc@telusplanet.net
www.vermilionchamber.ca

Viking Economic Development Committee (VEDC)
PO Box 369, Viking AB T0B 4N0 Canada
Tel: 780-336-3466; *Fax:* 780-336-2660
laura.arndt@town.viking.ab.ca
www.town.viking.ab.ca
Doug Lefsrud, Chair
Rod Krips, Town Manager

Vulcan & District Chamber of Commerce
PO Box 1161, 115 Centre St., Vulcan AB T0L 2B0 Canada
Tel: 403-485-2994; *Fax:* 403-485-2878
info@vulcantourism.com
www.vulcantourism.com

Wabamun District Chamber of Commerce Society
PO Box 29, Wabamun AB T0E 2K0 Canada
Tel: 780-892-4665
www.albertafirst.com/profiles/statspack/20590.html
Tom Harris, President

Wainwright & District Chamber of Commerce
PO Box 2997, Wainwright AB T9W 1S9 Canada
Tel: 780-842-4910; *Fax:* 780-842-6061
exec@wdchamber.com
www.wdchamber.com

Waterton Park Chamber of Commerce & Visitors Association
PO Box 55, Waterton Lakes National Park AB T0K 2M0 Canada
Tel: 403-859-2224; *Fax:* 403-859-2650
waterton.info@pc.gc.ca
www.watertonchamber.com
Rod Kretz, President

Westlock & District Chamber of Commerce
PO Box 5917, Westlock AB T7P 2P7 Canada

Wetaskiwin Chamber of Commerce (WCC)
4910 - 55A St., Wetaskiwin AB T9A 2R7 Canada
Tel: 780-352-8003; *Fax:* 780-352-6226
wcoc@incentre.net
www.wetaskiwinchamber.ca

Whitecourt & District Chamber of Commerce
PO Box 1011, 3002 - 33rd St., Whitecourt AB T7S 1N9 Canada
Tel: 780-778-5363; *Fax:* 780-778-2351
Toll-Free: 800-313-7383
manager@whitecourtchamber.com
www.whitecourtchamber.com
Affiliation(s): Alberta Chamber of Commerce

Worsley Chamber of Commerce
PO Box 181, Worsley AB T0H 3W0 Canada
Tel: 780-685-3943; *Fax:* 780-685-2115
Doug Allen, President

British Columbia

Abbotsford Chamber of Commerce
#207, 32900 South Fraser Way, Abbotsford BC V2S 5A1 Canada
Tel: 604-859-9651; *Fax:* 604-850-6880
acoc@telus.net
www.abbotsfordchamber.com

Alberni Valley Chamber of Commerce
2533 Port Alberni Hwy., Port Alberni BC V9Y 8P2 Canada
Tel: 250-724-6535; *Fax:* 250-724-6560
avcoc@alberni.net
www.avcoc.com

Armstrong-Spallumcheen Chamber of Commerce
PO Box 118, 3550 Bridge St., Armstrong BC V0E 1B0 Canada
Tel: 250-546-8155; *Fax:* 250-546-8868
armstrong_chamber@telus.net
aschamber.com

Bamfield Chamber of Commerce
Bamfield BC V0R 1B0 Canada
Tel: 250-728-3006
info@bamfieldchamber.com
www.bamfieldchamber.com
Affiliation(s): Pacific Rim Tourism Association

Barriere & District Chamber of Commerce
PO Box 1190, Barriere BC V0E 1E0 Canada
Tel: 250-672-9221; *Fax:* 250-672-2159
info@barrieredistrict.com
www.barrieredistrict.com/
Affiliation(s): Canadian Chamber of Commerce
Lorne Richardson, Manager & Marketing Coordinator

Bowen Island Chamber of Commerce
432 Cardena Rd., Bowen Island BC V0N 1G0 Canada
Tel: 604-947-9024; *Fax:* 604-947-0633
info@bowenisland.org
www.bowenisland.org

Burnaby Board of Trade (BBOT)
#201, 4555 Kingsway, Burnaby BC V5H 4T8 Canada
Tel: 604-412-0100; *Fax:* 604-412-0102
contact@burnabyboardoftrade.com
www.bbot.ca

Burns Lake & District Chamber of Commerce
PO Box 339, Burns Lake BC V0J 1E0 Canada
Tel: 250-692-3773; *Fax:* 250-692-3493
bldcoc@telus.net
www.burnslakechamber.ca

Cache Creek Chamber of Commerce
PO Box 460, Cache Creek BC V0K 1H0 Canada
Tel: 250-457-9668; *Fax:* 250-457-9669
jade@coppervalleybc.ca
Gordon Daily, President

Campbell River & District Chamber of Commerce
PO Box 400, 900 Alder St., Campbell River BC V9W 5B6 Canada
Tel: 250-287-4636; *Fax:* 250-286-6490
chamber@campbellriverchamber.ca
www.campbellriverchamber.ca

Castlegar & District Chamber of Commerce (CDCoC)
c/o Mark Melnyk, 652 - 18th St., Castlegar BC V1N 4B7 Canada
Tel: 250-365-6313; *Fax:* 250-365-5778
info@castlegar.com
www.castlegar.com

Chamber of Commerce of the City of Grand Forks
PO Box 1086, 1647 Central Ave., Grand Forks BC V0H 1H0 Canada
Tel: 250-442-2833; *Fax:* 250-442-5688
Toll-Free: 866-442-2833
manager@grandforkschamber.com
www.grandforkschamber.com

Chase & District Chamber of Commerce
PO Box 592, 400 Shuswap Ave., Chase BC V0E 1M0 Canada
Tel: 250-679-8432; *Fax:* 250-679-3120
admin@chasechamber.com
www.chasechamber.com/

Chemainus & District Chamber of Commerce
PO Box 575, 9796 Willow St., Chemainus BC V0R 1K0 Canada
Tel: 250-246-3944; *Fax:* 250-246-3251
ccoc@islandnet.com
www.chemainus.bc.ca

Chetwynd & District Chamber of Commerce
PO Box 870, Chetwynd BC V0C 1J0 Canada
Tel: 250-788-3345; *Fax:* 250-788-3655
chetcham@pris.bc.ca

Chilliwack Chamber of Commerce
#16, 45966 Yale Rd., Chilliwack BC V2P 2M3 Canada
Tel: 604-793-4323; *Fax:* 604-793-4303
info@chilliwackchamber.com
www.chilliwackchamber.com

Christina Lake Chamber of Commerce
Hwy. 3 & Kimura Rd., Christina Lake BC V0H 1E2 Canada
Tel: 250-447-6161
info@christinalake.com
www.christinalake.com

Clearwater & District Chamber of Commerce
PO Box 1988, RR#1, Clearwater BC V0E 1N0 Canada
Tel: 250-674-2646; *Fax:* 250-674-3693
info@clearwaterbcchamber.com
www.clearwaterbcchamber.com

Clinton & District Chamber of Commerce
PO Box 256, Clinton BC V0K 1K0 Canada
Tel: 250-459-2640; *Fax:* 250-459-2627

Cloverdale & District Chamber of Commerce
17687 - 56A Ave., Surrey BC V3S 1G4 Canada
Tel: 604-574-9802; *Fax:* 604-574-9122
clovcham@axion.net
www.cloverdale.bc.ca
Ben Wevers, President

Columbia Valley Chamber of Commerce (CVCC)
PO Box 1019, Invermere BC V0A 1K0 Canada
Tel: 250-342-2844; *Fax:* 250-342-3261
www.cvchamber.ca
Affiliation(s): British Columbia Chamber of Commerce

Comox Valley Chamber of Commerce (CVCC)
2040 Cliffe Ave., Courtenay BC V9N 2L3 Canada
Tel: 250-334-3234; *Fax:* 250-334-4908
Toll-Free: 888-357-4471
membership@comoxvalleychamber.com
www.comoxvalleychamber.com

Cowichan Lake District Chamber of Commerce
PO Box 824, 125C South Shore Rd., Lake Cowichan BC V0R 2G0 Canada
Tel: 250-749-3244; *Fax:* 250-749-0187
info@cowichanlake.ca
www.cowichanlake.ca
Affiliation(s): Canadian Chamber of Commerce
Jim Humphrey, President

Cranbrook & District Chamber of Commerce
PO Box 84, Cranbrook BC V1C 4H6 Canada
Tel: 250-426-5914; *Toll-Free:* 800-222-6174
cbkchamber@cyberlink.bc.ca
www.cranbrookchamber.com

Cumberland Chamber of Commerce
PO Box 250, 2680 Dunsmuir Ave., Cumberland BC V0R 1S0 Canada
Tel: 250-336-8313; *Fax:* 250-336-2455
cumbcham@shaw.ca
www.cumberlandbc.org
Affiliation(s): North By Northwest Tourism Association of BC

Dawson Creek & District Chamber of Commerce
10201 - 10th St., Dawson Creek BC V1G 3T5 Canada
Tel: 250-782-4868; *Fax:* 250-782-2371
info@dawsoncreekchamber.ca
www.dawsoncreekchamber.ca
Affiliation(s): BC Chamber of Commerce

Dease Lake & District Chamber of Commerce
PO Box 338, Dease Lake BC V0C 1L0 Canada
Tel: 250-771-3900; *Fax:* 250-771-3900
Lyonna Mroch, Secretary
Rich Mroch, President

Delta Chamber of Commerce
6201 - 60 Ave., Delta BC V4K 4E2 Canada
Tel: 604-946-4232; *Fax:* 604-946-5285
info@deltachamber.com
www.deltachamber.com

Discovery Islands Chamber of Commerce
PO Box 190, Quathiaski Cove BC V0P 1N0 Canada
Tel: 250-285-2724; *Toll-Free:* 866-285-2724
chamber@discoveryislands.ca
www.discoveryislands.ca/chamber

Duncan-Cowichan Chamber of Commerce (DCCC)
381 Trans-Canada Hwy., Duncan BC V9L 3R5 Canada
Tel: 250-748-1111; *Fax:* 250-746-8222
Toll-Free: 888-303-3337
manager@duncancc.bc.ca
www.duncancc.bc.ca

Elkford Chamber of Commerce
PO Box 220, 4A Front St., Elkford BC V0B 1H0 Canada
Tel: 250-865-4614; *Fax:* 250-865-2442
Toll-Free: 877-355-9453
info@tourismelkford.ca
www.tourismelkford.ca

Enderby & District Chamber of Commerce
PO Box 1000, Enderby BC V0E 1V0 Canada
Tel: 250-838-6727; *Fax:* 250-838-0123
Toll-Free: 877-213-6509
echamber@jetstream.net
www.enderby.com/chamber

Esquimalt Chamber of Commerce
PO Box 36019, 1153 Esquimalt Rd., Victoria BC V9A 7J5 Canada
Tel: 250-704-2525; *Fax:* 250-380-6932
info@esquimaltchamber.com
www.esquimaltchamber.com
Ed Williams, President

Fernie Chamber of Commerce
102 Commerce Rd., Fernie BC V0B 1M5 Canada
Tel: 250-423-6868; *Fax:* 250-423-3811
Toll-Free: 877-433-7643
info@ferniechamber.com
www.ferniechamber.com
Affiliation(s): Economic Development Association of BC

Fort Nelson & District Chamber of Commerce
PO Box 196, 5315B - 50th Ave. South, Fort Nelson BC V0C 1R0 Canada
Tel: 250-774-2956; *Fax:* 250-774-2958
info@fortnelsonchamber.com
www.fortnelsonchamber.com

Fort St. James Chamber of Commerce
PO Box 1164, Fort St James BC V0J 1P0 Canada
Tel: 250-996-7023; *Fax:* 250-996-7047
fsjchamb@fsjames.com
www.fortstjameschamber.com

Fort St. John & District Chamber of Commerce
9325 - 100 St., Fort St John BC V1J 4N4 Canada
Tel: 250-785-6037; *Fax:* 250-785-7181
info@fsjchamber.com
www.fsjchamber.com

Gabriola Island Chamber of Commerce
PO Box 249, #3, 575 North Rd., Gabriola BC V0R 1X0 Canada
Tel: 250-247-9332; *Fax:* 250-247-9332
Toll-Free: 888-284-9332
info@gabriolaisland.org, manager@gabriolaisland.org
www.gabriolaisland.org
Affiliation(s): Tourism Association of Vancouver Island
Ken Wur, President

Galiano Island Chamber of Commerce
PO Box 73, Galiano BC V0N 1P0 Canada
Tel: 250-539-2233
info@galianoisland.com
www.galianoisland.com
Ken Smith, President

Gibsons & District Chamber of Commerce
PO Box 1190, #21, 900 Gibsons Way, Gibsons BC V0N 1V0 Canada
Tel: 604-886-2325; *Fax:* 604-886-2379
gibsonsbcchamber@telus.net
www.gibsonsbc.ca/chamber

Gold River Chamber of Commerce
PO Box 39, Gold River BC V0P 1G0 Canada
Tel: 250-283-7333
Gabriella Pentz, President
Craig Scott, Vice-President

Golden & District Chamber of Commerce (GDCC)
PO Box 1320, #500, 10 North Ave., Golden BC V0A 1H0 Canada
Tel: 250-344-7125; *Fax:* 250-344-6688
Toll-Free: 800-622-4653
info@goldenchamber.bc.ca
www.goldenchamber.bc.ca

Greater Kamloops Chamber of Commerce
1290 Trans Canada Hwy., Kamloops BC V2C 6R3 Canada
Tel: 250-372-7722; *Fax:* 250-828-9500
mail@kamloopschamber.bc.ca
www.kamloopschamber.bc.ca

Greater Langley Chamber of Commerce
#1, 5761 Glover Rd., Langley BC V3A 8M8 Canada
Tel: 604-530-6656; *Fax:* 604-530-7066
chamber@langleychamber.com
www.langleychamber.com

Greater Nanaimo Chamber of Commerce
2133 Bowen Rd., Nanaimo BC V9S 1H8 Canada
Tel: 250-756-1191; *Fax:* 250-756-1584
info@nanaimochamber.bc.ca
www.nanaimochamber.bc.ca

Greater Vernon Chamber of Commerce (GVCC)
701 Hwy. 97 South, Vernon BC V1B 3W4 Canada
Tel: 250-545-0771; *Fax:* 250-545-3114
info@vernonchamber.ca
www.vernonchamber.ca
Affiliation(s): Canadian Chamber of Commerce

Greater Victoria Chamber of Commerce (GVCC)
#100, 852 Fort St., Victoria BC V8W 1H8 Canada
Tel: 250-383-7191; *Fax:* 250-385-3552
chamber@gvcc.org
www.victoriachamber.ca

Harrison Agassiz Chamber of Commerce
PO Box 429, Harrison Hot Springs BC V0M 1K0 Canada
Tel: 604-796-1133; *Fax:* 604-796-3694
www.harrison.ca

Hope & District Chamber of Commerce
PO Box 588, 895 - 3rd Ave., Hope BC V0X 1L0 Canada
Tel: 604-869-3111; *Fax:* 604-869-8208
info@hopechamber.bc.ca
www.hopechamber.bc.ca

Houston & District Chamber of Commerce
PO Box 396, 3289 Hwy. 16, Houston BC V0J 1Z0 Canada
Tel: 250-845-7640; *Fax:* 250-845-3682
info@houstonchamber.ca
www.houstonchamber.ca

Kaslo Chamber of Commerce
PO Box 329, Kaslo BC V0G 1M0 Canada
Toll-Free: 866-276-3212
info@kaslochamber.com
www.kaslochamber.com

Kelowna Chamber of Commerce
544 Harvey Ave., Kelowna BC V1Y 6C9 Canada
Tel: 250-861-3627; *Fax:* 250-861-3624
info@kelownachamber.org
www.kelownachamber.org
Affiliation(s): BC Chamber of Commerce

Kimberley Bavarian Society Chamber of Commerce (KBSCC)
270 Kimberley Ave., Kimberley BC V1A 3N3 Canada
Tel: 250-427-3666; *Fax:* 250-427-5378
Toll-Free: 866-913-3666
info@kimberleychamber.ca
www.kimberleychamber.ca

Kitimat Chamber of Commerce
PO Box 214, Kitimat BC V8C 2G7 Canada
Tel: 250-632-6294; *Fax:* 250-632-4685
Toll-Free: 800-664-6554
kitimatchamber@telus.net
www.visitkitimat.com

Kitsilano Chamber of Commerce (KCC)
PO Box 34369, Stn. D, Vancouver BC V6J 4P3 Canada
Tel: 604-731-4454; *Toll-Free:* 877-312-1898
admin@kitsilanochamber.com
www.kitsilanochamber.com/
Thomas B. DeSchutter, President

Kootenay Lake Chamber of Commerce
PO Box 120, Crawford Bay BC V0B 1E0 Canada
Tel: 250-227-9233
info@kootenaylake.bc.ca
www.kootenaylake.bc.ca

Ladysmith Chamber of Commerce
PO Box 598, 441B - 1st Ave., Ladysmith BC V9G 1A4 Canada
Tel: 250-245-2112; *Fax:* 250-245-2124
info@ladysmithcofc.com
www.ladysmithcofc.com
Affiliation(s): Cowichan Regional Valley

Lake Country Chamber of Commerce
#40, 9522 Main St., Lake Country BC V4V 2L9 Canada
Tel: 250-766-5670; *Fax:* 250-766-0170
Toll-Free: 888-766-5670
admin@lakecountrychamber.com
www.lakecountrychamber.com
Bill Clark, President
Linda Wilson, Manager

Likely & District Chamber of Commerce
PO Box 29, Likely BC V0L 1N0 Canada
Tel: 250-790-2127; *Fax:* 250-790-2323
chamber@likely-bc.ca
www.likely-bc.ca

Lillooet & District Chamber of Commerce
PO Box 650, Lillooet BC V0K 1V0 Canada
Tel: 250-256-3578; *Fax:* 250-256-4882
deverell@telus.net
www.lillooetchamberofcommerce.com

Lumby & District Chamber of Commerce
PO Box 534, Lumby BC V0E 2G0 Canada
Tel: 250-547-2300; *Fax:* 250-547-2300
lumbychamber@shaw.ca
www.monasheetourism.com
Stephanie Sexsmith, Manager
Bill Maltman, President

Lytton & District Chamber of Commerce
PO Box 460, Lytton BC V0K 1Z0 Canada
Tel: 250-455-2523; *Fax:* 250-455-6669
lyttoncc@goldtrail.com
www.coastandmountains.bc.ca/page.cfm/650
Affiliation(s): Vancouver Coast & Mountains Tourism Region

Mackenzie Chamber of Commerce
PO Box 880, Mackenzie BC V0J 2C0 Canada
Tel: 250-997-5459; *Fax:* 250-997-6117
Toll-Free: 877-622-5360
mackcoc@mackbc.com
www.mackenziechamber.bc.ca
Affiliation(s): Retail Merchants Association of BC

Maple Ridge Pitt Meadows Chamber of Commerce
22238 Lougheed Hwy., Maple Ridge BC V2X 2T2 Canada
Tel: 604-463-3366; *Fax:* 604-463-3201
www.ridgemeadowschamber.com
Affiliation(s): BC Chamber Executive; Canadian Chamber of Commerce; Southwestern BC Tourism

Mayne Island Community Chamber of Commerce
PO Box 2, Mayne BC V0N 2J0 Canada
Tel: 250-539-9815
info@mayneislandchamber.ca
www.mayneislandchamber.ca
Richard Iredale, President
Joanie McCorry, Manager

McBride & District Chamber of Commerce
PO Box 2, McBride BC V0J 2E0 Canada
Tel: 250-569-3366; *Fax:* 250-569-2376
Toll-Free: 866-569-3366
come2mcbride@telus.net
www.mcbridebc.info
Vincent de Niet, President

Merritt & District Chamber of Commerce
PO Box 1649, 2185B Voght St., Merritt BC V1K 1B8 Canada
Tel: 250-378-5634; *Fax:* 250-378-6561
manager@merrittchamber.com
www.merrittchamber.com

Mission Regional Chamber of Commerce
34033 Lougheed Hwy., Mission BC V2V 5X8 Canada
Tel: 604-826-6914; *Fax:* 604-826-5916
manager@missionchamber.bc.ca
www.missionchamber.bc.ca

Nakusp & District Chamber of Commerce
PO Box 387, 92 - 6th. Ave. NW, Nakusp BC V0G 1R0 Canada
Tel: 250-265-4234; *Fax:* 250-265-3808
Toll-Free: 800-909-8819
nakcom@telus.net
www.nakusparrowlakes.com
Affiliation(s): Tourism British Columbia
Kim Reich, President

Nelson & District Chamber of Commerce
255 Hall St., Nelson BC V1L 5X4 Canada
Tel: 250-352-3433; *Fax:* 250-352-6355
Toll-Free: 877-663-5706
info@discovernelson.com
www.discovernelson.com
Affiliation(s): British Columbia Chamber of Commerce; Canadian Chamber of Commerce
Cal Renwick, President

New Westminster Chamber of Commerce
601 Queens Ave., New Westminster BC V3M 1L1 Canada
Tel: 604-521-7781; *Fax:* 604-521-0057
nwcc@newwestchamber.com
www.newwestchamber.com

North Shuswap Chamber of Commerce
PO Box 101, Celista BC V0E 1L0 Canada
Tel: 250-955-2113; *Fax:* 250-955-2113
Toll-Free: 888-955-1488
requests@northshuswapbc.com
www.northshuswapbc.com

North Vancouver Chamber of Commerce (NVCC)
#102, 124 - 1st St. West, Vancouver BC V7M 3N3 Canada
Tel: 604-987-4488; *Fax:* 604-987-8272
info@nvchamber.bc.ca; events@nvchamber.ca
www.nvchamber.bc.ca

Okanagan Falls Chamber of Commerce
PO Box 246, Okanagan Falls BC V0H 1R0 Canada
okfalls@img.net
Kevin Therrien, President

Osoyoos Chamber of Commerce
PO Box 277, Osoyoos BC V0H 1V0 Canada
Tel: 250-495-7142; *Fax:* 250-495-7132
info@osoyoochamber.bc.ca
www.osoyoochamber.bc.ca

Parksville & District Chamber of Commerce
PO Box 99, 1275 East Island Hwy., Parksville BC V9P 2G3 Canada
Tel: 250-248-3613; *Fax:* 250-248-5210
www.parksvillechamber.com

Peachland Chamber of Commerce
5812 Beach Ave., Peachland BC V0H 1X7 Canada
Tel: 250-767-2455; *Fax:* 250-767-2420
Toll-Free: 866-955-2455
peachlandchamber@shawcable.com
www.peachlandchamber.bc.ca
Donna Weigelt, President

Pemberton Chamber of Commerce
PO Box 370, Pemberton BC V0N 2L0 Canada
Tel: 604-894-6477; *Fax:* 604-894-5571
info@pembertonchamber.com
www.pembertonchamber.com
Affiliation(s): Vancouver Board of Trade

Pender Harbour & Egmont Chamber of Commerce
PO Box 265, 1287 Madeira Park Rd., Madeira Park BC V0N 2H0 Canada
Tel: 604-883-2561; *Fax:* 604-883-2561
Toll-Free: 877-873-6337
chamber@penderharbour.ca
www.penderharbour.ca
Kerry Milligan, Secretary
Dave Milligan, President

Pender Island Chamber of Commerce
PO Box 123, Pender Island BC V0N 2M0 Canada
Tel: 250-629-3988; *Toll-Free:* 866-468-7924
travel@penderislandchamber.com
www.penderislandchamber.com

Penticton & Wine Country Chamber of Commerce
553 Railway St., Penticton BC V2A 8S3 Canada
Tel: 250-492-4103; *Fax:* 250-492-6119
Toll-Free: 800-663-5052
membership@penticton.org
www.penticton.org

Port Hardy & District Chamber of Commerce
PO Box 249, Port Hardy BC V0N 2P0 Canada
Tel: 250-949-7622; *Fax:* 250-949-6653
phcc@cablerocket.com
www.ph-chamber.bc.ca

Port McNeill & District Chamber of Commerce
PO Box 129, 1594 Beach Dr., Port McNeill BC V0N 2R0 Canada
Tel: 250-956-3131; *Fax:* 250-956-3132
Toll-Free: 888-956-3131
pmccc@island.net
www.portmcneill.net

Port Renfrew Chamber of Commerce
General Delivery, Port Renfrew BC V0S 1K0 Canada
Tel: 250-647-0009; *Fax:* 250-647-0058
prcc@portrenfrew.com
www.portrenfrewcommunity.com
Tim Cash, President
Brian Cameron, Vice-President

Powell River Chamber of Commerce
6807 Wharf St., Powell River BC V8A 2T9 Canada
Tel: 604-485-4051; *Fax:* 604-485-4272
office@powellriverchamber.com
www.powellriverchamber.com

Prince George Chamber of Commerce
890 Vancouver St., Prince George BC V2L 2P5 Canada
Tel: 250-562-2454; *Fax:* 250-562-6510
chamber@pgchamber.bc.ca
www.pgchamber.bc.ca

Prince Rupert & District Chamber of Commerce (PRDCC)
PO Box 158, #100, 215 Cow Bay Rd., Prince Rupert BC V8J 1A2 Canada
Tel: 250-624-2296; *Fax:* 250-624-6105
Toll-Free: 800-667-1994
manager@princerupertchamber.ca
www.princerupertchamber.ca

Princeton & District Chamber of Commerce
PO Box 540, Princeton BC V0X 1W0 Canada
Tel: 250-295-3103; *Fax:* 250-295-3255
chamber@nethop.net
www.princeton.ca

Qualicum Beach Chamber of Commerce
PO Box 159, 124 West 2nd Ave., Qualicum Beach BC V9K 1S7 Canada
Tel: 250-752-0960; *Fax:* 250-752-2923
chamber@qualicum.bc.ca
www.qualicum.bc.ca
Affiliation(s): Oceanside Tourism Association

Queen Charlotte Islands Chamber of Commerce
PO Box 448, Port Clements BC V0T 1R0 Canada
Tel: 250-557-4565; *Fax:* 250-557-4565
chamber@qcislands.net
www.qcislands.net/chamber

Quesnel & District Chamber of Commerce
679B, Hwy. 97 South, Quesnel BC V2J 4C7 Canada
Tel: 250-747-0125; *Fax:* 250-747-0126
qchamber@quesnelbc.com
www.quesnelchamber.com

Radium Hot Springs Chamber of Commerce
PO Box 225, Radium Hot Springs BC V0A 1M0 Canada
Tel: 250-347-9331; *Fax:* 250-347-9127
Toll-Free: 800-347-9704
info@RadiumHotSprings.com
www.RadiumHotSprings.com
Kent Kebe, Manager
Douglas McIntosh, President

Revelstoke Chamber of Commerce
PO Box 490, 204 Campbell Ave., Revelstoke BC V0E 2S0 Canada
Tel: 250-837-5345; *Fax:* 250-837-4223
revelstokeinfo@telus.net
revelstokechamber.com

Richmond Chamber of Commerce
South Tower, #101, 5811 Cooney Rd., Richmond BC V6X 3M1 Canada
Tel: 604-278-2822; *Fax:* 604-278-2972
rcc@richmondchamber.ca
www.richmondchamber.ca
Affiliation(s): Tourism Richmond; Sister Chamber - Kent, Washington

Rossland Chamber of Commerce
PO Box 1385, Rossland BC V0G 1Y0 Canada
Tel: 250-362-5666; *Fax:* 250-362-5399
commerce@rossland.com
www.rossland.com/about

Saanich Peninsula Chamber of Commerce (SPCOC)
#201, 2453 Beacon Ave., Sidney BC V8L 1X7 Canada
Tel: 250-656-3616; *Fax:* 250-656-7111
info@peninsulachamber.ca
www.peninsulachamber.ca

Salmo & District Chamber of Commerce
PO Box 400, 100 Fourth St., Salmo BC V0G 1Z0 Canada
Tel: 250-357-2596
www.salmo.net

Salmon Arm & District Chamber of Commerce (SACC)
PO Box 999, #101, 20 Hudson Ave. NE, Salmon Arm BC V1E 4P2 Canada
Tel: 250-832-6247; *Fax:* 250-832-8382
info@sachamber.bc.ca
www.sachamber.bc.ca

Salt Spring Island Chamber of Commerce
121 Lower Ganges Rd., Salt Spring Island BC V8K 2T1 Canada
Tel: 250-537-5252; *Fax:* 250-537-4276
Toll-Free: 866-216-2936
chamber@saltspring.com
www.saltspringtoday.com

Sechelt & District Chamber of Commerce
PO Box 360, #102 - 5700 Cowrie St., Sechelt BC V0N 3A0 Canada
Tel: 604-885-0662; *Fax:* 604-885-0691
Toll-Free: 877-633-2963
secheltchamber@dccnet.com
www.secheltchamber.bc.ca

Seton Portage/Shalalth District Chamber of Commerce
PO Box 2067, Seton Portage BC V0N 3B0 Canada
Tel: 250-259-8312; *Fax:* 250-259-8213
snor@uniserve.com
Ray Klassen, Vice-President

Sicamous & District Chamber of Commerce
PO Box 346, Sicamous BC V0E 2V0 Canada
Tel: 250-836-3313; *Fax:* 250-836-4368
sicamouschamber@cablelan.net
www.sicamouschamber.bc.ca

Slocan District Chamber of Commerce
PO Box 448, New Denver BC V0G 1S0 Canada
Tel: 250-358-2544; *Fax:* 250-358-7998
www.slocanlake.com/chamber.html

Smithers District Chamber of Commerce
PO Box 2379, Smithers BC V0J 2N0 Canada
Tel: 250-847-5072; *Fax:* 250-847-3337
Toll-Free: 800-542-6673
chamber@tourismsmithers.com
www.tourismsmithers.com/chamber
Affiliation(s): Northern BC Tourism Association

Sooke Harbour Chamber of Commerce
PO Box 18, 6716 Westcoast Rd., Sooke BC V0S 1N0 Canada
Tel: 250-642-6112
info@sookeharbourchamber.com
www.sookeharbourchamber.com

South Cariboo Chamber of Commerce
PO Box 2312, 100 Mile House BC V0K 2E0 Canada
Tel: 250-395-6124; *Fax:* 250-395-8974
manager@scariboochamber.org
www.scariboochamber.org
Affiliation(s): Canadian Chamber of Commerce

South Cowichan Chamber of Commerce (SCCC)
#368, 2720 Mill Bay Rd., Mill Bay BC V0R 2P1 Canada
Tel: 250-743-3566; *Fax:* 250-743-5332
info@southcowichanchamber.org
www.southcowichanchamber.org
Rosalie Power, Manager
Leslie Grills, President

South Okanagan Chamber Of Commerce
PO Box 460, 36205 - 93rd St., Oliver BC V0H 1T0 Canada
Tel: 250-498-6321; *Fax:* 250-498-3156
Toll-Free: 888-498-6321
www.sochamber.ca

South Shuswap Chamber of Commerce
PO Box 7, Blind Bay BC V0E 2W0 Canada
Tel: 250-675-3515; *Fax:* 250-675-3516
sorrentochamber@telus.net
www.southshuswapchamberofcommerce.org
Chris Emery, President
Nancy Kyle, Manager

Sparwood & District Chamber of Commerce
PO Box 1448, Aspen Dr., Sparwood BC V0B 2G0 Canada
Tel: 250-425-2423; *Fax:* 250-425-7130
Toll-Free: 877-485-8185
administrator@sparwoodchamber.bc.ca
www.sparwoodchamber.bc.ca

Squamish Chamber of Commerce
Squamish Adventure Centre, #102, 38551 Loggers Lane, Squamish BC V8B 0H2 Canada
Tel: 604-815-4994; *Fax:* 604-815-4998
Toll-Free: 866-333-2010
info@squamishchamber.com
www.squamishchamber.com

Stewart-Hyder International Chamber of Commerce
PO Box 306, Stewart BC V0T 1W0 Canada
Tel: 250-636-9224; *Fax:* 250-636-2199
Toll-Free: 888-366-5999
info@stewart-hyder.com
www.stewart-hyder.com

Summerland Chamber of Economic Development & Tourism (SCEDT)
PO Box 130, 15600 Hwy. 97, Summerland BC V0H 1Z0 Canada
Tel: 250-494-2686; *Fax:* 250-494-4039
info@summerlandchamber.com
www.summerlandchamber.com
Affiliation(s): Economic Development Association of BC; Thompson/Okanagan Tourism Association

Surrey Board of Trade (SBOT)
#101, 14439 - 104 Ave., Surrey BC V3R 1M1 Canada
Tel: 604-581-7130; *Fax:* 604-588-7549
Toll-Free: 866-848-7130
info@businessinsurrey.com
www.businessinsurrey.com

Tahsis Chamber of Commerce
PO Box 278, 36 Rugged Mountain Road, Tahsis BC V0P 1X0 Canada
Tel: 204-934-6425
info@tahsischamberofcommerce.com
www.tahsischamberofcommerce.com
Corrine Dahling, President
Jude Schooner, Secretary/Treasurer

Terrace & District Chamber of Commerce
4511 Keith Ave., Terrace BC V8G 1K1 Canada
Tel: 250-635-2063; *Fax:* 250-635-2573
Toll-Free: 800-499-1637
executivedirector@terracechamber.com
www.terracechamber.com

Tofino-Long Beach Chamber of Commerce
PO Box 249, Tofino BC V0R 2Z0 Canada
Tel: 250-725-3414; *Fax:* 250-725-3296
info@tourismtofino.com
www.tourismtofino.com

Trail & District Chamber of Commerce
#200, 1199 Bay Ave., Trail BC V1R 4A4
Tel: 250-368-3144; *Fax:* 250-368-6427
tcoc@netidea.com
www.trailchamber.com

Tri-Cities Chamber of Commerce Serving Coquitlam, Port Coquitlam & Port Moody
1209 Pinetree Way, Coquitlam BC V3B 7Y3 Canada
Tel: 604-464-2716; *Fax:* 604-464-6796
info@tricitieschamber.com
www.tricitieschamber.com

Ucluelet Chamber of Commerce (UCOC)
PO Box 428, #3, 1645 Cedar St., Ucluelet BC V0R 3A0 Canada
Tel: 250-726-4641; *Fax:* 250-726-4611
marny@ucluelet info.com
www.ucluelet info.com

Valemount & Area Chamber of Commerce
PO Box 690, Valemount BC V0E 2Z0 Canada
Tel: 250-566-0061; *Fax:* 250-566-4244
www.thevalleysentinel.com/chamber
Christine Latimer, President

Vanderhoof & District Chamber of Commerce
PO Box 126, 2353 Burrard Ave., Vanderhoof BC V0J 3A0 Canada
Tel: 250-567-2124; *Fax:* 250-567-3316
Toll-Free: 800-752-4094
chamber@hwy16.com
www.vanderhoofchamber.com
Affiliation(s): BC Chamber of Commerce

Wells & District Chamber of Commerce
PO Box 123, Wells BC V0K 2R0 Canada
Tel: 250-994-3223; *Fax:* 250-994-3223
Toll-Free: 877-451-9355
marketing@wellsbc.com
www.wellsbc.com

West Shore Chamber of Commerce
2830 Aldwynd Rd., Victoria BC V9B 3S7 Canada
Tel: 250-478-1130; *Fax:* 250-478-1584
chamber@westshore.bc.ca
www.westshore.bc.ca

West Vancouver Chamber of Commerce
1846 Marine Dr., West Vancouver BC V7V 1J6 Canada
Tel: 604-926-6614; *Fax:* 604-925-7220
info@westvanchamber.com
www.westvanchamber.com

Westbank & District Chamber of Commerce
#4, 2375 Pamela Rd., Westbank BC V4T 2H9 Canada
Tel: 250-768-3378; *Fax:* 250-768-3465
Toll-Free: 866-768-3378
chamber@westbankchamber.com
www.westbankchamber.com
Broc Braconnier, President
Leah Thordarson, Manager

Whistler Chamber of Commerce
#201, 4230 Gateway Dr., Whistler BC V0N 1B4 Canada
Tel: 604-932-5922; *Fax:* 604-932-3755
chamber@whistlerchamber.com
www.whistlerchamber.com

White Rock & South Surrey Chamber of Commerce
#101, 2430 King George Hwy., Surrey BC V4B 1H5 Canada
Tel: 604-536-6844; *Fax:* 604-536-4994
info@whiterockchamber.com
www.whiterockchamber.com
Affiliation(s): BC Tourism

Williams Lake & District Chamber of Commerce
1660 Broadway South, Williams Lake BC V2G 2W4 Canada
Tel: 250-392-5025; *Fax:* 250-392-4214
Toll-Free: 877-967-5253
info@williamslakechamber.com
www.williamslakechamber.com
Affiliation(s): BC Chamber of Commerce; Canadian Chamber of Commerce; Cariboo Chilcotin Coast Tourism Association

Zeballos Board of Trade
PO Box 208, Zeballos BC V0P 2A0 Canada
Tel: 250-761-4261; *Fax:* 250-761-4188
boardoftrade@zeballos.com
www.zeballos.com
Tom Weston, President
Debra Brown, Secretary

Manitoba

Altona & District Chamber of Commerce
PO Box 329, Altona MB R0G 0B0 Canada
Tel: 204-324-8793; *Fax:* 204-324-1314
chamber@shopaltona.com
www.shopaltona.com
Vic Loewen, President
Susan Yakabowich, Manager

Arborg Chamber of Commerce
PO Box 415, Arborg MB R0C 0A0 Canada
Tel: 204-376-2878; *Fax:* 204-376-2999
Lorne Floyd, President

Ashern & District Chamber of Commerce
PO Box 582, Ashern MB R0C 0E0 Canada
Tel: 204-768-2634; *Fax:* 204-768-2088
info@ashern.ca
www.ashern.ca

Assiniboia Chamber of Commerce (MB) (ACC)
PO Box 42122, Stn. Ferry Road, Winnipeg MB R3J 3X7 Canada
Tel: 204-774-4154; *Fax:* 204-774-4201
info@assiniboiacc.mb.ca
www.assiniboiacc.mb.ca

Beausejour & District Chamber of Commerce
PO Box 224, Beausejour MB R0E 0C0 Canada
Tel: 204-268-3502; *Fax:* 204-268-3502
chamber@mybeausejour.com
mybeausejour.com/chamber/index.php

Birtle & District Chamber of Commerce
PO Box 278, Birtle MB R0M 0C0 Canada
Tel: 204-842-3944
Alan Wong, Secretary

Steve Desjardins, President

Blue Water Chamber of Commerce
PO Box 11, St Georges MB R0E 1V0 Canada
Tel: 204-367-2762
Edward A Gaffray, President

Boissevain & District Chamber of Commerce
PO Box 734, Boissevain MB R0K 0E0 Canada
Tel: 204-534-6300; *Fax:* 204-534-6825

Brandon Chamber of Commerce
1043 Rosser Ave., Brandon MB R7A 0L5 Canada
Tel: 204-571-5340; *Fax:* 204-571-5347
info@brandonchamber.ca
www.brandonchamber.ca

Carberry & District Chamber of Commerce
PO Box 101, Carberry MB R0K 0H0 Canada
Tel: 204-834-6616
edo@townofcarberry.ca
Christinia Steen, President
Lori Scott, Secretary

Carman & Community Chamber of Commerce
PO Box 249, Carman MB R0G 0J0 Canada
Tel: 204-750-3050
ccchamber@gmail.com
www.carmanchamberofcommerce.com
Affiliation(s): Manitoba Chamber of Commerce

Chambre de commerce de Notre Dame
PO Box 107, Notre Dame de Lourdes MB R0G 1M0 Canada
Tel: 204-248-2582; *Fax:* 204-248-2731
Denis Collet, President
Joey Dupasquler, Secretary

La chambre de commerce de Saint-Malo & District
CP 328, Saint-Malo MB R0A 1T0 Canada
Joël Fouasse, Co-président
Gilles Maynard, Co-président

Chambre de commerce francophone de Saint-Boniface (CCFSB) / St-Boniface chamber of Commerce
CP 204, #212, 383, boul. Provencher, Saint-Boniface MB R2H 3B4 Canada
Tél: 204-235-1406; *Téléc:* 204-233-1017
info@ccfsb.mb.ca
www.ccfsb.mb.ca
Alain Laurencelle, Président

Churchill Chamber of Commerce
PO Box 176, Churchill MB R0B 0E0 Canada
Tel: 204-675-2022; *Toll-Free:* 888-389-2327
churchillchamber@mts.net
www.churchill.ca/chamber-of-commerce/

Crystal City & District Chamber of Commerce
PO Box 56, Crystal City MB R0K 0N0 Canada
Tel: 204-873-2523; *Fax:* 204-873-2456
chamberofcommerce@crystalcitymb.ca

Cypress River Chamber of Commerce
PO Box 261, Cypress River MB R0K 0P0 Canada
Tel: 204-743-2119; *Fax:* 204-743-2339
www.cypressriver.ca
Jim Cassels, President

Dauphin & District Chamber of Commerce
101 - 1st Ave. NW, #B, Dauphin MB R7N 1G8 Canada
Tel: 204-622-3140; *Fax:* 204-622-3141
dauphinchamber@mts.net

Deloraine & District Chamber of Commerce
PO Box 748, Deloraine MB R0M 0M0 Canada
Tel: 204-747-2842; *Fax:* 204-747-2856

Elie Chamber of Commerce
PO Box 175, Elie MB R0H 0H0 Canada
Tel: 204-353-2892; *Fax:* 204-353-2336

Elkhorn Chamber of Commerce
PO Box 141, Elkhorn MB R0M 0N0 Canada
Tel: 204-845-2388; *Fax:* 204-845-2073
Kelly Martin, Secretary
Sharlean Bickerton, President

Eriksdale & District Chamber of Commerce
PO Box 434, Eriksdale MB R0C 0W0 Canada
Tel: 204-739-2641
www.eriksdale.com
Phyllis Lamb, Secretary
Cindy Kinkead, President

Falcon/West Hawk Lakes Chamber of Commerce (FWHLCC)
PO Box 187, Falcon Beach MB R0E 0N0 Canada
Tel: 204-349-3134; *Fax:* 204-349-3134
info@chamber-southwhiteshell.ca
www.chamber-southwhiteshell.ca
Affiliation(s): Canadian Chamber of Commerce
Bob Harbottle, President

Fisher Branch Chamber of Commerce
PO Box 566, Fisher Branch MB R0C 0Z0 Canada
Tel: 204-372-6034; *Fax:* 204-372-8545
fisher01@mts.net
Darcy Plett, President

Flin Flon & District Chamber of Commerce
#228, 35 Main St., Flin Flon MB R8A 1J7 Canada
Tel: 204-687-4518; *Fax:* 204-687-4456
flinflonchamber@mts.net
www.cityofflinflon.com/chamber

Gilbert Plains & District Chamber of Commerce
PO Box 670, Gilbert Plains MB R0L 0X0 Canada
Tel: 204-548-2682; *Fax:* 204-548-2682
Brenda Kerns, President

Gillam Chamber of Commerce
PO Box 366, Gillam MB R0B 0L0 Canada
Tel: 204-652-5135; *Fax:* 204-652-5155
John Cullen, President

Grahamdale Chamber of Commerce
R.M. Of Grahamdale Administration Office, PO Box 160, 23 Government Rd., Moosehorn MB R0C 2E0 Canada
Tel: 204-768-2858; *Fax:* 204-768-3374
info@grahamdale.ca
www.grahamdale.ca
Karen Bittner, President

Grandview & District Chamber of Commerce
PO Box 28, Grandview MB R0L 0Y0 Canada
Tel: 204-546-2501
Linda Zazuliak, Secretary
Dennis Lukey, President

Grunthal & District Chamber of Commerce
PO Box 451, Grunthal MB R0A 0R0 Canada
Tel: 204-434-6750; *Fax:* 204-434-9353
leonard@emergencyvehicles.ca

Hamiota Chamber of Commerce
PO Box 403, Hamiota MB R0J 1Z0 Canada
Tel: 204-764-2884
info@hamiota.com
www.hamiota.com/business.html
Larry Oakden, President
Bonnie Michaudville, Secretary

Hartney & District Chamber of Commerce
PO Box 224, Hartney MB R0M 0X0 Canada
Tel: 204-858-2089; *Fax:* 204-858-2089
www.hartney.ca
Sharon Evans, Contact
Carol Thomas, President

Headingley Chamber of Commerce
5353 Portage Ave., Headingley MB R4H 1J9 Canada
Tel: 204-889-2132; *Fax:* 204-831-0816
dwhitermofheadingley@mts.net
www.rmofheadingley.ca/business/cofc.asp
Affiliation(s): Central Plains Development Corporation; White Horse Plains Development Corporation; Headingley Heritage Centre
Jill Ruth, President
Dave White, Executive Director

Killarney & District Chamber of Commerce
PO Box 809, Killarney MB R0K 1G0 Canada
Tel: 204-523-4202
killarneychamber@hotmail.com
Mark Witherspoon, Chair
Dale Banman, Executive Director

Lac du Bonnet & District Chamber of Commerce
PO Box 598, Lac du Bonnet MB R0E 1A0 Canada
Tel: 204-345-8194; *Fax:* 204-345-8194
kimbuhay@mts.net
www.lacdubonnetchamber.com
Affiliation(s): Manitoba Chambers of Commerce
Donna Tschetter, President
Kim Buhay, Manager

Landmark & Community Chamber of Commerce
PO Box 469, Landmark MB R0A 0X0 Canada
Tel: 204-355-5200
info@landmarkonline.ca
www.landmarkonline.ca
Randy Wolgemuth, President

Leaf Rapids Chamber of Commerce
PO Box 26, Leaf Rapids MB R0B 1W0 Canada
Tel: 204-473-2491; *Fax:* 204-473-2284
franklhd@mts.net
www.townofleafrapids.ca

Lundar Chamber of Commerce
PO Box 26, Lundar MB R0C 1Y0 Canada
Tel: 204-762-5611; *Fax:* 204-762-5551
Faye Goranson, President

MacGregor Chamber of Commerce
PO Box 685, MacGregor MB R0H 0R0 Canada
Tel: 204-685-2862; *Fax:* 204-685-2631
www.macgregorchamber.com

Melita & District Chamber of Commerce
PO Box 666, Melita MB R0M 1L0 Canada
Tel: 204-522-3285; *Fax:* 204-522-3536
ccagenci@mts.net

Minnedosa Chamber of Commerce
PO Box 857, Minnedosa MB R0J 1E0 Canada
Tel: 204-867-2951; *Fax:* 204-867-3641
chamber@minnedosachamber.ca
www.minnedosachamber.ca
Don Farr, President
Callie Mashtoler, Secretary

Morden Chamber of Commerce
311 North Railway St., Morden MB R6M 1S9 Canada
Tel: 204-822-5630; *Fax:* 204-822-2041
chamber@mordenmb.com
www.mordenchamber.com
Cheryl Link, Manager
Carol Fehr, President

Morris & District Chamber of Commerce
PO Box 98, Morris MB R0G 1K0 Canada
Tel: 204-746-6275; *Fax:* 204-746-6953

Neepawa & District Chamber of Commerce
PO Box 726, 282 Hamilton St., Neepawa MB R0J 1H0 Canada
Tel: 204-476-5292; *Fax:* 204-476-5231
Toll-Free: 877-633-7292
neepawachamber@mts.net
www.neepawachamber.com

Niverville Chamber of Commerce
PO Box 157, Niverville MB R0A 1E0 Canada
Tel: 204-388-4325
chamber@niverville.com
www.niverville.com
Debbie Pearson, President
Jeannine Funk, Contact

North Interlake Chamber of Commerce
PO Box 160, 23 Government Rd., Moosehorn MB R0C 2E0 Canada
Tel: 204-768-2858; *Fax:* 204-768-3374
rm606@tcmsnet.com
www.grahamdale.ca
Gayle James, President
Carol Thurman, Secretary

Oakville & District Chamber of Commerce
PO Box 263, Oakville MB R0H 0Y0 Canada
Tel: 204-267-2048; *Fax:* 204-267-7015
bingram@mts.net
Kam Blight, President
Barb Ingram, Contact

Pansy & District United Chamber of Commerce
PO Box 34, Pansy MB R0A 1J0 Canada
Tel: 204-425-3530; *Fax:* 204-425-3530

The Pas & District Chamber of Commerce
PO Box 996, The Pas MB R9A 1L1 Canada
Tel: 204-623-7256; *Fax:* 204-623-2589
tpinfo@mts.net
www.thepaschamber.com
Debbie Doucette, President

Pilot Mound & District Chamber of Commerce
PO Box 356, Pilot Mound MB R0G 1P0 Canada
Tel: 204-825-2587
chamberofcommerce@pilotmound.com
www.pilotmound.com

Pinawa Chamber of Commerce
PO Box 544, Pinawa MB R0E 1L0 Canada
Tel: 204-753-2747
chamber@granite.mb.ca
www.pinawachamber.com
Rhonda Henschell, Secretary
Marsha Sheppard, President

Piney & District Chamber of Commerce
PO Box 50, Sprague MB R0A 1Z0 Canada
Tel: 204-437-2259; *Fax:* 204-437-2561
Dennis Konchak, President

Plum Coulee & District Chamber of Commerce
PO Box 392, Plum Coulee MB R0G 1R0 Canada
Tel: 204-829-3419; *Fax:* 204-829-3436
wanderer@mts.net
June Letkeman, Secretary
June Alvinklassen, President

Portage & District Chamber of Commerce
11 - 2nd St. NE, Portage la Prairie MB R1N 1R8 Canada
Tel: 204-857-7778; *Fax:* 204-857-4095
info@portagechamber.com
www.portagechamber.com
Affiliation(s): Canadian Chamber of Commerce

Rivers & District Chamber of Commerce
PO Box 795, Rivers MB R0K 1X0 Canada
Tel: 204-328-7316; *Fax:* 204-328-4460
mbeever@mts.net
Marlin Beener, President
Jean Young, Manager

Riverton & District Chamber of Commerce
PO Box 258, Riverton MB R0C 2R0 Canada
Tel: 204-378-2084; *Fax:* 204-378-2085
berniced@mts.net
www.rivertoncanada.com
Bernice Danielson, President
Karen Donnellan-Fisher, Contact

Roblin & District Chamber of Commerce
PO Box 160, Roblin MB R0L 1P0 Canada
Tel: 204-937-3194
rdcoc@mts.net
www.roblinmanitoba.com

Rossburn & District Chamber of Commerce
PO Box 579, Rossburn MB R0J 1V0 Canada
Tel: 204-859-3334; *Fax:* 204-859-3313
wheatland@mts.net
Raymond Lysyshin, President
Val White, Secretary
Terence Waychyshin, First Vice President

Russell & District Chamber of Commerce
PO Box 155, Russell MB R0J 1W0 Canada
Tel: 204-773-2456
www.russellmb.com/chamber.html
Brent Havelange, President

St. Pierre Chamber of Commerce
PO Box 71, St Pierre Jolys MB R0A 1V0 Canada
Tel: 204-433-7123; *Fax:* 204-433-3135
st-pierre-jolys@mts.net
Sherry Stasiuk, Secretary
Luc Catellier, President

La Salle & District Chamber of Commerce
PO Box 608, La Salle MB R0G 1B0 Canada
Tel: 204-736-4555; *Fax:* 204-736-4363
Donna Bell, President
Ray Cormier, Treasurer

Selkirk & District Chamber of Commerce
100 Eaton Ave., Selkirk MB R1A 0W6 Canada
Tel: 204-482-7176; *Fax:* 204-482-5448
info@selkirkanddistrictchamber.ca
www.selkirkanddistrictchamber.ca

Shoal Lake & District Chamber of Commerce
PO Box 547, Shoal Lake MB R0J 1Z0 Canada
Tel: 204-759-3343; *Fax:* 204-759-2740
nsims@simsco.mb.ca
Tara Patterson, Contact
Norman Sims, President

Somerset & District Chamber of Commerce
PO Box 353, Somerset MB R0G 2L0 Canada
Tel: 204-744-2088; *Fax:* 204-744-2153
Affiliation(s): Manitoba Chamber of Commerce

Souris & Glenwood Chamber of Commerce
PO Box 939, Souris MB R0K 2C0 Canada
Tel: 204-483-3127; *Fax:* 204-483-2777
robbin2@mts.net
Affiliation(s): Manitoba Chamber of Commerce
Sande Denbow, Contact
Colleen Robbins, President

Ste Rose & District Chamber of Commerce
PO Box 688, Ste Rose du Lac MB R0L 1S0 Canada
Tel: 204-447-2196; *Fax:* 204-447-2692
storestarter@yahoo.ca
Trevor Gates, President
Monica Lambourne, Contact

Steinbach Chamber of Commerce
PO Box 1795, 225 Reimer Ave., Steinbach MB R5G 1N4 Canada
Tel: 204-326-9566; *Fax:* 204-346-6600
stbcofc@mts.net
www.steinbachchamberofcommerce.com

Stonewall & District Chamber of Commerce
PO Box 762, Stonewall MB R0C 2Z0 Canada
Tel: 204-467-8377
info@stonewallchamber.com
www.stonewallchamber.com

Swan River Chamber of Commerce
PO Box 1540, Swan River MB R0L 1Z0 Canada
Tel: 204-734-3102; *Fax:* 204-734-4342
srcc@svcn.mb.ca
Naomi Neufeld, President

Teulon Chamber of Commerce
PO Box 235, Teulon MB R0C 3B0 Canada
Tel: 204-294-6171; *Fax:* 204-886-3232
president@teulonchamber.ca
Michael Ledarney, President
Debra Osbak, Secretary

Thompson Chamber of Commerce
PO Box 363, Thompson MB R8N 1N2 Canada
Tel: 204-677-4155; *Fax:* 204-677-3434
Toll-Free: 888-307-0103
commerce@mts.net
www.thompson.ca

Treherne Chamber of Commerce
PO Box 344, Treherne MB R0G 2V0 Canada
Tel: 204-723-2774; *Fax:* 204-723-2719

Virden & District Chamber of Commerce
PO Box 899, 425 - 6th Ave. South, Virden MB R0M 2C0 Canada
Tel: 204-748-3955; *Fax:* 204-748-3467
virdencc@mts.net
Affiliation(s): Virden Wallace Community Development Corp.; Virden Employment Skills Centre Inc., Virden Agricultural Society; Virden Indoor Rodeo

Wasagaming Chamber of Commerce
PO Box 222, 110 Wasagaming Dr., Wasagaming MB R0J 2H0 Canada
Tel: 204-848-2742; *Fax:* 204-848-7712
info@discoverclearlake.com
www.discoverclearlake.com
Debb Geiler, President
Wayne Zachedniak, Treasurer

Winkler & District Chamber of Commerce
185 Main St., Winkler MB R6W 1B4 Canada
Tel: 204-325-9758; *Fax:* 204-325-8290
chamber@winkleronline.com
www.winklerchamber.com

Winnipeg Chamber of Commerce (WCC) / Chambre de commerce de Winnipeg
#100, 259 Portage Ave., Winnipeg MB R3B 2A9 Canada
Tel: 204-944-8484; *Fax:* 204-944-8492
info@winnipeg-chamber.com
www.winnipeg-chamber.com
Affiliation(s): Canadian Chamber of Commerce; Manitoba Chamber of Commerce

New Brunswick

Albert County Chamber of Commerce
PO Box 3051, Hillsborough NB E4H 4W5 Canada
Tel: 506-389-6002; *Fax:* 506-387-8331
kpower@nb.sympatico.ca
Brian Keirstead, President
Phyllis Sutherland, Secretary

Atlantic Provinces Chambers of Commerce (APCC) / Chambres de commerce des provinces de l'Atlantique
#21, 236 St. George St., Moncton NB E1C 1W1 Canada
Tel: 506-857-3980; *Fax:* 506-859-6131
grace@apcc.ca
www.apcc.ca
Bill Denyar, President & CEO
Jonathan T.T. Daniels, Chair

Bath Chamber of Commerce
163A Church St., Bath NB E7J 1A7 Canada
Tel: 506-278-5213; *Fax:* 506-278-5963

Bouctouche Chamber of Commerce / Chambre de commerce de Bouctouche
PO Box 338, #301, 59, boul Irving, Bouctouche NB E4S 3J6 Canada
Tel: 506-743-2411; *Fax:* 506-743-8991
chambouc@mon.auracom.com

Campbellton Regional Chamber of Commerce / Chambre de commerce régional de Campbellton
PO Box 236, 18 Water St., Campbellton NB E3N 3G4 Canada
Tel: 506-759-7856; *Fax:* 506-759-7557
crcc@nbnet.nb.ca
www.campbelltonregionalchamber.ca
Affiliation(s): NB Chamber of Commerce; Atlantic Chamber of Commerce

Central Carleton Chamber of Commerce
28 Palmer Rd., Waterville NB E7P 1B4 Canada
Tel: 506-375-4074
Dale Albright, President

Centreville Chamber of Commerce
PO Box 628, Centreville NB E7K 3H5 Canada
Tel: 506-276-4241; *Fax:* 506-276-9891
centreville.chamber@aernet.ca

Chambre de commerce de Clair
PO Box 1025, Clair NB E7A 2J5 Canada
Tel: 506-992-6030; *Fax:* 506-992-6041
info@chambrecommerceclair.com
www.chambrecommerceclair.com
Marie-Josée Michaud, Présidente

Chambre de commerce de Cocagne, Notre-Dame et Grande-Digue
CP 1090, Cocagne NB E4R 1N6 Canada
Tél: 506-576-6005; *Téléc:* 506-576-6073
Gilles Allain, Président

Chambre de commerce de Collette
60, rue des Arbres, Collette NB E4Y 1G4 Canada
Tél: 506-622-0752; *Téléc:* 506-622-0477
Maurice Desroches, Président

Chambre de commerce de Kent Centre Chamber of Commerce
#2, 9235 Main St., Richibucto NB E4W 4C6 Canada
Tel: 506-523-1443; *Fax:* 506-523-6520
kccc@richibucto.org

Chambre de commerce de la région d'Edmundston
1, ch Canada, Edmundston NB E3V 1T6 Canada
Tél: 506-737-1866; *Téléc:* 506-737-1862
info@ccedmundston.com
www.ccedmundston.com
Affiliation(s): Chambre de commerce du Nouveau-Brunswick; Chambre de commerce des Provinces Atlantiques; Chambre de commerce du Canada; Chambre de commerce Internationale

Chambre de commerce de la region de Cap-Pelé
CP 1219, Cap-Pelé NB E4N 3B1 Canada
Tél: 506-577-4560; *Téléc:* 506-577-8900
Marcel Doiron, Président
Stéphane Dallaire, Secrétaire

Chambre de commerce de Rogersville / Rogersville Chamber of Commerce
#5, 11101, rue Principale, Rogersville NB E4Y 2N2 Canada
Tél: 506-775-9378; *Téléc:* 506-775-1906

Chambre de Commerce de Saint Louis de Kent
#A, 83A Beauséjour, Saint-Louis-de-Kent NB E4X 1A6 Canada
Tel: 506-876-3475; *Fax:* 506-876-3477
René Côté, Présidente
Daniel Comeau, Secrétaire

Chambre de commerce de Saint-François
CP 378, Saint-François-de-Madawaska NB E7A 1G4 Canada
Tél: 506-992-6067; *Téléc:* 506-992-6049
cdecsf@nb.aibn.com
www.nbchamber.ca

Chambre de commerce de Saint-Quentin Inc.
144D, rue Canada, Saint-Quentin NB E8A 1G7 Canada
Tél: 506-235-3666; *Téléc:* 506-235-1804
n6chcomm@nb.aibn.com
www.saintquentin.nb.ca
Jean-Guy R. Michaud, Président
Joyce Somers, Secrétaire

Chambre de commerce de Shippagan inc.
227, boul J.D. Gauthier, Shippagan NB E8S 3H1 Canada
Tél: 506-336-2207
chambredecommerce@shippagan.com
Donald Hachey, Président

Chambre de commerce des Iles Lamèque et Miscou inc.
CP 2075, Lamèque NB E8T 3N5 Canada
Tél: 506-344-7148
www.lameque.ca

Chambre de commerce du Grand Caraquet Inc
#214, 220, boul St-Pierre ouest, Caraquet NB E1W 1B7 Canada
Tél: 506-727-2931; *Téléc:* 506-727-3191
chambre@nb.aira.com
www.acadie.net

Chambre de commerce du Rivière-du-Portage
5898B, RR#11, Rivière-du-Portage NB E9H 1X2 Canada
Tél: 506-393-1902
jetta@nbnet.nb.ca
www.nbchamber.ca

Chipman Chamber of Commerce
237 Main St., Chipman NB E4E 1E5 Canada
Tel: 506-339-1821; *Fax:* 506-339-1823
Brian Harris, Chairman-Elect

East Restigouche Chamber of Commerce
389 Adelaide St., Dalhousie NB E8C 1B5 Canada
Tel: 506-684-5571; *Fax:* 506-684-4717
Paul Hayes, President

Eastern Charlotte Chamber of Commerce
#2, 21 Main St., St George NB E5C 3H9 Canada
Tel: 506-456-3951
eccc@nbnet.nb.ca
Wanda MacLean, President
Irene Wright, Secretary

Florenceville Chamber of Commerce
PO Box 601, Florenceville NB E7L 1Y7 Canada
Tel: 506-392-0900; *Fax:* 506-392-0900

Fredericton Chamber of Commerce / La Chambre de Commerce de Fredericton
PO Box 275, 270 Rookwood Ave., Fredericton NB E3B 4Y9 Canada
Tel: 506-458-8006; *Fax:* 506-451-1119
fchamber@frederictonchamber.ca
www.frederictonchamber.ca

Gagetown & Area Chamber of Commerce
76 Babbit St., Gagetown NB E5M 1C8 Canada
Tel: 506-488-3281
Nancy MacQuade, President

Grand Falls/Grand Sault & District Chamber of Commerce
#300, 81 Burgess Street, Grand Falls NB E3Y 1C6 Canada
Tel: 506-473-1905; *Fax:* 506-475-7755
gfcocgs@nbnet.nb.ca
Côme Ouellette, President
Linda N. Martin, Staff

Grand Manan Chamber of Commerce
1141 Rte. 776, Grand Manan NB E5G 4K9 Canada
Tel: 506-662-3442; *Fax:* 506-662-3593
Toll-Free: 888-525-1655
info@grandmanannb.com
www.grandmanannb.com

Greater Bathurst Chamber of Commerce / Chambre de commerce du Grand Bathurst
CEI Bldg., 725 College St., Bathurst NB E2A 4B9 Canada
Tel: 506-548-8498; *Fax:* 506-548-2200
bathcham@nbnet.nb.ca
www.bathurstchamber.ca
Affiliation(s): Canadian Chamber of Commerce

Greater Hillsborough Chamber of Commerce
PO Box 3051, Hillsborough NB E4H 4W5 Canada
Tel: 506-734-2851; *Fax:* 506-734-2244
Carole Coleman, Director

Greater Miramichi Chamber of Commerce
PO Box 342, Miramichi NB E1N 3A7 Canada
Tel: 506-622-5522; *Fax:* 506-622-5959
mirchamber@nb.aibn.com
www.miramichichamber.com

Greater Moncton Chamber of Commerce (GMCC) / Chambre de commerce du Grand Moncton
#100, 910 Main St., Moncton NB E1C 1G6 Canada
Tel: 506-857-2883; *Fax:* 506-857-9209
info@gmcc.nb.ca
www.gmcc.nb.ca

Greater Sackville Chamber of Commerce
#87, 8 Main St., Sackville NB E4L 4A9 Canada
Tel: 506-364-8911; *Fax:* 506-364-8082
gscc@nbnet.nb.ca
www.sackvillechamber.ca

Rebecca Maclean, Staff
Lisa Smith, President
Wayne Harper, Secretary

Greater Woodstock Chamber of Commerce
#2, 220 King St., Woodstock NB E7M 1Z8 Canada
Tel: 506-325-9049; *Fax:* 506-328-4683
woodstockchamberofcommerce@nb.aibn.com
www.town.woodstock.nb.ca

Peter Clark, Contact
Jeanne Langille, President

Hampton Area Chamber of Commerce (HACC)
PO Box 1829, #2, 17 Centennial Rd., Hampton NB E5N 6N3 Canada
Tel: 506-832-2559; *Fax:* 506-832-2559
hacc@nbnet.nb.ca
www.hamptonareachamber.org

Kennebecasis Valley Chamber of Commerce
PO Box 4455, #8, 53C Clark Rd., Rothesay NB E2E 5X2 Canada
Tel: 506-849-2860; *Fax:* 506-847-0996
admin@kvbusiness.com
www.kvbusiness.com

Phil Brodersen, President
Scott Cochrane, Secretary-Treasurer
Ann-Marie O'Neill, Administrator

Mactaquac County Chamber of Commerce
PO Box 1163, Nackawic NB E6G 2N1 Canada
Tel: 506-575-9622; *Fax:* 506-575-2035
mccc@mactaquaccountry.com
www.mactaquaccountry.com

Melanie Sloat, President
Dora Boudreau, Secretary

Oromocto & Area Chamber of Commerce
Oromocto Mall, PO Box 20124, Oromocto NB E2V 2R6 Canada
Tel: 506-446-6043; *Fax:* 506-446-6925
oromotcochamber@nb.aibn.com
www.oromoctochamber.nb.ca

Perth-Andover & Area Chamber of Commerce
11640 Route 105, Kilburn NB E7H 4W3 Canada
Tel: 506-273-6375; *Fax:* 506-273-6915
Jeff Walters-Gray, President
Elizabeth Davenport, Secretary

River Valley Chamber of Commerce (RVCC)
PO Box 3123, Grand Bay-Westfield NB E5K 4V4 Canada
Tel: 506-738-8666; *Fax:* 506-738-3697

St. Andrews Chamber of Commerce
46 Reed Ave., St Andrews NB E5B 1A1 Canada
Tel: 506-529-3555; *Fax:* 506-529-8095
stachamb@nbnet.nb.ca
www.standrewsby-the-sea.ca

St. Martins & District Chamber of Commerce
229 Main St., St Martins NB E5R 1B7 Canada
Tel: 506-833-2019; *Fax:* 506-833-2028
fundytp@nbnet.nb.ca

Bruce Huttges, President
Brian Clark, Secretary

St. Stephen Area Chamber of Commerce
PO Box 457, 34 Milltown Blvd., St Stephen NB E3L 2X3 Canada
Tel: 506-466-7703; *Fax:* 506-466-7753
chamber.ststephen@nb.aibn.com
www.town.ststephen.nb.ca

Affiliation(s): Atlantic Chamber of Commerce; Canadian Chamber of Commerce

Sussex & District Chamber of Commerce
PO Box 5152, 66 Broad St., Sussex NB E4E 5L2 Canada
Tel: 506-433-1845; *Fax:* 506-433-1886
sdcc@nbnet.nb.ca
sdccinc.org

Affiliation(s): Atlantic Provinces Chambers of Commerce

Washademoak Region Chamber of Commerce
3359 Lower Cambridge, Cambridge-Narrows NB E4C 4P9 Canada
Tel: 506-488-2517; *Fax:* 506-488-2622
www.w-rcc.ca/frameset.html

Newfoundland and Labrador

Argentia Area Chamber of Commerce
PO Box 109, 1 O'Reilly St., Placentia NL A0B 2Y0 Canada
Tel: 709-227-0003; *Fax:* 709-227-0016
info@argentiachamber.org
www.argentiachamber.org

Arnolds Cove Area Chamber of Commerce
PO Box 411, Arnolds Cove NL A0B 1A0 Canada
Tel: 709-472-4151; *Fax:* 709-472-4182
Gloria Warren-Slade, President
Germaine Lynch, Treasurer

Baie Verte & Area Chamber of Commerce
PO Box 578, Baie Verte NL A0K 1B0 Canada
Tel: 709-532-4204; *Fax:* 709-532-4252
bvachamber@nf.aibn.com
www.bvachamber.com

Shannon Lewis, President

Bay St. George Chamber of Commerce
35 Carolina Ave., Stephenville NL A2N 3P8 Canada
Tel: 709-643-5854; *Fax:* 709-643-6398
bsgcoc@wec-center.nl.ca
www.bsgcc.org

Bonavista Area Chamber of Commerce (BACC)
PO Box 280, Bonavista NL A0C 1B0 Canada
Fax: 709-468-2495
info@bacc.ca
www.bacc.ca

Diane Thorpe, Secretary

Channel Port Aux Basques Chamber of Commerce
PO Box 1389, Channel-Port-aux-Basques NL A0M 1C0 Canada
Tel: 709-695-3688; *Fax:* 709-695-7925
pabchamber@thezone.net
www.pabchamber.com

Clarenville Area Chamber of Commerce
292A Memorial Dr., Clarenville NL A5A 1P1 Canada
Tel: 709-466-5800; *Fax:* 709-466-5803
Toll-Free: 866-466-5800
info@clarenvillechamber.net
www.clarenvilleareachamber.net

Conception Bay Area Chamber of Commerce
#3, 702 Conception Bay Hwy., Conception Bay South NL A1X 3A5 Canada
Tel: 709-834-5670; *Fax:* 709-834-5760
info@cbachamber.com
www.cbachamber.com

Deer Lake Chamber of Commerce
6 Cresent St., Deer Lake NL A8A 1H6 Canada
Tel: 709-635-3260; *Fax:* 709-635-5857
s-goulding@warp.nfld.net

Affiliation(s): Newfoundland Chambers of Commerce

Exploits Regional Chamber of Commerce
PO Box 272, 16 High St., Grand Falls-Windsor NL A2A 2J7 Canada
Tel: 709-489-7512; *Fax:* 709-489-7532
info@exploitschamber.com
www.exploitschamber.com

Gander & Area Chamber of Commerce (GACC)
109 Trans Canada Hwy., Gander NL A1V 1P6 Canada
Tel: 709-256-7110; *Fax:* 709-256-4080
ganderchamber@ganderchamber.nf.ca
www.ganderchamber.nf.ca

Greater Corner Brook Board of Trade
PO Box 475, 11 Confederation Dr., Corner Brook NL A2H 6E6 Canada
Tel: 709-634-5831; *Fax:* 709-639-9710
cbcc@thezone.net
www.gcbbt.com

Irish Loop Chamber of Commerce
PO Box 6, Trepassey NL A0A 4B0 Canada
Tel: 709-432-2662; *Fax:* 709-438-2892
Cathy Perry, President

Labrador North Chamber of Commerce (LNCC)
PO Box 460, Stn. B, 169 Hamilton River Rd., Happy Valley-Goose Bay NL A0P 1E0 Canada
Tel: 709-896-8787; *Fax:* 709-896-0585
Toll-Free: 877-920-8787
admin@chamberlabrador.com
www.chamberlabrador.com

Labrador South East Chamber of Commerce
PO Box 65, Port Hope Simpson NL A0K 4E0 Canada
Tel: 709-960-0510
bfgillis@nf.sympatico.ca

Blair Gillis, President
Sharon Penney, Secretary

Labrador Straits Chamber of Commerce
PO Box 179, Forteau NL A0K 2P0 Canada
Tel: 709-931-2073; *Fax:* 709-931-2073
chamber@labradorstraits.net
Kinza Trimm, Executive Director

Labrador West Chamber of Commerce
PO Box 273, Labrador City NL A2V 2K5 Canada
Tel: 709-944-3723; *Fax:* 709-944-4699
lwc@crrstv.net
www.labradorwestchamber.ca

Lewisporte & Area Chamber of Commerce
PO Box 953, Lewisporte NL A0G 3A0 Canada
Tel: 709-535-2500; *Fax:* 709-535-2482
lacc@superweb.ca
Cynthia Aylward, Executive Assistant

Marystown-Burin Area Chamber of Commerce
PO Box 728, Marystown NL A0E 2M0 Canada
Tel: 709-279-2080; *Fax:* 709-279-4492
chamber@mbacc.nf.ca
www.marystownburinchamber.com

Mike Graham, President
Kelly Pardy, Executive Director

Mount Pearl Chamber of Commerce
39 Commonwealth Ave., Mount Pearl NL A1N 1W7 Canada
Tel: 709-364-8513; *Fax:* 709-364-8500
info@mtpearlchamber.com
www.mtpearlchamber.com

Pasadena Chamber of Commerce
c/o The Venture Centre, PO Box 149, Pasadena NL A0L 1K0 Canada
Tel: 709-686-2078; *Fax:* 709-686-2081
Derrick Anthony, President

St Anthony & Area Chamber of Commerce
PO Box 650, St Anthony NL A0K 4S0 Canada
Tel: 709-454-8898
stanthonyandareachamber@yahoo.ca

Springdale & Area Chamber of Commerce
PO Box 37, 151 Main St., Springdale NL A0J 1T0 Canada
Tel: 709-673-3837; *Fax:* 709-673-3897
seabrightfinancial@aibn.com

Straits-St. Barbe Chamber of Commerce
PO Box 119, Flowers Cove NL A0K 2N0 Canada
Tel: 709-456-2592; *Fax:* 709-456-2592
straitsstbarbe@nf.aibn.com

Maggie Chambers, Secretary
Donna Doyle, President

Northwest Territories

Baffin Regional Chamber of Commerce (BRCC)
Igluvut Bldg., 2nd Fl., PO Box 59, Iqaluit NU X0A 0H0 Canada
Tel: 867-979-4656; *Fax:* 867-979-2929
www.baffinchamber.ca

Hal Timar, Executive Director
Chris West, President
Frank May, Sec.-Treas.

Iqaluit Chamber of Commerce
PO Box 1107, Iqaluit NU X0A 0H0 Canada
Tel: 867-979-4095
board@icoc.nu.ca
www.icoc.nu.ca
David Fulgham, 2nd Vice-President

Kivalliq Chamber of Commerce
PO Box 147, Rankin Inlet NU X0C 0G0 Canada
Tel: 867-645-2718; *Fax:* 867-645-2483
krmanson@arctic.ca
Ellie Camsill, President

Kugluktuk Chamber of Commerce
PO Box 307, Kugluktuk NU X0B 0E0 Canada
Tel: 867-982-3232; *Fax:* 867-982-3229
coptours@polarnet.ca
Rachel Horn, President
Ruth Palmer, Office Manager

Nova Scotia

Amherst & Area Chamber of Commerce
PO Box 283, Amherst NS B4H 3Z4 Canada
Tel: 902-667-8186; *Fax:* 902-667-2270
info@amherstchamber.ca
www.amherstchamber.ca
David McNarin, President
Debbie Allen, Staff

Antigonish Chamber of Commerce
21B James St., Antigonish NS B2G 1R6 Canada
Tel: 902-863-6308; *Fax:* 902-863-2656
contact@antigonishchamber.com
www.antigonishchamber.com

Barrington & Area Chamber of Commerce
PO Box 110, Barrington NS B0W 1E0 Canada
Tel: 902-637-2625; *Fax:* 902-637-2075
bcc@auracom.com
Wendy S. McGill, President
Debra Goreham, Staff

Bridgewater & Area Chamber of Commerce
PO Box 100, 200 North St., Bridgewater NS B4V 2W8 Canada
Tel: 902-543-4263; *Fax:* 902-527-1156
bacc@eastlink.ca
www.bridgewaterchamber.com
Ann O'Connell, Executive Director
Sandra Statton, President
Bernice Theriault, Secretary

Brier Island Chamber of Commerce
PO Box 74, Westport NS B0V 1H0 Canada
Tel: 902-839-2347; *Fax:* 902-839-2006
akicita@ns.sympatico.ca
Harold Graham, President
Joan Riday, Secretary

Central Annapolis Valley Chamber of Commerce
PO Box 395, 831 Main St., Kingston NS B0P 1R0 Canada
Tel: 902-765-0344; *Fax:* 902-765-0141
info@cavcoc.ca
www.cavcoc.ca
Affiliation(s): World Trade Centre

Chambre de commerce de Clare
CP 35, Pointe-de-l'Église NS B0W 1M0 Canada
Tél: 902-645-2368; *Téléc:* 902-645-2787
chambredecommerce@hotmail.com
www.commercedeclare.ca

Chester Municipal Chamber of Commerce
PO Box 831, #13, 4171 Hwy. 3, Chester NS B0J 1J0 Canada
Tel: 902-275-4709
info@chesterns.com
www.chesterns.com

East Hants & District Chamber of Commerce
PO Box 1053, Lantz NS B2S 3G6 Canada
Tel: 902-883-1010; *Fax:* 902-883-7862
info@ehcc.ca
www.ehcc.ca

Eastern Kings Chamber of Commerce (EKCC)
PO Box 314, Kentville NS B4N 3X1 Canada
Tel: 902-678-4634; *Fax:* 902-678-5448
ekccbob@ns.aliantzinc.ca
www.easternkingschamber.ns.ca

Fort Simpson Chamber of Commerce
PO Box 244, Fort Simpson NT X0E 0N0 Canada
Tel: 867-695-3555; *Fax:* 867-695-3313
commerce@fschamber.biz
www.fschamber.biz
Duncan Canvin, President

Fort Smith Chamber of Commerce
PO Box 121, Fort Smith NT X0E 0P0 Canada
Tel: 867-872-4213; *Fax:* 867-872-9450
Fred Daniels, Director

Halifax Chamber of Commerce
#200, 656 Windmill Rd., Dartmouth NS B3B 1B8 Canada
Tel: 902-468-7111; *Fax:* 902-468-7333
info@halifaxchamber.com
www.halifaxchamber.com
Social Media: www.facebook.com/halifaxchamberofcommerce
Valerie Payn, President
Jeff Forbes, Chair

Hay River Chamber of Commerce
10K Gagnier St., Hay River NT X0E 1G1 Canada
Tel: 867-874-2565; *Fax:* 867-874-3631
info@hayriverchamber.com
www.hayriverchamber.com
Brian Lefebvre, President

Mahone Bay & Area Chamber of Commerce
PO Box 59, Mahone Bay NS B0J 2E0 Canada
Tel: 902-624-6151; *Fax:* 902-624-6152
Toll-Free: 888-624-6151
info@mahonebay.com
www.mahonebay.com
Allan O'Brien, President
Ray Morin, Secretary
Marie Raymond, Staff

Norman Wells & District Chamber of Commerce
PO Box 400, Norman Wells NT X0E 0V0 Canada
Tel: 867-587-6609; *Fax:* 867-587-2865
Chris Buist, Contact

Northeast Highlands Chamber of Commerce
PO Box 125, Ingonish Beach NS B0C 1L0 Canada
Tel: 902-285-2289; *Fax:* 902-285-2285
alison.roper@pc.gc.ca
www.northeasthighlands.com
Walter Lauffer, President
Mary Sue Mackinnon, Staff
Ann Hussey, Secretary

Northumberland Central Chamber of Commerce
Lower Level, Northumberland Mall, 1111 Elgin St. West, Cobourg NS K9A 5H7 Canada
Tel: 905-372-5831; *Fax:* 905-372-2411
info@cobourgchamber.com
www.cobourgchamber.com
Publications: Chamber Spotlight, Business Directory

Pictou County Chamber of Commerce
East River Plaza, 980 East River Rd., New Glasgow NS B2H 3S5 Canada
Tel: 902-755-3463; *Fax:* 902-755-2848
info@pictouchamber.com
www.pictouchamber.com

Sheet Harbour & Area Chamber of Commerce
PO Box 239, Sheet Harbour NS B0J 3B0 Canada
Tel: 902-885-2595; *Fax:* 902-885-2708
shcoc@ns.sympatico.ca
coc.sheetharbour.ca

Shelburne & Area Chamber of Commerce
PO Box 1150, Shelburne NS B0T 1W0 Canada
Tel: 902-875-0224; *Fax:* 902-875-3214
info@shelburnechamber.com
www.shelburnechamber.com
Sam Stewart, President
Ron Chute, Secretary

South Queens Chamber of Commerce
PO Box 1378, Liverpool NS B0K 1K0 Canada
Tel: 902-354-4163; *Fax:* 902-354-7388
sqchambr@atcom.com
www.southqueenschamber.com

Springhill & Area Chamber of Commerce
PO Box 1030, Springhill NS B0M 1X0 Canada
Tel: 902-597-8462; *Fax:* 902-597-3839
audrey@surrette.com
Adrien Baillargeon, President
Carys Messinger, Secretary

Strait Area Chamber of Commerce
#2, 4 MacIntosh Ave., Port Hawkesbury NS B9A 3K5 Canada
Tel: 902-625-1588; *Fax:* 902-625-5985
straitareacoc@ns.sympatico.ca
www.straitchamber.ca
Affiliation(s): Atlantic Provinces Chamber of Commerce
Shannon MacDougall, Executive Director
Bob MacEachern, President

Sydney & Area Chamber of Commerce (SACC)
PO Box 131, 275 Charlotte Street, Sydney NS B1P 1C6 Canada
Tel: 902-564-6453; *Fax:* 902-539-7487
info@sydneyareachamber.ca
www.sydneyareachamber.ca
Anne Marie Singler, Executive Secretary

Truro & District Chamber of Commerce (TDCOC)
PO Box 54, 605 Prince St., Truro NS B2N 1G2 Canada
Tel: 902-895-6328; *Fax:* 902-897-6641
tdcoc@tru.eastlink.ca
www.trurochamber.com

West Hants Chamber of Commerce
PO Box 2188, Windsor NS B0N 2T0 Canada
Tel: 902-798-5106
info@whcc.ca
www.whcc.ca
Gordon Winstone, President
Richard Cole, Vice-President

Yarmouth & Area Chamber of Commerce (YCC)
PO Box 532, #205, 310 Forest St., Yarmouth NS B5A 4B4 Canada
Tel: 902-742-3074; *Fax:* 902-749-1383
info@yarmouthchamberofcommerce.com
www.yarmouthchamberofcommerce.com
Ken Wheelans, President
Chris Atwood, 1st Vice-President
Gurdeep Brar, 2nd Vice-President

Yellowknife Chamber of Commerce
#21, 4910 - 50th Ave., 3rd Fl., Yellowknife NT X1A 3S5 Canada
Tel: 867-920-4944; *Fax:* 867-920-4640
generalmanager@ykchamber.com
www.ykchamber.com

Ontario

1,000 Islands Gananoque Chamber of Commerce
10 King St. East, Gananoque ON K7G 1E6 Canada
Tel: 613-382-3250; *Fax:* 613-382-1585
Toll-Free: 800-561-1595
info@1000islandschamber.com
www.1000islandsgananoque.com
Affiliation(s): Travel Media Association of Canada

Aguasabon Chamber of Commerce
PO Box 695, Terrace Bay ON P0T 2W0 Canada
Tel: 807-825-4505; *Fax:* 807-825-9664
Toll-Free: 888-445-9999
info@sncfdc.com
John Lubberdink, Chair
Robert Kirkpatrick, Director

Alliston & District Chamber of Commerce
519 Victoria St. East, Alliston ON L9R 1K1 Canada
Tel: 705-435-7921; *Fax:* 705-435-0289
Toll-Free: 888-835-3092
info@adcc.ca
www.adcc.ca

Amherstburg Chamber of Commerce
PO Box 101, 268 Dalhousie St., Amherstburg ON N9V 2Z3 Canada
Tel: 519-736-2001; *Fax:* 519-736-9721
acoc@mnsi.net
www.amherstburgchamberofcommerce.ca
Ray Bezaire, President

Arthur & District Chamber of Commerce
PO Box 519, 146 George St., Arthur ON N0G 1A0 Canada
Tel: 519-848-5603; *Fax:* 519-848-5603
achamber@wightman.ca
Jamie Couper, President

Atikokan Chamber of Commerce
PO Box 997, Atikokan ON P0T 1C0 Canada
Tel: 807-597-1599; *Fax:* 807-597-2726
Toll-Free: 888-334-2332
info@atikokanchamber.com
www.atikokanchamber.com
Affiliation(s): Canadian Chamber of Commerce
Judi Nault, President
Nancy Jordan, Office Manager

Aurora Chamber of Commerce
#321, 6 - 14845 Yonge St., Aurora ON L4G 6H8 Canada
Tel: 905-727-7262; *Fax:* 905-841-6217
info@aurorachamber.on.ca
www.aurorachamber.on.ca

Bancroft & District Chamber of Commerce
PO Box 539, Bancroft ON K0L 1C0 Canada
Tel: 613-332-1513; *Fax:* 613-332-2119
chamber@commerce.bancroft.on.ca
www.commerce.bancroft.on.ca

Bayfield & Area Chamber of Commerce
PO Box 2065, Bayfield ON N0M 1G0 Canada
Tel: 519-565-2499; *Toll-Free:* 800-565-2499
info@villageofbayfield.com
www.villageofbayfield.com
Janet Snider, President

Beaverton District Chamber of Commerce
PO Box 29, Beaverton ON L0K 1A0 Canada
Tel: 705-426-2051
chamber@beavertononlakesimcoe.com
www.beavertononlakesimcoe.com
Affiliation(s): Ontario Chamber of Commerce

Belleville & District Chamber of Commerce (BCC)
PO Box 726, 5 East Moira St., Belleville ON K8N 5B3 Canada
Tel: 613-962-4597; *Fax:* 613-962-3911
Toll-Free: 888-852-9992
info@bellevillechamber.ca
www.bellevillechamber.ca

Blenheim & District Chamber of Commerce
PO Box 1089, c/o 127 Malborough St. North, Blenheim ON N0P 1A0 Canada
Tel: 519-676-6555; *Fax:* 519-676-2622

Blind River Chamber of Commerce (BRCC)
PO Box 998, Blind River ON P0R 1B0 Canada
Tel: 705-356-2555; *Fax:* 705-356-3911
Toll-Free: 800-563-8719
chamber@brchamber.ca
www.brchamber.ca
Affiliation(s): Algoma Kinniwabi Travel Association
Betty-Ann Dunbar, President

Blue Mountains Chamber of Commerce
PO Box 477, Thornbury ON N0H 2P0 Canada
Tel: 519-599-1200; *Fax:* 519-599-3971
info@bluemountainschamber.ca
www.bluemountainschamber.ca
George Matamoros, President

Bobcaygeon & Area Chamber of Commerce
PO Box 388, 21 Canal St. East, Bobcaygeon ON K0M 1A0 Canada
Tel: 705-738-2202; *Fax:* 705-738-1534
Toll-Free: 800-318-6173
chamber@bobcaygeon.org
www.bobcaygeon.org
Affiliation(s): Kawartha Lakes Associated Chambers of Commerce

Bracebridge Chamber of Commerce
#1, 1 Manitoba St., Bracebridge ON P1L 2A8 Canada
Tel: 705-645-5231; *Fax:* 705-645-7592
chamber@bracebridgechamber.com
www.bracebridgechamber.com

Bradford & District Chamber of Commerce (BDCC)
PO Box 59, 100 Dissette St., Bradford ON L3Z 2A7 Canada
Tel: 905-775-3037; *Fax:* 905-775-6357
info@bradfordchamber.on.ca

Brighton & District Chamber of Commerce
PO Box 880, 74 Main Street, Brighton ON K0K 1H0 Canada
Tel: 613-475-2775; *Fax:* 613-475-3777
Toll-Free: 877-475-2775
info@brightonchamber.ca
www.brightonchamber.ca
George Lucas, Administrator

Brockville & District Chamber of Commerce
#1, 3 Market St. West, Brockville ON K6V 7L2 Canada
Tel: 613-342-6553; *Fax:* 613-342-6849
info@brockvillechamber.com
www.brockvillechamber.com

Burlington Chamber of Commerce
#201, 414 Locust St., Burlington ON L7S 1T7 Canada
Tel: 905-639-0174; *Fax:* 905-333-3956
info@burlingtonchamber.com
www.burlingtonchamber.com

Caledon Chamber of Commerce
PO Box 626, Bolton ON L7E 5T5 Canada
Tel: 905-857-7393; *Fax:* 905-857-7405
Toll-Free: 888-599-9967
info@caledonchamber.com
www.caledonchamber.com
Affiliation(s): Canadian Chamber of Commerce; Ontario Chamber of Commerce
Kelly Darnley, President/CEO
Linda Bond, Chair

Caledonia Regional Chamber of Commerce
PO Box 2035, 1 Grand Trunk Lane, Caledonia ON N3W 2G6 Canada
Tel: 905-765-0377; *Fax:* 905-765-6730
crcc@mountaincable.net
www.caledonia-ontario.com
Barb Martindale, Executive Director

Cambridge Chamber of Commerce
750 Hespler Rd., Cambridge ON N3H 5L8 Canada
Tel: 519-622-2221; *Fax:* 519-622-0177
cchamber@cambridgechamber.com
www.cambridgechamber.com

Carleton Place & District Chamber of Commerce
132 Coleman St., Carleton Place ON K7C 4M7 Canada
Tel: 613-257-1976; *Fax:* 613-257-8170
manager@cpchamber.com
www.cpchamber.com

Cayuga & District Chamber of Commerce
PO Box 118, 6 Cayuga St. North, Cayuga ON N0A 1E0 Canada
Tel: 905-772-5954; *Fax:* 905-772-2680
info@cayugachamber.ca
www.cayugachamber.ca
Bernadine Tompkins, President

Central Bruce Peninsula Chamber of Commerce
c/o Tourist Information Center, 2866 Hwy. 6, Wiarton ON N0H 2TO Canada
Tel: 519-793-3178; *Fax:* 519-793-3296
info@centralbrucepeninsula.ca
www.centralbrucepeninsula.ca
Affiliation(s): Bruce Peninsula Tourism Association; Ontario Chamber of Commerce; Bruce County Tourism; Tobermory & District Chamber of Commerce; South Bruce Peninsula Chamber of Commerce; Sauble Beach Chamber of Commerce
Publications: Business Information Guide, Central Bruce Peninsula Chamber of Commerce Newsletter

Centre Wellington Chamber of Commerce
400 Tower St. South, Fergus ON N1M 2P7 Canada
Tel: 519-843-5140; *Fax:* 519-787-0983
Toll-Free: 877-242-6353
chamber@ferguselora.com
www.ferguselora.com
Affiliation(s): Canadian Chamber of Commerce

Chamber of Commerce of Brantford & Brant (BRCC)
PO Box 1294, 77 Charlotte St., Brantford ON N3T 5T6 Canada
Tel: 519-753-2617; *Fax:* 519-753-0921
chamber@brcc.ca
www.brcc.ca
Charlene Nicholson, Chief Executive Officer

Chatham-Kent Chamber of Commerce
54 Fourth St., Chatham ON N7M 2G2 Canada
Tel: 519-352-7540; *Fax:* 519-352-8741
info@chatham-kentchamber.ca
www.chatham-kentchamber.ca

Chesley & District Chamber of Commerce
PO Box 406, 112 - 1st Ave. South, Chesley ON N0G 1L0 Canada
Tel: 519-363-9837; *Fax:* 519-363-9838
cdcc@bmts.com
www.townofchesley.com
Stacy Charlton, Treasurer

Cobourg & District Chamber of Commerce
Northumberland Mall, 1111 Elgin St. West, Cobourg ON K9A 5H7 Canada
Tel: 905-372-5831; *Fax:* 905-372-2411
info@cobourgchamber.com
www.cobourgchamber.com

Collingwood Chamber of Commerce
PO Box 36, 25 Second St., Collingwood ON L9Y 1E4 Canada
Tel: 705-445-0221; *Fax:* 705-445-6858
info@collingwoodchamber.com
www.collingwoodchamber.com
Affiliation(s): Canadian Chamber of Commerce; Ontario Chamber of Commerce

Cornwall Chamber of Commerce
Commerce Court, #100, 113 Second St. East, Cornwall ON K6H 1Y5 Canada
Tel: 613-933-4004; *Fax:* 613-933-8466
www.cornwallchamber.com

Dryden District Chamber of Commerce (DDCC)
284 Government St., Dryden ON P8N 2P3 Canada
Tel: 807-223-2622; *Fax:* 807-223-2626
Toll-Free: 800-667-0935
chamber@mail.drytel.net
www.drydenchamber.ca
Affiliation(s): Sunset County Travel Association; Patricia Regional Tourist Council; Kenora District Camp Owners Association

Dunnville Chamber of Commerce
PO Box 124, 231 Chestnut St., Dunnville ON N1A 2X1 Canada
Tel: 905-774-3183; *Fax:* 905-774-9281
chamberofcommerce@mountaincable.net
www.dunnvillechamberofcommerce.ca

East Gwillimbury Chamber of Commerce
PO Box 199, 1590 Queensville Side Rd., Queensville ON L0G 1R0 Canada
Tel: 905-478-8447; *Fax:* 905-478-8786
info@egcoc.org
www.egcoc.org
Cindy Thiele, President

Eastern Ottawa Chamber of Commerce
#310, 2183 Ogilvie Rd., Gloucester ON K1J 1C8 Canada
Tel: 613-745-3578; *Fax:* 613-745-8575
info@easternottawa.com
www.easternottawa.com

Elliot Lake & District Chamber of Commerce
PO Box 81, Elliot Lake ON P5A 2J6 Canada
Tel: 705-848-3974; *Fax:* 705-848-7121
elchamber@onlink.net
www.elliotlakechamber.com

Emo Chamber of Commerce
PO Box 476, Emo ON P0W 1E0 Canada
Tel: 807-482-1811; *Fax:* 807-482-1813
vennechenko@sympatico.ca
www.twspemo.on.ca/chamber.html
Colleen Vennechenko, Contact
Paul Kyro, NOACC Representative
Dave Goodman, Vice-President

Englehart & District Chamber of Commerce
PO Box 171, Englehart ON P0J 1H0 Canada
Tel: 705-544-8580; *Fax:* 705-544-1964
deacon@ntl.sympatico.ca

Espanola & District Chamber of Commerce
30 McCulloch, Espanola ON P5E 1J1 Canada
Tel: 705-869-3351; *Fax:* 705-869-4601
rbheale@cyberbeach.net
Rob Heale, Contact

Fenelon Falls & District Chamber of Commerce
PO Box 28, 15 Oak St., Fenelon Falls ON K0M 1N0 Canada
Tel: 705-887-3409; *Fax:* 705-887-6912
info@fenelonfallschamber.com
www.fenelonfallschamber.com

Flamborough Chamber of Commerce (FCC)
PO Box 1030, Waterdown ON L0R 2H0 Canada
Tel: 905-689-7650; *Fax:* 905-689-1313
admin@flamboroughchamber.ca
www.flamboroughchamber.ca
Affiliation(s): Ontario & Canadian Chamber of Commerce

Fort Frances Chamber of Commerce
474 Scott St., Fort Frances ON P9A 1H2 Canada
Tel: 807-274-5773; *Fax:* 807-274-8706
Toll-Free: 800-820-3678
thefort@nwonet.net
www.fortfranceschamber.com
Affiliation(s): Ontario Chamber of Commerce; Canadian Chamber of Commerce

Georgina Chamber of Commerce
22937 Woodbine Ave., RR#2, Keswick ON L4P 3E9 Canada
Tel: 905-476-7870; *Fax:* 905-476-6700
Toll-Free: 888-436-7446
admin@georginachamber.com
www.georginachamber.com
Christine Thomas, General Manager
Dan Fellini, President

Geraldton & District Chamber of Commerce
PO Box 128, Geraldton ON P0T 1M0 Canada
Tel: 807-854-1925
ddumont42@sympatico.ca
www.gdcc-on.ca
Stephane Parent, President
Gerard Dufour, Secretary
Katherine Russwurm, NOACC Representative

Goderich & District Chamber of Commerce
56 East St., Goderich ON N7A 1N3 Canada
Tel: 519-440-0176; *Fax:* 519-440-0305
info@goderichchamber.ca
www.goderichchamber.ca

Gogama Chamber of Commerce
PO Box 73, 59 Poupore St., Gogama ON P0M 1W0 Canada
Tel: 705-894-2111
gogamachamber@vianet.ca
Eija MacDonald, Chair

Grand Bend & Area Chamber of Commerce
PO Box 248, #1, 81 Crescent St., Grand Bend ON N0M 1T0 Canada
Tel: 519-238-2001; *Fax:* 519-238-5201
Toll-Free: 888-338-2001
info@grandbendtourism.com
www.grandbendtourism.com

Gravenhurst Chamber of Commerce/Visitors Bureau
#685, 2 Muskoka Rd. North, Gravenhurst ON P1P 1N5 Canada
Tel: 705-687-4432; *Fax:* 705-687-4382
info@gravenhurstchamber.com
www.gravenhurstchamber.com

Greater Arnprior Chamber of Commerce (GACC)
PO Box 213, 16 Edward St., Arnprior ON K7S 3H2 Canada
Tel: 613-623-6817; *Fax:* 613-623-6826
arnpriorchamberofcommerce@bellnet.ca
www.gacc.ca
Lori Martin, Administrative Assistant
Joan Carey, President

Greater Barrie Chamber of Commerce
97 Toronto St., Barrie ON L4N 1V1 Canada
Tel: 705-721-5000; *Fax:* 705-726-0973
chadmin@barriechamber.com
www.barriechamber.com

Greater Dufferin Area Chamber of Commerce
PO Box 101, Hwy. 10, Orangeville ON L9W 2Z5 Canada
Tel: 519-941-0490; *Fax:* 519-941-0492
info@gdacc.ca
www.gdacc.ca
Affiliation(s): Ontario Chamber of Commerce; Canadian Chamber of Commerce

Greater Fort Erie Chamber of Commerce
#1, 660 Garrison Rd., Fort Erie ON L2A 6E2 Canada
Tel: 905-871-3803; *Fax:* 905-871-1561
info@forteriechamber.com
www.forteriechamber.com

Greater Innisfil Chamber of Commerce (GICC)
7896 Yonge St., Innisfil ON L9S 1L5 Canada
Tel: 705-431-4199; *Fax:* 705-431-8020
Toll-Free: 866-575-0008
info@innisfilchamber.com
www.innisfilchamber.com
Affiliation(s): Alcona Business Association; South Innisfil Business & Community Association; Cookstown Chamber of Commerce; 400 Industrial Group

Greater Kingston Chamber of Commerce (GKCC)
67 Brock St., Kingston ON K7L 1R8 Canada
Tel: 613-548-4453; *Fax:* 613-548-4743
bob@kingstonchamber.on.ca
www.kingstonchamber.on.ca

Greater Kitchener & Waterloo Chamber of Commerce
PO Box 2367, 80 Queen St. North, Kitchener ON N2H 6L4 Canada
Tel: 519-576-5000; *Fax:* 519-742-4760
Toll-Free: 888-672-4282
admin@greaterkwchamber.com
www.greaterkwchamber.com

Greater Nepean Chamber of Commerce
#1175, 2720 Queensview Dr., Ottawa ON K2B 1A5 Canada
Tel: 613-828-5556; *Fax:* 613-828-8022
info@nepeanchamber.com
www.nepeanchamber.com

Greater Oshawa Chamber of Commerce
#100, 44 Richmond St. West, Oshawa ON L1G 1C7 Canada
Tel: 905-728-1683; *Fax:* 905-432-1259
info@oshawachamber.com
www.oshawachamber.com
Affiliation(s): Ontario Chamber of Commerce; Canadian Chamber of Commerce

Greater Peterborough Chamber of Commerce (GPCC)
175 George St. North, Peterborough ON K9J 3G6 Canada
Tel: 705-748-9771; *Fax:* 705-743-2331
Toll-Free: 887-640-4037
info@peterboroughchamber.ca
www.peterboroughinfo.com

Greater Sudbury Chamber of Commerce / Chambre de commerce du Grand Sudbury
#1, 40 Elm St., Sudbury ON P3C 1S8 Canada
Tel: 705-673-7133; *Fax:* 705-673-2944
cofc@sudburychamber.ca
www.sudburychamber.ca

Grimsby & District Chamber of Commerce
424 South Service Rd., RR#2, Grimsby ON L3M 4E8 Canada
Tel: 905-945-8319; *Fax:* 905-945-1615
info@grimsbychamber.com
www.grimsbychamber.com

Guelph Chamber of Commerce (GCC)
PO Box 1268, #15, 485 Silvercreek Pkwy. North, Guelph ON N1H 6N6 Canada
Tel: 519-822-8081; *Fax:* 519-822-8451
chamber@guelphchamber.com
www.guelphchamber.com
Affiliation(s): Guelph Business Enterprise Centre; Guelph Partnership for Innovation

Hagersville & District Chamber of Commerce
PO Box 1090, 24 Parkview Rd., Hagersville ON N0A 1H0 Canada
Tel: 905-768-3384

Haliburton Highlands Chamber of Commerce
PO Box 147, 5 Bobcaygeon Rd., Minden ON K0M 2K0 Canada
Tel: 705-286-7160; *Fax:* 705-286-6016
Toll-Free: 877-811-6111
admin@hhchamber.on.ca
www.hhchamber.on.ca
Social Media:
www.facebook.com/people/Chamber-Staff/100000476011254

Halton Hills Chamber of Commerce
328 Guelph St., Halton Hills ON L7G 4B5 Canada
Tel: 905-877-7119; *Fax:* 905-877-5117
info@haltonhillschamber.on.ca
www.haltonhillschamber.on.ca

Hamilton Chamber of Commerce (HCC)
555 Bay St. North, Hamilton ON L8L 1H1 Canada
Tel: 905-522-1151; *Fax:* 905-522-1154
hdcc@hamiltonchamber.on.ca
www.hamiltonchamber.on.ca

Hanover Chamber of Commerce
#1, 214 - 10th St., Hanover ON N4N 1N7 Canada
Tel: 519-364-5777; *Fax:* 519-364-6949
koelschlagel@bdo.ca

Harrow & Colchester Chamber of Commerce
PO Box 888, Harrow ON N0R 1G0 Canada
Tel: 519-974-3200; *Fax:* 519-974-2222
chamber@harrowchamber.ca
www.harrowchamber.ca
Ginger Cooke, President

Havelock, Belmont, Methuen Chamber of Commerce
PO Box 779, Havelock ON K0L 1Z0 Canada
Tel: 705-778-2182; *Fax:* 705-778-2444
info@havelockchamber.com
www.havelockchamber.com
Rae McCutcheon, Secretary

Hawkesbury Chamber of Commerce / Chambre de Commerce de Hawkesbury
PO Box 36, 2 John St., Hawkesbury ON K6A 2R4 Canada
Tel: 613-632-8066; *Fax:* 613-632-3324
info@hcoc.ca
www.hcoc.ca
Richard Denis, President
Sylvain Labrie, Secretary-Treasurer

Hearst, Mattice - Val Côté Chamber of Commerce
PO Box 987, 523 Hwy. 11 East, Hearst ON P0L 1N0 Canada
Tel: 705-372-2838; *Fax:* 705-372-2840
Toll-Free: 800-655-5769
hearstcoc@hearst.ca
www.hearstcoc.com
Ghislain Jacques, President

Ingersoll District Chamber of Commerce
132 Thames St. South, Ingersoll ON N5C 2T4 Canada
Tel: 519-485-7333; *Fax:* 519-485-6606
info@ingersollchamber.com
www.ingersollchamber.com

Iroquois Falls & District Chamber of Commerce
PO Box 840, 727 Synagogue Ave., Iroquois Falls ON P0K 1G0 Canada
Tel: 705-232-4656
ifchamber@hotmail.com
www.iroquoisfallschamber.com

Kawartha Lakes Chamber of Commerce
Eastern Region, PO Box 537, 12 Queen St., Lakefield ON K0L 2H0 Canada
Tel: 705-652-6963; *Fax:* 705-652-9140
Toll-Free: 888-565-8888
info@kawarthachamber.ca
www.kawarthachamber.ca

Kenora & District Chamber of Commerce
PO Box 471, Kenora ON P9N 3X5 Canada
Tel: 807-467-4646; *Fax:* 807-468-3056
kenorachamber@kmts.ca
www.kenorachamber.com
Laurene Manson-Sillery, Chamber Manager

Kincardine & District Chamber of Commerce
PO Box 115, Kincardine ON N2Z 2Y6 Canada
Tel: 519-396-9333; *Fax:* 519-396-5529
kincardine.cofc@bmts.com
www.kincardinechamber.com

Kirkland Lake District Chamber of Commerce (KLCC)
PO Box 966, 400 Government Rd. West, Kirkland Lake ON P2N 3N1 Canada
Tel: 705-567-5444; *Fax:* 705-567-1666
klcofc@ntl.sympatico.ca
kirklandlakechamber.com
Affiliation(s): Ontario Chamber of Commerce

The Land of Nipigon Chamber of Commerce
PO Box 760, 22 Third Street, Nipigon ON P0T 2J0 Canada
Tel: 807-887-0740; *Fax:* 807-887-5117
Toll-Free: 877-596-1359
nipigonchamber@vianet.ca
www.nipigon.net
Judi Bernard, President
Rebecca Lawrence, Director

Leamington District Chamber of Commerce
PO Box 321, 21 Talbot St., Leamington ON N8H 1L1 Canada
Tel: 519-326-2721; *Fax:* 519-326-3204
christinec@leamingtonchamber.com
www.leamingtonchamber.com

Lincoln Chamber of Commerce
4800 South Service Rd., Beamsville ON L0R 1B0 Canada
Tel: 905-563-5044; *Fax:* 905-563-7098
lcoc@vaxxine.com
www.lincolnchamber.ca
Cathy McNiven, General Manager

London Chamber of Commerce
#101, 244 Pall Mall St., London ON N6A 5P6 Canada
Tel: 519-432-7551; *Fax:* 519-432-8063
gerry@londonchamber.com
www.londonchamber.com

Longlac Chamber of Commerce
PO Box 877, 112 Hamel Ave., Longlac ON P0T 1A0 Canada
Tel: 807-876-2273; *Fax:* 807-876-2575
Lorraine Gagnon, Contact
Wayne Morris, President

Lucknow & District Chamber of Commerce
PO Box 313, Lucknow ON N0G 2H0 Canada
Tel: 519-528-2099

Lyndhurst Seeleys Bay & District Chamber of Commerce
PO Box 89, RR#1, Lyndhurst ON K0E 1N0 Canada
Tel: 613-387-3847
info@lyndhurstseeleysbaychamber.com
www.lyndhurstseeleysbaychamber.com

Charlie Kellington, President
Charles Shaw, Treasurer

Manitoulin Chamber of Commerce
PO Box 307, 6062 Hwy. 542, Mindemoya ON P0P 1S0 Canada
Tel: 705-377-7501; *Fax:* 705-377-7501
Toll-Free: 800-698-6681
office@manitoulinchamber.com
www.manitoulinchamber.com
Bob Taylor, President

Manitouwadge Chamber of Commerce
PO Box 2030, 1 Mississauga Dr., Manitouwadge ON P0T 2C0 Canada
Tel: 807-826-3227; *Fax:* 807-826-4592

Marathon Chamber of Commerce
PO Box 988, Marathon ON P0T 2E0 Canada
Tel: 807-229-3100; *Fax:* 807-229-1486
Affiliation(s): Northwestern Ontario Associated Chambers of Commerce
Bob Hancherow, Contact
George Macey, NOACC Representative

Markdale Chamber of Commerce
PO Box 177, 19 Toronto St. North, Markdale ON N0C 1H0 Canada
Tel: 519-986-4612; *Fax:* 519-986-4612
Toll-Free: 888-986-4612
markdalechamber@cablerocket.com
www.village.markdale.on.ca

Maryborough Chamber of Commerce
PO Box 143, Moorefield ON N0G 2K0 Canada
Tel: 519-638-2971
dcraven@wightman.net

Meaford & District Chamber of Commerce
PO Box 4836, 16 Trowbridge St. West, Meaford ON N4L 1X6 Canada
Tel: 519-538-1640; *Fax:* 519-538-5493
Toll-Free: 877-538-1640
info@mdcc.ca
www.mdcc.ca

Milton Chamber of Commerce
#104, 251 Main St., Milton ON L9T 1P1 Canada
Tel: 905-878-0581; *Fax:* 905-878-4972
info@chamber.milton.on.ca
www.chamber.milton.on.ca
Sandy Martin, Executive Director

Minto Chamber of Commerce
PO Box 864, Harriston ON N0G 1Z0 Canada
Tel: 519-327-9619
info@mintochamber.on.ca
www.mintochamber.on.ca
John Burgess, President

Mount Forest District Chamber of Commerce
514 Main St. North, Mount Forest ON N0G 2L0 Canada
Tel: 519-323-4480; *Fax:* 519-323-1557
mfchamber@wightman.ca
www.mountforest.ca

Muskoka Lakes Chamber of Commerce
PO Box 536, 3181 Muskoka Rd. 169, Bala ON P0C 1A0 Canada
Tel: 705-762-5663; *Fax:* 705-762-5664
info@muskokalakeschamber.com
www.muskokalakeschamber.com
Tracy Owen, President
Jane Templeton, Manager

Napanee & District Chamber of Commerce
Napanee Business Centre, 47 Dundas St. East, Napanee ON K7R 1H7 Canada
Tel: 613-354-6601; *Fax:* 613-354-6848
Toll-Free: 877-354-6601
info@napaneechamber.ca
www.napaneechamber.ca
Dan Atkinson, President

Newmarket Chamber of Commerce
470 Davis Dr., Newmarket ON L3Y 2P3 Canada
Tel: 905-898-5900; *Fax:* 905-853-7271
info@newmarketchamber.com
www.newmarketchamber.com
Social Media: www.twitter.com/NewmarktChamber

Niagara Falls Chamber of Commerce
4056 Dorchester Rd., Niagara Falls ON L2E 6M9 Canada
Tel: 905-374-3666; *Fax:* 905-374-2972
info@niagarafallschamber.com
www.niagarafallschamber.com

Niagara on the Lake Chamber of Commerce
PO Box 1043, 26 Queen St., Niagara-on-the-Lake ON L0S 1J0 Canada
Tel: 905-468-1950; *Fax:* 905-468-4930
tourism@niagaraonthelake.com
www.niagaraonthelake.com

North Bay & District Chamber of Commerce
PO Box 747, 1375 Seymour St., North Bay ON P1B 8J8 Canada
Tel: 705-472-8480; *Fax:* 705-472-8027
Toll-Free: 888-249-8998
nbcc@northbaychamber.com
www.northbaychamber.com

North Grenville Chamber of Commerce
PO Box 1047, 5 Clothier St. East, Kemptville ON K0G 1J0 Canada
Tel: 613-258-4838; *Fax:* 613-258-3801
info@northgrenvillechamber.com
www.northgrenvillechamber.com

North Perth Chamber of Commerce
580 Main St., Listowel ON N4W 1A8 Canada
Tel: 519-291-1551; *Fax:* 519-291-4151
info@npchamber.com
www.npchamber.com

Northwestern Ontario Associated Chambers of Commerce (NOACC)
#102, 200 Syndicate Ave. South, Thunder Bay ON P7E 1C9 Canada
Tel: 807-624-2626; *Fax:* 807-622-7752
chamber@tb-chamber.on.ca
www.tb-chamber.on.ca
Affiliation(s): Ontario Chamber of Commerce

Oakville Chamber of Commerce
2521 Wyecroft Rd., Oakville ON L6L 6P8 Canada
Tel: 905-845-6613; *Fax:* 905-845-6475
inquiries@oakvillechamber.com
www.oakvillechamber.com
John Sawyer, President

Orillia & District Chamber of Commerce
150 Front St. South, Orillia ON L3V 4S7 Canada
Tel: 705-326-4424; *Fax:* 705-327-7841
orilinfo@orillia.com
www.orillia.com
Affiliation(s): Canadian Chamber of Commerce
Susan Lang, Managing Director

Orléans Chamber of Commerce / Chambre de commerce d'Orléans
2276A, boul St-Joseph, Orleans ON K1C 1E8 Canada
Tel: 613-824-9137; *Fax:* 613-824-0090
contact@orleanschamber.ca
www.orleanschamber.ca
Affiliation(s): National Capital Business Alliance

Oro-Medonte Chamber of Commerce
PO Box 100, 148 Line 7 South, Oro ON L0L 2X0 Canada
Tel: 705-487-7337; *Fax:* 705-487-0133
info@oromedontecc.com
www.oromedontecc.com
Carol Benedetti, Administrative Coordinator
Rick Dory, President
Anna Proctor, Vice-President
Bruce Chappell, Treasurer
Publications: Business / Membership Directory, Chamber Newsletter, Oro-Medonte Guide Map, North Simcoe Community News

Ottawa Chamber of Commerce (OCC)
1701 Woodward Dr., #LL-20, Ottawa ON K2C 0R4 Canada
Tel: 613-236-3631; *Fax:* 613-236-7498
info@ottawachamber.ca
www.ottawachamber.ca
Gail Logan, President

Owen Sound & District Chamber of Commerce
PO Box 1028, Owen Sound ON N4K 6K6 Canada
Tel: 519-376-6261; *Fax:* 519-376-5647
bert@oschamber.com
www.oschamber.com
David Moyer, President
Joanne Horton, Vice President

Paris Chamber of Commerce
c/o Williams Brant County Power, 65 Dundas St. East, Paris ON N3L 3H1 Canada
Tel: 519-758-5095
sinjsswint@rogers.com
www.pariscoc.ca
Tracey Palmer, President

Bryan Maude, President

Perth & District Chamber of Commerce
34 Herriott St., Perth ON K7H 1T2 Canada
Tel: 613-267-3200; *Fax:* 613-267-6797
Toll-Free: 888-319-3204
welcome@perthchamber.com
www.perthchamber.com
Social Media: www.twitter.com/perthchamber
Affiliation(s): Canadian Chamber of Commerce; Ontario Chamber of Commerce

Pointe-au-Baril Chamber of Commerce
PO Box 67, Pointe-au-Baril-Station ON P0G 1K0 Canada
Tel: 705-366-2331; *Fax:* 705-366-2331
info@pointeaubarilchamber.com
www.pointeaubarilchamber.com
Affiliation(s): Rainbow County Travel Association

Port Colborne-Wainfleet Chamber of Commerce
76 Main St. West, Port Colborne ON L3K 3V2 Canada
Tel: 905-834-9765; *Fax:* 905-834-1542
office@pcwchamber.com
www.pcwchamber.com

Port Hope & District Chamber of Commerce
58 Queen St., Port Hope ON L1A 3Z9 Canada
Tel: 905-885-5519; *Fax:* 905-885-1142
info@porthopechamber.com
www.porthopechamber.com

Prescott & District Chamber of Commerce
PO Box 2000, Prescott ON K0E 1T0 Canada
Tel: 613-925-2171; *Fax:* 613-925-4381
prescottchamber@xplornet.com
www.prescottanddistrictchamber.com

Prince Edward County Chamber of Tourism & Commerce (PECCTAC)
116 Main St., Picton ON K0K 2T0 Canada
Tel: 613-476-2421; *Fax:* 613-476-7461
Toll-Free: 800-640-4717
pec@reach.net
www.pecchamber.com

Quinte West Chamber of Commerce
97 Front St., Trenton ON K8V 4N6 Canada
Tel: 613-392-7635; *Fax:* 613-392-8400
Toll-Free: 800-930-3255
info@quintewestchamber.on.ca
www.quintewestchamber.on.ca
Suzanne Andrews, Manager

Rainy River & District Chamber of Commerce
PO Box 458, Rainy River ON P0W 1L0 Canada
Tel: 807-852-3343
www.rainyriver.ca/chamber
Susan Carpenter, President

Ramara & District Chamber of Commerce
PO Box 144, 2304 Highway 12, Brechin ON L0K 1B0 Canada
Tel: 705-484-2141; *Fax:* 705-484-0161
info@ramarachamber.com
www.ramarachamber.com
Walt Meyers, President

Red Lake Chamber of Commerce
PO Box 430, Red Lake ON P0V 2M0 Canada
Tel: 807-727-3722; *Fax:* 807-727-3285
chamber@goredlake.com

Renfrew & Area Chamber of Commerce
161 Raglan St. South, Renfrew ON K7V 1R2 Canada
Tel: 613-432-7015; *Fax:* 613-432-8645

Richmond Hill Chamber of Commerce (RHCOC)
376 Church St. South, Richmond Hill ON L4C 9V8 Canada
Tel: 905-884-1961; *Fax:* 905-884-1962
info@rhcoc.com
www.rhcoc.com
Affiliation(s): Toronto Board of Trade

Rideau Chamber of Commerce
PO Box 247, Manotick ON K4M 1A3 Canada
Tel: 613-692-6262; *Fax:* 613-822-4687
info@rideauchamber.com
www.rideauchamber.com
Affiliation(s): Ontario Chamber of Commerce

Ridgetown & District Chamber of Commerce
37 Main St. East, Ridgetown ON N0P 2C0 Canada
Tel: 519-674-0802; *Fax:* 519-674-0802
ridgetownchamber@sympatico.ca
www.ridgetown.com
Charlie Mitton, President
Sandra Dorner, General Manager

St Catharines-Thorold Chamber of Commerce
PO Box 940, #103, 1 St. Paul St., St Catharines ON L2R 6Z4 Canada
Tel: 905-684-2361; *Fax:* 905-684-2100
info@scchamberofcommerce.com
www.scthamber.com
Walter Sendzik, Executive Vice President

St. Catherine's-Thorold Chamber of Commerce
PO Box 940, #103, 1 St. Paul St., St Catharines ON L2R 36Z4 Canada
Tel: 905-684-2361; *Fax:* 905-684-2100
info@scchamberofcommerce.com
www.thoroldchamber.com, www.sctchamber.com

St Thomas & District Chamber of Commerce
555 Talbot St., St Thomas ON N5P 1C5 Canada
Tel: 519-631-1981; *Fax:* 519-631-0466
mail@stthomaschamber.on.ca
www.stthomaschamber.on.ca
Affiliation(s): Ontario Chamber of Commerce; Canadian Chamber of Commerce

Sarnia Lambton Chamber of Commerce
556 North Christina St., Sarnia ON N7T 5W6 Canada
Tel: 519-336-2400; *Fax:* 519-336-2085
info@sarnialambtonchamber.com
www.sarnialambtonchamber.com

Sauble Beach Chamber of Commerce
General Delivery, Sauble Beach ON N0H 2G0 Canada
Tel: 519-422-1262
info@saublebeach.com
www.saublebeach.com

Saugeen Shores Chamber Office
559 Goderich St., Port Elgin ON N0H 2C4 Canada
Tel: 519-832-2332; *Fax:* 519-389-3725
Toll-Free: 800-387-3456
portelgininfo@saugeenshores.ca
www.saugeenshores.ca

Sault Ste Marie Chamber of Commerce (SSMCOC)
334 Bay St., Sault Ste Marie ON P6A 1X1 Canada
Tel: 705-949-7152; *Fax:* 705-759-8166
comments@ssmcoc.com
www.ssmcoc.com

Scarborough Chamber of Commerce (SCC)
940 Progress Ave., Toronto ON M1G 3T5 Canada
Tel: 416-439-4140; *Fax:* 416-439-4147
gbailey@bot.com
www.bot.com

Scugog Chamber of Commerce
PO Box 1282, #G1, 181 Perry St., Port Perry ON L9L 1A7 Canada
Tel: 905-985-4971; *Fax:* 905-985-7698
info@scugogchamber.ca
www.scugogchamber.ca
Affiliation(s): Joint Chambers of Durham Region; Durham Network for Excellence; Tourism Durham; Tourist Association of Durham Region; Durham Home & Small Business Association

Simcoe & District Chamber of Commerce
95 Queensway West, Chamber Plaza, Simcoe ON N3Y 2M8 Canada
Tel: 519-426-5867; *Fax:* 519-428-7718
chamber@simcoechamber.on.ca
www.simcoechamber.on.ca

Sioux Lookout Chamber of Commerce
PO Box 577, 11 First Ave. South, Sioux Lookout ON P8T 1A8 Canada
Tel: 807-737-1937; *Fax:* 807-737-1778
chamber@siouxlookout.com
www.siouxlookout.com

South Bruce Peninsula Chamber of Commerce
PO Box 68, Wiarton ON N0H 2T0 Canada
Tel: 519-534-4009
info@wiartonchamber.ca
www.sbpcc.org
Affiliation(s): Wiarton BIA

South Dundas Chamber of Commerce
PO Box 288, Morrisburg ON K0C 1X0 Canada
Tel: 613-543-3443; *Fax:* 613-652-4120
info@southdundaschamber.com
sdcc.southdundas.com

South Huron Chamber of Commerce
PO Box 550, 414 Main St. South, Exeter ON N0M 1S6 Canada
Tel: 519-235-4520; *Fax:* 519-235-3141
office@shcc.on.ca
www.shcc.on.ca
Hugh McMaster, President

South Stormont Chamber of Commerce
PO Box 489, Ingleside ON K0C 1M0 Canada
Tel: 613-537-8344; *Fax:* 613-537-9439
info@sscc.on.ca
www.sscc.on.ca
Lesley O'Gorman, President

Southeast Georgian Bay Chamber of Commerce
PO Box 70, 99 Lone Pine Rd., Port Severn ON L0K 1S0 Canada
Tel: 705-756-4863
info@segbay.ca
www.segbay.ca
Marianne Braid, Manager

Southern Georgian Bay Chamber of Commerce / Chambre de Commerce de la Baie Georgienne Sud
208 King St., Midland ON L4R 4C9 Canada
Tel: 705-526-7884; *Fax:* 705-526-1744
info@sgbchamber.ca
www.southerngeorgianbay.on.ca
Social Media: twitter.com/sgbchamber

Stoney Creek Chamber of Commerce
21 Mountain Ave. South, Stoney Creek ON L8G 2V5 Canada
Tel: 905-664-4000; *Fax:* 905-664-7228
sccc@bellnet.ca
www.chamberstoneycreek.com
David Cage, Executive Director

Stratford & District Chamber of Commerce
55 Lorne Ave. East, Stratford ON N5A 6S4 Canada
Tel: 519-273-5250; *Fax:* 519-273-2229
info@stratfordchamber.com
www.stratfordchamber.com
Affiliation(s): Chamber of Commerce Executives of Canada

Tavistock Chamber of Commerce
PO Box 670, Tavistock ON N0B 2R0 Canada
Tel: 519-655-2277
b&croutly@rogers.com

Temagami & District Chamber of Commerce
PO Box 57, Stn. T, 7 Lakeshore Dr., Temagami ON P0H 2H0 Canada
Tel: 705-569-3344; *Fax:* 705-569-2834
Toll-Free: 800-661-7609
cofc@temagami.ca
www.temagamiinformation.com
Ann Richmond, Office Manager
Hendrika Krygsman, President

Thunder Bay Chamber of Commerce (TBCC)
#102, 200 Syndicate Ave. South, Thunder Bay ON P7E 1C9 Canada
Tel: 807-624-2626; *Fax:* 807-622-7752
chamber@tb-chamber.on.ca
www.tb-chamber.on.ca
Affiliation(s): Northwestern Ontario Associated Chambers of Commerce; Ontario Chamber of Commerce; Canadian Chamber of Commerce

Tilbury & District Chamber of Commerce
PO Box 1299, Tilbury ON N0P 2L0 Canada
Tel: 519-682-3040; *Fax:* 519-682-3123
tbia.dcc@pppoe.ca

Tillsonburg District Chamber of Commerce
PO Box 113, Tillsonburg ON N4G 4H3 Canada
Tel: 519-842-5571; *Fax:* 519-842-2941
srenken@ody.ca
www.tillsonburgchamber.ca

Timmins Chamber of Commerce / Chambre de Commerce de Timmins
PO Box 985, 76 McIntyre Rd., Timmins ON P4N 7H6 Canada
Tel: 705-360-1900; *Fax:* 705-360-1193
info@timminschamber.on.ca
www.timminschamber.on.ca

Tobermory & District Chamber of Commerce
PO Box 250, 7420 Hwy. 6, Tobermory ON N0H 2R0 Canada
Tel: 519-596-2452; *Fax:* 519-596-2452
chamber@tobermory.org
www.tobermory.org
Affiliation(s): Central Bruce Peninsula Chamber of Commerce; South Bruce Peninsula Chamber of Commerce; Manitoulin Chamber of Commerce; Manitoulin Tourism Association; Sauble Beach Chamber of Commerce

Trent Hills & District Chamber of Commerce
PO Box 376, 51 Grand Road, Campbellford ON K0L 1L0 Canada
Tel: 705-653-1551; *Fax:* 705-653-1629
Toll-Free: 888-653-1556
info@trenthillschamber.ca
www.trenthillschamber.ca
Nancy Allanson, Executive Director

Tri-Town & District Chamber of Commerce
PO Box 811, 883356 Hwy. 65 East, New Liskeard ON P0J 1P0 Canada
Tel: 705-647-5771; *Fax:* 705-647-8633
Toll-Free: 866-947-5753
chamber@ntl.sympatico.ca
www.tritownchamber.ca
Ken Laffernier, President

Tweed Chamber of Commerce
PO Box 988, Tweed ON K0K 3J0 Canada
Tel: 613-813-2784
www.tweed-chamber.ca
Richard Rashotte, President

Upper Ottawa Valley Chamber of Commerce
PO Box 1010, 611 TV Tower Rd., Pembroke ON K8A 6Y6 Canada
Tel: 613-732-1492; *Fax:* 613-732-5793
manager@upperottawavalleychamber.com
www.upperottawavalleychamber.com

Uxbridge Chamber of Commerce
#810, 2 Campbell Dr., Uxbridge ON L9P 0A3 Canada
Tel: 905-852-7683; *Fax:* 905-852-2517
www.uxcc.ca

Vaughan Chamber of Commerce (VCC)
#2, 25 Edilcan Dr., Vaughan ON L4K 3S4 Canada
Tel: 905-761-1366; *Fax:* 905-761-1918
Toll-Free: 888-828-4426
info@vaughanchamber.ca
www.vaughanchamber.ca

Walkerton & District Chamber of Commerce
PO Box 1344, 4 Park St., Walkerton ON N0G 2V0 Canada
Tel: 519-881-3413; *Fax:* 519-881-4009
Toll-Free: 888-820-9291
chamberinfo@wightman.ca
town.walkerton.on.ca/Chamber/chamber.html
Affiliation(s): Ontario Chamber of Commerce

Wasaga Beach Chamber of Commerce
PO Box 394, 550 River Rd. West, Wasaga Beach ON L9Z 1A4 Canada
Tel: 705-429-2247; *Fax:* 705-429-1407
Toll-Free: 866-292-7242
info@wasagainfo.com
www.wasagainfo.com
Affiliation(s): Canadian Chamber of Commerce; Ontario Chamber of Commerce
Trudie McCrea, Office Manager/Special Events Coord

The Welland/Pelham Chamber of Commerce
32 East Main St., Welland ON L3B 3W3 Canada
Tel: 905-732-7515; *Fax:* 905-732-7175
chamber.gurix.com

West Carleton District Chamber of Commerce
PO Box 179, Carp ON K0A 1L0 Canada
Tel: 613-839-5316; *Fax:* 613-839-1436
rosemarylyall@hotmail.com
Rose Lyall, Secretary

West Elgin Chamber of Commerce
PO Box 276, Rodney ON N0L 2C0 Canada
Tel: 519-785-2217
secretary@westelginchamber.ca
www.westelginchamber.ca
Ted Uffen, Secretary

West Grey Chamber of Commerce
PO Box 800, 625 Garafraxa Rd. North, Durham ON N0G 1R0 Canada
Tel: 519-369-5750; *Fax:* 519-369-5750
info@westgreychamber.ca
www.westgreychamber.ca
Affiliation(s): Durham Business Improvement Association

West Lincoln Chamber of Commerce
PO Box 555, 270 Station St., Smithville ON L0R 2A0 Canada
Tel: 905-957-1606; *Fax:* 905-957-4628
wloffice@westlincolnchamber.com
www.westlincolnchamber.com

Westport & Rideau Lakes Chamber of Commerce
PO Box 157, Westport ON K0G 1X0 Canada
Tel: 613-273-2929; *Fax:* 613-273-2929
wrlcc@rideau.net
www.westportrideaulakes.on.ca
Colin Horsfall, President

Whitby Chamber of Commerce (WCC)
128 Brock St. South, Whitby ON L1N 5Y4 Canada
Tel: 905-668-4506; *Fax:* 905-668-1894
info@whitbychamber.org
www.whitbychamber.org
Social Media: www.facebook.com/group.php?gid=25826309738

Whitchurch-Stouffville Chamber of Commerce
PO Box 1500, 6176 Main St., Stouffville ON L4A 8A4 Canada
Tel: 905-642-4227; *Fax:* 905-642-8966
chamber@whitchurchstouffville.ca
www.whitchurchstouffville.ca

Windsor-Essex Regional Chamber of Commerce
2575 Ouellette Place, Windsor ON N8X 1L9 Canada
Tel: 519-966-3696; *Fax:* 519-966-0603
info@windsorchamber.org
www.windsorchamber.org

Wingham & Area Chamber of Commerce
PO Box 1360, 273 Josephine St., Wingham ON N0G 2W0 Canada
Tel: 519-357-4990; *Fax:* 519-357-4847
wacc@scsinternet.com
Kerri Herrfort, Manager

Woodstock District Chamber of Commerce
#3, 425 Dundas St., Woodstock ON N4S 1B8 Canada
Tel: 519-539-9411; *Fax:* 519-456-1611
info@woodstockchamber.on.ca
www.woodstockchamber.on.ca

Zurich & Association District Chamber of Commerce
PO Box 189, Zurich ON N0M 2T0 Canada
Tel: 519-236-4717
www.zurich-ontario-canada.com

Prince Edward Island

Chambre de commerce acadienne et francophone de l'Ile-du-Prince-Édouard
PO Box 67, Wellington PE C0B 2E0 Canada
Tel: 902-854-3439; *Fax:* 902-854-3099

Greater Charlottetown Chamber of Commerce
PO Box 67, 127 Kent St., Charlottetown PE C1A 7K2 Canada
Tel: 902-628-2000; *Fax:* 902-368-3570
info@charlottetownchamber.com
www.charlottetownchamber.com
Social Media: www.facebook.com/group.php?gid=117356628329546
Affiliation(s): Atlantic Provinces Chamber of Commerce

Greater Summerside Chamber of Commerce (GSCC)
#10, 263 Harbour Dr., Summerside PE C1N 5P1 Canada
Tel: 902-436-9651; *Fax:* 902-436-8320
info@chamber.summerside.ca
www.chamber.summerside.ca

Kensington & Area Chamber of Commerce
PO Box 234, Kensington PE C0B 1M0 Canada
Tel: 902-836-3209
kacc@pei.aibn.com
www.kensington.ca/chamber

South Shore Chamber of Commerce
PO Box 127, Crapaud PE C0A 1J0 Canada
Tel: 902-437-2510
wiseone@isn.net
www.southshorechamber.pe.ca
Marion Miller, President

Southern Kings & Queens Chamber of Commerce (SKQCC)
PO Box 1593, Montague PE C0A 1R0 Canada
Tel: 902-838-4791; *Fax:* 902-838-0610

West Prince Chamber of Commerce
455 Main St., Alberton PE C0B 1B0 Canada
Tel: 902-853-4555

Québec

Chambre de commerce au Coeur de la Montérégie
675, rue St-Joseph, Marieville QC J3M 1H1 Canada
Tél: 450-460-4019; *Téléc:* 450-460-2362
ccmonteregie@qc.aira.com

Chambre de Commerce Bois-des-Filion - Lorraine
CP 72012, Bois-des-Filion QC J6Z 4N9 Canada
Tél: 450-471-4381
info@ccbdfl.com
www.ccbdfl.com

Chambre de commerce d'Amos-région
644, 1e rue ouest, Amos QC J9T 1V3 Canada
Tél: 819-732-8100; *Téléc:* 819-732-8101
www.ccar.qc.ca

Chambre de commerce de Beauceville
CP 5142, Beauceville QC G5X 2P5 Canada
Tél: 418-774-1020
cdecommercebeauceville@sogetel.net
Affiliation(s): Chambre de commerce du Québec; Chambre du commerce du Canada
Julien Boudreault, Président

Chambre de commerce de Bonaventure/St-Siméon/St-Élzear
CP 5006, 119, av Port-Royal, Bonaventure QC G0C 1E0 Canada
Tél: 418-392-9832
Pierre Gallant, Vice-président

Chambre de commerce de Brandon
117, rue Pacifique, Saint-Gabriel-de-Brandon QC J0K 2N0 Canada
Tél: 450-835-2105; *Téléc:* 450-835-2991
Ligne sans frais: 800-363-2788
france.brisebois@qc.aira.com
Affiliation(s): Chambre de commerce du Québec

Chambre de Commerce de Cap-des-Rosiers
1127, boul de Cap-des-Rosiers, Cap-des-Rosiers QC G4X 6G3 Canada

Chambre de commerce de Carleton
629, boul Perron, Carleton QC G0C 1J0 Canada
Tél: 418-364-1004

Chambre de commerce de Causapscal
5, rue St-Jacques sud, Causapscal QC G0J 1J0 Canada
Tél: 418-756-6048

Chambre de commerce de Charlevoix
658, rue Richelieu, La Malbaie QC G5A 2X1 Canada
Tél: 418-435-6187; *Téléc:* 418-665-0077
info@creezdesliens.com
www.creezdesliens.com

Chambre de commerce de Chibougamau
#4, 600, 3e rue, Chibougamau QC G8P 1P1 Canada
Tél: 418-748-4827
Affiliation(s): Chambre de Commerce du Québec et du Canada

Chambre de commerce de Cowansville et région
#100B, 104, rue du Sud, Cowansville QC J2K 2X2 Canada
Tél: 450-266-1665; *Téléc:* 450-266-4117
cccr@qc.aira.com
www.chambre-cowansville.com

Chambre de commerce de Danville-Shipton
CP 599, 52, rue Daniel Johnson, Danville QC J0A 1A0 Canada
Tél: 819-839-2475; *Téléc:* 819-839-2446
dgirard@interlinx.qc.ca
www.villededanville.com/chambre.html

Chambre de commerce de Disraéli
CP 5008, 846, av Champlain, Disraéli QC G0N 1E0 Canada
Tél: 418-449-2955; *Téléc:* 418-449-1669
chambcommdisraeli@tlb.sympatico.ca
www.villededisraeli.com/chambredecommerce/index.html

Chambre de commerce de Dolbeau-Mistassini
#300, 1341, boul Wallberg, Dolbeau-Mistassini QC G8L 1H3 Canada
Tél: 418-276-6638; *Téléc:* 418-276-9518
info@cdcdm.com
www.cdcdm.com

Chambre de commerce de East Angus et Région
221, St-Jean Ouest, East Angus QC J0B 1R0 Canada
Tél: 819-832-4950; *Téléc:* 819-832-1208
info@cceastangus.com
www.cceastangus.com

Chambre de commerce de Ferme-Neuve
125, 12e rue, Ferme-Neuve QC J0W 1C0 Canada
Tél: 819-587-2727; *Téléc:* 819-587-2747
c.ouellette@yahoo.ca

Chambre de Commerce de Fermont
CP 419, Fermont QC G0G 1J0 Canada
Tél: 418-287-3000; *Téléc:* 418-287-3001
chambre.commerce@diffusionfermont.ca
www.ccfermont.com

Chambre de commerce de Fleurimont
#204, 798, rue Du Conseil, Sherbrooke QC J1G 1L2 Canada
Tél: 819-565-7991; *Téléc:* 819-565-3160
info@ccfleurimont.com
www.ccfleurimont.com
François Desmarais, Directeur général

Chambre de commerce de Forestville
34, route 138 est, Forestville QC G0T 1E0 Canada
Tél: 418-587-6136
www.repertoire-chambres.fccq.ca

Chambre de commerce de Gatineau
#100, 45, rue de Villebois, Gatineau QC J8T 8J7 Canada
Tél: 819-243-2246; *Téléc:* 819-243-3346
ccgatineau@ccgatineau.ca
www.ccgatineau.ca
Karl Lavoie, Directeur général

Chambre de commerce de Hâvre-Saint-Pierre
1235, rue de la Digue, RC-1, Hâvre-Saint-Pierre QC G0G 1P0 Canada
Tél: 418-538-2576; *Téléc:* 418-538-3822
Richard Boudreau, Personne ressource

Chambre de commerce de Hemmingford / Hemmingford Chamber of Commerce
#6, 505, rue Frontière, Hemmingford QC J0L 1H0 Canada
Tél: 450-247-3310; *Téléc:* 450-247-2389
villagehford@b2b2c.ca
www.hemmingford.org

Chambre de Commerce de l'Assomption
CP 3027, 312, rue St-Jacques, L'Assomption QC J5W 4M9 Canada
Tél: 450-589-2405; *Téléc:* 450-589-9213
cclassomption@qc.aira.com
www.cclassomption.qc.ca
Ginette Blanchard, Directrice générale

Chambre de commerce de l'Est de la Beauce
CP 519, Saint-Prosper QC G0M 1Y0 Canada
Tél: 418-594-1219
info@ccestbeauce.com
www.ccestbeauce.com

Chambre de commerce de l'Est de Montréal
#201, 5790, av Pierre-de Coubertin, Montréal QC H1N 1R4 Canada
Tél: 514-354-5378; *Téléc:* 514-354-5340
info@ccemontreal.ca
www.ccemontreal.ca
Isabelle Foisy, Directrice générale

Chambre de commerce de l'Est de Portneuf
CP 4031, Pont-Rouge QC G3H 3R4 Canada
Tél: 418-873-4085; *Téléc:* 418-873-4599
ccep@globetrotter.net
www.portneufest.com
Chantal Trudeau, Directrice générale

Chambre de commerce de l'Ile d'Orléans (CCIO)
490, côte du Pont, Saint-Pierre-Ile-d'Orléans QC G0A 4E0 Canada
Tél: 418-828-0880; *Téléc:* 418-828-2335
Ligne sans frais: 866-941-9411
ccio@videotron.ca
www.cciledorleans.com
Affiliation(s): Chambre de commerce de Québec

Chambre de commerce de l'Ouest-de-l'Ile de Montréal
#602, 1000, boul Saint-Jean, Pointe-Claire QC H9R 5P1 Canada
Tél: 514-697-4228; *Téléc:* 514-697-2562
info@wimcc.ca
www.ccoim.ca

Chambre de commerce de la Haute-Gaspésie
CP 6014, Sainte-Anne-des-Monts QC G4V 2Y3 Canada
Tél: 418-763-2200; *Téléc:* 418-763-3473
dagneau.4@globetrotter.net
www.cchg.qc.ca
Carol Dagneau, Directeur général

Chambre de commerce de la Haute-Matawinie
521, rue Brassard, Saint-Michel-des-Saints QC J0K 3B0 Canada
Tél: 450-833-1334
infocchm@satelcom.qc.ca
www.haute-matawinie.com
France Chapdelaine, Directrice générale

Chambre de Commerce de la Jacques-Cartier
4517, rte de Fossambault, RR#3, Ste-Catherine-de-la-J-Cartier QC G0A 3M0 Canada
Tél: 418-875-4103; *Téléc:* 418-875-2913
Stéphanie Bérard, Secrétaire

Chambre de commerce de la MRC de la Matapédia
CP 5056, 123, rue Desbiens, 4e étage, Amqui QC G5J 3S5 Canada
Tél: 418-629-5765; *Téléc:* 418-629-5530
www.ccmrcmatapedia.qc.ca
Affiliation(s): Fédération des Chambres de commerce du Québec
Chantal St-Pierre, Directrice générale

Chambre de commerce de la MRC de Rivière-du-Loup
298, boul. Armand-Thériault, Rivière-du-Loup QC G5R 4C2 Canada
Tél: 418-862-5243; *Téléc:* 418-862-5136
info@ccmrcrdl.com
www.ccmrcrdl.com

Chambre de commerce de la région d'Acton
Édifice Gauthier, 1053, rue St-André, Acton Vale QC J0H 1A0 Canada
Tél: 450-546-0123; *Téléc:* 450-546-2709
ccracton@cooptel.qc.ca
www.chambredecommerce.info/

Chambre de commerce de la région d'Asbestos
332, 1re av, Asbestos QC J1T 1Y9 Canada
Tél: 819-879-5768; *Téléc:* 819-879-5871
ccra@qc.aira.com
www.lccra.com

Chambre de commerce de la région de Berthier / D'Autray
CP 482, Berthierville QC J0K 1A0 Canada
Tél: 450-836-4689; *Téléc:* 450-836-4926
ccregionberthier@hotmail.com
www.ccberthier-dautray.com

Chambre de commerce de la région de Mont-Joli
#304, 1553, boul. Jacques-Cartier, Mont-Joli QC G5H 2V9 Canada
Tél: 418-775-4366; *Téléc:* 418-775-4366

Chambre de commerce de la région de Salaberry-de-Valleyfield
#400, 100, rue Sainte-Cécile, Salaberry-de-Valleyfield QC J6T 1M1 Canada
Tél: 450-373-8789; *Téléc:* 450-373-8642
info@ccrsv.com
www.ccrsv.com

Chambre de commerce de la région de Weedon
280, 9e av, Weedon QC J0B 3J0 Canada
Tél: 819-560-8555; *Téléc:* 819-877-1111
admin@ccweedon.com
www.ccweedon.com
Affiliation(s): Chambre de Commerce du Québec

Chambre de commerce de Lac-Brome
CP 3654, 255-C ch Knowlton, Lac-Brome QC J0E 1V0 Canada
Tél: 450-242-2870; *Téléc:* 450-242-6896
Ligne sans frais: 877-242-2870
info@cclacbrome.com
www.cclacbrome.com

Chambre de commerce de Lévis
#225, 5700, rue JB Michaud, Lévis QC G6V 0B1 Canada
Tél: 418-837-3411; *Téléc:* 418-837-8497
cclevis@cclevis.com
www.cclevis.com

Chambre de commerce de Malartic
CP 368, Malartic QC J0Y 1Z0 Canada
Tél: 819-757-2332

Chambre de commerce de Manicouagan
#302, 67, place La Salle, Baie-Comeau QC G4Z 1K1 Canada
Tél: 418-296-2010; *Téléc:* 418-296-5397
info@ccmanic.qc.ca
www.ccmanic.qc.ca

Chambre de commerce de Mascouche
#240, 2822-A, ch Ste-Marie, Mascouche QC J7K 1N4 Canada
Tél: 450-966-1536; *Téléc:* 450-966-1531
info@ccmascouche.com
www.ccmascouche.com

Chambre de commerce de Mont-Laurier
445, du Pont, Mont-Laurier QC J9L 2R8 Canada
Tél: 819-623-3642; *Téléc:* 819-623-5220
ccml@mont-laurier.net
www.mont-laurier.net

Chambre de commerce de Montmagny
#1, 17, rue St-Jean Baptiste ouest, Montmagny QC G5V 3B4 Canada
Tél: 418-248-3111; *Téléc:* 418-241-5779

Chambre de commerce de Nicolet
30, rue Notre-Dame, Nicolet QC J3T 1G1 Canada
Tél: 819-293-4537; *Téléc:* 819-293-6092
chambre@chambre-cnicolet.org
www.chambre-cnicolet.org

Chambre de commerce de Port-Cartier
CP 82, Port-Cartier QC G5B 2G7 Canada
Tél: 418-766-8047; *Téléc:* 418-766-6367
popco@globetrotter.net

Chambre de commerce de Québec
17, rue St-Louis, Québec QC G1R 3Y8 Canada
Tél: 418-692-3853; *Téléc:* 418-694-2286
info@ccquebec.ca
www.ccquebec.ca
Affiliation(s): Chambre de commerce du Canada; Chambre de commerce du Québec
Alain Kirouac, Vice-président exécutif et directeu

Chambre de commerce de Rawdon
3590, rue Metcalfe, Rawdon QC J0K 1S0 Canada
Tél: 450-834-2282; *Téléc:* 450-834-3084
ccdr@bellnet.ca
www.chambrecommercerawdon.ca

Chambre de commerce de Saint-Bruno
CP 123, Saint-Bruno-de-Montarville QC J3V 4P8 Canada
Tél: 450-653-0585; *Téléc:* 450-653-6967
info@ccstbruno.ca
www.ccstbruno.ca
Affiliation(s): Chambre de commerce du Québec; Chambre de commerce du Canada

Chambre de commerce de Saint-Côme
1661-A rue Principale, Saint-Côme QC J0K 2B0 Canada
Tél: 450-883-2730; *Téléc:* 450-883-3455
info@stcomelanaudiere.com
www.stcomelanaudiere.com
Sylvain Bourque, Président

Chambre de commerce de Sainte-Adèle
100, rue Morin, Sainte-Adèle QC J8B 2P7 Canada
Tél: 450-229-2644; *Téléc:* 450-229-1436
chambredecommerce@sainte-adele.net
www.sainte-adele.net

Chambre de Commerce de Saint-Ephrem
CP 2015, Saint-Éphrem QC G0M 1R0 Canada
Tél: 418-484-2681
info@ccstephrem.com
www.ccstephrem.com

Chambre de commerce de Ste-Julienne
1799, rte 125, Sainte-Julienne QC J0K 2T0 Canada
Tél: 819-831-3551; *Téléc:* 819-831-3551
Nicole Bourgie, Secrétaire

Chambre de commerce de Ste-Justine
167, rte 204, Sainte-Justine QC G0R 1Y0 Canada
Tél: 418-383-5397; *Téléc:* 418-383-5398
sjustine@sogetel.net

Chambre de commerce de Sept-Iles
#237, 700, boul Laure, Sept-Iles QC G4R 1Y1 Canada
Tél: 418-968-3488; *Téléc:* 418-968-3432
cadoretd@cgocable.ca

Chambre de commerce de Sherbrooke
#402, 75, rue Wellington nord, Sherbrooke QC J1H 5A9 Canada
Tél: 819-822-6151; *Téléc:* 819-822-6156
info@ccsherbrooke.ca
www.ccsherbrooke.ca

Chambre de commerce de St-Côme-Linière
1614, 6e rue, Saint-Côme-Linière QC G0M 1J0 Canada
Tél: 418-685-2630; *Téléc:* 418-685-2630
chambredecommerce@stcomeliniere.com
www.stcomeliniere.com/c_ccommerce.php
Sylvain Bourque, Président

Chambre de commerce de St-Donat
536A, rue Principale, Saint-Donat-de-Montcalm QC J0T 2C0 Canada
Tél: 819-424-2833; *Téléc:* 819-424-4366
cc.st-donat@bellnet.ca

Chambre de commerce de St-Eugène-de-Guigues
CP 1013, 9, 1ere Avenue Ouest, Saint-Eugène-de-Guigues QC J0Z 3L0 Canada
Tél: 819-785-2057
Lillian Matteau, Secrétaire

Chambre de commerce de St-Frédéric
2166, rue Principale, Saint-Frédéric QC G0N 1P0 Canada
Tél: 418-426-3104; *Téléc:* 418-426-3357

Chambre de commerce de St-Georges
#310, 8585, boul Lacroix, Ville de Saint-Georges Beauce QC G5Y 5L6 Canada
Tél: 418-228-7879; *Téléc:* 418-228-8074
administration@ccstgeorges.com
www.ccstgeorges.com
Affiliation(s): Chambre de commerce du Québec; Chambre de commerce du Canada

Chambre de commerce de St-Jean-de-Dieu
CP 392, Saint-Jean-de-Dieu QC G0L 3M0 Canada
Tél: 418-963-3205

Chambre de commerce de St-Jules-de-Beauce
CP 81, 213, av Roy, Saint-Jules QC G0N 1R0 Canada
Tél: 418-397-1870

Chambre de commerce de St-Léonard
8370, boul. Lacordaire, Saint-Léonard QC H1R 3Y6 Canada
Tél: 514-325-4232; *Téléc:* 514-955-8544
tmelita@citenet.net
www.ccstleonard.qc.ca

Chambre de Commerce de Terrebonne
#301, 1025, montée Masson, Lachenaie QC J6W 5H9 Canada
Tél: 450-471-8779; *Téléc:* 450-471-5610
info@ccterrebonne.qc.ca
www.ccterrebonne.qc.ca
Affiliation(s): Chambre de commerce du Canada; Chambre de commerce du Québec; Chambre de commerce régionale de Lanaudière; Réseau canadien de centres de services aux entreprises; Centre local de développement économique des Moulins (CLDEM); Centre local d'emploi de Terrebonne; Société de développement touristique des Moulins; Conseil de développement bioalimentaire de Lanaudière.
Robert Lalancette, Directeur général

Chambre de commerce de Tring-Jonction
184, av Commerciale, Tring-Jonction QC G0N 1X0 Canada
Tél: 418-427-3320; *Téléc:* 418-427-1466
Danye Vachon, Secrétaire

Chambre de commerce de Valcourt et Région
CP 900, Valcourt QC J0E 2L0 Canada
Tél: 450-532-3041; *Téléc:* 450-532-3041
commerce@cooptel.qc.ca
Affiliation(s): Chambre de commerce régionale de l'Estrie

Chambre de commerce de Val-d'Or
400, 3e av, Val-d'Or QC J9P 1R9 Canada
Tél: 819-825-3703; *Téléc:* 819-825-8599
ccvd@cablevision.qc.ca
www.ccvd.qc.ca

Chambre de commerce de Villebois
3897, rue de l'Église, Villebois QC J0Z 3V0 Canada
Tél: 819-941-6302
www.villebois.qc.ca
Claude Côté, Président

Chambre de commerce de Ville-Marie
1, rue Industrielle, Ville-Marie QC J9V 1S3 Canada
Tél: 819-629-2918; *Téléc:* 819-622-1801
chambredecommerce-vill@cablevision.qc.ca

Chambre de commerce des Iles-de-la-Madeleine (CCIM)
Édifice Fernand Cyr, #103, 735, ch Principal, Cap-aux-Meules QC G4T 1G8 Canada
Tél: 418-986-4111; *Téléc:* 418-986-4112
info@ccim.qc.ca
www.ccim.qc.ca

Chambre de commerce du Centre-de-la-Mauricie
900, 6e Avenue, Shawinigan-Sud QC G9P 1S4 Canada
Tél: 819-536-0777; *Téléc:* 819-536-0039
info@cccmauricie.qc.ca
www.cccmauricie.qc.ca

Chambre de commerce du Grand Joliette
500, rue Dollard, Joliette QC J6E 4M4 Canada
Tél: 450-759-6363; *Téléc:* 450-759-5012
info@ccgj.qc.ca
www.ccgj.qc.ca

Chambre de commerce du Grand Paspébiac
CP 1232, 6, boul Gérard D. Lévesque est, Paspébiac QC G0C 2K0 Canada
Tél: 418-752-3330; *Téléc:* 418-752-3330

Chambre de commerce du Haut St-Maurice
547-C, rue Commerciale, La Tuque QC G9X 3A7 Canada
Tél: 819-523-9933

Chambre de commerce du Haut-Richelieu
#301, 929, boul Séminaire nord, Saint-Jean-sur-Richelieu QC J3A 1B6 Canada
Tél: 450-346-2544; *Téléc:* 450-346-3812
info@cchautrichelieu.qc.ca
www.cchautrichelieu.qc.ca

Chambre de commerce du Lac des Deux-Montagnes (Pointe-Calumet, Saint-Joseph-du-Lac, Oka & Saint-Placide)
#400, 190 - 41e av, Pointe-Calumet QC J0N 1G2 Canada
Tél: 450-472-7535; *Téléc:* 450-472-0229
c.c.lac2montagnes@videotron.ca
www.cclac2montagnes.com
Affiliation(s): Chambre de Commerce du Québec
Denise Lemay, Directrice générale

Chambre de commerce du Lac Robertson
CP 100, Tête-à-la-Baleine QC G0G 2W0 Canada
Tél: 418-773-2659; *Téléc:* 418-773-2526
Gérald Organ, Secrétaire

Chambre de commerce du Montréal métropolitain / Board of Trade of Metropolitan Montréal
Niveau plaza, #6000, 380, rue St-Antoine ouest, Montréal QC H3Y 3X7 Canada
Tél: 514-871-4000; *Téléc:* 514-871-1255
info@ccmm.qc.ca
www.ccmm.qc.ca

Chambre de commerce du Saguenay
194, rue Price ouest, Chicoutimi QC G7J 1H1 Canada
Tél: 418-543-5941; *Téléc:* 418-543-5576
info@ccchic.qc.ca
www.ccchic.qc.ca

Chambre de commerce du secteur de Normandin
1048, rue St-Cyrille, Normandin QC G8M 4R9 Canada
Tél: 418-274-2004; *Téléc:* 418-274-7171
ccnormandin@hotmail.com
www.ville.normandin.qc.ca

Chambre de commerce du Transcontinental
CP 2004, Rivière-Bleue QC G0L 2B0 Canada
Tél: 418-893-2347; *Téléc:* 418-893-2889
cctrans@globetrotter.net
pages.globetrotter.net/cctrans

Chambre de commerce Duparquet
CP 369, Duparquet QC J0Z 1W0 Canada
Tél: 819-948-2030

Chambre de commerce East Broughton
CP 916, East Broughton QC G0N 1G0 Canada
Tél: 418-427-5761; *Téléc:* 418-427-4032
cceastbroughton@globetrotter.net
Annie Roy, Secrétaire

Chambre de commerce et d'entreprises de Bellechasse
225A, rue Principale, Saint-Gervais QC G0R 3C0 Canada
Tél: 418-887-4075; *Téléc:* 418-887-4074
info@ccbellechasse.ca
www.ccbellechasse.ca

Chambre de commerce et d'industrie (St-Eustache / Deux-Montagnes / Ste-Marthe-sur-le-Lac)
67 A, boul. Industriel, Saint-Eustache QC J7R 5P2 Canada
Tél: 450-491-1991; *Téléc:* 450-491-1648
info@chambrecommerce.com
www.chambrecommerce.com

Chambre de commerce et d'industrie d'Abitibi-Ouest
#203, 99, 5e Av est, La Sarre QC J9Z 3A8 Canada
Tél: 819-333-9836; *Téléc:* 819-333-5737
ccao@ccao.qc.ca
www.ccao.qc.ca

Chambre de commerce et d'industrie d'Argenteuil
#225, 580, rue Principale, Lachute QC J8H 1Y7 Canada
Tél: 450-562-1947; *Téléc:* 450-562-1896
cci.argen@qc.aira.com
www.cciargenteuil.qc.ca
Suzanne Gaudet, Directrice générale

Chambre de commerce et d'industrie de Bécancour
1045, av Nicolas Perrot, Bécancour QC G9H 3B7 Canada
Tél: 819-294-6010; *Téléc:* 819-294-6020
info@ccibecancour.ca
www.ccibecancour.ca

Chambre de commerce et d'industrie de Châteauguay
#100, 15, boul Maple, Châteauguay QC J6J 3P7 Canada
Tél: 450-698-0027; *Téléc:* 450-698-0088
ccic@abacom.com
www.ccichateauguay.ca

Chambre de commerce et d'industrie de Drummond
CP 188, 234, rue Saint-Marcel, Drummondville QC J2B 6V7 Canada
Tél: 819-477-7822; *Téléc:* 819-477-2823
info@ccid.qc.ca
www.ccid.qc.ca

Chambre de commerce et d'industrie de la MRC de Maskinongé
396, Ste-Élisabeth, Louiseville QC J5V 1M7 Canada
Tél: 819-228-8582; *Téléc:* 819-228-8989
info@cci-maskinonge.ca
www.cci-maskinonge.ca
Marc H. Plante, Directeur général

Chambre de commerce et d'Industrie de la région de Coaticook (CCIRC)
150, rue Child, Coaticook QC J1A 2B3 Canada
Tél: 819-849-4733; *Téléc:* 819-849-6828
ccrc@abacom.com
www.ccircoaticook.ca

Chambre de commerce et d'industrie de la région de Richmond
CP 3119, Richmond QC J0B 2H0 Canada
Tél: 819-826-5854; *Téléc:* 819-826-2813
ch.commerce@ville.richmond.qc.ca
www.ville.richmond.qc.ca/chcom.htm

Chambre de commerce et d'industrie de la Rive-Sud
#101, 85, rue Saint-Charles ouest, Longueuil QC J4H 1C5 Canada
Tél: 450-463-2121; *Téléc:* 450-463-1858
info@ccirs.qc.ca
www.ccirs.qc.ca

Chambre de commerce et d'industrie de la Vallée-du-Richelieu
#102, 230, rue Brébeuf, Beloeil QC J3G 5P3 Canada
Tél: 450-464-3733; *Téléc:* 450-446-4163
www.ccivr.qc.ca

Chambre de commerce et d'industrie de Laval (CCIL)
#200, 1555, boul Chomedey, Laval QC H7V 3Z1 Canada
Tél: 450-682-5255; *Téléc:* 450-682-5735
info@ccilaval.qc.ca
www.ccilaval.qc.ca

Chambre de commerce et d'industrie de Maniwaki (CCIM)
171, rue Principale sud, Maniwaki QC J9E 1Z8 Canada
Tél: 819-449-6627; *Téléc:* 819-449-7667
Ligne sans frais: 866-449-6728
valeried@ccimki.ca
www.ccimaniwaki.com
Claude Benoit, Président
Sophie Beaudoin, Directrice générale

Chambre de commerce et d'industrie de Mirabel
#208, 13479, boul du Curé Labelle, Mirabel QC J7J 1L2 Canada
Tél: 450-433-1944; *Téléc:* 450-433-5168
info@ccmirabel.com

Chambre de commerce et d'industrie de Montréal-Nord (CRIMN)
#006A, 6000, boul Henri-Bourassa est, Montréal-Nord QC H1G 2T6 Canada
Tél: 514-329-4453; *Téléc:* 514-329-5373
info@ccimn.qc.ca
www.ccimn.qc.ca

Chambre de commerce et d'industrie de Rouyn-Noranda (CCIRN)
225, boul Rideau, Rouyn-Noranda QC J9X 5Y6 Canada
Tél: 819-797-2000; *Téléc:* 819-762-3091
reseau@ccirn.qc.ca
www.ccirn.qc.ca
Guy Veillet, Présidente

Chambre de commerce et d'industrie de St-Félicien
CP 34, 1209, boul Sacré-Coeur, Saint-Félicien QC G8K 2P8 Canada
Tél: 418-679-2097; *Téléc:* 418-679-4039
ccistfe@ville.stfelicien.qc.ca
www.chambre-sf.com

Chambre de commerce et d'industrie de St-Joseph-de-Beauce
165, av Taschereau, Saint-Joseph-de-Beauce QC G0S 2V0 Canada
Tél: 418-397-5980; *Téléc:* 418-397-5982

Chambre de commerce et d'industrie de St-Laurent
#204, 935, Décarie, Saint-Laurent QC H4L 3M3 Canada
Tél: 514-333-5222; *Téléc:* 514-333-0937
info@ccstl.qc.ca
www.ccstl.qc.ca

Chambre de commerce et d'industrie de Thetford Mines
81, rue Notre-Dame ouest, Thetford Mines QC G6G 1J4 Canada
Tél: 418-338-4551; *Téléc:* 418-335-2066
www.ccitm.com

Chambre de commerce et d'industrie de Varennes (CCIV)
266, rue Ste-Anne, local B, Varennes QC J3X 1R7 Canada
Tél: 450-652-4209; *Téléc:* 450-652-4244
info@cciv.ca
www.cciv.ca

Chambre de commerce et d'industrie de Ville de La Baie
285, boul Grande Baie nord, La Baie QC G7B 3K4 Canada
Tél: 418-544-9861

Chambre de commerce et d'industrie des Bois-Francs et de l'Érable
122, rue de l'Acqueduc, Victoriaville QC G6P 1M3 Canada
Tél: 819-758-6371; *Téléc:* 819-758-4604
ccibf@ccibf.com
www.ccibf.qc.ca

Chambre de commerce et d'industrie du bassin de Chambly (CCIB)
929, boul. de Périgny, Chambly QC J3L 5H5 Canada
Tél: 450-658-7598; *Téléc:* 450-658-6477
info@ccibc.qc.ca
www.ccibc.qc.ca

Chambre de commerce et d'industrie du secteur Roberval (CCISR)
CP 115, Roberval QC G8H 2N4 Canada
Tél: 418-275-3504; *Téléc:* 418-275-0851
info@ccisr.qc.ca
www.ccisr.qc.ca
Affiliation(s): Chambre de Commerce du Québec; Chambre de Commerce du Canada

Chambre de commerce et d'industrie Lac-Saint-Jean-Est
625, rue Bergeron ouest, Alma QC G8B 1V3 Canada
Tél: 418-662-2734; *Téléc:* 418-669-2220
cca@qc.aira.com
www.ccilacsaintjeanest.com

Chambre de commerce et d'industrie Magog-Orford
801, rue Principale Ouest, Magog QC J1X 2B4 Canada
Tél: 819-843-3494; *Téléc:* 819-843-4124
info@ccimo.qc.ca
www.ccimo.qc.ca

Chambre de commerce et d'industrie régionale de Saint-Léonard-d'Aston
#1, 370, rue Principale, Saint-Léonard-d'Aston QC J0C 1M0 Canada
Tél: 819-399-2020; *Téléc:* 819-399-3288
ccistl@tlb.sympatico.ca
www.ccst-leonard-daston.com
Marthe Proulx, Directrice générale

Chambre de commerce et d'industrie Sorel-Tracy métropolitain
CP 568, #112, 67, rue George, Sorel-Tracy QC J3P 1C2 Canada
Tél: 450-742-0018; *Téléc:* 450-742-7442
www.ccstm.qc.ca

Chambre de commerce et d'industrie St-Jérôme (CCISJ)
309, rue De Villemure, Saint-Jérôme QC J7Z 5J5 Canada
Tél: 450-431-4339; *Téléc:* 450-431-1677
rachel.roy@ccisj.qc.ca
www.ccisj.qc.ca
Jocelyne Légaré, Directrice générale

Chambre de commerce et d'industrie Vaudreuil-Dorion
#123, 421, av St-Charles, Vaudreuil-Dorion QC J7V 2M9 Canada
Tél: 450-424-6886; *Téléc:* 450-424-4989
ccvd@bellnet.ca
www.ccivd.com
Charles L. Milot, Directeur général

Chambre de commerce et d'industries de Trois-Rivières
CP 1045, 168, rue Bonaventure, Trois-Rivières QC G9A 5K4 Canada
Tél: 819-375-9628; *Téléc:* 819-375-9083
info@ccdtr.com
www.ccdtr.com

Chambre de commerce et de l'industrie du Haut St-Laurent
CP 1914, 8, rue King, Huntingdon QC J0S 1H0 Canada
Tél: 450-264-5252; *Téléc:* 450-264-5111
cdechsl@suroit.com
ww.cdechsl.com

Chambre de commerce et de l'industrie Les Maskoutains
780, av de L'Hôtel-de-ville, Saint-Hyacinthe QC J2S 5B2 Canada
Tél: 450-773-3474; *Téléc:* 450-773-9339
chambre@chambrecommerce.ca
www.chambrecommerce.ca
Nicole Laverrière, Directrice générale

Chambre de commerce et de l'industrie Rimouski-Neigette
CP 1296, #101, 125, rue de l'Évêché, Rimouski QC G5L 8M2 Canada
Tél: 418-722-4494; *Téléc:* 418-722-8402
info@ccrimouski.com
www.ccrimouski.com

Chambre de commerce et de tourisme de Gaspé
27, boul York est, Gaspé QC G4X 2K9 Canada
Tél: 418-368-8525; *Téléc:* 418-368-8549
info@cctgaspe.org
cctgaspe.org

Chambre de commerce et de tourisme de la Vallée de Saint-Sauveur/Piedmont
30, rue Filion, Saint-Sauveur QC J0R 1R0 Canada
Tél: 450-227-2564; *Téléc:* 450-227-6480
Ligne sans frais: 877-528-2553
info@valleesaintsauveur.com
www.valleesaintsauveur.com
Pierre Urquhart, Directeur général

Chambre de commerce et de tourisme de Murdochville
CP 879, #29, 635 - 5e rue, Murdochville QC G0E 1W0 Canada
Tél: 418-784-2577; *Téléc:* 418-784-2597
ccmurd.roy@globetrotter.net
www.ccmurdochville.com

Chambre de commerce et de tourisme de St-Adolphe-d'Howard
CP 326, Saint-Adolphe-d'Howard QC J0T 2B0 Canada
Ligne sans frais: 888-710-4636
info@st-adolphe.com
www.st-adolphe.com

Chambre de commerce et de'industrie du Sud-Ouest de Montréal
#32, 410, av Lafleur, Montréal QC H8R 3H6 Canada
Tél: 514-365-4575; *Téléc:* 514-365-0487
www.ccisom.ca
Affiliation(s): Chambre de commerce du Canada; Fédération des Chambres de commerce du Québec
Gilles Dubien, Directeur général

Chambre de commerce gaie du Québec (CCGQ) / The Québec Gay Chamber of Commerce
#302, 249, rue St-Jacques, Montréal QC H2Y 1M6 Canada
Tél: 514-522-1885; *Téléc:* 514-522-9468
Ligne sans frais: 888-595-8110
info@ccgq.ca
www.ccgq.ca

Chambre de commerce Haute-Yamaska et Région
650, rue Principale, Granby QC J2G 8L4 Canada
Tél: 450-372-6100; *Téléc:* 450-372-3161
info@chambredecommerce.org
www.chambredecommerce.org

Chambre de commerce Hemmingford—Napierville—Saint-Rémi
CP 3541, 1009, rue Notre-Dame, Saint-Rémi QC J0L 2L0 Canada
Tél: 450-615-0512; *Téléc:* 450-615-0612
info@ccsaint-remi.ca
www.ccsaint-remi.ca

Chambre de commerce juive / Jewish Chamber of Commerce
1, carré Cummings, Montréal QC H3W 1M6 Canada
Tél: 514-345-2645; *Téléc:* 514-345-2655
info@jccmontreal.com
www.jccmontreal.com
Elliot Greenstone, Coprésident
Heidi Minkoff, Coprésidente

Chambre de commerce Kamouraska-L'Islet (CCKL)
#208, 1000, 6e av, La Pocatière QC G0R 1Z0 Canada
Tél: 418-856-6227; *Téléc:* 418-856-6462
Ligne sans frais: 877-856-6227
cckl@qc.aira.com
www.cckl.org
Gabriel Hudon, Président

Chambre de commerce MRC du Rocher-Percé
CP 129, 35, rue Commerciale ouest, Chandler QC G0C 1K0 Canada
Tél: 418-689-6998
info@ccrocherperce.org
www.ccrocherperce.org
Sonya Cauvier, Directrice générale

Chambre de commerce Notre-Dame-du-Lac
CP 147, Notre-Dame-du-Lac QC G0L 1X0 Canada
Tél: 418-899-6987

Chambre de commerce Notre-Dame-du-Nord
CP 517, Notre-Dame-du-Nord QC J0Z 3B0 Canada
Tél: 819-723-2814; *Téléc:* 819-723-2899

Chambre de commerce Nouvelle Beauce
CP 684, #C, 700, rue Notre-Dame nord, Sainte-Marie QC G6E 2K9 Canada
Tél: 418-387-2006; *Téléc:* 418-387-8223
info@ccnb.ca
www.nouvellebeauce.com/site.asp

Chambre de commerce Pierre-Le Gardeur De Repentigny
#151, 534, rue Notre-Dame, Repentigny QC J6A 2T8 Canada
Tél: 450-581-3010; *Téléc:* 450-581-5069
info@ccrepentigny.qc.ca
www.ccrepentigny.qc.ca

Chambre de commerce région de Matane
CP 518, Matane QC G4W 3P5 Canada
Tél: 418-562-9344; *Téléc:* 418-562-7734
info@ccmatane.com
www.ccmatane.com

Chambre de commerce région de Mégantic
6346, rue Salaberry, Lac-Mégantic QC G6B 1J3 Canada
Tél: 819-583-5392; *Téléc:* 819-583-5457
info@ccrmeg.com
www.ccrmeg.com

Chambre de commerce régionale de St-Raymond (CCRSR)
#1, 100, av St-Jacques, Saint-Raymond QC G3L 3Y1 Canada
Tél: 418-337-4049; *Téléc:* 418-337-8017
ccrsr@cite.net
www.ccrsr.qc.ca

Chambre de commerce régionale de Windsor
13, rue de la Croix, Windsor QC J1S 2K3 Canada
Tél: 819-845-5646

Chambre de commerce régionale des entrepreneurs de Québec (CCREQ)
#3200, 2700, boul Laurier, Sainte-Foy QC G1V 4K5 Canada
Tél: 418-651-7181; *Téléc:* 418-651-5248
info@cceq.ca

Chambre de commerce Ste-Émélie-de-l'Énergie
CP 272, Sainte-Émélie-de-l'Énergie QC J0K 2K0 Canada
Tél: 450-886-1658
rlachance@simonlussier.com

Chambre de commerce Saint-Lin-Laurentides
CP 3340, #101, 704, rue St-Isidore, Saint-Lin-Laurentides QC J5M 2V2 Canada
Tél: 450-439-3704; *Téléc:* 450-439-2066
chambrecstlin@videotron.ca
André Corbeil, Président

Chambre de commerce secteur ouest de Portneuf
CP 2006, 295, rue Gauthier, local 2, Saint-Marc-des-Carrières QC G0A 4B0 Canada
Tél: 418-268-5447; *Téléc:* 418-268-3532
ccsop@globetrotter.net
www.portneufouest.com
Étienne Bourré-Denis, Personne ressource

Chambre de commerce St-Félix de Valois
15, ch Joliette, Saint-Félix-de-Valois QC J0K 2M0 Canada
Tél: 450-889-8161; *Téléc:* 450-889-1590
ccst-flx@megacom.net
www.stfelixdevalois.qc.ca
Josée Durand, Directrice générale

Chambre de commerce St-Jean-de-Matha
1159, rte Louis-Cyr, Saint-Jean-de-Matha QC J0K 2S0 Canada
Tél: 450-886-0599; *Téléc:* 450-886-3123
info@chambrematha.com
www.chambrematha.com

Chambre de commerce St-Martin de Beauce
CP 31, 60, 5e av ouest, Saint-Martin QC G0M 1B0 Canada
Tél: 418-382-5549
chambre@st-martin.qc.ca
www.st-martin.qc.ca
Affiliation(s): Chambre de commerce du Québec; Chambre de commerce du Canada

Chambre de commerce Vallée de la Missisquoi
858, rte de la Missisquoi, Bolton Centre QC J0E 1G0 Canada
Tél: 450-292-4217

Chambre de commerce Vallée de la Petite-Nation
185, rue Henri-Bourassa, Papineauville QC J0V 1R0 Canada
Tél: 819-427-8450; *Téléc:* 819-427-9849
ccvpn@videotron.ca
www.ccvpn.org

Chambre de commerce Ville de Mont-Tremblant
990, rue Lauzon, Mont-Tremblant QC J8E 3J5 Canada
Tél: 819-425-8441; *Téléc:* 819-425-7949
info@ccdemonttremblant.com
www.ccdemonttremblant.com

Jeune chambre de commerce de Montréal (JCCM)
#1220, 1010, rue Sherbrooke ouest, Montréal QC H3A 2R7 Canada
Tél: 514-845-4951; *Téléc:* 514-845-0587
vboilard@jccm.org
www.jccm.org

Jeune chambre de commerce de Québec
#249, 4600, boul Henri-Bourassa, Charlesbourg QC G1H 3A5 Canada
Tél: 418-622-6937; *Téléc:* 418-628-7777
jccq@jccq.qc.ca
www.jccq.qc.ca
Média social: www.facebook.com/group.php?gid=6715149631
Marie-Eve Goulet, Présidente

Regroupement des jeunes chambres de commerce du Québec (RJCCQ)
555, rue René-Lévesque Ouest, 9e étage, Montréal QC H2Z 1B1 Canada
Tél: 514-933-7595; *Téléc:* 514-844-0226
Ligne sans frais: 877-933-7595
info@rjccq.com
www.rjccq.com
Mèdia social: www.facebook.com/rjccq
Anthony Lacopo, Président

Saskatchewan

Assiniboia Chamber of Commerce (SK)
PO Box 1803, 110 - 4th Ave. West, Assiniboia SK S0H 0B0 Canada
Tel: 306-642-5553; *Fax:* 306-642-3529
aeda@assiniboia.net
Terry L. Sieffert, President
Sonia Dahlman, Treasurer
Bonnie Ruzicka, Executive Assistant

Battlefords Chamber of Commerce
PO Box 1000, North Battleford SK S9A 3E6 Canada
Tel: 306-445-6226; *Fax:* 306-445-6633
b.chamber@sasktel.net
www.battlefordschamber.com
Affiliation(s): Institution of Association Executives; Tourism Industry Association of Saskatchewan

Big River Chamber of Commerce
c/o Kangaroo Cottage, PO Box 351, Big River SK S0J 0E0 Canada
Tel: 306-469-2484; *Fax:* 306-469-2485
www.bigriver.ca

Biggar & District Chamber of Commerce
c/o Bear Hills R.D.C., PO Box 327, 117 - 3rd Ave. West, Biggar SK S0K 0M0 Canada
Tel: 306-948-2295; *Fax:* 306-948-5050
bearhills.rdc@sasktel.net
townofbiggar.com
Garry Faye, Co-Chair
Diane Koenders, Sec.-Treas.

Blaine Lake & District Chamber of Commerce
PO Box 178, Blaine Lake SK S0J 0J0 Canada
Tel: 306-497-2695; *Fax:* 306-497-2402
elhoe@sasktel.net
T.L. Bowie, President

Broadview Chamber of Commerce
PO Box 508, Broadview SK S0G 0K0 Canada
Tel: 306-696-3166

Canora & District Chamber of Commerce
PO Box 1409, Canora SK S0A 0L0 Canada
Tel: 306-563-4123; *Fax:* 306-563-4124

Carlyle Chamber of Commerce
PO Box 365, Carlyle SK S0C 0R0 Canada
Tel: 306-453-6718; *Fax:* 306-453-2910
blair.andrew@andrewagencies.com

Choiceland & District Chamber of Commerce
c/o Grow Plan Fertilizers Ltd., PO Box 339, 115 Railway Ave. West, Choiceland SK S0J 0M0 Canada
Tel: 306-428-2300; *Fax:* 306-428-2526
Frank H. Bond, President
Colleen F Digness, Secretary

Coronach Community Chamber of Commerce
PO Box 577, Coronach SK S0H 0Z0 Canada
Tel: 306-267-2077; *Fax:* 306-267-2047
marshalljackie@hotmail.com
Affiliation(s): Saskatchewan Chamber of Commerce

Debden & District Chamber of Commerce
PO Box 91, Debden SK S0J 0S0 Canada
Tel: 306-724-2266; *Fax:* 306-724-4505
p.demers@sasktel.net
Phil Demers, President
Denis Belair, Secretary

Eastend & District Chamber of Commerce
c/o L & E Farm Sales Ltd., PO Box 534, Eastend SK S0N 0T0 Canada
Tel: 306-295-3355; *Fax:* 306-295-3571

Eatonia & District Chamber of Commerce
PO Box 370, Eatonia SK S0L 0Y0 Canada
Tel: 306-967-2506; *Fax:* 306-967-2267
T. Drurey, President
Anne Rhodes, Secretary

Esterhazy & District Chamber of Commerce
PO Box 778, Esterhazy SK S0A 0X0 Canada
Tel: 306-745-5405; *Fax:* 306-745-6797
esterhazy.ed@sasktel.net

Estevan Chamber of Commerce
#303, 1133 - 4th St., Estevan SK S4A 0W6 Canada
Tel: 306-634-2828; *Fax:* 306-634-6729
estevanchamber@sasktel.net
www.estevanchamber.ca

Fort Qu'Appelle & District Chamber of Commerce
c/o Mission Ridge, PO Box 1273, Fort Qu'appelle SK S0G 1S0 Canada
Tel: 306-332-5717; *Fax:* 306-332-1287

Fox Valley Chamber of Commerce
c/o Double L. Farms, PO Box 133, Fox Valley SK S0N 0V0 Canada
Tel: 306-666-4447; *Fax:* 306-666-4448

Goodsoil & District Chamber of Commerce
PO Box 88, Main St., Goodsoil SK S0M 1A0 Canada
Tel: 306-238-2033; *Fax:* 306-238-4441
joan.baer@goodsoil.cu.sk.ca

Gravelbourg Chamber of Commerce
PO Box 85, Gravelbourg SK S0H 1X0 Canada
Tel: 306-648-3182; *Fax:* 306-648-2311
brouwerc@sasktel.net
G. Murray, Treasurer
Cees Brouwer, President

Greater Saskatoon Chamber of Commerce
#104, 202 - 4th Ave. North, Saskatoon SK S7K 0K1 Canada
Tel: 306-244-2151; *Fax:* 306-244-8366
chamber@eboardoftrade.com
www.eboardoftrade.com
Affiliation(s): Enterprise Centre; Leadership Saskatoon; Raj Manek Mentorship Program; Saskatchewan Agrivision Corporation; Saskatchewan Economic Development Authority; Saskatchewan Young Professionals & Entrepreneurs; Saskatoon Aboriginal Employment & Business Opportunities Inc., Saskatoon Air Services; Saskatoon Regional Economic Development Authority; Tourism Saskatoon; United Way of Saskatoon; Vision 2000

Herbert & District Chamber of Commerce
PO Box 700, Herbert SK S0H 2A0 Canada
Tel: 306-784-3475; *Fax:* 306-784-2801
marniescoffeeshop@sasktel.net

Hudson Bay Chamber of Commerce
PO Box 430, Hudson Bay SK S0E 0Y0 Canada
Tel: 306-865-2288; *Fax:* 306-865-2177

Humboldt & District Chamber of Commerce
PO Box 1440, Humboldt SK S0K 2A0 Canada
Tel: 306-682-4990; *Fax:* 306-682-5203
humboldtchamber@sasktel.net
www.humboldtchamber.ca

Indian Head Chamber of Commerce
PO Box 1233, Indian Head SK S0G 2K0 Canada
Tel: 306-695-2238; *Fax:* 306-695-2307
ihac@sasktel.net
Melanie Roth, Secretary

Kamsack & District Chamber of Commerce
PO Box 817, Kamsack SK S0A 1S0 Canada
Tel: 306-542-9694; *Fax:* 306-542-4396
becenko@sasktel.net
Jack Koreluik, President
Wendy Becenko, Secretary

Kelvington & District Chamber of Commerce
c/o Kelvington Radio, PO Box 667, 107 Main St., Kelvington SK S0A 1W0 Canada
Tel: 306-327-4656

Kenaston & District Chamber of Commerce
PO Box 70, Kenaston SK S0G 2N0 Canada
Tel: 306-252-2236; *Fax:* 306-252-2089

Kerrobert Chamber of Commerce
PO Box 408, Kerrobert SK S0L 1R0 Canada
Tel: 306-834-5423
kerrobert@sasktel.net

Kindersley Chamber of Commerce
PO Box 1537, Kindersley SK S0L 1S0 Canada
Tel: 306-463-2320; *Fax:* 306-463-2312
kindersleychamber@sasktel.net
www.kindersleychamber.com

Kinistino & District Chamber of Commerce
PO Box 803, Kinistino SK S0J 1H0 Canada
Tel: 306-864-2275

Kipling Chamber of Commerce
PO Box 700, Kipling SK S0G 2S0 Canada
Tel: 306-736-8520; *Fax:* 306-736-2260
ssauve.mib@sasktel.net

Lafleche & District Chamber of Commerce
PO Box 40, 41 Main St., Lafleche SK S0H 2K0 Canada
Tel: 306-472-3252; *Fax:* 306-472-5958
lgs.cga@sasktel.net
L. Sutherland, President
Twyla Verhelst, Secretary

Langenburg & District Chamber of Commerce
PO Box 610, Langenburg SK S0A 2A0 Canada
Tel: 306-743-2231; *Fax:* 306-743-2873

Macklin Chamber of Commerce
PO Box 642, Macklin SK S0L 2C0 Canada
Tel: 306-753-2221; *Fax:* 306-753-3585
macklin.coop@sasktel.net

Maidstone & District Chamber of Commerce
PO Box 300, Maidstone SK S0M 1M0 Canada
Tel: 306-893-2461; *Fax:* 306-893-4222
cheryl@elliottinsurance.ca

Maple Creek Chamber of Commerce
PO Box 1766, Maple Creek SK S0N 1N0 Canada
Tel: 306-558-7055; *Fax:* 306-662-2422
thedailygrind@sasktel.net

Meadow Lake & District Chamber of Commerce
c/o Northwest REDA, PO Box 1168, 106 - 1st St. East, Meadow Lake SK S9X 1Y8 Canada
Tel: 306-236-4447; *Fax:* 306-236-1833
mltouristinfo@sasktel.net
Affiliation(s): Northwest Regional Economic Development Authority

Melfort & District Chamber of Commerce
PO Box 2002, 102 Spruce Haven Rd., Melfort SK S0E 1A0 Canada
Tel: 306-752-4636; *Fax:* 306-752-9505
melfortchamber@sasktel.net
www.melfortchamber.com

Melville & District Chamber of Commerce
c/o Chamber Office, PO Box 429, 420 Main St., Melville SK S0A 2P0 Canada
Tel: 306-728-4177; *Fax:* 306-728-5911
melvillechamber@sasktel.net
www.melvillechamber.com

Moose Jaw & District Chamber of Commerce
88 Saskatchewan St. East, Moose Jaw SK S6H 0V4 Canada
Tel: 306-692-6414; *Fax:* 306-694-6463
chamber@mjchamber.com
www.mjchamber.com

Moosomin Chamber of Commerce
PO Box 819, Moosomin SK S0G 3N0 Canada
Tel: 306-435-2445; *Fax:* 306-435-3696
world_spectator@sasktel.net
www.moosomin.com/chamber

Nipawin & District Chamber of Commerce
PO Box 177, Nipawin SK S0E 1E0 Canada
Tel: 306-862-5252; *Fax:* 306-862-5350
info@nipawinchamber.ca
www.nipawinchamber.ca

Norquay & District Chamber of Commerce
PO Box 457, Norquay SK S0A 2V0 Canada
Tel: 306-594-2293; *Fax:* 306-594-2435
nnjohnson@sasktel.net

Outlook & District Chamber of Commerce
PO Box 431, Outlook SK S0L 2N0 Canada
Tel: 306-867-9580; *Fax:* 306-867-9559
www.town.outlook.sk.ca/chamber.htm

Paradise Hill Chamber of Commerce
PO Box 118, Paradise Hill SK S0M 2G0 Canada
Tel: 306-344-2188; *Fax:* 306-344-4799
George H Palen, President
Sheila M Phillips, Secretary

Prince Albert Chamber of Commerce
#347, 1084 Central Ave., Prince Albert SK S6V 7P3 Canada
Tel: 306-764-6222; *Fax:* 306-922-4727
pachamber@sasktel.net
www.princealbertchamber.com

Affiliation(s): Canadian Chamber of Commerce; Saskatchewan Chamber of Commerce

Radisson & District Chamber of Commerce
PO Box 397, Radisson SK S0K 3L0 Canada
Tel: 306-827-4801; *Fax:* 306-827-2336
Lloyd E. Lorass, President
Cheryl D. Hamilton, Secretary

Radville Chamber of Commerce
PO Box 799, Radville SK S0C 2G0 Canada
Tel: 306-869-2610; *Fax:* 306-869-2859
town.radville@sasktel.net

Redvers Chamber of Commerce
PO Box 602, Redvers SK S0C 2H0 Canada
Tel: 306-452-3155; *Fax:* 306-452-3155
rdaycare@sasktel.net
Tricia Martel, President
Tanis Chalmers, Director

Regina & District Chamber of Commerce
2145 Albert St., Regina SK S4P 2V1 Canada
Tel: 306-757-4658; *Fax:* 306-757-4668
info@reginachamber.com
www.reginachamber.com
Affiliation(s): Canadian Chamber of Commerce; Saskatchewan Chamber of Commerce

Regina Beach & District Chamber of Commerce
PO Box 606, Regina Beach SK S0G 4C0 Canada
Tel: 306-729-4596
J. Cumbers, President
D. Needham, Secretary

La Ronge & District Chamber of Commerce
PO Box 179, La Ronge SK S0J 1L0 Canada
Tel: 306-425-3056; *Toll-Free:* 866-527-6643
chamberofcommerce@townoflaronge.ca

Rosetown & District Chamber of Commerce
PO Box 744, Rosetown SK S0L 2V0 Canada
Tel: 306-882-1300; *Fax:* 306-882-1310
e2000@sasktel.net
www.rosetown.ca

St. Walburg Chamber of Commerce
PO Box 501, St Walburg SK S0M 2T0 Canada
Tel: 306-248-3244; *Fax:* 306-248-3988
townofstwalburg@sasktel.net
www.stwalburg.com

Shaunavon Chamber of Commerce
PO Box 820, Shaunavon SK S0N 2M0 Canada
Tel: 306-297-3462; *Fax:* 306-297-3420
www.shaunavon.com/chamber.htm

Spiritwood Chamber of Commerce
PO Box 429, Spiritwood SK S0J 2M0 Canada
Tel: 306-883-2267; *Fax:* 306-883-2136

Swift Current Chamber of Commerce
885 - 6th Ave. NE, Swift Current SK S9H 2M9 Canada
Tel: 306-773-7268; *Fax:* 306-773-5686
info@swiftcurrentchamber.ca
www.swiftcurrentchamber.ca
Affiliation(s): Saskatchewan Chamber of Commerce; Canadian Chamber of Commerce

Tisdale & District Chamber of Commerce
PO Box 219, Tisdale SK S0E 1T0 Canada
Tel: 306-873-4257; *Fax:* 306-873-4241
tisdalechamber@sasktel.net

Unity & District Chamber of Commerce
PO Box 834, Unity SK S0K 4L0 Canada
Tel: 306-228-2621
T.J. Schroh, President
Christine Gerein, Treasurer

Vonda Chamber of Commerce
c/o Vonda Hometown Insurance Brokers, PO Box 285, Vonda SK S0K 4N0 Canada
Tel: 306-258-2134; *Fax:* 306-258-2244
rlalonde@sasktel.net

Waskesiu Chamber of Commerce
PO Box 216, Waskesiu Lake SK S0J 2Y0 Canada
Tel: 306-663-5140; *Fax:* 306-663-5448
wakesiuchamber@sasktel.net
www.waskesiulake.ca

Watrous & District Chamber of Commerce
PO Box 906, Watrous SK S0K 4T0 Canada
Tel: 306-946-3353; *Fax:* 306-946-3966

Watson & District Chamber of Commerce
PO Box 686, Watson SK S0K 4V0 Canada
Tel: 306-287-3636; *Fax:* 306-287-3601

Weyburn Chamber of Commerce
#11, 3rd St. NE, Weyburn SK S4H OW5 Canada
Tel: 306-842-4738; *Fax:* 306-842-0520
manager@weyburnchamber.com
www.weyburnchamber.com
Affiliation(s): Saskatchewan Chamber of Commerce

Wolseley & District Chamber of Commerce
PO Box 519, Wolseley SK S0G 5H0 Canada
Tel: 306-698-2252; *Fax:* 306-698-2750

Wynyard & District Chamber of Commerce
PO Box 508, Wynyard SK S0A 4T0 Canada
Tel: 306-554-2224; *Fax:* 306-554-3226

Yorkton Chamber of Commerce
PO Box 1051, Hwy. 9 South, Yorkton SK S3N 2X3 Canada
Tel: 306-783-4368; *Fax:* 306-786-6978
yorktonchamber@sasktel.net
www.chamber.yorkton.sk.ca
Affiliation(s): Saskatchewan Economic Developers Association

Yukon Territory

Dawson City Chamber of Commerce
PO Box 1006, Dawson YT Y0B 1G0 Canada
Tel: 867-993-5274; *Fax:* 867-993-6817
dccc@dawson.net
Dina Grenon, President

St. Elias Chamber of Commerce
PO Box 5419, Haines Junction YT Y0B 1L0 Canada
Tel: 867-634-2916; *Fax:* 867-634-2034
kluaneridin@yknet.ca
Wade Istchenko, President

Silver Trail Chamber of Commerce
PO Box 268, Mayo YT Y0B 1M0 Canada
Tel: 867-996-2827
educate@nndfn.com
Nancy Hager, President

Southern Lakes Chamber of Commerce
PO Box 45, Carcross YT Y0B 1B0 Canada
Tel: 867-821-4372; *Fax:* 867-393-2436
president@southernlakeschamber.com
www.southernlakeschamber.com
Greg Kehoe, Contact

Teslin Regional Chamber of Commerce
PO Box 181, Teslin YT Y0A 1B0 Canada
Tel: 867-390-2521; *Fax:* 867-390-2687
wes.wirth@northwestel.net
Wes Wirth, President

Watson Lake Chamber of Commerce
PO Box 591, Watson Lake YT Y0A 1C0 Canada
Tel: 867-536-2240; *Fax:* 867-536-7294
wlchamberofcommerce@northwestel.net
Jennifer Anderson, Contact

Whitehorse Chamber of Commerce (WCC)
#101, 302 Steele St., Whitehorse YT Y1A 2C5 Canada
Tel: 867-667-7545; *Fax:* 867-667-4507
business@whitehorsechamber.ca
www.whitehorsechamber.ca
Affiliation(s): Yukon Chamber of Commerce; Tourism Industry Association of Yukon
Rick Karp, President

Credit Unions/Caisses Populaires

Credit unions and caisses populaires are owned and controlled by their members. These cooperative financial institutions are regulated at the provincial level. Credit unions, in most provinces, must engage external auditors to prepare financial statements. An annual inspection of credit unions is conducted by their provincial regulatory body.

The national trade association and central finance facility for Canadian credit unions is Credit Union Central of Canada. It is regulated under the Cooperative Credit Associations Act. In Québec, Mouvement des caisses Desjardins du Québec consists of a network of caisses. Fédération des caisses Desjardins du Québec is a cooperative which supports Mouvement des caisses Desjardins du Québec.

1st Choice Savings & Credit Union Ltd.
1320 - 3 Ave. South
Lethbridge, AB T1J 0K5
Tel: 403-320-4600; *Fax:* 403-329-6434
contact@1stchoicesavings.ca
www.1stchoicesavings.ca
Former Name: St. Patrick's Credit Union Ltd.; Southland Credit Union
Ownership: Public
Year Founded: 2001
Assets: $100-500 million

3M Employees' (London) Credit Union Limited
1840 Oxford St. East
London, ON N6A 4T1
Tel: 519-452-6765; *Fax:* 519-452-6023
cuca-corporate@mmm.com
www.3mcreditunion.com

Acadian Credit Union
PO Box 250
15089 Cabot Trail
Cheticamp, NS B0E 1H0
Tel: 902-224-2055; *Fax:* 902-224-3510
Toll-Free: 877-477-7724
www.acadiancreditu.ca
Social Media:
www.facebook.com/pages/Acadian-Credit-Union/144590197297;
www.twitter.com/AcadianCU
Former Name: Cheticamp Credit Union
Year Founded: 1936
Number of Employees: 12

ACE Credit Union Limited
#100, 2055 Albert St.
Regina, SK S4P 2T8
Tel: 306-337-1700; *Fax:* 306-337-1719
info@ace.cu.sk.ca
www.acecreditunion.com
Year Founded: 1973

Adjala Credit Union Limited
7320 St. James Lane
Colgan, ON L0G 1W0
Tel: 905-936-2761; *Fax:* 905-936-6391
Year Founded: 1946

Advance Savings Credit Union (ASCU)
Corporate Office
10 Record St.
Moncton, NB E1C 0B2
Tel: 506-853-1880; *Fax:* 506-382-3564
www.royal-cu.com
Former Name: Rexton Credit Union; Royal Credit Union; Trico Credit Union
Ownership: Member-owned
Year Founded: 2006
Assets: $50-100 million

Advantage Credit Union
PO Box 1657
118 Main St.
Melfort, SK S0E 1A0
Tel: 306-752-2744; *Fax:* 306-752-1919
www.advantagecu.com
Former Name: Melfort Credit Union Ltd.
Ownership: Member-owned
Year Founded: 1943

Affinity Credit Union
309 - 22nd St. East
Saskatoon, SK S7K 0G7
Tel: 306-934-4000; *Fax:* 306-934-5490
Toll-Free: 1-866-863-6237
questions@affinitycu.ca
www.affinitycu.com
Former Name: St. Mary's Credit Union Limited
Ownership: Member-owned
Year Founded: 1949
Assets: $1-10 billion

Agassiz Credit Union Limited
430 Stephen St.
Morden, MB R6M 1T6
Tel: 204-822-4485; *Fax:* 204-822-6155
Toll-Free: 1-877-822-4485
admin@agassizcu.mb.ca
www.agassizcu.mb.ca
Ownership: Member-owned

Airline Financial Credit Union Limited
#120, 5955 Airport Rd.
Mississauga, ON L4V 1R9
Tel: 905-673-7262; *Fax:* 905-676-8437
info@airlinecreditunion.com
www.airlinecreditunion.ca
Former Name: Airline (Malton) Credit Union Limited
Ownership: Member-owned
Year Founded: 1950
Number of Employees: 9
Assets: $10-50 million

Air-Toronto Credit Union
124 Florence Ave.
Toronto, ON M2N 1G3
Tel: 416-359-9685; *Fax:* 416-512-2497
Year Founded: 1959

Aldergrove Credit Union
2941 - 272nd St.
Aldergrove, BC V4W 3R3
Tel: 604-856-7724; *Fax:* 604-856-2565
www.aldergrovecu.ca
Former Name: Otter Farmers' Institute Credit Union
Year Founded: 1954

All Trans Financial Credit Union Limited
Administration Ctr.
#707, 3250 Bloor St. West
Toronto, ON M8X 2X9
Tel: 416-231-8400; *Fax:* 416-231-8296
info@alltrans.com
www.alltrans.com
Year Founded: 1993
Number of Employees: 18

L'Alliance des caisses populaires de l'Ontario limitée
PO Box 3500
1870 Bond St.
North Bay, ON P1B 4V6
Tel: 705-474-5634; *Fax:* 705-474-5326
support@acpol.com
www.caissealliance.com
Ownership: Member-owned.
Year Founded: 1979
Number of Employees: 240
Assets: $500m-1 billion
Revenues: $10-50 million

Alterna Savings & Credit Union Limited
400 Albert St.
Ottawa, ON K1R 5B2
Tel: 613-560-0100; *Fax:* 613-560-0177
Toll-Free: 877-560-0100
query@alterna.ca
www.alterna.ca
Other Contact Information: 416-252-5621 (Toronto phone)
Former Name: Civil Service Co-operative Credit Society Ltd.
Ownership: Member-owned
Year Founded: 2005
Number of Employees: 600+
Assets: $1-10 billion

Anishinabek Nation Credit Union (ANCU)
7 Shingwauk St.
Garden River, ON P6A 6Z8
Tel: 705-942-7655; *Fax:* 705-942-7613
Toll-Free: 866-775-2628
cu-info@ancu.ca
www.ancu.ca

Apex Credit Union Limited
Administration Office, TransCanada Centre
#210, 1440 - 52nd St. NE
Calgary, AB T2A 4T8
Tel: 403-974-8640; *Fax:* 403-282-3099
Toll-Free: 1-877-273-9247
www.apexcu.com
Ownership: Member-owned
Year Founded: 1940
Assets: $50-100 million

Apple Community Credit Union
406 North Cumberland St.
Thunder Bay, ON P7A 4P8
Tel: 807-345-8153; *Fax:* 807-343-9271
info@applecu.com
www.applecu.com
Ownership: Private

Arctic Credit Union Ltd.
800 Central Ave., 9th Fl.
Prince Albert, SK S6V 6Z2
Tel: 306-922-8252
Former Name: Arctic Savings & Credit Union Ltd.
Year Founded: 1939

Arnstein Community Credit Union Limited
PO Box 104
Port Loring, ON P0H 1Y0
Tel: 705-757-2662; *Fax:* 705-757-2662
Year Founded: 1962

Assiniboine Credit Union Limited (ACU)
Corporate Office
PO Box 2, Main Stn. Main
200 Main St., 6th Fl.
Winnipeg, MB R3C 2G1
Tel: 877-958-8588; *Fax:* 877-958-7348
cu@assiniboine.mb.ca
www.assiniboine.mb.ca
Other Contact Information: 1-877-957-1587 (TTY Line for Hearing Impaired)
Ownership: Member-owned
Year Founded: 1943
Number of Employees: 500
Assets: $1-10 billion

Austin Credit Union
PO Box 205
24 - 2nd Ave.
Austin, MB R0H 0H0
Tel: 204-385-6140; *Fax:* 204-637-2204
www.austincreditunion.com
Year Founded: 1949

Auto Workers (Ajax) Credit Union Limited
PO Box 21115
290 Harwood Ave. South
Ajax, ON L1S 2J1
Tel: 905-683-0791; *Fax:* 905-683-6047
Year Founded: 1968

Auto Workers' Community Credit Union Limited
322 King St. West
Oshawa, ON L1J 2J9
Tel: 905-728-5187; *Fax:* 905-728-8727
Toll-Free: 800-268-8771
information@awccu.com
www.awccu.com
Ownership: Private. Cooperative
Year Founded: 1938
Number of Employees: 70
Revenues: $100-500 million

Battle River Credit Union Ltd.
5007 - 51 St.
Camrose, AB T4V 1S6
Tel: 780-672-1175; *Fax:* 780-672-5996
brcu@battlerivercreditunion.com
www.battlerivercreditunion.com
Ownership: Member-owned
Year Founded: 1949
Number of Employees: 110
Assets: $100-500 million Year End: 20080930
Revenues: $1-5 million Year End: 20080930

Bay Credit Union Limited
142 Algoma St. South
Thunder Bay, ON P7B 3B8
Tel: 807-345-7612; *Fax:* 807-345-8939
Toll-Free: 1-877-249-7076
info@baycreditunion.com
www.baycreditunion.com

Bay St Lawrence Credit Union
PO Box 112
3020 Bay St. Lawrence Rd.
Dingwall, NS B0C 1G0
Tel: 902-383-2003
Year Founded: 1937
Number of Employees: 1

Bayshore Credit Union Ltd.
PO Box 878
191 North Front St.
Belleville, ON K8N 5B5
Tel: 613-966-5550; *Fax:* 613-966-9523
www.bayshorecu.com

Bayview Credit Union
#400, 57 King St.
Saint John, NB E2L 1G5
Tel: 506-634-1263; *Fax:* 506-634-1686
www.bayviewnb.com
Year Founded: 1938
Number of Employees: 115
Assets: $100-500 million

Beaubear Credit Union
PO Box 764
376 Water St.
Miramichi, NB E1V 3V4
Tel: 506-622-4532
mdaley@beaubear.creditu.net
www.beaubear.ca
Ownership: Member-owned
Year Founded: 1938
Assets: $10-50 million

Beaumont Credit Union Limited
5007 - 50th Ave.
Beaumont, AB T4X 1E7
Tel: 780-929-8561; *Fax:* 780-929-2999
Toll-Free: 800-307-8353
cberube@alberta-cu.com
www.beaumontcu.com
Other Contact Information: 1-800-561-7849 (Credit Card Balances); 306-566-1276 (Outside Canada)
Former Name: St Vital & Beaumont Savings & Credit Union
Year Founded: 1946

Beautiful Plains Credit Union
PO Box 99
239 Hamilton St.
Neepawa, MB R0J 1H0
Tel: 204-476-3341; *Fax:* 204-476-3609
info@bpcu.mb.ca
www.bpcu.mb.ca
Year Founded: 1955

Belgian-Alliance Credit Union
1177 Portage Ave.
Winnipeg, MB R3G 0T2
Tel: 204-927-0460; *Fax:* 204-927-0461
mail@alliancecu.ca
www.alliancecu.ca
Former Name: Alliance Credit Union; Adanac Credit Union Ltd; Communicators Credit Union; Progress Vera Credit Union
Year Founded: 2001

Bengough Credit Union Ltd.
260 Main St.
Bengough, SK S0C 0K0
Tel: 306-268-2930
info@bengough.cu.sk.ca
www.bengough.cu.sk.ca
Year Founded: 1943

Bergengren Credit Union
257 Main St.
Antigonish, NS B2G 2C1
Tel: 902-863-6600; *Fax:* 902-863-3031
Toll-Free: 888-273-3488
info@bergengrencu.com
www.bergengrencu.com
Year Founded: 1933
Number of Employees: 51

Blackville Credit Union
128 Main St.
Blackville, NB E9B 1P1
Tel: 506-843-2219; *Fax:* 506-843-6773
Year Founded: 1936

Bow Valley Credit Union Limited
PO Box 876
Cochrane, AB T4C 1A9
Tel: 403-932-4693; *Fax:* 403-932-9865
lbohn@bowvalleycu.com
www.bowvalleycu.com
Ownership: Member-owned

Brewers Warehousing Employees (Hamilton) Credit Union Limited
c/o Beer Store
673 Upper James St.
Hamilton, ON L9C 5R9
Tel: 905-574-7652; *Fax:* 905-574-7652

Brewers Warehousing Employees (Kitchener) Credit Union Limited
53 Filbert St.
Kitchener, ON N2H 1Y1
Tel: 519-576-7324

Brook Street Credit Union Ltd.
Millbrook Mall
PO Box 713
2 Herald Ave., Main Level
Corner Brook, NL A2H 6G7
Tel: 709-634-4632; *Toll-Free:* 866-273-3488
brookstreet@brookstreet.creditu.net
www.bscu.ca

Ownership: Member-owned
Year Founded: 1963
Assets: $10-50 million

Bruno Savings & Credit Union Limited
PO Box 158
511 Main St.
Bruno, SK S0K 0S0
Tel: 306-369-2901; Fax: 306-369-2225
www.brunocu.com
Ownership: Member-owned

Buduchnist Credit Union (BCU)
2280 Bloor St. West
Toronto, ON M6S 1N9
Tel: 416-763-6883; Fax: 416-763-4512
Toll-Free: 800-461-5941
info@buduchnist.com; help@buduchnist.com (Help Desk)
www.buduchnist.com
Other Contact Information: link@buduchnist.com (BCU Link); privacyofficer@buduchnist.com (Privacy Officer)
Ownership: Member-owned
Year Founded: 1952

Bulkley Valley Credit Union
PO Box 3637
3872 - 1st Ave.
Smithers, BC V0J 2N0
Tel: 250-847-3255; Fax: 250-847-3012
infoadmin@bvcu.com
www.bvcu.com

Caisse centrale Desjardins du Québec (CCD)
#600, 1170 rue Peel
Montréal, QC H3B 0B1
Tél: 514-281-7070; Téléc: 514-281-7083
www.desjardins.com/ccd
Ownership: Cooperatively owned by the Fédération des caisses Desjardins du Québec
Year Founded: 1979

Caisse Horizon Credit Union Ltd.
PO Box 147
Girouxville, AB T0H 1S0
Tel: 780-323-4600; Fax: 780-323-4545
Toll-Free: 866-758-6466
www.powerofmembers.ca
Also Known As: Horizon Credit Union
Ownership: Member-owned
Year Founded: 1956
Number of Employees: 58
Assets: $10-50 million

Caisse populaire de Saulnierville
RR#1
Saulnierville, NS B0W 2Z0
Tél: 902-769-2574; Téléc: 902-769-3555
Year Founded: 1953

Cambrian Credit Union Ltd.
Also listed under: Financing & Loan Companies
225 Broadway
Winnipeg, MB R3C 5R4
Tel: 204-925-2600; Fax: 204-231-1306
Toll-Free: 888-695-8900
ccuinfo@cambrian.mb.ca; ccuhead@cambrian.mb.ca
www.cambrian.mb.ca
Ownership: Member-owned
Year Founded: 1959
Assets: $1-10 billion

Campbell's Employees' (Toronto) Credit Union Limited
60 Birmingham St.
Toronto, ON M8V 2B8
Tel: 416-251-1117; Fax: 416-253-8669

Canada Safeway Limited Employees Savings & Credit Union
1822 - 10th Ave. SW
Calgary, AB T3C 0J8
Tel: 403-261-5681; Fax: 403-261-5748
Toll-Free: 877-723-2653
info@safewaycucalgary.com
www.safewaycucalgary.com
Ownership: Member-owned
Year Founded: 1952
Number of Employees: 10

Canadian Alternative Investment Cooperative
#111, 146 Laird Dr.
Toronto, ON M4G 3V7
Tel: 416-467-7797; Fax: 416-467-8946
Toll-Free: 866-241-2242
caic@caic.ca
www.caic.ca
Year Founded: 1984

Canadian General Tower Employees (Galt) Credit Union Limited
Cambridge Place
#117, 73 Water St. North
Cambridge, ON N1R 7L6
Tel: 519-623-2211; Fax: 519-623-2051
Ownership: Private
Number of Employees: 3

Canadian Transportation Employees' Credit Union Ltd.
PO Box 4
600 Ferguson Ave. North
Hamilton, ON L8L 4Z9
Tel: 905-523-7385; Fax: 905-523-7556
Number of Employees: 3

Carleton Pioneer Credit Union
#1, 106 Richmond St.
Woodstock, NB E7M 2N9
Tel: 506-328-8120; Fax: 506-328-3445
www.cpcu.coop
Year Founded: 1938
Number of Employees: 9

Carpathia Credit Union
952 Main St.
Winnipeg, MB R2W 3P4
Tel: 204-989-7400; Fax: 204-589-2529
info@carpathiacu.mb.ca
www.carpathiacu.mb.ca
Ownership: Member-owned
Year Founded: 1940
Assets: $100-500 million

Casera Credit Union
1300 Plessis Rd.
Winnipeg, MB R2C 2Y6
Tel: 204-958-6300; Fax: 204-222-6766
Toll-Free: 866-211-9233
www.caseracu.ca
Also Known As: Transcona Credit Union
Ownership: Member-owned
Year Founded: 1951

Cataract Savings & Credit Union Limited
7172 Dorchester Rd.
Niagara Falls, ON L2G 5V6
Tel: 905-357-5222; Fax: 905-357-9366
www.cataractsavings.on.ca
Year Founded: 1949

CBC (Nfld) Credit Union Ltd.
PO Box 12010, A Stn. A
29-31 Pippy Place
St. John's, NL A1B 3T8
Tel: 709-576-5407; Fax: 709-576-5409
cbccreditunion@cbccu.ca
www.cbccu.ca
Year Founded: 1965
Number of Employees: 3

CCB Employees' Credit Union Limited
46 Overlea Blvd.
Toronto, ON M4H 1B6
Tel: 416-424-6280; Fax: 416-701-1944
Year Founded: 1973
Number of Employees: 2
Revenues: Under $1 million

CCEC Credit Union
2250 Commercial Dr.
Vancouver, BC V5N 5P9
Tel: 604-254-4100; Fax: 604-254-6558
Toll-Free: 866-254-4100
info@ccec.bc.ca
www.ccec.bc.ca
Ownership: Cooperative
Year Founded: 1976

Central 1 Credit Union - British Columbia Region
1441 Creekside Dr.
Vancouver, BC V6J 4S7
Tel: 604-734-2511; Fax: 604-734-5055
info@central1.com
www.cucbc.com
Former Name: Credit Union Central of British Columbia
Ownership: Member credit unions
Year Founded: 1944
Number of Employees: 475
Assets: $1-10 billion
Revenues: $10-50 million

Central 1 Credit Union - Ontario Region
2810 Matheson Blvd. East
Mississauga, ON L4W 4X7
Tel: 905-238-9400; Fax: 905-238-8196
Toll-Free: 800-661-6813
customerservice@central1.com
www.ontariocreditunions.com
Other Contact Information: 905-629-5711 (Help Desk Phone)
Former Name: Credit Union Central of Ontario
Number of Employees: 125
Assets: $1-10 billion

Central Credit Union Limited
PO Box 279
512 Main St.
O'Leary, PE C0B 1V0
Tel: 902-859-2266; Fax: 902-859-3219
central.cu@central.creditu.net
www.centralcreditu.com
Ownership: Member-owned
Year Founded: 1969
Number of Employees: 17

Chinook Credit Union Ltd.
PO Box 1137
99 - 2nd St. West
Brooks, AB T1R 1B9
Tel: 403-362-4233; Fax: 403-362-4239
www.chinookcu.com
Former Name: Macleod Savings & Credit Union Ltd.
Ownership: Member-owned
Year Founded: 1941
Number of Employees: 160
Assets: $50-100 million

Church River Credit Union
305 Burnt Church Rd.
Burnt Church, NB E9G 4C8
Tel: 506-776-3247; Fax: 506-776-3247

Churchbridge Savings & Credit Union
PO Box 260
103 Vincent Ave. East
Churchbridge, SK S0A 0M0
Tel: 306-896-2544; Fax: 306-896-2325
Toll-Free: 877-890-2797
info@churchbridge.cu.sk.ca
www.churchbridgecu.ca
Year Founded: 1945

City Plus Credit Union Ltd.
Municipal Bldg.
PO Box 2100, M Stn. M
#8130, 800 MacLeod Trail SE, 5th Fl.
Calgary, AB T2P 2M5
Tel: 403-268-2626; Fax: 403-268-4886
main@cpcu.ca
www.cpcu.ca
Former Name: Calgary Civic Employees Credit Union Limited
Ownership: Private
Year Founded: 1942
Number of Employees: 5

City Savings Financial Services
6002 Yonge St.
Toronto, ON M2M 3V9
Tel: 416-225-7716; Fax: 416-225-7772
info@citysavingscu.com
www.citysavingscu.com
Former Name: City Savings & Credit Union Ltd.; The North York Municipal Employees' Credit Union
Year Founded: 1950

CN (London) Credit Union Limited
#301, 205 York St.
London, ON N6A 1B1
Tel: 519-667-2326; Fax: 519-434-5687
cncucindy@ody.ca
www.cncu.ca
Year Founded: 1945
Number of Employees: 4

CNR Employees (Lakehead Terminal) Credit Union Limited
417 Fort William Rd.
Thunder Bay, ON P7B 2Z5
Tel: 807-344-4096; Fax: 807-346-0595

Coady Credit Union
32 West Ave.
Glace Bay, NS B1A 6E9
Tel: 902-849-7610; *Fax:* 902-842-0911
Year Founded: 1933

Coast Capital Savings Credit Union
Corporate Head Office
15117 - 101 Ave.
Surrey, BC V3R 8P7
Tel: 604-517-7000; *Fax:* 604-517-7405
Toll-Free: 888-517-7000
info@coastcapitalsavings.com
www.coastcapitalsavings.com
Other Contact Information: 1-877-333-7736 (Technical Support); 604-517-7822 (Cantonese); 604-517-7823 (Mandarin); 604-517-7780 (Punjabi)
Ownership: Member-owned
Year Founded: 2000
Number of Employees: 2,000+

Coastal Community Credit Union
#21, 13 Victoria Cres.
Nanaimo, BC V9R 5B9
Tel: 250-741-3200; *Fax:* 250-741-3223
Toll-Free: 888-741-1010
www.cccu.ca
Other Contact Information: 1-888-741-4040 (Telephone Banking Toll-Free); 1-800-567-8111 (Lost Member Card, Canada & the USA); 1-800-567-8111 (Lost MasterCard, Canada & the USA)
Ownership: Member-owned
Year Founded: 1946
Number of Employees: 600+
Assets: $1-10 billion

Coastal Financial Credit Union
2 Collins St.
Yarmouth, NS B5A 3C3
Tel: 902-742-7322; *Fax:* 902-742-7476
rdoucette@coastalfinancial.ca
www.coastalfinancial.ca
Ownership: Member-owned
Year Founded: 2001
Number of Employees: 53
Assets: $50-100 million

Codroy Valley Credit Union
PO Box 29
Doyles, NL A0N 1J0
Tel: 709-955-2402; *Fax:* 709-955-3081
www.codroyvalleycu.com

College Hill Credit Union
c/o University of New Brunswick, McConnell Hall
PO Box 4400
#107, 19 Bailey Dr.
Fredericton, NB E3B 5A3
Tel: 506-455-3535
www.unb.ca/facilities/chcu

Columbia Valley Credit Union
PO Box 720
511 Main St.
Golden, BC V0A 1H0
Tel: 250-344-2282; *Fax:* 250-344-2117
Toll-Free: 888-298-1777
www.cvcu.bc.ca
Other Contact Information: 1-888-273-3488 (Online Banking Support); 1-866-344-7968 (Phone Banking)
Ownership: Member-owned
Year Founded: 1955
Assets: $100-500 million

Communication Technologies Credit Union Limited
Eaton Centre
PO Box 501
#102, 220 Yonge St.
Toronto, ON M5B 2H1
Tel: 416-598-1197; *Fax:* 416-598-0171
Toll-Free: 800-209-7444
member_services@comtechcu.com
www.comtechcu.com
Ownership: Member-owned
Number of Employees: 14
Assets: $50-100 million

Community Credit Union Ltd.
164 Main St.
Grunthal, MB R0A 0R0
Tel: 204-434-6338; *Fax:* 204-434-9074
grunthal@communitycu.mb.ca
www.communitycu.mb.ca

Community Credit Union of Cumberland Colchester Limited
PO Box 578
#201, 32 Church St.
Amherst, NS B4H 4B8
Tel: 902-667-7541; *Fax:* 902-667-0217
Toll-Free: 1-888-273-3488
www.communitycreditunion.ns.ca
Former Name: Amherst Credit Union; Colchester Credit Union
Ownership: Member-owned
Year Founded: 1999

Community First Credit Union Limited
289 Bay St.
Sault Ste Marie, ON P6A 1W7
Tel: 705-942-1000; *Fax:* 705-946-2363
www.communityfirst-cu.com
Year Founded: 1948

Community Savings Credit Union
Central City Tower
#1600, 13450 - 102nd Ave., 16th Fl.
Surrey, BC V3T 5X3
Tel: 604-654-2000; *Fax:* 604-586-5156
Toll-Free: 888-963-2000
www.comsavings.com
Former Name: IWA & Community Credit Union
Year Founded: 1944
Number of Employees: 500

Concentra Financial Corporate Banking
333 - 3rd Ave. North
Saskatoon, SK S7K 2M2
Toll-Free: 800-788-6311
servicecentre@concentrafinancial.ca
www.concentrafinancial.ca
Former Name: CUCORP Financial Services
Ownership: Private
Year Founded: 1997
Revenues: $1-10 billion

Conexus Credit Union
1960 Albert St.
Regina, SK S4P 2T4
Tel: 306-780-1750; *Toll-Free:* 800-667-7477
information@conexuscu.com
www.conexuscu.com
Former Name: Assiniboia Credit Union Ltd.
Number of Employees: 1,000

Copperfin Credit Union
346 - 2nd St. South
Kenora, ON P9N 1G5
Tel: 807-467-4400; *Fax:* 807-468-3500
Toll-Free: 888-710-6664
kenora@copperfin.ca
www.copperfin.ca
Former Name: Lakewood Credit Union Ltd.
Ownership: Member-owned
Year Founded: 1954
Number of Employees: 34

Cornerstone Credit Union Ltd.
PO Box 455
1202, 100th St.
Tisdale, SK S0E 1T0
Tel: 306-873-2616; *Fax:* 306-873-4322
reception@cornerstone.cu.sk.ca
www.cornerstonecu.ca
Former Name: Tisdale Credit Union Ltd.
Ownership: Private. Member-owned
Year Founded: 1943
Number of Employees: 30
Assets: $100-500 million
Revenues: $1-5 million

Credit Union Atlantic (CUA)
#350, 7105 Chebucto Rd.
Halifax, NS B3L 4W8
Tel: 902-492-6500; *Fax:* 902-492-6501
Toll-Free: 800-474-4282
www.cua.com
Other Contact Information: 902-493-4800 (Teleservice); 1-800-963-4848 (TeleService Toll Free); 1-800-561-7849 (MasterCard Inquiries); 1-800-567-8111 (Lost MasterCards)
Year Founded: 1948
Number of Employees: 115
Assets: $100-500 million

Credit Union Central Alberta Limited
#350N, 8500 MacLeod Trail South
Calgary, AB T2H 2N1
Tel: 403-258-5900; *Fax:* 403-253-7720
email@albertacentral.com
www.albertacentral.com
Ownership: Owned by the credit unions of Alberta
Number of Employees: 230
Assets: $1-10 billion

Credit Union Central of Canada (CUCC)
#500, 300 The East Mall
Toronto, ON M9B 6B7
Tel: 416-232-1262; *Fax:* 416-232-9196
cucc@cucentral.com
www.cucentral.ca
Ownership: Owned by the provincial credit union centrals
Year Founded: 1953

Credit Union Central of Manitoba (CUCM)
#400, 317 Donald St.
Winnipeg, MB R3B 2H6
Tel: 204-985-4700; *Fax:* 204-957-0217
cuinfo@cucm.org
www.creditunion.mb.ca
Former Name: Cooperative Credit Society of Manitoba Ltd.
Ownership: Member-owned
Year Founded: 1950
Assets: $10-100 billion

Credit Union Central of New Brunswick (CUCNB)
663 Pinewood Rd.
Riverview, NB E1B 5R6
Tel: 506-857-8184; *Toll-Free:* 800-332-3320
info@cucnb.nb.ca
www.creditunion.nb.ca
Year Founded: 1950

Credit Union Central of Nova Scotia
PO Box 9200
6074 Lady Hammond Rd.
Halifax, NS B3K 5N3
Tel: 902-453-0680; *Fax:* 902-455-2437
Toll-Free: 800-668-2879
info@cucns.ca; humanresources@cucns.ca;
communications@cucns.ca
www.ns-credit-unions.com
Year Founded: 1938

Credit Union Central of Prince Edward Island
PO Box 968
281 University Ave.
Charlottetown, PE C1A 7M4
Tel: 902-566-3350; *Fax:* 902-368-3534
website@cucpei.com
www.peicreditunions.com
Year Founded: 1936
Number of Employees: 200
Assets: $500m-1 billion

Creston & District Credit Union
PO Box 215
140 - 11th Ave. North
Creston, BC V0B 1G0
Tel: 250-428-5351; *Fax:* 250-428-5302
Toll-Free: 866-857-2802
cdcu@cdcu.com
www.cdcu.com
Ownership: Credit Union Central, BC
Year Founded: 1951

Croatian Toronto Credit Union Limited
19 Dundas St. West
Mississauga, ON L5B 1H2
Tel: 905-276-1962; *Fax:* 905-532-0846
info@coatiancreditunion.ca
www.croatiancreditunion.ca
Year Founded: 1958

Crocus Credit Union
1016 Rosser Ave.
Brandon, MB R7A 0L6
Tel: 204-729-4800; *Fax:* 204-729-4818
info@crocuscu.mb.ca
www.crocuscu.mb.ca
Other Contact Information: 1-800-567-8111 (Lost ATM Cards)
Former Name: Brandon Terminal Credit Union Society Limited
Ownership: Member-owned
Year Founded: 1952

Crosstown Civic Credit Union
171 Donald St.
Winnipeg, MB R3C 1M4
Tel: 204-942-1277; *Fax:* 204-947-3108
cu@crosstowncivic.mb.ca
www.crosstowncivic.mb.ca
Other Contact Information: 1-800-567-8111 (Lost ATM & Member Cards); 204-949-1048 (ExpressLine TeleService)
Ownership: Member-owned
Year Founded: 1943
Assets: $1-10 billion Year End: 20081231

Crosstown Civic Credit Union Ltd.
171 Donald St.
Winnipeg, MB R3C 1M4
Tel: 204-942-1277; *Fax:* 204-947-3108
cu@crosstowncivic.mb.ca
www.crosstowncivic.mb.ca
Former Name: Civic Credit Union Ltd.
Ownership: Member-owned
Year Founded: 1943

Cut Knife Credit Union Ltd.
PO Box 308
205 Broad St.
Cut Knife, SK S0M 0N0
Tel: 306-398-2544; *Fax:* 306-398-2744
Mitch.Rokochy@cutknife.cu.sk.ca
Year Founded: 1960
Number of Employees: 7

Cypress Credit Union Ltd.
PO Box 1060
115 Jasper St.
Maple Creek, SK S0N 1N0
Tel: 306-662-2683; *Fax:* 306-662-3859
Toll-Free: 877-353-6311
www.cypresscu.sk.ca

Dauphin Plains Credit Union
PO Box 340
505 Main St. North
Dauphin, MB R7N 2V2
Tel: 204-622-4500; *Fax:* 204-622-4530
Toll-Free: 1-866-372-4535
info@dauphinplainscu.mb.ca
www.dauphinplainscu.mb.ca
Year Founded: 1940

Desjardins Credit Union
Also listed under: *Credit Card Companies; Non-Depository Institutions*
East Tower, Whitby Mall
1615 Dundas St. East, 3rd Fl.
Whitby, ON L1N 2L1
Tel: 905-743-5790; *Fax:* 905-743-6156
Toll-Free: 888-283-8333
www.desjardins.com
Ownership: Member-owned
Year Founded: 2002

Desjardins Gestion d'actifs/ Desjardins Asset Management
Also listed under: *Credit Card Companies; Non-Depository Institutions*
95 St Clair Ave. West
Toronto, ON M4V 1N7

Diamond North Credit Union
PO Box 2074
Nipawin, SK S0E 1E0
Tel: 306-862-4651; *Fax:* 306-862-9611
Toll-Free: 877-881-2020
contactus@diamondnorthcu.com
www.diamondnorthcu.com, www.nipawincu.com
Other Contact Information: 306/862-2370 (Loans)
Year Founded: 2006
Assets: $100-500 million

Dodsland & District Credit Union Ltd.
PO Box 129
Dodsland, SK S0L 0V0
Tel: 306-356-2155; *Fax:* 306-356-2202
james.duncan@dodsland.cu.sk.ca
www.dodslandcreditunion.com
Year Founded: 1961
Number of Employees: 7

Dominion Credit Union
94 Commercial St.
Dominion, NS B1G 1B4
Tel: 902-849-8648; *Fax:* 902-842-0273
Year Founded: 1934

Domtar Newsprint Employees (Trenton) Credit Union Limited
PO Box 254
Trenton, ON K8V 5R5
Tel: 613-392-2426; *Fax:* 613-392-6851
ldwannamaker@sympatico.ca

DUCA Financial Services Credit Union Ltd.
5290 Yonge St.
Toronto, ON M2N 5P9
Tel: 416-223-8502; *Fax:* 416-223-2575
Toll-Free: 866-900-3822
duca.info@duca.com
www.duca.com
Former Name: Duca Community Credit Union Limited
Ownership: Member-owned
Year Founded: 1954
Number of Employees: 100
Assets: $500m-1 billion
Revenues: $10-50 million

Dundalk District Credit Union Limited
PO Box 340
79 Proton St. North
Dundalk, ON N0C 1B0
Tel: 519-923-2400; *Fax:* 519-923-2950
jmason@dundalkdistrictcreditunion.ca
www.dundalkdistrictcreditunion.ca
Year Founded: 1943
Number of Employees: 11
Assets: $10-50 million
Revenues: Under $1 million

Dunnville & District Credit Union Ltd.
208 Broad St. East
Dunnville, ON N1A 1G2
Tel: 905-774-7559; *Fax:* 905-774-4662
www.ddcu.com
Ownership: Member-owned
Number of Employees: 5

Dysart Credit Union Ltd.
PO Box 39
110 Main St.
Dysart, SK S0G 1H0
Tel: 306-432-2211
Year Founded: 1960

Eagle River Credit Union
PO Box 29
8 Branch Rd.
L'Anse au Loup, NL A0K 3L0
Tel: 709-927-5524; *Fax:* 709-927-5759
Toll-Free: 877-377-3728
aobrien@eagleriver.creditu.net
www.eaglerivercu.com
Year Founded: 1984
Number of Employees: 40
Assets: $10-50 million
Revenues: Under $1 million

East Coast Credit Union
Admin. Office
305 Granville St.
Port Hawkesbury, NS B9A 2M5
Tel: 902-625-5610
www.eastcoastcreditu.ca
Year Founded: 2003
Number of Employees: 104
Assets: $100-500 million

East Kootenay Community Credit Union
924 Baker St.
Cranbrook, BC V1C 1A5
Tel: 250-426-6666; *Fax:* 250-426-0879
Toll-Free: 866-960-6666
reception@ekccu.com
www.ekccu.com
Number of Employees: 30

EasternEdge Credit Union
PO Box 2110
10 Factory Lane
St. John's, NL A1C 5H6
Tel: 709-739-2920; *Fax:* 709-739-3728
Toll-Free: 800-716-7283
www.easternedgecu.com
Former Name: NewTel Credit Union
Year Founded: 1976
Assets: $10-50 million

Eckville District Savings & Credit Union Ltd.
PO Box 278
Eckville, AB T0M 0X0
Tel: 403-746-2288; *Fax:* 403-746-3737
info@eckvillecu.com
www.eckvillecu.com
Ownership: Private
Year Founded: 1943
Number of Employees: 9

Edson Savings & Credit Union
PO Box 6118
4912 - 2nd Ave.
Edson, AB T7E 1T6
Tel: 780-723-4468; *Fax:* 780-723-7973
edsoncu@alberta-cu.com
www.edsoncu.com
Year Founded: 1940

Electragas Credit Union
6070 Stairs St.
Halifax, NS B3K 2E5
Tel: 902-454-6843; *Fax:* 902-453-5161

Electric Employees Credit Union
10 Lanceleve Cres.
Albert Bridge, NS B1K 3J3
Tel: 902-564-9707; *Fax:* 902-564-0956

Enderby & District Credit Union
PO Box 670
703 Mill St.
Enderby, BC V0E 1V0
Tel: 250-838-6841; *Fax:* 250-838-9756
info@enderbycreditunion.com
www.enderbycreditunion.com

Entegra Credit Union
Corporate Head Office
1335 Jefferson Ave.
Winnipeg, MB R2P 1S7
Tel: 204-949-7744; *Fax:* 204-949-5865
info@entegra.ca
www.entegra.ca
Former Name: Holy Spirit Credit Union
Year Founded: 1960
Number of Employees: 47
Assets: $100-500 million

Envision Credit Union
6470 - 201st St.
Langley, BC V2Y 2X4
Tel: 604-539-7300; *Fax:* 604-539-7315
www.envisionfinancial.ca
Also Known As: Envision Financial
Ownership: Member-owned
Year Founded: 1946
Number of Employees: 779
Assets: $1-10 billion
Revenues: $100-500 million

Equity Financial Services
#3, 400 Eastern Ave.
Toronto, ON M4M 1B9
Tel: 416-463-3173; *Fax:* 416-465-9984
Toll-Free: 1-800-263-9793
info@equityfs.ca
www.equitycreditunion.ca
Former Name: Unilever Employees Credit Union Limited; Equity Credit Union

Erickson Credit Union Limited
PO Box 100
24 Main St. West
Erickson, MB R0J 0P0
Tel: 204-636-7771; *Fax:* 204-636-2498
info@ericksoncu.mb.ca
www.ericksoncu.mb.ca
Ownership: Member-owned
Year Founded: 1952

Eriksdale Credit Union Limited
PO Box 99, Railway Stn. Railway
Eriksdale, MB R0C 0W0
Tel: 204-739-2137; *Fax:* 204-739-5409
info@eriksdalecu.mb.ca
www.eriksdalecu.mb.ca
Ownership: Member-owned
Year Founded: 1972
Number of Employees: 29

Espanola & District Credit Union Limited
91 Centre St.
Espanola, ON P5E 1S4
Tel: 705-869-3001
www.espanolacu.com
Year Founded: 1958

Estonian (Toronto) Credit Union Limited
958 Broadview Ave.
Toronto, ON M4K 2R6
Tel: 416-465-4659; *Fax:* 416-465-8442
Toll-Free: 866-844-3828
info@estoniancu.com
www.estoniancu.com
Year Founded: 1954
Number of Employees: 12

ETCU Financial
1 East Mall Cres.
Toronto, ON M9B 6G8
Tel: 416-622-8500; *Fax:* 416-622-0610
Toll-Free: 877-337-8500
www.etcu.com
Former Name: Etobicoke Teachers' Credit Union Limited
Year Founded: 1951

Ethelbert Credit Union
109 Railway Ave.
Ethelbert, MB R0L 0T0
Tel: 204-742-3529

Fairview & District Savings & Credit Union Ltd.
PO Box 459
10300 - 110 St.
Fairview, AB T0H 1L0
Tel: 780-835-2914; *Fax:* 780-835-4214

Fédération des caisses Desjardins du Québec
100, av. des Commandeurs
Lévis, QC G6V 7N5
Tél: 418-835-8444; *Ligne sans frais:* 1-866-835-8444
www.desjardins.com
Former Name: Fédération des Caisses Populaires Desjardins du Québec

Fédération des caisses populaires acadiennes ltée
CP 5554
295, boul St-Pierre ouest
Caraquet, NB E1W 1B7
Tél: 506-726-4000; *Téléc:* 506-726-4001
info@acadie.com
www.acadie.com
Year Founded: 1946
Number of Employees: 227

Fédération des caisses populaires de l'Ontario
214 Montreal Rd.
Ottawa, ON K1L 8L8
Tél: 613-746-3276; *Téléc:* 613-746-6035
Ligne sans frais: 800-423-3276

Fédération des caisses populaires du Manitoba
#200, 605 Des Meurons St.
Winnipeg, MB R2H 2R1
Tél: 204-237-8988; *Téléc:* 204-233-6405
federation@caisse.biz
www.caisse.biz
Ownership: Member-owned
Year Founded: 1937
Number of Employees: 240

Fiberglas Employees (Guelph) Credit Union Limited
PO Box 3603
247 York Rd.
Guelph, ON N1E 3G4
Tel: 519-824-2212; *Fax:* 519-824-1390
fiberglascu@bellnet.ca
Year Founded: 1953
Number of Employees: 1

First Calgary Savings & Credit Union Limited
#200, 510 - 16th Ave. NE
Calgary, AB T2E 1K4
Tel: 403-230-2783; *Fax:* 403-276-6338
info@1stcalgary.com
www.1stcalgary.com
Ownership: Member-owned
Year Founded: 1987
Assets: $1-10 billion

FirstOntario Credit Union Limited
688 Queensdale Ave. East
Hamilton, ON L8V 1M1
Tel: 905-387-0770; *Toll-Free:* 888-283-7835
contact@firstontariocu.com
www.firstontariocu.com
Former Name: Avestel Family Savings Credit Union Limited; Family Savings & Credit Union Limited
Year Founded: 1940
Number of Employees: 300
Assets: $500m-1 billion

Flin Flon Credit Union
36 Main St.
Flin Flon, MB R8A 1J6
Tel: 204-687-6620
www.flinfloncu.mb.ca
Year Founded: 1940
Number of Employees: 3

Foam Lake Savings & Credit Union Ltd.
PO Box 160
326 Main St.
Foam Lake, SK S0A 1A0
Tel: 306-272-3385; *Fax:* 306-272-4948
info@foamlake.cu.sk.ca
www.foamlake.cu.sk.ca
Year Founded: 1941

Food Family Credit Union
2044 Danforth Ave.
Toronto, ON M4C 1J6
Tel: 416-424-4798; *Fax:* 416-424-4760
Toll-Free: 800-267-3663
info@foodfamilycreditunion.com
www.foodfamilycreditunion.com
Year Founded: 1964
Number of Employees: 3
Assets: $10-50 million

Forget Credit Union Ltd.
General Delivery
Stoughton, SK S0C 0X0
Tel: 306-457-2747
Year Founded: 1950

Fort Erie Community Credit Union Limited
1201 Garrison Rd.
Fort Erie, ON L2A 1N8
Tel: 905-994-1201; *Fax:* 905-994-1897
info@forteriecu.com
www.forteriecu.com

Fort York Community Credit Union Limited
Sunnyside East Wing
#207, 30 The Queensway
Toronto, ON M6R 1B5
Tel: 416-530-6474; *Fax:* 416-530-6763
fyinfo@fortyork.com
www.fortyork.com
Year Founded: 1950

Frontline Financial Credit Union
365 Richmond Rd.
Ottawa, ON K2A 0E7
Tel: 613-729-4312; *Fax:* 613-729-5075
www.911cu.com
Former Name: Ottawa Fire Fighters' Credit Union Ltd.
Year Founded: 1948

G & F Financial Group
Also listed under: *Financial Planning & Investment Management Companies; Insurance Companies*
7375 Kingsway
Burnaby, BC V3N 3B5
Tel: 604-517-5100; *Fax:* 604-659-4025
www.gffg.com
Former Name: Gulf & Fraser Fishermen's Credit Union
Year Founded: 1941
Number of Employees: 175
Assets: $500m-1 billion
Revenues: $1-5 million

Ganaraska Financial Services Group
17 Queen St.
Port Hope, ON L1A 2Y8
Tel: 905-885-8134; *Fax:* 905-885-8298
info@ganaraskacu.com
www.ganaraskacu.com
Former Name: Ganaraska Credit Union
Year Founded: 1945

Glace Bay Central Credit Union
598 Main St.
Glace Bay, NS B1A 4X8
Tel: 902-849-7512; *Fax:* 902-842-9201
www.glacebaycentralcreditunion.com
Year Founded: 1932

Goderich Community Credit Union Limited
PO Box 66
39 St. David St.
Goderich, ON N7A 3Y5
Tel: 519-524-8366; *Fax:* 519-524-1329
reception@gccu.on.ca
www.gccu.on.ca
Ownership: Member-owned
Year Founded: 1954
Number of Employees: 15

Goodsoil Credit Union Limited
PO Box 88
Goodsoil, SK S0M 1A0
Tel: 306-238-2033; *Fax:* 306-238-4441
info@goodsoil.cu.sk.ca
www.goodsoilcu.com
Ownership: Member-owned
Year Founded: 1946
Number of Employees: 7
Assets: $10-50 million
Revenues: Under $1 million

Goodyear Employees (Bowmanville) Credit Union Limited
371 Orange Cres.
Oshawa, ON L1G 5X2
Tel: 905-623-2606; *Fax:* 905-432-7590
Year Founded: 1966
Number of Employees: 1

Govan Credit Union Ltd.
PO Box 280
Govan, SK S0G 1Z0
Tel: 306-484-2177; *Fax:* 306-484-4333
Toll-Free: 866-298-1336
govancreditunion@govan.cu.sk.ca
www.govancreditunion.ca
Year Founded: 1940

Grand Forks District Savings Credit Union
PO Box 2500
447 Market Ave.
Grand Forks, BC V0H 1H0
Tel: 250-442-5511; *Fax:* 250-442-5644
Toll-Free: 866-442-5511
info@gfdscu.com
www.gfdscu.com
Year Founded: 1949

Grandview Credit Union
PO Box 159
405 Main St.
Grandview, MB R0L 0Y0
Tel: 204-546-5200; *Fax:* 204-546-5219
info@grandviewcu.mb.ca
www.grandviewcu.mb.ca

Greater Vancouver Community Credit Union
1801 Willingdon Ave.
Burnaby, BC V5C 5R3
Tel: 604-298-3344; *Fax:* 604-421-8949
info@gvccu.com
www.gvccu.com

Greater Victoria Savings Credit Union
1001 Blanshard St.
Victoria, BC V8W 2H4
Tel: 250-388-4408; *Fax:* 250-384-4232
www.vancity.com
Year Founded: 1940

Grey Bruce Health Services Credit Union Ltd.
1939 - 8 Ave. East
Owen Sound, ON N4K 3C4
Tel: 519-376-9336; *Fax:* 519-376-1719
creditunion@mbts.com
Former Name: Health Centre (Owen Sound) Employees Credit Union Limited
Year Founded: 1967

GSW (Fergus) Credit Union Limited
599 Hill St. West
Fergus, ON N1M 2X1
Tel: 519-843-1616; *Fax:* 519-787-5533
Year Founded: 1951
Number of Employees: 2

Hald-Nor Community Credit Union Limited
PO Box 2135
22 Caithness St. East
Caledonia, ON N3W 2G6
Tel: 905-765-4071; *Fax:* 905-765-0485
caledonia@hald-nor.on.ca
www.hald-nor.on.ca
Ownership: Member-owned
Year Founded: 1954
Assets: $50-100 million

Halifax Civic Credit Union
6070 Lady Hammond Rd.
Halifax, NS B3K 2R6
Tel: 902-455-5489; *Fax:* 902-453-5491
Year Founded: 1938

Hamilton Community Credit Union Limited
698 King St. East
Hamilton, ON L8M 1A3
Tel: 905-529-9445; *Fax:* 905-529-9016
hccu@sympatico.ca
www.hccu.on.ca
Number of Employees: 15

Health Care Credit Union Ltd.
PO Box 5375
800 Commissioners Rd. East
London, ON N6A 4G5
Tel: 519-685-8353; *Fax:* 519-685-8153
creditunion@lhsc.on.ca
www.lhsc.on.ca/cr_union/
Year Founded: 1949

Healthcare & Municipal Employees Credit Union (HMECU)
209 Limeridge Rd. East
Hamilton, ON L9A 2S6
Tel: 905-575-8888; *Fax:* 905-575-3104
Toll-Free: 866-808-2888
www.hmecu.com
Number of Employees: 9

Heritage Credit Union
#100, 630 - 17th St.
Castlegar, BC V1N 4G7
Tel: 250-365-7232; *Fax:* 250-365-2913
hcu@heritagecu.ca
www.heritagecu.ca
Former Name: Castlegar Savings Credit Union
Ownership: Member-owned
Year Founded: 1948
Assets: $50-100 million

Hir-Walk Employees' (Windsor) Credit Union Limited
2072 Riverside Dr. East
Windsor, ON N8Y 4S5
Tel: 519-561-5543; *Fax:* 519-971-5744
hir-walker.credit@bellnet.ca
Year Founded: 1949
Number of Employees: 4

Holy Angel's & St. Anne's Parish (St Thomas) Credit Union Limited
PO Box 20125
St Thomas, ON N5P 4H4
Tel: 519-633-1710; *Fax:* 519-633-4024
lphoffer@bellnet.ca

Holy Name Parish (Pembroke) Credit Union Limited
667 Front St.
Pembroke, ON K8A 6J4
Tel: 613-732-3181; *Fax:* 613-732-1903
Ownership: Member-owned
Year Founded: 1942
Number of Employees: 3
Assets: Under $1 million
Revenues: Under $1 million

Horizon Credit Union
PO Box 1900
136 - 3rd Ave. East
Melville, SK S0A 2P0
Tel: 306-728-5425; *Fax:* 306-728-4520
Toll-Free: 866-522-1880
info@horizon.cu.sk.ca
www.horizon.cu.sk.ca
Other Contact Information: Telephone Banking: 306/728-1880
Former Name: Melville District Credit Union Ltd.; Aspen Prairie Credit Union Ltd.
Ownership: Co-operative. Member-owned
Year Founded: 1949
Number of Employees: 49

Hudson Bay Credit Union Ltd.
PO Box 538
208 Churchill St.
Hudson Bay, SK S0E 0Y0
Tel: 306-865-2209; *Fax:* 306-865-2381
info@hudsonbay.cu.sk.ca
www.hudsonbaycu.com
Year Founded: 1954
Number of Employees: 17
Assets: $10-50 million
Revenues: $1-5 million

Industrial Savings & Credit Union Ltd.
PO Box 97
Hwy 16A & 17 St.
Edmonton, AB T5J 2G9
Tel: 780-410-5502; *Fax:* 780-410-5391
Year Founded: 1964

Inglewood Savings & Credit Union
1328 - 9th Ave. SE
Calgary, AB T2G 0T3
Tel: 403-265-5396; *Fax:* 403-265-1326
manager@inglewoodcu.com
www.inglewoodcu.com
Ownership: Member-owned
Year Founded: 1938
Assets: $10-50 million

Innovation Credit Union
PO Box 638
1202 - 102nd St.
North Battleford, SK S9A 2Y7
Tel: 306-446-7000; *Fax:* 306-445-6086
www.innovationcu.ca
Other Contact Information: 1-866-446-7001 (North Region Toll-Free); 1-800-381-5502 (South Region Toll-Free); 306-445-6086 (North Region Fax); 306-773-0294 (South Region Fax)
Year Founded: 2007

iNova Credit Union
PO Box 8153, A Stn. A
6175 Almon St.
Halifax, NS B3K 5L9
Tel: 902-453-1145; *Fax:* 902-453-0370
Toll-Free: 800-665-1145
www.nspostalcreditunion.com
Former Name: Nova Scotia Postal Employees Credit Union

Integris Credit Union
1532 - 6th Ave.
Prince George, BC V2L 5B5
Tel: 250-612-3456; *Fax:* 250-612-3450
www.integriscu.ca
Former Name: Prince George Savings Credit Union; Nechako Valley Credit Union; Quesnel & District Credit Union
Year Founded: 2004

Interior Savings Credit Union
#300, 678 Bernard Ave.
Kelowna, BC V1Y 6P3
Tel: 250-762-4355; *Fax:* 250-762-9581
info@interiorsavings.com
www.interiorsavings.com
Ownership: Member-owned
Assets: $100-500 million

Island Savings Credit Union
Also listed under: *Financing & Loan Companies*
#300, 499 Canada Ave.
Duncan, BC V9L 1T7
Tel: 250-748-4728; *Fax:* 250-748-8831
info@iscu.com
www.iscu.com
Social Media: www.twitter.com/Island_Savings XXÇ
Ownership: Member-owned
Year Founded: 1951
Number of Employees: 300
Assets: $500m-1 billion

Kawartha Credit Union Limited
PO Box 116
1054 Monaghan Rd.
Peterborough, ON K9J 6Y5
Tel: 705-743-3643; *Fax:* 705-749-1890
Toll-Free: 888-743-9966
info@kawarthacu.com
www.kawarthacu.com
Year Founded: 1952

Kellogg Employees Credit Union Limited
PO Box 5517
100 Kellogg Lane
London, ON N6A 4P9
Tel: 519-452-6414; *Fax:* 519-452-6316
kelloggcu@kelloggcu.com
www.kelloggcu.com
Year Founded: 1953
Number of Employees: 3
Revenues: $10-50 million

Kelvington Credit Union Ltd.
PO Box 459
Kelvington, SK S0A 1W0
Tel: 306-327-4728; *Fax:* 306-327-5100
info@kelvington.cu.sk.ca
www.kelvingtoncu.com
Year Founded: 1943

Kenaston Credit Union Ltd.
PO Box 70
607 - 3rd St.
Kenaston, SK S0G 2N0
Tel: 306-252-2160
garth.lewis@kenaston.cu.sk.ca
www.kenaston.cu.sk.ca

Kenora District Credit Union Limited
PO Box 2200
101 Park St.
Kenora, ON P9N 3X8
Tel: 807-467-4400; *Fax:* 807-468-6452
www.kdcu.on.ca

Kerrobert Credit Union Ltd.
PO Box 140
437 Pacific Ave.
Kerrobert, SK S0L 1R0
Tel: 306-834-2611; *Fax:* 306-834-5558
info@kerrobert.cu.sk.ca
www.kerrobert.cu.sk.ca
Year Founded: 1963

Khalsa Credit Union (Alberta) Limited
#604, 4656 Westwinds Dr. NE
Calgary, AB T3J 3Z5
Tel: 403-285-0707; *Fax:* 403-285-0771
khalsacu@telusplanet.net
www.khalsacu.ca
Year Founded: 1995
Number of Employees: 3
Assets: $1-5 million
Revenues: $1-5 million

King-York Newsmen Toronto Credit Union Limited
444 Front St. West
Toronto, ON M5V 2S9
Tel: 416-585-5110; *Fax:* 416-585-5534
credit-union@globeandmail.ca
Ownership: Private
Year Founded: 1955
Assets: $1-5 million
Revenues: $1-5 million

Kootenay Savings Credit Union
#300, 1199 Cedar Ave.
Trail, BC V1R 4B8
Tel: 250-368-2686; *Fax:* 250-368-5203
info@kscu.com
www.kscu.com
Ownership: Member-owned
Year Founded: 1969
Number of Employees: 208
Assets: $500m-1 billion

Korean (Toronto) Credit Union Limited
703 Bloor St. West
Toronto, ON M6G 1L5
Tel: 416-535-4511; *Fax:* 416-535-9323
ktcul@rogers.com
www.koreancu.com

Korean Catholic Church Credit Union Limited
849 Don Mills Rd., 2nd Fl.
Toronto, ON M3C 1W1
Tel: 416-447-7788; *Fax:* 416-447-5297
kcccu@on.aibn.com

Krek Slovenian Credit Union Ltd.
747 Brown's Line
Toronto, ON M8W 3V7
Tel: 416-252-6527; *Fax:* 416-252-2092
main@krek.ca
www.krek.ca

Former Name: John E. Krek's Slovenian (Toronto) Credit Union Limited
Ownership: Private
Year Founded: 1953
Number of Employees: 17
Assets: $50-100 million

Ladysmith & District Credit Union
PO Box 430
330 First Ave.
Ladysmith, BC V9G 1A3
Tel: 250-245-2247; *Fax:* 250-245-5913
info@ldcu.ca
www.ldcu.ca
Year Founded: 1944

LaFleche Credit Union Ltd.
105 Main St.
Lafleche, SK S0H 2K0
Tel: 306-472-5215; *Fax:* 306-472-5545
info@lafleche.cu.sk.ca
www.laflechecu.com
Ownership: Member-owned
Year Founded: 1938
Number of Employees: 12
Assets: $10-50 million

Lake View Credit Union
800 - 102nd Ave.
Dawson Creek, BC V1G 2B2
Tel: 250-782-4871; *Fax:* 250-782-5828
lvcu@lakeviewcreditunion.com
www.lakeviewcreditunion.com
Ownership: Private
Number of Employees: 36

Lakeland Credit Union
PO Box 8057
5016 - 50 Ave.
Bonnyville, AB T9N 2J3
Tel: 780-826-3377; *Fax:* 780-826-6322
admin@lakelandcreditunion.com
www.lakelandcreditunion.com

Lambton Financial Credit Union Ltd.
1295 London Rd.
Sarnia, ON N7S 1P6
Tel: 519-542-0483; *Fax:* 519-542-3778
Toll-Free: 866-380-8008
www.lambtonfinancial.ca
Former Name: Polysar Lambton Credit Union Limited
Ownership: Private
Year Founded: 1947
Number of Employees: 48
Assets: $100-500 million
Revenues: $5-10 million

Landis Credit Union Ltd.
PO Box 220
Landis, SK S0K 2K0
Tel: 306-658-2152; *Fax:* 306-658-2153
owen.nicklin@landis.cu.sk.ca
www.landis.cu.sk.ca
Year Founded: 1942
Number of Employees: 4
Assets: $5-10 million
Revenues: Under $1 million

Lasco Employees' (Whitby) Credit Union Limited
1801 Hopkins St. South
Whitby, ON L1N 5T1
Tel: 905-668-8811; *Fax:* 905-668-2807

Latvian Credit Union
4 Credit Union Dr.
Toronto, ON M4A 2N8
Tel: 416-922-2551; *Fax:* 416-922-2758
www.kredsab.ca
Ownership: Member-owned
Number of Employees: 12

Lear Seating Canada Employees' (Kitchener) Credit Union Ltd.
PO Box 758
530 Manitou Dr.
Kitchener, ON
Tel: 519-895-3213

Legacy Savings & Credit Union Ltd.
1940, 9 Ave.
Calgary, AB T2G 0V2
Tel: 403-265-6050; *Fax:* 403-265-8010
admin@legacysavings.com
www.legacysavings.com

Lethbridge Legion Savings & Credit Union Ltd.
324 Mayor Magrath Dr.
Lethbridge, AB T1J 3L7
Tel: 403-327-6417; *Fax:* 403-317-0122
Year Founded: 1958

Libro Financial Group
217 York St., 4th Fl.
London, ON N6A 5P9
Tel: 519-672-0124; *Fax:* 519-672-7831
Toll-Free: 800-361-8222
service@libro.ca
www.libro.ca
Former Name: St. Willibrod Credit Union Limited; St. Willibrod Community Credit Union Limited
Ownership: 47,000 owners
Year Founded: 1951
Number of Employees: 300
Assets: $1-10 billion
Revenues: $500m-1 billion

Lintlaw Credit Union Ltd.
PO Box 190
212 Main St.
Lintlaw, SK S0A 2H0
Tel: 306-325-2118; *Fax:* 306-325-4311
Year Founded: 1940

LIUNA Local 183 Credit Union Limited
#108, 1263 Wilson Ave.
Toronto, ON M3M 3G2
Tel: 416-242-6643; *Fax:* 416-242-7852
info@local183cu.ca
www.local183cu.ca

London Civic Employees' Credit Union Limited
343 Dundas St.
London, ON N6B 1V5
Tel: 519-661-4563; *Fax:* 519-663-9369
memberservices@lcecu.com
www.lcecu.com
Ownership: Private
Year Founded: 1948

London Fire Fighters' Credit Union Limited
400 Horton St. East
London, ON N6B 1L7
Tel: 519-661-5635; *Fax:* 519-661-5635
info@lfdcreditunion.com
www.lfdcreditunion.com
Ownership: Private
Number of Employees: 2

Macklin Credit Union Ltd.
PO Box 326
4809 Herald St.
Macklin, SK S0L 2C0
Tel: 306-753-2333; *Fax:* 306-753-2676
info@macklin.cu.sk.ca
www.macklin.cu.sk.ca
Number of Employees: 13

Main-à-Dieu Credit Union
2365 Louisbourg-Main-à-Dieu Rd.
Main-à-Dieu, NS B1C 1X2
Tel: 902-733-2555; *Fax:* 902-733-2301
Ownership: Member-owned
Year Founded: 1935
Number of Employees: 2
Assets: $1-5 million
Revenues: Under $1 million

Mankota Credit Union
Main St.
Mankota, SK S0H 2W0
Tel: 306-478-2284; *Fax:* 306-478-2277
info@mankota.cu.sk.ca
www.mankotacu.ca
Other Contact Information: Kikcaid Phone: 306-264-3822; Kincaid Office Fax: 306-264-5175
Number of Employees: 7

McMaster Savings & Credit Union Ltd.
Westdale Village
1005 King St. West
Hamilton, ON L8S 1L3
Tel: 905-522-2903; *Fax:* 905-522-4467
mscuwestdale@maccu.com
www.maccu.com
Ownership: Member-owned
Year Founded: 1936

Media Group Financial Credit Union Limited
369 York St.
London, ON N6A 4G1
Tel: 519-667-4505; *Fax:* 519-667-5522
creditunion@mediagroupfinancial.ca
www.mediagroupfinancial.ca

Me-Dian Credit Union
303 Selkirk Ave.
Winnipeg, MB R2W 2L8
Tel: 204-943-9111; *Fax:* 204-942-3698
www.me-diancu.mb.ca

The Medical-Dental Financial, Savings & Credit Limited
c/o Credential, Ontario Regl. Office
#200, 3430 South Service Rd.
Burlington, ON L7N 3T9
Tel: 905-632-9200; *Fax:* 905-632-0032

Member Savings Credit Union
55 Lakeshore Blvd. East
Toronto, ON M5E 1A4
Tel: 416-864-2461; *Fax:* 416-864-6858
Toll-Free: 888-560-2218
membercu@membercu.com
www.membercu.com
Year Founded: 1949
Assets: $50-100 million

MemberOne Credit Union Ltd.
PO Box 35
200 Front St. West, Concourse Level
Toronto, ON M5V 3K2
Tel: 416-344-4070; *Fax:* 416-344-4069
info@memberone.ca
www.memberone.ca
Former Name: WCB Credit Union Limited

Mendham-Burstall Credit Union
PO Box 69
Mendham, SK S0N 1P0
Tel: 306-628-3257; *Fax:* 306-628-4284
mendham@sasktel.net
Ownership: Member-owned
Assets: $10-50 million
Revenues: Under $1 million

Mennonite Savings & Credit Union (Ontario) Limited
1265 Strasburg Rd.
Kitchener, ON N2R 1S6
Tel: 519-746-1010; *Fax:* 519-746-1045
Toll-Free: 888-672-6728
info@mscu.com
www.mscu.com
Ownership: Member-owned
Year Founded: 1964
Number of Employees: 96
Assets: $500m-1 billion
Revenues: $50-100 million

Meridian Credit Union
College Park
777 Bay St., 26th Fl.
Toronto, ON M5G 2C8
Tel: 416-597-4400; *Fax:* 416-597-5068
Toll-Free: 866-592-2226
www.meridiancu.ca
Former Name: HEPCOE Credit Union Limited
Ownership: Member-owned
Year Founded: 2005
Number of Employees: 1,000
Assets: $1-10 billion

Midale Credit Union Ltd.
PO Box 418
211 Main St.
Midale, SK S0C 1S0
Tel: 306-458-2222; *Fax:* 306-458-2329
www.midalecu.com

Milestone Credit Union Ltd.
PO Box 144
118 Main St.
Milestone, SK S0G 3L0
Tel: 306-436-2002; *Fax:* 306-436-2114
info@milestone.cu.sk.ca
Former Name: Milestone Savings & Credit Union Ltd.

Minnedosa Credit Union
PO Box 459
60 Main St.
Minnedosa, MB R0J 1E0
Tel: 204-867-6350; *Fax:* 204-867-6391
Toll-Free: 877-663-7228
info@minnedosacu.mb.ca
www.minnedosacu.mb.ca
Year Founded: 1947
Number of Employees: 20

Miracle Credit Union Ltd.
#22, 86 Guided Crt.
Toronto, ON M9V 4K6
Tel: 416-740-7553; *Fax:* 416-740-3767
miracle@on.aibn.com
www.miraclecreditunion.ca

Mitchell & District Credit Union Limited
105 Ontario Rd.
Mitchell, ON N0K 1N0
Tel: 519-348-8448; *Fax:* 519-348-8009
mitchell@mitchellcu.ca
www.mitchellcu.ca
Ownership: Private
Year Founded: 1960
Number of Employees: 33
Assets: $50-100 million
Revenues: $1-5 million

Molson Brewery Employees Credit Union Limited
1 Carlingview Dr.
Toronto, ON M9W 5E5
Tel: 416-675-8710; *Fax:* 416-213-0518
www.virtualonecu.ca
Year Founded: 1956
Number of Employees: 2

Moore Employees' Credit Union Limited
6100 Vipond Dr.
Mississauga, ON L5T 2X1
Tel: 416-241-7132
sylvia_murphy@ca.moore.com
Year Founded: 1962

Motor City Community Credit Union Limited
6701 Tecumseh Rd. East
Windsor, ON N8T 1E8
Tel: 519-944-7333; *Fax:* 519-944-9765
info@mcccu.com
www.mcccu.com
Ownership: Member-owned
Assets: $100-500 million

Mount Lehman Credit Union
5889 Mount Lehman Rd.
Mount Lehman, BC V4X 1V7
Tel: 604-856-7761; *Fax:* 604-856-1429
info@mtlehman.com
www.mtlehman.com
Other Contact Information: MemberCall: 604-856-7726
Year Founded: 1942
Number of Employees: 12

Mountain View Credit Union Ltd.
PO Box 3752
4920 - 50 Ave.
Olds, AB T4H 1P5
Tel: 403-556-3306; *Fax:* 403-556-1050
mvcu@mvcu.ca
www.mvcu.ca
Ownership: Member-owned
Year Founded: 1977
Number of Employees: 1977
Assets: $100-500 million

Mouvement des caisses Desjardins du Québec
Also listed under: *Financing & Loan Companies; Insurance Companies*
100, av. des Commandeurs
Lévis, QC G6V 7N5
Tél: 418-835-8444; *Téléc:* 418-833-5873
www.desjardins.com
Ownership: Private
Year Founded: 1901
Number of Employees: 38,000
Assets: $10-50 million

Mozart Savings & Credit Union Limited
PO Box 96
Mozart, SK S0A 2S0
Tel: 306-554-2808; *Fax:* 306-554-2839
mozart@sasktel.net
Year Founded: 1940
Number of Employees: 3

Municipal Employees (Chatham) Credit Union Limited
301 Delaware Ave.
Chatham, ON N7L 2W9
Tel: 519-354-9182
Year Founded: 1954
Number of Employees: 2
Assets: $1-5 million
Revenues: Under $1 million

Nelson & District Credit Union
PO Box 350
501 Vernon St.
Nelson, BC V1L 5R2
Tel: 250-352-7207; *Fax:* 250-352-9663
Toll-Free: 877-352-7207
enrichingyourlife@nelsoncu.com
www.nelsoncu.com
Number of Employees: 50

New Brunswick Teachers' Association Credit Union
PO Box 752
650 Montgomery St.
Fredericton, NB E3B 5R6
Tel: 506-452-1724; *Fax:* 506-452-1732
Toll-Free: 800-565-5626
nbtacu@nbnet.nb.ca
www.nbtacu.nb.ca
Ownership: Private
Year Founded: 1971
Number of Employees: 12
Assets: $10-50 million

New Community Credit Union
321 - 20th St. West
Saskatoon, SK S7M 0X1
Tel: 306-653-1300; *Fax:* 306-653-4711
info@newcommunity.cu.sk.ca
www.newcommunitycu.com
Former Name: New Community Savings & Credit Union Ltd.
Year Founded: 1939

New Glasgow Credit Union
175 Victoria St.
New Glasgow, NS B2H 4V3
Tel: 902-752-3102; *Fax:* 902-755-5777

New Ross Credit Union
PO Box 32
56 Forties Rd.
New Ross, NS B0J 2M0
Tel: 902-689-2949; *Fax:* 902-689-2597
www.newrosscreditunion.ca
Year Founded: 1956

New Waterford Credit Union
3462 Plummer Ave.
New Waterford, NS B1H 1Z6
Tel: 902-862-6453; *Fax:* 902-862-9206
www.newwaterfordcreditunion.com
Year Founded: 1934
Number of Employees: 14
Assets: $10-50 million

Niverville Credit Union
PO Box 430
62 Main St.
Niverville, MB R0A 1E0
Tel: 204-388-4747; *Fax:* 204-388-9970
info@nivervillecu.mb.ca
www.nivervillecu.mb.ca
Year Founded: 1949

North Peace Savings & Credit Union
10344 - 100th St.
Fort St John, BC V1J 3Z1
Tel: 250-787-0361; *Fax:* 250-787-9704
Toll-Free: 800-561-7849
members@northpeacesavings.com
www.northpeacesavings.com
Ownership: Private
Number of Employees: 53

North Shore Credit Union
1112 Lonsdale Ave., 3rd Fl.
North Vancouver, BC V7M 2H2
Tel: 604-982-8000; *Fax:* 604-713-3035
Toll-Free: 880-713-6728
www.nscu.com
Year Founded: 1941

North Valley Credit Union Limited
PO Box 1389
516 Main St.
Esterhazy, SK S0A 0X0
Tel: 306-745-6615; *Fax:* 306-745-2858
Toll-Free: 866-533-6828
www.northvalleycu.com
Former Name: Esterhazy Credit Union Limited
Ownership: Member-owned
Year Founded: 1998
Number of Employees: 14

Northern Credit Union
Also listed under: *Financial Planning & Investment Management Companies*
681 Pine St.
Sault Ste Marie, ON P6B 3G2
Tel: 705-253-9868; *Fax:* 705-949-1056
www.northerncu.com
Year Founded: 1957
Assets: $500m-1 billion

Northern Lights Credit Union Limited
PO Box 876
97 Duke St.
Dryden, ON P8N 2Z5
Tel: 807-223-5358; *Fax:* 807-223-8650
kimf@nlcu.on.ca
www.nlcu.on.ca
Number of Employees: 57

Northern Savings Credit Union
138 Third Ave. West
Prince Rupert, BC V8J 1K8
Tel: 250-627-7571; *Fax:* 250-624-8297
info@northsave.com
www.northsave.com
Ownership: Member-owned

Northland Savings & Credit Union Limited
10 Cain Ave.
Kapuskasing, ON P5N 1S9
Tel: 705-335-2348; *Fax:* 705-337-1070
kapcu@ntl.sympatico.ca
Ownership: Member-owned
Year Founded: 1939

Northridge Savings & Credit Union Ltd.
9 Second Ave. North
Sudbury, ON P3B 3L7
Tel: 705-566-8540; *Fax:* 705-566-8480
www.northridgesavings.com

Oak Bank Credit Union
PO Box 217
686 Main St.
Oakbank, MB R0E 1J0
Tel: 204-444-7200; *Fax:* 204-444-3513
info@oakbankcu.mb.ca
www.oakbankcu.mb.ca
Year Founded: 1946

Ogema District Credit Union Ltd.
PO Box 339
Ogema, SK S0C 1Y0
Tel: 306-459-2266
info@ogema.cu.sk.ca
www.ogema.cu.sk.ca
Year Founded: 1950

Omista Credit Union
151 Cornhill St.
Moncton, NB E1C 6L3
Tel: 506-857-3222; *Fax:* 506-857-2235
cornhillst@omista.com
www.omista.com
Ownership: Member-owned

ONR Employees' (North Bay) Credit Union Limited
555 Oak St. East
North Bay, ON P1B 9E5
Tel: 705-472-1100; *Fax:* 705-472-0651
onrcu@ontc.on.ca
Year Founded: 1950

Ontario Civil Service Credit Union Limited
#1, 18 Grenville St.
Toronto, ON M4Y 3B3
Tel: 416-314-6772; *Fax:* 416-314-7805
Toll-Free: 888-516-6664
memberassistance@mycreditunion.ca
www.mycreditunion.ca
Ownership: Cooperative
Year Founded: 1945
Assets: $100-500 million

Revenues: $5-10 million

Ontario Educational Credit Union Limited
PO Box 360
#1, 6435 Edwards Blvd.
Mississauga, ON L5T 2P7
Tel: 905-795-1637; *Fax:* 905-795-0625
Toll-Free: 800-463-3602
www.oecu.on.ca
Year Founded: 1962
Number of Employees: 8

Ontario Provincial Police Association Credit Union Limited
123 Ferris Lane
Barrie, ON L4M 2Y1
Tel: 705-726-5656; *Fax:* 705-726-1449
Toll-Free: 800-461-4288
gd@oppacu.com
www.oppacu.com
Also Known As: O.P.P.A Credit Union
Year Founded: 1971

Osoyoos Credit Union
PO Box 360
8312 Main St.
Osoyoos, BC V0H 1V0
Tel: 250-495-6522; *Fax:* 250-495-3363
Toll-Free: 800-882-1966
contact@osoyooscreditunion.com
www.osoyooscreditunion.com
Ownership: Member-owned
Year Founded: 1946
Number of Employees: 20

Ottawa Police Credit Union Limited
#206, 474 Elgin St., 2nd Fl.
Ottawa, ON K2P 2J6
Tel: 613-236-1222; *Fax:* 613-567-3760
www.opcu.com
Former Name: Ottawa-Carleton Police Credit Union Limited
Ownership: Private.
Year Founded: 1955
Number of Employees: 5
Revenues: $10-50 million

Ottawa Women's Credit Union Limited
Co-operative House
271 Bank St.
Ottawa, ON K2P 1X5
Tel: 613-233-7711; *Fax:* 613-233-6413
info@owcu.on.ca
www.owcu.on.ca

PACE Savings & Credit Union Limited
#1, 8111 Jane St.
Vaughan, ON L4K 4L7
Tel: 905-738-8900; *Fax:* 905-738-8283
Toll-Free: 800-433-9122
pace.info@pacecu.com
www.pacecu.com
Ownership: Member-owned
Year Founded: 1984
Assets: $50-100 million
Revenues: $5-10 million

Parama Lithuanian Credit Union Limited
1573 Bloor St. West
Toronto, ON M6P 1A6
Tel: 416-532-1149; *Fax:* 416-532-5595
info@parama.ca
www.parama.net
Year Founded: 1952
Number of Employees: 30
Assets: $100-500 million

Pedeco (Brockville) Credit Union Limited
2337 Parkedale Ave.
Brockville, ON K6V 5W5
Tel: 613-342-4436; *Fax:* 613-342-6584
cmacdonald@ripnet.com
Year Founded: 1952

PenFinancial Credit Union
247 East Main St.
Welland, ON L3B 3X1
Tel: 905-735-4801; *Fax:* 905-735-2983
www.penfinancial.com
Former Name: St Catharines Civic Employees' Credit Union Ltd.
Year Founded: 1951
Number of Employees: 57
Assets: $100-500 million

Peterborough Community Credit Union Limited
PO Box 1600
167 Brock St.
Peterborough, ON K9J 7S4
Tel: 705-748-4481; *Fax:* 705-748-5520
www.pboccu.com
Year Founded: 1939

Peterborough Industrial Credit Union
890 High St.
Peterborough, ON K9J 5R2
Tel: 705-743-4651; *Fax:* 705-743-9889

Pierceland Credit Union Ltd.
PO Box 10
181 Main St.
Pierceland, SK S0M 2K0
Tel: 306-839-2071; *Fax:* 306-839-2292
info@pierceland.cu.sk.ca
Year Founded: 1941
Number of Employees: 8

Pincher Creek Credit Union Ltd.
PO Box 1660
750 Kettles St.
Pincher Creek, AB T0K 1W0
Tel: 403-627-4431; *Fax:* 403-627-5331
www.pinchercreek-creditunion.com
Ownership: Member-owned
Year Founded: 1944
Number of Employees: 5

Plainsview Credit Union
PO Box 150
600 Main St.
Kipling, SK S0G 2S0
Tel: 306-736-2549; *Fax:* 306-736-8290
info@plainsview.cu.sk.ca
www.plainsview.com

The Police Credit Union Ltd.
#303, 3650 Victoria Park Ave.
Toronto, ON M2H 3P7
Tel: 416-226-3353; *Fax:* 416-226-1565
Toll-Free: 800-561-2557
callcentre@tpcu.on.ca
www.tpcu.on.ca
Ownership: Member-owned
Year Founded: 1946

Porcupine Credit Union Ltd.
PO Box 189
150 McAllister Ave.
Porcupine Plain, SK S0E 1H0
Tel: 306-278-2181; *Fax:* 306-278-2944
info@porcupine.cu.sk.ca
www.porcupine.cu.sk.ca
Year Founded: 1946

Powell River Credit Union Financial Group
Also listed under: *Financial Planning & Investment Management Companies*
4721 Joyce Ave.
Powell River, BC V8A 3B5
Tel: 604-485-6206; *Fax:* 604-485-7112
Toll-Free: 800-393-6733
www.prcu.com
Year Founded: 1939
Number of Employees: 46
Assets: $100-500 million
Revenues: $5-10 million

Prairie Centre Credit Union
PO Box 940
Rosetown, SK S0L 2V0
Tel: 306-882-2693; *Fax:* 306-882-3326
comments@pccu.ca
www.pccu.ca
Ownership: Cooperative
Year Founded: 1993
Number of Employees: 75
Assets: $100-500 million
Revenues: $5-10 million

Prairie Diamond Credit Union
PO Box 819
123 Garfield St.
Davidson, SK S0G 1A0
Tel: 306-567-2931; *Fax:* 306-567-5503
info@prairiediamond.cu.sk.ca
www.affinitycu.ca
Year Founded: 1994

Prairie Pride Credit Union
PO Box 37
Alameda, SK S0C 0A0
Tel: 306-489-2131; *Fax:* 306-489-2188
info@prairiepride.cu.sk.ca
www.prairiepridecu.com
Former Name: Gainsborough Credit Union Ltd.
Year Founded: 2001
Number of Employees: 9

Prime Savings Credit Union
#201, 735 South Service Rd.
Stoney Creek, ON L8E 5Z2
Tel: 905-643-2879
www.primecu.com
Former Name: Industrial Family (Hamilton) Credit Union Ltd.

Princess Credit Union
22 Fraser Ave.
Sydney Mines, NS B1V 2B7
Tel: 902-736-9204; *Fax:* 902-736-2887

Progressive Credit Union
30 Hughes
Fredericton, NB E3A 2W3
Tel: 506-458-9145; *Fax:* 506-459-0106
www.progressivecu.nb.ca
Former Name: Capital Credit Union
Year Founded: 1949

Prosperity ONE Credit Union
44 Main St. East
Milton, ON L9T 1N3
Tel: 905-878-4168; *Fax:* 905-878-5500
info@prosperityone.ca
www.prosperityone.ca
Former Name: Halton Community Credit Union
Year Founded: 1957
Number of Employees: 36
Assets: $50-100 million

Province House Credit Union Ltd.
PO Box 1083
1724 Granville St.
Halifax, NS B3J 2X1
Tel: 902-424-5712; *Fax:* 902-424-3662
Toll-Free: 888-484-0880
info@provincehouse.com
www.provincehouse.com

Provincial Alliance Credit Union Limited
1201 Wilson Ave.
Toronto, ON M3M 1J8
Tel: 416-235-4373; *Fax:* 416-235-4225
Toll-Free: 877-523-7228
help@provincialalliance.com
www.provincialalliance.com
Year Founded: 1953
Number of Employees: 24

Public Service Credit Union Ltd.
403 Empire Ave.
St. John's, NL A1E 1W6
Tel: 709-579-8210; *Fax:* 709-579-8233
Toll-Free: 800-563-6755
pscuadmin@pscu.creditu.net
www.pscu.ca
Ownership: Cooperative
Year Founded: 1936
Number of Employees: 18
Assets: $10-50 million
Revenues: $1-5 million

Public Service Employees Credit Union
141 Weldon St.
Moncton, NB E1C 5W1
Tel: 506-853-8881; *Fax:* 506-856-8492
www.psecreditunion.ca

Quill Lake Credit Union Ltd.
PO Box 520
Quill Lake, SK S0A 3E0
Tel: 306-383-4155; *Fax:* 306-383-2622
www.quilllake.cu.sk.ca
Year Founded: 1946

QuintEssential Credit Union Limited
293 Sidney St.
Belleville, ON K8P 3Z4
Tel: 613-966-4111; *Fax:* 613-966-8909
info@qcu.ca
www.qcu.ca

Radville Credit Union Ltd.
PO Box 279
201 Main St.
Radville, SK S0C 2G0
Tel: 306-869-2215; *Fax:* 306-869-2891
info@radville.cu.sk.ca
www.radville.cu.sk.ca
Year Founded: 1943

Railway Employees' (Sarnia) Credit Union Limited
431 Russell St. South
Sarnia, ON N7T 3N1
Tel: 519-336-0093; *Fax:* 519-336-6945
info@recu.ca
www.recu.ca

Raymore Savings & Credit Union Ltd.
PO Box 460
121 Main St.
Raymore, SK S0A 3J0
Tel: 306-746-2160; *Fax:* 306-746-5811
Toll-Free: 866-612-2300
info@raymore.cu.sk.ca
www.raymorecu.com
Year Founded: 1949

RBW Employees' (Owen Sound) Credit Union Limited
2049 - 20th St.
Owen Sound, ON N4K 5R2
Tel: 519-376-8330; *Fax:* 519-376-1164
Number of Employees: 1

Reddy Kilowatt Credit Union Ltd.
Newfoundland Power Bldg.
PO Box 8910
50 Duffy Pl.
St. John's, NL A1B 3P6
Tel: 709-737-5624; *Fax:* 709-737-2937
Toll-Free: 800-409-2887
rkcu@reddykilowatt.creditu.net
www.reddyk.net
Year Founded: 1956
Number of Employees: 6

Resurrection Parish (Toronto) Credit Union Limited
3 Resurrection Rd.
Toronto, ON M9A 5G1
Tel: 416-532-3400; *Fax:* 416-532-4816
rpcul@rpcul.com
www.rpcul.com
Number of Employees: 13

River City Credit Union Ltd.
11715A - 108 Ave.
Edmonton, AB T5H 1B8
Tel: 780-496-3482; *Fax:* 780-496-3477
rivercity@alberta-cu.com
www.river-citycu.com
Former Name: Edmonton Civic Employees Credit Union Ltd.

Rochdale Credit Union Limited
943 Dundas St.
Woodstock, ON N4S 1H2
Tel: 519-539-4813; *Fax:* 519-539-8667
rochdale@rcu.com
www.rcu.com
Year Founded: 1942

Rocky Credit Union Ltd.
PO Box 1420
5035 - 49 St.
Rocky Mountain House, AB T4T 1B1
Tel: 403-845-2861; *Fax:* 403-845-7295
rockycu@alberta-cu.com
www.rockycreditunion.com
Ownership: Public
Year Founded: 1944
Number of Employees: 40
Assets: $100-500 million
Revenues: $1-5 million

Rorketon & District Credit Union
PO Box 10
691 Main St.
Rorketon, MB R0L 1R0
Tel: 204-732-2448; *Fax:* 204-732-2275
rorkinfo@rorketoncu.mb.ca
www.rorketoncu.mb.ca
Year Founded: 1961

Rosenort Credit Union Limited
PO Box 339
23 Main St.
Rosenort, MB R0G 1W0
Tel: 204-746-2355; *Fax:* 204-746-2541
Toll-Free: 800-265-7925
info@rcu.mb.ca
www.rcu.mb.ca
Year Founded: 1940
Assets: $50-100 million

Rossignol Credit Union
PO Box 310
Brooklyn, NS B0J 1H0
Tel: 902-354-2021
Ownership: Private
Year Founded: 1937
Number of Employees: 1
Assets: $1-5 million
Revenues: Under $1 million

Royglenor Savings & Credit Union Ltd.
Royal Alexander Hospital, Community Services Centre
#174, 10240 Kingsway Ave.
Edmonton, AB T5H 3V9
Tel: 780-474-7724; *Fax:* 780-474-9043
www.royglenorcu.ca
Year Founded: 1956

St Gregor Credit Union Ltd.
PO Box 128
2 Main St.
St Gregor, SK S0K 3X0
Tel: 306-366-2116; *Fax:* 306-366-2032

St. Joseph's Credit Union
PO Box 159
3552 Hwy. 206
Petit de Grat, NS B0E 2L0
Tel: 902-226-2288; *Fax:* 902-226-9855
Toll-Free: 866-876-3192
www.stjosephscreditu.ca
Year Founded: 1936
Number of Employees: 12

St. Mary's Paperworkers Credit Union
75 Huron St.
Sault Ste Marie, ON P6A 5P4
Tel: 705-541-2438; *Fax:* 705-942-6427
baile_s@stmarys-paper.com
Ownership: Private. Closed Bond.
Year Founded: 1953
Number of Employees: 1
Assets: Under $1 million
Revenues: Under $1 million

St. Stanislaus & St. Casimir's Polish Parishes Credit Union Ltd.
220 Roncesvalles Ave.
Toronto, ON M6R 2L7
Tel: 416-537-2181; *Fax:* 416-536-8525
info@polcu.com
www.polcan.com
Former Name: Polish (St Catharines) Credit Union Limited
Year Founded: 1951
Number of Employees: 3

Sandhills Credit Union
PO Box 249
Leader, SK S0N 1H0
Tel: 306-628-3687; *Fax:* 306-628-3674
info@sandhills.cu.sk.ca
www.sandhillscu.com
Ownership: Member-owned

Sandy Lake Credit Union
PO Box 129
102 Main St.
Sandy Lake, MB R0J 1X0
Tel: 204-585-2609; *Fax:* 204-585-2163
slcunion@slcu.mb.ca
www.slcu.mb.ca

Sanford Credit Union
7 Mellow St.
Sanford, MB R0G 2J0
Tel: 204-736-2373; *Fax:* 204-736-4108
info@sanfordcu.mb.ca
www.sanfordcu.mb.ca
Year Founded: 1950

Saskatoon City Employees Credit Union
222 - 3rd Ave. North
Saskatoon, SK S7K 0J5
Tel: 306-975-3280; *Fax:* 306-975-7806
www.scecu.com
Social Media: twitter.com/#!/scecu
Former Name: Saskatoon City Employee Credit Union Ltd.
Year Founded: 1947
Number of Employees: 9
Assets: $10-50 million
Revenues: $1-5 million

SaskCentral
PO Box 3030
2055 Albert St.
Regina, SK S4P 3G8
Tel: 306-566-1200; *Fax:* 306-566-1372
Toll-Free: 1-866-403-7499
info@saskcentral.com
www.saskcu.com
Ownership: Owned by Saskatchewan credit unions
Assets: $1-10 billion

Saugeen Community Credit Union Limited
PO Box 708
118 Queen St. South
Durham, ON N0G 1R0
Tel: 519-369-2931; *Fax:* 519-369-2994
durhamcu@saugeencreditunion.com
www.saugeencreditunion.com

Scarborough Hospitals Employees' Credit Union Ltd.
#504, 3050 Lawrence Ave. East
Toronto, ON M1O 2T7
Tel: 416-438-2911; *Fax:* 416-431-8131
fran.carolyn@sympatico.ca
Year Founded: 1964

Servus Credit Union
#300, 8723 - 82 Ave.
Edmonton, AB T6C 0Y9
Tel: 780-496-2000; *Fax:* 780-468-5220
Toll-Free: 877-496-2151
info@servuscu.ca; careers@servuscu.ca
www.servuscu.ca
Other Contact Information: askafinancialplanner@servuscu.ca (Financial Planning); 780-450-9647 (TTY for the hearing impaired)
Ownership: Member-owned
Year Founded: 1938
Assets: $1-10 billion

Sharons Credit Union
1055 Kingsway
Vancouver, BC V5V 3C7
Tel: 604-873-6490; *Fax:* 604-873-6498
sharons@sharonscu.ca
www.sharonscu.ca
Year Founded: 1988
Number of Employees: 30
Assets: $100-500 million

Shaunavon Credit Union
399 Centre St.
Shaunavon, SK S0N 2N0
Tel: 306-297-2635; *Fax:* 306-297-3137
Toll-Free: 800-667-0068
contactus@myscu.ca
www.myscu.ca
Also Known As: mySCU
Ownership: Member-owned
Year Founded: 1944

Shell Employees Credit Union Limited
PO Box 100, M Stn. M
Calgary, AB T2P 2H5
Tel: 403-691-3817; *Fax:* 403-262-4009
shellcu@shellcu.com
www.shellcu.com
Other Contact Information: Toll Free: 1-877-582-6222 (AB only)
Ownership: Member-owned
Year Founded: 1953

Sheridan Park Credit Union Ltd.
2251 Speakman Dr.
Mississauga, ON L5K 1B2
Tel: 905-823-1263; *Fax:* 905-823-8661
spcu@primus.ca
www.spcu.ca

Smiths Falls Community Credit Union Limited
1 Beckwith St. North
Smiths Falls, ON K7A 2B2
Tel: 613-283-3835; *Fax:* 613-283-9623

Year Founded: 1951

SOC Savings & Credit Union Ltd.
Eau Claire Place I
525 - 3 Ave. SW
Calgary, AB T2P 0G4
Tel: 403-509-4078; *Fax:* 403-509-4299

So-Use Credit Union
2265 Bloor St. West
Toronto, ON M6S 1P1
Tel: 416-763-5575; *Fax:* 416-761-9604
Toll-Free: 800-322-9274
so-use.info@so-use.com
www.so-use.com
Year Founded: 1950

South Calgary Savings & Credit Union Limited
4810 - 16th St. SW
Calgary, AB T2T 4J5
Tel: 403-243-5224; *Fax:* 403-287-9189
Ownership: Member-owned

South Interlake Credit Union Ltd.
233 Main St.
Selkirk, MB R1A 1S1
Tel: 204-785-7625; *Fax:* 204-785-7649
www.sicu.mb.ca
Ownership: Member-owned
Year Founded: 1944
Number of Employees: 106
Assets: $100-500 million

Southlake Regional Health Centre Employees' Credit Union Limited
596 Davis Dr.
Newmarket, ON L0G 1V0
Tel: 905-895-4521; *Fax:* 905-853-2218
Former Name: York County Hospital Employees' (Newmarket) Credit Union Limited
Number of Employees: 1

Southwest Regional Credit Union
1205 Exmouth St.
Sarnia, ON N7S 1W7
Tel: 519-383-8001; *Fax:* 519-383-8841
info@southwestcu.com
www.southwestcu.com
Year Founded: 1989
Number of Employees: 30

Spalding Savings & Credit Union Ltd.
111 Centre St.
Spalding, SK S0K 4C0
Tel: 306-872-2050; *Fax:* 306-872-2100
Year Founded: 1941

Spiritwood Credit Union Ltd.
PO Box 129
Spiritwood, SK S0J 2M0
Tel: 306-883-2250; *Fax:* 306-883-2223
Toll-Free: 877-288-1414
contactus@spiritwood.cu.sk.ca
www.spiritwoodcu.com
Ownership: Member-owned
Year Founded: 1938

Spruce Credit Union
879 Victoria St.
Prince George, BC V2L 2K7
Tel: 250-562-5415
sprucecu@cucbc.com
www.sprucecu.bc.ca
Number of Employees: 30
Assets: $50-100 million

Squamish Credit Union
PO Box 1940
38085 - 2nd St.
Squamish, BC V0N 3G0
Tel: 604-892-8355; *Fax:* 604-892-8377
Toll-Free: 877-892-5288
squamishsavings.com
Ownership: Private

Stanco Credit Union Ltd.
Chevron Plaza, Room 759
500 - 5 Ave. SW
Calgary, AB T2P 0L7
Tel: 403-234-5300; *Fax:* 403-234-5823
info@stancocu.com
www.stancocu.com
Number of Employees: 1
Assets: $1-5 million
Revenues: Under $1 million

Starbuck Credit Union
16 Main St.
Starbuck, MB R0G 2P0
Tel: 204-735-2394; *Fax:* 204-735-4020
Toll-Free: 866-398-9642
info@starbuckcreditunion.com
www.starbuckcreditunion.com
Year Founded: 1940
Assets: $50-100 million

Starnews Credit Union Limited
1 Yonge St.
Toronto, ON M5E 1E5
Tel: 416-366-5534; *Fax:* 416-366-6225
Toll-Free: 877-782-7639
inquiries@starnewscu.com
www.starnewscu.com

State Farm (Toronto) Credit Union Limited
333 First Commerce Dr.
Aurora, ON L4G 8A4
Tel: 905-750-4100; *Fax:* 905-750-4487
Year Founded: 1968

Steel Centre Credit Union
340 Prince St.
Sydney, NS B1P 5K9
Tel: 902-562-5559; *Fax:* 902-539-6024
www.sccu.ca
Year Founded: 1993

Steinbach Credit Union
305 Main St.
Steinbach, MB R5G 1B1
Tel: 204-326-3495; *Fax:* 204-326-3102
Toll-Free: 800-728-6440
scu@scu.mb.ca
www.scu.mb.ca
Ownership: Member-owned
Year Founded: 1941
Assets: $1-10 billion
Revenues: $50-100 million

Stoughton Credit Union Ltd.
PO Box 420
Stoughton, SK S0G 4T0
Tel: 306-457-2443; *Fax:* 306-457-2511
info@stoughton.cu.sk.ca
www.stoughtoncu.com
Year Founded: 1960
Number of Employees: 9
Assets: $10-50 million
Revenues: $1-5 million

Strathclair Credit Union
PO Box 246
Strathclair, MB R0J 2C0
Tel: 204-365-4700; *Fax:* 204-365-4710
info@strathclaircu.mb.ca
www.strathclaircu.mb.ca

Strathfiner Credit Union Ltd.
PO Box 1020
Edmonton, AB T5J 2M1
Tel: 780-449-8295; *Fax:* 780-449-8174
sfcu@datanet.ab.ca
Ownership: Member-owned. Closed bond.
Year Founded: 1954
Number of Employees: 1
Assets: $1-5 million
Revenues: Under $1 million

Sudbury Credit Union
Also listed under: *Financing & Loan Companies*
PO Box 662
1 Gribble St.
Copper Cliff, ON P0M 1N0
Tel: 705-682-0641; *Fax:* 705-682-1348
info@sudburycu.com
www.sudburycu.com
Former Name: Sudbury Regional Credit Union
Ownership: Member-owned
Year Founded: 1951
Assets: $100-500 million

Summerland & District Credit Union
PO Box 750
13601 Victoria Rd. North
Summerland, BC V0H 1Z0
Tel: 250-494-7181; *Fax:* 250-494-4261
sdcu@sdcu.com
www.sdcu.com
Year Founded: 1944
Number of Employees: 39

Sunnybrook Credit Union Limited
c/o Sunnybrook Health Sciences Centre
#CB02, 2075 Bayview Ave.
Toronto, ON M4N 3M5
Tel: 416-480-4467; *Fax:* 416-480-5908
info@sunnybrookcu.com
www.sunnybrookcu.com
Year Founded: 1950

SunRise Credit Union
356 South Railway St.
Boissevain, MB R0K 0E0
Tel: 204-534-2421; *Fax:* 204-534-6310
Former Name: Turtle Mountain Credit Union

Sunshine Coast Credit Union
Also listed under: *Financial Planning & Investment Management Companies*
PO Box 799
985 Sunshine Coast Hwy.
Gibsons, BC V0N 1V0
Tel: 604-886-2122; *Fax:* 604-886-0797
Toll-Free: 1-866-886-2132
administration@sunshineccu.net
www.sunshineccu.com
Ownership: Member-owned
Year Founded: 1941
Number of Employees: 83
Assets: $100-500 million
Revenues: $100-500 million

Superior Credit Union Limited
318 South Syndicate Ave.
Thunder Bay, ON P7E 1E3
Tel: 807-624-2255
info@supercu.com
www.supercu.com
Year Founded: 1997

Sydenham Community Credit Union Limited
32 Front St. East
Strathroy, ON N7G 1Y4
Tel: 519-245-2530; *Fax:* 519-245-0167
info@sydenhamccu.on.ca
www.sydenhamccu.on.ca
Year Founded: 1957

Sydney Credit Union
PO Box 1386
95 Townsend St.
Sydney, NS B1P 6K3
Tel: 902-562-5593; *Fax:* 902-539-8448
sydney@sydney.creditu.net
www.sydneycreditunion.com
Ownership: Member-owned
Year Founded: 1935

Taiwanese - Canadian Toronto Credit Union Limited
Also listed under: *Financing & Loan Companies*
Metro Square
#305, 3636 Steeles Ave. East
Markham, ON L3R 1K9
Tel: 905-944-0981; *Fax:* 905-944-0982
Toll-Free: 866-889-8893
tcu@on.aibn.com
www.tctcu.com
Ownership: Member-owned
Year Founded: 1978
Number of Employees: 5
Assets: $5-10 million
Revenues: Under $1 million

Talka Lithuanian Credit Union Limited
830 Main St. East
Hamilton, ON L8M 1L6
Tel: 905-544-7125; *Fax:* 905-544-7126
www.talka.ca
Former Name: Talka Hamilton Credit Union
Year Founded: 1955

Teachers Credit Union
75 James St. South
Hamilton, ON L8P 2Y9
Tel: 905-525-8090; *Fax:* 905-525-7422
Toll-Free: 877-427-1281
www.teacherscu.on.ca
Former Name: Hamilton Teachers Credit Union Limited
Ownership: Private

Teachers Plus Credit Union
36 Brookshire Ct.
Bedford, NS B4A 4E9
Tel: 902-477-5664; *Fax:* 902-477-4108
Toll-Free: 800-565-3103
info@teachersplus.ca
www.teachersplus.ca
Former Name: Nova Scotia Teachers Credit Union
Year Founded: 1956
Number of Employees: 11
Assets: $10-50 million

Thamesville Community Credit Union
84 London Rd.
Thamesville, ON N0P 2K0
Tel: 519-692-3855; *Fax:* 519-692-9532
info@thamesvillecu.ca
www.thamesvillecu.ca
Ownership: Member-owned
Year Founded: 1955

Thorold Community Credit Union
63 Front St. South
Thorold, ON L2V 3Z3
Tel: 905-227-1106; *Fax:* 905-227-1109
www.thoroldcu.com

Thunder Bay Elevators Employees' Credit Union Limited
417 Fort William Rd.
Thunder Bay, ON P7B 2Z5
Tel: 807-345-2471; *Fax:* 807-344-0829
elevatorcreditunion@tbaytel.net
Year Founded: 1953

Toronto Catholic School Board Employees' Credit Union Ltd.
80 Sheppard Ave. East
Toronto, ON M2N 6E8
Tel: 416-229-5315; *Fax:* 416-512-3427
tcsbecu-info@tcsbecu.com
www.tcsbecu.com
Former Name: Metropolitan Separate School Board Employees Credit Union Limited
Ownership: Private
Year Founded: 1972
Number of Employees: 7
Assets: $10-50 million

The Toronto Electrical Utilities Credit Union Limited
14 Carlton St.
Toronto, ON M5B 1K5
Tel: 416-542-2522; *Fax:* 416-542-2735
teucu@teucu.com
www.teucu.com
Ownership: Member-owned
Year Founded: 1941
Number of Employees: 8

Toronto Municipal Employees' Credit Union Limited
City Hall
PO Box 30
100 Queen St. West, Main Fl.
Toronto, ON M5H 2N2
Tel: 416-392-6868; *Fax:* 416-392-6895
www.tmecu.com
Year Founded: 1940

Tri-Island Credit Union
PO Box 580
1 Rink Rd.
Twillingate, NL A0G 4M0
Tel: 709-884-2704; *Fax:* 709-884-2026
www.triislandcu.com
Year Founded: 1986
Number of Employees: 10

Turtleford Credit Union Ltd.
PO Box 370
208 Main St.
Turtleford, SK S0M 2Y0
Tel: 306-845-2105; *Fax:* 306-845-3035
info@turtleford.cu.sk.ca
www.turtleford.cu.sk.ca

Twin Oak Credit Union Ltd.
PO Box 463
1045 Industry St.
Oakville, ON L6J 5A8
Tel: 905-845-3441; *Fax:* 905-845-2155
Toll-Free: 877-894-6625
industry@twinoakcu.com
www.twinoakcu.com
Year Founded: 1954

Number of Employees: 11
Assets: $10-50 million

Ukrainian (St Catharines) Credit Union Limited (USCCU)
118 Niagara St.
St Catharines, ON L2R 4L4
Tel: 905-684-5062; *Fax:* 905-684-3098
www.hroshi.com
Year Founded: 1946

Unigasco Credit Union Limited
40 Keil Dr. South
Chatham, ON N7M 3G8
Tel: 519-436-4590; *Fax:* 519-436-5451
Toll-Free: 800-592-9592
www.unigasco.com
Year Founded: 1952
Number of Employees: 23

Union Bay Credit Union
PO Box 158
313 McLeod Rd.
Union Bay, BC V0R 3B0
Tel: 250-335-2122; *Fax:* 250-335-2131
www.unionbaycreditunion.com
Ownership: Member-owned
Year Founded: 1944

United Employees Credit Union Limited
964 Eastern Ave.
Toronto, ON M4L 1A6
Tel: 416-461-9257; *Fax:* 416-461-8141
infounited@unitedcu.com
www.unitedcu.com
Year Founded: 1946
Number of Employees: 10

Unity Credit Union Ltd.
PO Box 370
120 - 2nd Ave. East
Unity, SK S0K 4L0
Tel: 306-228-2688; *Fax:* 306-228-2185
info@unity.cu.sk.ca
www.unity.cu.sk.ca
Year Founded: 1941
Number of Employees: 31
Assets: $50-100 million
Revenues: $1-5 million

Unity Savings & Credit Union Limited
Central Management Support Office, Bayridge Centre West
775 Strand Blvd.
Kingston, ON K7P 2S7
Tel: 613-389-9965
unityone@unitysavings.com
www.unitysavings.com
Number of Employees: 23

University Hospitals Staff Credit Union Ltd.
8440 - 112 St.
Edmonton, AB T6G 2B7
Tel: 780-407-8151; *Fax:* 780-407-7557
chauah@telus.net
Year Founded: 1949
Number of Employees: 3
Assets: $5-10 million
Revenues: Under $1 million

Utilities Employees' (Windsor) Credit Union Limited
4545 Rhodes Dr.
Windsor, ON N8W 5T1
Tel: 519-945-5141; *Fax:* 519-945-0347

Valley Credit Union
PO Box 70
5682 Hwy. #1
Waterville, NS B0P 1V0
Tel: 902-538-4510; *Fax:* 902-538-4529
www.valleycreditunion.com
Year Founded: 1994

Valley First Financial Group
184 Main St., 3rd Fl.
Penticton, BC V2A 8G7
Tel: 250-490-2720; *Fax:* 250-490-2721
Toll-Free: 800-567-8111
info@valleyfirst.com
www.valleyfirst.com
Also Known As: Valley Field Credit Union
Year Founded: 2001
Assets: $500m-1 billion

Van Tel/Safeway Credit Union
#2010, 4330 Kingsway
Burnaby, BC V5H 4G8
Tel: 604-656-6200; *Fax:* 604-656-6167
Toll-Free: 800-663-1557
Former Name: Van Tel Credit Union
Year Founded: 1940
Number of Employees: 70+
Assets: $100-500 million

Vancouver City Savings Credit Union
PO Box 2120, Terminal Stn. Terminal
183 Terminal Ave.
Vancouver, BC V6B 5R8
Tel: 604-877-7000; *Fax:* 604-877-7639
Toll-Free: 888-826-2489
vc_editor@vancity.com
www.vancity.com
Also Known As: VanCity Credit Union
Year Founded: 1946
Assets: $1-10 billion

Vanguard Credit Union
Also listed under: *Financing & Loan Companies; Investment Management*
PO Box 490
47 Main St.
Rossburn, MB R0J 1V0
Tel: 204-859-5010; *Fax:* 204-859-5020
contact@vanguardcu.mb.ca
www.vanguardcu.mb.ca
Ownership: Member-owned
Year Founded: 1947
Number of Employees: 92
Assets: $100-500 million
Revenues: $5-10 million

Vermilion Credit Union Ltd.
5019 - 50 Ave.
Vermilion, AB T9X 1A7
Tel: 780-853-2822; *Fax:* 780-853-4361
vermilion@alberta-cu.com
www.vermilioncreditunion.com

Vernon & District Credit Union
Also listed under: *Financing & Loan Companies; Investment Management*
3108 - 33rd Ave.
Vernon, BC V1T 2N7
Tel: 250-545-9251; *Fax:* 250-545-8166
Toll-Free: 888-339-8328
info@vdcu.com
www.vdcu.com
Ownership: Co-operative. Member-owned.
Year Founded: 1944
Number of Employees: 45
Assets: $100-500 million
Revenues: $10-50 million

Victory Community Credit Union
#102, 2100 Lawrence Ave. West
Toronto, ON M9N 3W3
Tel: 416-243-0686; *Fax:* 416-243-9614
creditunion@vccu.com
www.vccu.com
Year Founded: 1948
Number of Employees: 3
Revenues: $5-10 million

Victory Credit Union
PO Box 340
41 Water St.
Windsor, NS B0N 2T0
Tel: 902-798-1820; *Fax:* 902-798-1255
www.victorycreditunion.ca
Ownership: Cooperative
Number of Employees: 30
Revenues: $10-50 million

Virden Credit Union
PO Box 1660
220 - 7th Ave. South
Virden, MB R0M 2C0
Tel: 204-748-2907; *Fax:* 204-748-1081
Toll-Free: 888-748-2907
Year Founded: 1940
Number of Employees: 58
Assets: $100-500 million

Virtual One Credit Union Ltd.
15 Bronte College Ct.
Mississauga, ON L5B 0E7
Tel: 905-270-2223; *Fax:* 905-270-0902
info_cu@virtualonecu.com
www.virtualonecu.com

Year Founded: 1946
Assets: $50-100 million

Wainwright Credit Union
Administration Office
502 - 10 St.
Wainwright, AB T9W 1P4
Tel: 780-842-9184; *Fax:* 780-842-2855
www.wainwright-cu.com

Ownership: Member-owned
Year Founded: 1943
Number of Employees: 84
Assets: $100-500 million
Revenues: $10-50 million

Wallace Barnes Employees' Credit Union Limited
3100 Mainway Dr.
Burlington, ON L7M 1A3
Tel: 905-335-6688; *Fax:* 905-336-1336

Ownership: Private
Year Founded: 1943
Number of Employees: 1
Assets: Under $1 million
Revenues: Under $1 million

Westminster Savings Credit Union
Corporate Centre
#108, 960 Quayside Dr.
New Westminster, BC V3M 6G2
Tel: 604-517-0100; *Fax:* 604-528-3812
www.wscu.com

Ownership: Member-owned
Year Founded: 1944
Number of Employees: 357
Assets: $1-10 billion
Revenues: $50-100 million

Westoba Credit Union Limited
#C, 220 - 10th St.
Brandon, MB R7A 4E8
Tel: 204-729-2050; *Fax:* 204-729-8852
infowcul@westoba.com
www.westoba.com

Ownership: Member-owned
Year Founded: 1963
Number of Employees: 200
Assets: $500m-1 billion
Revenues: $10-50 million

Weyburn Credit Union Limited
PO Box 1117
221 Coteau Ave.
Weyburn, SK S4H 2L3
Tel: 306-842-6641; *Fax:* 306-842-6620
Toll-Free: 800-667-8842
info@weyburn.cu.sk.ca
www.weyburn.cu.sk.ca

Ownership: Member-owned
Year Founded: 1944
Assets: $1-5 million
Revenues: $1-5 million

Weymouth Credit Union
PO Box 411
4569 Hwy. #1
Weymouth, NS B0W 3T0
Tel: 902-837-4089; *Fax:* 902-837-4089

Williams Lake & District Credit Union
139 North 3rd Ave.
Williams Lake, BC V2G 2A5
Tel: 250-392-4135; *Fax:* 250-392-4361
info@wldcu.com
www.wldcu.com

Year Founded: 1952
Number of Employees: 12

Windsor Family Credit Union
2800 Tecumseth Rd East
Windsor, ON N8W 1G4
Tel: 519-974-3100; *Fax:* 519-974-4077
info@windsorfamily.com
www.windsorfamily.com

Winnipeg Police Credit Union Ltd.
300 William Ave.
Winnipeg, MB R3A 1P9
Tel: 204-944-1033; *Fax:* 204-949-0821
Toll-Free: 866-491-7122
www.policecu.mb.ca

Year Founded: 1949

York Credit Union
494 Queen St.
Fredericton, NB E3B 1B6
Tel: 506-458-8844; *Fax:* 506-452-8496
membersfirst@york.creditu.net
www.yorkcu.nb.ca

Year Founded: 1953

Your Credit Union Limited
14 Chamberlain Ave
Ottawa, ON K1S 1V9
Tel: 613-238-8001; *Fax:* 613-238-2149
Toll-Free: 800-379-7757
info@yourcu.com
www.yourcu.com

Ownership: Member-owned

Your Neighbourhood Credit Union Ltd.
5415 Tecumseh Rd. East
Windsor, ON N8T 1C5
Tel: 519-258-3890; *Fax:* 519-945-5933
info@yncu.com
www.yncu.com

Former Name: Windsor & Essex Educational Credit Union
Year Founded: 1953

Insurance Companies

Insurance companies are registered to conduct business under the federal Insurance Companies Act and/or corresponding provincial legislation. Life insurance companies are registered to underwrite life insurance, accident and sickness insurance and annuity business. Property and casualty insurance companies are registered to underwrite insurance other than life insurance.

Included in these listings are federally and provincially incorporated insurance companies, reinsurance companies, fraternal benefit societies and reciprocal exchanges, with the classes of insurance they offer.

*Companies marked with an * are provincially incorporated. For provincially incorporated companies not listed below, contact the government agency for each province. For further information, please see the "Government Quick Reference" guide at the beginning of Section 7, and check under "Insurance."*

Classes of insurance listed below include: Accident, Auto, Aircraft, Boiler & Machinery, Credit, Fidelity, Fire, Hail & Crop, Legal Expense, Liability, Life, Marine, Personal Accident & Sickness, Property, Reinsurance, Surety, and Theft.

Insurance Class Index

Accident
ACA Assurance
ACE INA Insurance
American Bankers Life Insurance Company of Florida
American Re-Insurance Company
Assumption Mutual Life Insurance Company
Ayr Farmers Mutual Insurance Company
Caisse Centrale de Réassurance
Canadian Professional Sales Association
CIGNA Life Insurance Company of Canada
The Citadel General Assurance Company
Connecticut General Life Insurance Co.
Constitution Insurance Company of Canada
Continental Casualty Company
CUMIS Life Insurance Company
Desjardins Financial Security
Echelon General Insurance Company
Empire Life Insurance Company
L'Entraide assurance, compagnie mutuelle
FaithLife Financial
Federated Insurance Company of Canada
Federation Insurance Company of Canada
Granite Insurance Company
The Guarantee Company of North America
Industrial Alliance Pacific Life Insurance Company
ING Insurance Company of Canada - Corporate Office (Western Region)
Life Insurance Company of North America
London & Midland General Insurance Company
The Nordic Insurance Company of Canada
Odyssey America Reinsurance Corp., Canadian Branch
Old Republic Insurance Company of Canada
Optimum Reassurance Company
Pacific Blue Cross
Peace Hills General Insurance Company
Pembridge Insurance Company
Promutuel Réassurance
Promutuel Vie inc
Québec Blue Cross
Saskatchewan Motor Club Insurance Company Ltd.
SGI CANADA Consolidated
Société de l'assurance automobile du Québec
South Easthope Mutual Insurance Co.
SSQ, Société d'assurances générales inc.
SSQ, Société d'assurance-vie inc
Tradition Mutual Insurance Company
Trillium Mutual Insurance Company
Union of Canada Life Insurance
Western Financial Group Inc.
Zurich Canada

Aircraft
ACE INA Insurance
American Home Assurance Company
Avemco Insurance Company
Aviation & General Insurance Company Limited
Aviva Canada Inc.
AXA Corporate Solutions Assurance
AXA General Insurance Company
AXA Insurance (Canada)
AXA Pacific Insurance Company
AXA RE
Berkley Insurance Company
Caisse Centrale de Réassurance
Canadian Universities Reciprocal Insurance Exchange
Chubb Insurance Company of Canada
Commonwealth Insurance Company
Continental Casualty Company
Co-operators General Insurance Company
Eagle Star Insurance Company Ltd.
Elite Insurance Company
Employers Insurance Company of Wausau
Employers Reinsurance Corporation
Everest Insurance Company of Canada
Everest Reinsurance Company
GCAN Insurance Company
General Reinsurance Corporation
Global Aerospace Underwriting Managers (Canada) Limited
Great American Insurance Company
Hannover Rückversicherungs AG
Hartford Fire Insurance Company
Henderson Insurance Inc.
Koch B&Y Insurance Services Ltd.
Liberty Mutual Insurance Company
Lloyd's Underwriters
Lombard General Insurance Company of Canada
Lombard Insurance Company
Mitsui Sumitomo Insurance Co., Limited.
NIPPONKOA Insurance Company, Limited
Odyssey America Reinsurance Corp., Canadian Branch
Old Republic Insurance Company of Canada
Omega General Insurance Company
Oxford Mutual Insurance Co.
Peace Hills General Insurance Company
The Personal Insurance Company
Revios Reinsurance
St. Paul Fire & Marine Insurance Company
SGI CANADA Consolidated
State Farm Fire & Casualty Company
TD General Insurance Company
Wedgwood Insurance Ltd.
Western Assurance Company
XL Reinsurance America Inc.

Auto
ACE INA Insurance
Alberta Motor Association Insurance Co.
Algoma Insurance Group Ltd.
Algoma Mutual Insurance Company
Alliance Assurance
Allstate Insurance Company of Canada
All-West Insurance Network
L'ALPHA, compagnie d'assurances inc.
Alpine Insurance & Financial Inc.
American Home Assurance Company
American Re-Insurance Company
The American Road Insurance Company
Astro Insurance 1000 Inc.
Atlantic Insurance Company Limited
Aviva Canada Inc.
AXA Corporate Solutions Assurance
AXA General Insurance Company
AXA Insurance (Canada)
AXA Pacific Insurance Company

AXA RE
Ayr Farmers Mutual Insurance Company
Bay of Quinte Mutual Insurance Co.
Belair Insurance Company Inc.
Berkley Insurance Company
Bertie & Clinton Mutual Insurance Co.
Brant Mutual Insurance Company
British Columbia Automobile Association Insurance Agency
Butler Byers Insurance Ltd.
CAA Insurance Company (Ontario)
Caisse Centrale de Réassurance
Canadian Northern Shield Insurance Company
Canadian Petroleum Insurance Exchange Ltd.
Canadian Professional Sales Association
La Capitale General Insurance Inc.
Caradoc Delaware Mutual Fire Insurance Company
Carleton Mutual Insurance Company
Cavell Insurance Company Limited
Certas Direct Insurance Company
Chubb Insurance Company of Canada
The Citadel General Assurance Company
Coachman Insurance Company
Coastal Community Insurance Services (2007) Ltd.
La Compagnie d'Assurance Missisquoi
Constitution Insurance Company of Canada
Continental Casualty Company
Co-operators General Insurance Company
COSECO Insurance Company
Cowan Insurance Group
Crowsnest Insurance Agencies Ltd.
CUMIS General Insurance Company
The CUMIS Group Limited
CUMIS Life Insurance Company
DaimlerChrysler Insurance Company
Desjardins assurances générales inc
The Dominion of Canada General Insurance Company
Dufferin Mutual Insurance Company
Dumfries Mutual Insurance Company
Eagle Star Insurance Company Ltd.
Ecclesiastical Insurance Office plc
Echelon General Insurance Company
Economical Mutual Insurance Company
Elite Insurance Company
Employers Insurance Company of Wausau
Employers Reinsurance Corporation
Erie Mutual Fire Insurance Co.
Everest Insurance Company of Canada
Everest Reinsurance Company
Farmers' Mutual Insurance Company (Lindsay)
Federal Insurance Company
Federated Insurance Company of Canada
Federation Insurance Company of Canada
Fenchurch General Insurance Company
First North American Insurance Company
Folksamerica Reinsurance Company
Formosa Mutual Insurance Co.
Fundy Mutual Insurance Company
GCAN Insurance Company
General Reinsurance Corporation
Germania Farmers' Mutual Fire Insurance Company
Gibb's Agencies (1997) Ltd.
Glengarry Farmers' Mutual Fire Insurance Co.
Gore Mutual Insurance Company
Granite Insurance Company
Great American Insurance Company
Grenville Mutual Insurance Co.
Grey & Bruce Mutual Insurance Co.
Le Groupe Estrie-Richelieu, compagnie d'assurance
The Guarantee Company of North America
Halwell Mutual Insurance Company
Hannover Rückversicherungs AG
Hartford Fire Insurance Company
Hay Mutual Insurance Company
Henderson Insurance Inc.
Howard Mutual Insurance Co.
Howick Mutual Insurance Company
Industrial Alliance Insurance & Financial Services Inc.
ING Insurance Company of Canada - Corporate Office (Central & Atlantic Region)
ING Insurance Company of Canada - Corporate Office (Western Region)
ING Novex Insurance Company of Canada
Innovative Insurance Corporation
Insurance Company of Prince Edward Island
Insurance Corporation of British Columbia
JEVCO Insurance Company
Kent & Essex Mutual Insurance Company
Kingsway Financial Services Inc.
Kingsway General Insurance Company
Kirkham Insurance (1984) Ltd.
Koch B&Y Insurance Services Ltd.
Lambton Mutual Insurance Company
Lanark Mutual Insurance Company
Lennox & Addington Fire Mutual Insurance Company
Liberty Mutual Insurance Company
Lloyd's Underwriters
Lombard General Insurance Company of Canada
Lombard Insurance Company
London & Midland General Insurance Company
Manitoba Public Insurance
Markel Insurance Company of Canada
McFarlane & Company
McKillop Mutual Insurance Company
Mennonite Mutual Insurance Co. (Alberta) Ltd.
Metro General Insurance Corp. Limited
Middlesex Mutual Insurance Co.
Millennium Insurance Corporation
Mitsui Sumitomo Insurance Co., Limited.
Motors Insurance Corporation
Munich Reinsurance Company of Canada
New India Assurance Company, Limited
NIPPONKOA Insurance Company, Limited
The Nordic Insurance Company of Canada
Norfolk Mutual Insurance Company
North Bleinheim Mutual Insurance Co.
North Blenheim Mutual Insurance Company
North Kent Mutual Fire Insurance Company
The North Waterloo Farmers Mutual Insurance Company
Odyssey America Reinsurance Corp., Canadian Branch
Old Republic Insurance Company of Canada
Ontario Mutual Insurance Association
Ontario School Boards' Insurance Exchange
Optimum Assurance Agricole inc
Optimum Général inc
Optimum Société d'Assurance inc
Oxford Mutual Insurance Co.
Pafco Insurance Company
PartnerRe SA
PC Financial Insurance Agency
Peace Hills General Insurance Company
Peel Mutual Insurance Co.
The Personal General Insurance Inc.
The Personal Insurance Company
Perth Insurance Company
Pilot Insurance Company
The Portage La Prairie Mutual Insurance Company
Primmum Insurance Company
Progressive Casualty Insurance Company
Protective Insurance Company
Québec Blue Cross
RBC General Insurance Company
RBC Insurance
Revios Reinsurance
St. Paul Fire & Marine Insurance Company
Saskatchewan Auto Fund
Saskatchewan Mutual Insurance Company
Scottish & York Insurance Co. Limited
Security National Insurance Company
SGI CANADA Consolidated
Société de l'assurance automobile du Québec
South Easthope Mutual Insurance Co.
SSQ Financial Group
SSQ, Société d'assurances générales inc.
SSQ, Société d'assurance-vie inc
Stanley Mutual Insurance Company
State Farm Fire & Casualty Company
State Farm Mutual Automobile Insurance Company
Suecia Reinsurance Company
TD General Insurance Company
TD Home & Auto Insurance Company
Thomson-Schindle-Green Insurance & Financial Services Ltd.
The Tokio Marine & Nichido Fire Insurance Co., Ltd.
Town & Country Mutual Insurance Company
Townsend Farmers' Mutual Fire Insurance Company
Traders General Insurance Company
Tradition Mutual Insurance Company
Trillium Mutual Insurance Company
Unified Assurance Company
L'Union Canadienne Compagnie d'Assurances
United General Insurance Corporation
Virginia Surety Company, Inc.
Wabisa Mutual Insurance Company
Waterloo Insurance Company
The Wawanesa Mutual Insurance Company
Wedgwood Insurance Ltd.
West Elgin Mutual Insurance Company
West Wawanosh Mutual Insurance Company
Western Assurance Company
Western Financial Group Inc.
Westland Insurance Group
Westminster Mutual Insurance Company
XL Insurance Company Limited
XL Reinsurance America Inc.
Yarmouth Mutual Fire Insurance Company
York Fire & Casualty Insurance Company
Zenith Insurance Company
Zurich Canada

Boiler & Machinery

ACE INA Insurance
Affiliated FM Insurance Company
Algoma Insurance Group Ltd.
Allstate Insurance Company of Canada
American Home Assurance Company
American Re-Insurance Company
The American Road Insurance Company
L'Assurance Mutuelle des Fabriques de Montréal
Atlantic Insurance Company Limited
Aviva Canada Inc.
AXA Corporate Solutions Assurance
AXA General Insurance Company
AXA Insurance (Canada)
AXA Pacific Insurance Company
AXA RE
Ayr Farmers Mutual Insurance Company
Bay of Quinte Mutual Insurance Co.
Belair Insurance Company Inc.
Berkley Insurance Company
Bertie & Clinton Mutual Insurance Co.
The Boiler Inspection & Insurance Company of Canada
Brant Mutual Insurance Company
Caisse Centrale de Réassurance
Canadian Farm Insurance Corporation
Caradoc Delaware Mutual Fire Insurance Company
Cavell Insurance Company Limited
Chubb Insurance Company of Canada
Commonwealth Insurance Company
La Compagnie d'Assurance Missisquoi
Continental Casualty Company
Co-operators General Insurance Company
CUMIS General Insurance Company
Desjardins assurances générales inc
Dufferin Mutual Insurance Company
Dumfries Mutual Insurance Company
Eagle Star Insurance Company Ltd.
Ecclesiastical Insurance Office plc
Economical Mutual Insurance Company
Elite Insurance Company
Employers Insurance Company of Wausau
Employers Reinsurance Corporation
Erie Mutual Fire Insurance Co.
Everest Insurance Company of Canada
Everest Reinsurance Company
Farmers' Mutual Insurance Company (Lindsay)
Federal Insurance Company
Federated Insurance Company of Canada
Federation Insurance Company of Canada
Fenchurch General Insurance Company
FM Global
Fundy Mutual Insurance Company
GCAN Insurance Company
General Reinsurance Corporation
Germania Farmers' Mutual Fire Insurance Company
Glengarry Farmers' Mutual Fire Insurance Co.
Grain Insurance & Guarantee Company
Granite Insurance Company
Great American Insurance Company
Grenville Mutual Insurance Co.
Grey & Bruce Mutual Insurance Co.
Le Groupe Estrie-Richelieu, compagnie d'assurance
The Guarantee Company of North America
Halwell Mutual Insurance Company
Hannover Rückversicherungs AG
Hartford Fire Insurance Company
Howick Mutual Insurance Company
ING Insurance Company of Canada - Corporate Office (Western Region)
ING Novex Insurance Company of Canada
Innovative Insurance Corporation
Kent & Essex Mutual Insurance Company
Lambton Mutual Insurance Company
Lanark Mutual Insurance Company
Liberty Mutual Insurance Company
Lloyd's Underwriters
Lombard General Insurance Company of Canada
Lombard Insurance Company
London & Midland General Insurance Company
Lumbermen's Underwriting Alliance
MAX Canada Insurance Company
McKillop Mutual Insurance Company
Mennonite Mutual Fire Insurance Company

Mitsui Sumitomo Insurance Co., Limited.
Motors Insurance Corporation
New India Assurance Company, Limited
NIPPONKOA Insurance Company, Limited
The Nordic Insurance Company of Canada
The North Waterloo Farmers Mutual Insurance Company
Odyssey America Reinsurance Corp., Canadian Branch
Omega General Insurance Company
Ontario School Boards' Insurance Exchange
Oxford Mutual Insurance Co.
Peace Hills General Insurance Company
Peel Mutual Insurance Co.
The Personal General Insurance Inc.
The Personal Insurance Company
Promutuel Réassurance
Red River Valley Mutual Insurance Company
Revios Reinsurance
St. Paul Fire & Marine Insurance Company
Saskatchewan Mutual Insurance Company
Scottish & York Insurance Co. Limited
SGI CANADA Consolidated
South Easthope Mutual Insurance Co.
Southeastern Mutual Insurance Company
Stanley Mutual Insurance Company
State Farm Fire & Casualty Company
TD General Insurance Company
Temple Insurance
Town & Country Mutual Insurance Company
Townsend Farmers' Mutual Fire Insurance Company
Tradition Mutual Insurance Company
Trillium Mutual Insurance Company
Virginia Surety Company, Inc.
The Wawanesa Mutual Insurance Company
West Wawanosh Mutual Insurance Company
Western Assurance Company
Western Financial Group Inc.
XL Insurance Company Limited
XL Reinsurance America Inc.
Zurich Canada

Credit

ACE INA Insurance
American Home Assurance Company
American Re-Insurance Company
The American Road Insurance Company
Assurance-Vie Banque Nationale
Assurant Solutions Canada
AXA Corporate Solutions Assurance
AXA Pacific Insurance Company
Berkley Insurance Company
Canadian Premier Life Insurance Company
CIGNA Life Insurance Company of Canada
Continental Casualty Company
CUMIS Life Insurance Company
Employers Reinsurance Corporation
L'Entraide assurance, compagnie mutuelle
Euler Hermes Canada
Everest Insurance Company of Canada
Everest Reinsurance Company
GCAN Insurance Company
General Reinsurance Corporation
Granite Insurance Company
The Guarantee Company of North America
Industrial Alliance Pacific Life Insurance Company
ING Insurance Company of Canada - Corporate Office (Western Region)
ING Novex Insurance Company of Canada
Lombard General Insurance Company of Canada
Lombard Insurance Company
Omega General Insurance Company
Peace Hills General Insurance Company
The PMI Group, Inc. Canada
Revios Reinsurance
Transatlantic Reinsurance Company
Zurich Canada

Fidelity

ACE INA Insurance
Affiliated FM Insurance Company
Allstate Insurance Company of Canada
American Home Assurance Company
American Re-Insurance Company
ATB Financial
Atlantic Insurance Company Limited
Aviva Canada Inc.
AXA Corporate Solutions Assurance
AXA General Insurance Company
AXA Insurance (Canada)
AXA Pacific Insurance Company
AXA RE
Ayr Farmers Mutual Insurance Company
Bay of Quinte Mutual Insurance Co.
Belair Insurance Company Inc.
Berkley Insurance Company
Bertie & Clinton Mutual Insurance Co.
Brant Mutual Insurance Company
Caisse Centrale de Réassurance
Canadian Farm Insurance Corporation
Cavell Insurance Company Limited
Chubb Insurance Company of Canada
The Citadel General Assurance Company
Commonwealth Insurance Company
La Compagnie d'Assurance Missisquoi
Constitution Insurance Company of Canada
Continental Casualty Company
Co-operators General Insurance Company
CUMIS General Insurance Company
CUMIS Life Insurance Company
Dufferin Mutual Insurance Company
Eagle Star Insurance Company Ltd.
Ecclesiastical Insurance Office plc
Echelon General Insurance Company
Elite Insurance Company
Employers Insurance Company of Wausau
Employers Reinsurance Corporation
Erie Mutual Fire Insurance Co.
Everest Reinsurance Company
Farmers' Mutual Insurance Company (Lindsay)
Federal Insurance Company
Federated Insurance Company of Canada
Federation Insurance Company of Canada
Folksamerica Reinsurance Company
GCAN Insurance Company
General Reinsurance Corporation
Germania Farmers' Mutual Fire Insurance Company
Glengarry Farmers' Mutual Fire Insurance Co.
Grain Insurance & Guarantee Company
Granite Insurance Company
Great American Insurance Company
Grenville Mutual Insurance Co.
The Guarantee Company of North America
Halwell Mutual Insurance Company
Hannover Rückversicherungs AG
Hartford Fire Insurance Company
Howard Mutual Insurance Co.
Howick Mutual Insurance Company
ING Insurance Company of Canada - Corporate Office (Western Region)
ING Novex Insurance Company of Canada
Kent & Essex Mutual Insurance Company
Lambton Mutual Insurance Company
Liberty Mutual Insurance Company
Lloyd's Underwriters
Lombard General Insurance Company of Canada
Lombard Insurance Company
London & Midland General Insurance Company
MAX Canada Insurance Company
McKillop Mutual Insurance Company
Mitsui Sumitomo Insurance Co., Limited.
NIPPONKOA Insurance Company, Limited
The Nordic Insurance Company of Canada
The North Waterloo Farmers Mutual Insurance Company
Omega General Insurance Company
Oxford Mutual Insurance Co.
Peace Hills General Insurance Company
Peel Mutual Insurance Co.
The Personal Insurance Company
Red River Valley Mutual Insurance Company
Revios Reinsurance
St. Paul Fire & Marine Insurance Company
Saskatchewan Mutual Insurance Company
Scottish & York Insurance Co. Limited
SGI CANADA Consolidated
State Farm Fire & Casualty Company
Suecia Reinsurance Company
Swiss Reinsurance Company Canada
TD General Insurance Company
Town & Country Mutual Insurance Company
Tradition Mutual Insurance Company
Trillium Mutual Insurance Company
Wabisa Mutual Insurance Company
West Elgin Mutual Insurance Company
West Wawanosh Mutual Insurance Company
Western Assurance Company
Western Financial Group Inc.
Western Surety Company
XL Reinsurance America Inc.
Zurich Canada

Fire

ACE INA Insurance
Affiliated FM Insurance Company
Alberta Motor Association Insurance Co.
Antigonish Farmers' Mutual Insurance Company
L'Assurance Mutuelle des Fabriques de Montréal
British Columbia Automobile Association Insurance Agency
Caisse Centrale de Réassurance
Carleton Mutual Insurance Company
The Citadel General Assurance Company
Clare Mutual Insurance Company
La Compagnie d'Assurance Missisquoi
Co-operators General Insurance Company
CUMIS General Insurance Company
CUMIS Life Insurance Company
The Dominion of Canada General Insurance Company
Echelon General Insurance Company
Federated Insurance Company of Canada
Federation Insurance Company of Canada
Germania Mutual Insurance Company
Glengarry Farmers' Mutual Fire Insurance Co.
Gore Mutual Insurance Company
Grain Insurance & Guarantee Company
Granite Insurance Company
Le Groupe Estrie-Richelieu, compagnie d'assurance
The Guarantee Company of North America
Hamilton Township Mutual Insurance Company
Hartford Fire Insurance Company
ING Insurance Company of Canada - Corporate Office (Western Region)
The Kings Mutual Insurance Company
Lloyd's Underwriters
Lombard Canada Ltd.
Lombard Insurance Company
London & Midland General Insurance Company
Mennonite Mutual Fire Insurance Company
Mennonite Mutual Insurance Co. (Alberta) Ltd.
The Mutual Fire Insurance Company of British Columbia
New India Assurance Company, Limited
Norfolk Mutual Insurance Company
North Kent Mutual Fire Insurance Company
The North Waterloo Farmers Mutual Insurance Company
Odyssey America Reinsurance Corp., Canadian Branch
Ontario School Boards' Insurance Exchange
Optimum Assurance Agricole inc
Peace Hills General Insurance Company
Prince Edward Island Mutual Insurance Company
Promutuel Réassurance
RBC General Insurance Company
Red River Valley Mutual Insurance Company
Revios Reinsurance
St. Paul Fire & Marine Insurance Company
Security National Insurance Company
Southeastern Mutual Insurance Company
SSQ, Société d'assurances générales inc.
SSQ, Société d'assurance-vie inc
State Farm Fire & Casualty Company
The Tokio Marine & Nichido Fire Insurance Co., Ltd.
The Wawanesa Mutual Insurance Company
Western Financial Group Inc.
Zurich Canada

Hail & Crop

ACE INA Insurance
Agriculture Financial Services Corporation
American Home Assurance Company
American Re-Insurance Company
Astro Insurance 1000 Inc.
Aviva Canada Inc.
AXA Corporate Solutions Assurance
AXA General Insurance Company
AXA Insurance (Canada)
AXA Pacific Insurance Company
AXA RE
Ayr Farmers Mutual Insurance Company
Berkley Insurance Company
Brant Mutual Insurance Company
Butler Byers Hail Insurance Ltd.
Cavell Insurance Company Limited
Clare Mutual Insurance Company
Continental Casualty Company
Co-operative Hail Insurance Company Ltd.
Co-operators General Insurance Company
Dumfries Mutual Insurance Company
Employers Reinsurance Corporation
Everest Insurance Company of Canada
Everest Reinsurance Company
Federation Insurance Company of Canada
Folksamerica Reinsurance Company
GCAN Insurance Company
General Reinsurance Corporation
Granite Insurance Company
Great American Insurance Company
The Guarantee Company of North America

Hannover Rückversicherungs AG
Hartford Fire Insurance Company
Hay Mutual Insurance Company
Henderson Insurance Inc.
Howard Mutual Insurance Co.
Howick Mutual Insurance Company
Lambton Mutual Insurance Company
Lanark Mutual Insurance Company
Lombard General Insurance Company of Canada
Lombard Insurance Company
Manitoba Agricultural Services Corporation - Insurance Corporate Office
McFarlane & Company
New India Assurance Company, Limited
North Kent Mutual Fire Insurance Company
The North Waterloo Farmers Mutual Insurance Company
Odyssey America Reinsurance Corp., Canadian Branch
Oxford Mutual Insurance Co.
Palliser Insurance Company Limited
Rain & Hail Insurance Corporation
Revios Reinsurance
Saskatchewan Crop Insurance Corporation
Saskatchewan Municipal Hail Insurance Association
Suecia Reinsurance Company
Thomson-Schindle-Green Insurance & Financial Services Ltd.
Town & Country Mutual Insurance Company
Townsend Farmers' Mutual Fire Insurance Company
Tradition Mutual Insurance Company
Trillium Mutual Insurance Company
West Elgin Mutual Insurance Company
Western Financial Group Inc.
XL Reinsurance America Inc.
Yarmouth Mutual Fire Insurance Company

Legal Expense

Allstate Insurance Company of Canada
Aviva Canada Inc.
AXA Corporate Solutions Assurance
AXA General Insurance Company
AXA Insurance (Canada)
AXA Pacific Insurance Company
Belair Insurance Company Inc.
Berkley Insurance Company
CAA Insurance Company (Ontario)
Caisse Centrale de Réassurance
La Compagnie d'Assurance Missisquoi
Constitution Insurance Company of Canada
Echelon General Insurance Company
Federation Insurance Company of Canada
Glengarry Farmers' Mutual Fire Insurance Co.
The Guarantee Company of North America
ING Insurance Company of Canada - Corporate Office (Western Region)
ING Novex Insurance Company of Canada
Lloyd's Underwriters
Lombard General Insurance Company of Canada
Lombard Insurance Company
The Nordic Insurance Company of Canada
Omega General Insurance Company
The Portage La Prairie Mutual Insurance Company
Scottish & York Insurance Co. Limited

Liability

ACE INA Insurance
ACE INA Life Insurance
Affiliated FM Insurance Company
Algoma Insurance Group Ltd.
Alliance Assurance
Allstate Insurance Company of Canada
All-West Insurance Network
Alpine Insurance & Financial Inc.
American Home Assurance Company
American Re-Insurance Company
The American Road Insurance Company
Amherst Island Mutual Insurance Company
L'Assurance Mutuelle des Fabriques de Montréal
Astro Insurance 1000 Inc.
Atlantic Insurance Company Limited
Aviation & General Insurance Company Limited
Aviva Canada Inc.
AXA Corporate Solutions Assurance
AXA General Insurance Company
AXA Insurance (Canada)
AXA Pacific Insurance Company
AXA RE
Ayr Farmers Mutual Insurance Company
Bay of Quinte Mutual Insurance Co.
Belair Insurance Company Inc.
Berkley Insurance Company
Bertie & Clinton Mutual Insurance Co.
The Boiler Inspection & Insurance Company of Canada
Brant Mutual Insurance Company
CAA Insurance Company (Ontario)
Caisse Centrale de Réassurance
Canadian Direct Insurance Incorporated
Canadian Farm Insurance Corporation
Canadian Lawyers Liability Assurance Society
Canadian Northern Shield Insurance Company
Canadian Petroleum Insurance Exchange Ltd.
Canadian Universities Reciprocal Insurance Exchange
Canassurance Insurance Company
Caradoc Delaware Mutual Fire Insurance Company
Cavell Insurance Company Limited
Certas Direct Insurance Company
Chubb Insurance Company of Canada
The Citadel General Assurance Company
Commonwealth Insurance Company
La Compagnie d'Assurance Missisquoi
Constitution Insurance Company of Canada
Continental Casualty Company
Crowsnest Insurance Agencies Ltd.
DaimlerChrysler Insurance Company
Desjardins assurances générales inc
The Dominion of Canada General Insurance Company
Dufferin Mutual Insurance Company
Dumfries Mutual Insurance Company
Eagle Star Insurance Company Ltd.
Ecclesiastical Insurance Office plc
Echelon General Insurance Company
Elite Insurance Company
Employers Insurance Company of Wausau
Employers Reinsurance Corporation
Erie Mutual Fire Insurance Co.
Everest Insurance Company of Canada
Everest Reinsurance Company
Farmers' Mutual Insurance Company (Lindsay)
Federal Insurance Company
Federated Insurance Company of Canada
Federation Insurance Company of Canada
Fenchurch General Insurance Company
Folksamerica Reinsurance Company
Frank Cowan Company Limited
Fundy Mutual Insurance Company
GCAN Insurance Company
General Reinsurance Corporation
Germania Farmers' Mutual Fire Insurance Company
Germania Mutual Insurance Company
Glengarry Farmers' Mutual Fire Insurance Co.
Global Aerospace Underwriting Managers (Canada) Limited
Gore Mutual Insurance Company
Grain Insurance & Guarantee Company
Granite Insurance Company
Great American Insurance Company
Grenville Mutual Insurance Co.
Grey & Bruce Mutual Insurance Co.
Le Groupe Estrie-Richelieu, compagnie d'assurance
The Guarantee Company of North America
Halwell Mutual Insurance Company
Hannover Rückversicherungs AG
Hartford Fire Insurance Company
Hay Mutual Insurance Company
Henderson Insurance Inc.
Howard Mutual Insurance Co.
Howick Mutual Insurance Company
ING Novex Insurance Company of Canada
Kent & Essex Mutual Insurance Company
The Kings Mutual Insurance Company
Kingsway General Insurance Company
Lambton Mutual Insurance Company
Lanark Mutual Insurance Company
Lawyers' Professional Indemnity Company
Legacy General Insurance Company
Lennox & Addington Fire Mutual Insurance Company
Liberty Mutual Insurance Company
Lloyd's Underwriters
Lombard General Insurance Company of Canada
Lombard Insurance Company
MAX Canada Insurance Company
McFarlane & Company
McKillop Mutual Insurance Company
Mennonite Mutual Insurance Co. (Alberta) Ltd.
Metro General Insurance Corp. Limited
Middlesex Mutual Insurance Co.
Mitsui Sumitomo Insurance Co., Limited.
Motors Insurance Corporation
Munich Reinsurance Company of Canada
Municipal Insurance Association of British Columbia
MUNIX Reciprocal
NIPPONKOA Insurance Company, Limited
The Nordic Insurance Company of Canada
North Bleinheim Mutual Insurance Co.
North Blenheim Mutual Insurance Company
North Kent Mutual Fire Insurance Company
The North Waterloo Farmers Mutual Insurance Company
Odyssey America Reinsurance Corp., Canadian Branch
Old Republic Insurance Company of Canada
Omega General Insurance Company
Ontario School Boards' Insurance Exchange
Optimum Général inc
Optimum Société d'Assurance inc
Oxford Mutual Insurance Co.
Peace Hills General Insurance Company
Peel Mutual Insurance Co.
The Personal General Insurance Inc.
The Personal Insurance Company
Pictou County Farmers' Mutual Fire Insurance Company
The Portage La Prairie Mutual Insurance Company
Premier Marine Insurance Managers Group
Prince Edward Island Mutual Insurance Company
Progressive Casualty Insurance Company
Promutuel Réassurance
Protective Insurance Company
Québec Blue Cross
RBC General Insurance Company
Real Estate Insurance Exchange
Red River Valley Mutual Insurance Company
Revios Reinsurance
St. Paul Fire & Marine Insurance Company
Saskatchewan Mutual Insurance Company
Scottish & York Insurance Co. Limited
SGI CANADA Consolidated
Southeastern Mutual Insurance Company
SSQ, Société d'assurances générales inc.
SSQ, Société d'assurance-vie inc
Stanley Mutual Insurance Company
State Farm Fire & Casualty Company
Suecia Reinsurance Company
TD General Insurance Company
TD Home & Auto Insurance Company
Thomson-Schindle-Green Insurance & Financial Services Ltd.
Town & Country Mutual Insurance Company
Townsend Farmers' Mutual Fire Insurance Company
Tradition Mutual Insurance Company
Trans Global Insurance Company
Trillium Mutual Insurance Company
Trisura Guarantee Insurance Company
Virginia Surety Company, Inc.
Wabisa Mutual Insurance Company
The Wawanesa Mutual Insurance Company
West Elgin Mutual Insurance Company
West Wawanosh Mutual Insurance Company
Western Assurance Company
Western Financial Group Inc.
Westland Insurance Group
Westminster Mutual Insurance Company
XL Insurance Company Limited
XL Reinsurance America Inc.
Yarmouth Mutual Fire Insurance Company
York Fire & Casualty Insurance Company
Zenith Insurance Company
Zurich Canada

Life

ACA Assurance
Acadia Life
ACTRA Fraternal Benefit Society
Aetna Life Insurance Company of Canada
AIG Assurance Canada
AIG Life Insurance Company of Canada
Alberta Motor Association Insurance Co.
Allianz Life Insurance Company of North America
Alpine Insurance & Financial Inc.
American Bankers Life Insurance Company of Florida
American Health & Life Insurance Company
American Income Life Insurance Company
AMEX Assurance Company
Assumption Mutual Life Insurance Company
Assurance-Vie Banque Nationale
AXA Equitable Life Insurance Company
AXA RE
BMO Life Insurance Company
British Columbia Automobile Association Insurance Agency
British Columbia Life & Casualty Company
Butler Byers Insurance Ltd.
CAA Insurance Company (Ontario)
Canada Life Financial Corporation
Canadian Premier Life Insurance Company
Canadian Professional Sales Association
Canadian Slovak League
Canassurance Insurance Company
La Capitale Civil Service Insurer Inc.
La Capitale Insurance & Financial Services

CIBC Life Insurance Company Limited
CIGNA Life Insurance Company of Canada
Clarica Life Insurance Co.
Combined Insurance Company of America
Connecticut General Life Insurance Co.
Co-operators General Insurance Company
Co-operators Life Insurance Company
Croatian Fraternal Union of America
The CUMIS Group Limited
CUMIS Life Insurance Company
Desjardins Financial Security
Empire Life Insurance Company
Employers Reassurance Corporation
L'Entraide assurance, compagnie mutuelle
The Equitable Life Insurance Company of Canada
L'Excellence, Compagnie d'assurance-vVie
FaithLife Financial
GAN Assurances Vie Compagnie française d'assurances vie mixte
General American Life Insurance Company
Gerber Life Insurance Company
The Grand Orange Lodge of British America Beneficent Fund
The Great-West Life Assurance Company
The Independent Order of Foresters
Industrial Alliance Insurance & Financial Services Inc.
Industrial Alliance Pacific Life Insurance Company
Insurance Company of Prince Edward Island
L'Internationale, compagnie d'assurance-vie
Knights of Columbus
Koch B&Y Insurance Services Ltd.
Life Insurance Company of North America
London & Midland General Insurance Company
London Life Insurance Company
Manitoba Blue Cross
Manufacturers Life Insurance Company
Manulife Canada Ltd.
Manulife Financial
Massachusetts Mutual Life Insurance Company
McFarlane & Company
MD Life Insurance Company
Medavie Blue Cross
Metropolitan Life Insurance Company, Canadian Branch
Minnesota Life Insurance Company
Munich Reinsurance Company - Canada Life
New India Assurance Company, Limited
The North West Commercial Travellers' Association of Canada
Optimum Reassurance Company
The Order of United Commercial Travelers of America
Pacific Blue Cross
PartnerRe SA
Penncorp Life Insurance Company
Primerica Life Insurance Company of Canada
Principal Life Insurance Company
Promutuel Vie inc
Québec Blue Cross
RBC Insurance
RBC Life Insurance Company
RBC Travel Insurance Company
Reliable Life Insurance Company
ReliaStar Life Insurance Company
Saskatchewan Blue Cross
SCOR Vie - Succursale du Canada
Scotia Life Insurance Company
Sons of Scotland Benevolent Association
SSQ Financial Group
SSQ, Société d'assurance-vie inc
The Standard Life Assurance Company of Canada
State Farm Life Insurance Company
Sun Life Assurance Company of Canada
Sun Life Financial Inc.
Supreme Council of the Royal Arcanum
La Survivance, compagnie mutuelle d'assurance vie
Swiss Re Frankona Rückversicherungs-Aktiengesellschaft
TD Life Insurance Company
Thomson-Schindle-Green Insurance & Financial Services Ltd.
Trans Global Life Insurance Company
Transamerica Life Canada
Ukrainian Fraternal Association of America
Ukrainian Fraternal Society of Canada
Ukrainian Mutual Benefit Association of Saint Nicholas of Canada
Ukrainian National Association
Union of Canada Life Insurance
L'Union-Vie, compagnie mutuelle d'assurance
United American Insurance Company
Unity Life of Canada
The Wawanesa Life Insurance Company
Wedgwood Insurance Ltd.
Western Financial Group Inc.
Western Life Assurance Company
Woman's Life Insurance Society

Marine

ACE INA Insurance
American Re-Insurance Company
Antigonish Farmers' Mutual Insurance Company
Avemco Insurance Company
Aviva Canada Inc.
AXA RE
Belair Insurance Company Inc.
Butler Byers Insurance Ltd.
CAA Insurance Company (Ontario)
Canadian Universities Reciprocal Insurance Exchange
Cavell Insurance Company Limited
Chubb Insurance Company of Canada
Commonwealth Insurance Company
Cowan Insurance Group
Ecclesiastical Insurance Office plc
Elite Insurance Company
Everest Insurance Company of Canada
Farmers' Mutual Insurance Company (Lindsay)
Federal Insurance Company
Formosa Mutual Insurance Co.
GCAN Insurance Company
Great American Insurance Company
Hamilton Township Mutual Insurance Company
Henderson Insurance Inc.
ING Insurance Company of Canada - Corporate Office (Specialty Lines)
Koch B&Y Insurance Services Ltd.
Lennox & Addington Fire Mutual Insurance Company
Lombard Canada Ltd.
Lombard Insurance Company
MAX Canada Insurance Company
NIPPONKOA Insurance Company, Limited
Pacific Coast Fishermen's Mutual Marine Insurance Company
Peace Hills General Insurance Company
Pembridge Insurance Company
Premier Marine Insurance Managers Group
Providence Washington Insurance Company
Revios Reinsurance
St. Paul Fire & Marine Insurance Company
Swiss Reinsurance Company Canada
The Tokio Marine & Nichido Fire Insurance Co., Ltd.
Trillium Mutual Insurance Company
Wedgwood Insurance Ltd.
Western Assurance Company
Zurich Canada

Personal Accident & Sickness

Acadia Life
ACE INA Life Insurance
ACTRA Fraternal Benefit Society
Aetna Life Insurance Company of Canada
AIG Assurance Canada
AIG Life Insurance Company of Canada
Alberta Blue Cross
Alberta Motor Association Insurance Co.
Allianz Life Insurance Company of North America
Allstate Insurance Company of Canada
American Bankers Life Insurance Company of Florida
American Home Assurance Company
American Income Life Insurance Company
American Re-Insurance Company
AMEX Assurance Company
Amherst Island Mutual Insurance Company
Assumption Mutual Life Insurance Company
Assurance-Vie Banque Nationale
Avemco Insurance Company
Aviva Canada Inc.
AXA Corporate Solutions Assurance
AXA Equitable Life Insurance Company
AXA General Insurance Company
AXA Insurance (Canada)
AXA Pacific Insurance Company
AXA RE
Ayr Farmers Mutual Insurance Company
Bay of Quinte Mutual Insurance Co.
Belair Insurance Company Inc.
Berkley Insurance Company
Bertie & Clinton Mutual Insurance Co.
BMO Life Insurance Company
Brant Mutual Insurance Company
British Columbia Automobile Association Insurance Agency
British Columbia Life & Casualty Company
Butler Byers Insurance Ltd.
CAA Insurance Company (Ontario)
Canadian Direct Insurance Incorporated
Canadian Farm Insurance Corporation
Canadian Premier Life Insurance Company
Canadian Professional Sales Association
Canassurance Insurance Company
La Capitale Insurance & Financial Services
Caradoc Delaware Mutual Fire Insurance Company
Cavell Insurance Company Limited
Chubb Insurance Company of Canada
CIBC Life Insurance Company Limited
CIGNA Life Insurance Company of Canada
The Citadel General Assurance Company
Clarica Life Insurance Co.
Combined Insurance Company of America
Connecticut General Life Insurance Co.
Continental Casualty Company
Co-operators General Insurance Company
Co-operators Life Insurance Company
Croatian Fraternal Union of America
The CUMIS Group Limited
CUMIS Life Insurance Company
Desjardins Financial Security
Dufferin Mutual Insurance Company
Eagle Star Insurance Company Ltd.
Echelon General Insurance Company
Elite Insurance Company
Empire Life Insurance Company
Employers Insurance Company of Wausau
Employers Reassurance Corporation
Employers Reinsurance Corporation
L'Entraide assurance, compagnie mutuelle
Erie Mutual Fire Insurance Co.
Everest Reinsurance Company
L'Excellence, Compagnie d'assurance-vVie
FaithLife Financial
Farmers' Mutual Insurance Company (Lindsay)
Federal Insurance Company
Fenchurch General Insurance Company
First North American Insurance Company
GCAN Insurance Company
General Reinsurance Corporation
Germania Farmers' Mutual Fire Insurance Company
Glengarry Farmers' Mutual Fire Insurance Co.
Global Aerospace Underwriting Managers (Canada) Limited
Gore Mutual Insurance Company
Granite Insurance Company
Great American Insurance Company
The Great-West Life Assurance Company
Green Shield Canada
Grenville Mutual Insurance Co.
Grey & Bruce Mutual Insurance Co.
The Guarantee Company of North America
Hannover Rückversicherungs AG
Hartford Fire Insurance Company
Howard Mutual Insurance Co.
Howick Mutual Insurance Company
The Independent Order of Foresters
Industrial Alliance Insurance & Financial Services Inc.
Industrial Alliance Pacific Life Insurance Company
ING Insurance Company of Canada - Corporate Office (Central & Atlantic Region)
ING Insurance Company of Canada - Corporate Office (Western Region)
ING Novex Insurance Company of Canada
L'Internationale, compagnie d'assurance-vie
Kent & Essex Mutual Insurance Company
Lambton Mutual Insurance Company
Legacy General Insurance Company
Lennox & Addington Fire Mutual Insurance Company
Liberty Mutual Insurance Company
Life Insurance Company of North America
Lloyd's Underwriters
Lombard General Insurance Company of Canada
Lombard Insurance Company
London & Midland General Insurance Company
London Life Insurance Company
Manitoba Blue Cross
Manufacturers Life Insurance Company
Massachusetts Mutual Life Insurance Company
McKillop Mutual Insurance Company
Medavie Blue Cross
Metropolitan Life Insurance Company, Canadian Branch
Mitsui Sumitomo Insurance Co., Limited.
Munich Reinsurance Company - Canada Life
New India Assurance Company, Limited
NIPPONKOA Insurance Company, Limited
Omega General Insurance Company
Ontario Blue Cross
Ontario Mutual Insurance Association
Optimum Reassurance Company
The Order of United Commercial Travelers of America
Oxford Mutual Insurance Co.
Pacific Blue Cross
PartnerRe SA
Penncorp Life Insurance Company
The Personal Insurance Company

Primerica Life Insurance Company of Canada
Principal Life Insurance Company
Promutuel Vie inc
Protective Insurance Company
Québec Blue Cross
RBC General Insurance Company
RBC Insurance
RBC Life Insurance Company
RBC Travel Insurance Company
Reliable Life Insurance Company
ReliaStar Life Insurance Company
Saskatchewan Blue Cross
SCOR Vie - Succursale du Canada
Scotia Life Insurance Company
SecuriCan General Insurance Company
Security National Insurance Company
The Sovereign General Insurance Company
SSQ Financial Group
SSQ, Société d'assurance-vie inc
The Standard Life Assurance Company of Canada
State Farm Mutual Automobile Insurance Company
Suecia Reinsurance Company
Sun Life Assurance Company of Canada
Supreme Council of the Royal Arcanum
La Survivance, compagnie mutuelle d'assurance vie
Swiss Re Frankona Rückversicherungs-Aktiengesellschaft
TD General Insurance Company
TD Life Insurance Company
Town & Country Mutual Insurance Company
Townsend Farmers' Mutual Fire Insurance Company
Trans Global Insurance Company
Trans Global Life Insurance Company
Transamerica Life Canada
Transatlantic Reinsurance Company
Ukrainian Mutual Benefit Association of Saint Nicholas of Canada
Ukrainian National Association
L'Union-Vie, compagnie mutuelle d'assurance
United American Insurance Company
Unity Life of Canada
Wabisa Mutual Insurance Company
The Wawanesa Life Insurance Company
West Elgin Mutual Insurance Company
West Wawanosh Mutual Insurance Company
Western Assurance Company
Western Financial Group Inc.
Western Life Assurance Company
XL Insurance Company Limited
XL Reinsurance America Inc.
Zenith Insurance Company
Zurich Canada

Property

ACE INA Insurance
Affiliated FM Insurance Company
Alberta Motor Association Insurance Co.
Algoma Insurance Group Ltd.
Algoma Mutual Insurance Company
Alliance Assurance
Allstate Insurance Company of Canada
All-West Insurance Network
L'ALPHA, compagnie d'assurances inc.
Alpine Insurance & Financial Inc.
American Home Assurance Company
American International Underwriters, Canada
American Re-Insurance Company
The American Road Insurance Company
Amherst Island Mutual Insurance Company
Antigonish Farmers' Mutual Insurance Company
L'Assurance Mutuelle des Fabriques de Montréal
Astro Insurance 1000 Inc.
Atlantic Insurance Company Limited
Aviva Canada Inc.
AXA Corporate Solutions Assurance
AXA General Insurance Company
AXA Insurance (Canada)
AXA Pacific Insurance Company
AXA RE
Ayr Farmers Mutual Insurance Company
Bay of Quinte Mutual Insurance Co.
Belair Insurance Company Inc.
Berkley Insurance Company
Bertie & Clinton Mutual Insurance Co.
The Boiler Inspection & Insurance Company of Canada
Brant Mutual Insurance Company
British Columbia Automobile Association Insurance Agency
Butler Byers Insurance Ltd.
CAA Insurance Company (Ontario)
Caisse Centrale de Réassurance
Canadian Direct Insurance Incorporated
Canadian Farm Insurance Corporation
Canadian Northern Shield Insurance Company
Canadian Petroleum Insurance Exchange Ltd.
Canadian Professional Sales Association
Canadian Universities Reciprocal Insurance Exchange
Canassurance Insurance Company
La Capitale General Insurance Inc.
Caradoc Delaware Mutual Fire Insurance Company
Carleton Mutual Insurance Company
Cavell Insurance Company Limited
Certas Direct Insurance Company
Chubb Insurance Company of Canada
The Citadel General Assurance Company
Clare Mutual Insurance Company
Coastal Community Insurance Services (2007) Ltd.
Commonwealth Insurance Company
La Compagnie d'Assurance Missisquoi
Constitution Insurance Company of Canada
Continental Casualty Company
Co-operators General Insurance Company
Co-operators Life Insurance Company
COSECO Insurance Company
Cowan Insurance Group
Crowsnest Insurance Agencies Ltd.
CUMIS General Insurance Company
The CUMIS Group Limited
CUMIS Life Insurance Company
DaimlerChrysler Insurance Company
Desjardins assurances générales inc
The Dominion of Canada General Insurance Company
Dufferin Mutual Insurance Company
Dumfries Mutual Insurance Company
Eagle Star Insurance Company Ltd.
Ecclesiastical Insurance Office plc
Echelon General Insurance Company
Economical Mutual Insurance Company
Elite Insurance Company
Employers Insurance Company of Wausau
Employers Reinsurance Corporation
Erie Mutual Fire Insurance Co.
Everest Insurance Company of Canada
Everest Reinsurance Company
Farmers' Mutual Insurance Company (Lindsay)
Federal Insurance Company
Federated Insurance Company of Canada
Federation Insurance Company of Canada
Fenchurch General Insurance Company
First North American Insurance Company
FM Global
Folksamerica Reinsurance Company
Formosa Mutual Insurance Co.
Fundy Mutual Insurance Company
GCAN Insurance Company
General Reinsurance Corporation
Germania Farmers' Mutual Fire Insurance Company
Germania Mutual Insurance Company
Gibb's Agencies (1997) Ltd.
Glengarry Farmers' Mutual Fire Insurance Co.
Global Aerospace Underwriting Managers (Canada) Limited
Gore Mutual Insurance Company
Grain Insurance & Guarantee Company
Granite Insurance Company
Great American Insurance Company
Grenville Mutual Insurance Co.
Grey & Bruce Mutual Insurance Co.
Le Groupe Estrie-Richelieu, compagnie d'assurance
The Guarantee Company of North America
Halwell Mutual Insurance Company
Hannover Rückversicherungs AG
Hartford Fire Insurance Company
Hay Mutual Insurance Company
Henderson Insurance Inc.
Howard Mutual Insurance Co.
Howick Mutual Insurance Company
ING Insurance Company of Canada - Corporate Office (Central & Atlantic Region)
ING Insurance Company of Canada - Corporate Office (Western Region)
ING Novex Insurance Company of Canada
Innovative Insurance Corporation
Insurance Company of Prince Edward Island
JEVCO Insurance Company
Kent & Essex Mutual Insurance Company
The Kings Mutual Insurance Company
Kingsway Financial Services Inc.
Kingsway General Insurance Company
Kirkham Insurance (1984) Ltd.
Lambton Mutual Insurance Company
Lanark Mutual Insurance Company
Legacy General Insurance Company
Lennox & Addington Fire Mutual Insurance Company
Liberty Mutual Insurance Company
Lloyd's Underwriters
Lombard General Insurance Company of Canada
Lombard Insurance Company
London & Midland General Insurance Company
Lumbermen's Underwriting Alliance
MAX Canada Insurance Company
McFarlane & Company
McKillop Mutual Insurance Company
Mennonite Mutual Fire Insurance Company
Mennonite Mutual Insurance Co. (Alberta) Ltd.
Metro General Insurance Corp. Limited
Middlesex Mutual Insurance Co.
Millennium Insurance Corporation
Mitsui Sumitomo Insurance Co., Limited.
Munich Reinsurance Company of Canada
MUNIX Reciprocal
The Mutual Fire Insurance Company of British Columbia
New India Assurance Company, Limited
NIPPONKOA Insurance Company, Limited
The Nordic Insurance Company of Canada
Norfolk Mutual Insurance Company
North Bleinheim Mutual Insurance Co.
North Blenheim Mutual Insurance Company
North Kent Mutual Fire Insurance Company
The North Waterloo Farmers Mutual Insurance Company
Odyssey America Reinsurance Corp., Canadian Branch
Old Republic Insurance Company of Canada
Omega General Insurance Company
Ontario Mutual Insurance Association
Ontario School Boards' Insurance Exchange
Optimum Assurance Agricole inc
Optimum Général inc
Optimum Société d'Assurance inc
Oxford Mutual Insurance Co.
PartnerRe SA
PC Financial Insurance Agency
Peace Hills General Insurance Company
Peel Mutual Insurance Co.
Pembridge Insurance Company
The Personal General Insurance Inc.
The Personal Insurance Company
Perth Insurance Company
Pictou County Farmers' Mutual Fire Insurance Company
Pilot Insurance Company
Pool Insurance Company
The Portage La Prairie Mutual Insurance Company
Premier Marine Insurance Managers Group
Primmum Insurance Company
Prince Edward Island Mutual Insurance Company
Progressive Casualty Insurance Company
Promutuel Réassurance
Protective Insurance Company
Providence Washington Insurance Company
RBC General Insurance Company
RBC Insurance
Red River Valley Mutual Insurance Company
Revios Reinsurance
Royal & SunAlliance Insurance Company of Canada
St. Paul Fire & Marine Insurance Company
Saskatchewan Mutual Insurance Company
Scottish & York Insurance Co. Limited
Security National Insurance Company
SGI CANADA Consolidated
South Easthope Mutual Insurance Co.
Southeastern Mutual Insurance Company
The Sovereign General Insurance Company
SSQ, Société d'assurances générales inc.
SSQ, Société d'assurance-vie inc
Stanley Mutual Insurance Company
State Farm Fire & Casualty Company
Suecia Reinsurance Company
Swiss Reinsurance Company Canada
TD General Insurance Company
TD Home & Auto Insurance Company
Temple Insurance
Thomson-Schindle-Green Insurance & Financial Services Ltd.
The Tokio Marine & Nichido Fire Insurance Co., Ltd.
Town & Country Mutual Insurance Company
Townsend Farmers' Mutual Fire Insurance Company
Traders General Insurance Company
Tradition Mutual Insurance Company
Trans Global Insurance Company
Transatlantic Reinsurance Company
Trillium Mutual Insurance Company
Unified Assurance Company
L'Union Canadienne Compagnie d'Assurances
Virginia Surety Company, Inc.
Wabisa Mutual Insurance Company
Waterloo Insurance Company
The Wawanesa Mutual Insurance Company

Wedgwood Insurance Ltd.
West Elgin Mutual Insurance Company
West Wawanosh Mutual Insurance Company
Western Assurance Company
Western Financial Group Inc.
Westland Insurance Group
Westminster Mutual Insurance Company
XL Insurance Company Limited
XL Reinsurance America Inc.
Yarmouth Mutual Fire Insurance Company
York Fire & Casualty Insurance Company
Zenith Insurance Company
Zurich Canada

Reinsurance

American Re-Insurance Company
General American Life Insurance Company
Kingsway Financial Services Inc.
Lloyd's Underwriters
London Life Insurance Company
Munich Reinsurance Company - Canada Life
Odyssey America Reinsurance Corp., Canadian Branch
Old Republic Insurance Company of Canada
Optimum Reassurance Company
Promutuel Réassurance
RGA Life Reinsurance Company of Canada
St. Paul Fire & Marine Insurance Company
SCOR Canada Reinsurance Company
SGI CANADA Consolidated
Suecia Reinsurance Company
Swiss Reinsurance Company Canada
The Toa Reinsurance Company of America
Transatlantic Reinsurance Company
L'Union-Vie, compagnie mutuelle d'assurance

Surety

ACE INA Insurance
Affiliated FM Insurance Company
Algoma Insurance Group Ltd.
Allstate Insurance Company of Canada
L'ALPHA, compagnie d'assurances inc.
American Home Assurance Company
American Re-Insurance Company
The American Road Insurance Company
Atlantic Insurance Company Limited
Aviva Canada Inc.
AXA Corporate Solutions Assurance
AXA General Insurance Company
AXA Insurance (Canada)
AXA Pacific Insurance Company
AXA RE
Belair Insurance Company Inc.
Berkley Insurance Company
CAA Insurance Company (Ontario)
Caisse Centrale de Réassurance
Canadian Farm Insurance Corporation
Cavell Insurance Company Limited
Certas Direct Insurance Company
Chubb Insurance Company of Canada
The Citadel General Assurance Company
Commonwealth Insurance Company
La Compagnie d'Assurance Missisquoi
Constitution Insurance Company of Canada
Continental Casualty Company
Co-operators General Insurance Company
DaimlerChrysler Insurance Company
Desjardins assurances générales inc
The Dominion of Canada General Insurance Company
Eagle Star Insurance Company Ltd.
Echelon General Insurance Company
Economical Mutual Insurance Company
Elite Insurance Company
Employers Insurance Company of Wausau
Employers Reinsurance Corporation
Everest Insurance Company of Canada
Everest Reinsurance Company
Federal Insurance Company
Federated Insurance Company of Canada
Federation Insurance Company of Canada
Fenchurch General Insurance Company
Folksamerica Reinsurance Company
GCAN Insurance Company
General Reinsurance Corporation
Grain Insurance & Guarantee Company
Granite Insurance Company
Great American Insurance Company
The Guarantee Company of North America
Hannover Rückversicherungs AG
Hartford Fire Insurance Company
ING Insurance Company of Canada - Corporate Office (Specialty Lines)
ING Insurance Company of Canada - Corporate Office (Western Region)
ING Novex Insurance Company of Canada
Kingsway General Insurance Company
Koch B&Y Insurance Services Ltd.
Liberty Mutual Insurance Company
Lloyd's Underwriters
Lombard General Insurance Company of Canada
Lombard Insurance Company
London & Midland General Insurance Company
McFarlane & Company
Mitsui Sumitomo Insurance Co., Limited.
NIPPONKOA Insurance Company, Limited
The Nordic Insurance Company of Canada
Odyssey America Reinsurance Corp., Canadian Branch
Omega General Insurance Company
Peace Hills General Insurance Company
The Personal General Insurance Inc.
The Personal Insurance Company
Progressive Casualty Insurance Company
Promutuel Réassurance
Red River Valley Mutual Insurance Company
Revios Reinsurance
St. Paul Fire & Marine Insurance Company
St. Paul Guarantee Insurance Company
Scottish & York Insurance Co. Limited
SGI CANADA Consolidated
State Farm Fire & Casualty Company
Swiss Reinsurance Company Canada
TD General Insurance Company
Transatlantic Reinsurance Company
Trisura Guarantee Insurance Company
The Wawanesa Mutual Insurance Company
Western Assurance Company
Western Financial Group Inc.
Western Surety Company
XL Insurance Company Limited
XL Reinsurance America Inc.
Zurich Canada

Theft

Algoma Insurance Group Ltd.
L'Assurance Mutuelle des Fabriques de Montréal
Canadian Petroleum Insurance Exchange Ltd.
The Citadel General Assurance Company
La Compagnie d'Assurance Missisquoi
Co-operators General Insurance Company
CUMIS General Insurance Company
CUMIS Life Insurance Company
The Dominion of Canada General Insurance Company
Federated Insurance Company of Canada
Germania Mutual Insurance Company
Glengarry Farmers' Mutual Fire Insurance Co.
Gore Mutual Insurance Company
Grain Insurance & Guarantee Company
Granite Insurance Company
The Guarantee Company of North America
Hartford Fire Insurance Company
ING Insurance Company of Canada - Corporate Office (Western Region)
Lanark Mutual Insurance Company
Lombard General Insurance Company of Canada
Lombard Insurance Company
London & Midland General Insurance Company
Mennonite Mutual Fire Insurance Company
Munich Reinsurance Company of Canada
North Kent Mutual Fire Insurance Company
Peace Hills General Insurance Company
Prince Edward Island Mutual Insurance Company
Promutuel Réassurance
RBC General Insurance Company
Red River Valley Mutual Insurance Company
SSQ Financial Group
SSQ, Société d'assurances générales inc.
The Wawanesa Mutual Insurance Company
Western Financial Group Inc.
Zurich Canada

Federal & Provincial Insurance Companies

ACA Assurance
3050, boul. St-Jean
Trois-Rivières, QC G9A 5E1
Tel: 819-377-1777; *Fax:* 819-377-3587
Toll-Free: 1-800-567-9455
infocan@aca-assurance.org
www.aca-assurance.org
Classes of Insurance: Accident, Life

ACE INA Insurance
130 King St. West, 12th Fl.
Toronto, ON M5X 1A6
Tel: 416-368-2911; *Fax:* 416-594-2600
www.ace-ina-canada.com
Classes of Insurance: Accident, Aircraft, Auto, Liability, Boiler & Machinery, Credit, Marine, Fidelity, Property, Fire, Surety, Hail & Crop

ACE INA Life Insurance/ Assurance-vie ACE INA
#1400, 25 York St.
Toronto, ON M5J 2V5
Tel: 416-368-2911; *Fax:* 416-594-2600
Classes of Insurance: Personal Accident & Sickness, Liability

ACTRA Fraternal Benefit Society (AFBS)
1000 Yonge St.
Toronto, ON M4W 2K2
Tel: 416-967-6600; *Fax:* 416-967-4744
Toll-Free: 800-387-8897
benefits@actrafrat.com
www.actrafrat.com
Classes of Insurance: Personal Accident & Sickness, Life

Affiliated FM Insurance Company
#500, 165 Commerce Valley Dr. West
Thornhill, ON L3T 7V8
Tel: 905-763-5555; *Fax:* 905-763-5556
www.affiliatedfm.ca
Classes of Insurance: Liability, Boiler & Machinery, Fidelity, Property, Fire, Surety

Agriculture Financial Services Corporation (AFSC)
5718 - 56 Ave.
Lacombe, AB T4J 1R5
Tel: 403-782-3000; *Fax:* 403-782-4226
www.afsc.ca
Classes of Insurance: Hail & Crop

AIG United Guaranty Mortgage Insurance Company Canada
#400, 1 Toronto St.
Toronto, ON M5C 2V6
Tel: 416-640-8924; *Fax:* 416-640-8948
Toll-Free: 866-414-9109
info@aigug.ca
www.aigug.ca
Other Contact Information: 1-877-244-8422 (Toll Free underwriting related inquiries)

Alberta Blue Cross
Blue Cross Place
10009 - 108th St. NW
Edmonton, AB T5J 3C5
Tel: 780-498-8000; *Fax:* 780-425-4627
Toll-Free: 800-661-6995
www.ab.bluecross.ca
Other Contact Information: Travel Coverage: 780/498-8550; Individual Health & Dental Plans: 780/498-8008; Group Sales: 780/498-8500
Classes of Insurance: Personal Accident & Sickness

Alberta Motor Association Insurance Co.
PO Box 8180, South Stn. South
Edmonton, AB T6H 5X9
Tel: 780-430-5555; *Toll-Free:* 800-615-5897
www.ama.ab.ca
Other Contact Information: Membership Inquiries Toll Free: 800-222-6400
Classes of Insurance: Personal Accident & Sickness, Auto, Life, Property, Fire

Algoma Insurance Group
#200, 855 Queen St. East
Sault Ste. Marie, ON P6A 2B3
Tel: 705-949-6555; *Fax:* 705-949-3513
info@algomains.com
www.algomains.com
Classes of Insurance: Auto, Liability, Boiler & Machinery, Property, Surety, Theft

Algoma Mutual Insurance Co.
131 Main St.
Thessalon, ON P0R 1L0
Tel: 705-842-3345; *Fax:* 705-842-3500
Toll-Free: 800-461-7260
www.amico.ca
Classes of Insurance: Auto, Property

Alliance Assurance
PO Box 7664
#200, 166 Broadway Blvd.
Grand Falls, NB E3Z 2J9
Tel: 506-473-9400; *Fax:* 506-473-9401
Toll-Free: 800-939-9400
gffax@alliance-assurance.com
www.alliance-assurance.com
Classes of Insurance: Auto, Liability, Property

Allianz Life Insurance Company of North America
#700, 2005 Sheppard Ave. East
Toronto, ON M2J 5B4
Fax: 416-502-2555
Classes of Insurance: Personal Accident & Sickness, Life

Allstate Insurance Company of Canada/ Allstate du Canada, Compagnie d'assurance
#100, 27 Allstate Pkwy.
Markham, ON L3R 5P8
Tel: 905-477-6900; *Fax:* 905-415-4831
Toll-Free: 800-255-7828
www.allstate.ca
Other Contact Information: Claims Toll Free Numbers: 800-387-0462 (AB, BC, MB, ON, SK); 800-463-2813 (QC); 800-561-7222 (NS, NB, PE, NL)
Classes of Insurance: Personal Accident & Sickness, Legal Expense, Auto, Liability, Boiler & Machinery, Fidelity, Property, Surety

L'ALPHA, compagnie d'assurances inc.
#119, 430, rue Saint-Georges
Drummondville, QC J2C 4H4
Tel: 819-474-7958; *Fax:* 819-477-6139
drummond@assurance-alpha.com
www.assurance-alpha.com/alpha.php
Classes of Insurance: Auto, Property, Surety

Alpine Insurance & Financial Inc.
#203, 1026 - 16th Ave. NW
Calgary, AB T2M 0K6
Tel: 403-270-8822; *Fax:* 403-270-0201
Toll-Free: 877-770-8822
calgary.info@alpineinsurance.ca
www.alpineinsurance.ca
Classes of Insurance: Auto, Liability, Life, Property

American Bankers Life Assurance Company of Florida
#500, 5160 Yonge St.
Toronto, ON M2N 7C7
Tel: 416-733-3360; *Fax:* 416-733-7826
Toll-Free: 800-561-3232
www.assurant.com.br/canada/
Classes of Insurance: Accident, Personal Accident & Sickness, Life

American Health & Life Insurance Company
201 Queens Ave.
London, ON N6A 1J1
Tel: 519-672-1070; *Fax:* 519-660-2625
Classes of Insurance: Life

American Home Assurance Company
145 Wellington St. West
Toronto, ON M5J 1H8
Tel: 416-596-3000
AHAC@aig.com
www.aigamericanhome.com
Classes of Insurance: Personal Accident & Sickness, Aircraft, Auto, Liability, Boiler & Machinery, Credit, Fidelity, Property, Surety, Hail & Crop

American Income Life Insurance Company
c/o McLean & Kerr
#2800, 130 Adelaide St. West
Toronto, ON M5H 3P5
Tel: 416-364-5371; *Fax:* 416-366-8571
Classes of Insurance: Personal Accident & Sickness, Life

American International Underwriters, Canada
145 Wellington St. West
Toronto, ON M5J 2T4
Tel: 416-596-3000
www.aig.com
Classes of Insurance: Property

American Re-Insurance Company
Munich Re Centre
390 Bay St., 22nd Fl.
Toronto, ON M5H 2Y2
Tel: 416-591-8668
Classes of Insurance: Accident, Personal Accident & Sickness, Auto, Liability, Boiler & Machinery, Credit, Marine, Fidelity, Property, Surety, Hail & Crop, Reinsurance

The American Road Insurance Company
#2, 1145 Nicholson Rd.
Newmarket, ON L3Y 9C3
Tel: 905-853-0858
Classes of Insurance: Auto, Liability, Boiler & Machinery, Credit, Property, Surety

AMEX Assurance Company/ AMEX Compagnie d'Assurance
c/o Focus Group Inc.
#500, 36 King St. East
Toronto, ON M5C 1E5
Tel: 416-361-1728; *Fax:* 416-361-6113
Classes of Insurance: Personal Accident & Sickness, Life

Amherst Island Mutual Insurance Company
RR#1
Stella, ON K0H 2S0
Tel: 613-389-2012; *Fax:* 613-389-9986
Classes of Insurance: Personal Accident & Sickness, Liability, Property

Antigonish Farmers' Mutual Insurance Company
188 Main St.
Antigonish, NS B2G 2B9
Tel: 902-863-3544; *Fax:* 902-863-0664
jchisolm@antigonish-mutual.com
www.antigonish-mutual.com
Other Contact Information: Toll Free (Maritimes only): 1-800-565-3544
Classes of Insurance: Marine, Property, Fire

Ascentus Insurance Ltd.
10 Wellington St. East
Toronto, ON M5E 1L5
Toll-Free: 888-877-1710
www.ascentusinsurance.ca
Other Contact Information: Claims: 1-877-275-3698

Assumption Mutual Life Insurance Company/ Assomption Compagnie Mutuelle d'Assurance-Vie
Assumption Place
PO Box 160
770 Main St.
Moncton, NB E1C 8L1
Tel: 506-853-6040; *Fax:* 506-853-5428
Toll-Free: 800-455-7337
comments@assumption.ca; financial.services@assumption.ca
www.assumption.ca
Other Contact Information: Group Insurance, Phone: 506-869-9797; Toll Free: 1-888-869-9797; Individual Insurance, Toll Free: 1-800-343-5622; Mortgage Loans, Phone: 506-869-9755
Classes of Insurance: Accident, Personal Accident & Sickness, Life

L'Assurance Mutuelle des Fabriques de Montréal
1071, rue de la Cathédrale
Montréal, QC H3B 2V4
Tel: 514-395-4969; *Fax:* 514-861-8921
Toll-Free: 800-567-6586
info.general@amf-mtl.com
Classes of Insurance: Liability, Boiler & Machinery, Property, Fire, Theft

Assurance-Vie Banque Nationale/ National Bank Life Insurance Company
1100, rue University, 11e étage
Montréal, QC H3B 2G7
Tél: 514-871-7500; *Téléc:* 514-394-6604
Ligne sans frais: 877-871-7500
assurances@nbc.ca
www.nbc.ca
Classes of Insurance: Personal Accident & Sickness, Life, Credit

Assurant Solutions Canada
#500, 5160 Yonge St.
Toronto, ON M2N 7C7
Tel: 416-733-3360; *Fax:* 416-733-7826
Toll-Free: 800-561-3232
shari.doherty@assurant.com
www.assurantsolutions.com/canada/
Classes of Insurance: Credit

Astro Insurance 1000 Inc.
#100, 542 - 7th St.
Lethbridge, AB T1J 2H1
Tel: 403-328-1000; *Fax:* 403-320-1962
astroins@astro-insurance.com
www.astro-insurance.com
Classes of Insurance: Auto, Liability, Property, Hail & Crop

Atlantic Insurance Company Limited
64 Commonwealth Ave.
Mount Pearl, NL A1N 1W8
Tel: 709-364-5209; *Fax:* 709-364-5262
Classes of Insurance: Auto, Liability, Boiler & Machinery, Fidelity, Property, Surety

Avemco Insurance Company
#401, 133 Richmond St. West
Toronto, ON M5H 2L3
Tel: 416-363-6103; *Fax:* 416-363-7454
Classes of Insurance: Personal Accident & Sickness, Aircraft, Marine

Aviation & General Insurance Company Limited
#201, 3650 Victoria Park Ave.
Toronto, ON M2H 3P7
Tel: 416-496-1148; *Fax:* 416-496-1089
Classes of Insurance: Aircraft, Liability,

AVie, Financial Security Advisors/ AVie, Cabinet de conseillers en sécurité financière
Édifice Martin-J.-Légère
CP 5554
295, boul St-Pierre ouest
Caraquet, NB E1W 1B7
Tél: 506-726-4203; *Téléc:* 506-726-8204
Ligne sans frais: 888-822-2343
www.acadie.com; www.assumption.ca
Classes of Insurance: Personal Accident & Sickness, Life

Aviva Canada Inc./ Aviva, Compagnie d'Assurance du Canada
2206 Eglinton Ave. East
Toronto, ON M1L 4S8
Tel: 416-288-1800; *Fax:* 416-288-5888
Toll-Free: 800-387-4518
www.avivacanada.com
Social Media: www.linkedin.com/companies/301062
Classes of Insurance: Personal Accident & Sickness, Aircraft, Legal Expense, Auto, Liability, Boiler & Machinery, Marine, Fidelity, Property, Surety, Hail & Crop

A-WIN Insurance Network
#200, 2417 - 51 Ave. SE
Calgary, AB T2C 0A2
Tel: 403-278-1050; *Fax:* 403-225-0515
info1@awinins.ca
www.awinins.ca
Classes of Insurance: Auto, Liability, Property

AXA Canada Inc.
#700, 2020, rue University
Montréal, QC H3A 2A5
Tel: 514-282-1914; *Fax:* 514-282-9588
www.axa.ca

AXA Corporate Solutions Assurance
#600, 2020, rue University
Montréal, QC H3A 2A5
Tel: 514-392-6033; *Fax:* 514-392-7392
www.axa-corporatesolutions.com
Classes of Insurance: Personal Accident & Sickness, Aircraft, Legal Expense, Auto, Liability, Boiler & Machinery, Credit, Fidelity, Property, Surety, Hail & Crop

AXA General Insurance Company/ AXA Assurances générales
#1400, 5700 Yonge St.
Toronto, ON M2M 4K2
Toll-Free: 877-292-4968
www.axa.ca
Classes of Insurance: Personal Accident & Sickness, Aircraft, Legal Expense, Auto, Liability, Boiler & Machinery, Fidelity, Property, Surety, Hail & Crop

AXA Insurance (Canada)/ AXA Assurances (Canada)
#1400, 5700 Yonge St.
Toronto, ON M2M 4K2
Toll-Free: 8770292-4968
av.operations@axa-assurances.ca
www.axa-insurance.ca; www.axa.ca
Classes of Insurance: Personal Accident & Sickness, Aircraft, Legal Expense, Auto, Liability, Boiler & Machinery, Fidelity, Property, Surety, Hail & Crop

AXA Pacific Insurance Company/ AXA Pacifique Compagnie d'Assurance
PO Box 22
999 Hastings St. West, 2nd Fl.
Vancouver, BC V6C 2W2
Tel: 604-669-4247; *Fax:* 604-682-6693
www.axa.ca

Classes of Insurance: Personal Accident & Sickness, Aircraft, Legal Expense, Auto, Liability, Boiler & Machinery, Credit, Fidelity, Property, Surety, Hail & Crop

AXA RE Canada
Place Montréal Trust
#2000, 1800, av. McGill College
Montréal, QC H3A 3J6
Tel: 514-842-9262; *Fax:* 514-842-9254
www.axa.com
Classes of Insurance: Personal Accident & Sickness, Aircraft, Auto, Liability, Boiler & Machinery, Life, Marine, Fidelity, Property, Surety, Hail & Crop

Ayr Farmers Mutual Insurance Company
PO Box 1170
1400 Northumberland St.
Ayr, ON N0B 1E0
Tel: 519-632-7413; *Fax:* 519-632-8908
Toll-Free: 800-265-8792
www.ayrmutual.com
Classes of Insurance: Accident, Personal Accident & Sickness, Auto, Liability, Boiler & Machinery, Fidelity, Property, Hail & Crop

Bay of Quinte Mutual Insurance Co.
PO Box 6050
13379 Loyalist Pkwy.
Picton, ON K0K 2T0
Tel: 613-476-2145; *Toll-Free:* 800-267-2126
info@bayofquintemutual.com
www.bayofquintemutual.com
Classes of Insurance: Personal Accident & Sickness, Auto, Liability, Boiler & Machinery, Fidelity, Property

Belair Insurance Company Inc./ La Compagnie d'Assurance Belair Inc.
#300, 7101, rue Jean-Talon est
Montréal, QC H1M 3T6
Tel: 514-270-9111; *Toll-Free:* 888-270-9111
belairdirect@belairdirect.com,
belairdirect.ontario@belairdirect.com
www.belairdirect.com
Other Contact Information: 888-280-8549, 888-270-9732 (Toll Free, Auto & Home); 1-877-874-5433 (Toll Free, Travel Insurance); 877-270-9124 (Toll Free, Claims Emergency)
Classes of Insurance: Personal Accident & Sickness, Legal Expense, Auto, Liability, Boiler & Machinery, Marine, Fidelity, Property, Surety

Berkley Insurance Company
#201, 3650 Victoria Park Ave.
Toronto, ON M2H 3P7
Tel: 416-496-1148; *Fax:* 416-496-1089
Classes of Insurance: Personal Accident & Sickness, Aircraft, Legal Expense, Auto, Liability, Boiler & Machinery, Credit, Fidelity, Property, Surety, Hail & Crop

Bertie and Clinton Mutual Insurance Company
1789 Merrittville Hwy., RR#2
Welland, ON L3B 5N5
Tel: 905-892-0606; *Fax:* 905-892-0365
Toll-Free: 800-263-0494
info@bertieandclinton.com
www.bertieandclinton.com
Classes of Insurance: Personal Accident & Sickness, Auto, Liability, Boiler & Machinery, Fidelity, Property

BMO Life Assurance Company of Canada
60 Yonge St.
Toronto, ON M5E 1H5
Tel: 416-596-3900; *Fax:* 416-596-4143
Toll-Free: 877-742-5244
www4.bmo.com
Classes of Insurance: Personal Accident & Sickness, Life

The Boiler Inspection & Insurance Company of Canada (BI&I)
18 King St. East
Toronto, ON M5C 1C4
Tel: 416-363-5491; *Fax:* 416-363-0538
corporate@biico.com
www.biico.com
Classes of Insurance: Liability, Boiler & Machinery, Property

Brant Mutual Insurance Company
207 Greenwich St.
Brantford, ON N3S 2X7
Tel: 519-752-0088; *Fax:* 519-752-7917
solutions@brantmutual.com
www.brantmutual.com
Classes of Insurance: Personal Accident & Sickness, Auto, Liability, Boiler & Machinery, Fidelity, Property, Hail & Crop

British Columbia Automobile Association Insurance Agency
4567 Canada Way
Burnaby, BC V5G 4T1
Tel: 604-268-5000; *Fax:* 604-268-5569
Toll-Free: 800-719-2224
www.bcaa.com
Other Contact Information: Claims: 604-268-5260; Toll Free, TeleCentre: 1-877-325-8888; Toll Free, BCAA Advantage Home Policy: 310-2345; Customer Contact Centre: 604 268-5555
Classes of Insurance: Personal Accident & Sickness, Auto, Life, Property, Fire

British Columbia Life & Casualty Company
PO Box 7000
Vancouver, BC V6B 4E1
Tel: 604-419-2000; *Fax:* 604-419-2990
Toll-Free: 888-275-4672
www.pbchbs.com
Classes of Insurance: Personal Accident & Sickness, Life

Butler Byers Hail Insurance Ltd.
PO Box 330
Saskatoon, SK S7K 3L5
Tel: 306-652-4245; *Fax:* 306-652-8472
Toll-Free: 800-997-4245
sbyers@butlerbyers.com
www.butlerbyers.com
Classes of Insurance: Hail & Crop

Butler Byers Insurance Ltd.
301 - 4th Ave. North
Saskatoon, SK S7K 2L8
Tel: 306-653-2233
www.butlerbyers.com
Classes of Insurance: Personal Accident & Sickness, Auto, Life, Marine, Property

CAA Insurance Company (Ontario)
60 Commerce Valley Dr. East
Thornhill, ON L3T 7P9
Tel: 905-771-3000; *Fax:* 905-771-3101
Toll-Free: 800-268-3750
info@caasco.ca
www.caasco.on.ca/insurance
Other Contact Information: 877-222-3939 (Auto & Property); 800-387-2656 (Claims); 866-999-4222 (Health & Dental); 877-942-4222 (Group Life)
Classes of Insurance: Personal Accident & Sickness, Legal Expense, Auto, Liability, Life, Marine, Property, Surety

Caisse Centrale de Réassurance
#2110, 181 University Ave.
Toronto, ON M5H 3M7
Tel: 416-644-0821
www.ccr.fr
Classes of Insurance: Accident, Aircraft, Legal Expense, Auto, Liability, Boiler & Machinery, Fidelity, Property, Fire, Surety

Canadian Direct Insurance Incorporated
#600, 750 Cambie St.
Vancouver, BC V6B 0A2
Tel: 604-699-3838; *Fax:* 604-699-3860
Toll-Free: 888-225-5234
insurancegeneral@canadiandirect.com
www.canadiandirect.com
Other Contact Information: 888-261-8888 (Toll Free, Claims)
Classes of Insurance: Personal Accident & Sickness, Liability, Property

Canadian Farm Insurance Corp. (CFIC)
#310, 13220 St. Albert Trail
Edmonton, AB T5L 4W1
Tel: 780-447-3276; *Fax:* 780-732-3607
Toll-Free: 877-909-3276
www.cdnfarmins.com
Other Contact Information: 24 hour Livestock Claims Assistance: 780-732-3692
Classes of Insurance: Personal Accident & Sickness, Liability, Boiler & Machinery, Fidelity, Property, Surety

Canadian Lawyers Insurance Association/ L'Association d'Assurance des Juristes Canadiens
#2900, 250 Yonge St.
Toronto, ON M5B 2L7
Tel: 416-408-3721; *Toll-Free:* 800-268-9484
info@clia.ca
www.clia.ca

Canadian Lawyers Liability Assurance Society (CLLAS)
c/o Torys LLP
#3000, 79 Wellington St. West
Toronto, ON M5K 1N2
Tel: 416-865-7337; *Fax:* 416-865-7380
cllas.ca
Classes of Insurance: Liability

Canadian Northern Shield Insurance Company (CNS)
#1900, 555 Hastings St. West
Vancouver, BC V6B 4N6
Tel: 604-662-2911; *Fax:* 604-662-5698
www.cns.ca
Classes of Insurance: Auto, Liability, Property

Canadian Petroleum Insurance Exchange Ltd. (CPIX)
#500, 717 - 7th Ave. SW
Calgary, AB T2P 0Z3
Tel: 403-261-6061; *Fax:* 403-261-6068
insurance@cpix.com
www.cpix.com
Social Media: www.linkedin.com/companies/415791
Classes of Insurance: Auto, Liability, Property, Theft

Canadian Premier Life Insurance Company
80 Tiverton Ct., 5th Fl.
Markham, ON L3R 0G4
Tel: 905-479-7500; *Fax:* 905-479-3224
Toll-Free: 800-598-6918
www.canadianpremier.ca
Classes of Insurance: Personal Accident & Sickness, Life, Credit

Canadian Professional Sales Association (CPSA)
#800, 310 Front St. West
Toronto, ON M5V 3B5
Tel: 416-408-2685; *Fax:* 416-408-2684
Toll-Free: 888-267-2772
www.cpsa.com
Classes of Insurance: Accident, Personal Accident & Sickness, Auto, Life, Property

Canadian Slovak League
#6, 259 Traders Blvd. East
Mississauga, ON L4Z 2E5
Tel: 905-735-5624
Classes of Insurance: Life

Canadian Universities Reciprocal Insurance Exchange (CURIE)
#901, 5500 North Service Rd.
Burlington, ON L7L 6W6
Tel: 905-336-3366; *Fax:* 905-336-3373
Toll-Free: 888-462-8743
inquiry@curie.org
www.curie.org
Classes of Insurance: Aircraft, Liability, Marine, Property

Canassurance Insurance Company
c/o Ontario Blue Cross
#610, 185 The West Mall
Toronto, ON M9C 5P1
Toll-Free: 866-732-2583
www.useblue.com
Classes of Insurance: Personal Accident & Sickness, Liability, Life, Property

La Capitale Civil Service Insurer Inc.
625, rue Saint-Amable
Québec, QC G1R 2G5
Tel: 418-643-3884; *Fax:* 418-646-0370
Toll-Free: 866-227-2606
www.lacapitale.com
Classes of Insurance: Life

La Capitale General Insurance Inc./ La Capitale assurances générales inc.
Édifice Hector-Fabre
CP 17100
525, boul. René-Lévesque est
Québec, QC G1K 9E2
Ligne sans frais: 888-522-5260
www.lacapitale.com
Other Contact Information: Claims: 800-461-0770
Classes of Insurance: Auto, Property

La Capitale Insurance & Financial Services/ La Capitale assurances et gestion du patrimoine
Édifice Le Delta II
#100, 2875, boul. Laurier
Québec, QC G1V 2M2
Tel: 418-644-4200; *Fax:* 418-644-5226
Toll-Free: 888-463-4856
collectif@lacapitale.com
www.lacapitale.com
Classes of Insurance: Personal Accident & Sickness, Life

Caradoc Delaware Mutual Fire Insurance Company
PO Box 460
22508 Adelaide Rd.
Mount Brydges, ON N0L 1W0
Tel: 519-264-2298; *Fax:* 519-264-9101
Toll-Free: 877-707-2298
info@cdmins.com
www.cdmins.com
Classes of Insurance: Personal Accident & Sickness, Auto, Liability, Boiler & Machinery, Property

Carleton Mutual Insurance Company
301 Main St.
Florenceville, NB E7L 3G5
Tel: 506-392-6041; *Fax:* 506-392-8243
Toll-Free: 800-561-1550
cmi@nb.aibn.com
www.carletonmutual.com
Classes of Insurance: Auto, Property, Fire

Cavell Insurance Company Limited
c/o D.M. Williams & Associates Ltd.
#201, 3650 Victoria Park Ave.
Toronto, ON M2H 3P7
Tel: 416-496-1148; *Fax:* 416-496-1089
Classes of Insurance: Personal Accident & Sickness, Auto, Liability, Boiler & Machinery, Marine, Fidelity, Property, Surety, Hail & Crop

Certas Direct Insurance Company/ Certas Direct, compagnie d'assurances
PO Box 3500
6300, boul. de la Rive-Sud
Lévis, QC G6V 6P9
Tel: 905-306-3900; *Fax:* 418-835-5599
Toll-Free: 800-565-6020
www.certas.ca
Classes of Insurance: Auto, Liability, Property, Surety

Chicago Title Insurance Company Canada
2700 Argentia Rd.
Mississauga, ON L5N 5V4
Tel: 905-816-4485; *Fax:* 902-816-4988
Toll-Free: 888-868-4853
info@chicagotitle.ca
www.ctic.ca

Chrysler Insurance Company (DCIC)
#400, East Tower, 2700 Matheson Blvd. East
Mississauga, ON L4W 4V9
Tel: 905-629-6066
www.insurance.chrysler.com
Classes of Insurance: Auto, Liability, Property, Surety

Chubb Insurance Company of Canada/ Chubb du Canada Compagnie d'Assurance
One Financial Place
1 Adelaide St. East
Toronto, ON M5C 2V9
Tel: 416-863-0550; *Fax:* 416-863-5010
www.chubb.com/international/canada
Classes of Insurance: Personal Accident & Sickness, Aircraft, Auto, Liability, Boiler & Machinery, Marine, Fidelity, Property, Surety

CIBC Life Insurance Company Limited/ Compagnie d'Assurance-Vie CIBC Limitée
#900, 3 Robert Speck Pkwy.
Mississauga, ON L4Z 2G5
Tel: 905-306-4904; *Fax:* 905-306-4957
Classes of Insurance: Personal Accident & Sickness, Life

CIGNA Life Insurance Company of Canada
PO Box 14
#606, 55 Town Centre Ct.
Toronto, ON M1P 4X4
Tel: 416-290-6666; *Fax:* 416-290-0732
www.cigna.com
Classes of Insurance: Accident, Personal Accident & Sickness, Life, Credit

The Citadel General Assurance Company
#1200, 1075 Bay St.
Toronto, ON M5S 2W5
Tel: 416-928-8500; *Fax:* 416-928-1553
cit-web-info@citadel.ca
www.citadel.ca
Classes of Insurance: Accident, Personal Accident & Sickness, Auto, Liability, Fidelity, Property, Fire, Surety, Theft

Clare Mutual Insurance Company
3300 Hwy. 1
Belliveau Cove, NS B0W 1J0
Tel: 902-837-4597; *Fax:* 902-837-7745
Toll-Free: 877-818-0887
www.claremutual.com
Classes of Insurance: Property, Fire, Hail & Crop

Coachman Insurance Company
802 The Queensway
Toronto, ON M8Z 1N5
Tel: 416-255-3417; *Fax:* 416-255-3347
Toll-Free: 800-361-2622
inquiries@coachmanins.com
www.coachmaninsurance.ca
Classes of Insurance: Auto

Coast Underwriters Limited
#1610, 200 Granville St.
Vancouver, BC V6C 1S4
Tel: 604-683-5631; *Fax:* 604-683-8561
www.coast-uw.com

Coastal Community Insurance Services (2007) Ltd.
#21, 13 Victoria Cres.
Nanaimo, BC V9R 5B9
Tel: 250-741-3200; *Toll-Free:* 888-741-1010
Classes of Insurance: Auto, Property

Combined Insurance Company of America/ Combined Assurances
PO Box 3720, MIP Stn. MIP
7300 Warden Ave., 3rd. Fl.
Markham, ON L3R 0X3
Tel: 905-305-1922; *Fax:* 905-305-8600
Toll-Free: 888-234-4466
www.combined.ca
Classes of Insurance: Personal Accident & Sickness, Life

Commonwealth Insurance Company
Bentall Tower III
PO Box 49115
#1500, 595 Burrard St.
Vancouver, BC V7X 1G4
Tel: 604-683-5511; *Fax:* 604-683-8968
info@commonw.com
www.commonw.com
Classes of Insurance: Aircraft, Liability, Boiler & Machinery, Marine, Fidelity, Property, Surety

La Compagnie d'Assurance Missisquoi/ The Missisquoi Insurance Company
#500, 1000, rue de la Gauchetière ouest
Montréal, QC H3B 4W5
Tél: 514-875-5790; *Téléc:* 514-875-9769
Ligne sans frais: 800-361-7573
Classes of Insurance: Legal Expense, Auto, Liability, Boiler & Machinery, Fidelity, Property, Fire, Surety, Theft

Connecticut General Life Insurance Co. (CGLIC)
c/o CIGNA Life Insurance Company of Canada
#606, 55 Town Centre Ct.
Toronto, ON M1P 4X4
Tel: 416-290-6666; *Fax:* 416-290-0732
Toll-Free: 800-668-7029
www.cigna.com
Classes of Insurance: Accident, Personal Accident & Sickness, Life

Constitution Insurance Company of Canada
#202, 1232C Lawrence Ave. East
Toronto, ON M3A 1B9
Tel: 416-585-9876; *Fax:* 416-595-5302
Classes of Insurance: Accident, Legal Expense, Auto, Liability, Fidelity, Property, Surety

Continental Casualty Company
#1500, 250 Yonge St.
Toronto, ON M5B 2L7
Tel: 416-542-7300; *Fax:* 416-542-7310
Toll-Free: 800-268-9399
www.cnacanada.ca/portal/
Classes of Insurance: Accident, Personal Accident & Sickness, Aircraft, Auto, Liability, Boiler & Machinery, Credit, Fidelity, Property, Surety, Hail & Crop

Co-operative Hail Insurance Company Ltd.
PO Box 777
2709 - 13th Ave.
Regina, SK S4P 3A8
Tel: 306-522-8891; *Fax:* 306-352-9130
info@coophail.com
www.coophail.com
Classes of Insurance: Hail & Crop

Co-operators General Insurance Company
Priory Sq., 7th Fl.
Guelph, ON N1H 6P8
Tel: 519-824-4400; *Fax:* 519-824-0599
Toll-Free: 877-795-7272
service@cooperators.ca
www.cooperators.ca
Classes of Insurance: Personal Accident & Sickness, Aircraft, Auto, Boiler & Machinery, Life, Fidelity, Property, Fire, Surety, Hail & Crop, Theft

Co-operators Life Insurance Company
1920 College Ave.
Regina, SK S4P 1C4
Tel: 306-347-6200; *Fax:* 306-347-6806
Toll-Free: 800-454-8061
service@cooperators.ca; phs_individual_life@cooperators.ca
www.cooperators.ca
Other Contact Information: Group Benefits, Toll Free: 1-800-667-8164; Fax: 306-761-7373; Email: group_client_services@cooperators.ca; Travel, Toll Free: 1-800-869-6747
Classes of Insurance: Personal Accident & Sickness, Life, Property

COSECO Insurance Company
5600 Cancross Ct.
Mississauga, ON L5R 3E9
Tel: 905-507-6156; *Fax:* 905-507-8661
service@cooperators.ca.
www.cooperators.ca
Classes of Insurance: Auto, Property

Cowan Insurance Group Ltd.
PO Box 1510
705 Fountain St. North
Cambridge, ON N1R 5T2
Tel: 519-650-6360; *Fax:* 519-650-6366
Toll-Free: 866-912-6926
infocib@cowangroup.ca
www.cowangroup.ca
Classes of Insurance: Auto, Marine, Property

Croatian Fraternal Union of America
c/o Deloitte & Touche
#1400, 181 Bay St.
Toronto, ON M5J 2V1
Tel: 416-601-6150; *Fax:* 416-601-6590
www.croatianfraternalunion.org
Classes of Insurance: Personal Accident & Sickness, Life

Crowsnest Insurance Agencies Ltd.
PO Box 88
12731 - 20th Ave.
Blairmore, AB T0K 0E0
Tel: 403-562-8822; *Fax:* 403-562-8239
Toll-Free: 800-361-8658
info@crowsnestinsurance.com
crowsnestinsurance.com
Classes of Insurance: Auto, Liability, Property

Culross Mutual Insurance Company (CMI)
PO Box 173
28 Clinton St.
Teeswater, ON N0G 2S0
Tel: 519-392-6260; *Fax:* 519-392-8177
Toll-Free: 888-800-8666
ken@culrossmutual.com
www.culrossmutual.com

CUMIS General Insurance Company
PO Box 5065
151 North Service Rd.
Burlington, ON L7R 4C2
Tel: 905-632-1221; *Fax:* 905-632-9412
Toll-Free: 800-263-9120
www.cumis.com
Classes of Insurance: Auto, Boiler & Machinery, Fidelity, Property, Fire, Theft

The CUMIS Group Limited
PO Box 5065
151 North Service Rd.
Burlington, ON L7R 4C2
Tel: 905-632-1221; *Fax:* 905-632-9412
Toll-Free: 800-263-9120
customer.service@cumis.com
www.cumis.com
Classes of Insurance: Personal Accident & Sickness, Auto, Life, Property

CUMIS Life Insurance Company
PO Box 5065
151 North Service Rd.
Burlington, ON L7R 4C2
Tel: 905-632-1221; *Fax:* 905-632-9412
Toll-Free: 800-263-9120
customer.service@cumis.com
www.cumis.com
Classes of Insurance: Accident, Personal Accident & Sickness, Auto, Life, Credit, Fidelity, Property, Fire, Theft

Desjardins assurances générales inc/ Desjardins General Insurance Inc.
PO Box 3500
6300, boul. de la Rive-Sud
Lévis, QC G6V 6P9
Tel: 418-835-4850; *Fax:* 418-835-5599
Toll-Free: 800-277-8726
www.desjardinsassurancesgenerales.com
Classes of Insurance: Auto, Liability, Boiler & Machinery, Property, Surety

Desjardins Financial Security (DFS)/ Desjardins Sécurité financière
200, av. des Commandeurs
Lévis, QC G6V 6R2
Toll-Free: 866-838-7553
info@desjardinssecuritefinanciere.com; grouppension@dsf.ca
www.dsf-dfs.com
Classes of Insurance: Accident, Personal Accident & Sickness, Life

Desjardins Groupe d'assurances générales inc/ Desjardins General Insurance Group Inc.
6300, boul. de la Rive-Sud
Lévis, QC G6V 6P9
Ligne sans frais: 888-277-8726
www.dgag.ca

The Dominion of Canada General Insurance Company/ Compagnie d'assurance générale dominion du Canada
165 University Ave.
Toronto, ON M5H 3B9
Tel: 416-362-7231; *Fax:* 416-362-9918
Toll-Free: 800-268-8447
www.thedominion.ca
Classes of Insurance: Auto, Liability, Property, Fire, Surety, Theft

Dufferin Mutual Insurance Company
712 Main St. East
Shelburne, ON L0N 1S0
Tel: 519-925-2026; *Fax:* 519-925-3357
Toll-Free: 800-265-9115
info@dufferinmutual.com
www.dufferinmutual.com
Classes of Insurance: Personal Accident & Sickness, Auto, Liability, Boiler & Machinery, Fidelity, Property

Dumfries Mutual Insurance Company
12 Cambridge St.
Cambridge, ON N1R 3R7
Tel: 519-621-4660; *Fax:* 519-740-8732
info@dumfriesmutual.com
www.dumfriesmutual.com
Classes of Insurance: Auto, Liability, Boiler & Machinery, Property, Hail & Crop

Eagle Star Insurance Company Ltd.
c/o Focus Group Inc.
#500, 36 King St. East
Toronto, ON M5C 1E5
Tel: 416-361-1728; *Fax:* 416-361-6113
www.eaglestar.ie
Classes of Insurance: Personal Accident & Sickness, Aircraft, Auto, Liability, Boiler & Machinery, Fidelity, Property, Surety

Ecclesiastical Insurance Office plc/ Société des Assurances écclésiastiques
PO Box 2004
#2200, 20 Eglinton Ave. West
Toronto, ON M4R 1K8
Tel: 416-484-4555; *Fax:* 416-484-6352
info@eccles-ins.com
www.eigcanada.com, www.ecclesiastical.co.uk
Classes of Insurance: Auto, Liability, Boiler & Machinery, Marine, Fidelity, Property,

Echelon General Insurance Company/ Echelon Compagnie d'Assurances Générale
#300, 2680 Matheson Blvd. East
Mississauga, ON L4W 0A5
Tel: 905-214-7880; *Fax:* 905-214-7893
Toll-Free: 800-324-3566
www.echelon-insurance.ca
Classes of Insurance: Accident, Personal Accident & Sickness, Legal Expense, Auto, Liability, Fidelity, Property, Fire, Surety

The Economical Insurance Group
PO Box 2000
111 Westmount St. South
Waterloo, ON N2J 4S4
Tel: 519-570-8200; *Fax:* 519-570-8389
Toll-Free: 800-265-2180
www.economicalinsurance.com

Economical Mutual Insurance Company
PO Box 2000
111 Westmount Rd. South
Waterloo, ON N2J 4S4
Tel: 519-570-8200; *Fax:* 519-570-8389
Toll-Free: 800-265-2180
www.economicalinsurance.com
Classes of Insurance: Auto, Boiler & Machinery, Property, Surety

Elite Insurance Company
2206 Eglinton Ave. East
Toronto, ON M1L 4S8
Tel: 416-288-1800; *Fax:* 416-288-5888
www.avivacanada.com
Other Contact Information: 800-590-5003 (Toll Free, After Hours Emergency Service, Atlantic Canada); 800-561-9899 (Toll Free, NB, 8am-5pm); 800-565-7153 (Toll Free, NS, PE, NL)
Classes of Insurance: Personal Accident & Sickness, Aircraft, Auto, Liability, Boiler & Machinery, Marine, Fidelity, Property, Surety

Employers Reinsurance Corporation
PO Box 50
#2200, 150 King St. West
Toronto, ON M5H 1J9
Tel: 416-217-5555; *Fax:* 416-217-5566
www.swissre.com
Classes of Insurance: Personal Accident & Sickness, Aircraft, Auto, Liability, Boiler & Machinery, Credit, Fidelity, Property, Surety, Hail & Crop

L'Entraide assurance, compagnie mutuelle/ L'Entraide Assurance Mutual Company
CP 70226, Québec-Centre Stn. Québec-Centre
520, boul. Charest est, 1er étage
Québec, QC G1K 7P5
Tél: 418-658-0663; *Téléc:* 418-658-5065
Ligne sans frais: 800-536-8724
service@lentraide.com
www.lentraide.com
Classes of Insurance: Accident, Personal Accident & Sickness, Life, Credit

The Equitable Life Insurance Company of Canada
1 Westmount Rd. North
Waterloo, ON N2J 4C7
Tel: 519-886-5110; *Fax:* 519-883-7400
Toll-Free: 800-265-8878
webmaster@equitable.ca
www.equitable.ca
Classes of Insurance: Life

Erie Mutual Fire Insurance Company
711 Main St. East
Dunnville, ON N1A 2W5
Tel: 905-774-8566; *Fax:* 905-774-6468
Toll-Free: 800-263-6484
www.eriemutual.com
Classes of Insurance: Personal Accident & Sickness, Auto, Liability, Boiler & Machinery, Fidelity, Property,

Euler Hermes Canada
#1702, 1155, boul. René-Lévesque ouest
Montréal, QC H3B 3Z7
Tel: 514-876-9656; *Fax:* 514-876-9658
Toll-Free: 877-509-3224
www.eulerhermes.ca
Social Media: twitter.com/#!/ehworldwide
Classes of Insurance: Credit

Everest Insurance Company of Canada/ La Compagnie d'assurance Everest du Canada
The Exchange Tower
PO Box 431
#2520, 130 King St. West
Toronto, ON M5X 1E3
Tel: 416-862-1228; *Fax:* 416-366-5899
www.everestre.com
Classes of Insurance: Aircraft, Auto, Liability, Boiler & Machinery, Credit, Marine, Property, Surety, Hail & Crop

Everest Reinsurance Company
The Exchange Tower
PO Box 431
#2520, 130 King St. West
Toronto, ON M5X 1E3
Tel: 416-862-1228; *Fax:* 416-366-5899
www.everestre.com
Classes of Insurance: Personal Accident & Sickness, Aircraft, Auto, Liability, Boiler & Machinery, Credit, Fidelity, Property, Surety, Hail & Crop

L'Excellence, Compagnie d'assurance-vie/ Excellence Life Insurance Company
#202, 5055, boul. Métropolitain est
Montréal, QC H1R 1Z7
Tel: 514-327-0020; *Toll-Free:* 800-465-5818
service@excellence.qc.ca
www.excellence.qc.ca
Classes of Insurance: Personal Accident & Sickness, Life

FaithLife Financial
470 Weber St. North
Waterloo, ON N2J 4G4
Tel: 519-886-4610; *Fax:* 519-886-0350
moreinfo@faithlifefinancial.ca
www.faithlifefinancial.ca
Classes of Insurance: Accident, Personal Accident & Sickness, Life

Farmers' Mutual Insurance Company (Lindsay)
PO Box 28
336 Angeline St. South
Lindsay, ON K9V 4R8
Tel: 705-324-2146; *Fax:* 705-324-2356
Toll-Free: 800-461-0310
www.farmerslindsay.com
Classes of Insurance: Personal Accident & Sickness, Auto, Liability, Boiler & Machinery, Marine, Fidelity, Property

Federal Insurance Company
One Financial Place
1 Adelaide St. East
Toronto, ON M5C 2V9
Tel: 416-863-0550; *Fax:* 416-863-5010
gdamiano@chubb.com
www.chubb.com/international/canada
Classes of Insurance: Personal Accident & Sickness, Auto, Liability, Boiler & Machinery, Marine, Fidelity, Property, Surety

Federated Insurance Company of Canada
PO Box 5800
717 Portage Ave.
Winnipeg, MB R3C 3C9
Tel: 204-786-6431; *Fax:* 204-784-6755
Toll-Free: 800-665-1934
webmaster@federated.ca
www.federated.ca
Classes of Insurance: Accident, Auto, Liability, Boiler & Machinery, Fidelity, Property, Fire, Surety, Theft

Federation Insurance Company of Canada/ La Fédération Compagnie d'Assurances du Canada
#500, 1000, rue de la Gauchetière ouest
Montréal, QC H3B 4W5
Tel: 514-875-5790; *Fax:* 514-875-9769
Toll-Free: 800-361-7573
www.federation.ca
Classes of Insurance: Accident, Legal Expense, Auto, Liability, Boiler & Machinery, Fidelity, Property, Fire, Surety, Hail & Crop

Fenchurch General Insurance Company (FGIC)
Promontory II
#115, 2655 North Sheridan Way
Mississauga, ON L5K 2P8
Tel: 905-822-2282; *Fax:* 905-822-1282
info@fenchurchgeneral.com
www.fenchurchgeneral.com
Classes of Insurance: Personal Accident & Sickness, Auto, Liability, Boiler & Machinery, Property, Surety

First Canadian Title
2235 Sheridan Garden Dr.
Oakville, ON L6J 7Y5
Tel: 905-287-1000; *Fax:* 905-287-2400
Toll-Free: 800-307-0370
www.firstcanadiantitle.com

First North American Insurance Company
#1600, 5650 Yonge St.
Toronto, ON M2M 4G4
Toll-Free: 800-668-0195
am_service@manulife.com
www.manulife.ca
Classes of Insurance: Personal Accident & Sickness, Auto, Property

FM Global
#500, 165 Commerce Valley Dr. West
Thornhill, ON L3T 7V8
Tel: 905-763-5555; *Fax:* 905-763-5556
www.fmglobal.com
Classes of Insurance: Boiler & Machinery, Property

FNF Canada
2700 Argentia Rd.
Mississauga, ON L5N 5V4
Tel: 905-821-2262; *Fax:* 905-821-7918
Toll-Free: 877-526-3232
info@fnf.ca
www.fnf.ca

Folksamerica Reinsurance Company
#1202, 80 Bloor St. West
Toronto, ON M5S 2V1
Tel: 416-928-2430; *Fax:* 416-928-2459
marketing@folksamerica.com
www.folksamerica.com
Classes of Insurance: Auto, Liability, Fidelity, Property, Surety, Hail & Crop

Fonds d'assurance responsabilité professionnelle de la Chambre des notaires du Québec
#1500, 1200, av. McGill College
Montréal, QC H3B 4G7
Tel: 514-871-4999; *Fax:* 514-879-1781
www.cdnq.org

Fonds d'assurance responsabilité professionnelle du Barreau du Québec
#300, 445, boul. Saint-Laurent
Montréal, QC H2Y 3T8
Tel: 514-954-3452; *Fax:* 514-954-3454
www.assurance-barreau.com
Other Contact Information: Toll Free: 1-800-361-8495, poste 3452

Frank Cowan Company Limited
4 Cowan St. East
Princeton, ON N0J 1V0
Tel: 519-458-4331; *Fax:* 519-458-4366
Toll-Free: 800-265-4000
mail@frankcowan.com
www.frankcowan.com
Classes of Insurance: Liability

Fundy Mutual Insurance Company
1022 Main St.
Sussex, NB E4E 2M3
Tel: 506-432-1535; *Fax:* 506-433-6788
Toll-Free: 800-222-9550
info@fundymutual.com
www.fundymutual.com
Classes of Insurance: Auto, Liability, Boiler & Machinery, Property

G & F Financial Group
7375 Kingsway
Burnaby, BC V3N 3B5
Tel: 604-517-5100; *Fax:* 604-659-4025
www.gffg.com

GAN Assurances Vie Compagnie française d'assurances vie mixte
#1470, 1155, rue Metcalfe
Montréal, QC H3B 2V6
Tel: 514-286-9007
eclark@bellnet.ca
Classes of Insurance: Life

GCAN Insurance Company (GCAN)/ GCAN compagnie d'assurances
#1000, 181 University Ave.
Toronto, ON M5H 3M7
Tel: 416-682-5300; *Fax:* 416-682-9213
central.office@gcan.ca
www.gcan.ca
Classes of Insurance: Personal Accident & Sickness, Aircraft, Auto, Liability, Boiler & Machinery, Credit, Marine, Fidelity, Property, Surety, Hail & Crop

General American Life Insurance Company (GALIC)
c/o RGA Life Reinsurance Company of Canada
#1000, 1255, rue Peel
Montréal, QC H3B 2T9
Tel: 514-985-5260; *Fax:* 514-985-3066
Toll-Free: 800-985-4326
mail@rgare.ca
Classes of Insurance: Life, Reinsurance

General Reinsurance Corporation
PO Box 471
#5705, 1 First Canadian Pl.
Toronto, ON M5X 1E4
Tel: 416-869-0490; *Fax:* 416-360-2020
AskGenRe@genre.com
www.genre.com
Classes of Insurance: Personal Accident & Sickness, Aircraft, Auto, Liability, Boiler & Machinery, Credit, Fidelity, Property, Surety, Hail & Crop

Genworth Financial Mortgage Insurance Company Canada
#300, 2060 Winston Park Dr.
Oakville, ON L6H 5R7
Toll-Free: 800-511-8888
mortgage.info@genworth.com
www.gemortgage.ca

Gerber Life Insurance Company
PO Box 22265, BRM B Stn. BRM B
Toronto, ON M7Y 4A1
Toll-Free: 800-518-8884
www.gerberlife.ca
Classes of Insurance: Life

Germania Farmers' Mutual Fire Insurance Co.
PO Box 30
403 Mary St.
Ayton, ON N0G 1C0
Tel: 519-665-7715; *Fax:* 519-665-7558
Toll-Free: 800-265-3433
info@germaniamutual.com
www.germaniamutual.com
Classes of Insurance: Personal Accident & Sickness, Auto, Liability, Boiler & Machinery, Fidelity, Property

Germania Mutual Insurance Company
127 Kaiser William Ave. East
Langenburg, SK S0A 2A0
Tel: 306-743-5363
germania@sasktel.net
Classes of Insurance: Liability, Property, Fire, Theft

Gibb's Agencies (1997) Ltd.
Main St.
Barons, AB T0L 0G0
Tel: 403-757-3820; *Fax:* 403-757-2083
Toll-Free: 888-974-4227
info@gibbsagencies.ca
www.gibbsagencies.com
Classes of Insurance: Auto, Property

Glengarry Farmers' Mutual Fire Insurance Co.
PO Box 159
3720 County Rd. 34
Alexandria, ON K0C 1A0
Tel: 613-525-2557; *Fax:* 613-525-5162
Toll-Free: 800-263-7684
glenins@glenins.ca
www.glenins.ca
Classes of Insurance: Personal Accident & Sickness, Legal Expense, Auto, Liability, Boiler & Machinery, Fidelity, Property, Fire, Theft

Global Aerospace Underwriting Managers (Canada) Limited
#200, 100 Renfrew Dr.
Markham, ON L3R 9R6
Tel: 905-479-2244; *Fax:* 905-479-0751
www.global-aero.co.uk
Classes of Insurance: Personal Accident & Sickness, Aircraft, Liability, Property

Gore Mutual Insurance Company
PO Box 70, Galt Stn. Galt
252 Dundas St.
Cambridge, ON N1R 5T3
Tel: 519-623-1910; *Toll-Free:* 800-265-8600
webserver@goremutual.ca
www.goremutual.ca
Classes of Insurance: Personal Accident & Sickness, Auto, Liability, Property, Fire, Theft

Grain Insurance and Guarantee Company
#1240, 1 Lombard Pl.
Winnipeg, MB R3B 0V9
Tel: 204-943-0721; *Fax:* 204-943-6419
Toll-Free: 800-665-3351
infowinnipeg@graininsurance.com
www.graininsurance.com
Classes of Insurance: Liability, Boiler & Machinery, Fidelity, Property, Fire, Surety, Theft

The Grand Orange Lodge of British America Beneficent Fund
94 Sheppard Ave. West
Toronto, ON M2N 1M5
Tel: 416-223-1690; *Fax:* 416-223-1324
Toll-Free: 800-565-6248
info@grandorangelodge.ca
www.grandorangelodge.ca
Classes of Insurance: Life

Granite Insurance Company
#200, 2 Eva Rd.
Toronto, ON M9C 2A8
Tel: 416-622-0660; *Fax:* 416-622-8809
Toll-Free: 800-342-5243
dsymons@gorancapital.com
Classes of Insurance: Accident, Personal Accident & Sickness, Auto, Liability, Boiler & Machinery, Credit, Fidelity, Property, Fire, Surety, Hail & Crop, Theft

Great American Insurance Company
c/o Cassels, Brock & Blackwell, Scotia Plaza
#2100, 40 King St. West
Toronto, ON M5H 3C2
Tel: 416-869-5300; *Fax:* 416-360-8877
Classes of Insurance: Personal Accident & Sickness, Aircraft, Auto, Liability, Boiler & Machinery, Marine, Fidelity, Property, Surety, Hail & Crop

The Great-West Life Assurance Company (GWL)/ Great-West, Compagnie d'Assurance Vie
100 Osborne St. North
Winnipeg, MB R3C 3A5
Tel: 204-946-1190; *Fax:* 204-946-4159
Toll-Free: 800-665-5758
webmaster@gwl.ca
www.greatwestlife.com; www.grsaccess.com
Other Contact Information: TTY, Toll Free: 1-800-990-6654
Classes of Insurance: Personal Accident & Sickness, Life

Green Shield Canada
PO Box 1606
8677 Anchor Dr.
Windsor, ON N9A 6W1
Tel: 519-739-1133; *Fax:* 519-739-0200
Toll-Free: 800-265-5615
www.greenshield.ca
Classes of Insurance: Personal Accident & Sickness

Grenville Mutual Insurance Company
PO Box 10
3005 County Rd. 21
Spencerville, ON K0E 1X0
Tel: 613-658-2013; *Fax:* 613-658-3374
Toll-Free: 800-267-4400
mail@grenvillemutual.com
www.grenvillemutual.com
Classes of Insurance: Personal Accident & Sickness, Auto, Liability, Boiler & Machinery, Fidelity, Property

Grey & Bruce Mutual Insurance Co.
517 - 10th St.
Hanover, ON N4N 1R4
Tel: 519-364-2250; *Fax:* 519-364-6067
Toll-Free: 800-265-5522
www.greybrucemutualinsurance.com
Classes of Insurance: Personal Accident & Sickness, Auto, Liability, Boiler & Machinery, Property

Le Groupe Estrie-Richelieu, compagnie d'assurance (GER)
770, rue Principale
Granby, QC J2G 2Y7
Tél: 450-378-0101; *Téléc:* 450-378-5189
ressources@ger.qc.ca
www.ger.qc.ca
Classes of Insurance: Auto, Liability, Boiler & Machinery, Property, Fire

Groupe Promutuel, Fédération de sociétés mutuelles d'assurance générale
1091, Grande Allée ouest
Québec, QC G1S 4Y7
Ligne sans frais: 866-999-2433
federation@promutuel.ca
www.promutuel.ca

The Guarantee Company of North America/ La Garantie, Compagnie d'Assurance de l'Amérique du Nord
Madison Centre
#1400, 4950 Yonge St.
Toronto, ON M2N 6K1
Tel: 416-223-9580; *Fax:* 416-223-6577
Toll-Free: 800-260-6617
www.gcna.com
Classes of Insurance: Accident, Personal Accident & Sickness, Legal Expense, Auto, Liability, Boiler & Machinery, Credit, Fidelity, Property, Fire, Surety, Hail & Crop, Theft

Halwell Mutual Insurance Company
PO Box 60
812 Woolwich St.
Guelph, ON N1H 6J6
Tel: 519-836-2860; *Fax:* 519-836-2831
Toll-Free: 800-267-5706
reception@halwellmutual.com
www.halwellmutual.com
Classes of Insurance: Auto, Liability, Boiler & Machinery, Fidelity, Property

Hamilton Township Mutual Insurance Company
PO Box 201
1176 Division St.
Cobourg, ON K9A 4K5
Tel: 905-372-0186; *Fax:* 905-372-1364
Toll-Free: 800-263-3935
info@htminsurance.ca
www.htminsurance.ca
Classes of Insurance: Marine, Fire

Hannover Rückversicherungs AG
#201, 3650 Victoria Park Ave.
Toronto, ON M2H 3P7
Tel: 416-496-1148; *Fax:* 416-496-1089
www.hannover-rueck.de
Classes of Insurance: Personal Accident & Sickness, Aircraft, Auto, Liability, Boiler & Machinery, Fidelity, Property, Surety, Hail & Crop

Hartford Fire Insurance Company
121 King St. West
Toronto, ON M5H 3T9
Tel: 416-733-9265; *Fax:* 416-733-0510
Toll-Free: 888-898-8334
Classes of Insurance: Personal Accident & Sickness, Aircraft, Auto, Liability, Boiler & Machinery, Fidelity, Property, Fire, Surety, Hail & Crop, Theft

Hay Mutual Insurance Company
PO Box 130
37868 Zurich-Hensall Rd.
Zurich, ON N0M 2T0
Tel: 519-236-4381; *Fax:* 519-236-7681
www.haymutual.on.ca
Classes of Insurance: Auto, Liability, Property, Hail & Crop

Henderson Insurance Inc.
339 Main St. North
Moose Jaw, SK S6H 0W2
Tel: 306-694-5959; *Fax:* 306-693-0117
Toll-Free: 888-661-5959
hii@hendersoninsurance.ca
www.hendersoninsurance.ca

Classes of Insurance: Aircraft, Auto, Liability, Marine, Property, Hail & Crop

Howard Mutual Insurance Co.
PO Box 398
20 Ebenezer St. West
Ridgetown, ON N0P 2C0
Tel: 519-674-5434; *Fax:* 519-674-2029
howardmutual.com
Classes of Insurance: Personal Accident & Sickness, Auto, Liability, Fidelity, Property, Hail & Crop

Howick Mutual Insurance Company
PO Box 30
1091 Centre St.
Wroxeter, ON N0G 2X0
Tel: 519-335-3561; *Fax:* 519-335-6416
Toll-Free: 800-265-3033
sedgar@howickmutual.com
www.howickmutual.com
Classes of Insurance: Personal Accident & Sickness, Auto, Liability, Boiler & Machinery, Fidelity, Property, Hail & Crop

Independent Order of Foresters
789 Don Mills Rd.
Toronto, ON M3C 1T9
Tel: 416-429-3000; *Toll-Free:* 800-828-1540
service@foresters.com; humanresources@foresters.com
www.foresters.biz
Other Contact Information: Member Benefits, Toll-Free Phone: 800-444-3043; Unity Life Policy Holders, E-mail: clientservice@unitylife.ca, Toll-Free Phone: 800-267-8777
Social Media: www.facebook.com/Foresters
Classes of Insurance: Personal Accident & Sickness, Life

Industrial Alliance Insurance & Financial Services Inc./ Industrielle Alliance Assurance et Services Financ
CP 1907, Terminus Stn. Terminus
1080, ch. Saint-Louis
Québec, QC G1K 7M3
Tél: 418-684-5000; *Ligne sans frais:* 800-463-6236
info@inalco.com, customers@inalco.com
www.inalco.com
Classes of Insurance: Personal Accident & Sickness, Auto, Life

Industrial Alliance Pacific Insurance & Financial Services Inc. (IAP)
PO Box 5900
2165 West Broadway
Vancouver, BC V6B 5H6
Tel: 604-734-1667; *Fax:* 604-734-8221
Toll-Free: 800-363-2166
intouch@iapacific.com
www.iaplife.com
Classes of Insurance: Accident, Personal Accident & Sickness, Life, Credit

Innovative Insurance Agencies
6351 Rideau Valley Dr. North
Ottawa, ON K4M 1B3
Fax: 613-692-0338
Toll-Free: 800-265-4275
info@innovativeinsurance.ca
www.innovativeinsurance.ca

Insurance Company of Prince Edward Island
14 Great George St.
Charlottetown, PE C1A 4J6
Tel: 902-368-3675; *Fax:* 902-626-3529
inquiries@icpei.ca
www.icpei.ca
Classes of Insurance: Auto, Life, Property

Insurance Corporation of British Columbia (ICBC)
151 West Esplanade
North Vancouver, BC V7M 3H9
Tel: 604-661-2800; *Fax:* 604-646-7400
Toll-Free: 800-663-3051
www.icbc.com
Classes of Insurance: Auto

Intact Insurance Company of Canada
700 University Ave., 15th Fl.
Toronto, ON M5G 0A1
Tel: 416-341-1464; *Fax:* 416-344-8030
Toll-Free: 877-341-1464
info@intact.net
www.intactinsurance.com
Classes of Insurance: Marine, Surety

Intact Insurance Company of Canada - Novex Group Insurance/ ING Novex Compagnie d'Assurance du Canada
700 University Ave., 15th Fl.
Toronto, ON M5G 0A1
Tel: 416-341-1464; *Fax:* 416-344-8030
Toll-Free: 877-341-1464
info@intact.net
www.intactinsurance.com
Classes of Insurance: Personal Accident & Sickness, Legal Expense, Auto, Liability, Boiler & Machinery, Credit, Fidelity, Property, Surety

L'Internationale, compagnie d'assurance-vie/ The International Life Insurance Company
CP 696
142, rue Hériot
Montréal, QC J2B 6W9
Tél: 514-281-0666; *Téléc:* 514-281-6340
Ligne sans frais: 800-310-2166
courrier@linternationale.qc.ca
www.linternationale.qc.ca
Classes of Insurance: Personal Accident & Sickness, Life

JEVCO Insurance Company/ La Compagnie d'Assurances JEVCO
#100, 5250, boul. Décarie
Montréal, QC H3X 2H9
Tel: 514-284-9350; *Fax:* 514-289-9257
Toll-Free: 800-361-8500
www.jevco.ca
Other Contact Information: 514-284-4823 (Commercial); 514-284-3805 (Claims); 514-284-3390 (Motoplan)
Classes of Insurance: Auto, Property

Johnston Meier Insurance Agencies Group
1944 Como Lake Ave.
Coquitlam, BC V3J 3R3
Tel: 604-937-3601; *Fax:* 604-937-5062
www.kbyinsurance.com
Classes of Insurance: Aircraft, Auto, Life, Marine, Surety

Kent & Essex Mutual Insurance Company
PO Box 356
10 Creek Rd.
Chatham, ON N7M 5K4
Tel: 519-352-3190; *Fax:* 519-352-5344
Toll-Free: 800-265-5206
info@kentesexmutual.com
www.kentessexmutual.com
Classes of Insurance: Personal Accident & Sickness, Auto, Liability, Boiler & Machinery, Fidelity, Property

The Kings Mutual Insurance Company
220 Commercial St.
Berwick, NS B0P 1E0
Tel: 902-538-3187; *Fax:* 902-538-7271
Toll-Free: 800-565-7220
info@kingsmutual.ns.ca
www.kingsmutual.ns.ca
Classes of Insurance: Liability, Property, Fire

Kingsway Financial Services Inc.
#800, 7210 Hurontario St.
Mississauga, ON L5W 0A9
Tel: 905-629-7888; *Fax:* 905-629-5008
info@kingsway-financial.com
www.kingsway-financial.com
Classes of Insurance: Auto, Property, Reinsurance

Kingsway General Insurance Company
#700, 7120 Hurontario St.
Mississauga, ON L5W 0B1
Tel: 905-677-8889; *Fax:* 905-677-5008
Toll-Free: 800-265-5458
kgmarketing@kingsway-general.com
www.kingsway-general.com
Classes of Insurance: Auto, Liability, Property, Surety

Kirkham Insurance
205 - 11th St. South
Lethbridge, AB T1J 4A6
Tel: 403-328-1228; *Fax:* 403-380-4051
Toll-Free: 800-256-2155
www.kirkhaminsurance.com
Classes of Insurance: Auto, Property

Knights of Columbus Insurance
c/o The Raymond Richer Agency
26 Davis Court
Hampton, ON L0B 1J0
Tel: 905-263-4212
www.kofc.org
Classes of Insurance: Life

Lambton Mutual Insurance Company
PO Box 520
7873 Confederation Line
Watford, ON N0M 2S0
Tel: 519-876-2304; *Fax:* 519-876-3940
Toll-Free: 800-561-4136
info@lambtonmutual.com
www.lambtonmutual.com
Classes of Insurance: Personal Accident & Sickness, Auto, Liability, Boiler & Machinery, Fidelity, Property, Hail & Crop

Lanark Mutual Insurance Company
96 South St., Scotch Line Rd.
Perth, ON K7H 0A2
Tel: 613-267-5554; *Fax:* 613-267-6793
Toll-Free: 800-267-7908
lmadmin@LanarkMutual.com
www.lanarkmutual.com
Classes of Insurance: Auto, Liability, Boiler & Machinery, Property, Hail & Crop, Theft

Lawyers' Professional Indemnity Company (LAWPRO)
PO Box 3
#3101, 250 Yonge St.
Toronto, ON M5B 2L7
Tel: 416-598-5800; *Fax:* 416-599-8341
Toll-Free: 800-410-1013
service@lawpro.ca
www.lawpro.ca
Classes of Insurance: Liability

Legacy General Insurance Company/ Compagnie d'Assurances Générales Legacy
80 Tiverton Ct., 5th Fl.
Markham, ON L3R 0G4
Tel: 905-479-7500; *Fax:* 905-479-3224
www.canadianpremier.ca
Classes of Insurance: Personal Accident & Sickness, Liability, Property

Lennox & Addington Mutual Insurance Company
PO Box 174
32 Mill St.
Napanee, ON K7R 3M3
Tel: 613-354-4810; *Fax:* 613-354-7112
Toll-Free: 800-267-7812
www.l-amutual.com
Classes of Insurance: Personal Accident & Sickness, Auto, Liability, Marine, Property

Liberty Mutual Insurance Company/ La Compagnie d'Assurance Liberté Mutuelle
Brookfield Place
#1000, 181 Bay St.
Toronto, ON M5J 2T3
Tel: 416-307-4353; *Fax:* 416-365-7281
www.libertymutual.com
Classes of Insurance: Personal Accident & Sickness, Aircraft, Auto, Liability, Boiler & Machinery, Fidelity, Property, Surety

Life Insurance Company of North America (LINA)
#606, 55 Town Centre Ct.
Toronto, ON M1P 4X4
Tel: 416-290-6666; *Fax:* 416-290-0726
www.cigna.com
Classes of Insurance: Accident, Personal Accident & Sickness, Life

Lloyd's Underwriters
#2220, 1155, rue Metcalfe
Montréal, QC H3B 2V6
Tel: 514-861-8361; *Fax:* 514-861-0470
Toll-Free: 877-455-6937
info@lloyds.ca
www.lloyds.com
Classes of Insurance: Personal Accident & Sickness, Aircraft, Legal Expense, Auto, Liability, Boiler & Machinery, Fidelity, Property, Fire, Surety, Reinsurance

Lombard General Insurance Company of Canada
105 Adelaide St. West
Toronto, ON M5H 1P9
Tel: 416-350-4400; *Fax:* 416-350-4412
Classes of Insurance: Personal Accident & Sickness, Aircraft, Legal Expense, Auto, Liability, Boiler & Machinery, Credit, Fidelity, Property, Surety, Hail & Crop, Theft

Lombard Insurance Company
105 Adelaide St. West
Toronto, ON M5H 1P9
Tel: 416-350-4400; *Fax:* 416-350-4412
www.lombard.ca
Classes of Insurance: Personal Accident & Sickness, Aircraft, Legal Expense, Auto, Liability, Boiler & Machinery, Credit, Marine, Fidelity, Property, Fire, Surety, Hail & Crop, Theft

London & Midland General Insurance Company
201 Queens Ave.
London, ON N6A 1J1
Tel: 519-672-1070; *Fax:* 519-660-2625
Toll-Free: 800-285-8623
Classes of Insurance: Accident, Personal Accident & Sickness, Auto, Boiler & Machinery, Life, Fidelity, Property, Fire, Surety, Theft

London Life Insurance Company/ London Life, Compagnie d'Assurance-Vie
255 Dufferin Ave.
London, ON N6A 4K1
Tel: 519-432-5281
corporate.information@londonlife.com
www.londonlife.com
Classes of Insurance: Personal Accident & Sickness, Life, Reinsurance

The Loyalist Insurance Company
#107, 911 Golf Links Rd.
Ancaster, ON L9K 1H9
Tel: 905-648-6767; *Fax:* 905-648-7220
info@loyalistinsurance.com
www.loyalistinsurance.com

Lumbermen's Underwriting Alliance
#300, 455, boul. Fénelon
Montréal, QC H9S 5T8
Tel: 514-631-2710; *Fax:* 514-631-9788
www.lumbermensunderwriting.com
Classes of Insurance: Boiler & Machinery, Property

Manitoba Agricultural Services Corporation - Insurance Corporate Office (MASC)
#400, 50 - 24th St. NW
Portage La Prairie, MB R1N 3V9
Tel: 204-239-3246; *Fax:* 204-239-3401
mailbox@masc.mb.ca
www.masc.mb.ca
Classes of Insurance: Hail & Crop

Manitoba Blue Cross
PO Box 1046
599 Empress St.
Winnipeg, MB R3C 2X7
Tel: 204-775-0151; *Fax:* 204-786-5965
Toll-Free: 888-873-2583
www.mb.bluecross.ca
Classes of Insurance: Personal Accident & Sickness, Life

Manitoba Public Insurance
PO Box 6300
Winnipeg, MB R3C 4A4
Tel: 204-985-7000; *Toll-Free:* 800-665-2410
www.mpi.mb.ca
Other Contact Information: TTY/TTY: 204-985-8832
Classes of Insurance: Auto

Manufacturers Life Insurance Company/ La Compagnie d'Assurance-Vie Manufacturers
200 Bloor St. East
Toronto, ON M4W 1E5
Toll-Free: 888-626-8543
www.manulife.ca
Classes of Insurance: Personal Accident & Sickness, Life,

Manulife Canada Ltd./ Manuvie Canada Ltée
PO Box 1669
500 King St. North
Waterloo, ON N2J 4Z6
Toll-Free: 888-626-8543
valued_customer_centre@manulife.com
www.manulife.ca
Classes of Insurance: Life

Manulife Financial
PO Box 1669
500 King St. North
Waterloo, ON N2J 4Z6
Toll-Free: 888-626-8543
valued_customer_centre@manulife.com
www.manulife.ca
Classes of Insurance: Life

Markel Insurance Company of Canada
#1500, 55 University Ave.
Toronto, ON M5J 2H7
Tel: 416-364-7800; *Fax:* 416-364-5655
Toll-Free: 888-627-5351
letstalk@markel.ca
www.markel.ca
Classes of Insurance: Auto

Massachusetts Mutual Life Insurance Company
c/o Cassels Brock & Blackwell LLP, Scotia Plaza
#2100, 40 King St. West
Toronto, ON M5H 3C2
Tel: 416-869-5745; *Fax:* 416-350-6955
www.massmutual.com
Classes of Insurance: Personal Accident & Sickness, Life

MAX Canada Insurance Company
140 Foundry St.
Baden, ON N3A 2P7
Fax: 519-634-5159
Toll-Free: 877-770-7729
www.mutualaidexchange.com
Classes of Insurance: Liability, Boiler & Machinery, Marine, Fidelity, Property

McFarlane & Company Financial Group Limited
#430, 999 - 8th St. SW
Calgary, AB T2R 1J5
Tel: 403-229-0466; *Fax:* 403-228-9784
Toll-Free: 888-224-0466
info@mcfarlaneco.com
www.mcfarlaneco.com
Classes of Insurance: Auto, Liability, Life, Property, Surety, Hail & Crop

McKillop Mutual Insurance Company
PO Box 819
91 Main St. South
Seaforth, ON N0K 1W0
Tel: 519-527-0400; *Fax:* 519-527-2777
Toll-Free: 800-463-9204
mckillo@tcc.on.ca
www.mckillopmutual.com
Classes of Insurance: Personal Accident & Sickness, Auto, Liability, Boiler & Machinery, Fidelity, Property

MD Life Insurance Company
1870 Alta Vista Dr.
Ottawa, ON K1G 6R7
Classes of Insurance: Life

Medavie Blue Cross
PO Box 220
644 Main St.
Moncton, NB E1C 8L3
Tel: 506-853-1811; *Fax:* 506-867-4651
Toll-Free: 800-667-4511
www.medavie.bluecross.ca
Other Contact Information: Group Benefits, Atlantic Provinces & Ontario: 1-888-227-3400; Group Benefits, Québec: 1-888-588-1212
Classes of Insurance: Personal Accident & Sickness, Life

Meloche Monnex Inc.
50, Place Crémazie, 12e étage
Montréal, QC H2P 1B6
Tel: 514-382-6060; *Fax:* 514-385-2162
www.melochemonnex.com

Mennonite Mutual Fire Insurance Company
PO Box 190
Waldheim, SK S0K 4R0
Tel: 306-945-2239; *Fax:* 306-945-4666
mmfi@sasktel.net
www.mmfi.com
Classes of Insurance: Boiler & Machinery, Property, Fire, Theft

Mennonite Mutual Insurance Co. (Alberta) Ltd. (MMI)
#300, 2946 - 32nd St. NE
Calgary, AB T1Y 6J7
Tel: 403-275-6996; *Fax:* 403-291-6733
Toll-Free: 866-222-6996
office@mmiab.ca
www.mmiab.ca
Classes of Insurance: Auto, Liability, Property, Fire

Metro General Insurance Corp.
T.D. Place
PO Box 548
#700, 140 Water St.
St. John's, NL A1C 5K9
Tel: 709-726-1922; *Fax:* 709-726-5207
Classes of Insurance: Auto, Liability, Property

Metropolitan Life Insurance Company, Canadian Branch
Constitution Square
#1750, 360 Albert St.
Ottawa, ON K1R 7X7
Tel: 613-237-7171; *Fax:* 613-237-7585
ldumas@metlife.com
www.metlife.com
Classes of Insurance: Personal Accident & Sickness, Life

Middlesex Mutual Insurance Co.
PO Box 100
13271 Ilderton Rd.
Ilderton, ON N0M 2A0
Tel: 519-666-0075; *Fax:* 519-666-0079
Toll-Free: 800-851-4045
mmic@middlesexmutual.on.ca
www.middlesexmutual.on.ca
Classes of Insurance: Auto, Liability, Property

Millennium Insurance Corporation
340 Sioux Rd.
Sherwood Park, AB T8A 3X6
Tel: 780-467-1500; *Fax:* 780-467-0004
Toll-Free: 866-467-1245
info@millenniuminsurance.ca
www.directinsure.net
Classes of Insurance: Auto, Property

Minnesota Life Insurance Company/ Compagnie d'Assurance-vie Minnesota
c/o McLean & Kerr LLP
#2800, 130 Adelaide St. West
Toronto, ON M5H 3P5
Tel: 416-364-5371; *Fax:* 416-366-8571
www.minnesotamutual.com
Classes of Insurance: Life

Mitsui Sumitomo Insurance Co., Limited.
Chubb Insurance Company of Canada, One Financial Place
#1500A, 1 Adelaide St. East
Toronto, ON M5C 2V9
Tel: 416-863-0550; *Fax:* 416-863-3144
www.ms-ins.com/english/index.html
Classes of Insurance: Personal Accident & Sickness, Aircraft, Auto, Liability, Boiler & Machinery, Fidelity, Property, Surety

Motors Insurance Corporation
#400, 8500 Leslie St.
Thornhill, ON L3T 7M8
Tel: 905-882-3900; *Fax:* 905-882-3955
Classes of Insurance: Auto, Liability, Boiler & Machinery

Mouvement des caisses Desjardins du Québec
100, av. des Commandeurs
Lévis, QC G6V 7N5
Tél: 418-835-8444; *Téléc:* 418-833-5873
www.desjardins.com

Munich Reinsurance Company - Canada Life
Munich Re Centre
390 Bay St., 26th Fl.
Toronto, ON M5H 2Y2
Tel: 416-359-2200; *Fax:* 416-361-0305
generalenquiries@munichre.ca
www.munichre.ca
Classes of Insurance: Personal Accident & Sickness, Life, Reinsurance

Munich Reinsurance Company of Canada
390 Bay St., 22nd Fl.
Toronto, ON M5H 2Y2
Tel: 416-366-9206; *Fax:* 416-366-4330
Toll-Free: 800-444-5321
www.mroc.com
Classes of Insurance: Auto, Liability, Property, Theft

Municipal Insurance Association of British Columbia (MIA)
#390, 1050 Homer St.
Vancouver, BC V6E 2W9
Tel: 604-683-6266; *Fax:* 604-683-6244
info@miabc.org
www.miabc.org
Classes of Insurance: Liability

MUNIX Reciprocal (MUNIX)
300-8616 51 Ave.
Edmonton, AB T6E 6E6
Tel: 780-433-4431; *Fax:* 780-409-4314
www.auma.ca
Classes of Insurance: Liability, Property

The Mutual Fire Insurance Company of British Columbia
#201, 9366 - 200A St.
Langley, BC V1M 4B3
Tel: 604-881-1250; *Fax:* 604-881-1440
www.mutualfirebc.com
Classes of Insurance: Property, Fire

La Mutuelle d'Église de l'Inter-ouest
180, boul. du Mont-Bleu
Gatineau, QC J8Z 3J5
Tél: 819-595-2678

The Nordic Insurance Company of Canada
181 University Ave., 7th Fl.
Toronto, ON M5H 3M7
Tel: 416-941-5151; *Fax:* 416-941-5322
Classes of Insurance: Accident, Legal Expense, Auto, Liability, Boiler & Machinery, Fidelity, Property, Surety

Norfolk Mutual Insurance Company
PO Box 515
33 Park Rd.
Simcoe, ON N3Y 4L5
Tel: 519-426-1294; *Fax:* 519-426-7594
Toll-Free: 800-304-5573
norins@norfolkmutualinsco.on.ca
www.norfolkmutualinsco.on.ca
Classes of Insurance: Auto, Property, Fire

North Bleinheim Mutual Insurance Co.
11 Baird St. North
Bright, ON N0J 1B0
Tel: 519-454-8661; *Fax:* 519-454-8785
Toll-Free: 800-665-6888
north.blenheim@sympatico.ca
www.northblenheim.omia.com
Classes of Insurance: Auto, Liability, Property

North Blenheim Mutual Insurance Company
11 Baird St. North
Bright, ON N0J 1B0
Tel: 519-454-8661; *Fax:* 519-454-8785
Toll-Free: 800-665-6888
info@northblenheim.com
www.northblenheim.ca
Classes of Insurance: Auto, Liability, Property

North Kent Mutual Fire Insurance Company
PO Box 478
29553 St. George St.
Dresden, ON N0P 1M0
Tel: 519-683-4484; *Fax:* 519-683-4509
Toll-Free: 888-736-4705
nkm@northkentmutual.com
www.nkmutual.com
Classes of Insurance: Auto, Liability, Property, Fire, Hail & Crop, Theft

The North Waterloo Farmers Mutual Insurance Company
100 Erb St. East
Waterloo, ON N2J 1L9
Tel: 519-886-4530; *Fax:* 519-746-0222
Toll-Free: 800-265-8813
insurance@nwfm.com
www.nwfm.com
Classes of Insurance: Auto, Liability, Boiler & Machinery, Fidelity, Property, Fire, Hail & Crop

The North West Commercial Travellers' Association of Canada (NWC)
PO Box 336
28 Queen Elizabeth Way
Winnipeg, MB R3C 2H6
Tel: 204-284-8900; *Fax:* 204-284-8909
Toll-Free: 800-665-6928
nwcta@nwcta.com
www.nwcta.com
Classes of Insurance: Life

OdysseyRe - Canadian Branch
#1600, 55 University Ave.
Toronto, ON M5J 2H7
Tel: 416-862-0162; *Fax:* 416-367-3248
www.odysseyre.com
Classes of Insurance: Accident, Aircraft, Auto, Liability, Boiler & Machinery, Property, Fire, Surety, Hail & Crop, Reinsurance

Old Republic Insurance Company of Canada/ L'Ancienne République, Compagnie d'Assurance du Ca
PO Box 557, LCD 1 Stn. LCD 1
100 King St. West
Hamilton, ON L8N 3K9
Tel: 905-523-5936; *Fax:* 905-528-4685
Classes of Insurance: Accident, Aircraft, Auto, Liability, Property, Reinsurance

Omega General Insurance Company
#500, 36 King St. East
Toronto, ON M5C 1E5
Tel: 416-361-1728; *Fax:* 416-361-6113
contactus@omegageneral.com
www.omegageneral.com
Classes of Insurance: Personal Accident & Sickness, Aircraft, Legal Expense, Liability, Boiler & Machinery, Credit, Fidelity, Property, Surety,

Ontario Blue Cross
#610, 185 The West Mall
Toronto, ON M9C 5P1
Tel: 416-626-1447; *Fax:* 416-626-0997
Toll-Free: 800-873-2583
bco.indhealth@ont.bluecross.ca
www.useblue.com
Classes of Insurance: Personal Accident & Sickness

Ontario Mutual Insurance Association
PO Box 3187
1305 Bishop St. North
Cambridge, ON N3H 4S6
Tel: 519-622-9220; *Fax:* 519-622-9227
information@omia.com
www.omia.com
Classes of Insurance: Personal Accident & Sickness, Auto, Property

Ontario School Boards' Insurance Exchange (OSBIE)
91 Westmount Rd.
Guelph, ON N1H 5J2
Tel: 519-767-2182; *Fax:* 519-767-0281
Toll-Free: 800-668-6724
info@osbie.on.ca
www.osbie.on.ca
Classes of Insurance: Auto, Liability, Boiler & Machinery, Property, Fire

Optimum Assurance Agricole inc/ Optimum Farm Insurance Inc.
#422, 25 rue des Forges
Trois-Rivières, QC G9A 6A7
Tel: 819-373-2040; *Fax:* 819-373-2801
www.optimum-general.com
Classes of Insurance: Auto, Property, Fire

Optimum Général inc/ Optimum General Inc.
#1500, 425, boul. de Maisonneuve ouest
Montréal, QC H3A 3G5
Tél: 514-288-8725; *Téléc:* 514-288-0760
www.optimum-general.com
Classes of Insurance: Auto, Liability, Property

Optimum Reassurance Company
#1200, 425, boul. de Maisonneuve ouest
Montréal, QC H3A 3G5
Tél: 514-288-1900; *Téléc:* 514-288-8099
www.optimumre.ca
Classes of Insurance: Accident, Personal Accident & Sickness, Life, Reinsurance

Optimum Société d'Assurance inc (OSA)/ Optimum Insurance Company Inc.
#1500, 425, boul. de Maisonneuve ouest
Montréal, QC H3A 3G5
Tel: 514-288-8711; *Fax:* 514-288-8269
Classes of Insurance: Auto, Liability, Property

The Order of United Commercial Travelers of America (UCT)
#300, 901 Centre St. North
Calgary, AB T2E 2P6
Tel: 403-277-0745; *Fax:* 403-277-6662
Toll-Free: 800-267-2371
www.uct.org
Classes of Insurance: Personal Accident & Sickness, Life

Ordre des Architectes du Québec
1825, boul. René-Lévesque ouest
Montréal, QC H3H 1R4
Tel: 514-937-6168; *Fax:* 514-933-0242
Toll-Free: 800-599-6168
info@oaq.com
www.oaq.com

Ordre des dentistes du Québec
625, boul. René-Lévesque ouest, 15e étage
Montréal, QC H3B 1R2
Tel: 514-875-8511; *Fax:* 514-393-9248
Toll-Free: 800-361-4887
www.odq.qc.ca

Oxford Mutual Insurance Company
PO Box 430
RR#4
Thamesford, ON N0M 2M0
Tel: 519-285-2916; *Fax:* 519-285-3099
Toll-Free: 800-461-6933
mail@oxfordmutual.com
www.oxfordmutual.com
Classes of Insurance: Personal Accident & Sickness, Aircraft, Auto, Liability, Boiler & Machinery, Fidelity, Property, Hail & Crop

Pacific Blue Cross
PO Box 7000
4250 Canada Way
Vancouver, BC V6B 4E1
Tel: 604-419-2000; *Fax:* 604-419-2990
Toll-Free: 800-487-3228
www.pac.bluecross.ca
Classes of Insurance: Accident, Personal Accident & Sickness, Life

Pacific Coast Fishermen's Mutual Marine Insurance Company
3757 Canada Way
Burnaby, BC V5G 1G5
Tel: 604-438-4240; *Fax:* 604-438-5756
info@mutualmarine.bc.ca
www.mutualmarine.bc.ca
Other Contact Information: Toll Free (BC only): 1-888-438-4242
Classes of Insurance: Marine

Pafco Insurance Company
#100, 27 Allstate Pkwy.
Markham, ON L3R 5P8
Tel: 905-513-4000; *Fax:* 905-513-4026
Toll-Free: 877-216-6973
contactus@pafco.ca
www.pafco.ca
Classes of Insurance: Auto

Palliser Insurance Company Limited
PO Box 1358
Saskatoon, SK S7H 3N9
Tel: 306-955-4814; *Fax:* 306-955-1317
info@palliserinsurance.com
www.palliserinsurance.com
Classes of Insurance: Hail & Crop

PartnerRe SA
PO Box 166
#2300, 130 King St. West
Toronto, ON M5X 1C7
Tel: 416-861-0033; *Fax:* 416-861-0200
Toll-Free: 800-363-6800
www.partnerre.com
Classes of Insurance: Personal Accident & Sickness, Auto, Life, Property

PC Financial Insurance Agency
2202 Eglinton Ave. East
Toronto, ON M1L 4S8
Toll-Free: 866-660-9035
talktous@homeauto.pcinsurance.ca
www.pcinsurance.ca
Other Contact Information: 1-866-472-2683 (Claims)
Classes of Insurance: Auto, Property

Peace Hills General Insurance Company
#300, 10709 Jasper Ave., 3rd Fl.
Edmonton, AB T5J 3N3
Tel: 780-424-3986; *Fax:* 780-424-0396
Toll-Free: 800-272-5614
phi@peacehillsinsurance.com
www.peacehillsinsurance.com
Classes of Insurance: Accident, Aircraft, Auto, Liability, Boiler & Machinery, Credit, Marine, Fidelity, Property, Fire, Surety, Theft,

Peel Maryborough Mutual Insurance Company
PO Box 190
103 Wellington St.
Drayton, ON N0G 1P0
Tel: 519-638-3304; *Fax:* 519-638-3521
Toll-Free: 800-265-2473
pmmutual@pmmutual.on.ca
www.pmmutual.on.ca

Peel Mutual Insurance Company
103 Queen St. West
Brampton, ON L6Y 1M3
Tel: 905-451-2386
info@peelmutual.com
www.peelmutual.com
Classes of Insurance: Auto, Liability, Boiler & Machinery, Fidelity, Property

Pembridge Insurance Company
#100, 27 Allstate Pkwy.
Markham, ON L3R 5P8
Tel: 905-513-4013; *Fax:* 905-513-4020
Toll-Free: 877-736-2743
www.pembridge.com
Classes of Insurance: Accident, Marine, Property

Penncorp Life Insurance Company
7150 Derrycrest Dr.
Mississauga, ON L5W 0E5
Fax: 905-795-2316
Toll-Free: 800-268-2835
cs@penncorp.ca
www.penncorp.ca
Classes of Insurance: Personal Accident & Sickness, Life

The Personal General Insurance Inc./ La Personnelle, assurances générales inc.
PO Box 3500
6300, boul. de la Rive-Sud
Lévis, QC G6V 6P9
Tel: 418-835-9040; *Fax:* 418-835-5599
Toll-Free: 800-463-6416
info@lapersonnelle.com
www.lapersonnelle.com
Classes of Insurance: Auto, Liability, Boiler & Machinery, Property, Surety

The Personal Insurance Company/ La Personnelle, compagnie d'assurances
PO Box 3500
6300, boul. de la Rive-Sud
Lévis, QC G6V 6P9
Tel: 905-306-3350; *Fax:* 418-835-5599
Toll-Free: 800-268-2620
www.thepersonal.com
Classes of Insurance: Personal Accident & Sickness, Aircraft, Auto, Liability, Boiler & Machinery, Fidelity, Property, Surety

Perth Insurance Company
#1600, 5700 Yonge St.
Toronto, ON M2M 4K2
Tel: 416-590-0038; *Toll-Free:* 800-268-8801
www.economicalinsurance.com
Classes of Insurance: Auto, Property

Pictou Mutual Insurance Company
PO Box 130
368 Faulkland St.
Pictou, NS B0K 1H0
Tel: 902-485-4542; *Fax:* 902-485-5136
Toll-Free: 888-485-4542
info@pictoumutual.com
www.pictoumutual.com
Classes of Insurance: Liability, Property

Pilot Insurance Company
2206 Eglinton Ave. East
Toronto, ON M1L 4S8
Tel: 416-288-1800; *Fax:* 416-288-5888
Toll-Free: 800-387-4518
www.avivacanada.com
Classes of Insurance: Auto, Property,

The PMI Group, Inc. Canada
520 Coronation Dr.
Toronto, ON M1E 5C7
Tel: 416-286-2176
www.pmicgroupinc.ca
Classes of Insurance: Credit

The Portage La Prairie Mutual Insurance Company
PO Box 340
749 Saskatchewan Ave. East
Portage La Prairie, MB R1N 3B8
Tel: 204-857-3415; *Fax:* 204-239-6655
Toll-Free: 800-567-7721
info@portagemutual.com
www.portagemutual.com
Classes of Insurance: Legal Expense, Auto, Liability, Property

Premier Marine Insurance Managers Group
#650, 625 Howe St.
Vancouver, BC V6C 2T6
Tel: 604-669-5211; *Fax:* 604-669-2667
www.premiermarine.com
Classes of Insurance: Liability, Marine, Property

Primerica Life Insurance Company of Canada
Plaza V
#300, 2000 Argentia Rd.
Mississauga, ON L5N 2R7
Tel: 905-812-2900; *Fax:* 905-813-5310
Toll-Free: 800-387-7876
www.primericacanada.ca
Classes of Insurance: Personal Accident & Sickness, Life

Primmum Insurance Company/ Primmum compagnie d'assurance
999, boul. de Maisonneuve ouest, 3e étage
Montréal, QC H3A 3L4
Tel: 514-954-2463; *Fax:* 514-874-0463
Toll-Free: 866-454-8911
www.primmum.com
Classes of Insurance: Auto, Property

Prince Edward Island Mutual Insurance Company
201 Water St.
Summerside, PE C1N 1B4
Tel: 902-436-2185; *Fax:* 902-436-0148
Toll-Free: 800-565-5441
protect@peimutual.com
www.peimutual.com
Classes of Insurance: Liability, Property, Fire, Theft

Principal Life Insurance Company/ Compagnie d'assurance-vie Principal
c/o John Milnes & Associates
1300 Bay St., 4th Fl.
Toronto, ON M5R 3K8
Tel: 416-964-0067; *Fax:* 416-964-3338
www.principal.com
Classes of Insurance: Personal Accident & Sickness, Life

Progressive Casualty Insurance Company
#1500-28, 5650 Yonge St.
Toronto, ON M2M 4G3
Tel: 416-499-6599; *Fax:* 416-499-7478
www.progressive.com
Classes of Insurance: Auto, Liability, Property, Surety

Promutuel Réassurance
1091, Grande Allée ouest
Québec, QC G1S 1Y7
Tel: 418-683-1212; *Fax:* 418-683-2559
Toll-Free: 800-463-4888
sylvain.fauchon@promutuel.ca
www.promutuel.ca
Classes of Insurance: Accident, Liability, Boiler & Machinery, Property, Fire, Surety, Theft, Reinsurance

Promutuel Vie inc
1091, Grande Allée ouest
Québec, QC G1S 4Y7
Tel: 418-683-1212; *Fax:* 418-683-2559
federation@promutuel.ca
www.promutuel.ca
Classes of Insurance: Accident, Personal Accident & Sickness, Life

Protective Insurance Company
c/o John Milnes & Associates
1300 Bay St., 4th Fl.
Toronto, ON M5R 3K8
Tel: 416-964-0067; *Fax:* 416-964-3338
www.protective.com
Classes of Insurance: Personal Accident & Sickness, Auto, Liability, Property

Québec Blue Cross/ Croix Bleue du Québec
#B9, 550, rue Sherbrooke ouest
Montréal, QC H3C 3S3
Tel: 514-286-8403; *Fax:* 514-286-8358
Toll-Free: 877-909-7686
info@qc.bluecross.ca, info@qc.croixbleue.ca
www.qc.bluecross.ca, www.qc.croixbleue.ca

Classes of Insurance: Accident, Personal Accident & Sickness, Auto, Liability, Life

Rain and Hail Insurance Corporation
#200, 4303 Albert St.
Regina, SK S4S 3R6
Tel: 306-584-8844; *Fax:* 306-584-3466
Toll-Free: 800-667-8084
regina@rainhail.com
www.rainhail.com/about/canada.htm
Classes of Insurance: Hail & Crop

RBC General Insurance Company/ Compagnie d'assurance generale RBC
6880 Financial Dr.
Mississauga, ON L5N 7Y5
Tel: 905-816-2452; *Fax:* 905-816-2450
Toll-Free: 800-769-2526
www.rbcinsurance.com
Classes of Insurance: Personal Accident & Sickness, Auto, Liability, Property, Fire, Theft

RBC Insurance
Tower 1
6880 Financial Dr.
Mississauga, ON L5N 7Y5
Tel: 905-949-3663; *Fax:* 905-813-4853
Toll-Free: 877-749-7224
www.rbcinsurance.com
Classes of Insurance: Personal Accident & Sickness, Auto, Life, Property

RBC Life Insurance Company
West Tower
6880 Financial Dr.
Mississauga, ON L5N 7Y5
Tel: 905-606-1473; *Fax:* 905-813-4850
Toll-Free: 877-519-9501
www.rbcinsurance.com
Other Contact Information: 866-223-7113 (Toll Free, New Life Insurance Inquiries); 800-461-1413 (Toll Free, Existing Life Insurance Inquiries)
Classes of Insurance: Personal Accident & Sickness, Life

RBC Travel Insurance Company
West Tower
6880 Financial Dr., 5th Fl.
Mississauga, ON L5N 7Y5
Tel: 905-816-2452; *Fax:* 905-813-4850
www.rbcinsurance.com/travel
Other Contact Information: Toll Free, Trip Cancellation Insurance Claim: 800-387-2487; Mail Address, Trip Cancellation Insurance Claim: PO Box 97, Stn. A, Mississauga, L5A 2Y9
Classes of Insurance: Personal Accident & Sickness, Life

Real Estate Insurance Exchange (REIX)
#205, 4954 Richard Rd. SW
Calgary, AB T3E 6L1
Tel: 403-228-2667; *Fax:* 403-229-3466
Toll-Free: 877-462-7349
info@reix.ca
www.reix.ca
Classes of Insurance: Liability

Red River Valley Mutual Insurance Co.
PO Box 940
245 Centre Ave. East
Altona, MB R0G 0B0
Tel: 204-324-6434; *Fax:* 204-324-1316
Toll-Free: 800-370-2888
info@redrivermutual.com
www.redrivermutual.com
Classes of Insurance: Liability, Boiler & Machinery, Fidelity, Property, Fire, Surety, Theft

Reliable Life Insurance Company
PO Box 557
100 King St. West
Hamilton, ON L8N 3K9
Tel: 905-523-5587; *Fax:* 905-522-7211
Toll-Free: 800-465-0661
service@reliablelifeinsurance.com
www.reliablelifeinsurance.com
Classes of Insurance: Personal Accident & Sickness, Life

ReliaStar Life Insurance Company/ Compagnie d'Assurance-Vie ReliaStar
c/o D.M. Williams & Assoc. Ltd.
#201, 3650 Victoria Park Ave.
Toronto, ON M2H 3P7
Tel: 416-496-1148
www.ing.com/us/reliastar
Classes of Insurance: Personal Accident & Sickness, Life

Revios Reinsurance
#1600, 480 University Ave.
Toronto, ON M5G 1V6
Tel: 416-598-4677; *Fax:* 416-599-6390
Classes of Insurance: Aircraft, Auto, Liability, Boiler & Machinery, Credit, Marine, Fidelity, Property, Fire, Surety, Hail & Crop

RGA Life Reinsurance Company of Canada/ RGA Compagnie de réassurance-vie du Canada
#1100, 55 University Ave.
Toronto, ON M5J 2H7
Tel: 416-682-0000; *Fax:* 416-777-9526
Toll-Free: 800-433-4326
www.rgare.com/global/canada.asp
Classes of Insurance: Reinsurance

Royal & SunAlliance Insurance Company of Canada
10 Wellington St. East
Toronto, ON M5E 1L5
Tel: 416-366-7511; *Fax:* 416-367-9869
Toll-Free: 800-268-8406
www.royalsunalliance.ca
Classes of Insurance: Property

St. Paul Guarantee Insurance Company
PO Box 6
#300, 20 Queen St. West
Toronto, ON M5H 3R3
Tel: 416-360-8183; *Fax:* 416-360-8267
www.stpaulguarantee.com
Other Contact Information: Toll Free: 1-800-387-1581, 1-800-330-5033
Classes of Insurance: Surety

Saskatchewan Auto Fund
2260 - 11th Ave.
Regina, SK S4P 0J9
Tel: 306-751-1200; *Fax:* 306-565-8666
www.sgi.sk.ca
Classes of Insurance: Auto

Saskatchewan Blue Cross
PO Box 4030
516 - 2nd Ave. North
Saskatoon, SK S7K 3T2
Tel: 306-244-2662; *Fax:* 306-652-5751
Toll-Free: 800-667-6853
www.sk.bluecross.ca
Classes of Insurance: Personal Accident & Sickness, Life

Saskatchewan Crop Insurance Corporation
PO Box 3000
484 Prince William Dr.
Melville, SK S0A 2P0
Tel: 306-728-7200; *Fax:* 306-728-7268
Toll-Free: 888-935-0000
customer.service@scic.gov.sk.ca
www.saskcropinsurance.com
Classes of Insurance: Hail & Crop

Saskatchewan Motor Club Insurance Company Ltd.
200 Albert St. North
Regina, SK S4R 5E2
Tel: 306-791-4321; *Fax:* 306-949-4461
www.caasask.sk.ca
Classes of Insurance: Accident

Saskatchewan Municipal Hail Insurance Association
2100 Cornwall St.
Regina, SK S4P 2K7
Tel: 306-569-1852; *Fax:* 306-522-3717
Toll-Free: 877-414-7644
smhi@smhi.ca
www.smhi.ca
Classes of Insurance: Hail & Crop

Saskatchewan Mutual Insurance Company (SMI)
279 - 3 Ave. North
Saskatoon, SK S7K 2H8
Tel: 306-653-4232; *Fax:* 306-653-3260
Toll-Free: 800-667-3067
headoffice@saskmutual.com
www.saskmutual.com
Classes of Insurance: Auto, Liability, Boiler & Machinery, Fidelity, Property

SCOR Canada Reinsurance Company/ SCOR Canada Compagnie de Réassurance
TD Canada Trust Tower, BCE Place
PO Box 615
#5000, 161 Bay St.
Toronto, ON M5J 2S1
Tel: 416-869-3670; *Fax:* 416-365-9393
Toll-Free: 800-268-8207
ca@scor.com
www.scor.com
Classes of Insurance: Reinsurance

SCOR Vie/ SCOR Life - Canada Branch
TD Canada Trust Tower, BCE Place, Succursale du Canada
#5100, 161 Bay St.
Toronto, ON M5J 2S1
Tel: 416-304-6536; *Fax:* 416-304-6574
cavie@scor.com
www.scor.com
Classes of Insurance: Personal Accident & Sickness, Life

Scotia Life Insurance Company/ Scotia-Vie Compagnie d'Assurance
#400, 100 Yonge St.
Toronto, ON M5H 1H1
Tel: 416-866-5412; *Fax:* 416-866-5810
Toll-Free: 800-387-9844
www.scotiabank.com
Classes of Insurance: Personal Accident & Sickness, Life

Scottish & York Insurance Co. Limited
2206 Eglinton Ave. East
Toronto, ON M1L 4S8
Tel: 416-288-1800; *Fax:* 416-288-5888
Toll-Free: 800-387-4518
info@avivacanada.com
www.avivacanada.com
Classes of Insurance: Legal Expense, Auto, Liability, Boiler & Machinery, Fidelity, Property, Surety

SecuriCan General Insurance Company
#200, 1200 Portage Ave.
Winnipeg, MB R3G 0T5
Toll-Free: 800-431-3132
info@securican.ca
www.securican.ca
Classes of Insurance: Personal Accident & Sickness

Security National Insurance Company/ Sécurité Nationale compagnie d'assurance
50, Place Crémazie, 12e étage
Montréal, QC H2P 1B6
Tel: 514-382-6060; *Fax:* 514-385-2162
Toll-Free: 800-361-3821
www.melochemonnex.com
Classes of Insurance: Personal Accident & Sickness, Auto, Property, Fire

SGI CANADA Consolidated
2260 - 11th Ave.
Regina, SK S4P 0J9
Tel: 306-751-1200; *Fax:* 306-565-8666
Toll-Free: 800-667-8015
sgiinquiries@sgi.sk.ca
www.sgi.sk.ca
Classes of Insurance: Accident, Aircraft, Auto, Liability, Boiler & Machinery, Fidelity, Property, Surety, Reinsurance

Société de l'assurance automobile du Québec
CP 19600, Terminus Stn. Terminus
333, boul. Jean-Lesage
Québec, QC G1K 8J6
Tél: 418-643-7620; *Ligne sans frais:* 800-361-7620
www.saaq.gouv.qc.ca
Other Contact Information: Montréal: 514/873-7620
Classes of Insurance: Accident, Auto

Sons of Scotland Benevolent Association
#202, 40 Eglinton Ave. East
Toronto, ON M4P 3A2
Tel: 416-482-1250; *Fax:* 416-482-9576
Toll-Free: 800-387-3382
info@sonsofscotland.com
www.sonsofscotland.com
Classes of Insurance: Life

South Easthope Mutual Insurance Co.
PO Box 33
62 Woodstock St.
Tavistock, ON N0B 2R0
Tel: 519-655-2011; *Fax:* 519-655-2021
seins@seins.on.ca
www.seins.on.ca

Classes of Insurance: Accident, Auto, Boiler & Machinery, Property

Southeastern Mutual Insurance Company
378 Coverdale Rd.
Riverview, NB E1B 3J7
Tel: 506-386-9002; *Fax:* 506-386-3325
Toll-Free: 800-561-7223
www.semutual.nb.ca
Classes of Insurance: Liability, Boiler & Machinery, Property, Fire

The Sovereign General Insurance Company
#140, 6700 Macleod Trail SE
Calgary, AB T2H 0L3
Tel: 403-298-4200; *Fax:* 403-298-4217
Toll-Free: 800-661-1652
www.cooperators.ca; www.sovereigngeneral.com
Classes of Insurance: Personal Accident & Sickness, Property

SSQ Financial Group
PO Box 10500, Sainte-Foy Stn. Sainte-Foy
2525, boul. Laurier
Québec, QC G1V 4H6
Tel: 418-651-7000; *Fax:* 418-688-7791
Toll-Free: 888-900-3457
communications@ssq.ca; mutuallife@ssq.ca
www.ssq.ca
Classes of Insurance: Personal Accident & Sickness, Auto, Life, Theft

SSQ, Société d'assurances générales inc./ SSQ General Insurance Company Inc.
Édifice Le Delta 2
CP 10530
2515, boul. Laurier
Québec, QC G1V 0A5
Tél: 418-683-0554; *Téléc:* 418-683-5603
Ligne sans frais: 800-463-2343
email@ssqgenerale.com
www.ssqgenerale.com
Classes of Insurance: Accident, Auto, Liability, Property, Fire, Theft

SSQ, Société d'assurance-vie inc/ SSQ, Life Insurance Company Inc.
CP 10500
2525, boul. Laurier
Québec, QC G1V 4H6
Tél: 418-651-7000; *Téléc:* 418-652-2739
www.ssq.ca
Classes of Insurance: Accident, Personal Accident & Sickness, Auto, Liability, Life, Property, Fire

The Standard Life Assurance Company of Canada
1245, rue Sherbrooke ouest, 17e étage
Montréal, QC H3G 1G3
Tel: 514-499-6844; *Fax:* 514-499-4466
Toll-Free: 888-841-6633
csc@standardlife.ca; information@standardlife.ca
www.standardlife.ca
Other Contact Information: Media Inquiries, E-mail: public.relations@standardlife.ca
Classes of Insurance: Personal Accident & Sickness, Life

Stanley Mutual Insurance Company
32 Irishtown Rd.
Stanley, NB E6B 1B6
Tel: 506-367-2273; *Fax:* 506-367-3076
Toll-Free: 800-442-9714
info@stanleymutual.com
www.stanleymutual.com
Classes of Insurance: Auto, Liability, Boiler & Machinery, Property

State Farm Canada
333 First Commerce Dr.
Aurora, ON L4G 8A4
Tel: 905-750-4100
www.statefarm.ca
Classes of Insurance: Aircraft, Auto, Liability, Boiler & Machinery, Fidelity, Property, Fire, Surety

Stewart Financial Services
1282 Cornwall Rd., #B
Oakville, ON L6J 7W5
Tel: 905-845-0990; *Fax:* 905-845-2882
Toll-Free: 888-845-0990
drew@stewartfinancial.ca
www.stewartfinancial.ca

Stewart Title Guaranty Company
North Tower, Royal Bank Plaza
#2200, 200 Bay St.
Toronto, ON M5J 2J2
Tel: 416-307-3300; *Fax:* 416-307-3305
Toll-Free: 888-667-5151
inquirycda@stewart.com
www.stewart.ca

Suecia Reinsurance Company
763 Pape Ave.
Toronto, ON M4K 3T2
Tel: 416-361-0056
Classes of Insurance: Personal Accident & Sickness, Auto, Liability, Fidelity, Property, Hail & Crop, Reinsurance

Sun Life Assurance Company of Canada
Corporate Office
150 King St. West
Toronto, ON M5H 1J9
Tel: 416-979-9966; *Fax:* 416-979-4853
corp_website@sunlife.com
www.sunlife.ca
Classes of Insurance: Personal Accident & Sickness, Life

Sun Life Financial Inc.
150 King St. West
Toronto, ON M5H 1J9
Tel: 416-979-9966; *Fax:* 416-979-4853
www.sunlife.com
Classes of Insurance: Life

Supreme Council of the Royal Arcanum
PO Box 990
#400, 21 King St. West
Hamilton, ON L8N 3R1
Tel: 905-528-8411; *Toll-Free:* 888-272-2686
www.royalarcanum.com
Classes of Insurance: Personal Accident & Sickness, Life

La Survivance, compagnie mutuelle d'assurance vie
CP 10 000
1555, rue Girouard ouest
Saint-Hyacinthe, QC J2S 7C8
Tél: 450-773-6051; *Téléc:* 450-773-6470
Ligne sans frais: 800-773-8404
info@lasurvivance.com
www.lasurvivance.com; www.lsmutual.com
Classes of Insurance: Personal Accident & Sickness, Life

Swiss Re Frankona Rückversicherungs-Aktiengesellschaft
#1000, 150 King St. West
Toronto, ON M5H 1J9
Tel: 416-814-2272; *Fax:* 416-364-7308
Classes of Insurance: Personal Accident & Sickness, Life

Swiss Reinsurance Company Canada
PO Box 50
#2200, 150 King St. West
Toronto, ON M5H 1J9
Tel: 416-408-0272; *Fax:* 416-408-4222
Toll-Free: 800-268-7116
www.swissre.com
Classes of Insurance: Marine, Fidelity, Property, Surety, Reinsurance

TD General Insurance Company
c/o Meloche Monnex Inc.
50, Place Crémazie, 12e étage
Montréal, QC H2P 1B6
www.tdcanadatrust.com/tdinsurance
Classes of Insurance: Personal Accident & Sickness, Aircraft, Auto, Liability, Boiler & Machinery, Fidelity, Property, Surety

TD Home & Auto Insurance Company/ Compagnie d'Assurance Habitation et Auto TD
2161 Yonge St., 4th Fl.
Toronto, ON M4S 3A6
Toll-Free: 800-338-0218
www.tdcanadatrust.com/tdinsurance, www.mytdigroup.com
Other Contact Information: 866-955-5558 (Toll Free, Quotes); 866-322-5854 (Toll Free, Client Services); 866-482-1919 (Toll Free, Claims)
Classes of Insurance: Auto, Liability, Property

TD Life Insurance Company/ TD, Compagnie d'assurance-vie
120 Adelaide St. West, 2nd Fl.
Toronto, ON M5H 1T1
Tel: 416-982-3006; *Fax:* 416-944-5859
Toll-Free: 877-397-4187
TD.InsuranceLifeAndHealth@td.com
www.tdcanadatrust.com/tdinsurance/life
Classes of Insurance: Personal Accident & Sickness, Life

Temple Insurance Company
390 Bay St., 20nd Fl.
Toronto, ON M5H 2Y2
Tel: 416-364-2851; *Fax:* 416-361-1163
Toll-Free: 877-364-2851
www.templeinsurance.ca
Classes of Insurance: Boiler & Machinery, Property

Thomson-Schindle-Green Insurance & Financial Services Ltd.
Chinook Place
#100, 623 - 4th St. SE
Medicine Hat, AB T1A 0L1
Tel: 403-526-3283; *Fax:* 403-526-8082
Toll-Free: 800-830-9423
tsg@tsginsurance.com
www.tsginsurance.com
Classes of Insurance: Auto, Liability, Life, Property, Hail & Crop

The Toa Reinsurance Company of America
PO Box 17
#2420, 401 Bay St.
Toronto, ON M5H 2Y4
Tel: 416-366-5888; *Fax:* 416-366-7444
info@toare.com
www.toare.com
Classes of Insurance: Reinsurance

The Tokio Marine & Nichido Fire Insurance Co., Ltd.
c/o Lombard Canada Ltd.
105 Adelaide St. West
Toronto, ON M5H 1P9
Tel: 416-350-4400; *Fax:* 416-350-4412
Classes of Insurance: Auto, Marine, Property, Fire

Town & Country Mutual Insurance
79 Caradoc St. North
Strathroy, ON N7G 2M5
Tel: 519-246-1132; *Fax:* 519-246-1115
Toll-Free: 888-868-5064
info@town-country-ins.ca
www.town-country-ins.ca
Classes of Insurance: Personal Accident & Sickness, Auto, Liability, Boiler & Machinery, Fidelity, Property, Hail & Crop

Townsend Farmers' Mutual Fire Insurance Company
Waterford Place Plaza
PO Box 1030
Waterford, ON N0E 1Y0
Tel: 519-443-7231; *Fax:* 519-443-5198
Toll-Free: 888-302-6052
farmins@townsendfarmers.com
www.townsendfarmers.com
Classes of Insurance: Personal Accident & Sickness, Auto, Liability, Boiler & Machinery, Property, Hail & Crop

Traders General Insurance Company/ Compagnie d'Assurance Traders Générale
2206 Eglinton Ave. East
Toronto, ON M1L 4S8
Tel: 416-288-1800; *Fax:* 416-288-5888
Toll-Free: 800-387-4518
info@avivacanada.com
www.avivacanada.com
Classes of Insurance: Auto, Property

Tradition Mutual Insurance Company
PO Box 10
264 Huron Rd.
Sebringville, ON N0K 1X0
Tel: 519-393-6402; *Fax:* 519-393-5185
Toll-Free: 800-263-1961
www.traditionmutual.com
Classes of Insurance: Accident, Auto, Liability, Boiler & Machinery, Fidelity, Property, Hail & Crop

Trans Global Insurance Company (TGI)
c/o Fraser Milner Cosgrain LLP, First Canadian Place
100 King St. West, 42nd Fl.
Toronto, ON T5X 1B2
Tel: 416-862-3418; *Fax:* 416-863-4592
Classes of Insurance: Personal Accident & Sickness, Liability, Property

Trans Global Life Insurance Company (TGLI)
c/o Fraser Milner Cosgrain LLP, First Canadian Place
100 King St. West, 42nd Fl.
Toronto, ON M5X 1B2
Tel: 416-862-3418; *Fax:* 416-863-4592
Classes of Insurance: Personal Accident & Sickness, Life

Transamerica Life Canada
5000 Yonge St.
Toronto, ON M2N 7J8
Tel: 416-883-5000; *Fax:* 416-883-5012
webmaster.canada@aegoncanada.ca
www.transamerica.ca
Classes of Insurance: Personal Accident & Sickness, Life

Transatlantic Reinsurance Company
145 Wellington St. West
Toronto, ON M5J 1H8
Tel: 416-596-3960; *Fax:* 416-971-8782
www.transre.com
Classes of Insurance: Personal Accident & Sickness, Credit, Property, Surety, Reinsurance

Travelers - Canada
PO Box 5
#200, 20 Queen St. West
Toronto, ON M5H 3R3
Tel: 416-366-8301; *Fax:* 416-366-0846
Toll-Free: 800-268-8481
www.travelerscanada.ca
Classes of Insurance: Aircraft, Auto, Liability, Boiler & Machinery, Marine, Fidelity, Property, Fire, Surety, Reinsurance

Trillium Mutual Insurance Company
1078 Bruce Rd. 12
Formosa, ON N0G 1W0
Tel: 519-367-5600; *Fax:* 519-367-5681
Toll-Free: 800-265-3020
admin@trilliummutual.com
www.trilliummutual.com
Classes of Insurance: Accident, Auto, Liability, Boiler & Machinery, Marine, Fidelity, Property, Hail & Crop

Trisura Guarantee Insurance Company
#1100, 70 York St.
Toronto, ON M5J 1S9
Tel: 416-214-2555; *Fax:* 416-214-9597
info@trisura.com
www.trisura.com
Classes of Insurance: Liability, Surety

Ukrainian Fraternal Association of America (UFA)
c/o Burns Hubley
#406, 2800 - 14 Ave.
Markham, ON L3R 0E4
Tel: 416-495-1755; *Fax:* 416-495-1838
Classes of Insurance: Life

Ukrainian Fraternal Society of Canada
235 McGregor St.
Winnipeg, MB R2W 4W5
Tel: 204-586-4482; *Fax:* 204-589-6411
Toll-Free: 800-988-8372
Classes of Insurance: Life,

Ukrainian Mutual Benefit Association of St. Nicholas of Canada
804 Selkirk Ave.
Winnipeg, MB R2W 2N6
Tel: 204-582-4882; *Fax:* 204-586-2095
Toll-Free: 866-582-4882
umbaofsn@mts.net
www.ukrainianmutual.com
Classes of Insurance: Personal Accident & Sickness, Life

Ukrainian National Association (UNA)
c/o Burns Hubley LLP
#406, 2800 - 14 Ave.
Markham, ON L3R 0E4
Tel: 416-495-1755; *Fax:* 416-495-1838
www.unamember.com
Classes of Insurance: Personal Accident & Sickness, Life

Unifund Assurance Company
PO Box 12049
95 Elizabeth Ave.
St. John's, NL A1B 1R7
Tel: 709-737-1500; *Fax:* 709-737-1580
unifund@johnson.ca
www.unifund.ca
Classes of Insurance: Auto, Property

L'Union Canadienne Compagnie d'Assurances
2475, boul. Laurier
Québec, QC G1T 1C4
Tel: 418-651-3551; *Toll-Free:* 800-463-3382
www.unioncanadienne.com
Classes of Insurance: Auto, Property

Union of Canada Life Insurance
PO Box 717, B Stn. B
325 Dalhousie St.
Ottawa, ON K1P 5P8
Tel: 613-241-3660; *Fax:* 613-241-7880
Toll-Free: 877-966-6676
union@on.aira.com
www.ucav.ca
Classes of Insurance: Accident, Life

L'Union-Vie, compagnie mutuelle d'assurance/ The Union Life, Mutual Assurance Company
CP 696
142, rue Hériot
Drummondville, QC J2B 6W9
Tél: 819-478-1315; *Téléc:* 819-474-1990
Ligne sans frais: 800-567-0988
www.union-vie.qc.ca
Classes of Insurance: Personal Accident & Sickness, Life, Reinsurance

United American Insurance Company (UA)
c/o McLean & Kerr LLP
#2800, 130 Adelaide St. West
Toronto, ON M5H 3P5
Tel: 416-369-6624; *Fax:* 416-366-8571
www.unitedamerican.com
Classes of Insurance: Personal Accident & Sickness, Life

United General Insurance Corporation
860 Prospect St.
Fredericton, NB E3B 2T8
Tel: 506-459-5120; *Fax:* 506-453-0882
don.dougherty@ugic.nb.ca
Classes of Insurance: Auto

Unity Life of Canada
#400, 100 Milverton Dr.
Mississauga, ON L5R 4H1
Tel: 905-219-8000; *Fax:* 905-219-8121
Toll-Free: 800-267-8777
info@unitylife.ca
www.unitylife.ca
Classes of Insurance: Personal Accident & Sickness, Life

Usborne & Hibbert Mutual Fire Insurance Company
507 Main St. South
Exeter, ON N0M 1S1
Tel: 519-235-0350; *Fax:* 519-235-3623
usborne@on.aibn.com
www.usborne-ins.com

Virginia Surety Company, Inc. (VCS)/ Compagnie de Sûreté Virginia Inc.
#201, 3650 Victoria Park Ave.
Toronto, ON M2H 3P7
www.thewarrantygroup.com
Classes of Insurance: Auto, Liability, Boiler & Machinery, Property

Wabisa Mutual Insurance Company
PO Box 621
35 Talbot St. East
Jarvis, ON N0A 1J0
Tel: 519-587-4454; *Fax:* 519-587-5470
wabisa@mountaincable.net
www.wabisa.omia.com
Classes of Insurance: Personal Accident & Sickness, Auto, Liability, Fidelity, Property

Waterloo Insurance Company
590 Riverbend Dr.
Kitchener, ON N2K 3S2
Tel: 519-570-8335; *Fax:* 519-570-8312
Toll-Free: 800-265-4562
www.economicalinsurance.com
Classes of Insurance: Auto, Property

The Wawanesa Life Insurance Company
#200, 191 Broadway
Winnipeg, MB R3C 3P1
Tel: 204-985-3940; *Fax:* 204-985-3872
Toll-Free: 800-263-6785
life@wawanesa.com
www.wawanesalife.com
Classes of Insurance: Personal Accident & Sickness, Life

The Wawanesa Mutual Insurance Company
#900, 191 Broadway
Winnipeg, MB R3C 3P1
Tel: 204-985-3923; *Fax:* 204-942-7724
www.wawanesa.com
Classes of Insurance: Auto, Liability, Boiler & Machinery, Property, Fire, Surety, Theft

Wedgwood Insurance Limited
PO Box 13370, A Stn. A
85 Thorburn Rd.
St. John's, NL A1B 4B7
Tel: 709-753-3210; *Fax:* 709-753-8238
Toll-Free: 800-706-2676
www.wedgwoodinsurance.com
Classes of Insurance: Aircraft, Auto, Life, Marine, Property

West Elgin Mutual Insurance Company
PO Box 130
274 Currie Rd.
Dutton, ON N0L 1J0
Tel: 519-762-3530; *Fax:* 519-762-3801
Toll-Free: 800-265-7635
info@westelgin.com
www.westelgin.com
Classes of Insurance: Personal Accident & Sickness, Auto, Liability, Fidelity, Property, Hail & Crop

West Wawanosh Mutual Insurance Company
PO Box 130
81 Southampton St., RR#1
Dungannon, ON N0M 1R0
Tel: 519-529-7921; *Fax:* 519-529-3211
Toll-Free: 800-265-5595
wawains@wwmic.com
www.wwmic.com
Classes of Insurance: Personal Accident & Sickness, Auto, Liability, Boiler & Machinery, Fidelity, Property

Western Assurance Company
Sheridan Insurance Centre
#1000, 2225 Erin Mills Pkwy.
Mississauga, ON L5K 2S9
Tel: 905-403-3318; *Fax:* 905-403-3319
Toll-Free: 877-263-4442
www.royalsunalliance.ca
Classes of Insurance: Personal Accident & Sickness, Aircraft, Auto, Liability, Boiler & Machinery, Marine, Fidelity, Property, Surety

Western Financial Group Inc.
1010 - 24 St. SE
High River, AB T1V 2A7
Tel: 403-652-2663; *Fax:* 403-652-2661
Toll-Free: 866-843-9378
info@westernfinancialgroup.net
www.westernfinancialgroup.net
Classes of Insurance: Accident, Personal Accident & Sickness, Auto, Liability, Boiler & Machinery, Life, Fidelity, Property, Fire, Surety, Hail & Crop, Theft

Western Life Assurance Company
1010 24th St. SE
High River, AB T1V 2A7
Tel: 403-652-2663; *Fax:* 403-652-2673
Toll-Free: 866-843-9378
info@westernlife.com
www.westernlifeassurance.net
Classes of Insurance: Personal Accident & Sickness, Life

Western Surety Company
PO Box 527
#2000, 1874 Scarth St.
Regina, SK S4P 2G8
Tel: 306-791-3735; *Fax:* 306-359-0929
Toll-Free: 800-475-4454
wscinfo@westernsurety.ca
www.westernsurety.ca
Classes of Insurance: Fidelity, Surety

Westland Insurance
#300, 5455 152nd St.
Surrey, BC V3S 5A5
Tel: 604-543-7788; *Toll-Free:* 800-899-3093
contactus@westland-insurance.com
www.westland-insurance.com
Classes of Insurance: Auto, Liability, Property

Westminster Mutual Insurance Company
14122 Belmont Rd.
Belmont, ON N0L 1B0
Tel: 519-644-1663; *Fax:* 519-644-0315
Toll-Free: 800-565-3523
westminster@westminstermutual.com
www.westminstermutual.com
Classes of Insurance: Auto, Liability, Property

Woman's Life Insurance Society
PO Box 234
1455 Lakeshore Rd.
Sarnia, ON N7S 2M4
Tel: 519-542-2826; *Fax:* 810-985-6970
Toll-Free: 800-521-9292
www.womanslifeins.com
Classes of Insurance: Life

XL Insurance Company Limited (XL)
#1802, 100 Yonge St.
Toronto, ON M5C 2W1
Tel: 416-928-5586; *Fax:* 416-928-8858
www.xlinsurance.com
Classes of Insurance: Personal Accident & Sickness, Auto, Liability, Boiler & Machinery, Property, Surety

XL Reinsurance America Inc.
Scotia Plaza
#1702, 100 Yonge St.
Toronto, ON M5C 2W1
Tel: 416-598-1084; *Fax:* 416-598-1980
www.xlre.com
Classes of Insurance: Personal Accident & Sickness, Aircraft, Auto, Liability, Boiler & Machinery, Fidelity, Property, Surety, Hail & Crop

Yarmouth Mutual Fire Insurance Company
1229 Talbot St. East
St Thomas, ON N5P 1G9
Tel: 519-631-1572; *Fax:* 519-631-6058
office@yarmouth-ins.com
www.yarmouth-ins.com
Classes of Insurance: Auto, Liability, Property, Hail & Crop

York Fire & Casualty Insurance Company
#400, 7120 Hurontario St.
Mississauga, ON L5W 0B2
Tel: 905-677-9777; *Toll-Free:* 800-676-0967
yfmarketing@york-fire.com
www.york-fire.com
Classes of Insurance: Auto, Liability, Property

Zenith Insurance Company/ Compagnie d'Assurance Zenith
c/o Lombard Canada Ltd.
105 Adelaide St. West, 3rd Fl.
Toronto, ON M5H 1P9
Tel: 416-350-4400; *Fax:* 416-350-4417
Toll-Free: 888-440-4876
inquiries@zenithinsurance.ca
www.zenithinsurance.ca
Classes of Insurance: Personal Accident & Sickness, Auto, Liability, Property

Zurich Canada
400 University Ave., 25th Fl.
Toronto, ON M5G 1S7
Tel: 416-586-3000; *Fax:* 416-586-2525
Toll-Free: 800-387-5454
zurich.information@zurich.com
www.zurichcanada.com
Classes of Insurance: Accident, Personal Accident & Sickness, Auto, Liability, Boiler & Machinery, Credit, Marine, Fidelity, Property, Fire, Surety, Theft,

Major Companies

Agriculture

AG Growth Income Fund
1301 Kenaston Blvd., Winnipeg, MB R3P 2P2
Tel: 204-489-1855; *Fax:* 204-488-6929
www.aggrowth.com
Ticker Symbol: AFN.UN
Company Type: Public
Profile: AG Growth Income Fund is involved in the manufacturing of grain handling, conditioning, & storage equipment. Products include belt conveyors, augers, grain storage bins, & grain aeration equipment.

Bennett Environmental Inc.
#208, 1540 Cornwall Rd., Oakville, ON L6J 7W5
Tel: 905-339-1540; *Fax:* 905-339-0016
Toll-Free: 800-386-1388
info@bennettenv.com
www.bennettenv.com
Ticker Symbol: BEV
Company Type: Public
Profile: The company is engaged in contaminated soil remediation.

James Richardson International
#2800, 1 Lombard Pl., Winnipeg, MB R3B 0X8
Tel: 204-934-5961; *Fax:* 204-942-4161
corporateaffairs@jri.ca
www.jri.ca
Company Type: Private
Profile: Offices of holding companies; Commodity contracts brokers and dealers

Newco Grain Ltd.
PO Box 717, Coaldale, AB T1M 1M6
Fax: 403-345-2040
Toll-Free: 800-661-2312
info@newcograin.com
www.newcograin.com
Company Type: Private
Profile: Newco Grain Ltd. purchases grains from producers throughout western Canada, & distributes these feed products.

Nexia Biotechnologies Inc.
c/o 70 St. George's Cres., Edmonton, AB T5N 3M7
Tel: 780-486-2317; *Fax:* 780-486-9411
www.nexiabiotech.com
Ticker Symbol: NBL
Company Type: Public
Profile: Nexia is involved in transgenic goat husbandry & related research

Ridley Inc.
Ridley Feed Operations, 34 Terracon Pl., Winnipeg, MB R2J 4G7
Tel: 507-388-9400; *Fax:* 507-388-9415
campbell@ridleyinc.com
www.ridleyinc.com
Ticker Symbol: RCL
Company Type: Public
Profile: The commercial animal nutrition company manufactures & distributes animal nutrition products. Products include feeds, supplements, health products, low-moisture blocks, & animal care & livestock handling equipment.

Stolt Sea Farm Inc.
#513, 4100 Yonge St., Toronto, ON M2P 2B5
Tel: 416-221-0404; *Fax:* 416-221-4010
info@stoltseafarm.com
www.stoltseafarm.com
Company Type: Private
Profile: Agricultural production & animal aquaculture; Commercial fishing in fish hatcheries & preserves

Thompsons Limited
2 Hyland Dr., Blenheim, ON N0P 1A0
Tel: 519-676-5411; *Fax:* 519-676-3185
Toll-Free: 800-265-5225
info@thompsonslimited.com
www.thompsonslimited.com
Company Type: Private
Profile: Thompsons Limited is a supplier of agricultural products & farm services to producers throughout Ontario, & a provider of grain handling facilities. Agricultural products include seed, fertilizer, & crop protectants. The company is also engaged in the purchasing, processing, packaging, & shipping of commercial corn, wheat, soybeans, & edible beans to both domestic & export markets.

United Farmers of Alberta Co-Operative Limited
PO Box 5350 A, #700, 4838 Richard Rd. SW, Calgary, AB T2H 2J9
Toll-Free: 866-333-3832
customer.support@ufa.com; grain@ufa.com
www.ufa.net
Company Type: Public
Profile: United Farmers of Alberta Co-Operative Limited has over 35 farm & ranch supply stores & more than 120 petroleum locations throughout Alberta. UFA is also a provider of construction services. The cooperative consists of over 110,000 members. United Farmers of Alberta Co-Operative Limited has an environmental program which involves the education of member-owners about environmentally sustainable farm practices, the replacement of older petroleum systems, the safe storage & distribution of crop-related chemicals, & the establishment of emergency response plans & training programs.

Viterra Inc.
2625 Victoria Ave., Regina, SK S4T 7T9
Tel: 306-569-4411; *Fax:* 306-569-4400
investor@viterra.ca
www.viterra.ca
Ticker Symbol: VT
Company Type: Public
Profile: Viterra is the owner & operator of a large grain handling network. The agri-business is also engaged in livestock, agri-food processing, sales, & financial products. Operations & distribution capabilities are located throughout Canada, as well as in the United States Singapore, & Japan.

Business & Computer Services

20-20 Technologies
#2020, 400 Armand-Frappier Blvd., Laval, QC H7V 4B4
Tel: 514-332-4110; *Fax:* 514-334-6043
investor@2020.net
www.2020technologies.com
Ticker Symbol: TWT
Company Type: Public
Profile: Provider of computer-aided design, sales & manufacturing software for the interior design industry

724 Solutions Inc.
4101 Yonge St., Toronto, ON M2P 1N6
Tel: 416-226-2900; *Fax:* 416-226-4456
www.724.com
Ticker Symbol: SVN
Company Type: Public
Profile: Computer integrated systems design; Prepackaged software; Computer related services

ACD Systems International Inc.
#200, 1312 Blanshard St., Victoria, BC V8W 2J1
Tel: 250-419-6700; *Fax:* 250-419-6745
www.acdcorporate.com
Ticker Symbol: ASA
Company Type: Public
Profile: Image management & technical illustration software

Actuate Corporation
Performance Management Center of Excellence, #600, 150 John St., Toronto, ON M5V 3E3
Tel: 416-537-9336; *Toll-Free:* 800-449-3804
PMinfo@actuate.com
www.actuate.com
Ticker Symbol: ACTU
Company Type: Public
Profile: Actuate provides a full range of Business Intelligence & Reporting Tools (BIRT), professional services, & support.

Aditya Birla Minacs
180 Duncan Mill Rd., 7th Floor, Toronto, ON M3B 1Z6
Tel: 416-380-3800; *Fax:* 416-380-3830
Toll-Free: 888-646-2271
info@minacs.adityabirla.com
www.minacs.adityabirla.com
Ticker Symbol: MXW
Company Type: Public
Profile: Business process outsourcing solutions in the following areas: contact center solutions, transaction & knowledge services, integrated marketing services & IT solutions & services

Adobe Systems Canada Inc.
343 Preston St., Ottawa, ON K1S 1N4
Tel: 613-940-3600; *Fax:* 613-594-8886
Toll-Free: 866-341-2256
info@adobe.com
www.adobe.com/ca
Company Type: Public
Profile: Imaging, design & document technology software

Advanced Micro Devices
1 Commerce Valley Dr. East, Markham, ON L3T 7X6
Tel: 905-882-2600; *Fax:* 905-882-2620
www.amd.com
Ticker Symbol: AMD
Company Type: Public
Profile: Computer integrated systems design; Commercial art & graphic design

Apple Canada Inc.
7495 Birchmount Rd., Markham, ON L3R 5G2
Tel: 905-513-5800; *Fax:* 905-477-8668
www.apple.ca
Company Type: Private
Profile: Computer integrated systems design; computer related services

Averna
#140, 87, rue Prince, Montréal, QC H3C 2M7
Tel: 514-842-7577; *Fax:* 514-842-7573
Toll-Free: 877-842-7577
info@averna.com; sales@averna.com
www.averna.com
Company Type: Public
Profile: The firm is engaged in test engineering. Averna works with OEMs in a variety of industries, in order to deliver solutions that have been tried & tested.

Axia NetMedia Corporation
#3300, 450 - 1st St. SW, Calgary, AB T2P 5H1
Tel: 403-538-4000; *Fax:* 403-538-4100
Toll-Free: 866-773-3348
info@axia.com; sales@axia.com
www.axia.com
Ticker Symbol: AXX
Company Type: Public
Profile: The company is a provider of real broadband Internet Protocol services & solutions. Axia NetMedia plans, designs, develops, & operates Open Access Next Generation Networks.

Belzberg Technologies Inc.
#3400, 40 King St. West, Toronto, ON M5H 3Y2
Tel: 416-360-1812; *Fax:* 416-360-0039
Toll-Free: 800-823-8631
sales@belzberg.com
www.belzberg.com
Ticker Symbol: BLZ
Company Type: Public
Profile: Provider of technology-based brokerage services

Book4golf Corporation
#302, 250 Ferrand Dr., Toronto, ON M3C 3G8
Tel: 416-421-5501; *Fax:* 416-429-8457
info@book4.com
www.book4golf.com
Company Type: Public
Profile: Information retrieval services; Prepackaged software; Travel agencies

Burntsand Inc
#600, 185 The East Mall, Toronto, ON M9C 5L5
Tel: 416-234-3800; *Fax:* 416-234-3801
info@burntsand.com
www.burntsand.com
Ticker Symbol: BRT
Company Type: Public
Profile: Computer integrated systems design

CDC Software
Guinness Tower, #800, 1055 West Hastings St., Vancouver, BC V6E 2E9
Tel: 604-699-8000; *Fax:* 604-699-8001
info@cdcsoftware.com
www.cdcsoftware.com
Company Type: Private
Profile: CDC Software provides enterprise software applications & services. Industries served include healthcare, financial services, & food & beverage.

Cedara Software, a Merge Healthcare Company
6509 Airport Rd., Mississauga, ON L4V 1S7
Tel: 905-672-2100; *Fax:* 905-672-2307
Toll-Free: 800-724-5970
www.cedara.com
Ticker Symbol: CDE
Company Type: Public
Profile: Prepackaged medical imaging software; Computer integrated systems design; Commercial physical & biological research

Certicom Corp.
5520 Explorer Dr., 4th Fl., Mississauga, ON L4W 5L1
Tel: 905-507-4220; *Fax:* 905-507-4230
Toll-Free: 800-561-6100
info@certicom.com
www.certicom.com
Company Type: Public
Profile: Manufacturers of computer peripheral equipment; programming services; integrated systems design

Compugen Systems Ltd.
25 Leek Cres., Richmond Hill, ON L4B 4B3
Tel: 905-707-2000; *Fax:* 905-707-2020
Toll-Free: 800-387-5045
info@compugen.com
www.compugen.com
Company Type: Private
Profile: Information technology service providers; PC systems integrators

Constellation Software Inc.
#1200, 20 Adelaide St. East, Toronto, ON M5C 2T6
Tel: 416-861-2279; *Fax:* 416-861-2287
info@csisoftware.com
www.csisoftware.com
Ticker Symbol: CSU
Company Type: Public
Profile: Constellation Software's area of expertise is the acquisition & management of industry specific software businesses. Specialized software solutions are provided to customers in more than 30 countries.

Corel Corporation
1600 Carling Ave., Ottawa, ON K1Z 8R7
Tel: 613-728-8200; *Fax:* 613-725-2691
Toll-Free: 800-772-6735
www.corel.com
Ticker Symbol: CRE
Company Type: Public
Profile: Software company selling to both consumers & corporations in 75 countries

CryptoLogic Limited
55 St. Clair Ave. West, 3rd Fl., Toronto, ON M4V 2Y7
Tel: 416-545-1455; *Fax:* 416-545-1454
info@cryptologic.com
www.cryptologic.com
Ticker Symbol: CRY
Company Type: Public
Profile: Through its wholly-owned subsidiary, WagerLogic Ltd., CryptoLogic Limited is engaged in online gaming software industry. The company serves the Internet gaming market around the world.

Cyberplex Inc.
#400, 1255 Bay St., Toronto, ON M5R 2A9
Tel: 416-597-8889; *Fax:* 416-597-2345
Toll-Free: 888-597-8889
investor@cyberplex.com
www.cyberplex.com
Ticker Symbol: CX
Company Type: Public
Profile: Web advertising solutions and online customer acquisition strategies

Cybersurf Corp.
#300, 1144 - 29 Ave. NE, Calgary, AB T2E 7P1
Tel: 403-777-2000; *Fax:* 403-777-2003
Toll-Free: 888-858-8958
investor.relations@cybersurf.com
www.cybersurf.com
Company Type: Public
Profile: Computer programming services; Information retrieval services; Computer related services

Dialogic Corporation
9800, boul Cavendish, 5th Fl., Montréal, QC H4M 2V9
Tel: 514-745-5500; *Fax:* 514-745-5588
www.dialogic.com
Company Type: Private
Profile: Prepackaged software; computer related services; manufacturers of computer terminals; IP Solutions

Diversinet Corp.
#1700, 2235 Sheppard Ave. East, Toronto, ON M2J 5B5
Tel: 416-756-2324; *Fax:* 416-756-7346
Toll-Free: 800-357-7050
info@diversinet.com
www.diversinet.com
Company Type: Public
Profile: Solutions for securing and provisioning mobile business applications in healthcare and financial services

Divestco Inc.
#700, 707 - 7th Ave. SW, Calgary, AB T2P 3H6
Tel: 403-237-9170; *Fax:* 403-269-7066
Toll-Free: 888-294-0081
info@divestco.com
www.divestco.com
Ticker Symbol: DVT
Company Type: Public
Profile: Divestco Inc. offers a portfolio of software, data, & consulting products & services. It serves the oil & gas industry.

EMJ, A Technology Solutions Division of SYNNEX
PO Box 1012 Main, Guelph, ON N1H 6N1
Fax: 877-801-6300
Toll-Free: 800-265-7212
info@emj.ca
www.emj.ca
Ticker Symbol: SNX
Company Type: Public
Profile: Niche market hardware and software products, including Auto-ID, Card Technology, Physical Security, Digital Signage, Video and Imaging, Kiosk solutions

Enghouse Systems Limited
#800, 80 Tiverton Ct., Markham, ON L3R 0G4
Tel: 905-946-3200; *Fax:* 905-946-3201
info@enghouse.com
www.enghouse.com
Ticker Symbol: ESL
Company Type: Public
Profile: Enghouse Systems Limited provides enterprise software solutions. The company's divisions include Syntellect & Asset Management. Syntellect specializes in interactive voice response & voice & speech enabled systems. The Asset Management group develops & sells geographic (GIS) based asset management solutions.

Envoy Capital Group Inc.
172 John St., Toronto, ON M5T 1X5
Tel: 416-593-1212; *Fax:* 416-593-4434
Toll-Free: 866-883-6869
info@envoy.to
www.envoy.to
Ticker Symbol: ECG
Company Type: Public
Profile: Advertising agencies; Commercial art & graphic design; Information retrieval services; Computer related services

Epic Data International Inc.
#300, 6300 River Rd., Richmond, BC V6X 1X5
Tel: 604-273-9146; *Fax:* 604-273-1830
Toll-Free: 877-332-3792
info@epicdata.com
www.epicdata.com
Ticker Symbol: EKD
Company Type: Public
Profile: Computer programming services; Prepackaged software

Gemcom Software International Inc.
PO Box 12507, #1100, West Hastings St., Vancouver, BC V6E 3X1
Tel: 604-684-6550; *Fax:* 604-684-3541
info@gemcomsoftware.com
www.gemcomsoftware.com
Company Type: Public
Profile: Gemcom Software International Inc. provides software & professional service solutions to the mining industry. Gemcom's technology & services help mining companies around the world increase productivity.

Hartco Corporation
9393, Louis H. Lafontaine, Montréal, QC H1J 1Y8
Tel: 514-354-3810; *Fax:* 514-354-1998
www.hartco.com
Ticker Symbol: HCI:UN
Company Type: Public
Profile: Computer integrated systems design; retails-computer & computer software stores; retails-miscellaneous retail stores

IBM Cognos
PO Box 9707 T, 3755 Riverside Dr., Ottawa, ON K1G 4K9
Tel: 613-738-1440; *Fax:* 613-738-0002
Toll-Free: 800-267-2777
www.cognos.com
Ticker Symbol: COGN
Company Type: Public
Profile: Business intelligence (BI) and performance planning software

Intrinsyc Software International Inc.
700 West Pender St., 10th Fl., Vancouver, BC V6C 1G8
Tel: 604-801-6461; *Fax:* 604-801-6417
Toll-Free: 800-474-7644
info@intrinsyc.com
www.intrinsyc.com
Ticker Symbol: ICS
Company Type: Public
Profile: Software solutions for mobile and embedded device development, and project management services to clients building wireless devices

L-1 Identity Solutions
505 Cochrane Dr., Markham, ON L3R 8E3
Tel: 905-940-7750; *Fax:* 905-940-7642
www.l1id.com
Ticker Symbol: ID
Company Type: Public
Profile: Security systems services; Patent owners & lessors

LGS Group Inc.
#400, 1300, René-Lévesque ouest, Montréal, QC H3G 2W6
Tel: 514-964-0939; *Fax:* 514-861-4114
infolgsmtl@lgs.com
www.lgs.com
Company Type: Private
Profile: Solutions for portals, content management, data warehousing, business intelligence, corporate and technological architecture, system implementation, security, work organization and change management. Offices in Montréal, Québec and Gatineau

Liquidation World Inc.
225 Henry Street, Brantford, ON N3S 7R4
Tel: 519-758-8878; *Fax:* 866-237-3778
investorinfo@liquidationworld.com
www.liquidationworld.com
Ticker Symbol: LQW
Company Type: Public
Profile: Business services (various)

Logibec Groupe Informatique Ltée
#1500, 700 Wellington St., Montréal, QC H3C 3S4
Tel: 514-766-0134; *Fax:* 514-766-9237
Toll-Free: 877-392-2486
marketing@logibec.com
www.logibec.com
Ticker Symbol: LGI
Company Type: Public
Profile: Logibec develops application software & implements information management systems. Management software is used by the health & social service sector. Related services include end-user training & system maintenance.

MacDonald, Dettwiler & Associates Ltd.
13800 Commerce Pkwy., Richmond, BC V6V 2J3
Tel: 604-278-3411; *Fax:* 604-278-1837
Toll-Free: 888-780-6444
info@mdacorporation.com
www.mdacorporation.com
Ticker Symbol: MDA
Company Type: Public
Profile: The company offers advanced information solutions to capture & process great amounts of data for business & government organizations. Products include tailored information services, complex operational systems, & electronic information products.

Mad Catz Interactive Inc.
Brookfield Place, #2500, 181 Bay St., Toronto, ON M5J 2T7
Tel: 416-368-4449; *Fax:* 416-368-7779
Toll-Free: 800-831-1442
mcz@jcir.com
www.madcatz.com
Ticker Symbol: MCZ
Company Type: Public
Profile: Mad Catz Interactive Inc. is a designer & marketer of accessories for video game systems. The company is also engaged in the publication of video game software. An example of Mad Catz' software is the GameShark brand of video game enhancements.

March Networks
303 Terry Fox Dr., Ottawa, ON K2K 3J1
Tel: 613-591-8181; *Fax:* 613-591-7337
Toll-Free: 800-563-5564
info@marchnetworks.com
www.marchnetworks.com
Ticker Symbol: MN
Company Type: Public
Profile: March Networks Corporation provides IP video software & systems for risk mitigation, loss prevention, & improved security. The company's business analysis applications are used by organizations such as financial institutions, transportation authorities, & retailers. March Networks is ISO-certified.

Maximizer Software Inc.
1090 West Pender St., 10th Fl., Vancouver, BC V6E 2N7
Tel: 604-601-8000; *Fax:* 604-601-8001
Toll-Free: 800-804-6299
info@maximizer.com
www.maximizer.com
Ticker Symbol: MAX
Company Type: Public
Profile: Maximizer Software provides accessible customer relationship management & mobile customer relationship management solutions. The company serves small & medium-sized businesses, as well as divisions of large organizations.

McKesson Canada
8625, rte Transcanadienne, Montréal, QC H4S 1Z6
Tel: 514-725-2100; *Fax:* 514-745-2300
communication@mckesson.ca
www.mckesson.ca
Company Type: Private
Profile: Provider of logistics services, software applications and automation solutions to the Canadian healthcare sector

Mediagrif Interactive Technologies Inc.
Le Bienville Phase III, #800, 1010, rue de Sérigny, Longueuil, QC J4K 5G7
Tel: 450-677-8797; *Fax:* 450-677-4612
info@mediagrif.com
www.mediagrif.com
Ticker Symbol: MDF
Company Type: Public
Profile: Established in 1996, Mediagrif Interactive Technologies Inc. operates e-business networks. Networks include Polygon, The Broker Forum, Telecom Finders, Global Wine & Spirits, & Power Source On-Line. The company's markets include North America, the Middle East, Europe, & Asia.

MediSolution Ltd.
110, boul Cremazie ouest, 10e étage, Montréal, QC H2P 1B9
Tel: 514-850-5000; *Fax:* 514-850-5005
Toll-Free: 800-361-4187
careers@medisolution.com
www.medisolution.com
Company Type: Private
Profile: The information technology company provides ERP software & services to the North American healthcare & service sectors.

Mercer LLC
Brookfield Place, PO Box 501, 161 Bay St., Toronto, ON M5J 2S5
Tel: 416-868-2000; *Fax:* 416-868-7671
www.mercer.com
Company Type: Private
Profile: The firm is engaged in human resources consulting & the provision of related financial advice, products, & services.

Microforum International
1 Woodborough Ave., Toronto, ON M6M 5A1
Tel: 416-657-8548; *Fax:* 416-657-8621
Toll-Free: 866-737-0577
info@microforum.com; fab@microforum.com
www.microforuminternational.com
Company Type: Private
Profile: Microforum International is a developer & publisher of mobile games. Mobile gaming solutions are provided to the following: network operators, handset manufactures, media companies, services providers, & brand owners.

Microsoft Canada Inc.
1950 Meadowvale Blvd., Mississauga, ON L5N 8L9
Tel: 905-568-0434; *Fax:* 905-568-1527
Toll-Free: 877-568-2495
www.microsoft.ca
Company Type: Private
Profile: Microsoft Canada Inc. is a provider of software, services, & Internet technologies for both personal & business computing.

Microtec Enterprises Inc.
4780, rue Saint-Felix, St-Augustin-de-Desmaures, QC G3A 2J9
Toll-Free: 888-864-7918
www.microtec.ca
Company Type: Private
Profile: Microtec is a large residential & commercial security monitoring company.

Mitel Networks Corporation
Corporate Headquarters, 350 Legget Dr., Kanata, ON K2K 2W7
Tel: 613-592-2122; *Fax:* 613-592-4784
Toll-Free: 800-267-6244
www.mitel.com
Company Type: Private
Profile: The organization provides a broad range of communications solutions, from basic business communications to tailored applications. Mitel is present in more than ninety countries.

MKS Inc.
410 Albert St., Waterloo, ON N2L 3V3
Tel: 519-884-2251; *Fax:* 519-884-8861
Toll-Free: 800-265-2797
info@mks.com
www.mks.com
Ticker Symbol: MKX
Company Type: Public
Profile: MKS Inc. is a global application lifecycle management technology company. Through a single enterprise application, the MKS Integrity product enables support for software-related activities & assets.

NBS Technologies Inc.
#400, 703 Evans Ave., Toronto, ON M9C 5E9
Tel: 416-621-1911; *Fax:* 416-621-8875
info@nbstech.com
www.nbstech.com
Ticker Symbol: MIS
Company Type: Public
Profile: NBS Technologies has a worldwide dealer network. Its Smart Card Solutions division develops & manufactures card personalization equipment & software, plus related products & services.

Netgraphe Inc
300, av Viger est, 7e étage, Montréal, QC H2X 3W4
Tel: 514-847-9155; *Fax:* 514-847-9151
info@canoe.quebecor.com
www2.canoe.com
Ticker Symbol: WWW
Company Type: Public
Profile: Information retrieval services; Computer programming services

Northcore Technologies Inc.
#300, 302 The East Mall, Toronto, ON M9B 6C7
Tel: 416-640-0400; *Toll-Free:* 888-287-7467
info@northcore.com
www.northcore.com
Ticker Symbol: NTI
Company Type: Public
Profile: Information retrieval services; Computer programming services; Retailing in miscellaneous stores

Nurun Inc.
711, rue de la Commune ouest, Montréal, QC H3C 1X6
Tel: 514-392-1900; *Fax:* 514-392-0911
Toll-Free: 877-696-1292
montreal@nurun.com
www.nurun.com
Ticker Symbol: IFN
Company Type: Private
Profile: Nurun Inc. is a global interactive marketing agency. Working with a great range of companies & organizations, Nurun executes & measures interactive programs that use technologies.

OnX Enterprise Solutions Inc.
155 Commerce Valley Dr. East, Thornhill, ON L3T 7T2
Tel: 905-482-2292; *Fax:* 905-482-2295
Toll-Free: 866-906-4669
www.onx.com
Ticker Symbol: ON
Company Type: Private
Profile: OnX Enterprise Solutions Ltd. delivers high-impact, vendor neutral IT solutions & services. Offices are located in Canada, the United States, & Europe.

Open Solutions Canada
#200, 13571 Commerce Pkwy., Richmond, BC V6V 2R2
Tel: 604-278-6470; *Fax:* 604-214-4900
www.ca.opensolutions.com
Company Type: Private
Profile: Open Solutions Canada serves the Canadian financial services industry by providing banking system outsourcing. The company designs, builds, integrates, & operates advanced banking & payment technologies. These technologies are used by financial institutions, retailers, independent sales organizations, processing centres, & third-party organizations.

Open Text Connectivity Solutions Group
38 Leek Cres., Richmond Hill, ON L4B 4N8
Tel: 905-762-6400; *Fax:* 905-762-6407
Toll-Free: 877-359-4866
conninfo@opentext.com
connectivity.opentext.com
Company Type: Public
Profile: Designer of computer integrated systems; Wholesaler of computers, peripheral equipment & business software

Open Text Corporation
275 Frank Tompa Dr., Waterloo, ON N2L 0A1
Tel: 519-888-7111; *Fax:* 519-888-0386
Toll-Free: 800-499-6544
sales@opentext.com; support@opentext.com
www.opentext.com
Ticker Symbol: OTC
Company Type: Public
Profile: Open Text Corporation provides Enterprise Content Management solutions to assist organizations manage their information assets.

Optimal Group Inc.
2 Place Alexis Nihon, #800, 3500, boul de Maisonneuve ouest, Montréal, QC H3Z 3C1
Tel: 514-738-8885; *Fax:* 514-738-2284
info@optimalgrp.com
www.optimalgrp.com
Ticker Symbol: OPMR
Company Type: Public
Profile: Operates The Optimal Payments group of companies (secure electronic payment & risk management solutions for businesses delivering goods & services over the Internet); & The WowWee group of companies (technology-based consumer robotic, toy & electronic products)

Optimal Payments
2 Place Alexis Nihon, #700, 3500, boul de Maisonneuve ouest, Montréal, QC H3Z 3C1
Tel: 514-380-2700; *Fax:* 514-380-2760
info@optimalpayments.com
www.optimalpayments.ca
Ticker Symbol: FIR
Company Type: Public
Profile: Customized solutions for payment processing. A subsidiary of CardOne Plus

Pason Systems Inc.
6130 - 3 St. SE, Calgary, AB T2H 1K4
Tel: 403-301-3400; *Fax:* 403-301-3499
InvestorRelations@pason.com
www.pason.com
Ticker Symbol: PSI
Company Type: Public
Profile: Pason Systems Inc. specializes in the design & manufacture of specialized rental drilling instrumentation systems. These systems are used by the oilfield industry on land based drilling & service rigs. Operations are located in Canada, the United States, Mexico, South America, & Australia.

Peer 1 Network Enterprises Inc.
#100, 555 West Hastings St., Vancouver, BC V6B 4N5
Tel: 604-683-7747; *Fax:* 604-683-4634
Toll-Free: 877-504-0091
investor@peer1.com
www.peer1.com
Ticker Symbol: PIX
Company Type: Public
Profile: PEER 1 Network Enterprises, Inc. is the parent company of PEER 1 Network Inc.. The company is an online information technology infrastructure provider.

Procom
#400, 2323 Yonge St., Toronto, ON M4P 2C9
Tel: 416-483-0766; *Fax:* 416-483-8102
Toll-Free: 800-461-4878
toronto@procom.ca; montreal@procom.ca
www.procom.ca
Company Type: Private
Profile: Procom is a vendor of information technology staffing services. The organization maintains ISO 9001:2000 certification for its management and quality processes.

Q - Media Solutions Corporation
13566 Maycrest Way, Richmond, BC V6V 2J7
Toll-Free: 800-690-5881
info@qmscorp.com
qmsfife.com
Company Type: Private
Profile: The supply chain services company works with technology companies to provide documentation, software, & accessory kits to customers. Q - Media Solutions' services include planning, materials procurement, media replication, printing, package assembly, inventory management, & e-commerce.

Rand Worldwide
5285 Solar Dr., Mississauga, ON L4W 5B8
Tel: 905-625-2000; *Fax:* 905-625-2012
Toll-Free: 877-726-3243
www.rand.com
Company Type: Private
Profile: Rand Worldwide provides technology solutions & professional services to assist organizations with information technology & engineering design requirements.

Reliance Protectron Security Services
8481, boul Langelier, Montréal, QC H1P 2C3
Tel: 514-323-5000; *Fax:* 514-323-6423
Toll-Free: 800-811-1818
www.protectron.com
Company Type: Private
Profile: Reliance Protectron Security Services is a security monitoring & installation company. The company serves residential, commercial, industrial, & wholesale subscribers throughout Canada.

Resolve Business Outsourcing Income Fund
#1600, 2 Robert Speck Pkwy., Mississauga, ON L4Z 1H8
Tel: 905-306-6200; *Fax:* 905-306-2904
Toll-Free: 866-678-6019
www.resolve.com
Ticker Symbol: RBO.UN
Company Type: Public
Profile: Resolve Business Outsourcing Income Fund is involved in business process outsourcing. The firm serves businesses & governments throughout Canada, the United States, & Mexico.

Roxio
c/o Sonic Solutions, #110, 101 Rowland Blvd., Novato, CA
Toll-Free: 877-697-6946
www.roxio.com
Company Type: Private
Profile: Roxio provides digital media creation applications for consumers. The division of Sonic Solutions also produces media products & services to help people in their creation, management, & sharing of digital media. Examples of products include Roxio Creator, Roxio Easy VHS to DVD, Roxio CinePlayer DVD Decoders, Roxio BackOnTrack Suite, Roxio Easy LP to MP3, & Easy DVD Copy 4 Premier.

Sandvine Corp.
408 Albert St., Waterloo, ON N2L 3V3
Tel: 519-880-2600; *Fax:* 519-884-9892
investor_relations@sandvine.com
www.sandvine.com
Ticker Symbol: SVC
Company Type: Public
Profile: Sandvine Corporation is a developer & marketer of broadband network management products. Products are used by residential broadband service providers. Sandvine Incorporated is the wholly owned operating subsidiary of Sandvine Corporation.

Sierra Systems Group Inc.
#2500, 1177 West Hastings St., Vancouver, BC V6E 2K3
Tel: 604-688-1371; *Fax:* 604-688-6482
Toll-Free: 877-688-1371
Marketing@SierraSystems.com
www.sierrasystems.com
Company Type: Private
Profile: Sierra Systems Group is an information technology & management consulting services company. Examples of the company's services include content & records management, human capital management, & finance & controlling. Sierra Systems serves the government, justice, transportation, health, energy, & financial services sectors.

Sun Microsystems of Canada Inc.
27 Allstate Pkwy., 7th Fl., Markham, ON L3R 5L7
Tel: 905-477-6745; *Fax:* 905-477-9423
ca.sun.com
Company Type: Private
Profile: Provides software solutions, systems, and services, including Java technology, Solaris OS and the MySQL database management system

SXC Health Solutions, Inc.
555 Industrial Dr., Milton, ON L9T 5E1
Tel: 905-876-4741; *Fax:* 905-878-8869
investors@sxc.com
www.sxc.com
Ticker Symbol: SXC
Company Type: Public
Profile: SXC Health Solutions Corp. serves the healthcare benefits management industry. Healthcare information technology solutions are among the professional services provided.

TECSYS Inc.
87, rue Prince, 5e étage, Montréal, QC H3C 2M7
Tel: 514-866-0001; *Fax:* 514-866-1805
Toll-Free: 800-922-8649
info@tecsys.com
www.tecsys.com
Ticker Symbol: TCS
Company Type: Public
Profile: Prepackaged software

TELUS Health Solutions
#600, 1000, rue de Sérigny, Longueuil, QC J4K 5B1
Tel: 450-928-6000; *Fax:* 450-928-6344
Toll-Free: 866-363-7447
www.telushealth.com
Ticker Symbol: IFM
Company Type: Public
Profile: Implementation of information communication technology processes for healthcare: claims & benefit management, electronic health records, centralized warehousing of health data, telehealth, & other information processing solutions

Teranet Income Fund
#600, 1 Adelaide St. East, Toronto, ON M5C 2V9
Tel: 416-360-5263; *Fax:* 416-360-5659
Toll-Free: 800-208-5263
info@teranet.ca
www.teranet.ca
Company Type: Public
Profile: The organization provides e-service solutions. Services are useful to the financial, legal, government, healthcare, & real estate markets. One of its applications, Teraview software, allows access to the Ontario Electronic Land Registration System.

The Descartes Systems Group Inc.
120 Randall Dr., Waterloo, ON N2V 1C6
Tel: 519-746-8110; *Fax:* 519-747-0082
Toll-Free: 800-419-8495
info@descartes.com
www.descartes.com
Ticker Symbol: DSG
Company Type: Public
Profile: Prepackaged software; Computer programming services

Ventyx
10271 Shellbridge Way, Richmond, BC V6X 2W8
Tel: 604-207-6000; *Fax:* 604-207-6060
Toll-Free: 800-294-6374
www.ventyx.com
Company Type: Public
Profile: Service delivery management solutions for utility, communications and other commercial field service organizations; services include asset management, mobile workforce management, customer care, energy trading and risk management, energy operations, and energy analytics

Chemicals

Abbott Laboratories Ltd.
PO Box 6150 Centre-Ville, 8401, rte Trans-Canada, Saint-Laurent, QC H4S 1Z1
Tel: 514-832-7000; *Fax:* 514-832-7800
Toll-Free: 800-361-7852
www.abbott.ca
Company Type: Public
Profile: Manufacturers of pharmaceutical preparations

Acetex Corporation
World Trade Centre, #750, 999 Canada Pl., Vancouver, BC V6C 3E1
Tel: 604-688-9600; *Fax:* 604-688-9620
invest@acetex.com
www.acetex.com
Company Type: Private
Profile: Manufacturers of various industrial organic chemicals, plastic materials, synthetic resins, & nonvulcanizable elastomers

Agrium Inc.
13131 Lake Fraser Dr. SE, Calgary, AB T2J 7E8
Tel: 403-225-7000; *Fax:* 403-225-7609
Toll-Free: 877-247-4861
investor@agrium.com
www.agrium.com
Ticker Symbol: AGU
Company Type: Public
Profile: Agrium Inc. produces & markets major agricultural nutrients throughout the world. The company also supplies specialty fertilizers across North America. In North & South America, Agrium is engaged in the retail supply of agricultural products & services.

Ambrilia Biopharma Inc.
1000, chemin du Golf, Verdun, QC H3E 1H4
Tel: 514-751-2003; *Fax:* 514-751-2502
info@ambrilia.com
www.ambrilia.com
Ticker Symbol: AMB
Company Type: Public
Profile: Commercial, physical & biological research

Angiotech Pharmaceuticals, Inc.
1618 Stanton St., Vancouver, BC V6A 1B6
Tel: 604-221-7676; *Fax:* 604-221-2330
info@angio.com
www.angiotech.com
Ticker Symbol: ANP
Company Type: Public
Profile: Commercial physical & biological research

Apotex Inc., Canada
150 Signet Dr., Toronto, ON M9L 1T9
Tel: 416-749-9300; *Fax:* 416-291-0049
Toll-Free: 800-268-4623
corpinfo@apotex.com
www.apotex.com
Company Type: Private
Profile: The largest Canadian-owned pharmaceutical company.

AstraZeneca Canada Inc.
1004 Middlegate Rd., Mississauga, ON L4Y 1M4
Tel: 905-277-7111; *Fax:* 905-270-3248
Toll-Free: 800-565-5877
customer.relations1@astrazeneca.com
www.astrazeneca.ca
Company Type: Private
Profile: Global pharmaceutical company; therapeutic areas include gastrointestinal, cardiovascular, infection, neuroscience, oncology & respiratory; drug discovery centre based in Montréal, QC

Atrium Innovations Inc.
1405, boul du Parc-Technologique, Québec, QC G1P 4P5
Tel: 418-652-1116; *Fax:* 418-652-0151
atrium@atrium-innov.com
www.atrium-bio.ca
Ticker Symbol: ATB
Company Type: Public
Profile: Atrium Innovations is engaged in the development & manufacture of products, which are marketed to the chemical, pharmaceutical, & nutrition industries.

Axcan Pharma Inc.
597, boul Laurier, Mont-Saint-Hilaire, QC J3H 6C4
Tel: 450-467-5138; *Fax:* 450-464-9979
Toll-Free: 800-565-3255
axcan@axcan.com
www.axcan.com
Ticker Symbol: AXP
Company Type: Public
Profile: Pharmaceutical company specializing in the field of gastroenterology; products are marketed in North America & the European Union

BASF Canada
100 Milverton Dr., 5th Fl., Mississauga, ON L5R 4H1
Tel: 289-360-1300; *Fax:* 289-360-6000
Toll-Free: 866-485-2273
noc_canada-webmaster@basf-corp.com
www.basf.ca
Company Type: Private
Profile: Manufacturers of: gum & wood chemicals, paints, lacquers, enamels & allied products, pesticides & agricultural chemicals, prepared feeds & feed ingredients for animals & fowls, industrial organic chemical, synthetic rubber, cyclic crudes, intermediates, organic dyes & pigments; Wholesalers of: chemicals & allied products, paints, agricultural products & nutrition, raw materials, reactants, solvents & catalysts, pigments, plastics, polyurethans, coatings

Baxter Corporation
#700, 4 Robert Speck Pkwy., Mississauga, ON L4Z 3Y4
Tel: 905-270-1125; *Fax:* 905-281-6560
Toll-Free: 800-387-8399
business_development_canada@baxter.com
www.baxter.ca
Company Type: Private
Profile: Wholesalers of professional equipment & supplies; Manufacturers of pharmaceutical preparations

Bayer Inc.
77 Belfield Rd., Toronto, ON M9W 1G6
Tel: 416-248-0771; *Toll-Free:* 800-622-2937
contactbayer@bayer.com
www.bayer.ca
Company Type: Private
Profile: Wholesalers of drugs, drug proprietaries & druggists' sundries, synthetic rubber, chemicals & allied products; Manufacturers of synthetic rubber; agriculture crop engineering

BioMS Medical Corp.
6030 - 88 Street, Edmonton, AB T6E 6G4
Tel: 780-413-7152; *Fax:* 780-408-3040
Toll-Free: 866-701-6603
info@biomsmedical.com
www.biomsmedical.com
Ticker Symbol: MS
Company Type: Public
Profile: Commercial physical & biological research

Bioniche Life Sciences Inc.
PO Box 1570, 231 Dundas St. East, Belleville, ON K8N 5J2
Tel: 613-966-8058; *Fax:* 613-966-4177
Toll-Free: 800-265-5464
info@bioniche.com
www.bioniche.com
Ticker Symbol: BNC
Company Type: Public
Profile: Manufacturers of pharmaceutical preparations; Commercial physical & biological research

Biovail Corporation
7150 Mississauga Rd., Mississauga, ON L5N 8M5
Tel: 905-286-3000; *Fax:* 905-286-3050
ir@biovail.com
www.biovail.com
Ticker Symbol: BVF
Company Type: Public
Profile: Biovail Corporation formulates, tests, registers, manufactures, & commercializes pharmaceutical products. Canada & the United States are the company's main markets.

Biovail Corporation
7150 Mississauga Rd., Mississauga, ON L5N 8M5
Tel: 905-286-3000; *Fax:* 905-286-3050
ir@biovail.com
www.biovail.com
Ticker Symbol: BVF
Company Type: Public
Profile: Manufacturers of pharmaceutical preparations; Wholesalers of drugs, drug proprietaries & druggists' sundries; Commercial physical & biological research; Patent owners & lessors

BXL Bulk Explosives Ltd
PO Box 5247 A, 5511 - 6 St. SE, Calgary, AB T2H 1X6
Tel: 403-255-7776; *Fax:* 403-255-2226
www.explosives.com
Company Type: Private
Profile: Wholesales-chemicals and allied products; Mfrs-explosives

Canexus Income Fund
#600, 801 - 7th Ave. SW, Calgary, AB T2P 3P7
Tel: 403-571-7300; *Fax:* 403-571-7800
canexus@canexus.ca
www.canexus.ca
Ticker Symbol: CUS.UN
Company Type: Public
Profile: Canexus Income Fund is an unincorporated open-ended trust. It is involved in the production of chlor-alkali & sodium chlorate products.

Cangene Corporation
#360, 180 Attwell Dr., Toronto, ON M9W 6A9
Tel: 416-675-8300; *Fax:* 416-675-8301
ir@cangene.com
www.cangene.com
Ticker Symbol: CNJ
Company Type: Public
Profile: Cangene Corporation's areas of expertise are the developing, manufacturing, & marketing of biotechnology products & specialty hyperimmune plasma. Research & development operations are located in Canada & the United States.

Cardiome Pharma Corp.
6190 Agronomy Rd., 6th Fl., Vancouver, BC V6T 1Z3
Tel: 604-677-6905; *Fax:* 604-677-6915
Toll-Free: 800-330-9928
phofman@cardiome.com
www.cardiome.com
Ticker Symbol: COM
Company Type: Public
Profile: Commercial physical & biological research

CCL Industries Inc.
#500, 105 Gordon Baker Rd., Toronto, ON M2H 3P8
Tel: 416-756-8500; *Fax:* 416-756-8555
ccl@cclind.com
www.cclind.com
Ticker Symbol: CCL
Company Type: Public
Profile: CCL Industries Inc. is engaged in the development & provision of specialty packaging for producers of consumer brands. Products include labelling, plastic tubes, & aluminum containers.

Chemtrade Logistics Income Fund
#301, 111 Gordon Baker Rd., Toronto, ON M2H 3R1
Tel: 416-496-5856; *Fax:* 416-496-9942
investor-relations@chemtradelogistics.com
www.chemtradelogistics.com
Ticker Symbol: CHE.UN
Company Type: Public
Profile: Chemtrade Logistics Income Fund supplies the following: sodium hydrosulphite, sulphuric acid, liquid sulphur dioxide, sodium chlorate, sulphur, & phosphorus pentasulphide. The organization is also a processor of spent acid & a producer of zinc oxide. Chemtrade distributes industrial chemicals & services to customers in North America & around the world.

DRAXIS Health, Inc.
#200, 6870 Goreway Dr., Mississauga, ON L4V 1P1
Tel: 905-677-5500; *Fax:* 905-677-5494
Toll-Free: 877-441-1984
requestforinfo@draxis.com
www.draxis.com
Company Type: Public
Profile: Manufacturers of pharmaceutical preparations; Wholesalers of drugs, drug proprietaries & druggists' sundries; Patent owners & lessors; Commercial physical & biological research

DuPont Canada
PO Box 2200 Streetsville, 7070 Mississauga Rd., Mississauga, ON L5M 2H3
Tel: 905-821-3300; *Fax:* 905-821-5057
Toll-Free: 800-387-2122
information@ca.dupont.com
www.ca.dupont.com
Ticker Symbol: DUP
Company Type: Public
Profile: Manufacturers of various industrial inorganic chemicals, manmade organic fibers & various organic chemicals; Wholesalers of chemicals & allied products

Eli Lilly Canada Inc.
3650 Danforth Ave., Toronto, ON M1N 2E8
Tel: 416-694-3221; *Fax:* 416-694-0487
Toll-Free: 800-268-4446
www.lilly.ca
Company Type: Private
Profile: Manufacturers of pharmaceutical preparations

Enerchem International Inc.
#1950, 777 - 8th Avenue SW, Calgary, AB T2P 3R5
Tel: 780-980-1682; *Fax:* 780-980-2610
investors@enerchem.com
www.enerchem.com
Ticker Symbol: ECH
Company Type: Public
Profile: Supplier of specialty chemicals & hydrocarbon-based well-servicing fluids to the oil & gas industry

GlaxoSmithKline Inc.
7333 Mississauga Rd. North, Mississauga, ON L5N 6L4
Tel: 905-819-3000; *Fax:* 905-819-3099
Toll-Free: 800-387-7374
www.gsk.ca
Company Type: Private
Profile: Commercial physical & biological research; Manufacturers of pharmaceutical preparations

Haemacure Corporation
#100, 215, ave Redfern, Montréal, QC H3Z 3L5
Tel: 514-282-3350; *Fax:* 514-282-3358
info@haemacurecorp.com
www.haemacure.com
Ticker Symbol: HAE
Company Type: Public
Profile: Manufacturers of pharmaceutical preparations; Commercial physical & biological research

Hanfeng Evergreen Inc.
#788, 20 Toronto St., Toronto, ON M5C 2B8
Tel: 416-368-8588; *Fax:* 416-849-0075
info@hanfengevergreen.com
www.hanfengevergreen.com
Ticker Symbol: HF
Company Type: Public
Profile: Hanfeng Evergreen Inc.'s area of expertise is the production of slow & controlled release (S&CR) fertilizers. The company's fertilizers are used by China's agricultural sector. Hanfeng Evergreen owns production facilities in China.

Intellipharmaceutics International Inc.
30 Worcester Rd., Toronto, ON M9W 5X2
Tel: 416-798-3001; *Fax:* 416-798-3007
info@intellipharmaceutics.com
www.intellipharmaceutics.com
Ticker Symbol: I
Company Type: Public
Profile: Intellipharmaceutics International Inc. designs, develops, & produces sophisticated controlled release pharmaceutical products. IntelliPharmaCeutics employs its patented HYPERMATRIX technology to bring finished drug products to market.

Kronos Canadian Systems Inc.
#800, 100 Milverton Dr., Mississauga, ON L5R 4H1
Tel: 905-568-0101; *Fax:* 905-568-8510
www.kronos.com/canada/
Company Type: Private
Profile: Employee management software & solutions

Labopharm Inc.
480, boul Armand-Frappier, Laval, QC H7V 4B4
Tel: 450-686-0207; *Fax:* 450-687-5860
Toll-Free: 888-686-1017
info@labopharm.com
www.labopharm.com
Ticker Symbol: DDS
Company Type: Public
Profile: Manufacturers of pharmaceutical preparations; Patent owners & lessors

Merck Canada
16711, rte Trans-Canada, Montréal, QC H9H 3L1
Tel: 514-428-8600; *Toll-Free:* 800-567-2594
servicesmf_customer@merck.com
www.merckfrosst.ca
Company Type: Private
Profile: Merck Canada is a research-driven pharmaceutical company. It researches, develops, manufactures, & markets innovative pharmaceutical, consumer. & animal health products. Merck also publishes resources that provide general health information to consumers. The company supports sustainable access to life-saving medicines in developing countries, through its partnership with Health Partners International of Canada.

Methanex Corporation
Waterfront Centre, #1800, 200 Burrard St., Vancouver, BC V6C 3M1
Tel: 604-661-2600; *Fax:* 604-661-2666
invest@methanex.com
www.methanex.com
Ticker Symbol: MX
Company Type: Public
Profile: Methanex Corporation is a producer & marketer of methanol.

Migao Corporation
#1108, 8 King St. East, Toronto, ON M5C 1B5
Tel: 416-869-1108; *Fax:* 416-869-1101
info@migaocorp.com
www.migaocorp.com
Ticker Symbol: MGO
Company Type: Public
Profile: Migao Corporation is the the owner & operator of fertilizer production plants. Plants are situated across the People's Republic of China. Products are used by Chinese domestic agricultural markets.

MIGENIX Inc.
#400, 1727 West Broadway, Vancouver, BC V6J 4W6
Tel: 604-221-9666; *Fax:* 604-221-9688
info@migenix.com
www.migenix.com
Ticker Symbol: MGI
Company Type: Public
Profile: MIGENIX Inc. develops & commercializes drugs for the treatment of infectious diseases.

Nova Chemicals Corporation
PO Box 2518, 1000 - 7th Ave. SW, Calgary, AB T2P 5C6
Tel: 403-750-3600;
invest@novachem.com; public@novachem.com
www.novachemicals.com
Company Type: Public
Profile: Chemicals & plastics are produced by the company.

Novartis Pharmaceuticals Canada Inc.
385, boul Bouchard, Montréal, QC H9S 1A9
Tel: 514-631-6775;
www.novartis.ca
Company Type: Private
Profile: Novartis Pharmaceuticals Canada is a healthcare company which is engaged in scientific research to discover, develop, & market innovative pharmaceutical products to prevent & cure diseases.

Nuvo Research Inc.
#10, 7560 Airport Rd., Mississauga, ON L4T 4H4
Tel: 905-673-6980; *Fax:* 905-673-1842
Toll-Free: 888-398-3463
www.nuvoresearch.com
Ticker Symbol: NRI
Company Type: Public
Profile: The Canadian pharmaceutical company is engaged in the research & development of drug products that are delivered to & through the skin, with the use of topical & transdermal drug delivery technologies.

Nymox Pharmaceutical Corporation
#306, 9900, boul Cavendish, Montréal, QC H4M 2V2
Fax: 514-332-2227
Toll-Free: 800-936-9669
info@nymox.com
www.nymox.com
Ticker Symbol: NYMX
Company Type: Public
Profile: Biopharmaceutical company specializing in research & development of therapeutics & diagnostics for an aging population

Oncolytics Biotech Inc
#210, 1167 Kensington Cres. NW, Calgary, AB T2N 1X7
Tel: 403-670-7377; *Fax:* 403-283-0858
info@oncolyticsbiotech.com
www.oncolyticsbiotech.com
Ticker Symbol: ONC
Company Type: Public
Profile: The biotechnology company develops oncolytic viruses as potential cancer therapeutics. Oncolytics Biotech's clinical program includes a range of human trials.

Oncothyreon Inc.
#500, 2601 Fourth Ave., Seattle, WA
Tel: 206-801-2100; *Fax:* 206-801-2101
ir@oncothyreon.com
www.oncothyreon.com
Ticker Symbol: ONTY
Company Type: Public
Profile: Commercial physical & biological research; Manufacturers of biological products; Wholesalers of drugs, drug proprietaries & druggists' sundries; Primary focus is on oncology products

Orbus Pharma Inc.
20 Konrad Cres., Markham, ON L3R 8T4
Tel: 905-943-9444; *Fax:* 905-943-9878
info@orbus.ca
www.orbus.ca
Ticker Symbol: ORB
Company Type: Public
Profile: Develops & manufactures off-patent generic drugs & drug delivery systems

Paladin Labs Inc.
#102, 6111, av Royalmount, Montréal, QC H4P 2T4
Tel: 514-340-1112; *Fax:* 514-344-4675
info@paladin-labs.com
www.paladin-labs.com
Ticker Symbol: PLB
Company Type: Public
Profile: The specialty pharmaceutical company acquires or in-licenses pharmaceutical products for the Canadian market.

Patheon Inc.
2100 Syntex Court, Mississauga, ON L5N 7K9
Tel: 905-821-4001; *Fax:* 905-812-6705
Toll-Free: 888-728-4366
patheon@patheon.com
www.patheon.com
Ticker Symbol: PTI
Company Type: Public
Profile: Manufacturers of pharmaceutical preparations; Testing laboratories

PFB Corporation
#100, 2886 Sunridge Way NE, Calgary, AB T1Y 7H9
Tel: 403-569-4300; *Fax:* 403-569-4075
mailbox@pfbcorp.com
www.pfbcorp.com
Ticker Symbol: PFB
Company Type: Public
Profile: Through its wholly-owned subsidiaries, PFB Corporation manufactures insulating building products, based on expanded polystyrene technology. Brands of insulating building products include Plasti-Fab EPS, Riverbend Timber Framing, Insulspan SIPS, & Advantage ICF. The company serves the construction, industrial, commercial, & residential markets throughout North America.

Pfizer Canada Inc.
17300, rte Trans-Canada, Montréal, QC H9R 2M5
Tel: 514-695-0500; *Toll-Free:* 877-633-2001
www.pfizer.ca
Ticker Symbol: PFE (NYSE)
Company Type: Public
Profile: Pfizer develops innovative medications & other products to prevent & treat diseases of both people & animals thoughout the world. Canadian locations include Kirkland, Quebec, where Pfizer Animal Health & Pfizer Global Pharmaceuticals are situated, as well as Calgary Alberta's distribution centre, & Mississauga Ontario's logistics centre. The company's environmental, health, & safety management system is consistent with international management standards, such as ISO 14001 & OHSAS 18001.

Pharmascience Inc.
#100, 6111, av Royalmount, Montréal, QC H4P 2T4
Tel: 514-340-9800; *Fax:* 514-342-7764
Toll-Free: 800-363-8805
Corporate-Affairs@pharmascience.com
www.pharmascience.com
Company Type: Private
Profile: Pharmascience Inc. consists of the following commercial business units: pharmaceutical products (generics), consumer products (OTC), international, & hospital & institutional products. Products include a great range of drug therapies, such as anti-infectives & cholestorol reduction agents, as well as non-prescription, over-the-counter products. These products are marketed & sold to retail pharmacies & hospitals in Canada & internationally.

PPG Canada Inc.
2450 Bristol Way, Oakville, ON L6H 6P6
Tel: 905-829-5074; *Fax:* 905-829-9498
www.ppg.com
Company Type: Private
Profile: PPG Canada is a manufacturer of coatings & specialty products & services. The manufacturer serves customers in the following areas: construction, industrial markets, consumer products, & transportation markets.

Procter & Gamble Inc.
PO Box 355 A, 4711 Yonge St., Toronto, ON M5W 1C5
Toll-Free: 800-668-1050
www.pg.com
Company Type: Private
Profile: Procter & Gamble is a consumer product company. Some of the brands offered by the company include Bounce, CoverGirl, Crest toothpastes & toothbrushes, Duracell, Gillette, Ivory, Mr. Clean, Pampers, Pringles, Swiffer, Tide, & Vicks. Proctor & Gamble supports environmental management actions & scientific research to reduce environmental impacts, & it also participates in waste reduction initiatives.

ProMetic Life Sciences Inc.
8168, ch Montview, Montréal, QC H4P 2L7
Tel: 514-341-2115; *Fax:* 514-341-6227
info@prometic.com; investor@prometic.com
www.prometic.com
Ticker Symbol: PLI
Company Type: Public
Profile: The biopharmaceutical company provides technologies for drug development, drug purification, the elimination of pathogens, & the study of proteins. ProMetic also develops therapeutic drugs for the treatment of nephrological & hematological disorders & cancer.

QLT Inc.
887 Great Northern Way, Vancouver, BC V5T 4T5
Tel: 604-707-7000; *Fax:* 604-707-7001
Toll-Free: 800-663-5486
corpcomm@qltinc.com
www.qltinc.com
Ticker Symbol: QLT
Company Type: Public
Profile: Global biopharmaceutical company; Develops treatments for eye diseases & dermatological & urological conditions

Ratiopharm Inc.
6755 Mississauga Rd., 4th Fl., Mississauga, ON L5N 7Y2
Tel: 905-858-9612; *Fax:* 905-858-9610
Toll-Free: 800-266-2584
clients@ratiopharm.ca
www.ratiopharm.ca
Company Type: Private
Profile: Ratiopharm provides Canadian pharmacists with a wide range of generic products. The company also offers pharmacists professional services, such as Rx solutions, a comprehensive technology & patient-focussed program.

Recochem Inc.
850, montée de Liesse, Montréal, QC H4T 1P4
Tel: 514-341-3550; *Fax:* 514-341-1292
Consumerinquiry@recochem.com
www.recochem.com
Company Type: Private
Profile: Manufacturers of various chemicals & chemical preparations, specialty cleaning, polishing & sanitation preparations

Rohm & Haas Canada Inc.
2 Manse Rd., Toronto, ON M1E 3T9
Tel: 416-284-4711; *Fax:* 416-287-4486
www.rohmhass.com
Company Type: Private
Profile: Rohm & Haas Canada Inc. is part of the architectural & functional coatings industry. It manufactures specialty chemical products that are used by industries such as the commercial & industrial paints & coatings sector, the industrial finishes sector, & printing inks & overprint varnishes companies. The Rohm & Haas facility in West Hill is the first chemical company to join Ontario's Environmental Leaders Program, because of its reduced emissions & its commitment to further reductions.

Sico Inc.
2505, rue de la Métropole, Longueuil, QC J4G 1E5
Tel: 514-527-5111; *Fax:* 514-651-1257
Toll-Free: 800-463-7426
info@sico.ca
www.sico.ca
Company Type: Private
Profile: Sico develops, manufactures, & markets paints, coatings, & related products. Markets include the architectural business & industry.

Theratechnologies Inc.
2310, boul Alfred-Nobel, Montréal, QC H4S 2A4
Tel: 514-336-7800; *Fax:* 514-336-7242
communications@theratech.com
www.theratech.com
Ticker Symbol: TH
Company Type: Public
Profile: Manufacturers of pharmaceutical preparations, in vitro & in vivo diagnostic substances, surgical & medical instruments & apparatus, dental equipment & supplies; Commercial physical & biological research; Wholesalers of drugs, drug proprietaries & druggists' sundries

Univar Canada Ltd.
9800 Van Horne Way, Richmond, BC V6X 1W5
Tel: 604-273-1441; *Fax:* 604-273-2046
www.univarcanada.com
Company Type: Private
Profile: Univar provides chemicals & related chemical distribution services.

Communications

Allstream Corp.
#1400, 200 Wellington St. West, Toronto, ON M5V 3G2
Tel: 204-225-5687; *Fax:* 204-949-1244
Toll-Free: 800-883-2054
brad.woods@mts.ca
www.allstream.com
Ticker Symbol: TEL
Company Type: Public
Profile: Telephone communications; Information retrieval services

Amtelecom Income Fund
PO Box 1800, 18 Sydenham St. East, Aylmer West, ON N5H 3E7
Tel: 519-773-8441; *Fax:* 519-765-3200
Toll-Free: 800-440-7472
info@amtelecom.ca
www.amtelecom.ca
Ticker Symbol: ATM
Company Type: Public
Profile: Cable & other pay television services; Telephone communications; Internet services

Astral Media Inc
Maison Astral, #1000, 2100, rue Sainte-Catherine ouest, Montréal, QC H3H 2T3
Tel: 514-939-5000; *Fax:* 514-939-1515
investorrelations@corp.astral.com
www.astral.com
Ticker Symbol: ACM
Company Type: Public
Profile: Astral Media focuses upon the following services: radio & outdoor advertising; & speciality, pay & pay-per-view television.

BCE Inc.
1 Carrefour Alexander-Graham-Bell, Montréal, QC H3B 3B3
Tel: 514-870-8276; *Fax:* 514-786-3970
Toll-Free: 800-339-6353
investor.relations@bce.ca
www.bce.ca
Ticker Symbol: BCE
Company Type: Public
Profile: Radiotelephone, telephone, telegraph & other message communications services; Miscellaneous publishing; Special trade electrical work; Electrical & electronic repair shops; Retail stores

BCE Inc.
#3700, 1000, rue de la Gauchetière ouest, Montréal, QC H3B 4Y7
Tel: 514-870-8777; *Fax:* 514-786-3970
Toll-Free: 800-339-6353
investor.relations@bce.ca
www.bce.ca
Ticker Symbol: BCE
Company Type: Public
Profile: BCE Inc. is a provider of communication services, such as internet access, IP-broadband services, phone services, direct-to-home satellite, & VDSL television services. Customers include residential & business customers across Canada.

Bell Aliant Inc.
PO Box 1430, Saint John, NB E2L 4K2
Tel: 877-248-3113; *Fax:* 506-694-2722
Toll-Free: 866-425-4268
investors@bell.aliant.ca
www.bellaliant.ca
Ticker Symbol: BA.UN
Company Type: Public
Profile: Offices of holding companies; Telephone & various other communications services; Computer related services

Canadian Broadcasting Corporation
PO Box 3220 C, Ottawa, ON K1Y 1E4
Tel: 613-288-6033; *Fax:* 613-724-5707
liaison@radio-canada.ca
www.cbc.ca
Company Type: Crown
Profile: Radio & television broadcasting stations; Theatrical producers & miscellaneous services; Motion picture & video tape production

CanWest Global Communications Corp.
CanWest Place, 201 Portage Ave., 31st Fl., Winnipeg, MB R3B 3L7
Tel: 204-956-2025; *Fax:* 204-947-9841
www.canwestglobal.com
Ticker Symbol: CGS
Company Type: Public
Profile: The international media company owns the Global Television Network. The company also holds interests in newspapers, specialty cable channels, radio networks, advertising, & websites. Business is conducted in Canada, the United States, the United Kingdom, Turkey, Singapore, Australia, & New Zealand.

Cogeco Cable Inc.
#1700, 5 Place Ville-Marie, Montréal, QC H3B 0B3
Tel: 514-764-4700; *Fax:* 514-874-2625
marie.carrier@cogeco.com
www.cogeco.ca
Ticker Symbol: CCA
Company Type: Public
Profile: The cable telecommunications company provides the following services: internet, telephony, audio, & analog & digital television.

COGECO Cable Inc.
#1700, 5, Place Ville-Marie, Montréal, QC H3B 0B3
Tel: 514-764-4700; *Fax:* 514-874-2625
marie.carrier@cogeco.com
www.cogecocable.com
Ticker Symbol: CCA
Company Type: Public
Profile: The cable operator provides analogue & digital video & audio services, high-speed Internet access, & digital telephony service to residential & commercial customers.

COGECO Inc.
#915, 5, Place Ville-Marie, Montréal, QC H3B 3P2
Tel: 514-874-2600; *Fax:* 514-874-2625
www.cogeco.com
Ticker Symbol: CGO
Company Type: Public
Profile: COGECO Inc. is a diversified telecommunication company which serves consumers & advertisers. It is engaged in broadcasting in Quebec & cable distribution in Canada & Portugal.

Copernic Inc.
388, rue St-Jacques ouest, 9e étage, Montréal, QC H2Y 1S1
Tel: 514-844-2700; *Fax:* 514-844-3532
Toll-Free: 888-844-2372
www.copernic.com
Ticker Symbol: CNIC
Company Type: Public
Profile: Software development; Internet, desktop and mobile search products; Web properties include mamma.com, and copernic.com

Corus Entertainment Inc.
Bay Wellington Tower, BCE Place, #1630, 181 Bay St., Toronto, ON M5J 2T3
Tel: 416-642-3770; *Fax:* 416-642-3779
investor.relations@corusent.com
www.corusent.com
Ticker Symbol: CJR
Company Type: Public
Profile: The media & entertainment company is engaged in the following services: television broadcasting, specialty television, pay television, specialty radio, digital audio services, advertising, children's animation, & children's book publishing. Some of the companies & brands that comprise Corus Entertainment include the following: W Network, YTV, Treehouse, TELETOON, Nelvana, & Kids Can Press.

Cossette Communication Group Inc.
#200, 801, Grande Allée ouest, Québec, QC G1S 1C1
Tel: 418-647-2727; *Fax:* 418-523-1689
infomaster@cossette.com
www.cossette.com
Ticker Symbol: KOS
Company Type: Public
Profile: Cossette Communication Group Inc. offers the following services: planning, researching, B2B communications, advertising, database marketing, direct marketing, ethnic marketing, alliance marketing, sports marketing, interactive marketing solutions, branding, sales promotion, product placement, & public relations. The full range of communication services are provided to clients of all sizes.

Cossette Communication Group Inc.
#200, 801 Grande Allee Ouest, Québec, QC G1S 1C1
Tel: 418-647-2727; *Fax:* 418-647-2564
investor@cossette.com
www.cossette.com
Ticker Symbol: KOS
Company Type: Public
Profile: The company offers a full range of communication services to clients of all sizes.

CTV Inc.
9 Channel Nine Ct., Scarborough, ON M1S 4B5
Tel: 416-332-5000; *Fax:* 416-332-5022
www.ctv.ca
Company Type: Public
Profile: Television broadcasting stations; Motion picture & video tape production

EastLink
PO Box 8660 A, NS, NL B3K 5M3
Tel: 709-754-3775; *Fax:* 709-754-3883
Toll-Free: 888-345-1111
www.eastlink.ca
Company Type: Private
Profile: EastLink services include telephone, high speed Internet, & cable & digital cable. Residential, business, & public sector customers are located throughout Canada.

Ericsson Canada Inc.
5255 Satellite Dr., Mississauga, ON L4W 5E3
Tel: 905-629-6700; *Fax:* 905-629-6701
www.ericsson.ca
Company Type: Private
Profile: Provides mobile internet, wireless, IP & data systems, & consulting services

General Dynamics Canada
3785 Richmond Rd., Ottawa, ON K2H 5B7
Tel: 613-596-7000; *Fax:* 613-596-7396
info@gdcanada.com
www.gdcanada.com
Company Type: Private
Profile: International supplier of maritime systems, integrating naval & airborne anti-submarine warfare systems

Glentel Inc.
8501 Commerce Ct., Burnaby, BC V5A 4N3
Tel: 604-415-6500; *Fax:* 604-415-6565
tskidmore@glentel.com
www.glentel.com
Ticker Symbol: GLN
Company Type: Public

Profile: Glentel Inc. is a provider of telecommunications services & solutions, through its retail & business operating divisions. Products & services include wireless devices, wireless engineering, & wireless asset monitoring. Locations across Canada are known as Glentel Wireless Business Centres, The Telephone Booth / La Cabine Telephonique, WIRELESS, & WirelessWave.

Manitoba Telecom Services Inc.
PO Box 6666, #MP18C, 333 Main St., Winnipeg, MB R3C 3V6
Tel: 204-941-8256; *Fax:* 204-772-6391
Toll-Free: 800-263-1174
investor.relations@mtsallstream.com
www.mts.ca
Ticker Symbol: MBT
Company Type: Public
Profile: Through its wholly-owned subsidiary MTS Allstream Inc., Manitoba Telecom Services Inc. provides television, voice, data, wireless, & wireline services. Both residential & business customers are served in Manitoba, while across Canada, business clients are served through a portfolio of information technology consulting & security services, as well as voice & data connectivity services.

Newfoundland Capital Corporation Limited
745 Windmill Rd., Dartmouth, NS B3B 1C2
Tel: 902-468-7557; *Fax:* 902-468-7558
ncc@ncc.ca
www.ncc.ca
Ticker Symbol: NCC
Company Type: Public
Profile: Newfoundland Capital Corporation Limited is the owner & operator of radio stations throughout Canada. Newcap Radio is a wholly owned subsidiary of Newfoundland Capital Corporation Limited. In addition to its involvement in radio broadcasting, Newfoundland Capital Corporation Limited also owns & operates the Glynmill Inn in Corner Brook, Newfoundland & Labrador.

Northwestel Inc.
PO Box 2727 Main, 301 Lambert St., Whitehorse, YT Y1A 4Y4
Tel: 867-668-5300; *Fax:* 867-668-7079
Toll-Free: 888-423-2333
customerservice@nwtel.ca
www.nwtel.ca
Company Type: Private
Profile: Northwestel is engaged in the communications & entertainment industry. It offers innovative technology to customers in northern Canada. The following are some of Northwestel's services: cable television; advanced data communications, including high speed internet in some areas; long distance communications by microwave radio; & satellite & fibre optic cable.

Rainmaker Entertainment Inc.
#500, 2025 West Broadway, Vancouver, BC V6J 1Z6
Tel: 604-714-2600; *Fax:* 604-714-2641
www.rainmaker.com
Ticker Symbol: RNK
Company Type: Public
Profile: Animated film production

Rogers Communications Inc.
333 Bloor St. East, 7th Floor, Toronto, ON M4W 1G9
Toll-Free: 888-764-3771
investor.relations@rogers.com
www.rogers.com
Ticker Symbol: RCI.A; RCI.B
Company Type: Private
Profile: Rogers Wireless is one of three business lines of Rogers Communications Inc., and Canada's largest wireless voice and data communications services provider

Rogers Communications Inc.
333 Bloor St. East, 7th Floor, Toronto, ON M4W 1G9
Toll-Free: 888-764-3771
investor.relations@rogers.com
www.rogers.com
Ticker Symbol: RCI.A; RCI.B
Company Type: Public
Profile: A diversified Canadian company with three main business lines: Rogers Wireless, Rogers Cable, and Rogers Media

SaskTel
PO Box 2121, Regina, SK S4P 4C5
Toll-Free: 866-727-5835
www.sasktel.com
Company Type: Crown
Profile: SaskTel is a full service communications provider in Saskatchewan. Communications products & services include voice, cellular, data, wireless data, messaging, internet, entertainment, & directory services.

Score Media Inc.
#425, 370 King St. West, Toronto, ON M5V 1J9
Tel: 416-977-6787; *Fax:* 416-977-7851
www.scoremedia.ca
Ticker Symbol: SCR
Company Type: Public
Profile: The media company delivers sports entertainment. Its primary asset is The Score Television Network, a national specialty television service. The company also operates a satellite radio network, known as Hardcore Sports Radio. Other assets include Score Mobile & theScore.com.

Shaw Communications Inc.
#900, 630 - 3rd Ave. SW, Calgary, AB T2P 4L4
Tel: 403-750-4500; *Fax:* 403-750-4501
angela.haigh@sjrb.ca
www.shaw.ca
Ticker Symbol: SJR
Company Type: Public
Profile: The communications company provides broadband cable television, internet, digital phone, telecommunications services, & satellite direct-to-home services.

Shaw Direct
Shaw Satellite G.P., #100, 2400 -32 Ave. NE, Calgary, AB T2E 9A7
Tel: 866-782-7932; *Fax:* 800-872-8219
investor.relations@sjrb.ca
www.shawdirect.ca
Company Type: Private
Profile: Shaw Direct supplies digital satellite television. The company offers more than 470 audio & video channels to over 870,000 subscribers. Subscribers also have access to pay per view movies & events.

Stratos Global Corporation
#210, 2650 Queensview Dr., Ottawa, ON K2B 8H6
Tel: 613-230-4544; *Fax:* 613-230-4212
Toll-Free: 877-995-9901
investor@stratosglobal.com
www.stratosglobal.com
Company Type: Public
Profile: Offices of holding companies; Radiotelephone & various other communications services

Tata Communications
1555, rue Carrie-Derick, Montréal, QC H3C 6W2
Tel: 514-868-7272; *Fax:* 514-868-7234
www.tatacommunications.com
Company Type: Public
Profile: Communications solutions and services, including transmission, IP, converged voice, mobility, managed network connectivity, hosting, storage, managed security, managed collaboration and business transformation, Internet, retail broadband, content services

Telesat Canada
1601 Telesat Ct., Gloucester, ON K1B 5P4
Tel: 613-748-0123; *Fax:* 613-748-8712
info@telesat.ca
www.telesat.ca
Company Type: Private
Profile: Telesat manages satellite communications & systems.

TELUS Corp.
555 Robson St., Vancouver, BC V6B 3K9
Tel: 800-667-4871; *Fax:* 604-899-9228
ir@telus.com
www.telus.com
Ticker Symbol: T
Company Type: Public
Profile: Communications products include internet protocol, data, voice, & video.

TVA Group Inc.
1600, boul de Maisonneuve est, Montréal, QC H2L 4P2
Tel: 514-526-9251; *Fax:* 514-598-6085
denis.rozon@tva.ca
www.tva.canoe.ca
Ticker Symbol: TVA
Company Type: Public
Profile: The integrated communications company provides the following services: broadcasting, publishing, & producting & distributing audiovisual products. TVA Group owns French-language television stations, plus a specialty channel. It also publishes French-language magazines. The TVA Films subsidiary serves both Canada's English & French-language markets.

Télébec
625, av Godefroy, Bécancour, QC G9H 1S3
Fax: 819-233-6877
Toll-Free: 888-835-3232
telebec@telebec.com
www.telebec.com
Ticker Symbol: BA.UN
Company Type: Public
Profile: Provides range of integrated telecommunications services in the province of Québec. A member of the Bell Aliant Group

Videon CableSystems, Inc.
#900, 630 - 3rd Ave. SW, Calgary, AB T2P 4L4
Tel: 403-750-4570; *Fax:* 403-750-7469
www.shaw.ca
Company Type: Public
Profile: Multi-system cable operator

Videotron Communications Ltd
300, av Viger est, Montréal, QC H2X 3W4
Tel: 514-281-1232; *Fax:* 514-985-8834
www.videotron.com
Company Type: Private
Profile: Cable & other pay television services; Television broadcasting stations; Communications services (various)

Construction

Aecon Group Inc.
#800, 20 Carlson Ct., Toronto, ON M9W 7K6
Tel: 416-293-7004; *Fax:* 416-293-0271
aecon@aecon.com
www.aecon.com
Ticker Symbol: ARE
Company Type: Public
Profile: Aecon Group is a construction & infrastructure development company. It serves both public & private sector clients through the provision of engineering, financing, procurement, construction, & project management services.

Badger Income Fund
#2820, 715 - 5th Ave. SW, Calgary, AB T2P 2X6
Tel: 403-264-8500; *Fax:* 403-228-9773
Toll-Free: 800-465-4273
rlynas@badgerinc.com
www.badgerinc.com
Ticker Symbol: BAD
Company Type: Public
Profile: Badger Income Fund is an open-ended trust. It is involved in non-destructive excavating & slot trenching services. Services are provided to industries, such as petroleum, industrial, utility, industrial, & transportation.

Bechtel Canada Inc.
#910, 1500, rue Univesité, Montréal, QC H3A 3S7
Tel: 514-871-1711; *Fax:* 514-871-1392
www.bechtel.com
Company Type: Private
Profile: Offices of holding companies; Management & public relations services; Engineering services

Bird Construction Income Fund
5403 Eglinton Ave. West, Toronto, ON M9C 5K6
Tel: 416-620-7122; *Fax:* 416-620-1516
investor.relations@bird.ca
www.bird.ca
Ticker Symbol: BDT.UN
Company Type: Public
Profile: The organization is a national general contractor in the residential, institutional, & industrial markets.

Carma Corporation
4906 Richard Rd. SW, Calgary, AB T3E 6L1
Tel: 403-231-8900; *Fax:* 403-231-8960
info@carma.ca
www.carma.ca
Company Type: Public
Profile: General contractors in residential buildings, & single family houses; Real estate land subdividers & developers

Churchill Corporation
11825 - 146 St., Edmonton, AB T5L 2J1
Tel: 780-454-3667; *Fax:* 780-488-0194
inquiries@churchill-cuq.com
www.churchillcorporation.com
Ticker Symbol: CUQ
Company Type: Public
Profile: The Churchill Corporation is a provider of building construction, industrial construction, & related maintenance services. It operates in western Canada. The Churchill Corporation's subsidiaries are as follows: Triton Projects, Laird Electric, Stuart Olson Construction Ltd., & Insulation Holdings Inc. The company has policies, procedures, training programs, &

compliance procedures in place to manage environmental issues & comply with legislation & regulations.

Dominion Construction Company Inc.
#130, 2985 Virtual Way, Vancouver, BC V5M 4X7
Tel: 604-631-1000; *Fax:* 604-631-1100
reception@dominionco.com
www.dominionco.com
Company Type: Private
Profile: General contractors in industrial & non-residential buildings & warehouses; Offices located in Vancouver, Calgary, Edmonton, Regina, Saskatoon, Swift Current, Winnipeg & Thunder Bay

Eastern Construction Company Ltd.
#1100, 505 Consumers Rd., Toronto, ON M2J 5G2
Tel: 416-497-7110; *Fax:* 416-497-7241
info@easternconstruction.com
www.easternconstruction.com
Company Type: Private
Profile: General contractors in industrial & non-residential buildings & warehouses

Ellis-Don Construction Ltd.
2045 Oxford St. West, London, ON N5V 2Z7
Tel: 519-455-6770; *Fax:* 519-455-2944
bwaltham@ellisdon.com
www.ellisdon.com
Company Type: Private
Profile: General contractors of industrial buildings & warehouses, residential & non-residential buildings

Finning International Inc.
Park Place, #1000, 666 Burrard St., Vancouver, BC V6C 2X8
Tel: 604-691-6444; *Fax:* 604-691-6440
investor_relations@finning.ca
www.finning.com
Ticker Symbol: FTT
Company Type: Public
Profile: The company sells, rents, & offers customer service for Caterpillar equipment. Business is conducted in Canada, South America, & the United Kingdom.

Fluor Canada Ltd.
Sundance Park, 55 Sunpark Plaza SE, Calgary, AB T2X 3R4
Tel: 403-537-4000; *Fax:* 403-537-4222
www.fluor.com/canada
Company Type: Private
Profile: Engineering, architectural & surveying services; Management & public relations services; Oil & gas field exploration services

Lafarge Canada Inc.
#900, 606, rue Cathcart, Montréal, QC H3B 1L7
Tel: 514-861-1411; *Fax:* 514-876-8900
www.lafarge-na.com
Company Type: Private
Profile: Manufacturer & supplier of construction materials, including aggregates; asphalt, paving & construction solutions; cement; concrete; gypsum; precast solutions; ductal; & pipe.

Ledcor Industries Inc.
#1200, 1067 West Cordova St., Vancouver, BC V61 1C7
Tel: 604-681-7500; *Fax:* 604-895-4385
info@ledcor.com
www.ledcor.com
Company Type: Private
Profile: General contractors in nonresidential, industrial buildings & warehouses; Highway, bridge, tunnel, elevated highway & street construction; Water, sewer, pipeline, communications, power line construct; Various heavy construction; Special trade construction in excavation work

Les Entreprises Kiewit ltée
4333, Grande-Allée, Boisbriand, QC J7H 1M7
Tel: 450-435-5756; *Fax:* 450-435-6764
info@kiewit.com
www.kiewit.ca
Company Type: Private
Profile: Offices of holding companies; Bridge, tunnel, elevated highway & various construction; Water, sewer, pipeline, communications & power line construction; Metal mining services in gold & copper ores; Coal mining services

Lockerbie & Hole Inc.
14940-121A Ave., Edmonton, AB T5V 1A3
Tel: 780-452-1250; *Fax:* 780-452-1284
Toll-Free: 800-417-2329
mail@lockerbiehole.com
www.lockerbiehole.com
Company Type: Private
Profile: Construction services to industrial, municipal, commercial & institutional markets

Maple Reinders Constructors Ltd.
2660 Argentia Rd., Mississauga, ON L5N 5V4
Tel: 905-821-4844; *Fax:* 905-821-4822
info@maple.ca
www.maple-reinders.com
Company Type: Private
Profile: The construction company is involved in green building in all regions of Canada.

Monarch Corporation
#200, 2550 Victoria Park Ave., Toronto, ON M2J 5A9
Tel: 416-491-7440;
www.monarchgroup.net
Company Type: Private
Profile: The construction company offers a range of housing options, from high-rise condominiums to single family homes.

PCL Constructors Inc.
5410 - 99 St., Edmonton, AB T6E 3P4
Tel: 780-733-5000; *Fax:* 780-733-5075
pclinfo@pcl.com
www.pcl.com
Company Type: Private
Profile: PCL Constructors provides full service building operations & civil work. Construction management services & general contracting services are available for industrial companies, such as oil & gas, pulp & paper, & mining industries.

Seacliff Construction Corp.
Oceanic Plaza, 1066 West Hastings St., 23rd Fl., Vancouver, BC V6E 3X2
Tel: 604-601-8206; *Fax:* 604-408-8893
info@seacliffconstruction.ca
www.seacliffconstruction.ca
Ticker Symbol: SDC
Company Type: Public
Profile: The diversified construction company provides services in the institutional infrastructure, light, & commercial sectors. Seacliff Construction's independently operated business units include Canem Systems & Dominion Construction. The company has locations in western Canada.

Steeplejack Industrial Group Inc.
8925 - 62 Ave., Edmonton, AB T6E 5L2
Tel: 780-465-9016; *Fax:* 780-466-8584
request@steeplejack.ca
www.steeplejack.ca
Company Type: Public
Profile: Offices of holding companies; Special trade contractors in plastering, drywall, acoustical & insulation

Stuart Olson Construction Ltd.
#400 4954 Richard Rd. SW, Calgary, AB T3E 6L1
Tel: 403-520-6565; *Fax:* 403-230-5323
info@stuartolson.com
www.stuartolson.com
Ticker Symbol: CUQ
Company Type: Private
Profile: General contractors in residential, non-residential & industrial buildings & warehouses

The Churchill Corporation
11825 - 149 St., Edmonton, AB T5L 2J1
Tel: 780-454-3667; *Fax:* 780-488-0194
inquiries@churchill-cuq.com
www.churchillcorporation.com
Ticker Symbol: CUQ
Company Type: Public
Profile: Commercial building & industrial construction, insulation, industrial electical, maintenance & related services

Viceroy Homes Limited
Corporate Headquarters, 414 Croft St. East, Port Hope, ON L1A 4H1
Tel: 905-885-8600;
info@viceroy.com; careers@viceroy.com
www.viceroy.com
Company Type: Private
Profile: Viceroy Homes Limited designs, engineers, & manufactures custom home packages for owners & professional contractors. Viceroy ships its home packages to clients throughout the world.

Winalta Inc.
Kalwin Business Park, 26302 Township Rd. 531A, Acheson, AB T7X 5A3
Tel: 780-960-6900; *Fax:* 780-960-9523
winalta@winaltainc.com
www.winaltainc.com
Ticker Symbol: WTA
Company Type: Public
Profile: Winalta Inc. is a land developer. The company is also involved in the production of manufacturered & modular homes & site built homes, as well as the manufacturing & renting of industrial trailers and camps. Operations take place in western Canada.

Distribution & Retail

A & B Sound Ltd.
13260 Delf Pl., Richmond, BC V6V 2A2
Tel: 604-303-2900; *Fax:* 604-303-2932
webfeedback@absound.ca
www.absound.ca
Company Type: Private
Profile: A & B Sound Ltd. is a retailer of consumer electronics, as well as music & movies.

Acklands-Grainger Inc.
90 West Beaver Creek Rd., Richmond Hill, ON L4B 1E7
Tel: 905-731-5516; *Fax:* 905-731-9677
Toll-Free: 800-668-8989
contact@agi.ca
www.acklandsgrainger.com
Company Type: Public
Profile: Distributes industrial, safety and fastener products, including hand tools, power tools, metalworking tools, electrical equipment, material handling equipment, shop equipment

Alimentation Couche-Tard inc
Tour B, #200, 1600, boul Saint-Martin est, Laval, QC H7G 4S7
Tel: 450-662-6632; *Fax:* 450-662-6633
info@couche-tard.com
www.couche-tard.com
Ticker Symbol: ATD
Company Type: Public
Profile: In eastern, central, & western Canada, as well as in the United States, Alimentation Couche-Tard operates convenience stores. Some of these stores include motor fuel dispensing. In Canada, the businesses operate under the brands Couche-Tard & Mac's.

Avon Canada Inc.
5500, aut Transcanadienne, Montréal, QC H9R 1B6
Tel: 514-695-3371; *Fax:* 514-630-5439
Toll-Free: 800-265-2866
questions@avon.com
www.avon.ca
Company Type: Private
Profile: Manufacturers of perfumes, cosmetics & other toilet preparations, costume jewelry & novelties; Retailing in miscellaneous retail stores

Birks & Mayors Inc.
1240 Phillips Sq., Montréal, QC H3B 3H4
Tel: 514-397-2511; *Fax:* 514-397-2537
mrabinovitch@birksandmayors.com
www.birksandmayors.com
Ticker Symbol: BMJ
Company Type: Public
Profile: Birks & Mayors Inc. designs, manufactures, & retails fine jewellery, silverware, timepieces, & gitware. Brand names include Birks, Brinkhaus, & Mayors. Retail stores are located in Canada & the United States.

Black Photo Corporation
371 Gough Rd., Markham, ON L3R 4B6
Tel: 905-475-2777; *Fax:* 905-475-8027
Toll-Free: 800-668-3826
support@blackphoto.com
www.blackphoto.com
Company Type: Private
Profile: Photograpy equipment & supplies retail stores

BMR Le Groupe
2375, rue de la Province, Longueuil, QC J4G 1G3
Tel: 450-463-2441; *Fax:* 450-463-1766
info@bmr-legroupe.com
www.bmr-legroupe.com
Company Type: Private
Profile: Wholesale distributor of brick, stone, lumber, plywood, millwork & related construction materials

BMTC Group Inc.
8500, Place Marien, Montréal, QC H1B 5W8
Tel: 514-648-5757; *Fax:* 514-881-4056
y.desgroseillers@braultmartineau.com
Ticker Symbol: GBT.A
Company Type: Public
Profile: BMTC Group is a holding company. Its subsidiaries include Ameublements Tanguay Inc. & Brault et Martineau Inc. These subsidiaries are engaged in the retail sale of furniture, electronic goods, & household appliances in Québec.

Calgary Co-Operative Association Ltd.
#110, 151 - 86th Ave. SE, Calgary, AB T2H 3A5
Tel: 403-219-6025; *Fax:* 403-299-5445
www.calgarycoop.com
Company Type: Private
Profile: The Calgary Co-Operative Association Ltd. offers a range of retail services in the Calgary area, including grocery, pharmacy, petroleum, liquor, & travel.

Canada Safeway Ltd.
1020 - 64 Ave. NE, Calgary, AB T2E 7V8
Tel: 403-730-3500; *Fax:* 403-730-3888
Toll-Free: 800-723-3929
www.safeway.com
Company Type: Private
Profile: Manufacturers of fluid milk, bread & other bakery products, various other food preparations; Retailing in grocery stores

Canadian Tire Corporation, Limited
PO Box 770 K, 2180 Yonge St., Toronto, ON M4V 2V8
Tel: 416-480-3000; *Fax:* 416-544-7715
investor.relations@cantire.com
www.canadiantire.ca
Ticker Symbol: CTC
Company Type: Public
Profile: Canadian Tire Corporation, Limited is engaged in retail, petroleum, & financial services.

Canon Canada Inc.
6390 Dixie Rd., Mississauga, ON L5T 1P7
Tel: 905-795-1111; *Fax:* 905-795-2130
hrmississauga@canada.canon.com
www.canon.ca
Company Type: Private
Profile: Wholesales-photographic equipment & supplies; Wholesales-commercial equipment; Retails-camera & photographic supply stores

Canpotex Limited
PO Box 1600, #400, 111 - 2nd Ave. South, Saskatoon, SK S7K 3R7
Tel: 306-931-2200; *Fax:* 306-653-5505
canpqlx.sasktelwebhosting.com
Company Type: Private
Profile: Exporter of Saskatchewan potash

CanWel Building Materials Income Fund
PO Box 10034, #1510, 700 West Georgia St., Vancouver, BC V7Y 1A1
Tel: 604-432-1400; *Fax:* 604-436-6670
info@canwel.com
www.canwel.com
Ticker Symbol: CWX.UN
Company Type: Public
Profile: CanWel Building Materials Income Fund is involved in the distribution of building materials & related products. Business is conducted throughout Canada.

CanWel, Hardware Division
PO Box 5485, 3232 White Oak Rd., London, ON N6A 4G8
Tel: 519-686-2200;
www.canwel.com
Ticker Symbol: CWX.UN
Company Type: Public
Profile: Wholesalers of hardware

Cara Operations Limited
6303 Airport Rd., Mississauga, ON L4V 1R8
Tel: 905-405-6500;
info@cara.com
www.cara.com
Ticker Symbol: CAO
Company Type: Public
Profile: Retail eating places & gift, novelty & souvenir shops, news dealers & newsstands

Cargill Ltd.
PO Box 5900, #300, 240 Graham Ave., Winnipeg, MB R3C 4C5
Tel: 204-947-0141; *Fax:* 204-947-6444
www.cargill.com
Company Type: Private
Profile: Wholesalers of grain & field beans, farm supplies, meat packing plants, sausages & other prepared meat products, prepared feeds & feed ingredients for animals & fowls, nitrogenous fertilizers, & phosphatic fertilizers

Cervus LP
#205, 120 Country Hills Landing NW, Calgary, AB T3K 5P3
Tel: 403-567-0339; *Fax:* 403-567-0392
www.cervuslp.com
Ticker Symbol: CVL.UN
Company Type: Public
Profile: Cervus LP retails agricultural & industrial equipment. The company acquires & operates dealerships, such as John Deere, Bobcat, JLG, & JCB Construction equipment dealerships. Business is conducted in western Canada.

Co-op Atlantic
PO Box 750, 123 Halifax St., Moncton, NB E1C 8N5
Tel: 506-858-6000; *Fax:* 506-858-6477
www.coopatlantic.ca
Profile: Wholesalers of general line groceries, farm supplies, grain & field beans, petroleum & petroleum products, hardware

Coast Wholesale Appliances Income Fund
8488 Main St., Vancouver, BC V5X 4W8
Tel: 604-321-6644; *Fax:* 604-321-6782
invest@coastappliances.com
www.coastappliances.com
Ticker Symbol: CWA.UN
Company Type: Public
Profile: Coast Wholesale Appliances Income Fund is an unincorporated, open-ended limited purpose trust. The Fund indirectly owns 65% of Coast Wholesale Appliances LP (Coast). Coast Wholesale Appliances Income Fund is involved in the supply of household appliances. It serves retail customers, plus developers & builders of single family & multi-family housing. There are locations across Canada.

Commercial Solutions Inc.
4203 - 95th St., Edmonton, AB T6E 5R6
Tel: 780-432-1611; *Fax:* 780-496-9172
info@csinet.ca
www.commercialsolutions.ca
Ticker Symbol: CSA
Company Type: Public
Profile: Commercial Solutions Inc. is a national distributor of the following products: forestry, mining & resource management equipment, bearing & power transmission supplies, & industrial safety equipment. In addition to these products & services, Commercial Solution Inc.'s group of companies also provides Business to Business services, such as electronic fund transfers, invoicing, & electronic data interchange. Commercial Solution Inc.'s subsidiaries are as follows: Cando Oilfield Supplies & Rentals Ltd., Commercial Bearing Service (1966) Ltd., & Impact Oilfield Supply Inc.. Divisions include Aim Supply, CFE Equipment, & Nisku Safety Service.

CoolBrands International Inc.
210 Shields Court, Markham, ON L3R 8V2
Tel: 905-479-8762; *Fax:* 905-479-5235
info@coolbrandsinternational.com
www.coolbrandsinc.com
Ticker Symbol: COB
Company Type: Public
Profile: Retailing in eating places; Wholesalers of dairy products, frozen specialties, frozen fruits, fruit juices & vegetables; Manufacturers of ice cream & frozen desserts

Coopérative fédérée de Québec
#200, 9001, boul de L'Acadie, Montréal, QC H4N 3H7
Tel: 514-384-6450; *Fax:* 514-384-7176
information@lacoop.coop
www.lacoop.coop
Company Type: NA
Profile: Wholesalers of meats & meat products, fresh fruits & vegetables, dairy products, petroleum & petroleum products

Costco Canada Inc.
415 West Hunt Club, Ottawa, ON K2E 1C5
Tel: 613-221-2000; *Fax:* 613-221-2001
www.costco.com
Company Type: Private
Profile: Bulk retail store that provides members with discounts on items

easyhome Ltd.
10239 - 178 St., Edmonton, AB T5S 1M3
Tel: 780-930-3000; *Fax:* 780-481-7426
leanne@easyhome.ca
www.easyhome.ca
Ticker Symbol: EH
Company Type: Public
Profile: easyhome Ltd. is a merchandise lease company. The company rents products, such as household furnishings, home entertainment products, electronics, appliances & computers. Customers may have the option to purchase products.

Forzani Group Ltd.
824 - 41 Ave. NE, Calgary, AB T2E 3R3
Tel: 403-717-1400; *Fax:* 403-717-1490
cjordan@forzani.com (Investor Relations)
www.forzanigroup.com
Ticker Symbol: FGL
Company Type: Public
Profile: The Forzani Group Ltd. is involved in the retail of sporting goods. Its stores operate under the following corporate banners: National Sports, Coast Mountain Sports, Sport Chek, & Sport Mart. Franchised banners feature the following: Nevada Bob's, Intersport, Econosport, Fitness Source, Sports Experts, Pegasus, & Atmosphere.

Future Shop Ltd.
8800 Glenlyon Pkwy., Burnaby, BC V5J 5K3
Tel: 604-435-8223; *Fax:* 604-412-5280
Toll-Free: 800-663-2275
service@futureshop.ca
www.futureshop.ca
Company Type: Private
Profile: Retailing in radio, television & consumer electronics stores, computer & computer software stores, household appliance stores

Futuremed Healthcare Income Fund
277 Basaltic Rd., Concord, ON L4K 5V3
Tel: 905-761-0068; *Fax:* 905-761-6079
Toll-Free: 800-387-7025
www.futuremed.ca
Ticker Symbol: FMD.UN
Company Type: Public
Profile: Futuremed Healthcare Income Fund is involved in the distribution of medical supplies, equipment, & specialized furniture to long-term care facilities.

GLV Inc.
#2100, 2001, av McGill College, Montréal, QC H3A 1G1
Tel: 514-284-2224; *Fax:* 514-284-2225
courrier@glv.com
www.glv.com
Ticker Symbol: GLV.A
Company Type: Public
Profile: GLV Inc. supplies technological solutions & services. Processes & equipment are used in pulp & paper production & for the treatment & recycling of municipal & industrial wastewater.

Grand & Toy Ltd.
33 Green Belt Dr., Toronto, ON M3C 1M1
Tel: 416-445-7255; *Fax:* 416-445-7741
generalinquiries@grandtoy.com
www.grandandtoy.com
Company Type: Private
Profile: Commercial supplier of office supplies, furniture & technology products

Groupe BMTC inc
8500, Place Marien, Montréal, QC H1B 5W8
Tel: 514-648-5757; *Fax:* 514-881-4056
service.clients@braultetmartineau.com
www.braultetmartineau.com
Ticker Symbol: GBT
Company Type: Public
Profile: Retailing furniture stores, household appliance stores, radio, television, & consumer electronics stores

Harry Rosen Inc.
#1600, 77 Bloor St. West, Toronto, ON M5S 1M2
Tel: 416-935-9200; *Fax:* 416-515-7067
www.harryrosen.com
Company Type: Private
Profile: Retail menswear

Harry Winston Diamond Corporation
PO Box 4569 A, Toronto, ON M5W 4T9
Tel: 416-362-2237; *Fax:* 416-362-2230
hw@harrywinston.com
investor.harrywinston.com
Ticker Symbol: HW
Company Type: Public
Profile: Harry Winston Diamond Corporation owns 40% interest in the Diavik Diamond Mine in the Northwest Territories. Rough diamonds are supplied to an international market. The specialist diamond enterprise is also the owner of a diamond jewelry & watch retailer, known as Harry Winston Inc. Retail salons are locatedd in cities around the world, such as Tokyo, Beijing, Paris, London, & New York.

Hart Stores Inc.
900, Place Paul Kane, Laval, QC H7C 2T2
Tel: 450-661-4155; *Fax:* 450-661-6531
hartstoresinfo@hartstores.com
www.hartstores.com
Ticker Symbol: HIS
Company Type: Public
Profile: Hart Stores Inc. operates a network of mid-sized department stores. Its stores are located in Newfoundland, Nova Scotia, New Brunswick, Quebec, & Ontario. Hart Stores Inc.'s banners include Bargain Giant, Géant des Aubaines, & Hart.

Haworth Canada
10 SMED Lane SE, Calgary, AB T2C 4T5
Tel: 403-203-6000; *Fax:* 403-203-6001
www.haworth.com
Company Type: Private
Profile: Haworth Canada manufactures & markets office furniture & workspaces. A factory is located in Quebec, and showrooms are situated in Toronto & Calgary.

Hudson's Bay Company
#500, 401 Bay St., Toronto, ON M5H 2Y4
Tel: 416-861-6112; *Fax:* 416-861-4720
Toll-Free: 866-746-7422
www.hbc.ca
Company Type: Public
Profile: Retailing in department stores; Short-term business credit institutions; Information retrieval services

Indigo Books & Music Inc.
#500, 468 King St. West, Toronto, ON M5V 1L8
Tel: 416-364-4499; *Fax:* 416-364-0355
Toll-Free: 800-832-9124
InvestorRelations@indigo.ca
www.chapters.indigo.ca
Ticker Symbol: IDG
Company Type: Public
Profile: The book retailer operates in all provinces & one territory, under the following names: Indigo, Coles, Chapters, & the World's Biggest Bookstore. Indigo also operates chapters.indigo.ca, to retail books, music, & movies online. Indigo Books & Music Inc. is implementing an environmental paper policy in conjunction with Markets Initiative.

Itochu Canada Ltd
World Trade Centre, #770, 999 Canada Pl., Vancouver, BC V6C 3E1
Tel: 604-331-5800; *Fax:* 604-688-9292
www.itochu.com
Company Type: Private
Profile: Wholesalers of electrical appliances, television & radio sets, commercial equipment, various durable & non-durable goods

Jace Holdings Ltd.
6649 Bulter Cres., Saanichton, BC V8M 1Z7
Tel: 250-483-1600; *Fax:* 250-483-1601
Toll-Free: 800-667-8280
info@thriftyfoods.com
www.thriftyfoods.com
Company Type: Private
Profile: Isle Three Holdings Ltd. provides retail grocery stores & bakeries.

Jean Coutu Group (PJC) Inc.
530, rue Bériault, Longueuil, QC J4G 1S8
Tel: 450-646-9760; *Fax:* 450-646-0550
www.jeancoutu.com
Ticker Symbol: PJC
Company Type: Public
Profile: Wholesalers of drugs, drug proprietaries & druggists' sundries; Retailing in drug stores & proprietary stores; Real estate operators of nonresidential buildings; Patent owners & lessors

Katz Group Canada Ltd.
Bell Tower, #1702, 10104 - 103 Ave., Edmonton, AB T5J 0H8
Tel: 780-990-0505; *Fax:* 780-702-0647
Toll-Free: 877-378-4100
esilverman@katzgroup.ca
www.katzgroup.ca
Company Type: Private
Profile: Encompasses more than 1,800 pharmacies across North America; Canadian pharmacies include Rexall Drug Stores, Pharma Plus, Rexall Pharma Plus, Medicine Shoppe Pharmacy, Guardian, I.D.A., Herbie's/Payless Drug & Food, & Meditrust Pharmacy

La Senza Corporation
1604, boul St-Régis, Montréal, QC H9P 1H6
Tel: 514-684-3651; *Fax:* 514-421-0381
Toll-Free: 888-527-3692
ir@lasenza.com
www.lasenza.com
Ticker Symbol: LTD
Company Type: Public
Profile: Retailing in women's clothing stores, women's accessory & specialty stores, miscellaneous apparel & accessory stores

Leon's Furniture Limited
PO Box 1100 B, 45 Gordon Mackay Rd., Toronto, ON M9L 2R8
Tel: 416-243-7880; *Fax:* 416-243-7890
investors@leons.ca
www.leons.ca
Ticker Symbol: LNF
Company Type: Public
Profile: Through a chain of retail facilities & franchises across Canada, Leon's Furniture Limited is engaged in the sale of home furnishings, electronics, & appliances.

Liquor Control Board of Ontario
55 Lakeshore Blvd. East, Toronto, ON M5E 1A4
Tel: 416-365-5900; *Fax:* 416-864-2596
Toll-Free: 800-668-5226
infoline@lcbo.com
www.lcbo.com
Company Type: Crown
Profile: Retailers in liquor stores

Loblaw Companies Limited
1 President's Choice Circle, Brampton, ON L6Y 5S5
Tel: 905-459-2500; *Fax:* 905-861-2206
investor@loblaw.ca
www.loblaw.com
Ticker Symbol: L
Company Type: Public
Profile: Loblaw Companies Limited operates the following grocery stores: Loblaws, Your Independent Grocer, The Real Canadian Superstore, Fortinos, Atlantic Superstore, Atlantic SaveEasy, No Frills, SuperValu, Valumart, Extra Foods, Shop Easy Foods, Provigo, Zehrs, Cash & Carry, & Maxi.

Loeb Canada Inc
5559 Dundas St. W., Toronto, ON M9B 1B9
Toll-Free: 877-335-5632
loeb@metro.ca
www.loeb.ca
Company Type: Private
Profile: Retails-miscellaneous general merchandise stores; Wholesales-tobacco and tobacco products; Wholesales-confectionery; Wholesales-drugs, drug proprietaries and druggists' sundries; Wholesales-groceries, general line; Retails-fruit and vegetable markets; Retails-meat and fish markets, and freezer provisioners; Retails-dairy products stores

Mark's Work Wearhouse Ltd.
#30, 1035 - 64 Ave. SE, Calgary, AB T2H 2J7
Tel: 403-255-9220; *Fax:* 403-255-6005
Toll-Free: 800-663-6275
www.marks.com
Company Type: Private
Profile: Incorporated on April 12, 1977, the company operates Mark's Work Wearhouse retail stores & has granted franchises to operate Mark's stores in Canada. There are currently 380 stores in Canada, selling a wide range of men's, women's, unisex leisure, casual & workwear clothes & footwear, healthwear & uniforms. In Quebec, Mark's corporate & franchise stores operate under the name L'Equipeur. The company employs approx. 4,600 people & is a wholly-owned subsidiary of CTC Acquisition, a wholly-owned subsidiary of Canadian Tire Corporation, Limited. Mark's was purchased by CT on Feb. 1, 2002, & is now a private company.

Marubeni Canada Ltd.
#600, 40 University Ave., Toronto, ON M5J 1T1
Tel: 416-368-1171; *Fax:* 416-947-9004
www.marubeni.com
Company Type: Private
Profile: Wholesalers of farm & garden machinery & equipment, automobile & other motor vehicles. Offices in Toronto & Vancouver

Metro Inc.
11011, boul Maurice-Duplessis, Montréal, QC H1C 1V6
Tel: 514-643-1000; *Fax:* 514-643-1215
finance@metro.ca
www.metro.ca
Ticker Symbol: MRU
Company Type: Public
Profile: Metro Inc. operates food retail stores in Ontario & Québec, under the following names: Metro, Super C, A&P, Loeb, Food Basics, Marché Richelieu, AMI, Les 5 Saisons, & GEM. The company also distributes pharmaceutical products under the following banners: Brunet, Clini-Plus, The Pharmacy, & Drug Basics.

Metro Inc.
PO Box 68 A, Toronto, ON M5A 1A6
Tel: 416-239-7171; *Fax:* 416-234-6581
Toll-Free: 877-763-7374
www.metro.ca
Company Type: Private
Profile: Offices of holding companies; Retailing in grocery stores

Mitsubishi Canada Limited
#2800, 200 Granville St., Vancouver, BC V6C 1G6
Tel: 604-654-8000; *Fax:* 604-654-8222
asako.a.suzuki@mitsubishicorp.com
www.mitsubishicorp.com
Company Type: Private
Profile: With corporate offices in Vancouver & Toronto, Mitsubishi Canada are wholesalers of automobiles & other motors vehicles, supplies & new parts; divisions in electrical machinery, & home appliances.

Mitsui & Co. (Canada) Ltd.
#1400, 20 Adelaide St. East, Toronto, ON M5C 2T6
Tel: 416-365-3800; *Fax:* 416-865-1486
www.mitsui.ca
Company Type: Private
Profile: Steel & metals; machinery; chemicals; energy; foods; consumer goods; transportation logistics

Nevada Bob's International Inc.
824 - 41st Ave. NE, Calgary, AB T2E 3R3
Tel: 403-717-1400; *Fax:* 403-717-1491
cjordan@forzani.com
www.nevadabobs.ca; www.forzanigroup.com
Ticker Symbol: FGL; NBC
Company Type: Public
Profile: Owns and operates golf specialty shops

New Brunswick Liquor Corporation
PO Box 20787, 170 Wilsey Rd., Fredericton, NB E3B 5B8
Tel: 506-452-6826; *Fax:* 506-462-2024
info@anbl.com
www.nbliquor.com
Company Type: Crown
Profile: A provincial Crown corporation responsible for the purchase, importation, distribution and retailing of all beverage alcohol in New Brunswick

North West Company Fund
Gibraltar House, 77 Main St., Winnipeg, MB R3C 2R1
Tel: 204-943-0881; *Fax:* 204-934-1455
Toll-Free: 800-563-0002
nwc@northwest.ca
www.northwest.ca
Ticker Symbol: NWF
Company Type: Public
Profile: North West Company Fund is involved in the retail of food & daily products & services. Business is carried out in northern Canada, Alaska, the South Pacific, & the Caribbean.

Olco Petroleum Group Inc.
2775, av Georges Vanier, Montréal, QC H1L 6J7
Tel: 514-645-6526; *Fax:* 514-645-8048
Toll-Free: 800-363-1120
www.olco.ca
Company Type: Private
Profile: OLCO is engaged in the supply & marketing of petroleum products. Products include gasoline, propane, kerosene, ultra low-sulphur diesel, furnace oils, & various grades of residual oils. Environmentally friendly products are promoted, such as reusable propane tanks.

Pantorama Industries Inc.
2, rue Lake, Montréal, QC H9B 3H9
Tel: 514-421-1850; *Fax:* 514-684-3159
www.pantorama.com
Ticker Symbol: PTA
Company Type: Private
Profile: Retailing in men's & boys' clothing & accessory stores, women's clothing stores & shoe stores

Parkland Income Fund
Riverside Office Plaza, #236, 4919 - 59th St., Red Deer, AB T4N 6C9
Tel: 403-357-6400; *Fax:* 403-352-0042
corpinfo@parkland.ca
www.parkland.ca
Ticker Symbol: PKI
Company Type: Public
Profile: The Fund is engaged in the operation of retail & wholesale fuels, as well as convenience store businesses. These operations are carried out through independent branded dealers & the following brands: Fas Gas, Fas Gas Plus, Race Trac Fuels, & Short Stop Food Stores. Fuel is transported through the Petrohaul division. Parkland has implemented risk mitigation programs & emergency response procedures to prevent environmental risk in the handling & transportation of fuels, propane, & other products. Business is conducted in Ontario, Manitoba, Saskatchewan, Alberta, British Columbia, & the Yukon Territory.

Pet Valu Canada Inc.
121 McPherson St., Markham, ON L3R 3L3
Tel: 905-946-1200; *Fax:* 905-946-0658
Toll-Free: 888-254-7824
hr@petvalue.com
www.petvalue.com
Ticker Symbol: PVC
Company Type: Public
Profile: Specialty retailer of pet food and pet-related supplies, with stores located in Ontario and Manitoba, as well as the US states of Maryland, Virginia, Pennsylvania and New Jersey

Pharmacy Won Inc.
7171 Yonge St., Thornhill, ON L3T 2A9
Tel: 905-886-7171; *Fax:* 905-886-9605
www.pharmacy2.ca
Company Type: Private
Profile: Retailing in drug stores & proprietary stores, grocery stores & miscellaneous general merchandise stores

Pharmasave Drugs National Ltd.
#201, 8411 - 200th St., Langley, BC V2Y 0E7
Tel: 604-455-2400; *Fax:* 604-455-2493
Toll-Free: 800-661-6106
info@bc.pharmasave.ca
www.pharmasave.com
Company Type: Private
Profile: Pharmasave Drugs National Ltd. is an independent pharmacy & drugstore retailer. Over 400 stores are located in nine provinces.

Premetalco Inc.
110 Belfield Rd., Toronto, ON M9W 1G1
Tel: 416-245-7386; *Fax:* 416-242-2839
Company Type: Private
Profile: Wholesales-metals service centers and offices; Wholesales-chemicals and allied products; Wholesales-construction materials; Mfrs-miscellaneous fabricated wire products

Provigo Inc.
400, av Sainte-Croix, Saint-Laurent, QC H4N 3L4
Tel: 514-383-8800; *Fax:* 514-383-3100
www.provigo.ca
Company Type: Private
Profile: The holding company is engaged in the wholesale & retail of groceries & general merchandise. Provigo owns or franchises supermarkets in Québec, under the Provigo banner. The company also owns or franchises discount stores, known as Maxi & Maxi & Cie.

Reitmans (Canada) Limited
250, rue Sauvé ouest, Montréal, QC H3L 1Z2
Tel: 514-384-1140; *Fax:* 514-385-2669
info@reitmans.com
www.reitmans.com
Ticker Symbol: RET
Company Type: Public
Profile: Reitmans (Canada) Ltd. is the operator of clothing stores, which specialize in both women's & men's fashions & accessories. Stores are operated under the following names: Reitmans, RW & Co., Smart Set, Cassis, Pennington Superstores, Addition-Elle, & Thyme Maternity.

Richelieu Hardware Ltd.
7900, boul Henri-Bourassa ouest, Montréal, QC H4S 1V4
Tel: 514-336-4144; *Fax:* 514-832-4002
Toll-Free: 866-832-4040
info@richelieu.com
www.richelieu.com
Ticker Symbol: RCH
Company Type: Public
Profile: Richelieu Hardware manufactures, imports, & distributes specialty hardware & complementary products. The company serves manufacturers & retailers throughout North America.

Ritchie Bros. Auctioneers Inc.
6500 River Rd., Richmond, BC V6X 4G5
Tel: 604-273-7564; *Fax:* 604-273-2405
Toll-Free: 800-663-1739
info@rbauction.com
www.rbauction.com
Ticker Symbol: RBA
Company Type: Public
Profile: The company is an auctioneer of industrial equipment for the agricultural, mining, petroleum, forestry, construction, transportation, marine, & material handling industries. Ritchie Bros. Auctioneers has locations worldwide.

Roadking Travel Centres Inc.
26 Strathmoor Dr., Sherwood Park, AB T8H 2B6
Tel: 780-464-1000; *Fax:* 780-464-1043
info@roadking.ca
www.roadking.ca
Ticker Symbol: RKG
Company Type: Public
Profile: Roadking Travel Centres Inc. operates travel facilities which offer hospitality & fuel services in Alberta. Centres include Roadking Inns, RK General Stores, RK Express Convenience Stores, restaurants, & fuel stations.

RONA Inc.
220, ch du Tremblay, Boucherville, QC J4B 8H7
Tel: 514-599-5100; *Fax:* 514-599-5161
investor.relations@rona.ca
www.rona.ca
Ticker Symbol: RON
Company Type: Public
Profile: Hardware, home renovation, & gardening products are distributed & retailed by RONA Inc.

Sears Canada Inc.
222 Jarvis St., Toronto, ON M5B 2B8
Tel: 416-941-4425; *Fax:* 416-941-4793
home@sears.ca
www.sears.ca
Ticker Symbol: SCC
Company Type: Public
Profile: Sears Canada Inc. is a general merchandise retailer, as well as a catalogue publisher.

Shnier
50 Kenview Blvd., Brampton, ON L6T 5S8
Tel: 905-789-3755; *Fax:* 905-789-3757
Toll-Free: 800-970-2000
www.shnier.ca
Company Type: Private
Profile: Markets floor covering products

Shoppers Drug Mart Corporation
243 Consumers Rd., Toronto, ON M2J 4W8
Tel: 416-493-1220; *Fax:* 416-491-1022
investorrelations@shoppersdrugmart.ca
www.shoppersdrugmart.ca
Ticker Symbol: SC
Company Type: Public
Profile: Shoppers Drug Mart Corporation licenses retail drug stores, which operate under the name Shoppers Drug Mart, & Pharmaprix in Quebec. Shoppers Home Health Care stores are also owned & operated by Shoppers Drug Mart Corporation. In addition to these retail establishments, Shoppers Drug Mart Corporation also owns a provider of pharmaceutical products & services to long-term care facilities, which operates under the name MediSystem Technologies Inc.

Sleep Country Canada Income Fund
#1, 140 Wendell Ave., Toronto, ON M9N 3R2
Tel: 416-242-4774; *Fax:* 416-242-9644
Toll-Free: 888-753-3788
investor@sleepcountry.ca
www.sleepcountry.ca
Company Type: Public
Profile: Sleep Country Canada Income Fund is engaged in the provision of mattresses & bedding related products. Its wholly-owned subsidiaries are as follows: Sleep Country Canada Inc., Sleep America, LLC, & Dormez-vous Sleep Centres Inc.

Sobeys Inc.
115 King St., Stellarton, NS B0K 1S0
Tel: 902-752-8371;
paul.jewer@sobeys.com
www.sobeys.com
Ticker Symbol: SBY
Company Type: Public
Profile: Sobeys is a national grocery retailer. Retail banners include Sobeys, Foodland, IGA, & Price Chopper. Its two operating divisions are Thrifty Foods & Lawtons Drugs.

Société des alcools du Québec
905, av de Lorimier, Montréal, QC H2K 3V9
Tel: 514-254-2711; *Fax:* 514-864-3532
Toll-Free: 866-873-2020
info@saq.com
www.saq.com
Company Type: Crown
Profile: Regulation, licensing & inspection of miscellaneous commercial sectors

Somerset Entertainment Income Fund
#600, 20 York Mills Rd., Toronto, ON M2P 2C2
Tel: 416-510-2800; *Fax:* 416-510-3070
information@somersetent.com
www.somersetent.com
Ticker Symbol: SOM.UN
Company Type: Public
Profile: Somerset Entertainment Income Fund is engaged in the production & distribution of specialty music. Music is sold internationally, through non-traditional retailers, using interactive displays.

Sony of Canada Ltd.
115 Gordon Baker Rd., Toronto, ON M2H 3R6
Tel: 416-499-1414; *Fax:* 416-497-1774
Toll-Free: 877-899-7669
general_enquiries@sony.ca
www.sony.ca
Company Type: Private
Profile: Sony of Canada Ltd. is an entertainment company that offers electronics, movies, music, & games. Examples of Sony products include BRAVIA televisions, VAIO computers, Blu-ray Disc players, Handycam Camcorders, broadcast cameras, Cyber-shot digital cameras, & IPELA security cameras. Sony of Canada Ltd. is headquartered in Toronto. Sales offices are located in Montréal, Québec & Vancouver British Columbia. Distribution centres are situated in Whitby, Ontario & Coquitlam, British Columbia.

Sterling Shoes Income Fund
2580 Viscount Way, Richmond, BC V6V 1N1
Tel: 604-270-6114; *Fax:* 604-278-7751
www.sterlingshoesincomefund.com
Ticker Symbol: SSI.UN
Company Type: Public
Profile: Through its interest in Sterling Shoes Limited Partnership, Sterling Shoes Income Fund is involved in the retailing of footwear. The following are the organization's retail banners: Sterling Shoes, Shoe Warehouse, Gia Shoes, Joneve Shoes, Freedman Shoes, & Sterling Outlet. There are more than 100 stores throughout Canada.

Summit Food Service Distributors Inc.
580 Industrial Rd., London, ON N5V 1V1
Fax: 519-453-5148
Toll-Free: 800-265-9267
headoffice@summitfoods.com
www.summitfoods.com
Company Type: Public
Profile: Wholesalers of packaged frozen foods & general line groceries

SunOpta Inc.
2838 Bovaird Dr. West, Brampton, ON L7A 0H2
Tel: 905-455-1990; *Fax:* 905-455-2529
info@sunopta.com
www.sunopta.com
Ticker Symbol: STKL
Company Type: Public
Profile: SunOpta Inc. is focused upon sourcing, processing, & distributing healthy, environmentally responsible products. Products include organic food supplements & health & beauty products. The company consists of the following business segments: SunOpta Food Group, SunOpta BioProcess Inc., & Opta Minerals Inc.

The Brick Group Income Fund
16930 - 114 Ave., Edmonton, AB T5M 3S2
Tel: 780-930-6000; *Fax:* 780-454-0969
Toll-Free: 877-843-2742
investor@thebrick.com
www.thebrick.com
Ticker Symbol: BRK.UN
Company Type: Public
Profile: The Brick Group Income Fund is an unincorporated, open-ended, limited purpose trust. The Fund indirectly acquired the limited partnership units of The Brick Warehouse LP. The Brick Warehouse LP owns the outstanding limited partnership units of United Furniture Warehouse LP (United Furniture) & the outstanding shares of First Oceans Trading Corporation. Through its subsidiaries, The Brick Group Income Fund is involved in retailing furniture, appliances, mattresses, & electronics.

The Winroc Corporation
4949 - 51 St. SE, Calgary, AB T2B 3S7
Tel: 403-236-5383; *Fax:* 403-279-0372
www.winroc.com
Company Type: Private
Profile: Wholesalers of construction materials; Retailing in lumber & other building materials dealers

Toshiba of Canada Ltd.
191 McNabb St., Markham, ON L3R 8H2
Tel: 905-470-3500; *Fax:* 905-470-3509
www.toshiba.ca
Company Type: Private
Profile: Wholesalers of office equipment, computers & peripheral equipment & software, electrical appliances, television & radio sets, electronic parts & equipment, medical, dental, hospital equipment & supplies

UAP Inc.
7025, rue Ontario est, Montréal, QC H1N 2B3
Tel: 514-256-5031; *Fax:* 514-256-8469
www.uapinc.com
Company Type: Private
Profile: Wholesales-motor vehicle supplies and new parts; Retails-auto and home supply stores

Uni-Select Inc.
170, boul Industriel, Boucherville, QC J4B 2X3
Tel: 450-641-2440; *Fax:* 450-449-4908
questions@uni-select.com
www.uni-select.com
Ticker Symbol: UNS
Company Type: Public
Profile: Uni-Select Inc. is a wholesale distributor & marketer of heavy duty tools, equipment, replacement parts, & accessories. The company serves the automotive industry.

Unilever Canada Inc.
PO Box 38, Saint John, NB E2L 3X1
Fax: 506-631-6424
Toll-Free: 800-565-7273
www.unilever.ca
Company Type: Private
Profile: Unilever supplies consumer products including foods, & home & personal care products.

United Furniture Warehouse Ltd.
16930 - 114th Ave., Edmonton, AB T5M 3S2
Fax: 780-454-0969
Toll-Free: 866-508-7766
vp@ufw.com
www.ufw.com
Company Type: Private
Profile: The home furnishing retailer has warehouse-style shopping operations in British Columbia, Alberta, Saskatchewan, Manitoba, & Ontario.

Wajax Income Fund
3280 Wharton Way, Mississauga, ON L4X 2C5
Tel: 905-212-3300; *Fax:* 905-624-6020
ir@wajax.com
www.wajax.com
Ticker Symbol: WJX
Company Type: Public
Profile: Through its subsidiaries, Wajax is involved in the sale & parts & service support of power systems, mobile equipment, & industrial components. Wajax serves the manufacturing, natural resources, utilities, construction, & industrial processing sectors. Branches are located throughout Canada.

Westfair Foods Ltd.
PO Box 300 M, 3225 - 12 St. NE, Calgary, AB T2P 2H9
Tel: 403-291-7700; *Fax:* 403-291-7899
www.loblaw.ca
Ticker Symbol: WF
Company Type: Public
Profile: Retailing in grocery stores; Wholesalers of general line groceries. The division serves Western Canada and Northern Ontario

Electronics & Electrical Equipment

Aastra Technologies Limited
155 Snow Blvd., Concord, ON L4K 4N9
Tel: 905-760-4200; *Fax:* 905-760-4233
investors@aastra.com
www.aastra.com
Ticker Symbol: AAH
Company Type: Public
Profile: The company develops, markets, & supports products for communication networks. Products include communication servers, gateways, wireless products, telephone terminals, & advanced software applications. Aastra Technologies Limited serves both the business & residential markets.

Ansen Corporation
100 Schneider Rd., Kanata, ON K2K 1Y2
Tel: 613-599-6277; *Fax:* 613-599-6146
www.ansencorp.com
Ticker Symbol: AGT
Company Type: Public
Profile: Manufacturers of various measuring & controlling devices, & printed circuit boards

Ballard Power Systems Inc.
9000 Glenlyon Parkway, Burnaby, BC V5J 5J8
Tel: 604-454-0900; *Fax:* 604-412-4700
investors@ballard.com
www.ballard.com
Ticker Symbol: BLD
Company Type: Public
Profile: Designers, developers & manufacturers of zero-emission proton exchange membrane fuel cells

Celestica Inc.
12 Concorde Place, 5th Fl., Toronto, ON M3C 3R8
Tel: 416-448-5800; *Fax:* 416-448-5527
Toll-Free: 888-899-9998
corpinfo@celestica.com
www.celestica.com
Ticker Symbol: CLS
Company Type: Public
Profile: Manufacturers of various electronic components, printed circuit boards; Wholesalers in electronic parts & equipment

Cinram International Inc.
2255 Markham Rd., Scarborough, ON M1B 2W3
Tel: 416-298-8190; *Fax:* 416-298-0612
lynefisher@cinram.com
www.cinram.com
Ticker Symbol: CRW
Company Type: Public
Profile: Manufacturers of phonograph records & prerecorded audio tapes & disks; Services allied to motion picture production; Motion picture & video tape distribution

CMC Electronics Inc.
600, boul Dr.-Frederik-Philips, Montréal, QC H4M 2S9
Tel: 514-748-3148; *Fax:* 514-748-3100
www.cmcelectronics.ca
Company Type: Private
Profile: Manufacturers of aviation electronics, communications solutions, custom electronic products, CPS OEM products; Marine & land electronics sales & service; Customer support; Calibration

COM DEV International Ltd.
155 Sheldon Dr., Cambridge, ON N1R 7H6
Tel: 519-622-2300; *Fax:* 519-622-1691
investor.relations@comdev.ca
www.comdev.ca
Ticker Symbol: CDV
Company Type: Public
Profile: COM DEV International engineers & manufactures custom-designed space hardware. The space technology company serves the commercial, civil, & military space hardware market. Facilities are located in Canada, the United States, & the United Kingdom.

Connex See Service
120 East Beaver Creek Rd., Richmond Hill, ON L4B 4V1
Tel: 905-944-6500; *Fax:* 905-944-6520
Toll-Free: 866-429-4625
central@connexservice.ca
www.connexservice.ca
Company Type: Public
Profile: Manufacturers of radio & television broadcasting & communications equipment

Coretec Inc.
8150 Sheppard Ave. East, Toronto, ON M1B 5K2
Tel: 416-208-2100; *Fax:* 416-208-2195
snemchin@coretec-inc.com
www.coretec-inc.com
Ticker Symbol: CYY
Company Type: Public
Profile: Manufacturers of printed circuit boards; Wholesalers of electronic parts & equipment

DALSA Corp.
605 McMurray Rd., Waterloo, ON N2V 2E9
Tel: 519-866-6000; *Fax:* 519-866-8023
sales.americas@dalsa.com
www.dalsa.com
Ticker Symbol: CRC
Company Type: Public
Profile: Designers, developers, and manufacturers of digital imaging products & solutions. In addition engineers semiconductor components.

Descartes Systems Group Inc.
120 Randall Dr., Waterloo, ON N2V 1C6
Tel: 519-746-8110; *Fax:* 519-747-0082
Toll-Free: 800-419-8495
info@descartes.com
www.descartes.com
Ticker Symbol: DSG
Company Type: Public
Profile: The Descartes Systems Group provides logistics management solutions. Solutions are used by the transportation logistics, distribution, manufacturing, & retail sectors.

Electrovaya Inc.
2645 Royal Windsor Dr., Mississauga, ON L5J 1K9
Tel: 905-855-4610; *Fax:* 905-822-7953
Toll-Free: 800-388-2865
customerservice@electrovaya.com
www.electrovaya.com
Ticker Symbol: EFL
Company Type: Public
Profile: Manufacturers of storage batteries

Evertz Technologies Limited
5288 John Lucas Dr., Burlington, ON L7L 5Z9
Tel: 905-335-3700; *Fax:* 905-335-3573
ir@evertz.com; sales@evertz.com
www.evertz.com
Ticker Symbol: ET
Company Type: Public
Profile: Evertz Technologies Limited is a high-technology company. It is engaged in the designing, manufacturing, & marketing of film production, post production, & broadcast equipment. This equipment is used in the film & television broadcast industry.

EXFO Electro-Optical Engineering Inc.
400, av Godin, Québec, QC G1M 2K2
Tel: 418-683-0211; *Fax:* 418-683-2170
Toll-Free: 800-663-3936
info@exfo.com; ir@exfo.com
www.exfo.com
Ticker Symbol: EXF
Company Type: Public
Profile: Test, measurement, & monitoring products are designed & manufactured by EXFO Electro-Optical Engineering Inc.. The company's test & service assurance solutions are used by the global telecommunications industry.

Gamecorp Ltd.
#102, 3565 King Rd., King City, ON L7B 1M3
Tel: 905-833-5844; *Fax:* 905-833-9847
jmoretto@gamecorp.comcom
www.gamecorp.com
Ticker Symbol: GGG
Company Type: Public
Profile: Manufacturers of telephone & telegraph apparatus; Computer integrated systems design

General Electric Canada Inc.
2300 Meadowvale Blvd., Mississauga, ON L5N 5P9
Tel: 905-858-5100; *Fax:* 905-858-5106
www.ge.com/ca/en/
Company Type: Private
Profile: Manufactured products & services include power generation, water processing, aircraft engines, medical imaging, security technology, business & consumer financing, & media content

Genesis Microchip (Canada) Co.
165 Commerce Valley Dr. West, Thornhill, ON L3T 7V8
Tel: 905-889-5400; *Fax:* 905-889-5422
sales-americas@gnss.com
www.gnss.com
Ticker Symbol: GNSS
Company Type: Public
Profile: Monitor products, analog video processors, digital TV processing

Gennum Corporation
4281 Harvester Road, Burlington, ON L7L 5M4
Tel: 905-632-2996; *Fax:* 905-632-2055
corporate@gennum.com
www.gennum.com
Ticker Symbol: GND
Company Type: Public
Profile: Manufacturers & marketers of semiconductor components, electrical subsystems & solutions for the global video, audio & data communications markets

Hammond Power Solutions Inc.
595 Southgate Dr., Guelph, ON N1G 3W6
Tel: 519-822-2441; *Fax:* 519-822-9701
cdncustservice@hammondpowersolutions.com
www.hammondpowersolutions.com
Ticker Symbol: HPS.A
Company Type: Public
Profile: Hammond Power Solutions Inc. engineers & manufactures custom & standard dry-type transformers & related magnetic products. The company's products are used by the global electrical industry.

Hemisphere GPS Inc.
4110 - 9 St. SE, Calgary, AB T2G 3C4
Tel: 403-259-3311; *Fax:* 403-259-8866
info@hemispheregps.com
www.hemispheregps.com
Company Type: Public
Profile: Manufacturers of precision commercial GPS (Global Positioning System) technology

Hewlett-Packard (Canada) Ltd.
5150 Spectrum Way, Mississauga, ON L4W 5G1
Tel: 905-206-4725; *Fax:* 905-206-4739
www.hp.ca
Company Type: Public
Profile: Hewlett-Packard (Canada) Ltd. is a technology solutions companys. It offers information technology infrastructure, personal computing & access devices, global services, imaging, & printing. for consumers & small & medium businesses.

Honeywell Ltd.
333 Unity Dr., Mississauga, ON L5L 3S6
Tel: 905-608-6000; *Fax:* 905-608-6001
www.honeywell.ca
Company Type: Private
Profile: Provides aerospace technology & manufacturing products & services, control technologies for buildings, homes & industry, automotive products, power generation systems, specialty chemicals, fibers, plastics & advanced materials

Hydrogenics Corporation
5985 McLaughlin Rd., Mississauga, ON L5R 1B8
Tel: 905-361-3660; *Fax:* 905-361-3626
investors@hydrogenics.com
www.hydrogenics.com
Ticker Symbol: HYG
Company Type: Public
Profile: Manufacturers of various electrical industrial apparatus, fuel cell systems for power generation; Fuel testing & diagnosis

L-3 Wescam
649 North Service Rd. West, Burlington, ON L7P 5B9
Tel: 905-633-4000; *Fax:* 905-633-4100
Toll-Free: 800-668-4355
Sales.Wescam@L-3com.com
www.wescam.com
Company Type: Public
Profile: Manufacturers of gyrostabilized imaging turrets, digital & analogue reception & custom fitted system integration

Miranda Technologies Inc.
3499, rue Douglas B. Floreani, Montréal, QC H4S 2C6
Tel: 514-333-1772; *Fax:* 514-333-9828
investorrelations@miranda.com
www.miranda.com
Ticker Symbol: MT
Company Type: Public
Profile: Miranda Technologies is a developer, manufacturer, & marketer of hardware & software. Products are used by the television broadcast industry.

Mitec Telecom Inc.
3299, boul. Jean-Baptiste-Deschamps, Lachine, QC H8T 3E4
Tel: 514-694-9000; *Fax:* 514-630-8600
sales@mitectelecom.com
www.mitectelecom.com
Ticker Symbol: MTM
Company Type: Public
Profile: The company is a designer, manufacturer, & supplier of frequency products & solutions. Products power infrastructure in wireless communications, broadcast networks, & satellite communications. Facilities are operated in the United States & China.

Mobile Knowledge Corp.
308 Legget Dr., Kanata, ON K2K 1Y6
Tel: 613-287-5020; *Fax:* 613-287-5021
Toll-Free: 866-624-5330
info@mobile-knowledge.com
www.mobile-knowledge.com
Company Type: Public
Profile: GPS, wireless and mobile data communications technology to serve the taxi, black car, and limousine industry

MOSAID Technologies Incorporated
#203, 11 Hines Rd., Ottawa, ON K2K 2X1
Tel: 613-599-9539; *Fax:* 613-591-8148
communications@mosaid.com
www.mosaid.com
Ticker Symbol: MSD
Company Type: Public
Profile: MOSAID Technologies Incorporated specializes in the development & licensing of patented intellectual property. Products include semiconductors, & wireless & wired communications systems.

Norsat International Inc.
#110, 4020 Viking Way, Richmond, BC V6V 2N2
Tel: 604-821-2800; *Fax:* 604-821-2801
info@norsat.com; sales@norsat.com
www.norsat.com
Ticker Symbol: NII
Company Type: Public
Profile: Norsat International, Inc. designs, engineers, & markets intelligent satellite solutions for high-speed data transmission. Examples of its portable satellite units include the GLOBETrekker & NewsLink models.

Nortel Networks Corporation
#100, 8200 Dixie Road, Brampton, ON L6T 5P6
Tel: 905-863-0000; *Fax:* 905-863-8423
Toll-Free: 888-901-7286
investor@nortel.com
www.nortelnetworks.com
Ticker Symbol: NT
Company Type: Public
Profile: Offices of holding companies; Manufacturers of telephone & telegraph apparatus, radio & television broadcasting & communications equipment; Wholesalers of electrical apparatus & equipment, wiring supplies; Commercial physical & biological research

Philips Electronics Canada
281 Hillmount Rd., Markham, ON L6C 2S3
Tel: 905-201-4100; *Fax:* 905-887-4241
Toll-Free: 888-744-5477
webmaster@philips.com
www.philips.ca
Company Type: Private
Profile: Philips Electronics manufactures & markets technological products in areas such as healthcare, household, entertainment, & personal care.

Research In Motion Limited
295 Phillip St., Waterloo, ON N2L 3W8
Tel: 519-888-7465; *Fax:* 519-888-7884
investor_relations@rim.com; help@rim.com
www.rim.com
Ticker Symbol: RIM
Company Type: Public
Profile: Research in Motion Ltd. designs, manufactures, & markets wireless solutions for the mobile communications market.

Sierra Wireless, Inc.
13811 Wireless Way, Richmond, BC V6V 3A4
Tel: 604-231-1100; *Fax:* 604-231-1109
info@sierrawireless.com
www.sierrawireless.com
Ticker Symbol: SW
Company Type: Public
Profile: Sierra Wireless, Inc. specializes in wireless solutions. It provides professional services to clients who require expertise in wireless design, integration, & carrier certification.

Softchoice Corporation
#200, 173 Dufferin St., Toronto, ON M6K 3H7
Tel: 416-588-9002; *Fax:* 416-588-9004
investor_relations@softchoice.com
www.softchoice.com
Ticker Symbol: SO
Company Type: Public
Profile: Softchoice Corporation provides technology solutions & services. Organizations & businesses are assisted with their software & hardware technology resources.

Sonepar Canada
#1840, 1, Place Ville-Marie, Montréal, QC H3B 4A9
Tel: 514-861-1155; *Fax:* 514-861-4453
www.sonepar.com
Company Type: Private
Profile: Electrical equipment, with emphasis on cable, wiring, fittings, HVAC & lighting. Sonepar Canada comprises Gescan, Texcan, Lumen, Osso Electric Supplies Inc., and Hagemeyer Canada Century Vallen divisions

Spectrum Signal Processing by Vecima
#300, 2700 Production Way, Burnaby, BC V5A 4X1
Tel: 604-421-5422; *Fax:* 604-421-1764
Toll-Free: 800-663-8986
sales@spectrumsignal.com
www.spectrumsignal.com
Ticker Symbol: VCM
Company Type: Public
Profile: Developer of software defined radio (SDR) solutions for communications and intelligence gathering applications (rugged and semi-rugged military communications, modem solutions for infrastructure, signals intelligence, radar/sonar, industrial computing, electronic warfare)

SR Telecom & Co.
3200, rue Guénette, Montréal, QC H4S 2G5
Tel: 514-335-1210;
www.srtelecom.com
Company Type: Private
Profile: SR Telecom & Co. provides WiMAX & WiMAX-based wireless technologies for mobile, nomadic, & fixed networks. Clients include telecommunications companies & independent operating companies that deliver Internet & broadband data services.

Tri-Vision International Ltd.
41 Pullman Ct., Toronto, ON M1X 1E4
Tel: 416-298-8551; *Fax:* 416-298-7976
Toll-Free: 888-298-8551
trivision@tri-vision.ca
www.tri-vision.ca
Ticker Symbol: TVL
Company Type: Public
Profile: Provides technologies & systems design, development & manufacture of hardward & software products for cable television & multimedia industries

TS Telecom Ltd.
180 Amber St., Markham, ON L3R 3J8
Tel: 905-470-2282; *Fax:* 905-470-2273
tsinfo@tstelecom.com
www.tstelecom.com
Ticker Symbol: TOM
Company Type: Public
Profile: Manufacturers of telephone & telegraph apparatus

Tundra Semiconductor Corp.
603 March Rd., Ottawa, ON K2K 2M5
Tel: 613-592-0714; *Fax:* 613-592-1320
Toll-Free: 800-267-7321
inquire@tundra.com
www.tundra.com
Ticker Symbol: TUN
Company Type: Public
Profile: Manufacturers of semiconductors & related devices; Wholesalers of electronic parts & equipment

Turbo Power Systems Inc.
#400, 350 Bay St., Toronto, ON M5H 2S6
Tel: 905-690-1722; *Fax:* 905-690-1721
rak@turbopowersystems.com
www.turbopowersystems.com
Company Type: Public
Profile: Development and manufacture of electrical machines used in distributed and other power generation applications

Vecima Networks Inc.
4210 Commerce Circle, Victoria, BC V8Z 6N6
Tel: 250-881-1982; *Fax:* 250-881-1974
invest@vecima.com
www.vecima.com
Ticker Symbol: VCM
Company Type: Public
Profile: Vecima Networks Inc. is a designer, manufacturer, & distributor of hardware products with embedded software that supports broadband access to cable, wireless, & telephony networks. Principal markets include Broadband Wireless & Converged Wired Solutions. Vecima Networks has ISO 9001:2000 certified manufacturing operations in Saskatoon, Saskatchewan.

Wi-LAN Inc.
#608, 11 Holland Ave., Ottawa, ON K1Y 4S1
Tel: 613-688-4330; *Fax:* 613-688-4894
info@wi-lan.com; ir@wi-lan.com
www.wi-lan.com
Ticker Symbol: WIN
Company Type: Public
Profile: The company is a technology innovation & licensing company. Wi-LAN Inc.'s patent portfolio applies to products in the communications & consumer electronics markets.

Wireless Matrix Corporation
#1A, 3751 North Fraser Way, Burnaby, BC V5J 5G4
Tel: 604-439-2444; *Fax:* 604-439-2447
Toll-Free: 888-843-8554
invest@wirelessmatrixcorp.com
www.wirelessmatrixcorp.com
Ticker Symbol: WRX
Company Type: Public
Profile: Wireless Matrix Corporation is engaged in the provision of software solutions to improve service fleet delivery metrics.

Zarlink Semiconductor Inc.
400 March Rd., Ottawa, ON K2K 3H4
Tel: 613-592-0200; *Fax:* 613-592-5470
Toll-Free: 800-325-4927
corporate@zarlink.com
www.zarlink.com
Ticker Symbol: ZL
Company Type: Public
Profile: Zarlink Semiconductor Inc. focuses upon manufacturing & distributing microelectronic components. Products are used in the medical device & communications markets.

Engineering & Management

ADS Inc.
485, des Érables, Saint-Elzéar, QC G0S 2J0
Tel: 418-387-3383; *Fax:* 418-387-8853
ads@adsinc.ca
www.adsinc.ca
Ticker Symbol: AAL
Company Type: Public
Profile: Offices of holding companies; Engineering services; General contractors in industrial buildings & warehouses

AECOM Canada Ltd.
#275, 3001 Wayburne Dr., Burnaby, BC V5G 4W3
Tel: 604-438-5311; *Fax:* 604-438-5587
info@aecom.com
www.aecom.com
Company Type: Private
Profile: AECOM provides professional technical & management support services. The company serves a great range of markets, such as the energy, water, environmental, & transporation industries. AECOM has more than seventy offices across Canada. An example of its work is the Distant Early Warning Line Project, which remediates landfills in the Canadian North.

AEterna Zentaris Inc.
1405 du Parc-Technologique Blvd., Québec, QC G1P 4P5
Tel: 418-652-8525; *Fax:* 418-652-0881
www.aeternazentaris.com
Ticker Symbol: AEL
Company Type: Public
Profile: Commercial physical & biological research

AMEC Inc.
4th Floor, 700 University Ave., Toronto, ON M5G 1X6
Tel: 416-592-2102; *Fax:* 416-592-8284
www.amec.com
Company Type: Private
Profile: Engineering & management services; Heavy construction; Water, sewer, pipeline, communications, power line construct; Refuse systems; Prepackaged software; Real estate, Land subdividers & developers; Manufacturers of general industrial machinery & equipment

Armtec Infrastructure Income Fund
#3, 370 Speedvale Ave. West, Guelph, ON N1H 7M7
Tel: 519-822-0210; *Fax:* 519-822-8894
www.armtecincomefund.com
Ticker Symbol: ARF.UN
Company Type: Public
Profile: Armtec Infrastructure Income Fund is an unincorporated, open-ended, limited purpose trust. It is involved in the manufacturing & marketing of engineered bridging solutions & drainage products. Products are used for infrastructure applications, such as residential & commercial building construction, agricultural drainage, & the natural resources industry.

Ausenco Sandwell
855 Homer St., Vancouver, BC V6B 2W2
Tel: 604-684-9311; *Fax:* 604-688-5913
info@ausencosandwell.com
www.ausenco.com
Company Type: Public
Profile: Engineering & project management services in the areas of: Energy (Oil & Gas, Biofuels, Renewable Energy, Power Generation & Transmission); Environment & Sustainability (Civil & Geotechnical Engineering, Waste Treatment, Mine Waste Management, Permitting, Water Management, Landfill Design); Minerals & Metals (Processing Facilities); Process Infrastructure (Ports, Rail, Pipelines, Materials Handling, Supply Chain Optimisation, Control Systems, Waste Water Treatment); & Program Management (Project Management, Logistics, Construction Management, Statutory Approvals, Stakeholder Relations). Offices in Vancouver, Calgary, Montreal & Burlington.

Avcorp Industries Inc.
10025 River Way, Delta, BC V4G 1M7
Tel: 604-582-1137; *Fax:* 604-582-2620
info@avcorp.com
www.avcorp.com
Ticker Symbol: AVP
Company Type: Public
Profile: Engineering services; Manufacturers of aircraft parts & auxiliary equipment, aircraft engines & engine parts

CAE Inc.
8585, ch de Côte-de-Liesse, Montréal, QC H4T 1G6
Tel: 514-341-6780; *Fax:* 514-341-7699
Toll-Free: 866-999-6223
investor.relations@cae.com
www.cae.com
Ticker Symbol: CAE
Company Type: Public
Profile: CAE Inc. serves the civil aviation & defense forces, through the provision of simulation & modelling technologies, as well as integrated training solutions. The company's civil aviation & military training centres are located throughout the world. CAE Inc. has been granted the BOMA Go Green plan certification, & has implemented environmental programs such as the management of residual materials, recycling, pollution prevention, & residue exchange.

Calian Technology Ltd.
2 Beaverbrook Rd., Ottawa, ON K2K 1L1
Tel: 613-599-8600; *Fax:* 613-592-7771
ir@calian.com
www.calian.com
Ticker Symbol: CTY
Company Type: Public
Profile: Calian Technologies Ltd. is comprised of a Technology Services Division & a Systems Engineering Division. It specializes in the satellite communications, telecommunications, manufacturing, defence, & aerospace markets. Technology services are sold to industry & government in Canada & internationally.

Cell-Loc Location Technologies Inc.
#1600, 37th St. SW, Calgary, AB T3C 3P1
Tel: 403-569-5700; *Fax:* 403-569-5701
investors@cell-loc.com
www.cell-loc.com
Ticker Symbol: XCT
Company Type: Public
Profile: Commercial physical & biological research; Patent owners & lessors

CGI Group Inc.
1130, rue Sherbrooke ouest, 7e étage, Montréal, QC H3A 2M8
Tel: 514-841-3200; *Fax:* 514-841-3299
www.cgi.com
Ticker Symbol: GIB
Company Type: Public
Profile: The information technology & business process services firm is engaged in the integration & customization of technologies & software applications, as well as the management of business processes & transactions.

Chromos Molecular Systems Inc.
PO Box 8, #220, 980 W 1st St., North Vancouver, BC V7P 3N4
Tel: 604-985-7100; *Fax:* 604-980-2501
info@chromos.com
www.chromos.com
Ticker Symbol: CHR
Company Type: Public
Profile: Commercial physical & biological research

ConjuChem Inc.
#3950, 225, President Kennedy Ave., Montréal, QC H2X 3Y8
Tel: 514-844-5558; *Fax:* 514-844-1119
lapointe@conjuchem.com
www.conjuchem.com
Ticker Symbol: CJB
Company Type: Public
Profile: Commercial physical & biological research

Conor Pacific Group Inc.
Four Bentall Centre, PO Box 49224, #3474, 1055 Dunsmuir St., Vancouver, BC V7X 1L2
Tel: 604-669-3373; *Fax:* 604-669-3353
bob.nowack@conorpacific.com
www.conorpacific.com
Company Type: Public
Profile: Refuse systems

CPI Plastics Group Limited
151 Courtney Park Dr. West, Mississauga, ON L5W 1Y5
Tel: 905-795-5505; *Fax:* 905-795-5523
Toll-Free: 800-663-9097
info@cpiplastics.com
www.cpiplastics.com
Ticker Symbol: CPI
Company Type: Public
Profile: Plastics processor & thermoplastic profile design, engineering & processing

CryoCath Technologies Inc.
16771, ch Sainte-Marie, Montréal, QC H9H 5H3
Tel: 514-694-1212; *Fax:* 514-694-6279
customerservice@cryocath.com
www.cryocath.com
Company Type: Public
Profile: Commercial physical & biological research; Manufacturers of surgical & medical instruments & apparatus

Cymat Corp.
#6320, 2 Danville Rd., Mississauga, ON L5T 2L7
Tel: 905-696-9900; *Fax:* 905-696-9300
info@cymat.com
www.cymat.com
Ticker Symbol: CYM
Company Type: Public
Profile: Commercial physical & biological research; Patent owners & lessors; Manufacturers of various primary metal products; Wholesalers of metals service centers & offices

Decoma International Inc.
50 Casmir Ct., Concord, ON L4K 4J5
Tel: 905-669-2888; *Fax:* 905-669-5075
info@decoma.com
www.decoma.com
Company Type: Private
Profile: Engineering services; Manufacturers of motor vehicle parts & accessories, automotive stampings, various plastics products, coating, engraving & allied services

GE Water & Process Technologies
3239 Dundas St. West, Oakville, ON L6M 4B2
Tel: 905-465-3030; *Fax:* 905-465-3050
www.zenon.com
Company Type: Private
Profile: ZENON is engaged in commercial physical & biological research. It manufactures various service industry machinery, general industrial machinery & equipment, & water treatment systems.

GENIVAR Income Fund
5858, ch de la Côte-des-Neiges, 4e étage, Montréal, QC H3S 1Z1
www.genivar.com
Ticker Symbol: GNV.UN
Company Type: Public
Profile: GENIVAR Income Fund is involved in consulting engineering. Projects are carried out in over 35 countries. Offices are located in Canada & the Caribbean. GENIVAR is an ISO 9001:2000 certified organization.

Hatch Ltd.
Sheridan Science & Technology Park, 2800 Speakman Dr., Mississauga, ON L5K 2R7
Tel: 905-855-7600; *Fax:* 905-855-8270
webmaster@hatch.ca
www.hatch.ca
Company Type: Private
Profile: The consulting & technical design firm serves the global mining & metals, energy & infrastructure sectors.

Helix BioPharma Corp.
#3, 305 Industrial Pkwy. South, Aurora, ON L4G 6X7
Tel: 905-841-2300; *Fax:* 905-841-2244
helix@helixbiopharma.com
www.helixbiopharma.com
Ticker Symbol: HBP
Company Type: Public
Profile: Commercial physical & biological research

Isotechnika Inc.
5120 - 75th St., Edmonton, AB T6E 6W2
Tel: 780-487-1600; *Fax:* 780-484-4105
Toll-Free: 888-487-9944
investorrelations@isotechnika.com
www.isotechnika.com
Ticker Symbol: ISA
Company Type: Public
Profile: Commercial physical & biological research; Manufacturers of pharmaceutical preparations, in-vitro & in-vivo diagnostic substances

KHD Humboldt Wedag International Ltd.
#1620, 400 Burrard St., Vancouver, BC V6C 3A6
Tel: 604-683-5767; *Fax:* 604-683-3205
www.khdhumboldt.com
Ticker Symbol: KHD
Company Type: Public
Profile: KHD Humboldt Wedag International Ltd. is engaged in designing & engineering services. It supplies proprietary technologies & equipment for the coal, cement, & minerals processing industry.

Linamar Corporation
287 Speedvale Ave. West, Guelph, ON N1H 1C5
Tel: 519-836-7550; *Fax:* 519-836-9175
investorrelations@linamar.com
www.linamar.com
Ticker Symbol: LNR
Company Type: Public
Profile: Highly engineered products are developed, designed, & produced by thie manufacturing company. Linamar Corporation's divisions, Driveline & Powertrain, are engaged in the manufacture of components, modules, & systems for the automotive industry, & mobile industrial markets.

Marsulex Inc.
#300, 111 Gordon Baker Rd., Toronto, ON M2H 3R1
Tel: 416-496-9655; *Fax:* 416-496-4155
Toll-Free: 800-387-5030
investor@marsulex.com
www.marsulex.com
Ticker Symbol: MLX
Company Type: Public
Profile: Marsulex Inc. provides the following industrial services: handling waste streams & industrial by-products; production of water treatment chemicals; environmental compliance solutions for air quality control; & production of sulphur-based industrial chemicals.

Neo Material Technologies Inc.
#1740, 121 King St. West, Toronto, ON M5H 3T9
Tel: 416-367-8588; *Fax:* 416-367-5471
info@neomaterials.com
www.neomaterials.com
Ticker Symbol: NEM
Company Type: Public
Profile: Through its business divisions, Performance Materials & Magnaquench, Neo Material Technologies Inc. produces, processes, & develops zirconium, neodymium-iron-boron magnetic powders, & rare earths based engineered materials & applications. The products are used in many high technology products.

Neurochem Inc.
275, boul Armand-Frappier, Laval, QC H7V 4A7
Tel: 450-680-4500; *Fax:* 450-680-4501
Toll-Free: 877-680-4500
webinfo@neurochem.com
www.neurochem.com
Ticker Symbol: NRM
Company Type: Public
Profile: Commercial physical & biological research

SNC-Lavalin Group Inc.
455, boul René-Lévesque ouest, Montréal, QC H2Z 1Z3
Tel: 514-393-1000; *Fax:* 514-866-0795
investors@snclavalin.com
www.snclavalin.com
Ticker Symbol: SNC
Company Type: Public
Profile: The international engineering & construction organization owns infrastructure, & is engaged in the provision of operation & maintenance services. Examples of services include project financing, project management, procurement, engineering, & construction. The group is involved in sectors such as pharmaceuticals, petroleum, agrifood, the environment, transit, power, & mining.

Stantec Inc.
10160 - 112th St., Edmonton, AB T5K 2L6
Tel: 780-917-7000; *Fax:* 780-917-7330
ir@stantec.com
www.stantec.com
Ticker Symbol: STN
Company Type: Public
Profile: Stantec Inc. offers professional consulting services for infrastructure & facilities projects. The following services are provided: planning, project management, project economics, surveying & geomatics, engineering, architecture, landscape architecture, environmental science, & interior design.

Stressgen Biotechnologies Corporation
#350, 4243 Glanford Ave., Victoria, BC V8Z 4B9
Tel: 250-744-2811; *Fax:* 250-744-3331
Toll-Free: 800-661-4978
www.stressgen.com
Company Type: Public
Profile: Commercial physical & biological research; Manufacturers of pharmaceutical preparations

Thallion Pharmaceuticals Inc.
7150, rue Alexander-Fleming, Montréal, QC H4S 2C8
Tel: 514-940-3600; *Fax:* 514-940-3622
info@thallion.com
www.thallion.com
Ticker Symbol: TLN
Company Type: Public
Profile: Commercial physical & biological research

The Goldfarb Corporation
#100, 18 Spadina Rd., Toronto, ON M5R 2S7
Tel: 416-229-2070; *Fax:* 416-229-5392
info@goldfarbcorp.com
www.goldfarbcorp.com
Company Type: Public
Profile: Management consulting services; Wholesalers of industrial & personal service paper; General automotive repair shops; Automotive exhaust system repair shops

Virtek Vision International Inc.
785 Bridge St., Waterloo, ON N2V 2K1
Tel: 519-746-7190; *Fax:* 519-746-3383
info@virtek.ca
www.virtek.ca
Company Type: Private
Profile: Virtek is a provider of precision laser-based templating, inspection, & CNC manufacturing solutions. The company serves customers in the automotive, aerospace, woodworking, metalworking, & transportation industries around the world.

Westaim Corporation
#1010, 144 - 4th Ave. SW, Calgary, AB T2P 3N4
Tel: 403-237-7272; *Fax:* 403-237-8181
info@westaim.com
www.westaim.com
Ticker Symbol: WED
Company Type: Public
Profile: Commercial physical & biological research; Patent owners & lessors

Finance

Accord Financial Corp.
#1803, 77 Bloor St. West, Toronto, ON M5S 1M2
Tel: 416-961-0007; *Fax:* 416-961-9443
info@accordfinancial.com
www.accordfinancial.com
Ticker Symbol: ACD
Company Type: Public
Profile: Through its subsidiaries, Accord Financial provides the following financial services to small & medium-sized businesses: record-keeping, financing, credit investigation, collection services, & guarantees.

AGF Management Limited
Toronto Dominion Bank Tower, 66 Wellington St. West, 31st Fl., Toronto, ON M5K 1E9
Tel: 416-367-1900; *Fax:* 905-214-8243
Toll-Free: 800-268-8583
tiger@agf.com
www.agf.com
Ticker Symbol: AGF
Company Type: Public
Profile: AGF Management Limited comprises AGF Asset Management, AGF Investment Management, & AGF Trust. The financial services company has offices throughout Canada, as well as subsidiaries internationally.

Allbanc Split Corp.
Scotia Plaza, PO Box 4085 A, 40 King St. West, 26th Fl., Toronto, ON M5W 2X6
Tel: 416-945-4171; *Fax:* 416-863-7425
mc_allbanc@scotiacapital.com
www.scotiamanagedcompanies.com
Ticker Symbol: ABK
Company Type: Public
Profile: Security brokers, dealers, & flotation companies; Unit investment trusts, certificate/closed-end management offices

Amalgamated Income Limited Partnership
#1, 606 Meredith Rd. NE, Calgary, AB T2E 5A8
Tel: 403-265-6540; *Fax:* 403-206-7185
Toll-Free: 888-708-5757
info@aiun.ca
www.aiun.ca
Ticker Symbol: AI
Company Type: Public
Profile: Security brokers, dealers & flotation companies

Amisk Inc.
#101, 3633 rue Panet, Jonquière, QC G7X 8T7
Tel: 418-546-1156; *Fax:* 418-546-0004
Company Type: Public
Profile: Miscellaneous business credit institutions

ATB Financial
9888 Jasper Ave. NW, Edmonton, AB T5J 1P1
Tel: 780-408-7000; *Fax:* 780-422-4178
Toll-Free: 800-332-8383
atbinfo@atb.com
www.atb.com
Company Type: Crown
Profile: Provincially chartered banks &/or trust companies

Aurquest Resources Inc.
Scotia Plaza, #3100, 40 King St. West, Toronto, ON M5H 3Y2
Tel: 416-744-7405; *Fax:* 416-744-7405
Company Type: Public
Profile: Security brokers, dealers, & flotation companies

AXA Canada
#700, 2020, rue University, Montréal, QC H3A 2A5
Tel: 514-282-1914; *Fax:* 514-282-9588
Toll-Free: 877-392-6323
www.axa.ca
Company Type: Private
Profile: Property/casualty insurance & financial services; other head offices in Toronto (416-928-8801), Vancouver (604-669-0595)

B2B Trust
#200, 130 Adelaide St. West, Toronto, ON M5H 3P5
Tel: 416-947-7427; *Fax:* 416-947-9476
Toll-Free: 800-263-8349
questions@b2btrust.com
b2btrust.com
Ticker Symbol: BBT
Company Type: Public
Profile: Enables non-bank partners to provide banking & other financial services to their customers

Bank of Canada
234 Wellington St., Ottawa, ON K1A 0G9
Tel: 613-782-8111; *Fax:* 613-782-7713
Toll-Free: 800-303-1282
info@bankofcanada.ca
www.bankofcanada.ca
Company Type: Crown
Profile: The Bank of Canada is a federal central bank.

BMO Financial Group
First Canadian Place, 100 King St. West, 18th Fl., Toronto, ON M5X 1A1
Tel: 416-867-6642; *Fax:* 416-867-3367
Toll-Free: 877-225-5266
feedback@bmo.com; remarque@bmo.com
www.bmo.com
Ticker Symbol: BMO
Company Type: Public
Profile: BMO Financial Group offers a wide range of financial products & services, including retail banking, investment banking, & wealth management.

Business Development Bank of Canada
BDC Bldg., #400, 5, Place Ville Marie, Montréal, QC H3B 5E7
Toll-Free: 877-232-2269
info@bdc.ca
www.bdc.ca
Ticker Symbol: BDB
Company Type: Crown
Profile: Federal & federally sponsored credit agency; management consulting services; business consulting services; operates 100 business centres across Canada

Canaccord Financial Inc.
Pacific Centre, PO Box 10337, #2200, 609 Granville St., Vancouver, BC V7Y 1H2
Tel: 604-643-7300; *Toll-Free:* 800-382-9280
scott_davidson@canaccord.com
www.canaccordfinancial.com
Ticker Symbol: CCI
Company Type: Public

Profile: The full service investment dealer conducts operations in the following sectors: capital markets, & private client services.

Canada Life Financial Corporation
330 University Ave., Toronto, ON M5G 1R8
Tel: 416-597-6981; *Fax:* 416-597-1940
Toll-Free: 888-252-1847
www.canadalife.com
Ticker Symbol: CL.PR.B
Company Type: Public
Profile: CLFC is the parent company of Canada Life Assurance Company which provides insurance, reinsurance services, unit trusts, & wealth management products & services. Clients are both individuals & groups in Canada, the United Kingdom, the United States, & the Republic of Ireland.

Canada Mortgage & Housing Corporation
700 Montreal Rd., Ottawa, ON K1A 0P7
Tel: 613-748-2000; *Fax:* 613-748-2098
chic@cmhc-schl.gc.ca
www.cmhc-schl.gc.ca
Company Type: Crown
Profile: Administration of housing programs

Canadian Imperial Bank of Commerce
Commerce Court West, 199 Bay St., Toronto, ON M5L 1A2
Tel: 416-980-2211; *Toll-Free:* 800-465-2422
investorrelations@cibc.com
www.cibc.com
Ticker Symbol: CM
Company Type: Public
Profile: CIBC provides financial products & services through CIBC Retail Markets and CIBC World Markets. Customers include individuals & small business clients, plus corporate & institutional clients.

Canadian Western Bank
#3000, 10303 Jasper Ave., Edmonton, AB T5J 3X6
Tel: 780-423-8865; *Fax:* 780-423-8899
Toll-Free: 800-663-1124
comments@cwbank.com
www.cwbankgroup.com
Ticker Symbol: CWB
Company Type: Public
Profile: The federally chartered, Schedule I bank provides personal & commercial banking services across western Canada. Subsidiaries of Canadian Western Bank include Valiant Trust Company & Canadian Western Trust. These subsidiaries offer both personal & corporate trust services. Canadian Direct Insurance Inc., another of Canadian Western Bank's subsidiaries, is engaged in the provision of personal home & automobile insurance.

Carfinco Income Fund
#300, 4245 - 97 St., Edmonton, AB T6E 5Y7
Tel: 780-413-7549; *Fax:* 780-450-1134
Toll-Free: 888-486-4356
carfinco@carfinco.com
www.carfinco.com
Ticker Symbol: CFN.UN
Company Type: Public
Profile: Carfinco Income Fund is a specialty finance income fund. It is involved in the provision of consumer car loans to borrowers who are unable to obtain financing through traditional sources.

Cash Store Financial Services Inc.
17631 - 103 Ave., Edmonton, AB T5S 1N8
Tel: 780-408-5110; *Fax:* 780-408-5122
information@csfinancial.ca
www.csfinancial.ca
Ticker Symbol: CSF
Company Type: Public
Profile: CFS provides alternative financial products & services. It serves clients who seek short term loans, & operates under the following banners: Instaloans; The Cash Store. It has a network of 570 branches across Canada.

Central 1 Credit Union
1441 Creekside Dr., Vancouver, BC V6J 4S7
Tel: 604-734-2511; *Fax:* 604-737-5055
Toll-Free: 800-661-6813
info@central1.com
www.central1.com
Company Type: Public
Profile: Provincially chartered credit union. Ontario regional office located at 2810 Matheson Blvd. E., Mississauga, ON L4W 4X7, (905) 238-9400.

Chrysler Financial Canada Inc.
2425 Matheson Blvd. East, 3rd Fl., Mississauga, ON L4W 5N7
Tel: 905-629-6000; *Toll-Free:* 800-263-6920
www.chryslerfinancial.ca
Company Type: Public
Profile: Personal credit & business credit institution

CI Financial Corp.
2 Queen St. East, 20th Fl., Toronto, ON M5C 3G7
Tel: 416-364-1145; *Fax:* 416-364-4990
Toll-Free: 800-268-9374
djamieson@ci.com
www.ci.com
Ticker Symbol: CIX
Company Type: Public
Profile: CI Financial Corp. is a wealth management firm & investment fund company. Through its wholly-owned subsidiaries, CI Investments Inc. & the Assante Corporation, CI Financial Income Fund manages mutual funds & other investment products.

Clairvest Group Inc.
#1700, 22 St. Clair Ave. East, Toronto, ON M4T 2S3
Tel: 416-925-9270; *Fax:* 416-925-5753
www.clairvest.com
Ticker Symbol: CVG
Company Type: Public
Profile: Clairvest Group Inc. is a private equity management firm. Through Clairvest Equity Partners, Clairvest Equity Partners III & IV, it provides equity financing to North American mid-market companies with a goal to build value in the businesses & generate financial returns for investors.

Clarke Inc.
6009 Quinpool Rd., 9th Fl., Halifax, NS B3K 5J7
Tel: 902-442-3000; *Fax:* 902-442-0187
www.clarkeinc.com
Ticker Symbol: CKI
Company Type: Public
Profile: Clarke Inc. is an activist catalyst investment company, with several wholly-owned operating companies & divisions. The company has a diversified portfolio of investments, with operating subsidiaries as follows: Clarke Transport Inc., Clarke Road Transport Inc., Clarke IT Solutions Inc., La Traverse Rivière-du-Loup - St. Siméon Ltée., CIS Shipping International Inc., & Granby Industries.

Coast Capital Savings Credit Union
15117 - 101 Ave., Surrey, BC V3R 8P7
Tel: 604-517-7000; *Toll-Free:* 888-517-7000
www.coastcapitalsavings.com
Company Type: Private
Profile: Coast Capital Savings Credit Union is a provincially chartered credit union in British Columbia.

Credit Union Central of Saskatchewan
PO Box 3030, 2055 Albert St., Regina, SK S4P 3G8
Tel: 306-566-1200; *Fax:* 306-566-1372
Toll-Free: 866-403-7499
info@saskcentral.com
www.saskcu.com; www.saskcentral.com
Company Type: Private
Profile: Credit Union Central of Saskatchewan is a provincially chartered credit union.

Davis + Henderson Corporation
#201, 939 Eglington Ave. East, Toronto, ON M4G 4H7
Tel: 416-696-7700; *Fax:* 416-696-8308
Toll-Free: 866-524-1470
investorrelations@dhltd.com
www.dhltd.com
Ticker Symbol: DHF.UN
Company Type: Public
Profile: The organization supplies financial services to financial organizations, including mortgage lenders/brokers, insurance companies, governments, & regional banks. It was recognized as one of Canada's Greenest Employers for 2010.

Desjardins Trust Inc.
PO Box 34, 1, Complexe Desjardins, Montréal, QC H5B 1E4
Tel: 514-286-9441; *Fax:* 514-286-1131
Toll-Free: 800-361-6840
www.desjardins.com
Company Type: Public
Profile: Federally chartered bank & trust company

Deutsche Bank AG, Canada Branch
Commerce Court West, PO Box 263, #4700, 199 Bay St., Toronto, ON M5L 1E9
Tel: 416-682-8400; *Fax:* 416-682-8383
www.db.com/canada
Company Type: Private
Profile: Federally chartered bank; branch of a foreign bank

DRI Capital Inc.
#200, 22 St. Clair Ave East, Toronto, ON M4T 2S5
Tel: 416-863-1865; *Fax:* 416-863-5161
info@dricapital.com
www.dricapital.com
Company Type: Private
Profile: Patent owners & lessors; Personal credit institutions

Equitable Group Inc.
#700, 30 St. Clair Ave. West, Toronto, ON M4V 3A1
Tel: 416-515-7000; *Fax:* 416-515-7001
Toll-Free: 866-407-0004
customerservice@equitabletrust.com
www.equitabletrust.com
Ticker Symbol: ETC
Company Type: Public
Profile: Through its wholly-owned subsidiary, The Equitable Trust Company, Equitable Group Inc. offers first mortgage financing & Guaranteed Investment Certificates to depositors. The Equitable Trust Company is a federally incorporated trust company.

Export Development Canada
151 O'Connor St., Ottawa, ON K1A 1K3
Tel: 613-598-2500; *Fax:* 613-237-2690
Toll-Free: 800-267-8510
www.edc.ca
Company Type: Crown
Profile: Export credit agency; offers assistance to Canadian exporters & investors to expand their international business

Farm Credit Canada
PO Box 4320, 1800 Hamilton St., Regina, SK S4P 4L3
Tel: 306-780-8100; *Fax:* 306-780-5456
Toll-Free: 888-332-3301
csc@fcc-fac.ca
www.fcc-fac.ca
Company Type: Crown
Profile: Federal & federally sponsored credit agencies

Fiera Capital Inc.
#800, 1501, av McGill College, Montréal, QC H3A 3M8
Tel: 514-954-3300; *Fax:* 514-954-5098
Toll-Free: 800-361-3499
info@fieracapital.com
www.fieracapital.com
Company Type: Private
Profile: Fiera Capital is an independent investment management firm. Its clientele consists of private clients, institutional investors, charitable organizations, & mutual funds.

Fiera Sceptre Inc.
#800, 1501, av McGill College, Montréal, QC H3A 3M8
Tel: 514-954-3300; *Fax:* 514-954-5098
Toll-Free: 800-361-3499
info@fierasceptre.ca
www.fierasceptre.ca
Ticker Symbol: FSZ
Company Type: Public
Profile: Fiera Sceptre is an an independent, full-service, investment management firm offering advice & asset management to such clients as corporations, governments, hospitals, charitable foundations, endowments, universities & unions. Regional offices in: Toronto, Waterloo, Vancouver.

Firm Capital Mortgage Investment Corp.
1244 Caledonia Rd., Toronto, ON M6A 2X5
Tel: 416-635-0221; *Fax:* 416-635-1713
mortgages@firmcapital.com
www.firmcapital.com
Ticker Symbol: FC
Company Type: Public
Profile: Through its mortgage banker, Firm Capital Corporation, Firm Capital Mortgage Investment Trust is a non-bank lender. It provides residential & commercial real estate finance.

Ford Credit Canada Limited
PO Box 5005, #800, 1275 North Service Rd., Oakville, ON L6M 3G4
Tel: 905-845-2511; *Fax:* 866-868-1213
Toll-Free: 800-263-0582
www.fordcredit.ca
Company Type: Public
Profile: Personal credit institution; Provides automotive financial services to manufacturers, dealers & customers

General Motors Acceptance Corp. of Canada Ltd.
Main Mailing Dept. CA1-002-002, 1908 Colonel Sam Dr., Oshawa, ON L1HÆ8P7
Tel: 416-234-6600; *Fax:* 416-234-6607
Toll-Free: 800-268-2508
www.gmcanada.com
Company Type: Public

Profile: Personal credit institutions; Short-term business credit institutions, except agricultural

Gluskin Sheff + Associates Inc.
Brookfield Place, PO Box 774, #4600, 181 Bay St., Toronto, ON M5J 2T3
Tel: 416-681-6000; *Fax:* 416-681-6060
Toll-Free: 866-681-6001
shareholders@gluskinsheff.com
www.gluskinsheff.com
Ticker Symbol: GS
Company Type: Public

Profile: The independent, wealth management firm serves institutional investors & private clients of high net worth.

GMP Capital Inc.
#300, 145 King St. West, Toronto, ON M5H 1J8
Tel: 416-367-8600; *Fax:* 416-367-8164
Toll-Free: 888-301-3244
corporatesecretary@gmpcapital.com
www.gmpcapital.com
Ticker Symbol: GMP
Company Type: Public

Profile: GMP Capital Inc. is a Canadian independent investment dealer. Through its subsidiaries, GMP Capital is involved in the following investment areas: alternative investments, capital markets, & wealth management. Individual, corporate, & institutional investor clients are served.

Great Eastern Corporation Limited
#2104, 1969 Upper Water St., Halifax, NS B3J 3R7
Tel: 902-423-8414; *Fax:* 902-422-7701
Ticker Symbol: GTN.PR.A
Company Type: Public

Profile: The organization is an investment holding company with a diversified investment portfolio.

Guardian Capital Group Limited
PO Box 201, #3100, Commerce Ct. West, Toronto, ON M5L 1E8
Tel: 416-364-8341; *Fax:* 416-364-9634
Toll-Free: 800-253-9181
www.guardiancapitallp.com
Ticker Symbol: GCG
Company Type: Public

Profile: Through its businesses, Guardian Capital Group Limited is involved in the distribution of mutual funds, institutional & high net worth investment management, as well as other financial services. Guardian Capital LP is a wholly-owned division of Guardian Capital Group Limited.

Home Capital Group Inc.
#2300, 145 King St. West, Toronto, ON M5H 1J8
Tel: 416-360-4663; *Fax:* 416-363-7611
Toll-Free: 800-990-7881
inquiry@homecapital.com
www.homecapital.com
Ticker Symbol: HCG.B
Company Type: Public

Profile: Home Capital Group Inc.'s subsidiary is Home Trust Company. It offers deposit services, retail credit, credit card issuing services, & mortgage lending. Offices are located in Nova Scotia, Québec, Ontario, Alberta, & British Columbia.

HSBC Bank Canada
#300, 885 West Georgia St., Vancouver, BC V6C 3E9
Tel: 604-685-1000; *Fax:* 604-641-2506
Toll-Free: 888-310-4722
hsbc_business_centre@hsbc.ca
www.hsbc.ca
Ticker Symbol: HSB
Company Type: Public

Profile: The company offers compleat banking & financial services.

IGM Financial Inc.
One Canada Centre, 447 Portage Ave., Winnipeg, MB R3C 3B6
Tel: 204-943-0361; *Fax:* 204-947-1659
www.igmfinancial.com
Ticker Symbol: IGM
Company Type: Public

Profile: IGM Financial Inc. is a managed asset, mutual fund, & personal financial services company. Its operating units include Investment Planning Counsel Inc., Mackenzie Financial Corporation, & Investors Group.

Investors Group Inc.
Canada Centre, #1, 447 Portage Ave., Winnipeg, MB R3C 3B6
Tel: 204-943-0361; *Fax:* 204-947-1659
Toll-Free: 888-746-6344
www.investorsgroup.com
Ticker Symbol: IGI
Company Type: Public

Profile: Provides personal financial planning services, mutual funds, other investment products including Registered Retirement Savings Plans, Registered Retirement Income Funds, Deferred Profit Sharing Plans, life and disability insurance, mortgages and Guaranteed Investment Certificates

Laurentian Bank of Canada
Tour Banque Laurentienne, #1660, 1981, av McGill College, Montréal, QC H3A 3K3
Tel: 514-284-4500; *Fax:* 514-284-3916
Toll-Free: 800-522-1846
www.laurentianbank.com
Ticker Symbol: LB
Company Type: Public

Profile: The schedule I chartered bank provides products & services across Canada through it bank branches, commercial banking centres, & brokerage offices.

LML Payment Systems Inc.
#1680, 1140 West Pender St., Vancouver, BC V6E 4G1
Tel: 604-689-4440; *Fax:* 604-689-4413
Toll-Free: 800-888-2260
info@lmlpayment.com
www.lmlpayment.com
Ticker Symbol: LMLP
Company Type: Public

Profile: Financial payment processor specializing in providing end-to-end cheque processing solutions to supermarkets, grocery stores, retailers

Macquarie Private Wealth Management
Bay Wellington Tower, Brookfield Place, #3200, 181 Bay St., Toronto, ON M5J 2T3
Tel: 416-864-3600; *Fax:* 416-864-9024
Toll-Free: 866-775-7704
www.macquarie.com
Company Type: Private

Profile: Macquarie's Banking & Financial Services Group in Canada comprises several businesses, including Macquarie Private Wealth Management, which offers clients tailored, independent investment advice. Macquarie Private Wealth Management has thirteen offices in Canada.

Manulife Financial Corporation
North Tower 3, 200 Bloor St. East, 2nd Fl., Toronto, ON M4W 1E5
Tel: 416-852-1189; *Fax:* 416-926-5410
Toll-Free: 877-308-7714
corporate_communications@manulife.com
www.manulife.ca
Ticker Symbol: MFC
Company Type: Public

Profile: Manulife Financial provides financial protection services & wealth management products.

MCAN Mortgage Corporation
#400, 200 King St. West, Toronto, ON M5H 3T4
Tel: 416-598-2665; *Fax:* 416-598-4142
Toll-Free: 800-387-4405
mcanexecutive@mcanmortgage.com
www.mcanmortgage.com
Ticker Symbol: MKP
Company Type: Public

Profile: MCAN Mortgage is a mortgage investment corporation. Funds are invested in a portfolio of mortgages, as well as other types of loans & investments, real estate, & marketable securities.

National Bank of Canada
Tour de la Banque Nationale, 600, rue de la Gauchetière ouest, Montréal, QC H3B 4L2
Tel: 514-394-5000; *Fax:* 514-394-6258
Toll-Free: 888-483-5628
investorrelations@nbc.ca
www.nbc.ca
Ticker Symbol: NA
Company Type: Public

Profile: Chartered under the Bank Act of Canada, the National Bank of Canada provides retail, commercial, corporate, international, & treasury banking services. Branches & offices are located across Canada & throughout the world. Subsidiaries of the National Bank of Canada are National Bank Financial & National Bank Trust.

Pyxis Capital Inc.
175 King St. East, 2nd Fl., Toronto, ON M5A 1J4
Tel: 416-867-9079; *Fax:* 416-867-1961
info@pyxiscapital.ca
Company Type: Public

Profile: Pyxis Capital is engaged in financial services.

Renasant Financial Partners Ltd.
#800, 55 City Centre Dr., Mississauga, ON L5B 1M3
Tel: 905-281-4760; *Fax:* 905-281-4761
www.renasant.ca
Ticker Symbol: REN
Company Type: Private

Profile: An independent, financial service provider undertaking debt & equity investments in private & public companies

Royal Bank of Canada
Royal Bank Plaza, PO Box 1, 200 Bay St., Toronto, ON M5J 2J5
Tel: 416-974-5151; *Fax:* 416-955-7800
invesrel@rbc.com
www.rbc.com
Ticker Symbol: RY
Company Type: Public

Profile: The Royal Bank of Canada is engaged in the following services: personal & commercial banking; corporate & investment banking, insurance; wealth management; & transaction processing services.

Royal Canadian Mint
320 Sussex Dr., Ottawa, ON K1A 0G8
Tel: 613-993-8990; *Fax:* 613-998-4130
Toll-Free: 800-267-1871
info@mint.ca
www.rcmint.ca
Company Type: Crown

Profile: The Royal Canadian Mint is a for-profit Crown Corporation. Its responsibilities include the production of circulation & non-circulation coins, management of the domestic coinage system, & the provision of advice to the Minister of Finance on matters related to coinage.

Scotiabank
Scotia Plaza, 40 King St. West, Toronto, ON M5H 1H1
Tel: 416-866-6161; *Fax:* 416-866-3750
investor.relations@scotiabank.com
www.scotiabank.com
Ticker Symbol: BNS
Company Type: Public

Profile: Scotiabank's range of services includes personal & commercial banking, corporate & investment banking services & products, as well as wealth management services.

Seamark Asset Management Ltd.
#310, 1801 Hollis St., Halifax, NS B3J 3N4
Tel: 902-423-9367; *Fax:* 902-423-1518
Toll-Free: 888-303-5055
information@seamark.ca
www.seamark.ca
Ticker Symbol: SM
Company Type: Public

Profile: Investment management firm focusing on enhancing assets over a long term period

Sentry Select Capital Inc.
The Exchange Tower, #2850, 130 King St. West, Toronto, ON M5X 1A4
Tel: 416-861-8729; *Fax:* 416-364-1197
Toll-Free: 888-246-6656
info@sentryselect.com
www.sentryselect.com
Ticker Symbol: SYI
Company Type: Public

Profile: Sentry Select Capital Inc. is a wealth management company. It offers investment products, such as mutual funds, closed-end trusts, & principal-protected notes. Offices are located in Toronto, Vancouver, & Montréal.

Split Yield Corporation
Royal Trust Tower, PO Box 341, #4500, 77 King St. West, Toronto, ON M5K 1K7
Tel: 416-304-4443; *Fax:* 416-304-4441
Toll-Free: 877-478-237
info@quadravest.com
www.quadravest.com
Ticker Symbol: YLD
Company Type: Public

Profile: Split Yield Corporation provides quarterly dividends to each class of shareholder. It returns the original issue price to each shareholder on the maturity of the company. To generate additional income, Split Yield Corporation writes covered call options. The company's investment manager is Quadravest Capital Management Inc.

Sprott Inc.
South Tower, Royal Bank Plaza, PO Box 27, #2700, 200 Bay St., Toronto, ON M5J 2J1
Tel: 416-362-7172; *Fax:* 416-943-6497
Toll-Free: 888-362-7172
ir@sprott.com
www.sprottinc.com
Ticker Symbol: SII
Company Type: Public
Profile: Sprott Inc. is an independent asset management firm operating through its four business units: Sprott Asset Management LP, Sprott Private Wealth LP, Sprott Consulting LP & Sprott U.S. Holdings Inc.

Sprott Resource Lending Corp.
Royal Bank Plaza, South Tower, PO Box 90, #2750, 200 Bay St., Toronto, ON M5J 2J2
Tel: 416-362-7172; *Toll-Free:* 888-362-7172
www.sprottlending.com
Company Type: Public
Profile: The firm is a natural resource lender, providing bridge financing to mid-cap & junior mining, oil & gas companies.

Sunwah International Limited
#1400, 8 King St. East, Toronto, ON M5C 1B5
Tel: 416-861-3099; *Fax:* 416-861-9027
info@kingswaygroup.ca
www.kingswaygroup.ca
Ticker Symbol: SWH
Company Type: Public
Profile: Boutique investment bank specializing in general business-to-Asia intermediation

TMX Group Inc.
The Exchange Tower, 130 King St. West, Toronto, ON M5X 1J2
Tel: 416-947-4670; *Fax:* 416-947-4662
Toll-Free: 888-873-8392
info@tmx.com
www.tmx.com
Ticker Symbol: X
Company Type: Public
Profile: TMX Group is the owner & operator of the Toronto Stock Exchange, the TSX Venture Exchange, the Natural Gas Exchange (NGX), & Shorcan Brokers Ltd. The Toronto Stock Exchange, a national stock exchange, serves the senior equity market. Another national stock exchange, the TSX Venture Exchange provides services for the public venture equity market. The Natural Gas Exchange is a North American exchange for the trading & clearing of natural gas & electricity contracts. Shorcan Brokers Ltd. is a fixed income inter-dealer broker. The Equicom Group Inc. is also owned by the TSX Group. It provides investor relations & corporate communications.

Toronto-Dominion Bank
Toronto-Dominion Centre, PO Box 1, 66 Wellington St. West, Toronto, ON M5K 1A2
Tel: 416-982-8222; *Toll-Free:* 866-756-8936
tdir@td.com; tdshinfo@td.com
www.td.com
Ticker Symbol: TD
Company Type: Public
Profile: Toronto-Dominion Bank & its subsidiaries are collectively known as TD Bank Group. This major Canadian bank offers a wide range of financial products & services through 4 business lines: Canadian Personal & Commercial Banking (TD Canada Trust, TD Insurance); Wealth Management (TD Waterhouse); Wholesale Banking (TD Securities); U.S. Personal and Commercial Banking (TD Bank).

Urbana Corporation
PO Box 47, #1702, 150 King St. West, Toronto, ON M5H 1J9
Tel: 416-595-9106; *Fax:* 416-862-2498
info@urbanacorp.com
www.urbanacorp.com
Ticker Symbol: URB.A
Company Type: Public
Profile: Urbana Corporation is a non-redeemable investment fund. Urbana seeks & acquires investments for capital appreciation & income.

Vancouver City Savings Credit Union
PO Box 2120 Terminal, Vancouver, BC V6B 5R8
Tel: 604-877-7000; *Toll-Free:* 888-826-2489
www.vancity.com
Company Type: Private
Profile: The credit union serves over 400,000 members at almost sixty locations throughout British Columbia.

West Street Capital Corporation
Brookfield Place, #300, 181 Bay St., Toronto, ON M5J 2T3
Tel: 416-359-8590; *Fax:* 416-365-9642
Company Type: Private
Profile: West Street Capital Corporation is an investment holding company. In 2009, West Street amalgamated with a wholly-owned subsidiary of Brookfield Asset Management Inc.

Western Financial Group Inc.
1010 - 24th St. SE, High River, AB T1V 2A6
Tel: 403-652-2663; *Fax:* 403-652-2661
Toll-Free: 866-843-9378
info@westernfg.ca
www.westernfinancialgroup.ca
Ticker Symbol: WES
Company Type: Public
Profile: Western Financial Group offers insurance, banking, & investment products to customers in western Canada through its business units: Network, Bank West, Western Life Assurance Co., & Marlin Travel.

Wilmington Capital Management Inc.
Brookfield Place, PO Box 762, #300, 181 Bay St., Toronto, ON M5J 2T3
Tel: 416-867-9370; *Fax:* 416-363-2856
www.wilmingtoncapital.com
Ticker Symbol: WCM
Company Type: Public
Profile: The Canadian investment company holds cash & marketable securities. Wilmington Capital Management also owns land lease properties.

Food, Beverages & Tobacco

A&W Revenue Royalties Income Fund
#300, 171 Esplanade West, North Vancouver, BC V7M 3K9
Tel: 604-988-2141; *Fax:* 604-988-5531
investorrelations@aw.ca
www.awincomefund.ca
Ticker Symbol: AW.UN
Company Type: Private
Profile: A&W Revenue Royalties Income Fund is a limited purpose trust. It invests in A&W Trade Marks Inc., which owns the trade-marks used in the A&W restaurant business in Canada. Through its subsidiary, A&W Trade Marks Inc., A&W Revenue Royalties licences trade-marks for royalty income.

Agropur cooperative
#600 - 101 boul. Roland-Therrien, Longueuil, QC J4H 4B9
Tel: 450-646-1010;
www.agropur.com
Company Type: NA
Profile: Manufacturers of fluid milk; creamery butter; natural, processed & imitation cheese; dry, condensed & evaporated dairy products; ice cream & frozen desserts

Andrew Peller Limited
697 South Service Rd., Grimsby, ON L3M 4E8
Tel: 905-643-4131; *Fax:* 905-643-4944
info@andrewpeller.com
www.andrewpeller.com
Ticker Symbol: ADW.A
Company Type: Public
Profile: Andrew Peller Limited is the owner of wineries located in Nova Scotia, Ontario, & British Columbia. Through Vineco International Products Ltd. & Winexpert Inc., Andrew Peller Limited is also engaged in the production & marketing of wine kit products. The company also markets craft beer, under the Granville Island brand. Products are sold predominantly in Canada.

Arctic Glacier Income Fund
625 Henry Ave., Winnipeg, MB R3A 0V1
Tel: 204-772-2473; *Fax:* 204-783-9857
Toll-Free: 888-573-9237
info@arcticglacierinc.com
www.arcticglacierinc.com
Ticker Symbol: AG.UN
Company Type: Public
Profile: Through its wholly-owned operating company, Arctic Glacier Inc., Arctic Glacier Income Fund produces, markets, & distributes packaged ice products. Products are marketed under the brand name, Arctic Glacier Premium Ice. Production & distribution take place throughout Canada, as well as in the western, central, & northeastern United States.

Barry Callebaut Canada Inc.
PO Box 398, 2950 rue Nelson, Saint-Hyacinthe, QC J2S 1Y7
Tél: 450-774-9131; *Téléc:* 450-774-8335
sthyacinthe@barry-callebaut.com
www.barry-callebaut.com
Company Type: Private
Profile: Producers of cocoa & chocolate products

Big Rock Brewery Income Trust
5555 - 76 Ave. SE, Calgary, AB T2C 4L8
Tel: 403-720-3239; *Fax:* 403-236-7523
Toll-Free: 800-242-3107
beer@bigrockbeer.com
www.bigrockbeer.com
Ticker Symbol: BR.UN
Company Type: Public
Profile: Manufacturers of malt beverages; Wholesalers of beer & ale

Boston Pizza Royalties Income Fund
5500 Parkwood Way, Richmond, BC V6V 2M4
Tel: 604-270-1108; *Fax:* 604-270-4168
investorrelations@bostonpizza.com
www.bpincomefund.com
Ticker Symbol: BPF.UN
Company Type: Public
Profile: Boston Pizza Royalties Income Fund is a limited purpose open-ended trust. Its purpose is to acquire certain trade marks & trade names used by Boston Pizza International Inc. (BPI) in its Boston Pizza restaurants in Canada.

Campbell Soup Company Ltd. of Canada
60 Birmingham St., Toronto, ON M8V 2B8
Tel: 416-251-1131; *Fax:* 416-253-8611
Toll-Free: 800-575-7687
www.campbellsoup.ca
Company Type: Private
Profile: Manufacturers of canned specialties, various food preparations, pickled fruits & vegetables, sauces, seasonings & dressings; Wholesalers of general line groceries

Canada Bread Company, Limited
Investor Relations Department, #1500, 30 St. Clair Ave. West, Toronto, ON M4V 3A2
Tel: 416-926-2000; *Fax:* 416-926-2018
Toll-Free: 800-465-5515
Investorrelations@mapleleaf.ca
www.canadabread.ca
Ticker Symbol: CBY
Company Type: Public
Profile: Canada Bread Company, Limited manufactures & markets the following products: fresh bakery products, such as bread, bagels, & sweet goods; frozen unbaked & partially baked products, such as bread, rolls, & bagels; & specialty pasta & sauces. Brand names include Olafson's, Ben's, POM, Dempster's, & Olivieri. Operations are located throughout North America & in the United Kingdom.

Chai-Na-Ta Corp.
CNT Nutraceuticals Ltd., #100, 12051 Horseshoe Way, Richmond, BC V7A 4V4
Tel: 604-272-4118; *Fax:* 604-272-4113
Toll-Free: 800-406-7668
info@chainata.com
www.chainata.com
Ticker Symbol: CCCFF
Company Type: Public
Profile: The world's largest grower and exporter of North American ginseng

Clearly Canadian Beverage Corporation
#11/12, 220 Viceroy Rd., Vaughan, ON L4K 3C2
Toll-Free: 800-735-7180
consumer.relations@clearly.ca
www.clearly.ca
Ticker Symbol: CCBEF
Company Type: Public
Profile: Marketer of bottled carbonated & noncarbonated waters; Patent owners & lessors

Corby Distilleries Limited
#1100, 225 King St. West, Toronto, ON M5V 3M2
Tel: 416-479-2400; *Fax:* 416-369-9809
investors@corby.ca
www.corby.ca
Ticker Symbol: CDL
Company Type: Public
Profile: Corby Distilleries is a marketer of distilled spirits, whiskies, & liqueurs produced in Canada. In addition, imported wines, gin, cognac, scotch, & liqueurs are marketed by the organization. Its owned brands include Wiser's Canadian whiskies & Seagram Coolers. Corby Distilleries represents international brands, such as Jameson Irish whiskey & Wyndham Estate wines, through its affiliation with Pernod Ricard.

Cott Corporation
6525 Viscount Road, Mississauga, ON L4V 1H6
Tel: 905-672-1900; *Fax:* 905-672-7504
investor_relations@cott.com
www.cott.com
Ticker Symbol: BCB
Company Type: Public
Profile: Manufacturers of retailer branded soft drinks & carbonated waters

Dover Industries Limited
4350 Harvester Rd., Burlington, ON L7L 5S4
Tel: 905-333-1515; *Fax:* 905-333-1584
info@dovergrp.com
www.dovergrp.com
Ticker Symbol: DVI
Company Type: Public
Profile: Dover Industries Ltd. is made up up a food products division & a paper products division. Dover Flour operates flour mills in Saskatchewan, Ontario, & Nova Scotia. Dover Cone produces ice cream cones. Dover Cup manufactures hot & cold paper cups & related food containers.

Farmers Cooperative Dairy Ltd.
PO Box 8118, Halifax, NS B3K 5Y6
Tel: 902-835-3373; *Fax:* 902-835-1583
Toll-Free: 800-565-1945
customer.services@farmersdairy.ca
www.farmersdairy.ca
Company Type: Private
Profile: Produces & distributes dairy & dairy-related products in Atlantic Canada

Forbes Medi-Tech Inc.
#200, 750 West Pender St., Vancouver, BC V6C 2T8
Tel: 604-689-5899; *Fax:* 604-689-7641
info@forbesmedi.com
www.forbesmedi.com
Ticker Symbol: FMI
Company Type: Public
Profile: Develops and markets a portfolio of nutraceutical products, including functional foods and supplements

FP Resources Limited
PO Box 550, 70 O'Leary Ave., St. John's, NL A1C 5L1
Tel: 709-570-0000; *Fax:* 709-570-0479
www.fpresources.ca
Company Type: Public
Profile: Harvests, processes, sources & markets seafood products

Freshxtend Technologies Corp.
#104, 334 East Kent Ave., Vancouver, BC V5X 4N6
Tel: 604-322-0759; *Fax:* 604-322-0487
Toll-Free: 800-269-5269
info@freshxtend.com
www.freshxtend.com
Ticker Symbol: FXT
Company Type: Public
Profile: A leading provider of natural life extension technologies to the fresh produce and flower industries

Gay Lea Foods Co-Operative Ltd.
5200 Orbitor Dr., Mississauga, ON L4W 5B4
Tel: 905-283-5300; *Fax:* 416-741-5384
Toll-Free: 800-268-0508
contact@gayleafoodmembers.com
www.gaylea.com
Company Type: Private
Profile: Manufacturers of fluid milk, creamery butter & dry, condensed & evaporated dairy products; Wholesalers of dairy products, groceries & related products

George Weston Limited
22 St Clair Ave. East, Toronto, ON M4T 2S7
Tel: 416-922-2500; *Fax:* 416-922-4395
investor@weston.ca
www.weston.ca
Ticker Symbol: WN
Company Type: Public
Profile: George Weston Limited consists of Weston Foods & Loblaws. Weston Foods is involved in the baking & dairy industries. Operated by Loblaw Companies Limited, Loblaws is engaged in food distribution. Loblaws also offers drug store merchandise & general merchandise, as well as financial products & services.

High Liner Foods Incorporated
PO Box 910, 100 Battery Point, Lunenburg, NS B0J 2C0
Tel: 902-634-8811; *Fax:* 902-634-4785
info@highlinerfoods.com
www.highlinerfoods.com
Ticker Symbol: HLF
Company Type: Public
Profile: High Liner Foods Incorporated specializes in processing & marketing prepared, frozen seafood products. Products are marketed under the following brands: High Liner, Sea Cuisine, Fisher Boy, Royal Sea, Mirabel, & FPI. Subsidiaries & divisions include High Liner Foods (USA) Incorporated & Fishery Products International (USA). The company serves the retail & food service markets throughout Canada, the United States, & Mexico.

Imperial Tobacco Canada Limited
3711, rue Saint-Antoine, Montréal, QC H4C 3P6
Tel: 514-932-6161; *Fax:* 514-932-3993
www.imperialtobaccocanada.com
Company Type: Private
Profile: Manufacturers of cigarettes, chewing & smoking tobacco & snuff; Wholesalers of tobacco & tobacco products

Kraft Canada Inc.
95 Moatfield Dr., Toronto, ON M3B 3L6
Tel: 416-441-5000; *Fax:* 416-441-5059
Toll-Free: 800-323-0768
www.kraftcanada.com
Company Type: Private
Profile: Manufacturers of natural, processed & imitation cheese; cereal breakfast foods; canned fruits, vegetables, preserves, jams & jellies; various food preparations; pickled fruits & vegetables, sauces, seasonings, dressings; roasted coffee; chocolate & cocoa products

Lassonde Industries Inc.
755, rue Principale, Rougemont, QC J0L 1M0
Tel: 450-469-4926; *Fax:* 450-469-1366
Toll-Free: 866-552-7643
info@lassonde.com
www.lassonde.com
Ticker Symbol: LAS
Company Type: Public
Profile: Through its subsidiaries, Lassonde Industries develops, manufactures, packages, & markets food products. The following products are manufactured: fruit juices, fruit beverages, canned corn, baked beans, barbecue sauces, dipping sauces, pasta sauces, meat marinades, bruschetta topping, tapenades, & fondue bouillon.

Leading Brands, Inc.
#1800, 1500 West Georgia, Vancouver, BC V6G 2Z6
Tel: 604-685-5200; *Fax:* 604-685-5249
Toll-Free: 866-685-5200
info@lbix.com
www.leadingbrandsinc.com
Company Type: Public
Profile: Manufacturers of bottled & canned soft drinks & carbonated waters; wholesalers of groceries & related products

Lilydale Co-Operative Ltd.
7727 - 127 Ave., Edmonton, AB T5C 1R9
Tel: 780-476-6261; *Fax:* 780-476-7253
webmaster@lilydale.com
www.lilydale.com
Company Type: NA
Profile: Wholesalers of poultry & poultry products

Liquor Stores Income Fund
#300, 10508 - 82 Ave., Edmonton, AB T6E 2A4
Tel: 780-944-9994; *Fax:* 780-702-1999
www.liquorstoresgp.ca
Ticker Symbol: LIQ.UN
Company Type: Public
Profile: Liquor Stores Income Fund is involved in the operation of retail liquor stores in Alberta.

Magnotta Winery Corporation
271 Chrislea Rd., Vaughan, ON L4L 8N6
Tel: 905-738-9463; *Fax:* 905-738-5551
Toll-Free: 800-461-9463
mailbox@magnotta.com
www.magnotta.com
Ticker Symbol: MGN
Company Type: Public
Profile: Magnotta Winery Corporation is licensed to produce & sell wine, beer & distilled products.

Maple Leaf Foods Inc.
#1500, 30 St Clair Ave. West, Toronto, ON M4V 3A2
Tel: 416-926-2000; *Fax:* 416-926-2018
Toll-Free: 800-268-3708
investorrelations@mapleleaf.ca
www.mapleleaf.ca
Ticker Symbol: MFI
Company Type: Public
Profile: Maple Leaf Foods products include fresh & prepared meats, poultry, seafood, fresh & frozen bakery goods, & animal feed. Products are sold to wholesale, retail, & industrial customers around the world. Maple Leaf Foods has operations in Canada, the United States, Europe, & Asia.

McCain Foods (Canada)
107 Main St., Florenceville, NB E7L 1B2
Tel: 800-563-7437; *Toll-Free:* 800-387-7321
www.mccain.ca
Company Type: Private
Profile: McCain Foods in Canada produces food products. Products include frozen foods, such as potato products & beverages, as well as specialty items under brand names such as Wong Wing Foods & Charcuterie la Tour Eiffel. Food products are distributed throughout Canada & internationally.

McDonald's Restaurants of Canada Ltd.
McDonald's Place, Toronto, ON M3C 3L4
Tel: 416-443-1000; *Fax:* 416-446-3443
www.mcdonalds.ca
Company Type: Private
Profile: McDonald's Canada consists of over 1,400 McDonald's restaurants across Canada. More than 77,000 Canadians are employed at McDonald's & its franchisees.

Molson Coors Brewing Company (Canada)
1555, rue Notre-Dame est, 4e étage, Montréal, QC H2L 2R5
Tel: 514-597-1786; *Toll-Free:* 800-566-1786
www.molsoncoorscanada.com
Ticker Symbol: TAP
Company Type: Public
Profile: Molson Coors Brewing Company (Canada) operates six breweries throughout Canada. Major markets are located in Canada, the United States, & the United Kingdom.

MTY Food Group Inc.
3465, boul Thimens, Montréal, QC H4R 1V5
Tel: 514-336-8885; *Fax:* 514-336-9222
info@mtygroup.com
www.mtygroup.com
Ticker Symbol: MTY
Company Type: Public
Profile: MTY Food Group is an operator & franchisor of quick service restaurants. Brands include Thai Express, Vanellis, Yogen Früz, & Cultures.

Nestlé Canada Inc.
25 Sheppard Ave. West, Toronto, ON M2N 6S8
Tel: 416-512-9000; *Fax:* 416-218-2654
Toll-Free: 800-387-4636
corporateaffairs@ca.nestle.com
www.nestle.ca
Company Type: Private
Profile: 27 facilities in Canada, including manufacturing sites, sales offices & distribution centres, employ 4,000 people; Producer of foods & beverages such as Carnation, Nescafé, Lean Cuisine, Good Start, Nestlé Baby Cereal, Powerbar, Nestlé Pure Life, Nestlé Drumstick, Kit Kat & Purina Beneful

Parmalat Canada Limite
Consumer Relations Department, 405 The West Mall, 10th Fl., Toronto, ON M9C 5J1
Tel: 416-626-1973; *Fax:* 416-620-3123
Toll-Free: 800-563-1515
www.parmalat.ca
Company Type: Private
Profile: Parmalat Canada produces & markets a variety of dairy products, fruit juices, table spreads, & cultured products to Canadians. Brand names include Balderson, Black Diamond, Beatrice, Astro, & Lantantia. Operating facilities are located across Canada.

PDM Royalties Income Fund
#400, 774 Main St., Moncton, NB E1C 9Y3
Tel: 506-853-0990; *Fax:* 506-853-4131
blane@imvescor.ca
www.pdmfund.com
Ticker Symbol: PDM.UN
Company Type: Public
Profile: PDM Royalties Income Fund is an open-ended, limited purpose trust. The Fund is the indirect owner of the trade marks & other intellectual property for Mikes, Scores, Pizza Delight, & Baton Rouge. They are licensed to Imvescor Inc., which operates restaurants under the brand names Mikes, Scores, Pizza Delight, & Baton Rouge.

Pizza Pizza Royalty Income Fund
580 Jarvis St., Toronto, ON M4Y 2H9
Tel: 416-967-1010; *Fax:* 416-967-5941
www.pizzapizzaroyaltyincomefund.com
Company Type: Public
Profile: Pizza Pizza Royalty Income Fund is a limited purpose, open-ended trust. The Fund acquired trademarks & trade names used by Pizza Pizza Limited in its restaurants. The trademarks are licensed to Pizza Pizza.

Premium Brands Income Fund
7720 Alderbridge Way, Richmond, BC V6X 2A2
Tel: 604-656-3100; *Fax:* 604-656-3170
investor@premiumbrandsgroup.com
www.premiumbrandsincomefund.com
Ticker Symbol: PBI.UN
Company Type: Public
Profile: Premium Brands Income Fund is the owner of branded specialty food businesses. Manufacturing & distribution facilities are situated in Manitoba, Saskatchewan, Alberta, British Columbia, & Washington. The following are the brands within the Fund's family of businesses: Quality Fast Foods, McSweeney's, B&C Foods, Bread Garden, Grimm's, Made-Rite, Harlan's, Stuyver's, Harvest, Centennial, Harlan's, Gloria's, Hempler's, & Hygaard.

Prime Restaurants Royalty Income Fund
#600, 10 Kingsbridge Garden Circle, Mississauga, ON L5R 3K6
Tel: 905-568-0000; *Fax:* 905-568-0080
www.primeincomefund.ca
Ticker Symbol: EAT.UN
Company Type: Public
Profile: Prime Restaurants Royalty Income Fund is a limited purpose trust. Its subsidiary is PRC Trademarks Inc.. The Fund receives royalties from pooled restaurants, under an agreement with Prime Restaurants of Canada Inc.. Prime Restaurants of Canada Inc. owns, operates, & franchises casual dining restaurants & pubs. Prime Restaurants of Canada's restaurants & pubs include Casey's, East Side Mario's, Bier Markt, Paddy Flaherty's & Fionn MacCool's.

Quaker Oats Company of Canada Ltd.
Consumer Relations, 14 Hunter St. East, Peterborough, ON K9J 7B2
Toll-Free: 800-267-6287
www.quakeroats.ca
Company Type: Private
Profile: Quaker Oats Company of Canada provides the following products: oatmeal, cereals, granola bars, portion & lite snacks, & baking mixes.

Rothmans Inc.
1500 Don Mills Rd., Toronto, ON M3B 3L1
Tel: 416-449-5525; *Fax:* 416-449-9601
ir@rothmansinc.ca
www.rothmansinc.ca
Ticker Symbol: ROC
Company Type: Public
Profile: The holding company owns 60% of Rothmans Bensons & Hedges Inc., which manufactures tobacco products.

Saputo Inc.
6869, boul Métropolitain est, Montréal, QC H1P 1X8
Tel: 514-328-6662; *Fax:* 514-328-3310
saputo@saputo.com
www.saputo.com
Ticker Symbol: SAP
Company Type: Public
Profile: Saputo Inc. is engaged in the production, commercialization, & distribution of dairy products & grocery products. The company's brands include the following: Saputo, Dairyland De Lucia, Frigo, Stella, HOP&GO!, Rondeau, Alexis de Portneuf, DuVillage de Warwick, La Paulina, Treasure Cave, Armstrong, Nutrilait, Vachon, & Ricrem. Production facilities are situated in five countries.

Schneider Corporation
PO Box 130, 321 Courtland Ave. East, Kitchener, ON N2G 3X8
Tel: 519-741-5000; *Fax:* 519-749-7420
Toll-Free: 877-567-5326
www.schneiders.ca
Company Type: Private
Profile: Schneider Foods is a producer of meats & food products, such as Schneiders sliced meats & Schneiders Lunchmate & SmartSnax.

Scotsburn Dairy Group
PO Box 340, Scotsburn, NS B0K 1R0
Tel: 902-485-8023; *Fax:* 902-485-4013
Toll-Free: 800-511-6455
consumerservices@scotsburn.com
www.scotsburn.com
Company Type: Private
Profile: Scotsburn Dairy Group manufactures & distributes ice cream & frozen novelties, such as fluid milk, ice cream, frozen yogourt, sherbet, sour cream, & butter. Retail customers are located throughout the world.

Second Cup Royalty Income Fund
6303 Airport Rd., Mississauga, ON L4V 1R8
Tel: 905-405-6500; *Fax:* 905-405-6777
investor@secondcup.com
www.secondcupincomefund.com
Ticker Symbol: SCU.UN
Company Type: Public
Profile: Second Cup Royalty Income Fund is an open-ended trust. Through its wholly-owned subsidiary, Second Cup Royalty Income Fund holds The Second Cup cafés' trademarks & other intellectual property & rights. These trademarks are licenced by the Fund to The Second Cup Ltd. The Second Cup Ltd. is a retailer & franchisor of specialty coffee cafés throughout Canada.

Sepp's Gourmet Foods Ltd.
529 Annance Ct., Delta, BC V3M 6Y7
Tel: 604-524-2540; *Fax:* 604-524-2941
dcullum@seppsfoods.com
www.seppsfoods.com
Company Type: Private
Profile: Sepp's Gourmet Foods Ltd. produces & markets food products. Products include frozen waffles, French toast, & wraps. The company serves the food service & retail grocery sectors in North America, South America, & Asia.

SIR Royalty Income Fund
#200, 5360 South Service Rd., Burlington, ON L7L 5L1
Tel: 905-681-2997; *Fax:* 905-681-0394
info@sircorp.com
www.sircorp.com
Ticker Symbol: SRV.UN
Company Type: Public
Profile: Trademarks related to SIR Corp.'s restaurant brands are used under a license agreement with SIR Royalty Limited Partnership. A royalty is paid by SIR Corp. to SIR Royalty Limited Partnership. SIR Royalty Income Fund has an investment in SIR Royalty Limited Partnership. The Fund receives distribution income from this investment. Distributions are paid to unitholders by the Fund on a monthly basis. SIR Corp.'s restaurant brands include Alice Fazooli's, Jack Astor's Bar & Grill, Canyon Creek Chop House, Far Nienter / Soul of the Vine, & Loose Moose Tap & Grill.

Sleeman Breweries Ltd.
551 Clair Rd. West, Guelph, ON N1L 1E9
Tel: 519-822-1834; *Fax:* 519-822-0148
Toll-Free: 800-268-8537
consumer.relations@sleeman.ca
www.sleeman.com
Company Type: Private
Profile: Sleeman Breweries Ltd. is a brewer & distributor of beer.

Smucker Foods of Canada Co.
Consumer Services Department, 80 Whitehall Dr., Markham, ON L3R 0P3
Toll-Free: 800-567-1897
www.smuckers.ca
Company Type: Private
Profile: Smucker Foods of Canada manufactures & markets products such as fruit spreads, peanut butter, ice cream toppings, condiments, & shortening & oils. Brand names include Smuckers, Crisco, Robin Hood, Five Roses, Europe's Best, Bick's, Red River, & Double Fruit Spreads.

Sodexo Canada Ltd.
3350 South Service Rd., Burlington, ON L7N 3M6
Tel: 514-866-7070; *Toll-Free:* 877-632-8592
Canada@sodexo.com
www.sodexoca.com
Company Type: Private
Profile: Sodexo Canada provides food & facilities management. Outsourcing solutions offered include food service, grounds keeping, housekeeping, laundry services, & plant operations & maintenance.

Sun-Rype Products Ltd.
1165 Ethel St., Kelowna, BC V1Y 2W4
Tel: 250-860-7973; *Fax:* 250-762-3611
info@sunrype.com
www.sunrype.com
Ticker Symbol: SRF
Company Type: Public
Profile: Sun-Rype manufactures & markets fruit juices & fruit snacks. Products include 100% Pure Not From Concentrate Apple Juice & Fruit to Go.

Swiss Water Decaffeinated Coffee Co. Income Fund
3131 Lake City Way, Burnaby, BS V5A 3A3
Tel: 604-420-4050; *Fax:* 604-420-8711
Toll-Free: 800-667-6181
info@swisswater.com
www.swisswater.com
Ticker Symbol: SWS.UN
Company Type: Public
Profile: Listed on the Toronto Stock Exchange in 2002, Swiss Water Decaffeinated Coffee Co. Income Fund is a limited purpose, open ended trust. Swiss Water Decaffeinated Coffee Company, Inc. (SWDCC) decaffeinates premium coffees. The organization is certified by the Organic Crop Improvement Association (OCIA), in accordance with National Organic Program (NOP) standards.

TDL Group Ltd.
874 Sinclair Rd., Oakville, ON L6K 2Y1
Tel: 905-845-6511; *Fax:* 905-845-0265
Toll-Free: 888-601-1616
customer_service@timhortons.com
www.timhortons.com
Company Type: Private
Profile: Retail eating places; head office of Tim Hortons

The Keg Royalties Income Fund
10100 Shellbridge Way, Richmond, BC V6X 2W7
Tel: 604-821-6416; *Fax:* 604-276-0138
www.kegincomefund.com
Ticker Symbol: KEG.UN
Company Type: Public
Profile: The Keg Royalties Income Fund is an unincorporated open-ended, limited purpose trust. The Fund is the owner of The Keg Rights LP, which owns the trademarks, names, & other intellectual property used by The Keg restaurants. The Keg Royalties Income Fund licenses Keg Restaurants Ltd. to use these rights.

The Spectra Hospitality Group Inc.
389 West 6th Ave., Vancouver, BC V5Y 1L1
Tel: 604-714-6500; *Fax:* 604-730-5508
www.spectragroup.com
Company Type: Public
Profile: Retailing in eating places, alcoholic beverage drinking places; Patent owners & lessors

Van Houtte Inc.
8300, 19e av, Montréal, QC H1Z 4J8
Tel: 514-593-7711; *Fax:* 514-593-8755
Toll-Free: 877-593-7722
www.vanhoutte.com
Company Type: Private
Profile: Van Houtte Inc. roasts, markets, & distributes gourmet, flavoured, organic, & fair trade coffees throughout North America. Other activities include offering a coffee service & manufacturing single-cup equipment. The company also markets & distributes a range of water filtration systems for businesses.

Vincor Canada
441 Courtneypark Dr. East, Mississauga, ON L5T 2V3
Tel: 905-564-6900; *Fax:* 905-564-6909
Toll-Free: 800-265-9463
www.vincorinternational.com
Company Type: Private
Profile: Vincor Canada produces & markets wine & related products throughout Canada. Products are produced at wineries in New Brunswick, Québec, Ontario, & British Columbia. Examples of Vincor Canada's brands include Inniskillin, Jackson-Triggs, & Sawmill Creek.

Forestry & Paper

3M Canada Company
300 Tartan Dr., London, ON N6A 4T1
Tel: 519-452-6765; *Fax:* 800-479-4453
Toll-Free: 888-364-3577
www.3m.ca
Ticker Symbol: 3M CO
Company Type: Private
Profile: Manufacturers of packaging paper & coated & laminated plastics film, adhesives & sealants, photographic equipment & supplies, orthopedic, prosthetic & surgical appliances & supplies

Abitibi-Consolidated Inc.
#800, 1155, rue Metcalfe, Montréal, QC H3B 5H2
Tel: 514-875-2160;
contact@abitibiconsolidated.com
www.abitibiconsolidated.com
Ticker Symbol: A
Company Type: Public
Profile: Manufacturers in paper mills, pulp mills, logging, sawmills & general planing mills

Ainsworth Lumber Co. Ltd.
Bentall 4, PO Box 49307, #3194, 1055 Dunsmuir St., Vancouver, BC V7X 1L3
Tel: 604-661-3200; *Fax:* 604-661-3201
info@ainsworth.ca
www.ainsworth.ca
Ticker Symbol: ANS
Company Type: Public
Profile: Manufacturers in logging, sawmills & general planing mills, hardwood & softwood veneer & plywood, reconstituted wood products, & various other wood products

Arbec Forest Products Inc.
#216, 8770, boul Langelier, St-Léonard, QC H1P 3C6
Tel: 514-327-3350; *Fax:* 514-327-1966
information@arbec.ca
www.arbec.ca
Ticker Symbol: ABR.SV.A
Company Type: Public
Profile: The manufacturer of softwood lumber carries on business through mills in Port-Cartier & in the Péribonka area.

Canfor Pulp Income Fund
#100, 1700 - 75 Ave. West, Vancouver, BC V6P 6G2
Tel: 604-661-5241; *Fax:* 604-661-5235
info@canfor.ca
www.canfor.com
Ticker Symbol: CFX.UN
Company Type: Public
Profile: Canfor Pulp Income Fund is an unincorporated, open-ended trust, which holds interest in the Canfor Pulp Limited Partnership. The Limited Partnership is an owner & operator of mills in British Columbia. NBSK pulp & fully bleached Kraft Paper are produced.

Cascades Inc.
PO Box 30, 404, boul Marie-Victorin, Kingsey Falls, QC J0A 1B0
Tél: 819-363-5100; *Téléc:* 819-363-5127
info@cascades.com
www.cascades.com
Ticker Symbol: CAS
Company Type: Public
Profile: Cascades Inc. is engaged in the production, transformation, & marketing of packaging & tissue products. Products are composed mainly of recycled fibres. Operations are situated throughout North America & Europe.

Catalyst Paper Corporation
3600 Lysander Lane, 2nd Fl., Richmond, BC V7B 1C3
Tel: 604-247-4400; *Fax:* 604-247-0551
contactus@catalystpaper.com
www.catalystpaper.com
Ticker Symbol: CTL
Company Type: Public
Profile: Producer of mechanical printing papers & deinked & market kraft pulp; Owner of Western Canada's largest paper recycling facility

Commonwealth Plywood Co. Ltd.
PO Box 90, 15 boul Labelle, Sainte-Thérèse, QC J7E 4H9
Tél: 450-435-6541; *Téléc:* 450-435-3814
info@commonwealthplywood.com
www.commonwealthplywood.com
Company Type: Private
Profile: Manufacturers of hardwood veneer & plywood, softwood veneer & plywood, millwork; in sawmills & planing mills; wholesalers hardwood & softwood lumber, plywood, millwork & wood panels

Concert Industries Ltd.
1680 rue Atmec, Gatineau, QC J8P 7G7
Tel: 819-669-8100; *Fax:* 819-669-8161
info@concert.ca
www.concert.ca
Company Type: Public
Profile: Manufacturers sanitary paper products

Domtar Inc.
395, boul de Maisonneuve ouest, Montréal, QC H3A 1L6
Tél: 514-848-5555; *Téléc:* 514-848-5638
ir@domtar.com
www.domtar.com
Ticker Symbol: UFS
Company Type: Public
Profile: Manager of forestland in Canada & the USA; Producer of lumber & other wood products; Manufacturer of business, commercial printing, publication, technical & specialty papers

Eacom Timber Corp.
#425, 5600 Parkwood Way, Richmond, BC V6V 2M2
Tel: 604-279-8511; *Fax:* 604-279-8711
Toll-Free: 800-315-3660
www.eacomtimber.com
Ticker Symbol: ETR
Company Type: Public
Profile: Forestry and lumber company.

Federated Co-Operatives Ltd.
PO Box 1050 Main, 401 - 22 St. East, Saskatoon, SK S7K 0H2
Tel: 306-244-3311; *Fax:* 306-244-3403
inquiries@fcl.ca
www.fcl.ca
Company Type: Private
Profile: Manufacturers in sawmills & planing mills, general; of millwork, prepared feeds & feed ingredients for animals & fowls, petroleum refining, dog & cat food; Wholesalers of general-line groceries & hardware; Retailing in lumber & other building materials dealers

Fortress Paper Ltd.
157 Chadwick Ct., 2nd Fl., North Vancouver, BC V7M 3K2
Tel: 604-904-2328; *Fax:* 604-988-5327
Toll-Free: 888-820-3888
info@fortresspaper.com
www.fortresspaper.com
Ticker Symbol: FTP
Company Type: Public
Profile: Fortress Paper is engaged in the production of security & other specialty papers. It operates the following paper mills: the Dresden mill in Germany, & the Landqart Mill in Switzerland. Products include banknotes, visa & passport papers, technical papers, & wallpaper base products.

Goodfellow Inc.
225, rue Goodfellow, Delson, QC J5B 1V5
Tel: 450-635-6511; *Fax:* 450-635-3730
Toll-Free: 800-361-6503
info@goodfellowinc.com
www.goodfellowinc.com
Ticker Symbol: GDL
Company Type: Public
Profile: Goodfellow Inc. re-manufactures, wholesales, & distributes wood & wood by-products, such as the following: dressed & rough lumber, sawn timber, composite & veneer based wood panel products, & prefinished & unfinished flooring. Customers are served in Canada & internationally. Goodfellow Inc. has implemented an environmental policy to conduct its business in an environmentally responsible manner.

Hardwoods Distribution Income Fund
#306, 9440 - 202 St., Langley, BC V1M 4A6
Tel: 604-881-1999; *Fax:* 604-881-1995
www.hardwoods-inc.com
Ticker Symbol: HWD.UN
Company Type: Public
Profile: The Hardwoods Distribution Income Fund is an unincorporated open-ended limited purpose trust. The Fund holds interest in the securities of Hardwoods Specialty LP & Hardwoods Specialty Products USLP. The businesses distribute hardwood lumber, plywood, & specialty wood products to the woodworking industry. Distribution centres are located in Canada & the United States.

International Forest Products Ltd.
Bentall Tower Four, PO Box 49114, #3500, 1055 Dunsmuir St., Vancouver, BC V7X 1H7
Tel: 604-689-6800; *Fax:* 604-689-6825
info@interfor.com
www.interfor.com
Ticker Symbol: IFP
Company Type: Public
Profile: Manufacturers in sawmills & general planing mills; of logging; special product sawmills; wholesalers of lumber, plywood, millwork & wood panels

Kitchen Craft of Canada Ltd.
1180 Springfield Rd., Winnipeg, MB R2C 2Z2
Tel: 204-224-3211; *Fax:* 800-665-3495
Toll-Free: 800-463-9707
sales@kitchencraft.com
www.kitchencraft.com
Company Type: Private
Profile: Kitchen Craft of Canada is a manufacturer of wood kitchen cabinets.

Kruger Inc.
3285, ch Bedford, Montréal, QC H3S 1G5
Tel: 514-737-1131; *Fax:* 514-343-3124
webadmin@kruger.com
www.kruger.com
Company Type: Private
Profile: Paperboard mills & paper mills; Manufacturers of packaging paper & plastics film, coated & laminated, corrugated & solid fiber boxes

Masonite International Corporation
6184, rue Notre-Dame, Lac-Mégantic, QC G6B 3B5
Tel: 819-683-1550; *Fax:* 819-583-5902
immirh@megantic.ca
www.masonite.com
Ticker Symbol: MHM
Company Type: Private
Profile: Masonite International Corporation designs & markets interior doors.

Norwall Group Inc.
1055 Clark Blvd., Brampton, ON L6T 3W4
Tel: 905-791-2787; *Fax:* 905-791-5281
Toll-Free: 800-268-0147
mmartin@norwallgroup.com
www.norwall.net
Ticker Symbol: NGI
Company Type: Public
Profile: Norwall Group Inc. is a manufacturer of residential wallcoverings & borders. Products are distributed to home centres, mass merchants, & specialty stores in Canada. In the United States, products are distributed through Norwall Group's wholly-owned operating subsidiary, Patton Wallcoverings.

PRT Forest Regeneration Income Fund
#101, 1006 Fort St., Victoria, BC V8V 3K4
Tel: 250-381-1404; *Fax:* 250-381-0252
Toll-Free: 866-553-8733
investor_relations@prtgroup.com
www.prtgroup.com
Ticker Symbol: PRT.UN
Company Type: Private
Profile: PRT produces forest seedlings in nurseries located in Canada & the USA.

Quebecor Inc.
612, rue Saint-Jacques, Montréal, QC H3C 4M8
Tel: 514-877-9777; *Fax:* 514-380-6097
webmaster@quebecor.com
www.quebecor.com
Ticker Symbol: QBR
Company Type: Public
Profile: Offices of holding companies; Manufacturers in pulp & paper mills, sawmills & planing mills; Newspaper, periodical & books: publishing & printing

Sino-Forest Corporation
#1208, 90 Burnhamthorpe Rd. West, Mississauga, ON L5B 3C3
Tel: 905-281-8889; *Fax:* 905-281-3338
info@sinoforest.com
www.sinoforest.com
Ticker Symbol: TRE
Company Type: Public
Profile: Sino-Forest Corporation is an owner & cultivator of forest plantation trees. The company manufactures engineered-wood products & sells standing timber & harvested logs. Operations are carried out in China.

St. Mary's Paper Corp.
75 Huron St., Sault Ste Marie, ON P6A 5P4
Tel: 705-942-6070; *Fax:* 705-541-2440
www.stmarys-paper.com
Company Type: Private
Profile: St. Marys Paper Corp. operates a paper mill in Sault Ste Marie, Ontario. It produces paper under the trade names Synpress, Sequence, & Sequel. The paper is sold mainly to magazine publishers & to retail companies for the production of catalogues.

Stella-Jones Inc.
#300, 3100 boul de la Côte-Vertu, Montréal, QC H4R 2J8
Tel: 514-934-8666; *Fax:* 514-934-5327
ir@stella-jones.com
www.stella-jones.com
Ticker Symbol: SJ
Company Type: Public
Profile: Stella-Jones specializes in the production & marketing of industrial treated wood products. Products include the following: treated wood for bridges; pressure treated railway ties; marine & foundation pilings; construction timbers; highway guardrail posts; & wood poles for electrical utilities & telecommunications companies.

Supremex Income Fund
7213, rue Cordner, Lasalle, QC H8N 2J7
Tel: 514-595-4045; *Fax:* 514-595-3092
investors@supremex.com
www.supremex.com
Ticker Symbol: SXP.UN
Company Type: Private

Profile: Supremex specializes in manufacturing & marketing stock & custom envelopes & related products. The company has an Enviro-logiX Program, which includes environmentally friendly bubble mailers, among other products.

Taiga Building Products Ltd.
PO Box 80329, #800, 4710 Kingsway, Burnaby, BC V5H 3X6
Tel: 604-438-1471; *Fax:* 604-439-4242
Toll-Free: 800-663-1470
invest@taigabuilding.com
www.taigabuilding.com
Ticker Symbol: TBL
Company Type: Public
Profile: Taiga Building Products Ltd. distributes building products, such as lumber, engineered wood, mouldings, siding, flooring, & polyethylene sheeting. It is also involved in the production of treated wood, which reduces the use of timber resources. The company's customers are most often industrial manufacturers & building supply dealers.

Tembec Inc.
#1050, 800, boul René-Lévesque ouest, Montréal, QC H3B 1X9
Tel: 514-871-0137; *Fax:* 514-397-0896
www.tembec.ca
Ticker Symbol: TMB
Company Type: Public
Profile: Forest products company with operations in North America & France

TimberWest Forest Corp.
PO Box 11101, #2300, 1055 West Georgia St., Vancouver, BC V6E 3P3
Tel: 604-654-4600; *Fax:* 604-654-4662
invest@timberwest.com
www.timberwest.com
Ticker Symbol: TWF
Company Type: Public
Profile: Manufacturers of logging; in sawmills & general planing mills; Forestry-timber tracts

Uniboard Canada Inc
#500, 2540, boul Daniel-Johnson, Laval, QC H7T 2S3
Tel: 450-682-5240; *Fax:* 450-682-0550
Toll-Free: 800-263-5240
sales.canada@uniboard.com
www.uniboard.com
Company Type: Private
Profile: Manufacturers in paperboard mills; of reconstituted wood products, converted paper & various paperboard products

West Fraser Timber Co. Ltd.
#501, 858 Beatty St., Vancouver, BC V6B 1C1
Tel: 604-895-2700; *Fax:* 604-681-6061
shareholder@westfraser.com
www.westfrasertimber.ca
Ticker Symbol: WFT
Company Type: Public
Profile: Manufacturers in pulp mills, paper mills, paperboard mills, sawmills & general planing mills; Retailers in hardware stores, lumber & other building materials dealers

Western Forest Products Inc.
435 Trunk Rd., Duncan, BC V9L 2P9
Tel: 250-748-3711; *Fax:* 250-748-6045
info@westernforest.com
www.westernforest.com
Ticker Symbol: WEF
Company Type: Public
Profile: Western Forest Products is a large woodland operator & lumber producer in the coastal region of British Columbia. Activities include timber harvesting, sawmilling logs into lumber & wood chips, value-added remanufacturing, & reforestation. Customers are served in North America & around the world.

Weyerhaeuser Company Limited
925 West Georgia St., 5th Fl., Vancouver, BC V6C 3L2
Tel: 604-661-8000; *Toll-Free:* 800-525-5440
www.weyerhaeuser.com
Company Type: Public
Profile: Weyerhaeuser is part of the forest products industry. The company grows & harvests trees & produces forestry products. Businesses include cellulose fibers, newsprint & specialty papers, hardwood products, & homes. It works to conduct its business in an environmentally sustainable & socially responsible manner.

Government Administration

Alberta Gaming & Liquor Commission
50 Corriveau Ave., St Albert, AB T8N 3T5
Tel: 780-447-8600; *Fax:* 780-447-8918
Toll-Free: 800-272-8876
aglc_feedback@aglc.gov.ab.ca
www.aglc.gov.ab.ca
Company Type: Crown
Profile: The agent of the Government of Alberta oversees games of chance, gambling & sale & distribution of liquor in the province.

British Columbia Lottery Corporation
74 West Seymour St., Kamloops, BC V2C 1E2
Tel: 250-828-5500; *Fax:* 250-828-5631
www.bclc.com
Company Type: Crown
Profile: BC Lottery Corp. is a gaming entertainment company.

Canada Post Corporation
2701 Riverside Dr., Ottawa, ON K1A 0B1
Tel: 613-734-8440; *Fax:* 613-734-6084
Toll-Free: 866-607-6301
service@canadapost.ca
www.canadapost.ca
Company Type: Crown
Profile: Canadian postal service

Loto-Québec
500, rue Sherbrooke ouest, Montréal, QC H3A 3G6
Tel: 514-282-8000; *Fax:* 514-873-8999
service_clientele@loto-quebec.com
www.loto-quebec.com
Company Type: Crown
Profile: Oversees games of chance & gambling; operates & monitors casinos, a video lottery terminal network, & network bingo activities

Manitoba Lotteries Corporation
830 Empress St., Winnipeg, MB R3G 3H3
Tel: 204-957-2500; *Fax:* 204-957-3991
communications@mlc.mb.ca
www.mlc.mb.ca
Company Type: Crown
Profile: Manitoba Lotteries Corporation is the owner & operator of the Video Lottery Terminal (VLT) Network, Club Regent Casino, & McPhillips Station Casino. The crown corporation also distributes & sells tickets for lotteries operated by the Western Canada Lottery Corporation.

Ontario Lottery and Gaming Corporation
#800, 70 Foster Dr., Sault Ste. Marie, ON P6A 6V2
Tel: 705-946-6464; *Toll-Free:* 800-387-0098
www.olg.ca
Company Type: Crown
Profile: Oversees games of chance & gambling; Operates & monitors casinos: charity, aboriginal & commercial; Operates slotmachines at race tracks

Holding & Other Investment

ACE Aviation Holding Inc.
5100, boul de Maisonneuve ouest, Montréal, QC H4Y 1H4
Tel: 514-422-5000; *Fax:* 514-422-5789
shareholders.actionnaires@aceaviation.com
www.aceaviation.com
Ticker Symbol: ACE
Company Type: Public
Profile: The investment holding company has interests in aviation companies such as Air Canada & Jazz Air.

AGF Master Limited Partnership
Toronto-Dominion Centre, PO Box 50, Toronto, ON M5K 1E9
Tel: 416-367-1900; *Fax:* 800-214-8243
Toll-Free: 800-268-8583
info@agf.com
www.agf.com
Ticker Symbol: AFP
Company Type: Public
Profile: Offices of holding companies

AIC Diversified Canada Split Corp.
1375 Kerns Rd., Burlington, ON L7R 4X8
Tel: 905-331-4286; *Fax:* 905-331-1321
Toll-Free: 800-263-2144
info@aic.com
www.aic.com
Ticker Symbol: ADC
Company Type: Public
Profile: Unit investment trusts, certificate/closed-end management offices

Argus Corporation Limited
10 Toronto St., Toronto, ON M5C 2B7
Tel: 416-363-8721; *Fax:* 416-363-4187
Ticker Symbol: AR
Company Type: Public
Profile: Offices of holding companies

Avenir Diversified Income Trust
#300, 808 - 1st St. SW, Calgary, AB T2P 1M9
Tel: 403-237-9949; *Fax:* 403-237-0903
info@avenirtrust.com
www.avenirtrust.com
Ticker Symbol: AVF.UN
Company Type: Public
Profile: The income trust has interests in the following sectors: financial services, energy, & real estate.

BAM Investments Corp.
Brookfield Place, #300, 181 Bay St., Toronto, ON M5J 2T3
Tel: 416-359-8620; *Fax:* 416-365-9642
Ticker Symbol: BNB
Company Type: Public
Profile: BAM Investments Corp. is a leveraged investment company. It has a principal holding in Brookfield Asset Management.

BAM Split Corp.
Brookfield Place, PO Box 762, #300, 181 Bay St., Toronto, ON M5J 2T3
Tel: 416-359-8620; *Fax:* 416-359-9642
www.bnnsplit.com
Ticker Symbol: BAM
Company Type: Public
Profile: Offices of holding companies

British Columbia Investment Management Corporation
PO Box 9910, Victoria, BC V8W 9R1
Tel: 250-356-0263; *Fax:* 250-387-7874
communications@bcimc.com
www.bcimc.com
Company Type: Public
Profile: Investment funds management, with clients including public sector pension plans, the Province of British Columbia, Crown corporations and publicly administered trust funds; pooled investment funds and segregated funds

Brookfield Asset Management
Brookfield Place, #300, 181 Bay St., Toronto, ON M5J 2T3
Tel: 416-363-9491; *Fax:* 416-365-9642
www.brookfield.com
Ticker Symbol: BAM
Company Type: Public
Profile: The global asset manager concentrates on property, infrastructure, & power assets.

C.I. Fund Management Inc.
2 Queen St. East, 20th Fl., Toronto, ON M5C 3G7
Tel: 416-364-1145; *Fax:* 416-364-6299
Toll-Free: 800-268-9374
service@ci.com
www.cifunds.com
Ticker Symbol: CIX
Company Type: Public
Profile: Management investment offices, open-end

Canada Trust Income Investments
c/o TD Asset Management Inc., Canada Trust Tower, 161 Bay St., 35th Fl., Toronto, ON M5J 2T2
Tel: 416-308-9049; *Fax:* 416-983-1729
Toll-Free: 866-888-3383
tdeft@tdam.com
www.tdcanadatrust.com
Company Type: Public
Profile: Unit investment trusts, certificate/closed-end management offices

Canadian Apartment Properties Real Estate Investment
#401, 11 Church St., Toronto, ON M5E 1W1
Tel: 416-861-9404; *Fax:* 416-861-9209
ir@capreit.net
www.capreit.net
Ticker Symbol: CAR
Company Type: Public
Profile: Real estate investment trusts

Canadian Real Estate Investment Trust
North Tower, #500, 175 Bloor St. East, Toronto, ON M4W 3R8
Tel: 416-628-7771; *Fax:* 416-628-7777
info@creit.ca
www.creit.ca
Ticker Symbol: REF
Company Type: Public
Profile: Canadian Real Estate Investment Trust is the owner of a portfolio of retail, office, & industrial properties.

Canadian Resources Income Trust
Scotia Plaza, PO Box 4085 A, #2600, 40 King St. West, Toronto, ON M5W 2X6
Tel: 416-863-7144; *Fax:* 416-863-7425
mc_carit@scotiacapital.com
Company Type: Public
Profile: Unit investment trusts, certificate/closed-end management offices

Canadian World Fund Limited
10 Toronto St., Toronto, ON M5C 2B7
Tel: 416-366-2931; *Fax:* 416-366-2729
Toll-Free: 866-443-6097
mma@mmainvestments.com
www.mmainvestments.com
Ticker Symbol: CWF
Company Type: Public
Profile: Unit investment trusts, certificate/closed-end management offices

Central Fund of Canada Limited
Hallmark Estates, #805, 1323 - 15th Ave. SW, Calgary, AB T3C 0X8
Tel: 403-228-5861; *Fax:* 403-228-2222
info@centralfund.com
www.centralfund.com
Ticker Symbol: CEF, CEF.A
Company Type: Public
Profile: A Canadian company that passively holds gold and silver bullion on a secure basis for investors

Chesswood Income Fund
4077 Chesswood Dr., Toronto, ON M3J 2R8
Tel: 416-386-3099; *Fax:* 416-386-3085
info@chesswoodfund.com
www.chesswoodfund.com
Ticker Symbol: CFU.UN
Company Type: Public
Profile: A financial services trust with operating businesses in both Canada & the USA

Cineplex Galaxy Income Fund
1303 Yonge St., Toronto, ON M4T 2Y9
Tel: 416-323-6600; *Fax:* 416-323-6633
pat.marshall@cineplex.com
www.cineplex.com
Ticker Symbol: CGX.UN
Company Type: Public
Profile: The unincorporated, open-ended limited purpose trust owns approximately 97% of Cineplex Entertainment Limited Partnership.

Citadel Diversified Investment Trust
#1006, 141 Adelaide St. West, Toronto, ON M5H 3L5
Tel: 416-361-9673; *Fax:* 416-361-0634
Toll-Free: 877-261-9674
investorrelations@citadelfunds.com
www.citadelfunds.com
Company Type: Public
Profile: Unit investment trusts, certificate/closed-end management offices

CML Healthcare Income Fund
#1, 60 Courtneypark Dr. West, Mississauga, ON L5W 0B3
Tel: 905-565-0043; *Fax:* 905-565-2844
Toll-Free: 800-263-0801
www.cmlhealthcare.com
Ticker Symbol: CLC
Company Type: Public
Profile: The open-ended investment trust is the owner of CML HealthCare Inc. The healthcare service provides laboratory testing & medical imaging services in Canada. HealthCare Income Fund also acquired American Radiology Services, Inc., which provides diagnostic medical imaging services in the United States.

Consolidated Mercantile Incorporated
106 Avenue Rd., Toronto, ON M5R 2H3
Tel: 416-920-0500; *Fax:* 416-920-7851
info@consolidatedmercantile.com
www.consolidatedmercantile.com
Ticker Symbol: CMC
Company Type: Public
Profile: Offices of holding companies; Manufacturers of wood household & office furniture, various plastics products; Real estate land subdividers & developers; Investment management in furniture specialty covers, packaging, & real estate industries

Consumers' Waterheater Income Fund
80 Allstate Pkwy., 2nd Fl., Markham, ON L3R 6H3
Tel: 905-943-6292; *Fax:* 905-943-6393
Toll-Free: 877-877-0142
info@consumerswaterheaters.com
www.consumerswaterheaters.com
Ticker Symbol: CWI.UN
Company Type: Public
Profile: Consumers Waterheater Income Fund is the owner of a portfolio of waterheaters, which are leased to residential customers in Ontario.

Counsel Corporation
Scotia Plaza, #3200, 40 King St. West, Toronto, ON M5H 3Y2
Tel: 416-866-3000; *Fax:* 416-866-3061
info@counselcorp.com
www.counselcorp.com
Ticker Symbol: CXS
Company Type: Public
Profile: Counsel Corporation is an international asset management firm. It strives to take advantage of corporate & real estate investment opportunities.

Crew Gold Corporation
#400, 837 West Hastings St., Vancouver, BC V6C 3N6
Tel: 604-683-7585; *Fax:* 604-682-0566
investorrelations@crewgold.com
www.crewgroup.com
Ticker Symbol: CRU
Company Type: Public
Profile: Offices of holding companies

DDJ High Yield Fund
CI Investments, 2 Queen St. East, 20th Fl., Toronto, ON M5C 3G7
Tel: 416-364-1145; *Fax:* 416-364-6299
Toll-Free: 800-268-9374
service@ci.com
www.ci.com
Ticker Symbol: HYB
Company Type: Public
Profile: Unit investment trusts, certificate/closed-end management offices

Dundee Corporation
Dundee Place, 1 Adelaide St. East, 28th Fl., Toronto, ON M5C 2V9
Tel: 416-863-6990; *Fax:* 416-363-4536
investor@dundeebancorp.com
www.dundeecorporation.com
Ticker Symbol: DC.A
Company Type: Public
Profile: The asset management company is engaged in real estate, private wealth management, & resources.

E-L Financial Corporation Limited
165 University Ave., 10th Fl., Toronto, ON M5H 3B8
Tel: 416-947-2578; *Fax:* 416-362-0792
Ticker Symbol: ELF
Company Type: Public
Profile: The investment & insurance holding company consists of the following subsidiaries: E-L Financial Services Ltd., The Dominion of Canada General Insurance Company, & The Empire Life Insurance Company.

Economic Investment Trust Limited
165 University Ave., 10th Fl., Toronto, ON M5H 3B8
Tel: 416-947-2578; *Fax:* 416-362-2592
Ticker Symbol: EVT
Company Type: Public
Profile: Unit investment trusts, certificate/closed-end management offices

Empire Company Limited
115 King St., Stellarton, NS B0K 1S0
Tel: 902-755-4440; *Fax:* 902-755-6477
ir-empire@sobeys.com
www.empireco.ca
Ticker Symbol: EMP
Company Type: Public
Profile: The Empire Company Limited is engaged in food retailing, through its majority ownership of Sobeys Inc. Through wholly-owned companies, Empire Company is also involved in real estate.

EnerVest Diversified Income Trust
350 - 7th Ave. SW, 39th Fl., Calgary, AB T2P 3N9
Tel: 403-571-5550; *Fax:* 403-571-5554
Toll-Free: 877-434-2796
info@enervest.com
www.enervest.com
Ticker Symbol: EIT
Company Type: Public
Profile: Unit investment trusts, certificate/closed-end management offices

Exchange Industrial Income Fund
1067 Sherwin Rd., Winnipeg, MB R3H 0T8
Tel: 204-982-1852; *Fax:* 204-982-1855
dspencer@eig.ca
www.eiif.ca
Ticker Symbol: EIF.UN
Company Type: Public
Profile: Exchange Industrial Income Fund is a Canadian business trust. The Fund seeks acquisition opportunities in well-established, profitable companies in the industrial products & transportation markets. The following are the Fund's subsidiaries: Overlanders Manufacturing, Water Blast Manufacturing, Jasper Tank, Stainless Fabrication, Inc., Perimeter Air, & Keewatin Air.

Fairfax Financial Holdings Limited
#800, 95 Wellington St. West, Toronto, ON M5J 2N7
Tel: 416-367-4941; *Fax:* 416-367-4946
www.fairfax.ca
Ticker Symbol: FFH
Company Type: Public
Profile: Through its subsidiaries, the financial services holding company is involved in insurance claims management, property & casualty insurance & reinsurance, & investment management. Subsidiaries include Northbridge Financial, Crum & Forster, Falcon Insurance, First Capital, OdysseyRe, Group Re, Hamblin Watsa Investment Counsel, & MFXchange.

First Asset Energy & Resource Fund
#1400, 95 Wellington St., Toronto, ON M5J 2N7
Tel: 416-642-1289; *Fax:* 416-362-2199
Toll-Free: 877-642-1289
info@firstasset.com
www.firstasset.com
Ticker Symbol: TRF.UN
Company Type: Public
Profile: Unit investment trusts, certificate/closed-end management offices

Forest & Marine Investments Ltd.
#500, 345 Wallace St., Nanaimo, BC V9R 5B6
Tel: 250-753-0141; *Fax:* 250-753-0173
Toll-Free: 877-772-0022
dhitch@forestandmarine.com
www.forestandmarine.com
Ticker Symbol: FME
Company Type: Public
Profile: Unit investment trusts, certificate/closed-end management offices

Freehold Royalty Trust
#400, 144 - 4th Ave. SW, Calgary, AB T2P 3N4
Tel: 403-221-0802; *Fax:* 403-221-0888
Toll-Free: 888-257-1873
ir@freeholdtrust.com
www.freeholdtrust.com
Ticker Symbol: FRU
Company Type: Public
Profile: Open-ended management investment offices; Oil royalty traders

Garbell Holdings Limited
Standard Life Centre, PO Box 35, #1770, 121 King St. West, Toronto, ON M5H 3T9
Tel: 416-947-1100; *Fax:* 416-947-0834
msimpson@garbell.on.ca
Company Type: Private
Profile: Garbell Holdings Limited is an investment holding company.

Gendis Inc.
1370 Sony Place, Winnipeg, MB R3C 3C3
Tel: 204-474-5200; *Fax:* 204-474-5201
finance@gendis.ca
www.gendis.ca
Ticker Symbol: GDS
Company Type: Public
Profile: Offices of holding companies; Management services

Glendale International Corp.
353 Iroquois Shore Rd., Oakville, ON L6H 1M3
Tel: 905-844-2870; *Fax:* 905-844-2907
info@glendaleint.com
www.glendaleint.com
Ticker Symbol: GIN
Company Type: Public
Profile: Glendale International Corp. manages a portfolio of companies involved in electronics, technology, & recreational vehicles.

GLP NT Corporation
Brookfield Place, PO Box 770, #300, 181 Bay St., Toronto, ON M5J 2T3
Tel: 416-369-8268; *Fax:* 416-363-2856
Ticker Symbol: GP
Company Type: Public
Profile: Offices of holding companies

Great-West Lifeco Inc.
100 Osborne St. North, Winnipeg, MB R3C 3A5
Tel: 204-946-8366; *Fax:* 204-946-4129
contactus@gwl.ca
www.greatwestlife.com
Ticker Symbol: GWO
Company Type: Public
Profile: The financial services holding company owns Great-West Life Assurance Co. of Winnipeg, Manitoba.

H&R Real Estate Investment Trust
#500, 3625 Dufferin St., Toronto, ON M3K 1N4
Tel: 416-635-7520; *Fax:* 416-398-0040
info@hr-reit.com
www.hr-reit.com
Ticker Symbol: HR
Company Type: Public
Profile: The organization is a real estate investment trust.

Halterm Income Fund
PO Box 1057, 577 Marginal Rd., Halifax, NS B3J 2X1
Tel: 902-421-1778; *Fax:* 902-429-3193
info@halterm.com
www.halterm.com
Ticker Symbol: HAL
Company Type: Public
Profile: Non-charitable, non-educational & non-religious trusts

IAT Air Cargo Facilities Income Fund
#2000, 5000 Miller Rd., Richmond, BC V7B 1K6
Tel: 604-249-5100; *Fax:* 604-249-5101
mmitchell@amb.com
www.iat-yvr.com
Ticker Symbol: ACF
Company Type: Public
Profile: Unit investment trusts, certificate/closed-end management offices

IBI Income Fund
230 Richmond St. West, 5th Fl., Toronto, ON M5V 1V6
Tel: 416-596-1930; *Fax:* 416-596-8024
www.ibigroup.com
Ticker Symbol: IBG.UN
Company Type: Public
Profile: IBI Income Fund holds interest in IBI Group. IBI Group provides service in the following areas of practice: facilities, systems, urban land, & transportation. Offices are situated in Canada, the United States, Europe, the Middle East, & Asia.

Income Financial Trust
Royal Trust Tower, PO Box 341, #4500, 77 King St. West, Toronto, ON M5K 1K7
Tel: 416-304-4440; *Fax:* 416-304-4441
Toll-Free: 877-478-2372
info@quadravest.com
www.quadravest.com
Ticker Symbol: INC
Company Type: Public
Profile: Unit investment trusts, certificate/closed-end management offices; Investors

iUnits S&P/TSE 60 Index Participation Fund
Barclays Global Investors Canada Limited, BCE Plac, PO Box 614, #2500, 161 Bay St., Toronto, ON M5J 2S1
Tel: 416-643-4080; *Fax:* 416-643-4039
Toll-Free: 877-468-6487
iunits@barclaysglobal.com
www.iunits.com
Ticker Symbol: XIU
Company Type: Public
Profile: Unit investment trusts, certificate/closed-end management offices

Labrador Iron Ore Royalty Income Fund
Scotia Plaza, PO Box 4085 A, 40 King St. West, 26th Fl., Toronto, ON M5W 2X6
Tel: 416-863-7133; *Fax:* 416-863-7425
www.labradorironore.com
Ticker Symbol: LIF
Company Type: Public
Profile: Labrador Iron Ore Royalty Income Fund is an unicorporated, limited purpose trust. Its wholly-owned subsidiaries include Hollinger-Hanna Limited & Labrador Mining Co Ltd. (Labmin). Through these subsidiaries, the Fund holds a 15.10% equity interest in Iron Ore Company of Canada (IOC).

Longview Capital Partners Inc.
1111 West Georgia St., 24th Fl., Vancouver, BC V6E 4M3
Tel: 604-681-5755; *Fax:* 604-684-2990
info@longviewcp.com
www.longviewcp.com
Ticker Symbol: LV
Company Type: Public
Profile: The global resource group's portfolio of companies includes over ten different mineral commodities. The company commenced a Corporate Social Responsibility program to assess the environmental, social, & financial impacts of its operations.

MINT Income Fund
c/o Middlefield Fund Management Limited, PO Box 192, One First Canadian Pl., 58th Fl., Toronto, ON M5X 1A6
Tel: 416-362-0714; *Fax:* 416-362-7925
Toll-Free: 888-890-1868
invest@middlefield.com
www.middlefield.com
Ticker Symbol: MIDUN
Company Type: Public
Profile: The closed-end investment trust invests in securities primarily of units of business trusts, power & pipeline trusts, & real estate investment trusts. It is managed by Middlefield Fund Management Limited.

Morgan Meighen & Associates
10 Toronto St., Toronto, ON M5C 2B7
Tel: 416-366-2931; *Fax:* 416-366-2729
Toll-Free: 866-443-6097
mma@mmainvestments.com
www.mmainvestments.com
Ticker Symbol: CGI
Company Type: Public
Profile: Unit investment trusts, certificate/closed-end management offices

Morguard Real Estate Investment Trust
#1000, 55 City Centre Dr., Mississauga, ON L5B 1M3
Tel: 905-281-4800; *Fax:* 905-281-4818
skaur@morguard.com
www.morguardreit.com
Ticker Symbol: MRT
Company Type: Public
Profile: The organization is a closed-end investment trust. The Morguard Real Estate Investment Trust has a portfolio of diversified real estate assets across Canada.

Mulvihill Capital Management Inc.
Standard Life Centre, #2600, 121 King St. West, Toronto, ON M5H 3T9
Tel: 416-681-3900; *Fax:* 416-681-3901
Toll-Free: 800-725-7172
info@mulvihill.com
www.mulvihill.com
Company Type: Private
Profile: Mulvihill Capital Management is registered as a mutual fund dealer, limited market dealer, & investment counselor throughout Canada.

Mulvihill Premier Canada Income Fund
Mulvihill Capital Management, #2600, 121 King St. West, Toronto, ON M5H 3T9
Tel: 416-681-3900; *Fax:* 416-681-3901
Toll-Free: 800-725-7172
hybrid@mulvihill.com
www.mulvihill.com
Ticker Symbol: GIP
Company Type: Public
Profile: Unit investment trusts, certificate/closed-end management offices

NAL Oil & Gas Trust
#1000, 550 - 6th Ave. SW, Calgary, AB T2P 0S2
Tel: 403-294-3600; *Fax:* 403-294-3601
Toll-Free: 888-223-8792
investor.relations@nal.ca
www.nal.ca
Ticker Symbol: NAE.UN
Company Type: Public
Profile: NAL Oil & Gas Trust is an open-end investment trust. The Trust's distributions are generated by acquiring, developing, producing, & marketing oil, natural gas, & natural gas liquids.

NewGrowth Corp.
Scotia Plaza, Scotia Managed Companies Admin. Inc., PO Box 4085 A, 40 King St. West, 26th Fl., Toronto, ON M5W 2X6
Tel: 416-862-3931; *Fax:* 416-863-7425
mc_newgrowth@scotiacapital.com
www.scotiamanagedcompanies.com
Ticker Symbol: NEW
Company Type: Public
Profile: The mutual fund corporation's investment portfolio consists of publicly-listed securities of selected Canadian chartered banks, pipelines, telecommunications companies, & utility issuers.

Northfield Capital Corporation
#301, 141 Adelaide St. West, Toronto, ON M5H 3L5
Tel: 416-628-5901; *Fax:* 416-628-5911
info@northfieldcapital.com
www.northfieldcapital.com
Ticker Symbol: NFD.A
Company Type: Public
Profile: Formed in 1981, the investment company owns interests in diverse business activities. Major oil, gas, minining, & viticulture holdings include Ground Star Resources, GoldCorp Inc., Queenston Mining Inc., FNX Mining Corporation, Guyana Goldfields Inc., White Pine Resources Inc., Bear Lake Gold Ltd., & The Grange of Prince Edward Inc.

Northland Power Income Fund
c/o Iroquois Falls Power Management Inc., 30 St Clair Ave. West, 17th Fl., Toronto, ON M4V 3A2
Tel: 416-962-6262; *Fax:* 416-962-6266
info@npifund.com
www.npifund.com
Ticker Symbol: NPI
Company Type: Public
Profile: Open-ended management investment offices; Owner & operator of independent power projects

Onex Corporation
PO Box 700, 161 Bay St., Toronto, ON M5J 2S1
Tel: 416-362-7711; *Fax:* 416-362-5765
info@onex.com
www.onex.com
Ticker Symbol: OCX
Company Type: Public
Profile: Through Onex Partners & ONCAP families of funds, Onex Corporation makes private equity investments. The company is also engaged in the management of alternative asset platforms, which focuses on real estate & distressed credit.

Oppenheimer Holdings Inc.
PO Box 2015, #1110, 20 Eglinton Ave. West, Toronto, ON M4R 1K8
Tel: 416-322-1515; *Fax:* 416-322-7007
investorrelations@opy.ca; info@opco.com
www.opco.com
Ticker Symbol: OPY
Company Type: Public
Profile: Oppenheimer Holdings Inc. is a holding company. Its subsidiaries provide the following financial services: investment banking, securities brokerage, asset management, & trust services. Offices are located in the United States, Latin America, England, & Israel.

Power Corp. of Canada
751, carré Victoria, Montréal, QC H2Y 2J3
Tel: 514-286-7400; *Fax:* 514-286-7424
www.powercorporation.com
Ticker Symbol: POW
Company Type: Public
Profile: The main subsidiaries of this diversified international management & holding company include Gesca Ltee., Power Financial Corp., & Power Technology Investment Corp.

Power Financial Corp.
751, carré Victoria, Montréal, QC H2Y 2J3
Tel: 514-286-7400; *Fax:* 514-286-7424
www.powerfinancial.com
Ticker Symbol: PWF
Company Type: Public
Profile: The holding & management company includes the following subsidiaries: IGM Financial Inc., Canada Life Assurance Company, Great-West Lifeco Inc., London Insurance Insurance Company, Investors Group Inc., Mackenzie Financial Corporation, & Putnam Investments, LLC.

Quadravest Capital Management Inc.
PO Box 341, #4500, 77 King St. West, Toronto, ON M5K 1K7
Tel: 416-304-4440; *Fax:* 416-304-4441
Toll-Free: 877-478-2372
info@quadravest.com
www.quadravest.com
Company Type: Public
Profile: Unit investment trusts, certificate/closed-end management offices

R Split II Corporation
Scotia Plaza, PO Box 4085 A, 40 King St. West, 26th Fl., Toronto, ON M5W 2X6
Tel: 416-945-5353; *Fax:* 416-863-7425
mc_rsplit2@scotiacapital.com
www.scotiamanagedcompanies.com
Ticker Symbol: RBS
Company Type: Public
Profile: Unit investment trusts, certificate/closed-end management offices; Investors

Ravensource Fund
Cinnamon Investments, 60 Bedford Rd., Toronto, ON M5R 2K2
Tel: 416-922-9096; *Fax:* 416-921-3551
www.ravensource.ca
Company Type: Public
Profile: This company is a closed end fund which focuses on troubled business enterprises, including small capitalization stocks, income trusts, defualted bonds and restricted securities.

Richards Packaging Income Fund
6095 Ordan Dr., Mississauga, ON L4T 2M7
Tel: 905-670-7760; *Fax:* 905-670-1961
www.richardspackaging.com
Ticker Symbol: RPI.UN
Company Type: Public
Profile: Richards Packaging Income Fund is an indirect owner of securities of Richards Packaging Inc. Richards Packaging is a plastic & glass container manufacturer & distributor. The company also distributes metal & plastic closures, as well as injection molded containers & packaging systems.

Rogers Sugar Income Fund
4026, rue Notre-Dame est, Montréal, QC H1W 2K3
Tel: 514-940-4350; *Fax:* 514-527-1610
infos@rogerssugar.com
www.rogerssugar.com
Ticker Symbol: RSI
Company Type: Public
Profile: The open-ended, limited purpose trust holds the common shares & notes of Lantic Sugar Limited. Lantic refines, processes, distributes, & markets sugar products throughout Canada.

SCI Income Trust
#251, 6900 Airport Rd., Mississauga, ON L4V 1E8
Tel: 905-671-1033; *Fax:* 905-671-0669
sci-investor-relations@simmonscanada.com
www.simmonscanada.com
Ticker Symbol: SMN.UN
Company Type: Public
Profile: Manufacturers of mattresses & foundations

Senvest Capital Inc.
#2400, 1000, rue Sherbrooke ouest, Montréal, QC H3A 3G4
Tel: 514-281-8082; *Fax:* 514-281-0166
www.senvest.com
Ticker Symbol: SEC
Company Type: Public
Profile: Senvest Capital Inc.'s subsidiaries are involved in following sectors: asset management, merchant banking, real estate, & electronic security.

Sonor Investments Limited
PO Box 104, #2120, 130 Adelaide St. West, Toronto, ON M5H 3P5
Tel: 416-369-1499; *Fax:* 416-369-0280
Ticker Symbol: SNI
Company Type: Public
Profile: Sonor Investments Limited is an investment holding company.

Superior Plus Income Fund
#2820, 605 - 5th Ave. SW, Calgary, AB T2P 3H5
Tel: 403-218-2954; *Fax:* 403-218-2973
info@superiorplus.com
www.superiorplus.ca
Ticker Symbol: SPB
Company Type: Public
Profile: The limited purpose trust holds securities of Superior Plus Inc.. Distributions are made to holders of trust units of the Fund.

The Data Group Income Fund
9195 Torbram Rd., Brampton, ON L6S 6H2
Tel: 905-791-3151; *Fax:* 905-791-3277
www.datagroup.ca
Ticker Symbol: DGI.UN
Company Type: Public
Profile: The Data Group Income Fund is the owner of The Data Group Limited Partnership. Document management solutions are provided, including printed products. Twenty-five facilities are operated throughout Canada.

The Health Care & Biotechnology Venture Fund
c/o Lumira Capital Corp., #770, 141 Adelaide St. West, Toronto, ON M5H 3L5
Tel: 416-675-7661; *Fax:* 416-213-4232
www.lumiracapital.com
Company Type: Public
Profile: Unit investment trusts, certificate/closed-end management offices; Investors

The Jim Pattison Group
#1800, 1067 West Cordova St., Vancouver, BC V6C 1C7
Tel: 604-688-6764; *Fax:* 604-687-2601
admin@jp-group.com
www.jimpattison.com
Company Type: Private
Profile: Periodical distribution; Radio & TV stations; Advertising display & signage; Retail food & fish harvesting & processing; Retail vehicle franchising; Export & financial services

Third Canadian General Investment Trust Limited
10 Toronto St., Toronto, ON M5C 2B7
Tel: 416-366-2931; *Fax:* 416-366-2729
Toll-Free: 866-443-6097
mma@mmainvestments.com
www.mmainvestments.com
Ticker Symbol: THD
Company Type: Public
Profile: Offices of holding companies; Unit investment trusts, certificate/closed-end management offices

Thirty-Five Split Corp.
Scotia Plaza, PO Box 4085 A, 40 King St. West, 26th Fl., Toronto, ON M5W 2X6
Tel: 416-945-4535; *Fax:* 416-863-7425
mc_thirtyfivesplit@scotiacapital.com
www.scotiamanagedcompanies.com
Ticker Symbol: TFS
Company Type: Public
Profile: Open-ended management investment offices

Triax Diversified High-Yield Trust
#1400, 95 Wellington St., Toronto, ON M5J 2N7
Tel: 416-362-2929; *Fax:* 416-362-2199
Toll-Free: 800-407-0287
info@triaxcapital.com
www.triaxcapital.com
Ticker Symbol: TRH
Company Type: Public
Profile: Unit investment trusts, certificate/closed-end management offices

Unique Broadband Systems, Inc.
8250 Lawson Rd., Milton, ON L9T 5C6
Tel: 905-660-8100; *Fax:* 905-669-0785
irinfo@uniquebroadband.com
www.uniquebroadband.com
Ticker Symbol: UBS
Company Type: Public
Profile: Unique Broadband Systems, Inc. is a publicly listed Canadian holding company.

United Corporations Limited
165 University Ave., 10th Fl., Toronto, ON M5H 3B8
Tel: 416-947-2578; *Fax:* 416-362-2592
www.ucorp.ca
Ticker Symbol: UNC
Company Type: Public
Profile: Unit investment trusts, certificate/closed-end management offices

Utility Corp.
Scotia Plaza, PO Box 4085 A, 40 King St. West, 26th Fl., Toronto, ON M5W 2X6
Tel: 416-863-7893; *Fax:* 416-863-7425
mc_utility@scotiacapital.com
www.scotiamanagedcompanies.com
Ticker Symbol: UTC
Company Type: Public
Profile: Utility Corp. is a mutual fund corporation whose investment portfolio consists of publicly listed securities of Canadian utility & telecommunications companies.

WesternOne Equity Income Fund
#910, 925 West Georgia St., Vancouver, BC V6C 3L2
Tel: 604-678-4042; *Fax:* 604-681-5969
info@weq.ca
www.weq.ca
Ticker Symbol: WEQ.UN
Company Type: Public
Profile: WesternOne Equity Income Fund is an unincorporated, open-ended trust. It invests in mainly small & medium sized equipment & infrastructure related businesses. The Fund's businesses are located primarily in Saskatchewan, Alberta, & British Columbia.

Westshore Terminals Income Fund
#1800, 1067 West Cordova St., Vancouver, BC V6C 1C7
Tel: 604-688-6764; *Fax:* 604-687-2601
www.westshore.com
Ticker Symbol: WTE
Company Type: Public
Profile: The open-ended trust owns all the limited partnership units of Westshore Terminals Limited Partnership. Westshore Terminals Limited is located in Roberts Bank, British Columbia, where it operates a coal storage & coal export facility. The Fund distributes available cash received from Westshore Terminals Limited to its unitholders. Westar Management Ltd. operates Westshore Terminals Limited for the Fund.

Insurance

Agriculture Financial Services Corporation
5718 - 56 Ave., Lacombe, AB T4L 1B1
Tel: 403-782-8200; *Fax:* 403-782-4226
Toll-Free: 800-396-0215
afsc.webmaster@afsc.ca
www.afsc.ca
Company Type: Crown
Profile: Fire, marine & casualty insurance; Agricultural services, farm management services

Aviva Canada Inc.
2206 Eglinton Ave. East, Toronto, ON M1L 4S8
Tel: 416-288-1800; *Toll-Free:* 800-387-4518
www.avivacanada.com
Company Type: Private
Profile: Property & casualty insurance group

Canada Deposit Insurance Corporation
PO Box 2340 D, 50 O'Connor St., 17th Fl., Ottawa, ON K1P 5W5
Fax: 613-996-6095
Toll-Free: 800-461-2342
info@cdic.ca
www.cdic.ca
Company Type: Crown
Profile: Various insurance carriers; Public finance, taxation, & monetary policy

Co-operators General Insurance Company
Service Quality Department, Priory Square, 130 MacDonell St., Guelph, ON N1H 6P8
Tel: 519-824-4400; *Fax:* 519-763-5152
Toll-Free: 800-265-2612
service@cooperators.ca
www.cooperators.ca
Ticker Symbol: CCS
Company Type: Public
Profile: Co-operators General Insurance Company provides home, automobile, farm, & commercial insurance services throughout Canada.

Cunningham Lindsey Group Inc.
#1000, 70 University Ave., Toronto, ON M5J 2M4
Tel: 416-596-8020; *Fax:* 416-596-6510
corpservices@cl-na.com
www.cunninghamlindsey.com
Ticker Symbol: LIN
Company Type: Public
Profile: Offices of holding companies; Insurance agents, brokers & service

Desjardins Financial Corporation
PO Box 10500 Desjardins, #2822, 1 complexe Desjardins, Montréal, QC H5B 1J1
Tel: 514-281-7070; *Fax:* 514-281-7083
info@desjardins.com
www.desjardins.com
Company Type: Public
Profile: Offices of holding companies; Life, fire, marine & casualty insurance

EGI Financial Holdings Inc.
#300, 2680 Matheson Blvd. East, Mississauga, ON L4W 0A5
Tel: 905-214-7880; *Fax:* 905-214-8028
www.egi.ca
Ticker Symbol: EFH
Company Type: Public
Profile: Through its subsidiary, Echelon General Insurance, EGI Financial is involved in the property & casualty insurance industry in Canada. Specialty general insurance products include non-standard automobile insurance.

Equitable Life Insurance Company of Canada
1 Westmount Rd. North, Waterloo, ON N2J 4C7
Tel: 519-886-5110; *Fax:* 519-883-7400
Toll-Free: 800-265-8878
headoffice@equitable.ca
www.equitable.ca
Company Type: Private
Profile: Individual life & health insurance & annuities, group life, health & pension plans; retirement savings; commercial mortgages & segregated funds

Gore Mutual Insurance Company
PO Box 70, 252 Dundas St. North, Cambridge, ON N1R 5T3
Tel: 519-623-1910; *Fax:* 800-601-9773
Toll-Free: 800-265-8600
www.goremutual.ca
Company Type: Private
Profile: Fire, marine surety & casualty insurance

Great-West Life Assurance Company
100 Osborne St. North, Winnipeg, MB R3C 3A5
Tel: 204-946-1190; *Fax:* 204-946-4129
www.greatwestlife.com.
Ticker Symbol: GWL
Company Type: Public
Profile: The insurance company serves individuals, families, businesses, & organizations. Great-West Life Assurance Company also supplies specialty general insurance & reinsurance.

Hub International Limited
8 Nelson St. West, 6th Fl., Brampton, ON L6X 4J2
Tel: 905-459-4000; *Fax:* 905-459-1401
Toll-Free: 800-387-2592
dennis.pauls@hubinternational.com
www.hubinternational.com
Company Type: Public
Profile: Insurance brokerage: property, casualty, life & health, employee benefits, investment & risk management & services

Industrial Alliance Insurance & Financial Services
PO Box 1907 Terminus, 1080, Grande Allée ouest, Québec, QC G1K 7M3
Tél: 418-684-5000; *Téléc:* 418-684-5294
Ligne sans frais: 800-463-6236
info@inalco.com; investors@inalco.com
www.inalco.com
Ticker Symbol: IAG
Company Type: Public
Profile: Industrial Alliance Insurance & Financial Services Inc. provides a great range of financial & insurance products & services, including life & health insurance, automobile & home insurance, RRSPs, savings & retirement plans, securities, mutual & segregated funds, & mortgage loans.

ING Canada Inc.
ING Tower, 700 University Ave., 15th Fl., Toronto, ON M5G 0A1
Tel: 416-341-1464; *Fax:* 416-941-5320
info@ingcanada.com
www.ingcanada.com
Ticker Symbol: IIC
Company Type: Private
Profile: Through its subsidiaries, ING Canada Inc. provides the following types of insurance: property, liability, & automobile. The property & casualty insurance provider serves both individuals & businesses.

Insurance Corporation of British Columbia
151 West Esplanade, North Vancouver, BC V7M 3H9
Tel: 604-661-2800; *Toll-Free:* 800-663-3051
www.icbc.com
Company Type: Crown
Profile: Automobile insurance

Kingsway Financial Services Inc.
#800, 7120 Hurontario, Mississauga, ON L5W 0A9
Tel: 905-696-1372; *Fax:* 905-696-1772
info@kingsway-financial.com
www.kingsway-financial.com
Ticker Symbol: KFS
Company Type: Public
Profile: Offices of holding companies; Fire, marine & casualty insurance

Lloyd's Canada Inc.
Royal Bank Plaza, South Tower, #2930, 200 Bay St., Toronto, ON M5J 2J2
Toll-Free: 877-455-6937
info@lloyds.ca; lineage@lloyds.ca
www.lloyds.com
Company Type: Private
Profile: With offices in Montréal & Toronto, Lloyd's Canada provides all classes of insurance & reinsurance, with the exception of life, title, mortgage, credit protection, home warranty (BC only), & crop hail insurance (QC only). Lloyd's expertise is in property, casualty & specialty classes of business insurance to the commercial market, notably to small & medium sized enterprises.

London Life Insurance Company
255 Dufferin Ave., London, ON N6A 4K1
Tel: 519-432-5281; *Fax:* 519-435-7077
www.londonlife.com
Company Type: Public
Profile: London Life Insurance Company provides financial security advice & planning for individuals, businesses, & organizations. Products include life insurance, mortgages, & group retirement plans.

MARSH Canada Limited
Brookfield Place, #1400, 161 Bay St., Toronto, ON M5J 2S4
Tel: 416-868-2600;
www.marsh.ca
Company Type: Private
Profile: The broker & risk advisor offers advice & transactional capabilities. Services include mergers & acquisitions, risk management services, & alternative risk financing.

Northbridge Financial Corporation
105 Adelaide St. West, 7th Fl., Toronto, ON M5H 1P9
Tel: 416-350-4300; *Fax:* 416-350-4307
investor.relations@norfin.com
www.norfin.com
Ticker Symbol: NB
Company Type: Public
Profile: Northbridge Financial Corporation provides automobile, property, general liability, & other commercial insurance products. Clients are businesses in Canada.

Optimum General Inc.
#1500, 425, boul de Maisonneuve ouest, Montréal, QC H3A 3G5
Tel: 514-288-8725; *Fax:* 514-288-0760
direction@optimum-general.com
www.optimum-general.com
Ticker Symbol: OGI
Company Type: Public
Profile: Automobile, personal property, commercial property and liability insurance

Royal & Sun Alliance Insurance Company of Canada
10 Wellington St. East, Toronto, ON M5E 1L5
Tel: 416-366-7511; *Fax:* 416-367-9869
Toll-Free: 800-268-8406
info@royalsunalliance.ca
www.royalsunalliance.ca
Company Type: Private
Profile: Automobile & personal property insurance; Marine, small business & custom risk products

SGI Canada
2260 - 11th Ave., Regina, SK S4P 0J9
Tel: 306-751-1200; *Toll-Free:* 800-667-8015
sgiinquiries@sgi.sk.ca
www.sgi.sk.ca
Company Type: Crown
Profile: SGI Canada sells property & casualty insurance products. The company operates in the following provinces: Alberta, Saskatchewan, Manitoba, Ontario, New Brunswick, Nova Scotia, & Prince Edward Island. In Saskatchewan, the compulsory auto insurance program is the Saskatchewan Auto Fund. The Fund operates both the drivers' licensing & the vehicle registration systems. SGI Canada works with motor licence issuing outlets in Saskatchewan, plus insurance brokers in numerous provinces. The company also operates the Coachman Insurance Company in Toronto, & is a partner of the Insurance Company of Prince Edward Island.

State Farm Group Insurance Company
333 First Commerce Dr., Aurora, ON L4G 8A4
Tel: 905-750-4573; *Fax:* 905-750-4834
info@statefarm.ca
www.statefarm.ca
Company Type: Private
Profile: Group of insurance companies

Sun Life Financial Inc.
150 King St. West, Toronto, ON M5H 1J9
Tel: 416-979-9966; *Fax:* 416-585-7892
Toll-Free: 877-786-5433
investor.relations@sunlife.com
www.sunlife.com
Ticker Symbol: SLF
Company Type: Public
Profile: Sun Life Financial serves both individuals & corporate customers. It offers customers a broad range of protection & wealth management products & services.

The CUMIS Group Limited
PO Box 5065, 151 North Service Rd., Burlington, ON L7R 4C2
Tel: 905-632-1221; *Fax:* 905-632-9412
Toll-Free: 800-263-9120
customer.service@cumis.com
www.cumis.com
Company Type: Private
Profile: Offices of holding companies; Life, accident, health, fire, marine & casualty insurance; Pension, health, & welfare funds

The Economical Insurance Group
PO Box 2000, 111 Westmount Rd. South, Waterloo, ON N2J 4S4
Tel: 519-570-8200; *Fax:* 519-570-8389
Toll-Free: 800-265-2180
www.economicalinsurance.com
Company Type: Private
Profile: Auto, property & casualty insurers

Wawanesa Insurance
#900, 191 Broadway, Winnipeg, MB R3C 3P1
Tel: 204-985-3923; *Fax:* 204-942-7724
www.wawanesa.com
Company Type: Private
Profile: Property & casualty insurer, owned by policyholders. Offices across Canada. The Wawanesa Life Insurance Company, and Wawanesa General Insurance (U.S.) are subsidiaries.

Workers' Compensation Board - Alberta
PO Box 2415, 9912 - 107 St., Edmonton, AB T5J 2S5
Tel: 780-498-3999; *Fax:* 780-498-7999
Toll-Free: 866-922-9221
www.wcb.ab.ca
Company Type: Private
Profile: Non-profit disability insurance system

Workplace Safety & Insurance Board of Ontario
200 Front St. West, Toronto, ON M5V 3J1
Tel: 416-344-1000; *Fax:* 416-344-4684
Toll-Free: 800-387-5540
wsibcomm@wsib.on.ca
www.wsib.on.ca
Company Type: Crown
Profile: Oversees workplace safety education & training, provides disability benefits

Machinery

Anchor Lamina Inc.
2590 Ouellette Ave., Windsor, ON N8X 1L7
Tel: 519-966-4431; *Fax:* 519-972-6862
Toll-Free: 800-265-5007
wineng@anchorlamina.com
www.anchorlamina.com
Company Type: Private
Profile: The company is a manufacturer of special dies & tools, die sets, jigs & fixtures, molds, & fabricated plate work.

Atlas Copco Canada Inc.
Atlas Copco Compressors Canada, 30, av Montrose, Dollard-des-Ormeaux, QC H9B 3J9
Tel: 514-421-4121; *Fax:* 514-421-1950
Toll-Free: 800-513-3782
compressors.canada@ca.atlascopco.com
www.atlascopco.com
Company Type: Private
Profile: International industrial company, publicly listed under the laws of Sweden, with locations and contacts across Canada. Products and services include compressed air and gas equipment, generators, construction and mining equipment, industrial tools, assembly systems

ATS Automation Tooling Systems Inc.
PO Box 32100, 250 Royal Oak Rd., Cambridge, ON N3H 4R6
Tel: 519-653-6500; *Fax:* 519-653-6533
info@atsautomation.com
www.atsautomation.com
Ticker Symbol: ATA
Company Type: Public

Profile: Producers of turn-key automated manufacturing & test systems, precision components, sub-assemblies, & solar power cells & panels

Bühler Industries Inc.
1260 Clarence Ave., Winnipeg, MB R3T 1T2
Tel: 204-661-8711; *Fax:* 204-654-2503
Toll-Free: 888-524-1003
info@buhler.com
www.buhler.com
Ticker Symbol: BUI
Company Type: Public
Profile: The company manufactures farm machinery & equipment. Agricultural products include Buhler Farm King Grain Handling & Compact Implements, Buhler Versatile Tractors, Buhler Inland Hay Tools, & Buhler Allied Front-End Loaders.

CE Franklin Ltd.
#1900, 300 - 5th Ave. SW, Calgary, AB T2P 3C4
Tel: 403-531-5600; *Fax:* 403-234-7698
ho-calgary@cefranklin.com
www.cefranklin.com
Ticker Symbol: CFT
Company Type: Public
Profile: CE Franklin Ltd. provides products & services to the oil & gas industry in Canada. Products include production equipment, pipes, valves, fittings, & flanges.

Collicutt Energy Services Ltd.
7550 Edgar Industrial Dr., Red Deer, AB T4P 3R2
Tel: 403-358-3200; *Fax:* 403-358-3210
Toll-Free: 888-323-2217
inquiries@collicutt.com
www.collicutt.com
Ticker Symbol: COH
Company Type: Public
Profile: Manufacturers of air & gas compressors; Wholesalers of industrial machinery & equipment; Engineering services; Various oil & gas field services

Eagle Precision Technologies Inc.
31 Adams Blvd., Brantford, ON N3S 7V8
Tel: 519-720-6800;
www.eaglept.com
Company Type: Public
Profile: Manufacturers of machine tools, metal forming & cutting types

Enerflex Systems Income Fund
4700 - 47 St. SE, Calgary, AB T2B 3R1
Tel: 403-236-6800; *Fax:* 403-236-6816
ir@enerflex.com
www.enerflex.com
Ticker Symbol: EFX
Company Type: Public
Profile: Enerflex Systems Income Fund supplies products & services to the international oil & gas production industry. Products include natural gas compression, power generation, & process equipment. Services include field maintenance & electrical, instrumentation, & controls services. In its operations, Enerflex follows industry & regional environmental guidelines, legislation, & regulations, & conducts environmental audits on a regular basis.

Exco Technologies Limited
130 Spy Ct., 2nd Fl., Markham, ON L3R 5H6
Tel: 905-477-3065; *Fax:* 905-477-2449
excotech@compuserve.com
www.excocorp.com
Ticker Symbol: XTC
Company Type: Public
Profile: Manufacturers of special dies & tools, die sets, jigs & fixtures, molds, cutting tools, mach tool accessories, measuring devices, various industrial & commercial machinery & equipment, motor vehicle parts & accessories

Foremost Industries LP
1225 - 64 Ave. NE, Calgary, AB T2E 8P9
Tel: 403-295-5800; *Fax:* 403-295-5832
Toll-Free: 800-661-9190
investorrelations@foremost.ca
www.foremost.ca
Ticker Symbol: FMO.UN
Company Type: Public
Profile: Foremost Income Fund is an unincorporated, open-ended unit trust, which holds manufacturing businesses. Through these holdings, Foremost is involved in the design, manufacture, sale, & service of oil treating systems, drilling equipment, petroleum storage tanks, gas separation equipment, compression equipment, pressure vessels, & off-road vehicles. Foremost Industries Ltd. is the administrator of the Fund.

Groupe Laperrière & Verreault inc
Le Bourg du Fleuve Bldg., #420, 25, rue Des Forges, Trois-Rivières, QC G9A 6A7
Tel: 819-371-8265; *Fax:* 819-373-4439
courrier@glv.com
www.glv.com
Ticker Symbol: GLV
Company Type: Public
Profile: Manufacturers of general industrial machinery & equipment, paper industries machinery; Special trade installation/erection of building equipment

Husky Injection Molding Systems Ltd.
500 Queen St. South, Bolton, ON L7E 5S5
Tel: 905-951-5000; *Fax:* 905-951-5337
Toll-Free: 888-884-8759
info@husky.ca
www.husky.ca
Company Type: Public
Profile: Manufacturers of special dies & tools, die sets, jigs & fixtures, molds, machine tools, metal cutting types; Wholesalers of various durable goods

IBM Canada Ltd.
3600 Steeles Ave. East, Markham, ON L3R 9Z7
Tel: 905-316-5000; *Fax:* 905-316-2535
Toll-Free: 800-426-4968
canada_int@vnet.ibm.com
www.ibm.com/ca/
Company Type: Private
Profile: Manufacturers of electronic computers, & calculating & accounting machines; Repair shops & various related services; equipment rental & leasing

Ingersoll Rand Canada Inc.
1076 Lakeshore Rd. E., Mississauga, ON L5E 1E4
Tel: 905-403-1800; *Fax:* 416-213-4616
IRS&SCanada@irco.com
www.irco.com
Company Type: Private
Profile: Manufacturers of general industrial machinery & equipment, pumps & pumping equipment, various special industry machinery, automatic controls regulating environment & appliances

Komatsu America Corp.
160 boul de l'Industrie, Candiac, QC J5R 1J3
Tel: 450-659-1961; *Fax:* 450-659-3557
www.komatsuamerica.com; www.komatsu.com
Company Type: Private
Profile: Manufacturer of construction, mining and compact construction equipment, with distributors across Canada

Luxell Technologies Inc.
2145 Meadowpine Blvd., Mississauga, ON L5N 6R8
Tel: 905-363-0325; *Fax:* 905-363-0336
info@luxell.com; careers@luxell.com
www.luxell.com
Company Type: Public
Profile: The company is engaged in the research & development of flat panel display enhancing technologies. Business activities are focussed on products & services for defence & aero-space applications, such as radar warning devices, field communications systems, & navigational displays.

NCR Canada Ltd.
6865 Century Ave., Mississauga, ON L5N 2E2
Tel: 905-826-9000;
www.ncr.com
Company Type: Private
Profile: NCR has evolved from the National Cash Register Company in 1884 into a global company providing solutions for payment & imaging, point-of-sale, e-Commece, & self-service. The company manufactures & supplies ATMs & cash dispensers, self-service kiosks for a number of sectors, cheque & document imaging systems, software for retailers & other industries, & printer consumables.

Pitney Bowes Canada Ltd.
#200, 314 Harwood Ave., Ajax, ON L1S 2J1
Toll-Free: 800-672-6937
MrBowes.Canada@pb.com
www.pitneybowes.ca
Company Type: Private
Profile: Pitney Bowes Canada's activities focus upon mailing technology. Products include innovations that copy, scan, print, fax, insert, & seal. With Pitney Bowes' services, companies are able to manage the flow of information, mail, documents, & packages.

Reko International Group Inc.
5390 Brendan Lane, Oldcastle, ON N0R 1L0
Tel: 519-737-6974; *Fax:* 519-737-6975
vpf@rekointl.com
www.rekointl.com
Ticker Symbol: REK
Company Type: Public
Profile: Manufacturers of special dies & tools, die sets, molds, jigs & fixtures; Engineering services

RPM Tech Inc.
184, rte 138, Cap-Santé, QC G0A 1L0
Tel: 418-285-1811; *Fax:* 418-285-4289
Toll-Free: 800-463-3882
info@grouperpmtech.com
www.grouperpmtech.com
Ticker Symbol: RP
Company Type: Public
Profile: Manufacturers of construction machinery & equipment, industrial trucks, tractors, trailers & stackers, mining machinery & equipment; Repair shops & various related services; Wholesalers of farm & garden machinery & equipment

Skyjack Inc.
55 Campbell Rd., Guelph, ON N1H 1B9
Tel: 519-837-0888; *Fax:* 519-837-8104
Toll-Free: 800-265-2738
skyjack@skyjack.com; service@skyjack.com
www.skyjackinc.com
Company Type: Public
Profile: Skyjack Inc. designs, manufactures, sells, & services self propelled aerial work platforms.

Strongco Income Fund
1640 Enterprise Rd., Mississauga, ON L4W 4L4
Tel: 905-565-1899; *Fax:* 905-565-1907
info@strongco.com
www.strongco.com
Ticker Symbol: SQP.UN
Company Type: Public
Profile: Strongco Income Fund is involved in multi-line equipment distribution in Canada. Mobile industrial equipment is sold, rented, & serviced. The equipment is used in the following sectors: mining, forestry, construction, road building, & utilities. Business divisions include Strongco Equipment/Cranes & Strongco Engineered Systems. Among the equipment manufacturers represented by Strongco are Cedarapids, Case, Volvo, & Manitowoc.

Tesco Corporation
6204 - 6A St. SE, Calgary, AB T2H 2B7
Tel: 403-692-5700; *Fax:* 403-692-5710
investor@tescocorp.com
www.tescocorp.com
Ticker Symbol: TESO
Company Type: Public
Profile: Tesco Corporation specializes in the design, manufacture, & service of technology. The company's technology based solutions are used in the upstream energy industry.

Toromont Industries Ltd.
Bldg. B, PO Box 5511, 3131 Hwy. 7 West, Concord, ON L4K 1B7
Tel: 416-667-5511; *Fax:* 416-667-5555
pjewer@toromont.com
www.toromont.com
Ticker Symbol: TIH
Company Type: Public
Profile: The company is engaged in the design, engineering, & sale of specialized equipment & other heavy equipment. Its business segments are the Equipment Group & the Compression Group. Toromont Industries has implemented environmental practices, such as technology to recycle energy, reduce greenhouse gas emissions, & cleanse oil of contaminants.

Weir Canada Inc.
2360 Millrace Ct., Mississauga, ON L4N 1W2
Tel: 905-812-7100; *Fax:* 905-812-1749
info@weirmaricas.com
www.weirservices.com
Company Type: Private
Profile: Manufacturers of pumps & pumping equipment, valves & pipe fittings, speed changers, industrial high-speed drives & gears, industrial trucks, tractors, trailers & stackers; Wholesalers of construction & mining machinery & equipment; Wholesalers of industrial machinery & equipment

Wenzel Downhole Tools Ltd.
#1000, 717 - 7th Ave. SW, Calgary, AB T2P 0Z3
Tel: 403-262-3050; *Fax:* 403-265-8154
handre@wenzel-downhole.com
www.downhole.com
Ticker Symbol: WZL
Company Type: Public
Profile: Manufacturers of oil & gas field machinery & equipment; Wholesalers of construction & mining machinery & equipment; Equipment rental & leasing

Westport Innovations Inc.
#101, 1750 West 75th Ave., Vancouver, BC V6P 6G2
Tel: 604-718-2000; *Fax:* 604-718-2001
info@westport.com
www.westport.com
Ticker Symbol: WPT
Company Type: Public
Profile: Develops technologies to allow commercial engine industry to shift from oil-based to gaseous fuels

Xerox Canada Inc.
5650 Yonge St., Toronto, ON M2M 4G7
Tel: 416-229-3769; *Fax:* 416-229-6826
Toll-Free: 800-275-9376
www.xerox.ca
Company Type: Public
Profile: To improve work processes, Xerox Canada provides document technologies, products, & services. The company has created waste-free products, & built in waste-free facilities, as part of its continuing remanufacturing initiatives.

Manufacturing, Miscellaneous

AFG Industries Ltd.
PO Box 628, 18544 - 9th Concession, Mount Albert, ON L0G 1M0
Tel: 905-738-9400; *Fax:* 905-738-1177
Toll-Free: 800-661-7214
www.afg.com
Company Type: Private
Profile: Manufacturers of flat glass, glass products (made of purchased glass); Wholesalers of construction materials

AirBoss of America Corp.
16441 Yonge St., Newmarket, ON L3X 2G8
Tel: 905-751-1188; *Fax:* 905-751-1101
info@airbossofamerica.com
www.airbossofamerica.com
Ticker Symbol: BOS
Company Type: Public
Profile: The company is a developer, manufacturer, & seller of rubber compounds & specialty rubber moulded products. Products are used in the industrial, transportation, & defense industries.

Amcor PET Packaging—North America
910 Central Pkwy. West, Mississauga, ON L5C 2V5
Tel: 905-275-1592; *Fax:* 905-275-1061
brigitte.sigwarth@amcor.com
www.amcor.com
Company Type: Private
Profile: Manufacturers of plastics packaging, rigid plastics & plastube packaging

Amisco Industries Ltd.
33 - 5e rue, L'Islet, QC G0R 2C0
Tel: 800-361-6360; *Fax:* 800-232-6614
info@amisco.com
www.amisco.com
Ticker Symbol: IAC
Company Type: Public
Profile: Manufacturers of metal & wood household furniture

Armstrong World Industries Canada Ltd
6911, boul Decarie, Montréal, QC H3W 3E5
Tel: 514-733-9981;
www.armstrong.com
Company Type: Private
Profile: Manufacturers of linoleum, asphalted-felt-base, & other hard floorings, & mineral wool; Wholesalers of construction materials & home furnishings; Miscellaneous nonmetallic minerals mining & quarrying

ART Advanced Research Technologies Inc.
2300, boul Alfred-Nobel, Montréal, QC H4S 2A4
Tel: 514-832-0777; *Fax:* 514-832-0778
info@art.ca
www.art.ca
Ticker Symbol: ARA
Company Type: Public
Profile: Canadian medical device company specializing in optical molecular imaging products for the healthcare & pharmaceutical industries.

Bestar Inc.
4220, rue Villeneuve, Lac-Mégantic, QC G6B 2C3
Fax: 819-583-5370
Toll-Free: 888-823-7827
service@bestar.ca
www.bestar.ca
Ticker Symbol: BES
Company Type: Public
Profile: Manufacturers of wood household furniture, wood tv, radio, phonograph & sewing machine cabinets; Wholesalers of furniture

Brampton Brick Limited
225 Wanless Dr., Brampton, ON L7A 1E9
Tel: 905-840-1011; *Fax:* 905-840-1535
investor.relations@bramptonbrick.com
www.bramptonbrick.com
Ticker Symbol: BBL
Company Type: Public
Profile: Brampton Brick Limited manufactures the following products: concrete interlocking paving stone, clay brick, retaining walls, & related items. In Ontario & Nova Scotia, the company operates facilities for the destruction of biomedical & pharmaceutical waste. Brampton Brick Limited is an ISO 9001 certified company.

BW Technologies Ltd.
2840 - 2 Ave. SE, Calgary, AB T2A 7X9
Tel: 403-248-9226; *Fax:* 403-273-3708
Toll-Free: 800-663-4164
info@gasmonitors.com
www.gasmonitors.com
Company Type: Public
Profile: Manufacturers of various measuring & controlling devices; Wholesalers of industrial machinery & equipment

Camco Inc.
PO Box 5345, #300, 5420 North Service Rd., Burlington, ON L7R 5B6
Tel: 905-315-2300; *Fax:* 905-315-2451
Toll-Free: 888-566-6667
InvestorRelations@mabe.ca
www.geappliances.ca
Company Type: Public
Profile: Manufacturers of household cooking equipment, household refrigerators & home & farm freezers, household laundry equipment, various household appliances; Wholesalers of electrical appliances, television & radio sets

CGC Inc.
350 Burnhamthorpe Rd. West, 5th Fl., Mississauga, ON L5B 3J1
Tel: 905-803-5600; *Fax:* 905-803-5688
Toll-Free: 800-565-6607
ckane@cgcinc.com
www.cgcinc.com
Company Type: Private
Profile: Manufacturers and distributors of gypsum wallboard products, interior finishing materials & suspended acoustical ceilings

Chevron Canada Limited
#1200, 1050 West Pender St., Vancouver, BC V6E 3T4
Tel: 604-668-5300; *Toll-Free:* 800-663-1650
www.chevron.ca
Ticker Symbol: CVX
Company Type: Private
Profile: The upstream operation, based in Calgary, is involved in exploration, production & marketing of crude oil, natural gas & natural gas liquids; the downstream operation, based in B.C., is a retail & commercial fuelling & lubricants distribution company with refining facility in Burnaby & an extensive retail network throughout Western Canada.

CVTech Group Inc.
1975, rue Jean-Bérimens Michaud, Drummondville, QC J2C 0H2
Tel: 819-479-7771; *Fax:* 819-479-8887
a.laramee@cvtech.ca
www.groupecvtech.com
Ticker Symbol: CVT
Company Type: Public
Profile: Through its subsidiaries, CVTech Group designs, manufactures, & sells continuously variable power transmission systems. The company's subsidiary, Thiro Ltd., is a general contracting firm, which specializes in the maintenance of transmission & distribution lines, electrical power houses, & substations.

Dorel Industries Inc.
#300, 1255, av Greene, Montréal, QC H3Z 2A4
Tel: 514-934-3034; *Fax:* 514-934-9379
info@dorel.com; ir@dorel.com
www.dorel.com
Ticker Symbol: DII
Company Type: Public
Profile: Dorel Industries Inc. designs, manufactures, & markets juvenile products, bicycles, & home furnishings. The company has facilities in seventeen countries, & sells its products throughout the world.

Dynetek Industries Ltd.
4410 - 46 Ave. SE, Calgary, AB T2B 3N7
Tel: 403-720-0262; *Fax:* 403-720-0263
Toll-Free: 888-396-3835
contactus@dynetek.com
www.dynetek.com
Ticker Symbol: DNK
Company Type: Public
Profile: Manufacturer and supplier of lightweight storage cyliners for compressed gases, and complete systems.

Empire Industries Ltd.
717 Jarvis Ave., Winnipeg, MB R2W 3B4
Tel: 204-589-9300; *Fax:* 204-582-8057
www.empind.com
Ticker Symbol: EIL
Company Type: Public
Profile: Empire Industries Ltd. is a designer & manufacturer of various industrial products & amusement park rides. The company is also engaged in erecting structural steel & offering structural & construction engineering services. Empire Industries Ltd. has a Health, Safety, & Environmental Policy, & adheres to regulations. Some of Empire Industries Ltd.'s subsidiaries include the following: Dynamic Structures, Empire Construction Services, Empire Iron Works, George Third & Son, Hopkins Steel Works, Lemax Machine & Welding, Parr Metal Fabricators, Sorge's Welding Ltd., Somerset Engineering, Tornado Technologies Inc., & Ward Industrial Equipment.

Essroc Canada Inc.
PO Box 620, Highway 49 South, Picton, ON K0K 2T0
Tel: 613-476-3233; *Fax:* 613-476-8130
info@essroc.com
www.essroc.com
Company Type: Private
Profile: Manufacturers of cement and other building materials

General Donlee Income Fund
9 Fenmar Dr., Toronto, ON M9L 1L5
Tel: 416-743-4417; *Fax:* 416-746-8998
info@generaldonlee.com
www.generaldonlee.com
Ticker Symbol: GDI.UN
Company Type: Public
Profile: General Donlee Income Fund is a trust that holds the securities of General Donlee Limited. General Donlee Limited manufactures precision-machined products. Products are used by the military, commercial, & general aviation industries, as well as the industrial products & power generation industries.

Global Alumina Corp.
245 Park Ave., 38th Fl., New York, NY
Tel: 212-351-0000; *Fax:* 212-351-0001
info@globalalumina.com
www.globalalumina.com
Ticker Symbol: GLA.U
Company Type: Public
Profile: Incorporated in New Brunswick in 2004, Global Alumina is involved in alumina production & sales. It is developing an alumina refinery in the bauxite-rich region of in the Republic of Guinea.

GSW Inc.
599 Hill St. West, Fergus, ON N1M 2X1
Tel: 519-843-1610; *Fax:* 519-787-5500
gswinfo@gsw-wh.com
www.gsw-wh.com
Company Type: Public
Profile: Offices of holding companies; Manufacturers of various household appliances, air-conditioning, warm air heating, refrigeration equipment, pumps & pumping equipment, fabricated plate work, various plastics products

Hanwei Energy Services Corp.
#902, 595 Howe St., Vancouver, BC V6C 2T5
Tel: 604-685-2239; *Fax:* 604-677-5579
info@hanweienergy.com
www.hanweienergy.com
Ticker Symbol: HE
Company Type: Public
Profile: Hanwei Energy Services develops, manufactures, & sells high pressure fiberglass reinforced plastic products.

Products are used mainly in the global energy sector. The company owns interest in Daqing Harvest Longwall High Pressure Pipe Co. Ltd. in China.

Heroux-Devtek Inc.
Tour Est, #658, 1111, rue Saint-Charles ouest, Longueuil, QC J4K 5G4
Tel: 450-679-3330; *Fax:* 450-679-3666
ir@herouxdevtek.com
www.herouxdevtek.com
Ticker Symbol: HRX
Company Type: Public
Profile: Heroux-Devtek Inc. develops, designs, manufactures, repairs, & overhauls systems & components. The company has three divisions: The Landing Gear Division; The Aerostructure Division; & The Gas Turbine Components Division. Products are used in the aerospace market in both the commercial & military sectors, & in the industrial market for power generation & other machinery applications.

Holcim (Canada) Inc.
2300 Steeles Ave. West, 4th Fl., Concord, ON L4K 5X6
Tel: 905-532-3000; *Fax:* 905-761-7200
communications-ca@holcim.com
www.holcim.ca
Company Type: Private
Profile: Holcim (Canada) Inc. is a producer & supplier of aggregates, concrete, & construction materials. It provides products & services for the construction industry throughout Canada. The building materials & construction company's divisions are Dufferin in Ontario & Demix in Québec. From Holcim's plant in Mississauga, Ontario, cement is shipped throughout Ontario, & to western Canada & the United States. From the Holcim plant in Joliette, Québec, cement is sent to locations in Québec, Atlantic Canada, & the United States.

Imax Corporation
Sheridan Science & Technology Park, 2525 Speakman Dr., Mississauga, ON L5K 1B1
Tel: 905-403-6500; *Fax:* 905-403-6474
info@imax.com
www.imax.com
Ticker Symbol: IMX
Company Type: Public
Profile: Manufacturers of photographic equipment & supplies; Motion picture & video tape production & distribution; Motion picture theatres

INSCAPE Corporation
67 Toll Rd., Holland Landing, ON L9N 1H2
Tel: 905-836-7676; *Fax:* 905-836-6000
info@inscapesolutions.com
www.inscapesolutions.com
Ticker Symbol: INQ
Company Type: Public
Profile: Manufacturers of wood & non-wood office furniture, wood & non-wood office & store fixtures & partitions; Wholesalers of furniture & office equipment

IPL Inc.
140, rue Commerciale, Saint-Damien, QC G0R 2Y0
Tel: 418-789-2880; *Fax:* 418-789-2185
Toll-Free: 600-463-7083
info-ipl@ipl-plastics.com
www.ipl-plastics.com
Ticker Symbol: IPI
Company Type: Public
Profile: IPL Inc. specializes in manufacturing injection & extrusion moulded plastic products. Products, such as material & handling crates & rigid packaging containers & pails, are used by the following industries: recycling, automotive, transportation, construction, petrochemical, chemical, food, fishing, & forestry. The company is an ISO 14001 certified organization

JDS Uniphase Canada Ltd.
#210, 362 Terry Fox Dr., Kanata, ON K2K 2P5
Tel: 613-599-4069; *Fax:* 613-271-2627
www.jdsu.com
Ticker Symbol: JDU
Company Type: Public
Profile: Designs & manufactures products for fiberoptic communications

Johnson Controls Ltd.
100 Townline Rd., Tillsonburg, ON N4G 2R7
Tel: 519-842-5971; *Fax:* 519-842-3443
www.jci.com
Company Type: Private
Profile: Special trade contracting in plumbing, heating & air-conditioning; Manufacturers of automatic controls regulating environments & appliances

Lear Canada Ltd.
PO Box 9758, 530 Manitou Dr., Kitchener, ON N2G 4C2
Tel: 519-895-1600; *Fax:* 519-895-3248
www.lear.com
Company Type: Private
Profile: Designs, tests & produces automotive interiors: seat systems, electronic products and electrical distribution systems

MAAX
600, rte Cameron, Sainte-Marie-de-Beauce, QC G6E 1B2
Fax: 418-387-8055
Toll-Free: 418-386-3487
www.maax.com
Company Type: Private
Profile: MAAX is a designer of bathroom products, such as bathtubs, showers, & medicine cabinets.

Magna International Inc.
337 Magna Dr., Aurora, ON L4G 7K1
Tel: 905-726-2462; *Fax:* 905-726-7164
www.magna.com
Ticker Symbol: MG.A
Company Type: Public
Profile: The automotive supplier designs, develops, & manufactures automotive systems, assemblies, modules, & components. Magna also engineers & assembles complete vehicles to sell to original equipment manufacturers of cars & trucks.

McCoy Corporation
#301, 9618 - 42 Ave., Edmonton, AB T6E 5Y4
Tel: 780-453-8451; *Fax:* 780-453-8756
www.mccoycorporation.ca
Ticker Symbol: MCB
Company Type: Public
Profile: McCoy Corporation serves the transportation industry & the oil & gas sector. The following are some of the products & services provided by McCoy Corporation: trailer mounted hydrovac & vacuum tanks; heavy duty trailer manufacturing; parts & service for heavy-duty trucks & trailers; hydraulic power tongs for rigs; & coatings for the prevention of corrosion.

Nestlé Purina Petcare Company
2500 Royal Windsor Dr., Mississauga, ON L5J 1K8
Tel: 905-822-1611; *Fax:* 905-855-5700
Toll-Free: 800-268-5345
www.purina.ca
Company Type: Private
Profile: The pet care company provides the following brands in North America: Puppy Chow, Dog Chow, Alpo, Busy Bones, T-Bonz, Beggin Strips, Beneful, Kitten Chow, Cat Chow, Luvs, Friskies, Fancy Feast, Maxx Multi Cat, Kitty Litter, Purina Veterinary Diets, Pro Plan, & Purina One.

NovAtel Inc.
1120 - 68 Ave. NE, Calgary, AB T2E 8S5
Tel: 403-295-4500; *Fax:* 403-295-4501
Toll-Free: 800-668-2835
sales@novatel.ca; support@novatel.com
www.novatel.com
Company Type: Private
Profile: NovAtel Inc. is an ISO 9001 certified company which provides Global Navigation Satellite System components & subsystems. Products include irmware, receivers, antennas, & enclosures, which are integrated into high precision positioning applications. Applications include Geographical Information System (GIS) mapping, surveying, port automation, & precision agriculture machine guidance.

Opta Minerals Inc.
PO Box 260, 407 Parkside Dr., Waterdown, ON L0R 2H0
Tel: 905-689-7361; *Fax:* 905-689-0604
Toll-Free: 888-689-6661
info@optaminerals.com
www.optaminerals.com
Ticker Symbol: OPM
Company Type: Public
Profile: Opta Minerals Inc. is engaged in the recycling, manufacturing, production, & distribution of industrial minerals, specialty sands, & related products. The company's products are used mainly in the following industries: steel, foundry, roof shingle granules, loose abrasive cleaning, & municipal water filtration. Opta Minerals production facilities are located in Ontario, Quebec, Michigan, New York, Louisiana, Virginia, Maryland, South Carolina, Indiana, Ohio, & Texas, as well as France & Slovakia.

Owens-Corning Canada LP
3450 McNicoll Ave., Toronto, ON M1V 1Z5
Tel: 416-292-4000; *Fax:* 416-412-6719
Toll-Free: 800-438-7465
non-managementdirectors@owenscorning.com
www.owenscorning.ca
Ticker Symbol: OC (NYSE: OC)
Company Type: Private
Profile: The home building products company is an innovator of glass fiber materials & glass fiber insulation. Glass fiber materials are used in applications such as automobiles, aircraft, boats, computers, telecommunications cables, & appliances.

Palliser Furniture Ltd
70 Lexington Park, Winnipeg, MB R2G 4H2
Tel: 204-988-5600; *Fax:* 204-663-1776
www.palliser.com
Company Type: Private
Profile: Manufacturers of wood household furniture

Polyair Inter Pack Inc.
330 Humberline Dr., Toronto, ON M9W 1R5
Tel: 416-679-6600; *Fax:* 416-740-7356
Toll-Free: 888-765-9247
marketing@polyair.com
www.polyair.com
Ticker Symbol: PPK
Company Type: Public
Profile: Manufacturers of plastic foam products, various plastics products, packaging paper & coated & laminated plastics film; Wholesalers of plastics materials & basic forms & shapes

PreMD Inc.
#242, 4211 Yonge St., Toronto, ON M2P 2A9
Tel: 416-222-3449; *Fax:* 416-222-4533
info@premdinc.com
www.premdinc.com
Company Type: Public
Profile: Acquires & develops technologies for non-invasive predictive medical tests that detect early stage cardiovascular disease and cancer

Premier Tech Ltd.
International Corporate Office, 1, av Premier, Rivière-du-Loup, QC G5R 6C1
Tel: 418-867-8883; *Fax:* 418-862-6642
info@premiertech.com
www.premiertech.com
Ticker Symbol: PTL
Company Type: Private
Profile: Premier Tech's develops, manufactures, & markets innovative solutions in the following areas: horticulture & agriculture, environmental technologies, & industrial equipment.

Royal Group, Inc.
1 Royal Gate Blvd., Woodbridge, ON L4L 8Z7
Tel: 905-264-0701; *Fax:* 905-264-0702
www.royalbuildingproducts.com
Company Type: Private
Profile: Royal Group Inc. produces & markets vinyl-based construction, building, & home improvement products. The company consists of the following divisions: Royal Building Products, Royal Pipe Systems, Royal Mouldings, Royal Window & Door Profiles, & Royal Outdoor Products. Royal Group has locations in both Canada & the Unitd States. Customers include construction, renovation, & remodeling industries.

SACO Smartvision Inc
7809 Trans Canada Hwy, Montréal, QC H4S 1L3
Tel: 514-745-0310; *Fax:* 514-745-0315
info@smartvision.com
www.smartvision.com
Ticker Symbol: SSV
Company Type: Public
Profile: Manufacturers of photographic equipment & supplies

Shermag Inc.
2171, rue King ouest, Sherbrooke, QC J1J 2G1
Tel: 819-566-1515; *Fax:* 819-566-4104
info@shermag.com
www.shermag.com
Ticker Symbol: SMG
Company Type: Public
Profile: Manufacturers of wood household furniture, sawmills & general planing mills

Siemens Canada Limited
2185 Derry Rd. West, Mississauga, ON L5N 7A6
Tel: 905-819-8000; *Fax:* 905-819-5777
Toll-Free: 888-303-3353
corporate.communications@siemens.com
www.siemens.ca
Company Type: Private

Profile: Provides innovative products and solutions in automation & control, power, transportation, medical, information & communications, & lighting

Sigma Industries Inc.
Tour Belle Cour, Place de la Cité, #380, 2590, boul Laurier, 3e étage, Québec, QC G1V 4M6
Tel: 418-780-3903; *Fax:* 418-780-3909
www.sigmaventures.ca
Ticker Symbol: SIC
Company Type: Public
Profile: Sigma Industries Inc. manufactures plastic composites & metal products. Its markets include machinery, heavy duty truck, coach, bus & transit, train & subway, forestry, agriculture, & alternative energy.

Tarkett Inc.
1001, rue Yamaska est, Farnham, QC J2N 1J7
Tel: 450-293-3173; *Fax:* 450-293-6644
Toll-Free: 800-465-4030
www.tarkett-floors.com
Company Type: Private
Profile: Manufacturers of linoleum, felt-base & other vinyl floorings, hardwood dimension & flooring mills; Wholesalers of home furnishings

Teknion Corporation
1150 Flint Rd., Toronto, ON M3J 2J5
Tel: 416-661-3370; *Fax:* 416-661-7970
info.can@teknion.com
www.teknion.com
Ticker Symbol: TKN
Company Type: Public
Profile: Manufacturers of wood & non-wood office furniture, public building & related furniture, wood & non-wood office & store fixtures, partitions, shelving etc.; Wholesalers of furniture

Trojan Technologies Inc.
3020 Gore Rd., London, ON N5V 4T7
Tel: 519-457-3400; *Fax:* 519-457-3030
Toll-Free: 888-220-6118
www.trojanuv.com
Company Type: Private
Profile: Trojan Technologies develops technology-based, environmentally responsible solutions to the water related problems of municipalities, industries, & residential consumers. For example, Trojan manufactures ultraviolet ray equipment for residential water disinfection applications.

VSM MedTech Ltd.
9 Burbidge St., Coquitlam, BC V6K 7B2
Tel: 604-472-2300; *Fax:* 604-472-2301
Toll-Free: 877-876-8484
corp@vsmmedtech.com
www.vsmmedtech.com
Ticker Symbol: VSM
Company Type: Public
Profile: Produces diagnostic medical devices for the evaluation & treatment of neurological disorders & cardiovascular disease

Winpak Ltd.
100 Saulteaux Cres., Winnipeg, MB R3J 3T3
Tel: 204-889-1015; *Fax:* 204-888-7806
info@winpak.com
www.winpak.com
Ticker Symbol: WPK
Company Type: Public
Profile: Manufacturing & distributing packaging materials & related packaging machines are the chief activities of Winpak Ltd. Products are used to protect perishable foods & beverages, as well as in health care applications. The company's facilities are located in Canada & the United States. Its services are offered in North America, Latin America, the Pacific Rim countries, & Europe.

Mining

Agnico-Eagle Mines Limited
#400, 145 King St. East, Toronto, ON M5C 2Y7
Tel: 416-947-1212; *Fax:* 416-367-4681
info@agnico-eagle.com
www.agnico-eagle.com
Ticker Symbol: AEM
Company Type: Public
Profile: Agnico-Eagle Mines Limited is an international gold production company, which carries out exploration & development activities. Operations are conducted in Canada, the United States, Mexico, & Finland.

Alamos Gold Inc.
#2010, 120 Adelaide St. West, Toronto, ON M5H 1T1
Tel: 416-368-9932; *Fax:* 416-368-2934
Toll-Free: 866-788-8801
info@alamosgold.com
www.alamosgold.com
Ticker Symbol: AGI
Company Type: Public
Profile: The mining company owns the Salamandra group of concessions. The group includes the Mulatos gold deposit in Sonora, Mexico.

Altius Minerals Corporation
PO Box 385, #300, 53 Bond St., St. John's, NL A1C 5J9
Tel: 709-576-3440; *Fax:* 709-576-3441
Toll-Free: 877-576-2209
info@altiusminerals.com
www.altiusminerals.com
Company Type: Public
Profile: Altius Minerals Corporation is a natural resource project generation & royalty business. The company has royalty interest or equity stakes in several natural resource projects.

Amerigo Resources Ltd.
Three Bentall Centre, PO Box 49298, #3083, 595 Burrard St., Vancouver, BC V7X 1L3
Tel: 604-681-2802; *Fax:* 604-682-2802
questions@amerigoresources.com
www.amerigoresources.com
Ticker Symbol: ARG
Company Type: Public
Profile: Amerigo Resources Ltd. specializes in the production of copper & molybdenum concentrates. The company is active in Chile. Amerigo's wholly-owned subsidiary is Minera Valle Central.

Andean American Mining Corp.
#1340, 1090 West Georgia St., Vancouver, BC V6E 3V7
Tel: 604-681-6186; *Fax:* 604-681-3652
IR@andeanamerican.com
www.andeanamerican.com
Ticker Symbol: AAG
Company Type: Public
Profile: Metal mining in gold, silver & copper ores

Anvil Mining Limited
#2001, 1, Place Ville Marie. 20e étage, Montréal, QC H3B 2C4
Tel: 514-448-6664; *Fax:* 514-448-6665
robertl@anvilmining.com
www.anvilmining.com
Ticker Symbol: AVM
Company Type: Public
Profile: The copper & silver producer focuses upon the exploration, acquisition, development, & mining of mineral properties.

Archon Minerals Ltd
#2801, 323 Jervis St., Vancouver, BC V6C 3P8
Tel: 604-682-3303; *Fax:* 604-682-2919
sblusson@shaw.ca
Ticker Symbol: ACS
Company Type: Public
Profile: Mining & quarrying of miscellaneous nonmetallic minerals

Arehada Mining Limited
#1000, 36 Toronto St., Toronto, ON M5C 2C5
Tel: 416-350-5133; *Fax:* 416-350-3510
info@arehada.com
www.arehadamining.com
Ticker Symbol: AHD
Company Type: Public
Profile: Arehada Mining Limited explores, develops, extracts, & refines base metals. Zinc & lead concentrates are produced & sold to smelters. Operations are carried out in Dongwuzhumuqinqi, Inner Mongolia, China.

Arizona Star Resource Corp.
Bldg. 152, #2700, 401 Bay St., Toronto, ON M5H 2Y4
Tel: 416-359-7800; *Fax:* 416-359-7801
pparisotto@coniston.ca
www.arizonastar.com
Ticker Symbol: AZS
Company Type: Public
Profile: Metal mining gold, copper & miscellaneous metal ores

Ashton Mining of Canada Inc.
#116, 980 West 1st St., North Vancouver, BC V7P 3N4
Tel: 604-983-7750; *Fax:* 604-987-7107
Ticker Symbol: ACA
Company Type: Public
Profile: Mining & quarrying of miscellaneous nonmetallic minerals

Atacama Minerals Corp.
#2101, 885 West Georgia St., Vancouver, BC V6C 3E8
Tel: 604-689-7842; *Fax:* 604-689-4250
atacama@namdo.com
www.atacama.com
Ticker Symbol: AAM
Company Type: Public
Profile: Mining & quarrying of potash, soda & borate minerals

Aurizon Mines Ltd.
#3120, 666 Burrard St., Vancouver, BC V6C 2X8
Tel: 604-687-6600; *Fax:* 604-687-3932
info@aurizon.com
www.aurizon.com
Ticker Symbol: ARZ
Company Type: Public
Profile: Aurizon Mines Ltd. specializes in gold exploration & production. Activity takes places in the Abitibi region of northwestern Quebec.

Azure Resources Corporation
#502, 815 Hornby St., Vancouver, BC V6Z 2E6
Tel: 604-684-2401; *Fax:* 604-684-2407
azu@azure-res.com
www.azure-res.com
Ticker Symbol: TMI
Company Type: Public
Profile: Azure Resources Corporation is engaged in the exploration of copper & gold & the production of diamonds. A copper & gold project is located in Gilgit, Pakistan, & a diamond exploration project is situated in Kokong, Botswana.

Banro Corporation
First Canadian Place, PO Box 419, #7070, 100 King St. West, Toronto, ON M5X 1E3
Tel: 416-366-2221; *Fax:* 416-366-7722
info@banro.com
www.banro.com
Ticker Symbol: BAA
Company Type: Public
Profile: Metal mining in gold ores

Barrick Gold Corporation
TD Canada Trust Tower, Brookfield Place, PO Box 212, #3700, 161 Bay St., Toronto, ON M5J 2S1
Tel: 416-861-9911; *Fax:* 416-861-2492
Toll-Free: 800-720-7415
investor@barrick.com
www.barrick.com
Ticker Symbol: ABX
Company Type: Public
Profile: The gold mining company explores, develops, & operates mines in five continents.

Breakwater Resources Ltd.
#950, 95 Wellington St. West, Toronto, ON M5J 2N7
Tel: 416-363-4798; *Fax:* 416-363-1315
investorinfo@breakwater.ca
www.breakwater.ca
Ticker Symbol: BWR
Company Type: Public
Profile: Breakwater Resources' area of expertise is the acquisition, exploration, development, & mining of base metal & precious metal deposits. Operations are carried out at the Myra Falls mine in British Columbia, the El Mochito mine in Honduras, & the El Toqui mine in Chile.

Caledonia Mining Corporation
#1201, 67 Yonge St., Toronto, ON M5E 1JB
Tel: 416-369-9835; *Fax:* 416-369-0449
info@caledoniamining.com
www.caledoniamining.com
Ticker Symbol: CAL
Company Type: Public
Profile: Metal mining in copper, gold, silver & ferroalloy ores; Mining & quarrying in miscellaneous nonmetallic minerals

Cameco Corporation
2121 - 11 St. West, Saskatoon, SK S7M 1J3
Tel: 306-956-6200; *Fax:* 306-956-6201
www.cameco.com
Ticker Symbol: CCO
Company Type: Public
Profile: The uranium producer conducts its exploration activities in North America, Australia, & Asia. Cameco Corp. holds a majority interest in Centerra Gold Inc. & a 31.6% interest in Bruce Power Limited Partnership.

Campbell Resources Inc.
#1101, 80 Berlioz Street, Montréal, QC H3E 1N9
Tel: 514-766-4517; *Fax:* 514-765-9810
afortier@campbellresources.com
www.campbellresources.com
Ticker Symbol: CCH
Company Type: Public
Profile: Metal mining in gold & copper ores

Canadian Royalties Inc.
2772 chemin Sullivan, Val-d'Or, QC J0Y 2N0
Tel: 819-824-1030; *Fax:* 819-824-1003
Toll-Free: 866-219-4678
info@canadianroyalties.com
www.canadianroyalties.com
Ticker Symbol: CZZ
Company Type: Public
Profile: Nickel exploration in Canada

Canadian Salt Company Limited
#700, 755, boul Saint-Jean, Montréal, QC H9R 5M9
Tel: 514-630-0900; *Fax:* 514-694-2451
tferrara@windsorsalt.com
www.windsorsalt.com
Company Type: Private
Profile: Manufacturing and sale of salt & salt products

Canarc Resource Corp.
#301, 700 West Pender St., Vancouver, BC V6C 1G8
Tel: 604-685-9700; *Fax:* 604-685-9744
Toll-Free: 877-684-9700
invest@canarc.net
www.canarc.net
Ticker Symbol: CCM
Company Type: Public
Profile: Metal mining in gold & silver ores

Capstone Mining Corp.
#1980, 1055 West Hastings St., Vancouver, BC V6E 2E9
Tel: 604-684-8894; *Fax:* 604-688-2180
Toll-Free: 866-684-8894
info@capstonemining.com
www.capstonemining.com
Ticker Symbol: CS
Company Type: Public
Profile: Capstone Mining Corp. operates silver, zinc, lead, & copper mines. Activities are focused in Zacatecas State, Mexico.

Claude Resources Inc.
#200, 224 - 4th Ave. South, Saskatoon, SK S7K 5M5
Tel: 306-668-7505; *Fax:* 306-668-7500
clauderesources@clauderesources.com
www.clauderesources.com
Ticker Symbol: CRJ
Company Type: Public
Profile: Metal mining in gold ores; Crude petroleum, natural gas & natural gas liquids extraction

Cogema Resources Inc.
PO Box 9204, 817 - 45 St. West, Saskatoon, SK S7K 3X5
Tel: 306-343-4500; *Fax:* 306-653-3883
Toll-Free: 888-992-7382
publicrelations@cogema.ca
www.cogema.ca
Company Type: Private
Profile: Metal mining in uranium, radium, vanadium & gold ores

Continental Minerals Corporation
#1020, 800 West Pender St., Vancouver, BC V6C 2V6
Tel: 604-684-6365; *Fax:* 604-684-8092
info@hdgold.com
www.hdgold.com/kmk/home.asp
Ticker Symbol: KMK
Company Type: Public
Profile: Exploration & mining company; Engaged in the advancement of the Xietongmen Project in Tibet, China

Crew Gold
#615, 800 West Pender St., Vancouver, BC V6C 2V6
Tel: 604-681-8003; *Fax:* 604-662-3180
Toll-Free: 800-444-9284
www.crewgroup.com
Ticker Symbol: CRU
Company Type: Public
Profile: Offices of holding companies; Mining & quarrying of gold

Crystallex International Corporation
#1210, 18 King St. East, Toronto, ON M5C 1C4
Tel: 416-203-2448; *Fax:* 416-203-0099
Toll-Free: 800-738-1577
info@crystallex.com
www.crystallex.com
Ticker Symbol: KRY
Company Type: Public
Profile: Metal mining in gold ores

Cumberland Resources Ltd.
One Bentall Centre, PO Box 72, #950, 505 Burrard St., Vancouver, BC V7X 1M4
Tel: 604-608-2557; *Fax:* 604-608-2559
Company Type: Public
Profile: Metal mining in gold ores

Denison Mines Corp.
Atrium on Bay, #402, 595 Bay St., Toronto, ON M5G 2C2
Tel: 416-979-1991; *Fax:* 416-979-5893
blazare@denisonmines.com
www.denisonmines.com
Ticker Symbol: DML
Company Type: Public
Profile: Denison Mines Corp. is a uranium exploration & production company. Its active uranium mines are located in Canada & the United States. Denison Environmental Services (DES) was established to provide mine decommissioning, long-term care, & maintenance services to closed mining facilities.

Denison Mines Corporation
Atrium On Bay, #402, 595 Bay St., Toronto, ON M5G 2C2
Tel: 416-979-1991; *Fax:* 416-979-5893
www.denisonmines.com
Ticker Symbol: DML
Company Type: Public
Profile: Metal mining in uranium, radium & vanadium ores

Dundee Precious Metals Inc.
South Tower, Royal Bank Plaza, #3060, 200 Bay St., Toronto, ON M5J 2J1
Tel: 416-365-5191; *Fax:* 416-365-9080
info@dundeeprecious.com
www.dundeeprecious.com
Ticker Symbol: DPM
Company Type: Public
Profile: Dundee Precious Metals Inc. acquires, explores, develops, & mines precious metals properties. The company is active in Nunavut, Armenia, Bulgaria, & Serbia.

East Asia Minerals Corporation
#1980, 1055 West Hastings St., Vancouver, BC V6E 2E9
Tel: 604-684-8894; *Fax:* 604-688-2180
patchettm@eaminerals.com
www.eaminerals.com
Ticker Symbol: EAS
Company Type: Public
Profile: The mineral acquisition & exploration company has gold & copper assets in Indonesia & uranium properties in Mongolia.

Eldorado Gold Corporation
Bentall 5, #1188, 550 Burrard St., Vancouver, BC V6C 2B5
Tel: 604-687-4018; *Fax:* 604-687-4026
Toll-Free: 888-353-8166
info@eldoradogold.com
www.eldoradogold.com
Ticker Symbol: ELD
Company Type: Public
Profile: Eldorado Gold Corporation specializes in the exploration & development of gold properties. The gold producer has properties in Brazil, Greece, Turkey, & China. Industry best practices are implemented in each region in an effort to minimize environmental impacts.

Elk Valley Coal Corporation
#1000, 205 - 9th Ave., Calgary, AB T2G 0R3
Tel: 403-260-9800; *Fax:* 403-265-8794
info@elkvalleycoal.ca
www.elkvalleycoal.ca
Company Type: Public
Profile: Coal mining in bituminous coal & lignite surface mining

Energold Drilling Corp.
#1100, 543 Granville St., Vancouver, BC V6C 1X8
Tel: 604-681-9501; *Fax:* 604-605-3816
info@energold.com
www.energold.com
Ticker Symbol: EGD
Company Type: Public
Profile: The contract diamond drilling company serves the international mining sector. The driller strives to operate in an environmentally & socially sensitive manner. Canada's E3 Environmental Excellence in Exploration chose one of Energold's drill programs as a case study.

European Goldfields Ltd.
Registered Office, Financial Plaza, #200, 204 Lambert St., Whitehorse, YT Y1A 3T2
info@egoldfields.com
www.egoldfields.com
Ticker Symbol: EGU
Company Type: Public
Profile: European Goldfields Limited is engaged in the acquisition, exploration, & development of mineral properties. Operations take place in Greece, Romania, & southeastern Europe. The company implemented environmental initiatives such as improving the distribution system of mine water, installing a sprinkler system, removing old mining debris & waste, & switching from tailings slurry disposal to dry fitter cake disposal.

Excellon Resources Inc.
#900, 20 Victoria St., Toronto, ON M5C 2N8
Tel: 416-364-1130; *Fax:* 416-364-6745
info@excellonresources.com
www.excellonresources.com
Ticker Symbol: EXN
Company Type: Public
Profile: The mineral exploration company is engaged in the production of silver, lead, & zinc. Its principal area of activity is Durango State, Mexico.

Farallon Resources Ltd.
#1020, 800 West Pender St., Vancouver, BC V6C 2V6
Tel: 604-684-6365; *Fax:* 604-684-8092
Toll-Free: 800-667-2114
info@hdgold.com
www.farallonresources.com
Ticker Symbol: FAN
Company Type: Public
Profile: Metal mining in gold, silver, lead & zinc ores

First Quantum Minerals Ltd.
#800, 543 Granville St., Vancouver, BC V6C 1X8
Tel: 604-688-6577; *Fax:* 604-688-3818
Toll-Free: 888-688-6577
info@fqml.com
www.first-quantum.com
Ticker Symbol: FM
Company Type: Public
Profile: Operations of the mining & metals company include mineral exploration, development, mining, smelting, & refining. First Quantum Minerals is engaged in copper & cobalt mining in Africa. The company also has interest in gold & cobalt production.

FNX Mining Company Inc.
#1500, 145 King St. West, Toronto, ON M5H 1J8
Tel: 416-628-5929; *Fax:* 416-360-0550
info@fnxmining.com
www.fnxmining.com
Ticker Symbol: FNX
Company Type: Public
Profile: Metal mining & metal mining services

FNX Mining Company Inc.
#1500, 145 King St. West, Toronto, ON M5H 2B7
Tel: 416-628-5929; *Fax:* 416-360-0550
info@fnxmining.com
www.fnxmining.com
Ticker Symbol: FNX
Company Type: Public
Profile: The company focuses upon the exploration, development, & production of copper, platinum, nickel, cobalt, gold, & palladium. Mining properties are situated in Sudbury, Ontario.

Formation Capital Corporation
#1510, 999 West Hastings St., Vancouver, BC V6C 2W2
Tel: 604-682-6229; *Fax:* 604-682-6205
inform@formcap.com
www.formcap.com
Ticker Symbol: FCO
Company Type: Public
Profile: Formation Capital Corporation's area of expertise is mineral exploration, mine development, & refining. It has interests in base, precious metal, & uranium projects. The company also owns a hydrometallurgical complex & precious metals refinery in the United States, through its wholly-owned subsidiary, Essential Metals Corporation. The following are Formation Capital Corporation's areas of activity: Canada, the United States, & Mexico.

Fronteer Development Group Inc.
#1650, 1055 West Hastings St., Vancouver, BC V6E 2E9
Tel: 604-632-4677; *Fax:* 604-632-4678
Toll-Free: 877-632-4677
info@fronteergroup.com
www.fronteergroup.com
Ticker Symbol: FRG
Company Type: Public
Profile: Fronteer Development Group is involved in exploration & development. Its portfolio includes the following: gold projects in Nevada; Aurora Energy Resources (42.2% interest); & gold & copper-gold projects in northwestern Turkey (40% interest).

Frontera Copper Corporation
#1000, 36 Toronto St., Toronto, ON M5C 2C5
Tel: 602-667-3202; *Fax:* 602-424-5490
info@fronteracopper.com
www.fronteracopper.com
Ticker Symbol: FCC
Company Type: Public
Profile: Frontera Copper Corporation is a Canadian copper cathode producer. Its' principle area of activity is the Piedras Verdes project in Sonora, Mexico.

Gabriel Resources Ltd.
#1501, 110 Yonge St., Toronto, ON M5C 1T4
Tel: 416-955-9200; *Fax:* 416-955-4661
info@gabrielresources.com
www.gabrielresources.com
Ticker Symbol: GBU
Company Type: Public
Profile: Metal mining in gold & silver ores

Gammon Gold Inc.
PO Box 2067 Summit Place, #402, 1601 Water St., Halifax, NS B3J 3P6
Tel: 902-468-0614; *Fax:* 902-468-0631
info@gammongold.com
www.gammongold.com
Ticker Symbol: GAM
Company Type: Public
Profile: Owns gold-silver deposits at Ocampo, Mexico

Glencairn Gold Corp.
#500, 6 Adelaide St. E, Toronto, ON M5C 1H6
Tel: 416-860-0919; *Fax:* 416-367-0182
Company Type: Public
Profile: Metal mining in gold & silver ores

GobiMin Inc.
#1250, 120 Adelaide St. West, Toronto, ON M5H 1T1
Tel: 416-915-0133; *Fax:* 416-915-2908
info@gobimin.com
www.gobimin.com
Ticker Symbol: GMN
Company Type: Public
Profile: GobiMin Inc. is engaged in mineral exploration & development. The junior mining company has nickel, copper, & sulphide operations in northwestern China. In addition to the Chinese properties, GobiMin has set up a joint venture for exploration of metal properties in Indonesia. GobiMin Inc.'s subsidiaries include Hami Jubao Resources Co. Ltd. & Xinjiang Yakesi Resources Co. Ltd.

Goldcorp Inc.
Park Place, #3400, 666 Burrard St., Vancouver, BC 86C 2X8
Tel: 604-696-3000; *Fax:* 604-696-3001
Toll-Free: 800-567-6223
info@goldcorp.com
www.goldcorp.com
Ticker Symbol: G
Company Type: Public
Profile: Goldcorp Inc. is a gold mining company. Its development projects & operations are located throughout North & South America.

Golden Queen Mining Co. Ltd.
6411 Imperial Ave., Vancouver, BC V7W 2J5
Tel: 604-921-7570; *Fax:* 604-921-9446
mintoexpl@telus.net
www.goldenqueen.com
Ticker Symbol: GQM
Company Type: Public
Profile: Metal mining in gold & silver ores

Great Basin Gold Ltd.
#1020, 800 West Pender St., Vancouver, BC V6C 2V6
Tel: 604-684-6365; *Fax:* 604-684-8092
Toll-Free: 800-667-2114
info@hdgold.com
www.greatbasingold.com
Ticker Symbol: GBG
Company Type: Public
Profile: Mid-tier gold producer with mines in South Africa and the United States

Harry Winston Diamond Corporation
PO Box 4569 A, Toronto, ON M5W 4T9
Tel: 416-362-2237; *Fax:* 416-362-2230
hw@harrywinston.com
www.harrywinston.com; investor.harrywinston.com
Ticker Symbol: ABZ
Company Type: Public
Profile: Mining & quarrying of miscellaneous nonmetallic minerals

High River Gold Mines Ltd.
#1700, 155 University Ave., Toronto, ON M5H 3B7
Tel: 416-947-1440; *Fax:* 416-360-0010
info@hrg.ca
www.hrg.ca
Ticker Symbol: HRG
Company Type: Public
Profile: Metal mining in gold ores

High River Gold Mines Ltd.
#1700, 155 University Ave., Toronto, ON M5H 3B7
Tel: 416-947-1440; *Fax:* 416-360-0010
highrivergold@hrg.ca
www.hrg.ca
Ticker Symbol: HRG
Company Type: Public
Profile: Metal mining in gold ores

Horizon North Logistics Inc.
#1600, 505 - 3rd St. SW, Calgary, AB T2P 3E6
Tel: 403-517-4654; *Fax:* 403-517-4678
Toll-Free: 888-366-5558
www.horizonnorth.ca
Ticker Symbol: HNL
Company Type: Public
Profile: Services are provided to natural resource development projects. Horizon North Logistics Inc.'s services include marine transportation & logistics, mobile structures, & matting solutions. Projects take place in oil & gas exploration & development areas & the oil sands of western & northern Canada & Alaska.

HudBay Minerals Inc.
Dundee Place, #2501, 1 Adelaide St. East, Toronto, ON M4S 2E2
Tel: 416-362-0615; *Fax:* 416-362-7844
investor.relations@hbms.ca
www.hudbayminerals.com
Ticker Symbol: HBM
Company Type: Private
Profile: Zinc, copper, & precious metals are produced by the mining & smelting company.

IAMGOLD Corporation
PO Box 153, #3200, 401 Bay St., Toronto, ON M5H 2Y4
Tel: 416-360-4710; *Fax:* 416-360-4750
Toll-Free: 888-464-9999
info@iamgold.com
www.iamgold.com
Ticker Symbol: IMG
Company Type: Public
Profile: Metal mining in gold & miscellaneous ores

IAMGOLD Corporation
PO Box 153, #3200, 401 Bay St., Toronto, ON M5H 2Y4
Tel: 416-360-4710; *Fax:* 416-360-4750
Toll-Free: 888-464-9999
info@iamgold.com
www.iamgold.com
Ticker Symbol: IMG
Company Type: Public
Profile: The company is engaged in metal mining in gold ores.

Imperial Metals Corporation
#200, 580 Hornby St., Vancouver, BC V6C 3B6
Tel: 604-669-8959; *Fax:* 604-687-4030
info@imperialmetals.com
www.imperialmetals.com
Ticker Symbol: III
Company Type: Public
Profile: Imperial Metals Corporation explores, develops, operates, & maintains mine properties.

Inco Limited
#1500, 145 King St. West, Toronto, ON M5H 4B7
Tel: 416-361-7511; *Fax:* 416-361-7781
inco@inco.com
www.inco.com
Company Type: Public
Profile: Metal mining in ferroalloy, copper & gold ores; Manufacturers of primary smelting & refining of nonferrous metals, various industrial inorganic chemicals, secondary smelting & refining of nonferrous metals, nonferrous forgings

Inmet Mining Corporation
#1000, 330 Bay St., Toronto, ON M5H 2S8
Tel: 416-361-6400; *Fax:* 416-368-4692
ir@inmetmining.com
www.inmetmining.com
Ticker Symbol: IMN
Company Type: Public
Profile: The mining company produces gold, copper, & zinc.

International Royalty Corporation
#104, Inverness Dr. East, Englewood, CO 80112
Tel: 303-799-9020; *Fax:* 303-799-9017
Toll-Free: 800-496-1629
info@internationalroyalty.com
www.internationalroyalty.com
Ticker Symbol: IRC
Company Type: Public
Profile: The global mineral royalty company holds more than 60 royalties. It is listed on the Toronto Stock Exchange. Its legal counsel & transfer agent are also in Toronto.

Ivanhoe Mines Ltd.
World Trade Centre, #654, 999 Canada Pl., Vancouver, BC V6C 3E1
Tel: 604-688-5755; *Fax:* 604-682-2060
Toll-Free: 888-273-9999
info@ivanhoemines.com
www.ivanhoemines.com
Ticker Symbol: IVN
Company Type: Public
Profile: Metal mining in copper, iron, gold, silver, lead & zinc ores

Ivernia Inc.
#300, 44 Victoria St., Toronto, ON M5C 1Y2
Tel: 416-867-9298; *Fax:* 416-867-9384
investor@ivernia.ca
www.ivernia.com
Ticker Symbol: IVW
Company Type: Public
Profile: Offices of holding companies; Metal mining in lead & zinc ores

Kinross Gold Corporation
Scotia Plaza, 40 King St. West, 52nd Fl., Toronto, ON M5H 3Y2
Tel: 416-365-5123; *Fax:* 416-363-6622
Toll-Free: 866-561-3636
info@kinross.com
www.kinross.com
Ticker Symbol: K
Company Type: Public
Profile: Kinross Gold Corporation explores, acquires, mines, & processes gold & silver ore in North & South America.

Kirkland Lake Gold Inc.
Macassa Mine, PO Box 370 Main, 1360 Government Road West, Kirkland Lake, ON P2N 3J1
Tel: 705-567-5208; *Fax:* 705-568-6444
info@klgold.com
www.klgold.com
Ticker Symbol: KGI
Company Type: Public
Profile: Gold mining

Lakota Resources Inc.
#600, 15 Toronto St., Toronto, ON M5C 2E3
Tel: 416-368-1447; *Fax:* 416-368-8957
info@lakotaresources.ca
www.lakotaresources.ca
Ticker Symbol: YLA
Company Type: Public
Profile: Gold exploration in Tanzania

Leader Mining International Inc.
#2806, 505 - 6th St. SW, Calgary, AB T2P 1X5
Tel: 403-234-7501; *Fax:* 403-539-9490
gen-info@leadermining.com
www.leadermining.com
Ticker Symbol: LMN
Company Type: Public
Profile: Magnesium & tantalum mining

Lundin Mining Corporation
PO Box 38, #1500, 150 King St. West, Toronto, ON M5H 1J9
Tel: 416-342-5560; *Fax:* 416-348-0303
info@lundinmining.com
www.lundinmining.com
Ticker Symbol: LUN
Company Type: Public
Profile: Lundin Mining Corporation is engaged in the exploration, mining, & production of base metal mineral resources, such as copper, nickel, zinc, & lead. Operations are located in Spain, Portugal, & Sweden. The corporation also holds a development project pipeline & an equity stake in a copper & cobalt project in the Democratic Republic of Congo.

Madison Minerals Inc.
Guinness Tower, #2000, 1055 West Hastings St., Vancouver, BC V6E 2E9
Tel: 604-331-8772; *Fax:* 604-331-8773
Toll-Free: 877-529-8475
dscott@mine-tech.com
www.madison-enterprises.com
Ticker Symbol: MNP
Company Type: Public
Profile: The company is engaged in metal mining of gold, silver & copper ores.

Magellan Minerals Ltd.
#1650, 409 Granville St., Vancouver, BC V6C 1T2
Tel: 604-676-5660; *Fax:* 604-676-5664
info@magellanminerals.com
www.magellanminerals.com
Company Type: Public
Profile: Acquisition, exploration & development of gold properties

Major Drilling Group International Inc.
#100, 111 St George St., Moncton, NB E1C 1T7
Tel: 506-857-8636; *Fax:* 506-857-9211
info@majordrilling.com
www.majordrilling.com
Ticker Symbol: MDI
Company Type: Public
Profile: Major Drilling Group International's drilling operations are carried out in the following areas: Canada, the United States, Central America, South America, Africa, Armenia, Indonesia, & Australia. Drilling services include geotechnical, environmental drilling, surface & underground coring, reverse circulation, & coal-bed methane. The company primarily serves the mining industry.

Mazarin Inc.
696, rue Monfette est, Thetford Mines, QC G6G 7G9
Tel: 418-338-3669; *Fax:* 418-338-0229
jleboutillier@mazarin-inc.com
Ticker Symbol: MAZ.H
Company Type: Public
Profile: The company manages several mining sites. Mazarin Inc. is also engaged in the development of tailings.

Mediterranean Resources Ltd.
#890, 885 Dunsmuir St., Vancouver, BC V6C 1N5
Tel: 604-669-3397; *Fax:* 604-669-3357
charpestad@medresources.ca
www.medresources.ca
Ticker Symbol: MNR
Company Type: Public
Profile: Mediterranean Resources Ltd. develops gold deposits in Turkey.

Metalex Ventures Ltd.
2600 B Enterprise Way, Kelowna, BC V1X 7Y5
Tel: 250-860-8599; *Fax:* 250-860-1362
www.metalexventures.com
Ticker Symbol: MTX
Company Type: Public
Profile: Exploration & mining diamonds in Ontario & Quebec and oversees projects in Angola, Greenland, Mali and Morocco

Minefinders Corporation Ltd.
#2288, 1177 West Hastings St., Vancouver, BC V6E 2K3
Tel: 604-687-6263; *Fax:* 604-687-6267
Toll-Free: 866-687-6263
ilianne@minefinders.com
www.minefinders.com
Ticker Symbol: MFL
Company Type: Public
Profile: Metal mining in gold & silver ores

Mountain Province Diamonds Inc.
PO Box 152, #2700, 401 Bay St., Toronto, ON M5H 2Y4
Tel: 416-361-3562; *Fax:* 416-603-8565
p.evans@mountainprovince.com
www.mountainprovince.com
Ticker Symbol: MPV
Company Type: Public
Profile: Mountain Province Diamonds Inc. is engaged in diamond exploration & development. The Gahcho Kué diamond project in the Northwest Territories is the company's main asset, in a joint venture partnership with De Beers Canada.

NEMI Northern Energy & Mining Inc.
2500 - 555 W. Hastings St., Vancouver, BC V6B 4N5
Tel: 604-689-0277; *Fax:* 604-688-5210
info@nemi-energy.com
www.nemi-energy.com
Ticker Symbol: NNE.A
Company Type: Public
Profile: Mine development company focused on the exploration and development of metallurgical coal assets in northeast British Columbia

Neo Material Technologies
#1740, 121 King St. West, Toronto, ON M5H 3T9
Tel: 416-367-8588; *Fax:* 416-367-5471
info@neomaterials.com
www.neomaterials.com
Ticker Symbol: NEM
Company Type: Public
Profile: Metal mining in miscellaneous ores; Manufacturing of various industrial inorganic chemicals

Nevsun Resources Ltd.
#800, 1075 West Georgia St., Vancouver, BC V6E 3C9
Tel: 604-623-4700; *Fax:* 604-623-4701
Toll-Free: 888-600-2200
nevsuninfo@nevsun.com
www.nevsun.com
Ticker Symbol: NSU
Company Type: Public
Profile: Metal mining in gold & miscellaneous metal ores

New Gold Inc.
#3110, 666 Burrard St., Vancouver, BC V6C 2X8
Tel: 604-639-0022; *Fax:* 604-696-4110
Toll-Free: 888-315-9715
info@newgold.com
www.newgold.com
Company Type: Public
Profile: The intermediate gold mining company has assets in Canada, Alaska, Mexico, Brazil, & Australia.

Newmont Mining Corporation of Canada Ltd.
Cambridge Bay Expediting Building, PO Box 1203, Cambridge Bay, NU X0B 0C0
Tel: 604-759-3450; *Fax:* 506-759-0318
canadahr@newmont.com
www.newmont.com
Ticker Symbol: NEM
Company Type: Public
Profile: Newmont Mining Corporation of Canada Ltd. is engaged in gold exploration & production. Current activity takes place in the Hope Bay greenstone belt area of the Arctic.

NGEx Resources Inc.
#2101, 885 West Georgia St., Vancouver, BC V6C 3E8
Tel: 604-689-7842; *Fax:* 604-689-4250
ngexresources@namdo.com
www.ngexresources.com
Ticker Symbol: NGQ
Company Type: Public
Profile: Metal mining in gold, copper, lead & zinc ores

Noranda Income Fund
c/o Xstrata Canada Inc., First Canadian Place, PO Box 403, #6900, 100 King St. West, Toronto, ON 5X 1E33
Tel: 416-775-1500; *Fax:* 416-775-1749
www.norandaincomefund.com
Ticker Symbol: NIF.UN
Company Type: Public
Profile: The Fund's main asset is Canadian Electrolytic Zinc Limited, a zinc processing facility in Salaberry-de-Valleyfield, Québec. The facility has obtained ISO 9001 & ISO 14001 certification to cover all environmental processes at the plant.

North American Palladium Ltd.
#2116, 130 Adelaide St. West, Toronto, ON M5H 3P5
Tel: 416-360-7590; *Fax:* 416-360-7709
info@napalladium.com
www.napalladium.com
Ticker Symbol: PDL
Company Type: Public
Profile: Metal mining in gold, copper, ferroalloy & miscellaneous metal ores

Northgate Minerals Corporation
#406, 815 Hornby St., Vancouver, BC V6Z 2E6
Tel: 604-681-4004; *Fax:* 604-681-4003
ngx@northgateminerals.com
www.northgateminerals.com
Ticker Symbol: NGX
Company Type: Public
Profile: Northgate Minerals Corp. is engaged in the production of gold & copper. The company's exploration properties, development projects, & mining operations are located in Canada & Australia.

Northrock Resources Inc.
Pacific Centre, PO Box Box 10322, #1588, 609 Granville St., Vancouver, BC V7Y 1G5
Tel: 604-689-7422; *Fax:* 604-689-7442
www.northrockresources.com
Ticker Symbol: NRK
Company Type: Public
Profile: The company is engaged in the exploration & development of mineral properties.

NovaGold Resources Inc
Granville Square, PO Box 24, #2300, 200 Granville St., Vancouver, BC V6C 1S4
Tel: 604-669-6227; *Fax:* 604-669-6272
Toll-Free: 866-669-6227
info@novagold.net
www.novagold.net
Ticker Symbol: NG
Company Type: Public
Profile: Metal mining-gold ores; Metal mining-miscellaneous metal ores

Olympus Pacific Minerals Inc.
#500, 10 King St. East, Toronto, ON M5C 1C3
Tel: 416-572-2525; *Fax:* 416-572-4202
Toll-Free: 888-902-5522
info@olympuspacific.com
www.olympuspacific.com
Ticker Symbol: OYM
Company Type: Public
Profile: Production & exploration for gold in Vietnam & SE Asia

Orsu Metals Corporation
c/o Vanguard Shareholder Solutions Inc., #1205, 1095 West Pender St., Vancouver, BC
Tel: 604-608-0824; *Fax:* 604-608-0854
Toll-Free: 866-448-0780
info@orsumetals.com
www.orsumetals.com
Ticker Symbol: OSU
Company Type: Public
Profile: Metal mining gold & silver ores; Oil royalty traders

Orvana Minerals Corp.
#1530, 320 Bay St., Toronto, ON M5H 4A6
Tel: 416-369-1629; *Fax:* 416-369-1402
mking@orvana.com
www.orvana.com
Ticker Symbol: ORV
Company Type: Public
Profile: The Canadian gold mining & exploration company evaluates, develops, & mines precious & base metals deposits. Orvana Minerals is the owner & operator of the Don Mario gold mine in Bolivia.

OZ Minerals Limited
#200, 1159 Alloy Dr., Thunder Bay, ON P7B 6M8
Tel: 807-346-1668; *Fax:* 807-345-8708
Toll-Free: 866-690-9653
www.ozminerals.com
Ticker Symbol: OZL.AX
Company Type: Public
Profile: Mining exploration & development, with operations around the world, including 2,600 km of exploration area in the Slave Region of Nunavut. Through the acquisition of Wolfden Resources Limited in 2007, OZ Minerals now owns the High Lake and Izok Lake projects

Pacific Rim Mining Corp.
#1050, 625 Howe St., Vancouver, BC V6C 2T6
Tel: 604-689-1976; *Fax:* 604-689-1978
Toll-Free: 888-775-7097
general@pacrim-mining.com
www.pacrim-mining.com
Ticker Symbol: PMU
Company Type: Public
Profile: Pacific Rim Mining is a gold exploration company. The company's main asset is the El Dorado gold project in El Salvador. Salvadoran & U.S. subsidiaries include Pac Rim Cayman LLC, Pacific Rim El Salvador, S.A. de C.V., & Dorado Exploraciones, S.A. de C.V..

Pan American Silver Corp.
#1500, 625 Howe St., Vancouver, BC V6C 2T6
Tel: 604-684-1175; *Fax:* 604-684-0147
info@panamericansilver.com
www.panamericansilver.com
Ticker Symbol: PAA
Company Type: Public
Profile: The silver producer conducts its mining & exploration activities in Mexico, Bolivia, Peru, & Argentina.

Pelangio Exploration Inc.
440 Harrop Dr., 2nd Fl, Milton, ON L9T 3H2
Tel: 905-875-3828; *Fax:* 905-875-3829
Toll-Free: 877-746-1632
info@pelangio.com
www.pelangio.com
Ticker Symbol: PX
Company Type: Public
Profile: Pelangio Exploration Inc. is a junior gold exploration company. Its exploration & development operations are conducted on mineral properties in Canada & Ghana.

Philex Gold Inc.
#1200, 95 Wellington St. West, Toronto, ON M5J 2Z9
Tel: 416-864-9700; *Fax:* 416-941-8852
www.philexgold.com
Ticker Symbol: PGI
Company Type: Public
Profile: Philex Gold is engaged in gold & copper exploration in the Philippines. The company's interests include the former Bulawan gold mine, the Silangan Project, the Lascogon, Danao, & other gold prospects. Philex adheres to the Community-Based Development & Environmental Management Program.

Potash Corporation of Saskatchewan Inc.
PCS Tower, #500, 122 - 1st Ave. South, Saskatoon, SK S7K 7G3
Tel: 306-933-8500; *Fax:* 306-652-2699
Toll-Free: 800-667-0403
corporate.relations@potashcorp.com
www.potashcorp.com
Ticker Symbol: POT
Company Type: Public
Profile: The fertilizer enterprise produces the following plant nutrients: potash, nitrogen, & phosphate. Potash Corporation of Saskatchewan supplies the agriculture, animal nutrition, & industrial chemical markets.

Quadra Mining Ltd.
Four Bentall Centre, PO Box 49185, #2414, 1055 Dunsmuir St., Vancouver, BC V7X 1K8
Tel: 604-689-8550; *Fax:* 604-689-8556
info@quadramining.com
www.quadramining.com
Ticker Symbol: QUA
Company Type: Public
Profile: Quadra Mining Ltd. owns & operates the Robinson copper mine in Nevada. The base metal producer also holds a 100% interest in the Carlota Copper Project, which is under construction in Arizona, plus an 82% interest in International Molybdenum & its Malmbjerg Project.

Redcorp Ventures Ltd.
#800, 1281 West Georgia St., Vancouver, BC V6E 3J7
Tel: 604-639-0135; *Fax:* 604-669-5330
Toll-Free: 888-669-4775
info@redcorp-ventures.com
www.redcorp-ventures.com
Ticker Symbol: RDV
Company Type: Public
Profile: The company is engaged in metal mining of gold, silver, copper, lead & zinc ores. It is listed on the TSX.

Rex Diamond Mining Corporation
#1900, 25 Adelaide St. East, Toronto, ON M5C 3A1
Tel: 416-867-8800;
info@rexmining.com
www.rexmining.com
Company Type: Public
Profile: Rex Diamond Mining Corporation is a Canadian incorporated, public company which is currently seeking new business opportunities.

Richmont Mines Inc.
110, av Principale, Rouyn-Noranda, QC J9X 4P2
Tel: 819-797-2465; *Fax:* 819-797-0166
info@richmont-mines.com
www.richmont-mines.com
Ticker Symbol: RIC
Company Type: Public
Profile: Richmont Mines Inc. specializes in gold exploration, development, & mining. Operations take place in Ontario, Quebec, & Newfoundland & Labrador.

Rochester Resources Ltd.
#1305, 1090 West Georgia St., Vancouver, BC V6E 3V7
Tel: 604-685-9316; *Fax:* 604-683-1585
info@rochesterresources.com
www.rochesterresources.com
Ticker Symbol: RCT
Company Type: Public
Profile: Rochester Resources Ltd. is engaged in the exploration & development of gold & silver properties. Operations take place in the state of Nayarit, Mexic, where the Mina Real Property & the Santa Fe Project are located.

Sabina Silver Corporation
#202, 930 West 1st St., North Vancouver, BC V7P 3N4
Tel: 604-998-4175; *Fax:* 604-998-1051
Toll-Free: 888-648-4218
info@sabinasilver.com
www.sabinasilver.com
Ticker Symbol: SBB
Company Type: Public
Profile: Sabina Silver Corporation specializes in acquiring, exploring, & developing precious metal properties. The company's assets are as follows: the Del Norte project in the Stewart-Eskay Creek Mining District; the Hackett River silver-zinc project in the Canadian Arctic; & many projects in the Red Lake gold camp.

Seabridge Gold Inc.
#400, 106 Front St. East, Toronto, ON M5A 1E1
Tel: 416-367-9292; *Fax:* 416-367-2711
info@seabridgegold.net
www.seabridgegold.net
Ticker Symbol: SEA
Company Type: Public
Profile: Has gold interests in North America; Does not operate mines

SEMAFO Inc.
#375, 750, boul Marcel-Laurin, Montréal, QC H4M 2M4
Tel: 514-744-4408; *Fax:* 514-744-2291
info@semafo.com
www.semafo.com
Ticker Symbol: SMF
Company Type: Public
Profile: Metal mining in gold, lead & zinc ores

Sherritt International Corporation
Investor Relations, 1133 Yonge St., 5th Fl., Toronto, ON M4T 2Y7
Tel: 416-924-4551; *Fax:* 416-924-5015
Toll-Free: 800-704-6698
info@sherritt.com; investor@sherritt.com
www.sherritt.com
Ticker Symbol: S
Company Type: Public
Profile: Sherrit International Corporation has interests in a nickel & cobalt metals business, thermal coal production, electricity generation, & oil & gas exploration, development, & production. The company conducts its operations in Canada & internationally.

Shore Gold Inc.
#300, 224 - 4th Ave. South, Saskatoon, SK S7K 5M5
Tel: 306-664-2202; *Fax:* 306-664-7181
shoregold@shoregold.com
www.shoregold.com
Ticker Symbol: SGF
Company Type: Public
Profile: Shore Gold Inc. specializes in mineral exploration & development. Operations take place in Saskatchewan.

Silver Standard Resources Inc.
#1180, 999 West Hastings St., Vancouver, BC V6C 2W2
Tel: 604-689-3846; *Fax:* 604-689-3847
Toll-Free: 888-338-0046
invest@silverstandard.com
www.silverstandard.com
Ticker Symbol: SSO
Company Type: Public
Profile: Metal mining in gold & silver ores

Silver Wheaton Corp.
#3150, 666 Burrard St., Vancouver, BC V6C 2X8
Tel: 604-684-9648; *Fax:* 604-684-3123
Toll-Free: 800-380-8687
info@silverwheaton.com
www.silverwheaton.com
Ticker Symbol: SLW
Company Type: Public
Profile: Silver Wheaton Corp. is engaged in silver production. The company purchases silver production from mines in the United States, Mexico, Peru, Sweden, & Greece.

Silvercorp Metals Inc.
#1378, 200 Granville St., Vancouver, BC V6C 1S4
Tel: 604-669-9397; *Fax:* 604-669-9387
Toll-Free: 888-224-1881
info@silvercorp.ca; ir@silvercorp.ca
www.silvercorp.ca
Ticker Symbol: SVM
Company Type: Public
Profile: Silvercorp Metals acquires, explores, & mines silver-related properties located in the People's Republic of China. The company has implemented a range of employee safety measures & environmental protection measures.

Southwestern Resources Corp.
PO Box 10102, #1650, 701 West Georgia St., Vancouver, BC V7Y 1C6
Tel: 604-669-2525; *Fax:* 604-688-5175
swg@swgold.com
www.swgold.com
Ticker Symbol: SWG
Company Type: Public
Profile: Metal mining in gold, silver & miscellaneous metal ores; Mining & quarrying of miscellaneous nonmetallic minerals

St. Andrew Goldfields Ltd.
#212, 1540 Cornwall Rd., Oakville, ON L6J 7W5
Tel: 905-815-9855; *Fax:* 905-815-9437
Toll-Free: 800-463-5139
info@standrewgoldfields.com
www.standrewgoldfields.com
Ticker Symbol: SAS
Company Type: Public
Profile: Metal mining of gold ores

Sterlite Gold Ltd.
PO Box 25, 199 Bay St., Toronto, ON M5L 1A9
Tel: 416-863-2753; *Fax:* 416-863-2653
Company Type: Private
Profile: Metal mining in gold & ferroalloy ores

Stratic Energy Corporation
#17, 100 - 6th Ave. SW, Calgary, AB T2P 0P5
Tel: 403-698-8897; *Fax:* 403-410-7797
yash.chapanery@straticenergy.com
www.straticenergy.com
Ticker Symbol: SE
Company Type: Public
Profile: Metal mining in gold ores

Tahera Diamond Corporation
PO Box 1020 T.D.C., 77 King St. West, Toronto, ON M5K 1P2
Tel: 416-777-1998; *Fax:* 416-777-1898
Toll-Free: 877-777-2004
investor_relations@tahera.com
www.tahera.com
Ticker Symbol: TAH
Company Type: Public
Profile: Publicly traded on the Toronto Stock Exchange, the company is a diamond mine explorer, developer, & operator.

Tan Range Exploration Corporation
#1400, 355 Burrard St., Vancouver, BC V6C 2G8
Tel: 604-669-5598; *Fax:* 604-669-8915
Toll-Free: 800-811-3855
investors@tanrange.com
www.tanrange.com
Ticker Symbol: TNX
Company Type: Public
Profile: Exploration & mining gold in Tanzania

Taseko Mines Limited
#200, 900 West Pender St., Vancouver, BC V6C 1L6
Tel: 604-684-6365; *Fax:* 604-684-8092
Toll-Free: 800-667-2114
info@hdgold.com
www.tasekomines.com
Ticker Symbol: TKO
Company Type: Public
Profile: Taseko Mines Limited is a mineral exploration & mining company. The company is engaged in the following main projects in British Columbia: the Prosperity gold-copper project; the Gibraltar copper-molybdenum mine; & the Harmony gold prospect.

Teck Cominco Ltd.
Bentall 5, #3300, 550 Burrard St., Vancouver, BC V6C 0B3
Tel: 604-699-4000; *Fax:* 604-699-4718
info@teck.com
www.teck.com
Ticker Symbol: TCK
Company Type: Public
Profile: The mining, smelting, & refining company produces zinc, copper, metallurgical coal, & gold.

Thompson Creek Metals Company Inc.
PO Box 118, #2010, 401 Bay St., Toronto, ON M5H 2Y4
Tel: 416-860-1438; *Fax:* 416-860-0813
info@tcrk.com
www.thompsoncreekmetals.com
Ticker Symbol: TCM
Company Type: Public
Profile: The molybdenum producer owns the Thompson Creek open-pit molybdenum mine & mill in Idaho, a metallurgical roasting facility in Pennsylvania, as well as 75% of northern British Columbia's Endako open-pit mine, mill, & roasting facility.

Tiberon Minerals Ltd.
Scotia Plaza, #1101, 100 Yonge St., Toronto, ON M5C 2W1
Tel: 416-214-1877; *Fax:* 416-214-0091
Toll-Free: 866-616-2404
info@tiberon.com
www.tiberon.com
Ticker Symbol: TBR
Company Type: Public
Profile: Exploration & production, mainly in Vietnam

TVI Pacific Inc.
#2000, 736 - 6th Ave. SW, Calgary, AB T2P 3T7
Tel: 403-265-4356; *Fax:* 403-264-7028
tvi-info@tvipacific.com
www.tvipacific.com
Ticker Symbol: TVI
Company Type: Public
Profile: Precious & base metal producer & explorer; contract drilling services in SE Asia & the Philippines

Uranium One Inc.
#900, 1285 West Pender Street, Vancouver, BC V6E 4B1
Tel: 604-601-5620; *Fax:* 604-601-5621
chris.sattler@uranium1.com
www.uranium1.com
Ticker Symbol: UUU
Company Type: Public
Profile: Metal mining in uranium, radium & vanadium ores

Uruguay Mineral Exploration
#101, Richmond St. East, Toronto, ON M5C 1N7
Tel: 416-848-7744; *Fax:* 416-848-0790
www.uruguayminerals.com
Ticker Symbol: UME
Company Type: Public
Profile: The gold exploration & production company is active in South America. Uruguay Mineral Exploration Inc. also has a portfolio of diamond & base metal prospects.

Vista Gold Corp.
Waterfront Centre, PO Box 48600, #900, 200 Burrard St., Vancouver, BC V7X 1T2
Tel: 720-981-1185; *Fax:* 720-981-1186
www.vistagold.com
Ticker Symbol: VGZ
Company Type: Public
Profile: Evaluates & acquires gold & precious metal projects

Wesdome Gold Mines Ltd.
#1305, 8 King St. East, Toronto, ON M5C 1B5
Tel: 416-360-3743; *Fax:* 416-360-7620
info@wesdome.com
www.wesdome.com
Ticker Symbol: WDO
Company Type: Public
Profile: Metal mining in gold ores

Western Copper Corporation
#2050, 1111 West Georgia St., Vancouver, BC V6E 4M3
Tel: 604-684-9497; *Fax:* 604-669-2926
Toll-Free: 888-966-9995
info@westerncoppercorp.com
www.westerncoppercorp.com
Ticker Symbol: WRN
Company Type: Public
Profile: Metal mining in copper ores

Xstrata Canada Corporation
PO Box 403, #6900, 100 King St. West, Toronto, ON M5X 1E3
Tel: 416-775-1556; *Fax:* 416-775-1740
info@xstrata.com
www.xstrata.com
Ticker Symbol: FAL
Company Type: Public
Profile: Xstrata is engaged in the production of thermal coal, copper, mined nickel, & zinc.

Yamana Gold Inc.
#1102, 150 York St., Toronto, ON M5H 3S5
Tel: 416-815-0220; *Fax:* 416-815-0021
investor@yamana.com
www.yamana.com
Ticker Symbol: YRI
Company Type: Public
Profile: Yamana Gold Inc. is engaged in the exploration & production of gold, copper, & other precious metals. Development projects & operating mines are located in Mexico, Central America, Brazil, & Argentina.

Oil & Gas

Addax Petroleum Corporation
#3400, 350 - 7th Ave. SW, Calgary, AB
Tel: 22 -702-9400; *Fax:* 22 -702-9590
investor.relations@addaxpetroleum.com
www.addaxpetroleum.com
Ticker Symbol: AXC
Company Type: Public
Profile: The oil & gas exploration & production company carries out activities in Africa & the Middle East.

Advantage Oil & Gas Ltd.
Canterra Tower, #700, 400 - 3rd Ave. SW, Calgary, AB T2P 4H2
Tel: 403-718-8000; *Fax:* 403-718-8300
Toll-Free: 866-393-0393
ir@advantageog.com; hr@advantageog.com
www.advantageog.com
Ticker Symbol: AAV
Company Type: Public
Profile: The intermediate oil & natural gas corporation has properties in western Canada, including the Montney natural gas resource at Glacier, Alberta.

Akita Drilling Ltd.
#900, 311 - 6 Ave. SW, Calgary, AB T2P 3H2
Tel: 403-292-7979; *Fax:* 403-292-7990
akitainfo@akita-drilling.com
www.akita-drilling.com
Ticker Symbol: AKT
Company Type: Public
Profile: Akita Drilling Ltd. serves the oil & gas industry by providing contract drilling services. Western Canada, Canada's northern territories, & Alaska are the principal areas of activity.

Apache Canada Ltd.
700 - 9 Ave. SW, Calgary, AB T2P 3V4
Tel: 403-261-1200; *Fax:* 403-266-5987
www.apachecorp.com
Company Type: Private
Profile: Crude petroleum & natural gas extraction; oil & gas fields exploration services

ARC Energy Trust
#2100, 440 - 2nd Ave. SW, Calgary, AB T2P 5E9
Tel: 403-503-8600; *Fax:* 403-509-6417
Toll-Free: 888-272-4900
ir@arcresources.com
www.arcenergytrust.com
Ticker Symbol: AET
Company Type: Public
Profile: ARC Energy Trust offers investors indirect ownership in oil & gas assets.

Argosy Energy Inc.
#2100, 500 - 4th Ave. SW, Calgary, AB T2P 2V6
Tel: 403-269-8846; *Fax:* 403-269-8366
investor@argosyenergy.com
www.argosyenergy.com
Ticker Symbol: GSY
Company Type: Public
Profile: Argosy Engery Inc. was formed in conjunction with Pengrowth Energy Trust's acquisition of Accrete Energy Inc.. The company commenced trading on the Toronto Stock Exchange in 2008. The junior oil & gas company acquires, explores, & develops oil & gas properties. Areas of operation include Claresholm, Granum, Pearce, Edson, & Saxon in southern & north central Alberta.

Barrick Energy Inc.
Watermark Tower, #1400, 530 - 8th Ave. SW, Calgary, AB T2P 3S8
Tel: 403-290-3400; *Fax:* 403-290-3447
www.barrick.com
Company Type: Public
Profile: Crude petroleum, natural gas & natural gas liquids extraction

Baytex Energy Ltd.
Bow Valley Square II, #2200, 205 - 5th Ave. SW, Calgary, AB T2P 2V7
Tel: 403-269-4282; *Fax:* 403-205-3845
Toll-Free: 800-524-5521
investor@baytex.ab.ca
www.baytex.ab.ca
Ticker Symbol: BTE.UN
Company Type: Public
Profile: The organization is a conventional oil & gas income trust. It is engaged in internal property development, maintenance of production, & delivery of consistent returns to unitholders. Baytex Energy Trust has a formal policy to ensure environmental health & safety policies are carried out in the course of its operations.

Baytex Energy Trust
Bow Valley Square II, 2200, 205 - 5th Ave. SW, Calgary, AB T2P 2V7
Tel: 403-269-4282; *Fax:* 403-205-3845
Toll-Free: 800-524-5521
helpdesk@baytex.ab.ca
www.baytex.ab.ca
Ticker Symbol: BTE.UN
Company Type: Public
Profile: Baytex Energy Trust is an energy income trust. Its portfolio of heavy oil, light oil, & natural gas assets is focused in the Western Canadian Sedimentary Basin & the United States. In addition to establishing its own health, safety and environmental policies & procedures, Baytex Energy Trust also participates in the Canadian Association of Petroleum Producer's Environment, Health, & Safety Stewardship program.

Berkana Energy Corp.
#2100, 801 - 6th Ave. SW, Calgary, AB T2P 3W2
Tel: 403-221-7700; *Fax:* 403-221-7719
info@berkanaenergy.com
www.berkanaenergy.com
Ticker Symbol: BEC
Company Type: Public
Profile: Crude petroleum, natural gas & natural gas liquids extraction

BJ Services Company Canada
4839 - 90 Ave. SE, Calgary, AB T2C 2S8
Tel: 403-531-5300; *Fax:* 403-236-8740
www.bjservices.com
Company Type: Private
Profile: Oil & gas field services; Manufacturers of oil & gas field machinery & equipment

Bonavista Energy Trust
#700, 311 - 6th Ave. SW, Calgary, AB T2P 3H2
Tel: 403-213-4300; *Fax:* 403-262-5184
inv_rel@bonavistaenergy.com
www.bonavistaenergy.com
Ticker Symbol: BNP.UN
Company Type: Public
Profile: Bonavista Energy Trust is an oil & gas royalty trust. Operations are carried out in Alberta, Saskatchewan, & northeastern British Columbia.

Bonterra Oil & Gas Ltd.
#901, 1015 - 4th St. SW, Calgary, AB T2R 1J4
Tel: 403-262-5307; *Fax:* 403-265-7488
info@bonterraenergy.com
www.bonterraenergy.com
Ticker Symbol: BNE
Company Type: Public
Profile: Bonterra Oil & Gas Ltd. is engaged in acquiring, exploring, & developing oil & natural gas properties. Activities are conducted in Saskatchewan & Alberta.

Bow Valley Energy Ltd.
#1200, 333 - 7th Ave. SW, Calgary, AB T2P 2Z1
Tel: 403-232-0292; *Fax:* 403-232-8920
bve@bvenergy.com
www.bvenergy.com
Ticker Symbol: BVX
Company Type: Public
Profile: The company is engaged in acquiring, exploring, & developing natural gas properties. Operations take place in Alaska & the United Kingdom.

Breaker Energy Ltd.
#2300, 635 - 8th Ave. SW, Calgary, AB T2P 3M3
Tel: 403-215-5264; *Fax:* 403-263-8665
info@breakerenergy.com
www.breakerenergy.com
Ticker Symbol: WAV.A
Company Type: Public
Profile: Breaker Energy Ltd. is a junior exploration & production company. Its specialty is the exploration, development, & production of oil & gas. Operations are carried out primarily in northern & southern Alberta, & northeastern British Columbia.

Brownstone Ventures Inc.
The Exchange Tower, #2500, 130 King Street West, Toronto, ON M5X 1A9
Tel: 416-941-8900; *Fax:* 416-941-1090
www.brownstoneventures.com
info@brownstoneventures.com
Ticker Symbol: BWN
Company Type: Public
Profile: Brownstone Ventures Inc. is a Canadian based investment company, which has direct interests in oil & gas assets. Its portfolio includes diverse energy-based projects throughout the world.

Calfrac Well Services Ltd.
411 - 8th Ave. SW, Calgary, AB T2P 1E3
Tel: 403-266-6000; *Fax:* 403-266-7381
Toll-Free: 866-770-3722
info@calfrac.com
www.calfrac.com
Ticker Symbol: CFW
Company Type: Public
Profile: Calfrac Well Services Ltd. is engaged in the provision of oilfield services, such as cementing, fracturing, & well stimulation services. Operations are situated in western Canada, the United States, Mexico, Argentina, & Russia.

Calpine Canada
#210, 1011 - 1st St., SW, Calgary, AB T2R 1J2
Tel: 403-296-1410; *Fax:* 403-266-3896
public-relations@calpine.com
www.calpine.com
Company Type: Public
Profile: Electricity production using natural gas, geothermal steam, geothermal energy

Calvalley Petroleum Inc.
#700, 600 - 6th Ave. SW, Calgary, AB T2P 0S5
Tel: 403-297-0490; *Fax:* 403-297-0499
inquiries@calvalleypetroleum.com
www.calvalleypetroleum.com
Ticker Symbol: CVI.A
Company Type: Public
Profile: Calvalley Petroleum's area of expertise is acquiring, exploring, & developing oil & gas properties. Activity takes place in the Republic of Yemen.

Canadex Resources Ltd.
10 Sun Pac Blvd., Brampton, ON L6S 4R5
Tel: 905-792-2700; *Fax:* 905-792-8490
Company Type: Public
Profile: Extraction of crude petroleum, natural gas & natural gas liquids; School buses; Local trucking with storage; General warehousing & storage; Truck rental & leasing

Canadian Energy Services L.P.
East Tower, Energy Plaza, #300, 311 - 6th Ave. SW, Calgary, AB T2P 3H2
Tel: 403-269-2800; *Fax:* 403-266-5708
Toll-Free: 888-785-6695
info@ceslp.ca
www.canadianenergyservices.ca
Ticker Symbol: CEU.UN
Company Type: Public
Profile: Canadian Energy Services L.P. is a designer of drilling fluid systems. Products are delivered to the oil & natural gas industry in the Western Canadian Sedimentary Basin & the United States. The company's subsidiary is AES Drilling Fluids, LLC.

Canadian Imperial Venture Corp.
Fortis Bldg., PO Box 6232, 139 Water St., St. John's, NL A1C 6J9
Tel: 709-739-6700; *Fax:* 709-739-6605
info@canadianimperial.com
www.canadianimperial.com
Ticker Symbol: CQV
Company Type: Public
Profile: Crude petroleum, natural gas & natural gas liquids extraction

Canadian Natural Resources Limited
#2500, 855 - 2nd St. SW, Calgary, AB T2P 4J8
Tel: 403-517-6700; *Fax:* 403-517-7370
ir@cnrl.com
www.cnrl.com
Ticker Symbol: CNQ
Company Type: Public
Profile: Canadian Natural Resources Limited is engaged in the exploration, development, & production of oil & natural gas. Operations are carried out in western Canada, the North Sea, & offshore west Africa.

Canadian Oil Sands Trust
First Canadian Centre, #2500, 350 - 7th Ave. SW, Calgary, AB T2P 3N9
Tel: 403-218-6200; *Fax:* 403-218-6201
investor_relations@cos-trust.com
www.cos-trust.com
Ticker Symbol: COS.UN
Company Type: Public
Profile: The trust holds a 36.74% working interest in the Syncrude Project.

Canadian Superior Energy Inc.
#2700, 605 - 5th Ave. SW, Calgary, AB T2P 3H5
Tel: 403-294-1411; *Fax:* 403-216-2374
www.cansup.com
Ticker Symbol: SNG
Company Type: Public
Profile: Extraction of crude petroleum, natural gas & natural gas liquids

Canetic Resources Trust
#1900, 255 - 5th Ave. SW, Calgary, AB T2P 3G6
Tel: 403-539-6300; *Fax:* 403-539-6499
Toll-Free: 877-539-6300
info@canetictrust.com
canetictrust.com
Ticker Symbol: CNE.UN
Company Type: Public
Profile: Unit investment trusts, certificate/closed-end management offices; Extraction of crude petroleum, natural gas & natural gas liquids

Cathedral Energy Services Trust
#1700, 715 - 5th Ave. SW, Calgary, AB T2P 2X6
Tel: 403-265-2560; *Fax:* 403-262-4682
www.cathedralenergyservices.com
Ticker Symbol: CET.UN
Company Type: Public
Profile: Cathedral Energy Services Income Trust is a limited purpose trust. The Trust is the owner of the securities of Cathedral Energy Services Ltd. & Cathedral Energy Services Limited Partnership. Cathedral is engaged in the provision of oilfield services to oil & natural gas companies. Activities take place in western Canada & the Rocky Mountain area of the United States.

CCS Income Trust
#2400, 530 - 8th Ave. SW, Calgary, AB T2P 3S8
Tel: 403-233-7565; *Fax:* 403-261-5612
info@ccsincometrust.com
www.ccsincometrust.com
Ticker Symbol: CCR
Company Type: Public
Profile: Various oil & gas fields services; Refuse systems

Celtic Exploration Ltd.
#500, 505 - 3rd St. SW, Calgary, AB T2P 3E6
Tel: 403-201-9153; *Fax:* 403-201-9163
invest@celticex.com
www.celticex.com
Ticker Symbol: CLT
Company Type: Public
Profile: Celtic Exploration Ltd. specializes in the exploration & production of oil & gas.

Centurion Energy International Inc.
Bow Valley Square II, #1700, 205 - 5th Ave. SW, Calgary, AB T2P 2V7
Tel: 403-263-6002;
Company Type: Public
Profile: Extraction of crude petroleum, natural gas & natural gas liquids

Compton Petroleum Corporation
East Tower, Fifth Avenue Place, #3300, 425 - 1st St. SW, Calgary, AB T2P 3L8
Tel: 403-237-9400; *Fax:* 403-237-9410
investorinfo@comptonpetroleum.com
www.comptonpetroleum.com
Ticker Symbol: CMT
Company Type: Public
Profile: Compton Petroleum Corporation explores for, develops, & produces natural gas, natural gas liquids, & crude oil. Activities are carried out in western Canada's sedimentary basin.

Connacher Oil & Gas Limited
#900, 332 - 6th Ave. SW, Calgary, AB T2P 0B2
Tel: 403-538-6201; *Fax:* 403-538-6225
inquiries@connacheroil.com
www.connacheroil.com
Ticker Symbol: CLL
Company Type: Public
Profile: Connacher Oil & Gas Limited is involved in the exploration, development, & production of oil & natural gas. The company's operations are carried out in western Canada, where its principal asset is oil sands leases in the Great Divide & Halfway Creek regions near Fort McMurray, Alberta. It is also the owner & operator of a refinery in Montana.

Conoco Phillips Canada
Gulf Canada Square, PO Box 130 M, 401 - 9 Ave. SW, Calgary, AB T2P 2H7
Tel: 403-233-4000; *Fax:* 403-233-5143
www.conocophillips.ca
Company Type: Private

Profile: Extraction of crude petroleum, natural gas & natural gas liquids

Corridor Resources Inc.
#301, 5475 Spring Garden Rd., Halifax, NS B3J 3T2
Tel: 902-429-4511; *Fax:* 902-429-0209
Toll-Free: 888-429-4511
info@corridor.ca
www.corridor.ca
Ticker Symbol: CDH
Company Type: Public
Profile: Corridor Resources Inc. is a junior resource company, which is engaged in the exploration & development of oil & gas properties. Activities are carried out onshore in Prince Edward Island, New Brunswick, & Québec, & offshore in the Gulf of St. Lawrence.

Crescent Point Energy Trust
#2800, 111 - 5th Ave. SW, Calgary, AB T2P 3Y6
Tel: 403-693-0020; *Fax:* 403-693-0070
www.crescentpointenergy.com
Ticker Symbol: CPG
Company Type: Public
Profile: Conventional oil & gas income trust

Crew Energy Inc.
#1400, 425 First St. SW, Calgary, AB T2P 3L8
Tel: 403-266-2088; *Fax:* 403-266-6259
investor@crewenergy.com
www.crewenergy.com
Ticker Symbol: CR
Company Type: Public
Profile: The junior oil & natural gas producer carries out its activities in northeastern British Columbia & central Alberta.

Destiny Resource Services Corp.
#300, 444 - 58th Ave. SE, Calgary, AB T2H 0P4
Tel: 403-237-6437; *Fax:* 403-233-8714
destiny@destiny-resources.com
www.destiny-resources.com
Ticker Symbol: DSC
Company Type: Public
Profile: Extraction services in drilling oil & gas wells; Oil & gas fields exploration services

Devon Canada Corporation
#2000, 400 - 3rd Ave. SW, Calgary, AB T2P 4H2
Tel: 403-232-7100; *Fax:* 403-232-7221
www.devonenergy.com
Ticker Symbol: DVN
Company Type: Public
Profile: Crude petroleum, natural gas & natural gas liquids extraction

Duvernay Oil Corp.
#1500, 202 - 6th Ave. SW, Calgary, AB T2P 2R9
Tel: 403-571-3600; *Fax:* 403-269-6510
Ticker Symbol: DDQ
Company Type: Public
Profile: Duvernay Oil acquires, explores, & develops crude oil & natural gas properties in the sedimentary basin of Alberta & northeastern British Columbia.

Enbridge Inc.
Fifth Avenue Place, #3000, 425 - 1st St. SW, Calgary, AB T2P 3L8
Tel: 403-231-3900; *Fax:* 403-231-3920
Toll-Free: 877-420-8800
investor.relations@enbridge.com
www.enbridge.com
Ticker Symbol: ENB
Company Type: Public
Profile: Enbridge Inc. is engaged in the following businesses: natural gas pipelines, crude oil & liquids pipelines, & natural gas distribution. The company;s pipeline system is located in Canada & the United States. International activity includes energy projects & renewable energy.

EnCana Corporation
PO Box 2850, #1800, 855 - 2nd St. SW, Calgary, AB T2P 2S5
Tel: 403-645-2000; *Fax:* 403-645-2091
investor.relations@encana.com
www.encana.com
Ticker Symbol: ECA
Company Type: Public
Profile: The company is engaged in oil & gas production.

Enerplus Resources Fund
The Dome Tower, #3000, 333 - 7th Ave. SW, Calgary, AB T2P 2Z1
Tel: 403-298-2200; *Fax:* 403-298-2211
investorrelations@enerplus.com
www.enerplus.com
Ticker Symbol: ERF.UN
Company Type: Public

Profile: Enerplus Resources Fund has a portfolio of oil & natural gas producing properties. Properties are situated in western Canada & the United States.

Ensign Energy Services Inc.
#1000, 400 - 5th Ave. SW, Calgary, AB T2P 0L6
Tel: 403-262-1361; *Fax:* 403-262-8215
info@ensignenergy.com
www.ensignenergy.com
Ticker Symbol: ESI
Company Type: Public
Profile: Oilfield services are provided throughout the world to the oil & natural gas industry. Some of Ensign Energy Services's principal operating subsidiaries include Arctic Ensign Drilling Ltd., Big Sky Drilling Inc., Encore Coring & Drilling Inc., Opsco Energy Industries Ltd., Rockwell Servicing Inc., & Gwich'in Ensign Oilfield Services Inc.

Enterra Energy Corp.
#2700, 500 - 4th Ave. SW, Calgary, AB T2P 2V6
Tel: 403-263-0262; *Fax:* 403-294-1197
Toll-Free: 877-263-0262
info@enterraenergy.com
www.enterraenergy.com
Company Type: Public
Profile: Crude petroleum, natural gas & natural gas liquids extraction

Eurogas Corporation
#250, 435 - 4 Ave. SW, Calgary, AB T2P 3A8
Tel: 403-264-4985; *Fax:* 403-262-8299
eurogas@eurogascorp.com
www.eurogascorp.com
Ticker Symbol: EUG
Company Type: Public
Profile: Extraction of crude petroleum, natural gas & natural gas liquids, natural gas storage

Eveready Inc.
14904 - 121A Ave., Edmonton, AB T5V 1A3
Tel: 780-451-6075; *Fax:* 780-451-2142
Toll-Free: 877-661-6689
investorrelations@evereadyinc.com
www.evereadyinc.com
Ticker Symbol: EIS
Company Type: Public
Profile: Eveready Inc. serves the energy, resource, & industrial sectors. The company provides industrial & oilfield maintenance & production services in Canada & internationally.

Fairborne Energy Ltd.
#3400, 450 - 1st St. SW, Calgary, AB T2P 5H1
Tel: 403-290-7750; *Fax:* 403-290-7724
info@fairborne-energy.com
www.fairborne-energy.com
Ticker Symbol: FEL
Company Type: Public
Profile: Fairborne Energy Ltd. develops oil & gas properties. The company's main operating areas are as follows: Central Alberta; West Pembina/Brazeau; Columbia/Harlech; Deep Basin; Peace River Arch in Alberta; & Sinclair in southwestern Manitoba. The company has implemented a comprehensive health, safety, & environmental program.

First Calgary Petroleums Ltd.
#500, 1414 - 8th St. SW, Calgary, AB T2R 1J6
Tel: 403-264-6697; *Fax:* 403-264-3955
info@fcpl.ca
www.fcpl.ca
Ticker Symbol: FCP
Company Type: Public
Profile: Extraction of crude petroleum, natural gas & natural gas liquids

Flint Energy Services Ltd.
Stock Exchange Bldg., #700, 300 - 5th Ave. SW, Calgary, AB T2P 3C4
Tel: 403-218-7100; *Fax:* 403-215-5481
gcocquyt@flint-energy.com
www.flint-energy.com
Ticker Symbol: FES
Company Type: Public
Profile: The company serves North America's energy & resource industries through the provision of integrated midstream production services. Flint Energy Services employs a Corporate Manager of Occupational Health, Safety & the Environment to monitor regulatory requirements & implement compliance procedures.

Fort Chicago Energy Partners L.P.
Livingston Place, #440, 222 - 3rd Ave. SW, Calgary, AB T2P 0B4
Tel: 403-296-0140; *Fax:* 403-213-3648
investor-relations@fortchicago.com
www.fortchicago.com
Ticker Symbol: FCE
Company Type: Public
Profile: Fort Chicago Energy Partners L.P. invests in natural gas liquids extraction, power, & pipeline transportation businesses throughout North America.

Galleon Energy Inc.
West Tower, Livingston Place, #400, 250 - 2nd St. SW, Calgary, AB T2P 0C1
Tel: 403-261-6012; *Fax:* 403-262-5561
information@galleonenergy.com
www.galleonenergy.com
Ticker Symbol: GO
Company Type: Public
Profile: Galleon Energy is a mid-sized oil & natural gas explorer & producer. It specializes in the acquisition, exploration, & development of petroleum & natural gas properties. Activities are carried out in western Canada.

Halliburton Canada Inc.
#1600, 645 - 7 Ave. SW, Calgary, AB T2P 4G8
Tel: 403-231-9300; *Fax:* 403-261-9420
www.halliburton.com
Company Type: Public
Profile: Offices of holding companies; Various & oil & gas fields services; Engineering services; Equipment rental & leasing

Harvest Energy Trust
Calgary Place, #2100, 330 - 5th Ave. SW, Calgary, AB T2P 0L4
Tel: 403-265-1178; *Fax:* 403-265-3490
www.harvestenergy.ca
Ticker Symbol: HTE.UN
Company Type: Private
Profile: Crude petroleum, natural gas & natural gas liquids extraction

Heritage Oil Corporation
#2000, 633 - 6th Avenue SW, Calgary, AB T2P 2Y5
Tel: 403-234-9974; *Fax:* 403-261-1941
info@heritageoilcorp.com
www.heritageoilcorp.com
Ticker Symbol: HOC.A
Company Type: Public
Profile: Oil & gas exploration, development & production in Africa & Middle East

Hunt Oil Company of Canada, Inc.
Transcanada Tower, #3100, 450 First St. SW, Calgary, AB T2P 5H1
Tel: 403-531-1430; *Fax:* 403-531-1539
Toll-Free: 877-444-9295
www.huntoil.com
Company Type: Private
Profile: Crude petroleum, natural gas & natural gas liquids extraction

Husky Energy Inc.
PO Box 6525 D, 707 - 8 Ave. SW, Calgary, AB T2P 3G7
Tel: 403-298-6111; *Fax:* 403-298-7464
investor.relations@huskyenergy.ca
www.huskyenergy.ca
Ticker Symbol: HSE
Company Type: Public
Profile: Husky Energy Inc. is engaged in the exploration & development of crude oil & natural gas, as well as the production, transportation & marketing of petroleum products.

Imperial Oil Limited
PO Box 2480 M, 237 Fourth Ave. SW, Calgary, AB T2P 3M9
Tel: 800-567-3776; *Fax:* 800-367-0585
www.imperialoil.ca
Ticker Symbol: IMO
Company Type: Public
Profile: The company is a producer of crude oil & natural gas. Imperial Oil also refines & markets petroleum products.

Integrated Production Services Ltd.
#1900, 840 - 7th Ave. SW, Calgary, AB T2P 3G2
Tel: 403-266-0908; *Fax:* 403-266-1639
www.ipsadvantage.com
Company Type: Private
Profile: Various oil & gas fields services

Inter Pipeline Fund
#2600, 237 - 4th Ave. SW, Calgary, AB T2P 4K3
Tel: 403-290-6000; *Fax:* 403-290-6092
Toll-Free: 866-716-7473
investorrelations@interpipelinefund.com
www.interpipelinefund.com
Ticker Symbol: IPL.UN
Company Type: Public
Profile: Services included petroleum transportation, bulk liquid storage & natural gas liquids extraction; Owner & operator of energy infrastructure assets in Western Canada, the United Kingdom, Germany & the Republic of Ireland

Ivanhoe Energy Inc.
#654, 999 Canada Place, Vancouver, BC V6C 3E1
Tel: 604-688-8323; *Fax:* 604-682-2060
info@ivanhoeenergy.com
www.ivanhoeenergy.com
Ticker Symbol: IE
Company Type: Public
Profile: Extraction of crude petroleum, natural gas & natural gas liquids

Jura Energy Corporation
#227, 200 Barclay Parade SW, Calgary, AB T2P 4R5
Tel: 403-266-6364; *Fax:* 403-266-6365
info@juraenergy.com
www.juraenergy.com
Ticker Symbol: JEC
Company Type: Public
Profile: Petroleum & natural gas exploration & production, primarily conducted in Pakistan

Kinder Morgan Canada
#2700, 300 - 5th Ave., Calgary, AB T2P 5J2
Tel: 403-514-6400; *Fax:* 403-514-6401
Toll-Free: 800-535-7219
info@kindermorgan.com
www.kindermorgan.com
Company Type: Public
Profile: Crude petroleum & refined petroleum pipelines

Nabors Drilling (Canada)
#2800, 500 - 4th Ave. SW, Calgary, AB T2P 2V6
Tel: 403-263-6777; *Fax:* 403-269-7352
ndl.marketing@nabors.com
www.nabors.com
Company Type: Private
Profile: Nabors is engaged in the exploration & development of oil, gas, & geothermal wells. A variety of land rigs & ancillary services are marketed by Nabors Canada throughout the country.

Nexen Inc.
801 - 7 Ave. SW, Calgary, AB T2P 3P7
Tel: 403-699-4000; *Fax:* 403-699-5800
ir@nexeninc.com
www.nexeninc.com
Ticker Symbol: NXY
Company Type: Public
Profile: The energy company carries out operations in the Athabasca oil sands of Alberta, the Gulf of Mexico, offshore West Africa, & the Middle East.

Niko Resources Ltd.
4600 Canterra Tower, #4600, 400 - 3 Ave. SW, Calgary, AB T2P 4H2
Tel: 403-262-1020; *Fax:* 403-263-2686
nikocalgary@nikoresources.com
www.nikoresources.com
Ticker Symbol: NKO
Company Type: Public
Profile: Extraction of crude petroleum, natural gas & natural gas liquids

North American Energy Partners Inc.
Zone 3, Acheson Industrial Area, #2, 53016 Hwy. 60, Acheson, AB T7X 5A7
Tel: 780-960-4531; *Fax:* 780-960-7103
IR@nacg.caca
www.nacg.ca
Ticker Symbol: NOA
Company Type: Public
Profile: North American Energy Partners Inc. is the corporate parent of North American Construction Group Inc. The following services are provided by North American Energy Partners Inc.: pipeline, piling, heavy construction, & mining. Large oil, natural gas, & resource companies are the main recipients of these services. The principal area of activity is the Canadian oil sands.

NuVista Energy Ltd.
#700, 311 - 6th Ave. SW, Calgary, AB T2P 3H2
Tel: 403-538-8500; *Fax:* 403-538-8505
inv_rel@nuvistaenergy.com
www.nuvistaenergy.com
Ticker Symbol: NVA
Company Type: Public
Profile: Nuvista Energy is a Canadian oil & gas company, which acquires, explores, & develops oil & gas properties. The company is active in the Western Canadian Sedimentary Basin.

Oilexco Inc.
#3200, 715 - 5th Ave. SW, Calgary, AB T2P 2X6
Tel: 403-262-5441; *Fax:* 403-263-3251
info@oilexco.com
www.oilexco.com
Ticker Symbol: OIL
Company Type: Public
Profile: Oilexco Inc. specializes in the exploration, development, & production of oil & gas.

Open Range Energy Corp.
#1100, 645 - 7 Ave. SW, Calgary, AB T2P 4G8
Tel: 403-262-2936; *Fax:* 403-262-3924
sbuick@tempestenergy.com
www.openrangeenergy.com
Ticker Symbol: ONR
Company Type: Public
Profile: Oil & gas exploration, development & production, primarily in Alberta

Pacific Northern Gas Ltd.
#950, 1185 West Georgia St., Vancouver, BC V6E 4E6
Tel: 604-691-5680; *Fax:* 604-697-6210
info@png.ca
www.png.ca
Ticker Symbol: PNG
Company Type: Public
Profile: Pacific Northern Gas delivers natural gas to its residential, commercial, & industrial customers. Customers are situated in west-central British Columbia. The company's subsidiary, Pacific Northern Gas (N.E.) Ltd., is engaged in the delivery of natural gas to customers in northeastern British Columbia.

Pacific Rubiales Energy
#1400, 220 Bay St., Toronto, ON M5J 2W4
Tel: 416-362-7735; *Fax:* 416-360-7783
www.petrorubiales.com
Ticker Symbol: PRE
Company Type: Public
Profile: Pacific Rubiales Energy is engaged in the production of heavy crude oil & natural gas. It is the owner of Meta Petroleum Limited, which is a Colombian oil operator.

Pan Orient Energy Corp.
#1505, 505 - 3rd St. SW, Calgary, AB T2P 3E6
Tel: 403-294-1770; *Fax:* 403-294-1780
www.panorient.ca
Ticker Symbol: POE
Company Type: Public
Profile: The oil & gas exploration & production company's areas of activity are western Canada & Thailand.

Pantera Drilling Income Trust
#600, 407 - 8th Ave. SW, Calgary, AB T2P 1E5
Tel: 403-515-8400; *Fax:* 403-515-8405
info@panteradrilling.com
www.panteradrilling.com
Ticker Symbol: RIG.UN
Company Type: Public
Profile: Pantera Drilling Income Trust is an open-ended, investment trust. The Trust is involved in the provision of contract drilling services. It serves oil & gas exploration & production companies in the Western Canadian Sedimentary Basin.

Paramount Resources Ltd.
Bankers Hall West, #4700, 888 - 3rd St. SW, Calgary, AB T2P 5C5
Tel: 403-290-3600; *Fax:* 403-262-7994
info@paramountres.com
www.paramountres.com
Ticker Symbol: POU
Company Type: Public
Profile: The oil & natural gas exploration, development, & production company carries out its operations in western Canada.

Peak Energy Services Trust Ltd.
#900, 222 - 3rd Ave. SW, Calgary, AB T2P 0B4
Tel: 403-543-7325; *Fax:* 403-543-7335
Toll-Free: 800-661-3803
mjhuber@pesl.com
www.peak-energy.com
Ticker Symbol: PES
Company Type: Public
Profile: Offices of holding companies; Various oil & gas fields services; Manufacturers of oil & gas field machinery & equipment; Equipment rental & leasing

Pebercan Inc.
#106, 750, boul Marcel Laurin, Saint-Laurent, QC H4M 2M4
Tel: 514-286-5200; *Fax:* 514-286-5177
info@pebercan.com
www.pebercan.com
Ticker Symbol: PBC
Company Type: Public
Profile: Pebercan Inc. is engaged in the exploration, development, & operation of oil & gas fields in the Republic of Cuba. Its wholly-owned subsidiary is Peberco Limited.

Pembina Pipeline Income Fund
#2000, 700 - 9th Ave. SW, Calgary, AB T2P 3V4
Tel: 403-231-7500; *Fax:* 403-237-0254
investor-relations@pembina.com
www.pembina.com
Ticker Symbol: PIF
Company Type: Public
Profile: Through its subsidiaries, Pembina Pipeline Income Fund is involved in the transportation of light conventional & synthetic crude oil, & condensate & natural gas liquids. Operations are carried out in western Canada.

Pengrowth Energy Trust
#2100, 222 - 3rd Ave. SW, Calgary, AB T2P 0B4
Tel: 403-233-0224; *Fax:* 866-433-5224
pengrowth@pengrowth.com
www.pengrowth.com
Ticker Symbol: PGF
Company Type: Public
Profile: The energy royalty trust invests in crude oil & natural gas properties.

Penn West Energy Trust
#200, 207 - 9th Ave. SW, Calgary, AB T2P 1K3
Tel: 403-777-2500; *Fax:* 403-777-2699
Toll-Free: 866-693-2707
investor_relations@pennwest.com
www.pennwest.com
Ticker Symbol: PWT.UN, PWE
Company Type: Public
Profile: Penn West Petroleum Ltd. is a conventional oil & natural gas producing income trust. It operates throughout the Western Canadian Sedimentary Basin. The organization strives to meet & exceed regulatory environmental codes & guidelines.

Petro-Canada
PO Box 2844, 150 - 6th Ave. SW, Calgary, AB T2P 3E3
Tel: 403-296-8000; *Fax:* 403-296-3030
investor@petro-canada.ca
www.petro-canada.ca
Ticker Symbol: PCA
Company Type: Public
Profile: Petro-Canada is engaged in the development, production, & marketing of crude oil & natural gas. Petroleum products are also refined & distributed by the company.

Petrobank Energy & Resources Ltd.
#2600, 240 - 4th Ave. SW, Calgary, AB T2P 4H4
Tel: 403-750-4400; *Fax:* 403-266-5794
ir@petrobank.com
www.petrobank.com
Ticker Symbol: PBG
Company Type: Public
Profile: The company is engaged in the acquisition, exploration, & development of natural gas & oil properties. Operations are carried out in western Canada & Colombia.

Petrolifera Petroleum Limited
#900, 332 - 6th Ave. SW, Calgary, AB T2P 0B2
Tel: 403-538-6201; *Fax:* 403-538-6225
inquiries@petrolifera.ca
www.petrolifera.ca
Ticker Symbol: PDP
Company Type: Public
Profile: The oil & natural gas exploration & production company is active in Peru, Argentina, & Columbia. Connacher Oil and Gas Limited owns part of Petrolifera's shares.

Peyto Energy Trust
#2900, 450 - 1st St. SW, Calgary, AB T2P 5H1
Tel: 403-261-6081; *Fax:* 403-261-8976
info@peyto.com
www.peyto.com
Ticker Symbol: PEY
Company Type: Public
Profile: The exploration & development of oil & gas properties take place in western Canada.

Phoenix Technology Income Fund
#630, 434 - 4th Ave. SW, Calgary, AB T2P 3A8
Tel: 403-543-4466; *Fax:* 403-543-4485
investor@phoenixcan.com
www.phoenixcan.com
Ticker Symbol: PHX.UN
Company Type: Public
Profile: Phoenix Technology Income Fund is involved in the provision of directional & horizontal drilling services & technology. The organization serves the oil & natural gas producing sectors in Canada & the United States. Phoenix Technology Income Fund works through the following companies: Phoenix Technology Services LP in Canada; & Nevis Energy Services Inc. in the United States.

Precision Drilling Trust
#4200, 150 - 6th Ave. SW, Calgary, AB T2P 3Y7
Tel: 403-716-4500; *Fax:* 403-264-0251
info@precisiondrilling.com
www.precisiondrilling.com
Ticker Symbol: PD.UN
Company Type: Public
Profile: The energy services company consists of the following business segments: contract drilling, & completion & production.

Progress Energy Resources Corp.
#1200, 205 - 5th Ave. SW, Calgary, AB T2P 2V7
Tel: 403-216-2510; *Fax:* 403-216-2514
ir@progressenergy.com
www.progressenergy.com
Ticker Symbol: PRQ
Company Type: Public
Profile: Progress Energy Resources Corp. is a natural gas & crude oil exploration & production organization.

Provident Energy Trust
#2100, 250 - 2nd St. SW, Calgary, AB T2P 0C1
Tel: 403-296-2233; *Fax:* 403-294-0111
info@providentenergy.com
www.providentenergy.com
Ticker Symbol: PVE.UN
Company Type: Public
Profile: The open-ended income trust has a diversified portfolio of energy infrastructure assets & upstream oil & gas assets.

Pulse Data Inc.
#2400, 639 - 5th Ave. SW, Calgary, AB T2P 0M9
Tel: 403-237-5559; *Fax:* 403-531-0688
Toll-Free: 877-460-5559
info@pulsedatainc.com
www.pulsedatainc.com
Ticker Symbol: PSD
Company Type: Public
Profile: Specializing in data ownership through acquisition, marketing & information management, with current focus on the energy sector

Sabretooth Energy Ltd.
#702, 2303 - 4th St. SW, Calgary, AB T2S 2S7
Tel: 403-229-3050; *Fax:* 403-229-0603
info@sabretooth.ca
www.sabretooth.ca
Ticker Symbol: SAB
Company Type: Public
Profile: Production of oil, natural gas, & natural gas liquids. The company holds interest in properties in Alberta & British Columbia

Savanna Energy Services Corp.
#1800, 311 - 6th Ave. SW, Calgary, AB T2P 3H2
Tel: 403-503-9990; *Fax:* 403-267-6749
Toll-Free: 877-568-2344
info@savannaenergy.com
www.savannaenergy.com
Ticker Symbol: SVY
Company Type: Public
Profile: The company is a North American energy services provider. Savanna Energy Services has partnerships with several Aboriginal communities in western Canada. It uses PLC-controlled service rigs & patented hybrid drilling rigs in its operations.

Saxon Energy Services Inc.
#1700, 700 - 4th Ave. SW, Calgary, AB T2P 3J4
Tel: 403-716-4150; *Fax:* 403-716-4151
www.saxonservices.com
Ticker Symbol: SES
Company Type: Public
Profile: Saxon Energy Services Inc. is engaged in oil & gas drilling, & well servicing. The company serves multinational & national oil & gas exploration & production companies. Saxon Energy Services is active in Canada, the United States, Mexico, Ecuador, Venezuela, & Columbia.

Schlumberger Canada Ltd.
525 - 3rd Ave. SW, Calgary, AB T2P 0G4
Tel: 403-509-4000; *Fax:* 403-509-4021
www.slb.com
Company Type: Private
Profile: Schlumberger Canada is an oilfield services provider, with offices in Calgary, Alberta & Mount Pearl, Newfoundland. It offers a great range of products & services, from well cementing to information management services. The company has research & engineering facilities throughout the world to develop innovative technology for the oil & gas industry. Schlumberger has high standards for health & safety & the protection of the environment in the communities in which it works.

ShawCor Ltd.
25 Bethridge Rd., Toronto, ON M9W 1M7
Tel: 416-743-7111; *Fax:* 416-743-9123
glove@shawcor.com
www.shawcor.com
Ticker Symbol: SCL.A
Company Type: Public
Profile: ShawCor Ltd. is a provider of technology-based products & services for the pipeline & pipe services market, as well as the petrochemical & industrial market. Facilities are located in over twenty countries.

Shell Canada Limited
PO Box 100 M, 400 - 4th Ave. SW, Calgary, AB T2P 2H5
Tel: 403-691-3537; *Fax:* 403-691-3696
Toll-Free: 800-661-1600
questions@shell.ca
www.shell.ca
Company Type: Private
Profile: Shell Canada is an integrated oil & gas company. The following are the company's activities: exploration & production of oil & gas; delivery of gas projects; production of petrochemicals for industrial customers; the sale of petroleum-based products for domestic, transport, & industrial use; & the extraction of bitumen, at the company's Athabasca Oil Sands Project in Alberta, & its conversion to synthetic crude oil.

Stoneham Drilling Trust
#1230, 335 - 8th Ave. SW, Calgary, AB T2P 1C9
Tel: 403-264-7777; *Fax:* 403-264-7766
bjones@stonehamdrilling.ca
www.stonehamdrilling.com
Ticker Symbol: SDG.UN
Company Type: Public
Profile: Contract drilling services are provided by Stoneham Drilling Trust. It serves oil & natural gas exploration & production companies in the Western Canada Sedimentary Basin & the Anadarko Basin of Oklahoma. The company's operating practices comply with provincial standards for oilfield waste management.

Storm Exploration Inc.
#800, 205 - 5th Ave. SW, Calgary, AB T2P 2V7
Tel: 403-264-3520; *Fax:* 403-264-3552
info@stormexploration.com
www.stormexploration.com
Ticker Symbol: SEO
Company Type: Public
Profile: Storm Exploration Inc. focuses upon exploring, acquiring, & developing oil & natural gas reserves in Alberta & British Columbia.

Suncor Energy Inc.
PO Box 38, 112 - 4 Ave. SW, Calgary, AB T2P 2V5
Tel: 403-269-8100; *Fax:* 403-269-6217
Toll-Free: 866-786-2671
info@suncor.com
www.suncor.com
Ticker Symbol: SU
Company Type: Public
Profile: Suncor Energy Inc. is engaged in natural gas production in western Canada, with a focus on the oil sands. Refinement & marketing operations are carried out in Ontario & Colorado. The company also invests in renewable energy, especially ethanol production & wind power.

Sword Energy Inc.
#400, 321 - 6th Ave. SW, Calgary, AB T2P 3H3
Tel: 403-294-1635; *Fax:* 403-232-1317
info@swordenergy.com
www.thunderenergy.com
Company Type: Public
Profile: Crude petroleum, natural gas & natural gas liquids extraction

Syncrude Canada Ltd.
PO Box 4023 Main, 9911 MacDonald Ave., Fort McMurray, AB T9H 3H5
Tel: 780-790-5911; *Fax:* 780-790-6215
Toll-Free: 800-667-9494
info@syncrude.com
www.syncrude.com
Company Type: Private
Profile: Crude petroleum & natural gas extraction

Talisman Energy Inc.
#3400, 888 - 3rd St. SW, Calgary, AB T2P 5C5
Tel: 403-237-1234; *Fax:* 403-237-1210
tlm@talisman-energy.com
www.talisman-energy.com
Ticker Symbol: TLM
Company Type: Public
Profile: Talisman Eenergy carries out its operations as an oil & gas producer in Canada. The company's subsidiaries has operations in the United States, Trinidad & Tobago, North Africa, the North Sea, Southeast Asia, & Australia.

Tanganyika Oil Company Ltd.
#700, 444 - 7th Ave. SW, Calgary, AB T2P 0X8
Tel: 403-663-2999; *Fax:* 403-261-1007
info@tanganyikaoil.com
www.tanganyikaoil.com
Ticker Symbol: TYK
Company Type: Public
Profile: The international oil & gas exploration, development, & production company has interests in properties in Syria.

TAQA North Ltd.
#5100, 150 - 6th Ave. SW, Calgary, AB T2P 3Y7
Tel: 403-724-5000; *Fax:* 403-724-5025
ir@taqaglobal.com
www.taqa.ae/en/canada.html
Company Type: Private
Profile: TAQA North Ltd. is engaged in oil & gas exploration. It is active in the following regions: the Northwest Territories, northern British Columbia & Alberta; west central & southern Alberta, & southeastern & southwestern Saskatchewan.

Taylor NGL Limited Partnership
#2200, 800 - 5th Ave. SW, Calgary, AB T2P 3T6
Tel: 403-781-8181; *Fax:* 403-777-1907
Company Type: Private
Profile: Extraction of natural gas liquids; Processing of natural gas

Terasen Gas Inc.
16705 Fraser Hwy., Surrey, BC V4N 0E8
Tel: 604-576-7000; *Toll-Free:* 800-773-7001
websupport@terasengas.com
www.terasengas.com
Company Type: Public
Profile: Natural gas transmission & distribution; Gas & other services combined; Refined petroleum pipelines

Total Energy Services Trust
#2550, 300 - 5th Ave. SW, Calgary, AB T2P 3C4
Tel: 403-216-3939; *Fax:* 403-234-8731
Toll-Free: 877-818-6825
investorrelations@totalenergy.ca
www.totalenergy.ca
Ticker Symbol: TOT
Company Type: Public
Profile: The oil & gas service income trust is involved in drilling & production services. Total Energy Services Trust serves western & northern Canada's oil & gas industry.

Trans Québec & Maritimes Pipeline Inc.
#525, 6300, av Auteuil, Brossard, QC J4Z 3P2
Tel: 450-462-5300; *Fax:* 450-462-5388
tqm@gazoductqm.com
www.gazoductqm.com
Company Type: Public
Profile: Natural gas transmission & distribution

TransCanada PipeLines Limited
450 - 1 St. SW, Calgary, AB T2P 5H1
Tel: 403-920-2000; *Fax:* 403-920-2200
Toll-Free: 800-661-3805
communications@transcanada.com
www.transcanada.com
Ticker Symbol: TCA
Company Type: Public
Profile: The energy infrastructure company is engaged in natural gas transmission & power services.

TransGlobe Energy Corporation
#2500, 605 - 5th Ave. SW, Calgary, AB T2P 3H5
Tel: 403-264-9888; *Fax:* 403-264-9898
contact@trans-globe.com
www.trans-globe.com
Ticker Symbol: TGL
Company Type: Public
Profile: TransGlobe Energy acquires, explores, & develops oil & gas properties. The Alberta-based oil & gas exploration & development company focuses its production activities in the Arab Republic of Egypt, & the Republic of Yemen.

Trican Well Service Ltd.
#2900, 645 - 7th Ave. SW, Calgary, AB T2P 4G8
Tel: 403-266-0202; *Fax:* 403-237-7716
info@trican.ca; sales@trican.ca
www.trican.ca
Ticker Symbol: TCW
Company Type: Public
Profile: Trican Well Service Ltd. is a provider of products, equipment, & services, which are employed in the exploration & development of oil & gas reserves. The company conducts its operations in Canada, the United States, & Russia.

Trinidad Drilling Ltd.
#2500, 700 - 9th Ave. SW, Calgary, AB T2P 3V4
Tel: 403-265-6525; *Fax:* 403-265-4168
info@trinidaddrilling.com
www.trinidaddrilling.com
Ticker Symbol: TDG
Company Type: Public
Profile: The company specializes in drilling, well servicing, & barge drilling operations within the North American oil & gas industry. Trinidad Drilling Ltd.incorporates environmental protection measures into its procedures for site inspections, products, equipment, & waste disposal.

True Energy Trust
#2300, 530 - 8th Avenue SW, Calgary, AB T2P 3S8
Tel: 403-266-8670; *Fax:* 403-264-8163
general.info@trueenergy.ab.ca
www.trueenergytrust.com
Ticker Symbol: TUI.UN
Company Type: Public

TUSK Energy Corp.
#1900, 700 - 4th Ave. SW, Calgary, AB T2P 3J4
Tel: 403-264-8875; *Fax:* 403-263-4247
tusk@tusk-energy.com
www.tusk-energy.com
Ticker Symbol: TSK
Company Type: Public
Profile: Crude petroleum, natural gas & natural gas liquids extraction

Ultra Petroleum Corp.
#1200, 363 North Sam Houston Pkwy. East, Houston, TX 77060
Tel: 281-876-0120; *Fax:* 281-876-2831
info@ultrapetroleum.com
www.ultrapetroleum.com
Ticker Symbol: UPL
Company Type: Public
Profile: Incorporated in British Columbia in 1979, Ultra Petroleum Corp. is engaged in the exploration & development of oil & gas properties in the Green River Basin of Wyoming. The company's transfer agent is Computershare Trust Company of Canada & Computershare Trust Company, Inc.

Ultramar Ltd.
2200, av McGill College, Montréal, QC H3A 3L3
Tel: 514-499-6111; *Toll-Free:* 800-363-6949
publicaffairs@ultramar.ca
www.ultramar.ca
Company Type: Private
Profile: Ultramar Ltd. is engaged in the provision of clean-burning, environmentally sound petroleum fuels at the industrial, commercial, & retail levels in North America. The company has a network of service stations, including car washes & stores, located throughout eastern Ontario, Québec, & the Atlantic provinces. Ultramar Ltd. also provides home heating & air conditioning services.

Union Gas Limited
PO Box 2001, 50 Keil Dr. North, Chatham, ON N7M 5M1
Tel: 519-352-3100; *Fax:* 519-436-4566
Toll-Free: 800-265-5230
customerrelations@uniongas.com
www.uniongas.com
Ticker Symbol: UNG
Company Type: Public
Profile: The natural gas storage, transmission, & distribution company provides services in northern, southwestern, & eastern Ontario to commercial, industrial, & residential customers. In Quebec, Ontario, & the United States, Union Gas Limited also offers natural gas storage & transportation services to other utilities.

UPI Energy LP
#200, #105 Silvercreek Pkwy. North, Guelph, ON N1H 8M1
Tel: 519-821-2667; *Fax:* 519-821-4919
Toll-Free: 800-396-2667
info@upi.on.ca; customers@upi.on.ca
www.upienergylp.com
Company Type: Public
Profile: UPI Energy LP provides environmentally friendly energy products & related services. Examples of products & services offered to farms & businesses include gasolines, diesel fuels, propane, & lubricants. The company serves consumers & motorists in rural Ontario.

UTS Energy Corporation
#1000, 350 - 7th Ave. SW, Calgary, AB T2P 3N9
Tel: 403-538-7030; *Fax:* 403-538-7033
mail@uts.ca
www.uts.ca
Ticker Symbol: UTS
Company Type: Public
Profile: The company is engaged in the exploration & development of oil sands leases, such as the Fort Hills Project.

Vermilion Energy Trust
#2800, 400 - 4th Ave. SW, Calgary, AB T2P 0J4
Tel: 403-269-4884; *Fax:* 403-264-6306
Toll-Free: 866-895-8101
investor_relations@vermilionenergy.com
www.vermilionenergy.com
Ticker Symbol: VET
Company Type: Public
Profile: The international energy trust is engaged in acquiring, developing, & optimizing producing properties. Activities take place in western Canada, western Europe, & Australia.

Vero Energy Inc.
#1400, 333 - 5th Ave. SW, Calgary, AB T2P 3B6
Tel: 403-218-2063; *Fax:* 403-218-2064
Toll-Free: 866-709-8376
general.info@veroenergy.ca
www.veroenergy.ca
Ticker Symbol: VRO
Company Type: Public
Profile: Vero Energy Inc. specializes in oil & natural gas exploration, development, & production.

Westcoast Energy Inc
#2600, 425 - 1st St. SW, Calgary, AB T2P 3L8
Tel: 403-699-1999; *Fax:* 403-699-1998
www.spectraenergy.com
Ticker Symbol: W.PR.J
Company Type: Public
Profile: Operating under the name, Spectra Energy Transmission, the company owns & operates businesses which are engaged in natural gas gathering, processing, storage, transmission, & distribution.

Winstar Resources Ltd.
#845, 401 - 9th Ave. SW, Calgary, AB T2P 3C5
Tel: 403-205-3722; *Fax:* 403-205-2722
Toll-Free: 800-875-1217
info@winstar.ca
www.winstar.ca
Ticker Symbol: WIX
Company Type: Public
Profile: Winstar Resources Ltd. is an oil & gas exploration & development company. Operations are carried out in Canada, Romania, Hungary, & Tunisia.

Zargon Energy Trust
#700, 333 - 5th Ave. SW, Calgary, AB T2P 3B6
Tel: 403-264-9992; *Fax:* 403-265-3026
zargon@zargon.ca
www.zargon.ca
Ticker Symbol: ZAR
Company Type: Public
Profile: Zargon Energy Trust is involved in oil & natural gas exploration, development, & production. The organization is active in the Alberta plains, west central Alberta, & the Williston Basin core area.

ZCL Composites Inc.
6907 - 36 St., Edmonton, AB T6B 2Z6
Fax: 780-466-6126
Toll-Free: 800-661-8265
ir@zcl.com
www.zcl.com
Ticker Symbol: ZCL
Company Type: Public
Profile: ZCL Composites Inc. designs, manufactures & distributes fiberglass tank systems. The environmentally friendly liquid handling solutions are used by the petroleum industry.

Port Authorities

Halifax Port Authority
PO Box 336, 1215 Marginal Rd., Halifax, NS B3H 4P8
Tel: 902-426-8222; *Fax:* 902-426-7335
www.portofhalifax.ca
Company Type: Crown
Profile: Cargo: Bulk Cargo (Oil, Fuel, Gypsum) - 8.8 million metric tones Breakbulk Cargo (Iron/Steel, Machinery, Rubber) - 136,000 metric tones Roll-on, Roll-off Cargo (Cars and Trucks) - 216,000 metric tones Containerized Cargo - 4.6 million metric tones

Hamilton Port Authority
605 James St. North, 6th Floor, Hamilton, ON L8L 1K1
Tel: 905-525-4330; *Fax:* 905-528-6554
Toll-Free: 800-263-2131
cargo@hamiltonport.ca
www.hamiltonport.ca
Company Type: Crown

Montreal Port Authority
Édifice du port de Montréal, 2100, av Pierre-Dupuy, Aile #1, Montréal, QC H3C 3R5
Tel: 514-283-7011; *Fax:* 514-283-0829
www.port-montreal.com
Company Type: Crown
Profile: The Montreal port offers year-round access to major markets in central Canada, & the midwestern & northeastern United States.

Nanaimo Port Authority
PO Box 131, 104 Front St., Nanaimo, BC V9R 5K4
Tel: 250-753-4146; *Fax:* 250-753-4899
info@npa.ca
www.npa.ca/en/index.htm
Company Type: Crown
Profile: The harbour, waters, & foreshore of the Georgia Strait are administered, controlled, & managed by the Nanimo Port Authority.

Port Alberni Port Authority
2750 Harbour Rd., Port Alberni, BC V9Y 7X2
Tel: 250-723-5312; *Fax:* 250-723-1114
bfilipchuk.papa@portalberni.ca
www.portalberniportauthority.ca
Company Type: Crown
Profile: Under the Canada Marine Act, the Port Alberni Port Authority has jurisdiction of the Alberni Inlet, from the Somass River to Tzartus Island. The Inlet offers a direct shipping route to the Pacific Rim & can accommodate Panama size vessels.

Port of Belledune
112, Shannon Dr., Belledune, NB E8G 2W2
Tel: 506-522-1200; *Fax:* 506-522-0803
info@portofbelledune.ca
www.portofbelledune.ca
Company Type: Crown
Profile: The Port of Belledune is a year-round marine transport facility, offering access to north-eastern & global markets. The port serves shipping companies, importers, & exporters.

Prince Rupert Port Authority
#200, 215 Cow Bay Rd., Prince Rupert, BC V8J 1A2
Tel: 250-627-8899; *Fax:* 250-627-8980
www.rupertport.com
Company Type: Crown
Profile: The Prince Rupert Port Authority operates the port in the Prince Rupert Harbour, under the Canada Marine Act, & Letters Patent issued under the Act. The Authority facilitates the movement of cargo & passengers through the port in a safe & environmentally sound manner. Its responsibilities include the planning, development, marketing, & management of the commercial port facilities.

Québec Port Authority
PO Box 80 Haute-Ville, 150, rue Dalhousie, Québec, QC G1R 4M8
Tel: 418-648-3640; *Fax:* 418-649-6414
marketing@portquebec.ca
www.portquebec.ca
Company Type: Crown
Profile: The Québec Port Authority is an independent federal agency which serves the economic interests of Québec & Canada by developing & promoting maritime trade. The port authority is involved in commercial exchanges with countries around the world.

Saguenay Port Authority
6600, rue Quai-Marcel-Dionne, La Baie, QC G7B 3N9
Tel: 418-697-0250; *Fax:* 418-697-0243
info@portsaguenay.ca
www.portsaguenay.ca
Company Type: Crown
Profile: Under the Canada Marine Act, the Saguenay Port Authority provides services that promote & expand Canada's foreign trade. The port authority also works to develop the port's hinterland, especially the area of Saguenay-Lac-Saint-Jean-Chibougamau-Chapais. The Saguenay Port Authority consists of the Grande-Anse Marine Terminal, for the reception & transshipment of general cargo, & the Albert Maltais Oil Terminal, for the reception of oil.

Saint John Port Authority
111 Water St., Saint John, NB E2L 0B1
Tel: 506-636-4869; *Fax:* 506-636-4443
port@sjport.com
www.sjport.com
Company Type: Crown
Profile: The Port of Saint John is an international seaport which accommodates a variety of shipping services, from shipping lines to cruise ships & ferry services. The port is important to New Brunswick's import & export trade, handling an average of 27 million metric tonnes of cargo each year.

Sept-Iles Port Authority
1 Quai Mgr-Blanche, Sept-Iles, QC G4R 5P3
Tel: 418-968-1231; *Fax:* 418-962-4445
www.portsi.com/eg/default.htm
Company Type: Crown

Toronto Port Authority
60 Harbour St., Toronto, ON M5J 1B7
Tel: 416-863-2000; *Fax:* 416-863-4830
www.torontoport.com
Company Type: Crown
Profile: Maintains a paved facility of over 50 acres centrally located, adjacent to downtown Toronto. The yard provides convenience, with excellent access to the railroads, as well as all major highways. This facility is fully bonded and has 24-hour security

Vancouver Fraser Port Authority
999 Canada Place, 100 The Pointe, Vancouver, BC V6C 3T4
Tel: 604-665-9000; *Fax:* 866-284-4271
www.nfpa.ca/engindex.html
Company Type: Crown
Profile: In 2008, the Vancouver Port Authority, the Fraser River Port Authority, & the North Fraser Port Authority combined to create the Vancouver Fraser Port Authority. The port authority offers twenty-eight marine cargo terminals, plus three Class 1 railroads to serve the international shipping community.

Windsor Port Authority
#502, 251 Goyeau St., Windsor, ON N9A 6V2
Tel: 519-258-5741; *Fax:* 519-258-5905
www.portwindsor.com
Company Type: Crown
Profile: Located on the Great Lakes / St. Lawrence Seaway System, the Windsor Port Authority carries out the following activities: administration of federal lands within the port; representation of port users at the municipal, provincial, & federal levels; facilitation of economic development & trade; development & promotion of the port; provision of general security; & ensuring safety & environmental responsibility in all operations.

Printing & Publishing

Canadian Bank Note Company, Limited
145 Richmond Rd., Ottawa, ON K1Z 1A1
Tel: 613-722-3421; *Fax:* 613-722-2548
headoffice@cbnco.com
www.cbnco.com
Ticker Symbol: CBK
Company Type: Public
Profile: Manufacturers of security-printed products; production divisions include: Lottery Systems, Identification Systems, Payment Systems, and Shareholder Services

Datamark Systems Group Inc.
2800, av Francis-Hughes, Laval, QC H7L 3Y7
Tel: 450-663-8716; *Fax:* 450-663-7720
Toll-Free: 888-360-0470
www.datamark.ca
Ticker Symbol: DMK
Company Type: Public
Profile: Manufacturers of manifold business forms, various, gravure & lithographic commercial printing

FP Newspapers Income Fund
1355 Mountain Ave., Winnipeg, MB R2X 3B6
Tel: 204-697-7364; *Fax:* 204-697-7344
www.fpnewspapers.com
Ticker Symbol: FP.UN
Company Type: Public
Profile: FP Newspapers Income Fund is an unincorporated, open-ended, limited purpose trust. It owns indirect interests in FP Canadian Newspapers Limited Partnership (FPLP). The Winnipeg Free Press & the Brandon Sun are two of the newspapers owned & published by FP Canadian Newspapers Limited Partnership.

Glacier Media Inc.
1970 Alberta St., Vancouver, BC V5Y 3X4
Tel: 604-872-8565; *Fax:* 604-879-1483
www.glacierventures.com
Ticker Symbol: GVC
Company Type: Public
Profile: Glacier Media Inc. provides information & related services through print, electronic, & online media. The Business & Professional Group consists of organizations such as CD-Pharma, Eco Log ERIS, & Fundata. The Newspaper & Trade Group is comprised of organizations such as Western Producer Publications, Farm Business Communications, & the Business Information Group.

GVIC Communications Corp.
275 West 4th Ave., Vancouver, BC V5Y 1G8
Tel: 604-872-8565; *Fax:* 604-879-1483
osmysnuik@madison.ca
Ticker Symbol: GCT
Company Type: Public
Profile: GVIC Communications is an information communications company. It owns local newspapers in western Canada, as well as trade, business, & professional information businesses.

Hollinger Inc.
#512, 120 Adelaide Street West, Toronto, ON M5H 1T1
Tel: 416-363-8721; *Fax:* 416-363-4187
www.hollingerinc.com
Ticker Symbol: HLG
Company Type: Public
Profile: Offices of holding companies; Information retrieval services; Media broadcasting; Publishing & printing of newspapers & periodicals

McGraw-Hill Ryerson Limited
300 Water St., Whitby, ON L1N 9B6
Tel: 905-430-5000; *Fax:* 905-430-5020
Toll-Free: 800-463-5885
gordond@mcgrawhill.ca
www.mcgrawhill.ca
Ticker Symbol: MHR
Company Type: Public
Profile: McGraw-Hill Ryerson publishes & distributes educational, technical, & professional books & reference materials. The publishing company also provides multi-media products & services.

MDC Partners
45 Hazelton Ave., Toronto, ON M5R 2E3
Tel: 416-960-9000; *Fax:* 416-960-9555
www.mdc-partners.com
Ticker Symbol: MDZ
Company Type: Public
Profile: A portfolio of marketing communications companies

Metro Label Company Inc.
99 Progress Ave., Toronto, ON M1B 6J1
Tel: 416-292-6600; *Fax:* 416-292-6133
Toll-Free: 800-668-4405
sales@metrolabel.com; jobs@metrolabel.com
www.metrolabel.com
Company Type: Private
Profile: Metro Label Company Inc. is a manufacturer of pressure sensitive labels.

PLM Group
210 Duffield Dr., Markham, ON L6G 1C9
Tel: 416-848-8500; *Fax:* 416-848-8501
Toll-Free: 866-848-8500
contact_us@plmgroup.com
www.plmgroup.com
Company Type: Private
Profile: The commercial printing company delivers innovative print solutions. PLM Group serves agencies & corporations such as those in the promotional & print-for-one markets. Brand names include Mailer Magic & Optium.

Pollard Banknote Income Fund
1499 Buffalo Pl., Winnipeg, MB R3T 1L7
Tel: 204-474-2323; *Fax:* 204-453-1375
winnipeg@pollardbanknote.com
www.pollardbanknote.com
Ticker Symbol: PBL.UN
Company Type: Public
Profile: Pollard Banknote Income Fund is an unincorporated, open-ended, limited purpose trust. It holds indirectly an investment in Pollard Holdings Limited Partnership. The Fund is involved in the printing of instant-win scratch tickets & break open/pull tab tickets, as well as the provision of related services to the lottery & charitable gaming industry.

Quebecor World Inc.
612, rue Saint-Jacques, Montréal, QC H3C 4M8
Tel: 514-954-0101; *Fax:* 514-954-9624
Toll-Free: 800-567-7070
webmaster@quebecorworldinc.com
www.quebecorworldinc.com
Ticker Symbol: IQW
Company Type: Public
Profile: Manufacturers of lithographic, gravure & various commercial printing, paper mills & book printing

Technicolor Canada Inc.
40 Lesmill Rd., Don Mills, ON M3B 2T5
Fax: 416-449-3001
www.technicolor.com
Company Type: Public
Profile: Full port production, transfer, editing, visual effects, lab service & audio

Thomson Reuters
Toronto-Dominion Bank Tower, 66 Wellington St. West, Toronto, ON M5K 1A1
Tel: 416-360-8700;
investor.relations@thomsonreuters.com
www.thomsonreuters.com
Ticker Symbol: TRI
Company Type: Public
Profile: Thomson Reuters provides intelligent information for businesses & professionals.

Torstar Corporation
#600, 1 Yonge St., Toronto, ON M5E 1P9
Tel: 416-869-4010; *Fax:* 416-869-4183
torstar@thestar.ca
www.torstar.com
Ticker Symbol: TS
Company Type: Public
Profile: The media company includes the following businesses: Star Media Group, which features the Toronto Star & Torstar Digital; Metroland Media Group, which publishes community & daily newspapers throughout Ontario; & Harlequin Enterprises, which publishes books for women. Torstar Corporation also owns parts of CTVglobemedia Inc. & Black Press.

Transcontinental Inc.
#3315, 1, Place Ville Marie, Montréal, QC H3B 3N2
Tel: 514-954-4000; *Fax:* 514-954-4016
info@transcontinental.ca
www.transcontinental.com
Ticker Symbol: TCL.A
Company Type: Public
Profile: The company is engaged in the printing & publishing of consumer magazines & community newspapers, as well as direct marketing, & distribution of advertising material. Transcontinental Inc. has worked to address environmental issues, by programs such as the implementation of the Transcontinental Paper Purchasing Policy.

Yellow Pages Income Fund
Ile des Soeurs, 16, Place du Commerce, Verdun, QC H3E 2A5
Tel: 514-934-2611; *Toll-Free:* 877-909-9356
ir.info@ypg.com
www.ypg.com
Ticker Symbol: YLO
Company Type: Public
Profile: Yellow Pages Income Fund indirectly holds 97% ownership interest in Yellow Pages Group & Trader Corporation. Yellow Pages Group publishes telephone directories. The Trader Corporation is engaged in print & online vertical media.

Real Estate

Accommodation and Real Estate Services
3350 Douglas St., Victoria, BC V8Z 3L1
Tel: 250-952-8500; *Fax:* 250-952-8295
ARES@gov.bc.ca
www.accommodationandrealestate.gov.bc.ca
Company Type: Crown
Profile: Real estate operators of nonresidential buildings; General contractors of nonresidential buildings; Real estate agents & managers; Management services

Allied Hotel Properties Inc.
#300, 515 West Pender St., Vancouver, BC V6B 6H5
Tel: 604-669-5335; *Fax:* 604-682-8131
info@alliedhotels.com
www.alliedhotels.com
Ticker Symbol: AHP
Company Type: Public
Profile: Allied Hotel Properties Inc. owns first class business hotels in Canadian urban centres. The organization's principal hotel properties are the Crowne Plaza Chateau Lacombe Hotel & the Crowne Plaza Toronto Don Valley Hotel.

Allied Properties Real Estate Investment Trust
255 Adelaide St. West, Toronto, ON M5H 1X9
Tel: 416-977-9002; *Fax:* 416-977-9053
info@alliedpropertiesreit.com
www.alliedpropertiesreit.com
Ticker Symbol: AP.UN
Company Type: Public
Profile: Allied Properties REIT is the owner of office properties. Properties are located in Winnipeg, Toronto, Montréal, & Québec.

Altus Group Income Fund
#7, 17075 Leslie St., Newmarket, ON L3Y 8E1
Tel: 905-953-9948; *Fax:* 905-953-0018
Toll-Free: 877-953-9948
info@altusgroup.com
www.altusgroupincomefund.com
Ticker Symbol: AIF.UN
Company Type: Public
Profile: Altus Group Income Fund is involved in the provision of independent real estate consulting & advisory services. The following are the organization's business units: cost consulting; research, valuation, & advisory; environmental & forestry services; & geomatics.

Amica Mature Lifestyles Inc.
1111 Melville St., 10th Fl., Vancouver, BC V6E 3V6
Tel: 604-608-6777; *Fax:* 604-608-6717
Toll-Free: 877-447-4827
mail@amica.ca
www.amica.ca
Ticker Symbol: ACC
Company Type: Public
Profile: Amica Mature Lifestyles Inc. is a designer, developer, manager, & marketer of seniors' retirement residences & services. Amica has locations in Ontario & British Columbia.

Anthem Works Ltd.
#300, 550 Burrard St., Vancouver, BC V6C 2B5
Tel: 604-689-3040; *Fax:* 604-689-5642
Toll-Free: 800-926-8436
info@anthemproperties.com
www.anthemproperties.com
Ticker Symbol: ANT
Company Type: Private
Profile: Real estate agents & managers; real estate land subdividers & developers

Artis Real Estate Investment Trust
#300, 360 Main St., Winnipeg, MB R3C 3Z3
Tel: 204-947-1250; *Fax:* 204-947-0453
info@artisreit.com
www.artisreit.com
Ticker Symbol: AX.UN
Company Type: Public
Profile: Artis REIT is an open-end real estate investment trust. It produces distributions for unitholders from its ownership & management of retail, commercial, & industrial properties. Properties are located in western Canada.

Aspen Properties Ltd.
#1200, 833 - 4th Ave. SW, Calgary, AB T2P 3T5
Tel: 403-216-2660; *Fax:* 403-216-2661
apl@aspenpropertiesltd.com
www.aspenpropertiesltd.com
Company Type: Private

Profile: Real estate agents & managers; Real estate land subdividers & developers

Bentall LP
Four Bentall Centre, PO Box 49001, #1800, 1055 Dunsmuir St., Vancouver, BC V7X 1B1
Tel: 604-661-5000; *Fax:* 604-661-5055
info@bentall.com
www.bentall.com
Company Type: Private
Profile: Provides real estate investment management services, property development & merchant banking

Berwick Retirement Communities Ltd.
1162 Fort St., Victoria, BC V8V 3K8
Tel: 250-385-1505; *Fax:* 250-385-9851
Toll-Free: 866-397-5463
mail@berwickrc.com
www.berwickrc.com
Ticker Symbol: BWK
Company Type: Public
Profile: Residential care; Real estate operators of non-apartment building dwellings

Boardwalk Real Estate Income Trust
#200, 1501 - 1st St. SW, Calgary, AB T2R 0W1
Tel: 403-531-9255; *Fax:* 403-531-9565
investor@bwalk.com
www.bwalk.com
Ticker Symbol: BEI.UN
Company Type: Public
Profile: Real estate operators of apartment buildings; Real estate real estate agents & managers

Boston Development Corp.
#201, 3550 Taylor St. East, Saskatoon, SK S7H 5H9
Tel: 306-955-6012; *Fax:* 306-955-3446
neil@bostoncorp.com
www.bostoncorp.com
Ticker Symbol: BTN
Company Type: Private
Profile: Real estate operators of apartment buildings

BPO Properties Ltd.
Brookfield Place, PO Box 770, #330, 181 Bay St., Toronto, ON M5J 2T3
Tel: 416-359-8555; *Fax:* 416-359-8596
info@bpoproperties.com
www.bpoproperties.com
Ticker Symbol: BPP
Company Type: Public
Profile: The Canadian commercial real estate company is engaged in the ownership, development, & management of office properties. BPO Properties has endeavoured to develop several environmental initiatives in its properties, such as energy savings programs, environmentally sensitive fittings & finishes, & recycling.

Brookfield Properties Corporation
Brookfield Place, #330, 181 Bay St., Toronto, ON M5J 2T3
Tel: 416-369-2300; *Fax:* 416-369-2301
melissa.coley@brookfieldproperties.com
www.brookfieldproperties.com
Ticker Symbol: BPO
Company Type: Public
Profile: The corporation owns, develops and manages office properties. Brookfield's portfolio includes the following places: Bankers Hall in Calgary, BCE Place in Toronto, World Financial Center in New York, & Bank of America Plaza in Los Angeles. The company is working towards developing properties that are sustainable & environmentally friendly, by ensuring that all future developments are built to a Leadership in Energy & Environmental Design (LEED) Gold standard.

Brookfield Real Estate Services Fund
39 Wynford Dr., Toronto, ON M3C 3K5
Tel: 416-510-5853; *Fax:* 416-446-0050
info@brookfieldres.com
www.brookfieldres.com
Ticker Symbol: BRE.UN
Company Type: Public
Profile: Brookfield Real Estate Services Fund is involved in the provision of services to residential real estate franchisees & agents across Canada. Cash flow is generated from franchise royalties & service fees from realtors. Realtors operate under the brand names Royal LePage, La Capitale Real Estate Network, & Johnston & Daniel.

Cadillac Fairview Corporation Limited
20 Queen St. West, 5th Fl., Toronto, ON M5H 3R4
Tel: 416-598-8200; *Fax:* 416-598-8607
www.cadillacfairview.com
Company Type: Private
Profile: Real estate operators of nonresidential buildings; Real estate agents & managers; Real estate land subdividers & developers

Calloway Real Estate Investment Trust
#200, 700 Applewood Cres., Vaughan, ON L4K 5X3
Tel: 905-326-6400; *Fax:* 905-326-0783
investorrelations@callowayreit.com
www.callowayreit.com
Ticker Symbol: CWT.UN
Company Type: Public
Profile: Calloway REIT is an unincorporated, open-end real estate investment trust. It focuses on owning & developing high quality retail properties. Its portfolio consists of leaseable area throughout Canada.

Charlwood Pacific Group
#900, 1199 West Pender St., Vancouver, BC V6E 2R1
Tel: 604-718-2600; *Fax:* 604-718-2678
Company Type: Private
Profile: Travel & real estate franchising company made up of brands such as Uniglobe Travel International, Century 21 Canada and Centum Financial Group.

CML Global Capital Ltd.
#1200, 833 - 4th Ave. SW, Calgary, AB T2P 3T5
Tel: 403-216-3850; *Fax:* 403-216-2661
Company Type: Private
Profile: Offices of holding companies; Real estate land subdividers & developers; Automobile parking

CMN International Inc.
#1910, 200 Granville St., Vancouver, BC V6C 2R6
Tel: 604-681-4111; *Fax:* 604-661-0849
www.colliersmn.com
Company Type: Public
Profile: Commercial real estate services: brokerage, property management, valuation and market research

Cominar Real Estate Investment Trust
455, rue du Marais, Québec, QC G1M 3A2
Tel: 418-681-8151; *Fax:* 418-681-2946
info@cominar.com
www.cominar.com
Ticker Symbol: CUF
Company Type: Public
Profile: The unincorporated closed-end investment trust owns & manages commercial property in the Quebec City, Montreal, & Ottawa region.

Consolidated HCI Holdings Corporation
#3, 100 Strada Dr., Woodbridge, ON L4L 5V7
Tel: 905-851-7741; *Fax:* 416-253-5074
ewdl@sympatico.ca
Ticker Symbol: CXA
Company Type: Public
Profile: The Ontario-based real estate company invests in syndicated mortgage loans. Through joint ventures, it is also engaged in housebuilding & the leasing of commercial & industrial properties.

Crombie Real Estate Investment Trust
115 King St., Stellarton, NS B0K 1S0
Tel: 902-755-8100; *Fax:* 902-752-5136
investing@crombie.ca
www.crombiereit.ca
Ticker Symbol: CRR.UN
Company Type: Public
Profile: Crombie REIT owns & manages properties across Saskatchewan, Ontario, Quebec, & Atlantic Canada. Office buildings & shopping centres are the organizations's main properties.

Dundee Real Estate Investment Trust
State Street Financial Centre, #1600, 30 Adelaide St. East, Toronto, ON M5C 3H1
Tel: 416-365-3535; *Fax:* 416-365-6565
info@dundeereit.com
www.dundeereit.com
Ticker Symbol: D.UN
Company Type: Public
Profile: Dundee REIT is engaged in acquiring, owning, managing, & leasing mid-sized urban & suburban offices & industrial properties across Canada.

Extendicare Real Estate Investment Trust
#700, 3000 Steeles Ave. East, Markham, ON L3R 9W2
Tel: 905-470-4000; *Fax:* 905-470-5588
hgould@extendicare.com
www.extendicare.com
Ticker Symbol: EXE
Company Type: Public
Profile: Through its wholly owned subsidiaries, Extendicare REIT owns & operates retirement, assisted living, & nursing homes. In Canada, Extendicare REIT's wholly owned subsidiary is Extendicare (Canada) Inc. (ECI), & its division is ParaMed Home Health Care.

First Capital Realty Inc.
#400, 85 Hanna Ave., Toronto, ON M6K 3S3
Tel: 416-504-4114; *Fax:* 416-941-1655
investor.relations@firstcapitalrealty.ca
www.firstcapitalrealty.ca
Ticker Symbol: FCR
Company Type: Public
Profile: First Capital Realty Inc. owns, develops, & operates shopping centres, anchored by supermarkets & drug stores. Properties are located mainly in metropolitan areas.

FirstService Corporation
#4000, 1140 Bay St., Toronto, ON M5S 2B4
Tel: 416-960-9500; *Fax:* 416-960-5333
info@firstservice.com
www.firstservice.com
Ticker Symbol: FSV
Company Type: Public
Profile: FirstService Corporation is involved in residential property management, property improvement services, & commerical real estate.

Genesis Land Development Corp.
#200, 3115 - 12 St. NE, Calgary, AB T2E 7J2
Tel: 403-265-8079; *Fax:* 403-266-0746
Toll-Free: 800-341-7211
genesis@genesisland.com
www.genesisland.com
Ticker Symbol: GDC
Company Type: Public
Profile: The community development company operates in British Columbia & Alberta. Most of the land is situated in & around Calgary. Activities include land development, single-family & multi-family home building, & commercial development & leasing.

Homburg Invest Inc.
#600, 1741 Brunswick St., Halifax, NS B3J 3X8
Tel: 902-468-3395; *Fax:* 902-468-2457
sjedynak@homburg.com
www.homburginvest.com
Ticker Symbol: HII
Company Type: Public
Profile: The company is the owner, developer, & operator of residential & commercial real estate, including townhouses, apartments, offices, & retail properties. Properties are located in Canada, the United States, Germany, & The Netherlands.

InnVest Real Estate Investment Trust
#700, 5090 Explorer Dr., Mississauga, ON L4W 4T9
Tel: 905-206-7100; *Fax:* 905-206-7114
Toll-Free: 877-209-3429
investor@innvestreit.com
www.innvestreit.com
Ticker Symbol: INN.UN
Company Type: Public
Profile: InnVest Real Estate Investment Trust holds a portfolio of hotels. The portfolio of limited service & full service hotel properties operate under the following brands: Holiday Inn, Radisson, Travelodge, Best Western, Comfort Inn, Quality Suites, Delta, & Hilton.

Intrawest ULC
#800, 200 Burrard St., Vancouver, BC V6C 3L6
Tel: 604-669-9777; *Fax:* 604-669-0605
intrainfo@intrawest.com
www.intrawest.com
Ticker Symbol: ITW
Company Type: Public
Profile: Development and management of experiential destination resorts

Ivanhoe Cambridge
Centre CDP Capital, #C-500, 1001 square Victoria, Montréal, QC H2Z 2B5
Tel: 514-841-7600; *Fax:* 514-841-7762
communications@ivanhoecambridge.com
www.ivanhoecambridge.com
Company Type: Private
Profile: Property owners, managers & developers of shopping centres in urban areas

King George Financial Corporation
#604, 905 West Pender St., Vancouver, BC V6C 1L6
Tel: 604-687-8882; *Fax:* 604-687-1476
billc@kinggeorge.ca
Ticker Symbol: KGF
Company Type: Public
Profile: Real estate-operators of nonresidential buildings; Real estate-operators of apartment buildings; Real estate-land subdividers & developers

Kruger Capital Corp.
#300, 550 Burrard St., Vancouver, BC V6C 2B5
Tel: 604-689-3040; *Fax:* 604-689-5642
Company Type: Public
Profile: Offices of holding companies; Real estate agents & managers

Madison Pacific Properties Inc.
389 West 6th Ave., Vancouver, BC V5Y 1L1
Tel: 604-732-6540; *Fax:* 604-732-6550
reception@madisonpacific.ca
www.madisonpacific.ca
Ticker Symbol: MPC
Company Type: Public
Profile: Madison Pacific Properties Inc. is a real estate investment & development company. Its properties are located in Greater Vancouver.

Mainstreet Equity Corp.
#100, 1122 - 8th Ave. SW, Calgary, AB T2P 1J5
Tel: 403-215-6060; *Fax:* 403-266-8867
mainstreet@mainst.biz
www.mainst.biz
Ticker Symbol: MEQ
Company Type: Public
Profile: Real estate operators of apartment buildings; Real estate agents & managers

Melcor Developments Ltd.
#900, 10310 Jasper Ave., Edmonton, AB T5J 1Y8
Tel: 780-423-6931; *Fax:* 780-426-1796
info@melcor.ca
www.melcor.ca
Ticker Symbol: MRD
Company Type: Public
Profile: Melcor Developments acquires land to develop & sell for multi-family sites, residential communities, & commercial sites. The organization is also the owner, developer, & manager of commercial income properties & golf courses.

MI Developments Inc.
455 Magna Dr., Aurora, ON L4G 7A9
Tel: 905-713-6322; *Fax:* 905-713-6332
ir@midevelopments.com
www.midevelopments.com
Ticker Symbol: MIM.A
Company Type: Public
Profile: The real estate company is the owner, leaser, developer, & manager of industrial & commercial properties. MI Developments Inc.'s real estate properties are located in North America & Europe. The company also holds a controlling interest in Magna Entertainment Corp.

Mont Saint-Sauveur International Inc.
350, av Saint-Denis, Saint-Sauveur, QC J0R 1R3
Tel: 450-227-4671; *Fax:* 450-227-2065
Toll-Free: 800-363-2426
webmaster@mssi.ca
www.montsaintsaveur.com
Ticker Symbol: MSX
Company Type: Public
Profile: Ski resorts, hotels & motels; real estate

Morguard Corporation
#1000, 55 City Centre Dr., Mississauga, ON L5B 1M3
Tel: 905-281-3800; *Fax:* 905-281-5890
info@morguard.com
www.morguard.com
Ticker Symbol: MRC
Company Type: Public
Profile: Morguard Corporation is a real estate & property management company. Through its investments in Morguard REIT & Revenue Properties Company Limited, the corporation has a diversified portfolio of residential, office, retail, & industrial properties owned or under management. Through Morguard Investments Limited, management services to institutional & other investors for residential & commercial real estate are offered.

MP Western Properties Inc.
389 West 6th Ave., Vancouver, BC V5Y 1L1
Tel: 604-732-6540; *Fax:* 604-732-6550
reception@madisonpacific.ca
Ticker Symbol: MPW.H
Company Type: Public
Profile: Real estate operators of nonresidential buildings; Real estate operators of apartment buildings; Real estate land subdividers & developers

Northern Property Real Estate Investment Trust
#110, 6131 - 6th St. SE, Calgary, AB T2H 1L9
Tel: 403-531-0720; *Fax:* 403-531-0727
info@npreit.com
www.npreit.com
Ticker Symbol: NPR
Company Type: Public
Profile: Northern Property Real Estate Investment Trust is an unincorporated, open-end real estate investment trust. The Trust invests in mainly residential income-producing properties. Commercial buildings & executive suites are also owned by the Trust. Properties are situated in Newfoundland & Labrador, Alberta, northeastern British Columbia, Nunavut & the Northwest Territories.

Oxford Properties Group Inc.
Oxford Tower, #1100, 130 Adelaide St. West, Toronto, ON M5H 3P5
Tel: 416-865-8300; *Fax:* 416-868-3751
www.oxfordproperties.com
Company Type: Private
Profile: Commercial real estate investment firm; Owner & manager of a portfolio of office, retail, industrial & multi-family residential properties across Canada; Holder of interests in real estate assets abroad

Pacific & Western Credit Corp.
#2002, 140 Fullarton St., London, ON N6A 5P2
Tel: 519-645-1919; *Fax:* 519-645-2060
investorrelations@pwbank.com
www.pwbank.com
Ticker Symbol: PWC
Company Type: Public
Profile: Banking & financial services

Parkbridge Lifestyle Communities Inc.
#700, 505 - 3rd St. SW, Calgary, AB T2P 3E6
Tel: 403-215-2100; *Fax:* 403-215-2115
info@parkbridge.ca
www.parkbridge.ca
Ticker Symbol: PRK
Company Type: Public
Profile: Parkbridge Lifestyle Communities Inc. owns, develops, & operates land use communities. Communities are located in British Columbia, Alberta, Ontario, & Quebec. Parkbridge specializes in the following sectors: marinas, family & senior communities, chalets, cottage & RV communities, & lifestyle communities.

Plazacorp Retail Properties Ltd.
#200, 527 Queen St., Fredericton, NB E3B 1B8
Tel: 506-451-1826; *Fax:* 506-451-1802
info@plaza.ca
www.plaza.ca
Ticker Symbol: PLZ
Company Type: Public
Profile: Plazacorp Retail Properties Ltd. is engaged in the acquisition, development, & re-development of enclosed mall shopping centres, strip centres, & freestanding retail properties. Operations take place in Ontario, Québec, New Brunswick, Nova Scotia, Prince Edward Island, & Newfoundland.

Retrocom Mid-Market Real Estate Investment Trust
PO Box 204, #214, 4025 Yonge St., Toronto, ON M2P 2E3
Tel: 416-741-7999; *Fax:* 416-741-7993
info@rmmreit.com
www.rmmreit.com
Ticker Symbol: RMM.UN
Company Type: Public
Profile: The Retrocom Mid-Market REIT acquires & owns mid-market commercial properties in cities throughout Canada.

Revenue Properties Company Limited
#800, 55 City Centre Dr., Mississauga, ON L5B 1M3
Tel: 905-281-3800; *Fax:* 905-281-5890
pmiatello@morguard.com
www.revprop.com
Ticker Symbol: RPC
Company Type: Public
Profile: Real estate operators of nonresidential buildings, apartment buildings & other dwellings; Land subdividers and developers

RioCan Real Estate Investment Trust
RioCan Yonge Eglinton Centre, PO Box 2386, #500, 2300 Yonge St., Toronto, ON M4P 1E4
Tel: 416-866-3033; *Fax:* 416-866-3020
Toll-Free: 800-465-2733
inquiries@riocan.com; ir@riocan.com
www.riocan.com
Ticker Symbol: REI
Company Type: Public
Profile: The Trust owns a portfolio of retail properties throughout Canada.

Royal Host Real Estate Investment Trust
#103, 808 - 42 Ave. SE, Calgary, AB T2G 1Y9
Tel: 403-259-9800; *Fax:* 403-259-8580
investorinfo@royalhost.com
www.royalhost.com
Ticker Symbol: RYL
Company Type: Public
Profile: The open-end unincorporated investment trust invests in & manages hotel properties. Royal Host REIT owns the master franchise rights for Thriftlodge & Travelodge in Canada.

United Communities Inc.
#200, 808 - 4 Ave. SW, Calgary, AB T2P 3E8
Tel: 403-265-6180; *Fax:* 403-265-6270
info@unitedcommunities.com
www.unitedcommunities.com
Company Type: Private
Profile: The real estate development company has operations in the following areas: Calgary & Edmonton, Alberta, Sacramento, California, & Kimberley, British Columbia. United Communities Inc. builds architecturally controlled & themed communities to satisfy the needs of families.

Wall Financial Corporation
#3502, 1088 Burrard St., Vancouver, BC V6Z 2R9
Tel: 604-893-7131; *Fax:* 604-893-7179
Ticker Symbol: WFC
Company Type: Public
Profile: The corporation is engaged in the following acitivites: real estate development; investment in properties; management of residential rental apartments & hotel properties; & development & construction of residential housing for resale.

Services, Miscellaneous

Arbor Memorial Services Inc.
#211, 2 Jane St., Toronto, ON M6S 4W8
Tel: 416-763-4531; *Fax:* 416-763-4821
lhowe@arbormemorial.com
www.arbormemorial.com
Ticker Symbol: ABO
Company Type: Public
Profile: Arbor Memorial Services Inc. is the owner of the following: reception centres, crematoria, funeral homes, & cemeteries. Services are available in all Canadian provinces, except Prince Edward Island & Newfoundland & Labrador.

Atlantic Lottery Corporation Inc.
PO Box 5500, 922 Main St., Moncton, NB E1C 8W6
Tel: 506-867-5825; *Toll-Free:* 800-561-3942
info@alc.ca
www.alc.ca
Company Type: Public
Profile: Amusement and recreation services (various)

BFI Canada Income Fund
#300, 135 Queens Plate Dr., Toronto, ON M9W 6V1
Tel: 416-741-5221; *Fax:* 416-741-4565
investorrelations@bficanada.com
www.bficanada.com
Ticker Symbol: BFC
Company Type: Public
Profile: The waste management company provides non-hazardous solid waste collection & landfill disposal services. BFI Canada serves residential, commercial, industrial, & municipal customers in Canada & the United States.

Boyd Group Income Fund
3570 Portage Ave., Winnipeg, MB R3K 0Z8
Tel: 204-895-1244; *Fax:* 204-895-1283
info@boydgroup.com
www.boydgroup.com
Ticker Symbol: BYD
Company Type: Public
Profile: Boyd Group Income Fund is an unincorporated, open-ended mutual fund trust. The Fund has an interest in the Boyd Group Inc. & its subsidiaries. Boyd Group Inc. operates collision repair facilities. Operations are situated in western Canada & the United States. The organization's trade names include Boyd Autobody & Glass & Service Collision Repair & Gerber Collision & Glass.

Canadian Commercial Corporation
50 O'Connor St., 11th Floor, Ottawa, ON K1A 0S6
Tel: 613-996-0034; *Fax:* 613-995-2121
Toll-Free: 800-748-8191
info@ccc.ca
www.ccc.ca
Company Type: Crown
Profile: The organization is engaged in the administration of general economic programs.

Canlan Ice Sports Corp
6501 Sprott St., Burnaby, BC V5B 3B8
Tel: 604-736-9152; *Fax:* 604-736-9170
info@icesports.com
www.canlanicesports.com
Ticker Symbol: ICE
Company Type: Public
Profile: Amusement and recreation services (various)

ClubLink Corporation
15675 Dufferin St., King City, ON L7B 1K5
Tel: 905-841-3730; *Fax:* 905-841-1134
Toll-Free: 800-661-1818
invest@clublink.ca
www.clublink.ca
Ticker Symbol: LNK
Company Type: Public
Profile: ClubLink Corporation owns, develops, & operates member golf clubs, daily fee golf clubs, & resorts.

Compass Group Canada
#400, 5560 Explorer Dr., Mississauga, ON L4W 5M3
Tel: 905-568-4636; *Fax:* 905-568-9392
Toll-Free: 905-568-9392
info@compass-canada.com
www.compass-canada.com
Company Type: Private
Profile: Catering & retail eating places

Fairmont Hotels & Resorts Inc.
Canadian Pacific Tower, PO Box 40 TD Centre, #1600, 100 Wellington St. West, Toronto, ON M5K 1B7
Tel: 416-874-2600; *Fax:* 416-874-2601
communications@fairmont.com
www.fairmont.com
Company Type: Public
Profile: Hotels & motels; Real estate operators of nonresidential buildings

First National AlarmCap
#810, 112 - 4th St. SW, Calgary, AB T2R 1M1
Tel: 403-299-2299; *Fax:* 403-299-2209
www.alarmcap.ca
Ticker Symbol: FNA.UN
Company Type: Public
Profile: First National AlarmCap Income Fund is involved in the provision of electronic security alarm monitoring & services. It indirectly owns & operates Microtec Security & Securex. The full-service alarm organization serves both residential & commercial subscribers.

Four Seasons Hotels Inc.
1165 Leslie St., Toronto, ON M3C 2K8
Tel: 416-449-1750; *Fax:* 416-441-4374
investors@fourseasons.com
www.fourseasons.com
Ticker Symbol: FSH
Company Type: Public
Profile: Hotels & motels

Gamehost Income Fund
#400, 4406 - 50 Ave., Red Deer, AB T4N 3Z5
Tel: 403-346-4545; *Fax:* 403-340-0683
info@gamehost.ca
www.gamehost.ca
Ticker Symbol: GH.UN
Company Type: Public
Profile: Gamehost Income Fund is an unincorporated open-ended limited purpose trust. It is involved in gaming, hospitality, & hotel services in Alberta. Operations include the Boomtown Casino in Fort McMurray, the Great Northern Casino in Grande Prairie, & Service Plus Inns & Suites in Grand Prairie. The Fund is also a joint venture partner in the Stampede Casino & the Deerfoot Inn & Casino Inc. in Calgary.

Garda World Security Corporation
1390, rue Barré, Montréal, QC H3C 1N4
Tel: 514-281-2811; *Fax:* 514-281-2860
Toll-Free: 800-859-1599
info@garda.ca
www.garda.ca
Ticker Symbol: GW
Company Type: Public
Profile: Garda World Security Corporation's areas of expertise are consulting, investigation & security. The firm's operations are located in Canada, the United States, Latin America, Europe, Africa, the Middle East, & Asia.

Great Canadian Gaming Corporation
#200, 13775 Commerce Pkwy., Richmond, BC V6V 2V4
Tel: 604-303-1000; *Fax:* 604-279-8605
info@gcgaming.com
www.gcgaming.com
Ticker Symbol: GC
Company Type: Public
Profile: Great Canadian Gaming Corporation is a gaming & entertainment operator. Operations include entertainment facilities, such as casinos, racetracks, & show theatres. Business is conducted in Nova Scotia, Ontario, British Columbia, & Washington State.

Helix Hearing Care of America Corp.
#203, 815 Taylor Creek Dr., Cumberland, ON K1C 1T1
Tel: 613-824-1154; *Fax:* 613-824-1109
info@helixhca.com
www.helixhca.com
Ticker Symbol: HCA
Company Type: Public
Profile: Hearing care practitioners: audiologists and hearing instrument specialists

K-Bro Linen Income Fund
#103, 15023 - 123 Ave., Edmonton, AB T5V 1J7
Tel: 780-453-5218; *Fax:* 780-455-6676
www.k-brolinen.com
Ticker Symbol: KBL.UN
Company Type: Public
Profile: Through its wholly-owned subsidiary, K-Bro Linen Systems, K-Bro Linen Income Fund is involved in the operation of laundry & linen processing facilities. It serves industrial & commercial sectors, such as hospitality & healthcare. Facilities are located in Toronto, Edmonton, Calgary, Vancouver, & Victoria.

Keystone North America Inc.
#1900, 400 North Ashley Dr., Tampa, FL
Tel: 813-225-4650; *Fax:* 813-225-4655
www.keystonenorthamerica.ca
Ticker Symbol: KNA.UN
Company Type: Public
Profile: Keystone North America Inc. owns & operates funeral homes & cemeteries in Ontario & the United States.

Lions Gate Entertainment Corp.
#2200, 1055 West Hastings St., Vancouver, BC V6E 2E9
Tel: 604-983-5555; *Fax:* 604-983-5554
pwilkes@lgf.com
www.lgf.com
Ticker Symbol: LGF
Company Type: Public
Profile: Lions Gate Entertainment Corp. is a developer, producer, & distributor of television, motion picture, family entertainment, home entertainment, video-on-demand, & digitally delivered content. The company is made up of the following operating divisions: Motion Pictures, Television, Animation, & Studio Facilities.

Lorus Therapeutics Inc.
2 Meridian Rd., Toronto, ON M9W 4Z7
Tel: 416-798-1200; *Fax:* 416-798-2200
info@lorusthera.com; ir@lorusthera.com
www.lorusthera.com
Ticker Symbol: LOR
Company Type: Public
Profile: The biopharmaceutical company is engaged in the research & development of anticancer therapies.

Loto-Québec
500, rue Sherbrooke ouest, Montréal, QC H3A 3G6
Tel: 514-282-8000; *Fax:* 514-873-8999
service_clientele@loto-quebec.com
www.loto-quebec.com
Company Type: Crown
Profile: Oversees games of chance & gambling; operates & monitors casinos, and a video lottery terminal network

MDS Inc.
West Tower, #300, 2700 Matheson Blvd. E., Mississauga, ON L4W 4V9
Tel: 416-675-6777; *Fax:* 416-675-0688
info@mdsinc.com
www.mdsinc.com
Ticker Symbol: MDS
Company Type: Public
Profile: MDS Inc. provides products & services for the development of drugs, & the diagnosis & treatment of disease. Products include radiotherapeutics, medical isotopes for molecular imaging, & analytical instruments.

Morneau Sobeco Income Fund
One Morneau Sobeco Centre, #700, 895 Don Mills Rd., Toronto, ON M3C 1W3
Tel: 416-445-2700; *Fax:* 416-445-4688
info@morneausobeco.com
www.morneausobeco.com
Ticker Symbol: MSI.UN
Company Type: Public
Profile: Morneau Sobeco Income Fund is involved in the provision of human resource consulting & outsourcing services. The firm assists employers with the management of pension & benefit plans for employees.

Newalta Income Fund
211 - 11th Ave. SW, Calgary, AB T2R 0C6
Tel: 403-806-7000; *Fax:* 403-806-7348
Toll-Free: 800-774-8466
info@newalta.com
www.newalta.com
Ticker Symbol: NAL
Company Type: Public
Profile: Newalta Income Fund is part of the Canadian industrial waste management & environmental services industry. Newalta is involved in the recovery of saleable products & recycling, as well as the environmentally sound disposal of solid, non-hazardous industrial waste.

Peace Arch Entertainment Group Inc.
#650, 1867 Yonge St., Toronto, ON M4S 1Y5
Tel: 416-783-8383; *Fax:* 416-783-8384
Toll-Free: 888-588-3608
ryon@trilogy-capital.com
www.peacearch.com
Ticker Symbol: PAE
Company Type: Public
Profile: Offices of holding companies; Motion picture & video tape production

Service Corporation International (Canada) Limited
1835 Hastings St. E., Vancouver, BC V5L 1T3
Tel: 604-806-4100; *Fax:* 604-806-4111
www.sci-corp.com
Company Type: Private
Profile: Network of funeral homes, crematoria & cemeteries

Speedy Corporation
#303, 21 St. Clair Ave. East, Toronto, ON M4T 1L9
Tel: 416-961-1133; *Toll-Free:* 800-387-1410
www.speedy.com
Ticker Symbol: SMK
Company Type: Private
Profile: Speedy specializes in services for cars, light trucks, & SUVs. The company also sells tires & conducts road safety inspections. Speedy Corporation has a wholly owned susidiary called Minute Muffler.

TLC Vision Corporation
#100, 5280 Solar Dr., Mississauga, ON L4W 5M8
Tel: 800-852-1033; *Fax:* 905-602-2025
Toll-Free: 877-852-2020
investor.relations@tlcvision.com
www.tlcv.com
Ticker Symbol: TLC
Company Type: Public
Profile: Offices & clinics of doctors of medicine

Waste Services, Inc.
#600, 1122 International Blvd., Burlington, ON L7L 6Z8
www.wasteservicesinc.com
Company Type: Private
Profile: Waste Services, Inc. is a non-hazardous solid waste services company. It provides collection, transfer, landfill disposal, & recycling services. The company serves residential, commercial, & industrial customers in Ontario, Saskatchewan, Alberta, British Columbia, & the United States.

Steel & Metal

ADF Group Inc.
300, rue Henry-Bessemer, Terrebonne, QC J6Y 1T3
Tel: 450-965-1911; *Fax:* 450-965-8558
infos@adfgroup.com
www.adfgroup.com
Ticker Symbol: DRX
Company Type: Public
Profile: ADF Group Inc. specializes in the design, engineering, fabrication & installation of steel superstructures, architectural, & miscellaneous metals. The company serves the non-residential construction market.

Alcan Inc.
1188 Sherbrook St., Montréal, QC H3A 3G2
Tel: 514-848-8000; *Fax:* 514-848-8115
media.relations@alcan.com
www.alcan.com
Ticker Symbol: AL
Company Type: Public
Profile: Manufacturers of aluminum sheet, plate & foil, aluminum rolling & drawing, primary production of aluminum, aluminum foundries, various industrial inorganic chemicals; Metal mining of miscellaneous metal ores

American Iron & Metal Co. Inc.
9100, boul Henri-Bourassa est, Montréal, QC H1E 2S4
Tel: 514-494-2000; *Fax:* 514-494-3008
info@scrapmetal.net
www.scrapmetal.net
Company Type: Private
Profile: The company is engaged in scrap metals recovery & recycling, providing reusable raw material for industry. ISO 9001:2000 registered.

Arcelor Mittal Dofasco Inc.
PO Box 2460, 1330 Burlington St. East, Hamilton, ON L8N 3J5
Tel: 905-544-3761; *Fax:* 905-545-3236
Toll-Free: 800-363-2726
general@dofasco.ca
www.dofasco.ca
Company Type: Public
Profile: Manufacturers of steel works, blast furnaces, coke ovens, rolling mills, cold-rolled steel sheet, strip & bars, steel pipe & tubes

Babcock & Wilcox Canada, Ltd.
581 Coronation Blvd., Cambridge, ON N1R 5V3
Tel: 519-621-2130; *Fax:* 519-621-9681
www.babcock.com/bwc
Company Type: Private
Profile: Manufacturers of fabricated plate work

Ball Packaging Products Canada, Inc.
1121 Walkers Line, Burlington, ON L7N 2G4
Tel: 905-335-4780; *Fax:* 905-319-4083
info@ball.com
www.ball.com
Company Type: Private
Profile: Ball Packaging Products Canada manufactures metal & plastic packaging for food & beverages. It is also involved in aerospace & other technologies.

Canam Group Inc.
#500, 11505 - 1e av, Saint-Georges, QC G5Y 7H5
Tel: 418-228-8031; *Fax:* 418-228-1750
infocanamcanada@canam.ws
www.canamgroup.ws
Ticker Symbol: CAM
Company Type: Public
Profile: Canam Group Inc. is engaged in the design & fabrication of construction products & solutions.

Crown Cork & Seal Canada Inc.
7900 Keele St., Concord, ON L4K 2A3
Tel: 905-669-1401; *Fax:* 905-669-1692
www.crowncork.com
Company Type: Private
Profile: Manufacturers of metal cans, crowns & closures

ESSAR Steel Algoma Inc.
105 West St., Sault Ste Marie, ON P6A 7B4
Tel: 705-945-2351; *Fax:* 705-945-2203
www.algoma.com
Ticker Symbol: AGA
Company Type: Public
Profile: The company manufactures steel works, blast furnaces, coke ovens, rolling mills, sheet & plate.

Flex-N-Gate Corporation Canada
538 Blanchard Park Dr., Tecumseh, ON N8N 2L9
Tel: 519-727-3931;
mchadwick@flexngate.com
www.flex-n-gate.com
Company Type: Private
Profile: Supplier of truck bumpers & accessories

Foster Wheeler Ltd.
#200, 4954 Richard Rd. SE, Calgary, AB T3E 6L1
Tel: 403-255-3447; *Fax:* 403-259-4558
rcampbell@fwfhl.com
www.fwc.com
Company Type: Private
Profile: Foster Wheeler Ltd. is a manufacturer of fabricated plate work, & general industrial machinery & equipment.

Garneau Inc.
2003 - 5 St., Nisku, AB T9E 7X4
Tel: 780-955-2396; *Fax:* 780-955-7715
darlened@garneau-inc.com
www.garneau-inc.com
Ticker Symbol: GAR
Company Type: Public
Profile: Manufacturers of coating, engraving & allied services, various fabricated metal products

Gerdau Ameristeel Corporation
Hopkins St. South, Whitby, ON L1N 5T1
Tel: 416-297-3700; *Fax:* 416-297-3740
Toll-Free: 800-263-2662
basmith@gerdauameristeel.com
www.gerdauameristeel.com
Ticker Symbol: GNA
Company Type: Public
Profile: Gerdau Ameristeel Corporation manufactures steel products for the automotive, construction, appliance, & machinery industries. Steel scrap is also sourced, traded, & processed by the company.

Groupe Bocenor inc
274, rue Duchesnay, Sainte-Marie, QC G6E 3C2
Tél: 418-387-7723; *Téléc:* 418-387-3904
corpo@bocenor.com
www.bocenor.com
Ticker Symbol: GBO
Company Type: Public
Profile: Manufacturers of metal doors, sash, frames, molding & trim, millwork, windows; Retail in lumber & other building materials dealers, hardware stores

H. Paulin & Co., Limited
55 Milne Ave., Toronto, ON M1L 4N3
Tel: 416-694-3351; *Fax:* 416-694-1869
Toll-Free: 800-268-4000
investor@hpaulin.com
www.hpaulin.com
Ticker Symbol: PAP
Company Type: Public
Profile: Manufacturers of bolts, nuts, screws, rivets, washers, valves & pipe fittings, various hardware; Wholesalers of motor vehicle supplies & new parts, industrial supplies; Collection of end cuts & short lengths for recycling

Haley Industries Limited
634 Magnesium Rd., Haley, ON K0J 1Y0
Tel: 613-432-8841; *Fax:* 613-432-0743
info.haley@magellan.aero
Company Type: Private
Profile: Manufacturers of aluminum foundries, primary smelting & refining of nonferrous metals

Harris Steel Group Inc.
#404, 4120 Yonge St., Toronto, ON M2P 2B8
Tel: 416-590-9549; *Fax:* 416-590-9560
info@harrissteel.com
www.harrissteel.com
Company Type: Private
Profile: Fabrication & processing steel training business; installation of steel products

ITW Canada
120 Travail Rd., Markham, ON L3S 3J1
Toll-Free: 800-387-9692
info@itwconstruction.ca
www.itw.com
Company Type: Private
Profile: Offices of holding companies; Manufacturers of various fabricated metal products; Wholesalers of industrial supplies, industrial machinery & equipment, chemicals & allied products

Martinrea International Inc.
30 Aviva Park Dr., Vaughan, ON L4L 9C7
Tel: 416-749-0314; *Fax:* 905-264-2937
info@martinrea.com; HR@martinrea.com
www.martinrea.com
Ticker Symbol: MRE
Company Type: Public
Profile: Martinrea International Inc. specializes in the production of metal parts, assemblies & modules, & fluid management systems. The company supplies the automotive industry & other industrial sectors. Divisions are located in Canada, the United States, Mexico, & Europe.

Meridian Lightweight Technologies Inc.
25 MacNab Ave., Strathroy, ON N7G 4H6
Tel: 519-246-9600; *Fax:* 519-245-6605
hr@meridian-mag.com
www.meridian-mag.com
Company Type: Private
Profile: The company is engaged in magnesium die casting design & manufacturing. Components & assemblies are supplied to the global automotive market.

QIT-Fer & Titane inc
1625, rue Marie-Victorin, Sorel-Tracy, QC J3R 1M6
Tel: 450-746-3000; *Fax:* 450-746-4438
info@qit.com
www.qit.com
Company Type: Private
Profile: Manufacturers of steel works, blast furnaces & coke ovens, rolling mills

Russel Metals Inc.
#210, 1900 Minnesota Ct., Mississauga, ON L5N 3C9
Tel: 905-819-7777; *Fax:* 905-819-7409
info@russelmetals.com
www.russelmetals.com
Ticker Symbol: RUS
Company Type: Public
Profile: The metal processor & distributor operates in North America. The company implemented environmental standards & an ongoing audit process.

Samuel Manu-Tech Inc.
#1500, 185 The West Mall, Toronto, ON M9C 5L5
Tel: 416-626-2190; *Fax:* 416-626-5969
smt@samuelmanutech.com
www.samuelmanutech.com
Ticker Symbol: SMT
Company Type: Public
Profile: Samuel Manu-Tech Inc. produces steel, plastic, & related industrial products. The company has locations in Canada, the United States, & Mexico.

TenarisAlgomaTubes
#800, 440 - 2nd Ave. SW, Calgary, AB T2P 5E9
Tel: 403-514-2276; *Fax:* 403-290-0619
www.tenaris.com
Company Type: Public
Profile: Manufacturers of fabricated pipe & pipe fittings; Wholesalers in metals service centres & offices

Timminco Limited
Sun Life Financial Tower, #2401, 150 King St. West, Toronto, ON M5H 1J9
Tel: 416-364-5171; *Fax:* 416-364-3451
info@timminco.com
www.timminco.com
Ticker Symbol: TIM
Company Type: Public
Profile: Manufacturers of rolling, drawing & extruding of nonferrous metals, secondary smelting & refining of nonferrous metals; Wholesalers of metals service centers & offices

Tree Island Wire Income Fund
3933 Boundary Rd., Richmond, BC V6V 1T8
Tel: 604-524-3744; *Fax:* 604-524-2657
Toll-Free: 800-663-0955
www.treeisland.com
Ticker Symbol: TIL.UN
Company Type: Public
Profile: Tree Island Wire Income Fund is an unincorporated open ended limited purpose trust. It owns Tree Island Industries Ltd.. The company serves the following industries: residential construction, commercial construction, industrial, & agriculture. Products include the following: bright, galvanized, & stainless steel wire; fabricated wire products, such as fencing; stucco; engineered structural mesh; & bulk, packaged, & collated nails.

U.S. Steel Canada
PO Box 2030, 386 Wilcox St., Hamilton, ON L8N 3T1
Tel: 905-528-2511; *Fax:* 905-308-7002
Toll-Free: 800-263-9305
infocanada@uss.com
www.ussteelcanaca.com
Company Type: Public
Profile: Manufacturers of steel works, blast furnaces, coke ovens, rolling mills, hot & cold-rolled steel sheet, bars, steel pipe & tubes, wire & wire products

Valdor Technology International Inc.
#480, 789 West Pender St., Vancouver, BC V6C 1H2
Tel: 604-687-3775; *Fax:* 604-689-7654
info@valdor.com; sales@valdor.com
www.valdortech.com
Ticker Symbol: VTI
Company Type: Public
Profile: Valdor Technology International is a high technology fiber optic components company. It specializes in designing & manufacturing optical & optoelectronic components, such as new generation fiber optic connectors. Connectors incorporate the environmentally friendly Impact Mount technology.

Velan Inc.
7007, ch de la Côte-de-Liesse, Montréal, QC H4T 1G2
Tel: 514-748-7743; *Fax:* 514-748-8635
sales@velan.com
www.velan.com
Ticker Symbol: VLN
Company Type: Public
Profile: Velan Inc. manufactures industrial steel valves. Manufacturing plants are located in Canada, the United States, Europe, & Asia. Velan valves are used in numerous industries, such as oil & gas, chemical & petrochemical, pulp & paper, mining, & power generation. The company also offers aftermarket services.

Vicwest Income Fund
1296 South Service Rd. West, Oakville, ON L6L 5T7
Tel: 905-469-5702; *Fax:* 905-825-1090
IR@vicwestfund.com
www.vicwestfund.com
Ticker Symbol: VIC.UN
Company Type: Public
Profile: Vicwest Income Fund is involved in supplying metal roofing, siding & other building products to the residential, commercial, institutional, & industrial sectors. The organization also supplies steel containers used in the petroleum, grain, & fertilizer industries.

Textiles, Apparel & Leather

Algo Group Inc.
5555, rue Cypihot, Montréal, QC H4S 1R3
Tel: 514-382-1240; *Fax:* 514-385-0163
info@algo.com
www.algo.com
Company Type: Public
Profile: Manufacturers of various men's & boys' clothing, women's, misses' & juniors' dresses, misses' & juniors' suits, skirts, coats & various outerwear; manufacturers of broadwoven fabric and manmade fiber & silk, home furnishings

Beaulieu Canada
335, rue de Roxton, Acton Vale, QC J0H 1A0
Tel: 450-546-5000; *Fax:* 450-546-5027
Toll-Free: 800-853-9048
beaulieucanada-com.rebeltrail.com
Company Type: Private
Profile: Manufacture & distribution of broadloom carpets

Consoltex Inc.
8555, rte Transcanadienne, Saint-Laurent, QC H4S 1Z6
Tel: 514-333-8800; *Fax:* 514-335-7013
Toll-Free: 800-736-2743
solutions@consoltex.com
www.consoltex.com
Company Type: Public
Profile: Offices of holding companies; Manufacturers of circular weft, knit fabric mills; Finishers of broadwoven fabrics of manmade fiber & silk; Wholesalers of piece goods, notions & other dry goods

Danier Leather Inc.
2650 St Clair Ave. West, Toronto, ON M6N 1M2
Tel: 416-762-8175; *Fax:* 416-762-4570
info@danier.com
www.danier.com
Ticker Symbol: DL
Company Type: Public
Profile: Manufacturers of leather & sheepskin-lined clothing, leather gloves & mittens, personal leather goods; Retailing luggage & leather goods stores

Gildan Activewear Inc.
600, boul de Maisonneuve ouest, Montréal, QC H3A 3J2
Tel: 514-735-2023; *Fax:* 514-735-6810
Toll-Free: 866-755-2023
info@gildan.com
www.gildan.com
Ticker Symbol: GIL
Company Type: Public
Profile: Gildan Activewear manufactures & markets activewear, athletic socks, & underwear. The company serves both North American & international markets.

Intertape Polymer Group Inc.
999 Cavendish Blvd. 2nd Fl., Montréal, QC H4M 2X5
Tel: 514-731-7591; *Fax:* 514-731-5039
info@intertapeipg.com
www.intertapepolymer.com
Ticker Symbol: ITP
Company Type: Public
Profile: Manufacturers of coated fabrics, not rubberized, packaging paper & plastics film, coated & laminated

Le Château Inc.
8300, boul Decarie, Montréal, QC H4P 2P5
Tel: 514-738-7000; *Fax:* 514-738-3670
comments@lechateau.ca
www.lechateau.ca
Ticker Symbol: CTU
Company Type: Public
Profile: Le Château Inc. is a designer & manufacturer of clothing. The company operates retail stores in Canada & United States. Le Château stores sell ladieswear, menswear, footwear, & accessories.

Transportation & Travel

Admiral Marine Inc.
#207-7035 Maxwell Rd., Mississauga, ON L5S 1R5
Tel: 905-564-8788; *Fax:* 905-564-1440
admiral@admiralmarine.ca
www.admiralmarine.ca
Company Type: Public
Profile: Canstar Ocean Line, through Admiral Marine, operate a regular break-bulk/conventional service from North America to Europe, with transshipment via Antwerp to Eastern Europe, the Middle East and Africa.

Air Canada
PO Box 14000 St-Laurent, Saint-Laurent, QC H4Y 1H4
Tel: 514-422-5000; *Fax:* 514-422-5909
denis.biro@aircanada.ca
www.aircanada.ca
Ticker Symbol: AC
Company Type: Public
Profile: The Canadian-based international air carrier provides scheduled & chartered air transportation for both passengers & cargo.

Algoma Central Corporation
#600, 63 Church St., St Catharines, ON L2R 3C4
Tel: 905-687-7888; *Fax:* 905-687-7840
svaughan@heenan.ca
www.algonet.com
Ticker Symbol: ALC
Company Type: Public
Profile: Algoma Central Corporation is a Canadian-flag ship owner on the Great Lakes - St. Lawrence Waterway. The company owns both dry-bulk carriers & product tankers. As well as the operation of vessels, ship & diesel engine repair & fabrication are part of Algoma Central's operations.

American Cartage Ltd.
#101 - 9366, 200A St., Langley, BC V1M 4B3
Tel: 604-513-3681; *Fax:* 604-513-3677
www.americancartage.com
Company Type: Private
Profile: American Cartage Ltd. delivers marine containers to & from Vancouver's waterfront terminals.

American President Lines Ltd.
#728, 185 The West Mall, Toronto, ON M9C 5L5
Tel: 416-620-7790; *Fax:* 416-620-7723
www.apl.com
Company Type: Public
Profile: APL provides customers around the world with container transportation services.

Atlas Cold Storage Income Trust
5255 Yonge St., Toronto, ON M2N 5P8
Tel: 416-512-2352; *Fax:* 416-512-2353
Toll-Free: 888-642-3333
inquiries@atlascold.com
www.atlascold.com
Ticker Symbol: FZR
Company Type: Public
Profile: Refrigerated warehousing & storage

ATS Andlauer Income Fund
ATS Toronto (Head Office), 96 Disco Rd., Toronto, ON M9W 0A3
Tel: 416-679-7979; *Fax:* 416-679-7845
www.ats.ca
Company Type: Public
Profile: ATS Andlauer Income Fund is involved in the provision of integrated trucking, courier, & air freight transportation & distribution solutions. It serves major consumer companies in Canada.

AutoCanada Income Fund
#200, 15505 Yellowhead Trail, Edmonton, AB T5H 3P9
Tel: 780-732-3135; *Fax:* 780-447-0651
yporter@autocan.ca
www.autocan.ca
Ticker Symbol: ACQ.UN
Company Type: Public
Profile: Through its interest in AutoCanada LP, AutoCanada Income Fund is involved in the operation & management of franchised automobile dealerships across Canada. Both sales & repair services are provided by AutoCanada.

Automodular Corporation
#420, 20 Toronto St., Toronto, ON M5C 2B8
Tel: 416-861-0662; *Fax:* 416-861-0063
info@Automodular.com; hr@Automodular.net
www.automodular.com
Ticker Symbol: AM
Company Type: Public
Profile: Automodular Corporation is engaged in automotive parts sequencing & sub-assembly. Components & modules are installed in vehicles made by North American Original Equipment Manufacturers in Canada & the United States.

Bombardier Inc.
800, boul René-Lévesque ouest, 29e étage, Montréal, QC H3B 1Y8
Tel: 514-861-9481; *Fax:* 514-861-2629
investors@bombardier.com
www.bombardier.com
Ticker Symbol: BBD
Company Type: Public
Profile: Bombardier Inc. manufactures transportation solutions, such as rail equipment & commercial aircraft.

British Columbia Ferry Services Inc.
1112 Fort St., Victoria, BC V8V 4V2
Tel: 250-386-3431; *Fax:* 250-388-7754
Toll-Free: 888-223-3779
www.bcferries.com
Company Type: Private
Profile: Operates a fleet of 36 ferries serving 47 destinations in British Columbia

British Columbia Railway Company
#600, 221 West Esplanade Ave, North Vancouver, BC V7M 3J3
Tel: 604-678-4735; *Fax:* 604-678-4736
westerhouts@bcrco.com
www.bcrco.com
Company Type: Crown
Profile: Offices of holding companies; Real estate operators of nonresidential buildings; Real estate agents & managers; Railroads, line-haul operating; Marine cargo handling

Bulk Carriers (PEI) Ltd.
PO Box 153, 779 Bannockburn Rd., Cornwall, PE C0A 1H0
Tel: 902-675-2600; *Fax:* 902-675-3100
info@bulkcarrierspei.com
www.bulkcarrierspei.com
Company Type: Private
Profile: With a fleet made up of reefer trailers, the company hauls mainly food products throughout Canada & the United States.

Canada Steamship Lines Inc.
759 Victoria Square, Montréal, QC H2Y 2K3
Tel: 514-982-3800; *Fax:* 514-982-3801
info@cslmtl.com
www.csl.ca
Company Type: Public

Canadian American Transportation Inc.
4 rue du Transport, Coteau-du-Lac, QC J0P 1B0
Tel: 450-763-6363; *Fax:* 450-763-2400
Toll-Free: 800-363-5313
cat@cat.ca
www.cat.ca
Company Type: Private
Profile: Canadian American Transportation Inc. offers logistics services & a partnership program with other transportation companies.

Canadian Helicopters Income Fund
1215, montee Pilon, Les Cèdres, QC J7T 1G1
Tel: 450-452-3000; *Fax:* 450-452-3057
www.canadianhelicopters.com
Ticker Symbol: CHL.UN
Company Type: Public
Profile: Through Canadian Helicopters Limited, Canadian Helicopters Income Fund is a helicopter transportation services company. In addition to transportation services, the company also operates flight schools & offers repair & maintenance services. Canadian Helicopters serves the following sectors: emergency medical services, mining, construction, oil & gas, infrastructure maintenance, & utilities.

Canadian National Railway Company
935, rue de la Gauchetière ouest, Montréal, QC H3B 2M9
Tel: 514-399-6591; *Fax:* 514-399-4296
Toll-Free: 888-888-5909
CNPQATL@cn.ca; CNON@cn.ca; CNSKMB@cn.ca
www.cn.ca
Ticker Symbol: CNR
Company Type: Public
Profile: Crossing the North American continent, the Canadian National Railway Company serves ports on the Atlantic, Pacific, & Gulf coasts.

Canadian Pacific Railway Limited
Gulf Canada Square, #500, 401 - 9th Ave. SW, Calgary, AB T2P 4Z4
Tel: 403-319-7000; *Fax:* 403-319-7567
Toll-Free: 888-333-6370
investor@cpr.ca
www.cpr.ca
Ticker Symbol: CP
Company Type: Public
Profile: The transcontinental carrier operates in Canada & the United States.

Cargojet Income Fund
#5&6, 350 Britannia Rd. East, Mississauga, ON L4Z 1X9
Tel: 905-501-7373; *Fax:* 905-501-8228
www.cargojet.com
Ticker Symbol: CJT.UN
Company Type: Public
Profile: Cargojet Income Fund is involved in the provision of overnight air cargo services.

Celtic Maritime
1066 Thierry, La Salle, QC H8N 2Y6
Tel: 514-932-6464; *Fax:* 514-932-6565
info@celticmaritime.com
www.celticmaritime.com
Company Type: Public

Challenger Motor Freight Inc.
300 Maple Grove Rd., Cambridge, ON N3E 1B7
Tel: 519-653-6226; *Fax:* 519-653-9810
Toll-Free: 800-265-6358
ginfo@challenger.com
www.challenger.com
Company Type: Private

CHC Helicopter Corporation
4740 Agar Dr., Richmond, BC V7B 1A3
Tel: 604-276-7500; *Fax:* 604-232-8359
communications@chc.ca
www.chc.ca
Company Type: Public
Profile: CHC Helicopter Corporation offers helicopter transportation services throughout the world. It specializes in offshore support to serve the oil & gas industry. Other services include search & rescue & helicopter training. Through its Heli-One division, leasing, logistics, repair, & overhaul services are available. CHC Helicopters's systems & procedures meet or exceed ISO 9001, ISO 14001, & OHSAS 18001 specifications.

Chrysler Canada Inc.
One Riverside Drive West, Windsor, ON N9A 5K3
Tel: 519-973-2000; *Fax:* 519-973-2950
www.chryslercanada.ca
Company Type: Private
Profile: Marketing & sale of Chrysler, Dodge & Jeep vehicles; Operates the Automotive Research & Development Centre with University of Windsor

Contrans Income Fund
1179 Ridgeway Rd., Woodstock, ON N4V 1E3
Tel: 519-421-4600; *Fax:* 519-539-9220
info@contrans.ca
www.contrans.ca
Ticker Symbol: CSS
Company Type: Public
Profile: The organization is involved in trucking & logistics services. Services are provided across Canada & the United States.

CRS-Express Inc.
2100, 95e rue, Saint-Georges, QC G5Y 8J3
Tel: 418-227-7379; *Fax:* 418-227-7381
Toll-Free: 800-807-7379
www.crs-express.com
Company Type: Private

CSL Group Inc.
759, carré Victoria, 6e étage, Montréal, QC H2Y 2K3
Tel: 514-982-3800; *Fax:* 514-982-3920
ships@cslmtl.com
www.csl.ca
Company Type: Private
Profile: Specializes in bulk transportation & self-loading technology

Discovery Air Inc.
106 Dickens St., Yellowknife, NT X1A 2R3
Fax: 519-913-2204
Toll-Free: 866-903-3247
www.discoveryair.com
Ticker Symbol: DA.A
Company Type: Public
Profile: Incorporated in 2004, Discovery Air Inc. created an alliance of aviation companies to provide safe, professional air transportation in selected niche markets. The following are Discovery Air's subsidiaries: Great Slave Helicopters Ltd., Discovery Mining Services Ltd., Hicks & Lawrence Limited, Top Aces Inc., & Air Tindi Ltd.

Essen Transport Ltd.
PO Box 2229, Winkler, MB R6W 4B9
Tel: 204-325-5200; *Fax:* 204-325-5252
Toll-Free: 800-760-3776
www.essentransport.com
Company Type: Private
Profile: Essen Transport Ltd. provides supply chain management. It uses logistics to track inbound & outbound shipments for companies in Canada and the United States.

F.K. Warren Ltd.
Cogswell Tower, #920, 2000 Barrington St., Halifax, NS B3J 2X1
Tel: 902-423-8136; *Fax:* 902-429-1326
www.fkwarren.ca
Company Type: Public
Profile: F.K. Warren provides a comprehensive range of Marine Agency Services at all ports throughout Atlantic Canada.

Fednav Limited
#3500, 1000, rue de la Gauchetière ouest, Montréal, QC H3B 4W5
Tel: 514-878-6500; *Fax:* 514-878-6642
info@fednav.com
www.fednav.com
Company Type: Private
Profile: Deep sea foreign transportation of freight; Freight transportation on the Great Lakes - St.Lawrence Seaway; Marine cargo handling

Ford Motor Company of Canada, Limited
PO Box 2000, The Canadian Rd., Oakville, ON L6J 5E4
Fax: 905-845-7016
Toll-Free: 800-565-3673
www.ford.ca
Company Type: Private
Profile: Manufacturers of motor vehicles & passenger car bodies; wholesalers of automobiles & other motor vehicles, motor vehicle supplies & new parts

General Motors of Canada Limited
Main Mailing Dept. CA1-002-002, 1908 Colonel Sam Dr., Oshawa, ON L1H 8P7
Tel: 905-644-5000; *Fax:* 905-644-6273
Toll-Free: 800-263-3777
www.gmcanada.com
Company Type: Private
Profile: Manufacturers of motor vehicles & passenger car bodies, truck & bus bodies, motor vehicle parts & accessories, railroad equipment

Ghost Transportation Services
715E-46th St. West, Saskatoon, SK S7L 6A1
Tel: 306-249-3515; *Fax:* 306-249-3335
customerservice@ghosttrans.com
www.ghosttrans.com
Company Type: Private
Profile: Ghost Transportation Services offers warehousing, shipment of raw materials, & transportation or distribution of finished products.

Global Railway Industries Ltd.
PO Box 5484, 1255 Brydges St., London, ON N5W 2C2
Tel: 585-419-9720; *Fax:* 585-385-6790
info@globalrailway.com
www.globalrailway.com
Ticker Symbol: GBI
Company Type: Public
Profile: Global Railway Industries Ltd. is a designer, manufacturer, & marketer of railway equipment. The company is also engaged in remanufacturing locomotives & repairing rail cars. Global Railway Industries Ltd.'s products are provided through the following operating subsidiaries: CAD Railway Industries Ltd., Bach-Simpson Corporation, & G&B Specialties, Inc.. Operations are located in Canada & the United States.

GN Transport
163 Bowes Rd., Concord, ON L4K 1H3
Tel: 905-760-2888; *Fax:* 905-760-2040
Toll-Free: 866-738-6661
info@gntransport.com
www.gntransport.com
Company Type: Private

Go Transport Ltd.
57 Braid St., New Westminster, BC V3L 3P2
Tel: 604-525-0840; *Fax:* 604-525-3684
Toll-Free: 888-363-6699
dispatch@gotransport.ca
www.gotransport.ca
Company Type: Private

Greyhound Canada Transportation Corp.
877 Greyhound Way SW, Calgary, AB T3C 3V8
Tel: 403-260-0877; *Fax:* 403-260-0779
canada.info@greyhound.ca
www.greyhound.ca
Company Type: Private
Profile: Intercity & rural bus transportation; travel agencies; courier services

Grimshaw Trucking LP
PO Box 960, 11510-151 St., Edmonton, AB T5M 3N6
Tel: 780-414-2880; *Fax:* 780-455-7818
Toll-Free: 888-414-2850
www.grimshaw-trucking.com
Company Type: Private
Profile: Grimshaw Trucking LP is a transportation company in western Canada.

Group Express Inc.
170 Main St. N., Alexandria, ON K0C 1A0
Tel: 613-525-1275; *Fax:* 613-525-1278
Toll-Free: 800-387-6691
traffic@groupexpress.ca
www.groupexpress.ca
Company Type: Private

Groupe Desgagnés Inc.
21 Marché-Champlain St., Québec, QC G1K 8Z8
Tel: 418-692-1000; *Fax:* 418-692-6044
info@degagnes.com
www.groupedesgagnes.com
Company Type: Public
Profile: Groupe Desgagnés' entire history has been marked by sustained, carefully orchestrated efforts that have helped ensure its growth & maintain its position as a shipping industry leader.

Harold Newell & Son Trucking Ltd.
R.R. #1, Barrington, NS B0W 1E0
Tel: 902-637-2243; *Fax:* 902-637-1563
trucking@ns.sympatico.ca
www.tcfb.com/trucking
Company Type: Private

Holmes Maritime Inc.
1345 Hollis St., Halifax, NS B3J 1T8
Tel: 902-422-0400; *Fax:* 902-422-9439
info@holmesmaritime.com
www.holmesmaritime.com
Company Type: Public
Profile: Holmes Maritime Inc. is a privately owned Canadian company, headquartered in Halifax, Nova Scotia. It provides port agency & logistics services to international ship owners & operators throughout eastern Canada & along the Great Lakes.

Honda Canada Inc.
715 Milner Ave., Toronto, ON M1B 2K8
Tel: 416-284-8110; *Fax:* 416-286-1322
Toll-Free: 888-946-6329
www.honda.ca
Company Type: Private
Profile: Manufacturers of motor vehicles & passenger car bodies; Wholesalers of automobiles & other motor vehicles, motor vehicle supplies & new parts

Hyundai Canada Inc.
75 Frontenac Dr., Markham, ON L3R 6H2
Tel: 905-948-6712; *Fax:* 905-477-3820
Toll-Free: 800-461-8242
cr@hyundaicanada.com
www.hyundaicanada.com
Company Type: Private
Profile: Wholesalers of motor vehicle supplies & new parts

Jay's Moving & Storage
PO Box 4560, Regina, SK S4P 3Y3
Tel: 306-569-9369; *Fax:* 306-721-4641
jaysreg@sasktel.net
Company Type: Private

Profile: Jay's Moving & Storage is a multi-branch moving & storage firm which serves the prairie provinces. A freight division provides services in Saskatchewan.

Jazz Air Income Fund
Halifax International Airport, 310 Goudey Dr., Enfield, NS B2T 1E4
Tel: 902-873-5094; *Fax:* 902-873-2098
www.flyjazz.ca
Ticker Symbol: JAZ.UN
Company Type: Public
Profile: Jazz Air Income Fund is an unincorporated, open-ended trust. Its purpose is to hold an interest in the outstanding limited partnership units of Jazz Air LP.

Kindersley Transport Inc.
660 Aldford Ave., Delta, BC V3M 6X1
Tel: 604-522-4002; *Fax:* 604-525-2955
customerservice@kindersleytransport.com
www.kindersleytransport.com
Company Type: Private
Profile: The fleet, based in western Canada, provides truckload & less-than-truckload services through a network of service centers in Canada & the United States.

KO Transport Inc.
651 Burlington St. E., Hamilton, ON L8L 4J5
Tel: 905-544-9000;
Company Type: Private
Profile: Established in 1933, KO Transport services the southern Ontario region & points beyond.

Kooi Trucking Inc.
PO Box 70, Scotland, ON N0E 1R0
Tel: 519-446-3333; *Fax:* 519-446-3999
info@kooitruckinginc.com
www.kooitruckinginc.com
Company Type: Private
Profile: Kooi Trucking Inc. is a freight company, which specializes in the transportatoin needs of North American importers & exporters.

Lark Transport Inc.
2880 Saskatchewan Ave. W., Portage La Prarie, MB R1N 3B9
Tel: 888-444-5257; *Fax:* 888-246-9365
www.larktransport.com
Company Type: Private
Profile: Lark Transport Inc. is a Canadian based freight transportation company.

Lighthouse Transport Services Ltd.
PO Box 38010, #2-150 Wright Ave., Dartmouth, NS B3B 1X2
Tel: 902-468-3696; *Fax:* 902-468-5267
Toll-Free: 800-770-5457
colleen@lighthousetransport.com
www.lighthousetransport.com
Company Type: Private
Profile: Lighthouse Transport Services Ltd. offers the following services: FTL & LTL transport, container transport, warehousing & crating, oversized cargo moves, pilot car services, flatbed moves, deconsolidations, & exclusive deliveries.

Logistec Corporation
#1500, 360, rue Saint-Jacques, Montréal, QC H2Y 1P5
Tel: 514-844-9381; *Fax:* 514-985-2314
corp@logistec.com
www.logistec.com
Ticker Symbol: LGT
Company Type: Public
Profile: Logistec Corporation & its subsidiaries serve the marine & industrial sectors. Cargo-handling services are offered at port terminals situated in eastern Canada & the United States, & on the Great Lakes. Other services include agency services to foreign ship-owners & operators at Canadian ports, marine transportation services, & on-site decontamination services.

Marine Atlantic Inc.
Baine Johnston Centre, #802, 10 Fort William Pl., St. John's, NL A1C 1K4
Tel: 709-772-8957; *Fax:* 709-772-8956
Toll-Free: 800-341-7981
info@marine-atlantic.ca
www.marine-atlantic.ca
Company Type: Crown
Profile: Deep sea domestic transportation of freight; Ferries; Various water transportation of passengers

Mazda Canada Inc.
55 Vogell Rd., Richmond Hill, ON L4B 3K5
Tel: 905-787-7000; *Fax:* 905-787-7125
Toll-Free: 800-263-4680
www.mazda.ca
Company Type: Private
Profile: Wholesalers of automobiles & other motor vehicles, motor vehicle supplies & new parts

Mercedes-Benz Canada Inc.
98 Vanderhoof Ave., Toronto, ON M4G 4C9
Toll-Free: 800-387-0100
www.mercedes-benz.ca
Company Type: Private
Profile: Wholesalers of automobiles & other motor vehicles, motor vehicle supplies & new parts; Retailers in new & used motor vehicle dealers

Montship Inc.
#1000, 360, rue Saint-Jacques, Montréal, QC H2Y 1R2
Tel: 514-286-4646; *Fax:* 514-286-4650
www.montship.ca
Company Type: Public
Profile: The Canadian shipping agent has the capability of handling most any type of cargo movement. Montship Inc. has six offices located across the country.

N.M. Paterson & Sons Limited
PO Box 24, GRP 210, RR2 ., Winnipeg, MB R3C 2E6
Tel: 204-694-4445; *Fax:* 204-694-4446
winnipeg_terminal@patersongrain.com
www.patersongrain.com
Company Type: Private
Profile: Freight transportation on the Great Lakes - St. Lawrence Seaway

NAV Canada
PO Box 3411 D, 77 Metcalfe St., Ottawa, ON K1P 5L6
Tel: 613-563-5588; *Fax:* 613-563-3426
Toll-Free: 800-876-4693
service@navcanada.ca
www.navcanada.ca
Company Type: Private
Profile: Canada's civil air navigation services provider. Provides air traffic control, flight information, weather briefings, aeronautical information services, airport advisory services and electronic aids to navigation

Nissan Canada Inc.
5290 Orbitor Dr., Mississauga, ON L4W 4Z5
Fax: 905-629-6553
Toll-Free: 800-387-0122
information.centre@nissancanada.com
www.nissan.ca
Company Type: Private
Profile: Manufacturers of motor vehicles & passenger car bodies; Provides vehicles to Meals-on-Wheels agencies

Oceanex Inc.
#2550, 630, boul René-Lévesque ouest, Montréal, QC H3B 1S6
Tel: 514-875-9244; *Fax:* 514-392-0200
bookings@oceanex.com
www.oceanex.com
Company Type: Public
Profile: Inter-modal transportation, with emphasis on container/roroship operations; door-to-door freight servies from any point of origin in North America to destinations in Newfoundland and Labrador

Overland West Freight Lines
#300, 10362 King George Hwy., Surrey, BC V3T 2W5
Tel: 604-580-4600; *Fax:* 604-580-4601
Toll-Free: 800-698-2111
admin@overlandwest.ca
www.overlandwest.ca
Company Type: Private
Profile: Overland West Freight Lines operates as a full service carrier in British Columbia. It serves the retail, commercial, municipal construction, forestry, & mineral sectors.

Pacific Coast Express Ltd.
10299 Grace Rd., Surrey, BC V3V 3V7
Tel: 604-582-3230; *Fax:* 604-588-7906
Toll-Free: 800-667-6061
service@pcx.ca; dispatch@pcx.ca
www.pcx.ca
Company Type: Private
Profile: Pacific Coast Express provides services related to the movement of goods across North America.

Phantom Freightlines
5300 - 86 Ave. SE, Calgary, AB T2C 47L
Tel: 403-219-1008; *Fax:* 403-219-1016
www.phantomfreightlines.com
Company Type: Private
Profile: Phantom Freightlines specializes in the transportation of time sensitive & delicate materials, such as flowers, & fresh & frozen goods. Business is conducted across Canada & the United States.

Premium Trucking Ltd.
PO Box 39, 449 Lower Rd., Arichat, NS B0E 1A0
Tel: 902-226-3474; *Fax:* 902-226-0026
www.premiumseafoods.ns.ca/ptrucking.php
Company Type: Private
Profile: Premium Trucking Ltd. transports fish & other products for Premium Seafoods Ltd. & for other companies that require dependable transportation services.

Prevost Car Inc.
35, boul Gagnon, Sainte-Claire, QC G0R 2V0
Tel: 418-883-3391; *Fax:* 418-883-4157
prevostcar@volvo.com
www.prevostcar.com
Company Type: Private
Profile: Manufacturers of intercity coaches & coach shells for motorhomes & specialty conversion

Public Storage Canadian Properties
One First Canadian Place, #6600, 100 King St. West, Toronto, ON M5X 1B8
Toll-Free: 866-772-2623
www.publicstoragecanada.com
Ticker Symbol: PUB
Company Type: Public
Profile: Public Storage Canadian Properties invests in self-storage facilities located throughout Canada. The facilities operate under the trade name "Public Storage". Canadian Mini-Warehouse Properties Company (CMP) is the General Partner of Public Storage Canadian Properties. CMP manages the facilities owned by Public Storage Canadian Properties.

Purolator Courier Ltd.
5995 Avebury Rd., Mississauga, ON L5R 3T8
Toll-Free: 888-744-7123
www.purolator.com
Company Type: Private
Profile: The courier company has facilities throughout Canada. Purolator also provides international delivery services.

Rigel Shipping Canada Inc.
PO Box 5151, Shediac, NB E4P 8T9
Tel: 506-533-9000; *Fax:* 506-533-9010
admin@rigelcanada.com
www.rigelcanada.com
Company Type: Private
Profile: Rigel Shipping Canada Inc. offers marine tanker solutions for petroleum & petro-chemical transportation. It serves the Canadian petroleum industry by providing safe, secure, & environmentally friendly shipping services.

Rockman Trucking Inc.
#56, 10765, ch de Côte-de-Liesse, Dorval, QC H9P 1A7
Tel: 514-422-1085; *Fax:* 514-422-1083
Toll-Free: 800-565-1085
info@rockman.ca
www.rockman.ca
Company Type: Private
Profile: The licensed Canadian trucking company is a container, truckload, & LTL carrier. Rockman Trucking offers shipping in Canada & to the United States.

Rolls Right Industries
2864 Norland Ave., Burnaby, BC V5B 3A6
Tel: 604-298-0080; *Fax:* 604-298-1366
info@rollsright.ca
www.rollsright.ca
Company Type: Private
Profile: The Canadian owned & operated carrier company has a fleet of more than eighty trucks. Rolls Right Industries provides truck & van delivery (LTL), trailer loads (FTL), & container hauling.

Seaway Marine Transport
#300, 20 Corporate Park Dr., St. Catharines, ON L2S 3W2
Tel: 905-988-2600; *Fax:* 905-988-1803
www.seawaymarinetransport.com
Company Type: Private
Profile: Seaway Marine Transport, Inc. manages a fleet of gearless bulk carriers & self-unloading vessels, which carry products such as iron ore, coal, potash, grain, gypsum, & salt. A grain marketing office is located in the Richardson Building in Winnipeg, Manitoba.

Shadow Lines Transportation Group
9818 - 198B St., Langley, BC V1M 2X5
Tel: 604-888-2928; *Fax:* 604-888-2794
Toll-Free: 800-663-1421
trucking@shadowlines.com
www.shadowlines.com
Company Type: Private
Profile: The transporation company operates from British Columbia to Ontario & throughout the United States. Shadow Lines Transportation Group's container fleet of trucks operates

from the Langley, British Columbia terminal, where it serves Vancouver, Seattle, & Tacoma ports. The company's divisions include Heavy Haul / Line Haul & Logistics Solutions. Offices are also located in Edmonton & Calgary, Alberta & Regina & Saskatoon, Saskatchewan.

Spar Aerospace Limited
Edmonton International Airport, PO Box 9864, Edmonton, AB T5J 2T2
Tel: 780-890-6300; *Fax:* 780-890-6652
www.spar.ca
Company Type: Private
Profile: Aviation services: aircraft programs; Component maintenance, repair & operation; Support services

Subaru Canada, Inc.
560 Suffolk Ct., Mississauga, ON L5R 4J7
Fax: 905-568-8087
Toll-Free: 800-894-4212
www.subaru.ca
Company Type: Private
Profile: Manufacturers & retailers of motor vehicles

The Toronto Transit Commission
1900 Yonge St., Toronto, ON M4S 1Z2
Tel: 416-393-4000; *Fax:* 416-482-0478
www.ttc.ca
Company Type: Crown
Profile: Operates & maintains the Toronto urban transit system: buses, subways, streetcars & trolleys, and Wheel-Trans accessible transit

TMT Freight System
14 Cadetta Rd., Brampton, ON L6T 3Z8
Tel: 905-794-9845; *Fax:* 905-794-9846
Toll-Free: 888-817-4410
info@tmtfreight.com
www.tmtfreight.com
Company Type: Private
Profile: TMT Freight System is a container carrier.

Toyota Canada Inc.
1 Toyota Pl., Toronto, ON M1H 1H9
Tel: 416-438-6320; *Fax:* 416-431-1867
Toll-Free: 888-869-6828
www.toyota.ca
Company Type: Private
Profile: Wholesalers of automobiles & other motor vehicles, motor vehicle supplies & new parts, industrial machinery & equipment

Transat A.T. Inc.
Place du Parc, #600, 300, rue Léo-Pariseau, Montréal, QC H2X 4C2
Tel: 514-987-1660; *Fax:* 514-987-8035
Toll-Free: 800-387-2672
info@transat.com
www.transat.com
Ticker Symbol: TRZ
Company Type: Public
Profile: Transat A.T. is an integrated tour operator, which organizes & markets holiday travel. Tour operators are based in Canada & France.

TransForce Income Fund
#300, 8585, rte Trans-Canada, Montréal, QC H4S 1Z6
Tel: 514-331-4000; *Fax:* 514-337-4200
administration@transforce.ca
www.transforce.ca
Ticker Symbol: TFI
Company Type: Public
Profile: The Fund invests in organizations that provide trucking & transportation logistics services.

TransForce Income Fund
#300, 8585 Trans-Canada Highway, Saint-Laurent, QC H4S 1Z6
Tel: 514-331-4000; *Fax:* 514-337-4200
administration@transforce.ca
www.transforce.ca
Company Type: Private
Profile: TransForce Income Fund invests in a network of independent operating companies. The Fund, through these subsidiaries, is involved in Canada's transportation & logistics industry.

Trappers Transport Ltd.
2475 Day St., Winnipeg, MB R2C 2Z2
Tel: 204-697-7647; *Fax:* 204-633-5569
info@trapperstransport.com
www.trapperstransport.com
Company Type: Private
Profile: Trappers Transport Ltd. specializes in the transportation of refrigerated LTL or full Loads throughout North America.

Tri-White Corporation
#1400, 1 University Ave., Toronto, ON M5J 2P1
Tel: 416-367-6877; *Fax:* 416-367-6890
www.tri-white.com
Ticker Symbol: TWH
Company Type: Public
Profile: Tri-White Corporation is the owner & operator of White Pass & Yukon Route. Port facilities, the passenger tourist railway, & related services operate in British Columbia, the Yukon Territory, & Alaska. Tri-White Corporation is also involved in merchant banking in Canada.

Trimac Income Fund
#1700, 800 - 5th Ave. SW, Calgary, AB T2P 5A3
Tel: 403-298-5100; *Fax:* 403-298-5146
investors@trimac.com
www.trimacincomefund.com
Ticker Symbol: TMA.UN
Company Type: Public
Profile: Trimac Income Fund is an unincorporated, open-ended limited purpose trust. Through its subsidiary, Trimac Transportation Services Limited Partnership, Trimac Income Fund is involved in the provision of bulk trucking services.

Uniglobe Travel International L.P.
#900, 1199 West Pender St., Vancouver, BC V6E 2R1
Tel: 604-718-2600; *Fax:* 604-718-2678
info@uniglobetravel.com
www.uniglobetravel.com
Company Type: Private
Profile: Travel franchise specializing in corporate travel services for small to medium accounts as well as individual travelers.

Upper Lakes Group Inc.
49 Jackes Ave., Toronto, ON M4T 1E2
Tel: 416-920-7610;
inquires@upperlakes.com
www.upperlakes.com
Company Type: Public
Profile: Upper Lakes Group Inc. moves, handles, & stores wet & dry bulk commodities & containerized cargoes. Areas of operation include the Great Lakes, Canada, & around the world. The company operates a large fleet of ships on the Great Lakes & the St. Lawrence Seaway, & it owns & operates grain terminal facilities throughout the Great Lakes & the St. Lawrence Seaway System. Upper Lakes Group Inc. is also involved in property development.

Vector Aerospace Corporation
#300, 105 Bedford Rd., Toronto, ON M5R 2K4
Tel: 416-925-1143; *Fax:* 416-925-7214
info@vectoraerospace.com
www.vectoraerospace.com
Ticker Symbol: RNO
Company Type: Public
Profile: Vector Aerospace Corporation provides aviation maintenance, repair & overhaul services. Services are offered to both commercial & military customers, with fixed wing & rotary wing aircraft. Facilities are located in Canada, the United States, & the United Kingdom.

VersaCold
2115 Commissioner St., Vancouver, BC V5L 1A6
Tel: 604-255-4656; *Fax:* 604-255-4330
Toll-Free: 800-563-2653
info@versacold.com
www.versacold.com
Company Type: Public
Profile: Refrigerated warehousing & logistics

VIA Rail Canada Inc.
Customer Relations, PO Box 8116 A, Montréal, QC H3C 3N3
Tel: 514-871-6000; *Fax:* 514-871-6104
Toll-Free: 888-842-7245
customer_relations@viarail.ca
www.viarail.ca
Company Type: Crown
Profile: On behalf of the Government of Canada, VIA Rail Canada operates a safe, efficient, & environmentally responsible passenger rail service. VIAÆRail serves 450 communities across Canada.

Vitran Corporation Inc.
#701, 185 The West Mall, Toronto, ON M9C 5L5
Tel: 416-596-7664; *Fax:* 416-596-8039
webmaster@vitran.com
www.vitran.com
Ticker Symbol: VTN
Company Type: Public
Profile: Vitran Corporation provides freight surface transportation & related logistics services in Canada & the United States. Services include logistics, less-than-truckload, & truckload services.

Volvo Cars of Canada Corp.
Customer Service, 175 Gordon Baker Rd., Toronto, ON M2H 2N7
Toll-Free: 800-663-8255
customerservice@volvo.com
www.volvocanada.com
Company Type: Private
Profile: Volvo Cars of Canada is an automotive manufacturer, which focuses on safety, quality, & environmental care.

Wallenius Wilhelmsen Logistics Vehicle Svs Canada Ltd
Annacis Auto Terminals, #100, 820 Dock Rd., Delta, BC V3M 6A3
Tel: 604-521-6681; *Fax:* 604-522-7783
cms@2wglobal.com
www.2wglobal.com
Company Type: Private
Profile: Wallenius Wilhelmsen Logistics is engaged in the provision of global factory-to-dealer transport solutions. The company serves the automotive, construction equipment, & agricultural industries. Innovative solutions have been developed to reduce the impact of the company's operations on the environment. In British Columbia, the company operates an automotive terminal located on the Fraser River. It handles Mercedes Benz, BMW, Subaru, Kia, Mitsubishi, Honda, Nissan, & Hyundai.

WestJet Airlines Ltd.
5055 - 11 St. NE, Calgary, AB T2E 8N4
Tel: 403-444-2600; *Fax:* 403-444-2261
investor_relations@westjet.com
www.westjet.com
Ticker Symbol: WJA
Company Type: Public
Profile: Scheduled passenger airline transportation is provided by WestJet Airlines.

World Point Terminals Inc.
#110, 1981, av McGill College, Montréal, QC H3A 3C1
Tel: 403-261-3700;
broy@wpo.ca
www.wpo.ca
Ticker Symbol: WPO
Company Type: Public
Profile: World Point Terminals Inc. & its subsidiaries are involved in the ownership & operation of oil terminaling facilities. The facilities tranship crude oil, refined petroleum, & other liquid products. Bulk storage is also offered. Liquid bulk storage & terminal facilities are situated in North America, the Bahamas, & the Netherlands.

Yanke Group of Companies
2815 Lorne Ave., Saskatoon, SK S7J 0S5
Tel: 306-955-4221; *Fax:* 306-955-5663
Toll-Free: 800-667-7988
yanke_sales@yanke.ca
www.yanke.ca
Company Type: Private
Profile: Yanke Group of Companies is an international transportation company. It offers eight terminals across Canada. The company specializes in moving products such as agri-chemicals, temperature sensitive commodities, hazardous materials, & food stuffs.

Zeena Transport
PO Box 759, Morden, MB R6M 1A7
Tel: 204-822-4915; *Fax:* 204-822-4687
info@zeenatransport.com
www.zeenatransport.com
Company Type: Private
Profile: Zeena Transport provides refrigerated & dry van service. The company also offers a brokerage service to ensure that freight is moved effectively.

Transportation Manufacturers & Services

Héroux-Devtek inc
Tour est, Complexe Saint-Charles, #658, 1111, rue Saint-Charles, Longueuil, QC J4K 5G4
Tel: 450-679-3330; *Fax:* 450-679-3666
ir@herouxdevtek.com
www.herouxdevtek.com
Ticker Symbol: HRX
Company Type: Public
Profile: Manufacturers of aircraft parts & auxiliary equipment; Wholesalers of transportation equipment & supplies; Airports, flying fields & airport terminal services

Magellan Aerospace Corporation
3160 Derry Rd. East, Mississauga, ON L4T 1A9
Tel: 905-677-1889; *Fax:* 905-677-5658
info@magellanaerospace.com
www.magellanaerospace.com
Ticker Symbol: MAL
Company Type: Public
Profile: Manufacturers of aircraft parts & auxiliary equipment, aircraft engines & engine parts

Northstar Aerospace
 # 3430, 695 Bishop St. N, Cambridge, ON N3H 4V2
Tel: 519-653-5774; *Fax:* 519-653-7190
infocambridge@nsaero.com
www.nsaero.com
Ticker Symbol: NAS
Company Type: Public
Profile: Manufacturers of motor vehicle parts & accessories, aircraft parts & auxiliary equipment, speed changers, industrial high-speed drives, gears, aircraft engines & engine parts; Airports, flying fields & airport terminal services

Pratt & Whitney Canada
1000, boul Marie-Victorin, Longueuil, QC J4G 1A1
Tel: 450-677-9411; *Toll-Free:* 800-268-8000
maria.mandato@pwc.ca (Media Relations)
www.pwc.ca
Company Type: Private
Profile: Pratt & Whitney Canada is a designer & manufacturer of aircraft engines. The company also sells, rents, & repairs its products. Pratt & Whitney Canada's new generation engines surpass ICAO standards for low emissions & low noise. With research & manufacturing facilities throughout Canada & around the globe, Pratt & Whitney Canada is a major research & development investor in the Canadian aerospace industry.

Rolls-Royce Canada Ltd.
9500, ch de Côte-de-Liesse, Montréal, QC H8T 1A2
Tel: 514-636-0964; *Fax:* 514-636-9969
www.rolls-royce.com
Company Type: Private
Profile: Canadian operations consist of engineering, repair, & overhaul within the diversified aerospace, industrial engine, & energy businesses. Facilities are situated in Montréal, Quebec & Vancouver, British Columbia. Customers include airlines, government bodies, & corporate operators around the world.

Wescast Industries Inc.
150 Savannah Oaks Dr., Brantford, ON N3T 5L8
Tel: 519-750-0000; *Fax:* 519-720-1629
investor.relations@wescast.com
www.wescast.com
Ticker Symbol: WCS.A
Company Type: Public
Profile: Manufacturers of motor vehicle regional parts & accessories; Wholesalers of motor vehicle supplies & new parts

Trucking Companies

AMJ Campbell Inc.
1445 Courtneypark Dr., Mississauga, ON L5T 2E3
Tel: 905-795-3785; *Fax:* 905-670-3787
www.amjcampbell.com
Ticker Symbol: AMJ
Company Type: Public
Profile: Local trucking with storage; Trucking, except local

Can-Truck Inc.
655 Bloor St. West, Oshawa, ON L1J 5Y6
Tel: 905-404-6622; *Fax:* 905-404-6620
donf@can-truck.com
www.can-truck.com
Company Type: Private
Profile: Concentrates mainly on truckload freight including consolation and distribution throughout North America

Canadian Freightways
Lake City Industrial Park, 7867 Express St., Burnaby, BC V5A 1S8
Tel: 604-420-4044; *Fax:* 604-420-4312
Toll-Free: 888-868-7923
http://cf.cfmvmt.com
Company Type: Private
Profile: North American Coverage: Canadian Freightways provides services to 25,000 points across Canada and the U.S. through an integrated network of regional carriers including sister companies Epic Express and Click Express and strategic partners Averitt Express, New England Motor Freight, Midwest Motor Express and the Connection Company. Regional Expertise: Each partner in their North American network is a regional specialist providing overnight and second day service within their region. Partners operate local Service Centers and are represented by professional drivers and sales teams in key economic communities.

Challenger Motor Freight Inc.
300 Maple Grove Rd., Cambridge, ON N3E 1B7
Tel: 519-653-6226; *Fax:* 519-653-9810
Toll-Free: 800-265-6358
info1@challenger.com
www.challenger.com
Company Type: Private
Profile: Challenger transports goods between Canada and anywhere in North America. Has a full range of transportation, warehousing and logistics services

International Truck and Engine Corporation Canada
5500 North Service Rd., 4th Fl., Burlington, ON L7L 5H7
Tel: 905-332-3323; *Fax:* 905-332-2965
www.internationaldelivers.com
Company Type: Private
Profile: Dealers of trucks, buses, vans: engines, parts, services & financing

Motrux Inc.
731 Belgrave Way, Delta, BC V3M 5R8
Tel: 604-527-1000; *Fax:* 604-527-1002
Toll-Free: 800-663-3436
info@motrux.com
www.motrux.com
Company Type: Private
Profile: Motrux is a carrier which serves a wide range of industries throughout North America. In addition to its head office in Delta, British Columbia, it also has an office in Oakville, Ontario.

Mullen Group Income Fund
PO Box 87, 1 Maple Leaf Rd., Aldersyde, AB T0L 0A0
Tel: 403-652-8888; *Fax:* 403-601-8301
ir@mullentransportation.com
www.mullen-group.com
Ticker Symbol: MTL
Company Type: Public
Profile: Offices of holding companies; Long-distance trucking; Local trucking with storage; Various oil & gas fields services

Polar Express Transportation Ltd.
#4, 10097 - 201 St., Langley, BC V1M 3G4
Tel: 604-888-3729; *Fax:* 604-888-3759
accounting@polarexpresstrans.com
www.polarexpresstrans.com
Company Type: Private
Profile: Polar Express Transportation is a Canadian & USA bonded carrier, which meets customers' distribution needs. Full & LTL loads are hauled between British Columbia, western Canada, & the United States.

Swift Dispatch Service Ltd.
32 West 5th Ave., Vancouver, BC V5Y 1H5
Tel: 604-873-5422; *Fax:* 604-879-2311
info@swiftdispatch.com
www.swiftdispatch.com
Company Type: Private

TLI FlatDecks Inc.
1260 Cliveden Ave., Delta, BC V3M 6Y1
Tel: 877-517-1177; *Fax:* 604-527-1175
www.tliflatdecks.net
Company Type: Private
Profile: The international flat deck specialized carrier is based in Delta BC. It services all North America.

Utilities

Algonquin Power Income Fund
2845 Bristol Circle, Oakville, ON L6H 7H7
Tel: 905-465-4500; *Fax:* 905-465-4514
apif@algonquinpower.com
www.algonquinpower.com
Ticker Symbol: APF
Company Type: Public
Profile: Algonquin Power Income Fund is an open-ended investment trust. It owns or has interests in a portfolio of renewable power & sustainable infrastructure assets throughout Canada & the United States. The Trust's facilities include the following: hydroelectric generation, wind energy, energy from waste, landfill gas, biomass-fired generation, natural gas cogeneration, water distribution, & wastewater treatment.

AltaGas Income Trust
#1700, 355 - 4th Ave. SW, Calgary, AB T2P 0J1
Tel: 403-691-7575; *Fax:* 403-691-7576
Toll-Free: 888-890-2715
feedback@altagas.ca
www.altagas.ca
Ticker Symbol: ALA
Company Type: Public
Profile: The energy infrastructure organization acquires, grows, & optimizes gas & power infrastructure. AltaGas Income Trust focuses upon renewable energy sources.

AltaGas Utility Group Inc.
#540, 355 - 4 Ave. SW, Calgary, AB T2P 0J1
Tel: 403-806-3310; *Fax:* 403-806-3311
information@altagasutility.com
www.altagasutilitygroup.com
Ticker Symbol: AUI
Company Type: Public
Profile: AltaGas Utility Group Inc. is involved in the natural gas distribution marketplace. The company invests in infrastructure-based utility & related businesses. It holds interest in the following companies: AltaGas Utilities Inc., Inuvik Gas Ltd., Heritage Gas Limited, & Ikhil Joint Venture.

ATCO Ltd.
#1400, 909 - 11th Ave. SW, Calgary, AB T2R 1N6
Tel: 403-292-7500; *Fax:* 403-292-7623
info@atco.com
www.atco.com
Ticker Symbol: ACO
Company Type: Public
Profile: The management holding company consists of the following main divisions: utilities, which includes natural gas & electricity transmission & distribution; power generation, which features the operation of hydroelectric, coal, & natural gas fired power plants; & global enterprises, which comprises ATCO Frontec, ATCO Midstream, ATCO Structures, ATCO Travel, ATCO I-Tek, & ATCO Noise Management.

Atomic Energy of Canada Limited
2251 Speakman Dr., Mississauga, ON L5K 1B2
Tel: 905-823-9040; *Fax:* 905-823-1290
Toll-Free: 866-886-2325
info@aecl.ca
www.aecl.ca
Company Type: Crown
Profile: Manufacturers of various industrial inorganic chemicals, measuring & controlling devices, special industry machinery; Commercial physical & biological research; Management services; Electric services

Bell Aliant Regional Communications Income Fund
1 Brunswick Sq., 5th Fl., Saint John, NB E2L 4L4
Tel: 877-248-3113; *Fax:* 877-498-2464
investors@bell.aliant.ca
www.bell.aliant.ca
Ticker Symbol: BA.UN
Company Type: Public
Profile: The wireline company operates in Atlantic Canada, Quebec, & Ontario.

Boralex Inc.
36, rue Lajeunesse, Kingsey Falls, QC J0A 1B0
Tel: 819-363-5860; *Fax:* 819-363-5866
info@boralex.com
www.boralex.com
Ticker Symbol: BLX
Company Type: Public
Profile: The electricity producer provides the following types of power generation: natural gas cogeneration, hydroelectric, wind power, & wood-residue.

BP Canada Energy Company
240-4th Ave., SW, Calgary, AB T2P 2H8
Tel: 403-233-1313;
www.bp.com
Company Type: Public
Profile: BP is an energy company which provides its customers with fuel for transportation, energy for heat & light, retail services, & petrochemical products.

Brantford Power Inc.
84 Market St. 3rd Fl., Brantford, ON N3T 5N8
Tel: 519-751-3522; *Fax:* 519-753-6130
brantfordpower@brantford.ca
www.brantfordpower.com
Company Type: Public
Profile: Brantford Power strives to provide safe, reliable, & competitively priced services to customers, while providing value for municipal shareholder.

British Columbia Hydro
6911 Southpoint Dr., Burnaby, BC V3N 4X8
Tel: 604-224-9376; *Fax:* 604-528-3137
Toll-Free: 800-224-9376
www.bchydro.com
Company Type: Crown
Profile: Electric services

British Columbia Utilities Commission
PO Box 250, 900 Howe St., Vancouver, BC V6Z 2N3
Tel: 604-660-4700; *Fax:* 604-660-1102
Toll-Free: 800-663-1385
commission.secretary@bcuc.com
www.bcuc.com
Company Type: Public
Profile: The British Columbia Utilities Commission is an independent regulatory agency of the Provincial Government. The Commission's primary responsibility is the regulation of British Columbia's natural gas & electricity utilities. It also regulates intra-provincial pipelines & universal compulsory automobile insurance.

Cambridge & North Dumfries Hydro Inc.
PO Box 1060, 1500 Bishop St., Cambridge, ON N1R 5X6
Tel: 519-621-3530; *Fax:* 519-621-0383
Company Type: Public
Profile: Cambridge & North Dumfries Hydro Inc. is a local distribution company which delivers electricity to the community on a not-for-profit basis. Local distribution rates are approved by the Ontario Energy Board.

Canadian Hydro Developers, Inc.
#500, 1324 - 17 Ave. SW, Calgary, AB T2T 5S8
Tel: 403-269-9379; *Fax:* 403-244-7388
canhydro@canhydro.com
www.canhydro.com
Ticker Symbol: KHD
Company Type: Public
Profile: Canadian Hydro Developers, Inc. owns, develops, & operates generating facilities, which are certified, or slated for certification, under Environment Canada's EcoLogo Program. Renewable power generation facilities are situated in Quebec, Ontario, Alberta, & British Columbia. The renewable generation portfolio includes water, wind, & biomass technologies. The company's wholly-owned subsidiary is Canadian Renewable Energy Corporation.

Canadian Utilities Limited
#1400, 909 - 11th Ave. SW, Calgary, AB T2R 1N6
Tel: 403-292-7500; *Fax:* 403-292-7623
investors@canadian-utilities.com
www.canadian-utilities.com
Ticker Symbol: CU
Company Type: Public
Profile: Part of the ATCO Group of Companies, Canadian Utilities Limited is engaged in natural gas & electricity transmission & distribution, as well as technology, logistics, & energy services.

CU Inc.
#1600, 909 - 11 Ave. SW, Calgary, AB T2R 1N6
Tel: 403-292-7500; *Fax:* 403-292-7532
www.canadian-utilities.com
Ticker Symbol: CIU.PR.A
Company Type: Public
Profile: A wholly owned subsidiary of Canadian Utilities Limited, CU Inc. is involved in natural gas & electricity transmission & distribution, as well as power generation. CU Inc.'s subsidiaries include CU Water Limited, ATCO Gas & Pipelines Ltd., ATCO Electric Ltd., & Alberta Power (2000) Ltd.

Emera Incorporated
Barrington Tower, Scotia Square, PO Box 910, 1894 Barrington St., 18th Fl., Halifax, NS B3J 2W5
Tel: 902-450-0507; *Fax:* 902-428-6112
Toll-Free: 888-450-0507
investors@emera.com
www.emera.com
Ticker Symbol: EMA
Company Type: Public
Profile: The holding company is involved in the energy sector. Emera Inc.'s subsidiaries include Bangor Hydro-Electric Company, Nova Scotia Power Inc., Emera Energy, Maritimes & Northeast Pipeline, Brunswick Pipeline, Emera Utility Services, & Grand Bahama Power Ltd.

Enbridge Income Fund
Fifth Avenue Place, #3000, 425 - 1st St. SW, Calgary, AB T2P 3L8
Tel: 403-231-3900; *Fax:* 403-231-3920
webmaster@enbridgeincomefund.com
www.enbridgeincomefund.com
Ticker Symbol: ENF.UN
Company Type: Public
Profile: The unincorporated, open-ended trust is the owner of the following organizations: Enbridge Pipelines (Saskatchewan) Inc. (Saskatchewan System); NRGreen Power Limited Partnership (50% interest); wind power projects; & Alliance Canada Pipeline (50% interest). Enbridge is also developing electrical generation opportunities with waste heat. Operations are conducted in western Canada.

Energy Savings Income Fund
#2630, 100 King St. West, Toronto, ON M5X 1E1
Tel: 416-367-2998; *Fax:* 416-367-4749
fundinfo@energysavingsincomefund.com
www.esif.ca
Ticker Symbol: SIF
Company Type: Public
Profile: The open-ended, limited purpose trust is involved in the sale of natural gas & electricity to both residential & commercial customers. Operating affiliates inlcude Ontario Energy Savings L.P., Energy Savings (Manitoba) L.P., Energy Savings (Quebec) L.P., ES (B.C.) Limited Partnership, Alberta Energy Savings L.P., Illinois Energy Savings Corp., New York Energy Savings Corp., Indiana Energy Savings Corp., & Energy Savings Texas Corp.

Enersource Hydro Mississauga
3240 Mavis Rd., Mississauga, ON L5C 3K1
Tel: 905-273-9050; *Fax:* 905-566-2731
info@enersource.com
www.enersource.com
Company Type: Private
Profile: Provides electricity to the City of Mississauga

ENMAX Corporation
141 - 50 Ave. SE, Calgary, AB T2G 4S7
Tel: 403-514-3000; *Fax:* 403-310-2010
Toll-Free: 877-571-7111
customercare@enmax.com
www.enmax.com
Company Type: Public
Profile: ENMAX Corporation provides electricity & natural gas energy services in Alberta.

EPCOR Power Equity Ltd.
Investor Relations, EPCOR Centre, 10065 Jasper Ave., Edmonton, AB T5J 3B1
Tel: 780-412-4297; *Fax:* 780-412-3808
Toll-Free: 866-896-4636
InvestorInquiries@epcorpowerlp.ca
www.epcor.ca
Ticker Symbol: EPP.PR.A
Company Type: Public
Profile: EPCOR's business & power generation assets, plus other assets in the United States, are indirectly held by EPCOR Power Equity Ltd.

EPCOR Power L.P.
EPCOR Centre, 10065 Jasper Ave., 20th Fl., Edmonton, AB T5J 3B1
Tel: 780-412-4297; *Fax:* 780-412-3808
Toll-Free: 866-896-4636
investorinquiries@epcorpowerlp.ca
www.epcorpowerlp.ca
Ticker Symbol: EP.UN
Company Type: Public
Profile: EPCOR Power L.P. is a limited partnership, which is involved in the generation of electricity & steam, through it ownership & operation of a portfolio power plants. Earnings & cash flows are derived from this activity. The Partnership's wholly-owned power generation assets are situated in Canada & the United States. The General Partner of the Partnership, EPCOR Power Services Ltd., is responsible for management of the Partnership.

Fortis Inc.
Fortis Bldg., PO Box 8837, #1201, 139 Water St., St. John's, NL A1B 3T2
Tel: 709-737-2800; *Fax:* 709-737-5307
investorrelations@fortisinc.com
www.fortisinc.com
Ticker Symbol: FTS
Company Type: Public
Profile: Fortis Inc. is an international distribution utility holding company, which serves gas & electricity customers. The company also owns hotels & commercial real estate in Canada.

FortisAlberta
320 17th Avenue SW, Calgary, AB T2S 2V1
Tel: 403-514-4000; *Fax:* 403-514-4001
Toll-Free: 866-717-3113
www.fortisalberta.com
Company Type: Public
Profile: FortisAlberta provides power to various communities in Alberta. It is affliated with the Fortis Family of Companies.

FortisOntario
PO Box 1218, 1130 Bertie St., Fort Erie, ON L2A 5Y2
Tel: 905-871-0330;
www.cornwallelectric.com
Company Type: Public
Profile: FortisOntario is an innovative growth company with core businesses focused on electricity distribution, transmission, & generation. It is 100% Canadian owned & is affliated with the Fortis Family of Companies.

Gaz Métro inc
1717, rue du Havre, Montréal, QC H2K 2X3
Tel: 514-598-3444; *Fax:* 514-598-3144
Toll-Free: 800-361-4005
info@gazmetro.com
www.gazmetro.com
Ticker Symbol: GZM
Company Type: Public
Profile: Offices of holding companies; Natural gas transmission & distribution; Retail in household appliance stores; Equipment rental & leasing

Gaz Métro Limited Partnership
1717, rue du Havre, Montréal, QC H2K 2X3
Tel: 514-598-3444; *Fax:* 514-598-3144
investors@gazmetro.com
www.gazmetro.com
Ticker Symbol: GZM
Company Type: Public
Profile: Gaz Métro Limited Partnership focuses upon the distribution of natural gas, through its interests in natural gas transmission companies. The company is also engaged in the sale of goods in the energy & fiber optics fields, as well as the diagnosis & rehabilitation of drinking water & wastewater infrastructures. In order to reduce greenhouse gas emissions, Gaz Métro has adopted an environmental policy, an environmental management system, & energy efficiency programs.

Great Lakes Hydro Income Fund
#200, 480, boul de la Cité, Gatineau, QC J8T 8R3
Tel: 819-561-2722; *Fax:* 819-561-7188
Toll-Free: 888-327-2722
unitholderenquiries@greatlakeshydro.com
www.greatlakeshydro.com
Ticker Symbol: GLH
Company Type: Public
Profile: Electric services; Open-ended management investment offices.

Grimsby Power Incorporated
231 Roberts Rd., Grimsby, ON L3M 5N2
Tel: 905-945-5437; *Fax:* 905-945-9933
info@grimsbypower.com
www.grimsbypower.com
Company Type: Public
Profile: Grimsby Power Incorporated provides customers in Grimsby with electricity.

Guelph Hydro Electric Systems Inc.
395 Southgate Dr., Guelph, ON N1G 4Y1
Tel: 519-822-3010; *Fax:* 519-822-0960
bbagley@guelphhydro.com
www.guelphhydro.com
Company Type: Public
Profile: Guelph Hydro Electric Systems Inc. is Guelph's and Rockwood's electricity distribution company. They deliver electricity, maintain the lines to homes and businesses provide 24-hr emergency service and ensure that the local distribution system meets Guelph's and Rockwood's growing needs.

Hydro One Inc.
483 Bay St., 15th Fl., Toronto, ON M5G 2P5
Tel: 416-345-6867; *Fax:* 416-345-6225
Toll-Free: 877-955-1155
investor.relations@hydroone.com
www.hydroone.com
Company Type: Public
Profile: HydroOne is the largest electricity delivery company in Ontario. It is a holding company for various subsidiaries. It provides electric services in Toronto.

Hydro-Québec
75, boul René-Lévesque ouest, Montréal, QC H2Z 1A4
Tel: 514-289-2211; *Fax:* 514-289-5773
Toll-Free: 800-790-2424
www.hydroquebec.com
Company Type: Crown
Profile: Electricity services in Quebec

Independent Electricity System Operator
PO Box 4474 A, Toronto, ON M5W 4E5
Tel: 905-403-6900; *Fax:* 905-403-6921
customer.relations@ieso.ca
www.ieso.ca
Company Type: Public
Profile: The IESO balances the supply of & demand for electricity in Ontario & then directs its flow across the province's transmission lines. The IESO works at the heart of Ontario's power system, connecting all participants that produce electricity, transmitters that send it across the province, retailers that buy & sell it, industries & businesses that use it in large quantities, & local distribution companies that deliver it to homes.

Innergex Renewable Energy Inc.
#1255, 1111, rue Saint-Charles ouest, Longueuil, QC J4K 5G4
Tel: 450-928-2550; *Fax:* 450-928-2544
jtrudel@innergex.com
www.innergex.com
Ticker Symbol: INE
Company Type: Public
Profile: Innergex Renewable Energy develops & operates renewable power generating facilities. If focuses upon the wind power & hydroelectric sectors.

Kenora Hydro Electric Corp. Ltd
City Hall, 1 Main St. South, Kenora, ON P9N 3X2
Tel: 807-467-2000;
service@kenora.ca
Company Type: Private
Profile: Distributes electricity to the towns of Kenora and Keewatin; has 12 employees dedicated to the delivery of electricity to its customers

Keyera Facilities Income Fund
#600, 144 - 4 Ave. SW, Calgary, AB T2P 3N4
Tel: 403-205-8300; *Fax:* 403-205-8303
ir@keyera.com
www.keyera.com
Ticker Symbol: KEY.UN
Company Type: Public
Profile: The Keyera Facilities Income Fund is an unincorporated open-ended trust. It owns 100% interest in Keyera Energy Canada Partnership. Keyera is engaged in the following activities: gathering & processing natural gas; storing & transporting natural gas liquids & crude oil; & marketing natural gas liquids.

London Hydro
111 Horton St., London, ON N6A 4J8
Tel: 519-661-5503; *Fax:* 519-661-5838
admin@londonhydro.com
www.londonhydro.com
Company Type: Public
Profile: The sole shareholder of London Hydro is the City of London. London Hydro provides London residents & businesses with electricity, through a network of overhead & underground power lines.

Manitoba Hydro
PO Box 815 Main, 360 Portage Ave., Winnipeg, MB R3C 2P4
Tel: 204-480-5900; *Fax:* 204-475-0069
Toll-Free: 888-624-9376
publicaffairs@hydro.mb.ca
www.hydro.mb.ca
Company Type: Crown
Profile: Manitoba Hydro is a major energy utility. It serves electric & natural gas customers in Manitoba.

Maritime Electric
c/o Island Customer Service Centre, PO Box 1328, 180 Kent St., Charlottetown, PE C1A 7N2
Fax: 902-629-3630
Toll-Free: 800-670-1012
customerservice@maritimeelectric.com
www.maritimeelectric.com
Company Type: Public
Profile: Maritime Electric operates according to the Electric Power Act & the Renewable Energy Act to deliver electricity on Prince Edward Island.

MAXIM Power Corp.
#1210, 715 - 5th Ave. SW, Calgary, AB T2P 2X6
Tel: 403-263-3021; *Fax:* 403-263-9125
maxim@maximpowercorp.com
www.maximpowercorp.com
Ticker Symbol: MXG
Company Type: Public
Profile: MAXIM Power Corp. is an independent power producer. The company is involved in the acquisition, development, ownership, & operation of environmentally responsible power projects. Its assets include coal & natural gas powered generators in western Canada, the United States, & France.

Medicine Hat Electric
2172 Brier Park Place NW, Medicine Hat, AB T1C 1S6
Tel: 403-529-8262; *Fax:* 403-502-8060
elecdist@medicinehat.ca
Company Type: Private
Profile: Responsible for providing electrical power, natural gas, water treatment & supply, and waste management services to the city of Medicine Hat

New Brunswick Power Distribution & Customer Svs. Corp
PO Box 2000, 515 King St., Fredericton, NB E3B 4X1
Tel: 506-458-4444; *Fax:* 506-458-4000
Toll-Free: 800-663-6272
customerservices@nbpower.com
www.nbpower.com
Company Type: Crown
Profile: NB Power provides safe & sustainable energy services to homes, businesses, & facilities in New Brunswick. Electricity is generated at sixteen facilities.

Newfoundland & Labrador Hydro
Hydro Place, PO Box 12400, 500 Columbus Dr., St.John's, NL A1B 4K7
Tel: 709-737-1400; *Fax:* 709-737-1800
Toll-Free: 888-737-1296
hydro@nlh.nl.ca; tenders@nlh.nl.ca
www.nlh.nl.ca
Company Type: Public
Profile: Newfoundland & Labrador Hydro is the primary generator of safe & reliable electricity to residents, utilities, & industries across the province. The company's assets include hydroelectric generating stations, high-voltage terminal stations, lower-voltage interconnected distribution stations, diesel plants, gas turbines, transmission & distribution lines, & an oil-fired plant.

Newfoundland Power Inc.
PO Box 8910, 55 Kenmount Rd., St. John's, NL A1B 3P6
Tel: 709-737-2802; *Fax:* 709-737-2903
Toll-Free: 800-663-2802
contactus@newfoundlandpower.com
www.newfoundlandpower.com
Company Type: Public
Profile: Newfoundland Power Inc. is engaged in the operation of an integrated generation, transmission, & distribution system. Safe, reliable electricity is supplied to the island portion of Newfoundland & Labrador.

Niagara Peninsula Energy Inc.
PO Box 120, 7447 Pin Oak Dr., Niagara Falls, ON L2E 6S9
Tel: 905-356-2681; *Fax:* 905-356-0118
Toll-Free: 877-270-3938
info@npei.ca
www.npei.ca
Company Type: Public
Profile: Niagara Peninsula Energy Inc. provides local electricity distribution & related services in the Township of West Lincoln, the City of Niagara Falls, the Town of Pelham, & the Town of Lincoln. It serves both business & residential customers.

Northwest Territories Power Corporation
4 Capital Dr., Hay River, NT X0E 1G2
Tel: 867-874-5200;
info@ntpc.com
www.ntpc.com
Company Type: Crown
Profile: Northwest Territories Power Corporation generates & delivers power across the Northwest Territories. The corporation operates 28 separate power systems. Northwest Territories Power Corporation attempts to reduce its environmental impact with natural gas engines in Inuvik, rather than shipping in diesel.

Nova Scotia Power Inc.
PO Box 910, #1800, 1894 Barrington St., Halifax, NS B3J 2W5
Tel: 902-450-0507; *Fax:* 902-428-6112
Toll-Free: 800-428-6230
investors@emera.com
www.nspower.ca
Ticker Symbol: NSI
Company Type: Public
Profile: Nova Scotia Power Inc. is engaged in the generation, transmission, & distribution of electric power across Nova Scotia.

Ontario Power Generation Inc.
700 University Ave., Toronto, ON M5G 1X6
Tel: 416-592-2555; *Toll-Free:* 877-592-2555
investor.relations@opg.com; media@opg.com
www.opg.com; mypowercareer@opg.com
Company Type: Crown
Profile: The electricity generation company operates in a safe & environmentally responsible manner to generate & sell electricity throughout Ontario. Assets include sixty-five hydroelectric generating stations, five fossil generating stations, & three nuclear generating stations.

Oshawa PUC Networks Inc.
100 Simcoe St. South, Oshawa, ON L1H 7M7
Tel: 905-723-4623; *Fax:* 905-743-5222
contactus@opuc.on.ca
www.opuc.on.ca
Company Type: Private
Profile: Oshawa PUC Networks distributes electricity to homes & businesses in Oshawa.

Peterborough Utilities Group
PO Box 4125 Main, 1867 Ashburnham Dr., Peterborough, ON K9J 6Z5
Tel: 705-748-9300; *Fax:* 705-748-6761
info@peterboroughutilities.ca
www.peterboroughutilities.ca
Company Type: Public
Profile: Peterborough Utilities Group delivers & sells utility-related products & services.

Powerex Corp.
#1400, 666 Burrard St., Vancouver, BC V6C 2X8
Tel: 604-891-5000; *Fax:* 604-891-6060
Toll-Free: 800-220-4907
Brian.Moghadam@powerex.com (Business Dev)
www.powerex.com
Company Type: Public
Profile: As a wholly-owned subsidiary of BC Hydro, Powerex markets BC Hydro's surplus electricity. Powerex is a participant in energy markets across North America, where it supplies & buys wholesale power, natural gas, ancillary services, & environmental products.

Saint John Energy
PO Box 850, Saint John, NB E2L 4C7
Tel: 506-658-5252; *Fax:* 506-658-0868
Toll-Free: 877-907-5550
www.sjenergy.com
Company Type: Private
Profile: Responsible for providing electricity to the city of Saint John. Other services include tree trimming, rental of water heaters, street light repair

Saskatoon Light & Power
322 Brand Rd., Saskatoon, SK S7K 0J5
Tel: 306-975-2414; *Fax:* 306-975-3057
www.city.saskatoon.sk.ca/org/electrical
Company Type: Private
Profile: Founded in 1906, Saskatoon Light & Power distributes electrical services to citizens & businesses of the Saskatoon area that lies roughly within the 1958 boundary. The utility is also responsible for the street light system for the city.

SaskEnergy Incorporated
1777 Victoria Ave., Regina, SK S4P 4K5
Tel: 306-777-9225; *Toll-Free:* 800-567-8899
www.saskenergy.com
Company Type: Crown
Profile: The natural gas distribution company is a provincial Crown corporation. SaskEnergy Incorporated delivers safe & environmentally friendly natural gas to customers throughout Saskatchewan. The company also works with independent natural gas retailers to offer natural gas appliances, maintenance, & financing.

Spectra Energy Inc.
#1000, 1055 West Georgia St., Vancouver, BC V6E 3K9
Tel: 604-488-8000; *Fax:* 604-488-8500
www.duke-energy.com
Company Type: Public
Profile: Natural gas transmission & distribution; Electric services; Crude petroleum, natural gas & natural gas liquids extraction; Natural gas transmission; Special warehousing & storage.

Terasen Gas
PO Box 6666 Terminal, Vancouver, BC V6B 6M9
Tel: 250-979-4900; *Fax:* 888-224-2720
Toll-Free: 888-224-2710
customerservice@tersengas.com
www.terasengas.com
Company Type: Public
Profile: Tersan Gas delivers natural gas & piped propane to homes & businesses throughout BC. It has approximately 900,000 customers in 125 communities & provides service to 95% of BC's natural gas customers.

Toronto Hydro Corporation
14 Carlton St., Toronto, ON M5B 1K5
Tel: 416-542-3100; *Fax:* 416-542-3452
contactus@torontohydro.com
www.torontohydro.com
Company Type: Crown
Profile: Offices of holding companies; Electric services; Natural gas distribution.

TransAlta Corporation
PO Box 1900 M, 110 - 12 Ave. SW, Calgary, AB T2P 2M1
Tel: 403-267-7110; *Fax:* 403-267-2590
investor_relations@transalta.com
www.transalta.com
Ticker Symbol: TA
Company Type: Public
Profile: TransAlta Corporation is engaged in coal & gas-fired generation. The company carries out its activities in Canada, the United States, Mexico, & Australia.

TransAlta Power, L.P.
PO Box 1900 M, 110 - 12 Ave. SW, Calgary, AB T2P 2M1
Tel: 403-267-7110; *Fax:* 403-267-2590
investor_relations@transalta.com
www.transalta.com
Ticker Symbol: TA
Company Type: Public
Profile: Unit investment trusts, certificate/closed-end management offices; Electric services

TransCanada Corp.
450 - 1 St. SW, Calgary, AB T2P 5H1
Tel: 403-920-2000; *Fax:* 403-920-2200
communications@transcanada.com
www.transcanada.com
Ticker Symbol: TRP
Company Type: Public
Profile: TransCanada Corporation is engaged in the pipelines & energy business. Pipelines are located in Canada, the United States, & Mexico. Power operations & natural gas storage are part of the energy segment.

Utilities Kingston
PO Box 790, Kingston, ON K7L 4X7
Tel: 613-456-0000;
info@utilitieskingston.com
www.utilitieskingston.com
Company Type: Private
Profile: Utilities Kingston is responsible for supplying, distributing and metering electricity and natural gas in the City Central. Also responsible for supplying, distributing and metering water and for collecting, pumping and treating sewage for the entire city of Kingston

Wellington North Power Inc.
PO Box 359, 290 Queen St. West, Mount Forest, ON N0G 1A0
Tel: 519-323-1710; *Fax:* 519-323-2425
wnp@wellingtonnorthpower.com
www.wellingtonnorthpower.com
Company Type: Public
Profile: The distribution company delivers electricity & maintains service to residents & businesses. Wellington North Power Inc. serves the areas of Arthur, Mount Forest, & Holstein in Ontario.

Westario Power Inc.
24 Eastridge Rd., RR#2, Walkerton, ON N0G 2V0
Tel: 519-507-6937; *Toll-Free:* 866-978-2746
customer.service@westario.com
www.westario.com
Company Type: Public
Profile: Westario Power Inc. is engaged in the safe & reliable delivery of electricity. It is owned by the municipalities it serves. FortisOntario also has a 10% interest in Westario Power.

Yukon Electrical Company Limited
#100, 1100 - 1st Ave., Whitehorse, YT Y1A 3T4
Tel: 867-633-7000; *Fax:* 867-668-6692
Toll-Free: 800-661-0513
www.yukonelectrical.com
Company Type: Private
Profile: The Yukon Electrical Company Limited is a private, investor-owned utility which provides electrical services to Yukoners. The company works to design & construct its facilities in a way that reduces pollution & the impact of operations upon the environment.

Stock Exchanges

Canadian National Stock Exchange (CNSX)
c/o CNSX Markets Inc.
220 Bay St., 9th Fl.
Toronto, ON M5J 2W4
Tel: 416-572-2000; *Fax:* 416-572-4160
www.cnsx.ca
Former Name: Canadian Trading & Quotation System Inc.
Also Known As: CNSX
Year Founded: 2004

Canadian Unlisted Board Inc.
The Exchange Tower, Trading Services, Toronto Stock Exchange
130 King St. West
Toronto, ON M5X 1J2
Tel: 416-947-4705; *Fax:* 416-947-4280
cubadmin@cub.ca
www.cub.ca
Also Known As: CUB
Year Founded: 2000

ICE Futures Canada, Inc.
Commodity Exchange Tower
#400, 360 Main St.
Winnipeg, MB R3C 3Z4
Tel: 204-925-5000; *Fax:* 204-943-5448
www.theice.com
Other Contact Information: 204-925-5017 (Phone, ICE Clear Canada)
Former Name: Winnipeg Commodity Exchange Inc.
Ownership: Wholly owned subsidiary of IntercontinentalExchange (ICE), Atlanta, GA, USA
Year Founded: 1887

Montréal Exchange Inc. (MX)/ Bourse de Montréal Inc.
Tour de la Bourse
CP 61
800, carré Victoria
Montréal, QC H4Z 1A9
Tél: 514-871-2424; *Téléc:* 514-871-3514
Ligne sans frais: 800-361-5353
info@m-x.ca; communications@m-x.ca; finances@m-x.ca; legal@m-x.ca
www.m-x.ca
Other Contact Information: 00.800.36.15.35.35 (Toll-free from Great Britain & France); rh@m-x.ca (HR); marketdata@m-x.ca (Market Data); reg@m-x.ca (Regulation / Registration)
Also Known As: MX
Year Founded: 1874

Natural Gas Exchange Inc. (NGX)
#2330, 140 - 4 St. SW
Calgary, AB T2P 3N3
Tel: 403-974-1700; *Fax:* 403-974-1719
Clearing@ngx.com; Marketing@ngx.com
www.ngx.com
Other Contact Information: Ops@ngx.com (NGX Help Desk & Operations)
Also Known As: NGX
Ownership: Wholly owned by TMX Group Inc., Toronto, ON.
Year Founded: 1994

NEX Board
PO Box 11633
#2700, 650 West Georgia St.
Vancouver, BC V6B 4N9
Tel: 604-689-3334; *Fax:* 604-844-7502
Toll-Free: 866-344-5639
nex@tsxventure.com
www.tsx.com/en/nex
Also Known As: NEX
Year Founded: 2003

TMX Group Inc.
PO Box 450
130 King St. West, 3rd Fl.
Toronto, ON M5X 1J2
Tel: 416-947-4670; *Fax:* 416-947-4662
Toll-Free: 888-873-8392
info@tsx.com (TSX); information@tsxventure.com (TSX Venture)
www.tsx.com
Other Contact Information: Couriered deliveries to TMX Group Inc.: c/o Plus One Inc., First Canadian Place, 77 Adelaide St. West, Toronto, ON, M5X 1A4
Former Name: TSX Group Inc.
Also Known As: TSX-X

The Toronto Stock Exchange (TSX)
The Exchange Tower
PO Box 450
130 King St. West, 3rd Fl.
Toronto, ON M5X 1J2
Tel: 416-947-4670; *Fax:* 416-947-4770
Toll-Free: 888-873-8392
info@tsx.com; listedissuers@tsx.com; issuersupport@tsxconnect.com
www.tsx.com
Other Contact Information: marketregs@tsx.com (Investor Services); disclosure@tsx.com (Compliance & disclosure); queries@tsxdatalinx.com (TSX Datalinx)
Also Known As: TSX
Ownership: Subsidiary of TMX Group Inc., Toronto, ON
Year Founded: 1861

TSX Venture Exchange
PO Box 450
130 King St. West, 3rd Fl.
Toronto, ON M5X 1J2
Tel: 416-365-2200; *Fax:* 416-365-2224
Toll-Free: 877-421-2369
information@tsxventure.com
www.tsxventure.com
Other Contact Information: 888-873-8392 (Toll Free, Business Development); complianceanddisclosure@tsxventure.com (E-mail, Concerns regarding listed issuers)
Former Name: Canadian Venture Exchange
Ownership: Subsidiary of TMX Group Inc., Toronto, ON

Trust Companies

Trust Companies are regulated under the federal Trust and Loan Companies Act and operate under either provincial or federal legislation. The business of trust companies includes activities like those of a bank, plus fiduciary functions.

AGF Trust Company
Toronto-Dominion Centre
66 Wellington St. West, 31st Fl.
Toronto, ON M5K 1E9
Tel: 416-216-5353; *Toll-Free:* 800-244-8457
trust@agf.com
www.agf.com/mortgages
Ownership: Wholly owned subsidiary of AGF Management Limited.
Year Founded: 1988

All Nations Trust Company
#208, 345 Yellowhead Hwy.
Kamloops, BC V2H 1H1
Tel: 250-828-9770; *Fax:* 250-372-2585
Toll-Free: 800-663-2959
antco@antco.bc.ca
www.antco.bc.ca
Ownership: Private
Year Founded: 1984
Number of Employees: 13

B2B Trust
130 Adelaide St. West
Toronto, ON M5H 3P5
Tel: 416-947-7427; *Fax:* 416-947-9476
Toll-Free: 800-263-8349
www.b2b-trust.com
Former Name: Sun Life Trust Company
Ownership: Private. Subsidiary of Laurentian Bank of Canada, Montréal, QC.
Year Founded: 1991
Number of Employees: 258
Assets: $1-10 billion
Revenues: $50-100 million

The Bank of Nova Scotia Trust Company
Scotia Plaza
44 King St. West
Toronto, ON M5H 1H1
Tel: 416-866-6161; *Fax:* 416-866-3750
Also Known As: Scotiatrust
Ownership: Private. Subsidiary of Bank of Nova Scotia
Year Founded: 1993
Number of Employees: 450

BMO Trust Company
55 Bloor St. West, 12th Fl.
Toronto, ON M4W 3N5
Tel: 416-867-6784
AATinvestmentservices@bmo.com
www.advisorsadvantagetrust.com
Former Name: The Trust Company of Bank of Montréal
Also Known As: Advisor's Advantage Trust
Ownership: Wholly owned subsidiary of Bank of Montréal. Member of BMO Financial Group.

BNY Trust Company of Canada
#1101, 4 King St. West
Toronto, ON M5H 1B6
www.bankofny.com
Ownership: Wholly owned subsidiary of the Bank of New York Company Inc.
Year Founded: 2001

The Canada Trust Company
Toronto Dominion Centre
PO Box 1, TD Centre Stn. TD Centre
55 King St. West, 12th Fl.
Toronto, ON M5K 1A2
Toll-Free: 888-222-3456
www.tdcanadatrust.com

Year Founded: 1855

Canadian Western Trust Co. (CWT)
#600, 750 Cambie St.
Vancouver, BC V6B 0A2
Tel: 604-685-2081; *Fax:* 604-669-6069
Toll-Free: 800-663-1124
informationservices@cwt.ca
www.cwt.ca
Ownership: Wholly owned subsidiary of Canadian Western Bank

CIBC Mellon Trust Company
320 Bay St., 4th Fl.
Toronto, ON M5H 4A6
Tel: 416-643-5000; *Fax:* 416-643-6409
www.cibcmellon.ca
Ownership: Parent companies are Canadian Imperial Bank of Commerce & Mellon Financial Corporation
Year Founded: 1978
Number of Employees: 350
Assets: $500m-1 billion

CIBC Trust Corporation
#900, 55 Yonge St.
Toronto, ON M5E 1J4
Toll-Free: 800-465-3863
www.cibc.com

Citizens Trust Company
#401, 815 West Hastings St.
Vancouver, BC V6B 1B4
Tel: 604-682-7171; *Fax:* 604-708-7790
Toll-Free: 800-663-1435
www.citizensbank.ca

Clarica Trustco Company
PO Box 1601, Waterloo Stn. Waterloo
227 King St. South
Waterloo, ON N2J 4C5
Toll-Free: 888-864-5463
service@clarica.com
www.clarica.ca
Former Name: Mutual Trust Co.
Ownership: Subsidiary of Sun Life Assurance Company of Canada
Year Founded: 1918

Community Trust Company
2271 Bloor St. West
Toronto, ON M6S 1P1
Tel: 416-763-2291; *Fax:* 416-763-2444
officepresident@communitytrust.ca
Ownership: Private
Year Founded: 1975

Computershare Trust Company of Canada
100 University Ave., 11th Fl.
Toronto, ON M5J 2Y1
Tél: 416-263-9200; *Téléc:* 416-263-9261
Ligne sans frais: 800-663-9097
www.computershare.com
Former Name: Montreal Trust
Ownership: Public. Listed on the Australian Stock Exchange
Year Founded: 2000
Number of Employees: 1,400
Revenues: $1-5 million

The Effort Trust Company
240 Main St. East
Hamilton, ON L8N 1H5
Tel: 905-528-8956; *Fax:* 905-528-8182
www.efforttrust.ca
Ownership: Private. Wholly owned subsidiary of Effort Corporation.
Year Founded: 1978
Number of Employees: 100
Assets: $100-500 million
Revenues: $10-50 million

The Equitable Trust Company
#700, 30 St. Clair Ave. West
Toronto, ON M4V 3A1
Tel: 416-515-7000; *Fax:* 416-515-7001
mortgage@equitabletrust.com
www.equitabletrust.com
Ownership: Wholly-owned subsidiary of Equitable Group Inc.
Year Founded: 1970

Equity Transfer & Trust Company
#400, 200 University Ave.
Toronto, ON M5H 4H1
Tel: 416-361-0152; *Fax:* 416-361-0470
Toll-Free: 866-393-4891
info@equitytransfer.com, trustservices@equitytransfer.com
www.equitytransfer.com
Other Contact Information: newbusiness@equitytransfer.com (New Business); investor@equitytransfer.com (Investor Inquiries); clientservices@equitytransfer.com (Client Services)
Ownership: Wholly owned subsidiary of Grey Horse Capital Corporation.
Year Founded: 1990

Fiduciary Trust Company of Canada
Also listed under: *Financial Planning & Investment Management Companies*
#3000, 350 Seventh Ave. SW
Calgary, AB T2P 3N9
Tel: 403-543-3950; *Fax:* 403-543-3955
Toll-Free: 800-574-3822
www.fiduciarytrust.ca
Former Name: Bissett & Associates Investment Management Ltd.
Year Founded: 1982

Home Trust Company
Also listed under: *Credit Card Companies*
#2300, 145 King St. West
Toronto, ON M5H 1J8
Tel: 416-360-4663; *Fax:* 416-360-0401
Toll-Free: 800-990-7881
inquiry@hometrust.ca
www.hometrust.ca
Ownership: Public. Principal subsidiary of Home Capital Group Inc.
Year Founded: 1977
Number of Employees: 296
Assets: $1-10 billion
Revenues: $100-500 million

HSBC Trust Company (Canada)
620, 885 West Georgia St.
Vancouver, BC V6C 3E9
Tel: 604-641-1122; *Fax:* 604-641-1138
Toll-Free: 888-887-3388
www.hsbc.ca
Ownership: Private. Wholly owned subsidiary of HSBC Bank Canada
Year Founded: 1972
Number of Employees: 28

IBT Trust Company (Canada)
PO Box 231, First Canadian Place Stn. First Canadian Place
#2800, 100 King St. West
Toronto, ON M5X 1C8
Tel: 416-363-6427; *Fax:* 416-861-8989
www.ibtco.com
Other Contact Information: 416-861-8983 (Sales phone)
Ownership: Subsidiary of Investors Bank & Trust, Boston, MA
Year Founded: 1993

Industrial Alliance Trust Inc.
1080, Grande Allée ouest
Québec, QC G1K 7M3
Tel: 418-684-5000
www.inalco.com
Former Name: Industrial-Alliance Trust Company
Year Founded: 2000

Investors Group Trust Co. Ltd./ La Compagnie de Fiducie du Groupe Investors Ltée
One Canada Centre
447 Portage Ave.
Winnipeg, MB R3C 3B6
Tel: 204-943-0361; *Fax:* 204-949-1340
Toll-Free: 888-746-6344
www.investorsgroup.com
Ownership: Subsidiary of Investors Group Inc.
Year Founded: 1968

Laurentian Trust of Canada Inc.
1981, av. McGill College
Montréal, QC H3A 3K3
Tel: 514-284-4500; *Fax:* 514-284-3396
mail@laurentianbank.ca
www.laurentianbank.com
Ownership: Private. Wholly owned subsidiary of the Laurentian Bank of Canada.
Year Founded: 1939
Assets: $500m-1 billion
Revenues: $10-50 million

LBC Trust
130 Adelaide St. West
Toronto, ON M5H 3P5
Toll-Free: 800-522-1846
www.laurentianbank.ca
Ownership: Wholly-owned subsidiary of Laurentian Bank

Legacy Private Trust
PO Box 1
#800, 1 Toronto St.
Toronto, ON M5C 2V6
Tel: 416-868-0001; *Fax:* 416-868-6541
rlw@legacyprivatetrust.com
www.legacyprivatetrust.com
Other Contact Information: 416-868-4205 (Corporate Secretary Phone)
Ownership: Private
Year Founded: 2002

Maple Trust Company/ Compagnie Maple Trust
TD Waterhouse Tower, Toronto-Dominion Centre
PO Box 349
#3500, 79 Wellington St. West
Toronto, ON M5K 1K7
Tel: 416-350-7400; *Fax:* 416-350-7441
Toll-Free: 800-307-8341
MTDepositServices@mapletrust.com
www.mapletrust.com
Other Contact Information: 416-350-7488 (Client Services Hotline); 416-350-7498 (Client Services Fax); MTMortgageAdministration@mapletrust.com (Mortgage Email)
Former Name: London Trust and Savings Corporation
Ownership: Private. Member of the Scotiabank Group.
Year Founded: 1999
Assets: $1-10 billion

Mennonite Trust Limited
PO Box 40
3005 Central Ave.
Waldheim, SK S0K 4R0
Tel: 306-945-2080; *Fax:* 306-945-2225
mtl@sasktel.ca
www.mennonitetrust.com
Year Founded: 1917

M.R.S. Trust Company
#2100, 777 Bay St.
Toronto, ON M5G 2N4
Tel: 416-964-0028; *Fax:* 416-413-1723
Toll-Free: 800-387-2087
accounthelp@mrs.com
www.mackenziefinancial.com
Other Contact Information: mortgages@mrs.com (Email MRS Mortgages); 888-677-5363 (Mortgage Toll-Free); 416-926-0570 (Mortgage Information Phone)
Former Name: Mackenzie Trust Company
Also Known As: MRS Trust
Ownership: Subsidiary of Mackenzie Financial Corporation.
Year Founded: 1979

NATCAN Trust Company
National Bank
1100, rue University, 12e étage
Montréal, QC H3B 2G7
Tel: 514-871-7633; *Fax:* 514-871-7580
Toll-Free: 800-235-5566
Ownership: Wholly owned by National Bank Acquisition Holding Inc.

National Bank Trust/ Trust Banque National
1100, rue University, 10e étage
Montréal, QC H3B 2G7
Tel: 514-871-7240; *Toll-Free:* 800-463-6643
www.nbc.ca

Northern Trust Company, Canada
PO Box 526
#1510, 145 King St. West
Toronto, ON M5H 1J8
Tel: 416-365-7161; *Fax:* 416-365-9484
www.ntrs.com
Ownership: Subsidiary of Northern Trust Company, Chicago, USA
Number of Employees: 31

Oak Trust Company
One London Place
#1770, 255 Queens Ave.
London, ON N6A 5R8
Tel: 519-433-6629; *Fax:* 519-433-6652
Toll-Free: 866-973-6631
www.oaktrust.ca
Other Contact Information: 519-979-2338 (Windsor/Essex Phone)

Year Founded: 2004

Olympia Trust Company
#2300, 125 - 9th Ave. SW
Calgary, AB T2G 0P6
Tel: 403-261-0900; *Fax:* 403-265-1455
Toll-Free: 800-727-4493
info@olympiatrust.com
www.olympiatrust.com
Ownership: Wholly owned subsidiary of Olympia Financial Group Inc.

Pacific Corporate Trust Company
510 Burrard St., 2nd Fl.
Vancouver, BC V6C 3B9
Tel: 604-689-9853; *Fax:* 604-689-8144
pacific@pctc.com
www.pctc.com
Former Name: Pacific Corporate Services Limited
Ownership: Private
Year Founded: 1981

Peace Hills Trust Company
Samson Mall, Samson Cree Nation Reserve
PO Box 60
Hobbema, AB T0C 1N0
Tel: 780-585-3013; *Fax:* 780-585-2216
pht@peacehills.com
www.peacehills.com
Ownership: Private
Year Founded: 1981
Number of Employees: 120
Assets: $100-500 million
Revenues: $10-50 million

Peoples Trust Company
Also listed under: *Financing & Loan Companies*
888 Dunsmuir St., 14th Fl.
Vancouver, BC V6C 3K4
Tel: 604-683-2881; *Fax:* 604-331-3469
people@peoplestrust.com
www.peoplestrust.com
Ownership: Private
Year Founded: 1985

RBC Dexia Investor Services Trust
Royal Trust Tower, Toronto Dominion Centre
77 King St. West, 35th Fl.
Toronto, ON M5W 1P9
Tel: 416-955-5907
www.rbcdexia-is.com
Ownership: Wholly-owned subsidiary of RBC Dexia Investor Services
Year Founded: 2006

ResMor Trust Company
Also listed under: *Financing & Loan Companies*
#400, 555 - 4th Ave. SW
Calgary, AB T2P 3E7
Tel: 403-539-4920; *Fax:* 403-539-4921
Toll-Free: 866-333-7030
www.resmor.com
Former Name: Equisure Trust Company
Ownership: Private. ResMor Capital Corporation.
Year Founded: 1964
Number of Employees: 195
Assets: $100-500 million
Revenues: $10-50 million

The Royal Trust Company
Also listed under: *Financial Planning & Investment Management Companies*
Royal Bank
1, Place Ville-Marie, 6e étage sud
Montréal, QC H3B 2B2
Tel: 514-874-7222; *Toll-Free:* 800-668-1990
tradvtor@rbc.com (East), tradvcal@rbc.com (West)
www.rbc.com
Other Contact Information: 866-553-5585 (Eastern Canada Toll Free); 888-299-5290 (Western Canada Toll Free); 866-474-4344 (Québec Toll Free); tradvmtl@rbc.com (Québec Email)
Ownership: Part of RBC Financial Group.
Year Founded: 1899

Standard Life Trust Company
#206, 1245, rue Sherbrooke ouest
Montréal, QC H3G 1G3
Toll-Free: 888-841-6633
www.standardlife.ca
Former Name: Bonaventure Trust Company of Canada
Ownership: Private
Year Founded: 1825

State Street Bank & Trust Company - Canada
Also listed under: *Foreign Banks: Schedule III*
#1100, 30 Adelaide St. East
Toronto, ON M5C 3G6
Tel: 416-362-1100; *Fax:* 416-956-2525
Toll-Free: 888-287-8639
www.statestreet.com
Former Name: State Street Trust Company Canada
Ownership: State Street Corporation
Year Founded: 1990
Number of Employees: 700

Sun Life Financial Trust Inc.
PO Box 1601, Waterloo Stn. Waterloo
227 King St. South
Waterloo, ON N2J 4C5
Toll-Free: 877-786-5433
www.sunlife.com

Trimark Trust/ Fiducie Trimark
#900, 5140 Yonge St.
Toronto, ON M2N 6X7
Tel: 416-590-0036; *Toll-Free:* 800-631-7008
inquiries@aimtrimark.com
www.aimtrimark.com
Former Name: Bayshore Trust
Ownership: AIM Trimark Investments, Toronto, ON.
Year Founded: 1977

The Trust Company of London Life
One Canada Centre
447 Portage Ave.
Winnipeg, MB R3C 3B6
Tel: 204-956-8470

Valiant Trust Company
#600, 750 Cambie St.
Vancouver, BC V6B 0A2
Tel: 604-699-4880; *Fax:* 604-681-3067
Toll-Free: 877-699-4880
inquiries@valianttrust.com
www.valianttrust.com
Ownership: Subsidiary of Canadian Western Bank

Western Pacific Trust Company
#500, 1130 West Pender St.
Vancouver, BC V6E 4A4
Tel: 604-683-0455; *Fax:* 604-669-6978
www.westernpacifictrust.com
Ownership: Public
Year Founded: 1964

SECTION 6
EDUCATION

Arranged by province, and each province includes the following categories. Each category is further arranged by specific subcategories, as applicable to each province.

Government Agencies

School Boards/Districts/Divisions
Public; Protestant; Catholic; French; School Authorities

Schools: Specialized
Charter; First Nations; Hearing Impaired; Distance Education; Special Education

Schools: Independent & Private

Universities & Colleges

Post Secondary/Technical

Alberta

Government Agencies

Edmonton: Alberta Advanced Education
Communications Branch
10155 - 102 St., 7th Fl., Edmonton, AB T5J 4L5, Canada
Tel: 780-422-4495; *Fax:* 780-422-1263
AdvanceEducation.Contact@gov.ab.ca
www.advancededucation.gov.ab.ca

School Boards/Districts/Divisions

Public

Airdrie: Rocky View School Division #41
2651 Chinook Winds Dr., Airdrie, AB T4B 0B4, Canada
Tel: 403-945-4000; *Fax:* 403-945-4001
www.rockyview.ab.ca

Enrollment: 16000
Sylvia Eggerer, Chair
seggerer@rockyview.ab.ca

Athabasca: Aspen View Regional Division #19
3600 - 48 Ave., Athabasca, AB T9S 1M8, Canada
Tel: 780-675-7080; *Fax:* 780-675-3660
Toll-Free: 1-888-488-0288
aspenview@aspenview.org
www.aspenview.org

Grades: Kindergarten - 12
Paul Ponich, Board Chair, 780-525-2288
paul.ponich@aspenview.org
Derm Madden, Superintendent, Schools
derm.madden@aspenview.org
Bernie Giacobbo, Associate Superintendent
bernie.giacobbo@aspenview.org
Brian LeMessurier, Associate Superintendent
brian.lemessurier@aspenview.org
Mark Francis, Director, Education Initiatives
mark.francis@aspenview.org
Dave Holler, Director, Business Services
dave.holler@aspenview.org

Barrhead: Pembina Hills Regional Division #7
5310 - 49 St., Barrhead, AB T7N 1P3, Canada
Tel: 780-674-8500; *Fax:* 780-674-3262
info@phrd.ab.ca
www.phrd.ab.ca

Enrollment: 4355
Richard Harvey, Superintendent

Bonnyville: Northern Lights School Division #69
6005 - 50 Ave., Bonnyville, AB T9N 2L4, Canada
Tel: 780-826-3145; *Fax:* 780-826-4600
www.nlsd.ab.ca

Grades: K.-12
Enrollment: 5885
This division is an amalgamation of the Lac La Biche School Division and the Lakeland Public School District.
Roger Nippard, Supt.
roger.nippard@nlsd.ab.ca
Beverley Topylki, Sec.-Treas.
beverley.topyki@nlsd.ab.ca

Brooks: Grasslands Regional Division #6
Also known as: Grasslands Public Schools
745 - 2nd Ave. East, Brooks, AB T1R 1L2, Canada
Tel: 403-793-6700; *Fax:* 403-362-8225
www.grasslands.ab.ca

Grades: Kindergarten - 12; Alternative Ed.
Number of Schools: 13 schools; 7 Hutterite colony schools
Susan Chomistek, Superintendent
Scott Brandt, Assistant Superintendent
David Steele, Deputy Superintendent
David Steele, Deputy Superintendent
Shane Harahus, Director, Finance
Michael Nielsen, Director, Technology
Alan Kloepper, Manager, Facilities & Maintenance

Calgary: Calgary Board of Education
515 Macleod Trail SE, Calgary, AB T2G 2L9, Canada
Tel: 403-294-8255
www.cbe.ab.ca
Other Information: Trustees: 403-294-8487; Aboriginal Education: 403-777-8970

Grades: Kindergarten - 12; Continuing Ed.
Enrollment: 102376
Number of Schools: 128 elementary schools; 26 junior high schools; 24 elementary / middle / junior high schools; 16 senior high schools; 14 unique settings; 6 junior / senior high schools; 4 outreach programs
Naomi Johnson, Chief Superintendent, Schools, 403-294-8100
David Stevenson, Deputy Chief Superintendent, Schools, 403-294-8100
Deborah Meyers, Chief Financial Officer, Business & Finance Services, 403-294-8392
Frank Coppinger, Superintendent, Facilities & Environment Servicess, 403-214-1119
Cathy Faber, Superintendent, Learning Innovation, 403-294-8154
John G. Johnston, Superintendent, Human Resources, 403-294-8189
Deborah Lewis, Superintendent, Learning Support, 403-294-8118
Diane Yee, Director, Area I, 403-777-8710
Susan Church, Director, Area II, 403-777-8720
Darlene Selby, Director, Area III, 403-777-6233
Jim Langley, Director, Area IV, 403-777-8750
Jane Rogerson, Director, Area V, 403-777-8780

Calgary: Francophone Regional Authority (South)
#230, 6940 Fisher Rd. SE, Calgary, AB T2H 0W3, Canada
Tel: 403-686-6998; *Fax:* 403-686-2914
Toll-Free: 1-877-245-7686

Enrollment: 2008
Number of Schools: 13
Anne-Marie Bocher, Contact, 403-686-6998
Diane Boutin, Contact
403-685-9881

Camrose: Battle River Regional Division #31
5402 - 48A Ave., Camrose, AB T4V 0L3, Canada
Tel: 780-672-6131; *Fax:* 780-672-6137
Toll-Free: 1-800-262-4869
www.brrd.ab.ca

Enrollment: 6700
Cheryl Smith, Board Chair, 780-678-3265
csmith@brsd.ab.ca
Dr. Larry Payne, Superintendent, Schools, 780-672-4718, ext. 5227
LPayne@brsd.ab.ca
Ray Bosh, Deputy Superintendent, Sc, 780-672-4718, ext. 5011
RBosh@brsd.ab.ca
Rick Jarret, Assistant Superintendent,, 780-672-4718, ext. 5238
RJarrett@brsd.ab.ca
Bill Schulte, Assistant Superintendent,, 780-672-4718, ext. 5229
BSchulte@brsd.ab.ca
Greg Friend, Director, Personnel, 780-672-4718, ext. 5247
GFriend@brsd.ab.ca
Brenda Johnson, Director, Transportation, 780-672-4718, ext. 5245
BJohnson@brsd.ab.ca
Maureen Parker, Director, Curriculum, 780-672-4718, ext. 5223
MParker@brsd.ab.ca
Percy Roberts, Director, Maintenance & O, 780-672-4718, ext. 5246
PRoberts@brsd.ab.ca
Diane Hutchinson, Coordinator, Communicatio, 780-672-4718, ext. 5248
DHutchinson@brsd.ab.ca

Canmore: Canadian Rockies Public Schools
618 - 7th St., Canmore, AB T1W 2H5, Canada
Tel: 403-609-6072; *Fax:* 403-609-6071
hr@crps.ab.ca (Human Resources)
www.crps.ab.ca

Grades: Kindergarten - 12
Enrollment: 2042
Number of Schools: 6
Brian Callaghan, Superintendent, Schools
D. MacKenzie, Secretary-Treasurer

Cardston: Westwind School Division #74
P.O. Box 10
445 Main St., Cardston, AB T0K 0K0, Canada
Tel: 403-653-4991; *Fax:* 403-653-4641
Toll-Free: 800-655-4991
www.westwind.ab.ca

Grades: Pre-K.-12
Enrollment: 4249
Ken Summerfeldt, Supt.
Dexter Durfey, Sec.-Treas.
Lance Miller, Chair., 403-634-4770

Claresholm: Livingstone Range School Division #68
P.O. Box 69
5202 - 5 St. East, Claresholm, AB T0L 0T0, Canada
Tel: 403-625-3356; *Fax:* 403-325-2424
Toll-Free: 800-310-6579
centraloffice@lrsd.ab.ca
www.lrsd.ab.ca

Grades: Pre.-12
Enrollment: 3845
Ellie Elliot, Supt. of Schools

Dunmore: Prairie Rose Regional Division #8
P.O. Box 204
918 - 2 Ave., Dunmore, AB T0J 1A0, Canada
Tel: 403-527-5516; *Fax:* 403-528-2264
www.prrd.ab.ca

Enrollment: 3380
Doug Nicholls, Superintendent

Edmonton: Edmonton School District #7
Centre for Education
One Kingsway Ave., Edmonton, AB T5H 4G9, Canada
Tel: 780-429-8000; *Fax:* 780-429-8318
info@epsb.ca
www.epsb.ca

Enrollment: 82447

Edmonton: Greater North Central Francophone Education Region No.2
Conseil scolaire Centre-Nord
#322, 8627 - 91st St. (Marie-Anne-Gaboury St.), Edmonton, AB T6C 3N1, Canada
Tel: 780-468-6440; *Fax:* 780-440-1631
Toll-Free: 1-800-248-6886
conseil@centrenord.ab.ca
www.centrenord.ab.ca

Grades: Kindergarten - 12
Enrollment: 2400
Number of Schools: 14 francophone (Catholic or public) schools
Claude Duret, Chair
cduret@centrenord.ab.ca
Henrie Lemire, Superintendent
hlemire@centrenord.ab.ca
Nicole Bugeaud, Associate Superintendent
nbugeaud@centrenord.ab.ca
Josée Devaney, Secretary-Treasurer
jdevaney@centrenord.ab.ca
Jean-Marc Cloutier, Director, Technological Services, 780-432-4654
jmcloutier@centrenord.ab.ca
Denise Lauzon Dempsey, Coordinator, Transportation
dldempsey@centrenord.ab.ca
Denise Lavallée, Coordinator, Communications
dlavallee@centrenord.ab.ca
Suzanne Amyotte, Associate, Human Ressources & Finance
samyotte@centrenord.ab.ca

Edson: Grande Yellowhead Public School Division No. 77
3656 - 1st Ave., Edson, AB T7E 1S8, Canada
Tel: 780-723-2414; *Fax:* 780-723-2414
Toll-Free: 1-800-723-2564
escgyrd@gyrd.ab.ca
www.gyrd.ab.ca

Grades: Elementary - Secondary
Enrollment: 5000
Number of Schools: 18. Number of Employees: 800
Dean Lindquist, Superintendent, Schools, 780-723-4471, ext. 103
deanlind@gyrd.ab.ca
Cory Gray, Deputy Superintendent, Leadership & Human Resources, 780-723-4471, ext. 106
corygray@gyrd.ab.ca
Ed Latka, Assistant Superintendent, Business Services, 780-723-4471, ext. 102
edlatk@gyrd.ab.ca
Nancy Spencer-Poitras, Assistant Superintendent, Learning Services, 780-723-4471, ext. 116
nancspen@gyrd.ab.ca
Ken Baluch, Director, Facility Services, 780-723-4471, ext. 119
kenbalu@gyrd.ab.ca
Leigh McDonald, Director, Transportation Services, 780-723-4471, ext. 121
leigmcdo@gyrd.ab.ca
Kathleen Gardiner, Manager, Financial Services, 780-723-4471, ext. 112
kathgard@gyrd.ab.ca
Nikki Gilks, Manager, Communications, 780-723-4471, ext. 142
nikkgilk@gyrd.ab.ca
Jody Beck, Supervisor, Learning Services - Student Programs, 780-723-4471
jodybeck@gyrd.ab.ca
Kurt Scobie, Supervisor, Learning Services - Special Programs, 780-865-5692
kurtscob@gyrd.ab.ca
Sharon Styles, Supervisor, Learning Services - Curriculum & Instruction, 780-723-4471
sharstyl@gyrd.ab.ca

Fort McMurray: Fort McMurray Public School District
District Office, Clearwater Public Education Cent
231 Hardin St., Fort McMurray, AB T9H 2G2, Canada
Tel: 780-799-7900
www.fortmcmurraypsd.sharpschool.com
Grades: ECS - 12
Number of Schools: 9 elementary schools; 3 high schools
Jeff Thompson, Board Chair, 780-743-3798, fax: 780-743-4542
Paula.Ogonoski@fmpsd.ab.ca
Dennis Parsons, Superintendent, Schools, 780-799-7903
Dennis.Parsons@fmpsd.ab.ca
Allan Kallal, Associate Superintendent, Business & Finance, 780-799-7908
Allan.Kallal@fmpsd.ab.ca
Phil Meagher, Associate Superintendent, Education & Administration, 780-799-7909
Phil.Meagher@fmpsd.ab.ca
Amgad Rushdy, Associate Superintendent, Human Resources & Administration, 780-799-7902
Amgad.Rushdy@fmpsd.ab.ca
Dr. Brenda Sautner, Director, Special Education, 780-792-5656
Brenda.Sautner@fmpsd.ab.ca
Leslie Ann Booker, Coordinator, Early Childhood Programs, 780-799-7928
Leslie.Booker@fmpsd.ab.ca
Ray Campbell, Coordinator, Education - Curriculum, 780-799-7925
Ray.Campbell@fmpsd.ab.ca
Lyndel Donald, Coordinator, Special Education Staffing, 780-788-8008
Lyndel.Donald@fmpsd.ab.ca
Malcolm Fedoretz, Coordinator, Student Information Systems, 780-799-7928
Malcolm.Fedoretz@fmpsd.ab.ca
Myrna Matheson, Coordinator, Literacy, 780-799-7906
Myrna.Matheson@fmpsd.ab.ca
Paula Ogonoski, Coordinator, Communications, 780-788-8009
Paula.Ogonoski@fmpsd.ab.ca
Ali Syed, Coordinator, Educational Technology, 780-799-7923
Ali.Syed@fmpsd.ab.ca
Lori Weinberger, Coordinator, District Numeracy, 780-788-8007
Lori.Weinberger@fmpsd.ab.ca

Fort Vermilion: Fort Vermilion School Division No. 52
P.O. Box 1
5213 River Rd., Fort Vermilion, AB T0H 1N0, Canada
Tel: 780-927-3766; *Fax:* 780-927-4625
info@fvsd.ab.ca
www.fvsd.ab.ca
Grades: Kindergarten - 12
Number of Schools: 15 schools; 4 learning stores (storefront schools)
Wally Schroeder, Chair
wallys@fvsd.ab.ca
Roger Clarke, Superintendent, Schools, 780-927-3766
rogerc@fvsd.ab.ca
Rick Cusson, Assistant Superintendent, Operations, 780-927-3766
rickc@fvsd.ab.ca
Kathryn Kirby, Assistant Superintendent, Teaching & Learning, 780-927-3766
kathrynk@fvsd.ab.ca
Bob Barrett, Manager, Information Technology, 780-926-4693
robertb@fvsd.ab.ca
Dan Dyck, Manager, Maintenance, 780-928-3013
dand@fvsd.ab.ca
Dave Elias, Manager, Transportation, 780-928-3860
davee@fvsd.ab.ca
Joanne Smith, Administrator, Payroll, 780-927-3766
joannes@fvsd.ab.ca

Grande Prairie: Grande Prairie School District
10213 - 99 St., Grande Prairie, AB T8V 2H3, Canada
Tel: 780-532-4491; *Fax:* 780-539-4265
www.gppsd.ab.ca
Grades: Kindergarten - 12
Enrollment: 6300
Number of Schools: 14
Karen Prokopowich, Chair, 780-532-1575
Chris Gonnet, Superintendent
chris.gonnet@gppsd.ab.ca
Dr. Roger Mestinsek, Deputy Superintendent
roger.mestinsek@gppsd.ab.ca
Lance Therrien, Assistant Superintendent, Curriculum
lance.therrien@gppsd.ab.ca
Christina Farquharson, Assistant Superintendent, Student Services
chris.farquharson@gppsd.ab.ca
Barry Bodner, Director, Operations
barry.bodner@gppsd.ab.ca
Frank Canavan, Director, Psychological Services
frank.canavan@gppsd.ab.ca
Sharron Graham, Director, Instruction
sharron.graham@gppsd.ab.ca
Sandy McDonald, Director, Education Technology
Sandy.McDonald@gppsd.ab.ca
Justin Vickers, Director, Information Technology
justin.vickers@gppsd.ab.ca
Wade Webb, Director, Finance
wade.webb@gppsd.ab.ca
Lorna Nordhagen, Manager, Human Resources
lorna.nordhagen@gppsd.ab.ca

Grande Prairie: Peace Wapiti Public School Division #76
8611A - 108 St., Grande Prairie, AB T8V 4C5, Canada
Tel: 780-532-8133; *Fax:* 780-532-4234
www.pwsd76.ab.ca
Enrollment: 5600
Sheldon Rowe, Superintendent

Hanna: Prairie Land Regional Division #25
P.O. Box 1400
Hanna, AB T0J 1P0, Canada
Tel: 403-854-4481; *Fax:* 403-854-2803
Toll-Free: 800-601-3898
lana.campbell@plrd.ab.ca
www.plrd.ab.ca
Enrollment: 1625
Wes Neumeier, Superintendent
wes.neumeier@plrd.ab.ca

High Prairie: High Prairie School Division #48
P.O. Box 870
High Prairie, AB T0G 1E0, Canada
Tel: 780-523-3337; *Fax:* 780-523-4639
Toll-Free: 877-523-3337
www.hpsd48.ab.ca
Enrollment: 3600
Laura Poloz, Superintendent
lpoloz@hpsd48.ab.ca

High River: Foothills School Division
P.O. Box 5700
120 - 5th Ave. West, High River, AB T1V 1M7, Canada
Tel: 403-652-3001; *Fax:* 403-652-4204
www.fsd38.ab.ca
Grades: Kindergarten - 12; French Immersion
Number of Schoools: 27
Doug Gardner, Chair, 403-652-7842
gardnerd@fsd38.ab.ca
Denise Rose, Chief Executive Officer & Superintendent, Schools, 403-652-6522
Del Litke, Deputy Superintendent
Louise Ascah, Manager, Communications, 403-652-6522

Innisfail: Chinook's Edge School Division #73
4904 - 50 St., Innisfail, AB T4G 1W4, Canada
Tel: 403-227-7070; *Fax:* 403-227-3652
Toll-Free: 1-800-561-922
division.office@chinooksedge.ab.ca
www.chinooksedge.ab.ca
Enrollment: 11000

Lethbridge: Lethbridge School District #51
433 - 15 St. South, Lethbridge, AB T1J 2Z5, Canada
Tel: 403-380-5300; *Fax:* 403-327-4387
www.lethsd.ab.ca
Grades: K-12
Enrollment: 8000
Gary Bartlett, Chair

Lethbridge: Palliser Regional Division #26
#101, 3305 - 18 Ave. North, Lethbridge, AB T1H 5S1, Canada
Tel: 403-328-4111; *Fax:* 403-380-6890
Toll-Free: 877-667-1234
www.pallisersd.ab.ca
Enrollment: 6300
Kevin Gietz, Superintendent

Lloydminster: Lloydminster School Division #99
5017 - 46 St., Lloydminster, AB T9V 1R4, Canada
Tel: 780-875-5541; *Fax:* 780-875-7829
www.lpsd.ca
Grades: K.-12
Enrollment: 3862
Dr. Michael Diachuk, Dir.
michael.diachuk@lpsd.ca
Walter Hardy, Supt. of Admin., 780-808-2523
walter.hardy@lpsd.ca

Medicine Hat: Medicine Hat School District #76
601 - 1 Ave. SW, Medicine Hat, AB T1A 4Y7, Canada
Tel: 403-528-6700; *Fax:* 403-529-5339
www.sd76.ab.ca
Grades: K.-12
Enrollment: 6275
Linda Rossler, Supt. of Schools
linda.rossler@sd76.ab.ca
Jerry Labossiere, Sec.-Treas.

Morinville: Sturgeon School Division #24
9820 - 104 St., Morinville, AB T8R 1L8, Canada
Tel: 780-939-4341; *Fax:* 780-939-5520
www.sturgeon.ab.ca
Grades: Kindergarten - 12
Enrollment: 5000
Number of Schools: 16 (including a school on the Morinville Hutterite Colony & a school operated in conjunction with the Oak Hill Boys' Ranch, plus 3 outreach learning centres)
Dr. Michèle Dick, Superintendent, 780-939-4341
mdick@sturgeon.ab.ca
Wolfgang Jeske, Director, Curriculum & Instruction

Nisku: Black Gold Regional Division #18
1101 - 5 St., 3rd Fl., Nisku, AB T9E 7N3, Canada
Tel: 780-955-6025; *Fax:* 780-955-6050
www.blackgold.ab.ca
Grades: Junior Kindergarten - Secondary
Barb Martinson, Chair, Board of Education
barb.martinson@blackgold.ca
Stuart Evans, Superintendent, 780-955-6026
stuart.evans@blackgold.ca
Neil Fenske, Associate Superintendent, 780-955-6028
neil.fenske@blackgold.ca
Dennis Nosyk, Associate Superintendent, 780-955-6032
dennis.nosyk@blackgold.ca
Dianne Butler, Director, Student Services, 780-955-6037
dianne.butler@blackgold.ca
Peter Balding, Administrator, Division Technology, 780-955-6037
dianne.butler@blackgold.ca
Dan Borys, Manager, Operations & Maintenance, 780-955-6068
dan.borys@blackgold.ca
Laurel Kvarnberg, Manager, Finance, 780-955-6059
laurel.kvarnberg@blackgold.ca
Sue Timmermans, Manager, Transportation, 780-955-6034
sue.timmermans@blackgold.ca
Warren Watson, Manager, Projects, 780-955-6062
warren.watson@blackgold.ca

Peace River: Northland School Division #61
P.O. Box 1400
9809 - 77 Ave., Peace River, AB T8S 1V2, Canada
Tel: 780-624-2060; *Fax:* 780-624-5914
Toll-Free: 800-362-1360
central.office@northland61.ab.ca
www.northland61.ab.ca
Grades: K.-12
Enrollment: 2600
Donald Tessier, Supt., ext. 6102
don.tessier@northland61.ab.ca
Dennis Walsh, Dir. of Finance, ext. 6141
dennis.walsh@northland61.ab.ca
Delores Pruden, Coordinator, Aboriginal Programs, ext. 6161

Peace River: Peace River School Division #10
10018 - 101 St., Peace River, AB T8S 2A5, Canada
Tel: 780-624-3601; *Fax:* 780-624-5941
peaceriversd@prsd.ab.ca
www.prsd.ab.ca
Enrollment: 3100
Nan Bartlett, Chair

Ponoka: Wolf Creek School Division #72
6000 Hwy. 2A, Ponoka, AB T4J 1P6, Canada
Tel: 403-783-3473; *Fax:* 403-783-3483
info@wolfcreek.ab.ca
www.wolfcreek.ab.ca
Grades: K.-12
Enrollment: 7500
Larry Jacobs, Supt.
ljacobs@wolfcreek.ab.ca
Joe Henderson, Sec.-Treas., 403-783-5441, ext. 1229
jhenderson@wolfcreek.ab.ca
Lorrie Jess, Chair

Red Deer: Red Deer School District #104
4747 - 53 St., Red Deer, AB T4N 2E6, Canada
Tel: 403-343-1405; *Fax:* 403-347-8190
info@rdpsd.ab.ca
www.rdpsd.ab.ca
Enrollment: 9000
Don Falk, Superintendent

Rocky Mountain House: Wild Rose School Division #66
4912 - 43 St., Rocky Mountain House, AB T4T 1P4, Canada
Tel: 403-845-3376; *Fax:* 403-845-3850
www.wrsd.ca

Grades: K.-12
Enrollment: 5469
Brian Celli, Supt.
brian.celli@wrsd.ca
Gordon Majeran, Sec.-Treas.
gordon.majeran@wrsd.ca
Keith Warren, Chair
keith.warren@wrsd.ca

Sherwood Park: Elk Island Public Schools Regional Division #14
683 Wye Rd., Sherwood Park, AB T8B 1N2, Canada
Tel: 780-464-3477; *Fax:* 780-417-8181
Toll-Free: 1-800-905-347
communications@ei.educ.ab.ca
www.ei.educ.ab.ca

Enrollment: 16200

St Isidore: Conseil scolaire du Nord-Ouest No. 1
P.O. Box 1220
St Isidore, AB T0H 3B0, Canada
Tél: 780-624-8855; *Téléc:* 780-624-8554
Ligne sans frais: 866-624-8855
conseil@csno.ab.ca
www.csno.ab.ca

Enrollment: 279

St Paul: East Central Francophone Education Region #3
P.O. Box 249
4537 - 50 Ave., St Paul, AB T0A 3A0, Canada
Tel: 780-645-3888; *Fax:* 780-645-2045
cen3@atrium.ca
www.cen3.ab.ca

Enrollment: 493

St Paul: St. Paul Education Regional Division #1
4313 - 48th Ave., St Paul, AB T0A 3A3, Canada
Tel: 780-645-3323; *Fax:* 780-645-5789
www.stpauleducation.ab.ca

Grades: Kindergarten - 12
Enrollment: 3988
Number of Schools: 18 (including 5 kindergarten to grade 12 schools, 2 Hutterite colonies, 2 outreach schools, & a virtual education campus). Number of Employees: 270 teaching staff; 346 support staff
Darrell Younghans, Chair, 780-943-2460
Glen Brodziak, Superintendent, 780-645-3323
Patricia Gervais, Assistant Superintendent, 780-645-3323
Patrick Rivard, Assistant Superintendent, 780-645-3323
Glenda Bristow, Coordinator, Program, 780-645-3323
Janice Muench, Coordinator, Special Education, 780-645-3323
Jean Champagne, Secretary-Treasurer, 780-645-3323

Stettler: Clearview School Division #71
4704 - 55 St., Stettler, AB T0C 2L2, Canada
Tel: 403-742-3331; *Fax:* 403-742-1388
www.clearview.ab.ca

Enrollment: 2628

Stony Plain: Parkland School Division #70
4603 - 48 St., Stony Plain, AB T7Z 2A8, Canada
Tel: 780-963-4010; *Fax:* 780-963-4169
www.psd70.ab.ca

Enrollment: 9454

Strathmore: Golden Hills School Division #75
435A Hwy. #1, Strathmore, AB T1P 1J4, Canada
Tel: 403-934-5121; *Fax:* 403-934-5125
Toll-Free: 1-800-320-3739
www.ghsd75.ca

Grades: ECS - 12
Ron Kenworthy, Chair, 403-823-8802, fax: 403-823-8819
ron.kenworthy@ghsd75.ca
Dianne McBeth, Superintendent, Schools, 403-934-5121, ext. 2013
Edwin Holt, Associate Superintendent, Schools, 403-934-5121, ext. 2016
Dr. Kandace Jordan, Associate Superintendent, Schools, 403-934-5121, ext. 2014
Bevan Daverne, Division Principal, 403-934-5121, ext. 2005
Richard Armstrong, Manager, Financial Services, 403-934-5121, ext. 2022
Don Hartman, Manager, Facilities & Maintenance, 403-934-5121, ext. 2053
Ken MacLean, Supervisor, Transportation, 877-442-4340
Tahra Sabir, Secretary-Treasurer, 403-934-5121, ext. 2024

Taber: Horizon School Division #67
6302 - 56 St., Taber, AB T1G 1Z9, Canada
Tel: 403-223-3547; *Fax:* 403-223-2999
www.horizon.ab.ca

Enrollment: 3500
Marie Logan, Chair

Wainwright: Buffalo Trail Public Schools Regional Division No. 28
Central Office
1041 - 10A St., Wainwright, AB T9W 2R4, Canada
Tel: 780-842-6144; *Fax:* 780-842-3255
www.btps.ca

Grades: Kindergarten - 12
Enrollment: 4500
Number of Schools: 19 schools, with varying grade combinations, from ECS to grade 12; 7 Hutterite Colony schools, 1 outreach site, 1 distance learning site. Number of Employees: 281 FTE teachers + 236 support staff
Darcy Eddleston, Chair, 780-745-2370
darcy.eddleston@btps.ca
Bob Allen, Superintendent, Schools, 780-842-6144
superintendent@btps.ca
Nick Radujko, Assistant Superintendent, 780-806-2059
nick.radujko@btps.ca
Bob Brown, Secretary-Treasurer, 780-806-2050
bob.brown@btps.ca
Daryl Hoey, Director, Technology, 780-806-2065
daryl.hoey@btps.ca
Randy Huxley, Director, Facilities, 780-806-2064
randy.huxley@btps.ca
Chrysti Mannix, Director, Transportation, 780-806-2051
chrysti.mannix@btps.ca
Shannon Melin, Director, Human Resources, 780-806-2062
shannon.melin@btps.ca
Crystal Tower, Director, Student Services, 780-806-2056
crystal.tower@btps.ca
Hugh Forrester, Curriculum Lead, 780-872-1885
hugh.forrester@btps.ca

Wetaskiwin: Wetaskiwin Regional Division #11
Also known as: Wetaskiwin Regional Public Schools
5515 - 47A Ave., Wetaskiwin, AB T9A 3S3, Canada
Tel: 780-352-6018; *Fax:* 780-352-7886
wrps@wrps.ab.ca
www.wrps.ab.ca

Grades: Pre-K.-12
Enrollment: 4081
Terry Pearson, Supt.
Sherri Senger, Dir., Bus. Services
Robert Reimer, Chair

Whitecourt: Northern Gateway Regional Division #10
P.O. Box 840
4104 Kepler St., Whitecourt, AB T7S 1M8, Canada
Tel: 780-778-2800; *Fax:* 780-778-6719
Toll-Free: 800-262-8674
www.ngrd.ab.ca

Grades: K.-12
Enrollment: 5300
Kevin Andrea, Supt.
Mike Gramatovich, Sec.-Treas.
mgramatovich@ngrd.ab.ca

Protestant

St Albert: St. Albert Protestant Separate School District #6
60 Sir Winston Churchill Ave., St Albert, AB T8N 0G4, Canada
Tel: 780-460-3712; *Fax:* 780-460-7686
www.spschools.org

Enrollment: 6600
Barry Wowk, Superintendent

Catholic

Bonnyville: Lakeland Roman Catholic Separate School District #150
4810 - 46 St., Bonnyville, AB T9N 1B5, Canada
Tel: 780-826-3764; *Fax:* 780-826-7576
www.lcsd150.ab.ca

Enrollment: 2200
Bernadette Provost, Superintendent

Calgary: Calgary Catholic School District
Catholic School Centre
1000 - 5th Ave. SW, Calgary, AB T2P 4T9, Canada
Tel: 403-500-2000
communications@cssd.ab.ca; trustees@cssd.ab.ca
www.cssd.ab.ca
Other Information: Communications: 403-500-2763; Trustees: 403-500-2761

Grades: Kindergarten - 12
Enrollment: 45066
Number of Schools: 52 elementary schools; 34 elementary / junior high schools; 9 senior high schools; 6 junior high schools; 2 junior / senior high schools; 2 congregated special education schools. Number of Employees: 3,143 instructional staff; 1,202 support staff; 314 caretaking staff; 144 exempt staff; 9 senior officers
Dr. Lucy Miller, EdD, Chief Superintendent
John Deausy, Superintendent, Finance & Business, & Secretary-Treasurer
Craig Foley, Superintendent, Human Resources
Judy MacKay, Superintendent, Specialized Schools/Instruction/Religious Ed.
Dr. Andra McGinn, Superintendent, Area A Schools
Luba Diduch, Superintendent, Area B Schools
Mark Rawlek, Superintendent, Area C Schools
Gary Strother, Superintendent, Area D Schools & Information Technology
Michael Barbero, Superintendent, Area E Schools & Support Services
Tania Younker, Director, Communications, 403-500-2763, fax: 403-500-2927
communications@cssd.ab.ca

Edmonton: Edmonton Catholic Separate School District #7
9807 - 106 St., Edmonton, AB T5K 1C2, Canada
Tel: 780-441-6000; *Fax:* 780-425-8759
www.ecsd.net

Enrollment: 32000

Fort McMurray: Fort McMurray Roman Catholic Board of Education
Fort McMurray Catholic Education Centre
9809 Main St., Fort McMurray, AB T9H 1T7, Canada
Tel: 780-799-5700; *Fax:* 780-799-5706
district@fmcsd.ab.ca
www.fmcsd.ab.ca
Other Information: Service Support Centre, Phone: 780-799-5714

Grades: Kindergarten - 12; French Immersion
Enrollment: 4300
Number of Schools: 9. Number of Employees: 260 teachers; 160 support staff
Geraldine Carbery, Chair
Kim Jenkins, Superintendent, Schools, 780-799-5799, ext. 5001
kjenkins@fmcsd.ab.ca
George McGuigan, Deputy Superintendent, 780-799-5799, ext. 5020
gmcguigan@fmcsd.ab.ca
Francois Gagnon, Associate Superintendent, Business & Finance, 780-799-5700
fgagnon@fmcsd.ab.ca
Norena Hart, Director, Facilities, 780-799-5714
NHart@fmcsd.ab.ca
Monica Mankowski, Director, Student Services, 780-799-5799, ext. 5041
mmankowski@fmcsd.ab.ca
Kathleen Murray House, Director, School Based Administration, & Mentor Principal, 780-799-5799, ext. 5001
kmurphy@fmcsd.ab.ca
Betty-Lou Cahill, Coordinator, Human Resources, 780-799-5799, ext. 5021
BCahill@fmcsd.ab.ca

Grande Prairie: Grande Prairie & District Catholic Schools
Catholic Education Centre
9902 - 101 St., Grande Prairie, AB T8V 2P4, Canada
Tel: 780-532-3013; *Fax:* 780-532-3430
Toll-Free: 1-800-661-2568
cec@gpcsd.ca (Catholic Ed. Ctr.); support@gpcsd.ca (Tech Support)
www.gpcsd.ca
Other Information: Transportation & Maintenance, Phone: 780-513-1220

Grades: JK - 12; French Immersion; Outreach
Enrollment: 3900
Number of Schools: 12. Number of Employees: 400
Karl Germann, Superintendent, Schools, 780-532-3013
Ed Buckle, Assistant Superintendent, Human Resources, 780-532-3013, ext. 121

Marlene Stefura, Assistant Superintendent, Curriculum & Assessment, 780-532-3013, ext. 122
Bryan Turner, Associate Superintendent, Business Operations, 780-532-3013, ext. 123
Pauline Ruel-Wyant, Director, Student Services, 780-532-3013, ext. 403
Clint Carrell, Administrator, Information Systems, 780-532-3013, ext. 300
John Dooley, Supervisor, Maintenance, 780-513-1220
Randy Lester, Supervisor, Transportation & Custodians, 780-513-1220

***Leduc:* St. Thomas Aquinas Roman Catholic Separate Regional Division #38**
4906 - 49th Ave., Leduc, AB T9E 6W6, Canada
Tel: 780-986-2500; *Fax:* 780-986-8620
Toll-Free: 1-800-583-0688
feedback@starcatholic.ab.ca
www.faithinyourfuture.ca

Grades: Kindergarten - 12; Catholicism
Enrollment: 2500
Number of Schools: 9 schools; 1 outreach centre. Number of Employees: 140 full-time teachers; 100 support staff
Maria Lentz, Board Chair
Jamie McNamara, Superintendent, Schools
jamie.mcnamara@starcatholic.ab.ca
Troy Davies, Assistant Superintendent
troy.davies@starcatholic.ab.ca
Jeanne Fontaine, Secretary-Treasurer
jeanne.fontaine@starcatholic.ab.ca
Tara-Ann Drexler, Coordinator, Transportation, & Accounting Clerk
tadrexler@starcatholic.ab.ca
Marilyn Kunitz, Coordinator, Student Services
marilyn.kunitz@starcatholic.ab.ca
Pius MacLean, Coordinator, Curriculum & Instruction
pius.maclean@starcatholic.ab.ca
Michael Marien, Coordinator, Faith Life & Curriculum
michael.marien@starcatholic.ab.ca
David Scribner, Coordinator, Facilites
david.scribner@starcatholic.ab.ca
Dan Svitich, Coordinator, Information Technology
david.scribner@starcatholic.ab.ca
Susan Baudin, Officer, Human Resouces & Payroll
susan.baudin@starcatholic.ab.ca
Wendy Hoguen, Liaison, Communications
wendy.hogue@starcatholic.ab.ca

***Lethbridge:* Holy Spirit Roman Catholic Separate Regional Division #4**
620 - 12B St. North, Lethbridge, AB T1H 2L7, Canada
Tel: 403-327-9555; *Fax:* 403-327-9595
www.holyspirit.ab.ca

Enrollment: 4400
Christopher Smeaton, Superintendent

***Lloydminster:* Lloydminster Roman Catholic Separate School Division #89**
6611B - 39th St., Lloydminster, AB T9V 2Z4, Canada
Tel: 780-808-8585; *Fax:* 780-808-8787
information@lcsd.ca
www.lcsd.ca

Grades: K.-12
Doug Robertson, Dir.
Tom Schinold, Supt. of Admin.
tschinold@lcsd.ca

***Medicine Hat:* Medicine Hat Catholic Separate School Regional Division #20**
1251 - 1 Ave. SW, Medicine Hat, AB T1A 8B4, Canada
Tel: 403-527-2292; *Fax:* 403-529-0917
Toll-Free: 866-864-0013
www.mhcbe.ab.ca

Grades: Pre-K.-12
Enrollment: 2800
David Leahy, Supt. of Schools

***Okotoks:* Christ the Redeemer Catholic Separate Regional Division #3**
46 Elma St. West, Okotoks, AB T1S 1J7, Canada
Tel: 403-938-2659; *Fax:* 403-938-4575
www.redeemer.ab.ca

Enrollment: 6200

***Peace River:* Holy Family Catholic Regional Division #37**
10307 - 99 St., Peace River, AB T8S 1R5, Canada
Tel: 780-624-3956; *Fax:* 780-624-1154
Toll-Free: 800-285-8712
www.hfcrd.ab.ca

Enrollment: 2000
Betty Turpin, Superintendent

***Red Deer:* Red Deer Catholic Regional Division #39**
5210 - 61 St., Red Deer, AB T4N 6N8, Canada
Tel: 403-343-1055; *Fax:* 403-347-6410
info@rdcrd.ab.ca
www.rdcrd.ab.ca

Enrollment: 5923
Paulette Hanna, Superintendent

***Sherwood Park:* Elk Island Catholic Separate Regional Division #41**
160 Festival Way, Sherwood Park, AB T8A 5Z2, Canada
Tel: 780-467-8896; *Fax:* 780-467-5469
www.eics.ab.ca

Enrollment: 5600

***Spruce Grove:* Evergreen Catholic Separate Regional Division No. 2**
Holy Trinity Church
P.O. Box 4265
200 Boundry Rd., 2nd Fl., Spruce Grove, AB T7X 3B4, Canada
Tel: 780-962-5627; *Fax:* 780-962-4664
Toll-Free: 1-800-825-7152
www.ecsrd.ca

Grades: ECS - 12
Enrollment: 3481
Number of Schools: 9
Gerald Bernakevitch, Board Chair
Dr. Cindi Vaselenak, Superintendent
Michael Hauptman, Deputy Superintendent
Sime Fatovic, Director, Facilities & Technology
Sheila Shumate, Director, Student Services
Karen Koester, Coordinator, Religious Education
Marlene Fehr, Treasurer
Al Brettnell, Network Administrator

***St Albert:* Greater St. Albert Catholic Schools**
6 St. Vital Ave., St Albert, AB T8N 1K2, Canada
Tel: 780-459-7711; *Fax:* 780-458-3213
pgerhardt@gsacrd.ab.ca (Exec. Asst, Office of the Superintendent)
www.gsacrd.ab.ca

Grades: Kindergarten - 12
Enrollment: 6251
Number of Schools: 17. Number of Employees: 666 staff in schools; 48 staff in division operations
David Keohane, Superintendent
dkeohane@gsacrd.ab.ca
Steve Bayus, Deputy Superintendent
sbayus@gsacrd.ab.ca
David Quick, Assistant Superintendent, Learning Services
dquick@gsacrd.ab.ca
Therese deChamplain-Good, Director, Curriculum & Instruction
tdecgood@gsacrd.ab.ca
Ren Giesbrecht, Director, Technology Services
rgiesbrecht@gsacrd.ab.ca
Tony McClellan, Director, Student Services
tmcclellan@gsacrd.ab.ca
Trevor Gough, Supervisor, Operations Services
tgough@gsacrd.ab.ca
Deb Schlag, Secretary-Treasurer
dschlag@gsacrd.ab.ca

***Wainwright:* East Central Alberta Catholic Separate School Regional Division #16**
1018 - 1st Ave., Wainwright, AB T9W 1G9, Canada
Tel.: 780-842-3992; *Fax:* 780-842-5322
www.ecacs16.ab.ca

Enrollment: 3300

***Whitecourt:* Living Waters Catholic Regional Division #42**
P.O. Box 1949
4204 Kepler St., Whitecourt, AB T7S 1P6, Canada
Tel: 780-778-5666; *Fax:* 780-778-2727
Toll-Free: 888-434-7348
www.livingwaters.ab.ca

Grades: Pre.-12
Enrollment: 1723

First Nations

***Brownvale:* Duncan's First Nation Education**
P.O. Box 148
Brownvale, AB T0H 0L0, Canada
Tel: 780-597-3777; *Fax:* 780-597-3920
www.duncansfn.ca

Duncan's First Nation is a small band situated southwest of Peace River, Alberta. A Child Development Centre offers daycare & a head start program. The head start program, for children from age three to five, includes a Cree language & cultural program. School buses transport Duncan's First Nation students to Berwyn, Grimshaw, & Peace River to enter a public school system.
Don Testawich, Chief, Duncan's First Nation

***Chard:* Chipewyan Prairie Dene First Nation Education Authority**
General Delivery, Chard, AB T0P 1G0, Canada
Tel: 780-559-2259; *Fax:* 780-559-2213

Number of Schools: 1

***Chateh:* Dene Tha' First Nation Education Department**
P.O. Box 120
Chateh, AB T0H 0S0, Canada
Tel: 780-321-3886; *Fax:* 780-321-3775
Toll-Free: 877-336-3842
info@denetha.ca
www.denetha.ca

Grades: Jr. Kindergarten-10; Dene language
Enrollment: 450
Number of Schools: 1 (Dene Tha' Community School). The Dene Tha' First Nation Education Department oversees education, counselling, transportation, & accommodation for Dene Tha' First Nation band members. Through its association with the North Peace Tribal Council, the Dene Tha' First Nation Education Department also directs post-secondary student services.
Adrienne Beaulieu, Coordinator, Post-Secondary Student Services, 780-926-2786, fax: 780-926-6652
Adrienne.Beaulieu@denetha.ca
Debbie Ahkimnachie, Clerk, Education Program, 780-321-3405
Debbie.Ahkimnachie@denetha.ca

***Duffield:* Paul Band Education Authority**
P.O. Box 89
Duffield, AB T0E 0N0, Canada
Tel: 780-892-2675; *Fax:* 780-892-4436

Grades: Pre.-12

***Enoch:* Kitaskinaw Education Authority**
P.O. Box 90
Enoch, AB T7X 3Y3, Canada
Tel: 780-470-5657

Grades: Nursery - 9
Number of Schools: 1 (Kitaskinaw School). The Kitaskinaw Education Authority oversees education for the Enoch Cree Nation.

***Fort Vermilion:* Tallcree First Nation School Division**
P.O. Box 310
Fort Vermilion, AB T0H 1N0, Canada
Tel: 780-927-3803
tallcreesd@gmail.com

Grades: K4 - 6
Enrollment: 100
Number of Schools: 2 (Chief Tallcree North School & Chief Tallcree South School)
Vic Dikaitis, Director, Education

***Goodfish:* Whitefish Lake Education Authority**
P.O. Box 274
Goodfish, AB T0A 1R0, Canada
Tel: 780-636-2525; *Fax:* 780-636-3101

Grades: Pre.-9

***Hobbema:* Kiseputinow Education Dept.**
P.O. Box 1290
Hobbema, AB T0C 1N0, Canada
Tel: 780-585-4065; *Fax:* 780-585-2037

Grades: Pre.-6

***Hobbema:* Nipisihkopahk Education Authority**
P.O. Box 658
Hobbema, AB T0C 1N0, Canada
Tel: 780-585-2211; *Fax:* 780-585-3857
www.wtc.ab.ca/nipisihkopahk

Grades: 1-12

***John D'Or Prairie:* Little Red River Board of Education**
P.O. Box 90
John D'Or Prairie, AB T0H 3X0, Canada
Tel: 780-759-3780; *Fax:* 780-759-3848
www.lrrbe.ab.ca

Grades: Kindergarten - 12; Special Ed.
Enrollment: 1050
Number of Schools: 3 (Jean Baptiste Sewepagaham School; John D'Or Prairie School; & Sister Gloria School). Number of Employees: 110+. The Little Red River Board of Education administers the provision of educational programming for First nation students of the Little Red River Cree Nation. Cultural programming is part of the students' education. The Board also offers adult upgrading & trades training.

Gloria Cardinal, Director, Education
glocardinal@gmail.com
Leah Blesse, Financial Controller

Lac La Biche: Beaver Lake Education Authority
P.O. Box 5000
Lac La Biche, AB T0A 2C0, Canada
Tel: 780-623-4549; Fax: 780-623-4523
amiskcommunityschool@yahoo.ca
www.beaverlakecreenation.ca
Other Information: Amisk Community School, Phone: 780-623-4548; Fax: 780-623-4659
Grades: Early Childhood Svs.-Jr. Secondary
Number of Schools: 1. The Beaver Lake Education Authority operates the Amisk Community School. The school is led by a nine member management team which is supervised by the Beaver Lake Cree Nation Band Council Education Portfolio Holder.
Councillor Germaine Anderson, Beaver Lake Cree Nation Council Education Portfolio Holder

Morinville: Alexander First Nation Education Authority
P.O. Box 3449
Morinville, AB T8R 1S3, Canada
Tel: 780-939-3868; Fax: 780-939-3991
The Alexander First Nation Education Authority operates the Kipohtakaw Education Centre.
Raymond Soetaert, Principal, Kipohtakaw Education Centre

Morley: Stoney Education Authority
P.O. Box 238
Morley, AB T0L 1N0, Canada
Tel: 403-881-2743; Fax: 403-881-4252
www.stoneynation.com
Grades: Kindergarten - 12; Stoney language
Enrollment: 1100
Number of Schools: 3 (Morley Community School; Ta Otha Community School; & Chief Jacob Bearspaw School). The Stoney Education Authority, located west of Calgary, Alberta, provides education to members of the Stoney Nakoda First Nation. Education includes cultural programs.
Nadeem Altaf, Administrator, Education, 403-881-2776

Rocky Mountain House: Sunchild First Nation Band Education Authority
P.O. Box 1149
Rocky Mountain House, AB T4T 1A8, Canada
Tel: 403-989-3476; Fax: 403-989-3614
Grades: Kindergarten - 12
Number of Schools: 1 (Sunchild First Nation School). Number of Employees: 50+ full-time & part-time personnel
Caroline Bigchild, Chair
Nelson Daychief, Director, Education
administrator@sunchildschool.com

Saddle Lake: Saddle Lake Education Authority
P.O. Box 130
Saddle Lake, AB T0A 3T0, Canada
Tel: 780-726-4009; Fax: 780-726-4141
Grades: 1-12

Siksika: Siksika Board of Education
P.O. Box 1099
Siksika, AB T0J 3W0, Canada
Tel: 403-734-5220; Fax: 403-734-2505
Grades: Pre.-12

Stand Off: Kainaiwa Board of Education
P.O. Box 240
Stand Off, AB T0L 1Y0, Canada
Tel: 403-737-3966; Fax: 403-737-2361
Grades: 7-12

Tsuu T'ina Sarcee: Tsuu T'ina Nation Board of Education
#250, 9911 Chiila Blvd. SW, Tsuu T'ina Sarcee, AB T2W 6H6, Canada
Tel: 403-238-5484
www.tsuutina.ca
Grades: K4 - 12; Adult Upgrading
Enrollment: 299
Number of Schools: 3 (Chiila Elementary School; Tsuu T'ina Junior Senior High School; & Tsuu T'ina Bullhead Adult Education Centre)

Valleyview: Sturgeon Lake First Nation, Band #154, Education Authority
P.O. Box 5
Valleyview, AB T0H 3N0, Canada
Tel: 780-524-4590
Grades: Kindergarten - 12
Enrollment: 230
Number of Schools: 1 (Sturgeon Lake School)

Wabasca: Bigstone Cree Nation Education Authority
P.O. Box 870
Wabasca, AB T0G 2K0, Canada
Tel: 780-891-3825; Fax: 780-891-3021
Toll-Free: 1-800-661-3891
www.bigstone.ca
Grades: Elementary
Enrollment: 247
Number of Schools: 1 (Oski Pasikoniwew Kamik, also known as the Bigstone Community School)
P. Ray Peters, Director, Education
ray.peters@bigstone.ca
Priscilla Auger, Counsellor, Post-Secondary Education, 877-458-2447, fax: 866-801-3021
priscilla.auger@bigstone.ca

Schools: Specialized

Charter

Calgary: Almadina Language Charter Academy
225 - 28 St. SE, Calgary, AB T2A 5K4, Canada
Tel: 403-543-5070; Fax: 403-543-5073
www.esl-almadina.com
Grades: 1-9
Enrollment: 600

Calgary: Calgary Arts Academy Society
4931 Grove Hill Rd. S.W., Calgary, AB T3E 4G4, Canada
Tel: 403-532-3020; Fax: 403-217-0965
info@calgaryartsacademy.com
www.calgaryartsacademy.com
Enrollment: 279

Calgary: Calgary Girls' School - Bel Aire Campus
1011 Beverley Blvd. SW, Calgary, AB T2V 2C4, Canada
Tel: 403-253-3785; Fax: 403-253-0430
www.calgarygirlsschool.com
Grades: 4-9
Lakeview Campus: 6304 Larkspur Way SW, (403) 220-0745.

Calgary: Calgary Girls' School - Lakeview Campus
6304 Larkspur Way SW, Calgary, AB T3E 5P7, Canada
Tel: 403-220-0745; Fax: 403-217-1371
www.calgarygirlsschool.com
Grades: 4-9
Enrollment: 460
Bel Aire Campus: 1011 Beverley Blvd. SW, (403) 253-3785.
Caroline Parker, Principal

Calgary: Calgary Science School Society
5915 Lewis Dr. SW, Calgary, AB T3E 5Z4, Canada
Tel: 403-282-2890; Fax: 403-282-2896
www.calgaryscienceschool.com
Enrollment: 343

Calgary: Foundations for the Future Charter Academy
Charter School Society
311, 5940 MacLeod Trail South, Calgary, AB T2H 2G4, Canada
Tel: 403-520-3206; Fax: 403-520-3209
www.ffca-calgary.com
Grades: 1-9
Enrollment: 1896

Calgary: Westmount Charter School Society
2519 Richmond Rd. SW, Calgary, AB T3E 4M2, Canada
Tel: 403-217-0426; Fax: 403-217-0252
admin@westmountcharter.com
www.westmountcharter.com
Grades: K-12
Enrollment: 880

Edmonton: Aurora Charter School Ltd.
8755 - 170 St., Edmonton, AB T5R 5Y6, Canada
Tel: 780-735-5502; Fax: 780-735-2598
aurorasc@telusplanet.net
www.auroraschool.com
Grades: 1-9
Enrollment: 437

Edmonton: Boyle Street Education Centre
10312 - 105 Ave., Edmonton, AB T5J 1E6, Canada
Tel: 780-428-1420; Fax: 780-429-1428
www.bsec.ab.ca
Grades: 7-12
Enrollment: 105

Edmonton: Suzuki Charter School Society
7211 - 96A Ave., Edmonton, AB T6B 1B5, Canada
Tel: 780-468-2598; Fax: 780-463-8630
www.suzukischool.ca
Grades: 1-6
Enrollment: 176

Fort McMurray: Moberly Hall School Society
194B Grenfell Cres., Fort McMurray, AB T9H 2M6, Canada
Tel: 780-743-8409; Fax: 780-743-9407
moberlyhall@shaw.ca
moberlyhallschool.com
Grades: 1-12
Enrollment: 85

Medicine Hat: Centre for Academic & Personal Excellence Institute - CAPE
830A Balmoral St. SE, Medicine Hat, AB T1A 0W9, Canada
Tel: 403-528-2983; Fax: 403-528-3048
tdininno@capeisgreat.org
www.capeisgreat.org
Grades: 1-9
Enrollment: 135

Sherwood Park: New Horizons Charter School Society
3 Spruce Ave., Sherwood Park, AB T8A 2B6, Canada
Tel: 780-467-6409; Fax: 780-417-1786
administration@newhorizons.ab.ca
www.newhorizons.ab.ca
Grades: K-9
Enrollment: 160

Wabamun: Mother Earth's Children's Charter School Society
P.O. Box 1150
Wabamun, AB T0E 2K0, Canada
Tel: 780-892-7222; Fax: 780-892-7223
admin@meccs.ca
www.meccs.ca

First Nations

Atikameg: Whitefish Lake First Nation
General Delivery, Atikameg, AB T0G 0C0, Canada
Tel: 780-767-3914; Fax: 780-767-3814
Grades: 1-12

Brocket: Peigan Band
P.O. Box 130
Brocket, AB T0K 0H0, Canada
Tel: 403-965-3910; Fax: 403-965-3713

Cadotte Lake: Woodland Cree First Nation
General Delivery, Cadotte Lake, AB T0H 0N0, Canada
Tel: 780-629-3803; Fax: 780-629-3898
Grades: Gr. 1-12

Chard: Chipewyan Prairie Dene High School (CPDHS)
Chipewyan Prairie Education Multi-Plex
General Delivery, Chard, AB T0P 1G0
Tel: 780-559-2478
Grades: Secondary
Enrollment: 30
The band operated high school is situated south of Fort McMurray, Alberta, where it provides education for the Chipewyan Prairie Dene First Nation.

Chateh: Dene Tha' Community School (DTCS)
P.O. Box 30
Chateh, AB T0H 0S0
Tel: 780-321-3940; Fax: 780-321-3800
reception@chateh-education.net; info@denetha.ca
www.denetha.ca
Grades: Jr. Kindergarten-10; Dene language
Enrollment: 450
Dene Tha' Community School provides education that follows Alberta's kindergarten to grade 10 curriculum, as well as programs such as an early literacy program, a special education program, & Dene language & culture programs.
Lori Aliche, Principal, 780-321-3940, fax: 780-926-0500
Virginia Alarcon, Vice-Principal, Junior High, 780-321-3940, fax: 780-926-1412
Rosalie Metchooyeah, Elder, 780-321-3940
Hayley Natannah, Office Manager, 780-321-3940
Hayley.Natannah@denetha.ca
Ann Austin, Librarian, 780-321-3940
Helen Metchooyeah, Instructor, Dene Language, 780-321-3940
Tyler Metchooyeah, Instructor, Dene, 780-321-3940
Shane Providence-Toho, Instructor, Dene, 780-321-3940

***Driftpile:* Driftpile Community School**
P.O. Box 240
Driftpile, AB T0G 0V0, Canada
Tel: 780-355-3615; *Fax:* 780-355-2135
www.driftpilecreenation.com
Grades: K-4, K-5 - 8; Cree language
Enrollment: 75
Driftpile Community School offers a full academic program, as well as a Cree language & cultural program with traditional music, folklore, & crafts.
Daisy McGee, Principal
Josephine Willier, Secretary
Janice Chalifoux, Family School Wellness Worker
Leonard Isadore, Contact, Cultural Appreciation

***Enoch:* Kitaskinaw School**
P.O. Box 90
Enoch, AB T7X 3Y3
Tel: 780-470-5657; *Fax:* 780-470-5687
Grades: Nursery - 9
Kitaskinaw School is part of the Kitaskinaw Education Authority. The school educates members of the Enoch Cree Nation.

***Enoch:* Yellowhead Tribal Council**
P.O. Box 150
Enoch, AB T7X 3Y3, Canada
Tel: 780-470-3454; *Fax:* 780-470-3541
Grades: 7-12

***Fox Lake:* Jean Baptiste Sewepagaham School**
P.O. Box 270
Fox Lake, AB T0H 1R0
Tel: 780-659-3820
jbssch@telusplanet.net
www.lrrbe.ab.ca
Grades: Kindergarten - 12; Cree language
Enrollment: 600
Jean Baptiste Sewepagaham School is one of three schools in the Little Red River Board of Education. The school serves members of the Little Red River Cree Nation, located approximately 125 kilometres east of High Level, Alberta.

***Frog Lake:* Frog Lake First Nation**
General Delivery, Frog Lake, AB T0A 1M0, Canada
Tel: 780-943-3918; *Fax:* 780-943-2336
Toll-Free: 1-800-816-873
Grades: Pre.-12; Special Ed.

***Garden River:* Sister Gloria School**
P.O. Box 90
Garden River, AB T0H 4G0
Tel: 780-659-3644; *Fax:* 780-659-3890
The Little Red River Board of Education consists of three schools, including Sister Gloria School. Sister Gloria School provides education to First Nation students of the Little Red River Cree Nation. The Alberta community is situated approximately 125 kilometres east of High Level.
Garry Wilson, Principal
wilson_garry@hotmail.com

***Glenevis:* Alexis Nakota Sioux First Nation School**
P.O. Box 27
Glenevis, AB T0E 0X0, Canada
Tel: 780-967-4878
www.alexised.ca
Grades: Elementary - Junior Secondary

***Hobbema:* Meskanahk Ka-Nipa-Wit School**
P.O. Box 129
Hobbema, AB T0C 1N0, Canada
Tel: 780-585-2799; *Fax:* 780-585-2264
Grades: Pre.-9

***Hobbema:* Miyo Wahkohtowin Community Education Authority**
P.O. Box 248
Hobbema, AB T0C 1N0, Canada
Tel: 780-585-2118; *Fax:* 780-585-2116
www.miyo.ca
Grades: Pre.-9

***Hythe:* Horse Lake First Nation**
P.O. Box 303
Hythe, AB T0H 2C0, Canada
Tel: 780-356-2248; *Fax:* 780-356-3666

***John D'Or Prairie:* John D'Or Prairie School**
P.O. Box 120
John D'Or Prairie, AB T0H 3X0
Tel: 780-759-3772
www.lrrbe.ab.ca
John D'Or Prairie School is part of the Little Red River Board of Education. Education is provided to the Little Red River Cree Nation, located approximately 865 kilometres north of Edmonton, Alberta.

***Kehewin:* Kehewin Cree Nation**
P.O. Box 30
Kehewin, AB T0A 1C0, Canada
Tel: 780-826-6200; *Fax:* 780-826-5919
Grades: Pre.-12

***Kinuso:* Swan River First Nation School**
P.O. Box 120
Kinuso, AB T0G 1K0
Tel: 780-775-2177; *Fax:* 780-775-2155
Grades: 7 - 12
Enrollment: 100
The Swan River First Nation School operates on the Swan River First Nation Reserve in Kinuso, Alberta.

***Lac La Biche:* Amisk Community School**
P.O. Box 5000
Lac La Biche, AB T0A 2C0
Tel: 780-623-4548; *Fax:* 780-623-4659
www.beaverlakecreenation.ca
Grades: Early Childhood Svs.-Jr. Secondary
Operated by the Beaver Lake Education Authority, the Amisk Community School provides education to the Beaver Lake Cree Nation.

***Lac La Biche:* Heart Lake First Nation**
P.O. Box 469
Lac La Biche, AB T0A 2C0, Canada
Tel: 780-623-2330; *Fax:* 780-623-3505
Grades: Pre.-12

***Longview:* Chief Jacob Bearspaw School**
P.O. Box 116
100 Center St. SW, Longview, AB T0L 1H0
Tel: 403-558-2480; *Fax:* 403-558-3618
www.stoney-nation.com
Chief Jacob Bearspaw School, located on the Eden Valley Reserve in Alberta, is part of the Stoney Education Authority.
Bill Shade, Principal

***Morley:* Morley Community School**
P.O. Box 238
Morley, Morley, AB T0L 1N0
Tel: 403-881-2755; *Fax:* 403-881-2333
www.stoney-nation.com
Grades: K4 - 12; Stoney language
The Stoney Education Authority oversees the Morley Community School. The First Nations school serves members of the Nakoda First Nation, situated west of Calgary, Alberta.

***Rocky Mountain House:* O'chiese Education Authority**
P.O. Box 337
Rocky Mountain House, AB T4T 1A3, Canada
Tel: 403-989-3911; *Fax:* 403-989-2122
Grades: K-12

***Rocky Mountain House:* Sunchild First Nation School**
P.O. Box 1149
Rocky Mountain House, AB T4T 1A8
Tel: 403-989-3476; *Fax:* 403-989-3614
www.sunchildschool.com
Grades: Kindergarten - 12
The Sunchild First Nation School is part of the Sunchild First Nation Band Education Authority.
Martin Sacher, Principal
sacher@sccyber.net
Susan Collicutt, Vice-Principal
collicutts@yahoo.ca

***Tsuu T'ina Sarcee:* Chiila Elementary School**
#250, 991 Chiila Blvd. SW, Tsuu T'ina Sarcee, AB T2W 6H6
Tel: 403-238-5484
www.tsuutina.ca
Grades: K4 - 5
Chiila Elementary School is part of the Tsuu T'ina Nation Board of Education.

***Tsuu T'ina Sarcee:* Tsuu T'ina Junior Senior High School**
#250, 991 Chiila Blvd. SW, Tsuu T'ina Sarcee, AB T2W 6H6
Tel: 403-251-9555; *Fax:* 403-251-9833
www.tsuutina.ca
Grades: 6 - 12
The Tsuu T'ina Nation Board of Education oversees the operations of the Tsuu T'ina Junior Senior High School.

***Valleyview:* Sturgeon Lake School**
P.O. Box 5
Valleyview, AB T0H 3N0
Tel: 780-524-4590; *Fax:* 780-524-3696
Grades: Kindergarten - 12
Enrollment: 230
The Sturgeon Lake School is part of the Sturgeon Lake First Nation, Band #154, Education Authority. The First Nation school serves the Sturgeon Lake Cree Nation.

***Wabasca:* Bigstone Cree Nation Community School Oski Pasikoniwew Kamik**
P.O. Box 930
Wabasca, AB T0G 2K0
Tel: 780-891-3830; *Fax:* 780-891-3831
www.bigstone.ca
Grades: Preschool - 6
Enrollment: 247
The Bigstone Community School operates under the direction of the Bigstone Cree Nation Education Authority. The school strives to maintain traditional values as its educational foundation.

Schools: Independent & Private

Catholic

***Calgary:* Clear Water Academy**
2521 Dieppe Ave. SW, Calgary, AB T3E 7J9, Canada
Tel: 403-217-8448; *Fax:* 403-217-8043
administration@clearwateracademy.com
www.clearwateracademy.com
Grades: Pre.-12
An independent Catholic school.
Paul Hudec, Principal

Special Education

***Edmonton:* Edmonton Academy**
10231 - 120 St., Edmonton, AB T5K 2A4, Canada
Tel: 780-482-5449; *Fax:* 780-482-0902
lizrich@telusplanet.net
www.edmontonacademy.com
Grades: 7-12
Founded in 1983; provides specialized teaching for students with learning disabilities.
Liz Richards, Executive Director

***Edmonton:* Elves Child Development Centre**
10825 - 142 St., Edmonton, AB T5N 3Y7, Canada
Tel: 780-454-5310; *Fax:* 780-454-5889
elvessoc@telusplanet.net
www.elves-society.com
Grades: Pre.-12
The Elves Special Needs Society offers programs for pre-school and older children, youth and adults who are severely developmentally delayed and/or medically fragile, as well as outreach to students unable to attend school for extended periods of time.
Cristina Molina, Executive Director

***Edmonton:* John Howard Society of Edmonton Alternative Learning Program**
#301, 10526 Jasper Ave., Edmonton, AB T5J 1Z7, Canada
Tel: 780-428-7590; *Fax:* 780-425-1549
info@edm.johnhoward.org
www.johnhoward.ab.ca; www.johnhoward.org
Grades: To Gr. 9
The Edmonton John Howard Society's Adult Transition Learning Centre offers courses to clients at every stage of learning, including: literacy, GED & college preparation, language arts, math & computer basics, personal development, & life skills (addictions, anger management, mental health; all aspects of employment preparation). The Centre is located at 10010 105th St., Suite 401, in Edmonton.

Independent & Private Schools

***Airdrie:* Airdrie Koinonia Christian School**
2104 Big Hill Springs Rd., RR#1, Airdrie, AB T4B 2A3, Canada
Tel: 403-948-5100; *Fax:* 403-948-5563
adminoffice@akcs.com
Grades: Pre.-12

***Banff:* Banff Mountain Academy**
P.O. Box 369 Main
1 Mount Norquay, Banff, AB T1L 1A5, Canada
Tel: 403-760-4101
Grades: 9-12
Enrollment: 40
Banff Mountain Academy is a residential, co-educational school. It offers a flexible program for athletes.

***Bow Island:* Cherry Coulee Christian Academy (CCCA)**
P.O. Box 10370
Bow Island, AB T0K 0G0, Canada
Tel: 403-545-2107; *Fax:* 403-545-2944
www.cherrycoulee.ca

Grades: Kindergarten - 9
Kim Dolan, Administrator

***Brant:* Brant Christian School**
P.O. Box 130
Brant, AB T0L 0L0, Canada
Tel: 403-684-3752; *Fax:* 403-684-3894
www.brantchristianschool.com

Grades: Kindergarten - 12
Corry Brown, Principal
Susan McLean, Librarian

***Brooks:* Newell Christian School (NCS)**
P.O. Box 100
Brooks, AB T1R 1B2, Canada
Tel: 403-378-4448; *Fax:* 403-378-3991
www.newellchristianschool.com

Grades: Kindergarten - 9
The Alberta curriculum is taught from a Christian perspective.
Dale Rempel, Chair
Ron Cousins, Principal

***Calgary:* Akiva Academy**
140 Haddon Rd. SW, Calgary, AB T2V 2Y3, Canada
Tel: 403-258-1312; *Fax:* 403-258-3812
office@akiva.ca
www.akiva.ca

Grades: Pre.-6
Jemmie Silver, Principal

***Calgary:* Banbury Crossroads Private School**
#201, 2451 Dieppe Ave. SW, Calgary, AB T3E 7K1, Canada
Tel: 403-270-7787; *Fax:* 403-270-7486
general@banburycrossroads.com
www.banburycrossroads.com
Banbury Crossroads Private School offers education to children aged 3 to 18.
Diane Swiatek, Principal
Karen Harrison, Vice Principal

***Calgary:* Bearspaw Christian School (BCS)**
15001 - 69th St. NW, Calgary, AB T3R 1C5, Canada
Tel: 403-295-2566; *Fax:* 403-275-8170
info@bearspawschool.com
www.bearspawschool.com

Grades: Kindergarten - 12
Enrollment: 500
Kelly Blake, President
kblake@bearspawschool.com
Judy Huffman, Principal
jhuffman@bearspawschool.com
Jennifer Lockhart, Vice Principal, Elementary
jlockhart@bearspawschool.com
Lara Melashenko, Vice Principal, Secondary
lmelashenko@bearspawschool.com

***Calgary:* Bethel Christian Academy**
2220 - 39th Ave. NE, Calgary, AB T2E 5T4, Canada
Tel: 403-735-3335; *Fax:* 403-219-3059
tbetts@encountergod.org
www.encountergod.org
Grades: Kindergarten - 12

***Calgary:* Calgary Academy**
9400 - 17th Ave. SW, Calgary, AB T3H 4A6, Canada
Tel: 403-686-6444; *Fax:* 403-240-3427
info@calgaryacademy.com; careers@calgaryacademy.com (Employment)
www.calgaryacademy.com
Grades: 2 - 12
Enrollment: 625
Peter Istvanffy, President/CEO
Joanne Endacott, Director, Admissions
jendacott@calgaryacademy.com

***Calgary:* Calgary Chinese Alliance School**
Calgary Chinese Alliance Church
150 Beddington Blvd. NE, Calgary, AB T3K 2E2, Canada
Tel: 403-274-6925; *Fax:* 403-275-7799
Grades: 10 - 12
Enrollment: 500
Alex Hung, President
Mimi Fong, Principal
mimiefong@hotmail.com

***Calgary:* Calgary Chinese Private School**
599 Northmount Dr. NW, Calgary, AB T2K 3J6, Canada
Tel: 403-264-2233; *Fax:* 403-263-3895
Grades: 10 - 12
The Calgary Chinese Private School works to maintain Chinese heritage & culture in the community.

***Calgary:* Calgary Christian School**
North Bldg.
5029 - 26th Ave. SW, Calgary, AB T3E 0R5, Canada
Tel: 403-242-2896; *Fax:* 403-242-6682
www.calgarychristianschool.com

Grades: Preschool - 12
Calgary Christian School has an elementary campus & a secondary campus.
Scott Hickling, Executive Director
Harry Fritschy, Principal, Elementary
Gwen Uittenbosch, Principal, Secondary
Glenda Jullion, Vice Principal, Elementary
Jason Kupery, Vice Principal, Secondary

***Calgary:* Calgary French & International School (CFIS)**
700 - 77th St. SW, Calgary, AB T3H 5R1, Canada
Tel: 403-240-1500; *Fax:* 403-249-5899
inquiries@cfis.com
www.cfis.com

Grades: Preschool - 12
Calgary French & International School offers French Immersion education.
John McVicar, Chair & President
societyboard@cfis.com
Dr. Richard Slevinsky, Headmaster, 403-240-1500, ext. 130
rslevinsky@cfis.com
Michele Gariépy, Vice Principal, Junior High School
mgariepy@cfis.com
Cecile Triggle, Vice Principal, Elementary School, 403-240-1500, ext. 210
ctriggle@cfis.com
Janice Jalving, Director, Child Care Centre, 403-246-4708
childcare@cfis.com
Katharine Ray, Officer, Admissions, 403-240-1500, ext. 329
kray@cfis.com

***Calgary:* Calgary Islamic Private School (CIS)**
2612 - 37th Ave. NE, Calgary, AB T1Y 5L2, Canada
Tel: 403-248-2773
www.calgaryislamicschool.com

Grades: Kindergarten - 9
Enrollment: 490
Calgary Islamic School offers the regular curriculum, as well as a Quran recitation & memorization curriculum, an Arabic language curriculum, an Islamic Studies curriculum.

***Calgary:* Calgary Jewish Academy (CJA)**
6700 Kootenay St. SW, Calgary, AB T2V 1P7, Canada
Tel: 403-253-3992; *Fax:* 403-255-0842
info@cja.ab.ca
www.cja.ab.ca

Grades: Preschool - 9
Ben Karmel, Principal
KarmelB@cja.ab.ca
Barbara Dare, Associate Principal, Alberta Curriculum
dareb@cja.ab.ca
Shoshana Kirmayer, Associate Principal, Judaic Studies
kirmayers@cja.ab.ca

***Calgary:* Calgary Quest School**
c/o Spruce Cliff Elementary
3405 Spruce Dr. SW, Calgary, AB T3C 0A5, Canada
Tel: 403-253-0003; *Fax:* 403-253-0025
info@calgaryquestschool.com
www.calgaryquestschool.com

Calgary Quest School offers a program for children with special challenges.
Kathy Peron, Chair

***Calgary:* Calgary Waldorf School**
515 Cougar Ridge Dr. SW, Calgary, AB T3H 5G9, Canada
Tel: 403-287-1868; *Fax:* 403-287-3414
info@calgarywaldorf.org
www.calgarywaldorf.org

Grades: Preschool - 9
Calgary Waldorf School also offers a Parent-and-Tot program.
Cathie Foote, School Administrator
Kathy Brunetta, Pedagogical Administrator
Dinah Clark, Financial Administrator
Laureen Loree, Principal
Sandra Langlois, Manager, Admissions & Facility

***Calgary:* The Chinese Academy**
John G. Diefenbaker Senior High School
6620 - 4th St. NW, Calgary, AB T2K 1C2, Canada
Tel: 403-777-7663; *Fax:* 403-777-7669
admin@chineseacademy.ca; chineseacademy@telus.net
www.chineseacademy.ca
Grades: Kindergarten - 12
Enrollment: 1925
Kindergarten, Level 1, begins for children aged 3.5 years at the Sir John A. Macdonald Junior High School, 6600 - 4th St. NW in Calgary. The goal of the school is to promote Chinese language & culture. Cantonese & Mandarin classes, as well as Chinese as a Second Language for beginners in Cantonese & Mandarin.
Martina Lui, President
Judy Fung, School Superintendent
Elaine Chan, BSc., M.A. (Ed. Admin.), Principal

***Calgary:* Chinook Winds Adventist Academy (CWAA)**
10101 - 2nd Ave. SW, Calgary, AB T3B 5T2, Canada
Tel: 403-286-5686; *Fax:* 403-247-1623
cwaa2@cwaa.net
www.cwaa.net

Grades: Kindergarten - 12
The Seventh-day Adventist school also features music, outdoor education, Bible instruction, & mission trips for senior high students.
Murray McLeod, BA, Principal
Marilyn Kelloway, BEd., Vice Principal
Samuel Millen, MDiv., Chaplain

***Calgary:* Community Connections School**
225 - 37 St. NW, Calgary, AB T2N 4N6, Canada
Tel: 403-283-6361; *Fax:* 403-283-5741
brenda@homeeducation.ca

Grades: 1-12

***Calgary:* Delta West Academy**
414 - 11A St. NE, Calgary, AB T2E 4P3, Canada
Tel: 403-290-0767; *Fax:* 403-290-0768
info@deltawestacademy.ca

Grades: Pre.-12; Special Ed.

***Calgary:* Eastside Christian Academy**
1320 Abbeydale Dr. SE, Calgary, AB T2A 7L8, Canada
Tel: 403-569-1039; *Fax:* 403-569-1023
admin@ecaab.ca

Grades: Pre.-12

***Calgary:* Edge School for Athletes**
700 - 77 St. SW, Calgary, AB T3H 5R1, Canada
Tel: 403-246-6432; *Fax:* 403-217-8463
Grades: 1-12

***Calgary:* Educere International College**
#1500, 910 - 7 Ave. SW, Calgary, AB T2P 3N8, Canada
Tel: 403-232-8551; *Fax:* 403-233-0239
educere@educere.ca

Grades: 10-12

***Calgary:* Equilibrium International Educational Institute**
707 - 14 St. NW, Calgary, AB T2N 2A4, Canada
Tel: 403-283-1111; *Fax:* 403-270-7786
school@equilibrium.ab.ca

Grades: 10-12

***Calgary:* Foothills Academy**
745 - 37 St. NW, Calgary, AB T2N 4T1, Canada
Tel: 403-270-9400; *Fax:* 403-270-9438
Grades: 1-12; Special Ed.

***Calgary:* Froebel's Garden of Children**
119 Pinetown Pl. NE, Calgary, AB T1Y 5J1, Canada
Tel: 403-280-4855
froebel@shaw.ca

Grades: Pre.-6

***Calgary:* Glenmore Christian Academy**
16520 - 24th St., Calgary, AB T2Y 4W2, Canada
Tel: 403-254-9050; *Fax:* 403-256-9695
admin@glenmorechristian.com
Grades: Pre.-9; Special Ed.
Derrick Mohamed, Principal

***Calgary:* Greek Community School**
1 Tamarac Cres. SW, Calgary, AB T3C 3B7, Canada
Tel: 403-246-4553; *Fax:* 403-246-8191
school@calgaryhellenic.com

Grades: 1-12

***Calgary:* Heritage Christian Academy**
2003 McKnight Blvd. NE, Calgary, AB T2E 6L2, Canada
Tel: 403-219-3201; *Fax:* 403-219-3210
hca@telus.net
www.hcacalgary.com

Grades: Pre.-12
Enrollment: 500
LaVerne Pue, Principal

***Calgary:* International School of Excellence**
3915 - 34 St. NE, Calgary, AB T1Y 6Z8, Canada
Tel: 403-234-0453; *Fax:* 403-250-2401
isoe@shaw.ca
Grades: Pre.-12

***Calgary:* Italian School of Calgary**
24 Beddington Way NE, Calgary, AB T3K 1N9, Canada
Tel: 403-264-6349
Grades: 7-12

***Calgary:* Janus Academy**
71 Edgebrook Circle NW, Calgary, AB T3A 5A4, Canada
Tel: 403-262-3333; *Fax:* 403-693-2345
Grades: Pre.-9

***Calgary:* Language School**
German Canadian Club
2626 - 23 St. NE, Calgary, AB T2E 8L2, Canada
Tel: 403-248-0994
Grades: 10-12

***Calgary:* LSC Calgary**
140 4th Ave. SW. Suite 300, North Tower, Calgary, AB T2P 3N3, Canada
Tel: 403-662-2200; *Fax:* 403-662-2201
calgary@lsc-canada.com
www.lsc-canada.com

***Calgary:* Lycée Louis Pasteur**
4099, boul Garrison sud-ouest, Calgary, AB T2T 6G2, Canada
Tél: 403-243-5420; *Téléc:* 403-287-2245
office@lycee.ca
www.lycee.ca
Grades: Mat./Prim.
Benjamin Orillon, Chef d'établissement

***Calgary:* Master's Academy**
4414 Crowchild Trail SW, Calgary, AB T2T 5J4, Canada
Tel: 403-242-7034; *Fax:* 403-242-4629
Grades: Pre.-12

***Calgary:* Menno Simons Christian School**
7000 Elkton Dr. SW, Calgary, AB T3H 4Y7, Canada
Tel: 403-531-0745; *Fax:* 403-531-0747
office@mennosimons.ab.ca
Grades: Pre.-9

***Calgary:* Montessori School of Calgary**
2201 Cliff St. SW, Calgary, AB T2S 2G4, Canada
Tel: 403-229-1011
msofc@telusplanet.net
www.montessorischoolofcalgary.com
Grades: Preschool / Elementary
Enrollment: 100
The children at the Montessori School of Calgary range in age from 2.5 to 12. Both the Montessori program & the Alberta Programme of Studies are followed.
Nancy Lowden, Head of School

***Calgary:* Mountain View Academy (MVA)**
#B4, 2452 Battleford Ave. SW, Calgary, AB T3E 7K9, Canada
Tel: 403-217-4346; *Fax:* 403-249-4312
www.mountainviewacademy.ca
Grades: Preschool - 12
Jitka Smuszko, Director
Lenka Popplestone, Principal
Colleen Ryan, Vice Principal
Jane Lizotte, Assistant Principal

***Calgary:* Renfrew Educational Services**
Main School & Administrative Centre
2050 - 21st St. NE, Calgary, AB T2E 6S5, Canada
Tel: 403-291-5038; *Fax:* 403-291-2499
renfrew@renfreweducation.org
www.renfreweducation.org
Grades: Preschool - Elementary
Enrollment: 700
Renfrew Educational Services offers specialized educational programs for preschool & elementary students. The not-for-profit society also develops programs for children with special needs.
Tom Buchanan, Chair
Janice McTighe, Executive Director
Kim LaCourse, Associate Executive Director
Cathy Gable, Director, Community Services
Mary lou Hill, Director, Education
Bruce Monnery, Director, Finance & Administration

***Calgary:* Rundle College Academy**
4330 - 16 St. SW, Calgary, AB T2J 4H9, Canada
Tel: 403-250-2965; *Fax:* 403-250-2914
www.rundle.ab.ca
Grades: 1-12

***Calgary:* Rundle College Elementary School**
2634 - 12 Ave. NW, Calgary, AB T2N 1K6, Canada
Tel: 403-282-8411; *Fax:* 403-282-4460
johnston@rundle.ab.ca
www.rundle.ab.ca
Grades: Pre.-6

***Calgary:* Rundle College Junior High School**
7375 - 17 Ave/ SW, Calgary, AB T3H 3W5, Canada
Tel: 403-250-7180; *Fax:* 403-250-7184
baird@rundle.ab.ca
Grades: 7-9

***Calgary:* Rundle College Senior High School**
7375 - 17 Ave. SW, Calgary, AB T3H 3W5, Canada
Tel: 403-250-7180; *Fax:* 403-250-7184
bridal@rundle.ab.ca
www.rundle.ab.ca
Grades: 7-12
Mr. Hauk, Headmaster
hauk@rundle.ab.ca

***Calgary:* St. John Bosco Private School**
712 Fortalice Cres. SE, Calgary, AB T2A 2E1, Canada
Tel: 403-248-3664; *Fax:* 403-273-8012
stjohnbosco@shaw.ca
www.stjohnboscoprivateschool.com
Grades: Pre.-9

***Calgary:* Third Academy**
B4 Bldg., Currie Barracks
2452 Battleford Ave. SW, Calgary, AB T3E 7K1, Canada
Tel: 403-288-5335; *Toll-Free:* 1-877-508-5335
info@thirdacademy.com
www.thirdacademy.com
Grades: 1 - 12
The Third Academy offers an Individualized Program Plan for students with special needs to remediate of compensate for their learning disorder. There is a Calgary North location, a Calgary South location, & a Red Deer location.
Jitka Smuszko, Chair
Dr. S. Lal Mattu, CEO & Founder
Sunil Mattu, LLB (Hons) Law, BEd, Chief Operating Officer
David Lambe, Vice President, Business & Community Relations.
Kathleen Colmant, Coordinator, Special Events
Rehana Mattu, BEd, Master Teacher
Liz Wray, Registrar

***Calgary:* The Timothy Centre for Scholarship**
P.O. Box 49096
7740 - 18th St. SE, Calgary, AB T2C 3W5, Canada
Tel: 403-230-0702
info@timothycentre.com
www.timothycentre.com
Grades: Kindergarten - 12
The Timothy Centre for Scholarship offers a classical Christian education for Calgary homeschoolers.
Laurel Roberts, Principal

***Calgary:* Trinity Christian School (TCS)**
#100, 295 Midpark Way SE, Calgary, AB T2X 2A8, Canada
Tel: 403-254-6682; *Fax:* 403-254-9843
trinity@tcskids.com
www.tcskids.com
Other Information: 403-254-6716 (Phone, Business Office)
Grades: Kindergarten - 9
Merle Rayner, Chair
James Sijpheer, Principal
james.sijpheer@tcskids.com
George Graffunder, Vice Principal
ggraffunder@tcskids.com
Tania Spears, Manager, Business
Sandy Stasko, Coordinator, Resources

***Calgary:* Truth Academy**
615 Northmount Dr. NW, Calgary, AB T2K 3J6, Canada
Tel: 403-282-0238; *Fax:* 403-289-8356
Grades: Preschool - 12

***Calgary:* Webber Academy**
1515 - 93rd St. SW, Calgary, AB T3H 4A8, Canada
Tel: 403-277-4700; *Fax:* 403-277-2770
www.webberacademy.ca
Grades: Junior Kindergarten - 12
Webber Academy is a coeducational, non-denominational university preparatory school.
Dr. Neil Webber, Head of School
nwebber@webberacademy.ca
Barbara Webber, Vice-President, Administration
bwebber@webberacademy.ca
Dianne Lever, Contact, Admissions
admissions@webberacademy.ca

***Calgary:* West Island College (WIC)**
7410 Blackfoot Trail SE, Calgary, AB T2H 1M5, Canada
Tel: 403-255-5300; *Fax:* 403-252-1434
office@westislandcollege.ab.ca
www.westislandcollege.ab.ca
Other Information: admissions@westislandcollege.ab.ca (E-mail, Admissions)
Grades: 7 - 12
West Island College provides pre-university training. Programs include English & French communication skills & the arts.
Carol Grant-Watt, Head of School, 403-255-5300, ext. 238
Boyd Belisle, Head, Junior School, 403-255-5300, ext. 277
Claire Allen, Director, International Studies, 403-255-5300, ext. 302
Scott Bennett, Director, Faculty Development, 403-255-5300, ext. 501
Roland Chalifoux, Director, Programme Studies, 403-255-5300, ext. 237
Todd Larsen, Director, Co-Curricular Programmes, 403-255-5300, ext. 231
Murray Marran, Director, Admissions & Bursar, 403-255-5300, ext. 285
Pierre Poitras, Director, Technology, 403-255-5300, ext. 260
Malcolm Rennie, Director, Post-Secondary Placement, 403-255-5300, ext. 286

***Canmore:* Mountain Gate Community School**
P.O. Box 8287
Canmore, AB T1W 2V1, Canada
Tel: 403-609-2105; *Fax:* 403-609-8355
mgsc@monarch.net
Grades: 1 - 6

***Cardston:* Red Crow Community College (RCCC)**
P.O. Box 1258
Cardston, AB T0K 0K0, Canada
Tel: 403-737-2400; *Fax:* 403-737-2101
Toll-Free: 866-937-2400
webmaster@redcrowcollege.com
www.redcrowcollege.com
Mi'Kai'sto Red Crow Community College is a post-secondary institution whcih offers Diploma, Degree and Masters programs. The College partners with Mount Royal, Lethbridge Community College, SAIT, the University of Lethbridge, & the University of Calgary.
Dr. Marie Smallface-Marule, President

***Caroline:* Living Faith Christian School**
P.O. Box 100
Caroline, AB T0M 0M0, Canada
Tel: 403-722-2225; *Fax:* 403-722-2459
lfcs@telusplanet.net
Grades: 1-12

***Champion:* Hope Christian School**
P.O. Box 235
Champion, AB T0L 0R0, Canada
Tel: 403-897-3019; *Fax:* 403-897-2392
hopec@telusplanet.net
Grades: 1-12

***Coaldale:* Coaldale Christian School**
2008 - 8 St., Coaldale, AB T1M 1L1, Canada
Tel: 403-345-4055; *Fax:* 403-345-6436
ccsoffic@telusplanet.net
Grades: Pre.-12; Special Ed.

***Cold Lake:* Lakeland Christian Academy**
P.O. Box 8397
Cold Lake, AB T9M 1N2, Canada
Tel: 780-639-2077; *Fax:* 780-639-4151
lca@hlvc.org
Grades: 1-12

***Cold Lake:* Trinity Christian School**
5731 - 50th Ave., Cold Lake, AB T9M-1T1, Canada
Tel: 780-594-2205; *Fax:* 780-594-3737
trinity@cablerocket.com
Grades: Preschool - 12
Richard Schienbein, Principal

***Devon:* Devon Christian School**
P.O. Box 5390
Devon, AB T9G 1Y1, Canada
Tel: 780-987-4157; *Fax:* 780-987-3323
dcs@devonchristianschool.com
Grades: Pre.-9

***Edmonton:* Alberta Centre for Chinese Studies**
13719 - 133 Ave., Edmonton, AB T5L 3T3, Canada
Tel: 780-453-3968
louisho@telus.net
Grades: 10-12

Edmonton: Columbus Academy
6770 - 129 Ave., Edmonton, AB T5C 1V7, Canada
Tel: 780-440-0708; *Fax:* 780-440-0760
cci@telusplanet.net
Grades: 7-12

Edmonton: Concordia Continuing Education High School
10537 - 44 St., Edmonton, AB T6A 1W1, Canada
Tel: 780-413-7800; *Fax:* 780-466-9394
gerrie.cameron@concordia.ab.ca
www.hs.concordia.ab.ca
Grades: 10-12

Edmonton: Concordia High School
7128 Ada Blvd., Edmonton, AB T5B 4E4, Canada
Tel: 780-479-9391; *Fax:* 780-479-5050
www.concordiahighschool.com
Grades: 10-12

Edmonton: Coralwood Adventist Academy
12218 - 135 St. NW, Edmonton, AB T5L 1X1, Canada
Tel: 780-454-2173; *Fax:* 780-455-6946
corlwood@telusplanet.net
Grades: Pre.-12

Edmonton: Dante Alighieri Italian School
c/o Archbishop O'Leary High
8760 - 132 Ave., Edmonton, AB T5E 0X8, Canada
Tel: 780-474-1787; *Fax:* 780-451-0669
aristidem@shaw.ca
Grades: 10-12

Edmonton: Don Bosco Academy
6770 - 129 Ave., Edmonton, AB T5C 1V7, Canada
Tel: 780-922-4790; *Fax:* 780-922-3290
admin@boscohomes.ca
Grades: 1-12

Edmonton: Edmonton Bible Heritage Christian School
13054 - 112 St. NW, Edmonton, AB T5E 6E6, Canada
Tel: 780-454-3672; *Fax:* 780-488-3672
Grades: 1-12

Edmonton: Edmonton Islamic Academy
14525 - 127 St., Edmonton, AB T6V 0B3, Canada
Tel: 780-454-4573; *Fax:* 780-454-3498
eia@islamicschool.ca
www.islamicacademy.ca
Grades: K.-9
Enrollment: 700
Abdullah A. Omar, Principal

Edmonton: Edmonton Menorah Academy
10735 McQueen Rd. NW, Edmonton, AB T5N 3L1, Canada
Tel: 780-451-1848; *Fax:* 780-451-2254
ema613@yahoo.ca
Grades: Pre.-9

Edmonton: Faith Lutheran School
11515 - 36 St., Edmonton, AB T5W 2A9, Canada
Tel: 780-496-9302; *Fax:* 780-496-3556
faithschool@shaw.ca
Grades: Pre.-9

Edmonton: German Language School Society of Edmonton
c/o Rio Terrace School
7608 - 154 St., Edmonton, AB T5R 1R7, Canada
Tel: 780-435-7540
kerstin.buelow@shaw.ca
www.germanschooledmonton.org
Grades: 10-12
Judith Meyers, Administrator
judith.meyers@gmx.de

Edmonton: Gil Vicente School
8830 - 132 Ave., Edmonton, AB T5E 0X8, Canada
Tel: 780-474-7242
cpereira@gsacrd.ab.ca
Grades: 10-12

Edmonton: Headway School Society of Alberta
3530 - 91 St., Edmonton, AB T6E 6P1, Canada
Tel: 780-461-7683; *Fax:* 780-485-0507
headway@telusplanet.net
www.members.shaw.ca/worman/
Grades: Pre.-12

Edmonton: Ivan Franko Ukrainian School
14535 - 52 St., Edmonton, AB T5A 4N1, Canada
Tel: 780-476-7529
lsukhy@hotmail.com
Grades: 10-12

Edmonton: Meadowlark Christian School
9825 - 158 St., Edmonton, AB T5P 2X4, Canada
Tel: 780-483-6476; *Fax:* 780-487-8992
mdlkchr@telusplanet.net
www.k-9christian.com
Grades: Pre.-9

Edmonton: Parkland Immanuel Christian School
21304 - 35 Ave. NW, Edmonton, AB T6M 2P6, Canada
Tel: 780-444-6443; *Fax:* 780-444-6448
info@parklandimmanuel.ca
www.parklandimmanuel.ca
Grades: Pre.-12

Edmonton: Phoenix Academy
6770 - 129 Ave., Edmonton, AB T5C 1V7, Canada
Tel: 780-440-0708; *Fax:* 780-440-0760
admin@boscohomes.ca
Grades: K.-12
School for students who struggle with behavioural disorders and learning disabilities

Edmonton: Progressive Academy
13212 - 106 Ave., Edmonton, AB T5N 1A3, Canada
Tel: 780-455-8344; *Fax:* 780-455-1425
info@progressiveacademy.ca
www.progressiveacademy.ca
Grades: Junior Kindergarten - 12
The school offers small classes & the flexibility for students to progress through grades at an irregular pace. Progressive Academy is licensed by Applied Scholastics International & accredited by Alberta Education.

Edmonton: St. George's Hellenic Language School
10831 - 124 St., Edmonton, AB T5M 0H4, Canada
Tel: 780-452-1455; *Fax:* 780-452-1455
Grades: 10-12

Edmonton: Solomon College
#228, 10621 - 100 Ave., Edmonton, AB T5J 0B3, Canada
Tel: 780-431-1515; *Fax:* 780-431-1644
info@solomoncollege.ca
www.solomoncollege.ca
Grades: 10-12

Edmonton: Tempo School
5603 - 148 St., Edmonton, AB T6H 4T7, Canada
Tel: 780-434-1190; *Fax:* 780-430-6209
admin@temposchool.org
www.temposchool.org
Grades: Pre.-12
Enrollment: 380
P. Mitchell, Headmaster

Edmonton: Victory Christian School (VCS)
11520 Ellerslie Rd., Edmonton, AB T6W 1A2, Canada
Tel: 780-988-5433; *Fax:* 780-988-5280
info@victorychristianschool.ca
www.victorychristianschool.ca
Grades: Preschool - 12
Enrollment: 120
Victory Christian School's preschool offers curriculum suited to the developmental stages of four year old children.

Edson: Yellowhead Koinonia Christian School
430 - 72 St., Edson, AB T7E 1N3, Canada
Tel: 780-723-3850; *Fax:* 780-723-7566
ykcs@yellowhead.com
Grades: Pre.-12

Fort McMurray: Fort McMurray Christian School
190 Tamarack Way, Fort McMurray, AB T9K 1A1, Canada
Tel: 780-743-1079; *Fax:* 780-743-1379
Grades: Pre.-9

Grande Prairie: Grande Prairie Christian School
8202 - 110 St., Grande Prairie, AB T8W 1M3, Canada
Tel: 780-539-4566; *Fax:* 780-539-4748
diana.krahn@gppsd.ab.ca
www.gppsd.ab.ca/school/gpchristian
Grades: Pre.-12
Enrollment: 220
John Bueckert, Principal

Grande Prairie: Hillcrest Christian School
10306 - 102 St., Grande Prairie, AB T8V 2W3, Canada
Tel: 780-539-9161; *Fax:* 780-532-6932
hcsgp@telus.net
Grades: Pre.-12

High Level: High Level Christian Academy
P.O. Box 1100
10701 - 100 Ave., High Level, AB T0H 1Z0, Canada
Tel: 780-926-2360; *Fax:* 780-926-3245
hlca@telusplanet.net
www.highlevelchristianacademy.ca
Grades: Pre.-12
Vera Bartlett, Vice Principal

Hobbema: Maskwachees Cultural School
P.O. Box 360
Hobbema, AB T0C 1N0, Canada
Tel: 780-585-3925; *Fax:* 780-585-2080
mcc@wtc.ab.ca
Grades: 10-12

Joussard: North Country School
1, Joussard, AB T0G 1J0, Canada
Tel: 780-776-2215
Grades: Kindergarten - 12

Kingman: Cornerstone Christian Academy
P.O. Box 99
Kingman, AB T0B 2M0, Canada
Tel: 780-672-7197; *Fax:* 780-608-1420
corner@cable-lynx.net
www.cornerstonekingman.ca
Grades: Pre.-12; Special Ed.
Core subjects are taught; Bible Studies.
Steve Ioanidis, Principal

Lacombe: Central Alberta Christian High School (CACHS)
22 Eagle Rd., Lacombe, AB T4L 1G7, Canada
Tel: 403-782-4535; *Fax:* 403-782-5425
office@cachs.ca
www.cachs.ca
Grades: Secondary
Bernie TenHove, Chair
Jack Vanden Pol, Principal
Wendy Barnes, Business Administrator
office@cachs.ca

Lacombe: College Heights Christian School
5201 College Ave., Lacombe, AB T4L 1Z6, Canada
Tel: 403-782-6212; *Fax:* 403-782-7507
Grades: Pre.-9

Lacombe: Lacombe Christian School
5206 - 58 St., Lacombe, AB T4L 1G9, Canada
Tel: 403-782-6531; *Fax:* 403-782-5760
office@lacs.ca
Grades: Pre.-9

Lacombe: Parkview Adventist Academy
5505 College Ave., Lacombe, AB T4L 2E7, Canada
Tel: 403-782-3381; *Fax:* 403-782-7308
www.paa.ca
Grades: 10-12
Christian boarding school affiliated with Canadian University College

Leduc: Covenant Christian School
P.O. Box 3827 Main
Leduc, AB T9E 6M7, Canada
Tel: 780-986-8353; *Fax:* 780-986-8360
www.covenantchristian.ca
Grades: Pre.-9; Special Ed.
Enrollment: 165
Christ-centered education within a curriculum of core subjects.
Gayle Monsma, Principal
gayle.monsma@blackgold.ca

Lethbridge: Immanuel Christian Elementary School
2010 - 5 Ave. North, Lethbridge, AB T1H 0N5, Canada
Tel: 403-317-7860; *Fax:* 403-317-7862
icesoffice@gmail.com
Grades: Pre.-6

Lethbridge: Immanuel Christian High School
802 - 6 Ave. North, Lethbridge, AB T1H 0S1, Canada
Tel: 403-328-4783; *Fax:* 403-327-6333
Grades: 7-12

Linden: Kneehill Christian School
P.O. Box 370
Linden, AB T0M 1J0, Canada
Tel: 403-546-3781; *Fax:* 403-546-3181
Grades: 1-9

***Medicine Hat:* Cornerstone Christian School**
P.O. Box 40043
355 Southridge Dr. SE, Medicine Hat, AB T1B 3M6, Canada
Tel: 403-529-6169; *Fax:* 403-529-6169
ccschool@canopycanada.net
Grades: Pre.-9

***Medicine Hat:* Medicine Hat Christian School**
68 Rice Dr. SE, Medicine Hat, AB T1B 3X2, Canada
Tel: 403-526-3246; *Fax:* 403-528-9048
mhcs@shockware.com
Grades: Pre.-9

***Monarch:* Calvin Christian School**
P.O. Box 40
Monarch, AB T0L 1M0, Canada
Tel: 403-381-3030; *Fax:* 403-381-4241
office@ccschool.ca

***Monarch:* Providence Christian School**
P.O. Box 68
Monarch, AB T0L 1M0, Canada
Tel: 403-381-4418; *Fax:* 403-381-4418
provchr@telusplanet.net
Grades: Preschool - 12

***Morinville:* Morinville Christian School**
10515 - 100 Ave., Morinville, AB T8R 1A2, Canada
Tel: 780-939-2987
mcfs@telus.net
www.morinvillechristian.com
Lou Brunelle, Director, School

***Neerlandia:* Covenant Canadian Reformed School**
P.O. Box 67
Neerlandia, AB T0G 1R0, Canada
Tel: 780-674-4774; *Fax:* 780-401-3295
ccrs@xplornet.com
www.ccrs.110mb.com
Grades: Pre.-12; Special Ed.
Enrollment: 170
Students are members of the Canadian Reformed or United Reformed churchesLocation: 3030 Township Rd. 615A, Neerlandia.
Harry VanDelden, Principal

***Okotoks:* Edison School**
Box 2, Site 11, RR#2, Okotoks, AB T1S 1A2, Canada
Tel: 403-938-7670; *Fax:* 403-938-7224
office@edisonschool.ca
Grades: Pre.-12

***Okotoks:* Strathcona-Tweedsmuir School**
RR#2, Okotoks, AB T1S 1A2, Canada
Tel: 403-938-4431; *Fax:* 403-938-8343
advancement@sts.ab.ca
www.sts.ab.ca
Grades: 1-12

***Olds:* Horizon School Special Education**
5401 - 53 St., Olds, AB T4H 1T3, Canada
Tel: 403-556-6310; *Fax:* 403-556-1640
shorizon@telusplanet.net
Grades: Pre., Special Ed.

***Olds:* Olds Koinonia Christian School**
P.O. Box 4039
Olds, AB T4H 1P7, Canada
Tel: 403-556-4038; *Fax:* 403-556-8770
www.oldskoinonia.com
Grades: Pre.-12
Enrollment: 300
Dwayne Brown, Administrator/Principal
dwaynebrown@chinooksedge.ab.ca

***Ponoka:* Ponoka Christian School**
6300 - 50 St., Ponoka, AB T4J 1V3, Canada
Tel: 403-783-6563; *Fax:* 403-783-6687
ponxsch@telus.net
www.ponokachristianschool.com
Grades: Pre.-9
Robert Morris, Principal

***Ponoka:* Woodlands Adventist School**
PO Box 16, Site 2, RR#3, Ponoka, AB T4J 1R3, Canada
Tel: 403-783-2640; *Fax:* 403-783-2640
woodlds@telusplanet.net
Grades: Pre.-9

***Purple Springs:* Tween Valley Christian School**
P.O. Box 96
Purple Springs, AB T0K 1X0, Canada
Tel: 403-223-9571; *Fax:* 403-224-9594
tvcs.principal@hotmail.com

Grades: 1 - 12

***Raymond:* Mennonite School**
P.O. Box 768
Raymond, AB T0K 2S0, Canada
Tel: 403-756-2277

***Red Deer:* Destiny Christian School Society**
Box 30, Site 4, RR#4, Red Deer, AB T4N 5E4, Canada
Tel: 403-343-6510; *Fax:* 403-343-8480
info@destinyschool.ca
Grades: Pre.-9

***Red Deer:* Koinonia Christian School of Red Deer**
6014 - 57 Ave., Red Deer, AB T4N 4S9, Canada
Tel: 403-346-1818; *Fax:* 403-347-3013
info@koinonia.ca
Grades: Pre.-12

***Red Deer:* Parkland School Special Education**
6016 - 45 Ave., Red Deer, AB T4N 3M4, Canada
Tel: 403-347-3911; *Fax:* 403-342-2677
prkland@shaw.ca
www.parklandschool.org
Grades: Special Ed.
Monica Lawes, Principal

***Red Deer:* South Side Christian School**
P.O. Box 219
Red Deer, AB T4N 5E8, Canada
Tel: 403-886-2266; *Fax:* 403-886-5026
office@southsidechristianschool.ca
www.southsidechristianschool.ca
Grades: Pre.-10
Affiliated with the Seventh-day Adventist Church

***Rimbey:* Echo Valley Christian School**
General Delivery, Rimbey, AB T0C 2J0, Canada
Tel: 403-843-4555
Grades: 1-9

***Rimbey:* Rimbey Christian School**
P.O. Box 90
4522 - 54th Ave., Rimbey, AB T0C 2J0, Canada
Tel: 403-843-4790; *Fax:* 403-843-3904
office@rimbeychristianschool.com
www.rimbeychristianschool.com
Grades: Kindergarten - 9
Enrollment: 84
The Alberta Provincial Program of Studies is taught from a Christian perspective.
Tambourine Simpson, Principal
principal@rimbeychristianschool.com

***Rocky Mountain House:* Rocky Christian School (RCS)**
5204 - 54 Ave., Rocky Mountain House, AB T4T 1S5, Canada
Tel: 403-845-3516; *Fax:* 403-845-4370
office@rockycs.com
www.rockycs.com
Grades: Kindergarten - 9
Enrollment: 105
The interdenominational school provides a Biblically based curriculum, which reflects Alberta Learning requirements.
Dave Simmelink, Chair
Rob Duiker, Principal

***Saddle Lake:* Saddle Lake Full Gospel School**
P.O. Box 69
Saddle Lake, AB T0A 3T0, Canada
Tel: 780-636-3736; *Fax:* 780-636-3994
slcs@telusplanet.net
Grades: 1-12

***Siksika:* Old Sun Community College**
P.O. Box 1250
Siksika, AB T0J 3W0, Canada
Tel: 403-734-3862; *Fax:* 403-734-5363
admin@oldsuncollege.net
www.oldsuncollege.net
Grades: College
Amelia Clark, B.A., M.A., President/Post-Secondary Director, 403-734-3862, ext. 222
amelia@oldsuncollege.net

***Slave Lake:* Slave Lake Koinonia Christian**
P.O. Box 1548
Slave Lake, AB T0G 2A0, Canada
Tel: 780-849-5400; *Fax:* 780-849-5460
koinonia@telusplanet.net
Grades: 1-9

***Spirit River:* Northern Lights School**
Box 19, Site 4, RR#1, Spirit River, AB T0H 3G0, Canada
Tel: 780-351-2242; *Fax:* 780-351-2280
Grades: 1 - 9
The Northern Lights Church of God in Christ Mennonite congregation operates the Northern Lights School.

***Spruce Grove:* Harvest Baptist Academy**
26404 Hwy.16 West, Spruce Grove, AB T7X 3H5, Canada
Tel: 780-960-0235; *Fax:* 780-960-9235
Toll-Free: 888-960-0235
hba@ibces.org
www.ibces.org
Grades: Pre.-12

***Spruce Grove:* Living Waters Christian Academy**
5 Grove Dr. West, Spruce Grove, AB T7X 3X8, Canada
Tel: 780-962-3331; *Fax:* 780-962-3958
www.lwca.ab.ca
Grades: Pre.-12

***St Paul:* Blue Quills First Nations College (BQFNC)**
P.O. Box 279
3 Airport Rd. North, St Paul, AB T0A 3A0, Canada
Tel: 780-645-4455; *Fax:* 780-645-5215
Toll-Free: 1-888-645-4455
www.bluequills.ca
Dr. Leona Makokis, BAdm, BEd, MA, EdD, President
Bernadine Houle-Steinhauer, BA, PRdip, Director, Special Projects
Dr. Patricia Makokis, EdD, Director, Curriculum Development
Dr. Halia Boychuk, BEd, MA, PhD, Coordinator, University Transfer
Sherri Chisan, BMgmt, MA, Coordinator, Leadership & Management
Sharon Steinhauer, BSW, RSW, Coordinator, Social Work Diploma
Lena Lapatrack, Registrar
registrar@bluequills.ca

***Stony Plain:* St. John's School of Alberta**
RR#5, Stony Plain, AB T7Z 1X5, Canada
Tel: 780-789-4826; *Fax:* 780-848-2395
info@sjsa.ab.ca
www.sjsa.ab.ca
Grades: 7-12

***Stony Plain:* St. Matthew Lutheran School**
5014 - 53 Ave., Stony Plain, AB T7Z 1R8, Canada
Tel: 780-963-2715; *Fax:* 780-963-7324
school@st-matthew.com
Grades: Pre.-9
Glen Schmitke, Principal
glen@st-matthew.com

***Sundre:* Olds Mountain View Christian School**
Box 2, Site 8, RR#2, Sundre, AB T4H 1P3, Canada
Tel: 403-556-1551; *Fax:* 403-556-5936
principal@omvcs.ca
www.omvcs.ca
Grades: K-12

***Sylvan Lake:* Lighthouse Christian School**
PO Box 1078, RR#1, Sylvan Lake, AB T4S 1X6, Canada
Tel: 403-887-2166; *Fax:* 403-887-5729
lightca@telusplanet.net
Grades: Pre.-12

***Three Hills:* Prairie Christian Academy Secondary School**
P.O. Box 68
Three Hills, AB T0M 2A0, Canada
Tel: 403-443-4220; *Fax:* 403-443-7005
pcasecondary@ghsd75.ca
pca.ghsd75.ca
Grades: 7-12

***Three Hills:* Prairie Christian Academy Elementary School**
P.O. Box 4451
1025 - 4th St. North, Three Hills, AB T0M 2N0, Canada
Tel: 403-443-3006; *Fax:* 403-443-3076
jsept@goldenhills-schools.com
www.pca3hills.ca
Grades: Pre.-9; Special Ed.

Post Secondary/Technical

***Calgary:* Columbia College**
802 Manning Rd. NE, Calgary, AB T2E 7N8, Canada
Tel: 403-235-9300; *Fax:* 403-272-3805
columbia@columbia.ab.ca
www.columbia.ab.ca

Grades: 10-12; Special Ed.
Adult education & continuing education. Professional programmes (business management, dental assisting, paramedic, health care aide, practical nurse); ESL; bridging programmes/university preparation; academic upgrading. ISO 9001:2000 certified.

Universities & Colleges

Universities

Athabasca: Athabasca University
1 University Dr., Athabasca, AB T9S 3A3, Canada
Tel: 780-675-6100; *Fax:* 780-675-6437
Toll-Free: 800-788-9041
www.athabascau.ca

Full Time Equivalency: 39700
An open university offering any student access to university-level study.
James D'Arcy, Registrar, 780-675-6302, fax: 780-675-6174
registrar@athabascau.ca
Dr Frits Pannekoek, President
auprez@athabascau.ca
Dr Margaret Haughey, Vice-Pres., Academic
mhaughey@athabascau.ca
Dr Ray Block, Vice-Pres., Finance/Admin.
rblock@athabascau.ca
Lori Van Rooijen, Vice-Pres., Advancement
loriv@athabascau.ca
Brian Stewart, Chief Information Officer
brians@athabascau.ca
Greg Wiens, Dir., Facilities/Services
gregw@athabascau.ca
David Hrenewich, Dir., Computing Services
daveh@athabascau.ca
Elizabeth Munroe, Assoc. Dir., Human Resources
elizabeth@athabascau.ca
Steve Schafer, Dir., Library Services
steves@athabascau.ca

Schools

Centre for Global & Social Analysis
Dr David Gregory, Chair
davidg@athabascau.ca

Centre for Distance Education
Dr Mohamed Ally, Director
mohameda@athabascau.ca

Centre for Innovative Management
Kay Devine, Director
kay_devine@mba.athabascau.ca

Centre for Language & Literature
Kathy Williams, Chair
kathyw@athabascau.ca

Centre for Science
Dr Norman Temple, Chair
normant@athabascau.ca

Centre for Nursing & Health Studies
Dr Donna Romyn, Dean, Health Disciplines
dromyn@athabascau.ca

Centre for Psychology
Dr Cheryl Kier, Chair
cherylk@athabascau.ca

Centre for State & Legal Studies
Dr Evelyn Ellerman, Co-Chair
evelyne@athabascau.ca
Dr Alvin Finkel, Co-Chair
alvinf@athabascau.ca

Centre for Work & Community Studies
Dr Lynda Ross, Chair
lyndar@athabascau.ca

Centre for Learning Accreditation
Dr Dianne Conrad, Director
diannec@athabascau.ca

Centre of Computing & Information Systems
Dr Kinshuk, Director
kinshuk@athabascau.ca

Centre for World Indigenous Knowledge
Dr Tracey Lindberg, Director
traceyl@athabascau.ca

Centre for Integrated Studies
Dr Mike Gismondi, Director
mikeg@athabascau.ca

Centre for Graduate Education in Applied Psychology
Dr Sandra Collins, Director
sandrac@athabascau.ca

Publications
The Voice Magazine
Published by the Athabasca University Students' Union
Tamra Ross, Editor-In-Chief
voice@voicemagazine.org

Calgary: The University of Calgary
2500 University Dr. NW, Calgary, AB T2N 1N4, Canada
Tel: 403-220-5110; *Fax:* 403-282-8413
www.ucalgary.ca

Full Time Equivalency: 24141
Joanne Cuthbertson, Chancellor
Jack Perraton, Chair
Harvey P. Weingarten, B.Sc., M.Sc., M.Phil., Ph, President & Vice-Chancellor
David B. Johnston, B.A., M.A., Registrar
Alan Harrison, Vice-President & Provost
Jonathan (Jake) Gebert, Interim Vice-President
Dennis R. Salahub, B.Sc., Ph.D., F.R.S.C., Vice-President
Dr. Ann Davies, Director
Rhonda M. Williams, B.A. (Hons.), Director
Roman Cooney, B.A., M.C.S., Vice-President

Faculties

Continuing Education
Dr. Scott McLean, Ph.D., Director

Education
Dr. Dennis Sumara, B.Ed., M.Ed., Ph.D., Dean

Engineering
M. Elizabeth Cannon, P.Eng, FCAE, FRSC, Dean

Environmental Design
Prof. Loraine Fowlow, Dean

Fine Arts
Ann E. Calvert, B.A., Dip.Ed., M.Ed., Ph., Dean

Graduate Studies & Assoc. Vice-President, Graduate & Post-Degree Progams
Dr. Fred Hall, Ph.D., Dean

Humanities
Dan Maher, Interim Dean

Law
Alastair R. Lucas, Q.C., Dean

Medicine
Dr. Tom Feasby, M.D., B.Sc., Dean

Nursing
Dianne Tapp, M.N., Ph.D., Dean

Kinesiology
Dr. Wayne Giles, Ph.D., Dean

Science
Dr. J.S. Murphree, B.Sc., Ph.D., Dean

Social Sciences
Dr. Kevin McQuillan, B.A., M.A., Ph.D., Dean

Social Work
Gayla Rogers, B.A., B.SW., R.SW., Ph.D., Dean

Communication & Culture
Wisdom Tettey, B.A. (Hons.), M.A., Ph.D., Interim Dean

Haskayne School of Business
Leonard Waverman, Dean

Publications
Alumni Magazine

The Gauntlet

Edmonton: University of Alberta
114 St. - 89 Ave., Edmonton, AB T6G 2E1, Canada
Tel: 780-492-3111
www.ualberta.ca

Full Time Equivalency: 36962
Linda Hughes, Chancellor
Dr. Indira Samarasekera, O.C., President & Vice-Chancellor
Brian Heidecker, Chair
Carl Amrhein, Ph.D., Provist & Vice-President
P. Clark, M.A., Vice-President
Sandra Conn, Vice-President
D. Hickey, P.Eng., Vice-President
Lee Elliott, Director
C. Byrne, M.B.A., Vice-Provost & Registrar
M. Craige, C.P.P., Director
T. Anderson, Director
K. Adams, Director
Frank Robinson, Interim Vice-Provost & Dean
L. Babiuk, Ph.D., Vice-President

Faculties

Agriculture, Forestry & Home Economics
John Kennelly, Ph.D., Dean

Arts
C. Skidmore, Ph.D., Interim Dean

Business
M. Percy, Ph.D., Dean

Education
Fern Snart, Ph.D., Dean

Engineering
D. Lynch, Ph.D., Dean

Extension
K. Campbell, Ph.D., Dean

Graduate Studies & Research
M. Shirvani, Ph.D., Dean

Law
P. Bryden, B.A., B.C.L., LL.M., Dean

Medicine & Dentistry
Philip Baker, D.M., FRCOG, Dean

Nursing
Dr. Anita Molzahn, Ph.D., Dean

Pharmacy & Pharmaceutical Sciences
F. Pasutto, Ph.D., Dean

Physical Education & Recreation
M. Mahon, Ph.D., Dean

Rehabilitation Medicine
M. Ferguson-Pell, Ph.D., Dean

School of Native Studies
E. Beilawski, Ph.D., Dean

Science
G. Taylor, Ph.D., Dean

Campus Saint-Jean
M. Arnal, Ph.D., Dean

Campuses

Augustana Faculty
R. Epp

St. Joseph's College
University of Alberta
Edmonton, AB T6G 2J5, Canada
Tel: 780-492-7681; *Fax:* 780-492-8145
www.ualberta.ca/~stjoseph
The College, located at the University of Alberta, was established by the Roman Catholic Archdiocese of Edmonton. It offers courses in Christian theology & philosophy.
Fr. Timothy Scott, President
timothy.scott@ualberta.ca
Kenneth J. Munro, Academic Dean
ken.munro@ualberta.ca

St. Stephen's College
University of Alberta Campus
8810, 112 St., Edmonton, AB T6G 1J6, Canada
Tel: 780-439-7311; *Fax:* 780-433-8875
Toll-Free: 1-800-661-4956
ststephn@ualberta.ca
www.ualberta.ca/st.stephens/
Earle Sharam, Dean
esharam@ualberta.ca
Shelley Westermann, Registrar
westerma@ualberta.ca

Publications
Gateway

New Trail
c/o Alumni Association
430 Athabasca Hall, Edmonton, AB T6G 2E8, Canada

Folio

Lethbridge: University of Lethbridge
4401 University Dr., Lethbridge, AB T1K 3M4, Canada
Tel: 403-329-2111; *Fax:* 403-329-2097
inquiries@uleth.ca
www.uleth.ca

Full Time Equivalency: 8000
Bill Cade, Ph.D., President & Vice-Chancellor
Chris Horbachewski, Vice-President
Seamus O'Shea, Vice-President
Andrew Hakin, Vice-President
Dennis Fitzpatrick, Vice-President
Daryl Schacher, Manager
Annette Bright, Manager
Nancy Walker, Vice-President

Faculties

Arts & Science
Chris Nicol, Dean

Education
Jane O'Dea, Dean

Fine Arts
Dr. Desmond Rochfort, Dean

Management
Murray Lindsay, Dean

Schools
Graduate Studies
Dr. Jo-Anne Fiske, Dean

Health Sciences
Christopher Hosgood, Dean

Publications
The Meliorist
Student newspaper at the University of Lethbridge

Colleges

Calgary: Alberta College of Art & Design (ACAD)
1407 - 14 Ave. NW, Calgary, AB T2N 4R3, Canada
Tel: 403-284-7600; *Fax:* 403-289-6682
registrar@acad.ca
www.acad.ca

Full Time Equivalency: 1115
Lance Carlson, President & CEO
lance.carlson@acad.ca
Marc Scholes, Dean of Undergraduate Studies
marc.scholes@acad.ca

Calgary: Ambrose Unviersity College
Canada Centre Building
#630, 833 - 4th Ave. SW, Calgary, AB T2P 3T5, Canada
Tel: 403-410-2000; *Fax:* 403-571-2556
Toll-Free: 800-461-1222
www.ambrose.edu

Full Time Equivalency: 508
Formerly Alliance University College/Nazarene University College
Dr. George Durance, President
Dr. R. Riley Coulter, President

Calgary: Bow Valley College
332 - 6 Ave. SE, Calgary, AB T2G 4S6, Canada
Tel: 403-410-1400; *Fax:* 403-297-4887
Toll-Free: 1-866-428-2669
info@bowvalleycollege.ca
www.bowvalleycollege.ca
TTY: 403-410-1412

Sharon Carry, President & CEO
Katherine Cormack, Director, Marketing, Communications & Recruitment
kcormack@bowvalleycollege.ca
Val Hoey, Director, Development

Calgary: Calgary Campus
2700 - 3rd Ave. SE, Calgary, AB T2A 7W4, Canada
Tel: 403-235-3450; *Toll-Free:* 800-363-5558
www.devry.edu/calgary

Calgary: St. Mary's University College
14500 Bannister Rd. SE, Calgary, AB T2X 1Z4, Canada
Tel: 403-531-9130; *Fax:* 403-531-9136
Tamara.Acheson@stmu.ab.ca
www.stmu.ab.ca

The post-secondary institution operates in the tradition of Catholic scholarship in Canada. Liberal arts & sciences are taught.
Most Rev. Frederick Henry, DD, Chancellor
Dr. Terrence Downey, Vice-Chancellor & President, 403-254-3701
Tamara Acheson, Registrar, 403-254-3732

Edmonton: Concordia University College of Alberta
7128 Ada Blvd., Edmonton, AB T5B 4E4, Canada
Tel: 780-479-8481; *Fax:* 780-474-1933
Toll-Free: 866-479-5200
www.concordia.ab.ca

Full Time Equivalency: 1700
Dr. Gerald Krispin, President
Dr. Richard Willie, Vice-President Academic & Provost
Patricia Warmington, Vice-President, Advancement
Jerry Reglin, Vice-President, Finance
Judy Kruse, Registrar

Edmonton: Grant MacEwan Community College
P.O. Box 1796
Edmonton, AB T5J 2P2, Canada
Tel: 780-497-5712; *Fax:* 780-497-5720
www.gmcc.ab.ca/

Full Time Equivalency: 40791
Enrolment figure includes full-time & part-time students
Dr. Paul Byrne, President

Edmonton: The King's University College
9125 - 50 St., Edmonton, AB T6B 2H3, Canada
Tel: 780-465-3500; *Fax:* 780-465-3534
Toll-Free: 800-661-8582
www.kingsu.ca

Full Time Equivalency: 652
Dr. J. Harry Fernhout, President

Edmonton: NorQuest College
Downtown Campus, Main Bldg.
10215 - 108 St., Edmonton, AB T5J 1L6, Canada
Tel: 780-644-6000; *Fax:* 780-644-6013
Toll-Free: 1-866-534-7218
info@norquest.ca
www.norquest.ca

Full Time Equivalency: 10800

Edmonton: Taylor University College & Seminary
11525 - 23 Ave., Edmonton, AB T6J 4T3, Canada
Tel: 780-431-5200; *Fax:* 780-436-9416
Toll-Free: 800-567-4988
admissions@taylor-edu.ca
www.taylor-edu.ca

David Williams, President
Craig Weston, Registrar
Terry Opperman, Director, Student Development
Tom Berekoff, Vice President of Development

Fort McMurray: Keyano College
8115 Franklin Ave., Fort McMurray, AB T9H 2H7, Canada
Tel: 780-791-4800; *Fax:* 780-791-1555
Toll-Free: 800-251-1408
www.keyanoc.ab.ca

Full Time Equivalency: 1200
5000 part-time enrollment
Jim Foote, President
Al Adibi, Vice-President, Finance & Administration
Marylea Jarvis, Vice-President, Instruction

Grande Prairie: Grande Prairie Regional College
10726 - 106 Ave., Grande Prairie, AB T8V 4C4, Canada
Tel: 780-539-2944; *Fax:* 780-539-2832
Toll-Free: 888-539-4772
studentinfo@gprc.ab.ca
www.gprc.ab.ca

Full Time Equivalency: 2000
Don Gnatiuk, President
dgnatiuk@gprc.ab.ca
Doug Hart, Vice-President, Special Projects
dhart@gprc.ab.ca

Lac La Biche: Portage College
P.O. Box 417
Lac La Biche, AB T0A 2C0, Canada
Tel: 780-623-5551; *Fax:* 780-623-5639
info@portagecollege.ca
www.portagecollege.ca

Business Career; Human Services; Native Arts & Culture; Health & Wellness; Trades & Technical; Academic Upgrading programs
William (Bill) Persley, President

Lacombe: Canadian University College
5415 College Ave., Lacombe, AB T4L 2E5, Canada
Tel: 403-782-3381; *Toll-Free:* 800-661-8129
admissions@cauc.ca
www.cauc.ca

Full Time Equivalency: 400
Lawrence Murrin, Registrar
lmurrin@cauc.ca

Lethbridge: Lethbridge College
3000 College Dr. South, Lethbridge, AB T1K 1L6, Canada
Tel: 403-320-3200; *Fax:* 403-320-1461
Toll-Free: 800-572-0103
info@lethbridgecollege.ab.ca
www.lethbridgecollege.ab.ca

Full Time Equivalency: 7200
Tracy L. Edwards, President, 403-320-3209
tracy.edwards@lethbridgecollege.ab.ca

Olds: Olds College
4500 - 50th St., Olds, AB T4H 1R6, Canada
Tel: 403-556-8281; *Fax:* 403-556-4711
Toll-Free: 1-800-661-6537
info@oldscollege.ca; library@oldscollege.ca
www.oldscollege.ca
Other Information: Continuing Education: 403-507-7956; Registrar: 403-556-8281

Full Time Equivalency: 1309
Olds College features the following schools: School of Agriculture, Business & Technology; School of Animal Science; School of Applied Arts & Career Studies; School of Horticulture; School of Land Sciences; School of Innovation; & Continuing Education.
Bill Quinney, Chair
H.J. (Tom) Thompson, President/CEO

Campuses
Calgary Campus
640 - 14th Ave. SE, Calgary, AB T2G 1E8

Slave Lake: Northern Lakes College
1201 Main St. SE, Slave Lake, AB T0G 2A3, Canada
Tel: 780-849-8600; *Fax:* 780-849-2570
Toll-Free: 1-866-652-3456
info@northernlakescollege.ca;
webmaster@northernlakescollege.ca
www.northernlakescollege.ca
Other Information: Grouard Phone: 780-751-3200; Library (Slave Lake): 780-849-8670

Distance learning is an important part of the college education. Northern Lakes College reaches full-time & part-time students in 30 rural communities in north central Alberta.
Trevor W. Gladue, Chair
Rick Neidig, President/CEO, 780-751-3260

Vermilion: Lakeland College
Also known as: Alberta/Saskatchewan Interprovincial Coll.
Vermillion Campus
5707 - 47 Ave. West, Vermilion, AB T9X 1K5, Canada
Tel: 780-853-8400; *Fax:* 780-853-7355
admissions@lakelandc.ab.ca
www.lakelandcollege.ca

Full Time Equivalency: 7000
Glenn Charlesworth, President & CEO

Campuses
Lloyminster Campus
2602-59 Ave. Bag 6000, Lloydminster, SK S9V 1Z3, Canada
Fax: 780-875-5136
Toll-Free: 1-800-661-6490
admissions@lakelandc.ab.ca
www.lakelandcollege.ca

Strathcona County Learning Centre
Broadmoore Place IV
#172, 2257 Premier Way, Sherwood Park, AB T8H 2M8, Canada
Toll-Free: 1-800-661-6490
admissions@lakelandc.ab.ca
www.lakelandcollege.ca

Post Secondary/Technical

Colleges

Calgary: Mount Royal College
Lincoln Park Campus
4825 Mount Royal Gate SW, Calgary, AB T3E 6K6, Canada
Tel: 403-440-6111; *Fax:* 403-440-5938
Toll-Free: 1-877-440-5001
externalrelations@mtroyal.ca; international@mtroyal.ca
www.mtroyal.ca

Enrollment: 11992
Sixty-eight credit programs are offered by the college.
Cathy Williams, Chair
Dr. David Marshall, President, 403-440-6393, fax: 403-440-6040
president@mtroyal.ca
Dr. Robin Fisher, Provost & Vice-President, Academic

Campuses
Holy Cross Campus
2204 - 2nd St. SW, Calgary, AB T2P 1S5
Tel: 403-503-4886

Sprinkbank Campus
143 MacLaurin Dr., Springbank, AB
Tel: 403-288-9551

Paul Tigchelaar, B.Sc., B.Ed., M.Ed., Principal
Grace Lo-Voo, B.Sc., M.Ed., Vice Principal
Dan Dowber, H.R. Management Diploma o, Director, Development
Elsy TerMaat, B.A., Business Administrator

Edmonton: Grant MacEwan University
City Centre Campus
10700 - 104 Ave., Edmonton, AB T5J 4S2, Canada
Tel: 780-497-5401; *Fax:* 780-497-5405
www.macewan.ca

Dr. Paul Byrne, President
byrnep@macewan.ca

Campuses
Alberta College Campus
10050 MacDonald Dr., Edmonton, AB T5J 0S3, Canada

Centre for the Arts
10045 - 156 St., Edmonton, AB T5P 2P7, Canada
Fax: 780-497-4300

City Centre Campus
10700 - 104 Ave., Edmonton, AB T5J 4S2, Canada
Fax: 780-497-5045

South Campus
7319 - 29 Ave., Edmonton, AB T6K 2P1, Canada
Fax: 780-497-4045

Publications
The Intercamp

The Interpreter
c/o Students' Association
P.O. Box 1796
Edmonton, AB T5J 2P2, Canada

The MacEwan Journalist
10700 - 104 St, Edmonton, AB T5J 4S2, Canada
Fax: 780-497-5630

Fort McMurray: Keyano College
8115 Franklin Ave., Fort McMurray, AB T9H 2H7, Canada
Tel: 780-791-4800; *Fax:* 780-791-1555
Toll-Free: 1-800-251-140
registrar@keyano.ca
www.keyano.ca

Jim Foote, President

Publications
Student Connection

Lethbridge: Lethbridge Community College
3000 College Dr. South, Lethbridge, AB T1K 1L6, Canada
Tel: 403-320-3200; *Fax:* 403-320-1461
Toll-Free: 1-800-572-010
info@lethbridgecollege.ab.ca
www.lethbridgecollege.ab.ca

Enrollment: 4100
Dr. Tracy Edwards, Ed.D., President/CEO

Medicine Hat: Medicine Hat College
299 College Dr. SE, Medicine Hat, AB T1A 3Y6, Canada
Tel: 403-529-3811; *Fax:* 403-504-3517
info@mhc.ab.ca
www.mhc.ab.ca

Ralph Weeks, Ph.D., President
weeks@mhc.ab.ca

Campuses
Brooks Campus
200 Horticultural Rd. East, Brooks, AB T1R 1E5, Canada
Fax: 403-362-1474

Publications
Express This

Red Deer: Red Deer College
P.O. Box 5005
100 College Blvd., Red Deer, AB T4N 5H5, Canada
Tel: 403-342-3300; *Fax:* 403-340-8940
www.rdc.ab.ca

Ron Woodward, President
ron.woodward@rdc.ab.ca

Publications
Bricklayer

Post Secondary/Technical

Banff: The Banff Centre
Also known as: Centre for Mountain Culture
P.O. Box 1020
Banff, AB T1L 1H5, Canada
Tel: 403-762-6100; *Fax:* 403-762-6444
www.banffcentre.ca
Other Information: Telex: Artsbanff 03-826657

Mary E. Hofstetter, President/CEO
Melanie Busby, Director

Banff: Banff Centre for Management
P.O. Box 1020 45
Banff, AB T0L 0C0, Canada
Tel: 403-762-6133; *Fax:* 403-762-6422
Toll-Free: 1-800-590-979
bcm@banffcentre.ca
www.banffcentre.ab.ca

Banff: Banff School of Advanced Management
P.O. Box 1020 5
Banff, AB T1L 1H5, Canada
Tel: 403-762-6127; *Fax:* 403-762-6499
Toll-Free: 1-888-762-612
bsam@banffcentre.ab.ca

Offers a 28-day executive development program for high potential & advancing managers

Calgary: CDI College of Business, Technology & Healthcare
Calgary City Centre
Trimac House
#100, 800 5th Ave. SW, Calgary, AB T2P 3T6OW7, Canada
Tel: 403-232-6410; *Fax:* 403-266-0830
www.cdicollege.com

Career training; 5 locations in Alberta

Calgary: Enform
1538 - 25 Ave. NE, Calgary, AB T2E 8Y3, Canada
Tel: 403-250-9606; *Fax:* 403-291-9408
Toll-Free: 1-800-667-555
pschoenhals@enform.ca
www.enform.ca

Paul Schoenhals, President/CEO

Calgary: The Southern Alberta Institute of Technology
Also known as: SAIT
1301 - 16th Ave. NW, Calgary, AB T2M 0L4, Canada
Tel: 403-284-7248; *Fax:* 403-284-7112
Toll-Free: 1-877-284-7248
advising@sait.ca
www.sait.ca

Canada's premier technical institute by 2010
Irene Lewis, President & CEO

Publications
The Emery Weal

Edmonton: The Northern Alberta Institute of Technology
11762 - 106 St., Edmonton, AB T5G 2R1, Canada
Tel: 780-471-7400; *Fax:* 780-471-8583
registrar@nait.ca
www.nait.ca

Campuses
Fairview Campus
P.O. Box 3000
11235 - 98 Ave., Fairview, AB T0H 1L0, Canada
Fax: 780-835-6698
Toll-Free: 1-888-999-7882

Grande Prairie Campus
10632 - 102 Ave., Grande Prairie, AB T8V 6J8, Canada
Fax: 780-539-2081

High Level Campus
P.O. Box 810
10901 - 93 St., High Level, AB T0H 1Z0, Canada
Fax: 780-926-2264

Peace River Campus
P.O. Box 3500
8106 - 99 Ave., Peace River, AB T8S 1V9, Canada
Fax: 780-624-4532

St. Albert Campus
506B St. Albert Rd., St Albert, AB T8N 5Z1, Canada
Fax: 780-458-6495

Publications
The Nugget

Edmonton: Northern Alberta Institute of Technology
11762 - 106 St. NW, Edmonton, AB T5G 3H1, Canada
Tel: 780-471-7400
www.nait.ab.ca/

D. Warwick, Environmental Training Coordinator, 780-471-7769
davew@nait.ab.ca

Grande Prairie: Mayfair College
#305, 9804 - 100 Ave., Grande Prairie, AB T8V 0T8, Canada
Tel: 780-539-5090; *Fax:* 780-539-7089
mayfair@telusplanet.net

Computer training.

Lloydminster: Reeves College
P.O. Box 51
5012 - 49 St., Lloydminster, AB S9V 0X9, Canada
Tel: 780-875-3308; *Fax:* 780-875-9209
www.reevescollege.ab.ca

Secretarial, accounting training; 4 campuses

Red Deer: Academy of Professional Hair Design
4929 - 49 St., Red Deer, AB T4N 1Z1, Canada
Tel: 403-347-2018; *Fax:* 403-342-4244
www.academyofprofessionalhairdesign.com

Esthetics, hair design.

Vermilion: Alberta Fire Training School
5704 - 47 Ave., Vermilion, AB T9X 1K4, Canada
Tel: 780-853-5800; *Fax:* 780-853-3008
Toll-Free: 1-888-863-238
aftsinfor@afts.ab.ca
www.afts.ab.ca

British Columbia

Government Agencies

Victoria: Ministry of Advanced Education
P.O. Box 9059 Prov Govt
Victoria, BC V8W 9E2, Canada
Fax: 250-356-2598
Toll-Free: 1-888-664-225
AVED.WEBMASTER@gov.bc.ca

Hon. Murray Coell, Minister
Moura Quayle, Deputy Minister

Victoria: Ministry of Education
Parliament Bldgs.
P.O. Box 9150 Prov Govt
Victoria, BC V8V 9H1, Canada
Tel: 250-356-8156; *Fax:* 250-356-5945

Hon. Shirley Bond, Minister

School Boards/Districts/Divisions

Public

Abbotsford: Abbotsford School District #34
2790 Tims St., Abbotsford, BC V2T 4M7, Canada
Tel: 604-859-4891; *Fax:* 604-852-8587
info@sd34.bc.ca
www.sd34.bc.ca
Other Information: Facilities, Phone: 604-852-9494; Fax: 604-852-4876

Grades: Kindergarten - Secondary
Enrollment: 18500
Julie MacRae, Superintendent, 604-859-4891, ext. 1230
Kevin Godden, Secretary-Treasurer, 604-859-4891, ext. 1241
Judy Chapman, Director, Curriculum, 604-504-0026
judy_chapman@sd34.bc.ca
Deb Peters, Director, Instruction, 604-504-4610
Debbie_PetersLSS@sd34.bc.ca
Lisa Pleadwell, Director, Finance, 604-859-4891, ext. 1287
Lisa_Pleadwell@sd34.bc.ca
Marnie Wright, Director, Human Resources, 604.859.4891, ext. 1249
marnie_wright@sd34.bc.ca
Dave Stephen, Manager, Communications, 604-859-4891, ext. 1206
dave_stephen@sd34.bc.ca

Ashcroft: Gold Trail School District #74
P.O. Box 250
400 Hollis Rd., Ashcroft, BC V0K 1A0, Canada
Tel: 250-453-9101; *Fax:* 250-453-2425
www.sd74.bc.ca

Grades: Kindergarten - Secondary
Enrollment: 1800
Number of Schools: 12. Number of Employees: 150 teachers & support staff
Valerie Adrian, Chair
vadrian@gw.sd74.bc.ca
Alison Sidow, Superintendent, Education, 250-453-9101, ext. 208
asidow@gw.sd74.bc.ca
Teresa Downs, District Principal, 250-453-9101, ext. 234
tdowns@gw.sd74.bc.ca
Marianne Munro, Manager, Information Technology, 250-453-9101, ext. 222
mmunro@gw.sd74.bc.ca
Patrice Barth, District Teacher, Learner Support, 250-453-9101, ext. 210
pbarth@gw.sd74.bc.ca
Wendy Blaskovic, District Resource Teacher, Trades, 250-453-9101, ext. 235
wblaskovic@gw.sd74.bc.ca
Lynda Minnabarriet, Secretary-Treasurer, 250-453-9101, ext. 200
lminnab@gw.sd74.bc.ca

Burnaby: **Burnaby School District #41**
5325 Kincaid St., Burnaby, BC V5G 1W2, Canada
Tel: 604-664-8441; *Fax:* 604-664-8382
www.sd41.bc.ca
Grades: Kindergarten - 12; Continuing Ed.
Enrollment: 24000
Number of Schools: 40 elementary schools (including 7 community schools); 8 secondary schools. Number of Employees: 4,000+
Diana Mumford, Chair, 604-434-9757
Claudio Morelli, Superintendent, Schools, 604-664-8393
claudio.morelli@sd41.bc.ca
Elliott Grieve, Associate Superintendent, 604-664-8385
Elliott.Grieve@sd41.bc.ca
Kevin Kaardal, Assistant Superintendent, 604-664-8377
kevin.kaardal@sd41.bc.ca
Gina Niccoli-Moen, Assistant Superintendent, 604-664-8365
Gina.Niccoli-Moen@sd41.bc.ca
Doug Berardine, Director, Employee Relations, 604-664-8362
doug.berardine@sd41.bc.ca
Bonda Bitzer, Director, Human Resources, 604-664-8353
Bonda.Bitzer@sd41.bc.ca
Phil Shepherd, Director, Facility Services, 604-664-8383
phil.shepherd@sd41.bc.ca
Greg Frank, Secretary-Treasurer, 604-664-8387
Greg.Frank@sd41.bc.ca

Campbell River: **Campbell River School District #72**
425 Pinecrest Rd., Campbell River, BC V9W 3P2, Canada
Tel: 250-830-2300; *Fax:* 250-287-2616
www.sd72.bc.ca
Grades: Kindergarten-12; Continuing Ed; ESL
Enrollment: 5874
Number of Schools: 15 elementary schools; 2 middle schools; 2 secondary schools. Number of Employees: 750
Tom Longridge, Superintendent, Schools, 250-830-2398
Jim Ansell, Assistant Superintendent, Schools, 250-830-2398
Nevenka Fair, Director, Instructional Programs, 250-830-2339
Sheila Johnsrude, Director, Student Services, 250-286-4400, ext. 2253
Diane Rhenisch, Director, Leadership Support, 250-830-2327
Yves Vachon, Manager, Human Resources, 250-830-2310
Geoff Wilson, Manager, Information Technology, 250-830-2390
Steve Woods, Manager, Operations, 250-830-2334
Greg Johnson, District Principal, Aboriginal Education, 250-923-4902, ext. 2216
Sean Toal, District Principal, Robron Centre, 250-923-4918
Lyle Boyce, Secretary-Treasurer, 250-830-2302
Ruth Kine, District Teacher Librarian, 250-830-2322

Chilliwack: **Chilliwack School District #33**
8430 Cessna Dr., Chilliwack, BC V2P 7K4, Canada
Tel: 604-792-1321; *Fax:* 604-792-9665
Enrollment: 12794
Jacquie Taylor, Supt.
jacquie_taylor@sd33.bc.ca
Jim Alkins, Sec.-Treas.
Brenda Point, Aboriginal Education Contact, 604-824-6173, fax: 604-824-0721
brenda_point@sd33.bc.ca

Coquitlam: **Coquitlam School District #43**
550 Poirier St., Coquitlam, BC V3J 6A7, Canada
Tel: 604-939-9201; *Fax:* 604-939-7828
Enrollment: 32838
Laureen Doerksen, Supt.
ldoerksen@sd43.bc.ca
Lorcan O'Melinn, Sec.-Treas.
Margaret Mary Deck, Aboriginal Education Contact, 604-945-7386, fax: 604-945-7395
mdeck@sd43.bc.ca

Courtenay: **Comox Valley School District #71**
607 Cumberland Rd., Courtenay, BC V9N 7G5, Canada
Tel: 250-334-5500; *Fax:* 250-334-4472
Enrollment: 9659
Bryan Morgan, Supt.
bryan.morgan@sd71.bc.ca
Len Ibbs, Sec.-Treas.
Lynn Joseph, Aboriginal Education Contact, 250-334-5502, fax: 250-334-4472

Cranbrook: **Southeast Kootenay School District #5**
940 Industrial Rd. No. 1, Cranbrook, BC V1C 4C6, Canada
Tel: 250-426-4201; *Fax:* 250-489-5460
www.sd5.bc.ca
Enrollment: 6204
Bill Gook, Superintendent
bill.gook@sd5.bc.ca
Robert Norum, Sec.-Treas.
Doug McPhee, Aboriginal Education Contact, 250-489-3480
doug.mcphee@sd5.bc.ca

Dawson Creek: **Peace River South School District #59**
11600, 7th St., Dawson Creek, BC V1G 4R8, Canada
Tel: 250-782-8571; *Fax:* 250-782-3204
www.sd59.bc.ca
Enrollment: 4855
Kathy Sawchuk, Superintendent
Gerry Slykhuis, Sec.-Treas.
Cammy-Jo Plummer, Aboriginal Education Contact

Dease Lake: **Stikine School District #87**
P.O. Box 190
Dease Lake, BC V0C 1L0, Canada
Tel: 250-771-4440; *Fax:* 250-771-4441
Grades: Kindergarten - 12; Alternative Ed.
Enrollment: 260
Number of Schools: 4 elementary schools; 3 high schools; 1 alternative school. Number of Employees: 71
Bryan Ennis, Superintendent, Schools
bennis@sd87.bc.ca

Delta: **Delta School District #37**
4585 Harvest Dr., Delta, BC V4K 5B4, Canada
Tel: 604-946-4101; *Fax:* 604-952-5375
Enrollment: 17426
Dr. John L. Anderson, Interim Supt.
jcalder@deltasd.bc.ca
Grant McRadu, Sec.-Treas.
Kathy Guild, Aboriginal Education Contact, 604-946-4101, fax: 604-946-7803
kguild@deltasd.bc.ca

Duncan: **Cowichan Valley School District #79**
2557 Beverly St., Duncan, BC V9L 2X3, Canada
Tel: 250-748-0321; *Fax:* 250-748-6591
Enrollment: 9801
Peter Porte, Supt.
pporte@sd79.bc.ca
Phil Turin, Sec.-Treas.
Ted Cadwallader, Aboriginal Education Contact, 250-748-0321, ext. ext.216, fax: 250-748-6591

Fort Nelson: **Fort Nelson School District #81**
P.O. Box 87
5104 Airport Dr., Fort Nelson, BC V0C 1R0, Canada
Tel: 250-774-2591; *Fax:* 250-774-2598
www.sd81.bc.ca
Grades: Kindergarten - 12
Enrollment: 889
Number of Schools: 5. Number of Employees: 100
Linda Dolen, Chair
ldolen@sd81.bc.ca
Diana Samchuck, Superintendent
dsamchuck@sd81.bc.ca
Ray Irwin, Director, Instruction
rirwin@sd81.bc.ca
Patti Burt, District Vice Principal, Technology / Distributed Learning
pburt@sd81.bc.ca
Margaret-Anne Hall, Secretary-Treasurer
mhall@sd81.bc.ca
Darryl Low, Supervisor, Maintenance
dlow@sd81.bc.ca

Fort St John: **Peace River North School District #60**
10112 - 105 Ave., Fort St John, BC V1J 4S4, Canada
Tel: 250-262-6000; *Fax:* 250-262-6048
www.prn.bc.ca
Enrollment: 5792
Larry Espe, Superintendent
lespe@prn.bc.ca
Doug Boyd, Sec.-Treas.
Brenda Paul, Aboriginal Education Contact, 250-785-8324, fax: 250-785-0846

Gibsons: **Sunshine Coast School District #46**
P.O. Box 220
494 South Fletcher Rd., Gibsons, BC V0N 1V0, Canada
Tel: 604-886-8811; *Fax:* 604-886-4652
Questions@sd46.bc.ca; board@sd46.bc.ca
www.sd46.bc.ca
Grades: Kindergarten - 12; Alternative Ed.
Enrollment: 3600
Number of Schools: 9 elementary schools; 4 secondary schools
Silas White, Chair
silas@nightwoodeditions.com
Deborah Palmer, Superintendent, Schools
dpalmer@sd46.bc.ca
Tom Hierck, Assistant Superintendent
thierck@sd46.bc.ca
Debbie Amaral, District Principal, Student Support Services
damaral@sd46.bc.ca
Kerry Mahlman, District Principal, Aboriginal Programs & Svs. & Partnerships
cmahlman@sd46.bc.ca
Maurice Arduin, Manager, Facilities & Transportation
marduin@sd46.bc.ca
Diane Ready, Secretary-Treasurer
dready@sd46.bc.ca
Tara Sweet, Officer, Human Resources
hr@sd46.bc.ca

Gold River: **Vancouver Island West School District #84**
P.O. Box 100
2 Hwy. 28, Gold River, BC V0P 1G0, Canada
Tel: 250-283-2241; *Fax:* 250-283-7352
www.sd84.bc.ca
Grades: Kindergarten - 12
Enrollment: 466
Number of Schools: 5
Jessie Smith, Chair
Lawrence Tarasoff, Superintendent, Schools, & Secretary-Treasurer
Annie James, Administrator, Human Resources

Grand Forks: **Boundary School District #51**
P.O. Box 640
1021 Central Ave., Grand Forks, BC V0H 1H0, Canada
Tel: 250-442-8258; *Fax:* 250-442-8800
info@sd51.bc.ca
www.sd51.bc.ca
Grades: Kindergarten - 12; Alternate Ed.
Teresa Rezansoff, Board Chair, 250-442-2240
teresa.rezansoff@sd51.bc.ca
Michael Strukoff, Superintendent, Schools
michael.strukoff@sd51.bc.ca
Jeanette Hanlon, Secretary-Treasurer
jeanette.hanlon@sd51.bc.ca
Maxine Ruzicka, Director, Instruction
maxine.ruzicka@sd51.bc.ca
Dean Higashi, Manager, Operations
dean.higashi@sd51.bc.ca
John Popoff, Manager, Technology
john.popoff@sd51.bc.ca

Hagensborg: **Central Coast School District #49**
PO Bag 130, Hagensborg, BC V0T 1H0, Canada
Tel: 250-982-2691; *Fax:* 250-982-2319
www.sd49.bc.ca
Grades: Kindergarten - 12
Enrollment: 200
Number of Schools: 5
Robyn Willis, Chair, Board of Trustees
rwillis@sd49.bc.ca
Denise Perry, CEO, Superintendent of Schools, & Secretary-Treasurer
dperry@sd49.bc.ca
Sheldon Lee, CMA, Director, Business Operations
Sheldon.Lee.SDBOC@telus.net
Lela Walkus, Coordinator, Aboriginal Studies
lwalkus@sd49.bc.ca
Jeremy Baillie, Principal, Sir Alexander Mackenzie Secondary School
jbaillie@sd49.bc.ca
Nam Nguyen, Principal, Bella Coola Elementary School
nnguyen@sd49.bc.ca
Erin Chapman, District Librarian
echapman@sd49.bc.ca
Debbie Gibson, Comptroller
dgibson@sd49.bc.ca
Mark Chatham, Lead Hand, Maintenance
mchatham@sd49.bc.ca
Stephen Sheppard, Lead Hand, Transportation
ssheppard@sd49.bc.ca

Hope: **Fraser Cascade School District No. 78**
650 Kawkawa Lake Rd., Hope, BC V0X 1L4, Canada
Tel: 604-869-2411; *Fax:* 604-869-7400
www.sd78.bc.ca
Other Information: Agassiz Phone: 604-796-2225
Grades: Kindergarten - 12
Number of Schools: 12
Linda McMullan, Chair
Dr. Karen Nelson, Superintendent, Schools
Dr. Scott Benwell, Assistant Superintendent
Natalie Lowe-Zucchet, CA, Secretary-Treasurer
Donna Barner, Speech Pathologist
Dan Landrath, Supervisor, Transportation
Mike Repstock, Supervisor, Maintenance
Pat Marsh, Assistant, First Nations Education

Invermere: Rocky Mountain School District #6
P.O. Box 430
620, 4th St., Invermere, BC V0A 1K0, Canada
Tel: 250-342-9243; Fax: 250-342-6966
www.sd6.bc.ca

Enrollment: 3823
Paul Carriere, Superintendent
pcarriere@sd6.bc.ca
Cameron Dow, Sec.-Treas.

Kamloops: Kamloops-Thompson School District #73
1383 - 9 Ave., Kamloops, BC V2C 3X7, Canada
Tel: 250-374-0679; Fax: 250-372-1183
www.sd73.bc.ca

Enrollment: 15087
Dr. Terry Sullivan, Superintendent
tsullivan@sd73.bc.ca
Jim Sheldon, Sec.-Treas.
Debora Draney, Aboriginal Education Principal, 250-374-0679

Kelowna: Central Okanagan School District #23
1940 Underhill St., Kelowna, BC V1X 5X7, Canada
Tel: 250-860-8888; Fax: 250-860-9799
www.sd23.bc.ca

Grades: Kindergarten - 12; Alternate Ed.
Rolli Cacchioni, Chair, 250-470-3216, fax: 250-860-9799
board@sd23.bc.ca
Hugh Gloster, Superintendent, 250-470-3256, fax: 250-860-9799
hgloster@sd23.bc.ca
Terry Lee Beaudry, Assistant Superintendent, 250-470-3225, fax: 250-870-5025
tbeaudry@sd23.bc.ca
Norm Bradley, Co-Director, Instruction K-12, 250-470-3271, fax: 250-870-5053
gthomson@sd23.bc.ca
Jim Colquhoun, Director, Human Resources - Labour Relations, 250-470-3237, fax: 250-870-5088
jcolquho@sd23.bc.ca
Alan Cumbers, Director, Operations, 250-491-4001, fax: 250-870-5094
acumbers@sd23.bc.ca
Ross Dumontet, Director, Instruction - Human Resources, 250-470-3237, fax: 250-870-5088
rdumonte@sd23.bc.ca
Lisa McCullough, Co-Director, Instruction K-12, 250-470-3210, fax: 250-870-5021
bbrowns@sd23.bc.ca
Peter Molloy, Director, Student Support Services, 250-470-3267, fax: 250-470-3272
bericksо@sd23.bc.ca
Jon Rever, Co-Director, Instruction K-12, 250-860-9729, ext. 4688, fax: 250-870-5086
lgradidg@sd23.bc.ca
Eileen Sadlowski, Director, Finance, 250-470-3224, fax: 250-470-3274
esadlows@sd23.bc.ca
Clara Sulz, Co-Director, Instruction K-12, 250-470-3217, fax: 250-870-5027
lpaziuk@sd23.bc.ca

Langley: Langley School District #35
4875 - 222 St., Langley, BC V3A 3Z7, Canada
Tel: 604-534-7891; Fax: 604-533-1115
www.sd35.bc.ca

Enrollment: 18000
Cheryle Beaumont, Superintendent
cbeaumont@sd35.bc.ca
Peter Greenwood, Sec.-Treas.
Dave Coutu, Aboriginal Program Administrator, 604-534-7891, fax: 604-532-1458
dcoutu@sd35.bc.ca

Maple Ridge: Maple Ridge School District #42
22225 Brown Ave., Maple Ridge, BC V2X 8N6, Canada
Tel: 604-463-4200; Fax: 604-463-4181
www.sd42.ca

Grades: K.-12
Enrollment: 15559
Jan Unwin, Supt.
junwin@sd42.ca
Wayne Jefferson, Sec.-Treas.
wjefferson@sd42.ca
Doug Hoey, Principal, Aboriginal Education, 604-466-6265
dhoey@sd42.ca

Merritt: Nicola-Similkameen School District #58
P.O. Box 4100 Main
1550 Chapman St., Merritt, BC V1K 1B8, Canada
Tel: 250-378-5161; Fax: 250-378-6263
www.sd58.bc.ca

Grades: K.-12
Enrollment: 2500
Dr Robert Peacock, Supt.
rpeacock@sd58.bc.ca
H. Bruce Tisdale, Sec.-Treas.
btisdale@sd58.bc.ca
Shelley Oppenheim-Lacerte, Principal, Aboriginal Education, ext. 1111
so-lacerte@sd58.bc.ca

Mission: Mission School District #75
33046 - 4 Ave., Mission, BC V2V 1S5, Canada
Tel: 604-826-6286; Fax: 604-826-4517
www.mpsd.ca

Grades: Pre-K.-12
Enrollment: 6311
Frank Dunham, Supt.
frank.dunham@mpsd.ca
Roy Daykin, Sec.-Treas.
roy.daykin@mpsd.ca
Colleen Hannah, Aboriginal Education Contact, 604-826-3103, fax: 604-820-2850
colleen.hannah@sd75.mission.bc.ca

Nakusp: Arrow Lakes School District #10
P.O. Box 340
98 - 6th Ave. NW, Nakusp, BC V0G 1R0, Canada
Tel: 250-265-3638; Fax: 250-265-3701
sdchanges@sd10.bc.ca
www.sd10production.bcelearner.ca

Grades: Kindergarten - 12
Enrollment: 589
Walter Posnikoff, District Superintendent & Secretary-Treasurer, 250-265-3638, ext. 25, fax: 250-265-3701
wposnikoff@sd10.bc.ca
George Harding, District Facilitator & Coordinator, Instruction & Programs, 250-265-3638, fax: 250-265-3081
gharding@sd10.bc.ca
Alistair Skey, Manager, District Technology, 250-265-3638, ext. 26, fax: 250-265-3701
askey@sd10.bc.ca
Natalie Verigin, District Financial Comptroller, 250-265-3638, fax: 250-265-3701
nverigin@sd10.bc.ca

Nanaimo: Nanaimo-Ladysmith School District #68
395 Wakesiah Ave., Nanaimo, BC V9R 3K6, Canada
Tel: 250-754-5521; Fax: 250-741-5248
info@sd68.bc.ca
www.sd68.bc.ca

Grades: Pre-K.-12
Enrollment: 14500
Michael J. Munro, Supt./CEO
mmunro@sd68.bc.ca
J. David Green, Sec.-Treas., 250-754-5521
dgreen@sd68.bc.ca
Stella Bates, District Principal, Aboriginal Education, 250-741-5318
sbates@sd68.bc.ca

Nelson: Kootenay Lake School District #8
570 Johnstone Rd., Nelson, BC V1L 6J2, Canada
Tel: 250-352-6681; Fax: 250-352-6686
www.sd8.bc.ca

Grades: K-12
Enrollment: 6113
Pat Dooley, Superintendent
Monica Schulte, Sec.-Treas.
Nancy Cobra, Aboriginal Education Co-ordinator, 250-428-2217, fax: 250-428-4990
ncobra@sd8.bc.ca

New Aiyansh: Nisga'a School District #92
P.O. Box 240
5201 Tait Ave., New Aiyansh, BC V0J 1A0, Canada
Tel: 250-633-2228; Fax: 250-633-2401
www.nisgaa.bc.ca

Grades: K.-12
Enrollment: 480
Keith Spencer, Supt., ext. 1102
kspencer@nisgaa.bc.ca
Bruce Matthews, Sec.-Treas., ext. 1104, fax: 250-633-2425
bmatthews@nisgaa.bc.ca
Tina Jules, Aboriginal Education Contact, ext. 1107
tjules@nisgaa.bc.ca

New Westminster: New Westminster School District #40
1001 Columbia St., New Westminster, BC V3M 1C4, Canada
Tel: 604-517-6240; Fax: 604-517-6390
district.sd40.bc.ca

Grades: K.-12
Enrollment: 6095
John Woudzia, Supt., 604-517-6328
rbennett@sd40.bc.ca
Brian Sommerfeldt, Sec.-Treas., 604-517-6320
bsommerfeldt@sd40.bc.ca
Bertha Lansdowne, Aboriginal Education Contact, 604-517-6316, fax: 604-517-6204
blansdow@sd40.bc.ca

North Vancouver: North Vancouver School District #44
721 Chesterfield Ave., North Vancouver, BC V7M 2M5, Canada
Tel: 604-903-3444; Fax: 604-903-3445
www.nvsd44.bc.ca

Grades: K.-12
Enrollment: 16917
John Lewis, Supt., 604-903-3449, fax: 604-903-3448
jlewis@nvsd44.bc.ca
Irene Young, Sec.-Treas.
iyoung@nvsd44.bc.ca
Brad Baker, Aboriginal Education Contact, 604-903-3463, fax: 604-903-3778
bbaker@nvsd44.bc.ca

Oliver: Okanagan Similkameen School District #53
P.O. Box 1770
35061, 101 St., Oliver, BC V0H 1T0, Canada
Tel: 250-498-3481; Fax: 250-498-4070
www.sd53.bc.ca

Enrollment: 2800
Juleen McElgunn, Superintendent
jmcelgunn@sd53.bc.ca
Richard Goodwein, Sec.-Treas.
Jim Insley, Asst. Superintendent, 250-498-3481, ext. 117

Parksville: Qualicum School District #69
P.O. Box 430
Parksville, BC V9P 2G5, Canada
Tel: 250-248-4241; Fax: 250-248-5767
www.sd69.bc.ca

Enrollment: 5322
Candice Morgan, Superintendent
cmorgan@sd69.bc.ca
Bernice Hannam, Sec.-Treas.
Rosie McLeod-Shannon, Aboriginal Education Contact, 250-954-3024, fax: 250-954-3027

Penticton: Okanagan Skaha School District #67
425 Jermyn Ave., Penticton, BC V2A 1Z4, Canada
Tel: 250-770-7700; Fax: 250-770-7730
sd67@summer.com
www.sd67.bc.ca

Enrollment: 7411
Wendy Hyer, Superintendent
whyer@summer.com
Ron Shongrunden, Sec.-Treas.
rs@summer.com
Kathy Pierre, Aboriginal Education Contact, 250-770-7703, fax: 250-770-7732

Port Alberni: School District #70 (Alberni)
4690 Roger St., Port Alberni, BC V9Y 3Z4, Canada
Tel: 250-723-3565; Fax: 250-723-0318
www.sd70.bc.ca

Grades: Kindergarten - Secondary
Cam Pinkerton, Superintendent, 250-720-2770
cpinkerton@sd70.bc.ca
Jerry Linning, Secretary-Treasurer, 250-720-2756
jlinning@sd70.bc.ca
Jack Hitchings, Director, Curriculum, 250-720-2779
Harry Eberts, Manager, Operations, 250-723-8821
heberts@sd70.bc.ca

Port Hardy: Vancouver Island North School District #85
Administration Office
P.O. Box 90
6975 Rupert St., Port Hardy, BC V0N 2P0, Canada
Tel: 250-949-6618; Fax: 250-949-8792
msalski@sd85.bc.ca
www.sd85.bc.ca

Grades: Kindergarten - 12
Enrollment: 1550
Number of Schools: 12
Kathy Bedard, Superintendent, Schools, & Chief Executive Officer, 250-949-6618, ext. 2236
kbedard@sd85.bc.ca
John Martin, Secretary-Treasurer, 250-949-6618, ext. 2222
jmartin@sd85.bc.ca
Katherine McIntosh, Director, Instruction (Curriculum), 250-949-6618, ext. 2234
kmcintosh@sd85.bc.ca
Kaleb Child, District Principal, FN Programs, Initiatives, & Assessment, 250-949-6618, ext. 2233
kchild@sd85.bc.ca

Wally Wright, District Principal, Special Programs, 250-949-6618, ext. 2229
wwright@sd85.bc.ca
Wendy Glos, Speech-Language Pathologist, 250-949-6618, ext. 2244
wglos@sd85.bc.ca
Jennifer Holme, District Teacher. Literacy & Early Learning, 250-949-6618, ext. 2228
jholme@sd85.bc.ca
Charleen Purdy, District Counsellor, Elementary Schools, 250-949-6618, ext. 2251
cpurdy@sd85.bc.ca
Randy Ball, Manager, Operations & Maintenance, 250-949-8155, ext. 229

Powell River: Powell River School District #47
4351 Ontario Ave., Powell River, BC V8A 1V3, Canada
Tel: 604-485-6271; *Fax:* 604-485-6435

Enrollment: 2500
Jay Yule, Superintendent
jyule@sd47.bc.ca
Steve Hopkins, Sec.-Treas.
Wayne Pielle, Aboriginal Education Contact, 604-485-6271, fax: 250-483-3127
wpielle@sd47.bc.ca

Prince George: Prince George School District #57
2100 Ferry Ave., Prince George, BC V2L 4R5, Canada
Tel: 250-561-6800; *Fax:* 250-561-6801
sd57@sd57.bc.ca
www.sd57.bc.ca

Enrollment: 15260
Brian Pepper, Superintendent
bpepper@sd57.bc.ca
Bryan Mix, Sec.-Treas.
Charlotte Henay, Aboriginal Education Contact, 250-561-6800, ext. ext.315, fax: 250-561-6820

Prince Rupert: Prince Rupert School District #52
634 - 6 Ave. East, Prince Rupert, BC V8J 1X1, Canada
Tel: 250-624-6717; *Fax:* 250-624-6517

Enrollment: 2937
Lynn Hauptman, Superintendent
Cam McIntyre, Sec.-Treas.
Debbie Leighton-Stephens, Aboriginal Education Contact, 250-627-1536, ext. ext.221, fax: 250-624-6572
debbiels@sd52.bc.ca

Queen Charlotte: Haida Gwaii / Queen Charlotte School District No. 50
P.O. Box 69
107 - 3rd Ave., Queen Charlotte, BC V0T 1S0, Canada
Tel: 250-559-8471; *Fax:* 250-559-8849
Toll-Free: 1-888-771-3131
trustees@sd50.bc.ca
www.sd50.bc.ca

Grades: Elementary-Secondary; Aboriginal Ed
Number of Schools: 6 (Agnes L. Mathers Elementary Jr. Secondary School; Sk'aadgaa Naay Elementary School; Queen Charlotte Secondary School; Port Clements Elementary School; Tahayghen Elementary School; George M. Dawson Secondary School)
Wayne Wilson, Chair, 250-559-4760, fax: 250-559-4773
wwilson@sd50.bc.ca
Angus Wilson, Superintendent, Schools
Ken Campbell, Secretary-Treasurer
Tawni Davidson, Coordinator, Early Learning
Alison Gear, Coordinator, Early Learning
Joanne Yovanovich, Principal, Aboriginal Education

Quesnel: Quesnel School District #28
401 North Star Rd., Quesnel, BC V2J 5K2, Canada
Tel: 250-992-8802; *Fax:* 250-992-7652
www.sd28.bc.ca

Enrollment: 4360
Sue-Ellen Miller, Superintendent
Teri Stoneman, Sec.-Treas.
Holly Toews, Aboriginal Education Contact

Revelstoke: Revelstoke School District #19
P.O. Box Bag 5800
1121 Vernon Ave., Revelstoke, BC V0E 2S0, Canada
Tel: 250-837-2101; *Fax:* 250-837-9335
www.sd19.bc.ca

Enrollment: 1200
Anne Cooper, Superintendent
acooper@sd19.bc.ca
Barbara Ross, Sec.-Treas.
Shan Jorgenson-Adam, Aboriginal Education Contact, 250-837-2101, fax: 250-837-9335

Richmond: French Education Authority of British Columbia
Conseil scholaire francophone de la Columbie-Britannique
#180, 10200 Shellbridge Way, Richmond, BC V6X 2W7, Canada
Tel: 604-214-2600; *Fax:* 604-214-9881
Toll-Free: 1-888-715-2200
info@csf.bc.ca
www.csf.bc.ca

Marie Bourgeois, President
Pierre Claveau, Director, Public Relations, 604-214-2617
pclaveau@csf.bc.ca

Richmond: Richmond School District #38
7811 Granville Ave., Richmond, BC V6Y 3E3, Canada
Tel: 604-668-6000; *Fax:* 604-668-6006
www.sd38.bc.ca

Enrollment: 23092
Monica Pamer, Superintendent
Mark De Mello, Sec.-Treas.
Mike Akiwenzie, Aboriginal Education Contact, 604-668-6068, fax: 604-668-6697
mike_akiwenzie@richmond.sd38.bc.ca

Saanichton: Saanich School District #63
2125 Keating Cross Rd., Saanichton, BC V8M 2A5, Canada
Tel: 250-652-7300; *Fax:* 250-652-6421
www.sd63.bc.ca

Enrollment: 9081
Dr. Keven Elder, Superintendent
kelder@sd63.bc.ca
Joan Axford, Sec.-Treas.
jaxford@sd63.bc.ca
Sheila Austin, Aboriginal Education Contact, 250-652-7331, fax: 250-652-7361
saustin@sd63.bc.ca

Salmon Arm: North Okanagan-Shuswap School District #83
P.O. Box 129
220 Shuswap St. NE, Salmon Arm, BC V1E 4N2, Canada
Tel: 250-832-2157; *Fax:* 250-832-9428
supt@sd83.bc.ca
www.sd83.bc.ca

Grades: K.-12
Enrollment: 6723
Doug Pearson, Supt.
supt@sd83.bc.ca
Bruce Hunt, Sec.-Treas., 250-804-7830
bhunt@sd83.bc.ca
Irene LaPierre, Principal, Aboriginal Education, 250-832-8223, fax: 250-832-4456
ilapierr@sd83.bc.ca

Salt Spring Island: Gulf Islands School District #64
112 Rainbow Rd., Salt Spring Island, BC V8K 2K3, Canada
Tel: 250-537-5548; *Fax:* 250-537-4200
dfennell@sd64.bc.ca ~~Assistant, Dawne Fennell)~~
~~www.sd64.bc.ca~~

Grades: Kindergarten-12; International Ed.
Number of Schools: 10 (Galiano Community; Mayne Island; Pender Islands; Saturna Island; Fernwood; Fulford Community; Phoenix; Gulf Islands Secondary; Salt Spring Elementary; Saltspring Island Middle)
May McKenzie, Chair, 250-539-2530
mayonmayne@shaw.ca
Jeff Hopkins, Superintendent
jhopkins@sd64.bc.ca
Sheila Miller, Director, Instruction, 250-537-9441, ext. 206
sheilamiller@sd64.bc.ca
Linda Underwood, Director, Human Resources
lunderwood@sd64.bc.ca
Rob Scotvold, Secretary-Treasurer
rscotvold@sd64.bc.ca
Dr. Holly Smith, District Psychologist, 250-537-9441
hsmith@sd64.bc.ca

Smithers: Bulkley Valley School District #54
P.O. Box 758
1235 Montreal St., Smithers, BC V0J 2N0, Canada
Tel: 250-877-6820; *Fax:* 250-877-6835
info@sd54.bc.ca; contact-sd54@sd54.bc.ca
www.sd54.bc.ca

Grades: Elementary - Secondary
Number of Schools: 7 elementary schools; 2 secondary schools
Les Kearns, Board Chair, 250-845-7859
Beverly Young, Superintendent, Schools
Chris van der Mark, Assistant Superintendent
Steven Richards, Secretary-Treasurer
Toni Perreault, Administrator, Human Resources
Barb Guillon, Administrator, Payroll

Ed Hildebrandt, Supervisor, Operations

Squamish: Howe Sound School District #48
P.O. Box 250
37866 Second Ave., Squamish, BC V8B 0A2, Canada
Tel: 604-892-5228; *Fax:* 604-892-1038
tfarina@sd48.bc.ca
www.sd48.bc.ca

Enrollment: 4536
Dr. Rick Erickson, Superintendent
ricke@sd48.bc.ca
John Hetherington, Sec.-Treas.
jhetherington@sd48.bc.ca
Juanita Coltman, Aboriginal Education Administrator
jcoltman@sd48.bc.ca

Surrey: Surrey School District #36
14225 - 56th Ave., Surrey, BC V3X 3A3, Canada
Tel: 604-596-7733; *Fax:* 604-596-4197
www.sd36.bc.ca

Grades: Kindergarten - 12; Adult Education
Enrollment: 67293
Number of Schools: 99 elementary schools; 19 secondary schools; 5 student learning centres; 4 adult education centres.
Number of Employees: 8,700 (including approximately 5,000 teachers)
Laurae McNally, Chair, 604-531-1091, fax: 604-542-2613
mcnally_laurae@sd36.bc.ca
Mike McKay, Superintendent, Schools, 604-596-7733, ext. 469
Sharon Cohen, Deputy Superintendent, 604-596-7733, ext. 469
Rick Fabbro, Assistant Superintendent, 604-596-7733, ext. 470
Alan Jones, Assistant Superintendent, 604-596-7733, ext. 471
John Ormond, Assistant Superintendent, 604-596-7733, ext. 478
David Paul, Assistant Superintendent, 604-596-7733, ext. 471
Rick Ryan, Assistant Superintendent, 604-596-7733, ext. 470
Brett Raycroft, District Principal, 604-596-7733, ext. 435
Wayne D. Noye, Secretary-Treasurer, 604-596-7733, ext. 416

Terrace: Coast Mountains School District #82
3211 Kenney St., Terrace, BC V8G 3E9, Canada
Tel: 250-635-4931; *Fax:* 250-635-4287

Enrollment: 6379
Randy Smalbrugge, Supt.
rsmalbrugge@cmsd.bc.ca
Marcel Aboriginal, Sec.-Treas.
Rob Greenwood, Aboriginal Education Contact, 250-638-4403, fax: 250-638-4287

Trail: Kootenay-Columbia School District #20
#120, 1290 Esplanade, Trail, BC V1R 4T2, Canada
Tel: 250-368-6434; *Fax:* 250-364-2470
Toll-Free: 888-316-3338
www.sd20.bc.ca

Enrollment: 4926
Jean Borsa, Superintendent
jborsa@sd20.bc.ca
Kim Morris, Sec.-Treas.
Christine Marsh, Aboriginal Education Program Coordinator, 250-364-1275, ext. 241

Vancouver: Vancouver School District #39
1580 West Broadway Ave., Vancouver, BC V6J 5K8, Canada
Tel: 604-713-5000; *Fax:* 604-713-5049
info@vsb.bc.ca
www.vsb.bc.ca

Grades: K.-12
Enrollment: 59182
Steve Cardwell, Supt., 604-713-5100, fax: 604-713-5412
scardwell@vsb.bc.ca
Brenda Ng, Sec.-Treas., 604-713-5080, fax: 604-713-5049
bng@vsb.bc.ca
Debra Martel, Aboriginal Education Contact, 604-713-5682, fax: 604-713-5076
dmartel@vsb.bc.ca

Vanderhoof: Nechako Lakes School District #91
P.O. Box 129
153 E. Connaught St., Vanderhoof, BC V0J 3A0, Canada
Tel: 250-567-2284; *Fax:* 250-567-4639
www.sd91.bc.ca

Grades: K.-12
Enrollment: 5500
Ray LeMoigne, Supt.
rlemoigne@mail.sd91.bc.ca
Sterling Olson, Sec.-Treas.
solson@mail.sd91.bc.ca
Libby McDiarmid, Aboriginal Education Contact, 250-567-2284, fax: 250-567-4639

***Vernon:* Vernon School District #22**
1401 - 15 St., Vernon, BC V1T 8S8, Canada
Tel: 250-542-3331; *Fax:* 250-549-9200
district_web@sd22.bc.ca
www.sd22.bc.ca

Grades: Pre-K.-12
Enrollment: 9047
Bev Rundell, Supt., 250-549-9226
brundell@sd22.bc.ca
Randy Hoffman, Sec.-Treas., 250-549-9205
rhoffman@sd22.bc.ca
Sandra Lynxleg, Aboriginal Education Contact, 250-542-3331
slynxleg@sd22.bc.ca

***Victoria:* Greater Victoria School District #61**
556 Boleskine Rd., Victoria, BC V8Z 1E8, Canada
Tel: 250-475-3212; *Fax:* 250-475-6161
Trustees@sd61.bc.ca
www.sd61.bc.ca
Other Information: Alternative Ed., Phone: 250-360-4321; Continuing Ed: 250-360-4332

Grades: Kindergarten - 12; Continuing Ed.
Enrollment: 20000
Number of Schools: 26 elementary schools; 10 middle schools; 7 secondary schools
Tom Ferris, Board Chair, 250-889-0689
tferris@sd61.bc.ca
John Gaiptman, Superintendent, Schools
Sherri Bell, Associate Superintendent
Pat Duncan, Associate Superintendent
Chris Harvey, Associate Superintendent
Deborah Courville, District Principal
Ted Pennell, Director, Information Technology
Jim Soles, Supervisor, Building Projects
Ross Walker, Supervisor, Construction
George Ambeault, Secretary-Treasurer

***Victoria:* Sooke School District #62**
3143 Jacklin Rd., Victoria, BC V9B 5R1, Canada
Tel: 250-474-9800; *Fax:* 250-474-9825
info@sd62.bc.ca
www.sd62.bc.ca

Enrollment: 8500
Jim Cambridge, Superintendent
jcambridge@sd62.bc.ca
David Lockyer, Sec.-Treas.
Kathleen King-Hunt, Aboriginal Education Contact, 250-474-9879, fax: 250-474-9825

***West Vancouver:* West Vancouver School District #45**
1075 - 21st St., West Vancouver, BC V7V 4A9, Canada
Tel: 604-981-1000; *Fax:* 604-981-1001
info@sd45.bc.ca
www.sd45.bc.ca

Grades: K.-12
Enrollment: 6758
Geoff Jopson, Supt., 604-981-1034
gjopson@sd45.bc.ca
Ellen Forsyth, Sec.-Treas., 604-981-1048
eforsyth@sd45.bc.ca
Jody Langlois, Aboriginal Education Contact, 604-981-1095, fax: 604-981-1096
jlanglois@sd45.bc.ca

***Williams Lake:* Cariboo-Chilcotin School District #27**
School Administration Office
350 - 2nd Ave. North, Williams Lake, BC V2G 1Z9, Canada
Tel: 250-398-3833; *Fax:* 250-392-3600
www.sd27.bc.ca

Grades: Kindergarten - 12; Adult Education
Enrollment: 6800
Number of Employees: 1,000+
Wayne Rodier, Chair, 250-305-7981
wayne.rodier@sd27.bc.ca
Diane Wright, Superintendent, Schools, 250-398-3824, fax: 250-392-3600
diane.wright@sd27.bc.ca
Harj Manhas, Assistant Superintendent, 250-398-3810, fax: 250-398-7871
harjinder.manhas@sd27.bc.ca
Mark Wintjes, Director, Instruction for Human Resources
mark.wintjes@sd27.bc.ca
Doug Gorcak, Manager, Facilities & Transportation, 250-398-3877, fax: 250-392-2202
doug.gorcak@sd27.bc.ca
Ken Matieshen, District Principal, Information Technology, 250-305-7955
Bonnie Roller, Secretary-Treasurer, 250-398-3801, fax: 250-392-3600
bonnie.roller@sd27.bc.ca

Schools: Specialized

Hearing Impaired

***Burnaby:* BC Provincial School for the Deaf**
c/o Burnaby South Secondary School
5455 Rumble St., Burnaby, BC V5J 2B7, Canada
Tel: 604-664-8560; *Fax:* 604-664-8561

Grades: 1-12
Enrollment: 75
M. Henderson, Principal
mhenders@south.sd41.bc.ca

Distance Education

***Chilliwack:* Fraser Valley Distance Education**
49520 Prairie Central Rd., Chilliwack, BC V2P 6H3, Canada
Tel: 604-794-7310; *Fax:* 604-795-8480
Toll-Free: 800-663-3381
www.fvdes.com

Grades: K.-12
Enrollment: 537
Trish Williams, Principal
twilliams@fvdes.com

***Courtenay:* North Island Distance Education**
2505 Smith Rd., Courtenay, BC V9J 1T6, Canada
Tel: 250-898-8999; *Fax:* 250-898-8883
Toll-Free: 800-663-7925
principal@nides.bc.ca
www.nides.bc.ca

Grades: K.-12
Enrollment: 466
Sheila Shanahan, Principal
sshanahan@nides.bc.ca

***Creston:* SelfDesign Learning Community**
P.O. Box 747
Creston, BC V0B 1G0, Canada
Tel: 604-224-3640; *Fax:* 604-224-3662
info@selfdesign.org
www.selfdesign.org

Grades: K.
Enrollment: 652
Brent Cameron, Principal
brentcameron@selfdesign.org

***Fort St John:* Northern BC Distance Education**
10511 - 99 Ave., Fort St John, BC V1J 1V6, Canada
Tel: 250-261-5660; *Fax:* 250-785-1188
Toll-Free: 800-663-9511
info@nbcdes.com
www.des.prn.bc.ca

Grades: K.-12
Enrollment: 228
Randy Pauls, Principal

***Grindrod:* Christian Homelearner's eStreams**
P.O. Box 162
Grindrod, BC V0E 1Y0, Canada
Tel: 250-838-5979; *Fax:* 250-838-5979
Toll-Free: 877-777-1547
info@estreams.ca
www.estreams.ca

Grades: K.-12
Enrollment: 211
H. Hunt, Principal

***Kelowna:* Heritage Christian Online School**
905 Badke Rd., Kelowna, BC V1X 5Z5, Canada
Tel: 250-862-2376; *Fax:* 250-762-9277
Toll-Free: 877-862-2375
info@onlineschool.ca
www.onlineschool.ca

Grades: K.-12
Enrollment: 864
Greg Bitgood, Superintendent

***Merritt:* South Central Interior Distance Education School**
P.O. Box 4700 Main
2475 Merritt Ave., Merritt, BC V1K 1B8, Canada
Tel: 250-378-4245; *Fax:* 250-378-1447
Toll-Free: 800-663-3536
www.scides.com

Grades: K.-12
Enrollment: 137
Al Mackay-Smith, Principal, 800-663-3536, ext. 1200

***Nelson:* Distance Education School of the Kootenays**
811 Stanley St., Nelson, BC V1L 1N8, Canada
Tel: 250-354-4311; *Fax:* 250-505-7007
Toll-Free: 800-663-4614
www.desk.bc.ca

Grades: K-12
Dan Dalgaard, Principal

***Prince George:* Central Interior Distance Education**
P.O. Box 7400
1270 - 2nd Ave., Prince George, BC V2L 3B3, Canada
Tel: 250-563-1818; *Fax:* 250-563-1150
Toll-Free: 800-661-7515
www.cides.sd57.bc.ca

Grades: K.-12
Enrollment: 188
Steve Fleck, Principal

***Salmon Arm:* Anchor Academy**
7201 Hurst Rd., Salmon Arm, BC V1E 4R8, Canada
Tel: 250-832-2754; *Fax:* 250-832-4379
Toll-Free: 888-917-3783
anchor@ark.net
www.ark.net

Grades: K.-12
Enrollment: 405
Howard Hunt, Principal & Missions Coordinator

***Surrey:* Traditional Learning Academy (DL)**
6225C - 136 St., Surrey, BC V3X 1H3, Canada
Tel: 604-572-3441; *Fax:* 604-572-7832
Toll-Free: 866-576-3001
principal@schoolathome.ca
www.schoolathome.ca

Grades: K.-12
Enrollment: 334
Karen Gledhill, Principal

***Terrace:* North Coast Distance Education**
P.O. Box 5000
3211 Kenney St., Terrace, BC V8G 5K2, Canada
Tel: 250-635-7944; *Fax:* 250-638-2399
Toll-Free: 800-663-3865
www.ncdes.ca

Grades: K.-12
Enrollment: 220
Cindy Sousa, Principal
Cindy.Sousa@cmsd.bc.ca

***Vancouver:* Vancouver Learning Network**
Also known as: Greater Vancouver Distance Education
530 East 41st Ave., Vancouver, BC V5W 1P3, Canada
Tel: 604-713-5520; *Fax:* 604-713-5528
vln@vsb.bc.ca
www.gvdes.com

Grades: K.-12
Enrollment: 578
Cindy Gauthier, Principal
cgauthier@gvdes.com

***Victoria:* South Island Distance Education**
4575 Wilkinson Rd., Victoria, BC V8Z 7E8, Canada
Tel: 250-704-4979; *Fax:* 250-479-9870
Toll-Free: 800-663-7610
sides@sides.ca
www.sides.sd63.bc.ca

Grades: K.-12
Enrollment: 626
Kevin White, Principal

Schools: Independent & Private

Catholic

***Burnaby:* Holy Cross Elementary**
1450 Delta Ave., Burnaby, BC V5B 3G2, Canada
Tel: 604-299-3530; *Fax:* 604-299-3534
hcoffice@telus.net
www.holycrosselementary.ca

Grades: K.-7
Enrollment: 224
Dino Alberti, Principal

***North Vancouver:* Holy Trinity Elementary School**
128 - 27 St. West, North Vancouver, BC V7N 2H1, Canada
Tel: 604-987-4454; *Fax:* 604-987-0360
holyt@telus.net
www.holytschool.org; www.holytrinityparish.ca

Grades: K.-7
Enrollment: 233
Kevin Smith, Principal

Penticton: **Holy Cross Elementary School**
1298 Main St., Penticton, BC V2A 5G2, Canada
Tel: 250-492-4480; *Fax:* 250-490-4602
www.holyc.com
Grades: K.-7
Enrollment: 145
Jeff Brophy, Principal

Port Coquitlam: **Archbishop Carney Regional Secondary School**
1335 Dominion Ave., Port Coquitlam, BC V3B 8G7, Canada
Tel: 604-942-7465; *Fax:* 604-942-5289
admin@acrss.org
www.acrss.org
Grades: 8-12
Enrollment: 720
Lorraine Paruzzolo, Principal
paruzzol@acrss.org

Powell River: **Assumption Catholic School**
7091 Glacier St., Powell River, BC V8A 1R8, Canada
Tel: 604-485-9894; *Fax:* 604-485-7984
assump.office@shaw.ca
www.assumpschool.com
Grades: K.-9
Enrollment: 186
Accredited by the B.C. Min. of Education. Curriculum includes math, sciences, social studies, physical education, languages, music, art, drama, & relgion.
Mimi Richardson, Principal

Surrey: **Cloverdale Catholic School**
17511 - 59th Ave., Surrey, BC V3S 1P3, Canada
Tel: 604-574-5151; *Fax:* 604-574-5160
office@ccsunited.ca
ccsunited.ca
Grades: Preschool; K.-7
Enrollment: 245
Jason Borkowski, Principal

Vancouver: **Corpus Christi School**
6344 Nanaimo St., Vancouver, BC V5P 4K7, Canada
Tel: 604-321-1117; *Fax:* 604-321-1410
mkcc@telus.net
www.corpuschristi-school.ca
Grades: K.-7
Enrollment: 241
Rosa Natola, Principal

First Nations

Iskut: **Klappan Independent Day School**
P.O. Box 60
Iskut, BC V0J 1K0, Canada
Tel: 250-234-3561; *Fax:* 250-234-3562
www.bced.gov.bc.ca
Grades: K.-9
Enrollment: 41
Serving students of Iskut First Nation.
Carolyn Ann Doody, Principal
carolyn_ann_doody@hotmail.com

Independent & Private Schools

100 Mile House: **Cariboo Christian School**
P.O. Box 670
550 Exeter Truck Rd., 100 Mile House, BC V0K 2E0, Canada
Tel: 250-395-4637
Grades: Kindergarten - 9

Abbotsford: **Abbotsford Christian School**
35011 Old Clayburn Rd., Abbotsford, BC V2S 7L7, Canada
Tel: 604-850-5730; *Fax:* 604-850-6978
administration@abbotsfordchristian.com
www.abbotsfordchristian.com
Grades: K.-12
Enrollment: 1014
Daryl Verbeek, Executive Director

Abbotsford: **Cornerstone Christian School**
P.O. Box 520 Main
Abbotsford, BC V2S 5Z5, Canada
Tel: 604-859-7867; *Fax:* 604-859-7860
principal@cornerstoneschool.ca
Grades: K.-12
Enrollment: 176
M. Dana, Principal

Abbotsford: **Dasmesh Punjabi School**
33094 South Fraser Way, Abbotsford, BC V2S 2A9, Canada
Tel: 604-852-8986; *Fax:* 604-852-8924
dastaff@telus.net
Grades: K.-10
Enrollment: 397
Dalip Singh Gill, Principal

Abbotsford: **Mennonite Educational Institute (MEI)**
4081 Clearbrook Rd., Abbotsford, BC V4X 2M8, Canada
Tel: 604-859-3700; *Fax:* 604-859-9206
www.meisoc.com
Grades: Preschool - 12
Enrollment: 1774
The British Columbia curriculum is taught from a Biblical perspective.
Tim Regehr, President
Peter Froese, Superintendent
Ernest Janzen, Principal, Elementary
Dave Loewen, Principal, Chilliwack
David Neufeld, Principal, Secondary
dneufeld@meisoc.com
Heather Smith, Principal, Middle
Jeff Gamache, Vice Principal, Elementary
Rick Thiessen, Vice Principal, Secondary
rthiessen@meisoc.com
Grant Wardle, Vice Principal, Middle
Mr. M. Friesen, Business Adminstrator

Abbotsford: **St. James School**
2767 Townline Rd., Abbotsford, BC V2T 5E1, Canada
Tel: 604-852-1788; *Fax:* 604-850-5376
Grades: K.-7
Enrollment: 219
J. Lindenbach, Principal
principal.stjames@shaw.ca

Abbotsford: **St. John Brebeuf**
2747 Townline Rd., Abbotsford, BC V2T 5E1, Canada
Tel: 604-855-0571; *Fax:* 604-855-0572
office@stjohnbrebeuf.com
www.stjohnbrebeuf.com
Grades: 8-12
Enrollment: 347
C. Blesch, Principal

Abbotsford: **Valley Christian School (VCS)**
32721 Cherry Ave., Abbotsford, BC V2V 2T8, Canada
Tel: 604-826-1388; *Fax:* 604-826-2744
info@valleychristianschool.ca
www.valleychristianschool.ca
Grades: Preschool - 9
The preschool program works with children, ages three & four. A home school program is supported by the interdenominational school.
Ken Keis, Chair, Board of Directors
Bill Humphreys, Principal
Bob Barclay, Business Administrator

Agassiz: **Agassiz Christian School**
7571 Morrow Rd., Agassiz, BC V0M 1A2, Canada
Tel: 604-796-9310; *Fax:* 604-796-9519
agchris@shawcable.com
Grades: K.-7
Enrollment: 58
J. Zuidhof, Principal

Agassiz: **Seabird Island Community School**
P.O. Box 930
5 Chowat Rd., Agassiz, BC V0M 1A0, Canada
Tel: 604-796-3061; *Fax:* 604-796-3068
principal@seabirdschool.ca
Grades: K.-12
Enrollment: 162
M. Point, Principal

Ahousat: **Maaqtusiis School**
General Delivery, Ahousat, BC V0R 1A0, Canada
Tel: 250-670-9589; *Fax:* 250-670-9543
Grades: K.-12
Enrollment: 217
Gregory Louie, Principal
gwl_princeapple@yahoo.com

Aldergrove: **Aldergrove Christian Academy**
4057 - 248 St., Aldergrove, BC V4W 1E3, Canada
Tel: 604-856-2577; *Fax:* 604-857-0088
academy@rosbc.com
Grades: K.-12
Enrollment: 335
G. Wickens, Principal

Aldergrove: **Fraser Valley Adventist Academy**
P.O. Box 249
Aldergrove, BC V4W 2T8, Canada
Tel: 604-607-3822; *Fax:* 604-856-1002
fvaa@fvaa.net
Grades: K.-12
Enrollment: 307
K. Honey, Principal

Alert Bay: **T'lisalagi'lakw School**
P.O. Box 50
Alert Bay, BC V0N 1A0, Canada
Tel: 250-974-5591; *Fax:* 250-974-2475
gloriaa@namgis.bc.ca
Grades: K.-11
Enrollment: 79
G. Alfred, Principal

Armstrong: **North Okanagan Junior Academy**
4699 South Grandview Flats Rd., Armstrong, BC V0E 1B5, Canada
Tel: 250-546-8330; *Fax:* 250-546-8343
info@noja.ca
www.noja.ca
The Academy is operated by the Seventh-day Adventist Church.
Marilyn Ilchuk, B.Sc., Principal
marilynilchuk@aol.com
Sharon Trussell, B.Sc., M.A., Vice Principal
shrbet@shaw.ca
Cameron Koronko, Pastor
koronkoc@hotmail.com

Bella Coola: **Acwsalcta Band School**
P.O. Box 778
Bella Coola, BC V0T 1C0, Canada
Tel: 250-799-5911; *Fax:* 250-799-5576
principal@acwsalcta.com
Grades: K.-12
Enrollment: 127
V. Latvala, Principal

Bowen Island: **Island Pacific School**
P.O. Box 128
671 Carter Rd., Bowen Island, BC V0N 1G0, Canada
Tel: 604-947-9311; *Fax:* 604-947-9366
info@islandpacific.org
Grades: 6-9
Enrollment: 50
E. Spear, Principal

Burnaby: **Deer Lake SDA School**
5550 Gilpin St., Burnaby, BC V5G 2H6, Canada
Tel: 604-434-5844; *Fax:* 604-434-5845
office@deerlakeschool.ca
Grades: K.-10
Enrollment: 192
C. Erickson, Principal

Burnaby: **John Knox Christian School**
8260 - 13 Ave., Burnaby, BC V3N 2G5, Canada
Tel: 604-522-1410; *Fax:* 604-522-4606
admin@johnknoxbc.org
Grades: K.-7
Enrollment: 310
A. Ferguson, Principal

Burnaby: **Kenneth Gordon School**
7855 Meadow Ave., Burnaby, BC V3N 2V8, Canada
Tel: 604-524-5224; *Fax:* 604-524-8297
Grades: Elem. Ungraded
Enrollment: 85
Eithne Harrison, Principal
joniharrison@shaw.ca

Burnaby: **Our Lady of Mercy School**
7481 - 10 Ave., Burnaby, BC V3N 2S1, Canada
Tel: 604-526-7121; *Fax:* 604-520-3194
admin@ourladyofmercy.ca
www.ourladyofmercy.ca
Grades: K.-7
Enrollment: 240
N. Grout, Principal

Burnaby: **St. Francis de Sales School**
6656 Balmoral St., Burnaby, BC V5E 1J1, Canada
Tel: 604-435-5311; *Fax:* 604-434-4798
Grades: K.-7
Enrollment: 217
Cecilia McLaren, Principal
cmclaren@cisva.bc.ca

Burnaby: **St. Helen's School**
3894 Triumph St., Burnaby, BC V5C 1Y7, Canada
Tel: 604-299-2234; *Fax:* 604-299-3565
sthelens@telus.net
Grades: K.-7
Enrollment: 352
Waldemar Sambor, Principal

Burnaby: **St. Michaels School**
9387 Holmes St., Burnaby, BC V3N 4C3, Canada
Tel: 604-526-9768; *Fax:* 604-540-9799
ckennedy@cisva.bc.ca

Grades: K.-7
Enrollment: 216
C. Kennedy, Principal

***Burnaby:* St. Thomas More Collegiate**
7450 - 12 Ave., Burnaby, BC V3N 2K1, Canada
Tel: 604-521-1801; *Fax:* 604-520-0725
www.stmc.bc.ca

Grades: 8-12
Enrollment: 666
D. Hall, Principal
principal@stmc.bc.ca

***Burnaby:* Vancouver Christian School, Carver Christian High School**
7650 Sapperton Ave., Burnaby, BC V3N 4E1
Tel: 604-523-1580; *Fax:* 604-523-9646
www.vancouverchristian.org; www.carverchristian.org
Grades: 9 - 12

***Campbell River:* Campbell River Christian School (CRCS)**
250 South Dogwood St., Campbell River, BC V9W 6Y7, Canada
Tel: 250-287-4266; *Fax:* 250-287-3130
crcs@oberon.ark.com
www.crcs.bc.ca

Grades: Kindergarten - 12
Neil Steinke, Principal
ns-admin-crcs@uniserve.com

***Chemainus:* St. Joseph's School**
9735 Elm St., Chemainus, BC V0R 1K0, Canada
Tel: 250-246-3191; *Fax:* 250-246-2921
sjc@cisdv.bc.ca

Grades: K.-7
Enrollment: 115
B. Cleary, Principal

***Chetwynd:* Peace Christian School**
P.O. Box 2050
5124, 46th Ave., Chetwynd, BC V0C 1J0, Canada
Tel: 250-788-2044; *Fax:* 250-788-2579
pcs@persona.ca

Grades: K.-10
Enrollment: 74
S. Lee, Principal

***Chilliwack:* Highroad Academy**
46641 Chilliwack Central Rd., Chilliwack, BC V2P 1K3, Canada
Tel: 604-792-4680; *Fax:* 604-792-2465
info@highroadacademy.com
www.highroadacademy.com

Grades: K.-12
Enrollment: 430
Dave Shinness, Principal
dshinness@highroadacademy.com

***Chilliwack:* John Calvin School**
4268 Stewart Rd., Chilliwack, BC V2R 5G3, Canada
Tel: 604-823-6814; *Fax:* 604-823-6791
office@jcss.ca

Grades: K.-7
Enrollment: 170
Pieter H. Torenvliet, Principal

***Chilliwack:* Mount Cheam Christian School**
48988 Yale Rd. East, Chilliwack, BC V2P 6H4, Canada
Tel: 604-794-3072; *Fax:* 604-794-3078
office@mccsbc.com

Grades: Kindergarten - 12
Enrollment: 360
Adrian Stoutjesdyk, B.Ed. M.Ed., Principal

***Chilliwack:* St. Mary's School**
8909 Mary St., Chilliwack, BC V2P 4J4, Canada
Tel: 604-792-7715; *Fax:* 604-792-7031
principalstmary@telus.net

Grades: K.-7
Enrollment: 183
M. McDermott, Principal

***Chilliwack:* Timothy Christian School**
50420 Castleman Rd., Chilliwack, BC V2P 6H4, Canada
Tel: 604-794-7114; *Fax:* 604-794-3520
office@tcs.chilliwack.bc.ca

Grades: Kindergarten - 12
Enrollment: 367
Doug Stam, Principal

***Chilliwack:* Unity Christian School, Elementary Campus (UCS)**
Elementary Campus
P.O. Box 371
9750 McNaught Rd., Chilliwack, BC V2P 6J4, Canada
Tel: 604-792-4171; *Fax:* 604-792-0640
elementary@unitychristian.ca; general@unitychristian.ca
www.unitychristian.ca

Grades: Preschool - 6
A Christ-centered education is provided by Unity Christian School.
Ed Noot, Principal
Jeanette Berkenbosch, Vice Principal

***Chilliwack:* Unity Christian School, Secondary Campus (UCS)**
Secondary Campus
P.O. Box 371
50950 Hack-Brown Rd., Chilliwack, BC V2P 6J4
Tel: 604-794-7797; *Fax:* 604-794-7667
general@unitychristian.ca
www.unitychristian.ca

Grades: 7 - 12
Unity Christian School offers a Christ-centered education.

***Cobble Hill:* Evergreen Independent School**
P.O. Box 166
Cobble Hill, BC V0R 1L0, Canada
Tel: 250-743-2433; *Fax:* 250-743-2570
evergreen@evergreenbc.net

Grades: K.-6
Enrollment: 63
J. Ovans, Principal

***Coquitlam:* Coquitlam College**
516 Brookmere Ave., Coquitlam, BC V3J 1W9, Canada
Tel: 604-939-6633; *Fax:* 604-939-0336
admiss@coquitlamcollege.com
www.coquitlamcollege.com

Grades: 11-12
Enrollment: 85
W. Eckford, Principal

***Coquitlam:* Eagle Ridge Montessori Elementary**
2541 Quay Pl., Coquitlam, BC V3S 3H7, Canada
Tel: 604-469-9166; *Fax:* 604-469-9168
info@ermontessori.com

Grades: K.-6
Enrollment: 38
V. Lawrie, Principal

***Coquitlam:* Mediated Learning Academy**
550 Thompson Ave., Coquitlam, BC V3J 3Z8, Canada
Tel: 604-937-3641; *Fax:* 604-937-3642
info@mediatedlearningacademy.org

Grades: K.-12
Enrollment: 84
K. Jeffrey, Principal

***Coquitlam:* Our Lady of Fatima School**
315 Walker St., Coquitlam, BC V3K 4C7, Canada
Tel: 604-936-4228; *Fax:* 604-936-4403
info@fatimaschool.ca
www.fatimaschool.ca

Grades: K.-7
Enrollment: 388
Maria Katsionis, Principal

***Coquitlam:* Queen of All Saints Elementary School (QAS)**
1405 Como Lake Ave., Coquitlam, BC V3J 3P4, Canada
Tel: 604-931-9071; *Fax:* 604-931-9089
queenofallsaintsschool@shawcable.com
www.queenofallsaintsschool.ca

Grades: Kindergarten - 7
Queen of All Saints Elementary School was established by the Roman Catholic Archdiocese of Vancouver. The school belongs to All Saints Parish.
Oscar Pozzolo, Principal
Mrs. J. Sussex, Vice Principal
Father Tien Tran, Pastor

***Coquitlam:* Traditional Learning Academy (TLA)**
1189 Rochester Ave., Coquitlam, BC V3K 2X3, Canada
Tel: 604-931-7265; *Fax:* 604-931-3432
tlaoffice@traditionallearning.com
www.traditionallearning.com
Other Information: tlaprincipal@traditionallearning.com (E-mail, Principal)
Traditional Learning Academy encourages students to know the Catholic faith.
Allan Garneau, Administrator

***Cranbrook:* Kootenay Christian Academy**
1200 Kootenay St. North, Cranbrook, BC V1C 5X1, Canada
Tel: 250-426-0166; *Fax:* 250-426-0186
kca12@shaw.ca

Grades: K.-9
Enrollment: 142
J. Markuson, Principal

***Cranbrook:* St. Mary's Catholic Independent School**
1701 - 5 St. South, Cranbrook, BC V1C 1K1, Canada
Tel: 250-426-5017; *Fax:* 250-426-5076
jmacneil@cintek.com

Grades: K.-6
Enrollment: 143
J. Macneil, Principal

***Dawson Creek:* Mountain Christian School (MCS)**
11501 - 17th St., Dawson Creek, BC V1G 4S7, Canada
Tel: 250-782-9528; *Fax:* 250-782-3888
mcs@shawcable.com
www.mcsed.ca

Grades: Kindergarten - 12
Enrollment: 94
Trevor Ragan, Principal

***Dawson Creek:* Notre Dame School**
925 - 104th Ave., Dawson Creek, BC V1G 2H8, Canada
Tel: 250-782-4923; *Fax:* 250-782-4388
www.notredamedc.org/notre-dame-school

Grades: Kindergarten - 7
Enrollment: 150
Notre Dame School provides a Catholic education.
Mrs. Terri Haynal, Principal

***Dawson Creek:* Ron Pettigrew Christian School**
1761 - 110th Ave., Dawson Creek, BC V1G 4X4, Canada
Tel: 250-782-4580; *Fax:* 250-782-9805
rpcs@pris.ca

Grades: Kindergarten - 12
Enrollment: 75
Phyllis Roch, Principal

***Delta:* Delta Christian School**
4789 - 53 St., Delta, BC V4K 2Y9, Canada
Tel: 604-946-2514; *Fax:* 604-946-2589
deltachristian@telus.net

Grades: K.-7
Enrollment: 169
G. de Vos, Principal

***Delta:* Immaculate Conception School**
8840 - 119 St., Delta, BC V4C 6M4, Canada
Tel: 604-596-6116; *Fax:* 604-596-4338
immaculate_conception_school@hotmail.com

Grades: K.-7
Enrollment: 473
W. MacCormack, Principal

***Delta:* Sacred Heart School**
P.O. Box 10 Main
3900 Arthur Dr., Delta, BC V4K 3N5, Canada
Tel: 604-946-2611; *Fax:* 604-946-0598
office@shsdelta.org
www.shsdelta.org

Grades: K.-7
Enrollment: 400
D. Schollen, Principal
dschollen@shsdelta.org

***Delta:* Southpointe Academy**
1741 - 56 St., Delta, BC V4L 2B2, Canada
Tel: 604-948-8826; *Fax:* 604-948-8853
school@spacademy.ca
www.southpointeacademy.ca

Grades: K.-12
Enrollment: 425
G. Baldwin, Principal
graham.baldwin@spacademy.ca

***Duncan:* Duncan Christian School**
495 Beech Ave., Duncan, BC V9L 3J8, Canada
Tel: 250-746-3654; *Fax:* 250-746-3615
office@duncanchristianschool.ca

Grades: K.-12
Enrollment: 276
C. Davis, Principal

***Duncan:* Island Oak High School**
P.O. Box 873 Main
Duncan, BC V9L 3Y2, Canada
Tel: 250-701-0400; *Fax:* 250-701-0400
mail@islandoak.org

Grades: 9-12
Enrollment: 40

R. Tibbetts, Principal

***Duncan:* Queen Margaret's School (QMS)**
660 Brownsey Ave., Duncan, BC V9L 1C2, Canada
Tel: 250-746-4185; *Fax:* 250-746-4187
www.qms.bc.ca

Grades: Junior Kindergarten - 12
Queen Margaret's School consists of a coeducational junior school for students from junior kindergarten to grade seven. The school also consists of an All-Girls High School, which offers a university preparatory program. An English as a Second Language Program is available for beginner & advanced students.
Michael DeBeck, Chair
Ms. Pat Rowantree, Head of School
prowantree@qms.bc.ca
Chad Holtum, Deputy Head, Operations
choltum@qms.bc.ca
Sharon Klein, Deputy Head, Student Life & Senior School Principal
sklein@qms.bc.ca
Stuart Hall, Junior School Principal
shall@qms.bc.ca
Celina Mason, Director, Residential Life & Student Support
Julie Scurr, Director, Finance & Privacy Officer
Shannon Peck, Coordinator, Admissions & Marketing
Cheryl Skinn, Coordinator, Student Life

***Duncan:* Queen of Angels Catholic School**
2085 Maple Bay Rd., Duncan, BC V9L 5L9, Canada
Tel: 250-746-5919; *Fax:* 250-746-8689
info@queenofangels.ca
www.queenofangels.ca

Grades: Preschool - 9
Tina Campagne, Chair, Local School Council
Art Therrien, Principal
Ciaran McLaverty, Vice Principal
Lana Durand, Coordinator, Special Education
Denika Osmond, Secretary

***Duncan:* Sunrise Waldorf School**
4344 Peters Rd., Duncan, BC V9L 6M3, Canada
Tel: 250-743-7253; *Fax:* 250-743-7245
mail@sunrisewaldorfschool.org
www.sunrisewaldorfschool.org

Grades: K.-8
Enrollment: 162
J. Canty, Principal

***Fernie:* Fernie Academy**
P.O. Box 2677
Fernie, BC V0B 1M0, Canada
Tel: 250-423-0212; *Fax:* 250-423-4799

Grades: K.-7
Enrollment: 97
J. Sombrowski, Principal
jsombrowski@fernieacademy.com

***Fort Nelson:* Chalo School**
Mile 293, RR#1, Fort Nelson, BC V0C 1R0, Canada
Tel: 250-774-7655; *Fax:* 250-774-7651
chalo@gmail.com
www.chaloschool.bc.ca

Grades: Preschool - 12
Enrollment: 200
Fort Nelson First Nation owns & operates Chalo School.
Celine Kotchea, Chair

***Fort St James:* Nak'albun Elementary School**
P.O. Box 1390
Fort St James, BC V0J 1P0, Canada
Tel: 250-996-8441; *Fax:* 250-996-2229
www.nakalbun.com

Grades: Kindergarten - 7
Enrollment: 60
The elementary school is operated under the jurisdiction of Nak'azdli Band.
Rick Aucoin, Principal
nkbprincipal@fsjames.com

***Fort St John:* Christian Life School**
8923 - 112th Ave., Fort St John, BC V1J 5H8, Canada
Tel: 250-785-1437; *Fax:* 250-785-4852
office@christianlifeschool.ca
www.christianlifeschool.ca

Grades: Kindergarten - 12; Christianity
Lynette Kovacs, Chair, 250-785-1437
Don Irwin, Principal
dirwin@christianlifeschool.ca

***Fort St John:* Maccabee Christian School**
P.O. Box 6771 Main
Fort St John, BC V1J 4J2, Canada
Tel: 250-772-5010; *Fax:* 250-772-5009

F. Roscher, Principal

***Fort Ware:* Aatse Davie School**
P.O. Box 79
Fort Ware, BC V0J 3B0, Canada
Tel: 250-471-2002; *Fax:* 250-471-2080
aatse@pris.bc.ca
www.kwadacha.com

Grades: K.-12
Enrollment: 84
The school serves the Kwadacha First Nation. In addition to the standard humanities & sciences curriculum, classes in the Tsek'ene language are taught.
Andreas Rohrbach, Principal

***Hazelton:* Kispiox Junior Secondary School**
RR#1, SK C 128, Hazelton, BC V0J 1Y0, Canada
Tel: 250-842-6148; *Fax:* 250-842-5799
kispiox@bc.firstnationschools.ca

Grades: K.-8
Enrollment: 86
R. Steinbeisser, Principal

***Houston:* Houston Christian School**
P.O. Box 237
Houston, BC V0J 1Z0, Canada
Tel: 250-845-7736; *Fax:* 250-845-7738
hcschool@telus.net

Grades: K.-12
Enrollment: 131
Jack Vanden Born, Principal

***Kamloops:* Kamloops Christian School**
750 Cottonwood Ave., Kamloops, BC V2B 3X2, Canada
Tel: 250-376-6900; *Fax:* 250-376-6904
heatherb@kamcs.org

Grades: K.-12
Enrollment: 363
T. Rogers, Principal

***Kamloops:* Our Lady of Perpetual Help School**
235 Poplar St., Kamloops, BC V2B 4B9, Canada
Tel: 250-376-2343; *Fax:* 250-376-2361
rose@olphschool.ca
www.olphschool.ca

Grades: K.-7
Enrollment: 181
Rose Nowicki, Principal
rose@olphschool.ca

***Kamloops:* St. Ann's Academy**
205 Columbia St., Kamloops, BC V2C 2S7, Canada
Tel: 250-372-5452; *Fax:* 250-372-5257
www.stannsacademy.bc.ca

Grades: K.-12
Enrollment: 480
S. Chisholm, Principal
principal@stannsacademy.bc.ca

***Kelowna:* First Lutheran Christian School**
4091 Lakeshore Rd., Kelowna, BC V1W 1V7, Canada
Tel: 250-764-3111; *Fax:* 250-764-3129

Grades: K.-6
Enrollment: 64
T. Hennig, Principal
thennig@firstlutheran.ca

***Kelowna:* Heritage Christian School**
907 Badke Rd., Kelowna, BC V1X 5Z5, Canada
Tel: 250-862-2377; *Fax:* 250-862-4943
office@heritagechristian.ca
www.heritagechristian.ca

Grades: K.-12
Enrollment: 308
Greg Bitgood, Principal
gbitgood@heritagechristian.ca

***Kelowna:* Immaculata Catholic Regional High School**
1493 K.L.O. Rd., Kelowna, BC V1W 3N8, Canada
Tel: 250-762-2730; *Fax:* 250-861-3028
secretary@immaculatakelowna.ca
www.immaculatakelowna.ca

Grades: Secondary; Religious Education
Enrollment: 350
Number of Employees: 26 (including 14 teachers)
John Campbell, B.Sc., Dip.Ed. M.Ed., Principal
principal@immaculatakelowna.ca
Edward Frison, B.Ed., Vice-Principal
vice_principal@immaculatakelowna.ca
Fr. Wayne Pfliger, Chaplain
chaplain@immaculatakelowna.ca
Mary Gallagher, B.Ed, Coordinator, Religious Education
religion@immaculatakelowna.ca
Nadine Casorso, Librarian
ncasorso@immaculatakelowna.ca
Chris Schmidt, Librarian
cschmidt@immaculatakelowna.ca
Lois Ehman, B.Ed., Contact, Special Education Department
lhorizons@immaculatakelowna.ca

***Kelowna:* Kelowna Christian School**
2870 Benvoulin Rd., Kelowna, BC V1W 2E3, Canada
Tel: 250-861-3238; *Fax:* 250-861-4844
berne.watters@kelownachristian.ca

Grades: K.-12
Enrollment: 802
B. Watters, Principal

***Kelowna:* Kelowna Christian School**
2870 Benvoulin Rd., Kelowna, BC V1W 2E3, Canada
Tel: 250-861-3238; *Fax:* 250-861-4844

Grades: K.-9
Enrollment: 195
B. Watters, Principal
berne.watters@kelownachristian.ca

***Kelowna:* Kelowna Waldorf School**
PO Box 29093, RPO Okanagan Mission, Kelowna, BC V1W 4A7, Canada
Tel: 250-764-4130; *Fax:* 250-764-4139
info@kelownawaldorfschool.com

Grades: K.-7
Enrollment: 107
D. Lane, Principal

***Kelowna:* Okanagan Adventist Academy**
1035 Hollywood Rd., Kelowna, BC V1X 4N3, Canada
Tel: 250-860-5305; *Fax:* 250-868-9703
okaa@shaw.ca
www.okaa.ca

Grades: K.-12
Enrollment: 135
Don Straub, Principal
dstraub@okaa.ca

***Kelowna:* St. Joseph Elementary School**
839 Sutherland Ave., Kelowna, BC V1Y 5X4, Canada
Tel: 250-763-3371; *Fax:* 250-763-2740
school@stjosephkelowna.ca
www.stjosephkelowna.ca

Grades: K.-7
Enrollment: 316
R. Smith, Principal

***Kelowna:* Vedanta Academy**
1180 Houghton Rd., Kelowna, BC V1X 2C9, Canada
Tel: 250-868-8816; *Fax:* 250-868-8836
www.vedantaacademy.com

Grades: Kindergarten - 12
C. Belliveau, Principal

***Kitimat:* St. Anthony's School**
1750 Nalabila Blvd., Kitimat, BC V8C 1E6, Canada
Tel: 250-632-6313; *Fax:* 250-632-6313
stanthonys@citywest.ca

Grades: K.-7
Enrollment: 150
Most Rev. P. Cornthwaite, Principal

***Ladysmith:* Stu"ate Lelum Secondary School**
P.O. Box 730
Ladysmith, BC V9G 1A5, Canada
Tel: 250-245-3522; *Fax:* 250-245-8263
len.merriman@cfnation.com

Grades: GA
Enrollment: 76
L. Merriman, Principal

***Langley:* Credo Christian Schools**
21846 - 52 Ave., Langley, BC V2Y 2M7, Canada
Tel: 604-530-5396; *Fax:* 604-530-8965
H.Moes@Credochs.com

Grades: K.-12
Enrollment: 470
H. Moes, Principal

***Langley:* Langley Christian School**
21789 - 50 Ave., Langley, BC V3A 3T2, Canada
Tel: 604-533-2222; *Fax:* 604-533-7276
elem@langleychristian.com

Grades: K.-12
Enrollment: 813
H. Vanderveen, Principal

Langley: Langley Montessori School
19785 - 55A Ave., Langley, BC V3A 3X1, Canada
Tel: 604-534-1556; *Fax:* 604-532-4358
langleymontessori@telus.net
Grades: K.
Enrollment: 65
U. Hodgson, Principal

Langley: St. Catherines School
20244 - 32 Ave., Langley, BC V2Z 2E1, Canada
Tel: 604-534-6564; *Fax:* 604-534-4871
www.stcatherines.ca
Grades: K.-7
Enrollment: 229
A. Castellon, Principal
acastellon@stcatherines.ca

Langley: Whytecliff Agile Learning Centre-Langley
20561 Logan Ave., Langley, BC V3A 7R3, Canada
Tel: 604-532-1268; *Fax:* 604-532-1269
mlinski@focusbc.org
Grades: 7-11
Enrollment: 49
M. Linski, Principal

Lantzville: Aspengrove School
7660 Clark Dr., Lantzville, BC V0R 2H0, Canada
Tel: 250-390-2201; *Fax:* 250-390-2281
cgrunlund@aspengroveschool.ca
aspengroveschool.ca
Grades: K.-12
Enrollment: 190
Accredited International Baccalaureate programs for primary and middle years; core academic subjects, as well as performing arts, physical and outdoor education, community service.
Zinda Fitzgerald, Head of School

Lax Kw'Alaams: Lax Kw Alaams Academy
11 Lagaic St., Lax Kw'Alaams, BC V0V 1H0, Canada
Tel: 604-625-3207; *Fax:* 604-625-3425
principal@laxkwalaamsacademy.net
Grades: K.-10
Enrollment: 152
S. Campbell, Principal

Lillooet: Fountainview Academy
P.O. Box 500
Lillooet, BC V0K 1V0, Canada
Tel: 250-256-5400; *Fax:* 250-256-5499
Grades: 9-12
Enrollment: 58
B. Corrigan, Principal
bcorrigan@fountainview.ca

Lister: Bountiful Elementary - Secondary School
P.O. Box 226
1070 JRB Rd., Lister, BC V0B 1Y0, Canada
Tel: 250-428-4679; *Fax:* 250-428-4789
bountifulschool@gmail.com
www.bountifulschool.org
Grades: Kindergarten - 12
Bountiful Elementary - Secondary School prrovides education for members of the FLDS faith.
Merrill R. Palmer, Principal

Lister: Mormon Hills Elementary Secondary School
P.O. Box 725
Lister, BC V0B 1Y0, Canada
Tel: 250-428-4800; *Fax:* 250-428-4810
mormonhillsschool@yahoo.ca
Grades: Kindergarten - 11
Enrollment: 191
Jeff Banman, Principal

Lytton: Stein Valley Nlakapamux School
PO Bag 300, Lytton, BC V0K 1Z0, Canada
Tel: 250-455-2522; *Fax:* 250-455-2512
steinvalleyschool@yahoo.com
Grades: K.-12
Enrollment: 109
C. Holmes, Principal

Mackenzie: Mackenzie Christian Academy
P.O. Box 2406
Mackenzie, BC V0J 2C0, Canada
Tel: 250-997-4000; *Fax:* 250-997-3800
ward@ljcc.ca
Grades: K.-8
Enrollment: 36
W. McGowan, Principal

Mansons Landing: Linnaea School
P.O. Box 98
Mansons Landing, BC V0P 1K0, Canada
Tel: 250-935-6747; *Fax:* 250-935-6413
school@linneafarm.org
Grades: K.-8
Enrollment: 57
D. Bracewell, Principal

Maple Ridge: James Cameron School
P.O. Box 157 Del Ctr.
Maple Ridge, BC V2X 7G1, Canada
Tel: 604-465-8444; *Fax:* 604-465-4561
jcsadmin@jcs.bc.ca
Grades: 2-7
Enrollment: 55
G. Storteboom, Principal

Maple Ridge: Maple Ridge Christian School
12140 - 203 St., Maple Ridge, BC V2X 2S5, Canada
Tel: 604-465-4442; *Fax:* 604-465-1685
jroxburgh@mrcs.ca
Grades: K.-12
Enrollment: 322
R. Roxburgh, Principal

Maple Ridge: Meadowridge School
12224 - 240th St., Maple Ridge, BC V4R 1N1, Canada
Tel: 604-467-4444; *Fax:* 604-467-4989
Grades: K.-12
Enrollment: 450
H. Burke, Principal
hburke@meadowridge.bc.ca

Maple Ridge: St. Patrick's School
22589 - 121 Ave., Maple Ridge, BC V2X 3T5, Canada
Tel: 604-467-1571; *Fax:* 604-467-2686
Grades: K.-7
Enrollment: 214
Irene Wihak, Principal
iwihak@cisva.bc.ca

Merritt: Lower Nicola Band School
181 Nawishaskin Lane, Merritt, BC V1K 1N2, Canada
Tel: 250-378-5527; *Fax:* 250-378-6389
Grades: K.-12
Enrollment: 60
D. Sterling, Principal
dsterling@lnib.net

Merville: Comox Valley Christian School
P.O. Box 425
Merville, BC V0R 2M0, Canada
Tel: 250-337-5335; *Fax:* 250-337-5632
cvcs4u@island.net
Grades: K.-9
Enrollment: 112
R. Janzen, Principal

Mill Bay: Brentwood College School
2735 Mount Baker Rd., Mill Bay, BC V0R 2P1, Canada
Tel: 250-743-5521; *Fax:* 250-743-2911
admissions@brentwood.bc.ca
www.brentwood.bc.ca
Grades: 9 - 12
Brentwood College School is a co-educational university prep school.
Andrea Pennells, Head, Brentwood College School
amp@brentwood.bc.ca
John Allpress, Deputy Head, Advancement
allpress@brentwood.bc.ca
Marius Felix, Assistant Head, Campus Life
marius.felix@brentwood.bc.ca
John Garvey, Assistant Head, Administration
garveyj@brentwood.bc.ca
Clayton Johnston, Director, Admissions
clayton.johnston@brentwood.bc.ca
Dave McCarthy, Director, Academics
mccarthd@brentwood.bc.ca
Gerry Pennells, Director, University Planning
pennells@brentwood.bc.ca

Milner: King's School
21783 - 76B Ave., Milner, BC V0X 1T0, Canada
Tel: 604-888-0969; *Fax:* 604-888-0977
school@tkc.com
Grades: K.-12
Enrollment: 141
P. Thomas, Principal

Nanaimo: Malaspina International High School
900 Fifth St., Nanaimo, BC V9R 5S5, Canada
Tel: 250-740-6317; *Fax:* 250-740-6470
lewist@mala.bc.ca
Grades: 10-12
Enrollment: 121
T. Lewis, Principal

Nanaimo: Nanaimo Christian School (NCS)
198 Holland Rd., Nanaimo, BC V9R 6W2, Canada
Tel: 250-754-4512; *Fax:* 250-754-4271
inquiries.ncs@shaw.ca
www.nanaimochristianschool.ca
Grades: Preschool - 12
John Reems, Principal
Brian De Schiffart, Vice Principal
Sue De Schiffart, Coordinator, Special Education

Nanoose Bay: Beacon Christian School
2210 Morello Rd., Nanoose Bay, BC V9P 9A9, Canada
Tel: 250-468-9433; *Fax:* 250-468-7748
beaconchristian@shaw.ca
Grades: Kindergarten - 3
Enrollment: 12
Barbara Judd, Principal
beacon.principal@shaw.ca

Nelson: Nelson Waldorf School
P.O. Box 165 Main
Nelson, BC V1L 5P9, Canada
Tel: 250-352-6919; *Fax:* 250-352-6887
info@nelsonwaldorf.org
www.nelsonwaldorf.org
Grades: Kindergarten - 8
The school offers Waldorf education to children in the West Kootenay area.
Beverley Barcham, General Administrator & Principal
Lisa Bramson, Coordinator, Special Needs
Diana Finley, Coordinator, Social Inclusion
Andromeda Drake, Bookkeeper

Nelson: St. Joseph's School
523 Mill St., Nelson, BC V1L 4S2, Canada
Tel: 250-352-3041; *Fax:* 250-352-9188
office@stjosephnelson.ca
www.stjosephnelson.ca
Grades: K.-6
Enrollment: 122
L. Luck, Principal

New Westminster: Purpose Independent Secondary School
Also known as: Purpose Young Adult Learning Centre
40 Begbie St., New Westminster, BC V3M 3L9, Canada
Tel: 604-526-2522; *Fax:* 604-526-6546
info@purposesociety.org
www.purposesociety.org/purpose
Grades: 10 - 12
The program at The Purpose School is designed for students, aged fifteen to nineteen, who are unable to succeed in the traditional school system. A Purpose Secondary School education leads to a Standard Dogwood Diploma.
Phill Esau, Principal

North Vancouver: Bodwell High School
955 Harbourside Dr., North Vancouver, BC V7P 3S4, Canada
Tel: 604-924-5056; *Fax:* 604-924-5058
www.bodwell.edu/highschool
Grades: 8 - 12
Bodwell High School is a co-educational day & boarding school.
Stephen Smith, B.A., Dip. Ed., M.A., M.E, Principal
Cathy Lee, B.S.Sc., M.S.W., Director, Admissions

North Vancouver: L'École française internationale de Vancouver
French International School of Vancouver
4343 Starlight Way, North Vancouver, BC V7N 3N8, Canada
Tél: 604-924-2457; *Téléc:* 604-924-4483
info@efiv.org
www.efiv.org
Grades: Mat./Prim.
Enrollment: 125
Programme du Ministère de l'Éducation Nationale Français, enrichi par des cours d'histoire, de géographie et des cultures du Canada.
Jérémy Harrison, Directeur (par intérim)

North Vancouver: Lions Gate Christian Academy
420 Seymour River Pl., North Vancouver, BC V7H 1S8, Canada
Tel: 604-984-8226; *Fax:* 604-984-8254
lgca@telus.net
Grades: K.-7
Enrollment: 181
D. North, Principal

North Vancouver: St. Edmund's School
535 Mahon Ave., North Vancouver, BC V7M 2R7, Canada
Tel: 604-988-7364; *Fax:* 604-988-7350
www.stedmunds.ca
Grades: K.-7
Enrollment: 204
Michael Field, Principal
mfield@stedmunds.ca

North Vancouver: St. Pius X Elementary School
1150 Mount Seymour Rd., North Vancouver, BC V7G 1R6, Canada
Tel: 604-929-0345; *Fax:* 604-929-5051
stpiusxschool@telus.net
Grades: K.-7
Enrollment: 227
Fabio Battisti, Principal

North Vancouver: St. Thomas Aquinas School
541 Keith Rd. West, North Vancouver, BC V7M 1M5, Canada
Tel: 604-987-4431; *Fax:* 604-987-7816
office@aquinas.org
www.aquinas.org
Grades: 8-12
Enrollment: 601
F. Dragojevich, Principal
dragojevich@aquinas.org

North Vancouver: Vancouver Waldorf School
2725 St. Christophers Rd. North, North Vancouver, BC V7K 2B6, Canada
Tel: 604-985-7435; *Fax:* 604-985-4948
reception@vws.ca
www.vws.ca
Other Information: board@vws.ca (E-mail, Board of Trustees)
Grades: Preschool - 12
Vancouver Waldorf School integrates the movement arts & artistic activities throughout the curriculum.
Rea Gill, Administrator
Robert Adams, Administrator, High School
Mary Paradis, Director, Development
Fiona Thatcher, Director, Admissions, 604-985-7435, ext. 200
admissions@vws.ca

Oliver: Sen Pok Chin
#2 McKinney Rd., Oliver, BC V0H 1T0, Canada
Tel: 250-498-2019; *Fax:* 250-498-3096
office@senpokchin.com
www.senpokchin.com
Grades: K.-7
Enrollment: 36
R. Laurie, Principal
principal@senpokchin.com

Penticton: Penticton Community Christian School
P.O. Box 910 Main
Penticton, BC V2A 6J9, Canada
Tel: 250-493-5233; *Fax:* 250-276-4124
office@pentictonchristianschool.ca
www.pentictonchristianschool.ca
Grades: K.-12
Enrollment: 54
K. Boehmer, Principal
kboehmer@pentictonchristianschool.ca

Port Alberni: Haahuupayak School
6000 Santu Dr., Port Alberni, BC V9Y 7M2, Canada
Tel: 250-724-5542; *Fax:* 250-724-7335
ha-ak-sap@hotmail.com
www.haahuupayak.com
Grades: K.-6
Enrollment: 79
Tricia McAuley, Principal

Port Alberni: Port Alberni Christian School
4283 Glenside Rd., Port Alberni, BC V9Y 5W9, Canada
Tel: 250-723-2700; *Fax:* 250-723-5799
Grades: K.-7
Enrollment: 36
M. Walker, Principal

Port Coquitlam: British Columbia Christian Academy
1019 Fernwood Ave., Port Coquitlam, BC V3B 5A8, Canada
Tel: 604-941-8426; *Fax:* 604-945-6455
admissions@bcchristianacademy.ca
www.bcchristianacademy.ca
Grades: Preschool - 12
British Columbia Christian Academy is an interdenominational Christian school.
Mr. I. Jarvie, Head Principal
ijarvie@bcchristianacademy.ca
Mr. T. Bryerton, Elementary Principal
tbryerton@bcchristianacademy.ca
Ms. T. Cota, Director, Preschool, Out Of School, Daycare
tcota@bcchristianacademy.ca
Mr. D. Dowell, Director, Foreign Studies & Continuing Education
ddowell@bcchristianacademy.ca
Ms. Tko, Librarian
library@bcchristianacademy.ca

Port Coquitlam: Hope Lutheran Elementary
3151 York St., Port Coquitlam, BC V3B 4A7, Canada
Tel: 604-942-5322; *Fax:* 604-942-5311
Grades: K.-8
Enrollment: 190
M. Towriss, Principal
mtowriss@hopelutheranschool.com

Port Coquitlam: Our Lady of the Assumption School
2255 Fraser Ave., Port Coquitlam, BC V3B 6G8, Canada
Tel: 604-942-5522; *Fax:* 604-942-8313
info@assumptionschool.com
www.assumptionschool.com
Grades: K.-7
Enrollment: 244
J. Brophy, Principal

Port Hardy: Avalon Adventist Junior Academy
P.O. Box 974
Port Hardy, BC V0N 2P0, Canada
Tel: 250-949-8243; *Fax:* 250-949-6770
www.aaja.ca
Grades: Kindergarten - 10
Wesley Bradford, P.E., Principal
wbradford@vandercook.edu
Karen Wallace, Vice Prinicipal
karenwallace1166@gmail.com

Port Hardy: Gwa'sala-'Nakwaxda'xw School
P.O. Box 1799
Port Hardy, BC V0N 2P0, Canada
Tel: 250-949-7743; *Fax:* 250-949-7422
www.gwanak.bc.ca
Grades: K.-7
Enrollment: 82
Independent First Nation's school
Barry Prong, Principal

Prince George: Cedars Christian School
701 North Nechako Rd., Prince George, BC V2K 1A2, Canada
Tel: 250-564-0707; *Fax:* 250-564-0729
www.cedars.bc.ca
Grades: Preschool - 12
Cedars Christian School is a non-denominational school.
Judy Serup, Chair

Prince George: Gateway Christian School
P.O. Box 1089
Prince George, BC V2L 4V2, Canada
Tel: 250-563-8585; *Fax:* 250-563-3488
gcsadmin@telus.net
Grades: K.-12
Enrollment: 126
M. Kostamo, Principal

Prince George: Immaculate Conception School
3285 Cathedral Ave., Prince George, BC V2N 5R2, Canada
Tel: 250-964-4362; *Fax:* 250-964-9465
iconceptoffice@shawcable.com
Grades: K.-7
Enrollment: 181
D. O'Callaghan, Principal

Prince George: Sacred Heart School
785 Patricia Blvd., Prince George, BC V2L 3V5, Canada
Tel: 250-563-5201; *Fax:* 250-563-5201
shspg@netbistro.com
www.shspg.com
Grades: K.-7
Enrollment: 104
K. Harnish, Principal
kharnish@netbistro.com

Prince George: St. Mary's School
1088 Gillett St., Prince George, BC V2M 2V3, Canada
Tel: 250-563-7502; *Fax:* 250-563-7818
coachbrent@stmaryspg.org
www.stmaryspg.org
Grades: K.-7
Enrollment: 199
B. Arsenault, Principal

Prince George: Westside Academy
3791 Hwy. 16 West, Prince George, BC V2N 5P8, Canada
Tel: 250-964-9600
waoffice@telus.net; webmaster@westsideacademy.ca
www.westsideacademy.ca
Grades: Kindergarten - 12
Westside Academy is a ministry of Westside Family Fellowship.
Robert Tower, School Principal
rob@westsideacademy.ca
Donna Rosenbaum, School Dean
drosenbaum@westsideacademy.ca
Shannon Dimler, School Secretary & Admissions Coordinator
shannon@westsideacademy.ca

Prince Rupert: Annunciation School
627 - 5 Ave. West, Prince Rupert, BC V8J 1V1, Canada
Tel: 250-624-5873; *Fax:* 250-627-4486
annun@citytel.net
Grades: K.-7
Enrollment: 197
M. McDermott, Principal

Quesnel: North Cariboo Christian School (NCCS)
2876 Red Bluff Rd., Quesnel, BC V2J 6C7, Canada
Tel: 250-747-4417; *Fax:* 250-747-4410
office@nccschool.ca
www.nccschool.ca
Grades: Kindergarten - 9
Enrollment: 63
The North Cariboo Christian School is a non-denominational school.
John Hengen, Principal

Quesnel: St. Ann's School
150 Sutherland Ave., Quesnel, BC V2J 2J5, Canada
Tel: 250-992-6237; *Fax:* 250-992-6234
principal.stanns@shawcable.com
Grades: K.-7
Enrollment: 71
R. Nieman, Principal

Richmond: BC Muslim School
12300 Blundell Rd., Richmond, BC V6W 1B3, Canada
Tel: 604-270-2511; *Fax:* 604-270-2679
admin@bcmuslimschool.ca
www.bcmuslimschool.ca
Grades: Kindergarten - 7
BC Muslim School offers an accredited Arabic program.
Farida Wahab, Principal

Richmond: Choice School
Main Campus
20451 Westminster Hwy. North, Richmond, BC V6V 1B3, Canada
Tel: 604-273-2418; *Fax:* 604-273-2419
info@choiceschool.org
www.choiceschool.org
Grades: Pre-Kindergarten - 8
Choice School offers gifted education to talented & gifted children.
Ken Affolder, Principal

Richmond: Cornerstone Christian Academy
7890 No. 5 Rd., Richmond, BC V6Y 2V2, Canada
Tel: 604-303-9181; *Fax:* 604-303-9187
cca@cebccanada.com
www.cebccanada.com
Grades: K.-7
Enrollment: 141
Associated with the Cornerstone Evangelical Baptist Church located on the same property.
W. Kushnir, Principal

Richmond: Richmond Christian School (RCS) Elementary School Campus
5240 Woodwards Rd., Richmond, BC V7E 1H1, Canada
Tel: 604-272-5720; *Fax:* 604-272-7370
info@richmondchristian.ca
www.richmondchristian.ca
Grades: Preschool - 5
Enrollment: 400
The Richmond Christian Elementary School is an independent school, which offers a Christ-centered curriculum.
Richard Macdonald, Chair
Roger Grose, Systems & Elementary Campus Principal
Hugh Mawby, Vice Principal, Elementary Campus
Aza Nakagawa, Business Manager
Darlene Neufeld, Coordinator, Educational Support Services
Judy Sawatsky, Secretary, Elementary Campus & Admissions

***Richmond:* Richmond Christian School (RCS) Middle School Campus**
10200 No. 5 Rd., Richmond, BC V7A 4E5
Tel: 604-274-1122; *Fax:* 604-274-1128
info@richmondchristian.ca
www.richmondchristian.ca
Grades: 6 - 8
Enrollment: 200
The Richmond Christian Middle School provides a Christ-centred community for students.

***Richmond:* Richmond Christian School (RCSS) Secondary School Campus**
10260 No. 5 Rd., Richmond, BC V7A 4E5
Tel: 604-274-1122; *Fax:* 604-274-1128
info@richmondchristian.ca
www.richmondchristian.ca
Grades: 9 - 12
Enrollment: 233
The Richmond Christian Secondary School is an independent school, where students grow academically, physically, & spiritually.

***Richmond:* Richmond Jewish Day School (RJDS)**
8760 No. 5 Rd., Richmond, BC V6Y 2V4, Canada
Tel: 604-275-3393; *Fax:* 604-275-9322
www.rjds.ca
Grades: Preschool - 7
Richmond Jewish Day School incorporates Hebrew & Judaic studies with the British Columbia curriculum.
Jeff Moss, Co-President, Board of Directors
Alan Seltzer, Co-President, Board of Directors
Rebecca Coen, Head of School
rcoen@rjds.ca
Dee Jacobs, Director, Preschool
djacobs@rjds.ca
Mary Jane Brown, Business Manager
mjbrown@rjds.ca
Malki Moshkovitz, Counsellor
mmoshkovitz@rjds.ca
Kelly Koyanagi, Administrative Assistant
kkoyanag@rjds.ca.ca

***Richmond:* St. Joseph the Worker School**
4451 Williams Rd., Richmond, BC V7E 1J7, Canada
Tel: 604-277-1115; *Fax:* 604-272-5214
office@stjo.richmond.bc.ca
Grades: K.-7
Enrollment: 222
M. Jacob, Principal

***Richmond:* St. Paul's School**
8251 St. Alban's Rd., Richmond, BC V6Y 2L2, Canada
Tel: 604-277-4487; *Fax:* 604-277-1810
principal@stpaulschool.ca
www.stpaulschool.ca
Grades: K.-7
Enrollment: 241
Nicole Regush, Principal

***Salmon Arm:* King's Christian School**
350B - 30th St. NE, Salmon Arm, BC V1E 1J2, Canada
Tel: 250-832-5200; *Fax:* 250-832-5201
info@kingschristianschool.com
Grades: K.-12
Enrollment: 214
D. Demeter, Principal

***Shawnigan Lake:* Maxwell International Baha'i School**
P.O. Box 1000
Shawnigan Lake, BC V0R 2W0, Canada
Tel: 250-743-7144; *Fax:* 250-743-3522
Grades: 7-12
Enrollment: 145
D. Vaillancourt, Principal
danv@maxwell.bc.ca

***Shawnigan Lake:* Shawnigan Lake School**
RR#1, 1975 Renfrew Rd., Shawnigan Lake, BC V0R 2W0, Canada
Tel: 250-743-5516; *Fax:* 250-743-6200
info@sls.bc.ca
Grades: 8-12
Enrollment: 444
D. Robertson, Principal

***Smithers:* Bulkley Valley Christian School (BVCS)**
Secondary Campus
P.O. Box 3635
Smithers, Smithers, BC V0J 2N0, Canada
Tel: 250-847-4238
www.bvcs.ca
Other Information: 250-857-9833 (Elementary); 250-847-4238 (Distributed Learning)
Grades: Elementary / Secondary
Bulkley Valley Christian School offers an program for international students.
Klaas Kort, Principal, Elementary Campus, 250-857-9833
Chris Steenhof, Principal, Distributed Learning, 250-847-4238
Hugo VanderHoek, Principal, Secondary Campus, 250-847-4238
Glenda Posthuma, Business Adminstrator, 250-847-4238
John Buikema, Director, Development, Academic Cousellor, & Teacher, 250-847-4238

***Smithers:* Ebenezer Canadian Reformed School**
P.O. Box 3700
1685 Lower Viewmount Rd., Smithers, BC V0J 2N0, Canada
Tel: 250-847-3492; *Fax:* 250-847-3912
ebenezer@bulkley.net
Grades: K.-12
Enrollment: 133
D. Stoffels, Principal

***Smithers:* Moricetown Elementary School**
#2, 205 Beaver Rd., RR#1, Smithers, BC V0J 2N1, Canada
Tel: 250-847-3166; *Fax:* 250-877-5092
school@moricetown.ca
www.moricetown.ca
Grades: Elementary

***Smithers:* St. Joseph's School**
P.O. Box 454
4054 Broadway Ave., Smithers, BC V0J 2N0, Canada
Tel: 250-847-9414; *Fax:* 250-847-9402
stjosephs@telus.net
Grades: K.-7
Enrollment: 191
S. Forbrigger, Principal

***South Hazelton:* Gitsegukla Elementary School**
21 Seymour Ave., RR#1, South Hazelton, BC V0J 2R0, Canada
Tel: 250-849-5739; *Fax:* 250-849-5276
roy.sakata@gitsegukla.org
www.gitsegukla.org
Grades: K.-7
Enrollment: 60
Tuskasa Sakata, Principal

***Summerland:* Glenfir School**
P.O. Box 1800
7808 Pierre Dr., Summerland, BC V0H 1Z0, Canada
Tel: 250-494-0004; *Fax:* 250-494-0058
Toll-Free: 1-866-494-0005
www.glenfir.com
Grades: Junior Kindergarten - 12
Dr. Justin Naude, Chair
justinnaude@shaw.ca
Craig Dunbar, Head of School
Mary Taylor, Managing Director
mtaylor@glenfir.com
Nikki Johnson, Director, Admissions
nikkijohnson@glenfir.com

***Surrey:* Bibleway Christian Academy (BCA)**
18603 - 60th Ave., Surrey, BC V3S 7P4, Canada
Tel: 604-576-8188; *Fax:* 604-576-1370
www.biblewayacademy.org
Grades: Kindergarten - 9
Julius Briner, President
Randall Timmermans, Principal

***Surrey:* Cornerstone Kindergarten**
14724 - 84 Ave., Surrey, BC V3S 2M5, Canada
Tel: 604-599-9918; *Fax:* 604-597-0468
corstone@telus.net
Grades: K.-7
Enrollment: 121
Rita Gausman, Principal

***Surrey:* Diamond Elementary**
18620 - 56th Ave., Surrey, BC V3S 1G1, Canada
Tel: 604-576-1146; *Fax:* 604-574-9831
relevantschool@shawlink.ca
Grades: K.-7
Enrollment: 159
Douglas Smith, Principal

***Surrey:* Fraser Valley Christian High School**
15353 - 92 Ave., Surrey, BC V3R 1C3, Canada
Tel: 604-581-1033; *Fax:* 604-581-1712
fvchs@fvchs.bc.ca
Grades: 8-12
Enrollment: 454
D. de Groot, Principal

***Surrey:* Heritage Christian School**
3487 King George Hwy., Surrey, BC V4P 1B7, Canada
Tel: 604-536-5967; *Fax:* 604-536-6073
hcs@telus.net
Grades: K.-12
Enrollment: 198
T. Bryerton, Principal

***Surrey:* Holy Cross Regional High School**
16193 - 88 Ave., Surrey, BC V4N 1G3, Canada
Tel: 604-581-3023; *Fax:* 604-583-4795
jfraser@idmail.com
Grades: 8-12
Enrollment: 797
Robert Dejulius, Principal

***Surrey:* Iqra School**
14590 - 116A Ave., Surrey, BC V3R 2V1, Canada
Tel: 604-583-7530; *Fax:* 604-583-7510
info@iqraschool.com
Grades: K.-8
Enrollment: 306
W. Ramadan, Principal

***Surrey:* Khalsa School (Surrey)**
6933 - 124th St., Surrey, BC V3W 3W6, Canada
Tel: 604-591-2248; *Fax:* 604-591-3396
Grades: K.-10
Enrollment: 1468
J. Bhatia, Principal
jsbhatia@khalsaschool.ca

***Surrey:* Our Lady of Good Counsel School**
10504 - 139 St., Surrey, BC V3T 4L5, Canada
Tel: 604-581-3154; *Fax:* 604-588-1633
olgcprincipal@shaw.ca
www.ourladyofgoodcounselschool.ca
Grades: K.-7
Enrollment: 245
G. Wright, Principal

***Surrey:* Pacific Academy**
10238 - 168 St., Surrey, BC V4N 1Z4, Canada
Tel: 604-581-5353; *Fax:* 604-581-0087
contact@papcs.com
www.pacificacademy.net
Grades: K.-12
Enrollment: 1450
Private Christian School
T. Kooy, Principal
tkooy@papcs.com

***Surrey:* Regent Christian Academy (RCA)**
15100 - 66A Ave., Surrey, BC V3S 2A6, Canada
Tel: 604-599-8171; *Fax:* 604-599-8175
www.regent.bc.ca
Grades: Preschool - 13
Enrollment: 550
Regent Christian Academy is a coeducational school, which offers primary, middle, high school, English as a Second Language, & international programs.
Paul Johnson, Principal
Linda Mehus-Barber, Administrator, Middle Division
Allan Visser, Administrator, International Division
Amanda Whone, Administrator, Primary Division
Maureen Sayler, Registrar & Secretary

***Surrey:* Relevant Schools' Society Relevant High School**
18620 Hwy. #10, Surrey, BC V3S 1G1, Canada
Tel: 604-574-4736; *Fax:* 604-574-9831
relevantschool@shawlink.ca
www.relevanthighschool.ca
Grades: 8 - 12
Relevant High School is coeducational, non-denominational secondary school.

***Surrey:* Relevant Schools' Society Diamond Elementary School**
18620 Hwy. #10, Surrey, BC V3S 1G1
Tel: 604-576-1146; *Fax:* 604-574-9831
diamondschool@shawlink.ca
www.relevanthighschool.ca
Grades: Kindergarten - 7

***Surrey:* Roots & Wings Montessori Place**
5438 - 152nd St., Surrey, BC V3S 5J9, Canada
Tel: 604-574-5399; *Fax:* 604-574-5319
info@rootsandwingsbc.com
www.rootsandwingsbc.com
Grades: Preschool - Elementary
Primary Montessori programs are offered for children between the ages of 2.5 & 5. The senior program at the school is designed for students from age 9 to 12.

***Surrey:* St. Bernadette School**
13130 - 65B Ave., Surrey, BC V3W 9M1, Canada
Tel: 604-596-1101; *Fax:* 604-596-1550
kkozack@cisva.bc.ca
Grades: K.-7
Enrollment: 227
K. Kozack, Principal

***Surrey:* Southridge Senior School**
2656 - 160 St., Surrey, BC V3S 0B7, Canada
Tel: 604-535-5056; *Fax:* 604-535-3676
Grades: 8-12
Enrollment: 260
M. Ayotte, Head of Senior School
mayotte@southridge.bc.ca

***Surrey:* Star of the Sea School**
15024 - 24 Ave., Surrey, BC V4A 2H8, Canada
Tel: 604-531-6316; *Fax:* 604-531-0171
www.starofthesea.bc.ca/school
Grades: K.-7
Enrollment: 316
L. Balsevich, Principal
lbalsevich@starofthesea.bc.ca

***Surrey:* Surrey Christian School**
9115 - 160 St., Surrey, BC V4N 2X7, Canada
Tel: 604-581-2474; *Fax:* 604-581-5211
primaryoffice@surreychristian.org
www.surreychristian.org
Grades: K.-8
Enrollment: 608
A. Stegeman, Principal

***Surrey:* White Rock Christian Academy**
2265 - 152 St., Surrey, BC V4A 4P1, Canada
Tel: 604-531-9186; *Fax:* 604-531-1727
wrca@wrca.bc.ca
Grades: K.-12
Enrollment: 308
L. Baerg, Principal

***Surrey:* William of Orange Christian School**
P.O. Box 34090
17790 Hwy. 10, Surrey, BC V3S 8C4, Canada
Tel: 604-576-2144; *Fax:* 604-576-0975
admin@wofo.org
Grades: K.-7
Enrollment: 106
J. Siebenga, Principal

***Surrey:* Zion Lutheran**
5950 - 179 St., Surrey, BC V3S 4J9, Canada
Tel: 604-576-6313; *Fax:* 604-576-1399
zionschool@telus.net
Grades: K.-9
Enrollment: 162
D. Davis, Principal

***Terrace:* Centennial Christian School**
3608 Sparks St., Terrace, BC V8G 2V6, Canada
Tel: 250-635-6173; *Fax:* 250-635-9385
ccs@telus.net
www.centennialchristian.ca
Grades: Preschool - 12
Curtis Tuininga, Principal
Edgars Veldman, Vice Principal

***Terrace:* Veritas Catholic School**
4836 Straume Ave., Terrace, BC V8G 4G3, Canada
Tel: 250-635-3035; *Fax:* 250-635-7588
www.veritascatholicschool.com
Grades: Kindergarten - 7
Colleen LeBlanc, Chair
Glen Palahicky, Principal
veritas.principal@telus.net
Isabel DeMedeiros, Secretary
veritas.class@telus.net

***Trail:* St. Michael's Elementary School**
1329 - 4 Ave., Trail, BC V1R 1S3, Canada
Tel: 250-368-6151; *Fax:* 250-368-9962
stmichaelsschool@shaw.ca
Grades: K.-7
Enrollment: 179
D. Nowicki, Principal

***Vancouver:* Blessed Sacrament School**
École Saint Sacrement
3020 Heather St., Vancouver, BC V5Z 3K3, Canada
Tel: 604-876-7211; *Fax:* 604-876-7280
admin@ess.vancouver.bc.ca
moodle.ess.vancouver.bc.ca/moodle
Grades: Kindergarten - 7
Michael Yaptinchay, Director
michael.yaptinchay@ess.vancouver.bc.ca

***Vancouver:* Canadian College International**
#200, 1050 Alberni St., Vancouver, BC V6E 1A3, Canada
Tel: 604-688-9366; *Fax:* 604-688-9322
study@canadiancollege.com
www.canadiancollege.com
Enrollment: 300
Jim Clark, President & Owner
jim.clark@canadiancollege.com
Jeff Carter, Director, Academic
jeff.carter@canadiancollege.com
Cindy Kwon, Director, Marketing
cindy.kwon@canadiancollege.com

***Vancouver:* Century High School (CHS)**
#300, 1788 West Broadway, Vancouver, BC V6J 1Y1, Canada
Tel: 604-730-8138; *Fax:* 604-731-9542
admission@centuryhighschool.ca
www.centuryhighschool.ca
Grades: 8 - 12

***Vancouver:* Columbia College**
#500, 555 Seymour St., Vancouver, BC V6B 6J9, Canada
Tel: 604-683-8360; *Fax:* 604-682-7191
admin@columbiacollege.ca
www.columbiacollege.ca
Enrollment: 57
A liberal arts college offering 1st & 2nd year university transfer courses, associate degrees, university preparation programmes, adult secondary school completion, & English language instruction geared to international students.
Dr. Trevor Toone, Principal

***Vancouver:* Crofton House School**
3200 - 41 Ave. West, Vancouver, BC V6N 3E1, Canada
Tel: 604-263-3255; *Fax:* 604-263-4941
www.croftonhouse.ca
Grades: Elem./Sec.; girls
Enrollment: 667
Patricia J. Dawson, Head of School
pdawson@croftonhouse.ca

***Vancouver:* Fraser Academy**
2294 - 10 Ave. West, Vancouver, BC V6K 2H8, Canada
Tel: 604-736-5575; *Fax:* 604-736-5578
enesling@fraser-academy.bc.ca
Grades: 1-12
Enrollment: 188
E. Nesling, Principal

***Vancouver:* Immaculate Conception School**
3745 - 28 Ave. West, Vancouver, BC V6S 1S6, Canada
Tel: 604-224-5012; *Fax:* 604-224-3721
chit-ics@shaw.ca
Grades: K.-7
Enrollment: 196
C. Riviere, Principal

***Vancouver:* Khalsa School (Vancouver)**
5987 Prince Albert St., Vancouver, BC V5W 3E2, Canada
Tel: 604-321-1226; *Fax:* 604-321-2709
khalsa13@telus.net
Grades: K.-7
Enrollment: 207
Amar Dhaliwal, Principal

***Vancouver:* King David High School**
5718 Willow St., Vancouver, BC V5Z 4S9, Canada
Tel: 604-263-9700; *Fax:* 604-263-4848
Grades: 8-12
Enrollment: 140
E. Seidelman, Principal
pseidelman@telus.net

***Vancouver:* Kingston High School**
2026 - 12th Ave. West, Vancouver, BC V6J 2G2, Canada
Tel: 604-738-6273; *Fax:* 604-738-6974
Grades: Gr. 10-12
Enrollment: 138
Dr. K. Skau, Principal
kskau@exchange.kingston.edu

***Vancouver:* Little Flower Academy**
4195 Alexandra St., Vancouver, BC V6J 4C6, Canada
Tel: 604-738-9016; *Fax:* 604-738-5749
lfa@lfabc.com
Grades: 8-12
Enrollment: 469
M. DeFreitas, Principal

***Vancouver:* LSC Vancouver**
570 Dusmuir St., Vancouver, BC V6B 1Y1, Canada
Tel: 604-683-1199; *Fax:* 604-683-6088
vancouver@lsc-canada.com
www.lsc-canada.com

***Vancouver:* Notre Dame Regional Secondary School**
2855 Parker St., Vancouver, BC V5K 2T8, Canada
Tel: 604-255-5454; *Fax:* 604-255-2115
www.ndrs.ca
Grades: 8 - 12
Enrollment: 620
Notre Dame Regional Secondary School is a Catholic school.
Mr. R. DesLauriers, Principal
Mr. R. Gabriele, Vice Principal
Mr. G. Oswald, Vice Principal
Mrs. M. Grant, Manager, Office

***Vancouver:* Our Lady of Perpetual Help School**
2550 Camosun St., Vancouver, BC V6R 3W6, Canada
Tel: 604-228-8811; *Fax:* 604-224-6822
Grades: K.-7
Enrollment: 406
Lora Clarke, Acting Principal

***Vancouver:* Our Lady of Sorrows School**
575 Slocan St., Vancouver, BC V5K 3X5, Canada
Tel: 604-253-2434; *Fax:* 604-253-1523
ourladyofsorrows1@telus.net
www.ourladyofsorrows.ca
Grades: K.-7
Enrollment: 231
P. Balletta, Principal

***Vancouver:* Pacific Spirit School**
Jericho Hill Centre
4196 West 4th Ave., Vancouver, BC V6J 4J5, Canada
Tel: 604-222-1900; *Fax:* 604-222-1934
info@pacificspiritschool.org
www.pacificspiritschool.org
Grades: K.-7
Enrollment: 227
Formerly Life Song School, Pacific Spirit School is the flagship for the New Learning Society, which promotes and supports the growth of the whole child.
Ingrid Price, Ph.D., Executive Director

***Vancouver:* Royal Canadian College**
8610 Ash St., Vancouver, BC V6P 3M2, Canada
Tel: 604-738-2221; *Fax:* 604-738-2282
info@royalcanadiancollege.com
Grades: 10-12
Enrollment: 52
H. Jiang, Principal

***Vancouver:* St. Andrew's School**
450 - 47th Ave. East, Vancouver, BC V5W 2B4, Canada
Tel: 604-325-6317; *Fax:* 604-325-0920
saintandrews@telus.net
Grades: K.-7
Enrollment: 227
M. Mailley, Principal

***Vancouver:* St. Anthony of Padua**
1370 - 73rd Ave. West, Vancouver, BC V6P 3E8, Canada
Tel: 604-261-4043; *Fax:* 604-261-4036
office@stanthonyofpaduaschool.ca
www.stanthonyofpaduaschool.ca
Grades: K.-7
Enrollment: 209
C. Kraemer, Principal

***Vancouver:* St. Augustine's School**
2145 - 8 Ave. West, Vancouver, BC V6K 2A5, Canada
Tel: 604-731-8024; *Fax:* 604-739-1712
info@faithandfoundation.com
www.faithandfoundation.com
Grades: K.-7
Enrollment: 224
Catherine Oberndorf, Principal

***Vancouver:* St. Francis of Assisi School**
870 Victoria Dr., Vancouver, BC V5L 4E7, Canada
Tel: 604-253-7311; *Fax:* 604-253-7375
sfaprincipal@telus.net

Grades: K.-7
Enrollment: 191
Joan Sandberg, Principal

***Vancouver:* St. Francis Xavier School**
428 Great Northern Way, Vancouver, BC V5T 4S5, Canada
Tel: 604-254-2714; *Fax:* 604-254-2514
sfxs@telus.net

Grades: K.-7
Enrollment: 327
B. Krivuzoff, Principal

***Vancouver:* St. George's School**
4175 - 29 Ave. West, Vancouver, BC V6S 1V1, Canada
Tel: 604-224-1304; *Fax:* 604-224-7066
sradmin@stgeorges.bc.ca
www.stgeorges.bc.ca

Grades: 1-12
Enrollment: 1123
Day and boarding school for boys
Nigel Toy, Headmaster

***Vancouver:* St. John's International**
1885 West Broadway, Vancouver, BC V6J 1Y5, Canada
Tel: 604-683-4572; *Fax:* 604-683-4679
general@stjohnsis.com
www.stjohnsis.com

Grades: 8-12
Enrollment: 76
L. Fast, Principal

***Vancouver:* St. John's School**
2215 - 10 Ave. West, Vancouver, BC V6K 2J1, Canada
Tel: 604-732-4434; *Fax:* 604-732-1074
info@stjohns.bc.ca
www.stjohns.bc.ca

Grades: K.-12
Enrollment: 342
University prep school
S. Hutchison, Headmaster
shutchison@stjohns.bc.ca

***Vancouver:* St. Joseph's School**
3261 Fleming St., Vancouver, BC V5N 3V6, Canada
Tel: 604-872-5715; *Fax:* 604-872-5700
stjosephsvancouver@telus.net
www.stjoesschool-vancouver.org

Grades: K.-7
Enrollment: 210
Dierdre O'Callaghan, Principal

***Vancouver:* St. Jude's School**
2953 - 15 Ave. East, Vancouver, BC V5M 2K7, Canada
Tel: 604-434-1633; *Fax:* 604-434-8677
stjude@shawcable.com

Grades: K.-7
Enrollment: 221
M. Perry, Principal

***Vancouver:* St. Mary's School**
5239 Joyce St., Vancouver, BC V5R 4G8, Canada
Tel: 604-437-1312; *Fax:* 604-437-1193

Grades: K.-7
Enrollment: 230
K. Smith, Principal
ksmith@cisva.bc.ca

***Vancouver:* St. Patrick Regional Secondary School**
115 - 11 Ave. East, Vancouver, BC V5T 2C1, Canada
Tel: 604-874-6422; *Fax:* 604-874-5176
administration@stpats.bc.ca

Grades: 8-12
Enrollment: 501
J. Bevacqua, Principal
jbevacqua@stpats.bc.ca

***Vancouver:* St. Patrick's Elementary School**
2850 Quebec St., Vancouver, BC V5T 3A9, Canada
Tel: 604-879-4411; *Fax:* 604-879-3737

Grades: K.-7
Enrollment: 249
M. Boreham, Principal
mboreham@shaw.ca

***Vancouver:* Stratford Hall**
3000 Commercial Dr., Vancouver, BC V5N 4E2, Canada
Tel: 604-436-0608; *Fax:* 604-436-0616
info@stratfordhall.ca
www.stratfordhall.ca

Grades: K.-12
Enrollment: 370
J. McConnell, Principal

***Vancouver:* Vancouver Christian School (VCS)**
3496 Mons Dr., Vancouver, BC V5M 3E6, Canada
Tel: 604-435-3113; *Fax:* 604-430-1591
office@vancouverchristian.org
www.vancouverchristian.org
Other Information: 604-523-1580 (Phone, Carver Christian High School)

Grades: Kindergarten - 12
Vancouver Christian School is an independent, interdenominational school. Grades nine to twelve are offered at Carver Christian High School.
Mrs. E. Freestone, Principal
Mrs. Wiebe, Vice Principal, Kindergarten - Grade 5
Miss Wong, Vice Principal, Grades 6 to 8

***Vancouver:* Vancouver College**
5400 Cartier St., Vancouver, BC V6M 3A5, Canada
Tel: 604-261-4285; *Fax:* 604-261-2284
info@vc.bc.ca
www.vc.bc.ca

Grades: Kindergarten - 12
Enrollment: 1000
Vancouver College consists of an elementary school, a middle school, & a senior school.
John McFarland, Principal
jmcfarland@vc.bc.ca
Mary-Joy Derouin, Assistant Principal, Senior School
Michel DesLauriers, Assistant Principal, Middle School
Barbara Seppelt, Assistant Principal, Elementary School
Kelly Lattimer, Business Manager
Ronith Cogswell, Athletic Director & Communications Officer
Mr. Kim Findlay, Chief Development Officer
Rev. John Horgan, Chaplain
Margaret Vossen, Registrar
Wade Anderson, Department Head, Physical Education
Monica Beck, Department Head, Student Services
Henry Budai, Department Head, Second Languages
Anne Field, Department Head, English
Br. Charles Gattone, Department Head, Religion
Marilia Marghetti, Department Head, Sciences
Enzo Nardi, Department Head, Mathematics
Larry Olson, Department Head, Applied / Fine Arts
Lilian Vernier, Department Head, Social Studies

***Vancouver:* Vancouver Hebrew Academy**
1545 West 62nd Ave., Vancouver, BC V6P 2E8, Canada
Tel: 604-266-1245; *Fax:* 604-264-0648
vha@vhebrewacademy.com
www.vhebrewacademy.com

Grades: Preschool - 10
Vancouver Hebrew Academy is an Orthodox Jewish school which offers Judaic & general studies.
Rabbi Don Pacht, Head of School
Patricia Haslop, Principal
Nancy Scambler, Administrative Secretary

***Vancouver:* Vancouver Montessori School**
8650 Barnard St., Vancouver, BC V6P 5G5, Canada
Tel: 604-261-0315
www.vancouvermontessorischool.com

Grades: Preschool - Elementary
Preschool (Casa) programs are available for three to six year old children. Elementary classes are offered for children from age six to twelve.
Prasannata Runkel, Principal
Roni (Bamendine) Jones, Administrator, School Operations
Chrystle Williams, Registrar & Administration Assistant

***Vancouver:* Vancouver Talmud Torah School (VTT)**
998 West 26th Ave., Vancouver, BC V5Z 2G1, Canada
Tel: 604-736-7307; *Fax:* 604-736-9754
info@talmudtorah.com
sites.google.com/a/vttschool.ca/vtt1/Home

Grades: Preschool - 7
Enrollment: 500
Vancouver Talmud Torah School is a Jewish day school.
Cathy Lowenstein, B.Ed., M.Ed., Principal
Janice St. Helene, Vice Principal, General Studies
Judith Wolfman, Vice Principal, Judaic Studies
Adam Gelmon, Director, Admissions & School-Wide Programs
Gaby Lutrin, Director, Preschool
Mark Maibauer, Director, Operations
Jessica Neville, Director, Student Services
Jennifer Shecter-Balin, Director, Communications

***Vancouver:* West Coast Christian School (WCCS)**
15 North Renfrew St., Vancouver, BC V5K 3N6, Canada
Tel: 604-255-2990; *Fax:* 604-255-2103
school@wccf.bc.ca
www.westcoastchristianschool.ca

Grades: Kindergarten - 12
Enrollment: 100
The school is a ministry of West Coast Christian Fellowship. It offers a Christian approach to learning.
David Ferguson, Principal
Marcellina Arnold, Secretary

***Vancouver:* West Point Grey Academy (WPGA)**
4125 West 8th Ave., Vancouver, BC V6R 4P9, Canada
Tel: 604-222-8750; *Fax:* 604-222-8756
admissions@wpga.ca
www.wpga.ca
Other Information: 604-224-1332 (Phone, Senior School)

Grades: Preschool - 12
Enrollment: 905
West Point Grey Academy demonstrates a belief in Humanism in its community of Renaissance learners. The pre-kindergarten class is for four year old children.
Robert Standerwick, Chair
boardchair@wpga.ca
Clive S.K. Austin, Headmaster
headmaster@wpga.ca
Stephen Anthony, Head, Senior School
headmaster@wpga.ca

***Vancouver:* York House School**
4176 Alexandra St., Vancouver, BC V6J 2V6, Canada
Tel: 604-736-6551; *Fax:* 604-736-6530
info@yorkhouse.ca

Grades: K.-12
Enrollment: 598
G. Ruddy, Principal

***Vanderhoof:* Northside Christian School**
3337 Voth Rd., RR#2, Vanderhoof, BC V0J 3A2, Canada
Tel: 250-567-9335; *Fax:* 250-567-9332
ncadmin@telus.net

Grades: 1 - 12
Enrollment: 67
Michael Shenk, Principal

***Vanderhoof:* Rainbow Christian School**
P.O. Box 710
2994 Burrard Ave., Vanderhoof, BC V0J 3A0, Canada
Tel: 250-567-3127; *Fax:* 250-567-3167
rcschool@telus.net

Grades: Kindergarten - 8
Enrollment: 80
The day school offers a Christ-centered learning environment.

***Vanderhoof:* St. Joseph's School**
P.O. Box 1429
Vanderhoof, BC V0J 3A0, Canada
Tel: 250-567-2794; *Fax:* 250-567-2333
gillis.stjoes1@telus.net

Grades: K.-7
Enrollment: 92
G. Gillis, Principal

***Vernon:* Pleasant Valley Christian Academy**
1802 - 45th Ave., Vernon, BC V1T 3M7, Canada
Tel: 250-545-7852; *Fax:* 250-545-9230
pvadmin@shaw.ca

Grades: K.-9
Enrollment: 30
Affiliated with the Seventh-day Adventist Church
R. Tiller, Principal

***Vernon:* St. James School**
2700 - 28 Ave., Vernon, BC V1T 1V7, Canada
Tel: 250-542-4081; *Fax:* 250-542-5696
principalsjs@shaw.ca

Grades: K.-7
Enrollment: 106
G. Higginson, Principal

***Vernon:* Vernon Christian School**
Elementary Campus
6890 Pleasant Valley Rd., Vernon, BC V1B 3R5, Canada
Tel: 250-545-7345; *Fax:* 250-545-0254
info@vcs.ca
www.vcs.ca

Grades: Kindergarten - 12
Enrollment: 350
TVernon Christian School is an interdenominational school. The school's secondary campus is located at 6920 Pleasant Valley Road.
Karen Wiseman, Chair
kwiseman@vcs.ca
Larry Simpson, Principal
lsimpson@vcs.ca
Matt Driediger, Assistant Principal, Secondary Campus
mdriediger@vcs.ca
Steve Onsorge, Assistant Principal, Elementary Campus
sonsorge@vcs.ca

***Victoria:* Christ Church Cathedral School (CCCS)**
Cathedral Memorial Hall
912 Vancouver St., Victoria, BC V8V 3V7, Canada
Tel: 250-383-5125; *Fax:* 250-383-5128
cathedralschool@cathedralschool.ca (office)
www.cathedralschool.ca
Grades: Kindergarten - 8
Enrollment: 155
Christ Church Cathedral School is an Anglican school attached to a cathedral.
Mary Hendy, President
Charles Peacock, Head of School
head@cathedralschool.ca
Tobi Blue, Assistant Head, Elementary Grades
Marylee McKeown, Assistant Head, Middle & Intermediate Grades

***Victoria:* Glenlyon Norfolk School**
801 Bank St., Victoria, BC V8S 4A8, Canada
Tel: 250-370-6800; *Fax:* 250-370-6840
gns@mygns.ca
www.glenlyonnorfolk.bc.ca
Grades: K.-12
Enrollment: 643
Simon Bruce-Lockhart, Head of School

***Victoria:* Greater Victoria Christian Academy**
98 Cadillac Ave., Victoria, BC V8Z 1T4, Canada
Tel: 250-475-2977; *Fax:* 250-475-2988
deborah.arcuri@gvca.ca
Grades: K.-12
Enrollment: 179
L. Makaroff, Principal

***Victoria:* Lakeview Christian School**
729 Cordova Bay Rd., Victoria, BC V8Y 1P7, Canada
Tel: 250-658-5082; *Fax:* 250-658-5072
lakeviewschool@shaw.ca
Grades: K.-7
Enrollment: 71
A. Oosterhof, Principal

***Victoria:* Lighthouse Christian Academy**
1289 Parkdale Dr., Victoria, BC V9B 4G9, Canada
Tel: 250-474-5311; *Fax:* 250-474-5021
info@lighthousechristianacademy.com
Grades: K.-9
Enrollment: 70
D. Hunwick, Principal

***Victoria:* Maria Montessori Academy**
4052 Wilkinson Rd., Victoria, BC V8Z 5A5, Canada
Tel: 250-479-4746; *Fax:* 250-744-1925
mma@montessori.bc.ca
Grades: K.-7
Enrollment: 95
B. McDermitt, Principal

***Victoria:* Pacific Christian School**
654 Agnes St., Victoria, BC V8Z 2E7, Canada
Tel: 250-479-9365; *Fax:* 250-479-3685
www.pacificchristian.ca
Grades: K.-12
Enrollment: 1000
B. Helmus, Principal
bhelmus@pacificchristian.ca

***Victoria:* St. Andrew's Regional High School**
880 Mckenzie Ave., Victoria, BC V8X 3G5, Canada
Tel: 250-479-1414; *Fax:* 250-479-5356
wjamieson@cisdv.bc.ca
www.standrewshigh.ca
Grades: 8-12
Enrollment: 469
W. Jamieson, Principal

***Victoria:* St. Andrew's School**
1002 Pandora Ave., Victoria, BC V8V 3P5, Canada
Tel: 250-382-3815; *Fax:* 250-385-3830
kpollard@cisdv.bc.ca
Grades: K.-7
Enrollment: 188
K. Pollard, Principal

***Victoria:* St. Joseph's Catholic School**
757 Burnside Rd. West, Victoria, BC V8Z 1M9, Canada
Tel: 250-479-1232; *Fax:* 250-479-1907
sdicastri@cisdv.bc.ca
Grades: K.-7
Enrollment: 203
S. Di Castri, Principal

***Victoria:* St. Margaret's School**
1080 Lucas Ave., Victoria, BC V8X 3P7, Canada
Tel: 250-479-7171; *Fax:* 250-479-3244
stmarg@stmarg.ca
www.stmarg.ca
Grades: K.-12
Enrollment: 325
L. Mcgregor, Principal
lmcgregor@stmarg.ca

***Victoria:* St. Michael's University School (Junior)**
820 Victoria Ave., Victoria, BC V8S 4N3, Canada
Tel: 250-598-3922; *Fax:* 250-592-0783
nrichards@smus.ca
www.smus.ca
Grades: K.-5
Enrollment: 160
University prep boarding school
Nancy Richards, Principal

***Victoria:* St. Michael's University School (Middle)**
3400 Richmond Rd., Victoria, BC V8P 4P5, Canada
Tel: 250-592-3549; *Fax:* 250-592-3942
www.smus.bc.ca
Grades: 6-8
Enrollment: 204
X. Abrioux, Principal
xabrioux@smus.bc.ca

***Victoria:* St. Michael's University School (Senior)**
3400 Richmond Rd., Victoria, BC V8P 4P5, Canada
Tel: 250-592-2411; *Fax:* 250-592-2812
www.smus.bc.ca
Grades: 9-12
Enrollment: 573
K. Roth, Principal
kathy.roth@smus.bc.ca

***Victoria:* St. Patrick's School**
2368 Trent St., Victoria, BC V8R 4Z3, Canada
Tel: 250-592-6713; *Fax:* 250-592-6717
pmckenna@cisdv.bc.ca
Grades: K.-7
Enrollment: 355
P. McKenna, Principal

***Victoria:* Selkirk Montessori School**
2970 Jutland Rd., Victoria, BC V8T 5K2, Canada
Tel: 250-384-3414; *Fax:* 250-384-3449
office@selkirkmontessori.ca
www.selkirkmontessori.ca
Grades: K.
Enrollment: 202
G. Henry, Interim Academic Head

***Victoria:* West-Mont School**
4075 Metchosin Rd., Victoria, BC V9C 4A4, Canada
Tel: 250-474-2626; *Fax:* 250-478-8944
info@west-mont.ca
www.west-mont.ca
Grades: Preschool - 7
West-Mont School provides a Montessori preschool to grade three. For students in grades four to seven, an enriched British Columbia curriculum is offered. The school is operated by the Western Communities Montessori Society.
Bruce Laurie, Principal
Cory Meausette, Vice Principal
Barbara Kennelly, Manager, Business
bkennelly@west-mont.ca
Barb Lewis, Head, Admissions
admissions@west-mont.ca

***Waglisla:* Bella Bella Community School (BBCS)**
General Delivery, Waglisla, BC V0T 1Z0, Canada
Tel: 250-957-2391; *Fax:* 250-957-2691
Brendah@bellabella.net
www.bellabella.ca
Grades: Nursery - Secondary
Brenda Humchitt, Principal
Jason Cobey, Vice Principal
Frances Brown, Head, Heiltsuk Language Program

***West Vancouver:* Collingwood School**
70 Morven Dr., West Vancouver, BC V7S 1B2, Canada
Tel: 604-925-3331; *Fax:* 604-925-3862
jonna.mcguinness@collingwood.org
Grades: K.-12
Enrollment: 1196
R. Wright, Principal

***West Vancouver:* Mulgrave School**
2330 Cypress Lane, West Vancouver, BC V7S 3H9, Canada
Tel: 604-922-3223; *Fax:* 604-922-3328
info@mulgrave.com
www.mulgrave.com
Grades: Kindergarten - 12
The coeducational, non-denominational school is an IB World School.
Donald Kirkwood, Chair
Tony Macoun, Head of School
tmacoun@mulgrave.com
Derek Muzyka, Head, Finance
dmuzyka@mulgrave.com
Graham Gilley, Director, Educational Technology
ggilley@mulgrave.com
Martin Jones, Director, Summer Camp Programmes
mjones@mulgrave.com
Luke Lawson, Director, University Counselling
Tony Macoun, Director, Advancement
tmacoun@mulgrave.com
Mark Steffens, Director, Community Relations
msteffens@mulgrave.com
Lesley Tetiker, Director, Admissions
ltetiker@mulgrave.com

***West Vancouver:* St. Anthony's School**
595 Keith Rd., West Vancouver, BC V7T 1L8, Canada
Tel: 604-922-0011; *Fax:* 604-922-3196
office@saswv.ca
www.saswv.ca
Grades: K.-7
Enrollment: 204
Laila Maravillas, Principal
principal@saswv.ca

***Westbank:* Our Lady of Lourdes Elementary School**
2547 Hebert Rd., Westbank, BC V4T 2J6, Canada
Tel: 250-768-9008; *Fax:* 250-768-0168
adminolol@telus.net
www.ourladyoflourdeswestbank.com
Grades: K.-7
Enrollment: 132
M. Manton, Principal

***Westbank:* Sensisyusten House of Learning**
1920 Quail Lane, Westbank, BC V4T 2H3, Canada
Tel: 250-768-2802; *Fax:* 250-768-5462
school@wfn.ca
Grades: K.-6
Enrollment: 36
R. Howardson, Principal

***Williams Lake:* Cariboo Adventist Academy**
1405 South Lakeside Dr., Williams Lake, BC V2G 3A7, Canada
Tel: 250-392-4741
cacademy@yahoo.com
www.caribooadventistacademy.ca
Grades: Kindergarten - 12
The Cariboo Adventist Academy is operated by the Seventh-day Adventist Church.

***Williams Lake:* Maranatha Christian School**
1278 Lakeview Cres., Williams Lake, BC V2G 1A3, Canada
Tel: 250-392-7410; *Fax:* 250-392-2823
maranatha@telus.net
Grades: K.-12
Enrollment: 128
C. Klaue, Principal

***Williams Lake:* Sacred Heart Catholic School**
455 Pigeon Ave., Williams Lake, BC V2G 4R5, Canada
Tel: 250-398-7770; *Fax:* 250-398-7725
principal.shcs@telus.net
Grades: K.-7
Enrollment: 84
Donna Ameerali, Principal

Universities & Colleges

Universities

***Abbotsford:* Summit Pacific College**
P.O. Box 1700
35235 Straiton Rd., Abbotsford, BC V2S 7E7, Canada
Tel: 604-853-7491; *Fax:* 604-853-8951
Toll-Free: 1-800-976-8388
www.summitpacific.ca
Formerly Western Pentecostal Bible College

Burnaby: Simon Fraser University
8888 University Dr., Burnaby, BC V5A 1S6, Canada
Tel: 604-291-3111
www.sfu.ca

Full Time Equivalency: 30313
Dr. Brandt C. Louie, Chancellor
Dr. Michael Stevenson, B.A., M.A, Ph.D., President & Vice-Chancellor
Dr. Jon Driver, Vice-President
Pat Hibbitts, B.A., M.B.A., Vice-President
Mario Pinto, Vice-President
William Krane, B.A., M.A., Ph.D., Assoc. Vice-President
Kate Ross, Registrar
Lynn Copeland, B.Sc., M.A., M.L.S., University Librarian & Dean
R. Szczotko, Manager
Biff Savoie, B.A., Director
Gregg Macdonald, B.A., M.A., Executive Director
Warren Gill, B.A., M.A., Ph.D., Vice-President
Joe Weinberg, Assoc. Vice-President
Judith Osborne, LL.B., M.A., LL.M., Vice-President
Joanne Curry, B.Sc., Ph.D., Executive Director
Cathy Daminato, Vice-President

Faculties
Applied Sciences
Brian Lewis, B.A., M.A., Ph.D., Dean

Arts
John T. Pierce, B.A., M.A., Ph.D., Dean

Business Administration
Daniel Shapiro, B.A., M.A., Ph.D., Dean

Continuing Studies
John Labrie, Ph.D., Dean

Education
Paul Shaker, B.A., M.A., Ph.D., Dean

Graduate Studies
Wade Parkhouse, B.P.E., M.P.E., Ph.D., Dean

Health Sciences
David MacLean, Ph.D., Dean

Science
Michael Plischke, B.Sc., M.Phil., Ph.D., Dean

Publications
Alumni Journal
c/o Simon Fraser University
8888 University Dr., Burnaby, BC V5A 1S6, Canada

The Peak

Kamloops: Thompson Rivers University
P.O. Box 3010
900 McGill Rd., Kamloops, BC V2C 5N3, Canada
Tel: 250-828-5000; *Fax:* 250-828-5086
Toll-Free: 800-663-1663
admissions@tru.ca
www.tru.ca

Full Time Equivalency: 7632
With distance-learning, enrolment figures swell to over 25,000 students.
The Hon Nancy Greene Raine, Chancellor
Dr Roger H. Barnsley, Interim President & Vice-chancellor, 250-828-5001
president@tru.ca
Dr Ulrich Scheck, Provost & Vice-Pres., Academic, 250-377-6126
uscheck@tru.ca
Cliff Neufeld, Vice-Pres., Admin. & Finance, 250-828-5012
Christopher Seguin, Vice-Pres., Advancement, 250-574-0474
cseguin@tru.ca
Judith Murray, Vice-Pres., Open Learning, 250-828-5007
judithmurray@tru.ca

Faculties
Arts
Tel: 250-371-5566; *Fax:* 250-371-5510
baadvising@tru.ca

Dr Michael Mehta, Dean, 250-852-7275
mmehta@tru.ca

Science
Dr Tom Dickinson, Dean, 250-852-7137
tdickinson@tru.ca

Human, Social, and Educational Development
Dr. Charles F. Webber, Dean, 250-828-5249
cwebber@tru.ca

Law
Chris Axworthy, QC, Dean, 250-852-7267
caxworthy@tru.ca

Schools
Business and Economics (SoBE)
Dr. Murray Young, Dean, 250-828-5217
myoung@tru.ca

Nursing
Barbara Paterson, Dean, 250-852-7288
bpaterson@tru.ca

Tourism
Harold Richins, Dean, 250-852-7138
hrichins@tru.ca

Trades & Technology
Lindsay Langill, Dean, 250-828-5110
lblangill@tru.ca

Campuses
100 Mile House Centre
P.O. Box 2109
485 South Birch Ave., 100 Mile House, BC V0K 2E0, Canada
Tel: 250-395-3115; *Fax:* 250-395-2894
Robin Bercowski, Coordinator
rbercowski@tru.ca

Ashcroft/Cache Creek Centre
P.O. Box 1419
310 Railway Ave., Ashcroft, BC V0K 1A0, Canada
Tel: 250-453-9999; *Fax:* 250-453-2518
Sloane Hammond, Coordinator
shammond@tru.ca

Barriere Centre
629 Barriere Town Rd., Barriere, BC V0E 1E0, Canada
Tel: 250-672-9875; *Fax:* 250-672-9875
Susan Ross, Coordinator
sross@tru.ca

Clearwater Centre
Also known as: North Thompson Community Skills Centre
751 Clearwater Village Rd., RR#1, Clearwater, BC V0E 1N0, Canada
Tel: 250-674-3530; *Fax:* 250-674-3540
Sylvia Arduini, Coordinator
sarduini@tru.ca

Lillooet Centre
P.O. Box 339
#10, 155 Main St., Lillooet, BC V0K 1V0, Canada
Tel: 250-256-4296; *Fax:* 250-256-4278
Jane Bryson, Coordinator
jbryson@tru.ca

Williams Lake Campus
1250 Western Ave., Williams Lake, BC V2G 1H7, Canada
Tel: 250-392-8000; *Fax:* 250-392-4984
Toll-Free: 800-663-4936
wlmain@tru.ca

Open Learning Division
P.O. Box 3010
900McGill Rd., Kamloops, BC V2C 5N3, Canada
Tel: 250-852-7000; *Fax:* 250-852-6405
Toll-Free: 1-800-663-1663
student@tru.ca

Publications
The Omega
Tel: 250-372-1272; *Fax:* 250-372-5331
theomega.ca

Sadie Cox, Editor-In-Chief
editorofomega@gmail.com

Langley: The Associated Canadian Theological Schools of Trinity Western University
Also known as: ACTS
7600 Glover Rd., Langley, BC V2Y 1Y1, Canada
Tel: 604-888-6045; *Fax:* 604-513-2045
acts@twu.ca

Langley: Canadian Baptist Seminary
7600 Glover Rd., Langley, BC V2Y 1Y1, Canada
Tel: 604-513-2015; *Fax:* 604-513-2078
canadianbaptistseminary.com

Full Time Equivalency: 23
This institution is one of six seminaries representative of other denominations forming a consortium called Associated Canadian Theological Seminaries (ACTS). It is located on the Trinity Western University campus.

Langley: Canadian Pentecostal Seminary
Fosmark Bldg.
7600 Glover Rd., Langley, BC V2Y 1Y1, Canada
Tel: 604-513-2161; *Fax:* 604-513-2078
cps@twu.ca
canadianpentecostalseminary.ca

This institution is in partnership with Trinity Western University, and with five other denominations, to form ACTS, the Associated Canadian Theological Schools. It is located on the Trinity Western U. campus.

Langley: Canadian Theological Seminary
7600 Glover Rd., Langley, BC V2Y 1Y1, Canada
Tel: 604-888-7511

Langley: Mennonite Brethren Biblical Seminary - BC
7600 Glover Rd., Langley, BC V2Y 1Y1, Canada
Tel: 604-513-2133

Langley: Northwest Baptist Seminary
P.O. Box 790
Langley, BC V1M 2S2, Canada
Tel: 604-888-3310

Langley: Trinity Western University
7600 Glover Rd., Langley, BC V2Y 1Y1, Canada
Tel: 604-888-7511; *Fax:* 604-513-2061
admissions@twu.ca
www.twu.ca

Full Time Equivalency: 2510
Dr Jonathan S. Raymond, President
president@twu.ca
Paul Weme, Vice-Pres., Strategic Advancement
paul.weme@twu.ca
David Coons, Vice-Pres., Developemnt
david.coons@twu.ca
Jim Poulsen, Vice-Pres., Finance
poulsen@twu.ca
Joan van Dyck, Vice-Pres., University Communications
joan.vandyck@twu.ca
Dennis Jameson, Provost
jameson@twu.ca
Alma Barranco-Mendoza, Exec. Dir., Information Technology
alma.barranco@twu.ca
Janis Ryder, Exec. Dir., Human Resources
janis.ryder@twu.ca
Scott Henderson, Dir., University Enterprises
scott.henderson@twu.ca
Grant McMillan, Registrar, 604-513-2070, fax: 604-513-2096
registrar@twu.ca

Faculties
Natural & Applied Sciences
Dr Ka Yin Leung, Dean
kayin.leung@twu.ca

Humanities & Social Sciences
Dr Robert K. Burkinshaw, Dean
burkinsh@twu.ca

Professional Studies & Performing Arts
David Squires, Dean
david.squires@twu.ca

Schools
Graduate Studies
Tel: 604-513-2019; *Fax:* 604-513-2064
Toll-Free: 888-468-6898
gradadmissions@twu.ca

Dr William R. Acton, Interim Dean
william.acton@twu.ca

Business
Andrea Soberg, Dean, 604-513-2137, fax: 604-513-2042
andreas@twu.ca

Education
Dr Kimberly Franklin, Dean, 604-513-2105
kimberly.franklin@twu.ca

Human Kinetics
Dr Blair Whitmarsh, Dean, 604-513-2121, ext. 2114
whitmars@twu.ca

Nursing
Dr Landa Terblanche, Dean, 604-888-7511, ext. 3268, fax: 604-513-2012
landa.terblanche@twu.ca

Affiliations
Associated Canadian Theological Seminaries of Trinity Western University (ACTS)
Also known as: ACTS Seminaries
7600 Glover Rd., Langley, BC V2Y 1Y1, Canada
Tel: 604-513-2044; *Fax:* 604-513-2078
acts@twu.ca
acts.twu.ca

Dr John W. Auxier, Acting President & Dean
auxier@twu.ca

Canadian Baptist Seminary
7600 Glover Rd., Langley, BC V2Y 1Y1, Canada
Tel: 604-513-2015; *Fax:* 604-513-2078
canadianbaptistseminary.com

Dr Ed Stuckey, Interim President
estuckey@journeycentre.ca
Cal Netterfield, D.Min., Vice-Pres., Development, ext. 3805
cal.netterfield@twu.ca
Dr Daryl Busby, Dean, ext. 3833
daryl@twu.ca
Wendell Phillips, Registrar, ext. 3807
phillips@twu.ca

Canadian Pentecostal Seminary
7600 Glover Rd., Langley, BC V2Y 1Y1, Canada
Tel: 604-513-2161; *Fax:* 604-513-2078
cps@twu.ca
canadianpentecostalseminary.ca

Dr. Jim Lucas, President
jim@clcc.ca
Dr Joanne Pepper, Dean

Mennonite Brethren Biblical Seminary - BC
7600 Glover Rd., Langley, BC V2Y 1Y1, Canada
Tel: 604-513-2044; *Fax:* 604-513-2078

Dr Lynn Jost, Acting-President

Northwest Baptist Seminary
7600 Glover Rd., Langley, BC V2Y 1Y1, Canada
Tel: 604-888-7592; *Fax:* 604-637-3212
www.nbseminary.ca

Dr Larry Perkins, President, ext. 3861
Loren Warkentin, Registrar, ext. 3866

Trinity Western Seminary
7600 Glover Rd., Langley, BC V2Y 1Y1, Canada
Tel: 604-513-2044; *Fax:* 604-513-2078

Dr John Auxier, Acting-President

Pacific Summit College
P.O. Box 1700
35235 Straiton Rd., Abbotsford, BC V2S 7E7, Canada
Tel: 604-853-7491; *Fax:* 604-853-8951
Toll-Free: 800-976-8388
pr@summitpacific.ca
www.summitpacific.ca

Formerly Western Pentecostal Bible College
Dr Dave Demchuk, President
ddemchuk@summitpacific.ca
Melody Deeley, Registrar
registrar@summitpacific.ca

North Vancouver: Capilano University

Lynmour Campus
2055 Purcell Way, North Vancouver, BC V7J 3H5, Canada
Tel: 604-986-1911; *Fax:* 604-984-4985
www.capilanou.ca
TTY: 604-990-7848

Full Time Equivalency: 14500
Peter Ufford, Chancellor
Dr. Kris Bulcroft, President/Vice-Chancellor, 604-984-4925
kbulcrof@capilanou.ca
Cindy Turner, VP, Finance & Administration, 604-984-4937
cturner@capilanou.ca
Dr Jacalyn Snodgrass, VP, Education - Academic & Arts Programs, 604-984-1740
jsnodgra@capilanou.ca
Catherine Vertesi, VP, Education - Mgmt. & International Programs, 604-990-7894
cvertesi@capilanou.ca
Dr Patrick Donahoe, VP, Student and Institutional Support, 604-984-4975
pdonahoe@capilanou.ca
Mike Arbogast, VP, Human Resources, 604-984-4991
marbogas@capilanou.ca
Cheryl Helm, Acting Registrar, 604-983-7506
chelm@capilanou.ca

Faculties

Arts & Science
Dr Robert Campbell, Dean, 604-984-4976
robertc@capilanou.ca

Business
Graham Fane, Dean, 604-984-4988
gfane@capilanou.ca

Fine & Applied Arts
Jennifer Moore, Dean, 604-990-7801
jmoore2@capilanou.ca

Health & Education
Jean Bennett, Dean, 604-990-7982
jbennett@capilanou.ca

Tourism & Outdoor Recreation
Dr Chris Bottrill, Dean, 604-983-7586
cbottril@capilanou.ca

Campuses

Squamish
P.O. Box 1538
1150 Carson Pl., Squamish, BC V8B 0B1, Canada
Tel: 604-892-5322; *Fax:* 604-892-9274
squamish@capilanou.ca

Sunshine Coast
P.O. Box 1609
5627 Inlet Ave., Sechelt, BC V0N 3A0, Canada
Tel: 604-885-9310; *Fax:* 604-885-9350

Publications

Capilano Courier

Prince George: University of Northern British Columbia (UNBC)

3333 University Way, Prince George, BC V2N 4Z9, Canada
Tel: 250-960-5555; *Fax:* 250-960-5794
www.unbc.ca

Full Time Equivalency: 3675
Dr. George Iwama, President
Nancy Black, Acting University Librarian
Dr. Mark R.T. Dale, Vice-President
John DeGrace, University Secretariat & Registrar
Eileen Bray, Vice-President
John DeGrace, Registrar
Dr. Gail Fondahl, Vice-President
Rob van Adrichem, Director

Faculties

Arts, Social & Health Sciences
Dr. John Young, Acting Dean

Graduate Programs
Dr. Ian Hartley, Dean

Science & Management
Dr. William McGill, Dean

Publications

Over the Edge
Student newspaper at the University of Northern British Columbia

Vancouver: University of British Columbia

2329 West Mall, Vancouver, BC V6T 1Z4, Canada
Tel: 604-822-2211
www.ubc.ca
Other Information: Telex: 04-51233

Full Time Equivalency: 48610
Bill Levine, Chair
Sarah Morgan-Silvester, Chancellor
Dr Stephen J. Toope, President & Vice-Chancellor, 604-822-8300, ext. 604-822-50
presidents.office@ubc.ca
Dr David H. Farrar, Provost & Vice-Pres., Academic, 604-822-4948
david.farrar@ubc.ca
Pierre Ouillet, Vice-Pres., Finance, Resources & Operations, 604-822-6317
carolina.cerna@ubc.ca
Barbara Miles, Vice-Pres., Development & Alumni Engagement, 604-822-1585
barbara.miles@ubc.ca
Stephen Owen, Vice-Pres., External, Legal & Community Relations, 604-822-5017
stephen.owen@ubc.ca
Dr John Hepburn, Vice-Pres., Research & International, 604-822-1995
vpr@exchange.ubc.ca
Brian D. Sullivan, Vice-Pres., Students, 604-822-3955
vpstudents@exchange.ubc.ca
James Ridge, Assoc. Vice-Pres. & Registrar, 604-822-3265
james.ridge@ubc.ca

Faculties

Applied Science
www.apsc.ubc.ca
Dr Tyseer Aboulnasr, Dean, 604-822-6413, fax: 604-822-7006
info@apsc.ubc.ca

Arts
www.arts.ubc.ca
Dr Gage Averill, Dean, 604-822-3751
mtw@mail.arts.ubc.ca

Dentistry
www.dentistry.ubc.ca
Dr Charles Shuler, Dean, 604-822-0738, fax: 604-822-4532
foddo@interchange.ubc.ca

Education
www.educ.ubc.ca
Dr Jon shapiro, Interim Dean, 604-822-5214, fax: 604-822-6501
jon.shapiro@ubc.ca

Forestry
www.forestry.ubc.ca
Dr John Innes, Dean, 604-822-3542
john.innes@ubc.ca

Graduate Studies
www.grad.ubc.ca
Barbara Evans, Dean, 604-827-5547
barbara.evans@ubc.ca

Land & Food Systems
www.landfood.ubc.ca
Murray B. Isman, Dean, 604-822-1219, fax: 604-822-6394
dean.landfood@ubc.ca

Law
www.law.ubc.ca
Mary Ann Bobinski, Dean, 604-822-6335
deansoffice@law.ubc.ca

Medicine
www.med.ubc.ca
Dr Gavin Stuart, Dean, 604-822-2421, fax: 604-822-6061
fomdo_reception@medd.med.ubc.ca

Pharmaceutical Sciences
www.pharmacy.ubc.ca
Robert Sindelar, Dean, 604-822-2343, fax: 604-822-3035
sindelar@interchange. ubc.ca

Sciences
www.science.ubc.ca
Dr Simon Peacock, Dean, 604-822-3336, fax: 604-822-5558
scidean@science.ubc.ca

Schools

Architecture & Landscape Architecture
Tel: 604-822-2779; *Fax:* 604-822-3808
arch1@interchange.ubc.ca; larc@interchange.ubc.ca
www.sala.ubc.ca

Leslie Van Duzer, Director
vanduzer@interchange.ubc.ca

Audiology & Speech Sciences
Tel: 604-822-5591; *Fax:* 604-822-6569
inquiry@audiospeech.ubc.ca
www.audiospeech.ubc.ca

Valter Ciocca, Director
director@audiospeech.ubc.ca

Community & Regional Planning
Tel: 604-822-3276; *Fax:* 604-822-3787
www.scarp.ubc.ca

Dr Penny Gurstein, Director
gurstein@interchange.ubc.ca

Continuing Studies
Tel: 604-822-1444; *Fax:* 604-822-1599
www.cstudies.ubc.ca

Dr Judith Plessis, Executive Director

Human Kinetics
Tel: 604-822-3838; *Fax:* 604-822-6842
www.hkin.educ.ubc.ca

Dr Robert E.C. Sparks, Director
robert.sparks@ubc.ca

Library, Archival & Information Studies
Tel: 604-822-2404; *Fax:* 604-822-6006
slais@interchange.ubc.ca
www.slais.ubc.ca

Terry Eastwood, Interim Director
eastwood@interchange.ubc.ca

Music
Tel: 604-822-3113; *Fax:* 604-822-4884
www.music.ubc.ca

Dr Richard Kurth, Director
richard.kurth@ubc.ca

Nursing
Tel: 604-822-7417; *Fax:* 604-822-7466
www.nursing.ubc.ca

Dr Sally Thorne, Director
sally.thorne@nursing.ubc.ca

Population & public Health
Tel: 604-822-2772; *Fax:* 604-822-4994
www.spph.ubc.ca

Dr Martin Schechter, Director
martin.schechter@ubc.ca

Journalism
Tel: 604-822-6688; *Fax:* 604-822-6707
journal@interchange.ubc.ca
www.journalism.ubc.ca
Dr Mary Lynn Young, Director

Social Work
Tel: 604-822-2255; *Fax:* 604-822-8656
www.socialwork.ubc.ca
Dr Kwong-leung Tang, Director
kltang@interchange.ubc.ca

Sauder School of Business
Tel: 604-822-8868; *Fax:* 604-822-8468
www.sauder.ubc.ca
Dr Daniel Muzyka, Dean
daniel.muzyka@sauder.ubc.ca

Environmental Health
Tel: 604-822-9595; *Fax:* 604-822-9588
soeh@interchange.ubc.ca
www.soeh.ubc.ca
Christie Hurrell, Exeuctive Director
hurrell@interchange.ubc.ca

College of Health Disciplines
Tel: 604-822-5571; *Fax:* 604-822-2495
chd@interchange.ubc.ca
www.health-disciplines.ubc.ca
Louise Nasmith, Principal
louise.nasmith@ubc.ca

College of Interdisciplinary Studies
www.cfis.ubc.ca
Michael Burgess, Principal, 604-827-5262
cfis.principal@ubc.ca

Campuses
UBC Okanagan Campus
3333 University Way, Kelowna, BC V1V 1V7, Canada
Tel: 250-807-8000; *Toll-Free:* 866-596-0767
askme@ubc
www.ubc.ca/okanagan

UBC Robson Square Campus
800 Robson St., Vancouver, BC V6Z 3B7
Tel: 604-822-3333; *Fax:* 604-822-0070
robson.info@ubc.ca
www.robsonsquare.ubc.ca

Great Northern Way Campus
577 Great Northern Way, Vancouver, BC V5T 1E1
Tel: 778-370-1001; *Fax:* 778-370-1045
admin@gnwc.ca
www.gnwc.ca

Affiliations
Regent College
5800 University Blvd., Vancouver, BC V6T 2E4, Canada
Tel: 604-224-3245; *Fax:* 604-224-3097
Toll-Free: 1-800-663-8664
admissions@regent-college.edu; registrar@regent-college.edu
www.regent-college.edu
Other Information: Regent Bookstore, Toll Free: 1-800-334-3279
Dr Rod J.K. Wilson, President
presidentsoffice@regent-college.edu

St. Mark's College
5935 Iona Dr., Vancouver, BC V6T 1J7, Canada
Tel: 604-822-4463; *Fax:* 604-822-4659
stmarks@stmarkscollege.ca
www.stmarkscollege.ca
Dr. J. Stapleton, Interim Principal
Dr. Marjorie Budnikas, Registrar
registrar@stmarkscollege.ca

Carey Theological College
5920 Iona Dr., Vancouver, BC V6T 1J6
Tel: 604-224-4308; *Fax:* 604-224-5014
info@careytheologicalcollege.ca
www.careycentre.com

Vancouver School of Theology
6000 Iona Dr., Vancouver, BC V6T 1L4
Tel: 604-822-0824; *Fax:* 604-822-9212
possibilities@vst.edu
www.vst.edu

Publications
Perspectives
perspectives.ubc.ca
An English-Chinese bilingual student paper
KaGeen Cheung, Editor-In-Chief
editor@perspectives.ubc.ca

Discorder Magazine
discorder.ca/discorder-magazine
Jordie Yow, Editor-In-Chief
editor.discorder@gmail.com

The Graduate Magazine
Published by the Graduate Student Society

The Point
thepoint@rec.ubc.ca
www.thepoint.ubc.ca
Focusing on recreational activities, health and lifestyle news

The Thunderbird
thethunderbird.ca
A student publication of the Graduate School of Journalism

The Ubyssey
ubyssey.ca
Justin McElroy, Coordinating Editor
coordinating@ubyssey.ca

Trek Magazine
www.alumni.ubc.ca/trekmagazine/index.php
Published by UBC Alumni Affairs
Chris Petty, Editor
chris.petty@ubc.ca

Victoria: Royal Roads University
2005 Sooke Rd., Victoria, BC V9B 5Y2, Canada
Tel: 250-391-2511; *Fax:* 250-391-2500
Toll-Free: 1-800-788-8028
info@royalroads.ca .ca
www.royalroads.ca

Full Time Equivalency: 4130
Royal Roads University offers: Doctoral degrees in Social Sciences; Masters degrees in Arts, Business Admin., Science; Bachelor degrees in Arts, Commerce, Science; Graduate Certificates; Graduate Diplomas.
Peter Robinson, Chair & Chancellor
Dr Allan Cahoon, President & Vice-Chancellor, 250-391-2517
allan.cahoon@royalroads.ca
Thomas Chase, Vice-Pres., Academic & Provost, 250-391-2545
thomas.chase@royalroads.ca
Dan Tulip, Vice-Pres. & CFO, 250-391-2521
dan.tulip@royalroads.ca
Cyndi McLeod, Vice-Pres., Marketing, Recruitment & Business Development, 250-391-2516
cyndi.mcleod@royalroads.ca
Steve Grundy, Registrar, CIO & Assoc. Vice-Pres., Program Development, 250-391-2606
steve.grundy@royalroads.ca

Victoria: University of Victoria
P.O. Box 1700 CSC
Victoria, BC V8W 2Y2, Canada
Tel: 250-721-7211; *Fax:* 250-721-7212
www.uvic.ca

Full Time Equivalency: 16961
Murray Farmer, B.A., Chancellor
David H. Turpin, B.Sc., Ph.D., President
James L. Cassels, B.A., LL.B., LL.M., Vice-President
Gayle Gorrill, B.B.A., C.A., C.B.V., Vice-President
Julia Eastman, B.A., M.A., Ph.D., University Secretary
Vacant, Administrative Registrar
Bruce Kilpatrick, B.A., Director
J. Howard Brunt, B.A., A.D.N., M.Sc.N., Ph, Vice-President
Valerie Kuehne, B.Sc.N., M.Ed., M.A., Ph., Vice-President

Faculties
Business
Ali Dastmalchian, B.Sc., M.Sc., Ph.D., Dean

Continuing Studies
Maureen MacDonald, B.A., LL.B., M.B.A., D.Ph, Dean

Education
Ted Riecken, B.A., M.Ed., Ph.D., Dean

Engineering
Thomas Tiedje, B.Sc., M.Sc., Ph.D., Dean

Fine Arts
Sarah Blackstone, B.A., M.A., Ph.D., Dean

Graduate Studies
Aaron H. Devor, B.A., M.A., Ph.D., Dean

Human & Social Development
Mary Ellen Purkis, B.S.N., M.Sc., Ph.D., Dean

Humanities
Andrew Rippin, B.A., M.A., Ph.D., Dean

Law
Donna Greschner, B.Comm., LL.B., Dean

Science
Tom Pedersen, B.Sc., Ph.D., Dean

Social Sciences
Peter Keller, B.A., M.A., Ph.D., Dean

Publications
The Martlet
Independent weekly student newspaper at the University of Victoria

The Ring
The University of Victoria's monthly newspaper

Standard
The University of Victoria's monthly newspaper

The UVic Torch
P.O. Box 3060
3775 Haro Rd, Victoria, BC V8W 3R4, Canada
Fax: 250-721-8955
Alumni magazine

Colleges

Castlegar: Selkirk College
Castlegar Campus
301 Frank Beinder Way, Castlegar, BC V1N 4L3, Canada
Tel: 250-365-6601; *Fax:* 250-365-6568
Toll-Free: 1-888-953-1133
www.selkirk.ca

The regional community college consists of the following schools: Kootenay School of the Arts; School of Adult Basic Education & Transitional Training; School of Business & Aviation; School of Digital Media & Music; School of Health & Human Services; School of Hospitality & Tourism; School of Industry & Trades Training; School of Renewable Resources; School of University Arts & Sciences; & Selkirk International.
Christian Schadendorf, Chair
Marilyn Luscombe, President

Campuses
Grand Forks Campus
486 - 72nd Ave., Grand Forks, BC V0H 1H0, Canada
Tel: 250-442-2704; *Fax:* 250-442-2877

Kaslo Centre
421 Front St., Kaslo, BC V0G 1M0, Canada
Tel: 250-353-2618; *Fax:* 250-353-7121

Kootenay School of the Arts (KSA) Campus
606 Victoria St., Nelson, BC V1L 4K9
Tel: 250-352-2821; *Fax:* 250-352-1625
Toll-Free: 1-877-552-2821

Nakusp Centre
311 Broadway, Nakusp, BC V0H 1R0, Canada
Tel: 250-265-4077; *Fax:* 250-265-3195
Other Information: Adult Basic Education: 250-265-3640

Silver King Campus
2001 Silver King Rd., Nelson, BC V1L 1C8, Canada
Tel: 250-352-6601; *Fax:* 250-352-3180
Toll-Free: 1-866-301-6601

Tenth Street Campus
820 Tenth St., Nelson, BC V1L 3C7, Canada
Tel: 250-352-6601; *Fax:* 250-352-5716
Toll-Free: 1-866-301-6601

Trail Campus
900 Helena St., Trail, BC V1R 4S6, Canada
Tel: 250-368-5236; *Fax:* 250-368-4983

Courtenay: North Island College
Comox Valley Campus
2300 Ryan Rd., Courtenay, BC V9N 8N6, Canada
Tel: 250-334-5000; *Fax:* 250-334-5018
Toll-Free: 800-715-0914
www.northislandcollege.ca

Full Time Equivalency: 8253
Dr. Lou Dryden, President
Susan Toresdahl, Director

Campuses
Campbell River Campus
1685 South Dogwood St., Campbell River, BC V9W 8C1, Canada
Tel: 250-923-9700; *Fax:* 250-923-9703
Toll-Free: 1-800-715-0914
www.northislandcollege.ca

Comox Valley Campus
2300 Ryan Rd., Courtenay, BC V9N 8N6, Canada
Tel: 250-334-5000; *Fax:* 250-334-5018
Toll-Free: 1-800-715-0914
www.northislandcollege.ca

Port Alberni Campus
3699 Roger St., Port Alberni, BC V9Y 8E3, Canada
Tel: 250-724-8711; *Fax:* 250-724-8700
Toll-Free: 1-800-715-0914
www.northislandcollege.ca

Port Hardy Campus
P.O. Box 901
9300 Trustee Rd., Port Hardy, BC V0N 2P0, Canada
Tel: 250-949-7912; *Fax:* 250-949-2617
Toll-Free: 1-800-715-0914
www.northislandcollege.ca

Vigar Vocational Centre
2780 Vigar Rd., Campbell River, BC V9W 6A3, Canada
Tel: 250-923-9794; *Fax:* 250-830-0816
Toll-Free: 1-800-715-0914
www.northislandcollege.ca

Tebo Vocational Centre
4781 Tebo Ave., Port Alberni, BC V9Y 6X7, Canada
Toll-Free: 1-800-715-0914
www.northislandcollege.ca

Cranbrook: College of the Rockies
P.O. Box 8500
2700 College Way, Cranbrook, BC V1C 5L7, Canada
Tel: 250-489-2751; *Fax:* 250-489-1790
Toll-Free: 1-877-489-2687
ask@cotr.bc.ca
www.cotr.bc.ca

Full Time Equivalency: 2000
Donna Kraus-Hagerman, Manager
Dr. Nick Rubidge, President

Campuses
Creston Campus
P.O. Box 1978
301-16th Ave., Creston, BC V0B 1G0, Canada
Tel: 250-428-5332; *Fax:* 250-428-4314
Toll-Free: 1-877-489-2687
creston@cotr.bc.ca
www.cotr.bc.ca/creston/

Invermere Campus
#2, 1535 - 14th St., RR#4, Invermere, BC V0A 1K4, Canada
Tel: 250-342-3210; *Fax:* 250-342-9221
Toll-Free: 1-877-489-2687
invermere@cotr.bc.ca
www.cotr.bc.ca/invermere/

Elk Valley-Fernie Campus
P.O. Box 1770
342-3rd Ave., Fernie, BC V0B 1M0, Canada
Tel: 250-423-4691; *Fax:* 250-423-3932
Toll-Free: 1-866-423-4691
fernie@cotr.bc.ca
www.cotr.bc.ca/fernie/

Golden Campus
P.O. Box 376
1305 South 9th St., Golden, BC V0A 1H0, Canada
Tel: 250-344-5901; *Fax:* 250-344-5745
Toll-Free: 1-877-489-2687
golden@cotr.bc.ca
www.cotr.bc.ca/golden/

Kimberley Campus
555 McKenzie St., Kimberley, BC V1A 2C1, Canada
Tel: 250-427-7116; *Fax:* 250-427-3034
Toll-Free: 1-877-489-2687
peet@cotr.bc.ca
http://www.cotr.bc.ca/kimberley/

Dawson Creek: Northern Lights College
Regional Administration
11401 - 8th St., Dawson Creek, BC V1G 4G2, Canada
Tel: 250-782-5251; *Fax:* 250-782-5233
Toll-Free: 1-866-463-6652
appinfo@nlc.bc.ca; webmaster@nlc.bc.ca
www.nlc.bc.ca

Kate O'Neil, Board Chair
D. Jean Valgardson, CEO
jvalgardson@nlc.bc.ca

Campuses
Atlin Campus
Also known as: Atlin Learning Centre
P.O. Box 29
Atlin, BC V0W 1A0
Tel: 250-651-7762
ljancek@nlc.bc.ca (Campus Clerk); dthorn@nlc.bc.ca (Literacy)
The campus offers continuing education in academic & pre-professional studies, development & upgrading, distance education, & industrial & workforce training.
Richard Macdonald, Chair
Roger Grose, Systems Principal
Bob White, Principal, Secondary Campus
Henry Au, Vice Principal, Secondary Campus
Aza Nakagawa, Business Manager
Blondie Enns, Secretary, High School

Chetwynd Campus
P.O. Box 1180
5132 - 50th St., Chetwynd, BC V0C 1J0, Canada
Tel: 250-788-2248; *Fax:* 250-788-9706
mmeunier@nlc.bc.ca (Administrator)

Enrollment: 400
Programs offered include applied business technology, teacher assistant training, social services worker training, forestry, hospitality & tourism operations, continuing education, adult basic education, university transfer, & adult special education.
Mark Meunier, Campus Administrator

Dawson Creek Campus
11401 - 8 St., Dawson Creek, BC V1G 4G2, Canada
Fax: 250-782-5251
Toll-Free: 250-784-7563
dpatterson@nlc.bc.ca (Administrator)
Other Information: Continuing Education Coordinator, Phone: 250-784-7509
The campus features technical, academic, trades, & vocational programs.
Doug Patterson, Campus Administrator

Dease Lake Campus
P.O. Box 220
Commercial Dr., Dease Lake, BC V0C 1L0
Tel: 250-771-5500; *Fax:* 250-771-5510
Toll-Free: 1-800-324-8203
mpharand@nlc.bc.ca (Stikine Administrator)
Enrollment: 625
The campus serves full-time & part-time vocational and continuing education students in Atlin, Telegraph Creek, Lower Post, Iskut, & Good Hope Lake.
Tiffany Scobie, Head of School, 905-565-8707, ext. 10
tscobie@rotherglen.com
Laura Rossi, Office Manager, 905-565-8707, ext. 10
lrossi@rotherglen.com

Fort Nelson Campus
P.O. Box 860
5201 Simpson Trail, Fort Nelson, BC V0C 1R0, Canada
Fax: 250-774-2741
Toll-Free: 250-774-2750
ssandvik@nlc.bc.ca (Administrator)
Continuing education programs are provided.
Vacant, Campus Administrator

Fort St. John Campus
P.O. Box 1000
9820 - 120 St., Fort St John, BC V1J 6K1, Canada
Tel: 250-785-6981; *Fax:* 250-785-1294
Enrollment: 1800
Academic, apprenticeship, career/technical, vocational, & international students students are served by the Fort St. John campus.
Ed Benoit, Campus Administrator

Hudson's Hope Campus
Also known as: Hudson's Hope Learning Centre
Perkes Centre
P.O. Box 268
10801 Dudley Dr., Hudson's Hope, BC
Tel: 250-783-5711; *Fax:* 250-783-5788
vrowsell@nlc.bc.ca (Continuing Education Coordinator)
Adult basic education & continuing education programs are offered in Hudson's Hope.
Jacinta Snyder, Head of School
jsnyder@rotherglen.com

Tumbler Ridge Campus
High School Bldg.
180 Southgate, Tumbler Ridge, BC V0C 2W0
Tel: 250-242-5591; *Fax:* 250-242-3109
mmeunier@nlc.bc.ca (Administrator)
Adult basic education is offered in Tumbler Ridge.
Tracey Chong, Administrator
tchong@rotherglen.com

Kelowna: Okanagan University College
North Kelowna Campus
3333 College Way, Kelowna, BC V1V 1V7, Canada
Tel: 250-762-5445; *Fax:* 250-470-6004
www.ouc.bc.ca/

Campuses
The Phoenix

Langley: Trinity Western Seminary
7600 Glover Rd., Langley, BC V2Y 1Y1, Canada
Tel: 604-513-2019; *Fax:* 604-513-2045
www.acts.twu.ca

Publications
Mars' Hill
Official student newspaper of Trinity Western University

Nanaimo: Vancouver Island University
900 - 5th St., Nanaimo, BC V9R 5S5, Canada
Tel: 250-753-3245; *Toll-Free:* 888-920-2221
info@viu.ca
www.viu.ca

Full Time Equivalency: 19124
Formerly Malaspina University College.
Ralph Nilson, President, 250-740-6102
ralph.nilson@viu.ca

Prince George: College of New Caledonia
3330 - 22 Ave., Prince George, BC V2N 1P8, Canada
Tel: 250-562-2131; *Fax:* 250-561-5861
Toll-Free: 1-800-371-811
www.cnc.bc.ca/

Full Time Equivalency: 5000
John Bowman, President
bowmanj@cnc.bc.ca

Surrey: Kwantlen Polytechnic University
12666 - 72nd Ave., Surrey, BC V3W 2M8, Canada
Tel: 604-599-2100; *Fax:* 604-599-2068
inquiry@kwantlen.ca
www.kwantlen.ca

Full Time Equivalency: 11000
Formerly known as Kwantlen University College; 6,000 part-time enrollment
David Atkinson, President, 604-599-2078
david.atkinson@kwantlen.ca
Joshua Mitchell, Director, Enrolment Services, 604-599-2474
joshua.mitchell@kwantlen.ca

Terrace: Northwest Community College
College Services
5331 McConnell Ave., Terrace, BC V8G 4X2, Canada
Tel: 250-635-6511; *Fax:* 250-635-5432
Toll-Free: 1-877-277-2288
www.nwcc.bc.ca

Stephanie Forsyth, President

Campuses
Hazelton Campus
P.O. Box 338
4815 Swannell Dr., Hazelton, BC V0J 1Y0, Canada
Tel: 250-842-5291; *Fax:* 250-842-5813
www.nwcc.bc.ca

Houston Campus
P.O. Box 1277
3221 - 14 St.W., Houston, BC V0J 1Z0, Canada
Tel: 250-845-7266; *Fax:* 250-845-5629
www.nwcc.bc.ca

Kitimat Campus
606 Mountainview Sq., Kitimat, BC V8C 2N2, Canada
Tel: 250-632-4766; *Fax:* 250-632-5069
www.nwcc.bc.ca

Prince Rupert Campus
353 - 5th St., Prince Rupert, BC V8J 3L6, Canada
Tel: 250-624-6054; *Fax:* 250-624-3923
www.nwcc.bc.ca

Queen Charlotte City Campus
P.O. Box 67
138 Bay St., Queen Charlotte Village, BC V0T 1S0, Canada
Tel: 250-559-8222; *Fax:* 250-559-8219
www.nwcc.bc.ca

Smithers Campus
P.O. Box 3606
3966 - 2nd Ave., Smithers, BC V0J 2N0, Canada
Tel: 250-847-4461; *Fax:* 250-847-4568
www.nwcc.bc.ca

Stewart Campus
P.O. Box 919
Stewart, BC V0T 1W0, Canada
Tel: 250-636-9184; *Fax:* 250-636-2770
www.nwcc.bc.ca

Terrace Campus
5331 McConnell Ave., Terrace, BC V8G 4X2, Canada
Tel: 250-635-6511; *Fax:* 250-638-5432

Masset Campus
P.O. Box 559
1730 Hodges, Masset, BC V0T 1M0, Canada
Tel: 250-626-3670; *Fax:* 250-626-3680
www.nwcc.bc.ca

Victoria: Camosun College
Lansdowne Campus, 3100 Foul Bay Rd., Victoria, BC V8P 5J2, Canada
Tel: 250-370-3000; *Fax:* 250-370-3551
Toll-Free: 877-554-7555
info@camosun.bc.ca
www.camosun.bc.ca/
Full Time Equivalency: 7200
Dr. Liz Ashton, President

Victoria: Lester B. Pearson College of the Pacific
650 Pearson College Dr., Victoria, BC V9C 4H7, Canada
Tel: 250-391-2411; *Fax:* 250-391-2412
admin@pearsoncollege.ca
www.pearsoncollege.ca
Full Time Equivalency: 200
David B. Hawley, College Director

Post Secondary/Technical

Universities

Abbotsford: University of the Fraser Valley
33844 King Rd., Abbotsford, BC V2S 7M8, Canada
Tel: 604-504-7441; *Fax:* 604-855-7614
Toll-Free: 888-504-7441
info@ufv.ca
www.ucfv.ca
Enrollment: 10000
Dr Brian Minter, Chancellor
Dr Mark Evered, President & Vice-Chancellor, 604-864-4608, fax: 604-853-7341
jill.smith@ufv.ca
Dr Brian Minter, Chancellor
Dr Eric Davis, Provost & Vice-Pres., Academic, 604-864-4642
eric.davis@ufv.ca
Eleanor Busse-Klassen, Exec. Ass't to Vice-Pres., Administration
eleanor.busse@ufv.ca
Bill Cooke, Registrar, ext. 2820
bill.cooke@ufv.ca

Faculties
Arts
Dr Jacqueline Nolte
jacqueline.nolte@ufv.ca

Science
Ora Stein, Interim Dean
ora.steyn@ufv.ca

Professional Studies
Dr Rosetta Khalideen, Dean
rosetta.khalideen@ufv.ca

Trades & Technology
Harv McCullough, Dean
harv.mccullough@ufv.ca

Access & Continuing Studies
Dr Karen Evans
karen.evans@ufv.ca

Schools
Graduate Studies
Yvon Dandurand, Assoc. Vice-President
yvon.dandurand@ufv.ca

Campuses
Chilliwack Campus
45635 Yale Rd., Chilliwack, BC V2P 6T4, Canada
Tel: 604-792-0025; *Fax:* 604-792-2388

Chilliwack, Trades & Tech Centre
Canada Education Park
5579 Tyson Rd., Chilliwack, BC V2R 0H9, Canada
Fax: 604-824-7931
Toll-Free: 888-504-7441

UFV Aerospace Centre
Abbotsford Airport
30645 Firecat Ave., Abbotsford, BC V2T 6H5, Canada
Fax: 604-852-7399
Toll-Free: 888-504-7441
aerospace@ufv.ca

Hope Centre
1250 7th Ave., Hope, BC V0X 1L4, Canada
Tel: 604-869-9991; *Fax:* 604-869-7431

Mission Campus
Heritage Park Centre
33700 Prentis Ave., Mission, BC V2V 7B1, Canada
Tel: 604-557-7603; *Fax:* 604-826-0681

Abbotsford, Marshall Rd. Annex
34194 Marshall Rd., Abbotsford, BC V2S 5E4
Tel: 604-851-6324

UFV India Office
SD College Chandigarh
Sector 32C, Chandigarth, UT, India
ufv.india@ufv.ca
www.ufv.ca/chandigarh
Other Information: (0)172 500 1048

Publications
The Cascade
ufvcascade.ca

Nanaimo: Vancouver Island University
900 Fifth St., Nanaimo, BC V9R 5S5, Canada
Tel: 250-753-3245; *Fax:* 250-740-6473
Toll-Free: 888-920-2221
info@viu.ca
www.viu.ca
Enrollment: 18000
VIU offers a variety of certificate, diploma, and degree programs.
Chief Shawn A. Atleo, Chancellor
Dr Ralph Nilson, President & Vice-chancellor, 250-740-6101, fax: 250-740-6555
president@viu.ca
Pat Eager, Vice-Pres., Admin. & Finance
ralph.nilson@viu.ca
David Witty, Vice-Pres., Academic & Provost
david.witty@viu.ca
Fred Jacklin, Registrar, 250-753-3245, ext. 2283
david.witty@viu.ca

Campuses
Cowichan Campus
222 Cowichan Way, Duncan, BC V9L 6P4, Canada
Tel: 250-746-3500; *Fax:* 250-746-3529

Parksville-Qualicum Centre
100 Jensen Ave. East, Parksville, BC V9P 2G3, Canada
Tel: 250-248-2096; *Fax:* 250-248-9792
pqcampus@viu.ca

Powell River Campus
3960 Selkirk Ave., Powell River, BC V8A 3C6, Canada
Tel: 604-485-2878; *Fax:* 604-485-2868
Toll-Free: 877-888-8890

Publications
Navigator
editor@thenav.ca
thenav.mala.bc.ca

Surrey: Kwantlen Polytechnic University
12666 - 72 Ave., Surrey, BC V3W 2M8, Canada
Tel: 604-599-2100; *Fax:* 604-599-2068
switchboard@kwantlen.ca
www.kwantlen.bc.ca
Enrollment: 17000
Arvinder Singh Bubber, Chancellor
David W. Atkinson, President & Vice-Chancellor, 604-599-2078, fax: 604-599-2235
sandy.kuzyk@kwantlen.ca
Judith McGillivray, Provost & Vice-Pres., Academic, 604-599-2363
judith.mcgillivray@kwantlen.ca
Robert Hensley, Registrar, 604-599-2018
robert.hensley@kwantlen.ca

Faculties
Humanities
Dr Mazen Guirguis, Dean, 604-599-2672
humanities.dean@kwantlen.ca

Social Sciences
Dr Robert Adamoski, Dean, 604-599-3068, fax: 604-599-2966
robert.adamoski@kwantlen.ca

Design
Barbara Duggan, Dean, 604-599-2525
barbara.duggan@kwantlen.ca

Community & Health Studies
Jean Nicolson-Church, Interim Dean, 604-599-2266
jean.nicolson-church@kwantlen.ca

Academic & Career Advancement
Dr Arthur Coren, Interim Dean, 604-599-3252
arthur.coren@kwantlen.ca

Trades & Technology
Wayne Tebb, Dean, 604-599-6101
wayne.tebb@kwantlen.ca

Science, Mathematics & Applied Sciences
Dr Brian G. Carr, Dean, 604-599-2244, fax: 604-599-2435
brian.carr@kwantlen.ca

Business
Dr Arthur Coren, Dean, 604-599-3252
arthur.coren@kwantlen.ca

Schools
Horticulture
David Davidson, Assoc. Dean, 604-599-3254
horticulture@kwantlen.ca

Campuses
Surrey Campus
12666 - 72 Ave., Surrey, BC V3T 5H8, Canada
Fax: 604-599-2068

Richmond Campus
8771 Lansdowne Rd., Richmond, BC V6X 3V8, Canada
Fax: 604-599-2578

Cloverdale Campus
5500 - 180 St., Surrey, BC V3S 4K5, Canada

Langley Campus
20901 Langley Bypass, Langley, BC V3A 8G9, Canada
Fax: 604-599-3242

Publications
Kwantlen Chronicle
www.kwantlenchronicle.ca

Colleges

Kelowna: Okanagan College
1000 KLO Rd., Kelowna, BC V1Y 4X8, Canada
Tel: 250-762-5445
www.okanagan.bc.ca
Enrollment: 4850
Jim Hamilton, President

Campuses
Penticton Campus
583 Duncan Ave. West, Penticton, BC V2A 8E1, Canada
Fax: 250-490-3950
Donna Lomas, Regional Dean

Salmon Arm Campus
P.O. Box 189
Salmon Arm, BC V1E 4N3, Canada
Fax: 250-804-8850
Lynda Wilson, Regional Dean

Kalamalka Campus
7000 College Way, Vernon, BC V1B 2N5, Canada
Fax: 250-545-3277
Tony Sellars, Regional Dean

South Kelowna Campus
1000 KLO Rd., Kelowna, BC V1Y 4X8, Canada
Heather Schneider, Regional Dean

Publications
The Phoenix

New Westminster: Douglas College
P.O. Box 2503
New Westminster, BC V3L 5B2, Canada
Tel: 604-527-5400; *Fax:* 604-527-5095
registrar@douglas.bc.ca
www.douglas.bc.ca/
Enrollment: 7000
Susan R. Witter, President

Campuses
New Westminster Campus
700 Royal Ave., New Westminster, BC V3M 5Z5, Canada

David Lam Campus
1250 Pinetree Way, Coquitlam, BC V3B 7X3, Canada

Publications
Other Press

North Vancouver: Capilano College
2055 Purcell Way, North Vancouver, BC V7J 3H5, Canada
Tel: 604-986-1911; *Fax:* 604-984-4985
switchboard@capcollege.bc.ca
www.capcollege.bc.ca
Enrollment: 5537
Dr. Greg Lee, B.Sc., M.Sc., Ph.D., President

Publications
Capilano Courier

Prince George: College of New Caledonia
3330 - 22nd Ave., Prince George, BC V2N 1P8, Canada
Tel: 250-562-2131; *Fax:* 250-561-5816
Toll-Free: 1-800-371-811
askcnc@cnc.bc.ca
www.cnc.bc.ca
Enrollment: 5250
John Bowman, President, 250-561-5825

Bruce Sutherland, Chair

Campuses

Lakes District Campus
Also known as: Burns Lake
P.O. Box 5000
545 Hwy. 16 West, Burns Lake, BC V0J 1E0, Canada
Tel: 250-692-1700; *Fax:* 250-692-1750
Toll-Free: 866-692-1943
lksdist@cnc.bc.ca
Joan Ragsdale, Director, 250-692-1715
ragsdale@cnc.bc.ca

Mackenzie Campus
P.O. Box 2110
540 Mackenzie Blvd., Mackenzie, BC V0J 2C0, Canada
Tel: 250-997-7200; *Fax:* 250-997-3779
cncmackenzie@cnc.bc.ca
Carole L'Herault, Director, 250-997-7203
lherault@cnc.bc.ca

Quesnel Campus
100 Campus Way, Quesnel, BC V2J 7K1, Canada
Tel: 250-991-7500; *Fax:* 250-991-7502
Toll-Free: 866-680-7523
quesnel@cnc.bc.ca
Lynda Williams, Associate Director, 250-991-7622
williamsl2@cnc.bc.ca

Nechako Campus
3231 Hospital Rd., Vanderhoof, BC V0J 3A2, Canada
Tel: 250-567-3200; *Fax:* 250-567-3217
nechako@cnc.bc.ca
Maureen Mallais, Director, 250-567-3200
mallais@cnc.bc.ca

Fort St. James Campus
P.O. Box 1557
179 Douglas St., Fort St. James, BC V0J 1P0
Tel: 250-996-7019; *Fax:* 250-996-7014
cncfsj@cnc.bc.ca
Ann McCormick, Campus Supervisor
mccormicka@cnc.bc.ca

Valemount Campus
P.O. Box 789
99 Gorse St., Valemount, BC V0E 2Z0, Canada
Tel: 250-566-4601; *Fax:* 250-566-4602
Toll-Free: 888-690-4422
valemount@cnc.bc.ca
Sandra Craig, Program Clerk
craigs@cnc.bc.ca

Fraser Lake Campus
298 McMillan Ave., Fraser Lake, BC V0J 1S0
Tel: 250-699-6249; *Fax:* 250-699-6247
cncfl@cnc.bc.ca
Wendy Galvin, Program Assistant
galvinw@cnc.bc.ca

Publications
The Confluence
cncsn@cnc.bc.ca

Vancouver: Langara College
100 West 49th Ave., Vancouver, BC V5Y 2Z6, Canada
Tel: 604-323-5511; *Fax:* 604-323-5555
geninfo@langara.bc.ca
www.langara.bc.ca
Enrollment: 12218
Linda Holmes, President

Publications
Gleaner
The Voice

Vancouver: Vancouver Community College
1155 East Broadway, Vancouver, BC V5T 4V5, Canada
Tel: 604-871-7000; *Fax:* 604-871-7100
www.vcc.ca
Dale Dorn, President
L. Martin, Vice-President
Alan Davis, Vice-President
Peter Legg, Interim Vice-President

Campuses

City Centre Campus
250 West Pender St., Vancouver, BC V6B 1S9, Canada
Fax: 604-443-8588

King Edward Campus
1155 East Broadway, Vancouver, BC V5T 4V5, Canada
Fax: 604-871-7100

Publications
The Gleaner
V.C.C. Voice
100 - 49th Ave. West, Vancouver, BC V5Y 2Z6, Canada

Victoria: Camosun College
Lansdowne Campus
3100 Foul Bay Rd., Victoria, BC V8P 5J2, Canada
Tel: 250-370-3550; *Fax:* 250-370-3551
www.camosun.bc.ca
Dr. Elizabeth Ashton, President

Campuses

Interurban Campus
4461 Interurban Rd., RR#3, Victoria, BC V9E 2C1, Canada
Fax: 250-370-3750

Publications
Nexus

Post Secondary/Technical

Burnaby: BC Institute of Technology
3700 Willingdon Ave., Burnaby, BC V5G 3H2, Canada
Tel: 604-434-5734; *Fax:* 604-431-6917
www.bcit.ca
Dr. Tony Knowles, President
Marshall Heinekey, Acting Vice President
Dr. Verna Magee-Shepherd, Vice President

Campuses

Burnaby Campus
3700 Willingdon Ave., Burnaby, BC V5G 3H2, Canada

Aircraft Technology Campus
5301 Airport Rd. South, Richmond, BC V7B 1B5, Canada

Downtown Campus
555 Seymour St., Vancouver, BC V6B 3H6, Canada

Marine Campus
265 West Esplanade, North Vancouver, BC V7M 1A5, Canada

Publications
Great Northern Way Campus
555 Great Northern Way, Vancouver, BC V5T 1E2, Canada

Burnaby: British Columbia Institute of Technology
3700 Willingdon Ave., Burnaby, BC V5G 3H2, Canada
Tel: 604-434-5734; *Fax:* 604-434-6243
www.bcit.bc.ca/

Burnaby: CDI College of Business, Technology & Healthcare
#211, 4603 Kingsway, Burnaby, BC V5H 4M4, Canada
Tel: 604-437-8585; *Fax:* 604-437-8595
www.cdicollege.com
Computers, accounting & business training; 7 locations across BC

Burnaby: Institute of Indigenous Government
#200, 4355 Mathissi Place, Burnaby, BC V5G 4S8, Canada
Tel: 604-602-9555; *Fax:* 604-602-3400
iig@all-nations.ca
www.all-nations.ca

Burnaby: Jennings Institute for Performing Artists Inc.
1870 Sperling Ave., Burnaby, BC V5B 4K5, Canada
Tel: 604-420-3213; *Fax:* 604-420-3210
forperformingartists@hotmail.com
Representation & management of performers, training in dance, music, drama, speech arts & theoretical subjects

Burnaby: Pacific Vocational College Ltd.
4064 McConnell Dr., Burnaby, BC V5A 3A8, Canada
Tel: 604-421-5255; *Fax:* 604-421-7445
pvc@telus.net
www.pacificvocationalcollege.com
Piping trades, gas fitting, sprinkler fitting, welding
Robert F. Bradbury, President

Burnaby: ProCare Institute Inc.
#240, 4411 Hastings St., Burnaby, BC V5C 2K1, Canada
Tel: 604-291-0030; *Fax:* 604-291-0003
Toll-Free: 1-800-282-003
procare@telus.net
www.procare.ca
Health care programs

Coquitlam: Barkel Business School Ltd.
#223, 3030 Lincoln Ave., Coquitlam, BC V3B 6B4, Canada
Tel: 604-464-8717; *Fax:* 604-942-6355
Secretarial, bookkeeping, computer training & management

Coquitlam: Personal Growth Consulting Training Centre
#4, 1111 Austin Ave., Coquitlam, BC V3K 3P4, Canada
Tel: 604-939-1760
breathwork.citysoup.ca
Susan Hewins, Master Teacher

Coquitlam: Sprott-Shaw Community College
#104, 2748 Lougheed Hwy., Coquitlam, BC V3B 6P2, Canada
Tel: 604-552-7686; *Fax:* 604-552-6986
Toll-Free: 1-800-310-447
info@sprott-shaw.com
www.sprottshaw.com
21 campuses in BC; 1 in Calgary; 1 in Edmonton; 3 international colleges in India & Jordan

Courtenay: Comox Valley Beauty School
911 McPhee Ave., Courtenay, BC V9N 3A1, Canada
Tel: 250-338-9982; *Fax:* 250-338-0199
cvbeautyschool.com/
Beauty, cosmetology, esthetics

Kelowna: Fine-Art Bartending School
2979 Pandosy St., Kelowna, BC V1Y 1W1, Canada
Tel: 250-363-6392; *Fax:* 250-860-0998
Toll-Free: 1-866-881-669
info@fineart.ca
www.fineart.ca

Kelowna: Kelowna College of Professional Counselling
#101, 251 Lawrence Ave., Kelowna, BC V1Y 6L2, Canada
Tel: 250-717-0412; *Fax:* 250-717-0427
Toll-Free: 1-800-667-327
cti@uniserve.com
www.counselortraining.com
Counselling practice training
Dr. Libby Stowers, Program Director

Kelowna: Trend College Kelowna Ltd.
546 Leon Ave., Kelowna, BC V1Y 6J6, Canada
Tel: 250-763-7400; *Fax:* 250-763-9948
Toll-Free: 1-888-763-740
info@trendcollege.com
www.trendcollege.com
Computer technology, business & management, specialty careers, health care, beauty & trade

Langley: New Directions
#101, 20570 - 56 Ave., Langley, BC V3A 3Z1, Canada
Tel: 604-530-4555
Career counselling, ESL, general upgrading, life skills
Annemieke Vrijmoed, ELSA Coordinator

Langley: RCABC Roofing Institute
9734 - 201st St., Langley, BC V1M 3E8, Canada
Tel: 604-882-9734; *Fax:* 604-882-1744
registrar@rcabc.org
www.rcabc.org
Roofing training
Brian Hofler, Exec. Vice-President

Maple Ridge: Justice Institute - Fire & Safety Training Centre
13500 - 256 St., Maple Ridge, BC V4R 1C9, Canada
Tel: 604-462-1000; *Fax:* 604-462-9149
www.jibc.bc.ca
Courses offered on marine & industrial firefighting, emergency response to incidents involving hazardous materials, fire service training from recruit to chief officer.
Dan Murphy, Manager

Maple Ridge: Ridge Meadows College
22610 Dewdney Trunk Rd., Maple Ridge, BC V2X 3J9, Canada
Tel: 604-466-6577; *Fax:* 604-467-7548
rmc@sd42.ca
www.rmcollege.ca
Business, Education, Health Care, Hospitality, Recreation, Trades & Corporate Contract Training: Admin. Asst., Computer Accounting, Family Daycare, ECE, SETA, TESL, Dental Reception, FoodSafe Programs, Home Health Aide, Medical Asst., Hospitality Operation.

Campuses

Arthur Peake Centre
23125 - 116th Ave., Maple Ridge, BC V2X 3M6, Canada
Fax: 604-467-4143

Thomas Haney Centre
23000C - 116th Ave., Maple Ridge, BC V2X 0T8, Canada
Fax: 604-463-5437

Merritt: **Nicola Valley Institute of Technology**
4155 Belshaw St., Merritt, BC V1K 1R1, Canada
Tel: 250-378-3300; *Fax:* 250-378-3332
Toll-Free: 1-877-682-330
www.nvit.bc.ca
Enrollment: 800
Certificate & diploma programs, adult basic education, collaborative degrees & on-campus, in-community & online delivery
Casey Sheridan, President
Ken Tourand, Director
Dr. Gerry William, Dean
Verna Billy-Minnabarriet, Dean

New Westminster: **Canadian Electrolysis College Ltd.**
712 - 6th St., New Westminster, BC V3L 3C5, Canada
Tel: 604-519-1101; *Toll-Free:* 1-888-561-441
www.canadianelectrolysis.com/
Electrolysis thermolysis, blend + multiple needle, & advanced computerized epilation; 13 weeks, 500 hrs.
Ruth Struve, Owner

New Westminster: **Justice Institute of B.C.**
715 McBride Blvd., New Westminster, BC V3L 5T4, Canada
Tel: 604-525-5422; *Fax:* 604-528-5518
Toll-Free: 1-88-865-7764
infodesk@jibc.ca
www.jibc.bc.ca
Jack McGee, President

Campuses

Chilliwack Campus
1092 Caen Rd., Chilliwack, BC V2R 5X6, Canada
Tel: 604-847-0881
infodesk@jibc.ca
www.jibc.ca

Downtown Vancouver
Education Centre
400 Burrard St., 18th Fl., Vancouver, BC V6C 3A6, Canada
Fax: 604-528-5653

Maple Ridge Campus
13500 - 256 St., Maple Ridge, BC V4R 1C9, Canada
Tel: 604-462-1000; *Fax:* 604-462-9149
infodesk@jibc.ca
www.jibc.ca

Okanagan Campus
825 Walrod St., Kelowna, BC V1Y 2S4, Canada
Tel: 250-469-6020; *Fax:* 250-469-6022
infodesk@jibc.ca
www.jibc.ca
Anyone shipping good to this campus should contact the Facilities Adinistrator at 250-469-6020.

Victoria Campus
#101, 910 Government St., Victoria, BC V8W 1X3, Canada
Tel: 250-405-3500; *Fax:* 250-405-3500
infodesk@jibc.ca
www.jibc.ca

North Vancouver: **Academy of Learning**
#300, 1221 Lonsdale Ave., North Vancouver, BC V7M 2H5, Canada
Tel: 604-987-4277; *Fax:* 604-987-4213
www.academyoflearning.com
Computer & business skills; 24 locations across BC

Port Moody: **BC Office**
#108, 135 Balmoral Dr., Port Moody, BC V3H 1X7, Canada
Tel: 604-461-7132
wmtcbc@telus.net
westernmontessori.ca

Campuses

AB Office
P.O. Box 1120
Bragg Creek, AB T0L 0K0, Canada
Tel: 403-949-2238; *Fax:* 403-949-2238
WMTCab@telus.net
westernmontessori.ca

Revelstoke: **Canadian Avalanche Association**
P.O. Box 2759
Revelstoke, BC V0E 2S0, Canada
Tel: 250-837-2435; *Fax:* 250-837-4624
canav@avalanche.ca
www.avalanche.ca
Other Information: Toll Free: 1-800-667-1105 (Voice Bulletins)
Observing weather, snowpack conditions, forecasting snow stability, organizing training courses in all aspects of avalanche hazard control for professionals

Richmond: **Automotive Training Centre**
#210, 13460 Smallwood Pl., Richmond, BC V6V 1W8, Canada
Tel: 604-270-6121; *Fax:* 604-270-6123
Toll-Free: 1-888-546-288
vancouver@autotrainingcentre.com
www.autotrainingcentre.com

Richmond: **Richmond Campus**
8057 Anderson Rd., Richmond, BC V6Y 1S2, Canada
Tel: 604-276-8202
www.hairdressing.ca
Hairstyling courses

Campuses

Maple Ridge Campus
11922 - 227 St., Maple Ridge, BC V2X 6J2, Canada
Tel: 604-467-0222; *Fax:* 604-467-0218
www.hairdressing.ca

New Westminster Campus
333 - 6th St., New Westminster, BC V3L 4H2, Canada
Tel: 604-520-3989
www.hairdressing.ca

Sechelt: **Sunshine Coast Computer College**
P.O. Box 2429
5797 Ebbtide St., Sechelt, BC V0N 3A0, Canada
Tel: 604-885-3386; *Fax:* 604-885-7123
b_pap@uniserve.com
www.homestead.com/computercollege/

Surrey: **Hilltop Security Academy**
#119, 9801 King George Hwy., Surrey, BC V3T 5H5, Canada
Tel: 604-930-8377
info@hilltopsecurity.com
www.hilltopsecurity.com/
Private security training; software quality assurance

Surrey: **West Coast College of Health Care**
#210, 2383 King George Hwy., Surrey, BC V4A 5A4, Canada
Tel: 604-951-6644; *Fax:* 604-951-6608
Toll-Free: 1-800-807-855
admin@westcoastcollege.com
www.westcoastcollege.com
Enrollment: 220
Pharmacy Technician, Community Support/Justice Worker, Veterinary Assistant, Medical Lab Assistant, Resident Care Attendant, Certified Dental Assistant

Vancouver: **Blanche Macdonald Centre**
#100, 555 West 12th Ave., Vancouver, BC V5Z 3X7, Canada
Tel: 604-685-0347; *Fax:* 604-669-1415
info@blanchemacdonald.com
www.blanchemacdonald.com
Fashion merchandising & design, make-up artistry, esthetics programs, professional nail technology programs

Vancouver: **BM Chan International Cosmetology College**
2951 Kingsway, Vancouver, BC V5R 5J4, Canada
Tel: 604-437-3109
info@bmchan.com
www.bmchan.com
Hair, esthetics & nail courses
Monita Chan, Founder/President/Director

Vancouver: **Canadian Business English Institute**
#400, 1130 West Pender St., Vancouver, BC V6E 4A4, Canada
Tel: 604-685-0291; *Fax:* 604-685-0294
info@cbei.com
www.cbei.com
ESL, TOEFL, business English, TEFL training, student internships

Vancouver: **Canadian Family Resource Institute & Career College**
L-1 Broadway Plaza
600 West Broadway, Vancouver, BC V5Z 4C2, Canada
Tel: 604-879-2291; *Fax:* 604-879-2082
info@fricollege.com
www.fricollege.com
Nurse's aides training

Vancouver: **Canadian Institute of Gemmology**
P.O. Box 57010
Vancouver, BC V5K 5G6, Canada
Tel: 604-530-8569; *Fax:* 604-530-8569
Toll-Free: 1-800-294-221
www.cigem.ca
Diamond grading, jewellery, history & design, gem identification

Vancouver: **Columbia Academy, Digital Entertainment & Communications Training**
1295 West Broadway, Vancouver, BC V6H 3X8, Canada
Tel: 604-736-3316; *Fax:* 604-731-5458
Toll-Free: 1-800-665-928
administration@columbia-academy.com
www.columbia-academy.com
10-month programs in Broadcast Performing Arts (Radio/TV), Audio Recording/Sound Design & Digital Video Production

Vancouver: **EJ Canada College**
520 Hornby St., Vancouver, BC V6C 2E7, Canada
Tel: 604-689-1079; *Fax:* 604-689-1649
info@ejcanadacollege.com
www.ejcanadacollege.com
ESL

Vancouver: **Emily Carr Institute of Art & Design**
1399 Johnston St., Vancouver, BC V6H 3R9, Canada
Tel: 604-844-3800; *Fax:* 604-844-3801
Toll-Free: 1-800-832-778
www.eciad.ca/
Enrollment: 1173
Dr. Ronald Burnett, President

Vancouver: **Erickson College**
2021 Columbia St., Vancouver, BC V5Y 3C9, Canada
Tel: 604-879-5600; *Toll-Free:* 1-800-665-694
info@erickson.edu
www.erickson.edu
Psychotherapy & counselling, personal & professional empowerment & growth
Marilyn Atkinson, President

Vancouver: **Eurocentres Vancouver**
#250, 815 West Hastings St., Vancouver, BC V6C 1B4, Canada
Tel: 604-688-7942; *Fax:* 604-688-7985
info@languagecanada.com
www.languagecanada.com
English as a Second Language training

Vancouver: **Gateway Careers Inc.**
395 West Broadway, Vancouver, BC V5Y 1A7, Canada
Tel: 604-738-0285; *Fax:* 604-738-0994
info@gatewaycareers.ca
www.gatewaycareers.ca
Resident care; long-term care aide training

Vancouver: **Granville Business College**
#725, 570 Dunsmuir St., Vancouver, BC V6B 1Y1, Canada
Tel: 604-683-8850; *Fax:* 604-682-7115
Toll-Free: 1-800-661-988
vetassistant@telus.net
www.vet-assistant.com
Veterinary Office Assistants

Vancouver: **Helen Lefeaux Inc. School of Fashion Design**
#100, 247 Abbott St., Vancouver, BC V6B 2K7, Canada
Tel: 604-687-3352; *Fax:* 604-687-3356
info@helenlefeaux.com
www.helenlefeaux.com
Fashion design

Vancouver: **Institute of Forest Engineering of BC**
Forintek Building University of British Columbia
2665 East Mall, Vancouver, BC V6T 1W5, Canada
Tel: 604-224-7800; *Fax:* 604-224-7010
ifebc@interchg.ubc.ca

Vancouver: **Joji's Academy of Hair Fashion International**
1126 Commercial Dr., Vancouver, BC V5L 3X2, Canada
Tel: 604-255-5809; *Fax:* 604-255-5803
enroll@jojishair.com
www.jojishairschool.com

Vancouver: **MTI Vancouver Campus**
#290, 220 Cambie St., Vancouver, BC V6B 2M9, Canada
Tel: 604-682-6020; *Fax:* 604-682-6468
Toll-Free: 1-866-682-6020
vancouver@mticc.com
www.metrocollege.net
ECCE; Residential Care; Long Term Care Aide; Community Support Worker; Internet Development; MCSE

Campuses

Surrey King George Campus
10072 King George Hwy., Surrey, BC V3T 2W4, Canada
Tel: 604-583-6020; *Fax:* 604-583-6019
surrey@mticc.com
www.metrocollege.net

Coquitlam Campus
#223- 3030 Lincoln Ave., Coquitlam, BC V3B 6B4, Canada
Tel: 604-464-8718; *Fax:* 604-942-6355
coquitlam@mticc.com
www.metrocollege.net

Burnaby Campus
#100-6446 Nelson Ave., Burnaby, BC V5H 3J5, Canada
Tel: 604-437-6030; *Fax:* 604-437-6036
burnaby@mticc.com
www.metrocollege.net

Chilliwack Campus
#107-7491 Vedder Rd., Chilliwack, BC V2R 4E7, Canada
Tel: 604-824-6081; *Fax:* 604-824-6084
chilliwack@mticc.com
www.metrocollege.net

Vancouver: Native Education Centre
285 East 5th Ave., Vancouver, BC V5T 1H2, Canada
Tel: 604-873-3772; *Fax:* 604-873-9152
admissions@necvancouver.org
www.necvancouver.org
Family counselling, ECE, office administration, criminal justice studies, aboriginal tourism & aboriginal land stewardship

Vancouver: Pacific Gateway Vancouver
1155 Robson St., 3rd Fl., Vancouver, BC V6E 1B5, Canada
Tel: 604-687-3595; *Fax:* 604-687-3586
info@pacificgateway.net
www.pacificgateway.net

Campuses
Brisbane Campus
Level 1, 232 Adelaise St., Brisbane, Queensland, Australia
Fax: 617-322- 027
study@pacificgateway.net.au
www.pacificgateway.net.au
Other Information: 61-7-3220-0144

Pacific Gateway Toronto
80 Bloor St. West, 9th Fl., Toronto, ON M5S 2V1, Canada
Tel: 416-413-0511; *Fax:* 416-413-9044
toronto@pacificgateway.net
www.pacificgateway.net

Pacific Gateway Victoria
1012 Douglas St., 3rd. Fl., Victoria, BC V8W 2C3, Canada
Tel: 250-381-6630; *Fax:* 250-381-6631
victoria@pacificgateway.net
www.pacificgateway.net

Sydney Campus
Level 7, 190 George St. The Rocks, Sydney NSW
Tel: 029-247-1744; *Fax:* 029-247-1644
study@pacificgateway.net.au
www.pacificgateway.net.au

Vancouver: Rhodes Wellness College
#280, 1125 Howe St., Vancouver, BC V6Z 2K8, Canada
Tel: 604-708-4416; *Fax:* 604-708-4418
admin@rhodescollege.ca
www.rhodescollege.ca
Wellness, lifeskills, coaching & counselling diplomas & certificates; PCTIA accredited

Vancouver: Spectrum College & Consulting Services Ltd.
#301, 1010 Beach Ave., Vancouver, BC V6E 1T7, Canada
Tel: 604-685-5100; *Fax:* 604-685-5199
flong@knowplace.ca
knowplace.ca
Provides online courses, workshops and conferences online

Vancouver: Tourism Training Institute
#301, 1245 West Broadway, Vancouver, BC V6H 1G7, Canada
Tel: 604-736-7008; *Fax:* 604-736-7723
info@tourismti.com
www.tourismti.com
Travel & tourism; hotel management; cruise hospitality

Vancouver: Vancouver Campus
#501-1755 West Broadway, Vancouver, BC V6J 4S5, Canada
Tel: 604-736-8000; *Fax:* 604-731-9819
Toll-Free: 1-800-668-9301
vancouver@tourismcollege.com
www.tourismcollege.com
Travel, tourism & hospitality

Campuses
Surrey
#320-10362 King, Surrey, BC V3R 8X8, Canada
Fax: 604-583-4092
www.tourismcollege.com

Vancouver: Vancouver Campus
#200, 1111 Melville St., Vancouver, BC V6E 3V6, Canada
Tel: 604-684-4467; *Fax:* 604-689-4430
Toll-Free: 1-87-STENBERG
vanadmin@stenbergcollege.com
www.stenbergcollege.com
Resident care attendant; community support worker; nursing unit clerk, medical office assistant; institutional aid; veterinary assistant; practical nursing program; automotive technician

Campuses
Surrey Campus at Central City
#750-13450 - 102nd Ave., Surrey, BC V3T 5X3, Canada
Tel: 604-580-2772; *Fax:* 604-580-2774
Toll-Free: 1-87-STENBERG
admin@stenbergcollge.com
www.stenbergcollege.com

Vancouver: Vancouver School of Theology
6000 Iona Dr., Vancouver, BC V6T 1L4, Canada
Tel: 604-822-9031; *Fax:* 604-822-9212
Toll-Free: 1-866-822-903
possibilities@vst.edu
www.vst.edu
Multi-denominational graduate school educating leaders for the church, service agencies & businesses
Rev. Dr. Wendy Fletcher, Principal

Vancouver: Western Imperial College of Canada
#201, 2460 Commercial Dr., Vancouver, BC V5H 4T9, Canada
Tel: 604-872-1236; *Fax:* 604-872-1275
teachabroad@telus.net
wiccbc.tripod.com/index.html
Specializes in offering Aspen University's Master's Degree Programs to international & North American students; also runs & manages ESL International - an educational centre that specializes in the training of individuals to teach English as a Second/For
Henry Yeo, Executive Director

Victoria: Academy of Excellence
#303, Goldstream Ave., Victoria, BC V9B 2W4, Canada
Tel: 604-386-7843; *Fax:* 250-386-0090
excellence@telus.net
www.academyofexcellencevictoria.com

Victoria: Aveda Institute Victoria
660 Johnson St., Victoria, BC V8W 1M6, Canada
Tel: 250-386-7985; *Fax:* 250-386-7945
admissions@pauldacostainstitute.ca
www.avedainstitutevictoria.ca
Enrollment: 81
Cosmetology & esthiology

Victoria: BC School of Art Therapy
1941 Lee Ave., Victoria, BC V8R 4W9, Canada
Tel: 250-598-6434; *Fax:* 250-598-6449
info@bcsat.com
bcsat.com
Graduate level clinical training in art therapy
Aira Welwood, Program Director

Victoria: Canadian Acupressure College Inc.
#301, 733 Johnson St., Victoria, BC V8W 3C7, Canada
Tel: 250-388-7475; *Fax:* 250-383-3647
Toll-Free: 1-877-909-224
cai@islandnet.com
www.acupressureshiatsuschool.com
Training in acupressure & shiatsu diploma programs

Victoria: Canadian College of Business & Language
16 Bastion Sq., Victoria, BC V8W 1H9, Canada
Tel: 250-383-3933; *Fax:* 250-383-2292
admin@cdncollege.bc.ca
www.canadiancollege.ca
Gerald La Belle, President

Victoria: Canadian College of Performing Arts
1701 Elgin Rd., Victoria, BC V8R 5L7, Canada
Tel: 250-595-9970; *Fax:* 250-595-0779
admin@ccpacanada.com
www.ccpacanada.com
Enrollment: 65
Two, 1-year extensive training programs in acting, voice, dance & career management

Victoria: Lester B. Pearson College of the Pacific
650 Pearson College Dr., Victoria, BC V9C 4H7, Canada
Tel: 250-391-2411; *Fax:* 250-391-2412
admin@pearsoncollege.ca
www.pearsoncollege.ca
Stuart Walker, Director

Victoria: Western Academy of Photography
755A Queens Ave., Victoria, BC V8T 1M2, Canada
Tel: 250-383-1522; *Fax:* 250-383-1534
wap-office@shaw.ca
www.westernacademyofphotography.com
Professional Photography & Journalism/Photojournalism

West Vancouver: ABC Occupational First Aid Training
1057 Millstream Rd., West Vancouver, BC V7S 2C8, Canada
Tel: 604-925-1057; *Fax:* 604-596-2999
www.abcfirstaidtraining.com
Industrial first aid
Alison Spears
alison_abc@shaw.ca

West Vancouver: The Anna Wyman School of Dance Arts
1457 Marine Dr., West Vancouver, BC V7T 1B8, Canada
Tel: 604-926-6535; *Fax:* 604-926-6912
info@annawyman.com
www.annawyman.com
Offering professional dance training to dedicated students for over 30 years

West Vancouver: Vancouver Art Therapy Institute
#350, 1425 Marine Dr., West Vancouver, BC V7T 1B9, Canada
Tel: 604-926-9381; *Fax:* 604-926-5728
vatimail@telus.net
www.vati.bc.ca

Manitoba

Government Agencies

Winnipeg: Manitoba Advanced Education & Training
Legislative Bldg.
#156, 450 Broadway, Winnipeg, MB R3C 0V8, Canada
Tel: 204-945-0825; *Fax:* 204-948-2216
www.edu.gov.mb.ca/aet/
Hon. Diane McGifford, Minister
Dwight Botting, Acting Deputy Minister

Winnipeg: Manitoba Education, Citizenship & Youth
#168, 450 Broadway, Winnipeg, MB R3C 0Y8, Canada
Tel: 204-945-3720; *Fax:* 204-945-1291
minedu@leg.gov.mb.ca
www.edu.gov.mb.ca
Gerald Farthing, Acting Deputy Minister
Hon. Peter Bjornson, Minister

School Boards/Districts/Divisions

Public

Altona: Border Land School Division
P.O. Box 390
120 - 9th St. NW, Altona, MB R0G 0B0, Canada
Tel: 204-324-6491; *Fax:* 204-324-1664
Toll-Free: 1-866-324-6491
www.borderland.ca
Other Information: Transportation Office: 204-427-2091; Maintenance: 204-324-9536
Grades: Kindergarten - 12; French Immersion
Krista Curry, Chief Executive Officer / Superintendent, 204-324-6491, ext. 1010, fax: 204-324-1664
Carol Braun, Assistant Superintendent, 204-324-6491, ext. 1011, fax: 204-324-1664
Anne Malyon, Secretary-Treasurer, 204-324-6491, ext. 1012, fax: 204-324-1664
Todd Nichols, Coordinator, Transportation, 204-427-2091, ext. 1510, fax: 204-427-2531
Julie Weber, Coordinator, Student Services, 204-427-2091, ext. 1013, fax: 204-427-2531

Beausejour: Sunrise School Division
Sunrise Education Center
P.O. Box 1206
344 Second St. North, Beausejour, MB R0E 0C0, Canada
Tel: 204-268-6500; *Fax:* 204-268-6545
Toll-Free: 1-866-444-5559
kwold@sunrisesd.ca (Kathy Wold, Reception)
www.sunrisesd.ca
Other Information: Transportation, Phone: 204-444-2498; Business, Fax: 204-268-4149
Grades: Kindergarten - 12; Adult Education
Number of Schools: 24
Don Nichol, Chair, 204-348-2818
dnichol@sunrisesd.ca

Wayne Leckie, Superintendent & Chief Executive Officer, 204-268-6507
wleckie@sunrisesd.ca
Paul Barnard, Assistant Superintendent, People Services, 204-268-6538
pbarnard@sunrisesd.ca
Paul Magnan, Assistant Superintendent, Student Learning, 204-268-6517
pmagnan@sunrisesd.ca
Lesley Eblie Trudel, Division Principal, Student Support Programs, 204-268-6535
leblie@sunrisesd.ca
Joan Badger, Leader, Middle Years & ICt Program, 204-268-6543
jbadger@sunrisesd.ca
Karen David, Leader, Early Years Program, 204-268-6527
kdavid@sunrisesd.ca
Kevin Doell, Leader, Music Program, 204-444-2473
kdoell@sunrisesd.ca
Marie Josee Morneau, Leader, Senior Years Program, 204-268-6532
mjmorneau@sunrisesd.ca
Fran King, Manager, Purchasing, 204-268-6531
fking@sunrisesd.ca
Roger Hardman, Secretary-Treasurer, 204-268-6514
rhardman@sunrisesd.ca

Birtle: Park West School Division
P.O. Box 68
1161 St. Claire St., Birtle, MB R0M 0C0, Canada
Tel: 204-842-2100; *Fax:* 204-842-2110
Toll-Free: 877-418-5320
cbonner@pwsd.ca
www.pwsd.ca

Enrollment: 1800
Joe Arruda, Chief Executive Officer

Brandon: Brandon School Division
Administration Office
1031 - 6th St., Brandon, MB R7A 4K5, Canada
Tel: 204-729-3100; *Fax:* 204-727-2217
info@brandonsd.mb.ca; human.resources@brandonsd.mb.ca
www.brandonsd.mb.ca

Grades: Kindergarten - 12; French Immersion
Enrollment: 7200
George Buri, Chair, 204-727-3156
buri.george@brandonsd.mb.ca
Dr. Donna Michaels, Chief Executive Officer & Superintendent of Schools
michaels.donna@brandonsd.mb.ca
Greg Malazdrewicz, Associate Superintendent
malazdrewicz.greg@brandonsd.mb.ca
Gerald F. Barnes, Secretary-Treasurer
barnes.gerald@brandonsd.mb.ca

Carman: Prairie Rose School Division
45 Main St. South, Carman, MB R0G 0J0, Canada
Tel: 204-745-2003; *Fax:* 204-745-3699
Toll-Free: 866-745-3699
prsd@prsdmb.ca
www.prsdmb.ca

Enrollment: 2278
Bruce Wood, Superintendent

Dauphin: Mountain View School Division
P.O. Box 715
Dauphin, MB R7N 3B3, Canada
Tel: 204-638-3001; *Fax:* 204-638-7250
www.mvsd.ca

Grades: K.-12
Enrollment: 3300
Jack Sullivan, Supt.
jsullivan@mvsd.ca
Bart Michaleski, Sec.-Treas.
michale@mvsd.ca

Eriksdale: Lakeshore School Division
P.O. Box 100
Eriksdale, MB R0C 0W0, Canada
Tel: 204-739-2101; *Fax:* 204-739-2145
admin@lakeshoresd.mb.ca
www.lakeshoresd.mb.ca

Enrollment: 1304
Janet Martell, Superintendent

Flin Flon: Flin Flon School Division
9 Terrace Ave., Flin Flon, MB R8A 1S2, Canada
Tel: 204-681-3413; *Fax:* 204-681-3417
www.ffsd.mb.ca

Grades: Kindergarten - 12; Alternative Ed.
Enrollment: 1378
Number of Schools: 3 elementary schools; 2 secondary schools
Trish Sattelberger, Chair
Blaine Veitch, Superintendent
bveitch@ffsd.mb.ca
Dean Grove, Assistant Superintendent
dgrove@ffsd.mb.ca
Debbie Bongfeldt, Secretary-Treasurer
dbongfeldt@ffsd.mb.ca
Bruce Fidler, Supervisor, Maintenance
bfidler@ffsd.mb.ca

Gimli: Evergreen School Division
Education Support Centre
P.O. Box 1200
140 Centre Ave. West, Gimli, MB R0C 1B0, Canada
Tel: 204-642-6260; *Fax:* 204-642-7273
info@esd.mb.ca
www.esd.mb.ca

Grades: Kindergarten - 12; Continuing Ed.
Enrollment: 1671
Number of Schools: 8. Number of Employees: 273
Ruth Ann Furgala, Chair, 204-378-2901
rfurgala@esd.mb.ca
Paul Cuthbert, Superintendent & Chief Executive Officer, 204-642-6278
pcuthbert@esd.mb.ca
Roza Gray, Assistant Superintendent, 204-642-6267
rgray@esd.mb.ca
Daniel Howe, Director, Operations, 204-642-6269
dhowe@esd.mb.ca
Fay Cassidy, Coordinator, Student Services, 204-642-6279
fcassidy@esd.mb.ca
Brenda Chapman, Officer, Safety, 204-641-1365
bchapman@esd.mb.ca
Charlie Grieve, Secretary-Treasurer, 204-642-6266
cgrieve@esd.mb.ca

Gladstone: Pine Creek School Division
P.O. Box 420
Gladstone, MB R0J 0T0, Canada
Tel: 204-385-2216; *Fax:* 204-385-2825
pcsddo@pinecreeksd.mb.ca
www.pinecreeksd.mb.ca

Enrollment: 1200
Brian Gouriluk, Superintendent
bgouriluk@pinecreeksd.mb.ca

Killarney: Turtle Mountain School Division
P.O. Box 280
435 Williams Ave., Killarney, MB R0K 1G0, Canada
Tel: 204-523-7531; *Fax:* 204-523-7269
dbo@tmsd.mb.ca
www.tmsd.mb.ca

Grades: Kindergarten - 12; Continuing Ed.
Number of Schools: 4 Hutterian schools; 1 elementary / middle years schools; 2 kindergarten to grade 12 schools; 2 adult education campuses
Larry Rainnie, Superintendent
lrainnie@tmsd.mb.ca
Tanya Edgar, Assistant Superintendent, Student Services
tedgar@tmsd.mb.ca
Kathy Siatecki, Secretary-Treasurer
Julie Dyck, Administrator, Payroll & Benefits
jdyck@tmsd.mb.ca
John Reimer, Supervisor, Transportation
jreimer@tmsd.mb.ca
Ken Rose, Supervisor, Buildings & Maintenance
krose@tmsd.mb.ca

Lorette: Division Scolaire franco-manitobaine
P.O. Box 204
1263, ch Dawson, Lorette, MB R0A 0Y0, Canada
Tél: 204-878-9399; *Téléc:* 204-878-9407
dsfm@atrium.ca

Enrollment: 4572
Gérard Auger, Supt.

Lorette: Seine River School Division
475A Senez St., Lorette, MB R0A 0Y0, Canada
Tel: 204-878-4713; *Fax:* 204-878-4717
www.srsd.mb.ca

Enrollment: 3500
Michael Borgfjord, Superintendent

McCreary: Turtle River School Division
P.O. Box 309
808 Burrows Rd., McCreary, MB R0J 1B0, Canada
Tel: 204-835-2067; *Fax:* 204-835-2426
trsd32.mb.ca

Grades: Kindergarten - 12
Enrollment: 771
Number of Schools: 7. Number of Staff: 63 teachers; 52 support staff
Allan Trotter, Chair, Board of Trustees
Bev Szymesko, Superintendent, Student Services
bevs@trsd32.mb.ca
Richard Bidzinski, Secretary-Treasurer
Richard@trsd32.mb.ca
Dean Bluhm, Supervisor, Transportation & Maintenance
deanb@trsd32.mb.ca
Shannon Desjardins, Accountant
shannon@trsd32.mb.ca
Helen Sommer, Speech / Language Pathologist
helen@trsd32.mb.ca
Jeff Fudge, Information & Communication Technology Technician
jeff@trsd32.mb.ca

Melita: Southwest Horizon School Division
P.O. Box 370
Melita, MB R0M 1L0, Canada
Tel: 204-483-5533; *Fax:* 204-483-5535
www.shsd.mb.ca

Enrollment: 1793
Brad Kyle, Superintendent

Minnedosa: Rolling River School Division
P.O. Box 1170
Minnedosa, MB R0J 1E0, Canada
Tel: 204-867-2754; *Fax:* 204-867-2037
rrsd@rrsd.mb.ca
www.rrsd.mb.ca

Enrollment: 1882
Reg Klassen, Superintendent
rklassen@rrsd.mb.ca

Morden: Western School Division
75 Thornhill St., #4, Morden, MB R6M 1P2, Canada
Tel: 204-822-4448; *Fax:* 204-822-4262
divoff@westernsd.mb.ca
www.westernsd.mb.ca

Grades: K.-12
Enrollment: 1600
Stephen Ross, Supt.
sross@westernsd.mb.ca
Carl Pedersen, Sec.-Treas.
cpedersen@westernsd.mb.ca
Dr David McAndrew, Chair
dmcandrew@westernsd.mb.ca

Morris: Red River Valley School Division
P.O. Box 400
233 Main St., Morris, MB R0G 1K0, Canada
Tel: 204-746-2317; *Fax:* 204-746-2785
rrvsd@rrvsd.ca
www.rrvsd.ca

Enrollment: 2196
Kelly Barkman, Superintendent

Neepawa: Beautiful Plains School Division
P.O. Box 700
Neepawa, MB R0J 1H0, Canada
Tel: 204-476-2388; *Fax:* 204-476-3606
bpsd@bpsd.mb.ca
www.bpsd.mb.ca

Grades: Kindergarten - 12; Special Ed.
Enrollment: 1500
Jason Young, Superintendent
jyoung@bpsd.mb.ca
Gord Olmstead, Secretary-Treasurer
golmstead@bpsd.mb.ca
Melanie Burnett, Coordinator, Student Services
mburnett@bpsd.mb.ca
Melanie Nordstrom, Coordinator, Technology
mordstrom@bpsd.mb.ca
Jennifer Donais, Speech Language Pathologist
jdonais@bpsd.mb.ca

Pilot Mound: Prairie Spirit School Division
P.O. Box 77
152 Broadway Ave. West, Pilot Mound, MB R0G 1P0, Canada
Tel: 204-825-2721; *Fax:* 204-825-2725
prspirit@mts.net
www.prairiespirit.mb.ca

Enrollment: 2479
Don Hurton, Superintendent

Pinawa: Whiteshell School District
P.O. Box 130
Pinawa, MB R0E 1L0, Canada
Tel: 204-753-8366; *Fax:* 204-753-2237
derousie@sdwhiteshell.mb.ca
sdwhiteshell.mb.ca

Grades: K.-12
Enrollment: 206

Bob Derousie, Supt./CEO
derousie@sdwhiteshell.mb.ca
Jenny Petersen, Sec.-Treas.
petersenj@sdwhiteshell.mb.ca
Rob Murray, Chair
murrayr@sdwhiteshell.mb.ca

***Portage la Prairie:* Portage la Prairie School Division**
535 - 3 St. NW, Portage la Prairie, MB R1N 2C4, Canada
Tel: 204-857-8756; *Fax:* 204-239-5998
div0024@merlin.mb.ca
www.plpsd.mb.ca

Enrollment: 3486
Hazen Barrett, Superintendent

***Selkirk:* Lord Selkirk School Division**
205 Mercy St., Selkirk, MB R1A 2C8, Canada
Tel: 204-482-5942; *Fax:* 204-482-3000
Toll-Free: 866-433-5942
lssd.boardoffice@lssd.ca
www.lssd.ca

Grades: K.-12
Enrollment: 5000
The schools celebrate the heritage and culture of the region - including the Brokenhead Ojibway Nation, the Scottish pioneers, the French Canadian voyageurs and the Ukrainian settlers.
Scott Kwasnitza, Supt./CEO
Bruce Cairns, Sec. Treas.

***Steinbach:* Hanover School Division**
5 Chrysler Gate, Steinbach, MB R5G 0E2, Canada
Tel: 204-326-6471; *Fax:* 204-326-9901
hsdadmin@hsd.ca
www.hsd.ca

Enrollment: 7400
Ken Klassen, Superintendent

***Stonewall:* Interlake School Division**
192 - 2nd Ave. North, Stonewall, MB R0C 2Z0, Canada
Tel: 204-467-5100; *Fax:* 204-467-8334
www.isd21.mb.ca

Enrollment: 3040
Ross Metcalfe, Superintendent
rmetcalfe@isd21.mb.ca

***Swan River:* Swan Valley School Division**
John Kastrukoff Building
1481 - 3rd St. North, Swan River, MB R0L 1Z0, Canada
Tel: 204-734-4531
www.svsd.ca

Grades: JK - 12; French Immersion
Number of Schools: 9
Bryon Fried, Chair
M. Marquis-Forster, Superintendent
R. Rausch, Secretary-Treasurer
D. Coulthart, Supervisor, Transportation
L. Delaurier, Supervisor, Maintenance
D. Burnside, Coordinator, Student Services

***The Pas:* Kelsey School Division**
P.O. Box 4700
322 Edwards Ave., The Pas, MB R9A 1R4, Canada
Tel: 204-623-6421; *Fax:* 204-623-7704
kelsey@merlin.mb.ca
www.ksd.mb.ca

Enrollment: 1733
Doug Long, Superintendent
douglong@ksd.mb.ca

***Thompson:* Mystery Lake School District**
408 Thompson Dr. North, Thompson, MB R8N 0C5, Canada
Tel: 204-677-6150; *Fax:* 204-677-9528
sdml@mysterynet.mb.ca
www.mysterynet.mb.ca

Grades: K.-12
Enrollment: 3000
Beverly Hammond, Supt./CEO
Arnie Assoignon, Sec.-Treas.
aassoignon@mysterynet.mb.ca

***Virden:* Fort la Bosse School Division**
P.O. Box 1420
523 - 9th Ave. South, Virden, MB R0M 2C0, Canada
Tel: 204-748-2692; *Fax:* 204-748-2436
flbsd@flbsd.mb.ca
www.flbsd.mb.ca

Grades: Kindergarten - 12
Enrollment: 1400
Number of Schools: 11
Gary E. Draper, Chair
Barry Pitz, Superintendent
Vaughn Wilson, Supervisor, Operations
Kent Reid, Secretary-Treasurer

Judy Dandridge, Coordinator, Student Services
Dr. Robert Paulet, School Psychologist

***Winkler:* Garden Valley School Division**
P.O. Box 1330
750 Triple E Blvd., Winkler, MB R6W 4B3, Canada
Tel: 204-325-8335; *Fax:* 204-325-4132
gvsd@gvsd.ca
www.gvsd.ca

Grades: Kindergarten - Secondary
Enrollment: 4100
Hilda Froese, Board Chair
Vern Reimer, Chief Executive Officer & Superintendent of Schools
Todd Monster, Assistant Superintendent
Debra Loewen, Assistant Superintendent, Student Services
Jenn Sager Hlady, Manager, Human Resources
Ken Bergen, Supervisor, Operations
Abe Wiebe, Supervisor, Capital Projects
James Reimer, Coordinator, Technology
Terry Penner, Secretary-Treasurer

***Winnipeg:* Frontier School Division**
30 Speers Rd., Winnipeg, MB R2J 1L9, Canada
Tel: 204-775-9741; *Fax:* 204-775-9940
frontier@frontiersd.mb.ca
www.frontiersd.mb.ca

Enrollment: 6869
Number of Schools: 41
Linda Ballantyne, Chair
Gordon Shead, Chief Superintendent
Bradley Hampson, Assistant Superintendent, Technology
Don McCaskill, Assistant Superintendent, Senior Years & Careers Program
Arnold Dysart, Superintendent, Area 1
Karen Crozier, Superintendent, Area 2
Cam Giavedoni, Superintendent, Area 3
Catherine Fidierchuk, Superintendent, Area 4
David Swanson, Superintendent, Area 5
Lena McAlinden, Director, Human Resources
Gerald Cattani, Secretary-Treasurer

***Winnipeg:* Louis Riel School Division**
900 St. Mary's Rd., Winnipeg, MB R2M 3R3, Canada
Tel: 204-257-7827; *Fax:* 204-256-8553
www.lrsd.net

Grades: K.-12
Enrollment: 14464
The is an amalgamation of the St. Boniface and St. Vital School Divisions.
Terry D. Borys, Supt./CEO

***Winnipeg:* Pembina Trails School Division**
181 Henlow Bay, Winnipeg, MB R3Y 1M7, Canada
Tel: 204-488-1757; *Fax:* 204-487-3667
ptsdwebinfo@pembinatrails.ca
www.pembinatrails.ca

Enrollment: 13385
Lawrence Lussier, Superintendent

***Winnipeg:* River East Transcona School Division**
589 Roch St., Winnipeg, MB R2K 2P7, Canada
Tel: 204-667-7130; *Fax:* 204-661-5618
www.retsd.mb.ca

Enrollment: 17000
Dennis Pottage, Superintendent

***Winnipeg:* St. James-Assiniboia School Division**
2574 Portage Ave., Winnipeg, MB R3J 0H8, Canada
Tel: 204-888-7951; *Fax:* 204-831-0859
inquiries@sjsd.net; mnachtigall@sjsd.net (administration & board)
www.sjsd.net
Other Information: Continuing Ed., Phone: 204-832-9637; Intl. Program: 204-837-1331

Grades: Kindergarten - Senior 4
Number of Schools: 15 early years schools; 6 middle years schools; 5 senior years schools
Bruce Chegus, Chair, 204-888-9498
bchegus@sjsd.net
Ron K. Weston, Chief Superintendent
Brett J. Lough, Assistant Superintendent, Administration, Planning & Research
Greg Mutter, Assistant Superintendent, Personnel & Human Resources
Tanis C.M. Pshebniski, Assistant Superintendent, Program & Curriculum
Dennis G. Dart, Manager, Facilities & Maintenance
Carrol A. Harvey, Manager, Human Resources (MANTE & excluded)
Cindy Labaty, Manager, Human Resources (CUPE)
P. Elsworth, Officer, Information
pelsworth@sjsd.net

B. Neufeld, Officer, Purchasing
bneufeld@sjsd.net
Michael J. Friesen, Secretary-Treasurer

***Winnipeg:* Seven Oaks School Division**
830 Powers St., Winnipeg, MB R2V 4E7, Canada
Tel: 204-586-8061; *Fax:* 204-589-2504
communitybeginshere@7oaks.org
www.7oaks.org

Enrollment: 8950
Brian O'Leary, Superintendent

***Winnipeg:* Winnipeg School Division**
1577 Wall St. East, Winnipeg, MB R3E 2S5, Canada
Tel: 204-775-0231; *Fax:* 204-772-6464
adminofc@wsd1.org
www.wsd1.org

Grades: Pre-K.-12
Enrollment: 32000
Pauline Clarke, Chief Supt.
pclarke@wsd1.org
Rene Appelmans, Sec.-Treas.
rappelmans@wsd1.org
Val Georges, Dir., Aboriginal Ed., 204-788-0203, fax: 204-772-3911
vgeorges@wsd1.org

First Nations

***Ebb & Flow:* Ebb & Flow Eduction Authority**
P.O. Box 160
Ebb & Flow, MB R0L 0R0
Tel: 204-448-2438; *Fax:* 204-448-2393
eandf@mts.net

Grades: Elementary - Secondary
Number of Schools: 1 (Ebb & Flow School). The Ebb & Flow Eduction Authority serves the Ebb & Flow First Nation in Manitoba
Arlene Mousseau, Director, Education

***Gods River:* Amos Okemow Memorial Education Authority**
Building 1D
103, Gods River, MB R0B 0N0, Canada
Tel: 204-366-2070; *Fax:* 204-366-2105

Grades: Kindergarten - 9
Enrollment: 170
The Amos Okemow Memorial Education Authority serves the Manto Sipi Cree Nation through operation of the Amos Okemow Memorial School. To continue their secondary school education, students must leave the community.
A. Jane Tuesday, Director, Education
ajanet25@hotmail.com
Alan Pogson, Principal

***Oxford House:* Oxford House First Nation Board of Education**
General Delivery, Oxford House, MB R0B 1C0
Tel: 204-538-2051

Grades: Elementary - S4
Enrollment: 675
Number of Schools: 2 (Oxford House Elementary School & 1972 Memorial High School). The Oxford House First Nation Board of Education serves the Bunibonibee Cree Nation of Oxford House, which is situated 600 km north of Winnipeg, Manitoba.
Alvin Grieves, Director, Education, Oxford House First Nation Board of Ed.
argrieves@hotmail.com

***Pelican Rapids:* Sapotaweyak Education Authority**
General Delivery, Pelican Rapids, MB R0L 1L0
Tel: 204-587-2045; *Fax:* 204-587-2341

Grades: Nursery - 12
Enrollment: 350
Number of Schools: 1 (Neil Dennis Kematch Memorial School). Number of Employees: 50. The Sapotaweyak Education Authority is responsible for the provision of education for the Sapotaweyak Cree Nation, near the towns of Swan River & The Pas in Manitoba.
Diane Genaille, Director, Education
school@ndkms.com

***Pine Falls:* Sagkeeng Education Authority**
P.O. Box 1610
Pine Falls, MB R0E 1M0, Canada
Tel: 204-367-2287; *Fax:* 204-367-4315
Toll-Free: 1-866-878-2911

Grades: Elementary - Secondary
Number of Schools: 3 (Anicinabe Community School; Sagkeeng Junior High School; & Sagkeeng Anicinabe High School)
Eva Courchene, Education Director
Alan Courchene, Principal, Sagkeeng Anicinabe High School, 204-367-2243, fax: 204-367-4566

Rick Fewchuck, Principal, Anicinabe Community School, 204-367-2285, fax: 204-367-9205
Claude Guimond, Principal, Sagkeeng Junior High School, 204-367-2588, fax: 204-367-9231

Winnipeg: **Southeast Tribal Division for Schools Inc.**
#301, 208 Edmonton St., Winnipeg, MB R3C 1R7, Canada
Tel: 204-943-7412; *Fax:* 204-947-8386

Schools: Specialized

First Nations

Beulah: **Chan Kagha Otina Dakota Wayawa Tipi School**
P.O. Box 40
Beulah, MB R0M 0B0, Canada
Tel: 204-568-4757; *Fax:* 204-568-4762
www.frontiersd.mb.ca
Grades: birdtailschool@gmail.ca
Enrollment: 130
The Chan Kagha Otina Dakota Wayawa Tipi School serves the Birdtail Sioux Dakota Nation. It is part of Manitoba's Frontier School Division.
Karen Crozier, Superintendent, Frontier School Division (Dauphin Area), 204-638-6839
jacqueline_birdtail@yahoo.ca
Michael Gamblin, Principal

Birch River: **Chief Charles Thomas Audy Memorial School**
P.O. Box 307
Birch River, MB R0L 0E0, Canada
Tel: 204-236-4783; *Fax:* 204-236-4779
Grades: Nursery - 8
Chief Charles Thomas Audy Memorial School serves the Wuskwi Sipihk First Nation.

Bloodvein: **Miskooseepi School**
General Delivery, Bloodvein, MB R0C 0J0, Canada
Tel: 204-395-2012; *Fax:* 204-395-2189
Grades: Pre.-9

Camperville: **Pine Creek School**
P.O. Box 130
Camperville, MB R0L 0J0, Canada
Tel: 204-524-2318; *Fax:* 204-524-2177
Grades: Pre.-11

Crane River: **Donald Ahmo School**
P.O. Box 91
Crane River, MB R0L 0M0, Canada
Tel: 204-732-2548; *Fax:* 204-732-2753
The Donald Ahmo School is a band-operated First Nation school which serves the O-Chi-Chak-Ko-Sipi First Nation in Crane River, Manitoba.
Peter McKay, Director, Education & Principal
mckay_pj@hotmail.com

Cross Lake: **Mikisew Middle School**
P.O. Box 370
Cross Lake, MB R0B 0J0, Canada
Tel: 204-676-3030; *Fax:* 204-676-2798
Grades: 5-8

Cross Lake: **Otter Nelson River**
P.O. Box 370
Cross Lake, MB R0B 0J0, Canada
Tel: 204-676-2050; *Fax:* 204-676-2464
sch1991@merlin.mb.ca
Grades: Pre.-12

Dakota Tipi: **Dakota Tipi School**
2000A Dakota Dr., Dakota Tipi, MB R1N 3P1, Canada
Tel: 204-857-7190
Enrollment: 60
Located outside the city of Portage La Prairie, Manitoba, the Dakota Tipi School is a First Nations band operated school. The school serves the Dakota Tipi First Nation.

Easterville: **Chemawawin School**
P.O. Box 10
Easterville, MB R0C 0V0, Canada
Tel: 204-329-2115; *Fax:* 204-329-2214
Located on the southern shore of Cedar Lake, 300 kilometres north of Winnipeg, Manitoba, the Chemawawin School provides education to the Chemawawin Cree Nation.
Melvin George, Director, Education
Amie Martin, Principal
amiemd@gmail.com

Ebb & Flow: **Ebb & Flow School**
P.O. Box 160
Ebb & Flow, MB R0L 0R0, Canada
Tel: 204-448-2012; *Fax:* 204-448-2393
eandf@mts.net
Grades: Elementary - Secondary
The Ebb & Flow School is a band-operated school in Manitoba which provides education to the Ebb & Flow First Nation.
Paul Monchka, Principal

Edwin: **Dakota Plains School**
P.O. Box 120
Edwin, MB R0H 0G0, Canada
Tel: 204-252-2895; *Fax:* 204-252-2188
Grades: Elementary
The Dakota Plains School serves the Dakota Plains Wahpeton Nation.
Donald R. Smoke, Director, Education

Elphinstone: **Keeseekoowenin School**
P.O. Box 129
Elphinstone, MB R0J 0N0, Canada
Tel: 204-625-2062; *Fax:* 204-625-2418
Grades: Pre.-8

Fairford: **Pinaymootang School**
Fairford Reserve
Fairford, MB R0C 0X0, Canada
Tel: 204-659-2045; *Fax:* 204-659-2270
sch1972@merlin.mb.ca
Grades: Pre.-12

Fisher River: **Charles Sinclair School**
P.O. Box 109
Fisher River, MB R0C 1S0, Canada
Tel: 204-645-2206; *Fax:* 204-645-2614
www.csschool.mb.ca
Part of the Fisher River Board of Education, Charles Sinclair School provides education to the Fisher River Cree Nation.
Davin Dumas, Principal, 204-645-2206, fax: 204-645-2614
davin@csschool.mb.ca
Jennifer Garson, Vice-Principal, 204-645-2206, fax: 204-645-2614
jennifer@csschool.mb.ca

Gillam: **Fox Lake Native Spiritual School**
P.O. Box 279
Gillam, MB R0B 0L0, Canada
Tel: 204-486-2307; *Fax:* 204-486-2606
Grades: Pre.-4

Ginew: **Ginew School**
P.O. Box 10
Ginew, MB R0A 2R0, Canada
Tel: 204-427-2490; *Fax:* 204-427-2398
Grades: Pre.-10

Gods Lake Narrows: **God's Lake Narrows First Nation School**
General Delivery, Gods Lake Narrows, MB R0B 0M0, Canada
Tel: 204-335-2003; *Fax:* 204-335-2440
Grades: Pre.-8

Gods River: **Amos Okemow Memorial School**
Building 1D
103, Gods River, MB R0B 0N0
Tel: 204-366-2312; *Fax:* 204-366-2105
Toll-Free: 866-896-4255
Grades: Kindergarten - 9
Enrollment: 170
Under the direction of the Amos Okemow Memorial Education Authority, the Amos Okemow Memorial School serves the Manto Sipi Cree Nation. Students must leave the community to continue their secondary school education.

Griswold: **Sioux Valley School**
P.O. Box 99
Griswold, MB R0M 0S0, Canada
Tel: 204-855-2536; *Fax:* 204-855-3204
sioux2@escape.ca
Grades: Pre.-12

Gypsumville: **Dauphin River School**
P.O. Box 140
Gypsumville, MB R0C 1J0, Canada
Tel: 204-659-5268; *Fax:* 204-659-5790
Grades: Elementary
Dauphin River First Nation is located at the junction of Dauphin River & Lake Winnipeg. A Dauphin River Mature Student Program is also available.

Gypsumville: **Lake St. Martin School**
P.O. Box 2020
Gypsumville, MB R0C 1J0, Canada
Tel: 204-659-2699; *Fax:* 204-659-5739
narrowsed@xplornet.ca
Grades: Nursery - 9
Enrollment: 120
The Lake St. Martin School provides elementary education to the Lake St. Martin First Nation in Manitoba's Interlake Region.
Roselyn Beardy, Principal

Gypsumville: **Little Saskatchewan School**
P.O. Box 5050
Gypsumville, MB R0C 1J0, Canada
Tel: 204-659-2672; *Fax:* 204-659-5763
sch1216@merlin.mb.ca
Grades: Pre.-10

Hodgson: **Lawrence Sinclair Memorial School**
P.O. Box 359
Hodgson, MB R0C 1N0, Canada
Tel: 204-394-2314; *Fax:* 204-394-2431
lawrencesinclairmemorialschool@hotmail.com
Grades: Nursery - 10
Lawrence Sinclair Memorial School is a band operated school which serves members of the Kinonjeoshtegon First Nation.
Adeline Traverse, Principal

Island Lake: **Garden Hill First Nations High School**
General Delivery, Island Lake, MB R0B 0T0, Canada
Tel: 204-456-2886; *Fax:* 204-456-2894
Grades: 7-12

Island Lake: **Kistiganwacheeng Elementary School**
General Delivery, Island Lake, MB R0B 0T0, Canada
Tel: 204-456-2391; *Fax:* 204-456-2350
Grades: Gr. N.-6

Lac Brochet: **Petit Casimir Memorial School**
General Delivery, Lac Brochet, MB R0B 2E0, Canada
Tel: 204-337-2278; *Fax:* 204-337-2078
Grades: Pre.-12

Marius: **Isaac Beaulieu Memorial**
Marius Post Office
Marius, MB R0H 0T0, Canada
Tel: 204-843-2407; *Fax:* 204-843-2269
sch1402@merlin.mb.ca
Grades: Pre.-12

Negginan: **Poplar River School**
Stn Negginan, Negginan, MB R0B 0Z0, Canada
Tel: 204-244-2113; *Fax:* 204-244-2259
prfn@mb.sympatico.ca
Grades: Pre.-9

Nelson House: **Nisichawayasihk Neyo Ohtinwak**
General Delivery, Nelson House, MB R0B 1A0, Canada
Tel: 204-484-2095; *Fax:* 204-484-2257
Grades: 9-12

Nelson House: **Otetiskewin Kiskinwamahtowekamik**
General Delivery, Nelson House, MB R0B 1A0, Canada
Tel: 204-484-2242; *Fax:* 204-484-2002
sch1413@merlin.mb.ca
Grades: Pre.-8

O'Hanly: **Little Black River School**
General Delivery, O'Hanly, MB R0E 1K0, Canada
Tel: 204-367-8298; *Fax:* 204-367-2266
Grades: Kindergarten - 12
Enrollment: 242
Members of the Little Black River First Nation are educated at the Little Black River School in O'Hanley, Manitoba. The First Nation community is situated approximately 150 kilometres north of Winnipeg.
Sheldon Kent, Chief

Opaskwayak: **Joe A. Ross School**
c/o Opaskwayak Education Authority
P.O. Box 10160
Opaskwayak, MB R0B 2J0, Canada
Tel: 204-623-4286; *Fax:* 204-623-4442
Grades: Pre.-12

Oxford House: **1972 Memorial High School**
General Delivery, Oxford House, MB R0B 1C0, Canada
Tel: 204-538-2020; *Fax:* 204-538-2075
Toll-Free: 1-888-377-8520
www.ohboe.ca
Other Information: Oxford House First Nation Bd. of Ed., Phone: 204-538-2051
Grades: 7 - S4
Enrollment: 225

Under the Oxford House First Nation Board of Education, the 1972 Memorial High School serves the Bunibonibee Cree Nation of Oxford House.
Alvin Grieves, Director, Education, Oxford House First Nation Board of Ed.
argrieves@hotmail.com
Lawrence Einarsson, Principal
l.einarsson@hotmail.com

***Oxford House:* Oxford House Elementary School**
General Delivery, Oxford House, MB R0B 1C0, Canada
Tel: 204-538-2318; *Fax:* 204-538-2782
Toll-Free: 1-888-377-8520
www.ohboe.ca
Other Information: Oxford House First Nation Bd. of Ed., Phone: 204-538-2051
Grades: Elementary
Enrollment: 450
Under the Oxford House First Nation Board of Education, the Oxford House Elementary School serves the Bunibonibee Cree Nation of Oxford House.
Alvin Grieves, Director, Education, Oxford House First Nation Board of Ed.
argrieves@hotmail.com
Wilfred Wood, Principal
wilfred.wood@ohboe.ca

***Peguis First Nation:* Peguis Central School**
P.O. Box 670
Peguis First Nation, MB R0C 3J0, Canada
Tel: 204-645-2164; *Fax:* 204-645-2270
Grades: 6-12

***Pelican Rapids:* Neil Dennis Kematch Memorial School (NDKMS)**
General Delivery, Pelican Rapids, MB R0L 1L0, Canada
Tel: 204-587-2045; *Fax:* 204-587-2341
school@ndkms.com
www.ndkms.com
Grades: Nursery - 12
Enrollment: 350
The Neil Dennis Kematch Memorial School serves the citizens of Sapotaweyak Cree First Nation in a community located approximately 120 kilometres north of Swan River, Manitoba. The school is administered by the Sapotaweyak Education Authority.
Lorna Carter, Principal
principal@ndkms.com

***Pine Falls:* Anicinabe Community School**
P.O. Box 219
Pine Falls, MB R0E 1M0
Tel: 204-367-2285; *Fax:* 204-367-9205
Anicinabe Community School serves the Sagkeeng First Nation. It operates under the direction of the Sagkeeng Education Authority.
Rick Fewchuck, Principal

***Pine Falls:* Sagkeeng Anicinabe High School**
P.O. Box 1610
Pine Falls, MB R0E 1M0
Tel: 204-367-2243; *Fax:* 204-367-4566
Grades: Secondary
The Sagkeeng Education Authority operates the Sagkeeng Anicinabe High School, which educates secondary school students of the Sagkeeng First Nation.
Alan Courchene, Principal

***Pine Falls:* Sagkeeng Junior High School**
P.O. Box 1610
Pine Falls, MB R0E 1M0
Tel: 204-367-2588; *Fax:* 204-367-9231
Sagkeeng Junior High School serves the Sagkeeng First Nation. The school operates under the Sagkeeng Education Authority.
Claude Guimond, Principal

***Pipestone:* Wambdi Iyotaka School**
P.O. Box 146
Pipestone, MB R0M 1T0, Canada
Tel: 204-854-2975; *Fax:* 204-854-2933
wambdi_iyotaka@live.ca
The Wambdi Iyotaka School serves members of the Canupawakpa Dakota Nation in Manitoba.
Anna Bone, Principal

***Portage la Prairie:* Long Plain School**
P.O. Box 430
Portage la Prairie, MB R1N 3B7, Canada
Tel: 204-252-2326; *Fax:* 204-252-2786
Grades: Pre.-9

***Pukatawagan:* Sakastew School**
P.O. Box 319
Pukatawagan, MB R0B 1G0, Canada
Tel: 204-553-2163; *Fax:* 204-553-2225
pukschol@cancom.net
Grades: K.-12

***Red Sucker Lake:* Red Sucker Lake School**
General Delivery, Red Sucker Lake, MB R0B 1H0, Canada
Tel: 204-469-5302; *Fax:* 204-469-5436
Grades: Pre.-12

***Scanterbury:* Sergeant Tommy Prince School**
General Delivery, Scanterbury, MB R0E 1W0, Canada
Tel: 204-766-2636; *Fax:* 204-766-2809
bone2@mb.sympatico.ca
Grades: K.-12

***Shamattawa:* Abraham Beardy Memorial School**
General Delivery, Shamattawa, MB R0B 1K0, Canada
Tel: 204-565-2022; *Fax:* 204-565-2122
Grades: Kindergarten - 10
Enrollment: 350
Abraham Beardy Memorial School serves the Cree First Nation of Shamattawa. To attend grades 11 & 12, students must enroll in educational institutions outside the community.
Ron Miles, Director, Education
Roberto Romero, Principal
r_romero@hotmail.com

***Shortdale:* Chief Clifford Lynxleg Anishinabe School**
General Delivery, Shortdale, MB R0L 1W0, Canada
Tel: 204-546-2641; *Fax:* 204-546-3120
Chief Clifford Lynxleg Anishinabe School is located on the Tootinawaziibeeng (Valley River) Reserve, where it provides education to the Tootinaowaziibeeng First Nation.
Madeline Whitehawk, Director, Education, & Principal
cclas@live.ca

***Split Lake:* Chief Sam Cook Mahmuwee Education Centre**
General Delivery, Split Lake, MB R0B 1P0, Canada
Tel: 204-342-2134; *Fax:* 204-342-2139
teduauthority@mts.net
Grades: Nursery - 12
Chief Sam Cook Mahmuwee Education Centre serves the Tataskweyak Cree Nation. The Tataskweyak reserve is located approximately 150 kilometres northeast of Thompson, Manitoba.
Alfred Beardy, Director, Education
Dan Beardy, Principal, Grades 7 - 12
Thelma Spence, Principal, Nursery - Grade 6
Blake Symons, Principal, Middle Years

***St Theresa Point:* St. Theresa Point School**
General Delivery, St Theresa Point, MB R0B 1J0, Canada
Tel: 204-462-2600; *Fax:* 204-462-2341
Grades: K.-12

***Swan Lake:* Indian Springs School**
P.O. Box 145
Swan Lake, MB R0G 2S0, Canada
Tel: 204-836-2332; *Fax:* 204-836-2317
isprings@mb.sympatico.ca
Grades: Pre.-8

***Tadoule Lake:* Peter Yassie Memorial School**
General Delivery, Tadoule Lake, MB R0B 2C0, Canada
Tel: 204-684-2279; *Fax:* 204-684-2130
Grades: K.-12

***Vogar:* Lake Manitoba School**
P.O. Box 1250
Vogar, MB R0C 3C0, Canada
Tel: 204-768-2728; *Fax:* 204-768-2194
Grades: Nursery - 8
Lake Manitoba School provides education to the Lake Manitoba First Nation.
Freda Missayabit, Principal

***Waasagomach:* George Knott School**
General Delivery, Waasagomach, MB R0B 1Z0, Canada
Tel: 204-457-2485; *Fax:* 204-457-2273
sch2067@merlin.mb.ca
Grades: Pre.-12

***Waywayseecappo:* Waywayseecappo Community School**
P.O. Box 9
Waywayseecappo, MB R0J 1S0, Canada
Tel: 204-859-2811; *Fax:* 204-859-2992
waywayschool@yahoo.ca
Grades: Nursery - 8
Enrollment: 457
Number of Employees: 21 teachers; 6 teacher assistants; 8 bus drivers; 3 custodians. The Waywayseecappo Community School is a band operated elementary school, which provides education to members of Manitoba's Waywayseecappo First Nation. The First Nation community is situated approximately thirty-four kilometres east of Russell. Secondary school students from Waywayseecappo First Nation are transported to Russell's Major Pratt School.
Patrick Anderson, Principal

***York Landing:* George Saunders Memorial School**
General Delivery, York Landing, MB R0B 2B0, Canada
Tel: 204-341-2118; *Fax:* 204-341-2235
Grades: Pre.-12

Special Education

***Brandon:* Child & Adolescent Treatment Centre**
1240 - 10th St., Brandon, MB R7A 7L6, Canada
Tel: 204-727-3445; *Fax:* 204-727-3451
Grades: 4-12

***Portage la Prairie:* Gladys Cook Educational Centre**
P.O. Box 1342
Portage la Prairie, MB R1N 3A9, Canada
Tel: 204-239-3029; *Fax:* 204-239-3025
sch1219@merlin.mb.ca
Grades: 1-12

***Winnipeg:* Behavioural Health Foundation**
35 av de la Digue, Winnipeg, MB R3V 1L6, Canada
Tel: 204-261-3312; *Fax:* 204-275-8847
Grades: K-S4

***Winnipeg:* Manitoba School for the Deaf**
242 Stradford St., Winnipeg, MB R2Y 2C9, Canada
Tel: 204-945-8934; *Fax:* 204-945-1767
sch1570@merlin.mb.ca
Grades: K.-12

***Winnipeg:* Manitoba Youth Centre**
170 Doncaster St., Winnipeg, MB R3N 1X9, Canada
Tel: 204-475-2010; *Fax:* 204-945-3112
sch1049@merlin.mb.ca
Grades: K.-12

***Winnipeg:* Marymound School**
442 Scotia St., Winnipeg, MB R2V 1X4, Canada
Tel: 204-336-5285; *Fax:* 204-338-4690
school@marymound.com
Grades: 3-10

***Winnipeg:* St. Amant School**
440 River Rd., Winnipeg, MB R2M 3Z9, Canada
Tel: 204-256-4301; *Fax:* 204-257-4349
Grades: K.-12

Schools: Independent & Private

Protestant

***Austin:* Edrans Christian School**
P.O. Box 1
RR #1, Austin, MB R0H 0C0, Canada
Tel: 204-466-2865; *Fax:* 204-466-2994
www.echurchnet.ca
Grades: K.-12
Dwight Kinley, Contact

***Stonewall:* Faith Academy - Stonewall Campus**
P.O. Box 1669
539 - 4th Ave. South, Stonewall, MB R0C 2Z0, Canada
Tel: 204-467-5833; *Fax:* 204-467-5833
www.faithacademy.ca
Grades: K.-8
Bill Cavey, Executive Director
FA_ceo@shaw.ca

***Winnipeg:* Faith Academy - Winnipeg Campus**
437 Matheson Ave., Winnipeg, MB R2W 0E1, Canada
Tel: 204-582-3400; *Fax:* 204-582-2616
www.faithacademy.ca
Grades: K.-12
Enrollment: 520
Faith Academy is a conservative, evangelical, Christian, revival-based educational institution open to any Manitoba student willing and able to follow the established school guide. Winnipeg Middle School located at 600 Jefferson Ave., (204) 338-6150; Pritchard Campus located at 220 Pritchard Ave., (204) 589-6885.
Bill Cavey, Executive Director
FA_ceo@shaw.ca

Catholic

Winnipeg: Holy Cross School
300 Dubuc St., Winnipeg, MB R2H 1E4, Canada
Tel: 204-237-4936; *Fax:* 204-237-7433
Grades: K.-8
Enrollment: 159
John Talaga, Principal

Independent & Private Schools

Altona: Sunflower Valley Christian School
P.O. Box 2484
Altona, MB R0G 0B0, Canada
Tel: 204-324-1564; *Fax:* 204-327-5505
Grades: 1-9

Arborg: Interlake Mennonite Fellowship School
P.O. Box 388
Arborg, MB R0C 0A0, Canada
Tel: 204-364-2328
Grades: K.-12

Arborg: Lake Centre Mennonite Fellowship School
P.O. Box 838
Arborg, MB R0C 0A0, Canada
Tel: 204-364-2201
Grades: 1-9

Arborg: Morweena Christian School (MCS)
P.O. Box 1030
Arborg, MB R0C 0A0, Canada
Tel: 204-364-2466; *Fax:* 204-364-3117
Grades: Kindergarten - 12

Austin: Austin Christian Academy
P.O. Box 460
Austin, MB R0H 0C0, Canada
Tel: 204-637-2303; *Fax:* 204-637-2529
aca@escape.ca
Grades: Kindergarten - 12
Enrollment: 50

Austin: Austin Mennonite School
P.O. Box 267
Austin, MB R0H 0C0, Canada
Tel: 204-637-2008
Grades: 1 - 12

Austin: Pine Creek School
Pine Creek Colony
P.O. Box 370
Austin, MB R0H 0C0, Canada
Tel: 204-466-2925; *Fax:* 204-466-2698
Grades: K.-10

Austin: Pine Creek School
P.O. Box 74
Austin, MB ROH OCO, Canada
Tel: 204-385-3025
Grades: K.-10

Beausejour: Willow Grove School
P.O. Box 59
Beausejour, MB R0E 0C0, Canada
Tel: 204-268-4035
Grades: 2-8

Birnie: Shady Oak Christian School
P.O. Box 14
Birnie, MB R0J 0J0, Canada
Tel: 204-966-3477; *Fax:* 204-966-3479
Grades: 1-9

Brandon: Christian Heritage School
Heritage Campus
2025 - 26 St., Brandon, MB R7B 3Y2, Canada
Tel: 204-725-3209; *Fax:* 204-728-9641
chs@westman.wave.ca
Grades: K.-8
Enrollment: 103

Carman: Dufferin Christian School
Box 1450, Carman, MB R0G 0J0, Canada
Tel: 204-745-2278; *Fax:* 204-745-3441
dufferin@mb.sympatico.ca
Grades: K.-12
Enrollment: 210

Cartwright: Cartwright Community Independent School (CCIS)
P.O. Box 419
Cartwright, MB R0K 0L0, Canada
Tel: 204-529-2357; *Fax:* 204-529-2455
Grades: 12 (Senior 4)

Cartwright: Rock Lake School
P.O. Box 69
Cartwright, MB R0K 0L0, Canada
Tel: 204-529-2349; *Fax:* 204-529-2184
Grades: 1 - 9

Elie: Huron Christian Academy
Elie, MB R0H 0H0, Canada
Tel: 204-353-4120
Grades: 1-12

Elie: Milltown Academy
P.O. Box 250
Elie, MB R0H 0H0, Canada
Tel: 204-353-4111; *Fax:* 204-353-2224
Grades: Kindergarten - 12

Elm Creek: Wingham HB School
P.O. Box 45
RR #1, Elm Creek, MB R0G 0N0, Canada
Tel: 204-436-3231; *Fax:* 204-436-3230
Grades: K.-12

Elma: Riverside School
P.O. Box 136
Elma, MB R0E 0Z0, Canada
Tel: 204-348-2686; *Fax:* 204-348-7181
Grades: 1 - 9

Elma: Twin Rivers Country School
P.O. Box 30
Elma, MB R0E 0Z0, Canada
Tel: 204-426-5611; *Fax:* 204-426-5611
Grades: 1 - 9

Fairford: Interlake Christian Academy
Fairford, MB R0C 0X0, Canada
Tel: 204-659-5359
Grades: 1-10

Grandview: Poplar Grove School
P.O. Box 70
Grandview, MB R0L 0Y0, Canada
Tel: 204-546-2691
Grades: 1-9

Gretna: Mennonite Collegiate Institute
P.O. Box 250
Gretna, MB R0G 0V0, Canada
Tel: 204-327-5891; *Fax:* 204-327-5872
mciblues@mb.sympatico.ca
Grades: 9-12
Enrollment: 170

Grunthal: Mennonite Christian Academy
P.O. Box 149
Grunthal, MB R0A 0R0, Canada
Tel: 204-434-9315
Grades: K.-11

Hodgson: Hodgson Christian Academy
P.O. Box 220
Hodgson, MB R0C 1N0, Canada
Tel: 204-372-8483
Grades: 1-9

Horndean: Horndean Christian Day School
P.O. Box 79
Horndean, MB R0G 0Z0, Canada
Tel: 204-829-3354
Grades: 1-10

Kenville: Riverdale School
RR#1, Kenville, MB R0L 0Z0, Canada
Tel: 204-539-2660
Grades: 1 - 9

Killarney: Lakeside Christian School
P.O. Box 894
Killarney, MB R0K 1G0, Canada
Tel: 204-523-8240; *Fax:* 204-523-8351
ics@mb.sympatico.ca
Grades: K.-9

Kleefeld: New Hope Christian School
P.O. Box 120
Kleefeld, MB R0A 0V0, Canada
Tel: 204-377-4204
Grades: 1 - 12

Kleefeld: Wild Rose School
P.O. Box 167
Kleefeld, MB R0A 0V0, Canada
Tel: 204-377-4778
Grades: 1-8

Kola: Kola Community School
P.O. Box 553
Kola, MB R0M 1B0, Canada
Tel: 204-556-2488; *Fax:* 204-556-2600
Grades: K.-1

Lorette: Daystar Christian Academy
PO Box 5, Grp. 100, RR#2, Lorette, MB R0A 0Y0, Canada
Tel: 204-878-3044
Grades: 2-9

MacGregor: Grace Christian Academy
P.O. Box 331
MacGregor, MB R0H 0R0, Canada
Tel: 204-685-2867; *Fax:* 204-685-2867
Grades: 1-12

MacGregor: H.B. Community Baker Colony School
P.O. Box 40
MacGregor, MB R0H 0R0, Canada
Tel: 204-252-2178; *Fax:* 204-252-2381
bakercs@mb.sympatico.ca
Grades: K.-12

Minnedosa: Odanah Colony School
P.O. Box 990
Minnedosa, MB R0J 1E0, Canada
Tel: 204-867-5074; *Fax:* 204-867-2037
Grades: K.-12

Neepawa: Living Hope School
P.O. Box 2158
Neepawa, MB R0J 1H0, Canada
Tel: 204-966-3274
Grades: 3-12

Pine Falls: Christian Faith Academy
P.O. Box 459
Pine Falls, MB R0E 1M0, Canada
Tel: 204-367-2056; *Fax:* 204-367-2056
cfa@granite.mb.ca
Grades: 1 - 12

Pine River: Pine River School
P.O. Box 242
Pine River, MB R0L 1M0, Canada
Tel: 204-263-2617; *Fax:* 204-263-2184
Grades: K.-9

Plum Coulee: Christ Full Gospel Academy
P.O. Box 107
75 Elm St., Plum Coulee, MB R0G 1R0, Canada
Tel: 204-829-3506; *Fax:* 204-829-7937
cfgf@mts.net
www.christfullgospel.org/main/academy.html
Other Information: 204-829-7937 (Phone, Pastor's study)
Grades: Kindergarten - 12
Christ Full Gospel Academy uses the Accelerated Christian Education curriculum.

Plum Coulee: Prairie Mennonite School
P.O. Box 53
Plum Coulee, MB R0G 1R0, Canada
Tel: 204-829-3336
Grades: 1-11

Portage la Prairie: Airport Colony School
P.O. Box 967
Portage la Prairie, MB R1N 3C4, Canada
Tel: 204-274-2412
Grades: K.-10
Location: NE 2-13-8 W, MacDonald, MB.

Portage la Prairie: Lighthouse Christian School
P.O. Box 1360
Portage la Prairie, MB R1N 3N9, Canada
Tel: 204-428-5332; *Fax:* 204-428-5386
Grades: K.-12

Portage la Prairie: Westpark School
P.O. Box 91
2375 Saskatchewan Ave. West, Portage la Prairie, MB R1N 3B2, Canada
Tel: 204-857-3726
office@westpark.mb.ca
www.westpark.mb.ca
Grades: Kindergarten - 12 (Senior 1 - 4)
Enrollment: 220
The school is a ministry of Portage Alliance Church.
Akaps Mweemba, Principal
Heather Boddy, Vice Principal

***Roblin:* Parkland Christian School**
P.O. Box 480
Roblin, MB R0L 1P0, Canada
Tel: 204-937-2870
Grades: 1-9

***Rosenort:* Prairie View School**
P.O. Box 117
112 River Rd. North, Rosenort, MB R0G 1W0, Canada
Tel: 204-746-8837; *Fax:* 204-746-8517
Grades: 1 - 9

***Sinclair:* Stony Creek School**
P.O. Box 5
Sinclair, MB R0M 2A0, Canada
Tel: 204-662-4409; *Fax:* 204-662-4539
Grades: 1-9

***Sperling:* Silverwinds School**
P.O. Box 130
Sperling, MB R0G 2M0, Canada
Tel: 204-626-3378; *Fax:* 204-626-3397
Grades: K.-12

***Ste. Anne:* Greenland School**
P.O. Box 224
RR#1, Ste. Anne, MB R5H 1R1, Canada
Tel: 204-355-4922; *Fax:* 204-355-9280
Grades: 1-9

***Steinbach:* Church of God Sunrise Academy**
P.O. Box 3368
Steinbach, MB R5G 1P6, Canada
Tel: 204-434-6643; *Fax:* 204-326-6681
Grades: K.-9

***Steinbach:* Country View School**
P.O. Box 3910
Steinbach, MB R5G 1P9, Canada
Tel: 204-326-1481
Grades: 1-9

***Steinbach:* Steinbach Christian Academy**
P.O. Box 20629
Steinbach, MB R5G 1S1, Canada
Tel: 204-326-5553
Grades: K.-12

***Steinbach:* Steinbach Christian High School**
50 Pth 12 North, Steinbach, MB R5G 1T4, Canada
Tel: 204-326-3537; *Fax:* 204-326-5164
schs@schs.ca
www.schs.ca
Grades: 7-12
Enrollment: 161
Christian High School with Mennonite affiliation

***Stonewall:* Northern Shield Academy**
P.O. Box 1039
Stonewall, MB R0C 2Z0, Canada
Tel: 204-467-5547; *Fax:* 204-467-2571
Grades: 6 - 12
Enrollment: 50
This is a private Christian school.

***Stuartburn:* Border View Christian Day School**
P.O. Box 11
Stuartburn, MB R0A 2B0, Canada
Tel: 204-427-2932
Grades: 1 - 10

***Swan River:* Community Bible Fellowship Christian School**
P.O. Box 1630
Swan River, MB R0L 1Z0, Canada
Tel: 204-734-2174; *Fax:* 204-734-5706
Grades: K.-8
Enrollment: 25

***Swan River:* Solid Rock Christian School**
P.O. Box 1239
Swan River, MB R0L 1Z0, Canada
Tel: 204-734-2651
Grades: K.-12

***Swan River:* Solid Rock Christian School**
P.O. Box 1239
Swan River, MB R0L 1Z0, Canada
Tel: 204-734-2651
Grades: K.-12

***Wawanesa:* Green Acres Colony High School**
P.O. Box 190
Wawanesa, MB R0K 2G0, Canada
Tel: 204-824-2340; *Fax:* 204-824-2112
Grades: 9-12

***Winkler:* Grace Valley Mennonite Academy**
P.O. Box 839
Winkler, MB R6W 4A9, Canada
Tel: 204-829-3301; *Fax:* 204-829-3038
Grades: 1-12

***Winkler:* Schoenweise Christian School**
P.O. Box 663
Group 11, Winkler, MB R6W 4A1, Canada
Tel: 204-325-5401
Grades: 1-11

***Winkler:* Valley Mennonite Academy**
P.O. Box 139
Grp. 7, RR#1, Winkler, MB R6W 4A1, Canada
Tel: 204-325-8172; *Fax:* 204-331-3199
Grades: Kindergarten - 12
Enrollment: 134
Two private schools are operated by the Valley Mennonite Academy.

***Winnipeg:* Alhijra Islamic School**
410 Desalaberry Ave., Winnipeg, MB R2L 0Y7, Canada
Tel: 204-489-1300; *Fax:* 204-489-1323
alhijraschool@hotmail.com
Grades: K.-9
Enrollment: 196

***Winnipeg:* Balmoral Hall School**
630 Westminster Ave., Winnipeg, MB R3C 3S1, Canada
Tel: 204-784-1600
www.balmoralhall.com
TTY: 1-866-373-2611
Grades: Nursery - 5
Balmoral Hall School specializes in education for girls. It also offers a child care program for girls, aged 2 & 3.
Corrine Scott, Chair
Dr. Linda Schwartz, Head
Tina Alto, Director, Advancement, 204-784-1600
Pamela McGhie, Director, Admissions, 204-784-1621

***Winnipeg:* Beautiful Savior Lutheran School (BSLS)**
52 Birchdale Ave., Winnipeg, MB R2H 1R9, Canada
Tel: 204-984-9600; *Fax:* 204-984-9607
admin@bsls.ca; admissions@bsls.ca; preschool@bsls.ca
www.bsls.ca
Grades: Nursery - 8
Beautiful Savior Lutheran School also offers a daycare program & before & after school care.
Jennifer McCrea, Principal
Heather Burnett, Director, Child Care Services

***Winnipeg:* Calvin Christian School**
Collegiate Campus
706 Day St., Winnipeg, MB R2C 1B6, Canada
Tel: 204-222-7910; *Fax:* 204-222-8511
www.calvinchristian.mb.ca
Other Information: 204-338-7981 (Elementary phone); 204-339-3280 (Elementary fax)
Grades: Kindergarten - 12
Rob Booy, Chair & Staff Liaison
David Taylor, Principal, Collegiate Campus
Hank Vande Kraats, Principal, Elementary Campus
Rod Harris, Vice Principal, Collegiate Campus
Maureen Vaags-Nyhof, Vice Principal, Elementary Campus

***Winnipeg:* Christ the King School**
12 Lennox Ave., Winnipeg, MB R2M 1A6, Canada
Tel: 204-257-0027; *Fax:* 204-257-2129
www.ctkschool.ca
Grades: Junior Kindergarten - 8
Brian Steeves, Chair
brian@steeves.ca
Maria Coutu, Principal
mcoutu@ctkschool.ca
Mrs. S. Finnigan, Accountant
sfinnigan@ctkschool.ca
Ms. S. Barnert, Administrative Secretary
sbarnert@ctkschool.ca

***Winnipeg:* The Collegiate at the University of Winnipeg**
515 Portage Ave., Winnipeg, MB R3B 2E9, Canada
Tel: 204-786-9221; *Fax:* 204-775-1942
collegiate@uwinnipeg.ca
www.uwinnipeg.ca/index/collegiate-index
Grades: 9 - 12
The independent secondary school is a division of The University of Winnipeg.
Robert Bend, Dean, 204-786-9843
r.bend@uwinnipeg.ca
Claude Garand, Associate Dean, 204-786-9842
c.garand@uwinnipeg.ca
Heather Singer, Associate Dean, 204-786-9258
h.singer@uwinnipeg.ca
Kathy Cullen, Registrar & International Student Advisor, 204-786-9901
k.cullen@uwinnipeg.ca

***Winnipeg:* Gray Academy of Jewish Education**
A100, 123 Doncaster St., Winnipeg, MB R3N 2B4, Canada
Tel: 204-477-7410; *Fax:* 204-477-7474
info@grayacademy.ca
www.grayacademy.ca
Grades: K.-12
The largest independent Jewish day school in Western Canada. Co-educational. General subjects & Jewish studies programmes.
Rory Paul, Head of School

***Winnipeg:* Holy Ghost School**
319 Selkirk Ave., Winnipeg, MB R2W 2L8, Canada
Tel: 204-582-1053; *Fax:* 204-582-4870
Grades: K.-8
Enrollment: 239

***Winnipeg:* Immaculate Heart of Mary School**
650 Flora Ave., Winnipeg, MB R2W 2S5, Canada
Tel: 204-582-5698; *Fax:* 204-586-6698
ihms@ihms.mb.ca
Grades: K.-8
Enrollment: 235

***Winnipeg:* Immanuel Christian School**
215 Rougeau Ave., Winnipeg, MB R2C 3Z9, Canada
Tel: 204-661-8937; *Fax:* 204-669-7013
sch1274@merlin.mb.ca
Grades: K.-12
Enrollment: 188

***Winnipeg:* Indian & Métis Holiness**
610 Selkirk Ave., Winnipeg, MB R2W 2N1, Canada
Tel: 204-586-9484
Grades: K.-10

***Winnipeg:* Islamic Academy of Manitoba**
Académie islamique du Manitoba
340 Provencher Blvd., Winnipeg, MB R2H 0G7, Canada
Tel: 204-231-4441; *Fax:* 204-231-3240
www.miaonline.org
Grades: K.-6
Program & instruction Arabic, English & French. Daily Qur'an studies.
Dr. Taib Soufi, Principal

***Winnipeg:* The King's School**
851 Panet Rd., Winnipeg, MB R2K 4C9, Canada
Tel: 204-989-6581; *Fax:* 204-989-6584
www.thekingsschool.ca
Grades: Kindergarten - 12
Enrollment: 250
The King's School is a co-educational school, which is a ministry of Gateway Christian Community Church.
Peter Todd, BA (Hons), PGCE, Principal

***Winnipeg:* The Laureate Academy**
100 Villa Maria Pl., Winnipeg, MB R3V 1A9, Canada
Tel: 204-831-7107; *Fax:* 204-885-3217
www.laureateacademy.com
Grades: Kindergarten - 12

***Winnipeg:* Linden Christian School**
877 Wilkes Ave., Winnipeg, MB R3P 1B8, Canada
Tel: 204-989-6730; *Fax:* 204-487-7068
Grades: K.-12
Enrollment: 741

***Winnipeg:* Mennonite Brethren Collegiate Institute**
180 Riverton Ave., Winnipeg, MB R2L 2E8, Canada
Tel: 204-667-8210; *Fax:* 204-661-5091
mbci@mbci.mb.ca
Grades: 1-12
Enrollment: 532

***Winnipeg:* Montessori Learning Centre (MLC)**
Asland School
170 Ashland Ave., Winnipeg, MB R3L 1L1, Canada
Tel: 204-475-1039; *Fax:* 204-452-4643
mlcmont@mts.net
www.mlcwinnipeg.ca
Grades: Preschool - Kindergarten
The Centre's preschool program is designed for children from age 3 to 5.

Winnipeg: Oholei Torah School
2095 Sinclair St., Winnipeg, MB R2V 3K2, Canada
Tel: 204-339-8737; *Fax:* 204-586-0487
sch1997@merlin.mb.ca

Grades: Gr. N.-8
Enrollment: 13

Winnipeg: Ohr Hatorah School
620 Brock St., Winnipeg, MB R3N 0Z4, Canada
Tel: 204-489-1147; *Fax:* 204-489-5899

Grades: Gr. N.-4

Winnipeg: Our Lady of Victory School
249 Arnold Ave., Winnipeg, MB R3L 0W4, Canada
Tel: 204-452-7632; *Fax:* 204-453-3081
olv@shawbiz.ca
www.victoryedu.com

Grades: Pre K.-8
Enrollment: 117
A. Cap, Principal

Winnipeg: Red River Valley Junior Academy (RRVJA)
56 Grey St., Winnipeg, MB R2L 1V3, Canada
Tel: 204-667-2383; *Fax:* 204-667-1396
info@rrvja.ca
www.rrvja.ca
Other Information: info@rrvja.ca

Grades: Junior Kindergarten - 10
Red River Valley Junior Academy is owned & operated by the Seventh Day Adventist Church.
Ian Mighty, M.A., B.Ed., PBCE, Admin., Principal
imight@rrvja.ca
Daniel NcGuire, B.Ed., Vice Principal & Middle Years Specialist
dmcguire@rrvja.ca
Lora Troop, Administrative Assistant
ltoop@rrvja.ca

Winnipeg: St. Aidan's Christian School
418 Aberdeen Ave., Winnipeg, MB R2W 1V7, Canada
Tel: 204-586-6792; *Fax:* 204-582-4729

Grades: K.-8
Enrollment: 30

Winnipeg: St. Alphonsus School
343 Munroe Ave., Winnipeg, MB R2K 1H2, Canada
Tel: 204-667-6271; *Fax:* 204-663-4187
info@stalphonsusschool.ca
www.stalphonsusschool.ca

Grades: K.-8
Enrollment: 230

Winnipeg: St. Boniface Diocesan High School
282 Dubuc St., Winnipeg, MB R2H 1E4, Canada
Tel: 204-987-1560; *Fax:* 204-237-9891
www.sbdhs.net
admin@sbdhs.net

Grades: S1-S4
Enrollment: 150
Jeff Beaudin, Principal

Winnipeg: St. Charles Interparochial School
331 St. Charles St., Winnipeg, MB R3K 1T6, Canada
Tel: 204-837-1520; *Fax:* 204-837-2326
sec@stccs.ca
www.stccs.ca

Grades: K.-8
Enrollment: 206
Dr. Penny Parzyjagla, Principal

Winnipeg: St. Edward's School
836 Arlington St., Winnipeg, MB R3E 2E4, Canada
Tel: 204-774-8773; *Fax:* 204-775-0011
sch1430@merlin.mb.ca

Grades: K.-6
Enrollment: 191

Winnipeg: St. Emile School
552 St. Anne's Rd., Winnipeg, MB R2M 3G4, Canada
Tel: 204-989-5020; *Fax:* 204-989-5026
www.stemileschool.ca

Grades: K.-8
Enrollment: 236

Winnipeg: St. Gerard School
40 Foster St., Winnipeg, MB R2L 1V7, Canada
Tel: 204-667-4862; *Fax:* 204-668-7932
stgerard@shaw.ca

Grades: Gr. N.-8
Enrollment: 240

Winnipeg: St. Ignatius School
239 Harrow St., Winnipeg, MB R3M 2Y3, Canada
Tel: 204-475-1386; *Fax:* 204-475-3961
sch1829@merlin.mb.ca

Grades: K.-8
Enrollment: 245

Winnipeg: St. John Brebeuf School
605 Renfrew St., Winnipeg, MB R3N 1J8, Canada
Tel: 204-489-2115; *Fax:* 204-489-6097
sch1729@merlin.mb.ca

Grades: K.-8
Enrollment: 221

Winnipeg: St. John's-Ravenscourt School
400 South Dr., Winnipeg, MB R3T 3K5, Canada
Tel: 204-477-2400; *Fax:* 204-477-2429
sch1155@merlin.mb.ca

Grades: K.-12
Enrollment: 780

Winnipeg: St. Joseph the Worker School
505 Brewster St., Winnipeg, MB R2C 2W6, Canada
Tel: 204-222-1841; *Fax:* 204-222-1769
stjoesch@mts.net
www.stjosephtheworkerschool.ca

Grades: K.-6
Enrollment: 129
Brian Hargrave, Principal

Winnipeg: St. Mary's Academy
550 Wellington Cres., Winnipeg, MB R3M 0C1, Canada
Tel: 204-477-0244; *Fax:* 204-453-2417

Grades: 7-12
Enrollment: 550

Winnipeg: St. Mary's Montessori School Inc.
150 Pacific Ave., Winnipeg, MB R3B 3K8, Canada
Tel: 204-956-1622; *Fax:* 204-956-7088

Grades: Gr. N.-K.
Enrollment: 74

Winnipeg: St. Maurice School
1639 Pembina Hwy., Winnipeg, MB R3T 2G6, Canada
Tel: 204-452-2873; *Fax:* 204-452-4050
admin@stmaurice.mb.ca
www.stmaurice.mb.ca

Grades: K.-12
Enrollment: 585
G. Caligiuri, Principal

Winnipeg: St. Michael's School
174 Maple St. North, Winnipeg, MB R2W 3L4, Canada
Tel: 204-334-8763

Grades: 1-12

Winnipeg: St. Paul's High School
2200 Grant Ave., Winnipeg, MB R3P 0P8, Canada
Tel: 204-831-2300; *Fax:* 204-831-2340
contact-us@stpauls.mb.ca
www.stpauls.mb.ca

Grades: 9-12
Enrollment: 582
Jesuit University prep school for boys
Tom Lussier, Principal

Winnipeg: Southeast College
1301 Lee Blvd., Winnipeg, MB R3T 5W8, Canada
Tel: 204-261-3551; *Fax:* 204-269-7880
ilinklater@secollege.ca
www.secollege.ca

Grades: S1-S4
Irene Linklater, Principal

Winnipeg: Springs Christian Academy
#2, 595 Lagimodiere Blvd., Winnipeg, MB R2J 3X2, Canada
Tel: 204-235-0863; *Fax:* 204-235-0390
sch1942@merlin.mb.ca
www.springschurch.com/sca

Grades: K.-12
Enrollment: 689
Affiliated with Springs Church

Winnipeg: Twelve Tribes School
89 East Gate, Winnipeg, MB R3C 2C2, Canada
Tel: 204-779-1118

Grades: 1 - 8

Winnipeg: Westgate Mennonite Collegiate
86 West Gate, Winnipeg, MB R3C 2E1, Canada
Tel: 204-775-7111; *Fax:* 204-786-1651
www.westgatemennonite.ca

Grades: 7 - 12
Enrollment: 315

The Christian school is based upon the Anabaptist Mennonite tradition.
Bob Hummelt, Principal

Winnipeg: Winnipeg Mennonite Elementary School
Bedson Campus
250 Bedson St., Winnipeg, MB R3K 1R7, Canada
Tel: 204-885-1032; *Fax:* 204-897-4068
wmes@wmes.ca

Grades: K.-8
Enrollment: 450

Winnipeg: Winnipeg Montessori School Inc.
1525 Willson Pl., Winnipeg, MB R3T 4H1, Canada
Tel: 204-452-3315; *Fax:* 204-452-3315
sch2093@merlin.mb.ca

Grades: Gr. N.-K.

Winnipeg: Winnipeg South Academy
870 Scotland Ave., Winnipeg, MB R3M 1X8, Canada
Tel: 204-488-5046; *Fax:* 204-452-6563

Grades: Gr. N.-4
Enrollment: 107

Universities & Colleges

Universities

Brandon: Brandon University
270 - 18th St., Brandon, MB R7A 6A9, Canada
Tel: 204-728-9520; *Fax:* 204-726-4573
www.brandonu.ca

Full Time Equivalency: 2625
Dr. Deborah C. Poff, Pres./Vice-Chancellor
president@brandonu.ca
Scott J.B. Lamont, Vice-Pres., Admin./Finance
lamont@brandonu.ca
Dr. Scott Grills, Vice-Pres., Academic
grillss@brandonu.ca
Bruce Strang, Dean, Arts
artsdean@brandonu.ca
Dr Cam Symons, Dean, Education
symonsc@Brandonu.ca
Dr W. Dean Care, Dean, Health Studies
cared@brandonu.ca
Dr Austin F. Gulliver, Dean, Science
gulliver@brandonu.ca
Dr. Lawrence VanBeek, Registrar, 204-727-7310
vanbeekl@brandonu.ca

Faculties

Arts
S. Grills, Dean

Education
Jerrie Storie, Acting Dean

Science
Dr. Austin Gulliver, Acting Dean

Student & International Affairs
Dr. Janet Wright, Dean

Schools

Health Studies
L. Ross, Dean

Music
G. Carruthers, Dean

Publications

Quill

Winnipeg: Canadian Mennonite University
500 Shaftsbury Blvd., Winnipeg, MB R3P 2N2, Canada
Tel: 204-487-3300; *Fax:* 204-487-3858
Toll-Free: 877-231-4570
info@cmu.ca
www.cmu.ca

Full Time Equivalency: 1600
Gerald Gerbrandt, President
ggerbrandt@cmu.ca
Earl Davey, Vice-Pres., Academic
edavey@cmu.ca
Wesley Toews, Registrar & Assistant VP
wtoews@cmu.ca
Gordon Matties, Dean, Humanities & Sciences
gmatties@cmu.ca
Dietrich Bartel, Dean, School of Music
dbartel@cmu.ca
Paul Redekop, Dean, Social Sciences
p.redekop@uwinnipeg.ca
Paul Kroeker, Dean, International Programs
pkroeker@cmu.ca
Ruth Taronno, Assoc. Vice-Pres., MSC
rtaronno@cmu.ca

Winnipeg: Prairie Theatre Exchange
300-393 Portage Ave., #Y, Winnipeg, MB R3B 2H6, Canada
Tel: 204-942-7291; *Fax:* 204-942-1774
www.pte.mb.ca

Winnipeg: Salvation Army William & Catherine Booth University College
Also known as: Booth College; Booth University College
447 Webb Pl., Winnipeg, MB R3B 2P2, Canada
Tel: 204-947-6701; *Fax:* 204-942-3856
Toll-Free: 877-942-6684
admissions@boothcollege.ca
www.boothcollege.ca
Full Time Equivalency: 500
Enrollment number includes on-campus and distance students.

Winnipeg: University College
#203, 220 Dysart Rd., Winnipeg, MB R3T 2M8, Canada
Tel: 204-474-9751; *Fax:* 204-261-0021
ucsecr@cc.umanitoba.ca
umanitoba.ca/colleges/uc/
Affiliated with the University of Manitoba

Winnipeg: University of Manitoba
134 Services Building
97 Dafoe Rd., Winnipeg, MB R3T 2N2, Canada
Tel: 204-474-8880
www.umanitoba.ca
Full Time Equivalency: 29932
William Norrie, C.M., O.M., Q.C., B.A., L, Chancellor
Dr. David T. Barnard, B.Sc., M.Sc., Ph.D., Dip., President & Vice-Chancellor
Bob Raeburn, B.Sc., Executive Assistant to the President
Deborah J. McCallum, B.Sc., Vice-President
Digvir Jayas, Ph.D., Vice-President
Joanne C. Keselman, B.A., M.A., Ph.D., Vice-President
P. Dueck, Director
Alan Simms, B.Comm.(Hons.), L.L.B., Assoc. Vice-President
Peter Cattini, B.Sc.(Hons.), Ph.D., Assoc. Vice-President
David R. Morphy, B.A., M.A., Ph.D., Vice-Provost
Karen R. Grant, B.A., M.A., Ph.D., Vice-Provost
Richard A. Lobdell, B.A., M.A., Ph.D., Vice-Provost
Terry Voss, B.Comm. (Hons.), C.H.R.P., Exec. Director
Karen Adams, B.A., M.L.S., Director
John G. Alho, B.A.(Hons.), Assoc. Vice-President
B. Hanchard, Manager
Peter A. Cattini, B.Sc., Ph.D., Assoc. Vice-President
Elaine V. Goldie, Cert.Ed., Vice-President
Gerry Miller, B.Sc., Exec. Director
A. Simms, L.L.B., Exec. Director
James S. Gardner, B.Sc., M.Sc., Ph.D., Exec. Director
Jeffrey M. Leclerc, B.Ed., University Secretary

Faculties

Agricultural & Food Sciences
Michael Trevan, Dean

Architecture
Richard Perron, Acting Dean

Arts
Richard Sigurdson, Dean

Continuing Education
A. Percival, Dean

Dentistry
Anthony Iacopino, Dean

Education
John Wiens, Dean

Engineering
Douglas Ruth, Dean

Environment
Clayton H. Riddell, Dean

Graduate Studies
Jay Doering, Dean

Human Ecology
Gustaaf P. Sevenhuysen, Dean

I.H. Asper School of Business
Glenn Feltham, Dean

Law
Chris Axworthy, Q.C., Dean

Medicine
Dean Sandham, Dean

Music
Edmund Dawe, Dean

Nursing
Ruth Anne Kinsman, Dean

Pharmacy
David M. Collins, Dean

Physical Education & Recreation Studies
Dr. Jane Watkinson, Dean

Science
Mark Whitmore, Dean

Social Work
Harvy Frankel, Dean

University 1
Christine Blais, Dean

Schools

Agriculture
Mervyn K. Pritchard, Director

Art
Prof. Celia Rabinovitch, Director

Dental Hygiene
Salme Lavigne, Director

Extended Education Division
Anne Percival, Director

Medical Rehabilitation
Emily Etcheverry, Director

Affiliations

Collège universitaire de Saint-Boniface
200, av de la Cathédrale, Winnipeg, MB R2H 0H7, Canada
Tel: 204-233-0210
Raymonde Gagné, B.A., Cert.Ed., M.B.A., Rectrice
rgagne@ustboniface.mb.ca

St. John's College
92 Dysart Rd., Winnipeg, MB R3T 2M5, Canada
Tel: 204-474-8531; *Fax:* 204-474-7610
Toll-Free: 1-800-432-1960
Stjohns_College@umanitoba.ca
www.umanitoba.ca/colleges/st_johns
Affiliated with the Anglican Church of Canada, St. John's College is located on the University of Manitoba campus.
Dr. Janet Hoskins, Warden & Vice-Chancellor
j_hoskins@umanitoba.ca
Erin Palamar, Registrar
e_palamar@umanitoba.ca

St. Paul's College
70 Dysart Rd., Winnipeg, MB R3T 2M6, Canada
Tel: 204-474-8575
stpauls@umanitoba.ca
www.umanitoba.ca/stpauls
The Roman Catholic College is located on the University of Manitoba campus.
Denic C. Bracken, Rector
bracken@cc.umanitoba.ca
Christine Butterill, Dean of Studies
butteri@cc.umanitoba.ca

University College
500 Dysart Rd., Winnipeg, MB R3T 2M8, Canada
Tel: 204-474-9388
Dr. Richard Sigurdson, B.A., M.A. Ph.D., Acting Provost

William & Catherine Booth Bible College
447 Webb Pl., Winnipeg, MB R3B 2P2, Canada
Tel: 204-947-6701
Dr. Donald Burke, President, 204-924-4868
president@boothcollege.ca
Denise Young, BBA, MPA, Director, College Admin., 204-924-4864
dyoung@boothcollege.ca
Deborah Knight, Financial Coordinator, 204-924-4853
dknight@boothcollege.ca

Prairie Theatre Exchange
300-393 Portage Ave., #Y, Winnipeg, MB R3B 2H6, Canada
Tel: 204-942-7291
Robert Metcalfe, Artistic Director
ad@pte.mb.ca

Publications

Alumni Journal
180 Dafoe Rd, Winnipeg, MB R3T 2N2, Canada

The Gradzette

The Manitoban

Winnipeg: University of Winnipeg
515 Portage Ave., Winnipeg, MB R3B 2E9, Canada
Tel: 204-786-7811
www.uwinnipeg.ca
Full Time Equivalency: 9460
Robert Silver, Chancellor
Lloyd Axworthy, President & Vice-Chancellor, 204-786-9214
president@uwinnipeg.ca
John Corlett, Vice-Pres., Academic, 204-786-9120
j.corlett@uwinnipeg.ca
Bill Balan, Vice-Pres., Finance & Administration, 204-786-9229
b.balan@uwinnipeg.ca
Laurel Repski, Vice-Pres., Human Resources, 204-789-1451
l.repski@uwinnipeg.ca
Neil Besner, Vice-Pres., Students & International, 204-786-8656
n.besner@uwinnipeg.ca

Faculties

Arts
David Fitzpatrick, Dean, 204-786-9943
d.fitzpatrick@uwinnipeg.ca

Business & Economics
Michael Benarroch, Dean, 204-786-9268
m.benarroch@uwinnipeg.ca

Education
Ken Mccluskey, Dean, 204-786-9470
k.mccluskey@uwinnipeg.ca

Science
Rodney Hanley, Dean, 204-786-9862
r.hanley@uwinnipeg.ca

Theology
Dr James Christie, Dean, 204-786-9247
j.christie@uwinnipeg.ca

Affiliations

Menno Simons College
520 Portage Ave., Winnipeg, MB R3C 0G2, Canada
Tel: 204-953-3855; *Fax:* 207-783-3699
msc@uwinnipeg.ca
mscollege.ca
A college of the Canadian Mennonite University, maintaining an affiliation with the University of Winnipeg. It is located on the campus of the U. of W.
Dr. Earl Davey, Vice-President, Academic (CMU), 204-953-3873
e.davey@uwinnipeg.ca
Dr. Paul Redekop, Dean, MSC/Faculty of Social Sciences (CMU), 204-953-3858
p.redekop@uwinnipeg.ca

Publications

The Uniter
Tel: 204-786-9790; *Fax:* 204-786-9497
uniter@uniter.ca
uniter.ca

Colleges

Brandon: Assiniboine Community College
1430 Victoria Ave. East, Brandon, MB R7A 2A9, Canada
Tel: 204-725-8700; *Fax:* 204-725-8740
Toll-Free: 1-800-862-6307
info@assiniboine.net
www.assiniboine.net
Full Time Equivalency: 2500
Joel Ward, President
wardj@assiniboine.net
Karen Barclay, Associate Registrar
barclay@assiniboine.net

Campuses

Parkland Campus
P.O. Box 4000
520 Whitmore Ave. East, Dauphin, MB R7N 2V5, Canada
Tel: 204-622-2023; *Fax:* 204-638-3941
info@assiniboine.net
www.assiniboine.net

Saint-Boniface: Collège universitaire de Saint-Boniface
200, av de la Cathédrale, Saint-Boniface, MB R2H 0H7, Canada
Tél: 204-233-0210; *Téléc:* 204-237-3240
Ligne sans frais: 1-888-233-5112
sci@ustboniface.mb.ca
www.ustboniface.mb.ca
Raymonde Gagné, B.A., Cert.Ed., M.B.A., Rectrice
rgagne@ustboniface.mb.ca

Saint-Boniface: École technique et professionnelle
c/o Collège universitaire de Saint-Boniface
200, av de la Cathédrale, Saint-Boniface, MB R2H 0H7, Canada
Tél: 204-233-0210; *Téléc:* 204-237-3240
Ligne sans frais: 1-888-233-5112
sci@ustboniface.mb.ca
www.ustboniface.mb.ca
Raymonde Gagné, Rectrice

The Pas: University College of the North
P.O. Box 3000
436 - 7 St. East, The Pas, MB R9A 1M7, Canada
Tel: 204-627-8500; *Fax:* 204-623-7316
Toll-Free: 866-627-8500
admissions@ucn.ca
www.ucn.ca
Full Time Equivalency: 3500
Denise K. Henning, President & Vice-Chancellor
Carol Girling, Registrar & Director, Enrolment Services, 204-627-8553
cgirling@ucn.ca

Winnipeg: Collège universitaire de Saint-Boniface
200, av de la Cathédrale, Winnipeg, MB R2H 0H7, Canada
Tél: 204-233-0210; *Téléc:* 204-237-3240
Ligne sans frais: 1-888-233-5112
sci@ustboniface.mb.ca
www.ustboniface.mb.ca

Publications
Le Réveil

Brandon: Office of the Fire Commissioner (Brandon)
1601 Vanhorne Ave. East, Brandon, MB R7A 7K2, Canada
Tel: 204-726-6855; *Fax:* 204-948-2089
Toll-Free: 1-800-282-806
firecomm@gov.mb.ca
www.firecomm.gov.mb.ca
The college is a broad-based emergency services training organizationwhich offers a full-time program for those interested in a career in the EMS field.
Rick Negrich, 204-945-3330

Winnipeg: Office of the Fire Commissioner (Winnipeg)
508-401 York Ave., Winnipeg, MB R3C 0P8, Canada
Tel: 204-945-3322; *Fax:* 204-948-2089
Toll-Free: 1-800-282-8069
firecomm@gov.mb.ca
www.firecomm.gov.mb.ca
The college is a broad-based emergency services training organizationwhich offers a full-time program for those interested in a career in the EMS field.

Winnipeg: Red River College of Applied Arts, Science & Technology
2055 Notre Dame Ave., Winnipeg, MB R3H 0J9, Canada
Tel: 204-632-3960
register@rrc.mb.ca; cde@rrc.mb.ca; intled@rrc.mb.ca
www.rrc.mb.ca
Full Time Equivalency: 32000
Al Morin, Chair
Jeff Zabudsky, PhD, President/CEO

Campuses
Gimli Campus
Gimli Industrial Park
P.O. Box 190
234 Tudor Lane, Gimli, MB R0C 1B0
Tel: 204-642-5496; *Fax:* 204-642-4189
gimli@rrc.mb.ca

Portage Campus
180 Centennaire Dr., Southport, MB R0H 1N0
Tel: 204-428-6322; *Fax:* 204-428-6337
portage@rrc.mb.ca

Steinbach Campus
#2, 385 Loewen Blvd., Steinbach, MB R5G 0B3
Tel: 204-320-2500; *Fax:* 204-346-0178
steinbach@rrc.mb.ca
The Steinbach Campus has community learning centres in Steinbach (204-320-2500) and in St. Pierre (204-433-7404).

Winkler Campus
#100, 561 Main St., Winkler, MB R6W 1E8
Tel: 204-325-9672; *Fax:* 204-325-4947
winkler@rrc.mb.ca; winklerlearningcentre@rrc.mb.ca
Other Information: Winkler Community Learning Centre, Phone: 204-325-4997

Winnipeg: St. Andrew's College
29 Dysart Rd., Winnipeg, MB R3T 2M7, Canada
Tel: 204-474-8895; *Fax:* 204-474-7624
st_andrews@umanitoba.ca
www.umanitoba.ca/colleges/st_andrews
Affiliated with the University of Manitoba, St. Andrew's College is an institution of the Ukrainian Orthodox Church of Canada. It works to promote spiritual, academic, cultural, & moral leadership.
His Eminence John Stinka, Chancellor
V. Rev. Fr. Roman Bozyk, Chair, Dean of Theology, Acting Principal, & Registrar

Post Secondary/Technical

Post Secondary/Technical

Winnipeg: Winnipeg Branch
300 Oak Point Hwy., Winnipeg, MB R2R 1V1, Canada
Tel: 204-925-1580; *Fax:* 204-925-1587
Toll-Free: 1-888-883-7483
learn@transportdriver.com
www.transportdriver.com
Class 1 air brake licence training

Brandon: Brandon Branch
1731 B Middleton Ave., Brandon, MB R7A 1A7, Canada
Tel: 204-729-0240; *Toll-Free:* 1-888-883-7483
learn@transportdriver.com
www.transportdriver.com

Dauphin: Academy of Learning
Village Mall
P.O. Box 603
1430 Main St. South, Dauphin, MB R7N 2V4, Canada
Tel: 204-622-9999; *Fax:* 204-622-9998
www.academyoflearning.com
Computer & business training; other locations in Brandon, Steinbach, Swan River, Winnipeg - North, Winnipeg - South

McCreary: Canadian College of Taxidermy
419 - First Ave., McCreary, MB R0J 1B0, Canada
Tel: 204-835-2639; *Fax:* 204-835-2764
tledoux@sympatico.ca

Otterburne: Providence College & Theological Seminary
Otterburne, MB R0A 1G0, Canada
Tel: 204-433-7488; *Fax:* 204-433-7158
Toll-Free: 1-800-668-776
info@prov.ca
www.prov.ca
Enrollment: 717
Institution for Christian higher education

Winnipeg: Canadian School of Floral Art
569 St. Mary's Rd., Winnipeg, MB R2M 3L6, Canada
Tel: 204-233-2426; *Fax:* 204-237-7301

Winnipeg: CDI College of Business, Technology & Healthcare
280 Main St., Winnipeg, MB R3C 1A9, Canada
Tel: 204-942-1773; *Fax:* 204-944-0752
Computer & business training

Winnipeg: European School of Esthetics
241 Vaughan St., Winnipeg, MB R3C 1T6, Canada
Tel: 204-943-3440
idonils.mts.net
www.idonails.ca
Esthetics

Winnipeg: Herzing College
723 Portage Ave., Winnipeg, MB R3G 0M8, Canada
Tel: 204-775-8175; *Fax:* 204-783-8107
info@wpg.herzing.edu
www.herzing.edu/winnipeg
Bill Riches, President

Winnipeg: Mid Ocean School of Media Arts
1588 Erin St., Winnipeg, MB R3E 2T1, Canada
Tel: 204-775-3308; *Fax:* 204-775-9231
info@midoceanschool.ca
www.midoceanschool.ca
Audio engineer, audio in media

Winnipeg: National Screen Institute
#206, 70 Arthur St., Winnipeg, MB R3B 1G7, Canada
Tel: 204-956-7800; *Fax:* 204-956-5811
info@nsi-canada.ca
www.nsi-canada.ca
Professional training & development for Canadian film & television writers, directors & producers
Susan Millican, CEO
Glynis Corkal, Manager
Paul Moreau, Director

Winnipeg: Panache Agency Models School
#106, 897 Corydon Ave., Winnipeg, MB R3M 0W7, Canada
Tel: 204-982-6150; *Fax:* 204-474-2687
panache_jane@mts.net
www.panachemanagement.com
Models training

Winnipeg: Patal Vocational Preparation Schools Ltd.
264 Portage Ave., Winnipeg, MB R3C 0B6, Canada
Tel: 204-944-8202; *Fax:* 204-944-8207
Toll-Free: 1-877-829-807
www.patalvocational.mb.ca
Life skills, upgrading, PC service, computerized accounting, purchasing/inventory, service/parts/inventory; internet technical support; customer service training for the customer contact industry; cooking

Winnipeg: Reimer Express Driver Training Institute Inc.
50 Milner St., Winnipeg, MB R2X 2X3, Canada
Tel: 204-958-5100; *Fax:* 204-958-3034
Toll-Free: 1-888-866-7623
wayne.hartle@reimerexpress.com
www.reimerdrivertraining.com
Class 1S driver training.
Wayne Hartle, Manager

Winnipeg: Robertson College Winnipeg
265 Notre Dame Ave., Winnipeg, MB R3B 1N9, Canada
Tel: 204-943-5661; *Fax:* 204-926-8320
Toll-Free: 1-877-880-8789
info@robertsoncollege.com
www.robertsoncollege.com
Wayne Palendat, Registrar

Campuses
Robertson College Calgary
Edinburgh Pl.
300-417 14th St. NW, Calgary, AB T2N 2A1, Canada
Tel: 403-920-0070; *Fax:* 403-543-1245
Toll-Free: 1-866-920-0070
Calgary@RobertsonCollege.com
www.robersoncollege.com

Robertson College Brandon
Town Centre
800 Rosser Ave., Brandon, MB R7A 6N5, Canada
Tel: 204-725-7205; *Fax:* 204-725-7218
Toll-Free: 1-877-757-7575
info@robertsoncollege.com
www.robertsoncollege.com

Winnipeg: School of Recording Arts of Manitoba
275 Selkirk Ave., Winnipeg, MB R2W 2L5, Canada
Tel: 204-586-8057; *Fax:* 204-582-8397
studio@magic.mb.ca, info@worldwidesunshine.com
www.sunshinerecords.com
Studio recording

Winnipeg: Scientific-Marvel School of Hairstyling & Esthetics
269 Kennedy St. 2nd Fl., Winnipeg, MB R3C 1T2, Canada
Tel: 204-943-2145; *Fax:* 204-943-2445
winnipeghairstylingesthetics@marvelschools.com
www.marvelschools.com
Skin care & hairstyling

Winnipeg: Winnipeg Campus
105-260 St. Mary Ave., Winnipeg, MB R3C 0M6, Canada
Tel: 204-925-2790
learn@anokiiwin.com
www.anokiiwin.com/learn
Aboriginally owned and operated training company committed to providing culturally sensitive, high quality training to First Nation communinities.

Campuses
Thompson Campus
203-3 Station Rd., Thompson, MB R8N 0R2, Canada
Tel: 204-778-5937
learn@anokiiwin.com
www.anokiiwin.com/learn
Aboriginally owned and operated training company committed to providing culturally sensitive, high quality training to First Nation communinities.

Winnipeg: Winnipeg Technical College
130 Henlow Bay, Winnipeg, MB R3Y 1G4, Canada
Tel: 204-989-6500; *Fax:* 204-488-4152
sch1956@merlin.mb.ca
Enrollment: 1200
Dave Thorlakson, Director

New Brunswick

Government Agencies

Fredericton: Department of Education
P.O. Box 6000
Place 2000, Fredericton, NB E3B 5H1, Canada
Tel: 506-453-3678; *Fax:* 506-453-3111
www.gnb.ca/000/index-e.asp
Barry Lydon, Director, 506-453-2155
barry.lydon@gnb.ca
Marcel Lavoie, Director, 506-453-2743
marcel.lavoie@gnb.ca

Fredericton: Department of Post-Secondary Education & Training (asp)
Chestnut Complex
P.O. Box 6000
Fredericton, NB E3B 5H1, Canada
Tel: 506-453-2597; *Fax:* 506-453-3618
www.gnb.ca/0105/index-e.asp
Margaret-Ann Blaney, Minister
Barbara Leger, Manager
Félixine Thériault, Administrator

School Boards/Districts/Divisions

Public

Campbellton: District Scolaire #5
21, rue King, Campbellton, NB E3N 1C5, Canada
Tel: 506-789-2255; *Fax:* 506-789-2269
Enrollment: 5934
Monelle Perron, Dir. de l'éducation
monelle.perron@gnb.ca
Jean-Guy Levesque, Dir. gén.
jean-guy.levesque@gnb.ca

Dalhousie: School District #15
464 Montgomery St., Dalhousie, NB E8C 2A6, Canada
Tel: 506-684-7557; *Fax:* 506-684-7552
Toll-Free: 888-950-1515
district15@gnb.ca
www.district15.nbed.nb.ca
Enrollment: 3982
Nancy Boucher, Director, Education
John McLaughlin, Superintendent
john.mclaughlin@gnb.ca

Dieppe: District Scolaire #1
425, rue Champlain, Dieppe, NB E1A 1P2, Canada
Tel: 506-856-3225; *Fax:* 506-856-3254
Enrollment: 7056
Anne-Marie LeBlanc, Dir. gén.
anne-marie.leblanc@gnb.ca
Maurice Langlais, Dir. de l'éducation
maurice.langlais@gnb.ca

Edmundston: District Scolaire #3
298, rue Martin, Edmundston, NB E3V 5E5, Canada
Tel: 506-737-4550; *Fax:* 506-737-4569
Enrollment: 6966
Bertrand Beaulieu, Dir. gén.
bertrand.beaulieu@gnb.ca
Lise Aubut, Dir. de l'éducation
lise.aubut@gnb.ca

Fredericton: School District #18
P.O. Box 10
1135 Prospect St., Fredericton, NB E3B 4Y4, Canada
Tel: 506-453-5454; *Fax:* 506-444-5264
www.district18.nbed.nb.ca
Enrollment: 12000
Dianne Wilkins, Director, Education
dianne.wilkins@gnb.ca
Alex Dingwall, Superintendent
alex.dingwall@gnb.ca

Miramichi: School District #16
78 Henderson St., Miramichi, NB E1N 2R7, Canada
Tel: 506-778-6075; *Fax:* 506-778-6090
www.district16.nbed.nb.ca
Enrollment: 8100
Richard Walsh, Director, Education
richard.walsh@gnb.ca
Laurie Keoughan, Superintendent
laurie.keoughan@gnb.ca

Moncton: School District #2
1077 St. George Blvd., Moncton, NB E1E 4C9, Canada
Tel: 506-856-3222; *Fax:* 506-856-3224
www.district2.nbed.nb.ca
Enrollment: 16000
Gregg Ingersoll, Director, Education
Gregg.Ingersoll@gnb.ca
Karen Branscombe, Superintendent
karen.branscombe@gnb.ca

Oromocto: School District #17
17 Miramichi Rd., Oromocto, NB E2V 2P6, Canada
Tel: 506-357-4010; *Fax:* 506-357-4011
Enrollment: 5200
David McTimoney, Superintendent
Rick Demmings, Director, Education

Richibucto: District Scolaire #11
#2, 10, rue Commerciale, Richibucto, NB E4W 3X6, Canada
Tél: 506-523-7655; *Téléc:* 506-523-7659
Enrollment: 6093
Ronald Caissie, Dir. gén.
ronald.caissie@gnb.ca
Yolande McLaughlin, Dir. de l'éducation
yolande.mclaughlin@gnb.ca

Rothesay: School District #6
70B Hampton Rd., Rothesay, NB E2E 5Y2, Canada
Tel: 506-847-6262; *Fax:* 506-847-6211
www.district6.nbed.nb.ca
Enrollment: 10200
Andrew Hopper, Director, Education
andrew.hopper@gnb.ca
Zoë Watson, Superintendent
zoe.watson@gnb.ca

Saint John: School District #8
490 Woodward Ave., Saint John, NB E2K 5N3, Canada
Tel: 506-658-5300; *Fax:* 506-658-5399
www.district8.nbed.nb.ca
Enrollment: 13000
Susan Tipper, Superintendent
susan.tipper@gnb.ca
Beverly MacDonald, Director, Education
bev.macdonald@gnb.ca

St Stephen: School District #10
11 School St., St Stephen, NB E3L 2N4, Canada
Tel: 506-466-7300; *Fax:* 506-466-7309
d10webadmin@gnb.ca
www.district10.nbed.nb.ca
Enrollment: 4340
Jenny MacDougall, Director, Education
Jenny.MacDougall@gnb.ca
Derek O'Brien, Superintendent
derek.o'brien@nbed.nb.ca

Tracadie-Sheila: District Scolaire #9
P.O. Box 3668 Bureau chef
3376, rue Principale, Tracadie-Sheila, NB E1X 1G5, Canada
Tél: 506-394-3400; *Téléc:* 506-394-3455
Enrollment: 7412
Philip Chiasson, Dir. de l'éducation
philip.chiasson@gnb.ca
Solange Haché, Dir. gén.
solange.hache@gnb.ca

Woodstock: School District #14
138 Chapel St., Woodstock, NB E7M 1H3, Canada
Tel: 506-325-4432; *Fax:* 506-325-4490
www.district14.nbed.nb.ca
Enrollment: 8511
Loree Kaye, Director, Education
loree.kaye@gnb.ca
Lisa Gallagher, Superintendent
lisa.gallagher@gnb.ca

Schools: Specialized

First Nations

Burnt Church: Burnt Church School
Also known as: Esgenoôpetitj School
626 Bayview Dr., Burnt Church, NB E9G 2A8, Canada
Tel: 506-776-1206; *Fax:* 506-776-1226
lflanagan@burntchurchschool.ca
burntchurchschool.ca
Grades: Kindergarten - 8
Enrollment: 120
The Burnt Church School, located northeast of the City of Miramichi, is part of School District #16. The school serves the Burnt Church First Nation.
Robert Bowes, Principal

Eel Ground: Eel Ground First Nation School
55 Church St., Eel Ground, NB E1V 4E6, Canada
Tel: 506-627-4615; *Fax:* 506-627-4624
www.eelgroundschool.ca
Grades: Kindergarten - 8; Mi'kmaq Language
Eel Ground First Nation School operates as part of School District #16 in Miramichi, New Brunswick. The school provides education to the Eel Ground First Nation, a Mi'kmaq community in northeastern New Brunswick.
Donald Donahue, Principal

Eel River Bar: Eel River Bar First Nation Pre-School
Eel River Bar First Nation
P.O. Box 4007
#201, 11 Main St., Eel River Bar, NB E8C 1A1, Canada
Tel: 506-684-6307; *Fax:* 506-684-6282
Grades: Pre-School (K4)
Eel River Bar First Nation Pre-School is a First Nations band operated school in a Mi'kmaq village on New Brunswick's north shore.
Priscilla Pictou, Principal

Elsipogtog: Elsipogotg School
356 Big Cove Rd., Elsipogtog, NB E4W 2S6, Canada
Tel: 506-523-8240; *Fax:* 506-523-8235
kitpo@nbnet.nb.ca
www.elsipogtogschool.ca
Grades: Kindergarten - 8
Part of Miramichi, New Brunswick's School District #16, the Elsipogtog School provides education to the Elsipogtog First Nation.
Levi Sock, Superintendent
Ivan Augustine, Principal
Stan Drillen, Vice-Principal
Laurie Donovan, Program Coordinator, Resources
lauried@elsipogtogschool.ca

Fredericton: Chief Harold Sappier Memorial Elementary School
c/o St. Mary's Maliseet First Nation
305 Maliseet Dr., Fredericton, NB E3A 5R8, Canada
Tel: 506-462-9683; *Fax:* 506-462-9686
chsmesjf@nb.aibn.com
www.firstnationhelp.com/stmarys
Grades: K4 - K5; 1 - 5; Maliseet Language
In addition to providing elementary education beginning with kindergarten, the Chief Harold Sappier Memorial Elementary School provides education about the Maliseet language & culture.
Allison Brooks, Principal
Judith Fullarton, Office Manager

Fredericton: Wulastukw Elementary School
Kingsclear First Nation
712 Church St., Fredericton, NB E3E 1K8, Canada
Tel: 506-363-3019
Grades: K4; 1-5
Enrollment: 45
Allan McIntyre, Principal

Red Bank: Metepanagiag - Red Bank School
1926 MicMac Rd., Red Bank, NB E9E 1B3, Canada
Tel: 506-836-6160
rbedu@nbt.aibn.com
Grades: K4; 1-6
Enrollment: 41
Maureen Donovan, Principal

Tobique First Nation: Mah-Sos School
270 Main St., Tobique First Nation, NB E7H 2Y8, Canada
Tel: 506-273-5407
Grades: K4; 1-5
Enrollment: 115
Paula Pirie, Principal
paula_pirie@hotmail.com

Woodstock First Nation: Woodstock First Nation Pre-School
6 Eagles Nest Dr., Woodstock First Nation, NB E7M 4J3, Canada
Tel: 506-328-4332
June Tomah, Principal
Janet Paul, Principal

Schools: Independent & Private

Independent & Private Schools

Fredericton: Devon Park Christian School
P.O. Box 3510 B
145 Clark St., Fredericton, NB E3A 5J8, Canada
Tel: 506-458-9379; *Fax:* 506-458-8702

Grades: K.-12
Enrollment: 179
Randy Fox, Principal

***Moncton:* Moncton Christian Academy (MCA)**
945 St. George Blvd., Moncton, NB E1E 2C9, Canada
Tel: 506-855-5403; *Fax:* 506-857-9016
www.monctonchristianacademy.com
Grades: Kindergarten - 12
Enrollment: 120
Moncton Christian Academy is an interdenominational school.
Willie Brownlee, Administrator
Esther Flanagan, Assistant

***Plaster Rock:* Apostolic Christian School**
123 Main St., Plaster Rock, NB E7G 2H2, Canada
Tel: 506-356-8690; *Fax:* 506-356-9996
Grades: K.-12
Enrollment: 64
Sanford Goodine, Principal

***Rothesay:* Rothesay Netherwood School (RNS)**
40 College Hill Rd., Rothesay, NB E2E 5H1, Canada
Tel: 506-847-8224; *Fax:* 506-848-0851
education@rns.cc; admission@rns.cc; bursar@rns.cc; alumni@rns.cc
www.rns.cc
Grades: 6 - 12
Rothesay Netherwood School is a day & boarding school.
Sylvia MacVey, Chair
Paul G. Kitchen, Head of School, 506-848-0863
kitchenp@rns.cc
Paul McLellan, Director, Senior School & Assistant Head of School, 506-848-0864
mclellanp@rns.cc
Dean Van Doleweerd, Director, Middle School & Assistant Head of School, 506-847-8224
vandoleweerdd@rns.cc
Jayne Fillman, Director, Admission, 506-848-0859
fillmanj@rns.cc
David Keeping, Director, Finance & Operations, 506-848-0855
keepingd@rns.cc
Linda MacDonald, Director, Residential Life, 506-848-8224
macdonaldl@rns.cc
Geoffrey McCullogh, Director, Athletics, 506-848-0852
mcculloghg@rns.cc
Brian Murray, Director, Student Life, 506-848-0876
murrayb@rns.cc
Tammy Earle, Head, Information Technology & Coordinator IB Diploma, 506-848-1739
earlet@rns.cc

***Rothesay:* Valley Christian Academy (VCA)**
P.O. Box 4722
30 Vincent Rd., Rothesay, NB E2E 5X4, Canada
Tel: 506-848-6373; *Fax:* 506-848-6379
vca@nbnet.nb.ca
www.valleychristianacademy.com
Grades: Preschool - 9
Valley Christian Academy is a ministry of Rothesay Baptist Church. The preschool accepts children as young as three years of age.
Elizabeth MacDonald, Principal
vcaprinc@nbnet.nb.ca

***Somerville:* Somerville Christian Academy**
2608, rte 103, Somerville, NB E7P 3A9, Canada
Tel: 506-375-4327; *Fax:* 506-375-4406
Grades: K.-5
Enrollment: 63
Angela Mabey, Principal

***Sussex:* Sussex Christian School**
45 Chapman Dr., Sussex, NB E4E 1M4, Canada
Tel: 506-433-4005; *Fax:* 506-433-3402
scs@sussexchristianschool.com
www.sussexchristianschool.com
Grades: Jr. K.-12
Enrollment: 67
Marsha Boyd-Mitchell, Principal

Universities & Colleges

Universities

***Fredericton:* Maritime College of Forest Technology**
Hugh John Flemming Forestry Centre
1350 Regent St., Fredericton, NB E3C 2G6, Canada
Tel: 506-458-0653; *Fax:* 506-458-0652
info@mcft.ca
www.mcft.ca
Full Time Equivalency: 150

***Fredericton:* St. Thomas University**
Fredericton, NB E3B 5G3, Canada
Tel: 506-452-0532; *Fax:* 506-452-0617
www.stu.ca
Most Rev. Faber MacDonald, B.Comm., Chancellor
Dr. Daniel W. O'Brien, B.Comm., M.S.W., Adv.Dip., President & Vice-Chancellor, 506-452-0537
obrien@stu.ca
Dr. Patrick Malcolmson, B.Ed., M.A., Ph.D., Vice-President, 506-452-0417
pmalcolm@stu.ca
Lawrence H. Durling, B.B.A., C.A., Vice-President, 506-452-0533
ldurling@stu.ca
Kathryn Monti, B.A., Director, 506-452-0532
monti@stu.ca
Derryl Smith, B.A., B.Ed., M.Ed., Director, 506-452-0539
dsmith@stu.ca
Robert B. Edgett, B.A., C.F.R.E., Director, 506-452-0512
Rev. John Keoughan, B.A., B.Ed., M.Ed., Chaplain, 506-452-0643
Reginald J. Gallant, B.B.A., C.A., Comptroller, 506-452-0631
gallant@stu.ca
Fred Wallace, Manager, 506-452-0606
Jane McGinn-Giberson, P.Eng., Director, 506-452-0638
jmcginn@stu.ca
Lawrence A. Batt, B.A., M.A., Registrar, 506-452-0530
lbatt@stu.ca
Peter Dielissen, ISP., Director, 506-460-0363
peterd@stu.ca
Kathy Wishart, B.A., B.Ed., Coordinator, 506-452-0529
wishart@stu.ca
Ilkay Silk, N.S.C.D., L.U.D., L.R.A.M, Coordinator, 506-452-0605
silk@stu.ca
Colleen Comeau, B.A., B.Ed., Director, 506-452-0630
ccomeau@stu.ca
Ryan Sullivan, B.A., Coordinator, 506-460-0343
sullivan@stu.ca
Karen Taylor, B.A., M.P.A., C.S.W., Director, 506-452-0445
taylor@stu.ca
Dale Dasset, B.A., Multimedia Coordinator, 506-460-0320
dasset@stthomas.ca
Jeffrey Carleton, B.A., M.A., Director, 506-452-0522
carleton@stu.ca

Publications
Aquinian

***Fredericton:* University of New Brunswick**
P.O. Box 4400 A
Fredericton, NB E3B 5A3, Canada
Tel: 506-453-4666; *Fax:* 506-453-5158
trudya@unb.ca
www.unb.ca
Full Time Equivalency: 9000
Richard J. Currie, O.C., M.B.A., L.L.D., P.E, Chancellor
John D. McLaughlin, B.Sc.E., M.Sc.E., Ph.D.,, President & Vice-Chancellor
jdm@unb.ca
Angelo Belcastro, B.A., B.PE., M.Sc., Ph.D., Vice-President
abelcas@unb.ca
Daniel V. Murray, C.A., B.Comm., Vice-President
dmurray@unb.ca
Larry J. Guitard, B.A., L.L.B., C.A., Asst. Vice-President, Finance & Corporate Services & Comptrol
lguitard@unb.ca
S. Strople, B.A., M.A., University Secretary
sstrople@unb.ca
David Hinton, B.Sc., M.Sc., Registrar
hinton@unb.ca
Peter McDougall, B.A., M.I.R., C.H.R.P., Associate Vice-President
pmcdouga@unb.ca
C. Anne Forrestall, B.A., M.A., Director
caf@unb.ca
W. Brewer, Procurement Manager
wbrewer@unb.ca
S. Fillmore, Manager
fillmore@unb.ca
Kathryn E. Hamer, B.A., M.A., Ph.D., Vice-President
khamer@unbsj.ca
Gregory Kealey, B.A., M.A., Ph.D., F.R.S., Vice-President
gkealey@unb.ca
Thomas Buckley, B.A., B.Ed., Registrar
buckleyt@unbsj.ca
K. Bonner, B.A., M.Ed., Director
kbonner@unbsj.ca
P. Joas, Manager
joas@unbsj.ca

Faculties
Arts
James Murray, B.A., M.A., Ph.D., Dean
arts@unb.ca
Arts (Saint John)
Robert MacKinnon, B.A., M.A., Ph.D., Dean
Business (Saint John)
Shelley Rinehart, B.A., M.B.A., Ph.D., Dean
Business Administration
Daniel Coleman, B.A., Ph.D., Dean
fadmin@unb.ca
Computer Science
Virendra Bhavsar, B.Eng., M.Tech., Ph.D., Dean
Education
Sharon Rich, Ed.D., M.Ed., B.A., Dean
educ@unb.ca
Engineering
David Coleman, B.Sc.E., Ph.D., P.Eng., M, Dean
deaneng@unb.ca
Forestry & Environmental Management
D. MacLean, B.Sc., Ph.D., Dean
forem@unb.ca
Kinesiology
Terry Haggerty, B.A., B.P.H.E., Dip.Educ., Dean
cls@unb.ca
Law
Philip Bryden, B.A., B.C.L., L.L.M., Dean
law@unb.ca
Nursing
C.H. Gibson, B.N., M.Sc.N., Ph.D., Dean
nursing@unb.ca
School of Graduate Studies
Gwendolyn Davies, B.A., M.A., Ph.D., Cert.E, Dean
gradschl@unb.ca
Science
A.R. Sharp, B.Sc., M.Sc., Ph.D., Dean
science@unb.ca
Science, Applied Science & Engineering (Saint John)
Deborah MacLatchy, B.Sc., Ph.D., Dean
sci-eng@unbsj.ca

Campuses
Renaissance College
P.O. Box 4400
Fredericton, NB E3B 5A3, Canada
Fax: 506-447-3274
Pierre Zundel, Dean
Saint John Campus
Saint John
P.O. Box 5050
Saint John, NB E2L 4L5, Canada
Fax: 506-648-5528
K.E. Hamer, Vice-President

Affiliations
Maritime College of Forest Technology
1350 Regent St., Fredericton, NB E3C 2G6, Canada
Tel: 506-458-0653; *Fax:* 506-458-0652
info@mcft.ca
www.mcft.ca
Robert A. Whitney, Acting Executive Director
rwhitney@mcft.ca
Jason A. Thibodeau, MFRS, Recruitment Officer
jthibodeau@mcft.ca

Publications
Baron (St. John campus)

Brunswickan

***Moncton:* Université de Moncton**
Campus de Moncton
Moncton, NB E1A 3E9, Canada
Tél: 506-858-4000; *Téléc:* 506-858-4544
Ligne sans frais: 1-800-363-8336
info@umoncton.ca
www.umoncton.ca
Une institution d'enseignement exclusivement de langue française; campus: Edmunston, Moncton et Shippagan
Louis R. Comeau, C.M., Chancelier
Yvon Fontaine, Recteur et Vice-Chancelier
recteur@umoncton.ca
Lynne Castonguay, Secrétaire générale
Nassir El-Jabi, Vice-recteur à l'administration et aux ressources humaines
eljabin@umoncton.ca

Linda Schofield, Dir. gén.
schofil@umoncton.ca
Daniel Godbout, Directeur
godboud@umoncton.ca
Roger Boulay, Directeur
boulayr@umoncton.ca
vacant, Bibliothécaire en chef
Janique Léger, Directrice
legerja@umoncton.ca
Rhéal Belliveau, Directeur
bellivr@umoncton.ca
Paul-Emile Benoit, Directeur
benoitpe@umoncton.ca
Thérèse Thériault, Directrice
theriat@umoncton.ca
Gaston LeBlanc, Doyen
Isabelle McKee-Allain, Doyenne
chiassz@umoncton.ca
Andrew Boghen, Doyen
Anne Lowe, Doyenne
Charles Bourque, Doyen
Lise Caron, Doyenne
Marie-France Albert, Doyenne
Paul Chiasson, Doyen
Régina Robichaud, Directrice
Sylvie Robichaud-Ekstrand, Directrice
Paul Bourque, Directeur
Normand Gionet, Directeur
Paul Albert, Vice-recteur
Jocelyne Roy-Vienneau, Vice-rectrice
Normand Gionet, Doyen (par intérim)
Nasser Baccouche, Directeur
Zénon Chiasson, Directeur
chiassz@umoncton.ca
Terrance J. LeBlanc, Director
leblanct@umoncton.ca
Marc Boudreau, Directeur
boudrema@umoncton.ca
Neil Boucher, Vice-recteur à l'enseignement et à la recherche
bouchen@umoncton.ca

Publications
Le Front

***Sackville:* Mount Allison University**
65 York St., Sackville, NB E4L 1E4, Canada
Tel: 506-364-2300
www.mta.ca

John L. Bragg, O.C., B. Comm., B.Ed., LL, Chancellor
Kenneth L. Ozmon, O.C., Ph.D., B.A., M.A., President & Vice-Chancellor
Brian G. Johnston, B. Comm., LL.B., Q.C., Chair
John F. Read, B.Sc., Ph.D., Vice-President
David Stewart, B.Sc., LL.B., Vice-President
Carrie MacMillan, B.A., M.A., Ph.D., Dean
Robert Summerby-Murray, B.A., M.A., Ph.D., A.T.C., Dean
Chris Parker, B.F.A., Registrar
Charles W. F. Hunter, B.A., M.A., B.Ed., Associate Vice-President
Margaret Beattie, B.Sc., M.Sc., Ph.D., Dean
Bruno Gnassi, B.A., M.A., M.L.S., University Librarian

Publications
Argosy Weekly

Colleges

***Bathurst:* New Brunswick Community College (Bathurst)**
Collège communautaire du Nouveau-Brunswick (Bathurst)
P.O. Box 266
725, rue du Collège, Bathurst, NB E2A 3Z2, Canada
Tel: 506-547-2145; *Fax:* 506-547-2741
Toll-Free: 1-800-552-5483
www.bathurst.ccnb.nb.ca

Jeanne A. Comeau, Principal
jeanne.a.comeau@gnb.ca

***Campbellton:* Collège communautaire du Nouveau-Brunswick - Campbellton**
P.O. Box 309
47, av Village, Campbellton, NB E3N 3G7, Canada
Tél: 506-789-2377; *Téléc:* 506-789-2433
Ligne sans frais: 1-888-648-4111
yves.chouinard2@gnb.ca
campbellton.ccnb.nb.ca

Yves Chouinard, Directeur général

***Dieppe:* Collège Communautaire du Nouveau-Brunswick - Dieppe**
505, rue du Collège, Dieppe, NB E1A 7H9, Canada
Tél: 506-856-2200; *Téléc:* 506-856-2847
Ligne sans frais: 1-800-561-7162
cheryl.mclaughlin-basque@gnb.ca
www.ccnb.nb.ca/college/campus/dieppe

Claude Allard, Directeur
claude.allard@gnb.ca

***Edmundston:* New Brunswick Community College (Edmundston)**
Collège communautaire du Nouveau-Brunswick (Edmundston)
225, rue Pouvoir, Edmundston, NB E3V 3K7, Canada
Tel: 506-735-2500; *Fax:* 506-735-2717
Toll-Free: 1-888-695-2262
infoccnb@gnb.ca
www.edmundston.ccnb.nb.ca

Richard Doiron, Principal
richard.doiron@gnb.ca

***Fredericton:* New Brunswick Community College (Fredericton)**
Collège communautaire du Nouveau-Brunswick (Fredericton)
P.O. Box 6000
457 Queen St., Fredericton, NB E3B 5H1, Canada
Tel: 506-453-2305; *Fax:* 506-457-7352
nbccd.email@gnb.ca
www.nbccd.nbcc.nb.ca

Bronwen Cunningham, Principal
bronwen.cunningham@gnb.ca

***Miramichi:* New Brunswick Community College (Miramichi)**
Collège communautaire du Nouveau-Brunswick (Miramichi)
P.O. Box 1053
80 University Ave., Miramichi, NB E1N 3W4, Canada
Tel: 506-778-6000; *Fax:* 506-778-6001
www.nbcc.ca

Karen White-O'Connell, Principal
karen.white-o'connell@gnb.ca

***Moncton:* New Brunswick Community College (Moncton)**
Collège communautaire du Nouveau-Brunswick (Moncton)
1234 Mountain Rd., Moncton, NB E1C 8H9, Canada
Tel: 506-856-2220; *Fax:* 506-856-3288
Toll-Free: 1-888-664-1477
student.services@gnb.ca
www.nbcc.nb.ca/

Full Time Equivalency: 3500
Darren Ros, Principal
darren.rose@gnb.ca

***Saint John:* New Brunswick Community College (Saint John)**
Collège communautaire du Nouveau-Brunswick (Saint John)
P.O. Box 2270
950 Grandview Ave., Saint John, NB E2L 3V1, Canada
Tel: 506-658-6600; *Fax:* 506-658-6792
studentservices.nbccsj@gnb.ca
www.nbcc.nb.ca

Annette Albert, Principal
annette.albert@gnb.ca

***Shippagan:* New Brunswick Community College (Péninsule acadienne)**
Collège communautaire du Nouveau-Brunswick (Péninsule acad
232A, avenue de l'Église, Shippagan, NB E8S 1P6, Canada
Tel: 506-336-3073; *Fax:* 506-336-3075
Toll-Free: 1-866-299-9900
info_ccnbpa@gnb.ca

Thérèse Finn-McGraw, Principal
therese.finn-mcgraw@gnb.ca

***St Andrews:* New Brunswick Community College (St. Andrews)**
Collège communautaire du Nouveau-Brunswick (St. Andrews)
99 Augustus St., St Andrews, NB E5B 2E9, Canada
Tel: 506-529-5024; *Fax:* 506-529-5078
webinquiries@gnb.ca
www.nbcc.nb.ca

Full Time Equivalency: 300
Diane Burt, Principal
diane.burt@gnb.ca

***Woodstock:* New Brunswick Community College (Woodstock)**
Collège communautaire du Nouveau-Brunswick (Woodstock)
100 Broadway St., Woodstock, NB E7M 5C5, Canada
Tel: 506-325-4400; *Fax:* 506-328-8426
debbie.antworth@gnb.ca
www.nbcc.nb.ca

Joy Dion, Principal
joy.dion@gnb.ca

Post Secondary/Technical

Post Secondary/Technical

***Fredericton:* Maritime Forest Ranger School**
1350 Regent St., Fredericton, NB E3C 2G6, Canada
Tel: 506-458-0199; *Fax:* 506-458-0652

Established 1946. Identical francophone program offered at the Bathurst, NB campus. A minimum 12-month pre-admission apprenticeship in woods work or forestry is required. In addition to course work, students are required to work a minimum 12-week practic
J.S. Hoyt, Director

***Fredericton:* New Brunswick Community Colleges**
Collèges communautaires du Nouveau-Brunswick
Woodstock Fredericton Campus
284 Smythe St., Fredericton, NB E3B 3C9, Canada
Tel: 506-453-3641; *Fax:* 506-453-7944
www.gov.nb.ca/ael/nbcc/

***Moncton:* McKenzie College**
100 Cameron St., Moncton, NB E1C 5Y6, Canada
Tel: 506-384-6460; *Fax:* 506-384-6224
info@mckenzie.edu
www.mckenzie.edu

Multimedia, animation & information technology training.

***Fredericton:* Atlantic Business College - Fredericton Campus**
1115 Regent St., Fredericton, NB E3B 3Z2, Canada
Tel: 506-450-1408; *Fax:* 506-450-8388
Toll-Free: 1-800-983-292
atlantic@abc.nb.ca
www.abc.nb.ca

Day school programs, continuing education courses, corporate training; also in Moncton.
Jacqueline Devine, Principal

***Moncton:* Moncton Campus**
100 Cameron St. 2nd Fl., Moncton, NB E1C 5Y6, Canada
Tel: 506-857-3011; *Fax:* 506-857-4885
Toll-Free: 1-800-442-3111
moncton@abc.nb.ca
www.abc.nb.ca
TTY: 1-800-442-3011

Day school programs, continuing education courses, corporate training; also in Moncton.

***Saint John:* Academy of Learning**
245 Union St., Saint John, NB E2L 1B2, Canada
Tel: 506-652-8973; *Fax:* 506-634-1997
learn@aolnb.com
ww.aolnb.com

Computer & business skills training; 2 other locations in New Brunswick
Sumbal Sheikh, Manager

Newfoundland & Labrador

Government Agencies

***St. John's:* Department of Education**
P.O. Box 8700
St. John's, NL A1B 4J6, Canada
Tel: 709-729-5097; *Fax:* 709-729-5896
education@gov.nl.ca
www.gov.nl.ca/edu

Rick Hayward, Asst. Deputy Minister, 709-729-3025
rhayward@gov.nl.ca
Rachelle Cochrane, Asst. Deputy Minister, 709-729-3026
rachellecochrane@gov.nl.ca
Tony Cornect, District Assistant, 709-729-5096
tonycornect@gov.nl.ca

School Boards/Districts/Divisions

Public

Corner Brook: Western School District
P.O. Box 368
10 Wellington St., Corner Brook, NL A2H 6G9, Canada
Tel: 709-637-4000; *Fax:* 709-634-1828
www.wnlsd.ca
Grades: K.-12
Enrollment: 14737
This district is an amalgation of school districts 2, 3, and 4.
Ross Elliott, PhD, Dir., 709-634-8349
Donald Brown, Chair

Gander: Nova Central - School District 3
203 Elizabeth Dr., Gander, NL A1V 1H6, Canada
Tel: 709-256-2547; *Fax:* 709-651-3044
www.ncsd.ca
Enrollment: 13000
Cynthia Fleet, Director, Education
cfleet@ncsd.ca

Happy Valley-Goose Bay: District Office (Lab. East)
P.O. Box 1810 B
16 Strathcona, Happy Valley-Goose Bay, NL A0P 1E0, Canada
Tel: 709-896-2431; *Fax:* 709-896-9638
bpardy@lsb.ca
www.lsb.ca
Cindy Fleet, Director

Regional Office (Lab.West)
669 Tamarack Dr., Labrador City, NL A2V 2V2, Canada
Tel: 709-944-7628; *Fax:* 709-944-3480
sthibeau@lsb.ca
www.lsb.ca

Happy Valley-Goose Bay: Labrador - School district 1
P.O. Box 1810 B
16 Strathcona St., Happy Valley-Goose Bay, NL A0P 1E0, Canada
Tel: 709-896-2431; *Fax:* 709-896-9638
www.lsb.ca
Grades: K-12
Enrollment: 5000
Bruce Vey, Director, Education
bvey@lsb.ca

St. Jean: Conseil scolaire francophone provincial de Terre-Neuve-et-Labrador
#212, 65, ch Ridge, St. Jean, NL A1B 4P5, Canada
Tél: 709-722-6324; *Téléc:* 709-722-6325
Ligne sans frais: 888-794-6324
conseil@csfp.nf.ca
www.csfp.nf.ca
Dr. Ahmed Derradji-Aouat, Président du Conseil

St. John's: Eastern - School District 4
#601 Atlantic Place
P.O. Box 64-66
215 Water St., St. John's, NL A1C 6C9, Canada
Tel: 709-758-2372; *Fax:* 709-758-2706
www.esdnl.ca
Dr. Darin King, Dir. of Education

Schools: Specialized

First Nations

Conne River: Se't A'newey Kina'magino'kuom School
Also known as: Ste. Anne's School
P.O. Box 100
Conne River, NL A0H 1J0, Canada
Tel: 709-882-2747; *Fax:* 709-882-2528
www.k12.nf.ca/stannes/
Grades: K.-12
Craig Benoit, Principal

Natuashish: Mushuau Innu Natuashish
P.O. Box 189
Natuashish, NL A0P 1A0, Canada
Tel: 709-478-8972; *Fax:* 709-478-8989
www.natuashish.K12.nf.ca
Robert Myers
rmyers122@hotmail.com

Hearing Impaired

St. John's: Newfoundland School for the Deaf
425 Topsail Rd., St. John's, NL A1E 5N7, Canada
Tel: 709-364-1234; *Fax:* 709-729-5848
regmacdonald@gov.nl.ca
www.nsd.nf.ca/
Grades: K.-3, 5, 7-12
Reginald MacDonald, Principal

Schools: Independent & Private

Independent & Private Schools

Churchill Falls: Eric G. Lambert All-Grade School
P.O. Box 40
Churchill Falls, NL A0R 1A0, Canada
Tel: 709-925-3371; *Fax:* 709-925-3364
aclarke@nlh.nf.ca
www.k12.nf.ca/eglambert
Grades: K.-12
Enrollment: 156
Adrian Clarke, Principal
aclarke@nlh.nf.ca

St. John's: Lakecrest - St. John's Independent School
58 Patrick St., St. John's, NL A1E 2S7, Canada
Tel: 709-738-1212; *Fax:* 709-738-1701
www.lakecrest.ca
Grades: K.-9
Enrollment: 129
Ron Pellerin, Principal

St. John's: St. Bonaventure's College
Bonaventure Ave., St. John's, NL A1C 6B3, Canada
Tel: 709-726-0024; *Fax:* 709-726-0148
principal@stbonaventurescollege.ca
www.stbonaventurescollege.ca/
Grades: K.-12
Enrollment: 325
Catholic school in the Jesuit tradition
Cecil Critch, Principal
ccritch@stbonaventurescollege.ca

Universities & Colleges

Universities

St. John's: Memorial University of Newfoundland
P.O. Box 4200
230 Elizabeth Ave., St. John's, NL A1C 5S7, Canada
Tel: 709-737-8000; *Fax:* 709-737-4569
www.mun.ca
Full Time Equivalency: 17300
The Hon. Edward Roberts, O.N.L., B.A., LL.B., LL.D, Official Visitor
Gen. Rick Hillier, Chancellor
Dr. H.E.A. Campbell, Acting President & Vice-Chancellor
Dr. Chris Loomis, Vice-President
vpacad@mun.ca
Kent Decker, B.Comm. (Hons.), C.A., Vice-President
kdecker@mun.ca
Christopher W. Loomis, B.Sc., M.Sc., Ph.D., Vice-President
cwloomis@mun.ca
Glenn Collins, B.Sc., B.Ed., M.Sc., Registrar
gcollins@mun.ca
Deborah Collis, Acting Director
dcollis@mun.ca
Robert E. Simmonds, QC, Chair
Wilf Nicholls, B.Sc., Ph.D., Director
John Hanchar, Ph.D., Director
Charles Randell, P.Eng., B.Eng., M.A.Sc.,, President/CEO
Bill Morrissey, B.A.(Ed.), M.Ed., Director
Kenneth M. LeDez, M.B., Ch.B., F.R.C.T.C., Director
Graham Mowbray, B.Sc., Director
Peter Cornish, B.Sc., M.A., Ph.D., Director
Karen Hollett, B.A., L.L.B., Director
Martin Lovelace, B.A., M.A., Ph.D., Director
Bonnie Simmons, B.Comm., M.B.A., Director
David King, B.Comm., M.B.A., C.A., President & CEO
Lisa Hollett, B.A., M.I.R., Director
James A. Tuck, A.B., Ph.D., F.R.S.C., Director
Ron Sparkes, Ed.D., Interim Director
Richard H. Ellis, B.A., M.L.S., University Librarian
rhellis@mun.ca
Heather Wareham, B.A., Archivist
Peter Pope, B.A., M.A., Ph.D., Director
B.J. Veitch, B.Eng., M.Eng., L.Tech.,, Director
Ian Fleming, Ph.D., Director
Barbara Cox, B.A., Director
Norman Lee, B.M.S., M.D., C.C.F.P., Director
Sheila Devine, B.A., B.Ed., LL.B., Director
Robert Sheppard, B.Eng., M.B.A., M.Eng., P, Director
Victoria Collins, B.A., Director
Darrell Miles, P.Eng., Director
L. Husa, M.V.Dr., Director
Susan Vaughan, B.A., M.B.A., Director
Georgina Hedges, M.D., Acting Chair
Michael Collins, M.Sc., M.Ed., Ph.D., Assoc. Vice-President
collinsm@mun.ca
Penny Blackwood, B.Sc., M.Sc., Ph.D., Director
Paul Chancey, B.Sc., B.Comm., Director
Gerald Pocius, B.Sc., M.A., Ph.D., Director
Robert Shea, B.A., B.S.W., M.Ed., R.S., Director
Keith Storey, B.A., M.A., Ph.D., Director
Christine Burke, B.Comm., M.B.A., Director
J. Beal (Britain), B.A.(Hons.), Ph.D., Director
Anthony B. Dickinson, B.Sc., B.Ed., M.Sc., M.A., Acting Exec. Director
James Feehan, B.A., M.Sc., Ph.D., Director
Claude Horlick, B.Comm., Director
Bruce Belbin, B.A., B.Ed., M.Ed., Director
Dr. Lilly Walker, B.A., M.A., Ph.D., Dean
lwalker@mun.ca
Robert Greenwood, B.A.(Hons.), M.A., Ph.D., Director

Faculties
Arts
Reeta Tremblay, Ph.D., Dean
Business Administration
Gary Gorman, B.B.A., M.B.A., Ph.D., Dean
Education
Alice Collins, B.A., B.Ed., M.A., Ph.D., Dean
Engineering & Applied Science
Ray Gosine, B.Eng., Ph.D., P.Eng., Dean
Graduate Studies
Chet Jablonski, B.Sc., Ph.D., F.C.I.C., Dean
Medicine
James Rourke, M.D., C.C.F.P. (EM), F.C., Dean
Science
Robert Lucas, B.Sc., M.Sc., D.Phil., F., Dean

Schools
Division of Lifelong Learning
Doreen Whalen, Dip. A.A., C.T.T., B.Voc., Director
Distance Education & Learning Technologies
Anne Marie Vaughan, B.A., B.Ed., M.Ed., M.A., Director
Human Kinetics & Recreation
Mary Bluechardt, B.P.H.D., M.Sc., Ph.D., Director
Marine Institute
Glenn Blackwood, B.Sc. (Hon.), M.A., Executive Director
Music
Tom Gordon, B.A., B.Mus., M.A., Ph.D., Director
Nursing
Sandra LeFort, B.A., B.N., M.N., Ph.D., Director
Pharmacy
Linda Hensman, B.Sc.(Pharm.), S.U.N.Y.,, Director
Social Work
Shelly Birnie-Lefcovitch, B.A., M.S.W., Ph.D., Director

Affiliations
Fisheries & Marine Institute of Memorial University of Newfoundland
P.O. Box 4920
St. John's, NL A1C 5R3, Canada
Tel: 709-778-0200; *Fax:* 709-778-0672
Toll-Free: 1-800-563-5799
public.relations@mi.mun.ca; admissions@mi.mun.ca
www.mi.mun.ca
Other Information: Registrar, Phone: 709-778-0492
Glenn Blackwood, Executive Director
Carey Bonnell, Head, MI School of Fisheries

Harlow Campus Trust
The Maltings, St. John's Walk, Market St., Old Harl, Essex, England
hcampus@hcampus.inty.net
www.mun.ca/harlow
Other Information: Phone: (0)1279-455900; Fax: (0)1279-455921
Sandra Wright, General Manager

Queen's College
c/o The Provost, Faculty of Theology
#3000, 210 Prince Philip Dr., St. John's, NL A1B 3R6, Canada
Tel: 709-753-0116; *Fax:* 709-753-1214
Toll-Free: 1-877-753-0116
queens@mun.ca
www.mun.ca/queens
The Rev. Dr. John Mellis, Provost & Vice-Chancellor & Associate Professor
jmellis@mun.ca

Sir Wilfred Grenfell College
1 University Dr., Corner Brook, NL A2H 6P9, Canada
Tel: 709-637-6200
info@swgc.mun.ca; helpdesk@swgc.mun.ca;
webadmin@swgc.mun.ca
www.swgc.mun.ca
The College features the following divisions: Arts, Fine Arts, Science, & Social Science.
E. Holly Pike, Ph.D., Acting Principal, 709-637-6200, ext. 6231
hpike@swgc.mun.ca

Publications
The Muse

Colleges

Stephenville: College of the North Atlantic
P.O. Box 5400
Stephenville, NL A2N 2Z6, Canada
Tel: 709-643-7701; *Fax:* 709-643-7808
Toll-Free: 888-982-2268
info@cna.nl.ca
www.cna.nl.ca
Full Time Equivalency: 20000
Bruce Hollett, Interim President, 709-643-7701, fax: 709-643-7808
bruce.hollet@cna.nl.
John Hutchings, Vice-Pres., Finance & Administration, 709-643-7704
john.hutchings@cna.nl.ca
Cyril Organ, Vice-Pres., Academic & Learner Services, 709-643-7732
cyril.organ@cna.nl.ca
Corinne Dunne, Vice-Pres., Development/College Advancement, 709-758-7652
corinne.dunne@cna.nl.ca
Greg Chaytor, Vice-Pres., Qatar Project, 709-643-7702
greg.chaytor@cna.nl.ca
Linda Dunne, Registrar, 709-643-0827, fax: 709-643-7843
linda.dunne@cna.nl.ca

Schools
Academics
Brenda Tobin, Dean, 709-292-5636, fax: 709-643-0518
Applied Arts
Brenda Tobin, Dean, 709-292-5636, fax: 709-489-0518
Business
Mary Vaughan, Dean, 709-649-7970, fax: 709-643-8454
Engineering Technology
Arthur Leung, Dean, 709-758-7100, fax: 709-758-7126
Health Sciences
Jane Gamberg, Dean, 709-758-7624, fax: 709-758-7634
Industrial Trades
Norris Eaton, Dean, 709-637-8523, fax: 709-634-8767
Information Technology
Mary Vaughan, Dean, 709-649-7970, fax: 709-643-8454
Tourism & Natural Resources
Brent Howell, Dean, 709-637-8608, fax: 709-634-2126

Campuses
Baie-Verte Campus
1 Terra Nova Rd., Baie Verte, NL A0K 1B0, Canada
Tel: 709-532-8066; *Fax:* 709-532-4624
Emily Foster, Campus Administrator, 709-532-8066, fax: 709-532-4624
emily.foster@cna.nl.ca

Bay St. George Campus - Headquarters
DSB Fowlow Bldg.
P.O. Box 5400
432 Massachussetts Dr., Stephenville, NL A2N 2Z6, Canada
Tel: 709-643-7838; *Fax:* 709-643-7734
Chris Dohaney, Campus Administrator, 709-643-7916, fax: 709-643-7827
chris.dohaney@cna.nl.ca

Bonavista Campus
P.O. Box 670
301 Confederation Dr., Bonavista, NL A0C 1B0, Canada
Tel: 709-468-2610; *Fax:* 709-468-2004
Marilyn Coles-Hayley, Campus Administrator, 709-468-1700, fax: 709-468-2004
marilyn.hayley@cna.nl.ca

Burin Campus
P.O. Box 370
105 Main St., Burin Bay, NL A0E 1G0, Canada
Tel: 709-891-5600; *Fax:* 709-891-2256
Toll-Free: 800-838-0976
ask.burin@cna.nl.ca
Mike Graham, Campus Administrator, 709-891-5602, fax: 709-891-2256
mike.graham@cna.nl.ca

Carbonear Campus
4 Pike's Lane, Carbonear, NL A1Y 1A7, Canada
Tel: 709-596-6139; *Fax:* 709-596-2688
Gary Myrden, Campus Administrator, 709-596-6139, fax: 709-596-2688
gary.myrden@cna.nl.ca

Clarenville Campus
69 Pleasant St., Clarenville, NL A5A 1V9, Canada
Tel: 709-466-6900; *Fax:* 709-466-2771
Maisie Caines, Campus Administrator, 709-466-6931, fax: 709-466-2771
maisie.caines@cna.nl.ca

Corner Brook Campus
P.O. Box 822
41 O'Connell Dr., Corner Brook, NL A2H 6H6, Canada
Tel: 709-637-8530; *Fax:* 709-634-2126
Chad Simms, Campus Administrator, 709-637-8549, fax: 709-634-2126
chad.simms@cna.nl.ca

Gander Campus
P.O. Box 395
1 Magee Rd., Gander, NL A1V 1W8, Canada
Tel: 709-651-4800; *Fax:* 709-651-3376
Bob Dwyer, Campus Administrator, 709-651-4803, fax: 709-651-3376
bob.dwyer@cna.nl.ca

Grand Falls-Windsor Campus
P.O. Box 413
5 Cromer Ave., Grand Falls-Windsor, NL A2A 1X3, Canada
Tel: 709-292-5600; *Fax:* 709-489-4180
Joan Pynn, Campus Administrator, 709-292-5625, fax: 709-489-5765
joan.pynn@cna.nl.ca

Happy Valley Campus
P.O. Box 1720 B
219 Hamilton River Rd., Happy Valley-Goose Bay, NL A0P 1E0, Canada
Tel: 709-896-6300; *Fax:* 709-896-3733
Paul Motty, Campus Administrator, 709-896-6312, fax: 709-896-9533
paul.motty@cna.nl.ca

Labrador West Campus
1 Campbell Dr., Labrador City, NL A2V 2Y1, Canada
Tel: 709-944-7210; *Fax:* 709-944-6581
Richard Sawyer, Campus Administrator, 709-944-6814, fax: 709-944-5413
richard.sawyer@cna.nl.ca

Placentia Campus
P.O. Box 190
1 Roosevelt Ave., Placentia, NL A0B 2Y0, Canada
Tel: 709-227-2037; *Fax:* 709-227-7185
Darrell Clarke, Campus Administrator, 709-227-2037, fax: 709-227-7185
darrell.clarke@cna.nl.ca

Port-aux-Basques Campus
P.O. Box 760
59 Grand Bay Rd., Port-aux-Basques, NL A0M 1C0, Canada
Tel: 709-695-3582; *Fax:* 709-695-2963
Mr Jan Peddle, Campus Administrator, 709-695-3582, fax: 709-695-2963
jan.peddle@cna.nl.ca

Prince Philip Drive Campus - St. John's
P.O. Box 1693
1 Prince Philip Dr., St. John's, NL A1C 5P7, Canada
Tel: 709-758-7284; *Fax:* 709-758-7304
Trudy Barnes, Campus Administrator, 709-758-7418, fax: 709-758-7235
trudy.barnes@cna.nl.ca

Ridge Road Campus
P.O. Box 1150
St. John's, NL A1C 6L8
Tel: 709-758-7000; *Fax:* 709-758-7059
John Oates, Campus Administrator, 709-758-7517, fax: 709-758-7126
john.oates@cna.nl.ca

Seal Cove Campus
P.O. Box 19003 Seal Cove
1670 Conception Bay Highway, Conception Bay South, NL A1X 5C7, Canada
Tel: 709-744-2047; *Fax:* 709-744-3929
Chris Patey, Campus Administrator, 709-744-1041, fax: 709-744-3929
chris.patey@cna.nl.ca

St. Anthony Campus
P.O. Box 550
83-93 East St., St Anthony, NL A0K 4S0, Canada
Tel: 709-454-3559; *Fax:* 709-454-8808
Fred Russell, Campus Administrator, 709-454-2884, fax: 709-454-8808
frederick.russell@cna.nl.ca

Qatar Campus
P.O. Box 24449
Doha, Qatar
Other Information: 974-495-2222

The Troubadour
Tel: 709-643-7746
the.troubador@cna.nl.ca
www.cna.nl.ca/troubadour

Post Secondary/Technical

Post Secondary/Technical

Badger: Central Training Academy
P.O. Box 400
6 - 3rd Ave., Badger, NL A0H 1A0, Canada
Tel: 709-539-5150; *Fax:* 709-539-5145
Toll-Free: 1-800-563-515
cta@nf.aibn.com
Training in commercial transport, heavy equipment operation

Bay Roberts: Canadian Training Institute
P.O. Box 479
Bay Roberts, NL A0A 1G0, Canada
Tel: 709-786-2400; *Fax:* 709-786-1215
Arthur Dominix

Conception Bay South: Woodford Training Centre Inc.
P.O. Box 17145 Kelligrews
Conception Bay South, NL A1X 3H1, Canada
Tel: 709-834-7000; *Fax:* 709-834-9663
info@woodfordtraining.com
www.woodfordtraining.com
Cosmetology & barbering
Sharon Woodford

Corner Brook: Corner Brook (VON)
Corner Brook District
31 Wellington St., Corner Brook, NL A2H 5H5, Canada
Tel: 709-634-2042; *Fax:* 709-634-2517
pitchere@von.ca
www.von.ca/branch/nf_cornerbrook/
Eileen Pitcher

Campuses
Gander District (VON)
Gander Medical Bldg.
177 Elizabeth Dr., Gander, NL A1V 1H6, Canada
Tel: 709-256-2924; *Fax:* 709-256-2905
vongander@nf.aibn.com
www.von.ca/branch/nf_gander

St.John's (VON)
39 Campbell Ave., St.John's, NF A1E 2Z3, Canada
Tel: 709-726-8597; *Fax:* 709-726-4228
von@nf.aibn.com
www.von.ca/branch/nf_stjohns

Corner Brook: Corner Brook Campus
2 University Dr., Corner Brook, NL A2H 5G4, Canada
Tel: 709-637-2100; *Fax:* 709-637-2123
www.academycanada.com
M.A.Ed. Michael Barrett, President

Campuses
St. John's Campus
167-169 Kenmount Rd., St. John's, NL A1B 3P9, Canada
Tel: 709-739-6767; *Fax:* 709-739-6797
www.academycanada.com

Trades College
37-45 Harding Rd., St. John's, NL A1C 5R4, Canada
Tel: 709-722-9151; *Fax:* 709-722-9197
www.academycanada.com

Creston: Centrac College of Business, Trades & Technology
P.O. Box 160
Creston, NL A0E 1K0, Canada
Tel: 709-891-1995; *Fax:* 709-891-5272
Toll-Free: 1-800-563-191
admissions@centraccollege.ca
www.centraccollege.ca

Gander: Centrac College of Business, Trades & Technology
P.O. Box 473
Gander, NL A1V 1W8, Canada
Tel: 709-256-2670; *Fax:* 709-256-3697
Toll-Free: 1-888-336-872
Campuses in Gander, Marystown, St. John's & Springdale.

Gander: Gander Flight Training
P.O. Box 355
Gander, NL A1V 1W7, Canada
Tel: 709-256-7484; *Fax:* 709-256-7953
Toll-Free: 1-888-926-766
admin@gft.ca
www.gft.ca
Patrick White, President & CEO

Grand Falls-Windsor: Corona Training Institute
P.O. Box 819
60 Hardy Ave., Grand Falls-Windsor, NL A2A 2P7, Canada
Tel: 709-489-7825; *Fax:* 709-489-5001
Toll-Free: 1-888-926-766
admin@coronacollege.com
www.coronacollege.com
Bernice Walker

Holyrood: Boilermakers Industrial Training Centre
P.O. Box 250
Holyrood, NL A0A 2R0, Canada
Tel: 709-229-7958; *Fax:* 709-229-7300
Tom Welsh

Holyrood: Operating Engineers, Education & Development Inc.
P.O. Box 389
Holyrood, NL A0A 2R0, Canada
Tel: 709-229-6464; *Fax:* 709-229-6469
oec@oecollege.com
www.oecollege.com
Larry Connolly

Lewisporte: DieTrac Technical Institute
P.O. Box 970
82 Premier Dr., Lewisporte, NL A0G 3A0, Canada
Tel: 709-535-0550; *Fax:* 709-535-6101
admin@dietrac.com
www.dietrac.com

Mount Pearl: Iron Workers Education & Training Co. Inc.
38 Sagona St., Mount Pearl, NL A1N 4R3, Canada
Tel: 709-747-2158; *Fax:* 709-747-1042
Tom Woodward

Paradise: Carpenters Millwrights College Inc.
P.O. Box 3040
Paradise, NL A1L 3W2, Canada
Tel: 709-364-5586; *Fax:* 709-364-5587
kpower@nlrc.ca
www.nlrc.ca
John Pitcher

St. John's: Association for New Canadians
P.O. Box 2031
St. John's, NL A1C 5R6, Canada
Tel: 709-722-9680; *Fax:* 709-754-4407
www.anc-nf.cc
ESL
Bridget Foster, Executive Director

St. John's: Atlantic Aviation Academy
St. John's International Airport
Hangar #2, St. John's, NL A1A 5B5, Canada
Tel: 709-576-3420; *Fax:* 709-576-3427
snoseworthy@provair.com

St. John's: Atlantic Construction Training Centre
P.O. Box 236
41-44 Harding Rd., St. John's, NL A1G 1H2, Canada
Tel: 709-726-6264; *Fax:* 709-726-6255
jpoirier@actc.nf.ca
John Poirier, Training Co-ordinator

St. John's: Avalon Educational Systems
65 Whiteway St., St. John's, NL A1B 1K5, Canada
Tel: 709-739-5507; *Fax:* 709-754-3212
Custom-designed programs

St. John's: Graduate Centre of Applied Technology
P.O. Box 6345 C
275 Duckworth St., St. John's, NL A1C 6J9, Canada
Tel: 709-758-5770; *Toll-Free:* 1-800-247-575
gcat@graduatecentre.com
www.graduatecentre.com
Cal Burton

St. John's: Highland College of Trades & Technology
P.O. Box 21323
St. John's, NL A1A 5G6, Canada
Tel: 709-747-0171; *Fax:* 709-747-0172
www.highlandcollege.com
Secina Brown

St. John's: Judy Knee Dance College Ltd.
27 Mayor Ave., St. John's, NL A1C 4N4, Canada
Tel: 709-579-3233; *Fax:* 709-579-3392
jknee@avint.net
Judy Knee

St. John's: Keyin College
KeyCorp Incorporated, Head Office Keyin College
P.O. Box 13609 A
44 Austin St., St. John's, NL A1B 4G1, Canada
Tel: 709-579-1061; *Fax:* 709-579-6002
Toll-Free: 1-800-563-8989
lori@keyin.com
www.coredynamic.com/keyin/about.asp
Industry-directed education
Gwen Tucker, Founder

Campuses

Carbonear Campus
81 LeMarchant St., Carbonear, NL A1Y 1A9, Canada
Tel: 709-596-6472; *Fax:* 709-596-0217
Toll-Free: 800-563-8989
margdrover@hotmail.com (Principal Margaret Drover)
www.coredynamic.com/keyin/about.asp
Ken Drover, Principal

Clarenville Campus
Cormack Bldg.
221B Memorial Dr., Clarenville, NL A5A 1R3, Canada
Tel: 709-466-7115; *Fax:* 709-466-1290
Toll-Free: 1-800-563-8989
paula@keyinclarenville.com (Principal Paula Benson)
www.coredynamic.com/keyin/about.asp
Paula Benson, Principal

Fortune Adult Learning Centre Campus
8 Benson St., Fortune, NL A0E 1P0, Canada
Tel: 709-279-5090; *Fax:* 709-279-5091
Toll-Free: 1-800-563-8989
marc.coady@personainternet.ca (Principal Marc Coady)
www.coredynamic.com/keyin/about.asp

Gander Campus
175 Airport Blvd., Gander, NL A1V 1K6, Canada
Tel: 709-651-8560; *Fax:* 709-651-8565
Toll-Free: 1-800-563-8989
ebabstock@keyincentral.nf.ca (Principal Elsie Babstock)
www.coredynamic.com/keyin/about.asp
Elise Babstock, Principal

Grand Falls-Windsor Campus
3 Hardy Ave., Grand Falls-Windsor, NL A2A 2P8, Canada
Tel: 709-489-8560; *Fax:* 709-489-8565
Toll-Free: 1-800-563-8989
bhanlon@keyincentral.nf.ca (Principal Bill Hanlon)
www.coredynamic.com/keyin/about.asp
Bill Hanlon, Principal

Lamaline Adult Learning Centre Campus
GLADA Bldg.
P.O. Box 39
Lamaline, NL A0E 2C0, Canada
Tel: 709-279-5090; *Fax:* 709-279-5091
Toll-Free: 1-800-563-8989
marc.coady@personainternet.com (Principal Marc Coady)
www.coredynamic.com/keyin/about.asp

Lewisporte Adult Learning Centre Campus
395 Main St., Lewisporte, NL A0G 3A0, Canada
Tel: 709-535-3946; *Fax:* 709-535-3946
Toll-Free: 1-800-563-8989
brian@keyincentral.nf.ca
www.coredynamic.com/keyin/about.asp
Brian Caravan, Principal

Marystown Campus
P.O. Box 1327
414 Ville Marie Dr., Marystown, NL A0E 2M0, Canada
Tel: 709-279-8090; *Fax:* 709-279-5091
Toll-Free: 1-800-563-8989
marc.coady@personainternet.com (Principal Marc Coady)
www.coredynamic.com/keyin/about.asp
Marc Coady, Principal

St. John's Campus
P.O. Box 13609 A
44 Austin St., St. John's, NL A1B 4G1, Canada
Tel: 709-579-1061; *Fax:* 709-579-6002
Toll-Free: 1-800-563-8989
lori@keyin.com (Principal Lori Caines)
www.coredynamic.com/keyin/about.asp

St. John's: Lawrence College Inc.
120 LeMarchant Rd., St. John's, NL A1C 2H2, Canada
Tel: 709-738-1053; *Fax:* 709-738-3350
Toll-Free: 1-888-738-105
Brenda Steele, Principal

St. John's: LeMoine's School of Hair Design
P.O. Box 5744
St. John's, NL A1C 5X3, Canada
Tel: 709-576-2148; *Fax:* 709-579-1134
lemoines@nl.rogers.com
www.lemoines.com
Hair dressing and esthetics school.
Allan LeMoine

St. John's: T & R Goldshield Security Services
300 Topsail Rd., St. John's, NL A1E 2B5, Canada
Tel: 709-726-0160; *Fax:* 709-726-0133
Don Ross

St.John's: United Association of Journeymen & Apprentices of the Plumbing and Pipefitti (UA)
P.O. Box 8583 A
St.John's, NL A1B 3P2, Canada
Tel: 709-747-0364; *Fax:* 709-747-2861
bshea@local74.nf.net (Betty Shea: Executive Secretary)
www.ualocal740.ca
Official name: "United Association of Journeymen & Apprentices of the Plumbing and Pipefitting Industry of the United States and Canada".
Larry Slaney

Northwest Territories

Government Agencies

Yellowknife: Department of Education, Culture & Employment
P.O. Box 1320
Yellowknife, NT X1A 2L9, Canada
Tel: 867-920-6240; *Fax:* 867-873-0338
www.ece.gov.nt.ca
Pauline Gordon, Asst. Deputy Minister
Dan Daniels, Deputy Minister

School Boards/Districts/Divisions

Public

Fort Simpson: Dehcho Divisional Education Council
P.O. Box 376
Fort Simpson, NT X0E 0N0, Canada
Tel: 867-695-7308
Nolan Swartzentruber, Supt.

Fort Smith: South Slave Divisional Education Council
P.O. Box 510
Fort Smith, NT X0E 0P0, Canada
Tel: 867-872-5701; *Fax:* 867-872-2150
jmurray@ssdec.nt.ca
www.ssdec.nt.ca
Curtis Brown, Superintendent
cbrown@ssdec.nt.ca

***Inuvik:* Beaufort Delta Divisional Education Council**
c/o Bag Service No. 12, Inuvik, NT X0E 0T0, Canada
Tel: 867-777-7136; *Fax:* 867-777-2469
www.bdec.nt.ca

Grades: Kindergarten - 12
Enrollment: 1800
Roy Cole, Superintendent, Schools, 867-777-7332
roy_cole@bdec.learnnet.nt.ca
Gayle Strikes With A Gun, Assistant Superintendent, 867-777-7176
gaylestrikeswithagun@bdec.learnnet.nt.ca
Grey Storey, Supervisor, Schools, 867-777-7131
greg_storey@bdec.learnnet.nt.ca
Austin Abbott, Coordinator, Skills Programs, 867-777-7367
austin_abbott@bdec.learnnet.nt.ca
Camellia Gray, Coordinator, Public Affairs, 867-777-7322
camellia_gray@bdec.learnnet.nt.ca
Liz Hansen, Coordinator, Gwich'in Aboriginal Language & Culture, 867-777-7101
liz_hansen@bdec.learnnet.nt.ca
Rose Marie Kirby, Coordinator, Inuvialuit Aboriginal Language & Culture, 867-777-7371
rosemarie_kirby@bdec.learnnet.nt.ca

***Norman Wells:* Sahtu Divisional Education Council**
P.O. Box 64
Norman Wells, NT X0E 0V0, Canada
Tel: 867-587-3450
info@sahtudec.ca
www.sahtudec.ca

Seamus Quigg, Superintendent

***Rae Edzo:* Tłįchǫ Community Services Agency**
Bag Service #5, Rae Edzo, NT X0E 0Y0, Canada
Tel: 867-392-3000; *Fax:* 867-392-3001
tcsa@tlicho.net
www.tlicho.ca

Lucy Lafferty, Superintendent

***Yellowknife:* Commission scolaire francophone des Territoires du Nord-Ouest**
P.O. Box 1980
4920, 51e Rue, Yellowknife, NT X1A 2P5, Canada
Tél: 867-873-6555; *Téléc:* 867-873-5644
csftno@gov.nt.ca
www.csftno.com

Philippe Brûlot, Directeur général

***Yellowknife:* Yellowknife Catholic Schools**
5124 - 49 St., Yellowknife, NT X1A 2P4, Canada
Tel: 867-766-7400; *Fax:* 867-766-7401
www.ycs.nt.ca

Grades: K.-12
Enrollment: 1450
Claudia Parker, Supt.
Mike Huvenaars, Asst. Supt., Business
Dianne Lafferty, Coordinator, Aboriginal Ed.

***Yellowknife:* Yellowknife Education District No. 1**
P.O. Box 788
5402 - 50th Ave., Yellowknife, NT X1A 2N6, Canada
Tel: 867-766-5050; *Fax:* 867-873-5051
yk1@yk1.nt.ca
www.yk1.nt.ca/#Scene_1

Grades: K.-12
Enrollment: 2000
Metro Huculak, Supt./CEO, 867-766-5064
metro.huculak@yk1.nt.ca
Metro Huculak, Supt./CEO, 867-766-5064
metro.huculak@yk1.nt.ca
Myrna Pokiak, Coordinator, Aboriginal Ed., 867-766-5054
myrna.pokiak@yk1.nt.ca

Universities & Colleges

Colleges

***Inuvik:* Aurora College**
P.O. Box 1290
199 McDougal, Inuvik, NT X0E 0P0, Canada
Tel: 867-872-7009; *Fax:* 867-872-4730
www.auroracollege.nt.ca

Maurice Evans, President

Campuses
Aurora Campus
P.O. Box 1008
Inuvik, NT X0E 0T0, Canada
Fax: 867-777-2850

Miki O'Kane, Campus Director

Thebacha Campus
P.O. Box 600
Fort Smith, NT X0E 0P0, Canada
Fax: 867-872-4511

Kathleen E. Purchase, Campus Director

Yellowknife Campus
Bag Service 9700, Yellowknife, NT X1A 2R3, Canada
Fax: 867-873-0333

Sarah Wright, Campus Director

Nova Scotia

Government Agencies

***Halifax:* Department of Education**
P.O. Box 578
2021 Brunswick St., Halifax, NS B3J 2S9, Canada
Tel: 902-424-5168; *Fax:* 902-424-0511
www.ednet.ns.ca

Margelaine Holding, Executive Director, 902-424-3927
Ann Blackwood, Director, 902-424-5745

School Boards/Districts/Divisions

Public

***Berwick:* Annapolis Valley Regional School Board**
P.O. Box 340
121 Orchard St., Berwick, NS B0P 1E0, Canada
Tel: 902-538-4600; *Fax:* 902-538-4630
Toll-Free: 1-800-850-3887
communications@avrsb.ednet.ns.ca
www.avrsb.ca

Grades: Elementary - Secondary
Enrollment: 16000
Margo Tait, Superintendent, Schools, 902-538-4606, fax: 902-538-4634
superintendent@avrsb.ednet.ns.ca
Allen Hume, Director, Human Resources, 902-538-4610, fax: 902-538-4635
allen.hume@avrsb.ca
Stuart Jamieson, Director, Finance & Operations, 902-538-4607, fax: 902-538-4657
stuart.jamieson@avrsb.ca
Dave Jones, Director, Programs & Services, 902-538-4611, fax: 902-538-4630
dave.jones@avrsb.ca

***Bridgewater:* South Shore Regional School Board**
130 North Park St., Bridgewater, NS B4V 4G9, Canada
Tel: 902-543-2468; *Fax:* 902-541-3051
Toll-Free: 888-252-2217
tsmith@ssrsb.ca
www.ssrsb.ca

Enrollment: 7400
Elliott Payzant, Chair
Nancy Pynch-Worthylake, Superintendent
npynch-worthylake@ssrsb.ca

***Dartmouth:* Halifax Regional School Board**
90 Alderney Dr., Dartmouth, NS B2Y 4S8, Canada
Tel: 902-464-2000
www.hrsb.ns.ca

Grades: Primary - 12
Enrollment: 52000
Number of Schools: 85 elementary schools; 28 junior high schools; 15 senior high schools; 9 primary to grade 9 schools.
Number of Employees: 8,000 (including 3,478 teachers & school administrators
Irvine Carvery, Chair, 902-464-2000, ext. 4445
icarvery@hrsb.ns.ca
Carole Olsen, Superintendent
Geoff Cainen, Director, Program
Mike Christie, Director, Human Resource Services
Charles Clattenburg, Director, Operations Services
Danielle McNeil-Hessian, Director, School Administration
Richard Morris, Director, Financial Services
Heather Chandler, Coordinator, Diversity Management
Gerard Costard, Coordinator, Information Technology
Doug Hadley, Coordinator, Communications
Kim Matheson, Coordinator, Policy & Research
Tracey O'Kroneg, Coordinator, Human Resource Services
Jim Gunn, Corporate Secretary

***Port Hastings:* Strait Regional School Board**
16 Cemetery Rd., Port Hastings, NS B9A 1K6, Canada
Tel: 902-625-2191; *Fax:* 902-625-2281
Toll-Free: 1-800-650-4448
srsb@srsb.ca; cathy.rankin@srsb.ca (Receptionist)
ls-strait.ednet.ns.ca/srsb/SRSBoard.nsf/MainFrameSet

Grades: Primary - 12
Number of Schools: 25
Mary Jess MacDonald, Chair
Jack Beaton, Superintendent, Schools, 902-625-7065
jack.beaton@srsb.ca
William J. Cormier, Director, Finance, 902-625-7050
william.cormier@srsb.ca
Terry Doyle, Director, Operations, 902-747-3647
terry.doyle@srsb.ca
Sherman England, Director, Human Resources, 902-625-7081
sherman.england@srsb.ca
Monica Williams, Director, Programs & Student Services, 902-625-7083
monica.williams@srsb.ca
Anita Cameron, Manager, Labour Relations, 902-747-3647
anita.cameron@srsb.ca
Tara Gaskell, Manager, Occupational Health & Safety Programs, 902-747-3647
tara.gaskell@srsb.ca
Deanna Gillis, Manager, Communications & Community Relations, 902-625-7093
deanna.gillis@srsb.ca
Shirley Hart, Manager, Purchasing, 902-625-7050
shirley.hart@srsb.ca
Carleton MacNeil, Manager, Facilities, 902-747-3647
carleton.macneil@srsb.ca
Philip Hall, Coordinator, Information Technology & Integration, 902-625-7083
philip.hall@srsb.ca
Kathy Rhodes-Langille, Coordinator, Race Relations & Cross Cultural Understanding, 902-625-7112
kathy.rhodeslangille@srsb.ca
Joan Bona, Board Secretary, 902-625-7065
joan.bona@srsb.ca

***Saulnierville:* Conseil scolaire acadien provincial**
P.O. Box 88
Saulnierville, NS B0W 2Z0, Canada
Tél: 902-769-5458; *Téléc:* 902-769-5459
Ligne sans frais: 888-533-2727
madeleine.ferron@csap.ednet.ns.ca
csap.ednet.ns.ca

Enrollment: 4059
Adresse civique: 9248, rte 1, La Butte, Meteghan River, N-É.
Darrell Samson, Directeur général
Madeleine Ferron, Secrétaire du Conseil
madeleine.ferron@csap.ednet.ns.ca

***Sydney:* Cape Breton-Victoria Regional School Board**
275 George St., Sydney, NS B1P 1J7, Canada
Tel: 902-564-8293; *Fax:* 902-564-0123
Grades: Elementary - Secondary; Adult Ed.
Enrollment: 16006
Number of Schools: 61
Lorne Green, Chair
Ed Davis, Superintendent
Charles Sheppard, Coordinator, School Services

***Truro:* Chignecto-Central Regional School Board**
60 Lorne St., Truro, NS B2N 3K3, Canada
Tel: 902-897-8900; *Fax:* 902-897-8989
Toll-Free: 1-800-770-000
www.ccrsb.ednet.ns.ca

Enrollment: 25722
Gary Miller, Supt.
Trudy Thompson, Chair

***Yarmouth:* Tri-County Regional School Board**
79 Water St., Yarmouth, NS B5A 1L4, Canada
Tel: 902-749-5696; *Fax:* 902-749-5697
Toll-Free: 1-800-915-0113
www.tcrsb.ca

Grades: Primary - 12
Number of Schools: 30
Faye Haley, Chair
Phil Landry, Superintendent, Schools, 902-749-5682
plandry@tcrsb.ca
Trevor Cunningham, Director, Programs & Student Services, 902-749-5675
tcunning@tcrsb.ca
Gerry Purdy, Director, Human Resources, 902-749-5684
gpurdy@tcrsb.ca
Steve Stoddart, Director, Operations, 902-749-5691
sstoddar@tcrsb.ca
Wade Tattrie, Director, Finance, 902-541-3009
wtattrie@ssrsb.ca
Steve Adams, Manager, Transportation, 902-749-2804
sadams@tcrsb.ca
Mark Albert, Manager, Technology Services, 902-749-5689
mark.albert@tcrsb.ca

Dave Buckland, Coordinator, Monitoring & Evaluation, 902-749-5814
dbuckland@tcrsb.ca
Craig Crosby, Coordinator, Property Services, 902-749-2827
ccrosby@tcrsb.ca
Jason Curtis, Coordinator, Information Systems, 902-749-5186
jcurtis@tcrsb.ca
Lisa Doucet, Coordinator, Student Services, 902-749-5196
ldoucet@tcrsb.ca
Steven Gaudet, Coordinator, French Programs, 902-749-5680
sgaudet@tcrsb.ca
Gerry Pitman, Coordinator, Community Learning, 902-749-5679
gpitman@tcrsb.ca
Gerry Randell, Coordinator, Programs 7 - 12, 902-749-5197
grandell@tcrsb.ca
Gerry Stockman, Coordinator, Programs P - 6, 902-749-2826
kstockman@tcrsb.ca

First Nations

Eskasoni: Eskasoni First Nation School Board
P.O. Box 7959
4645 Shore Rd., Eskasoni, NS B1W 1B8
Tel: 902-379-2507; *Fax:* 902-379-2273
www.eskasonischoolbd.com
eskasoni@schoolbd.ca
Grades: Day Care - Secondary; Mi'kmaq
Enrollment: 1249
Number of Schools: 4 (Eskasoni Ksite'taqnk Day Care; Eskasoni Unama'ki Training & Education Centre; Eskasoni Elementary & Middle School, & Chief Allison Bernard Memorial High School).
Number of Employees: 175. Situated on eastern Cape Breton Island, Eskasoni First Nation is a large Mi'kmaq community. Education in the community is directed by the Eskasoni First Nation School Board, which is overseen by the Eskasoni Band Council.
John F. Toney, Chair
Patricia Marshall, Director, Education, 902-379-2507, fax: 902-379-2273
patriciamarshall@schoolbd.ca
Patrick Johnson, Director, Mi'kmaq Student Services at Cape Breton University, 902-379-2507, fax: 902-379-2273
patriciamarshall@schoolbd.ca
Terry Lynn Marshall, Contact, Finance, 902-379-2507, fax: 902-379-2273
terrylynnmarshall@schoolbd.ca
Barbara Sylliboy, Contact, Language, 902-379-2507, fax: 902-379-2273
barbsylliboy@schoolbd.ca
Belinda Stevens, Clerk, Post-Secondary Program, 902-379-2507, fax: 902-379-2273
belindastevens@schoolbd.ca

Schools: Specialized

First Nations

Chapel Island: Mi'kmaway School
P.O. Box 538
RR#1, Richmond County, Chapel Island, NS B0E 3B0, Canada
Tel: 902-535-2307; *Fax:* 902-535-3428
mikmawey@auracom.com
www.kinu.ns.ca/chapel
Grades: Primary - 6; Mi'kmaq language
Enrollment: 73
The Mi'kmaway School is administered by the Potlotek Board of Education. The school serves the Chapel Island First Nation.
Nancy MacLeod, Director, Potlotek Education Office, fax: 902-535-3164
nmacleod@potlotek.ca

Eskasoni: Chief Allison Bernard Memorial High School
Also known as: Eskasoni High School
P.O. Box 7969
4673 Shore Rd., Eskasoni, NS B1W 1B8, Canada
Tel: 902-379-3000; *Fax:* 902-379-3011
www.eskasonischoolbd.com
Grades: 10 - 12; Mi'kmaq language & culture
Enrollment: 200
Chief Allison Bernard Memorial High School operates under the direction of the Eskasoni First Nation School Board. The First Nation secondary school is situated in the Mi'kmaq community of Eskasoni in Cape Breton Island. Chief Allison Bernard Memorial High School follows the Nova Scotia Curriculum Guide & also offers Mi'kmaq studies.
John Googoo, Principal
johndgoogoo@hotmail.com
Newell Johnson, Vice-Principal

Eskasoni: Eskasoni Elementary & Middle School
P.O. Box 7970
4675 Shore Rd., Eskasoni, NS B1W 1B8, Canada
Tel: 902-379-2825; *Fax:* 902-379-2886
eems@eskasonischool.ca
www.eskasonischool.ca
Grades: Kindergarten - 9; Mi'kmaq language
Eskasoni Elementary & Middle School is a Mi'kmaq First Nation school, which operates under the direction of the Eskasoni First Nation School Board. Mi'kmaq immersion classes are offered from kindergarten to grade 3.
Philomena Moore, Principal
philmoore46@hotmail.com
Cameron Frost, Vice-Principal

Eskasoni: Eskasoni Ksite'taqnk Day Care
c/o Eskasoni First Nation School Board
P.O. Box 7959
4645 Shore Rd., Eskasoni, NS B1W 1B8
Tel: 902-379-2017
www.eskasonischoolbd.com
Grades: Pre-School
Number of Employees: 1 coordinator, 6 early childhood educators; 1 cook / day care worker. The Eskasoni Ksite'taqnk Day Care operates under the administration of the Eskasoni First Nation School Board. The day care offers a Mi'kmaq educational program, taught in the Mi'kmaq language.
Miranda Bernard, Contact

Eskasoni: Eskasoni Unama'ki Training & Education Centre (TEC)
P.O. Box 7010
Eskasoni, NS B1L 1A1, Canada
Tel: 902-379-2758; *Fax:* 902-379-2586
www.unamakitec.ca; www.eskasonischoolbd.com
Grades: Adult & Alternative Education
Enrollment: 75
Number of Employees: 1 principal; 1 teaching vice-principal; 5 teachers; 1 guidance counsellor; 1 secretary; 1 teaching assistant; 1 janitor. Activities of the Unama'ki Training & Education Centre are guided by the Eskasoni First Nation School Board.
Michelle Marshall-Johnson, Principal
Joanne MacDonald, Vice-Principal

Micmac: Indian Brook School
Micmac Post Office, Micmac, NS B0N 1W0, Canada
Tel: 902-758-1229; *Fax:* 902-758-1492
Grades: K.-12
Randy Kelly, Principal
kellyr2@staff.ednet.ns.ca

Sydney: Membertou Elementary School
Wallace Bernard Memorial
45 Maillard St., Sydney, NS B1S 2P5, Canada
Tel: 902-562-2205; *Fax:* 902-562-4561
Grades: K.-6
Darrell Syms, Principal
dsyms@membertouschool.ca

Trenton: Pictou Landing First Nations Elementary School
P.O. Box 116
43 Maple St., Pictou Landing, Site 6, RR#2, Trenton, NS B0K 1X0, Canada
Tel: 902-755-9954; *Fax:* 902-752-4916
firstnationhelp.com/pictou
Grades: K.-6
Sheila Francis, Director
sheilaf@pchg.net

Wagmatcook: Wagmatcookewey School
P.O. Box 30018
Wagmatcook, NS B0E 3N0, Canada
Tel: 902-295-3491
wagmatco@auracom.com
Grades: Primary - 12; Mi'kmaq Studies
Located on the Wagmatcook First Nation Reserve in Cape Breton, Nova Scotia, the Wagmatcookewey School provides education to Mi'Kmaq First Nation students.
Wayne Morris, Principal

Whycocomagh: We'koqma'q Elementary School
P.O. Box 209
15 Reservation Rd., Whycocomagh, NS B0E 3M0, Canada
Tel: 902-756-9000; *Fax:* 902-756-2171
Grades: K.-6
Joanne Alex, Principal
joanna@wfnes.ca

Whycocomagh: We'koqma'q School Secondary Education
P.O. Box 209
9231 Trans Canada Hwy., Whycocomagh, NS B0E 3M0, Canada
Tel: 902-756-3002; *Fax:* 902-756-2017
Grades: 7-12
John Leonard, Principal
Lisa Lunney, Vice-Principal

Special Education

Halifax: Atlantic Provinces Special Education Authority (APSEA)
5940 South St., Halifax, NS B3H 1S6, Canada
Tel: 902-424-8500; *Fax:* 902-424-0543
apsea@apsea.ca
www.apsea.ca
Deborah Pottie, Supt.

Schools: Independent & Private

Independent & Private Schools

Bedford: Sandy Lake Academy
435 Hammond's Plains Rd., Bedford, NS B4B 1Y2, Canada
Tel: 902-835-8548; *Fax:* 902-835-9752
info@sandylakeacademy.ca
www.sandylakeacademy.ca
Grades: Pre.-12
Enrollment: 76
A Seventh-day Adventist Christian School
Chris Dupuis, Principal

Cambridge Station: Kings County Christian School
6185 Hwy. 1, RR#1, Cambridge Station, NS B0P 1G0, Canada
Tel: 902-679-6641
www.kccschool.ca
Grades: Pre.-9
Enrollment: 65
Barbara C. Billings, Principal

Halifax: Armbrae Academy
1400 Oxford St., Halifax, NS B3H 3Y8, Canada
Tel: 902-423-7920; *Fax:* 902-423-9731
office@armbrae.ns.ca
www.armbrae.ns.ca
Grades: Pre.-12
Enrollment: 245
Gary O'Meara, Headmaster
omeara@armbrae.ednet.ns.ca

Halifax: Halifax Christian Academy
114 Downs Ave., Halifax, NS B3N 1Y6, Canada
Tel: 902-475-1441; *Fax:* 902-477-4922
office@halifaxchristianacademy.ca
www.halifaxchristianacademy.ca
Grades: Pre.-12
Enrollment: 243
Jo-an Dennis, Principal

Halifax: Halifax Grammar School
945 Tower Rd., Halifax, NS B3H 2Y2, Canada
Tel: 902-423-9312; *Fax:* 902-423-9315
info@hgs.ns.ca
www.hgs.ns.ca
Grades: Pre.-12
Enrollment: 410
Blayne Addley, Headmaster

Halifax: Maritime Muslim Academy
6225 Chebucto Rd., Halifax, NS B3L 1K7, Canada
Tel: 902-429-9067; *Fax:* 902-429-0136
www.maritimemuslimacademy.ca/
Grades: Pre.-12; Islamic studies; Arabic la
Enrollment: 78
Dr. M.A. Salah, Principal

Halifax: Sacred Heart School of Halifax
5820 Spring Garden Rd., Halifax, NS B3H 1X8, Canada
Tel: 902-422-4459; *Fax:* 902-423-7691
admin@shsh.ca
www.sacredheartschool.ns.ca
Grades: Pre.-12
Enrollment: 444
Patricia Donnelly, Headmistress
pdonnelly@sacredheartschool.ns.ca

Halifax: Shambhala School
5450 Russell St., Halifax, NS B3K 1W9, Canada
Tel: 902-454-6100; *Fax:* 902-454-6157
director@shambhalaschool.org
www.shambhalaschool.org

Grades: Preschool - 12
Enrollment: 160
This is a non-denominational school, which offers an enriched curriculum.
Steve Mustain, Director

Tantallon: Crossroads Academy
15 French Village Station Rd., Tantallon, NS B3Z 1H3, Canada
Tel: 902-826-1805; *Fax:* 902-826-1867
ca@crossroadsacademy.ca
www.crossroadsacademy.ca/

Grades: Pre.-6
Sylvia Luffman, Principal

Truro: Colchester Christian Academy
P.O. Box 393
15 Elm St., Truro, NS B2N 5C5, Canada
Tel: 902-895-6520; *Fax:* 902-893-3727

Grades: Pre.-12
Enrollment: 132
Steve Vanderkwaak, Principal

Tusket: Living Waters Christian Academy
P.O. Box 175
Tusket, NS B0W 3M0, Canada
Tel: 902-648-2676; *Fax:* 902-648-2676

Grades: Pre.-9
Enrollment: 44
Mardee Nickerson, Acting Principal

Windsor: Kings-Edgehill School
33 King's-Edgehill Lane, Windsor, NS B0N 2T0, Canada
Tel: 902-798-2278; *Fax:* 902-798-2105
admissions@kes.ns.ca
www.kes.ns.ca

Grades: 1-12
Enrollment: 282
David R. Penaluna, Headmaster

Wolfville: Landmark East School
708 Main St., Wolfville, NS B4P 1G4, Canada
Tel: 902-542-2237; *Fax:* 902-542-4147
gmitchell@landmarkeast.org
www.landmarkeast.org

Grades: 4-12
Enrollment: 57
Tim Moore, Headmaster

Universities & Colleges

Universities

Antigonish: St. Francis Xavier University
P.O. Box 5000
Antigonish, NS B2G 2W5, Canada
Tel: 902-863-3300; *Fax:* 902-867-5153
admit@stfx.ca
www.stfx.ca
Other Information: Admissions: 902-867-2219

Full Time Equivalency: 4200
The university is primarily an undergraduate university, offering education in the arts, science, business & information systems, & applied programs.
Sean E. Riley, Ph.D., President
sriley@stfx.ca
Dr. Mary B. McGillivray, Vice-President, Academic & Provost
Peter Fardy, Vice-President, University Advancement
Ramsay Duff, Vice-President, Finance & Operations
Mary Coyle, Vice-President & Director, Coady International Institute
Danny McInnis, Acting Registrar
John Blackwell, Director, Research Grants
Lynne Murphy, Librarian

Faculties

Arts
Dr. Steve Baldner, Dean

Science
Dr. William Marshall, Dean

Students
Joe MacDonald, Dean

Schools

Coady International Institute
Mary Coyle, Director
mcoyle@stfx.ca

Enterprise Development Centre
Sue McNeil, Interim Director

Halifax: Atlantic School of Theology
660 Francklyn St., Halifax, NS B3H 3B5, Canada
Tel: 902-423-6939; *Fax:* 902-492-4048
www.astheology.ns.ca

Full Time Equivalency: 150
The Rev. Canon Eric Beresford, President, 902-423-6801
Rev. Dr. David MacLachlan, Academic Dean & Registrar, 902-496-7941
David Myatt, Chief Admin. Officer, 902-496-7946
Joyce Thomson, Library Director, 902-496-7948

Halifax: Dalhousie University
Henry Hicks Academic Administration Bldg.
6299 South St., Halifax, NS B3H 4H6, Canada
Tel: 902-494-2211; *Fax:* 902-494-1630
communications.marketing@dal.ca
www.dal.ca

Full Time Equivalency: 16000
Dalhousie University is a comprehensive teaching & research university located in Atlantic Canada. Dalhousie places special emphasis on Ocean Studies & Health Studies & has a growing involvement in Advanced Technical Studies.
Dr Fred Fountain, Chancellor
Dr Tom Traves, Vice-Chancellor & President, 902-494-2511, fax: 902-494-1658
tom.traves@dal.ca
Dr Carolyn Watters, Acting Vice-Pres., Academic & Provost, 902-494-2586
carolyn.watters@dal.ca
Ken Burt, Vice-Pres., Finance & Admin., 902-494-3862
ken.burt@dal.ca
Floyd Dykeman, Vice-Pres., External, 902-494-2238
floyd.dykeman@dal.ca
Dr Bonnie Neuman, Vice-Pres., Student Services, 902-494-8021
bonnie.neuman@dal.ca
Dr Martha Crago, Vice-Pres., Research, 902-494-8075, fax: 902-494-1595
martha.crago@dal.ca

Faculties

Architecture & Planning
Tel: 902-494-3971; *Fax:* 902-423-6672
arch.office@dal.ca
Christine Macy, Dean

Arts & Social Sciences
Tel: 902-494-1440; *Fax:* 902-494-1957
fass@dal.ca
Dr Robert Summerby-Murray, Dean

Computer Science
Tel: 902-494-2093; *Fax:* 902-492-1517
inquiries@cs.dal.ca
Dr Michael Shephard, Dean

Dentistry
Tel: 902-494-2824; *Fax:* 902-494-2527
Dr Thomas Boran, Dean
thomas.boran@dal.ca

Engineering
Tel: 902-494-6217; *Fax:* 902-429-3011
Dr L. Joshua Leon, Dean
joshua.leon@dal.ca

Graduate Studies
Tel: 902-494-2485; *Fax:* 902-494-8797
Sunny Marche, Acting Dean
sunny.marche@dal.ca

Health Professions
Tel: 902-494-3327; *Fax:* 902-494-1966
Dr William G. Webster, Dean
will.webster@dal.ca

Management
Tel: 902-494-2582; *Fax:* 902-494-1195
Peggy Cunningham, Dean
managementdean@dal.ca

Medicine
Tel: 902-494-6592; *Fax:* 902-494-7119
Dr Thomas J. Marrie, Dean
dean.medicine@dal.ca

Science
Tel: 902-494-3540; *Fax:* 902-494-1123
science@dal.ca
Chris Moore, Dean

Schools

Atlantic Health Promotion Research Centre
Tel: 902-494-2240; *Fax:* 902-494-3594
ahprc@dal.ca
Sandra J. Crowell, Managing Director

Business Administration
Tel: 902-494-7080; *Fax:* 902-494-1107
Dr Greg Hebb, Director
gregory.hebb@dal.ca

Canadian Institute of Fisheries Technology
Tel: 902-494-6030; *Fax:* 902-494-0219
cift@dal.ca
Dr Tom Gill, Director

Centre for Foreign Policy Studies
Tel: 902-494-3769; *Fax:* 902-494-3825
centre@dal.ca
David R. Black, Director

College of Continuing Education
Tel: 902-494-2526; *Fax:* 902-494-3662
ducceinf@dal.ca
Andrew Cochrane, Dean

College of Pharmacy
Tel: 902-494-2378; *Fax:* 902-494-1396
pharmacy@dal.ca
Rita Caldwell, Director

Dental Hygiene
Nancy Neish, Director, 902-494-8864
nancy.neish@dal.ca

Division of Medical Education
Tel: 902-494-1845; *Fax:* 902-494-2278
dme@dal.ca
Dr. Frank Blye, Director

Health & Human Performance
Tel: 902-494-2152; *Fax:* 902-494-5120
hahp@dal.ca
Dr Fred McGinn, Interim Director

Health Administration
Tel: 902-494-7097; *Fax:* 902-494-6849
healthadmin@dal.ca
Dr Joseph M. Byrne, Director

Human Communication Disorders
Tel: 902-494-7052; *Fax:* 902-494-5151
hucd@dal.ca
Dr. Joy Armson, Director

Information Management
Tel: 902-494-3656; *Fax:* 902-494-2451
sim@dal.ca
Fiona Black, Director

International Research & Development
Tel: 902-494-2038; *Fax:* 902-494-1216
ird@dal.ca
Pat Rodee, Director

Neuroscience Institute
Tel: 902-494-1251; *Fax:* 902-494-2050
neurosci@dal.ca
Dr Alan Fine, Director

Nursing
Tel: 902-494-2535; *Fax:* 902-494-3487
nursing@dal.ca
Dr. Patricia Sullivan, Director

Occupational Therapy
Tel: 902-494-8804; *Fax:* 902-494-1229
occupational.therapy@dal.ca
Dr Fazley Siddiq, Director

Physiotherapy
Tel: 902-494-2524; *Fax:* 902-494-1941
physiotherapy@dal.ca
Dr Sandy Rennie, Director

Public Administration
Tel: 902-494-3742; *Fax:* 902-494-7023
dalmpa@dal.ca

Resource & Environmental Studies
Tel: 902-494-3632; *Fax:* 902-494-3728
sres@dal.ca
Dr. Peter Duinker, Director

Schulich School of Law
Tel: 902-494-3495; *Fax:* 902-494-1316
Kim R. Brooks, Dean
lawdean@dal.ca

Social Work
Tel: 902-494-3760; *Fax:* 902-494-6709
social.work@dal.ca
Dr. Wanda Thomas Bernard, Director

Transition Year Program
Prof. Patricia Doyle-Bedwell, Director, 902-494-8810, fax: 902-494-2135
patricia.doyle.bedwell@dal.ca

Affiliations
Nova Scotia Agricultural College
P.O. Box 550
Truro, NS B2N 5E3, Canada
Tel: 902-893-6600
reg@nsac.ca
www.nsac.ns.ca

Full Time Equivalency: 900
NSAC has the following academic departments: Business & Social Sciences, Engineering, Environmental Sciences, & Plant & Animal Sciences; as well as, these academic units: Continuing & Distance Education, Research.
Carol Goodwin, Chair
Dr. Bernie Macdonald, Co-President & VP, Admin.
Dr. Leslie MacLaren, Co-President & VP, Academic

University of King's College
6350 Coburg Rd., Halifax, NS B3H 2A1, Canada
Tel: 902-422-1271; *Fax:* 902-423-3357
www.ukings.ns.ca

Full Time Equivalency: 1170
The Hon. Michael A. Meighen, QC, Chancellor
Dr William Barker, President & Vice-Chancellor, ext. 121
Elizabeth Yeo, Registrar, ext. 122
elizabeth.yeo@ukings.ns.ca

Publications
Dalhousie Gazette
6136 University Ave., Halifax, NS B3H 4J2
Tel: 902-128-0
www.dalgazette.com

Josh Boyter, Editor-In-Chief
editor.dalgazatte.com

Halifax: Mount Saint Vincent University
166 Bedford Hwy., Halifax, NS B3M 2J6, Canada
Tel: 902-457-6117; *Fax:* 902-457-6498
www.msvu.ca

Full Time Equivalency: 4900
Kathryn E. Laurin, M.Mus., President & Vice-Chancellor
Donna Woolcott, Vice-President
Brigitte MacInnes, Registrar
Amanda Whitewood, C.M.A., C.H.E., Vice-President
Sr. Donna Geernaert, Chancellor

Faculties
Arts & Sciences
Susan Mumm, Ph.D., Dean

Education
Jim Sharpe, Ph.D., Dean

Professional Studies
Mary Lyon, Ph.D., Dean

Publications
Jargon

Picaro

Halifax: NSCAD University
5163 Duke St., Halifax, NS B3J 3J6, Canada
Tel: 902-444-9600; *Fax:* 902-425-2420
admiss@nscad.ca
www.nscad.ca

Full Time Equivalency: 1025
Prof. David B. Smith, President
Kenn Gardner Honeychurch, Sr. Vice-President
Peter Flemming, Vice-President
Dr. Laurelle LeVert, Registrar & Director
Deborah Carver, Executive Director

Halifax: Saint Mary's University
923 Robie St., Halifax, NS B3H 3C3, Canada
Tel: 902-420-5400
public.affairs@smu.ca; webmaster@smu.ca; helpdesk@smu.ca
www.smu.ca
Other Information: Students Closure/Cancellation Hotline: 902-491-6263

Full Time Equivalency: 8500
Offering a wide range of both undergraduate & graduate programs, Saint Mary's University has a student-faculty ratio of 21-1.
Most Rev. Terrence Prendergast, Chancellor
Most Rev. Claude Champagne, Vice-Chancellor
Dr. J. Colin Dodds, President
Gabrielle Morrison, Vice-President, Administration
Dr. Terry Murphy, Vice-President, Academic & Research

Faculties
Arts
Dr. Esther Enns, Dean

Commerce
Dr. David Wicks, Dean

Continuing Education
Betty MacDonald, Director
betty.macdonald@smu.ca

Graduate Studies & Research
Dr. Kevin Vessey, Dean

Science
Dr. Malcolm Butler, Dean

Pointe-de-L'Église: Université Sainte-Anne
1695, Route 1, Pointe-de-L'Église, NS B0W 1M0, Canada
Tél: 902-769-2114; *Téléc:* 902-769-2930
Ligne sans frais: 1-888-338-8337
mario.dushesne@usaintanne.ca
www.usainteanne.ca

La seule institution d'enseignement post-secondaire de langue française en Nouvelle-Écosse. Programmes: administration des affaires, éducation, sciences humaines, science pures, programmes professionnels. Campus: Pointe-de-L'Église, Halifax, Petit-de-Grat, Saint-Joseph-du Moine, et Tusket
Christiane Rabier, Vice-rectrice (Enseignement et Recherche)
Murielle Comeau, Registraire
Éric Tufts, Vice-recteur (Administrations)
Hughie Batherson, Vice-recteur (Affaires étudiantes)
Allister Surette, Vice-recteur (Développement & partenariats)
André Roberge, Recteur
andre.roberge@usaintanne.ca

Campuses
Campus de Halifax
1589 Walnut St., Halifax, NS B3H 3S1, Canada
Tel: 902-424-2630; *Fax:* 902-424-3607
pachalifax@usainteanne.ca
www.usainteanne.ca

Donald Kenny, Contact

Campus de Petit-de-Grat
3433 rte 206, Petit-de-Grat, N.-É., NS B0E 2L0, Canada
Tel: 902-226-3900
lisa.berthier@usainteanne.ca
www.usainteanne.ca

Lisa Berthier

Campus de Saint-Joseph-du-Moine
12521 Cabot Trail, Grand-Étang, N.-É., NS B0E 3A0, Canada
Tel: 902-244-4100
rene.aucoin@usainteanne.ca
www.usaintanne.ca

René Aucoin, Contact

Campus de Wellington
48 Chemin Mill, Wellington, PE C0B 2E0, Canada
Tel: 902-854-7286
colette@socedipe.org
www.usainteanne.ca

Colette Aucoin, Contact

Campus de Tusket
1 Slocumb Cres., Tusket, NS B0W 3M0, Canada
Tel: 902-648-3524
peter.boudreau@usainteanne.ca
www.usainteanne.ca

Peter Boudreau, Contact

Sydney: Cape Breton University
P.O. Box 5300
1250 Grand Lake Rd., Sydney, NS B1P 6L2, Canada
Tel: 902-539-5300; *Fax:* 902-562-0119
Toll-Free: 888-959-9995
welcome@cbu.ca; registrar@cbu.ca
www.capebretonu.ca

Full Time Equivalency: 3110
The university is also home to Unama'ki College which offers Mi'kmaw programs and services, such as teacher training, court worker certification, business, Mi'kmaw language, health careers, and natural resources. Email: mci@cbu.ca
Annette Verschuren, Chancellor
H. John Harker, President & Vice-Chancellor, 902-563-1333
john_harker@cbu.ca
Gordon MacInnis, Vice-Pres., Finance & Operations, 902-563-1128
gordon_macinnis@cbu.ca
Robert Baily, Vice-Pres., Academic & Research, 902-563-1980
robert_bailey@cbu.ca
Roger Winn, Vice-Pres., Academic
roger_winn@cbu.ca
Brown Keith, Vice-Pres., External, 902-563-1859
keith_brown@cbu.ca
Dr Ross McCurdy, COO, 902-563-1392
ross_mccurdy@cbu.ca
Debbie Rudderham, CIO, 902-563-1446
debbie_rudderham@cbu.ca
Alexis Manley, Registrar/VP, Student Services, 902-563-1650
registrar@cbu.ca

Faculties
Arts & Social Studies
Dr Roderick Nicholls, Dean, 902-563-1354
rod_nicholls@cbu.ca

Science & Technology
Dr Allen Britten, Dean, 902-563-1262
allen_britten@cbu.ca

Schools
Shannon School of Business
John MacKinnon, Dean, 902-563-1221
john_mackinnon@cbu.ca

School of Professional & Graduate Studies
Robert Baily, Interim Dean, 902-563-1304
brenda_leloup@cbu.ca

Publications
Caper Times
Suzanne MacNeil, Editor-In-Chief, 902-563-1473
editor@capertimes.ca

The 60th Meridian

Wolfville: Acadia Divinity College
31 Horton Ave., Wolfville, NS B4P 2R6, Canada
Tel: 902-585-2210; *Fax:* 902-585-2233
Toll-Free: 866-875-8975
adc.acadiau.ca

Full Time Equivalency: 160
Dr Harry G. Gardner, President/Dean, Theology
Dr Bruce Fawcett, Academic Dean/Dir., Doctoral Studies
Shawna Peverill, Registrar, 902-585-2216
shawna.peverill@acadiau.ca

Wolfville: Acadia University
Wolfville, NS B4P 2R6, Canada
Tel: 902-542-2201; *Fax:* 902-585-1072
agi@acadiau.ca
www.acadiau.ca

Full Time Equivalency: 3620
Ray Ivany, Pres./Vice-Chancellor, ext. 1218
Dr. Tom Herman, Vice-Pres., Academic, ext. 1357
Dr Akivah Starkman, Vice-Pres., Admin.
Rosemary Jotcham, Registrar
registrar@acadiau.ca
Scott Roberts, Exec. Dir., Communications & Public Affairs, ext. 1705
scott.roberts@acadiau.ca

Faculties
Arts
Robert Perrins, B.A., M.A., Ph.D., Dean, ext. 1782

Professional Studies
Dr Heather Hemming, B.Sc., M.Sc., D.P.E., Dean, ext. 1133

Pure & Applied Science
Dr Peter Williams, B.Sc., M.Sc., Ph.D., Dean, ext. 1472

Theology
Dr Harry Gardner, B.A., B.D., Th.M., Ph.D., Dean, ext. 2212

Schools
Business Administration
Dr Ian Hutchinson, Director, ext. 1205

Computer Science
Dr Daniel Silver, Director, ext. 1331

Education
Dr. Ann Vibert, Director, ext. 1229

Engineering
Andrew Mitchell, Dip.Eng., B.Eng., M.A.Sc., Director, ext. 1206

Music
Dr Jeff Hennessy, Director, ext. 1512

Nutrition & Dietetics
Barb Anderson, Director, ext. 1346

Recreation, Management & Kinesiology
Dr Rene Murphy, Director, ext. 1559

Publications
The Athenaeum
The official student newspaper
Tim Hansen, Editor-in-Chief

Colleges

Halifax: Nova Scotia Community College (NSCC)
P.O. Box 220
Halifax, NS B3J 2M4, Canada
Tel: 902-491-4911; *Fax:* 902-491-3514
Toll-Free: 1-866-679-6722
admissions@nscc.ca
www.nscc.ca
Other Information: Toll Free Fax: 1-866-329-6722
TTY: 1-866-288-7034
The college has the following institutes: The Aviation Institute, located in the Halifax Regional Municipality at Shearwater, the Centre of Geographic Sciences in Lawrencetown, & the Nautical Institute in Port Hawkesbury & the School of Fisheries at Pictou.
Sandra Greer, Chair
Joan McArthur-Blair, President, 902-491-6701, fax: 902-491-4825
Ronald Farrell, Dean, Trades & Technology
Ken Jones, Dean, Business Development
Judith Limkilde, Dean, Health & Human Services
Claudine Lowry, Dean, Organizational Learning
George MacDonald, Dean, Access
Bruce Tawse, Dean, Applied Arts & New Media
Bill Walsh, Dean, Business

Campuses

Akerley Campus
21 Woodlawn Rd., Dartmouth, NS B3W 2R7, Canada
Tel: 902-491-4940; *Fax:* 902-491-4903
akadmissions@nscc.ca
Other Information: Centre for Student Success, Phone: 902-491-4940
Enrollment: 4000
Graham MacDermott, Principal

Amherst Community Learning Centre
Tel: 902-661-3180
Deborah.MacPhail@nscc.ca

Annapolis Valley Campus, Lawrencetown
50 Elliott Rd., Lawrencetown, NS B0S 1M0
Tel: 902-825-3491; *Fax:* 902-825-2285
avc.info@nscc.ca
www.annapolis.nscc.ca
Other Information: Centre for Student Success, Phone: 902-825-2930
Enrollment: 900
Jim Stanley, Principal

Annapolis Valley Campus, Middleton
295 Commercial St., Middleton, NS B0S 1P0, Canada
Tel: 902-825-3491
avc.info@nscc.ca
www.annapolis.nscc.ca
Other Information: Centre for Student Success, Phone: 902-825-2930
Enrollment: 900
The Applied Geomatics Research Centre is located at the Middleton location.
Jim Stanley, Principal

Burridge Campus
372 Pleasant St., Yarmouth, NS B5A 2L2, Canada
Tel: 902-742-0760; *Fax:* 902-749-2402
buadmissions@nscc.ca
www.burridge.nscc.ca
Other Information: Centre for Student Success, Phone: 902-742-0760
Enrollment: 950
Marcel Cottreau, Principal

Cumberland Campus
P.O. Box 550
1 Main St., Springhill, NS B0M 1X0, Canada
Tel: 902-597-3737; *Fax:* 902-597-8548
cuadmissions@nscc.ca
Other Information: Centre for Student Success, Phone: 902-597-4101
Enrollment: 400
Shelley Carter-Rose, Principal

Digby Community Learning Centre
Tel: 902-245-7211
Deborah.Fox@nscc.ca

Institute of Technology Campus
P.O. Box 2210
5685 Leeds St., Halifax, NS B3J 3C4, Canada
Tel: 902-491-6722; *Fax:* 902-491-4800
inadmissions@nscc.ca
Other Information: Centre for Student Success, Phone: 902-491-4752
Enrollment: 5200
Daurene Lewis, Principal

Kingstec Campus
236 Belcher St., Kentville, NS B4N 0A6, Canada
Tel: 902-678-7341; *Fax:* 902-679-1141
kiadmissions@nscc.ca
Other Information: Centre for Student Success, Phone: 902-679-7361; 902-679-7359
Enrollment: 1750
Don Bureaux, Principal

Liverpool Community Learning Centre
Tel: 902-543-8261
Cecile.Mansfield@nscc.ca

Lunenburg Campus
75 High St., Bridgewater, NS B4V 1V8, Canada
Tel: 902-543-4608; *Fax:* 902-543-0190
Toll-Free: 1-866-346-4608
luadmissions@nscc.ca
Other Information: Centre for Student Success, Phone: 902-543-2295
Enrollment: 850
Craig Collins, Principal

Marconi Campus
P.O. Box 1042
1240 Grand Lake Rd., Sydney, NS B1P 6J7, Canada
Tel: 902-563-2450; *Fax:* 902-563-3440
maadmissions@nscc.ca
Other Information: Centre for Student Success, Phone: 902-563-2464
Enrollment: 2300
Dave MacLean, Principal

New Glasgow Community Learning Centre
Tel: 902-755-7209
David.Freckelton@nscc.ca

Pictou Campus
P.O. Box 820
39 Acadia Ave., Stellarton, NS B0K 1S0, Canada
Tel: 902-752-2002; *Fax:* 902-752-5446
piadmissions@nscc.ca
Other Information: Centre for Student Success, Phone: 902-755-7299
Enrollment: 1675
Dave Freckelton, Principal

Shelburne Campus
P.O. Box 760
1575 Lake Rd., Shelburne, NS B0T 1W0, Canada
Tel: 902-875-8640; *Fax:* 902-875-3797
shadmissions@nscc.ca
Other Information: Centre for Student Success, Phone: 902-875-8640
Enrollment: 350
Marcel Cottreau, Principal

Strait Area Campus
226 Reeves St., Port Hawkesbury, NS B9A 2A2, Canada
Tel: 902-625-4017; *Fax:* 902-625-0193
stadmissions@nscc.ca
Other Information: Centre for Student Success, Phone: 902-625-4017
Enrollment: 800
The Nautical Institute is located on the Strait Area Campus.
Bert Lewis, Principal

Truro Campus
36 Arthur St., Truro, NS B2N 1X5, Canada
Tel: 902-893-5385; *Fax:* 902-893-5610
tradmissions@nscc.ca
www.truro.nscc.ca
Other Information: Centre for Student Success, Phone: 902-893-5346
Enrollment: 1300
Kevin Quinlan, Principal

Waterfront Campus
80 Mawiomi Pl., Dartmouth, NS B2Y 0A5
Tel: 902-491-1100; *Fax:* 902-491-1795
watadmissions@nscc.ca
Other Information: Centre for Student Success, Phone: 902-491-1793
Enrollment: 4300
Cathy MacLean, Principal

Halifax: University of King's College
6350 Coburg Rd., Halifax, NS B3H 2A1, Canada
Tel: 902-422-1271; *Fax:* 902-423-3357
www.ukings.ns.ca
Full Time Equivalency: 1100

Publications

Watch
Student newspaper at University of King's College

Post Secondary/Technical

Post Secondary/Technical

Bedford: C.L. Douglas & Associates Inc.
1142 Bedford Hwy., Bedford, NS B4A 1B8, Canada
Tel: 902-835-8880; *Fax:* 902-835-6751
info@cldouglas.com
www.cldouglas.com
Computer software, network management training.
Paul Cudmore

East Dover: Atlantic Home Building & Renovation Sector Council
53 Leary's Cove Rd., East Dover, NS B3Z 3W7, Canada
Tel: 902-852-2151; *Fax:* 902-852-3193
info@ahbrsc.com
www.ahbrsc.com/courses/index.html
Atlantic Home Warranty Program Training; Nova Scotia Home Builder's Association Certified Builder Training Program; Training for Employment Insurance Recipients; Renovation Sector Skills Development

Englishtown: Gaelic College of Celtic Arts & Crafts
P.O. Box 80
Englishtown, NS B0C 1H0, Canada
Tel: 902-295-3411; *Fax:* 902-295-2912
info@gaeliccollege.edu
www.gaeliccollege.edu

Halifax: Atlantic Media Institute (AMI)
#300, 7071 Bayers Rd., Halifax, NS B3L 2C2, Canada
Tel: 902-457-0002; *Fax:* 902-457-4503
ami@theami.com
www.theami.com

Halifax: CDI College of Business, Technology & Health Care
P.O. Box 111
5657 Spring Garden Rd., Halifax, NS B3J 3R4, Canada
Tel: 902-429-7373; *Fax:* 902-422-0576
Anne Miller

Halifax: Halifax Campus
800 Sackville Dr., Halifax, NS B4E 1R8, Canada
Tel: 902-865-8283; *Fax:* 902-865-0285
Toll-Free: 1-800-662-3991
halifax@thinksuccess.ca
www.thinksuccess.ca
Work related programs.
Hazel Matthews

Campuses

Truro Campus
100 Victoria St., Truro, NS B2N 1Y8, Canada
Tel: 902-893-2400; *Fax:* 902-893-7875
Toll-Free: 1-866-897-0349
Work related programs.

Halifax: Maritime Conservatory of Performing Arts
6199 Chebucto Rd., Halifax, NS B3L 1K7, Canada
Tel: 902-423-6995; *Fax:* 902-423-6029
admin@maritimeconservatory.com
www.maritimeconservatory.com
Ifan Williams, Director

North Sydney: Mactech Distance Education
P.O. Box 457
North Sydney, NS B2A 3M3, Canada
Fax: 902-794-1414
Toll-Free: 1-888-622-8324
administration@homeed.com
www.homeed.com
Distance education

Truro: Institute for Human Services Education
#1, 60 Lorne St., 2nd Fl., Truro, NS B2N 3K3, Canada
Tel: 902-893-3342; *Fax:* 902-895-4487
admin@inst-hse.ca
www.inst-hse.ca
Early Childhood Education Diploma, Public School Program Assistants Certificate, Special Education Diploma, Youth Worker Diploma
Kimberly Elliott, B.Comm., Executive Director
Anna MacDonell, CDSA IV, B.A., M.Ed., Program Director
Debbie Connoly, CDSA IV, BBA, Student Services Coordinator

Nunavut

Government Agencies

Iqaluit: **Department of Education**
P.O. Box 1000 980
Iqaluit, NU X0A 0H0, Canada
Tel: 867-975-5600; *Fax:* 867-975-5605
www.gov.nu.ca/education/eng/
Pam Hine, Deputy Minister

School Boards/Districts/Divisions

Public

Arctic Bay: **Arctic Bay District Education Authority**
P.O. Box 90
Arctic Bay, NU X0A 0A0, Canada
Tel: 867-439-8843
Grades: Kindergarten - 12

Arviat: **Arviat District Education Authority**
P.O. Box 180
Arviat, NU X0C 0E0, Canada
Tel: 867-857-2885; *Fax:* 867-857-2622

Baker Lake: **Baker Lake District Education Authority**
P.O. Box 119
Baker Lake, NU X0C 0A0, Canada
Tel: 867-793-4657; *Fax:* 867-793-4659

Baker Lake: **Kivalliq School Operations**
P.O. Box 90
Baker Lake, NU X0C 0A0, Canada
Tel: 867-793-2803; *Fax:* 867-793-2996
http://kivalliq.edu.nu.ca

Cambridge Bay: **Cambridge Bay District Education Authority**
Also known as: Ikaluktutiak District Education Authority
P.O. Box 9
Cambridge Bay, NU X0B 0C0, Canada
Tel: 867-983-2510; *Fax:* 867-983-2515
Karen Wilford, Chair

Cape Dorset: **Cape Dorset District Education Authority**
P.O. Box 210
Cape Dorset, NU X0A 0C0, Canada
Tel: 867-897-8826
Grades: Kindergarten - 12; Inuktitut

Chesterfield Inlet: **Chesterfield Inlet District Education Authority**
P.O. Box 6
Chesterfield Inlet, NU X0C 0B0, Canada
Tel: 867-898-9007; *Fax:* 867-898-9143
Annie Amuyak, Chair

Clyde River: **Clyde River District Education Authority**
General Delivery, Clyde River, NU X0A 0E0, Canada
Tel: 867-924-6309; *Fax:* 867-924-6247
Jacob Jaypoody

Coral Harbour: **Coral Harbour District Education Authority**
P.O. Box 129
Coral Harbour, NU X0C 0C0, Canada
Tel: 867-925-8637; *Fax:* 867-925-9000
Dino Bruce, Chair

Gjoa Haven: **Gjoa Haven District Education Authority**
General Delivery, Gjoa Haven, NU X0E 1J0, Canada
Tel: 867-360-7414; *Fax:* 867-360-7314
Raymond Kamookak, Chair

Grise Fiord: **Grise Fiord District Education Authority**
General Delivery, Grise Fiord, NU X0A 0J0, Canada
Tel: 867-980-9921

Hall Beach: **Hall Beach District Education Authority**
P.O. Box 83
Hall Beach, NU X0A 0K0, Canada
Tel: 867-928-8839
Grades: Kindergarten - 12

Igloolik: **Igloolik District Education Authority**
P.O. Box 150
Igloolik, NU X0A 0L0, Canada
Tel: 867-934-8909; *Fax:* 867-934-8571
Lucasi Ivvalu, Chair

Iqaluit: **Apex District Education Authority**
P.O. Box 1420
Iqaluit, NU X0A 0H0, Canada
Tel: 867-979-6597

Iqaluit: **La Commission scolaire francophone du Nunavut**
P.O. Box 11008
Iqaluit, NU X0A 1H0, Canada
Tél: 867-979-5849; *Téléc:* 867-979-5878
info.ecoletrois-soleils@csfn.ca
www.trois-soleils.ca
Martine St-Louis, Directrice

Iqaluit: **Iqaluit District Education Authority**
P.O. Box 235
Iqaluit, NU X0A 0H0, Canada
Tel: 867-979-5314; *Fax:* 867-979-0330
Christa Kunnuk, Chair

Kimmirut: **Kimmirut District Education Authority**
General Delivery, Kimmirut, NU X0A 0N0, Canada
Tel: 867-939-2221; *Fax:* 867-939-2334
Pudloo Akavak, Chair

Kugaaruk: **Kugaaruk District Education Authority**
c/o Kugaaruk Iliniarvik
P.O. Box 53
Kugaaruk, NU X0B 1K0, Canada
Tel: 867-769-6211; *Fax:* 867-769-6116
Remi Krikort, Chair

Kugluktuk: **Kitikmeot School Operations**
P.O. Box 287
Kugluktuk, NU X0B 0E0, Canada
Tel: 867-982-7220; *Fax:* 867-982-3054
kitikmeot.edu.nu.ca

Kugluktuk: **Kugluktuk District Education Authority**
P.O. Box 273
Kugluktuk, NU X0B 0E0, Canada
Tel: 867-982-5001; *Fax:* 867-982-5706
Simon Kuliktana, Chair

Pangnirtung: **Pangnirtung District Education Authority**
P.O. Box 54
Pangnirtung, NU X0A 0R0, Canada
Tel: 867-473-8810; *Fax:* 867-473-8718
Tim Evic, Chair

Pond Inlet: **Pond Inlet District Education Authority**
General Delivery, Pond Inlet, NU X0A 0S0, Canada
Tel: 867-899-8779; *Fax:* 867-899-8780
Norman Simonie, Chair

Pond Inlet: **Qikiqtani School Operations**
P.O. Box 429
Pond Inlet, NU X0A 0S0, Canada
Tel: 867-899-7350; *Fax:* 867-899-7334
qikiqtani.edu.nu.ca
Trudy Pettigrew, Executive Director

Qikiqtarjuaq: **Qikiqtarjuaq District Education Authority**
P.O. Box 7
Qikiqtarjuaq, NU X0A 0B0, Canada
Tel: 867-927-8938; *Fax:* 867-927-8067
Toomasie Newkingnak, Chair

Rankin Inlet: **Rankin Inlet District Education Authority**
PO Bag 002, Rankin Inlet, NU X0C 0G0, Canada
Tel: 867-645-2642; *Fax:* 867-645-2209
Darrin Nichol, Chair

Repulse Bay: **Repulse Bay District Education Authority**
P.O. Box 105
Repulse Bay, NU X0C 0H0, Canada
Tel: 867-462-4045; *Fax:* 867-462-4232
Elizabeth Kidlapik, Chair

Resolute Bay: **Resolute Bay District Education Authority**
P.O. Box 120
Resolute Bay, NU X0A 0V0, Canada
Tel: 867-252-3888; *Fax:* 867-252-3690
Zipporah K. Aronsen, Chair

Sanikiluaq: **Sanikiluaq District Education Authority**
General Delivery, Sanikiluaq, NU X0A 0W0, Canada
Tel: 867-266-8816; *Fax:* 867-266-8843
Lucassie Arragutainaq, Chair

Taloyoak: **Taloyoak District Education Authority**
c/o Netsilik Ilihakvik
P.O. Box 9
Taloyoak, NU X0B 1B0, Canada
Tel: 867-561-6706; *Fax:* 867-561-5036
Johnny Kootook, Chair

Whale Cove: **Whale Cove District Education Authority**
P.O. Box 90
Whale Cove, NU X0C 0J0, Canada
Tel: 867-896-9300; *Fax:* 867-896-9005
Grades: K.-12
Enrollment: 110
Imelda Angotialuk, Chair

Post Secondary/Technical

Post Secondary/Technical

Arviat: **Nunavut Arctic College**
Head Office
P.O. Box 230
Arviat, NU X0C 0E0, Canada
Tel: 867-857-8608; *Fax:* 867-857-8623
Toll-Free: 866-988-4636
www.arcticcollege.ca
Daniel Vandermeulen, President
dan.vandermeulen@arcticcollege.ca
Linda Pemik, Director, Academic Affairs, 867-857-8603, fax: 867-857-8623
linda.pemik@arcticcollege.ca
Penny Dominix-Nadeau, Registrar, 866-979-7222, fax: 867-979-7103
penny.dominix-nadeau@arcticcollege.ca

Campuses

Kitikmeot Campus - Cambridge Bay
P.O. Box 54
Cambridge Bay, NU X0B 0C0, Canada
Tel: 867-983-4107; *Fax:* 867-983-4106
Toll-Free: 866-988-4636
Fiona Buchan-Corey, Director

Kivalliq Campus - Rankin Inlet
P.O. Box 002
Rankin Inlet, NU X0C 0G0, Canada
Tel: 867-645-5500; *Fax:* 867-645-2387
Mike Shouldice, Director, 866-988-4636, fax: 867-645-2387

Nunatta Campus - Iqaluit
P.O. Box 600
Iqaluit, NU X0A 0H0, Canada
Tel: 867-979-7200; *Fax:* 867-979-7102
Peesee Pitsiulak-Stephens, Director, 867-979-7216, fax: 867-979-7102

Ontario

Government Agencies

Brampton: **Ontario Environmental Training Consortium (OETC)**
37 George St. North Suite 206, Brampton, ON L6X 1R5, Canada
Tel: 905-796-2851; *Fax:* 905-796-8744
Toll-Free: 1-877-796-2851
info@oetc.on.ca
www.oetc.on.ca
The OETC represents the Ontario Colleges of Applied Arts & Technology in developing & delivering province-wide environmental training, education & certification programs. OETC can provide a single point of contact with experts in all areas of environment
Gary Cronkwright, Executive Director

Toronto: **Ministry of Education & Training**
c/o Public Inquiries Unit
2nd Fl., 880 Bay St., Toronto, ON M7A 1N3, Canada
Tel: 416-325-2929; *Fax:* 416-325-4153
Toll-Free: 1-800-268-5755
info@edu.gov.on.ca
www.edu.gov.on.ca
TTY: 1-800-263-2892
Ginette Plourde, Director, 416-325-2127
Marie-Lison Fougère, Director, 416-325-2660

Campuses

Barrie
20 Rose St., 2nd Fl., Barrie, ON L4M 2T2, Canada
Fax: 705-725-7635
Toll-Free: 800-471-0713

London
#207, 217 York St., London, ON N6A 5P9, Canada
Fax: 519-667-9769
Toll-Free: 800-265-4221

North Bay/Sudbury
#211, 447 McKeown Ave., North Bay, ON P1B 9S9, Canada
Fax: 705-497-6896
Toll-Free: 800-461-9570

Ottawa
#504, 1580 Merivale Rd., Nepean, ON K2G 4B5, Canada
Fax: 613-225-2881
Toll-Free: 800-267-1067

Thunder Bay
#336, 435 James St. South, Thunder Bay, ON P7E 6S9, Canada
Fax: 807-475-1550
Toll-Free: 800-465-5020

Toronto & Area
880 Bay St., 2nd Fl., Toronto, ON M7A 1N3, Canada
Fax: 416-325-4190
Toll-Free: 800-268-5755

Toronto: Ministry of Training, Colleges & Universities
c/o Public Inquiries Unit
880 Bay St., 2nd Fl., Toronto, ON M7A 1N3, Canada
Tel: 416-325-2929; *Fax:* 416-325-6348
info@edu.gov.on.ca
www.edu.gov.on.ca
TTY: 1-800-263-289

Toronto: Ontario Agricultural Training Institute
#405, 491 Eglinton Ave. West, Toronto, ON M5N 1A8, Canada
Tel: 416-485-3677; *Fax:* 416-485-5661
Toll-Free: 1-800-668-628
infooati@oati.com

School Boards/Districts/Divisions

Public

Aurora: York Region District School Board
The Education Centre
60 Wellington St. West, Aurora, ON L4G 3H2, Canada
Tel: 905-727-3141; *Fax:* 905-727-1931
feedback@yrdsb.edu.on.ca
www.yrdsb.edu.on.ca

Grades: Pre-K.-12
Enrollment: 112000
Ken Thurston, Dir.
ken.thurston@yrdsb.edu.on.ca
Bruce Richardson, Assoc. Dir., Bus. Services
bruce.richardson@yrdsb.edu.on.ca
Diane Giangrande, Chair, 905-770-0826
diane.giangrande@yrdsb.edu.on.ca

Belleville: Hastings & Prince Edward District School Board
156 Ann St., Belleville, ON K8N 1N9, Canada
Tel: 613-966-1170; *Fax:* 613-966-6023
Toll-Free: 800-267-4350
information@hpedsb.on.ca
www.hpedsb.on.ca

Grades: JK-12
Enrollment: 15700
Kathy Soule, Director, Education
Carl Pitman, Chair

Brantford: Grand Erie District School Board
Education Centre
349 Erie Ave., Brantford, ON N3T 5V3, Canada
Tel: 519-756-6301; *Fax:* 519-756-9181
Toll-Free: 1-888-548-8878
www.granderie.ca

Grades: JK - 12; Special Ed; Continuing Ed.
Enrollment: 28226
Number of Schools: 64 elementary schools; 18 secondary schools
Jane Angus, Chair, 519-753-2530
jane.angus@granderie.ca
Jim Wibberley, Director, Education, & Secretary, 519-756-6301, ext. 281137
Sharon Bell, Manager, Human Resources, 519-756-6301, ext. 281289
Kevin Holly, Manager, Information Technology Services, 519-754-0696, ext. 287033
Kathy Kirby, Manager, Business Services, 519-754-0696, ext. 281123
Phil Kuckyt, Manager, Transportation Services, 519-751-7532, ext. 282202
Michael Tancredi, Manager, Facilities Services, 519-751-7532, ext. 281161
Wayne Hobbs, Executive Supervisor, Student Support Services, 519-754-0696, ext. 287237
Jamie Gunn, Treasurer, 519-756-6301, ext. 281142

Brockville: Upper Canada District School Board
Administration Building
225 Central Ave. West, Brockville, ON K6V 5X1, Canada
Tel: 613-342-0371; *Toll-Free:* 1-800-267-7131
inquiries@ucdsb.on.ca
www.ucdsb.on.ca

Grades: K-12; Alternative Ed; Continuing Ed
Enrollment: 30825
Number of Schools: 100 elementary & secondary schools (alternative & continuing education available at more than 30 campuses); Number of Employees: 5,000
David K. Thomas, Director, Education, 613-342-0371, ext. 1234, fax: 613-342-6084
david.thomas@ucdsb.on.ca
Ian Carswell, Associate Director, 613-342-0371, ext. 1397, fax: 613-342-0277
ian.carswell@ucdsb.on.ca
David Coombs, Superintendent, School Effectiveness, 613-933-5256, ext. 4279, fax: 613-933-5275
david.coombs@ucdsb.on.ca
Susan Edwards, Superintendent, Student Engagement, 877-485-1211
susan.edwards@ucdsb.on.ca
Rick Gales, Superintendent, Business, 613-342-0371, ext. 1255, fax: 613-343-0277
rick.gales@ucdsb.on.ca
Ted Kennedy, Superintendent, School Operations, 613-258-9393, ext. 2551, fax: 613-258-6321
ted.kennedy@ucdsb.on.ca
Linda Lumsden, Superintendent, School Effectiveness, 613-342-0371, ext. 1414, fax: 613-342-6084
linda.lumsden@ucdsb.on.ca
Charlotte Patterson, Superintendent, Human Resources, 613-342-0371, ext. 1240, fax: 613-342-0277
charlotte.patterson@ucdsb.on.ca
Jeremy Hobbs, Chief Information & Facilities Officer, 613-342-0371, ext. 1126, fax: 613-498-0291
jeremy.hobbs@ucdsb.on.ca
Terry Davies, Officer, Accountability & Alignment, 613-342-0371, ext. 1274, fax: 613-342-6084
terry.davies@ucdsb.on.ca
Terry Simzer, Manager, Communications, 613-342-0371, ext. 1119, fax: 613-342-0277
terry.simzer@ucdsb.on.ca
Frances Boomhouwer, Trustee Liaison, 613-342-0371, ext. 1279, fax: 613-342-6084
frances.boomhouwer@ucdsb.on.ca

Burlington: Halton District School Board
J.W. Singleton Education Centre
P.O. Box 5005 LCD 1
2050 Guelph Line, Burlington, ON L7R 3Z2, Canada
Tel: 905-335-3663; *Fax:* 905-335-9802
inquiry@haltonbus.ca (student transportation)
www.hdsb.ca
Other Information: Special Ed. Ctr., Student Svs., & Programs, Phone: 905-631-6120

Grades: Elementary - Secondary
Enrollment: 54000
Number of Schools: 80 elementary schools; 17 secondary schools. Number of Employees: 3,244 teachers; 1,350 non-teaching & support staff; 181 principals & vice-principals
Bruce Jones, Chair, 905-257-5926, fax: 905-257-5923
jonesbr@hdsb.ca
David Euale, Director, Education, fax: 905-335-4447
director@hdsb.ca
Ruth Peden, Acting Associate Director, Education, 905-335-3663, ext. 3352, fax: 905-335-4447
pedenr@hdsb.ca
Marnie Denton, Manager, Communication Services, fax: 905-335-4447
dentonm@hdsb.ca
Gail Gortmaker, Manager, Director's Office, fax: 905-335-4447
gortmakerg@hdsb.ca
Suzanne Muir, Coordinator, Diversity, 905-631-6120, ext. 434, fax: 905-335-4447
muirs@hdsb.ca
Jacki Oxley, Liaison, School & Community, fax: 905-335-4447
oxleyj@hdsb.ca

Chesley: Bluewater District School Board
P.O. Box 190
351 - 1st Ave. North, Chesley, ON N0G 1L0, Canada
Tel: 519-363-2014; *Fax:* 519-370-2909
Toll-Free: 1-800-661-7509
communications@bwdsb.on.ca
www.bwdsb.on.ca

Grades: Elementary - Secondary; Special Ed.
Enrollment: 19454
Jennifer Yenssen, Chair
Mary Ann Alton, Director, Education
Brenda Booth, Treasurer & Superintendent, Business
Marnie Coke, Superintendent, Elementary Education
Alana Murray, Superintendent, Secondary Education
Jean Stephenson, Superintendent, Student Success
Lori Wilder, Superintendent, Student Services
Jacqui Traverse-Thomas, Principal, Program
Richard Thomas, Coordinator, Communications

Fort Frances: Rainy River District School Board
522 Second St. East, Fort Frances, ON P9A 1N4, Canada
Tel: 807-274-9855; *Fax:* 807-274-5078
Toll-Free: 800-214-1753
www.rrdsb.com

Enrollment: 3080
Heather Campbell, Director, Education
Dan Belluz, Chair

Guelph: Upper Grand District School Board
Main Office
500 Victoria Rd. North, Guelph, ON N1E 6K2, Canada
Tel: 519-822-4420; *Fax:* 519-822-4487
Toll-Free: 1-800-321-4025
inquiry@ugdsb.on.ca
www.ugdsb.on.ca

Grades: JK - 12; Continuing Education
Martha Rogers, Director, Education, & Secretary-Treasurer, 519-822-4420, ext. 720
martha.rogers@ugdsb.on.ca
Maggie McFadzen, Officer, Communications, 519-822-4420, ext. 275, fax: 519-826-9534
maggie.mcfadzen@ugdsb.on.ca

Hamilton: Hamilton-Wentworth District School Board
P.O. Box 2558
100 Main St. West, Hamilton, ON L8N 3L1, Canada
Tel: 905-527-5092; *Fax:* 905-521-2536
www.hwdsb.on.ca

Enrollment: 50000
John Malloy, Director, Education
Jessica Brennan, Chair

Kenora: Keewatin-Patricia District School Board
100 First Ave. West, Kenora, ON P9N 3Z7, Canada
Tel: 807-468-5571; *Fax:* 807-468-3857
Toll-Free: 877-275-7771
www.kpdsb.on.ca

Enrollment: 7000
Larry Hope, Director, Education
David Penney, Chair

Kingston: Limestone District School Board
P.O. Box Bag 610
220 Portsmouth Ave., Kingston, ON K7L 4X4, Canada
Tel: 613-544-6920; *Fax:* 613-544-6804
Toll-Free: 800-267-0935
inq@limestone.on.ca
www.limestone.on.ca
Other Information: Automated: 613-544-6925
TTY: 613-548-0279

Grades: JK-12
Enrollment: 22000
Brenda Hunter, Director, Education
Helen Chadwick, Chair

Kitchener: Waterloo Region District School Board
51 Ardelt Ave., Kitchener, ON N2C 2R5, Canada
Tel: 519-570-0003; *Fax:* 519-742-1364
www.wrdsb.on.ca

Grades: Pre-K.-12
Enrollment: 60000
Linda Fabi, Dir., ext. 4222
Colin Harrington, Chair, ext. 4224

***Lindsay:* Trillium Lakelands District School Board**
Corporate Office
P.O. Box 420
300 County Rd. 36, Lindsay, ON K9V 4S4, Canada
Tel: 705-324-6776; *Fax:* 705-328-2036
Toll-Free: 1-888-526-5552
info@tldsb.on.ca
www.tldsb.on.ca
Other Information: Bracebridge Office, Phone: 705-645-8704; Haliburton: 705-457-1980
Grades: K-12; French Immersion; Adult Ed.
Enrollment: 18000
Number of Schools: 41 elementary schools; 7 secondary schools; 6 education centres. Number of Employees: 1,216 elementary school staff, including 772 teachers; 626 secondary school staff, including 440 teachers; 55 adult education centre staff, including 36 teachers; 158 other staff, including 26 teachers
Larry Hope, Director, Education, 705-324-6776
Bruce Barrett, Superintendent, Secondary School Improvement/Student Success, 705-324-6776
Kevin Cutler, Superintendent, Special Education, 705-645-8704
Bob Kaye, Superintendent, Business, 705-324-6776
Dianna Scates, Superintendent, ICT & Secondary Operations, 705-324-6776
Gale Sherin, Superintendent, Elementary School Improvement, 705-324-6776
Andrea Gillespie, District Principal, Elementary School Improvement, 705-645-8704
Greg Ingram, District Principal, Secondary School Improvement, 705-324-6776
Shelley Woon, District Principal, Special Education, 705-324-6776
Earl Manners, Administrator, Human Resources, 705-324-6776
Jeanne Pengelly, Officer, Communications, 888-526-5552, ext. 22129
jeanne.pengelly@tldsb.on.ca

***London:* Thames Valley District School Board**
P.O. Box 5888
1250 Dundas St., London, ON N5W 5P2, Canada
Tel: 519-452-2000; *Fax:* 519-452-2395
info@tvdsb.on.ca
www.tvdsb.on.ca
Grades: JK - 12; Adult Ed.; Alternative Ed.
Enrollment: 76864
Number of Schools: 148 elementary schools; 32 secondary schools. Number of Employees: 4,920 teachers; 297 principals & vice-principals; 2,645 support staff
Bill Tucker, Director, Education & Secretary, 519-452-2000, ext. 20001
Karen Dalton, Executive Superintendent, Operations, 519-452-2000, ext. 20083
Laura Elliott, Executive Superintendent, Program Services, 519-452-2000, ext. 20380
Brian Greene, Executive Superintendent, Business Services, & Treasurer, 519-452-2000, ext. 20343
Michael Sereda, Executive Superintendent, Human Resources, 519-452-2000, ext. 20254
C. Bourbonnais Macdonald, Superintendent, Education - Operations Services, 519-452-2000, ext. 20376
Karen Edgar, Superintendent, Education - Operations Svs. / Program Svs., 519-452-2000, ext. 20275
Lynne Griffith-Jones, Superintendent, Education - HR Services / Operations Services, 519-452-2000, ext. 20250
Scott Hughes, Superintendent, Education - Operations Svs. / Program Svs., 519-452-2000, ext. 20082
Marion Moynihan, Superintendent, Education - Operations Services, 519-452-2000, ext. 20075
Valerie Neilsen, Superintendent, Education - Operations Svs. / Program Svs., 519-452-2000, ext. 20387
Mary Ellen Smith, Superintendent, Education - Operations Services, 519-452-2000, ext. 20251
Barbara Sonier, Superintendent, Education - Operations Services, 519-452-2000, ext. 20078
Paul Tufts, Superintendent, Education - Operations Services, 519-452-2000, ext. 20073
Karen Wilkinson, Superintendent, Education - Operations Services, 519-452-2000, ext. 20501

***Marathon:* Superior-Greenstone District School Board**
12 Hemlo Dr., Postal Bag A, Marathon, ON P0T 2E0, Canada
Tel: 807-229-0436; *Fax:* 807-229-1471
boardoffice@sgdsb.on.ca
www.sgdsb.on.ca
Grades: Elementary - Secondary
Number of Schools: 12 elementary schools; 5 secondary schools
Julie Sparrow, Board Chair
jsparrow@sgdsb.on.ca
Patti Pella, Director, Education
ppella@sgdsb.on.ca
Cathy Tsubouchi, Superintendent, Business, & Treasurer
Wayne Chiupka, Manager, Plant Services
wchiupka@sgdsb.on.ca
Barb Draper, Coordinator, Human Resources
bdraper@sgdsb.on.ca
Val Newton, Coordinator, Student Success
vnewton@sgdsb.on.ca
Marc Paris, Coordinator, Maintenance & Safety
mparis@sgdsb.on.ca
Bradley Ross, Coordinator, Systems & Information Technology
bross@sgdsb.on.ca

***Midhurst:* Simcoe County District School Board**
1170 Hwy. 26, Midhurst, ON L0L 1X0, Canada
Tel: 705-728-7570; *Fax:* 705-728-2265
www.scdsb.on.ca
Enrollment: 50000
Kathi Wallace, Director, Education
Brad Saunders, Chair

***Mississauga:* Peel District School Board**
5650 Hurontario St., Mississauga, ON L5R 1C6, Canada
Tel: 905-890-1099; *Fax:* 905-890-6747
Toll-Free: 800-668-1146
communications@peelsb.com
www.peel.edu.on.ca
Enrollment: 150000
Tony Pontes, Director, Education
Janet McDougald, Chair

***Nepean:* Ottawa-Carleton District School Board**
133 Greenbank Rd., Nepean, ON K2H 6L3, Canada
Tel: 613-721-1820; *Fax:* 613-820-6968
www.ocdsb.edu.on.ca
Enrollment: 72436
Cathy Curry, Chair
Dr. Lyall M. Thompson, Director, Education

***North Bay:* Near North District School Board**
P.O. Box 3110
963 Airport Rd., North Bay, ON P1B 8H1, Canada
Tel: 705-472-8170; *Fax:* 705-472-9927
Toll-Free: 800-278-4922
info@nearnorthschools.ca
www.nearnorthschools.ca
Grades: Pre-K.-12
Enrollment: 4895
Heli Vail, Dir., ext. 5050
vailh@nearnorthschools.ca
Al Bottomley, Chair, 705-384-5267
bottomleya@nearnorthschools.ca

***Pembroke:* Renfrew County District School Board**
1270 Pembroke St. West, Pembroke, ON K8A 4G4, Canada
Tel: 613-735-0151; *Fax:* 613-735-6315
www.renfrew.edu.on.ca
Enrollment: 10537
Roger Clarke, Director, Education
Roy C. Reiche, Chair

***Peterborough:* Kawartha Pine Ridge District School Board**
P.O. Box 7190
1994 Fisher Dr., Peterborough, ON K9J 7A1, Canada
Tel: 705-742-9773; *Fax:* 705-742-7801
Toll-Free: 877-741-4577
kpr_info@kpr.edu.on.ca
www.kpr.edu.on.ca
Enrollment: 37156
W.R. (Rusty) Hick, Director, Education
Diane Lloyd, Chair

***Sarnia:* Lambton Kent District School Board**
P.O. Box 2091
200 Wellington St., Sarnia, ON N7T 7L2, Canada
Tel: 519-336-1500; *Fax:* 519-336-0992
Toll-Free: 800-754-7125
www.lkdsb.net
Enrollment: 24000
Jim Costello, Director
Carmen McGregor, Chair

***Sault Ste Marie:* Algoma District School Board**
Central Board Office, Education Centre
644 Albert St. East, Sault Ste Marie, ON P6A 2K7, Canada
Tel: 705-945-7111; *Toll-Free:* 1-888-393-3639
vanders@adsb.on.ca (Susan Vandermolen)
www.adsb.on.ca
Other Information: Northern Office: 705-856-2309; Eastern Office: 705-848-3661
Grades: Kindergarten - 12; Adult Education
Mario Turco, Director, Education
Wanda McQueen, Chair

***Seaforth:* Avon Maitland District School Board**
62 Chalk St. North, Seaforth, ON N0K 1W0, Canada
Tel: 519-527-0111; *Fax:* 519-527-0222
Toll-Free: 1-800-592-5437
info@fc.amdsb.ca
www.avonmaitland.on.ca
Grades: JK - Secondary; Continuing Ed.
Enrollment: 17000
Jenny Versteeg, Chair, Board of Trustees, 519-335-3623
jennvers@fc.amdsb.ca
Chuck Reid, Director, Education & Secretary of the Board, 519-527-0111, ext. 106
chucreid@fc.amdsb.ca
Mike Ash, Superintendent, Education - School Operations, 519-527-0111, ext. 113
Janet Baird-Jackson, Superintendent, Business, 519-527-0111, ext. 206
Jodie Baker, Superintendent, Education - Learning Services, 519-527-0111, ext. 109
Ted Doherty, Superintendent, Education - Human Resources, 519-527-0111, ext. 208
Patricia Stanley, Superintendent, Education - Curriculum & Assessment, 519-527-0111, ext. 116
Steve Howe, Manager, Communications, 519-527-0111, ext. 132

***St Catharines:* District School Board of Niagara**
191 Carleton St., St Catharines, ON L2R 7P4, Canada
Tel: 905-641-1550; *Fax:* 905-685-8511
www.dsbn.edu.on.ca
Enrollment: 15749
Warren Hoshizaki, Dir.
Kevin Maves, Chair

***Sudbury:* Rainbow District School Board**
69 Young St., Sudbury, ON P3E 3G5, Canada
Tel: 705-674-3171; *Fax:* 705-647-9112
Toll-Free: 866-421-2661
www.rainbowschools.ca
Enrollment: 14762
Norm Blaseg, Director, Education
Tyler Campbell, Chair

***Thunder Bay:* Lakehead District School Board**
The Jim McCuaig Education Centre
2135 Sills St., Thunder Bay, ON P7E 5T2, Canada
Tel: 807-625-5100; *Fax:* 807-622-0961
www.lakeheadschools.ca
Enrollment: 10906
Catherine Siemieniuk, Director, Education
Deborah Massaro, Chair

***Timmins:* District School Board Ontario North East**
P.O. Box 1020
Timmins, ON P4N 7H7, Canada
Tel: 705-360-1151; *Fax:* 705-268-7100
Toll-Free: 1-800-381-728
comments@dsb1.edu.on.ca
www.dsb1.edu.on.ca
Enrollment: 4316
Linda Knight, Dir.
Juergen Leukert, Chair

***Toronto:* Toronto District School Board**
5050 Yonge St., Toronto, ON M2N 5N8, Canada
Tel: 416-397-3000
communications@tdsb.on.ca
www.tdsb.on.ca
Other Information: Public Affairs, Phone: 416-395-2721
Grades: K - 12; Adult Ed.; French Immersion
Enrollment: 260000
Number of Schools: 565. Number of Employees: 37,000
Chris Spence, Director, Education
chris.spence@tdsb.on.ca
Sue Pfeffer, Superintendent, Region NE1, 416-396-9172
Sue.Pfeffer@tdsb.on.ca
Peter Chang, Superintendent, Region NE2, 416-396-9180
p.chang@tdsb.on.ca
Sandy Spyropoulos, Superintendent, Region NE3, 416-396-9176
sandy.spyropoulos@tdsb.on.ca
Colleen Russell, Superintendent, Region NE4, 416-396-9178
Colleen.Russell@tdsb.on.ca
Kathleen Meighan, Superintendent, Region NE5, 416-396-9174
Kathleen.Meighan@tdsb.on.ca
Johanne Messner, Superintendent, Region NE6, 416-396-9182
johanne.messner@tdsb.on.ca
Rauda Dickinson, Superintendent, Region SE1, 416-396-9186
Rauda.Dickinson@tdsb.on.ca

Kerry-Lynn Stadnyk, Superintendent, Region SE2, 416-396-9188
Kerry-Lynn.Stadnyk@tdsb.on.ca
Don McLean, Superintendent, Region SE3, 416-396-9190
Don.McLean@tdsb.on.ca
Allan Wolch, Superintendent, Region SE4, 416-396-9192
Allan.Wolch@tdsb.on.ca
Anne Kerr, Superintendent, Region SE5, 416-396-9194
Anne.Kerr@tdsb.on.ca
Kathy Cowan, Superintendent, Region SE6, 416-396-9196
Kathy.Cowan@tdsb.on.ca
Jim Spyropoulos, Superintendent, Region SW1, 416-394-2042
Jim.Spyropoulos@tdsb.on.ca
Manon Gardner, Superintendent, Region SW2, 416-394-2044
Manon.Gardner@tdsb.on.ca
Michael Smith, Superintendent, Region SW3, 416-394-2046
Michael.Smith@tdsb.on.ca
Ian Allison, Superintendent, Region SW4, 416-394-2048
Ian.Allison@tdsb.on.ca
Andrea Alimi, Superintendent, Region SW5, 416-394-2050
Andrea.Alimi@tdsb.on.ca
Karen Falconer, Superintendent, Region SW6, 416-394-2052
karen.falconer@tdsb.on.ca
Annie Appleby, Superintendent, Region NW1, 416-394-2028
Annie.Appleby@tdsb.on.ca
Glenford Duffus, Superintendent, Region NW2, 416-394-2030
Glenford.Duffus@tdsb.on.ca
John Chasty, Superintendent, Region NW3, 416-394-2032
john.chasty@tdsb.on.ca
Jeff Hainbuch, Superintendent, Region NW4, 416-394-2034
Jeff.Hainbuch@tdsb.on.ca
Leila Girdhar, Superintendent, Region NW5, 416-394-2036
Leila.Girdhar@tdsb.on.ca
Susan Winter, Superintendent, Region NW6, 416-394-2038
Susan.Winter@tdsb.on.ca

Whitby: Durham District School Board
400 Taunton Rd. East, Whitby, ON L1R 2K6, Canada
Tel: 905-666-5500; *Fax:* 905-666-6474
Toll-Free: 1-800-265-3968
douglas_karen@durham.edu.on.ca (Executive Assistant to Director)
www.durham.edu.on.ca
Other Information: Trustees' Administrative Assistant, Phone: 905-666-6363
TTY: 905-666-6943

Grades: K - 12; Special Ed.; Continuing Ed.
Enrollment: 69086
Number of Schools: 109 elementary schools; 26 secondary schools & learning centres. Number of Employees: 2,760 elementary teachers; 1,663 secondary teachers; 208 elementary administrators; 77 secondary administrators; 2,665 educational services staff (including educational assistants, clerical, custodial, maintenance, & lunchroom supervisors)
Martyn Beckett, Director, Education, 905-666-5500, fax: 905-666-6318
beckett_martyn@durham.edu.on.ca
Luigia Ayotte, Superintendent, Education (Programs), 905-666-5500, fax: 905-666-6946
ayotte_luigia@durham.edu.on.ca
John Beatty, Superintendent, Education (Brock, Uxbridge, & Scugog), 905-666-6905
beatty_john@durham.edu.on.ca
John Bowyer, Superintendent, Education (Whitby), 905-666-6373
bowyer_john@durham.edu.on.ca
Doug Crichton, Superintendent, Education (Special Education), 905-666-6371
crichton_doug@durham.edu.on.ca
Janet Edwards, Superintendent, Education (Ajax), 905-666-6379
edwards_janet@durham.edu.on.ca
Ed Hodgins, Superintendent, Education & Business, & Treasurer, 905-666-6402, fax: 905-666-6969
hodgins_ed@durham.edu.on.ca
Mark Joel, Superintendent, Education (Ops, Transportation & Leadership), 905-666-5500, fax: 905-666-6376
joel_mark@durham.edu.on.ca
Jeannine Joubert, Superintendent, Education (Oshawa), 905-666-6369
joubert_jeannine@durham.edu.on.ca
Lisa Millar, Superintendent, Education (Pickering), 905-666-6486
millar_lisa@durham.edu.on.ca
Lou Vavougios, Superintendent, Education (Employee Services), 905-666-6332, fax: 905-666-6908
vavougios_lou@durham.edu.on.ca
David Visser, Superintendent, Education (Facilities Services), 905-666-6426, fax: 905-666-6439
visser_david@durham.edu.on.ca
Denise Gilbert, Executive Director, Schoolhouse Playcare Centres, 905-666-6487
gilbert_denise@durham.edu.on.ca
Andrea Pidwerbecki, Manager, Communications, 905-666-6313
pidwerbecki_andrea@durham.edu.on.ca

Windsor: Greater Essex County District School Board
P.O. Box 210
451 Park St. West, Windsor, ON N9A 6K1, Canada
Tel: 519-255-3200
www.gecdsb.on.ca
Other Information: Adult & Continuing Education, Phone: 519-253-5006

Grades: Jr Kindergarten-12; Alternative Ed.
Enrollment: 35350
Number of Schools: 61 elementary schools; 16 secondary schools; 5 agency schools
Warren Kennedy, Director, Education, 519-255-3200, ext. 10250
Penny Allen, Superintendent, Business, 519-255-3200, ext. 10210
Paul Antaya, Superintendent, Secondary Schools, 519-255-3200, ext. 10254
Clara Howitt, Superintendent, Program & Instructional Services, 519-255-3200, ext. 10255
John Howitt, Superintendent, Operations & Information Technology, 519-255-3200, ext. 10253
Heather Liffiton, Superintendent, Education, 519-255-3200, ext. 10251
Terry Lyons, Superintendent, Accommodations & Safe Schools, 519-255-3200, ext. 10223
Donne Petryshyn, Superintendent, Human Resources, 519-255-3200, ext. 10264
Sharon Pyke, Superintendent, Special Education, 519-255-3200, ext. 10222
Mary Guthrie, Chief Information Officer, 519-255-3200, ext. 10260

Catholic

Aurora: York Catholic District School Board
320 Bloomington Rd. West, Aurora, ON L4G 0M1, Canada
Tel: 905-713-1211; *Fax:* 905-713-1272
www.ycdsb.ca

Grades: Pre-K.-12
Enrollment: 54580
Susan LaRosa, Dir.
susan.larosa@ycdsb.ca
John Sabo, Assoc. Dir./Board Treas., ext. 12300
john.sabo@ycdsb.ca
Elizabeth Crowe, Chair
elizabeth.crowe@ycdsb.ca

Barrie: Simcoe Muskoka Catholic District School Board
46 Alliance Blvd., Barrie, ON L4M 5K3, Canada
Tel: 705-722-3555; *Fax:* 705-722-6534
www.smcdsb.on.ca

Enrollment: 22000
Michael. O'Keefe, Director, Education
John Grisé, Chair

Brantford: Brant Haldimand Norfolk Catholic District School Board
P.O. Box 217
322 Fairview Dr., Brantford, ON N3T 5M8, Canada
Tel: 519-756-6505; *Fax:* 519-756-9913
webmaster@bhncdsb.ca
www.bhncdsb.edu.on.ca

Grades: Elementary - Secondary; Special Ed.
Enrollment: 10653
Number of Schools: 31 Catholic elementary schools; 3 Catholic secondary schools. Number of Employees: 700+ teachers; 300+ non-academic staff
June Szeman, Chair, 519-753-9198
jszeman@bhncdsb.ca
Cathy Horgan, Director, Education & Secretary, 519-756-6505, ext. 223
William Chopp, Superintendent, Education, 519-756-6505, ext. 244
Patricia (Trish) Kings, Superintendent, Education, 519-756-6505, ext. 242
Chris Roehrig, Superintendent, Education, 519-756-6505, ext. 240
Wally Easton, Associate Director, Corporate Services, & Treasurer, 519-756-6505, ext. 272
Mary Gallo, Principal, Secondary Program, 519-756-6505, ext. 251
Terre Slaght, Principal, Special Education Program, 519-759-8862, ext. 402
Leslie Telfer, Principal, School Effectiveness, 519-756-6505, ext. 264
Maureen Wills, Principal, Elementary Program, 519-756-6505, ext. 256
Tony Castagna, Manager, Information Technology, 519-758-5924, ext. 342
Paula Dunn, Manager, Human Resources, 519-756-6505, ext. 235
Phillip Kuckyt, Manager, Transportation Services, 519-751-7532, ext. 28220
Pat Petrella, Manager, Finance, 519-756-6505, ext. 228
Don Zelem, Manager, Facilities & Construction Projects, 519-759-3555, ext. 15
Tracey Austin, Coordinator, Communications & Community Relations, 519-756-6505, ext. 234
taustin@bhncdsb.ca

Burlington: Halton Catholic District School Board
Education Center
802 Drury Lane, Burlington, ON L7R 2Y2, Canada
Tel: 905-632-6300; *Fax:* 905-333-4661
Toll-Free: 1-800-741-8382
comments@hcdsb.org; communications@hcdsb.org; business@hcdsb.org
www.haltonrc.edu.on.ca
Other Information: Special Education Services, E-mail: speced@hcdsb.org

Grades: Elementary-Secondary; Continuing Ed
Enrollment: 29000
Number of Schools: 40 elementary schools; 8 secondary schools; 2 continuing education centres
Michael Pautler, Director, Education, 905-632-6314, ext. 110, fax: 905-333-4661
director@hcdsb.org
Erica vanRoosmalen, Chief Officer, Research & Development Services, 905-632-6314, ext. 367
Joseph O'Hara, Executive Officer, Human Resources, 905-632-6314, ext. 104
Giacomo Corbacio, Superintendent, Facilities Services, 905-632-6314, ext. 170
Jacqueline Herman, Superintendent, Education, 905-632-6314, ext. 161
John Langill, Superintendent, School Services, 905-632-6314, ext. 183
Richard MacDonald, Superintendent, Curriculum Services, 905-632-6314, ext. 122
Fiammetta Mazzetti, Superintendent, Education, 905-632-6314, ext. 216
Paul McMahon, Superintendent, Business Services, 905-632-6314, ext. 130
Suzanne Rossini, Superintendent, Special Education Services, 905-632-6314, ext. 128
James Rowles, Superintendent, Education, 905-632-6314, ext. 180
Mary Tessari, Superintendent, Education, Staff Dev. & Faith Formation Svs., 905-632-6314, ext. 118
Wayne Elshof, Senior Administrator, Information Technology, 905-632-6314, ext. 550
Scott Bland, Administrator, Planning Services, 905-632-6314, ext. 107
Christopher Jewell, Administrator, Communication Services, 905-632-6314, ext. 157

Dublin: Huron-Perth Catholic District School Board
P.O. Box 70
87 Mill St., Dublin, ON N0K 1E0, Canada
Tel: 519-345-2440; *Fax:* 519-345-2449
www.hpcdsb.edu.on.ca

Enrollment: 1753
Martha Dutrizac, Director, Education
Mike Miller, Chair

Dubreuilville: Conseil des écoles séparées catholiques de Dubreuilville
P.O. Box 69
149, av du Parc, Dubreuilville, ON P0S 1B0, Canada
Tél: 705-884-2309; *Téléc:* 705-884-2062
www.dubreuilville.ca

Enrollment: 138
Guy Pelletier, Président du Conseil

Fort Frances: Northwest Catholic District School Board
555 Flinders Ave., Fort Frances, ON P9A 3L2, Canada
Tel: 807-274-2931; *Fax:* 807-274-8792
www.tncdsb.on.ca

Enrollment: 1434
Mary-Catherine Kelly, Director, Education
Anne-Marie Fitzgerald, Chair
amfitzgerald@tncdsb.on.ca

Guelph: Wellington Catholic District School Board
75 Woolwich St., Guelph, ON N1H 6N6, Canada
Tel: 519-821-4600; *Fax:* 519-824-3088
andrew_duszczyszyn@wellingtoncssb.edu.on.ca
www.wellingtoncssb.edu.on.ca

Grades: Pre-K.-12
Enrollment: 61000
Don Drone, Dir., 519-821-4640, fax: 519-837-4156
ddrone@wellingtoncdsb.ca
Dan Duszczyszyn, Supt. of Corp. Services/Treas., fax: 519-837-4154
dduszczyszyn@wellingtoncdsb.ca
Rev Dennis J. Noon, Chair, 519-824-3951, fax: 519-824-1920
dnoon@dionet.ca

Hamilton: Hamilton-Wentworth Catholic District School Board
P.O. Box 2012
90 Mulberry St., Hamilton, ON L8N 3R9, Canada
Tel: 905-525-2930; *Fax:* 905-525-1724
www.hwcdsb.edu.on.ca/
Other Information: Summer fax: 905-525-2914

Grades: K-12
Enrollment: 30000
Patricia Amos, Director, Education, 905-525-2930, ext. 2180
Patrick J. Daly, Chair, 905-525-2930, ext. 2162

Hanover: Bruce-Grey Catholic District School Board
799 - 16th Ave., Hanover, ON N4N 3A1, Canada
Tel: 519-364-5820; *Fax:* 519-364-5882
bruce_grey@bgcdsb.org
www.bgcdsb.org

Grades: Kindergarten-12; Religious Ed.; ESL
Enrollment: 3524
Number of Schools: 13
Norman Bethune, Chair, 519-376-8315
Bruce MacPherson, Director, Education
Gerald Casey, Superintendent, Education
Catherine Montreuil, Superintendent, Education
Cathy Colton, Superintendent, Business
Jim Aitken, Supervisor, Maintenance
Joyce Benninger, Supervisor, Payroll & Health & Safety
Doreen Rogers, Coordinator, Community Relations & Outreach
Ann-Marie Deas, Social Worker
Alecia Lantz, Financial Analyst
Brenda Leahy, Speech Language Pathologist
Catherine Penner, Psychometrist

Kemptville: Catholic District School Board of Eastern Ontario
c/o Kemptville Board Office
P.O. Box 2222
2755 Hwy. 43, Kemptville, ON K0G 1J0, Canada
Tel: 613-258-7757; *Fax:* 613-258-7134
Toll-Free: 1-800-443-4562
mail@cdsbeo.on.ca
www.cdsbeo.on.ca
Other Information: Western Ed. Ctr.: 613-283-5007; Eastern Ed. Ctr.: 613-933-1720

Grades: Elementary - Secondary
Enrollment: 15000
Number of Schools: 40 elementary schools; 10 secondary schools. Number of Employees: 850 teachers; 450 support staff
Ronald Eamer, Chair, 613-931-2369
Ronald.Eamer@cdsbeo.on.ca
Dr. Donaleen Hawes, Superintendent, Education, 613-283-5007, ext. 234, fax: 613-283-5783
Donaleen.Hawes@cdsbeo.on.ca
Mark Musca, Superintendent, Human Resources, 613-258-7757, fax: 613-258-3610
Mark.Musca@cdsbeo.on.ca
Marg Shea-Lawrence, Superintendent, Religious & Family Life Education, 613-258-7757, ext. 207, fax: 613-258-3610
Marg.Shea@cdsbeo.on.ca
Bernie Kehoe, Manager, Plant & Maintenance, 613-258-7757, ext. 227, fax: 613-258-3610
Bernie.Kehoe@cdsbeo.on.ca
Nicole Makinson, Manager, Transportation & Assessment, 613-258-7757, ext. 107, fax: 613-258-3610
Nicole.Makinson@cdsbeo.on.ca
Bonnie Norton, Manager, Finance, 613-258-7757, ext. 238, fax: 613-258-3610
Bonnie.Norton@cdsbeo.on.ca
James Proulx, Manager, ICT Services, 613-258-7757, ext. 555, fax: 613-258-3610
James.Proulx@cdsbeo.on.ca
Sheila Farris, Supervising Principal, Student Success Initiative, 613-283-5007, fax: 613-283-5783
Sheila.Farris@cdsbeo.on.ca
Tom Jordan, Principal, Special Education, 613-283-5007, ext. 205, fax: 613-283-5783
Tom.Jordan@cdsbeo.on.ca
Jim Roberts, Principal, Religious Education, 613-258-7757, ext. 246, fax: 613-258-3610
jim.roberts@cdsbeo.on.ca
Charlotte Rouleau, Principal, Curriculum, 613-933-1720, ext. 377, fax: 613-933-7966
charlotte.rouleau@cdsbeo.on.ca

Kenora: Kenora Catholic District School Board
200 First St. North, Kenora, ON P9N 2K4, Canada
Tel: 807-468-9851; *Fax:* 807-468-8094
mcunningham@kcdsb.on.ca
www.kcdsb.on.ca

Enrollment: 1475
Phyllis Eikre, Director, Education
Darryl Michaluk, Chair

Kitchener: Waterloo Catholic District School Board
P.O. Box 91116
35 Weber St. W, #A, Kitchener, ON N2G 4G2, Canada
Tel: 519-578-3660; *Fax:* 519-578-5291
info@wcdsb.ca
www.wcdsb.ca

Grades: Pre-K.-12
Enrollment: 40000
Roger Lawler, Dir.
roger.lawler@wcdsb.ca
Shesh Maharaj, CFO
shesh.maharaj@wcdsb.ca
Wayne Buchholtz, Chair

L'Orignal: Conseil scolaire de district catholique de l'Est ontarien
875, ch de comté 17, L'Orignal, ON K0B 1K0, Canada
Tél: 613-675-4691; *Téléc:* 613-675-2921
Ligne sans frais: 800-204-4098
bur-central@csdceo.on.ca
www.csdceo.ca

Enrollment: 3718
Céline Cadieux, Directrice de l'éducation/Sec.
Michel Pilon, Président du Conseil

London: London District Catholic School Board
Catholic Education Centre
P.O. Box 5474
5200 Wellington Rd. South, London, ON N6A 4X5, Canada
Tel: 519-663-2088
communications@ldcsb.on.ca
www.ldcsb.on.ca

Grades: Jr Kindergarten - 12; Continuing Ed
Enrollment: 21000
Number of Schools: 48 elementary schools; 8 secondary schools
Bill Hall, Chair, Board of Trustees
Wilma de Rond, Director, Education, & Secretary-Treasurer, 519-663-2088, ext. 40002, fax: 519-663-9250
w.derond@ldcsb.on.ca
Terry Grand, Superintendent, Education
Vince MacDonald, Superintendent, Education
John Mombourquette, Superintendent, Education
Tamara Nugent, Superintendent, Education
Sharon Wright-Evans, Superintendent, Education

Mississauga: Dufferin-Peel Catholic District School Board
40 Matheson Blvd. West, Mississauga, ON L5R 1C5, Canada
Tel: 905-890-1221; *Fax:* 905-890-7610
www.dpcdsb.org

Enrollment: 80000
Michael Bator, Dir.
mike.bator@dpcdsb.org
Arthur Peters, Chair

Napanee: Algonquin & Lakeshore Catholic District School Board
151 Dairy Ave., Napanee, ON K7R 4B2, Canada
Tel: 613-354-2255; *Toll-Free:* 1-800-581-1116
www.alcdsb.on.ca
Other Information: info@alcdsb.on

Grades: Elementary - Secondary
Enrollment: 12397
Michael Schmitt, Director, Education, 613-354-6257, ext. 448
schmitt@alcdsb.on.ca
Bob Koubsky, Superintendent, Finance & Business Services, 613-354-6257, ext. 436
koubsky@alcdsb.on.ca
Lori Bryden, Coodinator, Student Services, 613-354-6257, ext. 434
bryden@alcdsb.on.ca
Bronek Korczynski, Coodinator, Religous & Family Life Education, 613-354-6257, ext. 462
Bronek.Korczynski@alcdsb.on.ca
Louise Lannan, Coodinator, Curriculum & Staff Development, 613-354-6257, ext. 402
lannan@alcdsb.on.ca

Nepean: Ottawa-Carleton Catholic District School Board
570 Hunt Club Rd. West, Nepean, ON K2G 3R4, Canada
Tel: 613-224-2222; *Fax:* 613-224-5063
www.occdsb.on.ca

Enrollment: 39000
Julian Hanlon, Director, Education & Sec.-Treas.
Gordon Butler, Chair

North Bay: Conseil scolaire catholique Franco-Nord
681-C, rue Chippewa ouest, North Bay, ON P1B 6G8, Canada
Tél: 705-472-1702; *Téléc:* 705-474-3824
information@franco-nord.ca
www.franco-nord.edu.on.ca

Enrollment: 3400
Cynthia Roveda, Directrice de l'éducation/Sec.-trésorière
Ronald Demers, Président du Conseil

North Bay: Nipissing-Parry Sound Catholic District School Board
1000 High St., North Bay, ON P1B 6P2, Canada
Tel: 705-472-1201; *Fax:* 705-472-0507
www.npsc.edu.on.ca

Grades: Pre_K.-12
Enrollment: 3438
Anna Marie Bitonti, Dir.
Joanne Bénard, Supt.
Donald B. Houle, Chair

Oshawa: Durham Catholic District School Board
650 Rossland Rd. West, Oshawa, ON L1J 7C4, Canada
Tel: 905-576-6150; *Fax:* 905-576-0953
www.durhamrc.edu.on.ca

Enrollment: 26069
Patricia Manson, Dir.
patricia.manson@idirect.com
Mary Ann Martin, Chair

Ottawa: Conseil des écoles catholiques du Centre-Est
4000, rue Labelle, Ottawa, ON K1J 1A1, Canada
Tél: 613-744-2555; *Téléc:* 613-746-3081
Ligne sans frais: 888-230-5131
ecolecatholique@ecolecatholique.ca
www.ceclf.edu.on.ca

Enrollment: 18000
Diane Doré, Présidente du Conseil
Bernard Roy, Directeur de l'éducation/Sec.-trésorier

Pembroke: Renfrew County Catholic District School Board
499 Pembroke St. West, Pembroke, ON K8A 5P1, Canada
Tel: 613-735-1031; *Fax:* 613-735-2649
Toll-Free: 800-267-0191
www.rccdsb.edu.on.ca

Enrollment: 5000
Michele Arbour, Director
Bob Schreader, Chair

Peterborough: Peterborough Victoria Northumberland & Clarington Catholic District School B
1355 Lansdowne St. West, Peterborough, ON K9J 7M3, Canada
Tel: 705-748-4861; *Fax:* 705-748-9734
Toll-Free: 800-461-8009
www.pvnccdsb.on.ca

Enrollment: 14678
John Mackle, Director, Education & Secretary-Treasurer
David Bernier, Chair

Sault Ste Marie: Huron-Superior Catholic District School Board
90 Ontario Ave., Sault Ste Marie, ON P6B 6G7, Canada
Tel: 705-945-5400; *Fax:* 705-945-5575
Toll-Free: 800-267-0754
www.hscdsb.on.ca

Enrollment: 6795
John Stadnyk, Director, Education
Marchy Bruni, Chair

Sudbury: Conseil scolaire catholique du Nouvel-Ontario
201, rue Jogues, Sudbury, ON P3C 5L7, Canada
Tél: 705-673-5626; *Téléc:* 705-669-1270
Ligne sans frais: 800-259-5567
info@nouvelon.ca
www.nouvelon.ca

Enrollment: 7500
Marcel Montpellier, Président du Conseil
Lyse-Anne Papineau, Directrice de l'éducation

***Sudbury:* Sudbury Catholic District School Board**
Catholic Education Centre
165A D'Youville St., Sudbury, ON P3C 5E7, Canada
Tel: 705-673-5620; *Fax:* 705-673-6670
employment@sudburycatholicschools.ca
www.scdsb.edu.on.ca
Other Information: Transportation, Phone: 705-521-1234
Grades: JK - 12; French Immersion; Adult Ed
Enrollment: 6595
Number of Schools: 20 elementary schools; 5 secondary schools (including an all-girls school & the St. Albert Adult Learning Centre)
Catherine McCullough, Director, Education, & Secretary of the Board, 705-673-5620, ext. 242, fax: 705-688-1781
Catherine.McCullough@sudburycatholicschools.ca
Rossella Bagnato, Superintendent, Special Education & Academic Programs, 705-673-5620, ext. 238, fax: 705-688-1781
Rossella.Bagnato@sudburycatholicschools.ca
Dennis Bazinet, Superintendent, Business & Finance, 705-673-5620, ext. 238, fax: 705-688-1781
Dennis.Bazinet@sudburycatholicschools.ca
Jean McHarg, Superintendent, Programs (K-12), 705-673-5620, ext. 238, fax: 705-688-1781
Jean.McHarg@sudburycatholicschools.ca
Roland Muzzatti, Superintendent, Student Success & 7-12 Schools, 705-673-5620, ext. 238, fax: 705-688-1781
Roland.Muzzatti@sudburycatholicschools.ca
Suzanne Dubien, Senior Manager, Human Resources, 705-673-5620, ext. 312
Denis Faucher, Manager, Facility Services, 705-673-5620, ext. 415
Gerry Robillard, Manager, Information Management Services, 705-673-5620, ext. 371
Gina Tullio, Coordinator, Outreach & Media Relations, 705-673-5620, ext. 244

***Terrace Bay:* Superior North Catholic District School Board**
P.O. Box 610
21 Simcoe Plaza, Terrace Bay, ON P0T 2W0, Canada
Tel: 807-825-3209; *Fax:* 807-825-3885
BoardOffice@sncdsb.on.ca; Board@sncdsb.on.ca
www.sncdsb.on.ca
Grades: Elementary; Religious Program
Number of Schools: 9 elementary schools
Valerie Pichette, Director, Education
vpichette@sncdsb.on.ca
Mary Anne Baker, Superintendent, Education
mbaker@sncdsb.on.ca
Sherry Bortolotti, Superintendent, School Effectiveness
sbortolotti@sncdsb.on.ca
Scott Adams, Manager, Finance
sadams@sncdsb.on.ca
Dan Bourgeault, Manager, Operations
dbourgeault@sncdsb.on.ca
Laureen Kay, Officer, Payroll & Human Resources, 807-825-3209, ext. 25, fax: 807-825-3885
lkay@sncdsb.on.ca
Maria Lapenskie, Officer, Transportation
mlapenskie@sncdsb.on.ca

***Thunder Bay:* Conseil scolaire de district catholique des Aurores boréales**
175, rue High nord, Thunder Bay, ON P7A 8C7, Canada
Tél: 807-344-2266; *Téléc:* 807-344-3734
Ligne sans frais: 800-367-0874
info@csdcab.on.ca
www.csdcab.on.ca
Enrollment: 652
Sylvianne Mauro, Directrice de l'éducation
Angèle Brunelle, Présidente du Conseil

***Thunder Bay:* Thunder Bay Catholic District School Board**
Catholic Education Centre
459 Victoria Ave. West, Thunder Bay, ON P7C 0A4, Canada
Tel: 807-625-1555
jsheriff@tbcdsb.on.ca nne Sheriff, Executive Assistant)
www.tbcdsb.on.ca
Grades: Jr. Kindergarten-12; Alternative Ed
Enrollment: 8606
Number of Schools: 16 elementary schools; 3 senior elementary schools; 2 secondary schools. Number of Employees: 366 elementary school teachers; 194 secondary school teachers; 283 non-teaching staff
John De Faveri, Director, Education, 807-625-1567, fax: 807-623-2167
jdefaver@tbcdsb.on.ca
Tom Mustapic, Associate Director & Superintendent, Business & Corporate Svs, 807-625-1508, fax: 807-625-1583
tmustapi@tbcdsb.on.ca
Rob Kruse, Superintendent, Education (St. Ignatius HS & St. Patrick HS), 807-625-1590, fax: 807-625-1560
dsebesta@tbcdsb.on.ca
Joan Powell, Superintendent, Education - Special Education & JK-8 Schools, 807-625-1573, fax: 807-625-1560
jpowell@tbcdsb.on.ca
David Bragnalo, Officer, Education, 807-625-1585, fax: 807-625-1560
dbragnal@tbcdsb.on.ca
Michael Thompson, Officer, Communications, 807-625-1587, fax: 807-623-2187
mthompso@tbcdsb.on.ca
Garry Grgurich, Manager, Employee Services, 807-625-1577, fax: 807-625-8601
jwillis@tbcdsb.on.ca

***Timmins:* Conseil des écoles séparées catholiques de Foleyet**
52, pl Theodore, Timmins, ON P4N 7P6, Canada
Tél: 705-267-3521; *Téléc:* 705-267-3691
www.afocsc.org
Enrollment: 15
Lisa Côté, Sec.-Treas.
Suzanne Roch, Chair

***Timmins:* Conseil scolaire catholique de district des Grandes Rivières**
896, promenade Riverside, Timmins, ON P4N 3W2, Canada
Tél: 705-267-1421; *Téléc:* 705-267-7247
www.cscdgr.on.ca
Enrollment: 2668
Isabelle Charbonneau, Présidente du Conseil
charbonneau@cscdgr.on.ca
Lorraine Presley, Directrice de l'éducation

***Timmins:* Northeastern Catholic District School Board**
101 Spruce St. North, Timmins, ON P4N 6M9, Canada
Tel: 705-268-7443; *Fax:* 705-267-3590
Toll-Free: 877-422-9322
www.ncdsb.on.ca
Grades: Pre-K.-12
Enrollment: 2373
Glenn Sheculski, Dir., fax: 705-268-7499
gsheculski@ncdsb.on.ca
Tricia Stefanic Weltz, Supt., fax: 705-266-9144
tricia.weltz@ncdsb.on.ca

***Toronto:* Conseil scolaire de district catholique Centre-Sud**
110, av Drewry, Toronto, ON M2M 1C8, Canada
Tél: 416-397-6564; *Téléc:* 416-397-6576
Ligne sans frais: 800-274-3764
commentaires@csdccs.edu.on.ca
www.csdccs.edu.on.ca
Enrollment: 12000
Réjean Sirois, Directeur de l'éducation/Sec.-trésorier
Mikale-Andrée Joly, Directrice des communications stratégiques

***Toronto:* Toronto Catholic District School Board**
80 Sheppard Ave. East, Toronto, ON M2N 6E8, Canada
Tel: 416-222-8282; *Fax:* 416-229-5345
webmaster@tcdsb.org; helpdesk@tcdsb.org (technical difficulties)
www.tcdsb.org
Other Information: Public Relations, Phone: 416-222-8282, ext. 5314
Grades: Kindergarten - 12; Adult Education
Enrollment: 93054
Number of Schools: 168 elementary schools; 31 secondary schools; 2 combined elementary & secondary (Cardinal Carter Academy for the Arts & St. Michael's Choir). Number of Employees: 5,997 teachers; 2,806 support & academic staff; 356 principals & vice-principals; 202 administrative personnel
Ann Perron, Director, Education, 416-222-8282, ext. 2296
ann.perron@tcdsb.org
Angela Gauthier, Associate Director, Academic Services, 416-222-8282, ext. 2641
angela.gauthier@tcdsb.org
Sandra Pessione, Associate Director, Business Services, CFO, & Treasurer, 416-222-8282, ext. 2641
sandra.pessione@tcdsb.org
Angelo Sangiorgio, Associate Director, Planning & Facilities, 416-222-8282, ext. 2349
Josie DiGiovanni, Superintendent, Curriculum & Accountability & Staff Dev., 416-222-8282, ext. 2490
josie.digiovanni@tcdsb.org
Lori DiMarco, Superintendent, Schools - Area 4ountability & Staff Dev., 416-222-8282, ext. 2267
lori.dimarco@tcdsb.org
Richard Francki, Superintendent, Facilities Services, 416-222-8282, ext. 2349
richard.francki@tcdsb.org
Geoffrey Grant, Superintendent, Schools - Area 8, 416-222-8282, ext. 2730
geoffrey.grant@tcdsb.org
Patrick Keyes, Superintendent, Student Success, Equity & Inclusive Education, 416-222-8282, ext. 5370
patrick.keyes@tcdsb.org
Rory McGuckin, Superintendent, Safe Schools & Parent & Community Engagement, 416-222-8282
rory.mcguckin@tcdsb.org
Michael McMorrow, Superintendent, Schools - Area 6, 416-222-8282, ext. 5371
michael.mcmorrow@tcdsb.org
Josie Nespolo, Superintendent, Schools - Area 2, 416-222-8282, ext. 2732
josephine.nespolo@tcdsb.org
Loretta Notten, Superintendent, Schools - Area 1, 416-222-8282, ext. 2732
loretta.notten@tcdsb.org
Anthony Petitti, Superintendent, Schools - Area 7, 416-222-8282, ext. 2730
anthony.petitti@tcdsb.org
Frank Piddisi, Superintendent, Special Services & Parent Engagement, 416-222-8282, ext. 2486
frank.piddisi@tcdsb.org
Gary Poole, Superintendent, Human Resources, 416-222-8282, ext. 2304
gary.poole@tcdsb.org
Vidyia Rego, Superintendent, Business Services, 416-222-8282, ext. 2257
vidyia.rego@tcdsb.org
Jim Saraco, Superintendent, Schools - Area 5, 416-222-8282, ext. 5371
jim.saraco@tcdsb.org
Doug Yack, Superintendent, Schools - Area 3, 416-222-8282, ext. 2267
douglas.yack@tcdsb.org
Barbara McMorrow, Executive Corporate Secretary & Board Liaison Officer, 416-222-8282, ext. 2080
barbara.mcmorrow@tcdsb.org
Mary Jo Dieghan, Coordinator, Communications, 416-222-8282, ext. 5314
maryjo.deighan@tcdsb.org; commdept@tcdsb.org

***Wallaceburg:* St. Clair Catholic District School Board**
Catholic Education Centre
420 Creek St., Wallaceburg, ON N8A 4C4, Canada
Tel: 519-627-6762; *Fax:* 519-627-8230
Toll-Free: 1-866-336-6139
media@st-clair.net
www.st-clair.ne
Grades: Elementary - Secondary
Number of Schools: 29 elementary schools; 3 secondary schools. Number of Employees: 1,100+
Anita Labadie, Chair, 519-360-9254
Paul Wubben, Director, Education, Chief Executive Officer, & Secretary, 519-627-6762, ext. 241
James McKenzie, Associate Director & Treasurer
Deb Crawford, Superintendent, Education
Dr. Frank Leddy, Superintendent, Education
Ann Sutton, Superintendent, Education
Steven Mitchell, Chief Information Officer
Carol Ann Bélanger, Assistant Superintendent, Catholic Curriculum
Lisa Demers, Principal, Special Education
Cindy Waddick, Leader, Elementary Chaplaincy
cindy.waddick@st-clair.net
Karen Dolson, Manager, Planning Services
Bruce Hannah, Manager, Facility Services
Amy Janssens, Manager, Financial Services
Todd Lozon, Supervisor, Communications & Community Relations, 519-627-6762, ext. 243
todd.lozon@st-clair.net

***Welland:* Niagara Catholic District School Board**
427 Rice Rd., Welland, ON L3C 7C1, Canada
Tel: 905-735-0240; *Fax:* 905-734-8828
info@ncdsb.com
www.niagararc.com
Grades: Pre-K.-12
Enrollment: 25000
John Crocco, Dir./Sec.-Treas., ext. 220
john.crocco@ncdsb.com
Kathy Burtnik, Chair

***Windsor:* Conseil scolaire de district des écoles catholiques du Sud-Ouest**
7515, promenade Forest Glade, Windsor, ON N8T 3P5, Canada
Tél: 519-948-9227; *Téléc:* 519-948-1091
Ligne sans frais: 888-768-2219
www.csdecso.on.ca
Enrollment: 1412

Janine Griffore, Directrice générale

***Windsor:* Windsor-Essex Catholic District School Board**
1325 California Ave., Windsor, ON N9B 3Y6, Canada
Tel: 519-253-2481; *Fax:* 519-253-8397
www.wecdsb.on.ca

Grades: Pre-K.-12
Enrollment: 27518
Joseph Berthiaume, Dir., ext. 1201
joseph_berthiaume@wecdsb.on.ca
Mario Iatonna, Supt. of Business, ext. 1211
mario_iatonna@wecdsb.on.ca
Fred Alexander, Chair, 519-735-8664
fred_alexander@wecdsb.on.ca

French

***North Bay:* Conseil scolaire public du Nord-Est de l'Ontario**
310, av Algonquin, North Bay, ON P1B 9T5, Canada
Tél: 705-472-3443; *Téléc:* 705-472-5757
Ligne sans frais: 888-591-5656
information@csdne.edu.on.ca
www.csdne.edu.on.ca

Enrollment: 1725
Timmins: 111, av Wilson, (705) 264-1119.
Roch Gallien, Directeur de l'éducation
Robert Poirier, Président du Conseil

***Ottawa:* Conseil des écoles publiques de l'Est de l'Ontario**
2445, boul Saint-Laurent, Ottawa, ON K1G 6C3, Canada
Tél: 613-747-3802; *Téléc:* 613-747-3810
Ligne sans frais: 888-332-3736
www.cepeo.on.ca

Rachid El Keurti, Directeur exécutif
rachid.elkeurti@cepeo.on.ca
Georges Orfal, Président du Conseil
georges.orfali@cepeo.on.ca

***Sudbury:* Conseil scolaire public Grand Nord de l'Ontario**
296, rue Van Horne, Sudbury, ON P3B 1H9, Canada
Tél: 705-671-1533; *Téléc:* 705-671-1720
Ligne sans frais: 800-465-5993
www.cspgno.ca

Enrollment: 902
Pierre Riopel, Directeur général (par intérim)
Jean-Marc Aubin, Président

***Toronto:* Conseil scolaire de district du Centre-Sud-Ouest**
116, Cornelius Pkwy., Toronto, ON M6L 2K5, Canada
Tél: 416-614-0844; *Téléc:* 416-397-2012
Ligne sans frais: 888-538-1702
www.csdcso.on.ca

Enrollment: 7700
Jean-Luc Bernard, Directeur de l'éducation
Ronald Marion, Président du Conseil

School Authorities

***Armstrong:* Northern District School Area Board**
P.O. Box 98
1 Hwy. 527, Armstrong, ON P0T 1A0, Canada
Tel: 807-583-2010; *Fax:* 807-583-2614
esip.edu.gov.on.ca/english/profiles/board_directory.asp?ID=B15245

Grades: Pre-K.-8
Enrollment: 123
Fred Porter, Supervisory Officer, 807-475-6989
fporter@resourcenorth.com
Yolanda Wanakamik, Chair

***Hornepayne:* Hornepayne Roman Catholic Separate School Board**
P.O. Box 430
200 Front St., Hornepayne, ON P0M 1Z0, Canada
Tel: 807-868-2010; *Fax:* 807-868-3026

Enrollment: 86
Julie Roy, Sec.
Carol MacEachern, Chair

***Madawaska:* Murchison & Lyell District School Area Board**
c/o G. Breshnahan, Major Lake Rd.
P.O. Box 10
Madawaska, ON K0J 2C0, Canada
Tel: 613-637-1349; *Fax:* 613-637-1349
esip.edu.gov.on.ca/english/profiles/board_directory.asp?ID=B15229

Grades: Pre-K.-8
Enrollment: 21
Elaine Hare, Vice-Chair/Trustee

***Mine Centre:* Mine Centre District Area School Board**
P.O. Box 128
Mine Centre, ON P0W 1H0, Canada
Tel: 807-599-2836; *Fax:* 807-599-2815
esip.edu.gov.on.ca/english/profiles/board_directory.asp?ID=B15172

Grades: Pre-K.-8
Enrollment: 84
Sheila McMillen, Sec.-Treas.
Genevieve Bliss, Chair

***Moose Factory:* Moose Factory Island District School Area Board**
P.O. Box 160
Moose Factory, ON P0L 1W0, Canada
Tel: 705-658-4571; *Fax:* 705-658-4768
esip.edu.gov.on.ca/english/profiles/board_directory.asp?ID=B15199

Grades: Pre-K.-8
Enrollment: 362
Brenda J. Chilton-Jeffries, Sec.-Treas.
Irene Hunter, Chair

***Moosonee:* James Bay Lowlands Secondary School Board**
P.O. Box 157
1 Keewatin Dr., Moosonee, ON P0L 1Y0, Canada
Tel: 705-336-2903; *Fax:* 705-336-0234

Enrollment: 179
Charles Faries, Adm.
Bernice Morrison, Chair

***Moosonee:* Moosonee District School Area Board**
P.O. Box 250
Moosonee, ON P0L 1Y0, Canada
Tel: 705-336-2300; *Fax:* 705-336-0334
esip.edu.gov.on.ca/english/profiles/board_directory.asp?ID=B15202

Grades: Pre-K.-8
Enrollment: 328
Barbara Faries, Sec.-Treas.
Dianne Wynne, Chair

***Moosonee:* Moosonee Roman Catholic Separate School Board**
P.O. Box 340
Moosonee, ON P0L 1Y0, Canada
Tel: 705-336-2605; *Fax:* 705-336-2881
esip.edu.gov.on.ca/english/profiles/board_directory.asp?ID=B16063

Grades: Pre-K-8
Enrollment: 109
Kathy Hallett, Supervisory Officer

***Oshawa:* Campbell Children's School Authority**
600 Towline Rd. South, Oshawa, ON L1H 7K6, Canada
Tel: 905-576-8403; *Fax:* 905-576-4414
ccs@grtc.ca

Grades: Specialized programs
Campbell Children's School serves students from the local district school boards with communication or multiple disabilities.
Lynda Schuler, Chair

***Ottawa:* Ottawa Children's Treatment Centre School Authority**
395 Smyth Rd., Ottawa, ON K2H 8L2, Canada
Tel: 613-737-0871; *Fax:* 613-523-5167

Enrollment: 23
Neil Wilson, Chair

***Parry Sound:* Parry Sound Roman Catholic Separate School Board**
#203, 60 James St., Parry Sound, ON P2A 1T5, Canada
Tel: 705-746-6231; *Fax:* 705-746-7568

Enrollment: 208
Brian McLeod, Chair

***Penetanguishene:* Penetanguishene Protestant Separate School Board**
2 Poyntz St., Penetanguishene, ON L9M 1M2, Canada
Tel: 705-549-6422; *Fax:* 705-549-2768
pssbp@bellnet.ca
www.pssb.ca

Enrollment: 261
Lynne Cousens, Chair

***Red Lake:* Red Lake Area Combined Roman Catholic Separate School Board**
P.O. Box 888
54 Discovery Rd., Red Lake, ON P0V 2M0, Canada
Tel: 807-727-3470; *Fax:* 807-727-3211

Enrollment: 119
Nora Kolmel, Secretary
Vaughan Blab, Chair

***St Catharines:* Niagara Peninsula Children's Centre School Authority**
567 Glenridge Ave., St Catharines, ON L2T 4C2, Canada
Tel: 905-688-3550; *Fax:* 905-688-1055
Toll-Free: 800-896-5496
info@npcc.on.ca
www.npcc.on.ca

Enrollment: 84
A non-profit, charitable organization aiming to provide programs and services to enable children and youth with physical or communicative challenges to maximize their independence.
Oksana Fisher, CEO
Tim Wright, Exec. Dir.

***Timmins:* Missarenda District School Area Board**
869 Denise St., Timmins, ON P6N 7M5, Canada
Tel: 705-268-6217; *Fax:* 705-268-6217
esip.edu.gov.on.ca/english/profiles/board_directory.asp?ID=B15180

Enrollment: 3
Jody Charette, Sec.
Lise Anglehart, Chair

***Toronto:* Bloorview School Authority**
150 Kilgour Rd., Toronto, ON M4G 1R8, Canada
Tel: 416-424-3831; *Fax:* 416-425-2981
school@bloorview.ca
www.bloorviewschool.ca

Bloorview School Authority provides school programs to children & youth with special needs.
Rachee Allen, Trustee
Dr. Doug Biggar, Trustee
Earl Campbell, Trustee
Mary Campbell, Trustee
Brenda Keleher, Trustee
James McCarron, Trustee
Richard Volpe, Trustee

***Waterloo:* KidsAbility School Authority Board**
500 Hallmark Dr., Waterloo, ON N2K 3P5, Canada
Tel: 519-886-8886; *Fax:* 519-885-6222
www.kidsability.ca

KidsAbility School Authority Board serves children with a wide range of special needs. Programs & services include a kindergarten program, individual education plans, composite classes, communication classes, & language classes.
Justin Heimpel, Chair
Linda Rogers, Principal & Secretary to the Board
Joanne Cotter, Secretary-Treasurer

***Windsor:* John McGivney Children's Centre School Authority**
3945 Matchette Rd., Windsor, ON N9C 4C2, Canada
Tel: 519-252-7281; *Fax:* 519-252-5873
www.jmccentre.ca

The John McGivney Children's Centre School Authority governs the John McGivney Children's Centre School, formerly known as the Children's Rehabilitation Centre School. The school provides a post trauma / post operative rehabilitation program for students from ages four to twenty-one, who live in Windsor / Essex County.
Carolyn Tavolieri, Chair
Adelina Irvine, Vice-Chair
Dr. Brenda Roberts-Santarossa, Secretary
Karen McConnell, Treasurer

First Nations

***Attawapiskat:* Attawapiskat First Nation Education Authority**
General Delivery, Attawapiskat, ON P0L 1A0, Canada
Tel: 705-997-2114; *Fax:* 705-997-2357
psinfo@afnea.com; recruit@afnea.com (Recruitment)
www.afnea.com

Grades: Junior Kindergarten-12; Special Ed.
Enrollment: 800
Number of Schools: 2 (J.R. Nakogee School & Vezina Secondary School)
John B. Nakogee, Director, Education
Andrew Hirst, Chair

Big Trout Lake: **Kitchenuhmaykoosib Education Authority**
General Delivery, Big Trout Lake, ON P0V 1G0, Canada
Tel: 807-537-2553; *Fax:* 807-537-2316
kifirstnation@knet.ca
www.bigtroutlake.firstnation.ca
Grades: Junior Kindergarten-11; Special Ed.
Enrollment: 275
Number of Schools: 1 (Aglace Chapman Education Centre).
Number of Employees: 30. The Kitchenuhmaykoosib Education Authority serves the Kitchenuhmaykoosib Inninnuwug First Nation, formerly known as Big Trout Lake First Nation, located north of Thunder Bay, Ontario. Secondary programs are also available through computer, radio, & television.

Christian Island: **Beausoleil First Nation Education Authority**
Administration Building
1 O'Gema St., Main Level, Christian Island, ON L0K 1C0, Canada
Tel: 705-247-2051; *Fax:* 705-247-2239
p.mcgregor@beausoleil-education.ca
www.beausoleil-education.ca
Grades: Junior Kindergarten - 8; Special Ed
Number of Schools: 1 (Christian Island Elementary School). The Beausoleil First Nation Education Authority serves the Chippewas of the Beausoleil First Nation by operating the Christian Island Elementary School. For secondary education, students attend high schools in the Simcoe County District School Board or the Simcoe Muskoka Catholic School Board.
Peggy McGregor, Director, Education
p.mcgregor@beausoleil-education.ca
Mike Lucas, Principal, Christian Island Elementary School
m.lucas@beausoleil-education.ca
Peter Dimoff, Manager, Human Resources
pdimoff@chimnissing.ca
Herb Connell, Coordinator, Adult Education, 705-247-2825
Karen King, Coordinator, Parental Engagement
Angela Phillips, Teacher, Special Education
Nancy Assance, Contact, Post-Secondary Student Assistance Program
n.assance@beausoleil-education.ca

Constance Lake: **Constance Lake First Nation Education Authority**
P.O. Box 4000
Constance Lake, ON P0L 1B0, Canada
Tel: 705-463-4511; *Fax:* 705-463-2222
www.clfn.on.ca
Grades: Daycare - JK - 12; Adult Education
Enrollment: 257
Number of Schools: 1 (Mamawmatawa Holistic Education Center). Located in the District of Cochrane, the Constance Lake First Nation Education Authority provides education to community members of Cree & Ojibway ancestry. The Constance Lake First Nation Education Authority is supported by the Matawa Education Department in Thunder Bay, Ontario.
Ronnie Martin, President, Board of Diretors
Ron Wesley, Councillor (Education, Day care, Finance, & Administration)
Ken Neegan, Administrator, Education
Veronica Ramadan, Manager, Finance
Lizzie Sutherland, Librarian & Secretary

Cornwall: **Ahkwesahsne Mohawk Board of Education**
P.O. Box 819
169 International Rd., Cornwall, ON K6H 5T7, Canada
Tel: 613-933-0409; *Fax:* 613-933-9262
www.akwesasne.ca
Grades: Pre-Kindergarten-8; Alternative Ed.
The Ahkwesahsne Mohawk Board of Education operates three elementary schools. Since the Ahkwesahsne Mohawk Board of Education does not have a secondary school, there is an agreement with the Upper Canada Public School Board to provide secondary education.
Barry M. Montour, Director, Education, 613-933-0409
bmontour@akwesasne.ca
Deborah Terrance, Associate Director
Lillian Macias, Coordinator, Curriculum, 613-933-3366
Val Mitchell, Coordinator, Alternative Education Program, 613-575-1969
Sandra Rourke, Coordinator, Student Services
Norma Sunday, Coordinator, Post Secondary Program
Alice King, Supervisor, Head Start Program
Dwayne Thomas, Supervisor, Transportation
Gerald Thompson, Supervisor, Operation & Maintenance
Anneke Fischer-Fey, Psychometrist, 613-932-3366

Deer Lake: **Deer Lake Education Authority**
P.O. Box 69
Deer Lake, ON P0V 1N0
Tel: 807-775-2055; *Fax:* 807-751-9225
www.deerlake.firstnation.ca
TTY: 1-888-751-9225
Grades: K4 - K5; 1 - 9; Special Education
Number of Schools: 1 (Deer Lake School). The Deer Lake Education Authority oversees education for the Deer Lake First Nation, an Oji-Cree community situated about 180 kilometres north of Red Lake, Ontario. Deer Lake School provides education to grade nine. The Authority coordinates the enrollment & boarding for students who leave the reserve for schooling beyond ninth grade, in places such as Ear Falls, Sioux Lookout, Red Lake, Thunder Bay, & Winnipeg.
Leonard Mamakeesic, Director, Education

Dinorwic: **Wabigoon Lake Ojibway Nation Education Authority**
P.O. Box 24
Site 112, Dinorwic, ON P0V 1P0, Canada
Tel: 807-938-6684; *Fax:* 807-938-1166
Grades: Junior Kindergarten - 8
Number of Schools: 1 (Wabsnki-Penasi School). Elementary education is provided in a school operated by the Wabigoon Lake Ojibway Nation. Secondary school students are bused to nearby Dryden, Ontario.

Eabamet Lake: **Eabametoong (Fort Hope) First Nation Education Authority**
P.O. Box 294
Eabamet Lake, ON P0T 1L0, Canada
Tel: 807-242-1305; *Fax:* 807-242-1313
efnea64@gmail.com
www.eabametoong.firstnation.ca
Other Information: Education Coordinator, Phone: 807-242-1305, ext. 24
Grades: Kindergarten - 10; Special Ed.
Enrollment: 380
Number of Schools: 1 (John C. Yesno Education Centre).
Number of Employees: 25 teachers; 10 teaching assistants & tutor escorts; 3 counsellors. Eabametoong (Fort Hope) is a fly-in Ojibwe First Nations community located approximately 360 kilometres northeast of Thunder Bay, Ontario. The Eabametoong (Fort Hope) First Nation Education Authority consists of a Board of Directors & a head office staff. The Matawa Education Department in Thunder, Bay, Ontario supports the education authority.
Sharon Allan, Education Coordinator, Eabametoong First Nation
sharon-nate@hotmail.com

Eagle River: **Migisi Sah Gai Gun Education Authority**
P.O. Box 10
Eagle River, ON P0V 1S0, Canada
Tel: 807-755-5350; *Fax:* 807-755-5696
Grades: Elem.
Enrollment: 44
Leonard Gardner, Dir.

Fort Albany: **Mundo Peetabeck Education Authority**
P.O. Box 31
Fort Albany, ON P0L 1H0, Canada
Tel: 705-278-3390; *Fax:* 705-278-1049
www.onlink.net/~stannes/staff/
Grades: Elem.
Enrollment: 150
Daniel Metatawabin, Administrator

Fort Severn: **Wasaho Education Authority**
General Delivery, Fort Severn, ON P0V 1W0, Canada
Tel: 807-478-9548; *Fax:* 807-478-2573
Enrollment: 120
Number of Schools: 1. The Wasaho Education Authority provides education to members of the Fort Severn First Nation. The Fort Severn First Nation Reserve is situated in northern Ontario, near the mouth of the Severn River.

Heron Bay: **Pic River First Nation Education Authority**
General Delivery, Heron Bay, ON P0T 1R0, Canada
Tel: 807-229-1749; *Fax:* 807-229-1944
Grades: Elem.
Enrollment: 94
Cindy Fisher, Dir.

Kasabonika: **Sineonokway Education Authority**
P.O. Box 102
Kasabonika, ON P0V 1Y0, Canada
Tel: 807-535-1117; *Fax:* 807-535-1152
Grades: Elem.
Enrollment: 250
Ida Morris, Chair
Josie Semple, Dir.

Kashechewan: **Hishkoonikun Education Authority**
P.O. Box 235
Kashechewan, ON P0L 1S0, Canada
Tel: 705-275-4538; *Fax:* 705-275-4515
Grades: Elem.
Enrollment: 500
Jonathan Solomon, Dir.
Elkina Hughie, Chair

Keewaywin: **Keewaywin Education Authority**
General Delivery, Keewaywin, ON P0V 3G0, Canada
Tel: 807-771-1125; *Fax:* 807-774-1067
Enrollment: 78
Lorraine Kakegamic, Dir.

Kejick: **Shoal Lake Chief & Council: Education Authority**
General Delivery, Kejick, ON P0X 1E0, Canada
Tel: 807-733-2315; *Fax:* 807-733-3115
Grades: Elem.
Enrollment: 50
Kelvin Redsky, Administrator

Kenora: **Northwest Angle #33 Education Authority**
P.O. Box 1490
Kenora, ON P9N 3X7, Canada
Tel: 807-733-2200; *Fax:* 807-733-3148
Grades: Elem.
Enrollment: 16
Josephine Sandy, Education Counsellor

Kingfisher: **Kingfisher Lake Education Authority**
General Delivery, Kingfisher, ON P0V 1Z0, Canada
Tel: 807-532-2067; *Fax:* 807-532-2153
Grades: Elem.
Enrollment: 100
Solomon Mamakwa, Dir.

Lac Seul: **Obishikokaang Education Authority**
General Delivery, Lac Seul, ON P0V 2A0, Canada
Tel: 807-582-3420; *Fax:* 807-582-3430
Grades: Elem./Sec.
Enrollment: 97
Karen Ningewance, Chair
Richard Morris, Dir.

Longlac: **Long Lake #58 & Ginoogaming First Nations Education Authority**
P.O. Box 89
Longlac, ON P0T 2A0
Tel: 807-876-4914
Grades: JK-12; Special Ed; Ojibway language
Enrollment: 173
Number of Schools: 2 (Migizsi Wazisin Elementary School & Nimiki Migizsi Secondary School). Number of Employees: 24 teachers, board administrative personnel, support staff, & custodial personnel. The Long Lake #58 & Ginoogaming First Nations Education Authority consists of three board members from Long Lake #58 First Nation & three board members from Ginoogaming First Nation (formerly the Long Lake #77 First Nation). Both First Nations are members of Matawa First Nations, so that educational support services for the Long Lake #58 & Ginoogaming First Nations Education Authority are provided by the Matawa Education Department in Thunder Bay, Ontario.
Claire Onabigon, Director, Education, 807-876-1270
conabigo@lakeheadu.ca
Fred Simoniatis, Principal

M'Chigeeng: **West Bay Board of Education**
P.O. Box 297
M'Chigeeng, ON P0P 1J0, Canada
Tel: 705-377-5611; *Fax:* 705-377-5080
Grades: Elem.
Enrollment: 180
Melvina Corbiere, Education Coordinator

MacDiarmid: **Rocky Bay First Nation Education Authority**
71 Macdonald Ave., MacDiarmid, ON P0T 2B0, Canada
Tel: 807-885-3401; *Fax:* 807-885-3266
Grades: Elem.
Enrollment: 41

Morson: **Big Grassy River (Mishkosiimiiniiziibig) Education Authority**
P.O. Box 453
Beach Rd., Morson, ON P0W 1J0, Canada
Tel: 807-488-5916; *Fax:* 807-488-5345
bgschool@bgfn.onca
www.bgfn.on.ca

Grades: Jr. Kindergarten - 8; Special Ed.
Enrollment: 61
Number of Schools: 1 (Pegamigaabo Elementary School)

Muncey: Chippewas of the Thames First Nation Board of Education
330 Chippewa Rd., Muncey, ON N0L 1Y0, Canada
Tel: 519-289-0621; *Fax:* 519-289-0633
www.chippewa-ed.on.ca

Grades: Elementary
Number of Schools: 1 elementary school (Antler River Elementary School)
Kristin Hendrick, Council Liaison
Joanne Henry, Coordinator, Eucation Administration
joann.henry@chippewa-ed.on.ca
Jody Joseph, Contact, Post-Secondary Program & Guidance, 519-289-0621, fax: 519-289-0633
postsecondary@chippewa-ed.on.ca
Starr McGahey-Albert, Contact, Education Finance
postsecondary@chippewa-ed.on.ca

Muskrat Dam: Muskrat Dam First Nation Education Authority
P.O. Box 140
Muskrat Dam, ON P0V 3B0, Canada
Tel: 807-471-2524; *Fax:* 807-471-2649
Other Information: Whasa Distant Education Centre, Phone: 807-471-2619

Grades: Junior Kindergarten - 8
Number of Schools: 1 (Samson Beardy Memorial School). The Muskrat Dam First Nation community is situated approximately 370 kilometres north of Sioux Lookout. Oji-Cee & English are spoken. The community features an elementary school, plus the Wahsa Distance Education Centre to support secondary & post-secondary students attending schools in towns & cities.
Vernon Morris, Chief, Muskrat Dam First Nation

New Osnaburgh: Mishkeegogamang Education Authority
General Delivery, New Osnaburgh, ON P0V 2H1, Canada
Tel: 807-928-2137; *Fax:* 807-928-2077

Grades: Elem./Sec.; 3 schools
Enrollment: 255
Ida Mackuck, Education Coordinator
Isabe Skunk, Secretary

North Spirit Lake: North Spirit Lake Education Authority
General Delivery, North Spirit Lake, ON P0V 2G0, Canada
Tel: 807-776-0001; *Fax:* 807-776-0003

Grades: Elem.
Enrollment: 50
Luke Rae, Dir.

Ogoki Post: Marten Falls (Ogoki) First Nation Education Authority
Education Administration Office
General Delivery, Ogoki Post, ON P0T 2L0, Canada
Tel: 807-349-2628; *Fax:* 807-349-2511

Grades: Kindergarten - 8
Number of Schools: 1 (Henry Coaster Memorial School). The Marten Falls (Ogoki) First Nation Education Authority offers elementary education in the Cree-Ojibwe community. Members of the First Nation board in Thunder Bay, Ontario to attend secondary school. The Matawa Education Department provides educational support services to the Marten Falls (Ogoki) First Nation Education Authority.
Maria Baxter, Education Administrator, 807-349-2509, fax: 807-349-2602
maria.baxter@martenfallsfn.ca

Pawitik: Whitefish Bay: Northwest Angle Education Authority
General Delivery, Pawitik, ON P0X 1L0, Canada
Tel: 807-226-5710; *Fax:* 807-226-1066

Grades: Elem./Sec.
Enrollment: 300
Isobel White, Dir.

Peawanuck: Weenusk First Nation Education Services
P.O. Box 2
Peawanuck, ON P0L 2H0, Canada
Tel: 705-473-2527; *Fax:* 705-473-2528

Grades: Elem.
Enrollment: 60
Abraham Hunter Sr., Chair
George Hunter, Dir.

Pikangikum: Pikangikum Education Authority
c/o Eenchokay Birchstick School
General Delivery, Pikangikum, ON P0V 2L0, Canada
Tel: 807-773-1093; *Fax:* 807-773-1014
http://forcedata.net/pea/

Grades: Elem./Sec.
Enrollment: 750
Charlie Pascal, Dir.
George Suggashie, Chair

Rama: Mnjikaning First Nation Education Authority
#200, 5884 Rama Rd., Rama, ON L0K 1T0, Canada
Tel: 705-325-3611; *Fax:* 705-327-7029

Enrollment: 126
Tracey Sharpe, Manager
Myrna Watson, Manager

Sandy Lake: Sandy Lake Board of Education
P.O. Box 8
Sandy Lake, ON P0V 1V0, Canada
Tel: 807-774-1135; *Fax:* 807-774-1166
www.sandylake.firstnation.ca

Grades: Kindergarten - 10; Adult Ed.
Enrollment: 514
Number of Schools: 3 (Thomas Fiddler Memorial Elementary School; Thomas Fiddler Memorial High School; Gabbius Goodman Memorial Adult Learning Centre). The Sandy Lake Board of Education oversees the management of schools which serve students of Sandy Lake First Nation.
Christina Meekis, Director, Education
Troy Kakepetum, Assistant Director, Education
Russell Kakepetum, Band Councillor, Education Portfolio
Florance Ballentyne, Officer, Finance

Sarnia: Aamjiwnaang First Nation Education Administration
978 Tashmoo Ave., Sarnia, ON N7T 7H5, Canada
Tel: 519-336-8410; *Fax:* 519-336-0382
www.aamjiwnaang.ca

Formerly Chippewas of Sarnia, the community of Aamjiwnaang First Nation is located in the city limits of Sarnia, Ontario.
Jodi Branton, Coordinator, Education Services, 519-336-0382, ext. 247
Diane Aiken, Assistant, Education Services, 519-336-0382, ext. 246

Sioux Lookout: Sioux Lookout Education Authority
P.O. Box 1118
Sioux Lookout, ON P8T 1B7, Canada
Tel: 807-727-1488; *Fax:* 807-737-1732

Enrollment: 600
Dennis Nestrovich, Dir.

Sioux Lookout: Windigo Education Authority
P.O. Box 299
Sioux Lookout, ON P8T 1A3, Canada
Tel: 807-737-1064; *Fax:* 807-737-3452
wea@windigo.on.ca
www.windigoeducation.on.ca

Grades: JK-8; Aboriginal language & culture
Enrollment: 445
Number of Schools: 4 (Michikan Lake School; Titotay Memorial School; Martin McKay Memorial School; & Bimaychikamah School). Windigo Education Authority consists of the following First Nation members: Bearskin Lake First Nation, Cat Lake First Nation, Sachigo Lake First Nation, & Slate Falls Nation. The language of each First Nation community is Ojibway or Oji-Cree.
Lana Bighead, Education Coordinator, Bimaychikamah School, 807-737-5701, fax: 807-347-1299
James Chapman, Education Coordinator, Martin McKay Memorial School, 807-595-2527, fax: 807-595-1119
Vince Ostberg, Education Coordinator, Michikan Lake School, 807-363-1011, fax: 807-363-2519
Marie Stewart, Education Coordinator, Titotay Memorial School, 807-347-2102, fax: 807-347-2057

Sioux Narrows: Northwest Angle #37 Education Authority
P.O. Box 267
Sioux Narrows, ON P0X 1N0, Canada
Tel: 807-733-3284; *Fax:* 807-226-1164

Southwold: Onyota'a:ka Kalthuny Nihtsla Tehatilihutakwas (OKT) Education Authority
RR#2, Southwold, ON N0L 2G0, Canada
Tel: 519-652-1580; *Fax:* 519-652-3219

Grades: Elem.
Enrollment: 185
Neil Cornelius, Chair
Lynda Doxtator, Education Adm.

Thunder Bay: Matawa Education Department
c/o Matawa First Nations Management
233 South Court St., Thunder Bay, ON P7B 2X9, Canada
Tel: 807-344-4575; *Fax:* 807-344-2977
Toll-Free: 1-800-463-2249
learningcentre@matawa.on.ca
www.education.matawa.on.ca

Grades: JK - Secondary; Adult Education
Number of Schools: 9 (Johnny Therriault School, Aroland First Nation; Mamawmatawa Holistic Education Centre, Constance Lake First Nation; John C. Yesno Education Centre, Eabametoong First Nation; Nibinamik Education Centre, Nibinamik First Nation; Migizi Wazisin Elementary School, Long Lake #58 First Nation; Henry Coaster Memorial School, Marten Falls First Nation; Nimiki Migizi Secondary School, Ginoogaming First Nation; Neskantaga Education Centre, Neskantaga First Nation; & Simon Jacob Memorial Education Centre, Webequie First Nation). The Matawa Education Department delivers educational support services to local education authorities. Education is provided at local Matawa First Nation schools in a culturally appropriate environment to meet the diverse needs of students. Post-secondary student support services, as well as alternative learning & adult education & training are also offered.
Murray L. Wavoose, Manager, Education Department
mwaboose@matawa.on.ca
Georgette O'Nabigon, Coordinator, Post Secondary Program
gonabigon@matawa.on.ca
Steve Chase, Developer, E-Learning
schase@matawa.on.ca

Tyendinaga Mohawk Territory: Tyendinaga Mohawk Education, Culture, & Language Department
Administration Building
13 Old York Rd., Tyendinaga Mohawk Territory, ON K0K 1X0, Canada
Tel: 613-396-3424; *Fax:* 613-396-3627

Educational programs available for the Mohawks of the Bay of Quinte include the Eksa'okon:'a Child Care Centre, the Tahatikonhsotontie Head Start Program, a Post-Secondary Education Program, a Native Student Liaison Program, an Employment & Training Program, the Ka:nhiote Public Library, & Mohawk Bus Lines. Mohawk language & cultural instruction is part of Tahatikonhsotontie Head Start, an early childhood education program.
Tracey Gazley, Manager, Tahatikonhsotontie Head Start Program, 613-396-6716
traceyg@mbq-tmt.org
Cheryl Lavigne, Manager, Day Care (Eksa'okon:'a Child Care Centre), 613-967-4401
daycare@tyendinaga.net
Bruce Maracle, Manager, Mohawk Bus Lines, 613-396-2000
Karen Lewis, Librarian, Ka:nhiote Public Library, 613-967-6264
karenl@tyendinaga.net
Patti Brinklow, Coordinator, Post-Secondary Education, 613-396-3424, ext. 119
pattig@mbq-tmt.org
Betty Maracle, Teacher, Culture, 613-396-6716
bettym@mbq-tmt.org
Melissa Maracle, Teacher, Mohawk Language
Sandra Sero, Counsellor, Employment & Training Program, 613-968-1122, ext. 141
sandys@mbq-tmt.org

Wallaceburg: Walpole Island Elementary School
RR#3, Wallaceburg, ON N8A 4K9, Canada
Tel: 519-627-0712; *Fax:* 519-627-8596

Grades: Junior Kindergarten - 8
The Walpole Island Elementary School is a First Nation operated school which serves members of the Walpole Island First Nation community. School employees are required to have knowledge & understanding of the Anishinaabeg culture. The education program is administered by the Walpole Island First Nation Board of Education. For secondary education, students from Walpole Island First Nation are transported to the nearby communities of Sarnia, Chatham, & Wallaceburg.

Wallaceburg: Walpole Island First Nation Board of Education
RR#3, Wallaceburg, ON N8A 4K9
Tel: 519-627-1481; *Fax:* 519-627-0440

Grades: Junior Kindergarten - 8
Number of Schools: 1 (Walpole Island Elementary School). Secondary school students from the Walpole Island First Nation community are transported to Chatham, Sarnia, & Wallaceburg to attend school.
Joseph Gilbert, Chief
Bill Tooshkenig, Chair
Cynthia Williams, Officer, Human Resources
cynthia.williams@wifn.org

***Weagamow Lake:* North Caribou Lake First Nation Education Office**
P.O. Box 155
Weagamow Lake, ON P0V 2Y0, Canada
Tel: 807-469-1222; *Fax:* 807-469-1351
Grades: Elem.
Enrollment: 136
Saul Williams, Dir.

***Webequie:* Webequie First Nation Education Authority**
P.O. Box 102
Webequie, ON P0T 3A0
Tel: 807-353-9942; *Fax:* 807-353-9966
webequieeducation@knet.ca
info@webequie.ca
Grades: K-10; Native Language; Special Ed.
Enrollment: 200
Number of Schools: 1 (Simon Jacob Memorial Education Centre). The Webequie First Nation Education Authority is located in a Oji-Cree community on the Winisk River in northern Ontario. The education authority receives educational support services from the Matawa Education Department in Thunder Bay, Ontario. Programs include special education, native education, distance education, & post-secondary education support services.
Ennis Jacob, Director, Education
ennisjacob@hotmail.com
Paul Quisses, Administrator, Finance

***Whitedog:* Wabaseemoong Education Authority**
General Delivery, Whitedog, ON P0X 1P0, Canada
Tel: 807-927-2062; *Fax:* 807-927-2176
Grades: JK - 12; Cultural activities
Enrollment: 300
Number of Schools: 1 (Wabaseemoong School). The Wabaseemoong Education Authority oversees education in the Wabaseemoong First Nation community located approximately 100 kilometres northwest of Kenora, Ontario.

***Wiarton:* Chippewas of Nawash Unceded First Nation Board of Education**
6 Harbour Rd., RR#5, Cape Croker Reserve, Wiarton, ON N0H 2T0, Canada
Tel: 519-534-0882; *Fax:* 519-534-5138
cnbdofed@bmts.com
www.nawash.ca
Number of Schools: 1. The board of education serves the Chippewas of Nawash Unceded First Nation band members of the Neyaashiinigmiing Indian Reserve No. 27. The reserve is situated on the eastern shore of the Saugeen (Bruce) Peninsula in Ontario, approximately 26 kilometres from Wiarton. The Chippewas of Nawash Unceded First Nation Board of Education strives to offer a culturally & community based education, based upon traditional values.
Pamela J. Keeshig, Chair & Curriculum & Program Development Portfolio Holder
Judy Nadjiwan, Education Administrator, 519-534-0882
nawashed.administrator@gbtel.ca
Jennifer Linklater, Coordinator, Nawash Post-Secondary Education Program
nawashed.postsec@gbtel.ca
Lisa Pedoniquotte, Education Counsellor, Secondary Student Services Program
nawashed.edcounsellor@gbtel.ca
Vanessa M. Keeshig, Contact, Administrative Support
nawashed.vkeeshig@gbtel.ca

***Wikwemikong:* Wikwemikong Board of Education**
P.O. Box 112
34 Henry St, Wikwemikong, ON P0P 2J0, Canada
Tel: 705-859-3864; *Fax:* 705-859-3787
speltier@wiky.net
Grades: Elem./Sec.; 3 schools
Enrollment: 486
Margaret Manitowabi, Chair
Sara Peltier, Dir.

***Wunnummin Lake:* Wunnumin Lake Education Authority**
P.O. Box 105
Wunnummin Lake, ON P0V 2Z0, Canada
Tel: 807-442-2559; *Fax:* 807-442-2627
Grades: Elem.
Enrollment: 146
Samuel Mamokwa, Chair
Matthew Angees, Dir.

Schools: Specialized

First Nations

Neskantaga First Nation Education Centre
P.O. Box 106
Lansdowne House,, ON P0T 1Z0
Tel: 807-479-1170; *Fax:* 807-479-1178
www.education.matawa.on.ca
Grades: JK - 9; Native culture & language
The Neskantaga First Nation Education Centre is situated in a community approximately 180 kilometres north of Pickle Lake in northern Ontario. The elementary school is a Matawa First Nations community school which receives educational support services from the Matawa Education Department.
Tony Sakanee, Member, Matawa Regional Committee on Education
tonysakanee@hotmail.com

***Aroland:* Johnny Therriault Memorial School**
c/o Aroland First Nation
General Delivery, Aroland, ON P0T 1B0
Tel: 807-329-5470; *Fax:* 807-329-5472
www.education.matawa.on.ca
Grades: Junior Kindergarten - 9
Enrollment: 120
The Johnny Therriault School serves the Aroland First Nation School, which is located approximately 350 kilometres northeast of Thunder Bay, Ontario. The school is supported by the Matawa Education Department. Tuition agreements are in place with the Superior-Greenstone District School Board, so that Aroland First Nation students can attend grades 10 to 12 in the communities of Nakina & Geraldton.
Sam Kashkeesh, Chief, Aroland First Nation
Patricia Magiskan, Member, Matawa Regional Committee on Education
Stephanie Ash, Communications Officer, Aroland First Nation, 807-767-4443

***Attawapiskat:* J.R. Nakogee Elementary School Also known as: Attawapiskat First Nation Elementary**
P.O. Box 15
Attawapiskat, ON P0L 1A0
Tel: 705-997-2114; *Fax:* 705-997-1259
www.afnea.com
Grades: Junior Kindergarten - 8; Special Ed
J.R. Nakogee Elementary School is located in the Ontario Cree fly-in only community of Attawapiskat. It is part of the Attawapiskat First Nation Education Authority.

***Attawapiskat:* Vezina Secondary School**
P.O. Box 219
Attawapiskat, ON P0L 1A0
Tel: 705-997-2117; *Fax:* 705-997-2357
www.afnea.com
Grades: 9 - 12
Attawapiskat First Nation Education Authority operates the high school on the west coast of James Bay.

***Bearskin Lake:* Michikan Lake School**
General Delivery, Bearskin Lake, ON P0V 1E0
www.windigoeducation.on.ca
Grades: JK-8; Aboriginal language & culture
Enrollment: 140
Operations of the Michikan Lake School are overseen by the Windigo Education Authority. The school provides elementary education to young people of the Bearskin Lake First Nation. The First Nation community is located about 425 kilometres north of Sioux Lookout, Ontario.
Nona Sinclair, Principal, 807-363-2570, fax: 807-363-1078

***Big Trout Lake:* Aglace Chapman Education Centre**
P.O. Box 168
Big Trout Lake, ON P0V 1G0, Canada
Tel: 807-537-2264; *Fax:* 807-537-1067
kifirstnation@knet.ca
www.aglacechapmaneducationcentre.myknet.org
Grades: Junior Kindergarten-11; Special Ed.
Enrollment: 275
The Kitchenuhmaykoosib Education Authority oversees operations of the Aglace Chapman Education Centre. The centre is located about 270 air miles north of Sioux Lookout, Ontario, where it provides education to the Kitchenuhmaykoosib Inninnuwug First Nation.

***Brantford:* Six Nations of the Grand River**
Indian & Northern Affairs
P.O. Box 1960
Brantford, ON N3T 5W5, Canada
Tel: 519-758-2405; *Fax:* 519-754-0639
Grades: Elem.; 5 schools
Enrollment: 1328
Kathy Knott

***Cat Lake:* Titotay Memorial School**
P.O. Box 80
Cat Lake, ON P0V 1J0
Tel: 807-347-2102; *Fax:* 807-347-2057
www.titotayschool.myknet.org; www.windigoeducation.on.ca
Grades: JK-8; Aboriginal language & culture
Enrollment: 135
The Titotay Memorial School is one of four schools within the Windigo Education Authority. The First Nation School provides elementary education to members of the Cat Lake First Nation. The school is situated about 180 kilometres north of Sioux Lookout, Ontario.
Ruby Keesiquayash, Principal, 807-347-2102, fax: 807-347-2057

***Christian Island:* Christian Island Elementary School**
67 Kate Kegwin St., Christian Island, ON L0K 1C0
Tel: 705-247-2011
l.monague@beausoleil-education.ca
ASSISTANT)
WWW.BEAUSOLEIL-EDUCATION.CA
Grades: Junior Kindergarten - 8; Special Ed
Under the Beausoleil First Nation Education Authority, the Christian Island Elementary School provides education to the Chippewas of the Beausoleil First Nation.
Mike Lucas, Principal
m.lucas@beausoleil-education.ca
Sylvia Norton-Sutherland, Native Student Advisor

***Constance Lake:* Mamawmatawa Holistic Education Center**
P.O. Box 4000
Constance Lake, ON P0L 1B0
Tel: 705-463-1199; *Fax:* 705-463-2077
www.clfn.on.ca
Grades: Daycare - JK - 12; Adult Education
Enrollment: 257
The Mamawmatawa Holistic Education Center educates members of the Constance Lake First Nation, who live west of Hearst, Ontario. The school operates under the direction of the Constance Lake First Nation Education Authority.
Zandra Bear-Lowen, Principal
Karen Wesley, Administrator, Daycare
Pamela Dalcourt, Teacher, Literacy Resources
Judy Hewitt, Teacher, Special Education
Florrie Sutherland, Teacher, Native Language
Vivian Bird, Counsellor, Attendance & Guidance
Linda Chum, Counsellor, Child & Youth
Leo Grezla, Counsellor, Guidance
Susan Sutherland, Contact, Adult Education, ILC, & Co-op

***Deer Lake:* Deer Lake School**
P.O. Box 69
Deer Lake, ON P0V 1N0, Canada
Tel: 807-775-2055; *Fax:* 807-775-2148
Toll-Free: 1-888-751-9225
www.dls.firstnationschools.ca
Grades: K4 - K5; 1 - 9; Special Education
The Deer Lake School also offers native language instruction.
Leonard Mamakeesic, Director, Education
Elizabeth Rae, Finance Officer
Loretta Cameron, Teacher, Special Education
Victoria Meekis, Senior Instructor, Native Language

***Dinorwic:* Wabsnki-Penasi School**
P.O. Box 24
Site 112, Dinorwic, ON P0V 1P0
Tel: 807-938-6684; *Fax:* 807-938-1166
Grades: Junior Kindergarten - 8
The First Nation elementary school is part of the Wabigoon Lake Ojibway Nation Education Authority. For secondary school education, students are transported thirty kilometres west to Dryden, Ontario.

***Fort Hope:* John C. Yesno Education Centre**
P.O. Box 297
Fort Hope, ON P0T 1L0, Canada
Tel: 807-242-8421; *Fax:* 807-242-1592
Grades: Kindergarten - 10; Special Ed.
Enrollment: 380
The John C. Yesno Education Centre serves the Eabametoong First Nation. The Ojibwe First Nations community is located on the north shore of northern Ontario's Eabamet Lake. Eabametoong First Nation students, continuing their education beyond tenth grade, attend schools in Thunder Bay, Sault Ste. Marie, & Sioux Lookout.

***Fort Severn:* Wasaho First Nations School**
P.O. Box 165
Fort Severn, ON P0V 1W0
Tel: 807-478-9548; *Fax:* 807-478-2573

Enrollment: 120
The Wasaho First Nations School is part of the Wasaho Education Authority. The school serves members of the Fort Severn First Nation in northern Ontario.

Longlac: **Migizi Wazisin Elementary School**
P.O. Box 240
Martin Rd., Longlac, ON P0T 2A0
Tel: 807-876-4482; *Fax:* 807-876-4128
www.education.matawa.on.ca
Grades: JK - 7; Special Ed; Native language
The Migizi Wazisin Elementary School is located in Long Lake #58 First Nation, an Anishinaabe (Ojibway) First Nation near Geraldton, Ontario. It serves students from both the Long Lake #58 First Nation & the Ginoogaming First Nation. Operations of the elementary school are administered by the Long Lake #58 & Ginoogaming First Nations Education Authority.

Longlac: **Nimiki Migizi Secondary School**
P.O. Box 360
100 Balsam St., Longlac, ON P0T 2A0
Tel: 807-876-1270; *Fax:* 807-876-4151
www.education.matawa.on.ca; www.ginoogaming.ca
Grades: 8 - 12; Ojibway language
The Nimiki Migizi Secondary School is located in the Ginoogaming First Nation, which is an Anishnawbe (Ojibway) First Nation near Geraldton, Ontario. The high school serves students from both the Ginoogaming First Nation & Long Lake #58 First Nation. Nimiki Migizi Secondary School operates with support from the Long Lake #58 & Ginoogaming First Nations Education Authority.

Muskrat Dam: **Samson Beardy Memorial School**
P.O. Box 43
Muskrat Dam, ON P0V 3B0
Tel: 807-471-2524; *Fax:* 807-471-2649
Grades: Junior Kindergarten - 8
The Samson Beardy Memorial School is a First Nation operated school administered by the Muskrat Dam First Nation Education Authority. Secondary & post-secondary students attend schools outside the remote First Nation community.

Nordegg: **Ta Otha Community School**
P.O. Box 39
Nordegg, ON T0M 2H0
Tel: 403-721-3989; *Fax:* 403-721-2174
www.stoney-nation.com
The Ta Otha School is part of the Stoney Education Authority. The school serves members of the Stoney Nakoda First Nation.

Ogoki Post: **Henry Coaster Memorial School**
General Delivery, Ogoki Post, ON P0T 2L0
Tel: 807-349-2509; *Fax:* 807-349-2511
maria.baxter@martenfallsfn.ca (Education Administrator)
www.education.matawa.on.ca
Grades: Junior Kindergarten - 8
Enrollment: 90
Henry Coaster Memorial School is located in Marten Falls Nation, on the north side of the Albany River in northern Ontario. The First Nation school offers traditional culture & language programming. The elementary school operates with support from the Marten Falls (Ogoki) First Nation Education Authority.

Sachigo Lake: **Martin McKay Memorial School**
General Delivery, Sachigo Lake, ON P0V 2P0, Canada
www.windigoeducation.on.ca
Grades: JK-8; Aboriginal language & culture
Enrollment: 115
The Martin McKay Memorial School serves students of the Sachigo Lake First Nation. The First Nation community is situated approximately 150 kilometres west of Big Trout Lake, Ontario. Activities of the Sachigo Lake First Nation school are administerd by the Windigo Education Authority.
Doug St. Laurent, Principal, 807-595-2526, fax: 807-595-1305

Sarnia: **Aamjiwnaang Junior Kindergarten (Aamjiwnaang Binoojiinyag Kino Maagewgamgoon**
1900 Virgil Ave., Sarnia, ON N7T 8A7
Tel: 519-344-4132; *Fax:* 519-344-6956
Grades: Junior Kindergarten
Under the Aamjiwnaang First Nation Education Administration, education is offered to members of the Aamjiwnaang First Nation.
Kim Henry, Principal
Muriel Joseph-Plain, Supervisor, 519-344-5831

Slate Falls: **Bimaychikamah School**
General Delivery, Slate Falls, ON P0V 3C0
Grades: JK-8; Aboriginal language & culture
Enrollment: 55
Education for members of the Slate Falls Nation is provided by the Bimaychikamah School. The elementary school is situated in the Slate Falls Nation community north of Sioux Lookout, Ontario. Operations of Bimaychikamah School are overseen by the Windigo Education Authority.
Mary Anne Ketchemonia, Principal, 807-737-5701, fax: 807-347-1299

Summer Beaver: **Nibinamik First Nation Education Centre**
General Delivery, Summer Beaver, ON P0T 3B0
Tel: 807-593-2195; *Fax:* 807-593-2198
www.education.matawa.on.ca
Grades: JK - 10; Native Language
The Nibinamik First Nation Education Centre is a Matawa First Nations community school which receives educational support services from the Matawa Education Department. The Nibinamik First Nation is located approximately 185 kilometres northwest of Pickle Lake in northern Ontario.

Whitedog: **Wabaseenmoong School**
General Delivery, Whitedog, ON P0X 1P0, Canada
Tel: 807-927-2062; *Fax:* 807-927-2176
Grades: JK - 12; Alternative Education
Enrollment: 300
Elementary & secondary education is provided to Wabaseemoong First Nation students living in a community situated about 100 kilometres northwest of Kenora, Ontario. The school focuses upon academics as well as cultural education. School activities are overseen by the Wabaseemoong Education Authority.
Ron R. McDonald, Principal, 807-927-2000, ext. 264

Wiarton: **Cape Croker Elementary School**
Also known as: Chippewas of Nawash Elementary School
17 School Rd., RR#5, Wiarton, ON N0H 2T0
Tel: 519-534-0719; *Fax:* 519-534-1592
ccfnes@bmts.com
www.nawash.ca
Grades: Pre-Kindergarten - 8
Part of the Chippewas of Nawash Unceded First Nation Board of Education, the Cape Croker Elementary School provides a culturally-based education, which includes the history of the Anishnabek, band sovereignty, & communication & language arts in Anishinaabemowin & English.
Judy Nadjiwan, Education Administrator, Board of Education, 519-534-0882
nawashed.administrator@gbtel.ca
Debra Chegahno, Prinicpal, Cape Croker Elementary School, 519-534-0719, fax: 519-534-1592
nawashed.principal@gbtel.ca
Juanita Pheasant, Ojibway Language Resource Teacher

Hearing Impaired

Belleville: **The Sir James Whitney School**
350 Dundas St. West, Belleville, ON K8P 1B2, Canada
Tel: 613-967-2823; *Fax:* 613-967-2841
Lauraine Milligan

Brantford: **The W. Ross Macdonald School**
350 Brant Ave., Brantford, ON N3T 3J9, Canada
Tel: 519-759-0730; *Fax:* 519-759-4741
Donald Neale

London: **The Robarts School**
P.O. Box 7300 E
1090 Highbury Ave., London, ON N5Y 4V9, Canada
Tel: 519-453-4400; *Fax:* 519-453-4193
Paul Cowley

Milton: **The Ernest C. Drury School**
255 Ontario St., Milton, ON L9T 2N5, Canada
Tel: 905-878-2851; *Fax:* 905-878-9261
Nancy Syer

Special Education

Belleville: **Sir James Whitney/Sagonaska School**
350 Dundas St. West, Belleville, ON K8P 1B2, Canada
Tel: 613-967-2830; *Fax:* 613-967-2482
Lindi Pierce, Principal

London: **The Amethyst School**
P.O. Box 7300
1090 Highbury Ave., London, ON N5Y 4V9, Canada
Tel: 519-453-4400; *Fax:* 519-453-2160
Clive Hodder, Principal

Milton: **E.C. Drury/Trillium Demonstration School Elementary**
347 Ontario St. South, Milton, ON L9T 3X9, Canada
Tel: 905-878-2851; *Fax:* 905-878-4278

Ottawa: **Centre Jules-Léger**
281, av Lanark, Ottawa, ON K1Z 6R8, Canada
Tél: 613-761-9300; *Téléc:* 613-761-9301
www.centrejulesleger.com
Other Information: ATS: 613-761-9302
Services aux enfants (et leurs familles) en difficultés d'apprentissage, avec ou sans déficit d'attention/hyperactivité, qui sont sourds ou malentendant, qui sont aveugles ou en basse vision, ou qui sont sourds et aveugles.
Lillian Patry, Surintendante

Schools: Independent & Private

Catholic

Richmond Hill: **Holy Trinity School**
c/o The Head of School
11300 Bayview Ave., Richmond Hill, ON L4S 1L4, Canada
Tel: 905-737-1114; *Fax:* 905-737-5187
Toll-Free: 866-727-7580
Grades: Elem./Sec.
Enrollment: 694
George Rutherford, Head of School

First Nations

Pikangikum: **Eenchokay Birchstick School**
General Delivery, Pikangikum, ON P0V 2L0, Canada
Tel: 807-773-5561; *Fax:* 807-773-5958
Grades: K./Elem./Sec.
Enrollment: 166
Serving students of the Pikangikum First Nation.
Jonah Strang, Chief, Pikangikum First Nation, 807-773-5578

Special Education

Richmond Hill: **Academy for Gifted Children**
Also known as: P.A.C.E.
12 Bond Cres., Richmond Hill, ON L4E 3K2, Canada
Tel: 905-773-0997; *Fax:* 905-773-4722
www.pace.on.ca
Grades: Elem./Sec.
Enrollment: 284
P.A.C.E. - Programming for Academic & Creative Excellence. A non-denominational, co-ed, private day school, with programmes focussing on basic skills, with a strong emphasis on math & science, accelerated learning & individual instruction.
Barbara Rosenberg, Founder & Principal

Independent & Private Schools

Ajax: **Faithway Baptist Church School**
1964 Salem Rd., Ajax, ON L1T 4V3, Canada
Tel: 905-686-0951; *Fax:* 905-686-1450
Grades: K./Elem./Sec.
Enrollment: 65
L. Homan

Ajax: **Montessori Learning Centre of Ajax**
Also known as: 849179 Ontario Inc.
250 Bayly St. West, Ajax, ON L1S 3V4, Canada
Tel: 905-428-3122
www.montessorilearningcentreofajax.ca
Grades: Preschool / Elementary
Montessori Learning Centre of Ajax offers a toddler program for children from 18 months to 3 years, as well as a Casa program for 3 to 6 year old children. Elementary education is provided for children from age 6 to 12.
Camilla Graziani, Principal

Ajax: **Pickering Christian School**
162 Rossland Rd. East, Ajax, ON L1T 4V2, Canada
Tel: 905-427-3120; *Fax:* 905-427-0211
office@pickeringcs.on.ca
www.pickeringcs.on.ca
Grades: Elem.
Enrollment: 219
Dr. Paul Douglas Ogborne, Principal

Alliston: **Alliston Community Christian School**
4428 Adjala-Tecumseth Townline, RR#4, Alliston, ON L9R 1V4, Canada
Tel: 705-434-2227; *Fax:* 705-435-0126
info@allistonchristianschool.com
www.allistonccs.ca
Grades: K./Elem.
Enrollment: 113
Cathy Lubbers, Principal

Ancaster: **Hamilton District Christian High School**
92 Glancaster Rd., RR#1, Ancaster, ON L9G 3K9, Canada
Tel: 905-648-6655; *Fax:* 905-648-3139
www.hdch.org
info@hdch.org
Grades: Sec.
Enrollment: 600
George VanKampen, Principal
gvankampen@hdch.org

Aurora: **Aurora Montessori School & Private School**
330 Industrial Pkwy. North, Aurora, ON L4G 4C3, Canada
Tel: 905-841-0065; *Fax:* 905-841-2022
info@auroramontessori.com;
admissions@auroramontessori.com
www.auroramontessori.com
Grades: 1-8
Aurora Montessori School & Private School also offers a toddler program for children from ages 18 months to 3 years. Casa programs are for children from ages 2.5 to 6 years.
Brenda Glashan, Principal

Aurora: **Foundations Private School**
81 Industrial Pkwy North, Aurora, ON L4G 4C4, Canada
Tel: 905-713-1141
Grades: Elem.
Enrollment: 159
Ellen Powers

Aurora: **St. Andrew's College**
15800 Yonge St. North, Aurora, ON L4G 3H7, Canada
Tel: 905-727-3178; *Fax:* 905-841-6911
info@sac.on.ca
www.sac.on.ca
Grades: 6-12
Enrollment: 560
All-boys boarding and day school
Kevin McHenry, Headmaster

Aylmer: **Immanuel Christian School Society**
75 Caverly Rd., Aylmer, ON N5H 2P6, Canada
Tel: 519-773-8476; *Fax:* 519-773-8315
Grades: K./Elem.
Enrollment: 152
Marianne Vangoor

Aylmer: **Mount Salem Christian School (MSCS)**
c/o Evangelical Mennonite Church
6576 Springfield Rd., RR#6, Aylmer, ON N5H 2R5, Canada
Tel: 519-765-3555; *Fax:* 519-765-3879
mscsch@amtelecom.net
www.mountsalemchristianschool.ca
Grades: Junior Kindergarten - 12
Mount Salem Christian School is an interdenominational school, using a BEKA curriculum.
Judy Wiebe, Principal

Aylmer: **Old Colony Christian School**
P.O. Box 127
Aylmer, ON N5H 2R8, Canada
Tel: 519-765-1138
Grades: Elem./Sec.
Enrollment: 288
Anna Ens

Bancroft: **Bancroft Christian Academy**
P.O. Box 657
160 South Baptiste Lake Rd., Bancroft, ON K0L 1C0, Canada
Tel: 613-332-3670
Grades: Elementary / Secondary

Barrie: **Heritage Christian Academy**
79 Ardagh Rd., Barrie, ON L4N 9B6, Canada
Tel: 705-733-0112; *Fax:* 705-733-2054
Grades: JK.-12
Enrollment: 75
Pastor Brett Pennell, Principal

Barrie: **Timothy Christian School**
750 Essa Rd., Barrie, ON L4N 9E9, Canada
Tel: 705-726-6621; *Fax:* 705-726-8571
tcsgen@timothychristianschool.ca
www.timothychristianschool.ca
Grades: Junior Kindergarten - 8
Timothy Christian School is an interdenominational school.
Kevin Eisses, Chair
Andrew Straatsma, Principal
Brenda Goodnough, Vice Principal
Ina VanHouten, Director, Development

Beamsville: **Great Lakes Christian College**
4875 King St., Beamsville, ON L0R 1B0, Canada
Tel: 905-563-5374; *Fax:* 905-563-0818
www.glchs.on.ca
Grades: Sec.
Enrollment: 130
Don Rose, President
drose@glchs.on.ca

Belleville: **Albert College**
160 Dundas St. West, Belleville, ON K8P 1A6, Canada
Tel: 613-968-5726; *Fax:* 613-968-9651
info@albertcollege.ca
www.albertc.on.ca
Grades: Elem./Sec.
Enrollment: 298
Heather Kidd, Director, Admission
hkidd@albertc.on.ca

Belleville: **Belleville District Christian School (BCS)**
18 Christian School Rd., RR#5, Belleville, ON K8N 4Z5, Canada
Tel: 613-962-7849; *Fax:* 613-962-6440
bellevillechristianschool@yahoo.com
www.bellevillechristianschool.ca
Grades: Junior Kindergarten - 8
Jennifer Richmond, Principal

Belleville: **Quinte Christian High School (QCHS)**
138 Wallbridge-Loyalist Rd., Belleville, ON K8N 4Z2, Canada
Tel: 613-968-7870; *Fax:* 613-968-7970
admin@qchs.ca; finance@qchs.ca
www.qchs.ca
Grades: Secondary
Johan Cooke, Principal

Bethany: **The Bethany Hills School**
P.O. Box 10
727 Bethany Hills Rd., Bethany, ON L0A 1A0, Canada
Tel: 705-277-2866; *Fax:* 705-277-2455
info1@bethanyhills.on.ca
www.bethanyhills.on.ca
Grades: Jr. K.-12
Enrollment: 80
Co-educational day school for all grades and girls-only boarding school for grades 7-12
Andrew Wallace

Bloomingdale: **Koinonia Christian Academy**
850 Sawmill Rd., Bloomingdale, ON N0B 1K0, Canada
Tel: 519-744-7447; *Fax:* 519-744-6745
Enrollment: 157
David J. Champion

Bolton: **Countryside Montessori Private School**
1 Loring Dr., Bolton, ON L7E 1Y1, Canada
Tel: 905-951-3359; *Fax:* 905-951-3920
Enrollment: 257
Rose Sampogna

Bowmanville: **Durham Christian High School**
340 Scugog St., Bowmanville, ON L1C 3K2, Canada
Tel: 905-623-5940; *Fax:* 905-623-6258
Grades: Sec.
Enrollment: 164
Fred Spoelstra

Bowmanville: **Knox Christian School**
410 Scugog St., RR#1, Bowmanville, ON L1C 3K2, Canada
Tel: 905-623-5871; *Fax:* 905-623-8877
Grades: K./Elem.
Enrollment: 339
George Petrusma

Brampton: **Brampton-Georgetown Montessori School (BGMS)**
1030 Queen St. West, Brampton, ON L6X 0B2, Canada
Tel: 905-457-2496
info@bgmschool.com
www.bgmschool.com
Grades: Casa / Elementary
Brampton-Georgetown Montessori School provides programs for children from ages 2.5 to 11.

Brampton: **Canada Christian Academy**
22 Abbey Rd., Brampton, ON L6W 2T8, Canada
Tel: 905-789-5841; *Fax:* 905-789-0645
www.canadachristianacademy.com
Grades: Junior Kindergarten - 12
Enrollment: 100

Brampton: **John Knox Christian School**
82 McLaughlin Rd. South, Brampton, ON L6Y 2C7, Canada
Tel: 905-451-3236; *Fax:* 905-451-3448
Grades: K./Elem.
Enrollment: 336
Ed Boelens

Brampton: **Rowntree Montessori School**
3 Sunforest Dr., Brampton, ON L6Z 2Z2, Canada
Tel: 905-790-3838; *Fax:* 905-790-5686
www.rowntreemontessori.com
Dr. Yamil H. Alonso

Brampton: **Tall Pines School**
8525 Torbram Rd., Brampton, ON L6T 5K4, Canada
Tel: 905-458-6770; *Fax:* 905-458-7967
info@tallpinesschool.com
www.tallpinesschool.com
Grades: Elem.
Enrollment: 519
Private Montessori and Progressive school
Elaine Flett, Principal

Brantford: **Braemar House School**
36 Baxter St., Brantford, ON N3R 2V8, Canada
Tel: 519-753-2929; *Fax:* 519-753-1235
admin@braemarhouseschool.ca
www.braemarhouseschool.ca
Grades: Junior Kindergarten - 8
Enrollment: 92
Braemar House School also offers a Montessori Casa program.
Annette Minutillo, Executive Director

Brantford: **Brantford Christian Collegiate**
North Park Plaza
P.O. Box 28116
452 Grey St., Brantford, ON N3R 7X5, Canada
Tel: 519-753-4900
information@brantfordchristiancollegiate.org
www.brantfordchristiancollegiate.org
Grades: 9 - 12
Jeff Gillmore, Principal
Rev. Ron Humphries, Faculty Member

Brantford: **Brantford Christian School (BCS)**
7 Calvin St., Brantford, ON N3S 3E4, Canada
Tel: 519-752-0433; *Fax:* 519-752-6088
www.bcsbrantford.ca
Grades: Junior Kindergarten - 8
Walter Hartholt, Principal
whartholt@bcsbrantford.ca
Heather Murray, Vice Principal
hmurray@bcsbrantford.ca
Audrey Reitsma, Vice Principal
areitsma@bcsbrantford.ca

Brantford: **Central Baptist Academy (CBA)**
300 Fairview Dr., Brantford, ON N3R 2X6, Canada
Tel: 519-754-4806; *Fax:* 519-754-4201
cbaoffice@centralbaptistbrantford.com
www.centralbaptistbrantford.com
Grades: Junior Kindergarten - 8
Rev. Minne Bouma, Principal

Brantford: **Montessori House of Children**
85 Charlotte St., Brantford, ON N3T 2X2, Canada
Tel: 519-759-7290; *Fax:* 519-759-6774
mails@montessorihouseofchildren.com
www.montessorihouseofchildren.com
Other Information: admissions@montessorihouseofchildren.com (Admission inquiries)
Brantford's Montessori House of Children provides programs for children from 2.5 to 9 years of age.
Nahida Hamam, Principal

Breslau: **St. John's-Kilmarnock School**
P.O. Box 179
2201 Shantz Station Rd., Breslau, ON N0B 1M0, Canada
Tel: 519-648-2183; *Fax:* 519-648-2186
info@sjkschool.org
www.sjkschool.org
Grades: Jr. K.-12
Enrollment: 505
Ian Hornsby

Breslau: **Woodland Christian High School**
1058 Spitzig Rd. R.R.# 1, Breslau, ON N0B 1M0, Canada
Tel: 519-648-2114; *Fax:* 519-648-3402
office@woodland.on.ca
www.woodland.on.ca
Grades: Sec.
Enrollment: 194
Gary VanArragon

Brockville: **Grenville Christian College**
P.O. Box 610
Brockville, ON K6V 5V8, Canada
Tel: 613-345-5521; *Fax:* 613-345-3826
Grades: K./Elem./Sec.
Enrollment: 301
Rev. Gordon G. Mintz, Head Master

***Burlington:* Burlington Christian Academy (BCA)**
521 North Service Rd. West, Burlington, ON L7P 5C3, Canada
Tel: 905-639-7364; *Fax:* 905-639-1657
info@burlingtonchristian.net
www.burlingtonchristian.net
Grades: Junior Kindergarten - 8
Enrollment: 130
Gord McNeice, Principal
Heather Crossing, Vice Principal (Part-time)
Jessica Purdy, Vice Principal (Part-time)
Jann Schlett, Coordinator, Advancement & Recruitment

***Burlington:* Halton Waldorf School (HWS)**
2193 Orchard Rd., Burlington, ON L7R 3X5, Canada
Tel: 905-331-4387; *Fax:* 905-331-3231
enrollment@haltonwaldorf.com
www.waldorfschool.net
Grades: Preschool - 8
Enrollment: 160
The school provides Waldorf education.

***Burlington:* John Calvin Christian School**
607 Dynes Rd., Burlington, ON L7N 2V4, Canada
Tel: 905-634-8015; *Fax:* 905-634-9772
Grades: K./Elem.
Enrollment: 141
Jane Holtvluwer

***Burlington:* Niagara Montessori School**
3132 South Dr., Burlington, ON L7N 1H7, Canada
Tel: 905-632-2374; *Fax:* 905-632-9959
Grades: Preschool - Kindergarten
The Montessori School offers programs for children from age 2.5 to 6.
Jacqueline Gaskin, Principal

***Burlington:* Trinity Christian School**
2170 Itabashi Way, Burlington, ON L7M 5B3, Canada
Tel: 905-634-3052; *Fax:* 905-634-9382
trinity@tcsonline.ca
www.tcsonline.ca
Grades: Junior Kindergarten - 8
Juliette Lamb, Chair
Rick Schenk, Principal
principal@tcsonline.ca
Sara Flokstra, Vice Principal
Cheri VanderBrook, Bookkeeper

***Caledon:* Brampton Christian School (BCS)**
12480 Hurontario St., Caledon, ON L7C 2B6, Canada
Tel: 905-846-3771; *Fax:* 905-843-2929
admin@bramptoncs.org
www.bramptoncs.org
Grades: Elementary/Junior High/Senior High
R. Andrews, Principal
randrews@bramptoncs.org
A. Cabral, Division Head, Senior High
afcabral@bramptoncs.org
C. Doggart, Division Head, Elementary
cdoggart@bramptoncs.org
J. Miller, Division Head, Junior High
jmiller@bramptoncs.org

***Cambridge:* Cambridge Christian School (CCS)**
229 Myers Rd., Cambridge, ON N1R 7H3, Canada
Tel: 519-623-2261; *Fax:* 519-623-4042
cc2@bellnet.ca
www.cambridgechristianschool.com
Grades: Kindergarten - 8
Derek Frank, Chair
Jules de Jager, Principal
ccsprincipal@bellnet.ca

***Cambridge:* Temple Baptist Christian Academy**
400 Holiday Inn Dr., Cambridge, ON N3C 3T1, Canada
Tel: 519-658-9001; *Fax:* 519-658-9426
academy@tbca.ca
www.tbca.ca
Grades: Jr. K-8
Enrollment: 267
Evelyn Hewitt, Principal

***Campbellville:* Hitherfield Preparatory School**
2439 - 10th Side Rd., Campbellville, ON L0P 1B0, Canada
Tel: 905-854-0890; *Fax:* 905-854-3155
Grades: Elem./Sec.
Enrollment: 115
Ann J. Scott

***Carp:* Venta Preparatory School**
2013 Old Carp Rd., Carp, ON K0A 1L0, Canada
Tel: 613-839-2175; *Fax:* 613-839-1956
info@ventapreparatoryschool.com
www.ventapreparatoryschool.com
Grades: 1 - 10
Venta Preparatory School is a day & boarding school. The maximum class size is twelve students.
Marilyn Mansfield, Principal, 613-839-2175, ext. 223
Sean Hopper, Dean, Students, 613-839-2175, ext. 225
Shaun Quinn, Director, Studies, 613-839-2175, ext. 224
Tracey Quinn, Director, Enrollment, 613-839-2175, ext. 240

***Chatham:* Chatham Christian High School (CCHS)**
475 Keil Dr. South, Chatham, ON N7M 6L8, Canada
Tel: 519-352-4980; *Fax:* 519-352-4041
chathamchristian@chathamchristian.ca
www.chathamchristian.ca
Other Information: rayverburg@chathamchristian.ca (Vice Principal)
Grades: 9 - 12
Enrollment: 140

***Chatham:* Chatham Christian School**
475 Keil Dr. South, Chatham, ON N7M 6L8, Canada
Tel: 519-352-4980; *Fax:* 519-352-4041
chathamchristian@chathamchristian.ca
www.chathamchristian.ca
Other Information: philteeuwsen@chathamchristian.ca (Head Administrator)
Grades: Junior Kindergarten - 8
Enrollment: 300

***Chatham:* Eben-Ezer Christian School**
485 McNaughton Ave. East, Chatham, ON N7L 2H2, Canada
Tel: 519-354-1142; *Fax:* 519-354-2159
Grades: Elem.
Enrollment: 51
Carlos Bos

***Clinton:* Clinton & District Christian School**
P.O. Box 658
87 Percival St., Clinton, ON N0M 1L0, Canada
Tel: 519-482-7851; *Fax:* 519-482-7448
Grades: K./Elem.
Enrollment: 205
Clarence Bos

***Cobourg:* Northumberland Christian School**
8861 Danforth Rd., RR#5, Cobourg, ON K9A 4J8, Canada
Tel: 905-372-8766; *Fax:* 905-372-6299
ncsoffice@bellnet.ca
www.northumberlandchristianschool.com
Grades: Junior Kindergarten - 8
Northumberland Christian School is an interdenominational school.
Cindy Warr

***Cookstown:* Thor College**
4073 - 4th Line Innisfil, Cookstown, ON L0L 1L0
Tel: 705-458-9705
www.thorcollege.ca
Grades: Preschool - 12
W.H. Madden, BA, BPHE, BEd, Director
Michael J. Madden, Headmaster

***Copetown:* Rehoboth Christian School - Copetown (RCS)**
P.O. Box 70
198 Inksetter Rd., Copetown, ON L0R 1J0, Canada
Tel: 905-627-5977; *Fax:* 905-628-4422
office@rehoboth.on.ca
www.rehoboth.on.ca
Grades: Kindergarten - 12
Rehoboth Free Reformed Christian School Society of Copetown owns & operates the school. Education is provided with a Reformed Christian view.
Jack Westerink, B.Sc., M.Sc., CSPC, Principal
jwesterink@rehoboth.on.ca
Dick Naves, B.A., C.S.P.C., Vice Principal
dnaves@rehoboth.on.ca

***Cornwall:* Islamic Institute Al-Rashid**
RR#1, Cornwall, ON K6H 5R5, Canada
Tel: 613-931-2895
Grades: Elem./Sec.
Enrollment: 66
M.M. Alam

***Deep River:* The Deep River Science Academy (DRSA)**
20 Forest Ave., Deep River, ON K0J 1P0, Canada
Tel: 613-584-4541
info@drsa.ca
www.drsa.ca
Grades: Secondary
The Deep River Science Academy partners with Atomic Energy of Canada, Ltd. to offer science camps. Students must have completed a grade 10 or higher science high school credit. Hhigh school credits are awarded.

***Deer Lake:* David Meekis Memorial School**
P.O. Box 69
Deer Lake, ON P0V 1N0, Canada
Tel: 807-775-2055; *Fax:* 807-775-2148
www.dmms.firstnationschools.ca/
Grades: Sec.
Enrollment: 236
Leonard Mamakeesic, Dir.

***Drayton:* Community Christian School (CCS)**
P.O. Box 141
35 High St., Drayton, ON N0G 1P0, Canada
Tel: 519-638-2935; *Fax:* 519-638-3373
ccsdray@bellnet.ca
www.ccsdray.org
Grades: Junior Kindergarten - 8

***Dresden:* Dresden Private Mennonite School**
P.O. Box 1210
RR#2, Dresden, ON N0P 1M0, Canada
Tel: 519-683-6610; *Fax:* 519-683-6610
Grades: Elem.
Enrollment: 69
Anna Friesen

***Dundas:* Calvin Christian School - Dundas**
542 Ofield Rd. North, Dundas, ON L9H 5E2, Canada
Tel: 905-627-1411; *Fax:* 905-627-8004
www.dccs.ca
Grades: Kindergarten - 8
Enrollment: 180
Rick Dykstra, Principal
rdykstra@dccs.ca
Mrs. I. Vos, Coordinator, Curriculum
ivos@dccs.ca
Corrie Zandstra, Administrator, Office
office@dccs.ca

***Dunnville:* Attercliffe Canadian Reformed Elementary School**
75785 Canborough Rd., RR#1, Dunnville, ON N1A 2W1, Canada
Tel: 905-774-9009
Grades: Kindergarten - 8
This is a coducational school.
Ed Slaa, Principal

***Dunnville:* Dunnville Christian School**
37 Robinson Rd, Dunnville, ON N1A 2W1, Canada
Tel: 905-774-5142; *Fax:* 905-774-5519
Grades: K./Elem.
Enrollment: 129
Arie Vanderstoel

***Etobicoke:* Al-Ashraf Islamic School**
23 Brydon Dr., Etobicoke, ON M9W 4M7, Canada
Tel: 416-740-1495
Grades: Elem./Sec.
Enrollment: 157
Riyad Khan, Principal

***Etobicoke:* Kingsway College School**
4600 Dundas St. West, Etobicoke, ON M9A 1A5, Canada
Tel: 416-234-5073; *Fax:* 416-234-8386
Grades: Elem.
Enrollment: 180
Glenn Zederayko

***Etobicoke:* Madresatul Banaat Almuslimaat**
10 Vulcan St., Etobicoke, ON M9W 1L2, Canada
Tel: 416-244-8600
Grades: Elem./Sec.
Enrollment: 152
Syed Quadri

***Etobicoke:* Richmond Hill Christian Academy**
Administration
96 Antioch Dr., Etobicoke, ON M9B 5V4, Canada
Tel: 416-621-4100; *Fax:* 416-621-0930
rhca@rogers.com
www.rhcaweb.ca
Other Information: 905-770-4055 (Phone, RHCA Campus); 905-770-6255 (Fax, Campus)
Grades: Junior Kindergarten - 8
Enrollment: 339
Richmond Hill Christian Academy is a non-denominational school, which is a member of the Association of Christian Schools International. The A Beka curriculum is used. Its campus is located at 9711 Bayview Avenue in Richmond Hill.
Brian R. Hayes, B.Com., C.F.A., Administrator
Madeline J. Hayes, B.A., M.Ed., Principal

***Fergus:* Emmanuel Christian High School**
RR#3, Fergus, ON N1M 2W4, Canada
Tel: 519-843-3029; *Fax:* 519-843-3029
Grades: Elem./Sec.
Enrollment: 110
Henk Nobel

***Fergus:* Maranatha Christian School**
RR#3, Fergus, ON N1M 2W4, Canada
Tel: 519-843-3029; *Fax:* 519-843-3029
Grades: Elem.
Enrollment: 146
Henk Nobel

***Fort Erie:* Niagara Christian Community of Schools (NCC)**
2619 Niagara Pkwy., Fort Erie, ON L2A 5M4, Canada
Tel: 905-871-6980; *Fax:* 905-871-9260
ncc@niagaracc.com
www.niagaracc.com
Grades: Junior Kindergarten - 12
Kevin Bayne, Principal, Secondary School
kbayne@niagaracc.com
Cari Dean, Principal, Elementary School & Middle School
cdean@niagaracc.com
Mark Thiessen, Principal, Secondary School
mthiess@niagaracc.com
Tom Auld, Director, Student Life
tomauld@niagaracc.com
Vivian Pengelly, Business Administrator
vivianp@niagaracc.com

***Fort Frances:* Lac La Croix High School**
P.O. Box 640
Fort Frances, ON P9A 3M9, Canada
Tel: 807-485-2402; *Fax:* 807-485-2558
Grades: 9-12

***Fort Frances:* Seven Generations Education Institute School**
P.O. Box 297
Fort Frances, ON P9A 3M6, Canada
Tel: 807-274-2796; *Fax:* 807-274-8761
www.7generations.org/
Dan Bird

***Fruitland:* John Knox Christian School**
795 Hwy. #8, Fruitland, ON L8E 5J3, Canada
Tel: 905-643-2460; *Fax:* 905-643-5875
www.nace.ca
Grades: K./Elem.
Enrollment: 185
The Niagara Ass'n for Christian Education (NACE).
Bonnie Desjardins, Principal
bdesjardins@nace.ca

***Georgetown:* Halton Hills Christian School**
11643 Trafalgar Rd., Georgetown, ON L7G 4S4, Canada
Tel: 905-877-4221; *Fax:* 905-877-1483
office@haltonhillschristianschool.org
www.haltonhillschristianschool.org
Grades: K./Elem.
Enrollment: 228
Formerly known as Georgetown District Christian School
Marianne Vangoor, Principal

***Gloucester:* Life Christian Academy**
2214 Innes Rd., Gloucester, ON K1B 4C4, Canada
Tel: 613-834-6588; *Fax:* 613-834-6589
Grades: Elem./Sec.
Enrollment: 130
Jason Courteau

***Grassy Narrows:* Sakatcheway-Anishinabe**
P.O. Box 213
General Delivery, Grassy Narrows, ON P0X 1B0, Canada
Tel: 807-925-2626; *Fax:* 807-925-2855

***Guelph:* Crestwicke Christian Academy**
400 Speedvale Ave. East, Guelph, ON N1E 1N9, Canada
Tel: 519-836-5395; *Fax:* 519-836-2139
Grades: K./Elem.
Enrollment: 330
Sharon Dow

***Guelph:* Elora Road Christian School**
5696 Wellington Rd.7, RR #5, Guelph, ON N1H 6J2, Canada
Tel: 519-824-1890; *Fax:* 519-821-3518
school@ercf.ca
www.eloraroad.ca
Grades: K./Elem.
Enrollment: 99
Jason Wryghte

***Guelph:* John Calvin Christian School**
286 Water St., Guelph, ON N1G 1B8, Canada
Tel: 519-824-8860; *Fax:* 519-824-2105
Grades: K./Elem.
Enrollment: 188
Jake Vriend

***Hamilton:* Calvin Christian School (CCS)**
547 West 5th St., Hamilton, ON L9C 3P7, Canada
Tel: 905-388-2645; *Fax:* 905-388-2769
www.ccshamilton.ca
Grades: Junior Kindergarten - 8
Enrollment: 450
Ted Postma, Principal

***Hamilton:* Columbia International College of Canada**
1003 Main St. West, Hamilton, ON L8S 4P3, Canada
Tel: 905-572-7883; *Fax:* 905-572-9332
Grades: Sec.
Enrollment: 1285
Anna Skholnik

***Hamilton:* Guido de Bres Christian High School**
P.O. Box 30013
1576 Upper James St., Hamilton, ON L9B 1K0, Canada
Tel: 905-574-4011; *Fax:* 905-574-8662
office@guidodebres.org
www.guidodebres.org
Grades: Sec.
Enrollment: 400
J.G. Vandooren, Principal

***Hamilton:* Hamilton Hebrew Academy Zichron Meir School**
60 Dow Ave., Hamilton, ON L8S 1W4, Canada
Tel: 905-528-0330; *Fax:* 905-528-0544
school@hamiltonhebrewacademy.ca
www.hamiltonhebrewacademy.ca
Grades: Elem.
Enrollment: 132
Rivka Shaffir, Principal
principal@hamiltonhebrewacademy.ca

***Hamilton:* Hillfield - Strathallan College**
299 Fennell Ave. West, Hamilton, ON L9C 1G3, Canada
Tel: 905-389-1367; *Fax:* 905-389-6366
Grades: K./Elem./Sec.
Enrollment: 1173
William Matthews

***Hamilton:* Islamic School of Hamilton (ISH)**
1545 Stonechurch Rd. East, Hamilton, ON L8W 3P8, Canada
Tel: 905-383-7786; *Fax:* 905-667-4797
Enrollment: 170
The school also teaches the Arabic language, Quran, & Islam Studies.
Zakir Patel, Principal

***Hamilton:* Southern Ontario College**
430 York Blvd., Hamilton, ON L8R 3K8, Canada
Tel: 905-546-1500; *Fax:* 905-538-5494
info@mysoc.ca
www.mysoc.ca
Grades: Sec.
Enrollment: 181
International Secondary School specializing in ESL and University prep.
Brian Inglis, Director

***Hamilton:* Timothy Canadian Reformed School**
430 East 25th St., Hamilton, ON L8V 3B4, Canada
Tel: 905-385-3953; *Fax:* 905-385-8073
Grades: Kindergarten - 8
The school is affiliated with the Canadian Reformed Church.
Hendrik Plug, Principal

***Hawkesville:* Countryside Christian School**
P.O. Box 67
Hawkesville, ON N0B 1X0, Canada
Tel: 519-699-5793; *Fax:* 519-699-4576
Grades: K./Elem./Sec.
Enrollment: 119
Howard Lichty

***Islington:* Kingsley Primary School**
516 The Kingsway, Islington, ON M9A 3W6, Canada
Tel: 416-233-0150; *Fax:* 416-233-5971
Grades: K./Elem.
Enrollment: 52
Ursula Morton

***Jarvis:* Jarvis District Christian School**
P.O. Box 520
Jarvis, ON N0A 1J0, Canada
Tel: 519-587-4444; *Fax:* 519-587-2985
Grades: K./Elem.
Enrollment: 178
Garry Glasbergen

***Jordan Station:* Heritage Christian School**
P.O. Box 400
2850 Fourth Ave., Jordan Station, ON L0R 1S0, Canada
Tel: 905-562-7303; *Fax:* 905-562-0020
Grades: Elem./Sec.
Enrollment: 501
Ben Harsvoort, Principal

***Jordan Station:* Jordan Christian School**
P.O. Box 69
4171 - 15 St. South, Jordan Station, ON L0R 1S0, Canada
Tel: 905-562-4023; *Fax:* 905-562-4024
Enrollment: 132
Mark Fintelman

***Kasabonika Lake:* Chief Simeon McKay Education Centre**
P.O. Box 120
Kasabonika Lake, ON P0V 1Y0, Canada
Tel: 807-535-2574; *Fax:* 807-535-1108

***King:* The Country Day School (CDS)**
13415 Dufferin St., King, ON L7B 1K5, Canada
Tel: 905-833-1220; *Fax:* 905-833-1350
www.cds.on.ca
Grades: Junior Kindergarten - 12
The co-educational school is non-denominational.
Paul C. Duckett, Headmaster
David Huckvale, Director, Admission

***King City:* St. Thomas of Villanova College School**
P.O. Box 133
2480 15th Sideroad, King City, ON L7B 1A4, Canada
Tel: 905-833-1909; *Fax:* 905-833-1915
www.villanovacollege.net
Grades: 5-12
Enrollment: 450
Paul Paradiso

***Kingston:* Kingston Christian School**
1212 Woodbine Rd., Kingston, ON K7L 4V2, Canada
Tel: 613-384-9572; *Fax:* 613-384-9580
Grades: K./Elem.
Enrollment: 145
Karl Reid

***Kingsville:* Old Colony Christian Academy**
Kingsville Campus
1521 County Rd. 4 West, RR#2, Kingsville, ON N9Y 2E5, Canada
Tel: 519-733-8308; *Fax:* 519-733-2167
Grades: Elem./Sec.
Enrollment: 194
Peter Klassen

***Kitchener:* Fellowship Christian School**
1780 Glascow St., Kitchener, ON N2G 3W7, Canada
Tel: 519-746-0008; *Fax:* 519-746-4206
Grades: Elem.
Enrollment: 84
Marilyn Lambert

***Kitchener:* Kitchener-Waterloo Montessori School**
194 Allen St. East, Kitchener, ON N2J 1K1, Canada
Tel: 519-742-1051; *Fax:* 519-742-1051
Grades: K./Elem.

***Kitchener:* Laurentian Hills Christian School**
11 Laurentian Dr., Kitchener, ON N2E 1C1, Canada
Tel: 519-576-6700; *Fax:* 519-576-2583
Grades: K./Elem.
Enrollment: 333
Hugo Marcus

***Kitchener:* Rockway Mennonite Collegiate Inc.**
110 Doon Rd., Kitchener, ON N2G 3C8, Canada
Tel: 519-743-5209; *Fax:* 519-743-5935
www.rockway.on.ca
Grades: 7 - 12
Enrollment: 350
Rockway Mennonite Collegiate is an inspected & accredited private school, with students from Mennonite congregations & Christian denominations.
Gloria Eby, Chair
Betsy Petker, Principal
Dennis Wikerd, Assistant Principal
Tom Bileski, Director, Community Relations
Bernie Burnett, Director, Development
Barry Bishop, Business Manager

***Kitchener:* Sunshine Montessori School**
10 Boniface Ave., Kitchener, ON N2C 1L9, Canada
Tel: 519-744-1423; *Fax:* 519-744-9929
admin@sunshinemontessori.on.ca
www.sunshinemontessori.on.ca
Grades: Jr. K.-8
Enrollment: 209
Roshmina Shamji, Principal/Administrator

***Kleinburg:* Calvary Christian School**
6950 Nashville Rd., Kleinburg, ON L0J 1C0, Canada
Tel: 905-893-7211
ccs.behosted.ca
Grades: Junior Kindergarten - 8
Garry Zondervan, Principal
LeeAnn Major, Head, Junior Department

***Lakefield:* Lakefield College School**
4391 County Rd. 29, Lakefield, ON K0L 2H0, Canada
Tel: 705-652-3324; *Fax:* 705-652-6320
www.lcs.on.ca
Grades: Elem./Sec.
Enrollment: 321
Founded 1879; co-ed boarding and day school, for grades 9-12 and 7-12 respectively; core academics, athletics, and co-curricular arts programmes.
David Thompson, Head of School
Kathy Green, Board Secretary
kgreen@lcs.on.ca

***Laurel:* Dufferin Area Christian School**
General Delivery, Laurel, ON L0N 1L0, Canada
Tel: 519-941-4368; *Fax:* 519-941-3748
Grades: Elem.
Enrollment: 122
Nick Mans

***Leamington:* United Mennonite Educational Institute (UMEI)**
614 Mersea Rd. 6, RR#5, Leamington, ON N8H 3V8, Canada
Tel: 519-326-7448; *Fax:* 519-326-0278
umei@mnsi.net
www.umei.on.ca
Grades: 9 - 12
United Mennonite Educational Institute is a secondary school which provides an education that incorporates an Anabaptist / Mennonite world view.
Victor J. Winter, Principal
umeiadmi@mnsi.net
Jane Klassen, Secretary

***Lindsay:* Heritage Christian School**
159 Colborne St. West, Lindsay, ON K9V 5Z8, Canada
Tel: 705-324-8363; *Fax:* 705-324-8363
hcs_office@bellnet.ca
Grades: K./Elem.
Enrollment: 102
John Frederick

***Listowel:* Listowel Christian School**
P.O. Box 151
Listowel, ON N4W 3H2, Canada
Tel: 519-291-3086; *Fax:* 519-291-3086
Grades: K./Elem.
Enrollment: 142
Garth Bierma

***London:* Al-Taqwa Islamic Schools**
Elementary School
35 Jim Ashton St., London, ON N5V 3H4, Canada
Tel: 519-951-1414; *Fax:* 519-951-1092
Toll-Free: 866-812-9127
ischool@altaqwa.org
www.altaqwa.org
Grades: Elem./Sec.
Enrollment: 163
The elementary school is located at 35 Jim Ashton St.; the secondary school is located at 1697 Trafalgar St., (519) 452-3366, secondary@altaqwa.org.
Siham Kaloti, Principal

***London:* Faith Community Christian School**
7 Howard Ave., London, ON N6P 1B3, Canada
Tel: 519-652-1250; *Fax:* 519-652-1296
Grades: K./Elem.
Enrollment: 85
Mel Finch

***London:* London Christian Academy (LCA)**
85 Charles St., London, ON N6H 1H1, Canada
Tel: 519-473-3332; *Fax:* 519-473-9843
www.londonchristianacademy.ca
Grades: Junior Kindergarten - 8
London Christian Academy is an interdenominational, Christian school.
Glen Smeltzer, Chair
chairman@londonchristianacademy.ca
Ron Hesman, Principal
principal@londonchristianacademy.ca
Steve Gaunt, Vice Principal
sgaunt@londonchristianacademy.ca

***London:* London Community Hebrew Day School**
247 Epworth Ave., London, ON N6A 2M2, Canada
Tel: 519-439-8419; *Fax:* 519-439-0404
Grades: K./Elem.
Enrollment: 75
Janet Nish-Lapidus

***London:* London District Christian Secondary School**
24 Braesyde Ave., London, ON N5W 1V3, Canada
Tel: 519-455-4360; *Fax:* 519-455-4364
Grades: Sec.
Enrollment: 363
Henry Kooy

***London:* London Islamic School**
151 Oxford St. West, London, ON N6H 1S3, Canada
Tel: 519-679-9920; *Fax:* 519-679-6842
Enrollment: 187
Patricia Zabian

***London:* London Parental Christian School**
202 Clarke Rd., London, ON N5W 5E4, Canada
Tel: 519-455-0360; *Fax:* 519-455-6717
Grades: K./Elem.
Enrollment: 217
Mary Haven

***London:* London Waldorf School**
7 Beaufort St., London, ON N6G 1A5, Canada
Tel: 519-858-8862; *Fax:* 519-858-8863
Grades: K./Elem.
Enrollment: 109
Peter von Holtzendorff

***London:* Matthews Hall Private School**
1370 Oxford St. West, London, ON N6H 1W2, Canada
Tel: 519-471-5942; *Fax:* 519-471-4765
Grades: K./Elem./Sec.
Enrollment: 233
Patricia Doig

***London:* Montessori House of Children**
711 Waterloo St., London, ON N6A 3W1, Canada
Tel: 519-433-9121; *Fax:* 519-433-8941
reception@montessori.on.ca
www.montessori.on.ca
Grades: 1 - 8
London's Montessori House of Children also offers a toddler program for children from 18 to 30 months & a Casa program, for children from ages 2.5 to 6.
Margaret Whitley, Director
mwhitley@montessori.on.ca
Kim Clarke, Coordinator, Communications
kclarke@montessori.on.ca
Kristen Crouse, Coordinator, Elementary & Junior High
kcrouse@montessori.on.ca
Marianne Rutledge, Coordinator, Admissions
registrar@montessori.on.ca
Kathy Work-Schlattman, Coordinator, Casa
kwork@montessori.on.ca
Shonagh Stevenson-Ramsay, Directress, Toddler Program
sstevenson@montessori.on.ca
Walter Iwanowski, Controller
wki@montessori.on.ca

***Lucknow:* Lucknow & District Christian School**
PO Box 550, Lucknow, ON N0G 2H0, Canada
Tel: 519-528-2016; *Fax:* 519-528-2095
Grades: K./Elem.
Lawrence Uyl

***Markham:* Somerset Academy**
7700 Brimley Rd., Markham, ON L3R 0E5, Canada
Tel: 905-940-8990; *Fax:* 905-940-8992
administration@somersetacademy.ca
www.somersetacademy.ca
Grades: Jr. K.-8
Enrollment: 172
Maureen VanLoon

***Markham:* Town Centre Montessori Private Schools (TCMPS)**
Main Campus
155 Clayton Dr., Markham, ON L3R 7P3, Canada
Tel: 905-470-1200; *Fax:* 905-470-0184
admin@tcmps.com
www.tcmps.com
Other Information: 905-474-3434 (Phone, Preschool & Grade 1)
Grades: Preschool - 8
The preschool program accepts children as young as two years of age.
Marianne Vanderlugt, Principal

***Markham:* Town Centre Private High School (TCPHS)**
155 Clayton Dr., Markham, ON L3R 7P3
Tel: 905-470-1200; *Fax:* 905-470-1721
www.tcphs.com
Grades: 9 - 12
This is a coeducational school which provides university bound & advanced placement courses.

***Markham:* Trillium School**
4277 - 14th Ave., Markham, ON L3R 0J2, Canada
Tel: 905-946-1181; *Fax:* 905-946-8267
info@trilliumschool.ca
www.trilliumschool.ca
Grades: Preschool - 8
Trillium School is a coeducational, non-denominational school. It features a pre-Casa program for toddlers & a Casa program.
Lily Moon, Principal

***Markham:* Wesley Christian Academy**
22 Heritage Rd., Markham, ON L3P 1M4, Canada
Tel: 905-201-8461; *Fax:* 905-201-6438
office@wesleychristianacademy.com
www.wesleychristianacademy.com
Grades: Senior Kindergarten - 8
Wesley Christian Academy offers an academic program within the context of Christian principles.

***Markham:* Wishing Well Montessori School**
#30, 455 Cochrane Dr., Markham, ON L3R 9R4, Canada
Tel: 905-470-9751; *Fax:* 905-470-0496
Grades: K./Elem.
Enrollment: 432
Connie Xuereb

***Metcalfe:* Community Christian School**
2681 Glen St., Metcalfe, ON K0A 2P0, Canada
Tel: 613-821-3669; *Fax:* 613-821-6135
info@communitychristianschool.ca
www.communitychristianschool.ca
Grades: Elem.
Enrollment: 77
Gayle Freeburn, Principal

***Millgrove:* Covenant Christian School**
P.O. Box 2
497 Millgrove Side Rd., Millgrove, ON L0R 1V0, Canada
Tel: 905-689-3191; *Fax:* 905-689-0191
covenant@on.aibn.com
Grades: Elem.
Enrollment: 119
George Hofsink, Principal

***Mississauga:* Bronte College of Canada**
88 Bronte College Ct., Mississauga, ON L5B 1M9, Canada
Tel: 905-270-7788; *Fax:* 905-270-7828
info@brontecollege.ca; admissions@brontecollege.ca
www.brontecollege.ca

Grades: 9 - 12
Bronte College of Canada is a co-educational, international day & boarding school. The school also offers University of Guelph & Bronte College first year university courses, an advanced placement program, & English as a Second Language (ESL).

Mississauga: Froebel Education Centre
1576 Dundas St. West, Mississauga, ON L5C 1E5, Canada
Tel: 905-277-9371; *Fax:* 905-277-9402
office@froebel.com
www.froebel.com
Grades: K.-8
Enrollment: 89
Education based on the principle's of Friedrich Froebel: working in partnership with the child's family, tranformation of creative play into creative work, & making connections with others, the world & God.
Barbara E. Corbett, B.A., Ed.D., Director, Education

Mississauga: IQRA Islamic School
5753 Coopers Ave., Mississauga, ON L4Z 1R9, Canada
Tel: 905-507-6688; *Fax:* 905-507-9243
Enrollment: 150
Ghzala Khan

Mississauga: ISNA Islamic School
1525 Sherway Dr., Mississauga, ON L4X 1C5, Canada
Tel: 905-272-4303; *Fax:* 905-272-4311
Grades: K./Elem.
Enrollment: 306
Osama Ghanim

Mississauga: Khalsa Community School
7280 Airport Rd., Mississauga, ON L4T 2H3, Canada
Tel: 905-678-0603; *Fax:* 905-678-9133
Enrollment: 187
Ripsodhak Grewal

Mississauga: Mentor College
Main Campus
40 Forest Ave., Mississauga, ON L5G 1L1, Canada
Tel: 905-271-3393; *Fax:* 905-271-8367
40forest@mentorcollege.edu (Main campus)
www.mentorcollege.edu
Other Information: 56cayuga@mentorcollege.edu (E-mail, Primary campus)
Grades: Junior Kindergarten - 12
Ken Philbrook, Director

Mississauga: Mississauga Christian Academy (MCA)
Gananoque Campus
2720 Gananoque Dr., Mississauga, ON L5N 2R2, Canada
Tel: 905-826-4114; *Fax:* 905-567-5874
office@mississaugachristianacademy.com
www.mississaugachristianacademy.com
Grades: Junior Kindergarten - 8
The Mississauga Christian Academy also operates a licensed day care.

Mississauga: Northstar Montessori
4900 Tomken Rd., Mississauga, ON L4W 1J8, Canada
Tel: 905-890-7827; *Fax:* 905-890-6771
admin@northstarmontessori.com
www.northstarmontessori.com
Grades: Preschool / Elementary
Northstar Montessori offers the following programs: toddlers, pre-Casa, primary, & elementary. Ages of children range from 18 months to 12 years.
Virginia Ramirez, Principal
Sherry Gosal, Vice Principal
Rick Ramirez, Manager, Business
Rose Sta. Ana, Office Administrator

Mississauga: Rotherglen School
Gooderham Estate Campus
929 Old Derry Rd., Mississauga, ON L5W 1A1
Tel: 905-565-8707; *Fax:* 905-565-0485
www.rotherglen.com
Grades: Preschool - 8
The Casa program is designed for children from age three to five. Rotherglen school has over 1,200 students who attend the school's four campuses.

Mississauga: Rotherglen School
Erin Mills Campus
3553 South Common Crt., Mississauga, ON L5L 2B3
Tel: 905-820-9445; *Fax:* 905-569-1569
www.rotherglen.com
Grades: Preschool - 6
The Erin Mills campus provides a Montessori program for its students, from Casa to grade six.

Mississauga: Sherwood Heights School
3065 Glen Erin Dr., Mississauga, ON L5L 1J3, Canada
Tel: 905-569-8999; *Fax:* 905-569-9034
info@sherwoodheights.com
www.sherwoodheights.com
Grades: Elem.
Enrollment: 206
Anthony H. Mutlak

Mississauga: Sommerville Manor Private School
1135 Central Pkwy. West, Mississauga, ON L5C 3J2, Canada
Tel: 905-277-1085; *Fax:* 905-277-3801
info@sommervillemanor.com
www.sommervillemanor.com
Grades: K.-8
Enrollment: 283
Winefride Johnson

Mississauga: Springfield Preparatory School
1444 Dundas Cres., Mississauga, ON L5C 1E9, Canada
Tel: 905-273-9717; *Fax:* 905-273-9717
info@springfieldprep.ca
www.springfieldprep.ca
Grades: Jr. K.-6
Enrollment: 66
Janet Murphy

Mississauga: TEAM School
Also known as: Tutorial & Educ. Assistance in Mississauga
275 Rudar Rd., Mississauga, ON L5A 1S2, Canada
Tel: 905-279-7200; *Fax:* 905-279-1561
www.teamschool.com
Grades: K./Elem./Spec. Ed.
Enrollment: 299
Chuck MacDonald, Principal

Mississauga: Toronto Ability School
1146 Clarkson Rd. North, Mississauga, ON L5J 2W2, Canada
Tel: 905-855-3800
Grades: Preschool - 8

Mississauga: White Oaks Montessori School Ltd.
Vanier Campus
1200 Vanier Dr., Mississauga, ON L5H 4C7, Canada
Tel: 905-278-4454; *Fax:* 905-278-5184
admin@woms.ca
www.woms.ca
Other Information: 905-855-2321 (Phone, Clarkson Campus)
Grades: Preschool - Elementary
White Oaks Montessori School is a fully accredited Canadian Council of Montessori Administrators school. The youngest children are offered toddler programs. Casa programs are provided for children from age three to five. The Clarkson Campus is located at the following address: 1338 Clarkson Road North, Mississauga.
Barbara S. Ward, AMI, Founder & Chief Administrative Officer
Irene Stathoukos, BSc., AMI, Principal
Daniel Ward, Information Technologist

Mount Forest: Farewell Parochial
9173 Concession 11, Mount Forest, ON N0G 2L0, Canada
Grades: Elem.
Florence Martin

Mount Hope: Grandview Adventist Academy
3975 Hwy. 6, Mount Hope, ON L0R 1W0, Canada
Tel: 905-679-4492; *Fax:* 905-679-4492
grandview@mountaincable.net
www.grandviewschool.ca
Grades: Elem./Sec.
Enrollment: 58
Gisela I. Hoelzel

Nepean: Ottawa Islamic School
10 Coral Ave., Nepean, ON K2E 5Z6, Canada
Tel: 613-727-5066; *Fax:* 613-727-8486
info@ottawaislamicschool.org
www.ottawaislamicschool.org
Grades: JK-12
Enrollment: 246
Mohamed Sheik Ahmed (Dalmar, Principal
msahmed@islamicschool.on.ca

Nepean: Rambam Day School
25 Esquimault Ave., Nepean, ON K2H 6Z5, Canada
Tel: 613-820-9484; *Fax:* 613-820-0029
www.rambam.ca
Other Information: 613-820-9484, ext. 348 (Phone, Admissions & Judaica)
Grades: Preschool - 8
The RAMBAM Day School offers general & Judaic studies, in Hebrew, French, & English.
Rabbi Dovid Hayes, Executive Director, 613-820-9484, ext. 350
Chana Hayes, Principal & Head, Judaica
Susan Spence, Vice Principal & Head, General Studies
Rabbi Yaakov Wilschanski, Educational Director, 613-820-9484, ext. 351

Nepean: Redeemer Christian High School (RCHS)
82 Colonnade Rd. North, Nepean, ON K2E 7L2, Canada
Tel: 613-723-9262; *Fax:* 613-723-9321
info@rchs.on.ca
www.rchs.on.ca
Grades: 9 - 12
Redeemer Christian High School offers a Christ-centered education. The school also provides programs for students with learning disabilities.
William Van Dyke, Principal
principal@rchs.on.ca
J. David Naftel, B.Ed., B.Sc., Vice Principal
dnaftel@rchs.on.ca
Mary Joustra, Contact, Finance & Admissions
info@rchs.on.ca
Cheryl Sullivan, Secretary
office@rchs.on.ca

Nestor Falls: Mikinaak Onigaming School
P.O. Box 160
Nestor Falls, ON P0X 1K0, Canada
Tel: 807-484-2162; *Fax:* 807-484-2737
Grades: Junior Kindergarten - 12
Enrollment: 100
Mikinaak Onigaming School is a band operated school, providing education for the Ojibways of Onigaming First Nation.
Owen Zoccole, Director, Education

Newmarket: Holland Marsh District Christian School
18955 Dufferin St., Newmarket, ON L3Y 4V9, Canada
Tel: 905-775-3701; *Fax:* 905-775-2395
Grades: K./Elem.
Enrollment: 279
Rod Berg

Newmarket: Newmarket & District Christian Academy (NDCA)
P.O. Box 297
221 Carlson Dr., Newmarket, ON L3Y 4X1, Canada
Tel: 905-895-1199; *Fax:* 905-895-4353
ndca@rogers.com
www.ndca.ca
Grades: Kindergarten - 8
Steve Klassen, Chair
Jane MacLachlan, Principal

Newmarket: Pickering College
16945 Bayview Ave., Newmarket, ON L3Y 4X2, Canada
Tel: 905-895-1700; *Fax:* 905-895-9076
Toll-Free: 877-895-1700
info@pickeringcollege.on.ca
www.pickeringcollege.on.ca
Grades: Jr. K.-University Prep
Enrollment: 415
Day and Boarding School
Peter C. Sturrup, Headmaster

Niagara Falls: Niagara Community Church School
9527 McLeod St., RR#2, Niagara Falls, ON L2E 6S5, Canada
Tel: 905-357-9519
Grades: Kindergarten - 8
Chris Schmoll, Principal

Nobleton: The Montessori Country School
Nobleton Campus
P.O. Box 455
6185 - 15th Sideroad, Nobleton, ON L0G 1N0, Canada
Tel: 905-859-4739; *Fax:* 905-859-5696
Toll-Free: 1-866-557-2272
admin@mcs-nobleton.com
www.montessoricountryschool.ca
Grades: Preschool / Elementary
The Montessori Country School offers a toddler program, a Casa program, & an elementary program. Children range in age from 12 months to 12 years.
Jack Rice, Director, Education
Joanne Hastie, Director, Curriculum & Instruction
Gregory Dixon, Administrator

North York: Scarborough Christian School
95 Jonesville Cres., North York, ON M4A 1H2, Canada
Tel: 416-750-7515; *Fax:* 905-750-7720
info@scarboroughchristianschool.com
www.scarboroughchristianschool.com
Grades: K./Elem./Sec.
Enrollment: 276
Martin D. Sandford, Principal

North York: Willow Wood School
55 Scarsdale Rd., North York, ON M3B 2R3, Canada
Tel: 416-444-7644; Fax: 416-444-1801
Grades: Elem./Sec./Spec. Ed.
Joy Kurtz

North York: Willowdale Christian School
60 Hilda Ave., North York, ON M2M 1V5, Canada
Tel: 416-222-1711; Fax: 416-222-1939
Grades: K./Elem.
Enrollment: 191
Mary Jansen

Norwich: Rehoboth Christian School - Norwich
P.O. Box 220
43 Main St. East, Norwich, ON N0J 1P0, Canada
Tel: 519-863-2403; Fax: 519-863-3984
office@rcsnorwich.com
Grades: Kindergarten - 12
Enrollment: 600
J. Heikoop, Principal
Martien Vanderspek, Vice Principal
mvanterspek@nor-del.com

Oakville: Al-Falah Islamic School
391 Burnhamthorpe Rd. East, Oakville, ON L6H 7B4, Canada
Tel: 905-257-5782; Fax: 905-257-0848
office@al-falah.org
www.al-falah.org
Grades: Elem.
Enrollment: 215
Accredited by the Ontario Min. of Education; curriculum also includes programmes in the arts, computers, physical education, Arabic language, & Quran studies.
Nafees Khan, Principal

Oakville: Appleby College
540 Lakeshore Rd. West, Oakville, ON L6K 3P1, Canada
Tel: 905-845-4681; Fax: 905-845-9828
info@appleby.on.ca
www.appleby.on.ca
Grades: Elem./Sec.
Enrollment: 740
Independent, co-educational school for boarding & day students in Grandes 7 through 12.
Guy S. McLean, Principal

Oakville: Chisholm Educational Centre
1484 Cornwall Rd., Oakville, ON L6J 7W5, Canada
Tel: 905-844-3240
www.chisholmcentre.com
Grades: Secondary / Post Secondary
Chisholm Educational Centre consists of the Academy High School & the Collegiate.
Dr. Howard Bernstein, C. Psych., Executive Director
Dr. Shirley Bryntwick, C. Psych., Director, Professional Services
Frances Hatcher, Dip. Math., Post Grad. Ed, Head, Chisholm Collegiate
C. David Jowett, M.Ed., Principal, Chisholm Academy
Sylvia Moyssakos, M.Sc.Ed., O.C.T., Head, Tutorial & Remedial Services
Karen Boyd, Manager, Office

Oakville: Dearcroft Montessori School
1167 Lakeshore Rd. East, Oakville, ON L6J 1L3, Canada
Tel: 905-844-2114; Fax: 905-844-3529
Grades: K./Elem.
Enrollment: 138
Barbara Phippen

Oakville: Fern Hill School
Oakville Campus
3300 Ninth Line Rd., Oakville, ON L6H 7A8, Canada
Tel: 905-257-0022
www.fernhillschool.com
Grades: Elem.
Enrollment: 542
Co-educational. Burlington Campus: 801 North Service Rd., (905) 634-8652.
Wendy Derrick, Director/Co-founder
Joanne McLean, Director/Co-founder

Oakville: Glenburnie School
2035 Upper Middle Rd. East, Oakville, ON L6J 7G6, Canada
Tel: 905-338-6236; Fax: 905-338-2654
admin@glenburnieschool.com
www.glenburnieschool.com
Grades: K./Elem.
Enrollment: 361
Melissa Leduc, Principal
mleduc@glenburnieschool.com

Oakville: John Knox Christian School
2232 Sheridan Garden Dr., Oakville, ON L6J 7T1, Canada
Tel: 905-829-8048; Fax: 905-829-8056
Grades: Elem.
Enrollment: 382
Lorna Keith

Oakville: John Knox Christian School
2232 Sheridan Garden Dr., Oakville, ON L6J 7T1, Canada
Tel: 905-829-8048; Fax: 905-829-8056
www.jkcs-oakville.org
Grades: K./Elem.
Enrollment: 256
William Barneveld

Oakville: King's Christian College
528 Burnhamthorpe Rd. West, Oakville, ON L6M 4K6, Canada
Tel: 905-257-5464
Grades: Sec.
Enrollment: 152
Jim Vanderkooy

Oakville: MacLachlan College
337 Trafalgar Rd., Oakville, ON L6J 3H3, Canada
Tel: 905-844-0372; Fax: 905-844-9369
Grades: Elem./Sec.
Enrollment: 375
John H. Bailey

Oakville: Oakville Christian School (OCS)
112 Third Line, Oakville, ON L6L 3Z6, Canada
Tel: 905-825-1247
ocsadmissions@ocsonline.org
www.ocsonline.org
Grades: Junior Kindergarten - 8
Enrollment: 245
Jeff Kennedy, Principal

Oakville: Rotherglen School
Oakville Elementary Campus
2050 Neyagawa Blvd., Oakville, ON L6H 6R2, Canada
Tel: 905-849-1897; Fax: 905-849-1354
www.rotherglen.com
Grades: 1 - 8
The school features the Rotherglen Education in Active Leadership initiative for its grade eight students. Over 1,200 students attend Rotherglen School's four campuses in Oakville & Mississauga.
Tracey Du Preez, Coordinator, Admissions
tdupreez@rotherglen.com

Oakville: Rotherglen School
Oakville Primary Campus
2045 Sixth Line, Oakville, ON L6H 1X9
Tel: 905-338-3528; Fax: 905-338-9599
www.rotherglen.com
Grades: Preschool - 1
The Casa program is designed for children as young as three years of age. The school includes students from age three to six.

Oakville: St. Mildred's - Lightbourn School
1080 Linbrook Rd., Oakville, ON L6J 2L1, Canada
Tel: 905-845-2386; Fax: 905-845-4799
info@smls.on.ca
www.smls.on.ca/
Grades: Jr. K.-12
Enrollment: 600
All-girls school
Jane Wightman, Principal
jwightman@smls.on.ca

Orangeville: Hillcrest School
#74A, 90 Lawrence Ave., Orangeville, ON L9W 4J3, Canada
Tel: 519-942-3251; Fax: 519-942-3251
Grades: K./Elem./Sec.
Enrollment: 66
Gail P. Hooper

Orangeville: The Maples Independent Country School
RR#4, Orangeville, ON L9W 2Z1, Canada
Tel: 519-942-3310; Fax: 519-942-8041
info@TheMaplesSchool.com
www.themaplesschool.com
Grades: Preschool - 8
Enrollment: 120

Orillia: Orillia Christian School
P.O. Box 862
505 Gill St., Orillia, ON L3V 6K8, Canada
Tel: 705-326-0532; Fax: 705-327-9856
www.ocswebsite.com
Grades: K./Elem.
Enrollment: 120
Bill Freeman

Oshawa: College Park Elementary School
220 Townline Rd. North, Oshawa, ON L1H 8L7, Canada
Tel: 905-723-0163; Fax: 905-723-2984
Grades: K./Elem.
Enrollment: 200
Cathy Dan, Principal

Oshawa: Durham Christian Academy
615 Ridgeway Ave., Oshawa, ON L1J 2W3, Canada
Tel: 905-436-6354; Fax: 905-436-9852
Grades: K./Elem.
Enrollment: 95
David Burns

Oshawa: Immanuel Christian School
849 Rossland Rd. West, Oshawa, ON L1J 8R5, Canada
Tel: 905-728-9071; Fax: 905-728-0604
Grades: K./Elem.
Enrollment: 143
Jasper Hoogendam, Principal

Oshawa: Kingsway College
1200 Leland Rd., Oshawa, ON L1K 2H4, Canada
Tel: 905-433-1144; Fax: 905-433-1156
Grades: Sec.
Enrollment: 186
John C. Janes

Ottawa: Abraar School
P.O. Box 332
1568 Merivale Rd., Ottawa, ON K2G 5Y7, Canada
Tel: 613-820-0044; Fax: 613-820-1495
info@abraarschool.com
www.abraarschool.com
Grades: Elem.
Enrollment: 212
Islamic school. Location: 1085 Grenon Ave., Ottawa.
Moussa Ouarou, Principal

Ottawa: Ashbury College
362 Mariposa Ave., Ottawa, ON K1M 0T3, Canada
Tel: 613-749-5954; Fax: 613-749-9724
Grades: Elem./Sec.
Enrollment: 648
Tam Mathews

Ottawa: Bishop Hamilton School
2199 Regency Terrace, Ottawa, ON K2C 1H2, Canada
Tel: 613-596-4013; Fax: 613-596-4971
bhswest@bhsmontessori.ca
www.bhsmontessori.ca
Grades: Toddler/Casa/Elementary/Junior High
Bishop Hamilton School is a Christian Montessori school for children from ages 18 months to 14 years.
Heather Smith, Chair
Alison Goss, B.A., AMI., M.Ed., Principal

Ottawa: Canadian Montessori Academy (CMA)
70 Fieldrow St., Ottawa, ON K2G 2Y7, Canada
Tel: 613-727-9427; Fax: 613-723-1035
info@montessori-academy.com;
office@montessori-academy.com
www.montessori-academy.com
Canadian Montessori Academy is a bilingual school, with both English & French Montessori teachers.
Renette Sasouni, Chief Administrative Officer
Sherie de Mel, Principal
Sabena de Mel, Vice Principal & Head, Primary Department
Jackie Lalumiere, Head, Infant / Toddler Department
Dylan McLaughlin, Head, Elementary & Middle School
Libby Glencross, Coordinator, Corpore Sano Programme

Ottawa: Counterpoint Academy Inc.
149 King George St., Ottawa, ON K1K 1V2, Canada
Tel: 613-748-1052; Fax: 613-748-8234
dpribyl@counterpointacademy.com
www.counterpointacademy.com
Grades: K.-6
Enrollment: 163
Enriched curriculum, including early literacy, spelling/phonics/grammar, writing skills, math, science, English & French language arts, public speaking, art, music, drama, computers, & physical education. Counterpoint Academy West: 35 Beaufort Dr., Kanata, (613) 271-6356 (Ms. C. Kim, B.A., B.Ed., Principal & Registrar). Day care centres at both locations.
Laura W. Tilson, B.A., B.Ed., M.Ed., Principal

Ottawa: Elmwood School
Rockcliffe Park
261 Buena Vista Rd., Ottawa, ON K1M 0V9, Canada
Tel: 613-749-6761; *Fax:* 613-741-8210
Grades: K./Elem./Sec.
Enrollment: 564
Helen Hirsh Spence

Ottawa: Fern Hill School (Ottawa) Inc.
50 Vaughan St., Ottawa, ON K1M 1X1, Canada
Tel: 613-746-0255; *Fax:* 613-746-7514
www.fernhillottawa.com
Grades: Pre./K./Elem.
Enrollment: 99
Enriched academic programme; before/after school care & after school programmes; Extended French programme.
Elizabeth Milligan, Principal
principal@fernhillottawa.com

Ottawa: Hillel Academy
31 Nadolny Sachs Private, Ottawa, ON K2A 1R9, Canada
Tel: 613-820-5602; *Fax:* 613-722-0020
Grades: K./Elem./Sec.
Enrollment: 421
Borch Perton

Ottawa: Joan of Arc Academy
2221 Elmira Dr., Ottawa, ON K2C 1H3, Canada
Tel: 613-728-6364; *Fax:* 613-728-2935
Grades: K./Elem.; Girls
Enrollment: 160
Suzanne Lebrun-Lamoureux

Ottawa: Lycée Claudel
1635, prom Riverside, Ottawa, ON K1G 0E5, Canada
Tél: 613-733-8522; *Téléc:* 613-733-3782
www.claudel.org
Grades: Mat./Prim./Sec.
Enrollment: 887
Joëlle Émorine, Proviseure
proviseure@claudel.org

Ottawa: Ottawa Christian School
2191 Benjamin Ave., Ottawa, ON K2A 1P6, Canada
Tel: 613-722-5836; *Fax:* 613-722-5836
info@ocschool.org
www.ocschool.org
Grades: K./Elem.
Enrollment: 237
Paul Triemstra, Principal

Ottawa: Ottawa Languages Institute Ltd.
1990 Leslie Ave., Ottawa, ON K1H 5M3, Canada
Tel: 613-521-3331; *Fax:* 613-521-6482
Grades: Sec.
Tin S. Yap

Ottawa: Ottawa Montessori School
335 Lindsay St., Ottawa, ON K1G 0L6, Canada
Tel: 613-521-5185; *Fax:* 613-521-6796
info@ottawamontessori.com
www.ottawamontessori.com/
Grades: K./Elem.
Enrollment: 400
Pat Gere, Dir.

Ottawa: Parsifal Waldorf School
1644 Bank St., Ottawa, ON K1V 7Y6, Canada
Tel: 613-733-2668; *Fax:* 613-733-6774
Grades: K./Elem.
Rachel Montgomery

Ottawa: Turnbull School
1132 Fisher Ave., Ottawa, ON K1Z 6P7, Canada
Tel: 613-729-9940; *Fax:* 613-729-1636
admin@turnbull.ca
www.turnbull.ca
Grades: Junior Kindergarten - 8
Mary Ann S. Turnbull, B.Sc. (Psychology), Director
Gareth Reid, Principal
Buddy Clinch, Vice Principal, Junior School
Craig Dunn, Vice Principal, Senior School
Liz Doran, Head, Academic Studies (Primary Division)
Christine Ferris, Head, Academic Studies (Senior Division)
Katie Horton, Head, Academic Studies (Junior Division)
Jane Minty, Head, School Life
Sally Swan, Head, Community Service
Joyce Walker-Steed, Registrar
jwalker-steed@turnbull.ca

Ottawa: Westboro Academy
Académie Westboro
200 Brewer Way, Ottawa, ON K1S 5R2, Canada
Tel: 613-737-9543
Westboro@WestboroAcademy.com
www.westboroacademy.com
Grades: Junior Kindergarten - 8
Westboro Academy is a coeducational school, which offers an enriched bilingual education.
Marcel Papineau, Principal

Owen Sound: Riverforest Montessori School
1595 - 3rd Ave. West, Owen Sound, ON N4K 4R2, Canada
Tel: 519-371-2313; *Fax:* 519-371-1178
riverforestmontessori@hotmail.com
www.riverforestmontessori.com
Grades: Preschool - 6
The Casa program is offered for children from age 2.5 to 6.

Owen Sound: Timothy Christian School (TCS)
1735 - 4th Ave. West, Owen Sound, ON N4K 4X7, Canada
Tel: 519-371-9151; *Fax:* 519-371-8607
timothy@timothycs.org
www.timothycs.org
Grades: Junior Kindergarten - 8
Matthew Bittel, Principal
Kendra VanSchepen, Bookkeeper

Pawitik: Baibombeh Anishinabe School
Whitefish Bay First Nation
General Delivery, Pawitik, ON P0X 1L0, Canada
Tel: 807-226-5698; *Fax:* 807-226-1089
bbbschool@hotmail.com; bbbschool@kmts.ca
www.kmts.ca/~baibombe
Grades: Junior Kindergarten - 12
Baibombeh Anishinabe School is a band operated Ojibway school.

Peterborough: Grace Christian Academy
575 Centreline, Peterborough, ON K9J 7Y4, Canada
Tel: 705-745-4400; *Fax:* 705-745-5427
Grades: K./Elem.
Enrollment: 92
Kim T. Bolton

Peterborough: Rhema Christian School
29 County Rd. 4, Peterborough, ON K9L 1B8, Canada
Tel: 705-743-1400; *Fax:* 705-743-1415
office@rhema.ca
www.rhema.ca
Grades: Junior Kindergarten - 8
Rhema Christian School is a day school which offers a Christ-centered education.
Joel Slofstra, Principal
Joel Slofstra, Principal
Joanne Brethour, Business Administrator
Rena Ridley, Office Administrator

Pickering: Blaisdale Montessori School
415 Toynevale Rd., Pickering, ON L1W 2G9, Canada
Tel: 905-509-5005; *Fax:* 905-509-1959
info@blaisdale.com
www.blaisdale.com
Grades: Toddler/Casa/Elementary/Renaissance
Blaisdale Montessori School offers programs for ages 12 months to 14 years, including pre-toddler.
Heather Wilson, Principal & Administrator, 905-509-5005, ext. 107
hwilson@blaisdale.com

Pickering: Montessori Learning Centre of Pickering (MLCP)
401 Kingston Rd., Pickering, ON L1V 1A3, Canada
Tel: 905-509-1722; *Fax:* 905-509-8283
info@montessorilearningcentre.com
www.mlcp.ca
Grades: Preschool / Elementary
Enrollment: 240
Montessori Learning Centre of Pickering provides the following programs: infants, pre-Casa, Casa, & elementary.

Picton: Sonrise Christian Academy
P.O. Box 845
58 Johnson St., Picton, ON K0K 2T0, Canada
Tel: 613-476-7883; *Fax:* 613-476-4202
office@sonrisechristianacademy.com
www.sonrisechristianacademy.com
Grades: Elem.
Enrollment: 62
Julie Scrivens, Principal

Poole: Fair Haven Christian Day School
RR#1, Poole, ON N0K 1S0, Canada
Tel: 519-595-4568
Grades: K./Elem.
Enrollment: 66
Howard Bean

Port Hope: Trinity College School (TCS)
55 Deblaquire St. North, Port Hope, ON L1A 4K7, Canada
Tel: 905-885-3217; *Fax:* 905-885-9690
info@tcs.on.ca; communications@tcs.on.ca;
admissions@tcs.on.ca
www.tcs.on.ca
Grades: 5 - 12
Enrollment: 600
The school is a coeducational boarding / day school. The senior school has approximately 500 students. Over 100 students attend the junior school.
Stuart K.C. Grainger, Headmaster
Jeffrey Prince, Secretary

Prince Albert: Scugog Christian School
P.O. Box 3308
14480 Old Simcoe Rd., Prince Albert, ON L9L 1C3, Canada
Tel: 905-985-3741; *Fax:* 905-985-7153
scugogchristianschool@powergate.ca
www.scugogchristianschool.com
Grades: K.-8
Enrollment: 53
Grace van Niejenhuis, Principal

Richmond Hill: Century Montessori School
Regent Campus
71 Regent St., Richmond Hill, ON L4C 9Y1, Canada
Tel: 905-737-9494; *Fax:* 905-737-1014
Info@CenturyMontessori.com
www.centurymontessori.com
Grades: Casa / PresSchool - 8
Century Montessori School offers education for children from age 2.5 to grade 8.

Richmond Hill: Richmond Hill Montessori & Elementary School (RHMS)
Hillsview Campus
118 Hillsview Dr., Richmond Hill, ON L4C 1T2, Canada
Tel: 905-508-2228; *Fax:* 905-508-2229
reception@rhms.org
www.rhms.org
Grades: Preschool - 8
The school's preschool program is Montessori based. The junior program includes three & four year old children. The senior program is designed for children who are four & five year olds.
Walter Ribeiro, Director
w.ribeiro@rhms.org
Janet Darbey, Principal, Hillsview Campus
jdarbey@rhms.org
Anita Gonzalez, Principal, 16th Avenue Campus
agonzalez@rhms.org
Dino D'Amato, Vice Principal, Hillsview Campus
ddamato@rhms.org
Rose Chitiz, Administrator
rchitiz@rhms.org
Catherine Evans, Administrator
cevans@rhms.org
Sarah Salvatore, Administrator
ssalvatore@rhms.org
Claude Rodrigues, Contact, Purchasing & Finance
crodrigues@rhms.org

Richmond Hill: Toronto Montessori Schools (TMS)
8569 Bayview Ave., Richmond Hill, ON L4B 3M7
Tel: 905-889-6882; *Fax:* 905-886-6516
admissions@torontomontessori.ca;
alumni@torontomontessori.ca
www.torontomontessori.ca
Other Information: tmshr@torontomontessori.ca (E-mail, Human Resources)
Grades: Preschool - 12

Rosseau: Rosseau Lake College (RLC)
1967 Bright St., Rosseau, ON P0C 1J0, Canada
Tel: 705-732-4351; *Fax:* 705-732-6319
Toll-Free: 800-265-0569
info@rlc.on.ca; advancement@rlc.on.ca; admissions@rlc.on.ca
www.rosseaulakecollege.com
Enrollment: 150
Rosseau Lake College is a coeducational day & boarding school. The average class size is twelve.
Graham Hookey, Head of School

Ruthven: Emmanuel Christian Academy
P.O. Box 34
294 County Rd. East, RR#2, Ruthven, ON N0P 2G0, Canada
Tel: 519-839-4874; *Fax:* 519-839-4875

Grades: K./Elem.
Enrollment: 22
Benna Nicolai

Sandy Lake: Thomas Fiddler Memorial Elementary School
P.O. Box 8
Sandy Lake, ON P0V 1V0, Canada
Tel: 807-744-4491; *Fax:* 807-774-1324
www.sandylake.firstnation.ca

Grades: Kindergarten - 6; Special Ed.
Enrollment: 390
Number of Employees: 53. The Thomas Fiddler Memorial Elementary School is part of the Sandy Lake Board of Education. The elementary school educates members of Sandy Lake First Nation. From kindergarten to grade four, Thomas Fiddler Memorial Elementary School provides a native immersion program.
Rose Yesno, Principal
roseyesno@hotmail.com
Doreen Fiddler, Social Counsellor
Andrew Mamakeesic, Social Counsellor

Sandy Lake: Thomas Fiddler Memorial High School
P.O. Box 8
Sandy Lake, ON P0V 1V0
Tel: 807-774-1229; *Fax:* 807-774-1228
www.sandylake.firstnation.ca

Grades: 7 - 10
Enrollment: 124
The activities of Thomas Fiddler Memorial High School are overseen by the Sandy Lake Board of Education. The secondary school serves students of the Sandy Lake First Nation.

Sarnia: Sarnia Christian School
1273 Exmouth St., Sarnia, ON N7S 1W9, Canada
Tel: 519-383-7750; *Fax:* 519-383-6304
info@sarniachristian.com
www.sarniachristian.com

Grades: K.-8
Enrollment: 164
Len Smit, Principal
len.smit@sarniachristian.com

Sarnia: Temple Christian Academy
1410 Quinn Dr., Sarnia, ON N7T 7H4, Canada
Tel: 519-542-9563; *Fax:* 519-542-9889
office@templechristianacademy.ca
www.templechristianacademy.ca

Grades: Jr. K.-8
Enrollment: 84
P. Wes Harding, Principal

Scarborough: Agbu Zaroukian School
930 Progress Ave., Scarborough, ON M1G 3T5, Canada
Tel: 416-439-3900; *Fax:* 416-431-2510

Grades: K./Elem.
Enrollment: 91
Hasmik Kurdian

Scarborough: Ellesmere Montessori School Incn Campus
37 Marchington Circle, Scarborough, ON M1R 3M6, Canada
Tel: 416-447-1059; *Fax:* 416-447-1059

Grades: K./Elem.
Enrollment: 76
Jill Weinberger

Scarborough: Ellington Montessori
2102 Lawrence Ave. East, Scarborough, ON M1R 2Z9, Canada
Tel: 416-759-8363; *Fax:* 416-759-2162

Grades: Elem.
Enrollment: 81
Deborah Renwick

Scarborough: Madinatul-Uloom Academy
670 Progress Ave, Scarborough, ON M1H 3A4, Canada
Tel: 416-332-1810

Grades: Elem./Sec.
Enrollment: 358
Mohammed Wajiduddin

Scarborough: Madison Academy
#1, 700 Progress Ave., Scarborough, ON M1H 2Z7, Canada
Tel: 416-439-8991

Grades: Sec.
Enrollment: 177
Sheileen Krone

Scarborough: Salaheddin Islamic School
741 Kennedy Rd., Scarborough, ON M1K 2C6, Canada
Tel: 416-264-9495

Grades: Elem.
Enrollment: 185
Laila Maarouf

Scarborough: Whitefield Christian Schools
5808 Finch Ave. East, Scarborough, ON M1B 4Y6, Canada
Tel: 416-297-1212; *Fax:* 416-291-4632

Grades: Elem.
Enrollment: 330
Dr. Ruth E. Slade

Sebringville: Stratford District Christian School
130 Huron Rd., RR#1, Sebringville, ON N0K 1X0, Canada
Tel: 519-393-5675; *Fax:* 519-393-6306

Grades: K./Elem.
Enrollment: 90
Edward J. Petrusma

Simcoe: Bethel Baptist Christian School
P.O. Box 752
4059 Hwy. #3 East, Simcoe, ON N3Y 4T2, Canada
Tel: 519-426-8421; *Fax:* 519-426-8426
www.bethelsimcoe.addr.com/school.html

Grades: Junior Kindergarten - 12
Dr. Michael Glowacki, Principal

Sioux Lookout: New Life Christian Academy
P.O. Box 697
28 - 1st Ave., Sioux Lookout, ON P8T 1B1, Canada
Tel: 807-737-0020; *Fax:* 807-737-4281

Sioux Lookout: Pelican Falls First Nation High School
P.O. Box 4127
Sioux Lookout, ON P8T 1J9, Canada
Tel: 807-737-1110; *Fax:* 807-737-1449
Toll-Free: 1-800-378-911
pelican@nnec.on.ca
www.nnec.on.ca/pffnhs/

Grades: Sec.
Enrollment: 143
Desta Buswa, Principal

Sioux Lookout: Wahsa Distance Education Centre
P.O. Box 1118
74 Front St., Sioux Lookout, ON P8T 1B7, Canada
Tel: 807-737-1488; *Fax:* 807-737-1732

Grades: 9 - 12
Enrollment: 950
The Wahsa Distance Education Centre allows students in northern Ontario communities across the Sioux Lookout District to complete their secondary school education at home. Courses & services are developed in consultation with First Nation communities. The Centre is operated by the Northern Nishnawbe Education Council.
Norma Kejick

Smithville: Covenant Christian School
6470 Regional Rd. #14, Smithville, ON L0R 2A0, Canada
Tel: 905-957-7796; *Fax:* 905-957-7794
www.nace.ca

Grades: Elem.
Enrollment: 226
The Niagara Ass'n for Christian Education (NACE).
Sid Bakker, Principal
sbakker@nace.ca

Smithville: John Calvin Private School
P.O. Box 280
320 Station St., Smithville, ON L0R 2A0, Canada
Tel: 905-957-2341; *Fax:* 905-957-2342

Grades: K./Elem.
Enrollment: 275
Frank C. Ludwig

Smithville: Smithville District Christian High School
P.O. Box 40
6488 Smithville Rd., Smithville, ON L0R 2A0, Canada
Tel: 905-957-3255; *Fax:* 905-957-3431
sdoffice@sdch.on.ca
www.sdch.on.ca

Grades: Sec.
Enrollment: 224
Ted Harris, Administrator

St Catharines: Beacon Christian Schools
Bldg. A & Bldg. B
300 Scott St., St Catharines, ON L2N 1J3, Canada
Tel: 905-937-7411; *Fax:* 905-937-1130
admissions@beaconchristian.org
www.beaconchristian.org

Grades: Elementary / Secondary
Dwayne Bulthuis, Principal, Secondary School
dbulthuis@beaconchristian.org
Karen Gerritsma, Principal, Elementary School
kgerritsma@beaconchristian.org
Ralph Pot, Vice Principal, Elementary School

St Catharines: Grey Gables School
1 Dexter St., St Catharines, ON L2S 2L4, Canada
Tel: 905-685-4577; *Fax:* 905-685-5102

Grades: K./Elem./Sec.
Enrollment: 176
Kathleen Miller

St Catharines: Ridley College
P.O. Box 3013
2 Ridley Rd., St Catharines, ON L2R 7C3, Canada
Tel: 905-684-1889; *Fax:* 905-684-8875
admission@ridleycollege,com
www.ridley.on.ca

Enrollment: 607
Ridley College is a university preparatory school, which features both a lower school & an uppper school. Boarding is available. Over 30% of students are international students.
John R. Anderson, President, Board of Governors
Jonathan Leigh, Headmaster
headmaster@ridleycollege.com
Brian Iggulden, Deputy Headmaster, 905-684-1889, ext. 2211
brian_iggulden@ridleycollege.com
Jay Goulart, Executive Director, Advancement
jay_goulart@ridleycollege.com
Cynthia A. Weedon, Executive Director, Finance & Operations
cynthia_weedon@ridleycollege.com
Don Rickers, Director, External Relations
don_rickers@ridleycollege.com
Stephen Clarke, Assistant Head, Academics, 905-684-1889, ext. 2301
stephen_clarke@ridleycollege.com
Margaret Lech, Assistant Headmaster, Student Affairs
margaret_lech@ridleycollege.com
James Milligan, Assistant Head, Lower School
jim_milligan@ridleycollege.com

St Catharines: St Catharines Montessori School
238 Geneva St., St Catharines, ON L2R 4P8, Canada
Tel: 905-684-6110
stcathmontessori@hotmail.com

Grades: K./Elem.
Susan Bowslaugh

St Catharines: Wheatley School of Montessori Education Inc.
497 Scott St., St Catharines, ON L2M 3X3, Canada
Tel: 905-641-3012; *Fax:* 905-641-1443
mail@wheatleyschool.com
www.wheatleyschool.com

Grades: Preschool - 8
The coeducational, non-denominational school provides Montessori programs for children from preschool to grade four. The Wheatley School's preschool program accepts children as young as two years of age. For upper elementary students in grades five to eight, a traditional, enriched program is offered.
Eda Varalli, Principal

St Thomas: Faith Christian Academy
109 Chestnut St., St Thomas, ON N5R 2B1, Canada
Tel: 519-633-0943; *Fax:* 519-633-6848

Grades: K./Elem.
Enrollment: 163
Barry E. Pearce

St Thomas: St. Thomas Community School
77 Fairview Ave., St Thomas, ON N5R 4X7, Canada
Tel: 519-633-0690; *Fax:* 519-633-0019
info@stthomaschristian.org
www.stthomaschristian.org

Grades: Jr. K.-8
Enrollment: 789
John Lunshof

Stittsville: Ottawa Waldorf School
1 Goulbourn St., Stittsville, ON K2S 1N9, Canada
Tel: 613-836-1547; *Fax:* 613-831-4447
ottawawaldorf@bellnet.ca
www.waldorf.cyberus.ca

Grades: K./Elem.
Enrollment: 91
Karen Ann McKinna

Stouffville: Stouffville Christian School
12485 Tenth Line, Stouffville, ON L4A 7X3, Canada
Tel: 905-640-3297; *Fax:* 905-640-7845
stouffville_cs@bellnet.ca
www.stouffvillechristianschool.org

Grades: Jr. K.-8
Enrollment: 70
Jake Vriend, Principal

Strathroy: Strathroy Community Christian School
7880 Walkers Dr., RR#2, Strathroy, ON N7G 3H4, Canada
Tel: 519-245-1934; *Fax:* 519-245-4424
sccs@sympatico.ca
www.sccs.ca

Grades: Jr. K.-8
Enrollment: 200
Henry Wiersema

Thornhill: As-Sadiq Islamic School
9000 Bathurst St., Thornhill, ON L4J 8A7, Canada
Tel: 905-771-9917; *Fax:* 905-771-9778

Enrollment: 165
William Lahey

Thornhill: Associated Hebrew Schools of Toronto — The Kamin Education Centre
300 Atkinson Ave., Thornhill, ON L4J 8A2, Canada
Tel: 905-889-3998; *Fax:* 905-889-5183
www.associatedhebrewschools.com

Grades: K./Elem.
Enrollment: 1415
Bet Hayeled: Eynat Katz, Vice Principal; Brenda Dzalov, Preschool Coordinator.
Sandy Rabinowitz, Principal
srabinowitz@ahschools.com

Thornhill: Central Montessori School of Thornhill (CMS)
72 Steels Ave. West, Thornhill, ON L4J 1A1, Canada
Tel: 416-889-0012; *Fax:* 905-889-0422
info@cmschool.net
www.cmschool.net

Grades: Toddlers - 8
Central Montessori School is a co-educational, non-denominational school. The early childhood education program is designed for children from 18 months to 2.5 years.
Minno Mohajer

Thornhill: The Leo Baeck Day School
North Campus
36 Atkinson Ave., Thornhill, ON L4J 8C9, Canada
Tel: 905-709-3636; *Fax:* 905-709-1999
info@leobaeck.ca
www.leobaeck.ca

Grades: Preschool - 8
The Leo Baeck Day School is a Reform Jewish day school. Students experience Judaism from a Reform perspective.
Brian Simon, President
board@leobaeck.ca
Dennis H. Grubbs, Interim Director of School
dgrubbs@leobaeck.ca
Robyn Buchmam, Director, Admission
rbuchman@leobaeck.ca
Howard Laderman, Principal, North Campus
hladerman@leobaeck.ca
Eric Petersiel, M.A., B. Ed., RJE, Principal, South Campus, 416-787-9899, fax: 416-787-9838
epetersiel@leobaeck.ca

Thornhill: Ner Israel Yeshiva College
250 Bathurst Glen Dr., Thornhill, ON L4J 8A7, Canada
Tel: 905-731-1224; *Fax:* 905-731-2104

The college provides undergraduate & graduate religious degrees.

Thornhill: Netivot HaTorah Day School
18 Atkinson Ave., Thornhill, ON L4J 8C8, Canada
Tel: 905-771-1234; *Fax:* 905-771-1807
webregistration@netivothatorah.com
www.netivot.com

Grades: Elementary
Enrollment: 600
Netivot HaTorah is an orthodox Jewish school. Its program includes Judaic & general studies.
Dr. Reuven Stern, Head of School
rstern@netivothatorah.com
Rabbi Elliott Diamond, Vice-Principal, Judaic Studies
ediamond@netivothatorah.com
Robyn Shiner, Vice-Principal, General Studies
rshiner@netivothatorah.com
Eileen Goldstein, Director, ECE Department
egoldstein@netivothatorah.com
Alan Steinfeld, Director, Development
asteinfeld@netivothatorah.com
Carol Weir, Director, Podolski NESS Department
cweir@netivothatorah.com

Thornhill: Or Haemet Sefaradic School
7026 Bathurst St., Thornhill, ON L4J 8K3, Canada
Tel: 905-669-7653; *Fax:* 905-669-5138
orhaemet@kehilacentre.com

Grades: K./Elem.
Enrollment: 181
Sarah Wasserman

Thornhill: Toronto Waldorf School (TWS)
9100 Bathurst St., Thornhill, ON L4J 8C7, Canada
Tel: 905-881-1611; *Fax:* 905-881-6710
www.torontowaldorfschool.com

Grades: Preschool - Secondary
Bill Harlow, Chair
Michèle Andrews, Administrative Director
Katharina Dannenberg, High School Administrator
Natalie Semenov, Financial Administrator
Darlene Gregoire, Manager, Business
Paul Sheardown, Manager, Facilities
Aileen Stewart, Coordinator, Admissions

Thorold: Grand River Academy of Christian Education
29 Claremont St., Thorold, ON L2V 1R4, Canada
Tel: 905-227-7507

Grades: Elem./Sec.
Enrollment: 125
Terrence Edwards

Thunder Bay: Thunder Bay Christian School (TBCS)
37 Cooper Rd., Thunder Bay, ON P7C 4V1, Canada
Tel: 807-939-1209; *Fax:* 807-939-2843
tbcs@tbaytel.net
www.tbaychristianschool.ca

Grades: Junior Kindergarten - 10
Enrollment: 165
Thunder Bay Christian School is an interdenominational school operated by parents.
Bea Hayen, Principal

Toronto: Alan Howard Waldorf School (AHWS)
250 Madison Ave., Toronto, ON M4V 2W6, Canada
Tel: 416-962-6447; *Fax:* 416-975-5513
admin@ahws.org
www.ahws.org

Grades: Elem.
Enrollment: 169
Einat Bar Yosef, Enrolment Manager
admissions@ahws.org

Toronto: Archer Preparatory College
1440 Don Mills Rd., Toronto, ON M3B 3M1, Canada
Tel: 416-512-7143
www.archereducation.com

Grades: 3 - 12
Archer Preparatory College was formerly Toronto Academic School. The coeducational high school is operated by Archer Education Group. Advanced academic programs are offered for students in grades three to eight. High school credits are offered for students in grades nine to twelve. English as a Second Language is also provided.
Ivan Davis, Principal

Toronto: ARS Armenian Private School
45 Hallcrown Pl., Toronto, ON M2J 4Y4, Canada
Tel: 416-491-2675; *Fax:* 416-491-8559
www.arsdayschool.ca

Grades: K.-12
Enrollment: 363
Armen Martirossian, Principal

Toronto: Associated Hebrew Schools of Toronto
Hurwich Education Centre
252 Finch Ave. West, Toronto, ON M2R 1M9, Canada
Tel: 416-494-7666; *Fax:* 416-494-2925
www.associatedhebrewschools.com

Grades: K.-8
Enrollment: 1700
A community day school with a focus on Torah-values & high academic standards. Locations in Toronto & Thornhill.
Dr. Mark Smiley, Director, Education
msmiley@ahschools.com

Toronto: Bais Yaakov Elementary School
15 Saranac Blvd., Toronto, ON M6A 2G4, Canada
Tel: 416-256-4436; *Fax:* 416-783-4688

Grades: Pre-school - 8
Enrollment: 400
Bais Yaakov Elementary School is a school for girls.
Magda Simon, Principal, 416-783-6181
Devorah Drebin, Junior High Principal, 416-783-6181

Toronto: Bannockburn School
12 Bannockburn Ave., Toronto, ON M5M 2M8, Canada
Tel: 416-789-7855; *Fax:* 416-789-7963
bannockburn@bannockburn.ca
www.bannockburn.ca

Grades: Toddler / Preschool / Elementary
Bannockburn School offers Montessori education.
Adalove Gorrie, Principal, Elementary Program, 416-789-7855, ext. 303
agorrie@bannockburn.caa
Helen Traicus, Vice Principal, Toddler & Primary Program, 416-789-7855, ext. 306
htraicus@bannockburn.ca
Terry Gorrie, Director, Business, 416-789-7855, ext. 302
tgorrie@bannockburn.ca

Toronto: Bayview Glen
275 Duncan Mill Rd., Toronto, ON M3B 3H9, Canada
Tel: 416-443-1030; *Fax:* 416-443-1032
jmaxwell@bayviewglen.ca
www.bvg.on.ca

Grades: Preschool - 12
Enrollment: 1011
Preschool education at Bayview Glen starts at age 2. The school includes lower school, prep school, & upper school.
Eileen Daunt, Head
Vince Haines, Director, Finance
vhaines@bayviewglen.ca
Dara Kazane, Director, Summer Camp
darak@bayviewglen.ca
Judy Maxwell, Director, Admissions
jmaxwell@bayviewglen.ca

Toronto: Beth Jacob High School
410 Lawrence Ave. West, Toronto, ON M5M 1C2, Canada
Tel: 416-787-4949; *Fax:* 416-787-0453

Grades: Secondary
Beth Jacob High School is a school for Orthodox Jewish girls.

Toronto: Bialik Hebrew Day School
2760 Bathurst St., Toronto, ON M6B 3A1, Canada
Tel: 416-783-3346
info@bialik.ca; boardsecretary@bialik.on.ca
www.bialik.ca

Grades: Junior kindergarten - 8
Enrollment: 800
Sonia Shron, Executive Director
Shana Harris, Head
Benjamin Cohen, Principal, General Studies
Simona Dayan, Principal, Jewish Studies
simona_dayan@bialik.on.ca
Anita Eckhaus, Vice Principal, Elementary Division
Rochelle Wise, Vice Principal, Preschool Division
Beverley Young, Vice Principal, Senior Division

Toronto: The Bishop Strachan School (BSS)
298 Lonsdale Rd., Toronto, ON M4V 1X2, Canada
Tel: 416-483-4325; *Fax:* 416-481-5632
strachan@bss.on.ca
www.bss.on.ca

Grades: Junior Kindergarten - 12
The Bishop Strachan School educates girls.
Kate Berghuis, Chair, Board of Governors
Sarah Kavanagh, Chair, Board of Trustees
Deryn Lavell, Head of School
Catherine Hart, Director, Admissions
admissions@bss.on.ca
Rachel Yeager, Director, Marketing & Communications
ryeager@bss.on.ca ca

Toronto: Bnei Akiva Schools
45 Canyon Ave., Toronto, ON M3H 3S4, Canada
Tel: 416-630-5434; *Fax:* 416-638-7905
bneiakivaschools.org

Grades: 9-12
Enrollment: 283
Bnei Akiva Schools serves the Jewish community.
Jeff Shumacher, President
Frank Samuels, Principal, General Studies
Rabbi Scot A. Berman, Headmaster
Jay Shiel, Director, Operations
Jerry Solomon, MSW, Director, Development

Toronto: Bond International College
720 Midland Ave., Toronto, ON M1K 4C9, Canada
Tel: 416-266-8878; *Fax:* 416-266-3898
info@bondcollege.com
www.bondcollege.com

Grades: Secondary
Bond International College prepares international students for

colleges & universities in Canada, the United States, the United Kingdom, & Australia.
Jeffrey Farber, Principal

Toronto: Branksome Hall
10 Elm Ave., Toronto, ON M4W 1N4, Canada
Tel: 416-920-9741; Fax: 416-920-5390
attendance@branksome.on.ca
www.branksome.on.ca

Grades: Junior Kindergarten - 12
Branksome Hall is an independent day & boarding school for girls & an International Baccalaureate (IB) World School.
Karen Murton, Principal
kmurton@branksome.on.ca
Sarah Craig, Head, Junior School
scraig@branksome.on.ca
Karrie Weinstock, Head, Senior / Middle School & Admissions
kweinstock@branksome.on.ca
Terence Carty, Director, Information Technology
tcarty@branksome.on.ca
Joanne Colwell, Director, Student Life
jcolwell@branksome.on.ca
Julia Drake, Director, Communications & Marketing
jdrake@branksome.on.ca
Rosemary Evans, Director, Academic Studies
revans@branksome.on.ca
Judy Gordon, Director, Finance & Administration
jgordon@branksome.on.ca
Nanci Smith, Director, Residence & Athletics
nsmith@branksome.on.ca

Toronto: Cambridge International College of Canada (CICC)
35 Ourland Ave., Toronto, ON M8Z 4E1, Canada
Tel: 416-252-9195

Grades: Secondary
The school for foreign students specializes in TOEFL / ESL & preparation courses for university.

Toronto: Cathedral Christian Academy
c/o The Prayer Palace Ministries
1111 Arrow Rd., Toronto, ON M9N 3B3, Canada
Tel: 416-241-1100; Fax: 416-241-4404
generalinfo@th[rayerpalace.com
www.theprayerpalace.com/cds

Grades: Junior Kindergarten - 12

Toronto: Children's Garden Junior School (CGS)
670 Eglinton Ave. East, Toronto, ON M4G 2K4, Canada
Tel: 416-423-5017
info@childrensgardenschool.com
www.childrensgardenschool.com

Grades: Pre- Kindergarten - 6
Kelly Shimizu, Director, Admissions, 416-423-5017, ext. 43
kshimizu@childrensgardenschool.com
Zandee Toovey, Executive Assistant, 416-423-5017, ext. 44
ztoovey@childrensgardenschool.com

Toronto: City Academy
3080 Yonge St., Toronto, ON M4N 3N1, Canada
Tel: 416-482-2521; Fax: 416-482-2496
info@cityacademy.ca
www.cityacademy.ca

Grades: Sec.
Enrollment: 230
Sheila Dever, Principal

Toronto: Community Hebrew Academy of Toronto (CHAT)
Also known as: TanenbaumCHAT
Wallenberg Campus
200 Wilmington Ave., Toronto, ON M3H 5J8, Canada
Tel: 416-636-5984; Fax: 416-636-7717
info@tanenbaumchat.org
www.chat-edu.ca

Grades: Sec.
Enrollment: 800
Co-educational high school of the Greater Toronto Jewish community. Campuses in Toronto and Vaughan. Programmes include core subjects and Jewish studies.
Paul Shaviv, M.A., M.Phil., Director, Education

Toronto: Crawford Adventist Academy
531 Finch Ave. West, Toronto, ON M2R 3X2, Canada
Tel: 416-633-0090; Fax: 416-633-0467

Grades: K./Elem./Sec.
Enrollment: 526
Vernon Langdon

Toronto: Crescent School
2365 Bayview Ave., Toronto, ON M2L 1A2, Canada
Tel: 416-449-2556; Fax: 416-449-7950
info@crescentschool.org
www.crescentschool.org

Grades: 3 - 12
Crescent School is a day school for boys.
Geoff Roberts, Headmaster
Mark Hord, Head, Middle School
Ross MacDonald, Head, Lower School
Christopher White, Director, Admissions

Toronto: Crestwood Preparatory College
217 Brookbanks Dr., Toronto, ON M3A 2T7, Canada
Tel: 416-391-1441; Fax: 416-444-0949
dcarrotte@crestwoodprepco.com
www.crestwoodprepco.com

Grades: Elem./Sec.
Enrollment: 391
Vince Pagano, Principal

Toronto: Crestwood School
411 Lawrence Ave. East, Toronto, ON M3C 1N9, Canada
Tel: 416-444-5858; Fax: 416-444-2127

Grades: Elem.
Enrollment: 416
Dalia Eisen

Toronto: De La Salle College
131 Farnham Ave., Toronto, ON M4V 1H7, Canada
Tel: 416-969-8771; Fax: 416-969-9175
info@delasalle.toronto.on.ca
www2.delasalle.toronto.on.ca/

Grades: Elem./Sec.
Enrollment: 578
Br. Domenic Viggiani

Toronto: Dominion College
343 Jones Ave., Toronto, ON M4J 3G4, Canada
Tel: 416-348-8708; Fax: 416-348-8805

Grades: Sec.
Enrollment: 83
David Tech

Toronto: Dr. Abraham Shore She'Arim Hebrew Day School
4588 Bathurst St., Toronto, ON M2R 1W6, Canada
Tel: 416-633-8247; Fax: 416-633-4783

Grades: Elem./Spec. Ed.
Enrollment: 67
Kathy Manoim

Toronto: Eitz Chaim Schools
475 Patricia Ave., Toronto, ON M2R 2N1, Canada
Tel: 416-225-1187; Fax: 416-225-3732

Grades: K./Elem./Sec.
Enrollment: 831
Robert W. Pletsch

Toronto: Fieldstone Day School
2999 Dufferin St., Toronto, ON M6B 3T4, Canada
Tel: 416-487-7381; Fax: 416-487-8190
office@fieldstonedayschool.org
www.fieldstonedayschool.org

Grades: K.-12
Enrollment: 244
Enriched curriculum.
Melissa Volekaert, Head of Lower School
mvol@fieldstonedayschool.org
Sue Johnson, Ass't Head of Lower School
sjohnson@fieldstonedayschool.org

Toronto: The Giles School
L'École Giles
80 Scarsdale Rd., Toronto, ON M3C 2C3, Canada
Tel: 416-446-0825; Fax: 416-446-0846
info@gilesschool.ca
www.gilesschool.ca

Grades: Pre-Kindergarten - 12
The Giles School is a co-educational school which offers an enriched French immersion program. Students are introduced to a third language in grade one.
Kemp Rickett, Headmaster
kemp_rickett@gilesschool.ca
Sue Vijh, Deputy Headmaster
sue_vijh@gilesschool.ca
Harry Giles, Director, Education
Rosine Dika Balotoken, Manager, Administration
rosine_dika@gilesschool.ca
Bob Spencer, Manager, Special Projects
rgspencer@rogers.com

Toronto: Great Lakes College of Toronto (GLCT)
Toronto Campus
323 Keele St., Toronto, ON M6P 2K6, Canada
Tel: 416-763-4121; Fax: 416-763-5225
query@glctschool.com
www.glctschool.com

Grades: 10 - 12
The school is an international high school, which offers a pre-university program. English as a Second Language courses are also provided.
Tom Tidey, B.A., M.Ed., Principal

Toronto: Havergal College
1451 Avenue Rd., Toronto, ON M5N 2H9, Canada
Tel: 416-483-3843; Fax: 416-483-6796
www.havergal.on.ca

Grades: K./Elem./Sec.
Enrollment: 956
University-preparatory day and boarding school for girls.
Dr. Susan R. Groesbeck, Principal

Toronto: Hawthorn School for Girls
101 Scarsdale Rd., Toronto, ON M3B 2R2, Canada
Tel: 416-444-3054; Fax: 416-449-2891
www.hawthornschool.com

Grades: Elem./Sec.
Enrollment: 222
Eliza Trotter, School Head

Toronto: High Park Centennial Montessori School
35 High Park Gdns., Toronto, ON M6R 1S8, Canada
Tel: 416-763-6097; Fax: 416-763-0380

Grades: K./Elem.
Enrollment: 332
Tracy Grisdale

Toronto: Humberside Montessori School
121 Kennedy Ave, Toronto, ON M6S 2X8, Canada
Tel: 416-762-8888; Fax: 416-766-1211

Grades: Elem./Ungraded
Enrollment: 81
Felix Bednarski

Toronto: Imperial College of Toronto
20 Queen Elizabeth Blvd., Toronto, ON M8Z 1L8, Canada
Tel: 416-251-4970; Fax: 416-251-0259

Grades: Sec.
Enrollment: 114
Jon Austin

Toronto: Institute of Child Study
45 Walmer Rd., Toronto, ON M5R 2X2, Canada
Tel: 416-934-4509; Fax: 416-978-6485

Grades: Elem.
Enrollment: 176
Elizabeth Morley

Toronto: Islamic Foundation School
441 Nugget Ave., Toronto, ON M1V 5E1, Canada
Tel: 416-321-3776; Fax: 416-321-1078

Grades: Elem.
Enrollment: 327
Yahya Qurechi

Toronto: The Japanese School of Toronto Shokokai Inc.
c/o McMurrich Junior Public Shool
115 Winnona Dr., Toronto, ON M6G 3S8, Canada
Tel: 416-656-4822; Fax: 416-658-8931
www.torontohoshuko.ca

This is a Japanese Saturday school

Toronto: Junior Academy
2454 Bayview Ave., Toronto, ON M2L 1A6, Canada
Tel: 416-425-4567; Fax: 416-425-7379
www.junioracademy.com

Grades: Kindergarten - 8
Pat Kendall, B.A., Graduate Diploma in, Administrator
Dianne Johnson, Principal
Julie Stewart, Vice Principal
Cathy Hibbert, Director, Physical Education
Susan Jones, Director, Middle School
Kris Potter, Director, Student Affairs

Toronto: Leonardo Da Vinci Academy of Arts & Sciences
100 Allanhurst Dr., Toronto, ON M9A 4K4, Canada
Tel: 416-247-6137; Fax: 416-247-6138
ldva@ldva.on.ca
www.ldva.on.ca/

Grades: K./Elem.
Salvatore Ritacca, Principal

Toronto: The Linden School
10 Rosehill Ave., Toronto, ON M4T 1G5, Canada
Tel: 416-966-4406
www.lindenschool.ca
Grades: 1 - 12
The Linden School provides education for girls.
Alana Bell, BA (Honours) (English), M, Co-Principal
Dawn Chan, B.Sc. (Biology), M.Sc. (S, Co-Principal
Ina Székely, B.A., M.A., B.Ed., Co-Principal
Kate Raven, B.A. (Honours), Post-Grad, Coordinator, Communications

Toronto: LSC Toronto
#400, 124 Eglinton Ave. West, Toronto, ON M4R 2G8, Canada
Tel: 416-488-2200; *Fax:* 416-488-2225
toronto@lsc-canada.com
www.lsc-canada.com
David S. Diplock, Director

Toronto: Lycée Français de Toronto
2327, rue Dufferin, Toronto, ON M6E 3S5, Canada
Tél: 416-924-1789; *Téléc:* 416-924-9078
samia.farahat@lft.ca
www.lft.ca
Grades: Prim./Sec.
Enrollment: 340
M. Dominique Duthel, Proviseur

Toronto: The Mabin School
50 Poplar Plains Rd., Toronto, ON M4V 2M8, Canada
Tel: 416-964-9594; *Fax:* 416-964-3643
admissions@mabin.com
www.mabin.com
Grades: Junior Kindergarten - 6
The Mabin School provides a full day, non-denominational program for girls & boys.
Lynn Seligman, Principal

Toronto: Maria Montessori School
125 Brentcliffe Rd., Toronto, ON M4G 3Y7, Canada
Tel: 416-423-9123; *Fax:* 416-423-7819
Grades: Elem.
Enrollment: 196
James Brand

Toronto: McDonald International Academy
920 Yonge St., 2nd Fl., Toronto, ON M4W 3C7, Canada
Tel: 416-322-1502; *Fax:* 416-322-5775
Enrollment: 753
Fraser Rose

Toronto: Metropolitan Preparatory Academy
49 Mobile Dr., Toronto, ON M4A 1H5, Canada
Tel: 416-285-0870; *Fax:* 416-285-0873
www.metroprep.com
Grades: 6 - 12
Metropolitan Preparatory Academy offers a middle & high school program for university-oriented students.
William Wayne McKelvey, Hons. B.A., M.A., Dip. Ed, Principal
Debra McKelvey-Cleveland, Vice Principal & Head, Guidance
dmckelvey@MetroPrep.com
Jason Van Allen, Administrator, Information Technology
lvanallen@MetroPrep.com

Toronto: Montcrest School
4 Montcrest Blvd., Toronto, ON M4K 1J7, Canada
Tel: 416-469-2008; *Fax:* 416-469-0934
info@montcrest.on.ca
www.montcrest.on.ca
Grades: Junior Kindergarten - 8
Enrollment: 300
Montcrest School is a co-educational, nondenominational school. The school also offers special education classes for students with learning disabilities.
Stephen Beatty, Head of School

Toronto: MPS Etobicoke (MPS)
Also known as: Mississauga Private School
30 Barrhead Cres., Toronto, ON M9W 3Z7, Canada
Tel: 416-745-1328; *Fax:* 416-745-4168
mpsinfo@rogers.com
www.mpsontario.com
Grades: Junior Kindergarten - 12
Gabrielle Bush, Director

Toronto: National Ballet School (NBS)
400 Jarvis St., Toronto, ON M4Y 2G6, Canada
Tel: 416-964-3780; *Fax:* 416-964-5133
Toll-Free: 1-800-387-0785
careers@nbs-enb.ca
www.nbs-enb.ca
The school offers elite ballet training, academic instruction, & residential care.
Judith Gelber, Chair
Jeff Melanson, Executive Director & Co-Chief Executive Officer
Mavis Staines, Artistic Director & Co-Chief Executive Officer
Katharine Harris, Officer, Media Relations & Communications, 416-964-3780, ext. 2117
kharris@nbs-enb.ca

Toronto: North Toronto Christian School (NTCS)
50 Page Ave., Toronto, ON M2K 2B4, Canada
Tel: 416-226-3366
www.yorkland.on.ca
Grades: Junior Kindergarten - 6
Enrollment: 380

Toronto: Northmount School
26 Mallard Rd., Toronto, ON M3B 1S3, Canada
Tel: 416-449-8823; *Fax:* 416-449-1244
Lolita.Pereira@northmount.com
www.northmount.com
Grades: Junior Kindergarten - 8
Northmount School specializes in the education of boys.
Dr. Carmen Mombourquette, Head of School

Toronto: P.T. Montessori School
280 Culford Rd., Toronto, ON M6L 2V3, Canada
Tel: 416-242-3725
ptmontessori@look.ca
Grades: Elem.
Enrollment: 51
Linda Harrison, Administrator

Toronto: People's Christian Academy
374 Sheppard Ave. East, Toronto, ON M2N 3B6, Canada
Tel: 416-222-3341; *Fax:* 416-222-3344
info@pca.ca
www.pca.ca
Grades: Jr. K.-12
Enrollment: 808
Rev. Reg Andrews, Director, Operations & Ministry

Toronto: Queensway Christian College School (QCC)
1536 The Queensway, Toronto, ON M8Z 1T5, Canada
Tel: 416-255-6033; *Fax:* 416-255-7389
www.qccollege.com
Grades: Junior Kindergarten - 12
Queensway Christian College os a non-denominational Christian school, which consists of a high school, a middle school, & a junior school.
David Broomer, Executive Director
John Allardyce, Supervising Principal
Tim Bramer, Elementary Vice Principal
Sue Broomer, Secretary

Toronto: Royal St. George's College
120 Howland Ave., Toronto, ON M5R 3B5, Canada
Tel: 416-533-9481; *Fax:* 416-533-0028
contactus@rsgc.on.ca
www.rsgc.on.ca/
Grades: Elem./Sec.; Boys
Enrollment: 430
Hal Hannaford

Toronto: St. Clement's School
21 St. Clement's Ave., Toronto, ON M4R 1G8, Canada
Tel: 416-483-4835; *Fax:* 416-483-8242
admissions@scs.on.ca
www.scs.on.ca/
Grades: 1-12
Enrollment: 450
All-girl's school affiliated with the Anglican church
Patricia Parisi, Principal

Toronto: St. Michael's College School
1515 Bathurst St., Toronto, ON M5P 3H4, Canada
Tel: 416-653-3180; *Fax:* 416-653-7704
info@smcsmail.com; privacyofficer@smcsmail.com (privacy officer)
www.stmichaelscollegeschool.com
Grades: 7-12
Enrollment: 1100
St. Michael's College School provides Catholic, Liberal Arts eductaion for young men.
Fr. Tim Scott, C.S.B., Chair, Board of Directors
Rev. John Malo, C.S.B., Superior
Fr. Joseph Redican, C.S.B., President, 416-653-3180, ext. 174
Terence Sheridan, Principal, 416-653-3180, ext. 139
Emile John, Vice-Principal, 416-653-3180, ext. 156
David Lee, Vice-Principal
Kimberley Bailey, Director, Advancement, 416-653-3180, ext. 118
Michael De Pellegrin, Director, Communications, 416-653-3180, ext. 292
Fr. John Malo, C.S.B., Director, Pastoral Care, 416-653-3180, ext. 229
Greg Paolini, Director, Admissions, 416-653-3180, ext. 195
Fr. John Reddy, C.S.B., Director, Faith Development, 416-653-3180, ext. 217
Bill Smith, Director, Plant, 416-653-3180, ext. 129
Gino Saccone, Corporate Controller, 416-653-3180, ext. 239

Toronto: School of Liberal Arts (SOLA)
#200, 36 Eglinton Ave. West, Toronto, ON M4R 1A1, Canada
Tel: 416-489-7652; *Fax:* 416-489-2074
www.solaprep.com
Grades: Sec.
Enrollment: 251
University Preparatory School
David L. Ferguson

Toronto: Shmuel Zahavy Cheder Chabad of Toronto
#203, 900 Alness St., Toronto, ON M3J 2H6, Canada
Tel: 416-663-1972; *Fax:* 416-650-9404
www.chederchabad.com
Students at Shmuel Zahavy Cheder Chabad of Toronto also receive education in Torah scholarship & classic Jewish values.
Rabbi Yona Shur, Director
Rabbi Baruch Zaltzman, Principal

Toronto: Sidney Ledson School Ltd.
#107, 220 Duncan Mill Rd., Toronto, ON M3B 3J5, Canada
Tel: 416-447-5355; *Fax:* 416-447-5283
www.sidneyledsoninstitute.com
Grades: K./Elem.
Enrollment: 50
Sidney Ledson

Toronto: Sterling Hall School of Toronto (SHS)
99 Cartwright Ave., Toronto, ON M6A 1V4, Canada
Tel: 416-785-3410; *Fax:* 416-785-6616
shsadmin@sterlinghall.com
www.sterlinghall.com
Grades: Junior Kindergarten - 8
Enrollment: 300
Sterling Hall School of Toronto educates boys.
Ian Robinson, Principal
Claire Reed, Director, Admissions
admissions@sterlinghall.com

Toronto: Sunnybrook School
469 Merton St., Toronto, ON M4S 1B4, Canada
Tel: 416-487-5308; *Fax:* 416-487-5381
sbmail@sunnybrookschool.com
www.sunnybrookschool.com
Grades: Jr. K.-6
Enrollment: 134
Dr. Irene Davy, Ph.D., Director

Toronto: Three Fishes Christian Elementary School
Miracle Family Temple
1100 Bellamy Rd. North, Toronto, ON M1H 1H2, Canada
Tel: 416-284-9003
3fishes@threefishes.org
www.threefishes.org
Grades: Junior Kindergarten - 8
Three Fishes Christian Elementary School offers a Christ-centered & academically demanding program.
Laurel Ann Mirams, Principal
dmirams@sympatico.ca

Toronto: Timothy Christian School (Rexdale) (TCS)
28 Elmhurst Dr., Toronto, ON M9W 2J5, Canada
Tel: 416-741-5770; *Fax:* 416-741-3359
www.timothycs.com
Grades: Junior Kindergarten - 8
Enrollment: 100
Timothy Christian School in Rexdale offers a Christ-centred education.
Margareth Lise, Principal
Bobbie Van Ysseldyk, Finance Administrator & Administrative Assistant

Toronto: Toronto Cheder School
3995 Bathurst St., Toronto, ON M3H 5V3, Canada
Tel: 416-636-2987
Enrollment: 200
Toronto Cheder School is an Orthodox school for boys.
Rabbi D. Engel, Principal

Toronto: Toronto French School (TFS)
Toronto Campus
306 Lawrence Ave. East, Toronto, ON M4N 1T7, Canada
Tel: 416-484-6533; *Fax:* 416-488-3090
admissions@tfs.ca
www.tfs.ca

Grades: Preschool - 12
Toronto French School is a co-educational, non-denominational school, which offers bilingual education.
Lena Sarkissian, Chair
board@tfs.ca
John Godfrey, Headmaster
Alain Delaune, Principal, Mississauga School
Heidi Gollert, Principal, Senior School
Mirna Hafez, Principal, Junior School

Toronto: The Toronto Heschel School
819 Sheppard Ave. West, Toronto, ON M3H 3J7, Canada
Tel: 416-635-1876; *Fax:* 416-635-1800
info@torontoheschel.org
www.torontoheschel.org

Grades: Junior Kindergarten - 8
Enrollment: 300
The Jewish day school combines the teaching of Judaism with a general studies curriculum.
Ashira Gobrin, Board Co-Chair
Ken Kraft, Board Co-Chair
Mark Abramsohn, Executive Director
Gail Baker, Head of School & Principal
Rav Eliot Feldman, Vice Principal
Greg Beiles, Director, Curriculum & Training

Toronto: United Synagogue Day School (USDS)
Administration House
3072 Bayview Ave., Toronto, ON M2N 5L3, Canada
Tel: 416-224-8737; *Fax:* 416-225-9108
admin.house@usds.ca; bathurst.campus@usds.ca (Bathurst Campus)
www.usds.ca
Other Information: bayview.campus@usds.ca (E-mail, Bayview Campus)

Grades: Preschool - 8
Enrollment: 700
United Synagogue Day School is a Conservative Jewish day school. It offers a program of Jewish & general studies.
Gail Silver, Principal, Bayview Campus, 416-225-1143, ext. 201
gails@usds.ca
Ashley Waltman, Principal, Bathurst Campus, 416-781-5658, ext. 301
awaltman@usds.ca
Sheila Miller, Director, Development, 416-224-8737, ext. 140
sheilam@usds.ca
Michele Viner, Director, Admissions, 416-224-8737, ext. 137
mviner@usds.ca

Toronto: University of Toronto Schools (UTS)
371 Bloor St. West, Toronto, ON M5S 2R7, Canada
Tel: 416-978-3212; *Fax:* 416-978-6775
info@utschools.ca
www.utschools.ca
Other Information: 416-946-7995 (Phone, Admissions); 416-978-7325 (Student Services)

Grades: 7 - 12
Enrollment: 640
UTS is a coeducational school, affiliated with the University of Toronto.
Robert E. Lord, Chair
UTSBoard@utschools.ca
Michaele Robertson, Principal

Toronto: Upper Canada College (UCC)
200 Lonsdale Rd., Toronto, ON M4V 1W6, Canada
Tel: 416-488-1125; *Fax:* 416-484-8611
admission@ucc.on.ca; administration@ucc.on.ca
www.ucc.on.ca
Other Information: 416-488-1125, ext. 2313 (Phone, Office of Advancement)

Grades: Senior Kindergarten - 12
The Preparatory School has over 400 boys from Senior Kindergarten to grade seven. The Upper School offers a five year secondary education.
Michael MacMillan, Chair, Board of Governors
Jim Power, Principal, 416-488-1125, ext. 4010
Steve Griffin, Head, Upper School
sgriffin@ucc.on.ca
David Matthews, Asst. Head, University Relations & Sec., Board of Governors, 416-488-1125, ext. 2260
dmatthews@ucc.on.ca
Andrea Aster, Associate Director, Marketing & Communications 416-488-1125, ext. 3355

Toronto: Yeshiva Bnei Zion of Bobov
44 Champlain Blvd., Toronto, ON M3H 2Z1, Canada
Tel: 416-633-6332; *Fax:* 416-633-6704

Grades: K./Elem.; Boys
Enrollment: 146
David Kessler

Toronto: Yeshiva Yesodei Hatorah
77 Glen Rush Blvd., Toronto, ON M5N 2T8, Canada
Tel: 416-787-1101; *Fax:* 416-787-9044

Grades: K./Elem.; Boys
Enrollment: 422
Rabbi Asher A. Bornstein

Toronto: Yeshivas Nachalas Zvi
475 Lawrence Ave. West, Toronto, ON M5M 1C6, Canada
Tel: 416-782-8912; *Fax:* 416-782-8517

Grades: Elem./Sec.
Enrollment: 90
Bruce Graham

Toronto: The York School
1320 Yonge St., Toronto, ON M4T 1X2, Canada
Tel: 416-926-1325
www.yorkschool.com
Other Information: 416-646-5275 (Phone, Admissions)

Grades: Junior Kindergarten - 12
Enrollment: 593
The York School is co-educational & non-denominational. It is an International Baccalaureate World School, which offers PYP, MYP, & Diploma programs.
Jason Hanson, Chair
Ezio Crescenzi, Head of School, 416-646-5271
ezio_crescenzi@tys.on.ca
Susan Charron, Principal, Lower School, 416-646-5273
susan_charron@tys.on.ca
David Hamilton, Principal, Upper School, 416-646-5272
david_hamilton@tys.on.ca
Marilyn Andrews, Director, External Relations
Conor Jones, Director, Admission
Robin Kester, Director, Advancement
Annette Whiteley, Director, Business & Finance

Toronto: The Yorkland School (TYS)
255 Yorkland Blvd., Toronto, ON M2J 1S3, Canada
Tel: 416-491-7667; *Fax:* 416-491-3806
admin@yorkland.on.ca
www.yorkland.on.ca

Grades: 7 - 12
The Yorkland School is the middle & upper school division of the North Toronto Christian School, The school is commited to Biblical principles & values. The Yorkland School helps its students achieve both academically & athletically.
Kevin Ko, Principal

Trenton: Trenton Christian School
340 Second Dug Hill Rd., Trenton, ON K8V 5P7, Canada
Tel: 613-392-3600; *Fax:* 613-392-6316
tcs@reach.net
www.trentonchristianschool.com

Grades: Junior Kindergarten - 8
Linda Wikkerink, Chair
Allen Bron, Principal
Laurie Tuckey, Vice Principal
Mrs. K. Whitley, Director, Development
tcsdvdr@reach.net

Unionville: Unionville Montessori School (UMS)
9302 Kennedy Rd., Unionville, ON L6C 1N6, Canada
Tel: 905-474-9888; *Fax:* 905-474-5767
www.unionvillemontessori.com

Grades: Preschool - 8
Unionville Montessori School is a coeducational, non-denominational school. The Casa program is available for children from age two to six.
Kevin R. McCarthy, Principal
B.A, B.Sc., M.Ed.

Utterson: Muskoka Christian School
P.O. Box 150
2483 Old Muskoka Rd., Utterson, ON P0B 1M0, Canada
Tel: 705-385-2847; *Fax:* 705-385-1756
mcs@muskoka.com
www.muskokachristianschool.com

Grades: Junior Kindergarten - 8
The school is owned and operated by the Muskoka Association for Christian Education.
Lauralyn Mercer, Principal

Vaughan: Community Hebrew Academy of Toronto (CHAT)
Also known as: Kimel Centre
Vaughan Campus
9600 Bathurst St., Vaughan, ON L4A 3Z8, Canada
Tel: 905-787-8772; *Fax:* 905-787-8773
info@tanenbaumchat.org
www.chat-edu.ca

Grades: Sec.
Enrollment: 600
Paul Shaviv, M.A., M.Phil., Director, Education

Wallaceburg: Wallaceburg Christian Private School (WCS)
693 Albert St., Wallaceburg, ON N8A 1Y8, Canada
Tel: 519-627-6013; *Fax:* 519-627-5051
admin@wallaceburgchristianschool.com
www.wallaceburgchristianschool.com

Grades: Junior Kindergarten - 8
The school is a member of the Ontario Alliance of Christian Schools & Christian Schools International. It is independent of the Ministry of Education, although the school is registerd with the Ministry.
Andy J. Alblas, Principal

Wasaga Beach: Silvercrest Christian School
3267 Mosley St., Wasaga Beach, ON L0L 2P0, Canada
Tel: 705-429-4303; *Fax:* 705-429-0417
silvercrest@rogers.com
www.silvercrestchristianschool.com

Grades: Jr. K.-8
Enrollment: 52
Heidi Kerssies, Principal

Waterloo: Kitchener Waterloo Bilingual School
600 Erb St. West, Waterloo, ON N2J 3Z4, Canada
Tel: 519-886-6510; *Fax:* 519-886-4053

Grades: K./Elem.
Enrollment: 320
Michel Poinot

Waterloo: St. Jude's School Inc.
420 Weber St., Waterloo, ON N2R 1K4, Canada
Tel: 519-888-0807; *Fax:* 519-884-0316
director2@stjudes.com
www.stjudes.com

Grades: 1-12
Enrollment: 172
Founded in 1980 for students with learning difficulties. Also offers an after-hours Tutoring School and Second Language School
Toni Fouse

Webequie: Simon Jacob Memorial Education Centre
P.O. Box 265
Webequie, ON P0T 3A0, Canada
Tel: 807-353-6491; *Fax:* 807-353-1306
www.education.matawa.on.ca

Grades: K-10; Native Language; Special Ed.
The Simon Jacob Memorial Education Centre serves members of the Webequie First Nation, in a community about 540 kilometres northeast of Thunder Bay, Ontario. The education centre operates on a schedule, which is sensitive to the Webequie First Nation culture. The school is administered by the Webequie First Nation Education Authority.
Mary Gardiner, Principal
Stephanie Jones, Teacher, Special Education
Lois Whitehead, Instuctor, Native Language

Wellandport: Robert Land Academy
6726 South Chippawa Rd., RR#3, Wellandport, ON L0R 2J0, Canada
Tel: 905-386-6203; *Fax:* 905-386-6607
www.robertlandacademy.com

Grades: 6 - 12
Enrollment: 165
Robert Land Academy is a highly structured military boarding school, which provides education for previously under-achieving boys with potential.
Major (retired) G. Scott Bowman, Founder & Headmaster

Wellandport: Wellandport Christian Private School
P.O. Box 123
84008 Wellandport Rd., Wellandport, ON L0R 2J0, Canada
Tel: 905-386-6272; *Fax:* 905-386-7184
wcs@wellandportchristianschool.ca
www.wellandportchristianschool.ca

Grades: Preschool - 8
Wellandport Christian Private School is a day school which offers Christ-centred programs. The Christian preschool program is for four year old children.

Wheatley: Old Colony Christian Academy
21311 Campbell Rd., RR#1, Wheatley, ON N0P 2P0, Canada
Tel: 519-825-9188; *Fax:* 519-825-9122

Grades: Elem.
Enrollment: 252
Abe Thiessen

Whitby: Trafalgar Castle School
401 Reynolds St., Whitby, ON L1N 3W9, Canada
Tel: 905-668-3358; *Fax:* 905-668-4136
www.castle-ed.com

Grades: 6 - 12
The day & boarding school educates young women.

Brian McClure, Principal, 905-668-3358, ext. 225
mcclureb@castle-ed.com
Gillian Martin, Vice Principal, School Life, 905-668-3358, ext. 228
mcclureb@castle-ed.com
Tim Southwell, Vice Principal, Academics, 905-668-3358, ext. 229
southwellt@castle-ed.com
Marguerita Dykstra, Director, Finance, 905-668-3358, ext. 232
dykstram@castle-ed.com
Martha Cassidy, Administrator, Office, 905-668-3358, ext. 221
cassidym@castle-ed.com
Rhonda Daley, Officer, Marketing & Development, 905-668-3358, ext. 247
daleyr@castle-ed.com
Irene Talent, Officer, Admissions & Administrative Assistant, 905-668-3358, ext. 227
talenti@castle-ed.com

***Whitby:* Whitby Montessori & Elementary School**
95 Taunton Rd. East, Whitby, ON L1R 3L3, Canada
Tel: 905-430-8201
Grades: Preschool - Elementary
Whitby Montessori & Elementary School educates children from age thirteen months to fourteen years.
Cathy Barber, Principal

***Williamsburg:* Timothy Christian School**
P.O. Box 179
12600 County Rd. 18, Williamsburg, ON K0C 2H0, Canada
Tel: 613-535-2687; *Fax:* 613-535-1074
www.tcswilliamsburg.ca
Grades: Junior Kindergarten - 8
Enrollment: 130
Gary Postma, Principal
Principal@tcswilliamsburg.ca
Truusje Berkelaar, Administrative Assistant
office@tcswilliamsburg.ca

***Windsor:* Académie Ste. Cécile International School**
925 Cousineau Rd., Windsor, ON N9G 1V8, Canada
Tel: 519-969-1291; *Fax:* 519-969-7953
info@stececile.ca
www.stececile.ca
Grades: Pre./Elem./Sec.
Enrollment: 250
Affiliated with the Univ. of Windsor. Programmes include the Ontario Sec. School Programme, the International Bacc. Programme, Advanced Placement; emphasis on music, dance, art, & performing arts, as well as programmes in technology; ESL, FSL & TOEFL courses; summer school.
Thérèse H. Gadoury, Principal

***Windsor:* An-Noor Private School**
1480 Janette Ave., Windsor, ON N8X 1Z4, Canada
Tel: 519-966-4422
Grades: Elem.
Enrollment: 158
Cassim Parak, Principal

***Windsor:* First Lutheran Christian Academy**
3850 Locke St., Windsor, ON N9G 1S1, Canada
Tel: 519-250-7888; *Fax:* 519-250-7715
Enrollment: 201
Suzanne Eberhard

***Windsor:* Maranatha Christian Academy**
939 Northwood St., Windsor, ON N9E 2B4, Canada
Tel: 519-966-7424; *Fax:* 519-966-9519
Grades: K./Elem.
Enrollment: 252
William Van Dyke

***Windsor:* Windsor Christian Fellowship Academy**
4490 - 7th Concession, RR#1, Windsor, ON N9A 6J3, Canada
Tel: 519-972-5986; *Fax:* 519-972-5643
Grades: Elem.
Enrollment: 81
Patti Banks

***Woodbridge:* Credo Christian Private School**
8260 Huntington Rd., RR#1, Woodbridge, ON L4L 1A5, Canada
Tel: 905-851-1620; *Fax:* 905-851-1620
Grades: K./Elem.
Enrollment: 74
L.P. Maat

***Woodbridge:* Maple Leaf Montessori School Inc.**
8286 Islington Ave., Woodbridge, ON L4L 1W8, Canada
Tel: 905-856-3359
Grades: Elem.
Enrollment: 178
Johanna Madeley

***Woodbridge:* Toronto District Christian High School**
377 Woodbridge Ave., Woodbridge, ON L4L 2V7, Canada
Tel: 905-851-1772; *Fax:* 905-851-9992
info@tdchristian.ca; admissions@tdchristian.ca
www.tdchristian.ca
Grades: Secondary
Ren Siebenga, Principal
principal@tdchristian.ca
Tim Bentum, Vice Principal, Admissions & Students
bentum@tdchristian.ca
Justin De Moor, Vice Principal, Communications
demoor@tdchristian.ca
William Groot, Vice Principal, Scheduling
groot@tdchristian.ca
Meg Cate, Financial Administrator
cate@tdchristian.ca

***Wunnummin Lake:* Lydia Lois Beardy Memorial School**
P.O. Box 108
General Delivery, Wunnummin Lake, ON P0V 2Z0, Canada
Tel: 807-442-2575; *Fax:* 807-442-2640
Grades: Elem./Sec.
Enrollment: 150
Mary Angees

***Wyoming:* John Knox Christian School of Wyoming**
P.O. Box 81
Wyoming, ON N0N 1T0, Canada
Tel: 519-845-3112; *Fax:* 519-845-1404
Grades: K./Elem.
Enrollment: 140
Ymko Boersma

Universities & Colleges

Universities

***Guelph:* University of Guelph**
50 Stone Rd. East, Guelph, ON N1G 2W1, Canada
Tel: 519-824-4120; *Fax:* 519-767-1693
www.uoguelph.ca
Full Time Equivalency: 19408
Pamela Wallin, O.C., S.O.M., Chancellor
chancellor@uoguelph.ca
Alastair J.S. Summerlee, President & Vice-Chancellor
president@uoguelph.ca
Maureen Mancuso, Provost & Vice-President (Academic)
Nancy Sullivan, Vice-President (Finance & Administration)
Martha Harley, Asst. Vice-President (Human Resources)
Brenda Whiteside, Assoc. Vice-President (Student Affairs)
Serge Desmarais, Assoc. Vice-President (Academic)
Michael Ridley, Chief Librarian & Chief Information Officer

Faculties
Arts
Jacqueline Murray, Dean
Biological Science
Michael Emes, Dean
Environmental Sciences
Josef Ackerman, Dean
Graduate Studies
Isobel Heathcote, Dean
Management & Economics
Chris McKenna, Dean
Ontario Agricultural College
Craig Pearson, Dean
Ontario Veterinary College
Elizabeth Stone, Interim Dean
Physical & Engineering Science
Peter Tremaine, Dean
Social & Applied Sciences
Alun Joseph, Dean

Schools
College d'Alfred
Marcel Couture, Acting Director
Engineering
Richard Zynter, Acting Director
Environmental Design & Rural Development
Robert Brown, Acting Director
Fine Arts & Music
John Kissick, Director
Hospitality & Tourism Management
Marion Joppe, Director
Kemptville College
Michael Goss, Director
Ridgetown College
Ron Pitblado, Acting Director
School of English & Theatre Studies
David Murray, Acting Director

Publications
At Guelph
Guelph Peak
The Ontarion

***Hamilton:* McMaster University**
1280 Main St. West, Hamilton, ON L8S 4L8, Canada
Tel: 905-525-9140; *Fax:* 905-521-9183
www.mcmaster.ca
Full Time Equivalency: 23325
Lynton (Red) Wilson, Chancellor, ext. 24340
Peter George, President & Vice-Chancellor, ext. 24340
Engineering
David S. Wilkinson, Dean
Graduate Studies
F.L. Hall, Dean
Health Sciences
John G. Kelton, Dean
Humanities
Suzanne Crosta, Dean
Science
John P. Capone, Dean
Social Sciences
Charlotte A.B. Yates, Dean

Schools
DeGroote School of Business
Paul Bates, Dean
Arts & Science Program
Gary Warner, Director
Indigenous Studies Program
Dawn Martin-Hill, Director
Institute on Globalization and the Human Condition
Robert O'Brien, Director

Affiliations
McMaster Divinity College
1280 Main St. W., Hamilton, ON L8S 4K1, Canada
Tel: 905-525-9140; *Fax:* 090-577-4782
divinity@mcmaster.ca
www.macdiv.ca
Full Time Equivalency: 300
Stanley E. Porter, Principal & Dean
Bill Marshall, Director, Finance, 905-525-9140, ext. 24685
marshaw@mcmaster.ca
Dr. Phil Zylla, Academic Dean, 905-525-9140, ext. 20104
zyllap@mcmaster.ca

Publications
Community Report
McMaster Times
vanraay@mcmaster.ca
Alumni magazine.
McMaster Update
c/o Office of Public Relations, Room 111, Chester
1280 Main St. West, Hamilton, ON L8S 4L9, Canada
Tel: 905-525-9140
update@mcmaster.ca

***Hearst:* Université de Hearst**
60, 9e Rue, Hearst, ON P0L 1N0, Canada
Tél: 705-372-1781; *Ligne sans frais:* 1-800-887-1781
info_gen@uhearst.ca
www.uhearst.ca

***Kemptville:* Kemptville Campus**
P.O. Box 2003
830 Prescott St., Kemptville, ON K0G 1J0, Canada
Tel: 613-258-8336; *Fax:* 613-258-8384
kcampus@kemptvillec.uoguelph.ca
www.kemptvillec.uoguelph.ca
Dr. Michael Goss

***Kingston:* Queen's University**
99 University Ave., Kingston, ON K7L 3N6, Canada
Tel: 613-533-2000; *Fax:* 613-533-6300
www.queensu.ca
Full Time Equivalency: 21607
David A. Dodge, Chancellor

Dr. Tom Williams, B.Sc., M.A., Ph.D., Principal & Vice-Chancellor
Leora Jackson, B.Sc.H, Rector
Sean Conway, B.A., Vice-Principal
Bill Bryck, Vice-Principal
Jo-Anne Brady, B.A., M.B.A., University Registrar
Georgina Moore, B.A., Secretary of the Senate, University & Board
Richard P. Seres, B.Comm., Director
Peggy Watkin, Secretary of the University Council
Mike Stefano, Director
Chris Tabor, Bookstore Manager
Dr. Patrick Deane, Ph.D., Vice-Principal
Dr. Kerry Rowe, B.Sc., B.E., Ph.D., D.Eng, Vice-Principal
Roderick Morrison, B.A., M.B.A., M.I.R., Vice-Principal

Faculties

Applied Science
Dr. K. Woodhouse, Ph.D., P.Eng., Dean

Arts & Science
Dr. A. MacLean, Ph.D., C.Psych., Dean

Business
Dr. David Saunders, Ph.D., Dean

Education
Dr. Rosa Bruno-Jofré, Ph.D., Dean

Graduate Studies & Research
Dr. J. Deakin, Ph.D., Dean

Health Sciences
Dr. David M.C. Walker, M.D., F.R.C.P.(C), Dean

Law
William F. Flanagan, J.D., D.E.A., LL.M., Dean

Schools

Centre for International Relations
Charles Pentland, B.A., M.A., Ph.D., Director

English
Amanda Marshall, Acting Co-Chair
Barbara Yates, Acting Co-Chair

Institute of Intergovernmental Relations
Sean Conway, Director

Music
Gordon E. Smith, A.R.C.T., B.A., M.A., Ph., Director

Nursing
Cynthia Baker, M.N., Ph.D., Director

Physical & Health Education
Janice Deakin, B.A., B.P.H.E., M.Sc., Director

Policy Studies
Arthur Sweetman, B.Eng., M.A., Ph.D., Director

Rehabilitation Therapy
Sandra J. Olney, B.Sc., Ph.D., M.Ed., Director

Theological College
Jean Stairs, Mus.Bac., M.Div., D.Min., Principal

Urban & Regional Planning
Hok-Lin Leung, B.Arch., M.C.P., M.Sc., P, Director

Computing
James Cordy, B.Sc., M.Sc., Ph.D., P.En, Director

Publications

antiThesis

Golden Words

Queen's Alumni Review
79 Stuart St, Kingston, ON K7L 3N6, Canada
Fax: 613-545-6777

Queen's Journal

Kingston: Royal Military College of Canada
Collège militaire royal du Canada

P.O. Box 17000 Forces
Kingston, ON K7K 7B4, Canada
Tel: 613-541-6000; *Fax:* 613-542-3565
Toll-Free: 1-866-762-2672
liaison@rmc.ca; transcripts@rmc.ca; webmaster@rmc.ca
www.rmc.ca
Other Information: Undergraduate Programs: 613-541-6000, ext. 6797

Individuals must be a Canadian citizen in possession of the necessary academic qualifications. Applicants must also be one of the following: an MOC ((Military Occupation Classification) qualified member of the Canadian Forces; an applicant for the Regular Officer Training Plan (ROTP) or the Reserve Entry Training Plan (RETP); an employee of the Department of National Defence; or the spouse of a member of the Canadian Forces.

Dr. Joel Sokolsky, BA, MA, PhD, Principal
principals.office@rmc.ca
Dr. James Downey, OC, PhD, DHL, DLitt, LLD, Chair
Brigadier-Gener Tom Lawson, O.M.M., C.D., Commandant
Colonel J.G.B. Ouellette, CD, Director, Cadets
Lieutenant-Colo R.R.(Rod) McDonald, CD, Registrar, 613-541-6000, ext. 4790

Faculties

Arts
J.J. Sokolsky, BA, MA, PhD, Dean
sokolsky-j@rmc.ca

Continuing Studies
M.A. Hennessy, BA, MA, PhD., Dean
hennessy-m@rmc.ca

Engineering
Dr. John A. Stewart, Dean
stewart_j@rmc.ca

Graduate Studies & Research
Dr. B.J. Fugère, Dean
fugere-j@rmc.ca

Science
Dr. Richard Marsden, Dean
marsden-r@rmc.ca

London: Brescia University College

1285 Western Rd., London, ON N6G 1H2, Canada
Tel: 519-432-8353; *Fax:* 519-858-5137
brescia@uwo.ca
www.brescia.uwo.ca

Full Time Equivalency: 1005
A women's university affiliated with the University of Western Ontario

London: Huron University College

1349 Western Rd., London, ON N6G 1H3, Canada
Tel: 519-438-7224; *Fax:* 519-438-3938
www.huronuc.on.ca

Full Time Equivalency: 1100

London: King's University College

266 Epworth Ave., London, ON N6A 2M3, Canada
Tel: 519-433-3491; *Fax:* 519-433-2227
Toll-Free: 1-800-265-4406
kings@uwo.ca
www.uwo.ca/kings/

Full Time Equivalency: 3650

London: University of Western Ontario

#2, 1151 Richmond St., London, ON N6A 5B8, Canada
Tel: 519-661-2111
www.uwo.ca

Full Time Equivalency: 25000
Dr. Amit Chakma, President & Vice-Chancellor
Frank Angeletti, Vice-Chair
Fred Longstaffe, Provost & Vice-President
Gitta Kulczycki, Vice-President
Ted Garrard, Vice-President
Ted Hewitt, Vice-President
Irene Birrell, Secretary
Valerie Smith, Director
G. Blazak, Director
D. Jones, Director
G.E. Hutchinson, Director
Therese Quigley, Director
S. Grindrod, Assoc. Vice-President
J. Schroeder, Director
Joyce Garnett, Director
V. Smith, Director
R. Moore, Director
Susan Hoddinott, Director
S. Bantock, Director
Michael Mics, Manager
D. Estok, Director
Alan Weedon, Vice-Provost
Carole A. Orchard, Director
Roma Harris, Vice-Provost & Registrar
Tyrrel de Langley, Director
D. Dawson, Director
Alex Navarre, Director
Steve Alb, Director
F. Bauer, Ombudsman
Michele Noble, Chair
John Thompson, Chancellor

Faculties

Arts & Humanities

Education
Julia O'Sullivan, Dean

Engineering
Amit Chakma, Dean

Graduate Studies
Alan C. Weedon, Dean

Health Sciences
William James Weese, Dean

Information & Media Studies
Dr. Thomas Carmichael, Dean

Law
Ian Holloway, Dean

Medicine & Dentistry
Carol Herbert, Dean

Music
Robert Wood, Dean

Richard Ivey School of Business
Carol Stephenson, Dean

Science
David M. Wardlaw, Dean

Social Science
Brian Timney, Dean

Schools

Applied Electrostatics Research Centre
I. Inculet, Director

Boundary Layer Wind Tunnel Laboratory
A.G. Davenport, Director

Canadian Centre for Activity & Aging
Clara Fitzgerald, Director

Centre for Cognitive Science
Z.W. Pylyshyn, Director

Centre for Health & Well-Being
W. Avison, Director

Centre for Interdisciplinary Studies in Chemical Physics
M. Stillman, Director

Centre for Mass Media Studies
A.M. Osler, Director

Centre for Research & Teaching of Canadian Native Languages
R. Darnell, Director

Centre for Studies in Family Medicine
M. Stewart, Director

Centre for the Study of International Economic Relations
J. Whalley, Director

Centre for the Study of Theory & Criticism
T. Rajan, Director

Centre for Textual Scholarship
R.J. Shroyer, Director

Centre for Women's Studies & Feminist Research
Katherine McKenna, Director

Chemical Reactor Engineering Centre
H. de Lasa, Director

Continuing Studies
Kim Miller, Acting Director

Geotechnical Research Centre
K. Lo, Director

International Centre for Olympic Studies
R. Barney, Director

John P. Robarts Research Institute
M. Poznansky, Director
poznansky@admin.rri.uwo.ca

London Museum of Archaeology
Robert Pearce, Director

National Centre for Management Research & Development
K. Hardy, Director

National Tax Centre
T.W. Edgar, Director

Population Studies Centre
Rajulton Fernando, Director

Research Centre in Tribology
W.K. Wan, Director

Surface Science Western
Leo Lau, Director

Affiliations

Brescia University College
1285 Western Rd., London, ON N6G 1H2, Canada
Tel: 519-432-8553; *Fax:* 519-679-6489
Dr Colleen Hanycz, Principal, ext. 28263
chanycz@uwo.ca
Dr John B. Mitchell, Academic Dean, ext. 28116
jbmitche@uwo.ca
Marianne Simm, Registrar, ext. 28266
msimm@uwo.ca

Huron University College
1349 Western Rd., London, ON N6G 1H3, Canada
Tel: 519-438-7224; *Fax:* 519-438-3938
Dr. Ramona Lumpkin, Principal, 519-438-7224, ext. 307
rlumpkin@huron.uwo.ca
Bonnie Crocker, Registrar, 519-438-7224, ext. 285
bcrocke2@huron.uwo.ca
Rev. Susan Baldwin, Acting Dean, 519-438-7224, ext. 251
ssteers2@huron.uwo.ca

King's College
266 Epworth Ave., London, ON N6A 2M3, Canada
Tel: 519-433-3491; *Fax:* 519-433-2227
Dr. Gerald Killan, Principal, 519-433-3491, ext. 4300
gkillian@uwo.ca
Dr. Desmond Dutrizac, Academic Dean, 519-433-3491, ext. 4303
dutrizac@uwo.ca
Marilyn Mason, Registrar, 519-433-3491, ext. 4308
mmason@uwo.ca

Publications

Alumni Gazette

The Gazette
Rm. 244, University Community Centre
London, ON N6A 3K7, Canada
Fax: 519-661-3816

Western Alumni Gazette
#11, Alumni Hall, University of Western Ontario
Richmond St. N, London, ON N6A 5B9, Canada
Fax: 519-661-3948

Western News

North Bay: Nipissing University
P.O. Box 5002
100 College Dr., North Bay, ON P1B 8L7, Canada
Tel: 705-474-3450; *Fax:* 705-474-1947
nuinfo@nipissingu.ca
www.nipissingu.ca

Full Time Equivalency: 4800
David Brian Liddle, Chancellor
Dr. Lesley Lovett-Doust, President & Vice-Chancellor
Peter Gavan, Chair
Vicky Paine-Mantha, Vice-Pres., Finance & Administration, ext. 4289
vickyp@nipissingu.ca
Dr. Katharine M. Bergman, Vice-Pres., Academic & Research, ext. 4254
kmb@nipissingu.ca
Lisa Drinkwalter, Acting Exec. Dir., University Advancement, ext. 4327
lisad@nipissingu.ca
Brian Nettlefold, Exec. Dir., Library Services, ext. 4220
briann@nipissingu.ca
Heather Brown, Associate Registrar, ext. 4521, fax: 705-495-1772
registrar@nipissingu.ca

Faculties

Applied & Professional Studies
Rick Vanderlee, Dean
rickv@nipissingu.ca

Arts & Science
Dr. Craig Cooper, Dean, ext. 4290
craigc@nipissingu.ca

Schulich School of Education
Dr. Sharon Rich, Dean
sharonr@nipissingu.ca

Campuses

Brantford
50 Wellington St., Brantford, ON N3T 2L6
Tel: 519-752-1524; *Fax:* 519-752-8372
brant@nipissingu.ca.
Dr Maria Cantalini-Williams, Interim Assoc. Dean
mariac@nipissingu.ca

Muskoka
125 Wellington St., Bracebridge, ON P1L 1E2
Tel: 705-645-2921; *Fax:* 705-645-2922
muskoka@nipissingu.ca

Jan Lucy, Campus Administrator
janl@nipissingu.ca

Oshawa: University of Ontario Institute of Technology (UOIT)
2000 Simcoe St. North, Oshawa, ON L1H 7K4, Canada
Tel: 905-721-8668; *Fax:* 905-721-3178
admissions@uoit.ca
www.uoit.ca

Full Time Equivalency: 6500
Hon. Perrin Beatty, B.A., Chancellor
Dr. Ronald Bordessa, B.A., Ph.D, L.LD. (Hons.), President & Vice-Chancellor, 905-721-8668, ext. 3212
ron.bordessa@uoit.ca
Richard Marceau, B.Eng., M.Sc.A., Ph.D., F, Provost, 905-721-8668, ext. 3147, fax: 905-721-3210
richard.marceau@uoit.ca
MaryLynn West-Moynes, B.Sc. (Hons.), M.A., Vice-President, External Relations, 905-721-8668, ext. 3135
marylynn.west-moynes@uoit.ca
Ralph Aprile, B.Tech., M.B.A., Vice-President, Facilities & Ancillary Services, 905-721-8668, ext. 3024
ralph.aprile@dc-uoit.ca
Tom Austin, B.A., C.M.A., Vice-President, Finance & CFO, 905-721-8668, ext. 3796
tom.austin@uoit.ca
Margaret Greenley, B.Ed., M.A., Vice-President, Student Affairs, 905-721-8668, ext. 2340
margaret.greenley@uoit.ca
Pamela Drayson, B.A., M.A., Ph.D., Chief Librarian, 905-721-8668, ext. 2348
pamela.drayson@uoit.ca
Victoria Choy, B.A. (Hons.), M.A., Registrar, 905-721-8668, ext. 2988
victoria.choy@uoit.ca

Faculties

Faculty of Business & Information Technology
2000 Simcoe St. N., Oshawa, ON L1H 7K4, Canada
Tel: 905-721-3181
www.businessandit.uoit.ca
Pamela Ritchie, B.A., M.Sc., Ph.D., Dean, 905-721-8668, ext. 3160
pamela.ritchie@uoit.ca

Faculty of Criminology, Justice, and Policy Studies (Social Sciences & Human
2000 Simcoe St. N., Oshawa, ON L1H 7K4, Canada
Tel: 905-721-3234
www.criminologyandjustice.uoit.ca/
Nawal Ammar, B.Sc. (Hons.), M.Sc., Ph., Dean, 905-721-8668, ext. 3159
nawal.ammar@uoit.ca

Faculty of Education
2000 Simcoe St. N., Oshawa, ON L1H 7K4, Canada
Tel: 905-721-3181
kim.mitchell@uoit.ca (Receptionist, Faculty of Education)
http://education.uoit.ca/
Jim Greenlaw, B.A., B.Ed., M.A.(T), Ph., Dean, 905.721.8668, ext. 3158
jim.greenlaw@uoit.ca

Faculty of Energy Systems & Nuclear Science
2000 Simcoe St. N., Oshawa, ON L1H 7K4, Canada
Tel: 905-721-8668; *Fax:* 905-721-3046
admissions@uoit.ca
nuclear.uoit.ca/
George Bereznai, B.Eng., M.Eng., Ph.D., Dean, 905-721-8668, ext. 3142
george.bereznai@uoit.ca

Faculty of Engineering & Applied Science
Ontario Power Generation Engineering Bldg.
2000 Simcoe St.N., Oshawa, ON L1H 7K4, Canada
Tel: 905-721-3268; *Fax:* 905-721-3370
engineering@uoit.ca
www.engineering.uoit.ca
George Bereznai, B.Eng., M.Eng., Ph.D., Dean, 905-721-8668, ext. 3142
george.bereznai@uoit.ca

Faculty of Health Sciences
2000 Simcoe St. N., Oshawa, ON L1H 7K4, Canada
Tel: 905-721-3166
viven.ricard@uoit.ca
www.healthsciences.uoit.ca
Mary Bluechardt, E.M.T., B.PHE, M.Sc., Ph., Dean, 905-721-8668, ext. 2518
mary.bluechardt@uoit.ca

Faculty of Science
Science Bldg. UA4000
2000 Simcoe St.N., Oshawa, ON L1H 7K4, Canada
Tel: 905-721-3050; *Fax:* 905-721-3304
facultyofscience@uoit.ca
www.science.uoit.ca
William Smith, B.A.Sc., M.A.Sc., M.Sc.,, Dean, 905-721-8668, ext. 3235
william.smith@uoit.ca

Office of Graduate Studies
Business and It Bldg.
2nd Fl., 2000 Simcoe St.N., Oshawa, ON L1H 7K4, Canada
Tel: 905-721-8668; *Fax:* 905-721-3242
gradstudies@uoit.ca
gradstudies.uoit.ca/

Address as of August 20th, 2007.
Brian Campbell, Dean, 905-721-8668, ext. 2650
brian.campbell@uoit.ca

Ottawa: Carleton University
1125 Colonel By Dr., Ottawa, ON K1S 5B6, Canada
Tel: 613-520-7400; *Fax:* 613-520-7858
info@carleton.ca
www.carleton.ca

Grades: 25200
Herb Gray, Chancellor
Dr. Roseann O'Reilly Runte, President & Vice-Chancellor, 613-520-3801
presidents_office@carleton.ca
Peter Ricketts, Provost & Vice-President, 613-520-3884
provost@carleton.ca
Duncan Watt, Vice-Pres., Finance & Administration, 613-520-3804
duncan_watt@carleton.ca
Kimberly Matheson, Vice-Pres., Research & International, 613-520-7838
vpri@carleton.ca
Gisele Samson-Verreault, Chair, 613-520-3811
governors@carleton.ca
Suzanne Blanchard, Registrar, 613-520-2874, fax: 613-520-4410
registrar@carleton.ca

Faculties

Arts & Social Sciences
John Osborne, Dean, 613-520-2355, fax: 613-520-4481
fassod@carleton.ca

Engineering & Design
Dr Rafik Goubran, Dean, 613-520-5790, fax: 613-520-7481
info_engdesign@carleton.ca

Graduate & Postdoctoral Affairs
John Shepard, Dean, 613-520-2525, fax: 613-520-4049
graduate_studies@carleton.ca

Public Affairs
John ApSimon, Interim Dean, 613-520-3741, fax: 613-520-3742
odfpa@carleton.ca

Science
Malcolm Butler, Dean, 613-520-4388, fax: 613-520-4389
odscience@carleton.ca

Azrieli School of Architecture & Urbanism
Sheryl Boyle, Director, 613-520-2855, fax: 613-520-2849
architecture@carleton.ca

Schools

School for Studies in Art & Culture
Brian Foss, Director, 613-520-2600, ext. 3791, fax: 613-520-3575
brian_foss@carleton.ca

Linguistics & Language Studies
Lynne Young, Acting Director, 613-520-6612, fax: 613-520-6641
slals@carleton.ca

Sprott School of Business
Dr. Jerry Tomberlin, Dean, 613-520-2388, fax: 613-520-4427
info@sprott.carleton.ca

Canadian Studies
André Loiselle, Director, 613-520-2366, fax: 613-520-3903
canadian_studies@carleton.ca

Computer Science
Dr Douglas Howe, Director, 613-520-4333, fax: 613-520-4334
howescs.carleton.ca

Technology, Society, Environment Studies
Dr. John Buschek, Chair, 613-520-4483
john_buschek@carleton.ca

Industrial Design
Thomas Garvey, Director, 613-520-5672, fax: 613-520-4465
diane_smyth@carleton.ca

Information Technology
Dr Anthony Whitehead, Director, 613-520-5644, fax: 613-520-6623
info@bitdegree.ca

Journalism & Communication
Christopher Waddell, Director, 613-520-7404, fax: 613-520-6690
journalism@carleton.ca

Norman Paterson School of International Affairs
Bryan Henderson, Director, 613-520-6655, fax: 613-520-2889
international_affairs@carleton.ca

Public Policy & Administration
Dr. Susan Phillips, Director, 613-520-2547, fax: 613-520-2551
sppa@carleton.ca

Social Work
Hugh Shewell, Director, 613-520-5601, fax: 613-520-7496
karen_spencer@carleton.ca

Mathematics & Statistics
Yiqiang Zhao, Director, 613-520-3531
ms-dir@math.carleton.ca

Institute for Comparative Studies in Literature, Art & Culture
Paul Théberge, Director, 613-520-2177
icslac@carleton.ca

Institute of African Studies
Blair Rutherford, Director, 613-520-2600, ext. 2220, fax: 613-520-2363
african_studies@carleton.ca

Institute of Cognitive Science
Dr Jo-Anne Lefevre, Director, 613-520-2368, fax: 613-520-3985
jo-anne_lefevre@carleton.ca

Institute of Interdisciplinary Studies
Fran Cherry, Director, 613-520-2368, fax: 613-520-3985
iis@carleton.ca

Pauline Jewett Institute of Women's & Gender Studies
Katharine Kelly, Director, 613-520-6645, fax: 613-520-2622
womens_studies@carleton.ca

Institute of Criminology & Criminal Justice
Joanna Pozzulo, Director, 613-520-2588, fax: 613-520-6654
criminology@carleton.ca

Institute of European, Russian & Eurasian Studies
Dr Jeff Sahadeo, Director, 613-520-2888, fax: 613-520-7501
jeff_sahadeo@carleton.ca

Institute of Political Economy
Prof Janet Siltanen, Director, 613-520-7414, fax: 613-520-2154
political_economy@carleton.ca

Institute of Biochemistry
John Vierula, Director, 613-520-2478, fax: 613-520-3539
biochem@carleton.ca

Institute of Environmental Science
Dr Frederick A. Michel, Director, 613-520-2600, ext. 4461, fax: 613-520-3422
environmentalscience@carelton.ca

Integrated Science Institute
Pam Wolff, Director, 613-520-2600, ext. 4461, fax: 613-520-3422
integratedscience@carleton.ca

Publications
Carleton University Magazine
Tel: 613-520-3636; *Fax:* 613-520-3587
advancement@carleton.ca
magazine.carleton.ca

Fateema Sayani, Editor
fateema_sayani@carleton.ca

The Charlatan
Tel: 613-520-6680
charlatan@charlatan.ca
www.charlatan.ca

An independent student newspaper since 1945
Julia Johnson, Editor-In-Chief
editor@charlatan.ca

Ottawa: Dominican University College
Collège Universitaire Dominicain
96 Empress Ave., Ottawa, ON K1R 7G3, Canada
Tel: 613-233-5696; *Fax:* 613-233-6064
info@dominicancollege.ca
www.collegedominicain.ca

Full Time Equivalency: 110
Yvon Pomerleau, O.P., Chancellor
Gabor Csepregi, President & Regent of Studies
Michel Gourges, O.P., Vice-President
Peter Foy, Sec.-Treas.
Francis Peddle, Master of Studies
Daniel Cadrin, Chair, Institute of Pastoral Studies
Marie-Thérèse Nadeau, C.N.D., Dean, Faculty of Theology
Jean-François Méthot, Dean, Philosophy

Ottawa: Saint Paul University
Université Saint-Paul
223 Main St., Ottawa, ON K1S 1C4, Canada
Tel: 613-236-1393; *Fax:* 613-782-3005
Toll-Free: 1-800-637-6859
info@ustpaul.ca; studentservices@ustpaul.ca;
bookstore@ustpaul.ca
www.ustpaul.ca

Federated with the University of Ottawa, the Catholic & bilingual institution offers faculties of Canon Law, Human Sciences, Philosophy, & Theology.
Rev. Dale Schlitt, Rector
Prof. Achiel Peelman, Acting Vice-Rector, Academic
Prof. Chantal Beauvais, Vice-Rector, Administration
Rev. Andrea Spatafora, Dean, Faculty of Theology

Ottawa: University of Ottawa
Université d'Ottawa
75 Laurier Ave E., Ottawa, ON K1N 6N5, Canada
Tel: 613-562-5700; *Fax:* 613-562-5103
Toll-Free: 1-877-868-8292
www.uottawa.ca

Full Time Equivalency: 35548
Huguette Labelle, O.C., B.Sc.N.Ed., B.Ed.,, Chancellor
Allan Rock, B.A., P.C., President & Vice-Chancellor
François Hule, Vice-President, Academic & Provost
Sylvie Lauzon, B.Sc., M.Sc., Ph.D., Assoc. Vice-President
Victor Simon, B.A., M.A., Vice-President
Louis de Melo, B.A., C.M.A., Vice-President
Pierre Mercier, B.A., M.A., Ph.D., Assoc. Vice-President
Pamela Harrod, Secretary
François Chapleau, B.Sc., M.Sc., Ph.D., Registrar & Assoc. Vice-President
Leslie Weir, B.A., M.L.S., Chief Librarian
Lyse Huot, B.A., Director
Kathryn Prud'homme, B.A., LL.B., Legal Counsel
Mona Nemer, Vice-President
Nicolas Georganas, Ph.D., F.I.E.E., F.R.S.Ca, Assoc. Vice-President
Adele Reinhart, B.A., M.A., Ph.D., Assoc. Vice-President
Paul Boult, B.A., Director

Faculties
Management
Micheál J. Kelly, A.B., M.A., Ph.D., Dean

Arts
Antoni Lewkowicz, B.A., M.A., Ph.D., Dean

Education
Marie Josée Berger, B.Ed., M.Ed. Ph.D., Dean

Engineering
Claude Laguë, Dean

Health Sciences
Denis Prud'homme, B.Sc., M.Sc., PR.D., M.D., Dean

Law, Common Law Section
Bruce Feldthusen, Dean

Law, Civil Law Section
Sébastien Grammond, Dean

Medicine
Jacques Bradwejn, Dean

Science
André Lalonde, B.Sc., M.Sc., Ph.D., Dean

Social Sciences
Catherine M. Lee, Ph.D., Acting Dean

Graduate Studies & Postdoctoral
Gary Slater, B.Sc., M.Sc., Ph.D., Dean

Publications
Tabaret Magazine

The Fulcrum

La Rotonde

Peterborough: Trent University
1600 West Bank Dr., Peterborough, ON K9J 7B8, Canada
Tel: 705-748-1011; *Fax:* 705-748-1246
Toll-Free: 1-888-739-8885
www.trentu.ca

Full Time Equivalency: 7475
David L. Morton, B.A., M.B.A., LL.D., Chair
Tom Jackson, O.C., LL.D (Hon.), Chancellor
Dr. Steven E. Franklin, Ph.D., President & Vice-Chancellor
Don F. O'Leary, B.B.A., Vice-President
Colin Taylor, M.A., Ph.D., Dean
Dianne Lister, Vice-President
Christopher Michael, B.A., LL.B., Registrar
Julie E. Smith, LL.B., Secretary of the Senate
Leonard Conolly, M.A., Ph.D.., Principal
Michael Peterman, A.B., M.A., Ph.D., Principal
Stephen Brown, M.A., Ph.D., F.S.A., Master
A.A. Krüger, STAATSEXAMEN, Principal
Ian Storey, M.A., Ph.D., Head
Dr. Jocelyn Aubrey, Assoc. Dean of Arts & Science
Garth Brownscombe, B.A., CGA, Director
Lorraine Hayes, B.Sc., Manager
Don Cumming, B.A., Senior Director
Bill Byrick, B.A., Director
D'Arcy Legros, Bookstore Manager
Dr. Christine McKinnon, B.A. (Hons.), B.Phil., D., Vice-President
James Parker, B.A., M.A., Ph.D., Assoc. Vice-President
David Poole, B.Sc., M.Sc., Ph.D., Associate Dean

Publications
Arthur

St Catharines: Brock University
500 Glenridge Ave., St Catharines, ON L2S 3A1, Canada
Tel: 905-688-5550; *Fax:* 905-688-2789
www.brocku.ca

Full Time Equivalency: 17493
Dr Ned Goodman, Chancellor
Dr Jack N. Lightstone, President & Vice-Chancellor
Dr Murray Knuttila, Provost/Vice-Pres., Academic
Steven Pillar, Vice-Pres., Finance/Admin.
David Petis, Vice-Pres., Advancement
Ian Brindle, Vice-Pres., Research
Barb Anderson, Registrar, ext. 3566
bdavis@brocku.ca

Faculties
Business
Barbara Sainty, Interim Dean, ext. 3182
bsainty@brocku.ca

Education
James Heap, Dean, ext. 5190
jheap@brocku.ca

Humanities
Rosemary Hale, Dean, ext. 4562
rhale@brocku.ca

Social Sciences
Thomas Dunk, Dean, ext. 3426
tdunk@brocku.ca

Mathematics & Sciences
Richard Cheel, Interim Dean, ext. 3421
dean.fms@brocku.ca

Applied Health Sciences
John Corlett, Dean, ext. 3385
john.corlett@brocku.ca

Graduate Studies
Marilyn Rose, Dean, ext. 5152
mrose@brocku.ca

Publications
Brock Press
Katherine Gottli, Editor-In-Chief, ext. 3269
editor@brockpress.com

Sudbury: Huntington University
935 Ramsey Lake Rd., Sudbury, ON P3E 2C6, Canada
Tel: 705-673-4126; *Fax:* 705-673-6917
Toll-Free: 800-461-6366
www.huntingtonu.ca

Liberal Arts University specializing in Communication Studies, Ethics, Gerontology, Religious studies and Theology.

Sudbury: Laurentian University of Sudbury
Université Laurentienne de Sudbury
935 Ramsey Lake Rd., Sudbury, ON P3E 2C6, Canada
Tel: 705-675-1151; *Fax:* 705-675-4891
Toll-Free: 800-461-4030
admissions@laurentian.ca
www.laurentian.ca

Full Time Equivalency: 8270
Teaching is in French & English. Certain faculties offer parallel programs in both languages.
Dominic Giroux, MBA, President
Susan Silverton, Ph.D., M.D., Vice-President
Harley d'Entremont, M.A., Ph.D., Vice-President
R. Bertoli, Director
D. Mayer, M.Sc., Assoc. Vice-President
R. Smith, B.Sc., Registrar
L. Bonin, B.A., M.L.S., Director
Gerry Labelle, B.Comm., C.A., Director

Faculties
Humanities & Social Sciences
Donald Dennie, B.A., M.A., Ph.D., Dean
Management
Huguette Blanco, M.B.A., Ph.D., Dean
Professional Schools
Anne-Marie Mawhiney, B.A., B.S.W., M.S.W., Ph., Dean
Sciences & Engineering
R. Haq, B.Sc., M.Sc., Ph.D., Dean
Schools
Commerce
Ozhand Ganjavi, M.M.Sc., Ph.D., Director
Education (English)
John Lundy, Ed.D., Director
Education (French)
Serge Demers, Ph.D., Director
Engineering
Anis Farah, Ph.D., Director
Graduate Studies
Paul Colilli, M.A., Ph.D., Director
Human Kinetics
Roger Couture, M.A., Ph.D., Director
Nursing
Sharolyn Mossey, M.Sc.N., Director
Social Work
Duncan Matheson, M.S.W., Ph.D., Director
Sports Administration
K. Lefroy, B.Ed., M.Ed., Ed.D., Director
Affiliations
University of Sudbury
Université de Sudbury
935 Ramsey Lake Rd., Sudbury, ON P3E 2C6, Canada
Tel: 705-673-5661; *Fax:* 705-673-4912
usudreg@usudbury.ca; usudburyalumni@usudbury.ca (Alumni)
www.usudbury.com
Other Information: Registrar, E-mail: registrar@usudbury.ca
Founded in 1913 as Collège du Sacré-Coeur, the University of Sudbury operates in the Jesuit tradition. The bilingual university is committed to the English, French, & First Nations cultures. Courses include Religious Studies, Philosophy, Communications, French-Canadian Folklore, & Native Studies.
André Lacroix, Q.C., LL.D., Chancellor
Robert L. Fabbro, LL.B., Chair, Board of Regents
Dr. Pierre Zundel, Ph.D., President & Vice-Chancellor
pzundel@usudbury.ca
Sylvie Renault, H.B.Com., Registrar & Director, Recruitment & Communications
srenault@usudbury.ca
Shelley R. Machum, B.Com., C.A., Treasurer & Director, Administrative Services
smachum@usudbury.ca
Gerry Copeman, B.A., S.T.B., B.Th., Director, Spiritual Services
gcopeman@usudbury.ca
Paul Laverdure, Ph.D., Director, Library Services
plaverdure@usudbury.ca
Rachel Haliburton, Chair, Philosophy
rhaliburton@usudbury.ca
Jack Laughlin, Chair, Religious Studies
jlaughlin@usudbury.ca
Roger Spielmann, Chair, Native Studies
rspielmann@usudbury.ca
Pierre Brideau, Manager, Facilities & Security
pbrideau@usudbury.ca
Huntington University
Ramsey Lake Rd., Sudbury, ON P3E 2C6, Canada
Tel: 705-673-4126
Kevin McCormick, President & Vice-Chancellor
kmccormick@huntingtonu.ca
Thorneloe University at Laurentian University
935 Ramsey Lake Rd., Sudbury, ON P3E 2C6, Canada
Tel: 705-673-1730; *Fax:* 705-673-4979
Toll-Free: 1-866-846-7635
smoores@laurentian.ca (Susan Moores, Administrative Secretary)
www.thorneloe.laurentian.ca
Affiliated with the Anglican Church, Thorneloe University features the departments of Religious Studies, Classical Studies, Theatre Arts, & Women's Studies.
The Rev. Dr. Robert A. Derrenbacker, PhD., President, Provost, & Chaplain
rderrenbacker@laurentian.ca
Dr. Ian Maclennan, Registrar
imaclennan@laurentian.ca
Adam Sauve, Dean
ay_sauve@laurentian.ca
David Macdonald, Coordinator, Distance Education & Learning Technologies, 705-673-1730, ext. 33, fax: 705-673-4979
dmacdonald@laurentian.ca
Janine Moutsatsos, Librarian
jmoutsatsos@laurentian.ca
Collège Universitaire de Hearst
Hearst, ON P0L 1N0, Canada
Tel: 705-372-1781
Raymond Tremblay, B.A., B.Sc., M.A., Ph.D., Recteur
Pierre Ouellette, B.A., M.A., Vice-recteur
Manon Cyr, B.A., M.B.A., Secrétaire générale
Publications
Lambda
L'Original déchainé

Sudbury: Thorneloe University
935 Ramsey Lake Rd., Sudbury, ON P3E 2C6, Canada
Tel: 705-673-1730; *Fax:* 705-673-4979
Toll-Free: 866-846-7635
smoores@laurentian.ca
thorneloe.laurentian.ca

Sudbury: University of Sudbury
Ramsey Lake Rd, Sudbury, ON P3E 2C6, Canada
Tel: 705-673-5661
registrar@usudbury.ca
www.usudbury.ca

Thunder Bay: Lakehead University
955 Oliver Rd., Thunder Bay, ON P7B 5E1, Canada
Tel: 807-343-8110; *Fax:* 807-343-8023
www.lakeheadu.ca
Full Time Equivalency: 8050
L.G. Everett, Chancellor
Frederick F. Gilbert, President & Vice-Chancellor
K. Roche, Registrar & Secretary of Senate
A.E. Deighton, University Librarian
R. Blais, Controller
G. Wojda, Director
J. Podd, Director
J. Smith, Director
C. Calvert, Director
K.L. Clarke, Director
T. Warden, Director
L. Hayes, Vice-President
E.G. Walsh, Executive Director
M. Pawlowski, Vice-President
B. Sabourin, Vice-Provost
E. Abaya, Director
B. Moore, Director
S. Jafri, Director
R. Wang, Vice-President
Faculties
Business Administration
B. Dadgostar, Dean
Education
J. O'Sullivan, Dean
Engineering
H.T. Saliba, Dean
Forestry & the Forest Environment
U. Runesson, Dean
Graduate & International Studies
P. Hicks, Dean
Northern Ontario School of Medicine
J. Lanphear, West Campus Dean
Professional Schools
I. Newhouse, Dean
Science & Environmental Studies
A.P. Dean, Dean
Schools
Kinesiology
J. Farrell, Director
Nursing
K. Poole, Director
Outdoor Recreation
B. Cuthbertson, Director
Social Work
D. Tranter, Director
Publications
The Argus

Toronto: Emmanuel College
75 Queen's Park Cres. East, Toronto, ON M5S 1K7, Canada
Tel: 416-585-4539; *Fax:* 416-585-4516
ec.office@utoronto.ca
www.vicu.utoronto.ca/emmanuel.htm
Full Time Equivalency: 173
Theological college affiliated with the United Church of Canada

Toronto: Innis College
2 Sussex Ave., Toronto, ON M5S 1J6, Canada
Tel: 416-978-2513; *Fax:* 416-978-5503
www.utoronto.ca/innis/
Full Time Equivalency: 1480
Constituent college of the University of Toronto
Janet Paterson, Principal, 416-978-2510
principal.innis@utoronto.ca
Donald Boere, Assistant Principal & Registrar, 416-978-2513
donald.boere@utoronto.ca

Toronto: Knox College
59 St. George St., Toronto, ON M5S 2E6, Canada
Tel: 416-978-4500; *Fax:* 416-971-2133
knox.college@utoronto.ca
www.utoronto.ca/knox/
Theological college at the University of Toronto affiliated with the Presbyterian Church in Canada

Toronto: Massey College
4 Devonshire Pl., Toronto, ON M5S 2E1, Canada
Tel: 416-978-2895; *Fax:* 416-946-7890
massey.porter@gmail.com
masseycollege.ca
Full Time Equivalency: 130

Toronto: Ontario College of Art & Design (OCAD)
100 McCaul St., Toronto, ON M5T 1W1, Canada
Tel: 416-977-6000; *Fax:* 416-977-0235
www.ocad.ca
Full Time Equivalency: 3467
Sara Diamond, President
Dr. Sarah McKinnon, Vice-President
Peter Caldwell, Vice-President
Josephine Polera, Director
Simone Jones, Asst. Dean
Dr. Anthony Cahalan, Dean
Blake Fitzpatrick, Dean
Wendy Coburn, Asst. Dean
Steve Quinlan, Asst. Dean
Peter Fraser, Director
Colleen Reid, Asst. Dean
Rosemary Donegan, Asst. Dean
Jill Patrick, Director
Alastair MacLeod, Director
Christine Swiderski, Exhibitions Coordinator
Cindy Ball, Director
Marian Ruston, Manager
Jan Sage, Director
Nicky Davis, Director
Peter Lashko, Director
Ted Rickard, Manager
Sarah Mulholand, Coordinator
Laura Matthews, Director
Charles Reeve, Curator
Lance Straun, Manager
Dr. Kathryn Shailer, Dean
Vladimir Spicanovic, Asst. Dean
Doreen Balabanoff, Asst. Dean

Toronto: Ryerson University
350 Victoria St., Toronto, ON M5B 2K3, Canada
Tel: 416-979-5000
inquire@ryerson.ca
www.ryerson.ca
Full Time Equivalency: 25600
Peter Lukasiewicz, Chair
G. Raymond Chang, Chancellor
Sheldon Levy, President & Vice-Chancellor
Sheldon Levy, Provost & Vice-President
Michael Dewson, Vice-Provost
Dr. Linda Grayson, Vice-President
Keith Alnwick, Registrar
Janice Winton, Executive Director
Marion Creery, Sr. Director
Renée Lemieux, Sr. Director
Shirley Lewchuk, Secretary of the Board of Governors
Ian Marlatt, Sr. Director
Peter Lukasiewicz, Vice-Chair
Dr. Anastasios (Tas) Venetsanopoulos, Vice-President
Judith Sandys, Assoc. Vice-President

<u>Faculties</u>
Arts
Dr. Carla Cassidy, Dean

Business
Dr. Ken Jones, Ph.D., Dean

Communication & Design
Dr. Daniel Doz, Dean

Community Services
Dr. Usha George, Ph.D., Dean

Engineering & Applied Science
Dr. Mohamed Lachemi, Interim Dean

Engineering & Applied Science, Research, Development & New Science Programs
Steven Liss, Assoc. Dean

Engineering & Applied Science, Undergraduate Programs & Student Affairs
Zouheir Fawaz, Assoc. Dean

The G. Raymond Chang School of Continuing Education
Anita Shilton, Dean

Graduate Studies

<u>Publications</u>
The Eyeopener

The Ryerson Rambler
350 Victoria St, Toronto, ON M5B 2K3, Canada

Ryersonian

NightViews

Toronto: University College
15 King's College Circle, Toronto, ON M5S 3H7, Canada
Tel: 416-978-3170; *Fax:* 416-978-6019

Toronto: University of Guelph Humber
207 Humber College Blvd., Toronto, ON M9W 5L7, Canada
Tel: 416-798-1331; *Fax:* 416-798-1991
info@guelphhumber.ca
www.guelphhumber.ca

John Walsh, Vice-Provost, Chief Academic & Executive Officer
Dalia Smith, Librarian
dalia.smith@guelphhumber.ca
Jock Phippen, Manager, Registrarial Services
jock.phippen@guelphhumber.ca
Gabrielle Bernardi-Dengo, Manager, Finance & Administration Services
gabrielle.bernardi-dengo@guelphhumber.ca

Toronto: University of Toronto
21 King's College Circle, Toronto, ON M5S 1A1, Canada
Tel: 416-978-2011
www.utoronto.ca

Full Time Equivalency: 45009
The Hon. David Peterson, Chancellor
Dr. David Naylor, President
Cheryl Misak, Vice-President & Provost
Edith Hillan, Vice-Provost
John Challis, Assoc. Provost & Vice-President
Safwat Zaky, Vice-Provost
Rivi Frankle, Asst. Vice-President & Chief Operations Officer
Angela Hildyard, Vice-President
Catherine J. Riggall, Vice-President
Tim McTiernan, Asst. Vice-President, Research & Executive Director
Joan E. Foley, University Ombudsperson
Karel Swift, University Registrar & Director
Avon McFarlane, Acting Asst. Vice-President
Catharine Whiteside, Vice-Provost
Robert Steiner, Asst. Vice-President
Jonathan Freedman, Deputy Provost
John F. (Jack) Petch, Chair of the Governing Council
Sheila Brown, CFO
Judith Wolfson, Vice-President

<u>Faculties</u>
Applied Science & Engineering
Prof. Cristina Amon, Dean

Architecture, Landscape & Design
George Baird, Dean

Arts & Science
Meric Gertler, Dean

Dentistry
Prof. David Mock, Dean

Forestry
Tattersall Smith, Dean

Information Studies
Ross Seamus, Dean

Law
Mayo Moran, Dean

Management
Roger L. Martin, Dean

Medicine
Catharine Whiteside, Dean

Music
Russell Hartenberger, Dean

Nursing
Sioban Nelson, Dean

OISE/UT
Jane Gaskell, Dean

Pharmacy
Henry Mann, Dean

Physical Education & Health
Bruce Kidd, Dean

School of Graduate Studies
Brian Corman, Dean

Social Work
Cheryl Regehr, Dean

<u>Schools</u>
Asian Institute
Joseph Wong, Director

Canadian Institute for Theoretical Astrophysics
Norm Murray, Director

Centre for Comparative Literature
Neil ten Kortenaar, Director

Centre for Environmental Studies
Ingrid Leman Stefanovic, Director

Centre for European, Russian, and Eurasian Studies
Jeffrey Kopstein, Director

Centre for Industrial Relations
Anil Verma, Interim Director

Centre for International Studies
Prof. Louis W. Pauly, Director

Centre for Medieval Studies
Andrew Orchard, Director

Centre for Reformation & Renaissance Studies
Olga Pugliese, Director

Centre for Research in Women's Health
Heather Maclean, Director

Centre for South Asian Studies
Chelva Kanaganayekam, Director

Centre for the Study of Pain
Michael Salter, Director

Centre for Urban & Community Studies
David Hulchanski, Director

Centre of Criminology
Anthony Doob, Acting Director

Computing in the Humanities & Social Sciences
Chris Leowski, Director

David Dunlap Observatory
Sold to Metrus Development in 2008, operated by The Royal Astronomical Society of Canada

Fields Institute for Research in Mathematical Sciences
Sold to Metrus Development in 2008, operated by The Royal Astronomical Society of Canada
Barbara Keyfitz, Director

Frank Iacobucci Centre for Italian Canadian Studies
Sold to Metrus Development in 2008, operated by The Royal Astronomical Society of Canada
Salvatore Bancheri, Acting Director

Graduate Centre for Study of Drama
Sold to Metrus Development in 2008, operated by The Royal Astronomical Society of Canada
Prof. John Astington, Director

Institute for Aerospace Studies
Sold to Metrus Development in 2008, operated by The Royal Astronomical Society of Canada
D.W. Zingg, Director

Institute for History & Philosophy of Science & Technology
Sold to Metrus Development in 2008, operated by The Royal Astronomical Society of Canada
Paul Thompson, Director

Institute for Human Development, Life Course & Aging
Sold to Metrus Development in 2008, operated by The Royal Astronomical Society of Canada
L. McDonald, Director

Institute for Policy Analysis
Sold to Metrus Development in 2008, operated by The Royal Astronomical Society of Canada
Wendy Dobson, Director

Institute for Women's Studies & Gender Studies
Sold to Metrus Development in 2008, operated by The Royal Astronomical Society of Canada
Bonnie McElhinny, Director

Institute of Aboriginal People's Health
Sold to Metrus Development in 2008, operated by The Royal Astronomical Society of Canada
Jeff Reading, Director

Institute of Biomaterials & Biomedical Engineering
Sold to Metrus Development in 2008, operated by The Royal Astronomical Society of Canada
Paul Santerre, Director

Institute of Child Study
Sold to Metrus Development in 2008, operated by The Royal Astronomical Society of Canada
Kang Lee, Director

Institute of Medical Science
Sold to Metrus Development in 2008, operated by The Royal Astronomical Society of Canada
Ori D. Rothstein, Director

Institute of Population & Public Health
Sold to Metrus Development in 2008, operated by The Royal Astronomical Society of Canada
John Frank, Director

Institute on Human Development, Child & Youth Health
Sold to Metrus Development in 2008, operated by The Royal Astronomical Society of Canada
Michael Kramer, Director

Knowledge Media Design Institute
Sold to Metrus Development in 2008, operated by The Royal Astronomical Society of Canada
Ron Baecker, Interim Director

Masters of Mathematical Finance
Sold to Metrus Development in 2008, operated by The Royal Astronomical Society of Canada
Robert Almgren, Director

McLuhan Program in Culture & Technology
Sold to Metrus Development in 2008, operated by The Royal Astronomical Society of Canada
Derrick de Kerckhove, Director

Museum Studies Program
Sold to Metrus Development in 2008, operated by The Royal Astronomical Society of Canada
John Fleming, Interim Director

Pontifical Institute of Medieval Studies
Sold to Metrus Development in 2008, operated by The Royal Astronomical Society of Canada
James K. McConica, Director

Toronto School of Theology
Sold to Metrus Development in 2008, operated by The Royal Astronomical Society of Canada
Alan Hayes, Director

Transitional Year Program
Sold to Metrus Development in 2008, operated by The Royal Astronomical Society of Canada
Rhonda Love, Director

U of T Joint Program in Transportation
Sold to Metrus Development in 2008, operated by The Royal Astronomical Society of Canada
Eric Miller, Director

<u>Affiliations</u>
University of Toronto Mississauga
Also known as: Erindale College
3359 Mississauga Rd., Mississauga, ON L5L 1C6, Canada
Tel: 905-569-4455
hrserv.utm@utoronto.ca (human resources)
www.utm.utoronto.ca
Other Information: Admissions, Phone: 905-828-5400; Public Affairs: 905-828-5214
Full Time Equivalency: 11430
The University of Toronto Mississauga provides undergraduate education to approximately 11,000 students & graduate studies to about 430 graduate students. With 14 academic departments, the school employs 700 faculty & staff.
Professor Hargurdeep Saini, Vice-President & Principal

Lynda Collins, Director, Human Resources, 905-828-5210
lynda.collins@utoronto.ca

Massey College
4 Devonshire Pl., Toronto, ON M5S 2E1, Canada
Tel: 416-978-2891; *Fax:* 416-946-7890
John Fraser, Master/CAO, 416-978-2549
Mary Graham, Registrar, 416-978-2891, fax: 416-971-3032
mary.graham@utoronto.ca
Anna Luengo, College Administrator, 416-978-6606
anna.luengo@utoronto.ca

New College
300 Huron, Toronto, ON M5S 3J6, Canada
Tel: 416-978-2460; *Fax:* 416-978-0554
Prof. Yves Roberge, Principal, 416-978-2461, fax: 416-978-4345
nc.principal@utoronto.ca
Prof. Cheryl Misak, Vice-Principal

University of Toronto Scarborough
1265 Military Trail, Toronto, ON M1C 1A4, Canada
Tel: 416-287-8872
stuaff@utsc.utoronto.ca (student affairs)
www.utsc.utoronto.ca
Full Time Equivalency: 10131
Number of Employees: 189 academic staff & librarians; 373 non-academic staff. Number of Programs: 242
Professor Franco J. Vaccarino, Vice-President, U of T, & Principal, U of T Scarborough
Professor Rick Halpern, Vice-Principal & Dean, Academic
deanadmin@utsc.utoronto.ca
Professor Malcolm Campbell, MA (Oxon), PhD, Vice-Principal, Research
vpresearch@utsc.utoronto.ca
Tom Nowers, Dean, Student Affairs
Professor William Gough, Vice-Dean, Graduate Education & Program Development
Professor John Scherk, Vice-Dean, Undergraduate
Lesley Lewis, Assistant Dean
Andrew Arifuzzaman, Chief Strategy Officer
Kim McLean, Chief Administrative Officer
Georgette Zinaty, Executive Director, Development & Alumni Relations
gzinaty@utsc.utoronto.ca
Kim Burbine Richard, Director, Human Resource Services
Rita Pearsall, Director, Enrollment Services
Professor John Bassili, Chair, Department of Psychology
Professor William Bowen, Chair, Department of Humanities
Professor Donald Cormack, Chair, Department of Physical & Environmental Sciences
Professor Vassos Hadzilacos, Chair, Department of Computer & Mathematical Sciences
Professor Michael Krashinsky, Chair, Department of Management
Professor Ted Relph, Chair, Department of Social Sciences
Professor Greg Vanlerberghe, Chair, Department of Biological Sciences

University College
15 King's College Circle, Toronto, ON M5S 3H7, Canada
Tel: 416-978-3170; *Fax:* 416-978-6019
Paul Perron, Principal

Woodsworth College
119 Saint George St., Toronto, ON M5S 1A1, Canada
Tel: 416-978-4444; *Fax:* 416-978-4088
Joseph R. Desloges, Principal
Mary Choi, CAO
Cheryl Shook, Registrar

St. Michael's College
81 St. Mary St., Toronto, ON M4S 1J4, Canada
Tel: 416-926-1300
www.utoronto.ca/stmikes
Fully federated with the University of Toronto, St. Michael's College has a large Faculty of Theology. It also features the Canadian Catholic Bioethics Institute & the Pontifical Institute of Mediaeval Studies.
Anne Anderson, Interim President
Mark McGowan, Principal

Trinity College in the University of Toronto
6 Hoskin Ave., Toronto, ON M5S 1H8, Canada
Tel: 416-978-2522; *Fax:* 416-978-2797
deanofstudents@trinity.utoronto.ca; chaplain@trinity.utoronto.ca
www.trinity.utoronto.ca
Other Information: Bursar's Office, E-mail: fees@trinity.utoronto.ca
Full Time Equivalency: 1840
Trinity College educates approximately 1,700 undergraduate students in the Faculty of Arts & Science, plus 140 students in the Faculty of Divinity. Founded in 1851, it is Canada's oldest Anglican theological school.
The Hon. Bill Graham, Chancellor
Professor Andy Orchard, Provost & Vice-Chancellor, 416-978-2689
provost@trinity.utoronto.ca
Bruce Bowden, B.A., M.A., Ph.D. (Tor.), Registrar & Director, Student Services, 416-978-2687, fax: 416-978-2831
bowden@trinity.utoronto.ca; registrar@trinity.utoronto.ca
Linda W. Corman, A.B. (Vassar), M.A. (Chi., College Librarian, 416-978-4398, fax: 416-978-2797
linda.corman@utoronto.ca
Jill Willard, Officer, Personnel
jwillard@trinity.utoronto.ca

Victoria University
73 Queen's Park Cres. East, Toronto, ON M5S 1K9, Canada
Tel: 416-585-4524; *Fax:* 416-585-4584
www.vicu.utoronto.ca
Paul W. Gooch, President, 416-585-4511
vic.president@utoronto.ca
Susan McDonald, Registrar, 416-585-4405
s.mcdonald@utoronto.ca
Kelly Castle, Dean of Students, 416-585-4495
jason.hunter@utoronto.ca

Emmanuel College
75 Queen's Park Cres. East, Toronto, ON M5S 1K7, Canada
Tel: 416-585-4539; *Fax:* 416-585-4516
ec.office@utoronto.ca
Mark G. Toulouse, Principal
Wanda Chin, Registrar
wanda.chin@utoronto.ca

Knox College
59 Saint George St., Toronto, ON M5S 2E6, Canada
Tel: 416-978-4500; *Fax:* 416-971-2133
Rev. Dr. J. Dorcas Gordon, Principal
Rev. Beth McCutcheon, Director, Academic Programs
mb.mccutcheon@utoronto.ca

Wycliffe College
5 Hoskin Ave., Toronto, ON M5S 1H7, Canada
Tel: 416-979-3535; *Fax:* 416-946-3545
Rev. Dr. George Sumner, Principal

Regis College
15 St. Mary St., Toronto, ON M4Y 2R5, Canada
Tel: 416-922-5474; *Fax:* 416-922-2898
www.regiscollege.ca
Regis is a Roman Catholic college in the Jesuit tradition. It is a federated college of the University of Toronto.
Very Reverend Adolfo Nicolas, S.J., Chancellor, Ecclesiastical Faculty
Joseph G. Schner, S.J., President & Rector

Publications

The Bulletin
Dept. of Public Affairs
21 King's College Circle, Toronto, ON M5S 1A1, Canada

The Newspaper
#245, 1 Spadina Cres, Toronto, ON M5S 1A1, Canada
Fax: 416-593-0552

The Toike Oike

University of Toronto Magazine
Dept. of Public Affairs
21 King's College Circle, Toronto, ON M5S 1A1, Canada
Fax: 416-978-7430

Varsity

Toronto: Victoria University
73 Queen's Park Cres., Toronto, ON M5S 1K7, Canada
Tel: 416-585-4508; *Fax:* 416-585-4459
vic.registrar@utoronto.ca
www.vicu.utoronto.ca
Full Time Equivalency: 2300
Although the university is located within the University of Toronto campus, it has its own independent administration, faculty and governing body.

Toronto: Woodsworth College
119 Saint George St., Toronto, ON M5S 1A9, Canada
Tel: 416-978-4444; *Fax:* 416-978-6111
wdwregistrar@utoronto.ca
wdw.utoronto.ca
Full Time Equivalency: 6000

Toronto: Wycliffe College
5 Hoskin Ave., Toronto, ON M5S 1H7, Canada
Tel: 416-979-3535; *Fax:* 416-946-3545
www.wycliffecollege.ca
Seminary at the University of Toronto affiliated with the Anglican Church of Canada

Toronto: York University
4700 Keele St., Toronto, ON M3J 1P3, Canada
Tel: 416-736-2100; *Fax:* 416-736-5700
www.yorku.ca
Full Time Equivalency: 45890
Marshall Cohen, Chair of the Board
Roland (Roy) McMurty, O.C., O.O., B.A., LL.B., Chancellor
Mahmoud Shoukri, B.Sc., M.Eng., Ph.D., President & Vice-Chancellor
S.M. Embleton, B.Sc., M.Sc., Ph.D., Vice-President
John Lennox, Assoc. Vice-President
G. Brewer, Vice-President
S. Shapson, B.Sc., M.A., Ph.D., Vice-President
H.I. Lewis, B.A., M.A., LL.B., University Secretary & General Counsel
Sylvia Schippke, Asst. Vice-President
Trudy Pound-Curtis, CFO & Asst. Vice-President
Michael Graham, Asst. Vice-President
P. Cantor, B.A., L.L.B., F.I.C.B., Chair
N. White, Director
Luana Jursza, CIO & Executive Director
Norman Ahmet, Asst. Vice-President
B. Purves, President
B. Miller, Director
J. Meikle, Director
P. Murray, B.P.H.E., M.Sc., Director
R. Woodhouse, Academic Director
T. Mohammed, B.Sc., M.Sc., P.Eng., Director
P. Monk, Director/Curator
M. Scheepers, B.A., Director
J. Briggs, Director
B. Bellissimo, Director
R. Thompson, B.A., Director
P. Yu, B.Sc., Director
K. Irani, B.E., P.Eng., Director
D.L. Glass, B.A., B.Ed., M.E.D., Director
E.S. Spence, Director
B. Abner, B.A., M.A., Assoc. Vice-President
M. Chan, Director
Robert J. Tiffin, Vice-President
C. Archer, University Librarian
N. Gouda, Director
Calum MacKechnie, Director
K. Swartz, B.A., B.S.W., M.S.W., Director
Joanne Duklas, University Registrar
B. Brown, Director
S. MacDonald, Director
R.A. Webb, Assoc. Vice-President
A. Shubert, Assoc. Vice-President
A. Wickens, Asst. Vice-President
S. Spence, Director
B. Woodward, Director
R. Faverin, Director
Suzanne MacDonald, Assoc. Vice-President

Faculties

Arts
Bob Drummond, Dean

Joseph E. Atkinson College
Rhonda Lenton, Dean

Education
Paul Axelrod, Dean

Environmental Studies
David Morley, Dean

Fine Arts
Phillip Silver, B.A., Dean

Glendon College
K. McRoberts, B.A., M.A., Ph.D., Principal

Graduate Studies
Ronald Pearlman, Dean

Health
Harvey Skinner, Dean

Law School, Osgoode Hall
Patrick Monahan, Dean

Schulich School of Business
Dezsö J. Horvath, Dean

Science & Engineering
Nick Cercone, Dean

Schools

Canadian Centre for German & European Studies
Kurt Huebner, Acting Director

Centre for Applied Sustainability
D.V.J. Bell, B.A., A.M., Ph.D., Director

Centre for Atmospheric Chemistry
G.W. Harris, B.Sc., Ph.D., Director

Centre for International & Security Studies
D.B. Dewitt, B.A., M.A., Ph.D., Director

Centre for Jewish Studies
M. Lockshin, Director

Centre for Practical Ethics
Shirley Katz, Acting Director

Centre for Public Law & Public Policy
Bruce Ryder, Director

Centre for Refugee Studies
Susan McGrath, Director

Centre for Research in Earth & Space Science
G.G. Shepherd, B.Sc., M.Sc., Ph.D., F.R., Director

Centre for Research in Mass Spectrometry
M. Siu, Director

Centre for Research on Latin America & the Caribbean
Viviana Patroni, Director

Centre for Research on Work & Society
N. Pupo, Director

Centre for Vision Research
J. Tsotsos, B.A., M.Sc., Ph.D., Director

Institute for Research & Innovation in Sustainability
David Wheeler, Director

Institute for Research on Learning Technologies
Ron Owston, Director

Institute for Social Research
M.D. Ornstein, B.Sc., Ph.D., Director

Jack & Mae Nathanson Centre for the Study of Organized Crime & Corruption
M. Beare, B.A., M.A., M.P.H.L., Ph., Director

La Marsh Centre for Research on Violence & Conflict Resolution
Anne Marie Wall, Acting Director

Robarts Centre for Canadian Studies
S. Feldman, Director

York Centre for Asian Research
P. Vandergeest, Director

York Centre for Feminist Research
V. Agnew, Director

York Institute for Health Research
M. Rioux, Director

Campuses
Glendon Campus
2275 Bayview Ave., Toronto, ON M4N 3M6, Canada

Publications
Atkinsonian

Excalibur

Lexicon

MacMedia (McLaughlin College)

Obiter Dicta (Osgoode Hall)

The Pro Tem (Glendon College)

Waterloo: Conrad Grebel University College
140 Westmount Rd. North, Waterloo, ON N2L 3G6, Canada
Tel: 519-885-0220; *Fax:* 519-885-0014
congreb@uwaterloo.ca
grebel.uwaterloo.ca

Full Time Equivalency: 3894

Waterloo: University of Waterloo
200 University Ave. West, Waterloo, ON N2L 3G1, Canada
Tel: 519-888-4567; *Fax:* 519-884-8009
www.uwaterloo.ca/

Full Time Equivalency: 26457
V. Prem Watsa, Chancellor
Bob Harding, Chair
D.L. Johnston, C.C., A.B., L.L.B., President & Vice-Chancellor
Bruce Mitchell, B.Sc., M.Sc., Ph.D., Vice-President
Meg Beckell, B.A., M.B.A., Vice-President
W.B. Mitchell, B.A., M.A., Ph.D., Associate Provost
P.D. Guild, B.A., M.A., D.Phil., Vice-President
A.C. Scott, B.A., Associate Provost
D.E. Huber, B.B.A., C.M.A., Vice-President
L.H.P. Claxton, B.A., B.L.S., M.L.S., Secretary of the University
K.A. Lavigne, B.A., Registrar
G. Cuthbert Brandt, B.A., M.A., Ph.D., Associate Vice-President
J.D. Walker, B.A., M.A.Sc., Director
J.A. George, B.Sc., M.Sc., Ph.D., F.R., Vice-President, University Research & Associate Provost

Faculties
Applied Health Sciences
R.C. Mannell, B.A., M.P.E., Ph.D., Dean

Arts
Ken Coates, Dean

Engineering
A.S. Sedra, B.Sc., M.A.Sc., Ph.D., Dean

Environmental Studies
H.S. (Deep) Saini, B.Sc., M.Sc., Ph.D., Dean

Graduate Studies
R. Bird, B.Sc., M.Sc., Ph.D., Dean

Mathematics
T.F. Coleman, Ph.D., Dean

Science
Terry McMahon, Dean

Affiliations
Conrad Grebel University College
Waterloo, ON N2L 3G6, Canada
Tel: 519-885-0220
Henry Paetkau, B.A., M.A., Ph.D., Principal, 519-885-0220, ext. 24237
cgcpres@uwaterloo.ca
E. Paul Penner, Dir., Operations, 519-885-0220, ext. 24231
eppenner@uwaterloo.ca
Dr James Pankratz, Academic Dean, 519-885-0220, ext. 24232
pankratz@uwaterloo.ca

Renison College
240 Westmount Rd. North, Waterloo, ON N2L 3G4, Canada
Tel: 519-884-4400; *Fax:* 519-884-5135
www.renison.uwaterloo.ca
College programs lead to a Bachelor of Arts or an Honours Bachelor of Social Work degree of the University of Waterloo.
John Crossley, B.A., M.A., Ph.D., Principal

St. Jerome's University
290 Westmount Rd. North, Waterloo, ON N2L 3G3, Canada
Tel: 519-884-8110; *Fax:* 519-884-5759
webmaster@sju.uwaterloo.ca
www.sju.ca

Full Time Equivalency: 1019
Federated with the University of Waterloo, St. Jerome's University is a public Catholic university. Education in the Arts & Mathematics is provided.
Peter Naus, Chancellor
David Perrin, President & Vice-Chancellor, 519-884-8111, ext. 28253
dperrin@sju-serv1.uwaterloo.ca

St. Paul's United College
University of Waterloo
190 Westmount Rd. North, Waterloo, ON N2L 3G5, Canada
Tel: 519-885-1460; *Fax:* 519-885-6364
stpauls@uwaterloo.ca
www.stpauls.uwaterloo.ca
The residential teaching institution is affiliated with the University of Waterloo. It features the international development program.
Dr. Mark Seasons, Chair
Graham Brown, Principal
ggbrown@uwaterloo.ca
Peter Frick, Academic Dean
Rod McAllister, Dean of Students

Publications
Imprint
Student newspaper at the University of Waterloo

UW Gazette
Newspaper published by the Office of Information and Public Affairs

Waterloo: Wilfrid Laurier University
75 University Ave. West, Waterloo, ON N2L 3C5, Canada
Tel: 519-884-0710; *Fax:* 519-886-9351
www.wlu.ca

Full Time Equivalency: 12239
Dr. Max Blouw, President
Dr. Deborah MacLatchy, Vice-President
dmaclatchy@wlu.ca
Jim Butler, Vice-President
jbutler@wlu.ca
Ray Darling, Registrar
rdarling@wlu.ca
Robert Donelson, Vice-President
rdonelson@wlu.ca
Sharon Brown, University Librarian
sbrown@wlu.ca

Faculties
Arts
Dr. David Docherty, Dean

Brantford Campus
73 George St., Brantford, ON N3T 2Y3, Canada
Tel: 519-756-8228; *Fax:* 519-759-2172
Dr. Bruce Arai, Dean
barai@wlu.ca

Graduate Studies & Research
73 George St., Brantford, ON N3T 2Y3, Canada
Tel: 519-756-8228; *Fax:* 519-759-2172
Dr. Joan Norris, Dean

Music
73 George St., Brantford, ON N3T 2Y3, Canada
Tel: 519-756-8228; *Fax:* 519-759-2172
Charles Morrison, Dean
cdmorris@wlv.ca

School of Business & Economics
73 George St., Brantford, ON N3T 2Y3, Canada
Tel: 519-756-8228; *Fax:* 519-759-2172
Ginny Dybenko, Dean
gdybenko@wlv.ca

Science
73 George St., Brantford, ON N3T 2Y3, Canada
Tel: 519-756-8228; *Fax:* 519-759-2172
Dr. Peter Tiidus, Acting Dean
ptiidus@wlv.ca

Social Work
73 George St., Brantford, ON N3T 2Y3, Canada
Tel: 519-756-8228; *Fax:* 519-759-2172
Lesley Cooper, Dean

Waterloo Lutheran Seminary
73 George St., Brantford, ON N3T 2Y3, Canada
Tel: 519-756-8228; *Fax:* 519-759-2172
Dr. David Pfrimmer, Principal-Dean
dpfrimmer@wlu.ca

Publications
The Cord Weekly
Student newspaper at Wilfrid Laurier University

Windsor: Iona College
208 Sunset Ave., Windsor, ON N9B 3A7, Canada
Tel: 519-253-3000; *Fax:* 519-973-7050
office@ionacollege.edu
www.ionacollege.edu
Affiliate College to the University of Windsor, affiliated with the United Church of Canada designed to promote theological educaion, social justice and Chaplaincy.
Rev. Dr. BoJeong Kim, Principal & Chaplain Emeritus
principal@ionacollege.edu
Rev. Dr. Lloyd Smith, Chancellor
Dr. Norman King, Director, School of Theology
theology@ionacollege.edu

Windsor: University of Windsor
401 Sunset Ave., Windsor, ON N9B 3P4, Canada
Tel: 519-253-3000
www.uwindsor.ca/

Full Time Equivalency: 13496
Plus 3,387 part-time students
Amanda Gellman, Vice-President, University Advancement

Faculties
Arts & Social Sciences
Cecil Houston, B.A., M.A., Ph.D., Dean

Education
Pat Rogers, B.A., M.Sc., Ph.D., Dean

Engineering
Graham Reader, B.Tech. (Hons.), B.A., Ph, Dean

Graduate Studies & Research
Jim Frank, Dean

Human Kinetics
Bob Boucher, B.H.K., M.H.K., Ph.D., Dean

Law
Bruce Elman, B.Sc., L.L.B., L.L.M., Dean

Nursing
Elaine Duffy, B.A.Sc., M.N., Ph.D., Reg, Dean

Odette School of Business
Dr. Allan Conway, Dean

Science
Richard Caron, Dean

Schools
Athletics & Recreational Services
Gord Grace, Head

Biological Sciences
William Crosby, Head

Chemistry & Biochemistry
Douglas Stephan, Head

Civil & Environmental Engineering
Ram Balachandar, B.E., Ph.D., P.Eng., Head

Classical & Modern Languages
Dietmar Lage, B.A., M.A., Ph.D., Head

Communication Studies
James Wittebols, Head

Dramatic Art
Lionel Walsh, Head

Earth Sciences
Ihsan Al-Aasm, Head

Economics, Mathematics & Statistics
Ronald Meng, Head

Electrical & Computer Engineering
Maher Sid-Ahmed, Head

English
Karl Jirgens, Head

History
Christina Simmons, Head

Industrial & Manufacturing Systems Engineering
Leo Oriet, Head

Intelligent Manufacturing Systems
Hoda ElMaraghy, B.Eng., M.Eng., Ph.D., Head
Waguih ElMaraghy, B.Eng., M.Eng., Ph.D., Head

Languages, Literatures, Cultures
Dietmar Lage, Head

Mechanical, Automotive & Materials Engineering
Robert Gaspar, B.A.Sc., M.A.Sc., Ph.D., Head

Philosophy
Jeffrey Noonan, Head

Physics
Gordon Drake, B.Sc., M.Sc., Ph.D., Head

Political Science
Tom Najem, Head

Psychology
Shelagh Towson, B.A., M.A., Ph.D., Head

Social Work
Brent Angell, Head

Sociology & Anthropology
Lynne Phillips, B.A., M.A., Ph.D., Head

Student Health Services
Maria Blass, M.D., Head

Visual Arts
Brenda Pelkey, Head

Women's Studies
Anne Forrest, Head

Affiliations

Assumption University
2629 Riverside Dr. West, Windsor, ON N9B 1B4, Canada
Tel: 519-973-7033; *Fax:* 519-973-7089
cbertrand@assumptionu.ca
www.assumptionu.ca

Most Rev. Ronald P. Fabbro, C.S.B., D.D.Bishop of Lon, Chancellor
Fr William A. Riefel, C.S.B., Treas./Dir., Operations
Dr. Lois Smedick, Chair
Rev. Dr. Paul Rennick, C.S.B., Pres./Vice-Chancellor
Dr Anne Snowdon, Dir., Centre for Religion & Culture
Anne Shore, Prog. Dir., Dept. of Theology

Canterbury College
2500 University Ave. West, Windsor, ON N9B 3Y1, Canada
Tel: 519-971-3646; *Fax:* 519-971-3645
canter@uwindsor.ca
www.uwindsor.ca/canterbury

Canterbury College offers the following courses: Doctor of Ministry Degree (in affiliation with Ashland Theological Seminary at Ashland University); certificate courses for the Anglican Community of Deacons & interested lay people; & professional courses for the community.
Dr. Gordon W.F. Drake, Principal
Crystal Martens, Head of College
Brenda Smith, Coordinator, Residence Admissions
brsmith@uwindsor.ca

Iona College
208 Sunset Ave., Windsor, ON N9B 3A7, Canada
Tel: 519-973-7039

Publications
The Lance

The Uniter

Colleges

Barrie: Georgian College
One Georgian Dr., Barrie, ON L4M 3X9, Canada
Tel: 705-728-1968; *Fax:* 705-722-5123
inquire@georgianc.on.ca
www.georgianc.on.ca

Full Time Equivalency: 9000
Plus 28,000 part-time & continuing education students
Brian Tamblyn, President

Campuses

Collingwood Campus
49 Huron St., Collingwood, ON L9Y 1L5, Canada

Midland Campus
649 Prospect Blvd., Midland, ON L4R 4L3, Canada

Muskoka Campus
4440 Ecclestone Dr., Bracebridge, ON P1L 1Z6, Canada

Orangeville Campus
5 Armstrong St., Orangeville, ON L9W 3H6, Canada

Orillia Campus
P.O. Box 2316
825 Memorial Ave., Orillia, ON L3V 6S2, Canada

Owen Sound Campus
1450 - 8th St. East, Owen Sound, ON N4K 5R4, Canada

Port Colborne Campus
2193 Barber Dr., Port Colborne, ON L3K 5X7, Canada

Publications
The Georgian Eye

Belleville: Loyalist College of Applied Arts & Technology
P.O. Box 4200
Wallbridge-Loyalist Rd., Belleville, ON K8N 5B9, Canada
Tel: 613-969-1913; *Fax:* 613-962-1376
Toll-Free: 888-569-2547
www.loyalistcollege.com

Jeff MacNab, Registrar, ext. 2366
jmacnab@loyalistc.on.ca
Aatos Lehtila, Dean, ext. ext-2332

Hamilton: Mohawk College
P.O. Box 2034
Hamilton, ON L8N 3T2, Canada
Tel: 905-575-1212; *Fax:* 905-575-2378
www.mohawkcollege.ca

Full Time Equivalency: 13000
Plus 40,000 part-time students
MaryLynn West-Moynes, President
Rosemary Knechtel, Vice President, Academic
Dale Schenk, Vice President, Finance & Administration

Campuses

Brantford Campus
411 Elgin St., Brantford, ON N3T 5V2, Canada
Fax: 519-758-6043

Fennell Campus
P.O. Box 2034
Fennell Ave. & West 5th, Hamilton, ON L8N 3T2, Canada
Fax: 905-575-2378

Mohawk - McMaster Institute for Applied Health Sciences
1400 Main St. West, Hamilton, ON L8S 1C7, Canada
Fax: 905-528-4198

Stoney Creek Campus
P.O. Box 9901
481 Barton St. East, Stoney Creek, ON L8G 3Y4, Canada
Fax: 905-575-2549

Wentworth Campus
196 Wentworth St. North, Hamilton, ON L8L 5V7, Canada
Fax: 905-523-8504

Publications
The Satellite

Kingston: St. Lawrence College
Also known as: Collège Saint-Laurent
100 Portsmouth Ave., Kingston, ON K7L 5A6, Canada
Tel: 613-544-5400; *Fax:* 613-545-3923
Toll-Free: 866-276-6601
dreamit@sl.on.ca
www.sl.on.ca

Full Time Equivalency: 6500
Chris Whitaker, President & CEO
Glenn Vollebregt, Sr. Vice-Pres., Finance & Administration, ext. 1591
Gordon MacDougall, Vice-Pres., Student Services & External Affairs, ext. 1298
Lorraine Carter, Vice-Pres., Academic, ext. 1446

Campuses

Brockville Campus
2288 Parkedale Ave., Brockville, ON K6V 5X3, Canada
Tel: 613-345-0660; *Fax:* 613-345-0124
Toll-Free: 888-622-8880

Beverlie Dietze, Campus Dean, ext. 3260
bdietze@sl.on.ca

Cornwall Campus
2 Belmont St., Cornwall, ON K6H 4Z1, Canada
Tel: 613-933-6080; *Fax:* 613-937-1524
Toll-Free: 866-276-6600

Don Fairweather, Campus Dean, ext. 2223
dfairweather@sl.on.ca

Kitchener: Conestoga College Institute of Technology & Advanced Learning
299 Doon Valley Dr., Kitchener, ON N2G 4M4, Canada
Tel: 519-748-5220; *Fax:* 519-748-3505
www.conestogac.on.ca/

Full Time Equivalency: 6900
With an additional 38,000 part-time students
Dr. John W. Tibbits, President
jtibbits@conestogac.on.ca

Publications
Spoke

London: Fanshawe College
P.O. Box 7005
1001 Fanshawe College Blvd., London, ON N5Y 5R6, Canada
Tel: 519-452-4430; *Fax:* 519-452-4420
www.fanshawec.ca

Full Time Equivalency: 15000
Plus 5,000 part-time students
Dr. Howard W. Rundle, President
hrundle@fanshawec.ca
Janice Lamoureux, Registrar
jlamoureux@fanshawec.ca

Publications
The Interrobang

North Bay: Canadore College of Applied Arts & Technology
P.O. Box 5001
100 College Dr., North Bay, ON P1B 8K9, Canada
Tel: 705-474-7600; *Fax:* 705-474-2384
info@canadorec.on.ca
www.canadorec.on.ca

Full Time Equivalency: 3500
Barbara Taylor, President & CEO

Oakville: Sheridan College Institute of Technology & Advanced Learning
Trafalgar Road Campus
1430 Trafalgar Rd., Oakville, ON L6H 2L1, Canada
Tel: 905-845-9430
infosheridan@sheridaninstitute.ca; tours@sheridaninstitute.ca
www1.sheridaninstitute.ca

Full Time Equivalency: 14472
The polytechnic institute offers pre-apprenticeship & apprenticeship training, one-year certificate & graduate certificates, two & three-year diplomas, & Bachelor's degrees in applied areas of study. Collaborative degree progrmas are provided through partnerships with the following universities: Brock University, University of Toronto at Mississauga, & York University.
Dr. Robert W. Turner, President/CEO

Campuses

Davis Campus
P.O. Box 7500
7899 McLaughlin Rd., Brampton, ON L6V 1G6, Canada
Fax: 905-459-7533

Skills Training Centre
407 Iroquois Shore Rd., Oakville, ON L6H 1M3, Canada
Fax: 905-845-9430

St. Joseph Secondary School
5555 Creditview Rd., Mississaugua, ON L5V 2B9, Canada
This is an additional continuing education location.

Oshawa: Durham College
P.O. Box 385
2000 Simcoe St. North, Oshawa, ON L1H 7L7, Canada
Tel: 905-721-2000; *Fax:* 905-721-3113
www.durhamcollege.ca

Full Time Equivalency: 6000
Plus 23,000 part-time enrolment
Don Lovisa, President
Ralph Aprile, Vice-President, Facilities & Ancillary Services
Ruth MacKay, Director, Institutional Research & Government Relations
David Chambers, President, Foundation & Vice-President, Advancement
Judy Robinson, Vice-President, Academic
Margaret Greenley, Vice-President, Student Affairs
Donna MacFarlane, Vice-President, Communications & Marketing
Ken Robb, Vice-President, Human Resources
Gerry Pinkney, Vice-President, Information Technology Services

Publications
The Chronicle
P.O. Box 385
Oshawa, ON L1H 7L7, Canada
Fax: 905-436-9774

Ottawa: Algonquin College of Applied Arts & Technology
1385 Woodroffe Ave., Ottawa, ON K2G 1V8, Canada
Tel: 613-727-4723; *Fax:* 613-727-7743
www.algonquincollege.com/
Full Time Equivalency: 16000
Robert Gillett, President

Peterborough: Sir Sandford Fleming College
Sutherland Campus
599 Brealey Dr., Peterborough, ON K9J 7B1, Canada
Tel: 705-749-5530; *Fax:* 705-749-5507
Toll-Free: 1-866-353-6464
info@flemingc.on.ca; admissions@flemingc.on.ca
www.flemingc.on.ca
Full Time Equivalency: 3500
The College consists of the following schools: School of Business & Technology; School of Environmental & Natural Resource Sciences; School of Health & Wellness; School of Interdisciplinary Studies; School of Law, Justice & Community Services; School of Continuing Education & Skilled Trades; & the Haliburton School of The Arts.
Murray Rodd, Chair
G.A. (Tony) Tilly, Ph.D., President

Campuses
Cobourg Campus
1005 Elgin St. West, Cobourg, ON K9A 5J4
Tel: 905-372-6865; *Toll-Free:* 1-866-353-6464
info@flemingc.on.ca
The Cobourg Campus offers academic upgrading & part time studies, as well as esthetician studies.

Frost Campus
P.O. Box 8000
200 Albert St. South, Lindsay, ON K9V 5E6, Canada
Tel: 705-324-9144; *Fax:* 705-878-9331
Toll-Free: 1-866-353-6464
Enrollment: 1500
The Frost Campus features Fleming College's School of Environmental & Natural Resource Sciences, The Centre for Alternative Wastewater Treatment, The Centre for Heavy Equipment Technology, & The Geomatics Institute.

Haliburton Campus
P.O. Box 839
297 College Dr., Haliburton, ON K0M 1S0, Canada
Tel: 705-457-1680; *Toll-Free:* 1-866-353-6464
info@flemingc.on.ca
The Haliburton Campus features the Haliburton School of The Arts & Fleming's Ecotourism & Adventure Tourism Management program.

McRae Campus
P.O. Box 4350
555 Bonnacord St., Peterborough, ON K9J 7B1
Tel: 705-749-5530; *Fax:* 705-741-3279
Toll-Free: 1-888-269-6929
info@flemingc.on.ca
This campus offers specialized programs in skilled trades, apprenticeships, & several part-time studies.
Michael N. Durisin, Chair
Dr. Glenn Zederayko, Head of Schools
Ann Bianco-Harvey, Director, Marketing & Communications
webmaster@torontomontessori.ca; editor@torontomontessori.ca
Silvana Fazzari, Director, Admissions, 905-889-6882, ext. 230
Sharron Cooper, Registrar, 905-889-6882, ext. 254

Norwood - Eastern Ontario Fire Academy
36 Industrial Dr., Norwood, ON K0L 2V0
Tel: 705-639-2121

Sarnia: Lambton College of Applied Arts & Technology
1457 London Rd., Sarnia, ON N7S 6K4, Canada
Tel: 519-542-7751; *Fax:* 519-541-2418
www.lambton.on.ca
Full Time Equivalency: 2500
Catherine Holden, Registrar, 519-542-7751, ext. 3310
cathie@lambton.on.ca
Tony Hanlon, President

Publications
Lion's Tale

Sault Ste Marie: Sault College of Applied Arts & Technology
443 Northern Ave., Sault Ste Marie, ON P6A 5L3, Canada
Tel: 705-759-2554; *Fax:* 705-759-3273
Toll-Free: 1-800-461-2260
studentrecruitment@saultcollege.ca; registrar@saultcollege.ca
www.saultcollege.ca
Full Time Equivalency: 6000
The College offers education & training to full-time & part-time students in post-secondary, apprenticeship, adult retraining, continuing education, & contract training programs.
Joe Nardi, Chair
Dr. Ron Common, President
Max S. Liedke, Sec.-Treas.

Sault Ste. Marie: Algoma University College
1520 Queen St. E, Sault Ste. Marie, ON P6A 2G4, Canada
Tel: 705-949-2301; *Fax:* 705-949-6583
Toll-Free: 888-254-6628
info@algomau.ca
www.algomau.ca
Full Time Equivalency: 1207
Became wholly independent as of June, 2008
Dr Richard Myers, President
Dr. Arthur H. Perlini, Academic Dean, ext. 4116
dean@algomau.ca.
David Marasco, Registrar, ext. 4218
registrar@algomau.ca

Scarborough: Centennial College of Applied Arts & Technology
P.O. Box 631 A
Scarborough, ON M1K 5E9, Canada
Tel: 416-289-5000; *Fax:* 416-439-7358
Toll-Free: 800-268-4419
www.centennialcollege.ca
Other Information: Telex: 06-963824
Full Time Equivalency: 40000
Ann Buller, President

Publications
Siren

Sudbury: Cambrian College of Applied Arts & Technology
1400 Barrydowne Rd., Sudbury, ON P3A 3V8, Canada
Tel: 705-566-8101; *Fax:* 705-524-7334
Toll-Free: 800-461-7145
info@cambriancollege.ca
www.cambriancollege.ca
Full Time Equivalency: 4300
Sylvia Barnard, President

Publications
The Shield

Thunder Bay: Confederation College
P.O. Box 398
1450 Nakina Dr., Thunder Bay, ON P7C 4W1, Canada
Tel: 807-475-6110; *Fax:* 807-623-4512
Toll-Free: 800-465-5493
www.confederationc.on.ca/
Full Time Equivalency: 4160
Plus 17,000 part-time & continuing education students
Patricia Lang, President, 807-475-6350
plang@confederationc.on.ca
Brian Campbell, Director, Resource Development, 807-475-6582
campbell@confederationc.on.ca
Reg Jones, Vice-President, Corporate Services, 807-475-6173
jones@confederationc.on.ca

Publications
Opus

Polar Press

Talon

Timmins: Northern College of Applied Arts & Technology
P.O. Box 3211
Timmins, ON P4N 8R6, Canada
Tel: 705-235-3211; *Fax:* 705-235-7279
hansonth@northernc.on.ca (Registrar)
www.northernc.on.ca

Toronto: Elliott Allen Institute for Theology & Ecology
81 St. Mary's St., Toronto, ON M5S 1J4, Canada
Tel: 416-926-1300; *Fax:* 416-926-7294
eaite.contact@utoronto.ca
www.utoronto.ca/stmikes/eaite/
Other Information: ext. 3408
Dr. Dennis Patrick O'Hara, Director, 416-926-1300, ext. 3408

Campuses
Theology & Ecology Certificate of Specialization
Eight courses & one seminar. The Institute cooperates with the Tornot School of Theology, Holy Cross Centre for Ecology Y spirituality, Institute for Environmental Studies (Universsity of Toronto), Transformative Learning Centres (OISE), Faculty of Enviornmental Studues (York University).

Toronto: George Brown College
P.O. Box 1015 B
Toronto, ON M5T 2T9, Canada
Tel: 416-415-2000; *Fax:* 416-415-4493
Toll-Free: 800-265-2002
info@georgebrown.ca
www.georgebrown.ca
Full Time Equivalency: 15000
Plus 60,000 part-time & continuing education students
Anne Sado, President

Publications
Dialog Newspaper

Toronto: Humber Institute of Technology and Advanced Learning
North Campus
205 Humber College Blvd., Toronto, ON M9W 5L7, Canada
Tel: 416-675-5005; *Fax:* 416-675-2427
enquiry@humber.ca
www.humber.ca
Full Time Equivalency: 29000
Over 65,000 Part-time enrollment
Michael Hatton, Vice-President, Academic, ext. 4510
michael.hatton@humber.ca
John Mason, Vice-President, Student & Corporate Services, ext. 5041
john.mason@humber.ca
Rani K. Dhaliwal, Vice-President, Finance & Administrative Services, ext. 5062
rani.dhaliwal@humber.ca
John Davies, President, ext. 5070
john.davies@humber.ca

Campuses
Humber Canadian Plastics Training Centre
#NB102, 205 Humber College Blvd., Toronto, ON M9W 5L7, Canada
Fax: 416-213-0927

Lakeshore Campus
3199 Lakeshore Blvd. West, Toronto, ON M8V 1K8, Canada
Fax: 416-252-8842

Sailing & Powerboating Centre (SPC)
Humber Bay Park West (Lakeshore Blvd. West of Park, Toronto, ON M8V 3X7, Canada
Fax: 416-252-5393

Transportation Training Centre (TTC)
55 Woodbine Downs Blvd., Toronto, ON M9W 6N5, Canada
Fax: 416-798-0307

Publications
Etcetera

Toronto: New College
300 Huron St., Toronto, ON M5S 3J6, Canada
Tel: 416-978-2460; *Fax:* 416-978-0554
newcollege.registrar@utoronto.ca
www.newcollege.utoronto.ca/site6.aspx
Full Time Equivalency: 4300

Toronto: Seneca College of Applied Arts & Technology
Newnham Campus
1750 Finch Ave. East, Toronto, ON M2J 2X5, Canada
Tel: 416-491-5050
admissions@senecac.on.ca; InternationalAdmissions@senecac.on.ca
www.senecac.on.ca
Other Information: Newnham Campus Library Circulation: 416.491.5050, ext. 2099
The polytechnic educational institution consists of the following faculties: Faculty of Applied Arts & Health Sciences; Faculty of Applied Science & Engineering Technology; Faculty of Business; Faculty of Information Arts & Technology; Faculty of Continuing Education & Training; & Faculty of Workforce Skills Development
Jean Anne McLeod, B.A. (Hon.), Chair
Dr. Rick Miner, President, 416-491-5050, ext. 2261, fax: 416-491-7745
president@senecac.on.ca

Campuses
Buttonville Campus
Hangers 6, 7, & 8, Buttonville Airport
P.O. Box 190
2833 16th Ave., Markham, ON L3R 0P8, Canada
Tel: 416-491-5050; *Fax:* 905-477-8103

Jane Campus
21 Beverley Hills Dr., Toronto, ON M3L 1A2, Canada
Tel: 416-491-5050; *Fax:* 416-235-0462

King Campus
13990 Dufferin St., King City, ON L7B 1B3, Canada
Tel: 905-833-3333
Other Information: King Campus Library, Circulation: 416-491-5050, ext. 5108

Markham Campus
10 Allstate Pkwy., Markham, ON L3R 5Y1, Canada
Tel: 416-491-5050

Newmarket Campus
Weston Produce Plaza
#3, 16655 Yonge St., Newmarket, ON L3X 1V6, Canada
Tel: 905-898-6199

Seneca @ York Campus
70 The Pond Rd., Toronto, ON M3J 3M6, Canada
Tel: 416-491-5050
Other Information: Student Services: 416-491-5050, ext. 3000

Yorkgate Campus
1 York Gate Blvd., Toronto, ON M3N 3A1, Canada
Tel: 416-493-4144

Welland: Niagara College
Welland Campus
300 Woodlawn Rd., Welland, ON L3C 7L3, Canada
Tel: 905-735-2211; *Fax:* 905-736-6020
infocentre@niagaracollege.ca (Welland Campus InfoCentre)
www.niagarac.on.ca
Other Information: Grimsby Phone: 905-563-3254
Full Time Equivalency: 6300
In addition to its full time student enrollment, the college has more than 15,000 continuing education registrants each year. Niagara College offers over 90 post-secondary diploma & graduate certificate programs, skills & apprenticeship training programs, plus two bachelor degree programs.
Jim Ryan, Chair
Dan Patterson, President, 905-641-2252, ext. 4040
dpatterson@niagaracollege.ca

Campuses
Maid of the Mist Campus
Also known as: Tourism Industry Development Centre
5881 Dunn St., Niagara Falls, ON L2G 2N9, Canada
Fax: 905-374-7454

Niagara-on-the-Lake Campus
135 Taylor Rd., Niagara-on-the-Lake, ON L0S 1J0, Canada
Fax: 905-641-2252

Ontario Street Satellite Site - Niagara Health System
155 Ontario St.,, St. Catharines, ON L2R 5K3
Tel: 905-641-2252

Windsor: St. Clair College
South Campus
2000 Talbot Rd. West, Windsor, ON N9A 6S4, Canada
Tel: 519-966-1656; *Fax:* 519-972-3811
Toll-Free: 1-800-387-0524
info@stclaircollege.ca
www.stclaircollege.ca
Full Time Equivalency: 5000
The College consists of the following schools of specialization: School of Liberal Arts & Sciences; School of Business & Information Technology; School of Academic Studies; School of Community Studies; School of Media, Art & Design; School of Engineering Technologies; School of Health Sciences; & School of Skilled Trades.
Vince Marcotte, Chair
John A. Strasser, Ph.D., President, 519-972-2701
jstrasser@stclaircollege.ca
Sherry Sharon, Registrar, 519-972-2727, ext. 4260
ssharon@stclaircollege.ca

Campuses
Thames Campus
1001 Grand Ave. West, Chatham, ON N7M 5W4, Canada
Tel: 519-354-9100; *Fax:* 519-354-6941
Toll-Free: 1-800-387-0524
info@stclaircollege.ca
Other Information: Registrar's Office: 519-354-9100, ext. 3238
The campus provides specialized training from the Schools of Business & Technology, & Health & Community Studies.

Wallaceburg Campus - James A. Burgess Skills Centre
920 Elgin St., Wallaceburg, ON N9A 3E1, Canada
Tel: 519-627-8336; *Fax:* 519-627-5950
Toll-Free: 1-800-387-0524
info@stclaircollege.ca
The campus features the Technical Industry Education Partnership.

Windsor - Riverside Dr. - St. Clair Centre for the Arts
201 Riverside Dr. West, Windsor, ON N9A 5K4
Tel: 519-252-8311; *Fax:* 519-973-4976
Toll-Free: 1-800-387-0524
info@stclaircollege.ca
Enrollment: 500
The campus features the School of Media, Art & Design.
Ed Noot, Principal
Mike Campbell, Vice Principal & Counsellor

Post Secondary/Technical

Post Secondary/Technical

Northern Ontario School of Medicine
Tel: 807-766-7300
noms@normed.ca
www.normed.ca
4-year MD program
Dr. Roger Strasser, Founding Dean

Campuses
East Campus (NORMED)
935 Ramsey Lake Rd., Sudbury, ON P3E 2C6, Canada
Tel: 705-675-4883; *Fax:* 705-675-4858
nos@normed.ca
www.normed.ca

West Campus (NORMED)
955 Oliver Rd., Thunder Bay, ON P7B 5E1, Canada
Tel: 807-766-7300; *Fax:* 807-766-7370
nos@normed.ca
www.normed.ca

Ajax: Diamond Institute of Business & Computer Technology
Ajax GO Station
100 Westney Rd. S., Ajax, ON L1S 7H3, Canada
Tel: 905-427-1922; *Fax:* 905-427-2558
Toll-Free: 1-888-25-LEARN
info@diamondinstitute.ca
www.diamondinstitute.ca
Computer service technician, computer service/network engineer, computer programmer/analyst.

Alfred: Collège d'Alfred de l'Université de Guelph
31, rue St-Paul, CP 580, Alfred, ON K0B 1A0, Canada
Tel: 613-679-2218; *Fax:* 613-679-2423
www.alfredc.uoguelph.ca
Agriculture, horticulture, techniques de diététique, développement international, techniques soins vétérinaires
Marcel Couture, Directeur

Ancaster: Redeemer University College
777 Garner Rd. East, Ancaster, ON L9K 1J4, Canada
Tel: 905-648-2131; *Fax:* 905-648-2134
mvanbev@redeemer.ca
www.redeemer.ca
Enrollment: 816
Justin D. Cooper, Ph.D., President
Jacob P. Ellens, Ph.D., Vice-President
William van Staalduinen, M.A., Vice-President
Ineke VanBruinessen, C.G.A., Senior Director
Marian Ryks-Szelekovszky, M.Ed., Senior Director, Admissions & Student Services
Mark Van Beveren, M.B.A., Media & Public Relations Director
Doug Loney, Ph.D., Dean
Doug Needham, Ph.D., Dean

Publications
The Crown

Belleville: Loyalist College
P.O. Box 4200
Belleville, ON K8N 5B9, Canada
Tel: 613-969-1913; *Fax:* 613-962-1376
liaison@loyalistc.on.ca
www.loyalistcollege.com
Douglas A.L. Auld, President

Publications
The Pioneer

Brantford: Medical Radiation Technology
c/o Ontario Association of Medical Radiation Tech
P.O. Box 1054
Brantford, ON N3T 5S7, Canada
Tel: 519-753-6037; *Fax:* 519-753-6408
Toll-Free: 1-800-387-467
inquiries@oamrt.on.ca
www.oamrt.on.ca

Burks Falls: Outward Bound Canada
996 Chetwynd Rd., RR#2, Burks Falls, ON P0A 1C0, Canada
Tel: 705-382-5454; *Fax:* 705-382-5959
Toll-Free: 1-888-688-9273
dave_wolfenden@outwardbound.ca (Exec.Dir.)
www.outwardbound.ca
Enrollment: 440
Fiona Hugh, Executive Director

Burlington: Charles Sturt University, Ontario
Bay Area Learning Centre
860 Harrington Ct., Burlington, ON L7N 3N4, Canada
Tel: 905-333-4955; *Fax:* 905-333-6562
canada@csu.edu.au
www.csu.edu.au
1-year teacher education program

Burlington: Luba Mera School of Aesthetics, Cosmetology & Aromatherapy
515 John St., Burlington, ON L7R 2L1, Canada
Tel: 905-681-7882; *Fax:* 905-681-1494
Toll-Free: 1-888-809-5559
info@lubamera.com
www.lubamera.com
Aesthetics training.

Burlington: Syms Travel School
Mount Royal Plaza
2049A Mount Forest Dr., Burlington, ON L7P 1H4, Canada
Tel: 905-335-0125; *Fax:* 905-335-4880
Toll-Free: 1-888-306-922
symsts@bellnet.ca
www.symstravelschool.ca
Travel industry training

Concord: RCC College of Technology
2000 Steeles Ave. West, Concord, ON L4K 4N1, Canada
Tel: 905-669-0544; *Fax:* 905-669-0551
Toll-Free: 1-800-268-9098
www.rcc.on.ca
Electronics & computer networks engineering technology training & programs

Dundas: Dundas Valley School of Art
21 Ogilvie St., Dundas, ON L9H 2S1, Canada
Tel: 905-628-6357; *Fax:* 905-628-1087
dvsa@cogeco.net
www.dvsa.ca
Arthur Greenblatt, Director

Guelph: Canadian Academy of Floral Art
#103, 355 Elmira Rd. North, Guelph, ON N1K 1S5, Canada
Tel: 519-836-5495; *Fax:* 519-836-7529
Toll-Free: 1-800-698-011
cafa@cafachat.com
www.cafachat.com
Floral designing & business program
Maija Asaris, Pres.

Guelph: OATI Learning Group
#101, 450 Speedvale Ave. West, Guelph, ON N1H 7Y6, Canada
Tel: 519-763-3160; *Fax:* 519-763-9585
info@oatilearninggroup.com
Ian Barrett, Executive Director

***Guelph:* Ontario Agricultural College**
OAC Dean's Office, Univ. of Guelph
103 Johnston Hall, Guelph, ON N1G 2W1, Canada
Tel: 519-824-4120; *Fax:* 519-766-1423
oacinfo@uoguelph.ca
www.oac.uoguelph.ca
Heather Renwick, Executive Assistant, 519-824-4120, ext. ext.56513
hrenwick@oac.uoguelph.ca
Dr. Craig J. Pearson, Dean, 519-824-4120, ext. ext.52285
cpearson@uoguelph.ca

***Hamilton:* Canadian Institute for NDE**
135 Fennell Ave. West, Hamilton, ON L8N 3T2, Canada
Tel: 905-387-1655; *Fax:* 905-574-6080
info@cinde.ca
www.cinde.ca
Nondestructive testing/nondestructive examination
Douglas Marshall, Managing Director

***Hamilton:* Grand Health Academy - Hamilton Campus - King Street East**
760 King St. East, Hamilton, ON L8M 1A6, Canada
Tel: 905-577-7707; *Fax:* 905-577-7738
info@grandhealthacademy.com
www.grandhealthacademy.com
Personal support worker; CPR; first-aid courses
Janine K. Grand-Wilewski, Director

***Hamilton:* Grand Health Academy - Hamilton - Concession Street**
574 Concession St., Hamilton, ON L8V 1B1, Canada
Tel: 905-385-7727; *Fax:* 905-385-7477
info@grandhealthacademy.com
www.grandhealthacademy.com

***Hamilton:* Medical Laboratory Technology**
The Canadian Society for Medical Laboratory Scien
P.O. Box 2830
Hamilton, ON L8N 3N8, Canada
Tel: 905-528-8642; *Fax:* 905-528-4968
kurtd@csmls.org
www.csmls.org
Kurt H. Davis, Executive Director

***London:* AlphaLogic Career College**
280 King Edward Ave., London, ON N5Z 3V3, Canada
Tel: 519-858-0010; *Fax:* 519-858-0089
info@alphalogic.net
www.alphalogic.net
Computer software applications, information technology programs
Jerry Vandergoot, President

***London:* Elegance Schools Inc.**
#302, 219 Oxford St. West, London, ON N6H 1S5, Canada
Tel: 519-434-1181; *Fax:* 519-434-1182
elegance@eleganceschools.on.ca
www.eleganceschools.on.ca
Esthetics & electrolysis.
Lisa Hakim, Director

***London:* St. Peter's Seminary**
1040 Waterloo St. North, London, ON N6A 3Y1, Canada
Tel: 519-432-1824; *Fax:* 519-432-0964
stpeters@uwo.ca
www.stpetersseminary.ca
Rev. W.T. McGrattan, B.E.Sc., M.Div., S.T.L., Rector
Rev. T.F. O'Connor, M.A., M.T.S., M.Th., Spiritual Director
Rev. Brian Dunn, Dean
Rev. John Comiskey, B.A., M.Div., H.E.L., H.E, Vice Rector & Registrar
Gabriella Catolino, D.M.C., M.Div., Executive Director

***London:* Westervelt College**
1060 Wellington Rd., London, ON N6E 3W5, Canada
Tel: 519-668-2000; *Fax:* 519-668-1616
Toll-Free: 1-877-668-200
info@westerveltcollege.com
www.westerveltcollege.com
Business, travel, law, policing & computers
Donna M. Doerr, President & Chair

***Markham:* CMS Training**
#725, 7305 Woodbine Ave., Markham, ON L3R 3V7, Canada
Tel: 416-236-6332; *Toll-Free:* 1-800-477-957
www.cmstraining.com
Home study in computer programming

***Mississauga:* Credit Institute of Canada**
#216C, 219 Dufferin St., Mississauga, ON M6K 3J1, Canada
Tel: 905-572-2615; *Fax:* 905-572-2619
generalinformation@creditedu.org
www.creditedu.org
E. Keith Devolin, President & Dean
Geoff Wilkinson, General Manager

***Burlington:* HBI College - Burlington Campus (HBI)**
#26, 460 Brant St., Burlington, ON L7R 4B6, Canada
Tel: 905-637-3415; *Fax:* 905-637-2843
info@hbicollege.com
www.hbicollege.com
Administrative & computer programs.

***Mississauga:* HBI College - Mississauga Campus (HBI)**
Mississauga Executive Centre
Suite 120, 2 Robert Speck Parkway, Mississauga, ON L4Z 1H8, Canada
Tel: 905-949-9900
infogta@hbicollege.com
www.hbicollege.com
Administrative & computer programs.

***Mississauga:* The Investment Funds Institute of Canada**
3660 Huronatrio St., Mississauga, ON L5B 3C4, Canada
Tel: 416-865-1237; *Toll-Free:* 1-888-865-2437
ifse@ifse.ca
www.myinvestmentfunds.ca; www.cifp.ca
Keith Costello, Managing Director

Campuses
Québec Branch
#1800, 1010, rue Sherbrooke ouest, Montréal, QC H3A 2R7, Canada
Fax: 514-985-5113

***Mississauga:* Quality Management Institute (QMI)**
#300, 90 Burnhamthorpe Rd. West, Mississauga, ON L5B 3C3, Canada
Tel: 905-272-3920; *Fax:* 905-272-3942

Campuses
Calgary Office
Manulife Centre
#710, 603 - 7 Ave. SW, Calgary, AB T2P 2T5, Canada
Fax: 403-261-4075

Moncton Office
#400, 1133 George St., Moncton, NB E1E 4E1, Canada
Fax: 506-858-9302

Montréal Office
865, rue Ellingham, Pointe-Claire, QC H9R 5E8, Canada
Fax: 514-694-9697

Vancouver Office
13799 Commerce Pkwy., Richmond, BC V6V 2N9, Canada
Fax: 604-244-6810

***Niagara Falls:* Niagara Parks Botanical Gardens & School of Horticulture**
P.O. Box 150
Niagara Falls, ON L2E 6T2, Canada
Tel: 905-356-8554; *Fax:* 905-356-5488
schoolofhorticulture@niagaraparks.com
www.niagaraparks.com; www.schoolofhorticulture.com
Tom Laviolette, Supt.
Liz Klose, Supt.

***North Bay:* Canadore College of Applied Arts & Technology**
P.O. Box 5001
100 College Dr., North Bay, ON P1B 8K9, Canada
Tel: 705-474-7600; *Fax:* 705-474-2384
info@canadorec.on.ca
www.canadorec.on.ca
Enrollment: 2977
Barbara Taylor, President

***North York:* Tyndale University College & Seminary**
25 Ballyconnor Ct., North York, ON M2M 4B3, Canada
Tel: 416-226-6380; *Fax:* 416-226-6746
Toll-Free: 1-877-896-3253
info@tyndale.ca; admissions@tyndale.ca
www.tyndale.ca
A Christian College and Seminary whose mission is to educate and equip Christians to serve the world with passion for Jesus Christ.
Archie McLean, Chair
Dr. Brian C. Stiller, President
The Hon. Jake Epp, Chancellor

***Ohsweken:* Six Nations Polytechnic**
P.O. Box 700
Ohsweken, ON N0A 1M0, Canada
Tel: 519-445-0023; *Fax:* 519-445-4416
www.snpolytechnic.com
Linda Staats, CEO

***Ottawa:* Algonquin Careers Academy**
1644 Bank St., Ottawa, ON K1V 7Y6, Canada
Tel: 613-722-7811; *Fax:* 613-722-4494
Toll-Free: 1-888-722-781
www.algonquinacademy.com
Travel & Hospitality; Healthcare; Business

***Ottawa:* Canadian Police College**
Collège canadien de police
P.O. Box 8900
Ottawa, ON K1G 3J2, Canada
Tel: 613-993-9500; *Fax:* 613-990-9738
cpc-cpc@rcmp.gc.ca
www.cpc.gc.ca
Mike Saunders, Director general

***Ottawa:* La Cité collégiale**
801, promenade de l'Aviation, Ottawa, ON K1K 4R3, Canada
Tel: 613-742-2483; *Fax:* 613-742-2481
Toll-Free: 1-800-267-2483
info@lacitec.on.ca
www.lacitecollegiale.com
Enrollment: 3500
Andrée Lortie, Président

***Ottawa:* International Academy Health Education Centre**
380 Forest St., Ottawa, ON K2B 8E6, Canada
Tel: 613-820-0318; *Fax:* 613-820-7478
Toll-Free: 1-800-267-873
info@intlacademy.com
www.intlacademy.com
Nutrition; herbs; iridology; reflexology; aromatherapy; homeopathy; shiatsu/accupressure; massage
Dorothy Marshall, Ph.D., N.D., C.H.H.P., N., Executive Director

***Ottawa:* International Academy of Natural Health Sciences**
380 Forest St., Ottawa, ON K2B 8E6, Canada
Tel: 613-820-0318; *Fax:* 613-820-7478
Toll-Free: 1-800-267-873
naturalhealth@intlacademy.com
www.intlacademy.com
Nutrition; herbs; iridology; reflexology

***Ottawa:* Mican Business College**
1825 Woodward Dr., Ottawa, ON K2C 0P9, Canada
Tel: 613-224-6211; *Fax:* 613-224-2739
nicki@lcancollege.com
www.micancollege.com
Nicki Wilmore, President

***Ottawa:* Natural Resources Canada Industrial Energy Efficiency Initiative, Industrial, Commercial & Institution**
Office of Energy Efficiency
580 Booth St., 18th Fl., Ottawa, ON K1A 0E4, Canada
Tel: 613-995-6839; *Fax:* 613-947-4121
www.emr.ca/home/nrcanhpe.htm
Philip B. Jago, Chief
pjago@nrcan.gc.ca

***Ottawa:* Ottawa School of Art**
35 George St., Ottawa, ON K1N 8W5, Canada
Tel: 613-241-7471; *Fax:* 613-241-4391
info@artottawa.ca
www.artottawa.ca
Fine arts training.
Jeff Stellick, Executive Director

***Ottawa:* Pères Montfortains (Residence des étudiants)**
463 Riverdale Ave., Ottawa, ON K1S 1S1, Canada
Tel: 613-731-2271
Cor Kauffman, s.m.m., Superior

***Ottawa:* Transport Canada Training Institute**
c/o Coast Guard Emergencies, Canada Bldg.
#941, 344 Slater, Ottawa, ON K1A 0N7, Canada
Tel: 613-990-3400; *Fax:* 613-995-4700

***Ottawa:* Versailles Academy of Make-Up Arts, Esthetics, Hair**
#1, 1930 Bank St., Ottawa, ON K1V 7Z8, Canada
Tel: 613-521-4155; *Fax:* 613-521-6945
www.versaillesacademy.com
Cosmetic, esthetic & hair trades courses since 1981

***Ottawa:* Willis College of Business & Technology**
85 O'Connor St., Ottawa, ON K1P 5M6, Canada
Tel: 613-233-1128; *Fax:* 613-233-9286
ottawa@williscollege.com
www.williscollege.com
E-business & IT training.

Rima Aristocrat, President/CEO

Owen Sound: Creative Career Systems Inc.
RR#5, Owen Sound, ON N4K 5N7, Canada
Tel: 519-376-7396; Fax: 519-376-6772
Toll-Free: 1-800-463-045
info@creative.on.ca
www.creative.on.ca
Health care aide program.

Pickering: Pickering Campus
#220, 1099 Kingston Rd., Pickering, ON L1V 1B5, Canada
Tel: 905-427-3010; Fax: 905-420-6752
geninfo@staff.dbcc.on.ca
www.dbcc.on.ca
Business; Information Technology; Health Care; Corporate Training
Farid Jenabieh, President

Campuses

Oshawa Campus
#111, 50 Richmond St., Oshawa, ON L1G 7C7, Canada
Tel: 905-443-3010; Fax: 905-443-3011
geninfo@staff.dbcc.on.ca
www.dbcc.on.ca
Business; Information Technology; Health Care; Corporate Training

Toronto Campus
#203, 1457 McCowan Rd., Scarborough, ON M1E 2S2, Canada
Tel: 416-724-1053; Fax: 416-724-5258
geninfo@staff.dbcc.on.ca
www.dbcc.on.ca
Business; Information Technology; Health Care; Corporate Training

Richmond Hill: Academy of Learning
10235 Yonge St., Richmond Hill, ON L4C 3B4, Canada
Tel: 905-508-5791; Fax: 905-508-9409
www.academyoflearning.com
Computer & business skills training; 40 locations across Ontario

Ridgetown: Ridgetown College - University of Guelph
Ridgetown, ON N0P 2C0, Canada
Tel: 519-674-1500; Fax: 519-674-1515
Ron E. Pitblado, B.Sc.(Agr.), M.Sc., Ph.D., Acting Director
rpitblad@ridgetownc.uoguelph.ca
J.M. Brooks, Executive Officer
jbrooks@ridgetownc.uoguelph.ca

Scarborough: St. Augustine's Seminary of Toronto
2661 Kingston Rd., Scarborough, ON M1M 1M3, Canada
Tel: 416-261-7207; Fax: 416-261-2529
info@staugustines.on.ca
www.staugustines.on.ca
Enrollment: 95
Rev. Msgr. A. Robert Nusca, B.A., M.Div., S.T.B., S.S, Rector
Rev. Thomas A. Lynch, B.A., M.Div., S.T.L., S.T, Dean

Scarborough: Scarborough Campus
1371 Neilson Rd., Suite 413, Scarborough, ON M1B 4Z8, Canada
Tel: 416-283-8252; Fax: 416-283-3796
admin.scar@cjcollege.com
www.cjcollege.com
Health care related program.
Cynthia Cooper, President

Campuses

Etobicoke Campus
365 Evans Ave., Etobicoke, ON M8Z 1K2, Canada
Fax: 416-247-8927

Scarborough: Toronto Institute of Pharmaceutical Technology
#200, 55 Town Centre Ct., Scarborough, ON M1P 4X4, Canada
Tel: 416-296-1478; Fax: 416-296-7077
info@tipt.com
www.tipt.com
Alexander MacGregor, Dean

Sudbury: Collège Boréal
21, boul Lasalle, Sudbury, ON P3A 6B1, Canada
Tel: 705-560-6673; Fax: 705-560-7641
Toll-Free: 1-800-361-667
www.borealc.on.ca
Enrollment: 1500
Denis Hubert, Président

Timmins: Northern College
P.O. Box 3211
Hwy. 101 East, South Porcupine, Timmins, ON P4N 8R6, Canada
Tel: 705-235-3211; Fax: 705-235-7279
Toll-Free: 1-866-736-587
info@northern.on.ca
www.northernc.on.ca
Enrollment: 1489
Michael Hill, President, fax: 705-235-7277

Campuses

Haileybury Campus
640 Latchford, Haileybury, ON P0J 1K0, Canada
Fax: 705-672-2014
www.northernc.on.ca

Kirkland Lake Campus
140 Government Rd. East, Kirkland Lake, ON P2N 3L8, Canada
Fax: 705-568-8186

Timmins Campus
P.O. Box 3211
Hwy. 101 East, South Porcupine, Timmins, ON P4N 8R6, Canada
Fax: 705-235-7279

Toronto: Benns International Schools Inc.
#490, 20 Eglinton Ave. East, Toronto, ON M4P 1A9, Canada
Tel: 416-489-8246; Fax: 416-489-1662
benns@tesolandtesl.com
www.tesolandtesl.com
Enrollment: 125
TESL & ECE teacher training
Sandra Benns

Toronto: Canadian Business College
Head Office
2 Bloor St. West, 22nd Fl., Toronto, ON M4W 3E2, Canada
Tel: 416-925-9929; Fax: 416-925-9220
Toll-Free: 1-888-925-992
www.cbstraining.com
Business, technology, health care & digital graphics

Toronto: Canadian Churches' Forum for Global Ministries
47 Queen's Park Cres. East, Toronto, ON M5S 2C3, Canada
Tel: 416-924-9351; Fax: 416-978-7821
director@ccforum.ca
www.ccforum.ca
Cross cultural orientation programs for church related personnel & volunteers involved in global mission & ministry

Toronto: The Canadian College of Naturopathic Medicine
1255 Sheppard Ave. East, Toronto, ON M2K 1E2, Canada
Tel: 416-498-1255; Fax: 416-498-1576
Toll-Free: 1-866-241-226
info@ccnm.edu
www.ccnm.edu
Naturopathic medical education, research & clinical practice; 4,500+ hours of classroom & clinical training
Catherine Kenwell, Director
Bob Bernhardt, President & CEO

Toronto: Canadian Institute of Health Care & Business
#303, 7 Hayden St., Toronto, ON M4Y 2P2, Canada
Tel: 416-925-4417
best-care@sympatico.ca
www.infobest-care.com
Personal Support Worker; Live-in Caregiver; Travel & Tourism; Pharmacy Technician

Toronto: Canadian Jewellers Institute (CJI)
#600, 27 Queen St. East, Toronto, ON M5C 2M6, Canada
Tel: 416-368-7616; Fax: 416-368-1986
Toll-Free: 1-800-580-0942
cji@canadianjewellers.com
www.canadianjewellers.com/html/cji.htm
Wide range of jewellry education.

Toronto: Canadian Memorial Chiropractic College
6100 Leslie St., Toronto, ON M2H 3J1, Canada
Tel: 416-482-2340; Fax: 416-482-9745
communications@cmcc.ca
www.cmcc.ca
Undergraduate and graduate Chiropractic College.
J.A. Moss, D.C., M.B.A., President
president@cmcc.ca

Toronto: Canadian School of Private Investigation & Security Ltd.
2828 Dufferin St., Toronto, ON M6B 3S3, Canada
Tel: 416-785-5701; Fax: 416-785-6064
cspis@cspis.com
www.cspis.com
Private investigation, paralegal, security, law enforcement & police foundations training.
Carl Franco, Founder & Principle Instructor

Toronto: Canadian Securities Institute
200 Wellington St. W., 15th Fl., Toronto, ON M5V 3C7, Canada
Tel: 416-364-9130; Fax: 866-866-2660
Toll-Free: 1-866-866-2601
customer_support@csi.ca
www.csi.ca

Campuses

Montréal Office
1155, rue University, Suite 600, Montréal, QC H3B 3A7, Canada
Fax: 866-866-2660
Toll-Free: 1-866-866-2601
customer_support@csi.ca
www.csi.ca

Toronto: CDI College of Business, Technology & Healthcare
#200, 424 Yonge St., Toronto, ON M5B 2H4, Canada
Tel: 416-963-8633; Fax: 416-963-5919
Computers, accounting & business training; 23 locations across Ontario

Toronto: The Certified General Accountants Association of Ontario
240 Eglinton Ave. East, Toronto, ON M4P 1K8, Canada
Tel: 416-322-6520; Fax: 416-322-5594
Toll-Free: 1-800-668-1454
info@cga-ontario.org
www.cga-ontario.org/

Toronto: Commercial Business College
2327 Dufferin St., 1st Fl., Toronto, ON M6E 3S5, Canada
Tel: 416-480-1545
info@policefoundations-cbc.com
Police & law enforcement courses

Toronto: Complections International - The Make-Up School
85 St. Nicholas St., Toronto, ON M4Y 1W8, Canada
Tel: 416-968-6739; Fax: 416-968-7340
info@complectionsmake-up.com
www.complectionsmake-up.com
Professional make-up artistry training for stage, TV & film, special effects & fashion

Toronto: Constellation College of Hospitality
808 Mount Pleasant Rd., Toronto, ON M4P 2L2, Canada
Tel: 416-675-2175; Fax: 416-675-6477
admiss@constellationcollege.com
www.constellationcollege.com
Hotel & Restaurant Operations; Culinary Arts
Sharon Turner, Director

Toronto: Frontier College
35 Jackes Ave., Toronto, ON M4T 1E2, Canada
Tel: 416-923-3591; Fax: 416-323-3522
Toll-Free: 1-800-555-652
information@frontiercollege.ca
www.frontiercollege.ca
Volunteer-based, literacy organization.
John Daniel O'Leary, President

Toronto: The Glenn Gould School of the Royal Conservatory of Music
90 Croatia St., Toronto, ON M6H 1K9, Canada
Tel: 416-408-2824; Fax: 416-408-3096
glenngouldschool@rcmusic.ca
www.rcmusic.ca
Enrollment: 130
Professional training in music performance & pedagogy at the bachelor & graduate levels
Rennie Regehr, Dean

Toronto: Global Village
#202, 180 Bloor St. West, Toronto, ON M5S 2V6, Canada
Tel: 416-968-1405; Fax: 416-968-6667
toronto@gvenlish.com
www.gvenglish.com
Geneviève Bouchard, Director

Toronto: Granton Institute of Technology
263 Adelaide St. West, Toronto, ON M5H 1Y3, Canada
Tel: 416-977-3929; *Fax:* 416-977-5612
info@grantoninstitute.com
www.grantoninstitute.com
Distance education courses

Toronto: Herzing College
#202, 220 Yonge St., Toronto, ON M5B 2H1, Canada
Tel: 416-599-6996; *Fax:* 416-599-0192
mark@tor.herzing.edu
www.herzing.edu/toronto
Information technology programs (programming, networking, database management & microprocessor technology), healthcare & legal.

Toronto: Institute of Technical Trades Ltd.
749 Warden Ave., Toronto, ON M1L 4A8, Canada
Tel: 416-750-1950; *Fax:* 416-750-4702
technicaltrade@rogers.com
www.technicaltrade.ca
Welding & CNC machine setup operation.

Toronto: International Academy of Design & Technology
39 John St., Toronto, ON M5V 3G6, Canada
Tel: 041-692-2366; *Toll-Free:* 1-800-361-6664
www.iadt.ca
Accredited diploma programs in Computer Graphics, Interior Design, Multimedia Web Design & Development & Network & Internet Technologies.

Toronto: National Institute of Broadcasting
1498 Yonge St., Toronto, ON M4T 1Z6, Canada
Tel: 416-922-2556; *Fax:* 416-922-5470
Toll-Free: 1-800-216-6247
info@nibtv.com
www.nibtraining.com
Radio & television broadcast training.

Toronto: New Skills Health College
720 Midland Ave., Toronto, ON M1K 4C9, Canada
Tel: 416-261-8988; *Fax:* 416-261-8488
Toll-Free: 1-877-227-229
info@newskillshealth.ca
www.newskillshealth.ca
Personal Support Worker diploma program

Toronto: Ontario Institute for Studies in Education
252 Bloor St. West, Toronto, ON M5S 1V6, Canada
Tel: 416-923-6641; *Fax:* 416-926-4725
www.oise.utoronto.ca
Jane Gaskell, Dean

Toronto: The RCM Community School at The Royal Conservatory of Music
90 Croatia St., Toronto, ON M6H 1K9, Canada
Tel: 416-408-2825; *Fax:* 416-408-3096
communityschool@rcmusic.ca
www.rcmusic.ca
Enrollment: 6000
Music lessons for people of all ages & levels of ability; recognized for its Early Childhood Education programs & its commitment to life-long learning
Jeff Melanson, Dean

Toronto: Rets PLC Training
2084 Danforth Ave., Toronto, ON M4C 1J9, Canada
Tel: 416-698-5287; *Fax:* 416-689-5288
rets@canada.com
www.rets.ca
PLC automation; engineering technology; government regulated & approved.

Toronto: The Royal Conservatory of Music
90 Croatia St., Toronto, ON M6H 1K9, Canada
Tel: 416-408-2824; *Fax:* 416-408-3096
www.rcmusic.ca
The largest & oldest independent arts educator in Canada, committed to developing human potential through leadership in music & arts education
Peter Simon, President

Toronto: St. Basil's College
95 St. Joseph St., Toronto, ON M5S 2R9, Canada
Tel: 416-925-4368
Part of the University of Toronto.

Toronto: School of Makeup Art Ltd.
25 Yorkville Ave., Toronto, ON M4W 1L1, Canada
Tel: 416-340-1300; *Fax:* 416-640-4491
info@schoolofmakeup.com
www.schoolofmarkupart.com
Professional make-up training: beauty; film & TV; special effects.

Toronto: Shiatsu School of Canada Inc.
547 College St., Toronto, ON M6G 1A9, Canada
Tel: 416-323-1818; *Fax:* 416-323-1681
Toll-Free: 1-800-263-170
info@shiatsucanada.com
www.shiatsucanada.com
2,200-hour program has the highest standard in the world outside of Japan
Enza Ierullo, Director

Toronto: The Society of Management Accountants of Ontario
#300, 70 University Ave., Toronto, ON M5J 2M4, Canada
Tel: 416-977-7741; *Fax:* 416-977-6079
Toll-Free: 1-800-387-299
www.cma-canada.org/ontario/default.asp
David Hipgrave, President & CEO

Toronto: Sutherland Chan School & Teaching Clinic
#400, 330 Dupont St., Toronto, ON M5R 1V9, Canada
Tel: 416-924-1107; *Fax:* 416-924-9413
admissions@sutherland-chan.com
www.sutherland-chan.com
Massage therapy.
Grace Chan, President
Nicole Blake Perryman, Admissions & Student Services Coordinator

Toronto: Toronto Art Therapy Institute
216 St. Clair Ave. West, Toronto, ON M4V 1R2, Canada
Tel: 416-924-6221; *Fax:* 416-924-0156
info@tati.on.ca
www.tati.on.ca
Gilda Grossman, M.S.W., R.S.W., R.C.A.T., Director

Toronto: Toronto Baptist Seminary & Bible College
130 Gerrard St. East, Toronto, ON M5A 3T4, Canada
Tel: 416-925-3263; *Fax:* 416-925-8305
info@tbs.edu
www.tbs.edu
Michael Haykin, Principal

Toronto: Toronto Campus
Head Office
#300, 700 Lawrence Ave. West, Toronto, ON M6A 3B4, Canada
Tel: 416-630-8021; *Fax:* 416-630-9790
Toll-Free: 1-877-736-3349
dboyes@medixschool.ca
www.medixschool.ca
Health care programs
Randy Henry, President

Campuses
Brantford Campus
39 King George Rd., Brantford, ON N3R 5K2, Canada
Tel: 519-752-4859; *Fax:* 519-752-2217
Toll-Free: 1-877-736-3349
www.medixschool.ca

Kitchener
#14, 248 Stirling Ave., Kitchener, ON N2G 4L1, Canada
Tel: 519-895-0013; *Fax:* 519-772-0107
Toll-Free: 1-877-736-3349
www.medixschool.ca

London
1299 Oxford St. East, London, ON N5Y 4W5, Canada
Tel: 519-659-4822; *Fax:* 519-659-2516
Toll-Free: 1-877-736-3349
www.medixschool.ca

Scarborough
#205, 2130 Lawrence Avenue East, Scarborough, ON M1R 3A6, Canada
Tel: 416-701-1201; *Fax:* 416-701-0855
Toll-Free: 1-877-736-3349
www.medixschool.ca

Toronto: Toronto Centre
152 Norseman St., Toronto, ON M8Z 2R4, Canada
Tel: 416-231-7227; *Fax:* 416-231-2753
Toll-Free: 1-800-458-7473
toronto@autotrainingcentre.com
www.autotrainingcentre.com
Private college specializing in automotive training

Campuses
Montreal Campus
3900, rue Jean-Talon est, Montréal, QC H3R 2G8, Canada
Tel: 514-725-6026; *Fax:* 514-725-1630
Toll-Free: 1-877-725-6026
Montreal@AutoTraiingCentre.com
www.autotrainingcentre.com

Richmond Campus
210-13460 Smallwood Place, Richmond, BC V6V 1W8, Canada
Tel: 604-270-6121; *Fax:* 604-270-6123
Toll-Free: 1-888-546-2886
Vancouver@AutoTrainingCentre.com
www.autotrainingcentre.com

Surrey Campus
#4 12372 - 84th Ave., Surrey, BC V3W 0J5, Canada
Tel: 604-270-6121; *Fax:* 604-270-6123
Toll-Free: 1-888-546-2886
Surry@AutoTrainingCentre.com
www.autotrainingcentre.com

Toronto: Toronto Office (iitravel)
#302, 1240 Bay St., Toronto, ON M5R 2A7, Canada
Tel: 416-924-2271; *Fax:* 416-924-5667
iit@ica.net
www.iitravel.com
Travel & tourism training including "Learning at Seas Seminars".

Campuses
Brampton Campus
#200, 341 Main St. North, Brampton, ON L6X 1N5, Canada
Fax: 905-459-7463
Travel & tourism training including "Learning at Seas Seminars".

London Campus
2031 Dundas St. East, London, ON N5V 1P6, Canada
Fax: 519-452-1058
Travel & tourism training including "Learning at Seas Seminars".

Mississauga Campus
1550 South Gatway Rd. Suite 310, Mississauga, ON L4W 5G6, Canada
Tel: 905-624-8600; *Fax:* 905-624-4992
iit@ica.net
www.iitravel.com
Travel & tourism training including "Learning at Seas Seminars".

Scarborough Campus
#309, 80 Corporate Dr., Scarborough, ON M1H 3G5, Canada
Tel: 416-924-9132; *Fax:* 416-289-3342
iit@ica.net
www.ittravel.com
Travel & tourism training including "Learning at Seas Seminars".

Toronto: Toronto School
5 Park Home Ave., 6th Fl., Toronto, ON M2N 6L4, Canada
Tel: 416-223-7855; *Fax:* 416-224-1641
toronto@omnicomtrans.com
www.omnicomtrans.com
Ivan Markiet, Director

Campuses
Calgary School
#100, 840 - 6 Ave. SW, Calgary, AB T2P 3E5, Canada
Tel: 403-265-6936; *Fax:* 403-265-6926
calgary@omnicomstudy.com
www.omnicomstudy.com

Toronto: Townshend College of Business & Computers
#202, 1711 McCowan Rd., Toronto, ON M1S 2Y3, Canada
Tel: 416-297-5627; *Fax:* 416-297-0210
info@townshendcollege.com
www.townshendcollege.com
Accounting, payroll, administration, healthcare & technology training programs
Jerry Townshend, Dir. of Education
Sandra Townshend, Principal

Toronto: Travel Training Career Centre Ltd.
#201, 16 Spadina Rd., Toronto, ON M5R 2S7, Canada
Tel: 416-481-2265; *Fax:* 416-487-5428
travelcollege@sympatico.ca
www.travelcollege.ca
Travel & tourism industry courses, customer service.

Toronto: Trebas Institute
149 College St., Toronto, ON M5T 1P5, Canada
Tel: 416-966-3066; *Fax:* 416-966-0030
info@trebas.com
www.trebas.com
Enrollment: 400
Audio Engineering & Production/DJ Arts, Entertainment Management, Film/Television Production
Peter Di Santo, Director

Toronto: Yorkville College
2nd Fl., 1835 Yonge St., Toronto, ON M5S 1X8, Canada
Tel: 416-929-0121; *Toll-Free:* 1-888-868-9688
mail@yorkvillecollege.com
www.yorkvillecollege.com
Computer & technical programs.

Fred Fisher, President

***Waterloo:* Shad International**
8 Young St. East, Waterloo, ON N2J 2L3, Canada
Tel: 519-884-8844; *Fax:* 519-884-8191
info@shad.ca
www.shad.ca
Four week summer enrichment program for students in grades 11 or 12, secondaire V or CEGEP I for Quebec students, or the international equivalent. The program includes the sciences, technology, and entrepreneurship.
Barry Bisson, President
Mary Dever, National Director of Development

***Windsor:* MicroAge Learning Centre**
#920, 4510 Rhodes Dr., Windsor, ON N8W 5K5, Canada
Tel: 519-945-9900; *Fax:* 519-945-9777
Toll-Free: 1-800-946-266
info@learning-centre.com
www.learning-centre.com
Software training.

Prince Edward Island

Government Agencies

***Charlottetown:* Department of Education**
P.O. Box 2000
Charlottetown, PE C1A 7N8, Canada
Tel: 902-368-4600; *Fax:* 902-368-4663
www.gov.pe.ca/educ/
Clayton Coe, Acting Director
Imelda M. Arsenault, Director, 902-368-4477
Carolyn Simpson, Administrator

School Boards/Districts/Divisions

Public

***Abram Village:* French Language School Board of Prince Edward Island**
La Commission scolaire de langue française de l'le-du-Prin
P.O. Box 124
1596 rte. 124, Abram Village, PE C0B 2E0, Canada
Tel: 902-854-2975; *Fax:* 902-854-2981
cslf@edu.pe.ca
www.edu.pe.ca/cslf
Grades: 1 - 12
Number of Schools: 6
Robert Maddix, Chair
Gilles Benoit, Chief Executive Officer
gjbenoit@edu.pe.ca
Paul Cyr, Director, Instruction
pacyr@edu.pe.ca
Louise Gallant, Director, Accounting
lzgallant@edu.pe.ca
Brad Samson, Director, Administration
blsamson@edu.pe.ca
Michel Gagnon, Manager, Information Systemes & Communications
mgagnon@edu.pe.ca
Élise Milligan, Secretary
emmilligan@edu.pe.ca

***Charlottetown:* Eastern School District**
P.O. Box 8600
Charlottetown, PE C1A 8V7, Canada
Tel: 902-368-6990; *Fax:* 902-368-6960
Enrollment: 14309
David MacDonald, Secretary
Dr. Robert Clow, Chair
Mary Lou Morrison, Director
Ronald Lee, Vice-Chair
Ricky Hood, Director

***Summerside:* Western School Board**
272 MacEwen Rd., Summerside, PE C1N 2P7, Canada
Tel: 902-888-8400; *Fax:* 902-888-8449
www.edu.pe.ca/wsb
Grades: K.-12
Enrollment: 6244
Dale Sabean, Supt.
dcsabean@edu.pe.ca
Harvey MacEwen, Dir., Bus. Services
hfmacewen@edu.pe.ca
Gary Doucette, Chair

Schools: Specialized

First Nations

***Lennox Island:* John J. Sark Memorial School**
P.O. Box 124
Lennox Island, PE C0B 1P0, Canada
Tel: 902-831-2777; *Fax:* 902-831-3153
johnjsms@auracom.com
www.lennoxisland.com/portal/com_education.htm
Grades: K.-6
Alan Gillis, Director

Schools: Independent & Private

Independent & Private Schools

***Charlottetown:* Fair Isle Adventist School**
20 Lapthorne Ave., Charlottetown, PE C1A 2M2, Canada
Tel: 902-894-9301
Grades: 1-9; Seventh-day Adventist
Enrollment: 7
Deanna Fall

***Charlottetown:* Full Circle Co-operative**
219 Kent St., Charlottetown, PE C1A 1P1, Canada
Tel: 902-628-6174
fullcircleloop@easlink.ca
users.eastlink.ca/~fullcirclecoop/
Grades: 5-12
Enrollment: 15
Scott Davidson, B.A., B.Ed., Principal

***Charlottetown:* Grace Christian School**
50 Kirkdale Rd., Charlottetown, PE C1E 1N6, Canada
Tel: 902-628-1668; *Fax:* 902-628-1668
gbc@gracechristianschool.ca
www.gracechristianschool.ca
Grades: K.-12
Enrollment: 190
A ministry of Grace Baptist Church
Jason Biech, Principal
principal@gracechristianschool.ca

***Charlottetown:* Immanuel Christian School**
65 Kirkwood Dr., Charlottetown, PE C1A 8C3, Canada
Tel: 902-628-6465
ics@pei.aibn.com
www.immanuelchristianschool.ca/
Grades: K-9
Enrollment: 28
Ruth Van Eyk, Principal

Universities & Colleges

Universities

***Charlottetown:* University of Prince Edward Island**
550 University Ave., Charlottetown, PE C1A 4P3, Canada
Tel: 902-566-0439; *Fax:* 902-566-0420
www.upei.ca
Full Time Equivalency: 3500
H. Wade MacLaughlan, B.B.A., LL.B., LL.M., President & Vice-Chancellor
William G. (Bill Andrew, Chancellor
Fred Hyndman, Chair of the Board
Alan Buchannan, B.A., M.A., Registrar & University Secretary
Dr. Rosemary Herbert, Ph.D., Acting Vice-President
Roger Cook, Purchasing Agent
Kevin Rogers, Manager
Kevin Lewis, B.B.A., M.B.A., Chief Development Officer
Gary Bradshaw, Vice-President
Katherine Schultz, Vice-President
Mark Leggott, B.Sc., M.Sc, M.L.I.S., University Librarian

Faculties
Arts
Richard Kurial, B.A., M.A., Ph.D., Dean
Business Administration
Roberta MacDonald, B.A., Dean
Education
J. Tim Goddard, Ph.D., Dean
Nursing
Dr. Kim Critchley, Dean
Science
Christian Lacroix, B.Sc., M.Sc., Dean
Veterinary Medicine
Dr. Donald L. Reynolds, Dean

Publications
The Cadre
Panther Prints
X-Press

Post Secondary/Technical

Post Secondary/Technical

***Charlottetown:* Holland College of Applied Arts and Technology**
Administrative Services
140 Weymouth St., Charlottetown, PE C1A 4Z1, Canada
Tel: 902-629-4217; *Fax:* 902-629-4239
info@hollandc.pe.ca
www.hollandc.pe.ca/
Alex MacAulay, President

Campuses
Atlantic Police Academy
P.O. Box 156
Slemon Park, PE C0A 2A0, Canada
Fax: 902-888-6725
Marine Training Centre
100 Water St., Summerside, PE C1N 1A9, Canada
Fax: 902-888-6404
Royalty Centre
40 Enman Cres., Charlottetown, PE C1E 1E6, Canada
Fax: 902-566-9323
Souris Centre
Main St. Plaza
P.O. Box 429
Souris, PE C0B 2B0, Canada
Fax: 902-687-3543
East Prince Centre
223 Water St., Summerside, PE C1N 1B4, Canada
Fax: 902-888-6402
Montague Centre
Montague, PE C0A 1R0, Canada
Fax: 902-838-3518
Atlantic Technology Centre
140 Weymouth St., Charlottetown, PE C1A 4Z1, Canada
Culinary Institute of Canada
4 Sydney St., Charlottetown, PE C1A 1E9, Canada
Fax: 902-894-6801
Toll-Free: 877-475-2844
Tourism and Culinary Centre
4 Sydney St., Charlottetown, PE C1A 1E9, Canada
Fax: 902-894-6801
Toll-Free: 877-475-2844
Charlottetown Centre
140 Weymouth St., Charlottetown, PE C1A 4Z1, Canada
Fax: 902-566-9505
Georgetown Centre
117 Kent St., Georgetown, PE C0A 1L0, Canada
Fax: 902-652-2424
Atlantic Technology Centre
140 Weymouth St., Charlottetown, PE C1A 4Z1, Canada
Assessment & Counselling Service
140 Weymouth St., Charlottetown, PE C1A AZ1, Canada
Fax: 902-566-9639
Toll-Free: 800-446-5265

Publications
The Surveyor

***Summerside:* The College of Piping & Celtic Performing Arts of Canada**
619 Water St. East, Summerside, PE C1N 4H8, Canada
Tel: 902-436-5377; *Fax:* 902-436-4930
Toll-Free: 1-877-224-747
info@collegeofpiping.com
www.collegeofpiping.com
Scott MacAulay, Director

Québec

Government Agencies

***Québec:* Ministère de l'Éducation, du Loisir et du Sport**
Direction des communications
1035, rue De La Chevrotière, 28e étage, Québec, QC G1R 5A5, Canada
Tél: 418-643-7095; *Téléc:* 418-646-6561
Ligne sans frais: 866-747-6626
www.mels.gouv.qc.ca
Line Beauchamp, Ministre
Christiane Barbe, Sous-ministre

Campuses

Directions régionales 1 & 11: Bas St-Laurent/Gaspésie-Iles-de-la-Madeleine
337, rue Moreault, bureau 2.04, 2e étage, Rimouski, QC G5L 0A5, Canada
Tel: 418-727-3600; *Fax:* 418-727-3557
dr-01@mels.gouv.qc.ca
Gérard Bédard, Directeur régional

Direction régionale 2: Saguenay—Lac-Saint-Jean
2220, rue Saint-David, Jonquière, QC G7X 0L3, Canada
Tel: 418-695-7982; *Fax:* 418-695-7990
dr-02@mels.gouv.qc.ca
François Paquette, Directeur régional

Directions régionales 3 & 12: Capitale-Nationale et Chaudière-Appalaches
1020, rte de l'Église, 3e étage, Québec, QC G1V 3V9, Canada
Tel: 418-643-7934; *Fax:* 418-643-0972
dr-03-mels.gouv.qc.ca
Marie-Sylvie Descôteau, Directrice régionale

Directions régionales 4 & 17: Mauricie et Centre-du-Québec
Édifice Capitanal
#213, 100, rue Laviolette, Trois-Rivières, QC G9A 5S9, Canada
Tel: 819-371-6711; *Fax:* 819-371-6075
dr-04@mels.gouv.qc.ca
Claude Lamarre, Directeur régional

Direction régionale 5: Estrie
#3.05, 200, rue Belvédère nord, Sherbrooke, QC J1H 4A9, Canada
Tel: 819-820-3382; *Fax:* 819-820-3947
dr-05@mels.gouv.qc.ca
Diane Lamothe, Directrice régionale

Direction régionale 6: Montréal
600, rue Fullum, 10e étage, Montréal, QC H2K 4L1, Canada
Tel: 514-873-4630; *Fax:* 514-873-0620
dr-063@mels.gouv.qc.ca
Gilles Lamirande, Directeur régional

Direction régionale 7: Outaouais
170, rue de l'Hôtel-de-Ville, 4e étage, Gatineau, QC J8X 4C2, Canada
Tel: 819-772-3382; *Fax:* 819-772-3955
dr-07@mels.gouv.qc.ca
Hélène Audet, Directrice régionale

Directions régionales 8 & 10: Abitibi-Témiscamingue et Nord-du-Québec
215, boul Rideau, 1er étage, Rouyn-Noranda, QC J9X 5Y6, Canada
Tel: 819-763-3001; *Fax:* 819-763-3017
dr-08@mels.gouv.qc.ca
Louise Bilodeau, Directrice régionale (par intérim)

Direction régionale 9: Côte-Nord (Services adm. et gén.)
Édifice Paul-Provencher
#1.812, 625, boul Laflèche, Baie-Comeau, QC G5C 1C5, Canada
Tel: 418-295-4400; *Fax:* 418-295-4467
dr09-bc@mels.gouv.qc.ca
Lucy de Mendonça, Directrice régionale

Direction régionale 9: Côte-Nord (Services éducatifs)
#201, 106, rue Napoléon, Sept-Iles, QC G4R 3L7, Canada
Tel: 418-964-8420; *Fax:* 418-964-8504
dr09-si@mels.gouv.qc.ca
Lucy de Mendoça, Directrice régionale

Directions régionales 13, 14 et 15: Laval, Lanaudière, et Laurentides
#200, 300, rue Sicard, Sainte-Thérèse, QC J7E 3X5, Canada
Tel: 450-430-3611; *Fax:* 450-430-4005
dr-061@mels.gouv.qc.ca
Lauraine Langlois, Directrice régionale

Direction régionale 16: Montérégie
Édifice Montval
201, place Charles-Le Moyne, 6e étage, Longueuil, QC J4K 2T5, Canada
Tel: 450-928-7438; *Fax:* 450-928-7451
dr-062@mels.gouv.qc.ca
Francis Culée, Directeur régional

School Boards/Districts/Divisions

Public

***Aylmer:* Commission scolaire Western Québec Western Québec School Board**
15, rue Katimavik, Aylmer, QC J9J 0E9, Canada
Tél: 819-684-2336; *Téléc:* 819-684-1328
Ligne sans frais: 800-363-9111
wqsb@wqsb.qc.ca
www.wqsb.qc.ca
Michael Dawson, Directeur général

***Châteauguay:* Commission scolaire New Frontiers New Frontiers School Board**
214, rue McLeod, Châteauguay, QC J6J 2H4, Canada
Tél: 450-691-1440; *Téléc:* 450-691-0643
secgen@csnewfrontiers.qc.ca
www.csnewfrontiers.qc.ca
Wayne Goldthorp, Directeur général

***Dorval:* Commission scolaire Lester-B.-Pearson Lester B. Pearson School Board**
1925, av Brookdale, Dorval, QC H9P 2Y7, Canada
Tél: 514-422-3000
info@lbpsb.qc.ca
www.lbpsb.qc.ca
Robert T. Mills, Directeur général

***Magog:* Commission scolaire Eastern Townships Eastern Townships School Board**
#205, 101, rue Du Moulin, Magog, QC J1X 6H8, Canada
Tél: 819-868-3100; *Téléc:* 819-868-2286
priests@etsb.qc.ca
www.etsb.qc.ca
Chantal C. Beaulieu, Directrice générale

***Montréal:* Commission scolaire English-Montréal English Montréal School Board**
6000, av Fielding, Montréal, QC H3X 1T4, Canada
Tél: 514-483-7200; *Téléc:* 514-483-7324
webmaster@emsb.qc.ca
www.emsb.qc.ca
Robert Stocker, Directeur général

***New Carlisle:* Commission scolaire Eastern Shores Eastern Shores School Board**
40, rue Mount Sorrel, New Carlisle, QC G0C 1Z0, Canada
Tél: 418-752-2247; *Téléc:* 418-752-6447
info@essb.qc.ca
www.essb.qc.ca
Dave Royal, Directeur général
dave.royal@essb.qc.ca

***Québec:* Commission scolaire Central Québec Central Québec School Board**
2046, ch Saint-Louis, Québec, QC G1T 1P4, Canada
Tél: 418-688-8730; *Téléc:* 418-682-5891
Ligne sans frais: 800-249-5573
cqsb@dqsb.qc.ca
www.cqsb.qc.ca
Ronald Corriveau, Directeur général

***Rosemère:* Commission scolaire Sir-Wilfrid-Laurier Sir Wilfrid Laurier School Board**
235, montée Lesage, Rosemère, QC J7A 4Y6, Canada
Tél: 450-621-5600; *Téléc:* 450-621-7929
Ligne sans frais: 866-621-5600
www.swlauriersb.qc.ca
Anne-Marie Lepage, Directrice générale

***Saint-Lambert:* Commission scolaire Riverside Riverside School Board**
299, boul Sir Wilfrid-Laurier, Saint-Lambert, QC J4R 2V7, Canada
Tél: 450-672-4010; *Téléc:* 450-465-8809
rsb@rsb.qc.ca
www.rsb.qc.ca
Stephen Lessard, Directeur général
slessard@rsb.qc.ca

French

***Alma:* Commission scolaire du Lac-Saint-Jean**
350, boul Champlain sud, Alma, QC G8B 5W2, Canada
Tél: 418-669-6000; *Téléc:* 418-669-6351
www.cslacst-jean.qc.ca
Eric Blackburn, Directeur général
dglstjean@cslacst-jean.qc.ca

***Amos:* Commission scolaire Harricana**
341, rue Principale nord, Amos, QC J9T 2L8, Canada
Tél: 819-732-6561; *Téléc:* 819-732-1623
communications@csharricana.qc.ca
www.csharricana.qc.ca
Guy Baril, Directeur général

***Amqui:* Commission scolaire des Monts-et-Marées**
93, rue du Parc, Amqui, QC G5J 2L8, Canada
Tél: 418-629-6200; *Téléc:* 418-629-6234
www.csmm.qc.ca
Centre de services de Matane: 530, av Saint-Jérôme, 418-566-2500.
Pierre Berthelet, Directeur général

***Baie-Comeau:* Commission scolaire de l'Estuaire**
771, boul Joliet, Baie-Comeau, QC G5C 1P3, Canada
Tél: 418-589-0806; *Téléc:* 418-589-2711
Ligne sans frais: 877-589-0806
www.csestuaire.qc.ca
Alain Ouellet, Directeur général

***Beauharnois:* Commission scolaire de la Vallée-des-Tisserands**
630, rue Ellice, Beauharnois, QC J6N 3S1, Canada
Tél: 450-225-2788; *Téléc:* 450-225-0691
Ligne sans frais: 877-225-2788
info@csvt.qc.ca
www.csvt.qc.ca
Carole Houle, Directrice générale
dg@csvt.qc.ca

***Beauport:* Commission scolaire des Premières-Seigneuries**
643, av du Cénacle, Beauport, QC G1E 1B3, Canada
Tél: 418-666-4666; *Téléc:* 418-666-9783
sic@csdps.qc.ca
www.csdps.qc.ca
Serge Pelletier, Directeur général
dg@csdps.qc.ca

***Bonaventure:* Commission scolaire René-Lévesque**
145, av Louisbourg, Bonaventure, QC G0C 1E0, Canada
Tél: 418-534-3003; *Téléc:* 418-534-3220
www.cs-renelevesque.qc.ca
Chantal Bourdages, Directrice générale

***Cabano:* Commission scolaire du Fleuve-et-des-Lacs**
14, rue du Vieux-Chemin, Cabano, QC G0L 1E0, Canada
Tél: 418-854-2370; *Téléc:* 418-854-2715
info@csfl.qc.ca
www.csfl.qc.ca
Serge Pelletier, Directeur général

***Chibougamau:* Commission scolaire de la Baie-James**
596, 4e rue, Chibougamau, QC G8P 1S3, Canada
Tél: 418-748-7621; *Téléc:* 418-748-2440
www.csbj.qc.ca
Michèle Perron, Directrice générale

***Chicoutimi:* Commission scolaire des Rives-du-Saguenay**
36, rue Jacques-Cartier est, Chicoutimi, QC G7H 1W2, Canada
Tél: 418-698-5000; *Téléc:* 418-698-5262
www.csrsaguenay.qc.ca
Centre de services La Baie: 3111, rue Mgr Dufour, La Baie, 418-544-3307. Service informatique: 475, rue Lafontaine, Chicoutimi, 418-541-7799.
Yvon Pelletier, Directeur général

***Donnacona:* Commission scolaire de Portneuf**
310, rue de l'Église, Donnacona, QC G3M 1Z8, Canada
Tél: 418-285-2600; *Téléc:* 418-285-2738
www.csportneuf.qc.ca
Jean-Pierre Soucy, Directeur général
jeanpsoucy@csdp.qc.ca

Drummondville: **Commission scolaire des Chênes**
P.O. Box 846
457, rue des Écoles, Drummondville, QC J2B 6X1, Canada
Tél: 819-478-6700; *Téléc:* 819-478-6777
commentaires@csdeschenes.qc.ca
www.csdeschenes.qc.ca
Yvan Aubé, Directeur général

East Angus: **Commission scolaire des Hauts-Cantons**
308, rue Palmer, East Angus, QC J0B 1R0, Canada
Tél: 819-832-4953; *Téléc:* 819-832-4863
www.cshc.qc.ca
Bernard Lacroix, Directeur général

Gaspé: **Commission scolaire des Chic-Chocs**
102, rue Jacques-Cartier, Gaspé, QC G4X 2S9, Canada
Tél: 418-368-3499; *Téléc:* 418-368-6531
commission.scolaire@cschic-chocs.net
www.cschic-chocs.net
Jean Letarte, Directeur général

Gatineau: **Commission scolaire au Coeur-des-Vallées**
582, rue MacLaren est, Gatineau, QC J8L 2W2, Canada
Tél: 819-986-8511; *Téléc:* 819-986-9283
Ligne sans frais: 800-958-9966
info@cscv.qc.ca
www.cscv.qc.ca
Maurice Groulx, Directeur général

Gatineau: **Commission scolaire des Draveurs**
200, boul Maloney est, Gatineau, QC J8P 1K3, Canada
Tél: 819-663-9221; *Téléc:* 819-663-6176
reception@csdraveurs.qc.ca
www.csdraveurs.qc.ca
François Jetté, Directeur général
dg@csdraveurs.qc.ca

Gatineau: **Commission scolaire des Portages-de-l'Outaouais**
225, rue St-Rédempteur, Gatineau, QC J8X 2T3, Canada
Tél: 819-771-4548; *Téléc:* 819-771-6964
www.cspo.qc.ca
Jean-Claude Bouchard, Directeur général
dgcspo@cspo.qc.ca

Granby: **Commission scolaire du Val-des-Cerfs**
P.O. Box 9000
55, rue Court, Granby, QC J2G 9H7, Canada
Tél: 450-372-0221; *Téléc:* 450-372-3150
descerfs@csvdc.qc.ca
www.csvdc.qc.ca
André Messier, Directeur général

Ha@vre-Saint-Pierre: **Commission scolaire de la Moyenne-Côte-Nord**
1235, rue de la Digue, Ha@vre-Saint-Pierre, QC G0G 1P0, Canada
Tél: 418-538-3044; *Téléc:* 418-538-3268
www.csmcn.qc.ca
Marius Richard, Directeur général

Jonquière: **Commission scolaire De La Jonquière**
P.O. Box 1600
3644, rue St-Jules, Jonquière, QC G7X 7X4, Canada
Tél: 418-542-7551; *Téléc:* 418-542-1505
info@csjonquiere.qc.ca
www.csjonquiere.qc.ca
Raynald Thibeault, Directeur général

L'Étang-du-Nord: **Commission scolaire des Iles**
1419, ch de l'Étang-du-Nord, L'Étang-du-Nord, QC G4T 3B9, Canada
Tél: 418-986-5511; *Téléc:* 418-986-3552
info@csdesiles.qc.ca
www.csdesiles.qc.ca
Diane Arsenault, Directrice générale

La Malbaie: **Commission scolaire de Charlevoix**
575, boul de Comporté, La Malbaie, QC G5A 1T5, Canada
Tél: 418-665-3765; *Téléc:* 418-665-6805
www.cscharlevoix.qc.ca
Robert Labbé, Directeur général
robert.labbe@cscharlevoix.qc.ca

La Prairie: **Commission scolaire des Grandes-Seigneuries**
50, boul Taschereau, La Prairie, QC J5R 4V3, Canada
Tél: 514-380-8899; *Téléc:* 514-380-8345
www.csdgs.qc.ca
Michelle Fournier, Directrice générale
directiongenerale@csdgs.qc.ca

La Sarre: **Commission scolaire du Lac-Abitibi**
500, rue Principale, La Sarre, QC J9Z 2A2, Canada
Tél: 819-333-5411; *Téléc:* 819-333-3044
www.csdla.qc.ca
Huguette Théberge, Directrice générale

Laval: **Commission scolaire de Laval**
955, boul Saint-Martin ouest, Laval, QC H7S 1M5, Canada
Tél: 450-662-7000; *Téléc:* 450-625-2042
www2.cslaval.qc.ca
Claude Sabourin, Directeur général
directiongenerale@cslaval.qc.ca

Longueuil: **Commission scolaire Marie-Victorin**
13, rue St-Laurent est, Longueuil, QC J4H 4B7, Canada
Tél: 450-670-0730; *Téléc:* 450-670-0902
info@csmv.qc.ca
www.csmv.qc.ca
André Byette, Directeur général

Magog: **Commission scolaire des Sommets**
449, rue Percy, Magog, QC J1X 1B5, Canada
Tél: 819-847-1610; *Téléc:* 819-847-2065
Ligne sans frais: 888-847-1610
info@csdessommets.qc.ca
www.csdessommets.qc.ca
Christian Provencher, Directeur général

Maniwaki: **Commission scolaire des Hauts-Bois-de-l'Outaouais**
331, rue du Couvent, Maniwaki, QC J9E 1H5, Canada
Tél: 819-449-7866; *Téléc:* 819-449-2636
Ligne sans frais: 888-831-9606
info@cshbo.qc.ca
www.cshbo.qc.ca
Harold Sylvain, Directeur général

Mont-Laurier: **Commission scolaire Pierre-Neveu**
525, rue de la Madone, Mont-Laurier, QC J9L 1S4, Canada
Tél: 819-623-4310; *Téléc:* 819-623-7979
Ligne sans frais: 866-334-4114
cspn@cspn.qc.ca
www.cspn.qc.ca
Normand Bélanger, Directeur général
belanger.normand@cspn.qc.ca

Montmagny: **Commission scolaire de la Côte-du-Sud**
157, rue Saint-Louis, Montmagny, QC G5V 4N3, Canada
Tél: 418-248-1001
info@cscotesud.qc.ca
www.cscotesud.qc.ca
Jocelyn Carrier, Directeur général

Montréal: **Commission scolaire de la Pointe-de-l'Ile**
550, 53e av, Montréal, QC H1A 2T7, Canada
Tél: 514-642-9520; *Téléc:* 514-642-1590
www.cspi.qc.ca
Antonio Bernardelli, Directeur général

Montréal: **Commission scolaire de Montréal**
3737, rue Sherbrooke est, Montréal, QC H1X 3B3, Canada
Tél: 514-596-6000; *Téléc:* 514-596-7570
info@csdm.qc.ca
www.csdm.qc.ca
Gilles Petitclerc, Directeur général

Nicolet: **Commission scolaire de la Riveraine**
375, rue de Monseigneur-Brunault, Nicolet, QC J3T 1Y6, Canada
Tél: 819-293-5821; *Téléc:* 819-293-8691
csdlrweb@admin.csriveraine.qc.ca
www.csriveraine.qc.ca
Jean-René Dubois, Directeur général

Québec: **Commission scolaire de la Capitale**
1900, rue Côté, Québec, QC G1N 3Y5, Canada
Tél: 418-686-4040; *Téléc:* 418-686-4032
adm2@cscapitale.qc.ca
www.cscapitale.qc.ca
Berthe Bernatchez, Directrice générale

Québec: **Commission scolaire des Découvreurs**
945, av Wolfe, Québec, QC G1V 4E2, Canada
Tél: 418-652-2121; *Téléc:* 418-652-2146
www.csdecou.qc.ca
Reynald Deraspe, Directeur général
dirgen@csdecou.qc.ca

Repentigny: **Commission scolaire des Affluents**
80, rue Jean-Baptiste-Meilleur, Repentigny, QC J6A 6C5, Canada
Tél: 450-492-9400; *Téléc:* 450-492-3720
info@csaffluents.qc.ca
www.csaffluents.qc.ca
Thomas Duzyk, Directeur général
thomas.duzyk@dg.csaffluents.qc.ca

Rimouski: **Commission scolaire des Phares**
435, av Rouleau, Rimouski, QC G5L 8V4, Canada
Tél: 418-723-5927; *Téléc:* 418-724-3350
dgphares@csphares.qc.ca
www.csphares.qc.ca
Jacques Poirier, Directeur général
jpoirier@csphares.qc.ca

Rivière-du-Loup: **Commission scolaire de Kamouraska—Rivière-du-Loup**
464, rue Lafontaine, Rivière-du-Loup, QC G5R 3C2, Canada
Tél: 418-868-8201; *Téléc:* 418-862-0964
web.cskamloup.qc.ca
Yvan Tardif, Directeur général

Roberval: **Commission scolaire du Pays-des-Bleuets**
828, boul Saint-Joseph, Roberval, QC G8H 2L5, Canada
Tél: 418-275-4136; *Téléc:* 418-275-6217
www.cspaysbleuets.qc.ca
Secteur Dolbeau-Mistassini: 1950, boul Sacré-Coeur, Dolbeau-Mistassini, 418-276-2012.
Serge Bergeron, Directeur général

Rouyn-Noranda: **Commission scolaire de Rouyn-Noranda**
P.O. Box 908
70, rue des Oblats est, Rouyn-Noranda, QC J9X 5C9, Canada
Tél: 819-762-8161; *Téléc:* 819-764-7170
dgcsrn@csrn.qc.ca
www.csrn.qc.ca
Richard Gauthier, Directeur général

Saint-Eustache: **Commission scolaire de la Seigneurie-des-Mille-Iles**
430, boul Arthur-Sauvé, Saint-Eustache, QC J7R 6V6, Canada
Tél: 450-974-7000; *Téléc:* 450-974-6977
info@cssmi.qc.ca
www.cssmi.qc.ca
Jean-François Lachance, Directeur général

Saint-Félix-de-Valois: **Commission scolaire des Samares**
4671, rue Principale, Saint-Félix-de-Valois, QC J0K 2M0, Canada
Tél: 450-758-3500; *Téléc:* 450-889-8604
sq@cssamares.qc.ca
www.cssamares.qc.ca
Richard Fiset, Directeur général

Saint-Hyacinthe: **Commission scolaire de Saint-Hyacinthe**
2255, av Sainte-Anne, Saint-Hyacinthe, QC J2S 5H7, Canada
Tél: 450-773-8401; *Téléc:* 450-773-3262
webcorp.cssh.qc.ca
Yvan Gauthier, Directeur général
yvan.gauthier@cssh.qc.ca

Saint-Jean-sur-Richelieu: **Commission scolaire des Hautes-Rivières**
210, rue Notre-Dame, Saint-Jean-sur-Richelieu, QC J3B 6N3, Canada
Tél: 450-359-6411; *Téléc:* 450-359-4623
casegen@csdhr.qc.ca
www.csdhr.qc.ca
Mme Claude Boivin, Directrice générale

Saint-Jérôme: **Commission scolaire de la Rivière-du-Nord**
995, rue Labelle, Saint-Jérôme, QC J7Z 5N7, Canada
Tél: 450-438-3131; *Téléc:* 450-436-5277
csrdn@csrdn.qc.ca
www.csrdn.qc.ca
Centre administratif II: 795, rue Melançon, 450-438-3131.
Lise Allaire, Directrice générale

Saint-Laurent: **Commission scolaire Marguerite-Bourgeoys**
1100, boul de la Côte-Vertu, Saint-Laurent, QC H4L 4V1, Canada
Tél: 514-855-4500; *Téléc:* 514-855-4749
www.csmb.qc.ca

Yves Sylvain, Directeur général

***Saint-Romuald:* Commission scolaire des Navigateurs**
1860, 1e rue, Saint-Romuald, QC G6W 5M6, Canada
Tél: 418-839-0500; *Téléc:* 418-839-0536
dg@csnavigateurs.qc.ca
www.csdn.qc.ca
Joanne Plourde, Directrice générale

***Sainte-Agathe-des-Monts:* Commission scolaire des Laurentides**
13, rue Saint-Antoine, Sainte-Agathe-des-Monts, QC J8C 2C3, Canada
Tél: 819-326-0333; *Téléc:* 819-326-2121
beattiej@cslaurentides.qc.ca
www.cslaurentides.qc.ca
Claude Pouliot, Directeur général

***Sept-Iles:* Commission scolaire du Fer**
30, rue Comeau, Sept-Iles, QC G4R 4N2, Canada
Tél: 418-968-9901; *Téléc:* 418-962-7760
www.csdufer.qc.ca
Robert Smith, Directeur général

***Sept-Iles:* Commission scolaire du Littoral**
789, rue Beaulieu, Sept-Iles, QC G4R 1P8, Canada
Tél: 418-962-5559; *Téléc:* 418-968-2942
Ligne sans frais: 877-745-7226
www.csdulittoral.qc.ca
Lucy de Mendonça, Administratrice
dglittoral@csdulittoral.qc.ca

***Shawinigan:* Commission scolaire de l'Énergie**
P.O. Box 580
2072, rue Gignac, Shawinigan, QC G9N 6V7, Canada
Tél: 819-539-6971; *Téléc:* 819-539-7797
cse@csenergie.qc.ca
www.csenergie.qc.ca
Denis Lemaire, Directeur général

***Sherbrooke:* Commission scolaire de la Région-de-Sherbrooke**
2955, boul de l'Université, Sherbrooke, QC J1K 2Y3, Canada
Tél: 819-822-5540; *Téléc:* 819-822-5530
www.csrs.qc.ca
Claude St-Cyr, Directeur général

***Sorel-Tracy:* Commission scolaire de Sorel-Tracy**
41, av de l'Hôtel-Dieu, Sorel-Tracy, QC J3P 1L1, Canada
Tél: 450-746-3990; *Téléc:* 450-746-4474
www.cs-soreltracy.qc.ca
Jean Morin, Directeur général
dgen@cs-soreltracy.qc.ca

***St-Bruno-de-Montarville:* Commission scolaire des Patriotes**
1740, rue Roberval, St-Bruno-de-Montarville, QC J3V 3R3, Canada
Tél: 450-441-2919; *Téléc:* 450-441-0838
courriel@csp.qc.ca
www.csp.qc.ca
Normande Lemieux, Directrice générale

***St-Georges:* Commission scolaire de la Beauce-Etchemin**
1925, 118e rue, St-Georges, QC G5Y 7R7, Canada
Tél: 418-228-5541; *Téléc:* 418-228-5549
secretariat.general@csbe.qc.ca
www.csbe.qc.ca
Normand Lessard, Directeur général

***Thetford Mines:* Commission scolaire des Appalaches**
650, rue Lapierre, Thetford Mines, QC G6G 7P1, Canada
Tél: 418-338-7800; *Téléc:* 418-338-7845
ghebert@csappalaches.qc.ca
www.csappalaches.qc.ca
Camil Turmel, Directeur général

***Trois-Rivières:* Commission scolaire du Chemin-du-Roy**
1515, rue Ste-Marguerite, Trois-Rivières, QC G9A 5E7, Canada
Tél: 819-379-6565; *Téléc:* 819-379-2068
info@csduroy.qc.ca
www.csduroy.qc.ca
Michel Morin, Directeur général
dgduroy@csduroy.qc.ca

***Val-d'Or:* Commission scolaire de l'Or-et-des-Bois**
799, boul Forest, Val-d'Or, QC J9P 2L4, Canada
Tél: 819-825-4220; *Téléc:* 819-825-5305
info@csob.qc.ca
www.csob.qc.ca
Jean Denommé, Directeur général

***Vaudreuil-Dorion:* Commission scolaire des Trois-Lacs**
400, av St-Charles, Vaudreuil-Dorion, QC J7V 6B1, Canada
Tél: 514-477-7000
dgenerale@cstrois-lacs.qc.ca
www.cstrois-lacs.qc.ca
Sophie Proulx, Directrice générale

***Victoriaville:* Commission scolaire des Bois-Francs**
40, boul Bois-Francs nord, Victoriaville, QC G6P 6S5, Canada
Tél: 819-758-6453; *Téléc:* 819-758-4925
info@csbf.qc.ca
www.csbf.qc.ca
François Labbé, Directeur général

***Ville-Marie:* Commission scolaire du Lac-Témiscamingue**
2, rue Maisonneuve, Ville-Marie, QC J9V 1V4, Canada
Tél: 819-629-2472; *Téléc:* 819-629-2791
courrier@cslactem.qc.ca
www.cslactem.qc.ca
Éric Larivière, Directeur général
eric.lariviere@cslactem.qc.ca

First Nations

***Lac-Simon:* Conseil de l'Éducation du Lac-Simon**
1013, av Amikwiche, Lac-Simon, QC J0Y 3M0, Canada
Tél: 819-736-2121
ecole_amikwiche@hotmail.com
Grades: Elem./Sec.

***Mistissini:* Commission scolaire Crie Cree School Board**
203, rue Principale, Mistissini, QC G0W 1C0, Canada
Tél: 418-923-2764; *Téléc:* 418-923-2072
www.cscree.qc.ca
Abraham Jolly, Directeur général
ajolly@cscree.qc.ca

***Saint-Laurent:* Commission scolaire Kativik Kativik School Board**
#400, 9800, boul Cavendish, Saint-Laurent, QC H4M 2V9, Canada
Tél: 514-482-8220; *Téléc:* 514-482-8496
www.kativik.qc.ca
Annie Grenier, Directrice générale

Schools: Cégep

Cégep

***Baie-Comeau:* Cégep de Baie-Comeau**
537, boul Blanche, Baie-Comeau, QC G5C 2B2, Canada
Tél: 418-589-5707; *Téléc:* 418-589-9842
Ligne sans frais: 1-800-463-2030
fraduval@cegep-baie-comeau.qc.ca
www.cegep-baie-comeau.qc.ca
Grades: Préuniv., Techniques, Form. cont.
Danielle Delorme, Directrice générale

Publications
D.E.C. express

***Chicoutimi:* Cégep de Chicoutimi**
534, rue Jacques-Cartier est, Chicoutimi, QC G7H 1Z6, Canada
Tél: 418-549-9520; *Téléc:* 418-549-1315
dirgene@cegep-chicoutimi.qc.ca
www.cegep-chicoutimi.qc.ca
Grades: Préuniv., Techniques, Form. cont.
Ginette Sirois, Directrice générale

Publications
La Grenouille

Le Nénu phare

***Drummondville:* Cégep de Drummondville**
960, rue St-Georges, Drummondville, QC J2C 6A2, Canada
Tél: 819-478-4671; *Téléc:* 819-474-6859
dg@cdrummond.qc.ca
www.cdrummond.qc.ca
Grades: Préuniv., Techniques
Enrollment: 1900
Normand W. Bernier, Directeur général

Publications
Mouton Noir

***Gaspé:* Cégep de la Gaspésie et des Iles**
96, rue Jacques-Cartier, Gaspé, QC G4X 2S8, Canada
Tél: 418-368-2201; *Téléc:* 418-368-7003
Ligne sans frais: 1-866-424-3341
infogaspe@cgaspesie.qc.ca
www.cgaspesie.qc.ca
Grades: Préuniv., Techniques, Form. cont.
Enrollment: 1140
Roland Auger, Directeur général

***Gatineau:* Cégep de l'Outaouais**
Campus Gabrielle-Roy
333, boul de la Cité-des-Jeunes, Gatineau, QC J8Y 6M4, Canada
Tél: 819-770-4012; *Téléc:* 819-770-8167
www.cegepoutaouais.qc.ca
Enrollment: 4418
Marielle Poirier, Directrice générale
dirgen@cegepoutaouais.qc.ca

Publications
La Brise

L'Entremetteur

***Granby:* Cégep de Granby Haute-Yamaska**
P.O. Box 7000
235, rue St-Jacques, Granby, QC J2G 9H7, Canada
Tél: 450-372-6614; *Téléc:* 450-372-6565
lfalvarez@cegepgranby.qc.ca
www.cegepgranby.qc.ca
Marie-Johanne Lacroix, Directrice générale

Publications
de Fouille-moi

***Jonquière:* Cégep de Jonquière**
2505, rue St-Hubert, Jonquière, QC G7X 7W2, Canada
Tél: 418-547-2191; *Téléc:* 418-547-3359
cegep@cjonquiere.qc.ca
www.cjonquiere.qc.ca
Michel Gravel, Directeur général

Publications
La Pige

***La Pocatière:* Cégep de La Pocatière**
140, 4e av, La Pocatière, QC G0R 1Z0, Canada
Tél: 418-856-1525; *Téléc:* 418-856-4589
information@cegeplapocatiere.qc.ca
www.cegeplapocatiere.qc.ca
Enrollment: 900
Claude Harvey, Directeur général

Publications
Le Nordet

***Lasalle:* Cégep André-Laurendeau**
1111, rue Lapierre, Lasalle, QC H8N 2J4, Canada
Tél: 514-364-3320; *Téléc:* 514-364-7130
courrier@claurendeau.qc.ca
www.claurendeau.qc.ca
Grades: Préuniv., Tech., Form. continue
Enrollment: 2700
Hervé Pilon, Directeur général

Publications
Vox-Populi

***Lévis:* Cégep de Lévis-Lauzon**
205, rte Mgr Bourget, Lévis, QC G6V 6Z9, Canada
Tél: 418-833-5110; *Téléc:* 418-833-7323
julie.talbot@clevislauzon.qc.ca
www.clevislauzon.qc.ca
Enrollment: 2885
Guy Demers, Directeur général

Publications
Le Forcep

***Matane:* Cégep de Matane**
616, av St-Rédempteur, Matane, QC G4W 1L1, Canada
Tél: 418-562-1240; *Téléc:* 418-566-2115
information@cegep-matane.qc.ca
www.cegep-matane.qc.ca
Émery Béland, Directeur général

Publications
La Criée

***Montréal:* Cégep de Saint-Laurent**
625, av Ste-Croix, Montréal, QC H4L 3X7, Canada
Tél: 514-747-6521; *Téléc:* 514-748-1249
webmestre@cegep-st-laurent.qc.ca
www.cegep-st-laurent.qc.ca
Enrollment: 2500
Paul-Émile Bourque, Directeur général
pebourque@cegep-st-laurent.qc.ca

Publications
La Minerve

***Montréal:* Cégep du Vieux Montréal**
255, rue Ontario est, Montréal, QC H2X 1X6, Canada
Tél: 514-982-3437; *Téléc:* 514-982-3400
gestionnairew3@cvm.qc.ca
www.cvm.qc.ca
Enrollment: 6000
Jacques Roussil, Directeur général
jroussil@cvm.qc.ca

Publications
Le République

***Montréal:* Cégep Marie-Victorin**
7000, rue Marie-Victorin, Montréal, QC H1G 2J6, Canada
Tél: 514-325-0150; *Téléc:* 514-328-3830
promotion@collegemv.qc.ca
www.collegemv.qc.ca
Enrollment: 3082
Nicole Rouillier, Directrice générale

***Québec:* Cégep de Sainte-Foy**
2410, ch Ste-Foy, Québec, QC G1V 1T3, Canada
Tél: 418-659-6600; *Téléc:* 418-659-4563
info@cegep-ste-foy.qc.ca
www.cegep-ste-foy.qc.ca
Grades: Préuniv., Techniques, Form. cont.
Enrollment: 8000
Denis Juneau, Directeur général

Publications
Éclosion

***Québec:* Cégep François-Xavier-Garneau**
1660, boul de l'Entente, Québec, QC G1S 4S3, Canada
Tél: 418-688-8310; *Téléc:* 418-681-9384
communications@cegep-fxg.qc.ca
www.cegep-fxg.qc.ca
Grades: Préuniv., Bacc. int'l, Tech.
Enrollment: 9000
Yves Blouin, Directeur général

Publications
La Crise

***Québec:* Cégep Limoilou**
1300, 8e av, Québec, QC G1J 5L5, Canada
Tél: 418-647-6600; *Téléc:* 418-647-6798
info@climoilou.qc.ca
www.climoilou.qc.ca
Enrollment: 4470
Pierre Malouin, Directeur général

Publications
L'Interdit

***Repentigny:* Cégep régional de Lanaudière**
781, rue Notre-Dame, Repentigny, QC J5Y 1B4, Canada
Tél: 450-470-0911; *Téléc:* 450-581-1567
infocom@collanaud.qc.ca
www.collanaud.qc.ca
Bernard Lachance, Directeur général

Campuses
L'Assomption
180, rue Dorval, L'Assomption, QC J5W 6C1, Canada
Fax: 450-589-8926

Joliette
20, rue Saint-Charles sud, Joliette, QC J6E 4T1, Canada
Fax: 450-759-4468

Terrebonne
2505, boul des Entreprises, Terrebonne, QC J6X 5S5, Canada

Publications
L'Alinéa

***Rimouski:* Cégep de Rimouski**
60, rue de l'Évêché ouest, Rimouski, QC G5L 4H6, Canada
Tél: 418-723-1880; *Téléc:* 418-724-4961
infoscol@cegep-rimouski.qc.ca
www.cegep-rimouski.qc.ca
Enrollment: 4000
Jean-Pierre Villeneuve, Directeur général

Publications
Le Calvaire

***Rivière-du-Loup:* Cégep de Rivière-du-Loup**
80, rue Frontenac, Rivière-du-Loup, QC G5R 1R1, Canada
Tél: 418-862-6903; *Téléc:* 418-862-4959
sercom@cegep-rdl.qc.ca
www.cegep-rdl.qc.ca
Grades: Préuniv., Techniques, Form. cont.
Enrollment: 2200
André Morin, Directeur général

Publications
L'Ulcère

***Rouyn-Noranda:* Cégep de l'Abitibi-Témiscamingue**
425, boul du Collège, Rouyn-Noranda, QC J9X 5E5, Canada
Tél: 819-762-0931; *Téléc:* 819-762-2071
Ligne sans frais: 1-866-234-3728
cegepat.qc.ca
Grades: Préuniv., Techniques, Form. cont.
Enrollment: 2400
Daniel Marcotte, Directeur général
daniel.marcotte@cegepat.qc.ca

Publications
Le Profane

***Saint-Félicien:* Cégep de St-Félicien**
P.O. Box 7300
1105, boul Hamel, Saint-Félicien, QC G8K 2R8, Canada
Tél: 418-679-5412; *Téléc:* 418-679-0238
info@cstfelicien.qc.ca
www.cstfelicien.qc.ca
Grades: Préuniv., Techniques
Enrollment: 1000
Louis Lefebvre, Directeur général

Publications
Le Sentier

***Saint-Hyacinthe:* Cégep de Saint-Hyacinthe**
3000, av Boullé, Saint-Hyacinthe, QC J2S 1H9, Canada
Tél: 450-773-6800; *Téléc:* 450-773-9971
info@cegepsth.qc.ca
www.cegepsth.qc.ca
Grades: Préuniv., Techniques, Form. cont.
Enrollment: 3200
Roger Sylvestre, Directeur général

Publications
L'Électic

***Saint-Jean-sur-Richelieu:* Cégep Saint-Jean-sur-Richelieu**
P.O. Box 1018
30, boul du Séminaire, Saint-Jean-sur-Richelieu, QC J3B 7B1, Canada
Tél: 450-347-5301; *Téléc:* 450-347-3329
communications@cstjean.qc.ca
www.cstjean.qc.ca
Grades: Préuniv., Techniques, Form. cont.
Enrollment: 3600
Chantal Denis, Directrice générale

Publications
L'Hermes

***Saint-Jérôme:* Cégep de Saint-Jérôme**
455, rue Fournier, Saint-Jérôme, QC J7Z 4V2, Canada
Tél: 450-436-1580; *Téléc:* 450-436-1756
communications-et-promotion@cstj.qc.ca
www.cegep-st-jerome.qc.ca
Enrollment: 3300
Serge Tessier, Directeur général

***Sainte-Anne-de-Bellevue:* Cégep John Abbott College**
21275, rue Lakeshore, Sainte-Anne-de-Bellevue, QC H9X 3L9, Canada
Tél: 514-457-6610; *Téléc:* 514-457-4730
webmaster@johnabbott.qc.ca
www.johnabbott.qc.ca
Enrollment: 7600
Keith W. Henderson, Directeur général

Publications
Bandersnatch

***Sept-Iles:* Cégep de Sept-Iles**
175, rue De La Vérendrye, Sept-Iles, QC G4R 5B7, Canada
Tél: 418-962-9848; *Téléc:* 418-962-2458
info@cegep-sept-iles.qc.ca
www.cegep-sept-iles.qc.ca
Donald Bhérer, Directeur général
donald.bherer@cegep-sept-iles.qc.ca

Publications
D'Épiderme

***Sherbrooke:* Cégep de Sherbrooke**
475, rue du Cégep, Sherbrooke, QC J1E 4K1, Canada
Tél: 819-564-6350; *Téléc:* 819-564-1579
communications@cegepsherbrooke.qc.ca
www.cegepsherbrooke.qc.ca
Grades: Préuniv., Techniques, Form. cont.
Enrollment: 6000
Sylvain Saint-Cyr, Directeur général

Publications
in Extremis

***Sorel-Tracy:* Cégep de Sorel-Tracy**
3000, boul Tracy, Sorel-Tracy, QC J3R 5B9, Canada
Tél: 450-742-6651; *Téléc:* 450-742-1878
info@cegep-sorel-tracy.qc.ca
www.cegep-sorel-tracy.qc.ca
Grades: Préuniv., Techniques, Form. cont.
Fabienne Desroches, Directrice générale

Publications
L'Exemplaire

***St-Georges:* Cégep Beauce-Appalaches**
1055, 116e rue, St-Georges, QC G5Y 3G1, Canada
Tél: 418-228-8896; *Téléc:* 418-228-0562
info@cegepbceapp.qc.ca
www.cegepbceapp.qc.ca
Enrollment: 1424
Charles Garneau, Directeur général
cgarneau@cegepbceapp.qc.ca

***Thetford Mines:* Cégep de Thetford**
671, boul Frontenac ouest, Thetford Mines, QC G6G 1N1, Canada
Tél: 418-338-8591; *Téléc:* 418-338-6691
www.cegep-ra.qc.ca
Enrollment: 1000
François Dornier, Directeur général

***Trois-Rivières:* Cégep de Trois-Rivières**
P.O. Box 97
3500, rue De Courval, Trois-Rivières, QC G9A 5E6, Canada
Tél: 819-376-1721; *Téléc:* 819-693-8023
webmestre@cegeptr.qc.ca
www.cegeptr.qc.ca
Grades: Préuniv., Techniques, Form. cont.
Enrollment: 9475
Jean-Denis Leduc, Directeur général

Publications
La Gifle

***Victoriaville:* Cégep de Victoriaville**
475, rue Notre-Dame est, Victoriaville, QC G6P 4B3, Canada
Tél: 819-758-6401; *Téléc:* 819-758-6026
Ligne sans frais: 1-888-284-9476
information@cgpvicto.qc.ca
www.cgpvicto.qc.ca
Vincent Guay, Directeur général
guay.vincent@cgpvicto.qc.ca

Publications
La Réplique

Schools: Specialized

First Nations

***Betsiamites:* École Nussim du conseil de bande de Betsiamites**
P.O. Box 70
4, rue Pulis, Betsiamites, QC G0H 1B0, Canada
Tél: 418-567-2215
Grades: K./Elem.

***Betsiamites:* École secondaire Uashkaikan du conseil de bande de Betsiamites**
63, rue Messek, Betsiamites, QC G0H 1B0, Canada
Tél: 418-567-2271
Grades: Sec.

***Côte-Nord-du-Golfe-du-Saint-Lau:* École Olamen du Conseil des Montagnais (La Romaine)**
P.O. Box 222
Côte-Nord-du-Golfe-du-Saint-Lau, QC G0G 1M0, Canada
Tél: 418-229-2450
Grades: K./Elem./Sec.

***Kawawachikamach:* École Jimmy Sandy Memorial**
P.O. Box 5115
Kawawachikamach, QC G0G 2Z0, Canada
Tél: 418-585-3811
Grades: K./Elem./Sec.

***Manawan:* École Otapi**
470, rue Otapi, Manawan, QC J0K 1M0, Canada
Tél: 819-971-1379
lucpatin@hotmail.com
www.monecole-myschool.com/otapi/
Grades: Sec.

***Manawan:* École Simon P. Ottawa**
150, rue Wapoc, Manawan, QC J0K 1M0, Canada
Tél: 819-971-8817; *Téléc:* 819-871-8872
Grades: K./Elem./Sec.

***Mashteuiatsh:* École Amishk**
1725, rue Amishk, Mashteuiatsh, QC G0W 2H0, Canada
Tél: 418-275-2473
Grades: K./Elem.

***Mashteuiatsh:* École secondaire Kassinu Mamu**
1711, rue Amishk, Mashteuiatsh, QC G0W 2H0, Canada
Tél: 418-275-2473
kassinumamu@monecole-myschool.com
www.monecole-myschool.com/kassinumamu/
Grades: Sec.

***Natashquan:* École Uauitshitun Natashquan**
Pointe-Parent
Natashquan, QC G0G 2E0, Canada
Tél: 418-726-3368
Grades: K./Elem./Sec.

***Obedjiwan:* École primaire Niska**
70, rue Niska, Obedjiwan, QC G0W 3B0, Canada
Tél: 819-974-8842
Grades: K./Elem.

***Obedjiwan:* École secondaire Mikisiw**
92, rue Tcikatnaw, Obedjiwan, QC G0W 3B0, Canada
Tél: 819-974-1221
Grades: Sec.

***Pikogan:* École Mikwan**
P.O. Box 36
RR#4, Pikogan, QC J9T 3A3, Canada
Tél: 819-732-5213
ecole@pikogan.com
Grades: Gr. K./Elem.

***Sept-Iles:* École Johnny-Pilot du conseil des Montagnais de Sept-Iles et Maliotenam**
1, rue Ukuiass, Sept-Iles, QC G4R 5V2, Canada
Tél: 418-968-1550
Grades: K./Elem.

***Sept-Iles:* École Manikanetish du conseil des Montagnais de Sept-Iles et Maliotenam**
P.O. Box 8000
1, rue Ukuiass, Sept-Iles, QC G4R 2N5, Canada
Tél: 418-968-1550
Grades: Sec.

***Sept-Iles:* École Tshishteshinu du conseil des Montagnais de Sept-Iles et Maliotenam**
P.O. Box 430
Sept-Iles, QC G0G 2B0, Canada
Tél: 418-927-2956
Grades: K./Elem.

***Shefferville:* Kanatamat Tsitipenitamunu**
P.O. Box 1000
224, rue Lorraine, Shefferville, QC G0G 2T0, Canada
Tél: 418-585-2116
Grades: K./Elem./Sec.

***St-Augustin:* École Pakuashipi**
P.O. Box 68
St-Augustin, QC G0G 2R0, Canada
Tél: 418-947-2729
Grades: Gr. K./Elem./Sec.

***Wendake:* École Hetaie**
20, rue de l'Ours, Wendake, QC G0A 4V0, Canada
Tél: 418-842-3740
Grades: K./Elem.

***Weymontachie:* École primaire Seskitin**
P.O. Box 214 A
Weymontachie, QC G0X 3R0, Canada
Tél: 819-666-2226
ericniquay@hotmail.com
http://www.monecole-myschool.com/seskitin/
Grades: Elem.

***Weymontachie:* École secondaire Waratinak**
P.O. Box 222 B
Weymontachie, QC G0X 3R0, Canada
Tél: 819-666-2232
waratinak@monecole-myschool.com
www.monecole-myschool.com/waratinak/

Schools: Independent & Private

Catholic

***Ayer's Cliff:* Collège Notre-Dame des Servites**
470, rue Main, Ayer's Cliff, QC J0B 1C0, Canada
Tél: 819-838-4221; *Téléc:* 819-838-4222
courrier@cnds.qc.ca
www.cnds.qc.ca
Grades: Sec.; Pens. & Ext.
Confessionnelle catholique.
Éric Faucher, Directeur général
dirgen@cnds.qc.ca

***Baie-Comeau:* École secondaire Jean-Paul II**
20, av de Ramezay, Baie-Comeau, QC G4Z 1B2, Canada
Tél: 418-296-6212; *Téléc:* 418-296-3654
admjpii@globetrotter.net
www.jpii.ca
Grades: Sec.
Dorsay Talaï, Directrice générale

***Coaticook:* Collège Rivier**
343, rue St-Jacques nord, Coaticook, QC J1A 2R2, Canada
Tél: 819-849-4833; *Téléc:* 819-849-3621
crivier@crivier.qc.ca
www.crivier.qc.ca
Grades: Sec.; Pens. & Ext.
Enrollment: 250
École catholique, privée et mixte.
Benoit Hélie, Directeur général

***Dolbeau-Mistassini:* Juvénat Saint-Jean**
200, boul Wallberg, Dolbeau-Mistassini, QC G8L 6A5, Canada
Tél: 418-276-3340; *Téléc:* 418-276-1757
juvenatstjean@hotmail.com
www.juvenatstjean.ca
Grades: Sec.; Pens. & Ext.
Marc Tremblay, Directeur général

***Grenville-sur-la-Rouge:* Séminaire du Sacré-Coeur**
2738, rte 148, Grenville-sur-la-Rouge, QC J0V 1B0, Canada
Tél: 819-242-0957; *Téléc:* 819-242-4089
administration@seminairedusacrecoeur.qc.ca
www.seminairedusacrecoeur.qc.ca
Grades: Sec.; Pens. & Ext.
Richard Dupuis, Directeur

***Lan-Saint-Jean:* Séminaire Marie-Reine-du-Clergé**
1569, rte 169 Métabetchouan-Lac-à-la-Croix, Lan-Saint-Jean, QC G8G 1A8, Canada
Tél: 418-349-2816; *Téléc:* 418-349-8055
direction@smrc.qc.ca
www.smrc.qc.ca
Grades: Sec.; Pens. & Ext.
Jacques Ménard, Directeur général

***Lévis:* École Sainte-Famille (Fraternité St-Pie X) inc.**
10425, boul de la Rive-Sud, Lévis, QC G6V 7M5, Canada
Tél: 418-837-3028; *Téléc:* 418-837-7070
fspx@ecolestefamille.ca
Grades: Prim./Sec.
Jean de l'Estourbeillon, Directeur

***Montréal:* Collège de Montréal**
1931, rue Sherbrooke ouest, Montréal, QC H3H 1E3, Canada
Tél: 514-933-7397; *Téléc:* 514-933-3225
cdm@college-montreal.qc.ca
www.college-montreal.qc.ca
Grades: Sec.
École catholique privée.
Jacques Giguère, Directeur général

***Montréal:* École Augustin Roscelli inc.**
11960, boul de l'Acadie, Montréal, QC H3M 2T7, Canada
Tél: 514-334-0057; *Téléc:* 514-334-4060
info@ecoleaugustinroscelli.com
www.ecoleaugustinroscelli.com
Grades: Mat./Prim.
École Catholique, privée, mixte.
Sr. Rosa Rossi, Soeur Supérieure

***Montréal:* École Marie-Clarac**
3530, boul Gouin est, Montréal, QC H1H 1B7, Canada
Tél: 514-322-1161; *Téléc:* 514-322-4364
dcormier@marie-clarac.qc.ca
www.ecolemarie-clarac.qc.ca
Grades: Mat./Prim./Sec.; mixte; filles
Enrollment: 1300
Garderie et préscolaire/primaire (mixte); secondaire (filles); dirigée par les Soeurs de Charité de Sainte-Marie.
Sr. Martine Côté, Directrice générale

***Montréal:* École Saint-Joseph (1985) inc.**
4080, rue De Lorimier, Montréal, QC H2K 3X7, Canada
Tél: 514-526-8288; *Téléc:* 514-526-5498
secretariat@stjoseph.qc.ca
www.stjoseph.qc.ca
Grades: Mat./Prim.
Marc Tremblay, Directeur général
mtremblay@stjoseph.qc.ca

***Montréal:* Externat Mont-Jésus-Marie**
2755, ch de la Côte-Ste-Catherine, Montréal, QC H3T 1B5, Canada
Tél: 514-272-1035
www.montjesusmarie.com
Grades: Mat./Prim.
Sylvie Gagné, Directrice générale

***Montréal:* Pensionnat du Saint-Nom-de-Marie**
628, ch de la Côte Ste-Catherine, Montréal, QC H2V 2C5, Canada
Tél: 514-735-5261; *Téléc:* 514-735-5266
admission@psnm.qc.ca
www.psnm.qc.ca
Grades: Sec.; filles; Pens. & Ext.
Enrollment: 1020
Sr. Kathleen Caissy, Directrice
kcaissy@psnm.qc.ca

***Montréal:* The Sacred Heart School of Montreal**
3635, av Atwater, Montréal, QC H3H 1Y4, Canada
Tel: 514-937-2845; *Fax:* 514-937-8214
admissions@sacredheart.qc.ca
www.sacredheart.qc.ca
Grades: Sec.; Girls; Eng.; Res & Day
One of Canada's oldest, independent Catholic schools for girls.
Mr. Shawn O'Donnell, Head of School

***Montréal-Nord:* École secondaire Marie-Victorin inc.**
10748, boul Saint-Vital, Montréal-Nord, QC H1H 4T3, Canada
Tél: 514-322-8111; *Téléc:* 512—
dg@marievictorin.qc.ca
www.marievictorin.qc.ca
Grades: Sec.
Louise Bergeron, Directrice
Publications
Le Matulu

***Québec:* Collège Jésus-Marie de Sillery**
2047, ch St-Louis, Québec, QC G1T 1P3, Canada
Tél: 418-687-9250; *Téléc:* 418-687-9847
dir.gen@cjmds.qc.ca
www.cjmds.qc.ca
Grades: Prim./Sec.; filles; Pens. & Ext.
Dirigé par la Congrégation des Religieuses de Jésus-Marie; programme enrichi au primaire, programme d'éducation internationale au secondaire.
Sr. Odile Fortin, Directrice

***Québec:* Collège Saint-Charles-Garnier**
1150, boul René-Lévesque ouest, Québec, QC G1S 1V7, Canada
Tél: 418-681-0107; *Téléc:* 418-681-9631
cscg@collegegarnier.qc.ca
www.collegegarnier.qc.ca
Grades: Sec.
Propriétaire du Collège des Jésuites.
Mario Gagnon, Directeur général
mgagnon@collegegarnier.qc.ca

***Québec:* Externat Saint-Coeur de Marie**
30, av des Cascades, Québec, QC G1E 2J8, Canada
Tél: 418-663-0605; *Téléc:* 418-663-9484
richard.morin@pscm.ca
www.pscm.ca
Grades: Prim.; Pens. & Ext.
Enrollment: 411
Richard Morin, Directeur général

***Rosemère:* Externat Sacré-Coeur**
535, rue Lefrançois, Rosemère, QC J7A 4R5, Canada
Tél: 450-621-6720; *Téléc:* 450-621-1525
courrier@externat.qc.ca
www.externat.qc.ca
Grades: Sec.
Enrollment: 1000
Denyse Hébert, Directrice générale

***Saint-Augustin-de-Desmaures:* Séminaire Saint-François**
4900, rue Saint-Félix, Saint-Augustin-de-Desmaures, QC G3A 1X3, Canada
Tél: 418-872-0611; *Téléc:* 418-872-5845
l.lessard@ss-f.com
www.ss-f.com
Grades: Sec.; Pens. & Ext.
Père Jean-Marc Boulé, Directeur général/Directeur des élèves
jmb@ss-f.com

***Saint-Hyacinthe:* École secondaire Saint-Joseph de Saint-Hyacinthe**
2875, av Bourdages nord, Saint-Hyacinthe, QC J2S 5S3, Canada
Tél: 450-774-3775; *Téléc:* 450-774-6340
www.essj.qc.ca
Grades: Sec.; Pens. & Ext.
Pierre Duclos, Directeur général
pduclos@essj.qc.ca

***Saint-Laurent:* École bilingue Notre-Dame de Sion**
1775, boul Décarie, Saint-Laurent, QC H4L 3N5, Canada
Tél: 514-747-3895; *Téléc:* 514-747-5492
cnicolet@ebnds.ca
www.ebnds.ca
Grades: Mat./Prim.; Fr./Angl.
Véronique Lemieux-Boyer, Directrice générale

***Saint-Michel-de-Bellechasse:* Collège Dina-Bélanger**
1, rue St-Georges, Saint-Michel-de-Bellechasse, QC G0R 3S0, Canada
Tél: 418-884-2360; *Téléc:* 418-884-3274
colldb@globetrotter.net
www.collegedina-belanger.qc.ca
Grades: Sec.; Pens. & Ext.
Enrollment: 300
Dirigé par les Relgieuses de Jésus-Marie.
Sr Yvette Rioux, Directrice générale

***Sherbrooke:* Collège du Sacré-Coeur**
155, rue Belvédère nord, Sherbrooke, QC J1H 4A7, Canada
Tél: 819-569-9457; *Téléc:* 819-820-0636
info@cscoeur.ca
www.college-sacre-coeur.qc.ca
Grades: Sec.; filles
Enrollment: 500
Daniel Léveillé, Directeur général

***St-Bruno-de-Montarville:* Séminaire Sainte-Trinité**
1475, ch des Vingt, St-Bruno-de-Montarville, QC J3V 4P6, Canada
Tél: 450-653-2409; *Téléc:* 450-441-4786
secretariat@ste-trinite.qc.ca
www.ste-trinite.qc.ca
Grades: Sec.
Guy Saumure, Directeur général

***Trois-Rivières:* Séminaire Saint-Joseph**
858, rue Laviolette, Trois-Rivières, QC G9A 5S3, Canada
Tél: 819-376-4459; *Téléc:* 819-378-0607
andrem@ssj.qc.ca
www.ssj.qc.ca
Grades: Sec.; garçons; Pens. & Ext.
Michel Trépanier, Directeur général

Special Education

***Montréal:* L'École à Pas de Géant (Montréal)**
Giant Steps School (Montréal)
5460, av Connaught, Montréal, QC H4V 1X7, Canada
Tél: 514-935-1911
info@giantstepsmontreal.com
giantstepsmontreal.com
Grades: Mat./Prim./Sec; Éd. spéc.
Favoriser l'éducation et l'insertion scolaire et sociale des jeunes autistes.
Pierre Martin, Président, Conseil d'administration

***Montréal:* École orale de Montréal pour les sourds inc.**
Montreal Oral School for the Deaf Inc.
4670, rue Sainte-Catherine ouest, Montréal, QC H3Z 1S5, Canada
Tél: 514-488-4946; *Téléc:* 514-488-0802
info@montrealoralschool.com
www.montrealoralschool.com
Grades: Mat./Prim.; Éd. spéc.
Mission: enseigner aux enfants sourds à parler & à communiquer verbalement. Programmes d'études et programmes d'intégration; services cliniques; counseling.
Martha Pérusse, Directrice

***Montréal:* École Peter Hall inc.**
Peter Hall School
Campus Côte-Vertu & Centre administratif
840, boul de la Côte-Vertu, Montréal, QC H4L 1Y4, Canada
Tél: 514-747-4075; *Téléc:* 514-747-0164
cote-vertu@peterhall.qc.ca
www.peterhall.qc.ca
Grades: Mat./Prim./Sec.; Fr./Angl.;Éd.Spec.
Services éducatifs pour des élèves de 4 à 21 ans présentant une déficience intellectuelle. Campus Ouimet: 1200, rue Ouimet, St-Laurent, 514-748-1050, courriel: ouimet@peterhall.qc.ca.
Jean Laliberté, Directeur général

***Saint-Laurent:* Summit School**
École le Sommet
1750, rue Deguire, Saint-Laurent, QC H4L 1M7, Canada
Tel: 514-744-2867; *Fax:* 514-744-6410
admin@summit-school.com
www.summit-schol.com
Grades: Pre./Elem./Sec.; Spec. Ed.; Eng.
Enrollment: 450
Educational services for special needs students, from ages 4 to 21, with developmental disabilities such as autism, behavioral disturbances and other associated problems.
Lucy Orsini, Registrar

Independent & Private Schools

***Baie-d'Urfé:* École internationale allemande Alexander von Humboldt inc. (AvH)**
Alexander von Humboldt German International School Inc.
216, rue Victoria, Baie-d'Urfé, QC H9X 2H9, Canada
Tél: 514-457-2886; *Téléc:* 514-457-2885
avh@avh.montreal.qc.ca
www.avh.montreal.qc.ca
Grades: Mat./Prim./Sec.; Deutsche/Fr./Eng.
Environnement multilingue: allemand, anglais, français; sciences naturelles & sociales; arts; Dipl. d'études sec. du Québec & bacc. allemand international; Deutsches Sprachdiplom der Kultusministerkonferenz.
Dr. Jörg Klinkert, Directeur

***Beauceville:* École Jésus-Marie de Beauceville**
670, 9e av est, Beauceville, QC G5X 3P6, Canada
Tél: 418-774-3709; *Téléc:* 418-774-5749
secretariat@ejm.qc.ca
ww.ejm.qc.ca
Grades: Sec.; Pens. & Ext.
Enrollment: 80
Monique Lambert, Directrice générale

***Boisbriand:* L'Académie des jeunes filles Beth Tziril**
241, av Beth Halevy, Boisbriand, QC J7E 4H4, Canada
Tél: 450-419-4085; *Téléc:* 418-434-5440
cpetash@yahoo.com
Grades: Mat./Prim./Sec.
Abraham Halpern, Directeur

***Boucherville:* École Les Trois Saisons**
570, boul de Mortagne, Boucherville, QC J4B 5E4, Canada
Tél: 450-641-2000
3saisons@biz.videotron.ca
Grades: Prim.
Monique Mathieu, Directrice générale

***Brossard:* Académie Marie-Laurier**
Marie-Laurier Academy
1555, av Stravinski, Brossard, QC J4X 2H5, Canada
Tél: 450-923-2787; *Téléc:* 450-923-2291
academie@marielaurier.com
www.marielaurier.com
Grades: Mat./Prim./Sec.; Fr./Angl.
Enseignement bilingue.
Monique Bergeron, Directrice

***Châteauguay:* Collège Héritage de Châteauguay inc.**
P.O. Box 80036
270, boul d'Youville, Châteauguay, QC J6J 5X2, Canada
Tél: 450-692-5578; *Téléc:* 450-692-5579
info@collegeheritage.ca
www.collegeheritage.ca
Grades: Prim./Sec.
Enrollment: 570
Jean-Guy Brais, Directeur

***Chicoutimi:* École Apostolique de Chicoutimi (2A3)**
913, rue Jacques-Cartier est, Chicoutimi, QC G7H 2A3, Canada
Tél: 418-549-3302; *Téléc:* 418-615-2030
ecole.apostolique@globetrotter.net
www.soeursantoniennes.org
Grades: Prim.
Janick Dumas, Directrice

***Chicoutimi:* Le Lycée du Saguenay**
658, rue Racine est, Chicoutimi, QC G7H 1V1, Canada
Tél: 418-543-4448; *Téléc:* 418-543-1716
Grades: Sec.
Jean-François Gagné, Directeur

***Chicoutimi:* Séminaire de Chicoutimi**
679, rue Chabanel, Chicoutimi, QC G7H 1Z7, Canada
Tél: 418-549-0190; *Téléc:* 418-549-1524
lycee.seminaire@lyce-sdec.qc.ca
www.sdec.qc.ca
Grades: Sec.
Marcel Bergeron, Directeur

***Compton:* École primaire Des Arbrisseaux**
6288, rte Louis-S.-St-Laurent, Compton, QC J0B 1L0, Canada
Tél: 819-835-9503; *Téléc:* 819-835-9506
direction@arbrisseaux.qc.ca
www.arbrisseaux.qc.ca
Grades: Prim.; Pens. & Ext.
Brigitte Raymond, Directrice

***Côte Saint-Luc:* L'Académie Hébraïque Inc.**
Hebrew Academy
5700, av Kellert, Côte Saint-Luc, QC H4W 1T4, Canada
Tél: 514-489-5321; *Téléc:* 514-489-8607
www.ha-mtl.org
Grades: Mat./Prim./Sec.; Angl./Fr.
Linda Lehrer, Directrice
director@ha-montreal.org

***Dollard-des-Ormeaux:* Collège de l'Ouest de l'Ile**
West Island College
851, rue Tecumseh, Dollard-des-Ormeaux, QC H9B 2L2, Canada
Tél: 514-683-4660; *Téléc:* 514-683-1702
office@westislandcollege.qc.ca
www.westislandcollege.qc.ca
Grades: Sec.; Fr./Angl.
Martin Bailly, Directeur des services éducatifs

***Dollard-des-Ormeaux:* Emmanuel Christian School**
École chrétienne Emmanuel
4698, boul St-Jean, Dollard-des-Ormeaux, QC H9H 4S5, Canada
Tel: 514-696-6430; *Fax:* 514-696-3687
ladirection@emmanuelchristianschool.qc.ca
www.emmanuelchristianschool.qc.ca
Grades: Pre./Elem./Sec.; Eng./Fr.
Enrollment: 300
A Christian education, with instruction in English & French.
Jack Bauer, Director

***Dollard-des-Ormeaux:* Hebrew Foundation School**
École de formation hébraïque
2, rue Hope, Dollard-des-Ormeaux, QC H9A 2V5, Canada
Tel: 514-684-6270; *Fax:* 514-684-1998
hebrewfoundation@total.net
206.132.176.122/BJEC_HebrewFoundation/index.php
Grades: Pre./Elem.; Eng./Fr.
Programmes include M.E.L.S. French Immersion, traditional Jewish subjects, as well as the standard curriculum, dance & visual arts; instruction in English, French & Hebrew.
Rabbi Zev Lanton, Principal

***Dorval:* Queen of Angels Academy**
100, boul Bouchard, Dorval, QC H9S 1A7, Canada
Tel: 514-636-0900
jdion@qaa.qc.ca
www.qaa.qc.ca
Grades: Sec.; Girls; Eng.
Joanne Dion, Directrice

Drummondville: **Collège Saint-Bernard**
25, av des Frères, Drummondville, QC J2B 6A2, Canada
Tél: 819-478-3330; *Téléc:* 819-478-2582
csb@csb.qc.ca
www.csb.qc.ca
Grades: Prim./Sec.; Pens. & Ext.
Alexandre Cusson, Directeur général

Gatineau: **Collège Saint-Alexandre**
2425, rue Saint-Louis, Gatineau, QC J8V 1E7, Canada
Tél: 819-561-3812; *Téléc:* 819-561-5205
www.college-stalexandre.qc.ca
Grades: Sec.
Mario Vachon, Directeur général
mario.vachon@i-alex.qc.ca

Gatineau: **Collège Saint-Joseph de Hull**
174, rue Notre-Dame-de-l'Ile, Gatineau, QC J8X 3T4, Canada
Tél: 819-776-3123; *Téléc:* 819-776-0992
direction@collegestjoseph.ca
www.collegestjoseph.ca
Grades: Sec.; filles
Sandra Beauchamp, Directrice générale

Gatineau: **École Montessori de l'Outaouais inc.**
161, rue Principale, Gatineau, QC J9H 7H4, Canada
Tél: 819-682-3299; *Téléc:* 819-682-7484
info.montessori@videotron.ca
www.montessori-outaouais.qc.ca
Grades: Mat./Prim.
Paul Dumetz, Directeur

Granby: **Collège Mont-Sacré-Coeur**
210, rue Denison est, Granby, QC J2G 8E3, Canada
Tél: 450-372-6882; *Téléc:* 450-372-9219
info@college-msc.qc.ca
www.college-msc.qc.ca
Grades: Sec.
Enrollment: 870
Programme Exploration; Programme sports instensifs; Programme anglais intensif.
Claude Lacroix, S.C., Directeur général

Granby: **École secondaire du Verbe Divin**
P.O. Box 786
1021, rue Cowie, Granby, QC J2G 8W8, Canada
Tél: 450-378-1074; *Téléc:* 450-378-4566
pedagogie@verbedivin.com
www.verbedivin.com
Grades: Sec.
Programmes - Immersion anglaise; Sports-Élite; Arts-Élite; Voyages; Programme Découverte.
Pierre Labbé, Directeur

Joliette: **Académie Antoine Manseau**
P.O. Box 410
20, rue St-Charles-Borromée sud, Joliette, QC J6E 3Z9, Canada
Tél: 450-753-4271; *Téléc:* 450-753-3661
courier@aamanseau.qc.ca
www.amanseau.qc.ca
Grades: Sec.
Alain Bergmans, Directeur général

Joliette: **École les Mélèzes**
393, rue de Lanaudière, Joliette, QC J6E 3L9, Canada
Tél: 450-752-4433; *Téléc:* 450-752-4337
info@lesmelezes.qc.ca
www.lesmelezes.qc.ca
Grades: Mat./Prim.; filles; Pens. & Ext.
Renée Champagne, Directrice générale

Kirkland: **Académie Marie-Claire**
18190, boul Elkas, Kirkland, QC H9J 3Y4, Canada
Tél: 514-697-9995; *Téléc:* 514-697-5575
academie@academiemarieclaire.qc.ca
www.academiemarie-claire.qc.ca
Grades: Mat./Prim.
1ère année à 6ème année. Enseignement bilingue.
Marie-Claire Martin, Directrice

Kirkland: **Kuper Academy**
#2 & #4, 2975, rue Edmond, Kirkland, QC H9H 5K5, Canada
Tel: 514-426-3007; *Fax:* 514-426-0377
admissions@kuperacademy.ca
www.kuperacademy.ca
Grades: K./Prim./Sec.; Eng.
Liberal arts, mathematics, sciences, social sciences, & creative & performing arts.
Joan Salette, Director

L'Assomption: **Collège de l'Assomption**
270, boul de l'Ange-Gardien, L'Assomption, QC J5W 1R7, Canada
Tél: 450-589-5621; *Téléc:* 450-589-2910
dirgen@classomption.qc.ca
www.classomption.qc.ca
Grades: Sec.
Robert Corriveau, Directeur général

La Pocatière: **Collège de Sainte-Anne-de-la-Pocatière**
100, 4e av, La Pocatière, QC G0R 1Z0, Canada
Tél: 418-856-3012; *Téléc:* 418-856-5611
info@leadercsa.com
www.leadercsa.com
Grades: Sec.; Pens. & Ext.
Enrollment: 600
Le programme Leader est offert.
Martine Dubé, Directrice générale

La Prairie: **Collège Jean de la Mennais**
870, ch de St-Jean, La Prairie, QC J5R 2L5, Canada
Tél: 450-659-7657; *Téléc:* 450-659-3717
administration@jeandelamennais.qc.ca
www.jeandelamennais.qc.ca
Grades: Prim./Sec.
Enrollment: 1400
Serge Courtemanche, Directeur général

Laval: **Académie Lavalloise**
5290, boul des Laurentides Auteuil, Laval, QC H7K 2J8, Canada
Tél: 450-628-1430; *Téléc:* 450-628-1431
info@academielavalloise.com
www.academielavalloise.com
Grades: Mat./Prim.
Enrollment: 300
David C. Zakaïb, Directeur
david.zakaib@academielavalloise.com

Laval: **Collège Laval**
275, rue Laval, Laval, QC H7C 1W8, Canada
Tél: 450-661-7714; *Téléc:* 450-661-7146
secretariat@collegelaval.qc.ca
www.collegelaval.qc.ca
Grades: Sec.
Centre sportif, salle de théâtre, laboratoires informatiques, bibliothèque.
Richard Roy, Directeur

Laval: **Collège Letendre**
1000, boul de l'Avenir, Laval, QC H7N 6J6, Canada
Tél: 450-688-9933; *Téléc:* 450-688-3591
info@collegeletendre.qc.ca
www.collegeletendre.com
Grades: Sec.
Yves Legault, Directeur

Laval: **École Charles-Perrault (Laval)**
1750, boul de la Concorde est, Laval, QC H7G 2E7, Canada
Tél: 450-975-2233; *Téléc:* 450-975-2248
direction@charles-perrault-laval.com
www.ecolecharlesperrault.com/laval/
Grades: Mat./Prim./Sec.
Enrollment: 380
Denis Faber, Directeur général (Pierrefonds)

Laval: **École Démosthène**
1565, boul Saint-Martin ouest, Laval, QC H7S 1N1, Canada
Tél: 450-972-1800; *Téléc:* 450-972-1345
Grades: Mat./Prim.
Enrollment: 218
École privée de la communauté greque orthodoxe de Laval; formation générale; langues d'enseignement: française, greque.
Liza Henry, Directrice
liza.demonsthene@videotron.ca

Laval: **École Notre-Dame de Nareg**
555, 67E Av, Laval, QC H7V 2M3, Canada
Tél: 450-680-1168
naregvarjaran@hotmail.com
Grades: Mat./Prim.
L'Abbé Paul Kazandjian, Directeur

Lévis: **Juvénat Notre-Dame du Saint-Laurent**
30, rue du Juvénat, Lévis, QC G6V 6P5, Canada
Tél: 418-839-9592; *Téléc:* 418-839-5605
juvenat@jnd.qc.ca
www.jnd.qc.ca
Grades: Sec.
Claude Gélinas, Directeur général
cgelinas@jnd.qc.ca

Longueuil: **Collège Charles-Lemoyne inc. Administration générale/Campus Longueuil**
901, ch Tiffin, Longueuil, QC J4P 3G6, Canada
Tél: 514-875-0505; *Téléc:* 450-463-4494
college@cclemoyne.edu
www.cclemoyne.edu
Grades: Sec.
Enrollment: 2700
Campus Longueuil II: 2301, boul Fernand-Lafontaine; Campus Ville de Sainte-Catherine: 125, place Charles-Lemoyne.
Réjean Palardy, Directeur général

Longueuil: **Collège Français - Primaire Longueuil**
1391, rue Beauregard, Longueuil, QC J4K 2M3, Canada
Tél: 514-495-2581; *Téléc:* 514-279-5131
info@collegefrancais.ca
www.collegefrancais.ca
Grades: Mat./Prim.

Longueuil: **Collège Notre-Dame-de-Lourdes**
845, ch Tiffin, Longueuil, QC J4P 3G5, Canada
Tél: 450-670-4740; *Téléc:* 450-670-2800
collegendl@ndl.qc.ca
www.ndl.qc.ca
Grades: Sec.
Enrollment: 950
Lucie D'Amour, Directrice générale

Mont-Saint-Hilaire: **Collège Saint-Hilaire inc.**
800, rue Rouillard, Mont-Saint-Hilaire, QC J3G 4S6, Canada
Tél: 450-467-7001; *Téléc:* 450-467-9040
info@csh.qc.ca
www.csh.qc.ca
Grades: Sec.
Enrollment: 600
Diane Lavoie, Directrice générale

Montebello: **Sedbergh School**
École Sedbergh
810, Côte Azélie, Montebello, QC J0V 1L0, Canada
Tel: 819-423-5523; *Fax:* 819-423-5769
admissions@sedbergh.com
www.sedberghschool.ca
Grades: Elem./Sec.; Eng.; Res. & Day
Enrollment: 80
A co-educational boarding school, with a focus on academics, athletics & outdoor programs, & environmental education.
Andrew Blair, Headmaster

Montréal: **Académie Beth Rivkah**
5001, rue Vézina, Montréal, QC H3W 1C2, Canada
Tél: 514-731-3681; *Téléc:* 514-342-4956
info@bethrivkah.com
www.bethrivkah.com
Grades: Mat./Prim./Sec.; filles
Enrollment: 500
Une école pour filles juives, fondée en 1956 par le Rebbe Menachem Schneerson de Loubavitch.
Rabbin Leib Kramer, Directeur

Montréal: **Académie Kells**
Kells Academy
6865, boul Maisonneuve ouest, Montréal, QC H4B 1T1, Canada
Tél: 514-485-8565; *Téléc:* 514-485-8505
kadmin@kells.ca
www.kells.ca
Grades: Prim./Sec.; Fr./Angl.; Éd. spéc.
École mixte. Enseignement bilingue.
Irene Woods, Directrice

Montréal: **Académie Louis-Pasteur**
7220, rue Marie-Victorin, Montréal, QC H1G 2J5, Canada
Tél: 514-322-6123; *Téléc:* 514-322-6787
info@academielouispasteur.com
www.academielouispasteur.com
Grades: Mat./Prim.
École primaire privée qui accueille des enfants de la maternelle à la 6e année.
Gisèle Bisaillon, Directrice générale

Montréal: **Académie Michèle-Provost inc.**
1517, av des Pins ouest, Montréal, QC H3G 1B3, Canada
Tél: 514-934-0596; *Téléc:* 514-934-2390
info@academiemicheleprovost.qc.ca
www.academiemicheleprovost.qc.ca
Grades: Prim./Sec.; Pens. & Ext.
Michèle Provost, Directrice
m.provost@academiemicheleprovost.qc.

Montréal: Académie Saint-Louis de France
4430, rue Bélanger est, Montréal, QC H1T 1B3, Canada
Tél: 514-725-0340; *Téléc:* 514-725-1460
pascal.foucault@academiesldf.ca
academiestlouisdefrance.googlepages.com
Grades: Mat./Prim.
Pascal Foucault, Directeur

Montréal: Centennial Academy
L'Académie Centennale
3641, av Prud'homme, Montréal, QC H4A 3H6, Canada
Tel: 514-486-5533; *Fax:* 514-486-1401
aburgos@centennial.qc.ca
www.centennial.qc.ca
Grades: Sec.; Eng.
Angéla Burgos, Directrice

Montréal: Centre d'intégration scolaire inc.
6361, 6e av, Montréal, QC H1Y 2R7, Canada
Tél: 514-374-8490; *Téléc:* 514-374-3978
pallard@cisi.qc.ca
www.cisi.qc.ca
Grades: Prim./Sec.; Éd. spéc.
Patrice Allard, Directeur général

Montréal: Centre François-Michelle
10095, rue Meunier, Montréal, QC H3L 2Z1, Canada
Tel: 514-381-4418; *Fax:* 514-381-2895
dsormany@francois-michelle.qc.ca
www.francois-michelle.qc.ca
Grades: Mat./Prim./Sec.; Éd. spéc.
Danielle Sormany, Directrice générale

Montréal: Collège Beaubois
4901, rue du Collège Beaubois, Montréal, QC H8Y 3T4, Canada
Tél: 514-684-7642; *Téléc:* 514-684-3011
info@collegebeaubois.qc.ca
www.collegebeaubois.qc.ca
Grades: Mat./Prim./Sec.
Daniel Trottier, Directeur général

Montréal: Collège Charlemagne inc.
5000, rue Pilon, Montréal, QC H9K 1G4, Canada
Tél: 514-626-7060; *Téléc:* 514-626-1654
admin@collegecharlemagne.com
www.collegecharlemagne.com
Grades: Mat./Prim./Sec.
Julie Beaudet, Directrice générale
jbeaudet@collegecharlemagne.com
Claudette Bélanger, Registraire
cbelanger@collegecharlemagne.com

Montréal: Collège Français - Secondaire Montréal
185, av Fairmount ouest, Montréal, QC H2T 2M6, Canada
Tél: 514-495-2581; *Téléc:* 514-279-2823
info@collegefrancais.ca
www.collegefrancais.ca
Grades: Sec.; Pens. & Ext.
Colette Portal, Directrice

Montréal: Collège international Marie de France
4635, ch Queen Mary, Montréal, QC H3W 1W3, Canada
Tél: 514-737-1177; *Téléc:* 514-737-0789
college@mariedefrance.qc.ca
www.mariedefrance.qc.ca
Grades: Mat./Prim./Sec.
Enrollment: 1800
Brigitte Peytier, Directrice générale

Montréal: Collège Jean-Eudes
3535, boul Rosemont, Montréal, QC H1X 1K7, Canada
Tél: 514-376-5740; *Téléc:* 514-376-4325
info@jeaneudes.qc.ca
www.jeaneudes.qc.ca
Grades: Sec.
Enrollment: 1700
Louis Laliberté, Directeur général
llaliberte@jeaneudes.qc.ca

Montréal: Collège Mont-Royal
2165, rue Baldwin, Montréal, QC H1L 5A7, Canada
Tél: 514-351-7851; *Téléc:* 514-351-3124
mradm@collegemont-royal.qc.ca
www.collegemont-royal.qc.ca
Grades: Sec.
Anne-Marie Blais, Directrice générale

Montréal: Collège Mont-Saint-Louis
1700, boul Henri-Bourassa est, Montréal, QC H2C 1J3, Canada
Tél: 514-382-1560; *Téléc:* 514-382-5886
jldesrosiers@msl.qc.ca
www.msl.qc.ca
Grades: Sec.
André Lacroix, Directeur général
alacroix@msl.qc.ca

Montréal: Collège Notre-Dame
3791, ch Queen Mary, Montréal, QC H3V 1A8, Canada
Tél: 514-739-3371; *Téléc:* 514-739-4833
info@collegenotre-dame.qc.ca
www.collegenotre-dame.qc.ca
Grades: Sec.; Pens. & Ext.
Yvon Lafrenière, Directeur général

Montréal: College Prep International
7475, rue Sherbrooke ouest, Montréal, QC H4B 1S3, Canada
Tel: 514-489-7287; *Fax:* 514-489-7280
info@prepinternational.com
www.prepinternational.com
Grades: Elem./Sec.; Eng.
A private, non-sectarian & co-educational school.
Ursulene T. Mora, CEO

Montréal: Collège rabbinique du Canada
6405, av Westbury, Montréal, QC H3W 2X5, Canada
Tél: 514-735-2201; *Téléc:* 514-345-0275
nicoleytt@vl.videotron.ca
Grades: Mat./Prim./Sec.; garçons
Enrollment: 350
École juive orthodoxe.
Linda Rosenblum, Directrice
lindaytt@vl.videotron.ca

Montréal: Collège Rachel
5030, rue Jeanne-Mance, Montréal, QC H2V 4J8, Canada
Tél: 514-287-1944; *Téléc:* 514-287-7523
collegerachel@qc.aira.com
www.collegerachel.qc.ca
Grades: Sec.
Enrollment: 250
Véronique Geoffrion, Directrice générale

Montréal: Collège Regina Assumpta
1750, rue Sauriol est, Montréal, QC H2C 1X4, Canada
Tél: 514-382-4121; *Téléc:* 514-387-7825
info@reginaassumpta.qc.ca
www.reginaassumpta.qc.ca
Grades: Sec.
Enrollment: 2200
Programme de musique; danse; centre culturel & sportif; chapelle.
Pierre Carle, Directeur général

Montréal: Collège Reine-Marie
9300, boul Saint-Michel, Montréal, QC H1Z 3H1, Canada
Tél: 514-382-0484; *Téléc:* 514-858-1401
secretariat@reine-marie.qc.ca
www.reine-marie.qc.ca
Grades: Sec.; filles
Enrollment: 500
Johanne Kenyon, Directrice générale

Montréal: Collège Sainte-Anne de Lachine
1250, boul St-Joseph, Montréal, QC H8S 2M8, Canada
Tél: 514-637-3571; *Téléc:* 514-637-8906
lariviered@college-sainte-anne.qc.ca
www.college-sainte-anne.qc.ca
Grades: Sec.
Ugo Cavenaghi, M.Éd., M.B.A., Directeur général
cavenaghiu@college-sainte-anne.qc.ca

Montréal: Collège Sainte-Marcelline
9155, boul Gouin ouest, Montréal, QC H4K 1C3, Canada
Tél: 514-334-9651; *Téléc:* 514-334-0210
information@college.marcelline.qc.ca
college.marcelline.qc.ca
Grades: Mat./Prim/Sec.
Enseignement préscolaire et primaire pour garçons et filles; et l'enseignement secondaire pour filles.
Sr. Marielle Dion, Directrice

Montréal: Collège St-Jean-Vianney
12630, boul Gouin est, Montréal, QC H1C 1B9, Canada
Tél: 514-648-3821; *Téléc:* 514-648-8401
college@st-jean-vianney.qc.ca
www.st-jean-vianney.qc.ca
Grades: Sec.
Enrollment: 1350
Yves Lacroix, Directeur général

Montréal: Collège Ville-Marie
2850, rue Sherbrooke est, Montréal, QC H2K 1H3, Canada
Tél: 514-525-2516; *Téléc:* 514-525-7675
college@cvmarie.qc.ca
www.cvmarie.qc.ca
Grades: Sec.
Programme d'Éducation internationale.
Hélène Sirois, Directrice générale

Montréal: L'école Ali Ibn Abi Talib
1610, rue de Beauharnois ouest, Montréal, QC H4N 1J5, Canada
Tél: 514-744-0801; *Téléc:* 514-387-3457
info@ecoleali.com
www.ecoleali.com
Grades: Mat./Prim./Sec.
Bilal Jundi, Directeur

Montréal: L'École arménienne Sourp Hagop
3400, rue Nadon, Montréal, QC H4J 1P5, Canada
Tél: 514-332-1373; *Téléc:* 514-332-8303
direction@sourphagop.com
www.sourphagop.com
Grades: Mat./Prim./Sec.
Enrollment: 700
Hagop Boulgarian, Directeur

Montréal: École au Jardin Bleu inc.
1690, rue Sauvé est, Montréal, QC H2C 2A8, Canada
Tél: 514-388-4949; *Téléc:* 514-388-1970
ecole@ecoleaujardinbleu.ca
www.ecoleaujardinbleu.ca
Grades: Mat./Prim.
École privée française d'allégeance catholique.
Nicole Auclair Normand, Directrice

Montréal: École Charles-Perrault (Pierrefonds)
106, rue Cartier, Montréal, QC H8Y 1G8, Canada
Tél: 514-684-5043; *Téléc:* 514-684-5048
info@ecolecharlesperrault.com
www.ecolecharlesperrault.com/pierrefonds/
Grades: Mat./Prim.
Denis Faber, Directeur général

Montréal: L'École des Premières Lettres
5155, av de Gaspé, Montréal, QC H2T 2A1, Canada
Tél: 514-272-2229; *Téléc:* 514-272-3330
info@premiereslettres.com
www.premiereslettres.com
Grades: Mat./Prim.
Anne Deguilhem, Directrice
adeguilhem@premiereslettres.com

Montréal: École Maïmonide
Campus Jacob Safra
1900, rue Bourdon, Montréal, QC H4M 2X7, Canada
Tél: 514-744-5300; *Téléc:* 514-744-4838
admin@maimonide.ca
www.maimonide.ca
Grades: Mat./Prim./Sec.
École de la communauté Sépharade de Montréal. Campus Parkhaven: 5615, rue Parkhaven, Côte Saint-Luc, 514-488-9224 (Michelle Serano, Directrice).
Lucienne Azoulay, Directrice générale

Montréal: École Montessori Ville-Marie inc.
6520, boul Gouin ouest, Montréal, QC H4K 1B2, Canada
Tél: 514-335-6688; *Téléc:* 514-333-8988
emvm76@hotmail.com
ecolemontessorivillemarie.org
Grades: Mat./Prim.
Campus Saint-Laurent: 760, rue St-Germain; Campus Laval-Duvernay: 755, rue Roland-Forget. Enseignement bilingue.
Claudette Debbané, Directrice

Montréal: École Pasteur
12345, av de la Miséricorde, Montréal, QC H4J 2E8, Canada
Tél: 514-331-0850; *Téléc:* 514-331-2312
www.ecolepasteur.qc.ca
Grades: Mat./Prim./Sec.
Enrollment: 800
Volta Ramirez, Directeur général

Montréal: École première Mesifta du Canada
2355, av Ekers, Montréal, QC H3S 1C6, Canada
Tél: 514-738-1738
eelbaz@myway.com
Grades: Mat./Prim./Sec.
École juive.
Rabbin Chesky Buchinger, Directeur général

Montréal: École primaire Socrates
Socrates School
5777, av Wilderton, Montréal, QC H3S 2K8, Canada
Tél: 514-738-2421; *Téléc:* 514-906-0764
www.hcm-chm.org
Grades: Mat./Prim.
Langues d'enseignement: française, greque et anglaise.

Chris Adamopoulos, Directeur général
chis.adamopoulos@hcm-chm.org

***Montréal:* École Rudolf Steiner de Montréal**
4855, av Kensington, Montréal, QC H3X 3S6, Canada
Tél: 514-481-5686; *Téléc:* 514-481-5072
info@ersm.org
www.ersm.org
Grades: Mat./Prim./Sec.
Pédagogie Waldorf.
Anne Lange, Directrice

***Montréal:* École Sainte-Anne**
6855, 13e av, Montréal, QC H1X 2Z3, Canada
Tél: 514-725-4179; *Téléc:* 514-725-9962
admin@ecolesainte-anne.qc.ca
Grades: Mat./Prim.
Sr. Monique Cloutier, Directrice

***Montréal:* École secondaire Duval**
260, boul Henri-Bourassa est, Montréal, QC H3L 1B8, Canada
Tél: 514-382-6070; *Téléc:* 514-382-7207
info@ecoleduval.com
www.ecoleduval.com
Grades: Sec.
École sec. pour élèves qui ont abandonné leurs études régulières mais désirent obtenir leur diplôme dans les plus brefs délais, ou qui désirent satisfaire aux préalables d'un programme ou suivre un cours pour l'admission au collégial; cours individualisés ou cours de groupe.
Jacques Duval, Directeur

***Montréal:* École secondaire Jeanne-Normandin**
690, boul Crémazie est, Montréal, QC H2P 1E9, Canada
Tél: 514-381-3945; *Téléc:* 514-381-1695
mtremblay@jeanne-normandin.qc.ca
www.jeanne-normandin.qc.ca
Grades: Sec.; filles
Marie Robert, Directrice générale

***Montréal:* Les écoles communautaires Skver**
1235, av Ducharme, Montréal, QC H2V 1E2, Canada
Tél: 514-274-6133; *Téléc:* 514-274-1468
Grades: Mat./Prim./Sec.; Fr./Eng.
Ruth Bensimhon, Directrice
bensimhon@btmtl.ca

***Montréal:* Écoles musulmanes de Montréal**
Campus Secondaire
2255, boul Cavendish, Montréal, QC H4B 2L7, Canada
Tél: 514-484-5084; *Téléc:* 514-484-5439
info@emms.ca
www.emms.ca
Grades: Prim./Sec.
Campus Primaire: 7445, av Chester, (514) 484-8845 (Radjouh Idriss, directeur).
Fouzi Belaiboud, Directeur, Campus Secondaire

***Montréal:* Greaves Adventist Academy**
2330, av West Hill, Montréal, QC H4B 2S3, Canada
Tel: 514-486-5092; *Fax:* 514-486-0515
www.greavesadventistacademy.com
Grades: Pre./Elem./Sec.; Eng.

***Montréal:* Jewish People's Schools & Peretz Schools Inc.**
Les Écoles juives populaires et Les Écoles Peretz inc.
Also known as: JPPS-Bialik
Head Office
6502, ch Kildare, Montréal, QC H4W 3B8, Canada
Tel: 514-731-2944; *Fax:* 514-731-0343
info@jppsbialik.ca
www.jppsbialik.ca
Grades: Pre./Elem./Sec.; Eng./Fr.
One educational system retaining the names of both founding schools, united in 1971. JPPS-Bialik is a Jewish day school system in Montréal, comprising: Bialik High School, 6500, ch Kildare, 514-481-2736; JPPS Elementary School, 5170, av Van Horne, 514-731-6456; and JPPS Children's Centre, 7950 ch Wavell, 514-488-1232. Instruction in English, French & Hebrew, with language programmes in French, Hebrew, Yiddish; mathematics, sciences & technology, Judaic Studies, Social Sciences, Arts; athletics; library.
Arnold Cohen, President
Elaine Wisenthal Milech, Principal, Bialik High School
Ms. Randy Zucker, Director, JPPS Children's Centre
Adina Matas, Principal/Educational Director, JPPS

***Montréal:* Lower Canada College**
4090, av Royale, Montréal, QC H4A 2M5, Canada
Tel: 514-482-9916; *Fax:* 514-482-0195
admin@lcc.ca
www.lcc.ca
Grades: Sec.; Eng./Fr.
Christopher J. Shannon, Headmaster

***Montréal:* Loyola High School**
7272, rue Sherbrooke ouest, Montréal, QC H4B 1R2, Canada
Tel: 514-486-1101; *Fax:* 514-486-7266
admin@loyola.ca
www.loyola.ca/index.htm
Grades: Sec.; Boys; Eng.
Éric McLean, Directeur

***Montréal:* LSC Montréal**
1610 Ste-Catherine W. Suite 401, Montréal, QC H3H 2S2, Canada
Tel: 514-939-9911; *Fax:* 514-939-2223
montreal@lsc-canada.com
www.lsc-canada.com

***Montréal:* Pensionnat Notre-Dame-des-Anges**
5680, boul Rosemont, Montréal, QC H1T 2H2, Canada
Tél: 514-254-6447; *Téléc:* 514-254-6261
pnda@pnda.qc.ca
www.pnda.qc.ca/
Grades: Prim.
France Mailloux, Directrice générale

***Montréal:* The Priory School inc.**
3120 The Boulevard, Montréal, QC H3Y 1R9, Canada
Tel: 514-935-5966; *Fax:* 514-935-1428
info@priory.qc.ca
www.priory.qc.ca
Grades: Pre./Elem.; Eng.
John Marinelli, Directeur

***Montréal:* St. George's School of Montreal**
3100, The Boulevard, Montréal, QC H3Y 1R9, Canada
Tel: 514-937-9289; *Fax:* 514-933-3621
www.stgeorges.qc.ca
Grades: Pre./Elem./Sec.; Eng.
A co-educational, non-denominational school.
James A. Officer, Head of School
james.officer@stgeorges.qc.ca

***Montréal:* Solomon Schechter Academy**
Académie Solomon Schechter
5555, ch de la Côte-St-Luc, Montréal, QC H3X 2C9, Canada
Tel: 514-485-0866; *Fax:* 514-485-2267
info@solomonschechter.ca
www.ssa.koumbit.org
Grades: Pre./Prim.; Eng./Fr.
Committed to the values of Conservative Judaism; affiliated with the Shaare Zion Synagogue. Pre-Kindergarten to Gr. 6. Instruction in English, French & Hebrew.
Dr. Shimshon Hamerman, B.A., M.Sc., Ph.D., Principal

***Montréal:* Trafalgar School for Girls**
3495, rue Simpson, Montréal, QC H3G 2J7, Canada
Tel: 514-935-2644; *Fax:* 514-935-2359
admin1@trafalgar.qc.ca
www.trafalgar.qc.ca/
Grades: Sec.; Girls; Eng.
Geoffrey Dowd, Director

***Montréal:* United Talmud Torahs of Montréal**
Talmud Torahs Unis de Montréal
Herzliah High School, Snowdon Campus
4840, av Saint-Kevin, Montréal, QC H3W 1P2, Canada
Tel: 514-739-2294; *Fax:* 514-739-2296
www.herzliahsnowdon.qc.ca
Grades: Pre./Elem./Sec.; Eng./Fr.
Instruction in Hebrew, French & English; college preparatory programme; Judaic Studies; athletics; arts; library.
Linda Leiberman, Campus Director
lleiberman@utt.qc.ca

***Montréal:* Villa Maria**
4245, boul Décarie, Montréal, QC H4A 3K4, Canada
Tel: 514-484-4950; *Fax:* 514-484-4492
secretariat@villamaria.qc.ca
www.villamaria.qc.ca
Grades: Sec.; Girls; Eng./Fr.
Enrollment: 600
Committed to students' proficiency in French & English; programmes include languages; arts (visual arts, drama, music); mathematics & sciences; technology; social sciences; ethics & religious culture; physical education & health.
Claire Drolet, Director General

***Montréal:* Yechivat or Torah**
4605, rue Mackenzie, Montréal, QC H3W 1B2, Canada
Tel: 514-341-9459; *Fax:* 514-341-0594
jhassan-yavne@qc.aira.com
Grades: Pre./Elem./Sec.
Irène Waller, Directrice

***Montréal:* Yeshiva Gedola Merkaz Hatorah Section anglaise**
6155, ch Deacon, Montréal, QC H3S 2P4, Canada
Tel: 514-735-6611; *Fax:* 513-343-0083
Grades: Pre./Elem./Sec.; Eng./Fr.
Rabbin Moshe Glustein, Directeur

***Montréal-Nord:* Centre Académique Fournier**
10339, av du Parc-Georges, Montréal-Nord, QC H1H 4Y4, Canada
Tél: 514-321-2642; *Téléc:* 514-321-0278
paola.gravino@academiefournier.qc.ca
www.academiefournier.qc.ca
Grades: Prim./Sec.; Éd. spéc.
Paola Gravino, Directrice générale
paola.gravino@academiefournier.qc.ca

***Montréal-Nord:* École Michelet**
10550, av Pelletier, Montréal-Nord, QC H1H 3R5, Canada
Tél: 514-321-9551; *Téléc:* 514-321-9111
michelet@qc.aira.com
www.ecolemichelet.com
Grades: Prim.
Lucienne Mortier, Directrice

***Nicolet:* Collège Notre-Dame-de-l'Assomption**
225, rue St-Jean-Baptiste, Nicolet, QC J3T 0A2, Canada
Tél: 819-293-4500; *Téléc:* 819-293-2099
snault@cnda.qc.ca
www.cnda.qc.ca
Grades: Sec.; Pens. & Ext.
École privée mixte.
Robert Cyr, Directeur général

***Outremont:* Belz Community School**
École communautaire Belz
Also known as: Belz Girls School
1495, av Ducharme, Outremont, QC H2V 1E8, Canada
Tel: 514-271-0611; *Fax:* 514-271-9329
belz@belzschool.org
Grades: Pre./Elem./Sec.; Fr./Eng.; girls
Belz Boys School: 6508, Durocher, Outremont, (514) 270-5086.
Helen Liberman, Principal

***Outremont:* Beth Jacob School Inc.**
École Beth Jacob inc.
1750, av Glendale, Outremont, QC H2V 1B3, Canada
Tel: 514-739-3614; *Fax:* 514-739-0172
bjdrh@hotmail.com
Grades: Pre./Elem./Sec.; Eng./Fr.; Girls
Rabbin S. Aisenstark, Directeur

***Outremont:* Collège Stanislas**
780, boul Dollard, Outremont, QC H2V 3G5, Canada
Tél: 514-273-9521; *Téléc:* 514-273-3409
direction@stanislas.qc.ca
www.stanislas.qc.ca
Grades: Mat./Prim./Sec./Coll.
Enrollment: 2150
Henri-Laurent Brusa, Directeur général

***Outremont:* École Buissonnière, centre de formation artistique inc.**
215, av de l'Épée, Outremont, QC H2V 3T3, Canada
Tél: 514-272-4739; *Téléc:* 514-907-5094
infos@ecolebuissonniere.ca
www.ecolebuissonniere.ca
Grades: Mat./Prim.
Intégration des arts aux programmes du Min. de l'Éducation; arts plastiques, musique, danse, art dramatique.
Hélène Bourduas, Directrice générale

***Québec:* Académie Saint-Louis (Québec)**
1500, rue de La Rive-Boisée sud, Québec, QC G2C 2B3, Canada
Tél: 418-845-5121; *Téléc:* 418-845-5244
www.aslouis.qc.ca
Grades: Sec.
Enrollment: 800
Programmes: Concentration Langues; Études-Sports: Hockey, Golf, Natation, Football, Cheerleading, et Soccer féminin.
Jocelyn Lee, Directeur général

Québec: Centre Psycho-Pédagogique de Québec inc. (École Saint-François)
1000, rue du Joli-Bois, Québec, QC G1V 3Z6, Canada
Tél: 418-650-1171; *Téléc:* 418-650-1145
adm@cppq.qc.ca
www.cppq.qc.ca
Grades: Prim./Sec./; Éd. spéc.
Enrollment: 200
Favoriser l'intégration sociale de filles et garçons présentant des difficultés d'adaptation scolaire.
Jean-Marie Guay, Directeur

Québec: Collège de Champigny
1400, rte de l'Aéroport, Québec, QC G2G 1G6, Canada
Tél: 418-872-0508; *Téléc:* 418-872-1002
www.collegedechampigny.com
Grades: Sec.
Robert Laperle, Directeur
rlaperle@collegechampigny.com

Québec: L'École des Ursulines de Québec et de Loretteville
P.O. Box 820
4, rue du Parloir, Québec, QC G1R 4S7, Canada
Tél: 418-692-2612; *Téléc:* 418-692-1240
secrectariat_euq@ursulinesquebec.com
www.ursulinesquebec.com
Grades: Prim./Sec.; filles; Pens. & Ext.
Enrollment: 580
Loretteville: 63, rue Racine, (418) 842-2949.
Serge Goyette, Directeur

Québec: École Montessori de Québec inc.
1265, av Du Buisson, Québec, QC G1T 2C4, Canada
Tél: 418-688-7646; *Téléc:* 418-687-5282
montessori_qc@yahoo.ca
www.montessori-qc.net
Grades: Mat./Prim.
Benoît Dubuc, Directeur

Québec: École Saint-Louis-de-Gonzague
980, rue Richelieu, Québec, QC G1R 1L5, Canada
Tél: 418-692-1072; *Téléc:* 418-692-5965
secretariat@eslg.qc.ca
www.eslg.qc.ca
Grades: Prim.; garçons
Enrollment: 300
Programme d'éducation internationale.
Patrick L'Heureux, Directeur général
dirgen@eslg.qc.ca

Québec: École secondaire François-Bourrin
50, av des Cascades, Québec, QC G1E 6B3, Canada
Tél: 418-661-6978; *Téléc:* 418-661-4778
efb@fbourrin.qc.ca
www.fbourrin.qc.ca
Grades: Sec.
M. Magella Beaulieu, Directeur général

Québec: Externat Saint-Jean-Eudes
650, av du Bourg-Royal, Québec, QC G2L 1M8, Canada
Tél: 418-627-1550; *Téléc:* 418-627-0770
info@sje.qc.ca
www.sje.qc.ca
Grades: Sec.
Édouard Malenfant, Directeur général

Québec: Externat St-Jean-Berchmans
2303, ch Saint-Louis, Québec, QC G1T 1R5, Canada
Tél: 418-687-5871; *Téléc:* 418-687-5886
sec@externatsjb.com
www.externatsjb.com
Grades: Mat./Prim.
Alain Roy, Directeur général

Québec: Institut St-Joseph
Pavillon Saint-Vallier
550, ch Ste-Foy, Québec, QC G1S 2J5, Canada
Tél: 418-688-0736; *Téléc:* 418-688-0737
jean-guy_lussier@fc.st-joseph.qc.ca
www.st-joseph.qc.ca
Grades: Mat./Prim.
Jean-Guy Lussier, Directeur général

Québec: Le Petit Séminaire de Québec
6, rue de la Vielle-Université, Québec, QC G1R 5X8, Canada
Tél: 418-694-1020; *Téléc:* 418-694-1072
admission@psq.qc.ca
www.psq.qc.ca
Grades: Sec.
Réjean Lemay, Directeur général

Québec: Séminaire des Pères Maristes
2315, ch Saint-Louis, Québec, QC G1T 1R5, Canada
Tél: 418-651-4944; *Téléc:* 418-651-6841
spmecole@spmaristes.qc.ca
www.spmaristes.qc.ca
Grades: Sec.
Jean-François Bussières, Directeur général

Rawdon: Collège Champagneur
3713, rue Queen, Rawdon, QC J0K 1S0, Canada
Tél: 450-834-5401; *Téléc:* 450-834-6500
direction@champagneur.qc.ca
www.champagneur.qc.ca
Grades: Sec.; Pens. & Ext.
Privée mixte.
Richard Fiola, Directeur
brab@pandore.qc.ca

Rawdon: École et Pensionnat Marie-Anne
4567, rue du Mont-Pontbriand, Rawdon, QC J0K 1S0, Canada
Tél: 450-834-4668; *Téléc:* 450-834-2800
ema@intermonde.net
www.ecolemarieanne.qc.ca
Grades: Mat./Prim.; Pens. & Ext.
Carole Lalancette, Directrice

Repentigny: Académie François-Labelle
1227, rue Notre-Dame, Repentigny, QC J5Y 3H2, Canada
Tél: 450-582-2020; *Téléc:* 450-582-9732
afl@classomption.qc.ca
www.academiefrancoislabelle.qc.ca
Grades: Mat./Prim.
Michèle Beaudry, Directrice générale

Repentigny: Centre Académique de Lanaudière
930, boul L'Assomption, Repentigny, QC J6A 5H5, Canada
Tél: 450-654-5026
drn@lecadl.com
www.lecadl.com
Grades: Mat./Prim.
Denise Normandin, Directrice

Rigaud: Collège Bourget
65, rue St-Pierre, Rigaud, QC J0P 1P0, Canada
Tél: 450-451-0815; *Téléc:* 450-451-4171
dg@collegebourget.qc.ca
www.collegebourget.qc.ca
Grades: Prim./Sec.; Pens. & Ext.
Jean-Marc St-Jacques, c.s.v., Directeur général

Rivière-du-Loup: Collège Notre-Dame
P.O. Box 820
56, rue Saint-Henri, Rivière-du-Loup, QC G5R 3Z5, Canada
Tél: 418-862-8257; *Téléc:* 418-862-8495
info@collegenotredame.ca
collegenotredame.ca
Grades: Sec.
Abbé Fernand Chouinard, Directeur général

Saint-Augustin-de-Desmaures: Collège Saint-Augustin
4950, rue Lionel-Groulx, Saint-Augustin-de-Desmaures, QC G3A 1V2, Canada
Tél: 418-872-0954; *Téléc:* 418-872-8249
fouc@globetrotter.net
Grades: Sec.; Pens. & Ext.
Charles Fournier, Directeur

Saint-Bruno-de-Montarville: Pensionnat des Sacrés-Coeurs
1575, ch des Vingt, Saint-Bruno-de-Montarville, QC J3V 4P6, Canada
Tél: 450-653-3681; *Téléc:* 450-653-0816
info@psscc.qc.ca
www.psscc.qc.ca
Grades: Mat./Prim.; Pens. & Ext.
Guy Saumure, Directeur général

Saint-Gabriel-de-Valcartier: École secondaire Mont-Saint-Sacrement
200, boul St-Sacrement, Saint-Gabriel-de-Valcartier, QC G0A 4S0, Canada
Tél: 418-844-3771; *Téléc:* 418-844-2926
secretariat@mss.qc.ca
www.mss.qc.ca
Grades: Sec.
Programme Baccalauréat international; Programme Magellan.
Pierre Lantier, Directeur général

Saint-Guillaume: Juvénat Saint-Louis-Marie
96, rue Saint-Jean-Baptiste, Saint-Guillaume, QC J0C 1L0, Canada
Tél: 819-396-2076; *Téléc:* 819-396-3331
info@juvenat.ca
www.juvenat.ca
Grades: Sec.; Pens. & Ext.
Martin Girard, Directeur

Saint-Hyacinthe: Collège Antoine-Girouard
700, rue Girouard est, Saint-Hyacinthe, QC J2S 2Y2, Canada
Tél: 514-773-4334; *Téléc:* 450-773-8011
admin@antoine-girouard.qc.ca
www.antoine-girouard.qc.ca
Grades: Sec.
M. Dominique Lestage, Directeur général

Saint-Hyacinthe: Collège Saint-Maurice
630, rue Girouard ouest, Saint-Hyacinthe, QC J2S 2Y3, Canada
Tél: 450-773-7478; *Téléc:* 450-773-1413
info.college@csm.qc.ca
www.csm.qc.ca
Grades: Sec.; filles; Pens. & Ext.
École secondaire pour filles; Programme d'éducation internationale.
Jean-Pierre Jeannotte, Directeur général

Saint-Hyacinthe: La Petite Académie
1090, av Pratte, Saint-Hyacinthe, QC J2S 4B6, Canada
Tél: 450-771-0644; *Téléc:* 450-771-7242
info@lapetiteacademie.qc.ca
www.lapetiteacademie.qc.ca
Grades: Mat./Prim.
Lise Thiboutot, Directrice générale

Saint-Jacques: Collège Esther-Blondin
101, rue Ste-Anne, Saint-Jacques, QC J0K 2R0, Canada
Tél: 450-839-3672; *Téléc:* 450-839-3951
admin@collegeblondin.qc.ca
www.collegeblondin.qc.ca
Grades: Sec.; Pens. & Ext.
Enrollment: 1100
Membre, Soc. des établissements du bacc. international du Québec, et Org. du bacc. international; le collège est reconnu École Verte Brundtland.
Julie Pothier, Directrice générale

Saint-Jean-sur-Richelieu: École secondaire Marcellin-Champagnat
14, ch des Patriotes est, Saint-Jean-sur-Richelieu, QC J2X 5P9, Canada
Tél: 450-347-5343; *Téléc:* 450-347-2423
webmaster@esmc.qc.ca
www.esmc.qc.ca
Grades: Sec.
F. Jacques Bélisle, Directeur général

Saint-Jérôme: Académie Lafontaine
2171, boul Maurice, Saint-Jérôme, QC J7Y 4M7, Canada
Tél: 450-431-3733; *Téléc:* 450-431-7390
info@academielafontaine.qc.ca
www.academielafontaine.qc.ca
Grades: Mat./Prim./Sec.
Camps du jour; piscine; cantine.
Claude Potvin, Directeur général

Saint-Lambert: Collège Durocher Saint-Lambert
Pavillon Durocher
857, rue Riverside, Saint-Lambert, QC J4P 1C2, Canada
Tél: 450-465-7213; *Téléc:* 450-465-0860
johanne.tremblay@cdsl.qc.ca
www.cdsl.qc.ca
Grades: Sec.
Enrollment: 2230
Pavillon Saint-Lambert: 375, rue Riverside, 450-671-5585.
Carmen Poirier, Directrice générale

Saint-Laurent: École Alex Manoogian
755, rue Manoogian, Saint-Laurent, QC H4N 1Z5, Canada
Tél: 514-744-5636; *Téléc:* 514-744-2785
armenque@qc.aira.com
www.alexmanoogian.qc.ca
Grades: Mat./Prim./Sec.; Fr./Eng./Armenian
Enrollment: 550
La première école arménienne au Canada; école privée.
Dr. Robert Marc Kechayan, Directeur

Saint-Laurent: École Vanguard Québec ltée (École primaire interculturelle)
Vanguard Québec School
1150, rue Deguire, Saint-Laurent, QC H4L 1M2, Canada
Tél: 514-747-3711; *Téléc:* 514-747-2831
cccaputo@vanguardquebec.qc.ca
www.vanguardquebec.qc.ca
Grades: Prim./Sec.; Fr./Angl.; Éd. spéc.
Services adaptés à des élèves présentant des difficultés graves d'apprentissage. École Vanguard Primaire Interculturelle: 1150, rue Deguire, (514) 747-3711 (Denise Bédard, directrice). École Vanguard Secondaire Francophone: 83, boul des Prairies, Laval, (450) 972-6268 (François Papineau, directeur). École Vanguard Secondaire Interculturelle: 175, rue Metcalfe, (514) 932-9770 (Maryse Bessette, directrice).
Carolyn Coffin-Caputo, Directrice générale, 514-747-5500

Saint-Laurent: Education Plus
1275, rue Hodge, Saint-Laurent, QC H4N 2B1, Canada
Tel: 514-733-9600; *Fax:* 514-733-3060
www.edplus.ca
Grades: Grs. 10 & 11
Enrollment: 40
Relationship-based education, flexible structure, informal environment; Life Skills courses; drama; arts; English & French language skills.
James Watts, Director
j.watts@sympatico.ca

Sainte-Thérèse: Académie Ste-Thérèse
Campus Ste-Thérèse
425, rue Blainville est, Sainte-Thérèse, QC J7E 1N7, Canada
Tél: 450-434-1130; *Téléc:* 450-434-0010
infostetherese@academie.ste-therese.com
www.academie.ste-therese.com
Grades: Mat./Prim./Sec.; Pens. & Ext.
Campus Rosemère: 1, ch des Écoliers, Rosemère, 450-434-1130.
Rose De Angelis, Directrice générale

Sept-Iles: Institut d'enseignement de Sept-Iles inc.
737, av Gamache, Sept-Iles, QC G4R 2J8, Canada
Tél: 418-962-9104; *Téléc:* 418-962-8561
direction@ecolepriveesi.com
ecolepriveesi.com
Grades: Sec.
Richard Savignac, Directeur général

Shawinigan: Institution secondaire Montfort
1805, rang St-Mathieu est, Shawinigan, QC G9N 6T5, Canada
Tél: 819-536-2544; *Téléc:* 819-536-3609
montfort@bellnet.ca
Grades: Sec.
Guy Lefort, Directeur

Shawinigan: Séminaire Sainte-Marie
5655, boul des Hêtres, Shawinigan, QC G9N 4V9, Canada
Tél: 819-539-5493; *Téléc:* 819-539-1749
apsssm@ssm1950.qc.ca
www.seminairestemarie.com
Grades: Prim./Sec.
Marc St-Onge, Directeur général

Sherbrooke: Bishop's College School, Inc. (BCS)
P.O. Box 5001 Lennoxville
80, ch Moulton Hill, Sherbrooke, QC J1M 1Z8, Canada
Tel: 819-566-0227; *Fax:* 819-822-8917
admissions@bishopscollegeschool.com
www.bishopscollegeschool.com
Grades: 7-12
Bishop's College School is a bilingual boarding & day school.
Ian Watt, Headmaster, 819-566-0227, ext. 201
Charles de Sainte Marie, Director, Development, 819-566-0227, ext. 203
François de Sainte Marie, Director, Finance & Operations, 819-566-0227, ext. 205
Valerie Scullion, Director, Admissions, 819-566-0227, ext. 248

Sherbrooke: Collège du Mont-Sainte-Anne
2100, ch Ste-Catherine, Sherbrooke, QC J1N 3V5, Canada
Tél: 819-823-3003; *Téléc:* 819-569-9636
Ligne sans frais: 877-823-3003
msa@collegemsa.qc.ca
www.college-mont-sainte-anne.qc.ca
Grades: Sec.; garçons; Pens. & Ext.
André Ricard, Directeur général

Sherbrooke: Collège Mont Notre-Dame de Sherbrooke inc.
114, rue de la Cathédrale, Sherbrooke, QC J1H 4M1, Canada
Tél: 819-563-4104; *Téléc:* 819-563-8689
cmnd@mont-notre-dame.qc.ca
www.mont-notre-dame.qc.ca
Grades: Mat./Prim./Sec; filles
Programme d'éducation international; école de musique; école de danse; Espagnol; sports.
Richard Custeau, Directeur général

Sherbrooke: École Plein Soleil (Association coopérative)
300, rue de Montréal, Sherbrooke, QC J1H 1E5, Canada
Tél: 819-569-8359; *Téléc:* 819-569-3979
info@pleinsoleil.qc.ca
www.pleinsoleil.qc.ca
Grades: Mat./Prim.
Programme d'éducation internationale.
Marie-Josée Mayrand, Directrice générale
mjmayrand@pleinsoleil.qc.ca

Sherbrooke: École secondaire de Bromptonville
125, rue du Frère-Théode, Sherbrooke, QC J1C 0S3, Canada
Tél: 819-846-2738; *Téléc:* 819-846-4808
esb@esb-fsc.ca
www.esb.bromptonville.qc.ca
Grades: Sec.; garçons; Pens. & Ext.
Fr. Jean-Guy Beaulieu, Directeur général
dirgen@esb-fsc.ca

Sherbrooke: Séminaire de Sherbrooke
195, rue Marquette, Sherbrooke, QC J1H 1L6, Canada
Tél: 819-563-2050; *Téléc:* 819-562-8261
courrier@seminaire-sherbrooke.qc.ca
www.seminaire-sherbrooke.qc.ca
Grades: Sec.
Secondaire et collégial; formation continue.
André Métras, Recteur-Directeur général

Sherbrooke: Séminaire Salésien
135, rue Don Bosco nord, Sherbrooke, QC J1L 1E5, Canada
Tél: 819-566-2222; *Téléc:* 819-566-6969
salesien@seminairesalesien.org
www.seminairesalesien.org
Grades: Sec.
Raymond Lepage, Directeur

St-Augustin-de-Desmaures: Réseau VISION Également connu sous le nom de: Écoles VISION Schools
Maître Franchiseur Vision inc.
4920, rue Pierre-Georges-Roy, St-Augustin-de-Desmaures, QC G3A 1V7, Canada
Tél: 418-653-3547; *Téléc:* 418-653-6435
Ligne sans frais: 866-553-3547
info@visionschools.com
www.visionschools.com
Grades: Mat./Prim./Sec.
Le réseau regroupe huit écoles VISION (immersion) et deux écoles Once Upon a Time (préscolaire; apprentissage de l'anglais ou de l'espagnol).
Richard Dumais, Président

Stanstead: Stanstead College
450, rue Dufferin, Stanstead, QC J0B 3E0, Canada
Tel: 819-876-2223; *Fax:* 819-876-5891
admissions@stansteadcollege.com
www.stansteadcollege.com
Grades: Sec.; Eng.; Res. & Day
Enrollment: 200
Co-educational; curriculum/instruction in English, with programmes in French, arts, music, drama; athletics.
Michael Wolfe, Headmaster

Terrebonne: Collège Saint-Sacrement
901, rue St-Louis, Terrebonne, QC J6W 1K1, Canada
Tél: 450-471-6615; *Téléc:* 450-471-5904
css@collegesaintsacrement.qc.ca
www.collegesaintsacrement.qc.ca
Grades: Sec.
Luc St-Louis, Directeur général
lst-louis@collegesaintsacrement.qc.ca

Trois-Rivières: Collège Marie-de-l'Incarnation
725, rue Hart, Trois-Rivières, QC G9A 5S3, Canada
Tél: 819-379-3223; *Téléc:* 819-379-3226
ecole@cmitr.qc.ca
www.cmitr.qc.ca
Grades: Mat./Prim./Sec.; Pens. & Ext.
École pour filles; école de musique.
Martine Talbot, Directrice, Services éducatifs du secondaire
martine.talbot@cmitr.qc.ca
Carolyne Gagnon, Directrice, Services éducatifs du préscolaire & du primaire
carolyne.gagnon@cmitr.qc.ca

Trois-Rivières: Institut secondaire Keranna (1992) inc.
6205, boul des Chenaux, Trois-Rivières, QC G9A 5S3, Canada
Tél: 819-378-4833; *Téléc:* 819-378-2417
keranna@keranna.qc.ca
keranna.qc.ca
Grades: Sec.; filles; Pens. & Ext.
Julie L'Heureux, Directrice générale

Trois-Rivières: Val Marie
88, ch du Passage, Trois-Rivières, QC G8T 2M3, Canada
Tél: 819-379-8040; *Téléc:* 819-378-8559
sgoyette@ecolevalmarie.qc.ca
www.ecolevalmarie.qc.ca
Grades: Mat./Prim.; Pens. & Ext.
Serge Goyette, Directeur

Val-Morin: Académie Laurentienne
1200, 14e av, Val-Morin, QC J0T 2R0, Canada
Tél: 819-322-2913; *Téléc:* 819-322-7086
info@al.qc.ca
www.academielaurentienne.com
Grades: Prim./Sec.; Pens. & Ext.
Programmes académiques et sportifs; installations sportives: piscines, palestre, gymnase double; terrains de jeux, de tennis; centre équestre.
Guy Richard, Directeur
richard.guy@al.qc.ca

Varennes: Centre Éducatif Chante Plume
104, boul de la Marine, Varennes, QC J3X 1Z5, Canada
Tél: 450-652-6869; *Téléc:* 450-652-5773
varennes@visionschools.com
varennes.visionschools.com
Grades: Mat./Prim.
Colette Cardin, Directrice

Varennes: Collège Saint-Paul
235, rue Sainte-Anne, Varennes, QC J3X 1P9, Canada
Tél: 450-652-2941; *Téléc:* 450-652-4461
reception@college-st-paul.qc.ca
www.college-st-paul.qc.ca
Grades: Sec.
Programme de formation générale; Programme d'éducation internationale.
André Langevin, Directeur général

Victoriaville: Collège Clarétain
663, rue Gamache, Victoriaville, QC G6R 0W3, Canada
Tél: 819-752-4571; *Téléc:* 819-752-4572
administration@collegeclaretain.com
www.collegeclaretain.com
Grades: Sec.; Pens. & Ext.
École privée mixte.
Jean-Roch Gagné, Directeur général

Waterville: Collège François-Delaplace
365, rue Compton est, Waterville, QC J0B 3H0, Canada
Tél: 819-837-2882; *Téléc:* 819-837-0625
dir@college-francois-delaplace.qc.ca
www.college-francois-delaplace.qc.ca
Grades: Sec.; filles
École Verte Brundtland; école secondaire privée pour filles (pensionnaires & externes).
Josée Hamel, Directrice générale

Westmount: The Akiva School
450, av Kensington, Westmount, QC H3Y 3A2, Canada
Tel: 514-939-2430; *Fax:* 514-939-2432
suzanna@akivaschool.com
www.akivaschool.com
Grades: Pre-K./Gr. 6; Eng./Fr./Hebrew
Jewish community school; programmes include English Language Arts, Français, Judaic Studies, Music, Mathematics, Art, Media & Technology, Physical Education, & Ethics & Religious Cultures.
Frances Levy, Head of School

Westmount: Miss Edgar's & Miss Cramp's School (ECS)
525, av Mount Pleasant, Westmount, QC H3Y 3H6, Canada
Tel: 514-935-6357; *Fax:* 514-935-1099
www.ecs.qc.ca
Grades: Pre./Elem./Sec.; Girls; Eng.
Enrollment: 344
University-preparatory programme, to Gr. 11; French immersion junior school; arts, athletics, math, sciences, languages, citizenship education; extended day programme; library.

Katherine Nikidis, B.Ed., MHSc, Head of School
nikidisk@ecs.qc.ca

Westmount: Selwyn House
École Selwyn House
95, ch Côte-St-Antoine, Westmount, QC H3Y 2H8, Canada
Tel: 514-931-9481; *Fax:* 514-931-6118
admission@selwyn.ca
www.selwyn.ca

Grades: Pre./Elem./Sec.; Eng.; Boys
Enrollment: 570
Hal Hannford, Headmaster

Westmount: The Study
3233, The Boulevard, Westmount, QC H3Y 1S4, Canada
Tel: 514-935-9352; *Fax:* 514-935-1721
info@thestudy.qc.ca
www.thestudy.qc.ca

Grades: Pre./Elem./Sec.; Eng.; Girls
Committed to best practices in education, with a focus on proficiency in both English & French, academics & athletics. The school is the first in Québec to introduce a Mandarin language program at the primary level.
Elizabeth Falco, M.Ed., MBA, Head of School

Westmount: Villa Sainte-Marcelline
815, av Upper Belmont, Westmount, QC H3Y 1K5, Canada
Tél: 514-488-2528; *Téléc:* 514-488-5384
srmathilde@villa.marcelline.qc.ca

Grades: Mat./Prim./Sec.; filles
Sr. Mathilde Fantone, Directrice

Universities & Colleges

Universities

Chicoutimi: Université du Québec à Chicoutimi
555, boul de l'Université, Chicoutimi, QC G7H 2B1, Canada
Tél: 418-545-5011; *Téléc:* 418-545-5012
info_programmes@uqac.ca
www.uqac.ca

Publications
La Petite Caisse

Gatineau: Université du Québec en Outaouais
Pavillion Alexandre-Taché
283, boul Alexandre-Taché, Gatineau, QC J9A 1L8, Canada
Tél: 819-595-3900; *Téléc:* 819-595-3924
Ligne sans frais: 1-800-567-1283
questions@uqo.ca
www.uqo.ca

Full Time Equivalency: 5200

Publications
Le Canard Déchaine
Le Virus

Laval: Institut Armand-Frappier
531, boul des Prairies, Laval, QC H7V 1B7, Canada
Tél: 450-687-5010; *Téléc:* 450-686-5501
www.iaf.inrs.ca

Lennoxville: Université Bishop's
P.O. Box 5000
Lennoxville, QC J1M 1Z7, Canada
Tél: 819-822-9600; *Téléc:* 819-822-9661
Ligne sans frais: 1-800-567-279
liaison@ubishops.ca
www.ubishops.ca

Full Time Equivalency: 2206
Scott Griffin, B.A., D.C.L., Chancellor
Philip Matthews, B.A., LL.B., President of Corporation
Yves Jodoin, B.A., B.Sp. Adm., M.B.A., Registrar
Joan Stadelman, B.Sc., M.Sc., Vice-President of Corporation
Sam Elkas, Chair
Robert Poupart, B.A., B.Ph., M.Ps., D.Ps., Principal & Vice-Chancellor
Mark McLaughlin, B.B.A., C.A., Vice-Principal
Tony Addona, B.Sc., Dip.Ed., M.Sc., Director
Cathy Beauchamp, B.A., Dip.Ed., M.A., Ph.D, Director
Hans Rouleau, B.A., Liaison Coordinator
Damien Roy, B.A., Director
Suzanne Meeson, B.B.A., Continuing Education Coordinator
Pam McPhail, B.A., Director
Matt McBrine, B.A., Alumni Relations Coordinator
Patricia MacAulay, Manager
Jonathan Rittenhouse, B.A., M.A., Ph.D., Vice-Principal

Faculties
Business Administration
W. Robson, B.Com., M.B.A., Dean

Humanities
Stephen Sheeran, B.A., M.A., Dean

Natural Sciences & Mathematics
Brad Willms, B.Math, M.M. Ph.D., Dean

Social Sciences
Andrew Johnson, B.A., M.A., Ph.D., Dean

Student Affairs
Bruce Stevenson, B.A., Dip.Ed., M.Ed., Dean

Williams School of Business
Sylvie Béquet, M.Sc., Dean

Publications
The Campus

Montréal: Concordia University
Université Concordia
Sir George Williams Campus
1455, boul de Maisonneuve ouest, Montréal, QC H3G 1M8, Canada
Tel: 514-848-2424
www.concordia.ca

Full Time Equivalency: 44000
Please refer to main French record for more details.
Judith Woodsworth, President & Vice-Chancellor
David Graham, Provost & Vice-President, Academic
Kathy Assayag, Vice-President, Advancement and Alumni Relations
Bram Freedman, Vice-President, External Relations and Secretary-General
Patrick Kelley, CFO
Louise Dandurand, Vice-President, Research and Graduate Studies
Michael Di Grappa, Vice-President, Services
Philippe Beauregard, CCO

Faculties
Arts & Science
Dr. David Graham, Dean

Engineering & Computer Science
Nabil Esmail, Dean

Fine Arts
Catherine Wild, Dean

Graduate Studies & Research
Elizabeth Saccà, Dean

John Molson School of Business (JMSB)
Jerry Tomberlin, Dean

Campuses
Loyola Campus
7141, rue Sherbrooke ouest, Montréal, QC H4B 1R6, Canada

Sir George Williams Campus
1455, boul de Maisonneuve ouest, Montréal, QC H3G 1M8, Canada

Publications
Concordia University Magazine
Office of Alumni Affairs
#BC-101, 1455, boul de Maisonneuve ouest, Montréal, QC H3G 1M8, Canada
Fax: 514-848-2826

The Concordian
The Link
The Sting
Thursday Report
CAS

Montréal: École de technologie supérieure
1100, rue Notre-Dame ouest, Montréal, QC H3C 1K3, Canada
Tél: 514-396-8800; *Téléc:* 514-396-8950
Ligne sans frais: 1-888-394-7888
admission@etsmtl.ca
www.etsmtl.ca

Full Time Equivalency: 4800

Publications
Le Jets

Montréal: HEC Montréal
Également connu sous le nom de: École des Hautes Études Commerciales
Université de Montréal
3000, ch de la Côte-Sainte-Catherine, Montréal, QC H3T 2A7, Canada
Tél: 514-340-6000; *Téléc:* 514-340-6411
webmestre@hec.ca
www.hec.ca

Full Time Equivalency: 12000
HEC Montréal est la première école de gestion au Canada. Affaires internationales; finance; gestion des opérations/logistique; gestion des ressources humaines; management; marketing; méthodes quantitatives de gestion; sciences comptables; technologies de l'information; économie appliquée. Édifice Decelles: 5255, av Decelles. Campus Laval: 2572, boul Daniel-Johnson, (450) 973-7741. Campus Longueuil: 101, place Charles-Lemoyne, (450) 651-5458. Bureau international à Paris: 15, rue du Louvre, 75001 Paris, 33(0)1 42 33 43 40.
Michel Patry, Directeur

Montréal: McGill University
845, rue Sherbrooke ouest, Montréal, QC H3A 2T5, Canada
Tel: 514-398-4455; *Fax:* 514-398-4455
www.mcgill.ca

Full Time Equivalency: 32510
Arnold Steinberg, Chancellor
Robert Rabinovitch, Ph.D., M.A., B.Com., Chair of Board
Heather Munroe-Blum, O.C. Ph.D. FRSC, Principal & Vice-Chancellor
Anthony C. Masi, Provost
Morty Yalovsky, Vice-Principal
Sylvia Franke, CIO
Denis Therien, Vice-Principal
Johanne Pelletier, Secretary General
Sylvia Franke, Registrar & Exec. Director
Jennifer Robinson, Assoc. Vice-Principal
Kim Bartlett, Director
Howard Tontini, Director
Ann Dowsett Johnston, Vice-Principal

Faculties
Agricultural & Environmental Sciences
Chandra A. Madramootoo, B.Sc., M.Sc., Ph.D., Dean

Arts
John Galaty, Dean

Centre for Continuing Education
Robin Eley, Director

Dentistry
James Percy Lund, B.D.S., Ph.D., Dean

Education
Dr. Roger Slee, Dean

Engineering
Pierre Christophe, Dean

Graduate & Post-Doctoral Studies
Dr. James Nemes, Dean

Law
Prof. Nicholas Kasirer, Dean

Management
Peter Todd, Dean

Medicine
Abraham Fuks, B.Sc., M.D., C.M., Dean

Music
Don McLean, Dean

Religious Studies
B. Barry Levy, B.A., B.R.E., M.A., Ph.D., Dean

Science
Martin Grant, Dean

Schools
Architecture
David Covo, B.Sc.Arch., M.B.Arch., O., Director

Communication Sciences & Disorders
Dr. Shari R. Baum, Director

Computer Science
Sue Whitesides, Director

Dietetics & Human Nutrition
Dr. Kristine G. Koski, Director

International Executive Institute
Peter Todd, Director

Library & Information Studies
France Bouthillier, Director

Nursing
Dr. Hélène Ezer, Acting Director

Physical & Occupational Therapy
Dr. Maureen J. Simmonds, Director

Social Work
Dr. Wendy Thomson, Director

Urban Planning
David Brown, Director

Affiliations
Macdonald Campus
21111, ch Bord-du-Lac, Sainte-Anne-de-Bellevue, QC H9X 3V9, Canada
Tel: 514-398-7707; *Fax:* 514-398-7766
info.macdonald@mcgill.ca
www.mcgill.ca/macdonald/
Established in 1905, Macdonald College began as Canada's foremost institution for agricultural education. In 1972, it became the Macdonald Campus of McGill University & is the home of the University's Faculty of Agricultural & Environmental Sciences, the McGill School of Environment, & the School of Dietetics & Human Nutrition. Programmes leading to the degree of B.Sc.(Agr.), as well as graduate programs in agriculture, food, natural sciences, applied economics, environment, & engineering are offered.
Chandra A. Madramootoo, B.Sc., M.Sc., Ph.D., Dean, Fac. of Agricultural & Environmental Sciences

The Montreal Diocesan Theological College
3475, rue University, Montréal, QC H3A 2A8, Canada
Tel: 514-849-3004; *Fax:* 514-849-4113
info@dio-mdtc.ca
www.dio-mdtc.ca
An Anglican theological college founded in 1873. Affiliated with McGill Univ. & l'Univ. de Montréal. Degree courses: B.Th., Dip.Min, M.Div. Advanced degrees, offered through McGill: S.T.M, M.A., Ph.D. Distance education courses leading to the Cert. in Theology, or Licentiate in Theology also available.
The Rev. Canon John Simons, Principal

The Presbyterian College
Collège Presbytérien
3495, rue University, Montréal, QC H3A 2A8, Canada
Tel: 514-288-5256; *Fax:* 514-288-8072
email@presbyteriancollege.ca
www.presbyteriancollege.ca
Founded in 1867 & affiliated with McGill Univ.
Rev. Dr. John A. Vissers, B.A., M.Div., Th.M., Th.D, Principal
jvissers@presbyteriancollege.ca
Rev. Dr. Dale Woods, B.A., M.C.S., M.Div., D.M, Director, Pastoral Studies
dwoods@presbyteriancollege.ca

Royal Victoria College
3425, rue University, Montréal, QC H3A 2A8, Canada
Tel: 514-398-6378; *Fax:* 514-398-4445
www.mcgill.ca/residences/undergraduate/tour/rvc/
Full Time Equivalency: 266
Royal Victoria College is McGill's only all women's residence.

The United Theological College
Le Séminaire Uni
3521, rue University, Montréal, QC H3A 2A9, Canada
Tel: 514-849-2042; *Toll-Free:* 888-849-2042
admin@utc.ca
www.utc.ca
A college of the United Church of Canada, committed to the training of persons, regardless of race, economic status, sexual orientation & gender identity, for various Christian ministries. Instruction in English & French is offered.
Philip L. Joudrey, M.Div., D.Min., Principal
pjoudrey@utc.ca
Michael Ryneveld, Registrar
mryneveld@utc.ca
Elisabeth Jones, M.Div., Th.M, Director, Studies
erjones@utc.ca

Publications
Debit Memo

The Faucet

The McGill News
c/o Graduates' Society
3605 Mountain St, Montréal, QC H3G 2M1, Canada
Fax: 514-398-7338

The Reporter

The Tablet

Montréal: Télé-Université (Montréal)
#100, 4750, Henri-Julien, Montréal, QC H2T 3E4, Canada
Tél: 514-843-2015; *Téléc:* 514-843-2160
Ligne sans frais: 1-800-665-4333
info@teluq.ugam.ca
www.teluq.uquebec.ca
20,000 students in distance learning

Montréal: The United Theological College Le Séminaire Uni
3521, rue University, Montréal, QC H3A 2A9, Canada
Tel: 514-849-2042; *Fax:* 514-849-8634
Toll-Free: 888-849-2042
admin@utc.ca
www.utc.ca

Montréal: Université de Montréal
Pavillon J-A.-DeSève
P.O. Box 6205
2332, boul Édouard-Montpetit, Montréal, QC H3C 3T5, Canada
Tél: 514-343-7076; *Téléc:* 514-343-5788
www.umontreal.ca
Full Time Equivalency: 55000
Facultés: Aménagement; Arts/Sciences; Droit; Éducation permanente; Études supérieures/postdoctorales; Médecine; Médecine dentaire; Médecine vétérinaire; Musique; Pharmacie; Sciences de l'éducation; Sciences infirmières; Théologie; Kinésiologie; Optometrie; Santé publique. Campus régionaux: Terrebonne; Ville de Laval; Longueuil; Québec.
Guy Breton, Recteur, 514-343-6776
guy.breton@umontreal.ca

Affiliations
École Polytechnique de Montréal
Également connu sous le nom de: Polytechnique Montréal
P.O. Box 6079 Centre-ville
Montréal, QC H3C 3A7, Canada
Tél: 514-340-4711
www.polymtl.ca
Full Time Equivalency: 4000
Fondée en 1873, Le Polytechnique est une école d'ingénierie de classe internationale; programmes au baccalauréat, cycles supérieurs, formation continue; recherche; l'École se trouve à 2900, boul Édouard-Montpetit, Campus de l'Univ. de Montréal, 2500 ch de Polytechnique.
Christophe Guy, ing., Ph.D., MACG, Directeur général

HEC Montréal
Également connu sous le nom de: École des Hautes Études Commerciales
3000, ch de la Côte-Sainte-Catherine, Montréal, QC H3T 2A7, Canada
Tél: 514-340-6000; *Téléc:* 514-340-6411
www.hec.ca
Michel Patry, Directeur

Circuit
Presses de l'Université de Montréal
P.O. Box 6128 Centre-ville
Montréal, QC H3C 3J7
Tel: 514-343-6388; *Fax:* 514-343-5727
info@revuecircuit.ca
www.pum.umontreal.ca; www.revuecircuit.ca
Circuit, créée en 1989, publie des articles sur la musique contemporaine québécoise et internationale. Trois fois par année.
Jonathan Goldman, Rédacteur en chef

Études françaises
Presses de l'Université de Montréal
P.O. Box 6128 Centre-ville
Montréal, QC H3C 3J7
Tel: 514-343-6933; *Fax:* 514-343-2232
www.pum.umontreal.ca
Fondée en 1965; littératures de langue française, québécoises et internationales; critique et théorie. Trois fois par année.
Francis Gingras, Directeur

Pigeon Dissident
#A-2412, 3200, rue Jean-Brillant, Montréal, QC H3T 1N8
Tel: 514-343-6111; *Fax:* 514-343-5929
info@pigeondissident.com
www.pigeondissident.com
Le journal des étudiants de la Faculté de droit, l'Université de Montréal. Six fois par année.
Takwa Souissi, Rédactrice en chef

Quartier Libre
P.O. Box 6128 Centre-ville
2350, boul Édouard-Montpetit, Montréal, QC H3C 3J7
Tel: 514-343-7630; *Fax:* 514-343-7744
quartierlibre@hotmail.com
www.ql.umontreal.ca
Quartier Libre est le journal des étudiants de l'Université de Montréal, publié par Les Publications du Quartier Libre, une corporation sans but lucratif créée par des étudiants en 1992. Le version papier (bimensuel) est distribué gratuitement sur tout le campus de l'UM et dans ses environs.
Mikaëlle Monfort, Directrice
monfortmikaelle@hotmail.com

Montréal: Université du Québec à Montréal (UQAM)
P.O. Box 8888 Centre-Ville
Montréal, QC H3C 3P8, Canada
Tél: 514-987-3000
general@uqam.ca
www.uqam.ca

Publications
L'Action

Journal U.Q.A.M

Le Temporel

Transactions

Unité

Uquam

Suites

Québec: École nationale d'administration publique
555, boul Charest est, Québec, QC G1K 9E5, Canada
Tél: 418-641-3000; *Téléc:* 418-641-3060
info@enap.ca
www.enap.ca
Full Time Equivalency: 1832
Campus: Québec, Montréal, Gatineau, Saguenay, Trois-Rivières

Québec: Institut national de la recherche scientifique (INRS)
490, rue de la Couronne, Québec, QC G1K 9A9, Canada
Tél: 418-654-4677; *Téléc:* 418-654-2525
lise.roy@adm.inrs.ca
www.inrs.uquebec.ca

Québec: Université du Québec
475, rue de l'Église, Québec, QC G1K 9H7, Canada
Tél: 418-657-3551; *Téléc:* 418-657-2132
cscuq@uqss.uquebec.ca
www.uquebec.ca
Guy Massicotte, Directeur
Pierre Moreau, Président
Michel Quimper, Secrétaire général
Serge Cabana, Directeur
Pierre Chenard, Directeur

Affiliations
Université du Québec en Abitibi-Témiscamingue
445, boul de l'Université, Rouyn-Noranda, QC J9X 5E4, Canada
Tél: 819-762-0971; *Téléc:* 819-797-4727
www.uqat.ca
Johanne Jean, Rectrice
Jean Turgeon, Secrétaire généal

Université du Québec à Chicoutimi
555, boul de l'Université, Chicoutimi, QC G7H 2B1, Canada
Tél: 418-545-5011; *Téléc:* 418-545-5012
www.uqac.uquebec.ca
Michel Belley, Recteur

Université du Québec en Outaouais
Pavillion Alexandre-Taché
P.O. Box 1250 Hull
283, boul Alexandre-Taché, Gatineau, QC J8X 3X7, Canada
Tél: 819-595-3900; *Téléc:* 819-595-3924
www.uqo.ca
Jean Vaillancourt, Recteur

Université du Québec à Montréal
P.O. Box 8888 Centre-Ville
Montréal, QC H3C 3P8, Canada
Tél: 514-987-3000
www.uqam.ca
Claude Corbo, Recteur

Université du Québec à Rimouski
300, allée des Ursulines, Rimouski, QC G5L 3A1, Canada
Tél: 418-723-1986
uqar@uqar.qc.ca
www.uqar.qc.ca
Michel Ringuet, Recteur

Université du Québec à Trois-Rivières
P.O. Box 500 Bureau-chef
3351, boul des Forges, Trois-Rivières, QC G9A 5H7, Canada
Tél: 819-376-5011; *Téléc:* 819-376-5012
www.uqtr.ca
Ghislain Bourque, Recteur

École nationale d'administration publique
555, boul Charest est, Québec, QC G1K 9E5, Canada
Tél: 418-641-3000; *Téléc:* 418-641-3055
www.enap.ca
Marcel Proulx, Directeur général

École de technologie supérieure
1100, rue Notre-Dame ouest, Montréal, QC H3C 1K3, Canada
Tél: 514-396-8800; *Téléc:* 514-396-8950
www.etsmtl.ca
Yves Beauchamp, Directeur général

Institut Armand-Frappier
531, boul des Prairies, Laval, QC H7V 1B7, Canada
Tél: 450-687-5010; *Téléc:* 450-686-5501
www.iaf.inrs.ca

Institut national de la recherche scientifique (INRS)
490, rue de la Couronne, Québec, QC G1K 9A9, Canada
Tél: 418-654-4677; *Téléc:* 418-654-2525
Lise Roy, Communications
lise.roy@adm.inrs.ca
Yvonne Boisvert, Registraire
yvonne.boisvert@adm.inrs.ca

Télé-université
P.O. Box 4800 Terminus
455, rue de l'Église, Québec, QC G1K 9H5, Canada
Tél: 418-657-2747; *Téléc:* 418-657-2094
info@teluq.uquebec.ca
www.teluq.uquebec.ca/
Louise Bertrand, Directrice générale

Télé-Université (Montréal)
#100, 4750, Henri-Julien, Montréal, QC H2T 3E4, Canada
Tél: 514-843-2015; *Téléc:* 514-843-2160

Publications
Réseau/U.Q. Network

Québec: Université Laval
Cité universitaire, Québec, QC G1K 7P4, Canada
Tél: 418-656-3333; *Téléc:* 418-656-5920
Ligne sans frais: 1-877-785-2825
info@ulaval.ca
www.ulaval.ca
Full Time Equivalency: 38500
Première université francophone d'Amerique, ouverte sur le monde et animée d'une culture de l'exigence, l'Université Laval contribue au développement de la société par la formation de personnes compétentes, responsables et promotrice de changement, par l'avancement et le partage des connaissances, dans un environnement dynamique de recherche et de création
Denis Brière, Recteur

Campuses
Service des communications
Pavillon Alphonse-Desjardins.
#3577, Université de Laval, Laval, QC G1K 7P4, Canada
Fax: 418-656-2809
Richard Fournier, Directeur

Publications
Au Fil des Evénements
#214, Tour des Arts, Québec, QC G1K 7P4, Canada
Fax: 418-529-0649

Impact Campus

Rimouski: Université du Québec à Rimouski
P.O. Box 3300 A
300, allée des Ursulines, Rimouski, QC G5L 3A1, Canada
Tél: 418-723-1986; *Téléc:* 041-872-4152
Ligne sans frais: 1-800-511-3382
uqar@uqar.qc.ca
www.uqar.ca

Publications
U.Q.A.R. Information

Uquarium

Rouyn-Noranda: Université du Québec en Abitibi-Témiscamingue
445, boul de l'Université, Rouyn-Noranda, QC J9X 5E4, Canada
Tél: 819-762-0971; *Téléc:* 819-797-4727
www.uqat.ca

Publications
Le Voyeur

Sainte-Anne-de-Bellevue: Macdonald Campus
21111, ch Bord-du-Lac, Sainte-Anne-de-Bellevue, QC H9X 3V9, Canada
Tel: 514-398-7707; *Fax:* 514-398-7766
info.macdonald@mcgill.ca
www.mcgill.ca/macdonald/
Houses McGill University's Faculty of Agricultural & Environmental Sciences.

Sherbrooke: Bishop's University
2600 College St., Sherbrooke, QC J1M 1Z7, Canada
Tel: 819-822-9600; *Fax:* 819-822-9661
www.ubishops.ca
Full Time Equivalency: 2263
Michael Goldbloom, Principal/Vice-Chancellor, ext. 2611
principal@ubishops.ca
Isabelle Goyette, Dir., Finance, ext. 2656
isablle.goyette@ubishops.ca
Yves Jodoin, Registrar/Sec.-General, ext. 2676
yves.jodoin@ubishops.ca

Sherbrooke: Université de Sherbrooke
2500, boul de l'Université, Sherbrooke, QC J1K 2R1, Canada
Tél: 819-821-7686
information@usherbrooke.ca
www.usherbrooke.ca
Denis Marceau, Vice-recteur
Edwin Bourget, Vice-recteur
Jean Desclos, Vice-recteur
Martin Buteau, Vice-recteur
Roger Noël, Doyen
Bruno-Marie Béchard, Recteur
Luce Samoisette, Rectrice adjointe et vice-rectrice à l'administration
Daniel Proulx, Doyen
Céline Garant, Doyenne
Paul Deshaies, Doyen
Linda Bellalite, Doyenne
Dr. Réjean Hébert, Doyen
Donald Thomas, Doyen
Gérard Lachiver, Doyen
Marc Dumas, Doyen
Sylvie Belzile, Directrice
Jacques Labrecque, Directeur
Christian Gagnon, Directeur
Serge Cabana, Directeur
Renald Mercier, Directeur
René Alarie, Directeur
Luc Bédard, Directeur
Pierre Lemieux, Directeur
France Myette, Registraire
Lise Grenier, Directrice
Gilles Bilodeau, Directeur
Daniel Dupont, Directeur
Mario Laforest, Directeur
Michèle Desrochers, Directrice
Denis Marceau, Directeur (par interim)
Serge Fortier, Directeur
François Dubé, Directeur (par intérim)

Publications
Bilan

La Sagace

Liaison

Sommets
2500, boul de l'Université, Sherbrooke, QC J1K 2R1, Canada
Fax: 819-821-7900

Trois-Rivières: Université du Québec à Trois-Rivières
P.O. Box 500
3351, boul des Forges, Trois-Rivières, QC G9A 5H7, Canada
Tél: 819-376-5011; *Téléc:* 819-376-5210
Ligne sans frais: 1-800-365-0922
communications@uqtr.ca
www.uqtr.ca
Full Time Equivalency: 11000

Publications
En Tete

Le Voyeur

Colleges

Alma: Collège d'Alma
675, boul Auger ouest, Alma, QC G8B 2B7, Canada
Tél: 418-668-2387; *Téléc:* 418-668-7336
college@calma.qc.ca
www.calma.qc.ca
Grades: Préuniv., Techniques, Form. cont.
Jean Paradis, Directeur générale

Publications
Le Majeur

Gatineau: Heritage College
325, boul Cité des Jeunes, Gatineau, QC J8Y 6T3, Canada
Tel: 819-778-2270; *Fax:* 819-778-7364
www.cegep-heritage.qc.ca
Full Time Equivalency: 1387
Career Programs (Nursing; Early Childhood Ed.; New Media & Publication Design; Electronics; Computer Science); Pre-University Programs: Liberal Arts, Sciences, Commerce, Social Sciences, Visual Arts; Continuing Ed.: French as a Second Language; Distance Education; Corporate Training.
Louise Brunet, Director General
dg@cegep-heritage.qc.ca

La Pocatière: Institut de technologie agroalimentaire
Campus de La Pocatière
401, rue Poiré, La Pocatière, QC G0R 1Z0, Canada
Tél: 418-856-1110; *Téléc:* 418-856-1719
scitalp@mapaq.gouv.qc.ca
www.ita.qc.ca
Full Time Equivalency: 1000
Spécialisé en agroalimentaire; Campus de Saint-Hyacinthe: 3230, rue Sicotte, (450) 778-6504; Collège Macdonald, Univ. McGill.
Rosaire Ouellet, Directeur général

Campuses
Campus de Saint-Hyacinthe
P.O. Box 70
3230, rue Sicotte, Saint-Hyacinthe, QC J2S 7B3, Canada
Tel: 450-778-6504; *Fax:* 450-778-6536
ita.st.hyacinthe@mapaq.gouv.qc.ca
www.ita.qc.ca

Laval: Collège Montmorency
475, boul de l'Avenir, Laval, QC H7N 5H9, Canada
Tél: 450-975-6100; *Téléc:* 450-975-6116
info.programmes@cmontmorecy.qc.ca
www.cmontmorency.qc.ca
Denyse Blanchet, Directrice générale

Publications
Le Zèle

Lévis: Collège de Lévis
9, rue Monseigneur Gosselin, Lévis, QC G6V 5K1, Canada
Tél: 418-833-1249; *Téléc:* 418-833-1974
info@collegedelevis.qc.ca
www.collegedelevis.qc.ca
Grades: Sec.
David Lehoux, Directeur général

Publications
Le Script

Longueuil: Collège Édouard-Montpetit
945, ch de Chambly, Longueuil, QC J4H 3M6, Canada
Tél: 450-679-2631; *Téléc:* 450-679-5570
communications@college-em.qc.ca
www.college-em.qc.ca
Serge Brasset, Directeur général

Publications
Le Motdit

Montréal: Collège Ahuntsic
9155, rue St-Hubert, Montréal, QC H2M 1Y8, Canada
Tél: 514-389-5921; *Téléc:* 514-389-5762
www.collegeahuntsic.qc.ca
Full Time Equivalency: 10100
Roch Tremblay, Directeur général

Publications
L'Attribut

Le Misanthrope

Montréal: Collège Dawson
3040, rue Sherbrooke ouest, Montréal, QC H3Z 1A4, Canada
Tél: 514-931-8731; *Téléc:* 514-931-5181
www.dawsoncollege.qc.ca
Full Time Equivalency: 10000
Richard Filion, Dir. gén.

Publications
Plant

Montréal: Collège de Bois-de-Boulogne
10555, av de Bois-de-Boulogne, Montréal, QC H4N 1L4, Canada
Tél: 514-332-3000; *Téléc:* 514-332-5857
communications@bdeb.qc.ca
www.bdeb.qc.ca
Grades: Préuniv., Techniques, Form. cont.
Maurice Piché, Directeur général

Publications
L'Infomane

Montréal: Collège de Maisonneuve
3800, rue Sherbrooke est, Montréal, QC H1X 2A2, Canada
Tél: 514-254-7131; *Téléc:* 514-253-7637
communic@cmaisonneuve.qc.ca
www.cmaisonneuve.qc.ca

Grades: Préuniv., Techniques
Full Time Equivalency: 3398
Pierre Harrison, Directeur général

Publications
Le Trait d'Union

Montréal: **Collège de Rosemont**
6400, 16e av, Montréal, QC H1X 2S9, Canada
Tél: 514-376-1620; *Téléc:* 514-376-1440
regist@crosemont.qc.ca
www.crosemont.qc.ca
Patricia Hanigan, Directrice générale

Publications
République étudiante

Montréal: **Collège Jean-de-Brébeuf inc.**
3200, ch Côte Ste-Catherine, Montréal, QC H3T 1C1, Canada
Tél: 514-342-9342; *Téléc:* 514-342-6607
diradm@brebeuf.qc.ca
www.brebeuf.qc.ca
Grades: Sec., Collégial
Michel April, Directeur, Services administratifs

Publications
Le Grafitti

Montréal: **École Polytechnique de Montréal**
Également connu sous le nom de: Polytechnique de Montréal
Université de Montréal
2900, boul Édouard-Montpetit, Montréal, QC H3T 1J4, Canada
Tél: 514-340-4711
www.polymtl.ca
Full Time Equivalency: 4000
Fondée en 1873, le Polytechnique est une école d'ingénierie de classes internationale; programmes au baccalauréat, cycles supérieures, formation continue; recherche. Adresse postale: CP 6079, succ. Centre-ville, Montréal, QC H3C 3A7.

Publications
Le Polyscope

Montréal: **HEC Montréal**
Également connu sous le nom de: École des Hautes Études Commerciales
3000, ch de la Côte-Sainte-Catherine, Montréal, QC H3T 2A7, Canada
Tél: 514-340-6000; *Téléc:* 514-340-6411
webmestre@hec.ca
www.hec.ca
Grades: Bacc., MBA, LL.M., M.Sc., Ph.D.
Full Time Equivalency: 12000
La première école de gestion au Canada, fondée en 1907

Publications
Le Caducée
#310, 3333 Queen Mary Rd, Montréal, QC H3V 1A2, Canada
Fax: 514-340-6508
L'Intérêt

Montréal: **Institut de tourisme et d'hôtellerie du Québec**
3535, rue Saint-Denis, Montréal, QC H2X 3P1, Canada
Tel: 514-282-5108; *Fax:* 514-282-5126
administration@ithq.qc.ca
www.ithq.qc.ca
Lucille Daoust, Directrice

Montréal: **The Montreal Diocesan Theological College**
3475, rue University, Montréal, QC H3A 2A8, Canada
Tel: 514-849-3004; *Fax:* 514-849-4113
info@dio-mdtc.ca
www.dio-mdtc.ca

Montréal: **The Presbyterian College**
Collège Presbytérien
3495, rue University, Montréal, QC H3A 2A8, Canada
Tel: 514-288-5256; *Fax:* 514-288-8072
email@presbyteriancollege.ca
www.presbyteriancollege.ca
Full Time Equivalency: 70

Québec: **Direction générale du Conservatoire de musique et d'art dramatique du Québec**
Bloc C
225, Grande Allée est, 3e étage, Québec, QC G1R 5G5, Canada
Tél: 418-380-2327; *Téléc:* 418-380-2328
info@conservatoire.gouv.qc.ca
www.conservatoire.gouv.qc.ca

Campuses
Conservatoire de musique de Saguenay
202, rue Jacques-Cartier est, Chicoutimi, QC G7H 6R8, Canada
Fax: 418-698-3521
info@conservatoire.gouv.qc.ca
www.conservatoire.gouv.qc.ca/saguenay/index.asp
Jacques Clément, Directeur

Conservatoire de musique de Gatineau
430, boul Alexandre-Taché, Gatineau, QC J9A 1M7, Canada
Tel: 819-772-3283; *Fax:* 819-772-3346
info@conservatoire.gouv.qc.ca
www.conservatoire.gouv.qc.ca/gatineau/index.asp
Danielle Dubé, Directrice

Conservatoire de musique de Montréal
4750, av Henri-Julien, Montréal, QC H2T 2C8, Canada
Tel: 514-873-4031; *Fax:* 514-873-4601
info@conservatoire.gouv.qc.ca
http://www.conservatoire.gouv.qc.ca/montreal/index.asp
Isolde Lagacé, Directrice

Conservatoire de musique de Québec
270, rue St-Amable, Québec, QC G1R 5G1, Canada
Tel: 418-643-2190; *Fax:* 418-644-9658
info@conservatoire.gouv.qc.ca
www.conservatoire.gouv.qc.ca/quebec/index.asp
André Picard, Directeur

Conservatoire de musique de Rimouski
22, rue Sainte-Marie, Rimouski, QC G5L 4E2, Canada
Tel: 418-727-3706; *Fax:* 418-727-3818
info@conservatoire.gouv.qc.ca
www.conservatoire.gouv.qc.ca/rimouski/
Benoît Plourde, Directeur

Conservatoire de musique de Trois-Rivières
587, rue Radisson, Trois-Rivières, QC G9A 2C8, Canada
Fax: 819-371-6955
info@conservatoire.gouv.qc.ca
www.conservatoire.gouv.qc.ca/trois-rivieres
Pierre Normandin, Directeur

Conservatoire de musique de Val-d'Or
88, rue Allard, Val-d'Or, QC J9P 2Y1, Canada
Tel: 819-354-4585; *Fax:* 819-354-4297
info@conservatoire.gouv.qc.ca
www.conservatoire.gouv.qc.ca/val-dor/
Jean Saint-Jules, Directeur

Conservatoire d'art dramatique de Montréal
4750, av Henri-Julien, Montréal H2T 2C8, Canada
Tel: 514-873-4283; *Fax:* 514-873-4601
info@conservatoire.gouv.qc.ca
www.conservatoire.gouv.qc.ca/cadm/
Gilbert Lepage, Directeur

Conservatoire d'art dramatique de Québec
31, rue Mont-Carmel, Québec, QC G1R 4A6, Canada
Fax: 418-646-9255
info@conservatoire.gouv.qc.ca
www.conservatoire.gouv.qc.ca/cadq/
André Jean, Directeur (par intérim)

Saint-Laurent: **Vanier College**
821, av Ste-Croix, Saint-Laurent, QC H4L 3X9, Canada
Tel: 514-744-7500; *Fax:* 514-744-7505
info@vaniercollege.qc.ca
www.vaniercollege.qc.ca
Full Time Equivalency: 6100
An English Cégep.
Gilbert Héroux, Dir. gén.
John McMahon, Dean

Publications
The Echo
Vanier Phoenix
The Vanier Vandoo

Sainte-Geneviève: **Collège Gérald-Godin**
15615, boul Gouin ouest, Sainte-Geneviève, QC H9H 5K8, Canada
Tél: 514-626-2666; *Téléc:* 514-626-6866
information@cgodin.qc.ca
www.college-gerald-godin.qc.ca
Full Time Equivalency: 1125
Pierre Schetagne, Directeur général

Sainte-Thérèse: **Le Collège Lionel-Groulx**
100, rue Duquet, Sainte-Thérèse, QC J7E 3G6, Canada
Tél: 450-430-3120; *Téléc:* 450-971-7883
info@clg.qc.ca
www.clg.qc.ca

Grades: Préuniv., Techniques, Form. cont.
Full Time Equivalency: 4109
Monique Laurin, Directrice générale

Publications
L'Écorché

Salaberry-de-Valleyfield: **Collège de Valleyfield**
169, rue Champlain, Salaberry-de-Valleyfield, QC J6T 1X6, Canada
Tél: 450-373-9441; *Téléc:* 450-377-7719
courrier@colval.qc.ca
www.colval.qc.ca
Jacques Turgeon, Directeur général

Publications
Pars ailleurs

Shawinigan: **Collège Shawinigan**
P.O. Box 610
2263, av du Collège, Shawinigan, QC G9N 6V8, Canada
Tél: 819-539-6401; *Téléc:* 819-539-8819
information@collegeshawinigan.qc.ca
www.collegeshawinigan.qc.ca
Full Time Equivalency: 1500
Jean Lefebvre, Directeur général par intérim

Publications
Journal l'actif

Sherbrooke: **Champlain Regional College**
P.O. Box 5000
1301, boul Portland, Sherbrooke, QC J1H 5N1, Canada
Tél: 819-564-3600; *Téléc:* 819-564-3639
lmillette@abacom.com
www.champlaincollege.qc.ca
Gerald R. Cutting, Directeur général

Campuses
Campus Lennoxville
P.O. Box 5003
2580 College St., Lennoxville, QC J1M 0C8, Canada
Tel: 819-564-3666; *Fax:* 819-564-5171
admissions@crc-lennox.qc.ca
www.crc-lennox.qc.ca

Campus St. Lambert
900, av Riverside, Saint-Lambert, QC J4P 3P2, Canada
Tel: 450-672-7360; *Fax:* 450-672-9299
InfoCenter@champlaincollege.qc.ca
www.champlainonline.com

Campus St. Lawrence
790, rue Nérée-Tremblay, Sainte-Foy, QC G1V 4K2, Canada
Tel: 418-656-6921; *Fax:* 418-656-6925
slcegep@slc.qc.ca
www.slc.qc.ca

Post Secondary/Technical

Post Secondary/Technical

Brossard: **Academy of Arts & Design**
Académie des arts et de design
7305, Marie-Victorin, 2e étage, Brossard, QC J4W 1A6, Canada
Tel: 514-875-9777; *Toll-Free:* 800-268-9777
www.aadmtl.com
Fashion Design, Fashion Merchandising, Interior Design, Advertising & Web Design, Animation Design. Instruction in French & English.
Serge Landry, Directeur général

Drummondville: **Collège Ellis**
235, rue Moisan, Drummondville, QC J2C 1W9, Canada
Tél: 819-477-3113; *Téléc:* 819-477-4556
www.ellis.qc.ca
Les installations du Pensionnat de Drummondville passent au Collège Ellis en 2006. Campus Trois-Rivières: 90, rue Dorval, (819) 691-2600.
Alain Scalzo, Directeur général

Laval: **Collège CDI Administration. Technologie. Santé (ICD)**
#400, 3, place Laval, Laval, QC H7N 1A2, Canada
Tél: 450-662-9090; *Téléc:* 450-662-0741
Ligne sans frais: 1-800-961-417
martin.gascon@cdi.ca
www.cicdi.ca
Enrollment: 380
Martin Gascon, Directeur

Campuses
Montréal
#700, 416, boul de Maisonneuve ouest, Montréal, QC H3A 1L2, Canada
Fax: 514-849-9034

Québec
#20, 905, av Honoré-Mercier, Québec, QC G1R 5M6, Canada
Fax: 418-694-9082

Montréal: Les Ateliers de danse moderne de Montréal
#201, 372, rue Ste-Catherine ouest, Montréal, QC H3B 1A2, Canada
Tél: 514-866-9814; *Téléc:* 514-866-5887
reception@ladmmi.com
www.ladmmi.com
Christine Bouchard, Directrice générale

Montréal: CDI College of Business, Technology & Healthcare
416, boul De Maisonneuve ouest, 7e étage, Montréal, QC H3A 1L2, Canada
Tel: 514-849-4757; *Fax:* 514-849-9034
www.cdicollege.com
Computers, accounting & business training; 5 locations across Québec

Montréal: Collège André-Gasset
1001 Crémazie est, Montréal, QC H2M 1M3, Canada
Tel: 514-381-4293; *Fax:* 514-381-7421
inform@grasset.qc.ca
www.grasset.qc.ca/index.htm
Pascal Nadon

Montréal: Collège d'enseignement en immobilier inc.
255, boul Crémazie est, Montréal, QC H2M 1M2, Canada
Tél: 514-905-1551; *Téléc:* 514-904-1453
info@enseignementimmobilier.com
Shirley Soulard, Directeur général
ssoulard@enseignementimmobilier.com

Montréal: Collège d'informatique Marsan
1001, boul de Maisonneuve est, 9e étage, Montréal, QC H2L 4P9, Canada
Tél: 514-525-3030; *Téléc:* 514-525-3314
info@collegemarsan.qc.ca
www.collegemarsan.qc.ca
Carlos Richer, Directeur général

Montréal: Collège de photographie Marsan
1001, boul de Maisonneuve est, 9e étage, Montréal, QC H2L 4P9, Canada
Tél: 514-525-2352; *Téléc:* 514-525-3314
info@collegemarsan.qc.ca
www.collegemarsan.qc.ca
Carlos Richer, Directeur général

Montréal: College Inter Dec
2120, rue Ste-Catherine ouest, Montréal, QC H3H 1M7, Canada
Tel: 514-939-4444; *Fax:* 514-939-0762
InterdecInfo@clasalle.com
www.interdec.qc.ca
Chrystel Jacquot-Donnat, Dir.

Montréal: Collège Jean-de-Brébeuf
3200, ch Sainte-Catherine, Montréal, QC H3T 1C1, Canada
Tel: 514-342-1320; *Fax:* 514-342-7169
sadm@brebeuf.qc.ca
www.brebeuf.qc.ca
Jean-Claude Gaudet, Directeur général

Montréal: Collège LaSalle
2000, rue Sainte-Catherine ouest, Montréal, QC H3H 2T2, Canada
Tel: 514-939-2006; *Fax:* 514-939-2015
admission@clasalle.com
www.clasalle.qc.ca/fr/index.html
Jacques Marchand, Directeur général

Montréal: Collège Salette
418, rue Sherbrooke Est, 3e étage, Montréal, QC H2L 1J6, Canada
Tel: 514-388-5725; *Fax:* 514-388-5957
info@collegesalette.qc.ca
www.collegesalette.qc.ca
Graphic design & computer graphics

Montréal: L'École Du Show-Business
#3010, 5505, boul Saint-Laurent, Montréal, QC H2T 1S6, Canada
Tel: 514-271-2244; *Fax:* 514-271-2434
info@ecoledushowbusiness.com
www.ecoledushowbusiness.com
Richard Blin, Directeur général

Montréal: École nationale de cirque National Circus School
8181, 2e av, Montréal, QC H1Z 4N9, Canada
Tél: 514-982-0859; *Téléc:* 514-982-6025
info@enc.qc.ca
www.enc.qc.ca
Marc Lalonde, Dir.

Montréal: École nationale de l'humour
2120, rue Sherbrooke est, 7e étage, Montréal, QC H2K 1C3, Canada
Tél: 514-849-7876; *Téléc:* 514-849-3307
humour@enh.qc.ca
www.enh.qc.ca
Formation professionnelle aux humoristes & aux auteurs. Reconnue par le Min. de l'Éducation, du Loisir & du Sport du Québec.
Louise Richer, Directrice générale

Montréal: École supérieure de ballet contemporain
4816, rue Rivard, Montréal, QC H2J 2N6, Canada
Tel: 514-849-4929; *Fax:* 514-849-6107
info@enbc.org
www.enbc.org
Didier Chirpaz, Dir. gén.

Montréal: Herzing College
1616, boul René-Lévesque ouest, Montréal, QC H3H 1P8, Canada
Tel: 450-686-7494; *Fax:* 450-933-6182
info@mtl.herzing.edu
www.herzing.edu/campus_info/
Career training programs
Hayat Drinali, Directeur général

Montréal: Institut de création artistique et de recherche en infographie ICARI inc.
55, av Mont Royal ouest, 5e étage, Montréal, QC H2T 2S6, Canada
Tel: 514-982-0922; *Fax:* 514-982-0288
info@icari.com
www.icari.qc.ca
Mariam Ladha, Directrice générale

Montréal: Institut supérieur d'informatique I.S.I.
#100, 255, boul Crémazie est, Montréal, QC H2M 1M2, Canada
Tel: 514-842-2426; *Fax:* 514-842-2084
info@isi-mtl.com
www.isi-mtl.com
Henriette Morin

Montréal: Institut supérieur de design de mode I.S.D.M. inc.
6920, rue St-Hubert, 2e étage, Montréal, QC H2S 2H2, Canada
Tel: 514-274-1092; *Fax:* 514-270-0333
info@isdm-mode.com
www.isdm-mode.com
Phuc Tran-Huu, Directeur général
phuctran@aei.ca

Montréal: Institut Teccart (2003)
3030, rue Hochelaga, Montréal, QC H1W 1G2, Canada
Tel: 514-526-2501; *Fax:* 514-526-9192
nehajibi@teccart.qc.ca
www.teccart.qc.ca
Nour-Eddine Hajibi

Montréal: The International College of Spiritual & Psychic Sciences
P.O. Box 1445 H
1974, boul de Maisonneuve ouest, Montréal, QC H3G 2N3, Canada
Tél: 514-937-8359; *Téléc:* 514-937-5380
iiihs@iiihs.org
www.iiihs.org
Dr. Marilyn Zwaig Rossner, Ph.D., Dean
mrossner@iiihs.org

Montréal: Marianopolis College
3880, Côte-des-Neiges, Montréal, QC H3H 1W1, Canada
Tel: 514-931-8792; *Fax:* 514-931-8790
www.marianopolis.edu
Sr. Françoise Boisvert, Dir. gén.

Publications
The Papercut

Montréal: National Theatre School of Canada École nationale de théâtre du Canada
5030, rue St-Denis, Montréal, QC H2J 2L8, Canada
Tel: 514-842-7954; *Fax:* 514-842-5661
Toll-Free: 1-866-547-732
info@ent-nts.qc.ca
www.ent-nts.qc.ca
Enrollment: 160
Offers training in acting, playwriting, directing, set & costume design & technical production in both English & French.
Simon Brault, O.C., CEO

Montréal: Trebas Institute Institut Trebas
Tour Est
550, rue Sherbrooke ouest, 6e étage, Montréal, QC H3A 1B9, Canada
Tel: 514-845-4141; *Fax:* 514-845-2581
infomtl@trebas.com
www.trebas.com
Enrollment: 200
David P. Leonard, Président

Outremont: École de Musique Vincent d'Indy
628, ch Côte Ste-Catherine, Outremont, QC H2V 2C5, Canada
Tél: 514-735-5261; *Téléc:* 514-735-5266
info@isdm-mode.com
www.emvi.qc.ca
Kathleen Caissy, Directrice générale

Québec: Collège Mérici
755, ch St-Louis, Québec, QC G1S 1C1, Canada
Tel: 418-683-1591; *Fax:* 418-682-8938
information@college-merici.qc.ca
www.college-merici.qc.ca
Pierre L'Heureux, Directeur général

Québec: Collège radio télévision de Québec inc.
751, côte d'Abraham, Québec, QC G1R 1A2, Canada
Tél: 418-647-2095; *Téléc:* 418-522-5456
christian.lavoie@crtq.net
www.crtq.net
Christian Lavoie, Dir.

Québec: L'École de danse de Québec
#214, 310, boul Langelier, Québec, QC G1K 5N3, Canada
Tel: 418-649-4715; *Fax:* 418-649-4702
info.edq@qc.aira.com
www.ecolededansedequebec.qc.ca
Professional training in contemporary dance performance, 3-year, full-time, post-secondary level
Dominique Turcotte, Director

Saint-Hubert: Académie de l'Entrepreneurship Québécois inc.
4619, rue de Niverville, Saint-Hubert, QC J3Y 9G6, Canada
Tél: 450-676-5826; *Téléc:* 450-676-2261
info@academieentrepreneurship.com
www.academieentrepreneurship.com
Johanne Bouchard

Trois-Rivières: Collège Laflèche
1687, boul du Carmel, Trois-Rivières, QC G8Z 3R8, Canada
Tel: 819-375-7346; *Fax:* 819-375-7347
college@clafleche.qc.ca
www.clafleche.qc.ca
Marcel Côté, Directeur général

Verdun: Collège de l'immobilier du Québec
600, ch du Golf, Verdun, QC H3E 1A8, Canada
Tel: 514-762-1862; *Fax:* 514-762-4975
francine.forget@cigm.qc.ca
www.collegeimmobilier.com
Francine Forget, Directrice générale

Ville Mont-Royal: Collège Technique de Montréal
#204, Royalmount, Ville Mont-Royal, QC H4P 1H7, Canada
Tél: 514-932-6444; *Téléc:* 514-932-6448
info@mtccollege.com
www.mtccollege.com

Westmount: International Career School Canada ICS Canada
#610, 245 Victoria Ave., Westmount, QC H3Z 2M6, Canada
Tel: 514-482-6951; *Fax:* 514-482-6868
Toll-Free: 1-888-427-2400
info@icslearn.ca
www.icslearn.ca
Enrollment: 12875
At-home training in 50 career fields.

Saskatchewan

Government Agencies

***Regina:* Saskatchewan Advanced Education & Employment**
2220 College Ave., Regina, SK S4P 4V9, Canada
Tel: 306-787-6030; *Fax:* 306-798-2045
Toll-Free: 1-888-775-327
www.aee.gov.sk.ca

***Regina:* Saskatchewan Learning**
2220 College Ave., Regina, SK S4P 4V9, Canada
Tel: 306-787-6030; *Fax:* 306-798-2045
Toll-Free: 1-888-775-3276
learninginquiry@sasked.gov.sk.ca
www.sasklearning.gov.sk.ca

Campuses
Region One
4635 Wascana Parkway, Regina, SK S4P 3A3, Canada
Tel: 306-798-6071; *Fax:* 306-787-6139
Tom Chell, Regional Director
Region Two
350 Cheadle St. West, Swift Current, SK S9H 4G3, Canada
Tel: 306-778-8249; *Fax:* 306-778-8583
Wanda Biffart, Regional Director
Region Three
4635 Wascana Pkwy., Regina, SK S4P 3V7, Canada
Tel: 306-787-6075; *Fax:* 306-787-6139
Wayne Back, Regional Director
Region Four
Sturdy Stone Bldg.
122 - 3 Ave. North, 8th Fl., Saskatoon, SK S7K 2H6, Canada
Tel: 306-933-5028; *Fax:* 306-933-7469
Crandall Hrynkiw, Regional Director
Region Five
P.O. Box 6500
107 Crawford Ave. East, Melfort, SK S0E 1A0, Canada
Tel: 306-752-6166; *Fax:* 306-752-6168
Darlene Thompson, Regional Director
Region Six
1146 - 102 St., North Battleford, SK S9A 1E9, Canada
Tel: 306-446-7435; *Fax:* 306-446-7586
Dr. Lois Duffee, Regional Director
Northern Region Office- La Ronge
P.O. Box 5000
La Ronge, SK S0J 1L0, Canada
Tel: 306-425-4380; *Fax:* 306-425-4383
Toll-Free: 1-800-667-4380
Kevin (Toby Greschner, Regional Director

School Boards/Districts/Divisions

Public

***Creighton:* Creighton School Division #111**
P.O. Box 158
325 Main St., Creighton, SK S0P 0A0, Canada
Tel: 306-688-5825; *Fax:* 306-688-3131
Enrollment: 394
Austin Gerein, Dir.
Shirley Owen, Sec.-Treas.

***Englefeld:* Engelfeld Protestant Separate School Division #132**
P.O. Box 100
Englefeld, SK S0K 1N0, Canada
Tel: 306-287-3568; *Fax:* 306-287-3569
Enrollment: 107
Jim Martin, Sec.-Treas.
Harvey Bowers, Dir.

***Ile-a-la-Crosse:* Ile a la Crosse School Division #112**
P.O. Box 89
Ile-a-la-Crosse, SK S0M 1C0, Canada
Tel: 306-833-2141; *Fax:* 306-833-2104
Enrollment: 469
Christine Arnett, Sec.-Treas.
carnett@icsd.ca
Lon Borgerson, Director, Education
lborgerson@icsd.ca

***La Ronge:* Northern Lights School Division #113**
Bag Service #6500, La Ronge, SK S0J 1L0, Canada
Tel: 306-425-3302; *Fax:* 306-425-3377
centraloffice@nlsd113.net
www.nlsd113.com
Grades: K.-12
Enrollment: 4168
Ralph Pilz, Dir.
ralphpilz@nlsd113.net
Charlie McCloud, Sec.-Treas.
charliemccloud@nlsd113.net
Julius Park, First Nations/Metis Education Consultant
juliuspark@nlsd113.net

***Langian:* Horizon School Division #205**
P.O. Box 100
110 main st., Langian, SK S0K 2M0, Canada
Tel: 306-365-4888; *Fax:* 306-365-2808
Toll-Free: 877-365-4888
www.hzsd.ca
Enrollment: 6992
Marc Danylchuk, Director, Education
Philip Benson, Sec.-Treas.

***Melfort:* North East School Division #200**
P.O. Box 6000
402 Main St., Melfort, SK S0E 1A0, Canada
Tel: 306-752-5741; *Fax:* 306-752-1933
Toll-Free: 888-752-5741
www.nesd.ca
Grades: Pre-K.-12
Enrollment: 5317
Don Rempel, Dir.
Ralph Paquin, Supt. of Bus. Admin., 306-752-1211, fax: 306-752-4580

***Melville:* St. Henry's Roman Catholic Separate School Division #5**
P.O. Box 1930
633 Main St., Melville, SK S0A 2P0, Canada
Tel: 306-728-4426; *Fax:* 306-728-2351
Enrollment: 309
This division amalgamated with Yorkton RCSSD #86, St. Theodore RCSSD #138 Melville Rural RCSSD #217 and Yorkton Rural RCSSD #216 to form the new Christ the Teacher Roman Catholic Separate School Division #212.
Brian Boechler, Dir.
Wilfred Hotsko, Sec.-Treas.

***Moose Jaw:* Holy Trinity Roman Catholic Separate School Division #22**
P.O. Box 1087
502 - 6 Ave. NE, Moose Jaw, SK S6H 4P8, Canada
Tel: 306-694-5333; *Fax:* 306-692-2238
www.htcsd.ca
Enrollment: 2080
Celeste York, Director, Education
Gerry Gieni, Sec.-Treas.

***Moose Jaw:* Prairie South School Division #210**
15 Thatcher Dr. East, Moose Jaw, SK S6J 1L8, Canada
Tel: 306-694-1200; *Fax:* 306-694-4955
Toll-Free: 877-434-1200
www.prairiesouth.ca
Enrollment: 6931
Brenda Edwards, Director, Education
Gordon Stewart, Chair

***North Battleford:* Living Sky School Division #202**
509 Pioneer Ave., North Battleford, SK S9A 4A5, Canada
Tel: 306-937-7702; *Fax:* 306-445-4332
office@lskysd.ca
www.lskysd.ca
Grades: K.-12
Enrollment: 5550
Ron Ford, Dir., 306-937-7909
ron.ford@lskysd.ca
Ray Kopera, CFO, 306-937-7702
ray.kopera@lskysd.ca

***North Battleford:* North West Roman Catholic Separate School Division #16**
9301 - 19 Ave., North Battleford, SK S9A 3N5, Canada
Tel: 306-445-6158; *Fax:* 306-445-3993
loccsd@loccsd.ca
www.loccsd.ca
Grades: Pre-K.-12
Enrollment: 1968
This school division is an amalgamation of 4 boards: North Battleford RCSSD#16, Wilkie St. George RCSSD#85, Unity RCSSD#88 and Spiritwood RCSSD#82.
Herb Sutton, Dir.
h.sutton@loccsd.ca
Guy Denton, Supt. of Admin.
g.denton@loccsd.ca

***Prince Albert:* Prince Albert Roman Catholic Separate School Division #6**
118 - 11 St. East, Prince Albert, SK S6V 1A1, Canada
Tel: 306-953-7500; *Fax:* 306-763-1723
info@cec.pacsd6.sk.ca
www.pacsd6.sk.ca
Enrollment: 3121
Tim Jelinski, Director, Education
Don Orr, Sec.-Treas.

***Prince Albert:* Saskatchewan Rivers School Division #119**
545 - 11 St. East, Prince Albert, SK S6V 1B1, Canada
Tel: 306-764-1571; *Fax:* 306-763-4460
www.srsd119.ca
Enrollment: 9200
Dr. William O. Cooke, Director, Education
D. A.. Moniuk, Sec.-Treas.

***Regina:* Division scolaire francophone #310**
#200, 3850 Hillsdale St., Regina, SK S4S 7J5, Canada
Tel: 306-757-7541; *Fax:* 306-757-2040
www.dsf.sk.ca/
Enrollment: 1095
Denis Ferré, Dir.
Lise Gareau, Sec.-Treas.

***Regina:* Prairie Valley School Division #208**
P.O. Box 1937
3080 Albert St. North, Regina, SK S4P 3E1, Canada
Tel: 306-949-3366; *Fax:* 306-543-1771
reception@pvsd.ca
www.pvsd.ca
Enrollment: 8292
Ben J. Grebinski, Director
Michael Back, Sec.-Treas.

***Regina:* Regina Roman Catholic Separate School Division #81**
2160 Cameron St., Regina, SK S4T 2V6, Canada
Tel: 306-791-7200; *Fax:* 306-347-7699
rcs@rcs.sk.ca
www.rcsd.ca
Grades: K-12
Enrollment: 10000
Gwen Keith, Director
Curt Van Parys, Sec.-Treas.

***Regina:* Regina School Division #4**
1600 - 4 Ave., Regina, SK S4R 8C8, Canada
Tel: 306-523-3000; *Fax:* 306-532-3031
info@rbe.sk.ca
www.rbe.sk.ca
Enrollment: 20678
Don Hoium, Director
Debra Burnett, Sec.-Treas.

***Rosetown:* Sun West School Division #207**
P.O. Box 700
Rosetown, SK S0L 2V0, Canada
Tel: 306-882-2677; *Fax:* 306-882-3366
Toll-Free: 1-866-375-2677
info@sunwestsd.ca
www.sunwestsd.ca
Grades: Kindergarten - 12
Enrollment: 4500
Number of Schools: 14 kindergarten to grade 12 schools; 15 Hutterite colony schools; 7 elementary schools; 3 secondary schools; 1 distance education centre
Lorne Ulven, Chair
Janet Casswell-Beckmann, Director, Education, 306-882-2677
janet.casswell-beckmann@sunwestsd.ca
Tony Baldwin, Superintendent, Education
Cheryl Bashutski, Superintendent, Education
Tracy Dollansky, Superintendent, Education
Lynne Dressler, Superintendent, Education
Maureen Sample, Superintendent, Business
Mike Fedyk, Officer, Communications
Michelle Leith, Officer, Human Resources
Doug Klassen, Supervisor, Technology
Earl McKnight, Supervisor, Transportation
Rob Minion, Supervisor, Facilities
Rhonda Saathoff, Supervisor, Business

***Saskatoon:* Greater Saskatoon Catholic Schools**
420 - 22nd St. East, Saskatoon, SK S7K 1X3, Canada
Tel: 306-659-7000
info@gscs.sk.ca
www.scs.sk.ca
Other Information: Learning Services, Phone: 306-659-2010; HR Services: 306-659-2012
Grades: K-12; French, Cree, & Ukrainian
Enrollment: 15000

Number of Schools: 37 elementary schools; 6 secondary schools; 2 associate schools (Co-manager of Humboldt Collegiate Institute, with Horizon School Division). Number of Employees: 1,900+
Diane Boyko, Board Chair, 306-382-2832
DLBoyko@gscs.sk.ca
Beverley Hanson, Director, Education, 306-659-7001
Darryl Bazylak, Superintendent, Education, 306-659-7040
Al Boutin, Superintendent, Human Resource Services, 306-659-7048
Greg Chatlain, Superintendent, Education, 306-659-7090
Dr. Donald Lloyd, Superintendent, Administrative Services, 306-659-7021
Gordon Martell, Superintendent, Education, 306-659-7056
John McAuliffe, Superintendent, Education, 306-659-7044
Joanne Weninger, Superintendent, Education, 306-659-7041
Donella Hoffman, Consultant, Communications, 306-659-7077
dhoffman@gscs.sk.ca

Saskatoon: Saskatoon School Division #13
310 - 21st St. East, Saskatoon, SK S7K 1M7, Canada
Tel: 306-683-8200; *Fax:* 306-657-3900
totht@spsd.sk.ca
www.spsd.sk.ca
Enrollment: 20000
George Rathwell, Director, Education
Garry Benning, Chief Financial Officer

Swift Current: Chinook School Division No. 211
P.O. Box 1809
Swift Current, SK S9H 4J8, Canada
Tel: 306-778-9200; *Fax:* 306-773-8011
Enrollment: 6329
Liam Choo-Foo, Director
Rod Quintin, Sec.-Treas.

Turtleford: Northwest School Division #203
P.O. Box 280
Turtleford, SK S0M 2Y0, Canada
Tel: 306-845-2150; *Fax:* 306-845-3392
www.nwsd.ca
Enrollment: 4910
Glen Winkler, Director, Education
Greg Gerwing, Sec.-Treas.

Viscount: St. Alphonse Roman Catholic Separate School Division #2
P.O. Box 71
Viscount, SK S0K 4M0, Canada
Tel: 306-944-4446; *Fax:* 306-944-4446
Enrollment: 21
Joseph Kammermayer, Dir.
Mary Comeault, Sec.-Treas.

Warman: Prairie Spirit School Division #206
P.O. Box 809
121 Klassen St. East, Warman, SK S0K 4S0, Canada
Tel: 306-683-2800; *Fax:* 306-934-8221
www.spiritsd.ca
Enrollment: 8787
Evelyn Novak, Director, Education
Jim Shields, Superintendent

Weyburn: Holy Family R.C.S.S.D. #140
110 Souris Ave., 3rd Fl., Weyburn, SK S4H 2Z8, Canada
Tel: 306-842-7025; *Fax:* 306-842-7033
www.holyfamilyrcssd.ca
Enrollment: 981
Shelley Rowein, Director, Education
Bruno Tuchscherer, Chair

Weyburn: South East Cornerstone School Division #209
80A - 18 St. NE, Weyburn, SK S4H 2W4, Canada
Tel: 306-848-0080; *Fax:* 306-848-4747
Toll-Free: 888-938-0080
contactus@cornerstonesd.ca
www.cornerstonesd.ca
Enrollment: 7862
Marc Casavant, Director, Education
Lionel Diederichs, Chief Financial Officer

Yorkton: Christ the Teacher RCSSD No. 212
45A Palliser Way, Yorkton, SK S3N 4C5, Canada
Tel: 306-783-8787; *Fax:* 306-783-4992
www.christtheteacher.ca
Grades: Pre-K.-12
Enrollment: 1800
This division is an amalgamation of St. Henry's RCSSD #5, Yorkton RCSSD #86, St. Theodore RCSSD #138, Melville Rural RCSSD #217 and Yorkton Rural RCSSD #216.
Darrell Zaba, Dir.
Wilfred Hotsko, Sec.-Treas.
Del Killick, Chair

Yorkton: Good Spirit School Division #204
Fairview Education Centre
63 King St. East, Yorkton, SK S3N 0T7, Canada
Tel: 306-786-5500; *Fax:* 306-783-0355
Toll-Free: 1-866-390-0773
feedback@mail.gssd.ca
www.gssd.ca
Other Information: GSSD Distance Learning Center, Toll-Free Phone: 1-877-988-1122
Grades: Junior Kindergarten - 12
Enrollment: 5935
Number of Schools: 28
Raymond Sass, Chair
Dwayne Reeve, Director, Education
Juanita Brown, Assistant Superintendent, Learning
Withman Jaigobin, Superintendent, Schools
Thom Koroluk, Superintendent, Student Services
Susan Maserek, Superintendent, Schools
Alan Sharp, Superintendent, Program Development
Sherry Todosichuk, Superintendent, Business Administration

Yorkton: Yorkton Roman Catholic Separate School Division #86
259 Circlebrooke Dr., Yorkton, SK S3N 2S8, Canada
Tel: 306-783-8787; *Fax:* 306-783-4992
Enrollment: 1451
This division amalgamated with St. Henry's RCSSD #5 in Melville, St. Theodore RCSSD #138 in Theodore, and the two rural divisions around the cities of Yorkton and Melville to become Christ the Teacher Roman Catholic Separate School Division #212.
Brian Boechler, Dir.
Wilfred R. Maier, Sec.-Treas.
Tim Molnar, Chair

Protestant

Englefeld: Englefeld Protestant Separate School District #132
P.O. Box 190
Englefeld, SK S0K 1N0, Canada
Tel: 306-287-3568; *Fax:* 306-287-3569
Enrollment: 113
Harvey Bowers, Dir.
Jim Martin, Sec.-Treas.

Schools: Specialized

Special Education

Pilot Butte: Schaller School
P.O. Box 570
Pilot Butte, SK S0G 3Z0, Canada
Tel: 306-781-1829; *Fax:* 306-757-0599
Grades: K.-12
Enrollment: 192
Marion MacIver, Principal

Regina: Cornwall Alternative School
40 Dixon Cres., Regina, SK S4N 1V4, Canada
Tel: 306-522-0044; *Fax:* 306-359-0720
unis.ca@sasktel.net
www.saskschools.ca/schoolinfo/44.htm
Enrollment: 30
Eunice Cameron, Principal
eunice@sk.sympatico.ca

Saskatoon: Radius Community Centre for Education & Employment
P.O. Box 1812
#6 Bateman Crest., Saskatoon, SK S7H 3C2, Canada
Tel: 306-665-0362; *Fax:* 306-665-5579
info@radiuscentre.com
www.radiuscentre.com
Gail McKenzie-Wilcox, Principal

Schools: Independent & Private

Independent & Private Schools

Battleford: Heritage Christian School
P.O. Box 490
11 - 20th St. West, Battleford, SK S0M 0E0, Canada
Tel: 306-446-3188; *Fax:* 306-446-3187
hcs@bsd.sk.ca
Grades: K.-12; Days only
Enrollment: 59
Peter Halvorsen, Principal

Caronport: Caronport High School (CHS)
c/o Briercrest College & Seminary
510 College Dr., Caronport, SK S0H 0S0, Canada
Tel: 306-756-3200
info@briercrest.ca
www.briercrest.ca/chs
Grades: 9 - 12
Deborah Ike, Principal
deborahi@briercrest.ca
David Frostad, Vice Principal
dfrostad@briercrest.ca
George Willatt, Vice Principal
gwillatt@briercrest.ca
Vi Thiessen, Office Administrator
vthiessen@briercrest.ca

Moose Jaw: Cornerstone Christian School
43 Iroquois St. East, Moose Jaw, SK S6H 4S9, Canada
Tel: 306-693-2937
office@ccsmj.ca
www.ccsmj.ca
Grades: K.-12; Day only
Enrollment: 300
Scott Robertson, Principal

Outlook: Lutheran Collegiate Bible Institute
P.O. Box 459
Outlook, SK S0L 2N0, Canada
Tel: 306-867-8971; *Fax:* 306-867-9947
lcbi@outlet.sk.ca
www.lcbi.sk.ca
Grades: 10-12; Residential only
Philip Guebert, Principal

Pilot Butte: Schaller School
P.O. Box 570
Pilot Butte, SK S0G 3Z0, Canada
Tel: 306-781-1838; *Fax:* 306-757-0599
Grades: K.-12
Enrollment: 190
Marion MacIver, Principal

Prince Albert: Rivier Academy
1405 Bishop Pascal Pl., Prince Albert, SK S6V 5J1, Canada
Tel: 306-764-6289; *Fax:* 306-763-1442
rivier.academy_rivier@saskschools.ca
www.saskschools.ca/~rivier
Grades: 7 - 12
An associate school of the Prince Albert Roman Catholic School Division 6, Rivier Academy is an independent, Catholic high school for young women. It provides a full course, as prescribed by Saskatchewan Learning.
Sr. Mary Woodward, Principal
Claude Jalbert, Vice Principal

Regina: Harvest City Christian Academy
Harvest City Church
2202 - 8th Ave. North, Regina, SK S4R 7T9, Canada
Tel: 306-569-1935; *Fax:* 306-359-9047
hcc.office@harvestcity.sk.ca
www.harvestcity.sk.ca
Grades: K.-12 (Non-Denom.); Day only
Enrollment: 172
Todd Harrison, Principal

Regina: Luther College High School
1500 Royal St., Regina, SK S4T 5A5, Canada
Tel: 306-791-9150
Grades: 9-12
Berbel Knoll, Principal

Regina: Regina Christian School (RCS)
2505 - 23rd Ave., Regina, SK S4S 7K7, Canada
Tel: 306-775-0919; *Fax:* 306-775-3070
office@reginachristianschool.org
www.reginachristianschool.org
Other Information: development@reginachristianschool.org (E-mail, Development)
Grades: Preschool - 12
Enrollment: 504
The interdenominational school's academic program is offered with an evangelical Christian view.
Darryl Brown, Board Chair
Rod Rilling, B.Ed., B.A. (Hons), Principal
principal@reginachristianschool.org
Krista Munson, B.Ed., B.A., Vice Principal
krista.munson@rbe.sk.ca
Doreen Brace, B.Ed., Learning Leader & Resource Teacher
doreen.brace@rbe.sk.ca

***Regina:* Regina Huda School**
40 Sheppard St., Regina, SK S4R 3M6, Canada
Tel: 306-565-1988
www.hudaschool.regina.sk.ca

Grades: Preschool - 12
Regina Huda School strives to preserve the Islamic identity, by offering Islamic & Arabic studies for the Muslim community.
Dr. Ayman Aboguddah, Board President
aboguddah@gmail.com
Twila Wilson, Principal
twila.wilson@rbe.sk.ca
Diane Szabo, School Secretary
secretary@hudaschool.regina.sk.ca

***Rosthern:* Rosthern Junior College**
410 - 6th Ave., Rosthern, SK S0K 3R0, Canada
Tel: 306-232-4222; *Fax:* 306-232-5250
office@rjc.sk.ca
www.rjc.sk.ca

Grades: 10 - 12
The Christian secondary school operates within a Mennonite school community, for students of any faith. Completion of enriched courses leads to a Saskatchewan senior matriculation.
Gail Schellenberg, Principal
Lloyd Schmidt, Academic Coordinator
Holly Epp, Dean, Women
Matt Love, Dean, Men
Kathy Powley, Dean, Women
Graeme Rinholm, Dean, Men
Dave Feick, Contact, Admissions & Relations
Dave Feick, Contact, Admissions

***Saskatoon:* Christian Centre Academy (CCA)**
102 Pinehouse Dr., Saskatoon, SK S7K 5H7, Canada
Tel: 306-242-7141
academy@christiancentre.ca
www.christiancentre.ca/academy

Grades: Kindergarten - 12
The Accelerated Christian Education curriculum is used from kindergarten to grade 9 at the Christian Centre Academy. From grade 10 to 12, Saskatchewan Association of Independent Church Schools materials are used.

***Saskatoon:* Saskatoon Christian School**
Site 510, Box 8, RR#5, Saskatoon, SK S7K 3J8, Canada
Tel: 306-343-1494; *Fax:* 306-343-0366
ssce@saskatoonchristianschool.ca
www.saskatoonchristianschool.ca

Grades: K.-12; Day only
Doug Wiebe, Principal
wiebedo@spsd.sk.ca

***Wilcox:* Athol Murray College of Notre Dame**
P.O. Box 100
49 Main St., Wilcox, SK S0G 5E0, Canada
Tel: 306-732-2080; *Fax:* 306-732-4409
info@notredame.ca
www.notredame.sk.ca

Grades: 9-12
Enrollment: 350
Athol Murray College of Notre Dame is an international coeducational & residential college preparatory school. It is dedicated to Catholic Christian education.
Rob Palmarin, B.Ed., M.Th., President, 306-732-1230
Bob Baumuller, B.Ed., Director, Student Services, 306-732-1221
Dave Kenney, B.A., M.Ed., Director, Admissions, MarComm, & Alumni Relations, 306-732-2080, ext. 221
Hugh Lambert, B.Ed, B.Sc., Director, Academics, 306-732-2080, ext. 143

Universities & Colleges

Universities

***Caronport:* Briercrest College & Seminary**
510 College Dr., Caronport, SK S0H 0S0, Canada
Tel: 306-756-3200; *Fax:* 306-756-5500
Toll-Free: 800-667-5199
info@briercrest.ca
www.briercrest.ca

Full Time Equivalency: 640
The institution also operates the Caronport High School.

***Regina:* Campion College**
University of Regina
3737 Wascana Pkwy., Regina, SK S4S 0A2, Canada
Tel: 306-586-4242; *Fax:* 306-359-1200
Toll-Free: 800-667-7282
campion.college@uregina.ca
www.campioncollege.sk.ca

Full Time Equivalency: 1000

***Regina:* First Nations University of Canada**
1 First Nations Way, Regina, SK S4S 7K2, Canada
Tel: 306-790-5950; *Fax:* 306-790-5999
www.firstnationsuniversity.ca

Full Time Equivalency: 760

***Regina:* Luther College**
University of Regina Campus
Regina, SK S4S 0A2, Canada
Tel: 306-585-5333; *Fax:* 306-585-2949
Toll-Free: 800-588-4378
www.luthercollege.edu

Full Time Equivalency: 1000
While administratively independent, Luther is academically integrated with the University of Regina.

***Regina:* The University of Regina**
3737 Wascana Pkwy., Regina, SK S4S 0A2, Canada
Tel: 306-585-4402; *Fax:* 306-585-4997
communications@uregina.ca
www.uregina.ca

Full Time Equivalency: 11554
Lt. Gov. The Ho L.M. Haverstock, Visitor
Garth Fredrickson, Chairman
William F. Ready, Chancellor
Dr. Vianne Timmins, B.A., B.Ed., M.Ed., Ph.D., President & Vice-Chancellor
Dr. Gary Boire, Ph.D., Vice-President
Dave Button, M.Sc., P.Eng., P.M.P., Vice-President
Annette Revet, B.Sc.(Hons.), MBA, University Secretary
Barbara Pollock, B.A., B.Ed., Vice-President
Bev Liski, Registrar
Dr. Lynn Wells, B.A. (Hons.), M.A., Ph.D., Assoc. Vice-President
John D. Smith, Assoc. Vice-President
Allan Cahoon, B.A., M.Sc., Ph.D., Vice-President
Kelly Kummerfield, B.Admin., Assoc. Vice-President
Nelson Wagner, Assoc. Vice-President
Dale Schoffer, Assoc. Vice-President

Faculties
Arts
Dr. Lynn Wells, B.A. (Hons.), M.A., Ph.D., Acting Dean
Business Administration
Dr. Anne Lavack, Ph.D, Dean
Education
Dr. James McNinch, B.A., Ph.D., Dean
Engineering
Dr. Paitoon Tontiwachwuthikul, B.A., B.Eng. (Hons.), M.E, Dean
Fine Arts
Dr. Sheila Petty, B.A. (Hons.), L ès L, M è, Dean
Graduate Studies & Research
Dr. Rodney A. Kelln, B.Sc. (Hons.), Ph.D., Dean
Kinesiology & Health Studies
Dr. Craig Chamberlin, B.P.E., M.P.E., Ph.D., Dean
Science
Dr. Brien Maguire, B.Sc., M.Sc., Ph.D., Dean
Social Work
Dr. David Schantz, Ph.D., Dean

Schools
Canadian Plains Research Center
Dr. Polo Diaz, Ph.D., Executive Director
Centre for Continuing Education/Conservatory of Performing Arts
Dr. Harvey King, Ph.D., Director
Counselling Services
Dr. Brian Sveinson, B.A., M.A., Ph.D., Director
Graduate School of Business
Anne Lavack, B.Sc., M.B.A., Ph.D., Director
Graduate School of Public Policy
Dr. Michael Atkinson, B.A., M.A., Ph.D., Executive Director
School of Journalism
Mitch Diamantopoulos, B.A. Hons., M.A., Department Head

Affiliations
Campion College
c/o University of Regina
3737 Wascana Pkwy., Regina, SK S4S 0A2, Canada
Tel: 306-586-4242; *Fax:* 306-359-1200
Toll-Free: 1-800-667-7282
campion.college@uregina.ca
www.campioncollege.sk.ca

Enrollment: 1000
Number of Employees: 21 full-time professors; 12 full-time staff members; 1 campus minister
Fr. Benjamin Fiore, SJ, Ph.D., President, 306-359-1212
benjamin.fiore@uregina.ca
Fred Marcia, Exec. Dir., Administrative Services, 306-359-1231
fred.marcia@uregina.ca
Joanne Kozlowski, Dir., Admissions & Communications, 306-359-1244
joanne.kozlowski@uregina.ca
Kenneth Yanko, Dir. Facilities & Operations, 306-359-1249
ken.yanko@uregina.ca
Stephanie Molloy, Dir., Pastoral Studies, 306-359-1235
stephanie.molloy@uregina.ca
Frank Obrigewitsch, Dean, 306-359-1237
frank.obrigewitsch@uregina.ca
Nancy McNeill, Coordinator, Library, 306-359-1233
nancy.mcneill@uregina.ca
Deborah Morrison, Registrar, 306-359-1226
deborah.morrison@uregina.ca

First Nations University of Canada
1 First Nations Way, Regina, SK S4S 7K2, Canada
Tel: 306-790-5950; *Fax:* 306-790-5999
tpelletier@firstnationsuniversity.ca (Communications)
www.firstnationsuniversity.ca
Other Information: Human Resources, E-mail: mseveright@firstnationsuniversity.ca

Enrollment: 2190
At the First Nations University of Canada, students have the opportunity to learn in an environment of First Nations languages, traditions, & values.
Dr. Shauneen Pete, President, 306-790-5950, ext. 2105
spete@firstnationsuniversity.ca
Dr. Herman Michell, Vice-President, Academic
Joely BigEagle, Chair
Tina Pelletier, Officer, Communications

Gabriel Dumont Institute
#2, 604 - 22nd St. West, Saskatoon, SK S7M 5W1, Canada
Tel: 306-242-5297; *Fax:* 306-242-0002
www.gdins.org

Luther College
c/o University of Regina
Regina, SK S4S 0A2, Canada
Tel: 306-585-5333
www.luthercollege.edu/

Bruce Perlson, President, 306-585-5024
bruce.perlson@luthercollege.edu
Mark Duke, Dir. of Finance, 306-585-5023
mark.duke@luthercollege.edu
Mary Vetter, Academic Dean, 306-585-5036
mary.vetter@luthercollege.edu

Publications
The Carillon

Cityside
Regina, SK S4S 0A2, Canada

***Saskatoon:* College of Emmanuel & St. Chad**
Also known as: University of Emmanuel College
114 Seminary Cres., Saskatoon, SK S7N 0X3, Canada
Tel: 306-975-3753; *Fax:* 306-934-2683
emmanuel.stchad@usask.ca
www.usask.ca/stu/emmanuel

***Saskatoon:* Lutheran Theological Seminary**
114 Seminary Cres., Saskatoon, SK S7N 0X3, Canada
Tel: 306-966-7850; *Fax:* 306-966-7852
lutheran.seminary@usask.ca
www.usask.ca/stu/luther

Full Time Equivalency: 142
Theological college at the University of Saskatchewan affiliated with the Evangelical Lutheran Church in Canada

***Saskatoon:* St. Thomas More College**
1437 College Dr., Saskatoon, SK S7N 0W6, Canada
Tel: 306-966-8900; *Fax:* 306-966-8904
Toll-Free: 800-667-2019
info@stmcollege.ca
stmcollege.ca

Full Time Equivalency: 2294

***Saskatoon:* University of Saskatchewan**
105 Admin. Place, Saskatoon, SK S7N 5A2, Canada
Tel: 306-966-4343; *Fax:* 306-966-4530
www.usask.ca

Full Time Equivalency: 15228
The Hon. G. Barnhart, Lt. Governor of Saskatche, Visitor
Dr. Vera Pezer, Ph.D., Chancellor
Art Dumont, B.E.(ME), Chair
R.P. MacKinnon, Q.C., B.A., LL.B., LL.M., President
Dr. Brett Fairbairn, B.A. (Hons.), D.Phil., Provost & Vice-President
Richard Florizone, B.Sc., M.Sc., Ph.D., Vice-President
L. Pennock, B.A., M.A., Ph.D., University Secretary

Kelly McInnes, B.Sc., B.Ed., Registrar
L. Kennedy, B. Comm., C.A., Assoc. Vice-President & Controller
Karen Chad, Ph.D., Acting Vice-President
R. Bunt, B.Sc., M.Sc., Ph.D., Assoc. Vice-President
D. Hannah, B.Ed., M.Ed. Ph.D., Assoc. Vice-President
Jim Germida, B.S., M.S., Ph.D., Vice-Provost
Barb Daigle, B.Comm., M.B.A., C.H.R.P., Assoc. Vice-President

Faculties

Agriculture
Dr. G.J. Scoles, B.Sc., M.Sc., Ph.D., Acting Dean

Arts & Science
J. Dillon, A.R.C.T., B.Sc., M.Sc., P, Dean

Commerce
G.E. Isaac, B.A., M.A., Ph.D., Dean

Dentistry
G. Uswak, Dean

Education
C. Reynolds, B.A., M.A., Ph.D., Dean

Engineering
J.A. Kozinski, B.S., M.Eng., Ph.D., Dean

Extension
W. Archer, B.A., B.Ed., M.A., Ph.D., Dean

Graduate Studies & Research
L. Martz, B.Sc., M.Sc., Ph.D., Dean

Kinesiology
Carol Rodgers, Ph.D., B.P.E., M.H.K., Dean

Law
B. Cotter, B.Comm., LL.B., LL.M., Dean

Medicine
W. Albritton, M.D., Ph.D., FRCPC, Dean

Nursing
L. Butler, B.S.N., M.N., Ph.D., Dean

Pharmacy & Nutrition
D.K.J. Gorecki, B.S.P., Ph.D., Dean

Physical Therapy & Interprofessional Health Sciences Education
E.L. Harrison, Assoc. Dean

Veterinary Medicine
C. Rhodes, B.Sc., D.V.M., M.Sc., Dean

Schools

Physical Therapy
A. Busch, B.P.T., M.Sc., Ph.D., Director

Affiliations

Briercrest Bible College & Biblical Seminary
510 College Dr., Caronport, SK S0H 0S0, Canada
Tel: 306-756-3200
Dr Dwayne Uglem, President
Glenn Werner, Chair

Central Pentecostal College
1303 Jackson Ave., Saskatoon, SK S7H 2M9, Canada
Tel: 306-374-6655; *Fax:* 306-373-6968
Dr. Gordon Griesbrecht, President
Deborah McConkey, Registrar
Dr. David Munk, B.A., B.R.E., M.A., Ph.D., Academic Dean

College of Emmanuel & St. Chad
1337 College Dr, Saskatoon, SK S7N 0W6, Canada
Tel: 306-975-3753; *Fax:* 306-934-2683
The Rev Derek Hoskin, Chancellor
Rev. Dr Bill Richards, Vice-Chancellor
The Rt. Rev Greg Kerr-Wilson, President
The Rt. Rev. Dr Jane Alexander, Vice-President
Colleen Walker, Registrar
colleen.walker@usask.ca

Gabriel Dumont College
#2, 604 - 22nd St. West, Saskatoon, SK S7M 5W1, Canada
Tel: 306-934-4941; *Fax:* 306-242-0002
www.gdins.org/GDC.shtml
Geordy McCaffrey, Executive Director, 306-657-2231
geordy.mccaffrey_dti@sasktel.net

Lutheran Theological Seminary
114 Seminary Cres., Saskatoon, SK S7N 0X3, Canada
Tel: 306-966-7850; *Fax:* 306-966-7852
Kevin Ogilvie, President
Gordon Jensen, Dean of Studies
Susan Avant, Registrar
Debbie Thiessen, Office Manager

St. Andrew's College
1121 College Dr., Saskatoon, SK S7N 0W3, Canada
Tel: 306-966-8970; *Fax:* 306-966-8981
Toll-Free: 1-877-644-8970
standrews.registrar@usask.ca
www.usask.ca/stu/standrews
The College is a theological school of The United Church of Canada.
Vic Wiebe, Chair
vbwiebe@sasktel.net
Laura Balas, Acting Principal, 306-966-8975
laura.balas@usask.ca

St. Peter's College
P.O. Box 40
Muenster, SK S0K 2Y0, Canada
Tel: 306-682-7888; *Fax:* 306-682-4402
spc@stpeters.sk.ca
www.stpeterscollege.ca
Affiliated with the University of Saskatchewan, the College provides Arts & Science, Agriculture, & Commerce courses to first and second year students.
Robert Harasymchuk, President
Grant McConnell, Coordinator, Fine Arts, Conexus Community Art Gallery
Barbara Langhorst, Coordinator, Humanities, Academic Centre for Excellence

St. Thomas More College
1437 College Dr., Saskatoon, SK S7N 0W6, Canada
Tel: 306-966-8900; *Fax:* 306-966-8904
Toll-Free: 1-800-667-2019
www.stmcollege.ca
Enrollment: 2000
St. Thomas More College is a Catholic, liberal arts college, federated with the University of Saskatchewan. The college has 31 full-time tenure track faculty, 3 full-time term faculty, & 42 sessional faculty.
George Smith, President, 306-966-8903
gsmith@stmcollege.ca
Carl Still, Dean & Associate Professor, 306-966-8950
cstill@stmcollege.ca
Patricia McDougall, Associate Dean & Associate Professor, 306-966-8919
pmcdougall@stmcollege.ca
Derrin Raffey, Chief Financial Officer & Director, Administration, 306-966-8912
draffey@stmcollege.ca
Rod Antonichuk, Director, External Relations, 306-966-2955
rantonichuk@stmcollege.ca
Donna Brockmeyer, Director, Library, 306-966-8962
dbrockmeyer@stmcollege.ca
Kathie Jeffrey, Manager, Human Resources, 306-966-6467
kjeffrey@stmcollege.ca
Kerry Stefaniuk, Manager, Accounting, 306-966-2191
kstefaniuk@stmcollege.ca
Stacy Stillwell, Manager, Information Technology, 306-966-8920
sstillwell@stmcollege.ca
Richard Medernach, Coordinator, Student Services, 306-966-8946
rmedernach@stmcollege.ca
Luke Muller, Coordinator, Development & Alumni Affairs, 306-966-8918
lmuller@stmcollege.ca
David Peacock, Coordinator, Engaged Learning, 306-966-4828
dpeacock@stmcollege.ca
Gertrude Rompre, Campus Minister, 306-966-8929
grompre@stmcollege.ca

Publications

The Green & White
234 Kirk Hall, Saskatoon, SK S7N 0W0, Canada
Fax: 306-966-8717

The Sheaf

Colleges

***Saskatoon:* Gabriel Dumont Institute**
#2, 604 - 22nd St. West, Saskatoon, SK S7M 5W1, Canada
Tel: 306-934-4941; *Fax:* 306-244-0252
Toll-Free: 888-344-0445
general@gdi.gdins.org
www.gdins.org
Has partnerships with University of Saskatchewan & University of Regina; Educational arm of the Métis Nation-Saskatchewan

***Saskatoon:* Horizon College & Seminary**
Also known as: Central Pentecostal College
1303 Jackson Ave., Saskatoon, SK S7H 2M9, Canada
Tel: 306-374-6655; *Fax:* 306-373-6968
inquiries@horizon.edu
www.horizon.edu

Post Secondary/Technical

Post Secondary/Technical

***Air Ronge:* Northlands College**
P.O. Box 1000
Air Ronge, SK S0J 3G0, Canada
Tel: 306-425-4480; *Fax:* 306-425-3002
Toll-Free: 1-888-311-1185
www.northlandscollege.sk.ca
Program Centers are located in La Ronge (306-425-4353), Buffalo Narrows (306-235-1765), & Creighton (306-688-8838).
Bill McLaughlin, CEO, 306-425-4273

***Biggar:* Prairie West Regional College**
P.O. Box 700
701 Dominion St., Biggar, SK S0K 0M0, Canada
Tel: 306-948-3363; *Fax:* 306-948-2094
rosetown.office@prairiewestcollege.ca
www.prairiewestcollege.ca
Bruce Probert, CEO

***Humboldt:* Carlton Trail Regional College**
P.O. Box 720
623 - 7 St., Humboldt, SK S0K 2A0, Canada
Tel: 306-682-2623; *Fax:* 306-682-3101
Toll-Free: 1-800-667-2623
humboldt@ctrc.sk.ca
www.ctrc.sk.ca/ctrc/
Rob Barber, CEO

***Melville:* Parkland Regional College**
P.O. Box 790
200 Block 9th Ave. East, Melville, SK S0A 2P0, Canada
Tel: 306-728-4471; *Fax:* 306-728-2576
Toll-Free: 1-866-783-6766
info@parklandcollege.sk.ca
www.parklandcollege.sk.ca
Fay Myers, CEO

***North Battleford:* North West Regional College**
10702 Diefenbaker Dr., North Battleford, SK S9A 4A8, Canada
Tel: 306-937-5100; *Fax:* 306-445-1575
www.nwrc.sk.ca
Enrollment: 823
Bryan Nylander, CEO

***Regina:* Academy of Learning**
2721 Avonhurst Dr., Regina, SK S4R 3J3, Canada
Tel: 306-757-8973; *Fax:* 306-757-2544
admissions@aolregina.com
www.aolregina.com
Office admin.; accounting; IT training; other locations in: Lloydminster, Estevan, Fort Qu'Appelle, Moose Jaw, North Battleford, Meadow Lake, Prince Albert, Saskatoon, Yorkton & Swift Current
Chris Bourassa, Director
cbourassa@aolregina.com

***Regina:* INtouch Career Advancement Training**
633 Park St., Regina, SK S4N 5N1, Canada
Tel: 306-781-0366; *Fax:* 306-781-0369
info@intouchcareercollege.com
www.intouchcareercollege.com
Academic upgrading, employment preparation, computer education & business programs
Donna Singer, Principal
dsinger@intouchcareercollege.com

***Saskatoon:* Academy of Fashion Design**
218-B Ave. B South, Saskatoon, SK S7M 1M4, Canada
Tel: 306-978-9088; *Fax:* 306-933-9362
Toll-Free: 1-877-978-9088
fashiondesign@sasktel.net
www.aofdesign.com
Heather J. Brigidear, Principal & Manager

***Saskatoon:* CDI College of Business, Technology & Healthcare**
#107, 119 4th Ave. South, Saskatoon, SK S7K 5X2, Canada
Tel: 306-244-8585; *Fax:* 306-244-0788
www.cdicollege.com
Computer Programming, Networking Technology & Business Applications programs; also Regina campus
Peter Hubbs, Director
peter.hubbs@cdi.ca

***Saskatoon:* McKay Career Training Inc.**
226 - 20th St. East, Saskatoon, SK S7K 0A6, Canada
Tel: 306-652-7878; *Fax:* 306-653-1808
Toll-Free: 1-800-205-8140
registrar@careercampus.ca
www.careercampus.ca
Medical & veterinary office assistant, graphic art/electronic prepress, multi media, massage therapy.
Gordon McKay

***Saskatoon:* Redhouse College of Animation**
148 2nd Ave. North, Saskatoon, SK S7K 2B2, Canada
Tel: 306-668-0013; *Fax:* 306-668-0073
Toll-Free: 1-877-264-6867
info@redhousecollege.com
www.redhousecollege.com
Three year animation program which includes basic animation principles and the process of writing, directing, and animating ones own film.
Gord Groat, Principal & Manager

***Saskatoon:* Regency College**
233-4th Ave. South, Saskatoon, SK S7K 1N1, Canada
Tel: 306-651-1700; *Fax:* 306-651-1702
Toll-Free: 1-800-667-4771
regencycollege@sasktel.net
www.regencycollege.com
Private vocational college which specializes in training hospitality industry and business employees.
Karen Butcher, Principal & Manager

***Saskatoon:* Saskatchewan Indian Institute of Technologies**
c/o Asimakaniseekan Askiy Reserve
#118, 335 Packham Ave., Saskatoon, SK S7N 4S1, Canada
Tel: 306-244-4444; *Fax:* 306-244-1391
www.siit.sk.ca
Ray Ahenakew, Acting President
Paul Ledoux, Registrar
Darlene Arcand, Director, Admission

***Saskatoon:* Saskatchewan Institute of Applied Science & Technology (SIAST)**
Administrative Offices
400-119, 4th Ave. South, Saskatoon, SK S7K 5X2, Canada
Tel: 306-933-7331; *Fax:* 306-933-7323
Toll-Free: 1-866-467-4278
HR.Admin.Offices@siast.sk.ca
www.siast.sk.ca
Dr. Bob McCulloch, President & CEO
Claude Naud, Vice-President
Patricia Gillies, Director
Cheryl McMillan, Acting CFO

Campuses

SIAST Kelsey Campus
P.O. Box 1520
Saskatoon, SK S7K 3R5, Canada
Tel: 306-933-7331; *Fax:* 306-933-8403
Toll-Free: 1-866-467-4278
HR.Kelsey@siast.sk.ca
www.siast.sk.ca
Gerry Bonsal, Director

SIAST Palliser Campus
P.O. Box 1420
Moose Jaw, SK S6H 4R4, Canada
Tel: 306-694-3200; *Fax:* 306-693-3271
Toll-Free: 1-866-467-4278
palliserjobs@siat.sk.ca
www.siast.sk.ca
Don Shanner, Director

SIAST Wascana Campus
HR.Wascana@siast.sk.ca
P.O. Box 556
Regina, SK S4P 3A3, Canada
Tel: 306-798-4356; *Fax:* 306-798-8113
Toll-Free: 1-866-467-4278
HR.Wascana@siast.sk.ca
www.siast.sk.ca
Noel Selinger, Director

SIAST Woodland Campus
P.O. Box 3003
1100 - 15 St. East, Prince Albert, SK S6V 6G1, Canada
Tel: 306-953-7094; *Fax:* 306-953-7168
Toll-Free: 1-866-467-4278
HR.Woodland@siast.sk.ca
www.siast.sk.ca
Larry Fladager, Director

***Saskatoon:* Saskatchewan Institute of Applied Science & Technology**
Administrative Offices, S.J. Cohen Centre
#400, 119 4th Ave. South, Saskatoon, SK S7K 5X2, Canada
Tel: 306-933-7331
www.siast.sk.ca

***Saskatoon:* Saskatoon Business College**
221 Third Ave. North, Saskatoon, SK S7K 2H7, Canada
Tel: 306-244-6333; *Fax:* 306-652-4888
Toll-Free: 1-800-679-771
www.saskbusinesscollege.com
Business, health care, computer courses
Beth Shewkenek, Principal & Manager

***Saskatoon:* Saskatoon Campus**
1223 Idylwyld Dr. North, Saskatoon, SK S7L 1A1, Canada
Tel: 306-955-4412; *Fax:* 306-955-5337
Toll-Free: 1-866-755-5551
info@newmediacampus.com
www.newmediacampus.com
Multimedia; 3D animation.
Gary Lawrence, Principal

Campuses

Regina Campus
1831 College Ave., 3rd Fl., Regina, SK S4P 4V5, Canada
Fax: 306-721-1461
info@newmediacampus.com
www.newmediacampus.com
Janea Bailey, Principal

***Saskatoon:* Universal Career College**
226 - 20th St. East, Saskatoon, SK S7K 0A6, Canada
Tel: 306-652-7878; *Fax:* 306-653-1808
Toll-Free: 1-800-205-8140
registrar@careercampus.ca
www.careercampus.ca
Office & business management, travel & tourism
Laurette McCaig, Manager

***Saskatoon:* Western Academy Broadcasting College**
1222 Alberta Ave., Saskatoon, SK S7K 4E5, Canada
Tel: 306-665-1771; *Fax:* 306-244-1219
wabc@shaw.ca
www.wabcwesternacademy.com
Don Scott, Manager

***Swift Current:* Cypress Hills Regional College**
P.O. Box 5000
129 - 2 Ave. NE, Swift Current, SK S9H 4G3, Canada
Tel: 306-773-1531; *Fax:* 306-773-2384
Toll-Free: 1-866-296-2472
info@cypresshillscollege.sk.ca
www.cypresshillscollege.sk.ca
Mark Frison, CEO

***Gravelbourg:* Gravelbourg Campus**
P.O. Box 652
7 Athabasca St., Gravelbourg, SK S0H 1X0, Canada
Tel: 306-648-3244; *Fax:* 306-648-2983
Toll-Free: 1-866-296-2472
margarets@cypresshillscollege.sk.ca (Attn: Margaret Schafer)
www.cypresshillscottage.sk.ca

***Maple Creek:* Maple Creek Campus**
P.O. Box 1738
20 Pacific Ave., Maple Creek, SK S0N 1N0, Canada
Tel: 306-662-3829; *Fax:* 306-662-3849
Toll-Free: 1-866-296-2472
path@cypresshillscollege.sk.ca (Attn: Pat Hlady)
www.cypresshillscollege.sk.ca

***Shaunavon:* Shaunavon Campus**
P.O. Box 1478
23-4th Ave. W., Shaunavon, SK S0N 2M0, Canada
Tel: 306-297-3462; *Fax:* 306-297-3420
Toll-Free: 1-866-296-2472
maryjaneb@cypresshillcollege.sk.ca (Attn: Mary Jane Benesh)
www.cypresshillscollege.sk.ca

***Nipawin:* Nipawin Campus**
P.O. Box 2225
501 - 6th St. East, Nipawin, SK S0E 1E0, Canada
Tel: 306-862-9833; *Fax:* 306-862-4940
crc.nipawin@cumberlandcollege.sk.ca
www.cumberlandcollege.sk.ca
Valerie Mushinski, CEO

***Melfort:* Melfort Campus**
P.O. Box 2320
400 Burns Ave. E., Melfort, SK S0E 1A0, Canada
Tel: 306-752-2786; *Fax:* 306-752-3484
crc.melfort@cumberlandcollege.sk.ca
www.cumberlandcollege.sk.ca

***Hudson Bay:* Hudson Bay Campus**
P.O. Box 207
501 Prince St., Hudson Bay, SK S0E 0Y0, Canada
Tel: 306-865-2175; *Fax:* 306-865-2314
crc.hudsonbay@cumberlandcollege.sk.ca
www.cumberlandcollege.sk.ca

***Tisdale:* Tisdale Campus**
800-101 St., Tisdale, SK S0E 1T0, Canada
Tel: 306-873-2525; *Fax:* 306-873-4450
tisdale@cumberlandcollege.sk.ca
www.cumberlandcollege.sk.ca

***Weyburn:* Southeast Regional College**
P.O. Box 2003
629 King St., Weyburn, SK S4H 0M4, Canada
Tel: 306-848-2520; *Fax:* 306-848-2517
Toll-Free: 1-866-999-7372
www.southeastcollege.org
Graham Mickleborough, President

Yukon Territory

Government Agencies

***Whitehorse:* Department of Education**
P.O. Box 2703
1000 Lewes Blvd., Whitehorse, YT Y1A 2C6, Canada
Tel: 867-667-5141; *Fax:* 867-393-6254
contact.education@gov.yk.ca
www.education.gov.yk.ca
Brent Slobodin, Asst. Deputy Minister
Lee Kubica, Supt. of Schools/Asst. Deputy Minister
John Edzerza, Minister

School Boards/Districts/Divisions

Public

***Whitehorse:* Yukon Francophone School Board**
P.O. Box 3983
3151C - 3rd Ave., Whitehorse, YT Y1A 5M6, Canada
Tel: 867-667-8680; *Fax:* 867-393-6946
Toll-Free: 800-661-0408
Grades: Pre-K.-12
Enrollment: 165
The board operates the Yukon's only French first language school, École Émilie-Tremblay.
André Bourcier, President

Universities & Colleges

Colleges

***Whitehorse:* Yukon College**
P.O. Box 2799
500 College Dr., Whitehorse, YT Y1A 5K4, Canada
Tel: 867-668-8800; *Fax:* 867-668-8890
Toll-Free: 800-661-0504
www.yukoncollege.yk.ca
Terry Weninger, President
Karen Barnes, Vice-President (Education & Training)
Wayne Coghill, Director, Administrative Services
Jock Bryce, Director, Human Resources

Overseas Schools/Programs

***Antigua:* Picadilly: Island Academy**
Medical School Rd., Picadilly, Antigua
Tel: 026-856-2620; *Fax:* 026-846-3758
mwayne@hotmail.com
Accredited with the Ontario Ministry of Education (allowing the school to offer the Ontario Secondary School Diploma). Island Academy opened its doors to students in September, 2001 at Piccadilly, Antigua
Wayne MacInnis, Principal

***Canada:* Beijing: Beijing Tsinghua Zhiqing High School**
North Road of Zhongguancun, Beijing 100086, Canada
Tel: 086-106-2974; *Fax:* 086-106-2976
sotino@sina.com

Canada: Vancouver: Dalian Maple Leaf International School
#400-601 Broadway West, Vancouver, BC V5Z 4C2, Canada
Tel: 604-675-6910; *Fax:* 604-675-6911
don@mapleleafschool.com
http://mapleleafschools.org
Grades: 9-12
Enrollment: 1616
Maple Leaf Educational Systems is a Chinese firm that currently operates 12 schools in China enrolling approximately 5,000 students. Maple Leaf's High Schools (Grade 10-12) programs and its Foreign Nationals Schools (K-9) are taught in English by British Columbia, Canada certified teachers. These programs are inspected and certified by British Columbia's Ministry of Eductation. Grade 12 graduates receive both the Chinese and British Columbia graduation certificates
C. Savage, Principal

Canada: Vancouver: Grand Canadian Academy
2026 West 12th Ave., Vancouver, BC V6J 2G2, Canada
Tel: 604-738-6273; *Fax:* 604-738-6974
office@gcahighschool.ca
www.gcahighschool.ca
Grades: 10-12
Enrollment: 135
Certified by the Ministry of Education, Province of British Columbia. British Columbia's High School Graduation Program includes Grades 10, 11 and 12. Courses numbered 10, 11 and 12 earn credits toward graduation. To graduate, students must complete a minimum of 80 credits over the three-year Graduation Program
G. Batt, Principal

Canada: Vancouver: Jiangdu International School
c/o 1262 - 13th Ave. East, Vancouver, BC V5T 2M1, Canada
Tel: 604-874-3386; *Fax:* 604-874-3386
quincy_dai@yahoo.ca
Grades: 11
Enrollment: 13
Dr. R. Fransila, Principal

Canada: Vancouver: Shanxi Sino-Canadian School
c/o 1719 Trutch St., Vancouver, BC V6K 4G2, Canada
Tel: 604-738-5777; *Fax:* 604-737-9969
pm83@hotmail.com
Grades: 10
Enrollment: 50
Offers B.C. Grade 10,11, & 12
P. McManus, Principal

Canada: Harrison Hot Springs: Sino-Canadian High School
c/o PO Box 523, Harrison Hot Springs, BC V0M 1K0, Canada
Tel: 604-796-2368; *Fax:* 604-796-2378
butcherm218@yahoo.com
Grades: 10-12
Enrollment: 287
A. Butcher, Principal

China: Jiangmen City: Boren Sino - Canadian School
65 Shuanglong Ave., Jiangmen City, China
Tel: 086-750-3217; *Fax:* 086-750-3219
mryan1274@hotmail.com
Boren Sino-Canadian School is a privately funded education initiative with authorization from the Ministries of Education in the provinces of Guangdong, The People's Republic of China, and Ontario, Canada. As such, it adheres strictly to curricular re quirements and grants education credits in the pursuit of high school diplomas in both countries. The Chinese curriculum is designed to prepare students for national academic examinations qualifying students for university and college entrance. At the same time, the Ontario curriculum of the school is both demanding and exciting and requires a high level of aptitude and dedication
Carol Dubeau, Principal

China: Quanzhou City: The Canadian Trillium College
#7 High School, 46 Tian Hou Rd., Quanzhou City, China
Tel: 086-595-2203; *Fax:* 086-595-2202
CTC is a private Canadian School that offers an Ontario Secondary School curriculum to students in China. After passing their Chinese Middle School program and completing the necessary Ontario Secondary School courses students may be granted an Ontario Secondary School Diploma (OSSD). The granting of an OSSD is based on the total educational experience the student has acquired over their entire educational history in China
Don Folz, Principal

China: Changsha: Changjun Education Group, Changsha, Hunan, China
9th Section of Wang Yue Village, Changsha, China
Tel: 086-731-8883; *Fax:* 086-731-8883
Caifanganne@yahoo.com.cn

China: Ranghulu District, Daqing: Daqing - Bond International College Daqing High School
192 Zhongyong Da Jie, Ranghulu District, Daqing, China
Tel: 086-459-6346; *Fax:* 045-963-4652

China: Tianjin: Harbor View School
#71, 3rd Avenue South, Tianjin, China
Tel: 086-226-2226; *Fax:* 086-222-4992
liling@thehomeworld.com.cn
Harbor View School is a private-run boarding school owned and managed by Home World Corporation and certified with the Ministry of Education of Ontario. The school has been approved by the Tianjin Education Committee under whose great support - in cooperation with various other administrative departments in TEDA - was founded under its new name and in its new location in the year 2000. Harbor View School received the consent of the Tianjin Education Committee and was licensed as a private school in March and April of 2001. Construction was completed on June 10th 2003
Bill McInerney

China: Huanggu District, Shenyang: Liaodong Canadian International School of China Sino-Canadian Campus of Liaoning Province Shiyan High School
89 Huanghe South St., Huanggu District, Shenyang, China
Tel: 086-417-2615; *Fax:* 086-417-2615
jennysue0104@hotmail.com
Canadian international school in China, located in Yingkou

China: Longkou: Shandong Canada China Donghai School
Donghai Development Zone
P.O. Box 265713
Longkou, China
Tel: 086-535-8606; *Fax:* 086-535-8606
Terry Lynch, Principal

China: Shenzhen City, Futian District: Shenzhen Fujing Foreign Language School
Jingtian North, Futian District, Shenzhen City, Futian District, China
Tel: 086-755-3910; *Fax:* 086-755-3921
sunwenjin0208@hotmail.com
Enrollment: 108
The International Program at Fujing Foreign Languages School is accredited with the Ministry of Education and Training, Ontario and can grant credits leading to the Ontario Secondary School Diploma. All teachers teaching Ontario credit courses are qualified Ontario teachers. The program is inspected annually by the Ministry to ensure that all credit courses follow the prescribe Ontario courses of study and that assessment and evaluation follows the expectations of the Ministry as defined in the Ministry document, Ontario Secondary Schools, Program and Diploma Requirements, 1999. They offer a Dual Diploma Program which is currently in its third year of operation at Fujing Foreign Languages School. The purpose of the program is to provide Chinese students who wish to study abroad an opportunity to receive both their Chinese Diploma and the Ontario Secondary School Diploma
James Fish, Principal

China: WuQing District, Tianjin: Yinghua - Bond International College
P.O. Box 307100
Yong Yang West Road, WuQing District, Tianjin, China
Tel: 086-225-9611; *Fax:* 086-225-9611
elizabeth.jarrell@hotmail.com
Elizabeth Jarrell

China 510520: Guangzhou, Guangdong Province: Huamei-Bond International College
Longdong, Tianhe District, Guangzhou, Guangdong Province, China 510520
Tel: 085-227-8229; *Fax:* 086-208-7210
hmoacprincipal@yahoo.com
Huamei-Bond International College (HBIC) is operated jointly by Bond International College (Toronto) and Huamei International School (China). HBIC is accredited by and inspected by the Ontario Ministry of Education, Canada. The school offers Ontario secondary school academic courses as well as a Chinese high school curriculum leading to an Ontario Secondary School Diploma and a Chinese High School Diploma. With these two diplomas, graduates can apply directly to universities in China or overseas
Jim Burns, Principal
burnsjamesW@hotmail.com

Egypt: Zone 4, New Greater Cairo: Canadian International School
El Tagamosa El Khames, Zone 4, New Greater Cairo, Egypt
Tel: 001-120-2758; *Fax:* 001-120-2758
ser.sha@ie-eg.com
CISE is a Junior Kindergarten to Grade Twelve International School in Cairo (Kattameya - New Cairo) approved by the Egyptian Ministry of Education and licensed as a Canadian School by the Ontario Ministry of Education. Its administration and over 85% of its teachers are trained and licensed (certified) in Canada. The school uses a Canadian curriculum, teaching and classroom management techniques and Canadian learning materials (text books, computer software and audio-visual aids). The school opened its doors in September 2002
John Trafford, Principal

Hong Kong: Aberdeen: Canadian International School
36 Nam Long Shan Rd., Aberdeen, Hong Kong
Tel: 085-225-2570; *Fax:* 085-225-2575
schoolinfo@cdnis.edu.hk
www.cdnis.edu.hk
Enrollment: 1332
Offers kindergarten, primary & secondary education
Barbara McKenzie, Principal

Hong Kong: Quarry Bay: Delia School of Canada
Tai Fung Rd., Taikoo Shing, Quarry Bay, Hong Kong
Tel: 085-228-8441; *Fax:* 085-228-8578
dscstk@delia.edu.hk
www.delia.edu.hk
Enrollment: 909
Delia School of Canada is a private school. Delia School of Canada is a member of the Delia Group of Schools. It follows the curriculum offered in Ontario. Delia School of Canada is accredited with the Ministry of Education in Ontario and registered with the Hong Kong Education and Manpower Bureau. The school meets the appropriate regulations put forth by the Education Department of Ontario and the Hong Kong Education and Manpower Bureau. Delia School of Canada was established in 1987
Jack Merner Saddler, Principal

Hong Kong: Shamshuipo, Kowloon: Phoenix International School
5 Tonkin St., Shamshuipo, Kowloon, Hong Kong
Tel: 085-227-0822; *Fax:* 085-227-0820
info@phoenix.edu.hk
Enrollment: 369
Hugh McKeown, Principal

India: Bangalore 560 092: Canadian International School
14/1 Kodighalli Main Rd., Sahakar Nagar, Bangalore 560 092, India
Tel: 091-803-4384; *Fax:* 091-803-4364
csib@vsnl.com
Enrollment: 212
Provides a learning experience to mainly expatriate and Indian students, representing over 25 nationalities from Pre indergarten to Grade 12. The school is accredited by the International Baccalaureate Organization and Ontario Ministry of Education, and is a member of the Council of International Schools
Brian Tinker, Principal

Italy: Lanciano, Chieti: Canadian College Italy - The Renaissance
via Cavour 13, Lanciano, Chieti, Italy
Tel: 039-087-2714; *Fax:* 039-087-2450
cciren@tin.it
www.ccilanciano.com
Enrollment: 115
CCI debuted among Europe's private schools as the first private school in Italy to offer a Canadian high school program. The School offers grades 10 through high school graduation, and students may enroll for a single semester or for up to three academic years (two semesters per year). CCI is inspected by the province of Ontario, whose requirements parallel or exceed most other North American jurisdictions, and is a member of ECIS, the European Council of International Schools
Marisa DiCarlo D'Alessandr, Principal

Japan: Saitama 359-0027, Tokyo: Columbia International School of Japan
153 Matsugo, Tokorozawa, Saitama 359-0027, Tokyo, Japan
Tel: 042-946-1911; *Fax:* 042-946-1955
office@columbia-ca.co.jp
Enrollment: 112
Prepares students for the post secondary education overseas with a world recognized and accepted Ontario Secondary School Diploma (grade 12) of Canada. CIS admits students regardless of their nationality nor ethnic origin. CIS is accredited and

annually inspected by the Ontario Ministry of Education, and follows the Ontario curriculum
Barrie McCliggott, Principal

Malaysia: Petaling Jaya, Selanger Darul E: Canadian International Matriculation Programme Sunway College

P.O. Box 46150
No. 5 Jalan Kolej, Bandar Sunway, Petaling Jaya, Selanger Darul E, Malaysia
Tel: 060-374-9186; *Fax:* 060-356-3586
rosemaryg@sunway.edu.my

Enrollment: 649
CIMP is an Ontario Curriculum, developed according to the requirements of the Ontario Ministry of Education, Canada. It is identical to the programme offered in Ontario, which upon completion, students will receive the Ontario Secondary School Diploma (OSSD). Establised in 1990, the Canadian International Matriculation Programme (CIMP) has grown to become the largest Canadian Matriculation programme in the world
Rosemary Gannon, Principal

Malaysia: Selangor: Taylor's College International Canadian Pre-University

No. 1, Jalan SS15/8, 47500 Subang Jaya, Selangor, Malaysia
Tel: 060-356-3626; *Fax:* 060-356-3452
admission@taylors.edu.my

Enrollment: 490
For over three decades, Taylor's University College has been recognised as Malaysia's leading private college of higher learning. International Canadian Pre-University (ICPU) programme: Students choose this programme for its flexibility and wide-ranging subjects. Accepted for university entry internationally, ICPU students at Taylor's University College are constantly exposed to the latest developments in education and the global experiences provided by a team of qualified Malaysian and Canadian lecturers
Frank Meagher, Principal

Netherlands: AFNORTH International School

Ferdinand Bolstraat 1, 6445EE Brunssum,, Netherlands
Tel: 000-314-5527; *Fax:* 000-314-5527
Charmaine.Martel@eu.dodea.edu

Enrollment: 215
The AFNORTH International School was founded in September 1967 and provides education for about 1400 Children of Allied Forces Northern Europe (AFNORTH) and other NATO personnel serving at the Headquarters and nearby commands
Charmaine Martel, Principal

Netherlands Antilles: St. Maarten: Caribbean International Academy

#4 Tigres Rd., Dutch Lowlands, St. Maarten, Netherlands Antilles
Tel: 001-159-9545; *Fax:* 001-159-9545
admission@carib-international.org

To meet the Ministry of Ontario OSSD (Ontario Secondary School Diploma) graduation requirements, the Principal of the school and 80% of the secondary teaching staff must be certified by the Ontario College of Teachers. Opened in September 2003
Liz Shuttleworth

Rep. Of Trinidad & Tob: Montrose, Chaguanas: Trillium International School

#6 Maraj St., Montrose, Chaguanas, Rep. Of Trinidad & Tob
A private school offering the Ontario Ministry of Education Curriculum to Elementary and Secondary school students

Singapore: Singapore 289 759: Canadian International School

71 Bukit Tinggi Rd., Singapore 289 759, Singapore
Tel: 065-687-5151; *Fax:* 065-687-5151
secondary@cis.edu.sg
www.cis.edu.sg

Enrollment: 977
Accredited by the Ontario Ministry of Education, and the International Baccalaureate programmes. Their graduates receive the Ontario Secondary Diploma or the IB Diploma, both of which are recognized around the world by major universities. Associate member in the Council of International Schools (CIS)
James Dalziel, Principal

Switzerland: Neuchâtel: Neuchâtel Jr. College

P.O. Box 2002
Crêt-Taconnet, 4, Neuchâtel, Switzerland
Tel: 041-327-2527; *Fax:* 041-327-2442
principal@njc.ch
www.njc.ch/school/

Enrollment: 116
Member of the Canadian Association of Independent Schools (CAIS). Neuchâtel Junior College is a Swiss non-profit foundation of the Ville de Neuchâtel. As such, NJC has a governing council comprising two Boards of Governors, one in Switzerland (Le Conseil de Fondation), and the other in Canada. The members of the Conseil are appointed by the Neuchâtel City Council and come largely from the fields of education and business. The Canadian Board members are alumni of NJC and/or parents of recent students. The Boards are responsible for the selection of the Principal, the financial operation of the College, and the general direction of NJC's curricular and extra-curricular programs. All members of both Boards act on a volunteer basis
Norman Southward, Principal

Trinidad: Petit Valley: Maple Leaf International School

Alyce Heights Dr., Alyce Glen, Petit Valley, Trinidad
Tel: 086-863-2957; *Fax:* 086-863-3306
mlis@tstt.net.tt
www.mapleleaf-school.com

Enrollment: 509
Maple Leaf International School opened on September 5, 1994 and offers a Canadian International Education Program in Port of Spain, Trinidad. The curriculum follows the guidelines established by the Province of Ontario Ministry of Education and Training, offering advanced level courses leading to university and college entrance. Maple Leaf is a private coeducational school that accepts students from Junior Kindergarten (3 years of age) through to Grade 12 (age 19)
Janet Pomeroy, Principal

United Arab Emirates: Abu Dhabi: The Sheikh Zayed Private Academy for Girls

P.O. Box 42989
Abu Dhabi, United Arab Emirates
Tel: 097-1 2- 446; *Fax:* 097-1 2- 443
tszpaafg@emirates.net.ae
www.szpag.com

The Sheikh Zayed Private Academy for Girls is a school based in Abu Dhabi providing international education for students from KG1 through to Year 12. The Academy offers a holistic, international education programme based on the Canadian Curriculum
Natalie Little, Principal

Yemen: Sana: Canadian International School

P.O. Box 16621
Hadda Street - Diplomatic Area in front of Al Rahma, Sana, Yemen
Tel: 097-641-8510; *Fax:* 097-651-8510

SECTION 7
GOVERNMENT
FEDERAL & PROVINCIAL

Listings in this section are as current as possible at time of publication. For appointments made and results of elections held after publication, please refer to Canada's Information Resource Centre (CIRC), if your library subscribes to this online database.

Government Quick Reference Guide

ABORIGINAL AFFAIRS

Aboriginal Affairs & Northern Development Canada, 10 Wellington St., North Tower, Gatineau, QC K1A 0H4
819-997-0380, Fax: 866-817-3977, 800-567-9604, infopubs@aadnc-aandc.gc.ca

Canadian Heritage, 15 Eddy St., Gatineau, QC K1A 0M5
819-997-0055, 866-811-0055, info@pch.gc.ca

Office of Intergovernmental Affairs, c/o Privy Council Office, #1000, 85 Slater St., Ottawa, ON K1A 0A3
613-957-5153, Fax: 613-957-5043, info@pco-bcp.gc.ca

Specific Claims Tribunal Canada, #400, 427 Laurier Ave. West, PO Box 31, Ottawa, ON K1R 7Y2
613-947-0751, Fax: 613-943-0586, info@sct-trp.ca

Alberta

Alberta Aboriginal Relations, Deputy Minister's Office, Commerce Place, 10155 - 102 St., 19th Fl., Edmonton, AB T5J 4G8
780-427-8407

Métis Settlements Appeal Tribunal, 14605 - 134 St., Edmonton, AB T5L 4S9
780-422-1541, Fax: 780-422-0019, 800-661-8864

British Columbia

Ministry of Aboriginal Relations & Reconciliation, 2957 Jutland Rd., PO Box 9100 Prov Govt,Victoria, BC V8W 9B1
250-387-6121, 800-663-7867, abrinfo@gov.bc.ca

Manitoba

Manitoba Aboriginal & Northern Affairs, 59 Elizabeth Dr., PO Box 37, Thompson, MB R8N 1X4
204-677-6607, Fax: 204-677-6753, amartin@gov.mb.ca

Aboriginal Affairs Secretariat, #200, 500 Portage Ave., Winnipeg, MB R3C 3X1
204-945-2510, Fax: 204-945-3689

New Brunswick

Aboriginal Affairs Secretariat, Kings Place, #237, 440 King St., PO Box 6000, Fredericton, NB E3B 5H1
506-462-5177, Fax: 506-444-5142

Newfoundland & Labrador

Department of Labrador & Aboriginal Affairs, Confederation Bldg., East Block, 6th Fl., PO Box 8700, St. John's, NL A1B 4J6
709-729-4776, Fax: 709-729-4900, 877-788-8822, laa@gov.nl.ca

Northwest Territories

Department of Aboriginal Affairs & Intergovernmental Relations, 4910 - 52nd St., PO Box 1320, Yellowknife, NT X1A 2L9
867-873-7143, Fax: 867-873-0233, 877-838-8194, nancy_gardiner@gov.nt.ca

Nunavut

Department of Culture, Language, Elders & Youth, PO Box 1000 800,Iqaluit, NU X0A 0H0
867-975-5500, Fax: 867-975-5504, 866-934-2035

Ontario

Ministry of Aboriginal Affairs, 160 Bloor St. East, 4th & 9th Fl., Toronto, ON M7A 2E6
416-326-4740, Fax: 416-326-4017

Quebec

Secrétariat aux affaires autochtones, 905, av Honoré-Mercier, 1er étage, Québec, QC G1R 5M6
418-643-3166, Fax: 418-646-4918

Saskatchewan

Saskatchewan First Nations & Métis Relations, #1020, 1855 Victoria Ave., Regina, SK S4P 3T2
306-787-6250, Fax: 306-798-0083

ACTS & REGULATIONS

Justice Canada, East Memorial Bldg., 284 Wellington St., Ottawa, ON K1A 0H8
613-957-4222, Fax: 613-954-0811, webadmin@justice.gc.ca

New Brunswick

Legislative Services, Centennial Bldg., #418, 670 King St., PO Box 6000, Fredericton, NB E3B 5H1
506-453-2855, Fax: 506-457-7342

Newfoundland & Labrador

Department of Justice, Confederation Bldg., East Block, 4th Fl., PO Box 8700, St. John's, NL A1B 4J6
709-729-2869, Fax: 709-729-0469, justice@gov.nl.ca

Department of Transportation & Works, Confederation Bldg., West Block, 6th Fl., PO Box 8700, St. John's, NL A1B 4J6
709-729-3679, Fax: 709-729-4285, twminister@gov.nl.ca

Northwest Territories

Department of Justice, Courthouse, 4903 - 49th St., 6th Fl., PO Box 1320, Yellowknife, NT X1A 2L9
867-920-6197

Nova Scotia

Department of Service Nova Scotia & Municipal Relations, 1505 Barrington St., PO Box 216, Halifax, NS B3J 3K5
902-424-5200, Fax: 902-424-0581, 800-670-4357, askus@gov.ns.ca

Ontario

Ministry of the Attorney General, McMurtry-Scott Bldg., 720 Bay St., 11th Fl., Toronto, ON M5G 2K1
416-326-2220, Fax: 416-326-4007, 800-518-7901

Quebec

Les Publications du Québec, #500, 1000 rte de l'Église, Québec, QC G1V 3V9
418-643-5150, Fax: 418-643-6177, 800-463-2100, publicationsduquebec@cspq.gouv.qc.ca

Yukon Territory

Yukon Justice, Andrew Philipsen Law Centre, 2134 Second Ave., PO Box 2703, Whitehorse, YT Y1A 2C6
867-667-3033, Fax: 867-393-5790, jus.msb@gov.yk.ca

AGRICULTURE

See Also: Land Resources

Agriculture & Agri-Food Canada, 1341 Baseline Rd., Ottawa, ON K1A 0C5
613-773-1000, Fax: 613-773-2772, 866-345-7972, info@agr.gc.ca

Canadian Grain Commission, #600, 303 Main St., Winnipeg, MB R3C 3G8
204-983-2770, Fax: 204-983-2751, 800-853-6705, contact@grainscanada.gc.ca

Canadian Wheat Board, 423 Main St., PO Box 816 Main,Winnipeg, MB R3C 2P5
204-983-0239, Fax: 204-983-3841, 800-275-4292, questions@cwb.ca; farmerservice@cwb.ca

National Farm Products Council, Canada Bldg., 344 Slater St., 10th Fl., Ottawa, ON K1R 7Y3
613-995-6752, Fax: 613-995-2097, fpcc-cpac@agr.gc.ca

Plant Biotechnology Institute, 110 Gymnasium Pl., Saskatoon, SK S7N 0W9
306-975-5248, Fax: 306-975-4839, pbi-info@nrc-cnrc.gc.ca

Alberta

Agricultural Products Marketing Council, JG O'Donoghue Bldg., 7000 - 113 St., 3rd Fl., Edmonton, AB T6H 5T6
780-427-2164, Fax: 780-422-9690

Alberta Agriculture & Rural Development, J.G. O'Donoghue Bldg., #100A, 7000 - 113th St., Edmonton, AB T6H 5T6
780-427-2727, duke@gov.ab.ca

British Columbia

Ministry of Agriculture, PO Box 9120 Prov Govt,Victoria, BC V8W 9E2
250-387-5121, Fax: 250-387-1522

Manitoba

Agricultural Societies, 1129 Queens Ave., Brandon, MB R7A 1L9
204-726-6195, Fax: 204-726-6260

Manitoba Agriculture, Food & Rural Initiatives, Norquay Bldg., 401 York Ave., Winnipeg, MB R3C 0P8

Food Development Centre, 810 Phillips St., PO Box 1240, Portage la Prairie, MB R1N 3J9
204-239-3150, Fax: 204-239-3180, 800-870-1044

New Brunswick

Department of Agriculture, Aquaculture & Fisheries, PO Box 6000, Fredericton, NB E3B 5H1
506-453-2666, Fax: 506-453-7170, DAAF-MAAP@gnb.ca

Newfoundland & Labrador

Agrifoods Development, Provincial Agriculture Bldg., Brookfield Rd., PO Box 8700, St. John's, NL A1B 4J6
709-729-6588, Fax: 709-729-2674

Northwest Territories

Department of Environment & Natural Resources, PO Box 1320, Yellowknife, NT X1A 2L9

Nova Scotia

Department of Agriculture, 1741 Brunswick St., 3rd Fl., PO Box 2223, Halifax, NS B3J 3C4
902-424-4560, Fax: 902-424-4671

Ontario

Ministry of Agriculture, Food & Rural Affairs, Ontario Government Bldg., 1 Stone Rd. West, Guelph, ON N1G 4Y2
519-826-3100, 888-466-2372

Prince Edward Island

Prince Edward Island Department of Agriculture, Jones Bldg., 11 Kent St., PO Box 2000, Charlottetown, PE C1A 7N8
902-368-4880, Fax: 902-368-4857

Quebec

Ministère de l'Agriculture, des Pêcheries et de l'Alimentation, 200, ch Sainte-Foy, Québec, QC G1R 4X6
418-380-2110, 888-222-6272

Saskatchewan

Saskatchewan Agriculture, Walter Scott Bldg., 3085 Albert St., Regina, SK S4S 0B1
866-457-2377, aginfo@gov.sk.ca

AGRICULTURE & FOOD

Agriculture & Agri-Food Canada, 1341 Baseline Rd., Ottawa, ON K1A 0C5
613-773-1000, Fax: 613-773-2772, 866-345-7972, info@agr.gc.ca

Agriculture Policy & Regulatory Division, Jones Bldg., 11 Kent St., 5th Fl., Charlottetown, PE C1A 7N8

Market & Industry Services Branch, Tower 5, 1341 Baseline Rd., Ottawa, ON K1A 0C5
613-759-1000, Fax: 613-773-1755

Plant Biotechnology Institute, 110 Gymnasium Pl., Saskatoon, SK S7N 0W9
306-975-5248, Fax: 306-975-4839, pbi-info@nrc-cnrc.gc.ca

Research Branch, Tower 5, 1341 Baseline Rd., Ottawa, ON K1A 0C5
613-759-1000, Fax: 613-773-1866

Strategic Policy Branch, Tower 7, 1341 Baseline Rd., Ottawa, ON K1A 0C5
613-759-1000, Fax: 613-773-2111

Alberta

Agricultural Products Marketing Council, JG O'Donoghue Bldg., 7000 - 113 St., 3rd Fl., Edmonton, AB T6H 5T6
780-427-2164, Fax: 780-422-9690

Alberta Agriculture & Rural Development, J.G. O'Donoghue Bldg., #100A, 7000 - 113th St., Edmonton, AB T6H 5T6
780-427-2727, duke@gov.ab.ca

Alberta Livestock & Meat Agency, Ellwood Office Park South, #101, 1003 Ellwood Rd. SW, Edmonton, AB T6X 0B3
780-638-1699, Fax: 780-638-6495, info@almaltd.ca

Irrigation Council, Provincial Bldg., 200 - 5 Ave. South, 3rd Fl., Lethbridge, AB T1J 4L1
403-381-5176, Fax: 403-382-4406

British Columbia

Agricultural Land Commission, #133, 4940 Canada Way, Burnaby, BC V5G 4K6
604-660-7000, Fax: 604-660-7033, ALCBurnaby@Victoria1.gov.bc.ca

Ministry of Agriculture, PO Box 9120 Prov Govt,Victoria, BC V8W 9E2
250-387-5121, Fax: 250-387-1522

Manitoba

Agricultural Societies, 1129 Queens Ave., Brandon, MB R7A 1L9
204-726-6195, Fax: 204-726-6260

Manitoba Agriculture, Food & Rural Initiatives, Norquay Bldg., 401 York Ave., Winnipeg, MB R3C 0P8

Farm Lands Ownership Board, #812, Norquay Bldg., 401 York Ave., Winnipeg, MB R3C 0P8
204-945-3149, Fax: 204-945-1489, 800-282-8069, robert.mckenzie@gov.mb.ca

Farm Machinery Board, Norquay Bldg., #812, 401 York Ave., Winnipeg, MB R3C 0P8
204-945-3856, Fax: 204-948-2844, randy.ozunko@gov.mb.ca

Manitoba Agricultural Services Corporation, #100, 1525 First St. South, Brandon, MB R7A 7A1
204-726-6850, Fax: 204-726-6849, mailbox@masc.mb.ca

New Brunswick

New Brunswick Farm Products Commission, c/o Department of Agriculture, Aquaculture & Fisheries, PO Box 6000, Fredericton, NB E3B 5H1
506-453-3647, Fax: 506-444-5969

Newfoundland & Labrador

Agrifoods Development, Provincial Agriculture Bldg., Brookfield Rd., PO Box 8700, St. John's, NL A1B 4J6
709-729-6588, Fax: 709-729-2674

Department of Natural Resources, Natural Resources Bldg., 50 Elizabeth Ave., 7th Fl., PO Box 8700, St. John's, NL A1B 4J6
709-729-2920, Fax: 709-729-0059

Nova Scotia

Department of Agriculture, 1741 Brunswick St., 3rd Fl., PO Box 2223, Halifax, NS B3J 3C4
902-424-4560, Fax: 902-424-4671

Ontario

AGRICORP, 1 Stone Rd. West, 3rd Fl., PO Box 3660 Central, Guelph, ON N1H 8M4
Fax: 519-826-4118, 888-247-4999, cac@agricorp.com

Agricultural Research Institute of Ontario, 1 Stone Rd. West, 2nd Fl., Guelph, ON N1G 4Y2
519-826-4199, Fax: 519-826-4211

Agriculture, Food & Rural Affairs Tribunal, 1 Stone Rd. West, 2nd Fl., Guelph, ON N1G 4Y2
519-826-3433, Fax: 519-826-4232, appeals.tribunal@omafra.gov.on.ca

Ministry of Agriculture, Food & Rural Affairs, Ontario Government Bldg., 1 Stone Rd. West, Guelph, ON N1G 4Y2
519-826-3100, 888-466-2372

Prince Edward Island

Agricultural Insurance Corporation, 29 Indigo Cres., PO Box 1600, Charlottetown, PE C1A 7N3
902-368-4842, Fax: 902-368-6677

BIO FOOD TECH, 101 Belvedere Ave., PO Box 2000, Charlottetown, PE C1A 7N8
902-368-5548, Fax: 902-368-5549, 877-368-5548, biofoodtech@biofoodtech.ca

Prince Edward Island Department of Agriculture, Jones Bldg., 11 Kent St., PO Box 2000, Charlottetown, PE C1A 7N8
902-368-4880, Fax: 902-368-4857

Quebec

Ministère de l'Agriculture, des Pêcheries et de l'Alimentation, 200, ch Sainte-Foy, Québec, QC G1R 4X6
418-380-2110, 888-222-6272

Commission de protection du territoire agricole du Québec, 200, ch Ste-Foy, 2e étage, Québec, QC G1R 4X6
418-643-3314, Fax: 418-643-2261, 800-667-5294, info@cptaq.gouv.qc.ca

Régie des marchés agricoles et alimentaires du Québec, 201, boul Crémazie est, 5e étage, Montréal, QC H2M 1L3
514-873-4024, Fax: 514-873-3984

Saskatchewan

Saskatchewan Agriculture, Walter Scott Bldg., 3085 Albert St., Regina, SK S4S 0B1
866-457-2377, aginfo@gov.sk.ca

Saskatchewan Crop Insurance Corporation, 484 Prince William Dr., PO Box 3000, Melville, SK S0A 2P0
306-728-7200, Fax: 306-728-7202, 888-935-0000, customer.service@scic.gov.sk.ca

Yukon Territory

Yukon Environment, PO Box 2703, Whitehorse, YT Y1A 2C6
867-667-5652, Fax: 867-393-7197, environment.yukon@gov.yk.ca

AIR POLLUTION

See Also: Environment

Clean Energy Division, Centre West Building, 10035 - 108 St., 8th Fl., Edmonton, AB T5J 3E1

Environmental Stewardship Branch, 351 boul St-Joseph, Gatineau, QC K1A 0H3
819-997-1575, Fax: 819-953-9452

Integrated Environmental Policy Division, 77 Wellesley St. West, 11th Fl., Toronto, ON M7A 2T5
416-314-6338, Fax: 416-314-6346

International Joint Commission, 234 Laurier Ave. West, 22nd Fl., Ottawa, ON K1P 6K6
613-947-1420, Fax: 613-993-5583, beckhoffb@ottawa.ijc.org

Alberta

Alberta Environment, South Tower, Petroleum Plaza, 9915 - 108 St., 10th Fl., Edmonton, AB T5K 2G8
780-427-2700, Fax: 780-422-4086, env.infocent@gov.ab.ca

British Columbia

Ministry of Environment, PO Box 9339 Prov Govt,Victoria, BC V8W 9M1
250-387-1161, Fax: 250-387-5669, envmail@gov.bc.ca

Manitoba

Manitoba Conservation, 200 Saulteaux Cres., Winnipeg, MB R3J 3W3
204-945-6784, 800-214-6497, mincon@leg.gov.mb.ca

New Brunswick

Department of Natural Resources, Hugh John Flemming Forestry Centre, PO Box 6000, Fredericton, NB E3B 5H1
506-453-3826, Fax: 506-444-4367, dnrweb@gnb.ca

Department of the Environment, Marysville Place, 20 McGloin St., PO Box 6000, Fredericton, NB E3B 5H1
506-453-2690, Fax: 506-457-7800, env-info@gnb.ca

Environmental Management, Marysville Place, 20 McGloin St., PO Box 6000, Fredericton, NB E3B 5H1
506-444-5119, Fax: 506-457-7333, env-info@gnb.ca

Sciences & Planning, Marysville Place, 20 McGloin St., 2nd Fl., PO Box 6000, Fredericton, NB E3B 5H1
506-453-2862, Fax: 506-453-2265

Newfoundland & Labrador

Department of Environment & Conservation, Confederation Bldg., West Block, 4th Fl., PO Box 8700, St. John's, NL A1B 4J6
709-729-2664, Fax: 709-729-6639, 800-563-6181, info@gov.nl.ca

Northwest Territories

Department of Environment & Natural Resources, PO Box 1320, Yellowknife, NT X1A 2L9

Nova Scotia

Department of Environment, 5151 Terminal Rd., 5th Fl., PO Box 442, Halifax, NS B3J 2P8
902-424-3600, Fax: 902-424-0503, 877-936-8476

Nunavut

Department of Environment, PO Box 1000 1300,Iqaluit, NU X0A 0H0
867-975-7700, Fax: 867-975-7742, environment@gov.nu.ca

Ontario

Ministry of Environment, 135 St. Clair Ave. West, Toronto, ON M4V 1P5
416-325-4000, Fax: 416-325-3159, 800-565-4923

Prince Edward Island

Prince Edward Island Department of Environment, Energy, & Forestry, Jones Bldg., 11 Kent St., 4th Fl., PO Box 2000, Charlottetown, PE C1A 7N8
902-368-5000, Fax: 902-368-5830

Quebec

Ministère du Développement durable, de l'Environnement et des Parcs, Édifice Marie-Guyart, 675, boul René-Lévesque est, 29e étage, Québec, QC G1R 5V7
418-521-3830, Fax: 418-646-5974, 800-561-1616, info@mddep.gouv.qc.ca

Saskatchewan

Saskatchewan Environment, 3211 Albert St., 2nd Fl., Regina, SK S4S 5W6
306-787-2584, Fax: 306-787-9544, 800-567-4224, Centre.Inquiry@gov.sk.ca

Yukon Territory

Yukon Environment, PO Box 2703, Whitehorse, YT Y1A 2C6
867-667-5652, Fax: 867-393-7197, environment.yukon@gov.yk.ca

AIRPORTS & AVIATION

See Also: Transportation

Canadian Air Transport Security Authority, 99 Bank St., 13th Fl., Ottawa, ON K1P 6B9
Fax: 613-990-1295, 888-294-2202

Institute for Aerospace Research, 1200 Montreal Rd., Ottawa, ON K1A 0R6
613-990-0765, Fax: 613-952-7214

Transport Canada, Place de Ville, 330 Sparks St., Tower C, Ottawa, ON K1A 0N5
613-990-2309, Fax: 613-954-4731, 866-995-9737

Transportation Appeal Tribunal of Canada, #1201, 333 Laurier Ave. West, 12th Fl., Ottawa, ON K1A 0N5
613-990-6906, Fax: 613-990-9153, info@tatc.gc.ca

Newfoundland & Labrador

Department of Transportation & Works, Confederation Bldg., West Block, 6th Fl., PO Box 8700, St. John's, NL A1B 4J6
709-729-3679, Fax: 709-729-4285, twminister@gov.nl.ca

Northwest Territories

Airports, YK Centre, 4922 - 28th St., 4th fl., PO Box 1320, Yellowknife, NT X1A 2L9
867-873-7725, Fax: 867-873-0297

Department of Transportation, Lahm Ridge Bldg., 4501 50 Ave., PO Box 1320, Yellowknife, NT X1A 2L9
867-920-3460, Fax: 867-873-0363

Nunavut

Department of Community & Government Services, W.G. Brown Bldg., 4th Fl., PO Box 1000 700,Iqaluit, NU X0A 0H0
867-975-5400, Fax: 867-975-5305

Ontario

Ministry of Transportation, Ferguson Block, 77 Wellesley St. West, 3rd Fl., Toronto, ON M7A 1Z8
416-235-4686, Fax: 905-704-2001, 800-268-4686

Saskatchewan

Saskatchewan Highways & Infrastructure, Victoria Tower, 1855 Victoria Ave., Regina, SK S4P 3T2
306-787-4800, communications@highways.gov.sk.ca

Yukon Territory

Yukon Highways & Public Works, PO Box 2703, Whitehorse, YT Y1A 2C6
867-393-7193, Fax: 867-393-6218, 800-661-0408, hpw-info@gov.yk.ca

APPRENTICESHIP PROGRAMS

Canadian Council of Directors of Apprenticeship, 140 Promenade du Portage, 5th Fl, Phase IV, Gatineau, QC K1A 0J9
819-953-7443, Fax: 819-994-0202, redseal-sceaurouge@hrsdc-rhdcc.gc.ca

Alberta

Alberta Advanced Education & Technology, Legislature Bldg., #324, 10800 - 97 Ave., Edmonton, AB T5K 2B6
780-422-5400

Community, Learner & Industry Connections Division, Phipps-McKinnon Bldg., 10020 - 101A Ave., 5th Fl., Edmonton, AB T5J 3G2

New Brunswick

Apprenticeship & Occupational Certification Board, PO Box 6000, Fredericton, NB E3B 5H1
506-453-2260, Fax: 506-453-5317

Department of Post-Secondary Education, Training & Labour, Chestnut Complex, 470 York St., PO Box 6000, Fredericton, NB E3B 5H1
506-453-2597, Fax: 506-453-3618, dpetlinfo@gnb.ca

Northwest Territories

Northwest Territories Apprenticeship, Trade & Occupations Certification Board, PO Box 1320, Yellowknife, NT X1A 2L9
867-873-7357, Fax: 867-873-0200

Prince Edward Island

SkillsPEI, Atlantic Technology Centre, #212, 90 University Ave., Charlottetown, PE C1A 4K9
902-368-4260, Fax: 902-368-6340, 877-491-4766

Quebec

Conseil consultatif du travail et de la main d'oeuvre, #9.400, 500, boul René-Lévesque ouest, Montréal, QC H2Z 1W7
514-873-2880, Fax: 514-873-1129, cctm@cctm.gouv.qc.ca

Saskatchewan

Saskatchewan Advanced Education, Employment & Immigration, 1945 Hamilton St., Regina, SK S4P 2C8
306-787-9478, aeeinquiry@gov.sk.ca

Yukon Territory

Yukon Education, PO Box 2703, Whitehorse, YT Y1A 2C6
867-667-5141, Fax: 867-393-6254, contact.education@gov.yk.ca

ARCTIC & NORTHERN AFFAIRS

Aboriginal Affairs & Northern Development Canada, 10 Wellington St., North Tower, Gatineau, QC K1A 0H4
819-997-0380, Fax: 866-817-3977, 800-567-9604, infopubs@aadnc-aandc.gc.ca

Canadian Polar Commission, Constitution Square, #1710, 360 Albert St., Ottawa, ON K1R 7X7
613-943-8605, Fax: 613-943-8607, 888-765-2701, mail@polarcom.gc.ca

British Columbia

Northern Development Initiative Trust, #301, 1268 Fifth Ave., Prince George, BC V2L 3L2
250-561-2525, Fax: 250-561-2563, info@northerndevelopment.bc.ca

Manitoba

Manitoba Aboriginal & Northern Affairs, 59 Elizabeth Dr., PO Box 37, Thompson, MB R8N 1X4
204-677-6607, Fax: 204-677-6753, amartin@gov.mb.ca

Newfoundland & Labrador

Department of Labrador & Aboriginal Affairs, Confederation Bldg., East Block, 6th Fl., PO Box 8700, St. John's, NL A1B 4J6
709-729-4776, Fax: 709-729-4900, 877-788-8822, laa@gov.nl.ca

Northwest Territories

Department of Environment & Natural Resources, PO Box 1320, Yellowknife, NT X1A 2L9

Nunavut

Department of Executive & Intergovernmental Affairs, 1084 Aeroplex bldg., PO Box 1000 200,Iqaluit, NU X0A 0H0
867-975-6000, Fax: 867-975-6099

Ontario

Northern Development Division, Roberta Bondar Place, #200, 70 Foster Dr., Sault Ste Marie, ON P6A 6V8
705-945-5900, Fax: 705-945-5931, 800-461-2287

Ministry of Northern Development, Mines & Forestry, 99 Wellesley St. West, Toronto, ON M7A 1W3
416-327-0633, Fax: 416-327-0651

Yukon Territory

Yukon Economic Development, PO Box 2703, Whitehorse, YT Y1A 2C6
867-393-7191, Fax: 867-393-6412, 800-661-0408, ecdev@gov.yk.ca

ARTS & CULTURE

Canada Council for the Arts, 350 Albert St., PO Box 1047, Ottawa, ON K1P 5V8
613-566-4414, Fax: 613-566-4390, 800-263-5588

Canada Place Corporation, 504 - 999 Canada Place, Vancouver, BC V6C 3E1
604-775-7200, Fax: 604-775-6251, admin@canadaplace.ca

Canadian Artists & Producers Professional Relations Tribunal, C.D. Howe Bldg., 240 Sparks St., 1st Fl., West Tower, Ottawa, ON K1A 1A1
613-996-4052, Fax: 613-947-4125, 800-263-ARTS, info@capprt-tcrpap.gc.ca

Canadian Broadcasting Corporation, 181 Queen St., PO Box 3220 C,Ottawa, ON K1Y 1E4
613-288-6033, liaison@radio-canada.ca

Canadian Heritage, 15 Eddy St., Gatineau, QC K1A 0M5
819-997-0055, 866-811-0055, info@pch.gc.ca

Canadian Museum of Civilization Corporation, 100 Laurier St., Gatineau, QC K1A 0M8
819-776-7000, Fax: 819-776-8300, 800-555-5621, web@civilization.ca

Canadian Museum of Nature, PO Box 3443 D,Ottawa, ON K1P 6P4
613-566-4700, Fax: 613-364-4021, 800-263-4433

Library of Parliament, Parliamentary Bldgs., 111 Wellington St., Ottawa, ON K1A 0A9
613-992-4793, Fax: 613-943-6383, 866-599-4999

National Arts Centre, 53 Elgin St., PO Box 1534 B,Ottawa, ON K1P 5W1
613-947-7000, Fax: 613-996-9578, info@nac-cna.ca

National Film Board of Canada, 3155, rue Côte de Liesse, CP 1600 Centre-ville,Saint-Laurent, QC H4N 2N4
514-283-9000, Fax: 514-283-7564, 800-267-7710

National Gallery of Canada, 380 Sussex Dr., PO Box 427 A,Ottawa, ON K1N 9N4
613-990-1985, Fax: 613-993-4385, 800-319-2787, info@gallery.ca; info@beaux-arts.ca

Parks Canada, 25 Eddy St., Gatineau, QC K1A 0M5
613-860-1251, 888-773-8888, information@pc.gc.ca

Telefilm Canada, #500, 360, rue Saint-Jacques, Montréal, QC H2Y 1P5
514-283-6363, Fax: 514-283-2365, 800-567-0890, info@telefilm.gc.ca

British Columbia

Islands Trust, #200, 1627 Fort St., Victoria, BC V8R 1H8
250-405-5151, Fax: 250-405-5155, information@islandstrust.bc.ca

Ministry of Social Development, PO Box 9058 Prov Govt,Victoria, BC V8W 9E1
250-356-7750, Fax: 250-356-7292, SD.Minister@gov.bc.ca

Manitoba

Communications Services Manitoba, 155 Carlton St., 10th Fl., Winnipeg, MB R3C 3H8
204-945-3765, Fax: 204-948-2147

Manitoba Culture, Heritage, Tourism & Sport, Legislative Building, #118, 450 Broadway Ave., Winnipeg, MB R3C 0V8
204-945-3729, Fax: 204-945-5223, mincht@leg.gov.mb.ca

Heritage Grants Advisory Council, 213 Notre Dame Ave., 3rd Fl., Winnipeg, MB R3B 1N3
204-945-2213, Fax: 204-948-2086

Le Centre Culturel franco-manitobain/Franco-Manitoban Cultural Centre, 340, boul Provencher, St Boniface, MB R2H 0G7
204-233-8972, Fax: 204-233-3324, ccfm@ccfm.mb.ca

Manitoba Arts Council, #525, 93 Lombard Ave., Winnipeg, MB R3B 3B1
204-945-2237, Fax: 204-945-5925, 866-994-2787, info@artscouncil.mb.ca

Manitoba Centennial Centre Corporation, 555 Main St., Winnipeg, MB R3B 1C3
204-956-1360, Fax: 204-944-1390

Manitoba Film Classification Board, #216, 301 Weston St., Winnipeg, MB R3E 3H4
204-945-8962, Fax: 204-945-0890, 866-612-2399, mfcb@gov.mb.ca

Manitoba Heritage Council, 213 Notre Dame Ave., Main Fl., Winnipeg, MB R3B 1N3
204-945-2118, Fax: 204-948-2384, hrb@gov.mb.ca

Manitoba Museum, 190 Rupert Ave., Winnipeg, MB R3B 0N2
204-956-2830, Fax: 204-942-3679, info@manitobamuseum.mb.ca

Multiculturalism Secretariat, 213 Notre Dame Ave., 4th Fl., Winnipeg, MB R3B 1N3
204-945-1156, Fax: 204-948-2323

New Brunswick

Department of Social Development, Sartain MacDonald Bldg., 551 King St., PO Box 6000, Fredericton, NB E3B 5H1
506-453-2001, Fax: 506-453-7478, sd-ds@gnb.ca

Department of Wellness, Culture & Sport, Place 2000, 250 King St., 4th Fl., PO Box 6000, Fredericton, NB E3B 5H1
506-453-2909, Fax: 506-453-6548

Ministerial Advisory Committee on Multiculturalism, PO Box 6000, Fredericton, NB E3B 5H1

New Brunswick Arts Board, 61 Carleton St., Fredericton, NB E3B 3T2
506-444-4444, Fax: 506-444-5543, 1-866-460-2787

New Brunswick Film, Place 2000, 250 King St., 4th Fl., PO Box 6000, Fredericton, NB E1B 5H1
506-453-2555, Fax: 506-453-2416, nbfilm@gnb.ca

Newfoundland & Labrador

Department of Tourism, Culture & Recreation, Confederation Bldg., West Block, 2nd Fl., PO Box 8700, St. John's, NL A1B 4J6
709-729-0862, Fax: 709-729-0870, tcrinfo@gov.nl.ca

Provincial Information & Library Resources Board, 48 St. George's Ave, Stephenville, NL A2H 1K9
709-643-0900, Fax: 709-643-0925

Northwest Territories

Department of Education, Culture & Employment, PO Box 1320, Yellowknife, NT X1A 2L9
867-669-2399, Fax: 867-873-0431, 866-606-5627

NWT Arts Council, PO Box 1320 Main, Yellowknife, NT X1A 2L9
867-920-6370, Fax: 867-873-0205

Nova Scotia

Culture Division, #601, 1800 Argyle St., PO Box 456, Halifax, NS B3J 2R5
902-424-4510, Fax: 902-424-0710, culture@gov.ns.ca

Department of Education, Trade Mart Bldg., #402-2021 Brunswick St., PO Box 578, Halifax, NS B3J 2S9
902-424-5168, Fax: 902-424-0680

Film Nova Scotia, Collins Bank Bldg., 1869 Upper Water St., 3rd Fl., Halifax, NS B3J 1S9
902-424-7177, Fax: 902-424-0617, 888-360-2111

Nova Scotia Tourism Partnership Council, World Trade & Convention Centre, #603, 1800 Argyle St., Halifax, NS B3J 3N8
902-424-0048, Fax: 902-424-0723

Nunavut

Department of Culture, Language, Elders & Youth, PO Box 1000 800,Iqaluit, NU X0A 0H0
867-975-5500, Fax: 867-975-5504, 866-934-2035

Ontario

Ontario Heritage Trust, 10 Adelaide St. East, Toronto, ON M5C 1J3
416-325-5000, Fax: 416-325-5071

Ontario Library Service - North, 334 Regent St., Sudbury, ON P3C 4E2
705-675-6467, Fax: 705-675-2285, 800-461-6348

Ontario Media Development Corporation, South Tower, #501, 175 Bloor St. East, Toronto, ON M4W 3R8
416-314-6858, Fax: 416-314-6876, mail@omdc.on.ca

Ontario Northland, 555 Oak St. East, North Bay, ON P1B 8L3
705-472-4500, Fax: 705-472-4267, 800-363-7512, info@ontarionorthland.ca

Ontario Place Corporation, 955 Lake Shore Blvd. West, Toronto, ON M6K 3B9
416-314-9900, Fax: 416-314-9992

Ontario Tourism Marketing Partnership Corporation, #900,10 Dundas St. East, Toronto, ON M7A 2A1
416-212-0757, Fax: 416-325-6004, 800-668-2746

Ontario Trillium Foundation, 800 Bay St., 5th Fl., Toronto, ON M5S 3A9
416-963-4927, Fax: 416-963-8781, 800-263-2887, trillium@trilliumfoundation.org

Ottawa Convention Centre, 55 Colonel By Dr., Ottawa, ON K1N 9J2
613-563-1984, Fax: 613-563-7646

Royal Ontario Museum, 100 Queen's Park Cres., Toronto, ON M5S 2C6
416-586-5549, Fax: 416-586-5685, info@rom.on.ca

Southern Ontario Library Service, #902, 111 Peter St., Toronto, ON M5V 2H1
416-961-1669, Fax: 416-961-5122, 800-387-5765

Ministry of Tourism & Culture, Hearst Block, 900 Bay St., 9th Fl., Toronto, ON M7A 2E1
416-326-9326, Fax: 416-314-7854, 800-668-2746

Prince Edward Island

Prince Edward Island Department of Community Services, Seniors, & Labour, Jones Bldg., 11 Kent St., 2nd Fl., PO Box 2000, Charlottetown, PE C1A 7N8
902-620-3777, Fax: 902-368-4740, 866-594-3777

Quebec

Bibliothèque et Archives nationales du Québec (BAnQ), 475, boul De Maisonneuve est, Montréal, QC H2L 5C4
514-873-1100, Fax: 514-873-9312, 800-363-9028

Commission des biens culturels du Québec, Bloc A-RC, 225, Grande Allée est, Québec, QC G1R 5G5
418-643-8378, Fax: 418-643-8591, info@cbcq.gouv.qc.ca

Conseil des arts et des lettres du Québec, 79, boul René-Lévesque est, 3e étage, Québec, QC G1R 5N5
418-643-1707, Fax: 418-643-4558, 800-897-1707, info@calq.gouv.qc.ca

Conseil des relations interculturelles, #10.04, 500, boul René-Lévesque ouest, Montréal, QC H2Z 1W7
514-873-5634, Fax: 514-873-3469, info@conseilinterculturel.gouv.qc.ca

Ministère de la Culture, des Communications & de la Condition féminine, 225, Grande Allée est, Québec, QC G1R 5G5
888-380-8882

Curateur public du Québec, 600, boul René-Lévesque ouest, Montréal, QC H3B 4W9
514-873-4074, Fax: 514-873-5033, 800-363-9020

Musée d'art contemporain de Montréal, 185, rue Ste-Catherine ouest, Montréal, QC H2X 3X5
514-847-6226, Fax: 514-847-6290, info@macm.org

Musée de la civilisation, 85, rue Dalhousie, CP 155 B,Québec, QC G1K 7A6
418-643-2158, Fax: 418-646-9705, 866-710-8031, mcqweb@mcq.org

Musée national des beaux-arts du Québec, Parc des Champs-de-Bataille, 1, av Wolfe-Montcalm, Québec, QC G1R 5H3
418-643-2150, Fax: 418-646-3330, 866-220-2150, webmestre@mnba.qc.ca

Régie du cinéma, #100, 390, rue Notre-Dame ouest, Montréal, QC H2Y 1T9
514-873-2371, Fax: 514-873-8874, 800-463-2463, regieducinema@rcq.gouv.qc.ca

Secrétariat à la politique linguistique, 225 Grande-Allée est, 4e étage, Québec, QC G1R 5G5
418-643-4248, Fax: 418-646-7832, info@spl.gouv.qc.ca

Société de développement des entreprises culturelles, #800, 215, rue Saint-Jacques, Montréal, QC H2Y 1M6
514-841-2200, Fax: 514-841-8606, 800-363-0401, info@sodec.gouv.qc.ca

Société de la Place des Arts de Montréal, 260, boul de Maisonneuve ouest, Montréal, QC H2X 1Y9
514-285-4200, Fax: 514-285-1968, info@pda.qc.ca

Société de télédiffusion du Québec (Télé-Québec), 1000, rue Fullum, Montréal, QC H2K 3L7
514-521-2424, Fax: 514-873-2601, 800-361-4362, info@telequebec.tv

Société du Grand Théâtre de Québec, 269, boul René-Lévesque est, Québec, QC G1R 2B3
418-643-8111, gtq@grandtheatre.qc.ca

Saskatchewan

Saskatchewan Archives Board, University of Regina, 3303 Hillsdale St., PO Box 1665, Regina, SK S4P 3C6
306-787-4068, Fax: 306-787-1197, info.regina@archives.gov.sk.ca

Royal Saskatchewan Museum, 2445 Albert St., Regina, SK S4P 4W7
306-787-2815, Fax: 306-787-2820, rsminfo@gov.sk.ca

Sask Film, 1831 College Ave., Regina, SK S4P 4V5
306-798-9800, Fax: 306-798-7768, 800-561-9933

Saskatchewan Archives Board, University of Regina, 3303 Hillsdale St., PO Box 1665, Regina, SK S4P 3C6
306-787-4068, Fax: 306-787-1197, info.regina@archives.gov.sk.ca

Saskatchewan Communications Network, #313E, 2440 Broad St., Regina, SK S4P 0A5
306-779-2726, Fax: 306-545-8649, inquiries@scn.ca

Saskatchewan Film & Video Classification Board, #500, 1919 Saskatchewan Dr., Regina, SK S4P 4H2
306-787-5550, Fax: 306-787-9779, 888-374-4636

Saskatchewan Tourism, Parks, Culture & Sport, 1919 Saskatchewan Dr., 4th Fl., Regina, SK S4P 4H2
306-787-5729, Fax: 306-787-8560, info@cyr.gov.sk.ca

Wanuskewin Heritage Park, RR#4 Penner Rd., Saskatoon, SK S7K 3J7
306-931-6767, Fax: 306-931-4522, roxanne.parker@wanuskewin.com

Yukon Territory

Yukon Tourism & Culture, 100 Hanson St., Whitehorse, YT Y1A 2C6
867-667-5036, Fax: 867-667-3546

AUDITORS-GENERAL

Auditor General of Canada, 240 Sparks St., Ottawa, ON K1A 0G6
613-995-3708, Fax: 613-957-0474, 888-761-5953, communications@oag-bvg.gc.ca; infomedia@oag-bvg.gc.ca

Alberta

Alberta Office of the Auditor General, 9925 - 109 St., 8th Fl., Edmonton, AB T5K 2J8
780-427-4222, Fax: 780-422-9555, info@oag.ab.ca

British Columbia

Office of the Auditor General, PO Box 9036 Prov Govt,Victoria, BC V8W 9A2
250-419-6100, Fax: 250-387-1230

Manitoba

Office of the Auditor General, #500, 330 Portage Ave., Winnipeg, MB R3C 0C4
204-945-3790, Fax: 204-945-2169, oag.contact@oag.mb.ca

New Brunswick

Office of the Auditor General, HSBC Place, 520 King St., 6th Fl., Fredericton, NB E3B 6G3
506-453-2243, Fax: 506-453-3067

Newfoundland & Labrador

Office of the Auditor General, PO Box 8700, St. John's, NL A1B 4J6
709-729-2695, Fax: 709-729-5970, oagmail@oag.nl.ca

Nova Scotia

Office of the Auditor General, #302, 1888 Brunswick St., Halifax, NS B3J 3J8
902-424-5907, Fax: 902-424-4350

Ontario

Office of the Auditor General, Atrium on Bay, #1530, 20 Dundas St. West, PO Box 105, Toronto, ON M5G 2C2
416-327-2381, Fax: 416-327-9862, comments@auditor.on.ca

Prince Edward Island

Office of the Auditor General, Shaw Bldg., 105 Rochford St. North, 2nd Fl., Charlottetown, PE C1A 7N8
902-368-4520, Fax: 902-368-4598, www.assembly.pe.ca

Quebec
Vérificateur général du Québec, 750, boulevard Charest est, 3e étage, Québec, QC G1K 9J6
418-691-5900, Fax: 418-644-4460, verificateur.general@vgq.gouv.qc.ca

Saskatchewan
Provincial Auditor Saskatchewan, #1500, 1920 Broad St., Regina, SK S4P 3V2
306-787-6398, Fax: 306-787-6383, info@auditor.sk.ca

AUTOMOBILE INSURANCE

See Also: Insurance (Life, Fire Property)

Alberta
Alberta Automobile Insurance Rate Board, Canadian Western Bank Place, #2440, 10303 Jasper Ave., Edmonton, AB T5J 3N6
780-427-5428, Fax: 780-638-4254, airb@gov.ab.ca

British Columbia
Insurance Corporation of British Columbia, 151 West Esplanade, North Vancouver, BC V7M 3H9
604-661-2800, 800-663-3051

Manitoba
Manitoba Public Insurance, #B100, 234 Donald St., PO Box 6300, Winnipeg, MB R3C 4A4
204-985-7000, Fax: 204-985-3525, 800-665-2410

New Brunswick
Department of Justice & Consumer Affairs, Centennial Bldg., 670 King St., PO Box 6000, Fredericton, NB E3B 5H1
506-462-5100, Fax: 506-453-3651, justice.comments@gnb.ca

Northwest Territories
Department of Finance, Arthur Laing Building, 5th Fl., 5003 - 49th St., PO Box 1320, Yellowknife, NT X1A 2L9
867-873-7117, Fax: 867-873-0414

Nova Scotia
Nova Scotia Utility & Review Board, Summit Place, 1601 Lower Water St., 3rd Fl., Halifax, NS B3J 3P6
902-424-4448, Fax: 902-424-3919, uarb.board@gov.ns.ca

Ontario
Financial Services Commission of Ontario, New York City Ctr., 5160 Yonge St., 17th Fl., PO Box 85, Toronto, ON M2N 6L9
416-250-7250, Fax: 416-590-7070, 800-668-0128

Quebec
Société de l'assurance automobile du Québec, 333, boul Jean-Lesage, CP 19600 Terminus, Québec, QC G1K 8J6
418-643-7620, Fax: 418-644-0339, 800-361-7620, courrier@saaq.gouv.qc.ca

Saskatchewan
Saskatchewan Government Insurance, 2260 - 11th Ave., Regina, SK S4P 0J9
306-751-1200, Fax: 306-787-7477, 800-667-8015, sgiinquiries@sgi.sk.ca

Yukon Territory
Yukon Justice, Andrew Philipsen Law Centre, 2134 Second Ave., PO Box 2703, Whitehorse, YT Y1A 2C6
867-667-3033, Fax: 867-393-5790, jus.msb@gov.yk.ca

BANKING & FINANCIAL INSTITUTIONS

Bank of Canada, 234 Wellington St., Ottawa, ON K1A 0G9
613-782-7902, Fax: 613-782-7713, 800-303-1282, info@bankofcanada.ca; communications@bankofcanada.ca (Media)

Business Development Bank of Canada, #400, 5, Place Ville-Marie, Montréal, QC H3B 5E7
514-283-5904, Fax: 514-283-5626, 877-232-2269

Canada Deposit Insurance Corporation, 50 O'Connor St., 17th Floor, PO Box 2340 D,Ottawa, ON K1P 5W5
Fax: 613-996-6095, 800-461-2342, info@cdic.ca; info@sadc.ca

Finance Canada, L'esplanade Laurier, 140 O'Connor St., Ottawa, ON K1A 0G5
613-992-1573, Fax: 613-943-0938, finpub@fin.gc.ca

Financial Consumer Agency of Canada, 427 Laurier Ave. West, 6th Fl., Ottawa, ON K1R 1B9
Fax: 613-941-1436, info@fcac-acfc.gc.ca

Office of the Superintendent of Financial Institutions, Kent Square, 255 Albert St., Ottawa, ON K1A 0H2
613-990-7788, Fax: 613-990-5591, 800-385-8647, information@osfi-bsif.gc.ca

Provincial-Local Finance Division, College Park, 777 Bay St., 10th Fl., Toronto, ON M5G 2C8
416-327-0264, Fax: 416-325-7644

Treasury & Risk Management, Terrace Building, 9515 - 107 St., 3rd Fl., Edmonton, AB T5K 2C3

Alberta
ATB Financial, 9888 Jasper Ave., Edmonton, AB T5J 1P1
403-245-8110, 800-332-8383

Credit Union Deposit Guarantee Corporation, #2000, 10104 - 103 St., Edmonton, AB T5J 0H8
780-428-6680, Fax: 780-428-7571, 800-661-0351, mail@cudgc.ab.ca

Alberta Finance & Enterprise, Terrace Building, #426, 9515 - 107 St., Edmonton, AB T5K 2C3
780-427-3035, Fax: 780-427-1147, tra.revenue@gov.ab.ca

British Columbia
Ministry of Finance, PO Box 9417 Prov Govt,Victoria, BC V8W 9V1
250-387-3751, Fax: 250-387-5594, Fin.Minister@gov.bc.ca

Financial Institutions Commission, #1200, 13450 - 102 Ave., Surrey, BC V3T 5X3
604-953-5300, Fax: 604-953-5301, 866-206-3030, FICOM@ficombc.ca; HR@ficombc.ca

Manitoba
Credit Union Deposit Guarantee Corporation, #390, 200 Graham Ave., Winnipeg, MB R3C 4L5
204-942-8480, Fax: 204-947-1723, 800-697-4447, mail@cudgc.com

Financial Institutions Regulation Branch, #1115, 405 Broadway, Winnipeg, MB R3C 3L6
204-945-2542, Fax: 204-948-2268

New Brunswick
New Brunswick Credit Union Deposit Insurance Corp., PO Box 6000, Fredericton, NB E3B 5H1
506-457-4852, Fax: 506-453-7474

Newfoundland & Labrador
Credit Union Deposit Guarantee Corporation, PO Box 340, Marystown, NL A0E 2M0
709-279-0170, Fax: 709-279-0177, 877-279-0170

Northwest Territories
Department of Finance, Arthur Laing Building, 5th Fl., 5003 - 49th St., PO Box 1320, Yellowknife, NT X1A 2L9
867-873-7117, Fax: 867-873-0414

Nunavut
Nunavut Business Credit Corporation, Parnaivak Bldg., #100, PO Box 2548, Iqaluit, NU X0A 0H0
867-975-7891, Fax: 867-975-7897, 800-758-0038, credit@nbcc.nu.ca

Ontario
Deposit Insurance Corporation of Ontario, #700, 4711 Yonge St., Toronto, ON M2N 6K8
416-325-9444, Fax: 416-325-9722, 800-268-6653

Ministry of Finance, Frost Bldg. South, 7 Queen's Park Cres., 7th Fl., Toronto, ON M7A 1Y7
Fax: 866-888-3850, 800-263-7965, financecommunications.fin@ontario.ca

Financial Services Commission of Ontario, New York City Ctr., 5160 Yonge St., 17th Fl., PO Box 85, Toronto, ON M2N 6L9
416-250-7250, Fax: 416-590-7070, 800-668-0128

Ministry of Revenue, Frost Bldg. South, 7 Queen's Park Cres., 6th Fl., Toronto, ON M7A 1Y7
Fax: 866-888-3850, 866-668-8297

Quebec
Caisse de dépôt et placement du Québec, 1000, place Jean-Paul-Riopelle, Montréal, QC H2Z 2B3
514-842-3261, Fax: 514-842-4833, 866-330-3936, info@lacaisse.com

Registraire des entreprises, 787, boul Lebourgneuf, Québec, QC G2J 1C3
418-644-4545, Fax: 418-528-5703, 877-644-4545, registre@servicesquebec.gouv.qc.ca

Saskatchewan
Saskatchewan Finance, 2350 Albert St., Regina, SK S4P 4A6
306-787-6768, Fax: 306-787-0241, communications@finance.gov.sk.ca

Saskatchewan Financial Services Commission, #601, 1919 Saskatchewan Dr., Regina, SK S4P 4H2
306-787-5645, Fax: 306-787-5899

Yukon Territory
Yukon Finance, PO Box 2703, Whitehorse, YT Y1A 2C6
867-667-5343, Fax: 867-393-6217, fininfo@gov.yk.ca

BILINGUALISM

Canadian Heritage, 15 Eddy St., Gatineau, QC K1A 0M5
819-997-0055, 866-811-0055, info@pch.gc.ca

Office of the Commissioner of Official Languages, 344 Slater St., 3rd fl., Ottawa, ON K1A 0T8
613-996-6368, Fax: 613-993-5082, 877-996-6368

Manitoba
Le Centre Culturel franco-manitobain/Franco-Manitoban Cultural Centre, 340, boul Provencher, St Boniface, MB R2H 0G7
204-233-8972, Fax: 204-233-3324, ccfm@ccfm.mb.ca

Northwest Territories
Office of the Languages Commissioner, Laing Bldg., 5003 - 49 St., Yellowknife, NT X1A 2P4
867-873-7034, Fax: 867-873-0357, 800-661-0889, langcom@gov.nt.ca

Nunavut
Department of Culture, Language, Elders & Youth, PO Box 1000 800,Iqaluit, NU X0A 0H0
867-975-5500, Fax: 867-975-5504, 866-934-2035

Ontario
Office of Francophone Affairs, #200, 777 Bay St., Toronto, ON M7A 0A2
416-325-4949, Fax: 416-325-4980, 800-268-7507, ofa@ontario.ca

Quebec
Secrétariat à la politique linguistique, 225 Grande-Allée est, 4e étage, Québec, QC G1R 5G5
418-643-4248, Fax: 418-646-7832, info@spl.gouv.qc.ca

BIOTECHNOLOGY

Biotechnology Research Institute, 6100, av Royalmount, Montréal, QC H4P 2R2
514-496-6100, Fax: 514-496-1928, bri-info@cnrc-nrc.gc.ca

Plant Biotechnology Institute, 110 Gymnasium Pl., Saskatoon, SK S7N 0W9
306-975-5248, Fax: 306-975-4839, pbi-info@nrc-cnrc.gc.ca

BOARDS OF REVIEW

Advertising Review Board, Macdonald Block, #M2-56, 900 Bay St., 2nd Fl., Toronto, ON M7A 1N3
416-327-2183, Fax: 416-327-2179

Canada Industrial Relations Board, 240 Sparks St., 4th Fl. West, Ottawa, ON K1A 0X8
Fax: 613-941-4461, 800-575-9696, info@cirb-ccri.gc.ca

Canadian International Trade Tribunal, Standard Life Centre, 333 Laurier Ave. West, 15 Floor, Ottawa, ON K1A 0G7
613-990-2452, Fax: 613-990-2439, secretary@citt-tcce.gc.ca

Canadian Nuclear Safety Commission, 280 Slater St., PO Box 1046 B,Ottawa, ON K1P 5S9
613-995-5894, Fax: 613-995-5086, 800-668-5284

Commission for Public Complaints Against the Royal Canadian Mounted Police, National Intake Office, PO Box 88689, Surrey, BC V3W 0X1
Fax: 613-952-8045, 800-665-6878, org@cpc-cpp.gc.ca

Immigration & Refugee Board of Canada, Canada Bldg, 344 Slater St., 12th Fl., Ottawa, ON K1A 0K1
613-995-6486, Fax: 613-943-1550, contact@irb-cisr.gc.ca

Mackenzie Valley Environmental Impact Review Board, 200 Scotia Centre, #5102, 50th Ave., PO Box 938, Yellowknife, NT X1A 2N7
867-766-7050, Fax: 867-766-7074, 866-912-3472

Merchant Seamen Compensation Board, Secretary, Merchant Seamen Compensation Board, Phase II, Place du Portage, 10th Fl., Ottawa, ON K1A 0J2
819-953-8001, Fax: 819-994-5368

National Energy Board, 444 - 7 Ave. SW, Calgary, AB T2P 0X8
403-292-4800, Fax: 403-292-5503, 800-899-1265, info@neb-one.gc.ca

Nunavut Impact Review Board, PO Box 1360, Cambridge Bay, NU X0B 0C0
867-983-4600, Fax: 867-983-2594, 866-233-3033, info@nirb.ca

Nunavut Water Board, PO Box 119, Gjoa Haven, NU X0B 1J0
867-360-6338, Fax: 867-360-6369

Patented Medicine Prices Review Board, Standard Life Centre, #1400, 333 Laurier Ave. West, PO Box L40, Ottawa, ON K1P 1C1
613-954-8299, Fax: 613-952-7626, 877-861-2350, pmprb@pmprb-cepmb.gc.ca

Porcupine Caribou Management Board, PO Box 31723, Whitehorse, YT Y1A 6L3
867-633-4780, Fax: 867-393-3904, pcmb@taiga.net

Public Service Staffing Tribunal, 240 Sparks St., 6th Fl., Ottawa, ON K1A 0A5
613-949-6516, Fax: 613-949-6551, 866-637-4491, info@psst-tdfp.gc.ca

Royal Canadian Mounted Police External Review Committee, PO Box 1159 B, Ottawa, ON K1P 5R2
613-998-2134, Fax: 613-990-8969, org@erc-cee.gc.ca

Rural & Co-operatives Secretariat, Tower 7, 1341 Baseline Rd., Ottawa, ON K1A 0C5
613-759-1000, Fax: 613-773-2727

Security Intelligence Review Committee, Jackson Bldg., 122 Bank St., 4th Fl., PO Box 2430 D,Ottawa, ON K1P 5W5
613-990-8441, Fax: 613-990-5230, ellardm@sirc-csars.gc.ca

Veterans Review & Appeal Board, Daniel J. MacDonald Bldg., 161 Grafton St., PO Box 9900, Charlottetown, PE C1A 8V7
902-566-8751, Fax: 902-566-7850, 800-450-8006, vrab_tacra@vac-acc.gc.ca

Alberta
Alberta Review Board, Oxford Tower, 10235 - 101 St., 11th Fl., Edmonton, AB T5J 3E9

British Columbia
British Columbia Review Board, #1020, 510 Burrard St., Vancouver, BC V6C 3A8
604-660-8789, Fax: 604-660-8809, 877-305-2277

Manitoba
Manitoba Review Board, 408 York Ave., 2nd Fl., Winnipeg, MB R3C 0P9
204-945-4438, Fax: 204-945-5751
Northwest Territories
Legal Services Board of the Northwest Territories, PO Box 1320, Yellowknife, NT X1A 2L9
867-873-7450, Fax: 867-873-5320
Territorial Board of Revision, #400, 5201 - 50th Ave., PO Box 1320, Yellowknife, NT X1A 2L9
867-873-7125, Fax: 867-873-0609
Ontario
Animal Care Review Board, 77 Grenville St., 8th Fl., Toronto, ON M5S 1B3
416-314-3509, Fax: 416-314-3518
Medical Eligibility Committee, 370 Select Dr., PO Box 168, Kingston, ON K7M 8T4
613-548-6405
Ontario Municipal Board & Board of Negotiation, 655 Bay St., 15th Fl., Toronto, ON M5G 1E5
416-326-6800, Fax: 416-326-5370, 866-887-8820
Ontario Review Board, 151 Bloor St. West, 10th Fl., Toronto, ON M5S 2T5
416-327-8866, Fax: 416-327-8867
Quebec
Bureau d'audiences publiques sur l'environnement, Édifice Lomer-Gouin, #2.10, 575, rue Saint-Amable, Québec, QC G1R 6A6
418-643-7447, Fax: 418-643-9474, 800-463-4732, communication@bape.gouv.qc.ca
Saskatchewan
Public & Private Rights Board, #323, 3085 Albert St., Regina, SK S4S 0B1
306-787-4071, Fax: 306-787-0088
Saskatchewan Film & Video Classification Board, #500, 1919 Saskatchewan Dr., Regina, SK S4P 4H2
306-787-5550, Fax: 306-787-9779, 888-374-4636
Surface Rights Board of Arbitration, 113 - 2nd Ave. East, PO Box 1597, Kindersley, SK S0L 1S0
306-463-5447, Fax: 306-463-5449, surfacerightsboard@gov.sk.ca

BROADCASTING
Canadian Broadcasting Corporation, 181 Queen St., PO Box 3220 C,Ottawa, ON K1Y 1E4
613-288-6033, liaison@radio-canada.ca
Canadian Radio-Television & Telecommunications Commission, Central Building, 1, Promenade du Portage, Les Terrasses de la Chaudière, Gatineau, QC J8X 4B1
819-997-0313, Fax: 819-994-0218, 877-249-2782
Alberta
Alberta Public Affairs Bureau, Park Plaza, 10611 - 98 Ave., 6th Fl., Edmonton, AB T5K 2P7
780-427-2754, Fax: 780-422-4168
Manitoba
Manitoba News Media Services, #29, Legislative Bldg., 450 Broadway, Winnipeg, MB R3C 0V8
204-945-3746, Fax: 204-945-3988, nmservices@leg.gov.mb.ca
New Brunswick
Communications New Brunswick, Wilcom Bldg., 225 King St., 2nd Fl., PO Box 6000, Fredericton, NB E3B 5H1
506-453-2240, Fax: 506-453-5329
Nova Scotia
Communications Nova Scotia, 1723 Hollis St., 3rd Fl., PO Box 608, Halifax, NS B3J 2R7
902-424-7690, Fax: 902-424-0515
Quebec
Société de télédiffusion du Québec (Télé-Québec), 1000, rue Fullum, Montréal, QC H2K 3L7
514-521-2424, Fax: 514-873-2601, 800-361-4362, info@telequebec.tv
Saskatchewan
Saskatchewan Communications Network, #313E, 2440 Broad St., Regina, SK S4P 0A5
306-779-2726, Fax: 306-545-8649, inquiries@scn.ca

BUDGET PLANNING
Alberta
Enterprise Division, Commerce Place, 10155 - 102 St., 6th Fl., Edmonton, AB T5J 4L6
British Columbia
Provincial Treasury, PO Box 9414 Prov Govt,Victoria, BC V8V 9V1
250-387-4541, Fax: 250-356-3041
New Brunswick
Budget & Financial Management, Centennial Bldg., #250, 670 King St., PO Box 6000, Fredericton, NB E3B 5H1
506-453-2808, Fax: 506-444-4499
Northwest Territories
Department of Finance, Arthur Laing Building, 5th Fl., 5003 - 49th St., PO Box 1320, Yellowknife, NT X1A 2L9
867-873-7117, Fax: 867-873-0414
Financial Management Board Secretariat, c/o Secretary of the FMB / Comptroller General, 5003 - 49 St., PO Box 1320, Yellowknife, NT X1A 2L9
Nova Scotia
Department of Finance, Provincial Bldg., 1723 Hollis St., 7th Fl., PO Box 187, Halifax, NS B3J 2N3
902-424-5554, Fax: 902-424-0635, FinanceWeb@gov.ns.ca
Nunavut
Department of Finance, Bldg. 1079, 1st Fl., PO Box 1000 330,Iqaluit, NU X0A 0H0
867-975-5800, Fax: 867-975-5805

BUSINESS & FINANCE
Atlantic Canada Opportunities Agency, Blue Cross Centre, 644 Main St., 3rd Fl., PO Box 6051, Moncton, NB E1C 9J8
506-851-2271, Fax: 506-851-7403, 800-561-7862, information@acoa-apeca.gc.ca
Auditor General of Canada, 240 Sparks St., Ottawa, ON K1A 0G6
613-995-3708, Fax: 613-957-0474, 888-761-5953, communications@oag-bvg.gc.ca; infomedia@oag-bvg.gc.ca
Bank of Canada, 234 Wellington St., Ottawa, ON K1A 0G9
613-782-7902, Fax: 613-782-7713, 800-303-1282, info@bankofcanada.ca; communications@bankofcanada.ca (Media)
Business Development Bank of Canada, #400, 5, Place Ville-Marie, Montréal, QC H3B 5E7
514-283-5904, Fax: 514-283-5626, 877-232-2269
Calgary, #2403, 308-4th Ave. SW, Calgary, AB T2P 0H7
403-817-6700, Fax: 403-817-6701
Canada Business, 235 Queen St., Ottawa, ON K1A 0H5
888-576-4444
Canada Deposit Insurance Corporation, 50 O'Connor St., 17th Floor, PO Box 2340 D,Ottawa, ON K1P 5W5
Fax: 613-996-6095, 800-461-2342, info@cdic.ca; info@sadc.ca
Canada Economic Development for Québec Regions, Édifice Dominion Square, #900, 1255, rue Peel, Montréal, QC H3B 2T9
514-283-6412, Fax: 514-283-3302, 866-385-6412
Canada Investment & Savings, #900, 110 Yonge St., Toronto, ON M5C 1T4
416-952-1252, Fax: 416-952-1270, 800-575-5151, csb@csb.gc.ca
Canada Mortgage & Housing Corporation, 700 Montreal Rd., Ottawa, ON K1A 0P7
613-748-2000, Fax: 613-748-2098, 800-668-2642, chic@cmhc-schl.gc.ca
Canada Pension Plan Investment Board, #2600, 1 Queen St. East, PO Box 101, Toronto, ON M5C 2W5
416-868-4075, Fax: 416-868-8689, 866-557-9510, csr@cppib.ca
Canada Revenue Agency, 875 Heron Rd., Ottawa, ON K1A 0L5
800-267-6999
Canadian Commercial Corporation, 50 O'Connor St., 11th Fl., Ottawa, ON K1A 0S6
613-996-0034, Fax: 613-995-2121, 800-748-8191
Canadian International Development Agency, 200, Promenade du Portage, Gatineau, QC K1A 0G4
819-997-5456, Fax: 819-953-6088, 800-230-6349, info@acdi-cida.gc.ca
Competition Bureau, Place du Portage, Phase I, 50 Victoria Street, Ottawa, ON K1A 0C9
819-997-4282, Fax: 819-997-0324, 800-348-5358
Competition Tribunal, Thomas D'Arcy McGee Bldg., #600, 90 Sparks St., Ottawa, ON K1P 5B4
613-957-3172, Fax: 613-957-3170, tribunal@ct-tc.gc.ca
Corporate Support Division, Telus Plaza NT, 10025 Jasper Ave., 19th Fl., Edmonton, AB T5J 1S6
Electronic Commerce Branch, 300 Slater St., Ottawa, ON K1A 0C8
613-954-5031, Fax: 613-954-2340, 800-328-6189
Enterprise Cape Breton Corporation, Silicon Island, 70 Crescent St., Sydney, NS B1S 2Z7
902-564-3600, Fax: 902-564-3825, 800-705-3926, information@ecbc-secb.gc.ca
Export Development Canada, 151 Slater St., Ottawa, ON K1A 1K3
613-598-2500, Fax: 613-598-3811, 800-267-8510
Farm Credit Canada, 1800 Hamilton St., PO Box 4320, Regina, SK S4P 4L3
306-780-8100, Fax: 306-780-8919, 888-332-3301, csc@fcc-fac.ca
Finance Canada, L'esplanade Laurier, 140 O'Connor St., Ottawa, ON K1A 0G5
613-992-1573, Fax: 613-943-0938, finpub@fin.gc.ca
Office of the Superintendent of Financial Institutions, Kent Square, 255 Albert St., Ottawa, ON K1A 0H2
613-990-7788, Fax: 613-990-5591, 800-385-8647, information@osfi-bsif.gc.ca
Financial Transactions & Reports Analysis Centre of Canada, 234 Laurier Ave. West, 24th Fl., Ottawa, ON K1P 1H7
Fax: 613-943-7931, 866-346-8722, guidelines-lignesdirectrices@fintrac-canafe.gc.ca
Foreign Affairs & International Trade Canada, 125 Sussex Dr., Ottawa, ON K1A 0G2
613-944-4000, Fax: 613-996-9709, 800-267-8376, enqserv@international.gc.ca
Freshwater Fish Marketing Corporation, 1199 Plessis Rd., Winnipeg, MB R2C 3L4
204-983-6601, Fax: 204-983-6497, sandi.cain@freshwaterfish.com
Global Operations, 125 Sussex Dr,, Ottawa, ON K1A 0G2
613-944-2697, Fax: 613-996-1667
Industry Canada, C.D. Howe Building, 235 Queen St., Ottawa, ON K1A 0H5
613-954-5031, Fax: 613-954-2340, 800-328-6189, info@ic.gc.ca
Législation & enquêtes, 3800, rue de Marly, Secteur 5-1-9, Québec, QC G1X 4A5
418-652-6844, Fax: 418-643-9381
National Round Table on the Environment & Economy, #200, 344 Slater St., Ottawa, ON K1R 7Y3
613-992-7189, Fax: 613-992-7385, admin@nrtee-trnee.ca
North American Free Trade Agreement (NAFTA) Secretariat, Canadian Section, #705, 90 Sparks St., Ottawa, ON K1P 5B4
613-992-9388, Fax: 613-992-9392, webmaster@nafta-alena.gc.ca
Public Sector Pension Investment Board, #200, 440 Laurier Ave. West, Ottawa, ON K1R 7X6
613-782-3095, Fax: 613-782-6864, info@investpsp.ca
Royal Canadian Mint, 320 Sussex Dr., Ottawa, ON K1A 0G8
613-993-3500, Fax: 613-993-4092, 800-267-1871
Statistics Canada, R.H. Coats Bldg., Tunney's Pasture, 150 Tunney's Pasture Driveway, Ottawa, ON K1A 0T6
613-951-8116, Fax: 877-287-4369, 800-263-1136, infostats@statcan.ca
Treasury & Risk Management, Terrace Building, 9515 - 107 St., 3rd Fl., Edmonton, AB T5K 2C3
Treasury Board of Canada, 140 O'Connor St., Ottawa, ON K1A 0R5
613-957-2400, Fax: 613-941-4000, 877-636-0656
Western Economic Diversification Canada, Canada Place, #1500, 9700 Jasper Ave. NW, Edmonton, AB T5J 4H7
780-495-4164, Fax: 780-495-4557, 888-338-9378
Alberta
Agricultural Products Marketing Council, JG O'Donoghue Bldg., 7000 - 113 St., 3rd Fl., Edmonton, AB T6H 5T6
780-427-2164, Fax: 780-422-9690
Alberta Automobile Insurance Rate Board, Canadian Western Bank Place, #2440, 10303 Jasper Ave., Edmonton, AB T5J 3N6
780-427-5428, Fax: 780-638-4254, airb@gov.ab.ca
Alberta Capital Finance Authority, Canadian Western Bank Place, #2450, 10303 Jasper Ave., Edmonton, AB T5J 3N6
780-427-9711, Fax: 780-422-2175, webacfa@gov.ab.ca
Alberta Securities Commission, #600, 250 - 5th St. SW, Calgary, AB T2P 0R4
403-297-6454, Fax: 403-297-6156, 877-355-0585, inquiries@asc.ca; media@asc.ca; complaints@asc.ca
ATB Financial, 9888 Jasper Ave., Edmonton, AB T5J 1P1
403-245-8110, 800-332-8383
Alberta Office of the Auditor General, 9925 - 109 St., 8th Fl., Edmonton, AB T5K 2J8
780-427-4222, Fax: 780-422-9555, info@oag.ab.ca
Credit Union Deposit Guarantee Corporation, #2000, 10104 - 103 St., Edmonton, AB T5J 0H8
780-428-6680, Fax: 780-428-7571, 800-661-0351, mail@cudgc.ab.ca
Alberta Finance & Enterprise, Terrace Building, #426, 9515 - 107 St., Edmonton, AB T5K 2C3
780-427-3035, Fax: 780-427-1147, tra.revenue@gov.ab.ca
Intergovernmental Relations, Commerce Place, 10155 - 102 St., 12th Fl., Edmonton, AB T5J 4G8
780-427-6706, Fax: 780-427-0939,
Occupational Health & Safety Advisory Council, PO Box 697, Halifax, NS B3J 2T8
902-424-2484, Fax: 902-424-5640
British Columbia
Asia Pacific Foundation of Canada, #220, 890 West Pender St., Vancouver, BC V6C 1J9
604-684-5986, Fax: 604-681-1370, info@asiapacific.ca; researchgrants@asiapacific.ca
Auditor Certification Board, PO Box 9431 Prov Govt, Victoria, BC V8W 9V3
250-356-8658, Fax: 250-356-9422, Kelly.Fitzsimonds@gov.bc.ca

Office of the Auditor General, PO Box 9036 Prov Govt,Victoria, BC V8W 9A2
250-419-6100, Fax: 250-387-1230
British Columbia Innovation Council, 1188 West Georgia St., 9th Fl., Vancouver, BC V6E 4A2
604-683-2724, Fax: 604-683-6567, 800-665-7222, info@bcic.ca
British Columbia Pension Corporation, 2995 Jutland Rd., PO Box 9460, Victoria, BC V8W 9V8
250-387-1002, Fax: 250-953-0429, 800-663-8823, PensionCorp@pensionsbc.ca; Retired.Members@pensionsbc.ca
British Columbia Securities Commission, Pacific Centre, 701 West Georgia St., 12th Fl., PO Box 10142, Vancouver, BC V7Y 1L2
604-899-6500, Fax: 604-899-6506, 800-373-6393, inquiries@bcsc.bc.ca
Crown Agencies Resource Office, PO Box 9469 Prov Govt, Victoria, BC V8V 9V8
250-387-8770, Fax: 250-387-9061, CAS@gov.bc.ca
Ministry of Finance, PO Box 9417 Prov Govt,Victoria, BC V8W 9V1
250-387-3751, Fax: 250-387-5594, Fin.Minister@gov.bc.ca
Financial Institutions Commission, #1200, 13450 - 102 Ave., Surrey, BC V3T 5X3
604-953-5300, Fax: 604-953-5301, 866-206-3030, FICOM@ficombc.ca; HR@ficombc.ca
Insurance Corporation of British Columbia, 151 West Esplanade, North Vancouver, BC V7M 3H9
604-661-2800, 800-663-3051
Insurance Council of British Columbia, #300, 1040 West Georgia St., PO Box 7, Vancouver, BC V6E 4H1
604-688-0321, Fax: 604-662-7767, 877-688-0321
International Financial Centre British Columbia, Park Place, #1170, 666 Burrard St., Vancouver, BC V6C 2X8
604-683-6626, Fax: 604-683-6646, info@ifcvancouver.com
Office of the Superintendent of Motor Vehicles, PO Box 9254 Prov Govt,Victoria, BC V8W 9J2
250-387-7747, Fax: 250-387-4891, OSMV.Mailbox@gov.bc.ca
Public Sector Employers' Council Secretariat, #210, 880 Douglas St., PO Box 9400 Prov Govt, Victoria, BC V8V 9V1
250-387-0842, Fax: 250-387-6258
Ministry of Social Development, PO Box 9058 Prov Govt,Victoria, BC V8W 9E1
250-356-7750, Fax: 250-356-7292, SD.Minister@gov.bc.ca
Timber Export Advisory Committee, PO Box 9514 Prov Govt, Victoria, BC V8W 9C2
250-387-8916, Fax: 250-387-5050

Manitoba

Office of the Auditor General, #500, 330 Portage Ave., Winnipeg, MB R3C 0C4
204-945-3790, Fax: 204-945-2169, oag.contact@oag.mb.ca
Claimant Adviser Office, #200, 330 Portage Ave., Winnipeg, MB R3C 0C4
204-945-7413, Fax: 204-948-3157
Communities Economic Development Fund, #100, 23 Station Rd., Thompson, MB R8N 0N6
204-778-4138, Fax: 204-778-4313, 800-561-4315
Manitoba Competitiveness, Training & Trade, International Business Centre, The Paris Building, 259 Portage Ave., Winnipeg, MB R3B 3P4
204-945-2475, Fax: 204-945-3977, minctt@leg.gov.mb.ca
Comptroller Division, #715, 401 York Ave., Winnipeg, MB R3C 0P8
204-945-4920, Fax: 204-945-2394
Credit Union Deposit Guarantee Corporation, #390, 200 Graham Ave., Winnipeg, MB R3C 4L5
204-942-8480, Fax: 204-947-1723, 800-697-4447, mail@cudgc.com
Crown Corporations Council, #1130, 444 St. Mary Ave., Winnipeg, MB R3C 3T1
204-949-5270, Fax: 204-949-5283, crowncc@mts.net
Manitoba Development Corporation, #555, 155 Carlton St., Winnipeg, MB R3C 3H8
204-945-7626, Fax: 204-945-1193
Federal-Provincial Relations & Research Division, #910, 386 Broadway, Winnipeg, MB R3C 3R6
204-945-3757, Fax: 204-945-5051
Manitoba Finance, #109, Legislative Bldg., Winnipeg, MB R3C 0V8
204-945-3754, Fax: 204-945-8316, minfin@leg.gov.mb.ca
Heritage Grants Advisory Council, 213 Notre Dame Ave., 3rd Fl., Winnipeg, MB R3B 1N3
204-945-2213, Fax: 204-948-2086
Manitoba Public Insurance, #B100, 234 Donald St., PO Box 6300, Winnipeg, MB R3C 4A4
204-985-7000, Fax: 204-985-3525, 800-665-2410
Manitoba Intergovernmental Affairs, #301, 450 Broadway Ave., Winnipeg, MB R3C 0V8
Fax: 204-945-1383, mnia@leg.gov.mb.ca
Manitoba Agricultural Services Corporation, #100, 1525 First St. South, Brandon, MB R7A 7A1
204-726-6850, Fax: 204-726-6849, mailbox@masc.mb.ca
Manitoba Bureau of Statistics, #824, 155 Carlton St., Winnipeg, MB R3C 3H9
204-945-2406, Fax: 204-945-0695
Manitoba Round Table for Sustainable Development, #160, 123 Main St., Winnipeg, MB R3C 1A5
204-945-1671, Fax: 204-948-2357, mrtsd@gov.mb.ca
Manitoba Securities Commission, #500, 400 St. Mary Ave., Winnipeg, MB R3C 4K5
204-945-2548, Fax: 204-945-0330, 800-655-5244, securities@gov.mb.ca
Mineral Resources Division, #360, 1395 Ellice Ave., Winnipeg, MB R3G 3P2
Fax: 204-945-8427
Pension Commission of Manitoba, #1004, 401 York Ave., Winnipeg, MB R3C 0P8
204-945-2740, Fax: 204-948-2375, pensions@gov.mb.ca
Manitoba Treasury Board Secretariat, #200, 386 Broadway, Winnipeg, MB R3C 3R6
204-945-4150, Fax: 204-948-4878

New Brunswick

Office of the Auditor General, HSBC Place, 520 King St., 6th Fl., Fredericton, NB E3B 6G3
506-453-2243, Fax: 506-453-3067
Communications, Centennial Bldg., 670 King St., 5th Fl., PO Box 6000, Fredericton, NB E3B 5H1
506-453-3707, Fax: 506-453-3993
Office of the Comptroller, Centennial Bldg., 670 King St., Fredericton, NB E3B 1G1
506-453-2565, Fax: 506-453-2917, wwwooc@gnb.ca
Department of Business New Brunswick, Centennial Bldg., 670 King St., PO Box 6000, Fredericton, NB E3B 5H1
506-453-3707, Fax: 506-453-3993, investnb@gnb.ca
Department of Finance, 670 King St., PO Box 6000, Fredericton, NB E3B 5H1
506-453-2451, Fax: 506-457-4989, wwwfin@gnb.ca
Department of Supply & Services, PO Box 6000, Fredericton, NB E3B 5H1
506-453-3742, Fax: 506-444-4400, Reception.Marysville@gnb.ca
Finance & Administration, Centennial Bldg., #375, 670 King St., PO Box 6000, Fredericton, NB E3B 5H1
506-453-2451, Fax: 506-444-4724
New Brunswick Credit Union Deposit Insurance Corp., PO Box 6000, Fredericton, NB E3B 5H1
506-457-4852, Fax: 506-453-7474
New Brunswick Expropriations Advisory Office, Phoenix Square Bldg., 371 Queen St., Fredericton, NB E3B 1B1
506-453-7771, Fax: 506-453-9600
New Brunswick Farm Products Commission, c/o Department of Agriculture, Aquaculture & Fisheries, PO Box 6000, Fredericton, NB E3B 5H1
506-453-3647, Fax: 506-444-5969
New Brunswick Investment Management Corporation, York Tower, #581, 440 King St., Fredericton, NB E3B 5H8
506-444-5800, Fax: 506-444-5025, comments@nbimc.com
New Brunswick Lotteries & Gaming Corporation, Centennial Bldg., 670 King St., PO Box 6000, Fredericton, NB E3B 5H1
506-444-3468, Fax: 506-444-5818
New Brunswick Municipal Finance Corporation, #376, 670 King St., PO Box 6000, Fredericton, NB E3B 5H1
506-453-3952, Fax: 506-453-2053
New Brunswick Round Table on Environment & Economy, 20 McGloin St., PO Box 6000, Fredericton, NB E3B 5H1
506-453-3703, Fax: 506-453-3876
Regional Development Corporation, RDC Bldg., 836 Churchill Row, PO Box 428, Fredericton, NB E3B 5R4
506-453-2277, Fax: 506-453-7988

Newfoundland & Labrador

Office of the Auditor General, PO Box 8700, St. John's, NL A1B 4J6
709-729-2695, Fax: 709-729-5970, oagmail@oag.nl.ca
Credit Union Deposit Guarantee Corporation, PO Box 340, Marystown, NL A0E 2M0
709-279-0170, Fax: 709-279-0177, 877-279-0170
Department of Business, Confederation Bldg., East Block, 6th Fl., PO Box 8700, St. John's, NL A1B 4J6
709-729-3254, Fax: 709-729-3306, business@gov.nl.ca
Department of Finance, Confederation Bldg., PO Box 8700, St. John's, NL A1B 4J6
709-729-6165, Fax: 709-729-2070, finance@gov.nl.ca
Department of Innovation, Trade & Rural Development, West Block, Confederation Bldg., PO Box 8700, St. John's, NL A1B 4J6
709-729-7000, Fax: 709-729-0654, intrd@gov.nl.ca
Department of Labrador & Aboriginal Affairs, Confederation Bldg., East Block, 6th Fl., PO Box 8700, St. John's, NL A1B 4J6
709-729-4776, Fax: 709-729-4900, 877-788-8822, laa@gov.nl.ca
Ireland Business Partnership, PO Box 8700, St. John's, NL A1B 4J6
709-729-1684, Fax: 709-729-7234, ibp@gov.nl.ca
Newfoundland & Labrador Municipal Financing Corporation, Confederation Bldg., PO Box 8700, St. John's, NL A1B 4J6
709-729-6686, Fax: 709-729-2095

Northwest Territories

Department of Finance, Arthur Laing Building, 5th Fl., 5003 - 49th St., PO Box 1320, Yellowknife, NT X1A 2L9
867-873-7117, Fax: 867-873-0414
Department of Public Works & Services, PO Box 1320, Yellowknife, NT X1A 2L9
Financial Management Board Secretariat, c/o Secretary of the FMB / Comptroller General, 5003 - 49 St., PO Box 1320, Yellowknife, NT X1A 2L9

Nova Scotia

Office of the Auditor General, #302, 1888 Brunswick St., Halifax, NS B3J 3J8
902-424-5907, Fax: 902-424-4350
Department of Economic & Rural Development, Centennial Building, #600, 1660 Hollis St., PO Box 2311, Halifax, NS B3J 1V7
902-424-0377, Fax: 902-424-0500, comm@gov.ns.ca
Department of Finance, Provincial Bldg., 1723 Hollis St., 7th Fl., PO Box 187, Halifax, NS B3J 2N3
902-424-5554, Fax: 902-424-0635, FinanceWeb@gov.ns.ca
Nova Scotia Business Inc., World Trade & Convention Centre, #701, 1800 Argyle St., PO Box 2374, Halifax, NS B3J 3N8
902-424-6650, Fax: 902-424-5739, 800-260-6682, info@nsbi.ca

Nunavut

Department of Finance, Bldg. 1079, 1st Fl., PO Box 1000 330,Iqaluit, NU X0A 0H0
867-975-5800, Fax: 867-975-5805
Nunavut Legal Registries Division, Brown Bldg., 1st Fl., PO Box 1000 570,Iqaluit, NU X0A 0H0
Fax: 867-975-6594

Ontario

Agriculture, Food & Rural Affairs Tribunal, 1 Stone Rd. West, 2nd Fl., Guelph, ON N1G 4Y2
519-826-3433, Fax: 519-826-4232, appeals.tribunal@omafra.gov.on.ca
Office of the Auditor General, Atrium on Bay, #1530, 20 Dundas St. West, PO Box 105, Toronto, ON M5G 2C2
416-327-2381, Fax: 416-327-9862, comments@auditor.on.ca
Ministry of Consumer Services, Mowat Block, 900 Bay St., 6th Fl., Toronto, ON M7A 1L2
416-327-8300, Fax: 416-326-1947, 866-665-0662, infomcs@ontario.ca
Deposit Insurance Corporation of Ontario, #700, 4711 Yonge St., Toronto, ON M2N 6K8
416-325-9444, Fax: 416-325-9722, 800-268-6653
HR Ontario, Whitney Block, #5320, 99 Wellesley St. West, Toronto, ON M7A 1N3
416-212-2057, Fax: 416-325-6317
Ministry of Economic Development & Innovation, Hearst Block, 900 Bay St., 8th Fl., Toronto, ON M7A 2E1
416-325-6666, Fax: 416-325-6688, 866-668-4249, info@edt.gov.on.ca
Ministry of Finance, Frost Bldg. South, 7 Queen's Park Cres., 7th Fl., Toronto, ON M7A 1Y7
Fax: 866-888-3850, 800-263-7965, financecommunications.fin@ontario.ca
Financial Services Commission of Ontario, New York City Ctr., 5160 Yonge St., 17th Fl., PO Box 85, Toronto, ON M2N 6L9
416-250-7250, Fax: 416-590-7070, 800-668-0128
Ministry of Government Services, Whitney Block, #4320, 99 Wellesley St. West, 4th Fl., Toronto, ON M7A 1W3
416-326-1234, Fax: 416-327-3790, 800-268-1142
Grain Financial Protection Board, 1 Stone Rd. West, 1st Fl. Northeast, PO Box 3660 Central, Guelph, ON N1H 8M4
519-826-3949, Fax: 519-826-3367
Licence Appeal Tribunal, 20 Dundas St. West, 5th Fl., Toronto, ON M5G 2C2
416-314-4260, Fax: 416-314-4270, 800-255-2214
Liquor Control Board of Ontario, 55 Lake Shore Blvd. East, Toronto, ON M5E 1A4
416-365-5900, Fax: 416-864-2476, 800-668-5226, infoline@lcbo.com
Livestock Financial Protection Board, 1 Stone Rd. West, 5th Fl. Northwest, Guelph, ON N1G 4Y2
519-826-3886, Fax: 519-826-4375
Metro Toronto Convention Centre Corporation, 255 Front St. West, Toronto, ON M5V 2W6
416-585-8000, Fax: 416-585-8224, info@mtcc.com
Normal Farm Practices Protection Board, 1 Stone Rd. West, 3rd Fl., Guelph, ON N1G 4Y2
Fax: 519-826-3259, 877-424-1300
Ontario Electricity Financial Corporation, #1400, 1 Dundas St. West, Toronto, ON M7A 1Y7
416-325-8000, Fax: 416-325-8005

Ontario Farm Products Marketing Commission, 1 Stone Rd. West, 5th Fl. Southwest, Guelph, ON N1G 4Y2
519-826-4220, Fax: 519-826-3400
Ontario Financing Authority, #1400, 1 Dundas St. West, Toronto, ON M7A 1Y7
416-325-8000, Fax: 416-325-8005
Ontario Food Terminal Board, 165 The Queensway, Toronto, ON M8Y 1H8
416-259-5479, Fax: 416-259-4303
Ontario Place Corporation, 955 Lake Shore Blvd. West, Toronto, ON M6K 3B9
416-314-9900, Fax: 416-314-9992
Ontario Securities Commission, #1903, 20 Queen St. West, PO Box 55, Toronto, ON M5H 3S8
416-597-0681, Fax: 416-593-8241
Ottawa Convention Centre, 55 Colonel By Dr., Ottawa, ON K1N 9J2
613-563-1984, Fax: 613-563-7646
Pay Equity Commission, #300, 180 Dundas St. West, Toronto, ON M7A 2S6
416-314-1896, Fax: 416-314-8741, 800-387-8813
Ministry of Revenue, Frost Bldg. South, 7 Queen's Park Cres., 6th Fl., Toronto, ON M7A 1Y7
Fax: 866-888-3850, 866-668-8297
Stadium Corporation of Ontario Ltd., 33 King St. West, 6th Fl., Oshawa, ON L1H 8H5
416-314-5158, Fax: 905-433-6688

Prince Edward Island

Agricultural Insurance Corporation, 29 Indigo Cres., PO Box 1600, Charlottetown, PE C1A 7N3
902-368-4842, Fax: 902-368-6677
Charlottetown Area Development Corporation, 4 Pownal St., PO Box 786, Charlottetown, PE C1A 7L9
902-892-5341, Fax: 902-368-1935
Office of the Auditor General, Shaw Bldg., 105 Rochford St. North, 2nd Fl., Charlottetown, PE C1A 7N8
902-368-4520, Fax: 902-368-4598, www.assembly.pe.ca
Prince Edward Island Department of Innovation & Advanced Learning, Shaw Bldg., 105 Rochford St., 5th Fl., PO Box 2000, Charlottetown, PE C1A 7N8
902-368-4240, Fax: 902-368-4242
Prince Edward Island Lending Agency, Homburg Financial Tower, 98 Fitzroy St., 2nd Fl., Charlottetown, PE C1A 1R7
902-368-6200, Fax: 902-368-6201

Quebec

Autorité des marchés financiers, Tour de la Bourse, 800, Square Victoria, 22e étage, Montréal, QC H4Z 1G3
514-395-0337, Fax: 514-873-3090, 877-525-0337
Caisse de dépôt et placement du Québec, 1000, place Jean-Paul-Riopelle, Montréal, QC H2Z 2B3
514-842-3261, Fax: 514-842-4833, 866-330-3936, info@lacaisse.com
Ministère des Finances, Édifice Gérard-D.-Levesque, 12, rue Saint-Louis, Québec, QC G1R 5L3
418-528-9323, Fax: 418-646-1631, info@finances.gouv.qc.ca
Fonds de la recherche en santé du Québec, #800, 500, rue Sherbrooke ouest, Montréal, QC H3A 3C6
514-873-2114, Fax: 514-873-8768
Innovatech Québec, #410, 888, rue St-Jean, Québec, QC G1R 5H6
418-528-9770, Fax: 418-528-9783, 866-605-1676
Investissement Québec, #1500, 600, rue de la Gauchetière ouest, Montréal, QC H3B 4L8
514-873-4664, 866-870-0437
Le Protecteur du Citoyen, #1.25, 525, boul René-Lévesque est, Québec, QC G1R 5Y4
418-643-2688, Fax: 418-643-8759, 800-463-5070, protecteur@protecteurducitoyen.qc.ca
Loto-Québec, 500, rue Sherbrooke ouest, Montréal, QC H3A 3G6
514-282-8000, Fax: 514-873-8999
Registraire des entreprises, 787, boul Lebourgneuf, Québec, QC G2J 1C3
418-644-4545, Fax: 418-528-5703, 877-644-4545, registre@servicesquebec.gouv.qc.ca
Ministère des Relations internationales, Édifice Hector-Fabre, 525, boul Réne-Lévesque est, Québec, QC G1R 5R9
418-649-2300, Fax: 418-649-2656
Revenu Québec, Direction des relations publiques/Communications, 3800, rue de Marly, Québec, QC G1X 4A5
418-652-6831, Fax: 418-646-0167
Régie des rentes du Québec, CP 5200, Sainte-Foy, QC G1K 7S9
418-643-5185, 800-463-5185, rrq@rrq.gouv.qc.ca
Société du Centre des congrès de Québec, 1000, boul René-Lévesque est, Québec, QC G1R 5T8
418-644-4000, Fax: 418-644-6455, 888-679-4000
Secrétariat du Conseil du trésor, 875, Grande Allée est, 5e étage, secteur 500, Québec, QC G1R 5R8
418-643-1529, Fax: 418-643-9226, 866-552-5158, communication@sct.gouv.qc.ca
Vérificateur général du Québec, 750, boulevard Charest est, 3e étage, Québec, QC G1K 9J6
418-691-5900, Fax: 418-644-4460, verificateur.general@vgq.gouv.qc.ca

Saskatchewan

Provincial Auditor Saskatchewan, #1500, 1920 Broad St., Regina, SK S4P 3V2
306-787-6398, Fax: 306-787-6383, info@auditor.sk.ca
Board of Revenue Commissioners, #480, 2151 Scarth St., Regina, SK S4P 2H8
306-787-6221, Fax: 306-787-1610
Crown Investments Corporation of Saskatchewan, #400, 2400 College Ave., Regina, SK S4P 1C8
306-787-6851, Fax: 306-787-8125
Saskatchewan Energy & Resources, #300, 2103 - 11th Ave., Regina, SK S4P 3Z8
306-787-2528, webmasterer@gov.sk.ca
Saskatchewan Finance, 2350 Albert St., Regina, SK S4P 4A6
306-787-6768, Fax: 306-787-0241, communications@finance.gov.sk.ca
Saskatchewan Government Insurance, 2260 - 11th Ave., Regina, SK S4P 0J9
306-751-1200, Fax: 306-787-7477, 800-667-8015, sgiinquiries@sgi.sk.ca
Saskatchewan Crop Insurance Corporation, 484 Prince William Dr., PO Box 3000, Melville, SK S0A 2P0
306-728-7200, Fax: 306-728-7202, 888-935-0000, customer.service@scic.gov.sk.ca
Saskatchewan Development Fund Corporation, #400, 2400 College Ave., Regina, SK S4P 1C8
306-787-1645, Fax: 306-787-8125
Saskatchewan Financial Services Commission, #601, 1919 Saskatchewan Dr., Regina, SK S4P 4H2
306-787-5645, Fax: 306-787-5899
Saskatchewan Trade & Export Partnership, #320, 1801 Hamilton St., PO Box 1787, Regina, SK S4P 3C6
306-787-9210, Fax: 306-787-6666, inquire@sasktrade.sk.ca

Yukon Territory

Yukon Finance, PO Box 2703, Whitehorse, YT Y1A 2C6
867-667-5343, Fax: 867-393-6217, fininfo@gov.yk.ca
Yukon Lottery Commission, 312 Wood St., Whitehorse, YT Y1A 2E6
867-633-7890, Fax: 867-668-7561, lotteriesyukon@gov.yk.ca

BUSINESS DEVELOPMENT

See Also: Industry; Science & Technology

Atlantic Canada Opportunities Agency, Blue Cross Centre, 644 Main St., 3rd Fl., PO Box 6051, Moncton, NB E1C 9J8
506-851-2271, Fax: 506-851-7403, 800-561-7862, information@acoa-apeca.gc.ca
Business Development Bank of Canada, #400, 5, Place Ville-Marie, Montréal, QC H3B 5E7
514-283-5904, Fax: 514-283-5626, 877-232-2269
Canada Business, 235 Queen St., Ottawa, ON K1A 0H5
888-576-4444
Canada Economic Development for Québec Regions, Édifice Dominion Square, #900, 1255, rue Peel, Montréal, QC H3B 2T9
514-283-6412, Fax: 514-283-3302, 866-385-6412
Enterprise Cape Breton Corporation, Silicon Island, 70 Crescent St., Sydney, NS B1S 2Z7
902-564-3600, Fax: 902-564-3825, 800-705-3926, information@ecbc-secb.gc.ca
Export Development Canada, 151 Slater St., Ottawa, ON K1A 1K3
613-598-2500, Fax: 613-598-3811, 800-267-8510
Global Operations, 125 Sussex Dr,, Ottawa, ON K1A 0G2
613-944-2697, Fax: 613-996-1667
Industry Canada, C.D. Howe Building, 235 Queen St., Ottawa, ON K1A 0H5
613-954-5031, Fax: 613-954-2340, 800-328-6189, info@ic.gc.ca
Market & Industry Services Branch, Tower 5, 1341 Baseline Rd., Ottawa, ON K1A 0C5
613-759-1000, Fax: 613-773-1755
Western Economic Diversification Canada, Canada Place, #1500, 9700 Jasper Ave. NW, Edmonton, AB T5J 4H7
780-495-4164, Fax: 780-495-4557, 888-338-9378

British Columbia

Asia Pacific Foundation of Canada, #220, 890 West Pender St., Vancouver, BC V6C 1J9
604-684-5986, Fax: 604-681-1370, info@asiapacific.ca; researchgrants@asiapacific.ca
British Columbia Innovation Council, 1188 West Georgia St., 9th Fl., Vancouver, BC V6E 4A2
604-683-2724, Fax: 604-683-6567, 800-665-7222, info@bcic.ca
British Columbia Progress Board, 1188 West Georgia St., 9th Fl., Vancouver, BC V6E 4A2
604-775-1664, ideas@bcprogressboard.com
Columbia Basin Trust, Southwest Basin, #300, 445 - 13 Ave., Castlegar, BC V1N 1G1
250-365-6633, 800-505-8998, cbt@cbt.org
International Financial Centre British Columbia, Park Place, #1170, 666 Burrard St., Vancouver, BC V6C 2X8
604-683-6626, Fax: 604-683-6646, info@ifcvancouver.com
Ministry of Jobs, Tourism, & Innovation, PO Box 9071 Prov Govt,Victoria, BC V8W 9E9
250-356-2771, Fax: 250-356-3000, JTI.Minister@gov.bc.ca
Northern Development Initiative Trust, #301, 1268 Fifth Ave., Prince George, BC V2L 3L2
250-561-2525, Fax: 250-561-2563, info@northerndevelopment.bc.ca
Small Business BC, #82, 601 West Cordova St., Vancouver, BC V6B 1G1
604-775-5525, Fax: 604-775-5520, 800-667-2272, askus@smallbusinessbc.ca
Ministry of Social Development, PO Box 9058 Prov Govt,Victoria, BC V8W 9E1
250-356-7750, Fax: 250-356-7292, SD.Minister@gov.bc.ca

Manitoba

Manitoba Competitiveness, Training & Trade, International Business Centre, The Paris Building, 259 Portage Ave., Winnipeg, MB R3B 3P4
204-945-2475, Fax: 204-945-3977, minctt@leg.gov.mb.ca
Manitoba Development Corporation, #555, 155 Carlton St., Winnipeg, MB R3C 3H8
204-945-7626, Fax: 204-945-1193

New Brunswick

Department of Business New Brunswick, Centennial Bldg., 670 King St., PO Box 6000, Fredericton, NB E3B 5H1
506-453-3707, Fax: 506-453-3993, investnb@gnb.ca
Regional Development Corporation, RDC Bldg., 836 Churchill Row, PO Box 428, Fredericton, NB E3B 5R4
506-453-2277, Fax: 506-453-7988

Newfoundland & Labrador

Department of Business, Confederation Bldg., East Block, 6th Fl., PO Box 8700, St. John's, NL A1B 4J6
709-729-3254, Fax: 709-729-3306, business@gov.nl.ca
Department of Innovation, Trade & Rural Development, West Block, Confederation Bldg., PO Box 8700, St. John's, NL A1B 4J6
709-729-7000, Fax: 709-729-0654, intrd@gov.nl.ca
Department of Labrador & Aboriginal Affairs, Confederation Bldg., East Block, 6th Fl., PO Box 8700, St. John's, NL A1B 4J6
709-729-4776, Fax: 709-729-4900, 877-788-8822, laa@gov.nl.ca
Ireland Business Partnership, PO Box 8700, St. John's, NL A1B 4J6
709-729-1684, Fax: 709-729-7234, ibp@gov.nl.ca

Northwest Territories

Department of Industry, Tourism & Investment, PO Box 1320, Yellowknife, NT X1A 2L9
Fax: 867-873-0306, info@iti.ca

Nova Scotia

Department of Economic & Rural Development, Centennial Building, #600, 1660 Hollis St., PO Box 2311, Halifax, NS B3J 1V7
902-424-0377, Fax: 902-424-0500, comm@gov.ns.ca
InNOVACorp, #1400, 1801 Hollis St., Halifax, NS B3J 3N4
902-424-8670, Fax: 902-424-4679, 800-565-7051, communications@innovacorp.ca
Nova Scotia Business Inc., World Trade & Convention Centre, #701, 1800 Argyle St., PO Box 2374, Halifax, NS B3J 3N8
902-424-6650, Fax: 902-424-5739, 800-260-6682, info@nsbi.ca
Trade Centre Limited, 1800 Argyle St., PO Box 955, Halifax, NS B3J 2V9
902-421-8686, Fax: 902-422-2922

Nunavut

Department of Economic Development & Transportation, Bldg. 1104 A, Inuksugait Plaza, PO Box 1000 1500,Iqaluit, NU X0A 0H0
867-975-7800, Fax: 867-975-7870, 888-975-5999, edt@gov.nu.ca

Ontario

Ministry of Consumer Services, Mowat Block, 900 Bay St., 6th Fl., Toronto, ON M7A 1L2
416-327-8300, Fax: 416-326-1947, 866-665-0662, infomcs@ontario.ca
Ministry of Economic Development & Innovation, Hearst Block, 900 Bay St., 8th Fl., Toronto, ON M7A 2E1
416-325-6666, Fax: 416-325-6688, 866-668-4249, info@edt.gov.on.ca
Northern Development Division, Roberta Bondar Place, #200, 70 Foster Dr., Sault Ste Marie, ON P6A 6V8
705-945-5900, Fax: 705-945-5931, 800-461-2287
Ministry of Research & Innovation, Ferguson Block, 56 Wellesley St. West, 7th Fl., Toronto, ON M7A 2E7
416-325-5181, Fax: 416-325-3877, 866-446-5216,

Prince Edward Island
Charlottetown Area Development Corporation, 4 Pownal St., PO Box 786, Charlottetown, PE C1A 7L9
902-892-5341, Fax: 902-368-1935
Innovation PEI, 94 Euston St., PO Box 910, Charlottetown, PE C1A 7L9
902-368-6300, Fax: 902-368-6301, 800-563-3734
Prince Edward Island Department of Innovation & Advanced Learning, Shaw Bldg., 105 Rochford St., 5th Fl., PO Box 2000, Charlottetown, PE C1A 7N8
902-368-4240, Fax: 902-368-4242
Prince Edward Island Lending Agency, Homburg Financial Tower, 98 Fitzroy St., 2nd Fl., Charlottetown, PE C1A 1R7
902-368-6200, Fax: 902-368-6201

Quebec
Ministère du Développement économique, de l'Innovation et de l'Exportation, 710, place D'Youville, 3e étage, Québec, QC G1R 4Y4
418-691-5950, Fax: 418-644-0118, 866-680-1884

Saskatchewan
Saskatchewan Energy & Resources, #300, 2103 - 11th Ave., Regina, SK S4P 3Z8
306-787-2528, webmasterer@gov.sk.ca
Enterprise Saskatchewan, #200, 3085 Albert St., Regina, SK S4S 0B1
306-787-4484, Fax: 306-798-0629, 800-265-2001, webmaster@enterprisesask.ca; invest@enterprisesask.ca

Yukon Territory
Yukon Development Corporation, #2 Miles Canyon Rd., PO Box 5920, Whitehorse, YT Y1A 6S7
867-393-5337, Fax: 867-393-5401
Yukon Economic Development, PO Box 2703, Whitehorse, YT Y1A 2C6
867-393-7191, Fax: 867-393-6412, 800-661-0408, ecdev@gov.yk.ca

BUSINESS REGULATIONS

Canada Revenue Agency, 875 Heron Rd., Ottawa, ON K1A 0L5
800-267-6999
Industry Canada, C.D. Howe Building, 235 Queen St., Ottawa, ON K1A 0H5
613-954-5031, Fax: 613-954-2340, 800-328-6189, info@ic.gc.ca

Alberta
Strategic Planning & Financial Services, Commerce Place, 10155 - 102 St., 13th Fl., Edmonton, AB T5J 4G8
780-422-8545

British Columbia
Corporate & Ministry Support Services, PO Box 9415 Prov Govt,Victoria, BC V8W 9V1

Manitoba
Companies Office, #1010, 405 Broadway, Winnipeg, MB R3C 3L6
204-945-2500, Fax: 204-945-1459, companies@gov.mb.ca

Nova Scotia
Nova Scotia Business Inc., World Trade & Convention Centre, #701, 1800 Argyle St., PO Box 2374, Halifax, NS B3J 3N8
902-424-6650, Fax: 902-424-5739, 800-260-6682, info@nsbi.ca

Nunavut
Department of Finance, Bldg. 1079, 1st Fl., PO Box 1000 330,Iqaluit, NU X0A 0H0
867-975-5800, Fax: 867-975-5805

Ontario
ServiceOntario, College Park, 777 Bay St., 15th fl., Toronto, ON M7A 2J3
416-326-1234, Fax: 416-326-1313, 800-267-8097

Quebec
Registraire des entreprises, 787, boul Lebourgneuf, Québec, QC G2J 1C3
418-644-4545, Fax: 418-528-5703, 877-644-4545, registre@servicesquebec.gouv.qc.ca

CABINETS & EXECUTIVE COUNCILS

See Also: Government (General Information); Parliament
The Canadian Ministry, Information Service, Parliament of Canada, Ottawa, ON K1A 0A9
613-992-4793, 866-599-4999, info@parl.gc.ca

Alberta
Executive Council, Legislature Building, 10800 - 97 Ave., Edmonton, AB T5K 2B6
780-427-2711

British Columbia
Executive Council, Parliament Bldgs., Victoria, BC V8V 1X4

Manitoba
Executive Council, Legislative Building, 450 Broadway Ave., Winnipeg, MB R3C 0V8

New Brunswick
Executive Council, Centennial Bldg., 670 King St., PO Box 6000, Fredericton, NB E3B 5H1
506-453-2144, Fax: 506-453-7407, david.alward@gnb.ca

Newfoundland & Labrador
Executive Council, c/o Communications Branch, East Block, Confederation Bldg., 10th Fl., St. John's, NL A1B 4J6
709-729-5645, info@gov.nl.ca

Northwest Territories
Executive Council, PO Box 1320, Yellowknife, NT X1A 2L9
executive@gov.nt.ca

Nova Scotia
Executive Council, One Government Place, 1700 Granville St., 5th Fl., PO Box 2125, Halifax, NS B3J 3B7
902-424-5970, Fax: 902-424-0667, execounc@gov.ns.ca

Nunavut
Executive Council, Legislative Bldg., 2nd Fl., Box 2410, Iqaluit, NU X0A 0H0
867-975-5090, Fax: 867-975-5095

Ontario
Executive Council, Whitney Block, Queen's Park, 99 Wellesley St. West, 6th Fl., Toronto, ON M7A 1A1
416-325-5721, Fax: 416-314-1551

Prince Edward Island
Executive Council, Shaw Bldg., 5th Fl., PO Box 2000, Charlottetown, PE C1A 7N8
902-368-4502, Fax: 902-368-6118

Quebec
Ministère du Conseil exécutif, 875, Grande Allée est, Québec, QC G1R 4Y8
418-646-3021, Fax: 418-528-9242

Saskatchewan
Executive Council, Legislative Bldg., 2405 Legislative Dr., Regina, SK S4S 0B3
306-787-7448, admin.ec@gov.sk.ca

Yukon Territory
Executive Council, #2071, 2nd Ave., Whitehorse, YT Y1A 2C6
867-667-5393, Fax: 867-393-6214, eco@gov.yk.ca

CANADIANS & SOCIETY

Aboriginal Affairs & Northern Development Canada, 10 Wellington St., North Tower, Gatineau, QC K1A 0H4
819-997-0380, Fax: 866-817-3977, 800-567-9604, infopubs@aadnc-aandc.gc.ca
Beverly & Qamanirjuaq Caribou Management Board, Secretariat, PO Box 629, Stonewall, MB R0C 2Z0
204-467-2438, caribounews@arctic-caribou.com
Canada Council for the Arts, 350 Albert St., PO Box 1047, Ottawa, ON K1P 5V8
613-566-4414, Fax: 613-566-4390, 800-263-5588
Canada Lands Company Ltd., #1200, 1 University Ave., Toronto, ON M5J 2P1
416-952-6111, Fax: 416-952-6115, 888-252-5263
Canadian Heritage, 15 Eddy St., Gatineau, QC K1A 0M5
819-997-0055, 866-811-0055, info@pch.gc.ca
Canadian Human Rights Commission, 344 Slater St., 8th Fl., Ottawa, ON K1A 1E1
613-995-1151, Fax: 613-996-9661, 888-214-1090
Canadian Human Rights Tribunal, 160 Elgin St., 11th Fl., Ottawa, ON K1A 1J4
613-995-1707, Fax: 613-995-3484, registrar@chrt-tcdp.gc.ca
Canadian Race Relations Foundation, #701, 4576 Yonge St., Toronto, ON M2N 6N4
416-952-3500, Fax: 416-952-3326, 888-240-4936
Citizenship & Immigration Canada, Jean Edmonds, South Tower, 365 Laurier Ave. West, Ottawa, ON K1A 1L1
613-954-9019, Fax: 613-954-2221, 888-242-2100
First Nations Tax Commission, #321, 345 Yellowhead Hwy, Kamloops, BC V2H 1H1
250-828-9857, Fax: 250-828-9858, mailkamloops@fntc.ca
Foreign Affairs & International Trade Canada, 125 Sussex Dr., Ottawa, ON K1A 0G2
613-944-4000, Fax: 613-996-9709, 800-267-8376, enqserv@international.gc.ca
Government of Canada, c/o Canada Enquiry Centre, Service Canada, Ottawa, ON K1A 0J9
613-941-1827, 800-622-6232, sitecanadasite@canada.gc.ca
Historic Sites & Monuments Board of Canada, Terrasses de la Chaudière, 25 Eddy St., Gatineau, QC K1A 0M5
Fax: 819-934-1115, 855-283-8730, hsmbc-clmhc@pc.gc.ca
Human Resources & Skills Development Canada, 140 Promenade du Portage, Gatineau, QC K1A 0J9
Immigration & Refugee Board of Canada, Canada Bldg, 344 Slater St., 12th Fl., Ottawa, ON K1A 0K1
613-995-6486, Fax: 613-943-1550, contact@irb-cisr.gc.ca
National Advisory Council on Aging, Jeanne Mance Bldg., 8th Fl., Postal Locator 1908 A1, Ottawa, ON K1A 0K9
613-957-1968, Fax: 613-957-7627
National Battlefields Commission, 390, av de Bernières, Québec, QC G1R 2L7
418-648-3506, Fax: 418-648-3638, information@ccbn-nbc.gc.ca
National Capital Commission, #202, 40 Elgin St., Ottawa, ON K1P 1C7
613-239-5555, Fax: 613-239-5063, 800-704-8227, info@ncc-ccn.ca
National Round Table on the Environment & Economy, #200, 344 Slater St., Ottawa, ON K1R 7Y3
613-992-7189, Fax: 613-992-7385, admin@nrtee-trnee.ca
Office of the Prime Minister (Conservative Party of Canada), Langevin Block, 80 Wellington St., Ottawa, ON K1A 0A2
613-992-4211, Fax: 613-941-6900, pm@pm.gc.ca
Office of the Commissioner of Official Languages, 344 Slater St., 3rd fl., Ottawa, ON K1A 0T8
613-996-6368, Fax: 613-993-5082, 877-996-6368
Passport Canada, Le 70 Crémazie, 70 Crémazie St., Gatineau, QC K1A 0G3
Fax: 819-953-5856, 800-567-6868
Porcupine Caribou Management Board, PO Box 31723, Whitehorse, YT Y1A 6L3
867-633-4780, Fax: 867-393-3904, pcmb@taiga.net
Privacy Commissioner of Canada, Tower B, Place de Ville, 112 Kent St., 3rd Fl., Ottawa, ON K1A 1H3
613-947-1698, Fax: 613-947-6850, 800-282-1376
Social Sciences & Humanities Research Council of Canada, Constitution Sq., 350 Albert St., PO Box 1610 B,Ottawa, ON K1P 6G4
613-992-0691, Fax: 613-992-1787, info@sshrc.ca
Specific Claims Tribunal Canada, #400, 427 Laurier Ave. West, PO Box 31, Ottawa, ON K1R 7Y2
613-947-0751, Fax: 613-943-0586, info@sct-trp.ca
Status of Women Canada, 123 Slater St., 10th Fl., Ottawa, ON K1P 1H9
613-995-7835, Fax: 613-947-0761, 866-902-2719, infonational@swc-cfc.gc.ca
Veterans Affairs Canada, 161 Grafton St., PO Box 7700, Charlottetown, PE C1A 8M9
902-566-8888, 866-522-2111, information@vac-acc.gc.ca
Veterans Review & Appeal Board, Daniel J. MacDonald Bldg., 161 Grafton St., PO Box 9900, Charlottetown, PE C1A 8V7
902-566-8751, Fax: 902-566-7850, 800-450-8006, vrab_tacra@vac-acc.gc.ca

Alberta
Alberta Labour Relations Board, Labour Building, 10808 - 99 Ave., 5th Fl., Edmonton, AB T5K 0G5
780-422-5926, Fax: 780-422-0970, 800-463-2572, alrbinfo@lab.gov.ab.ca
Alberta Sport, Recreation, Parks, & Wildlife Foundation, Standard Life Centre, #903, 10405 Jasper Ave., 9th Fl., Edmonton, AB T5J 4R7
780-415-1167, Fax: 780-415-0308
Alberta Children & Youth Services, Communications, Sterling Place, 9940 - 106 St., 12th Fl., Edmonton, AB T5K 2N2
780-422-3004, Fax: 780-422-3071, cs.communications@gov.ab.ca
Alberta Health & Wellness, PO Box 1360 Main,Edmonton, AB T5J 2N3
780-427-7164, Fax: 780-427-1171
Premier's Council on the Status of Persons with Disabilities, HSBC Building, 10055 - 106 St., 11th Fl., Edmonton, AB T5J 1G3
780-422-1095, 800-272-8841, pcspd@gov.ab.ca
Alberta Seniors & Community Supports, Communications, Standard Life Centre, 10405 Jasper Ave., 3rd Fl., Edmonton, AB T5J 4R7
780-415-9950, Fax: 780-644-1227, 866-477-8589, seniors.communications@gov.ab.ca
Seniors Advisory Council for Alberta, Standard Life Centre, #600, 10405 Jasper Ave., 6th Fl., Edmonton, AB T5J 4R7
780-422-2321, Fax: 780-422-8762, saca@gov.ab.ca
Alberta Tourism, Parks, & Recreation, Communications Branch, Commerce Place, 10155 - 102 St., 6th Fl., Edmonton, AB T5J 4L6
780-644-5589, TPR.Communications@gov.ab.ca

British Columbia
British Columbia Treaty Commission, #700, 1111 Melville St., Vancouver, BC V6E 3V6
604-482-9200, Fax: 604-482-9222, 800-665-8330, info@bctreaty.net
Ministry of Children & Family Development, PO Box 9770 Prov Govt,Victoria, BC V8W 9S5
250-387-7027, 877-387-7027, MCF.CorrespondenceManagement@gov.bc.ca
Ministry of Community, Sport & Cultural Development, PO Box 9056 Prov Govt,Victoria, BC V8W 9E2
250-387-2283, Fax: 250-387-4312
Local Government, PO Box 9490 Prov Govt,Victoria, BC V8W 9N7
250-356-6575, Fax: 250-387-7973

Native Economic Development Advisory Board, c/o Director, Economic Initiatives, PO Box 9100 Prov Govt, Victoria, BC V8W 9B1
250-387-2536, Fax: 250-356-9467

Manitoba

Manitoba Aboriginal & Northern Affairs, 59 Elizabeth Dr., PO Box 37, Thompson, MB R8N 1X4
204-677-6607, Fax: 204-677-6753, amartin@gov.mb.ca

Aboriginal Affairs Secretariat, #200, 500 Portage Ave., Winnipeg, MB R3C 3X1
204-945-2510, Fax: 204-945-3689

Communications Services Manitoba, 155 Carlton St., 10th Fl., Winnipeg, MB R3C 3H8
204-945-3765, Fax: 204-948-2147

Communities Economic Development Fund, #100, 23 Station Rd., Thompson, MB R8N 0N6
204-778-4138, Fax: 204-778-4313, 800-561-4315

Manitoba Culture, Heritage, Tourism & Sport, Legislative Building, #118, 450 Broadway Ave., Winnipeg, MB R3C 0V8
204-945-3729, Fax: 204-945-5223, mincht@leg.gov.mb.ca

Manitoba Family Services & Housing, #219, 114 Garry St., Winnipeg, MB R3C 4V6
204-945-3242, Fax: 204-945-2156, minfam@leg.gov.mb.ca

Heritage Grants Advisory Council, 213 Notre Dame Ave., 3rd Fl., Winnipeg, MB R3B 1N3
204-945-2213, Fax: 204-948-2086

Manitoba Human Rights Commission, 175 Hargrave St., 7th Fl., Winnipeg, MB R3C 3R8
204-945-3007, Fax: 204-945-1292, 888-884-8681, hrc@gov.mb.ca

Le Centre Culturel franco-manitobain/Franco-Manitoban Cultural Centre, 340, boul Provencher, St Boniface, MB R2H 0G7
204-233-8972, Fax: 204-233-3324, ccfm@ccfm.mb.ca

Manitoba Centennial Centre Corporation, 555 Main St., Winnipeg, MB R3B 1C3
204-956-1360, Fax: 204-944-1390,

Manitoba Film Classification Board, #216, 301 Weston St., Winnipeg, MB R3E 3H4
204-945-8962, Fax: 204-945-0890, 866-612-2399, mfcb@gov.mb.ca

Manitoba Heritage Council, 213 Notre Dame Ave., Main Fl., Winnipeg, MB R3B 1N3
204-945-2118, Fax: 204-948-2384, hrb@gov.mb.ca

Multiculturalism Secretariat, 213 Notre Dame Ave., 4th Fl., Winnipeg, MB R3B 1N3
204-945-1156, Fax: 204-948-2323

Primary Care & Healthy Living, 300 Carlton St., 2nd Floor, Winnipeg, MB R3B 3M9

Manitoba Seniors & Healthy Aging Secretariat, #822, 155 Carlton St., Winnipeg, MB R3C 3H8
204-945-6565, Fax: 204-948-2514, 800-665-6565, seniors@gov.mb.ca

New Brunswick

Department of Health, PO Box 5100, Fredericton, NB E3B 5G8
506-457-4800, Fax: 506-453-5243, dh-ms@dh-ms.ca

Department of Intergovernmental Affairs, Centennial Bldg., #274, 670 King St., PO Box 6000, Fredericton, NB E3B 5H1
506-444-5418, Fax: 506-453-2995, iga@gnb.ca

Department of Social Development, Sartain MacDonald Bldg., 551 King St., PO Box 6000, Fredericton, NB E3B 5H1
506-453-2001, Fax: 506-453-7478, sd-ds@gnb.ca

Premier's Council on the Status of Disabled Persons, Kings Place, #648, 440 King St., Fredericton, NB E3B 5H8
506-444-3000, Fax: 506-444-3001, 800-442-4412, pcsdp@gnb.ca

New Brunswick Human Rights Commission, PO Box 6000, Fredericton, NB E3B 5H1
506-453-2301, Fax: 506-453-2653, 888-471-2233, hrc.cdp@gnb.ca

Ministerial Advisory Committee on Multiculturalism, PO Box 6000, Fredericton, NB E3B 5H1

Regional Development Corporation, RDC Bldg., 836 Churchill Row, PO Box 428, Fredericton, NB E3B 5R4
506-453-2277, Fax: 506-453-7988

New Brunswick Advisory Council on Youth, Frederick Square, #130, 77 Westmorland St., PO Box 6000, Fredericton, NB E3B 5H1
506-453-3271, Fax: 506-444-4413, 888-830-5588, nbacy-ccjnb@gnb.ca

Newfoundland & Labrador

C.A. Pippy Park Commission, Mount Scio House, 15 Mount Scio Rd., St. John's, NL A1B 3T2
709-737-3655, Fax: 709-737-3303, info@pippypark.com

Department of Human Resources, Labour & Employment, Confederation Bldg., PO Box 8700, St. John's, NL A1B 4J6
709-729-2480, Fax: 709-729-6996, hreweb@gov.nl.ca

Department of Labrador & Aboriginal Affairs, Confederation Bldg., East Block, 6th Fl., PO Box 8700, St. John's, NL A1B 4J6
709-729-4776, Fax: 709-729-4900, 877-788-8822, laa@gov.nl.ca

Department of Tourism, Culture & Recreation, Confederation Bldg., West Block, 2nd Fl., PO Box 8700, St. John's, NL A1B 4J6
709-729-0862, Fax: 709-729-0870, tcrinfo@gov.nl.ca

Newfoundland & Labrador Human Rights Commission, PO Box 8700, St. John's, NL A1B 4J6
709-729-2709, Fax: 709-729-0790, 800-563-5808, humanrights@mail.gov.nl.ca

Provincial Advisory Council on the Status of Women, #103, 15 Hallett Cres., St. John's, NL A1B 4C4
709-753-7270, Fax: 709-753-2606, 877-753-7270, info@pacsw.ca

Northwest Territories

Department of Aboriginal Affairs & Intergovernmental Relations, 4910 - 52nd St., PO Box 1320, Yellowknife, NT X1A 2L9
867-873-7143, Fax: 867-873-0233, 877-838-8194, nancy_gardiner@gov.nt.ca

Department of Municipal & Community Affairs, PO Box 1320, Yellowknife, NT X1A 2L9
867-873-7118, Fax: 867-873-0309

Office of the Languages Commissioner, Laing Bldg., 5003 - 49 St., Yellowknife, NT X1A 2P4
867-873-7034, Fax: 867-873-0357, 800-661-0889, langcom@gov.nt.ca

Status of Women Council of the Northwest Territories, PO Box 1320, Yellowknife, NT X1A 2L9
867-920-6177, Fax: 867-873-0285, 888-234-4485, council@statusofwomen.nt.ca

Nova Scotia

Department of Community Services, Nelson Place, 5675 Spring Garden Rd., 8th Fl., PO Box 696, Halifax, NS B3J 2T7
902-424-4304, Fax: 902-428-0618

Nova Scotia Human Rights Commission, Joseph Howe Bldg., 1690 Hollis St., 6th Fl., Halifax, NS B3J 3C4
902-424-4111, Fax: 902-424-0596, hrcinquiries@gov.ns.ca

Nova Scotia Advisory Commission on AIDS, Dennis Bldg., 1740 Granville St., 6th Fl., Halifax, NS B3J 1X5
902-424-5730, Fax: 902-424-4727, AIDS@gov.ns.ca

Nova Scotia Disabled Persons Commission, Dartmouth Professional Center, #104, 277 Pleasant St., Dartmouth, NS B2Y 4B7
902-424-8280, Fax: 902-424-0592, 800-565-8280

Pay Equity Commission, 5151 Terminal Rd., 6th Fl., PO Box 697, Halifax, NS B3J 2T8
902-424-2385, Fax: 902-424-0575

Seniors' Secretariat, Dennis Bldg., 1740 Granville St., 4th Fl., PO Box 2065, Halifax, NS B3J 2Z1
902-424-0065, Fax: 902-424-0561, 800-670-0065, seniors@gov.ns.ca

Department of Service Nova Scotia & Municipal Relations, 1505 Barrington St., PO Box 216, Halifax, NS B3J 3K5
902-424-5200, Fax: 902-424-0581, 800-670-4357, askus@gov.ns.ca

Nova Scotia Advisory Council on the Status of Women, 1700 Granville St., PO Box 943, Halifax, NS B3J 2V9
902-424-7660, women@gov.ns.ca

Nunavut

Nunavut Impact Review Board, PO Box 1360, Cambridge Bay, NU X0B 0C0
867-983-4600, Fax: 867-983-2594, 866-233-3033, info@nirb.ca

Nunavut Planning Commission, PO Box 2101, Cambridge Bay, NU X0B 0C0
867-983-4625, Fax: 867-983-4626

Nunavut Water Board, PO Box 119, Gjoa Haven, NU X0B 1J0
867-360-6338, Fax: 867-360-6369

Ontario

Ministry of Aboriginal Affairs, 160 Bloor St. East, 4th & 9th Fl., Toronto, ON M7A 2E6
416-326-4740, Fax: 416-326-4017

Citizenship & Immigration Division, 400 University Ave., 3rd Fl., Toronto, ON M7A 2R9
416-314-7541, Fax: 416-314-7599

Ministry of Citizenship & Immigration, 400 University Ave., 6th Fl., Toronto, ON M7A 2R9
416-327-2422, Fax: 416-314-4965, 800-267-7329

Ministry of Community & Social Services, Hepburn Block, 80 Grosvenor St., 6th Fl., Toronto, ON M7A 1E9
416-325-5666, Fax: 416-325-5172, 888-789-4199

Office of Francophone Affairs, #200, 777 Bay St., Toronto, ON M7A 0A2
416-325-4949, Fax: 416-325-4980, 800-268-7507, ofa@ontario.ca

Ministry of Government Services, Whitney Block, #4320, 99 Wellesley St. West, 4th Fl., Toronto, ON M7A 1W3
416-326-1234, Fax: 416-327-3790, 800-268-1142

Ontario Human Rights Commission, 180 Dundas St. West, 7th Fl., Toronto, ON M7A 2R9
416-326-9511, Fax: 416-314-4494, 800-387-9080

Information & Privacy Commissioner of Ontario, #1400, 2 Bloor St. East, Toronto, ON M4W 1A8
416-326-3333, Fax: 416-325-9195, 800-387-0073, info@ipc.on.ca

Ontario Heritage Trust, 10 Adelaide St. East, Toronto, ON M5C 1J3
416-325-5000, Fax: 416-325-5071

Ontario Northland, 555 Oak St. East, North Bay, ON P1B 8L3
705-472-4500, Fax: 705-472-4267, 800-363-7512, info@ontarionorthland.ca

Royal Ontario Museum, 100 Queen's Park Cres., Toronto, ON M5S 2C6
416-586-5549, Fax: 416-586-5685, info@rom.on.ca

Social Benefits Tribunal, 1075 Bay St., 7th Fl., Toronto, ON M5S 2B1
416-326-0978, Fax: 416-325-5135, 800-753-3895

Ontario Women's Directorate, 777 Bay St., 6th Fl., Toronto, ON M7A 2J4
416-314-0300, Fax: 416-314-0247, 866-510-5902, owd@ontario.ca

Prince Edward Island

Prince Edward Island Human Rights Commission, 53 Water St., PO Box 2000, Charlottetown, PE C1A 7N8
902-368-4180, Fax: 902-368-4236, 800-237-5031

Prince Edward Island Department of Community Services, Seniors, & Labour, Jones Bldg., 11 Kent St., 2nd Fl., PO Box 2000, Charlottetown, PE C1A 7N8
902-620-3777, Fax: 902-368-4740, 866-594-3777

Quebec

Secrétariat aux affaires autochtones, 905, av Honoré-Mercier, 1er étage, Québec, QC G1R 5M6
418-643-3166, Fax: 418-646-4918

Secteur du Québec de la Force terrestre, Montréal, QC
514-252-2777

Commission administrative des régimes de retraite et d'assurances (Québec), 475, rue Saint-Amable, Québec, QC G1R 5X3
418-643-4881, Fax: 418-644-3839, 800-463-5533

Commission des biens culturels du Québec, Bloc A-RC, 225, Grande Allée est, Québec, QC G1R 5G5
418-643-8378, Fax: 418-643-8591, info@cbcq.gouv.qc.ca

Conseil des arts et des lettres du Québec, 79, boul René-Lévesque est, 3e étage, Québec, QC G1R 5N5
418-643-1707, Fax: 418-643-4558, 800-897-1707, info@calq.gouv.qc.ca

Conseil des relations interculturelles, #10.04, 500, boul René-Lévesque ouest, Montréal, QC H2Z 1W7
514-873-5634, Fax: 514-873-3469, info@conseilinterculturel.gouv.qc.ca

Conseil du statut de la femme, #300, 800, place D'Youville, 3e étage, Québec, QC G1R 6E2
418-643-4326, Fax: 418-643-8926, 800-463-2851, csf@csf.gouv.qc.ca

Ministère de la Culture, des Communications & de la Condition féminine, 225, Grande Allée est, Québec, QC G1R 5G5
888-380-8882

Curateur public du Québec, 600, boul René-Lévesque ouest, Montréal, QC H3B 4W9
514-873-4074, Fax: 514-873-5033, 800-363-9020

Ministère de l'Emploi et de la Solidarité sociale, 425, rue St-Amable, 4e étage, Québec, QC G1R 4Z1
418-643-4721, 888-643-4721,

Fonds québécois de la recherche sur la société et la culture, #470, 140, Grande Allée est, Québec, QC G1R 5M8
418-643-7582, Fax: 418-644-5248, fqrsc@fqrsc.gouv.qc.ca

Ministère de l' Immigration et des Communautés culturelles, Édifice Gérald-Godin, 360, rue McGill, Montréal, QC H2Y 2E9
514-864-9191, Fax: 514-864-2899, 877-864-9191

Office des personnes handicapées du Québec, 309, rue Brock, Drummondville, QC J2B 1C5
Fax: 819-475-8753, 800-567-1465, michael.magner@ophq.gouv.qc.ca

Ministère des Relations internationales, Édifice Hector-Fabre, 525, boul Réne-Lévesque est, Québec, QC G1R 5R9
418-649-2300, Fax: 418-649-2656

Ministère de la Santé et des Services sociaux, Direction des communications, 1075, ch Sainte-Foy, 16e étage, Québec, QC G1S 2M1
418-643-9395, Fax: 418-643-4768, regisseur.web@msss.gouv.qc.ca

Secrétariat aux affaires intergouvernementales canadiennes, 875, Grande Allée est, 3e étage, Québec, QC G1R 4Y8
418-643-4011, Fax: 418-528-0052

Secrétariat à la politique linguistique, 225 Grande-Allée est, 4e étage, Québec, QC G1R 5G5
418-643-4248, Fax: 418-646-7832, info@spl.gouv.qc.ca

Société de développement des entreprises culturelles, #800, 215, rue Saint-Jacques, Montréal, QC H2Y 1M6
514-841-2200, Fax: 514-841-8606, 800-363-0401, info@sodec.gouv.qc.ca

Tribunal administratif du Québec, 575, rue Saint-Amable, Québec, QC G1R 5R4
418-643-3418, Fax: 418-643-5335

Saskatchewan

Saskatchewan First Nations & Métis Relations, #1020, 1855 Victoria Ave., Regina, SK S4P 3T2
306-787-6250, Fax: 306-798-0083

Saskatchewan Government Services, 1920 Rose St., Regina, SK S4P 0A9
306-787-6911, Fax: 306-787-1061, GSReception@gs.gov.sk.ca

Saskatchewan Human Rights Commission, Saskatoon Office, Sturdy Stone Bdg., #816, 122 - 3 Ave. North, 8th Fl., Saskatoon, SK S7K 2H6
306-933-5952, Fax: 306-933-7863, 800-667-9249, shrc@gov.sk.ca

Information & Privacy Commissioner of Saskatchewan, #503, 1801 Hamilton St., Regina, SK S4P 4B4
306-787-8350, Fax: 306-798-1603, 877-748-2298, webmaster@oipc.sk.ca

Saskatchewan Heritage Foundation, 1919 Saskatchewan Dr., 9th Fl., Regina, SK S4P 4H2
306-787-4188, Fax: 306-787-0069

Saskatchewan Social Services, 1920 Broad St., Regina, SK S4P 3V6
306-787-3700, 866-221-5200, socialservicesinquiry@gov.sk.ca

Saskatchewan Tourism, Parks, Culture & Sport, 1919 Saskatchewan Dr., 4th Fl., Regina, SK S4P 4H2
306-787-5729, Fax: 306-787-8560, info@cyr.gov.sk.ca

Yukon Territory

Yukon Community Services, PO Box 2703, Whitehorse, YT Y1A 2C6
867-667-5811, Fax: 867-393-6295, 800-661-0408, inquiry@gov.yk.ca

Yukon Health & Social Services, PO Box 2703, Whitehorse, YT Y1A 2C6
867-667-3673, Fax: 867-667-3096, hss@gov.yk.ca

Yukon Women's Directorate, #1, 404 Hason St., Whitehorse, YT Y1A 1Y8
867-667-3030, Fax: 867-393-6270

Yukon Human Rights Commission, #101, 9010 Quartz St., Whitehorse, YT Y1A 2Z5
867-667-6226, Fax: 867-667-2662, 800-661-0535, humanrights@yhrc.yk.ca

CAREER PLANNING

Alberta

Workforce Supports Division, Labour Building, 10808 - 99 Ave., 10th Fl., Edmonton, AB T5K 0G5
780-722-0010

Ontario

Ministry of Training, Colleges & Universities, Mowat Block, 900 Bay St., 14th Fl., Toronto, ON M7A 1L2
416-325-2929, Fax: 416-325-6348, 800-387-5514, information.met@ontario.ca

Saskatchewan

Saskatchewan Education, 2220 College Ave., Regina, SK S4P 4V9
linquiry@gov.sk.ca

CENSORSHIP (MEDIA)

Canadian Broadcasting Corporation, 181 Queen St., PO Box 3220 C,Ottawa, ON K1Y 1E4
613-288-6033, liaison@radio-canada.ca

Canadian Radio-Television & Telecommunications Commission, Central Building, 1, Promenade du Portage, Les Terrasses de la Chaudière, Gatineau, QC J8X 4B1
819-997-0313, Fax: 819-994-0218, 877-249-2782

Manitoba

Manitoba Film Classification Board, #216, 301 Weston St., Winnipeg, MB R3E 3H4
204-945-8962, Fax: 204-945-0890, 866-612-2399, mfcb@gov.mb.ca

Nunavut

Department of Community & Government Services, W.G. Brown Bldg., 4th Fl., PO Box 1000 700,Iqaluit, NU X0A 0H0
867-975-5400, Fax: 867-975-5305

Quebec

Régie du cinéma, #100, 390, rue Notre-Dame ouest, Montréal, QC H2Y 1T9
514-873-2371, Fax: 514-873-8874, 800-463-2463, regieducinema@rcq.gouv.qc.ca

Saskatchewan

Saskatchewan Film & Video Classification Board, #500, 1919 Saskatchewan Dr., Regina, SK S4P 4H2
306-787-5550, Fax: 306-787-9779, 888-374-4636

CHEMICALS

Institute for Chemical Process & Environmental Technology, Bldg. M-12, 1200 Montreal Rd., Ottawa, ON K1A 0R6
613-993-4041, Fax: 613-957-8231

CHILD WELFARE

See Also: Day Care Services

Prince Edward Island

Children's Secretariat, c/o Sarah Henry, Education & Early Childhood Development, 161 St. Peters Rd., PO Box 2000, Charlottetown, PE C1A 7N8

Office of the Child & Youth Advocate, Peace Hills Trust Tower, 10011 - 109 St., 8th Fl., Edmonton, AB T5J 3S8
780-422-6056, Fax: 780-644-8833, 800-661-3446

New Brunswick

Program Design & Quality Management, Sartain MacDonald Bldg., #4007, 551 King St., PO Box 6000, Fredericton, NB E3B 5H1
506-453-2181, Fax: 506-453-3829

Northwest Territories

Department of Health & Social Services, Centre Square Tower, PO Box 1320, Yellowknife, NT X1A 2L9
Fax: 867-873-0266

Nunavut

Department of Health & Social Services, PO Box 1000 1000,Iqaluit, NU X0A 0H0
867-975-5700, Fax: 867-975-5705

Ontario

Ministry of Children & Youth Services, 56 Wellesley St. West, 14th Fl., Toronto, ON M5S 2G3
Fax: 416-325-5191, 866-821-7770,

CITIZENSHIP

Immigration & Refugee Board of Canada, Canada Bldg, 344 Slater St., 12th Fl., Ottawa, ON K1A 0K1
613-995-6486, Fax: 613-943-1550, contact@irb-cisr.gc.ca

Manitoba

Manitoba Education, Citizenship & Youth, #168, Legislative Bldg., 450 Broadway, Winnipeg, MB R3C 0V8
204-945-3720, Fax: 204-945-1291, minedu@leg.gov.mb.ca

Ontario

Ministry of Citizenship & Immigration, 400 University Ave., 6th Fl., Toronto, ON M7A 2R9
416-327-2422, Fax: 416-314-4965, 800-267-7329

CLIMATE & WEATHER

Canadian Space Agency, John H. Chapman Space Centre, 6767, rte de l'Aéroport, Saint-Hubert, QC J3Y 8Y9
450-926-4800, Fax: 450-926-4352, promo@asc-csa.gc.ca

CLIMATE CHANGE

Manitoba

Energy Climate Change & Green Strategy Initiatives Branch, #1202 - 155 Carlton St., Winnipeg, MB R3C 3H8
204-945-7382, Fax: 204-948-3739, ccinfo@gov.mb.ca

Quebec

Ministère du Développement durable, de l'Environnement et des Parcs, Édifice Marie-Guyart, 675, boul René-Lévesque est, 29e étage, Québec, QC G1R 5V7
418-521-3830, Fax: 418-646-5974, 800-561-1616, info@mddep.gouv.qc.ca

COAL

See Also: Energy

Alberta

Energy Resources Conservation Board, #1000, 250 - 5 Ave. SW, Calgary, AB T2P 0R4
403-297-8311, Fax: 403-297-7336, 855-297-8311, inquiries@ercb.ca; infoservices@ercb.ca; ADR@ercb.ca

New Brunswick

New Brunswick Power Group of Companies, 515 King St., PO Box 2000, Fredericton, NB E3B 4X1
506-458-4444, Fax: 506-458-4000, questions@nbpower.com

Ontario

Ontario Power Generation, 700 University Ave., Toronto, ON M5G 1X6
416-592-2555, 877-592-2555, webmaster@opg.com

Saskatchewan

Saskatchewan Power Corporation (SaskPower), 2025 Victoria Ave., Regina, SK S4P 0S1
306-566-3306, Fax: 800-757-6937, 888-757-6937

COMMUNICATIONS

See: Telecommunications

Canada Post Corporation, Corporate Secretariat, 2701 Riverside Dr., Ottawa, ON K1A 0B1
866-607-6301

Canadian Broadcasting Corporation, 181 Queen St., PO Box 3220 C,Ottawa, ON K1Y 1E4
613-288-6033, liaison@radio-canada.ca

Canadian Radio-Television & Telecommunications Commission, Central Building, 1, Promenade du Portage, Les Terrasses de la Chaudière, Gatineau, QC J8X 4B1
819-997-0313, Fax: 819-994-0218, 877-249-2782

Communications Research Centre Canada, 3701 Carling Ave., PO Box 11490 H, Ottawa, ON K2H 8S2
613-991-3313, Fax: 613-998-5355, info@crc.gc.ca

Global Operations, 125 Sussex Dr., Ottawa, ON K1A 0G2
613-944-2697, Fax: 613-996-1667

Institute for Information Technology, Bldg. M-50, 1200 Montreal Rd., Ottawa, ON K1A 0R6
613-991-3373, Fax: 613-952-0074, 877-672-2672

Spectrum, Information Technologies & Telecommunications, Journal Tower North, 300 Slater St., 20th Fl., Ottawa, ON K1A 0C8
613-998-0368, Fax: 613-952-1203

Alberta

Alberta Public Affairs Bureau, Park Plaza, 10611 - 98 Ave., 6th Fl., Edmonton, AB T5K 2P7
780-427-2754, Fax: 780-422-4168

Manitoba

Communications Services Manitoba, 155 Carlton St., 10th Fl., Winnipeg, MB R3C 3H8
204-945-3765, Fax: 204-948-2147

Manitoba News Media Services, #29, Legislative Bldg., 450 Broadway, Winnipeg, MB R3C 0V8
204-945-3746, Fax: 204-945-3988, nmservices@leg.gov.mb.ca

Manitoba Telecom Services Inc., 333 Main St., PO Box 6666, Winnipeg, MB R3C 3V6
204-941-4111, Fax: 204-772-6391

New Brunswick

Communications New Brunswick, Wilcom Bldg., 225 King St., 2nd Fl., PO Box 6000, Fredericton, NB E3B 5H1
506-453-2240, Fax: 506-453-5329

Legislative Services, Centennial Bldg., #418, 670 King St., PO Box 6000, Fredericton, NB E3B 5H1
506-453-2855, Fax: 506-457-7342

Northern Development, Harbourview Place, 275 Main St., Bathurst, NB E2A 1A9
506-547-2227, Fax: 506-547-2269

Ontario

Ontario Library Service - North, 334 Regent St., Sudbury, ON P3C 4E2
705-675-6467, Fax: 705-675-2285, 800-461-6348

Quebec

Ministère de la Culture, des Communications & de la Condition féminine, 225, Grande Allée est, Québec, QC G1R 5G5
888-380-8882

Saskatchewan

Saskatchewan Communications Network, #313E, 2440 Broad St., Regina, SK S4P 0A5
306-779-2726, Fax: 306-545-8649, inquiries@scn.ca

Saskatchewan Telecommunications (SaskTel), 2121 Saskatchewan Dr., 7th Fl., Regina, SK S4P 4C3
306-777-3737, 800-727-5835, corporate.comments@sasktel.sk.ca

COMMUNITY & MUNICIPAL DEVELOPMENT

Atlantic Canada Opportunities Agency, Blue Cross Centre, 644 Main St., 3rd Fl., PO Box 6051, Moncton, NB E1C 9J8
506-851-2271, Fax: 506-851-7403, 800-561-7862, information@acoa-apeca.gc.ca

Canada Economic Development for Québec Regions, Édifice Dominion Square, #900, 1255, rue Peel, Montréal, QC H3B 2T9
514-283-6412, Fax: 514-283-3302, 866-385-6412,

Canadian Tourism Commission, Four Bentall Centre, #1400, 1055 Dunsmuir St., PO Box 49230, Vancouver, BC V7X 1L2
604-638-8300

Western Economic Diversification Canada, Canada Place, #1500, 9700 Jasper Ave. NW, Edmonton, AB T5J 4H7
780-495-4164, Fax: 780-495-4557, 888-338-9378

Alberta

Alberta Tourism, Parks, & Recreation, Communications Branch, Commerce Place, 10155 - 102 St., 6th Fl., Edmonton, AB T5J 4L6
780-644-5589, TPR.Communications@gov.ab.ca

British Columbia

Local Government, PO Box 9490 Prov Govt,Victoria, BC V8W 9N7
250-356-6575, Fax: 250-387-7973

Manitoba

Manitoba Aboriginal & Northern Affairs, 59 Elizabeth Dr., PO Box 37, Thompson, MB R8N 1X4
204-677-6607, Fax: 204-677-6753, amartin@gov.mb.ca

Community Land Use Planning Services, #604, 800 Portage Ave., Winnipeg, MB R3G 0N4
Provincial-Municipal Support Services, #508, 800 Portage Ave., Winnipeg, MB R3G 0N4

New Brunswick
Regional Development Corporation, RDC Bldg., 836 Churchill Row, PO Box 428, Fredericton, NB E3B 5R4
506-453-2277, Fax: 506-453-7988

Newfoundland & Labrador
Department of Health & Community Services, West Block, Confederation Bldg., PO Box 8700, St. John's, NL A1B 4J6
709-729-5021, Fax: 709-729-5824, healthinfo@gov.nl.ca

Northwest Territories
Department of Municipal & Community Affairs, PO Box 1320, Yellowknife, NT X1A 2L9
867-873-7118, Fax: 867-873-0309

Nova Scotia
Department of Service Nova Scotia & Municipal Relations, 1505 Barrington St., PO Box 216, Halifax, NS B3J 3K5
902-424-5200, Fax: 902-424-0581, 800-670-4357, askus@gov.ns.ca

Nunavut
Department of Community & Government Services, W.G. Brown Bldg., 4th Fl., PO Box 1000 700,Iqaluit, NU X0A 0H0
867-975-5400, Fax: 867-975-5305

Ontario
Ministry of Municipal Affairs & Housing, College Park, 777 Bay St., 17th Fl., Toronto, ON M5G 2E5
416-585-7041, Fax: 416-585-6470, 866-220-2290, mininfo@ontario.ca

Prince Edward Island
SkillsPEI, Atlantic Technology Centre, #212, 90 University Ave., Charlottetown, PE C1A 4K9
902-368-4260, Fax: 902-368-6340, 877-491-4766

Quebec
Ministère des Affaires municipales et Occupation du territoire, Aile Chaveau, 10, rue Pierre-Olivier-Chauveau, 3e étage, Québec, QC G1R 4J3
418-691-2019, Fax: 418-643-7385, communications@mamrot.gouv.qc.ca
Ministère du Développement économique, de l'Innovation et de l'Exportation, 710, place D'Youville, 3e étage, Québec, QC G1R 4Y4
418-691-5950, Fax: 418-644-0118, 866-680-1884

Saskatchewan
Enterprise Saskatchewan, #200, 3085 Albert St., Regina, SK S4S 0B1
306-787-4484, Fax: 306-798-0629, 800-265-2001, webmaster@enterprisesask.ca; invest@enterprisesask.ca

COMMUNITY FINANCING

Atlantic Canada Opportunities Agency, Blue Cross Centre, 644 Main St., 3rd Fl., PO Box 6051, Moncton, NB E1C 9J8
506-851-2271, Fax: 506-851-7403, 800-561-7862, information@acoa-apeca.gc.ca
Business Development Bank of Canada, #400, 5, Place Ville-Marie, Montréal, QC H3B 5E7
514-283-5904, Fax: 514-283-5626, 877-232-2269
Canada Economic Development for Québec Regions, Édifice Dominion Square, #900, 1255, rue Peel, Montréal, QC H3B 2T9
514-283-6412, Fax: 514-283-3302, 866-385-6412
Canada Investment & Savings, #900, 110 Yonge St., Toronto, ON M5C 1T4
416-952-1252, Fax: 416-952-1270, 800-575-5151, csb@csb.gc.ca
Finance Canada, L'esplanade Laurier, 140 O'Connor St., Ottawa, ON K1A 0G5
613-992-1573, Fax: 613-943-0938, finpub@fin.gc.ca
Provincial-Local Finance Division, College Park, 777 Bay St., 10th Fl., Toronto, ON M5G 2C8
416-327-0264, Fax: 416-325-7644
Western Economic Diversification Canada, Canada Place, #1500, 9700 Jasper Ave. NW, Edmonton, AB T5J 4H7
780-495-4164, Fax: 780-495-4557, 888-338-9378

Alberta
Alberta Capital Finance Authority, Canadian Western Bank Place, #2450, 10303 Jasper Ave., Edmonton, AB T5J 3N6
780-427-9711, Fax: 780-422-2175, webacfa@gov.ab.ca

Manitoba
Communities Economic Development Fund, #100, 23 Station Rd., Thompson, MB R8N 0N6
204-778-4138, Fax: 204-778-4313, 800-561-4315
Provincial-Municipal Support Services, #508, 800 Portage Ave., Winnipeg, MB R3G 0N4

New Brunswick
New Brunswick Municipal Finance Corporation, #376, 670 King St., PO Box 6000, Fredericton, NB E3B 5H1
506-453-3952, Fax: 506-453-2053

Newfoundland & Labrador
Newfoundland & Labrador Municipal Financing Corporation, Confederation Bldg., PO Box 8700, St. John's, NL A1B 4J6
709-729-6686, Fax: 709-729-2095

Nova Scotia
Nova Scotia Municipal Finance Corporation, Maritime Centre, 1505 Barrington St., 10th Fl. South, PO Box 850 M, Halifax, NS B3J 2V2
902-424-4590, Fax: 902-424-0525

Prince Edward Island
SkillsPEI, Atlantic Technology Centre, #212, 90 University Ave., Charlottetown, PE C1A 4K9
902-368-4260, Fax: 902-368-6340, 877-491-4766

Quebec
Ministère des Affaires municipales et Occupation du territoire, Aile Chaveau, 10, rue Pierre-Olivier-Chauveau, 3e étage, Québec, QC G1R 4J3
418-691-2019, Fax: 418-643-7385, communications@mamrot.gouv.qc.ca

Yukon Territory
Yukon Economic Development, PO Box 2703, Whitehorse, YT Y1A 2C6
867-393-7191, Fax: 867-393-6412, 800-661-0408, ecdev@gov.yk.ca

COMMUNITY SERVICES

Alberta
Alberta Tourism, Parks, & Recreation, Communications Branch, Commerce Place, 10155 - 102 St., 6th Fl., Edmonton, AB T5J 4L6
780-644-5589, TPR.Communications@gov.ab.ca

British Columbia
Ministry of Community, Sport & Cultural Development, PO Box 9056 Prov Govt,Victoria, BC V8W 9E2
250-387-2283, Fax: 250-387-4312

Manitoba
Local Government Development Division, 59 Elizabeth Dr., PO Box 33, Thompson, MB R8N 1X4
204-677-6794, Fax: 204-677-6525

New Brunswick
Department of Social Development, Sartain MacDonald Bldg., 551 King St., PO Box 6000, Fredericton, NB E3B 5H1
506-453-2001, Fax: 506-453-7478, sd-ds@gnb.ca

Newfoundland & Labrador
Department of Health & Community Services, West Block, Confederation Bldg., PO Box 8700, St. John's, NL A1B 4J6
709-729-5021, Fax: 709-729-5824, healthinfo@gov.nl.ca

Northwest Territories
Department of Municipal & Community Affairs, PO Box 1320, Yellowknife, NT X1A 2L9
867-873-7118, Fax: 867-873-0309

Nova Scotia
Department of Community Services, Nelson Place, 5675 Spring Garden Rd., 8th Fl., PO Box 696, Halifax, NS B3J 2T7
902-424-4304, Fax: 902-428-0618

Nunavut
Department of Community & Government Services, W.G. Brown Bldg., 4th Fl., PO Box 1000 700,Iqaluit, NU X0A 0H0
867-975-5400, Fax: 867-975-5305

Ontario
Ministry of Community & Social Services, Hepburn Block, 80 Grosvenor St., 6th Fl., Toronto, ON M7A 1E9
416-325-5666, Fax: 416-325-5172, 888-789-4199

Prince Edward Island
Prince Edward Island Department of Community Services, Seniors, & Labour, Jones Bldg., 11 Kent St., 2nd Fl., PO Box 2000, Charlottetown, PE C1A 7N8
902-620-3777, Fax: 902-368-4740, 866-594-3777

Saskatchewan
Saskatchewan Social Services, 1920 Broad St., Regina, SK S4P 3V6
306-787-3700, 866-221-5200, socialservicesinquiry@gov.sk.ca

Yukon Territory
Yukon Community Services, PO Box 2703, Whitehorse, YT Y1A 2C6
867-667-5811, Fax: 867-393-6295, 800-661-0408, inquiry@gov.yk.ca

CONFLICT OF INTEREST

Office of the Conflict of Interest & Ethics Commissioner, Commissioner's Office, 66 Slater St., 22nd Fl., Ottawa, ON K1A 0A6
613-995-0721, Fax: 613-995-7308, ciec-ccie@parl.gc.ca

Alberta
Alberta Office of the Ethics Commissioner, #1250, 9925 - 109 St. NW, Edmonton, AB T5K 2J8
780-422-2273, Fax: 780-422-2261, generalinfo@ethicscommissioner.ab.ca

British Columbia
Office of the Conflict of Interest Commissioner, #101, 431 Menzies St., Victoria, BC V8V 1X4
250-356-0750, Fax: 250-356-6580, conflictofinterest@coibc.ca

Ontario
Office of the Integrity Commissioner, #2101, 2 Bloor St. East, Toronto, ON M4W 1A8
416-314-8983, Fax: 416-314-8987, integrity.mail@oico.on.ca

CONSERVATION & ECOLOGY

See Also: Heritage Resources; Natural Resources

Canadian Heritage, 15 Eddy St., Gatineau, QC K1A 0M5
819-997-0055, 866-811-0055, info@pch.gc.ca
Canadian Polar Commission, Constitution Square, #1710, 360 Albert St., Ottawa, ON K1R 7X7
613-943-8605, Fax: 613-943-8607, 888-765-2701, mail@polarcom.gc.ca
Commission for Environmental Cooperation, Secretariat, #200, 393, rue St-Jacques ouest, Montréal, QC H2Y 1N9
514-350-4300, Fax: 514-350-4314, info@cec.org
Environment Canada, 10 Wellington St., Gatineau, QC K1A 0H3
819-997-2800, Fax: 819-994-1412, 800-668-6767, enviroinfo@ec.gc.ca
Fisheries Resource Conservation Council, PO Box 2001 D, Ottawa, ON K1P 5W3
613-998-0433, Fax: 613-998-1146, info@frcc-ccrh.ca
Forestry Division, Petroleum Plaza ST, 9915 - 108 St. 11th Fl., Edmonton, AB T5K 2G8
Integrated Environmental Policy Division, 77 Wellesley St. West, 11th Fl., Toronto, ON M7A 2T5
416-314-6338, Fax: 416-314-6346
Land Use Secretariat, Centre West Building, 10035 - 108 St., Edmonton, AB T5J 3E1
780-644-7972, Fax: 780-644-1034, luf@gov.ab.ca
Natural Resources Canada, 580 Booth St., Ottawa, ON K1A 0E4
613-995-0947, Fax: 613-992-7211
Parks Canada, 25 Eddy St., Gatineau, QC K1A 0M5
613-860-1251, 888-773-8888, information@pc.gc.ca

Alberta
Alberta Environmental Appeals Board, Peace Hills Trust Tower, #306, 10011 - 109 St., Edmonton, AB T5J 3S8
780-427-6207, Fax: 780-427-4693
Alberta Used Oil Management Association, Empire Building, #1008, 10080 Jasper Ave., Edmonton, AB T5J 1V9
780-414-1510, Fax: 780-414-1519, 866-414-1510, reception@usedoilrecycling.ca
Beverage Container Management Board, #750, 10707 - 100 Ave., Edmonton, AB T5J 3M1
780-424-3193, Fax: 780-428-4620, 888-424-7671
Alberta Environment, South Tower, Petroleum Plaza, 9915 - 108 St., 10th Fl., Edmonton, AB T5K 2G8
780-427-2700, Fax: 780-422-4086, env.infocent@gov.ab.ca
Natural Resources Conservation Board, Sterling Place, 9940 - 106 St., Edmonton, AB T5K 2N2
780-422-1977, Fax: 780-427-0607, 866-383-6722, info@nrcb.gov.ab.ca
Special Areas Board, Special Areas Board Administration, 212 - 2nd Ave. West, PO Box 820, Hanna, AB T0J 1P0
403-854-5600, Fax: 403-854-5527, specarea@telus.net

British Columbia
British Columbia Assessment Authority, #400, 3450 Uptown Blvd., Victoria, BC V8Z 0B9
250-595-6211, Fax: 250-595-6222, info@bcassessment.ca
Ministry of Environment, PO Box 9339 Prov Govt,Victoria, BC V8W 9M1
250-387-1161, Fax: 250-387-5669, envmail@gov.bc.ca
Environmental Appeal Board, 747 Fort St., 4th Fl., PO Box 9425 Prov Govt, Victoria, BC V8W 3E9
250-387-3464, Fax: 250-356-9923, eabinfo@gov.bc.ca
Environmental Stewardship Division, PO Box 9339 Prov Govt,Victoria, BC V8W 9M1
250-356-0121, Fax: 250-387-5669
Forest Practices Board, 1675 Douglas St., 3rd Fl., PO Box 9905 Prov Govt, Victoria, BC V8W 9R1
250-213-4700, Fax: 250-213-4725, 800-994-5899, fpboard@gov.bc.ca
Fraser Basin Council, Central Office, 470 Granville St., 1st Fl., Vancouver, BC V6C 1V5
604-488-5350, Fax: 604-488-5351, info@fraserbasin.bc.ca
North Area, 1011 - 4 Ave., 5th Fl., Prince George, BC V2L 3H9
250-565-6100
Surface Rights Board, #10, 10551 Shellbridge Way, Richmond, BC V6X 2W9
604-775-1740, Fax: 604-775-1742, 888-775-1740, office@surfacerightsboard.bc.ca

Manitoba
Clean Environment Commission, #305, 155 Carlton St., Winnipeg, MB R3C 3H8
204-945-0594, Fax: 204-945-0090

Manitoba Conservation, 200 Saulteaux Cres., Winnipeg, MB R3J 3W3
204-945-6784, 800-214-6497, mincon@leg.gov.mb.ca

Ecological Reserves Advisory Committee, c/o Manitoba Conservation, Parks & Natural Areas Branch, 200 Saulteaux Cres., Winnipeg, MB R3J 3W3
204-945-4148, Fax: 204-945-0012, hhernandez@gov.mb.ca

Manitoba Conservation Districts Commission, Secretariat c/o Planning & Coordination Branch, 123 Main St., PO Box 20000, Neepawa, MB R0J 1H0
204-476-7033, Fax: 204-476-7539, whildebran@gov.mb.ca

New Brunswick

Assessment & Planning Appeal Board, #201, 435 King St., PO Box 6000, Fredericton, NB E3B 5H1
506-453-2126, Fax: 506-444-4881

Department of the Environment, Marysville Place, 20 McGloin St., PO Box 6000, Fredericton, NB E3B 5H1
506-453-2690, Fax: 506-457-7800, env-info@gnb.ca

Newfoundland & Labrador

Department of Environment & Conservation, Confederation Bldg., West Block, 4th Fl., PO Box 8700, St. John's, NL A1B 4J6
709-729-2664, Fax: 709-729-6639, 800-563-6181, info@gov.nl.ca

Northwest Territories

Department of Environment & Natural Resources, PO Box 1320, Yellowknife, NT X1A 2L9

Nova Scotia

Department of Natural Resources, Founder's Square, 1701 Hollis St., 3rd Fl., PO Box 698, Halifax, NS B3J 2T9
902-424-5935, Fax: 902-424-0594, 800-565-2224

Ontario

Ministry of Environment, 135 St. Clair Ave. West, Toronto, ON M4V 1P5
416-325-4000, Fax: 416-325-3159, 800-565-4923

Ministry of Natural Resources, Whitney Block, #6630, 99 Wellesley St. West, 6th Fl., Toronto, ON M7A 1W3
800-667-1940

Niagara Escarpment Commission, 232 Guelph St., Georgetown, ON L7G 4B1
905-877-5191, Fax: 905-873-7452

Prince Edward Island

Environmental Advisory Council, PO Box 2000, Charlottetown, PE C1A 7N8

Prince Edward Island Department of Environment, Energy, & Forestry, Jones Bldg., 11 Kent St., 4th Fl., PO Box 2000, Charlottetown, PE C1A 7N8
902-368-5000, Fax: 902-368-5830

Prince Edward Island Department of Tourism & Culture, PO Box 2000, Charlottetown, PE C1A 7N8
902-368-5540, Fax: 902-368-5277, tpswitch@gov.pe.ca

Quebec

Comité consultatif de l'environnement Kativik, CP 930, Kuujjuaq, QC J0M 1C0
819-964-2961, Fax: 819-964-0694

Ministère du Développement durable, de l'Environnement et des Parcs, Édifice Marie-Guyart, 675, boul René-Lévesque est, 29e étage, Québec, QC G1R 5V7
418-521-3830, Fax: 418-646-5974, 800-561-1616, info@mddep.gouv.qc.ca

Fondation de la faune du Québec, Place Iberville II, #420, 1175, av Lavigerie, Québec, QC G1V 4P1
418-644-7926, Fax: 418-643-7655, 877-639-0742, ffq@fondationdelafaune.qc.ca

Société de développement de la Baie James, 110, boul Matagami, CP 970, Matagami, QC J0Y 2A0
819-739-4717, Fax: 819-739-4329, mat@sdbj.gouv.qc.ca

Société québécoise de récupération et de recyclage, #200, 420, boul Charest est, Québec, QC G1K 8M4
418-643-0394, Fax: 418-643-6507, 866-523-8290, info@recyc-quebec.gouv.qc.ca

Saskatchewan

Saskatchewan Assessment Management Agency, #200, 2201 - 11th Ave., Regina, SK S4P 0J8
306-924-8000, Fax: 306-924-8070, 800-667-7262, info.request@sama.sk.ca

Saskatchewan Environment, 3211 Albert St., 2nd Fl., Regina, SK S4S 5W6
306-787-2584, Fax: 306-787-9544, 800-567-4224, Centre.Inquiry@gov.sk.ca

Saskatchewan Conservation Data Centre, 3211 Albert St., Regina, SK S4S 5W6
306-787-9038, Fax: 306-787-9544

Saskatchewan Watershed Authority, 111 Fairford St. East, Moose Jaw, SK S6H 7X9
306-694-3900, Fax: 306-694-3465, comm@swa.ca

Yukon Territory

Alsek Renewable Resource Council, PO Box 2077, Haines Junction, YT Y0B 1L0
867-634-2524, Fax: 867-634-2527

Carmacks Renewable Resource Council, PO Box 122, Carmacks, YT Y0B 1C0
867-863-6838, Fax: 867-863-6429, carmacksrrc@northwestel.net

Dawson District Renewable Resource Council, PO Box 1380, Dawson City, YT Y0B 1G0
867-993-6976, Fax: 867-993-6093, dawsonrrc@northwestel.net

Yukon Environment, PO Box 2703, Whitehorse, YT Y1A 2C6
867-667-5652, Fax: 867-393-7197, environment.yukon@gov.yk.ca

Mayo District Renewable Resources Council, PO Box 249, Mayo, YT Y0B 1M0
867-996-2942, Fax: 867-996-2948, mayorrc@yknet.yk.ca

North Yukon Renewable Resources Council, PO Box 80, Old Crow, YT Y0B 1N0
867-966-3034, Fax: 867-966-3036, vgrrc@yknet.yk.ca

Selkirk Renewable Resources Council, PO Box 32, Pelly Crossing, YT Y0B 1P0
867-537-3937, Fax: 867-537-3939, selkirkrrc@yknet.yk.ca

Teslin Renewable Resource Council, PO Box 186, Teslin, YT Y0A 1B0
867-390-2323, Fax: 867-390-2919, teslinrrc@northwestel.net

Yukon Land Use Planning Council, #201, 307 Jarvis St., Whitehorse, YT Y1A 2H3
867-667-7397, Fax: 867-667-4624, ylupc@planyukon.ca

CONSTRUCTION

Canada Mortgage & Housing Corporation, 700 Montreal Rd., Ottawa, ON K1A 0P7
613-748-2000, Fax: 613-748-2098, 800-668-2642, chic@cmhc-schl.gc.ca

Defence Construction Canada, Constitution Square, 350 Albert St., 19th Fl., Ottawa, ON K1A 0K3
613-998-9548, Fax: 613-998-1061, 800-514-3555, info@dcc-cdc.gc.ca

Infrastructure Canada, #1100, 180 Kent Street, Ottawa, ON K1P 0B6
613-948-1148, Fax: 613-946-9888, 800-622-6232, info@infc.gc.ca

Institute for Research in Construction, Bldg. M-24, 1500 Montreal Rd., Ottawa, ON K1A 0R6
613-993-2607, Fax: 613-952-7673, Irc.Client-Services@nrc-cnrc.gc.ca

Policy & Corporate Services Division, Twin Atria Building, 4999 - 98 Ave., 3rd Fl., Edmonton, AB T6B 2X3

Alberta

Alberta Infrastructure, Infrastructure Building, 6950 - 113 St., Edmonton, AB T6H 5V7
780-415-0507, Fax: 780-427-2187, Infra.Contact.Us.m@gov.ab.ca

Manitoba

Construction & Maintenance Branch, #1610, 215 Garry St., Winnipeg, MB R3C 3Z1
Fax: 204-945-3841

Newfoundland & Labrador

Department of Transportation & Works, Confederation Bldg., West Block, 6th Fl., PO Box 8700, St. John's, NL A1B 4J6
709-729-3679, Fax: 709-729-4285, twminister@gov.nl.ca

Nunavut

Department of Community & Government Services, W.G. Brown Bldg., 4th Fl., PO Box 1000 700,Iqaluit, NU X0A 0H0
867-975-5400, Fax: 867-975-5305

Ontario

Building Code Commission, 777 Bay St., 2nd Fl., Toronto, ON M5G 2E5
416-585-6666, Fax: 416-585-7531

Building Materials Evaluation Commission, 777 Bay St., 2nd Fl., Toronto, ON M5G 2E5
416-585-4234, Fax: 416-585-7531,

Quebec

Commission de la construction du Québec, 3530, rue Jean-Talon ouest, Montréal, QC H3R 2G3
514-341-7740, Fax: 514-341-6354, 888-842-8282

Régie du bâtiment du Québec, 545, boul Crémazie est, 4e étage, Montréal, QC H2M 2V2
514-873-0976, Fax: 514-864-2903, 800-361-0761, crc@rbq.gouv.qc.ca

CONSUMER PROTECTION

See Also: Public Safety

Financial Consumer Agency of Canada, 427 Laurier Ave. West, 6th Fl., Ottawa, ON K1R 1B9
Fax: 613-941-1436, info@fcac-acfc.gc.ca

HR Ontario, Whitney Block, #5320, 99 Wellesley St. West, Toronto, ON M7A 1N3
416-212-2057, Fax: 416-325-6317

Alberta

Registry Services, Telus Plaza South, 10020 - 100 St., 29th Fl., Edmonton, AB T5J 0N3

Nova Scotia

Department of Service Nova Scotia & Municipal Relations, 1505 Barrington St., PO Box 216, Halifax, NS B3J 3K5
902-424-5200, Fax: 902-424-0581, 800-670-4357, askus@gov.ns.ca

Nunavut

Department of Community & Government Services, W.G. Brown Bldg., 4th Fl., PO Box 1000 700,Iqaluit, NU X0A 0H0
867-975-5400, Fax: 867-975-5305

CORONERS

British Columbia

Coroners Service of British Columbia, Metrotower II, #800, 4720 Kingsway, Burnaby, BC V5H 4N2
604-660-7745, Fax: 604-660-7766, BC.CorSer@gov.bc.ca

Manitoba

Office of the Chief Medical Examiner, #210, 1 Wesley Ave., Winnipeg, MB R3C 4C6
204-945-2088, Fax: 204-945-2442, 800-282-9069

Nova Scotia

Office of the Chief Medical Examiner, Halifax Insurance Bldg., #701, 5670 Spring Garden Rd., Halifax, NS B3J 1H7
902-424-2722, Fax: 902-424-0607

Nunavut

Office of the Chief Coroner, PO Box 1000 590, Iqaluit, NU X0A 0H0

Quebec

Bureau du coroner, Édifice le Delta 2, #390, 2875, boul Laurier, Québec, QC G1V 5B1
418-643-1845, Fax: 418-643-6174, 866-312-7051, clientele.coroner@msp.gouv.qc.ca

CORRECTIONAL SERVICES

Alberta

Corporate Services Division, John E. Brownlee Building, 10365 - 97 St., 9th Fl., Edmonton, AB T5J 3W7

Office of the Correctional Investigator, PO Box 3421 D,Ottawa, ON K1P 6L4
Fax: 613-990-9091, 877-885-8848, org@oci-bec.gc.ca

Correctional Service Canada, 340 Laurier Ave. West, Ottawa, ON K1A 0P9
613-992-5891, Fax: 613-943-1630

British Columbia

Corrections Branch, PO Box 9278 Prov Govt,Victoria, BC V8W 9J7
250-387-5059, Fax: 250-387-5698

Manitoba

Corrections Division, #810, 405 Broadway Ave., Winnipeg, MB R3C 3L6
204-945-7291

Nunavut

Baffin Correctional Centre, 1550 Federal Rd., PO Box 368, Iqaluit, NU X0A 0H0
867-979-8100, Fax: 867-979-4646

Saskatchewan

Saskatchewan Corrections, Public Safety & Policing, 1874 Scarth St., Regina, SK S4P 4B3
306-787-7872, communicationsCPSP@gov.sk.ca

CRIMES COMPENSATION

Communications Branch, 284 Wellington St., Ottawa, ON K1A 0H8
Fax: 613-941-2329

Alberta

Criminal Injuries Review Board, #1502, 10025 - 102A Ave., Edmonton, AB T5J 2Z2
780-427-7330, Fax: 780-427-7347

Manitoba

Compensation for Victims of Crime, 1410 - 405 Broadway, Winnipeg, MB R3C 3L6
204-945-0899, Fax: 204-948-3071, 800-262-9344

Northwest Territories

Victims Assistance Committee, c/o Community Justice Division, PO Box 1320, Yellowknife, NT X1A 2L9
867-920-6911, Fax: 867-873-0199

Ontario

Criminal Injuries Compensation Board, 439 University Ave., 4th Fl., Toronto, ON M5G 1Y8
416-326-2900, Fax: 416-326-2883, 800-372-7463, info.cicb@ontario.ca

Office for Victims of Crime, 700 Bay St., 3rd Fl., Toronto, ON M5G 1Z6
416-326-1682, Fax: 416-326-4497, 887-435-7661

Victims & Vulnerable Persons Division, 18 King St. E, 7th Fl., Toronto, ON M5C 1C4
416-325-3265, Fax: 416-212-1091

CULTURE & HERITAGE

See: Arts & Culture

Aboriginal Affairs & Northern Development Canada, 10 Wellington St., North Tower, Gatineau, QC K1A 0H4
819-997-0380, Fax: 866-817-3977, 800-567-9604, infopubs@aadnc-aandc.gc.ca
Canadian Heritage, 15 Eddy St., Gatineau, QC K1A 0M5
819-997-0055, 866-811-0055, info@pch.gc.ca
Corporate & Financial Services Division, Jones Bldg., 11 Kent St., 2nd Fl., PO Box 2000, Charlottetown, PE C1A 7N8
Fax: 902-894-0242,
Historic Sites & Monuments Board of Canada, Terrasses de la Chaudière, 25 Eddy St., Gatineau, QC K1A 0M5
Fax: 819-934-1115, 855-283-8730, hsmbc-clmhc@pc.gc.ca

Alberta
Alberta Sport, Recreation, Parks, & Wildlife Foundation, Standard Life Centre, #903, 10405 Jasper Ave., 9th Fl., Edmonton, AB T5J 4R7
780-415-1167, Fax: 780-415-0308
Alberta International & Intergovernmental Relations, Commerce Place, 10155 - 102 St., 12th Fl., Edmonton, AB T5J 4G8
780-422-1510, Fax: 780-427-0699

British Columbia
Ministry of Community, Sport & Cultural Development, PO Box 9056 Prov Govt,Victoria, BC V8W 9E2
250-387-2283, Fax: 250-387-4312

Manitoba
Manitoba Culture, Heritage, Tourism & Sport, Legislative Building, #118, 450 Broadway Ave., Winnipeg, MB R3C 0V8
204-945-3729, Fax: 204-945-5223, mincht@leg.gov.mb.ca
Manitoba Heritage Council, 213 Notre Dame Ave., Main Fl., Winnipeg, MB R3B 1N3
204-945-2118, Fax: 204-948-2384, hrb@gov.mb.ca

New Brunswick
Department of Wellness, Culture & Sport, Place 2000, 250 King St., 4th Fl., PO Box 6000, Fredericton, NB E3B 5H1
506-453-2909, Fax: 506-453-6548

Newfoundland & Labrador
Department of Tourism, Culture & Recreation, Confederation Bldg., West Block, 2nd Fl., PO Box 8700, St. John's, NL A1B 4J6
709-729-0862, Fax: 709-729-0870, tcrinfo@gov.nl.ca

Northwest Territories
Department of Aboriginal Affairs & Intergovernmental Relations, 4910 - 52nd St., PO Box 1320, Yellowknife, NT X1A 2L9
867-873-7143, Fax: 867-873-0233, 877-838-8194, nancy_gardiner@gov.nt.ca
Department of Education, Culture & Employment, PO Box 1320, Yellowknife, NT X1A 2L9
867-669-2399, Fax: 867-873-0431, 866-606-5627

Nova Scotia
Culture Division, #601, 1800 Argyle St., PO Box 456, Halifax, NS B3J 2R5
902-424-4510, Fax: 902-424-0710, culture@gov.ns.ca

Ontario
Ontario Trillium Foundation, 800 Bay St., 5th Fl., Toronto, ON M5S 3A9
416-963-4927, Fax: 416-963-8781, 800-263-2887, trillium@trilliumfoundation.org

Saskatchewan
Saskatchewan First Nations & Métis Relations, #1020, 1855 Victoria Ave., Regina, SK S4P 3T2
306-787-6250, Fax: 306-798-0083
Saskatchewan Government Services, 1920 Rose St., Regina, SK S4P 0A9
306-787-6911, Fax: 306-787-1061, GSReception@gs.gov.sk.ca

CURRENCY
Bank of Canada, 234 Wellington St., Ottawa, ON K1A 0G9
613-782-7902, Fax: 613-782-7713, 800-303-1282, info@bankofcanada.ca; communications@bankofcanada.ca (Media)
Royal Canadian Mint, 320 Sussex Dr., Ottawa, ON K1A 0G8
613-993-3500, Fax: 613-993-4092, 800-267-1871

CUSTOMS
Canada Border Services Agency, Headquarters, 191 Laurier Ave. West, Ottawa, ON K1A 0L8
800-461-9999, Contact@cbsa.gc.ca; communications@ps.gc.ca (Public Safety)

DAIRY INDUSTRY
Canadian Dairy Commission, Central Experimental Farm, NCC Driveway, Bldg. 55, 960 Carling Ave., Ottawa, ON K1A 0Z2
613-792-2000, Fax: 613-792-2009, cdc-ccl@cdc-ccl.gc.ca

Manitoba
Manitoba Milk Prices Review Commission, c/o Boards, Commissions & Legislation Branch, #812, 401 York Ave., Winnipeg, MB R3C 0P8
204-945-3854, Fax: 204-948-2844, randy.ozunko@gov.mb.ca

Prince Edward Island
Prince Edward Island Department of Agriculture, Jones Bldg., 11 Kent St., PO Box 2000, Charlottetown, PE C1A 7N8
902-368-4880, Fax: 902-368-4857

DANGEROUS GOODS & HAZARDOUS MATERIALS
See Also: Occupational Safety; Waste Management
Hazardous Materials Information Review Commission, 427 Laurier Ave. West, 7th Fl., Ottawa, ON K1A 1M3
613-993-4331, Fax: 613-993-4686, hmirc-ccrmd@hc-sc.gc.ca

British Columbia
Ministry of Transportation & Infrastructure, PO Box 9850 Prov Govt,Victoria, BC V8W 9T5
250-387-3198, Fax: 250-356-7706, tran.webmaster@gov.bc.ca

Northwest Territories
Department of Transportation, Lahm Ridge Bldg., 4501 50 Ave., PO Box 1320, Yellowknife, NT X1A 2L9
867-920-3460, Fax: 867-873-0363

Nova Scotia
Department of Transportation & Infrastructure Renewal, Johnston Bldg., 1672 Granville St., 2nd Fl., PO Box 186, Halifax, NS B3J 2N2
902-424-2297, Fax: 902-424-0532, tpwpaff@gov.ns.ca

Ontario
Ministry of Transportation, Ferguson Block, 77 Wellesley St. West, 3rd Fl., Toronto, ON M7A 1Z8
416-235-4686, Fax: 905-704-2001, 800-268-4686

Prince Edward Island
Prince Edward Island Department of Transportation & Infrastructure Renewal, Jones Bldg., 11 Kent St., 3rd Fl., PO Box 2000, Charlottetown, PE C1A 7N8
902-368-5100, Fax: 902-368-5395

Quebec
Ministère du Développement durable, de l'Environnement et des Parcs, Édifice Marie-Guyart, 675, boul René-Lévesque est, 29e étage, Québec, QC G1R 5V7
418-521-3830, Fax: 418-646-5974, 800-561-1616, info@mddep.gouv.qc.ca

Saskatchewan
Saskatchewan Highways & Infrastructure, Victoria Tower, 1855 Victoria Ave., Regina, SK S4P 3T2
306-787-4800, communications@highways.gov.sk.ca

Yukon Territory
Yukon Highways & Public Works, PO Box 2703, Whitehorse, YT Y1A 2C6
867-393-7193, Fax: 867-393-6218, 800-661-0408, hpw-info@gov.yk.ca

DAY CARE SERVICES
See Also: Child Welfare

Ontario
Ministry of Children & Youth Services, 56 Wellesley St. West, 14th Fl., Toronto, ON M5S 2G3
Fax: 416-325-5191, 866-821-7770

DEBT MANAGEMENT
Finance Canada, L'esplanade Laurier, 140 O'Connor St., Ottawa, ON K1A 0G5
613-992-1573, Fax: 613-943-0938, finpub@fin.gc.ca

British Columbia
Provincial Treasury, PO Box 9414 Prov Govt,Victoria, BC V8V 9V1
250-387-4541, Fax: 250-356-3041

New Brunswick
Treasury, Centennial Bldg., #376, 670 King St., PO Box 6000, Fredericton, NB E3B 5H1
506-453-3952, Fax: 506-453-2053

DEFENCE
See Also: Emergency Response; Public Safety
Canadian Forces Grievance Board, 60 Queen St., 10th Fl., Ottawa, ON K1P 5Y7
613-996-8529, Fax: 613-996-6491, 877-276-4193
Defence Construction Canada, Constitution Square, 350 Albert St., 19th Fl., Ottawa, ON K1A 0K3
613-998-9548, Fax: 613-998-1061, 800-514-3555, info@dcc-cdc.gc.ca
Defence Research & Development Canada, 305 Rideau St., Ottawa, ON K1A 0K2
613-992-7237, info@drdc-rddc.gc.ca
Military Police Complaints Commission, 270 Albert St., 10th Fl., Ottawa, ON K1P 5G8
613-947-5625, Fax: 613-947-5713, 800-632-0566, commission@mpcc-cppm.gc.ca
National Defence Canada, Major-General George R. Pearkes Bldg., 101 Colonel By Dr., Ottawa, ON K1A 0K2
613-995-2534, Fax: 613-992-4739, 800-856-8488

DISABLED PERSONS SERVICES
Canadian Human Rights Commission, 344 Slater St., 8th Fl., Ottawa, ON K1A 1E1
613-995-1151, Fax: 613-996-9661, 888-214-1090
Health System Strategy & Policy Division, Hepburn Block, 80 Grosvenor St., 8th Fl., Toronto, ON M7A 1R3
416-327-8295, Fax: 416-327-5109

Alberta
Persons with Developmental Disabilities Community Boards, c/o PDD Program Branch, Peace Hills Trust Tower, 10011 - 109 St., 4th Fl., Edmonton, AB T5J 3S8
780-427-1177, Fax: 780-427-1220, 800-310-0000, PDDinfo@gov.ab.ca
Premier's Council on the Status of Persons with Disabilities, HSBC Building, 10055 - 106 St., 11th Fl., Edmonton, AB T5J 1G3
780-422-1095, 800-272-8841, pcspd@gov.ab.ca
Alberta Seniors & Community Supports, Communications, Standard Life Centre, 10405 Jasper Ave., 3rd Fl., Edmonton, AB T5J 4R7
780-415-9950, Fax: 780-644-1227, 866-477-8589, seniors.communications@gov.ab.ca

Manitoba
Disabilities Issues Office, #630, 240 Graham Ave., Winnipeg, MB R3C 0J7
204-945-7613, Fax: 204-948-2896, dio@gov.mb.ca

New Brunswick
Premier's Council on the Status of Disabled Persons, Kings Place, #648, 440 King St., Fredericton, NB E3B 5H8
506-444-3000, Fax: 506-444-3001, 800-442-4412, pcsdp@gnb.ca

Nova Scotia
Nova Scotia Disabled Persons Commission, Dartmouth Professional Center, #104, 277 Pleasant St., Dartmouth, NS B2Y 4B7
902-424-8280, Fax: 902-424-0592, 800-565-8280

Nunavut
Department of Culture, Language, Elders & Youth, PO Box 1000 800,Iqaluit, NU X0A 0H0
867-975-5500, Fax: 867-975-5504, 866-934-2035

Quebec
Office des personnes handicapées du Québec, 309, rue Brock, Drummondville, QC J2B 1C5
Fax: 819-475-8753, 800-567-1465, michael.magner@ophq.gouv.qc.ca

DISCRIMINATION & EMPLOYMENT EQUITY
Canadian Human Rights Commission, 344 Slater St., 8th Fl., Ottawa, ON K1A 1E1
613-995-1151, Fax: 613-996-9661, 888-214-1090
Canadian Human Rights Tribunal, 160 Elgin St., 11th Fl., Ottawa, ON K1A 1J4
613-995-1707, Fax: 613-995-3484, registrar@chrt-tcdp.gc.ca

Alberta
Alberta Labour Relations Board, Labour Building, 10808 - 99 Ave., 5th Fl., Edmonton, AB T5K 0G5
780-422-5926, Fax: 780-422-0970, 800-463-2572, alrbinfo@lab.gov.ab.ca

British Columbia
British Columbia Human Rights Tribunal, #1170, 605 Robson St., Vancouver, BC V6B 5J3
604-775-2000, Fax: 604-775-2020, 888-440-8844, BCHumanRightsTribunal@gov.bc.ca

Manitoba
Manitoba Human Rights Commission, 175 Hargrave St., 7th Fl., Winnipeg, MB R3C 3R8
204-945-3007, Fax: 204-945-1292, 888-884-8681, hrc@gov.mb.ca

New Brunswick
New Brunswick Human Rights Commission, PO Box 6000, Fredericton, NB E3B 5H1
506-453-2301, Fax: 506-453-2653, 888-471-2233, hrc.cdp@gnb.ca

Newfoundland & Labrador
Newfoundland & Labrador Human Rights Commission, PO Box 8700, St. John's, NL A1B 4J6
709-729-2709, Fax: 709-729-0790, 800-563-5808, humanrights@mail.gov.nl.ca

Nova Scotia
Nova Scotia Human Rights Commission, Joseph Howe Bldg., 1690 Hollis St., 6th Fl., Halifax, NS B3J 3C4
902-424-4111, Fax: 902-424-0596, hrcinquiries@gov.ns.ca

Ontario
Ontario Human Rights Commission, 180 Dundas St. West, 7th Fl., Toronto, ON M7A 2R9
416-326-9511, Fax: 416-314-4494, 800-387-9080

Prince Edward Island
Prince Edward Island Human Rights Commission, 53 Water St., PO Box 2000, Charlottetown, PE C1A 7N8
902-368-4180, Fax: 902-368-4236, 800-237-5031,

Quebec
Commission de l'équité salariale, 200, ch Ste-Foy, 4e étage, Québec, QC G1R 6A1
418-528-8765, Fax: 418-528-6999, 888-528-8765, equite.salariale@ces.gouv.qc.ca

Saskatchewan
Saskatchewan Human Rights Commission, Saskatoon Office, Sturdy Stone Bdg., #816, 122 - 3 Ave. North, 8th Fl., Saskatoon, SK S7K 2H6
306-933-5952, Fax: 306-933-7863, 800-667-9249, shrc@gov.sk.ca

Yukon Territory
Yukon Human Rights Commission, #101, 9010 Quartz St., Whitehorse, YT Y1A 2Z5
867-667-6226, Fax: 867-667-2662, 800-661-0535, humanrights@yhrc.yk.ca

DIVORCE

Justice Canada, East Memorial Bldg., 284 Wellington St., Ottawa, ON K1A 0H8
613-957-4222, Fax: 613-954-0811, webadmin@justice.gc.ca

DRIVERS' LICENCES

Alberta
Strategic Planning & Financial Services, Commerce Place, 10155 - 102 St., 13th Fl., Edmonton, AB T5J 4G8
780-422-8545

British Columbia
Ministry of Transportation & Infrastructure, PO Box 9850 Prov Govt,Victoria, BC V8W 9T5
250-387-3198, Fax: 250-356-7706, tran.webmaster@gov.bc.ca

Manitoba
Manitoba Infrastructure & Transportation, Legislative Building, #203, 450 Broadway Ave., Winnipeg, MB R3C 0V8
204-945-3723, Fax: 204-945-7610

Northwest Territories
Road Licensing & Safety, 4510 - 50 Ave., 1st fl., PO Box 1320, Yellowknife, NT X1A 2L9
867-873-7972, Fax: 867-873-0120

Nova Scotia
Registry of Motor Vehicles, 1505 Barrington St., 8th Fl. North, PO Box 2734, Halifax, NS
902-424-7801, Fax: 902-424-0772, 800-898-7668

Ontario
Licence Appeal Tribunal, 20 Dundas St. West, 5th Fl., Toronto, ON M5G 2C2
416-314-4260, Fax: 416-314-4270, 800-255-2214
Ministry of Transportation, Ferguson Block, 77 Wellesley St. West, 3rd Fl., Toronto, ON M7A 1Z8
416-235-4686, Fax: 905-704-2001, 800-268-4686

Prince Edward Island
Prince Edward Island Department of Transportation & Infrastructure Renewal, Jones Bldg., 11 Kent St., 3rd Fl., PO Box 2000, Charlottetown, PE C1A 7N8
902-368-5100, Fax: 902-368-5395

Quebec
Société de l'assurance automobile du Québec, 333, boul Jean-Lesage, CP 19600 Terminus, Québec, QC G1K 8J6
418-643-7620, Fax: 418-644-0339, 800-361-7620, courrier@saaq.gouv.qc.ca

Saskatchewan
Saskatchewan Government Insurance, 2260 - 11th Ave., Regina, SK S4P 0J9
306-751-1200, Fax: 306-787-7477, 800-667-8015, sgiinquiries@sgi.sk.ca

Yukon Territory
Driver Control Board, 2130 Second Ave., 3rd Fl., PO Box 2703, Whitehorse, YT Y1A 2C6
867-667-5111, Fax: 867-667-3609, dcb@gov.yk.ca

DRUGS & ALCOHOL

See Also: Liquor Control
Canadian Centre on Substance Abuse, #500, 75 Albert St., Ottawa, ON K1P 5E7
613-235-4048, Fax: 613-235-8101, info@ccsa.ca

Alberta
Alberta Health Services, Corporate Office, North Tower, Seventh Street Plaza, 10030 - 107th St. NW, 14th Fl., Edmonton, AB T5J 3E4
780-342-2000, Fax: 780-342-2060, 888-342-2471, ahsb.admin@albertahealthservices.ca

British Columbia
Ministry of Health, 1515 Blanshard St., Victoria, BC V8W 3C8
250-952-1742, Fax: 250-356-9587, 800-465-4911, hlth.health@gov.bc.ca

Quebec
Bureau des projets Centres hospitaliers universitaires de Montréal, CHUM, CUSM et CHU Sainte-Justine, #10.049, 2021, rue Union, Montréal, QC H3A 2S9
514-864-9883, Fax: 514-873-7362, info.construction3chu@msss.gouv.qc.ca
Ministère de la Santé et des Services sociaux, Direction des communications, 1075, ch Sainte-Foy, 16e étage, Québec, QC G1S 2M1
418-643-9395, Fax: 418-643-4768, regisseur.web@msss.gouv.qc.ca

ECONOMIC DEVELOPMENT

See: Business Development

Prince Edward Island
Summerside Regional Development Corporation Ltd., 268 Water St., Summerside, PE C1N 1B6
902-436-2246, Fax: 902-436-9269, acroken@srdcpei.com

Prince Edward Island
Innovation PEI, 94 Euston St., PO Box 910, Charlottetown, PE C1A 7L9
902-368-6300, Fax: 902-368-6301, 800-563-3734

EDUCATION

Canada School of Public Service, 373 Sussex Dr., Ottawa, ON K1N 6Z2
819-953-5400, Fax: 819-953-7953, 866-703-9598, info@csps-efpc.gc.ca
Canadian Council of Directors of Apprenticeship, 140 Promenade du Portage, 5th Fl, Phase IV, Gatineau, QC K1A 0J9
819-953-7443, Fax: 819-994-0202, redseal-sceaurouge@hrsdc-rhdcc.gc.ca
Canadian Forces College, Toronto, ON
416-482-6800
Canadian Police College, PO Box 8900, Ottawa, ON K1G 3J2
613-993-9500, Fax: 613-990-9738, cpc-ccp@rcmp-grc.gc.ca
Children's Secretariat, c/o Sarah Henry, Education & Early Childhood Development, 161 St. Peters Rd., PO Box 2000, Charlottetown, PE C1A 7N8
RCMP Training Academy, 6101 Dewdney Ave., Regina, SK S4P 3J7
306-780-5002, Fax: 306-780-7940,
Royal Military College, Kingston, ON
613-541-6000

Alberta
Alberta Advanced Education & Technology, Legislature Bldg., #324, 10800 - 97 Ave., Edmonton, AB T5K 2B6
780-422-5400
Alberta Apprenticeship & Industry Training Board, Commerce Place, 10155 - 102nd St., 10th Fl., Edmonton, AB T5J 4L5
780-427-8765, Fax: 780-422-7376
Alberta Council on Admissions & Transfer, Commerce Place, 10155 - 102 St., 11th Fl., Edmonton, AB T5J 4L5
780-422-9021, Fax: 780-422-3688, acat@gov.ab.ca
Alberta Enterprise Corporation Board, Alberta Enterprise Corporation, #1100, 10830 Jasper Ave., Edmonton, AB T5J 2B3
780-392-3901
Alberta Innovates - Technology Futures, 250 Karl Clark Rd., Edmonton, AB T6N 1E4
780-450-5111, Fax: 780-450-5333, referral@albertainnovates.ca
Campus Alberta Quality Council, Commerce Place, 10155 - 102 St., 11th Fl., Edmonton, AB T5J 4L5
780-427-8921, Fax: 780-427-4185, caqc@gov.ab.ca
Community, Learner & Industry Connections Division, Phipps-McKinnon Bldg., 10020 - 101A Ave., 5th Fl., Edmonton, AB T5J 3G2
Council on Alberta Teaching Standards, 10044 - 108 St., Edmonton, AB T5J 5E6
780-427-2045, Fax: 780-422-4199
Alberta Education, Commerce Place, 10155 - 102 St., 7th Fl., Edmonton, AB T5J 4L5
780-427-7219, Fax: 780-427-0591

British Columbia
Ministry of Advanced Education, PO Box 9059 Prov Govt,Victoria, BC V8W 9E2
250-952-6508, Fax: 250-356-6942, ALMD.WEBMASTER@gov.bc.ca
Auditor Certification Board, PO Box 9431 Prov Govt, Victoria, BC V8W 9V3
250-356-8658, Fax: 250-356-9422, Kelly.Fitzsimonds@gov.bc.ca
Degree Quality Assessment Board, Degree Quality Assessment Board Secretariat, PO Box 9177 Prov Govt, Victoria, BC V8W 9H8
250-387-5163, DQABsecretariat@gov.bc.ca
Ministry of Education, PO Box 9146 Prov Govt,Victoria, BC V8W 9H1
250-387-1977, Fax: 250-387-3200, 888-879-1166
Leading Edge Endowment Fund Board, 1188 West Georgia St., 9th Fl., Vancouver, BC V6E 4A2
604-438-3220, contact@leefbc.ca
Private Career Training Institutions Agency, #300, 5172 Kingsway, Burnaby, BC V5H 2E8
604-660-4400, Fax: 604-660-3312, 800-661-7441, info@pctia.bc.ca

Manitoba
Manitoba Advanced Education & Literacy, Legislative Building, #162, 450 Broadway Ave., Winnipeg, MB R3C 0V8
204-945-0825, Fax: 204-948-2216, minaed@leg.gov.mb.ca
Division du Bureau de l'éducation française, #509, 1181 av Portage, Winnipeg, MB R3C 0T3
204-945-6916, Fax: 204-945-1625
Manitoba Education, Citizenship & Youth, #168, Legislative Bldg., 450 Broadway, Winnipeg, MB R3C 0V8
204-945-3720, Fax: 204-945-1291, minedu@leg.gov.mb.ca
Manitoba Education, Research & Learning Information Networks, #100 - 135 Innovation Dr., University of Manitoba, Winnipeg, MB R3T 6A8
204-474-7800, Fax: 204-474-7830, 800-430-6404
Public Schools Finance Board, #506, 1181 Portage Ave., Winnipeg, MB R3G 0T3
204-945-6628, Fax: 204-948-2001
School Programs Division, #307, 1181 Portage Ave., Winnipeg, MB R3G 0T3
Fax: 204-945-8303

New Brunswick
Apprenticeship & Occupational Certification Board, PO Box 6000, Fredericton, NB E3B 5H1
506-453-2260, Fax: 506-453-5317
Department of Education, Place 2000, 250 King St., PO Box 6000, Fredericton, NB E3B 5H1
506-453-3678, Fax: 506-453-3325, edcommunication@gnb.ca
Department of Post-Secondary Education, Training & Labour, Chestnut Complex, 470 York St., PO Box 6000, Fredericton, NB E3B 5H1
506-453-2597, Fax: 506-453-3618, dpetlinfo@gnb.ca

Newfoundland & Labrador
Department of Education, West Block, Confederation Bldg., 100 Prince Philip Dr., 3rd Fl., PO Box 8700, St. John's, NL A1B 4J6
709-729-5097, Fax: 709-729-5896, education@gov.nl.ca

Northwest Territories
Aurora Research Institute, 191 MacKenzie Rd., PO Box 1450, Inuvik, NT X0E 0T0
867-777-3298, Fax: 867-777-4264, webmaster@nwtresearch.com
Department of Education, Culture & Employment, PO Box 1320, Yellowknife, NT X1A 2L9
867-669-2399, Fax: 867-873-0431, 866-606-5627

Nova Scotia
Council of Atlantic Ministers of Education & Training, PO Box 2044, Halifax, NS B3J 2Z1
902-424-5352, Fax: 902-424-8976, camet_camef@cap-cpma.ca
Department of Education, Trade Mart Bldg., #402-2021 Brunswick St., PO Box 578, Halifax, NS B3J 2S9
902-424-5168, Fax: 902-424-0680
Nova Scotia Apprenticeship Board, 2021 Brunswick St., PO Box 578, Halifax, NS B3J 2S9
902-424-0872, Fax: 902-424-0488, 800-494-5651, bedgoomm@gov.ns.ca

Nunavut
Department of Education, Sivummut Bldg., 2nd Fl., PO Box 1000 910,Iqaluit, NU X0A 0H0
867-975-5600, Fax: 867-975-5605

Ontario
Academic & Experience Requirements Committee of the Association of Ontario Land Surveyors, 1043 McNicoll Ave., Toronto, ON M1W 3W6
416-491-9020, Fax: 416-491-2576
College of Veterinarians of Ontario, 2106 Gordon St., Guelph, ON N1L 1G6
519-824-5600, Fax: 519-824-6497, 800-424-2856, inquiries@cvo.org
Ministry of Education, Mowat Block, 900 Bay St., 22nd. Fl., Toronto, ON M7A 1L2
416-325-2929, Fax: 416-325-2934, 800-387-5514, info@edu.gov.on.ca
Elementary/Secondary Business & Finance Division, Mowat Block, 900 Bay St., 20th fl., Toronto, ON M7A 1L2
416-325-6127, Fax: 416-325-9560

Learning & Curriculum Division, Mowat Block, 900 Bay st., 22nd fl., Toronto, ON M7A 1L2
416-325-2135, Fax: 416-327-1182

Ontario Graduate Scholarship Program Selection Board, 189 Red River Rd., 4th Fl., PO Box 4500, Thunder Bay, ON P7B 6G9
807-343-7257, Fax: 807-343-7278, 800-465-3957

Ontario Student Assistance Appeal Board, Mowat Block, 900 Bay St., 7th Fl., Toronto, ON M7A 1L2
416-314-0714, Fax: 416-325-3096

Post-secondary Education Quality Assessment Board, #1511, 2 Carlton St., Toronto, ON M5B 1J3
416-212-1230, Fax: 416-212-6620

Ministry of Training, Colleges & Universities, Mowat Block, 900 Bay St., 14th Fl., Toronto, ON M7A 1L2
416-325-2929, Fax: 416-325-6348, 800-387-5514, information.met@ontario.ca

Prince Edward Island

Prince Edward Island Athletic Association, #101, 250 Water St., Summerside, PE C1N 1B6
902-438-4846, Fax: 902-438-4884

Prince Edward Island Department of Education & Early Childhood Development, Holman Centre, #101, 250 Water St., Summerside, PE C1N 1B6
902-438-4130, Fax: 902-438-4062

Quebec

Comité-conseil sur les programmes d'études, 1035, de la Chevrotière, 17e étage, Québec, QC G1R 5A5
418-646-0133, Fax: 418-643-0056, ccpe@mels.gouv.qc.ca

Commission consultative de l'enseignement privé, 1035, rue de la Chevrotière, 14e étage, Québec, QC G1R 5A5
418-646-1249, Fax: 418-643-7752, commission.consultative@mels.gouv.qc.ca

Commission d'évaluation de l'enseignement collégial, 800, place d'Youville, 18e étage, Québec, QC G1R 5P4
418-643-9938, Fax: 418-643-9019, info@ceec.gouv.qc.ca

Commission de l'éducation en langue anglaise, 600, rue Fullum, 9e étage, Montréal, QC H2K 4L1
514-873-5656, Fax: 514-864-4181, cela-abee@mels.gouv.qc.ca

Conseil supérieur de l'éducation, #180, 1175, av Lavigerie, Québec, QC G1V 5B2
418-643-3850, Fax: 418-644-2530, panorama@cse.gouv.qc.ca

Ministère de l'Éducation, du Loisir et du Sport, 1035, rue De La Chevrotière, 28e étage, Québec, QC G1R 5A5
418-643-7095, Fax: 418-646-6561, 866-747-6626

Saskatchewan

Saskatchewan Advanced Education, Employment & Immigration, 1945 Hamilton St., Regina, SK S4P 2C8
306-787-9478, aeeinquiry@gov.sk.ca

Saskatchewan Education, 2220 College Ave., Regina, SK S4P 4V9
linquiry@gov.sk.ca

Saskatchewan Research Council, #125, 15 Innovation Blvd., Saskatoon, SK S7N 2X8
306-933-5400, Fax: 306-933-7446, info@src.sk.ca

Yukon Territory

Yukon Education, PO Box 2703, Whitehorse, YT Y1A 2C6
867-667-5141, Fax: 867-393-6254, contact.education@gov.yk.ca

EDUCATION & TRAINING

Human Resources & Skills Development Canada, 140 Promenade du Portage, Gatineau, QC K1A 0J9

Department of Labour & Advanced Education, 5151 Terminal Rd., 6th Fl., PO Box 697, Halifax, NS B3J 2T8
902-424-5301, Fax: 902-424-0575

Alberta

Alberta Employment & Immigration, Minister's Office, Legislature Building, #418, 10800 - 97 Ave., Edmonton, AB T5K 2B6
780-644-5135, 866-644-5135, eii.communications@gov.ab.ca

British Columbia

Ministry of Labour, Citizens' Services & Open Government, PO Box 9056 Prov Govt,Victoria, BC V8W 9K4
250-952-7623, Fax: 250-387-4312, 800-663-7867, LCTZ.Minister@gov.bc.ca

Private Career Training Institutions Agency, #300, 5172 Kingsway, Burnaby, BC V5H 2E8
604-660-4400, Fax: 604-660-3312, 800-661-7441, info@pctia.bc.ca

New Brunswick

Department of Post-Secondary Education, Training & Labour, Chestnut Complex, 470 York St., PO Box 6000, Fredericton, NB E3B 5H1
506-453-2597, Fax: 506-453-3618, dpetlinfo@gnb.ca

Northwest Territories

Department of Education, Culture & Employment, PO Box 1320, Yellowknife, NT X1A 2L9
867-669-2399, Fax: 867-873-0431, 866-606-5627

Ontario

Ministry of Labour, 400 University Ave., 14th Fl., Toronto, ON M7A 1T7
416-326-7160, 800-531-5551

Saskatchewan

Saskatchewan Advanced Education, Employment & Immigration, 1945 Hamilton St., Regina, SK S4P 2C8
306-787-9478, aeeinquiry@gov.sk.ca

ELECTED OFFICIALS & CONSTITUENCIES

41st Parliament - Canada, House of Commons, Parliament Buildings, Ottawa, ON K1A 0A6

Alberta

Twenty-seventh Legislature - Alberta, Legislature Bldg., 10800 - 97 Ave., Edmonton, AB T5K 2B6
780-427-2826, laocommunications@assembly.ab.ca

British Columbia

Thirty-Ninth Legislature - British Columbia, Parliament Bldgs., Victoria, BC V8V 1X4
250-387-3785, Fax: 250-387-0942, ClerkHouse@leg.bc.ca

Manitoba

Fortieth Legislature - Manitoba, Legislative Building, 450 Broadway Ave., Winnipeg, MB R3C 0V8
204-945-3636, Fax: 204-948-2507, clerkla@leg.gov.mb.ca

New Brunswick

Fifty-seventh Legislature - New Brunswick, Legislative Assembly of New Brunswick, 706 Queen St., PO Box 6000, Fredericton, NB E3B 5H1
506-453-2506, Fax: 506-453-7154

Newfoundland & Labrador

Forty-seventh House of Assembly - Newfoundland & Labrador, PO Box 8700, St. John's, NL A1B 4J6
709-729-3405, ClerkHOA@gov.nl.ca

Northwest Territories

Seventeenth Legislature - Northwest Territories, PO Box 1320, Yellowknife, NT X1A 2L9
867-669-2200, Fax: 867-920-4735, 800-661-0784

Nova Scotia

Sixty-first Assembly - Nova Scotia, Province House, PO Box 1617, Halifax, NS B3J 2Y3
902-424-5978, Fax: 902-424-0632

Nunavut

Second Legislature - Nunavut, PO Box 1200, Iqaluit, NU X0A 0H0

Ontario

Fortieth Parliament - Ontario, Clerk's Office, Legislative Bldg., Queen's Park, Toronto, ON M7A 1A2
416-325-7500, Fax: 416-325-7489

Prince Edward Island

Sixty-fourth General Assembly - Prince Edward Island, Province House, 165 Richmond St., 1st Fl., PO Box 2000, Charlottetown, PE C1A 7N8
902-368-5970, Fax: 902-368-5175, 877-315-5518

Quebec

Trente-neuvième assemblée nationale, Hôtel du Parlement, 1045, rue des Parlementaires, Québec, QC G1A 1A4
418-643-7239, Fax: 418-646-4271, 866-337-8837

Saskatchewan

Twenty-sixth Legislature - Saskatchewan, #123, Legislative Bldg., 2405 Legislative Dr., Regina, SK S4S 0B3
306-787-2376, Fax: 306-787-1558, info@legassembly.sk.ca

Yukon Territory

Thirty-third Legislative Assembly - Yukon Territory, Yukon Legislative Assembly Office, 2071 Second Ave., PO Box 2703, Whitehorse, YT Y1A 2C6
867-667-5498

ELECTIONS

Elections Canada, The Jackson Bldg., 257 Slater St., Ottawa, ON K1A 0M6
613-993-2975, Fax: 613-954-8584, 800-463-6868

Alberta

Alberta Office of the Chief Electoral Officer / Elections Alberta, 11510 Kingsway Ave., 1st Fl., Edmonton, AB T5G 2Y5
780-427-7191, Fax: 780-422-2900, info@electionsalberta.ab.ca

British Columbia

Elections British Columbia, PO Box 9275 Prov Govt,Victoria, BC V8W 9J6
250-387-5305, Fax: 250-387-3578, 800-661-8683, electionsbc@elections.bc.ca

Manitoba

Elections Manitoba, #120, 200 Vaughan St., Winnipeg, MB R3C 1T5
204-945-3225, Fax: 204-945-6011, 866-628-6837, election@elections.mb.ca

New Brunswick

Office of the Chief Electoral Officer, PO Box 6000, Fredericton, NB E3B 5H1
506-453-2218, Fax: 506-457-4926, 800-308-2922,

Newfoundland & Labrador

Office of the Chief Electoral Officer, 39 Hallett Cr., St. John's, NL A1B 4C4
709-729-0712, Fax: 709-729-0679, 877-729-7987, enl@gov.nl.ca

Northwest Territories

Elections NWT/Plebiscite Office, YK Centre East, #7, 4915-48th St., 3rd Fl., Yellowknife, NT X1A 3S4
867-920-6999, Fax: 867-873-0366, 800-661-0796, electionsnwt@gov.nt.ca

Nova Scotia

Elections Nova Scotia, #6-7037 Mumford Rd., PO Box 2246, Halifax, NS B3J 2J1
902-424-8584, Fax: 902-424-6622, 800-565-1504, elections@gov.ns.ca

Nunavut

Legislative Assembly, 926 Federal Rd., PO Box 1200, Iqaluit, NU X0A 0H0
867-975-5000, Fax: 867-975-5190, 877-334-7266, leginfo@assembly.nu.ca

Ontario

Elections Ontario, 51 Rolark Dr., Toronto, ON M1R 3B1
416-326-6300, Fax: 416-326-6200, 888-668-8683, info@elections.on.ca

Prince Edward Island

Elections Prince Edward Island, J. Angus MacLean Bldg., 94 Great George St., 1st Fl., PO Box 774, Charlottetown, PE C1A 7L3
902-368-5895, Fax: 902-368-6500, 888-234-8783

Quebec

Directeur général des Élections du Québec, Édifice René-Lévesque, 3460, rue de La Pérade, Québec, QC G1X 3Y5
418-528-0422, Fax: 418-643-7291, 888-353-2846, info@electionsquebec.qc.ca

Saskatchewan

Elections Saskatchewan, 1702 Park St., Regina, SK S4N 6B2
306-787-4000, Fax: 306-787-4052, 877-958-8683, info@elections.sk.ca

EMERGENCY MEASURES

Environment Canada, 10 Wellington St., Gatineau, QC K1A 0H3
819-997-2800, Fax: 819-994-1412, 800-668-6767, enviroinfo@ec.gc.ca

National Search & Rescue Secretariat, #400, 275 Slater St., Ottawa, ON K1A 0K2
613-992-0054, Fax: 613-996-3746, 800-727-9414, inquiry@nss.gc.ca

Public Safety Canada, 269 Laurier Ave. West, Ottawa, ON K1A 0P8
613-944-4875, Fax: 613-954-5186, 800-830-3118, communications@ps.gc.ca

Alberta

Alberta Environment, South Tower, Petroleum Plaza, 9915 - 108 St., 10th Fl., Edmonton, AB T5K 2G8
780-427-2700, Fax: 780-422-4086, env.infocent@gov.ab.ca

British Columbia

British Columbia Provincial Emergency Program, Block A, #200, 2261 Keating Cross Rd., Saanichton, BC V8M 2A5
250-952-4913, Fax: 250-952-4888, 888-257-4777

Manitoba

Emergency Measures Organization, 405 Broadway Ave., 15th Floor, Winnipeg, MB R3C 3L6
204-945-4772, Fax: 204-945-4929, 888-267-8298, emo@gov.mb.ca

New Brunswick

New Brunswick Emergency Measures Organization, Victoria Health Centre, 65 Brunswick Ave., Fredericton, NB E3B 1G5
506-453-2133, Fax: 506-453-5513, 800-561-4034, emo@gnb.ca

Newfoundland & Labrador

Newfoundland & Labrador Fire & Emergency Services, 25 Hallett Cres., PO Box 8700, St. John's, NL A1B 4J6
709-729-3703, Fax: 709-729-3757

Nova Scotia

Nova Scotia Emergency Management Office, PO Box 2581, Halifax, NS B3J 3N5
902-424-5620, Fax: 902-424-5376, 866-424-5620, emo@gov.ns.ca

Nunavut

Nunavut Emergency Management, PO Box 1000 700,Iqaluit, NU X0A 0H0
867-975-5403, Fax: 867-979-4221, 800-693-1666

Ontario
Emergency Management Ontario, 77 Wellesley St. W, PO Box 222, Toronto, ON M7A 1N3
416-314-3723, Fax: 416-314-3758

Saskatchewan
Emergency Management & Fire Safety, #100, 1855 Victoria Ave., Regina, SK S4P 3T2
306-787-8568, Fax: 306-787-1694

Yukon Territory
Emergency Measures Organization, PO Box 2703, Whitehorse, YT Y1A 2C6
867-667-5220, Fax: 867-393-6266, 800-661-0408, emo.yukon@gov.yk.ca

EMPLOYMENT

Alberta
Alberta Employment & Immigration, Minister's Office, Legislature Building, #418, 10800 - 97 Ave., Edmonton, AB T5K 2B6
780-644-5135, 866-644-5135, eii.communications@gov.ab.ca

Manitoba
Manitoba Labour & Immigration, Legislative Building, 317, 450 Broadway Ave., Winnipeg, MB R3C 0V8
204-945-4079, Fax: 204-945-8312, minlab@leg.gov.mb.ca

New Brunswick
Office of Human Resources, Centennial Bldg, #345, 670 King St., PO Box 6000, Fredericton, NB E3B 5H1
506-453-2264, Fax: 506-453-7195

Newfoundland & Labrador
Department of Human Resources, Labour & Employment, Confederation Bldg., PO Box 8700, St. John's, NL A1B 4J6
709-729-2480, Fax: 709-729-6996, hreweb@gov.nl.ca

Northwest Territories
Department of Human Resources, PO Box 1320, Yellowknife, NT X1A 2L9
867-920-3409, Fax: 867-873-0306, 866-475-8162

Nunavut
Department of Human Resources, PO Box 1000 400,Iqaluit, NU X0A 1H0
Fax: 867-975-6216, 888-668-9993, gnhr@gov.nu.ca

Quebec
Ministère de l'Emploi et de la Solidarité sociale, 425, rue St-Amable, 4e étage, Québec, QC G1R 4Z1
418-643-4721, 888-643-4721
Emploi-Québec, 425, rue St-Amable, #RC 175, Québec, QC G1R 4Z1
418-643-4721, 888-643-4721
Ministère du Travail, 200, ch Sainte-Foy, 5e étage, Québec, QC G1R 5S1
418-644-4545, Fax: 418-528-0559, 800-643-4817,

Saskatchewan
Saskatchewan Advanced Education, Employment & Immigration, 1945 Hamilton St., Regina, SK S4P 2C8
306-787-9478, aeeinquiry@gov.sk.ca

EMPLOYMENT INSURANCE

Canada Employment Insurance Commission, 140, Promenade du Portage, Phase IV, Gatineau, QC K1A 0J9
800-206-7218

Saskatchewan
Saskatchewan Labour Relations & Workplace Safety, #300, 1870 Albert St., Regina, SK S4P 4W1
306-787-7404, webmaster@lab.gov.sk.ca

ENERGY

See Also: Natural Resources
Canadian Nuclear Safety Commission, 280 Slater St., PO Box 1046 B,Ottawa, ON K1P 5S9
613-995-5894, Fax: 613-995-5086, 800-668-5284
Indian Oil & Gas Canada, #100, 9911 Chiila Blvd., Tsuu T'ina (Sarcee), AB T2W 6H6
403-292-5625, Fax: 403-292-5618, ContactIOGC@inac-ainc.gc.ca
Lands, Minerals & Petroleum Division, Hugh John Flemming Forestry Centre, PO Box 6000, Fredericton, NB E3B 5H1
506-453-2684, Fax: 506-453-2930, dnrweb@gnb.ca
National Energy Board, 444 - 7 Ave. SW, Calgary, AB T2P 0X8
403-292-4800, Fax: 403-292-5503, 800-899-1265, info@neb-one.gc.ca

Alberta
Energy Resources Conservation Board, #1000, 250 - 5 Ave. SW, Calgary, AB T2P 0R4
403-297-8311, Fax: 403-297-7336, 855-297-8311, inquiries@ercb.ca; infoservices@ercb.ca; ADR@ercb.ca
Alberta Energy, North Petroleum Plaza, 9945 - 108 St., Edmonton, AB T5K 2G6
780-427-8050, Fax: 780-422-0698, Library.Energy@gov.ab.ca

British Columbia
Ministry of Energy & Mines, PO Box 9053 Prov Govt,Victoria, BC V8W 9E2
250-387-5896, Fax: 250-356-2965
British Columbia Hydro, 333 Dunsmuir St., Vancouver, BC V6B 5R3
604-224-9376, 800-224-9376
Oil & Gas Commission, #100, 10003 - 110 Ave., Fort St John, BC V1J 6M7
250-794-5200, Fax: 250-794-5375
Powerex Corp., #1400, 666 Burrard St., Vancouver, BC V6C 2X8
604-891-5000, Fax: 604-891-6060, 800-220-4907, Brian.Moghadam@powerex.com
Powertech Labs Inc., 12388 - 88 Ave., Surrey, BC V8W 7R7
604-590-7500, Fax: 604-590-6611
British Columbia Utilities Commission, 900 Howe St., 6th Fl., PO Box 250, Vancouver, BC V6Z 2N3
604-660-4700, Fax: 604-660-1102, 800-663-1385, commission.secretary@bcuc.com

Manitoba
Manitoba Hydro, PO Box 815 Main,Winnipeg, MB R3C 2P4
204-474-3311, Fax: 204-475-0069, publicaffairs@hydro.mb.ca
Petroleum, #360, 1395 Ellice Ave., Winnipeg, MB R3G 3P2
204-945-6577, Fax: 204-945-0586
Manitoba Science, Technology, Energy & Mines, #333, 450 Broadway, Winnipeg, MB R3C 0V8

New Brunswick
Department of Energy, Brunswick Square, #100M, 1 Germain St., Saint John, NB E2L 4V1
506-658-3180, Fax: 506-658-3191, DOEweb@gnb.ca
Department of Natural Resources, Hugh John Flemming Forestry Centre, PO Box 6000, Fredericton, NB E3B 5H1
506-453-3826, Fax: 506-444-4367, dnrweb@gnb.ca
Efficiency NB, #101, 33 Charlotte St., Saint John, NB E2L 2H3
506-643-7826, Fax: 506-643-7835, 866-643-8833
New Brunswick Power Group of Companies, 515 King St., PO Box 2000, Fredericton, NB E3B 4X1
506-458-4444, Fax: 506-458-4000, questions@nbpower.com

Newfoundland & Labrador
Canada-Newfoundland Offshore Petroleum Board, TD Place, 140 Water St., 5th Fl., St. John's, NL A1C 6H6
709-778-1400, Fax: 709-778-1473, information@cnlopb.nl.ca
Churchill Falls (Labrador) Corporation Limited, Hydro Place, 500 Columbus Dr., PO Box 12500, St. John's, NL A1B 4K7
709-737-1859, Fax: 709-737-1816
Newfoundland & Labrador Hydro, Hydro Place, Columbus Dr., PO Box 12400, St. John's, NL A1B 4K7
709-737-1400, Fax: 709-737-1800, hydro@nlh.nl.ca
Newfoundland & Labrador Board of Commissioners of Public Utilities, PO Box 21040, St. John's, NL A1A 5B2
709-726-8600, Fax: 709-726-9604, 866-782-0006, ito@pub.nf.ca
Twin Falls Power Corporation, PO Box 12500, St. John's, NL A1B 3T5

Northwest Territories
Department of Environment & Natural Resources, PO Box 1320, Yellowknife, NT X1A 2L9
Northwest Territories Power Corporation, 4 Capital Dr., Hay River, NT X0E 1G2
867-874-5200, Fax: 867-874-5251, info@ntpc.com

Nova Scotia
Canada-Nova Scotia Offshore Petroleum Board, TD Centre, 1791 Barrington St., 6th Fl., Halifax, NS B3J 3K9
902-422-5588, Fax: 902-422-1799, postmaster@cnsopb.ns.ca
Department of Energy, Bank of Montreal Bldg., #400, 5151 George St., PO Box 2664, Halifax, NS B3J 3P7
902-424-4575, Fax: 902-424-0528, energyinfo@gov.ns.ca
Nova Scotia Utility & Review Board, Summit Place, 1601 Lower Water St., 3rd Fl., PO Box 1692 M,Halifax, NS B3J 3S3
902-424-4448, Fax: 902-424-3919, uarb.board@gov.ns.ca

Ontario
Ministry of Energy, Hearst Block, 900 Bay St., 4th Fl., Toronto, ON M7A 2E1
416-327-6758, Fax: 416-325-8440, 888-668-4636, write2us@ontario.ca
Ministry of Environment, 135 St. Clair Ave. West, Toronto, ON M4V 1P5
416-325-4000, Fax: 416-325-3159, 800-565-4923
Hydro One Inc., North Tower, 483 Bay St., Toronto, ON M5G 2P5
416-345-5000, 877-955-1155, customercommunications@HydroOne.com
Independent Electricity System Operator, PO Box 4474 A,Toronto, ON M5W 4E5
905-403-6900, Fax: 905-403-6921, 888-448-7777, customer.relations@ieso.ca
Ontario Energy Board, #2700, 2300 Yonge St., Toronto, ON M4P 1E4
416-481-1967, Fax: 416-440-7656, 888-632-6273
Ontario Power Authority, #1600, 120 Adelaide St. West, Toronto, ON M5H 1T1
416-967-7474, Fax: 416-967-1947, 800-797-9604, info@powerauthority.on.ca
Ontario Power Generation, 700 University Ave., Toronto, ON M5G 1X6
416-592-2555, 877-592-2555, webmaster@opg.com

Prince Edward Island
Prince Edward Island Department of Environment, Energy, & Forestry, Jones Bldg., 11 Kent St., 4th Fl., PO Box 2000, Charlottetown, PE C1A 7N8
902-368-5000, Fax: 902-368-5830
Prince Edward Island Energy Corporation, Jones Bldg., 11 Kent St., 4th Fl., PO Box 2000, Charlottetown, PE C1A 7N8

Quebec
Agence de l'efficacité énergétique, 5700, 4e av ouest, Québec, QC G1H 6R1
418-627-6379, Fax: 418-643-5828, 877-727-6655, efficaciteenergetique@mrnf.gouv.qc.ca
Hydro-Québec, 75, boul René-Lévesque ouest, Montréal, QC H2Z 1A4
514-289-2211
Régie de l'énergie, Tour de la Bourse, #2.55, 800, Place Victoria, Montréal, QC H4Z 1A2
514-873-2452, Fax: 514-873-2070, 888-873-2452, secretariat@regie-energie.qc.ca
Société d'énergie de la Baie-James, 888, de Maisonneuve est, 6e étage, Montréal, QC H2L 5B2
514-286-2020

Saskatchewan
Saskatchewan Energy & Resources, #300, 2103 - 11th Ave., Regina, SK S4P 3Z8
306-787-2528, webmasterer@gov.sk.ca
Saskatchewan Power Corporation (SaskPower), 2025 Victoria Ave., Regina, SK S4P 0S1
306-566-3306, Fax: 800-757-6937, 888-757-6937
SaskEnergy Incorporated, 1777 Victoria Ave., Regina, SK S4P 4K5
306-777-9225, 800-567-8899

Yukon Territory
Yukon Energy, Mines & Resources, PO Box 2703, Whitehorse, YT Y1A 2C6
867-667-3130, Fax: 867-456-3965, 800-661-0408, emr@gov.yk.ca

ENGINEERING & CONSULTING

Canadian Environmental Assessment Agency, Place Bell Canada, 160 Elgin St., 22nd Fl., Ottawa, ON K1A 0H3
613-957-0700, Fax: 613-957-0862, 866-582-1884, info@ceaa-acee.gc.ca
Defence Construction Canada, Constitution Square, 350 Albert St., 19th Fl., Ottawa, ON K1A 0K3
613-998-9548, Fax: 613-998-1061, 800-514-3555, info@dcc-cdc.gc.ca
Natural Sciences & Engineering Research Council of Canada, Constitution Square, Tower II, 350 Albert St., Ottawa, ON K1A 1H5
613-995-4273, Fax: 613-943-1624, marie-josee.duval@nserc-crsng.gc.ca

British Columbia
Transportation Policy & Programs Department, PO Box 9850 Prov Govt,Victoria, BC V8W 9T5
250-387-5062, Fax: 250-387-6431

Manitoba
Manitoba Infrastructure & Transportation, Legislative Building, #203, 450 Broadway Ave., Winnipeg, MB R3C 0V8
204-945-3723, Fax: 204-945-7610

Northwest Territories
Highways & Marine, 4510 - 50 Ave., 2nd fl., PO Box 1320, Yellowknife, NT X1A 2L9
867-920-8771, Fax: 867-873-0288

Saskatchewan
Saskatchewan Highways & Infrastructure, Victoria Tower, 1855 Victoria Ave., Regina, SK S4P 3T2
306-787-4800, communications@highways.gov.sk.ca

ENVIRONMENT

Environment Canada, 10 Wellington St., Gatineau, QC K1A 0H3
819-997-2800, Fax: 819-994-1412, 800-668-6767, enviroinfo@ec.gc.ca
National Round Table on the Environment & Economy, #200, 344 Slater St., Ottawa, ON K1R 7Y3
613-992-7189, Fax: 613-992-7385, admin@nrtee-trnee.ca

Alberta
Alberta Environment, South Tower, Petroleum Plaza, 9915 - 108 St., 10th Fl., Edmonton, AB T5K 2G8
780-427-2700, Fax: 780-422-4086, env.infocent@gov.ab.ca

Alberta Sustainable Resource Development, Information Centre, Great West Life Building, 9920 - 108 St., Main Fl., Edmonton, AB T5K 2M4
780-944-0313, Fax: 780-427-4407, 877-944-0313, srd.infocent@gov.ab.ca

British Columbia

British Columbia Environmental Assessment Office, 836 Yates St., 1st Fl., PO Box 9426 Prov Govt,Victoria, BC V8W 9V1
250-356-7479, Fax: 250-356-6448, eaoinfo@gov.bc.ca

Ministry of Environment, PO Box 9339 Prov Govt,Victoria, BC V8W 9M1
250-387-1161, Fax: 250-387-5669, envmail@gov.bc.ca

Manitoba

Manitoba Conservation, 200 Saulteaux Cres., Winnipeg, MB R3J 3W3
204-945-6784, 800-214-6497, mincon@leg.gov.mb.ca

Manitoba Water Stewardship, 200 Saulteaux Cres., PO Box 11, Winnipeg, MB R3J 3W3
204-945-6398, 800-282-8069, wsd@gov.mb.ca

New Brunswick

Department of the Environment, Marysville Place, 20 McGloin St., PO Box 6000, Fredericton, NB E3B 5H1
506-453-2690, Fax: 506-457-7800, env-info@gnb.ca

Newfoundland & Labrador

Department of Environment & Conservation, Confederation Bldg., West Block, 4th Fl., PO Box 8700, St. John's, NL A1B 4J6
709-729-2664, Fax: 709-729-6639, 800-563-6181, info@gov.nl.ca

Northwest Territories

Department of Environment & Natural Resources, PO Box 1320, Yellowknife, NT X1A 2L9

Nova Scotia

Department of Environment, 5151 Terminal Rd., 5th Fl., PO Box 442, Halifax, NS B3J 2P8
902-424-3600, Fax: 902-424-0503, 877-936-8476

Nunavut

Department of Environment, PO Box 1000 1300,Iqaluit, NU X0A 0H0
867-975-7700, Fax: 867-975-7742, environment@gov.nu.ca

Ontario

Ministry of Environment, 135 St. Clair Ave. West, Toronto, ON M4V 1P5
416-325-4000, Fax: 416-325-3159, 800-565-4923

Environmental Commissioner of Ontario, #605, 1075 Bay St., Toronto, ON M5S 2B1
416-325-3377, Fax: 416-325-3370, 800-701-6454, commissioner@eco.on.ca

Prince Edward Island

Prince Edward Island Department of Environment, Energy, & Forestry, Jones Bldg., 11 Kent St., 4th Fl., PO Box 2000, Charlottetown, PE C1A 7N8
902-368-5000, Fax: 902-368-5830

Quebec

Bureau d'audiences publiques sur l'environnement, Édifice Lomer-Gouin, #2.10, 575, rue Saint-Amable, Québec, QC G1R 6A6
418-643-7447, Fax: 418-643-9474, 800-463-4732, communication@bape.gouv.qc.ca

Ministère du Développement durable, de l'Environnement et des Parcs, Édifice Marie-Guyart, 675, boul René-Lévesque est, 29e étage, Québec, QC G1R 5V7
418-521-3830, Fax: 418-646-5974, 800-561-1616, info@mddep.gouv.qc.ca

Saskatchewan

Saskatchewan Environment, 3211 Albert St., 2nd Fl., Regina, SK S4S 5W6
306-787-2584, Fax: 306-787-9544, 800-567-4224, Centre.Inquiry@gov.sk.ca

ENVIRONMENT DEPARTMENTS/MINISTRIES

Environment Canada, 10 Wellington St., Gatineau, QC K1A 0H3
819-997-2800, Fax: 819-994-1412, 800-668-6767, enviroinfo@ec.gc.ca

Alberta

Alberta Environment, South Tower, Petroleum Plaza, 9915 - 108 St., 10th Fl., Edmonton, AB T5K 2G8
780-427-2700, Fax: 780-422-4086, env.infocent@gov.ab.ca

British Columbia

Ministry of Environment, PO Box 9339 Prov Govt,Victoria, BC V8W 9M1
250-387-1161, Fax: 250-387-5669, envmail@gov.bc.ca

Manitoba

Manitoba Conservation, 200 Saulteaux Cres., Winnipeg, MB R3J 3W3
204-945-6784, 800-214-6497, mincon@leg.gov.mb.ca

New Brunswick

Department of the Environment, Marysville Place, 20 McGloin St., PO Box 6000, Fredericton, NB E3B 5H1
506-453-2690, Fax: 506-457-7800, env-info@gnb.ca

Newfoundland & Labrador

Department of Environment & Conservation, Confederation Bldg., West Block, 4th Fl., PO Box 8700, St. John's, NL A1B 4J6
709-729-2664, Fax: 709-729-6639, 800-563-6181, info@gov.nl.ca

Northwest Territories

Department of Environment & Natural Resources, PO Box 1320, Yellowknife, NT X1A 2L9

Nova Scotia

Department of Environment, 5151 Terminal Rd., 5th Fl., PO Box 442, Halifax, NS B3J 2P8
902-424-3600, Fax: 902-424-0503, 877-936-8476

Nunavut

Department of Environment, PO Box 1000 1300,Iqaluit, NU X0A 0H0
867-975-7700, Fax: 867-975-7742, environment@gov.nu.ca

Ontario

Ministry of Environment, 135 St. Clair Ave. West, Toronto, ON M4V 1P5
416-325-4000, Fax: 416-325-3159, 800-565-4923

Prince Edward Island

Prince Edward Island Department of Environment, Energy, & Forestry, Jones Bldg., 11 Kent St., 4th Fl., PO Box 2000, Charlottetown, PE C1A 7N8
902-368-5000, Fax: 902-368-5830

Quebec

Ministère du Développement durable, de l'Environnement et des Parcs, Édifice Marie-Guyart, 675, boul René-Lévesque est, 29e étage, Québec, QC G1R 5V7
418-521-3830, Fax: 418-646-5974, 800-561-1616, info@mddep.gouv.qc.ca

Saskatchewan

Saskatchewan Environment, 3211 Albert St., 2nd Fl., Regina, SK S4S 5W6
306-787-2584, Fax: 306-787-9544, 800-567-4224, Centre.Inquiry@gov.sk.ca

Yukon Territory

Yukon Environment, PO Box 2703, Whitehorse, YT Y1A 2C6
867-667-5652, Fax: 867-393-7197, environment.yukon@gov.yk.ca

ENVIRONMENTAL ASSESSMENT

Canadian Environmental Assessment Agency, Place Bell Canada, 160 Elgin St., 22nd Fl., Ottawa, ON K1A 0H3
613-957-0700, Fax: 613-957-0862, 866-582-1884, info@ceaa-acee.gc.ca

Land & Environment Division, Jones Bldg., 11 Kent St., 3rd Fl., PO Box 2000, Charlottetown, PE C1A 7N8
902-368-5221, Fax: 902-368-5395

British Columbia

British Columbia Environmental Assessment Office, 836 Yates St., 1st Fl., PO Box 9426 Prov Govt,Victoria, BC V8W 9V1
250-356-7479, Fax: 250-356-6448, eaoinfo@gov.bc.ca

New Brunswick

Environmental Management, Marysville Place, 20 McGloin St., PO Box 6000, Fredericton, NB E3B 5H1
506-444-5119, Fax: 506-457-7333, env-info@gnb.ca

EROSION CONTROL

Prince Edward Island

Agriculture Policy & Regulatory Division, Jones Bldg., 11 Kent St., 5th Fl., Charlottetown, PE C1A 7N8

Research Branch, Tower 5, 1341 Baseline Rd., Ottawa, ON K1A 0C5
613-759-1000, Fax: 613-773-1866

Quebec

Commission de protection du territoire agricole du Québec, 200, ch Ste-Foy, 2e étage, Québec, QC G1R 4X6
418-643-3314, Fax: 418-643-2261, 800-667-5294, info@cptaq.gouv.qc.ca

Saskatchewan

Saskatchewan Agriculture, Walter Scott Bldg., 3085 Albert St., Regina, SK S4S 0B1
866-457-2377, aginfo@gov.sk.ca

EXPORT DEVELOPMENT

Business Development Bank of Canada, #400, 5, Place Ville-Marie, Montréal, QC H3B 5E7
514-283-5904, Fax: 514-283-5626, 877-232-2269

Export Development Canada, 151 Slater St., Ottawa, ON K1A 1K3
613-598-2500, Fax: 613-598-3811, 800-267-8510

Global Operations, 125 Sussex Dr,, Ottawa, ON K1A 0G2
613-944-2697, Fax: 613-996-1667

Industry Canada, C.D. Howe Building, 235 Queen St., Ottawa, ON K1A 0H5
613-954-5031, Fax: 613-954-2340, 800-328-6189, info@ic.gc.ca

Western Economic Diversification Canada, Canada Place, #1500, 9700 Jasper Ave. NW, Edmonton, AB T5J 4H7
780-495-4164, Fax: 780-495-4557, 888-338-9378

New Brunswick

Northern Development, Harbourview Place, 275 Main St., Bathurst, NB E2A 1A9
506-547-2227, Fax: 506-547-2269

Ontario

Ministry of Economic Development & Innovation, Hearst Block, 900 Bay St., 8th Fl., Toronto, ON M7A 2E1
416-325-6666, Fax: 416-325-6688, 866-668-4249, info@edt.gov.on.ca

Saskatchewan

Saskatchewan Energy & Resources, #300, 2103 - 11th Ave., Regina, SK S4P 3Z8
306-787-2528, webmasterer@gov.sk.ca

Saskatchewan Trade & Export Partnership, #320, 1801 Hamilton St., PO Box 1787, Regina, SK S4P 3C6
306-787-9210, Fax: 306-787-6666, inquire@sasktrade.sk.ca

EXPROPRIATION

Canada Lands Company Ltd., #1200, 1 University Ave., Toronto, ON M5J 2P1
416-952-6111, Fax: 416-952-6115, 888-252-5263

Justice Canada, East Memorial Bldg., 284 Wellington St., Ottawa, ON K1A 0H8
613-957-4222, Fax: 613-954-0811, webadmin@justice.gc.ca

National Defence Canada, Major-General George R. Pearkes Bldg., 101 Colonel By Dr., Ottawa, ON K1A 0K2
613-995-2534, Fax: 613-992-4739, 800-856-8488

Alberta

Land Compensation Board, 1229 - 91 St. SW, Edmonton, AB T6X 1E9
srb.lcb@gov.ab.ca

Manitoba

Manitoba Land Value Appraisal Commission, 800 Portage Ave., Winnipeg, MB R3G 0N4
204-945-2941, Fax: 204-948-2235

New Brunswick

New Brunswick Expropriations Advisory Office, Phoenix Square Bldg., 371 Queen St., Fredericton, NB E3B 1B1
506-453-7771, Fax: 506-453-9600

Quebec

Ministère de la Justice, Édifice Louis-Philippe-Pigeon, 1200, rte de l'Église, Québec, QC G1V 4M1
418-643-5140, 866-536-5140, informations@justice.gouv.qc.ca

Ministère des Transports, 700, boul René-Lévesque est, 28e étage, Québec, QC G1R 5H1
418-643-6980, Fax: 418-643-2033, 888-355-0511, communications@mtq.gouv.qc.ca

Saskatchewan

Public & Private Rights Board, #323, 3085 Albert St., Regina, SK S4S 0B1
306-787-4071, Fax: 306-787-0088

FAMILY BENEFITS

See Also: Income Security; Social Services

Alberta

Alberta Children & Youth Services, Communications, Sterling Place, 9940 - 106 St., 12th Fl., Edmonton, AB T5K 2N2
780-422-3004, Fax: 780-422-3071, cs.communications@gov.ab.ca

British Columbia

Ministry of Children & Family Development, PO Box 9770 Prov Govt,Victoria, BC V8W 9S5
250-387-7027, 877-387-7027, MCF.CorrespondenceManagement@gov.bc.ca

Manitoba

Manitoba Family Services & Housing, #219, 114 Garry St., Winnipeg, MB R3C 4V6
204-945-3242, Fax: 204-945-2156, minfam@leg.gov.mb.ca

New Brunswick

Department of Social Development, Sartain MacDonald Bldg., 551 King St., PO Box 6000, Fredericton, NB E3B 5H1
506-453-2001, Fax: 506-453-7478, sd-ds@gnb.ca

Family Income Security Appeal Board, PO Box 6000, Fredericton, NB E3B 5H1
506-525-4007, Fax: 506-525-4008

Newfoundland & Labrador

Department of Human Resources, Labour & Employment, Confederation Bldg., PO Box 8700, St. John's, NL A1B 4J6
709-729-2480, Fax: 709-729-6996, hreweb@gov.nl.ca

Northwest Territories

Department of Education, Culture & Employment, PO Box 1320, Yellowknife, NT X1A 2L9
867-669-2399, Fax: 867-873-0431, 866-606-5627

Quebec

Ministère de l'Emploi et de la Solidarité sociale, 425, rue St-Amable, 4e étage, Québec, QC G1R 4Z1
418-643-4721, 888-643-4721

Ministère de la Famille et des Aînés, 425, rue Saint-Amable, 1er étage, Québec, QC G1R 4Z1
877-216-6202

FEDERAL-PROVINCIAL AFFAIRS

Canadian Intergovernmental Conference Secretariat, 222 Queen St., 10th Fl., PO Box 488 A,Ottawa, ON K1N 8V5
613-995-2341, Fax: 613-996-6091, info@scics.gc.ca

Office of Intergovernmental Affairs, c/o Privy Council Office, #1000, 85 Slater St., Ottawa, ON K1A 0A3
613-957-5153, Fax: 613-957-5043, info@pco-bcp.gc.ca

Alberta

Alberta International & Intergovernmental Relations, Commerce Place, 10155 - 102 St., 12th Fl., Edmonton, AB T5J 4G8
780-422-1510, Fax: 780-427-0699

British Columbia

Intergovernmental Relations Secretariat, PO Box 9333 Prov Govt,Victoria, BC V8W 9N3
250-387-0752, Fax: 250-387-1920, igrs@gov.bc.ca

New Brunswick

Department of Intergovernmental Affairs, Centennial Bldg., #274, 670 King St., PO Box 6000, Fredericton, NB E3B 5H1
506-444-5418, Fax: 506-453-2995, iga@gnb.ca

Newfoundland & Labrador

Intergovernmental Affairs Secretariat, Confederation Bldg., East Block, 7th Fl., PO Box 8700, St. John's, NL A1B 4J6
709-729-3164, Fax: 709-729-5038, iga@gov.nl.ca

Northwest Territories

Department of Aboriginal Affairs & Intergovernmental Relations, 4910 - 52nd St., PO Box 1320, Yellowknife, NT X1A 2L9
867-873-7143, Fax: 867-873-0233, 877-838-8194, nancy_gardiner@gov.nt.ca

Nova Scotia

Department of Intergovernmental Affairs, Duke Tower, 5251 Duke St., 5th Fl., PO Box 1617, Halifax, NS B3J 2Y3
Fax: 902-424-0728, iga@gov.ns.ca

Nunavut

Department of Executive & Intergovernmental Affairs, 1084 Aeroplex bldg., PO Box 1000 200,Iqaluit, NU X0A 0H0
867-975-6000, Fax: 867-975-6099

Ontario

Ministry of Intergovernmental Affairs, 77 Wellesley St. West, Toronto, ON M7A 1N3
416-325-4800, Fax: 416-325-4787

Quebec

Secrétariat aux affaires intergouvernementales canadiennes, 875, Grande Allée est, 3e étage, Québec, QC G1R 4Y8
418-643-4011, Fax: 418-528-0052

FILM PRODUCTION & COLLECTIONS

Canadian Broadcasting Corporation, 181 Queen St., PO Box 3220 C,Ottawa, ON K1Y 1E4
613-288-6033, liaison@radio-canada.ca

National Film Board of Canada, 3155, rue Côte de Liesse, CP 1600 Centre-ville,Saint-Laurent, QC H4N 2N4
514-283-9000, Fax: 514-283-7564, 800-267-7710

Telefilm Canada, #500, 360, rue Saint-Jacques, Montréal, QC H2Y 1P5
514-283-6363, Fax: 514-283-2365, 800-567-0890, info@telefilm.gc.ca

Manitoba

Manitoba Film & Sound Recording Development Corporation, #410, 93 Lombard Ave., Winnipeg, MB R3B 3B1
204-947-2040, Fax: 204-956-5261, carole@mbfilmsound.mb.ca

New Brunswick

New Brunswick Film, Place 2000, 250 King St., 4th Fl., PO Box 6000, Fredericton, NB E1B 5H1
506-453-2555, Fax: 506-453-2416, nbfilm@gnb.ca

Newfoundland & Labrador

Newfoundland & Labrador Film Development Corporation, 12 King's Bridge Rd., St. John's, NL A1C 3K3
709-738-3456, Fax: 709-739-1680, 877-738-3456, info@nlfdc.ca

Nova Scotia

Film Nova Scotia, Collins Bank Bldg., 1869 Upper Water St., 3rd Fl., Halifax, NS B3J 1S9
902-424-7177, Fax: 902-424-0617, 888-360-2111

Ontario

Ontario Media Development Corporation, South Tower, #501, 175 Bloor St. East, Toronto, ON M4W 3R8
416-314-6858, Fax: 416-314-6876, mail@omdc.on.ca

Saskatchewan

Sask Film, 1831 College Ave., Regina, SK S4P 4V5
306-798-9800, Fax: 306-798-7768, 800-561-9933

FINANCE

See Also: Banking & Financial Institutions

Finance Canada, L'esplanade Laurier, 140 O'Connor St., Ottawa, ON K1A 0G5
613-992-1573, Fax: 613-943-0938, finpub@fin.gc.ca

Alberta

Alberta Finance & Enterprise, Terrace Building, #426, 9515 - 107 St., Edmonton, AB T5K 2C3
780-427-3035, Fax: 780-427-1147, tra.revenue@gov.ab.ca

Occupational Health & Safety Advisory Council, PO Box 697, Halifax, NS B3J 2T8
902-424-2484, Fax: 902-424-5640

British Columbia

Ministry of Finance, PO Box 9417 Prov Govt,Victoria, BC V8W 9V1
250-387-3751, Fax: 250-387-5594, Fin.Minister@gov.bc.ca

Manitoba

Manitoba Finance, #109, Legislative Bldg., Winnipeg, MB R3C 0V8
204-945-3754, Fax: 204-945-8316, minfin@leg.gov.mb.ca

New Brunswick

Department of Finance, 670 King St., PO Box 6000, Fredericton, NB E3B 5H1
506-453-2451, Fax: 506-457-4989, wwwfin@gnb.ca

Newfoundland & Labrador

Department of Finance, Confederation Bldg., PO Box 8700, St. John's, NL A1B 4J6
709-729-6165, Fax: 709-729-2070, finance@gov.nl.ca

Northwest Territories

Department of Finance, Arthur Laing Building, 5th Fl., 5003 - 49th St., PO Box 1320, Yellowknife, NT X1A 2L9
867-873-7117, Fax: 867-873-0414

Nova Scotia

Department of Finance, Provincial Bldg., 1723 Hollis St., 7th Fl., PO Box 187, Halifax, NS B3J 2N3
902-424-5554, Fax: 902-424-0635, FinanceWeb@gov.ns.ca

Nunavut

Department of Finance, Bldg. 1079, 1st Fl., PO Box 1000 330,Iqaluit, NU X0A 0H0
867-975-5800, Fax: 867-975-5805

Ontario

Ministry of Finance, Frost Bldg. South, 7 Queen's Park Cres., 7th Fl., Toronto, ON M7A 1Y7
Fax: 866-888-3850, 800-263-7965, financecommunications.fin@ontario.ca

Ministry of Revenue, Frost Bldg. South, 7 Queen's Park Cres., 6th Fl., Toronto, ON M7A 1Y7
Fax: 866-888-3850, 866-668-8297

Prince Edward Island

Prince Edward Island Department of Finance & Municipal Affairs, Shaw Bldg., 95 Rochford St. South, 2nd Fl., PO Box 2000, Charlottetown, PE C1A 7N8
902-368-4000, Fax: 902-368-5544

Quebec

Ministère des Finances, Édifice Gérard-D.-Lévesque, 12, rue Saint-Louis, Québec, QC G1R 5L3
418-528-9323, Fax: 418-646-1631, info@finances.gouv.qc.ca

Saskatchewan

Saskatchewan Finance, 2350 Albert St., Regina, SK S4P 4A6
306-787-6768, Fax: 306-787-0241, communications@finance.gov.sk.ca

Yukon Territory

Yukon Finance, PO Box 2703, Whitehorse, YT Y1A 2C6
867-667-5343, Fax: 867-393-6217, fininfo@gov.yk.ca

FINANCING & LOANS

See Also: Investment

Business Development Bank of Canada, #400, 5, Place Ville-Marie, Montréal, QC H3B 5E7
514-283-5904, Fax: 514-283-5626, 877-232-2269

Canada Mortgage & Housing Corporation, 700 Montreal Rd., Ottawa, ON K1A 0P7
613-748-2000, Fax: 613-748-2098, 800-668-2642, chic@cmhc-schl.gc.ca

Farm Credit Canada, 1800 Hamilton St., PO Box 4320, Regina, SK S4P 4L3
306-780-8100, Fax: 306-780-8919, 888-332-3301, csc@fcc-fac.ca

Alberta

Alberta Capital Finance Authority, Canadian Western Bank Place, #2450, 10303 Jasper Ave., Edmonton, AB T5J 3N6
780-427-9711, Fax: 780-422-2175, webacfa@gov.ab.ca

ATB Financial, 9888 Jasper Ave., Edmonton, AB T5J 1P1
403-245-8110, 800-332-8383

British Columbia

International Financial Centre British Columbia, Park Place, #1170, 666 Burrard St., Vancouver, BC V6C 2X8
604-683-6626, Fax: 604-683-6646, info@ifcvancouver.com

Provincial Treasury, PO Box 9414 Prov Govt,Victoria, BC V8V 9V1
250-387-4541, Fax: 250-356-3041

Manitoba

Manitoba Agricultural Services Corporation, #100, 1525 First St. South, Brandon, MB R7A 7A1
204-726-6850, Fax: 204-726-6849, mailbox@masc.mb.ca

New Brunswick

New Brunswick Electric Finance Corporation, #376, 670 King St., PO Box 6000, Fredericton, NB E3B 5H1
506-453-3952, Fax: 506-453-2053,

Newfoundland & Labrador

Department of Finance, Confederation Bldg., PO Box 8700, St. John's, NL A1B 4J6
709-729-6165, Fax: 709-729-2070, finance@gov.nl.ca

Northwest Territories

Department of Industry, Tourism & Investment, PO Box 1320, Yellowknife, NT X1A 2L9
Fax: 867-873-0306, info@iti.ca

Nova Scotia

Nova Scotia Farm Loan Board, PO Box 550, Truro, NS B2N 5E3
902-893-6506, Fax: 902-895-7693, flb@gov.ns.ca

Nunavut

Nunavut Business Credit Corporation, Parnaivak Bldg., #100, PO Box 2548, Iqaluit, NU X0A 0H0
867-975-7891, Fax: 867-975-7897, 800-758-0038, credit@nbcc.nu.ca

Ontario

Ontario Electricity Financial Corporation, #1400, 1 Dundas St. West, Toronto, ON M7A 1Y7
416-325-8000, Fax: 416-325-8005

Ontario Financing Authority, #1400, 1 Dundas St. West, Toronto, ON M7A 1Y7
416-325-8000, Fax: 416-325-8005

Prince Edward Island

Prince Edward Island Lending Agency, Homburg Financial Tower, 98 Fitzroy St., 2nd Fl., Charlottetown, PE C1A 1R7
902-368-6200, Fax: 902-368-6201

Quebec

Caisse de dépôt et placement du Québec, 1000, place Jean-Paul-Riopelle, Montréal, QC H2Z 2B3
514-842-3261, Fax: 514-842-4833, 866-330-3936, info@lacaisse.com

Investissement Québec, #1500, 600, rue de la Gauchetière ouest, Montréal, QC H3B 4L8
514-873-4664, 866-870-0437

La financière agricole de Québec, 1400, boul de la Rive-Sud, Saint-Romuald, QC G6W 8K7
418-838-5602, Fax: 418-833-3871, 800-749-3646, financiereagricole@fadq.qc.ca

Saskatchewan

Saskatchewan Trade & Export Partnership, #320, 1801 Hamilton St., PO Box 1787, Regina, SK S4P 3C6
306-787-9210, Fax: 306-787-6666, inquire@sasktrade.sk.ca

Yukon Territory

Yukon Economic Development, PO Box 2703, Whitehorse, YT Y1A 2C6
867-393-7191, Fax: 867-393-6412, 800-661-0408, ecdev@gov.yk.ca

FIRE PREVENTION

British Columbia

Emergency Management BC, PO Box 9223 Prov Govt,Victoria, BC V8W 9J1
250-953-4002, Fax: 250-953-4081, BC.CorSer@gov.bc.ca (Coroner); OFC@gov.bc.ca (Fire Commissioner)

Manitoba

Office of the Fire Commissioner, #508, 401 York Ave., Winnipeg, MB R3C 0P8
204-945-3322, Fax: 204-948-2089, 800-282-8069, firecomm@gov.mb.ca

Newfoundland & Labrador

Eastern Waste Management Commission, #200, 120 Lemarchant Rd., St. John's, NL A1C 2H2
709-579-7960, Fax: 709-579-5392, info@easternwaste.ca

Northwest Territories

Department of Municipal & Community Affairs, PO Box 1320, Yellowknife, NT X1A 2L9
867-873-7118, Fax: 867-873-0309

Nunavut

Nunavut Emergency Management, PO Box 1000 700,Iqaluit, NU X0A 0H0
867-975-5403, Fax: 867-979-4221, 800-693-1666

Ontario

Fire Safety Commission, Place Nouveau Bldg., 5775 Yonge St., 7th Fl., Toronto, ON M2M 4J1
416-325-3100, Fax: 416-314-1217

Quebec
Commissariat des incendies, 455, rue Dupont, Québec, QC G1K 6N2
418-529-5706, Fax: 418-529-9922, cdelage@notarius.net
Yukon Territory
Fire Marshal's Office, PO Box 2703, Whitehorse, YT Y1A 2C6
867-667-5811, Fax: 867-393-6295, inquiry@gov.yk.ca

FIREARMS

Canada Firearms Program, Ottawa, ON K1A 0R2
Fax: 613-825-0297, 800-731-4000, cfp-pcaf@rcmp-grc.gc.ca
British Columbia
Ministry of the Attorney General, PO Box 9044 Prov Govt,Victoria, BC V8W 9E2
250-387-1866, Fax: 250-387-6411

FISHERIES

Fisheries & Oceans Canada, 200 Kent St., Ottawa, ON K1A 0E6
613-993-0999, Fax: 613-990-1866, info@dfo-mpo.gc.ca
Fisheries Resource Conservation Council, PO Box 2001 D, Ottawa, ON K1P 5W3
613-998-0433, Fax: 613-998-1146, info@frcc-ccrh.ca
Freshwater Fish Marketing Corporation, 1199 Plessis Rd., Winnipeg, MB R2C 3L4
204-983-6601, Fax: 204-983-6497, sandi.cain@freshwaterfish.com
Gulf Fisheries Centre, 343, av Université, 5th Fl., Moncton, NB E1C 9B6
506-851-3886, Fax: 506-851-7732
British Columbia
Ministry of Agriculture, PO Box 9120 Prov Govt,Victoria, BC V8W 9E2
250-387-5121, Fax: 250-387-1522
Parks & Protected Areas Division, PO Box 9339 Prov Govt,Victoria, BC V8W 9M9
Fax: 250-953-3414
New Brunswick
Department of Agriculture, Aquaculture & Fisheries, PO Box 6000, Fredericton, NB E3B 5H1
506-453-2666, Fax: 506-453-7170, DAAF-MAAP@gnb.ca
Department of Business New Brunswick, Centennial Bldg., 670 King St., PO Box 6000, Fredericton, NB E3B 5H1
506-453-3707, Fax: 506-453-3993, investnb@gnb.ca
Newfoundland & Labrador
Department of Fisheries & Aquaculture, Petten Bldg., 30 Strawberry Marsh Rd., PO Box 8700, St. John's, NL A1B 4J6
709-729-3723, Fax: 709-729-6082, fisheries@gov.nl.ca
Northwest Territories
Department of Environment & Natural Resources, PO Box 1320, Yellowknife, NT X1A 2L9
Nova Scotia
Fisheries & Aquaculture Loan Board, 1741 Brunswick St., 3rd Fl., PO Box 2223, Halifax, NS B3J 3C4
902-424-0318, Fax: 902-424-3502
Department of Fisheries & Aquaculture, 1741 Brunswick St., 3rd Fl., PO Box 2223, Halifax, NS B3J 3C4
902-424-4560, Fax: 902-424-4671
Ontario
Ontario Fish & Wildlife Heritage Commission, Robinson Pl., 300 Water St., PO Box 7000, Peterborough, ON K9J 8M5
705-755-1905, Fax: 705-755-1900
Prince Edward Island
Prince Edward Island Department of Agriculture, Jones Bldg., 11 Kent St., PO Box 2000, Charlottetown, PE C1A 7N8
902-368-4880, Fax: 902-368-4857

FISHERIES & WILDLIFE

Beverly & Qamanirjuaq Caribou Management Board, Secretariat, PO Box 629, Stonewall, MB R0C 2Z0
204-467-2438, caribounews@arctic-caribou.com
Fisheries & Oceans Canada, 200 Kent St., Ottawa, ON K1A 0E6
613-993-0999, Fax: 613-990-1866, info@dfo-mpo.gc.ca
Natural Resources Canada, 580 Booth St., Ottawa, ON K1A 0E4
613-995-0947, Fax: 613-992-7211
Porcupine Caribou Management Board, PO Box 31723, Whitehorse, YT Y1A 6L3
867-633-4780, Fax: 867-393-3904, pcmb@taiga.net
Alberta
Alberta Environment, South Tower, Petroleum Plaza, 9915 - 108 St., 10th Fl., Edmonton, AB T5K 2G8
780-427-2700, Fax: 780-422-4086, env.infocent@gov.ab.ca
British Columbia
Ministry of Environment, PO Box 9339 Prov Govt,Victoria, BC V8W 9M1
250-387-1161, Fax: 250-387-5669, envmail@gov.bc.ca
Manitoba
Endangered Species Advisory Committee, 200 Saulteaux Cres., PO Box 24, Winnipeg, MB R3J 3W3
204-945-7465, Fax: 204-945-3077
Manitoba Habitat Heritage Corporation, #200, 1555 St. James St., Winnipeg, MB R3H 1B5
204-784-4350, Fax: 204-784-7359, mhhc@mhhc.mb.ca
New Brunswick
Department of Agriculture, Aquaculture & Fisheries, PO Box 6000, Fredericton, NB E3B 5H1
506-453-2666, Fax: 506-453-7170, DAAF-MAAP@gnb.ca
Newfoundland & Labrador
Department of Fisheries & Aquaculture, Petten Bldg., 30 Strawberry Marsh Rd., PO Box 8700, St. John's, NL A1B 4J6
709-729-3723, Fax: 709-729-6082, fisheries@gov.nl.ca
Forestry Services, Fortis Bldg., PO Box 2006, Corner Brook, NL A2H 6J8
709-637-2284, Fax: 709-634-4378
Northwest Territories
Department of Environment & Natural Resources, PO Box 1320, Yellowknife, NT X1A 2L9
Nova Scotia
Department of Natural Resources, Founder's Square, 1701 Hollis St., 3rd Fl., PO Box 698, Halifax, NS B3J 2T9
902-424-5935, Fax: 902-424-0594, 800-565-2224
Ontario
Ministry of Natural Resources, Whitney Block, #6630, 99 Wellesley St. West, 6th Fl., Toronto, ON M7A 1W3
800-667-1940
Prince Edward Island
Prince Edward Island Department of Environment, Energy, & Forestry, Jones Bldg., 11 Kent St., 4th Fl., PO Box 2000, Charlottetown, PE C1A 7N8
902-368-5000, Fax: 902-368-5830
Prince Edward Island Department of Tourism & Culture, PO Box 2000, Charlottetown, PE C1A 7N8
902-368-5540, Fax: 902-368-5277, tpswitch@gov.pe.ca
Quebec
Ministère de l'Agriculture, des Pêcheries et de l'Alimentation, 200, ch Sainte-Foy, Québec, QC G1R 4X6
418-380-2110, 888-222-6272
Yukon Territory
Yukon Environment, PO Box 2703, Whitehorse, YT Y1A 2C6
867-667-5652, Fax: 867-393-7197, environment.yukon@gov.yk.ca
Yukon Fish & Wildlife Management Board, 106 Main St., 2nd Fl., Whitehorse, YT Y1A 5P7
867-667-3754, Fax: 867-393-6947, officemanager@yfwmb.ca

FOOD

See: Agriculture; Nutrition
Prince Edward Island
BIO FOOD TECH, 101 Belvedere Ave., PO Box 2000, Charlottetown, PE C1A 7N8
902-368-5548, Fax: 902-368-5549, 877-368-5548, biofoodtech@biofoodtech.ca

FOREST RESOURCES

Alberta
Alberta Innvoates - Bio Solutions, Phipps McKinnon Bldg., 10020 - 101A Ave., Edmonton, AB T5J 3G2
780-427-1956, Fax: 780-427-3252, 877-828-0444, bio@albertainnovates.ca
Forestry Division, Petroleum Plaza ST, 9915 - 108 St. 11th Fl., Edmonton, AB T5K 2G8
British Columbia
Ministry of Forests, Lands & Natural Resource Operations, PO Box 9049 Prov Govt,Victoria, BC V8W 9E2
250-387-4809, Fax: 250-387-1040
New Brunswick
Forest Protection Limited, 2502 Hwy. 102, Lincoln, NB E3B 7E6
506-446-6930, Fax: 506-446-6934, info@forestprotectionlimited.com
New Brunswick Forest Products Commission, PO Box 6000, Fredericton, NB E3B 5H1
506-453-2196, Fax: 506-457-4966
Newfoundland & Labrador
Forestry Services, Fortis Bldg., PO Box 2006, Corner Brook, NL A2H 6J8
709-637-2284, Fax: 709-634-4378,
Nova Scotia
NS Primary Forest Products Marketing Board, #804, 45 Alderney Dr., Dartmouth, NS B2Y 2N6
902-424-7598, Fax: 902-424-6965
Nunavut
Department of Environment, PO Box 1000 1300,Iqaluit, NU X0A 0H0
867-975-7700, Fax: 867-975-7742, environment@gov.nu.ca
Ontario
Algonquin Forestry Authority - Huntsville, 222 Main St. West, Huntsville, ON P1H 1Y1
705-789-9647, Fax: 705-789-3353, info@algonquinforestry.on.ca
Algonquin Forestry Authority - Pembroke, Victoria Centre, 84 Isabella St., 2nd Fl., Pembroke, ON K8A 5S5
613-735-0173, Fax: 613-735-4192, info@algonquinforestry.on.ca
Quebec
Forêt Québec, 880, ch Ste-Foy, #RC 120, Québec, QC G1S 4X4
418-627-8652, Fax: 418-528-1278, foretquebec@mrnf.gouv.qc.ca
Yukon Territory
Yukon Energy, Mines & Resources, PO Box 2703, Whitehorse, YT Y1A 2C6
867-667-3130, Fax: 867-456-3965, 800-661-0408, emr@gov.yk.ca
Yukon Environment, PO Box 2703, Whitehorse, YT Y1A 2C6
867-667-5652, Fax: 867-393-7197, environment.yukon@gov.yk.ca

FORESTRY & PAPER

Natural Resources Canada, 580 Booth St., Ottawa, ON K1A 0E4
613-995-0947, Fax: 613-992-7211
Alberta
Alberta Innvoates - Bio Solutions, Phipps McKinnon Bldg., 10020 - 101A Ave., Edmonton, AB T5J 3G2
780-427-1956, Fax: 780-427-3252, 877-828-0444, bio@albertainnovates.ca
Forestry Division, Petroleum Plaza ST, 9915 - 108 St. 11th Fl., Edmonton, AB T5K 2G8
British Columbia
Forest Practices Board, 1675 Douglas St., 3rd Fl., PO Box 9905 Prov Govt, Victoria, BC V8W 9R1
250-213-4700, Fax: 250-213-4725, 800-994-5899, fpboard@gov.bc.ca
Ministry of Forests, Lands & Natural Resource Operations, PO Box 9049 Prov Govt,Victoria, BC V8W 9E2
250-387-4809, Fax: 250-387-1040
Timber Export Advisory Committee, PO Box 9514 Prov Govt, Victoria, BC V8W 9C2
250-387-8916, Fax: 250-387-5050
New Brunswick
Forest Protection Limited, 2502 Hwy. 102, Lincoln, NB E3B 7E6
506-446-6930, Fax: 506-446-6934, info@forestprotectionlimited.com
New Brunswick Forest Products Commission, PO Box 6000, Fredericton, NB E3B 5H1
506-453-2196, Fax: 506-457-4966
Newfoundland & Labrador
Department of Natural Resources, Natural Resources Bldg., 50 Elizabeth Ave., 7th Fl., PO Box 8700, St. John's, NL A1B 4J6
709-729-2920, Fax: 709-729-0059
Forestry Services, Fortis Bldg., PO Box 2006, Corner Brook, NL A2H 6J8
709-637-2284, Fax: 709-634-4378
Nova Scotia
Department of Natural Resources, Founder's Square, 1701 Hollis St., 3rd Fl., PO Box 698, Halifax, NS B3J 2T9
902-424-5935, Fax: 902-424-0594, 800-565-2224
Ontario
Algonquin Forestry Authority - Huntsville, 222 Main St. West, Huntsville, ON P1H 1Y1
705-789-9647, Fax: 705-789-3353, info@algonquinforestry.on.ca
Algonquin Forestry Authority - Pembroke, Victoria Centre, 84 Isabella St., 2nd Fl., Pembroke, ON K8A 5S5
613-735-0173, Fax: 613-735-4192, info@algonquinforestry.on.ca
Ministry of Natural Resources, Whitney Block, #6630, 99 Wellesley St. West, 6th Fl., Toronto, ON M7A 1W3
800-667-1940
Quebec
Ministère du Développement durable, de l'Environnement et des Parcs, Édifice Marie-Guyart, 675, boul René-Lévesque est, 29e étage, Québec, QC G1R 5V7
418-521-3830, Fax: 418-646-5974, 800-561-1616, info@mddep.gouv.qc.ca
Saskatchewan
Saskatchewan Environment, 3211 Albert St., 2nd Fl., Regina, SK S4S 5W6
306-787-2584, Fax: 306-787-9544, 800-567-4224, Centre.Inquiry@gov.sk.ca
Yukon Territory
Yukon Environment, PO Box 2703, Whitehorse, YT Y1A 2C6
867-667-5652, Fax: 867-393-7197, environment.yukon@gov.yk.ca

GEOLOGICAL SERVICES

Geological Survey of Canada, 601 Booth St., Ottawa, ON K1A 0E8
613-996-3919, Fax: 613-943-8742, esic@nrcan.gc.ca

Alberta

Energy Resources Conservation Board, #1000, 250 - 5 Ave. SW, Calgary, AB T2P 0R4
403-297-8311, Fax: 403-297-7336, 855-297-8311, inquiries@ercb.ca; infoservices@ercb.ca; ADR@ercb.ca

British Columbia

Ministry of Energy & Mines, PO Box 9053 Prov Govt,Victoria, BC V8W 9E2
250-387-5896, Fax: 250-356-2965

Manitoba

Manitoba Geological Survey, #360, 1394 Ellice Ave., Winnipeg, MB R3G 3P2
Fax: 204-945-1406, 800-223-5215, minesinfo@gov.mb.ca

Nova Scotia

Nova Scotia Geomatics Centre, 160 Willow St., Amherst, NS B4H 3W5
902-667-7231, Fax: 902-667-6008, 800-798-0706, geoinfo@gov.ns.ca

GOVERNMENT

41st Parliament - Canada, House of Commons, Parliament Buildings, Ottawa, ON K1A 0A6

Aboriginal Affairs & Northern Development Canada, 10 Wellington St., North Tower, Gatineau, QC K1A 0H4
819-997-0380, Fax: 866-817-3977, 800-567-9604, infopubs@aadnc-aandc.gc.ca

Auditor General of Canada, 240 Sparks St., Ottawa, ON K1A 0G6
613-995-3708, Fax: 613-957-0474, 888-761-5953, communications@oag-bvg.gc.ca; infomedia@oag-bvg.gc.ca

Bank of Canada, 234 Wellington St., Ottawa, ON K1A 0G9
613-782-7902, Fax: 613-782-7713, 800-303-1282, info@bankofcanada.ca; communications@bankofcanada.ca (Media)

Business Development Bank of Canada, #400, 5, Place Ville-Marie, Montréal, QC H3B 5E7
514-283-5904, Fax: 514-283-5626, 877-232-2269

Canada Economic Development for Québec Regions, Édifice Dominion Square, #900, 1255, rue Peel, Montréal, QC H3B 2T9
514-283-6412, Fax: 514-283-3302, 866-385-6412

Canada Lands Company Ltd., #1200, 1 University Ave., Toronto, ON M5J 2P1
416-952-6111, Fax: 416-952-6115, 888-252-5263

Canada Revenue Agency, 875 Heron Rd., Ottawa, ON K1A 0L5
800-267-6999

Canadian Intergovernmental Conference Secretariat, 222 Queen St., 10th Fl., PO Box 488 A,Ottawa, ON K1N 8V5
613-995-2341, Fax: 613-996-6091, info@scics.gc.ca

Canadian Nuclear Safety Commission, 280 Slater St., PO Box 1046 B,Ottawa, ON K1P 5S9
613-995-5894, Fax: 613-995-5086, 800-668-5284

Defence Construction Canada, Constitution Square, 350 Albert St., 19th Fl., Ottawa, ON K1A 0K3
613-998-9548, Fax: 613-998-1061, 800-514-3555, info@dcc-cdc.gc.ca

Elections Canada, The Jackson Bldg., 257 Slater St., Ottawa, ON K1A 0M6
613-993-2975, Fax: 613-954-8584, 800-463-6868

Finance Canada, L'esplanade Laurier, 140 O'Connor St., Ottawa, ON K1A 0G5
613-992-1573, Fax: 613-943-0938, finpub@fin.gc.ca

First Nations Tax Commission, #321, 345 Yellowhead Hwy, Kamloops, BC V2H 1H1
250-828-9857, Fax: 250-828-9858, mailkamloops@fntc.ca

Foreign Affairs & International Trade Canada, 125 Sussex Dr., Ottawa, ON K1A 0G2
613-944-4000, Fax: 613-996-9709, 800-267-8376, enqserv@international.gc.ca

Government of Canada, c/o Canada Enquiry Centre, Service Canada, Ottawa, ON K1A 0J9
613-941-1827, 800-622-6232, sitecanadasite@canada.gc.ca

Governor General & Commander-in-Chief of Canada, Rideau Hall, 1 Sussex Dr., Ottawa, ON K1A 0A1
613-993-8200, Fax: 613-998-8760, 800-465-6890, info@gg.ca

House of Commons, Canada, House of Commons, Centre Block, Parliament Buildings, 111 Wellington St., Ottawa, ON K1A 0A6
613-992-4793, 866-599-4999, info@parl.gc.ca

Industry Canada, C.D. Howe Building, 235 Queen St., Ottawa, ON K1A 0H5
613-954-5031, Fax: 613-954-2340, 800-328-6189, info@ic.gc.ca

International Development Research Centre, 150 Kent St., PO Box 8500, Ottawa, ON K1G 3H9
613-236-6163, Fax: 613-238-7230, info@idrc.ca

Justice Canada, East Memorial Bldg., 284 Wellington St., Ottawa, ON K1A 0H8
613-957-4222, Fax: 613-954-0811, webadmin@justice.gc.ca

National Defence Canada, Major-General George R. Pearkes Bldg., 101 Colonel By Dr., Ottawa, ON K1A 0K2
613-995-2534, Fax: 613-992-4739, 800-856-8488

North American Free Trade Agreement (NAFTA) Secretariat, Canadian Section, #705, 90 Sparks St., Ottawa, ON K1P 5B4
613-992-9388, Fax: 613-992-9392, webmaster@nafta-alena.gc.ca

Office of Intergovernmental Affairs, c/o Privy Council Office, #1000, 85 Slater St., Ottawa, ON K1A 0A3
613-957-5153, Fax: 613-957-5043, info@pco-bcp.gc.ca

Office of Protocol, 125 Sussex Dr., Ottawa, ON K1A 0G2
613-996-8683, Fax: 613-943-1075

Office of the Leader, Bloc Québécois, Centre Block, Ottawa, ON K1A 0A6
613-992-6779, Fax: 613-954-2121

Office of the Leader, Green Party of Canada, Confederation Building,, #518, 244 Wellington St., Ottawa, ON K1A 0A6
613-996-1119, Fax: 613-996-0850, 866-868-3447, leader@greenparty.ca; info@greenparty.ca

Office of the Leader, Official Opposition (New Democratic Party), 111 Wellington St., Ottawa, ON K1A 0A6
613-995-7224, Fax: 613-995-4565

Office of the Prime Minister (Conservative Party of Canada), Langevin Block, 80 Wellington St., Ottawa, ON K1A 0A2
613-992-4211, Fax: 613-941-6900, pm@pm.gc.ca

Office of the Commissioner of Official Languages, 344 Slater St., 3rd fl., Ottawa, ON K1A 0T8
613-996-6368, Fax: 613-993-5082, 877-996-6368

Privy Council Office, #1000, 85 Sparks St., Ottawa, ON K1A 0A3
613-957-5153, Fax: 613-997-5043, info@pco-bcp.gc.ca

Public Service Commission, West Tower, 300 Laurier Ave. West, Ottawa, ON K1A 0M7
613-992-9562, Fax: 613-992-9352, infocom@psc-cfp.gc.ca

Public Service Staffing Tribunal, 240 Sparks St., 6th Fl., Ottawa, ON K1A 0A5
613-949-6516, Fax: 613-949-6551, 866-637-4491, info@psst-tdfp.gc.ca

Public Works & Government Services Canada, Place du Portage, Phase III, 11, rue Laurier, Ottawa, ON K1A 0S5
questions@tpsgc-pwgsc.gc.ca

Royal Canadian Mint, 320 Sussex Dr., Ottawa, ON K1A 0G8
613-993-3500, Fax: 613-993-4092, 800-267-1871

Senate of Canada, Ottawa, ON K1A 0A4
613-995-1900, 800-267-7362, sencom@sen.parl.gc.ca

Statistics Canada, R.H. Coats Bldg., Tunney's Pasture, 150 Tunney's Pasture Driveway, Ottawa, ON K1A 0T6
613-951-8116, Fax: 877-287-4369, 800-263-1136, infostats@statcan.ca

The Canadian Ministry, Information Service, Parliament of Canada, Ottawa, ON K1A 0A9
613-992-4793, 866-599-4999, info@parl.gc.ca

Treasury Board of Canada, 140 O'Connor St., Ottawa, ON K1A 0R5
613-957-2400, Fax: 613-941-4000, 877-636-0656

Alberta

Alberta Apprenticeship & Industry Training Board, Commerce Place, 10155 - 102nd St., 10th Fl., Edmonton, AB T5J 4L5
780-427-8765, Fax: 780-422-7376

Alberta Gaming & Liquor Commission, 50 Corriveau Ave., St. Albert, AB T8N 3T5
780-447-8600, Fax: 780-447-8916, 800-272-8876

Alberta Pensions Services Corporation, 5103 Windermere Blvd. SW, Edmonton, AB T6W 0S9
780-427-2782, 800-661-8198, memberservices@apsc.ca; employerservices@apsc.ca; pay@apsc.ca

Alberta Review Board, Oxford Tower, 10235 - 101 St., 11th Fl., Edmonton, AB T5J 3E9

Alberta Office of the Auditor General, 9925 - 109 St., 8th Fl., Edmonton, AB T5K 2J8
780-427-4222, Fax: 780-422-9555, info@oag.ab.ca

Alberta Office of the Chief Electoral Officer / Elections Alberta, 11510 Kingsway Ave., 1st Fl., Edmonton, AB T5G 2Y5
780-427-7191, Fax: 780-422-2900, info@electionsalberta.ab.ca

Alberta Office of the Ethics Commissioner, #1250, 9925 - 109 St. NW, Edmonton, AB T5K 2J8
780-422-2273, Fax: 780-422-2261, generalinfo@ethicscommissioner.ab.ca

Executive Council, Legislature Building, 10800 - 97 Ave., Edmonton, AB T5K 2B6
780-427-2711

Alberta Finance & Enterprise, Terrace Building, #426, 9515 - 107 St., Edmonton, AB T5K 2C3
780-427-3035, Fax: 780-427-1147, tra.revenue@gov.ab.ca

Government of Alberta, PO Box 1333, Edmonton, AB T5J 2N2
780-427-2711, Fax: 780-422-2852

Alberta Office of the Information & Privacy Commissioner, Office of the Information & Privacy Commissioner (Edmonton), #410, 9925 - 109 St., 4th Fl., Edmonton, AB T5K 2J8
780-422-6860, Fax: 780-422-5682, 888-878-4044, generalinfo@oipc.ab.ca

Alberta Infrastructure, Infrastructure Building, 6950 - 113 St., Edmonton, AB T6H 5V7
780-415-0507, Fax: 780-427-2187, Infra.Contact.Us.m@gov.ab.ca

Alberta International & Intergovernmental Relations, Commerce Place, 10155 - 102 St., 12th Fl., Edmonton, AB T5J 4G8
780-422-1510, Fax: 780-427-0699

Legislative Assembly of Alberta, Legislature Annex, 9718 - 107 St., Edmonton, AB T5K 1E4
780-427-2826, Fax: 780-427-1623, laocommunications@assembly.ab.ca

Office of the Lieutenant Governor, Office of the Lieutenant Governor of AB, Legislature Bldg., 10800 - 97 Ave., 3rd Fl., Edmonton, AB T5K 2B6
780-427-7243, Fax: 780-422-5134, ltgov@gov.ab.ca

Alberta Municipal Affairs, Communications Branch, Commerce Place, 10155 - 102 St., 18th Fl., Edmonton, AB T5J 4L4
780-427-2732, Fax: 780-422-1419, comments@gov.ab.ca

Occupational Health & Safety Advisory Council, PO Box 697, Halifax, NS B3J 2T8
902-424-2484, Fax: 902-424-5640

Alberta Office of the Ombudsman, Canadian Western Bank Building, #2800, 10303 Jasper Ave. NW, 28th Fl., Edmonton, AB T5J 5C3
780-427-2756, Fax: 780-427-2759, 888-455-2756, info@ombudsman.ab.ca

Office of the Premier, Office of the Premier, Legislature Building, #307, 10800 - 97 Ave., Edmonton, AB T5K 2B6
780-427-2251, Fax: 780-427-1349

Alberta Public Affairs Bureau, Park Plaza, 10611 - 98 Ave., 6th Fl., Edmonton, AB T5K 2P7
780-427-2754, Fax: 780-422-4168

Registry Services, Telus Plaza South, 10020 - 100 St., 29th Fl., Edmonton, AB T5J 0N3

Special Areas Board, Special Areas Board Administration, 212 - 2nd Ave. West, PO Box 820, Hanna, AB T0J 1P0
403-854-5600, Fax: 403-854-5527, specarea@telus.net

Twenty-seventh Legislature - Alberta, Legislature Bldg., 10800 - 97 Ave., Edmonton, AB T5K 2B6
780-427-2826, laocommunications@assembly.ab.ca

British Columbia

Agricultural Land Commission, #133, 4940 Canada Way, Burnaby, BC V5G 4K6
604-660-7000, Fax: 604-660-7033, ALCBurnaby@Victoria1.gov.bc.ca

British Columbia Treaty Commission, #700, 1111 Melville St., Vancouver, BC V6E 3V6
604-482-9200, Fax: 604-482-9222, 800-665-8330, info@bctreaty.net

Office of the Auditor General, PO Box 9036 Prov Govt,Victoria, BC V8W 9A2
250-419-6100, Fax: 250-387-1230

British Columbia Assessment Authority, #400, 3450 Uptown Blvd., Victoria, BC V8Z 0B9
250-595-6211, Fax: 250-595-6222, info@bcassessment.ca

Office of the Conflict of Interest Commissioner, #101, 431 Menzies St., Victoria, BC V8V 1X4
250-356-0750, Fax: 250-356-6580, conflictofinterest@coibc.ca

Court Services Branch, PO Box 9249 Prov Govt,Victoria, BC V8W 9J2
250-356-1550, Fax: 250-356-8152

Crown Agencies Resource Office, PO Box 9469 Prov Govt, Victoria, BC V8V 9V8
250-387-8770, Fax: 250-387-9061, CAS@gov.bc.ca

Elections British Columbia, PO Box 9275 Prov Govt,Victoria, BC V8W 9J6
250-387-5305, Fax: 250-387-3578, 800-661-8683, electionsbc@elections.bc.ca

Executive Council, Parliament Bldgs., Victoria, BC V8V 1X4

Government of British Columbia, Parliament Bldgs., Victoria, BC V8V 1X4
EnquiryBC@gov.bc.ca

Office of the Information & Privacy Commissioner for British Columbia, 947 Fort St., 4th Fl., PO Box 9038 Prov Govt,Victoria, BC V8W 9A4
250-387-5629, Fax: 250-387-1696, 800-663-7867, info@oipc.bc.ca

Legislative Assembly & Independent Offices, Clerk's Office, #221, Parliament Bldgs., Victoria, BC V8V 1X4
250-387-3785, Fax: 250-387-0942, ClerkHouse@leg.bc.ca

Office of the Lieutenant Governor, Government House, 1401 Rockland Ave., Victoria, BC V8S 1V9
250-387-2080, Fax: 250-387-2078, ghinfo@gov.bc.ca

Office of the Ombudsperson, 947 Fort St., 2nd Fl., PO Box 9039 Prov Govt,Victoria, BC V8W 9A5
250-387-5855, Fax: 250-387-0198, 800-567-3247, systems@bcombudsperson.ca (Information technology inquiries)

Office of the Premier, West Annex, Parliament Bldgs., PO Box 9041 Prov Govt,Victoria, BC V8W 9E1
250-387-1715, Fax: 250-387-0087, premier@gov.bc.ca

BC Public Service Agency, #4, 810 Blanshard St., PO Box 9404 Prov Govt,Victoria, BC V8W 9V1
250-387-0518, Fax: 250-356-7074
Shared Services BC, Chief Operating Office, PO Box 9412 Prov Govt,Victoria, BC V8W 9V1
250-952-6861, Fax: 250-387-5693
Thirty-Ninth Legislature - British Columbia, Parliament Bldgs., Victoria, BC V8V 1X4
250-387-3785, Fax: 250-387-0942, ClerkHouse@leg.bc.ca
British Columbia Utilities Commission, 900 Howe St., 6th Fl., PO Box 250, Vancouver, BC V6Z 2N3
604-660-4700, Fax: 604-660-1102, 800-663-1385, commission.secretary@bcuc.com

Manitoba

Aboriginal Affairs Secretariat, #200, 500 Portage Ave., Winnipeg, MB R3C 3X1
204-945-2510, Fax: 204-945-3689
Office of the Auditor General, #500, 330 Portage Ave., Winnipeg, MB R3C 0C4
204-945-3790, Fax: 204-945-2169, oag.contact@oag.mb.ca
Civil Service Commission Board, #935, 155 Carlton St., Winnipeg, MB R3C 3H8
204-945-1435, Fax: 204-945-1486
Manitoba Civil Service Commission, #935, 155 Carlton St., Winnipeg, MB R3C 3H8
204-945-2332, Fax: 204-945-1486, 800-282-8069, cschrp@gov.mb.ca
Crown Corporations Council, #1130, 444 St. Mary Ave., Winnipeg, MB R3C 3T1
204-949-5270, Fax: 204-949-5283, crowncc@mts.net
Elections Manitoba, #120, 200 Vaughan St., Winnipeg, MB R3C 1T5
204-945-3225, Fax: 204-945-6011, 866-628-6837, election@elections.mb.ca
Executive Council, Legislative Building, 450 Broadway Ave., Winnipeg, MB R3C 0V8
Federal-Provincial Relations & Research Division, #910, 386 Broadway, Winnipeg, MB R3C 3R6
204-945-3757, Fax: 204-945-5051
Fortieth Legislature - Manitoba, Legislative Building, 450 Broadway Ave., Winnipeg, MB R3C 0V8
204-945-3636, Fax: 204-948-2507, clerkla@leg.gov.mb.ca
Government of Manitoba, Legislative Building, Rm. 237, Winnipeg, MB R3C 0V8
204-945-3636, Fax: 204-948-2507, clerkla@leg.gov.mb.ca
Manitoba Intergovernmental Affairs, #301, 450 Broadway Ave., Winnipeg, MB R3C 0V8
Fax: 204-945-1383, mnia@leg.gov.mb.ca
Legislative Assembly, c/o Clerk's Office, Legislative Bldg., #237, 450 Broadway, Winnipeg, MB R3C 0V8
204-945-3636, Fax: 204-948-2507, clerkla@leg.gov.mb.ca
Office of the Lieutenant Governor, Legislative Building, #235, 450 Broadway Ave., Winnipeg, MB R3C 0V8
204-945-2753, Fax: 204-945-4329, ltgov@leg.gov.mb.ca
Local Government Development Division, 59 Elizabeth Dr., PO Box 33, Thompson, MB R8N 1X4
204-677-6794, Fax: 204-677-6525
Manitoba Civil Service Commission, #935, 155 Carlton St., Winnipeg, MB R3C 3H8
204-945-2332, Fax: 204-945-1486, cschrp@gov.mb.ca
Manitoba Land Value Appraisal Commission, 800 Portage Ave., Winnipeg, MB R3G 0N4
204-945-2941, Fax: 204-948-2235
Manitoba Municipal Board, #1144, 363 Broadway, Winnipeg, MB R3C 3N9
204-945-2941, Fax: 204-948-2235
Mineral Resources Division, #360, 1395 Ellice Ave., Winnipeg, MB R3G 3P2
Fax: 204-945-8427
Manitoba News Media Services, #29, Legislative Bldg., 450 Broadway, Winnipeg, MB R3C 0V8
204-945-3746, Fax: 204-945-3988, nmservices@leg.gov.mb.ca
Manitoba Office of the Ombudsman, 750 - 500 Portage Ave., Winnipeg, MB R3C 3X1
204-982-9130, Fax: 204-942-7803, 800-665-0531, ombudsma@ombudsman.mb.ca
Office of the Premier, Legislative Building, #204, 450 Broadway Ave., Winnipeg, MB R3C 0V8
204-945-3714, Fax: 204-949-1484, premier@leg.gov.mb.ca
Provincial-Municipal Support Services, #508, 800 Portage Ave., Winnipeg, MB R3G 0N4
Residential Tenancies Commission, #1650, 155 Carlton St., Winnipeg, MB R3C 3H8
204-945-2028, Fax: 204-945-5453, 800-782-8403, rtc@gov.mb.ca
Manitoba Treasury Board Secretariat, #200, 386 Broadway, Winnipeg, MB R3C 3R6
204-945-4150, Fax: 204-948-4878

New Brunswick

Office of the Auditor General, HSBC Place, 520 King St., 6th Fl., Fredericton, NB E3B 6G3
506-453-2243, Fax: 506-453-3067
Communications, Centennial Bldg., 670 King St., 5th Fl., PO Box 6000, Fredericton, NB E3B 5H1
506-453-3707, Fax: 506-453-3993
Communications New Brunswick, Wilcom Bldg., 225 King St., 2nd Fl., PO Box 6000, Fredericton, NB E3B 5H1
506-453-2240, Fax: 506-453-5329
Office of the Comptroller, Centennial Bldg., 670 King St., Fredericton, NB E3B 1G1
506-453-2565, Fax: 506-453-2917, wwwooc@gnb.ca
Department of Intergovernmental Affairs, Centennial Bldg., #274, 670 King St., PO Box 6000, Fredericton, NB E3B 5H1
506-444-5418, Fax: 506-453-2995, iga@gnb.ca
Department of Supply & Services, PO Box 6000, Fredericton, NB E3B 5H1
506-453-3742, Fax: 506-444-4400, Reception.Marysville@gnb.ca
Office of the Chief Electoral Officer, PO Box 6000, Fredericton, NB E3B 5H1
506-453-2218, Fax: 506-457-4926, 800-308-2922
Executive Council, Centennial Bldg., 670 King St., PO Box 6000, Fredericton, NB E3B 5H1
506-453-2144, Fax: 506-453-7407, david.alward@gnb.ca
Fifty-seventh Legislature - New Brunswick, Legislative Assembly of New Brunswick, 706 Queen St., PO Box 6000, Fredericton, NB E3B 5H1
506-453-2506, Fax: 506-453-7154
Finance & Administration, Centennial Bldg., #375, 670 King St., PO Box 6000, Fredericton, NB E3B 5H1
506-453-2451, Fax: 506-444-4724
Government of New Brunswick, PO Box 6000, Fredericton, NB E3B 5H1
Legislative Assembly of New Brunswick, Centre Block, Legislative Bldg., 706 Queen St., PO Box 6000, Fredericton, NB E3B 5H1
506-453-2506, Fax: 506-453-7154, wwwleg@gnb.ca
Office of the Lieutenant-Governor, Old Government House, 51 Woodstock Rd., PO Box 6000, Fredericton, NB E3B 5H1
506-453-2505, Fax: 506-444-5280
Office of the Ombudsman, 767 Brunswick St., PO Box 6000, Fredericton, NB E3B 5H1
506-453-2789, Fax: 506-453-5599, 800-465-1100, nbombud@gnb.ca
Office of the Premier, Centennial Bldg., 670 King St., PO Box 6000, Fredericton, NB E3B 5H1
506-453-2144, Fax: 506-453-7407, premier@gnb.ca

Newfoundland & Labrador

Office of the Auditor General, PO Box 8700, St. John's, NL A1B 4J6
709-729-2695, Fax: 709-729-5970, oagmail@oag.nl.ca
Department of Government Services, PO Box 8700, St. John's, NL A1B 4J6
709-729-4834, gsinfo@gov.nl.ca
Department of Municipal Affairs, West Block, Main Fl., Confederation Bldg., PO Box 8700, St. John's, NL A1B 4J6
709-729-3046, Fax: 709-729-0943, mainfo@gov.nl.ca
Office of the Chief Electoral Officer, 39 Hallett Cr., St. John's, NL A1B 4C4
709-729-0712, Fax: 709-729-0679, 877-729-7987, enl@gov.nl.ca
Executive Council, c/o Communications Branch, East Block, Confederation Bldg., 10th Fl., St. John's, NL A1B 4J6
709-729-5645, info@gov.nl.ca
Forty-seventh House of Assembly - Newfoundland & Labrador, PO Box 8700, St. John's, NL A1B 4J6
709-729-3405, ClerkHOA@gov.nl.ca
Government of Newfoundland & Labrador, Confederation Bldg., St. John's, NL A1B 4J6
info@gov.nl.ca
House of Assembly, c/o Clerk's Office, Confederation Bldg., PO Box 8700, St. John's, NL A1B 4J6
709-729-3405, Fax: 709-729-4820
Office of the Lieutenant Governor, Government House, Military Rd., PO Box 5517, St. John's, NL A1C 5W4
709-729-4494, Fax: 709-729-2234, governmenthouse@gov.nl.ca
Newfoundland & Labrador Municipal Financing Corporation, Confederation Bldg., PO Box 8700, St. John's, NL A1B 4J6
709-729-6686, Fax: 709-729-2095
Office of the Premier, East Block, Confederation Bldg., 8th F., PO Box 8700, St. John's, NL A1B 4J6
709-729-3570, Fax: 709-729-5875, premier@gov.nl.ca

Northwest Territories

Office of the Commissioner, #803 Northwest Tower, PO Box 1320, Yellowknife, NT X1A 2L9
867-873-7400, Fax: 867-873-0223, 888-270-3318, commissioner@gov.nt.ca
Department of Aboriginal Affairs & Intergovernmental Relations, 4910 - 52nd St., PO Box 1320, Yellowknife, NT X1A 2L9
867-873-7143, Fax: 867-873-0233, 877-838-8194, nancy_gardiner@gov.nt.ca
Department of Public Works & Services, PO Box 1320, Yellowknife, NT X1A 2L9
Executive Council, PO Box 1320, Yellowknife, NT X1A 2L9
executive@gov.nt.ca
Financial Management Board Secretariat, c/o Secretary of the FMB / Comptroller General, 5003 - 49 St., PO Box 1320, Yellowknife, NT X1A 2L9
Government of the Northwest Territories, PO Box 1320, Yellowknife, NT X1A 2L9
Legislative Assembly, c/o Clerk's Office, PO Box 1320, Yellowknife, NT X1A 2L9
867-669-2299, Fax: 867-920-4735, 800-661-0784
Office of the Premier, Legislative Assembly Bldg., PO Box 1320, Yellowknife, NT X1A 2L9
867-669-2311, Fax: 867-873-0385, premier@gov.nt.ca
Seventeenth Legislature - Northwest Territories, PO Box 1320, Yellowknife, NT X1A 2L9
867-669-2200, Fax: 867-920-4735, 800-661-0784

Nova Scotia

Office of the Auditor General, #302, 1888 Brunswick St., Halifax, NS B3J 3J8
902-424-5907, Fax: 902-424-4350
Council of Atlantic Premiers, Council Secretariat, #1006, 5161 George St., PO Box 2044, Halifax, NS B3J 2Z1
902-424-7590, Fax: 902-424-8976, info@cap-cpma.ca
Crown Land Information Management Centre, Founders Square, #501, 1701 Hollis St., PO Box 698, Halifax, NS B3J 2T9
902-424-3171
Elections Nova Scotia, #6-7037 Mumford Rd., PO Box 2246, Halifax, NS B3J 2J1
902-424-8584, Fax: 902-424-6622, 800-565-1504, elections@gov.ns.ca
Executive Council, One Government Place, 1700 Granville St., 5th Fl., PO Box 2125, Halifax, NS B3J 3B7
902-424-5970, Fax: 902-424-0667, execounc@gov.ns.ca
Government of Nova Scotia, Province House, 1726 Hollis St., Halifax, NS B3J 2T3
Legislative House of Assembly, c/o Clerk's Office, Province House, 1st Fl., PO Box 1617, Halifax, NS B3J 2Y3
902-424-5978, Fax: 902-424-0632
Office of the Lieutenant Governor, Government House, 1451 Barrington St., Halifax, NS B3J 1Z2
902-424-7001, Fax: 902-424-0537, lgoffice@gov.ns.ca
Office of the Ombudsman, #700, 5670 Spring Garden Rd., PO Box 2152, Halifax, NS B3J 3B7
902-424-6780, Fax: 902-424-6675, 800-670-1111, ombudsman@gov.ns.ca
Office of the Premier, One Government Place, 1700 Granville St., 7th Fl., PO Box 726, Halifax, NS B3J 2T3
902-424-6600, Fax: 902-424-7648, 800-267-1993, premier@gov.ns.ca
Department of Service Nova Scotia & Municipal Relations, 1505 Barrington St., PO Box 216, Halifax, NS B3J 3K5
902-424-5200, Fax: 902-424-0581, 800-670-4357, askus@gov.ns.ca
Sixty-first Assembly - Nova Scotia, Province House, PO Box 1617, Halifax, NS B3J 2Y3
902-424-5978, Fax: 902-424-0632
Nova Scotia Treasury & Policy Board, 1700 Granville St., 5th Fl., PO Box 1617, Halifax, NS B3J 2Y3
902-424-8910, Fax: 902-424-7638, TBenquiries@gov.ns.ca
Nova Scotia Utility & Review Board, Summit Place, 1601 Lower Water St., 3rd Fl., PO Box 1692 M,Halifax, NS B3J 3S3
902-424-4448, Fax: 902-424-3919, uarb.board@gov.ns.ca

Nunavut

Department of Community & Government Services, W.G. Brown Bldg., 4th Fl., PO Box 1000 700,Iqaluit, NU X0A 0H0
867-975-5400, Fax: 867-975-5305
Department of Culture, Language, Elders & Youth, PO Box 1000 800,Iqaluit, NU X0A 0H0
867-975-5500, Fax: 867-975-5504, 866-934-2035
Department of Education, Sivummut Bldg., 2nd Fl., PO Box 1000 910,Iqaluit, NU X0A 0H0
867-975-5600, Fax: 867-975-5605
Department of Environment, PO Box 1000 1300,Iqaluit, NU X0A 0H0
867-975-7700, Fax: 867-975-7742, environment@gov.nu.ca
Department of Executive & Intergovernmental Affairs, 1084 Aeroplex bldg., PO Box 1000 200,Iqaluit, NU X0A 0H0
867-975-6000, Fax: 867-975-6099
Department of Finance, Bldg. 1079, 1st Fl., PO Box 1000 330,Iqaluit, NU X0A 0H0
867-975-5800, Fax: 867-975-5805
Department of Health & Social Services, PO Box 1000 1000,Iqaluit, NU X0A 0H0
867-975-5700, Fax: 867-975-5705

Department of Human Resources, PO Box 1000 400,Iqaluit, NU X0A 1H0
Fax: 867-975-6216, 888-668-9993, gnhr@gov.nu.ca
Department of Justice, Sivummut, 1st Fl., PO Box 1000 500,Iqaluit, NU X0A 0H0
867-975-6170, Fax: 867-975-6195, justice@gov.nu.ca
Nunavut Emergency Management, PO Box 1000 700,Iqaluit, NU X0A 0H0
867-975-5403, Fax: 867-979-4221, 800-693-1666
Nunavut Impact Review Board, PO Box 1360, Cambridge Bay, NU X0B 0C0
867-983-4600, Fax: 867-983-2594, 866-233-3033, info@nirb.ca
Nunavut Planning Commission, PO Box 2101, Cambridge Bay, NU X0B 0C0
867-983-4625, Fax: 867-983-4626
Executive Council, Legislative Bldg., 2nd Fl., Box 2410, Iqaluit, NU X0A 0H0
867-975-5090, Fax: 867-975-5095
Government of the Nunavut Territory, PO Box 1200, Iqaluit, NU X0A 0H0
888-252-9869, info@gov.nu.ca
Legislative Assembly, 926 Federal Rd., PO Box 1200, Iqaluit, NU X0A 0H0
867-975-5000, Fax: 867-975-5190, 877-334-7266, leginfo@assembly.nu.ca
Office of the Commissioner, PO Box 2379, Iqaluit, NU X0A 0H0
867-975-5120, Fax: 867-975-5123, nunavutcommissioner@gov.nu.ca
Office of the Premier, Legislative Assembly Bldg., 2nd Fl., PO Box 2410, Iqaluit, NU X0A 0H0
867-975-5050, Fax: 867-975-5051
Second Legislature - Nunavut, PO Box 1200, Iqaluit, NU X0A 0H0

Ontario

Office of the Auditor General, Atrium on Bay, #1530, 20 Dundas St. West, PO Box 105, Toronto, ON M5G 2C2
416-327-2381, Fax: 416-327-9862, comments@auditor.on.ca
Cancer Care Ontario, 620 University Ave., 15th Fl., Toronto, ON M5G 2L7
416-971-9800, Fax: 416-971-6888
Elections Ontario, 51 Rolark Dr., Toronto, ON M1R 3B1
416-326-6300, Fax: 416-326-6200, 888-668-8683, info@elections.on.ca
Executive Council, Whitney Block, Queen's Park, 99 Wellesley St. West, 6th Fl., Toronto, ON M7A 1A1
416-325-5721, Fax: 416-314-1551
Fortieth Parliament - Ontario, Clerk's Office, Legislative Bldg., Queen's Park, Toronto, ON M7A 1A2
416-325-7500, Fax: 416-325-7489
Government of Ontario, Queen's Park, Toronto, ON M7A 1A2
416-326-1234, 800-267-8097
Office of the Integrity Commissioner, #2101, 2 Bloor St. East, Toronto, ON M4W 1A8
416-314-8983, Fax: 416-314-8987, integrity.mail@oico.on.ca
Ministry of Intergovernmental Affairs, 77 Wellesley St. West, Toronto, ON M7A 1N3
416-325-4800, Fax: 416-325-4787,
Legislative Assembly, c/o Clerk's Office, #104, Legislative Bldg., Queen's Park, Toronto, ON M7A 1A2
416-325-7500, Fax: 416-325-7489, assemblyinternet@ontla.ola.org
Office of the Lieutenant Governor, Room 131, Legislative Bldg., Queen's Park, Toronto, ON M7A 1A1
416-325-7780, Fax: 416-325-7787, ltgov@gov.on.ca
Ministry of Municipal Affairs & Housing, College Park, 777 Bay St., 17th Fl., Toronto, ON M5G 2E5
416-585-7041, Fax: 416-585-6470, 866-220-2290, mininfo@ontario.ca
Niagara Falls Bridge Commission, PO Box 395, Niagara Falls, ON L2E 6T8
905-354-5641, Fax: 905-353-6644
Office of the Ombudsman, Bell Trinity Sq., South Tower, 483 Bay St., 10th Fl., Toronto, ON M5G 2C9
416-586-3300, Fax: 416-586-3485, 800-263-1830, info@ombudsman.on.ca
Ontario Mental Health Foundation, 441 Jarvis St., 2nd Fl., Toronto, ON M4Y 2G8
416-920-7721, Fax: 416-920-0026, grants@omhf.on.ca
Ontario Northland, 555 Oak St. East, North Bay, ON P1B 8L3
705-472-4500, Fax: 705-472-4267, 800-363-7512, info@ontarionorthland.ca
Ontario Pension Board, Sun Life Bldg., #2200, 200 King St. West, Toronto, ON M5H 3X6
416-364-8558, Fax: 416-364-7578, 800-668-6203, office.services@opb.on.ca
Ottawa Office, #1209, 350 Sparks St., Ottawa, ON K1R 7S8
613-233-9890, Fax: 613-233-2543
Office of the Premier, Legislative Bldg., #281, 1 Queen's Park Cres. South, Toronto, ON M7A 1A1
416-325-1941, Fax: 416-325-3745

Prince Edward Island

Elections Prince Edward Island, J. Angus MacLean Bldg., 94 Great George St., 1st Fl., PO Box 774, Charlottetown, PE C1A 7L3
902-368-5895, Fax: 902-368-6500, 888-234-8783
Executive Council, Shaw Bldg., 5th Fl., PO Box 2000, Charlottetown, PE C1A 7N8
902-368-4502, Fax: 902-368-6118
Government of Prince Edward Island, Island Information Service, PO Box 2000, Charlottetown, PE C1A 7N8
902-368-4000, island@gov.pe.ca
Legislative Assembly, Province House, 165 Richmond St., 1st Fl., PO Box 2000, Charlottetown, PE C1A 7N8
902-368-5970, Fax: 902-368-5175, 877-315-5518, legislativelibrary@assembly.pe.ca
Office of the Premier, Shaw Bldg., 95 Rochford St. South, 5th Fl., PO Box 2000, Charlottetown, PE C1A 7N8
902-368-4501, Fax: 902-368-6118
Sixty-fourth General Assembly - Prince Edward Island, Province House, 165 Richmond St., 1st Fl., PO Box 2000, Charlottetown, PE C1A 7N8
902-368-5970, Fax: 902-368-5175, 877-315-5518

Quebec

Ministère des Affaires municipales et Occupation du territoire, Aile Chaveau, 10, rue Pierre-Olivier-Chauveau, 3e étage, Québec, QC G1R 4J3
418-691-2019, Fax: 418-643-7385, communications@mamrot.gouv.qc.ca
Bureau du coroner, Édifice le Delta 2, #390, 2875, boul Laurier, Québec, QC G1V 5B1
418-643-1845, Fax: 418-643-6174, 866-312-7051, clientele.coroner@msp.gouv.qc.ca
Centre de recherche industrielle du Québec, 333, rue Franquet, Québec, QC G1P 4C7
418-659-1550, Fax: 418-652-2251, 800-667-2386, infocriq@criq.qc.ca
Comité de déontologie policière, Tour du Saint-Laurent, #A-200, 2525, boul Laurier, 2e étage, Québec, QC G1V 4Z6
418-646-1936, Fax: 418-528-0987, comite.deontologie@msp.gouv.qc.ca
Commissaire à la déontologie policière, #1-40, 1200, rte de l'Église, Québec, QC G1V 4Y9
418-643-7897, Fax: 418-528-9473, 877-237-7897, deontologie-policiere.quebec@msp.gouv.qc.ca
Commissariat des incendies, 455, rue Dupont, Québec, QC G1K 6N2
418-529-5706, Fax: 418-529-9922, cdelage@notarius.net
Commission de la fonction publique (Québec), 800, Place d'Youville, 7e étage, Québec, QC G1R 3P4
418-643-1425, Fax: 418-643-7264, 800-432-0432, cfp@cfp.gouv.qc.ca
Commission québecoise des libérations conditionnelles, #1.32A, 300, boul Jean-Lesage, Québec, QC G1K 8K6
418-646-8300, Fax: 418-643-7217, cqlc@msp.gouv.qc.ca
Ministère du Conseil exécutif, 875, Grande Allée est, Québec, QC G1R 4Y8
418-646-3021, Fax: 418-528-9242
Direction générale de la Sûreté du Québec, 1701, rue Parthenais, Montréal, QC H2K 3S7
514-598-4141, Fax: 514-598-4242
Commission des droits de la personne et des droits de la jeunesse, 360, rue St-Jacques, 2e étage, Montréal, QC H2Y 1P5
514-873-5146, Fax: 514-873-6032, 800-361-6477, accueil@cdpdj.qc.ca
Ministère du Développement économique, de l'Innovation et de l'Exportation, 710, place D'Youville, 3e étage, Québec, QC G1R 4Y4
418-691-5950, Fax: 418-644-0118, 866-680-1884
Commission de la fonction publique, 800, place D'Youville, 7e étage, Québec, QC G1R 3P4
418-643-1425, Fax: 418-643-7264, 800-432-0432, cfp@cfp.gouv.qc.ca
Gouvernement du Québec, Hôtel du Parlement, 1045, rue des Parlementaires, Québec, QC G1A 1A3
418-643-7239, Fax: 418-646-4271, 866-337-8837
Ministère de l' Immigration et des Communautés culturelles, Édifice Gérald-Godin, 360, rue McGill, Montréal, QC H2Y 2E9
514-864-9191, Fax: 514-864-2899, 877-864-9191
Institut de la statistique du Québec, 200, ch Ste-Foy, 1er étage, Québec, QC G1R 5T4
418-691-2401, Fax: 418-643-4129, 800-463-4090, direction@stat.gouv.qc.ca
Investissement Québec, #1500, 600, rue de la Gauchetière ouest, Montréal, QC H3B 4L8
514-873-4664, 866-870-0437
L'Assemblée nationale, Hôtel du Parlement, 1045, rue des Parlementaires, Québec, QC G1A 1A3
418-643-7239, Fax: 418-646-4271, 866-337-8837, responsable.contenu@assnat.qc.ca
Cabinet du Lieutenant-gouverneur, Édifice André-Laurendeau, 1050, rue des Parlementaires R.C., Québec, QC G1A 1A1
418-643-5385, Fax: 418-644-4677, 866-791-0766
Cabinet du premier ministre, Édifice Honoré-Mercier, 835, boul René-Lévesque est, 3e étage, Québec, QC G1A 1B4
418-643-5321, Fax: 418-643-3924
Ministère des Relations internationales, Édifice Hector-Fabre, 525, boul Réne-Lévesque est, Québec, QC G1R 5R9
418-649-2300, Fax: 418-649-2656
Ministère des Ressources naturelles et de la Faune, 880, ch Sainte-Foy, Québec, QC G1S 4X4
418-627-8600, Fax: 418-644-6513, 866-248-6936, services.clientele@mrnf.gouv.qc.ca
Régie des alcools, des courses et des jeux, 560, boul Charest est, Québec, QC G1K 3J3
418-643-7667, Fax: 418-643-5971, 800-363-0320
Secrétariat aux affaires intergouvernementales canadiennes, 875, Grande Allée est, 3e étage, Québec, QC G1R 4Y8
418-643-4011, Fax: 418-528-0052
Société des alcools du Québec, 905, av De Lorimier, Montréal, QC H2K 3V9
514-873-2020, Fax: 514-873-6788, 866-873-2020, info@saq.com
Trente-neuvième assemblée nationale, Hôtel du Parlement, 1045, rue des Parlementaires, Québec, QC G1A 1A4
418-643-7239, Fax: 418-646-4271, 866-337-8837
École nationale de police du Québec, 350, rue Marguerite-d'Youville, Nicolet, QC J3T 1X4
819-293-8631, Fax: 819-293-8630, courriel@enpq.qc.ca
Directeur général des Élections du Québec, Édifice René-Lévesque, 3460, rue de La Pérade, Québec, QC G1X 3Y5
418-528-0422, Fax: 418-643-7291, 888-353-2846, info@electionsquebec.qc.ca

Saskatchewan

Provincial Auditor Saskatchewan, #1500, 1920 Broad St., Regina, SK S4P 3V2
306-787-6398, Fax: 306-787-6383, info@auditor.sk.ca
Board of Revenue Commissioners, #480, 2151 Scarth St., Regina, SK S4P 2H8
306-787-6221, Fax: 306-787-1610
Saskatchewan Communications Network, #313E, 2440 Broad St., Regina, SK S4P 0A5
306-779-2726, Fax: 306-545-8649, inquiries@scn.ca
Elections Saskatchewan, 1702 Park St., Regina, SK S4N 6B2
306-787-4000, Fax: 306-787-4052, 877-958-8683, info@elections.sk.ca
Executive Council, Legislative Bldg., 2405 Legislative Dr., Regina, SK S4S 0B3
306-787-7448, admin.ec@gov.sk.ca
Government of Saskatchewan, Regina, SK S4S 0B3
Saskatchewan Government Services, 1920 Rose St., Regina, SK S4P 0A9
306-787-6911, Fax: 306-787-1061, GSReception@gs.gov.sk.ca
Legislative Assembly, c/o Clerk's Office, Legislative Bldg., #123, 2405 Legislative Dr., Regina, SK S4S 0B3
306-787-2376, Fax: 306-787-1558, info@legassembly.sk.ca
Office of the Lieutenant Governor, Government House, 4607 Dewdney Ave., Regina, SK S4T 1B7
306-787-4070, Fax: 306-787-7716, lgo@ltgov.sk.ca
Ombudsman Saskatchewan, #150, 2401 Saskatchewan Dr., Regina, SK S4P 4H8
306-787-6211, Fax: 306-787-9090, 800-667-7180, ombreg@ombudsman.sk.ca
Office of the Premier, Legislative Bldg., #226, 2405 Legislative Dr., Regina, SK S4S 0B3
306-787-9433, Fax: 306-787-0885, premier@gov.sk.ca
Saskatchewan Public Service Commission, 2100 Broad St., Regina, SK S4P 1Y5
306-787-7853, 866-319-5999, psc.webmaster@gov.sk.ca; inquiry@psc.gov.sk.ca
Saskatchewan Development Fund Corporation, #400, 2400 College Ave., Regina, SK S4P 1C8
306-787-1645, Fax: 306-787-8125
Saskatchewan Tourism, Parks, Culture & Sport, 1919 Saskatchewan Dr., 4th Fl., Regina, SK S4P 4H2
306-787-5729, Fax: 306-787-8560, info@cyr.gov.sk.ca
Twenty-sixth Legislature - Saskatchewan, #123, Legislative Bldg., 2405 Legislative Dr., Regina, SK S4S 0B3
306-787-2376, Fax: 306-787-1558, info@legassembly.sk.ca

Yukon Territory

Office of the Commissioner, Closeleigh Manor, 1098 First Ave., Whitehorse, YT Y1A 0C1
867-667-5121, Fax: 867-393-6201, commissioner@gov.yk.ca
Executive Council, #2071, 2nd Ave., Whitehorse, YT Y1A 2C6
867-667-5393, Fax: 867-393-6214, eco@gov.yk.ca
Government of the Yukon Territory, PO Box 2703, Whitehorse, YT Y1A 2C6
867-667-5811, 800-661-0408

Legislative Assembly, 2071 Second Ave., PO Box 2703, Whitehorse, YT Y1A 2C6
867-667-5498, Fax: 867-393-6280

Office of the Premier, 2071 Second Ave., PO Box 2703, Whitehorse, YT Y1A 1B2
867-667-8660, Fax: 867-393-6252, premier@gov.yk.ca

Yukon Public Service Commission, Yukon Government Administration Building, #2071-2nd Ave., PO Box 2703, Whitehorse, YT Y1A 2C6
867-667-5653, Fax: 867-667-5755, 800-661-0408, PSCWebsite@gov.yk.ca

Thirty-third Legislative Assembly - Yukon Territory, Yukon Legislative Assembly Office, 2071 Second Ave., PO Box 2703, Whitehorse, YT Y1A 2C6
867-667-5498

GOVERNMENT (GENERAL INFORMATION)

Aboriginal Affairs & Northern Development Canada, 10 Wellington St., North Tower, Gatineau, QC K1A 0H4
819-997-0380, Fax: 866-817-3977, 800-567-9604, infopubs@aadnc-aandc.gc.ca

Auditor General of Canada, 240 Sparks St., Ottawa, ON K1A 0G6
613-995-3708, Fax: 613-957-0474, 888-761-5953, communications@oag-bvg.gc.ca; infomedia@oag-bvg.gc.ca

Canada Business, 235 Queen St., Ottawa, ON K1A 0H5
888-576-4444

Citizenship & Immigration Canada, Jean Edmonds, South Tower, 365 Laurier Ave. West, Ottawa, ON K1A 1L1
613-954-9019, Fax: 613-954-2221, 888-242-2100

Communications & Consultations Branch, Tower 7, 1341 Baseline Rd., Ottawa, ON K1A 0C7
613-759-1000, Fax: 613-773-2772

Communications Branch, 284 Wellington St., Ottawa, ON K1A 0H8
Fax: 613-941-2329

Consultations & Communications Branch, East Tower, 140 O'Connor St., 19th Fl., Ottawa, ON K1A 0G5
613-992-1573, finpub@fin.gc.ca

Correctional Service Canada, 340 Laurier Ave. West, Ottawa, ON K1A 0P9
613-992-5891, Fax: 613-943-1630

Environment Canada, 10 Wellington St., Gatineau, QC K1A 0H3
819-997-2800, Fax: 819-994-1412, 800-668-6767, enviroinfo@ec.gc.ca

Fisheries & Oceans Canada, 200 Kent St., Ottawa, ON K1A 0E6
613-993-0999, Fax: 613-990-1866, info@dfo-mpo.gc.ca

Foreign Affairs & International Trade Canada, 125 Sussex Dr., Ottawa, ON K1A 0G2
613-944-4000, Fax: 613-996-9709, 800-267-8376, enqserv@international.gc.ca

Health Canada, Tunney's Pasture, Ottawa, ON K1A 0K9
613-957-2991, Fax: 613-941-5366, 866-225-0709, info@hc-sc.gc.ca

House of Commons, Canada, House of Commons, Centre Block, Parliament Buildings, 111 Wellington St., Ottawa, ON K1A 0A6
613-992-4793, 866-599-4999, info@parl.gc.ca

Human Resources & Skills Development Canada, 140 Promenade du Portage, Gatineau, QC K1A 0J9

Industry Canada, C.D. Howe Building, 235 Queen St., Ottawa, ON K1A 0H5
613-954-5031, Fax: 613-954-2340, 800-328-6189, info@ic.gc.ca

National Defence Canada, Major-General George R. Pearkes Bldg., 101 Colonel By Dr., Ottawa, ON K1A 0K2
613-995-2534, Fax: 613-992-4739, 800-856-8488

Office of the Prime Minister (Conservative Party of Canada), Langevin Block, 80 Wellington St., Ottawa, ON K1A 0A2
613-992-4211, Fax: 613-941-6900, pm@pm.gc.ca

Service Canada, 140, Promenade du Portage, Gatineau, QC K1A 0J9
800-622-6232

Statistics Canada, R.H. Coats Bldg., Tunney's Pasture, 150 Tunney's Pasture Driveway, Ottawa, ON K1A 0T6
613-951-8116, Fax: 877-287-4369, 800-263-1136, infostats@statcan.ca

Transport Canada, Place de Ville, 330 Sparks St., Tower C, Ottawa, ON K1A 0N5
613-990-2309, Fax: 613-954-4731, 866-995-9737

Treasury Board of Canada, 140 O'Connor St., Ottawa, ON K1A 0R5
613-957-2400, Fax: 613-941-4000, 877-636-0656

Veterans Affairs Canada, 161 Grafton St., PO Box 7700, Charlottetown, PE C1A 8M9
902-566-8888, 866-522-2111, information@vac-acc.gc.ca

Alberta

Alberta Public Affairs Bureau, Park Plaza, 10611 - 98 Ave., 6th Fl., Edmonton, AB T5K 2P7
780-427-2754, Fax: 780-422-4168

Alberta Service Alberta, Government of Alberta, PO Box 1333, Edmonton, AB T5J 2N2
780-427-4088, service.alberta@gov.ab.ca

British Columbia

Business & Workforce Transformation, PO Box 9029 Prov Govt,Victoria, BC V8V 1T7
250-953-3470, Fax: 250-356-7391

New Brunswick

Communications New Brunswick, Wilcom Bldg., 225 King St., 2nd Fl., PO Box 6000, Fredericton, NB E3B 5H1
506-453-2240, Fax: 506-453-5329

Newfoundland & Labrador

Department of Government Services, PO Box 8700, St. John's, NL A1B 4J6
709-729-4834, gsinfo@gov.nl.ca

Nova Scotia

Department of Service Nova Scotia & Municipal Relations, 1505 Barrington St., PO Box 216, Halifax, NS B3J 3K5
902-424-5200, Fax: 902-424-0581, 800-670-4357, askus@gov.ns.ca

Nunavut

Department of Executive & Intergovernmental Affairs, 1084 Aeroplex bldg., PO Box 1000 200,Iqaluit, NU X0A 0H0
867-975-6000, Fax: 867-975-6099

Ontario

ServiceOntario, College Park, 777 Bay St., 15th fl., Toronto, ON M7A 2J3
416-326-1234, Fax: 416-326-1313, 800-267-8097

Quebec

Services Québec, Bureau de la qualité, 800, place D'Youville, 20e étage, Québec, QC G1R 3P4
418-644-4545, 877-644-4545

Yukon Territory

Government Inquiry Office, Yukon Government Administration Building, 2071 Second Ave., PO Box 2703, Whitehorse, YT Y1A 2C6
867-667-5811, information@gov.yk.ca

GRANTS & SUBSIDIES

See Also: Student Aid

Atlantic Canada Opportunities Agency, Blue Cross Centre, 644 Main St., 3rd Fl., PO Box 6051, Moncton, NB E1C 9J8
506-851-2271, Fax: 506-851-7403, 800-561-7862, information@acoa-apeca.gc.ca

Business Development Bank of Canada, #400, 5, Place Ville-Marie, Montréal, QC H3B 5E7
514-283-5904, Fax: 514-283-5626, 877-232-2269

Canada Council for the Arts, 350 Albert St., PO Box 1047, Ottawa, ON K1P 5V8
613-566-4414, Fax: 613-566-4390, 800-263-5588

Canada Economic Development for Québec Regions, Édifice Dominion Square, #900, 1255, rue Peel, Montréal, QC H3B 2T9
514-283-6412, Fax: 514-283-3302, 866-385-6412

Canada Mortgage & Housing Corporation, 700 Montreal Rd., Ottawa, ON K1A 0P7
613-748-2000, Fax: 613-748-2098, 800-668-2642, chic@cmhc-schl.gc.ca

Canadian Institutes of Health Research, 160 Elgin St., 9th Fl., Ottawa, ON K1A 0W9
613-941-2672, Fax: 613-954-1800, 888-603-4178, info@cihr-irsc.gc.ca

International Development Research Centre, 150 Kent St., PO Box 8500, Ottawa, ON K1G 3H9
613-236-6163, Fax: 613-238-7230, info@idrc.ca

National Film Board of Canada, 3155, rue Côte de Liesse, CP 1600 Centre-ville,Saint-Laurent, QC H4N 2N4
514-283-9000, Fax: 514-283-7564, 800-267-7710

Natural Sciences & Engineering Research Council of Canada, Constitution Square, Tower II, 350 Albert St., Ottawa, ON K1A 1H5
613-995-4273, Fax: 613-943-1624, marie-josee.duval@nserc-crsng.gc.ca

Western Economic Diversification Canada, Canada Place, #1500, 9700 Jasper Ave. NW, Edmonton, AB T5J 4H7
780-495-4164, Fax: 780-495-4557, 888-338-9378

Alberta

Local Government Services Division, Commerce Place, 10155 - 102 St., 17th Fl., Edmonton, AB T5J 4L4

Newfoundland & Labrador

Newfoundland & Labrador Municipal Financing Corporation, Confederation Bldg., PO Box 8700, St. John's, NL A1B 4J6
709-729-6686, Fax: 709-729-2095

Nova Scotia

Department of Finance, Provincial Bldg., 1723 Hollis St., 7th Fl., PO Box 187, Halifax, NS B3J 2N3
902-424-5554, Fax: 902-424-0635, FinanceWeb@gov.ns.ca

Saskatchewan

Saskatchewan Energy & Resources, #300, 2103 - 11th Ave., Regina, SK S4P 3Z8
306-787-2528, webmasterer@gov.sk.ca

HAZARDOUS MATERIALS

Hazardous Materials Information Review Commission, 427 Laurier Ave. West, 7th Fl., Ottawa, ON K1A 1M3
613-993-4331, Fax: 613-993-4686, hmirc-ccrmd@hc-sc.gc.ca

Institute for Chemical Process & Environmental Technology, Bldg. M-12, 1200 Montreal Rd., Ottawa, ON K1A 0R6
613-993-4041, Fax: 613-957-8231

British Columbia

British Columbia Provincial Emergency Program, Block A, #200, 2261 Keating Cross Rd., Saanichton, BC V8M 2A5
250-952-4913, Fax: 250-952-4888, 888-257-4777

Manitoba

Emergency Measures Organization, 405 Broadway Ave., 15th Floor, Winnipeg, MB R3C 3L6
204-945-4772, Fax: 204-945-4929, 888-267-8298, emo@gov.mb.ca

Ontario

Ministry of Environment, 135 St. Clair Ave. West, Toronto, ON M4V 1P5
416-325-4000, Fax: 416-325-3159, 800-565-4923

Pesticides Advisory Committee, 135 St. Clair Ave. West, 15th Fl., Toronto, ON M4V 1P5
416-314-9230, Fax: 416-314-9237

HEALTH

Canadian Centre for Occupational Health & Safety, 135 Hunter St. East, Hamilton, ON L8N 1M5
905-572-2981, Fax: 905-572-2206, 800-668-4284

Canadian Centre on Substance Abuse, #500, 75 Albert St., Ottawa, ON K1P 5E7
613-235-4048, Fax: 613-235-8101, info@ccsa.ca

Canadian Food Inspection Agency, 1400 Merivale Rd., Ottawa, ON K1A 0Y9
613-225-2342, Fax: 613-228-6601, 800-442-2342

Children's Secretariat, c/o Sarah Henry, Education & Early Childhood Development, 161 St. Peters Rd., PO Box 2000, Charlottetown, PE C1A 7N8

Corporate Support Division, Telus Plaza NT, 10025 Jasper Ave., 19th Fl., Edmonton, AB T5J 1S6

Hazardous Materials Information Review Commission, 427 Laurier Ave. West, 7th Fl., Ottawa, ON K1A 1M3
613-993-4331, Fax: 613-993-4686, hmirc-ccrmd@hc-sc.gc.ca

Health Canada, Tunney's Pasture, Ottawa, ON K1A 0K9
613-957-2991, Fax: 613-941-5366, 866-225-0709, info@hc-sc.gc.ca

Health Services Information & Information Technology Cluster, 56 Wellesley St. West, 10th Fl., Toronto, ON M5S 2S3
416-314-4243, Fax: 416-314-0289

Health System Strategy & Policy Division, Hepburn Block, 80 Grosvenor St., 8th Fl., Toronto, ON M7A 1R3
416-327-8295, Fax: 416-327-5109

Health Workforce Division, Telus Plaza NT, 10025 Jasper Ave., 10th Fl., Edmonton, AB T5J 1S6

National Advisory Council on Aging, Jeanne Mance Bldg., 8th Fl., Postal Locator 1908 A1, Ottawa, ON K1A 0K9
613-957-1968, Fax: 613-957-7627

Patented Medicine Prices Review Board, Standard Life Centre, #1400, 333 Laurier Ave. West, PO Box L40, Ottawa, ON K1P 1C1
613-954-8299, Fax: 613-952-7626, 877-861-2350, pmprb@pmprb-cepmb.gc.ca

Public Health Agency of Canada, 130 Colonnade Rd., Ottawa, ON K1A 0K9

Ste-Anne's Hospital, 305 boul des Anciens-Combattants, Sainte-Anne-de-Bellevue, QC H9X 1Y9
514-457-3440, 800-361-9287, steanne@vac-acc.gc.ca

Alberta

Alberta Health Services, Corporate Office, North Tower, Seventh Street Plaza, 10030 - 107th St. NW, 14th Fl., Edmonton, AB T5J 3E4
780-342-2000, Fax: 780-342-2060, 888-342-2471, ahsb.admin@albertahealthservices.ca

Alberta Health & Wellness, PO Box 1360 Main,Edmonton, AB T5J 2N3
780-427-7164, Fax: 780-427-1171

Health Quality Council of Alberta, #210, 811 - 14 St. NW, Calgary, AB T2N 2A4
403-297-8162, Fax: 403-297-8258, info@hqca.ca

Occupational Health & Safety Council, Labour Building, 10808 - 99 Ave., 9th Fl., Edmonton, AB T5K 0G5
780-415-8690, 866-415-8690

Office of the Chief Medical Officer of Health, Telus Plaza NT, 10025 Jasper Ave., 24th Fl., Edmonton, AB T5J 1S6
780-427-5263

Premier's Council on the Status of Persons with Disabilities, HSBC Building, 10055 - 106 St., 11th Fl., Edmonton, AB T5J 1G3
780-422-1095, 800-272-8841, pcspd@gov.ab.ca
Alberta Seniors & Community Supports, Communications, Standard Life Centre, 10405 Jasper Ave., 3rd Fl., Edmonton, AB T5J 4R7
780-415-9950, Fax: 780-644-1227, 866-477-8589, seniors.communications@gov.ab.ca
Seniors Advisory Council for Alberta, Standard Life Centre, #600, 10405 Jasper Ave., 6th Fl., Edmonton, AB T5J 4R7
780-422-2321, Fax: 780-422-8762, saca@gov.ab.ca

British Columbia

Ministry of Health, 1515 Blanshard St., Victoria, BC V8W 3C8
250-952-1742, Fax: 250-356-9587, 800-465-4911, hlth.health@gov.bc.ca

Manitoba

Addictions Foundation of Manitoba, 1031 Portage Ave., Winnipeg, MB R3G 0R8
204-944-6200, Fax: 204-786-7768, library@afm.mb.ca
Manitoba Health & Healthy Living, #100, 300 Carlton St., Winnipeg, MB R3B 3M9
204-786-7191, minhlt@leg.gov.mb.ca
Manitoba Council on Aging, #822, 155 Carlton St., Winnipeg, MB R3C 3H8
204-945-6565, Fax: 204-948-2514, 800-665-6565
Manitoba Drug Standards & Therapeutics Committee, #1014, 300 Carlton St., Winnipeg, MB R3B 3M9
204-786-7317, Fax: 204-942-2030
Office of the Chief Medical Examiner, #210, 1 Wesley Ave., Winnipeg, MB R3C 4C6
204-945-2088, Fax: 204-945-2442, 800-282-9069
Primary Care & Healthy Living, 300 Carlton St., 2nd Floor, Winnipeg, MB R3B 3M9

New Brunswick

Department of Health, PO Box 5100, Fredericton, NB E3B 5G8
506-457-4800, Fax: 506-453-5243, dh-ms@dh-ms.ca
Premier's Council on the Status of Disabled Persons, Kings Place, #648, 440 King St., Fredericton, NB E3B 5H8
506-444-3000, Fax: 506-444-3001, 800-442-4412, pcsdp@gnb.ca
Workplace Health, Safety & Compensation Commission of New Brunswick, 1 Portland St., PO Box 160, Saint John, NB E2L 3X9
506-632-2200, 800-222-9775, communications@ws-ts.nb.ca

Newfoundland & Labrador

Department of Health & Community Services, West Block, Confederation Bldg., PO Box 8700, St. John's, NL A1B 4J6
709-729-5021, Fax: 709-729-5824, healthinfo@gov.nl.ca
Newfoundland & Labrador Health Boards Associations, Beothuck Bldg., 20 Crosbie Pl., 2nd Fl., St. John's, NL A1B 3Y8
709-364-7701, Fax: 709-364-6460

Northwest Territories

Department of Health & Social Services, Centre Square Tower, PO Box 1320, Yellowknife, NT X1A 2L9
Fax: 867-873-0266

Nova Scotia

Department of Health & Wellness, Joseph Howe Bldg., 1690 Hollis St., 4th Fl., PO Box 488, Halifax, NS B3J 2R8
902-424-5818, Fax: 902-424-0730, 800-387-6665, DoHweb@gov.ns.ca
Nova Scotia Advisory Commission on AIDS, Dennis Bldg., 1740 Granville St., 6th Fl., Halifax, NS B3J 1X5
902-424-5730, Fax: 902-424-4727, AIDS@gov.ns.ca
Office of the Chief Medical Examiner, Halifax Insurance Bldg., #701, 5670 Spring Garden Rd., Halifax, NS B3J 1H7
902-424-2722, Fax: 902-424-0607

Nunavut

Department of Culture, Language, Elders & Youth, PO Box 1000 800,Iqaluit, NU X0A 0H0
867-975-5500, Fax: 867-975-5504, 866-934-2035
Department of Health & Social Services, PO Box 1000 1000,Iqaluit, NU X0A 0H0
867-975-5700, Fax: 867-975-5705
Office of the Chief Coroner, PO Box 1000 590, Iqaluit, NU X0A 0H0

Ontario

Cancer Care Ontario, 620 University Ave., 15th Fl., Toronto, ON M5G 2L7
416-971-9800, Fax: 416-971-6888
Consent & Capacity Board, 151 Bloor St. West, 10th Fl., Toronto, ON M5S 2T5
416-327-4142, Fax: 416-924-8873, 866-777-7391
Ministry of Health & Long-Term Care, Hepburn Block, 80 Grosvenor St., 10th Fl, Toronto, ON M7A 2C4
416-327-4327, 800-268-1153
Health Boards Secretariat, 151 Bloor St. West, 9th Fl., Toronto, ON M5S 2T5
416-327-8512, Fax: 416-327-8524, 866-282-2179
Ministry of Health Promotion & Sport, College Park, 777 Bay Street, 18th Fl., Toronto, ON M7A 1S5
416-326-8475, Fax: 416-326-4864, info@mhp.gov.on.ca
Medical Eligibility Committee, 370 Select Dr., PO Box 168, Kingston, ON K7M 8T4
613-548-6405
Ontario Mental Health Foundation, 441 Jarvis St., 2nd Fl., Toronto, ON M4Y 2G8
416-920-7721, Fax: 416-920-0026, grants@omhf.on.ca
Ontario Review Board, 151 Bloor St. West, 10th Fl., Toronto, ON M5S 2T5
416-327-8866, Fax: 416-327-8867
Pesticides Advisory Committee, 135 St. Clair Ave. West, 15th Fl., Toronto, ON M4V 1P5
416-314-9230, Fax: 416-314-9237
Trillium Gift of Life Network, #900, 522 University Ave., Toronto, ON M5G 1W7
416-363-4001, Fax: 416-363-4002, 800-263-2833

Prince Edward Island

BIO FOOD TECH, 101 Belvedere Ave., PO Box 2000, Charlottetown, PE C1A 7N8
902-368-5548, Fax: 902-368-5549, 877-368-5548, biofoodtech@biofoodtech.ca
Health PEI, 16 Garfield St., PO Box 2000, Charlottetown, PE C1A 7N8
902-368-6130, Fax: 902-368-6136, healthinput@gov.pe.ca
Prince Edward Island Department of Health & Wellness, 105 Rochford St. North, 4th Fl., PO Box 2000, Charlottetown, PE C1A 7N8
902-368-6414, Fax: 902-368-4121

Quebec

Agence d'évaluation des technologies et des modes d'intervention en santé, #10.083, 2021, av Union, Montréal, QC H3A 2S9
514-873-2563, Fax: 514-873-1369
Bureau des projets Centres hospitaliers universitaires de Montréal, CHUM, CUSM et CHU Sainte-Justine, #10.049, 2021, rue Union, Montréal, QC H3A 2S9
514-864-9883, Fax: 514-873-7362, info.construction3chu@msss.gouv.qc.ca
Bureau du coroner, Édifice le Delta 2, #390, 2875, boul Laurier, Québec, QC G1V 5B1
418-643-1845, Fax: 418-643-6174, 866-312-7051, clientele.coroner@msp.gouv.qc.ca
Commissaire à la santé et du bien-être, #700, 1020, rte de l'Église, Québec, QC G1V 3V9
418-643-3040, Fax: 418-644-0654, csbe@csbe.gouv.qc.ca
Commission de la santé et de la sécurité du travail, 425, rue du Pont, CP 4900 Terminus, Québec, QC G1K 7S6
418-266-4000, Fax: 418-266-4015, 888-999-2778
Conseil du médicament, #100, 1195, av Lavigerie, 1er étage, Québec, QC G1V 4N3
418-644-8103, Fax: 418-644-8120, cdm@cdm.gouv.qc.ca
Corporation d'hébergement du Québec, 2535, boul Laurier, 5e étage, Québec, QC G1V 4M3
418-644-3600, Fax: 418-644-3609, clientele.sante@siq.gouv.qc.ca
Fonds de la recherche en santé du Québec, #800, 500, rue Sherbrooke ouest, Montréal, QC H3A 3C6
514-873-2114, Fax: 514-873-8768
Institut national de santé publique du Québec, 945, av Wolfe, Québec, QC G1V 5B3
418-650-5115, Fax: 418-646-9328, info@inspq.qc.ca
Régie de l'assurance maladie du Québec, 1125, Grande Allée ouest, Québec, QC G1S 1E7
418-646-4636
Commission de la santé et de la sécurité du travail du Québec, 524, rue Bourdages, CP 1200 Terminus postal,Québec, QC G1K 7E2
418-266-4850, Fax: 418-266-4669, 866-302-2778
Ministère de la Santé et des Services sociaux, Direction des communications, 1075, ch Sainte-Foy, 16e étage, Québec, QC G1S 2M1
418-643-9395, Fax: 418-643-4768, regisseur.web@msss.gouv.qc.ca
Secrétariat à l'accès aux services en langue anglaise et aux communautés ethnoculturelles, #1.03, 201 boul Crémazie est, 1er étage, Montréal, QC H2M 1L2
514-873-5163, Fax: 514-873-9876
Urgences-santé Québec, 3232, rue Bélanger, Montréal, QC H1Y 3H5
514-723-5600, info@urgences-sante.qc.ca

Saskatchewan

Health Quality Council, 241, 111 Research Dr., Saskatoon, SK S7N 3R2
306-668-8810, Fax: 306-668-8820, info@hqc.sk.ca
Saskatchewan Health, T.C. Douglas Bldg., 3475 Albert St., Regina, SK S4S 6X6
306-787-0146, 800-667-7766, info@health.gov.sk.ca

Yukon Territory

Yukon Health & Social Services, PO Box 2703, Whitehorse, YT Y1A 2C6
867-667-3673, Fax: 867-667-3096, hss@gov.yk.ca

HEALTH & SAFETY

Alberta

Alberta Workers' Compensation Board, 9912 - 107 St., Edmonton, AB T5J 2S5
780-498-3999, Fax: 780-427-5863, 866-922-9221
Canadian Centre for Occupational Health & Safety, 135 Hunter St. East, Hamilton, ON L8N 1M5
905-572-2981, Fax: 905-572-2206, 800-668-4284
Canadian Coast Guard, Centennial Towers, #6S018, 200 Kent St., Ottawa, ON K1A 0E6
613-993-0999, Fax: 613-990-1866, info@dfo-mpo.gc.ca
Canadian Environmental Assessment Agency, Place Bell Canada, 160 Elgin St., 22nd Fl., Ottawa, ON K1A 0H3
613-957-0700, Fax: 613-957-0862, 866-582-1884, info@ceaa-acee.gc.ca
Canadian Food Inspection Agency, 1400 Merivale Rd., Ottawa, ON K1A 0Y9
613-225-2342, Fax: 613-228-6601, 800-442-2342
Canadian Food Inspection Agency, 1400 Merivale Rd., Ottawa, ON K1A 0Y9
613-225-2342, Fax: 613-228-6601, 800-442-2342
Hazardous Materials Information Review Commission, 427 Laurier Ave. West, 7th Fl., Ottawa, ON K1A 1M3
613-993-4331, Fax: 613-993-4686, hmirc-ccrmd@hc-sc.gc.ca
Health Canada, Tunney's Pasture, Ottawa, ON K1A 0K9
613-957-2991, Fax: 613-941-5366, 866-225-0709, info@hc-sc.gc.ca
Human Resources & Skills Development Canada, 140 Promenade du Portage, Gatineau, QC K1A 0J9
Department of Labour & Advanced Education, 5151 Terminal Rd., 6th Fl., PO Box 697, Halifax, NS B3J 2T8
902-424-5301, Fax: 902-424-0575,
National Defence Canada, Major-General George R. Pearkes Bldg., 101 Colonel By Dr., Ottawa, ON K1A 0K2
613-995-2534, Fax: 613-992-4739, 800-856-8488
Policy & Corporate Services Division, Twin Atria Building, 4999 - 98 Ave., 3rd Fl., Edmonton, AB T6B 2X3
Public Safety Canada, 269 Laurier Ave. West, Ottawa, ON K1A 0P8
613-944-4875, Fax: 613-954-5186, 800-830-3118, communications@ps.gc.ca
Transportation Safety Board of Canada, 200 Promenade du Portage, 4th Fl., Ottawa, ON K1A 1K8
819-994-3741, Fax: 819-997-2239, 800-387-3557

Alberta

Alberta Employment & Immigration, Minister's Office, Legislature Building, #418, 10800 - 97 Ave., Edmonton, AB T5K 2B6
780-644-5135, 866-644-5135, eii.communications@gov.ab.ca
Alberta Health & Wellness, PO Box 1360 Main,Edmonton, AB T5J 2N3
780-427-7164, Fax: 780-427-1171
Occupational Health & Safety Council, Labour Building, 10808 - 99 Ave., 9th Fl., Edmonton, AB T5K 0G5
780-415-8690, 866-415-8690
Transportation Safety Board, North Office, Twin Atria Building, 4999 - 98 Ave., Main Fl., Edmonton, AB T6B 2X3
780-427-7178, Fax: 780-422-9739

British Columbia

Ministry of Health, 1515 Blanshard St., Victoria, BC V8W 3C8
250-952-1742, Fax: 250-356-9587, 800-465-4911, hlth.health@gov.bc.ca
Ministry of Labour, Citizens' Services & Open Government, PO Box 9056 Prov Govt,Victoria, BC V8W 9K4
250-952-7623, Fax: 250-387-4312, 800-663-7867, LCTZ.Minister@gov.bc.ca
British Columbia Provincial Emergency Program, Block A, #200, 2261 Keating Cross Rd., Saanichton, BC V8M 2A5
250-952-4913, Fax: 250-952-4888, 888-257-4777
Workers' Compensation Board of British Columbia, PO Box 5350 Terminal,Vancouver, BC V6B 5L5
604-276-3100, Fax: 604-276-3247, 888-621-7233

Manitoba

Advisory Council on Workplace Safety & Health, #200, 401 York Ave., Winnipeg, MB R3C 0P8
204-945-3446, Fax: 204-945-4556
Emergency Measures Organization, 405 Broadway Ave., 15th Floor, Winnipeg, MB R3C 3L6
204-945-4772, Fax: 204-945-4929, 888-267-8298, emo@gov.mb.ca
Manitoba Health & Healthy Living, #100, 300 Carlton St., Winnipeg, MB R3B 3M9
204-786-7191, minhlt@leg.gov.mb.ca
Manitoba Labour & Immigration, Legislative Building, 317, 450 Broadway Ave., Winnipeg, MB R3C 0V8
204-945-4079, Fax: 204-945-8312, minlab@leg.gov.mb.ca

Workplace Safety & Health Division, #200, 401 York Ave., Winnipeg, MB R3C 0P8
204-945-3446, Fax: 204-948-2209, wshcompl@gov.mb.ca

New Brunswick

Department of Health, PO Box 5100, Fredericton, NB E3B 5G8
506-457-4800, Fax: 506-453-5243, dh-ms@dh-ms.ca

Department of Post-Secondary Education, Training & Labour, Chestnut Complex, 470 York St., PO Box 6000, Fredericton, NB E3B 5H1
506-453-2597, Fax: 506-453-3618, dpetlinfo@gnb.ca

Workplace Health, Safety & Compensation Commission of New Brunswick, 1 Portland St., PO Box 160, Saint John, NB E2L 3X9
506-632-2200, 800-222-9775, communications@ws-ts.nb.ca

Newfoundland & Labrador

Department of Environment & Conservation, Confederation Bldg., West Block, 4th Fl., PO Box 8700, St. John's, NL A1B 4J6
709-729-2664, Fax: 709-729-6639, 800-563-6181, info@gov.nl.ca

Department of Health & Community Services, West Block, Confederation Bldg., PO Box 8700, St. John's, NL A1B 4J6
709-729-5021, Fax: 709-729-5824, healthinfo@gov.nl.ca

Newfoundland & Labrador Fire & Emergency Services, 25 Hallett Cres., PO Box 8700, St. John's, NL A1B 4J6
709-729-3703, Fax: 709-729-3757

Newfoundland & Labrador Workplace Health, Safety & Compensation Commission, 146 - 148 Forest Rd., PO Box 9000, St. John's, NL A1A 3B8
709-778-1000, Fax: 709-738-1714, 800-563-9000, general.inquiries@whscc.nl.ca

Northwest Territories

Department of Health & Social Services, Centre Square Tower, PO Box 1320, Yellowknife, NT X1A 2L9
Fax: 867-873-0266

Northwest Territories & Nunavut Workers' Safety & Compensation Commission, Centre Square Tower, 5022 - 49th St., 5th Fl., PO Box 8888, Yellowknife, NT X1A 2R3
867-920-3888, Fax: 867-873-4596, 800-661-0792

Nova Scotia

Nova Scotia Emergency Management Office, PO Box 2581, Halifax, NS B3J 3N5
902-424-5620, Fax: 902-424-5376, 866-424-5620, emo@gov.ns.ca

Department of Health & Wellness, Joseph Howe Bldg., 1690 Hollis St., 4th Fl., PO Box 488, Halifax, NS B3J 2R8
902-424-5818, Fax: 902-424-0730, 800-387-6665, DoHweb@gov.ns.ca

Ontario

Ministry of Government Services, Whitney Block, #4320, 99 Wellesley St. West, 4th Fl., Toronto, ON M7A 1W3
416-326-1234, Fax: 416-327-3790, 800-268-1142

Ministry of Health & Long-Term Care, Hepburn Block, 80 Grosvenor St., 10th Fl, Toronto, ON M7A 2C4
416-327-4327, 800-268-1153

Ministry of Labour, 400 University Ave., 14th Fl., Toronto, ON M7A 1T7
416-326-7160, 800-531-5551

Road User Safety Division, Bldg A, #191, 1201 Wilson Ave., Downsview, ON M3M 1J8
416-235-2999, Fax: 416-235-4153

Prince Edward Island

Prince Edward Island Department of Health & Wellness, 105 Rochford St. North, 4th Fl., PO Box 2000, Charlottetown, PE C1A 7N8
902-368-6414, Fax: 902-368-4121

Prince Edward Island Workers Compensation Board, 14 Weymouth St., PO Box 757, Charlottetown, PE C1A 7L7
902-368-5680, Fax: 902-368-5696, 800-237-5049

Quebec

Commission de la santé et de la sécurité du travail du Québec, 524, rue Bourdages, CP 1200 Terminus postal,Québec, QC G1K 7E2
418-266-4850, Fax: 418-266-4669, 866-302-2778

Ministère de la Santé et des Services sociaux, Direction des communications, 1075, ch Sainte-Foy, 16e étage, Québec, QC G1S 2M1
418-643-9395, Fax: 418-643-4768, regisseur.web@msss.gouv.qc.ca

Ministère de la Sécurité publique, Tour des Laurentides, 2525, boul Laurier, 5e étage, Québec, QC G1V 2L2
418-643-2112, Fax: 418-646-6168, 866-644-6826

Ministère du Travail, 200, ch Sainte-Foy, 5e étage, Québec, QC G1R 5S1
418-644-4545, Fax: 418-528-0559, 800-643-4817

Saskatchewan

Saskatchewan Health, T.C. Douglas Bldg., 3475 Albert St., Regina, SK S4S 6X6
306-787-0146, 800-667-7766, info@health.gov.sk.ca

Saskatchewan Labour Relations & Workplace Safety, #300, 1870 Albert St., Regina, SK S4P 4W1
306-787-7404, webmaster@lab.gov.sk.ca

Yukon Territory

Emergency Measures Organization, PO Box 2703, Whitehorse, YT Y1A 2C6
867-667-5220, Fax: 867-393-6266, 800-661-0408, emo.yukon@gov.yk.ca

Yukon Health & Social Services, PO Box 2703, Whitehorse, YT Y1A 2C6
867-667-3673, Fax: 867-667-3096, hss@gov.yk.ca

Yukon Workers' Compensation Health & Safety Board, 401 Strickland St., Whitehorse, YT Y1A 5N8
867-667-5645, Fax: 867-393-6279, 800-661-0443, worksafe@gov.yk.ca

HEALTH CARE INSURANCE

Health Canada, Tunney's Pasture, Ottawa, ON K1A 0K9
613-957-2991, Fax: 613-941-5366, 866-225-0709, info@hc-sc.gc.ca

Health Services Information & Information Technology Cluster, 56 Wellesley St. West, 10th Fl., Toronto, ON M5S 2S3
416-314-4243, Fax: 416-314-0289

Health Workforce Division, Telus Plaza NT, 10025 Jasper Ave., 10th Fl., Edmonton, AB T5J 1S6

British Columbia

Medical Services Commission, 1515 Blanshard St., 3rd Fl., Victoria, BC V8W 3C8
250-952-3073, Fax: 250-952-3131

Newfoundland & Labrador

Department of Health & Community Services, West Block, Confederation Bldg., PO Box 8700, St. John's, NL A1B 4J6
709-729-5021, Fax: 709-729-5824, healthinfo@gov.nl.ca

Northwest Territories

Department of Health & Social Services, Centre Square Tower, PO Box 1320, Yellowknife, NT X1A 2L9
Fax: 867-873-0266

Nunavut

Department of Health & Social Services, PO Box 1000 1000,Iqaluit, NU X0A 0H0
867-975-5700, Fax: 867-975-5705

Prince Edward Island

Prince Edward Island Department of Health & Wellness, 105 Rochford St. North, 4th Fl., PO Box 2000, Charlottetown, PE C1A 7N8
902-368-6414, Fax: 902-368-4121

Quebec

Régie de l'assurance maladie du Québec, 1125, Grande Allée ouest, Québec, QC G1S 1E7
418-646-4636

HEALTH SERVICES

See Also: Health Care Insurance; Occupational Safety

Canadian Centre for Occupational Health & Safety, 135 Hunter St. East, Hamilton, ON L8N 1M5
905-572-2981, Fax: 905-572-2206, 800-668-4284

Canadian Institutes of Health Research, 160 Elgin St., 9th Fl., Ottawa, ON K1A 0W9
613-941-2672, Fax: 613-954-1800, 888-603-4178, info@cihr-irsc.gc.ca

Health Canada, Tunney's Pasture, Ottawa, ON K1A 0K9
613-957-2991, Fax: 613-941-5366, 866-225-0709, info@hc-sc.gc.ca

Health Services Information & Information Technology Cluster, 56 Wellesley St. West, 10th Fl., Toronto, ON M5S 2S3
416-314-4243, Fax: 416-314-0289

Ste-Anne's Hospital, 305 boul des Anciens-Combattants, Sainte-Anne-de-Bellevue, QC H9X 1Y9
514-457-3440, 800-361-9287, steanne@vac-acc.gc.ca

Alberta

Alberta Health & Wellness, PO Box 1360 Main,Edmonton, AB T5J 2N3
780-427-7164, Fax: 780-427-1171

British Columbia

Ministry of Health, 1515 Blanshard St., Victoria, BC V8W 3C8
250-952-1742, Fax: 250-356-9587, 800-465-4911, hlth.health@gov.bc.ca

Medical Services Commission, 1515 Blanshard St., 3rd Fl., Victoria, BC V8W 3C8
250-952-3073, Fax: 250-952-3131

Manitoba

Manitoba Health & Healthy Living, #100, 300 Carlton St., Winnipeg, MB R3B 3M9
204-786-7191, minhlt@leg.gov.mb.ca

Manitoba Healthy Child Office, #219, 114 Garry St., Winnipeg, MB R3C 1G1
204-945-2266, 888-848-0140, healthychild@gov.mb.ca

Manitoba Health Appeal Board, #4011, 300 Carlton St., Winnipeg, MB R3B 3M9
204-788-6704, Fax: 204-948-2024, 866-744-3257

New Brunswick

Department of Health, PO Box 5100, Fredericton, NB E3B 5G8
506-457-4800, Fax: 506-453-5243, dh-ms@dh-ms.ca

Newfoundland & Labrador

Department of Health & Community Services, West Block, Confederation Bldg., PO Box 8700, St. John's, NL A1B 4J6
709-729-5021, Fax: 709-729-5824, healthinfo@gov.nl.ca

Northwest Territories

Department of Health & Social Services, Centre Square Tower, PO Box 1320, Yellowknife, NT X1A 2L9
Fax: 867-873-0266

Nova Scotia

Department of Health & Wellness, Joseph Howe Bldg., 1690 Hollis St., 4th Fl., PO Box 488, Halifax, NS B3J 2R8
902-424-5818, Fax: 902-424-0730, 800-387-6665, DoHweb@gov.ns.ca

Nunavut

Department of Health & Social Services, PO Box 1000 1000,Iqaluit, NU X0A 0H0
867-975-5700, Fax: 867-975-5705

Ontario

Ministry of Health Promotion & Sport, College Park, 777 Bay Street, 18th Fl., Toronto, ON M7A 1S5
416-326-8475, Fax: 416-326-4864, info@mhp.gov.on.ca

Prince Edward Island

Health PEI, 16 Garfield St., PO Box 2000, Charlottetown, PE C1A 7N8
902-368-6130, Fax: 902-368-6136, healthinput@gov.pe.ca

Prince Edward Island Department of Health & Wellness, 105 Rochford St. North, 4th Fl., PO Box 2000, Charlottetown, PE C1A 7N8
902-368-6414, Fax: 902-368-4121

Quebec

Institut national de santé publique du Québec, 945, av Wolfe, Québec, QC G1V 5B3
418-650-5115, Fax: 418-646-9328, info@inspq.qc.ca

Ministère de la Santé et des Services sociaux, Direction des communications, 1075, ch Sainte-Foy, 16e étage, Québec, QC G1S 2M1
418-643-9395, Fax: 418-643-4768, regisseur.web@msss.gouv.qc.ca

Saskatchewan

Saskatchewan Health, T.C. Douglas Bldg., 3475 Albert St., Regina, SK S4S 6X6
306-787-0146, 800-667-7766, info@health.gov.sk.ca

HERITAGE RESOURCES

See Also: Land Resources; Parks

Canadian Heritage, 15 Eddy St., Gatineau, QC K1A 0M5
819-997-0055, 866-811-0055, info@pch.gc.ca

Parks Canada, 25 Eddy St., Gatineau, QC K1A 0M5
613-860-1251, 888-773-8888, information@pc.gc.ca

Manitoba

Manitoba Culture, Heritage, Tourism & Sport, Legislative Building, #118, 450 Broadway Ave., Winnipeg, MB R3C 0V8
204-945-3729, Fax: 204-945-5223, mincht@leg.gov.mb.ca

Heritage Grants Advisory Council, 213 Notre Dame Ave., 3rd Fl., Winnipeg, MB R3B 1N3
204-945-2213, Fax: 204-948-2086

Manitoba Heritage Council, 213 Notre Dame Ave., Main Fl., Winnipeg, MB R3B 1N3
204-945-2118, Fax: 204-948-2384, hrb@gov.mb.ca

Nova Scotia

Heritage Division, 1747 Summer St., Halifax, NS B3H 3A6
902-424-7344, Fax: 902-424-0560, 800-632-1114, heritage@gov.ns.ca

Nunavut

Department of Culture, Language, Elders & Youth, PO Box 1000 800,Iqaluit, NU X0A 0H0
867-975-5500, Fax: 867-975-5504, 866-934-2035

Ontario

Conservation Review Board, 400 University Ave. 4th Fl., Toronto, ON M7A 2R9
416-314-7137, Fax: 416-314-7175, conservation.review.board@ontario.ca

Ontario Heritage Trust, 10 Adelaide St. East, Toronto, ON M5C 1J3
416-325-5000, Fax: 416-325-5071

Prince Edward Island

Child & Family Services Division, Jones Bldg., 11 Kent St., 2nd Fl., PO Box 2000, Charlottetown, PE C1A 7N8
902-368-5294

Quebec

Commission des biens culturels du Québec, Bloc A-RC, 225, Grande Allée est, Québec, QC G1R 5G5
418-643-8378, Fax: 418-643-8591, info@cbcq.gouv.qc.ca

Saskatchewan
Saskatchewan Archives Board, University of Regina, 3303 Hillsdale St., PO Box 1665, Regina, SK S4P 3C6
306-787-4068, Fax: 306-787-1197, info.regina@archives.gov.sk.ca
Saskatchewan Heritage Foundation, 1919 Saskatchewan Dr., 9th Fl., Regina, SK S4P 4H2
306-787-4188, Fax: 306-787-0069
Saskatchewan Tourism, Parks, Culture & Sport, 1919 Saskatchewan Dr., 4th Fl., Regina, SK S4P 4H2
306-787-5729, Fax: 306-787-8560, info@cyr.gov.sk.ca

Yukon Territory
Yukon Tourism & Culture, 100 Hanson St., Whitehorse, YT Y1A 2C6
867-667-5036, Fax: 867-667-3546

HISTORY & ARCHIVES

Canada Council for the Arts, 350 Albert St., PO Box 1047, Ottawa, ON K1P 5V8
613-566-4414, Fax: 613-566-4390, 800-263-5588
Library & Archives Canada, 395 Wellington St., Ottawa, ON K1A 0N4
613-996-5115, Fax: 613-995-6274, 866-578-7777, reference@lac-bac.ca
Library of Parliament, Parliamentary Bldgs., 111 Wellington St., Ottawa, ON K1A 0A9
613-992-4793, Fax: 613-943-6383, 866-599-4999

Alberta
Recreation & Sport Development Division, Standard Life Centre, 10405 Jasper Ave., 9th Fl., Edmonton, AB T5J 4R7

Nova Scotia
Culture Division, #601, 1800 Argyle St., PO Box 456, Halifax, NS B3J 2R5
902-424-4510, Fax: 902-424-0710, culture@gov.ns.ca

Ontario
Information, Privacy & Archives Division, 134 Ian Macdonald Blvd., Toronto, ON M7A 2C5
416-327-1600, Fax: 416-327-1999, 800-668-9933

Quebec
Bibliothèque et Archives nationales du Québec (BAnQ), 475, boul De Maisonneuve est, Montréal, QC H2L 5C4
514-873-1100, Fax: 514-873-9312, 800-363-9028

Saskatchewan
Saskatchewan Archives Board, University of Regina, 3303 Hillsdale St., PO Box 1665, Regina, SK S4P 3C6
306-787-4068, Fax: 306-787-1197, info.regina@archives.gov.sk.ca

HOSPITALS

See Also: Health Care Insurance

Alberta
Alberta Health & Wellness, PO Box 1360 Main,Edmonton, AB T5J 2N3
780-427-7164, Fax: 780-427-1171

British Columbia
Ministry of Health, 1515 Blanshard St., Victoria, BC V8W 3C8
250-952-1742, Fax: 250-356-9587, 800-465-4911, hlth.health@gov.bc.ca
Hospital Appeal Board, 747 Fort St., 4th Fl., PO Box 9425 Prov Govt, Victoria, BC V8W 9V1
250-387-3464, Fax: 250-356-9923, 800-663-7867, hab@gov.bc.ca

Northwest Territories
Department of Health & Social Services, Centre Square Tower, PO Box 1320, Yellowknife, NT X1A 2L9
Fax: 867-873-0266

Nunavut
Department of Health & Social Services, PO Box 1000 1000,Iqaluit, NU X0A 0H0
867-975-5700, Fax: 867-975-5705

Prince Edward Island
Prince Edward Island Department of Health & Wellness, 105 Rochford St. North, 4th Fl., PO Box 2000, Charlottetown, PE C1A 7N8
902-368-6414, Fax: 902-368-4121

Quebec
Ministère de la Santé et des Services sociaux, Direction des communications, 1075, ch Sainte-Foy, 16e étage, Québec, QC G1S 2M1
418-643-9395, Fax: 418-643-4768, regisseur.web@msss.gouv.qc.ca

HOUSING

Canada Mortgage & Housing Corporation, 700 Montreal Rd., Ottawa, ON K1A 0P7
613-748-2000, Fax: 613-748-2098, 800-668-2642, chic@cmhc-schl.gc.ca

British Columbia
Local Government, PO Box 9490 Prov Govt,Victoria, BC V8W 9N7
250-356-6575, Fax: 250-387-7973

Manitoba
Employment, Income & Housing Division, #201, 280 Broadway Ave., Winnipeg, MB R3C 0R8
Manitoba Housing Authority - Public Housing, #2100, 185 Smith St., Winnipeg, MB R3C 3G4
204-945-4663, Fax: 204-948-2013, 800-661-4663

New Brunswick
Department of Local Government, Marysville Place, 20 McGloin St., PO Box 6000, Fredericton, NB E3B 5H1
506-453-2807, Fax: 506-453-3988
Department of Social Development, Sartain MacDonald Bldg., 551 King St., PO Box 6000, Fredericton, NB E3B 5H1
506-453-2001, Fax: 506-453-7478, sd-ds@gnb.ca

Newfoundland & Labrador
Newfoundland & Labrador Housing Corporation, Sir Brian Dunfield Bldg., 2 Canada Dr., PO Box 220, St. John's, NL A1C 5J2
709-724-3000, Fax: 709-724-3250

Northwest Territories
Northwest Territories Housing Corporation, Scotia Centre, 5102 50th Ave., PO Box 2100, Yellowknife, NT X1A 2P6
867-873-7853, Fax: 867-873-9426,

Nova Scotia
Department of Service Nova Scotia & Municipal Relations, 1505 Barrington St., PO Box 216, Halifax, NS B3J 3K5
902-424-5200, Fax: 902-424-0581, 800-670-4357, askus@gov.ns.ca

Nunavut
Department of Community & Government Services, W.G. Brown Bldg., 4th Fl., PO Box 1000 700,Iqaluit, NU X0A 0H0
867-975-5400, Fax: 867-975-5305
Nunavut Housing Corporation, PO Box 480, Arviat, NU X0C 0E0
867-857-3000, Fax: 867-857-3040

Quebec
Société d'habitation du Québec, Aile St-Amable, 1054, rue Louis-Alexandre-Taschereau, 3e étage, Québec, QC G1R 5E7
418-643-4035, Fax: 418-643-2533, 800-463-4315

Yukon Territory
Yukon Housing Corporation, 410H Jarvis St., PO Box 2703, Whitehorse, YT Y1A 2H5
867-667-5759, Fax: 867-667-3664, 800-661-0408, ykhouse@housing.yk.ca

HUMAN RIGHTS

See Also: Boards of Review

Canadian Human Rights Commission, 344 Slater St., 8th Fl., Ottawa, ON K1A 1E1
613-995-1151, Fax: 613-996-9661, 888-214-1090
Canadian Human Rights Tribunal, 160 Elgin St., 11th Fl., Ottawa, ON K1A 1J4
613-995-1707, Fax: 613-995-3484, registrar@chrt-tcdp.gc.ca

British Columbia
British Columbia Human Rights Tribunal, #1170, 605 Robson St., Vancouver, BC V6B 5J3
604-775-2000, Fax: 604-775-2020, 888-440-8844, BCHumanRightsTribunal@gov.bc.ca

Manitoba
Manitoba Human Rights Commission, 175 Hargrave St., 7th Fl., Winnipeg, MB R3C 3R8
204-945-3007, Fax: 204-945-1292, 888-884-8681, hrc@gov.mb.ca

New Brunswick
New Brunswick Human Rights Commission, PO Box 6000, Fredericton, NB E3B 5H1
506-453-2301, Fax: 506-453-2653, 888-471-2233, hrc.cdp@gnb.ca

Newfoundland & Labrador
Newfoundland & Labrador Human Rights Commission, PO Box 8700, St. John's, NL A1B 4J6
709-729-2709, Fax: 709-729-0790, 800-563-5808, humanrights@mail.gov.nl.ca

Nova Scotia
Nova Scotia Human Rights Commission, Joseph Howe Bldg., 1690 Hollis St., 6th Fl., Halifax, NS B3J 3C4
902-424-4111, Fax: 902-424-0596, hrcinquiries@gov.ns.ca

Ontario
Ontario Human Rights Commission, 180 Dundas St. West, 7th Fl., Toronto, ON M7A 2R9
416-326-9511, Fax: 416-314-4494, 800-387-9080

Prince Edward Island
Prince Edward Island Human Rights Commission, 53 Water St., PO Box 2000, Charlottetown, PE C1A 7N8
902-368-4180, Fax: 902-368-4236, 800-237-5031

Quebec
Commission des droits de la personne et des droits de la jeunesse, 360, rue St-Jacques, 2e étage, Montréal, QC H2Y 1P5
514-873-5146, Fax: 514-873-6032, 800-361-6477, accueil@cdpdj.qc.ca

Saskatchewan
Saskatchewan Human Rights Commission, Saskatoon Office, Sturdy Stone Bdg., #816, 122 - 3 Ave. North, 8th Fl., Saskatoon, SK S7K 2H6
306-933-5952, Fax: 306-933-7863, 800-667-9249, shrc@gov.sk.ca

Yukon Territory
Yukon Human Rights Board of Adjudication, #202, 407 Black St., Whitehorse, YT Y1A 2N2
867-667-5412, Fax: 867-633-6952, beyondwords@northwestel.net
Yukon Human Rights Commission, #101, 9010 Quartz St., Whitehorse, YT Y1A 2Z5
867-667-6226, Fax: 867-667-2662, 800-661-0535, humanrights@yhrc.yk.ca

HYDRO, ELECTRIC POWER

National Energy Board, 444 - 7 Ave. SW, Calgary, AB T2P 0X8
403-292-4800, Fax: 403-292-5503, 800-899-1265, info@neb-one.gc.ca

Alberta
Energy Resources Conservation Board, #1000, 250 - 5 Ave. SW, Calgary, AB T2P 0R4
403-297-8311, Fax: 403-297-7336, 855-297-8311, inquiries@ercb.ca; infoservices@ercb.ca; ADR@ercb.ca

British Columbia
British Columbia Hydro, 333 Dunsmuir St., Vancouver, BC V6B 5R3
604-224-9376, 800-224-9376
Powertech Labs Inc., 12388 - 88 Ave., Surrey, BC V8W 7R7
604-590-7500, Fax: 604-590-6611

Manitoba
Manitoba Hydro, PO Box 815 Main,Winnipeg, MB R3C 2P4
204-474-3311, Fax: 204-475-0069, publicaffairs@hydro.mb.ca

New Brunswick
New Brunswick Electric Finance Corporation, #376, 670 King St., PO Box 6000, Fredericton, NB E3B 5H1
506-453-3952, Fax: 506-453-2053
New Brunswick Power Group of Companies, 515 King St., PO Box 2000, Fredericton, NB E3B 4X1
506-458-4444, Fax: 506-458-4000, questions@nbpower.com

Newfoundland & Labrador
Churchill Falls (Labrador) Corporation Limited, Hydro Place, 500 Columbus Dr., PO Box 12500, St. John's, NL A1B 4K7
709-737-1859, Fax: 709-737-1816
Newfoundland & Labrador Hydro, Hydro Place, Columbus Dr., PO Box 12400, St. John's, NL A1B 4K7
709-737-1400, Fax: 709-737-1800, hydro@nlh.nl.ca
Twin Falls Power Corporation, PO Box 12500, St. John's, NL A1B 3T5

Northwest Territories
Northwest Territories Power Corporation, 4 Capital Dr., Hay River, NT X0E 1G2
867-874-5200, Fax: 867-874-5251, info@ntpc.com

Nova Scotia
Nova Scotia Utility & Review Board, Summit Place, 1601 Lower Water St., 3rd Fl., PO Box 1692 M,Halifax, NS B3J 3S3
902-424-4448, Fax: 902-424-3919, uarb.board@gov.ns.ca

Ontario
Hydro One Inc., North Tower, 483 Bay St., Toronto, ON M5G 2P5
416-345-5000, 877-955-1155, customercommunications@HydroOne.com
Independent Electricity System Operator, PO Box 4474 A,Toronto, ON M5W 4E5
905-403-6900, Fax: 905-403-6921, 888-448-7777, customer.relations@ieso.ca
Ontario Power Authority, #1600, 120 Adelaide St. West, Toronto, ON M5H 1T1
416-967-7474, Fax: 416-967-1947, 800-797-9604, info@powerauthority.on.ca
Ontario Power Generation, 700 University Ave., Toronto, ON M5G 1X6
416-592-2555, 877-592-2555, webmaster@opg.com

Quebec
Hydro-Québec, 75, boul René-Lévesque ouest, Montréal, QC H2Z 1A4
514-289-2211
Société d'énergie de la Baie-James, 888, de Maisonneuve est, 6e étage, Montréal, QC H2L 5B2
514-286-2020

Saskatchewan
Saskatchewan Power Corporation (SaskPower), 2025 Victoria Ave., Regina, SK S4P 0S1
306-566-3306, Fax: 800-757-6937, 888-757-6937

IMMIGRATION

See Also: Citizenship

Citizenship & Immigration Canada, Jean Edmonds, South Tower, 365 Laurier Ave. West, Ottawa, ON K1A 1L1
613-954-9019, Fax: 613-954-2221, 888-242-2100

Immigration & Refugee Board of Canada, Canada Bldg, 344 Slater St., 12th Fl., Ottawa, ON K1A 0K1
613-995-6486, Fax: 613-943-1550, contact@irb-cisr.gc.ca

Passport Canada, Le 70 Crémazie, 70 Crémazie St., Gatineau, QC K1A 0G3
Fax: 819-953-5856, 800-567-6868

Manitoba
Immigration & Multiculturalism Division, 213 Notre Dame Ave., 5th Floor, Winnipeg, MB R3B 1N3
204-945-6300, Fax: 204-948-2148, immigratemanitoba@gov.mb.ca

Prince Edward Island
Island Investment Development Inc., 94 Euston St., 2nd Fl., Charlottetown, PE C1A 7M8
902-620-3628, Fax: 902-368-5886, peinominee@gov.pe.ca

IMPORTS

See Also: Trade

Canada Border Services Agency, Headquarters, 191 Laurier Ave. West, Ottawa, ON K1A 0L8
800-461-9999, Contact@cbsa.gc.ca; communications@ps.gc.ca (Public Safety)

Canadian International Trade Tribunal, Standard Life Centre, 333 Laurier Ave. West, 15 Floor, Ottawa, ON K1A 0G7
613-990-2452, Fax: 613-990-2439, secretary@citt-tcce.gc.ca

North American Free Trade Agreement (NAFTA) Secretariat, Canadian Section, #705, 90 Sparks St., Ottawa, ON K1P 5B4
613-992-9388, Fax: 613-992-9392, webmaster@nafta-alena.gc.ca

New Brunswick
Investment, Export & Business Development, Centennial Bldg., 670 King St., 5th Fl., PO Box 6000, Fredericton, NB E3B 5H1
506-453-2875, Fax: 506-444-4277

Quebec
Revenu Québec, Direction des relations publiques/Communications, 3800, rue de Marly, Québec, QC G1X 4A5
418-652-6831, Fax: 418-646-0167

INCOME SECURITY

See Also: Social Services

Alberta
Workforce Supports Division, Labour Building, 10808 - 99 Ave., 10th Fl., Edmonton, AB T5K 0G5
780-722-0010

Manitoba
Employment, Income & Housing Division, #201, 280 Broadway Ave., Winnipeg, MB R3C 0R8

New Brunswick
Family Income Security Appeal Board, PO Box 6000, Fredericton, NB E3B 5H1
506-525-4007, Fax: 506-525-4008

Ontario
Ministry of Community & Social Services, Hepburn Block, 80 Grosvenor St., 6th Fl., Toronto, ON M7A 1E9
416-325-5666, Fax: 416-325-5172, 888-789-4199

Yukon Territory
Yukon Health & Social Services, PO Box 2703, Whitehorse, YT Y1A 2C6
867-667-3673, Fax: 867-667-3096, hss@gov.yk.ca

INCORPORATION OF COMPANIES & ASSOCIATIONS

Alberta
Strategic Planning & Financial Services, Commerce Place, 10155 - 102 St., 13th Fl., Edmonton, AB T5J 4G8
780-422-8545

New Brunswick
Service New Brunswick, Westmorland Place, #200, 82 Westmorland St., PO Box 1998, Fredericton, NB E3B 5G4
506-457-3581, Fax: 506-457-7520, 888-762-8600, snb@snb.ca

Northwest Territories
Department of Justice, Courthouse, 4903 - 49th St., 6th Fl., PO Box 1320, Yellowknife, NT X1A 2L9
867-920-6197

Nova Scotia
Department of Economic & Rural Development, Centennial Building, #600, 1660 Hollis St., PO Box 2311, Halifax, NS B3J 1V7
902-424-0377, Fax: 902-424-0500, comm@gov.ns.ca

Registry of Joint Stock Companies, Maritime Centre, 1505 Barrington St., 9th Fl., Halifax, NS B3J 2Y4
902-424-7770, Fax: 902-424-4633, 800-225-8227, joint-stock@gov.ns.ca

Nunavut
Nunavut Legal Registries Division, Brown Bldg., 1st Fl., PO Box 1000 570,Iqaluit, NU X0A 0H0
Fax: 867-975-6594

Ontario
ServiceOntario, College Park, 777 Bay St., 15th fl., Toronto, ON M7A 2J3
416-326-1234, Fax: 416-326-1313, 800-267-8097

Quebec
Registraire des entreprises, 787, boul Lebourgneuf, Québec, QC G2J 1C3
418-644-4545, Fax: 418-528-5703, 877-644-4545, registre@servicesquebec.gouv.qc.ca

Yukon Territory
Yukon Community Services, PO Box 2703, Whitehorse, YT Y1A 2C6
867-667-5811, Fax: 867-393-6295, 800-661-0408, inquiry@gov.yk.ca

INDUSTRY

See Also: Business Development

Agriculture & Agri-Food Canada, 1341 Baseline Rd., Ottawa, ON K1A 0C5
613-773-1000, Fax: 613-773-2772, 866-345-7972, info@agr.gc.ca

Atlantic Canada Opportunities Agency, Blue Cross Centre, 644 Main St., 3rd Fl., PO Box 6051, Moncton, NB E1C 9J8
506-851-2271, Fax: 506-851-7403, 800-561-7862, information@acoa-apeca.gc.ca

Canada Mortgage & Housing Corporation, 700 Montreal Rd., Ottawa, ON K1A 0P7
613-748-2000, Fax: 613-748-2098, 800-668-2642, chic@cmhc-schl.gc.ca

Canadian Dairy Commission, Central Experimental Farm, NCC Driveway, Bldg. 55, 960 Carling Ave., Ottawa, ON K1A 0Z2
613-792-2000, Fax: 613-792-2009, cdc-ccl@cdc-ccl.gc.ca

Canadian Food Inspection Agency, 1400 Merivale Rd., Ottawa, ON K1A 0Y9
613-225-2342, Fax: 613-228-6601, 800-442-2342

Canadian Grain Commission, #600, 303 Main St., Winnipeg, MB R3C 3G8
204-983-2770, Fax: 204-983-2751, 800-853-6705, contact@grainscanada.gc.ca

Canadian International Development Agency, 200, Promenade du Portage, Gatineau, QC K1A 0G4
819-997-5456, Fax: 819-953-6088, 800-230-6349, info@acdi-cida.gc.ca

Canadian International Trade Tribunal, Standard Life Centre, 333 Laurier Ave. West, 15 Floor, Ottawa, ON K1A 0G7
613-990-2452, Fax: 613-990-2439, secretary@citt-tcce.gc.ca

Canadian Nuclear Safety Commission, 280 Slater St., PO Box 1046 B,Ottawa, ON K1P 5S9
613-995-5894, Fax: 613-995-5086, 800-668-5284

Canadian Radio-Television & Telecommunications Commission, Central Building, 1, Promenade du Portage, Les Terrasses de la Chaudière, Gatineau, QC J8X 4B1
819-997-0313, Fax: 819-994-0218, 877-249-2782

Canadian Space Agency, John H. Chapman Space Centre, 6767, rte de l'Aéroport, Saint-Hubert, QC J3Y 8Y9
450-926-4800, Fax: 450-926-4352, promo@asc-csa.gc.ca

Canadian Tourism Commission, #1400, 1055 Dunsmuir St., PO Box 49230, Vancouver, BC V7X 1L2
604-638-8300

Canadian Wheat Board, 423 Main St., PO Box 816 Main,Winnipeg, MB R3C 2P5
204-983-0239, Fax: 204-983-3841, 800-275-4292, questions@cwb.ca; farmerservice@cwb.ca

Centre for Surface Transportation Technology, 2320 Lester Rd., Ottawa, ON K1V 1S2
613-998-9639, Fax: 613-957-0831, inquiries.cstt@nrc-cnrc.gc.ca

Communications Research Centre Canada, 3701 Carling Ave., PO Box 11490 H, Ottawa, ON K2H 8S2
613-991-3313, Fax: 613-998-5355, info@crc.gc.ca

Competition Bureau, Place du Portage, Phase I, 50 Victoria Street, Ottawa, ON K1A 0C9
819-997-4282, Fax: 819-997-0324, 800-348-5358

Competition Tribunal, Thomas D'Arcy McGee Bldg., #600, 90 Sparks St., Ottawa, ON K1P 5B4
613-957-3172, Fax: 613-957-3170, tribunal@ct-tc.gc.ca

Defence Construction Canada, Constitution Square, 350 Albert St., 19th Fl., Ottawa, ON K1A 0K3
613-998-9548, Fax: 613-998-1061, 800-514-3555, info@dcc-cdc.gc.ca

Enterprise Cape Breton Corporation, Silicon Island, 70 Crescent St., Sydney, NS B1S 2Z7
902-564-3600, Fax: 902-564-3825, 800-705-3926, information@ecbc-secb.gc.ca

Environmental Sciences & Standards Division, 135 St. Clair Ave. West, 14th Fl., Toronto, ON M4V 1P5
416-314-6357, Fax: 416-314-6358

Export Development Canada, 151 Slater St., Ottawa, ON K1A 1K3
613-598-2500, Fax: 613-598-3811, 800-267-8510

Farm Credit Canada, 1800 Hamilton St., PO Box 4320, Regina, SK S4P 4L3
306-780-8100, Fax: 306-780-8919, 888-332-3301, csc@fcc-fac.ca

Office of the Superintendent of Financial Institutions, Kent Square, 255 Albert St., Ottawa, ON K1A 0H2
613-990-7788, Fax: 613-990-5591, 800-385-8647, information@osfi-bsif.gc.ca

Fisheries & Oceans Canada, 200 Kent St., Ottawa, ON K1A 0E6
613-993-0999, Fax: 613-990-1866, info@dfo-mpo.gc.ca

Foreign Affairs & International Trade Canada, 125 Sussex Dr., Ottawa, ON K1A 0G2
613-944-4000, Fax: 613-996-9709, 800-267-8376, enqserv@international.gc.ca

Freshwater Fish Marketing Corporation, 1199 Plessis Rd., Winnipeg, MB R2C 3L4
204-983-6601, Fax: 204-983-6497, sandi.cain@freshwaterfish.com

Hazardous Materials Information Review Commission, 427 Laurier Ave. West, 7th Fl., Ottawa, ON K1A 1M3
613-993-4331, Fax: 613-993-4686, hmirc-ccrmd@hc-sc.gc.ca

Health System Strategy & Policy Division, Hepburn Block, 80 Grosvenor St., 8th Fl., Toronto, ON M7A 1R3
416-327-8295, Fax: 416-327-5109

Indian Oil & Gas Canada, #100, 9911 Chiila Blvd., Tsuu T'ina (Sarcee), AB T2W 6H6
403-292-5625, Fax: 403-292-5618, ContactIOGC@inac-ainc.gc.ca

Industry Canada, C.D. Howe Building, 235 Queen St., Ottawa, ON K1A 0H5
613-954-5031, Fax: 613-954-2340, 800-328-6189, info@ic.gc.ca

Institute for Aerospace Research, 1200 Montreal Rd., Ottawa, ON K1A 0R6
613-990-0765, Fax: 613-952-7214

Institute for Information Technology, Bldg. M-50, 1200 Montreal Rd., Ottawa, ON K1A 0R6
613-991-3373, Fax: 613-952-0074, 877-672-2672

National Energy Board, 444 - 7 Ave. SW, Calgary, AB T2P 0X8
403-292-4800, Fax: 403-292-5503, 800-899-1265, info@neb-one.gc.ca

National Farm Products Council, Canada Bldg., 344 Slater St., 10th Fl., Ottawa, ON K1R 7Y3
613-995-6752, Fax: 613-995-2097, fpcc-cpac@agr.gc.ca

National Film Board of Canada, 3155, rue Côte de Liesse, CP 1600 Centre-ville,Saint-Laurent, QC H4N 2N4
514-283-9000, Fax: 514-283-7564, 800-267-7710

National Research Council Canada, Bldg. M-58, 1200 Montreal Rd., Ottawa, ON K1A 0R6
613-993-9101, Fax: 613-952-7928, 877-672-2672, info@nrc-cnrc.gc.ca

National Round Table on the Environment & Economy, #200, 344 Slater St., Ottawa, ON K1R 7Y3
613-992-7189, Fax: 613-992-7385, admin@nrtee-trnee.ca

Natural Resources Canada, 580 Booth St., Ottawa, ON K1A 0E4
613-995-0947, Fax: 613-992-7211

Natural Sciences & Engineering Research Council of Canada, Constitution Square, Tower II, 350 Albert St., Ottawa, ON K1A 1H5
613-995-4273, Fax: 613-943-1624, marie-josee.duval@nserc-crsng.gc.ca

North American Free Trade Agreement (NAFTA) Secretariat, Canadian Section, #705, 90 Sparks St., Ottawa, ON K1P 5B4
613-992-9388, Fax: 613-992-9392, webmaster@nafta-alena.gc.ca

Office of the Conflict of Interest & Ethics Commissioner, Commissioner's Office, 66 Slater St., 22nd Fl., Ottawa, ON K1A 0A6
613-995-0721, Fax: 613-995-7308, ciec-ccie@parl.gc.ca

Patented Medicine Prices Review Board, Standard Life Centre, #1400, 333 Laurier Ave. West, PO Box L40, Ottawa, ON K1P 1C1
613-954-8299, Fax: 613-952-7626, 877-861-2350, pmprb@pmprb-cepmb.gc.ca

Spectrum, Information Technologies & Telecommunications, Journal Tower North, 300 Slater St., 20th Fl., Ottawa, ON K1A 0C8
613-998-0368, Fax: 613-952-1203

Standards Council of Canada, #200, 270 Albert St., Ottawa, ON K1P 6N7
613-238-3222, Fax: 613-569-7808, info@scc.ca
Telefilm Canada, #500, 360, rue Saint-Jacques, Montréal, QC H2Y 1P5
514-283-6363, Fax: 514-283-2365, 800-567-0890, info@telefilm.gc.ca
Western Economic Diversification Canada, Canada Place, #1500, 9700 Jasper Ave. NW, Edmonton, AB T5J 4H7
780-495-4164, Fax: 780-495-4557, 888-338-9378

Alberta

Alberta Agriculture & Rural Development, J.G. O'Donoghue Bldg., #100A, 7000 - 113th St., Edmonton, AB T6H 5T6
780-427-2727, -310-3276, duke@gov.ab.ca
Alberta Gaming & Liquor Commission, 50 Corriveau Ave., St. Albert, AB T8N 3T5
780-447-8600, Fax: 780-447-8916, 800-272-8876
Alberta Grains Council, JG O'Donoghue Bldg., 7000 - 113 St., 3rd Fl., Edmonton, AB T6H 5T6
780-427-7329, Fax: 780-422-9690
Alberta Innovates - Energy & Environmental Solutions, AMEC Place, #2540, 801 - 6th Ave. SW, Calgary, AB T2P 3W2
403-297-7089, ees@albertainnovates.ca
Alberta Livestock & Meat Agency, Ellwood Office Park South, #101, 1003 Ellwood Rd. SW, Edmonton, AB T6X 0B3
780-638-1699, Fax: 780-638-6495, info@almaltd.ca
Community, Learner & Industry Connections Division, Phipps-McKinnon Bldg., 10020 - 101A Ave., 5th Fl., Edmonton, AB T5J 3G2
Energy Resources Conservation Board, #1000, 250 - 5 Ave. SW, Calgary, AB T2P 0R4
403-297-8311, Fax: 403-297-7336, 855-297-8311, inquiries@ercb.ca; infoservices@ercb.ca; ADR@ercb.ca
Alberta Energy, North Petroleum Plaza, 9945 - 108 St., Edmonton, AB T5K 2G6
780-427-8050, Fax: 780-422-0698, Library.Energy@gov.ab.ca
Alberta Environment, South Tower, Petroleum Plaza, 9915 - 108 St., 10th Fl., Edmonton, AB T5K 2G8
780-427-2700, Fax: 780-422-4086, env.infocent@gov.ab.ca
Intergovernmental Relations, Commerce Place, 10155 - 102 St., 12th Fl., Edmonton, AB T5J 4G8
780-427-6706, Fax: 780-427-0939
Land Compensation Board, 1229 - 91 St. SW, Edmonton, AB T6X 1E9
srb.lcb@gov.ab.ca

British Columbia

Agricultural Land Commission, #133, 4940 Canada Way, Burnaby, BC V5G 4K6
604-660-7000, Fax: 604-660-7033, ALCBurnaby@Victoria1.gov.bc.ca
Ministry of Agriculture, PO Box 9120 Prov Govt,Victoria, BC V8W 9E2
250-387-5121, Fax: 250-387-1522
British Columbia Farm Industry Review Board, 780 Blanshard St., PO Box 9129 Prov Govt, Victoria, BC V8W 9B5
250-356-8945, Fax: 250-356-5131, firb@gov.bc.ca
Ministry of Energy & Mines, PO Box 9053 Prov Govt,Victoria, BC V8W 9E2
250-387-5896, Fax: 250-356-2965
Financial Institutions Commission, #1200, 13450 - 102 Ave., Surrey, BC V3T 5X3
604-953-5300, Fax: 604-953-5301, 866-206-3030, FICOM@ficombc.ca; HR@ficombc.ca
Forest Practices Board, 1675 Douglas St., 3rd Fl., PO Box 9905 Prov Govt, Victoria, BC V8W 9R1
250-213-4700, Fax: 250-213-4725, 800-994-5899, fpboard@gov.bc.ca
Ministry of Forests, Lands & Natural Resource Operations, PO Box 9049 Prov Govt,Victoria, BC V8W 9E2
250-387-4809, Fax: 250-387-1040
British Columbia Hydro, 333 Dunsmuir St., Vancouver, BC V6B 5R3
604-224-9376, 800-224-9376
Industry Training Authority, #1223, 13351 Commerce Pkwy., Richmond, BC V6V 2X7
604-214-8700, Fax: 604-214-8701, 866-660-6011, info@itabc.ca; customerservice@itabc.ca
Insurance Council of British Columbia, #300, 1040 West Georgia St., PO Box 7, Vancouver, BC V6E 4H1
604-688-0321, Fax: 604-662-7767, 877-688-0321
Ministry of Jobs, Tourism, & Innovation, PO Box 9071 Prov Govt,Victoria, BC V8W 9E9
250-356-2771, Fax: 250-356-3000, JTI.Minister@gov.bc.ca
Ministry of Labour, Citizens' Services & Open Government, PO Box 9056 Prov Govt,Victoria, BC V8W 9K4
250-952-7623, Fax: 250-387-4312, 800-663-7867, LCTZ.Minister@gov.bc.ca
Oil & Gas Commission, #100, 10003 - 110 Ave., Fort St John, BC V1J 6M7
250-794-5200, Fax: 250-794-5375
Real Estate Council of British Columbia, #900, 750 West Pender St., Vancouver, BC V6C 2T8
604-683-9664, Fax: 604-683-9017, 877-683-9664, info@recbc.ca
British Columbia Utilities Commission, 900 Howe St., 6th Fl., PO Box 250, Vancouver, BC V6Z 2N3
604-660-4700, Fax: 604-660-1102, 800-663-1385, commission.secretary@bcuc.com

Manitoba

Manitoba Aboriginal & Northern Affairs, 59 Elizabeth Dr., PO Box 37, Thompson, MB R8N 1X4
204-677-6607, Fax: 204-677-6753, amartin@gov.mb.ca
Advisory Council on Workplace Safety & Health, #200, 401 York Ave., Winnipeg, MB R3C 0P8
204-945-3446, Fax: 204-945-4556
Agricultural Societies, 1129 Queens Ave., Brandon, MB R7A 1L9
204-726-6195, Fax: 204-726-6260
Manitoba Agriculture, Food & Rural Initiatives, Norquay Bldg., 401 York Ave., Winnipeg, MB R3C 0P8
Community & Economic Development Committee of Cabinet Secretariat, #648, 155 Carlton St., Winnipeg, MB R3C 3H8
204-945-8221, Fax: 204-945-8229
Manitoba Competitiveness, Training & Trade, International Business Centre, The Paris Building, 259 Portage Ave., Winnipeg, MB R3B 3P4
204-945-2475, Fax: 204-945-3977, minctt@leg.gov.mb.ca
Crown Corporations Council, #1130, 444 St. Mary Ave., Winnipeg, MB R3C 3T1
204-949-5270, Fax: 204-949-5283, crowncc@mts.net
Manitoba Development Corporation, #555, 155 Carlton St., Winnipeg, MB R3C 3H8
204-945-7626, Fax: 204-945-1193
Manitoba Education, Citizenship & Youth, #168, Legislative Bldg., 450 Broadway, Winnipeg, MB R3C 0V8
204-945-3720, Fax: 204-945-1291, minedu@leg.gov.mb.ca
Employment, Income & Housing Division, #201, 280 Broadway Ave., Winnipeg, MB R3C 0R8
Farm Lands Ownership Board, #812, Norquay Bldg., 401 York Ave., Winnipeg, MB R3C 0P8
204-945-3149, Fax: 204-945-1489, 800-282-8069, robert.mckenzie@gov.mb.ca
Farm Machinery Board, Norquay Bldg., #812, 401 York Ave., Winnipeg, MB R3C 0P8
204-945-3856, Fax: 204-948-2844, randy.ozunko@gov.mb.ca
Manitoba Hydro, PO Box 815 Main,Winnipeg, MB R3C 2P4
204-474-3311, Fax: 204-475-0069, publicaffairs@hydro.mb.ca
Manitoba Labour & Immigration, Legislative Building, 317, 450 Broadway Ave., Winnipeg, MB R3C 0V8
204-945-4079, Fax: 204-945-8312, minlab@leg.gov.mb.ca
Manitoba Lotteries Corporation, 830 Empress St., Winnipeg, MB R3G 3H3
204-957-2500, Fax: 204-957-3991, 800-265-2912, communications@casinosofwinnipeg.com
Manitoba Agricultural Services Corporation, #100, 1525 First St. South, Brandon, MB R7A 7A1
204-726-6850, Fax: 204-726-6849, mailbox@masc.mb.ca
Manitoba Bureau of Statistics, #824, 155 Carlton St., Winnipeg, MB R3C 3H9
204-945-2406, Fax: 204-945-0695
Manitoba Habitat Heritage Corporation, #200, 1555 St. James St., Winnipeg, MB R3H 1B5
204-784-4350, Fax: 204-784-7359, mhhc@mhhc.mb.ca
Manitoba Labour Board, A.A. Heaps Bldg., #402, 258 Portage Ave., Winnipeg, MB R3C 0B6
204-945-3783, Fax: 204-945-1296, mlb@gov.mb.ca
Manitoba Minimum Wage Board, 614 - 401 York Ave., Winnipeg, MB R3C 0P8
204-945-4889, Fax: 204-948-2085, mw@gov.mb.ca
Public Utilities Board, #400, 330 Portage Ave., Winnipeg, MB R3C 0C4
204-945-2638, Fax: 204-945-2643, 866-854-3698, publicutilities@gov.mb.ca
Taxicab Board, #200, 301 Weston St., Winnipeg, MB R3E 3H4
Fax: 204-948-2315
Tourism Secretariat & Travel Manitoba, 155 Carlton St., 7th Fl., Winnipeg, MB R3C 3H8
800-665-0040
Manitoba Workers' Compensation Board, 333 Broadway Ave., Winnipeg, MB R3C 4W3
204-954-4321, Fax: 204-954-4999, 800-362-3340, wcb@wcb.mb.ca
Workplace Safety & Health Division, #200, 401 York Ave., Winnipeg, MB R3C 0P8
204-945-3446, Fax: 204-948-2209, wshcompl@gov.mb.ca

New Brunswick

Board of Examiners under the Scaler's Act, 1350 Regent St. South, PO Box 6000, Fredericton, NB E3B 5H1
506-453-2441, Fax: 506-453-6689
Communications, Centennial Bldg., 670 King St., 5th Fl., PO Box 6000, Fredericton, NB E3B 5H1
506-453-3707, Fax: 506-453-3993
Department of Agriculture, Aquaculture & Fisheries, PO Box 6000, Fredericton, NB E3B 5H1
506-453-2666, Fax: 506-453-7170, DAAF-MAAP@gnb.ca
Department of Business New Brunswick, Centennial Bldg., 670 King St., PO Box 6000, Fredericton, NB E3B 5H1
506-453-3707, Fax: 506-453-3993, investnb@gnb.ca
Department of Natural Resources, Hugh John Flemming Forestry Centre, PO Box 6000, Fredericton, NB E3B 5H1
506-453-3826, Fax: 506-444-4367, dnrweb@gnb.ca
Department of Social Development, Sartain MacDonald Bldg., 551 King St., PO Box 6000, Fredericton, NB E3B 5H1
506-453-2001, Fax: 506-453-7478, sd-ds@gnb.ca
Department of the Environment, Marysville Place, 20 McGloin St., PO Box 6000, Fredericton, NB E3B 5H1
506-453-2690, Fax: 506-457-7800, env-info@gnb.ca
Forest Protection Limited, 2502 Hwy. 102, Lincoln, NB E3B 7E6
506-446-6930, Fax: 506-446-6934, info@forestprotectionlimited.com
Investment, Export & Business Development, Centennial Bldg., 670 King St., 5th Fl., PO Box 6000, Fredericton, NB E3B 5H1
506-453-2875, Fax: 506-444-4277
New Brunswick Liquor Corporation, 170 Wilsey Rd., PO Box 20787, Fredericton, NB E3B 5B8
506-452-6826, Fax: 506-462-2024, info@anbl.com
New Brunswick Farm Products Commission, c/o Department of Agriculture, Aquaculture & Fisheries, PO Box 6000, Fredericton, NB E3B 5H1
506-453-3647, Fax: 506-444-5969
New Brunswick Film, Place 2000, 250 King St., 4th Fl., PO Box 6000, Fredericton, NB E1B 5H1
506-453-2555, Fax: 506-453-2416, nbfilm@gnb.ca
New Brunswick Industrial Development Board, Business New Brunswick, Centennial Bldg., 670 King St., PO Box 6000, Fredericton, NB E3B 5H1
506-453-4200, Fax: 506-444-4182
New Brunswick Real Estate Association, #1, 22 Durelle St., Fredericton, NB E3C 1N8
506-459-8055, Fax: 506-459-8057, 800-762-1677, info@nbrea.ca
New Brunswick Round Table on Environment & Economy, 20 McGloin St., PO Box 6000, Fredericton, NB E3B 5H1
506-453-3703, Fax: 506-453-3876
New Brunswick Power Group of Companies, 515 King St., PO Box 2000, Fredericton, NB E3B 4X1
506-458-4444, Fax: 506-458-4000, questions@nbpower.com
Regional Development Corporation, RDC Bldg., 836 Churchill Row, PO Box 428, Fredericton, NB E3B 5R4
506-453-2277, Fax: 506-453-7988
New Brunswick Research & Productivity Council, 921 College Hill Rd., Fredericton, NB E3B 6Z9
506-452-1212, Fax: 506-452-1395, info@rpc.ca
Workplace Health, Safety & Compensation Commission of New Brunswick, 1 Portland St., PO Box 160, Saint John, NB E2L 3X9
506-632-2200, 800-222-9775, communications@ws-ts.nb.ca

Newfoundland & Labrador

Canada-Newfoundland Offshore Petroleum Board, TD Place, 140 Water St., 5th Fl., St. John's, NL A1C 6H6
709-778-1400, Fax: 709-778-1473, information@cnlopb.nl.ca
Department of Fisheries & Aquaculture, Petten Bldg., 30 Strawberry Marsh Rd., PO Box 8700, St. John's, NL A1B 4J6
709-729-3723, Fax: 709-729-6082, fisheries@gov.nl.ca
Department of Innovation, Trade & Rural Development, West Block, Confederation Bldg., PO Box 8700, St. John's, NL A1B 4J6
709-729-7000, Fax: 709-729-0654, intrd@gov.nl.ca
Department of Labrador & Aboriginal Affairs, Confederation Bldg., East Block, 6th Fl., PO Box 8700, St. John's, NL A1B 4J6
709-729-4776, Fax: 709-729-4900, 877-788-8822, laa@gov.nl.ca
Department of Natural Resources, Natural Resources Bldg., 50 Elizabeth Ave., 7th Fl., PO Box 8700, St. John's, NL A1B 4J6
709-729-2920, Fax: 709-729-0059
Newfoundland & Labrador Housing Corporation, Sir Brian Dunfield Bldg., 2 Canada Dr., PO Box 220, St. John's, NL A1C 5J2
709-724-3000, Fax: 709-724-3250
Newfoundland & Labrador Hydro, Hydro Place, Columbus Dr., PO Box 12400, St. John's, NL A1B 4K7
709-737-1400, Fax: 709-737-1800, hydro@nlh.nl.ca
Labour Relations Board, Beothuck Bldg., 20 Crosbie Pl., 5th Fl., PO Box 8700, St. John's, NL A1B 4J6
709-729-2707, Fax: 709-729-5738, lrb@gov.nl.ca
Newfoundland & Labrador Liquor Corporation, 90 Kenmount Rd., PO Box 8750 A, St. John's, NL A1B 3V1
709-724-1100, Fax: 709-754-0321, info@nfliquor.com

Newfoundland & Labrador Municipal Financing Corporation, Confederation Bldg., PO Box 8700, St. John's, NL A1B 4J6
709-729-6686, Fax: 709-729-2095
Professional Fish Harvesters Certification Board, 368 Hamilton Ave., PO Box 8541, St. John's, NL A1B 3P2
709-722-8170, Fax: 709-722-8201, pfh@pfhcb.com
Newfoundland & Labrador Board of Commissioners of Public Utilities, PO Box 21040, St. John's, NL A1A 5B2
709-726-8600, Fax: 709-726-9604, 866-782-0006, ito@pub.nf.ca

Northwest Territories

Department of Environment & Natural Resources, PO Box 1320, Yellowknife, NT X1A 2L9
Department of Industry, Tourism & Investment, PO Box 1320, Yellowknife, NT X1A 2L9
Fax: 867-873-0306, info@iti.ca
Highways & Marine, 4510 - 50 Ave., 2nd fl., PO Box 1320, Yellowknife, NT X1A 2L9
867-920-8771, Fax: 867-873-0288
Northwest Territories Housing Corporation, Scotia Centre, 5102 50th Ave., PO Box 2100, Yellowknife, NT X1A 2P6
867-873-7853, Fax: 867-873-9426
Northwest Territories Liquor Commission, #201, 31 Capital Dr., Hay River, NT X0E 1G2
867-874-2100, Fax: 867-874-2180
Northwest Territories Liquor Licensing & Enforcement, #210, 31 Capital Dr., Hay River, NT X0E 1G2
867-874-2906, Fax: 867-874-6011
Northwest Territories Power Corporation, 4 Capital Dr., Hay River, NT X0E 1G2
867-874-5200, Fax: 867-874-5251, info@ntpc.com

Nova Scotia

Department of Agriculture, 1741 Brunswick St., 3rd Fl., PO Box 2223, Halifax, NS B3J 3C4
902-424-4560, Fax: 902-424-4671
Canada-Nova Scotia Offshore Petroleum Board, TD Centre, 1791 Barrington St., 6th Fl., Halifax, NS B3J 3K9
902-422-5588, Fax: 902-422-1799, postmaster@cnsopb.ns.ca
Crane Operators Appeal Board, 5151 Terminal Rd., 7th Fl., PO Box 697, Halifax, NS B3J 2T8
902-424-8595, Fax: 902-424-0217, fernanfs@gov.ns.ca
Department of Economic & Rural Development, Centennial Building, #600, 1660 Hollis St., PO Box 2311, Halifax, NS B3J 1V7
902-424-0377, Fax: 902-424-0500, comm@gov.ns.ca
Film Nova Scotia, Collins Bank Bldg., 1869 Upper Water St., 3rd Fl., Halifax, NS B3J 1S9
902-424-7177, Fax: 902-424-0617, 888-360-2111
InNOVACorp, #1400, 1801 Hollis St., Halifax, NS B3J 3N4
902-424-8670, Fax: 902-424-4679, 800-565-7051, communications@innovacorp.ca
Nova Scotia Liquor Corporation, Bayers Lake Business Park, 93 Chain Lake Dr., Halifax, NS B3S 1A3
902-450-6752, 800-567-5874
Department of Natural Resources, Founder's Square, 1701 Hollis St., 3rd Fl., PO Box 698, Halifax, NS B3J 2T9
902-424-5935, Fax: 902-424-0594, 800-565-2224
Nova Scotia Farm Loan Board, PO Box 550, Truro, NS B2N 5E3
902-893-6506, Fax: 902-895-7693, flb@gov.ns.ca
Trade Centre Limited, 1800 Argyle St., PO Box 955, Halifax, NS B3J 2V9
902-421-8686, Fax: 902-422-2922
Nova Scotia Utility & Review Board, Summit Place, 1601 Lower Water St., 3rd Fl., PO Box 1692 M,Halifax, NS B3J 3S3
902-424-4448, Fax: 902-424-3919, uarb.board@gov.ns.ca
Waterfront Development Corporation Ltd., 1751 Lower Water St., 2nd Fl., Halifax, NS B3J 1S5
902-422-6591, Fax: 902-422-7582, info@wdcl.ca

Nunavut

Department of Economic Development & Transportation, Bldg. 1104 A, Inuksugait Plaza, PO Box 1000 1500,Iqaluit, NU X0A 0H0
867-975-7800, Fax: 867-975-7870, 888-975-5999, edt@gov.nu.ca
Nunavut Liquor Licensing Board, Bag 002, Rankin Inlet, NU X0C 0G0
Fax: 867-645-3327

Ontario

AGRICORP, 1 Stone Rd. West, 3rd Fl., PO Box 3660 Central, Guelph, ON N1H 8M4
Fax: 519-826-4118, 888-247-4999, cac@agricorp.com
Agricultural Research Institute of Ontario, 1 Stone Rd. West, 2nd Fl., Guelph, ON N1G 4Y2
519-826-4199, Fax: 519-826-4211
Ministry of Agriculture, Food & Rural Affairs, Ontario Government Bldg., 1 Stone Rd. West, Guelph, ON N1G 4Y2
519-826-3100, 888-466-2372
Building Code Commission, 777 Bay St., 2nd Fl., Toronto, ON M5G 2E5
416-585-6666, Fax: 416-585-7531
Building Materials Evaluation Commission, 777 Bay St., 2nd Fl., Toronto, ON M5G 2E5
416-585-4234, Fax: 416-585-7531
Ministry of Consumer Services, Mowat Block, 900 Bay St., 6th Fl., Toronto, ON M7A 1L2
416-327-8300, Fax: 416-326-1947, 866-665-0662, infomcs@ontario.ca
Corporate Services Division, Hearst Block, 900 Bay St., 7th fl., Toronto, ON M7A 2E1
416-325-6486, Fax: 416-325-6392
Ministry of Economic Development & Innovation, Hearst Block, 900 Bay St., 8th Fl., Toronto, ON M7A 2E1
416-325-6666, Fax: 416-325-6688, 866-668-4249, info@edt.gov.on.ca
Ministry of Environment, 135 St. Clair Ave. West, Toronto, ON M4V 1P5
416-325-4000, Fax: 416-325-3159, 800-565-4923
Environmental Commissioner of Ontario, #605, 1075 Bay St., Toronto, ON M5S 2B1
416-325-3377, Fax: 416-325-3370, 800-701-6454, commissioner@eco.on.ca
Ministry of Government Services, Whitney Block, #4320, 99 Wellesley St. West, 4th Fl., Toronto, ON M7A 1W3
416-326-1234, Fax: 416-327-3790, 800-268-1142
Hydro One Inc., North Tower, 483 Bay St., Toronto, ON M5G 2P5
416-345-5000, 877-955-1155, customercommunications@HydroOne.com
Independent Electricity System Operator, PO Box 4474 A,Toronto, ON M5W 4E5
905-403-6900, Fax: 905-403-6921, 888-448-7777, customer.relations@ieso.ca
Ministry of Labour, 400 University Ave., 14th Fl., Toronto, ON M7A 1T7
416-326-7160, 800-531-5551
Ministry of Municipal Affairs & Housing, College Park, 777 Bay St., 17th Fl., Toronto, ON M5G 2E5
416-585-7041, Fax: 416-585-6470, 866-220-2290, mininfo@ontario.ca
Ministry of Natural Resources, Whitney Block, #6630, 99 Wellesley St. West, 6th Fl., Toronto, ON M7A 1W3
800-667-1940
Ministry of Northern Development, Mines & Forestry, 99 Wellesley St. West, Toronto, ON M7A 1W3
416-327-0633, Fax: 416-327-0651
Office of the Employer Advisor, #704, 151 Bloor St. West., Toronto, ON M5S 1S4
416-327-0020, Fax: 416-327-0726, 800-387-0774
Ontario Media Development Corporation, South Tower, #501, 175 Bloor St. East, Toronto, ON M4W 3R8
416-314-6858, Fax: 416-314-6876, mail@omdc.on.ca
Ontario Power Generation, 700 University Ave., Toronto, ON M5G 1X6
416-592-2555, 877-592-2555, webmaster@opg.com
ServiceOntario, College Park, 777 Bay St., 15th fl., Toronto, ON M7A 2J3
416-326-1234, Fax: 416-326-1313, 800-267-8097
Ministry of Tourism & Culture, Hearst Block, 900 Bay St., 9th Fl., Toronto, ON M7A 2E1
416-326-9326, Fax: 416-314-7854, 800-668-2746
Workplace Safety & Insurance Board, 200 Front St. West, Ground Fl., Toronto, ON M5V 3J1
416-344-1000, Fax: 416-344-4684, 800-387-0750

Prince Edward Island

Advisory Council on the Status of Women, Sherwood Business Centre, 161 St. Peter's Rd., Main Level, PO Box 2000, Charlottetown, PE C1A 7N8
902-368-4510, Fax: 902-368-3269, peistatusofwomen@eastlink.ca
Agricultural Insurance Corporation, 29 Indigo Cres., PO Box 1600, Charlottetown, PE C1A 7N3
902-368-4842, Fax: 902-368-6677
Anne of Green Gables Licensing Authority Inc., 94 Euston, PO Box 910, Charlottetown, PE C1A 7L9
902-569-7787, Fax: 902-368-6301, kobaker@gov.pe.ca; aggla@bellnet.ca
BIO FOOD TECH, 101 Belvedere Ave., PO Box 2000, Charlottetown, PE C1A 7N8
902-368-5548, Fax: 902-368-5549, 877-368-5548, biofoodtech@biofoodtech.ca
Charlottetown Area Development Corporation, 4 Pownal St., PO Box 786, Charlottetown, PE C1A 7L9
902-892-5341, Fax: 902-368-1935
Grain Elevators Corporation, 7 Gerald McCarville Dr., PO Box 250, Kensington, PE C0B 1M0
902-836-8935, Fax: 902-836-8926
Innovation PEI, 94 Euston St., PO Box 910, Charlottetown, PE C1A 7L9
902-368-6300, Fax: 902-368-6301, 800-563-3734
Prince Edward Island Department of Agriculture, Jones Bldg., 11 Kent St., PO Box 2000, Charlottetown, PE C1A 7N8
902-368-4880, Fax: 902-368-4857
Prince Edward Island Department of Innovation & Advanced Learning, Shaw Bldg., 105 Rochford St., 5th Fl., PO Box 2000, Charlottetown, PE C1A 7N8
902-368-4240, Fax: 902-368-4242
Prince Edward Island Department of Tourism & Culture, PO Box 2000, Charlottetown, PE C1A 7N8
902-368-5540, Fax: 902-368-5277, tpswitch@gov.pe.ca
Prince Edward Island Department of Transportation & Infrastructure Renewal, Jones Bldg., 11 Kent St., 3rd Fl., PO Box 2000, Charlottetown, PE C1A 7N8
902-368-5100, Fax: 902-368-5395
Prince Edward Island Liquor Control Commission, 3 Garfield St., PO Box 967, Charlottetown, PE C1A 7M4
902-368-5710, Fax: 902-368-5735
Prince Edward Island Workers Compensation Board, 14 Weymouth St., PO Box 757, Charlottetown, PE C1A 7L7
902-368-5680, Fax: 902-368-5696, 800-237-5049
SkillsPEI, Atlantic Technology Centre, #212, 90 University Ave., Charlottetown, PE C1A 4K9
902-368-4260, Fax: 902-368-6340, 877-491-4766

Quebec

Agence de l'efficacité énergétique, 5700, 4e av ouest, Québec, QC G1H 6R1
418-627-6379, Fax: 418-643-5828, 877-727-6655, efficaciteenergetique@mrnf.gouv.qc.ca
Ministère de l'Agriculture, des Pêcheries et de l'Alimentation, 200, ch Sainte-Foy, Québec, QC G1R 4X6
418-380-2110, 888-222-6272
Centre de recherche industrielle du Québec, 333, rue Franquet, Québec, QC G1P 4C7
418-659-1550, Fax: 418-652-2251, 800-667-2386, infocriq@criq.qc.ca
Comité conjoint de chasse, de pêche et de piégeage, #C220, 383 rue Saint-Jacques, Montréal, QC H2Y 1N9
514-284-2151, Fax: 514-284-0039, infohftcc@cccpp-hftcc.com
Commission de protection du territoire agricole du Québec, 200, ch Ste-Foy, 2e étage, Québec, QC G1R 4X6
418-643-3314, Fax: 418-643-2261, 800-667-5294, info@cptaq.gouv.qc.ca
Conseil consultatif du travail et de la main d'oeuvre, #9.400, 500, boul René-Lévesque ouest, Montréal, QC H2Z 1W7
514-873-2880, Fax: 514-873-1129, cctm@cctm.gouv.qc.ca
Ministère de la Culture, des Communications & de la Condition féminine, 225, Grande Allée est, Québec, QC G1R 5G5
888-380-8882
Ministère du Développement durable, de l'Environnement et des Parcs, Édifice Marie-Guyart, 675, boul René-Lévesque est, 29e étage, Québec, QC G1R 5V7
418-521-3830, Fax: 418-646-5974, 800-561-1616, info@mddep.gouv.qc.ca
Ministère du Développement économique, de l'Innovation et de l'Exportation, 710, place D'Youville, 3e étage, Québec, QC G1R 4Y4
418-691-5950, Fax: 418-644-0118, 866-680-1884
Hydro-Québec, 75, boul René-Lévesque ouest, Montréal, QC H2Z 1A4
514-289-2211
Innovatech Québec, #410, 888, rue St-Jean, Québec, QC G1R 5H6
418-528-9770, Fax: 418-528-9783, 866-605-1676
Investissement Québec, #1500, 600, rue de la Gauchetière ouest, Montréal, QC H3B 4L8
514-873-4664, 866-870-0437
La financière agricole de Québec, 1400, boul de la Rive-Sud, Saint-Romuald, QC G6W 8K7
418-838-5602, Fax: 418-833-3871, 800-749-3646, financiereagricole@fadq.qc.ca
Office de la sécurité du revenu des chasseurs et piégeurs cris, Édifice Champlain, #1110, 2700, boul Laurier, Québec, QC G1V 4K5
418-643-7300, Fax: 418-643-6803, 800-363-1560, courrier@osrcpc.ca
Régie des marchés agricoles et alimentaires du Québec, 201, boul Crémazie est, 5e étage, Montréal, QC H2M 1L3
514-873-4024, Fax: 514-873-3984
Régie du bâtiment du Québec, 545, boul Crémazie est, 4e étage, Montréal, QC H2M 2V2
514-873-0976, Fax: 514-864-2903, 800-361-0761, crc@rbq.gouv.qc.ca
Société d'habitation du Québec, Aile St-Amable, 1054, rue Louis-Alexandre-Taschereau, 3e étage, Québec, QC G1R 5E7
418-643-4035, Fax: 418-643-2533, 800-463-4315
Société de développement des entreprises culturelles, #800, 215, rue Saint-Jacques, Montréal, QC H2Y 1M6
514-841-2200, Fax: 514-841-8606, 800-363-0401, info@sodec.gouv.qc.ca
Société des alcools du Québec, 905, av De Lorimier, Montréal, QC H2K 3V9
514-873-2020, Fax: 514-873-6788, 866-873-2020, info@saq.com

Société québécoise de récupération et de recyclage, #200, 420, boul Charest est, Québec, QC G1K 8M4
418-643-0394, Fax: 418-643-6507, 866-523-8290, info@recyc-quebec.gouv.qc.ca

Ministère du Tourisme, #400, 900, boul René-Lévesque est, Québec, QC G1R 2B5
418-643-5959, Fax: 418-646-8723, 800-482-2433

Saskatchewan

Agri-Food Council, #302, 3085 Albert St., Regina, SK S4S 0B1
306-787-5978, Fax: 306-787-5134, corey.ruud@gov.sk.ca

Saskatchewan Agriculture, Walter Scott Bldg., 3085 Albert St., Regina, SK S4S 0B1
866-457-2377, aginfo@gov.sk.ca

Crown Investments Corporation of Saskatchewan, #400, 2400 College Ave., Regina, SK S4P 1C8
306-787-6851, Fax: 306-787-8125

Saskatchewan Energy & Resources, #300, 2103 - 11th Ave., Regina, SK S4P 3Z8
306-787-2528, webmasterer@gov.sk.ca

Saskatchewan Environment, 3211 Albert St., 2nd Fl., Regina, SK S4S 5W6
306-787-2584, Fax: 306-787-9544, 800-567-4224, Centre.Inquiry@gov.sk.ca

Farm Stress Unit, #125, 3085 Albert St., Regina, SK S4S 0B1
306-787-5196, Fax: 306-798-3042, 800-667-4442

Labour Relations Board, #1600, 1920 Broad St., Regina, SK S4P 3V2
306-787-2406, Fax: 306-787-2664

Saskatchewan Liquor & Gaming Authority, 2500 Victoria Ave., PO Box 5054, Regina, SK S4P 3M3
306-787-4213, inquiry@slga.gov.sk.ca

Saskatchewan Power Corporation (SaskPower), 2025 Victoria Ave., Regina, SK S4P 0S1
306-566-3306, Fax: 800-757-6937, 888-757-6937

Prairie Agricultural Machinery Institute, Hwy 5 West, PO Box 1150, Humboldt, SK S0K 2A0
306-682-2555, Fax: 306-682-5080, 800-567-7264, humboldt@pami.ca

Saskatchewan Crop Insurance Corporation, 484 Prince William Dr., PO Box 3000, Melville, SK S0A 2P0
306-728-7200, Fax: 306-728-7202, 888-935-0000, customer.service@scic.gov.sk.ca

Saskatchewan Lands Appeal Board, #202, 3085 Albert St., Regina, SK S4S 0B1
306-787-4693, Fax: 306-787-1315, Donald.Brooks@gov.sk.ca

Saskatchewan Trade & Export Partnership, #320, 1801 Hamilton St., PO Box 1787, Regina, SK S4P 3C6
306-787-9210, Fax: 306-787-6666, inquire@sasktrade.sk.ca

Saskatchewan Workers' Compensation Board, #200, 1881 Scarth St., Regina, SK S4P 4L1
306-787-4370, Fax: 306-787-7582, 800-667-7590, internet_clientsvc@wcbsask.com

SaskEnergy Incorporated, 1777 Victoria Ave., Regina, SK S4P 4K5
306-777-9225, 800-567-8899

Saskatchewan Water Corporation (SaskWater), #200, 111 Fairford St. East, Moose Jaw, SK S6H 1C8
Fax: 306-694-3207, 888-230-1111, comm@saskwater.com; customerservice@saskwater.com

Saskatchewan Workers' Compensation Board, #200, 1881 Scarth St., Regina, SK S4P 4L1
306-787-4370, Fax: 306-787-4311, 800-667-7590, internet_clientsvc@wcbsask.com

Yukon Territory

Yukon Development Corporation, #2 Miles Canyon Rd., PO Box 5920, Whitehorse, YT Y1A 6S7
867-393-5337, Fax: 867-393-5401

Yukon Economic Development, PO Box 2703, Whitehorse, YT Y1A 2C6
867-393-7191, Fax: 867-393-6412, 800-661-0408, ecdev@gov.yk.ca

Yukon Environment, PO Box 2703, Whitehorse, YT Y1A 2C6
867-667-5652, Fax: 867-393-7197, environment.yukon@gov.yk.ca

Yukon Housing Corporation, 410H Jarvis St., PO Box 2703, Whitehorse, YT Y1A 2H5
867-667-5759, Fax: 867-667-3664, 800-661-0408, ykhouse@housing.yk.ca

Yukon Liquor Corporation, 9031 Quartz Rd., Whitehorse, YT Y1A 4P9
867-667-5245, Fax: 867-393-6306, yukon.liquor@gov.yk.ca

Yukon Tourism & Culture, 100 Hanson St., Whitehorse, YT Y1A 2C6
867-667-5036, Fax: 867-667-3546

INDUSTRY & TRADE

Atlantic Canada Opportunities Agency, Blue Cross Centre, 644 Main St., 3rd Fl., PO Box 6051, Moncton, NB E1C 9J8
506-851-2271, Fax: 506-851-7403, 800-561-7862, information@acoa-apeca.gc.ca

Business Development Bank of Canada, #400, 5, Place Ville-Marie, Montréal, QC H3B 5E7
514-283-5904, Fax: 514-283-5626, 877-232-2269

Corporate Services Division, PO Box 2000, Charlottetown, PE C1A 7N8

Defence Construction Canada, Constitution Square, 350 Albert St., 19th Fl., Ottawa, ON K1A 0K3
613-998-9548, Fax: 613-998-1061, 800-514-3555, info@dcc-cdc.gc.ca

Export Development Canada, 151 Slater St., Ottawa, ON K1A 1K3
613-598-2500, Fax: 613-598-3811, 800-267-8510

Foreign Affairs & International Trade Canada, 125 Sussex Dr., Ottawa, ON K1A 0G2
613-944-4000, Fax: 613-996-9709, 800-267-8376, enqserv@international.gc.ca

Industrial Materials Institute, 75, boul de Mortagne, Boucherville, QC J4B 6Y4
450-641-5000, Fax: 450-641-5101, Imi-Info@cnrc-nrc.gc.ca

Industry Canada, C.D. Howe Building, 235 Queen St., Ottawa, ON K1A 0H5
613-954-5031, Fax: 613-954-2340, 800-328-6189, info@ic.gc.ca

Institute for Research in Construction, Bldg. M-24, 1500 Montreal Rd., Ottawa, ON K1A 0R6
613-993-2607, Fax: 613-952-7673, Irc.Client-Services@nrc-cnrc.gc.ca

London - Centre for Automotive Materials & Manufacturing, 800 Collip Circle, London, ON N6G 4X8
519-430-7166, Fax: 519-430-7064, John.Lyons@nrc-cnrc.gc.ca

Market & Industry Services Branch, Tower 5, 1341 Baseline Rd., Ottawa, ON K1A 0C5
613-759-1000, Fax: 613-773-1755

Standards Council of Canada, #200, 270 Albert St., Ottawa, ON K1P 6N7
613-238-3222, Fax: 613-569-7808, info@scc.ca

Western Economic Diversification Canada, Canada Place, #1500, 9700 Jasper Ave. NW, Edmonton, AB T5J 4H7
780-495-4164, Fax: 780-495-4557, 888-338-9378

British Columbia

Timber Export Advisory Committee, PO Box 9514 Prov Govt, Victoria, BC V8W 9C2
250-387-8916, Fax: 250-387-5050

Manitoba

Manitoba Competitiveness, Training & Trade, International Business Centre, The Paris Building, 259 Portage Ave., Winnipeg, MB R3B 3P4
204-945-2475, Fax: 204-945-3977, minctt@leg.gov.mb.ca

New Brunswick

Board of Examiners under the Scaler's Act, 1350 Regent St. South, PO Box 6000, Fredericton, NB E3B 5H1
506-453-2441, Fax: 506-453-6689

Department of Business New Brunswick, Centennial Bldg., 670 King St., PO Box 6000, Fredericton, NB E3B 5H1
506-453-3707, Fax: 506-453-3993, investnb@gnb.ca

New Brunswick Industrial Development Board, Business New Brunswick, Centennial Bldg., 670 King St., PO Box 6000, Fredericton, NB E3B 5H1
506-453-4200, Fax: 506-444-4182

Regional Development Corporation, RDC Bldg., 836 Churchill Row, PO Box 428, Fredericton, NB E3B 5R4
506-453-2277, Fax: 506-453-7988

Newfoundland & Labrador

Department of Innovation, Trade & Rural Development, West Block, Confederation Bldg., PO Box 8700, St. John's, NL A1B 4J6
709-729-7000, Fax: 709-729-0654, intrd@gov.nl.ca

Department of Labrador & Aboriginal Affairs, Confederation Bldg., East Block, 6th Fl., PO Box 8700, St. John's, NL A1B 4J6
709-729-4776, Fax: 709-729-4900, 877-788-8822, laa@gov.nl.ca

Northwest Territories

Department of Environment & Natural Resources, PO Box 1320, Yellowknife, NT X1A 2L9

Nova Scotia

Department of Agriculture, 1741 Brunswick St., 3rd Fl., PO Box 2223, Halifax, NS B3J 3C4
902-424-4560, Fax: 902-424-4671

Department of Economic & Rural Development, Centennial Building, #600, 1660 Hollis St., PO Box 2311, Halifax, NS B3J 1V7
902-424-0377, Fax: 902-424-0500, comm@gov.ns.ca

Pay Equity Commission, 5151 Terminal Rd., 6th Fl., PO Box 697, Halifax, NS B3J 2T8
902-424-2385, Fax: 902-424-0575

Workers' Compensation Board of Nova Scotia, 5668 South St., PO Box 1150, Halifax, NS B3J 2Y2
902-491-8999, Fax: 902-491-8002, 800-870-3331, info@wcb.gov.ns.ca

Ontario

Ministry of Economic Development & Innovation, Hearst Block, 900 Bay St., 8th Fl., Toronto, ON M7A 2E1
416-325-6666, Fax: 416-325-6688, 866-668-4249, info@edt.gov.on.ca

Ministry of Northern Development, Mines & Forestry, 99 Wellesley St. West, Toronto, ON M7A 1W3
416-327-0633, Fax: 416-327-0651

Prince Edward Island

Prince Edward Island Department of Innovation & Advanced Learning, Shaw Bldg., 105 Rochford St., 5th Fl., PO Box 2000, Charlottetown, PE C1A 7N8
902-368-4240, Fax: 902-368-4242

Quebec

Commission des lésions professionnelles, #700, 900, Place d'Youville, Québec, QC G1R 3P7
418-644-7777, Fax: 418-644-6443, 800-463-1591

Innovatech Québec, #410, 888, rue St-Jean, Québec, QC G1R 5H6
418-528-9770, Fax: 418-528-9783, 866-605-1676

Saskatchewan

Saskatchewan Energy & Resources, #300, 2103 - 11th Ave., Regina, SK S4P 3Z8
306-787-2528, webmasterer@gov.sk.ca

Saskatchewan Trade & Export Partnership, #320, 1801 Hamilton St., PO Box 1787, Regina, SK S4P 3C6
306-787-9210, Fax: 306-787-6666, inquire@sasktrade.sk.ca

Tourism Saskatchewan, #189, 1621 Albert St., Regina, SK S4P 2S5
306-787-9600, 877-237-2273

Yukon Territory

Yukon Development Corporation, #2 Miles Canyon Rd., PO Box 5920, Whitehorse, YT Y1A 6S7
867-393-5337, Fax: 867-393-5401

INFORMATION & PRIVACY COMMISSIONER

Office of the Information Commissioner of Canada, Place de Ville, Tower B, 112 Kent St., 7th Fl., Ottawa, ON K1A 1H3
613-995-2410, Fax: 613-947-7294, 800-267-0441, general@oic-ci.gc.ca

Privacy Commissioner of Canada, Tower B, Place de Ville, 112 Kent St., 3rd Fl., Ottawa, ON K1A 1H3
613-947-1698, Fax: 613-947-6850, 800-282-1376

Ontario

Information & Privacy Commissioner of Ontario, #1400, 2 Bloor St. East, Toronto, ON M4W 1A8
416-326-3333, Fax: 416-325-9195, 800-387-0073, info@ipc.on.ca

Saskatchewan

Information & Privacy Commissioner of Saskatchewan, #503, 1801 Hamilton St., Regina, SK S4P 4B4
306-787-8350, Fax: 306-798-1603, 877-748-2298, webmaster@oipc.sk.ca

INFORMATION RESOURCES

Industry Canada, C.D. Howe Building, 235 Queen St., Ottawa, ON K1A 0H5
613-954-5031, Fax: 613-954-2340, 800-328-6189, info@ic.gc.ca

Public Works & Government Services Canada, Place du Portage, Phase III, 11, rue Laurier, Ottawa, ON K1A 0S5
questions@tpsgc-pwgsc.gc.ca

Statistics Canada, R.H. Coats Bldg., Tunney's Pasture, 150 Tunney's Pasture Driveway, Ottawa, ON K1A 0T6
613-951-8116, Fax: 877-287-4369, 800-263-1136, infostats@statcan.ca

New Brunswick

Service New Brunswick, Westmorland Place, #200, 82 Westmorland St., PO Box 1998, Fredericton, NB E3B 5G4
506-457-3581, Fax: 506-457-7520, 888-762-8600, snb@snb.ca

Nova Scotia

Nova Scotia Geomatics Centre, 160 Willow St., Amherst, NS B4H 3W5
902-667-7231, Fax: 902-667-6008, 800-798-0706, geoinfo@gov.ns.ca

Ontario

Ontario Geographic Names Board, Robinson Place, 300 Water St., 2nd Fl., PO Box 7000, Peterborough, ON K9J 8M5
705-755-2134

Science & Information Resources Division, Roberta Bondar Pl., #400, 70 Foster Dr., Sault Ste Marie, ON P6A 6V5
705-755-2000, Fax: 705-755-2802, 800-667-1940

Saskatchewan

Saskatchewan Conservation Data Centre, 3211 Albert St., Regina, SK S4S 5W6
306-787-9038, Fax: 306-787-9544

INSURANCE

New Brunswick

New Brunswick Insurance Board, Saint John Mercantile Centre, #600, 55 Union St., Saint John, NB E2L 5B7
506-643-7710, Fax: 506-652-5011, info@nbib-canb.org

INSURANCE (LIFE, FIRE, PROPERTY)

See Also: Automobile Insurance; Health Care Insurance

Canada Deposit Insurance Corporation, 50 O'Connor St., 17th Floor, PO Box 2340 D,Ottawa, ON K1P 5W5
Fax: 613-996-6095, 800-461-2342, info@cdic.ca; info@sadc.ca

Office of the Superintendent of Financial Institutions, Kent Square, 255 Albert St., Ottawa, ON K1A 0H2
613-990-7788, Fax: 613-990-5591, 800-385-8647, information@osfi-bsif.gc.ca

Office of Budget & Fiscal Planning, Terrace Building, 9515 - 107 St., 4th Fl., Edmonton, AB T5K 2C3

British Columbia

Insurance Council of British Columbia, #300, 1040 West Georgia St., PO Box 7, Vancouver, BC V6E 4H1
604-688-0321, Fax: 604-662-7767, 877-688-0321

Manitoba

Financial Institutions Regulation Branch, #1115, 405 Broadway, Winnipeg, MB R3C 3L6
204-945-2542, Fax: 204-948-2268

Manitoba Public Insurance, #B100, 234 Donald St., PO Box 6300, Winnipeg, MB R3C 4A4
204-985-7000, Fax: 204-985-3525, 800-665-2410

Manitoba Agricultural Services Corporation, #100, 1525 First St. South, Brandon, MB R7A 7A1
204-726-6850, Fax: 204-726-6849, mailbox@masc.mb.ca

New Brunswick

New Brunswick Credit Union Deposit Insurance Corp., PO Box 6000, Fredericton, NB E3B 5H1
506-457-4852, Fax: 506-453-7474

New Brunswick Insurance Board, Saint John Mercantile Centre, #600, 55 Union St., Saint John, NB E2L 5B7
506-643-7710, Fax: 506-652-5011, info@nbib-canb.org

Northwest Territories

Department of Finance, Arthur Laing Building, 5th Fl., 5003 - 49th St., PO Box 1320, Yellowknife, NT X1A 2L9
867-873-7117, Fax: 867-873-0414

Nova Scotia

Nova Scotia Utility & Review Board, Summit Place, 1601 Lower Water St., 3rd Fl., Halifax, NS B3J 3P6
902-424-4448, Fax: 902-424-3919, uarb.board@gov.ns.ca

Ontario

Deposit Insurance Corporation of Ontario, #700, 4711 Yonge St., Toronto, ON M2N 6K8
416-325-9444, Fax: 416-325-9722, 800-268-6653

Financial Services Commission of Ontario, New York City Ctr., 5160 Yonge St., 17th Fl., PO Box 85, Toronto, ON M2N 6L9
416-250-7250, Fax: 416-590-7070, 800-668-0128

Prince Edward Island

Agricultural Insurance Corporation, 29 Indigo Cres., PO Box 1600, Charlottetown, PE C1A 7N3
902-368-4842, Fax: 902-368-6677

Quebec

Commission administrative des régimes de retraite et d'assurances (Québec), 475, rue Saint-Amable, Québec, QC G1R 5X3
418-643-4881, Fax: 418-644-3839, 800-463-5533

Saskatchewan

Saskatchewan Government Insurance, 2260 - 11th Ave., Regina, SK S4P 0J9
306-751-1200, Fax: 306-787-7477, 800-667-8015, sgiinquiries@sgi.sk.ca

Saskatchewan Crop Insurance Corporation, 484 Prince William Dr., PO Box 3000, Melville, SK S0A 2P0
306-728-7200, Fax: 306-728-7202, 888-935-0000, customer.service@scic.gov.sk.ca

Saskatchewan Financial Services Commission, #601, 1919 Saskatchewan Dr., Regina, SK S4P 4H2
306-787-5645, Fax: 306-787-5899

INTELLECTUAL PROPERTY

London - Centre for Automotive Materials & Manufacturing, 800 Collip Circle, London, ON N6G 4X8
519-430-7166, Fax: 519-430-7064, John.Lyons@nrc-cnrc.gc.ca

INTERGOVERNMENTAL AFFAIRS

See: Federal-Provincial Affairs; International Affairs

Canadian Tourism Commission, Four Bentall Centre, #1400, 1055 Dunsmuir St., PO Box 49230, Vancouver, BC V7X 1L2
604-638-8300

INTERNATIONAL AFFAIRS

See Also: Trade

Canadian International Development Agency, 200, Promenade du Portage, Gatineau, QC K1A 0G4
819-997-5456, Fax: 819-953-6088, 800-230-6349, info@acdi-cida.gc.ca

Canadian International Trade Tribunal, Standard Life Centre, 333 Laurier Ave. West, 15 Floor, Ottawa, ON K1A 0G7
613-990-2452, Fax: 613-990-2439, secretary@citt-tcce.gc.ca

Canadian Tourism Commission, Four Bentall Centre, #1400, 1055 Dunsmuir St., PO Box 49230, Vancouver, BC V7X 1L2
604-638-8300

Foreign Affairs & International Trade Canada, 125 Sussex Dr., Ottawa, ON K1A 0G2
613-944-4000, Fax: 613-996-9709, 800-267-8376, enqserv@international.gc.ca

International Development Research Centre, 150 Kent St., PO Box 8500, Ottawa, ON K1G 3H9
613-236-6163, Fax: 613-238-7230, info@idrc.ca

National Defence Canada, Major-General George R. Pearkes Bldg., 101 Colonel By Dr., Ottawa, ON K1A 0K2
613-995-2534, Fax: 613-992-4739, 800-856-8488

Alberta

Alberta International & Intergovernmental Relations, Commerce Place, 10155 - 102 St., 12th Fl., Edmonton, AB T5J 4G8
780-422-1510, Fax: 780-427-0699,

British Columbia

Intergovernmental Relations Secretariat, PO Box 9333 Prov Govt,Victoria, BC V8W 9N3
250-387-0752, Fax: 250-387-1920, igrs@gov.bc.ca

Manitoba

Manitoba Intergovernmental Affairs, #301, 450 Broadway Ave., Winnipeg, MB R3C 0V8
Fax: 204-945-1383, mnia@leg.gov.mb.ca

New Brunswick

Department of Intergovernmental Affairs, Centennial Bldg., #274, 670 King St., PO Box 6000, Fredericton, NB E3B 5H1
506-444-5418, Fax: 506-453-2995, iga@gnb.ca

Ontario

Ministry of Intergovernmental Affairs, 77 Wellesley St. West, Toronto, ON M7A 1N3
416-325-4800, Fax: 416-325-4787

Quebec

Ministère des Relations internationales, Édifice Hector-Fabre, 525, boul Réne-Lévesque est, Québec, QC G1R 5R9
418-649-2300, Fax: 418-649-2656

INTERNATIONAL AID

Canadian International Development Agency, 200, Promenade du Portage, Gatineau, QC K1A 0G4
819-997-5456, Fax: 819-953-6088, 800-230-6349, info@acdi-cida.gc.ca

International Development Research Centre, 150 Kent St., PO Box 8500, Ottawa, ON K1G 3H9
613-236-6163, Fax: 613-238-7230, info@idrc.ca

INVESTMENT

See Also: Business Development; Industry

Canada Economic Development for Québec Regions, Édifice Dominion Square, #900, 1255, rue Peel, Montréal, QC H3B 2T9
514-283-6412, Fax: 514-283-3302, 866-385-6412

Canada Investment & Savings, #900, 110 Yonge St., Toronto, ON M5C 1T4
416-952-1252, Fax: 416-952-1270, 800-575-5151, csb@csb.gc.ca

Canada Pension Plan Investment Board, #2600, 1 Queen St. East, PO Box 101, Toronto, ON M5C 2W5
416-868-4075, Fax: 416-868-8689, 866-557-9510, csr@cppib.ca

Finance Canada, L'esplanade Laurier, 140 O'Connor St., Ottawa, ON K1A 0G5
613-992-1573, Fax: 613-943-0938, finpub@fin.gc.ca

Global Operations, 125 Sussex Dr,, Ottawa, ON K1A 0G2
613-944-2697, Fax: 613-996-1667

Industry Canada, C.D. Howe Building, 235 Queen St., Ottawa, ON K1A 0H5
613-954-5031, Fax: 613-954-2340, 800-328-6189, info@ic.gc.ca

Public Sector Pension Investment Board, #200, 440 Laurier Ave. West, Ottawa, ON K1R 7X6
613-782-3095, Fax: 613-782-6864, info@investpsp.ca

Tax & Revenue Administration, Sir Frederick W. Haultain Building, 9811 - 109 St., 2nd Fl., Edmonton, AB T5K 2L5
780-427-3044

Alberta

Intergovernmental Relations, Commerce Place, 10155 - 102 St., 12th Fl., Edmonton, AB T5J 4G8
780-427-6706, Fax: 780-427-0939

British Columbia

Forestry Innovation Investment Ltd., #1200, 1130 West Pender St., Vancouver, BC V6E 4A4
604-685-7507, Fax: 604-685-5373, info@bcfii.ca

Labour Market & Immigration Division, PO Box 9213, Vancouver, BC V8W 9J1
250-953-3585, Fax: 250-356-0033

New Brunswick

Investment, Export & Business Development, Centennial Bldg., 670 King St., 5th Fl., PO Box 6000, Fredericton, NB E3B 5H1
506-453-2875, Fax: 506-444-4277

New Brunswick Investment Management Corporation, York Tower, #581, 440 King St., Fredericton, NB E3B 5H8
506-444-5800, Fax: 506-444-5025, comments@nbimc.com

Northwest Territories

Department of Industry, Tourism & Investment, PO Box 1320, Yellowknife, NT X1A 2L9
Fax: 867-873-0306, info@iti.ca

Nova Scotia

InNOVACorp, #1400, 1801 Hollis St., Halifax, NS B3J 3N4
902-424-8670, Fax: 902-424-4679, 800-565-7051, communications@innovacorp.ca

Prince Edward Island

Charlottetown Area Development Corporation, 4 Pownal St., PO Box 786, Charlottetown, PE C1A 7L9
902-892-5341, Fax: 902-368-1935

Prince Edward Island Lending Agency, Homburg Financial Tower, 98 Fitzroy St., 2nd Fl., Charlottetown, PE C1A 1R7
902-368-6200, Fax: 902-368-6201

Quebec

Investissement Québec, #1500, 600, rue de la Gauchetière ouest, Montréal, QC H3B 4L8
514-873-4664, 866-870-0437

JUSTICE DEPARTMENTS

Justice Canada, East Memorial Bldg., 284 Wellington St., Ottawa, ON K1A 0H8
613-957-4222, Fax: 613-954-0811, webadmin@justice.gc.ca

Alberta

Alberta Justice & Attorney General, Communications, Bowker Building, 9833 - 109 St., 3rd Fl., Edmonton, AB T5K 2E8
780-427-2745

British Columbia

Ministry of the Attorney General, PO Box 9044 Prov Govt,Victoria, BC V8W 9E2
250-387-1866, Fax: 250-387-6411

Manitoba

Manitoba Justice, Legislative Building, #104, 405 Broadway Ave., Winnipeg, MB R3C 3L6
204-945-3728, Fax: 204-945-2517, minjus@gov.mb.ca

New Brunswick

Department of Justice & Consumer Affairs, Centennial Bldg., 670 King St., PO Box 6000, Fredericton, NB E3B 5H1
506-462-5100, Fax: 506-453-3651, justice.comments@gnb.ca

Newfoundland & Labrador

Department of Justice, Confederation Bldg., East Block, 4th Fl., PO Box 8700, St. John's, NL A1B 4J6
709-729-2869, Fax: 709-729-0469, justice@gov.nl.ca

Northwest Territories

Department of Justice, Courthouse, 4903 - 49th St., 6th Fl., PO Box 1320, Yellowknife, NT X1A 2L9
867-920-6197

Nova Scotia

Department of Justice, 5151 Terminal Rd., 4th Fl., PO Box 7, Halifax, NS B3J 2L6
902-424-4030, Fax: 902-424-0510, justweb@gov.ns.ca

Nunavut

Department of Justice, Sivummut, 1st Fl., PO Box 1000 500,Iqaluit, NU X0A 0H0
867-975-6170, Fax: 867-975-6195, justice@gov.nu.ca

Ontario

Ministry of the Attorney General, McMurtry-Scott Bldg., 720 Bay St., 11th Fl., Toronto, ON M5G 2K1
416-326-2220, Fax: 416-326-4007, 800-518-7901

Prince Edward Island

Prince Edward Island Department of Justice & Public Safety, Shaw Bldg., 95 Rochford St. South, 4th Fl., PO Box 2000, Charlottetown, PE C1A 7N8

Quebec

Ministère de la Justice, Édifice Louis-Philippe-Pigeon, 1200, rte de l'Église, Québec, QC G1V 4M1
418-643-5140, 866-536-5140, informations@justice.gouv.qc.ca

Saskatchewan

Saskatchewan Justice & Attorney General, 1874 Scarth St., Regina, SK S4P 4B3
306-787-8971, communications@justice.gov.sk.ca

Yukon Territory

Yukon Justice, Andrew Philipsen Law Centre, 2134 Second Ave., PO Box 2703, Whitehorse, YT Y1A 2C6
867-667-3033, Fax: 867-393-5790, jus.msb@gov.yk.ca

LABOUR

Canada Industrial Relations Board, 240 Sparks St., 4th Fl. West, Ottawa, ON K1A 0X8
Fax: 613-941-4461, 800-575-9696, info@cirb-ccri.gc.ca

Canadian Artists & Producers Professional Relations Tribunal, C.D. Howe Bldg., 240 Sparks St., 1st Fl., West Tower, Ottawa, ON K1A 1A1
613-996-4052, Fax: 613-947-4125, 800-263-ARTS, info@capprt-tcrpap.gc.ca

Canadian Council of Directors of Apprenticeship, 140 Promenade du Portage, 5th Fl, Phase IV, Gatineau, QC K1A 0J9
819-953-7443, Fax: 819-994-0202, redseal-sceaurouge@hrsdc-rhdcc.gc.ca

Commission des relations du travail, 900, boul René-Lévesque est, 5e étage, Québec, QC G1R 6C9
418-643-3208, Fax: 418-643-8946, 866-864-3646, crtm@crt.gouv.qc.ca

Human Resources & Skills Development Canada, 140 Promenade du Portage, Gatineau, QC K1A 0J9

Department of Labour & Advanced Education, 5151 Terminal Rd., 6th Fl., PO Box 697, Halifax, NS B3J 2T8
902-424-5301, Fax: 902-424-0575

Merchant Seamen Compensation Board, Secretary, Merchant Seamen Compensation Board, Phase II, Place du Portage, 10th Fl., Ottawa, ON K1A 0J2
819-953-8001, Fax: 819-994-5368

National Joint Council, C.D. Howe Bldg., 240 Sparks St. West, 7th Fl., PO Box 1525 B,Ottawa, ON K1P 5V2
613-990-1805, Fax: 613-990-7071, email.courrier@njc-cnm.gc.ca

Public Service Commission, West Tower, 300 Laurier Ave. West, Ottawa, ON K1A 0M7
613-992-9562, Fax: 613-992-9352, infocom@psc-cfp.gc.ca

Public Service Labour Relations Board, CD Howe Building, 240 Sparks St., 6th Fl., PO Box 1525 B, Ottawa, ON K1P 5V2
613-990-1800, Fax: 613-990-1849, 866-931-3454, mail.courrier@pslrb-crtfp.gc.ca

Public Service Staffing Tribunal, 240 Sparks St., 6th Fl., Ottawa, ON K1A 0A5
613-949-6516, Fax: 613-949-6551, 866-637-4491, info@psst-tdfp.gc.ca

Workers' Compensation Appeals Tribunal, #1002, 5670 Spring Garden Rd., Halifax, NS B3J 1H6
902-424-2250, Fax: 902-424-2321, 800-274-8281

Alberta

Alberta Apprenticeship & Industry Training Board, Commerce Place, 10155 - 102nd St., 10th Fl., Edmonton, AB T5J 4L5
780-427-8765, Fax: 780-422-7376

Alberta Labour Relations Board, Labour Building, 10808 - 99 Ave., 5th Fl., Edmonton, AB T5K 0G5
780-422-5926, Fax: 780-422-0970, 800-463-2572, alrbinfo@lab.gov.ab.ca

Community, Learner & Industry Connections Division, Phipps-McKinnon Bldg., 10020 - 101A Ave., 5th Fl., Edmonton, AB T5J 3G2

Alberta Employment & Immigration, Minister's Office, Legislature Building, #418, 10800 - 97 Ave., Edmonton, AB T5K 2B6
780-644-5135, 866-644-5135, eii.communications@gov.ab.ca

Health Quality Council of Alberta, #210, 811 - 14 St. NW, Calgary, AB T2N 2A4
403-297-8162, Fax: 403-297-8258, info@hqca.ca

Occupational Health & Safety Council, Labour Building, 10808 - 99 Ave., 9th Fl., Edmonton, AB T5K 0G5
780-415-8690, 866-415-8690

British Columbia

British Columbia Labour Relations Board, Oceanic Plaza, #600, 1066 West Hastings St., Vancouver, BC V6E 3X1
604-660-1300, Fax: 604-660-1892, information@lrb.bc.ca

Employment Standards Tribunal, Oceanic Plaza, #650, 1066 West Hastings St., Vancouver, BC V6E 3X1
604-775-3512, Fax: 604-775-3372, registrar.est@bcest.bc.ca

Ministry of Labour, Citizens' Services & Open Government, PO Box 9056 Prov Govt,Victoria, BC V8W 9K4
250-952-7623, Fax: 250-387-4312, 800-663-7867, LCTZ.Minister@gov.bc.ca

Workers' Compensation Appeal Tribunal, #150, 4600 Jacombs Rd., Richmond, BC V6V 3B1
604-664-7800, Fax: 604-664-7898, 800-663-2782

Workers' Compensation Board of British Columbia, PO Box 5350 Terminal,Vancouver, BC V6B 5L5
604-276-3100, Fax: 604-276-3247, 888-621-7233

Manitoba

Advisory Council on Workplace Safety & Health, #200, 401 York Ave., Winnipeg, MB R3C 0P8
204-945-3446, Fax: 204-945-4556

Civil Service Commission Board, #935, 155 Carlton St., Winnipeg, MB R3C 3H8
204-945-1435, Fax: 204-945-1486

Manitoba Civil Service Commission, #935, 155 Carlton St., Winnipeg, MB R3C 3H8
204-945-2332, Fax: 204-945-1486, 800-282-8069, cschrp@gov.mb.ca

Manitoba Education, Citizenship & Youth, #168, Legislative Bldg., 450 Broadway, Winnipeg, MB R3C 0V8
204-945-3720, Fax: 204-945-1291, minedu@leg.gov.mb.ca

Manitoba Labour & Immigration, Legislative Building, 317, 450 Broadway Ave., Winnipeg, MB R3C 0V8
204-945-4079, Fax: 204-945-8312, minlab@leg.gov.mb.ca

Manitoba Civil Service Commission, #935, 155 Carlton St., Winnipeg, MB R3C 3H8
204-945-2332, Fax: 204-945-1486, cschrp@gov.mb.ca

Manitoba Labour Board, A.A. Heaps Bldg., #402, 258 Portage Ave., Winnipeg, MB R3C 0B6
204-945-3783, Fax: 204-945-1296, mlb@gov.mb.ca

Manitoba Minimum Wage Board, 614 - 401 York Ave., Winnipeg, MB R3C 0P8
204-945-4889, Fax: 204-948-2085, mw@gov.mb.ca

Pension Commission of Manitoba, #1004, 401 York Ave., Winnipeg, MB R3C 0P8
204-945-2740, Fax: 204-948-2375, pensions@gov.mb.ca

Manitoba Workers' Compensation Board, 333 Broadway Ave., Winnipeg, MB R3C 4W3
204-954-4321, Fax: 204-954-4999, 800-362-3340, wcb@wcb.mb.ca

Workplace Safety & Health Division, #200, 401 York Ave., Winnipeg, MB R3C 0P8
204-945-3446, Fax: 204-948-2209, wshcompl@gov.mb.ca

New Brunswick

Apprenticeship & Occupational Certification Board, PO Box 6000, Fredericton, NB E3B 5H1
506-453-2260, Fax: 506-453-5317

Department of Post-Secondary Education, Training & Labour, Chestnut Complex, 470 York St., PO Box 6000, Fredericton, NB E3B 5H1
506-453-2597, Fax: 506-453-3618, dpetlinfo@gnb.ca

Workplace Health, Safety & Compensation Commission of New Brunswick, 1 Portland St., PO Box 160, Saint John, NB E2L 3X9
506-632-2200, 800-222-9775, communications@ws-ts.nb.ca

Newfoundland & Labrador

Department of Human Resources, Labour & Employment, Confederation Bldg., PO Box 8700, St. John's, NL A1B 4J6
709-729-2480, Fax: 709-729-6996, hreweb@gov.nl.ca

Labour Relations Board, Beothuck Bldg., 20 Crosbie Pl., 5th Fl., PO Box 8700, St. John's, NL A1B 4J6
709-729-2707, Fax: 709-729-5738, lrb@gov.nl.ca

Newfoundland & Labrador Workplace Health, Safety & Compensation Commission, 146 - 148 Forest Rd., PO Box 9000, St. John's, NL A1A 3B8
709-778-1000, Fax: 709-738-1714, 800-563-9000, general.inquiries@whscc.nl.ca

Northwest Territories

Department of Education, Culture & Employment, PO Box 1320, Yellowknife, NT X1A 2L9
867-669-2399, Fax: 867-873-0431, 866-606-5627

Northwest Territories Apprenticeship, Trade & Occupations Certification Board, PO Box 1320, Yellowknife, NT X1A 2L9
867-873-7357, Fax: 867-873-0200

Northwest Territories & Nunavut Workers' Safety & Compensation Commission, Centre Square Tower, 5022 - 49th St., 5th Fl., PO Box 8888, Yellowknife, NT X1A 2R3
867-920-3888, Fax: 867-873-4596, 800-661-0792

Nova Scotia

Nova Scotia Advisory Board on Colleges & Universities, 2021 Brunswick St., PO Box 2086 M, Halifax, NS B3J 3B7
Fax: 902-424-0651

Pay Equity Commission, 5151 Terminal Rd., 6th Fl., PO Box 697, Halifax, NS B3J 2T8
902-424-2385, Fax: 902-424-0575

Workers' Advisers Program, #502, 5670 Spring Garden Rd., PO Box 1063, Halifax, NS B3J 2X1
902-424-5050, Fax: 902-424-0530, 800-774-4712

Workers' Compensation Board of Nova Scotia, 5668 South St., PO Box 1150, Halifax, NS B3J 2Y2
902-491-8999, Fax: 902-491-8002, 800-870-3331, info@wcb.gov.ns.ca

Nunavut

Department of Human Resources, PO Box 1000 400,Iqaluit, NU X0A 1H0
Fax: 867-975-6216, 888-668-9993, gnhr@gov.nu.ca

Ontario

Ministry of Education, Mowat Block, 900 Bay St., 22nd. Fl., Toronto, ON M7A 1L2
416-325-2929, Fax: 416-325-2934, 800-387-5514, info@edu.gov.on.ca

Ministry of Labour, 400 University Ave., 14th Fl., Toronto, ON M7A 1T7
416-326-7160, 800-531-5551

Office of the Employer Advisor, #704, 151 Bloor St. West., Toronto, ON M5S 1S4
416-327-0020, Fax: 416-327-0726, 800-387-0774

Office of the Worker Advisor, #1300, 123 Edward St., Toronto, ON M5G 1E2
416-325-8570, Fax: 416-325-4830, 800-435-8980

Ontario Labour Relations Board, 505 University Ave., 2nd Fl., Toronto, ON M5G 2P1
416-326-7500, Fax: 416-326-7531, 877-339-3335

Pay Equity Commission, #300, 180 Dundas St. West, Toronto, ON M7A 2S6
416-314-1896, Fax: 416-314-8741, 800-387-8813

Ministry of Training, Colleges & Universities, Mowat Block, 900 Bay St., 14th Fl., Toronto, ON M7A 1L2
416-325-2929, Fax: 416-325-6348, 800-387-5514, information.met@ontario.ca

Workplace Safety & Insurance Board, 200 Front St. West, Ground Fl., Toronto, ON M5V 3J1
416-344-1000, Fax: 416-344-4684, 800-387-0750

Prince Edward Island

Advisory Council on the Status of Women, Sherwood Business Centre, 161 St. Peter's Rd., Main Level, PO Box 2000, Charlottetown, PE C1A 7N8
902-368-4510, Fax: 902-368-3269, peistatusofwomen@eastlink.ca

Prince Edward Island Workers Compensation Board, 14 Weymouth St., PO Box 757, Charlottetown, PE C1A 7L7
902-368-5680, Fax: 902-368-5696, 800-237-5049

Workers Compensation Appeal Tribunal, 161 St. Peters Rd., 1st Fl., PO Box 2000, Charlottetown, PE C1A 7N8

Quebec

Commission de l'équité salariale, 200, ch Ste-Foy, 4e étage, Québec, QC G1R 6A1
418-528-8765, Fax: 418-528-6999, 888-528-8765, equite.salariale@ces.gouv.qc.ca

Commission de la construction du Québec, 3530, rue Jean-Talon ouest, Montréal, QC H3R 2G3
514-341-7740, Fax: 514-341-6354, 888-842-8282

Commission des lésions professionnelles, #700, 900, Place d'Youville, Québec, QC G1R 3P7
418-644-7777, Fax: 418-644-6443, 800-463-1591

Commission des normes du travail, Hall Est, 400, boul Jean-Lesage, 7e étage, Québec, QC G1K 8W1
418-644-0817, Fax: 418-643-5132, 800-563-9058

Commission des partenaires du marché du travail, 800, rue du Square-Victoria, 28e étage, CP 100, Montréal, QC H4Z 1B7
514-873-5252, Fax: 514-864-8005, partenaires@mess.gouv.qc.ca

Conseil consultatif du travail et de la main d'oeuvre, #9.400, 500, boul René-Lévesque ouest, Montréal, QC H2Z 1W7
514-873-2880, Fax: 514-873-1129, cctm@cctm.gouv.qc.ca

Conseil des services essentiels du Québec, #9.100, 500, boul René-Lévesque ouest, 9e étage, CP 38, Montréal, QC H2Z 1W7
514-873-7246, Fax: 514-873-3839, 800-337-7246, info@cses.gouv.qc.ca

Office des professions du Québec, 800, place D'Youville, 10e étage, Québec, QC G1R 5Z3
418-643-6912, Fax: 418-643-0973, 800-643-6912, courrier@opq.gouv.qc.ca

Régie du bâtiment du Québec, 545, boul Crémazie est, 4e étage, Montréal, QC H2M 2V2
514-873-0976, Fax: 514-864-2903, 800-361-0761, crc@rbq.gouv.qc.ca

Commission de la santé et de la sécurité du travail du Québec, 524, rue Bourdages, CP 1200 Terminus postal,Québec, QC G1K 7E2
418-266-4850, Fax: 418-266-4669, 866-302-2778

Ministère du Travail, 200, ch Sainte-Foy, 5e étage, Québec, QC G1R 5S1
418-644-4545, Fax: 418-528-0559, 800-643-4817

Saskatchewan

Saskatchewan Education, 2220 College Ave., Regina, SK S4P 4V9
linquiry@gov.sk.ca

Saskatchewan Labour Relations & Workplace Safety, #300, 1870 Albert St., Regina, SK S4P 4W1
306-787-7404, webmaster@lab.gov.sk.ca

Labour Relations Board, #1600, 1920 Broad St., Regina, SK S4P 3V2
306-787-2406, Fax: 306-787-2664

Minimum Wage Board, #400, 1870 Albert St., Regina, SK S4P 4W1

Office of the Worker's Advocate, #300, 1870 Albert St., Regina, SK S4P 4W1
306-787-2456, Fax: 306-787-0249, 877-787-2456

Saskatchewan Public Service Commission, 2100 Broad St., Regina, SK S4P 1Y5
306-787-7853, 866-319-5999, psc.webmaster@gov.sk.ca; inquiry@psc.gov.sk.ca
Saskatchewan Workers' Compensation Board, #200, 1881 Scarth St., Regina, SK S4P 4L1
306-787-4370, Fax: 306-787-7582, 800-667-7590, internet_clientsvc@wcbsask.com
Saskatchewan Workers' Compensation Board, #200, 1881 Scarth St., Regina, SK S4P 4L1
306-787-4370, Fax: 306-787-4311, 800-667-7590, internet_clientsvc@wcbsask.com

Yukon Territory
Yukon Public Service Commission, Yukon Government Administration Building, #2071-2nd Ave., PO Box 2703, Whitehorse, YT Y1A 2C6
867-667-5653, Fax: 867-667-5755, 800-661-0408, PSCWebsite@gov.yk.ca
Yukon Workers' Compensation Health & Safety Board, 401 Strickland St., Whitehorse, YT Y1A 5N8
867-667-5645, Fax: 867-393-6279, 800-661-0443, worksafe@gov.yk.ca

LAND RESOURCES

See Also: Agriculture; Forest Resources; Parks
Canada Lands Company Ltd., #1200, 1 University Ave., Toronto, ON M5J 2P1
416-952-6111, Fax: 416-952-6115, 888-252-5263
Land Use Secretariat, Centre West Building, 10035 - 108 St., Edmonton, AB T5J 3E1
780-644-7972, Fax: 780-644-1034, luf@gov.ab.ca
Natural Resources Canada, 580 Booth St., Ottawa, ON K1A 0E4
613-995-0947, Fax: 613-992-7211
Parks Canada, 25 Eddy St., Gatineau, QC K1A 0M5
613-860-1251, 888-773-8888, information@pc.gc.ca

Alberta
Special Areas Board, Special Areas Board Administration, 212 - 2nd Ave. West, PO Box 820, Hanna, AB T0J 1P0
403-854-5600, Fax: 403-854-5527, specarea@telus.net

British Columbia
Strategic Industry Partnerships Division, PO Box 9120 Prov Govt,Victoria, BC V8W 9B4
250-356-1122, Fax: 250-356-7279

Manitoba
Farm Lands Ownership Board, #812, Norquay Bldg., 401 York Ave., Winnipeg, MB R3C 0P8
204-945-3149, Fax: 204-945-1489, 800-282-8069, robert.mckenzie@gov.mb.ca
Manitoba Conservation Districts Commission, Secretariat c/o Planning & Coordination Branch, 123 Main St., PO Box 20000, Neepawa, MB R0J 1H0
204-476-7033, Fax: 204-476-7539, whildebran@gov.mb.ca
Manitoba Land Value Appraisal Commission, 800 Portage Ave., Winnipeg, MB R3G 0N4
204-945-2941, Fax: 204-948-2235

New Brunswick
Service New Brunswick, Westmorland Place, #200, 82 Westmorland St., PO Box 1998, Fredericton, NB E3B 5G4
506-457-3581, Fax: 506-457-7520, 888-762-8600, snb@snb.ca

Northwest Territories
Department of Environment & Natural Resources, PO Box 1320, Yellowknife, NT X1A 2L9
Department of Municipal & Community Affairs, PO Box 1320, Yellowknife, NT X1A 2L9
867-873-7118, Fax: 867-873-0309

Nunavut
Department of Environment, PO Box 1000 1300,Iqaluit, NU X0A 0H0
867-975-7700, Fax: 867-975-7742, environment@gov.nu.ca

Prince Edward Island
Prince Edward Island Department of Environment, Energy, & Forestry, Jones Bldg., 11 Kent St., 4th Fl., PO Box 2000, Charlottetown, PE C1A 7N8
902-368-5000, Fax: 902-368-5830

Quebec
Commission de protection du territoire agricole du Québec, 200, ch Ste-Foy, 2e étage, Québec, QC G1R 4X6
418-643-3314, Fax: 418-643-2261, 800-667-5294, info@cptaq.gouv.qc.ca
Foncier Québec, 5700, 4e av ouest, Québec, QC G1H 6R1
418-643-3582, Fax: 418-528-8721, 866-226-0977, assistance.clientele@mrnf.registrefoncier.gouv.qc.ca
Territoire, #A313, 5700, 4e av ouest, Québec, QC G1H 6R1
418-627-6256, Fax: 418-528-2075

Saskatchewan
Saskatchewan Lands Appeal Board, #202, 3085 Albert St., Regina, SK S4S 0B1
306-787-4693, Fax: 306-787-1315, Donald.Brooks@gov.sk.ca

Yukon Territory
Yukon Land Use Planning Council, #201, 307 Jarvis St., Whitehorse, YT Y1A 2H3
867-667-7397, Fax: 867-667-4624, ylupc@planyukon.ca

LAND TITLES

See Also: Real Estate
Canada Lands Company Ltd., #1200, 1 University Ave., Toronto, ON M5J 2P1
416-952-6111, Fax: 416-952-6115, 888-252-5263

British Columbia
British Columbia Assessment Authority, #400, 3450 Uptown Blvd., Victoria, BC V8Z 0B9
250-595-6211, Fax: 250-595-6222, info@bcassessment.ca

New Brunswick
Service New Brunswick, Westmorland Place, #200, 82 Westmorland St., PO Box 1998, Fredericton, NB E3B 5G4
506-457-3581, Fax: 506-457-7520, 888-762-8600, snb@snb.ca

Nova Scotia
Registry of Deeds, PO Box 2205, Halifax, NS B3J 3C4
Fax: 902-424-5872

Nunavut
Nunavut Legal Registries Division, Brown Bldg., 1st Fl., PO Box 1000 570,Iqaluit, NU X0A 0H0
Fax: 867-975-6594

LANDLORD & TENANT REGULATIONS

Alberta
Alberta Justice & Attorney General, Communications, Bowker Building, 9833 - 109 St., 3rd Fl., Edmonton, AB T5K 2E8
780-427-2745

Northwest Territories
Northwest Territories Housing Corporation, Scotia Centre, 5102 50th Ave., PO Box 2100, Yellowknife, NT X1A 2P6
867-873-7853, Fax: 867-873-9426

Nunavut
Nunavut Housing Corporation, PO Box 480, Arviat, NU X0C 0E0
867-857-3000, Fax: 867-857-3040

Prince Edward Island
Prince Edward Island Regulatory & Appeals Commission, National Bank Tower, #501, 134 Kent St., PO Box 577, Charlottetown, PE C1A 7L1
902-892-3501, Fax: 902-566-4076, 800-501-6268, info@irac.pe.ca

Quebec
Régie du logement du Québec, Pyramide Ouest, #2095, 5199, rue Sherbrooke est, Montréal, QC H1T 3X1
514-873-2245, Fax: 514-864-8077, 800-683-2245

Saskatchewan
Provincial Mediation Board, #120, 2151 Scarth St., Regina, SK S4P 2H8
306-787-5387, Fax: 306-787-5574, 877-787-5408

LANDS & SOILS

Aboriginal Affairs & Northern Development Canada, 10 Wellington St., North Tower, Gatineau, QC K1A 0H4
819-997-0380, Fax: 866-817-3977, 800-567-9604, infopubs@aadnc-aandc.gc.ca
Agriculture & Agri-Food Canada, 1341 Baseline Rd., Ottawa, ON K1A 0C5
613-773-1000, Fax: 613-773-2772, 866-345-7972, info@agr.gc.ca
Canada Centre for Remote Sensing - Geomatics Canada, 588 Booth St., Ottawa, ON K1A 0Y7
613-995-0947, Fax: 613-947-1382
Natural Resources Canada, 580 Booth St., Ottawa, ON K1A 0E4
613-995-0947, Fax: 613-992-7211

Alberta
Irrigation Council, Provincial Bldg., 200 - 5 Ave. South, 3rd Fl., Lethbridge, AB T1J 4L1
403-381-5176, Fax: 403-382-4406
Land Compensation Board, 1229 - 91 St. SW, Edmonton, AB T6X 1E9
srb.lcb@gov.ab.ca

British Columbia
Ministry of Environment, PO Box 9339 Prov Govt,Victoria, BC V8W 9M1
250-387-1161, Fax: 250-387-5669, envmail@gov.bc.ca
Forest Practices Board, 1675 Douglas St., 3rd Fl., PO Box 9905 Prov Govt, Victoria, BC V8W 9R1
250-213-4700, Fax: 250-213-4725, 800-994-5899, fpboard@gov.bc.ca
Timber Export Advisory Committee, PO Box 9514 Prov Govt, Victoria, BC V8W 9C2
250-387-8916, Fax: 250-387-5050

Manitoba
Manitoba Geological Survey, #360, 1394 Ellice Ave., Winnipeg, MB R3G 3P2
Fax: 204-945-1406, 800-223-5215, minesinfo@gov.mb.ca

New Brunswick
Assessment & Planning Appeal Board, #201, 435 King St., PO Box 6000, Fredericton, NB E3B 5H1
506-453-2126, Fax: 506-444-4881
Department of Natural Resources, Hugh John Flemming Forestry Centre, PO Box 6000, Fredericton, NB E3B 5H1
506-453-3826, Fax: 506-444-4367, dnrweb@gnb.ca
Department of the Environment, Marysville Place, 20 McGloin St., PO Box 6000, Fredericton, NB E3B 5H1
506-453-2690, Fax: 506-457-7800, env-info@gnb.ca

Newfoundland & Labrador
Department of Government Services, PO Box 8700, St. John's, NL A1B 4J6
709-729-4834, gsinfo@gov.nl.ca

Northwest Territories
Department of Environment & Natural Resources, PO Box 1320, Yellowknife, NT X1A 2L9

Nova Scotia
Department of Natural Resources, Founder's Square, 1701 Hollis St., 3rd Fl., PO Box 698, Halifax, NS B3J 2T9
902-424-5935, Fax: 902-424-0594, 800-565-2224

Prince Edward Island
Prince Edward Island Department of Environment, Energy, & Forestry, Jones Bldg., 11 Kent St., 4th Fl., PO Box 2000, Charlottetown, PE C1A 7N8
902-368-5000, Fax: 902-368-5830
Prince Edward Island Department of Tourism & Culture, PO Box 2000, Charlottetown, PE C1A 7N8
902-368-5540, Fax: 902-368-5277, tpswitch@gov.pe.ca

Quebec
Ministère du Développement durable, de l'Environnement et des Parcs, Édifice Marie-Guyart, 675, boul René-Lévesque est, 29e étage, Québec, QC G1R 5V7
418-521-3830, Fax: 418-646-5974, 800-561-1616, info@mddep.gouv.qc.ca
Territoire, #A313, 5700, 4e av ouest, Québec, QC G1H 6R1
418-627-6256, Fax: 418-528-2075

Saskatchewan
Saskatchewan Assessment Management Agency, #200, 2201 - 11th Ave., Regina, SK S4P 0J8
306-924-8000, Fax: 306-924-8070, 800-667-7262, info.request@sama.sk.ca

Yukon Territory
Carmacks Renewable Resource Council, PO Box 122, Carmacks, YT Y0B 1C0
867-863-6838, Fax: 867-863-6429, carmacksrrc@northwestel.net
Yukon Environment, PO Box 2703, Whitehorse, YT Y1A 2C6
867-667-5652, Fax: 867-393-7197, environment.yukon@gov.yk.ca
Selkirk Renewable Resources Council, PO Box 32, Pelly Crossing, YT Y0B 1P0
867-537-3937, Fax: 867-537-3939, selkirkrrc@yknet.yk.ca
Yukon Land Use Planning Council, #201, 307 Jarvis St., Whitehorse, YT Y1A 2H3
867-667-7397, Fax: 867-667-4624, ylupc@planyukon.ca

LAW & JUSTICE

Auditor General of Canada, 240 Sparks St., Ottawa, ON K1A 0G6
613-995-3708, Fax: 613-957-0474, 888-761-5953, communications@oag-bvg.gc.ca; infomedia@oag-bvg.gc.ca
Canadian Forces Grievance Board, 60 Queen St., 10th Fl., Ottawa, ON K1P 5Y7
613-996-8529, Fax: 613-996-6491, 877-276-4193
Canadian Human Rights Commission, 344 Slater St., 8th Fl., Ottawa, ON K1A 1E1
613-995-1151, Fax: 613-996-9661, 888-214-1090
Canadian Human Rights Tribunal, 160 Elgin St., 11th Fl., Ottawa, ON K1A 1J4
613-995-1707, Fax: 613-995-3484, registrar@chrt-tcdp.gc.ca
Canadian International Trade Tribunal, Standard Life Centre, 333 Laurier Ave. West, 15 Floor, Ottawa, ON K1A 0G7
613-990-2452, Fax: 613-990-2439, secretary@citt-tcce.gc.ca
Canadian Judicial Council, 150 Metcalfe St., 15th Fl., Ottawa, ON K1A 0W8
613-288-1566, Fax: 613-288-1575, info@cjc-ccm.gc.ca
Canadian Police College, PO Box 8900, Ottawa, ON K1G 3J2
613-993-9500, Fax: 613-990-9738, cpc-ccp@rcmp-grc.gc.ca
Canadian Radio-Television & Telecommunications Commission, Central Building, 1, Promenade du Portage, Les Terrasses de la Chaudière, Gatineau, QC J8X 4B1
819-997-0313, Fax: 819-994-0218, 877-249-2782
Canadian Security Intelligence Service, PO Box 9732 T,Ottawa, ON K1G 4G4
613-993-9620, Fax: 613-231-0612

Commission for Public Complaints Against the Royal Canadian Mounted Police, National Intake Office, PO Box 88689, Surrey, BC V3W 0X1
Fax: 613-952-8045, 800-665-6878, org@cpc-cpp.gc.ca
Copyright Board of Canada, #800, 56 Sparks St., Ottawa, ON K1A 0C9
613-952-8621, Fax: 613-952-8630, secretariat@cb-cda.gc.ca
Corporate & Financial Services Division, Jones Bldg., 11 Kent St., 2nd Fl., PO Box 2000, Charlottetown, PE C1A 7N8
Fax: 902-894-0242
Office of the Correctional Investigator, PO Box 3421 D,Ottawa, ON K1P 6L4
Fax: 613-990-9091, 877-885-8848, org@oci-bec.gc.ca
Correctional Service Canada, 340 Laurier Ave. West, Ottawa, ON K1A 0P9
613-992-5891, Fax: 613-943-1630
Defence Research & Development Canada, 305 Rideau St., Ottawa, ON K1A 0K2
613-992-7237, info@drdc-rddc.gc.ca
Environmental Sciences & Standards Division, 135 St. Clair Ave. West, 14th Fl., Toronto, ON M4V 1P5
416-314-6357, Fax: 416-314-6358
Office of the Commissioner for Federal Judicial Affairs, 99 Metcalfe St., 8th Fl., Ottawa, ON K1A 1E3
613-995-5140, Fax: 613-995-5615, 877-583-4266, info@fja.gc.ca
Financial Transactions & Reports Analysis Centre of Canada, 234 Laurier Ave. West, 24th Fl., Ottawa, ON K1P 1H7
Fax: 613-943-7931, 866-346-8722, guidelines-lignesdirectrices@fintrac-canafe.gc.ca
Immigration & Refugee Board of Canada, Canada Bldg, 344 Slater St., 12th Fl., Ottawa, ON K1A 0K1
613-995-6486, Fax: 613-943-1550, contact@irb-cisr.gc.ca
International Joint Commission, 234 Laurier Ave. West, 22nd Fl., Ottawa, ON K1P 6K6
613-947-1420, Fax: 613-993-5583, beckhoffb@ottawa.ijc.org
Justice Canada, East Memorial Bldg., 284 Wellington St., Ottawa, ON K1A 0H8
613-957-4222, Fax: 613-954-0811, webadmin@justice.gc.ca
Legal Services Division, Bowker Building, 9833 - 109 St., 2nd Fl., Edmonton, AB T5K 2E8
780-422-0500
Législation & enquêtes, 3800, rue de Marly, Secteur 5-1-9, Québec, QC G1X 4A5
418-652-6844, Fax: 418-643-9381
Military Police Complaints Commission, 270 Albert St., 10th Fl., Ottawa, ON K1P 5G8
613-947-5625, Fax: 613-947-5713, 800-632-0566, commission@mpcc-cppm.gc.ca
National Parole Board, 410 Laurier Ave. West, Ottawa, ON K1A 0R1
613-954-7474, Fax: 613-995-4380, 800-874-2652, info@npb-cnlc.gc.ca
Office of the Conflict of Interest & Ethics Commissioner, Commissioner's Office, 66 Slater St., 22nd Fl., Ottawa, ON K1A 0A6
613-995-0721, Fax: 613-995-7308, ciec-ccie@parl.gc.ca
Passport Canada, Le 70 Crémazie, 70 Crémazie St., Gatineau, QC K1A 0G3
Fax: 819-953-5856, 800-567-6868
Privacy Commissioner of Canada, Tower B, Place de Ville, 112 Kent St., 3rd Fl., Ottawa, ON K1A 1H3
613-947-1698, Fax: 613-947-6850, 800-282-1376
RCMP Training Academy, 6101 Dewdney Ave., Regina, SK S4P 3J7
306-780-5002, Fax: 306-780-7940
Royal Canadian Mounted Police, 1200 Vanier Pkwy., Ottawa, ON K1A 0R2
613-993-7267, Fax: 613-993-0260
Royal Canadian Mounted Police External Review Committee, PO Box 1159 B, Ottawa, ON K1P 5R2
613-998-2134, Fax: 613-990-8969, org@erc-cee.gc.ca
Security Intelligence Review Committee, Jackson Bldg., 122 Bank St., 4th Fl., PO Box 2430 D,Ottawa, ON K1P 5W5
613-990-8441, Fax: 613-990-5230, ellardm@sirc-csars.gc.ca
Transportation Appeal Tribunal of Canada, #1201, 333 Laurier Ave. West, 12th Fl., Ottawa, ON K1A 0N5
613-990-6906, Fax: 613-990-9153, info@tatc.gc.ca
Transportation Safety Board of Canada, 200 Promenade du Portage, 4th Fl., Ottawa, ON K1A 1K8
819-994-3741, Fax: 819-997-2239, 800-387-3557
Veterans Review & Appeal Board, Daniel J. MacDonald Bldg., 161 Grafton St., PO Box 9900, Charlottetown, PE C1A 8V7
902-566-8751, Fax: 902-566-7850, 800-450-8006, vrab_tacra@vac-acc.gc.ca
Workers' Compensation Appeals Tribunal, #1002, 5670 Spring Garden Rd., Halifax, NS B3J 1H6
902-424-2250, Fax: 902-424-2321, 800-274-8281,

Alberta

Alberta Gaming & Liquor Commission, 50 Corriveau Ave., St. Albert, AB T8N 3T5
780-447-8600, Fax: 780-447-8916, 800-272-8876
Alberta Review Board, Oxford Tower, 10235 - 101 St., 11th Fl., Edmonton, AB T5J 3E9
Criminal Injuries Review Board, #1502, 10025 - 102A Ave., Edmonton, AB T5J 2Z2
780-427-7330, Fax: 780-427-7347
Alberta Office of the Ethics Commissioner, #1250, 9925 - 109 St. NW, Edmonton, AB T5K 2J8
780-422-2273, Fax: 780-422-2261, generalinfo@ethicscommissioner.ab.ca
Judicial Council, Law Courts, Provincial Court of Alberta, 1A Sir Winston Churchill Sq., 6th Fl., Edmonton, AB T5J 0R2
780-427-6330, Fax: 780-427-2077
Alberta Justice & Attorney General, Communications, Bowker Building, 9833 - 109 St., 3rd Fl., Edmonton, AB T5K 2E8
780-427-2745
Land Compensation Board, 1229 - 91 St. SW, Edmonton, AB T6X 1E9
srb.lcb@gov.ab.ca
Law Enforcement Review Board, City Centre Place, #1502, 10025 - 102A Ave., Edmonton, AB T5J 2Z2
780-422-9376, Fax: 780-422-4782, lerb@gov.ab.ca
Alberta Office of the Ombudsman, Canadian Western Bank Building, #2800, 10303 Jasper Ave. NW, 28th Fl., Edmonton, AB T5J 5C3
780-427-2756, Fax: 780-427-2759, 888-455-2756, info@ombudsman.ab.ca
Public Security Division, John E. Brownlee Building, 10365 - 97 St., 10th Fl., Edmonton, AB T5J 3W7
780-427-7952, Fax: 780-427-1194, bill.meade@gov.ab.ca
Registry Services, Telus Plaza South, 10020 - 100 St., 29th Fl., Edmonton, AB T5J 0N3
Alberta Solicitor General & Public Security, Communications, John E. Browntree Building, 10365 - 97 St., 9th Fl., Edmonton, AB T5J 3W7
780-427-3441, Fax: 780-427-2789

British Columbia

Ministry of the Attorney General, PO Box 9044 Prov Govt,Victoria, BC V8W 9E2
250-387-1866, Fax: 250-387-6411
British Columbia Office of the Police Complaint Commissioner, #501, 947 Fort St., PO Box 9895 Prov Govt, Victoria, BC V8W 9T8
250-356-7458, Fax: 250-356-6503, 877-999-8707, info@opcc.bc.ca
British Columbia Review Board, #1020, 510 Burrard St., Vancouver, BC V6C 3A8
604-660-8789, Fax: 604-660-8809, 877-305-2277
Office of the Conflict of Interest Commissioner, #101, 431 Menzies St., Victoria, BC V8V 1X4
250-356-0750, Fax: 250-356-6580, conflictofinterest@coibc.ca
Court Services Branch, PO Box 9249 Prov Govt,Victoria, BC V8W 9J2
250-356-1550, Fax: 250-356-8152
Judicial Council of British Columbia, Pacific Centre, #602, 700 West Georgia St., PO Box 10287, Vancouver, BC V7Y 1E8
604-660-2864, Fax: 604-660-1108, info@provincialcourt.bc.ca
Legal Services Society, #400, 510 Burrard St., Vancouver, BC V6C 3A8
604-601-6000
Management Services Branch, PO Box 9256 Prov Govt,Victoria, BC V8W 9J4
250-387-5258, Fax: 250-387-0081
Office of the Representative for Children & Youth, #201, 546 Yates St., Victoria, BC V8W 1K8
250-356-6710, Fax: 250-356-0837, 800-476-3933, rcy@rcybc.ca
Office of the Ombudsperson, 947 Fort St., 2nd Fl., PO Box 9039 Prov Govt,Victoria, BC V8W 9A5
250-387-5855, Fax: 250-387-0198, 800-567-3247, systems@bcombudsperson.ca (Information technology inquiries)
Public Guardian & Trustee of British Columbia, #700, 808 West Hastings St., Vancouver, BC V6C 3L3
604-660-4444, Fax: 604-660-0374, 800-663-7867, mail@trustee.bc.ca
Surface Rights Board, #10, 10551 Shellbridge Way, Richmond, BC V6X 2W9
604-775-1740, Fax: 604-775-1742, 888-775-1740, office@surfacerightsboard.bc.ca

Manitoba

Advisory Council on Workplace Safety & Health, #200, 401 York Ave., Winnipeg, MB R3C 0P8
204-945-3446, Fax: 204-945-4556
Office of the Auditor General, #500, 330 Portage Ave., Winnipeg, MB R3C 0C4
204-945-3790, Fax: 204-945-2169, oag.contact@oag.mb.ca
Automobile Injury Compensation Appeal Commission, #301, 428 Portage Ave.., Winnipeg, MB R3C 0E2
204-945-4155, Fax: 204-948-2402, autoinjury@gov.mb.ca
Compensation for Victims of Crime, 1410 - 405 Broadway, Winnipeg, MB R3C 3L6
204-945-0899, Fax: 204-948-3071, 800-262-9344
Comptroller Division, #715, 401 York Ave., Winnipeg, MB R3C 0P8
204-945-4920, Fax: 204-945-2394
Highway Traffic Board/Motor Transport Board, #200, 301 Weston St., Winnipeg, MB R3E 3H4
204-945-8912, Fax: 204-783-6529
Manitoba Human Rights Commission, 175 Hargrave St., 7th Fl., Winnipeg, MB R3C 3R8
204-945-3007, Fax: 204-945-1292, 888-884-8681, hrc@gov.mb.ca
Manitoba Justice, Legislative Building, #104, 405 Broadway Ave., Winnipeg, MB R3C 3L6
204-945-3728, Fax: 204-945-2517, minjus@gov.mb.ca
Law Enforcement Review Agency, #420, 155 Carlton St., Winnipeg, MB R3C 3H8
204-945-8667, Fax: 204-948-1014, 800-282-8069, lera@gov.mb.ca
Law Reform Commission, #432, 405 Broadway, Winnipeg, MB R3C 3L6
204-945-2896, Fax: 204-948-2184, lawreform@gov.mb.ca
Legal Aid Manitoba, 402 - 294 Portage Ave., Winnipeg, MB R3C 0B9
204-985-8500, Fax: 204-944-8582, 800-261-2960, info@legalaid.mb.ca
License Suspension Appeal Board/Medical Review Committee, #200, 301 Weston St., Winnipeg, MB R3E 3H4
204-945-7350, Fax: 204-948-2682
Manitoba Film Classification Board, #216, 301 Weston St., Winnipeg, MB R3E 3H4
204-945-8962, Fax: 204-945-0890, 866-612-2399, mfcb@gov.mb.ca
Manitoba Labour Board, A.A. Heaps Bldg., #402, 258 Portage Ave., Winnipeg, MB R3C 0B6
204-945-3783, Fax: 204-945-1296, mlb@gov.mb.ca
Manitoba Land Value Appraisal Commission, 800 Portage Ave., Winnipeg, MB R3G 0N4
204-945-2941, Fax: 204-948-2235
Manitoba Liquor Control Commission, 1555 Buffalo Pl., PO Box 1023, Winnipeg, MB R3C 2X1
204-284-2501, Fax: 204-475-7666, info@mlcc.mb.ca
Manitoba Minimum Wage Board, 614 - 401 York Ave., Winnipeg, MB R3C 0P8
204-945-4889, Fax: 204-948-2085, mw@gov.mb.ca
Manitoba Review Board, 408 York Ave., 2nd Fl., Winnipeg, MB R3C 0P9
204-945-4438, Fax: 204-945-5751
Manitoba Securities Commission, #500, 400 St. Mary Ave., Winnipeg, MB R3C 4K5
204-945-2548, Fax: 204-945-0330, 800-655-5244, securities@gov.mb.ca
Office of the Chief Medical Examiner, #210, 1 Wesley Ave., Winnipeg, MB R3C 4C6
204-945-2088, Fax: 204-945-2442, 800-282-9069
Office of the Fire Commissioner, #508, 401 York Ave., Winnipeg, MB R3C 0P8
204-945-3322, Fax: 204-948-2089, 800-282-8069, firecomm@gov.mb.ca
Office of the Public Trustee, #500, 155 Carlton St., Winnipeg, MB R3C 5R9
204-945-2700, Fax: 204-948-2251, publictrustee@gov.mb.ca
Manitoba Office of the Ombudsman, 750 - 500 Portage Ave., Winnipeg, MB R3C 3X1
204-982-9130, Fax: 204-942-7803, 800-665-0531, ombudsma@ombudsman.mb.ca
Residential Tenancies Commission, #1650, 155 Carlton St., Winnipeg, MB R3C 3H8
204-945-2028, Fax: 204-945-5453, 800-782-8403, rtc@gov.mb.ca
Manitoba Workers' Compensation Board, 333 Broadway Ave., Winnipeg, MB R3C 4W3
204-954-4321, Fax: 204-954-4999, 800-362-3340, wcb@wcb.mb.ca
Workplace Safety & Health Division, #200, 401 York Ave., Winnipeg, MB R3C 0P8
204-945-3446, Fax: 204-948-2209, wshcompl@gov.mb.ca

New Brunswick

Assessment & Planning Appeal Board, #201, 435 King St., PO Box 6000, Fredericton, NB E3B 5H1
506-453-2126, Fax: 506-444-4881
Board of Examiners under the Scaler's Act, 1350 Regent St. South, PO Box 6000, Fredericton, NB E3B 5H1
506-453-2441, Fax: 506-453-6689
Department of Justice & Consumer Affairs, Centennial Bldg., 670 King St., PO Box 6000, Fredericton, NB E3B 5H1
506-462-5100, Fax: 506-453-3651, justice.comments@gnb.ca

Department of Public Safety, 364 Argyle St., PO Box 6000, Fredericton, NB E3B 5H1
506-453-3992, Fax: 506-453-3870, DPS-MSP.Information@gnb.ca

New Brunswick Human Rights Commission, PO Box 6000, Fredericton, NB E3B 5H1
506-453-2301, Fax: 506-453-2653, 888-471-2233, hrc.cdp@gnb.ca

New Brunswick Liquor Corporation, 170 Wilsey Rd., PO Box 20787, Fredericton, NB E3B 5B8
506-452-6826, Fax: 506-462-2024, info@anbl.com

New Brunswick Real Estate Association, #1, 22 Durelle St., Fredericton, NB E3C 1N8
506-459-8055, Fax: 506-459-8057, 800-762-1677, info@nbrea.ca

Office of the Ombudsman, 767 Brunswick St., PO Box 6000, Fredericton, NB E3B 5H1
506-453-2789, Fax: 506-453-5599, 800-465-1100, nbombud@gnb.ca

New Brunswick Police Commission, Fredericton City Centre, #202, 435 King St., Fredericton, NB E3B 1E5
506-453-2069, Fax: 506-457-3542, nbpc@gnb.ca

Workplace Health, Safety & Compensation Commission of New Brunswick, 1 Portland St., PO Box 160, Saint John, NB E2L 3X9
506-632-2200, 800-222-9775, communications@ws-ts.nb.ca

Newfoundland & Labrador

Department of Justice, Confederation Bldg., East Block, 4th Fl., PO Box 8700, St. John's, NL A1B 4J6
709-729-2869, Fax: 709-729-0469, justice@gov.nl.ca

Newfoundland & Labrador Human Rights Commission, PO Box 8700, St. John's, NL A1B 4J6
709-729-2709, Fax: 709-729-0790, 800-563-5808, humanrights@mail.gov.nl.ca

Newfoundland & Labrador Legal Aid Commission, #300, 251 Empire Ave., PO Box 399 C, St. John's, NL A1C 5J9
709-753-7863, Fax: 709-753-6226, 800-563-9911, nlac@legalaid.nl.ca

Royal Newfoundland Constabulary Public Complaints Commission, Bally Rou Place, #E-160, 280 Torbay Rd., St. John's, NL A1A 3W8
709-729-0950, Fax: 709-729-1302, rnccomplaintscommission@gov.nl.ca

Northwest Territories

Assessment Appeal Tribunal of the Northwest Territories, #400, 5201 - 50th Ave., PO Box 1320, Yellowknife, NT X1A 2L9
867-873-7125, Fax: 867-873-0609

Department of Justice, Courthouse, 4903 - 49th St., 6th Fl., PO Box 1320, Yellowknife, NT X1A 2L9
867-920-6197

Judicial Council, PO Box 550, Yellowknife, NT X1A 2N4
867-873-7105, Fax: 867-873-0287

Legal Services Board of the Northwest Territories, PO Box 1320, Yellowknife, NT X1A 2L9
867-873-7450, Fax: 867-873-5320

Northwest Territories Liquor Commission, #201, 31 Capital Dr., Hay River, NT X0E 1G2
867-874-2100, Fax: 867-874-2180

Northwest Territories Liquor Licensing & Enforcement, #210, 31 Capital Dr., Hay River, NT X0E 1G2
867-874-2906, Fax: 867-874-6011

Northwest Territories Liquor Licensing Board, #210, 31 Capital Dr., Hay River, NT X0E 1G2
867-874-2906, Fax: 867-874-6011, delilah_st-arneault@gov.nt.ca

Territorial Board of Revision, #400, 5201 - 50th Ave., PO Box 1320, Yellowknife, NT X1A 2L9
867-873-7125, Fax: 867-873-0609

Victims Assistance Committee, c/o Community Justice Division, PO Box 1320, Yellowknife, NT X1A 2L9
867-920-6911, Fax: 867-873-0199

Northwest Territories & Nunavut Workers' Safety & Compensation Commission, Centre Square Tower, 5022 - 49th St., 5th Fl., PO Box 8888, Yellowknife, NT X1A 2R3
867-920-3888, Fax: 867-873-4596, 800-661-0792

Nova Scotia

Nova Scotia Human Rights Commission, Joseph Howe Bldg., 1690 Hollis St., 6th Fl., Halifax, NS B3J 3C4
902-424-4111, Fax: 902-424-0596, hrcinquiries@gov.ns.ca

Department of Justice, 5151 Terminal Rd., 4th Fl., PO Box 7, Halifax, NS B3J 2L6
902-424-4030, Fax: 902-424-0510, justweb@gov.ns.ca

Nova Scotia Legal Aid Commission, #102, 137 Chain Lake Dr., Halifax, NS B3S 1B3
902-420-6573, Fax: 902-420-3471, nsla.exec@ns.sympatico.ca

Nova Scotia Police Commission, #300, 1601 Lower Water St., PO Box 1573, Halifax, NS B3J 2Y3
902-424-3246, Fax: 902-424-3919, uarb.polcom@gov.ns.ca

Office of the Chief Medical Examiner, Halifax Insurance Bldg., #701, 5670 Spring Garden Rd., Halifax, NS B3J 1H7
902-424-2722, Fax: 902-424-0607

Office of the Ombudsman, #700, 5670 Spring Garden Rd., PO Box 2152, Halifax, NS B3J 3B7
902-424-6780, Fax: 902-424-6675, 800-670-1111, ombudsman@gov.ns.ca

Pay Equity Commission, 5151 Terminal Rd., 6th Fl., PO Box 697, Halifax, NS B3J 2T8
902-424-2385, Fax: 902-424-0575

Workers' Compensation Board of Nova Scotia, 5668 South St., PO Box 1150, Halifax, NS B3J 2Y2
902-491-8999, Fax: 902-491-8002, 800-870-3331, info@wcb.gov.ns.ca

Nunavut

Baffin Correctional Centre, 1550 Federal Rd., PO Box 368, Iqaluit, NU X0A 0H0
867-979-8100, Fax: 867-979-4646

Department of Justice, Sivummut, 1st Fl., PO Box 1000 500,Iqaluit, NU X0A 0H0
867-975-6170, Fax: 867-975-6195, justice@gov.nu.ca

Legal Services Board of Nunavut, PO Box 125, Gjoa Haven, NU X0A 0H0
Fax: 867-360-6112

Nunavut Legal Registries Division, Brown Bldg., 1st Fl., PO Box 1000 570,Iqaluit, NU X0A 0H0
Fax: 867-975-6594

Nunavut Liquor Licensing Board, Bag 002, Rankin Inlet, NU X0C 0G0
Fax: 867-645-3327

Office of the Chief Coroner, PO Box 1000 590, Iqaluit, NU X0A 0H0

Young Offenders, 1548 Federal Rd., PO Box 1439, Iqaluit, NU X0A 0H0
867-979-4452, Fax: 867-979-5506

Ontario

Alcohol & Gaming Commission of Ontario, 90 Sheppard Ave. East, Toronto, ON M2N 0A4
416-326-8700, Fax: 416-326-5555, 800-522-2876

Assessment Review Board, Eaton Tower, #1500, 655 Bay St., Toronto, ON M5G 1E5
416-212-6349, Fax: 416-314-3717, 866-448-2248, assessment.review.board@ontario.ca

Association of Ontario Land Surveyors, 1043 McNicoll Ave., Toronto, ON M1W 3W6
416-491-9020, Fax: 416-491-2576

Ministry of the Attorney General, McMurtry-Scott Bldg., 720 Bay St., 11th Fl., Toronto, ON M5G 2K1
416-326-2220, Fax: 416-326-4007, 800-518-7901

Chief Inquiry Officer - Expropriations Act, McMurtry-Scott Bldg., 720 Bay St., 8th Fl., Toronto, ON M7A 2S9
416-314-2226

Ministry of Community Safety & Correctional Services, George Drew Bldg., 25 Grosvenor St., 18th Fl., Toronto, ON M7A 1Y6
416-326-5000, Fax: 416-326-0498, 866-517-0571, mcscs.feedback@ontario.ca

Criminal Injuries Compensation Board, 439 University Ave., 4th Fl., Toronto, ON M5G 1Y8
416-326-2900, Fax: 416-326-2883, 800-372-7463, info.cicb@ontario.ca

Ontario Human Rights Commission, 180 Dundas St. West, 7th Fl., Toronto, ON M7A 2R9
416-326-9511, Fax: 416-314-4494, 800-387-9080

Information & Privacy Commissioner of Ontario, #1400, 2 Bloor St. East, Toronto, ON M4W 1A8
416-326-3333, Fax: 416-325-9195, 800-387-0073, info@ipc.on.ca

Office of the Integrity Commissioner, #2101, 2 Bloor St. East, Toronto, ON M4W 1A8
416-314-8983, Fax: 416-314-8987, integrity.mail@oico.on.ca

Judicial Appointments Advisory Committee, McMurtry-Scott Bldg., 720 Bay St., 3rd Fl., Toronto, ON M7A 2S9
416-326-4060, Fax: 416-212-7316

Legal Aid Ontario, #404, 375 University Ave., Toronto, ON M5G 2G1
416-979-1446, Fax: 416-979-8669, 800-668-8258, info@lao.on.ca

Licence Appeal Tribunal, 20 Dundas St. West, 5th Fl., Toronto, ON M5G 2C2
416-314-4260, Fax: 416-314-4270, 800-255-2214

Liquor Control Board of Ontario, 55 Lake Shore Blvd. East, Toronto, ON M5E 1A4
416-365-5900, Fax: 416-864-2476, 800-668-5226, infoline@lcbo.com

Office for Victims of Crime, 700 Bay St., 3rd Fl., Toronto, ON M5G 1Z6
416-326-1682, Fax: 416-326-4497, 887-435-7661

Office of the Ombudsman, Bell Trinity Sq., South Tower, 483 Bay St., 10th Fl., Toronto, ON M5G 2C9
416-586-3300, Fax: 416-586-3485, 800-263-1830, info@ombudsman.on.ca

Ontario Civilian Police Commission, 250 Dundas St. West, 6th Fl., Toronto, ON M7A 2T3
416-314-3004, Fax: 416-314-0198, 888-515-5005

Ontario Labour Relations Board, 505 University Ave., 2nd Fl., Toronto, ON M5G 2P1
416-326-7500, Fax: 416-326-7531, 877-339-3335

Ontario Municipal Board & Board of Negotiation, 655 Bay St., 15th Fl., Toronto, ON M5G 1E5
416-326-6800, Fax: 416-326-5370, 866-887-8820

Ontario Parole Board, #1803, 415 Yonge St., Toronto, ON M5B 2E7
416-325-4480, Fax: 416-325-4485, 888-579-2888

Ontario Police Arbitration Commission, George Drew Bldg., 25 Grosvenor St., 1st Fl., Toronto, ON M7A 1Y6
416-314-3520, Fax: 416-314-3522

Ontario Review Board, 151 Bloor St. West, 10th Fl., Toronto, ON M5S 2T5
416-327-8866, Fax: 416-327-8867

OPSEU Pension Trust, #1200, 1 Adelaide St. East, Toronto, ON M5C 3A7
416-681-6161, Fax: 416-681-6175, 800-637-0024

Road User Safety Division, Bldg A, #191, 1201 Wilson Ave., Downsview, ON M3M 1J8
416-235-2999, Fax: 416-235-4153

ServiceOntario, College Park, 777 Bay St., 15th fl., Toronto, ON M7A 2J3
416-326-1234, Fax: 416-326-1313, 800-267-8097

Social Benefits Tribunal, 1075 Bay St., 7th Fl., Toronto, ON M5S 2B1
416-326-0978, Fax: 416-325-5135, 800-753-3895,

Workplace Safety & Insurance Board, 200 Front St. West, Ground Fl., Toronto, ON M5V 3J1
416-344-1000, Fax: 416-344-4684, 800-387-0750

Prince Edward Island

Advisory Council on the Status of Women, Sherwood Business Centre, 161 St. Peter's Rd., Main Level, PO Box 2000, Charlottetown, PE C1A 7N8
902-368-4510, Fax: 902-368-3269, peistatusofwomen@eastlink.ca

Prince Edward Island Human Rights Commission, 53 Water St., PO Box 2000, Charlottetown, PE C1A 7N8
902-368-4180, Fax: 902-368-4236, 800-237-5031

Office of the Auditor General, Shaw Bldg., 105 Rochford St. North, 2nd Fl., Charlottetown, PE C1A 7N8
902-368-4520, Fax: 902-368-4598, www.assembly.pe.ca

Prince Edward Island Liquor Control Commission, 3 Garfield St., PO Box 967, Charlottetown, PE C1A 7M4
902-368-5710, Fax: 902-368-5735

Prince Edward Island Workers Compensation Board, 14 Weymouth St., PO Box 757, Charlottetown, PE C1A 7L7
902-368-5680, Fax: 902-368-5696, 800-237-5049

Prince Edward Island Regulatory & Appeals Commission, National Bank Tower, #501, 134 Kent St., PO Box 577, Charlottetown, PE C1A 7L1
902-892-3501, Fax: 902-566-4076, 800-501-6268, info@irac.pe.ca

Workers Compensation Appeal Tribunal, 161 St. Peters Rd., 1st Fl., PO Box 2000, Charlottetown, PE C1A 7N8

Quebec

Bureau du coroner, Édifice le Delta 2, #390, 2875, boul Laurier, Québec, QC G1V 5B1
418-643-1845, Fax: 418-643-6174, 866-312-7051, clientele.coroner@msp.gouv.qc.ca

Comité de déontologie policière, Tour du Saint-Laurent, #A-200, 2525, boul Laurier, 2e étage, Québec, QC G1V 4Z6
418-646-1936, Fax: 418-528-0987, comite.deontologie@msp.gouv.qc.ca

Commissaire à la déontologie policière, #1-40, 1200, rte de l'Église, Québec, QC G1V 4Y9
418-643-7897, Fax: 418-528-9473, 877-237-7897, deontologie-policiere.quebec@msp.gouv.qc.ca

Commissariat des incendies, 455, rue Dupont, Québec, QC G1K 6N2
418-529-5706, Fax: 418-529-9922, cdelage@notarius.net

Commission des lésions professionnelles, #700, 900, Place d'Youville, Québec, QC G1R 3P7
418-644-7777, Fax: 418-644-6443, 800-463-1591

Commission des services juridiques, Tour de l'Est, #1404, 2, Complexe Desjardins, Montréal, QC H5B 1B3
514-873-3562, Fax: 514-873-8762, info@csj.qc.ca

Commission québecoise des libérations conditionnelles, #1.32A, 300, boul Jean-Lesage, Québec, QC G1K 8K6
418-646-8300, Fax: 418-643-7217, cqlc@msp.gouv.qc.ca

Conseil de la justice administrative, #RC-01, 575, rue Saint-Amable, Québec, QC G1R 2G4
418-644-6279, Fax: 418-528-8471, 888-848-2581, courrier@cja.gouv.qc.ca

Conseil de la magistrature, #5.12, 300, boul Jean-Lesage, Québec, QC G1K 8K6
418-644-2196, Fax: 418-528-1581, information@cm.gouv.qc.ca

Direction générale de la Sûreté du Québec, 1701, rue Parthenais, Montréal, QC H2K 3S7
514-598-4141, Fax: 514-598-4242

Commission des droits de la personne et des droits de la jeunesse, 360, rue St-Jacques, 2e étage, Montréal, QC H2Y 1P5
514-873-5146, Fax: 514-873-6032, 800-361-6477, accueil@cdpdj.qc.ca
Fonds d'aide aux recours collectifs, #10.30, 1, rue Notre-Dame est, Montréal, QC H2Y 1B6
514-393-2087, Fax: 514-864-2998, farc@justice.gouv.qc.ca
Ministère de la Justice, Édifice Louis-Philippe-Pigeon, 1200, rte de l'Église, Québec, QC G1V 4M1
418-643-5140, 866-536-5140, informations@justice.gouv.qc.ca
Le Protecteur du Citoyen, #1.25, 525, boul René-Lévesque est, Québec, QC G1R 5Y4
418-643-2688, Fax: 418-643-8759, 800-463-5070, protecteur@protecteurducitoyen.qc.ca
Registraire des entreprises, 787, boul Lebourgneuf, Québec, QC G2J 1C3
418-644-4545, Fax: 418-528-5703, 877-644-4545, registre@servicesquebec.gouv.qc.ca
Régie des alcools, des courses et des jeux, 560, boul Charest est, Québec, QC G1K 3J3
418-643-7667, Fax: 418-643-5971, 800-363-0320
Société des alcools du Québec, 905, av De Lorimier, Montréal, QC H2K 3V9
514-873-2020, Fax: 514-873-6788, 866-873-2020, info@saq.com
Société québécoise d'information juridique, 715, carré Victoria, 8e étage, Montréal, QC H2Y 2H7
514-842-8741, Fax: 514-844-8984, 800-363-6718, info@soquij.qc.ca
Ministère de la Sécurité publique, Tour des Laurentides, 2525, boul Laurier, 5e étage, Québec, QC G1V 2L2
418-643-2112, Fax: 418-646-6168, 866-644-6826
Tribunal administratif du Québec, 575, rue Saint-Amable, Québec, QC G1R 5R4
418-643-3418, Fax: 418-643-5335
Vérificateur général du Québec, 750, boulevard Charest est, 3e étage, Québec, QC G1K 9J6
418-691-5900, Fax: 418-644-4460, verificateur.general@vgq.gouv.qc.ca
École nationale de police du Québec, 350, rue Marguerite-d'Youville, Nicolet, QC J3T 1X4
819-293-8631, Fax: 819-293-8630, courriel@enpq.qc.ca

Saskatchewan

Agricultural Implements Board, #202, 3085 Albert St., Regina, SK S4S 0B1
306-787-4693, Fax: 306-787-1315
Saskatchewan Human Rights Commission, Saskatoon Office, Sturdy Stone Bdg., #816, 122 - 3 Ave. North, 8th Fl., Saskatoon, SK S7K 2H6
306-933-5952, Fax: 306-933-7863, 800-667-9249, shrc@gov.sk.ca
Information & Privacy Commissioner of Saskatchewan, #503, 1801 Hamilton St., Regina, SK S4P 4B4
306-787-8350, Fax: 306-798-1603, 877-748-2298, webmaster@oipc.sk.ca
Saskatchewan Justice & Attorney General, 1874 Scarth St., Regina, SK S4P 4B3
306-787-8971, communications@justice.gov.sk.ca
Law Reform Commission of Saskatchewan, c/o University of Saskatchewan, College of Law, #209, 15 Campus Drive, Saskatoon, SK S7N 5A6
306-966-1625, Fax: 306-966-5900, director.research@sasklawreform.com
Saskatchewan Liquor & Gaming Authority, 2500 Victoria Ave., PO Box 5054, Regina, SK S4P 3M3
306-787-4213, inquiry@slga.gov.sk.ca
Ombudsman Saskatchewan, #150, 2401 Saskatchewan Dr., Regina, SK S4P 4H8
306-787-6211, Fax: 306-787-9090, 800-667-7180, ombreg@ombudsman.sk.ca
Provincial Mediation Board, #120, 2151 Scarth St., Regina, SK S4P 2H8
306-787-5387, Fax: 306-787-5574, 877-787-5408
Public & Private Rights Board, #323, 3085 Albert St., Regina, SK S4S 0B1
306-787-4071, Fax: 306-787-0088
Saskatchewan Farm Land Security Board, #207, 3988 Albert St., Regina, SK S4S 3R1
306-787-5047, Fax: 306-787-8599
Saskatchewan Farm Security Programs, #207, 3988 Albert St., Regina, SK S4S 3R1
306-787-5047, Fax: 306-787-8599
Saskatchewan Film & Video Classification Board, #500, 1919 Saskatchewan Dr., Regina, SK S4P 4H2
306-787-5550, Fax: 306-787-9779, 888-374-4636
Saskatchewan Financial Services Commission, #601, 1919 Saskatchewan Dr., Regina, SK S4P 4H2
306-787-5645, Fax: 306-787-5899
Saskatchewan Legal Aid Commission, #502, 201 - 21 St. East, Saskatoon, SK S7K 0B8
306-933-5300, Fax: 306-933-6764, 800-667-3764
Saskatchewan Public Complaints Commission, #300, 1919 Saskatchewan Dr., Regina, SK S4P 4H2
306-787-6519, Fax: 306-787-6528, 866-256-6194
Surface Rights Board of Arbitration, 113 - 2nd Ave. East, PO Box 1597, Kindersley, SK S0L 1S0
306-463-5447, Fax: 306-463-5449, surfacerightsboard@gov.sk.ca
Saskatchewan Workers' Compensation Board, #200, 1881 Scarth St., Regina, SK S4P 4L1
306-787-4370, Fax: 306-787-4311, 800-667-7590, internet_clientsvc@wcbsask.com

Yukon Territory

Driver Control Board, 2130 Second Ave., 3rd Fl., PO Box 2703, Whitehorse, YT Y1A 2C6
867-667-5111, Fax: 867-667-3609, dcb@gov.yk.ca
Law Society of Yukon - Discipline Committee, #202, 302 Steele St., Whitehorse, YT Y1A 3W8
867-668-4231, Fax: 867-667-7556, lsy@yknet.yk.ca
Law Society of Yukon - Executive, #202, 302 Steele St., Whitehorse, YT Y1A 2C5
867-668-4231, Fax: 867-667-7556, info@lawsocietyyukon.com
Yukon Liquor Corporation, 9031 Quartz Rd., Whitehorse, YT Y1A 4P9
867-667-5245, Fax: 867-393-6306, yukon.liquor@gov.yk.ca
Yukon Workers' Compensation Health & Safety Board, 401 Strickland St., Whitehorse, YT Y1A 5N8
867-667-5645, Fax: 867-393-6279, 800-661-0443, worksafe@gov.yk.ca
Yukon Human Rights Board of Adjudication, #202, 407 Black St., Whitehorse, YT Y1A 2N2
867-667-5412, Fax: 867-633-6952, beyondwords@northwestel.net
Yukon Human Rights Commission, #101, 9010 Quartz St., Whitehorse, YT Y1A 2Z5
867-667-6226, Fax: 867-667-2662, 800-661-0535, humanrights@yhrc.yk.ca
Yukon Judicial Council, PO Box 31222, Whitehorse, YT Y1A 5P7
867-667-5438, Fax: 867-393-6400, courtservices@gov.yk.ca
Yukon Law Foundation, PO Box 31789, Whitehorse, YT Y1A 6L3
867-668-4231, Fax: 867-667-7556, lsy@yknet.yk.ca
Yukon Legal Services Society/Legal Aid, #203, 2131 - 2nd Ave., Whitehorse, YT Y1A 1C3
867-667-5210, Fax: 867-667-8649, 800-661-0408, legalaid@yknet.yk.ca

LEGAL & REGULATORY

Canadian Coast Guard, Centennial Towers, #6S018, 200 Kent St., Ottawa, ON K1A 0E6
613-993-0999, Fax: 613-990-1866, info@dfo-mpo.gc.ca
Commission for Environmental Cooperation, Secretariat, #200, 393, rue St-Jacques ouest, Montréal, QC H2Y 1N9
514-350-4300, Fax: 514-350-4314, info@cec.org
Institute for National Measurement Standards, Bldg. M-36, 1500 Montreal Rd., Ottawa, ON K1A 0R6
613-998-7018, Fax: 613-954-1473, alexandra.shaw@nrc-cnrc.gc.ca
Standards Council of Canada, #200, 270 Albert St., Ottawa, ON K1P 6N7
613-238-3222, Fax: 613-569-7808, info@scc.ca
Standards Council of Canada, #200, 270 Albert Street, Ottawa, ON K1P 6N7
613-238-3222, Fax: 613-569-7808, info@scc.ca

British Columbia

Surface Rights Board, #10, 10551 Shellbridge Way, Richmond, BC V6X 2W9
604-775-1740, Fax: 604-775-1742, 888-775-1740, office@surfacerightsboard.bc.ca

New Brunswick

Board of Examiners under the Scaler's Act, 1350 Regent St. South, PO Box 6000, Fredericton, NB E3B 5H1
506-453-2441, Fax: 506-453-6689
Environmental Management, Marysville Place, 20 McGloin St., PO Box 6000, Fredericton, NB E3B 5H1
506-444-5119, Fax: 506-457-7333, env-info@gnb.ca

Northwest Territories

Assessment Appeal Tribunal of the Northwest Territories, #400, 5201 - 50th Ave., PO Box 1320, Yellowknife, NT X1A 2L9
867-873-7125, Fax: 867-873-0609

Nova Scotia

Crane Operators Appeal Board, 5151 Terminal Rd., 7th Fl., PO Box 697, Halifax, NS B3J 2T8
902-424-8595, Fax: 902-424-0217, fernanfs@gov.ns.ca
Pay Equity Commission, 5151 Terminal Rd., 6th Fl., PO Box 697, Halifax, NS B3J 2T8
902-424-2385, Fax: 902-424-0575
Workers' Advisers Program, #502, 5670 Spring Garden Rd., PO Box 1063, Halifax, NS B3J 2X1
902-424-5050, Fax: 902-424-0530, 800-774-4712
Workers' Compensation Board of Nova Scotia, 5668 South St., PO Box 1150, Halifax, NS B3J 2Y2
902-491-8999, Fax: 902-491-8002, 800-870-3331, info@wcb.gov.ns.ca

Ontario

Ministry of Community Safety & Correctional Services, George Drew Bldg., 25 Grosvenor St., 18th Fl., Toronto, ON M7A 1Y6
416-326-5000, Fax: 416-326-0498, 866-517-0571, mcscs.feedback@ontario.ca
Environmental Commissioner of Ontario, #605, 1075 Bay St., Toronto, ON M5S 2B1
416-325-3377, Fax: 416-325-3370, 800-701-6454, commissioner@eco.on.ca
Environmental Review Tribunal, #1500, 655 Bay St., Toronto, ON M5G 1E5
416-212-6349, Fax: 416-314-4506, 866-448-2248, erttribunalsecretary@ontario.ca
Road User Safety Division, Bldg A, #191, 1201 Wilson Ave., Downsview, ON M3M 1J8
416-235-2999, Fax: 416-235-4153

Prince Edward Island

Prince Edward Island Regulatory & Appeals Commission, National Bank Tower, #501, 134 Kent St., PO Box 577, Charlottetown, PE C1A 7L1
902-892-3501, Fax: 902-566-4076, 800-501-6268, info@irac.pe.ca

LEGAL AID SERVICES

Alberta

Court Services Division, Bowker Building, 9833 - 109 St., 2nd Fl., Edmonton, AB T5K 2E8
780-427-4992, Fax: 780-422-6613

British Columbia

Legal Services Society, #400, 510 Burrard St., Vancouver, BC V6C 3A8
604-601-6000

Manitoba

Legal Aid Manitoba, 402 - 294 Portage Ave., Winnipeg, MB R3C 0B9
204-985-8500, Fax: 204-944-8582, 800-261-2960, info@legalaid.mb.ca

New Brunswick

Department of the Attorney General, Centennial Bldg., #412, 670 King St., PO Box 6000, Fredericton, NB E3B 5H1
506-453-3132, Fax: 506-453-3651, justice.comments@gnb.ca

Newfoundland & Labrador

Newfoundland & Labrador Legal Aid Commission, #300, 251 Empire Ave., PO Box 399 C, St. John's, NL A1C 5J9
709-753-7863, Fax: 709-753-6226, 800-563-9911, nlac@legalaid.nl.ca

Northwest Territories

Legal Services Board of the Northwest Territories, PO Box 1320, Yellowknife, NT X1A 2L9
867-873-7450, Fax: 867-873-5320

Nova Scotia

Nova Scotia Legal Aid Commission, #102, 137 Chain Lake Dr., Halifax, NS B3S 1B3
902-420-6573, Fax: 902-420-3471, nsla.exec@ns.sympatico.ca

Ontario

Legal Aid Ontario, #404, 375 University Ave., Toronto, ON M5G 2G1
416-979-1446, Fax: 416-979-8669, 800-668-8258, info@lao.on.ca

Quebec

Fonds d'aide aux recours collectifs, #10.30, 1, rue Notre-Dame est, Montréal, QC H2Y 1B6
514-393-2087, Fax: 514-864-2998, farc@justice.gouv.qc.ca

Saskatchewan

Saskatchewan Legal Aid Commission, #502, 201 - 21 St. East, Saskatoon, SK S7K 0B8
306-933-5300, Fax: 306-933-6764, 800-667-3764

Yukon Territory

Yukon Legal Services Society/Legal Aid, #203, 2131 - 2nd Ave., Whitehorse, YT Y1A 1C3
867-667-5210, Fax: 867-667-8649, 800-661-0408, legalaid@yknet.yk.ca

LEGISLATIVE ASSEMBLIES/NATIONAL ASSEMBLIES/HOUSE OF COMMONS

House of Commons, Canada, House of Commons, Centre Block, Parliament Buildings, 111 Wellington St., Ottawa, ON K1A 0A6
613-992-4793, 866-599-4999, info@parl.gc.ca

Alberta
Legislative Assembly of Alberta, Legislature Annex, 9718 - 107 St., Edmonton, AB T5K 1E4
780-427-2826, Fax: 780-427-1623, laocommunications@assembly.ab.ca

British Columbia
Legislative Assembly & Independent Offices, Clerk's Office, #221, Parliament Bldgs., Victoria, BC V8V 1X4
250-387-3785, Fax: 250-387-0942, ClerkHouse@leg.bc.ca

Manitoba
Legislative Assembly, c/o Clerk's Office, Legislative Bldg., #237, 450 Broadway, Winnipeg, MB R3C 0V8
204-945-3636, Fax: 204-948-2507, clerkla@leg.gov.mb.ca

New Brunswick
Legislative Assembly of New Brunswick, Centre Block, Legislative Bldg., 706 Queen St., PO Box 6000, Fredericton, NB E3B 5H1
506-453-2506, Fax: 506-453-7154, wwwleg@gnb.ca

Newfoundland & Labrador
House of Assembly, c/o Clerk's Office, Confederation Bldg., PO Box 8700, St. John's, NL A1B 4J6
709-729-3405, Fax: 709-729-4820

Northwest Territories
Legislative Assembly, c/o Clerk's Office, PO Box 1320, Yellowknife, NT X1A 2L9
867-669-2299, Fax: 867-920-4735, 800-661-0784

Nova Scotia
Legislative House of Assembly, c/o Clerk's Office, Province House, 1st Fl., PO Box 1617, Halifax, NS B3J 2Y3
902-424-5978, Fax: 902-424-0632

Nunavut
Legislative Assembly, 926 Federal Rd., PO Box 1200, Iqaluit, NU X0A 0H0
867-975-5000, Fax: 867-975-5190, 877-334-7266, leginfo@assembly.nu.ca

Ontario
Legislative Assembly, c/o Clerk's Office, #104, Legislative Bldg., Queen's Park, Toronto, ON M7A 1A2
416-325-7500, Fax: 416-325-7489, assemblyinternet@ontla.ola.org

Prince Edward Island
Legislative Assembly, Province House, 165 Richmond St., 1st Fl., PO Box 2000, Charlottetown, PE C1A 7N8
902-368-5970, Fax: 902-368-5175, 877-315-5518, legislativelibrary@assembly.pe.ca

Quebec
L'Assemblée nationale, Hôtel du Parlement, 1045, rue des Parlementaires, Québec, QC G1A 1A3
418-643-7239, Fax: 418-646-4271, 866-337-8837, responsable.contenu@assnat.qc.ca

Saskatchewan
Legislative Assembly, c/o Clerk's Office, Legislative Bldg., #123, 2405 Legislative Dr., Regina, SK S4S 0B3
306-787-2376, Fax: 306-787-1558, info@legassembly.sk.ca

Yukon Territory
Legislative Assembly, 2071 Second Ave., PO Box 2703, Whitehorse, YT Y1A 2C6
867-667-5498, Fax: 867-393-6280

LEISURE CRAFT & VEHICLE REGULATIONS

Alberta
Strategic Planning & Financial Services, Commerce Place, 10155 - 102 St., 13th Fl., Edmonton, AB T5J 4G8
780-422-8545

Northwest Territories
Road Licensing & Safety, 4510 - 50 Ave., 1st fl., PO Box 1320, Yellowknife, NT X1A 2L9
867-873-7972, Fax: 867-873-0120

Nova Scotia
Department of Transportation & Infrastructure Renewal, Johnston Bldg., 1672 Granville St., 2nd Fl., PO Box 186, Halifax, NS B3J 2N2
902-424-2297, Fax: 902-424-0532, tpwpaff@gov.ns.ca
Registry of Motor Vehicles, 1505 Barrington St., 8th Fl. North, PO Box 2734, Halifax, NS
902-424-7801, Fax: 902-424-0772, 800-898-7668

Ontario
Ministry of Transportation, Ferguson Block, 77 Wellesley St. West, 3rd Fl., Toronto, ON M7A 1Z8
416-235-4686, Fax: 905-704-2001, 800-268-4686

Quebec
Ministère des Transports, 700, boul René-Lévesque est, 28e étage, Québec, QC G1R 5H1
418-643-6980, Fax: 418-643-2033, 888-355-0511, communications@mtq.gouv.qc.ca

Saskatchewan
Saskatchewan Government Insurance, 2260 - 11th Ave., Regina, SK S4P 0J9
306-751-1200, Fax: 306-787-7477, 800-667-8015, sgiinquiries@sgi.sk.ca

LIBRARIES

Library & Archives Canada, 395 Wellington St., Ottawa, ON K1A 0N4
613-996-5115, Fax: 613-995-6274, 866-578-7777, reference@lac-bac.ca
Library of Parliament, Parliamentary Bldgs., 111 Wellington St., Ottawa, ON K1A 0A9
613-992-4793, Fax: 613-943-6383, 866-599-4999

New Brunswick
Legislative Assembly of New Brunswick, Centre Block, Legislative Bldg., 706 Queen St., PO Box 6000, Fredericton, NB E3B 5H1
506-453-2506, Fax: 506-453-7154, wwwleg@gnb.ca

Newfoundland & Labrador
Provincial Information & Library Resources Board, 48 St. George's Ave, Stephenville, NL A2H 1K9
709-643-0900, Fax: 709-643-0925

Nova Scotia
Legislative House of Assembly, c/o Clerk's Office, Province House, 1st Fl., PO Box 1617, Halifax, NS B3J 2Y3
902-424-5978, Fax: 902-424-0632

Nunavut
Department of Culture, Language, Elders & Youth, PO Box 1000 800,Iqaluit, NU X0A 0H0
867-975-5500, Fax: 867-975-5504, 866-934-2035

Ontario
Ontario Library Service - North, 334 Regent St., Sudbury, ON P3C 4E2
705-675-6467, Fax: 705-675-2285, 800-461-6348
Southern Ontario Library Service, #902, 111 Peter St., Toronto, ON M5V 2H1
416-961-1669, Fax: 416-961-5122, 800-387-5765

Quebec
Bibliothèque et Archives nationales du Québec (BAnQ), 475, boul De Maisonneuve est, Montréal, QC H2L 5C4
514-873-1100, Fax: 514-873-9312, 800-363-9028

Saskatchewan
Saskatchewan Tourism, Parks, Culture & Sport, 1919 Saskatchewan Dr., 4th Fl., Regina, SK S4P 4H2
306-787-5729, Fax: 306-787-8560, info@cyr.gov.sk.ca

LIQUOR CONTROL

See Also: Drugs & Alcohol

Alberta
Alberta Gaming & Liquor Commission, 50 Corriveau Ave., St. Albert, AB T8N 3T5
780-447-8600, Fax: 780-447-8916, 800-272-8876,

British Columbia
Liquor Distribution Branch, 3200 East Broadway, Vancouver, BC V5M 1Z6
604-252-3000, Fax: 604-252-3026

Manitoba
Manitoba Liquor Control Commission, 1555 Buffalo Pl., PO Box 1023, Winnipeg, MB R3C 2X1
204-284-2501, Fax: 204-475-7666, info@mlcc.mb.ca

New Brunswick
New Brunswick Liquor Corporation, 170 Wilsey Rd., PO Box 20787, Fredericton, NB E3B 5B8
506-452-6826, Fax: 506-462-2024, info@anbl.com

Newfoundland & Labrador
Newfoundland & Labrador Liquor Corporation, 90 Kenmount Rd., PO Box 8750 A, St. John's, NL A1B 3V1
709-724-1100, Fax: 709-754-0321, info@nfliquor.com

Northwest Territories
Northwest Territories Liquor Commission, #201, 31 Capital Dr., Hay River, NT X0E 1G2
867-874-2100, Fax: 867-874-2180
Northwest Territories Liquor Licensing & Enforcement, #210, 31 Capital Dr., Hay River, NT X0E 1G2
867-874-2906, Fax: 867-874-6011
Northwest Territories Liquor Licensing Board, #210, 31 Capital Dr., Hay River, NT X0E 1G2
867-874-2906, Fax: 867-874-6011, delilah_st-arneault@gov.nt.ca

Nova Scotia
Nova Scotia Liquor Corporation, Bayers Lake Business Park, 93 Chain Lake Dr., Halifax, NS B3S 1A3
902-450-6752, 800-567-5874

Nunavut
Nunavut Liquor Licensing Board, Bag 002, Rankin Inlet, NU X0C 0G0
Fax: 867-645-3327

Ontario
Alcohol & Gaming Commission of Ontario, 90 Sheppard Ave. East, Toronto, ON M2N 0A4
416-326-8700, Fax: 416-326-5555, 800-522-2876
Liquor Control Board of Ontario, 55 Lake Shore Blvd. East, Toronto, ON M5E 1A4
416-365-5900, Fax: 416-864-2476, 800-668-5226, infoline@lcbo.com

Prince Edward Island
Prince Edward Island Liquor Control Commission, 3 Garfield St., PO Box 967, Charlottetown, PE C1A 7M4
902-368-5710, Fax: 902-368-5735

Quebec
Régie des alcools, des courses et des jeux, 560, boul Charest est, Québec, QC G1K 3J3
418-643-7667, Fax: 418-643-5971, 800-363-0320
Société des alcools du Québec, 905, av De Lorimier, Montréal, QC H2K 3V9
514-873-2020, Fax: 514-873-6788, 866-873-2020, info@saq.com

Saskatchewan
Saskatchewan Liquor & Gaming Authority, 2500 Victoria Ave., PO Box 5054, Regina, SK S4P 3M3
306-787-4213, inquiry@slga.gov.sk.ca

Yukon Territory
Yukon Liquor Corporation, 9031 Quartz Rd., Whitehorse, YT Y1A 4P9
867-667-5245, Fax: 867-393-6306, yukon.liquor@gov.yk.ca

LOTTERIES & GAMING

Alberta
Alberta Gaming & Liquor Commission, 50 Corriveau Ave., St. Albert, AB T8N 3T5
780-447-8600, Fax: 780-447-8916, 800-272-8876

British Columbia
British Columbia Lottery Corporation, 74 West Seymour St., Kamloops, BC V2C 1E2
250-828-5500, Fax: 250-828-5631, 866-815-0222

Manitoba
Manitoba Lotteries Corporation, 830 Empress St., Winnipeg, MB R3G 3H3
204-957-2500, Fax: 204-957-3991, 800-265-2912, communications@casinosofwinnipeg.com
Manitoba Gaming Control Commission, #800, 215 Garry St., Winnipeg, MB R3C 3P3
204-954-9400, Fax: 204-954-9450, 800-782-0363, information@mgcc.mb.ca

New Brunswick
New Brunswick Lotteries & Gaming Corporation, Centennial Bldg., 670 King St., PO Box 6000, Fredericton, NB E3B 5H1
506-444-3468, Fax: 506-444-5818

Newfoundland & Labrador
Department of Government Services, PO Box 8700, St. John's, NL A1B 4J6
709-729-4834, gsinfo@gov.nl.ca

Nunavut
Department of Community & Government Services, W.G. Brown Bldg., 4th Fl., PO Box 1000 700,Iqaluit, NU X0A 0H0
867-975-5400, Fax: 867-975-5305

Ontario
Alcohol & Gaming Commission of Ontario, 90 Sheppard Ave. East, Toronto, ON M2N 0A4
416-326-8700, Fax: 416-326-5555, 800-522-2876
Ontario Lottery & Gaming Corporation, Roberta Bondar Pl., #800, 70 Foster Dr., Sault Ste Marie, ON P6A 6V2
705-946-6464, Fax: 416-224-7000, 800-387-0098

Quebec
Loto-Québec, 500, rue Sherbrooke ouest, Montréal, QC H3A 3G6
514-282-8000, Fax: 514-873-8999
Régie des alcools, des courses et des jeux, 560, boul Charest est, Québec, QC G1K 3J3
418-643-7667, Fax: 418-643-5971, 800-363-0320

Saskatchewan
Saskatchewan Liquor & Gaming Authority, 2500 Victoria Ave., PO Box 5054, Regina, SK S4P 3M3
306-787-4213, inquiry@slga.gov.sk.ca

Yukon Territory
Yukon Lottery Commission, 312 Wood St., Whitehorse, YT Y1A 2E6
867-633-7890, Fax: 867-668-7561, lotteriesyukon@gov.yk.ca

MAPS, CHARTS & AERIAL PHOTOGRAPHS

Canada Centre for Remote Sensing - Geomatics Canada, 588 Booth St., Ottawa, ON K1A 0Y7
613-995-0947, Fax: 613-947-1382

Nova Scotia
Nova Scotia Geomatics Centre, 160 Willow St., Amherst, NS B4H 3W5
902-667-7231, Fax: 902-667-6008, 800-798-0706, geoinfo@gov.ns.ca
Ontario
Association of Ontario Land Surveyors, 1043 McNicoll Ave., Toronto, ON M1W 3W6
416-491-9020, Fax: 416-491-2576,

MARINE NAVIGATION

Atlantic Pilotage Authority, Cogswell Tower, #910, 2000 Barrington St., Halifax, NS B3J 3K1
902-426-2550, Fax: 902-426-4004, 877-272-3477, dispatch@atlanticpilotage.com
Great Lakes Pilotage Authority, 202 Pitt St., 2nd fl., PO Box 95, Cornwall, ON K6H 5R9
613-933-2991, Fax: 613-932-3793, administration@glpa-apgl.com
Pacific Pilotage Authority Canada, #1000, 1130 Pender St. West, Vancouver, BC V6E 4A4
604-666-6771, Fax: 604-666-1647, info@ppa.gc.ca
St. Lawrence Seaway Management Corporation, 202 Pitt St., Cornwall, ON K6J 3P7
613-932-5170, Fax: 613-932-7286, marketing@seaway.ca

MINERALS & MINING

New Brunswick
Lands, Minerals & Petroleum Division, Hugh John Flemming Forestry Centre, PO Box 6000, Fredericton, NB E3B 5H1
506-453-2684, Fax: 506-453-2930, dnrweb@gnb.ca
Resource Development Policy Division, Petroleum Plaza NT, 9945 - 108 St., Edmonton, AB T5K 2G6
British Columbia
Mines & Mineral Resources, PO Box 9319 Prov Govt,Victoria, BC V8W 9N3
Manitoba
Mines Branch, #360, 1395 Ellice Ave., Winnipeg, MB R3G 3P2
Fax: 204-948-2578
Mining Board, #360, 1395 Ellice Ave., Winnipeg, MB R3G 3P2
204-489-0018
Northwest Territories
Department of Industry, Tourism & Investment, PO Box 1320, Yellowknife, NT X1A 2L9
Fax: 867-873-0306, info@iti.ca
Nova Scotia
Department of Energy, Bank of Montreal Bldg., #400, 5151 George St., PO Box 2664, Halifax, NS B3J 3P7
902-424-4575, Fax: 902-424-0528, enérgyinfo@gov.ns.ca
Nunavut
Department of Environment, PO Box 1000 1300,Iqaluit, NU X0A 0H0
867-975-7700, Fax: 867-975-7742, environment@gov.nu.ca
Ontario
Mines & Minerals Division, Willet Green Miller Centre, 933 Ramsey Lake Rd., Sudbury, ON P3E 6B5
705-670-5755, Fax: 705-670-5818, 888-415-9845
Quebec
Mines, Centre de service des Mines, 1685, boul Wilfrid Hamel ouest, 1er étage, Québec, QC G1N 3Y7
418-627-6278, Fax: 418-644-8960, 800-363-7233, service.mines@mrnf.gouv.qc.ca
Énergie, #B401, 5700, 4e av ouest, Québec, QC G1H 6R1
418-627-6377, Fax: 418-643-0701
Saskatchewan
Saskatchewan Energy & Resources, #300, 2103 - 11th Ave., Regina, SK S4P 3Z8
306-787-2528, webmasterer@gov.sk.ca
Yukon Territory
Yukon Energy, Mines & Resources, PO Box 2703, Whitehorse, YT Y1A 2C6
867-667-3130, Fax: 867-456-3965, 800-661-0408, emr@gov.yk.ca

MINES & MINERALS

New Brunswick
Lands, Minerals & Petroleum Division, Hugh John Flemming Forestry Centre, PO Box 6000, Fredericton, NB E3B 5H1
506-453-2684, Fax: 506-453-2930, dnrweb@gnb.ca
Resource Development Policy Division, Petroleum Plaza NT, 9945 - 108 St., Edmonton, AB T5K 2G6
Alberta
Alberta Sport, Recreation, Parks, & Wildlife Foundation, Standard Life Centre, #903, 10405 Jasper Ave., 9th Fl., Edmonton, AB T5J 4R7
780-415-1167, Fax: 780-415-0308
British Columbia
Ministry of Energy & Mines, PO Box 9053 Prov Govt,Victoria, BC V8W 9E2
250-387-5896, Fax: 250-356-2965
Manitoba
Manitoba Geological Survey, #360, 1394 Ellice Ave., Winnipeg, MB R3G 3P2
Fax: 204-945-1406, 800-223-5215, minesinfo@gov.mb.ca
Mining Board, #360, 1395 Ellice Ave., Winnipeg, MB R3G 3P2
204-489-0018
Northwest Territories
Department of Environment & Natural Resources, PO Box 1320, Yellowknife, NT X1A 2L9
Ontario
Mines & Minerals Division, Willet Green Miller Centre, 933 Ramsey Lake Rd., Sudbury, ON P3E 6B5
705-670-5755, Fax: 705-670-5818, 888-415-9845
Ministry of Northern Development, Mines & Forestry, 99 Wellesley St. West, Toronto, ON M7A 1W3
416-327-0633, Fax: 416-327-0651
Quebec
Mines, Centre de service des Mines, 1685, boul Wilfrid Hamel ouest, 1er étage, Québec, QC G1N 3Y7
418-627-6278, Fax: 418-644-8960, 800-363-7233, service.mines@mrnf.gouv.qc.ca

MINIMUM WAGES

See Also: Labour
British Columbia
Ministry of Labour, Citizens' Services & Open Government, PO Box 9056 Prov Govt,Victoria, BC V8W 9K4
250-952-7623, Fax: 250-387-4312, 800-663-7867, LCTZ.Minister@gov.bc.ca
Quebec
Commission des normes du travail, Hall Est, 400, boul Jean-Lesage, 7e étage, Québec, QC G1K 8W1
418-644-0817, Fax: 418-643-5132, 800-563-9058
Saskatchewan
Minimum Wage Board, #400, 1870 Albert St., Regina, SK S4P 4W1

MULTICULTURALISM

Canadian Race Relations Foundation, #701, 4576 Yonge St., Toronto, ON M2N 6N4
416-952-3500, Fax: 416-952-3326, 888-240-4936
Manitoba
Manitoba Ethnocultural Advisory & Advocacy Council, 215 Notre Dame Ave. 4th Fl., Winnipeg, MB R3B 1N3
204-945-2339, Fax: 204-948-2323, 800-665-8332, meaac@gov.mb.ca
Multiculturalism Secretariat, 213 Notre Dame Ave., 4th Fl., Winnipeg, MB R3B 1N3
204-945-1156, Fax: 204-948-2323
New Brunswick
Ministerial Advisory Committee on Multiculturalism, PO Box 6000, Fredericton, NB E3B 5H1
Northwest Territories
Department of Education, Culture & Employment, PO Box 1320, Yellowknife, NT X1A 2L9
867-669-2399, Fax: 867-873-0431, 866-606-5627
Nova Scotia
Department of Communities, Culture & Heritage, World Trade & Convention Centre, 1800 Argyle St., 6th Fl., PO Box 456, Halifax, NS B3J 3N8
902-424-4510, Fax: 902-424-0710, culture@gov.ns.ca
Prince Edward Island
Prince Edward Island Department of Education & Early Childhood Development, Holman Centre, #101, 250 Water St., Summerside, PE C1N 1B6
902-438-4130, Fax: 902-438-4062
Quebec
Conseil des relations interculturelles, #10.04, 500, boul René-Lévesque ouest, Montréal, QC H2Z 1W7
514-873-5634, Fax: 514-873-3469, info@conseilinterculturel.gouv.qc.ca
Ministère de la Culture, des Communications & de la Condition féminine, 225, Grande Allée est, Québec, QC G1R 5G5
888-380-8882

MUNICIPAL & RURAL AFFAIRS

Aboriginal Affairs & Northern Development Canada, 10 Wellington St., North Tower, Gatineau, QC K1A 0H4
819-997-0380, Fax: 866-817-3977, 800-567-9604, infopubs@aadnc-aandc.gc.ca
Canada Economic Development for Québec Regions, Édifice Dominion Square, #900, 1255, rue Peel, Montréal, QC H3B 2T9
514-283-6412, Fax: 514-283-3302, 866-385-6412
Canada Mortgage & Housing Corporation, 700 Montreal Rd., Ottawa, ON K1A 0P7
613-748-2000, Fax: 613-748-2098, 800-668-2642, chic@cmhc-schl.gc.ca
Mackenzie Valley Environmental Impact Review Board, 200 Scotia Centre, #5102, 50th Ave., PO Box 938, Yellowknife, NT X1A 2N7
867-766-7050, Fax: 867-766-7074, 866-912-3472
Nunavut Impact Review Board, PO Box 1360, Cambridge Bay, NU X0B 0C0
867-983-4600, Fax: 867-983-2594, 866-233-3033, info@nirb.ca
Nunavut Planning Commission, PO Box 2101, Cambridge Bay, NU X0B 0C0
867-983-4625, Fax: 867-983-4626
Alberta
Alberta Agriculture & Rural Development, J.G. O'Donoghue Bldg., #100A, 7000 - 113th St., Edmonton, AB T6H 5T6
780-427-2727, -310-3276, duke@gov.ab.ca
Alberta Municipal Affairs, Communications Branch, Commerce Place, 10155 - 102 St., 18th Fl., Edmonton, AB T5J 4L4
780-427-2732, Fax: 780-422-1419, comments@gov.ab.ca
Municipal Government Board, Commerce Place, 10155 - 102 St., 15th Fl., Edmonton, AB T5J 4L4
780-427-4864, Fax: 780-427-0986, mgbmail@gov.ab.ca
Alberta Tourism, Parks, & Recreation, Communications Branch, Commerce Place, 10155 - 102 St., 6th Fl., Edmonton, AB T5J 4L6
780-644-5589, TPR.Communications@gov.ab.ca
British Columbia
Local Government, PO Box 9490 Prov Govt,Victoria, BC V8W 9N7
250-356-6575, Fax: 250-387-7973
Manitoba
Manitoba Aboriginal & Northern Affairs, 59 Elizabeth Dr., PO Box 37, Thompson, MB R8N 1X4
204-677-6607, Fax: 204-677-6753, amartin@gov.mb.ca
Community Land Use Planning Services, #604, 800 Portage Ave., Winnipeg, MB R3G 0N4
Manitoba Intergovernmental Affairs, #301, 450 Broadway Ave., Winnipeg, MB R3C 0V8
Fax: 204-945-1383, mnia@leg.gov.mb.ca
Manitoba Municipal Board, #1144, 363 Broadway, Winnipeg, MB R3C 3N9
204-945-2941, Fax: 204-948-2235
New Brunswick
Assessment & Planning Appeal Board, #201, 435 King St., PO Box 6000, Fredericton, NB E3B 5H1
506-453-2126, Fax: 506-444-4881
Department of Health, PO Box 5100, Fredericton, NB E3B 5G8
506-457-4800, Fax: 506-453-5243, dh-ms@dh-ms.ca
Regional Development Corporation, RDC Bldg., 836 Churchill Row, PO Box 428, Fredericton, NB E3B 5R4
506-453-2277, Fax: 506-453-7988
Newfoundland & Labrador
Department of Health & Community Services, West Block, Confederation Bldg., PO Box 8700, St. John's, NL A1B 4J6
709-729-5021, Fax: 709-729-5824, healthinfo@gov.nl.ca
Department of Labrador & Aboriginal Affairs, Confederation Bldg., East Block, 6th Fl., PO Box 8700, St. John's, NL A1B 4J6
709-729-4776, Fax: 709-729-4900, 877-788-8822, laa@gov.nl.ca
Department of Municipal Affairs, West Block, Main Fl., Confederation Bldg., PO Box 8700, St. John's, NL A1B 4J6
709-729-3046, Fax: 709-729-0943, mainfo@gov.nl.ca
Northwest Territories
Department of Municipal & Community Affairs, PO Box 1320, Yellowknife, NT X1A 2L9
867-873-7118, Fax: 867-873-0309
Nova Scotia
Department of Service Nova Scotia & Municipal Relations, 1505 Barrington St., PO Box 216, Halifax, NS B3J 3K5
902-424-5200, Fax: 902-424-0581, 800-670-4357, askus@gov.ns.ca
Department of Transportation & Infrastructure Renewal, Johnston Bldg., 1672 Granville St., 2nd Fl., PO Box 186, Halifax, NS B3J 2N2
902-424-2297, Fax: 902-424-0532, tpwpaff@gov.ns.ca
Ontario
Ministry of Agriculture, Food & Rural Affairs, Ontario Government Bldg., 1 Stone Rd. West, Guelph, ON N1G 4Y2
519-826-3100, 888-466-2372
Ministry of Municipal Affairs & Housing, College Park, 777 Bay St., 17th Fl., Toronto, ON M5G 2E5
416-585-7041, Fax: 416-585-6470, 866-220-2290, mininfo@ontario.ca
Northern Development Division, Roberta Bondar Place, #200, 70 Foster Dr., Sault Ste Marie, ON P6A 6V8
705-945-5900, Fax: 705-945-5931, 800-461-2287

Ministry of Northern Development, Mines & Forestry, 99 Wellesley St. West, Toronto, ON M7A 1W3
416-327-0633, Fax: 416-327-0651

Prince Edward Island

Prince Edward Island Department of Transportation & Infrastructure Renewal, Jones Bldg., 11 Kent St., 3rd Fl., PO Box 2000, Charlottetown, PE C1A 7N8
902-368-5100, Fax: 902-368-5395

Quebec

Ministère des Affaires municipales et Occupation du territoire, Aile Chaveau, 10, rue Pierre-Olivier-Chauveau, 3e étage, Québec, QC G1R 4J3
418-691-2019, Fax: 418-643-7385, communications@mamrot.gouv.qc.ca

Comité consultatif de l'environnement Kativik, CP 930, Kuujjuaq, QC J0M 1C0
819-964-2961, Fax: 819-964-0694,

Commission municipale du Québec, Mezzanine, aile Chauveau, 10, rue Pierre-Olivier-Chauveau, Québec, QC G1R 4J3
418-691-2014, Fax: 418-644-4676, 866-353-6767, cmq@mamr.gouv.qc.ca

Ministère du Développement économique, de l'Innovation et de l'Exportation, 710, place D'Youville, 3e étage, Québec, QC G1R 4Y4
418-691-5950, Fax: 418-644-0118, 866-680-1884

Yukon Territory

Yukon Community Services, PO Box 2703, Whitehorse, YT Y1A 2C6
867-667-5811, Fax: 867-393-6295, 800-661-0408, inquiry@gov.yk.ca

MUNICIPAL AFFAIRS

Prince Edward Island

Prince Edward Island Department of Finance & Municipal Affairs, Shaw Bldg., 95 Rochford St. South, 2nd Fl., PO Box 2000, Charlottetown, PE C1A 7N8
902-368-4000, Fax: 902-368-5544

Alberta

Alberta Municipal Affairs, Communications Branch, Commerce Place, 10155 - 102 St., 18th Fl., Edmonton, AB T5J 4L4
780-427-2732, Fax: 780-422-1419, comments@gov.ab.ca

British Columbia

Local Government, PO Box 9490 Prov Govt,Victoria, BC V8W 9N7
250-356-6575, Fax: 250-387-7973

Manitoba

Manitoba Aboriginal & Northern Affairs, 59 Elizabeth Dr., PO Box 37, Thompson, MB R8N 1X4
204-677-6607, Fax: 204-677-6753, amartin@gov.mb.ca

Manitoba Intergovernmental Affairs, #301, 450 Broadway Ave., Winnipeg, MB R3C 0V8
Fax: 204-945-1383, mnia@leg.gov.mb.ca

Local Government Development Division, 59 Elizabeth Dr., PO Box 33, Thompson, MB R8N 1X4
204-677-6794, Fax: 204-677-6525

Manitoba Municipal Board, #1144, 363 Broadway, Winnipeg, MB R3C 3N9
204-945-2941, Fax: 204-948-2235

Provincial-Municipal Support Services, #508, 800 Portage Ave., Winnipeg, MB R3G 0N4

New Brunswick

Department of Local Government, Marysville Place, 20 McGloin St., PO Box 6000, Fredericton, NB E3B 5H1
506-453-2807, Fax: 506-453-3988

Regional Development Corporation, RDC Bldg., 836 Churchill Row, PO Box 428, Fredericton, NB E3B 5R4
506-453-2277, Fax: 506-453-7988

Newfoundland & Labrador

Department of Municipal Affairs, West Block, Main Fl., Confederation Bldg., PO Box 8700, St. John's, NL A1B 4J6
709-729-3046, Fax: 709-729-0943, mainfo@gov.nl.ca

Newfoundland & Labrador Municipal Financing Corporation, Confederation Bldg., PO Box 8700, St. John's, NL A1B 4J6
709-729-6686, Fax: 709-729-2095

Northwest Territories

Department of Municipal & Community Affairs, PO Box 1320, Yellowknife, NT X1A 2L9
867-873-7118, Fax: 867-873-0309

Nova Scotia

Nova Scotia Municipal Finance Corporation, Maritime Centre, 1505 Barrington St., 10th Fl. South, PO Box 850 M, Halifax, NS B3J 2V2
902-424-4590, Fax: 902-424-0525

Department of Service Nova Scotia & Municipal Relations, 1505 Barrington St., PO Box 216, Halifax, NS B3J 3K5
902-424-5200, Fax: 902-424-0581, 800-670-4357, askus@gov.ns.ca

Nunavut

Department of Community & Government Services, W.G. Brown Bldg., 4th Fl., PO Box 1000 700,Iqaluit, NU X0A 0H0
867-975-5400, Fax: 867-975-5305

Ontario

Economic Development Division, 1 Stone Road W., 2nd Fl., Guelph, ON N1G 4Y2
519-826-6636, Fax: 519-826-4328

Ministry of Municipal Affairs & Housing, College Park, 777 Bay St., 17th Fl., Toronto, ON M5G 2E5
416-585-7041, Fax: 416-585-6470, 866-220-2290, mininfo@ontario.ca

Prince Edward Island

Prince Edward Island Department of Community Services, Seniors, & Labour, Jones Bldg., 11 Kent St., 2nd Fl., PO Box 2000, Charlottetown, PE C1A 7N8
902-620-3777, Fax: 902-368-4740, 866-594-3777

Quebec

Ministère des Affaires municipales et Occupation du territoire, Aile Chaveau, 10, rue Pierre-Olivier-Chauveau, 3e étage, Québec, QC G1R 4J3
418-691-2019, Fax: 418-643-7385, communications@mamrot.gouv.qc.ca

MUSEUMS

Canadian Heritage, 15 Eddy St., Gatineau, QC K1A 0M5
819-997-0055, 866-811-0055, info@pch.gc.ca

Canadian Museum of Civilization Corporation, 100 Laurier St., Gatineau, QC K1A 0M8
819-776-7000, Fax: 819-776-8300, 800-555-5621, web@civilization.ca

Canadian Museum of Nature, PO Box 3443 D,Ottawa, ON K1P 6P4
613-566-4700, Fax: 613-364-4021, 800-263-4433

National Gallery of Canada, 380 Sussex Dr., PO Box 427 A,Ottawa, ON K1N 9N4
613-990-1985, Fax: 613-993-4385, 800-319-2787, info@gallery.ca; info@beaux-arts.ca

Alberta

Recreation & Sport Development Division, Standard Life Centre, 10405 Jasper Ave., 9th Fl., Edmonton, AB T5J 4R7

Manitoba

Manitoba Museum, 190 Rupert Ave., Winnipeg, MB R3B 0N2
204-956-2830, Fax: 204-942-3679, info@manitobamuseum.mb.ca

Newfoundland & Labrador

Department of Fisheries & Aquaculture, Petten Bldg., 30 Strawberry Marsh Rd., PO Box 8700, St. John's, NL A1B 4J6
709-729-3723, Fax: 709-729-6082, fisheries@gov.nl.ca

Nova Scotia

Culture Division, #601, 1800 Argyle St., PO Box 456, Halifax, NS B3J 2R5
902-424-4510, Fax: 902-424-0710, culture@gov.ns.ca

Ontario

Royal Ontario Museum, 100 Queen's Park Cres., Toronto, ON M5S 2C6
416-586-5549, Fax: 416-586-5685, info@rom.on.ca

Quebec

Ministère de la Culture, des Communications & de la Condition féminine, 225, Grande Allée est, Québec, QC G1R 5G5
888-380-8882

Musée d'art contemporain de Montréal, 185, rue Ste-Catherine ouest, Montréal, QC H2X 3X5
514-847-6226, Fax: 514-847-6290, info@macm.org

Musée de la civilisation, 85, rue Dalhousie, CP 155 B,Québec, QC G1K 7A6
418-643-2158, Fax: 418-646-9705, 866-710-8031, mcqweb@mcq.org

Musée national des beaux-arts du Québec, Parc des Champs-de-Bataille, 1, av Wolfe-Montcalm, Québec, QC G1R 5H3
418-643-2150, Fax: 418-646-3330, 866-220-2150, webmestre@mnba.qc.ca

Saskatchewan

Royal Saskatchewan Museum, 2445 Albert St., Regina, SK S4P 4W7
306-787-2815, Fax: 306-787-2820, rsminfo@gov.sk.ca

Western Development Museum, 2935 Melville St., Saskatoon, SK S7J 5A6
306-934-1400, Fax: 306-934-4467, 800-363-6345, info@wdm.ca

Yukon Territory

Yukon Tourism & Culture, 100 Hanson St., Whitehorse, YT Y1A 2C6
867-667-5036, Fax: 867-667-3546

NATIVE PEOPLES & NORTHERN AFFAIRS

British Columbia

North Area, 1011 - 4 Ave., 5th Fl., Prince George, BC V2L 3H9
250-565-6100

New Brunswick

Aboriginal Affairs Secretariat, Kings Place, #237, 440 King St., PO Box 6000, Fredericton, NB E3B 5H1
506-462-5177, Fax: 506-444-5142

Yukon Territory

Yukon Development Corporation, #2 Miles Canyon Rd., PO Box 5920, Whitehorse, YT Y1A 6S7
867-393-5337, Fax: 867-393-5401

Yukon Land Use Planning Council, #201, 307 Jarvis St., Whitehorse, YT Y1A 2H3
867-667-7397, Fax: 867-667-4624, ylupc@planyukon.ca

NATURAL RESOURCES

Canadian Museum of Nature, PO Box 3443 D,Ottawa, ON K1P 6P4
613-566-4700, Fax: 613-364-4021, 800-263-4433

Fish & Wildlife Division, Petroleum Plaza ST, 9915 - 108 St., 11th Fl., Edmonton, AB T5K 2G8

Natural Resources Canada, 580 Booth St., Ottawa, ON K1A 0E4
613-995-0947, Fax: 613-992-7211

Alberta

Natural Resources Conservation Board, Sterling Place, 9940 - 106 St., Edmonton, AB T5K 2N2
780-422-1977, Fax: 780-427-0607, 866-383-6722, info@nrcb.gov.ab.ca

Alberta Sustainable Resource Development, Information Centre, Great West Life Building, 9920 - 108 St., Main Fl., Edmonton, AB T5K 2M4
780-944-0313, Fax: 780-427-4407, 877-944-0313, srd.infocent@gov.ab.ca

British Columbia

Ministry of Energy & Mines, PO Box 9053 Prov Govt,Victoria, BC V8W 9E2
250-387-5896, Fax: 250-356-2965

Ministry of Environment, PO Box 9339 Prov Govt,Victoria, BC V8W 9M1
250-387-1161, Fax: 250-387-5669, envmail@gov.bc.ca

Ministry of Forests, Lands & Natural Resource Operations, PO Box 9049 Prov Govt,Victoria, BC V8W 9E2
250-387-4809, Fax: 250-387-1040

Manitoba

Manitoba Conservation, 200 Saulteaux Cres., Winnipeg, MB R3J 3W3
204-945-6784, 800-214-6497, mincon@leg.gov.mb.ca

Manitoba Conservation Districts Commission, Secretariat c/o Planning & Coordination Branch, 123 Main St., PO Box 20000, Neepawa, MB R0J 1H0
204-476-7033, Fax: 204-476-7539, whildebran@gov.mb.ca

New Brunswick

Department of Natural Resources, Hugh John Flemming Forestry Centre, PO Box 6000, Fredericton, NB E3B 5H1
506-453-3826, Fax: 506-444-4367, dnrweb@gnb.ca

Newfoundland & Labrador

Department of Natural Resources, Natural Resources Bldg., 50 Elizabeth Ave., 7th Fl., PO Box 8700, St. John's, NL A1B 4J6
709-729-2920, Fax: 709-729-0059

Northwest Territories

Department of Environment & Natural Resources, PO Box 1320, Yellowknife, NT X1A 2L9

Nova Scotia

Department of Natural Resources, Founder's Square, 1701 Hollis St., 3rd Fl., PO Box 698, Halifax, NS B3J 2T9
902-424-5935, Fax: 902-424-0594, 800-565-2224

Nunavut

Department of Environment, PO Box 1000 1300,Iqaluit, NU X0A 0H0
867-975-7700, Fax: 867-975-7742, environment@gov.nu.ca

Ontario

Ministry of Natural Resources, Whitney Block, #6630, 99 Wellesley St. West, 6th Fl., Toronto, ON M7A 1W3
800-667-1940

Ministry of Northern Development, Mines & Forestry, 99 Wellesley St. West, Toronto, ON M7A 1W3
416-327-0633, Fax: 416-327-0651

Prince Edward Island

Prince Edward Island Department of Agriculture, Jones Bldg., 11 Kent St., PO Box 2000, Charlottetown, PE C1A 7N8
902-368-4880, Fax: 902-368-4857

Prince Edward Island Department of Environment, Energy, & Forestry, Jones Bldg., 11 Kent St., 4th Fl., PO Box 2000, Charlottetown, PE C1A 7N8
902-368-5000, Fax: 902-368-5830

Quebec

Ministère du Développement durable, de l'Environnement et des Parcs, Édifice Marie-Guyart, 675, boul René-Lévesque est, 29e étage, Québec, QC G1R 5V7
418-521-3830, Fax: 418-646-5974, 800-561-1616, info@mddep.gouv.qc.ca

Ministère des Ressources naturelles et de la Faune, 880, ch Sainte-Foy, Québec, QC G1S 4X4
418-627-8600, Fax: 418-644-6513, 866-248-6936, services.clientele@mrnf.gouv.qc.ca

Saskatchewan

Saskatchewan Energy & Resources, #300, 2103 - 11th Ave., Regina, SK S4P 3Z8
306-787-2528, webmasterer@gov.sk.ca

Saskatchewan Environment, 3211 Albert St., 2nd Fl., Regina, SK S4S 5W6
306-787-2584, Fax: 306-787-9544, 800-567-4224, Centre.Inquiry@gov.sk.ca

Yukon Territory

Yukon Energy, Mines & Resources, PO Box 2703, Whitehorse, YT Y1A 2C6
867-667-3130, Fax: 867-456-3965, 800-661-0408, emr@gov.yk.ca

Yukon Environment, PO Box 2703, Whitehorse, YT Y1A 2C6
867-667-5652, Fax: 867-393-7197, environment.yukon@gov.yk.ca

NUCLEAR ENERGY

Canadian Nuclear Safety Commission, 280 Slater St., PO Box 1046 B,Ottawa, ON K1P 5S9
613-995-5894, Fax: 613-995-5086, 800-668-5284

Alberta

Alberta Energy, North Petroleum Plaza, 9945 - 108 St., Edmonton, AB T5K 2G6
780-427-8050, Fax: 780-422-0698, Library.Energy@gov.ab.ca

Ontario

Ontario Power Generation, 700 University Ave., Toronto, ON M5G 1X6
416-592-2555, 877-592-2555, webmaster@opg.com

Quebec

Hydro-Québec, 75, boul René-Lévesque ouest, Montréal, QC H2Z 1A4
514-289-2211

NUTRITION

Alberta

Health Workforce Division, Telus Plaza NT, 10025 Jasper Ave., 10th Fl., Edmonton, AB T5J 1S6

Research Branch, Tower 5, 1341 Baseline Rd., Ottawa, ON K1A 0C5
613-759-1000, Fax: 613-773-1866

Manitoba

Manitoba Healthy Child Office, #219, 114 Garry St., Winnipeg, MB R3C 1G1
204-945-2266, 888-848-0140, healthychild@gov.mb.ca

Primary Care & Healthy Living, 300 Carlton St., 2nd Floor, Winnipeg, MB R3B 3M9

Newfoundland & Labrador

Department of Health & Community Services, West Block, Confederation Bldg., PO Box 8700, St. John's, NL A1B 4J6
709-729-5021, Fax: 709-729-5824, healthinfo@gov.nl.ca

Northwest Territories

Department of Health & Social Services, Centre Square Tower, PO Box 1320, Yellowknife, NT X1A 2L9
Fax: 867-873-0266

Nunavut

Department of Health & Social Services, PO Box 1000 1000,Iqaluit, NU X0A 0H0
867-975-5700, Fax: 867-975-5705

Ontario

Ministry of Health & Long-Term Care, Hepburn Block, 80 Grosvenor St., 10th Fl, Toronto, ON M7A 2C4
416-327-4327, 800-268-1153

Prince Edward Island

Prince Edward Island Department of Health & Wellness, 105 Rochford St. North, 4th Fl., PO Box 2000, Charlottetown, PE C1A 7N8
902-368-6414, Fax: 902-368-4121

Quebec

Ministère de la Santé et des Services sociaux, Direction des communications, 1075, ch Sainte-Foy, 16e étage, Québec, QC G1S 2M1
418-643-9395, Fax: 418-643-4768, regisseur.web@msss.gouv.qc.ca

Saskatchewan

Saskatchewan Health, T.C. Douglas Bldg., 3475 Albert St., Regina, SK S4S 6X6
306-787-0146, 800-667-7766, info@health.gov.sk.ca

OCCUPATIONAL SAFETY

See Also: Dangerous Goods & Hazardous Materials

Canadian Centre for Occupational Health & Safety, 135 Hunter St. East, Hamilton, ON L8N 1M5
905-572-2981, Fax: 905-572-2206, 800-668-4284

Alberta

Occupational Health & Safety Council, Labour Building, 10808 - 99 Ave., 9th Fl., Edmonton, AB T5K 0G5
780-415-8690, 866-415-8690

Workplace Standards Delivery Division, Labour Building, 10808 - 99 Ave., 9th Fl., Edmonton, AB T5K 0G5
780-415-9533

British Columbia

Ministry of Labour, Citizens' Services & Open Government, PO Box 9056 Prov Govt,Victoria, BC V8W 9K4
250-952-7623, Fax: 250-387-4312, 800-663-7867, LCTZ.Minister@gov.bc.ca

Workers' Compensation Board of British Columbia, PO Box 5350 Terminal,Vancouver, BC V6B 5L5
604-276-3100, Fax: 604-276-3247, 888-621-7233

Manitoba

Advisory Council on Workplace Safety & Health, #200, 401 York Ave., Winnipeg, MB R3C 0P8
204-945-3446, Fax: 204-945-4556

Workplace Safety & Health Division, #200, 401 York Ave., Winnipeg, MB R3C 0P8
204-945-3446, Fax: 204-948-2209, wshcompl@gov.mb.ca

New Brunswick

Workplace Health, Safety & Compensation Commission of New Brunswick, 1 Portland St., PO Box 160, Saint John, NB E2L 3X9
506-632-2200, 800-222-9775, communications@ws-ts.nb.ca

Newfoundland & Labrador

Newfoundland & Labrador Workplace Health, Safety & Compensation Commission, 146 - 148 Forest Rd., PO Box 9000, St. John's, NL A1A 3B8
709-778-1000, Fax: 709-738-1714, 800-563-9000, general.inquiries@whscc.nl.ca

Northwest Territories

Northwest Territories & Nunavut Workers' Safety & Compensation Commission, Centre Square Tower, 5022 - 49th St., 5th Fl., PO Box 8888, Yellowknife, NT X1A 2R3
867-920-3888, Fax: 867-873-4596, 800-661-0792

Nova Scotia

Workers' Compensation Board of Nova Scotia, 5668 South St., PO Box 1150, Halifax, NS B3J 2Y2
902-491-8999, Fax: 902-491-8002, 800-870-3331, info@wcb.gov.ns.ca

Ontario

Workplace Safety & Insurance Board, 200 Front St. West, Ground Fl., Toronto, ON M5V 3J1
416-344-1000, Fax: 416-344-4684, 800-387-0750

Prince Edward Island

Prince Edward Island Workers Compensation Board, 14 Weymouth St., PO Box 757, Charlottetown, PE C1A 7L7
902-368-5680, Fax: 902-368-5696, 800-237-5049

Quebec

Commission des lésions professionnelles, #700, 900, Place d'Youville, Québec, QC G1R 3P7
418-644-7777, Fax: 418-644-6443, 800-463-1591

Commission de la santé et de la sécurité du travail du Québec, 524, rue Bourdages, CP 1200 Terminus postal,Québec, QC G1K 7E2
418-266-4850, Fax: 418-266-4669, 866-302-2778

Saskatchewan

Office of the Worker's Advocate, #300, 1870 Albert St., Regina, SK S4P 4W1
306-787-2456, Fax: 306-787-0249, 877-787-2456

Saskatchewan Workers' Compensation Board, #200, 1881 Scarth St., Regina, SK S4P 4L1
306-787-4370, Fax: 306-787-4311, 800-667-7590, internet_clientsvc@wcbsask.com

Yukon Territory

Yukon Workers' Compensation Health & Safety Board, 401 Strickland St., Whitehorse, YT Y1A 5N8
867-667-5645, Fax: 867-393-6279, 800-661-0443, worksafe@gov.yk.ca

OCCUPATIONAL TRAINING

Canada School of Public Service, 373 Sussex Dr., Ottawa, ON K1N 6Z2
819-953-5400, Fax: 819-953-7953, 866-703-9598, info@csps-efpc.gc.ca

Alberta

Community, Learner & Industry Connections Division, Phipps-McKinnon Bldg., 10020 - 101A Ave., 5th Fl., Edmonton, AB T5J 3G2

British Columbia

Ministry of Labour, Citizens' Services & Open Government, PO Box 9056 Prov Govt,Victoria, BC V8W 9K4
250-952-7623, Fax: 250-387-4312, 800-663-7867, LCTZ.Minister@gov.bc.ca

Manitoba

Manitoba Advanced Education & Literacy, Legislative Building, #162, 450 Broadway Ave., Winnipeg, MB R3C 0V8
204-945-0825, Fax: 204-948-2216, minaed@leg.gov.mb.ca

New Brunswick

Department of Post-Secondary Education, Training & Labour, Chestnut Complex, 470 York St., PO Box 6000, Fredericton, NB E3B 5H1
506-453-2597, Fax: 506-453-3618, dpetlinfo@gnb.ca

Office of Human Resources, Centennial Bldg, #345, 670 King St., PO Box 6000, Fredericton, NB E3B 5H1
506-453-2264, Fax: 506-453-7195

Ontario

Ministry of Training, Colleges & Universities, Mowat Block, 900 Bay St., 14th Fl., Toronto, ON M7A 1L2
416-325-2929, Fax: 416-325-6348, 800-387-5514, information.met@ontario.ca

Quebec

École nationale de police du Québec, 350, rue Marguerite-d'Youville, Nicolet, QC J3T 1X4
819-293-8631, Fax: 819-293-8630, courriel@enpq.qc.ca

École nationale des pompiers du Québec, #3.08, 2800, boul Saint-Martin ouest, Laval, QC H7T 2S9
450-680-6800, Fax: 450-680-6818, 866-680-3677

OCEANOGRAPHY

Bayfield Institute, 867 Lakeshore Rd., PO Box 5050, Burlington, ON L7R 4A6
905-336-6240

Bedford Institute of Oceanography, 1 Challenger Dr., PO Box 1006, Dartmouth, NS B2Y 4A2
902-426-3492, Fax: 902-426-8484

Fisheries & Oceans Canada, 200 Kent St., Ottawa, ON K1A 0E6
613-993-0999, Fax: 613-990-1866, info@dfo-mpo.gc.ca

Institut Maurice-Lamontagne, 850, rte de le Mer, CP 1000, Mont-Joli, QC G5H 3Z4
418-775-0555, Fax: 418-775-0730

Institute for Marine Biosciences, 1411 Oxford St., Halifax, NS B3H 3Z1
902-426-8332, Fax: 902-426-9413, communications.imb@nrc-cnrc.gc.ca

Institute for Ocean Technology, Kerwin Pl. & Arctic Ave., PO Box 12093, St. John's, NL A1B 3T5
709-772-4939, Fax: 709-772-2462, Noel.Murphy@nrc-cnrc.gc.ca

Institute of Ocean Sciences, 9860 West Saanich Rd., PO Box 6000, Sidney, BC V8L 4B2
250-363-6517, Fax: 250-363-6390

OIL & NATURAL GAS RESOURCES

See Also: Energy; Natural Resources

Indian Oil & Gas Canada, #100, 9911 Chiila Blvd., Tsuu T'ina (Sarcee), AB T2W 6H6
403-292-5625, Fax: 403-292-5618, ContactIOGC@inac-ainc.gc.ca

Lands, Minerals & Petroleum Division, Hugh John Flemming Forestry Centre, PO Box 6000, Fredericton, NB E3B 5H1
506-453-2684, Fax: 506-453-2930, dnrweb@gnb.ca

National Energy Board, 444 - 7 Ave. SW, Calgary, AB T2P 0X8
403-292-4800, Fax: 403-292-5503, 800-899-1265, info@neb-one.gc.ca

Oil & Gas Mineral Resources, #300, 211 Main St., Whitehorse, YT Y1A 2B2
867-667-5087, Fax: 867-393-6262, oilandgas@gov.yk.ca

Alberta

Energy Resources Conservation Board, #1000, 250 - 5 Ave. SW, Calgary, AB T2P 0R4
403-297-8311, Fax: 403-297-7336, 855-297-8311, inquiries@ercb.ca; infoservices@ercb.ca; ADR@ercb.ca

Alberta Energy, North Petroleum Plaza, 9945 - 108 St., Edmonton, AB T5K 2G6
780-427-8050, Fax: 780-422-0698, Library.Energy@gov.ab.ca

British Columbia

Ministry of Energy & Mines, PO Box 9053 Prov Govt,Victoria, BC V8W 9E2
250-387-5896, Fax: 250-356-2965

Oil & Gas Commission, #100, 10003 - 110 Ave., Fort St John, BC V1J 6M7
250-794-5200, Fax: 250-794-5375

British Columbia Utilities Commission, 900 Howe St., 6th Fl., PO Box 250, Vancouver, BC V6Z 2N3
604-660-4700, Fax: 604-660-1102, 800-663-1385, commission.secretary@bcuc.com

Manitoba

Petroleum, #360, 1395 Ellice Ave., Winnipeg, MB R3G 3P2
204-945-6577, Fax: 204-945-0586

Surface Rights Board, #360, 1395 Ellice Ave., Winnipeg, MB R3G 3P2
204-945-0731, Fax: 204-948-2578, 800-282-8069, bmiskimmin@gov.mb.ca

Newfoundland & Labrador
Canada-Newfoundland Offshore Petroleum Board, TD Place, 140 Water St., 5th Fl., St. John's, NL A1C 6H6
709-778-1400, Fax: 709-778-1473, information@cnlopb.nl.ca

Nova Scotia
Canada-Nova Scotia Offshore Petroleum Board, TD Centre, 1791 Barrington St., 6th Fl., Halifax, NS B3J 3K9
902-422-5588, Fax: 902-422-1799, postmaster@cnsopb.ns.ca
Nova Scotia Utility & Review Board, Summit Place, 1601 Lower Water St., 3rd Fl., PO Box 1692 M,Halifax, NS B3J 3S3
902-424-4448, Fax: 902-424-3919, uarb.board@gov.ns.ca

Nunavut
Department of Environment, PO Box 1000 1300,Iqaluit, NU X0A 0H0
867-975-7700, Fax: 867-975-7742, environment@gov.nu.ca

Ontario
Ministry of Natural Resources, Whitney Block, #6630, 99 Wellesley St. West, 6th Fl., Toronto, ON M7A 1W3
800-667-1940

Saskatchewan
SaskEnergy Incorporated, 1777 Victoria Ave., Regina, SK S4P 4K5
306-777-9225, 800-567-8899

OIL SPILLS

Canadian Coast Guard, Centennial Towers, #6S018, 200 Kent St., Ottawa, ON K1A 0E6
613-993-0999, Fax: 613-990-1866, info@dfo-mpo.gc.ca

Newfoundland & Labrador
Canada-Newfoundland Offshore Petroleum Board, TD Place, 140 Water St., 5th Fl., St. John's, NL A1C 6H6
709-778-1400, Fax: 709-778-1473, information@cnlopb.nl.ca

OMBUDSMEN

Office of the Correctional Investigator, PO Box 3421 D,Ottawa, ON K1P 6L4
Fax: 613-990-9091, 877-885-8848, org@oci-bec.gc.ca
Office of the Commissioner of Official Languages, 344 Slater St., 3rd fl., Ottawa, ON K1A 0T8
613-996-6368, Fax: 613-993-5082, 877-996-6368
Privacy Commissioner of Canada, Tower B, Place de Ville, 112 Kent St., 3rd Fl., Ottawa, ON K1A 1H3
613-947-1698, Fax: 613-947-6850, 800-282-1376

Alberta
Alberta Office of the Ombudsman, Canadian Western Bank Building, #2800, 10303 Jasper Ave. NW, 28th Fl., Edmonton, AB T5J 5C3
780-427-2756, Fax: 780-427-2759, 888-455-2756, info@ombudsman.ab.ca

British Columbia
Office of the Ombudsperson, 947 Fort St., 2nd Fl., PO Box 9039 Prov Govt,Victoria, BC V8W 9A5
250-387-5855, Fax: 250-387-0198, 800-567-3247, systems@bcombudsperson.ca (Information technology inquiries)

Manitoba
Manitoba Office of the Ombudsman, 750 - 500 Portage Ave., Winnipeg, MB R3C 3X1
204-982-9130, Fax: 204-942-7803, 800-665-0531, ombudsma@ombudsman.mb.ca

New Brunswick
Office of the Ombudsman, 767 Brunswick St., PO Box 6000, Fredericton, NB E3B 5H1
506-453-2789, Fax: 506-453-5599, 800-465-1100, nbombud@gnb.ca

Nova Scotia
Office of the Ombudsman, #700, 5670 Spring Garden Rd., PO Box 2152, Halifax, NS B3J 3B7
902-424-6780, Fax: 902-424-6675, 800-670-1111, ombudsman@gov.ns.ca

Ontario
Office of the Ombudsman, Bell Trinity Sq., South Tower, 483 Bay St., 10th Fl., Toronto, ON M5G 2C9
416-586-3300, Fax: 416-586-3485, 800-263-1830, info@ombudsman.on.ca

Quebec
Le Protecteur du Citoyen, #1.25, 525, boul René-Lévesque est, Québec, QC G1R 5Y4
418-643-2688, Fax: 418-643-8759, 800-463-5070, protecteur@protecteurducitoyen.qc.ca

Saskatchewan
Ombudsman Saskatchewan, #150, 2401 Saskatchewan Dr., Regina, SK S4P 4H8
306-787-6211, Fax: 306-787-9090, 800-667-7180, ombreg@ombudsman.sk.ca

PARKS & RECREATION

Canadian Heritage, 15 Eddy St., Gatineau, QC K1A 0M5
819-997-0055, 866-811-0055, info@pch.gc.ca
Corporate Services Division, PO Box 2000, Charlottetown, PE C1A 7N8
Historic Sites & Monuments Board of Canada, Terrasses de la Chaudière, 25 Eddy St., Gatineau, QC K1A 0M5
Fax: 819-934-1115, 855-283-8730, hsmbc-clmhc@pc.gc.ca
Parks Canada, 25 Eddy St., Gatineau, QC K1A 0M5
613-860-1251, 888-773-8888, information@pc.gc.ca

Alberta
Alberta Sport, Recreation, Parks, & Wildlife Foundation, Standard Life Centre, #903, 10405 Jasper Ave., 9th Fl., Edmonton, AB T5J 4R7
780-415-1167, Fax: 780-415-0308
Parks Division, Oxbridge Place, 9820 - 106 St., 2nd Fl., Edmonton, AB T5K 2J6
780-427-3582, Fax: 780-427-5980, 866-427-3582
Special Areas Board, Special Areas Board Administration, 212 - 2nd Ave. West, PO Box 820, Hanna, AB T0J 1P0
403-854-5600, Fax: 403-854-5527, specarea@telus.net

British Columbia
Ministry of Environment, PO Box 9339 Prov Govt,Victoria, BC V8W 9M1
250-387-1161, Fax: 250-387-5669, envmail@gov.bc.ca

Manitoba
Manitoba Competitiveness, Training & Trade, International Business Centre, The Paris Building, 259 Portage Ave., Winnipeg, MB R3B 3P4
204-945-2475, Fax: 204-945-3977, minctt@leg.gov.mb.ca
Ecological Reserves Advisory Committee, c/o Manitoba Conservation, Parks & Natural Areas Branch, 200 Saulteaux Cres., Winnipeg, MB R3J 3W3
204-945-4148, Fax: 204-945-0012, hhernandez@gov.mb.ca

New Brunswick
Department of Business New Brunswick, Centennial Bldg., 670 King St., PO Box 6000, Fredericton, NB E3B 5H1
506-453-3707, Fax: 506-453-3993, investnb@gnb.ca
Department of Tourism & Parks, Centennial Bldg., 670 King St., Fredericton, NB E3B 1G1
506-444-5205, Fax: 506-457-4984, taponlinedirectory@gnb.ca

Newfoundland & Labrador
Department of Tourism, Culture & Recreation, Confederation Bldg., West Block, 2nd Fl., PO Box 8700, St. John's, NL A1B 4J6
709-729-0862, Fax: 709-729-0870, tcrinfo@gov.nl.ca

Northwest Territories
Department of Environment & Natural Resources, PO Box 1320, Yellowknife, NT X1A 2L9

Nova Scotia
Department of Economic & Rural Development, Centennial Building, #600, 1660 Hollis St., PO Box 2311, Halifax, NS B3J 1V7
902-424-0377, Fax: 902-424-0500, comm@gov.ns.ca

Nunavut
Department of Environment, PO Box 1000 1300,Iqaluit, NU X0A 0H0
867-975-7700, Fax: 867-975-7742, environment@gov.nu.ca

Ontario
Ministry of Economic Development & Innovation, Hearst Block, 900 Bay St., 8th Fl., Toronto, ON M7A 2E1
416-325-6666, Fax: 416-325-6688, 866-668-4249, info@edt.gov.on.ca

Prince Edward Island
Prince Edward Island Department of Innovation & Advanced Learning, Shaw Bldg., 105 Rochford St., 5th Fl., PO Box 2000, Charlottetown, PE C1A 7N8
902-368-4240, Fax: 902-368-4242
Prince Edward Island Department of Tourism & Culture, PO Box 2000, Charlottetown, PE C1A 7N8
902-368-5540, Fax: 902-368-5277, tpswitch@gov.pe.ca

Quebec
Ministère du Développement durable, de l'Environnement et des Parcs, Édifice Marie-Guyart, 675, boul René-Lévesque est, 29e étage, Québec, QC G1R 5V7
418-521-3830, Fax: 418-646-5974, 800-561-1616, info@mddep.gouv.qc.ca
Société des établissements en plein air du Québec, Place de la Cité, Tour Cominar, #250, 2640, boul Laurier, 2e étage, Québec, QC G1V 5C2
418-890-6527, Fax: 418-528-6025, 800-665-6527, inforeservation@sepaq.com

Saskatchewan
Tourism Saskatchewan, #189, 1621 Albert St., Regina, SK S4P 2S5
306-787-9600, 877-237-2273

Yukon Territory
Yukon Tourism & Culture, 100 Hanson St., Whitehorse, YT Y1A 2C6
867-667-5036, Fax: 867-667-3546,

PARLIAMENT

See Also: Government (General Information; Protocol (State)
41st Parliament - Canada, House of Commons, Parliament Buildings, Ottawa, ON K1A 0A6
Library of Parliament, Parliamentary Bldgs., 111 Wellington St., Ottawa, ON K1A 0A9
613-992-4793, Fax: 613-943-6383, 866-599-4999
Office of the Leader, Bloc Québécois, Centre Block, Ottawa, ON K1A 0A6
613-992-6779, Fax: 613-954-2121
Office of the Leader, Green Party of Canada, Confederation Building,, #518, 244 Wellington St., Ottawa, ON K1A 0A6
613-996-1119, Fax: 613-996-0850, 866-868-3447, leader@greenparty.ca; info@greenparty.ca
Office of the Leader, Official Opposition (New Democratic Party), 111 Wellington St., Ottawa, ON K1A 0A6
613-995-7224, Fax: 613-995-4565
Office of the Prime Minister (Conservative Party of Canada), Langevin Block, 80 Wellington St., Ottawa, ON K1A 0A2
613-992-4211, Fax: 613-941-6900, pm@pm.gc.ca
Privy Council Office, #1000, 85 Sparks St., Ottawa, ON K1A 0A3
613-957-5153, Fax: 613-997-5043, info@pco-bcp.gc.ca
The Canadian Ministry, Information Service, Parliament of Canada, Ottawa, ON K1A 0A9
613-992-4793, 866-599-4999, info@parl.gc.ca

Alberta
Legislative Assembly of Alberta, Legislature Annex, 9718 - 107 St., Edmonton, AB T5K 1E4
780-427-2826, Fax: 780-427-1623, laocommunications@assembly.ab.ca

British Columbia
Legislative Assembly & Independent Offices, Clerk's Office, #221, Parliament Bldgs., Victoria, BC V8V 1X4
250-387-3785, Fax: 250-387-0942, ClerkHouse@leg.bc.ca

Manitoba
Legislative Assembly, c/o Clerk's Office, Legislative Bldg., #237, 450 Broadway, Winnipeg, MB R3C 0V8
204-945-3636, Fax: 204-948-2507, clerkla@leg.gov.mb.ca

New Brunswick
Legislative Assembly of New Brunswick, Centre Block, Legislative Bldg., 706 Queen St., PO Box 6000, Fredericton, NB E3B 5H1
506-453-2506, Fax: 506-453-7154, wwwleg@gnb.ca

Northwest Territories
Legislative Assembly, c/o Clerk's Office, PO Box 1320, Yellowknife, NT X1A 2L9
867-669-2299, Fax: 867-920-4735, 800-661-0784

Nova Scotia
Legislative House of Assembly, c/o Clerk's Office, Province House, 1st Fl., PO Box 1617, Halifax, NS B3J 2Y3
902-424-5978, Fax: 902-424-0632

Nunavut
Legislative Assembly, 926 Federal Rd., PO Box 1200, Iqaluit, NU X0A 0H0
867-975-5000, Fax: 867-975-5190, 877-334-7266, leginfo@assembly.nu.ca

Ontario
Legislative Assembly, c/o Clerk's Office, #104, Legislative Bldg., Queen's Park, Toronto, ON M7A 1A2
416-325-7500, Fax: 416-325-7489, assemblyinternet@ontla.ola.org

Prince Edward Island
Legislative Assembly, Province House, 165 Richmond St., 1st Fl., PO Box 2000, Charlottetown, PE C1A 7N8
902-368-5970, Fax: 902-368-5175, 877-315-5518, legislativelibrary@assembly.pe.ca

Quebec
L'Assemblée nationale, Hôtel du Parlement, 1045, rue des Parlementaires, Québec, QC G1A 1A3
418-643-7239, Fax: 418-646-4271, 866-337-8837, responsable.contenu@assnat.qc.ca

Saskatchewan
Legislative Assembly, c/o Clerk's Office, Legislative Bldg., #123, 2405 Legislative Dr., Regina, SK S4S 0B3
306-787-2376, Fax: 306-787-1558, info@legassembly.sk.ca

Yukon Territory
Legislative Assembly, 2071 Second Ave., PO Box 2703, Whitehorse, YT Y1A 2C6
867-667-5498, Fax: 867-393-6280

PAROLE BOARDS

See Also: Correctional Services

Alberta

Criminal Justice Division, Bowker Building, 9833 - 109 St., 2nd Fl., Edmonton, AB T5K 2E8

National Parole Board, 410 Laurier Ave. West, Ottawa, ON K1A 0R1
613-954-7474, Fax: 613-995-4380, 800-874-2652, info@npb-cnlc.gc.ca

Manitoba

Corrections Division, #810, 405 Broadway Ave., Winnipeg, MB R3C 3L6
204-945-7291

New Brunswick

Department of Public Safety, 364 Argyle St., PO Box 6000, Fredericton, NB E3B 5H1
506-453-3992, Fax: 506-453-3870, DPS-MSP.Information@gnb.ca

Ontario

Ontario Parole Board, #1803, 415 Yonge St., Toronto, ON M5B 2E7
416-325-4480, Fax: 416-325-4485, 888-579-2888

Quebec

Commission québecoise des libérations conditionnelles, #1.32A, 300, boul Jean-Lesage, Québec, QC G1K 8K6
418-646-8300, Fax: 418-643-7217, cqlc@msp.gouv.qc.ca

PASSPORT INFORMATION

See Also: Citizenship; Immigration

Passport Canada, Le 70 Crémazie, 70 Crémazie St., Gatineau, QC K1A 0G3
Fax: 819-953-5856, 800-567-6868

PATENTS & COPYRIGHT

Copyright Board of Canada, #800, 56 Sparks St., Ottawa, ON K1A 0C9
613-952-8621, Fax: 613-952-8630, secretariat@cb-cda.gc.ca

PAY EQUITY

Human Resources & Skills Development Canada, 140 Promenade du Portage, Gatineau, QC K1A 0J9

British Columbia

Employment Standards Tribunal, Oceanic Plaza, #650, 1066 West Hastings St., Vancouver, BC V6E 3X1
604-775-3512, Fax: 604-775-3372, registrar.est@bcest.bc.ca

Ministry of Labour, Citizens' Services & Open Government, PO Box 9056 Prov Govt,Victoria, BC V8W 9K4
250-952-7623, Fax: 250-387-4312, 800-663-7867, LCTZ.Minister@gov.bc.ca

New Brunswick

Office of Human Resources, Centennial Bldg, #345, 670 King St., PO Box 6000, Fredericton, NB E3B 5H1
506-453-2264, Fax: 506-453-7195

Nova Scotia

Pay Equity Commission, 5151 Terminal Rd., 6th Fl., PO Box 697, Halifax, NS B3J 2T8
902-424-2385, Fax: 902-424-0575

Ontario

Pay Equity Commission, #300, 180 Dundas St. West, Toronto, ON M7A 2S6
416-314-1896, Fax: 416-314-8741, 800-387-8813

Prince Edward Island

Workers Compensation Appeal Tribunal, 161 St. Peters Rd., 1st Fl., PO Box 2000, Charlottetown, PE C1A 7N8

Quebec

Commission de l'équité salariale, 200, ch Ste-Foy, 4e étage, Québec, QC G1R 6A1
418-528-8765, Fax: 418-528-6999, 888-528-8765, equite.salariale@ces.gouv.qc.ca

PENSIONS

Canada Pension Plan Investment Board, #2600, 1 Queen St. East, PO Box 101, Toronto, ON M5C 2W5
416-868-4075, Fax: 416-868-8689, 866-557-9510, csr@cppib.ca

Finance Canada, L'esplanade Laurier, 140 O'Connor St., Ottawa, ON K1A 0G5
613-992-1573, Fax: 613-943-0938, finpub@fin.gc.ca

Office of the Superintendent of Financial Institutions, Kent Square, 255 Albert St., Ottawa, ON K1A 0H2
613-990-7788, Fax: 613-990-5591, 800-385-8647, information@osfi-bsif.gc.ca

Nova Scotia Pension Agency, Purdy's Landing, #400, 1949 Upper Water St., PO Box 371, Halifax, NS B3J 3N3
PensionsInfo@gov.ns.ca

Office of the Commissioner of Review Tribunals, PO Box 8250 T, Ottawa, ON K1G 5S5
613-954-1313, Fax: 613-946-1588, 800-363-0076, info@ocrt-bctr.gc.ca

Pension Appeals Board, PO Box 8567 T, Ottawa, ON K1G 3H9
613-995-0612, Fax: 613-995-6834, 888-640-8001, info@pab-cap.gc.ca

Public Sector Pension Investment Board, #200, 440 Laurier Ave. West, Ottawa, ON K1R 7X6
613-782-3095, Fax: 613-782-6864, info@investpsp.ca

Veterans Review & Appeal Board, Daniel J. MacDonald Bldg., 161 Grafton St., PO Box 9900, Charlottetown, PE C1A 8V7
902-566-8751, Fax: 902-566-7850, 800-450-8006, vrab_tacra@vac-acc.gc.ca

Alberta

Alberta Pensions Services Corporation, 5103 Windermere Blvd. SW, Edmonton, AB T6W 0S9
780-427-2782, 800-661-8198, memberservices@apsc.ca; employerservices@apsc.ca; pay@apsc.ca

British Columbia

British Columbia Pension Corporation, 2995 Jutland Rd., PO Box 9460, Victoria, BC V8W 9V8
250-387-1002, Fax: 250-953-0429, 800-663-8823, PensionCorp@pensionsbc.ca; Retired.Members@pensionsbc.ca

Manitoba

Pension Commission of Manitoba, #1004, 401 York Ave., Winnipeg, MB R3C 0P8
204-945-2740, Fax: 204-948-2375, pensions@gov.mb.ca

Teachers' Retirement Allowances Fund Board, #330 Johnston Terminal, 35 Forks Market Rd., Winnipeg, MB R3C 4S8
204-949-0048, Fax: 204-944-0361

Ontario

Financial Services Commission of Ontario, New York City Ctr., 5160 Yonge St., 17th Fl., PO Box 85, Toronto, ON M2N 6L9
416-250-7250, Fax: 416-590-7070, 800-668-0128

Ontario Pension Board, Sun Life Bldg., #2200, 200 King St. West, Toronto, ON M5H 3X6
416-364-8558, Fax: 416-364-7578, 800-668-6203, office.services@opb.on.ca

OPSEU Pension Trust, #1200, 1 Adelaide St. East, Toronto, ON M5C 3A7
416-681-6161, Fax: 416-681-6175, 800-637-0024

Quebec

Commission administrative des régimes de retraite et d'assurances (Québec), 475, rue Saint-Amable, Québec, QC G1R 5X3
418-643-4881, Fax: 418-644-3839, 800-463-5533

Régie des rentes du Québec, CP 5200, Sainte-Foy, QC G1K 7S9
418-643-5185, 800-463-5185, rrq@rrq.gouv.qc.ca

Saskatchewan

Crown Investments Corporation of Saskatchewan, #400, 2400 College Ave., Regina, SK S4P 1C8
306-787-6851, Fax: 306-787-8125

Saskatchewan Financial Services Commission, #601, 1919 Saskatchewan Dr., Regina, SK S4P 4H2
306-787-5645, Fax: 306-787-5899

PESTICIDES, HERBICIDES

Farm Financial Programs Branch, Tower 7, 1341 Baseline Rd., Ottawa, ON K1A 0C5
613-759-1000, Fax: 613-773-2121

Pest Management Regulatory Agency, 2720 Riverside Dr., Ottawa, ON K1A 0K9
613-736-3401, Fax: 613-736-3798

New Brunswick

Environmental Management, Marysville Place, 20 McGloin St., PO Box 6000, Fredericton, NB E3B 5H1
506-444-5119, Fax: 506-457-7333, env-info@gnb.ca

Ontario

Pesticides Advisory Committee, 135 St. Clair Ave. West, 15th Fl., Toronto, ON M4V 1P5
416-314-9230, Fax: 416-314-9237

PIPELINES

Alberta

Energy Resources Conservation Board, #1000, 250 - 5 Ave. SW, Calgary, AB T2P 0R4
403-297-8311, Fax: 403-297-7336, 855-297-8311, inquiries@ercb.ca; infoservices@ercb.ca; ADR@ercb.ca

Alberta Energy, North Petroleum Plaza, 9945 - 108 St., Edmonton, AB T5K 2G6
780-427-8050, Fax: 780-422-0698, Library.Energy@gov.ab.ca

British Columbia

British Columbia Hydro, 333 Dunsmuir St., Vancouver, BC V6B 5R3
604-224-9376, 800-224-9376,

New Brunswick

Lands, Minerals & Petroleum Division, Hugh John Flemming Forestry Centre, PO Box 6000, Fredericton, NB E3B 5H1
506-453-2684, Fax: 506-453-2930, dnrweb@gnb.ca

National Energy Board, 444 - 7 Ave. SW, Calgary, AB T2P 0X8
403-292-4800, Fax: 403-292-5503, 800-899-1265, info@neb-one.gc.ca

Northwest Territories

Department of Environment & Natural Resources, PO Box 1320, Yellowknife, NT X1A 2L9

Nova Scotia

Department of Energy, Bank of Montreal Bldg., #400, 5151 George St., PO Box 2664, Halifax, NS B3J 3P7
902-424-4575, Fax: 902-424-0528, energyinfo@gov.ns.ca

Nova Scotia Utility & Review Board, Summit Place, 1601 Lower Water St., 3rd Fl., PO Box 1692 M,Halifax, NS B3J 3S3
902-424-4448, Fax: 902-424-3919, uarb.board@gov.ns.ca

Saskatchewan

SaskEnergy Incorporated, 1777 Victoria Ave., Regina, SK S4P 4K5
306-777-9225, 800-567-8899

POLICING SERVICES

Royal Canadian Mounted Police, 1200 Vanier Pkwy., Ottawa, ON K1A 0R2
613-993-7267, Fax: 613-993-0260

Alberta

Public Security Division, John E. Brownlee Building, 10365 - 97 St., 10th Fl., Edmonton, AB T5J 3W7
780-427-7952, Fax: 780-427-1194, bill.meade@gov.ab.ca

British Columbia

Management Services Branch, PO Box 9256 Prov Govt,Victoria, BC V8W 9J4
250-387-5258, Fax: 250-387-0081

Manitoba

Manitoba Justice, Legislative Building, #104, 405 Broadway Ave., Winnipeg, MB R3C 3L6
204-945-3728, Fax: 204-945-2517, minjus@gov.mb.ca

Law Enforcement Review Agency, #420, 155 Carlton St., Winnipeg, MB R3C 3H8
204-945-8667, Fax: 204-948-1014, 800-282-8069, lera@gov.mb.ca

New Brunswick

New Brunswick Police Commission, Fredericton City Centre, #202, 435 King St., Fredericton, NB E3B 1E5
506-453-2069, Fax: 506-457-3542, nbpc@gnb.ca

Newfoundland & Labrador

Royal Newfoundland Constabulary Public Complaints Commission, Bally Rou Place, #E-160, 280 Torbay Rd., St. John's, NL A1A 3W8
709-729-0950, Fax: 709-729-1302, rnccomplaintscommission@gov.nl.ca

Nova Scotia

Nova Scotia Police Commission, #300, 1601 Lower Water St., PO Box 1573, Halifax, NS B3J 2Y3
902-424-3246, Fax: 902-424-3919, uarb.polcom@gov.ns.ca

Nunavut

Department of Justice, Sivummut, 1st Fl., PO Box 1000 500,Iqaluit, NU X0A 0H0
867-975-6170, Fax: 867-975-6195, justice@gov.nu.ca

Ontario

Ontario Provincial Police, Lincoln M. Alexander Bldg., 777 Memorial Ave., Orillia, ON L3V 7V3
705-329-6111, 888-310-1122

Quebec

Direction générale de la Sûreté du Québec, 1701, rue Parthenais, Montréal, QC H2K 3S7
514-598-4141, Fax: 514-598-4242

Saskatchewan

Saskatchewan Public Complaints Commission, #300, 1919 Saskatchewan Dr., Regina, SK S4P 4H2
306-787-6519, Fax: 306-787-6528, 866-256-6194

Yukon Territory

Yukon Justice, Andrew Philipsen Law Centre, 2134 Second Ave., PO Box 2703, Whitehorse, YT Y1A 2C6
867-667-3033, Fax: 867-393-5790, jus.msb@gov.yk.ca

POLITICS & SOCIETY

Auditor General of Canada, 240 Sparks St., Ottawa, ON K1A 0G6
613-995-3708, Fax: 613-957-0474, 888-761-5953, communications@oag-bvg.gc.ca; infomedia@oag-bvg.gc.ca

Canadian International Development Agency, 200, Promenade du Portage, Gatineau, QC K1A 0G4
819-997-5456, Fax: 819-953-6088, 800-230-6349, info@acdi-cida.gc.ca

Commission for Environmental Cooperation, Secretariat, #200, 393, rue St-Jacques ouest, Montréal, QC H2Y 1N9
514-350-4300, Fax: 514-350-4314, info@cec.org

Finance Canada, L'esplanade Laurier, 140 O'Connor St., Ottawa, ON K1A 0G5
613-992-1573, Fax: 613-943-0938, finpub@fin.gc.ca
Foreign Affairs & International Trade Canada, 125 Sussex Dr., Ottawa, ON K1A 0G2
613-944-4000, Fax: 613-996-9709, 800-267-8376, enqserv@international.gc.ca
International Development Research Centre, 150 Kent St., PO Box 8500, Ottawa, ON K1G 3H9
613-236-6163, Fax: 613-238-7230, info@idrc.ca
International Joint Commission, 234 Laurier Ave. West, 22nd Fl., Ottawa, ON K1P 6K6
613-947-1420, Fax: 613-993-5583, beckhoffb@ottawa.ijc.org
National Capital Commission, #202, 40 Elgin St., Ottawa, ON K1P 1C7
613-239-5555, Fax: 613-239-5063, 800-704-8227, info@ncc-ccn.ca
National Defence Canada, Major-General George R. Pearkes Bldg., 101 Colonel By Dr., Ottawa, ON K1A 0K2
613-995-2534, Fax: 613-992-4739, 800-856-8488
National Round Table on the Environment & Economy, #200, 344 Slater St., Ottawa, ON K1R 7Y3
613-992-7189, Fax: 613-992-7385, admin@nrtee-trnee.ca
Public Safety Canada, 269 Laurier Ave. West, Ottawa, ON K1A 0P8
613-944-4875, Fax: 613-954-5186, 800-830-3118, communications@ps.gc.ca
Public Works & Government Services Canada, Place du Portage, Phase III, 11, rue Laurier, Ottawa, ON K1A 0S5
questions@tpsgc-pwgsc.gc.ca
Strategic Policy Branch, Tower 7, 1341 Baseline Rd., Ottawa, ON K1A 0C5
613-759-1000, Fax: 613-773-2111

Alberta
Alberta International & Intergovernmental Relations, Commerce Place, 10155 - 102 St., 12th Fl., Edmonton, AB T5J 4G8
780-422-1510, Fax: 780-427-0699
Alberta Public Affairs Bureau, Park Plaza, 10611 - 98 Ave., 6th Fl., Edmonton, AB T5K 2P7
780-427-2754, Fax: 780-422-4168

British Columbia
Ministry of Community, Sport & Cultural Development, PO Box 9056 Prov Govt,Victoria, BC V8W 9E2
250-387-2283, Fax: 250-387-4312

Manitoba
Manitoba Round Table for Sustainable Development, #160, 123 Main St., Winnipeg, MB R3C 1A5
204-945-1671, Fax: 204-948-2357, mrtsd@gov.mb.ca

New Brunswick
Department of Supply & Services, PO Box 6000, Fredericton, NB E3B 5H1
506-453-3742, Fax: 506-444-4400, Reception.Marysville@gnb.ca
New Brunswick Round Table on Environment & Economy, 20 McGloin St., PO Box 6000, Fredericton, NB E3B 5H1
506-453-3703, Fax: 506-453-3876

Newfoundland & Labrador
Department of Government Services, PO Box 8700, St. John's, NL A1B 4J6
709-729-4834, gsinfo@gov.nl.ca
Department of Transportation & Works, Confederation Bldg., West Block, 6th Fl., PO Box 8700, St. John's, NL A1B 4J6
709-729-3679, Fax: 709-729-4285, twminister@gov.nl.ca

Northwest Territories
Department of Aboriginal Affairs & Intergovernmental Relations, 4910 - 52nd St., PO Box 1320, Yellowknife, NT X1A 2L9
867-873-7143, Fax: 867-873-0233, 877-838-8194, nancy_gardiner@gov.nt.ca
Department of Public Works & Services, PO Box 1320, Yellowknife, NT X1A 2L9

Nova Scotia
Nova Scotia Emergency Management Office, PO Box 2581, Halifax, NS B3J 3N5
902-424-5620, Fax: 902-424-5376, 866-424-5620, emo@gov.ns.ca

Ontario
Environmental Commissioner of Ontario, #605, 1075 Bay St., Toronto, ON M5S 2B1
416-325-3377, Fax: 416-325-3370, 800-701-6454, commissioner@eco.on.ca
Environmental Review Tribunal, #1500, 655 Bay St., Toronto, ON M5G 1E5
416-212-6349, Fax: 416-314-4506, 866-448-2248, erttribunalsecretary@ontario.ca

Prince Edward Island
Prince Edward Island Department of Health & Wellness, 105 Rochford St. North, 4th Fl., PO Box 2000, Charlottetown, PE C1A 7N8
902-368-6414, Fax: 902-368-4121

Saskatchewan
Saskatchewan First Nations & Métis Relations, #1020, 1855 Victoria Ave., Regina, SK S4P 3T2
306-787-6250, Fax: 306-798-0083
Saskatchewan Government Services, 1920 Rose St., Regina, SK S4P 0A9
306-787-6911, Fax: 306-787-1061, GSReception@gs.gov.sk.ca

Yukon Territory
Emergency Measures Organization, PO Box 2703, Whitehorse, YT Y1A 2C6
867-667-5220, Fax: 867-393-6266, 800-661-0408, emo.yukon@gov.yk.ca

POPULATION

See Also: Statistics

Statistics Canada, R.H. Coats Bldg., Tunney's Pasture, 150 Tunney's Pasture Driveway, Ottawa, ON K1A 0T6
613-951-8116, Fax: 877-287-4369, 800-263-1136, infostats@statcan.ca

Alberta
Registry Services, Telus Plaza South, 10020 - 100 St., 29th Fl., Edmonton, AB T5J 0N3

Manitoba
Manitoba Bureau of Statistics, #824, 155 Carlton St., Winnipeg, MB R3C 3H9
204-945-2406, Fax: 204-945-0695

Nunavut
Department of Executive & Intergovernmental Affairs, 1084 Aeroplex bldg., PO Box 1000 200,Iqaluit, NU X0A 0H0
867-975-6000, Fax: 867-975-6099

Quebec
Institut de la statistique du Québec, 200, ch Ste-Foy, 1er étage, Québec, QC G1R 5T4
418-691-2401, Fax: 418-643-4129, 800-463-4090, direction@stat.gouv.qc.ca

POSTAL SERVICE

Canada Post Corporation, Corporate Secretariat, 2701 Riverside Dr., Ottawa, ON K1A 0B1
866-607-6301

PREMIERS & LEADERS

See Also: Cabinets & Executive Councils; Government (General Info)

Office of the Prime Minister (Conservative Party of Canada), Langevin Block, 80 Wellington St., Ottawa, ON K1A 0A2
613-992-4211, Fax: 613-941-6900, pm@pm.gc.ca

Alberta
Office of the Premier, Office of the Premier, Legislature Building, #307, 10800 - 97 Ave., Edmonton, AB T5K 2B6
780-427-2251, Fax: 780-427-1349

British Columbia
Office of the Premier, West Annex, Parliament Bldgs., PO Box 9041 Prov Govt,Victoria, BC V8W 9E1
250-387-1715, Fax: 250-387-0087, premier@gov.bc.ca

Manitoba
Office of the Premier, Legislative Building, #204, 450 Broadway Ave., Winnipeg, MB R3C 0V8
204-945-3714, Fax: 204-949-1484, premier@leg.gov.mb.ca

New Brunswick
Office of the Premier, Centennial Bldg., 670 King St., PO Box 6000, Fredericton, NB E3B 5H1
506-453-2144, Fax: 506-453-7407, premier@gnb.ca

Newfoundland & Labrador
Office of the Premier, East Block, Confederation Bldg., 8th F., PO Box 8700, St. John's, NL A1B 4J6
709-729-3570, Fax: 709-729-5875, premier@gov.nl.ca

Northwest Territories
Office of the Premier, Legislative Assembly Bldg., PO Box 1320, Yellowknife, NT X1A 2L9
867-669-2311, Fax: 867-873-0385, premier@gov.nt.ca

Nova Scotia
Office of the Premier, One Government Place, 1700 Granville St., 7th Fl., PO Box 726, Halifax, NS B3J 2T3
902-424-6600, Fax: 902-424-7648, 800-267-1993, premier@gov.ns.ca

Nunavut
Office of the Premier, Legislative Assembly Bldg., 2nd Fl., PO Box 2410, Iqaluit, NU X0A 0H0
867-975-5050, Fax: 867-975-5051

Ontario
Office of the Premier, Legislative Bldg., #281, 1 Queen's Park Cres. South, Toronto, ON M7A 1A1
416-325-1941, Fax: 416-325-3745

Prince Edward Island
Office of the Premier, Shaw Bldg., 95 Rochford St. South, 5th Fl., PO Box 2000, Charlottetown, PE C1A 7N8
902-368-4501, Fax: 902-368-6118

Quebec
Cabinet du premier ministre, Édifice Honoré-Mercier, 835, boul René-Lévesque est, 3e étage, Québec, QC G1A 1B4
418-643-5321, Fax: 418-643-3924

Saskatchewan
Office of the Premier, Legislative Bldg., #226, 2405 Legislative Dr., Regina, SK S4S 0B3
306-787-9433, Fax: 306-787-0885, premier@gov.sk.ca

Yukon Territory
Office of the Premier, 2071 Second Ave., PO Box 2703, Whitehorse, YT Y1A 1B2
867-667-8660, Fax: 867-393-6252, premier@gov.yk.ca

PROPERTY ASSESSMENT

Alberta
Registry Services, Telus Plaza South, 10020 - 100 St., 29th Fl., Edmonton, AB T5J 0N3

British Columbia
British Columbia Assessment Authority, #400, 3450 Uptown Blvd., Victoria, BC V8Z 0B9
250-595-6211, Fax: 250-595-6222, info@bcassessment.ca

New Brunswick
Assessment & Planning Appeal Board, #201, 435 King St., PO Box 6000, Fredericton, NB E3B 5H1
506-453-2126, Fax: 506-444-4881

Newfoundland & Labrador
Department of Municipal Affairs, West Block, Main Fl., Confederation Bldg., PO Box 8700, St. John's, NL A1B 4J6
709-729-3046, Fax: 709-729-0943, mainfo@gov.nl.ca

Northwest Territories
Assessment Appeal Tribunal of the Northwest Territories, #400, 5201 - 50th Ave., PO Box 1320, Yellowknife, NT X1A 2L9
867-873-7125, Fax: 867-873-0609

Prince Edward Island
Prince Edward Island Regulatory & Appeals Commission, National Bank Tower, #501, 134 Kent St., PO Box 577, Charlottetown, PE C1A 7L1
902-892-3501, Fax: 902-566-4076, 800-501-6268, info@irac.pe.ca

Saskatchewan
Saskatchewan Assessment Management Agency, #200, 2201 - 11th Ave., Regina, SK S4P 0J8
306-924-8000, Fax: 306-924-8070, 800-667-7262, info.request@sama.sk.ca

PROTOCOL (STATE)

See Also: Parliament

Governor General & Commander-in-Chief of Canada, Rideau Hall, 1 Sussex Dr., Ottawa, ON K1A 0A1
613-993-8200, Fax: 613-998-8760, 800-465-6890, info@gg.ca
Office of Protocol, 125 Sussex Dr., Ottawa, ON K1A 0G2
613-996-8683, Fax: 613-943-1075

Prince Edward Island
Office of the Lieutenant Governor, Government House, PO Box 846, Charlottetown, PE C1A 7L9
902-368-5480, Fax: 902-368-5481

PUBLIC SAFETY

See Also: Occupational Safety

Canadian Coast Guard, Centennial Towers, #6S018, 200 Kent St., Ottawa, ON K1A 0E6
613-993-0999, Fax: 613-990-1866, info@dfo-mpo.gc.ca
Canadian Security Intelligence Service, PO Box 9732 T,Ottawa, ON K1G 4G4
613-993-9620, Fax: 613-231-0612
Canadian Transportation Agency, Les Terrasses de la Chaudière, 15, rue Eddy, Gatineau, QC J8X 4B3
Fax: 819-997-6727, 888-222-2592, info@otc-cta.gc.ca
Communications Security Establishment, 1500 Bronson Avenue, PO Box 9703 Terminal, Ottawa, ON K1A 0K2
613-991-7600, Fax: 613-991-8514
National Defence Canada, Major-General George R. Pearkes Bldg., 101 Colonel By Dr., Ottawa, ON K1A 0K2
613-995-2534, Fax: 613-992-4739, 800-856-8488
Office of the Communications Security Establishment Commissioner, PO Box 1984 B, Ottawa, ON K1P 5R5
613-992-3044
Prince Edward Island Department of Justice & Public Safety, Shaw Bldg., 95 Rochford St. South, 4th Fl., PO Box 2000, Charlottetown, PE C1A 7N8
Public Safety Canada, 269 Laurier Ave. West, Ottawa, ON K1A 0P8
613-944-4875, Fax: 613-954-5186, 800-830-3118, communications@ps.gc.ca
Royal Canadian Mounted Police, 1200 Vanier Pkwy., Ottawa, ON K1A 0R2
613-993-7267, Fax: 613-993-0260

Alberta
Public Security Division, John E. Brownlee Building, 10365 - 97 St., 10th Fl., Edmonton, AB T5J 3W7
780-427-7952, Fax: 780-427-1194, bill.meade@gov.ab.ca

British Columbia
Ministry of Public Safety & Solicitor General, PO Box 9290 Prov Govt,Victoria, BC V8W 9J7
250-387-6121, 800-663-7867, pssgwebfeedback@gov.bc.ca

New Brunswick
Department of Public Safety, 364 Argyle St., PO Box 6000, Fredericton, NB E3B 5H1
506-453-3992, Fax: 506-453-3870, DPS-MSP.Information@gnb.ca

Northwest Territories
Department of Justice, Courthouse, 4903 - 49th St., 6th Fl., PO Box 1320, Yellowknife, NT X1A 2L9
867-920-6197

Nunavut
Department of Justice, Sivummut, 1st Fl., PO Box 1000 500,Iqaluit, NU X0A 0H0
867-975-6170, Fax: 867-975-6195, justice@gov.nu.ca

Quebec
Ministère de la Sécurité publique, Tour des Laurentides, 2525, boul Laurier, 5e étage, Québec, QC G1V 2L2
418-643-2112, Fax: 418-646-6168, 866-644-6826

Saskatchewan
Saskatchewan Corrections, Public Safety & Policing, 1874 Scarth St., Regina, SK S4P 4B3
306-787-7872, communicationsCPSP@gov.sk.ca

PUBLIC SERVICES

Canada Deposit Insurance Corporation, 50 O'Connor St., 17th Floor, PO Box 2340 D,Ottawa, ON K1P 5W5
Fax: 613-996-6095, 800-461-2342, info@cdic.ca; info@sadc.ca

Canada Post Corporation, Corporate Secretariat, 2701 Riverside Dr., Ottawa, ON K1A 0B1
866-607-6301

Canadian Broadcasting Corporation, 181 Queen St., PO Box 3220 C,Ottawa, ON K1Y 1E4
613-288-6033, liaison@radio-canada.ca

Canadian Centre for Occupational Health & Safety, 135 Hunter St. East, Hamilton, ON L8N 1M5
905-572-2981, Fax: 905-572-2206, 800-668-4284

Canadian Coast Guard, Centennial Towers, #6S018, 200 Kent St., Ottawa, ON K1A 0E6
613-993-0999, Fax: 613-990-1866, info@dfo-mpo.gc.ca

Canadian Security Intelligence Service, PO Box 9732 T,Ottawa, ON K1G 4G4
613-993-9620, Fax: 613-231-0612

Citizenship & Immigration Canada, Jean Edmonds, South Tower, 365 Laurier Ave. West, Ottawa, ON K1A 1L1
613-954-9019, Fax: 613-954-2221, 888-242-2100

Commission for Public Complaints Against the Royal Canadian Mounted Police, National Intake Office, PO Box 88689, Surrey, BC V3W 0X1
Fax: 613-952-8045, 800-665-6878, org@cpc-cpp.gc.ca

Corporate & Financial Services Division, Jones Bldg., 11 Kent St., 2nd Fl., PO Box 2000, Charlottetown, PE C1A 7N8
Fax: 902-894-0242,

Correctional Service Canada, 340 Laurier Ave. West, Ottawa, ON K1A 0P9
613-992-5891, Fax: 613-943-1630

Health Services Information & Information Technology Cluster, 56 Wellesley St. West, 10th Fl., Toronto, ON M5S 2S3
416-314-4243, Fax: 416-314-0289

Health Workforce Division, Telus Plaza NT, 10025 Jasper Ave., 10th Fl., Edmonton, AB T5J 1S6

Human Resources & Skills Development Canada, 140 Promenade du Portage, Gatineau, QC K1A 0J9

Immigration & Refugee Board of Canada, Canada Bldg, 344 Slater St., 12th Fl., Ottawa, ON K1A 0K1
613-995-6486, Fax: 613-943-1550, contact@irb-cisr.gc.ca

Legal Services Division, Bowker Building, 9833 - 109 St., 2nd Fl., Edmonton, AB T5K 2E8
780-422-0500

MERX, PO Box 11684 Centre-ville,Montreal, QC H3C 6H4
Fax: 888-235-5800, merx@merx.com

Military Police Complaints Commission, 270 Albert St., 10th Fl., Ottawa, ON K1P 5G8
613-947-5625, Fax: 613-947-5713, 800-632-0566, commission@mpcc-cppm.gc.ca

National Capital Commission, #202, 40 Elgin St., Ottawa, ON K1P 1C7
613-239-5555, Fax: 613-239-5063, 800-704-8227, info@ncc-ccn.ca

National Defence Canada, Major-General George R. Pearkes Bldg., 101 Colonel By Dr., Ottawa, ON K1A 0K2
613-995-2534, Fax: 613-992-4739, 800-856-8488

National Parole Board, 410 Laurier Ave. West, Ottawa, ON K1A 0R1
613-954-7474, Fax: 613-995-4380, 800-874-2652, info@npb-cnlc.gc.ca

National Search & Rescue Secretariat, #400, 275 Slater St., Ottawa, ON K1A 0K2
613-992-0054, Fax: 613-996-3746, 800-727-9414, inquiry@nss.gc.ca

Public Service Commission, West Tower, 300 Laurier Ave. West, Ottawa, ON K1A 0M7
613-992-9562, Fax: 613-992-9352, infocom@psc-cfp.gc.ca

Public Service Staffing Tribunal, 240 Sparks St., 6th Fl., Ottawa, ON K1A 0A5
613-949-6516, Fax: 613-949-6551, 866-637-4491, info@psst-tdfp.gc.ca

Public Works & Government Services Canada, Place du Portage, Phase III, 11, rue Laurier, Ottawa, ON K1A 0S5
questions@tpsgc-pwgsc.gc.ca

Royal Canadian Mounted Police, 1200 Vanier Pkwy., Ottawa, ON K1A 0R2
613-993-7267, Fax: 613-993-0260

Royal Canadian Mounted Police External Review Committee, PO Box 1159 B, Ottawa, ON K1P 5R2
613-998-2134, Fax: 613-990-8969, org@erc-cee.gc.ca

Security Intelligence Review Committee, Jackson Bldg., 122 Bank St., 4th Fl., PO Box 2430 D,Ottawa, ON K1P 5W5
613-990-8441, Fax: 613-990-5230, ellardm@sirc-csars.gc.ca

Veterans Affairs Canada, 161 Grafton St., PO Box 7700, Charlottetown, PE C1A 8M9
902-566-8888, 866-522-2111, information@vac-acc.gc.ca

Veterans Review & Appeal Board, Daniel J. MacDonald Bldg., 161 Grafton St., PO Box 9900, Charlottetown, PE C1A 8V7
902-566-8751, Fax: 902-566-7850, 800-450-8006, vrab_tacra@vac-acc.gc.ca

Alberta
Alberta Capital Finance Authority, Canadian Western Bank Place, #2450, 10303 Jasper Ave., Edmonton, AB T5J 3N6
780-427-9711, Fax: 780-422-2175, webacfa@gov.ab.ca

Alberta Health Services, Corporate Office, North Tower, Seventh Street Plaza, 10030 - 107th St. NW, 14th Fl., Edmonton, AB T5J 3E4
780-342-2000, Fax: 780-342-2060, 888-342-2471, ahsb.admin@albertahealthservices.ca

Alberta Labour Relations Board, Labour Building, 10808 - 99 Ave., 5th Fl., Edmonton, AB T5K 0G5
780-422-5926, Fax: 780-422-0970, 800-463-2572, alrbinfo@lab.gov.ab.ca

Alberta Pensions Services Corporation, 5103 Windermere Blvd. SW, Edmonton, AB T6W 0S9
780-427-2782, 800-661-8198, memberservices@apsc.ca; employerservices@apsc.ca; pay@apsc.ca

Alberta Children & Youth Services, Communications, Sterling Place, 9940 - 106 St., 12th Fl., Edmonton, AB T5K 2N2
780-422-3004, Fax: 780-422-3071, cs.communications@gov.ab.ca

Energy Resources Conservation Board, #1000, 250 - 5 Ave. SW, Calgary, AB T2P 0R4
403-297-8311, Fax: 403-297-7336, 855-297-8311, inquiries@ercb.ca; infoservices@ercb.ca; ADR@ercb.ca

Alberta Infrastructure, Infrastructure Building, 6950 - 113 St., Edmonton, AB T6H 5V7
780-415-0507, Fax: 780-427-2187, Infra.Contact.Us.m@gov.ab.ca

Alberta Municipal Affairs, Communications Branch, Commerce Place, 10155 - 102 St., 18th Fl., Edmonton, AB T5J 4L4
780-427-2732, Fax: 780-422-1419, comments@gov.ab.ca

Municipal Government Board, Commerce Place, 10155 - 102 St., 15th Fl., Edmonton, AB T5J 4L4
780-427-4864, Fax: 780-427-0986, mgbmail@gov.ab.ca

Public Security Division, John E. Brownlee Building, 10365 - 97 St., 10th Fl., Edmonton, AB T5J 3W7
780-427-7952, Fax: 780-427-1194, bill.meade@gov.ab.ca

Alberta Tourism, Parks, & Recreation, Communications Branch, Commerce Place, 10155 - 102 St., 6th Fl., Edmonton, AB T5J 4L6
780-644-5589, TPR.Communications@gov.ab.ca

British Columbia
British Columbia Assessment Authority, #400, 3450 Uptown Blvd., Victoria, BC V8Z 0B9
250-595-6211, Fax: 250-595-6222, info@bcassessment.ca

British Columbia Transit, 520 Gorge Rd. East, Victoria, BC V8W 2P3
250-385-2551, Fax: 250-995-5639

Ministry of Children & Family Development, PO Box 9770 Prov Govt,Victoria, BC V8W 9S5
250-387-7027, 877-387-7027, MCF.CorrespondenceManagement@gov.bc.ca

British Columbia Ferry Services Inc., #500, 1321 Blanshard St., Victoria, BC V8W 0B7
250-381-1401, 888-223-3779

Local Government, PO Box 9490 Prov Govt,Victoria, BC V8W 9N7
250-356-6575, Fax: 250-387-7973

Management Services Branch, PO Box 9256 Prov Govt,Victoria, BC V8W 9J4
250-387-5258, Fax: 250-387-0081

Office of the Representative for Children & Youth, #201, 546 Yates St., Victoria, BC V8W 1K8
250-356-6710, Fax: 250-356-0837, 800-476-3933, rcy@rcybc.ca

British Columbia Provincial Emergency Program, Block A, #200, 2261 Keating Cross Rd., Saanichton, BC V8M 2A5
250-952-4913, Fax: 250-952-4888, 888-257-4777

BC Public Service Agency, #4, 810 Blanshard St., PO Box 9404 Prov Govt,Victoria, BC V8W 9V1
250-387-0518, Fax: 250-356-7074

Shared Services BC, Chief Operating Office, PO Box 9412 Prov Govt,Victoria, BC V8W 9V1
250-952-6861, Fax: 250-387-5693

Manitoba
Advisory Council on Workplace Safety & Health, #200, 401 York Ave., Winnipeg, MB R3C 0P8
204-945-3446, Fax: 204-945-4556

Office of the Auditor General, #500, 330 Portage Ave., Winnipeg, MB R3C 0C4
204-945-3790, Fax: 204-945-2169, oag.contact@oag.mb.ca

Automobile Injury Compensation Appeal Commission, #301, 428 Portage Ave.., Winnipeg, MB R3C 0E2
204-945-4155, Fax: 204-948-2402, autoinjury@gov.mb.ca

Civil Service Commission Board, #935, 155 Carlton St., Winnipeg, MB R3C 3H8
204-945-1435, Fax: 204-945-1486

Manitoba Civil Service Commission, #935, 155 Carlton St., Winnipeg, MB R3C 3H8
204-945-2332, Fax: 204-945-1486, 800-282-8069, cschrp@gov.mb.ca

Credit Union Deposit Guarantee Corporation, #390, 200 Graham Ave., Winnipeg, MB R3C 4L5
204-942-8480, Fax: 204-947-1723, 800-697-4447, mail@cudgc.com

Manitoba Culture, Heritage, Tourism & Sport, Legislative Building, #118, 450 Broadway Ave., Winnipeg, MB R3C 0V8
204-945-3729, Fax: 204-945-5223, mincht@leg.gov.mb.ca

Emergency Measures Organization, 405 Broadway Ave., 15th Floor, Winnipeg, MB R3C 3L6
204-945-4772, Fax: 204-945-4929, 888-267-8298, emo@gov.mb.ca

Employment, Income & Housing Division, #201, 280 Broadway Ave., Winnipeg, MB R3C 0R8

Manitoba Family Services & Housing, #219, 114 Garry St., Winnipeg, MB R3C 4V6
204-945-3242, Fax: 204-945-2156, minfam@leg.gov.mb.ca

Manitoba Health & Healthy Living, #100, 300 Carlton St., Winnipeg, MB R3B 3M9
204-786-7191, minhlt@leg.gov.mb.ca

Manitoba Human Rights Commission, 175 Hargrave St., 7th Fl., Winnipeg, MB R3C 3R8
204-945-3007, Fax: 204-945-1292, 888-884-8681, hrc@gov.mb.ca

Manitoba Hydro, PO Box 815 Main,Winnipeg, MB R3C 2P4
204-474-3311, Fax: 204-475-0069, publicaffairs@hydro.mb.ca

Manitoba Infrastructure & Transportation, Legislative Building, #203, 450 Broadway Ave., Winnipeg, MB R3C 0V8
204-945-3723, Fax: 204-945-7610

Manitoba Public Insurance, #B100, 234 Donald St., PO Box 6300, Winnipeg, MB R3C 4A4
204-985-7000, Fax: 204-985-3525, 800-665-2410

Manitoba Justice, Legislative Building, #104, 405 Broadway Ave., Winnipeg, MB R3C 3L6
204-945-3728, Fax: 204-945-2517, minjus@gov.mb.ca

Manitoba Labour & Immigration, Legislative Building, 317, 450 Broadway Ave., Winnipeg, MB R3C 0V8
204-945-4079, Fax: 204-945-8312, minlab@leg.gov.mb.ca

Local Government Development Division, 59 Elizabeth Dr., PO Box 33, Thompson, MB R8N 1X4
204-677-6794, Fax: 204-677-6525,

Manitoba Bureau of Statistics, #824, 155 Carlton St., Winnipeg, MB R3C 3H9
204-945-2406, Fax: 204-945-0695

Manitoba Film Classification Board, #216, 301 Weston St., Winnipeg, MB R3E 3H4
204-945-8962, Fax: 204-945-0890, 866-612-2399, mfcb@gov.mb.ca

Manitoba Housing & Renewal Corporation, 280 Broadway, Winnipeg, MB R3C 0R8
204-945-4895, Fax: 204-945-5710

Manitoba Housing Authority - Public Housing, #2100, 185 Smith St., Winnipeg, MB R3C 3G4
204-945-4663, Fax: 204-948-2013, 800-661-4663

Manitoba Labour Board, A.A. Heaps Bldg., #402, 258 Portage Ave., Winnipeg, MB R3C 0B6
204-945-3783, Fax: 204-945-1296, mlb@gov.mb.ca
Manitoba Land Value Appraisal Commission, 800 Portage Ave., Winnipeg, MB R3G 0N4
204-945-2941, Fax: 204-948-2235
Manitoba Minimum Wage Board, 614 - 401 York Ave., Winnipeg, MB R3C 0P8
204-945-4889, Fax: 204-948-2085, mw@gov.mb.ca
Manitoba News Media Services, #29, Legislative Bldg., 450 Broadway, Winnipeg, MB R3C 0V8
204-945-3746, Fax: 204-945-3988, nmservices@leg.gov.mb.ca
Office of the Fire Commissioner, #508, 401 York Ave., Winnipeg, MB R3C 0P8
204-945-3322, Fax: 204-948-2089, 800-282-8069, firecomm@gov.mb.ca
Primary Care & Healthy Living, 300 Carlton St., 2nd Floor, Winnipeg, MB R3B 3M9
Provincial-Municipal Support Services, #508, 800 Portage Ave., Winnipeg, MB R3G 0N4
Public Utilities Board, #400, 330 Portage Ave., Winnipeg, MB R3C 0C4
204-945-2638, Fax: 204-945-2643, 866-854-3698, publicutilities@gov.mb.ca
Manitoba Seniors & Healthy Aging Secretariat, #822, 155 Carlton St., Winnipeg, MB R3C 3H8
204-945-6565, Fax: 204-948-2514, 800-665-6565, seniors@gov.mb.ca
Manitoba Telecom Services Inc., 333 Main St., PO Box 6666, Winnipeg, MB R3C 3V6
204-941-4111, Fax: 204-772-6391
Manitoba Workers' Compensation Board, 333 Broadway Ave., Winnipeg, MB R3C 4W3
204-954-4321, Fax: 204-954-4999, 800-362-3340, wcb@wcb.mb.ca
Workplace Safety & Health Division, #200, 401 York Ave., Winnipeg, MB R3C 0P8
204-945-3446, Fax: 204-948-2209, wshcompl@gov.mb.ca

New Brunswick

Communications New Brunswick, Wilcom Bldg., 225 King St., 2nd Fl., PO Box 6000, Fredericton, NB E3B 5H1
506-453-2240, Fax: 506-453-5329
Department of Health, PO Box 5100, Fredericton, NB E3B 5G8
506-457-4800, Fax: 506-453-5243, dh-ms@dh-ms.ca
Department of Post-Secondary Education, Training & Labour, Chestnut Complex, 470 York St., PO Box 6000, Fredericton, NB E3B 5H1
506-453-2597, Fax: 506-453-3618, dpetlinfo@gnb.ca
Department of Social Development, Sartain MacDonald Bldg., 551 King St., PO Box 6000, Fredericton, NB E3B 5H1
506-453-2001, Fax: 506-453-7478, sd-ds@gnb.ca
Premier's Council on the Status of Disabled Persons, Kings Place, #648, 440 King St., Fredericton, NB E3B 5H8
506-444-3000, Fax: 506-444-3001, 800-442-4412, pcsdp@gnb.ca
Family Income Security Appeal Board, PO Box 6000, Fredericton, NB E3B 5H1
506-525-4007, Fax: 506-525-4008
New Brunswick Human Rights Commission, PO Box 6000, Fredericton, NB E3B 5H1
506-453-2301, Fax: 506-453-2653, 888-471-2233, hrc.cdp@gnb.ca
Legislative Services, Centennial Bldg., #418, 670 King St., PO Box 6000, Fredericton, NB E3B 5H1
506-453-2855, Fax: 506-457-7342
New Brunswick Municipal Finance Corporation, #376, 670 King St., PO Box 6000, Fredericton, NB E3B 5H1
506-453-3952, Fax: 506-453-2053
Office of the Ombudsman, 767 Brunswick St., PO Box 6000, Fredericton, NB E3B 5H1
506-453-2789, Fax: 506-453-5599, 800-465-1100, nbombud@gnb.ca
New Brunswick Power Group of Companies, 515 King St., PO Box 2000, Fredericton, NB E3B 4X1
506-458-4444, Fax: 506-458-4000, questions@nbpower.com

Newfoundland & Labrador

C.A. Pippy Park Commission, Mount Scio House, 15 Mount Scio Rd., St. John's, NL A1B 3T2
709-737-3655, Fax: 709-737-3303, info@pippypark.com
Department of Government Services, PO Box 8700, St. John's, NL A1B 4J6
709-729-4834, gsinfo@gov.nl.ca
Department of Human Resources, Labour & Employment, Confederation Bldg., PO Box 8700, St. John's, NL A1B 4J6
709-729-2480, Fax: 709-729-6996, hreweb@gov.nl.ca
Department of Municipal Affairs, West Block, Main Fl., Confederation Bldg., PO Box 8700, St. John's, NL A1B 4J6
709-729-3046, Fax: 709-729-0943, mainfo@gov.nl.ca
Department of Transportation & Works, Confederation Bldg., West Block, 6th Fl., PO Box 8700, St. John's, NL A1B 4J6
709-729-3679, Fax: 709-729-4285, twminister@gov.nl.ca
Eastern Waste Management Commission, #200, 120 Lemarchant Rd., St. John's, NL A1C 2H2
709-579-7960, Fax: 709-579-5392, info@easternwaste.ca
Newfoundland & Labrador Fire & Emergency Services, 25 Hallett Cres., PO Box 8700, St. John's, NL A1B 4J6
709-729-3703, Fax: 709-729-3757
Income & Employment Support Appeal Board, Confederation Bldg., PO Box 8700, St. John's, NL A1B 4J6
709-729-2479, Fax: 709-729-5139
Newfoundland & Labrador Legal Aid Commission, #300, 251 Empire Ave., PO Box 399 C, St. John's, NL A1C 5J9
709-753-7863, Fax: 709-753-6226, 800-563-9911, nlac@legalaid.nl.ca
Newfoundland & Labrador Liquor Corporation, 90 Kenmount Rd., PO Box 8750 A, St. John's, NL A1B 3V1
709-724-1100, Fax: 709-754-0321, info@nfliquor.com
Newfoundland & Labrador Public Service Commission, 2 Canada Dr., 3rd Fl., PO Box 8700, St. John's, NL A1B 4J6
709-729-5810, Fax: 709-729-6234
Royal Newfoundland Constabulary Public Complaints Commission, Bally Rou Place, #E-160, 280 Torbay Rd., St. John's, NL A1A 3W8
709-729-0950, Fax: 709-729-1302, rnccomplaintscommission@gov.nl.ca

Northwest Territories

Department of Health & Social Services, Centre Square Tower, PO Box 1320, Yellowknife, NT X1A 2L9
Fax: 867-873-0266
Department of Municipal & Community Affairs, PO Box 1320, Yellowknife, NT X1A 2L9
867-873-7118, Fax: 867-873-0309
Department of Public Works & Services, PO Box 1320, Yellowknife, NT X1A 2L9
Northwest Territories Housing Corporation, Scotia Centre, 5102 50th Ave., PO Box 2100, Yellowknife, NT X1A 2P6
867-873-7853, Fax: 867-873-9426
Northwest Territories Power Corporation, 4 Capital Dr., Hay River, NT X0E 1G2
867-874-5200, Fax: 867-874-5251, info@ntpc.com
Victims Assistance Committee, c/o Community Justice Division, PO Box 1320, Yellowknife, NT X1A 2L9
867-920-6911, Fax: 867-873-0199
Northwest Territories Water Board, 125 Mackenzie Rd., PO Box 2531, Yellowknife, NT X0E 0T0
867-678-2942, Fax: 867-678-2943, info@nwtwb.com

Nova Scotia

Department of Community Services, Nelson Place, 5675 Spring Garden Rd., 8th Fl., PO Box 696, Halifax, NS B3J 2T7
902-424-4304, Fax: 902-428-0618
Nova Scotia Emergency Management Office, PO Box 2581, Halifax, NS B3J 3N5
902-424-5620, Fax: 902-424-5376, 866-424-5620, emo@gov.ns.ca
Department of Health & Wellness, Joseph Howe Bldg., 1690 Hollis St., 4th Fl., PO Box 488, Halifax, NS B3J 2R8
902-424-5818, Fax: 902-424-0730, 800-387-6665, DoHweb@gov.ns.ca
Nova Scotia Disabled Persons Commission, Dartmouth Professional Center, #104, 277 Pleasant St., Dartmouth, NS B2Y 4B7
902-424-8280, Fax: 902-424-0592, 800-565-8280
Nova Scotia Legal Aid Commission, #102, 137 Chain Lake Dr., Halifax, NS B3S 1B3
902-420-6573, Fax: 902-420-3471, nsla.exec@ns.sympatico.ca
Nova Scotia Police Commission, #300, 1601 Lower Water St., PO Box 1573, Halifax, NS B3J 2Y3
902-424-3246, Fax: 902-424-3919, uarb.polcom@gov.ns.ca
Department of Transportation & Infrastructure Renewal, Johnston Bldg., 1672 Granville St., 2nd Fl., PO Box 186, Halifax, NS B3J 2N2
902-424-2297, Fax: 902-424-0532, tpwpaff@gov.ns.ca
Workers' Advisers Program, #502, 5670 Spring Garden Rd., PO Box 1063, Halifax, NS B3J 2X1
902-424-5050, Fax: 902-424-0530, 800-774-4712

Nunavut

Department of Community & Government Services, W.G. Brown Bldg., 4th Fl., PO Box 1000 700,Iqaluit, NU X0A 0H0
867-975-5400, Fax: 867-975-5305
Department of Finance, Bldg. 1079, 1st Fl., PO Box 1000 330,Iqaluit, NU X0A 0H0
867-975-5800, Fax: 867-975-5805
Department of Health & Social Services, PO Box 1000 1000,Iqaluit, NU X0A 0H0
867-975-5700, Fax: 867-975-5705,
Nunavut Emergency Management, PO Box 1000 700,Iqaluit, NU X0A 0H0
867-975-5403, Fax: 867-979-4221, 800-693-1666

Ontario

Advertising Review Board, Macdonald Block, #M2-56, 900 Bay St., 2nd Fl., Toronto, ON M7A 1N3
416-327-2183, Fax: 416-327-2179
Ministry of the Attorney General, McMurtry-Scott Bldg., 720 Bay St., 11th Fl., Toronto, ON M5G 2K1
416-326-2220, Fax: 416-326-4007, 800-518-7901
Ministry of Community & Social Services, Hepburn Block, 80 Grosvenor St., 6th Fl., Toronto, ON M7A 1E9
416-325-5666, Fax: 416-325-5172, 888-789-4199
Ministry of Community Safety & Correctional Services, George Drew Bldg., 25 Grosvenor St., 18th Fl., Toronto, ON M7A 1Y6
416-326-5000, Fax: 416-326-0498, 866-517-0571, mcscs.feedback@ontario.ca
Deposit Insurance Corporation of Ontario, #700, 4711 Yonge St., Toronto, ON M2N 6K8
416-325-9444, Fax: 416-325-9722, 800-268-6653
Fire Safety Commission, Place Nouveau Bldg., 5775 Yonge St., 7th Fl., Toronto, ON M2M 4J1
416-325-3100, Fax: 416-314-1217
Human Rights Tribunal of Ontario, 655 Bay St., 14th Fl., Toronto, ON M7A 2A3
416-326-1312, Fax: 416-326-2027, 866-598-0322, hrto.tdpo@ontario.ca
Hydro One Inc., North Tower, 483 Bay St., Toronto, ON M5G 2P5
416-345-5000, 877-955-1155, customercommunications@HydroOne.com
Independent Electricity System Operator, PO Box 4474 A,Toronto, ON M5W 4E5
905-403-6900, Fax: 905-403-6921, 888-448-7777, customer.relations@ieso.ca
Ministry of Municipal Affairs & Housing, College Park, 777 Bay St., 17th Fl., Toronto, ON M5G 2E5
416-585-7041, Fax: 416-585-6470, 866-220-2290, mininfo@ontario.ca
Office of the Employer Advisor, #704, 151 Bloor St. West., Toronto, ON M5S 1S4
416-327-0020, Fax: 416-327-0726, 800-387-0774
Office of the Worker Advisor, #1300, 123 Edward St., Toronto, ON M5G 1E2
416-325-8570, Fax: 416-325-4830, 800-435-8980
Ontario Pension Board, Sun Life Bldg., #2200, 200 King St. West, Toronto, ON M5H 3X6
416-364-8558, Fax: 416-364-7578, 800-668-6203, office.services@opb.on.ca
Ontario Power Generation, 700 University Ave., Toronto, ON M5G 1X6
416-592-2555, 877-592-2555, webmaster@opg.com
Public Safety Division, George Drew bldg, 25 Grosvenor St., 12th fl., Toronto, ON M7A 2H3
416-314-3000, Fax: 416-314-4037
Social Benefits Tribunal, 1075 Bay St., 7th Fl., Toronto, ON M5S 2B1
416-326-0978, Fax: 416-325-5135, 800-753-3895
Southern Ontario Library Service, #902, 111 Peter St., Toronto, ON M5V 2H1
416-961-1669, Fax: 416-961-5122, 800-387-5765
Ministry of Transportation, Ferguson Block, 77 Wellesley St. West, 3rd Fl., Toronto, ON M7A 1Z8
416-235-4686, Fax: 905-704-2001, 800-268-4686

Prince Edward Island

Island Waste Management Corporation, 110 Watts Ave., Charlottetown, PE C1E 2C1
902-894-0330, Fax: 902-894-0331, 888-280-8111, reception@iwmc.pe.ca; info@iwmc.pe.ca
Prince Edward Island Department of Community Services, Seniors, & Labour, Jones Bldg., 11 Kent St., 2nd Fl., PO Box 2000, Charlottetown, PE C1A 7N8
902-620-3777, Fax: 902-368-4740, 866-594-3777
Prince Edward Island Department of Health & Wellness, 105 Rochford St. North, 4th Fl., PO Box 2000, Charlottetown, PE C1A 7N8
902-368-6414, Fax: 902-368-4121
SkillsPEI, Atlantic Technology Centre, #212, 90 University Ave., Charlottetown, PE C1A 4K9
902-368-4260, Fax: 902-368-6340, 877-491-4766

Quebec

Ministère des Affaires municipales et Occupation du territoire, Aile Chaveau, 10, rue Pierre-Olivier-Chauveau, 3e étage, Québec, QC G1R 4J3
418-691-2019, Fax: 418-643-7385, communications@mamrot.gouv.qc.ca
Bureau des projets Centres hospitaliers universitaires de Montréal, CHUM, CUSM et CHU Sainte-Justine, #10.049, 2021, rue Union, Montréal, QC H3A 2S9
514-864-9883, Fax: 514-873-7362, info.construction3chu@msss.gouv.qc.ca
Commissariat des incendies, 455, rue Dupont, Québec, QC G1K 6N2
418-529-5706, Fax: 418-529-9922, cdelage@notarius.net

Commission administrative des régimes de retraite et d'assurances (Québec), 475, rue Saint-Amable, Québec, QC G1R 5X3
418-643-4881, Fax: 418-644-3839, 800-463-5533
Commission de la fonction publique (Québec), 800, Place d'Youville, 7e étage, Québec, QC G1R 3P4
418-643-1425, Fax: 418-643-7264, 800-432-0432, cfp@cfp.gouv.qc.ca
Commission municipale du Québec, Mezzanine, aile Chauveau, 10, rue Pierre-Olivier-Chauveau, Québec, QC G1R 4J3
418-691-2014, Fax: 418-644-4676, 866-353-6767, cmq@mamr.gouv.qc.ca
Conseil des services essentiels du Québec, #9.100, 500, boul René-Lévesque ouest, 9e étage, CP 38, Montréal, QC H2Z 1W7
514-873-7246, Fax: 514-873-3839, 800-337-7246, info@cses.gouv.qc.ca
Ministère de l'Emploi et de la Solidarité sociale, 425, rue St-Amable, 4e étage, Québec, QC G1R 4Z1
418-643-4721, 888-643-4721
Hydro-Québec, 75, boul René-Lévesque ouest, Montréal, QC H2Z 1A4
514-289-2211
Institut de la statistique du Québec, 200, ch Ste-Foy, 1er étage, Québec, QC G1R 5T4
418-691-2401, Fax: 418-643-4129, 800-463-4090, direction@stat.gouv.qc.ca
Office des personnes handicapées du Québec, 309, rue Brock, Drummondville, QC J2B 1C5
Fax: 819-475-8753, 800-567-1465, michael.magner@ophq.gouv.qc.ca
Palais des congrès de Montréal, 159, rue Saint-Antoine ouest, 9é étage, Montréal, QC H2Z 1H2
514-871-8122, Fax: 514-871-9389, 800-268-8122, info@congresmtl.com
Régie de l'assurance maladie du Québec, 1125, Grande Allée ouest, Québec, QC G1S 1E7
418-646-4636
Régie du logement du Québec, Pyramide Ouest, #2095, 5199, rue Sherbrooke est, Montréal, QC H1T 3X1
514-873-2245, Fax: 514-864-8077, 800-683-2245
Ministère de la Santé et des Services sociaux, Direction des communications, 1075, ch Sainte-Foy, 16e étage, Québec, QC G1S 2M1
418-643-9395, Fax: 418-643-4768, regisseur.web@msss.gouv.qc.ca
Société d'habitation du Québec, Aile St-Amable, 1054, rue Louis-Alexandre-Taschereau, 3e étage, Québec, QC G1R 5E7
418-643-4035, Fax: 418-643-2533, 800-463-4315
Société de l'assurance automobile du Québec, 333, boul Jean-Lesage, CP 19600 Terminus, Québec, QC G1K 8J6
418-643-7620, Fax: 418-644-0339, 800-361-7620, courrier@saaq.gouv.qc.ca
Société immobilière du Québec, 1075, rue de l'Amérique-Française, 1er étage, Québec, QC G1R 5P8
418-646-1766, Fax: 418-646-6911, 877-747-9911, courrier@siq.gouv.qc.ca
Ministère de la Sécurité publique, Tour des Laurentides, 2525, boul Laurier, 5e étage, Québec, QC G1V 2L2
418-643-2112, Fax: 418-646-6168, 866-644-6826
Urgences-santé Québec, 3232, rue Bélanger, Montréal, QC H1Y 3H5
514-723-5600, info@urgences-sante.qc.ca
Vérificateur général du Québec, 750, boulevard Charest est, 3e étage, Québec, QC G1K 9J6
418-691-5900, Fax: 418-644-4460, verificateur.general@vgq.gouv.qc.ca
École nationale des pompiers du Québec, #3.08, 2800, boul Saint-Martin ouest, Laval, QC H7T 2S9
450-680-6800, Fax: 450-680-6818, 866-680-3677

Saskatchewan

Saskatchewan Assessment Management Agency, #200, 2201 - 11th Ave., Regina, SK S4P 0J8
306-924-8000, Fax: 306-924-8070, 800-667-7262, info.request@sama.sk.ca
Provincial Auditor Saskatchewan, #1500, 1920 Broad St., Regina, SK S4P 3V2
306-787-6398, Fax: 306-787-6383, info@auditor.sk.ca
Crown Investments Corporation of Saskatchewan, #400, 2400 College Ave., Regina, SK S4P 1C8
306-787-6851, Fax: 306-787-8125
Saskatchewan Government Insurance, 2260 - 11th Ave., Regina, SK S4P 0J9
306-751-1200, Fax: 306-787-7477, 800-667-8015, sgiinquiries@sgi.sk.ca
Ombudsman Saskatchewan, #150, 2401 Saskatchewan Dr., Regina, SK S4P 4H8
306-787-6211, Fax: 306-787-9090, 800-667-7180, ombreg@ombudsman.sk.ca
Saskatchewan Power Corporation (SaskPower), 2025 Victoria Ave., Regina, SK S4P 0S1
306-566-3306, Fax: 800-757-6937, 888-757-6937
Saskatchewan Legal Aid Commission, #502, 201 - 21 St. East, Saskatoon, SK S7K 0B8
306-933-5300, Fax: 306-933-6764, 800-667-3764
SaskEnergy Incorporated, 1777 Victoria Ave., Regina, SK S4P 4K5
306-777-9225, 800-567-8899
Saskatchewan Social Services, 1920 Broad St., Regina, SK S4P 3V6
306-787-3700, 866-221-5200, socialservicesinquiry@gov.sk.ca
Saskatchewan Water Corporation (SaskWater), #200, 111 Fairford St. East, Moose Jaw, SK S6H 1C8
Fax: 306-694-3207, 888-230-1111, comm@saskwater.com; customerservice@saskwater.com

Yukon Territory

Yukon Community Services, PO Box 2703, Whitehorse, YT Y1A 2C6
867-667-5811, Fax: 867-393-6295, 800-661-0408, inquiry@gov.yk.ca
Emergency Measures Organization, PO Box 2703, Whitehorse, YT Y1A 2C6
867-667-5220, Fax: 867-393-6266, 800-661-0408, emo.yukon@gov.yk.ca
Yukon Health & Social Services, PO Box 2703, Whitehorse, YT Y1A 2C6
867-667-3673, Fax: 867-667-3096, hss@gov.yk.ca
Yukon Housing Corporation, 410H Jarvis St., PO Box 2703, Whitehorse, YT Y1A 2H5
867-667-5759, Fax: 867-667-3664, 800-661-0408, ykhouse@housing.yk.ca
Yukon Public Service Commission, Yukon Government Administration Building, #2071-2nd Ave., PO Box 2703, Whitehorse, YT Y1A 2C6
867-667-5653, Fax: 867-667-5755, 800-661-0408, PSCWebsite@gov.yk.ca
Yukon Utilities Board, #19, 1114 - 1st Ave., PO Box 31728, Whitehorse, YT Y1A 6L3
867-667-5058, Fax: 867-667-5059, yub@utilitiesboard.yk.ca

PUBLIC TRUSTEE

British Columbia

Public Guardian & Trustee of British Columbia, #700, 808 West Hastings St., Vancouver, BC V6C 3L3
604-660-4444, Fax: 604-660-0374, 800-663-7867, mail@trustee.bc.ca

Manitoba

Office of the Public Trustee, #500, 155 Carlton St., Winnipeg, MB R3C 5R9
204-945-2700, Fax: 204-948-2251, publictrustee@gov.mb.ca

New Brunswick

Department of Justice & Consumer Affairs, Centennial Bldg., 670 King St., PO Box 6000, Fredericton, NB E3B 5H1
506-462-5100, Fax: 506-453-3651, justice.comments@gnb.ca

Newfoundland & Labrador

Department of Justice, Confederation Bldg., East Block, 4th Fl., PO Box 8700, St. John's, NL A1B 4J6
709-729-2869, Fax: 709-729-0469, justice@gov.nl.ca

Nova Scotia

Public Trustee Office, #405, 5670 Spring Garden Rd., PO Box 685, Halifax, NS B3J 2T3
902-424-7760, Fax: 902-424-0616, PublicTrusteeHCD@gov.ns.ca (Health Care Decisions Division)

Quebec

Curateur public du Québec, 600, boul René-Lévesque ouest, Montréal, QC H3B 4W9
514-873-4074, Fax: 514-873-5033, 800-363-9020

PUBLIC UTILITIES

Alberta

Energy Resources Conservation Board, #1000, 250 - 5 Ave. SW, Calgary, AB T2P 0R4
403-297-8311, Fax: 403-297-7336, 855-297-8311, inquiries@ercb.ca; infoservices@ercb.ca; ADR@ercb.ca

British Columbia

British Columbia Hydro, 333 Dunsmuir St., Vancouver, BC V6B 5R3
604-224-9376, 800-224-9376
British Columbia Transmission Corporation, Four Bentall Centre, #1100, 1055 Dunsmuir St., PO Box 49260, Vancouver, BC V7X 1V5
604-699-7539, Interconnections@bchydro.com (transmission interconnections)
British Columbia Utilities Commission, 900 Howe St., 6th Fl., PO Box 250, Vancouver, BC V6Z 2N3
604-660-4700, Fax: 604-660-1102, 800-663-1385, commission.secretary@bcuc.com

Manitoba

Manitoba Hydro, PO Box 815 Main,Winnipeg, MB R3C 2P4
204-474-3311, Fax: 204-475-0069, publicaffairs@hydro.mb.ca
Public Utilities Board, #400, 330 Portage Ave., Winnipeg, MB R3C 0C4
204-945-2638, Fax: 204-945-2643, 866-854-3698, publicutilities@gov.mb.ca

New Brunswick

NB Board of Commissioners of Public Utilities, #1400, 15 Market Sq., PO Box 5001, Saint John, NB E2L 4Y9
506-658-2504, Fax: 506-643-7300, 866-766-2782, general@pub.nb.ca
New Brunswick Power Group of Companies, 515 King St., PO Box 2000, Fredericton, NB E3B 4X1
506-458-4444, Fax: 506-458-4000, questions@nbpower.com

Newfoundland & Labrador

Churchill Falls (Labrador) Corporation Limited, Hydro Place, 500 Columbus Dr., PO Box 12500, St. John's, NL A1B 4K7
709-737-1859, Fax: 709-737-1816
Newfoundland & Labrador Hydro, Hydro Place, Columbus Dr., PO Box 12400, St. John's, NL A1B 4K7
709-737-1400, Fax: 709-737-1800, hydro@nlh.nl.ca
Newfoundland & Labrador Board of Commissioners of Public Utilities, PO Box 21040, St. John's, NL A1A 5B2
709-726-8600, Fax: 709-726-9604, 866-782-0006, ito@pub.nf.ca

Northwest Territories

Northwest Territories Power Corporation, 4 Capital Dr., Hay River, NT X0E 1G2
867-874-5200, Fax: 867-874-5251, info@ntpc.com
Northwest Territories Water Board, 125 Mackenzie Rd., PO Box 2531, Yellowknife, NT X0E 0T0
867-678-2942, Fax: 867-678-2943, info@nwtwb.com

Nova Scotia

Nova Scotia Utility & Review Board, Summit Place, 1601 Lower Water St., 3rd Fl., PO Box 1692 M,Halifax, NS B3J 3S3
902-424-4448, Fax: 902-424-3919, uarb.board@gov.ns.ca

Ontario

Hydro One Inc., North Tower, 483 Bay St., Toronto, ON M5G 2P5
416-345-5000, 877-955-1155, customercommunications@HydroOne.com
Independent Electricity System Operator, PO Box 4474 A,Toronto, ON M5W 4E5
905-403-6900, Fax: 905-403-6921, 888-448-7777, customer.relations@ieso.ca
Ontario Power Generation, 700 University Ave., Toronto, ON M5G 1X6
416-592-2555, 877-592-2555, webmaster@opg.com

Prince Edward Island

Prince Edward Island Regulatory & Appeals Commission, National Bank Tower, #501, 134 Kent St., PO Box 577, Charlottetown, PE C1A 7L1
902-892-3501, Fax: 902-566-4076, 800-501-6268, info@irac.pe.ca

Quebec

Hydro-Québec, 75, boul René-Lévesque ouest, Montréal, QC H2Z 1A4
514-289-2211
Régie de l'énergie, Tour de la Bourse, #2.55, 800, Place Victoria, Montréal, QC H4Z 1A2
514-873-2452, Fax: 514-873-2070, 888-873-2452, secretariat@regie-energie.qc.ca

Saskatchewan

Saskatchewan Power Corporation (SaskPower), 2025 Victoria Ave., Regina, SK S4P 0S1
306-566-3306, Fax: 800-757-6937, 888-757-6937
SaskEnergy Incorporated, 1777 Victoria Ave., Regina, SK S4P 4K5
306-777-9225, 800-567-8899
Saskatchewan Water Corporation (SaskWater), #200, 111 Fairford St. East, Moose Jaw, SK S6H 1C8
Fax: 306-694-3207, 888-230-1111, comm@saskwater.com; customerservice@saskwater.com

Yukon Territory

Yukon Utilities Board, #19, 1114 - 1st Ave., PO Box 31728, Whitehorse, YT Y1A 6L3
867-667-5058, Fax: 867-667-5059, yub@utilitiesboard.yk.ca

PUBLIC WORKS

Public Works & Government Services Canada, Place du Portage, Phase III, 11, rue Laurier, Ottawa, ON K1A 0S5
questions@tpsgc-pwgsc.gc.ca

Alberta
Alberta Infrastructure, Infrastructure Building, 6950 - 113 St., Edmonton, AB T6H 5V7
780-415-0507, Fax: 780-427-2187, Infra.Contact.Us.m@gov.ab.ca

British Columbia
Ministry of Labour, Citizens' Services & Open Government, PO Box 9056 Prov Govt,Victoria, BC V8W 9K4
250-952-7623, Fax: 250-387-4312, 800-663-7867, LCTZ.Minister@gov.bc.ca

Manitoba
Manitoba Infrastructure & Transportation, Legislative Building, #203, 450 Broadway Ave., Winnipeg, MB R3C 0V8
204-945-3723, Fax: 204-945-7610

Newfoundland & Labrador
Department of Transportation & Works, Confederation Bldg., West Block, 6th Fl., PO Box 8700, St. John's, NL A1B 4J6
709-729-3679, Fax: 709-729-4285, twminister@gov.nl.ca

Northwest Territories
Department of Public Works & Services, PO Box 1320, Yellowknife, NT X1A 2L9

Nova Scotia
Department of Transportation & Infrastructure Renewal, Johnston Bldg., 1672 Granville St., 2nd Fl., PO Box 186, Halifax, NS B3J 2N2
902-424-2297, Fax: 902-424-0532, tpwpaff@gov.ns.ca

Nunavut
Department of Community & Government Services, W.G. Brown Bldg., 4th Fl., PO Box 1000 700,Iqaluit, NU X0A 0H0
867-975-5400, Fax: 867-975-5305

Prince Edward Island
Prince Edward Island Department of Transportation & Infrastructure Renewal, Jones Bldg., 11 Kent St., 3rd Fl., PO Box 2000, Charlottetown, PE C1A 7N8
902-368-5100, Fax: 902-368-5395

Quebec
Ministère des Services gouvernementaux, 875, Grande Allée est, 4e étage - Secteur 500, Québec, QC G1R 5R8
418-643-1529, Fax: 418-643-9226, communication@sct.gouv.qc.ca

Yukon Territory
Yukon Highways & Public Works, PO Box 2703, Whitehorse, YT Y1A 2C6
867-393-7193, Fax: 867-393-6218, 800-661-0408, hpw-info@gov.yk.ca

PUBLICATIONS

Public Works & Government Services Canada, Place du Portage, Phase III, 11, rue Laurier, Ottawa, ON K1A 0S5
questions@tpsgc-pwgsc.gc.ca

Manitoba
Statutory Publications, #20, 200 Vaughan St., Winnipeg, MB R3C 1T5
204-945-3101, Fax: 204-945-7172, 800-321-1203, statpub@gov.mb.ca

New Brunswick
Legislative Services, Centennial Bldg., #418, 670 King St., PO Box 6000, Fredericton, NB E3B 5H1
506-453-2855, Fax: 506-457-7342

Newfoundland & Labrador
Office of the Queen's Printer, Queen's Printer-Earl Tucker, Ground Fl., Confederation Blg., PO Box 8700, St. John's, NL A1B 4J6
709-729-3649, Fax: 709-729-1900, queensprinter@gov.nl.ca

Nova Scotia
Communications Nova Scotia, 1723 Hollis St., 3rd Fl., PO Box 608, Halifax, NS B3J 2R7
902-424-7690, Fax: 902-424-0515

Department of Service Nova Scotia & Municipal Relations, 1505 Barrington St., PO Box 216, Halifax, NS B3J 3K5
902-424-5200, Fax: 902-424-0581, 800-670-4357, askus@gov.ns.ca

Nunavut
Legislative Assembly, 926 Federal Rd., PO Box 1200, Iqaluit, NU X0A 0H0
867-975-5000, Fax: 867-975-5190, 877-334-7266, leginfo@assembly.nu.ca

Quebec
Ministère de la Culture, des Communications & de la Condition féminine, 225, Grande Allée est, Québec, QC G1R 5G5
888-380-8882

Yukon Territory
Yukon Highways & Public Works, PO Box 2703, Whitehorse, YT Y1A 2C6
867-393-7193, Fax: 867-393-6218, 800-661-0408, hpw-info@gov.yk.ca

PURCHASING

MERX, PO Box 11684 Centre-ville,Montreal, QC H3C 6H4
Fax: 888-235-5800, merx@merx.com

Alberta
Alberta Infrastructure, Infrastructure Building, 6950 - 113 St., Edmonton, AB T6H 5V7
780-415-0507, Fax: 780-427-2187, Infra.Contact.Us.m@gov.ab.ca

British Columbia
Ministry of Labour, Citizens' Services & Open Government, PO Box 9056 Prov Govt,Victoria, BC V8W 9K4
250-952-7623, Fax: 250-387-4312, 800-663-7867, LCTZ.Minister@gov.bc.ca

Manitoba
Government Services, Legislative Bldg., #332, 450 Broadway, Winnipeg, MB R3C 0V8

Newfoundland & Labrador
Department of Government Services, PO Box 8700, St. John's, NL A1B 4J6
709-729-4834, gsinfo@gov.nl.ca

Northwest Territories
Department of Public Works & Services, PO Box 1320, Yellowknife, NT X1A 2L9

Nunavut
Department of Community & Government Services, W.G. Brown Bldg., 4th Fl., PO Box 1000 700,Iqaluit, NU X0A 0H0
867-975-5400, Fax: 867-975-5305

Prince Edward Island
Prince Edward Island Department of Transportation & Infrastructure Renewal, Jones Bldg., 11 Kent St., 3rd Fl., PO Box 2000, Charlottetown, PE C1A 7N8
902-368-5100, Fax: 902-368-5395

RAIL TRANSPORTATION

See Also: Transportation

Transportation Safety Board of Canada, 200 Promenade du Portage, 4th Fl., Ottawa, ON K1A 1K8
819-994-3741, Fax: 819-997-2239, 800-387-3557

Via Rail Canada Inc., #500, 3, Place Ville-Marie, Montréal, QC H3B 2C9
514-871-6000, Fax: 514-871-6104, 888-842-7245,

Manitoba
Manitoba Infrastructure & Transportation, Legislative Building, #203, 450 Broadway Ave., Winnipeg, MB R3C 0V8
204-945-3723, Fax: 204-945-7610

New Brunswick
Department of Transportation, Kings Pl., 440 King St., PO Box 6000, Fredericton, NB E3B 5H8
506-453-3939, Fax: 506-453-2900, Transportation.Web@gnb.ca

Newfoundland & Labrador
Department of Transportation & Works, Confederation Bldg., West Block, 6th Fl., PO Box 8700, St. John's, NL A1B 4J6
709-729-3679, Fax: 709-729-4285, twminister@gov.nl.ca

Nova Scotia
Department of Transportation & Infrastructure Renewal, Johnston Bldg., 1672 Granville St., 2nd Fl., PO Box 186, Halifax, NS B3J 2N2
902-424-2297, Fax: 902-424-0532, tpwpaff@gov.ns.ca

Ontario
Metrolinx, #600, 20 Bay St., Toronto, ON M5J 2W3
416-869-3200, Fax: 416-869-3525, 888-438-6646

Quebec
Société du port ferroviaire Baie-Comeau-Hauterive, 18, rte Maritime, Baie-Comeau, QC G4Z 2L6
418-296-6785, Fax: 418-296-2377, societeduport@globetrotter.net

Ministère des Transports, 700, boul René-Lévesque est, 28e étage, Québec, QC G1R 5H1
418-643-6980, Fax: 418-643-2033, 888-355-0511, communications@mtq.gouv.qc.ca

Saskatchewan
Saskatchewan Highways & Infrastructure, Victoria Tower, 1855 Victoria Ave., Regina, SK S4P 3T2
306-787-4800, communications@highways.gov.sk.ca

REAL ESTATE

See Also: Land Titles

Canada Mortgage & Housing Corporation, 700 Montreal Rd., Ottawa, ON K1A 0P7
613-748-2000, Fax: 613-748-2098, 800-668-2642, chic@cmhc-schl.gc.ca

Alberta
Strategic Planning & Financial Services, Commerce Place, 10155 - 102 St., 13th Fl., Edmonton, AB T5J 4G8
780-422-8545

British Columbia
Real Estate Council of British Columbia, #900, 750 West Pender St., Vancouver, BC V6C 2T8
604-683-9664, Fax: 604-683-9017, 877-683-9664, info@recbc.ca

New Brunswick
New Brunswick Real Estate Association, #1, 22 Durelle St., Fredericton, NB E3C 1N8
506-459-8055, Fax: 506-459-8057, 800-762-1677, info@nbrea.ca

Nova Scotia
Department of Service Nova Scotia & Municipal Relations, 1505 Barrington St., PO Box 216, Halifax, NS B3J 3K5
902-424-5200, Fax: 902-424-0581, 800-670-4357, askus@gov.ns.ca

Nunavut
Nunavut Legal Registries Division, Brown Bldg., 1st Fl., PO Box 1000 570,Iqaluit, NU X0A 0H0
Fax: 867-975-6594

Ontario
Ontario Realty Corporation, #2000, 1 Dundas St. West, Toronto, ON M5G 2L5
416-327-3937, Fax: 416-327-1906, 877-863-9672, feedback@ontariorealty.ca

Quebec
Société immobilière du Québec, 1075, rue de l'Amérique-Française, 1er étage, Québec, QC G1R 5P8
418-646-1766, Fax: 418-646-6911, 877-747-9911, courrier@siq.gouv.qc.ca

REAL ESTATE

Ontario
Ontario Realty Corporation, #2000, 1 Dundas St. West, Toronto, ON M5G 2L5
416-327-3937, Fax: 416-327-1906, 877-863-9672, feedback@ontariorealty.ca

RECREATION

See Also: Tourism & Tourist Information

Canada Place Corporation, 504 - 999 Canada Place, Vancouver, BC V6C 3E1
604-775-7200, Fax: 604-775-6251, admin@canadaplace.ca

Canadian Heritage, 15 Eddy St., Gatineau, QC K1A 0M5
819-997-0055, 866-811-0055, info@pch.gc.ca

Canadian Tourism Commission, #1400, 1055 Dunsmuir St., PO Box 49230, Vancouver, BC V7X 1L2
604-638-8300

National Battlefields Commission, 390, av de Bernières, Québec, QC G1R 2L7
418-648-3506, Fax: 418-648-3638, information@ccbn-nbc.gc.ca

Parks Canada, 25 Eddy St., Gatineau, QC K1A 0M5
613-860-1251, 888-773-8888, information@pc.gc.ca

Alberta
Alberta Gaming & Liquor Commission, 50 Corriveau Ave., St. Albert, AB T8N 3T5
780-447-8600, Fax: 780-447-8916, 800-272-8876

Alberta Sport, Recreation, Parks, & Wildlife Foundation, Standard Life Centre, #903, 10405 Jasper Ave., 9th Fl., Edmonton, AB T5J 4R7
780-415-1167, Fax: 780-415-0308

British Columbia
British Columbia Lottery Corporation, 74 West Seymour St., Kamloops, BC V2C 1E2
250-828-5500, Fax: 250-828-5631, 866-815-0222

Office of the Superintendent of Motor Vehicles, PO Box 9254 Prov Govt,Victoria, BC V8W 9J2
250-387-7747, Fax: 250-387-4891, OSMV.Mailbox@gov.bc.ca

Ministry of Social Development, PO Box 9058 Prov Govt,Victoria, BC V8W 9E1
250-356-7750, Fax: 250-356-7292, SD.Minister@gov.bc.ca

Manitoba
Manitoba Competitiveness, Training & Trade, International Business Centre, The Paris Building, 259 Portage Ave., Winnipeg, MB R3B 3P4
204-945-2475, Fax: 204-945-3977, minctt@leg.gov.mb.ca

Manitoba Lotteries Corporation, 830 Empress St., Winnipeg, MB R3G 3H3
204-957-2500, Fax: 204-957-3991, 800-265-2912, communications@casinosofwinnipeg.com

Manitoba Horse Racing Commission, c/o Boards, Commissions & Legislation Branch, #812, 401 York Ave., Winnipeg, MB R3C 0P8
204-945-4495, Fax: 204-948-2844, gordon.mackenzie@gov.mb.ca

Tourism Secretariat & Travel Manitoba, 155 Carlton St., 7th Fl., Winnipeg, MB R3C 3H8
800-665-0040

New Brunswick
Department of Business New Brunswick, Centennial Bldg., 670 King St., PO Box 6000, Fredericton, NB E3B 5H1
506-453-3707, Fax: 506-453-3993, investnb@gnb.ca
Department of Wellness, Culture & Sport, Place 2000, 250 King St., 4th Fl., PO Box 6000, Fredericton, NB E3B 5H1
506-453-2909, Fax: 506-453-6548
Investment, Export & Business Development, Centennial Bldg., 670 King St., 5th Fl., PO Box 6000, Fredericton, NB E3B 5H1
506-453-2875, Fax: 506-444-4277,
New Brunswick Lotteries & Gaming Corporation, Centennial Bldg., 670 King St., PO Box 6000, Fredericton, NB E3B 5H1
506-444-3468, Fax: 506-444-5818

Newfoundland & Labrador
C.A. Pippy Park Commission, Mount Scio House, 15 Mount Scio Rd., St. John's, NL A1B 3T2
709-737-3655, Fax: 709-737-3303, info@pippypark.com
Department of Tourism, Culture & Recreation, Confederation Bldg., West Block, 2nd Fl., PO Box 8700, St. John's, NL A1B 4J6
709-729-0862, Fax: 709-729-0870, tcrinfo@gov.nl.ca

Ontario
Alcohol & Gaming Commission of Ontario, 90 Sheppard Ave. East, Toronto, ON M2N 0A4
416-326-8700, Fax: 416-326-5555, 800-522-2876
Ministry of Economic Development & Innovation, Hearst Block, 900 Bay St., 8th Fl., Toronto, ON M7A 2E1
416-325-6666, Fax: 416-325-6688, 866-668-4249, info@edt.gov.on.ca
Metro Toronto Convention Centre Corporation, 255 Front St. West, Toronto, ON M5V 2W6
416-585-8000, Fax: 416-585-8224, info@mtcc.com
Niagara Parks Commission, Oak Hall Administration Bldg., 7400 Portage Rd. South, PO Box 150, Niagara Falls, ON L2E 6T2
905-356-2241, Fax: 905-354-6041, 877-642-7275
Ontario Lottery & Gaming Corporation, Roberta Bondar Pl., #800, 70 Foster Dr., Sault Ste Marie, ON P6A 6V2
705-946-6464, Fax: 416-224-7000, 800-387-0098
Ontario Place Corporation, 955 Lake Shore Blvd. West, Toronto, ON M6K 3B9
416-314-9900, Fax: 416-314-9992
Ottawa Convention Centre, 55 Colonel By Dr., Ottawa, ON K1N 9J2
613-563-1984, Fax: 613-563-7646
St. Lawrence Parks Commission, RR#1, Morrisburg, ON K0C 1X0
613-543-3704, Fax: 613-543-2847, 800-437-2233
Ministry of Tourism & Culture, Hearst Block, 900 Bay St., 9th Fl., Toronto, ON M7A 2E1
416-326-9326, Fax: 416-314-7854, 800-668-2746

Prince Edward Island
Maritime Provinces Harness Racing Commission, 5 Gerald McCarville Dr., PO Box 128, Kensington, PE C0B 1M0
902-836-5500, Fax: 902-836-5320
Prince Edward Island Department of Community Services, Seniors, & Labour, Jones Bldg., 11 Kent St., 2nd Fl., PO Box 2000, Charlottetown, PE C1A 7N8
902-620-3777, Fax: 902-368-4740, 866-594-3777
Prince Edward Island Department of Innovation & Advanced Learning, Shaw Bldg., 105 Rochford St., 5th Fl., PO Box 2000, Charlottetown, PE C1A 7N8
902-368-4240, Fax: 902-368-4242
Prince Edward Island Department of Tourism & Culture, PO Box 2000, Charlottetown, PE C1A 7N8
902-368-5540, Fax: 902-368-5277, tpswitch@gov.pe.ca

Quebec
Comité conjoint de chasse, de pêche et de piégeage, #C220, 383 rue Saint-Jacques, Montréal, QC H2Y 1N9
514-284-2151, Fax: 514-284-0039, infohftcc@cccpp-hftcc.com
Loto-Québec, 500, rue Sherbrooke ouest, Montréal, QC H3A 3G6
514-282-8000, Fax: 514-873-8999
Régie des alcools, des courses et des jeux, 560, boul Charest est, Québec, QC G1K 3J3
418-643-7667, Fax: 418-643-5971, 800-363-0320
Société des établissements en plein air du Québec, Place de la Cité, Tour Cominar, #250, 2640, boul Laurier, 2e étage, Québec, QC G1V 5C2
418-890-6527, Fax: 418-528-6025, 800-665-6527, inforeservation@sepaq.com

Saskatchewan
Saskatchewan Liquor & Gaming Authority, 2500 Victoria Ave., PO Box 5054, Regina, SK S4P 3M3
306-787-4213, inquiry@slga.gov.sk.ca
Saskatchewan Science Centre, 2903 Powerhouse Dr., Regina, SK S4N 0A1
306-522-4629, 800-667-6300, info@sasksciencecentre.com
Saskatchewan Tourism, Parks, Culture & Sport, 1919 Saskatchewan Dr., 4th Fl., Regina, SK S4P 4H2
306-787-5729, Fax: 306-787-8560, info@cyr.gov.sk.ca
Western Development Museum, 2935 Melville St., Saskatoon, SK S7J 5A6
306-934-1400, Fax: 306-934-4467, 800-363-6345, info@wdm.ca

Yukon Territory
Yukon Tourism & Culture, 100 Hanson St., Whitehorse, YT Y1A 2C6
867-667-5036, Fax: 867-667-3546
Yukon Lottery Commission, 312 Wood St., Whitehorse, YT Y1A 2E6
867-633-7890, Fax: 867-668-7561, lotteriesyukon@gov.yk.ca

RECYCLING

Alberta
Alberta Recycling Management Authority, Scotia Tower 1, #1310, 10060 Jasper Ave., PO Box 189, Edmonton, AB T5J 2J1
780-990-1111, Fax: 780-990-1122, 888-999-8762, info@albertarecycling.ca

Newfoundland & Labrador
Multi-Materials Stewardship Board, PO Box 8131 A, St. John's, NL A1B 3M9
709-753-0948, Fax: 709-753-0974, 800-901-6672, inquiries@mmsb.nl.ca

RESEARCH & DEVELOPMENT

Bayfield Institute, 867 Lakeshore Rd., PO Box 5050, Burlington, ON L7R 4A6
905-336-6240
Bedford Institute of Oceanography, 1 Challenger Dr., PO Box 1006, Dartmouth, NS B2Y 4A2
902-426-3492, Fax: 902-426-8484
Biotechnology Research Institute, 6100, av Royalmount, Montréal, QC H4P 2R2
514-496-6100, Fax: 514-496-1928, bri-info@cnrc-nrc.gc.ca
Canada Centre for Remote Sensing - Geomatics Canada, 588 Booth St., Ottawa, ON K1A 0Y7
613-995-0947, Fax: 613-947-1382
Canadian Hydraulics Centre, 1200 Montreal Rd., Ottawa, ON K1A 0R6
613-993-9381, Fax: 613-952-7679, info.chc@nrc-cnrc.gc.ca
Canadian Space Agency, John H. Chapman Space Centre, 6767, rte de l'Aéroport, Saint-Hubert, QC J3Y 8Y9
450-926-4800, Fax: 450-926-4352, promo@asc-csa.gc.ca
Centre for Surface Transportation Technology, 2320 Lester Rd., Ottawa, ON K1V 1S2
613-998-9639, Fax: 613-957-0831, inquiries.cstt@nrc-cnrc.gc.ca
Fisheries Resource Conservation Council, PO Box 2001 D, Ottawa, ON K1P 5W3
613-998-0433, Fax: 613-998-1146, info@frcc-ccrh.ca
Freshwater Institute, 501 University Cres., Winnipeg, MB R3T 2N6
204-983-5000, Fax: 204-983-6285
Herzberg Institute of Astrophysics, 5071 West Saanich Rd., Victoria, BC V9E 2E7
250-363-0001, Fax: 250-363-0045, hia-www@nrc-cnrc.gc.ca
Industrial Materials Institute, 75, boul de Mortagne, Boucherville, QC J4B 6Y4
450-641-5000, Fax: 450-641-5101, lmi-Info@cnrc-nrc.gc.ca
Institut Maurice-Lamontagne, 850, rte de le Mer, CP 1000, Mont-Joli, QC G5H 3Z4
418-775-0555, Fax: 418-775-0730
Institute for Aerospace Research, 1200 Montreal Rd., Ottawa, ON K1A 0R6
613-990-0765, Fax: 613-952-7214
Institute for Biological Sciences, Bldg. M-54, 1200 Montreal Rd., Ottawa, ON K1A 0R6
613-993-5812, Fax: 613-957-7867
Institute for Chemical Process & Environmental Technology, Bldg. M-12, 1200 Montreal Rd., Ottawa, ON K1A 0R6
613-993-4041, Fax: 613-957-8231
Institute for Marine Biosciences, 1411 Oxford St., Halifax, NS B3H 3Z1
902-426-8332, Fax: 902-426-9413, communications.imb@nrc-cnrc.gc.ca
Institute for National Measurement Standards, Bldg. M-36, 1500 Montreal Rd., Ottawa, ON K1A 0R6
613-998-7018, Fax: 613-954-1473, alexandra.shaw@nrc-cnrc.gc.ca
Institute for Ocean Technology, Kerwin Pl. & Arctic Ave., PO Box 12093, St. John's, NL A1B 3T5
709-772-4939, Fax: 709-772-2462, Noel.Murphy@nrc-cnrc.gc.ca
Institute for Research in Construction, Bldg. M-24, 1500 Montreal Rd., Ottawa, ON K1A 0R6
613-993-2607, Fax: 613-952-7673, Irc.Client-Services@nrc-cnrc.gc.ca
Institute of Ocean Sciences, 9860 West Saanich Rd., PO Box 6000, Sidney, BC V8L 4B2
250-363-6517, Fax: 250-363-6390,
London - Centre for Automotive Materials & Manufacturing, 800 Collip Circle, London, ON N6G 4X8
519-430-7166, Fax: 519-430-7064, John.Lyons@nrc-cnrc.gc.ca
National Institute of Nanotechnology, Bldg. NINT, University of Alberta, 11421 Saskatchewan Dr., Edmonton, AB T6G 2M9
780-641-1600, Fax: 780-641-1601, nintinfo@nrc.gc.ca
National Research Council Canada, Bldg. M-58, 1200 Montreal Rd., Ottawa, ON K1A 0R6
613-993-9101, Fax: 613-952-7928, 877-672-2672, info@nrc-cnrc.gc.ca
Natural Sciences & Engineering Research Council of Canada, Constitution Square, Tower II, 350 Albert St., Ottawa, ON K1A 1H5
613-995-4273, Fax: 613-943-1624, marie-josee.duval@nserc-crsng.gc.ca
Pacific Biological Station, 3190 Hammond Bay Rd., Nanaimo, BC V9T 6N7
250-756-7000, Fax: 250-756-7053
Plant Biotechnology Institute, 110 Gymnasium Pl., Saskatoon, SK S7N 0W9
306-975-5248, Fax: 306-975-4839, pbi-info@nrc-cnrc.gc.ca
Research Branch, Tower 5, 1341 Baseline Rd., Ottawa, ON K1A 0C5
613-759-1000, Fax: 613-773-1866
St. Andrews Biological Station, 531 Brandy Cove Rd., St Andrews, NB E5B 2L9
506-529-8854, Fax: 506-529-5862, XMARSABS@mar.dfo-mpo.gc.ca

Alberta
Alberta Innovates - Energy & Environmental Solutions, AMEC Place, #2540, 801 - 6th Ave. SW, Calgary, AB T2P 3W2
403-297-7089, ees@albertainnovates.ca

British Columbia
Powertech Labs Inc., 12388 - 88 Ave., Surrey, BC V8W 7R7
604-590-7500, Fax: 604-590-6611

New Brunswick
New Brunswick Research & Productivity Council, 921 College Hill Rd., Fredericton, NB E3B 6Z9
506-452-1212, Fax: 506-452-1395, info@rpc.ca
Service New Brunswick, Westmorland Place, #200, 82 Westmorland St., PO Box 1998, Fredericton, NB E3B 5G4
506-457-3581, Fax: 506-457-7520, 888-762-8600, snb@snb.ca

Newfoundland & Labrador
Department of Innovation, Trade & Rural Development, West Block, Confederation Bldg., PO Box 8700, St. John's, NL A1B 4J6
709-729-7000, Fax: 709-729-0654, intrd@gov.nl.ca

Northwest Territories
Aurora Research Institute, 191 MacKenzie Rd., PO Box 1450, Inuvik, NT X0E 0T0
867-777-3298, Fax: 867-777-4264, webmaster@nwtresearch.com

Ontario
Ministry of Research & Innovation, Ferguson Block, 56 Wellesley St. West, 7th Fl., Toronto, ON M7A 2E7
416-325-5181, Fax: 416-325-3877, 866-446-5216
Science & Information Resources Division, Roberta Bondar Pl., #400, 70 Foster Dr., Sault Ste Marie, ON P6A 6V5
705-755-2000, Fax: 705-755-2802, 800-667-1940

Prince Edward Island
Agricultural Insurance Corporation, 29 Indigo Cres., PO Box 1600, Charlottetown, PE C1A 7N3
902-368-4842, Fax: 902-368-6677
BIO FOOD TECH, 101 Belvedere Ave., PO Box 2000, Charlottetown, PE C1A 7N8
902-368-5548, Fax: 902-368-5549, 877-368-5548, biofoodtech@biofoodtech.ca

Quebec
Centre de recherche industrielle du Québec, 333, rue Franquet, Québec, QC G1P 4C7
418-659-1550, Fax: 418-652-2251, 800-667-2386, infocriq@criq.qc.ca
Fonds de la recherche en santé du Québec, #800, 500, rue Sherbrooke ouest, Montréal, QC H3A 3C6
514-873-2114, Fax: 514-873-8768
Fonds québécois de la recherche sur la nature et les technologies, #450, 140, Grande Allée est, Québec, QC G1R 5M8
418-643-8560, Fax: 418-643-1451, info@fqrnt.gouv.qc.ca
Innovatech Québec, #410, 888, rue St-Jean, Québec, QC G1R 5H6
418-528-9770, Fax: 418-528-9783, 866-605-1676

Saskatchewan
Saskatchewan Power Corporation (SaskPower), 2025 Victoria Ave., Regina, SK S4P 0S1
306-566-3306, Fax: 800-757-6937, 888-757-6937
Saskatchewan Research Council, #125, 15 Innovation Blvd., Saskatoon, SK S7N 2X8
306-933-5400, Fax: 306-933-7446, info@src.sk.ca

ROUND TABLES

National Round Table on the Environment & Economy, #200, 344 Slater St., Ottawa, ON K1R 7Y3
613-992-7189, Fax: 613-992-7385, admin@nrtee-trnee.ca

Manitoba

Manitoba Round Table for Sustainable Development, #160, 123 Main St., Winnipeg, MB R3C 1A5
204-945-1671, Fax: 204-948-2357, mrtsd@gov.mb.ca

New Brunswick

New Brunswick Round Table on Environment & Economy, 20 McGloin St., PO Box 6000, Fredericton, NB E3B 5H1
506-453-3703, Fax: 506-453-3876

SALES TAX

British Columbia

Employment & Labour Market Services Division, PO Box 9762 Prov Govt,Victoria, BC V8W 1A4
250-356-0050, Fax: 250-953-3928

Financial Sector Regulation & Policy, Terrace Building, 9515 - 107 St., 4th Fl., Edmonton, AB T5K 2C3

Secretariat to Commission on the Reform of Ontario's Public Services, Frost Bldg. South, 7 Queen's Park Cres., 1st Fl., Toronto, ON M7A 1YA
416-326-9847, Fax: 416-212-7767

Manitoba

Taxation Division, #101, 401 York Ave., Winnipeg, MB R3C 0P8
204-945-6444, Fax: 204-948-2360

New Brunswick

Revenue & Taxation, Centennial Bldg., #671, 670 King St., PO Box 3000, Fredericton, NB E3B 5G5
506-444-2826, Fax: 506-444-4920

Northwest Territories

Department of Finance, Arthur Laing Building, 5th Fl., 5003 - 49th St., PO Box 1320, Yellowknife, NT X1A 2L9
867-873-7117, Fax: 867-873-0414

Nova Scotia

Tax Commission, Maritime Centre, 1505 Barrington St., 8th St., PO Box 1003, Halifax, NS B3J 2X1
902-424-6300, Fax: 902-424-7434, 800-565-4357

Nunavut

Department of Finance, Bldg. 1079, 1st Fl., PO Box 1000 330,Iqaluit, NU X0A 0H0
867-975-5800, Fax: 867-975-5805

Quebec

Centre de perception fiscale et des biens non réclamés, 3800, rue de Marly, Secteur 6-4-3, Québec, QC G1X 4A5

SCHOOL BOARDS

See: Education

Prince Edward Island

Eastern School District, PO Box 8600, Charlottetown, PE C1A 8V7
902-368-6990, Fax: 902-368-6960

French Language School Board, 1596, rte 124, Abram-Village, PE C0B 2E0
902-854-2975, Fax: 902-854-2981, cslf@edu.pe.ca

Western School Board of Prince Edward Island, Summerside Office, 272 MacEwen Dr., Summerside, PE C1N 2P7
902-888-8400, Fax: 902-888-8449

SCIENCE & NATURE

Aboriginal Affairs & Northern Development Canada, 10 Wellington St., North Tower, Gatineau, QC K1A 0H4
819-997-0380, Fax: 866-817-3977, 800-567-9604, infopubs@aadnc-aandc.gc.ca

Agriculture & Agri-Food Canada, 1341 Baseline Rd., Ottawa, ON K1A 0C5
613-773-1000, Fax: 613-773-2772, 866-345-7972, info@agr.gc.ca

Beverly & Qamanirjuaq Caribou Management Board, Secretariat, PO Box 629, Stonewall, MB R0C 2Z0
204-467-2438, caribounews@arctic-caribou.com

Canada Centre for Remote Sensing - Geomatics Canada, 588 Booth St., Ottawa, ON K1A 0Y7
613-995-0947, Fax: 613-947-1382

Canadian Institutes of Health Research, 160 Elgin St., 9th Fl., Ottawa, ON K1A 0W9
613-941-2672, Fax: 613-954-1800, 888-603-4178, info@cihr-irsc.gc.ca

Canadian Nuclear Safety Commission, 280 Slater St., PO Box 1046 B,Ottawa, ON K1P 5S9
613-995-5894, Fax: 613-995-5086, 800-668-5284

Canadian Polar Commission, Constitution Square, #1710, 360 Albert St., Ottawa, ON K1R 7X7
613-943-8605, Fax: 613-943-8607, 888-765-2701, mail@polarcom.gc.ca

Canadian Space Agency, John H. Chapman Space Centre, 6767, rte de l'Aéroport, Saint-Hubert, QC J3Y 8Y9
450-926-4800, Fax: 450-926-4352, promo@asc-csa.gc.ca

Centre for Surface Transportation Technology, 2320 Lester Rd., Ottawa, ON K1V 1S2
613-998-9639, Fax: 613-957-0831, inquiries.cstt@nrc-cnrc.gc.ca

Commission for Environmental Cooperation, Secretariat, #200, 393, rue St-Jacques ouest, Montréal, QC H2Y 1N9
514-350-4300, Fax: 514-350-4314, info@cec.org

Ecosystems & Fisheries Management, 200 Kent St., Ottawa, ON K1A 0E6

Electronic Commerce Branch, 300 Slater St., Ottawa, ON K1A 0C8
613-954-5031, Fax: 613-954-2340, 800-328-6189

Environment Canada, 10 Wellington St., Gatineau, QC K1A 0H3
819-997-2800, Fax: 819-994-1412, 800-668-6767, enviroinfo@ec.gc.ca

Environmental Sciences & Standards Division, 135 St. Clair Ave. West, 14th Fl., Toronto, ON M4V 1P5
416-314-6357, Fax: 416-314-6358

Fisheries & Oceans Canada, 200 Kent St., Ottawa, ON K1A 0E6
613-993-0999, Fax: 613-990-1866, info@dfo-mpo.gc.ca

Fisheries Resource Conservation Council, PO Box 2001 D, Ottawa, ON K1P 5W3
613-998-0433, Fax: 613-998-1146, info@frcc-ccrh.ca

Geological Survey of Canada, 601 Booth St., Ottawa, ON K1A 0E8
613-996-3919, Fax: 613-943-8742, esic@nrcan.gc.ca

Hazardous Materials Information Review Commission, 427 Laurier Ave. West, 7th Fl., Ottawa, ON K1A 1M3
613-993-4331, Fax: 613-993-4686, hmirc-ccrmd@hc-sc.gc.ca

Indian Oil & Gas Canada, #100, 9911 Chiila Blvd., Tsuu T'ina (Sarcee), AB T2W 6H6
403-292-5625, Fax: 403-292-5618, ContactIOGC@inac-ainc.gc.ca

Institute for Aerospace Research, 1200 Montreal Rd., Ottawa, ON K1A 0R6
613-990-0765, Fax: 613-952-7214

Institute for Information Technology, Bldg. M-50, 1200 Montreal Rd., Ottawa, ON K1A 0R6
613-991-3373, Fax: 613-952-0074, 877-672-2672

International Development Research Centre, 150 Kent St., PO Box 8500, Ottawa, ON K1G 3H9
613-236-6163, Fax: 613-238-7230, info@idrc.ca

Mackenzie Valley Environmental Impact Review Board, 200 Scotia Centre, #5102, 50th Ave., PO Box 938, Yellowknife, NT X1A 2N7
867-766-7050, Fax: 867-766-7074, 866-912-3472

National Energy Board, 444 - 7 Ave. SW, Calgary, AB T2P 0X8
403-292-4800, Fax: 403-292-5503, 800-899-1265, info@neb-one.gc.ca

National Research Council Canada, Bldg. M-58, 1200 Montreal Rd., Ottawa, ON K1A 0R6
613-993-9101, Fax: 613-952-7928, 877-672-2672, info@nrc-cnrc.ca

National Round Table on the Environment & Economy, #200, 344 Slater St., Ottawa, ON K1R 7Y3
613-992-7189, Fax: 613-992-7385, admin@nrtee-trnee.ca

Natural Resources Canada, 580 Booth St., Ottawa, ON K1A 0E4
613-995-0947, Fax: 613-992-7211

Natural Sciences & Engineering Research Council of Canada, Constitution Square, Tower II, 350 Albert St., Ottawa, ON K1A 1H5
613-995-4273, Fax: 613-943-1624, marie-josee.duval@nserc-crsng.gc.ca

Nunavut Impact Review Board, PO Box 1360, Cambridge Bay, NU X0B 0C0
867-983-4600, Fax: 867-983-2594, 866-233-3033, info@nirb.ca

Nunavut Water Board, PO Box 119, Gjoa Haven, NU X0B 1J0
867-360-6338, Fax: 867-360-6369

Pest Management Regulatory Agency, 2720 Riverside Dr., Ottawa, ON K1A 0K9
613-736-3401, Fax: 613-736-3798

Porcupine Caribou Management Board, PO Box 31723, Whitehorse, YT Y1A 6L3
867-633-4780, Fax: 867-393-3904, pcmb@taiga.net

Renewable Resources, Hugh John Flemming Forestry Centre, Suite 310, Fl 3rd, PO Box 6000, Fredericton, NB E3B 5H1
506-453-2684, Fax: 506-453-2684, dnrweb@gnb.ca

Science Sector, 200 Kent St., Ottawa, ON K1A 0E6

Social Sciences & Humanities Research Council of Canada, Constitution Sq., 350 Albert St., PO Box 1610 B,Ottawa, ON K1P 6G4
613-992-0691, Fax: 613-992-1787, info@sshrc.ca

Alberta

Access Advisory Council, Sterling Place, 9940 - 106 St., 4th Fl., Edmonton, AB
780-644-3183

Alberta Agriculture & Rural Development, J.G. O'Donoghue Bldg., #100A, 7000 - 113th St., Edmonton, AB T6H 5T6
780-427-2727, -310-3276, duke@gov.ab.ca

Alberta Environmental Appeals Board, Peace Hills Trust Tower, #306, 10011 - 109 St., Edmonton, AB T5J 3S8
780-427-6207, Fax: 780-427-4693

Alberta Innovates - Energy & Environmental Solutions, AMEC Place, #2540, 801 - 6th Ave. SW, Calgary, AB T2P 3W2
403-297-7089, ees@albertainnovates.ca

Alberta Innovates - Health Solutions, #1500, 10104 - 103 Ave., Edmonton, AB T5J 4A7
780-423-5727, Fax: 780-429-3509, 877-423-5727, health@albertainnovates.ca

Alberta Livestock & Meat Agency, Ellwood Office Park South, #101, 1003 Ellwood Rd. SW, Edmonton, AB T6X 0B3
780-638-1699, Fax: 780-638-6495, info@almaltd.ca

Alberta Recycling Management Authority, Scotia Tower 1, #1310, 10060 Jasper Ave., PO Box 189, Edmonton, AB T5J 2J1
780-990-1111, Fax: 780-990-1122, 888-999-8762, info@albertarecycling.ca

Alberta Research & Innvoation Authority, Phipps-McKinnon Bldg., #500, 101A Ave., Edmonton, AB T5J 3G2
780-427-1488, Fax: 780-427-0979, aria@albertainnovates.ca

Alberta Sport, Recreation, Parks, & Wildlife Foundation, Standard Life Centre, #903, 10405 Jasper Ave., 9th Fl., Edmonton, AB T5J 4R7
780-415-1167, Fax: 780-415-0308

Alberta Used Oil Management Association, Empire Building, #1008, 10080 Jasper Ave., Edmonton, AB T5J 1V9
780-414-1510, Fax: 780-414-1519, 866-414-1510, reception@usedoilrecycling.ca

Beverage Container Management Board, #750, 10707 - 100 Ave., Edmonton, AB T5J 3M1
780-424-3193, Fax: 780-428-4620, 888-424-7671

Alberta Energy, North Petroleum Plaza, 9945 - 108 St., Edmonton, AB T5K 2G6
780-427-8050, Fax: 780-422-0698, Library.Energy@gov.ab.ca

Alberta Environment, South Tower, Petroleum Plaza, 9915 - 108 St., 10th Fl., Edmonton, AB T5K 2G8
780-427-2700, Fax: 780-422-4086, env.infocent@gov.ab.ca

Irrigation Council, Provincial Bldg., 200 - 5 Ave. South, 3rd Fl., Lethbridge, AB T1J 4L1
403-381-5176, Fax: 403-382-4406

Land Compensation Board, 1229 - 91 St. SW, Edmonton, AB T6X 1E9
srb.lcb@gov.ab.ca

Natural Resources Conservation Board, Sterling Place, 9940 - 106 St., Edmonton, AB T5K 2N2
780-422-1977, Fax: 780-427-0607, 866-383-6722, info@nrcb.gov.ab.ca

Special Areas Board, Special Areas Board Administration, 212 - 2nd Ave. West, PO Box 820, Hanna, AB T0J 1P0
403-854-5600, Fax: 403-854-5527, specarea@telus.net

Alberta Sustainable Resource Development, Information Centre, Great West Life Building, 9920 - 108 St., Main Fl., Edmonton, AB T5K 2M4
780-944-0313, Fax: 780-427-4407, 877-944-0313, srd.infocent@gov.ab.ca

British Columbia

Agricultural Land Commission, #133, 4940 Canada Way, Burnaby, BC V5G 4K6
604-660-7000, Fax: 604-660-7033, ALCBurnaby@Victoria1.gov.bc.ca

Ministry of Agriculture, PO Box 9120 Prov Govt,Victoria, BC V8W 9E2
250-387-5121, Fax: 250-387-1522

British Columbia Farm Industry Review Board, 780 Blanshard St., PO Box 9129 Prov Govt, Victoria, BC V8W 9B5
250-356-8945, Fax: 250-356-5131, firb@gov.bc.ca

Emergency Management BC, PO Box 9223 Prov Govt,Victoria, BC V8W 9J1
250-953-4002, Fax: 250-953-4081, BC.CorSer@gov.bc.ca (Coroner); OFC@gov.bc.ca (Fire Commissioner)

Ministry of Energy & Mines, PO Box 9053 Prov Govt,Victoria, BC V8W 9E2
250-387-5896, Fax: 250-356-2965

Ministry of Environment, PO Box 9339 Prov Govt,Victoria, BC V8W 9M1
250-387-1161, Fax: 250-387-5669, envmail@gov.bc.ca

Environmental Appeal Board, 747 Fort St., 4th Fl., PO Box 9425 Prov Govt, Victoria, BC V8W 3E9
250-387-3464, Fax: 250-356-9923, eabinfo@gov.bc.ca

Environmental Protection Division, PO Box 9339, Victoria, BC V8W 9M1
250-387-1288, Fax: 250-387-5669

Environmental Stewardship Division, PO Box 9339 Prov Govt,Victoria, BC V8W 9M1
250-356-0121, Fax: 250-387-5669

Forest Appeals Commission, 747 Fort St., 4th Fl., PO Box 9425 Prov Govt, Victoria, BC V8W 9V1
250-387-3464, Fax: 250-356-9923, facinfo@gov.bc.ca
Forest Practices Board, 1675 Douglas St., 3rd Fl., PO Box 9905 Prov Govt, Victoria, BC V8W 9R1
250-213-4700, Fax: 250-213-4725, 800-994-5899, fpboard@gov.bc.ca
Forestry Innovation Investment Ltd., #1200, 1130 West Pender St., Vancouver, BC V6E 4A4
604-685-7507, Fax: 604-685-5373, info@bcfii.ca
Ministry of Forests, Lands & Natural Resource Operations, PO Box 9049 Prov Govt,Victoria, BC V8W 9E2
250-387-4809, Fax: 250-387-1040
Fraser Basin Council, Central Office, 470 Granville St., 1st Fl., Vancouver, BC V6C 1V5
604-488-5350, Fax: 604-488-5351, info@fraserbasin.bc.ca
Islands Trust, #200, 1627 Fort St., Victoria, BC V8R 1H8
250-405-5151, Fax: 250-405-5155, information@islandstrust.bc.ca
Oil & Gas Commission, #100, 10003 - 110 Ave., Fort St John, BC V1J 6M7
250-794-5200, Fax: 250-794-5375
Timber Export Advisory Committee, PO Box 9514 Prov Govt, Victoria, BC V8W 9C2
250-387-8916, Fax: 250-387-5050

Manitoba

Manitoba Aboriginal & Northern Affairs, 59 Elizabeth Dr., PO Box 37, Thompson, MB R8N 1X4
204-677-6607, Fax: 204-677-6753, amartin@gov.mb.ca
Aboriginal Affairs Secretariat, #200, 500 Portage Ave., Winnipeg, MB R3C 3X1
204-945-2510, Fax: 204-945-3689
Agricultural Societies, 1129 Queens Ave., Brandon, MB R7A 1L9
204-726-6195, Fax: 204-726-6260
Manitoba Agriculture, Food & Rural Initiatives, Norquay Bldg., 401 York Ave., Winnipeg, MB R3C 0P8
Clean Environment Commission, #305, 155 Carlton St., Winnipeg, MB R3C 3H8
204-945-0594, Fax: 204-945-0090
Manitoba Conservation, 200 Saulteaux Cres., Winnipeg, MB R3J 3W3
204-945-6784, 800-214-6497, mincon@leg.gov.mb.ca
Ecological Reserves Advisory Committee, c/o Manitoba Conservation, Parks & Natural Areas Branch, 200 Saulteaux Cres., Winnipeg, MB R3J 3W3
204-945-4148, Fax: 204-945-0012, hhernandez@gov.mb.ca
Endangered Species Advisory Committee, 200 Saulteaux Cres., PO Box 24, Winnipeg, MB R3J 3W3
204-945-7465, Fax: 204-945-3077
Farm Lands Ownership Board, #812, Norquay Bldg., 401 York Ave., Winnipeg, MB R3C 0P8
204-945-3149, Fax: 204-945-1489, 800-282-8069, robert.mckenzie@gov.mb.ca
Farm Machinery Board, Norquay Bldg., #812, 401 York Ave., Winnipeg, MB R3C 0P8
204-945-3856, Fax: 204-948-2844, randy.ozunko@gov.mb.ca
Manitoba Hydro, PO Box 815 Main,Winnipeg, MB R3C 2P4
204-474-3311, Fax: 204-475-0069, publicaffairs@hydro.mb.ca
Local Government Development Division, 59 Elizabeth Dr., PO Box 33, Thompson, MB R8N 1X4
204-677-6794, Fax: 204-677-6525
Manitoba Habitat Heritage Corporation, #200, 1555 St. James St., Winnipeg, MB R3H 1B5
204-784-4350, Fax: 204-784-7359, mhhc@mhhc.mb.ca

New Brunswick

Board of Examiners under the Scaler's Act, 1350 Regent St. South, PO Box 6000, Fredericton, NB E3B 5H1
506-453-2441, Fax: 506-453-6689
Department of Agriculture, Aquaculture & Fisheries, PO Box 6000, Fredericton, NB E3B 5H1
506-453-2666, Fax: 506-453-7170, DAAF-MAAP@gnb.ca
Department of Natural Resources, Hugh John Flemming Forestry Centre, PO Box 6000, Fredericton, NB E3B 5H1
506-453-3826, Fax: 506-444-4367, dnrweb@gnb.ca
Department of the Environment, Marysville Place, 20 McGloin St., PO Box 6000, Fredericton, NB E3B 5H1
506-453-2690, Fax: 506-457-7800, env-info@gnb.ca
Forest Protection Limited, 2502 Hwy. 102, Lincoln, NB E3B 7E6
506-446-6930, Fax: 506-446-6934, info@forestprotectionlimited.com
New Brunswick Farm Products Commission, c/o Department of Agriculture, Aquaculture & Fisheries, PO Box 6000, Fredericton, NB E3B 5H1
506-453-3647, Fax: 506-444-5969
New Brunswick Round Table on Environment & Economy, 20 McGloin St., PO Box 6000, Fredericton, NB E3B 5H1
506-453-3703, Fax: 506-453-3876
Northern Development, Harbourview Place, 275 Main St., Bathurst, NB E2A 1A9
506-547-2227, Fax: 506-547-2269
New Brunswick Research & Productivity Council, 921 College Hill Rd., Fredericton, NB E3B 6Z9
506-452-1212, Fax: 506-452-1395, info@rpc.ca
Service New Brunswick, Westmorland Place, #200, 82 Westmorland St., PO Box 1998, Fredericton, NB E3B 5G4
506-457-3581, Fax: 506-457-7520, 888-762-8600, snb@snb.ca

Newfoundland & Labrador

C.A. Pippy Park Commission, Mount Scio House, 15 Mount Scio Rd., St. John's, NL A1B 3T2
709-737-3655, Fax: 709-737-3303, info@pippypark.com
Canada-Newfoundland Offshore Petroleum Board, TD Place, 140 Water St., 5th Fl., St. John's, NL A1C 6H6
709-778-1400, Fax: 709-778-1473, information@cnlopb.nl.ca
Department of Environment & Conservation, Confederation Bldg., West Block, 4th Fl., PO Box 8700, St. John's, NL A1B 4J6
709-729-2664, Fax: 709-729-6639, 800-563-6181, info@gov.nl.ca
Department of Fisheries & Aquaculture, Petten Bldg., 30 Strawberry Marsh Rd., PO Box 8700, St. John's, NL A1B 4J6
709-729-3723, Fax: 709-729-6082, fisheries@gov.nl.ca
Department of Innovation, Trade & Rural Development, West Block, Confederation Bldg., PO Box 8700, St. John's, NL A1B 4J6
709-729-7000, Fax: 709-729-0654, intrd@gov.nl.ca
Department of Natural Resources, Natural Resources Bldg., 50 Elizabeth Ave., 7th Fl., PO Box 8700, St. John's, NL A1B 4J6
709-729-2920, Fax: 709-729-0059
Professional Fish Harvesters Certification Board, 368 Hamilton Ave., PO Box 8541, St. John's, NL A1B 3P2
709-722-8170, Fax: 709-722-8201, pfh@pfhcb.com

Northwest Territories

Aurora Research Institute, 191 MacKenzie Rd., PO Box 1450, Inuvik, NT X0E 0T0
867-777-3298, Fax: 867-777-4264, webmaster@nwtresearch.com
Department of Environment & Natural Resources, PO Box 1320, Yellowknife, NT X1A 2L9

Nova Scotia

Department of Agriculture, 1741 Brunswick St., 3rd Fl., PO Box 2223, Halifax, NS B3J 3C4
902-424-4560, Fax: 902-424-4671
Canada-Nova Scotia Offshore Petroleum Board, TD Centre, 1791 Barrington St., 6th Fl., Halifax, NS B3J 3K9
902-422-5588, Fax: 902-422-1799, postmaster@cnsopb.ns.ca
Crown Land Information Management Centre, Founders Square, #501, 1701 Hollis St., PO Box 698, Halifax, NS B3J 2T9
902-424-3171
Department of Natural Resources, Founder's Square, 1701 Hollis St., 3rd Fl., PO Box 698, Halifax, NS B3J 2T9
902-424-5935, Fax: 902-424-0594, 800-565-2224
Nova Scotia Farm Loan Board, PO Box 550, Truro, NS B2N 5E3
902-893-6506, Fax: 902-895-7693, flb@gov.ns.ca
Nova Scotia Geomatics Centre, 160 Willow St., Amherst, NS B4H 3W5
902-667-7231, Fax: 902-667-6008, 800-798-0706, geoinfo@gov.ns.ca

Nunavut

Department of Environment, PO Box 1000 1300,Iqaluit, NU X0A 0H0
867-975-7700, Fax: 867-975-7742, environment@gov.nu.ca

Ontario

Advisory Council on Drinking Water Quality & Testing Standards, 40 St. Clair Ave. West, 3rd Fl., Toronto, ON M4V 1M2
416-212-7779, Fax: 416-212-7595
Ministry of Agriculture, Food & Rural Affairs, Ontario Government Bldg., 1 Stone Rd. West, Guelph, ON N1G 4Y2
519-826-3100, 888-466-2372
Algonquin Forestry Authority - Huntsville, 222 Main St. West, Huntsville, ON P1H 1Y1
705-789-9647, Fax: 705-789-3353, info@algonquinforestry.on.ca
Algonquin Forestry Authority - Pembroke, Victoria Centre, 84 Isabella St., 2nd Fl., Pembroke, ON K8A 5S5
613-735-0173, Fax: 613-735-4192, info@algonquinforestry.on.ca
Animal Care Review Board, 77 Grenville St., 8th Fl., Toronto, ON M5S 1B3
416-314-3509, Fax: 416-314-3518
Association of Ontario Land Surveyors, 1043 McNicoll Ave., Toronto, ON M1W 3W6
416-491-9020, Fax: 416-491-2576
Cancer Care Ontario, 620 University Ave., 15th Fl., Toronto, ON M5G 2L7
416-971-9800, Fax: 416-971-6888
Conservation Review Board, 400 University Ave. 4th Fl., Toronto, ON M7A 2R9
416-314-7137, Fax: 416-314-7175, conservation.review.board@ontario.ca
Ministry of Environment, 135 St. Clair Ave. West, Toronto, ON M4V 1P5
416-325-4000, Fax: 416-325-3159, 800-565-4923
Environmental Commissioner of Ontario, #605, 1075 Bay St., Toronto, ON M5S 2B1
416-325-3377, Fax: 416-325-3370, 800-701-6454, commissioner@eco.on.ca
Environmental Review Tribunal, #1500, 655 Bay St., Toronto, ON M5G 1E5
416-212-6349, Fax: 416-314-4506, 866-448-2248, erttribunalsecretary@ontario.ca
Lake of the Woods Control Board, c/o Executive Engineer, Ottawa, ON K1A 0H3
Fax: 819-953-4666, 800-661-5922, secretariat@lwcb.ca
Livestock Medicines Advisory Committee, 1 Stone Rd. West, 3rd Fl. Northeast, Guelph, ON N1G 4Y2
519-826-4110, Fax: 519-826-3254
Mines & Minerals Division, Willet Green Miller Centre, 933 Ramsey Lake Rd., Sudbury, ON P3E 6B5
705-670-5755, Fax: 705-670-5818, 888-415-9845
Ministry of Natural Resources, Whitney Block, #6630, 99 Wellesley St. West, 6th Fl., Toronto, ON M7A 1W3
800-667-1940
Niagara Parks Commission, Oak Hall Administration Bldg., 7400 Portage Rd. South, PO Box 150, Niagara Falls, ON L2E 6T2
905-356-2241, Fax: 905-354-6041, 877-642-7275
Ministry of Northern Development, Mines & Forestry, 99 Wellesley St. West, Toronto, ON M7A 1W3
416-327-0633, Fax: 416-327-0651
Ontario Clean Water Agency, 1 Yonge St., 17th Fl., Toronto, ON M5E 1E5
416-314-5600, Fax: 416-314-8300, 800-667-6292
Ontario Fish & Wildlife Heritage Commission, Robinson Pl., 300 Water St., PO Box 7000, Peterborough, ON K9J 8M5
705-755-1905, Fax: 705-755-1900
Ontario Geographic Names Board, Robinson Place, 300 Water St., 2nd Fl., PO Box 7000, Peterborough, ON K9J 8M5
705-755-2134
Ontario Moose & Bear Allocation Advisory Committee, PO Box 964, Sioux Lookout, ON P8T 1B3
807-737-2615, Fax: 807-737-4173
Ontario Science Centre, 770 Don Mills Rd., Toronto, ON M3C 1T3
416-696-1000, Fax: 416-696-3124
Pesticides Advisory Committee, 135 St. Clair Ave. West, 15th Fl., Toronto, ON M4V 1P5
416-314-9230, Fax: 416-314-9237
Rabies Advisory Committee, Trent University Science Complex, PO Box 4840, Peterborough, ON K9J 8N8
705-755-2270
Royal Botanical Gardens, 680 Plains Rd. West, Burlington, ON L7T 4H4
905-527-1158, Fax: 905-577-0375, 800-694-4769
Science & Information Resources Division, Roberta Bondar Pl., #400, 70 Foster Dr., Sault Ste Marie, ON P6A 6V5
705-755-2000, Fax: 705-755-2802, 800-667-1940
Science North, 100 Ramsey Lake Rd., Sudbury, ON P3E 5S9
705-522-3701, Fax: 705-522-4954
Shibogama Interim Planning Board, PO Box 105, Wunnumin, ON P0V 2Z0
807-442-2559, Fax: 807-442-2627
St. Lawrence Parks Commission, RR#1, Morrisburg, ON K0C 1X0
613-543-3704, Fax: 613-543-2847, 800-437-2233
Windigo Interim Planning Board, PO Box 299, Sioux Lookout, ON P8T 1A3
807-737-1585, Fax: 807-737-3133

Prince Edward Island

Agricultural Insurance Corporation, 29 Indigo Cres., PO Box 1600, Charlottetown, PE C1A 7N3
902-368-4842, Fax: 902-368-6677
Grain Elevators Corporation, 7 Gerald McCarville Dr., PO Box 250, Kensington, PE C0B 1M0
902-836-8935, Fax: 902-836-8926
Prince Edward Island Department of Agriculture, Jones Bldg., 11 Kent St., PO Box 2000, Charlottetown, PE C1A 7N8
902-368-4880, Fax: 902-368-4857
Prince Edward Island Energy Corporation, Jones Bldg., 11 Kent St., 4th Fl., PO Box 2000, Charlottetown, PE C1A 7N8

Quebec

Ministère de l'Agriculture, des Pêcheries et de l'Alimentation, 200, ch Sainte-Foy, Québec, QC G1R 4X6
418-380-2110, 888-222-6272
Bureau d'audiences publiques sur l'environnement, Édifice Lomer-Gouin, #2.10, 575, rue Saint-Amable, Québec, QC G1R 6A6
418-643-7447, Fax: 418-643-9474, 800-463-4732, communication@bape.gouv.qc.ca

Comité consultatif de l'environnement Kativik, CP 930, Kuujjuaq, QC J0M 1C0
819-964-2961, Fax: 819-964-0694
Fondation de la faune du Québec, Place Iberville II, #420, 1175, av Lavigerie, Québec, QC G1V 4P1
418-644-7926, Fax: 418-643-7655, 877-639-0742, ffq@fondationdelafaune.qc.ca
Fonds québécois de la recherche sur la nature et les technologies, #450, 140, Grande Allée est, Québec, QC G1R 5M8
418-643-8560, Fax: 418-643-1451, info@fqrnt.gouv.qc.ca
Ottawa River Regulation Planning Board, 351 St Joseph Blvd., Hull, QC J8Y 3Z5
613-994-7079, 800-778-1246, secretariat@ottawariver.ca
Ministère des Ressources naturelles et de la Faune, 880, ch Sainte-Foy, Québec, QC G1S 4X4
418-627-8600, Fax: 418-644-6513, 866-248-6936, services.clientele@mrnf.gouv.qc.ca
Régie de l'énergie, Tour de la Bourse, #2.55, 800, Place Victoria, Montréal, QC H4Z 1A2
514-873-2452, Fax: 514-873-2070, 888-873-2452, secretariat@regie-energie.qc.ca
Société de développement de la Baie James, 110, boul Matagami, CP 970, Matagami, QC J0Y 2A0
819-739-4717, Fax: 819-739-4329, mat@sdbj.gouv.qc.ca

Saskatchewan

Agri-Food Council, #302, 3085 Albert St., Regina, SK S4S 0B1
306-787-5978, Fax: 306-787-5134, corey.ruud@gov.sk.ca
Agricultural Implements Board, #202, 3085 Albert St., Regina, SK S4S 0B1
306-787-4693, Fax: 306-787-1315
Saskatchewan Agriculture, Walter Scott Bldg., 3085 Albert St., Regina, SK S4S 0B1
866-457-2377, aginfo@gov.sk.ca
Enterprise Saskatchewan, #200, 3085 Albert St., Regina, SK S4S 0B1
306-787-4484, Fax: 306-798-0629, 800-265-2001, webmaster@enterprisesask.ca; invest@enterprisesask.ca
Saskatchewan Environment, 3211 Albert St., 2nd Fl., Regina, SK S4S 5W6
306-787-2584, Fax: 306-787-9544, 800-567-4224, Centre.Inquiry@gov.sk.ca
Farm Stress Unit, #125, 3085 Albert St., Regina, SK S4S 0B1
306-787-5196, Fax: 306-798-3042, 800-667-4442
Health Quality Council, 241, 111 Research Dr., Saskatoon, SK S7N 3R2
306-668-8810, Fax: 306-668-8820, info@hqc.sk.ca
Prairie Agricultural Machinery Institute, Hwy 5 West, PO Box 1150, Humboldt, SK S0K 2A0
306-682-2555, Fax: 306-682-5080, 800-567-7264, humboldt@pami.ca
Saskatchewan Research Council, #125, 15 Innovation Blvd., Saskatoon, SK S7N 2X8
306-933-5400, Fax: 306-933-7446, info@src.sk.ca
Saskatchewan Conservation Data Centre, 3211 Albert St., Regina, SK S4S 5W6
306-787-9038, Fax: 306-787-9544
Saskatchewan Crop Insurance Corporation, 484 Prince William Dr., PO Box 3000, Melville, SK S0A 2P0
306-728-7200, Fax: 306-728-7202, 888-935-0000, customer.service@scic.gov.sk.ca
Saskatchewan Farm Land Security Board, #207, 3988 Albert St., Regina, SK S4S 3R1
306-787-5047, Fax: 306-787-8599,
Saskatchewan Farm Security Programs, #207, 3988 Albert St., Regina, SK S4S 3R1
306-787-5047, Fax: 306-787-8599
Saskatchewan Lands Appeal Board, #202, 3085 Albert St., Regina, SK S4S 0B1
306-787-4693, Fax: 306-787-1315, Donald.Brooks@gov.sk.ca
Saskatchewan Watershed Authority, 111 Fairford St. East, Moose Jaw, SK S6H 7X9
306-694-3900, Fax: 306-694-3465, comm@swa.ca
Surface Rights Board of Arbitration, 113 - 2nd Ave. East, PO Box 1597, Kindersley, SK S0L 1S0
306-463-5447, Fax: 306-463-5449, surfacerightsboard@gov.sk.ca

Yukon Territory

Alsek Renewable Resource Council, PO Box 2077, Haines Junction, YT Y0B 1L0
867-634-2524, Fax: 867-634-2527
Carmacks Renewable Resource Council, PO Box 122, Carmacks, YT Y0B 1C0
867-863-6838, Fax: 867-863-6429, carmacksrrc@northwestel.net
Dawson District Renewable Resource Council, PO Box 1380, Dawson City, YT Y0B 1G0
867-993-6976, Fax: 867-993-6093, dawsonrrc@northwestel.net
Yukon Development Corporation, #2 Miles Canyon Rd., PO Box 5920, Whitehorse, YT Y1A 6S7
867-393-5337, Fax: 867-393-5401
Yukon Environment, PO Box 2703, Whitehorse, YT Y1A 2C6
867-667-5652, Fax: 867-393-7197, environment.yukon@gov.yk.ca
Mayo District Renewable Resources Council, PO Box 249, Mayo, YT Y0B 1M0
867-996-2942, Fax: 867-996-2948, mayorrc@yknet.yk.ca
North Yukon Renewable Resources Council, PO Box 80, Old Crow, YT Y0B 1N0
867-966-3034, Fax: 867-966-3036, vgrrc@yknet.yk.ca
Selkirk Renewable Resources Council, PO Box 32, Pelly Crossing, YT Y0B 1P0
867-537-3937, Fax: 867-537-3939, selkirkrrc@yknet.yk.ca
Teslin Renewable Resource Council, PO Box 186, Teslin, YT Y0A 1B0
867-390-2323, Fax: 867-390-2919, teslinrrc@northwestel.net
Yukon Fish & Wildlife Management Board, 106 Main St., 2nd Fl., Whitehorse, YT Y1A 5P7
867-667-3754, Fax: 867-393-6947, officemanager@yfwmb.ca
Yukon Land Use Planning Council, #201, 307 Jarvis St., Whitehorse, YT Y1A 2H3
867-667-7397, Fax: 867-667-4624, ylupc@planyukon.ca

SCIENCE & TECHNOLOGY

See Also: Business Development

Bedford Institute of Oceanography, 1 Challenger Dr., PO Box 1006, Dartmouth, NS B2Y 4A2
902-426-3492, Fax: 902-426-8484
Biotechnology Research Institute, 6100, av Royalmount, Montréal, QC H4P 2R2
514-496-6100, Fax: 514-496-1928, bri-info@cnrc-nrc.gc.ca
Canada Centre for Remote Sensing - Geomatics Canada, 588 Booth St., Ottawa, ON K1A 0Y7
613-995-0947, Fax: 613-947-1382
Canadian Food Inspection Agency, 1400 Merivale Rd., Ottawa, ON K1A 0Y9
613-225-2342, Fax: 613-228-6601, 800-442-2342
Canadian Hydraulics Centre, 1200 Montreal Rd., Ottawa, ON K1A 0R6
613-993-9381, Fax: 613-952-7679, info.chc@nrc-cnrc.gc.ca
Canadian Institutes of Health Research, 160 Elgin St., 9th Fl., Ottawa, ON K1A 0W9
613-941-2672, Fax: 613-954-1800, 888-603-4178, info@cihr-irsc.gc.ca
Canadian Space Agency, John H. Chapman Space Centre, 6767, rte de l'Aéroport, Saint-Hubert, QC J3Y 8Y9
450-926-4800, Fax: 450-926-4352, promo@asc-csa.gc.ca
Environmental Sciences & Standards Division, 135 St. Clair Ave. West, 14th Fl., Toronto, ON M4V 1P5
416-314-6357, Fax: 416-314-6358
Freshwater Institute, 501 University Cres., Winnipeg, MB R3T 2N6
204-983-5000, Fax: 204-983-6285
Herzberg Institute of Astrophysics, 5071 West Saanich Rd., Victoria, BC V9E 2E7
250-363-0001, Fax: 250-363-0045, hia-www@nrc-cnrc.gc.ca
Industrial Materials Institute, 75, boul de Mortagne, Boucherville, QC J4B 6Y4
450-641-5000, Fax: 450-641-5101, Imi-Info@cnrc-nrc.gc.ca
Institut Maurice-Lamontagne, 850, rte de le Mer, CP 1000, Mont-Joli, QC G5H 3Z4
418-775-0555, Fax: 418-775-0730
Institute for Biological Sciences, Bldg. M-54, 1200 Montreal Rd., Ottawa, ON K1A 0R6
613-993-5812, Fax: 613-957-7867
Institute for Chemical Process & Environmental Technology, Bldg. M-12, 1200 Montreal Rd., Ottawa, ON K1A 0R6
613-993-4041, Fax: 613-957-8231
Institute for Marine Biosciences, 1411 Oxford St., Halifax, NS B3H 3Z1
902-426-8332, Fax: 902-426-9413, communications.imb@nrc-cnrc.gc.ca
Institute for National Measurement Standards, Bldg. M-36, 1500 Montreal Rd., Ottawa, ON K1A 0R6
613-998-7018, Fax: 613-954-1473, alexandra.shaw@nrc-cnrc.gc.ca
Institute for Ocean Technology, Kerwin Pl. & Arctic Ave., PO Box 12093, St. John's, NL A1B 3T5
709-772-4939, Fax: 709-772-2462, Noel.Murphy@nrc-cnrc.gc.ca
Institute for Research in Construction, Bldg. M-24, 1500 Montreal Rd., Ottawa, ON K1A 0R6
613-993-2607, Fax: 613-952-7673, Irc.Client-Services@nrc-cnrc.gc.ca
Institute of Ocean Sciences, 9860 West Saanich Rd., PO Box 6000, Sidney, BC V8L 4B2
250-363-6517, Fax: 250-363-6390
International Development Research Centre, 150 Kent St., PO Box 8500, Ottawa, ON K1G 3H9
613-236-6163, Fax: 613-238-7230, info@idrc.ca
National Research Council Canada, Bldg. M-58, 1200 Montreal Rd., Ottawa, ON K1A 0R6
613-993-9101, Fax: 613-952-7928, 877-672-2672, info@nrc-cnrc.gc.ca
Natural Sciences & Engineering Research Council of Canada, Constitution Square, Tower II, 350 Albert St., Ottawa, ON K1A 1H5
613-995-4273, Fax: 613-943-1624, marie-josee.duval@nserc-crsng.gc.ca
Pacific Biological Station, 3190 Hammond Bay Rd., Nanaimo, BC V9T 6N7
250-756-7000, Fax: 250-756-7053
Plant Biotechnology Institute, 110 Gymnasium Pl., Saskatoon, SK S7N 0W9
306-975-5248, Fax: 306-975-4839, pbi-info@nrc-cnrc.gc.ca
Science Sector, 200 Kent St., Ottawa, ON K1A 0E6
Spectrum, Information Technologies & Telecommunications, Journal Tower North, 300 Slater St., 20th Fl., Ottawa, ON K1A 0C8
613-998-0368, Fax: 613-952-1203
St. Andrews Biological Station, 531 Brandy Cove Rd., St Andrews, NB E5B 2L9
506-529-8854, Fax: 506-529-5862, XMARSABS@mar.dfo-mpo.gc.ca

Alberta

Alberta Innovates - Energy & Environmental Solutions, AMEC Place, #2540, 801 - 6th Ave. SW, Calgary, AB T2P 3W2
403-297-7089, ees@albertainnovates.ca

British Columbia

Leading Edge Endowment Fund Board, 1188 West Georgia St., 9th Fl., Vancouver, BC V6E 4A2
604-438-3220, contact@leefbc.ca
Powertech Labs Inc., 12388 - 88 Ave., Surrey, BC V8W 7R7
604-590-7500, Fax: 604-590-6611

Manitoba

Industrial Technology Centre, #200, 78 Innovation Dr., Winnipeg, MB R3T 6C2
Manitoba Education, Research & Learning Information Networks, #100 - 135 Innovation Dr., University of Manitoba, Winnipeg, MB R3T 6A8
204-474-7800, Fax: 204-474-7830, 800-430-6404
Manitoba Science, Technology, Energy & Mines, #333, 450 Broadway, Winnipeg, MB R3C 0V8

New Brunswick

Northern Development, Harbourview Place, 275 Main St., Bathurst, NB E2A 1A9
506-547-2227, Fax: 506-547-2269
New Brunswick Research & Productivity Council, 921 College Hill Rd., Fredericton, NB E3B 6Z9
506-452-1212, Fax: 506-452-1395, info@rpc.ca
Sciences & Planning, Marysville Place, 20 McGloin St., 2nd Fl., PO Box 6000, Fredericton, NB E3B 5H1
506-453-2862, Fax: 506-453-2265

Northwest Territories

Aurora Research Institute, 191 MacKenzie Rd., PO Box 1450, Inuvik, NT X0E 0T0
867-777-3298, Fax: 867-777-4264, webmaster@nwtresearch.com

Nova Scotia

InNOVACorp, #1400, 1801 Hollis St., Halifax, NS B3J 3N4
902-424-8670, Fax: 902-424-4679, 800-565-7051, communications@innovacorp.ca

Ontario

Ontario Science Centre, 770 Don Mills Rd., Toronto, ON M3C 1T3
416-696-1000, Fax: 416-696-3124
Ministry of Research & Innovation, Ferguson Block, 56 Wellesley St. West, 7th Fl., Toronto, ON M7A 2E7
416-325-5181, Fax: 416-325-3877, 866-446-5216
Science North, 100 Ramsey Lake Rd., Sudbury, ON P3E 5S9
705-522-3701, Fax: 705-522-4954

Prince Edward Island

Prince Edward Island Department of Environment, Energy, & Forestry, Jones Bldg., 11 Kent St., 4th Fl., PO Box 2000, Charlottetown, PE C1A 7N8
902-368-5000, Fax: 902-368-5830

Quebec

Centre de recherche industrielle du Québec, 333, rue Franquet, Québec, QC G1P 4C7
418-659-1550, Fax: 418-652-2251, 800-667-2386, infocriq@criq.qc.ca
Fonds québécois de la recherche sur la nature et les technologies, #450, 140, Grande Allée est, Québec, QC G1R 5M8
418-643-8560, Fax: 418-643-1451, info@fqrnt.gouv.qc.ca

Saskatchewan

Saskatchewan Research Council, #125, 15 Innovation Blvd., Saskatoon, SK S7N 2X8
306-933-5400, Fax: 306-933-7446, info@src.sk.ca

Yukon Territory
Yukon Energy, Mines & Resources, PO Box 2703, Whitehorse, YT Y1A 2C6
867-667-3130, Fax: 867-456-3965, 800-661-0408, emr@gov.yk.ca

SECURITIES ADMINISTRATION

See Also: Finance

Alberta
Alberta Securities Commission, #600, 250 - 5th St. SW, Calgary, AB T2P 0R4
403-297-6454, Fax: 403-297-6156, 877-355-0585, inquiries@asc.ca; media@asc.ca; complaints@asc.ca

British Columbia
British Columbia Securities Commission, Pacific Centre, 701 West Georgia St., 12th Fl., PO Box 10142, Vancouver, BC V7Y 1L2
604-899-6500, Fax: 604-899-6506, 800-373-6393, inquiries@bcsc.bc.ca

Manitoba
Manitoba Securities Commission, #500, 400 St. Mary Ave., Winnipeg, MB R3C 4K5
204-945-2548, Fax: 204-945-0330, 800-655-5244, securities@gov.mb.ca

New Brunswick
New Brunswick Securities Commission, #300, 85 Charlotte St., Saint John, NB E2L 2J2
506-658-3060, Fax: 506-658-3059, 866-933-2222, information@nbsc-cvmnb.ca

Northwest Territories
Department of Justice, Courthouse, 4903 - 49th St., 6th Fl., PO Box 1320, Yellowknife, NT X1A 2L9
867-920-6197

Ontario
Ontario Securities Commission, #1903, 20 Queen St. West, PO Box 55, Toronto, ON M5H 3S8
416-597-0681, Fax: 416-593-8241

Quebec
Autorité des marchés financiers, Tour de la Bourse, 800, Square Victoria, 22e étage, Montréal, QC H4Z 1G3
514-395-0337, Fax: 514-873-3090, 877-525-0337

Saskatchewan
Saskatchewan Financial Services Commission, #601, 1919 Saskatchewan Dr., Regina, SK S4P 4H2
306-787-5645, Fax: 306-787-5899

SENIOR CITIZENS SERVICES

National Advisory Council on Aging, Jeanne Mance Bldg., 8th Fl., Postal Locator 1908 A1, Ottawa, ON K1A 0K9
613-957-1968, Fax: 613-957-7627

Office of the Commissioner of Review Tribunals, PO Box 8250 T, Ottawa, ON K1G 5S5
613-954-1313, Fax: 613-946-1588, 800-363-0076, info@ocrt-bctr.gc.ca

Alberta
Alberta Seniors & Community Supports, Communications, Standard Life Centre, 10405 Jasper Ave., 3rd Fl., Edmonton, AB T5J 4R7
780-415-9950, Fax: 780-644-1227, 866-477-8589, seniors.communications@gov.ab.ca

Seniors Advisory Council for Alberta, Standard Life Centre, #600, 10405 Jasper Ave., 6th Fl., Edmonton, AB T5J 4R7
780-422-2321, Fax: 780-422-8762, saca@gov.ab.ca

Manitoba
Manitoba Seniors & Healthy Aging Secretariat, #822, 155 Carlton St., Winnipeg, MB R3C 3H8
204-945-6565, Fax: 204-948-2514, 800-665-6565, seniors@gov.mb.ca

New Brunswick
New Brunswick Advisory Council on Seniors, #620, 440 King St., Fredericton, NB E3B 5H8
506-444-5757, Fax: 506-446-784, 888-762-5411

Program Design & Quality Management, Sartain MacDonald Bldg., #4007, 551 King St., PO Box 6000, Fredericton, NB E3B 5H1
506-453-2181, Fax: 506-453-3829

Nova Scotia
Seniors' Secretariat, Dennis Bldg., 1740 Granville St., 4th Fl., PO Box 2065, Halifax, NS B3J 2Z1
902-424-0065, Fax: 902-424-0561, 800-670-0065, seniors@gov.ns.ca

Nunavut
Department of Culture, Language, Elders & Youth, PO Box 1000 800,Iqaluit, NU X0A 0H0
867-975-5500, Fax: 867-975-5504, 866-934-2035

Ontario
Office of the Chief Information Officer, Mowat Block, 900 Bay St. 3rd FL, Toronto, ON M7A 1L2
416-325-4598

Quebec
Ministère de la Famille et des Aînés, 425, rue Saint-Amable, 1er étage, Québec, QC G1R 4Z1
877-216-6202

Ministère de la Santé et des Services sociaux, Direction des communications, 1075, ch Sainte-Foy, 16e étage, Québec, QC G1S 2M1
418-643-9395, Fax: 418-643-4768, regisseur.web@msss.gouv.qc.ca

Yukon Territory
Yukon Health & Social Services, PO Box 2703, Whitehorse, YT Y1A 2C6
867-667-3673, Fax: 867-667-3096, hss@gov.yk.ca

SEXUALLY TRANSMITTED DISEASE CONTROL

See Also: AIDS

Prince Edward Island
Prince Edward Island Department of Health & Wellness, 105 Rochford St. North, 4th Fl., PO Box 2000, Charlottetown, PE C1A 7N8
902-368-6414, Fax: 902-368-4121,

SOCIAL AFFAIRS

Ontario
Ontario Trillium Foundation, 800 Bay St., 5th Fl., Toronto, ON M5S 3A9
416-963-4927, Fax: 416-963-8781, 800-263-2887, trillium@trilliumfoundation.org

SOCIAL SERVICES

See Also: Community Services

Alberta
Alberta Children & Youth Services, Communications, Sterling Place, 9940 - 106 St., 12th Fl., Edmonton, AB T5K 2N2
780-422-3004, Fax: 780-422-3071, cs.communications@gov.ab.ca

Alberta Seniors & Community Supports, Communications, Standard Life Centre, 10405 Jasper Ave., 3rd Fl., Edmonton, AB T5J 4R7
780-415-9950, Fax: 780-644-1227, 866-477-8589, seniors.communications@gov.ab.ca

British Columbia
British Columbia College of Social Workers, #302, 1765 West 8th Ave., Vancouver, BC V6J 5C6
604-737-4916, Fax: 604-737-6809, info@bccsw.ca

Ministry of Community, Sport & Cultural Development, PO Box 9056 Prov Govt,Victoria, BC V8W 9E2
250-387-2283, Fax: 250-387-4312

Manitoba
Social Services Appeal Board, 175 Hargrave St., 7th Fl., Winnipeg, MB R3C 3R8
204-945-3003, Fax: 204-945-1736, 800-282-8069

New Brunswick
Department of Social Development, Sartain MacDonald Bldg., 551 King St., PO Box 6000, Fredericton, NB E3B 5H1
506-453-2001, Fax: 506-453-7478, sd-ds@gnb.ca

Newfoundland & Labrador
Department of Human Resources, Labour & Employment, Confederation Bldg., PO Box 8700, St. John's, NL A1B 4J6
709-729-2480, Fax: 709-729-6996, hreweb@gov.nl.ca

Northwest Territories
Department of Health & Social Services, Centre Square Tower, PO Box 1320, Yellowknife, NT X1A 2L9
Fax: 867-873-0266

Nunavut
Department of Health & Social Services, PO Box 1000 1000,Iqaluit, NU X0A 0H0
867-975-5700, Fax: 867-975-5705

Ontario
Operations Division, Hepburn Block, 80 Grosvenor St., 6th Fl., Toronto, ON M7A 1E9
416-325-5581, Fax: 416-325-5432

Quebec
Ministère de la Santé et des Services sociaux, Direction des communications, 1075, ch Sainte-Foy, 16e étage, Québec, QC G1S 2M1
418-643-9395, Fax: 418-643-4768, regisseur.web@msss.gouv.qc.ca

Saskatchewan
Saskatchewan Social Services, 1920 Broad St., Regina, SK S4P 3V6
306-787-3700, 866-221-5200, socialservicesinquiry@gov.sk.ca

SOIL RESOURCES

Soils & Crops Research & Development Centre, 2560, boul Hochelaga, Québec, QC G1V 2J3
418-657-7980, Fax: 418-648-2402

Quebec
Commission de protection du territoire agricole du Québec, 200, ch Ste-Foy, 2e étage, Québec, QC G1R 4X6
418-643-3314, Fax: 418-643-2261, 800-667-5294, info@cptaq.gouv.qc.ca

SOLICITORS GENERAL

Alberta
Alberta Solicitor General & Public Security, Communications, John E. Browntree Building, 10365 - 97 St., 9th Fl., Edmonton, AB T5J 3W7
780-427-3441, Fax: 780-427-2789

British Columbia
Ministry of Public Safety & Solicitor General, PO Box 9290 Prov Govt,Victoria, BC V8W 9J7
250-387-6121, 800-663-7867, pssgwebfeedback@gov.bc.ca

Manitoba
Manitoba Justice, Legislative Building, #104, 405 Broadway Ave., Winnipeg, MB R3C 3L6
204-945-3728, Fax: 204-945-2517, minjus@gov.mb.ca

Newfoundland & Labrador
Department of Justice, Confederation Bldg., East Block, 4th Fl., PO Box 8700, St. John's, NL A1B 4J6
709-729-2869, Fax: 709-729-0469, justice@gov.nl.ca

Nova Scotia
Department of Justice, 5151 Terminal Rd., 4th Fl., PO Box 7, Halifax, NS B3J 2L6
902-424-4030, Fax: 902-424-0510, justweb@gov.ns.ca

Ontario
Ministry of Community Safety & Correctional Services, George Drew Bldg., 25 Grosvenor St., 18th Fl., Toronto, ON M7A 1Y6
416-326-5000, Fax: 416-326-0498, 866-517-0571, mcscs.feedback@ontario.ca

Quebec
Ministère de la Sécurité publique, Tour des Laurentides, 2525, boul Laurier, 5e étage, Québec, QC G1V 2L2
418-643-2112, Fax: 418-646-6168, 866-644-6826

Yukon Territory
Yukon Justice, Andrew Philipsen Law Centre, 2134 Second Ave., PO Box 2703, Whitehorse, YT Y1A 2C6
867-667-3033, Fax: 867-393-5790, jus.msb@gov.yk.ca

SPACE & ASTRONOMY

Canadian Space Agency, John H. Chapman Space Centre, 6767, rte de l'Aéroport, Saint-Hubert, QC J3Y 8Y9
450-926-4800, Fax: 450-926-4352, promo@asc-csa.gc.ca

Herzberg Institute of Astrophysics, 5071 West Saanich Rd., Victoria, BC V9E 2E7
250-363-0001, Fax: 250-363-0045, hia-www@nrc-cnrc.gc.ca

Institute for Aerospace Research, 1200 Montreal Rd., Ottawa, ON K1A 0R6
613-990-0765, Fax: 613-952-7214,

SPORTS

See: Recreation

Prince Edward Island
Prince Edward Island Athletic Association, #101, 250 Water St., Summerside, PE C1N 1B6
902-438-4846, Fax: 902-438-4884

STANDARDS

Institute for National Measurement Standards, Bldg. M-36, 1500 Montreal Rd., Ottawa, ON K1A 0R6
613-998-7018, Fax: 613-954-1473, alexandra.shaw@nrc-cnrc.gc.ca

Standards Council of Canada, #200, 270 Albert St., Ottawa, ON K1P 6N7
613-238-3222, Fax: 613-569-7808, info@scc.ca

STATISTICS

See Also: Vital Statistics

Statistics Canada, R.H. Coats Bldg., Tunney's Pasture, 150 Tunney's Pasture Driveway, Ottawa, ON K1A 0T6
613-951-8116, Fax: 877-287-4369, 800-263-1136, infostats@statcan.ca

British Columbia
Shared Services BC, Chief Operating Office, PO Box 9412 Prov Govt,Victoria, BC V8W 9V1
250-952-6861, Fax: 250-387-5693

Manitoba
Manitoba Bureau of Statistics, #824, 155 Carlton St., Winnipeg, MB R3C 3H9
204-945-2406, Fax: 204-945-0695

Nunavut
Department of Executive & Intergovernmental Affairs, 1084 Aeroplex bldg., PO Box 1000 200,Iqaluit, NU X0A 0H0
867-975-6000, Fax: 867-975-6099

Prince Edward Island
Prince Edward Island Department of Health & Wellness, 105 Rochford St. North, 4th Fl., PO Box 2000, Charlottetown, PE C1A 7N8
902-368-6414, Fax: 902-368-4121

Quebec
Institut de la statistique du Québec, 200, ch Ste-Foy, 1er étage, Québec, QC G1R 5T4
418-691-2401, Fax: 418-643-4129, 800-463-4090, direction@stat.gouv.qc.ca

STATISTICS (ENVIRONMENTAL)

Statistics Canada, R.H. Coats Bldg., Tunney's Pasture, 150 Tunney's Pasture Driveway, Ottawa, ON K1A 0T6
613-951-8116, Fax: 877-287-4369, 800-263-1136, infostats@statcan.ca

STUDENT AID

Nunavut
Department of Education, Sivummut Bldg., 2nd Fl., PO Box 1000 910,Iqaluit, NU X0A 0H0
867-975-5600, Fax: 867-975-5605

Quebec
Aide financière aux études, 1035, rue De La Chevrotière, Québec, QC G1R 5A5
418-643-3750, 877-643-3750

Saskatchewan
Saskatchewan Education, 2220 College Ave., Regina, SK S4P 4V9
linquiry@gov.sk.ca

SUSTAINABLE DEVELOPMENT

Manitoba
Manitoba Round Table for Sustainable Development, #160, 123 Main St., Winnipeg, MB R3C 1A5
204-945-1671, Fax: 204-948-2357, mrtsd@gov.mb.ca

Quebec
Ministère du Développement durable, de l'Environnement et des Parcs, Édifice Marie-Guyart, 675, boul René-Lévesque est, 29e étage, Québec, QC G1R 5V7
418-521-3830, Fax: 418-646-5974, 800-561-1616, info@mddep.gouv.qc.ca

TAXATION

See Also: Sales Tax
Canada Revenue Agency, 875 Heron Rd., Ottawa, ON K1A 0L5
800-267-6999
Financial Sector Regulation & Policy, Terrace Building, 9515 - 107 St., 4th Fl., Edmonton, AB T5K 2C3
First Nations Tax Commission, #321, 345 Yellowhead Hwy, Kamloops, BC V2H 1H1
250-828-9857, Fax: 250-828-9858, mailkamloops@fntc.ca
Secretariat to Commission on the Reform of Ontario's Public Services, Frost Bldg. South, 7 Queen's Park Cres., 1st Fl., Toronto, ON M7A 1YA
416-326-9847, Fax: 416-212-7767

Manitoba
Taxation Division, #101, 401 York Ave., Winnipeg, MB R3C 0P8
204-945-6444, Fax: 204-948-2360

New Brunswick
Revenue & Taxation, Centennial Bldg., #671, 670 King St., PO Box 3000, Fredericton, NB E3B 5G5
506-444-2826, Fax: 506-444-4920

Nova Scotia
Tax Commission, Maritime Centre, 1505 Barrington St., 8th St., PO Box 1003, Halifax, NS B3J 2X1
902-424-6300, Fax: 902-424-7434, 800-565-4357

Quebec
Centre de perception fiscale et des biens non réclamés, 3800, rue de Marly, Secteur 6-4-3, Québec, QC G1X 4A5

Saskatchewan
Board of Revenue Commissioners, #480, 2151 Scarth St., Regina, SK S4P 2H8
306-787-6221, Fax: 306-787-1610,

TELECOMMUNICATIONS

See Also: Broadcasting
Canadian Broadcasting Corporation, 181 Queen St., PO Box 3220 C,Ottawa, ON K1Y 1E4
613-288-6033, liaison@radio-canada.ca
Canadian Radio-Television & Telecommunications Commission, Central Building, 1, Promenade du Portage, Les Terrasses de la Chaudière, Gatineau, QC J8X 4B1
819-997-0313, Fax: 819-994-0218, 877-249-2782
Communications Research Centre Canada, 3701 Carling Ave., PO Box 11490 H, Ottawa, ON K2H 8S2
613-991-3313, Fax: 613-998-5355, info@crc.gc.ca
Spectrum, Information Technologies & Telecommunications, Journal Tower North, 300 Slater St., 20th Fl., Ottawa, ON K1A 0C8
613-998-0368, Fax: 613-952-1203

Manitoba
Manitoba Telecom Services Inc., 333 Main St., PO Box 6666, Winnipeg, MB R3C 3V6
204-941-4111, Fax: 204-772-6391

Prince Edward Island
Prince Edward Island Department of Innovation & Advanced Learning, Shaw Bldg., 105 Rochford St., 5th Fl., PO Box 2000, Charlottetown, PE C1A 7N8
902-368-4240, Fax: 902-368-4242

Quebec
Ministère de la Culture, des Communications & de la Condition féminine, 225, Grande Allée est, Québec, QC G1R 5G5
888-380-8882
Société de télédiffusion du Québec (Télé-Québec), 1000, rue Fullum, Montréal, QC H2K 3L7
514-521-2424, Fax: 514-873-2601, 800-361-4362, info@telequebec.tv

Saskatchewan
Saskatchewan Telecommunications (SaskTel), 2121 Saskatchewan Dr., 7th Fl., Regina, SK S4P 4C3
306-777-3737, 800-727-5835, corporate.comments@sasktel.sk.ca

TOURISM & TOURIST INFORMATION

Canadian Tourism Commission, #1400, 1055 Dunsmuir St., PO Box 49230, Vancouver, BC V7X 1L2
604-638-8300
Canadian Tourism Commission, Four Bentall Centre, #1400, 1055 Dunsmuir St., PO Box 49230, Vancouver, BC V7X 1L2
604-638-8300
Charlottetown Civic Centre Management Inc., 46 Kensington Rd., Charlottetown, PE C1A 5H7
902-629-6600, Fax: 902-629-6650
Parks Canada, 25 Eddy St., Gatineau, QC K1A 0M5
613-860-1251, 888-773-8888, information@pc.gc.ca

Manitoba
Tourism Secretariat & Travel Manitoba, 155 Carlton St., 7th Fl., Winnipeg, MB R3C 3H8
800-665-0040

New Brunswick
Department of Tourism & Parks, Centennial Bldg., 670 King St., Fredericton, NB E3B 1G1
506-444-5205, Fax: 506-457-4984, taponlinedirectory@gnb.ca

Newfoundland & Labrador
Department of Tourism, Culture & Recreation, Confederation Bldg., West Block, 2nd Fl., PO Box 8700, St. John's, NL A1B 4J6
709-729-0862, Fax: 709-729-0870, tcrinfo@gov.nl.ca

Northwest Territories
Department of Industry, Tourism & Investment, PO Box 1320, Yellowknife, NT X1A 2L9
Fax: 867-873-0306, info@iti.ca

Ontario
Ministry of Tourism & Culture, Hearst Block, 900 Bay St., 9th Fl., Toronto, ON M7A 2E1
416-326-9326, Fax: 416-314-7854, 800-668-2746

Prince Edward Island
Prince Edward Island Department of Tourism & Culture, PO Box 2000, Charlottetown, PE C1A 7N8
902-368-5540, Fax: 902-368-5277, tpswitch@gov.pe.ca

Quebec
Société des établissements en plein air du Québec, Place de la Cité, Tour Cominar, #250, 2640, boul Laurier, 2e étage, Québec, QC G1V 5C2
418-890-6527, Fax: 418-528-6025, 800-665-6527, inforeservation@sepaq.com
Ministère du Tourisme, #400, 900, boul René-Lévesque est, Québec, QC G1R 2B5
418-643-5959, Fax: 418-646-8723, 800-482-2433

Saskatchewan
Tourism Saskatchewan, #189, 1621 Albert St., Regina, SK S4P 2S5
306-787-9600, 877-237-2273

Yukon Territory
Yukon Tourism & Culture, 100 Hanson St., Whitehorse, YT Y1A 2C6
867-667-5036, Fax: 867-667-3546

TRADE

See Also: Business Development; Imports
Business Development Bank of Canada, #400, 5, Place Ville-Marie, Montréal, QC H3B 5E7
514-283-5904, Fax: 514-283-5626, 877-232-2269
Canadian Commercial Corporation, 50 O'Connor St., 11th Fl., Ottawa, ON K1A 0S6
613-996-0034, Fax: 613-995-2121, 800-748-8191
Canadian International Trade Tribunal, Standard Life Centre, 333 Laurier Ave. West, 15 Floor, Ottawa, ON K1A 0G7
613-990-2452, Fax: 613-990-2439, secretary@citt-tcce.gc.ca
Canadian Wheat Board, 423 Main St., PO Box 816 Main,Winnipeg, MB R3C 2P5
204-983-0239, Fax: 204-983-3841, 800-275-4292, questions@cwb.ca; farmerservice@cwb.ca
Commission for Environmental Cooperation, Secretariat, #200, 393, rue St-Jacques ouest, Montréal, QC H2Y 1N9
514-350-4300, Fax: 514-350-4314, info@cec.org
Export Development Canada, 151 Slater St., Ottawa, ON K1A 1K3
613-598-2500, Fax: 613-598-3811, 800-267-8510
Global Operations, 125 Sussex Dr,, Ottawa, ON K1A 0G2
613-944-2697, Fax: 613-996-1667
International Trade Canada, 125 Sussex Dr., Ottawa, ON K1A 0G2
613-944-4000
Market & Industry Services Branch, Tower 5, 1341 Baseline Rd., Ottawa, ON K1A 0C5
613-759-1000, Fax: 613-773-1755
North American Free Trade Agreement (NAFTA) Secretariat, Canadian Section, #705, 90 Sparks St., Ottawa, ON K1P 5B4
613-992-9388, Fax: 613-992-9392, webmaster@nafta-alena.gc.ca

Alberta
Intergovernmental Relations, Commerce Place, 10155 - 102 St., 12th Fl., Edmonton, AB T5J 4G8
780-427-6706, Fax: 780-427-0939

British Columbia
Asia Pacific Trade Council, Robson Square, c/o Asia Pacific Business Centre, #288, 800 Hornby St., Vancouver, BC V6Z 2C5
604-660-9727, 888-880-2742
Labour Market & Immigration Division, PO Box 9213, Vancouver, BC V8W 9J1
250-953-3585, Fax: 250-356-0033
Ministry of Social Development, PO Box 9058 Prov Govt,Victoria, BC V8W 9E1
250-356-7750, Fax: 250-356-7292, SD.Minister@gov.bc.ca

Manitoba
Manitoba Competitiveness, Training & Trade, International Business Centre, The Paris Building, 259 Portage Ave., Winnipeg, MB R3B 3P4
204-945-2475, Fax: 204-945-3977, minctt@leg.gov.mb.ca

New Brunswick
Department of Business New Brunswick, Centennial Bldg., 670 King St., PO Box 6000, Fredericton, NB E3B 5H1
506-453-3707, Fax: 506-453-3993, investnb@gnb.ca

Newfoundland & Labrador
Department of Innovation, Trade & Rural Development, West Block, Confederation Bldg., PO Box 8700, St. John's, NL A1B 4J6
709-729-7000, Fax: 709-729-0654, intrd@gov.nl.ca

Nova Scotia
Department of Economic & Rural Development, Centennial Building, #600, 1660 Hollis St., PO Box 2311, Halifax, NS B3J 1V7
902-424-0377, Fax: 902-424-0500, comm@gov.ns.ca

Prince Edward Island
Prince Edward Island Department of Innovation & Advanced Learning, Shaw Bldg., 105 Rochford St., 5th Fl., PO Box 2000, Charlottetown, PE C1A 7N8
902-368-4240, Fax: 902-368-4242

Quebec
Ministère du Développement économique, de l'Innovation et de l'Exportation, 710, place D'Youville, 3e étage, Québec, QC G1R 4Y4
418-691-5950, Fax: 418-644-0118, 866-680-1884
Ministère des Relations internationales, Édifice Hector-Fabre, 525, boul Réne-Lévesque est, Québec, QC G1R 5R9
418-649-2300, Fax: 418-649-2656

Saskatchewan
Saskatchewan Trade & Export Partnership, #320, 1801 Hamilton St., PO Box 1787, Regina, SK S4P 3C6
306-787-9210, Fax: 306-787-6666, inquire@sasktrade.sk.ca

Yukon Territory
Yukon Economic Development, PO Box 2703, Whitehorse, YT Y1A 2C6
867-393-7191, Fax: 867-393-6412, 800-661-0408, ecdev@gov.yk.ca

TRADE-MARKS

See: Patents & Copyright

Prince Edward Island

Anne of Green Gables Licensing Authority Inc., 94 Euston, PO Box 910, Charlottetown, PE C1A 7L9
902-569-7787, Fax: 902-368-6301, kobaker@gov.pe.ca; aggla@bellnet.ca

TRAINING, ENVIRONMENTAL

Alberta

Community, Learner & Industry Connections Division, Phipps-McKinnon Bldg., 10020 - 101A Ave., 5th Fl., Edmonton, AB T5J 3G2

TRANSPORTATION

Atlantic Pilotage Authority, Cogswell Tower, #910, 2000 Barrington St., Halifax, NS B3J 3K1
902-426-2550, Fax: 902-426-4004, 877-272-3477, dispatch@atlanticpilotage.com

Canadian Air Transport Security Authority, 99 Bank St., 13th Fl., Ottawa, ON K1P 6B9
Fax: 613-990-1295, 888-294-2202

Canadian Coast Guard, Centennial Towers, #6S018, 200 Kent St., Ottawa, ON K1A 0E6
613-993-0999, Fax: 613-990-1866, info@dfo-mpo.gc.ca

Canadian Transportation Agency, Les Terrasses de la Chaudière, 15, rue Eddy, Gatineau, QC J8X 4B3
Fax: 819-997-6727, 888-222-2592, info@otc-cta.gc.ca

Centre for Surface Transportation Technology, 2320 Lester Rd., Ottawa, ON K1V 1S2
613-998-9639, Fax: 613-957-0831, inquiries.cstt@nrc-cnrc.gc.ca

Federal Bridge Corporation Limited, #1210, 55 Metcalfe St., Ottawa, ON K1P 6L5
613-993-6880, Fax: 613-993-6945, info@federalbridge.ca

Great Lakes Pilotage Authority, 202 Pitt St., 2nd fl., PO Box 95, Cornwall, ON K6H 5R9
613-933-2991, Fax: 613-932-3793, administration@glpa-apgl.com

Institute for Aerospace Research, 1200 Montreal Rd., Ottawa, ON K1A 0R6
613-990-0765, Fax: 613-952-7214

Laurentian Pilotage Authority Canada, #1501, 555, boul René-Lévesque ouest, Montréal, QC H2Z 1B1
514-283-6320, Fax: 514-496-2409, administration@apl.gc.ca

Marine Atlantic Inc., Baine Johnston Centre, #302, 10 Fort William Place, St. John's, NL A1C 1K4
709-772-8957, Fax: 709-772-8956, 800-341-7981, info@marine-atlantic.ca

Old Port of Montréal Corporation Inc., 333, rue de la Commune ouest, Montréal, QC H2Y 2E2
514-283-5256, information@oldportofmontreal.com

Pacific Pilotage Authority Canada, #1000, 1130 Pender St. West, Vancouver, BC V6E 4A4
604-666-6771, Fax: 604-666-1647, info@ppa.gc.ca

Parc Downsview Park Inc., #1, 35 Carl Hall Rd., Toronto, ON M3K 2B6
416-952-2222, Fax: 416-952-2225, info@downsviewpark.ca

Policy & Corporate Services Division, Twin Atria Building, 4999 - 98 Ave., 3rd Fl., Edmonton, AB T6B 2X3

St. Lawrence Seaway Management Corporation, 202 Pitt St., Cornwall, ON K6J 3P7
613-932-5170, Fax: 613-932-7286, marketing@seaway.ca

Transport Canada, Place de Ville, 330 Sparks St., Tower C, Ottawa, ON K1A 0N5
613-990-2309, Fax: 613-954-4731, 866-995-9737

Transportation & Civil Engineering Division, Twin Atria Building, 4999 - 98 Ave., 2nd Fl., Edmonton, AB T6B 2X3
780-422-2184, Fax: 780-415-1268

Transportation Appeal Tribunal of Canada, #1201, 333 Laurier Ave. West, 12th Fl., Ottawa, ON K1A 0N5
613-990-6906, Fax: 613-990-9153, info@tatc.gc.ca

Transportation Safety Board of Canada, 200 Promenade du Portage, 4th Fl., Ottawa, ON K1A 1K8
819-994-3741, Fax: 819-997-2239, 800-387-3557

Transportation Safety Services Division, Twin Atria Building, 4999 - 98 Ave., Main Fl., Edmonton, AB T6B 2X3
780-427-8901, Fax: 780-415-0782, 800-666-5036

Via Rail Canada Inc., #500, 3, Place Ville-Marie, Montréal, QC H3B 2C9
514-871-6000, Fax: 514-871-6104, 888-842-7245

Alberta

Alberta Automobile Insurance Rate Board, Canadian Western Bank Place, #2440, 10303 Jasper Ave., Edmonton, AB T5J 3N6
780-427-5428, Fax: 780-638-4254, airb@gov.ab.ca

Alberta Infrastructure, Infrastructure Building, 6950 - 113 St., Edmonton, AB T6H 5V7
780-415-0507, Fax: 780-427-2187, Infra.Contact.Us.m@gov.ab.ca

Transportation Safety Board, North Office, Twin Atria Building, 4999 - 98 Ave., Main Fl., Edmonton, AB T6B 2X3
780-427-7178, Fax: 780-422-9739

British Columbia

British Columbia Ferry Commission, PO Box 35119 Hillside, Victoria, BC V8T 5G2
250-590-2770, info@bcferrycommission.com

British Columbia Transit, 520 Gorge Rd. East, Victoria, BC V8W 2P3
250-385-2551, Fax: 250-995-5639

British Columbia Ferry Services Inc., #500, 1321 Blanshard St., Victoria, BC V8W 0B7
250-381-1401, 888-223-3779

Passenger Transportation Board, #202, 940 Blanshard St., PO Box 9850 Prov Govt, Victoria, BC V8W 9T5
250-953-3777, Fax: 250-953-3788, ptboard@gov.bc.ca

Ministry of Transportation & Infrastructure, PO Box 9850 Prov Govt,Victoria, BC V8W 9T5
250-387-3198, Fax: 250-356-7706, tran.webmaster@gov.bc.ca

Transportation Policy & Programs Department, PO Box 9850 Prov Govt,Victoria, BC V8W 9T5
250-387-5062, Fax: 250-387-6431,

Manitoba

Highway Traffic Board/Motor Transport Board, #200, 301 Weston St., Winnipeg, MB R3E 3H4
204-945-8912, Fax: 204-783-6529

Manitoba Infrastructure & Transportation, Legislative Building, #203, 450 Broadway Ave., Winnipeg, MB R3C 0V8
204-945-3723, Fax: 204-945-7610

License Suspension Appeal Board/Medical Review Committee, #200, 301 Weston St., Winnipeg, MB R3E 3H4
204-945-7350, Fax: 204-948-2682

Taxicab Board, #200, 301 Weston St., Winnipeg, MB R3E 3H4
Fax: 204-948-2315

New Brunswick

Department of Transportation, Kings Pl., 440 King St., PO Box 6000, Fredericton, NB E3B 5H8
506-453-3939, Fax: 506-453-2900, Transportation.Web@gnb.ca

New Brunswick Transportation Authority, Kings Place, 440 King St., PO Box 6000, Fredericton, NB E3B 5H1
506-453-3939, Fax: 506-453-2900

Newfoundland & Labrador

Department of Transportation & Works, Confederation Bldg., West Block, 6th Fl., PO Box 8700, St. John's, NL A1B 4J6
709-729-3679, Fax: 709-729-4285, twminister@gov.nl.ca

Northwest Territories

Department of Transportation, Lahm Ridge Bldg., 4501 50 Ave., PO Box 1320, Yellowknife, NT X1A 2L9
867-920-3460, Fax: 867-873-0363

Highways & Marine, 4510 - 50 Ave., 2nd fl., PO Box 1320, Yellowknife, NT X1A 2L9
867-920-8771, Fax: 867-873-0288

Nova Scotia

Department of Transportation & Infrastructure Renewal, Johnston Bldg., 1672 Granville St., 2nd Fl., PO Box 186, Halifax, NS B3J 2N2
902-424-2297, Fax: 902-424-0532, tpwpaff@gov.ns.ca

Nunavut

Department of Community & Government Services, W.G. Brown Bldg., 4th Fl., PO Box 1000 700,Iqaluit, NU X0A 0H0
867-975-5400, Fax: 867-975-5305

Department of Economic Development & Transportation, Bldg. 1104 A, Inuksugait Plaza, PO Box 1000 1500,Iqaluit, NU X0A 0H0
867-975-7800, Fax: 867-975-7870, 888-975-5999, edt@gov.nu.ca

Ontario

Licence Appeal Tribunal, 20 Dundas St. West, 5th Fl., Toronto, ON M5G 2C2
416-314-4260, Fax: 416-314-4270, 800-255-2214

Metrolinx, #600, 20 Bay St., Toronto, ON M5J 2W3
416-869-3200, Fax: 416-869-3525, 888-438-6646

Niagara Falls Bridge Commission, PO Box 395, Niagara Falls, ON L2E 6T8
905-354-5641, Fax: 905-353-6644

Ontario Highway Transport Board, 151 Bloor St. West, 10th Fl., Toronto, ON M5S 2T5
416-326-6732, Fax: 416-326-6738, ohtb@mto.gov.on.ca

Owen Sound Transportation Company Ltd., 717875, Hwy. 6, Owen Sound, ON N4K 5N7
519-376-8740, 800-265-3163

Road User Safety Division, Bldg A, #191, 1201 Wilson Ave., Downsview, ON M3M 1J8
416-235-2999, Fax: 416-235-4153

Ministry of Transportation, Ferguson Block, 77 Wellesley St. West, 3rd Fl., Toronto, ON M7A 1Z8
416-235-4686, Fax: 905-704-2001, 800-268-4686

Prince Edward Island

Prince Edward Island Department of Transportation & Infrastructure Renewal, Jones Bldg., 11 Kent St., 3rd Fl., PO Box 2000, Charlottetown, PE C1A 7N8
902-368-5100, Fax: 902-368-5395

Quebec

Abitibi-Témiscamingue-Nord-du-Québec, 80, av Québec, Rouyn-Noranda, QC J9X 6R1
819-763-3271, Fax: 819-763-3493, dat@mtq.gouv.qc.ca

Bas-Saint-Laurent-Gaspésie-Iles-de-la-Madeleine, #101, 92, 2e rue ouest, Rimouski, QC G5L 8E6
418-727-3674, Fax: 418-727-3673, dtbgi@mtq.gouv.qc.ca

Capitale-Nationale, 475, boul de l'Atrium, 2e étage, Québec, QC G1H 7H9
418-643-1911, Fax: 418-646-0003, dcnat@mtq.gouv.qc.ca

Chaudière-Appalaches, 1156, boul de la Rive-Sud, Saint-Romuald, QC G6W 5M6
418-839-5581, Fax: 418-834-7338, dtca@mtq.gouv.qc.ca

Commission des transports du Québec, 200, ch Sainte-Foy, 7e étage, Québec, QC G1R 5V5
Fax: 418-644-8034, 888-461-2433, courrier@ctq.gouv.qc.ca

Côte-Nord, #110, 625, boul Laflèche, Baie-Comeau, QC G5C 1C5
418-295-4765, Fax: 418-295-4766, cotenord@mtq.gouv.qc.ca

Est-de-la-Montérégie, 201, place Charles-Lemoyne, 5e étage, Longueuil, QC J4K 2T5
450-677-3413, Fax: 450-442-1317, dtem@mtq.gouv.qc.ca

Estrie, #2.02, 200, rue Belvédère nord, Sherbrooke, QC J1H 4A9
819-820-3280, Fax: 819-820-3118, dte@mtq.gouv.qc.ca

Laurentides-Lanaudière, 222, rue Saint-Georges, 2e étage, Saint-Jérôme, QC J7Z 4Z9
450-569-3057, Fax: 450-569-3072, dll@mtq.gouv.qc.ca

Laval-Mille-îles, 1725, boul Le Corbusier, Laval, QC H7S 2K7
450-680-6330, Fax: 450-973-4959, dtlmi@mtq.gouv.qc.ca

Mauricie-Centre-du-Québec, 100, rue Laviolette, 4e étage, Trois-Rivières, QC G9A 5S9
819-371-6896, Fax: 819-371-6136, dmcq@mtq.gouv.qc.ca

Ouest-de-la-Montérégie, #200, 180, boul d'Anjou, Châteauguay, QC J6K 1C4
450-698-3400, Fax: 450-698-3452, dtom@mtq.gouv.qc.ca

Outaouais, #5.110, 170, rue de l'Hôtel-de-Ville, Gatineau, QC J8X 4C2
819-772-3849, Fax: 819-772-3338, dto@mtq.gouv.qc.ca

Saguenay-Lac-Saint-Jean-Chibougamau, 3950, boul Harvey, Jonquière, QC G7X 8L6
418-695-7916, Fax: 418-695-7926, dt.slsjc@mtq.gouv.qc.ca

Société de l'assurance automobile du Québec, 333, boul Jean-Lesage, CP 19600 Terminus, Québec, QC G1K 8J6
418-643-7620, Fax: 418-644-0339, 800-361-7620, courrier@saaq.gouv.qc.ca

Société des traversiers du Québec, 250, rue Saint-Paul, Québec, QC G1K 9K9
418-643-2019, Fax: 418-643-7308, 877-787-7483, stq@traversiers.gouv.qc.ca

Société du port ferroviaire Baie-Comeau-Hauterive, 18, rte Maritime, Baie-Comeau, QC G4Z 2L6
418-296-6785, Fax: 418-296-2377, societeduport@globetrotter.net

Ministère des Transports, 700, boul René-Lévesque est, 28e étage, Québec, QC G1R 5H1
418-643-6980, Fax: 418-643-2033, 888-355-0511, communications@mtq.gouv.qc.ca

île-de-Montréal, 500, boul René-Lévesque ouest, 12e étage, CP 5, Montréal, QC H2Z 1W7
514-873-7781, Fax: 514-864-3867, dtim@mtq.gouv.qc.ca

Saskatchewan

Saskatchewan Highways & Infrastructure, Victoria Tower, 1855 Victoria Ave., Regina, SK S4P 3T2
306-787-4800, communications@highways.gov.sk.ca

Saskatchewan Highway Traffic Board, 1550 Saskatchewan Dr., Regina, SK S4P 0E4
306-775-6674, contactus@highwaytrafficboard.sk.ca

Yukon Territory

Yukon Community Services, PO Box 2703, Whitehorse, YT Y1A 2C6
867-667-5811, Fax: 867-393-6295, 800-661-0408, inquiry@gov.yk.ca

Driver Control Board, 2130 Second Ave., 3rd Fl., PO Box 2703, Whitehorse, YT Y1A 2C6
867-667-5111, Fax: 867-667-3609, dcb@gov.yk.ca

Yukon Highways & Public Works, PO Box 2703, Whitehorse, YT Y1A 2C6
867-393-7193, Fax: 867-393-6218, 800-661-0408, hpw-info@gov.yk.ca

TRANSPORTATION OF DANGEROUS GOODS

Nova Scotia

Department of Transportation & Infrastructure Renewal, Johnston Bldg., 1672 Granville St., 2nd Fl., PO Box 186, Halifax, NS B3J 2N2
902-424-2297, Fax: 902-424-0532, tpwpaff@gov.ns.ca

Ontario

Road User Safety Division, Bldg A, #191, 1201 Wilson Ave., Downsview, ON M3M 1J8
416-235-2999, Fax: 416-235-4153,

Prince Edward Island
Prince Edward Island Department of Transportation & Infrastructure Renewal, Jones Bldg., 11 Kent St., 3rd Fl., PO Box 2000, Charlottetown, PE C1A 7N8
902-368-5100, Fax: 902-368-5395

Saskatchewan
Saskatchewan Highways & Infrastructure, Victoria Tower, 1855 Victoria Ave., Regina, SK S4P 3T2
306-787-4800, communications@highways.gov.sk.ca

TRAPPING & FUR INDUSTRY

Ontario
Ontario Moose & Bear Allocation Advisory Committee, PO Box 964, Sioux Lookout, ON P8T 1B3
807-737-2615, Fax: 807-737-4173

Quebec
Comité conjoint de chasse, de pêche et de piégeage, #C220, 383 rue Saint-Jacques, Montréal, QC H2Y 1N9
514-284-2151, Fax: 514-284-0039, infohftcc@cccpp-hftcc.com

Office de la sécurité du revenu des chasseurs et piègeurs cris, Édifice Champlain, #1110, 2700, boul Laurier, Québec, QC G1V 4K5
418-643-7300, Fax: 418-643-6803, 800-363-1560, courrier@osrcpc.ca

Saskatchewan
Saskatchewan Environment, 3211 Albert St., 2nd Fl., Regina, SK S4S 5W6
306-787-2584, Fax: 306-787-9544, 800-567-4224, Centre.Inquiry@gov.sk.ca

TREASURY SERVICES

See Also: Finance

Ontario
Office of the Budget & Treasury Board, Frost Bldg. South, 95 Grosvenor St., 4th Fl., Toronto, ON M7A 1Z1
416-325-7620, Fax: 416-212-7767

Treasury Board of Canada, 140 O'Connor St., Ottawa, ON K1A 0R5
613-957-2400, Fax: 613-941-4000, 877-636-0656

British Columbia
Provincial Treasury, PO Box 9414 Prov Govt,Victoria, BC V8V 9V1
250-387-4541, Fax: 250-356-3041

New Brunswick
Treasury, Centennial Bldg., #376, 670 King St., PO Box 6000, Fredericton, NB E3B 5H1
506-453-3952, Fax: 506-453-2053

Nova Scotia
Nova Scotia Treasury & Policy Board, 1700 Granville St., 5th Fl., PO Box 1617, Halifax, NS B3J 2Y3
902-424-8910, Fax: 902-424-7638, TBenquiries@gov.ns.ca

Nunavut
Department of Finance, Bldg. 1079, 1st Fl., PO Box 1000 330,Iqaluit, NU X0A 0H0
867-975-5800, Fax: 867-975-5805

Quebec
Secrétariat du Conseil du trésor, 875, Grande Allée est, 5e étage, secteur 500, Québec, QC G1R 5R8
418-643-1529, Fax: 418-643-9226, 866-552-5158, communication@sct.gouv.qc.ca

URBAN RENEWAL & DESIGN

See Also: Municipal Affairs

Alberta
Local Government Services Division, Commerce Place, 10155 - 102 St., 17th Fl., Edmonton, AB T5J 4L4

Newfoundland & Labrador
Newfoundland & Labrador Housing Corporation, Sir Brian Dunfield Bldg., 2 Canada Dr., PO Box 220, St. John's, NL A1C 5J2
709-724-3000, Fax: 709-724-3250

Northwest Territories
Department of Municipal & Community Affairs, PO Box 1320, Yellowknife, NT X1A 2L9
867-873-7118, Fax: 867-873-0309

Ontario
Ministry of Municipal Affairs & Housing, College Park, 777 Bay St., 17th Fl., Toronto, ON M5G 2E5
416-585-7041, Fax: 416-585-6470, 866-220-2290, mininfo@ontario.ca

Prince Edward Island
SkillsPEI, Atlantic Technology Centre, #212, 90 University Ave., Charlottetown, PE C1A 4K9
902-368-4260, Fax: 902-368-6340, 877-491-4766

Quebec
Société d'habitation du Québec, Aile St-Amable, 1054, rue Louis-Alexandre-Taschereau, 3e étage, Québec, QC G1R 5E7
418-643-4035, Fax: 418-643-2533, 800-463-4315

VETERANS AFFAIRS

Ste-Anne's Hospital, 305 boul des Anciens-Combattants, Sainte-Anne-de-Bellevue, QC H9X 1Y9
514-457-3440, 800-361-9287, steanne@vac-acc.gc.ca

Veterans Affairs Canada, 161 Grafton St., PO Box 7700, Charlottetown, PE C1A 8M9
902-566-8888, 866-522-2111, information@vac-acc.gc.ca

VICE-REGAL REPRESENTATIVES

Governor General & Commander-in-Chief of Canada, Rideau Hall, 1 Sussex Dr., Ottawa, ON K1A 0A1
613-993-8200, Fax: 613-998-8760, 800-465-6890, info@gg.ca

Alberta
Office of the Lieutenant Governor, Office of the Lieutenant Governor of AB, Legislature Bldg., 10800 - 97 Ave., 3rd Fl., Edmonton, AB T5K 2B6
780-427-7243, Fax: 780-422-5134, ltgov@gov.ab.ca

British Columbia
Office of the Lieutenant Governor, Government House, 1401 Rockland Ave., Victoria, BC V8S 1V9
250-387-2080, Fax: 250-387-2078, ghinfo@gov.bc.ca

Manitoba
Office of the Lieutenant Governor, Legislative Building, #235, 450 Broadway Ave., Winnipeg, MB R3C 0V8
204-945-2753, Fax: 204-945-4329, ltgov@leg.gov.mb.ca

New Brunswick
Office of the Lieutenant-Governor, Old Government House, 51 Woodstock Rd., PO Box 6000, Fredericton, NB E3B 5H1
506-453-2505, Fax: 506-444-5280,

Newfoundland & Labrador
Office of the Lieutenant Governor, Government House, Military Rd., PO Box 5517, St. John's, NL A1C 5W4
709-729-4494, Fax: 709-729-2234, governmenthouse@gov.nl.ca

Northwest Territories
Office of the Commissioner, #803 Northwest Tower, PO Box 1320, Yellowknife, NT X1A 2L9
867-873-7400, Fax: 867-873-0223, 888-270-3318, commissioner@gov.nt.ca

Nova Scotia
Office of the Lieutenant Governor, Government House, 1451 Barrington St., Halifax, NS B3J 1Z2
902-424-7001, Fax: 902-424-0537, lgoffice@gov.ns.ca

Nunavut
Office of the Commissioner, PO Box 2379, Iqaluit, NU X0A 0H0
867-975-5120, Fax: 867-975-5123, nunavutcommissioner@gov.nu.ca

Ontario
Office of the Lieutenant Governor, Room 131, Legislative Bldg., Queen's Park, Toronto, ON M7A 1A1
416-325-7780, Fax: 416-325-7787, ltgov@gov.on.ca

Prince Edward Island
Office of the Lieutenant Governor, Government House, PO Box 846, Charlottetown, PE C1A 7L9
902-368-5480, Fax: 902-368-5481

Quebec
Cabinet du Lieutenant-gouverneur, Édifice André-Laurendeau, 1050, rue des Parlementaires R.C., Québec, QC G1A 1A1
418-643-5385, Fax: 418-644-4677, 866-791-0766

Saskatchewan
Office of the Lieutenant Governor, Government House, 4607 Dewdney Ave., Regina, SK S4T 1B7
306-787-4070, Fax: 306-787-7716, lgo@ltgov.sk.ca

Yukon Territory
Office of the Commissioner, Closeleigh Manor, 1098 First Ave., Whitehorse, YT Y1A 0C1
867-667-5121, Fax: 867-393-6201, commissioner@gov.yk.ca

VIOLENCE

See Also: policing Services

Alberta
Alberta Children & Youth Services, Communications, Sterling Place, 9940 - 106 St., 12th Fl., Edmonton, AB T5K 2N2
780-422-3004, Fax: 780-422-3071, cs.communications@gov.ab.ca

New Brunswick
Department of Social Development, Sartain MacDonald Bldg., 551 King St., PO Box 6000, Fredericton, NB E3B 5H1
506-453-2001, Fax: 506-453-7478, sd-ds@gnb.ca

Nova Scotia
Department of Community Services, Nelson Place, 5675 Spring Garden Rd., 8th Fl., PO Box 696, Halifax, NS B3J 2T7
902-424-4304, Fax: 902-428-0618

VITAL STATISTICS

Vital Statistics, 254 Portage Ave., Winnipeg, MB R3C 0B8
204-945-3701, Fax: 204-948-3128, 800-282-8063, vitalstats@gov.mb.ca

Northwest Territories
Vital Statistics, Bag #9, Inuvik, NT X0E 0T0
867-777-7400, Fax: 867-777-3197, 800-661-0830, hsa@gov.nt.ca

Nova Scotia
Vital Statistics, Joseph Howe Bldg., 1690 Hollis St., Ground Floor, PO Box 157, Halifax, NS B3J 2M9
902-424-4071, Fax: 902-424-0678, 877-848-2578, vstat@gov.ns.ca

Prince Edward Island
Prince Edward Island Department of Health & Wellness, 105 Rochford St. North, 4th Fl., PO Box 2000, Charlottetown, PE C1A 7N8
902-368-6414, Fax: 902-368-4121

Quebec
Directeur de l'état civil, 2535, boul Laurier, Québec, QC G1V 5C5
418-643-3900, Fax: 418-646-3255, 800-567-3900, etatcivil@gouv.qc.ca

WASTE & GARBAGE

Newfoundland & Labrador
Department of Government Services, PO Box 8700, St. John's, NL A1B 4J6
709-729-4834, gsinfo@gov.nl.ca

Department of Municipal Affairs, West Block, Main Fl., Confederation Bldg., PO Box 8700, St. John's, NL A1B 4J6
709-729-3046, Fax: 709-729-0943, mainfo@gov.nl.ca

Ontario
Ministry of Environment, 135 St. Clair Ave. West, Toronto, ON M4V 1P5
416-325-4000, Fax: 416-325-3159, 800-565-4923

Quebec
Bureau d'audiences publiques sur l'environnement, Édifice Lomer-Gouin, #2.10, 575, rue Saint-Amable, Québec, QC G1R 6A6
418-643-7447, Fax: 418-643-9474, 800-463-4732, communication@bape.gouv.qc.ca

Société québécoise de récupération et de recyclage, #200, 420, boul Charest est, Québec, QC G1K 8M4
418-643-0394, Fax: 418-643-6507, 866-523-8290, info@recyc-quebec.gouv.qc.ca

WASTE MANAGEMENT

See Also: Dangerous Goods & Hazardous Materials

Alberta
Alberta Recycling Management Authority, Scotia Tower 1, #1310, 10060 Jasper Ave., PO Box 189, Edmonton, AB T5J 2J1
780-990-1111, Fax: 780-990-1122, 888-999-8762, info@albertarecycling.ca

Alberta Used Oil Management Association, Empire Building, #1008, 10080 Jasper Ave., Edmonton, AB T5J 1V9
780-414-1510, Fax: 780-414-1519, 866-414-1510, reception@usedoilrecycling.ca

Beverage Container Management Board, #750, 10707 - 100 Ave., Edmonton, AB T5J 3M1
780-424-3193, Fax: 780-428-4620, 888-424-7671

Alberta Environment, South Tower, Petroleum Plaza, 9915 - 108 St., 10th Fl., Edmonton, AB T5K 2G8
780-427-2700, Fax: 780-422-4086, env.infocent@gov.ab.ca

New Brunswick
Department of Local Government, Marysville Place, 20 McGloin St., PO Box 6000, Fredericton, NB E3B 5H1
506-453-2807, Fax: 506-453-3988,

Newfoundland & Labrador
Multi-Materials Stewardship Board, PO Box 8131 A, St. John's, NL A1B 3M9
709-753-0948, Fax: 709-753-0974, 800-901-6672, inquiries@mmsb.nl.ca

Northwest Territories
Department of Municipal & Community Affairs, PO Box 1320, Yellowknife, NT X1A 2L9
867-873-7118, Fax: 867-873-0309

Ontario
Integrated Environmental Policy Division, 77 Wellesley St. West, 11th Fl., Toronto, ON M7A 2T5
416-314-6338, Fax: 416-314-6346

Prince Edward Island
Island Waste Management Corporation, 110 Watts Ave., Charlottetown, PE C1E 2C1
902-894-0330, Fax: 902-894-0331, 888-280-8111, reception@iwmc.pe.ca; info@iwmc.pe.ca
Quebec
Société québécoise de récupération et de recyclage, #200, 420, boul Charest est, Québec, QC G1K 8M4
418-643-0394, Fax: 418-643-6507, 866-523-8290, info@recyc-quebec.gouv.qc.ca
Saskatchewan
Saskatchewan Environment, 3211 Albert St., 2nd Fl., Regina, SK S4S 5W6
306-787-2584, Fax: 306-787-9544, 800-567-4224, Centre.Inquiry@gov.sk.ca
Yukon Territory
Yukon Environment, PO Box 2703, Whitehorse, YT Y1A 2C6
867-667-5652, Fax: 867-393-7197, environment.yukon@gov.yk.ca

WATER & WASTEWATER

Bedford Institute of Oceanography, 1 Challenger Dr., PO Box 1006, Dartmouth, NS B2Y 4A2
902-426-3492, Fax: 902-426-8484
Canadian Hydraulics Centre, 1200 Montreal Rd., Ottawa, ON K1A 0R6
613-993-9381, Fax: 613-952-7679, info.chc@nrc-cnrc.gc.ca
Environment Canada, 10 Wellington St., Gatineau, QC K1A 0H3
819-997-2800, Fax: 819-994-1412, 800-668-6767, enviroinfo@ec.gc.ca
Fisheries & Oceans Canada, 200 Kent St., Ottawa, ON K1A 0E6
613-993-0999, Fax: 613-990-1866, info@dfo-mpo.gc.ca
Freshwater Institute, 501 University Cres., Winnipeg, MB R3T 2N6
204-983-5000, Fax: 204-983-6285
Institut Maurice-Lamontagne, 850, rte de le Mer, CP 1000, Mont-Joli, QC G5H 3Z4
418-775-0555, Fax: 418-775-0730
Institute for Marine Biosciences, 1411 Oxford St., Halifax, NS B3H 3Z1
902-426-8332, Fax: 902-426-9413, communications.imb@nrc-cnrc.gc.ca
Institute for Ocean Technology, Kerwin Pl. & Arctic Ave., PO Box 12093, St. John's, NL A1B 3T5
709-772-4939, Fax: 709-772-2462, Noel.Murphy@nrc-cnrc.gc.ca
Institute of Ocean Sciences, 9860 West Saanich Rd., PO Box 6000, Sidney, BC V8L 4B2
250-363-6517, Fax: 250-363-6390
Alberta
Alberta Environment, South Tower, Petroleum Plaza, 9915 - 108 St., 10th Fl., Edmonton, AB T5K 2G8
780-427-2700, Fax: 780-422-4086, env.infocent@gov.ab.ca
Irrigation Council, Provincial Bldg., 200 - 5 Ave. South, 3rd Fl., Lethbridge, AB T1J 4L1
403-381-5176, Fax: 403-382-4406
British Columbia
Ministry of Environment, PO Box 9339 Prov Govt,Victoria, BC V8W 9M1
250-387-1161, Fax: 250-387-5669, envmail@gov.bc.ca
British Columbia Utilities Commission, 900 Howe St., 6th Fl., PO Box 250, Vancouver, BC V6Z 2N3
604-660-4700, Fax: 604-660-1102, 800-663-1385, commission.secretary@bcuc.com
Manitoba
Manitoba Conservation, 200 Saulteaux Cres., Winnipeg, MB R3J 3W3
204-945-6784, 800-214-6497, mincon@leg.gov.mb.ca
Manitoba Water Services Board, PO Box 22080, Brandon, MB R7A 6Y9
204-726-6076, Fax: 204-726-6290
New Brunswick
Department of Natural Resources, Hugh John Flemming Forestry Centre, PO Box 6000, Fredericton, NB E3B 5H1
506-453-3826, Fax: 506-444-4367, dnrweb@gnb.ca
Department of the Environment, Marysville Place, 20 McGloin St., PO Box 6000, Fredericton, NB E3B 5H1
506-453-2690, Fax: 506-457-7800, env-info@gnb.ca
Newfoundland & Labrador
Department of Environment & Conservation, Confederation Bldg., West Block, 4th Fl., PO Box 8700, St. John's, NL A1B 4J6
709-729-2664, Fax: 709-729-6639, 800-563-6181, info@gov.nl.ca
Newfoundland & Labrador Board of Commissioners of Public Utilities, PO Box 21040, St. John's, NL A1A 5B2
709-726-8600, Fax: 709-726-9604, 866-782-0006, ito@pub.nf.ca
Northwest Territories
Department of Environment & Natural Resources, PO Box 1320, Yellowknife, NT X1A 2L9
Northwest Territories Water Board, 125 Mackenzie Rd., PO Box 2531, Yellowknife, NT X0E 0T0
867-678-2942, Fax: 867-678-2943, info@nwtwb.com
Nova Scotia
Department of Natural Resources, Founder's Square, 1701 Hollis St., 3rd Fl., PO Box 698, Halifax, NS B3J 2T9
902-424-5935, Fax: 902-424-0594, 800-565-2224
Nova Scotia Utility & Review Board, Summit Place, 1601 Lower Water St., 3rd Fl., PO Box 1692 M,Halifax, NS B3J 3S3
902-424-4448, Fax: 902-424-3919, uarb.board@gov.ns.ca
Waterfront Development Corporation Ltd., 1751 Lower Water St., 2nd Fl., Halifax, NS B3J 1S5
902-422-6591, Fax: 902-422-7582, info@wdcl.ca
Nunavut
Nunavut Water Board, PO Box 119, Gjoa Haven, NU X0B 1J0
867-360-6338, Fax: 867-360-6369
Ontario
Ministry of Environment, 135 St. Clair Ave. West, Toronto, ON M4V 1P5
416-325-4000, Fax: 416-325-3159, 800-565-4923
Lake of the Woods Control Board, c/o Executive Engineer, Ottawa, ON K1A 0H3
Fax: 819-953-4666, 800-661-5922, secretariat@lwcb.ca
Ministry of Natural Resources, Whitney Block, #6630, 99 Wellesley St. West, 6th Fl., Toronto, ON M7A 1W3
800-667-1940
Ontario Clean Water Agency, 1 Yonge St., 17th Fl., Toronto, ON M5E 1E5
416-314-5600, Fax: 416-314-8300, 800-667-6292
Walkerton Clean Water Centre, 20 Ontario Rd., PO Box 160, Walkerton, ON N0G 2V0
519-881-2003, Fax: 519-881-4947, 866-515-0550, inquiry@wcwc.ca
Prince Edward Island
Prince Edward Island Department of Environment, Energy, & Forestry, Jones Bldg., 11 Kent St., 4th Fl., PO Box 2000, Charlottetown, PE C1A 7N8
902-368-5000, Fax: 902-368-5830
Prince Edward Island Department of Tourism & Culture, PO Box 2000, Charlottetown, PE C1A 7N8
902-368-5540, Fax: 902-368-5277, tpswitch@gov.pe.ca
Quebec
Ministère du Développement durable, de l'Environnement et des Parcs, Édifice Marie-Guyart, 675, boul René-Lévesque est, 29e étage, Québec, QC G1R 5V7
418-521-3830, Fax: 418-646-5974, 800-561-1616, info@mddep.gouv.qc.ca
Saskatchewan
Saskatchewan Environment, 3211 Albert St., 2nd Fl., Regina, SK S4S 5W6
306-787-2584, Fax: 306-787-9544, 800-567-4224, Centre.Inquiry@gov.sk.ca
Saskatchewan Watershed Authority, 111 Fairford St. East, Moose Jaw, SK S6H 7X9
306-694-3900, Fax: 306-694-3465, comm@swa.ca
Saskatchewan Water Corporation (SaskWater), #200, 111 Fairford St. East, Moose Jaw, SK S6H 1C8
Fax: 306-694-3207, 888-230-1111, comm@saskwater.com; customerservice@saskwater.com
Yukon Territory
Yukon Environment, PO Box 2703, Whitehorse, YT Y1A 2C6
867-667-5652, Fax: 867-393-7197, environment.yukon@gov.yk.ca

WATER RESOURCES

See Also: Oceanography
Drinking Water Management Division, 135 St. Clair Ave. West, Toronto, ON M4V 1P5
416-314-4475, Fax: 416-314-6935
Energy & Minerals Division, Jones Bldg., 4th Fl., Charlottetown, PE C1A 7N8
902-894-0288, Fax: 902-894-0290
Environmental Protection & Audit Division, 3211 Albert St., 5th Fl., Regina, SK S4S 5W6
306-787-2947
Environmental Stewardship Branch, 351 boul St-Joseph, Gatineau, QC K1A 0H3
819-997-1575, Fax: 819-953-9452
Freshwater Institute, 501 University Cres., Winnipeg, MB R3T 2N6
204-983-5000, Fax: 204-983-6285
Integrated Environmental Policy Division, 77 Wellesley St. West, 11th Fl., Toronto, ON M7A 2T5
416-314-6338, Fax: 416-314-6346
International Joint Commission, 234 Laurier Ave. West, 22nd Fl., Ottawa, ON K1P 6K6
613-947-1420, Fax: 613-993-5583, beckhoffb@ottawa.ijc.org
Monitoring & Science Division, Petroleum Plaza ST, 9915 - 108 St., 10th Fl., Edmonton, AB T5K 2G8
Alberta
Alberta Environment, South Tower, Petroleum Plaza, 9915 - 108 St., 10th Fl., Edmonton, AB T5K 2G8
780-427-2700, Fax: 780-422-4086, env.infocent@gov.ab.ca
British Columbia
Environmental Protection Division, PO Box 9339, Victoria, BC V8W 9M1
250-387-1288, Fax: 250-387-5669
Water Stewardship Division, PO Box 9339 Prov Govt,Victoria, BC V8W 9M1
Fax: 250-387-6003
Manitoba
Manitoba Water Services Board, PO Box 22080, Brandon, MB R7A 6Y9
204-726-6076, Fax: 204-726-6290
Office of Drinking Water, 1007 Century St., Winnipeg, MB R3H 0W4
204-945-5762, Fax: 204-945-1365
Manitoba Water Stewardship, 200 Saulteaux Cres., PO Box 11, Winnipeg, MB R3J 3W3
204-945-6398, 800-282-8069, wsd@gov.mb.ca
New Brunswick
Department of Local Government, Marysville Place, 20 McGloin St., PO Box 6000, Fredericton, NB E3B 5H1
506-453-2807, Fax: 506-453-3988
Department of the Environment, Marysville Place, 20 McGloin St., PO Box 6000, Fredericton, NB E3B 5H1
506-453-2690, Fax: 506-457-7800, env-info@gnb.ca
Environmental Management, Marysville Place, 20 McGloin St., PO Box 6000, Fredericton, NB E3B 5H1
506-444-5119, Fax: 506-457-7333, env-info@gnb.ca
Sciences & Planning, Marysville Place, 20 McGloin St., 2nd Fl., PO Box 6000, Fredericton, NB E3B 5H1
506-453-2862, Fax: 506-453-2265
Northwest Territories
Northwest Territories Water Board, 125 Mackenzie Rd., PO Box 2531, Yellowknife, NT X0E 0T0
867-678-2942, Fax: 867-678-2943, info@nwtwb.com
Nova Scotia
Department of Agriculture, 1741 Brunswick St., 3rd Fl., PO Box 2223, Halifax, NS B3J 3C4
902-424-4560, Fax: 902-424-4671
Nunavut
Department of Health & Social Services, PO Box 1000 1000,Iqaluit, NU X0A 0H0
867-975-5700, Fax: 867-975-5705
Nunavut Water Board, PO Box 119, Gjoa Haven, NU X0B 1J0
867-360-6338, Fax: 867-360-6369
Ontario
Advisory Council on Drinking Water Quality & Testing Standards, 40 St. Clair Ave. West, 3rd Fl., Toronto, ON M4V 1M2
416-212-7779, Fax: 416-212-7595
Ontario Clean Water Agency, 1 Yonge St., 17th Fl., Toronto, ON M5E 1E5
416-314-5600, Fax: 416-314-8300, 800-667-6292
Walkerton Clean Water Centre, 20 Ontario Rd., PO Box 160, Walkerton, ON N0G 2V0
519-881-2003, Fax: 519-881-4947, 866-515-0550, inquiry@wcwc.ca
Quebec
Ministère du Développement durable, de l'Environnement et des Parcs, Édifice Marie-Guyart, 675, boul René-Lévesque est, 29e étage, Québec, QC G1R 5V7
418-521-3830, Fax: 418-646-5974, 800-561-1616, info@mddep.gouv.qc.ca
Saskatchewan
Saskatchewan Environment, 3211 Albert St., 2nd Fl., Regina, SK S4S 5W6
306-787-2584, Fax: 306-787-9544, 800-567-4224, Centre.Inquiry@gov.sk.ca
Saskatchewan Watershed Authority, 111 Fairford St. East, Moose Jaw, SK S6H 7X9
306-694-3900, Fax: 306-694-3465, comm@swa.ca
Saskatchewan Water Corporation (SaskWater), #200, 111 Fairford St. East, Moose Jaw, SK S6H 1C8
Fax: 306-694-3207, 888-230-1111, comm@saskwater.com; customerservice@saskwater.com
Yukon Territory
Yukon Environment, PO Box 2703, Whitehorse, YT Y1A 2C6
867-667-5652, Fax: 867-393-7197, environment.yukon@gov.yk.ca

WEIGHTS & MEASURES

Standards Council of Canada, #200, 270 Albert St., Ottawa, ON K1P 6N7
613-238-3222, Fax: 613-569-7808, info@scc.ca

WILDLIFE RESOURCES

Alberta
Fish & Wildlife Division, Petroleum Plaza ST, 9915 - 108 St., 11th Fl., Edmonton, AB T5K 2G8

Alberta
Alberta Sport, Recreation, Parks, & Wildlife Foundation, Standard Life Centre, #903, 10405 Jasper Ave., 9th Fl., Edmonton, AB T5J 4R7
780-415-1167, Fax: 780-415-0308

British Columbia
Environmental Stewardship Division, PO Box 9339 Prov Govt,Victoria, BC V8W 9M1
250-356-0121, Fax: 250-387-5669

Manitoba
Endangered Species Advisory Committee, 200 Saulteaux Cres., PO Box 24, Winnipeg, MB R3J 3W3
204-945-7465, Fax: 204-945-3077,

Newfoundland & Labrador
Forestry Services, Fortis Bldg., PO Box 2006, Corner Brook, NL A2H 6J8
709-637-2284, Fax: 709-634-4378

Nunavut
Department of Environment, PO Box 1000 1300,Iqaluit, NU X0A 0H0
867-975-7700, Fax: 867-975-7742, environment@gov.nu.ca

Ontario
Ministry of Environment, 135 St. Clair Ave. West, Toronto, ON M4V 1P5
416-325-4000, Fax: 416-325-3159, 800-565-4923
Ontario Fish & Wildlife Heritage Commission, Robinson Pl., 300 Water St., PO Box 7000, Peterborough, ON K9J 8M5
705-755-1905, Fax: 705-755-1900

Quebec
Fondation de la faune du Québec, Place Iberville II, #420, 1175, av Lavigerie, Québec, QC G1V 4P1
418-644-7926, Fax: 418-643-7655, 877-639-0742, ffq@fondationdelafaune.qc.ca
Ministère des Ressources naturelles et de la Faune, 880, ch Sainte-Foy, Québec, QC G1S 4X4
418-627-8600, Fax: 418-644-6513, 866-248-6936, services.clientele@mrnf.gouv.qc.ca

WOMEN'S ISSUES

See Also: Pay Equity
Status of Women Canada, 123 Slater St., 10th Fl., Ottawa, ON K1P 1H9
613-995-7835, Fax: 613-947-0761, 866-902-2719, infonational@swc-cfc.gc.ca

Alberta
Alberta Tourism, Parks, & Recreation, Communications Branch, Commerce Place, 10155 - 102 St., 6th Fl., Edmonton, AB T5J 4L6
780-644-5589, TPR.Communications@gov.ab.ca

Manitoba
Manitoba Women's Advisory Council, #301, 155 Carlton St., Winnipeg, MB R3C 3H8
204-945-6281, Fax: 204-945-6511, 800-282-8069, 001women@gov.mb.ca
Status of Women, #409, 401 York Ave., Winnipeg, MB R3C 0P8
204-945-3476, Fax: 204-945-0013, 800-263-0234, mwd@gov.mb.ca

New Brunswick
Department of Social Development, Sartain MacDonald Bldg., 551 King St., PO Box 6000, Fredericton, NB E3B 5H1
506-453-2001, Fax: 506-453-7478, sd-ds@gnb.ca
New Brunswick Advisory Council on the Status of Women, 236 King St., Fredericton, NB E3B 1E2
506-444-4101, Fax: 506-444-4318, 800-332-3087, acswcccf@gnb.ca

Newfoundland & Labrador
Provincial Advisory Council on the Status of Women, #103, 15 Hallett Cres., St. John's, NL A1B 4C4
709-753-7270, Fax: 709-753-2606, 877-753-7270, info@pacsw.ca

Nova Scotia
Nova Scotia Advisory Council on the Status of Women, 1700 Granville St., PO Box 943, Halifax, NS B3J 2V9
902-424-7660, women@gov.ns.ca

Nunavut
Department of Culture, Language, Elders & Youth, PO Box 1000 800,Iqaluit, NU X0A 0H0
867-975-5500, Fax: 867-975-5504, 866-934-2035

Ontario
Ontario Women's Directorate, 777 Bay St., 6th Fl., Toronto, ON M7A 2J4
416-314-0300, Fax: 416-314-0247, 866-510-5902, owd@ontario.ca

Quebec
Ministère de la Famille et des Aînés, 425, rue Saint-Amable, 1er étage, Québec, QC G1R 4Z1
877-216-6202

Yukon Territory
Yukon Women's Directorate, #1, 404 Hason St., Whitehorse, YT Y1A 1Y8
867-667-3030, Fax: 867-393-6270

WORKERS' COMPENSATION

Merchant Seamen Compensation Board, Secretary, Merchant Seamen Compensation Board, Phase II, Place du Portage, 10th Fl., Ottawa, ON K1A 0J2
819-953-8001, Fax: 819-994-5368

Alberta
Appeals Commission for Alberta Workers' Compensation, Energy Square Building, #901, 10109 - 106th St., Edmonton, AB T5J 3L7
780-412-8700, Fax: 780-412-8701, webmaster1@appealscommission.ab.ca

British Columbia
Workers' Compensation Appeal Tribunal, #150, 4600 Jacombs Rd., Richmond, BC V6V 3B1
604-664-7800, Fax: 604-664-7898, 800-663-2782
Workers' Compensation Board of British Columbia, PO Box 5350 Terminal,Vancouver, BC V6B 5L5
604-276-3100, Fax: 604-276-3247, 888-621-7233

Manitoba
Manitoba Workers' Compensation Board, 333 Broadway Ave., Winnipeg, MB R3C 4W3
204-954-4321, Fax: 204-954-4999, 800-362-3340, wcb@wcb.mb.ca

New Brunswick
Workplace Health, Safety & Compensation Commission of New Brunswick, 1 Portland St., PO Box 160, Saint John, NB E2L 3X9
506-632-2200, 800-222-9775, communications@ws-ts.nb.ca

Newfoundland & Labrador
Newfoundland & Labrador Workplace Health, Safety & Compensation Commission, 146 - 148 Forest Rd., PO Box 9000, St. John's, NL A1A 3B8
709-778-1000, Fax: 709-738-1714, 800-563-9000, general.inquiries@whscc.nl.ca

Northwest Territories
Northwest Territories & Nunavut Workers' Safety & Compensation Commission, Centre Square Tower, 5022 - 49th St., 5th Fl., PO Box 8888, Yellowknife, NT X1A 2R3
867-920-3888, Fax: 867-873-4596, 800-661-0792

Nova Scotia
Workers' Compensation Board of Nova Scotia, 5668 South St., PO Box 1150, Halifax, NS B3J 2Y2
902-491-8999, Fax: 902-491-8002, 800-870-3331, info@wcb.gov.ns.ca

Ontario
Workplace Safety & Insurance Board, 200 Front St. West, Ground Fl., Toronto, ON M5V 3J1
416-344-1000, Fax: 416-344-4684, 800-387-0750

Prince Edward Island
Prince Edward Island Workers Compensation Board, 14 Weymouth St., PO Box 757, Charlottetown, PE C1A 7L7
902-368-5680, Fax: 902-368-5696, 800-237-5049

Quebec
Commission des lésions professionnelles, #700, 900, Place d'Youville, Québec, QC G1R 3P7
418-644-7777, Fax: 418-644-6443, 800-463-1591
Commission de la santé et de la sécurité du travail du Québec, 524, rue Bourdages, CP 1200 Terminus postal,Québec, QC G1K 7E2
418-266-4850, Fax: 418-266-4669, 866-302-2778

Saskatchewan
Saskatchewan Workers' Compensation Board, #200, 1881 Scarth St., Regina, SK S4P 4L1
306-787-4370, Fax: 306-787-4311, 800-667-7590, internet_clientsvc@wcbsask.com

Yukon Territory
Yukon Workers' Compensation Health & Safety Board, 401 Strickland St., Whitehorse, YT Y1A 5N8
867-667-5645, Fax: 867-393-6279, 800-661-0443, worksafe@gov.yk.ca

YOUNG OFFENDERS

Justice Canada, East Memorial Bldg., 284 Wellington St., Ottawa, ON K1A 0H8
613-957-4222, Fax: 613-954-0811, webadmin@justice.gc.ca

Alberta
Alberta Justice & Attorney General, Communications, Bowker Building, 9833 - 109 St., 3rd Fl., Edmonton, AB T5K 2E8
780-427-2745

British Columbia
Ministry of the Attorney General, PO Box 9044 Prov Govt,Victoria, BC V8W 9E2
250-387-1866, Fax: 250-387-6411
Office of the Representative for Children & Youth, #201, 546 Yates St., Victoria, BC V8W 1K8
250-356-6710, Fax: 250-356-0837, 800-476-3933, rcy@rcybc.ca

Northwest Territories
Department of Justice, Courthouse, 4903 - 49th St., 6th Fl., PO Box 1320, Yellowknife, NT X1A 2L9
867-920-6197

Nova Scotia
Department of Justice, 5151 Terminal Rd., 4th Fl., PO Box 7, Halifax, NS B3J 2L6
902-424-4030, Fax: 902-424-0510, justweb@gov.ns.ca

Nunavut
Young Offenders, 1548 Federal Rd., PO Box 1439, Iqaluit, NU X0A 0H0
867-979-4452, Fax: 867-979-5506

Ontario
Ministry of the Attorney General, McMurtry-Scott Bldg., 720 Bay St., 11th Fl., Toronto, ON M5G 2K1
416-326-2220, Fax: 416-326-4007, 800-518-7901

YOUTH SERVICES

Alberta
Office of the Child & Youth Advocate, Peace Hills Trust Tower, 10011 - 109 St., 8th Fl., Edmonton, AB T5J 3S8
780-422-6056, Fax: 780-644-8833, 800-661-3446

British Columbia
Provincial Services, PO Box 9717 Prov Govt,Victoria, BC V8W 9S1
250-387-0978, Fax: 250-356-2079

New Brunswick
New Brunswick Advisory Council on Youth, Frederick Square, #130, 77 Westmorland St., PO Box 6000, Fredericton, NB E3B 5H1
506-453-3271, Fax: 506-444-4413, 888-830-5588, nbacy-ccjnb@gnb.ca

Nunavut
Department of Culture, Language, Elders & Youth, PO Box 1000 800,Iqaluit, NU X0A 0H0
867-975-5500, Fax: 867-975-5504, 866-934-2035

Ontario
Ministry of Children & Youth Services, 56 Wellesley St. West, 14th Fl., Toronto, ON M5S 2G3
Fax: 416-325-5191, 866-821-7770

Quebec
Ministère de la Santé et des Services sociaux, Direction des communications, 1075, ch Sainte-Foy, 16e étage, Québec, QC G1S 2M1
418-643-9395, Fax: 418-643-4768, regisseur.web@msss.gouv.qc.ca

ZONING

Alberta
Local Government Services Division, Commerce Place, 10155 - 102 St., 17th Fl., Edmonton, AB T5J 4L4

British Columbia
Ministry of Community, Sport & Cultural Development, PO Box 9056 Prov Govt,Victoria, BC V8W 9E2
250-387-2283, Fax: 250-387-4312

Manitoba
Manitoba Municipal Board, #1144, 363 Broadway, Winnipeg, MB R3C 3N9
204-945-2941, Fax: 204-948-2235

New Brunswick
Department of Local Government, Marysville Place, 20 McGloin St., PO Box 6000, Fredericton, NB E3B 5H1
506-453-2807, Fax: 506-453-3988

Quebec
Commission municipale du Québec, Mezzanine, aile Chauveau, 10, rue Pierre-Olivier-Chauveau, Québec, QC G1R 4J3
418-691-2014, Fax: 418-644-4676, 866-353-6767, cmq@mamr.gouv.qc.ca

Government of Canada

c/o Canada Enquiry Centre, Service Canada, Ottawa, ON K1A 0J9
613-941-1827
800-622-6232
sitecanadasite@canada.gc.ca
www.canada.gc.ca
TTY: 800-926-9105

All political authority in Canada is divided between the federal & provincial governments, according to the provisions of the Constitution Act, 1867. Local municipalities are a concern of the provinces, & derive their authority from Acts of provincial legislation. The Parliament of Canada consists of Her Majesty Queen Elizabeth II (represented in Canada by the Governor General, His Excellency the Right Honourable David Johnston), an Upper House called the Senate, & an elected House of Commons.

Governor General & Commander-in-Chief of Canada / Gouverneur général et Commandant en chef du Canada

Rideau Hall, 1 Sussex Dr., Ottawa, ON K1A 0A1
613-993-8200 Fax: 613-998-8760
800-465-6890
info@gg.ca
www.gg.ca

Canada is a constitutional monarchy. Under the terms of its Constitution, Her Majesty Queen Elizabeth II is the Head of State. The duties of the Head of State are undertaken by the Governor General as the Crown's representative. He is also Commander-in-Chief of the Canadian Forces, Chancellor & Principal Companion of the Order of Canada, Chancellor & Commander of the Order of Military Merit, & Head of the Canadian Heraldic Authority. The Office of the Governor General encompasses a number of responsibilities, both constitutional & traditional in nature. The Governor General of Canada exercises powers & responsibilities belonging to the Sovereign, with the advice of members of the Privy Council. He is involved in the promotion of Canadian sovereignty at home & represents Canada abroad. Canadian values, diversity, inclusion, culture, & heritage are promoted by the Governor General. National honours, decorations, & awards to recognize people who have demonstrated excellence, valour, bravery, or exceptional dedication to service are presented by the Governor General.

Governor General, Rt. Hon. David Johnston, C.C.
613-993-8200, Fax: 613-993-1967
Secretary to the Governor General, Stephen Wallace
613-993-0259, Fax: 613-993-1967
Director General, Corporate Services, Fady Abdul-Nour
613-991-9091, Fax: 613-998-8762
Superintendent, Associated Services - Security, Sylvian Côté
613-993-9332, Fax: 613-993-8641

The Chancellery of Honours / Chancellerie
1 Sussex Dr., Ottawa, ON K1A 0A1
613-998-8732 Fax: 613-991-1681

Deputy Secretary & Deputy Herald Chancellor, Office of the Secretary to the Governor General, The Chancellery of Honours, Emmanuelle Sajous
613-998-8731, Fax: 613-991-1681
Director, Honours, Office of the Secretary to the Governor General, Honours Directorate, Gabrielle Lappa
613-991-0894, Fax: 613-991-1681
Chief Herald of Canada & Director, Office of the Secretary to the Governor General, The Canadian Heraldic Authority, Claire Boudreau
613-991-2227, Fax: 613-990-5818
Deputy Chief Herald of Canada & Assistant Director, Office of the Secretary to the Governor General, Bruce Patterson
613-991-2229, Fax: 613-990-5818

Policy, Program & Protocol Branch / Politique, programme et protocole
1 Sussex Dr., Ottawa, ON K1A 0A1

Deputy Secretary, Patricia Jaton
613-990-9006, Fax: 613-993-4728
Chief, Visitor Services & Exhibits, Dominique Bergeron
613-993-0311, Fax: 613-993-1656
Director, Security & Logistics, Sylvie Beaudry
613-993-0439, Fax: 613-993-4728
Acting Director, Public Affairs, Annabelle Cloutier
613-993-8158, Fax: 613-998-1664
Director, Events & Visitor Services, Christine MacIntyre
613-993-1901, Fax: 613-991-5113
Director, Policy, Planning, & Correspondence, Duncan Mousseau
613-993-1934, Fax: 613-993-1552
Director, Household Services, Philippe Wettel
613-990-7629, Fax: 613-998-5579

Privy Council Office (PCO) / Bureau du Conseil privé (BCP)

#1000, 85 Sparks St., Ottawa, ON K1A 0A3
613-957-5153 Fax: 613-997-5043
info@pco-bcp.gc.ca
www.pco-bcp.gc.ca
TTY: 613-957-5741
Other Communication: Media Phone: 613-957-5420

The Privy Council Office provides non-partisan advice & information from across the Public Service to the Prime Minister, the Cabinet, & its decision-making structures. The key roles of the Privy Council are as follows: advising the Prime Minister & supporting the Cabinet; managing the Cabinet's decision-making system & facilitating its efficient & effective functioning on a daily basis; & providing public service leadership, including the management of the appointments process for Crown corporations & agencies, & senior positions in federal departments. The Privy Council is led by the Clerk of the Privy Council. A member of the Privy Council is awarded the title, "Honourable", for life. The Governor General, the Prime Minister, & the Chief Justice of Canada are accorded the title, "The Right Honourable", for life.

Acts Administered:
Canadian Transportation Accident Investigation & Safety Board Act
National Round Table on the Environment & the Economy Act
Oaths of Allegiance Act
Parliamentary Employment & Staff Relations Act
Public Service Staff Relations Act
Representation Act, 1985

President, Queen's Privy Council for Canada; Minister, Intergovernmental Affairs, Hon. Peter Penashue
613-943-1838, Fax: 613-992-3700, peter.penashue@parl.gc.ca
Leader of the Government in the House of Commons (PCO Minister), Hon. Peter Van Loan
613-996-7752, Fax: 613-992-8351, peter.vanloan@parl.gc.ca; info@pco-bcp.gc.ca, Other Communications: Department Phone: 613-957-5153
Leader of the Government in the Senate (PCO Minister), Hon. Marjory LeBreton
613-943-0756, 800-267-7362, Fax: 613-943-1493, lebrem@sen.parl.gc.ca; Marjory.LeBreton@pco-bcp.gc.ca
Minister of State (Democratic Reform) (PCO Minister), Hon. Tim Uppal
613-995-5609, Fax: 613-943-6976, tim.uppal@parl.gc.ca
Minister of State; Chief Government Whip (PCO Minister), Hon. Gordon O'Connor, B.A., B.Sc.
613-992-1119, Fax: 613-992-1043, gordon.oconnor@parl.gc.ca
Clerk of the Privy Council & Secretary to the Cabinet, Wayne Wouters
613-957-5400, Fax: 613-957-5729, info@clerk.gc.ca
National Security Advisor to the Prime Minister, Stephen Rigby
613-957-5056, Fax: 613-957-5277
Special Advisor, Human Smuggling & Illegal Migration, Ward Elcock
613-952-6732, Fax: 613-952-6794
Deputy Minister, Afghanistan Task Force, Greta Bossenmaier
613-952-4900, Fax: 613-952-4924
Deputy Minister, Intergovernmental Affairs & Associate Secretary to the Cabinet, Janice Charette
613-957-5466, Fax: 613-957-5089
Deputy Secretary to the Cabinet, Foreign & Defence Policy Advisor to the Prime Minister, Vacant
Other Communications: Office Manager Phone: 613-957-5476
Deputy Secretary to the Cabinet, Senior Personnel & Public Service Renewal, Patricia Hassard
613-957-5360, Fax: 613-957-5006
Deputy Secretary to the Cabinet, Operations, Michael Martin
613-957-5417, Fax: 613-957-5637
Deputy Secretary to the Cabinet, Plans & Consultation, William Pentney
613-957-5462, Fax: 613-957-5487
Deputy Secretary to the Cabinet, Legislation & House Planning, & Machinery of Government, Counsel to the Clerk of the Privy Council, Yvan Roy
613-957-5792, Fax: 613-952-4955
Executive Director, Administrative Services Review, Wilma Vreeswijk
613-996-6538, Fax: 613-995-3506

Privy Council Members & Date When Sworn In
Hon. Paul Theodore Hellyer, Apr. 26, 1957
H.R.H. Prince Phillip, The Duke of Edinburg, Oct. 14, 1957
Rt. Hon. Martial Asselin, Mar. 18, 1963
Hon. Allan Joseph MacEachen, Apr. 22, 1963
Hon. Yvon Dupuis, Feb. 3, 1964
Rt. Hon. John Napier Turner, Dec. 18, 1965
Rt. Hon. Joseph Jacques Jean Chrétien, Apr. 4, 1967
Hon. Alexander Bradshaw Campbell, Jul. 5, 1967
Hon. Donald Stovel Macdonald, Apr. 20, 1968
Hon. Jean-Eudes Dubé, Jul. 6, 1968
Hon. Otto Emil Lang, Jul. 6, 1968
Rt. Hon. Herbert Eser Gray, Oct. 20, 1969
Hon. Robert D. George Stanbury, Oct. 20, 1969
Hon. Alastair William Gillespie, Aug. 12, 1971
Hon. Patrick Morgan Mahoney, Jan. 28, 1972
Hon. Eugene Francis Whelan, Nov. 27, 1972
Hon. William Warren Allmand, Nov. 27, 1972
Hon. James Hugh Faulkner, Nov. 27, 1972
Hon. André Ouellet, Nov. 27, 1972
Hon. Marc Lalonde, Nov. 27, 1972
Hon. J. Judd Buchanan, Aug. 8, 1974
Hon. Pierre Juneau, Aug. 29, 1975
Hon. Marcel Lessard, Sep. 26, 1975
Hon. Leonard Stephen Marchand, Sep. 15, 1976
Hon. Monique Bégin, Sep. 15, 1976
Hon. Jean-Jacques Blais, Sep. 15, 1976
Hon. Francis Fox, Sep. 15, 1976
Hon. Anthony Chisholm Abbott, Sep. 15, 1976
Hon. Iona Campagnolo, Sep. 15, 1976
Hon. Norman A. Cafik, Sep. 16, 1977
Hon. J. Gilles Lamontagne, Jan. 19, 1978
Hon. John M. Reid, Nov. 24, 1978
Hon. Pierre De Bané, Nov. 24, 1978
Rt. Hon. Charles Joseph Clark, Jun. 4, 1979
Hon. Flora Isabel MacDonald, Jun. 4, 1979
Hon. James Aloysius McGrath, Jun. 4, 1979
Hon. John Carnell Crosbie, Jun. 4, 1979
Hon. David Samuel Horne MacDonald, Jun. 4, 1979
Hon. Lincoln MacCauley Alexander, Jun. 4, 1979
Hon. Roch LaSalle, Jun. 4, 1979
Rt. Hon. Donald Frank Mazankowski, Jun. 4, 1979
Hon. Elmer MacIntosh MacKay, Jun. 4, 1979
Hon. Arthur Jacob Epp, Jun. 4, 1979
Hon. John Allen Fraser, Jun. 4, 1979
Hon. William H. Jarvis, Jun. 4, 1979
Hon. Sinclair McKnight Stevens, Jun. 4, 1979
Hon. John Wise, Jun. 4, 1979
Hon. Ronald George Atkey, Jun. 4, 1979
Hon. David Edward Crombie, Jun. 4, 1979
Hon. Henry Perrin Beatty, Jun. 4, 1979
Hon. J. Robert Howie, Jun. 4, 1979
Hon. Michael Holcombe Wilson, Jun. 4, 1979
Hon. Gerald Augustine Regan, Mar. 3, 1980
Hon. Robert Phillip Kaplan, Mar. 3, 1980
Hon. James Sydney Clark Fleming, Mar. 3, 1980
Hon. William H. Rompkey, Mar. 3, 1980
Hon. Pierre Bussières, Mar. 3, 1980
Hon. Charles Lapointe, Mar. 3, 1980
Hon. Edward C. Lumley, Mar. 3, 1980
Hon. Yvon Pinard, Mar. 3, 1980
Hon. Donald James Johnston, Mar. 3, 1980
Hon. Lloyd Axworthy, Mar. 3, 1980
Hon. Paul James Cosgrove, Mar. 3, 1980
Hon. Judith A. Erola, Mar. 3, 1980
Hon. Jacob Austin, Sep. 22, 1981
Hon. Serge Joyal, Sep. 22, 1981
Hon. Robert Gordon Robertson, Mar. 2, 1982
Hon. John Edward Broadbent, Apr. 17, 1982
Hon. William Grenville Davis, Apr. 17, 1982
Hon. E. Peter Lougheed, Apr. 17, 1982
Hon. William Richards Bennett, Apr. 17, 1982
Hon. John MacLennan Buchanan, Apr. 17, 1982
Hon. Alfred Brian Peckford, Apr. 17, 1982
Hon. James Matthew Lee, Apr. 17, 1982
Hon. Howard Russell Pawley, Apr. 17, 1982
Hon. David Michael Collenette, Aug. 12, 1983
Hon. Céline Hervieux-Payette, Aug. 12, 1983
Hon. Roger Simmons, Aug. 12, 1983
Hon. David Paul Smith, Aug. 12, 1983
Hon. Roy MacLaren, Aug. 17, 1983
Hon. Peter Michael Pitfield, Apr. 19, 1984
Rt. Hon. Martin Brian Mulroney, May 7, 1984
Rt. Hon. Edward Richard Schreyer, Jun. 3, 1984
Hon. Herb Breau, Jun. 30, 1984
Hon. Joseph Roger Rémi Bujold, Jun. 30, 1984
Hon. Jean-C. Lapierre, Jun. 30, 1984
Hon. Ralph Ferguson, Jun. 30, 1984
Hon. Robert Carman Coates, Sep. 17, 1984
Hon. Jack Burnett Murta, Sep. 17, 1984
Hon. Harvie Andre, Sep. 17, 1984
Hon. Otto John Jelinek, Sep. 17, 1984
Hon. Charles James Mayer, Sep. 17, 1984
Hon. Thomas Edward Siddon, Sep. 17, 1984
Hon. William Hunter McKnight, Sep. 17, 1984
Hon. Rev. Walter Franklin McLean, Sep. 17, 1984
Hon. Thomas Michael McMillan, Sep. 17, 1984
Hon. Patricia Carney, Sep. 17, 1984
Hon. André Bissonnette, Sep. 17, 1984
Hon. Suzanne Blais-Grenier, Sep. 17, 1984
Hon. Benoît Bouchard, Sep. 17, 1984
Hon. Andrée Champagne, Sep. 17, 1984
Hon. Michel Côté, Sep. 17, 1984
Hon. James Francis Kelleher, Sep. 17, 1984

Hon. Marcel Masse, Sep. 17, 1984
Hon. Barbara Jean McDougall, Sep. 17, 1984
Hon. Monique Vézina, Sep. 17, 1984
Hon. Saul Mark Cherniack, Nov. 30, 1984
Hon. Paule Gauthier, Nov. 30, 1984
Hon. Stewart Donald McInnes, Aug. 20, 1985
Hon. Frank Oberle, Nov. 20, 1985
Hon. Gordon F. Joseph Osbaldeston, Feb. 13, 1986
Hon. Lowell Murray, Jun. 30, 1986
Hon. Paul Wyatt Dick, Jun. 30, 1986
Hon. Pierre H. Cadieux, Jun. 30, 1986
Hon. Jean J. Charest, Jun. 30, 1986
Hon. Thomas Hockin, Jun. 30, 1986
Hon. Monique Landry, Jun. 30, 1986
Hon. Bernard Valcourt, Jun. 30, 1986
Hon. Gerry Weiner, Jun. 30, 1986
Hon. John William Bosley, Jun. 30, 1987
Hon. Douglas Grinslade Lewis, Aug. 27, 1987
Hon. Pierre Blais, Aug. 27, 1987
Hon. Lucien Bouchard, Mar. 31, 1988
Hon. Gerry St. Germain, Mar. 31, 1988
Hon. John Horton McDermid, Sep. 15, 1988
Hon. Shirley Martin, Sep. 15, 1988
Hon. Mary Collins, Jan. 30, 1989
Hon. Alan Redway, Jan. 30, 1989
Hon. William Charles Winegard, Jan. 30, 1989
Rt. Hon. A. Kim Campbell, Jan. 30, 1989
Hon. Gilles Loiselle, Jan. 30, 1989
Hon. Marcel Danis, Feb. 23, 1990
Hon. Audrey McLaughlin, Jan. 10, 1991
Hon. Pauline Browes, Apr. 21, 1991
Hon. J.J. Michel Robert, Dec. 5, 1991
Hon. Marcel Prud'homme, Jul. 1, 1992
Hon. Lorne Edmund Nystrom, Jul. 1, 1992
Hon. David Alexander Colville, Jul. 1, 1992
Hon. Paul Desmarais, Jul. 1, 1992
Hon. John Charles Polanyi, Jul. 1, 1992
Hon. Maurice F. Strong, Jul. 1, 1992
Hon. Antonine Maillet, Jul. 1, 1992
Hon. Richard Cashin, Jul. 1, 1992
Hon. Paul M. Tellier, Jul. 1, 1992
Hon. David Robert Peterson, Jul. 1, 1992
Hon. Conrad M. Black, Jul. 1, 1992
Hon. Charles Rosner Bronfman, Oct. 21, 1992
Hon. Pierre H. Vincent, Jan. 4, 1993
Hon. James Stewart Edwards, Jun. 25, 1993
Hon. Robert Douglas Nicholson, Jun. 25, 1993
Hon. Barbara Jane Sparrow, Jun. 25, 1993
Hon. Peter L. McCreath, Jun. 25, 1993
Hon. Ian Angus Ross Reid, Jun. 25, 1993
Hon. Larry Schneider, Jun. 25, 1993
Hon. Garth Turner, Jun. 25, 1993
Hon. David Anderson, Nov. 4, 1993
Hon. Ralph Edward Goodale, Nov. 4, 1993
Hon. David Charles Dingwall, Nov. 4, 1993
Hon. Ron Irwin, Nov. 4, 1993
Hon. Brian Tobin, Nov. 4, 1993
Hon. Joyce Fairbairn, Nov. 4, 1993
Hon. Sheila Maureen Copps, Nov. 4, 1993
Hon. Sergio Marchi, Nov. 4, 1993
Hon. John Manley, Nov. 4, 1993
Hon. Diane Marleau, Nov. 4, 1993
Rt. Hon. Paul Martin, Nov. 4, 1993
Hon. Douglas Young, Nov. 4, 1993
Hon. Michel Dupuy, Nov. 4, 1993
Hon. Arthur C. Eggleton, Nov. 4, 1993
Hon. Marcel Massé, Nov. 4, 1993
Hon. Anne McLellan, Nov. 4, 1993
Hon. Allan Rock, Nov. 4, 1993
Hon. Fernand Robichaud, Nov. 4, 1993
Hon. Ethel Blondin-Andrew, Nov. 4, 1993
Hon. Lawrence MacAulay, Nov. 4, 1993
Hon. Christine Stewart, Nov. 4, 1993
Hon. Raymond Chan, Nov. 4, 1993
Hon. Jon Gerrard, Nov. 4, 1993
Hon. Douglas Peters, Nov. 4, 1993
Hon. Alfonso Gagliano, Sep. 15, 1994
Hon. Lucienne Robillard, Feb. 22, 1995
Hon. Fred J. Mifflin, Jan. 25, 1996
Hon. Jane Stewart, Jan. 25, 1996
Hon. Stéphane Dion, Jan. 25, 1996
Hon. Pierre Pettigrew, Jan. 25, 1996
Hon. Martin Cauchon, Jan. 25, 1996
Hon. Hedy Fry, Jan. 25, 1996
Hon. James Andrew Grant, Sep. 30, 1996
Hon. Don Boudria, Oct. 4, 1996
Hon. Bernard Alasdair Graham, Jun. 11, 1997
Hon. Lyle Vanclief, Jun. 11, 1997
Hon. Herb Dhaliwal, Jun. 11, 1997
Hon. David Kilgour, Jun. 11, 1997
Hon. James Scott Peterson, Jun. 11, 1997
Hon. Andy Scott, Jun. 11, 1997
Hon. Andrew Mitchell, Jun. 11, 1997
Hon. Gilbert Normand, Jun. 18, 1997
Hon. Bob Rae, Apr. 30, 1998
Hon. Claudette Bradshaw, Nov. 23, 1998
Hon. Jocelyne Bourgon, Dec. 14, 1998
Hon. Raymond A. Speaker, Jun. 9, 1999
Hon. Frank Joseph McKenna, Jun. 9, 1999
Hon. George Baker, Aug. 3, 1999
Hon. Maria Minna, Aug. 3, 1999
Hon. Elinor Caplan, Aug. 3, 1999
Hon. Denis Coderre, Aug. 3, 1999
Hon. Robert Daniel Nault, Aug. 3, 1999
Hon. J. Bernard Boudreau, Oct. 4, 1999
Rt. Hon. Beverley M. McLachlin, Jan. 12, 2000
Hon. Sharon Carstairs, Jan. 9, 2001
Hon. Robert G. Thibault, Jan. 9, 2001
Hon. Rey Pagtakhan, Jan. 9, 2001
Hon. Gary Albert Filmon, Oct. 4, 2001
Hon. Susan Whelan, Jan. 15, 2002
Hon. Maurizio Bevilacqua, Jan. 15, 2002
Hon. Paul DeVillers, Jan. 15, 2002
Hon. Gar Knutson, Jan. 15, 2002
Hon. Denis Paradis, Jan. 15, 2002
Hon. Claude Drouin, Jan. 15, 2002
Hon. John McCallum, Jan. 15, 2002
Hon. Stephen Owen, Jan. 15, 2002
Hon. William Graham, Jan. 16, 2002
Hon. Gerry Byrne, Jan. 16, 2002
Hon. Jean Augustine, May 26, 2002
Hon. Arnold Wayne Easter, Oct. 22, 2002
Hon. Baljit Singh Chadha, Feb. 20, 2003
Hon. Steven W. Mahoney, Apr. 11, 2003
Hon. Roy J. Romanow, Nov. 13, 2003
Hon. Stan Kazmierczak Keyes, Dec. 12, 2003
Hon. Robert Speller, Dec. 12, 2003
Hon. Giuseppe (Joseph) Volpe, Dec. 12, 2003
Hon. Geoff Regan, Dec. 12, 2003
Hon. Tony Valeri, Dec. 12, 2003
Hon. David Pratt, Dec. 12, 2003
Hon. Jacques Saada, Dec. 12, 2003
Hon. Irwin Cotler, Dec. 12, 2003
Hon. Judy Sgro, Dec. 12, 2003
Hon. Hélène Chalifour Scherrer, Dec. 12, 2003
Hon. Ruben John Efford, Dec. 12, 2003
Hon. Liza Frulla, Dec. 12, 2003
Hon. Joseph Robert Comuzzi, Dec. 12, 2003
Hon. Albina Guarnieri, Dec. 12, 2003
Hon. Joseph McGuire, Dec. 12, 2003
Hon. Mauril Bélanger, Dec. 12, 2003
Hon. Carolyn Bennett, Dec. 12, 2003
Hon. M. Aileen Carroll, Dec. 12, 2003
Hon. André Harvey, Dec. 12, 2003
Hon. Susan Barnes, Dec. 12, 2003
Hon. David Price, Dec. 12, 2003
Hon. Jim Karygiannis, Dec. 12, 2003
Hon. Shawn Murphy, Dec. 12, 2003
Hon. Joseph Louis Jordan, Dec. 12, 2003
Hon. Roger Gallaway, Dec. 12, 2003
Hon. Paul Bonwick, Dec. 12, 2003
Hon. Eleni Bakopanos, Dec. 12, 2003
Hon. Georges Farrah, Dec. 12, 2003
Hon. Mark Eyking, Dec. 12, 2003
Hon. Dan McTeague, Dec. 12, 2003
Hon. Walt Lastewka, Dec. 12, 2003
Hon. Brenda Kay Chamberlain, Dec. 12, 2003
Hon. Larry Bagnell, Dec. 12, 2003
Hon. John Harvard, Dec. 12, 2003
Hon. Gurbax Singh Malhi, Dec. 12, 2003
Hon. Yvon Charbonneau, Dec. 12, 2003
Hon. Joseph Frank Fontana, Dec. 12, 2003
Hon. Jerry Pickard, Dec. 12, 2003
Hon. John McKay, Dec. 12, 2003
Hon. Scott Brison, Dec. 12, 2003
Hon. John Ferguson Godfrey, Dec. 12, 2003
Hon. Andrew Telegdi, Jan. 30, 2004
Hon. Rev. William Alexander Blaikie, Feb. 19, 2004
Hon. Grant Hill, Feb. 19, 2004
Rt. Hon. Stephen Joseph Harper, May 4, 2004
Hon. Joseph Marin Jacques Olivier, May 5, 2004
Hon. Ujjal Dosanjh, Jul. 20, 2004
Hon. Ken Dryden, Jul. 20, 2004
Hon. David Emerson, Jul. 20, 2004
Hon. Tony Ianno, Jul. 20, 2004
Hon. Peter Adams, Jul. 20, 2004
Hon. Sarmite Bulte, Jul. 20, 2004
Hon. Roy Cullen, Jul. 20, 2004
Hon. Marlene Jennings, Jul. 20, 2004
Hon. Dominic LeBlanc, Jul. 20, 2004
Hon. Judi Longfield, Jul. 20, 2004
Hon. Paul Macklin, Jul. 20, 2004
Hon. Keith P. Martin, Jul. 20, 2004
Hon. Karen Redman, Jul. 20, 2004
Hon. Raymond Simard, Jul. 20, 2004
Hon. Patricia Ann Torsney, Jul. 20, 2004
Hon. Bryon Wilfert, Jul. 20, 2004
Hon. Belinda Stronach, May 17, 2005
Hon. Aldéa Landry, Q.C., Jun. 24, 2005
Rt. Hon. Adrienne Clarkson, Oct. 3, 2005
Hon. Navdeep Bains, Oct. 7, 2005
Hon. Anita Neville, Oct. 7, 2005
Hon. Charles Hubbard, Oct. 7, 2005
Hon. Jean-Pierre Blackburn, Feb. 6, 2006
Hon. Greg Thompson, Feb. 6, 2006
Hon. Marjory LeBreton, Feb. 6, 2006
Hon. Monte Solberg, Feb. 6, 2006
Hon. Charles (Chuck) Strahl, Feb. 6, 2006
Hon. Gary Lunn, Feb. 6, 2006
Hon. Peter Gordon MacKay, Feb. 6, 2006
Hon. Loyola Hearn, Feb. 6, 2006
Hon. Stockwell Burt Day, Feb. 6, 2006
Hon. Carol Skelton, Feb. 6, 2006
Hon. Vic Toews, Feb. 6, 2006
Hon. Rona Ambrose, Feb. 6, 2006
Hon. Michael D. Chong, Feb. 6, 2006
Hon. Diane Finley, Feb. 6, 2006
Hon. Gordon O'Connor, Feb. 6, 2006
Hon. Beverley J. (Bev) Oda, Feb. 6, 2006
Hon. John Baird, Feb. 6, 2006
Hon. Maxime Bernier, Feb. 6, 2006
Hon. Lawrence Cannon, Feb. 6, 2006
Hon. Tony Clement, Feb. 6, 2006
Hon. James Michael (Jim) Flaherty, Feb. 6, 2006
Hon. Josée Verner, Feb. 6, 2006
Hon. Jim Prentice, Feb. 6, 2006
Hon. Michael Fortier, Feb. 6, 2006
Hon. John Reynolds, Feb. 6, 2006
Hon. Jay D. Hill, Feb. 16, 2006
Hon. Peter Van Loan, Nov. 27, 2006
Hon. Jason Kenney, Jan. 4, 2007
Hon. Gerry Ritz, Jan. 4, 2007
Hon. Helena Guergis, Jan. 4, 2007
Hon. Christian Paradis, Jan. 4, 2007
Hon. Daniel Philip Hays, Jan. 22, 2007
Hon. James Abbott, Oct. 15, 2007
Hon. Diane Ablonczy, Aug. 14, 2007
Hon. James Moore, Jun. 25, 2008
Hon. Denis Losier, Sep. 3, 2008
Hon. Arthur Thomas Porter, Sep. 3, 2008
Hon. Leona Aglukkaq, Oct. 30, 2008
Hon. Keith Ashfield, Oct. 30, 2008
Hon. Steven John Fletcher, Oct. 30, 2008
Hon. Gary Goodyear, Oct. 30, 2008
Hon. Peter Kent, Oct. 30, 2008
Hon. Denis Lebel, Oct. 30, 2008
Hon. Rob Merrifield, Oct. 30, 2008
Hon. Lisa Raitt, Oct. 30, 2008
Hon. Gail Shea, Oct. 30, 2008
Hon. Lynn Yelich, Oct. 30, 2008
Hon. Leonard Joseph Gustafson, Jan. 8, 2009
Hon. Frances Lankin, Jan. 22, 2009
Hon. Kevin Lynch, May 11, 2009
Hon. Rob Moore, Jan. 19, 2010
Hon. Michael Grant Ignatieff, May 7, 2010
Hon. Philippe Couillard, Jun. 21, 2010
Hon. John Duncan, Aug. 6, 2010
Hon. Rick Casson, Oct. 1, 2010
Hon. Laurie Hawn, Oct. 1, 2010
Hon. Julian Fantino, Jan. 4, 2011
Hon. Ted Menzies, Jan. 4, 2011
Hon. Steven Blaney, May 18, 2011
Hon. Edward Fast, May 18, 2011
Hon. Bal Gosal, May 18, 2011
Hon. Joe Oliver, May 18, 2011
Hon. Peter Penashue, May 18, 2011
Hon. Tim Uppal, May 18, 2011
Hon. Alice Wong, May 18, 2011

Associated Agencies, Boards & Commissions:
- Office of Intergovernmental Affairs / Affaires intergouvernementales

Senate of Canada / Sénat du Canada

Ottawa, ON K1A 0A4
613-995-1900
800-267-7362
sencom@sen.parl.gc.ca
www.sen.parl.gc.ca
Other Communication: Twitter: twitter.com/@SenateCA

Senators are appointed by the Governor General, upon the recommendation of the Prime Minister of Canada. Senators hold their positions only until they attain the age of seventy-five years. To be eligible for appointment, a senatorial candidate must be a Canadian citizen, & be at least thirty years of age. The person must own $4,000 of equity in land in his or her province or territory, & have a personal net worth of at least $4,000. A senator must also be a resident of the province or territory for which he or she is appointed. The main tasks of the Senate are as follows: to examinine bills; to approve, reject, or amend legislation; to investigate policy matters & to present recommendations; & to examine the government's spending proposals. No bill may become law unless it is passed by the Senate. The main thrust of the Senate's work is carried out in committees, where bills are interpreted & reviewed clause by clause, & evidence is heard from groups & individuals who may be affected by the particular bill under review. Senators' committees, or study groups, investigate key issues, such as poverty, terrorism, literacy, children's rights, Aboriginal peoples, constitutional affairs, & foreign affairs. The Senate reports produced from these investiga tions have proved to be valuable, & have often led to changes in government policy or legislation. The Speaker of the Senate is appointed by the Governor General, upon the recommendation of the Prime Minister. The Senate, as originally constituted at Confederation, consisted of 72 members. Through the addition of new provinces & territories, & the general growth of Canada, the Senate now has 105 regular members. By provinces & territories, representation in the Senate of Canada is as follows (October 2011): Alberta 6; British Columbia 6; Manitoba 6; New Brunswick 10; Newfoundland & Labrador 6; Northwest Territories 1; Nova Scotia 10; Nunavut 1; Ontario 24: Prince Edward Island 4; Québec 24: Saskatchewan 6; & Yukon 1; Total 105. By party affiliation, representation is as follows (October 2011): Conservative 54; Liberal 43; Independent 2; Progressive Conservative 1; Vacant seats 5; Total 105.

Speaker of the Senate, Hon. Noël Kinsella
613-992-4416, 800-267-7362, Fax: 613-992-9772, kinsen@sen.parl.gc.ca

Leader of the Government in the Senate, Hon. Marjory LeBreton
613-943-0756, 800-267-7362, Fax: 613-943-1493, lebrem@sen.parl.gc.ca

Leader of the Opposition, Hon. James S. Cowan
613-995-4268, 800-267-7362, Fax: 613-995-4287, cowanj@sen.parl.gc.ca

Deputy Leader of the Government, Hon. Claude Carrignan
613-992-0240, 800-267-7362

Deputy Leader of the Opposition, Hon. Claudette Tardif
613-947-3589, 800-267-7362, Fax: 613-947-3609, tardic@sen.parl.gc.ca

Government Whip, Hon. Elizabeth Marshall
613-943-4011, 800-267-7362, Fax: 613-943-4013, marshe@sen.parl.gc.ca

Opposition Whip, Hon. Jim Munson
613-947-2504, 800-267-7362, Fax: 613-947-2506, munsoj@sen.parl.gc.ca

Senators, with appointment year, political affiliation & contact information

Hon. Raynell Andreychuk, 1993, Conservative Party
613-947-2239, 800-267-7362, Fax: 613-947-2241, andrer@sen.parl.gc.ca

Hon. W. David Angus, 1993, Conservative Party
613-947-3193, 800-267-7362, Fax: 613-947-3195, anguswd@sen.parl.gc.ca

Hon. Salma Ataullahjan, 2010, Conservative Party
613-947-5906, 800-267-7362, Fax: 613-947-5908

Hon. George S. Baker, 2002, Liberal
613-947-2517, 800-267-7362, Fax: 613-947-1525, bakerg@sen.parl.gc.ca

Hon. Tommy Banks, 2000, Liberal
613-995-1889, 800-267-7362, Fax: 613-995-1938, gautht@sen.parl.gc.ca (Thérèsa Gauthier, Executive Assistant)

Hon. Pierre-Hugues Boisvenu, 2010, Conservative Party
613-943-4030, 800-267-7362, Fax: 613-943-4029, boisvp@sen.parl.gc.ca

Hon. David Braley, 2010, Conservative Party
613-943-0040, 800-267-7362, Fax: 613-943-0083, braled@sen.parl.gc.ca

Hon. Patrick Brazeau, 2008, Conservative Party
613-947-4231, 800-267-7362, Fax: 613-947-4228, brazep@sen.parl.gc.ca

Hon. Bert Brown, 2007, Conservative Party
613-944-3434, 800-267-7362, Fax: 613-944-3438, brownb@sen.parl.gc.ca

Hon. Catherine S. Callbeck, 1997, Liberal
613-943-0686, 800-267-7362, Fax: 613-943-0693, callbc@sen.parl.gc.ca

Hon. Larry W. Campbell, 2005, Liberal
613-995-4050, 800-267-7362, Fax: 613-995-4056, campbel@sen.parl.gc.ca

Hon. Claude Carignan, 2009, Conservative Party
613-992-0240, 800-267-7362, Fax: 613-992-0246, carigc@sen.parl.gc.ca

Hon. Sharon Carstairs, 1994, Liberal
613-947-7123, 800-267-7362, Fax: 613-947-7125, carsts@sen.parl.gc.ca

Hon. Andrée Champagne, 2005, Conservative Party
613-995-3999, 800-267-7362, Fax: 613-995-4034, champa@sen.parl.gc.ca

Hon. Maria Chaput, 2002, Liberal
613-943-2435, 800-267-7362, Fax: 613-943-2482, chapum@sen.parl.gc.ca

Hon. Ethel M. Cochrane, 1986, Conservative Party
613-992-1577, 800-267-7362, Fax: 613-995-6691, cochre@sen.parl.gc.ca

Hon. Gerald J. Comeau, 1990, Conservative Party
613-943-1448, 800-267-7362, Fax: 613-943-1556, comeag@sen.parl.gc.ca

Hon. Anne C. Cools, 1984, Independent
613-992-2808, 800-267-7362, Fax: 613-992-8513, coolsa@sen.parl.gc.ca

Hon. Jane Marie Cordy, 2000, Liberal
613-995-8409, 800-267-7362, Fax: 613-995-8432, cordyj@sen.parl.gc.ca

Hon. James S. Cowan, 2005, Liberal
613-995-4268, 800-267-7362, Fax: 613-995-4287, cowanj@sen.parl.gc.ca

Hon. Roméo Dallaire, 2005, Liberal
613-995-4191, 800-267-7362, Fax: 613-995-4219, dallar@sen.parl.gc.ca

Hon. Dennis Dawson, 2005, Liberal
613-995-3978, 800-267-7362, Fax: 613-995-3998, dawsod@sen.parl.gc.ca

Hon. Joseph A. Day, 2001, Liberal
613-992-0833, 800-267-7362, Fax: 613-992-1175, dayja@sen.parl.gc.ca

Hon. Pierre De Bané, 1984, Liberal
613-992-8289, 800-267-7362, Fax: 613-995-6709, debanp@sen.parl.gc.ca

Hon. Jacques Demers, 2009, Conservative Party
613-992-0151, 800-267-7362, Fax: 613-992-0128, tessil@sen.parl.gc.ca

Hon. Consiglio Di Nino, 1990, Conservative Party
613-992-3756, 800-267-7362, Fax: 613-943-1883, dininc@sen.parl.gc.ca

Hon. Fred Dickson, 2009, Conservative Party
613-947-4130, 800-267-7362, Fax: 613-947-4134, johnse@sen.parl.gc.ca

Hon. Percy E. Downe, 2003, Liberal
613-943-8107, 800-267-7362, Fax: 613-943-8109, downep@sen.parl.gc.ca

Hon. Michael Duffy, 2009, Conservative Party
613-947-4163, 800-267-7362, Fax: 613-947-4157, mikeduffy@sen.parl.gc.ca

Hon. Lillian Eva Dyck, 2005, Liberal
613-995-4318, 800-267-7362, Fax: 613-995-4331, dyckli@sen.parl.gc.ca

Hon. Nicole Eaton, 2009, Conservative Party
613-947-4047, 800-267-7362, Fax: 613-947-4044, eatonn@sen.parl.gc.ca

Hon. Art Eggleton, 2005, Liberal
613-995-4230, 800-267-7362, Fax: 613-995-4237, egglea@sen.parl.gc.ca

Hon. Joyce Fairbairn, 1984, Liberal
613-996-4382, 800-267-7362, Fax: 613-995-3223, fairbj@sen.parl.gc.ca

Hon. Doug Finley, 2009, Conservative Party
613-992-0172, 800-267-7362, Fax: 613-992-0169, finled@sen.parl.gc.ca

Hon. Suzanne Fortin-Duplessis, 2009, Conservative Party
613-947-4036, 800-267-7362, Fax: 613-947-4004, fortis@sen.parl.gc.ca

Hon. Francis Fox, 2005, Liberal
613-943-3626, 800-267-7362, Fax: 613-943-3628, foxf@sen.parl.gc.ca

Hon. Joan Fraser, 1998, Liberal
613-943-9556, 800-267-7362, Fax: 613-943-9558, frasej@sen.parl.gc.ca

Hon. Linda Frum, 2009, Conservative Party
613-992-0310, 800-267-7362, Fax: 613-992-0316, fruml@sen.parl.gc.ca

Hon. George Furey, 1999, Liberal
613-943-7805, 800-267-7362, Fax: 613-943-7807, fureyg@sen.parl.gc.ca

Hon. Irving R. Gerstein, 2009, Conservative Party
613-947-4041, 800-267-7362, Fax: 613-947-4039

Hon. Stephen Greene, 2009, Conservative Party
613-947-4210, 800-267-7362, Fax: 613-947-4224, greens@sen.parl.gc.ca

Hon. Mac Harb, 2003, Liberal
613-996-2379, 800-267-7362, Fax: 613-996-2318, harbm@sen.parl.gc.ca

Hon. Céline Hervieux-Payette, 1995, Liberal
613-947-8008, 800-267-7362, Fax: 613-947-8010, hervic@sen.parl.gc.ca

Hon. Leo Housakos, 2009, Conservative Party
613-947-4237, 800-267-7362, Fax: 613-947-4239, lacomd@sen.parl.gc.ca

Hon. Elizabeth Hubley, 2001, Liberal
613-992-1177, 800-267-7362, Fax: 613-992-1516, hublee@sen.parl.gc.ca

Hon. Mobina S.B. Jaffer, 2001, Liberal
613-992-0189, 800-267-7362, Fax: 613-992-0673, jaffem@sen.parl.gc.ca

Hon. Janis G. Johnson, 1990, Conservative Party
613-943-1430, 800-267-7362, Fax: 613-992-5029, johnsj@sen.parl.gc.ca

Hon. Serge Joyal, 1997, Liberal
613-943-0434, 800-267-7362, Fax: 613-943-0441, joyals@sen.parl.gc.ca

Hon. Colin Kenny, 1984, Liberal
613-996-2877, 800-267-7362, Fax: 613-996-3737, kennyco@sen.parl.gc.ca

Hon. Noël A. Kinsella, 1990, Conservative Party
613-992-4416, 800-267-7362, Fax: 613-992-9772, kinsen@sen.parl.gc.ca

Hon. Vim Kochhar, 2010, Conservative Party
613-943-4023, 800-267-7362, Fax: 613-943-4025, kochhv@sen.parl.gc.ca

Hon. Daniel Lang, 2009, Conservative Party
613-947-4050, 800-267-7362, Fax: 613-947-4049, langd@sen.parl.gc.ca

Hon. Marjory LeBreton, 1993, Conservative Party
613-943-0756, 800-267-7362, Fax: 613-943-1493, lebrem@sen.parl.gc.ca; Marjory.LeBreton@pco-bcp.gc.ca

Hon. Rose-Marie Losier-Cool, 1995, Liberal
613-947-8011, 800-267-7362, Fax: 613-947-8013, losier@sen.parl.gc.ca

Hon. Sandra M. Lovelace Nicholas, 2005, Liberal
613-943-3635, 800-267-7362, Fax: 613-943-3637, smithc@sen.parl.gc.ca

Hon. Michael L. MacDonald, 2009, Conservative Party
613-995-1866, 800-267-7362, Fax: 613-995-1853

Hon. Frank W. Mahovlich, 1998, Liberal
613-943-2065, 800-267-7362, Fax: 613-943-2067, mahovf@sen.parl.gc.ca

Hon. Fabian Manning, 2009, Conservative Party
613-947-4203, 800-267-7362, Fax: 613-947-4170, mannif@sen.parl.gc.ca

Hon. Elizabeth (Beth) Marshall, 2010, Conservative Party
613-943-4011, 800-267-7362, Fax: 613-943-4013, marshe@sen.parl.gc.ca

Hon. Yonah Martin, 2009, Conservative Party
613-947-4078, 800-267-7362, Fax: 613-947-4082, martin@sen.parl.gc.ca

Hon. Paul J. Massicotte, 2003, Liberal
613-943-8110, 800-267-7362, Fax: 613-943-8129, massip@sen.parl.gc.ca

Hon. Elaine McCoy, 2005, Progressive Conservative
613-995-4293, 800-267-7362, Fax: 613-995-4304, mccoye@sen.parl.gc.ca

Hon. Michael A. Meighen, 1990, Conservative Party
613-943-1421, 800-267-7362, Fax: 613-943-1565, meighen@sen.parl.gc.ca

Hon. Terry M. Mercer, 2003, Liberal
613-996-2657, 800-267-7362, Fax: 613-947-2345, mercet@sen.parl.gc.ca

Hon. Pana Merchant, 2002, Liberal
613-944-7777, 800-267-7362, Fax: 613-944-7778, merchp@sen.parl.gc.ca

Hon. Don Meredith, 20110705, 2010, Conservative Party
613-996-8572, 800-267-7362, Fax: 613-996-8570, meredd@sen.parl.gc.ca

Hon. Grant Mitchell, 2005, Liberal
613-995-4254, 800-267-7362, Fax: 613-995-4265, mitchg@sen.parl.gc.ca

Hon. Percy Mockler, 2009, Conservative Party
613-947-4225, 800-267-7362, Fax: 613-947-4227, mocklp@sen.parl.gc.ca

Hon. Wilfred P. Moore, 1996, Liberal
613-947-1921, 800-267-7362, Fax: 613-943-1995, moorew@sen.parl.gc.ca

Hon. Jim Munson, 2003, Liberal
613-947-2504, 800-267-7362, Fax: 613-947-2506, munsoj@sen.parl.gc.ca

Hon. Lowell Murray, 1979, Progressive Conservative
613-995-2407, 800-267-7362, Fax: 613-947-4730, murral@sen.parl.gc.ca

Hon. Richard Neufeld, 2009, Conservative Party
613-947-4055, 800-267-7362, Fax: 613-947-4065, neufer@sen.parl.gc.ca
Hon. Pierre Claude Nolin, 1993, Conservative Party
613-943-1451, 800-267-7362, Fax: 613-943-1792, nolinp@sen.parl.gc.ca
Hon. Kelvin Kenneth Ogilvie, 2009, Conservative Party
613-992-0331, 800-267-7362, Fax: 613-992-0334, nolinp@sen.parl.gc.ca
Hon. Donald H. Oliver, 1990, Conservative Party
613-943-1445, 800-267-7362, Fax: 613-943-1502, olived@sen.parl.gc.ca
Hon. Dennis Glen Patterson, 2009, Conservative Party
613-992-0480, 800-267-7362, Fax: 613-992-0495, patted@sen.parl.gc.ca
Hon. Lucie Pépin, 1997, Liberal
613-996-1726, 800-267-7362, Fax: 613-996-8392, pepinl@sen.parl.gc.ca
Hon. Robert W. Peterson, 2005, Liberal
613-995-4220, 800-267-7362, Fax: 613-995-4229, russem@sen.parl.gc.ca
Hon. Donald Neil Plett, 2009, Conservative Party
613-992-0180, 800-267-7362, Fax: 613-992-0186, plettd@sen.parl.gc.ca
Hon. Rose-May Poirier, 2010, Conservative Party
613-943-4027, 800-267-7362, Fax: 613-943-4026, poirir@sen.parl.gc.ca
Hon. Marie-P. Poulin (Charette), 1995, Liberal
613-947-8005, 800-267-7362, Fax: 613-947-8007, poulim@sen.parl.gc.ca
Hon. Vivienne Poy, 1998, Liberal
613-943-7854, 800-267-7362, Fax: 613-943-7856, poyv@sen.parl.gc.ca
Hon. Nancy Greene Raine, 2009, Conservative Party
613-947-4052, 800-267-7362, Fax: 613-947-4054, rainen@sen.parl.gc.ca
Hon. Pierrette Ringuette, 2002, Liberal
613-943-2248, 800-267-7362, Fax: 613-943-2245, ringup@sen.parl.gc.ca
Hon. Michel Rivard, 2009, Conservative Party
613-947-4107, 800-267-7362, Fax: 613-947-4110, rivarm@sen.parl.gc.ca
Hon. Jean-Claude Rivest, 1993, Independent
613-947-2236, 800-267-7362, Fax: 613-947-2238, jcrivest@sen.parl.gc.ca
Hon. Fernand Robichaud, 1997, Liberal
613-943-0675, 800-267-7362, Fax: 613-943-0677
Hon. Bob Runciman, 2010, Conservative Party
613-943-4020, 800-267-7362, Fax: 613-943-4022, runcib@sen.parl.gc.ca
Hon. Nancy Ruth, 2005, Conservative Party
613-995-4174, 800-267-7362, Fax: 613-995-4188, mcgeed@sen.parl.gc.ca
Hon. Gerry St. Germain, 1993, Conservative Party
613-947-2242, 800-267-7362, Fax: 613-947-2244, stgerg@sen.parl.gc.ca
Hon. Hugh Segal, 2005, Conservative Party
613-995-4059, 800-267-7362, Fax: 613-995-5259, kfl@sen.parl.gc.ca
Hon. Judith Seidman, 2009, Conservative Party
613-992-0110, 800-267-7362, Fax: 613-992-0118, seidmj@sen.parl.gc.ca
Hon. Nick G. Sibbeston, 1999, Liberal
613-943-7790, 800-267-7362, Fax: 613-943-7792, sibnic@sen.parl.gc.ca
Hon. David P. Smith, Q.C., 2002, Liberal
613-944-4079, 800-267-7362, Fax: 613-944-4083, smithd@sen.parl.gc.ca
Hon. Larry Smith, 2011, Conservative Party
613-996-8555, 800-267-7362, Fax: 613-996-8565
Hon. Carolyn Stewart Olsen, 2009, Conservative Party
613-992-0121, 800-267-7362, Fax: 613-992-0124, stewac@sen.parl.gc.ca
Hon. Terry Stratton, 1993, Conservative Party
613-947-2224, 800-267-7362, Fax: 613-943-1563, stratt@sen.parl.gc.ca
Hon. Claudette Tardif, 2005, Liberal
613-947-3589, 800-267-7362, Fax: 613-947-3609, tardic@sen.parl.gc.ca
Hon. David Tkachuk, 1993, Conservative Party
613-947-3196, 800-267-7362, Fax: 613-947-3198, tkachd@sen.parl.gc.ca
Hon. Josée Verner, 2011, Conservative Party
613-996-6999, 800-267-7362, Fax: 613-996-7004, vernej@sen.parl.gc.ca
Hon. John D. Wallace, 2009, Conservative Party
613-947-4240, 800-267-7362, Fax: 613-947-4252, wallaj@sen.parl.gc.ca
Hon. Pamela Wallin, 2009, Conservative Party
613-947-4097, 800-267-7362, Fax: 613-947-4091, wallinp@sen.parl.gc.ca
Hon. Charlie Watt, 1984, Liberal
613-992-2981, 800-267-7362, Fax: 613-990-5453, wattc@sen.parl.gc.ca
Hon. Rod A.A. Zimmer, 2005, Liberal
613-995-4043, 800-267-7362, Fax: 613-995-4046, zimmer@sen.parl.gc.ca

Clerk of the Senate & Clerk of the Parliaments
Parliament Hill, Centre Block, #185-S, Ottawa, ON K1A 0A4

Clerk of the Senate & Clerk of the Parliaments, Gary W. O'Brien
613-992-2493
Usher of the Black Rod, Kevin MacLeod
613-992-8483
Director, Information Services Directorate, Hélène Bouchard
613-993-5299, Fax: 613-992-7963
Director, Legislative Systems & Broadcasting Division, Diane Boucher
613-992-1222
Director, Human Resources Directorate, Linda Dodd
613-996-1096
Director, Audit & Planning, Jill Anne Joseph
613-944-4070, Fax: 613-943-4610
Director, Finance & Procurement Directorate, Nicole Proulx
613-943-0197, Fax: 613-943-4610
Acting Manager, Media Relations & Communications, Karen Schwinghamer
613-995-3232

Parliamentary Precinct Services
Chambers Bldg., 40 Elgin St., 13th Fl., Ottawa, ON K1A 0A4

Director General, Gilles Duguay
613-992-4787

House of Commons, Canada / Chambre des communes

House of Commons, Centre Block, Parliament Buildings, 111 Wellington St., Ottawa, ON K1A 0A6

613-992-4793
866-599-4999
info@parl.gc.ca
www.parl.gc.ca
TTY: 613-995-2266

The House of Commons is the major law-making unit in Canada. The 308 members of the House represent each constituency, or riding, across Canada.

Members are elected in general elections, held at least once every five years. During general elections, one candidate per riding is elected, based on the largest number of votes, even if his or her vote is less than half the total. When a member resigns or dies between general elections, a by-election is held. The party that wins the largest number of seats in the general election usually forms the government. The party with the second largest number of votes becomes the Official Opposition. A minority government is created when one particular party holds no clear majority of seats in the House. In this case, the government is usually led by the party with the most seats in Parliament, providing it can sustain the support from other minor parties that enable it to pass legislation.

Any bills within federal jurisdiction must be passed by a majority of House members to become law. Members usually vote on proposed legislation according to party affiliation. They may vote against their party. They may also leave their elected party to sit as an independent within the House.

The Speaker of the House of Commons is a Member of Parliament, who is selected by fellow Members of Parliament through a secret ballot process. The Speaker's roles are to ensure that all procedures & rules are followed in the House, & to oversee administration in the House.

Officers & Officials of the House of Commons

Speaker of the House, Hon. Andrew Scheer, Conservative Party
613-992-4593, Fax: 613-996-3120, andrew.scheer@parl.gc.ca; info@andrewscheer.ca, Other Communications: Speaker's Office: 613-992-5042; Fax: 613-995-4253
Social Media: twitter.com/andrewscheer, www.facebook.com/AndrewScheerMP
Note: Web Site: www.parl.gc.ca/About/House/Speaker/index-e.html
Chair, Committees of the Whole of the House of Commons; Deputy Speaker, Denise Savoie, B.A., M.A., M.Ed., New Democratic Party
613-996-2358, Fax: 613-952-1458, denise.savoie@parl.gc.ca
Social Media: twitter.com/denisesavoie, www.facebook.com/DeniseSavoieVictoria
Deputy Chair, Committees of the Whole, Barry Devolin, B.A., M.A., Conservative Party
613-992-2474, Fax: 613-996-9656, barry.devolin@parl.gc.ca
Social Media: twitter.com/BarryDevolin_MP
Assistant Deputy Chair, Committees of the Whole, Bruce Stanton, Conservative Party
613-992-6582, Fax: 613-996-3128, bruce.stanton@parl.gc.ca
Social Media: twitter.com/bruce_stanton, www.facebook.com/pages/Bruce-Stanton/6236822310 www.linkedin.com/pub/bruce-stanton/28/19/95
Leader of the Government in the House of Commons; House Leader, Conservative Party, Hon. Peter Van Loan, P.C., B.A., LL.B., M.A., M.Sc.Pl., Conservative Party
613-996-7752, Fax: 613-992-8351, peter.vanloan@parl.gc.ca, Other Communications: Office of Leader of Government in HoC: 613-995-7226
Note: Web Site: www.houseleader.gc.ca/index.asp?lang=eng&page=Team-equipe&doc=bio/bio-eng.htm
House Leader, the Official Opposition; House Leader, New Democratic Party, Thomas J. Mulcair, B.C.L., LL.B., New Democratic Party
613-995-7691, Fax: 613-995-0114, thomas.mulcair@parl.gc.ca, Other Communications: House Leader, Phone: 613-992-6030; Fax: 613-995-9696
House Leader, Liberal Party, Marc Garneau, C.C., C.D., B.Sc., Ph.D., F.C.A.S.I., Liberal
613-996-7267, Fax: 613-995-8632, marc.garneau@parl.gc.ca, Other Communications: House Leader, Phone: 613-995-2727
Social Media: twitter.com/MarcGarneau, www.facebook.com/pages/Marc-Garneau/21128206560
House Leader, Bloc Québécois (Acting), Louis Plamondon, B.A.Ped., B.A.An, BQ
613-995-9241, Fax: 613-995-6784, louis.plamondon@parl.gc.ca; louis.plamondon.c1@parl.gc.ca
Social Media: www.facebook.com/LouisPlamondonBQ www.linkedin.com/pub/louis-plamondon/36/b11/771
Chief Government Whip; Whip, Conservative Party of Canada, Hon. Gordon O'Connor, P.C., B.A., B.Sc., Conservative Party
613-992-1119, Fax: 613-992-1043, gordon.oconnor@parl.gc.ca, Other Communications: Chief Government Whip, Phone: 613-995-2291
Social Media: www.facebook.com/pages/Gordon-OConnor/228442573837062?sk=info
Chief Opposition Whip; Whip, New Democratic Party, Chris Charlton, B.A., M.A., New Democratic Party
613-995-9389, Fax: 613-992-7802, chris.charlton@parl.gc.ca; chris.charlton.c1@parl.gc.ca, Other Communications: Opposition Whip: 613-992-0336; Fax: 613-992-1160
Social Media: twitter.com/ChrisCharltonMP, www.facebook.com/pages/Chris-Charlton/25222718654www.linkedin.com/pub/chris-charlton/8/8aa/4b9
Whip, Liberal Party, Judy Foote, B.A., B.Ed, Liberal
613-992-8655, Fax: 613-992-5324, Judy.Foote@parl.gc.ca, Other Communications: Whip, Phone: 613-995-7774; Fax: 613-992-1065
Social Media: twitter.com/JudyFoote, www.facebook.com/pages/Judy-Foote/36948418784
Caucus Chair, Conservative Party, Guy Lauzon, Conservative Party
613-992-2521, Fax: 613-996-2119, guy.lauzon@parl.gc.ca; info@guylauzon.ca
Caucus Chair, New Democratic Party, Nycole Turmel, New Democratic Party
613-992-7550, Fax: 613-992-7599, nycole.turmel@parl.gc.ca; Nycole.Turmel.c1@parl.gc.ca, Other Communications: NDP Caucus Chair, Phone: 613-996-6417
Social Media: twitter.com/nycole_turmel, www.facebook.com/profile.php?id=100002634121396
Caucus Chair, Liberal Party, Francis Scarpaleggia, B.A., M.A., M.B.A., Liberal
613-995-8281, Fax: 613-995-0528, francis.scarpaleggia@parl.gc.ca
Social Media: twitter.com/scarpaleggiamp, www.facebook.com/Fscarpaleggia
Responsible, Conservative Party Research Office, Right Hon. Stephen Harper, P.C., B.A., M.A., Conservative Party
613-992-4211, Fax: 613-941-6900, stephen.harper@parl.gc.ca; pm@pm.gc.ca, Other Communications: Research Bureau: 613-996-5084;Fax: 613-943-8727
Social Media: twitter.com/pmharper, www.facebook.com/group.php?gid=338690276206
Responsible, New Democratic Party Research Office, Vacant, New Democratic Party
Responsible, Liberal Party Research Office, Hon. Ralph Goodale, P.C., B.A., LL.B., Liberal
613-996-4743, Fax: 613-996-9790, ralph.goodale@parl.gc.ca; goodale@sasktel.net, Other Communications: Research Bureau: 613-996-6740; Fax: 613-996-2551
Social Media: twitter.com/RalphGoodale, www.facebook.com/ralphgoodale
Clerk, House of Commons, Audrey Elizabeth O'Brien
613-992-2986, Fax: 613-995-6668
Deputy Clerk, House of Commons, Marc Bosc
613-992-3156, Fax: 613-995-1449
Law Clerk & Parliamentary Counsel, Robert R. Walsh
613-992-3156, Fax: 613-992-4441
Sergeant-at-Arms, Kevin M. Vickers
613-992-2637, Fax: 613-995-4901

Finance Services

Chief Financial Officer, Mark Watters
613-996-0485, Fax: 613-995-4970
Chief Acquisitions Officer, Khalil Ibrahim
613-996-2214, Fax: 613-992-3037

Head, Corporate Services, Murray Hodgins
613-996-6065, Fax: 613-995-3072
Manager, Accounting, Nathalie Charpentier
613-947-0946, Fax: 613-995-3072
Manager, Materiel Management & Warehousing, Stéphanie Charron
613-947-2485, Fax: 613-943-8353
Manager, Financial Planning, Céline Laflamme
613-995-1508, Fax: 613-947-3571
Manager, Standards & Performance Management, Dominique Lalonde
613-947-6756, Fax: 613-992-3037
Manager, Corporate Policy Services, James MacKay
613-992-1678, Fax: 613-947-3571
Manager, Contracting Services, Ghislaine Parent
613-943-0838, Fax: 613-992-3037
Manager, Policy Services for Members, Jane Princi
613-995-1618, Fax: 613-947-3571

Human Resources, Corporate Planning, & Communications Services

Chief Human Resources Officer, Kathryn Butler Malette
613-992-0100, Fax: 613-947-0001
Director, Human Resources Strategies & Development, Marie-Andrée Bourgouin
613-947-1175, Fax: 613-992-2599
Head, Corporate Communications, Léonie Bouvier
613-992-9216, Fax: 613-995-3052
Head, Payroll Services & Benefits, Michel Fortin
613-996-8768
Head, Corporate Planning, Kevin Whitehouse
613-947-6776, Fax: 613-996-1698
Manager, Health, Safety & Environment, Sandra Benoît
613-992-1379, Fax: 613-943-0848
Manager, Learning & Growth, Louise Chevrier
613-943-4516, Fax: 613-992-2599
Manager, Staffing, Classification & Compensation, Pierre Côté
613-995-6075, Fax: 613-995-1470
Manager, Administration, Planning, IM, & HR Systems, Sylvie Farrell
613-992-2737, Fax: 613-947-0001
Manager, Labour Relations & Compensation, Chantal Paquette
613-943-1500, Fax: 613-943-9772
Senior Communications Officer, Valérie Gervais
613-944-6475, Fax: 613-995-3052
Senior Administrative Assistant, Employee Relations & Human Resources Services, Alda Da Silva
613-995-3878, Fax: 613-943-9772

Information Services

613-995-9631 Fax: 613-947-3547

Chief Information Officer, Louis Bard
613-995-8884, Fax: 613-947-3547
Chief, Application Architecture & Development, Soufiane Ben Moussa
613-943-1465, Fax: 613-943-1810
Chief, Publishing Service, Kim Buzzetti
613-947-4911, Fax: 613-996-9496
Chief, Information Management, Leslie Hamel
613-944-5227, Fax: 613-944-4118
Chief, Telecommunications, Sophie Hart
613-947-6550, Fax: 613-995-4774
Chief, Finance, Administration, & Planning, Stéphane Jacques
613-996-4994, Fax: 613-943-7890
Chief, Application Maintenance & Support Operations, Roger Roy
613-996-4494, Fax: 613-943-1810
Chief, Reporting Services, Bruce Young
613-995-1542, Fax: 613-991-1851
Director, IT Operations, Stéphan Aubé
613-992-7449, Fax: 613-947-6292
Director, Printing Services, Benoit Giroux
613-992-7398, Fax: 613-996-1589
Director, Parliamentary Publications, Michel Roy
613-992-2420, Fax: 613-996-9496
Acting Deputy Director, IT Operations, Réal Charlebois
613-947-0145, Fax: 613-947-6292
Manager, IT Project Management Office, Jean Forgues
613-947-2397, Fax: 613-996-1414
Manager, Resources Applications, Michelle Guay-Leblanc
613-992-3944, Fax: 613-943-1713
Acting Manager, IT Security, Christopher Karson
613-947-7960, Fax: 613-947-6292
Manager, Television & Radio Services, Jean Leduc
613-992-8102
Manager, Information Services Procurement Services, Christine Lemieux
613-943-5727, Fax: 613-943-7890
Acting Manager, Event Support, François Patenaude
613-995-1973, Fax: 613-992-4897
Television Producer, Multimedia Services, Alain Bourque
613-992-1266, Fax: 613-995-3053
Television Producer, Multimedia Services, Pierre Ménard
613-947-3405

Law Clerk & Parliamentary Counsel

Law Clerk & Parliamentary Counsel, Robert Walsh
613-996-1057, Fax: 613-992-4441
Chief, Administrative Services, Suzanne Dupuis
613-947-1997, Fax: 613-947-5556
Deputy Law Clerk & Parliamentary Counsel, Richard Denis
613-943-2601, Fax: 613-947-5556

Office of the Clerk & Secretariat

Clerk of the House of Commons, Audrey O'Brien
613-992-2986, Fax: 613-995-6668
Director, Audit & Review, Marie Nadeau
613-996-2106, Fax: 613-943-2710
Director, Audit & Review, Jennifer Wall
613-944-4080, Fax: 613-943-2710
Manager, Office of the Clerk, Suzanne Verville
613-992-2986, Fax: 613-995-6668
Coordinator, Member's Orientation & Election Readiness Secretariat, Lyne Crêtes
613-992-8282, Fax: 613-995-6668
Senior Administrative Coordinator, Anne-Marie Wszol
613-996-1796, Fax: 613-995-6668
Senior Auditor, Michèle Serano
613-995-1749, Fax: 613-943-2710
Risks & Controls Officer, Céline Gauthier
613-943-9768, Fax: 613-943-2710

Parliamentary Precinct Services

613-995-7521 Fax: 613-995-4901

Sergeant-at-Arms of the House of Commons, Kevin Vickers
613-992-2637, Fax: 613-995-4901
Deputy Sergeant-at-Arms & Director General, John Janusz
613-995-7020, Fax: 613-947-0692
Sergeant, Scanner Operations, Robert Couture
613-996-9362, Fax: 613-947-9681
Sergeant, Chamber Security & Ceremonial Unit, Gérard Dignard
613-992-7081, Fax: 613-947-3115
Executive Director to the Sergeant-At-Arms, Josée Knight
613-943-0473, Fax: 613-995-4901
Director General, Parliamentary Accommodation, Michel Séguin
613-996-7077, Fax: 613-995-7888
Chief, Parking Operations, Denis Deschambault
613-947-5667, Fax: 613-947-0653
Chief, Postal, Distribution, Messenger, & Transportation Services, Robert Frenette
613-996-1021, Fax: 613-996-0221
Chief, Press Gallery, Terry Guillon
613-992-4511, Fax: 613-995-5795
Chief, Finance, Administration, & Planning, Brenda Hayter
613-995-4704, Fax: 613-995-7888

Procedural Services

Deputy Clerk, Marc Bosc
613-992-3156, Fax: 613-995-1449
Principal Clerk, Information Management, Colette Labrecque-Riel
613-944-5652, Fax: 613-992-9427
Principal Clerk, Committees & Legislative Services Directorate, Jeffrey LeBlanc
613-943-9484, Fax: 613-947-0309
Principal Clerk, Committees & Legislative Services Directorate, Ian McDonald
613-995-0516, Fax: 613-947-0309
Principal Clerk, Journals Branch, Pierre Rodrigue
613-996-1086, Fax: 613-947-5582
Clerk Assistant, House Proceedings, Beverley Isles
613-943-6703, Fax: 613-995-2997
Manager, Resource Planning & Administration, Committees & Legislative Services Directorate, Jeannette Goneau
613-995-9200, Fax: 613-947-0309
Manager, Administration & Finance, Office of the Clerk Assistant, Lynda Tremblay
613-996-6599, Fax: 613-995-2997
Program Administrator, Parliamentary Internship Program, JoAnne Cartwright
613-943-1228, Fax: 613-995-5357
Administration Officer, Canadian Study of Parliament Group, Table Research Branch, Dany Lamarque
613-995-4033, Fax: 613-943-9949
Coordinator, Page Program, Lisa Chartier-Derouin
613-947-3568, Fax: 613-947-2029

Committees of the House of Commons / Comités de la chambre des communes
Committees Directorate, House of Commons, 131 Queen St., 6th Fl., Ottawa, ON K1A 0A6

613-992-3150 Fax: 613-947-3089
cmteweb@parl.gc.ca
www.parl.gc.ca/committeebusiness

A committee consists of parliamentarians from the House of Commons, the Senate, or both. Committee members are selected for study & consideration of matters, including bills. Items for consideration by committess are referred by the House of Commons or the Senate.
Types of committees include the following: Committees of the Whole; Joint Committees; Legislative Committees; Liaison Committee; Standing Committees; & Special Committees.
The following are the House of Commons Committees:
Aboriginal Affairs & Northern Development;
Access to Information, Privacy, & Ethics;
Agriculture & Agri-Food;
Canadian Heritage;
Citizenship & Immigration;
Environment & Sustainable Development;
Finance;
Fisheries & Oceans;
Foreign Affairs & International Development;
Government Operations & Estimates;
Health;
Human Resources, Skills & Social Development, & the Status of Persons with Disabilities;
Industry, Science, & Technology;
International Trade;
Justice & Human Rights;
Liaison;
National Defence;
Natural Resources;
Official Languages;
Public Accounts;
Public Safety & National Security;
Status of Women;
Transport, Infrastructure, & Communities; &
Veterans Affairs.

Principal Clerk, Committees Directorate & Legislative Services, Jeffrey LeBlanc
613-943-9484, Fax: 613-947-0309
Principal Clerk, Committees Directorate & Legislative Services, Ian McDonald
613-995-0516, Fax: 613-947-0309
Clerk, Aboriginal Affairs & Northern Development Committee (Standing Committee), Jean-Marie David
613-996-1173, Fax: 613-992-7974, aano@parl.gc.ca
Clerk, Access to Information, Privacy, & Ethics Committee (Standing Committee), Chad Mariage
613-992-1240, Fax: 613-992-9069, ethi@parl.gc.ca
Clerk, Agriculture & Agri-Food Committee (Standing Committee), David-Andrés Novoa
613-947-6732, Fax: 613-943-0307, agri@parl.gc.ca
Clerk, Canadian Heritage Committee (Standing Committee), Christine Holke David
613-947-6729, Fax: 613-996-1626, chpc@parl.gc.ca
Clerk, Citizenship & Immigration Committee (Standing Committee), Julie Lalande Prud'homme
613-995-8525, Fax: 613-996-1962, cimm@parl.gc.ca
Clerk, Environment & Sustainable Development Committee (Standing Committee), Marie-France Renaud
613-992-5023, Fax: 613-996-1626, envi@parl.gc.ca
Clerk, Finance Committee (Standing Committee), Guyanne L. Desforges
613-992-9753, Fax: 613-996-1626, fina@parl.gc.ca
Clerk, Fisheries & Oceans Committee (Standing Committee), Georges Etoka
613-996-3105, Fax: 613-996-1626, fopo@parl.gc.ca
Clerk, Foreign Affairs & International Development Committee (Standing Committee), Miriam Burke
613-996-1540, Fax: 613-992-7974, faae@parl.gc.ca
Clerk, Government Operations & Estimates Committee (Standing Committee), Marc-Olivier Girard
613-995-9469, Fax: 613-992-9069, oggo@parl.gc.ca
Clerk, Health Committee (Standing Committee), Mariane Beaudin
613-995-4108, Fax: 613-992-7974, hesa@parl.gc.ca
Clerk, Human Resources, Skills, & Social Development & the Status of Persons with Disabilities Committee (Standing Committee), Evelyn Lukyniuk
613-996-1542, Fax: 613-996-1626, huma@parl.gc.ca
Clerk, Industry, Science, & Technology Committee (Standing Committee), Jean Michel Roy
613-947-1971, Fax: 613-996-1626, indu@parl.gc.ca
Clerk, International Trade Committee (Standing Committee), Paul Cardegna
613-944-4364, Fax: 613-992-7974, ciit@parl.gc.ca
Clerk, Justice & Human Rights Committee (Standing Committee), Jean-François Pagé
613-996-1553, Fax: 613-992-1962, just@parl.gc.ca
Clerk, Liaison Committee (Standing Committee), André Gagnon
613-947-5623, Fax: 613-947-0309, liai@parl.gc.ca
Clerk, National Defence Committee (Standing Committee), Jean-François Lafleur
613-995-9461, Fax: 613-947-9670, nddn@parl.gc.ca
Clerk, Natural Resources Committee (Standing Committee), Andrew Lauzon
613-995-0047, Fax: 613-996-1626, rnnr@parl.gc.ca
Clerk, Official Languages Committee (Standing Committee), Simon Larouche
613-947-8891, Fax: 613-996-1962, lang@parl.gc.ca
Clerk, Procedure & House Affairs Committee (Standing Committee), Michelle Tittley
613-996-0506, Fax: 613-996-1626, proc@parl.gc.ca

Clerk, Public Accounts Committee (Standing Committee), Joann Garbig
613-996-1664, Fax: 613-996-1626, pacp@parl.gc.ca
Clerk, Public Safety & National Security Committee (Standing Committee), Andrew Bartholomew Chaplin
613-944-5635, Fax: 613-992-7974, secu@parl.gc.ca
Clerk, Status of Women Committee (Standing Committee), Julie-Anne Macdonald
613-995-6119, Fax: 613-992-7974, fewo@parl.gc.ca
Clerk, Transport, Infrastructure, & Communities Committee (Standing Committee), Alexandre Roger
613-996-4663, Fax: 613-996-1626, tran@parl.gc.ca
Clerk, Veterans Affairs Committee (Standing Committee), Cynara Corbin
613-944-9354, Fax: 613-996-6616, acva@parl.gc.ca

Office of the Prime Minister (Conservative Party of Canada) / Cabinet du Premier ministre

Langevin Block, 80 Wellington St., Ottawa, ON K1A 0A2
613-992-4211 Fax: 613-941-6900
pm@pm.gc.ca
www.pm.gc.ca
TTY: 613-957-5741

The Prime Minister is the Head of Government in Canada & usually the leader of the party in power in the House of Commons.
The Prime Minister recommends the appointment of the Governor General to the monarchy, & is responsible for selecting a team of ministers, who are then appointed by the Governor General to the Queen's Privy Council. In addition, he or she also controls the appointment of senators, judges, & parliamentary secretaries. It is customary that the Prime Minister is also appointed to the Imperial Privy Council & is thus titled, "The Right Honourable". The Prime Minister has the right to dissolve parliament & can therefore control the timing of general elections.
The Prime Minister's Office is a central agency which features the executive staff of the Prime Minister, such as partisan political advisors & administrators, who provide support to the Prime Minister exclusively.

Prime Minister, Right Hon. Stephen Joseph Harper, P.C., B.A., M.A.
613-992-4211, Fax: 613-941-6900, stephen.harper@parl.gc.ca; pm@pm.gc.ca
Social Media: twitter.com/pmharper
Chief of Staff, Nigel Wright
613-992-4211
Parliamentary Secretary to the Prime Minister, Dean Del Mastro, B. Comm. (Hons.)
613-992-4211, dean.delmastro@parl.gc.ca
Social Media: www.twitter.com/mpdeandelmastro, www.facebook.com/deandelmastro
Principal Secretary, Raymond Novak
613-992-4211
Director, Tour & Scheduling, Deborah Campbell
613-952-4959
Director, Personnel & Administration, Policy, Rachel Curran
613-952-6874
Director, Communications, Angelo Persichilli
613-992-4211
Acting Director, Appointments, Derek Vanstone
613-992-4211
Director, Issues Management, Chris Woodcock
613-960-4019

Office of the Leader, Official Opposition (New Democratic Party)

111 Wellington St., Ottawa, ON K1A 0A6
613-995-7224 Fax: 613-995-4565
www.npd.ca

Jack Layton, Former Leader of the Official Opposition & Leader of the New Democratic Party died on August 22, 2011.
Nycole Turmel continues her work at the interim leader, until a permanent successor is elected.

Interim Leader, Official Opposition; Interim Party Leader, New Democratic Party; NDP Caucus Chair, Nycole Turmel
613-992-7550, Fax: 613-992-7599, nycole.turmel@parl.gc.ca
Social Media: twitter.com/nycole_turmel, www.facebook.com/profile.php?id=100002634121396
Director, Leader's Affairs, Emily Watkins
613-995-8469, Fax: 613-947-0868
Senior Press Secretary; Principal Secretary for Québec, Karl Bélanger
613-995-6767, Fax: 613-947-0868
Director, Strategic Communications, NDP Research Bureau, Kathleen Monk
613-995-0628, Fax: 613-995-4565
Director, Parliamentary Affairs, NDP Research Bureau, Peter Puxley
613-996-1420, Fax: 613-995-4565
Director, Operations & Community Outreach, NDP Research Bureau, Nathan Rotman
613-996-9449, Fax: 613-995-4565
Director, Operations, NDP Research Bureau, Jess Turk-Browne
613-995-8242, Fax: 613-996-7114

Office of the Leader, Liberal Party of Canada / Liberal Research Bureau

Centre Block, Ottawa, K1A 0A6
613-996-6740 Fax: 613-996-2551
www.liberal.ca

The former leader of the Liberal Party of Canada, Michael Ignatieff resigned in May 2011, following the general election. Later that month, Bob Rae was selected as the Interim Leader of the Liberal Party of Canada. He leads the party as it rebuilds before the next permanent leader is chosen.

Interim Party Leader, Liberal Party of Canada, Hon. Robert "Bob" Keith Rae, P.C., O.C., O.Ont., Q.C., B.A., B.Ph., LL.B.
613-996-6740, Fax: 613-996-2551, bob.rae@parl.gc.ca; info@bobrae.ca
Social Media: twitter.com/bobraemp, www.facebook.com/pages/Bob-Rae/8034824801
Chief of Staff, Peter Donolo
613-996-6740, Fax: 613-947-0310
Chief Operating Officer, Patricia Sorbara
613-995-0741, Fax: 613-996-2551
Principal Secretary, Patrick Parisot
613-996-6740
Director, Policy & the Liberal Research Bureau, Brian Bohunicky
613-947-6727, Fax: 613-996-2551
Director & Senior Advisor, Québec, Brigitte Legault
613-947-5334, Fax: 613-996-2551
Director, Policy & Liberal Research Bureau, Michael McNair
613-996-9614, Fax: 613-996-2551
Team Lead, Communications, Sheamus Murphy
613-995-6715, Fax: 613-996-2551

Office of the Leader, Bloc Québécois / Bureau du chef, Bloc Québécois

Centre Block, Ottawa, ON K1A 0A6
613-992-6779 Fax: 613-954-2121
www.blocquebecois.org

Following the May 2011 general election, Gilles Duceppe resigned as leader of the separatist Bloc Québécois party. A new leader will have to be elected to replace Duceppe.

Acting House Leader, Bloc Québécois; Chair, Bloc Québécois Caucus, Louis Plamondon, B.A.Ped., B.A.An
613-995-9241, Fax: 613-995-6784, louis.plamondon@parl.gc.ca
Social Media: www.facebook.com/LouisPlamondonBQ
Director, Communications, France Amyot
613-995-0531, Fax: 613-947-3373
Director, Administration, Josée Bergeron
613-943-0884, Fax: 613-995-1134
Director, Research, Benoît Cyr
613-995-7525, Fax: 613-996-3682
Coordinator, Bloc Québécois Caucus, Mireille Beaudin
613-947-4446, Fax: 613-947-4464

Office of the Leader, Green Party of Canada

Confederation Building,, #518, 244 Wellington St., Ottawa, ON K1A 0A6
613-996-1119 Fax: 613-996-0850
866-868-3447
leader@greenparty.ca; info@greenparty.ca
www.greenparty.ca
Other Communication: Media Requests, Phone: 613-562-4916, ext. 239

Elizabeth May was elected the Leader of the Green Party of Canada in 2006. In the May 2011 election, May became the first Green Party candidate to be elected to the House of Commons.

The Canadian Ministry / The Cabinet

Information Service, Parliament of Canada, Ottawa, ON K1A 0A9
613-992-4793
866-599-4999
info@parl.gc.ca
www.parl.gc.ca
TTY: 613-995-2266

The Canadian Ministry, or Cabinet, is the most significant of all federal government committees or councils. Cabinet members are selected & led by the Prime Minister. They must also be or become members of the Queen's Privy Council.
Cabinet ministers determine specific policies & are responsible for them in the House of Commons. The Cabinet is responsible for initiating all public bills in the House of Commons, & in some instances can create regulations that have the strength of law, termed decisions of the Governor-in-Council.
Cabinet meetings are usually closed to the public, allowing members to discuss their opinions on particular policy in secret. Once decided, members usually support all policy uniformly. If a minister is unable to support the Ministry, he or she is obligated to resign. Ministers are responsible to Parliament for their actions & the actions of their department.
The mailing address for all Cabinet members on Parliament Hill in Ottawa is as follows: House of Commons, Parliament Buildings, Ottawa, Ontario, K1A 0A6.
Members of the The Canadian Ministry are presented in order of precedence:

Members of The Canadian Ministry (Cabinet)
Prime Minister, Right Hon. Stephen Joseph Harper, P.C., B.A., M.A., Calgary Southwest, Alberta
613-992-4211, Fax: 613-941-6900, pm@pm.gc.ca; stephen.harper@parl.gc.ca, Other Communications: PM's Office, Phone: 613-992-4211; Fax: 613-995-0101
Social Media: twitter.com/pmharper, www.facebook.com/group.php?gid=338690276206
Note: Web Sites: www.pm.gc.ca (Prime Minister of Canada);www.conservative.ca/leader/stephen_harper (Party Web Site)
Minister, Justice; Attorney General of Canada, Hon. Robert Douglas Nicholson, P.C., Q.C., B.A., LL.B., Niagara Falls, Ontario
613-995-1547, Fax: 613-992-7910, rob.nicholson@parl.gc.ca, Other Communications: Justice, Phone: 613-992-4621; Fax: 613-990-7255, TTY: 613-992-4556
Note: Web Sites: www.canada.justice.gc.ca/eng/mag-mpg/index.html (Department of Justice Canada); www.robnicholson.ca (Personal Web Site)
Leader of the Goverment in the Senate, Hon. Marjory LeBreton, P.C.
613-943-0756, 800-267-7362, Fax: 613-943-1493, Marjory.LeBreton@pco-bcp.gc.ca; lebrem@sen.parl.gc.ca
Note: Web Site: www.pco-bcp.gc.ca/lgs/default.asp?Language=E&Page=home
Minister, National Defence, Hon. Peter Gordon MacKay, Central Nova, Nova Scotia
613-992-6022, Fax: 613-992-2337, dnd_mdn@forces.gc.ca; peter.mackay@parl.gc.ca, Other Communications: DND, Phone: 613-996-3100; Fax: 613-995-8189, TTY: 800-467-9877
Social Media: twitter.com/MacKayCPC
Note: Web Sites: www.forces.gc.ca/site/minister-ministre/index-eng.asp?WT.svl=minísterLef (Department of National Defence & the Canadian Forces); www.petermackay.ca (Personal Web Site)
Minister, Public Safety, Hon. Vic Toews, P.C., B.A., LL.B., Provencher, Manitoba
613-992-3128, 800-830-3118, Fax: 613-995-1049, vic.toews@parl.gc.ca; communications@ps.gc.ca, Other Communications: Public Safety Canada, Phone: 613-991-2924, TTY: 866-865-5667
Note: Web Sites: www.publicsafety.gc.ca/abt/wwa/min-eng.aspx (Public SafetyCanada); www.victoews.com (Personal Web Site)
Minister, Public Works & Government Services; Minister for Status of Women, Hon. Rona Ambrose, P.C., B.A., M.A., Edmonton - Spruce Grove, Alberta
613-996-9778, 866-902-2719, Fax: 613-996-0785, Rona.Ambrose@tpsgc-pwgsc.gc.ca;minister-ministre@swc-cfc.gc.ca, Other Communications: Status of Women: 819-956-4000; Fax: 613-995-1761, TTY: 613-996-1322
Social Media: twitter.com/MP_RonaAmbrosewww.linkedin.com/pub/rona-ambrose/16/bb0/668
Note: Web Sites: www.tpsgc-pwgsc.gc.ca/apropos-about/mnstr-eng.html (Public Works & Government Services Canada); www.swc-cfc.gc.ca/abu-ans/min/index-eng.html (Status of Women Canada); www.ronaambrose.com (PersonalWeb Site)
Minister, Human Resources & Skills Development, Hon. Diane Finley, P.C., B.A., M.B.A., Haldimand - Norfolk, Ontario
613-996-4974, 800-622-6232, Fax: 613-996-9749, diane.finley@hrsdc-rhdcc.gc.ca; diane.finley@parl.gc.ca, Other Communications: HR & Skills Dev.: 819-994-2482; Fax: 819-994-0448, TTY: 800-926-9105
Note: Web Site: www.hrsdc.gc.ca/eng/corporate/ministers/index.shtml (Human Resources & Skills Development Canada); www.dianefinley.ca (Personal Web Site)
Minister, International Cooperation, Hon. Beverley "Bev" J. Oda, P.C., B.A., Durham, Ontario
613-992-2792, 800-230-6349, Fax: 613-992-2794, bev.oda@parl.gc.ca, Other Communications: CIDA, Phone: 819-953-6238; Fax: 819-953-8525, TTY: 819-953-5023
Note: Web Sites: www.acdi-cida.gc.ca/acdi-cida/acdi-cida.nsf/eng/NIC-5494720-J79 (Canadian International Development Agency); www.international.gc.ca/ministers-ministres/index.aspx?view=d (Foreign Affairs & International Trade); www.bevoda.ca (Personal)
Minister, Foreign Affairs, Hon. John Baird, P.C., B.A. (Hons.), Ottawa West - Nepean, Ontario

613-996-0984, 800-267-8376, Fax: 613-996-9880, john.baird@parl.gc.ca, Other Communications: Foreign Affairs, Phone: 613-995-1851, TTY: 613-944-9136
Social Media: twitter.com/JohnBairdOWN
Note: Web Sites: www.international.gc.ca/ministers-ministres/John_Baird.aspx?lang=eng&view=d (Foreign Affairs& International Trade Canada); www.johnbaird.com (Personal Web Site)

Minister, Federal Economic Development Initiative for Northern Ontario; President, Treasury Board, Hon. Tony Clement, P.C., B.A., LL.B., Parry Sound - Muskoka, Ontario
613-944-7740, 877-333-6673, Fax: 613-992-5092, tony.clement@parl.gc.ca, Other Communications: FedNor, Fax: 613-941-4553
Social Media: twitter.com/TonyclementCPC
Note: Web Sites: www.ic.gc.ca/eic/site/ic1.nsf/eng/06510.html (FedNor, Industry Canada); www.tonyclement.ca (Personal Web Site)

Minister, Finance, Hon. James "Jim" Michael Flaherty, P.C., B.A., LL.B., Whitby - Oshawa, Ontario
613-992-6344, Fax: 613-992-8320, jim.flaherty@parl.gc.ca, Other Communications: Finance Communications, Phone: 613-992-1573, TTY: 613-995-1455
Social Media: twitter.com/JimFlaherty, www.facebook.com/pages/Jim-Flaherty/49500135386
Note: Web Sites: www.fin.gc.ca/comment/minfin-eng.asp (Department of Finance Canada); www.jimflaherty.com (Personal Web Site)

Leader, Government in the House of Commons, Hon. Peter Van Loan, P.C., B.A., LL.B., M.A., M.Sc.Pl., York - Simcoe, Ontario
613-996-7752, Fax: 613-992-8351, peter.vanloan@parl.gc.ca, Other Communications: Office of Leader of Government in HoC: 613-995-7226
Note: Web Sites: www.houseleader.gc.ca/index.asp?lang=eng&page=Team-equipe&doc=bio/bio-eng.htm (Leader of the Government in the House of Commons); www.petervanloan.com (Personal Web Site)

Minister, Citizenship, Immigration, & Multiculturalism, Hon. Jason Kenney, P.C., Calgary Southeast, Alberta
613-992-2235, Fax: 613-992-1920, Minister@cic.gc.ca; jason.kenney@parl.gc.ca, Other Communications: Citizenship & Immigration, Phone: 613-954-1064
Social Media: twitter.com/kenneyjason, www.facebook.com/pages/Jason-Kenney/29829307640
Note: Web Sites: www.cic.gc.ca/english/department/minister/index.asp (Citizenship &Immigration Canada); www.jasonkenney.com (Personal Web Site)

Minister, Agriculture & Agri-Food; Minister, Canadian Wheat Board, Hon. Gerry Ritz, P.C., Battlefords - Lloydminster, Saskatchewan
613-995-7080, Fax: 613-996-8472, gerry.ritz@parl.gc.ca, Other Communications: Agriculture & Agri-Food Canada, Fax: 613-773-1081
Note: Web Sites: www4.agr.gc.ca/AAFC-AAC/display-afficher.do?id=1203439690684&lang=eng (Agriculture & Agri-FoodCanada); www.gerryritzmp.com (Personal Web Site)

Minister, Industry; Minister of State, Agriculture, Hon. Christian Paradis, P.C., Mégantic - L'Érable, Québec
613-995-1377, Fax: 613-943-1562, minister.industry@ic.gc.ca; ParadC@parl.gc.ca, Other Communications: Agriculture & Agri-Food Canada, Fax: 613-773-1081
Social Media: twitter.com/christianparad
Note: Web Sites: www.ic.gc.ca/eic/site/ic1.nsf/eng/h_00279.html (Industry Canada); www4.agr.gc.ca/AAFC-AAC/display-afficher.do?id=1262962138890&lang=eng (Agriculture & Agri-Food Canada); www.christianparadis.com (Personal Web Site)

Minister, Canadian Heritage & Official Languages, Hon. James Moore, P.C., B.A., Port Moody - Westwood - Port Coquitlam, British Columbia
613-992-9650, 866-811-0055, Fax: 613-992-9868, james.moore@pch.gc.ca; james.moore@parl.gc.ca, Other Communications: Canadian Heritage: 819-997-7788; Fax: 819-994-1267, TTY: 888-997-3123
Social Media: twitter.com/JamesMoore_org, www.facebook.com/jamesmoore.org
Note: Web Sites: www.pch.gc.ca/pc-ch/minstr/moore/index-eng.cfm (Canadian Heritage); www.jamesmoore.org (Personal Web Site)

Minister, Transport, Infrastructure, & Communities; Minister, Economic Development Agency of Canada for the Regions of Québec, Hon. Denis Lebel, P.C., Roberval - Lac-Saint-Jean, Québec
613-996-6236, 866-995-9737, Fax: 613-996-6252, denis.lebel@parl.gc.ca, Other Communications: Economic Development: 514-283-6412; Fax: 514-496-5096, TTY: 888-675-6863
Social Media: www.facebook.com/pages/Denis-Lebel/137888079554744
Note: Web Sites: www.tc.gc.ca/eng/minister-menu.htm (Transport Canada); www.dec-ced.gc.ca/eng/minister/index.html (Canada Economic Development for Québec Regions); www.denislebel.com (Personal Web Site)

Minister, Health; Minister, Canadian Northern Economic Development Agency, Hon. Leona Aglukkaq, P.C., Nunavut
613-992-2848, 800-567-9604, Fax: 613-996-9764, Minister_Ministre@hc-sc.gc.ca; leona.aglukkaq@parl.gc.ca, Other Communications: Northern Economic Dev. Agency, Fax: 1-866-817-3977, TTY: 866-553-0554
Social Media: twitter.com/leonaaglukkaq
Note: Web Sites: www.hc-sc.gc.ca/ahc-asc/minist/index-eng.php (Health Canada); www.north.gc.ca/minstr-eng.asp (Canadian Northern Economic Development Agency); www.leonaaglukkaq.ca/EN/5215/ (Personal Web Site)

Minister, Fisheries & Oceans; Minister, Atlantic Gateway, Hon. Keith Ashfield, P.C., Fredericton, New Brunswick
613-992-1067, Fax: 613-996-9955, Min@dfo-mpo.gc.ca; keith.ashfield@parl.gc.ca, Other Communications: Fisheries & Oceans, Phone: 613-992-3474, TTY: 800-465-7735
Social Media: twitter.com/KeithAshfield11
Note: Web Sites: www.dfo-mpo.gc.ca/minister-ministre/bio-eng.htm (Fisheries & OceansCanada); www.atlanticgateway.gc.ca (Canada's Atlantic Gateway); www.keithashfield.ca (Personal Web Site)

Minister, Environment, Hon. Peter Kent, P.C., Thornhill, Ontario
613-992-0253, Fax: 613-992-0887, Minister@ec.gc.ca; peter.kent@parl.gc.ca, Other Communications: Environment, Phone: 819-997-1441; Fax: 819-953-0279
Social Media: twitter.com/ec_minister; www.twitter.com/mpPeterKent, www.facebook.com/apps/application.php?id=135514873168072
Note: Web Sites: www.peterkent.ca (Personal Web Site); www.ec.gc.ca/default.asp?lang=En&n=B6832638-1 (EnvironmentCanada); Twitter (French): www.twitter.com/ministre_ec

Minister, Labour, Hon. Lisa Raitt, P.C., B.Sc., M.Sc., LL.B., Halton, Ontario
613-996-7046, Fax: 613-992-0851, lisa.raitt@hrsdc-rhdcc.gc.ca; lisa.raitt@parl.gc.ca, Other Communications: Labour, Phone: 819-953-5646; Fax: 819-994-5168
Social Media: twitter.com/lraitt, www.facebook.com/lisaraitt
Note: Web Sites: www.hrsdc.gc.ca/eng/corporate/labour/minister/index.shtml (Labour, Human Resources &Skills Development Canada); www.lisaraittmp.ca (Personal Web Site)

Minister, National Revenue, Hon. Gail Shea, P.C., Egmont, Prince Edward Island
613-992-9223, Fax: 613-992-1974, gail.shea@parl.gc.ca; sheag1B@parl.gc.ca, Other Communications: Cda Revenue Agency: 613-995-2960; Fax: 613-952-6608, TTY: 800-665-0354
Social Media: twitter.com/CPCGailShea
Note: Web Sites: www.cra-arc.gc.ca/gncy/mnstr/menu-eng.html (Canada Revenue Agency); www.gailshea.ca (Personal Web Site)

Minister, Aboriginal Affairs & Northern Development, Hon. John Duncan, P.C., B.Sc.F., Vancouver Island North, British Columbia
613-992-2503, 800-567-9604, Fax: 613-996-3306, john.duncan@parl.gc.ca, Other Communications: Aboriginal Affairs: 819-997-0002; Fax: 819-953-4941, TTY: 866-553-0554
Note: Web Sites: www.ainc-inac.gc.ca/ai/min/index-eng.asp (Aboriginal Affairs & Northern Development Canada); www.johnduncanmp.com (Personal Web Site)

Minister, Veteran Affairs, Hon. Steven Blaney, P.C., M.B.A., Lévis - Bellechasse, Québec
613-992-7434, 866-522-2122, Fax: 613-995-6856, steven.blaney@parl.gc.ca; blanes1@parl.gc.ca, Other Communications: Veteran Affairs: 613-996-4649; Fax: 613-996-0287
Social Media: twitter.com/steven_blaney, www.facebook.com/people/Steven-Blaney/557166646
Note: Web Sites: www.veterans.gc.ca/eng/sub.cfm?source=department/blaney-corner (Veteran Affairs Canada);www.stevenblaney.ca (Personal Web Site)

Minister, International Trade; Minister, Asia-Pacific Gateway, Hon. Edward Fast, P.C., LL.B., Abbotsford, British Columbia
613-995-0183, Fax: 613-996-9795, ed.fast@parl.gc.ca; faste@parl.gc.ca; ed@edfast.ca, Other Communications: International Trade: 613-992-7332; Fax: 613-996-8924
Note: Web Sites: www.international.gc.ca/commerce/edward_fast.aspx?lang=eng (Foreign Affairs & International Trade Canada); www.edfast.ca (Personal Web Site)

Minister, Natural Resources, Hon. Joe Oliver, P.C., B.A., BCL, MBA, Eglinton - Lawrence, Ontario
613-992-6361, Fax: 613-992-9791, Minister.Ministre@NRCan-RNCan.gc.ca; joe.oliver@parl.gc.ca, Other Communications: Natural Resources: 613-996-2007; Fax: 613-996-4516
Social Media: twitter.com/joeoliver1, www.facebook.com/profile.php?id=707035179www.linkedin.com/pub/joseph-oliver/4/267/73b
Note: Web Sites: www.nrcan.gc.ca/com/deptmini/minmin/minmin-biobio-eng.php (NaturalResources Canada); www.joeoliver.ca (Personal Web Site)

Minister, Intergovernmental Affairs; President, Queen's Privy Council for Canada, Hon. Peter Penashue, P.C., Labrador, Newfoundland & Labrador
613-996-4630, Fax: 613-996-7132, peter.penashue@parl.gc.ca, Other Communications: Intergovernmental Affairs,Phone: 613-943-1838
Social Media: twitter.com/PeterPenashue, www.facebook.com/peterpenashue
Note: Web Site: www.pco-bcp.gc.ca/aia/index.asp?lang=eng&page=min (Intergovernmental Affairs)

Associate Minister, National Defence, Hon. Julian Fantino, P.C., C.O.M., O. Ont., Vaughan, Ontario
613-996-4971, Fax: 613-996-4973, Dnd_amnd@forces.gc.ca; julian.fantino@parl.gc.ca, Other Communications: Defence, Phone: 613-996-3100; Fax: 613-992-0028, TTY: 800-467-9877
Social Media: twitter.com/JulianFantino
Note: Web Sites: www.forces.gc.ca/site/minister-ministre/am-ma/index-eng.asp (National Defence & the Canadian Forces); www.julianfantino.ca (Personal Web Site)

Minister of State, Atlantic Canada Opportunities Agency (ACOA); Minister of State, La Francophonie, Hon. Bernard Valcourt, P.C., Q.C., B.A., LL.B., DHC, Madawaska - Restigouche, New Brunswick
613-995-0581, 800-561-7862, Fax: 613-996-9736, bernard.valcourt@parl.gc.ca; bvalcourt2011@hotmail.com, Other Communications: ACOA, Phone: 613-941-7241; Fax: 613-996-9736, TTY: 877-456-6500
Social Media: twitter.com/b_valcourt, www.facebook.com/pages/Bernard-Valcourt/214030968613999
Note: Web Sites: www.acoa-apeca.gc.ca/English/WhoWeAre/OurPeople/Pages/Minister.aspx?ProgramID= Atlantic Canada Opportunities Agency; www.bernardvalcourt.ca (Personal Web Site)

Minister of State, Hon. Gordon O'Connor, P.C., B.A., B.Sc., Carleton - Mississippi Mills, Ontario
613-992-1119, Fax: 613-992-1043, gordon.oconnor@parl.gc.ca, Other Communications: Minister of State, Phone: 613-995-2291
Social Media: www.facebook.com/pages/Gordon-OConnor/228442573837062?sk=info
Note: Web Site: www.gordonoconnor.ca (Personal Web Site)

Minister of State, Small Business & Tourism, Hon. Maxime Bernier, P.C., B.Comm., LL.B., Beauce, Québec
613-992-8053, Fax: 613-995-0687, mossbt.industry@ic.gc.ca; maxime.bernier@parl.gc.ca, Other Communications: Small Business: 613-943-6183; Fax: 613-990-4056
Note: Web Sites: www.ic.gc.ca/eic/site/ic1.nsf/eng/00097.html (IndustryCanada); www.maximebernier.com (Personal Web Site)

Minister of State, Foreign Affairs (Americas & Consular Affairs), Hon. Diane Ablonczy, P.C., B.Ed., LL.B., Calgary - Nose Hill, Alberta
613-996-2756, 800-267-8376, Fax: 613-992-2537, diane.ablonczy@parl.gc.ca; Calgary@ablonczy.com, Other Communications: ForeignAffairs, Phone: 613-944-2300, TTY: 613-944-9136
Social Media: twitter.com/dianeablonczymp
Note: Web Sites: www.international.gc.ca/ministers-ministres/Diane_Ablonczy.aspx?lang=eng&view=d (Foreign Affairs & International Trade Canada); www.dianeablonczy.com (Personal Web Site)

Minister of State, Western Economic Diversification, Hon. Lynne Yelich, P.C., Blackstrap, Saskatchewan
613-995-5653, Fax: 613-995-0126, Lynne.Yelich@parl.gc.ca, Other Communications: Western Diversification, Phone: 613-952-2768, TTY: 877-303-3388
Social Media: twitter.com/Lynne_Yelich, www.facebook.com/pages/Lynne-Yelich/64666054978
Note: Web Sites: www.wd.gc.ca/eng/43.asp (Western Economic DiversificationCanada); www.lynneyelich.com (Personal Web Site)

Minister of State, Transport, Hon. Steven John Fletcher, P.C., B.Sc., M.B.A., Charleswood - St. James - Assiniboia, Manitoba
613-995-5609, Fax: 613-992-3199, steven.fletcher@parl.gc.ca, Other Communications: Transport, Phone: 613-991-0700; Fax: 613-995-0327

Social Media: twitter.com/stevenjfletcher, www.facebook.com/StevenFletcherMP
Note: Web Sites: www.tc.gc.ca/eng/minister-state.htm (Transport Canada); www.stevenfletcher.com (PersonalWeb Site)

Minister of State, Science & Technology; Minister of State, Federal Economic Development Agency for Southern Ontario, Hon. Dr. Gary Goodyear, P.C., D.C.,F.C.C.S.S., Cambridge, Ontario
613-996-1307, Fax: 613-996-8340, mosst.industry@ic.gc.ca; gary.goodyear@parl.gc.ca, Other Communications: Industry, Phone: 613-947-2956; Fax: 613-943-7598
Note: Web Sites: www.ic.gc.ca/eic/site/ic1.nsf/eng/02933.html (Industry Canada); www.garygoodyear.com (Personal Web Site)

Minister of State, Finance, Hon. Ted Menzies, P.C., Macleod, Alberta
613-995-8471, Fax: 613-996-9770, ted.menzies@fin.gc.ca; ted.menzies@parl.gc.ca, Other Communications: Finance, Phone: 613-996-7861; Fax: 613-995-5176
Social Media: twitter.com/TedMenzies
Note: Web Sites: www.fin.gc.ca/comment/state-etat-eng.asp (Department of Finance Canada); www.tedmenzies.ca (Personal Web Site)

Minister of State, Democratic Reform, Hon. Tim Uppal, P.C., Edmonton - Sherwood Park, Alberta
613-995-3611, Fax: 613-995-3612, tim.uppal@parl.gc.ca, Other Communications: Democratic Reform: 613-992-3689; Fax: 613-947-8077
Social Media: twitter.com/TimUppal_MP, www.facebook.com/profile.php?id=560835735
Note: Web Sites: www.timuppal.ca (Personal Web Site); www.democraticreform.gc.ca/index.asp?lang=eng&page=min (Democratic Reform)

Minister of State, Seniors, Hon. Alice Wong, P.C., Ph.D., Richmond, British Columbia
613-995-2021, 800-622-6232, Fax: 613-995-2174, alice.wong@parl.gc.ca; alice.wong.c1@parl.gc.ca, Other Communications: Seniors Canada, Fax: 613-957-1602, TTY: 800-926-9105
Social Media: twitter.com/AliceWongCanada, www.facebook.com/profile.php?id=100002648510727
Note: Web Sites: www.hrsdc.gc.ca/eng/corporate/ministers/index.shtml (Human Resources & Skills Development Canada); www.seniors.gc.ca/h.4m.2@.jsp (Seniors Canada); www.alicewong.ca (Personal Web Site)

Minister of State, Sport, Hon. Bal Gosal, P.C., Bramalea - Gore - Malton, Ontario
613-992-9105, Fax: 613-947-0443, bal.gosal@pch.gc.ca; bal.gosal@parl.gc.ca, Other Communications: Sport, Phone: 819-934-1122; Fax: 819-953-8055
Social Media: twitter.com/MinStateSport, www.facebook.com/pages/Bal-Gosal/155006724554020
Note: Web Sites: www.pch.gc.ca/pc-ch/minstr/gosal/biograph-eng.cfm (Canadian Heritage); www.electbalgosal.ca (Personal Web Site)

41st Parliament - Canada

House of Commons, Parliament Buildings, Ottawa, ON K1A 0A6

www.parl.gc.ca

Members of the House of Commons are elected by the people. The Speaker is elected by the House.
Last General Election: May 2, 2011.
Political Party Leaders (August 2011):
Conservative Party of Canada - The Right Hon. Stephen Joseph Harper;
New Democratic Party - Nycole Turmel (Interim Leader);
Liberal Party of Canada - The Hon. Robert "Bob" Keith Rae (Interim Leader);
Bloc Québécois - Louis Plamondon (Chair, Bloc Québécois Caucus);
Green Party of Canada - Elizabeth May.
Representation in the House of Commons by province is as follows (August 2011):
Alberta - Conservative Party of Canada 27, New Democratic Party 1, Total 8;
British Columbia - Conservative Party of Canada 21, New Democratic Party 12, Liberal Party of Canada 2, Green Party of Canada 1, Total 36;
Manitoba - Conservative Party of Canada 11, New Democratic Party 2, Liberal Party of Canada 1, Total 14;
New Brunswick - Conservative Party of Canada 8, New Democratic Party 1, Liberal Party of Canada 1, Total 10;
Newfoundland & Labrador - Conservative Party of Canada 1, New Democratic Party 2, Liberal Party of Canada 4, Total 7;
Northwest Territories - New Democratic Party 1, Total 1;
Nova Scotia - Conservative Party of Canada 4, New Democratic Party 3, Liberal Party of Canada 4, Total 11;
Nunavut - Conservative Party of Canada 1, Total 1
Ontario - Conservative Party of Canada 73, New Democratic Party 21, Liberal Party of Canada 11, Vacant 1, Total 106;
Prince Edward Island - Conservative Party of Canada 1, Liberal Party of Canada 3, Total 4;
Québec - Conservative Party of Canada 5, New Democratice Party 59, Liberal Party of Canada 7, Bloc Québécois 4, Total 75;
Saskatchewan - Conservative Party of Canada 13, Liberal Party of Canada 1, Total 14;
Yukon - Conservative Party of Canada 1, Total 1.
Representation in the House of Commons by party affiliation is as follows (August 2011):
Conservative Party of Canada 166;
New Democratic Party 102;
Liberal Party of Canada 34;
Bloc Québécois 4;
Green Party of Canada 1;
Vacant 1;
Total 308.
Indemnities, Salaries, & Allowances (2011):
The basic sessional indemnity for each member of the House of Commons is $157,731. In addition to the indemnity, members who occupy certain positions in the House of Commons receive additional remuneration.
Prime Minister: $157,731, plus a car allowance of $2,112;
Minister $75,516, plus a car allowance of $2,122;
Minister of State: $56,637;
Secretary of State: $56,637;
Parliamentary Secretary: $15,834;
Speaker of the House of Commons: $75,516, plus a car allowance of $1,061, & a rent allowance of $3,000;
Deputy Speaker of the House of Commons: $39,179, plus a rent allowance of $1,500;
Leader of the Opposition in the House of Commons: $75,516, plus a car allowance of $2,122;
Leaders of Other Parties: $53,694;
Opposition House Leader: $39,179;
House Leader of Other Parties: $15,834;
Deputy House Leaders of Government & Official Opposition: $15,834;
Deputy House Leaders of Other Parties: $5,684;
Chief Government Whip: $28,420;
Chief Opposition Whip: $28,420;
Whip of Other Parties: $11,165;
Chief Government Whip's Assistant: $11,165;
Deputy Whip of the Official Opposition: $11,165;
Deputy Whip of Other Parties: $5,684;
Caucus Chair of the Government & the Official Opposition: $11,165;
Caucus Chair of Other Parties: $5,684;
Deputy Chair, Committees of the Whole: $15,834;
Assistant Deputy Chair, Committees of the Whole: $15,834;
Chair of Standing & Standing Joint Committee (excluding the Liaison Committee & the Standing Joint Committee on the Library of Parliament): $11,165
Vice-Chair of Standing & Standing Joint Committee (excluding the Liaison Committee & the Standing Joint Committee on the Library of Parliament): $5,684.
Mail may be sent postage-free to any Member of Parliament at the following address: House of Commons, Parliament Buildings, Ottawa, Ontario, K1A 0A6.
The following is a list of Members of Parliament, as of August 2011, with their constituency, party affiliation, federal electoral district population, & contact information:

Members with Party Affiliation, Riding, & Contact Information

Minister of State, Foreign Affairs (Americas & Consular Affairs), Hon. Diane Ablonczy, P.C., B.Ed., LL.B., Calgary - Nose Hill, Alberta, Conservative Party
613-996-2756, Fax: 613-992-2537, diane.ablonczy@parl.gc.ca; Calgary@ablonczy.com, Other Communications: Constituency Phone: 403-282-7980; Fax: 613-992-2537
Social Media: twitter.com/dianeablonczymp
Note: Web Sites: www.dianeablonczy.com (PersonalWeb Site); www.international.gc.ca/ministers-ministres/Diane_Ablonczy.aspx?lang=eng&view=d (Foreign Affairs & International Trade Canada)

Parliamentary Secretary to Minister, Veteran Affairs, Eve Adams, B.A., Mississauga - Brampton South, Ontario, Conservative Party
613-995-7784, Fax: 613-996-9817, eve.adams@parl.gc.ca, Other Communications: Constituency Phone: 905-625-1201;Fax: 905-625-1485
Social Media: twitter.com/MPEveAdams, www.facebook.com/eve.adams.mpwww.linkedin.com/in/eveadamsmississauga
Note: Web Site: www.voteadams.ca

Mark Adler, York Centre, Ontario, Conservative Party
613-941-6339, Fax: 613-941-2421, mark.adler@parl.gc.ca, Other Communications: Constituency Phone: 416-638-3700; Fax: 416-638-1407
Social Media: twitter.com/MarkAdlerMP
Note: Web Site: www.markadler.ca

Minister, Health; Minister, Canadian Northern Economic Development Agency, Hon. Leona Aglukkaq, P.C., Nunavut, Conservative Party
613-992-2848, 866-267-7701, Fax: 613-996-9764, leona.aglukkaq@parl.gc.ca; Minister_Ministre@hc-sc.gc.ca, Other Communications: Constituency Phone: 867-979-4193; Fax: 867-979-4196
Social Media: twitter.com/leonaaglukkaq
Note: Web Site: www.leonaaglukkaq.ca/EN/5215/ (Personal Web Site); www.hc-sc.gc.ca/ahc-asc/minist/index-eng.php (Health Canada); www.north.gc.ca/minstr-eng.asp (Canadian Northern Economic Development Agency)

Dan Albas, Okanagan - Coquihalla, British Columbia, Conservative Party
613-995-1702, Fax: 613-995-1154, dan.albas@parl.gc.ca, Other Communications: Constituency Phone: 250-770-4480; Fax: 250-770-4484
Social Media: twitter.com/DanAlbaswww.linkedin.com/in/danalbas
Note: Web Site: www.danalbas.com

Harold Albrecht, D.D.S., Kitchener - Conestoga, Ontario, Conservative Party
613-992-4633, Fax: 613-992-9932, harold.albrecht@parl.gc.ca, Other Communications: Constituency Phone: 519-578-3777; Fax: 519-578-0138
Note: Web Site: www.haroldalbrechtmp.ca

Parliamentary Secretary to the Minister, National Defence, Chris Alexander, Ajax - Pickering, Ontario, Conservative Party
613-995-8042, Fax: 613-996-1289, chris.alexander@parl.gc.ca
Social Media: twitter.com/calxandr
Note: Web Site: www.chrisalexander.ca

Malcolm Allen, Welland, Ontario, New Democratic Party
613-995-0988, Fax: 613-995-5245, malcolm.allen@parl.gc.ca; malcolm.allen.c1@parl.gc.ca, Other Communications: Constituency Phone: 905-788-2204; Fax: 905-788-0071
Social Media: twitter.com/Malcolm_AllenMP, www.facebook.com/malcolmallennmp
Note: Web Site: malcolmallen.ca

Mike Allen, B.Admin., M.B.A. (Hons.), Tobique - Mactaquac, New Brunswick, Conservative Party
613-947-4431, 800-671-6160, Fax: 613-947-4434, mike.allen@parl.gc.ca, Other Communications: Constituency Phone: 506-473-6632; Fax: 506-473-3926
Social Media: twitter.com/mpmikea, www.facebook.com/mike.allen.mpwww.linkedin.com/pub/mike-allen/27/53a/232
Note: Web Site: www.mikeallen.ca

Chair, Standing Committee on Foreign Affairs & International Development, Dean Allison, B.A., Niagara West - Glanbrook, Ontario, Conservative Party
613-995-2772, 877-563-7900, Fax: 613-992-2727, Allison.D@parl.gc.ca;info@deanallison.ca, Other Communications: Constituency Phone: 905-563-7900; Fax: 905-563-7500
Social Media: twitter.com/DeanAllisonMP
Note: Web Site: www.deanallison.ca

Stella Ambler, BSc. (Hons.), Mississauga South, Ontario, Conservative Party
613-992-4848, Fax: 613-996-3267, stella.ambler@parl.gc.ca; Stella@StellaAmbler.com, Other Communications: Constituency Phone: 905-486-1706
Social Media: www.facebook.com/pages/Stella-Ambler/135858743139392
Note: Web Site: www.stellaambler.com

Minister, Public Works & Government Services Canada; Minister, Status of Women, Hon. Rona Ambrose, P.C., B.A., M.A., Edmonton - Spruce Grove, Alberta, Conservative Party
613-996-9778, Fax: 613-996-0785, rona.ambrose@parl.gc.ca;ambror1a@parl.gc.ca, Other Communications: Constituency Phone: 780-495-7705; Fax: 780-495-7741
Social Media: twitter.com/MP_RonaAmbrosewww.linkedin.com/pub/rona-ambrose/16/bb0/668
Note: Web Site: www.ronaambrose.com (Personal Web Site);www.tpsgc-pwgsc.gc.ca/apropos-about/mnstr-eng.html (Public Works & Government Services Canada); www.swc-cfc.gc.ca/abu-ans/min/index-eng.html (Status of Women Canada)

Rob Anders, B.A., Calgary West, Alberta, Conservative Party
613-992-3066, Fax: 613-992-3256, rob.anders@parl.gc.ca; robanders@telus.net, Other Communications: Constituency Phone: 403-292-6666; Fax: 403-292-6670
Social Media: www.linkedin.com/pub/rob-anders/28/173/8b6
Note: Web Site: www.robanders.com

Parliamentary Secretary to the Minister, Natural Resources & for the Canadian Wheat Board, David Anderson, B.A., M.Div, Cypress Hills - Grasslands, Saskatchewan, Conservative Party
613-992-0657, Fax: 613-992-5508, david.anderson@parl.gc.ca;david.anderson1@sasktel.net, Other Communications: Constituency Phone: 306-778-4480; Fax: 306-778-6981

Social Media: twitter.com/DavidAndersonSK
Note: Web Site: www.davidanderson.ca

Scott Andrews, B.A., Avalon, Newfoundland & Labrador, Liberal
613-992-4133, 866-883-3424, Fax: 613-992-7277, scott.andrews@parl.gc.ca, Other Communications: Constituency Phone: 709-834-3424; Fax: 709-834-3628
Social Media: twitter.com/ScottAndrewsMP, www.facebook.com/pages/Scott-Andrews/26946316089
Note: Web Site: www.scottandrews.ca

Charlie Angus, Timmins - James Bay, Ontario, New Democratic Party
613-992-2919, Fax: 613-995-0747, charlie.angus@parl.gc.ca; Angus.C@parl.gc.ca, Other Communications: Constituency Phone: 705-567-2747; Fax: 705-567-5232
Social Media: twitter.com/CharlieAngusMP, www.facebook.com/profile.php?id=568261214&sk=info
Note: Web Site: www.charlieangus.ndp.ca

Scott Armstrong, B.A., M.A., Ph.D., Cumberland - Colchester - Musquodoboit Valley, Nova Scotia, Conservative Party
613-992-3366, Fax: 613-992-7220, scott.armstrong@parl.gc; armsts@parl.gc.ca; armsts2@parl.gc.ca, Other Communications: Constituency Phone: 902-893-2455; Fax: 902-893-1959
Social Media: twitter.com/SArmstrongCCMV, www.facebook.com/people/Scott-Armstrong/523045844www.linkedin.com/pub/scott-armstrong/37/b0/1b4
Note: Web Site: www.scottarmstrongmp.ca

Minister, Fisheries & Oceans, Hon. Keith Ashfield, P.C., Fredericton, New Brunswick, Conservative Party
613-992-1067, Fax: 613-996-9955, keith.ashfield@parl.gc.ca, Other Communications: Constituency Phone: 506-452-4110; Fax: 506-452-4076
Social Media: twitter.com/KeithAshfield11
Note: Web Sites: www.keithashfield.ca (Personal Web Site); www.dfo-mpo.gc.ca/minister-ministre/bio-eng.htm (Fisheries & Oceans Canada)

Chair, Standing Committee on the Status of Women, Niki Ashton, B.A., M.A., Churchill, Manitoba, New Democratic Party
613-992-3018, 866-785-0522, Fax: 613-996-5817, niki.ashton@parl.gc.ca, Other Communications: Constituency Toll-Free Phone: 1-866-669-7770
Social Media: www.facebook.com/niki.ashton
Note: Web Site: www.nikiashton.ndp.ca

Jay Aspin, Nipissing - Timiskaming, Ontario, C
613-995-6255, 800-461-1394, Fax: 613-996-7993, jay.aspin@parl.gc.ca, Other Communications: Constituency Phone: 705-647-6262; Fax: 705-647-6299
Social Media: twitter.com/JayAspin
Note: Web Site: www.jayaspin.ca

Alex Atamanenko, B.A., M.A., British Columbia Southern Interior, British Columbia, New Democratic Party
613-996-8036, 800-667-2393, Fax: 613-943-0922, alex.atamanenko@parl.gc.ca; atamaa1@parl.gc.ca, Other Communications: Constituency Phone: 250-365-2792; Fax: 250-365-2793
Social Media: www.facebook.com/pages/Alex-Atamanenko-MP/180017678676108
Note: Web Site: www.alexndp.ca

Robert Aubin, Trois-Rivières, Québec, New Democratic Party
613-992-2349, Fax: 613-995-9498, robert.aubin@parl.gc.ca, Other Communications: Constituency Phone: 819-371-5901; Fax: 819-371-5912
Note: Web Site: www.robertaubin.ndp.ca

Paulina Ayala, Honoré-Mercier,Québec, New Democratic Party
613-995-0580, Fax: 613-992-1710, Paulina.Ayala@parl.gc.ca
Note: Web Site: www.paulinaayala.ndp.ca

Minister, Foreign Affairs, Hon. John Baird, P.C., B.A. (Hons.), Ottawa West - Nepean, Ontario, Conservative Party
613-996-0984, Fax: 613-996-9880, john.baird@parl.gc.ca; bairdj1@parl.gc.ca, Other Communications: Constituency Phone: 613-990-7720; Fax: 613-993-6501
Social Media: twitter.com/JohnBairdOWN
Note: Web Site: www.johnbaird.com (Personal Web Site); www.international.gc.ca/ministers-ministres/John_Baird.aspx?lang=eng&view=d (Foreign Affairs & International Trade Canada)

Joyce Bateman, Winnipeg South Centre, Manitoba, Conservative Party
613-992-9475, Fax: 613-992-9586, joyce.bateman@parl.gc.ca, Other Communications: Constituency Phone: 204-983-1355; Fax: 204-984-3979
Note: Web Site: www.joycebateman.ca

Hon. Mauril Bélanger, P.C., B.A., Ottawa - Vanier, Ontario, Liberal
613-992-4766, Fax: 613-992-6448, mauril.bélanger@parl.gc.ca; BelanM1@parl.gc.ca, Other Communications: Constituency Phone: 613-947-7961; Fax: 613-947-7963
Note: Web Site: www.mauril.ca

André Bellavance, B.A., Richmond - Arthabaska, Québec, BQ
613-995-1554, 877-751-1375, Fax: 613-995-2026, andré.bellavance@parl.gc.ca; bellaa1@parl.gc.ca, Other Communications: Constituency Phone: 819-751-1375; Fax: 819-751-5517
Note: Web Site: www.andrebellavance.qc.ca

Hon. Dr. Carolyn Bennett, P.C., M.D., St. Paul's, Ontario, Liberal
613-995-9666, Fax: 613-947-4622, carolyn.bennett@parl.gc.ca, Other Communications: Constituency Phone: 416-952-3990; Fax: 416-952-3995
Social Media: twitter.com/Carolyn_Bennett, www.facebook.com/carolyn.bennett.stpaulswww.linkedin.com/pub/carolyn-bennett/13/a3/811
Note: Web Site: www.carolynbennett.liberal.ca

Chair, Standing Committee on Natural Resources, Leon Earl Benoit, Vegreville - Wainwright, Alberta, Conservative Party
613-992-4171, 800-463-1194, Fax: 613-996-9011, leon.benoit@parl.gc.ca; benoil1@parl.gc.ca, Other Communications: Constituency Phone: 780-763-6130;Fax: 780-763-6132
Social Media: www.linkedin.com/pub/leon-benoit/17/b6a/a9a
Note: Web Site: www.leonbenoit.ca

Tyrone Benskin, Jeanne-Le Ber, Québec, New Democratic Party
613-995-6403, tyrone.benskin@parl.gc.ca
Social Media: www.facebook.com/pages/Tyrone-Benskin/105638686181284
Note: Web Site: www.tyronebenskin.ndp.ca

Minister of State, Small Business & Tourism, Hon. Maxime Bernier, P.C., B.Comm., LL.B., Beauce, Québec, Conservative Party
613-992-8053, 888-470-2171, Fax: 613-995-0687, maxime.bernier@parl.gc.ca; bernim1a@parl.gc.ca, Other Communications: ConstituencyPhone: 418-227-2171; Fax: 418-227-3093
Note: Web Sites: www.maximebernier.com (Personal Web Site); www.ic.gc.ca/eic/site/ic1.nsf/eng/00097.html (Industry Canada)

Dennis Fraser Bevington, B.A., Western Arctic, Northwest Territories, New Democratic Party
613-992-4587, 800-661-0802, Fax: 613-992-1586, dennis.bevington@parl.gc.ca, Other Communications: Constituency Phone: 867-873-6995; Fax: 867-920-4233
Social Media: twitter.com/nwtdennis, www.facebook.com/pages/Dennis-Bevington/28453715670
Note: Web Site: www.dennisbevington.ca

Chair, Standing Committee on National Defence, James Bezan, Selkirk - Interlake, Manitoba, Conservative Party
613-992-2032, 888-247-9606, Fax: 613-992-6224, james.bezan@parl.gc.ca; office@jamesbezan.com, Other Communications: Constituency Phone: 204-785-6151; Fax: 204-785-6153
Social Media: twitter.com/jamesbezan, www.facebook.com/jamesbezan
Note: Web Site: www.jamesbezan.com

Denis Blanchette, Louis-Hébert, Québec, New Democratic Party
613-995-4995, Fax: 613-996-8292, denis.blanchette@parl.gc.ca, Other Communications: Constituency Phone: 418-648-3244
Social Media: twitter.com/DenisBlanchette, www.facebook.com/pages/Denis-Blanchette/13256142620
Note: Web Site: www.denisblanchette.npd.ca

Lysane Blanchette-Lamothe, Pierrefonds - Dollard, Québec, New Democratic Party
613-992-2689, Fax: 613-996-8478, lysane.blanchette-Lamothe@parl.gc, Other Communications: Constituency Phone: 514-624-5725
Social Media: www.facebook.com/LysanePierrefondsDollard
Note: Web Site: www.lysaneblanchettelamothe.ndp.ca

Minister, Veteran Affairs, Hon. Steven Blaney, P.C., M.B.A., Lévis - Bellechasse, Québec, Conservative Party
613-992-7434, 877-630-0500, Fax: 613-995-6856, steven.blaney@parl.gc.ca; blanes1@parl.gc.ca, Other Communications: Constituency Phone: 418-830-0500; Fax: 418-830-0504
Social Media: twitter.com/steven_blaney, www.facebook.com/people/Steven-Blaney/557166646
Note: Web Sites: www.stevenblaney.ca (Personal Web Site);www.veterans.gc.ca/eng/sub.cfm?source=department/blaney-corner (Veteran Affairs Canada)

Kelly Block, Saskatoon - Rosetown - Biggar, Saskatchewan, Conservative Party
613-995-1551, 888-590-6555, Fax: 613-943-2010, kelly.block@parl.gc.ca, Other Communications: Constituency Phone: 306-975-6555; Fax: 306-975-5786
Social Media: twitter.com/KellyBlockcpc, www.facebook.com/group.php?gid=75570595197
Note: Web Site: www.kellyblock.ca

Françoise Boivin, B.A., LL.L., Gatineau, Québec, New Democratic Party
613-992-4351, Fax: 613-992-1037, françoise.boivin@parl.gc.ca, Other Communications: Constituency Phone: 819-561-5555; Fax: 819-561-0005
Social Media: twitter.com/FBoivinNPD, www.facebook.com/francoiseboivingatineau
Note: Web Site: www.francoiseboivin.com

Charmaine Borg, Terrebonne -Blainville, Québec, New Democratic Party
613-947-4788, Fax: 613-947-4879, charmaine.borg@parl.gc.ca
Social Media: twitter.com/mpcharmaineborg
Note: Web Site: www.charmaineborg.ndp.ca

Ray Boughen, B.Sc., B.Ed., M.Sc., Palliser, Saskatchewan, Conservative Party
613-992-9115, Fax: 613-992-0131, ray.boughen@parl.gc.ca; ray.boughen.c1@parl.gc.ca, Other Communications: Constituency Phone: 306-691-3577; Fax: 306-691-3579
Note: Web Site: rayboughen.ca/index.php?docID=9

Alexandre Boulerice, Rosemont - La Petite-Patrie, Québec, New Democratic Party
613-992-0423, Fax: 613-992-0878, alexandre.boulerice@parl.gc.ca, Other Communications: Constituency Phone: 514-729-5342; Fax: 514-729-5875
Social Media: twitter.com/alexboulerice, www.facebook.com/pages/Alexandre-Boulerice-NPD/26089638685
Note: Web Site: www.alexandreboulerice.ndp.ca

Marjolaine Boutin-Sweet, Hochelaga, Québec, New Democratic Party
613-947-4576, Fax: 613-947-4579, marjolaine.boutin-sweet@parl.gc.ca, Other Communications: Constituency Phone: 514-283-2655; Fax: 514-283-6485
Social Media: twitter.com/marjboutinsweet, www.facebook.com/marjolaineboutinsweet
Note: Web Site: www.marjolaineboutinsweet.ndp.ca

Tarik Brahmi, Saint-Jean, Québec, New Democratic Party
613-992-5296, Fax: 613-992-9849, tarik.brahmi@parl.gc.ca, Other Communications: Constituency Phone: 450-357-9100; Fax: 450-357-9109
Social Media: twitter.com/TarikBrahmi
Note: Web Site: www.tarikbrahmi.ndp.ca

Peter Braid, B.A., Kitchener - Waterloo, Ontario, Conservative Party
613-996-5928, Fax: 613-992-6251, peter.braid@parl.gc.ca; peter.braid.c1@parl.gc.ca, Other Communications: Constituency Phone: 519-746-1573; Fax: 519-746-6436
Social Media: twitter.com/peterbraid, www.facebook.com/PeterBraid?ref=tswww.linkedin.com/pub/peter-braid/5/311/b1b
Note: Web Site: www.peterbraid.ca

Garry W. Breitkreuz, Yorkton - Melville, Saskatchewan, Conservative Party
613-992-4394, 800-667-6606, Fax: 613-992-8676, garry.breitkreuz@parl.gc.ca; garry.breitkreuz.c1@parl.gc.ca, Other Communications: Constituency Phone: 306-782-3309; Fax: 306-786-7207
Note: Web Site: www.garrybreitkreuz.com

Hon. Scott Brison, P.C., B.Comm., Kings - Hants, Nova Scotia, Liberal
613-995-8231, Fax: 613-996-9349, Brison.S@parl.gc.ca; kings.hants@ns.sympatico.ca, Other Communications: Constituency Phone: 902-542-4010; Fax: 902-542-4184
Social Media: twitter.com/scottbrisonwww.linkedin.com/pub/scott-brison/9/a43/1a6
Note: Web Site: www.brison.ca

Ruth Ellen Brosseau, Berthier - Maskinongé, Québec, New Democratic Party
613-992-5681, Fax: 613-992-7276, RuthEllen.Brosseau@parl.gc.ca; RuthEllen.Brosseau.c1@parl.gc.ca, Other Communications: Constituency Phone: 819-228-1210; Fax: 819-228-1181
Social Media: twitter.com/RE_Brosseau
Note: Web Site: www.ruthellenbrosseau.ndp.ca

Gordon Brown, B.A. (Hons), Leeds - Grenville, Ontario, Conservative Party
613-992-8756, 866-498-3096, Fax: 613-996-9171, gord.brown@parl.gc.ca; gord@gordbrownmp.ca, Other Communications: Constituency Phone: 613-498-3096; Fax: 613-498-3100
Note: Web Site: www.gordbrown.com

Parliamentary Secretary to the Minister, International Cooperation, Lois Brown, Newmarket - Aurora, Ontario, Conservative Party
613-992-9310, Fax: 613-992-9407, lois.brown@parl.gc.ca, Other Communications: Constituency Phone: 905-953-7515; Fax: 905-953-7527
Social Media: twitter.com/MPLoisBrown
Note: Web Site: www.loisbrown.ca

Patrick W. Brown, LL.B., Barrie, Ontario, Conservative Party
613-992-3394, Fax: 613-996-7923, patrick.brown@parl.gc.ca; barrie@servingbarrie.com, Other Communications: Constituency Phone: 705-726-5959; Fax: 705-726-3340
Social Media: twitter.com/brownbarrie
Note: Web Site: www.servingbarrie.com

Rod Bruinooge, B.A., Winnipeg South, Manitoba, Conservative Party
613-995-7517, Fax: 613-943-1466, rod.bruinooge@parl.gc.ca; Rod@bruinooge.com, Other Communications: Constituency Phone: 204-984-6787; Fax:

204-984-6792
Social Media: twitter.com/rodbruinooge, www.facebook.com/people/Rodney-Bruinooge/874415143
Note: Web Site: www.bruinooge.ca

Brad Butt, Mississauga - Streetsville, Ontario, Conservative Party
613-943-1766, Fax: 613-943-1768, Brad.Butt@parl.gc.ca, Other Communications: Constituency Phone: 905-812-1811; Fax: 905-812-8464
Social Media: twitter.com/buttbrad
Note: Web Site: www.bradbutt.ca

Hon. Gerry Byrne, P.C., B.Sc., Humber - St. Barbe - Baie Verte, Newfoundland & Labrador, Liberal
613-996-5511, 800-563-9934, Fax: 613-996-9632, gerry.byrne@parl.gc.ca; info@gerrybyrne.ca, Other Communications: Constituency Phone: 709-637-4540; 709-637-4537
Social Media: twitter.com/Gerry_Byrne
Note: Web Site: www.gerrybyrne.liberal.ca

Parliamentary Secretary to the Minister, Canadian Heritage, Paul Calandra, Oak Ridges - Markham, Ontario, Conservative Party
613-992-3640, Fax: 613-992-3642, paul.calandra@parl.gc.ca, Other Communications: Constituency Phone: 905-640-1125; Fax: 905-640-1182
Social Media: twitter.com/paulCalandra, www.facebook.com/pages/Paul-Calandra/97706410091www.linkedin.com/pub/paul-calandra/25/149/697
Note: Web Site: www.paulcalandra.com

Blaine Calkins, B.Sc., Wetaskiwin, Alberta, Conservative Party
613-995-8886, 800-665-0865, Fax: 613-996-9860, blaine.calkins@parl.gc.ca; calkib1@parl.gc.ca, Other Communications: Constituency Phone: 403-783-5530; Fax: 403-783-5532
Social Media: twitter.com/blainecalkinsmp, www.facebook.com/pages/Blaine-Calkins/208129505866377
Note: Web Site: www.blainecalkinsmp.ca

Ronald Cannan, Kelowna - Lake Country, British Columbia, Conservative Party
613-992-7006, Fax: 613-992-7636, ron.cannan@parl.gc.ca; ron@cannan.ca, Other Communications: Constituency Phone: 250-470-5075; Fax: 250-470-5077
Social Media: twitter.com/RonCannanwww.linkedin.com/pub/ron-cannan/18/227/242
Note: Web Site: www.cannan.ca

John Carmichael, B.A., Don Valley West, Ontario, Conservative Party
613-992-2855, Fax: 613-995-1635, john.carmichael@parl.gc.ca, Other Communications: Constituency Phone: 416-467-7275
Social Media: twitter.com/JohnBCarmichael, www.facebook.com/votecarmichaelwww.linkedin.com/pub/john-carmichael/2/11b/b41
Note: Web Site: www.johncarmichael.ca

Guy Caron, B.A., M.A., Rimouski-Neigette- Témiscouata - Les Basques, Québec, New Democratic Party
613-992-5302, Fax: 613-996-8298, guy.caron@parl.gc.ca
Social Media: twitter.com/GuyCaronNPD
Note: Web Site: www.guycaron.ndp.ca

Parliamentary Secretary to the Minister, Health, Dr. Colin Carrie, B.Sc. (Hons.), D.C., Oshawa, Ontario, Conservative Party
613-996-4756, Fax: 613-992-1357, colin.carrie@parl.gc.ca; colin@colincarriemp.ca, Other Communications: ConstituencyPhone: 905-440-4868; Fax: 905-440-4872
Social Media: twitter.com/ColinCarrie, www.facebook.com/people/Colin-Carrie/100001599242478
Note: Web Site: www.colincarriemp.ca

Sean Casey, Q.C., B.B.A., LL.B., Charlottetown, Prince Edward Island, Liberal
613-996-4714, Fax: 613-995-7685, sean.casey@parl.gc.ca, Other Communications: Constituency Phone: 902-566-7770; Fax: 902-566-7780
Social Media: twitter.com/SeanCaseyMP, www.facebook.com/pages/Sean-Casey/162651190466584www.linkedin.com/pub/sean-casey/36/17/608
Note: Web Site: www.seancasey.ca

Andrew Cash, Davenport,Ontario, New Democratic Party
613-992-2576, Fax: 613- 99-5820, andrew.cash@parl.gc.ca; cash@cashfortoronto.ca
Social Media: twitter.com/Cash4TO, www.facebook.com/cashfortoronto
Note: Web Site: www.cashfortoronto.ca

Chief Opposition Whip; Whip, New Democratic Party, Chris Charlton, B.A., M.A., Hamilton Mountain, Ontario, New Democratic Party
613-995-9389, 866-878-5191, Fax: 613-992-7802, chris.charlton@parl.gc.ca; chris.charlton.c1@parl.gc.ca, Other Communications: ConstituencyPhone: 905-574-3331; Fax: 905-574-4980
Social Media: twitter.com/ChrisCharltonMP, www.facebook.com/pages/Chris-Charlton/25222718654www.linkedin.com/pub/chris-charlton/8/8aa/4b9
Note: Web Site: www.chrischarlton.ca

Sylvain Chicoine, Châteauguay - Saint-Constant, Québec, New Democratic Party
613-996-7265, Fax: 613-996-9287, sylvain.chicoine@parl.gc.ca, Other Communications: Constituency Phone: 450-691-7044; Fax: 450-691-3114
Social Media: twitter.com/sylvainchicoine, www.facebook.com/group.php?gid=120841667990877
Note: Web Site: www.www.sylvainchicoine.ndp.ca

Robert Chisholm, B.A., M.A., Dartmouth- Cole Harbour, Nova Scotia, New Democratic Party
613-995-9378, Fax: 613-995-9379, robert.chisholm@parl.gc.ca
Social Media: twitter.com/RobertNDP, www.facebook.com/RobertNDP
Note: Web Site: www.robertchisholm.ndp.ca

Corneliu Chisu, B.Eng., M.Eng., Pickering - Scarborough East, Ontario, Conservative Party
613-995-8082, Fax: 613-993-6587, corneliu.chisu@parl.gc.ca, Other Communications: Constituency Phone: 416-287-0110; Fax: 416-287-6160
Social Media: twitter.com/cchisu, www.facebook.com/group.php?gid=229465150409635
Note: Web Site: www.electchisu.ca

Chair, Standing Committee on Official Languages, Hon. Michael D. Chong, P.C., Wellington - Halton Hills, Ontario, Conservative Party
613-992-4179, 866-878-5556, Fax: 613-996-4907, michael.chong@parl.gc.ca, Other Communications: Constituency Phone: 905-702-2597; Fax: 905-702-2564
Social Media: www.linkedin.com/pub/michael-chong/15/632/353
Note: Web Site: www.michaelchong.ca

François Choquette, Drummond, Québec, New Democratic Party
613-947-4550, Fax: 613-947-4551, francois.choquette@parl.gc.ca, Other Communications: Constituency Phone: 819-477-3611; Fax: 819-477-7116
Note: Web Site: www.francoischoquette.ndp.ca

Olivia Chow, B.A. (Hons.), Trinity - Spadina, Ontario, New Democratic Party
613-992-2352, Fax: 613-992-6301, olivia.chow@parl.gc.ca, Other Communications: Constituency Phone: 416-533-2710; Fax: 416-533-2236
Social Media: twitter.com/oliviachow, www.facebook.com/pages/Olivia-Chow/15535160141www.linkedin.com/pub/olivia-riding-1-chow/6/845/202
Note: Web Site: www.oliviachow.ca

Chair, Standing Committee on Public Accounts, David Christopherson, Hamilton Centre, Ontario, New Democratic Party
613-995-1757, Fax: 613-992-8356, david.christopherson@parl.gc.ca; hamilton@davidchristopherson.ca, Other Communications: ConstituencyPhone: 905-526-0770; Fax: 905-526-9943
Social Media: www.facebook.com/DavidChristophersonNDP
Note: Web Site: www.davidchristopherson.ndp.ca

Rob Clarke, Desnethé - Missinippi - Churchill River, Saskatchewan, Conservative Party
613-995-8321, 866-400-2334, Fax: 613-995-7697, rob.clarke@parl.gc.ca; rob.clarke.c1@parl.gc.ca, Other Communications: Constituency Phone: 306-425-2643; Fax: 306-425-2677
Social Media: twitter.com/rob_clarke_mp, www.facebook.com/pages/Rob-Clarke/123498939689
Note: Web Site: www.robclarkemp.ca

Ryan Cleary, St. John's South - Mount Pearl, Newfoundland & Labrador, New Democratic Party
613-992-0927, Fax: 613-995-7858, ryan.cleary@parl.gc.ca, Other Communications: Constituency Phone: 709-772-4608
Social Media: twitter.com/ClearyNDP, www.facebook.com/pages/Ryan-Cleary/218945144787655
Note: Web Site: www.www.ryancleary.ndp.ca

Minister, Federal Economic Development Initiative for Northern Ontario; President, Treasury Board, Hon. Tony Clement, P.C., B.A., LL.B., Parry Sound - Muskoka, Ontario, Conservative Party
613-944-7740, Fax: 613-992-5092, tony.clement@parl.gc.ca; Clemet1@parl.gc.ca; Clemet2@parl.gc.ca, Other Communications: Constituency Phone: 705-789-4640; Fax: 705-789-8857
Social Media: twitter.com/TonyclementCPC
Note: Web Sites: www.ic.gc.ca/eic/site/ic1.nsf/eng/06510.html (FedNor, Industry Canada); www.tonyclement.ca (Personal Web Site)

Hon. Denis Coderre, Bourassa, Québec, Liberal
613-995-6108, Fax: 613-995-9755, denis.coderre@parl.gc.ca; coderd1@parl.gc.ca, Other Communications: Constituency Phone: 514-323-1212; Fax: 514-323-2875
Social Media: twitter.com/DenisCoderrewww.linkedin.com/pub/denis-coderre/12/451/97a
Note: Web Site: www.deniscoderre.liberal.ca

Deputy House Leader of the Official Opposition, Joe Comartin, LL.B., Windsor - Tecumseh, Ontario, New Democratic Party
613-947-3445, Fax: 613-947-3448, joe.comartin@parl.gc.ca; comarj1@parl.gc.ca, Other Communications: Constituency Phone: 519-988-1826;Fax: 519-988-0152
Social Media: twitter.com/joecomartin, www.facebook.com/joecomartin
Note: Web Site: www.joecomartin.ca

Raymond Côté, B.A., Beauport - Limoilou, Québec, New Democratic Party
613-992-4406, Fax: 613-992-4544, raymond.cote@parl.gc.ca, Other Communications: Constituency Phone: 418-663-2113; Fax: 418-663-2988
Social Media: twitter.com/RCoteBL2011
Note: Web Site: www.raymondcote.ndp.ca

Hon. Irwin Cotler, P.C., O.C., B.A., B.C.L., LL.M., LL.D., Ph.D., Mount Royal, Québec, Liberal
613-995-0121, Fax: 613-992-6762, irwin.cotler@parl.gc.ca, Other Communications: Constituency Phone: 514-283-0171; Fax: 514-283-2407
Note: Web Site: www.irwincotler.liberal.ca

Jean Crowder, B.A., Nanaimo - Cowichan, British Columbia, New Democratic Party
613-943-2180, 866-609-9998, Fax: 613-993-5577, jean.crowder@parl.gc.ca, Other Communications: Constituency Phone: 250-746-4896; Fax: 250-746-2354
Social Media: twitter.com/JeanCrowder, www.facebook.com/jeancrowder
Note: Web Site: www.jeancrowder.ca

Chair, Standing Committee on Access to Information, Privacy, & Ethics, Nathan Cullen, B.A., Skeena - Bulkley Valley, British Columbia, New Democratic Party
613-993-6654, Fax: 613-993-9007, nathan.cullen@parl.gc.ca; info@nathancullen.ca, Other Communications: Constituency Phone: 250-877-4140; Fax: 250-877-4141
Social Media: twitter.com/nathancullen, www.facebook.com/nathan.cullen1www.linkedin.com/pub/nathan-cullen/21/24a/a36
Note: Web Site: www.nathancullen.com

Rodger Cuzner, B.A., Cape Breton - Canso, Nova Scotia, Liberal
613-992-6756, 866-282-0699, Fax: 613-992-4053, rodger.cuzner@parl.gc.ca; cuzner1@parl.gc.ca, Other Communications: Constituency Phone: 902-842-9763; Fax: 902-842-9025
Social Media: twitter.com/RodgerCuzner, www.facebook.com/rodger.cuzner
Note: Web Site: www.rodgercuzner.liberal.ca

Joe Daniel, B.Sc., M.Eng., Don Valley East, Ontario, Conservative Party
613-995-4988, Fax: 613-995-1686, joe.daniel@parl.gc.ca; joedanieldve@gmail.com, Other Communications: Constituency Phone: 647-624-6678; 647-624-6678
Social Media: www.facebook.com/pages/Joe-Daniel/162888397199
Note: Web Site: www.joedaniel.ca

Patricia Davidson, Sarnia - Lambton, Ontario, Conservative Party
613-957-2649, Fax: 613-957-2655, patricia.davidson@parl.gc.ca; davidp1@parl.gc.ca, Other Communications: Constituency Phone: 519-383-6600; Fax: 519-383-0609
Note: Web Site: www.patriciadavidson.ca

Don Davies, Vancouver Kingsway, British Columbia, New Democratic Party
613-943-0267, Fax: 613-943-0219, don.davies@parl.gc.ca, Other Communications: Constituency Phone: 604-775-6263; Fax: 604-775-6284
Social Media: twitter.com/dondavies, www.facebook.com/DonDaviesNDPwww.linkedin.com/pub/don-davies/30/3ab/934
Note: Web Site: www.dondavies.ndp.ca

Libby Davies, Vancouver East, British Columbia, New Democratic Party
613-992-6030, Fax: 613-995-7412, libby.davies@parl.gc.ca, Other Communications: Constituency Phone: 604-775-5800; Fax: 604-775-5811
Social Media: twitter.com/LibbyDavies, www.facebook.com/pages/Libby-Davies/7154945923?ref=nf
Note: Web Site: www.libbydavies.ca

Anne-Marie Day, Charlesbourg - Haute-Saint-Charles, Québec, New Democratic Party
613-995-8857, Fax: 613-995-1625, anne-marie.day@parl.gc.ca, Other Communications: Constituency Phone: 418-624-0022; Fax: 418-624-1095
Social Media: twitter.com/AnneMarieDay, www.facebook.com/pages/Anne-Marie-Day-NPD/191889404181173
Note: Web Site: www.annemarieday.ndp.ca

Parliamentary Secretary to the Minister, Foreign Affairs, Bob Dechert, Mississauga - Erindale, Ontario, Conservative Party
613-995-7321, Fax: 613-992-6708, bob.dechert@parl.gc.ca; bob.dechert.c1@parl.gc.ca, Other Communications: Constituency Phone: 905-897-1952; Fax: 905-897-6117
Note: Web Site: www.bobdechertmp.ca

Parliamentary Secretary to the Prime Minister & to the Minister, Intergovernmental Affairs, Dean Del Mastro, B. Comm.

(Hons.), Peterborough, Ontario, Conservative Party
613-995-6411, Fax: 613-996-9800,
dean.delmastro@parl.gc.ca; delmad1@parl.gc.ca, Other Communications: Constituency Phone: 705-745-2108; Fax: 705-741-4123
Social Media: twitter.com/mpdeandelmastro, www.facebook.com/deandelmastro
Note: Web Site: www.deandelmastro.ca

Deputy Chair, Committees of the Whole, Barry Devolin, B.A., M.A., Haliburton - Kawartha Lakes - Brock, Ontario, Conservative Party
613-992-2474, 866-688-9881, Fax: 613-996-9656,
barry.devolin@parl.gc.ca, Other Communications: Constituency Phone: 705-324-2400; Fax: 705-324-0880
Social Media: twitter.com/BarryDevolin_MP
Note: Web Site: www.barrydevolin.ca

Paul Dewar, B.A., B.Ed., Ottawa Centre, Ontario, New Democratic Party
613-996-5322, Fax: 613-996-5323, paul.dewar@parl.gc.ca; pauldewar@ndp.ca, Other Communications: Constituency Phone: 613-946-8682; Fax: 613-946-8680
Social Media: twitter.com/PaulDewar, www.facebook.com/pages/Paul-Dewar/21201054432
Note: Web Site: www.pauldewar.ca

Hon. Stéphane Dion, P.C., B.A., M.A., Ph.D., Saint-Laurent - Cartierville, Québec, Liberal
613-996-5789, Fax: 613-996-6562,
stephane.dion@parl.gc.ca; dions1@parl.gc.ca, Other Communications: Constituency Phone: 514-335-6655; Fax: 514-335-2712
Social Media: www.facebook.com/pages/Stephane-Dion/7874631159
Note: Web Site: www.stephanedion.liberal.ca

Pierre Dionne Labelle, Rivière-du-Nord, Québec, New Democratic Party
613-992-3257, Fax: 613-992-2156,
Pierre.DionneLabelle@parl.gc.ca, Other Communications: Constituency Phone: 450-565-0061; Fax: 450-565-0118
Note: Web Site: www.pierredionnelabelle.ndp.ca

Fin Donnelly, New Westminster - Coquitlam, British Columbia, New Democratic Party
613-947-4455, Fax: 613-947-4458, fin.donnelly@parl.gc.ca; Donnelly.F@parl.gc.ca, Other Communications: Constituency Phone: 604-664-9229; Fax: 604-664-9231
Social Media: twitter.com/FinDonnelly, www.facebook.com/pages/Fin-Donnelly/107434010722www.linkedin.com/pub/fin-donnelly/4/968/919
Note: Web Site: www.findonnelly.ca

Rosane Doré Lefebvre, B.A., Alfred-Pellan, Québec, New Democratic Party
613-992-0611, Fax: 613-992-8556,
rosane.dorelefebvre@parl.gc.ca, Other Communications: Constituency Phone: 450-661-4117; Fax: 450-661-5623
Social Media: twitter.com/RosaneDL, www.facebook.com/rosane.npd
Note: Web Site: www.rosanedorelefebvre.ndp.ca

Earl Dreeshen, Red Deer, Alberta, Conservative Party
613-995-0590, Fax: 613-995-6831,
earl.dreeshen@parl.gc.ca; Dreese1@parl.gc.ca, Other Communications: Constituency Phone: 403-347-7426; Fax: 403-347-7423
Social Media: twitter.com/earl_dreeshen, www.facebook.com/pages/Earl-Dreeshen/1040077593
Note: Web Site: www.earldreeshen.ca

Matthew Dubé, Chambly - Borduas, Québec, New Democratic Party
613-992-6035, Fax: 613-995-6223,
matthew.dube@parl.gc.ca, Other Communications: Constituency Phone: 450-441-7802; Fax: 450-441-3674
Social Media: twitter.com/MattDube, www.facebook.com/matthewdube.chamblyborduas
Note: Web Site: www.matthewdube.ndp.ca

Minister, Aboriginal Affairs & Northern Development, Hon. John Duncan, P.C., B.Sc.F., Vancouver Island North, British Columbia, Conservative Party
613-992-2503, 800-667-8404, Fax: 613-996-3306,
john.duncan@parl.gc.ca, Other Communications: Constituency Phone: 250-338-9381; Fax: 250-338-9361
Note: Web Sites: www.johnduncanmp.com (Personal Web Site); www.ainc-inac.gc.ca/ai/min/index-eng.asp (Aboriginal Affairs & Northern Development Canada)

Kirsty Duncan, B.A., PhD, Etobicoke North, Ontario, Liberal
613-995-4702, Fax: 613-995-8359, kirsty.duncan@parl.gc.ca, Other Communications: Constituency Phone: 416-747-6003; Fax: 416-747-8295
Social Media: twitter.com/KirstyDuncanMP, www.facebook.com/pages/Kirsty-Duncan/12293731397
Note: Web Site: www.kirstyduncan.liberal.ca

Linda Francis Duncan, B.A., LL.B., LL.M., Edmonton - Strathcona, Alberta, New Democratic Party
613-995-7325, Fax: 613-995-5342, linda.duncan@parl.gc.ca; duncal1@parl.gc.ca, Other Communications: Constituency Phone: 780-495-8404; Fax: 780-495-8403
Social Media: twitter.com/LindaDuncanMP, www.facebook.com/pages/Linda-Duncan/31779288732
Note: Web Site: www.lindaduncan.ndp.ca,www.edmontonstrathcona.ca/linda.html

Pierre-Luc Dusseault, Sherbrooke, Québec, New Democratic Party
613-943-7896, Fax: 613-943-7902,
pierre-luc.dusseault@parl.gc.ca, Other Communications: Constituency Phone: 819-564-4200; Fax: 819-564-3745
Social Media: twitter.com/PLDusseault, www.facebook.com/PLDusseault
Note: Web Site: www.www.pierrelucdusseault.ndp.ca

Parliamentary Secretary to the Minister, Citizenship & Immigration, Richard Dykstra, B.A., St. Catharines, Ontario, Conservative Party
613-992-3352, Fax: 613-947-4402, rick.dykstra@parl.gc.ca; info@rickdykstra.ca, Other Communications: Constituency Phone: 905-934-6767; Fax: 905-934-1577
Social Media: twitter.com/RickDykstra, www.facebook.com/RickDykstraMP
Note: Web Site: www.rickdykstra.ca

Hon. Arnold Wayne Easter, P.C., Dipl.T., LL.D. (Hon.), Malpeque, Prince Edward Island, Liberal
613-992-2406, Fax: 613-995-7408, wayne.easter@parl.gc.ca; eastew1@parl.gc.ca, Other Communications: Constituency Phone: 902-964-2428; Fax: 902-964-3242
Social Media: twitter.com/WayneEaster
Note: Web Site: www.wayneeaster.com

Hon. Mark Eyking, P.C., Sydney - Victoria, Nova Scotia, Liberal
613-995-6459, Fax: 613-995-2963, mark.eyking@parl.gc.ca, Other Communications: Constituency Phone: 902-567-6275; Fax: 902-564-2479
Note: Web Site: www.markeyking.liberal.ca

Associate Minister of National Defence, Hon. Julian Fantino, P.C., C.O.M., O. Ont., Vaughan, Ontario, Conservative Party
613-996-4971, Fax: 613-996-4973, julian.fantino@parl.gc.ca; fantij@parl.gc.ca, Other Communications: ConstituencyPhone: 905-303-5000; Fax: 905-303-5002
Social Media: twitter.com/JulianFantino
Note: Web Sites: www.julianfantino.ca (Personal Web Site); www.forces.gc.ca/site/minister-ministre/am-ma/index-eng.asp (National Defence & the Canadian Forces)

Minister, International Trade; Minister, Asia-Pacific Gateway, Hon. Edward Fast, P.C., LL.B., Abbotsford, British Columbia, Conservative Party
613-995-0183, Fax: 613-996-9795, ed.fast@parl.gc.ca; faste@parl.gc.ca; ed@edfast.ca, Other Communications: Constituency Phone: 604-557-7888; Fax: 604-557-9918
Note: Web Sites: www.edfast.ca (Personal Web Site);www.international.gc.ca/commerce/edward_fast.aspx?lang=eng (Foreign Affairs & International Trade Canada)

Parliamentary Secretary to the Minister of Justice, Kerry-Lynne Findlay, Q.C., B.A., LL.B., Delta - Richmond East, British Columbia, Conservative Party
613-992-2957, Fax: 613-992-3589,
kerry-lynne.findlay@parl.gc.ca, Other Communications: Constituency Phone: 604-940-8040; Fax: 604-940-8041
Social Media: twitter.com/KLDF2011
Note: Web Site: www.kerrylynnefindlay.ca

Minister, Human Resources & Skills Development, Hon. Diane Finley, P.C., B.A., M.B.A., Haldimand - Norfolk, Ontario, Conservative Party
613-996-4974, Fax: 613-996-9749, diane.finley@parl.gc.ca; diane.finley@hrsdc-rhdcc.gc.ca, Other Communications: Constituency Phone: 519-426-3400; Fax: 519-426-0003
Note: Web Sites: www.dianefinley.ca (Personal Web Site);www.hrsdc.gc.ca/eng/corporate/ministers/index.shtml (Human Resources & Skills Development Canada)

Minister, Finance, Hon. James "Jim" Michael Flaherty, P.C., B.A., LL.B., Whitby - Oshawa, Ontario, Conservative Party
613-992-6344, Fax: 613-992-8320, jim.flaherty@parl.gc.ca; jim@jimflahertymp.ca, Other Communications: Constitutency Phone: 905-665-8182; Fax: 905-665-8124
Social Media: twitter.com/JimFlaherty, www.facebook.com/pages/Jim-Flaherty/49500135386
Note: Web Sites: www.jimflaherty.com (Personal Web Site); www.fin.gc.ca/comment/minfin-eng.asp (Department ofFinance Canada)

Minister of State, Transport, Hon. Steven John Fletcher, P.C., B.Sc., M.B.A., Charleswood - St. James - Assiniboia, Manitoba, Conservative Party
613-995-5609, Fax: 613-992-3199,
steven.fletcher@parl.gc.ca, Other Communications: Constituency Phone: 204-984-6432; Fax: 204-984-6451
Social Media: twitter.com/stevenjfletcher, www.facebook.com/StevenFletcherMP
Note: Web Sites: www.stevenfletcher.com (Personal Web Site); www.tc.gc.ca/eng/minister-state.htm (Transport Canada)

Whip, Liberal Caucus, Judy Foote, B.A., B.Ed, Random - Burin - St. George's, Newfoundland & Labrador, Liberal
613-992-8655, Fax: 613-992-5324, Judy.Foote@parl.gc.ca, Other Communications: Constituency Phone: 709-832-1383; Fax: 709-832-1380
Social Media: twitter.com/JudyFoote, www.facebook.com/pages/Judy-Foote/36948418784
Note: Web Site: www.judyfoote.liberal.ca

Jean-François Fortin, B.A., Haute-Gaspésie - La Mitis - Matane - Matapédia, Québec, Bloc Quebecois
613-995-1013, Fax: 613-995-5184,
jean-francois.fortin@parl.gc.ca, Other Communications: Constituency Phone: 418-562-0343; Fax: 418-562-7655
Social Media: twitter.com/fortjf, www.facebook.com/JFFortin.Bloc
Note: Web Site: www.jffortin.info

Mylène Freeman, B.A., Argenteuil -Papineau - Mirabel, Quebec, Liberal
613-992-0902, Fax: 613-992-2935,
mylene.freeman@parl.gc.ca
Social Media: twitter.com/MyleneFreemanwww.linkedin.com/in/mylenefreeman
Note: Web Site: www.mylenefreeman.ndp.ca

Hon. Hedy Fry, P.C., M.D., L.R.C.P.S.I., L.M., Vancouver Centre, British Columbia, Liberal
613-992-3213, Fax: 613-995-0056, hedy.fry@parl.gc.ca, Other Communications: Constituency Phone: 604-666-0135; Fax: 604-666-0114
Social Media: twitter.com/hedyfry, www.facebook.com/pages/Dr-Hedy-Fry/6172639058
Note: Web Site: www.hedyfry.com

Royal Galipeau, Ottawa - Orléans, Ontario, Conservative Party
613-995-1800, Fax: 613-995-6298,
royal.galipeau@parl.gc.ca; galipr1@parl.gc.ca, Other Communications: Constituency Phone: 613-995-1800; Fax: 613-590-1201
Social Media: twitter.com/GalipeauOrleans, www.facebook.com/royal.galipeau
Note: Web Site: www.royalgalipeau.ca

Cheryl Gallant, Renfrew - Nipissing - Pembroke, Ontario, Conservative Party
613-992-7712, 866-295-7165, Fax: 613-995-2561,
cheryl.gallant@parl.gc.ca; gallac1@parl.gc.ca, Other Communications: Constituency Phone: 613-732-4404; Fax: 613-732-4697
Social Media: twitter.com/cherylgallant, www.facebook.com/CherylGallantwww.linkedin.com/pub/cheryl-gallant/36/336/366
Note: Web Site: www.cherylgallant.com

House Leader, Liberal Party, Marc Garneau, C.C., C.D., B.Sc., Ph.D., F.C.A.S.I., Westmount - Ville-Marie, Québec, Liberal
613-996-7267, Fax: 613-995-8632,
marc.garneau@parl.gc.ca, Other Communications: Constituency Phone: 514-283-2013; Fax: 514-283-9790
Social Media: twitter.com/MarcGarneau, www.facebook.com/pages/Marc-Garneau/21128206560
Note: Web Site: www.marcgarneau.liberal.ca

Randall Garrison, Esquimalt - Juan de Fuca, British Columbia, New Democratic Party
613-996-2625, Fax: 613-996-9779,
randall.garrison@parl.gc.ca, Other Communications: Constituency Phone: 250-474-6505; 250-216-3926
Social Media: twitter.com/r_garrisonwww.linkedin.com/pub/randall-garrison/15/922/193
Note: Web Site: www.randallgarrison.ca

Réjean Genest, Shefford, Québec, New Democratic Party
613-992-5279, Fax: 613-992-7871, rejean.genest@parl.gc.ca
Note: Web Site: www.rejeangenest.ndp.ca

Jonathan Genest-Jourdain, Manicouagan, Québec, New Democratic Party
613-992-2363, Fax: 613-996-7954,
jonathan.genest-jourdain@parl.gc.ca, Other Communications: Constituency Phone: 418-538-1632; Fax: 418-538-1736
Note: Web Site: www.jonathangenestjourdain.ndp.ca

Alain Giguère, Marc-Aurèle-Fortin, Québec, New Democratic Party
613-992-2617, Fax: 613-992-6069, alain.giguere@parl.gc.ca, Other Communications: Constituency Phone: 450-965-0548; Fax: 450-965-3221
Note: Web Site: www.alaingiguere.ndp.ca

Parm Gill, Brampton - Springdale, Ontario, Conservative Party
613-995-4843, Fax: 613-995-7003, parm.gill@parl.gc.ca, Other Communications: Constituency Phone: 905-840-0505; Fax: 905-840-1778
Social Media: twitter.com/ParmGill, www.facebook.com/profile.php?id=539745780&ref=ts
Note: Web Site: www.parmgillmp.ca

Parliamentary Secretary to the Minister, Finance, Shelly Glover, Saint Boniface, Manitoba, Conservative Party
613-995-0579, Fax: 613-996-7571, shelly.glover@parl.gc.ca, Other Communications: Constituency Phone: 204-983-3183; Fax: 204-983-4274
Social Media: www.facebook.com/MPShellyGlover
Note: Web Site: www.shellyglover.ca

Yvon Godin, Acadie - Bathurst, New Brunswick, New Democratic Party
613-992-2165, Fax: 613-992-4558, yvon.godin@parl.gc.ca,

Other Communications: Constituency Phone: 506-548-7511; Fax: 506-548-7418
Social Media: www.facebook.com/pages/Yvon-Godin/78947535300
Note: Web Site: www.yvongodin.ndp.ca

Parliamentary Secretary to the Minister, Justice, Robert Goguen, Q.C., B.B.A, LL.B., Moncton - Riverview - Dieppe, New Brunswick, Conservative Party
613-992-8072, Fax: 613-992-8083, robert.goguen@parl.gc.ca, Other Communications: Constituency Phone: 506-382-7175
Social Media: twitter.com/robertrgoguen, www.facebook.com/VoteGoguen
Note: Web Site: www.www.robertgoguen.ca

Peter Goldring, Edmonton East, Alberta, Conservative Party
613-992-3821, Fax: 613-992-6898, peter.goldring@parl.gc.ca; goldrp1@parl.gc.ca, Other Communications: Constituency Phone: 780-495-3261; Fax: 780-495-5142
Note: Web Site: www.petergoldring.com

Responsible, Liberal Party Research Office, Hon. Ralph Goodale, P.C., B.A., LL.B., Wascana, Saskatchewan, Liberal
613-996-4743, Fax: 613-996-9790, ralph.goodale@parl.gc.ca; goodale@sasktel.net, Other Communications: ConstituencyPhone: 306-585-2202; Fax: 306-585-2280
Social Media: twitter.com/RalphGoodale, www.facebook.com/ralphgoodale
Note: Web Site: www.ralphgoodale.liberal.ca

Minister of State, Science & Technology & Federal Economic Development Agency for Southern Ontario, Hon. Dr. Gary Goodyear, P.C., D.C.,F.C.C.S.S., Cambridge, Ontario, Conservative Party
613-996-1307, Fax: 613-996-8340, gary.goodyear@parl.gc.ca; info@garygoodyear.com, Other Communications: Constituency Phone: 519-624-7440; Fax: 519-624-3517
Note: WebSites: www.garygoodyear.com (Personal Web Site); www.ic.gc.ca/eic/site/ic1.nsf/eng/02933.html (Industry Canada)

Minister of State, Sport, Hon. Bal Gosal, P.C., Bramalea - Gore - Malton, Ontario, Conservative Party
613-992-9105, Fax: 613-947-0443, bal.gosal@parl.gc.ca; bal.gosal@pch.gc.ca, Other Communications: Constituency Phone: 905-790-9211; Fax: 905-790-9507
Social Media: twitter.com/MinStateSport, www.facebook.com/pages/Bal-Gosal/155006724554020
Note: Web Sites: www.electbalgosal.ca (Personal Web Site); www.pch.gc.ca/pc-ch/minstr/gosal/biograph-eng.cfm (Canadian Heritage)

Parliamentary Secretary to the Minister, Public Works & Government Services, for Official Languages, & for the Economic Development Agency for the Regions of Québec, Jacques Gourde, Lotbinière - Chutes-de-la-Chaudière,Québec, Conservative Party
613-992-2639, Fax: 613-992-1018, jacques.gourde@parl.gc.ca, Other Communications: Constituency Phone: 418-836-0970; Fax: 418-836-6177
Social Media: twitter.com/JacquesGourde, www.facebook.com/jacques.gourde
Note: Web Sites: www.jacquesgourde.ca; www.tpsgc-pwgsc.gc.ca/apropos-about/scrtr-eng.html

Claude Gravelle, Nickel Belt, Ontario, New Democratic Party
613-995-9107, 800-267-4829, Fax: 613-995-9109, claude.gravelle@parl.gc.ca, Other Communications: Constituency Phone: 705-897-2222; Fax: 705-897-2223
Social Media: www.facebook.com/pages/Claude-Gravelle/35478778040
Note: Web Site: www.claudegravelle.ndp.ca

Nina Grewal, B.A., Fleetwood - Port Kells, British Columbia, Conservative Party
613-996-2205, Fax: 613-995-7139, nina.grewal@parl.gc.ca; grewan1@parl.gc.ca, Other Communications: Constituency Phone: 604-501-5900; Fax: 604-501-5901
Social Media: twitter.com/MPNinaGrewal, www.facebook.com/NinaGrewalMP
Note: Web Site: www.ninagrewal.ca

Sadia Groguhé, Saint-Lambert,Québec, New Democratic Party
613-998-5961, Fax: 613-954-0707, sadia.groguhe@parl.gc.ca
Note: Web Site: www.sadiagroguhe.ndp.ca

Prime Minister; Responsible, Conservative Party Research Office, Right Hon. Stephen Joseph Harper, P.C., B.A., M.A., Calgary Southwest, Alberta, Conservative Party
613-992-4211, Fax: 613-941-6900, stephen.harper@parl.gc.ca;pm@pm.gc.ca, Other Communications: Constituency Phone: 403-253-7990; Fax: 403-253-8203
Social Media: twitter.com/pmharper, www.facebook.com/group.php?gid=338690276206
Note: Web Sites: www.pm.gc.ca ((Prime Minister of Canada);www.conservative.ca/leader/stephen_harper (Party Web Site); Facebook: www.facebook.com/pmharper?ref=ts

Dan Harris, Scarborough Southwest, Ontario, New Democratic Party
613-995-0284, Fax: 613-996-6309, dan.harris@parl.gc.ca, Other Communications: Constituency Phone: 416-261-8613; Fax: 416-261-5268
Social Media: twitter.com/danharrisndp, www.facebook.com/pages/Dan-Harris/141741619229068
Note: Web Site: www.danharris.ndp.ca

Jack Harris, Q.C., B.A., LL.B., LL.M., St. John's East, Newfoundland & Labrador, New Democratic Party
613-996-7269, Fax: 613-992-2178, jack.harris@parl.gc.ca, Other Communications: Constituency Phone: 709-772-7171; Fax: 709-772-7175
Social Media: twitter.com/JackHarrisNDP, www.facebook.com/pages/Jack-Harris/38470344017
Note: Web Site: www.jackharris.ndp.ca

Richard M. Harris, Cariboo - Prince George, British Columbia, Conservative Party
613-995-6704, 800-668-4282, Fax: 613-996-9850, richard.harris@parl.gc.ca; harrir1@parl.gc.ca, Other Communications: Constituency Phone: 250-564-7771; Fax: 250-564-6224
Note: Web Site: www.dickharris.ca

Sana Hassainia, Verchères- Les Patriotes, Québec, New Democratic Party
613-996-2998, Fax: 613-995-1062, sana.hassainia@parl.gc.ca
Social Media: twitter.com/sanouchkawww.linkedin.com/pub/sana-hassainia/21/690/915
Note: Web Site: www.sanahassainia.ndp.ca

Member, Treasury Board Sub-Committee on the Strategic & Operating Review, Hon. Laurie Hawn, P.C., Edmonton Centre, Alberta, Conservative Party
613-992-4524, Fax: 613-943-0044, laurie.hawn@parl.gc.ca;Laurie.Hawn.C1@parl.gc.ca, Other Communications: Constituency Phone: 780-442-1888; Fax: 780-442-1891
Social Media: www.facebook.com/mplauriehawnwww.linkedin.com/pub/laurie-hawn/29/573/203
Note: Web Site: www.lauriehawnmp.ca

Bryan Hayes, Sault Ste. Marie, Ontario, Conservative Party
613-992-9723, Fax: 613-992-1954, bryan.hayes@parl.gc.ca, Other Communications: Constituency Phone: 705-941-2900; Fax: 705-941-2903
Social Media: www.facebook.com/group.php?gid=177199632299222
Note: Web Site: www.bryanhayes.ca

Russ Hiebert, B.A., M.B.A., LL.B., South Surrey - White Rock - Cloverdale, British Columbia, Conservative Party
613-947-4497, Fax: 613-947-4500, russ.hiebert@parl.gc.ca; info@russhiebert.ca, Other Communications: Constituency Phone: 604-542-9495; Fax: 604-542-9496
Social Media: twitter.com/HiebertRuss, www.facebook.com/russhiebert
Note: Web Site: www.russhiebert.ca

Jim Hillyer, Lethbridge, Alberta, Conservative Party
613-996-0633, Fax: 613-995-5752, jim.hillyer@parl.gc.ca; hillyer@jimhillyer.com, Other Communications: Constituency Phone: 403-320-0070
Note: Web Site: www.jimhillyer.com

Randy Hoback, Prince Albert, Saskatchewan, Conservative Party
613-995-3295, Fax: 613-995-6819, randy.hoback@parl.gc.ca; hobacr1@parl.gc.ca; hobacr2@parl.gc.ca, Other Communications: Constituency Phone: 306-953-8622; Fax: 306-953-8625
Social Media: twitter.com/RandyHobackMP, www.facebook.com/randyhobackmp
Note: Web Site: www.randyhobackmp.ca

Parliamentary Secretary to the Minister, Public Safety, Candice Hoeppner, Portage - Lisgar, Manitoba, Conservative Party
613-995-9511, 866-856-2090, Fax: 613-947-0313, candice.hoeppner@parl.gc.ca; candice.hoeppner.c1a@parl.gc.ca, Other Communications: Constituency Phone: 204-822-7440; Fax: 204-822-7445
Social Media: twitter.com/CHoeppnerMP, www.facebook.com/pages/Candice-Hoeppner/144290685591209
Note: Web Site: www.candicehoeppner.com

Ed Holder, B.A., London West, Conservative Party
613-996-6674, Fax: 613-996-6772, ed.holder@parl.gc.ca, Other Communications: Constituency Phone: 519-473-5955; Fax: 519-473-7333
Social Media: twitter.com/EdHolder_MP, www.facebook.com/group.php?gid=111702495519652www.linkedin.com/pub/ed-holder/23/b96/92b
Note: Web Site: www.edholder.ca

Ted Hsu, B.Sc., Ph.D., Kingston & the Islands, Ontario, Liberal
613-996-1955, Fax: 613-996-1958, ted.hsu@parl.gc.ca, Other Communications: Constituency Phone: 613-542-3243; Fax: 613-542-5461
Social Media: twitter.com/tedhsu, www.facebook.com/tedhsu75www.linkedin.com/in/tedhsu
Note: Web Site: www.tedhsu.ca

Carol Hughes, Algoma - Manitoulin - Kapuskasing, Ontario, New Democratic Party
613-996-5376, 800-463-3335, Fax: 613-995-6661, carol.hughes@parl.gc.ca, Other Communications: Constituency Phone: 705-848-8080; Fax: 705-848-1818
Social Media: twitter.com/CarolHughesMP, www.facebook.com/pages/Carol-Hughes/38326584416
Note: Web Site: www.carolhughes.ndp.ca

Bruce Hyer, M.Sc.F., Thunder Bay - Superior North, Ontario, New Democratic Party
613-996-4792, 888-266-8004, Fax: 613-996-9785, bruce.hyer@parl.gc.ca, Other Communications: Constituency Phone: 807-345-1818; Fax: 807-345-4752
Social Media: twitter.com/brucehyer, www.facebook.com/brucehyer
Note: Web Site: www.brucehyer.ca

Pierre Jacob, Brome - Missisquoi, Québec, New Democratic Party
613-947-8185, Fax: 613-947-8188, pierre.jacob@parl.gc.ca, Other Communications: Constituency Phone: 450-266-6062; Fax: 450-266-6064
Note: Web Site: www.pierrejacob.ndp.ca

Roxanne James, Scarborough Centre, Ontario, Conservative Party
613-992-6823, Fax: 613-943-1045, roxanne.james@parl.gc.ca, Other Communications: Constituency Phone: 416-752-2358; Fax: 416-752-4624
Note: Web Site: www.roxannejames.ca

Brian Jean, B.Sc., M.B.A., LL.B., Fort McMurray - Athabasca, Alberta, Conservative Party
613-992-1154, 877-532-6272, Fax: 613-992-4603, brian.jean@parl.gc.ca; brian.jean.c1@parl.gc.ca, Other Communications: Constituency Phone: 780-743-2201; Fax: 780-743-2287
Social Media: twitter.com/BrianJean_MP
Note: Web Site: www.brianjean.ca

Peter Julian, B.A., Burnaby - New Westminster, British Columbia, New Democratic Party
613-992-4214, Fax: 613-947-9500, peter.julian@parl.gc.ca; peter.julian.c1@parl.gc.ca, Other Communications: Constituency Phone: 604-775-5707; Fax: 604-775-5743
Social Media: twitter.com/MPJulian, www.facebook.com/MPPeterJulian
Note: Web Site: www.peterjulian.ndp.ca

Parliamentary Secretary to the Minister, Fisheries & Oceans & for the Asia-Pacific Gateway, Randy Kamp, B.A., Pitt Meadows - Maple Ridge - Mission, British Columbia, Conservative Party
613-947-4613, 888-255-8140, Fax: 613-947-4615, randy.kamp@parl.gc.ca;randy@randykamp.com, Other Communications: Constituency Phone: 604-466-2761; Fax: 604-466-7593
Social Media: twitter.com/RandyKamp_com
Note: Web Sites: www.randykamp.com;www.dfo-mpo.gc.ca/minister-ministre/bio-kamp-eng.htm

Hon. Jim Karygiannis, P.C., B.A.Sc, F.B.A., Scarborough - Agincourt, Ontario, Liberal
613-992-4501, Fax: 613-995-1612, jim.karygiannis@parl.gc.ca; jim@karygiannismp.com, Other Communications: Constituency Phone: 416-321-5454; Fax: 416-321-5456
Social Media: twitter.com/jimkarygiannis
Note: Web Site: www.karygiannismp.com

Parliamentary Secretary to the Minister, International Trade, for the Atlantic Canada Opportunities Agency & for the Atlantic Gateway, Gerald Keddy, B.A., South Shore - St. Margaret's, NovaScotia, Conservative Party
613-996-0877, 888-816-4446, Fax: 613-996-0878, gerald.keddy@parl.gc.ca; keddyg@ns.sympatico.ca, Other Communications: Constituency Phone: 902-527-5655; Fax: 902-527-5656
Social Media: twitter.com/GeraldKeddywww.linkedin.com/pub/gerald-keddy/27/540/9b3
Note: Web Sites: www.geraldkeddymp.ca; www.international.gc.ca/commerce/Gerald_Keddy.aspx

Matthew Kellway, Beaches - East York, Ontario, New Democratic Party
613-992-2115, Fax: 613-996-7942, matthew.kellway@parl.gc.ca, Other Communications: Constituency Phone: 416-467-0860; Fax: 416-467-0905
Social Media: twitter.com/MatthewKellway, www.facebook.com/matthewkellwaywww.linkedin.com/pub/matthew-kellway/19/976/763
Note: Web Site: www.matthewkellway.ndp.ca

Minister, Citizenship, Immigration, & Multiculturalism, Hon. Jason Kenney, P.C., Calgary Southeast, Alberta, Conservative Party
613-992-2235, Fax: 613-992-1920, jason.kenney@parl.gc.ca; calgary@jasonkenney.com, Other Communications: ConstituencyPhone: 403-225-3480; Fax: 403-225-3504
Social Media: twitter.com/kenneyjason, www.facebook.com/pages/Jason-Kenney/29829307640

Note: Web Sites: www.jasonkenney.com (Personal Web Site); www.cic.gc.ca/english/department/minister/index.asp
Minister, the Environment, Hon. Peter Kent, P.C., Thornhill, Ontario, Conservative Party
613-992-0253, Fax: 613-992-0887, peter.kent@parl.gc.ca; Minister@ec.gc.ca, Other Communications: Constituency Phone: 905-886-9911; Fax: 905-886-5267
Social Media: twitter.com/mpPeterKent; twitter.com/ec_minister, www.facebook.com/apps/application.php?id=135514873168072
Note: Web Sites: www.peterkent.ca (Personal Web Site); www.ec.gc.ca/default.asp?lang=En&n=B6832638-1 (Environment Canada); Twitter (French): www.twitter.com/ministre_ec
Chair, Standing Committee on Veterans Affairs, Greg Kerr, B.A., B.Ed., West Nova, Nova Scotia, Conservative Party
613-995-5711, 866-280-5302, Fax: 613-996-9857, greg.kerr@parl.gc.ca, Other Communications: Constituency Phone: 902-742-6808; Fax: 902-742-6815
Social Media: twitter.com/MPGregKerr, www.facebook.com/MPGregKerr
Note: Web Site: www.gregkerrmp.ca
Chair, Standing Committee on Human Resources, Skills, & Social Development, & the Status of Persons with Disabilities, Ed Komarnicki, Souris - Moose Mountain, Saskatchewan, Conservative Party
613-992-7685, 866-249-4697, Fax: 613-995-8908, ed.komarnicki@parl.gc.ca; komare1@parl.gc.ca; komare2@parl.gc.ca, Other Communications: Constituency Phone: 306-842-9000; Fax: 306-842-3854
Note: WebSite: www.edkom.ca
Daryl Kramp, Prince Edward - Hastings, Ontario, Conservative Party
613-992-5321, Fax: 613-996-8652, daryl.kramp@parl.gc.ca; daryl.kramp.c1@parl.gc.ca, Other Communications: Constituency Phone: 613-969-3800; Fax: 613-969-3803
Social Media: twitter.com/darylkramp
Note: Web Site: www.darylkramp.ca
Parliamentary Secretary to the Minister, Industry, Mike Lake, B.Comm., Edmonton - Mill Woods - Beaumont, Alberta, Conservative Party
613-995-8695, 866-670-0966, Fax: 613-995-6465, mike.lake@parl.gc.ca; LakeM@parl.gc.ca, Other Communications: Constituency Phone: 780-495-2149;Fax: 780-495-2147
Social Media: twitter.com/MikeLakeMP, www.facebook.com/MikeLakeMP
Note: Web Site: www.mikelake.ca
Deputy House Leader, Liberal Party, Kevin Lamoureux, Winnipeg North, Manitoba, Liberal
613-996-6417, Fax: 613-996-9713, kevin.lamoureux@parl.gc.ca, Other Communications: Constituency Phone: 204-984-1767; Fax: 204-984-1766
Social Media: www.facebook.com/gokevin.ca
Note: Web Site: www.kevinlamoureux.liberal.ca
François Lapointe, Montmagny - L'Islet - Kamouraska - Rivière-du-Loup, Québec, New Democratic Party
613-995-0265, Fax: 613-943-1229, francois.lapointe@parl.gc.ca, Other Communications: Constituency Phone: 418-248-1211; Fax: 418-248-1244
Social Media: twitter.com/F_Lapointe
Note: Web Site: www.francoislapointe.ndp.ca
Jean-François Larose, Repentigny, Québec, New Democratic Party
613-992-5257, Fax: 613-996-4338, jean-francois.larose@parl.gc.ca, Other Communications: Constituency Phone: 450-581-3896; Fax: 450-581-9958
Social Media: twitter.com/LaroseJF, www.facebook.com/pages/Jean-Francois-Larose/239453629399576
Note: Web Site: www.jeanfrancoislarose.ndp.ca
Alexandrine Latendresse, Louis-Saint-Laurent, Québec, New Democratic Party
613-996-4151, Fax: 613-954-2269, alexandrine.latendresse@parl.gc.ca, Other Communications: Constituency Phone: 418-626-5522; Fax: 418-626-5646
Social Media: www.facebook.com/pages/Alexandrine-Latendresse/25741845826
Note: Web Site: www.alexandrinelatendresse.ndp.ca
Caucus Chair, Conservative Party, Guy Lauzon, Stormont - Dundas - South Glengarry, Ontario, Conservative Party
613-992-2521, 888-805-2515, Fax: 613-996-2119, guy.lauzon@parl.gc.ca; info@guylauzon.ca, Other Communications: Constituency Phone: 613-937-3331; Fax: 613-937-3251
Note: Web Site: www.guylauzon.ca
Hélène Laverdière, Laurier - Sainte-Marie, Québec, New Democratic Party
613-992-6779, Fax: 613-995-8461, helene.laverdiere@parl.gc.ca
Social Media: www.facebook.com/Helene.Laverdiere.deputee
Note: Web Site: www.helenelaverdiere.ndp.ca
Minister, Transport, Infrastructure, & Communities; Minister, Economic Development Agency of Canada for the Regions of Québec, Hon. Denis Lebel, P.C., Roberval - Lac-Saint-Jean, Québec, Conservative Party
613-996-6236, 800-667-2768, Fax: 613-996-6252, denis.lebel@parl.gc.ca, Other Communications: Constituency Phone: 418-275-2768; Fax: 418-275-6535
Social Media: www.facebook.com/pages/Denis-Lebel/137888079554744
Note: Web Sites: www.denislebel.com (Personal Web Site); www.tc.gc.ca/eng/minister-menu.htm (Transport Canada); www.dec-ced.gc.ca/eng/minister/index.html (Canada Economic Development for Québec Regions)
Hon. Dominic Leblanc, P.C., B.A., LL.B., LL.M., Beauséjour, New Brunswick, Liberal
613-992-1020, 800-432-0311, Fax: 613-992-3053, dominic.leblanc@parl.gc.ca, Other Communications: Constituency Phone: 506-533-5700; Fax: 506-533-5888
Social Media: www.facebook.com/pages/Dominic-LeBlanc/19671249720
Note: Web Site: www.dominicleblanc.ca
Hélène LeBlanc, LaSalle - Émard, Québec, New Democratic Party
613-943-6636, Fax: 613-943-6637, helene.leblanc@parl.gc.ca, Other Communications: Constituency Phone: 514-363-0954; Fax: 514-367-5533
Social Media: twitter.com/HeleneLeBlanc, www.facebook.com/group.php?gid=196692170380605
Note: Web Site: www.heleneleblanc.ndp.ca
Ryan Leef, Yukon, Conservative Party
613-995-9368, Fax: 613-995-0945, ryan.leef@parl.gc.ca, Other Communications: Constituency Phone: 867-668-6565; Fax: 867-668-6570
Social Media: www.facebook.com/group.php?gid=192960574077986
Note: Web Site: www.voteryanleef.ca
Parliamentary Secretary to the Minister, Human Resources & Skills Development & to the Minister, Labour, Dr. Kellie Leitch, O.Ont., M.D., M.B.A., F.R.C.S. (C), Simcoe - Grey, Ontario, Conservative Party
613-992-4224, Fax: 613-992-2164, kellie.leitch@parl.gc.ca
Social Media: www.facebook.com/KellieLeitch#!/profile.php?id=731715176www.linkedin.com/pub/dr-k-kellie-leitch/17/584/96
Note: Web Site: www.kellieleitch.ca
Parliamentary Secretary to the Minister, Agriculture, Pierre Lemieux, B.Eng., M.Sc., Glengarry - Prescott - Russell, Ontario, Conservative Party
613-992-0490, 800-990-0490, Fax: 613-996-9123, pierre.lemieux@parl.gc.ca, Other Communications: Constituency Phone: 613-632-4162;Fax: 613-632-5668
Note: Web Site: www.pierrelemieux.ca
Megan Leslie, B.A. (Hons), LL.B., Halifax, Nova Scotia, New Democratic Party
613-995-7614, Fax: 613-992-8569, megan.leslie@parl.gc.ca, Other Communications: Constituency Phone: 902-426-8691; Fax: 902-426-8693
Social Media: twitter.com/meganleslieMP, www.facebook.com/MeganLeslieMPwww.linkedin.com/pub/megan-leslie/1a/369/886
Note: Web Site: www.meganleslie.ndp.ca
Parliamentary Secretary for Multiculturalism, Chungsen Leung, B.A., M.Sc., Willowdale, Ontario, Conservative Party
613-992-4964, Fax: 613-992-1158, chungsen.leung@parl.gc.ca; info@chungsenleung.ca, Other Communications: Constituency Phone: 416-223 2858; Fax: 416-223 9715
Social Media: twitter.com/csleungmp, www.facebook.com/Chungsen.CS.Leungwww.linkedin.com/in/csleung
Note: Web Site: www.chungsenleung.ca
Laurin Liu, Rivière-des-Mille-Iles, Québec, New Democratic Party
613-992-7330, Fax: 613-992-2602, laurin.liu@parl.gc.ca, Other Communications: Constituency Phone: 450-473-4864; Fax: 450-473-9043
Social Media: twitter.com/laurinliu, www.facebook.com/group.php?gid=229547190392110
Note: Web Site: www.laurinliu.ndp.ca
Wladyslaw Lizon, Mississauga East - Cooksville, Ontario, Conservative Party
613-996-0420, Fax: 613-996-0279, wladyslaw.lizon@parl.gc.ca, Other Communications: Constituency Phone: 905-566-0009; Fax: 905-566-0017
Social Media: www.facebook.com/VoteLizon
Note: Web Site: www.wladyslawlizon.ca
Ben Lobb, B.Sc. Admin., Huron - Bruce, Ontario, Conservative Party
613-992-8234, Fax: 613-995-6350, ben.lobb@parl.gc.ca, Other Communications: Constituency Phone: 519-524-6560; Fax: 519-612-1141
Note: Web Site: www.benlobb.com
Parliamentary Secretary to the Leader of the Government in the House of Commons, Tom Lukiwski, Regina - Lumsden - Lake Centre, Saskatchewan, Conservative Party
613-992-4573, 888-790-4747, Fax: 613-996-6885, tom.lukiwski@parl.gc.ca, Other Communications: Constituency Phone: 306-790-4747; Fax: 613-996-6885
Social Media: twitter.com/TomLukiwski, www.facebook.com/TomLukiwski
Note: Web Site: www.tomlukiwski.com
Dr. James Lunney, B.Sc., D.C., Nanaimo - Alberni, British Columbia, Conservative Party
613-992-5243, 866-390-7550, Fax: 613-992-9112, james.lunney@parl.gc.ca, Other Communications: Constituency Phone: 250-390-7550; Fax: 250-390-7551
Social Media: twitter.com/jameslunneymp
Note: Web Site: www.jameslunneymp.ca
Hon. Lawrence Macaulay, P.C., Cardigan, Prince Edward Island, Liberal
613-995-9325, Fax: 613-995-2754, lawrence.macaulay@parl.gc.ca, Other Communications: Constituency Phone: 902-838-4139; Fax: 902-838-3790
Social Media: www.facebook.com/lawrence.macaulay
Note: Web Site: www.lawrencemacaulay11.com
Minister, National Defence, Hon. Peter Gordon MacKay, Central Nova, Nova Scotia, Conservative Party
613-992-6022, Fax: 613-992-2337, peter.mackay@parl.gc.ca, Other Communications: Constituency Phone: 902-752-0226; Fax: 902-752-0284
Social Media: twitter.com/MacKayCPC
Note: Web Sites: www.petermackay.ca (Personal Web Site); www.forces.gc.ca/site/minister-ministre/index-eng.asp?WT.sv l=ministerLeft ((Department of National Defence &the Canadian Forces)
Chair, Standing Committee on Justice & Human Rights, Dave MacKenzie, Oxford, Ontario, Conservative Party
613-995-4432, Fax: 613-995-4433, dave.mackenzie@parl.gc.ca, Other Communications: Constituency Phone: 519-421-7214; Fax: 519-421-9704
Note: Web Site: www.davemackenzie.ca
Hoang Mai, Brossard - La Prairie,Québec, New Democratic Party
613-995-9301, Fax: 613-992-7273, hoang.mai@parl.gc.ca
Social Media: twitter.com/hoangmai_npdwww.linkedin.com/pub/hoang-mai/10/635/232
Note: Web Site: www.hoangmai.ndp.ca
Wayne Marston, Hamilton East - Stoney Creek, Ontario, New Democratic Party
613-992-6535, Fax: 613-992-7764, wayne.marston@parl.gc.ca, Other Communications: Constituency Phone: 905-662-4763; Fax: 905-662-2285
Social Media: twitter.com/WMarstonNDP, www.facebook.com/wayne.marston
Note: Web Site: www.waynemarston.ca
Chair, Standing Committee on Government Operations & Estimates, Pat Martin, Winnipeg Centre, Manitoba, New Democratic Party
613-992-5308, Fax: 613-992-2890, pat.martin@parl.gc.ca, Other Communications: Constituency Phone: 204-984-1675; Fax: 204-984-1676
Social Media: twitter.com/PatMartinMP, www.facebook.com/pages/Pat-Martin/6587713095
Note: Web Site: www.patmartin.ca
Brian Masse, B.A. (Hons.), Windsor West, Ontario, New Democratic Party
613-996-1541, Fax: 613-992-5397, brian.masse@parl.gc.ca, Other Communications: Constituency Phone: 519-255-1631; Fax: 519-255-7913
Social Media: twitter.com/BrianMasseMP, www.facebook.com/brianmassemp
Note: Web Site: www.brianmasse.ca
Irene Mathyssen, B.A. (Hons), B.Ed., London - Fanshawe, Ontario, New Democratic Party
613-995-2901, Fax: 613-943-8717, irene.mathyssen@parl.gc.ca, Other Communications: Constituency Phone: 519-685-4745; Fax: 519-685-1462
Social Media: twitter.com/irenemathyssen, www.facebook.com/pages/Irene-Mathyssen/7711496179
Note: Web Site: www.irenemathyssen.ca
Leader, Green Party of Canada, Elizabeth May, O.C., LL.B., Saanich - Gulf Islands, British Columbia, G
613-996-1119, Fax: 613-996-0850, elizabeth.may@parl.gc.ca, Other Communications: Constituency Phone: 250-657-2000; Fax: 250-657-2004
Social Media: twitter.com/elizabethmay, www.facebook.com/ElizabethMayGreenLeaderwww.linkedin.com/pub/elizabeth-may/3/a91/69
Note: Web Site: www.elizabethmay.ca
Colin Mayes, Okanagan - Shuswap, British Columbia, Conservative Party
613-995-9095, 800-665-5040, Fax: 613-992-3195, colin.mayes@parl.gc.ca, Other Communications: Constituency Phone: 250-260-5020; Fax: 250-260-5025
Note: Web Site: www.colinmayes.ca
Hon. John McCallum, P.C., B.A., Ph.D., Markham - Unionville, Ontario, Liberal

613-996-3374, Fax: 613-992-3921, john.mccallum@parl.gc.ca, Other Communications: Constituency Phone: 905-479-8100; Fax: 905-479-3440
Social Media: twitter.com/JohnMcCallumMP, www.facebook.com/McCallumj1www.linkedin.com/pub/john-mccallum/24/78a/217
Note: Web Site: www.johnmccallum.liberal.ca

Phil McColeman, Brant, Ontario, Conservative Party
613-992-3118, Fax: 613-992-6382, phil.mccoleman@parl.gc.ca, Other Communications: Constituency Phone: 519-754-4300; Fax: 519-751-8177
Social Media: twitter.com/Phil4Brant, www.facebook.com/profile.php?id=544956732
Note: Web Site: www.philmccolemanmp.ca

David McGuinty, B.A., LL.B, LL.M., Ottawa South, Ontario, Liberal
613-992-3269, Fax: 613-995-1534, david.mcguinty@parl.gc.ca, Other Communications: Constituency Phone: 613-990-8640; Fax: 613-990-2592
Social Media: twitter.com/DavidMcGuinty, www.facebook.com/davidmcguinty
Note: Web Site: www.davidmcguinty.liberal.ca

Hon. John McKay, P.C., B.A., LL.B., Scarborough - Guildwood, Ontario, Liberal
613-992-1447, Fax: 613-992-8968, john.mckay@parl.gc.ca, Other Communications: Constituency Phone: 416-283-1226; Fax: 416-283-7935
Social Media: twitter.com/honjohnmckaymp, www.facebook.com/honjohnmckaymp
Note: Web Site: www.johnmckaymp.on.ca

Parliamentary Secretary to the Minister, National Revenue, Cathy McLeod, Kamloops - Thompson - Cariboo, British Columbia, Conservative Party
613-995-6931, 877-619-3332, Fax: 613-995-9897, cathy.mcleod@parl.gc.ca, Other Communications: Constituency Phone: 250-851-4991; Fax: 250-851-4994
Social Media: twitter.com/Cathy_McLeod, www.facebook.com/cathymcleodMP
Note: Web Site: www.cathymcleod.com

Costas Menegakis, Richmond Hill, Ontario, Conservative Party
613-992-3802, Fax: 613-996-1954, costas.menegakis@parl.gc.ca; costas.menegakis.c1@parl.gc.ca, Other Communications: Constituency Phone: 905-770-4440; Fax: 905-770-2221
Social Media: www.facebook.com/pages/Costas-Menegakis/121337297944082
Note: Web Site: www.costasmenegakis.ca

Minister of State, Finance, Hon. Ted Menzies, P.C., Macleod, Alberta, Conservative Party
613-995-8471, 866-636-9437, Fax: 613-996-9770, ted.menzies@parl.gc.ca; ted.menzies@fin.gc.ca, Other Communications: Constituency Phone: 403-625-5532; Fax: 403-625-5592
Social Media: twitter.com/TedMenzies
Note: Web Sites: www.tedmenzies.ca (Personal Web Sites); www.fin.gc.ca/comment/state-etat-eng.asp (Department of Finance Canada

Chair, Standing Committee on International Trade, Hon. Rob Merrifield, P.C., Yellowhead, Alberta, Conservative Party
613-992-1653, 800-268-7117, Fax: 613-992-3459, rob.merrifield@parl.gc.ca, Other Communications: Constituency Phone: 780-723-6068; Fax: 780-723-5060
Note: Web Site: www.merrifieldmp.com

Élaine Michaud, B.A., Portneuf - Jacques-Cartier, Quebec, New Democratic Party
613-992-2798, Fax: 613-995-1637, elaine.michaud@parl.gc.ca, Other Communications: Constituency Phone: 418-873-5010; Fax: 418-873-5031
Social Media: www.facebook.com/group.php?gid=219072564786090
Note: Web Site: www.elainemichaud.ndp.ca

Chair, Standing Committee on Agriculture & Agri-Food, Larry Miller, Bruce - Grey - Owen Sound, Ontario, Conservative Party
613-996-5191, Fax: 613-952-0979, larry.miller@parl.gc.ca, Other Communications: Constituency Phone: 519-371-1059; Fax: 519-371-1752
Note: Web Site: www.larrymiller.ca

Christine Moore, Abitibi-Témiscamingue, Quebec, New Democratic Party
613-996-3250, 800-567-6433, Fax: 613-992-3672, christine.moore@parl.gc.ca; christine.moore.c1@parl.gc.ca, Other Communications: Constituency Phone: 819-762-3733; Fax: 819-762-8732
Social Media: www.facebook.com/group.php?gid=146347468767378
Note: Web Site: www.christinemoore.ndp.ca

Minister, Canadian Heritage & Official Languages, Hon. James Moore, P.C., B.A., Port Moody - Westwood - Port Coquitlam, British Columbia, Conservative Party
613-992-9650, Fax: 613-992-9868, james.moore@parl.gc.ca; james.moore@pch.gc.ca, Other Communications: Constituency Phone: 604-937-5650; Fax: 604-937-5601
Social Media: twitter.com/JamesMoore_org, www.facebook.com/jamesmoore.org
Note: Web Sites: www.jamesmoore.org (Personal Web Site);www.pch.gc.ca/pc-ch/minstr/moore/index-eng.cfm (Canadian Heritage)

Chair, Standing Committee on Canadian Heritage, Hon. Rob Moore, P.C., B.B.A., LL.B., Fundy Royal, New Brunswick, Conservative Party
613-996-2332, 866-433-4677, Fax: 613-995-4286, rob.moore@parl.gc.ca, Other Communications: Constituency Phone: 506-832-4200; Fax: 506-832-4235
Social Media: twitter.com/RobMoore_CPC
Note: Web Site: www.robmooremp.com

Dany Morin, Chicoutimi - Le Fjord, Québec, New Democratic Party
613-992-7207, 866-599-4999, Fax: 613-992-0431, dany.morin@parl.gc.ca, Other Communications: Constituency Phone: 418-698-5648; Fax: 418-698-5611
Social Media: twitter.com/drdanymorin
Note: Web Site: www.danymorin.ndp.ca

Isabelle Morin, Notre-Dame-de-Grâce - Lachine, Québec, New Democratic Party
613-995-2251, Fax: 613-996-1481, isabelle.morin@parl.gc.ca, Other Communications: Constituency Phone: 514-654-0841
Social Media: twitter.com/IsabelleMorinMP, www.facebook.com/IsabelleMorinMP
Note: Web Site: www.isabellemorin.ndp.ca

Marc-André Morin, Laurentides - Labelle, Québec, New Democratic Party
613-992-2289, Fax: 613-992-9864, marc-andre.morin@parl.gc.ca, Other Communications: Constituency Phone: 819-326-5098; Fax: 819-326-8262
Note: Web Site: www.marcandremorin.ndp.ca

Marie-Claude Morin, Saint-Hyacinthe - Bagot, Québec, New Democratic Party
613-996-4585, Fax: 613-992-1815, marie-claude.morin@parl.gc.ca, Other Communications: Constituency Phone: 450-771-0505; Fax: 450-771-0767
Social Media: www.facebook.com/profile.php?id=100000609131071
Note: Web Site: www.marieclaudemorin.ndp.ca

Maria Mourani, B.A., M.A., Ahuntsic, Québec, BQ
613-992-0983, Fax: 613-992-1932, maria.mourani@parl.gc.ca, Other Communications: Constituency Phone: 514-383-3709; Fax: 514-383-3589
Social Media: www.facebook.com/group.php?gid=2314743183
Note: Web Site: www.mariamourani.org

Thomas J. Mulcair, B.C.L., LL.B., Outremont, Québec, New Democratic Party
613-995-7691, Fax: 613-995-0114, thomas.mulcair@parl.gc.ca, Other Communications: Constituency Phone: 514-736-2727; Fax: 514-736-2726
Note: Web Site: www.www.thomasmulcair.ndp.ca

Joyce Murray, Vancouver Quadra, British Columbia, Liberal
613-992-2430, Fax: 613-995-0770, joyce.murray@parl.gc.ca, Other Communications: Constituency Phone: 604-664-9220; Fax: 604-664-9221
Social Media: twitter.com/joycemurray, www.facebook.com/mpjoycemurraywww.linkedin.com/pub/joyce-murray/31/144/b64
Note: Web Site: www.joycemurray.liberal.ca

Pierre Nantel, Longueuil - Pierre-Boucher, Québec, New Democratic Party
613-992-8514, Fax: 613-992-2744, pierre.nantel@parl.gc.ca, Other Communications: Constituency Phone: 450-928-4288; Fax: 450-928-4293
Social Media: twitter.com/pierrenantel, www.facebook.com/pierrenantel
Note: Web Site: www.pierrenantel.ndp.ca

Peggy Nash, B.A. (Hons.), Parkdale - High Park, Ontario, New Democratic Party
613-992-2936, Fax: 613-995-1629, peggy.nash@parl.gc.ca, Other Communications: Constituency Phone: 416-769-5072; Fax: 416-769-8343
Social Media: twitter.com/peggynash_, www.facebook.com/pages/Peggy-Nash/120766445468
Note: Web Site: www.peggynash.ndp.ca

Jamie Nicholls, B.A., M.A., Vaudreuil - Soulanges, Quebec, New Democratic Party
613-957-3744, Fax: 613-952-0874, jamie.nicholls@parl.gc.ca
Social Media: twitter.com/JPNichollsNPD, www.facebook.com/pages/Jamie-Nicholls/158685237528810 www.linkedin.com/pub/jamie-nicholls/11/76/452
Note: Web Site: www.jamienicholls.ndp.ca

Attorney General of Canada; Minister, Justice, Hon. Robert Douglas Nicholson, P.C., Q.C., B.A., LL.B., Niagara Falls, Ontario, Conservative Party
613-995-1547, Fax: 613-992-7910, rob.nicholson@parl.gc.ca, Other Communications: Constituency Phone: 905-353-9590; Fax: 905-353-9588
Note: Web Sites: www.robnicholson.ca (Personal Web Site); www.canada.justice.gc.ca/eng/mag-mpg/index.html (Department of Justice Canada)

Rick Norlock, Northumberland - Quinte West, Ontario, Conservative Party
613-992-8585, Fax: 613-995-7536, rick.norlock@parl.gc.ca; rick@ricknorlock.ca, Other Communications: Constituency Phone: 905-372-8757; Fax: 905-372-1500
Social Media: twitter.com/RickNorlock, www.facebook.com/group.php?gid=27428322342
Note: Web Site: www.ricknorlock.ca

José Nunez-Melo, B. Gest., Laval, Québec, New Democratic Party
Fax: 613-996-1195, jose.nunez-melo@parl.gc.ca, Other Communications: Constituency Phone: 450-686-2562; Fax: 450-686-0450
Social Media: www.facebook.com/profile.php?id=1585725906
Note: Web Site: www.josenunezmelo.ndp.ca

Parliamentary Secretary to the Minister, Foreign Affairs, Deepak Obhrai, Calgary East, Alberta, Conservative Party
613-947-4566, Fax: 613-947-4569, deepak.obhrai@parl.gc.ca; deepak@deepakobhrai.com, Other Communications: Constituency Phone: 403-207-3030; Fax: 403-207-3035
Social Media: twitter.com/deepakobhrai, www.facebook.com/profile.php?id=1058993450
Note: Web Site: www.deepakobhrai.com;www.international.gc.ca/ministers-ministres/deepak_obhrai.aspx?view=d

Minister of State; Chief Government Whip; Whip, Conservative Party of Canada, Hon. Gordon O'Connor, P.C., B.A., B.Sc., Carleton - Mississippi Mills, Ontario, Conservative Party
613-992-1119, Fax: 613-992-1043, gordon.oconnor@parl.gc.ca, Other Communications: Constituency Phone: 613-592-3469; Fax: 613-592-4756
Social Media: www.facebook.com/pages/Gordon-OConnor/228442573837062?sk=info
Note: Web Site: www.gordonoconnor.ca (Personal Web Site)

Minister, International Cooperation, Hon. Beverley J. (Bev) Oda, P.C., B.A., Durham, Ontario, Conservative Party
613-992-2792, 866-436-1141, Fax: 613-992-2794, bev.oda@parl.gc.ca, Other Communications: Constituency Phone: 905-697-1699; Fax: 905-697-1678
Note: Web Sites: www.bevoda.ca (Personal Web Site); www.acdi-cida.gc.ca/acdi-cida/acdi-cida.nsf/eng/NIC-5494720-J79 (CanadianInternational Development Agency)

Minister, Natural Resources, Hon. Joe Oliver, P.C., B.A., BCL, MBA, Eglinton - Lawrence, Ontario, Conservative Party
613-992-6361, Fax: 613-992-9791, joe.oliver@parl.gc.ca; Minister.Ministre@NRCan-RNCan.gc.ca, Other Communications: Constituency Phone: 416-781-5583; Fax: 416-781-5586
Social Media: twitter.com/joeoliver1, www.facebook.com/profile.php?id=707035179www.linkedin.com/pub/joseph-oliver/4/267/73b
Note: Web Sites: www.joeoliver.ca (Personal Web Site); www.nrcan.gc.ca/com/deptmini/minmin/minmin-biobio-eng.php (Natural Resources Canada)

Tilly O'Neill-Gordon, Miramichi, Conservative Party
613-992-5335, Fax: 613-996-8418, tilly.oneillgordon@parl.gc.ca, Other Communications: Constituency Phone: 506-778-8448; Fax: 506-778-8150
Social Media: www.facebook.com/profile.php?id=1048071578
Note: Web Site: www.tillygordon.ca

Ted Opitz, Etobicoke Centre, Ontario, Conservative Party
613-947-5000, Fax: 613-947-4276, ted.opitz@parl.gc.ca, Other Communications: Constituency Phone: 416-249-7322; Fax: 416-249-6117
Social Media: twitter.com/TedOpitz, www.facebook.com/profile.php?id=720902831&sk=infowww.linkedin.com/pub/ted-opitz/13/a61/84b
Note: Web Site: www.tedopitz.ca

Deputy Whip, Massimo Pacetti, B.Comm., F.C.G.A., Saint-Léonard - Saint-Michel, Québec, Liberal
613-995-9414, Fax: 613-992-8523, massimo.pacetti@parl.gc.ca, Other Communications: Constituency Phone: 514-256-4548; Fax: 416-256-8828
Social Media: www.facebook.com/pages/Massimo-Pacetti/22800125080www.linkedin.com/pub/massimo-pacetti/29/264/535
Note: Web Site: www.massimopacetti.liberal.ca

Annick Papillon, B.A., Québec,Quebec, New Democratic Party
613-992-8865, Fax: 613-995-2805, annick.papillon@parl.gc.ca
Note: Web Site: www.annickpapillon.ndp.ca

Minister, Industry; Minister of State, Agriculture, Hon. Christian Paradis, P.C., Mégantic - L'Érable, Québec, Conservative Party
613-995-1377, Fax: 613-943-1562, christian.paradis@parl.gc.ca; paradc1@parl.gc.ca, Other Communications: ConstituencyPhone: 418-338-2903; Fax: 418-338-3631
Social Media: twitter.com/christianparad
Note: Web Sites: www.christianparadis.com;

www.ic.gc.ca/eic/site/ic1.nsf/eng/h_00279.html;www4.agr.gc.ca/AAFC-AAC/display-afficher.do?id=1262962138890&lang=eng
Claude Patry, Jonquière - Alma, Quebec, New Democratic Party
613-995-8425, Fax: 613-947-2748, claude.patry@parl.gc.ca, Other Communications: Constituency Phone: 418-695-7554; Fax: 418-695-4467
Note: Web Site: www.claudepatry.ndp.ca
LaVar Payne, Medicine Hat, Alberta, Conservative Party
613-992-4516, Fax: 613-992-6181, lavar.payne@parl.gc.ca; paynel1@parl.gc.ca; paynel2@parl.gc.ca, Other Communications: Constituency Phone: 403-528-4698; Fax: 403-528-4365
Social Media: twitter.com/LaVarMP, www.facebook.com/profile.php?id=733796432www.linkedin.com/pub/lavar-payne/16/318/767
Note: Web Site: www.lavarpayne.ca
Ève Péclet, La Pointe-de-l'Ile, Québec, New Democratic Party
613-995-6327, Fax: 613-996-5173, eve.peclet@parl.gc.ca, Other Communications: Constituency Phone: 514-645-0101; Fax: 514-645-0032
Note: Web Site: www.evepeclet.ndp.ca
Minister, Intergovernmental Affairs; President, Queen's Privy Council for Canada, Hon. Peter Penashue, P.C., Labrador, Newfoundland & Labrador, Conservative Party
613-996-4630, Fax: 613-996-7132, peter.penashue@parl.gc.ca, Other Communications: ConstituencyPhone: 709-927-5210; Fax: 709-927-5830
Social Media: twitter.com/PeterPenashue, www.facebook.com/peterpenashue
Note: Web Site: www.pco-bcp.gc.ca/aia/index.asp?lang=eng&page=min (Intergovernmental Affairs)
Manon Perreault, Montcalm, Québec, New Democratic Party
613-992-0164, manon.perreault@parl.gc.ca
Social Media: twitter.com/MPerreaultNPD
Note: Web Site: www.manonperreault.ndp.ca
François Pilon, Laval - Les Iles, Québec, New Democratic Party
613-992-2659, Fax: 613-992-9469, francois.pilon@parl.gc.ca, Other Communications: Constituency Phone: 450-689-5124; Fax: 450-689-5092
Social Media: twitter.com/francoispilon
Note: Web Site: www.francoispilon.ndp.ca
Acting House Leader, Bloc Québécois; Chair, Bloc Québécois Caucus, Louis Plamondon, B.A.Ped., B.A.An, Bas-Richelieu - Nicolet - Bécancour, Quebec, BQ
613-995-9241, Fax: 613-995-6784, louis.plamondon@parl.gc.ca;louis.plamondon.c1@parl.gc.ca, Other Communications: Constituency Phone: 450-742-0479; Fax: 450-742-1976
Social Media: www.facebook.com/LouisPlamondonBQwww.linkedin.com/pub/louis-plamondon/36/b11/771
Note: Web Site: www.louisplamondon.com
Parliamentary Secretary to the Minister, Transport, Infrastructure & Communities, and for the Federal Economic Development Agency for Southern Ontario, Pierre Poilievre, Nepean - Carleton, Ontario, Conservative Party
613-992-2772, Fax: 613-992-1209, pierre.poilievre@parl.gc.ca, Other Communications: Constituency Phone: 613-990-4300; Fax: 613-990-4333
Social Media: www.facebook.com/pierre.poilievre
Note: Web Site: www.resultsforyou.ca
Chair, Standing Committee on Procedure & House Affairs, Joe Preston, Elgin - Middlesex - London, Ontario, Conservative Party
613-990-7769, Fax: 613-996-0194, joe.preston@parl.gc.ca; joe@joeprestonmp.ca, Other Communications: Constituency Phone: 519-637-2255; Fax: 519-637-3358
Social Media: twitter.com/Joe_Preston, www.facebook.com/Burgerguywww.linkedin.com/pub/joe-preston/12/1a4/5a
Note: Web Site: www.joeprestonmp.ca
Anne Minh-Thu Quach, Beauharnois - Salaberry, Québec, New Democratic Party
613-995-2540, Fax: 613-941-3300, anneminh-thu.quach@parl.gc.ca; anneminh-thu.quach.A1@parl.gc.ca, Other Communications: Constituency Phone: 450-371-0644; Fax: 450-371-3330
Social Media: twitter.com/AnneMTQuach, www.facebook.com/group.php?gid=248314418518470
Note: Web Site: www.anneminhthuquach.ndp.ca
Interim Party Leader, Liberal Party of Canada, Hon. Robert "Bob" Keith Rae, P.C., O.C., O.Ont., Q.C., B.A., B.Ph., LL.B., Toronto Centre, Ontario, Liberal
613-992-5234, Fax: 613-996-9607, bob.rae@parl.gc.ca;info@bobrae.ca, Other Communications: Constituency Phone: 416-954-2222; Fax: 416-954-9649
Social Media: twitter.com/bobraemp, www.facebook.com/pages/Bob-Rae/8034824801
Note: Web Site: www.bobrae.ca
John Rafferty, B.A., B.E., Thunder Bay - Rainy River, Ontario, New Democratic Party
613-992-3061, 800-667-6186, Fax: 613-995-3515, Rae.B@parl.gc.ca, Other Communications: Constituency Phone: 416-954-2222; Fax: 416-954-9649
Social Media: twitter.com/JohnRaffertyMP, www.facebook.com/pages/John-Rafferty/19098359045
Note: Web Site: www.johnrafferty.ndp.ca
Minister, Labour, Hon. Lisa Raitt, P.C., B.Sc., M.Sc., LL.B., Halton, Ontario, Conservative Party
613-996-7046, Fax: 613-992-0851, lisa.raitt@parl.gc.ca; lisa.raitt@hrsdc-rhdcc.gc.ca, Other Communications: Constituency Phone: 905-693-0166;Fax: 905-693-0704
Social Media: twitter.com/lraitt, www.facebook.com/lisaraitt
Note: Web Sites: www.lisaraittmp.ca (Personal Web Site); www.hrsdc.gc.ca/eng/corporate/labour/minister/index.shtml (Labour, Human Resources & SkillsDevelopment Canada)
Chair, Standing Committee on Finance, James Rajotte, B.A., Edmonton - Leduc, Alberta, Conservative Party
613-992-3594, Fax: 613-992-3616, james.rajotte@parl.gc.ca, Other Communications: Constituency Phone: 780-495-4351; Fax: 780-495-4485
Social Media: twitter.com/JamesRajotte, www.facebook.com/group.php?gid=134492869959367www.linkedin.com/pub/james-rajotte/31/695/a57
Note: Web Site: www.jamesrajottemp.ca
Brent Rathgeber, Q.C., B.A., LL.B., Edmonton - St. Albert, Alberta, Conservative Party
613-996-4722, Fax: 613-995-8880, brent.rathgeber@parl.gc.ca; brent.rathgeber.c1@parl.gc.ca, Other Communications: Constituency Phone: 780-459-0809; Fax: 780-460-1246
Social Media: twitter.com/brentrathgeber, www.facebook.com/profile.php?id=531147984
Note: Web Site: www.brentrathgeber.ca
Mathieu Ravignat, M.A. (Political Science), Pontiac, Québec, New Democratic Party
613-992-5516, Fax: 613-992-6802, mathieu.ravignat@parl.gc.ca; mathieu.ravignat.c1@parl.gc.ca, Other Communications: Constituency Phone: 819-281-2626; Fax: 819-281-2755
Social Media: twitter.com/MathieuRavignat, www.facebook.com/mathieu.ravignat
Note: Web Site: www.mathieuravignat.ndp.ca
Francine Raynault, Joliette,Québec, New Democratic Party
613-996-6910, Fax: 613-995-2818, francine.raynault@parl.gc.ca
Social Media: www.facebook.com/profile.php?id=100002301630440
Note: Web Site: www.francineraynault.ndp.ca
Hon. Geoff Regan, P.C., B.A., LL.B., Halifax West, Nova Scotia, Liberal
613-996-3085, Fax: 613-996-6988, geoff.regan@parl.gc.ca; geoff@geoffregan.ca, Other Communications: Constituency, Phone: 902-426-2217; Fax: 902-426-8339
Social Media: twitter.com/geoffregan, www.facebook.com/pages/Geoff-Regan/19891033712
Note: Web Site: www.geoffregan.ca
Scott Reid, B.A., M.A., Lanark - Frontenac - Lennox - Addington, Ontario, Conservative Party
613-947-2277, 866-277-1577, Fax: 613-947-2278, scott.reid@parl.gc.ca, Other Communications: Constituency Phone: 613-257-8130; Fax: 613-257-4371
Social Media: www.facebook.com/profile.php?id=650980283&sk=info
Note: Web Site: www.scottreid.ca
Parliamentary Secretary to the Minister, Environment, Michelle Rempel, Calgary Centre-North, Alberta, Conservative Party
613-992-4275, Fax: 613-947-9475, michelle.rempel@parl.gc.ca, Other Communications: Constituency Phone: 403-216-7777; Fax: 403-230-4368
Social Media: twitter.com/MichelleRempel; twitter.com/MPRempelOffice, www.facebook.com/group.php?gid=126806667378661
Note: Web Site: www.michellerempel.ca
Blake Richards, Wild Rose, Alberta, Conservative Party
613-996-5152, 800-667-0410, Fax: 613-947-4601, blake.richards@parl.gc.ca; blake@blakerichards.ca, Other Communications: Constituency Phone: 403-948-5103; Fax: 403-948-0879
Social Media: twitter.com/BlakeRichardsMP, www.facebook.com/vote.blake
Note: Web Site: www.blakerichards.ca
Lee Richardson, Calgary Centre, Alberta, Conservative Party
613-995-1561, Fax: 613-995-1862, Rickford.G@parl.gc.ca; lee@leerichardson.ca, Other Communications: Constituency Phone: 403-244-1880; Fax: 403-245-3468
Social Media: www.facebook.com/pages/Lee-Richardson/22844654968
Note: Web Site: www.leerichardson.ca
Parliamentary Secretary to the Minister, Aboriginal Affairs & Northern Development, the Canadian Northern Economic Development Agency, & for the Federal Economic DevelopmentInitiative for Northern Ontario, Greg Rickford, MBA, Kenora, Ontario, Conservative Party
613-996-1161, 866-710-0008, Fax: 613-996-1759, greg.rickford@parl.gc.ca, Other Communications: Constituency Phone: 807-468-2170; Fax: 807-468-4896
Social Media: twitter.com/gregrickford
Note: Web Site: www.gregrickford.ca
Minister, Agriculture & Agri-Food; Minister for the Canadian Wheat Board, Hon. Gerry Ritz, P.C., Battlefords - Lloydminster, Saskatchewan, Conservative Party
613-995-7080, Fax: 613-996-8472, gerry.ritz@parl.gc.ca, Other Communications: Constituency Phone: 306-445-2004; Fax: 306-445-0207
Note: Web Site: www.gerryritzmp.com (Personal Web Site);www4.agr.gc.ca/AAFC-AAC/display-afficher.do?id=1203439690684&lang=eng
Jean Rousseau, B.Sc., Compton - Stanstead, Québec, New Democratic Party
613-995-2024, Fax: 613-992-1696, jean.rousseau@parl.gc.ca, Other Communications: Constituency Phone: 819-347-2598; Fax: 819-347-3583
Note: Web Site: www.jeanrousseau.ndp.ca
Romeo Saganash, Abitibi - Baie-James - Nunavik - Eeyou, Quebec, New Democratic Party
613-992-3030, Fax: 613-996-0828, romeo.saganash@parl.gc.ca, Other Communications: Constituency Phone: 819-824-2942; Fax: 819-824-2958
Social Media: twitter.com/RomeoSaganash, www.facebook.com/RomeoSaganash
Note: Web Site: www.romeosaganash.ndp.ca
Jasbir Sandhu, B.A., M.B.A., Surrey North, British Columbia, New Democratic Party
613-992-2922, Fax: 613-992-0252, jasbir.sandhu@parl.gc.ca, Other Communications: Constituency Phone:
Social Media: twitter.com/jasbirsandhu, www.facebook.com/sandhuj
Note: Web Site: www.jasbirsandhu.ndp.ca
Deputy Speaker; Chair, Committees of the Whole, Denise Savoie, B.A., M.A., M.Ed., Victoria, British Columbia, New Democratic Party
613-996-2358, Fax: 613-952-1458, denise.savoie@parl.gc.ca, Other Communications: Constituency Phone: 250-363-3600; Fax: 250-363-8422
Social Media: twitter.com/denisesavoie, www.facebook.com/DeniseSavoieVictoria
Note: Web Site: www.denisesavoie.ca
Parliamentary Secretary to the President, Treasury Board & for Western Economic Diversification, Andrew Saxton, B.A., North Vancouver, British Columbia, Conservative Party
613-995-1225, Fax: 613-992-7319, andrew.saxton@parl.gc.ca, Other Communications: Constituency Phone: 604-775-6333; Fax: 604-775-6332
Social Media: twitter.com/AndrewSaxton1, www.facebook.com/andrewsaxtonjrwww.linkedin.com/pub/andrew-saxton-jr/0/6b5/5a4
Note: Web Site: www.andrewsaxton.ca
Caucus Chair, Liberal Party, Francis Scarpaleggia, B.A., M.A., M.B.A., Lac-Saint-Louis, Québec, Liberal
613-995-8281, Fax: 613-995-0528, francis.scarpaleggia@parl.gc.ca, Other Communications: Constituency Phone: 514-695-6661; Fax: 514-695-3708
Social Media: twitter.com/scarpaleggiamp, www.facebook.com/Fscarpaleggia
Note: Web Site: www.scarpaleggia.ca
Speaker of the House of Commons, Hon. Andrew Scheer, Regina - Qu'Appelle, Saskatchewan, Conservative Party
613-992-4593, Fax: 613-996-3120, andrew.scheer@parl.gc.ca; info@andrewscheer.ca, Other Communications: Constituency Phone: 306-790-4727; Fax: 306-790-4728
Social Media: twitter.com/andrewscheer, www.facebook.com/AndrewScheerMP
Note: Web Site: www.andrewmp.ca
Gary Schellenberger, Perth - Wellington, Ontario, Conservative Party
613-992-6124, 866-303-1400, Fax: 613-998-7902, gary.schellenberger@parl.gc.ca, Other Communications: Constituency Phone: 519-273-1400; Fax: 519-273-9045
Social Media: twitter.com/GSchellenberger, www.facebook.com/gschellenberger
Note: Web Site: www.schellenberger.ca
Kyle Seeback, B.A., LL.B., Brampton West, Ontario, Conservative Party
613-995-5381, Fax: 613-995-6796, kyle.seeback@parl.gc.ca, Other Communications: Constituency Phone: 905-846-0076; Fax: 905-846-3901
Social Media: twitter.com/KyleSeeback
Note: Web Site: www.kyleseeback.com
Djaouida Sellah, Saint-Bruno - Saint-Hubert, Québec, New Democratic Party
613-996-2416, Fax: 613-995-6973, djaouida.sellah@parl.gc.ca, Other Communications: Constituency Phone: 450-926-5980; Fax: 450-926-5985
Social Media: twitter.com/DSellahNPD, www.facebook.com/pages/Djaouida-Sellah/198674956848267
Note: Web Site: www.djaouidasellah.ndp.ca

Hon. Judy Sgro, P.C., York West, Ontario, Liberal
613-992-7774, Fax: 613-947-8319, judy.sgro@parl.gc.ca, Other Communications: Constituency Phone: 416-744-1882; Fax: 416-952-1696
Social Media: twitter.com/JudySgro, www.facebook.com/pages/Judy-Sgro/29642650496www.linkedin.com/in/judysgro
Note: Web Site: www.judysgro.co

Minister, National Revenue, Hon. Gail Shea, P.C., Egmont, Prince Edward Island, Conservative Party
613-992-9223, Fax: 613-992-1974, gail.shea@parl.gc.ca; sheag1B@parl.gc.ca, Other Communications: Constituency Phone: 902-432-6899; Fax: 902-432-6853
Social Media: twitter.com/CPCGailShea
Note: Web Sites: www.gailshea.ca (Personal Web Site); www.cra-arc.gc.ca/gncy/mnstr/menu-eng.html (Canada Revenue Agency)

Bev Shipley, Lambton - Kent - Middlesex, Ontario, Conservative Party
613-947-4581, 800-586-4614, Fax: 613-947-4584, bev.shipley@parl.gc.ca, Other Communications: Constituency Phone: 519-245-6561; Fax: 519-245-6736
Social Media: twitter.com/VoteBevShipley, www.facebook.com/profile.php?id=674005042
Note: Web Site: www.bevshipley.ca

Devinder Shory, Calgary Northeast, Alberta, Conservative Party
613-947-4487, Fax: 613-947-4490, devinder.shory@parl.gc.ca, Other Communications: Constituency Phone: 403-291-0018; Fax: 403-291-9516
Social Media: twitter.com/NortheastShory, www.facebook.com/mpshory
Note: Web Site: www.devindershory.ca

Scott Simms, B.Comm., Bonavista - Gander - Grand Falls - Windsor, Newfoundland & Labrador, Liberal
613-996-3935, 888-489-1901, Fax: 613-996-7622, scott.simms@parl.gc.ca, Other Communications: Constituency Phone: 709-256-3130; Fax: 709-256-3169
Social Media: twitter.com/Scott_Simms, www.facebook.com/MPScottSimms
Note: Web Site: www.scottsimms.com

Jinny Jogindera Sims, B.Ed., Newton - North Delta, British Columbia, New Democratic Party
613-992-0666, Fax: 613-992-1965, jinny.sims@parl.gc.ca, Other Communications: Constituency Phone: 604-598-2200; Fax: 604-598-2212
Social Media: www.facebook.com/jinnysims
Note: Web Site: www.jinnysims.ndp.ca

Rathika Sitsabaiesan, Scarborough - Rouge River, Ontario, New Democratic Party
613-996-9681, Fax: 613-996-6643, rathika.sitsabaiesan@parl.gc.ca
Social Media: twitter.com/rathikas, www.facebook.com/rathikaspage
Note: Web Site: www.rathika.ca

Chair, Standing Committee on Health, Joy Smith, B.Ed., M.Ed. (Hons.), Kildonan - St. Paul, Manitoba, Conservative Party
613-992-7148, Fax: 613-996-9125, joy.smith@parl.gc.ca; joy@joysmith.ca, Other Communications: Constituency Phone: 204-984-6322; Fax: 204-984-6415
Note: Web Site: www.joysmith.ca

Robert Sopuck, B.Sc., M.Sc., Dauphin - Swan River - Marquette, Manitoba, Conservative Party
613-992-3176, Fax: 613-992-0930, robert.sopuck@parl.gc.ca; info@robertsopuck.ca, Other Communications: Constituency Phone: 204-622-4659; Fax: 204-622-4654
Social Media: www.facebook.com/pages/Robert-Sopuck/126578207395867
Note: Web Site: www.robertsopuck.ca

Chair, Standing Committee on Public Safety & National Security, Kevin Sorenson, Crowfoot, Alberta, Conservative Party
780-608-4600, 800-665-4358, Fax: 613-947-4611, kevin.sorenson@parl.gc.ca, Other Communications: Constituency Phone: 780-608-4600; Fax: 780-608-4603
Note: Web Site: www.kevinsorenson.ca

Assistant Deputy Chair, Committees of the Whole, Bruce Stanton, Simcoe North, Ontario, Conservative Party
613-992-6582, 800-265-6228, Fax: 613-996-3128, bruce.stanton@parl.gc.ca, Other Communications: Constituency Phone: 705-327-0513; Fax: 705-327-8310
Social Media: twitter.com/bruce_stanton, www.facebook.com/pages/Bruce-Stanton/6236822310www.linkedin.com/pub/bruce-stanton/28/19/95
Note: Web Site: www.brucestanton.ca

Lise St-Denis, B.A., M.A., M.Ed., Saint-Maurice - Champlain, Québec, New Democratic Party
613-995-4895, Fax: 613-996-6883, lise.st-denis@parl.gc.ca; Lise.St-Denis.C1@parl.gc.ca, Other Communications: Constituency Phone: 819-538-5291; Fax: 819-538-7624
Note: Web Site: www.lisestdenis.ndp.ca

Kennedy Stewart, B.A., M.A., Ph.D., Burnaby -Douglas, British Columbia, New Democratic Party
613-996-5597, Fax: 613-992-5501, kennedy.stewart@parl.gc.ca
Social Media: twitter.com/kennedystewart, www.facebook.com/kennedy.stewart www.linkedin.com/pub/kennedy-stewart/14/817/540
Note: Web Site: www.kennedystewart.ca

Peter Stoffer, Sackville - Eastern Shore, Nova Scotia, New Democratic Party
613-995-5822, 888-701-5557, Fax: 613-996-9655, peter.stoffer@parl.gc.ca, Other Communications: Constituency Phone: 902-861-2311; Fax: 902-861-4620
Note: Web Site: www.peterstoffer.ndp.ca

Brian Storseth, Westlock - St. Paul, Alberta, Conservative Party
613-996-1783, 800-667-8450, Fax: 613-995-1415, brian.storseth@parl.gc.ca; brian@brianstorseth.ca, Other Communications: Constituency Phone: 780-349-8333; Fax: 780-349-8340
Social Media: twitter.com/BrianStorseth, www.facebook.com/Brian.Storseth.MP
Note: Web Site: www.brianstorseth.ca

Mark Strahl, Chilliwack - Fraser Canyon, British Columbia, Conservative Party
613-992-2940, 800-667-2808, Fax: 613-944-9376, mark.strahl@parl.gc.ca, Other Communications: Constituency Phone: 604-847-9711; Fax: 604-847-9744
Social Media: twitter.com/markstrahl, www.facebook.com/pages/Mark-Strahl/223322794358475
Note: Web Site: www.markstrahl.com

Mike Sullivan, York South - Weston, Ontario, New Democratic Party
613-995-0777, Fax: 613-992-2949, mike.sullivan@parl.gc.ca, Other Communications: Constituency Phone: 416-656-2526
Social Media: twitter.com/mdsullivan, www.facebook.com/group.php?gid=161602783896439
Note: Web Site: www.mikesullivan.ca

Chair, Standing Committee on Industry, Science, & Technology, David Sweet, Ancaster - Dundas - Flamborough - Westdale, Ontario, Conservative Party
613-996-4984, Fax: 613-996-4986, David.Sweet@parl.gc.ca; David.Sweet.c1@parl.gc.ca, Other Communications: Constituency Phone: 905-627-9169; Fax: 905-627-3803
Social Media: twitter.com/DavidSweetMP, www.facebook.com/pages/David-Sweet/14043761823
Note: Web Site: www.davidsweet.ca/cms

Glenn Thibeault, Sudbury, Ontario, New Democratic Party
613-996-8962, Fax: 613-995-2569, glenn.thibeault@parl.gc.ca, Other Communications: Constituency Phone: 705-673-7107; Fax: 705-673-0944
Social Media: twitter.com/GlennThibeault, www.facebook.com/glennthibeaultmp
Note: Web Site: www.glennthibeault.ndp.ca

Chair, Standing Committee on Citizenship & Immigration, David Allan Tilson, Q.C., B.A.. LL.B., Dufferin - Caledon, Ontario, Conservative Party
613-995-7813, Fax: 613-992-9789, david.tilson@parl.gc.ca;david.tilson.c1@parl.gc.ca, Other Communications: Constituency Phone: 519-941-1832; Fax: 519-941-8660
Social Media: twitter.com/davidtilson
Note: Web Site: www.davidtilson.ca

Lawrence Toet, Elmwood - Transcona, Manitoba, Conservative Party
613-995-6339, Fax: 613-995-6688, lawrence.toet@parl.gc.ca; lawrence@lawrencetoet.ca, Other Communications: Constituency Phone: 204-984-2499; Fax: 204-984-2502
Social Media: www.facebook.com/pages/Lawrence-Toet/254206521258405
Note: Web Site: www.lawrencetoet.ca

Minister, Public Safety, Hon. Vic Toews, P.C., B.A., LL.B., Provencher, Manitoba, Conservative Party
613-992-3128, Fax: 613-995-1049, vic.toews@parl.gc.ca, Other Communications: Constituency Phone: 204-326-9889; Fax: 204-346-9874
Note: Web Sites: www.victoews.com (Personal Web Site); www.publicsafety.gc.ca/abt/wwa/min-eng.aspx (Public Safety Canada)

Deputy Opposition Whip, Philip Toone, Gaspésie - Iles-de-la-Madeleine, Québec, New Democratic Party
613-992-6188, 866-368-1855, Fax: 613-992-6194, philip.toone@parl.gc.ca, Other Communications: Constituency Phone: 418-368-1855; Fax: 418-368-1925
Social Media: www.facebook.com/pages/Philip-Toone/243294132367236
Note: Web Site: www.philiptoone.ndp.ca

Jonathan Tremblay, Montmorency - Charlevoix - Haute-Côte-Nord, Québec, New Democratic Party
613-995-9732, 866-660-6776, Fax: 613-996-2656, jonathan.tremblay@parl.gc.ca, Other Communications: Constituency Phone: 418-660-6776; Fax: 418-660-6777
Social Media: twitter.com/Jonathan_tremb
Note: Web Site: www.jonathantremblay.ca

Brad Trost, B.A., B.Sc., Saskatoon - Humboldt, Saskatchewan, Conservative Party
613-992-8052, Fax: 613-996-9899, brad.trost@parl.gc.ca, Other Communications: Constituency Phone: 306-975-6133; Fax: 306-975-6670
Social Media: twitter.com/BradTrostCPC, www.facebook.com/pages/Brad-Trost-MP/183289298385094
Note: Web Site: www.bradtrost.ca

Bernard Trottier, B.Sc.Eng., MBA, Etobicoke - Lakeshore, Ontario, Conservative Party
613-995-9364, Fax: 613-992-5880, bernard.trottier@parl.gc.ca, Other Communications: Constituency Phone: 416-251-5510; Fax: 416-251-2845
Social Media: twitter.com/btrottier, www.facebook.com/pages/Bernard-Trottier/128026606262?ref=tswww.linkedin.com/pub/bernard-trottier/3/b47/836
Note: Web Site: www.bernardtrottiermp.ca

Justin Trudeau, B.A., B.Ed., Papineau, Québec, Liberal
613-995-8872, Fax: 613-995-9926, justin.trudeau@parl.gc.ca, Other Communications: Constituency Phone: 514-277-6020; Fax: 514-277-3454
Social Media: twitter.com/justinpjtrudeau, www.facebook.com/pages/Justin-Trudeau/21751825648
Note: Web Site: www.justin.ca

Parliamentary Secretary for Status of Women, Susan Truppe, London North Centre, Ontario, Conservative Party
613-992-0805, Fax: 613-992-9613, susan.truppe@parl.gc.ca; susan.truppe.c1@parl.gc.ca, Other Communications: Constituency Phone: 519-663-9777;Fax: 519-663-2238
Social Media: twitter.com/susantruppe, www.facebook.com/group.php?gid=222527324455927www.linkedin.com/pub/susan-truppe/1b/3a5/a30
Note: Web Site: www.susantruppe.ca

Interim Leader, Official Opposition; Interim Party Leader, New Democratic Party; Caucus Chair, NDP, Nycole Turmel, Hull - Aylmer, Quebec, New Democratic Party
613-992-7550, Fax: 613-992-7599, nycole.turmel@parl.gc.ca;Nycole.Turmel.c1@parl.gc.ca, Other Communications: Constituency Phone: 819-994-8844; Fax: 819-994-8557
Social Media: twitter.com/nycole_turmel, www.facebook.com/profile.php?id=100002634121396
Note: Web Site: www.nycoleturmel.ndp.ca

Chair, Standing Committee on Transport, Infrastructure, & Communities, Mervin C. Tweed, Brandon - Souris, Manitoba, Conservative Party
613-995-9372, 866-558-0555, Fax: 613-992-1265, merv.tweed@parl.gc.ca; merv.tweed.c1@parl.gc.ca, Other Communications: Constituency Phone: 204-726-7600; Fax: 204-726-7699
Note: Web Site: www.mervtweed.com

Minister of State, Democratic Reform, Hon. Tim Uppal, P.C., Edmonton - Sherwood Park, Alberta, Conservative Party
613-995-3611, Fax: 613-995-3612, tim.uppal@parl.gc.ca, Other Communications: Constituency Phone: 780-467-4944; Fax: 780-449-1471
Social Media: twitter.com/TimUppal_MP, www.facebook.com/profile.php?id=560835735
Note: Web Sites: www.timuppal.ca (Personal Web Site); www.democraticreform.gc.ca/index.asp?lang=eng&page=min (Democratic Reform)

Minister of State, Atlantic Canada Opportunities Agency; Minister of State, La Francophonie, Hon. Bernard Valcourt, P.C., Q.C., B.A., LL.B., DHC, Madawaska - Restigouche, New Brunswick, Conservative Party
613-995-0581, Fax: 613-996-9736, bernard.valcourt@parl.gc.ca; bvalcourt2011@hotmail.com, Other Communications: Constituency Phone: 506-739-4600; Fax: 506-739-4607
Social Media: twitter.com/b_valcourt, www.facebook.com/pages/Bernard-Valcourt/214030968613999
Note: Web Sites: www.bernardvalcourt.ca (Personal Web Site); www.acoa-apeca.gc.ca/English/WhoWeAre/OurPeople/Pages/Minister.aspx?ProgramID= (Atlantic Canada Opportunities Agency)

Frank Valeriote, Guelph, Ontario, Liberal
613-996-4758, Fax: 613-996-9922, frank.valeriote@parl.gc.ca, Other Communications: Constituency Phone: 519-837-8276; Fax: 519-837-8443
Social Media: twitter.com/FrankValeriote, www.facebook.com/FrankValeriote
Note: Web Site: www.frankvaleriote.ca

Dave Van Kesteren, Chatham-Kent - Essex, Ontario, Conservative Party
613-992-2612, Fax: 613-992-1852, dave.vankesteren@parl.gc.ca, Other Communications: Constituency Phone: 519-358-7555; Fax: 519-358-1428
Social Media: www.facebook.com/davevankesteren
Note: Web Site: www.davevankesteren.ca

Leader of the Government in the House of Commons; House Leader, Conservative Party, Hon. Peter Van Loan, P.C., B.A., LL.B., M.A., M.Sc.Pl., York - Simcoe, Ontario, Conservative Party
613-996-7752, 877-738-3748, Fax: 613-992-8351, peter.vanloan@parl.gc.ca, Other Communications: Constituency Phone: 905-898-1600; Fax: 905-898-4600
Note: Web Site: www.petervanloan.com (Personal Web Site); www.houseleader.gc.ca/index.asp?lang=eng&page=Team-eq

uipe&doc=bio/bio-eng.htm (Leader of the Government in the House of Commons)

Maurice Vellacott, B.R.E., M.Div., D.Min., Saskatoon - Wanuskewin, Saskatchewan, Conservative Party
613-992-1899, 888-844-8886, Fax: 613-992-3085, maurice.vellacott@parl.gc.ca, Other Communications: Constituency Phone: 306-975-4725; Fax: 306-975-4728
Note: Web Site: www.mauricevellacott.ca

Mike Wallace, B.A., Burlington, Ontario, Conservative Party
613-995-0881, Fax: 613-995-1091, mike.wallace@parl.gc.ca; mike.wallace.c1@parl.gc.ca, Other Communications: Constituency Phone: 905-639-5757; Fax: 905-639-6031
Social Media: twitter.com/MikeWallaceMPwww.linkedin.com/pub/mike-wallace/1b/843/9b1
Note: Web Site: www.mikewallacemp.ca

Chair, Standing Committee on Environment & Sustainable Development, Mark Warawa, Langley, British Columbia, Conservative Party
613-992-1157, Fax: 613-943-1823, mark.warawa@parl.gc.ca, Other Communications: Constituency Phone: 604-534-5955; Fax: 604-534-5970
Social Media: twitter.com/MPmarkwarawa, www.facebook.com/markwarawa
Note: Web Site: www.markwarawa.com

Chair, Standing Committee on Aboriginal Affairs & Northern Development, Chris Warkentin, Peace River, Alberta, Conservative Party
613-992-5685, 800-667-0456, Fax: 613-947-4782, chris.warkentin@parl.gc.ca;chris.warkentin.c1@parl.gc.ca, Other Communications: Constituency Phone: 780-538-1677; Fax: 780-538-9257
Social Media: twitter.com/chriswarkentin, www.facebook.com/chriswarkentin
Note: Web Site: www.chriswarkentin.ca

Jeff Watson, Essex, Ontario, Conservative Party
613-992-1812, 866-776-5333, Fax: 613-995-0033, jeff.watson@parl.gc.ca, Other Communications: Constituency Phone: 519-776-4700; Fax: 519-776-1383
Social Media: www.facebook.com/JeffWatsonEssex
Note: Web Site: www.jeffwatsonmp.ca

John Weston, West Vancouver - Sunshine Coast - Sea to Sky Country, British Columbia, Conservative Party
613-947-4617, 800-665-6004, Fax: 613-947-4620, john.weston@parl.gc.ca, Other Communications: Constituency Phone: 604-981-1790; Fax: 604-981-1794
Social Media: twitter.com/JohnWestonMP, www.facebook.com/JohnWestonMP
Note: Web Site: www.johnweston.ca

Chair, Standing Committee on Fisheries & Oceans, Rodney Weston, Saint John, New Brunswick, Conservative Party
613-947-2700, Fax: 613-947-4574, rodney.weston@parl.gc.ca, Other Communications: Constituency Phone: 506-657-2500; Fax: 506-657-2504
Social Media: twitter.com/rodneywestonsj
Note: Web Site: www.rodneyweston.ca

David Wilks, Kootenay - Columbia, British Columbia, Conservative Party
613-995-7246, Fax: 613-996-9923, david.wilks@parl.gc.ca; david.wilks.c1@parl.gc.ca, Other Communications: Constituency Phone: 250-417-2250; Fax: 250-417-2253
Social Media: twitter.com/DavidJohnWilks, www.facebook.com/david.wilks
Note: Web Site: www.david-wilks.ca

John Williamson, B.A., MSc., New Brunswick Southwest, New Brunswick, Conservative Party
613-995-5550, 888-350-4734, Fax: 613-995-5226, john.williamson@parl.gc.ca; john.williamson.c1@parl.gc.ca, Other Communications: Constituency Phone: 506-466-3928; Fax: 506-466-2813
Social Media: www.facebook.com/pages/John-Williamson/172576949462450
Note: Web Site: www.votejohnwilliamson.ca

Minister of State, Seniors, Hon. Alice Wong, P.C., Ph.D., Richmond, British Columbia, Conservative Party
613-995-2021, 877-775-5790, Fax: 613-995-2174, alice.wong@parl.gc.ca; alice.wong.c1@parl.gc.ca, Other Communications: Constituency Phone: 604-775-5790; Fax: 604-775-6291
Social Media: twitter.com/AliceWongCanada, www.facebook.com/profile.php?id=100002648510727
Note: Web Sites: www.alicewong.ca (Personal Web Site); www.hrsdc.gc.ca/eng/corporate/ministers/index.shtml (Human Resources &Skills Development Canada); www.seniors.gc.ca/h.4m.2@.jsp (Seniors Canada)

Stephen Woodworth, LL.B., Kitchener Centre, Ontario, Conservative Party
613-995-8913, Fax: 613-996-7329, stephen.woodworth@parl.gc.ca, Other Communications: Constituency Phone: 519-741-2001; Fax: 519-579-2404
Social Media: twitter.com/WoodworthMP, www.facebook.com/WoodworthKitchenerCentrewww.linkedin.com/pub/stephen-woodworth/2b/84b/38
Note: Web Site: www.stephenwoodworth.ca

Minister of State, Western Economic Diversification, Hon. Lynne Yelich, P.C., Blackstrap, Saskatchewan, Conservative Party
613-995-5653, Fax: 613-995-0126, Lynne.Yelich@parl.gc.ca, Other Communications: Constituency Phone: 306-975-6472; Fax: 306-975-6492
Social Media: twitter.com/Lynne_Yelich, www.facebook.com/pages/Lynne-Yelich/64666054978
Note: Web Sites: www.lynneyelich.com (Personal Web Site); www.wd.gc.ca/eng/43.asp (Western Economic DiversificationCanada)

Terence H. Young, B.A., Oakville, Ontario, Conservative Party
613-995-4014, Fax: 613-992-0520, terence.young@parl.gc.ca, Other Communications: Constituency Phone: 905-338-2008
Social Media: twitter.com/TerenceYoungMP, www.facebook.com/TerenceYoungMP
Note: Web Site: www.terenceyoung.com

Wai Young, B.A., Vancouver South, British Columbia, Conservative Party
613-995-7052, Fax: 613-995-2962, Wai.Young@parl.gc.ca; info@waiyoung.ca, Other Communications: Constituency Phone: 604-775-5323; Fax: 604-775-5420
Social Media: twitter.com/WaiYoungMP, www.facebook.com/WaiYoungVancouverSouthwww.linkedin.com/pub/wai-young/2/4a7/a9a
Note: Web Site: www.waiyoung.ca

Bob Zimmer, B.A., Prince George - Peace River, British Columbia, Conservative Party
613-947-4524, Fax: 613-613-9474, Bob.Zimmer@parl.gc.ca, Other Communications: Constituency Phone: 250-561-7982; Fax: 250-561-7983
Social Media: twitter.com/ZimmerBob, www.facebook.com/group.php?gid=165836856816065www.linkedin.com/pub/bob-zimmer/26/a21/ba6
Note: Web Site: www.bobzimmer.ca

Member of Parliament, Vacant, Toronto - Danforth, Ontario

Federal Government Departments & Agencies / Agences et departements du gouvernement fédéral

Editor's Note: The entries listed below are entered alphabetically, using applied titles as registered by the Federal Identity Program. Cross references are used to help you to locate the entry quickly. The two departments that incorporate Department of as part of their applied titles (Department of Finance Canada; Department of Justice Canada) are nevertheless listed alphabetically under Finance & Justice.

Aboriginal Affairs & Northern Development Canada (AANDC) / Affaires autochtones et Dévelopment du Nord Canada (AADNC)

10 Wellington St., North Tower, Gatineau, QC K1A 0H4
819-997-0380 Fax: 866-817-3977
800-567-9604
infopubs@aadnc-aandc.gc.ca
www.aadnc-aandc.gc.ca
TTY: 866-553-0554

AANDC supports First Nations, Inuit & Métis people in their effort to develop healthy, sustainable communities and achieve their economic & social aspirations. This mandate is derived largely from the Department of Indian & Northern Development Act, the Indian Act, territorial acts & legal obligations arising from section 91 (24) of the Constitution Act, 1867. The department administers over 50 statutes.

Acts Administered:

(An Act to confirm an) Agreement between the Governments of Canada & the province of New Brunswick respecting the Indian Reserves
(An Act to confirm an) Agreement between the Governments of Canada & the province of Nova Scotia respecting the Indian Reserves
Alberta Natural Resources Act
Arctic Waters Pollution Prevention Act (jointly with Transport Canada & Natural Resources)
British Columbia Indian Cut-off Lands Settlement Act
British Columbia Indian Lands Settlement Act
British Columbia Treaty Commission Act
Canada Lands Surveys Act (jointly Natural Resources)
Canada Mining Regulations
Canada Oil & Gas Drilling & Production Regulations
Canada Oil & Gas Land Regulations
Canada Oil & Gas Operations Act (jointly with Natural Resources)
Canada Petroleum Resources Act (jointly with Natural Resources)
Canada - Yukon Oil & Gas Accord Implementation Act
Canadian Polar Commission Act
Caughnawaga Indian Reserve Act
Claim Settlements (Alberta & Saskatchewan) Implementation Act
Condominium Ordinance Validation Act
Cree-Naskapi (of Québec) Act
Crown Waiver Orders
Department of Indian & Northern Affairs Development Act
Dominion Water Power Act
Fort Nelson Indian Reserve Minerals Revenue Sharing Act
Government Employees Land Acquisition Orders
Grassy Narrows & Islington Indian Band Mercury Pollution Claims Settlement Act
Gwich'in Land Claim Settlement Act
Indian Act
Indian Lands Agreement (1986) Act
Indian Oil & Gas Act
Indian Reserve Waste Disposal Regulations
Indian (Soldier Settlement) Act
James Bay & Northern Quebec Native Claims Settlement Act
Kanesatake Interim Land Base Governance Act
Kelowna Accord Implementation Act
Labrador Inuit Land Claims Agreement Act
Land Titles Repeal Act
Maanulth First Nations Final Agreement Act
Mackenzie Valley Resource Management Act
Manitoba Claim Settlements Implementation Act
Manitoba Natural Resources Act
Manitoba Supplementary Provisions Act
Natural Resources Transfer (School Lands) Amendments, Alberta, Manitoba & Saskatchewan
Nelson House First Nation Flooded Land Act
Nisga'a Final Agreement Act
Northern Canada Power Commission (Share Issuance & Sale Authorization) Act
Northern Canada Power Commission Yukon Assets Disposal Authorization Act
Northwest Territories Act
Northwest Territories Mining Districts Order & Nunavut Mining District
Northwest Territories Waters Act
Nunavik Inuit Land Claims Agreement Act
Nunavut Act
Nunavut Land Claims Agreement Act
Nunavut Waters & Nunavut Surface Rights Tribunal Act, 2002
Oil & Gas Land Orders
Orders Authorizing Acquisition of Interest in Certain Lands
Orders Respecting Withdrawal from Disposal of Certain Lands
Pictou Landing Indian Band Agreement Act
Polar Bear Pass Withdrawal Order
Railway Belt Act
Railway Belt & Peace River Block Act
Railway Belt Water Act
Reservations to Crown Waiver Orders
St. Peter's Reserve Act
St. Regis Islands Act
Sahtu Dene & Metis Land Claim Settlement Act
Saskatchewan Natural Resources Act
Saskatchewan Treaty Land Entitlement Act
Sechelt Indian Band Self-Government Act
(An Act for the) Settlement of Certain Questions Between the Governments of Canada & Ontario Respecting the Indian Reserve Lands Act
Songhees Indian Reserve Act
Specific Claims Tribunal Act
Split Lake Cree First Nation Flooded Land Act
Territorial Coal Regulations
Territorial Dredging Regulations
Territorial Land Titles Offices Regulations
Territorial Land Use Regulations
Territorial Lands Act
Territorial Lands Act Exclusion Orders
Territorial Lands Regulations
Territorial Quarrying Regulations
Tlicho Land Claims & Self-Government Act
Tsawwassen First Nation Final Agreement Act
Westbank First Nation Self-Government Act
Western Arctic (Inuvialuit) Claims Settlement Act
Withdrawal of Certain Lands from Disposal Orders
Withdrawals of Disposal Orders
York Factory First Nation Flooded Land Act
Yukon Act
Yukon Environmental & Socio-Economic Assessment Act, 2003
Yukon First Nations Land Claims Settlement Act
Yukon First Nations Self-Government Act
Yukon Surface Rights Board Act

Minister, Indian Affairs & Northern Development; Minister of the Canadian Northern Economic Development Agency;, Federal Interlocutor for Métis & Non-Status Indians, Hon. John Duncan, B.Sc.F.
613-992-2503, Fax: 613-996-3306, Duncan.J@parl.gc.ca; Minister@ainc-inac.gc.ca, Other Communications: Indian Affairs & Northern Development: 819-997-0002

Parliamentary Secretary to the Minister of Aboriginal Affairs & Northern Development, Rod Bruinooge
613-995-7517, Fax: 613-943-4666

Deputy Minister, Michael Wernick
819-997-0133, Fax: 819-953-2251

Associate Deputy Minister, Colleen Swords
819-934-0583, Fax: 819-953-2251

Director General, Communications, Dianne Clarke
819-994-7526, Fax: 819-953-9465
Director General, Office of the Federal Interlocutor, Allan MacDonald
613-992-8186, Fax: 613-947-7580
Senior General Counsel, Legal Services, Andrew Saranchuk
819-994-4141, Fax: 819-953-7693
Director, Policy, Kym Purchase
819-997-0002, Fax: 819-953-4941

Associated Agencies, Boards & Commissions:

• Beverly & Qamanirjuaq Caribou Management Board Secretariat
PO Box 629
Stonewall, MB R0C 2Z0
204-467-2438
caribounews@arctic-caribou.com
www.arctic-caribou.com
Group of hunters, biologists & wildlife managers working together to conserve Canada's vast Beverly & Qamanirjuaq caribou herds for the welfare of traditional caribou-using communities in northern Manitoba, Saskatchewan, Northwest Territories & Nunavut.

• First Nations Tax Commission (FNTC) / Commission de la fiscalité des premières nations (CFPN)
#321, 345 Yellowhead Hwy
Kamloops, BC V2H 1H1
250-828-9857 Fax: 250-828-9858
mailkamloops@fntc.ca
www.fntc.ca
Other Communication: National Capital Region Email: mail@fntc.ca
The FNTC operates in the larger context of First Nation issues which goes beyond property tax. The FNTC is concerned with reducing the barriers to economic development on First Nation lands, increasing investor certainty, and enabling First Nations to be part of their regional economies. The FNTC is working to fill the institutional vacuum that has prevented First Nations from participating in the market economy and creating a national regulatory framework for First Nation tax systems that meets or beats the standards of provinces.

• Indian Oil & Gas Canada (IOGC) / Pétrole et gaz des Indiens du Canada
#100, 9911 Chiila Blvd.
Tsuu T'ina (Sarcee), AB T2W 6H6
403-292-5625 Fax: 403-292-5618
ContactIOGC@inac-ainc.gc.ca
www.pgic-iogc.gc.ca
Indian Oil and Gas Canada (IOGC) is an organization committed to managing and regulating oil and gas resources on First Nation reserve lands. It is a special operating agency within Aboriginal Affairs & Northern Development Canada.

• Mackenzie Valley Environmental Impact Review Board
200 Scotia Centre
#5102, 50th Ave.
PO Box 938
Yellowknife, NT X1A 2N7
867-766-7050 Fax: 867-766-7074 866-912-3472
www.reviewboard.ca
In 1998, the Mackenzie Valley Environmental Impact Review Board was established under the Mackenzie Valley Resources Management Act. The co-management Review Board is made up of members nominated by First Nations & federal & territorial governments. Board members represent the interests of all residents of the Mackenzie Valley.

• Nunavut Impact Review Board
PO Box 1360
Cambridge Bay, NU X0B 0C0
867-983-4600 Fax: 867-983-2594 866-233-3033
info@nirb.ca
www.nirb.ca
An institution of the government established under the Nunavut Land Claims Agreement to conduct environmental & socio-economic assessments. The NIRB process involves participation by members of the community, Inuit organizations, the Government of Nunavut & the Government of Canada through the entire environmental assessment. Under the Canadian Environmental Assessment Act, the federal departments with specific responsibilities for the project must ensure that the requirements of the Act are met throughout the assessment process. This open process facilitates sound environmental stewardship & promotes economic & sustainable development.

• Nunavut Planning Commission
PO Box 2101
Cambridge Bay, NU X0B 0C0
867-983-4625 Fax: 867-983-4626
www.nunavut.ca
Responsible for land use planning & environmental reporting & management in Nunavut.

• Nunavut Water Board
PO Box 119
Gjoa Haven, NU X0B 1J0
867-360-6338 Fax: 867-360-6369
www.nunavutwaterboard.org
Responsible for the regulation, use & management of water in the Nunavut Settlement Area.

• Porcupine Caribou Management Board
PO Box 31723
Whitehorse, YT Y1A 6L3
867-633-4780 Fax: 867-393-3904
pcmb@taiga.net
taiga.net/pcmb
Works to manage the Porcupine Caribou herd, one of the largest herds of migratory caribou in North America, & to protect & maintain its habitat.

Chief Financial Officer Sector / Secteur du dirigeant principal des finances
819-953-1201 Fax: 819-953-4094

Chief Financial Officer, Susan MacGowan
819-956-8188, Fax: 819-956-8193
Chief Information Officer, Information Management Branch, Tim Eryou
819-994-3334, Fax: 819-956-8739
Director General, Planning & Resource Management, Pamela D'Eon
819-994-6649, Fax: 819-953-8475
Director General, Corporate Accounting & Materiel Management, Andrew Francis
819-994-6649, Fax: 819-953-8475
Director, Corporate Accounting & Reporting Directorate, Eva Jacobs
819-934-0564, Fax: 819-953-3915

Education & Social Development Programs & Partnerships / Secteur des programmes et des partenariats en matière d'éducation et de dévelopment social
Fax: 819-953-4094

Assistant Deputy Minister, Françoise Ducros
819-997-0020, Fax: 819-953-4094
Director General, Education Branch, Kathleen Keenan
613-995-9392, Fax: 613-995-9393
Director General, Social Policy & Programs Branch, Sheilagh Murphy
613-947-6508, Fax: 613-947-9242
Manager, Resources Planning & Management Directorate, Syndie Régimbal
819-994-4406, Fax: 819-953-7627

Lands & Economic Development / Terres et Développement économique
Fax: 819-953-0248

Manages land-related statutory duties under the Indian Act & duties related to transferring land management services to First Nations. The Environment Directorate maintains an Inventory of Contaminated Sites on reserve land & coordinates remediation planning; responsible for the design & implementation of the Indian & Inuit Affairs Program Environmental Stewardship Strategy Action Plan; development of First Nations capacity, tools & enabling legislation in order that First Nations undertake their own environmental protection initiatives; supports First Nation, Métis & Inuit communities in efforts to promote environmental stewardship in a manner that is consistent with the principles of sustainable development.
Assistant Deputy Minister, Sara Filbee
819-997-0114, Fax: 819-953-0248
Director General, Community Opportunities Branch, Andrew Beynon
819-953-0517, Fax: 819-953-0649
Director General, Policy & Coordination, Allan Clarke
819-953-3004, Fax: 819-997-7054
Director General, Aboriginal Entrepreneurship Branch, Nicole Ladouceur
819-953-0622, Fax: 819-997-7223

Northern Affairs / Affaires du Nord
819-994-0044 Fax: 819-953-6121

Supports northern political & economic development through the management of federal interests; promotes sustainable development of the North's natural resources & northern communities. Works toward the devolution of all province-like responsibilities to northern governments of NWT, Nunavut & the Yukon. Develops & coordinates policies & programs related to northern environment & conservation, like the federal Northern Affairs Program Sustainable Development Strategy, the cleanup of northern hazardous waste sites, climate change & interdepartmental liaison with key policy departments like Environment Canada. Northern Contaminants Program is managed by AANDC in partnership with the federal departments of Health, Environment & Fisheries & Oceans, the territorial governments, Aboriginal organizations & university researchers, & its aim is to work toward reducing & eliminating, where possible, contaminants in traditionally harvested foods. The Northern Information Network is designed to link users to information about the Yukon, the Northwest Territories & Nunavut for more effective decision-making in areas such as resource management & economic development. NIN supports various research initiatives about the North, including project impact assessme nts, sustainable development strategies, wildlife management planning, land use planning & emergency preparedness. NIN has a directory of geo-referenced databases, provides a forum for discussion & has information & research documents pertaining to the North.
Assistant Deputy Minister, Janet King
819-953-3760, Fax: 819-953-6121
Director General, Northern Oil & Gas Branch, Mimi Fortier
819-953-9393, Fax: 819-934-6375
Director General, Natural Resources & Environment Branch, Paula Isaak
819-997-9381, Fax: 819-953-8766
Acting Director General, Northern Policy & Science Integration Branch, John Kozij
819-997-9449, Fax: 819-997-0552
Director General, Devolution & Territorial Relations, Stephen Van Dine
819-997-0223, Fax: 819-953-9323
Executive Director, IPY 2012 Conference Secretariat, Julie Boyer
613-995-6575, Fax: 613-995-7038
Director, Strategic Management Directorate, Trevor Thibault
819-934-9886, Fax: 819-934-9888

Policy & Strategic Direction / Politique et direction stratégique
Fax: 819-953-5082

Senior Assistant Deputy Minister, Jean-François Tremblay
819-994-7555, Fax: 819-953-5082
Director General, Strategic Planning & Analysis Branch, Claudine Gagnon
819-994-7213, Fax: 819-953-0239
Director General, Strategic Policy & Research Branch, Nicole Kennedy
819-953-3088, Fax: 819-994-7860
Director General, External Relations & Gender Issues Branch, Line Paré
819-997-8212, Fax: 819-934-7192
Director General, Litigation Management & Resolution Branch, Daniel Ricard
819-953-4968, Fax: 819-997-1679
Director General, Policy Services Branch, Jill Wherrett
819-997-8359, Fax: 819-953-3320
Policy Analyst, Federal Relations & Issues Management, Nicholas Charney
819-994-2658, Fax: 819-953-4366

Regional Operations / Opérations régionales
Fax: 819-953-9406

Senior Assistant Deputy Minister, Ron Hallman
819-953-5577, Fax: 819-953-9406
Director General, Governance Branch, Brenda Kustra
819-997-8154, Fax: 819-997-9541
Director General, Community Infrastructure Branch, Gail Mitchell
819-953-4636, Fax: 819-997-3107

Resolution & Individual Affairs / Résolution et affaires individuelles
Fax: 613-996-2811

Assistant Deputy Minister, Élisabeth Châtillon
613-996-2845, Fax: 613-996-2811
Director General, Kathryn Bruce
613-947-6537, Fax: 613-996-2808
Director General, Settlement Agreement Operations, Marielle Doyon
613-996-2890, Fax: 613-996-3053
Director General, Individual Affairs Branch, Ray Hatfield
819-953-2605, Fax: 819-953-3371
Director General, Settlement Agreement Policy & Partnerships, Aideen Nabigon
613-947-5209, Fax: 613-996-2456
Executive Director, Secure Certificate of Indian Status, Claudia Ferland
819-934-7852, Fax: 819-953-9395
General Counsel & Director, Aboriginal Children's Issues, Caroline Clark
613-996-0140, Fax: 613-996-1810
Manager, Business Integration & Modernization, Francine Duval
800-567-9604, Fax: 819-953-9395

Treaties & Aboriginal Government / Traités et gouvernement autochtone
Fax: 819-953-3246

Senior Assistant Deputy Minister, Patrick Borbey
819-953-3180, Fax: 819-953-3246
Director General, Policy Development & Coordination Branch, Perry Billingsley
819-953-4315, Fax: 819-953-3855
Director General, Negotiations - West, Anita Boscariol
604-775-7144, Fax: 604-775-7149
Director General, Specific Claims Branch, Anik Dupont
819-994-2323, Fax: 819-994-4123
Director General, Implementation Branch, Stephen Gagnon
819-994-3434, Fax: 819-953-6430
Director General, Negotiations - Central, Joëlle Montminy
819-953-4365, Fax: 819-956-7011
Director General, Negotiations - East, Michael Nadler
819-994-7521, Fax: 819-953-6768

Director General, Financial Management & Strategic Services, Tony Richard
819-997-9757, Fax: 819-994-0273

Regional Offices:
Alberta
Canada Pl., #620, 9700 Jasper Ave., Edmonton, AB T5J 4G2
780-495-2773 Fax: 780-495-4354
Regional Director General, George Arcand Jr.
780-495-2835, Fax: 780-495-4354
Atlantic
40 Havelock St., PO Box 160, Amherst, NS B4H 3Z3
902-661-6201 Fax: 902-661-6237
Regional Director General, Ian Gray
902-661-6262, Fax: 902-661-6237
British Columbia
#600, 1138 Melville St., Vancouver, BC V6E 4S3
604-775-5100 Fax: 604-775-7149 Toll-Free: 866-553-0554
Regional Director General, Eric Magnuson
604-666-5201, Fax: 604-775-7149
Manitoba
#200, 365 Hargrave St., Winnipeg, MB R3B 3A3
204-983-2474 Fax: 866-817-3977 Toll-Free: 800-567-9604
Regional Director General, Anna Fontaine
204-983-2474, Fax: 204-983-2936
Northwest Territories
#4914, 50th St., PO Box 1500, Yellowknife, NT X1A 2R3
867-669-2500 Fax: 867-669-2709
Regional Director General, Trish Merrithew-Mercredi
867-669-2501, Fax: 867-669-2703
Nunavut
PO Box 2200, Iqaluit, NU X0A 0H0
867-975-4500 Fax: 867-975-4560
nuinfo@ainc-inac.gc.ca
Regional Director General, Robin Aitken
867-975-4501, Fax: 867-975-4560
Director, Contaminated Sites, Natalie Plato
867-975-4730
Ontario
25 St. Clair Ave. East, 8th Fl., Toronto, ON M4T 1M2
416-973-6234 Fax: 416-954-6201 TTY: 866-553-0554
800-567-9604
Regional Director General, Joanne Wilkinson
416-973-6201, Fax: 416-954-4326
Québec
#400, 320, rue St-Joseph est, Québec, QC G1K 9J2
418-648-3270 Fax: 866-817-3977 TTY: 866-553-0554
800-567-9604
Regional Director General, Pierre Nepton
418-648-3270, Fax: 418-648-2266
Saskatchewan
#200, 1 First Nations Way, Regina, SK S4S 7K5
306-780-5945 Fax: 306-780-5733
Other Communication: 306-780-5392
Regional Director General, Riel Bellegarde
306-780-6486, Fax: 306-780-7305
Yukon
#415C, 300 Main St., Whitehorse, YT Y1A 2B5
867-667-3888 Fax: 867-667-3801
800-661-0451
ytinfo@inac-ainc.gc.ca
Regional Director General, Kerry Newkirk
867-667-3300, Fax: 867-667-3801
Director, Environment, Michelle Edwards
867-393-7934, Fax: 867-667-3861
Director, Governance, Dionne Savill
867-667-3398, Fax: 867-667-3801

Agriculture & Agri-Food Canada/Agriculture et Agro-alimentaire Canada

1341 Baseline Rd., Ottawa, ON K1A 0C5
613-773-1000, Fax: 613-773-2772, 866-345-7972
TTY: 613-773-2700
Agriculture & Agri-Food Canada is responsible for all matters related to agriculture.
Acts Administered:
Agricultural Marketing Programs Act
Agricultural Products Marketing Act
Animal Pedigree Act
Canada Grain Act
Canadian Agricultural Loans Act
Canadian Dairy Commission Act
Canadian Wheat Board Act
Department of Agriculture & Agri-Food Act
Experimental Farm Stations Act
Farm Debt Mediation Act
Farm Credit Canada Act
Farm Income Protection Act
Farm Products Agencies Act
Prairie Farm Rehabilitation Act
Minister, Agriculture & Agri-Food; Minister, Canadian Wheat Board, Hon. Gerry Ritz
613-773-1059, Fax: 613-773-1060, Ritz.G@parl.gc.ca
Parliamentary Secretary to the Minister, David Anderson
613-773-1059, Fax: 613-992-5508, david.anderson@agr.gc.ca
Parliamentary Secretary to the Minister of Agriculture, Pierre Lemieux
613-773-1059, Fax: 613-996-9123, lemieuxp@agr.gc.ca
Chief of Staff, Aaron Gairdner
613-773-1059, Fax: 613-773-1060, aaron.gairdner@agr.gc.ca
Director, Issues Management, Steven Barrett
613-773-1059, Fax: 613-773-1081, steven.barrett@agr.gc.ca
Director, Communications, Meagan Murdoch
613-773-1059, Fax: 613-773-1060, meagan.murdoch@agr.gc.ca
Director, Policy, Mindy Pearce
613-773-1059, Fax: 613-773-1081, mindy.pearce@agr.gc.ca
Regional Affairs Director, Andrea Smotra
306-780-8236, Fax: 306-780-7292, andrea.smotra@agr.gc.ca
Director of Operations to the Ministry of State, Margaux Stastny
613-773-1063, Fax: 613-773-1081, margaux.stastny@agr.gc.ca
Senior Policy Advisor, Jim Scott
613-773-1059, Fax: 613-773-1060, jim.scott@agr.gc.ca
Policy Advisor, Karla House
613-773-1059, Fax: 613-773-1060, karla.house@agr.gc.ca
Policy Advisor, Matthew J McBain
613-773-1059, Fax: 613-773-1060, matthewj.mcbain@agr.gc.ca
Policy Advisor, Tyler McCann
613-773-1059, Fax: 613-773-1081, tyler.mccann@agr.gc.ca
Policy Advisor, Dustin Pike
613-773-1059, Fax: 613-773-1060, dustin.pike@agr.gc.ca
Regional Communications Advisor, Danielle Maier
306-780-8236, Fax: 306-780-7292, danielle.maier@agr.gc.ca

Agri-Environment Services Branch (AESB)
Tower 4, 1341 Baseline Rd., Ottawa, ON K1A 0C5
613-759-1000 Fax: 613-773-1211
www4.agr.gc.ca/AAFC-AAC/display-afficher.do?id=1187362338955&lang
Other Communication: Agroforestry Development Centre, Phone: 1-866-766-2284, Fax: 306-695-2568; Canada-Manitoba Crop Diversification Centre, Phone: 204-834-6000, Fax: 204-834-3777
The Agri-Environment Services Branch integrates the following components: Prairie Farm Rehabilitation Administration; National Land & Water Information Service; & Agri-Environmental Policy Bureau. The mission of the branch is to deliver innovative environmental solutions to the agriculture & agri-food sector. Applied Technology Development Centres of the Agri-Environment Services Branch include the following: Agroforestry Development Centre (formerly known as the Prairie Farm Rehabilitation Administration); Canada-Saskatchewan Irrigation Diversification Centre; & the Canada-Manitoba Crop Diversification Centre.
Assistant Deputy Minister, Jamshed Merchant
613-773-1200, Fax: 613-773-1211, jamshed.merchant@agr.gc.ca
Director General, Agri-Environmental Knowledge, Innovation, & Technology Directorate, Dr. Richard Butts
506-452-4802, Fax: 506-474-7533, richard.butts@agr.gc.ca
Acting Director General, Agri-Environmental Adaptation & Practice Change Directorate, Alan Parkinson
306-780-5081, Fax: 306-780-6533, alan.parkinson@agr.gc.ca
Director General, Agri-Environmental Policy & Strategic Priorities Directorate, Greg Strain
613-773-1207, Fax: 613-773-1222, greg.strain@agr.gc.ca

Communications & Consultations Branch
Tower 7, 1341 Baseline Rd., Ottawa, ON K1A 0C7
613-759-1000 Fax: 613-773-2772
Assistant Deputy Minister, Jodi Redmond
613-773-2922, Fax: 613-773-2772, jodi.redmond@agr.gc.ca
Director General, Communications Services, Jane Taylor
613-773-2840, Fax: 613-773-2772, jane.taylor@agr.gc.ca
Director, E-Communications, Joan Anderson
613-773-2601, Fax: 613-773-2398, joan.anderson@agr.gc.ca
Director, Strategic & Ministerial Communications, Steven Jurgutis
613-773-2760, Fax: 613-773-2772, steven.jurgutis@agr.gc.ca
Director, Regions, Outreach & Events, Darell M. Pack
613-773-2755, Fax: 613-773-2772, darell.pack@agr.gc.ca
Director, Translation & Revision Services, Caroline Rahal
613-773-0986, Fax: 613-773-2397, caroline.rahal@agr.gc.ca

Corporate Management
Tower 4, 1341 Baseline Rd., Ottawa, ON K1A 0C5
613-759-1000 Fax: 613-773-0911
Assistant Deputy Minister, Pierre Corriveau
613-773-1330, Fax: 613-773-1233, pierre.corriveau@agr.gc.ca
Director General, Asset Management & Capital Planning, Lynden Hillier
613-773-0923, Fax: 613-773-0966, lynden.hillier@agr.gc.ca
Director General, Finance & Resource Management Services, Bev Levere
613-773-1332, Fax: 613-773-0777, bev.levere@agr.gc.ca
Acting Director General, Strategic Management, Debbie Winker
613-773-1344, Fax: 613-773-0911, debbie.winker@agr.gc.ca
Acting Executive Director, Canadian Pari-Mutuel Agency, Steve Suttie
613-949-0726, Fax: 613-949-0750, steve.suttie@agr.gc.ca
Acting Associate Executive Director, Management Services, Ron Nichol
613-949-0723, Fax: 613-759-0750, ron.nichol@agr.gc.ca

Deputy Minister's Office / Bureau du sous-ministre
Tower 7, 1341 Baseline Rd., Ottawa, ON K1A 0C5
613-759-1011 Fax: 613-759-1040
The Deputy Minister's Office oversees the following organizations: Corporate Secretariat; Food Safety Review Secretariat; & Portfolio Coordination Secretariat.
Deputy Minister, Agriculture & Agri-Food Canada, John Knubley
613-773-1101, Fax: 613-773-1040, john.knubley@agr.gc.ca
Associate Deputy Minister, Agriculture & Agri-Food Canada, Claude Carrière
613-773-1011, Fax: 613-773-1061, claude.carriere@agr.gc.ca
Executive Director, Portfolio Coord. Secretariat, Todd F. Hunter
613-773-1062, Fax: 613-773-1051, todd.hunter@agr.gc.ca
Executive Director, Food Safety Review Secretariat, Anna Romano
613-773-2128, Fax: 613-773-2939, anna.romano@agr.gc.ca
Manager, Parliamentary Relations Office, Kristen Bassett
613-773-1019, Fax: 613-773-1051, kristen.bassett@agr.gc.ca
Manager, Finance & Administration, Corporate Secretariat, Jeanne Johnson
613-773-1057, Fax: 613-773-1061, jeanne.johnson@agr.gc.ca

Farm Financial Programs Branch / Direction générale des programmes de financement agricoles
Tower 7, 1341 Baseline Rd., Ottawa, ON K1A 0C5
613-759-1000 Fax: 613-773-2121
The Farm Financial Programs Branch of Agriculture & Agri-Food Canada oversees the following organizations: Agriculture Transformation Programs Directorate; Business Risk Management Program Development; Centre of Program Excellence (COPE); Farm Income Programs Directorate; Finance & Renewal Programs Directorate; & Service Policy & Transformation Directorate.
Assistant Deputy Minister, Farm Financial Programs Branch, Rita Moritz
613-773-2815, Fax: 613-773-2121, rita.moritz@agr.gc.ca
Acting Director General, Finance & Renewal Programs Directorate, Sean Malone
613-773-2005, Fax: 613-773-2099, sean.malone@agr.gc.ca
Director General, Centre of Program Excellence (COPE), Ray Edwards
613-773-0612, Fax: 613-773-1911, ray.edwards@agr.gc.ca
Director General, Business Risk Management Program Development, Danny Foster
613-773-2100, Fax: 613-773-2198, danny.foster@agr.gc.ca
Acting Director General, Farm Income Programs Directorate, Patti Miller
204-984-5645, Fax: 204-983-7557, patti.miller@agr.gc.ca
Director General, Agriculture Transformation Programs Directorate, Linda Parsons
613-773-1900, Fax: 613-773-1911, linda.parsons@agr.gc.ca
Executive Director, Grants & Contributions Delivery Project, Johanne Y. Langevin
613-773-2006, Fax: 613-773-2121, johanne.langevin@agr.gc.ca

Human Resources Branch / Direction générale des ressources humaines
Tower 1, 560 Rochester St., Ottawa, ON K1A 0C5
613-759-1000 Fax: 613-759-7105
Assistant Deputy Minister, Human Resources, Johanne Bélisle
613-759-1196, Fax: 613-759-7105, johanne.belisle@agr.gc.ca
Acting Director General, Planning, Policy & Workplace Programs, Scott Aughey
613-759-6527, scott.aughey@agr.gc.ca
Director General, Planning, Policy, & Workplace Programs, Catherine Conrad
613-715-5056, Fax: 613-715-5150, catherine.conrad@agr.gc.ca
Director General, Workplace Relations, Caroline Dunn
613-715-5260, Fax: 613-759-6143, caroline.dunn@agr.gc.ca
Acting Director General, Client Services, Maureen Meaney
613-759-6231, Fax: 613-715-5244, maureen.meaney@agr.gc.ca
Senior Director, Learning, Development, & Official Languages, Laurie Hunter
613-759-7434, Fax: 613-792-3426, laurie.hunter@agr.gc.ca
Acting Senior Director, Staffing & Recruitment, Strategic Resources, Brian McCarthy
613-759-6683, Fax: 613-759-7767, brian.mccarthy@agr.gc.ca

Senior Director, Organizational Effectiveness & Compensation, Client Services, Michael Morin
613-694-2578, Fax: 613-759-7471, michael.morin@agr.gc.ca

Information Systems Branch / Direction générale des systèmes d'information
Tower 4, 1341 Baseline Rd., Ottawa, ON K1A 0C5
613-759-1000 Fax: 613-773-0676

The Information Systems Branch of Agriculture & Agri-Food Canada is reponsible for the following organizations: Applications Development Directorate; Information Management Services; IT Operations; & the Strategic Management Directorate.

Chief Information Officer, Peter Bruce
613-773-1395, Fax: 613-773-0676, peter.bruce@agr.gc.ca
Director General, IT Operations, Gail Eagen
613-773-0400, Fax: 613-773-0444, gail.eagen@agr.gc.ca
Director General, Applications Development Directorate, Angus Howieson
613-759-7735, Fax: 613-759-6045, angus.howieson@agr.gc.ca
Director General, Information Management Services, Jeff Lamirande
613-773-0304, Fax: 613-773-0666, jeff.lamirande@agr.gc.ca
Acting Director General, Strategic Management Directorate, Rama Rai
613-773-0615, Fax: 613-773-0666, rama.rai@agr.gc.ca
Director, Canadian Agriculture Library, Danielle Jacques
613-773-1448, Fax: 613-773-1499, danielle.jacques@agr.gc.ca
Director, Programs & Corporate Applications, Cameron MacDonald
613-759-6940, Fax: 613-694-2353, cameron.macdonald@agr.gc.ca

Legal Services / Services juridiques
Tower 7, 1341 Baseline Rd., Ottawa, ON K1A 0C5
613-759-1000 Fax: 613-773-2929

General Counsel & Executive Director, Louise Sénéchal
613-773-2901, Fax: 613-773-2929, louise.senechal@agr.gc.ca
Business Manager, Aysha Johnson
613-773-2915, Fax: 613-773-2929, aysha.johnson@agr.gc.ca
Information Specialist, Aurora Bravar
613-773-2920, Fax: 613-773-2929, aurora.bravara@agr.gc.ca
Senior Counsel, Duane Schippers
613-773-2913, Fax: 613-773-2929, duane.schippers@agr.gc.ca
Senior Counsel, Theresa Siok
613-773-2914, Fax: 613-773-2929, theresa.siok@agr.gc.ca

Market & Industry Services Branch (MISB) / Direction générale des services à l'industrie et aux marchés
Tower 5, 1341 Baseline Rd., Ottawa, ON K1A 0C5
613-759-1000 Fax: 613-773-1711
Other Communication: Government of Canada Export Services Information, Toll-Free Phone: 1-888-576-4444

The Market & Industry Services Branch of Agriculture & Agri-Food Canada oversees the following organizations: Bilateral Relations & Technical Trade Policy Directorate; Food Value Chain Bureau; International Markets Bureau; Market Access Secretariat; Negotiations & Multilateral Trade Policy Directorate; & the Operations Directorate. The Operations Directorate operates regional offices throughout Canada, which provide access to market & trade programs & services. Marketing & trade officers offer the following information: statistics by country & product; market access advice; investment opportunities; regulatory issues; export counselling; & news about promotional events.

Assistant Deputy Minister, Steve Tierney
613-773-1790, Fax: 613-773-1755, steve.tierney@agr.gc.ca
Director General, Multilateral Relations, Policy & Engagemnent Directorate, Blair Coomber
613-773-1600, Fax: 613-773-1616, blair.coomber@agr.gc.ca
Director General & Chief Agriculture Negotiator, Trade Agreements & Negotiations, Gilles Gauthier
613-773-0985, Fax: 613-773-1755, gilles.gauthier@agr.gc.ca
Director General, Market Access Secretariat, Fred Gorrell
613-773-1512, Fax: 613-773-0199, fred.gorrell@agr.gc.ca
Director General, Operations Directorate, Dr. Jaspinder Komal
613-773-1501, Fax: 613-773-1500, jaspinder.komal@agr.gc.ca
Director General, Sector Development & Analysis Directorate, Susie Miller
613-773-1750, Fax: 613-773-0300, susie.miller@agr.gc.ca
Director General, International Markets Bureau, Paul Murphy
613-773-1517, Fax: 613-773-1500, paul.murphy@agr.gc.ca

Market & Industry Services Branch Regional Offices:

Alberta & Territories Regional Office
#720, 9700 Jasper Ave., Edmonton, AB T5J 4G5
780-495-4141 Fax: 780-495-3324

Regional Director, Rodney Dlugos
780-495-5525, Fax: 780-495-3324, rodney.dlugos@agr.gc.ca
Deputy Director, Janet Dorey
780-495-5526, Fax: 780-495-3324, janet.dorey@agr.gc.ca

Atlantic Regional Office
#405, 1791 Barrington St., PO Box 248, Halifax, NS B3J 2N7
902-426-3198 Fax: 902-426-3439

The Atlantic Regional Office in Halifax, Nova Scotia, is the headquarters for the following operations: New Brunswick Operations (Phone: 506-452-3706, Fax: 506-452-3509); Newfoundland & Labrador Operations (Phone: 709-772-4063, Fax: 709-772-4803); Nova Scotia Operations (Phone: 902-896-0332, Fax: 902-896-0100); & Prince Edward Island Operations (Phone: 902-566-7300, Fax: 902-566-7316).

Regional Director, Janet Steele
902-426-7171, Fax: 902-426-3439, janet.steele@agr.gc.ca
Deputy Director, Prince Edward Island Operations, Heath Coles
902-566-7305, Fax: 902-566-7316, heath.coles@agr.gc.ca
Deputy Director, Newfoundland & Labrador Operations, Brian Goldsworthy
709-772-4055, Fax: 709-772-4803, brian.goldsworthy@agr.gc.ca
Acting Deputy Director, New Brunswick Operations, Dino Kubik
506-452-3753, Fax: 506-452-3509, dino.kubik@agr.gc.ca
Deputy Director, Nova Scotia Operations, Shelley Manning
902-896-0098, Fax: 902-896-0100, shelley.manning@agr.gc.ca

British Columbia Regional Office
#420, 4321 Stillcreek Dr., Burnaby, BC V5C 6S7
604-666-6344 Fax: 604-666-7235

Regional Director, John Berry
604-666-6344, Fax: 604-666-7235, john.berry@agr.gc.ca
Deputy Director, Michelle Soucie
604-666-3054, Fax: 604-666-7235, michelle.soucie@agr.gc.ca

Manitoba Regional Office
303 Main St., Winnipeg, MB R3C 3G7
204-983-3032 Fax: 204-983-4583

Acting Regional Director, Bob Nawolsky
204-983-3891, Fax: 204-983-4583, bob.nawolsky@agr.gc.ca
Acting Deputy Director, Ron Wonneck
204-983-4596, Fax: 204-983-4583, ron.wonneck@agr.gc.ca

Ontario Regional Office
174 Stone Rd. West, Guelph, ON N1G 4S9
519-837-9400 Fax: 519-837-9782

Acting Regional Director, Marg Bancroft
519-837-5821, Fax: 519-837-9782, marg.bancroft@agr.gc.ca
Deputy Director, Karl Michelazzi
519-780-8097, Fax: 519-837-9782, karl.michelazzi@agr.gc.ca
Deputy Director, Bill Robinson
519-837-5822, Fax: 519-837-9782, bill.robinson@agr.gc.ca

Québec Regional Office
2001, rue Université, 7e étage, Montréal, QC H3A 3N2
514-283-8888 Fax: 514-496-3966

Regional Director, Sandra Gagné
514-315-6170, Fax: 514-496-3966, sandra.gagne@agr.gc.ca
Regional Deputy Director, Scott Patterson
514-315-6171, Fax: 514-496-3966, scott.patterson2@agr.gc.ca

Saskatchewan Regional Office
1800 Hamilton St., Regina, SK S4P 4K7
306-780-5545 Fax: 306-780-7360

Regional Director, Dean L. Vey
306-780-7065, Fax: 306-780-7360, dean.vey@agr.gc.ca
Deputy Director, Wendy Collinge
306-780-5452, Fax: 306-780-7360, wendy.collinge@agr.gc.ca
Deputy Director, Markets & Trade, Gavin M. Conacher
306-780-5216, Fax: 306-780-7360, gavin.conacher@agr.gc.ca

Regional Coordination & Correspondence
613-759-7558 Fax: 613-773-1500

Deputy Director, Regional Coordination & Correspondence, Josy Parrotta-Marck
613-773-1876, Fax: 613-773-1500, josy.parrotta-marck@agr.gc.ca
Senior Commerce Officer, Nathalie Bradbury
613-773-0843, Fax: 613-773-1500, nathalie.bradbury@agr.gc.ca

Office of Audit & Evaluation
Tower 4, 1341 Baseline Rd., Ottawa, ON K1A 0C5
613-759-1000 Fax: 613-773-0660

Agriculture & Agri-Food Canada's Office of Audit & Evaluation is responsible for the following services: evaluation; governance & review; & internal audit & assurance.

Chief Audit & Evaluation Executive, Graham Barr
613-773-0650, Fax: 613-773-0660, graham.barr@agr.gc.ca
Director, Governance & Review Services, Jennifer Moher
613-773-1773, Fax: 613-773-0660, jennifer.moher@agr.gc.ca
Director, Evaluation Services, Sally Scott
613-773-0655, Fax: 613-773-0660, sally.scott@agr.gc.ca
Director, Internal Audit, Lyne Castonguay
613-773-0669, Fax: 613-773-0660, lyne.castonguay@agr.gc.ca

Canada-Saskatchewan Irrigation Diversification Centre
901 McKenzie St. South, PO Box 700, Outlook, SK S0L 2N0
306-867-5400 Fax: 306-867-9656
csidc@agr.gc.ca

Manitoba
#200, 303 Main St., Winnipeg, MB R3C 3G7
204-984-3695 Fax: 204-983-2178

Manitoba Crop Diversification Centre
PO Box 309, Carberry, MB R0K 0H0
204-834-6005 Fax: 204-834-3777

Northern Alberta & BC
Canada Place, #945, 9700 Jasper Ave. NW, Edmonton, AB T5J 4C3
780-495-3307 Fax: 780-495-4504

Northern Saskatchewan
#1101, 11 Innovation Blvd., Saskatoon, SK S7N 3H5
306-975-4693 Fax: 306-975-4594

Agroforestry Development Centre
PO Box 940, Indian Head, SK S0G 2K0
306-695-2284 Fax: 306-695-2568

Southern Alberta
Harry Hays Bldg., #600, 138 - 4 Ave. SE, Calgary, AB T2G 4Z2
403-292-5638 Fax: 403-292-5659

Southern Saskatchewan
#603, 1800 Hamilton St., Regina, SK S4P 4L2
306-780-5150 Fax: 306-780-6778

Research Branch / Direction générale de la recherche
Tower 5, 1341 Baseline Rd., Ottawa, ON K1A 0C5
613-759-1000 Fax: 613-773-1866

Agriculture & Agri-Food Canada's Research Branch consists of the following organizations: Innovation Directorate; International Scientific Cooperation Bureau; Land Resources; Science Centres Directorate, Science Partnerships Directorate; & Science Policy & Planning. Scientists from Agriculture & Agri-Food Canada work on projects to benefit the agricultural & agri-food sector at research centres located across Canada.

Acting Assistant Deputy Minister, Jody Aylard
613-773-1860, Fax: 613-773-1866, jody.aylard@agr.gc.ca
Director General, Science Policy & Planning, Dr. Christiane Deslauriers, PhD
613-773-1870, Fax: 613-773-1877, christiane.deslauriers@agr.gc.ca
Director General, Science Partnerships Directorate, Dr. Stephen D. Morgan Jones, PhD
403-317-2200, Fax: 403-317-2197, steve.morganjones@agr.gc.ca
Director General, Science Centres Directorate, Dr. Gilles Saindon, PhD
613-773-1843, Fax: 613-773-1844, gilles.saindon@agr.gc.ca
Director, Multilateral Science Relations, International Scientific Cooperation Bureau, Brad Fraleigh
613-773-1838, Fax: 613-773-1822, brad.fraleigh@agr.gc.ca
Chief Scientist, International Scientific Cooperation Bureau, Dr. Yvon Martel, PhD
613-773-1830, Fax: 613-773-1833, yvon.martel@agr.gc.ca
Chief Officer for Scientific Relations, China, International Scientific Cooperation Bureau, Jianqiang (Joe) Zhou, PhD
613-759-1744, Fax: 613-773-1833, joe.zhou@agr.gc.ca

Research Centres:

Atlantic Food & Horticulture Research Centre
32 Main St., Kentville, NS B4N 1J5
902-679-5333 Fax: 902-679-2311

Manager, Research, Dr. D. Mark Hodges, PhD
902-679-5544, Fax: 902-679-5784, mark.hodges@agr.gc.ca
Manager, Farm, Innovation & Renewal, David L. Bowlby
902-679-5589, Fax: 902-670-0004, david.bowlby@agr.gc.ca
Science Director, Crop Production Systems, Peter Hicklenton
902-679-5760, Fax: 902-679-5344, peter.hicklenton@agr.gc.ca

Brandon Research Centre
RR#3, PO Box 1000A, Brandon, MB R7A 5Y3
204-726-7650 Fax: 204-728-3858

Manager, Research, Dr. Fernando Selles, PhD
204-578-3539, Fax: 204-578-3528, fernando.selles@agr.gc.ca
Manager, Farm, Clay Jackson
204-578-3610, Fax: 204-578-3522, clayton.jackson@agr.gc.ca

Cereal Research Centre
195 Dafoe Rd., Winnipeg, MB R3T 2M9
204-983-5533 Fax: 204-983-4604

Manager, Research, Dr. David Wall
204-983-0099, Fax: 204-984-6333, david.wall@agr.gc.ca

Science Director, Water & Soil Resources, Dr. Johanne B. Boisvert, PhD
204-983-0466, Fax: 204-983-4604,
johanne.boisvert@agr.gc.ca

Crops & Livestock Research Centre
440 University Ave., Charlottetown, PE C1A 4N6
902-566-6800 Fax: 902-566-6821

The Crops and Livestock Research Centre (CLRC) in Charlottetown, Prince Edward Island is one of Agriculture and Agri-Food Canada's network of 19 research centres. The Centre's mandate is to develop scientific knowledge and new technologies in agriculture with the prime focus on Prince Edward Island and Atlantic Canada.

Manager, Research, Dr. Maria Rodriguez
902-566-6817, Fax: 902-566-6821,
maria.rodriguez@agr.gc.ca
Manager, Research Operations, Roddy C. Pratt
902-672-6426, Fax: 902-566-6821, roddy.pratt@agr.gc.ca

Dairy & Swine Research & Development Centre
2000, rue College, CP 90 Lennoxville, Sherbrooke, QC J1M 1Z3
819-565-9171 Fax: 819-564-5507

The Dairy & Swine Research & Development Centre oversees the operations of the Beef Research Farm in Kapuskasing, Ontario, as well as the Office of Intellectual Property & Commercialization in Sherbrooke, Québec.

Manager, Research, Dr. Alain Giguère
819-565-9174, Fax: 819-564-5407,
alain.giguere@agr.gc.cagc.ca
Science Director, Livestock Production Systems, Dr. Jacques Surprenant, PhD, MPA
819-565-9174, Fax: 819-564-4974,
jacques.surprenant@agr.gc.ca
Head Herdsman, Kapuskasing Beef Research Farm, Maurice Portelance
705-335-6148, Fax: 705-337-6000,
maurice.portelance@agr.gc.ca

Eastern Cereal & Oilseed Research Centre
960 Carling Ave., Ottawa, ON K1A 0C6
613-759-1858 Fax: 613-759-1970

Manager, Research, Dr. Marc Savard
613-759-1683, Fax: 613-759-1970, marc.savard@agr.gc.ca
Manager, Research Support, Ron Wheeler
613-759-1544, Fax: 613-952-6438, ron.wheeler@agr.gc.ca
Science Director, Food & Health, Dr. Michèle Marcotte, PhD, Eng
613-759-1525, Fax: 613-759-1970,
michele.marcotte@agr.gc.ca

Food Research & Development Centre
3600, boul Casavant ouest, Saint-Hyacinthe, QC J2S 8E3
450-773-1105 Fax: 450-773-8461

Manager, Research, Dr. Christian J. Toupin, PhD
450-768-3331, Fax: 450-773-2888,
christian.toupin@agr.gc.ca
Science Director, Food Production, Safety, & Quality, Gabriel Piette
450-768-3304, Fax: 450-773-2888, gabriel.piette@agr.gc.ca

Greenhouse & Processing Crops Research Centre
2585 Country Rd. 20, Harrow, ON N0R 1G0
519-738-2251 Fax: 519-738-2929

Manager, Research, Ranjana Sharma
519-738-1208, Fax: 519-738-2929,
ranjana.sharma@agr.gc.ca
Manager, Integrated Services, Adrian Lancop
519-738-1210, Fax: 519-738-2929, adrian.lancop@agr.gc.ca
Science Director, Integrated Pest Management, Environmental Health, Dr. Gary Whitfield
519-738-1218, Fax: 519-738-3756, gary.whitfield@agr.gc.ca

Guelph Food Research Centre
93 Stone Rd. West, Guelph, ON N1G 5C9
519-829-2400 Fax: 519-829-2600

Manager, Research, Dr. Punidadas Piyasena
519-780-8063, Fax: 519-829-2602, puni.piyasena@agr.gc.ca
Science Director, Gabriel Piette
450-768-3304, Fax: 450-773-2888, gabriel.pietter@agr.gc.ca

Horticulture Research & Development Centre
430, boul Gouin, Saint-Jean-sur-Richelieu, QC J3B 3E6
450-346-4494 Fax: 450-346-7740

Manager, Research, Roger Chagnon
450-515-2001, Fax: 450-346-7908, roger.chagnon@agr.gc.ca
Science Director, Jacques Surprenant
819-565-9174, Fax: 450-346-7908,
jacques.suprenant@agr.gc.ca
Manager, Greenhouse, Guy Boulet
450-515-2016, Fax: 450-346-7740, guy.boulet@agr.gc.ca

Lacombe Research Centre
6000 C & E Trail, Lacombe, AB T4L 1W1
403-782-8100 Fax: 403-782-6120

The Lacombe Research Centre is responsible for the operations of research farms in Beaverlodge & Fort Vermilion in Alberta.

Manager, Research, Rick Lawrence
403-782-8110, Fax: 403-782-4308, rick.lawrence@agr.gc.ca
Science Director, Paul McCaughey
306-956-7211, Fax: 306-956-7248,
paul.mccaughey@agr.gc.ca
Manager, Farm, Ken B. Grimson
403-782-8139, Fax: 403-782-8186, ken.grimson@agr.gc.ca
Foreman, Fort Vermilion Research Farm, Joe Unruh
780-927-3253, Fax: 780-927-3330, joe.unruh@agr.gc.ca

Lethbridge Research Centre
5403 - 1st Ave. South, PO Box 3000, Lethbridge, AB T1J 4B1
403-327-4561 Fax: 403-382-3156

The Lethbridge Research Centre oversees the operations of the Onefour Research Substation, the Stavely Research Substation, & the Vauxhall Research Substation in Alberta.

Manager, Research, Dr. Brian Freeze, PhD
403-317-3445, Fax: 403-317-2211, brian.freeze@agr.gc.ca
Manager, Facility, Donavan T. Casson
403-317-2233, Fax: 403-317-3491,
donavan.casson@agr.gc.ca
Manager, Feed Mill, Dave Dancoisne
403-317-3383, Fax: 403-382-3156,
dave.dancoisne@agr.gc.ca
Manager, Stavely Research Substation Site, Albert J. Middleton
403-549-2152, Fax: 403-549-3744,
albert.middleton@agr.gc.ca
Manager, Vauxhall Research Substation Site, Jim Sukeroff
403-654-2255, Fax: 403-654-4243, jim.sukeroff@agr.gc.ca
Manager, Onefour Research Substation Site, Ian Walker
403-868-2364, Fax: 403-868-2489, ian.walker@agr.gc.ca
Science Director, Crop Genetic Enhancement, Dr. Jeff Stewart
403-317-2208, Fax: 403-317-2197, jeff.stewart@agr.gc.ca

Pacific Agri-Food Research Centre (PARC)
4200 Hwy. 97, PO Box 5000, Summerland, BC V0H 1Z0
250-494-7711 Fax: 250-494-0755

The Pacific Agri-Food Research Centre oversees the following organizations: the Agassiz Site, the Kamloops Range Research Unit, & the Summerland Site.

Research Manager, Summerland Site, Kenna MacKenzie
250-494-6358, Fax: 250-494-6415,
kenna.mackenzie@agr.gc.ca
Research Manager, Agassiz Site, Sankaran KrishnaRaj
604-796-1709, Fax: 604-796-0359,
sankaran.krishnaraj@agr.gc.ca
Facility Manager, Kamloops Range Research Unit, Larry Maio
250-554-5227, Fax: 250-554-5229, larry.maio@agr.gc.ca
Integrated Services Manager, Summerland Site, Bruce Jensen
250-494-6357, Fax: 250-494-0755, bruce.jensen@agr.gc.ca
Field Services Manager, Summerland Site, Mark Neufield
250-494-6427, Fax: 250-494-0755, mark.neufield@agr.gc.ca
Grounds & Greenhouse Manager, Summerland Site, David Weir
250-494-6387, Fax: 250-494-0755, david.weir@agr.gc.ca

Potato Research Centre
850 Lincoln Rd., PO Box 20280, Fredericton, NB E3B 4Z7
506-452-3260 Fax: 506-452-3316

The Potato Research Centre is also responsible for the Senator Hervé J. Michaud Research Farm, located in Bouctouche, New Brunswick.

Manager, Research, Edward Hurley
506-452-4845, Fax: 506-452-3212,
jacques.millette@agr.gc.ca
Manager, Facilities, Sean Brown
506-452-4839, Fax: 506-452-3316, sean.brown@agr.gc.ca
Manager, Integrated Services, Senator Hervé J Michaud Research Farm, Louise Boucher
506-743-1140, Fax: 506-743-8316, louise.boucher@agr.gc.ca
Manager, Farm, Larry McMillan
506-452-4838, Fax: 506-452-3316, larry.mcmillan@agr.gc.ca

Saskatoon Research Centre
107 Science Pl., Saskatoon, SK S7N 0X2
306-956-7200 Fax: 306-956-7247

Manager, Research, Dr. Felicitas Katepa-Mupondwa
306-956-2489, Fax: 306-956-7248,
felicitas.katepa-mupondwa@agr.gc.ca
Science Director, Bioproducts Platforms & Genomics, Dr. Paul McCaughey
306-956-7211, Fax: 306-956-7248,
paul.mccaughey@agr.gc.ca

Semiarid Prairie Agricultural Research Centre
PO Box 1030, Swift Current, SK S9H 3X2
306-778-7200 Fax: 306-778-3188

The Semiarid Prairie Agricultural Research Centre is responsible for the operations of research farms in Indian Head & Regina, Saskatchewan.

Manager, Research, Bruce McArthur
306-778-7270, Fax: 306-778-3186,
bruce.mcarthur@agr.gc.ca
Manager, Integrated Services, Debbie Biese
306-778-7223, Fax: 306-778-3188, debbie.biese@agr.gc.ca
Manager, Regina Research Farm, Myron Knelsen
306-780-7426, Fax: 306-780-5501, myron.knelsen@agr.gc.ca
General Supervisor, Indian Head Research Farm, Danny Petty
306-695-4200, Fax: 306-695-3445, danny.petty@agr.gc.ca

Soils & Crops Research & Development Centre
2560, boul Hochelaga, Québec, QC G1V 2J3
418-657-7980 Fax: 418-648-2402

The Soils & Crops Research & Development Centre is also responsible for a research farm in Normandin, Québec.

Manager, Research, Genevieve Levasseur
418-210-5002, Fax: 418-648-7231,
genevieve.levasseur@agr.gc.ca
Science Director, Claudel Lemieux
418-210-5003, Fax: 418-648-7231,
claudel.lemieux@agr.gc.ca
Manager, Integrated Services, Normandin Research Farm, Mario Fortin
418-274-5881, Fax: 418-274-3386, mario.fortin@agr.gc.ca
Chief, Greenhouse, Normand Charest
418-210-5014, Fax: 418-648-2402,
normand.charest@agr.gc.ca

Southern Crop Protection & Food Research Centre
1391 Sandford St., London, ON N5V 4T3
519-457-1470 Fax: 519-457-3997

The Southern Crop Protection & Food Research Centre oversees the operations of research farms in Delhi & Vineland, Ontario, as well as an Office of Intellectual Property & Commercialization in London, Ontario.

Manager, Research, Southern Crop Protection & Food Research Centre, Dr. Karl Volkmar
519-457-1470, Fax: 519-457-3503, karl.volkmar@agr.gc.ca
Manager, Research, Vineland Research Farm, Antonet Svircev
604-796-1709, Fax: 604-796-0359,
antonet.svircev@agr.gc.ca
Manager, Facility, Joe Pratt
519-457-1470, Fax: 519-457-3997, joe.pratt@agr.gc.ca
Supervisor, Farm Services, Delhi Research Farm, Albert Asztalos
519-582-1950, Fax: 519-582-4223, albert.asztalos@agr.gc.ca

Rural & Co-operatives Secretariat / Le Secrétariat aux affaires rurales et aux coopératives
Tower 7, 1341 Baseline Rd., Ottawa, ON K1A 0C5
613-759-1000 Fax: 613-773-2727

Executive Director, Michaela Huard
613-773-2916, Fax: 613-773-2727,
michaela.huard@agr.gc.ca
Associate Executive Director, Christine Burton
613-773-2955, Fax: 613-773-2727,
christine.burton@agr.gc.ca
Director, Partnerships & Programs, Louise Boudreau
613-773-2988, Fax: 613-773-2198,
louise.boudreau@agr.gc.ca
Manager, Program Development & Implementation, Partnerships & Programs, Lawrence Euteneier
613-773-2943, Fax: 613-773-2198,
lawrence.euteneier@agr.gc.ca
Manager, Financial Services, Theresa Hedquist
613-773-2947, Fax: 613-773-2727,
theresa.hedquist@agr.gc.ca
Manager, Co-op Policy & Research Unit, Co-operative Policy & Research, Anne Marie McInnis
613-773-2971, Fax: 613-773-2199,
anne-marie.mcinnis@agr.gc.ca
Manager, Partnerships & Programs, Alain Roy
613-773-2925, Fax: 613-773-2198, alain.roy@agr.gc.ca
Officer, Rural Communications, Lauraine Watson
204-983-8376, Fax: 204-983-8357,
lauraine.watson@agr.gc.ca

Strategic Policy Branch / Direction générale des politiques stratégiques
Tower 7, 1341 Baseline Rd., Ottawa, ON K1A 0C5
613-759-1000 Fax: 613-773-2111

The Strategic Policy Branch of Agriculture & Agri-Food Canada includes the following organizations: Policy Development & Analysis Directorate; Policy, Planning, & Integration Directorate; & the Research & Analysis Directorate.

Assistant Deputy Minister, Greg Meredith
613-773-2930, Fax: 613-773-2121, greg.meredith@agr.gc.ca
Director General, Policy Development & Analysis Directorate, Paul Martin
613-773-2700, Fax: 613-773-2111, paul.martin@agr.gc.ca
Director General, Research & Analysis Directorate, Andrew Goldstein
613-773-0259, Fax: 613-773-2444,
andrew.goldstein@agr.gc.ca
Manager, Branch Planning & Resource Management, Taryn Barone
613-773-2301, Fax: 613-773-2333, taryn.barone@agr.gc.ca
Senior Policy Advisor, Lisa Foss
613-773-1563, Fax: 613-773-2121, lisa.foss@agr.gc.ca
Executive Assistant to the ADM, Louise Galipeau
613-773-2145, Fax: 613-773-2121,
louise.galipeau@agr.gc.ca

Atlantic Canada Opportunities Agency (ACOA) / Agence de promotion économique du Canada atlantique (APECA)

Blue Cross Centre, 644 Main St., 3rd Fl., PO Box 6051, Moncton, NB E1C 9J8

506-851-2271 Fax: 506-851-7403
800-561-7862
information@acoa-apeca.gc.ca
www.acoa-apeca.gc.ca
TTY: 877-456-6500

Other Communication: Secure fax: 506-875-1301; Access to information / privacy: 506-851-6202

The role of the Atlantic Canada Opportunities Agency is the development of opportunities for economic growth in Atlantic Canada. The agency achieves its mission in the following ways: assisting businesses to become more innovative, productive, & competitive; promoting the strengths of Atlantic Canada; & helping communities to develop more diversified local economies.

Minister of State (Atlantic Canada Opportunities Agency), Hon. Bernard Valcourt
613-941-7241, Fax: 613-952-6393, bvalcourt2011@hotmail.com

President, Paul J. LeBlanc
506-851-6128, Fax: 506-851-7403

Senior Vice-President, David Slade
506-851-6141

Vice-President, Finance & Corporate Services, Denise Frenette
506-851-6438

Director General, Human Resources, Kent Estabrooks
506-851-3070

Director General, Communications, Susan Wisking
506-851-7731, Fax: 613-952-6393, Other Communications: Alternate tel: 613-960-9010

Director, Regional Operations, Peter Hogan
902-426-1288

Director, Energy, Environment Policy, & Coordination, Daniel McCarthy
613-952-8216

Regional Offices:

New Brunswick Regional Office
570 Queen St., 3rd Fl., PO Box 578, Fredericton, NB E3B 5A6

506-452-3184 Fax: 506-452-3285
800-561-4030
TTY: 877-456-6500

The New Brunswick Regional Office oversees operations at the following offices: Campbellton (Phone: 506-789-4735); Edmundston (Phone: 506-735-4236); Fundy Region (Phone: 506-636-4485); Miramichi (506-778-1909); Northeast (Phone: 506-548-7420); Northwest (Phone: 506-473-5556); Southeast (Phone: 506-851-6432); Southwest (506-452-3135); & Tracadie-Sheila (506-395-1025).

Vice-President, New Brunswick, Janet Gagnon
506-452-3342

Executive Director, New Brunswick Federal Council, Raymond Gallant
506-452-4986

Director, Business Programs, André Charron
506-452-2413

Director, Communications, Patricia Field
506-452-4287

Director, Financial Management Services, David Hubbard
506-452-2423

Director, Policy, Advocacy, & Coordination, Gail Moser
506-452-3155

Newfoundland & Labrador Regional Office
John Cabot Building, 10 Barter's Hill, 11th Fl., PO Box 1060 C, St. John's, NL A1C 5M5

709-772-2751 Fax: 709-772-2712
800-668-1010
TTY: 877-456-6500

The Newfoundland & Labrador Regional Office oversees the following offices throughout the province: Clarenville (Phone: 709-466-5980); Corner Brook (Phone: 709-637-4477); Gander (Phone: 709-651-4457); Grand Bank (Phone: 709-832-2517); Grand Falls-Windsor (Phone: 709-489-6600); & Labrador (709-896-2648).

Vice-President, Newfoundland & Labrador, Paul Mills
709-772-4150

Director General, Policy, Advocacy, & Coordination, David Collins
709-772-2334

Executive Director, Federal / Regional Council, Mark Butler
709-772-2781

Director, Communications, Julie Afonso
709-772-2984

Director, Community Development, John Kennedy
709-772-2741

Director, Financial Management Services, Francis Mackey
709-772-6286

Director, Enterprise Development, Kenneth Martin
709-772-0212

Nova Scotia Regional Office
#600, 1801 Hollis St., PO Box 2284 C, Halifax, NS B3J 3C8

902-426-6743 Fax: 902-426-2054
800-565-1228
TTY: 877-456-6500

The Nova Scotia Regional Office of the Atlantic Canada Opportunities Agency oversees the following offices throughout Nova Scotia: Antigonish (Phone: 902-867-6075); Bridgewater (Phone: 902-541-5543); Church Point Office (Phone: 902-260-3590); Kentville (902-679-5356); Pictou (Phone: 902-755-3746); Truro (902-895-2743), & Yarmouth (Phone: 902-742-0809).

Vice-President, Nova Scotia (acting), Peter Hogan
902-426-1288

Director General, Regional Operations, Peter Hogan
902-426-1288

Director, Finance & Management Services, Nancy Ives
902-426-5968

Director, Intergovernmental Affairs & Coordination, Lisa Muton
902-426-4820

Director, Communications, Alexander Smith
902-426-9417, Fax: 902-426-5843

Prince Edward Island Regional Office
Royal Bank Building, 100 Sydney St., 3rd Floor, PO Box 40, Charlottetown, PE C1A 7K2

902-566-7492 Fax: 902-566-7098
800-871-2596
TTY: 877-456-6500

The Prince Edward Island Regional Office oversees the Summerside District Office (Phone: 902-888-4145).

Vice-President, Prince Edward Island & Tourism, Patrick Dorsey
902-368-0760

Director General, Enterprise Development & Policy, Wayne Hooper
902-626-2877, Fax: 902-566-7098

Director General, Atlantic Tourism, Robert McCloskey
902-626-2479, Fax: 902-566-7098

Executive Director, Prince Edward Island Federal Council, Catherine MacInnis
902-368-0889, Fax: 902-566-7489

Director, Corporate Programs & Services, Lynne Beairsto
902-566-7499

Director, Infrastructure Programs, Pat MacAulay
902-626-2794

Director, Communicatons, Cindy Roy
902-566-7569, Fax: 902-566-7098

Director, Trade & Business Programs, Douglas Smith
902-368-0890

Ottawa Office
60 Queen Street, 4th Fl., PO Box 1667 B, Ottawa, ON K1P 5R5

613-954-2422 Fax: 613-954-0429

Enterprise Cape Breton Corporation (ECBC) / Société d'expansion du Cap-Breton
Silicon Island, 70 Crescent St., PO Box 1750, Sydney, NS B1P 6T7

902-564-3600 Fax: 902-564-3825
800-705-3926
information@ecbc-secb.gc.ca
www.ecbc-secb.gc.ca

As the principal federal organization for economic development on Cape Breton Island, ECBC focuses on the major issues affecting the economy of the area. In partnership with all levels of government, the private sector, and other community stakeholders, ECBC promotes and assists the financing and development of communities and industry with a view to creating sustainable wealth on Cape Breton Island. In addition to its own programs, ECBC is responsible for the delivery of ACOA's programs on Cape Breton Island.

Chair, Paul J. LeBlanc
506-851-6128, Fax: 506-851-7403

Chief Executive Officer, John Lynn
902-564-3508, Fax: 902-564-2760

Atlantic Pilotage Authority (APA) / Administration de pilotage de l'Atlantique

Cogswell Tower, #910, 2000 Barrington St., Halifax, NS B3J 3K1

902-426-2550 Fax: 902-426-4004
877-272-3477
dispatch@atlanticpilotage.com
www.atlanticpilotage.com

Other Communication: Toll-Free Fax: 1-877-745-3477; Fax to Email Direct: 1-866-774-2477

The Federal Crown Corporation is responsible for the safe & efficient operation, maintenance, & administration of marine pilotage service to Atlantic Canada.

Chief Executive Officer, R.A. Anthony McGuinness
902-426-2553

Chief Financial Officer, Peter L. MacArthur
902-426-8657

Director, Operations, Patrick Gates
902-426-6389

Auditor General of Canada / Vérificateur général du Canada

240 Sparks St., Ottawa, ON K1A 0G6

613-995-3708 Fax: 613-957-0474
888-761-5953
communications@oag-bvg.gc.ca; infomedia@oag-bvg.gc.ca
www.oag-bvg.gc.ca
TTY: 613-954-8042

Other Communication: Media Relations, Phone: 613-952-0213, ext. 6292; Publications, Toll-Free Phone: 1-888-761-5953; Work Opportunities, E-mail: emplo@oag-bvg.gc.ca

The Office of the Auditor General of Canada was established in 1878. Today, the head office in Ottawa & regional offices in Halifax, Montréal, Edmonton, & Vancouver employ approximately 650 employees. The Office of the Auditor General of Canada provides objective, fact-based information required by Parliament to hold the federal government accountable for its stewardship of public funds. An Officer of Parliament, the Auditor General of Canada is responsible for auditing the following organizations: federal government departments; federal government agencies; most Crown corporations; many federal organizations; the government of the Yukon; the government of the Northwest Territories; & the government of Nunavut. The Auditor General, Sheila Fraser, reports publicly to the House of Commons about matters she believes should be brought to the attention of the House of Commons. stainable development matters that she believes should be brought to the attention of the House of Commons. The report can include chapters on audits & studies, sustainable development strategies, & environmental petitions

Interim Auditor General, John Wiersema
613-952-0213

Chief Information Officer & Assistant Auditor General, Ira Greenblatt
613-952-0213

Assistant Auditor General, IC, Aboriginal Issues, HRMA, Nunavut, Industry, & NRC, Ronnie Campbell
613-952-0213

Assistant Auditor General, Crown Corporations Group, Nancy Cheng
613-952-0213, Fax: 613-941-8284

Assistant Auditor General, Yukon & the Northwest Territories, Andrew Lennox
613-952-0213

Assistant Auditor General, CBSA, CIDA, CSIS, CIC, CSC, IRB, Justice, Public Safety, & RCMP, Wendy Loschiuk
613-952-0213

Assistant Auditor General, CDIC, CMHC, OP, FI, EDC, FCC, IDRC, & PSPIB, Clyde MacLellan
613-952-0213

Assistant Auditor General, Health Canada, SC, CFIA, AAFC, & Fisheries & Oceans, Neil Maxwell
613-952-0213

Assistant Auditor General, CRA, AA, FS, Separate Opinions, Income Tax, GST, & Performance Reporting, Marian McMahon
613-952-0213

Assistant Auditor General, HRSDC, Small Entities, Crown Corporations, & Other Entities, Sylvain Ricard
613-952-0213

Assistant Auditor General, Canadian Heritage Arts & Culture, Museums, NAC, CBC, TC, CATSA, VIA Rail, NCC, NRTEE, & ILO, John Rossetti
613-952-0213

Assistant Auditor General, Corporate Services, Lyn Sachs
613-952-0213

Principal, National Defence, Veteran Affairs Canada, Foreign Affairs, & International Trade Canada, Jerome Berthelette
613-952-0213

Principal, Practice Review & Internal Audit, & Strategic Planning, Julie Charron
613-952-0213

Principal, Forensic Audit Section, Linda Drainville
613-952-0213

Principal, Parliamentary Liaison & International Relations, Jocelyne Therrien
613-952-0213

Principal, Communications, Susan Wheeler
613-952-0213

Regional Offices:

Edmonton
Manulife Place, #2460, 10180 - 101st St., Edmonton, AB T5J 3S4

780-495-2028 Fax: 780-495-2031

Principal, Guy LeGras
780-495-2029

Director, David Irving
780-495-6338

Halifax/Dartmouth
Centennial Building, #414, 1660 Hollis St., Halifax, NS B3J 1V7
902-426-7721 Fax: 902-426-8591
Principal, Heather McManaman
902-426-7728
Director, Glenn Doucette
902-426-2097
Director, Paul Kelly
902-426-6512

Montréal
#545, 1255, rue Peel, Montréal, QC H3B 2T9
514-283-6086 Fax: 514-283-1715
Principal, René Béliveau
514-283-8324
Director, Jean-Pierre Morin
514-283-8136
Director, Tina Swiderski
514-283-7793

Vancouver
#210, 351 Abbott St., Vancouver, BC V6B 0G6
604-666-3596 Fax: 604-666-6162
Principal, Eric Hellsten
604-666-7600

Bank of Canada / Banque du Canada

234 Wellington St., Ottawa, ON K1A 0G9
613-782-7902 Fax: 613-782-7713
800-303-1282
info@bankofcanada.ca; communications@bankofcanada.ca (Media)
www.bankofcanada.ca
TTY: 888-418-1461
Other Communication: Access to information & privacy issues, E-mail: ATIP-AIPRP@bankofcanada.ca; Publications, E-mail: publications@bankofcanada.ca

Founded in 1934, the Bank of Canada was orignially a privately owned corporation. It became a Crown corporation, belonging to the federal government, in 1938. As Canada's central bank, the role of the Bank of Canada is the promotion of the economic & financial welfare of the nation. The following are the main responsibilities of the Bank of Canada: Canada's financial system; monetary policy; funds management; & bank notes. The Governor & Senior Deputy of the Bank of Canada are appointed by the Bank's Board of Directors, with the approval of the Cabinet. Regional offices of the Bank of Canada are located in the following cities: Halifax (Phone: 902-420-4600); Montréal (Phone: 514-496-4800); Toronto (Phone: 416-542-1251); Calgary (Phone: 403-215-6700); Vancouver (Phone: 604-643-6227); & New York (Phone: 212-596-1673).

Governor, Mark J. Carney
Senior Deputy Governor, Tiff Macklem
Deputy Governor, Jean Boivin
Deputy Governor, Agathe Côté
Deputy Governor, Timothy Lane
Deputy Governor, John Murray
Special Adviser to the Governor, Timothy Hodgson
General Counsel & Corporate Secretary, Executive & Legal Services, W. John Jussup
Interim Chief, Information Technology Services, Dale Fleck
Chief, International Economic Analysis, Donald Coletti
Chief, Currency, Gerry T. Gaetz
Chief, Financial Markets, Donna Howard
Chief, Canadian Economic Analysis, Sharon Kozicki
Chief, Corporate Services, Colleen Leighton
Chief, Funds Management & Banking, Ron Morrow
Chief Internal Auditor, Carmen Prévost Vierula
Chief, Communications, Jill Vardy
Chief, Financial Services; Chief Accountant, Sheila Vokey
Chief, Financial Stability, Mark Zelmer
Chief Librarian, Information Resource Centre, Beverly Graham
613-782-8466, Fax: 613-782-7387, ref1@bankofcanada.ca
Director, Data & Statistics Office, Dinah Maclean
Archivist, Jane Boyko
613-782-8673, Fax: 613-782-7387, archives@bankofcanada.ca

Business Development Bank of Canada (BDC) / Banque de développement du Canada (BDC)

#400, 5, Place Ville-Marie, Montréal, QC H3B 5E7
514-283-5904 Fax: 514-283-5626
877-232-2269
www.bdc.ca
Other Communication: Toll-Free Fax 1-877-329-9232; Corporate Financing (Québec & Atlantic Regions), Fax: 514-283-8410

The Business Development Bank of Canada is a financial institution which is wholly owned by the Goverment of Canada. It was created by an Act of Parliament in 1944. The Bank is governed by an independent Board of Directors, & reports to the Minister of Industry. The mission of the Business Development Bank of Canada is to assist in the establishment & development of Canadian businesses in all industries. The Bank focuses its efforts on small & medium-sized enterprises. The following services are carried out by the Business Development Bank of Canada: consulting services; flexible financing, such as long term business financing & subordinate financing; & venture capital. Branches of the Business Development Bank of Canada are located throughout Canada. Smaller communities are served by satellite branches, consultants, & travelling account managers.

Chair, John A. MacNaughton
President & Chief Executive Officer, Jean-René Halde
Executive Vice-President & Chief Financial Officer, Paul Buron
Executive Vice-President, Financing & Consulting, Edmée Métivier
Senior Vice President, Financing & Consulting, Québec, Patrice Bernard
Senior Vice President, Human Resources, Mary Karamanos
Senior Vice President, Financing & Consulting, Ontario, Peter Lawler
Senior Vice President, Strategy & Corporate Development, Jérôme Nycz
Senior Vice President, Legal Affairs; Corporate Secretary, Louise Paradis
Senior Vice President, Financing & Consulting, Atlantic, Terry Quinn
Senior Vice President, Credit Risk Management, André St-Pierre
National Vice President, Subordinate Financing, Roger Giraldeau
National Vice President, Subordinate Financing, Eastern Quebec, Montréal, North-Shore, & South-Shore, Danielle Landry
Vice President, Corporate Relations, Michel Bergeron
Vice President, Venture Capital, Charles Cazabon
Vice President, Securitization, Paula Cruickshank
Vice President, Information & Communication Technologies, Glen R. Egan
Vice President, Energy, Environment, Electronic, & Materials, Robert Inglese
Vice President, Consulting, Bruce McConnell
Vice President, Fund Investments, Frank Pho

Alberta Branches:

Calgary Area Branch
Barclay Centre, #110, 444 - 7 Ave. SW, Calgary, AB T2P 0X8
403-292-5600 Fax: 403-292-6616
Other Communication: Subordinate Financing (Prairies & Northwest Territories), Phone: 403-292-5000, Fax: 403-292-5862

Calgary North Branch
#100, 1935 - 32 Ave. NE, Calgary, AB T2E 7C8
403-292-5333 Fax: 403-292-6651

Calgary South Branch
#200, 6700 MacLeod Trail SE, Calgary, AB T2H 0L3
403-292-8882 Fax: 403-292-4345

Edmonton Branch
#200, 10665 Jasper Ave., Edmonton, AB T5J 3S9
780-495-2277 Fax: 780-495-6616

Edmonton South Branch
#201, 4628 Calgary Trail NW, Edmonton, AB T6H 6A1
780-495-7200 Fax: 780-495-7198

Grande Prairie Branch
#203, 10625 West Side Dr., Grande Prairie, AB T8V 8E6
780-532-8875 Fax: 780-539-5130

Lethbridge Branch
520 - 5th Ave. South, Lethbridge, AB T1J 0T8
403-382-3000 Fax: 403-382-3162

Medicine Hat Branch
#101, 2248 - 13th Ave. SE, Medicine Hat, AB T1A 8G6
403-527-2601 Fax: 403-528-6899
Office by appointment.

Red Deer Branch
#107, 4815 - 50th Ave., Red Deer, AB T4N 4A5
403-340-4203 Fax: 403-340-4243

British Columbia Branches:

Edmonton West Branch
236 Mayfield Common, Edmonton, AB T5P 4B3
780-442-7312 Fax: 780-495-3102

Cranbrook Branch
205B Cranbrook St. North, Cranbrook, BC V1C 3R1
250-417-2200 Fax: 250-417-2213

Fort St. John Branch
#7, 10230 - 100th St., Fort St. John, BC V1J 3Y9
250-787-0622 Fax: 250-787-9423

Kamloops Branch
205 Victoria St., Kamloops, BC V2C 2A1
250-851-4900 Fax: 250-851-4925

Kelowna Branch
313 Bernard Ave., Kelowna, BC V1Y 6N6
250-470-4802 Fax: 250-470-4832

Langley Branch
#101B, 6424 - 200th St., Langley, BC V2Y 2T3
604-532-5150 Fax: 604-532-5166

Nanaimo Branch
#500, 6581 Aulds Rd., Nanaimo, BC V9T 6J6
250-390-5757 Fax: 250-390-5753

North Vancouver Branch
#3, 221 West Esplanade, North Vancouver, BC V7M 3J3
604-666-7703 Fax: 604-666-1957

Prince George Branch
#150, 177 Victoria St., Prince George, BC V2L 5R8
250-561-5323 Fax: 250-561-5512

Surrey Branch
#160, 10362 King George Blvd., Surrey, BC V3T 2W5
604-586-2400 Fax: 604-586-2430

Terrace Branch
3233 Emerson St., Terrace, BC V8G 5L2
250-615-5300 Fax: 250-615-5320

Vancouver Branch
One Bentall Centre, #2100, 505 Burrard St., PO Box 6, Vancouver, BC V7X 1M6
604-666-7850 Fax: 604-666-1068
Other Communication: Subordinate Financing (British Columbia & Yukon), Phone: 604-666-7875, Fax: 604-666-8482; Corporate Financing (Western Canada), Phone: 604-666-1068

Victoria Branch
990 Fort St., Victoria, BC V8V 3K2
250-363-0161 Fax: 250-363-8029

Nelson Branch
#1, 619B Front St., Nelson, BC V1L 4B6
250-352-3837 Fax: 250-352-3809
Office by appointment.

Manitoba Branches:

South Vancouver Branch
#101, 5811 Cooney Rd., Richmond, BC V6X 3M1
604-666-7850 Fax: 604-666-1068
Office by appointment.

Brandon Branch
#10, 940 Princess Ave., Brandon, MB R7A 0P6
204-726-7570 Fax: 204-726-7555

Vernon Branch
#302, 3105 - 33rd St., Vernon, BC V1T 9P7
250-260-5061 Fax: 250-260-5011
Office by appointment.

Winnipeg Branch
#1100, 155 Carlton St., Winnipeg, MB R3C 3H8
204-983-7900 Fax: 204-983-0870

Tri-Cities Branch
#370, 2755 Lougheed Highway, Port Coquitlam, BC V3B 5Y9
604-927-1400 Fax: 604-927-1415

Winnipeg West Branch
#200, 1655 Kenaston Blvd., Winnipeg, MB R3P 2M4
204-983-6530 Fax: 204-983-6531

New Brunswick Branches:

Bathurst Branch
#205, 275 Main St., Bathurst, NB E2A 1A9
506-548-7360 Fax: 506-548-7381

Edmundston Branch
#407, 121, rue de l'Église, Edmundston, NB E3V 1J9
506-739-8311 Fax: 506-735-0019
Office by appointment.

Fredericton Branch
#504, 570 Queen St., PO Box 754, Fredericton, NB E3B 5B4
506-452-3030 Fax: 506-452-2416

Moncton Branch
766 Main St., Moncton, NB E1C 1E6
506-851-6120 Fax: 506-851-6033

Saint John Branch
53 King St., Saint John, NB E2L 1G5
506-636-4751 Fax: 506-636-3892

Newfoundland & Labrador Branches:

Corner Brook Branch
4 Herald Ave., 1st Fl., Corner Brook, NL A2H 4B4
709-637-4515 Fax: 709-637-4522

Grand Falls-Windsor Branch
42 High St., PO Box 744, Grand Falls-Windsor, NL A2A 2M4
709-489-2181 Fax: 709-489-6569

St. John's Branch
215 Water St., PO Box 520, St. John's, NL A1C 5K4
709-722-5505 Fax: 709-772-2516

Northwest Territories Branches:

Yellowknife & Nunavut Branch
4912 - 49th St., Yellowknife, NT X1A 1P3
867-873-3565 Fax: 867-873-3501

Nova Scotia Branches:

Halifax Branch
#1400, 2000 Barrington St., Halifax, NS B3J 2Z7
902-426-7850 Fax: 902-426-6783
Vice-President & Area Manager, Craig Levangie
902-426-7865, craig.levangie@bdc.ca

Sydney Branch
#117, 275 Charlotte St., Sydney, NS B1P 1C6
902-564-7700 Fax: 902-564-3975

Truro Branch
622 Prince St., PO Box 1378, Truro, NS B2N 5N2
902-895-6377 Fax: 902-893-7957
Senior Manager, Business Development, Matthew Fraser
902-895-6378, matthew.fraser@bdc.ca

Yarmouth Branch
103 Water St., PO Box 98, Yarmouth, NS B5A 4B1
902-742-7119 Fax: 902-742-8180

Ontario Branches:

Barrie Branch
#301, 151 Ferris Lane, PO Box 876, Barrie, ON L4M 4Y6
705-725-2533 Fax: 705-739-0467

Brampton Branch
#100, 24 Queen St. East, Brampton, ON L6V 1A3
905-450-9845 Fax: 905-450-7514

Burlington / Halton Branch
#401, 4145 North Service Rd., Burlington, ON L7L 6A3
905-315-9230 Fax: 905-315-9243

Durham (Whitby) Branch
400 Dundas St. West, Whitby, ON L1N 2M7
905-666-6694 Fax: 905-666-1059

Hamilton Branch
#1900, 25 Main St. West, Hamilton, ON L8P 1H1
905-572-2954 Fax: 905-572-4282

Kenora Branch
227 - 2nd St. South, Kenora, ON P9N 1G1
807-467-3535 Fax: 807-467-3533

Kingston Branch
#201, 1000 Gardiners Rd., Kingston, ON K7P 3C4
613-389-0999 Fax: 613-389-2543

Kitchener-Waterloo Branch
#110, 50 Queen St. North, Kitchener, ON N2H 6P4
519-571-6676 Fax: 519-571-6685

London Branch
380 Wellington St., London, ON N6A 5B5
519-645-4229 Fax: 519-645-5450
Other Communication: Subordinate Financing (Southwestern Ontario), Phone: 519-675-3114, Fax: 519-645-5989

Markham Branch
3130 Hwy. 7 East, Markham, ON L3R 5A1
905-305-6867 Fax: 905-305-1969

Mississauga Branch
#100, 4310 Sherwoodtowne Blvd., Mississauga, ON L4Z 4C4
905-566-6417 Fax: 905-566-6425

North Bay Branch
222 McIntyre St. West, North Bay, ON P1B 2Y8
705-495-5700 Fax: 705-495-5707

Ottawa Branch
55 Metcalfe St., Ground Fl., Ottawa, ON K1P 6L5
613-995-0234 Fax: 613-995-9045
Other Communication: Subordinate Financing (Ottawa & Atlantic Regions), Phone: 613-995-4084, Fax: 613-943-9866

Peterborough Branch
340 George St. North, 4th Fl., PO Box 1419, Peterborough, ON K9J 7H6
705-750-4800 Fax: 705-750-4808

Sault Ste Marie Branch
153 Great Northern Rd., Sault Ste Marie, ON P6B 4Y9
705-941-3030 Fax: 705-941-3040

St Catharines Branch
#100, 39 Queen St., PO Box 1193, St Catharines, ON L2R 7A7
905-988-2874 Fax: 905-988-2890

Stratford Branch
516 Huron St., Stratford, ON N5A 5T7
519-271-5650 Fax: 519-271-8472

Sudbury Branch
#10, 233 Brady St., Sudbury, ON P3B 4H5
705-670-6482 Fax: 705-670-6387

Thunder Bay Branch
#102, 1136 Alloy Dr., Thunder Bay, ON P7B 6M9
807-346-1780 Fax: 807-346-1790

Timmins Branch
#202, 85 Pine St. South, Timmins, ON P4N 2K1
705-267-1246 Fax: 705-268-5437
Office by appointment.

Toronto Branch
#1200, 121 King St. West, Toronto, ON M5H 3T9
416-973-0341 Fax: 416-954-5009
The King Street West branch offers corporate financing for the Greater Toronto Area.

Vaughan Branch
#600, 3901 Hwy. 7 West, Vaughan, ON L4L 8L5
905-264-2100 Fax: 905-264-2122

Windsor Branch
#200, 2485 Ouellette Ave., Windsor, ON N8X 1L5
519-257-6808 Fax: 519-257-6811

Belleville Branch
284B Wallbridge-Loyalist Rd., Belleville, ON K8N 5B3
613-969-4009 Fax: 613-969-4018
Office by appointment.

Prince Edward Island Branches

Brantford Branch
#10, 330 West St., Brantford, ON N3R 7V5
519-751-3005 Fax: 519-751-3006
Office by appointment.

Charlottetown Branch
#230, 119 Kent St., PO Box 488, Charlottetown, PE C1A 7L1
902-566-7454 Fax: 902-566-7459

Québec Branches:

Chatham Branch
62 Keil Dr. South, Chatham, ON N7M 3G8
519-380-8886 Fax: 519-380-8850
Office by appointment.

Brossard Branch
#200, 4255, boul Lapinière, Brossard, QC J4Z 0C7
450-926-7220 Fax: 450-926-7221

Etobicoke Branch
#1001, 1243 Islington Ave., Toronto, ON M8X 1Y9
416-954-2604 Fax: 416-954-2631
Other Communication: Subordinate Financing (Greater Toronto Area), Phone: 416-952-6291, Fax: 416-954-2630

Chaudière - Appalaches (Saint-Romuald) Regional Branch
#100, 1175, boul de la Rive sud, Saint-Romuald, QC G6W 5M6
418-834-5144 Fax: 418-834-1855

Guelph Branch
#100, 120 Research Lane, Guelph, ON N1G 0B5
519-826-2663 Fax: 519-826-2662

Des Moulins - Lanaudière (Terrebonne) Regional Branch
2785, boul des Plateaux, Terrebonne, QC J6X 4J9
450-964-8778 Fax: 450-964-8773

North York Branch
#502, Islington Ave. West, North York, ON M3J 3H7
416-736-3420 Fax: 416-736-3425

Drummondville Branch
1010, boul René-Lévesque, Drummondville, QC J2C 5W4
819-478-4951 Fax: 819-478-5864

Ottawa West Branch
#100, 700 Silver Seven Rd., Kanata, ON K2V 1C3
613-592-2968 Fax: 613-592-5053

Gatineau Branch
#104, 259, boul St-Joseph, Gatineau, QC J8Y 6T1
819-997-4434 Fax: 819-997-4435

Owen Sound Branch
173 - 8th St. East, Owen Sound, ON N4K 5N3
519-371-5666 Fax: 519-371-1707
Office by appointment.

Granby Branch
#302, 155, rue St-Jacques, Granby, QC J2G 9A7
450-372-5202 Fax: 450-372-2423

Sarnia Branch
1086 Modeland Rd., Sarnia, ON N7S 6L2
519-383-1848 Fax: 519-383-1849
Office by appointment.

Laval Branch
#100, 2525, Daniel-Johnson, Laval, QC H7T 1S9
450-973-3727 Fax: 450-973-6860

Scarborough Branch
#112, 305 Milner Ave., Toronto, ON M1B 3V4
416-954-0709 Fax: 416-954-0716

Boucherville Branch
1570 Ampère St, Boucherville, QC J4B 7L4
450-928-4120 Fax: 450-928-4127

Montréal Branch
#12525, 5, Place Ville-Marie, Montréal, QC H3B 2G2
514-496-7966 Fax: 514-496-7974
Other Communication: Subordinate Financing (Montréal), Phone: 514-496-0626, Fax: 514-496-1020; Subordinate Financing (North-Shore & South-Shore), Phone: 514-283-8265, Fax: 514-496-1020

Pointe-Claire Branch
#110, 755, boul St-Jean, Pointe-Claire, QC H9R 5M9
514-697-8014 Fax: 514-697-3160

Québec Branch
1134, Grande-Allée ouest, Québec, QC G1S 1E5
418-648-3972 Fax: 418-648-5525
Other Communication: Subordinate Financing (Eastern Quebec), Phone: 418-648-5517, Fax: 418-649-6301

Québec North West Branch
#310, 1165, boul Lebourgneuf, Québec, QC G2K 2C9
418-648-4740 Fax: 418-648-4745

Rimouski Branch
391, boul Jessop, Rimouski, QC G5L 1M9
418-722-3300 Fax: 418-722-3362

Rouyn-Noranda Branch
#301, 139, boul Québec, Rouyn-Noranda, QC J9X 6M8
819-764-6701 Fax: 819-764-5472

Saint-Jérôme Branch
#102, 55, rue Castonguay, Saint-Jérôme, QC J7Y 2H9
450-432-7111 Fax: 450-432-8366

Saint-Laurent Branch
#160, 3100, boul de la Côte-Vertu, Saint-Laurent, QC H4R 2J8
514-496-7500 Fax: 514-496-7510

Montreal East Branch
6347, rue Jean-Talon est, Saint-Léonard, QC H1S 3E7
514-251-2818 Fax: 514-251-2758

Sherbrooke Branch
2532, rue King ouest, Sherbrooke, QC J1J 2E8
819-564-5700 Fax: 819-564-4276

Thérèse-de-Blainville (Boisbriand) Regional Branch
3000, rue Cours le Corbusier, Boisbriand, QC J7G 3E8
450-420-4900 Fax: 450-420-4904

Trois-Rivières Branch
#150, 1500, rue Royale, Trois-Rivières, QC G9A 6E6
819-371-5215 Fax: 819-371-5220

Saguenay / Lac St-Jean Branch
#210, 325 des Saguenéens St, Chicoutimi, QC G7H 6K9
418-698-5599 Fax: 418-698-5678

Regina
#320, 2220 - 12th Ave., Regina, SK S4P 0M8
306-780-6478 Fax: 306-780-7516

Saskatoon
135 - 21st St. East, Main Fl., Saskatoon, SK S7K 0B4
306-975-4822 Fax: 306-975-5955

Yukon Branches:

Prince Albert Branch
#1, 1499 - 10th Ave. E, Prince Albert, SK S6V 7S6
306-953-8599 Fax: 306-953-1343
Office by appointment.

Whitehorse
#202, 204 Lambert St., Whitehorse, YT Y1A 1Z4
867-633-7510 Fax: 867-667-4058

Saskatchewan Branches:

Vaudreuil-Soulanges
450 Aimé-Vincent Street, Vaudreuil-Dorion, QC J7V 5V5
450-455-9370 Fax: 450-455-8126
Office by appointment.

Legal Services
Executive Director, Christine Calvé
514-283-2997, Fax: 514-283-1549

Communications
Director General, Jean-Pierre Thibault
514-283-8817, Fax: 514-283-7951

Corporate Services
Executive Director, Pierre Bordeleau
514-283-4565, Fax: 514-283-1549

Business Development & North Business Office
Director, Sophie Legendre
514-283-8866, Fax: 514-283-3637

Infrastructure Directorate
Director, Lucie Perreault
514-283-1333, Fax: 514-283-4131

Regional Coherence
Director General, Jacques Langelier
514-283-3628, Fax: 514-283-7491
Atlantic Region
Queen Square, #600, 45 Alderney Drive, Dartmouth, NS B2Y 2N6
Fax: 902-426-7397
800-575-9696
Senior Industrial Relations Officer (Registrar), David Gooch
Regional Director, Peter Suchanek
Quebec Region
#910, 1501, avenue McGill College, Montréal, QC H3A 3M8
Fax: 514-283-3590
800-575-9696
Regional Director, Jean Gosselin
Western Region
#501, 300 West Georgia St., Vancouver, BC V6B 6B4
Fax: 604-666-6071
800-575-9696
Regional Director, Tom Panelli
Western Satellite Office
#304, 400 St. Mary Avenue, Winnipeg, MA R3C 4K5
Fax: 204-983-3170
800-575-9696
Senior Industrial Relations Officer, John Taggart

Communications
Director, Case Management Services, Justine Abel
613-947-5432, Fax: 613-995-9493
Communications Officer, Joanne Maisonneuve
613-992-4001, Fax: 613-947-5407
Communications Officer, Natalie Ouellette
613-947-5386
Information Officer, Joanne Leclair
613-947-5392, Fax: 613-947-5407

Legal Services
General Counsel & Director of Legal Services, David Demirkan
613-944-5809, Fax: 613-947-5460
Senior Counsel, Marie-Claude Grignon
514-283-3571, Fax: 514-283-3590
Senior Counsel, Susan Nicholas
613-947-5456, Fax: 613-947-5460

Canada Border Services Agency (CBSA) / Agence des services frontaliers du Canada (ASFC)

Headquarters, 191 Laurier Ave. West, Ottawa, ON K1A 0L8
800-461-9999
Contact@cbsa.gc.ca; communications@ps.gc.ca (Public Safety)
www.cbsa-asfc.gc.ca
TTY: 866-335-3237
Other Communication: Border Information Service, Service in French, Toll-Free Phone: 1-800-959-2036; Public Safety Canada, Phone: 613-944-4875, Toll-Free: 1-800-830-3118

Established in 2003, as a response to the need for increased border services, the Canada Border Services Agency ensures the security & prosperity of Canada. The agency is responsible for managing the access of people & goods to & from Canada. To carry out its mission, Canada Border Services Agency administers more than ninety pieces of legislation. Some of the agencies duties include the following: managing over 100 border crossings; offering services at points throughout Canada & internationally; operating detention centres across the nation; conducting marine operations at the ports of Prince Rupert, Vancouver, Montréal, & Halifax; managing postal services at major mail centres in Montréal, Toronto, & Vancouver; & forming part of more than twenty Integrated Border Enforcement Teams across Canada.

Acts Administered:
Access to Information Act
Act to Establish the Canada Border Services Agency
Aeronautics Act
Anti-Personnel Mines Convention Implementation Act (through EIPA)
Blue Water Bridge Authority Act
Bretton Woods & Related Agreements Act
Canada Agricultural Products Act
Canada Customs & Revenue Agency Act
Canada Grain Act
Canada Post Corporation Act
Canada Shipping Act
Canada-Chile Free Trade Agreement Implementation Act
Canada-Costa Rica Free Trade Agreement Implementation Act
Canada-Israel Free Trade Agreement Implementation Act
Canada-United States Free Trade Agreement Implementation Act
Canadian Dairy Commission Act
Canadian Environmental Protection Act, 1999
Canadian Food Inspection Agency Act
Canadian International Trade Tribunal Act
Canadian Wheat Board Act
Carriage by Air Act
Chemical Weapons Convention Implementation Act (through EIPA)
Civil International Space Station Agreement Implementation Act
Coastal Fisheries Protection Act
Coasting Trade Act
Consumer Packaging & Labelling Act
Controlled Drug & Substances Act
Convention on International Trade in Endangered Species of Wild Fauna & Flora
Copyright Act
Criminal Code
Cultural Property Export & Import Act
Customs Act
Customs & Excise Offshore Application Act
Customs Tariff Act
Defence Production Act
Department of Health Act
Department of Industry Act
Energy Administration Act
Energy Efficiency Act
Excise Act
Excise Act, 2001
Excise Tax Act
Explosives Act
Export Act
Export & Import of Rough Diamonds Act
Export & Import Permits Act
Federal-Provincial Fiscal Arrangements Act
Feeds Act
Fertilizers Act
Financial Administration Act
Firearms Act
Fish Inspection Act
Fisheries Act
Foods & Drugs Act
Foreign Missions & International Organizations Act
Freshwater Fish Marketing Act
Hazardous Products Act
Health of Animals Act
Immigration & Refugee Protection Act
Importation of Intoxicating Liquors Act
Integrated Circuit Topography Act
International Boundary Commission Act
Manganese-based Fuel Additives Act
Meat Inspection Act
Motor Vehicle Fuel Consumption Standards Act (not in force)
Motor Vehicle Safety Act
National Energy Board Act
Navigable Waters Protection Act
North American Free Trade Agreement Implementation Act
Nuclear Energy Act
Nuclear Safety & Control Act
Pest Control Products Act
Pilotage Act
Plant Breeders' Rights Act
Plant Protection Act
Precious Metals Marking Act
Preclearance Act
Privacy Act
Privileges & Immunities (North Atlantic Organization Act)
Proceeds of Crime (Money Laundering) & Terrorist Financing Act
Quarantine Act
Quebec Harbour, Port Warden Act
Radiation Emitting Devices Act
Radiocommunication Act
Seeds Act
Special Economic Measures Act
Special Import Measures Act
Statistics Act
Telecommunications Act
Textile Labelling Act
Trade-Marks Act
Transportation of Dangerous Goods Act, 1992
United Nations Act
United States Wreckers Act
Visiting Forces Act
Wild Animals & Plant Protection & Regulation of International & Interprovincial Trade Act
Agriculture & Agri-Food Administrative Monetary Penalties Act
Citizenship Act

Minister, Public Safety, Hon. Vic Toews
613-992-3128, Fax: 613-995-1049, Toews.V@parl.gc.ca
President, Luc Portelance
613-952-3200, Fax: 613-948-3177
Executive Vice-President, Malcolm Brown
613-952-3200, Fax: 613-952-1851
Associate Vice-President, Martin Bolduc
613-952-5269, Fax: 613-948-7130
Regional Director General, Niagara Region, Rick Comerford
905-994-6000, Fax: 905-994-6010, Other Communications: Executive Assistant, Phone: 905-994-6002
Regional Director General, Windsor - St. Clair Region, Pete Diponio
519-967-4010
Regional Director General, Atlantic Region, Diane Giffin-Boudreau
902-426-2914, Other Communications: Administrative Assistant, Phone: 902-426-2914
Regional Director General, Pacific Region, Roslyn MacVicar
604-666-0760, Other Communications: Executive Assistant, Phone: 604-666-3305
Regional Director General, Northern Ontario Region, Denis R. Vinette
613-991-0566, Other Communications: Executive Assistant, Phone: 613-991-0565
Regional Director General, Greater Toronto Area Region, Goran Vragrovic
905-803-5595
Director, Prairie Region, Edmonton District, Bill Axten
780-890-8040
Director, Atlantic Region, Southern New Brunswick & Prince Edward Island District, Don Collins
506-636-4506, Other Communications: Administrative Assistant, Phone: 506-426-4501
Director, Atlantic Region, Northwestern New Brunswick District, John Dolimount
506-324-8663, Other Communications: Administrative Assistant, Phone: 506-324-8660
Director, Prairie Region, Calgary District, Paul Dumouchel
403-292-5690, Fax: 403-292-4840
Director, Pacific Region, Metro Vancouver District, John Dyck
604-775-6790, Fax: 604-775-6792
Director, Atlantic Region, Newfoundland & Labrador Districtt, John Fagan
709-772-2719, Other Communications: Administrative Assistant, Phone: 709-772-4335
Director, Northern Ontario Region, Northwest District, Gary Flanagan
705-941-3052, Fax: 705-941-3060
Director, Pacific Region, Vancouver Airport District, Sari Hellsten
604-666-1800, Fax: 604-666-1812, Other Communications: Executive Assistant, Phone: 604-666-9337
Director, Prairie Region, Southern Alberta District, Kevin Hewson
403-344-2061
Director, Québec Region, Montérégie District, Claire Jacques
450-246-2272
Director, Prairie Region, Southern Manitoba District, Darlene Klips
204-373-2352, Fax: 204-373-2007
Director, Pacific Region, Okanagan & Kootenay District, Glyn Lee
250-770-4512, Fax: 250-482-5983
Director, Atlantic Region, Nova Scotia District, Andrew LeFrank
902-426-1784
Director, Prairie Region, Winnipeg & Northwest Territories District, Barry Lutz
204-983-3770, Fax: 204-984-3106
Director, Northern Ontario Region, St. Lawrence District, Darko Nikolic
613-382-8495, Fax: 613-382-4366
Director, Pacific Region, West Coast & Yukon District, Ivan Peterson
250-363-3365, Fax: 250-363-8261
Director, Québec Region, St-Lawrence District, Danielle Petitclerc
514-350-6100, Fax: 514-283-8591, Other Communications: Executive Assistant, Phone: 514-350-6100
Director, Québec Region, Airports District, Pierre Provost
514-633-7702
Director, Pacific Region, Pacific Highway District, Kim Scoville
778-538-3602, Fax: 604-541-5968, Other Communications: Executive Assistant, Phone: 778-545-5559
Director, Prairie Region, Saskatchewan District, Mike Shoobert
306-780-7356, Fax: 306-780-8222

Director, Northern Ontario Region, Ottawa District, Debbie Zion
613-991-1214, Fax: 613-991-1407

Programs Branch
191 Laurier Ave. West, 15th Fl., Ottawa, ON K1A 0L8
The Programs Branch of the Canadian Border Services Agency is responsible for the following offices & directorates: Anti-Dumping & Countervailing Directorate; Border Programs Directorate; Business Systems Support Directorate; eManifest & Major Projects Directorate; International & Partnerships Directorate; Office of the Vice President & Associate Vice President; Planning & Performance Management Directorate; Post-Border Programs Directorate; Pre-Border Programs Directorate; Risk Assessment Programs Directorate; Trade Programs & CBSA Assessment Revenue Management Directorate
Vice-President, Programs Branch, Cathy Munroe
613-954-7220, Other Communications: Executive Assistant, Phone: 613-954-7287
Associate Vice-President, David Vigneault
613-952-2531
Director General, Planning & Performance Management Directorate, Tim Coughlin
613-946-3183, Fax: 613-952-2468
Director General, Trade Programs & CBSA Assessment Revenue Management Directorate, Mike Feniak
613-948-1838
Director General, Anti-Dumping & Countervailing Directorate, Daniel Giasson
613-954-1642
Director General, International & Partnerships Directorate, Chris Henderson
613-957-6623
Director General, Business Systems Support Directorate, Rachelle May
613-954-1909
Director General, eManifest & Major Projects Directorate, Bruna Rados
613-954-2157
Director General, Border Programs Directorate, Maureen Tracy
613-954-6431

Comptrollership Branch
219 Laurier Ave. West, 9th Fl., Ottawa, ON K1A 0L8
Canada Border Services Agency's Comptrollership Branch consists of the following divisions & directorates: Agency Comptroller Directorate; Deputy Chief Financial Officer & Resource Management Directorate; Infrastructure & Environmental Operations Directorate; Infrastructure & Environmental Operations Directorate; Security & Professional Standards Directorate; Vice-President's Office
Vice-President, Comptrollership Branch, Sylvain St-Laurent
613-948-8604, Fax: 613-948-8825
Director General; Deputy Chief Financial Officer, Simon Bonk
613-941-6388
Director General, Infrastructure & Environmental Operations Directorate, David Champagne
613-948-9717
Director General, Agency Comptroller Directorate, Terry Perkins
613-946-9337
Senior Director, Strategic Financial Planning & Oversight Division, Marc Monette
613-948-8606
Director, Asset Management & Planning Division, Rachelle Beaudry
613-960-8508
Director, HQ - Accomodations Division, Hélène Louise Gauthier
613-941-6616
Director, Corporate Accounting Division, Gaetan Gervais
613-948-9288
Director, Corporate Client Services Division, Rachelle Laurin
613-941-6597
Director, Environmental Programs Division, Kelly Marsden
613-954-3982
Director, Personnel Security & Professional Standards Division, Ken McCarthy
613-941-7244
Director, Infrastructure Delivery & Coordination Division, Hal Parker
613-946-9121
Director, Infrastructure & Information Security Division, Pierre Rivard
613-948-9355, Fax: 613-941-6008

Human Resources Branch
99 Metcalfe St., 3rd Fl., Ottawa, ON K1A 0L8
The Human Resources Branch consists of the following offices and directorates: Client Services Directorate; Corporate Human Resources Programs Directorate; Executive Group Services, Leadership & Talent Management Directorate; Labour Relations & Compensation Directorate; Strategic Branch Integration & Renewal Directorate; Training & Learning Directorate; Vice-President's Office; Workplace Development, Ethics & Employee Support Division
Vice-President, Human Resources Branch, Camille Therriault-Power
613-948-3180, Fax: 613-952-1783
Director General, Labour Relations & Compensation Directorate, Patti Bordeleau
613-948-9861
Director General, Client Services Directorate, Beverley Boyd
613-948-1164
Director General, Training & Learning Directorate, Michael Gardiner
613-946-4280
Director General, Executive Group Services, Leadership & Talent Management Directorate, France Guèvremont
613-948-9828
Director General, Corporate Human Resources Programs Directorate, Scott Taymun
613-957-3511
Director General, Strategic Branch Integration & Renewal Directorate, Lilia Trombetti
613-954-7504

Information, Science & Technology Branch
191 Laurier Ave. West, 7th Fl., Ottawa, ON K1A 0L8
The Canada Border Services Agency Information, Science, & Technology Branch includes the following offices and directorates: Enterprise Architecture & Information Management Directorate; Infrastructure Services Directorate; Planning & Portfolio Management Directorate; Science & Engineering Directorate; Solutions Directorate; Vice-President's Office.

Operations Branch
191 Laurier Ave. West, 18th Fl., Ottawa, ON K1A 0L8
The Operations Branch of the Canada Border Services Agency is responsible for the following offices and directorates: Border Operations Centre & Major Events Directorate; Border Operations Directorate; International Operations Directorate; Vice-President's Office.
Vice-President, Operations Branch, Pierre Sabourin
613-948-4445, Fax: 613-948-7130
Associate Vice-President, Martin Bolduc
613-952-5269, Fax: 613-948-7130
Director General, Border Operations Centre & Major Events Directorate, Megan Imrie
613-952-2728, Fax: 613-941-9866
Director, Border Operations Directorate, Glenda Lavergne
613-954-6990, Fax: 613-957-9723
Director, Operational Performance & Readiness Directorate, Arming Task Force, Arianne Reza
613-948-1846, Fax: 613-952-0777

Canada Business (CBSC) / Entreprises Canada (CSEC)

235 Queen St., Ottawa, ON K1A 0H5
888-576-4444
www.canadabusiness.ca
TTY: 800-457-8466

Canada Business provides a wide range of information on government services, programs & regulations to Canadian business people. The base framework is an organized network of centres across Canada, one in each province & territory. The network of Canada Business is expanding to include regional access partners in many other communities across Canada. The centres offer various products and services aimed at helping clients obtain quick, accurate & comprehensive business information. Each centre exists as a result of cooperative arrangements between federal & provincial governments, & the private sector in some cases. Administration & management of the CBSC varies depending on location between the following federal agencies: Western Economic Diversification (WD), Industry Canada, the Canada Economic Development for Quebec Regions (CEDQR) & the Atlantic Canada Opportunities Agency (ACOA). The Federal Business Information System (BIS) is a collection of information on business-related programs, services & selected regulations which are accessible through the CBSC & on the CBSC web site (www.cbsc.org). The Federal BIS acts as a single window for individuals or businesses to access relevant information from all federal departments
Senior Project Manager, Canada Business Network Operations, Laura Collier
613-952-5888, Fax: 613-954-5463
Project Manager, Canada Business Network Operations, Louise Cardinal
613-946-1613, Fax: 613-954-5463

Regional Offices:

The Business Link Business Service Centre
#100, 10237 - 104 St. NW, Edmonton, AB T5J 1B1
780-422-7722 Fax: 780-422-0055
800-272-9675
TTY: 800-457-8466
Other Communication: Library Phone: 780-422-7780

Small Business BC
82 - 601 West Cordova St., Vancouver, BC V6B 1G1
604-775-5525 Fax: 604-775-5520
800-667-2272
askus@smallbusinessbc.ca
www.smallbusinessbc.ca
TTY: 800-457-8466

Canada/Manitoba Business Service Centre
#250, 240 Graham Ave., PO Box 2609, Winnipeg, MB R3C 0J7
204-984-2272 Fax: 204-983-3852
800-665-2019
TTY: 800-457-8466

Canada/New Brunswick Business Service Centre
Barker House, #102, 570 Queen St., Fredericton, NB E3B 6Z6
506-444-6140 Fax: 506-444-6172
888-576-4444
TTY: 800-457-8466

Canada/Newfoundland & Labrador Business Service Centre
90 O'Leary Ave., PO Box 8687 A, St. John's, NL A1B 3T1
709-772-6022 Fax: 709-772-6090
800-668-1010
TTY: 800-457-8466

Canada/NWT Business Service Centre
#701, 5201 - 50 Ave., Yellowknife, NT X1A 3S9
876-873-7958 Fax: 876-873-7960
800-661-0599
TTY: 800-457-8466

Canada/Nova Scotia Business Service Centre (CNSBSC)
1575 Brunswick St., Halifax, NS B3J 2G1
902-426-8604
888-576-4444
TTY: 800-457-8466

Canada/Nunavut Business Service Centre
Inuksugait Plaza, PO Box 1000 1198, Iqaluit, NU X0A 0H0
867-975-7860 Fax: 867-975-7885
877-499-5199
TTY: 800-457-8466
Other Communication: Rankin Inlet, Phone: 867-645-8450, Fax: 867-645-8455; Cambridge Bay, Phone: 867-983-2095, Fax: 967-983-2075

Canada/Ontario Business Service Centre (COBSC)
151 Yonge St., 3rd Fl., Toronto, ON M5C 2W7
888-745-8888
www.cbo-eco.ca/en/locations.cfm
TTY: 800-457-8466

Canada/Prince Edward Island Business Service Centre (CPEIBSC)
100 Sydney St., 3rd Fl., PO Box 40, Charlottetown, PE C1A 7K2
902-368-0771
888-576-4444
TTY: 800-457-8466

Canada/Saskatchewan Business Service Centre (CSBSC)
#2, 345 3rd Ave. South, Saskatoon, SK S7K 1M6
306-956-2323 Fax: 306-956-2328
800-667-4374
TTY: 800-457-8466

Canada/Yukon Business Service Centre
#101, 307 Jarvis St., Whitehorse, YT Y1A 2H3
867-667-2000 Fax: 867-667-2001
800-661-0543
TTY: 800-457-8466

Info entrepreneurs
#W204, 380, rue St-Antoine ouest, local 6000, Montréal, QC H2Y 3X7
514-496-4636 Fax: 514-496-5934
888-576-4444
http: //infoentrepreneurs.org
TTY: 800-457-8466
Other Communication: Toll Free Fax: 1-888-417-0442

Canada Council for the Arts / Conseil des Arts du Canada

350 Albert St., PO Box 1047, Ottawa, ON K1P 5V8
613-566-4414 Fax: 613-566-4390
800-263-5588
www.canadacouncil.ca

The Canada Council for the Arts is a national arm's-length agency created by an Act of Parliament in 1957. According to the Canada Council Act, the role of the Council is to foster & promote the study & enjoyment of, & the production of works in the arts. To fulfill this mandate, the Council offers a broad range of grants & services to professional Canadian artists & arts organizations in dance, interdisciplinary work & performance art, media arts, music, interdisciplinary work, theatre, visual arts, &

writing & publishing. The Council awards more than 100 prizes every year. It administers the Killam Program of scholarly awards, the Governor General's Literary Awards & the Governor General's Awards in Visual & Media Arts. The Canadian Commission for UNESCO & the Public Lending Right Commission operate under its aegis.

Director & CEO, Robert Sirman
613-566-4414

Chair, Joseph L. Rotman
613-566-4414, Other Communications: Toll-Free: 1-800-263-5588

Vice-Chair, Simon Brault
613-566-4414, Other Communications: Toll-Free: 1-800-263-5588

Manager, Public Relations Team, Marketing Communications, Grace Thrasher
613-566-4414

Canada Deposit Insurance Corporation (CDIC) / Société d'assurance-dépôts du Canada (SADC)

50 O'Connor St., 17th Floor, PO Box 2340 D, Ottawa, ON K1P 5W5

Fax: 613-996-6095
800-461-2342
info@cdic.ca; info@sadc.ca
www.cdic.ca; www.sadc.ca

Other Communication: Toll Free: 1-800-461-7232 (French)

CDIC, a Crown corporation established in 1967, ensures eligible deposits in member institutions (banks, trust companies, loan companies & cooperative credit associations) in case a member becomes insolvent. Funding is provided by its member institutions through premiums paid on insured deposits. Reports to government through the Minister of Finance. CDIC responsibilities include: providing deposit insurance in case of member failure; contributing to the stability of the Canadian financial system.

Chair, Bryan P. Davies

President / CEO, Michèle Bourque

Vice-President, Insurance & Risk Assessment, Jeffery A. Johnson

Vice-President, Corporate Affairs/General Counsel & Corporate Secretary, M. Claudia Morrow

Vice-President, Finance & Administration / CFO, Thomas J. Vice

Canada Economic Development for Québec Regions / Développement économique Canada pour les régions du Québec

Édifice Dominion Square, #900, 1255, rue Peel, Montréal, QC H3B 2T9

514-283-6412 Fax: 514-283-3302
866-385-6412
www.dec-ced.gc.ca

Defines federal objectives relating to development opportunities & delivers business assistance programs for small- & medium-sized businesses in Qu,bec for innovation, entrepreneurial & market development purposes. Supports a series of programs for appropriate environmental initiatives in various regions of Québec. The agency fosters alliances among the various environmental industry stakeholders including small- & medium-sized enterprises & industrial associations. Goals include a strengthening of existing & new partnerships, & an improvement of access to government programs. The agency also provides a significant amount of support for research & development in areas of environmental technology, demonstration, marketing & transfer projects. Supports initiatives that contribute to making Montréal an industrial centre of excellence in the environment. Aids small- & medium-sized firms in gaining access to federal procurement process, & encourages training & education focusing on business management. Helps business develop export markets through cooperative efforts with Industry Canada & Foreign Affairs & International Trade Canada

Minister Responsible, Hon. Christian Paradis
613-995-1377, Fax: 613-943-1562, Paradis.C@parl.gc.ca

Minister of State, Economic Development Agency of Canada for the Regions of Québec, Hon. Denis Lebel
613-996-6236, Fax: 613-996-6252, Lebel.D@parl.gc.ca; denis.lebel@dec-ced.gc.ca, Other Communications: Economic Development Agency (QC): 514-496-1282

President, Suzanne Vinet
514-283-4843, Fax: 514-283-7778

Chief of Staff, Yan Plante
819-997-3319, Fax: 819-997-4469

Vice-President, Policy & Planning, Rita Tremblay
514-283-1294, Fax: 514-283-5940

Operations

Vice-President, Thao Pham
514-283-3510, Fax: 514-283-4547

Director, Infrastructure, Lucie Perreault
514-283-1333, Fax: 514-283-4131

Regional Offices:

Abitibi-Témiscamingue
906, 5e av, Val-d'Or, QC J9P 1B9
819-825-5260 Fax: 819-825-3245
800-567-6451

Regional Director, Sandra Lafleur
819-825-5260, Fax: 819-825-3245

Bas St-Laurent
Édifice Trust général du Canada, #310, 2, rue Saint-Germain Est, Rimouski, QC G5L 8T7
418-722-3282 Fax: 418-722-3285
800-463-9073

Regional Director, Pierre Roberge
418-722-3255, Fax: 418-722-3285

Centre-du-Québec
#105, 1100 boul René-Lévesque, Drummondville, QC J2C 5W4
819-478-4664 Fax: 819-478-4666
800-567-1418

Regional Director, Georges Arseneau
819-478-4664, Fax: 819-478-4666

Côte-Nord
#202B, 701, boul Laure, PO Box 698, Sept-Iles, QC G4R 4K9
418-968-3426 Fax: 418-968-0806
800-463-1707

Regional Director, Thomas Szalay
418-968-3426, Fax: 418-968-0806

Estrie
Place Andrew Paton, #100, 202, rue Wellington nord, Sherbrooke, QC J1H 5C6
819-564-5904 Fax: 819-564-5912
800-567-6084

Regional Director, Mariette Larochelle
819-564-5904, Fax: 819-564-5912

Gaspésie-Iles-de-la-Madeleine
Place Jacques-Cartier, 120, rue de la Reine, 3e étage, Gaspé, QC G4X 2S1
418-368-5870 Fax: 418-368-6256
866-368-0044

Regional Director, France Simard
418-368-5879, Fax: 418-368-6256

Ile-de-Montréal
Édifice Dominion Square, #900, 1255, rue Peel, Montréal, QC H3B 2T9
514-283-2500 Fax: 514-496-8310
800-322-4636

Regional Director, Marie-José Reid
514-283-8153, Fax: 514-469-8310

Laval - Laurentides - Lanaudière
#410, 2990, av Pierre-Péladeau, Laval, QC H7T 3B3
450-973-6844 Fax: 450-973-6851
800-430-6844

Regional Director, Carole Hart
450-973-6845, Fax: 450-973-6851

Mauricie
Immeuble Bourg du Fleuve, #413, 25, rue des Forges, Trois-Rivières, QC G9A 2G4
819-371-5182 Fax: 819-371-5186
800-567-8637

Regional Director, Pierre Lacoursière
819-371-5182, Fax: 819-371-5186

Montérégie
Place Agropur, #400, 101, boul Roland-Therrien, Longueuil, QC J4H 4B9
450-928-4088 Fax: 450-928-4097
800-284-0335

Regional Director, Charles Lambert
450-928-4088, Fax: 450-928-4097

Nord-du-Québec
Édifice Dominion Square, #900, 1255 rue Peel, Montréal, QC H3B 2T9
514-283-8131 Fax: 514-283-3637
800-561-0633

Regional Director, Sophie Legendre
514-283-8866, Fax: 514-283-3637

Outaouais
#202, 259 boul Saint-Joseph, Gatineau, QC J8Y 6T1
819-994-7442 Fax: 819-994-7846
800-561-4353

Regional Director, Marc Boily
819-994-7442, Fax: 819-994-7846, Other Communications: Administrative Assistant, Phone: 819-944-7442

Québec - Chaudière - Appalaches
Place Iberville IV, #030, 2954, boul Laurier, Québec, QC G1V 4T2
418-648-4826 Fax: 418-648-7291
800-463-5204

Regional Director, Christian Audet
418-648-4451, Fax: 418-648-7291

Policy, Research & Programs

Vice-President, Policy & Planning, Rita Tremblay
514-283-1294, Fax: 514-283-5940

Director General, Jean Pierre Lavoie
514-283-2664, Fax: 514-283-8429

Director, Special Projects, Keltoum Bouhabel
514-496-1299, Fax: 514-284-8429

Chief, Coordination & Administrative Services, Simon Labrecque
514-283-2664, Fax: 514-283-8429

Saguenay - Lac-Saint-Jean
#203, 100, rue Saint-Joseph sud, Alma, QC G8B 7A6
418-668-3084 Fax: 418-668-7584
800-463-9808

Regional Director, Donald Hudon
418-668-3084, Fax: 418-688-7584

Canada Industrial Relations Board (CIRB) / Conseil canadien des relations industrielles (CCRI)

240 Sparks St., 4th Fl. West, Ottawa, ON K1A 0X8

Fax: 613-941-4461
800-575-9696
info@cirb-ccri.gc.ca
www.cirb-ccri.gc.ca
TTY: 800-855-0511

The Board is an independent, administrative, quasi-judicial tribunal which administers Part I & certain provisions of Part II of the Canada Labour Code. Its responsibilities include the granting or revoking of collective bargaining rights, the mediation & adjudication of unfair labour practice complaints, the determination of unlawful strikes & lockouts & other matters.

Chair, Elizabeth MacPherson
613-947-5366, Fax: 613-947-3894

Vice-Chairperson, Graham Clarke
613-992-3979, Fax: 613-947-5407

Vice-Chairperson, Louise Fecteau
613-992-3979, Fax: 514-283-3590

Vice-Chairperson, Judith F. MacPherson
613-992-3979, Fax: 613-947-5407

Vice-Chairperson, William G. McMurray
613-992-3979, Fax: 613-947-5407

Vice-Chairperson, Claude Roy
613-992-3979, Fax: 514-283-3590, Other Communications: Executive Assistant, Phone: 613-944-6204

Acting Regional Director & Registrar, Andrew Boyle
613-947-5457, Fax: 613-941-4461

Research & Information Services Clerk, Marie-France Grenier
613-947-5391, Fax: 613-947-5407

Canada Lands Company Ltd. (CLCL) / Société immobilière du Canada limitée (SICL)

#1200, 1 University Ave., Toronto, ON M5J 2P1

416-952-6111 Fax: 416-952-6115
888-252-5263
www.clcl.ca

CLCL is a Crown corporation with a mandate to enhance the quality of life of the communities in which it conducts business, to generate best value for the taxpayer through the orderly disposal of strategic real estate properties no longer required by the federal government, as well as the management of certain other select properties. The agency reports to government through the Minister of Transport, Infrastructure & Communities.

President / CEO, Mark B. Laroche

Vice President, Strategic Acquisitions, Public & Government Affairs, Gordon McIvor
gmcivor@clc.ca

Old Port of Montréal Corporation Inc. / Société du Vieux port de Montréal

333, rue de la Commune ouest, Montréal, QC H2Y 2E2
514-283-5256
information@oldportofmontreal.com
www.quaysoftheoldport.com/home.html

Parc Downsview Park Inc.

#1, 35 Carl Hall Rd., Toronto, ON M3K 2B6
416-952-2222 Fax: 416-952-2225
info@downsviewpark.ca
www.downsviewpark.ca/

Chair, David Soknacki

Canada Mortgage & Housing Corporation (CMHC) / Société canadienne d'hypothèques et de logement (SCHL)

700 Montreal Rd., Ottawa, ON K1A 0P7
613-748-2000 Fax: 613-748-2098
800-668-2642
chic@cmhc-schl.gc.ca
www.cmhc.ca; www.schl.ca
TTY: 613-748-2447
Other Communication: Canadian Housing Information Centre: 613-748-2367

CMHC works closely with a network of professional associations, groups & institutions concerned with regional planning & the residential sector. It prepares various research projects for the examination of relationships between urban areas, housing & sustainable development issues. Involved in numerous technical research projects addressing interrelationships between housing, energy & resource use. Through its research & information transfer function, CMHC will undertake initiatives such as identifying approaches & solutions that lead to more sustainable & healthy communities, examining barriers to potential development of brownfield sites. CMHC will focus on ways to reduce residential energy consumption in multiple-unit housing, educate consumers on energy-saving changes to homes. The Net Zero Healthy Healthy Housing Initiative combines passive solar, energy-efficient design, construction & appliances, integrated with renewable energy systems, to achieve net zero energy consumption on an annual basis, significantly reducing environmental impacts & GHG emissions. Twenty demonstration projects across Canada are underway.

Acts Administered:
CMHC Act
National Housing Act (NHA)

Minister Responsible, Minister of Human Resources & Skills Development, Hon. Diane Finley
Chair, Dino Chiesa
President / CEO, Karen Kinsley
613-748-2186
Vice-President, Corporate Services & CFO, Marc Joyal
613-748-2958
Vice-President, Assisted Housing, Sharon Matthews
613-748-2251
Vice-President, Insurance Underwriting, Servicing & Policy, Mark McInnis
613-748-2134
Vice-President, Insurance Product & Business Development, Pierre Serré
613-748-2818
Vice-President, Policy & Planning, Douglas A. Stewart
613-748-2553
Vice-President, Human Resources, Gail Tolley
613-748-2082
Executive Director, CMHC International, André Asselin
613-748-2347
Executive Director, Communications, Peter De Barros
613-748-2143
Executive Director, Corporate Marketing, Charles Chenard
613-748-2505
Director, Risk Management, David Dmytryk
613-748-2409
Director, Audit & Evaluation Services, Serge Gaudet
613-748-4099

Atlantic Region
Barrington Tower, 9th Fl., 1894 Barrington St., Halifax, NS B3J 2A8
902-426-3530 Fax: 902-426-9991
TTY: 800-309-3388

General Manager, Christina Haddad
416-218-3321
Principal, Marketing, Info & Communications, Emily Poitras-Benedict
902-426-8127

British Columbia
#200, 1111 West Georgia St., Vancouver, BC V6E 4S4
604-731-5733 Fax: 604-737-4139
TTY: 800-309-3388

General Manager, Charles MacArthur
604-737-4150
Manager, Business Development & Marketing, Marcia Freeman
604-666-2529
Senior Consultant, Communications & Marketing, Tracy Wells
604-737-4162

Ontario
#300, 100 Sheppard Ave. East, Toronto, ON M2N 6Z1
416-221-2642 Fax: 416-218-3310
866-389-1742
TTY: 900-309-3388

General Manager, Peter Friedmann
416-218-3300
Senior Consultant, Communications & Marketing, Michele McMaster
416-218-3452

Prairie & Territories Region
#200, 1000 - 7 Ave. SW, Calgary, AB T2P 5L5
403-515-3000 Fax: 403-515-2930
877-499-7245
TTY: 800-309-3388

General Manager, Gordon McHugh
403-515-3001
Senior Consultant, Communications & Marketing, Kimberlee Jones
403-515-3048

Québec
1100, boul René-Levesque ouest, 1er étage, Montréal, QC H3B 5J7
514-283-2222
888-772-0772
TTY: 800-309-3388

General Manager, Sylvie Crispo
514-283-3023
Director, Communications & Marketing, Lise Hamilton
514-283-3151

Canada Pension Plan Investment Board / Office d'investissement du Régime de pensions du Canada

#2600, 1 Queen St. East, PO Box 101, Toronto, ON M5C 2W5
416-868-4075 Fax: 416-868-8689
866-557-9510
csr@cppib.ca
www.cppib.ca
TTY: 416-868-6035

The CPP Investment Board is a Crown corporation created as part of 1997 reforms designed to ensure the soundness & sustainability of the CPP. The Board operates under similar investment rules as other pension plans in Canada, which require the prudent management of pension plan assets in the interests of plan contributors & beneficiaries.

Chair, Board of Directors, Robert Astley
President/CEO, David Denison
Executive Vice-President, Investments, Mark Wiseman
Senior Vice-President, Private Investments, André Bourbonnais
Senior Vice-President/General Counsel & Corporate Secretary, John H. Butler
Senior Vice-President, Real Estate Investments, Graeme Eadie
Vice-President, Head of Quantitative Research, Sterling Gunn
Senior Vice-President, Communications & Stakeholder Relations, Michel Leduc
Senior Vice-President, Human Resources, Saylor Millitz-Lee
Senior Vice-President, Chief Investment Strategist, Donald M. Raymond
Senior Vice-President/COO, Benita M. Warmbold
Senior Vice-President, Public Market Investments, Eric M. Wetlaufer
Senior Vice-President/CFO, Nicholas Zelenczuk

Canada Place Corporation / Corporation Place du Canada

504 - 999 Canada Place, Vancouver, BC V6C 3E1
604-775-7200 Fax: 604-775-6251
admin@canadaplace.ca
www.canadaplace.ca
Other Communication: Media, Filming & Public Relations, Phone: 604-775-6245, Fax: 604-775-6215, Email: media@canadaplace.ca

The Corporation is the landlord & in charge of property management at Canada Place in Vancouver, which includes a cruise ship facility, a trade & convention centre, a hotel, an IMAX theatre, & a parking structure

Chair, Robin Wilson
President/CEO, Michael J. Shardlow
Chief Operating Officer, Andrew Mann
Director, Communications & Public Affairs, Robyn McVicker
Director, Facilities, Andy O'Neill

Canada Post Corporation / Société canadienne des postes

Corporate Secretariat, 2701 Riverside Dr., Ottawa, ON K1A 0B1
866-607-6301
www.canadapost.ca; www.postescanada.ca
TTY: 800-267-2797
Other Communication: Postal Security, Phone: 1-800-267-1177

Federal commercial Crown corporation responsible for Canada's postal system. Reports to government through the Minister of Transport, Infrastructure & Communities. For postal rates, codes, abbreviations & other general information; see Postal Information in the main Index.

President/CEO, Deepak Chopra
Chief Financial Officer, Wayne Cheeseman
Chief Operating Officer, Jacques Côté
Senior Vice-President, Direct Marketing, Advertising & Publishing Business, Laurene Cihosky
Senior Vice-President, Postal Transformation, Cal Hart
Senior Vice-President, Operations, Douglas Jones
Senior Vice-President, Human Resources, André Joron
Senior Vice-President, Sales, Peter V. Melanson
Senior Vice-President/Chief Customer Officer, Louis O'Brien
Senior Vice-President, Parcels, Marvin Rosenzweig
Senior Vice-President, Transaction Mail, Mary Traversy
Senior Vice-President, Chief Information Technology Officer, André Turgeon
Senior Vice-President, Strategy, Philip Ventura
Vice-President/General Counsel, Corporate Secretary & Compliance, Bonnie Boretsky
Vice-President, Real Estate, Murray Dea
Vice-President, Customer Service, Stephen Edmondson
Vice-President, Engineering & Postal Transformation, John Farnand
Vice-President, Pension Fund/Chief Investment Officer, Douglas Greaves
Vice-President, Finance & Comptroller, Barbara MacKenzie
Vice-President, Government Relations & Policy, Susan Margles
Vice-President, General Business Sales, Serge Pitre
Vice-President, Communications & Public Affairs, Jo-Anne Polak
Vice-President, Mail Processing & Network, Brian Wilson

ePost / Postel
#1300, 393 University Ave., Toronto, ON M5G 2P7
877-376-1212
service@to.epost.ca

Office of the Ombudsman / Bureau de l'ombudsman
PO Box 90026, Ottawa, ON K1V 1J8
Fax: 800-204-4193
800-204-4198
www.ombudsman.postescanadapost.ca

Ombudsman, Nicole Goodfellow

Canada Post Communications Offices:

Atlantic Division
6175 Almon St., Halifax, NS B3K 5N2
902-494-4711

Huron Division
951 Highbury Ave., London, ON N5Y 1B0
519-457-5362 Fax: 519-457-5346

Pacific Division
PO Box 2110 STN Terminal, Vancouver, BC V6B 4Z3
604-662-1592 Fax: 604-662-1710

Prairie Division
#1300, 10020 - 101A Ave., Edmonton, AB T5J 4J4
780-944-3137 Fax: 780-944-3140

Québec Division
#503, 300, rue St-Paul, Québec, QC G1K 3W0
418-694-3161 Fax: 418-694-6993

Greater Toronto Area & Regions
4567 Dixie Rd., Mississauga, ON L4W 1S2
905-214-9595 Fax: 905-214-9244

Canada Revenue Agency (CRA) / Agence du revenu du Canada

875 Heron Rd., Ottawa, ON K1A 0L5
800-267-6999
www.cra-arc.gc.ca
TTY: 800-665-0354
Other Communication: Individual Income Tax Enquiries: 1-800-959-8281; Telerefund: 1-800-959-1956; Business & Self-Employed Individuals: 1-800-959-5525; GST/HST Credit: 1-800-959-1953

The Canada Revenue Agency administers tax laws for the Canadian federal government & for most provincial & territorial governments. The Agency is also responisible for various social & economic benefit & incentive programs, which are delivered through the tax system.

Acts Administered:
Canada Pension Plan Act, Part I
Customs Act
Customs & Excise Offshore Application Act
Customs Tariff Act
Department of National Revenue Act
Excise Act
Excise Tax Act
Special Import Measures Act
Unemployment Insurance Act, Part III & VII

Minister, National Revenue; Minister, Fisheries & Oceans, Hon. Gail Shea
613-995-2960, Fax: 613-952-6608, Shea.G@parl.gc.ca

Commissioner & CEO, Linda Lizotte-MacPherson
613-957-3688

Appeals Branch / Direction générale des appels
Asst. Commissioner, Anne-Marie Lévesque
613-960-2388, Fax: 613-952-5965
Director General, Taxpayer Relief & Service Complaints, Lynn Atkinson
613-960-2232, Fax: 613-952-5825
Director General, Tax & Charities Appeals, John Crowley
613-960-2307, Fax: 613-941-8088
Director General, Program Management & Analysis, Sylvain St-Denis
613-960-2374, Fax: 613-952-4281
Director, CPP/EI Appeals, Natalie Stibernik
613-960-2205

Assessment & Benefit Services Branch / Direction générale des services de cotisation et de prestations
Asst. Commissioner, Arlene E. White
613-954-6614, Fax: 613-954-4434
Deputy Asst. Commissioner, Dave J. Bennett
613-941-5007, Fax: 613-954-4434
Director General, Individual Returns, Nathalie Dumais
613-957-7497, Fax: 613-941-2090
Director General, Business Returns, Ted Gallivan
613-954-7979
Director General, Benefit Programs, Cynthia Leblanc
613-957-9338, Fax: 613-946-6719
Director General, Horizontal Integration & Management Services, Sue Wormington
613-954-5755, Fax: 613-957-3365

Compliance Programs Branch / Programmes d'observation de la législation
Fax: 613-952-6772
Asst. Commissioner, Terrance I. McAuley
613-957-3709, Fax: 613-952-6772
Deputy Asst. Commissioner, Richard Montroy
613-957-3585, Fax: 613-952-6772
Director General, International & Large Business, Lucie Bergevin
613-952-7472, Fax: 613-941-9673
Director General, Audit Professional Services, Susan Betts
613-948-4744, Fax: 613-946-0044
Director General, Scientific Research & Experimental Development, Hélène Dompierre
613-946-3447, Fax: 613-952-8071
Director General, Small & Medium Enterprises, Jim Gauvreau
613-941-6756
Director General, Business Transformation & Corporate Management Directorate, Martin Leigh
613-941-5126, Fax: 613-960-0328, Other Communications: Alternate Telephone: 613-791-6880
Director General, Compliance Strategy, Claude St-Pierre
613-957-3648, Fax: 613-946-5931
Director General, Enforcement & Disclosures, Luc Vadnais
613-957-7780, Fax: 613-941-9606

Corporate Audit & Evaluation Branch / Direction générale de la vérification et de l'évaluation de l'entreprise
Chief Audit Executive & Director General, Program Evaluation, Patricia A. MacDonald
613-957-7522, Fax: 613-952-0512
Director, Internal Audit, Corporate Function, Annie Boudreau
613-957-7552, Fax: 613-941-3657
Director, Professional Practice & Corporate Services, Maura Butko
613-954-7840, Fax: 613-948-2314
Director, Internal Audit, Tax Operations, Gita Ghatt
613-941-5664
Director, Program Evaluation, Myles Kennedy
613-954-7881

Enterprise Risk Management Branch / Direction générale de la gestion des risques de l'entreprise
Asst. Commissioner & Chief Risk Officer, Brian Philbin
613-960-5536, Fax: 613-960-5557
Director, Enterprise Risk Management, Valérie Bournival
613-960-5534, Fax: 613-960-5557
Special Advisor to the Asst. Commissioner & CRO, Johanne Raby
613-960-5535, Fax: 613-960-5557

Finance & Administration Branch / Direction générale des finances et de l'administration
Asst. Commissioner & Chief Financial Officer, Filipe Dinis
613-946-1763, Fax: 613-948-5776
Director General, Security & Internal Affairs, Thérèse Awada
613-948-2449, Fax: 613-952-2019
Director General, Financial Administration, Michel Bernard
613-957-7343, Fax: 613-952-3087
Director General, Resource Management, Judy Cosby
613-947-3262, Fax: 613-941-2264
Director General, Real Property & Service Integration, Bill Doering
613-954-8330
Director General, Administration, Dennis Quinn
613-947-3262, Fax: 613-941-2264
Acting Director General, Strategic Management & Program Support, Michael K. Walker
613-957-7502, Fax: 613-957-7613

Human Resources Branch / Direction générale des ressources humaines
Fax: 613-957-2306
Asst. Commissioner, Cheryl Fraser
613-954-8200, Fax: 613-952-8557
Deputy Asst. Commissioner, Dan Danagher
613-946-4527, Fax: 613-952-8557
Director General, Strategic Business Integration, Claude Bourget
613-954-8166
Director General, Training & Learning, Karen Butcher
613-954-7573, Fax: 613-941-9411
Director General, Training & Learning, Judith Farley
613-954-7573, Fax: 613-941-9411
Director General, Human Resources Operations, Claire Lavoie
613-957-2319, Fax: 613-954-7214
Director General, Employment Programs, Anuradha Marisetti
613-954-1623, Fax: 613-954-4194
Director General, Executive Personnel, Monique Potvin
613-957-7623, Fax: 613-941-5132
Director General, Workplace Relations & Compensation, Claude P. Tremblay
613-954-8150

Information Technology Branch / Direction générale de l'informatique
Fax: 613-957-9058
Asst. Commissioner & Chief Information Officer, Peter Poulin
613-954-8983, Fax: 613-957-9058
Deputy Asst. Commissioner, Keith Barrass
613-948-2780
Director General, Technology Services, Annette Butikofer
613-948-0814, Fax: 613-948-0487
Director General, Branch Business Management, Denis Lafrenière
613-946-9473, Fax: 613-946-4992
Director General, Operations Services, Lorne Leech
613-948-0976
Director General, Data & Assurance Services, Randall Rennie
613-948-0396
Director, Distributed Services, Richard St-Jean
613-946-4741, Fax: 613-946-4992

Legal Services Branch / Direction générale des services juridiques
Fax: 613-954-6282
Senior General Counsel, Charles McNab
613-957-2358
Senior General Counsel, Jean-Marc Raymond
613-954-5881

Legislative Policy & Regulatory Affairs / Politiques législatives et affaires réglementaires
Asst. Commissioner, Brian McCauley
613-957-3708, Fax: 613-957-2067
Special Advisor to the Asst. Commissioner, Terry de March
613-941-1647, Fax: 613-954-2586
Director General, Income Tax Rulings, Wayne Adams
613-957-2132, Fax: 613-957-2088
Director General, Excise & GST/HST Rulings, Pierre Bertrand
613-948-4398, Fax: 613-941-4451
Director General, Charities, Cathy Hawara
613-954-0931, Fax: 613-954-2586
Director General, Registered Plans, Danielle Laflèche
613-954-0933, Fax: 613-952-1343
Director General, Legislative Policy, Mickey Sarazin
613-957-2061, Fax: 613-954-0896
Director, Planning & Management Services Division, Sherry Sharpe
613-957-2375, Fax: 613-952-8674

Public Affairs Branch / Direction générale des affaires publiques
Asst. Commissioner, Sandra Lavigne
613-957-3508, Fax: 613-954-7955
Director General, Ministerial Services & Operations, Louise Dorval
613-957-8438, Fax: 613-941-0914
Director General, Communications, Michel Hébert
613-948-4847
Director, Policies & Standards, Geneviève Binet
613-957-3265, Fax: 613-954-6441
Director, Access to Information & Privacy, Marie-Claude Juneau
613-960-5378, Fax: 613-941-9395
Director, Branch Services, Patrick Mineault
613-941-6865, Fax: 613-952-7939
Director, Electronic & Print Media, Christiane Séguin
613-960-5523

Strategy & Integration Branch / Direction generale de la strategie et de l'integration
Asst. Commissioner, Catherine Bennett
613-952-3660, Fax: 613-941-3438
Director General, Corporate Tax Administration for Ontario Directorate, Marilyn Gaudet
613-960-5687, Fax: 613-960-5700
Director General, Client Relations, Mireille Éthier
613-941-9964, Fax: 613-941-0181
Director General, Planning & Management Services Division, Rob Schumacher
613-941-0798, Fax: 613-946-3312
Director General, Corporate Planning, Governance & Measurement, Normand Théberge
613-954-6082, Fax: 613-952-0061
Director General, Statistics & Information Management, Patricia Whitridge
613-957-8706, Fax: 613-952-6715
Director, Strategic Policy, Maxine Ifill
613-941-6216, Fax: 613-946-8914
Director, Provincial Sales Tax Administration Reform Directorate, Cary O'Brien
613-948-5319, Fax: 613-960-5700

Taxpayer Services & Debt Management / Services aux contribuables et gestion des créances
Asst. Commissioner, Vacant
Deputy Asst. Commissioner, Danielle Morin
613-941-9801, Fax: 613-952-6395
Director General, Debt Management Research & Analytics, Richard Denis
613-957-1863, Fax: 613-948-3162, Other Communications: Alternative Telephone: 613-859-8175
Director General, Taxpaper Services, Marj Ogden
613-957-9362, Fax: 613-941-5100, Other Communications: Executive Assistant, Phone: 613-957-7849
Director General, Accounts Receivable Directorate, Michael Snaauw
613-954-1532

Tax Services Offices
800-959-8281
TTY: 800-665-0354
Other Communication: For Business or Self-Employed, Toll-Free: 1-800-959-5525

Atlantic Region

Bathurst
201 George St., PO Box 8888, Bathurst, NB E2A 4L8
Fax: 506-548-7176

Charlottetown
161 St. Peters Rd., PO Box 8500, Charlottetown, PE C1A 8L3
Fax: 902-566-7197

Nova Scotia
1557 Hollis St., PO Box 638, Halifax, NS B3J 2T5
Fax: 902-426-7170

Moncton
50 King St., PO Box 1070, Moncton, NB E1C 8P2
Fax: 506-851-7018

Newfoundland & Labrador
Sir Humphrey Gilbert Building, 165 Duckworth St., PO Box 12075, St. John's, NL A1B 4R5
Fax: 709-754-5928

Saint John
126 Prince William St., Saint John, NB E2L 4H9
Fax: 506-636-5200

Northern Ontario Region

Barrie
81 Mulcaster St., Barrie, ON L4M 6T7
Fax: 705-721-0056

Belleville
11 Station St., Belleville, ON K8N 2S3
Fax: 613-969-7845

Kingston
31 Hyperion Ct., PO Box 2600, Kingston, ON K7L 5P3
Fax: 613-545-3272

Ottawa & Nunavut
333 Laurier Ave. West, Ottawa, ON K1A 0L9
Fax: 613-238-7125

Ottawa Technology Centre
875 Heron Rd., Ottawa, ON K1A 1A2
Fax: 613-739-1147

Peterborough
185 King St. West, Peterborough, ON K9J 8M3
Fax: 705-876-6422

Sudbury
1050 Notre Dame Ave., Sudbury, ON P3A 5C1
Fax: 705-671-3994

Thunder Bay
130 South Syndicate Ave., Thunder Bay, ON P7E 1C7
Fax: 807-622-8512

Pacific Region

Burnaby-Fraser
9737 King George Blvd., PO Box 9070 Main, Surrey, BC V3T 5W6
Fax: 604-587-2010

Northern BC & Yukon
280 Victoria St., Prince George, BC V2L 4X3
Fax: 250-561-7869

Southern Interior
277 Winnipeg St., Penticton, BC V2A 1N6
Fax: 250-492-8346

Vancouver
1166 West Pender St., Vancouver, BC V6E 3H8
Fax: 604-689-7536

Vancouver Island
1415 Vancouver St., Victoria, BC V8V 3W4
Fax: 250-363-8188

Prairie Region

Edmonton & NWT
#10, 9700 Jasper Ave., Edmonton, AB T5J 4C8
Fax: 780-495-3533

Lethbridge
#200, 419 - 7 St. South, Lethbridge, AB T1J 4A9
Fax: 403-382-4765

Red Deer
4996 - 49 Ave., Red Deer, AB T4N 6X2
Fax: 403-341-7053

Regina
#260, 1783 Hamilton St., Regina, SK S4P 2B6
Fax: 306-757-1412

Saskatoon
340 - 3rd Ave. North, Saskatoon, SK S7K 0A8
Fax: 306-652-3211

Calgary
220 - 4 Ave. SE, Calgary, AB T2G 0L1
Fax: 403-264-5843

Winnipeg
325 Broadway, Winnipeg, MB R3C 4T4
Fax: 204-984-5164

Brandon
1039 Princess Ave., Winnipeg, MB R7A 4J5
Fax: 204-726-7868

Southern Ontario Region

Hamilton
55 Bay St., PO Box 2220, Hamilton, ON L8N 3E1
Fax: 905-546-1615

Kitchener-Waterloo
166 Frederick St., Kitchener, ON N2G 4N1
Fax: 519-579-4532

London
451 Talbot St., London, ON N6A 5E5
Fax: 519-645-4029

St Catharines
32 Church St., PO Box 3038, St Catharines, ON L2R 3B9
Fax: 905-688-5996

Toronto Centre
1 Front St. West, Toronto, ON M5J 2X6
Fax: 416-360-8908

Toronto East
#427, 200 Town Centre Ct., Toronto, ON M1P 4Y3
Fax: 416-973-5126

Toronto North
5001 Yonge St., Toronto, ON M2N 6R9
Fax: 416-512-2558

Toronto West
5800 Hurontario St., Mississauga, ON L5R 4B4
Fax: 905-566-6182

Windsor
185 Ouellette Ave., Windsor, ON N9A 5S8
Fax: 519-257-6558

Québec Region

Chicoutimi
100, rue Lafontaine, Chicoutimi, QC G7H 6X2
Fax: 418-698-6387

Laval
3400, av Jean-Béraud, Laval, QC H7T 2Z2
Fax: 514-956-7071

Montérégie-Rive-Sud
3250, boul Lapinière, Brossard, QC J4Z 3T8
Fax: 450-926-7100

Montréal
305, boul René-Lévesque ouest, Montréal, QC H2Z 1A6
Fax: 514-496-1309

Outaouais
1100, boul Maloney ouest, Gatineau, ON K1A 1L4
Fax: 819-994-1103

Québec
165, rue de la Pointe-aux-Lièvres sud, Québec, QC G1K 7L3
Fax: 418-649-6478

Rimouski
#101, 180, av de la Cathédrale, Rimouski, QC G5L 5H9
Fax: 418-722-3027

Rouyn-Noranda
44, av du Lac, Rouyn-Noranda, QC J9X 6Z9
Fax: 819-797-8366

Sherbrooke
50, Place de la Cité, CP 1300, Sherbrooke, QC J1H 5L8
Fax: 819-821-8582

Trois-Rivières
#111, 25, rue des Forges, Trois-Rivières, QC G9A 2G4
Fax: 819-371-2744

Canada School of Public Service (CCMD) / École de la fonction publique du Canada (EEPC)

373 Sussex Dr., Ottawa, ON K1N 6Z2
819-953-5400 Fax: 819-953-7953
866-703-9598
info@csps-efpc.gc.ca
www.csps-efpc.gc.ca
TTY: 819-934-6194
Other Communication: Toll-Free Fax: 1-866-944-0454

Learning provider for the Public Service of Canada. The School brings together three well-established federal public service learning organizations: the Canadian Centre for Management Development, & from the Public Service Commission, Training & Development Canada & Language Training Canada. Contributes to building & maintaining a modern, high-quality, professional public service that is at the leading-edge of knowledge in modern public administration & public sector management. Through up-to-date adult learning techniques, it provides public servants across the country with access to the common learning opportunities they require to effectively serve Canada & Canadians

Acts Administered:
Canadian Centre for Management Development Act

Deputy Minister/President, Guy McKenzie
613-992-8165, Fax: 613-943-1038,
guy.mckenzie@csps-efpc.gc.ca

President Emeritus, Jocelyne Bourgon
613-943-4311, Fax: 613-947-3130

Vice-President, Strategic Directions, Program Development & Marketing, Michele Brenning
613-943-0321, Fax: 613-947-3706, Other Communications: Executive Assistant, Phone: 613-943-4296

Vice-President & Chief Financial Officer, Corporate Management & Registration Services, Chantale Cousineau-Mahoney
613-947-1098, Fax: 613-995-5652, Other Communications: Executive Assistant, Phone: 613-947-4357

Vice-President, Penny Gotzaman
613-995-4035, Fax: 613-943-7873

Acting Vice-President, Program Operations, Jayne Huntley
613-943-0250, Fax: 613-992-3663

Director General, Functional Communities, Authority Delegation & Orientation, Élise Boisjoly
819-934-7692, Fax: 819-953-2392, Other Communications: Executive Assistant, Phone: 819-994-5734

Director General, Physical Infrastructure & Administration, Alain Dorion
613-943-8917, Fax: 613-995-0331

Director General, Strategic Directions, Innovation & Program Development, Jean-François Fleury
613-992-8346, Fax: 613-943-4312

Director General, Language Training, Patricia Jaton
819-994-5641, Fax: 819-953-7298

Director General, Registration Services & ILMS, Steven McLaughlin
819-934-8279, Fax: 819-934-8300, Other Communications: Executive Assistant, Phone: 819-934-8258

Director General, Marketing, Communications & Engagement, Marie-Claude Petit
613-943-4304, Fax: 613-943-5651

Director General, Leadership & Professional Development, Sandra Webber
613-996-5489, Fax: 613-947-0490, Other Communications: Executive Assistant, Phone: 613-996-0295

Canadian Artists & Producers Professional Relations Tribunal / Tribunal canadien des relations professionnelles artistes-producteurs

C.D. Howe Bldg., 240 Sparks St., 1st Fl., West Tower, Ottawa, ON K1A 1A1
613-996-4052 Fax: 613-947-4125
800-263-ARTS
info@capprt-tcrpap.gc.ca
www.capprt-tcrpap.gc.ca

The Tribunal administers legislation providing a framework for professional relations between self-employed artists & the producers in the federal jurisdiction who use their services.

Acts Administered:
The Status of the Artist Act

Executive Director & General Counsel, Diane Chartrand
613-947-4263, Fax: 613-947-4125,
chartrand.diane@capprt-tcrpap.gc.ca

Administrative & Financial Officer, Sylvie Besner
613-947-4264, Fax: 613-947-4125,
besner.sylvie@capprt-tcrpap.gc.ca, TTY: 800-267-6511

Administration & Communication Officer, Manon Allaire
613-947-9607, Fax: 613-947-4125,
allaire.manon@capprt-tcrpap.gc.ca, TTY: 800-267-6511

Director, Planning, Research & Communication, Brian K. Stewart
613-996-4053, Fax: 613-947-4125,
stewart.brianK@capprt-tcrpap.gc.ca, TTY: 800-267-6511

Manager, Corporate Services, Karen Berndt
613-996-4054, Fax: 613-947-4125, TTY: 800-267-6511

Registrar & Legal Counsel, Steve Joanisse
613-947-8413, Fax: 613-947-4125,
joanisse.steve@capprt-tcrpap.gc.ca, TTY: 800-267-6511

Canadian Broadcasting Corporation (CBC) / Société Radio-Canada (SRC)

181 Queen St., PO Box 3220 C, Ottawa, ON K1Y 1E4
613-288-6033
liaison@radio-canada.ca
www.cbc.radio-canada.ca
Other Communication: Toll Free: 1-866-306-4636

The Canadian Broadcasting Corporation (CBC) is a Crown corporation governed by the 1991 Broadcasting Act & subject to regulations of the Canadian Radio-television & Telecommunications Commission (CRTC). The CBC operates four national radio networks, CBC Radio One & CBC Radio Two in English, & La Radio de Radio-Canada & Espace musique in French, featuring information & general interest programs as well as classical music & cultural programs; two self-supporting specialty cable television services, CBC Newsworld in English & Le Réseau de l'information (RDI) in French which feature news & information programs 24 hours a day, seven days a week; & radio & television services for Canada's North in English, French & eight aboriginal languages. CBC also provides, on behalf of the Government of Canada, an international shortwave radio service, Radio Canada International, which broadcasts in seven languages.

Chair, Board of Directors, Timothy W. Casgrain
President/CEO, Hubert T. Lacroix
Executive Vice-President, French Services, Sylvain Lafrance
Executive Vice-President, English Services, Kirstine Stewart
Senior Vice-President, Corporate Secretary & Business Partnerships, Michel Tremblay
Vice President, Real Estate, Legal Services & General Counsel; Interim Vice-President, People & Culture, Maryse Bertrand
Vice-President, Brand, Communications & Corporate Affairs, Real Estate Division, William B. Chambers
Vice-President & Chief Regulatory Officer, Steven Guiton
Vice-President & Chief Financial Officer, Suzanne Morris

CBC Ombudsman

Ombudsman, CBC, English Services, Kirk LaPointe
416-205-2825, Fax: 416-205-2978, ombudsman@cbc.ca
Ombudsman, Radio-Canada, French Services, Julie Miville-Dechêne
514-597-4757, 877-846-4737, Fax: 514-597-5253,
ombudsman@radio-canada.ca

Radio Canada International

1400, boul René-Lévesque est, CP 6000, Montréal, QC H2L 2M2
514-597-7500
info@rcinet.ca
www.rcinet.ca

Radio Canada International produces daily and weekly programs in English, French, Spanish, Russian, Mandarin, Arabic and Portuguese. A wide variety of programs produced by CBC/Radio-Canada are also available. RCI also produces weekly and monthly short features and interviews for broadcast on numerous partner stations in English, French, Spanish, Russian and Mandarin. Radio Canada International is a member of several international organizations, such as NABA (North American Broadcasters Association), CBA (Commonwealth Broadcasting Association), CBU (Caribbean Broadcasting Union), ABU (Asia-Pacific Broadcasting Union) and DRM (Digital Radio Mondiale). RCI is an associate member of the UER (European Broadcasting Union).

CBC/Radio-Canada - English Services
250 Front St. W., PO Box 500 A, Toronto, ON M5W 1E6
866-306-4636
www.cbc.ca/contact/
TTY: 866-220-6045

CBC/Radio-Canada - French Services
1400, boul René-Lévesque est, CP 6000, Montréal, QC H3C 3A8
514-597-6000
866-306-4636
auditoire@radio-canada.ca
www.radio-canada.ca/

CBC Regional Offices:

Alberta (English & French)
10062 - 102nd Ave., PO Box 555, Edmonton, AB T5J 2P4
780-468-7500
www.cbc.ca/edmonton/contact/

British Columbia (English & French)
PO Box 4600, Vancouver, BC V6B 4A2
604-662-6000
866-306-4636
www.cbc.ca/bc/contact/

CBC North
PO Box 160, Yellowknife, NT X1A 2N2
867-920-5400
www.cbc.ca/north/contact/

Manitoba (English & French)
541 Portage Ave., Winnipeg, MB R3B 2G1
204-788-3222
www.cbc.ca/manitoba/contact/
TTY: 866-220-6045

Maritimes (English)
PO Box 3000, Halifax, NS B3J 3E9
902-420-8311
www.cbc.ca/ns/contact/

Atlantic Provinces (French Services) / Radio-Canada Acadie
250, av Université, Moncton, NB E1C 8N8
506-853-6666
Other Communication: www.cbc.ca/nb/contact/

Newfoundland (English)
PO Box 12010 A, St. John's, NL A1B 3T8
709-576-5000
www.cbc.ca/nl/contact/

Canadian Broadcasting Centre
250 Front St. W., PO Box 500 A, Toronto, ON M5W 1E6
416-205-3311
www.cbc.ca/toronto/contact/

Ottawa Production Centre
181 Queen St., PO Box 3220 C, Ottawa, ON K1Y 1E4
613-288-6000
www.cbc.ca/ottawa/contact/

Québec (English) / Maison de Radio-Canada
1400, boul René-Lévesque est, CP 6000, Montréal, QC H3C 3A8
514-597-6000
www.cbc.ca/montreal/contact/

Québec (French) / Société Radio-Canada
880, rue Saint-Jean, CP 18800, Québec, QC G1K 9L4
800-267-1341

Saskatchewan (English & French)
2440 Broad St., Regina, SK S4P 4A1
306-347-9540
www.cbc.ca/sask/contact/

Prince Edward Island (English & French)
430 University Ave., PO Box 2230, Charlottetown, PE C1A 8B9
902-629-6400
866-306-4636
www.cbc.ca/pei/contact/

Canadian Centre for Occupational Health & Safety (CCOHS) / Centre canadien d'hygiène et de sécurité au travail (CCHST)

135 Hunter St. East, Hamilton, ON L8N 1M5
905-572-2981 Fax: 905-572-2206
800-668-4284
www.ccohs.ca

Provides occupational health & safety & environmental information in the form of publications, responses to inquiries & a computerized information service available in various formats. Topics include: environmental acts & regulations; occupational & environmental health data; toxic effects of chemical substances; transport of dangerous goods; chemical evaluation; hazardous substances; & domestic substances listed under the Canadian Environmental Protection Act; biological hazards; ergonomics

President/CEO, S. Len Hong
905-572-2981
Vice-President, Dr. Patabendi K. Abeytunga
905-572-2981
Controller, Bonnie Easterbrook
905-572-2981
Manager, Computer Systems & Services, David Brophy
905-572-2981
Manager, General Health & Safety Services, Norma Gibson-MacDonald
905-572-2981
Manager, Communications, Eleanor Westwood
905-572-2981

Canadian Centre on Substance Abuse (CCSA) / Centre canadien de lutte contre l'alcoolisme et les toxicomanies (CCLAT)

#500, 75 Albert St., Ottawa, ON K1P 5E7
613-235-4048 Fax: 613-235-8101
info@ccsa.ca
www.ccsa.ca
Other Communication: Publications, Email: publications@ccsa.ca

CCSA is a non-profit organization working to minimize the harm associated with the use of alcohol, tobacco, & other drugs.

Acts Administered:
CCSA Act

Interim Chair, Beverly Clarke
CEO, Michel Perron
613-235-4048
Deputy CEO, Rita Notarandrea
613-235-4048
Director, Research & Knowledge Exchange, Cheryl Arratoon
613-235-4048
Director, Partnerships & Priorities, Rhowena Nebre Martin
613-235-4048
Director, Human Resources, Sherry Read
613-235-4048
Director, Finance, Anne Richer
613-235-4048

Canadian Commercial Corporation (CCC) / Corporation commerciale canadienne

50 O'Connor St., 11th Fl., Ottawa, ON K1A 0S6
613-996-0034 Fax: 613-995-2121
800-748-8191
www.ccc.ca

A Crown Corporation mandated to facilitate international trade, particularly in government markets. CCC specializes in international procurement markets for Canadian companies & provides services to help them win, negotiate & manage export contracts. As prime contractor, CCC offers a government-to-government agreement that simplifies customer access to Canadian technology & expertise. CCC contracts have a government guarantee for performance.

Chair, Robert C. Kay
President/CEO, Marc Whittingham
613-996-0042, Fax: 613-992-2134, Other Communications: Alternative Telephone: 613-996-0043
Vice-President, Business Development & Sales, Pierre Alarie
613-943-0953, Fax: 613-995-2121
Vice-President, Strategy & Organizational Development, Mariette Fyfe-Fortin
613-943-4360, Fax: 613-995-2121
Vice-President, Contract Management & Procurement, Jacques Greffe
613-996-0161, Fax: 613-995-2121
Vice-President/Legal General Counsel & Corporate Secretary, Legal Services, Tamara Parschin-Rybkin, Q.C.
613-992-4419, Fax: 613-947-3903
Vice-President/CFO, Risk & Finance, Martin Zablocki
613-992-9638, Fax: 613-995-2121

Canadian Dairy Commission (CDC) / Commission canadienne du lait (CCL)

Central Experimental Farm, NCC Driveway, Bldg. 55, 960 Carling Ave., Ottawa, ON K1A 0Z2
613-792-2000 Fax: 613-792-2009
cdc-ccl@cdc-ccl.gc.ca
www.cdc.ca
TTY: 613-792-2082
Other Communication: Special Milk Class Permits, Phone: 613-792-2057; Dairy Imports & Exports, Phone: 613-792-2010

The federal Crown corporation serves the interests of all dairy stakeholders, including producers, processors, further processors, exporters, consumers & governments. The following are the key objectives of the CDC: providing efficient milk & cream producers with the opportunity to obtain a fair return for their labour & investment; & ensuring an adequate supply of high quality dairy products for consumers.

CEO, John Core
613-792-2060, Fax: 613-792-2064, jcore@agr.gc.ca
Chair, Randy Williamson
Commissioner, Gilles Martin
Senior Director, Policy & Corporate Affairs, Gilles Froment
613-792-2030, Fax: 613-792-2009, gfroment@agr.gc.ca
Senior Director, Finance & Operations, Gaëtan Paquette
613-792-2070, Fax: 613-792-2009, gpaquette@agr.gc.ca
Director, Audit, Robert Hansis
613-792-2050, Fax: 613-792-2009, rhansis@agr.gc.ca

Canadian Environmental Assessment Agency (CEAA) / Agence canadienne d'évaluation environnementale (ACEE)

Place Bell Canada, 160 Elgin St., 22nd Fl., Ottawa, ON K1A 0H3
613-957-0700 Fax: 613-957-0862
866-582-1884
info@ceaa-acee.gc.ca
www.ceaa-acee.gc.ca

The Canadian Environmental Assessment Agency (CEAA) was established to administer the Canadian Environmental Assessment Act (the Act). The environmental assessment process identifies the environmental effects of proposed projects & measures to address those effects, in support of sustainable development. CEAA promotes environmental assessment as a tool to protect & sustain a healthy environment in harmony with a growing economy. The CEAA advocates high-quality environmental assessments by assisting federal departments & agencies with training & guidance & by investing in the research & development of best practices. CEAA provides administrative support to mediators & review panels & ensures that the public has opportunities to participate effectively in the environmental assessment process. Public participation strengthens the quality & credibility of environmental assessments by providing local & traditional knowledge, & insight into possible environmental effects. A publicly accessible master index of environmental assessments carried out by federal departments is available in the Canadian Environmental Assessment Registry (projects beginning before November 2003 are available in the Federal Environmental Assessment Index) located on the CEAA we b site. In addition, CEAA's participant funding program provides limited funds to ensure that interested individuals & groups have the opportunity to participate in mediations & panel reviews.
Accountable to the Minister of the Environment

President, Elaine Feldman
613-948-2671, Fax: 613-948-2208, elaine.feldman@ceaa-acee.gc.ca
Vice-President, Policy Development, Helen Cutts
613-948-2662, Fax: 613-957-0897, helen.cutts@ceaa-acee.gc.ca
Vice-President, Operations, Yves Leboeuf
613-948-2665, Fax: 613-957-0935, yves.leboeuf@ceaa-acee.gc.ca
Executive Director, Project Reviews, Steve Burgess
613-948-2663, Fax: 613-957-0941, steve.burgess@ceaa-acee.gc.ca
Director General, Corporate Services, Richard Gagné
613-957-0467, Fax: 613-957-0946, richard.gagne@ceaa-acee.gc.ca
Director, Operational Support, Andrée Chevrier
613-957-0641, Fax: 613-948-1354, andree.chevrier@ceaa-acee.gc.ca
Director, Communications, Charlene Gaudet
613-957-0712, Fax: 613-957-0946, charlene.gaudet@ceaa-acee.gc.ca
Director, Legislative & Regulatory Affairs, John McCauley
613-948-1785, Fax: 613-957-0897, john.mccauley@ceaa-acee.gc.ca
Director, Finance & Administration, Daniel Nadeau
613-948-2677, Fax: 613-957-0862, daniel.nadeau@ceaa-acee.gc.ca
Director, Human Resources, Brigitte Schryer
613-954-2201, Fax: 613-957-0858, brigitte.schryer@ceaa-acee.gc.ca

Senior Policy Analyst, Legislative & Regulatory Affairs, Natalie Deschamps
613-957-0366, Fax: 613-857-0366,
natalie.deschamps@ceaa-acee.gc.ca
General Counsel & Executive Director, Legal Services, Irene V. Gendron
613-957-0735, Fax: 613-957-0942

Regional Offices:

Alberta & Northwest Territories
61 Airport Rd. NW, Edmonton, AB T5G 0W6
780-495-2037 Fax: 780-495-2876

Ontario
#907, 55 St. Clair Ave. East, Toronto, ON M4T 1M2
416-952-1576 Fax: 416-952-1573

Pacific & Yukon
#410, 701 Georgia St. West, Vancouver, BC V7Y 1K8
604-666-2431 Fax: 604-666-6990

Prairie Region
#101, 167 Lobard Ave., Winnipeg, MB R3B OT6
204-983-5127 Fax: 204-983-7174

Québec
1141, rte de l'Église, 2e étage, CP 9514 Ste-Foy, Québec, QC G1V 4B8
418-649-6444 Fax: 418-649-6443

Canadian Food Inspection Agency (CFIA) / Agence canadienne d'inspection des aliments (ACIA)

1400 Merivale Rd., Ottawa, ON K1A 0Y9
613-225-2342 Fax: 613-228-6601
800-442-2342
www.inspection.gc.ca
TTY: 800-465-7735
Other Communication: Atlantic Area, Phone: 506-851-7400; Ontario Area: 519-837-9400; Québec Area: 514-283-8888; Western Area: 403-292-4301

The agency is responsible for all inspection services related to food safety, economic fraud, trade-related requirements, & animal & plant health programs.

Acts Administered:
Agriculture & Agri-Food Administration Monetary Penalties Act
Canada Agricultural Products Act
Canadian Food Inspection Agency Act
Consumer Packaging & Labelling Act
Feeds Act
Fertilizers Act
Fish Inspection Act
Food & Drugs Act
Health of Animals Act
Meat Inspection Act
Plant Breeders' Rights Act
Plant Protection Act
Seeds Act
Acts Administered in Part by the Canadian Food Inspection Agency

President, Carole Swan
613-773-6000, Fax: 613-773-6060,
carole.swan@inspection.gc.ca
Executive Vice-President, Office of the President, Mary Komarynsky
613-773-6500, Fax: 613-773-6060,
Mary.Komarynsky@inspection.gc.ca
Vice-President, Operations, Stephen Baker
613-773-5700, Fax: 613-773-5671,
Stephen.Baker@inspection.gc.ca
Vice-President, Human Resources, Omer Boudreau
613-773-5725, Fax: 613-773-5795,
Omer.Boudreau@inspection.gc.ca
Vice-President, Policy & Programs, Neil Bouwer
613-773-5734, Fax: 613-773-5791,
Neil.Bouwer@inspection.gc.ca
Vice-President, Science, Martine Dubuc
613-773-5722, Fax: 613-773-5797,
Martine.Dubuc@inspection.gc.ca
Vice-President, Corporate Management, Peter Everson
613-773-5759, Fax: 613-773-5792,
Peter.Everson@inspection.gc.ca
Vice-President, Inspection Modernization, Cameron Prince
613-773-7030, Fax: 613-773-5671,
Cameron.Prince@inspection.gc.ca
Vice-President, Information Management & Information Technology, Kevin Radford
613-773-5545, Fax: 613-773-5580,
Kevin.Radford@inspection.gc.ca
Vice-President, Public Affairs Branch, George W. Shaw
613-773-5776, Fax: 613-773-5559,
George.Shaw@inspection.gc.ca
Vice-President, Business Transformation, Bill Teeter
613-221-3125, Fax: 613-221-3158,
Bill.Teeter@inspection.gc.ca
Assoc. Vice-President, Integration & Management Services, Jim Butcher
613-773-6298, Fax: 613-773-5791,
Jim.Butcher@inspection.gc.ca
Executive Director, Strategic Communication, Laurel Herwig
613-773-5501, Fax: 613-773-5618,
Laurel.Herwig@inspection.gc.ca
Executive Director, Corporate Secretariat, Veronica McGuire
613-773-5751, Fax: 613-773-5791,
Veronica.McGuire@inspection.gc.ca
Executive Director, Audit, Evaluation & Risk Oversight, Brian Smithon
613-773-5349, Fax: 613-773-5696,
Brian.Smith@inspection.gc.ca
Director, Executive Support & Coordination, Aline Dimitri
613-773-5542, Fax: 613-773-5606,
Aline.Dimitri@inspection.gc.ca
Director, Corporate Planning & Reporting, Everett Ethier
613-221-7571, Fax: 613-221-5270,
Everett.Ethier@inspection.gc.ca

Canadian Forces Grievance Board / Comité des griefs des Forces canadiennes

60 Queen St., 10th Fl., Ottawa, ON K1P 5Y7
613-996-8529 Fax: 613-996-6491
877-276-4193
www.cfgb-cgfc.gc.ca
TTY: 877-986-1666
Other Communication: Secure Fax: 613-995-8129

An administrative tribunal with quasi-judicial powers, independent from the Department of National Defence (DND) & the Canadian Forces (CF). The Board was created on March 1, 2000, in accordance with legislation enacted in December 1998 that contained amendments to the National Defence Act. The Board conducts objective & transparent reviews of grievances with due respect to fairness & equity for each individual member of the CF, regardless of rank or position. It plays a unique role within the military grievance review process because it ensures that the rights of CF personnel are considered fairly & impartially in the best interests of both parties concerned, thus balancing the rights of the grievor against the legal & operational requirements of the CF.

Acts Administered:
National Defence Act, ch. N-5, sec. 29
Queen's Regulation & Orders for the Canadian Forces, Ch. 7

Chair, Bruno Hamel
613-996-6453, Fax: 613-995-8129, Other Communications: Executive Assistant, Phone: 613-996-8621
Vice-Chair, James Price
613-996-8628, Fax: 613-996-6491
Executive Director, Corporate Services, Anne Sinclair
613-996-7027, Fax: 613-996-6491, Other Communications: Executive Assistant, Phone: 613-995-7992
Director, Operations/General Counsel, Caroline Maynard
613-995-5552, Fax: 613-996-6491, Other Communications: Executive Assistant, Phone: 613-995-5127
Senior Legal Counsel, Legal Services, Ann Boivin
613-995-5599, Fax: 613-996-6491
Registrar, Andrée-Anne Paquette
613-995-5126, Fax: 613-996-6491

Canadian Grain Commission (CGC) / Commission canadienne des grains (CCG)

#600, 303 Main St., Winnipeg, MB R3C 3G8
204-983-2770 Fax: 204-983-2751
800-853-6705
contact@grainscanada.gc.ca
www.grainscanada.gc.ca
TTY: 866-317-4289
Other Communication: Grain Sanitation & Infestation Control Industry Services, Fax: 204-984-7550; Licensing & Security Unit, Fax: 204-983-4654; Statistics Unit, Phone: 204-983-2739

The CGC is Canada's official grain quality assurance agency. The CGC offers a wide range of programs & services. It regulates grain handling in Canada & establishes & maintains quality standards for Canadian grains. Responsibilities are as follows: officially inspecting & grading grain; weighing grain at terminal & transfer elevators; licensing grain elevators & dealers; conducting & publishing statistical & economic studies; & performing basic & applied research on Canadian grain.

Acts Administered:
Canada Grain Act

Chief Commissioner, Elwin Mermanson
204-983-2735, Fax: 204-983-2751
Commissioner, Murdoch MacKay
204-983-2732, Fax: 204-983-2751
Asst. Chief Commissioner, Jim Smolik
204-983-2730, Fax: 204-983-2751
Chief Financial Officer, Cheryl Blahey
204-984-7042, Fax: 204-984-7213
Chief Informatics Officer, Karl Daher
204-984-6948, Fax: 204-983-0248
Chief Operating Officer, Gordon Miles
204-983-2731, Fax: 204-983-2751
Director, Grain Research Laboratory, Peter Burnett
204-983-2764
Director, Corporate Services, Sandy HayGlass
204-983-2752, Fax: 204-983-0248
Director, Industry Services, Jim Stuart
204-983-1549, Fax: 204-983-7550
Coordinator, Communications, Louise Worster
204-983-2748

Canadian Museum of Nature (CMN) / Musée Canadien de la Nature (MCN)

PO Box 3443 D, Ottawa, ON K1P 6P4
613-566-4700 Fax: 613-364-4021
800-263-4433
www.nature.ca
TTY: 613-566-4770
Other Communication: Toll-Free TTY: 1-866-600-8801

A diverse natural history collection encompassing some 10 million specimens, & thousands of species. Provides access to specimens & data for research & access to knowledge on biodiversity, biosystematics & the environment. Carries out research on management & care of collections & employs a staff of researchers working on national & international projects. Through public programs, CMN communicates knowledge & promotes understanding of science & nature to diverseaudiences. It includes permanent, special & travelling exhibits, curriculum-based & interpretive programs, & print, electronic, audiovisual & multimedia publications.

Canadian Heritage / Patrimoine canadien

15 Eddy St., Gatineau, QC K1A 0M5
819-997-0055
866-811-0055
info@pch.gc.ca
www.pch.gc.ca
TTY: 888-997-3123

Canadian Heritage works to achieve a more cohesive & creative nation. Goals of the department are for Canadians to express & share their cultural experiences with others in their own country & globally & for Canadians to live in an inclusive society with intercultural understanding & citizen participation.
Responsibilities are carried out by the following sectors: Citizenship & Heritage; Cultural Affairs; International & Intergovernmental Affairs & Sport; Planning & Corporate Affairs; & Public & Regional Affairs.

Acts Administered:
An Act to Incorporate the Jules & Paul-Émile Léger Foundation
Broadcasting Act
Canada Council for the Arts Act
Canadian Charter of Rights & Freedoms
Canadian Radio-television & Telecommunications Commission
Copyright Act
Cultural Property Export & Import Act
Department of Canadian Heritage Act
Fitness & Amateur Sport Act
Foreign Publishers Advertising Services Act
Holidays Act
Income Tax Act
Investment Canada Act
Laurier House Act
Library & Archives of Canada Act
Lieutenant Governors Superannuation Act
Museums Act
National Anthem Act
National Arts Centre Act
National Battlefields at Québec Act
National Film Act
National Horse of Canada Act
National Sports of Canada Act
National Symbol of Canada Act
Official Languages Act
Parliamentary Employment & Staff Relations Act
Physical Activity & Sport Act
Public Servants Disclosure Protection Act
Public Service Employment Act
Public Service Labour Relations Act
Salaries Act
Sir John A. Macdonald Day & the Sir Wilfred Laurier Day Act
Status of the Artist Act
Telefilm Canada Act
Trademarks Act

Minister, Canadian Heritage & Official Languages, Hon. James Moore
819-997-7788, Fax: 819-994-1267, james.moore@pch.gc.ca
Minister of State (Status of Women), Hon. Rona Ambrose
819-956-4000, Fax: 613-995-1761,
minister-ministre@swc-cfc.gc.ca
Minister of State (Sport), Hon. Bal Gosal
819-934-1122, Fax: 819-953-8055, bal.gosal@pch.gc.ca
Deputy Minister, Daniel Jean
819-994-1132, Fax: 819-997-0979, Daniel.Jean@pch.gc.ca

Liaison & Agenda Officer, Associate Deputy Minister's Office, Joanne Courchesne
819-997-1356, Fax: 819-997-2978, Joanne.Courchesne@pch.gc.ca
Director, Communications, James Maunder
819-997-7788, Fax: 819-994-1267, James.Maunder@pch.gc.ca

Associated Agencies, Boards & Commissions:
- Canada Council for the Arts / Conseil des Arts du Canada
350 Albert St.
PO Box 1047
Ottawa, ON K1P 5V8
613-566-4414 Fax: 613-566-4390 800-263-5588
www.canadacouncil.ca
- Canada Science & Technology Museum Corporation / Musée des sciences et de la technologie du Canada
- Canadian Broadcasting Corporation (CBC) / Société Radio-Canada (SRC)
- Canadian Museum of Civilization (CMC) / Musée canadien des civilisations
- Canadian Museum of Nature (CMN) / Musée canadien de la nature (MCN)
- Canadian Museum of Civilization (CMC) / Musée canadien des civilisations
- Canadian Museum of Nature (CMN) / Musée canadien de la nature (MCN)
- Canadian Radio-television & Telecommunications Commission (CRTC) / Conseil de la radiodiffusion et des télécommunications canadiennes
- Library & Archives Canada
- National Arts Centre (NAC) / Centre national des Arts (CNA)
- National Battlefields Commission / Commission des champs de bataille nationaux
- National Film Board of Canada / Office national du film du Canada
- National Gallery of Canada / Musée des Beaux-Arts du Canada
- National Gallery of Canada / Musée des beaux-arts du Canada
- Public Service Commission of Canada / Commission de la fonction publique du Canada
- Status of Women Canada / Condition féminine Canada
- Telefilm Canada / Téléfilm Canada

Citizenship & Heritage Sector / Citoyenneté et patrimoine
Asst. Deputy Minister, Tom Scrimger
819-997-2832, Fax: 819-994-5032, Tom.Scrimger@pch.gc.ca
Director General, Canadian Heritage Information Network (CHIN), Gabrielle Blais
819-997-0091, Fax: 819-994-9555, Gabrielle.Blais@pch.gc.ca
Director General, Canadian Conservation Institute & Chief Operating Officer, Jeanne E. Inch
613-998-3721, Fax: 613-952-1431, jeanne.inch@pch.gc.ca
Director General, Strategic Management & Human Rights, Martha LaBarge
819-997-1588, Fax: 819-997-0329, Martha.Labarge@pch.gc.ca
Director General, Citizen Participation, Michel Lemay
819-953-5999, Fax: 819-953-3515, Michel.Lemay@pch.gc.ca
Director General, Official Languages Support Programs, Hubert Lussier
819-994-0943, Fax: 819-953-9353, Hubert.Lussier@pch.gc.ca
Director General, Aboriginal Affairs, Patricia Neri
819-994-6035, Fax: 819-934-6704, patricia.neri@pch.gc.ca
Director, Heritage Group, Pierre Derome
819-956-5555, Fax: 819-934-3201, Pierre.Derome@pch.gc.ca

Regional Offices:

Atlantic
#106, 1045 Main St., Moncton, NB E1C 1H1
506-851-7066 Fax: 506-851-7079
866-811-0055
pch-atlan@pch.gc.ca
TTY: 888-997-3123
Regional Executive Director, Paul Landry
506-851-7069, Fax: 506-851-7079, Paul.Landry@pch.gc.ca

Ontario
#400, 150 John St., Toronto, ON M5V 3T6
416-954-0395 Fax: 416-954-2909
866-811-0055
pch-ontario@pch.gc.ca
TTY: 888-997-3123
Executive Director, Marie Moliner
416-954-0396, Fax: 416-954-2909, marie.moliner@pch.gc.ca

Prairies & Northern Region
#510, 240 Graham Ave., PO Box 2160, Winnipeg, MB R3C 3R5
204-983-3601 Fax: 204-984-6996
866-811-0055
pnr-rpn@pch.gc.ca
TTY: 888-997-3123
Regional Executive Director, Louis Chagnon
204-983-0261, Fax: 204-984-2303, Louis.Chagnon@pch.gc.ca

Québec
Complexe Guy-Favreau, Tour Ouest, 200, boul René-Lévesque ouest, 6e étage, Montréal, QC H2Z 1X4
514-283-5191
866-811-0055
pch-qc@pch.gc.ca
TTY: 888-997-3123
Regional Executive Director, Marc Lemay
514-283-5797, Fax: 514-283-8762, Marc.Lemay@pch.gc.ca

Western
#400, 300 West Georgia St., Vancouver, BC V6B 6C6
604-666-0176 Fax: 604-666-3508
866-811-0055
wr-ro@pch.gc.ca
TTY: 888-997-3123
Other Communication: LAN Fax: 604-666-8801
Regional Executive Director, Patrick Tobin
604-666-2060, Fax: 604-666-6040, Patrick.Tobin@pch.gc.ca

Canadian Human Rights Commission / Commission canadienne des droits de la personne

344 Slater St., 8th Fl., Ottawa, ON K1A 1E1
613-995-1151 Fax: 613-996-9661
888-214-1090
www.chrc-ccdp.ca
TTY: 888-643-3304

The Commission administers the Canadian Human Rights Act which applies to federal government departments & agencies, & businesses under federal jurisdiction. The Commission accepts complaints of discrimination based on race, national or ethnic origin, colour, religion, age, sex, marital & family status, pardoned offence, disability & sexual orientation. It also administers the Employment Equity Act to remove barriers for four designated groups: women, Aboriginal peoples, persons with disabilities & members of visible minorities. Collect calls accepted throughout Canada.

Chief Commissioner, Jennifer Lynch, QC
613-943-9144
Deputy Chief Commissioner, David Langtry
613-943-9148
Secretary General, Karen Mosher
613-943-9134
Director General, Knowledge Center, Linda Dabros
613-943-9153
Director General, Dispute Resolution Branch, Ian Fine
613-943-9090
Director General, Discrimination Prevention Branch, Myriam Montrat
613-943-9155
Director General, Corporate Management Branch, Heather Throop
613-943-9033, Fax: 613-941-6808
Director, Outreach & Communications Branch, David Gollob
613-943-9138

Regional Offices:

Western Region
Canada Place, #1645, 9700 Jasper Ave., PO Box 21, Edmonton, AB T5J 4C3
780-495-4040 Fax: 780-495-4044
888-214-1090
TTY: 780-495-4108
Other Communication: Toll-Free TYY: 1-888-643-3304
Regional Manager, Hilda Andresen
780-495-5936, Fax: 780-495-4044

Eastern Region
#903, 425, boul de Maisonneuve ouest, Montréal, QC H3A 3G5
514-283-5218 Fax: 514-283-5084
888-214-1090
TTY: 514-283-1869
Other Communication: Toll-Free TTY: 1-888-643-3304
Regional Manager, Michel Bibeau
514-496-2932, Fax: 514-283-5084

National Aboriginal Initiative
#750, 175 Hargrave St., Winnipeg, MA RC3 3R8
204-983-2189 Fax: 204-983-6132
866-772-4880
TTY: 866-772-4840
Director, Sherri Helgason
204-983-4648

Canadian Human Rights Tribunal (CHRT) / Tribunal canadien des droits de la personne (TCDP)

160 Elgin St., 11th Fl., Ottawa, ON K1A 1J4
613-995-1707 Fax: 613-995-3484
registrar@chrt-tcdp.gc.ca
www.chrt-tcdp.gc.ca
TTY: 613-947-1070

Quasi-judicial body that adjudicates complaints of discrimination referred to it by the Canadian Human Rights Commission & determines whether the activities violate the Canadian Human Rights Act.

Acts Administered:
Canadian Human Rights Act
Employment Equity Act

Chair, Shirish P. Chotalia
613-995-1707, Fax: 613-995-3484
Vice-Chair, Susheel Gupta
613-995-1707, Fax: 613-995-3484
Executive Directory & Registrar, Frederick Gloade
613-947-1028, Fax: 613-995-3484, Frederick.Gloade@chrt-tcdp.gc.ca
Director, Registry Operations, Michelle Costello
613-947-1122, Fax: 613-947-3484, michelle.costello@chrt-tcdp.gc.ca
Director, Financial Services, Doreen Dyet
613-947-1169, Fax: 613-995-3484
Director, Administrative Services, Bernard Fournier
613-947-1038, Fax: 613-995-3484, bernard.fournier@chrt-tcdp.gc.ca
Director, Information Technology Services, Julie Sibbald
613-947-1185, julie.sibbald@chrt-tcdp.gc.ca

Canadian Institutes of Health Research (CIHR) / Instituts de recherche en santé du Canada (IRSC)

160 Elgin St., 9th Fl., Ottawa, ON K1A 0W9
613-941-2672 Fax: 613-954-1800
888-603-4178
info@cihr-irsc.gc.ca
www.cihr-irsc.gc.ca

Promotes health research excellence in Canada through training & funding programs in basic, clinical, health systems & services, & population health research. Research is carried out in universities, in the health sciences faculties, affiliated hospitals & institutions & other faculties where research projects are highly relevant to human health. University-Industry programs create the opportunity for collaboration between Canadian companies & researchers conducting research in Canadian universities or affiliated institutions. Also manages the health-related Networks of Centres of Excellence.

President, Alain Beaudet
613-954-1808
Executive Vice-President, Christine Fitzgerald
613-957-6134
Vice-President, Knowledge Translation & Public Outreach, Ian Graham
613-948-2318
Executive Director, Secretariat on Research Ethics, Susan Zimmerman
613-947-7148
Director, PAN - Institute Affairs & Initiatives, Terry Campbell
613-960-6211
Director, Ethics Office, Geneviève Dubois-Flynn
613-954-1801
Director, Human Resources, Diane Massicotte
613-957-8762
Director, Evaluations, Internal Audit & Risk Management, Martin Rubenstein
613-941-3557
Director, Communications & Marketing, Karen Spierkel
613-954-1812

Canadian Intergovernmental Conference Secretariat (CICS) / Secrétariat des conférences intergouvernementales canadiennes

222 Queen St., 10th Fl., PO Box 488 A, Ottawa, ON K1N 8V5
613-995-2341 Fax: 613-996-6091
info@scics.gc.ca
www.scics.gc.ca

CICS is a conference support body which provides the administrative services required for the planning & the conduct of federal-provincial-territorial & provincial-territorial conferences at the First Ministers, ministers & deputy ministers level. The agency is at the disposal of individual federal, provincial & territorial government departments which may be called upon to organize & chair such meetings.

Secretary, André M. McArdle
Director, Corporate Services, Anik Lapointe
Director, Information Services, Bernard Latulippe
Director, Conference Services, Louise Seaward-Gagnon
Louise.Seaward-Gagnon@scics.gc.ca

Canadian International Development Agency (CIDA) / Agence canadienne de développement international (ACDI)

200, Promenade du Portage, Gatineau, QC K1A 0G4
819-997-5456 Fax: 819-953-6088
800-230-6349
info@acdi-cida.gc.ca
www.acdi-cida.gc.ca
TTY: 819-953-5023
Other Communication: Toll-Free TDD: 1-800-331-5018

Major agency responsible for delivering most of Canada's foreign aid. CIDA is committed to supporting sustainable development in developing countries to meet the needs of current & future generations. The mission statement demands that criteria of sustainability be integrated into each project undertaken by the Agency in order to improve the economic, social, cultural, ecological & political condition of the world's developing nations. Many of the projects CIDA supports are aimed directly at the environment. Projects include reforestation & watershed rehabilitation, small scale fishing development (to increase output & food), water projects (to improve health), increased food production, improved rural quality, & supply & generation of electricity. Various other projects help nations develop the legal & administrative framework needed to promote environmentally sustainable development.In February, 2004, the Agency released its Sustainable Development Strategy 2004-2006: Enabling Change." This strategy sets out a number of key directions for the Agency to achieve sustainable development. The $100-million five-year Canada Climate Change Development Fund was extended to 2005-2006

Minister, International Cooperation, Hon. Beverley J. (Bev) Oda
819-953-6238, Fax: 819-953-8525
Parliamentary Secretary to the Minister of International Cooperation, Hon. Lois Brown
613-992-9310, Fax: 613-992-9407
Chief of Staff, Neil Desai
819-953-6238
Administrative Officer, Claudine Taillefer
819-997-6912
Senior Vice-President, Geographic Programs Branch, Hau Sing Tse
819-997-1665
Acting Vice-President, Afghanistan & Pakistan Task Force, Francoise Ducros
819-997-1408
Vice-President, Multilateral & Global Programs Branch, Diane Jacovella
819-997-7537, Fax: 819-953-5348
Vice-President, Pan Geographic Programs, Nadia Kostiuk
819-997-1643
Vice-President, Strategic Policy & Performance Branch, Vincent Rigby
819-997-6133, Fax: 819-997-9049
Acting Director General, Communications Branch, Bernard Etzinger
819-953-9574
Acting Director General, Human Resources Branch, Sheila Tenasco-Banerjee
819-934-4682
Director General, Multilateral Development Institutions Directorate, Paul Samson
819-994-3967
Director General, Strategic Planning & Operations Directorate, Naresh Singh
819-956-8266
Acting Chief Information Officer, Jacques Mailloux
819-994-3855

Canadian International Trade Tribunal / Tribunal canadien du commerce extérieur

Standard Life Centre, 333 Laurier Ave. West, 15 Floor, Ottawa, ON K1A 0G7
613-990-2452 Fax: 613-990-2439
secretary@citt-tcce.gc.ca
www.citt-tcce.gc.ca

The Tribunal is an independent, quasi-judicial body, which carries out both judicial & advisory functions relating to trade remedies for the North American Free Trade Agreement. In this capacity, the Tribunal succeeds the Procurement Review Board of Canada. Reports to government through the Minister of Finance.

Acts Administered:
Canadian International Trade Tribunal Act
Customs Act
Excise Tax Act
Special Import Measures Act
Acting Chair, Serge Fréchette
613-990-2432, Fax: 613-990-9881, Other Communications: Executive Assistant, Phone: 613-990-9881
Vice-Chair, Diane Vincent
613-990-1476, Fax: 613-990-9881
Secretary, Dominique Laporte
613-993-3595, Fax: 613-998-1322, Other Communications: Executive Assistant, Phone: 613-949-2309
Director General, Research, Rose Ritcey
613-990-8718, Fax: 613-990-2431, Other Communications: Executive Assistant, Phone: 613-990-8145
General Counsel, Reagan Walker
613-991-9247, Fax: 613-990-7132, Other Communications: Executive Assistant, Phone: 613-993-4372

Canadian Judicial Council / Conseil canadien de la magistrature

150 Metcalfe St., 15th Fl., Ottawa, ON K1A 0W8
613-288-1566 Fax: 613-288-1575
info@cjc-ccm.gc.ca
www.cjc-ccm.gc.ca/

The members of the Council include the Chief Justice of Canada (who acts as Chair), the Chief Justices & Associate Chief Justices of each Superior Court or Branch or Division thereof, the senior judges of the Supreme Court of the Yukon Territory, the Supreme Court of the Northwest Territories & the Nunavut Court of Justice, the Chief Judge & Associate Chief Judge of the Tax Court of Canada, & the Chief Justice of the Court Martial Court of Canada.

Executive Director & Senior General Counsel, Norman Sabourin
Senior Administrative Officer, Odette Dagenais
General Counsel, Julie Durette
Director, Committees Management, Caroline Collard
Director, Communications & Strategic Issues, Johanna Laporte

Canadian Nuclear Safety Commission (CNSC) / Commission canadienne de sûreté nucléaire (CCSN)

280 Slater St., PO Box 1046 B, Ottawa, ON K1P 5S9
613-995-5894 Fax: 613-995-5086
800-668-5284
www.nuclearsafety.gc.ca

Federal agency which regulates activities involving nuclear energy & prescribed substances in the interests of health & safety for workers & the public. Areas covered under the AECB's licensing process include the nuclear fuel cycle (from mining to waste disposal), heavy water plants, research reactors & accelerators, & radioisotopes. Operations ensure that the use of nuclear energy in Canada does not pose undue risk to health, safety, security & the environment. The Research & Support Program (RSP) augments & extends the AECB's regulatory program beyond the capability of in-house resources. It produces pertinent & independent information that will assist the Board & its staff in making sound, timely & credible decisions on regulating nuclear facilities & materials. The nine sectors of the program include: safety of nuclear facilities; radioactive waste management; health physics; physical security; development of regulatory processes; & social services

President, Michael Binder
613-992-8828, Fax: 613-995-5086
Executive Vice-President/Chief Regulatory Operations Officer, Ramzi Jammal
613-947-8899, Fax: 613-995-5086, Other Communications: Executive Assistant, Phone: 613-947-8896
Vice-President/CSB & Chief Financial Officer, Corporate Services Branch, Michel Cavallin
613-995-0104, Fax: 613-995-5086, Other Communications: Executive Assistant, Phone: 613-992-4543
Vice-President, Technical Support Branch, Terry Jamieson
613-947-8931, Fax: 613-995-5086, Other Communications: Executive Assistant, Phone: 613-996-0260
Vice-President, Regulatory Affairs, Gordon White
613-943-7662, Fax: 613-995-5086, Other Communications: Executive Assistant, Phone: 613-996-9505
Director General, Security & Safeguards, Raoul R. Awad
613-992-2943, Fax: 613-995-5086
Director General, Strategic Planning, Jason K. Cameron
613-947-3773, Fax: 613-995-5086
Director General, Finance & Administration, Stéphane Cyr
613-995-8273, Fax: 613-995-5086
Director General, Regulatory Policy, Mark Dallaire
613-947-3728, Fax: 613-995-5086
Director General, Nuclear Cycle & Facilities Regulation, Peter H. Elder
613-943-8948, Fax: 613-995-5086
Director General, Assessment & Analysis, Gerry Frappier
613-995-2031, Fax: 613-995-5086
Director General, Safety Management, Kathleen Heppell-Masys
613-991-3220, Fax: 613-995-5086
Director General, Regulatory Improvement & Major Projects Management, Barclay Howden
613-943-0179, Fax: 613-995-5086
Director General, Nuclear Substance Regulation, André Régimbald
613-993-7699, Fax: 613-995-5086
Director General, Information Management & Technology, Hugh Robertson
613-949-9498, Fax: 613-995-5086
Director General, Power Reactor Regulation, Greg Rzentkowski
613-995-2655, Fax: 613-995-5086
Director General, Environmental & Radiation Protection & Assessment, Patsy Thompson
613-947-3352, Fax: 613-995-5086

Canadian Museum of Civilization Corporation (CMC) / Musée canadien des civilisations

100 Laurier St., Gatineau, QC K1A 0M8
819-776-7000 Fax: 819-776-8300
800-555-5621
web@civilization.ca
www.civilization.ca
TTY: 819-776-7003

Canadian Polar Commission (CPC) / Commission canadienne des affaires polaires (CCAP)

Constitution Square, #1710, 360 Albert St., Ottawa, ON K1R 7X7
613-943-8605 Fax: 613-943-8607
888-765-2701
mail@polarcom.gc.ca
www.polarcom.gc.ca

Mandated to enhance the public's awareness of polar regions & to foster both international & domestic liaison & cooperation in circumpolar research & technology development. One of the Commission's main objectives in the short term is focus on climate change & energy. Maintains the Canadian Polar Information System (CPIS) which, in addition to polar data & information, includes services such as the Polar Science Forum, Researcher's Directory, Researcher's Toolbox, & links to International Partners. In September 2005, the federal government announced it will provide $150 million in new funding over six years for International Polar Year 2007-2008, an international research program.

Chair, Bernard Funston
Executive Director, Steven Bigras
613-943-8606, steven.bigras@polarcom.gc.ca
Manager, Information, John Bennett
613-943-0716, Fax: 613-943-8607, john.bennett@polarcom.gc.ca
Senior Science Advisor, Jean-Marie Beaulieu
613-947-9108, Fax: 613-943-8607, jean-marie.beaulieu@polarcom.gc.ca
Executive Secretary, Sandy Bianchini
613-943-8605
Financial Analyst, Tom Egan
613-943-0718, Fax: 613-943-8607
Polar Research Analyst, Laurie Buckland
laurie.buckland@polarcom.gc.ca

Canadian Race Relations Foundation (CRRF) / Fondation canadienne des relations raciales (TCRR)

#701, 4576 Yonge St., Toronto, ON M2N 6N4
416-952-3500 Fax: 416-952-3326
888-240-4936
www.crr.ca
Other Communication: Toll-Free Fax: 1-888-399-0333

Crown corporation operating at arms length from the federal government from which it receives no funding. The Foundation is committed to building a national framework for the fight against racism in Canadian society.

Acts Administered:
Canadian Race Relations Foundation Act
Executive Director, Ayman Al-Yassini
416-952-3500, Fax: 416-952-3326
Director, Finance & Administration, Arsalan Tavassoli
416-952-5063, Fax: 416-952-3326

Canadian Radio-Television & Telecommunications Commission (CRTC) / Conseil de la radiodiffusion et des télécommunications Canadiennes

Central Building, 1, Promenade du Portage, Les Terrasses de la Chaudière, Gatineau, QC J8X 4B1
819-997-0313 Fax: 819-994-0218
877-249-2782
www.crtc.gc.ca
TTY: 819-994-0423
Other Communication: Toll-Free TTY: 1-877-909-2782

The CRTC is vested with the authority to regulate & supervise all aspects of the Canadian broadcasting system, as well as to regulate telecommunications common carriers & service providers that fall under federal jurisdiction. Reports to Parliament through the Minister of Canadian Heritage.

Acts Administered:
Bell Canada Act
Broadcasting Act

Canadian Radio-television & Telecommunications Commission Act
Telecommunications Act
Chair, Konrad W. von Finckenstein
819-997-3430, Fax: 819-953-1555
Vice-Chair, Telecommunications, Leonard Katz
819-997-4644, Fax: 819-997-4923
Vice-Chair, Broadcasting, Tom Pentefountas
819-997-8766, Fax: 819-997-4923
Commissioner, Michel Morin
819-953-4375, Other Communications: Executive Assistant, Phone: 819-997-3917
Commissioner, Marc Patrone
819-953-9958, Other Communications: Executive Assistant, Phone: 819-997-4126
Commissioner, Alberta/Northwest Territories Regions, Peter Menzies
819-953-5241, Fax: 819-994-0218
Commissioner, Atlantic/Nunavut Regions, Elizabeth A. Duncan
819-997-4764, Fax: 819-997-4923, Other Communications: Executive Assistant, Phone: 819-997-3917
Commissioner, British Columbia/Yukon Regions, Stephen B. Simpson
819-953-6026, Other Communications: Executive Assistant, Phone: 819-997-3917
Commissioner, Manitoba/Saskatchewan Regions, Candice J. Molnar
306-780-3423
Commissioner, Ontario Region, Rita Cugini
819-997-2431, Fax: 819-994-0218
Commissioner, Québec Region, Suzanne Lamarre
819-934-6347, Fax: 819-997-3917
Executive Director, Policy Development & Research, Namir Anani
819-997-4534, Fax: 819-994-0218
Executive Director, Broadcasting, Scott Hutton
819-997-4573, Fax: 819-994-0218
Executive Director, Telecommunications, John Traversy
819-953-5889, Fax: 819-997-4550
Acting Director General, Strategic Communications & Parliamentary Affairs, Sally Southey
819-997-9372, Fax: 819-997-4245
Director General, Finance & Administrative Service, Jim Stefanik
819-997-0108, Fax: 819-953-5107
Secretary General, Corporate & Operations, Robert A. Morin
819-994-0233, Fax: 819-994-0218
Senior General Counsel, John Keogh
819-953-3990, Fax: 819-953-0589

Regional Offices:

Alberta
#403, 100 4th Ave. SW., Calgary, AB T2P 3N2
403-292-6660 Fax: 403-292-6686
Administrative Officer, Margot Anderson

British Columbia
#290, 858 Beatty St., Vancouver, BC V6B 1C1
604-666-2111 Fax: 604-666-8322
Administrative Officer, Jo-Anne Platt
604-666-2111

Manitoba
#1810, 275 Portage Ave., Winnipeg, MB R3B 2B3
204-983-6306 Fax: 204-983-6317
Acting Director, Western & Northern Region, Cheryl Grossi
204-983-6599, Fax: 204-983-6317, TTY: 877-249-2782
Administrative Officer, Judy Henry
204-983-6306

Nova Scotia
Metropolitan Place, #1410, 99 Wyse Rd., Dartmouth, NS B3A 4S5
902-426-7997 Fax: 902-426-2721
Manager, Eastern & Atlantic Regions, Donna Shewfelt
902-426-7268, Fax: 902-426-2721
Administrative Officer, Diane Mallet
902-426-7997

Ontario
#624, 55 St. Clair Ave. East, Toronto, ON M4T 1M2
416-954-6271
Administrative Officer, Andrea Mullin
416-954-6271

Québec
#504, 205, av Viger ouest, Montréal, QC H2Z 1G2
514-283-6607
Administrative Officer, Monique Cyr
514-496-4077

Saskatchewan
Cornwall Professional Bldg., #620, 2220 12th Ave., Regina, SK S4P 0M8
306-780-3422
Administrative Officer, Janet LaBar
306-780-3422

Canadian Security Intelligence Service (CSIS) / Service canadien du renseignement de sécurité

PO Box 9732 T, Ottawa, ON K1G 4G4
613-993-9620 Fax: 613-231-0612
www.csis.gc.ca
TTY: 613-991-9228

Acts Administered:
Canadian Security Intelligence Service Act
Charities Registration (Security Information) Act
Citizenship Act
Employment Equity Act
Immigration & Refugee Protection Act
Proceeds of Crime (Money Laundering) & Terrorist Financing Act
Anti-terrorism Act
Security of Information Act
Public Safety Act
Director, Richard B. Fadden
613-842-1200
Deputy Director, Charles Bisson
613-231-0986
Chief Financial Officer, Laura Danagher
613-842-1191
Chief Information Officer, Susan Brown
613-842-1531

Canadian Space Agency (CSA) / Agence spatiale canadienne (ASC)

John H. Chapman Space Centre, 6767, rte de l'Aéroport, Saint-Hubert, QC J3Y 8Y9
450-926-4800 Fax: 450-926-4352
promo@asc-csa.gc.ca
www.asc-csa.gc.ca
Other Communication: Client Services, Phone: 450-926-4351

Established in 1989, & responsible for coordinating all civil, space-related policies & programs on behalf of the Government of Canada. Scientific research & industrial development in earth observation, space science & exploration, satellite communications, & space awareness & learning. RADARSAT International (RSI) develops products & services demanded by world markets. RADARSAT-1, the first Canadian commercial Earth Observation (EO) satellite, is uniquely capable of responding to disasters around the world. The system can support the operational mapping & monitoring of natural disasters in four critical ways: prevention, preparedness, emergency response & recovery. Moreover, the development of the high performance RADARSAT-2 to be launched in 2007, will further enhance Canada's competitive position. RADARSAT-2 will offer improved quality of data images to meet the growing world demand of Earth observation information. The SCISAT satellite is used in ozone depletion research.

Acts Administered:
Canadian Space Agency Act
Minister, Industry; Minister Responsible, Canadian Space Agency, Hon. Christian Paradis
613-995-9001, Fax: 613-992-0302, Minister.Industry@ic.gc.ca
President & Chief Astronaut, Steven MacLean
450-926-4301, Fax: 450-926-4315
Vice-President, Chummer Farina
613-998-5284, Fax: 613-990-4994
Chief Financial Officer, Marie-Claude Guerard
450-926-4407, Fax: 450-926-4424
Chief Information Officer, Charles Ouellette
450-926-4851
Chief, Management & Liaison Services, Agathe Jérôme
613-991-3250, Fax: 613-990-4994
Chief, Human Resources Officer, Yves Saulnier
450-926-4815, Fax: 450-926-5194
Chief of the Astronauts, Jean-Marc Comtois
450-926-4755
Director General, Space Science, David Kendall
450-926-4770, Fax: 450-926-4766
Director General, Space Exploration, Gilles Leclerc
450-926-4606, Fax: 450-926-4323
Director General, Corporate Services, Benoît Marcotte
450-926-4667, Fax: 450-926-4612

Canadian Tourism Commission (CTC) / Commission canadienne du tourisme (CCT)

Four Bentall Centre, #1400, 1055 Dunsmuir St., PO Box 49230, Vancouver, BC V7X 1L2
604-638-8300
www.canadatourism.com

A Crown corporation owned entirely by the Canadian government, the Commission seeks to promote a thriving tourism industry in Canada, & encourage relationships between the private sector and the governments of Canada at all levels.
Chair, Steve Allan
President/Chief Executive Officer, Michele McKenzie
Senior Vice-President, Marketing Strategy & Communications, Greg Klassen
Senior Vice-President, Corporate Affairs/Corporate Secretary, Chantal Péan
Vice-President, Finance/Chief Financial Officer, Lena Bullock
Vice-President, International, Charles McKee
Vice-President, Strategy & Corporate Communications, Paul Nursey

Canadian Transportation Agency (CTA) / Office des transports du Canada (OTC)

Les Terrasses de la Chaudière, 15, rue Eddy, Gatineau, QC J8X 4B3
Fax: 819-997-6727
888-222-2592
info@otc-cta.gc.ca
www.cta-otc.gc.ca
TTY: 800-669-5575

Responsible for the economic regulation of transportation in Canada. The agency requires that all applications for new railway lines, modifications to existing railway lines, disputed railway crossings at grade, grade separation, utility crossings & private crossings be accompanied by an environment impact assessment

Acts Administered:
Canada Transportation Act
Canada Marine Act
Pilotage Act
Coasting Trade Act
Railway Safety Act
Chair/Chief Executive Officer, Geoffrey C. Hare
819-997-9233, Fax: 819-953-9979, geoffrey.hare@otc-cta.gc.ca
Vice-Chair, John Scott
819-953-8915, Fax: 819-953-9979, john.scott@otc-cta.gc.ca
Director General, Industry Regulation & Determinations Branch, Ghislain Blanchard
819-953-4657, Fax: 819-994-8807, ghislain.blanchard@otc-cta.gc.ca
Director General, Dispute Resolution Branch, Nina Frid
819-953-5074, Fax: 819-953-5562, nina.frid@otc-cta.gc.ca
Director General, Corporate Management Branch, Arun Thangaraj
819-997-6764, Fax: 819-953-9842
Senior Director, Regulatory Approvals & Compliance Directorate, Carole Girard
819-997-8761, Fax: 819-953-5562, carole.girard@otc-cta.gc.ca
Director, Communications Directorate, Jacqueline Bannister
819-953-7666, Fax: 819-953-8353, jacqueline.bannister@otc-cta.gc.ca
Director, Rail, Air & Marine Disputes Directorate, Joseph Dion
819-953-0327, Fax: 819-953-8353, joseph.dion@otc-cta.gc.ca
Senior Counsel, Legal Services, Claude Jacques
819-997-9323, Fax: 819-953-9269, claude.jacques@otc-cta.gc.ca

Regional Enforcement Officers:

Atlantic
#109, 1045 Main St., Moncton, NB E1C 1H1
506-851-6950 Fax: 506-851-2518
sap-amp@otc-cta.gc.ca

Central
#702, 269 Main St., PO Box 27007 Winnipeg Square, Winnipeg, MB R3C 4T3
204-984-6092 Fax: 204-984-6093
sap-amp@otc-cta.gc.ca

Ontario
#300, 4900 Yonge St., Toronto, ON M2N 6A5
416-952-7895 Fax: 416-952-7897
sap-amp@otc-cta.gc.ca

Pacific
#560, 800 Burrard St., Vancouver, BC V6Z 2V8
604-666-0620 Fax: 604-666-1267
sap-amp@otc-cta.gc.ca
Enforcement Officer, Wayne Wooldridge

Québec
#510, 101, boul Roland-Therrien, Longueuil, QC J4H 4B9
450-928-4173 Fax: 450-928-4174
sap-amp@otc-cta.gc.ca
Enforcement Officer, Richard Laliberté

Western
#1100, 9700 Jasper Ave. NW, Edmonton, AB T5J 4C3
780-495-6618 Fax: 780-495-5639
sap-amp@otc-cta.gc.ca
Enforcement Officer, Linda Brooklyn

Canadian Wheat Board (CWB) / Commission canadienne du blé

423 Main St., PO Box 816 Main, Winnipeg, MB R3C 2P5
204-983-0239 Fax: 204-983-3841
800-275-4292
questions@cwb.ca; farmerservice@cwb.ca
www.cwb.ca
Other Communication: Media relations, Phone: 204-983-3101; Government relations, Phone: 204-984-8167

The market agency serves farmers in Western Canada who grow wheat, durum wheat, & barley. The Canadian Wheat Board's main function is to market these grains in Canada & abroad.

Acts Administered:
Canadian Wheat Board Act

Minister, Agriculture & Agri-Food; Minister, Canadian Wheat Board, Hon. Gerry Ritz
613-995-7080, Fax: 613-996-8472
President/Chief Executive Officer, Ian White
Chair, Allen Oberg
780-582-2171, Fax: 780-582-4127, allen_oberg@cwb.ca
Chief Financial Officer, Brita Chell
Chief Information Officer, Information & Technology, Graham Paul
Chief Operating Officer, Ward Weisensel
Vice-President, Farmer Relations & Public Affairs, Dave Burrows
Vice-President, People & Organizational Services, Diane Wiesenthal

Regional & Overseas Offices:

Ottawa
21 Florence St., Ottawa, ON K2P 0W6
613-236-3633 Fax: 613-236-5749

China
Tower B, Beijing COFCO Plaza, #708, 8 Jianguomen Nei St., Beijing, 100005 China
Other Communication: 011-86-10-6526-3908; Fax: 011-86-10-6526-3907

Japan
Tomoecho Annex 2, 4 Fl., 3-8-27 Toranomon, Minato-ku, Tokyo, 105-0001 Japan
Other Communication: 011-81-3-5425-1055; Fax: 011-81-3-5425-0036

Citizenship & Immigration Canada / Citoyenneté et Immigration Canada

Jean Edmonds, South Tower, 365 Laurier Ave. West, Ottawa, ON K1A 1L1
613-954-9019 Fax: 613-954-2221
888-242-2100
www.cic.gc.ca
TTY: 888-576-8502

The Department of Citizenship & Immigration administers Canada's citizenship & immigration policies, procedures & service. The department is responsible for the following: examining immigrants, visitors & people claiming refugee status at land borders, seaports & airports; processing applications for permanent residence, extensions of visitor status requests & sponsorships for relatives & refugees overseas; admitting students, temporary workers & qualified business immigrants; investigating & removing people who are in Canada illegally; working with & helping fund a network of settlement agencies & services to help immigrants adapt to & participate in day-to-day Canadian life; promoting the acceptance of immigrants by Canadians; cooperating with various levels of government on enforcement, program development & the delivery of services; accepting applications & verifying the eligibility & documentation of applicants; granting citizenship & administration of the Oath of numerous community facilities across Canada; confirming Canadian citizenship status &; issuing proofs of citizenship to Canadians. The Immigration & Refugee Board reports to Parliament through the minister.

Acts Administered:
Citizenship Act
Immigration Act
Immigration & Refugee Protection Act

Minister, Citizenship, Immigration, & Multiculturalism, Hon. Jason Kenney
613-992-2235, Fax: 613-992-1920, jason.kenney@parl.gc.ca; Minister@cic.gc.ca
Parliamentary Secretary Assistant, Andrea Khanjin
613-954-1064, Fax: 613-957-2688
Special Assistant for Multiculturalism, Felix Wong
613-954-1064
Deputy Minister, Neil Yeates
613-954-3501
Director, Audit, Jacques Marquis
613-946-5651, Fax: 613-952-6556

Canada Immigration Centres & Citizenship Offices / Centres d'immigration et de citoyenneté
Immigration visa offices are located in most Canadian Embassies & Consulates abroad. Immigration centres are located at most ports of entry in Canada, & citizenship & immigration offices in major cities throughout the country. For specific addresses & other information contact 1-888-242-2100.

Office of the Asst. Deputy Attorney General / Bureau du Sous-procureur général adjoint
Asst. Deputy Attorney General, Micheline Van-Erum
613-957-4811, Fax: 613-941-1221
Senior Counsel, Legal Services, Deborah Horowitz
613-946-9980, Fax: 613-941-1221
General Counsel, Legal Services, Deen Olsen
613-946-9992, Fax: 613-941-1221

Office of the Assistant Deputy Minister, Operations / Bureau de la sous-ministre adjointe, Opérations
Asst. Deputy Minister, Claudette Deschênes
613-954-5335, Fax: 613-957-8887

Office of the Assistant Deputy Minister, Corporate Services / Bureau de la sous-ministre adjointe, Services ministériels
Asst. Deputy Minister, Manon Brassard
613-957-3338, Fax: 613-954-7360
Chief Technology Officer, Wade Daley
613-941-0015, Fax: 613-954-6209
Chief Information Officer/Director General, David Adamson
613-954-2700, Fax: 613-954-6209
Director General, Administration, Security & Accommodation, Bob Lanouette
613-954-4223, Fax: 613-954-3754
Director General, Human Resources, Diane Mikaelsson
613-941-7788, Fax: 613-957-3882
Director General, Global Case Management System, Soyoung Park
613-946-3901, Fax: 613-946-0581
Director General, Corporate Affairs, Dr. Raman Srivastava
613-941-7018, Fax: 613-957-5946

Office of the Assistant Deputy Minister, Chief Financial Officer / Bureau de la sous-ministre adjointe, administrateur principal des finances
Asst. Deputy Minister/Chief Financial Officer, Mark G. Watters
613-954-4443, Fax: 613-946-6048

Office of the Assistant Deputy Minister, Strategic & Program Policy / Cabinet du sous-ministre adjoint, Politiques stratégiques et de programmes
Asst. Deputy Minister, Les Linklater
613-954-7353, Fax: 613-946-6048
Director General, Refugees, Sarita Bhatla
613-957-5874, Fax: 613-957-5869
Director General, Admissibility, Alain Desruisseaux
613-954-6132, Fax: 613-952-9187
Director General, International & Intergovernmental Relations, Brian Grant
613-957-5878, Fax: 613-957-5913
Director General, Strategic Policy, Sandra Harder
613-957-5948, Fax: 613-954-5896
Director General, Research & Evaluation, Ümit Kiziltan
613-954-6526, Fax: 613-957-5936
Director General, Information Sharing Project Branch, Stéphane Larue
613-948-2473
Director General, Immigration, David Manicom
613-941-8989, Fax: 613-941-9323
Director General, Foreign Credentials Referral Office, Corinne Prince St-Amand
613-941-2769, Fax: 613-941-5314
Director General, Integration, Deborah Tunis
613-957-3257, Fax: 613-954-9144
Director, Policy & Knowledge Development, Mondher BenHassine
613-991-2241, Fax: 613-991-2485
Executive Head, Metropolis Project, Julie Boyer
613-957-5966, Fax: 613-957-5968
Executive Head, Metropolis Project, Howard Duncan
613-957-5916, Fax: 613-957-5968
Director General, Deborah Tunis
613-957-3257, Fax: 613-954-9144
Director, Horizontal Policy Development & Coordination, Angela Connidis
613-946-0572, Fax: 613-954-9144
Director, Integrated Business Services, François Des Rosiers
613-957-6527, Fax: 613-952-7416

Office of the Conflict of Interest & Ethics Commissioner / Commissariat aux conflits d'intérêts et à l'éthique

Commissioner's Office, 66 Slater St., 22nd Fl., Ottawa, ON K1A 0A6
613-995-0721 Fax: 613-995-7308
ciec-ccie@parl.gc.ca
www.ciec-ccie.gc.ca

The Conflict of Interest & Ethics Commissioner is an independent Officer of Parliament. Responsibilities include assisting elected & appointed officials to avoid conflicts between their private interests & public duties.

Acts Administered:
Conflict of Interest Act
Conflict of Interest Code for Members of the House of Commons

Conflict of Interest & Ethics Commissioner, Mary E. Dawson
613-995-0721, Fax: 613-995-7308
Executive Advisor, Robert LeBlond
613-995-5764, Fax: 613-995-7308
Assistant Commissioner, Advisory & Compliance, Lyne Robinson-Dalpé
613-996-6020, Fax: 613-995-7308
Director, Corporate Management, Denise Benoit
613-996-6025, Fax: 613-995-7308
Director, Reports & Investigations, Eppo Maertens
613-943-3763, Fax: 613-995-7308
Director, Policy, Research, & Communications, Sherry Perreault
613-996-4880, Fax: 613-995-7308
General Counsel, Legal Services, Nancy Bélanger
613-996-6028, Fax: 613-995-7308
Director General, Sarita Bhatla
613-957-5874, Fax: 613-957-5869
Acting Director, Asylum Policy & Programs, Jennifer Irish
613-941-8331, Fax: 613-941-6413
Director, Refugee Program Support, Josée Brennan
613-952-2119, Fax: 613-941-2960
Director, Resettlement, Debra Pressé
613-957-5833, Fax: 613-957-5836
Senior Policy Analyst, Horizontal Policy & International Protection Development, Jessie Thomson
613-960-7628, Fax: 613-957-5869

Copyright Board of Canada / Commission du droit d'auteur du Canada

#800, 56 Sparks St., Ottawa, ON K1A 0C9
613-952-8621 Fax: 613-952-8630
secretariat@cb-cda.gc.ca
www.cb-cda.gc.ca

The Board is an economic regulatory body empowered to establish, either mandatorily or at the request of an interested party, the royalties to be paid for the use of copyrighted works, when the administration of such copyright is entrusted to a collective-administration society. The Board also has the right to supervise agreements between users & licensing bodies & issues licences when the copyright owner cannot be located.

Chair, William J. Vancise
613-952-8621
Vice-Chair & Chief Executive Officer, Claude Majeau
613-952-8621
Acting Secretary General, Gilles McDougall
613-952-8624, gilles.mcdougall@cb-cda.gc.ca
General Counsel, Mario Bouchard
613-954-6470, mario.bouchard@cb-cda.gc.ca
Director, Research & Analysis, Vacant
613-946-4457

Office of the Correctional Investigator / L'Enquêteur correctionnel Canada

PO Box 3421 D, Ottawa, ON K1P 6L4
Fax: 613-990-9091
877-885-8848
org@oci-bec.gc.ca
www.oci-bec.gc.ca

Investigates complaints from inmates in Canadian institutions. Reports on problems inmates have that fall within the responsibility of the Department of Public Safety & Emergency Preparedness & meet certain conditions.

Acts Administered:
Corrections and Conditional Release Act (Part III)

Correctional Investigator, Howard Sapers
613-990-2689
Executive Director, Dr. Ivan Zinger
613-990-2690
Director of Investigations, Marie-France Kingsley
613-998-6960
Director of Investigations, Paul McKenzie
613-990-2691
Director, Policy & Research, David Hooey
613-990-2693
Director, Corporate Services & Planning, Manuel Marques
613-990-2692

Correctional Service Canada (CSC) / Service correctionnel Canada

340 Laurier Ave. West, Ottawa, ON K1A 0P9
613-992-5891 Fax: 613-943-1630
www.csc-scc.gc.ca

An agency within Public Safety & Emergency Preparedness Canada responsible for the administration of sentences with respect to convicted offenders sentenced to two or more years as decided by the federal courts, & certain provincial inmates who have been transferred to a federal institution. CSC is also responsible for the supervision of inmates who have been granted conditional release by the authority of the National Parole Board.

Acts Administered:
Corrections & Conditional Release Act
Criminal Code
Extradition Act
Old Age Security Act
Prisons & Reformatories Act
Transfer of Offenders Act

Chief Executive Officer, CORCAN, John Sargent
613-996-4530, Fax: 613-947-8875
Commissioner, Don Head
613-995-5781, Fax: 613-943-1630
Senior Deputy Commissioner, Vacant
Deputy Commissioner, Women, Jennifer Oades
613-992-6067, Fax: 613-992-4692
Asst. Commissioner, Corporate Services, Liette Dumas-Sluyter
613-996-4242, Fax: 613-992-8443
Asst. Commissioner, Human Resource Management, Fraser Macaulay
613-995-8899, Fax: 613-992-9208
Asst. Commissioner, Health Services, Leslie MacLean
613-995-8023, Fax: 613-995-6277
Asst. Commissioner, Policy & Research, Ian McCowan
613-996-2180, Fax: 613-995-3603
Executive Director & General Counsel, Legal Services, Carole Johnson
613-992-9009, Fax: 613-995-9971
Asst. Commissioner, Correctional Operations & Programs, Chris Price
613-943-0499, Fax: 613-996-6174
Asst. Commissioner, Communications & Engagements, Elizabeth Van Allen
613-995-6867, Fax: 613-947-0091

Regional Headquarters:

Atlantic
1045 Main St., 2nd Fl., Moncton, NB E1C 1H1
506-851-6313 Fax: 506-851-6316
Deputy Commissioner, Thérèse Leblanc
506-851-6377, Fax: 506-851-2418

Associated Agencies, Boards & Commissions:
• New Brunswick Agricultural Insurance Commission / Commission de L'assurance Agricole du Nouveau-Brunswick
c/o Department of Agriculture, Aquaculture & Fisheries
PO Box 6000
Fredericton, NB E3B 5H1
506-453-2185 Fax: 506-453-7406
daa-maa@gnb.ca
Agricultural Insurance Commission is responsible for administering the delivery to producers of an agricultural insurance plan to provide insurance protection against losses of production. This plan is funded through producer premiums and through contributions from the Province of New Brunswick and the Government of Canada.

Ontario
440 King St. West, PO Box 1174, Kingston, ON K7L 4Y8
613-536-4527 Fax: 613-545-8684
Assistant Commissioner, Lori MacDonald
613-545-8131, Fax: 613-545-8684

Pacific
32560 Simon Ave., 2nd Fl., PO Box 4500, Abbotsford, BC V2T 5L7
604-870-2500 Fax: 604-870-2430
Deputy Commissioner, Anne Kelly
604-870-2501, Fax: 604-870-2430

Prairies
2313 Hanselman Pl., PO Box 9223, Saskatoon, SK S7K 6A9
306-975-4850 Fax: 306-975-4435
Regional Director, Darcy Emann
306-975-5026

Québec
3, pl Laval, 2e étage, Laval, QC H7N 1A2
450-967-3333 Fax: 450-967-3326
Regional Director, Youssef Mani
450-664-6640, Fax: 450-664-6641

District Offices:

Northern/Interior Area
#203, 1635 Abbott St., Kelowna, BC V1Y 1A9
250-470-5166 Fax: 250-470-5173

Central Ontario
#215, 180 Dundas St. West, Toronto, ON M5G 1Z8
416-973-2393 Fax: 416-973-1779

East & West Québec
#202, 212, boul. Curé-Labelle, Sainte-Thérèse, QC J7E 2X7
450-435-3932 Fax: 450-420-7600
Acting District Director, Lise Bouthillier

Northeast Ontario
191 Gilmour St., Ottawa, ON K2P 0N8
613-996-7011 Fax: 613-954-1687

Fraser Valley
#100, 32544 George Ferguson Way, Abbotsford, BC V2T 4Y1
604-870-2730 Fax: 604-870-2731

Hamilton & Niagara
55 Bay St. North, 2nd Fl., Hamilton, ON L8R 3P7
905-572-2695 Fax: 905-572-2072

Manitoba/Sask/Northwestern Ontario
#102, 123 Main St., Winnipeg, MB R3C 1A3
204-983-4306 Fax: 204-983-5869

Montréal-Métropolitan
#917, Tour Ouest, 200, boul René-Lévesque ouest, Montréal, QC H2Z 1X4
514-283-1776 Fax: 514-283-1783

New Brunswick & PEI
1 Factory Lane, 1st Fl., Moncton, NB E1C 9M3
506-851-3038 Fax: 506-851-2057

Newfoundland & Labrador
531 Charter Ave., St. John's, NL A1A 1P7
709-772-5359 Fax: 709-772-6415

Northern Alberta, NWT
9530 - 101 Ave., 2nd Fl., Edmonton, AB T5H 0B3
780-495-4900 Fax: 780-495-4975

Ottawa
191 Gilmour St., Ottawa, ON K2P 0N8
613-996-7011 Fax: 613-954-1687

Nova Scotia
#102, 2131 Gottingen St., Halifax, NS B3K 5Z7
902-426-3408 Fax: 902-426-6579

Nunavut
1043 Woodhouse St., Iqaluit, NU X0A 0H0
867-979-8892 Fax: 867-979-7441

Saskatchewan
#603, 230 - 22 St. East, Saskatoon, SK S7K 0E9
306-975-4070 Fax: 306-975-4532

Southern Alberta
#140, 1925 - 18 Ave. NE, Calgary, AB T2E 7T8
403-292-5522 Fax: 403-292-5510

Vancouver Area
#401, 877 Expo Blvd., Vancouver, BC V6B 1K9
604-666-8004 Fax: 604-666-2000

Vancouver Island
#200, 256 Wallace St., Nanaimo, BC V9R 5B3
250-754-0264 Fax: 250-754-0266
District Director, Dave Keating

Western Ontario
#117, 255 Woodlawn Rd. West, Guelph, ON N1H 8J1
519-826-2139 Fax: 519-826-2143

Defence Construction Canada (DCC) / Construction de Défense Canada (CDC)

Constitution Square, 350 Albert St., 19th Fl., Ottawa, ON K1A 0K3
613-998-9548 Fax: 613-998-1061
800-514-3555
info@dcc-cdc.gc.ca
www.dcc-cdc.gc.ca

Federal government crown corporation responsible for the contracting & supervising of major military construction & maintenance projects required by National Defence. Services include construction, project management, environmental services & operational support services. DCC provides environmental science & environmental engineering services to help fulfill the Department of National Defence's sustainable development strategy, including: environmental impact & site assessment; environmental site remediation; environmental support for project & program management; sustainable development strategy support services; policy, compliance & advisory services; site decommissioning services; facility deconstruction & demolition; firing range decommissioning; waste management auditing & planning; waste reduction planning; landfill inventories & investigations; hazardous waste management; UST removals; training & education; ISO 14000 environmental management systems; environmental CIS applications; environmental checklists for property transactions & decommissioning; environmental monitoring & compliance auditing; designated substances inventories; environmental disclosures reporting; treatment & disposal facilities conceptual designs; environmental contrac ting & contract management; energy conservation. Projects include: the DEW (Distant Early Warning) Line cleanup, a dismantling of the DEW sites, scheduled for completion in 2012, & a major environmental project in the Canadian Arctic; green demolition at CFB Comox; biodiesel pilot program at 4 Wing Cold Lake, launched in 2005

President/CEO, James S. Paul
613-998-9541, Fax: 613-998-1218
Senior Vice-President, Operations, Ron de Vries, P.Eng
613-998-9543, Fax: 613-998-1218
Vice-President, Operations, Steve Irwin, P.Eng
613-949-7721, Fax: 613-998-1218
Vice-President, Operations, Randy McGee, P.Eng., GSC
613-949-0052, Fax: 613-998-1218
Vice-President, Corporate Services & CFO, Angelo Ottoni, C.A.
613-998-1001
Director, Atlantic Region, Business Operations - Atlantic Region, Ross Welsman, P.Eng., PMP, 20110705
902-426-5640, Fax: 902-426-9655
Manager, Operations Coordination, Business Operations - Atlantic Region, George Theoharopoulos
902-426-4040, Fax: 902-426-9655
Director, Ontario Region, Environmental Services - Ontario, John Graham, P.Eng., PMP, 20110705
613-384-1256, Fax: 613-384-7747
Manager, Environmental Services - Ontario, Dennis Katic
613-384-1256, Fax: 613-384-7747
Director, Quebec Region, Environmental Services - Québec, Marc Lanteigne, P.Eng., 20110705
514-496-2729, Fax: 514-283-8347
Manager, Environmental Services - Québec, Alain Dufresne
514-283-8165, Fax: 514-283-8347
Director, Western Region, Environmental Services - Western Region, Stephen G. Karpyshin, P.Eng., 20110706
780-495-2555, Fax: 780-495-5959
Manager, Environmental Services - Western Region, Sabrina Rock
780-495-3979, Fax: 780-495-5959
Director, Contract Services, Contract Services, Melinda Nycholat, P.Eng., PMP, 20110706
613-991-9313, Fax: 613-998-9547
Executive Administrative Assistant, Claire Péladeau
613-991-3475, Fax: 613-998-1218

Environmental Protection Review Canada / Révision de la protection de l'environnement Canada

240 Sparks St., 1st Fl. West, Ottawa, ON K1A 1A1
613-995-7599 Fax: 613-992-4918
eprc-rpec@eprc-rpec.gc.ca
www.eprc-rpec.gc.ca

Environmental Protection Review Canada is a group of expert adjudicators, entirely separate from Environment Canada, that conducts reviews of Environmental Protection Compliance Orders (EPCOs). Under the Canadian Environmental Protection Act, 1999 (CEPA, 1999), enforcement officers have the power to issue EPCOs to prevent a violation, to stop an on-going violation or to require that violations be corrected. Any person who has been issued an EPCO may ask for an independent review conducted by a Review Officer. Review Officers have the authority to confirm or cancel an EPCO. They may also amend, suspend, add or delete a term or condition of the Order. The decisions of Review Officers may be appealed to the Federal Court, Trial Division.

Chief Review Officer, Allan Pope
613-997-4060, Fax: 613-992-4918
Review Officer, Louis LaPierre, Ph.D.
506-863-2056, Fax: 506-863-2000, lapierl@umoncton.ca

Defence Research & Development Canada / Recherche et développement pour la défense Canada

305 Rideau St., Ottawa, ON K1A 0K2
613-992-7237
info@drdc-rddc.gc.ca
www.drdc-rddc.gc.ca
TTY: 800-467-9877

Provides research & development both nationally & internationally by providing the Canadian Forces with relevant & timely technologies, while at the same time offering attractive collaborative opportunities to other government departments, the private sector, academia & international allies.

CEO, Dr. Marc Fortin
613-996-2020

Director General, Science & Technology Operations, Richard Williams
613-992-5776
Director General, Corporate Services, Colin McEwan
613-992-6105
Director General, Research & Development Programs, Maria Rey
613-998-2303, Fax: 613-993-6095

Elections Canada / Élections Canada

The Jackson Bldg., 257 Slater St., Ottawa, ON K1A 0M6
613-993-2975 Fax: 613-954-8584
800-463-6868
www.elections.ca
TTY: 800-361-8935

The Chief Electoral Officer of Canada is responsible for the conduct of federal elections & referendums in Canada & for ensuring that all provisions of the Canada Elections Act are complied with & enforced. Major activities include the maintenance of the National Register of Electors, the production of lists of electors, the training of returning officers, the revisions of polling division boundaries & the acquisition of election materials & supplies. Elections Canada is also responsible for the compilation & publishing of statutory & statistical reports, & the provision of advice & assistance to Parliament, as required. The agency also implements public education & information programs. As well, its mandate includes the registration of political parties & third parties engaged in election advertising, & the certification of statutory payments to be made to auditors, political parties, & candidates under the election expenses provisions of the Act. Following each decennial census, the Chief Electoral Officer must calculate the number of electoral districts to be assigned to each province according to rules contained in s. 51 of the Constitution Act, prepare population distribution maps for use by the ten electoral boundaires commission s (one per province) that are directly responsible for readjusting federal electroal boundaries & publish their reports.

Chief Electoral Officer, Marc Mayrand
613-993-5755, Fax: 613-993-5380
Chief of Staff, Office of the CEO, Vivian Cousineau, 20110706
613-993-3748, Fax: 613-993-5380
Deputy Chief Information Officer, Pierre LaFrance
613-993-4121, Fax: 613-990-3662
Commissioner, Canada Elections, William H. Corbett
613-998-4051, Fax: 613-990-4877
General Counsel, Canada Elections, Johanne Gauthier, 20110706
613-998-4051, Fax: 613-990-4877
Acting Chief Financial Officer, Finance, Internal Audit & Administration, Brian Berry
613-998-8440, Fax: 613-993-8517
Deputy Chief Electoral Officer, Electoral Events, Rennie Molnar
613-949-3125, Fax: 613-954-2874, Other Communications: Administrative Assistant, Gargi Bose: 613-990-3440
Acting Director, Outreach, Communications & Research, Marc Lamontagne
613-990-2979, Fax: 613-954-8584
Director/General Counsel, Electoral Affairs, Michèle René de Cotret
613-990-7239, Fax: 613-993-5880
Chief Information Officer, Stéphane Cousineau
613-991-2401
Deputy Chief Electoral Officer, Policy, Planning & Public Affairs, Belaineh Deguefé, 20110706
613-991-4640
Deputy Chief Electoral Officer, Political Financing, François Bernier, 20110706
613-998-0670, Fax: 613-990-7241, Other Communications: Executive Assistant, Lyne Michaud: 613-990-7241
Chief Human Resources Officer, Human Resources, Pierrette Lacroix, 20110706
613-998-5262, Fax: 613-998-7561
Senior General Counsel/Senior Director, Stéphane Perrault, 20110706
613-990-6846, Fax: 613-993-5880

Environment Canada (EC) / Environnement Canada

10 Wellington St., Gatineau, QC K1A 0H3
819-997-2800 Fax: 819-994-1412
800-668-6767
enviroinfo@ec.gc.ca
www.ec.gc.ca
TTY: 819-994-0736
Other Communication: Environmental Emergencies (24-hour): |819/997-3742; TTY: 819/994-0736

Fosters a national capacity for sustainable development in cooperation with other governments, departments of government & the private sector that will result in a safe & healthy environment & a sound & prosperous economy by: undertaking & promoting programs to augment understanding of the environment; supporting environmentally responsible public & private decision-making; warning Canadians of risks to & from the environment; engaging Canadians as partners in measurably beneficial action to conserve, protect & restore the integrity of Canada's environment for the benefit of present & future generations.

Acts Administered:
Antarctic Environmental Protection Act
Canada Emission Reduction Incentives Agency Act
Canada Water Act
Canada Wildlife Act
Administration, Management & Control of Certain Public Lands
Wildlife Area Regulations
Canadian Environment Week Act
Canadian Environmental Assessment Act
Canada Port Authority Environmental Assessment Regulations
Comprehensive Study List Regulation
Exclusion List Regulation
Federal Authorities Regulations
Inclusion List Regulation
Law List Regulation
Projects Outside Canada Environmental Assessment Regulations
Canadian Environmental Protection Act
Alberta Equivalency Order
Asbestos Mines & Mills Release Regulations
Benzene in Gasoline Regulations
Chlor-Alkali, Mercury Release Regulations
Chlorobiphenyls Regulations
Clean Air Act
Contaminated Fuel Regulations
Disposal at Sea Regulations
Environmental Emergency Regulations
Export Control List of Notification Regulations
Export & Import of Hazardous Wastes Regulations
Export of Substances under the Rotterdam Convention Regulations
Federal Halocarbon Regulations
Federal Mobile PCB Treatment & Destruction Regulations
Federal Registration of Storage Tank Systems for Petroleum Products & Allied Petroleum Products on Federal Lands or Aboriginal Lands Regulations
Fuels Information Regulations, No. 1
Gasoline & Gasoline Blend Dispensing Flow Rate Regulations
Gasoline Regulations
Interprovincial Movement of Hazardous Waste Regulations
List of Hazardous Waste Authorities
List of Toxic Substances Authorities
Masked Name Regulations
New Substances Fees Regulations
New Substances Notification Regulations
Off-Road Small Spark-Ignition Engine Emission Regulations
On-Road Vehicle & Engine Emission Regulations
Ozone Depleting Substances Regulations
PCB Waste Export Regulations
Persistence & Bioaccumulation Regulations
Phosphorus Concentration Regulations
Prohibition of Certain Toxic Substances
Pulp & Paper Mill Defoamer & Wood Chip Regulations
Pulp & Paper Mill Effluent Chlorinated Dioxins & Furans Regulations
Regulations respecting Applications for Permits for Disposal at Sea
Rules for Procedures for Boards of Review
Secondary Lead Smelter Release Regulations
Solvent Degreasing Regulations
Sulphur in Diesel Fuel Regulations
Sulphur in Gasoline Regulations
Storage of PCB Material Regulations
Tetrachloroethylene (Use in Dry Cleaning & Reporting Requirements) Regulations
Tributyltetradeclyphosphonium Chloride Regulations
Vinyl Chloride Release Regulations
Department of the Environment Act
Kemano Completion Project Guidelines Order
Greenhouse Gas Technology Investment Fund Act
International River Improvements Act
Lac Seul Conservation Act
Lake of the Woods Control Board Act
Manganese-Based Fuel Additives Act
Migratory Birds Convention Act
Migratory Bird Regulations
Migratory Bird Sanctuary Regulations
National Wildlife Week Act
Species at Risk Act, 2002
Weather Modification Information Act
Wild Animal & Plant Protection & Regulation of International & Interprovincial Trade Act
Acts Administered in Part by Environment Canada
Auditor General Act (Treasury Board)
Energy Supplies Emergency Act (National Research)
Fisheries Act (Fisheries & Oceans)
Chlor-alkali Mercury Liquid Effluent Regulations
Meat & Poultry Products Plant Liquid Effluent Regulations
Metal Mining Effluent Regulations
Petroleum Refinery Liquid Effluent Regulations
Port Alberni Pulp & Paper Effluent Regulations
Potato Processing Plant Liquid Effluent Regulations
Pulp & Paper Effluent Regulations
James Bay & Northern Québec Native Claims Settlement Act
Motor Vehicle Safety Act (Transport)
Resources & Technical Surveys Act (Natural Resources/Fisheries & Oceans)
Acts in which Environment Canada Provides Assistance
Arctic Waters Pollution Prevention Act
Arctic Shipping Pollution Prevention Regulations
Arctic Waters Pollution Prevention Regulations
Atomic Energy Control Act
Transport Packaging of Radioactive Materials Regulations
Uranium & Thorium Mining Regulations
Canada Agricultural Products Act
Canada Shipping Act
Air Pollution Regulations
Dangerous Chemicals & Noxious Liquid Substances Regulations
Garbage Pollution Prevention Regulations
Great Lakes Sewage Pollution Prevention Regulations
Non-Pleasure Craft Sewage Pollution Prevention Regulations
Oil Pollution Prevention Regulations
Pleasure Craft Sewage Pollution Prevention Regulations
Pollutant Discharge Reporting Regulations
Pollutant Substances Regulations
Ship-Source Oil Pollution Fund Regulations
Canada-Chile Free Trade Agreement Implementation Act (International Trade)
Canada-Newfoundland Atlantic Accord Implementation Act
Newfoundland Offshore Area Oil & Gas Operations Regulations
Newfoundland Offshore Area Petroleum Geophysical Operations Regulations
Newfoundland Offshore Area Petroleum Production & Conservation Regulations
Newfoundland Offshore Certificate of Fitness Regulations
Newfoundland Offshore Petroleum Drilling Regulations
Newfoundland Offshore Petroleum Installations Regulations
Canada-Nova Scotia Offshore Petroleum Resources Accord Implementation Act
Nova Scotia Offshore Petroleum Drilling Regulations
Emergency Preparedness Act (National Defence)
Hazardous Products Act (Health Canada)
Controlled Products Regulations
International Boundary Waters Treaty Act (Foreign Affairs)
North American Free Trade Agreement Implementation Act
Nuclear Energy Act (Natural Resources)
Pest Control Products Act & Regulations (Health Canada)
Transportation of Dangerous Goods Act & Regulations (Transport Canada)
Environment Canada Related Acts & Regulations
Agricultural & Rural Development Act (Agriculture & Agri-Foods)
Alternative Fuels Act & Regulations (Treasury Board)
Canada Marine Act (Transport Canada)
Canada Oil & Gas Operations Act (Indian & Northern Affairs/Natural Resources)
Canada Oil & Gas Certificate of Fitness Regulations
Canada Oil & Gas Drilling Regulations
Canada Oil & Gas Geophysical Operations Regulations
Canada Oil & Gas Operations Regulations
Canada Oil & Gas Production & Conservation Regulations
Canada Petroleum Resources Act (Indian Affairs & Northern Development/Natural Resouces)
Environmental Studies Research Fund Regions Regulations
Canadian Transportation Accident Investigation & Safety Board Act (Privy Council)
Transportation Safety Board Regulations
Food & Drugs Act (Agriculture & Agri-Foods/Health Canada)
Mackenzie Valley Resource Management Act (Indian & Northern Affairs)
National Energy Board Act (Natural Resources/Transport Canada)
Electricity Regulations
Oil & Gas Regulations
Onshore Pipeline Regulations
Rules of Practice & Procedure
National Round Table on the Environment & the Economy Act (Prime Minister)
Northern Pipeline Act (Natural Resources)
Northern Pipeline Socio-Economic & Environmental Terms & Conditions (Northern BC, Southern BC, AB, SK & Swift River Portion in BC)
Oceans Act (Fisheries & Oceans)

Minister, Environment, Hon. Peter Kent
819-997-1441, Fax: 819-953-0279, minister@ec.gc.ca
Director, Parliamentary Affairs, Lori Dawe
819-997-1441
Deputy Minister, Paul Boothe
819-997-4203, Fax: 819-953-6897
Associate Deputy Minister, Vacant
819-953-2832
Acting Director General, Audit & Evaluation, Robert D'Aoust
819-953-5471, Fax: 819-953-2459
Director General, Communications Branch, David Henley
819-997-6820, Fax: 819-953-1599

Director General, Corporate Secretariat, Pierre Bernier
819-953-2743, Fax: 819-953-0749
Acting Asst. Deputy Minister, George Enei
819-994-3634, Fax: 819-934-7975

Environmental Stewardship Branch / Direction générale de l'intendance environnementale
351 boul St-Joseph, Gatineau, QC K1A 0H3
819-997-1575 Fax: 819-953-9452
Assessment & management of risk associated with domestic & international sources of pollution. The range of activity is broad, assessment of substances & practices that pose a risk to the environment, development & implementation of environmental protection measures including pollution prevention, regulations, permits & technology advancement & ensuring compliance with federal pollution & wildlife laws. These activities lead to improvements in environmental quality which helps to support the health of Canadians & their economic security.
Asst. Deputy Minister, Coleen Volk
819-953-1711, Fax: 819-953-9452
Assoc. Asst. Deputy Minister, Mike Beale
819-956-9500
Director General, Canadian Wildlife Service, Virginia Poter
819-994-1360, Fax: 819-953-7177
Director General, Chemicals Sector, Margaret Kenny, 20110711
819-934-4960, Fax: 819-953-3213
Director General, Energy & Transportation, Steve McCauley
819-997-1298, Fax: 819-953-9547
Director General, Environmental Protection Operations, Sue Milburn-Hopwood
819-934-5666, Fax: 819-934-6531
Executive Director, Habitat & Ecosystem Conservation, Robert McLean
819-997-1303, Fax: 819-994-4445
Director General, Public & Resources Sectors, Randall Meades
819-934-4205
Director General, Strategic Priorities, Louise Métivier
819-994-5022, Fax: 819-953-7941

Enforcement Branch / Direction générale de l'application de la loi
351 boul St-Joseph, Gatineau, QC K1A 0H3
819-997-2019 Fax: 819-997-0086
The Branch is built around the principle of ensuring that companies & individuals comply with the pollution prevention & conservation goals of environmental & wildlife protection acts & regulations. Enforcement is delivered through the work of in-the-field enforcement officers across Canada working through the Environmental Enforcement Directorate & The Wildlife Enforcement Directorate. Their work is carried out in cooperation with other federal, provincial & territorial governments & with international organizations involved in enforcement such as the United States Fish & Wildlife Service, the United States Environmental Protection Agency & Interpol.

Finance Branch / Direction générale des finances
819-953-7026 Fax: 819-953-4064
Acting Asst. Deputy Minister, Carol Najm
819-953-4736
Director General, Assets, Contracting & Environmental Management, Karen Anderson
819-997-2991, Fax: 819-997-1781
Acting Director General, Corporate Management, Karen Turcotte
819-953-5842
Acting Director General, Finance Directorate, Randy Larkin
819-953-9569, Fax: 819-953-2459
Acting Director General, Integrated Enterprise Services, Cheryl Bertrand
819-953-8911, Fax: 819-953-4064

International Affairs / Direction générale des affaires internationales
819-997-4882 Fax: 819-953-5981
Asst. Deputy Minister, Dan McDougall
819-934-6020, Fax: 819-953-9412
Director General, Americas, Dean Knudson
819-994-1670, Fax: 819-997-0199
Director General, Climate Change International, Stephen de Boer
819-953-6830, Fax: 819-953-9333
Director General, Multilateral & Bilateral Affairs, France Jacovella
819-956-5263, Fax: 819-994-6227
Director, Partnerships Division, Darren Goetze
819-953-9525, Fax: 819-953-9333

Legal Services / Services juridiques
819-953-3680 Fax: 819-953-9110

Meteorological Service of Canada (MSC) / Le service météorologique du Canada
819-997-2696 Fax: 819-994-8841
The Meteorological Service of Canada monitors water quantities, provides information & conducts research on climate, atmospheric science, air quality, ice & other environmental issues.
Asst. Deputy Minister, David Grimes
613-943-5585, Fax: 613-943-5737
Director General, Business Policy, Danielle Lacasse
613-943-5532, Fax: 613-995-0389
Director General, Weather & Environmental Monitoring, Jim Abraham
416-739-4965, Fax: 416-739-4261
Director General, Weather & Environmental Monitoring, Michel Jean
514-421-4601, Fax: 514-421-7250
Director General, Weather & Environmental Prediction & Services, Diane E. Campbell
613-947-9200, Fax: 613-943-6440

Science & Technology Branch / Direction générale des sciences et de la technologie
819-994-4751 Fax: 819-997-1541
Asst. Deputy Minister, Brian Gray
819-934-6851
Director General, Atmospheric Science & Technology, Charles A. Lin
416-739-4995, Fax: 416-739-4265
Acting Director General, Science & Risk Assessment, George Enei
819-997-4977, Fax: 819-953-5371
Director General, Science & Technology Strategies, Dr. Javier A. Gracia-Garza
819-953-3090, Fax: 819-953-9029
Director General, Water Science & Technology, Dr. John H. Carey
905-336-4625
Director General, Wildlife & Landscape Science, Dan Wicklum
613-998-0329

Strategic Policy / Direction générale de la politique stratégique
819-953-4818 Fax: 819-953-5981
Asst. Deputy Minister, Michael Keenan
819-953-4818, Fax: 819-953-5981
Executive Asst. to the ADM, Anne Morin, 20110713
819-997-8382, Fax: 819-953-5981
Manager, ADM's Office, Juie Philippe, 20110713
819-953-2667, Fax: 819-953-5981
Correspondence Officer, Suzanne Beaudoin, 20110713
819-953-1494, Fax: 819-953-5981
Administrative Assistant, Ashley Russell, 20110713
819-934-0000, Fax: 819-953-5981
Director General, Economic Analysis Directorate, Tony Young
819-953-7624, Fax: 819-953-5916
Director General, Strategic Information & Integration, Brenda McKelvey
819-934-6028, Fax: 819-994-8864
Director General, Strategic Policy Directorate, Lawrence Hanson
819-934-4149, Fax: 819-953-4679

Environment Canada Regional Directors General:

Atlantic
Queen Sq., 45 Alderney Dr., Dartmouth, NS B2Y 2N6
902-426-7231 Fax: 902-426-6348
15th.reception@ec.gc.ca
atlantic-web1.ns.ec.gc.ca/index_e.html
TTY: 819-994-0736
Regional Director General, Daniel Lebel
902-426-6700, Fax: 902-426-5168

Pacific & Yukon
201, 401 Burrard St., Vancouver, BC V6C 3S5
604-664-9145 Fax: 604-664-9190
greenlane.pyr@ec.gc.ca
www.pyr.ec.gc.ca
Regional Director General, Paul Kluckner
604-664-9145, Fax: 604-664-9190
Pacific Environment Centre Office
604-666-8425

Ontario
4905 Dufferin St., Toronto, ON M3H 5T4
416-739-4826 Fax: 416-739-4776
enviroinfo.ontario@ec.gc.ca
www.on.ec.gc.ca
Acting Regional Director General, Michael Goffin
416-739-4666, Fax: 416-739-4691

Prairie & Northern
Twin Atria Bldg., #200, 4999 - 98 Ave., Edmonton, AB T6B 2X3
780-951-8869 Fax: 780-495-3086
Acting Regional Director General, Mike Norton
780-951-8869, Fax: 780-495-2758

Québec
1141, rte de l'Église, 6e étage, CP 10100, Québec, QC G1V 4H5
418-648-4077 Fax: 418-648-4613
800-463-4311
quebec.lavoieverte@ec.gc.ca
Regional Director General, Philippe Morel
418-648-4077, Fax: 418-649-6213

Commission for Environmental Cooperation (CEC) / Commission coopération environnementale

Secretariat, #200, 393, rue St-Jacques ouest, Montréal, QC H2Y 1N9
514-350-4300 Fax: 514-350-4314
info@cec.org
www.cec.org
The Commission for Environmental Cooperation (CEC) is an international organization created by Canada, Mexico & the United States under the North American Agreement on Environmental Cooperation (NAAEC). The CEC was established to address regional environmental concerns, help prevent potential trade & environmental conflicts & to promote the effective enforcement of environmental law. The Agreement complements the environmental provisions of the North American Free Trade Agreement (NAFTA).
Executive Director, Evan Lloyd
514-350-4303, melhadj@cec.org
Legal Officer, Submission on Enforcement Matters Unit, Paolo Solano
514-350-4321, psolano@cec.org
Legal Officer, Submission on Enforcement Matters Unit, Paolo Solano
514-350-4321, psolano@cec.org
Program Manager, Air Quality & PRTR, Orlando Cabrera-Rivera
514-350-4323, ocabrera@cec.org
Program Manager, Chemicals Management, Ned T. Brooks
514-350-4372, nbrooks@cec.org
Program Manager, Environmental Information, Karen Richardson
514-350-4326, krichardson@cec.org
Program Manager, Environmental Law, Marco Antonio Heredia Fragoso
514-350-4302, maheredia@cec.org
Council Secretary, Nathalie Daoust
514-350-4310, ndaoust@cec.org

Export Development Canada (EDC) / Exportation et développement Canada (SEE)

151 Slater St., Ottawa, ON K1A 1K3
613-598-2500 Fax: 613-598-3811
800-267-8510
www.edc.ca
TTY: 866-574-0451
A financial services corporation assisting Canadian business to succeed in foreign markets. EDC provides a wide range of financial solutions to exporters across Canada & their customers around the world. The corporation's risk management services include: export-credit insurance protecting exporters against losses due to non-payment relating to commercial & political risks; & flexible medium- or long-term financing & guarantees. As a financially self-sustaining Crown corporation, EDC operates on commercial principles, charging fees & premiums for its products & interest on its loans. EDC is governed by a board of directors composed of representatives from both the private & public sectors, & reports to Parliament through the minister for international trade. An Environmental Review Directive is used to assess the environmental impacts of projects EDC is asked to support. EDC pursues an international multilateral consensus on environmental review practices so that all exporters are subject to the same rules. EDC has adopted & implemented the OECD Recommendation on Common Approaches on Environment & Officially Supported Export Credits. EDC has signed the UNEP Statement of Financial Institutions. Through the EnviroExport initiative, EDC helps Canadia n environmental exporters succeed internationally through financing products. Where EDC is considering providing financing support, political risk insurance or equity to the sponsor of a Category A project under the Environmental Review Directive, EDC will seek consent to inform the public on its website that it is considering support to such a project.
President/CEO, Stephen S. Poloz
Senior Vice-President, Business Development, Benoit Daignault
Senior Vice-President, Human Resources & Corporate Services, Susanne Laperle
Senior Vice-President, Business Solutions & Technology, Sherry L. Noble
Senior Vice-President, Financing Products Group, Rajesh Sharma
Senior Vice-President, Insurance, Pierre Gignac
Senior Vice-President, Legal Services & Secretary, Jim McArdle
Senior Vice-President/CFO, Finance, Ken Kember
Media Contact, Phil Taylor
613-598-2904, ptaylor@edc.ca

EDC Regional Offices:

Calgary
#2403, 308-4th Ave. SW, Calgary, AB T2P 0H7
403-817-6700 Fax: 403-817-6701

Edmonton
#1150, 10810 - 101 St., Edmonton, AB T5J 3S4
780-702-5233 Fax: 780-702-5235

Halifax
Tower 2, #1605, 1969 Upper Water St., Halifax, NS B3J 3R7
902-442-5205 Fax: 902-442-5204

London
#1512, 148 Fullarton St., London, ON N6A 5P3
519-963-5400 Fax: 519-963-5407

Moncton
#400, 735 Main St., Moncton, NB E1C 1E5
506-851-6066 Fax: 506-851-6406

Montréal
Tour de la Bourse, #4520, 800, Victoria Square, CP 124, Montréal, QC H4Z 1C3
514-908-9200 Fax: 514-878-9891

Québec
D-3, #600, 2875, boul Laurier, Québec, QC G1V 2M2
418-577-7408 Fax: 418-577-7419

St. John's
90 O'Leary Ave., St. John's, NL A1B 2C7
709-772-8808 Fax: 709-772-8693

Toronto
#3120, 155 Wellington St. West, Toronto, ON M5V 3L3
416-349-6515 Fax: 416-349-6516

Vancouver
Bentall Four, #400, 1055 Dunsmuir St., PO Box 49086, Vancouver, BC V7X 1G4
604-638-6950 Fax: 604-638-6955

Winnipeg
Commodity Exchange Tower, #2075, 360 Main St., Winnipeg, MB R3C 3Z3
204-975-5090 Fax: 204-975-5094

Farm Credit Canada / Financement agricole Canada

1800 Hamilton St., PO Box 4320, Regina, SK S4P 4L3
306-780-8100 Fax: 306-780-8919
888-332-3301
csc@fcc-fac.ca
www.fcc-fac.com
TTY: 306-780-6974

Federal Crown corporation reporting to Parliament through the Minister of Agriculture & Agri-Food. Under the Farm Credit Canada Act FCC offers financing to primary producers & agribusiness through 100 offices in rural communities across Canada.

President/CEO, Greg Stewart, P.Ag.
Executive Vice-President/CFO, Moyez Somani, CMA, MBA, FCMA
Executive Vice-President/COO, Operations, Rémi Lemoine, MBA, FCI
Senior Vice-President, Marketing, Lyndon Carlson, P.Ag.
Senior Vice-President, Strategy, Knowledge & Reputation, Kellie Garrett, ABC, MA
Senior Vice-President, Human Resources, Greg Honey
Senior Vice-President, Portfolio & Credit Risk, Michael Hoffort, P.Ag.

Office of the Commissioner for Federal Judicial Affairs / Bureau du Commissaire à la magistrature fédérale

99 Metcalfe St., 8th Fl., Ottawa, ON K1A 1E3
613-995-5140 Fax: 613-995-5615
877-583-4266
info@fja.gc.ca
www.fja.gc.ca

Commissioner, William Brooks
wbrooks@cmf.gc.ca
Deputy Commissioner, Marc A. Giroux
mgiroux@cmf.gc.ca
Executive Editor, Federal Court Reports, François Boivin
Executive Director & Senior General Counsel, Canadian Judicial Counsel, Norman Sabourin
Executive Director, Judicial Appointments & Senior Legal Counsel, Véronique Joly
Director, International Programs, Oleg Shakov
Chief, Administrative Services, Anne Barnabé
Director, Information Management & Information Technologies, Normand Bernier
Director, Judges Language Training, Reina Boyce
Director, Compensation, Benefits & Human Resources, Nikki Clemenhagen
Director, Finance & Administration, Wayne Osborne
Legal Counsel, Simon-Pierre Lessard
Director, Strategic Planning & Innovation, Nicole Sayed

Finance Canada / Finances Canada

L'esplanade Laurier, 140 O'Connor St., Ottawa, ON K1A 0G5
613-992-1573 Fax: 613-943-0938
finpub@fin.gc.ca
www.fin.gc.ca
TTY: 613-995-1455
Other Communication: Library Services: 613-995-5877

The Department of Finance Canada is responsible for providing the federal government with analysis & advice on financial & economic issues. It also monitors & researches the performance of the Canadian economy's major factors (output, growth, employment, income, price stability, monetary policy, & long-term change). Interacting with various other federal departments & agencies, the Department encourages coordination in all federal initiatives with an impact on the economy. Emphasis is placed on consulting with the public regarding policy directions & options.

Acts Administered:
Air Canada Public Participation Act
Air Travellers Security Charge Act
An Act Respecting Payments to a Trust Established to Provide Provinces & Territories with Funding for Community Development
An Act Respecting the Provision of Funding for Diagnostic & Medical Equiment
Bank of British Columbia Business Continuation Act
Bank of Canada Act
Bank for International Settlements (Immunity) Act
Beechwood Power Project Act
Bills of Exchange Act
Borrowing Authority Act
Bretton Woods & Related Agreements Act
Budget Implementation Acts & Acts Implementing Measures Announced in Economic Statements
Canada Deposit Insurance Corporation Act
Canada Employment Insurance Financing Board Act
Canada Health Care, Early Childhood Development & Other Social Services Funding Act
Canada-Newfoundland Atlantic Accord Implementation Act
Canada-Nova Scotia Offshore Petroleum Resources Accord Implementation Act
Canada Pension Plan Act
Canada Pension Plan Investment Board Act
Canada-US Free Trade Agreement Implementation Act
Canadian Commercial Bank Financial Assistance Act
Canadian International Trade Tribunal Act
Canadian Payments Act
Canadian Securities Regulation Regime Transition Office Act
Co-operative Credit Associations Act
Crown Corporations Dissolution or Transfer Authorization Act
Currency Act
Customs & Excise Offshore Application Act
Customs Tariff Act
Depository Bills & Notes Act
Diplomatic Service (Special) Superannuation Act
Economic Development Agency of Canada for Regions of Quebec Act
Eldorado Nuclear Limited Reorganization & Divestiture Act
Energy Costs Assistance Measures Act
European Bank for Reconstruction & Development Agreement Act
Excise Tax Act, 2001
Export Credits Insurance, Parts I & II
Federal-Provincial Fiscal Arrangements Act
Federal-Provincial Fiscal Revisions Act
Financial Administration Act
Financial Consumer Agency of Canada Act
Financial Institutions & Deposit Insurance System Amendment Act
Financial Institutions Depositors Compensation Act
First Nations Goods & Services Tax Act
First Nations Sales Tax Act
Garnishment, Attachment, & Pension Diversion Act
Halifax Relief Commission Pension Continuation Act
Income Tax Act
Income Tax Conventions Interpretation Act
Insurance Companies Act
Interest Act
Newfoundland Additional Finance Assistance Act
Nordion & Theatronics Divestiture Authorization Act
Nova Scotia & Newfoundland & Labrador Additional Fiscal Equalization Offset
Office of the Superintendent of Financial Institutions Act
Oil Export Tax Act
Payment Card Networks Act
Payment Clearing & Settlement Act
Pension Benefits Standards Act
Petro-Canada Public Participation Act
Prince Edward Island Subsidy Act
Proceeds of Crime (Money Laundering) & Terrorist Financing Act
Provincial Subsidies Act
Special Import Measures Act
Spending Control Act
Supplementary Fiscal Equalization Payments Act, 1982-87
Tax-Back Guarantee Act
Tax Convention Acts
Teleglobe Canada Reorganization & Divestiture Act
Telesat Canada Reorganization & Divestiture Act
Trust & Loan Companies Act

Minister, Finance, Hon. James Michael (Jim) Flaherty, B.A., LL.B.
613-992-6344, Fax: 513-992-8320, FlaheJ@parl.gc.ca; jflaherty@fin.gc.ca
Minister of State (Finance), Ted Menzies
613-996-7861, Fax: 613-995-5176, ted.menzies@fin.gc.ca
Deputy Minister, Michael Horgan
613-992-4925, Fax: 613-952-9569
Associate Deputy Minister & G-7 Deputy for Canada, Paul Rochon
613-943-2314, Fax: 613-952-9569
Associate Deputy Minister, Louise Levonian
613-996-1963, Fax: 613-952-9569
Assistant Deputy Minister, Denis Gauthier
613-992-1527, Fax: 613-992-0387

Associated Agencies, Boards & Commissions:
- Auditor General of Canada / Vérificateur Général du Canada
- Bank of Canada / Banque du Canada
- Canada Deposit Insurance Corporation / Société d'assurance-dépôts du Canada
- Canada Investment & Savings (CI&S) / Placements Épargne Canada (PEC)
#900, 110 Yonge St.
Toronto, ON M5C 1T4
416-952-1252 Fax: 416-952-1270 800-575-5151
csb@csb.gc.ca
www.csb.gc.ca
- Canada Revenue Agency / Agence du revenu du Canada
- Financial Consumer Agency of Canada / Agence de la consommation en matière financière du Canada
- Financial Transactions & Reports Analysis Centre of Canada (FINTRAC) / Centre d'analyse des opérations et déclarations financières du Canada (CANAFE)
234 Laurier Ave. West, 24th Fl.
Ottawa, ON K1P 1H7
Fax: 613-943-7931 866-346-8722
guidelines-lignesdirectrices@fintrac-canafe.gc.ca
www.fintrac.gc.ca
Created in 2000, FINTRAC is Canada's financial intelligence unit, a specialized agency created to collect, analyze & disclose financial information & intelligence on suspected money laundering & terrorist activities financing.
- Office of the Superintendent of Financial Institutions / Bureau du surintendant des institutions financières Canada

Consultations & Communications Branch / Direction des consultations et des communications

East Tower, 140 O'Connor St., 19th Fl., Ottawa, ON K1A 0G5
613-992-1573
finpub@fin.gc.ca
TTY: 613-995-1455

General Director, Jean-Michel Catta
613-992-1369, Fax: 613-943-0938
Assistant Deputy Minister, Alan Freeman
613-992-9194, Fax: 613-943-0938
Director, Public Affairs & Operations, David Gamble
613-992-7763

Corporate Services Branch / Direction des services ministériels

Provides joint services for the federal Treasury Board Secretariat & Finance Canada.
Acting Assistant Deputy Minister, Sherry Harrison
613-995-1408, Fax: 613-995-1408
Executive Director/CIO, Information Management & Technology, Robert Aubé
613-996-0313, Fax: 613-943-2077
Executive Director, Human Resources Division, Edward Poznanski
613-992-1105, Fax: 613-943-2807

Tax Policy Branch / Direction de la politique de l'impôt

Acting Assistant Deputy Minister, Nancy Horsman
613-992-1630, Fax: 613-996-1630
General Director, Tax Policy, Brian Ernewein
613-992-3045, Fax: 613-996-0660
Director, Personal Income Tax, Sean Keenan
613-992-6729, Fax: 613-943-5597
Director, Tax Legislation, Gerald Lalonde
613-992-0405, Fax: 613-992-4450
Director, Intergovernmental Tax Policy, Evaluation & Research, Kei Moray
613-947-3341, Fax: 613-947-1677
Director, Sales Tax Division, Lise Potvin
613-992-6298, Fax: 613-995-8970
Director, Business Income Tax Division, Geoff Trueman
613-992-1008, Fax: 613-943-2486

Acting General Director, Tax Policy, Baxter Williams
613-992-2555, Fax: 613-996-0660

Financial Consumer Agency of Canada (FCAC) / Agence de la consommation en matière financière du Canada (ACFC)

427 Laurier Ave. West, 6th Fl., Ottawa, ON K1R 1B9
Fax: 613-941-1436
info@fcac-acfc.gc.ca
www.fcac-acfc.gc.ca
TTY: 866-914-6097
Other Communication: Toll-Free: 1-866-461-FCAC (3222) for services in English; 1-866-461-ACFC (2232) for services in French; www.twitter.com/fcacan

Created by Parliament in 2001, the Financial Consumer Agency of Canada (FCAC) exists to protect Canada's financial consumers; to make them aware of their rights & responsibilities; & to inform Canadians about the financial products & services available to them. The FCAC ensures that the nearly 500 federally regulated financial institutions respect the consumer provisions in the laws that govern them & monitors the voluntary codes of conduct financial institutions have adopted. As well as informing people about their rights as financial consumers, the FCAC provides information & tools to help consumers shop around for the best financial product/service for their situation. As of July 2010, the FCAc oversees payment card network operators and their commerical practices.

Acts Administered:
Bank Act
Co-operative Credit Associations Act
Financial Consumer Agency of Canada Act
Green Shield Canada Act
Insurance Companies Act
Payment Card Network Act
Trust & Loan Companies Act

Commissioner, Ursula Menke
613-941-4300
Deputy Commissioner, Lucie Tedesco
613-941-4335
Senior Counsel, Legal Services, Joseph de Pencier
613-941-1425
Director, Marketing & Communications, André-Marc Allain
613-941-4770
Director, Corporate & Administrative Services, Martin Pachéco
613-941-4239
Director, Financial Literacy & Consumer Education, Jane Rooney
613-941-1528
Director, Compliance & Enforcement Research, John Rossi
613-941-3929
Director, Research, Vacant

Office of the Superintendent of Financial Institutions (OSFI) / Bureau du surintendant des institutions financières Canada

Kent Square, 255 Albert St., Ottawa, ON K1A 0H2
613-990-7788 Fax: 613-990-5591
800-385-8647
information@osfi-bsif.gc.ca
www.osfi-bsif.gc.ca
TTY: 613-943-3980

Responsible for regulating & supervising financial institutions & pension plans under federal jurisdiction. Included under federal jurisdiction are: banks, some insurance companies, trust companies, loan companies, cooperative credit associations, & fraternal benefit societies. OSFI monitors & examines these institutions & pension plans for solvency, liquidity, & compliance with legislation, regulations & Office guidelines. Provides actuarial services & advice to the Government of Canada. Reports to government through the Minister of Finance.

Superintendent, Julie Dickson
613-990-3667, Fax: 613-993-6782, julie.dickson@osfi-bsif.gc.ca
Director, Security Services, Raymond Bullard
613-990-7781, Fax: 613-990-0081, raymond.bullard@osfi-bsif.gc.ca
Communications Officer, Léonie Roux
613-949-8942, Fax: 613-660-5591, leonie.roux@osfi-bsif.gc.ca

Audit & Consulting Services / Services de vérification et de consultation

Fax: 416-954-3169
Capital Consultant, Robert J. Hanna
613-990-7278, Fax: 613-993-6525, bob.hanna@osfi-bsif.gc.ca

Corporate Services Sector / Secteur des services intégrés

Fax: 613-949-3968
Other Communication: Alt. Fax: 613-993-6782
Assistant Superintendent, Gary Walker
613-990-8761, Fax: 613-990-6328, gary.walker@osfi-bsif.gc.ca
Managing Director, Finance & Corporate Planning, Michele Bridges
613-991-4607, Fax: 613-990-6328, michele.briddges@osfi-bsif.gc.ca
Director, Communications & Consultations, Margaret Pearcy
613-993-0577, Fax: 613-990-5591, margaret.pearcy@osfi-bsif.gc.ca

Office of the Chief Actuary / Bureau de l'actuaire en chef

Fax: 613-990-9900
Chief Actuary, Jean-Claude Ménard
613-990-7577, Fax: 613-990-9900, jean-claude.menard@osfi-bsif.gc.c

Regulation Sector / Secteur de la réglementation

Fax: 613-993-6525
Assistant Superintendent, Mark White
416-973-1655, Fax: 416-973-1655, mark.white@osfi-bsif.gc.ca
Senior Director, Actuarial, Stuart Wason
416-973-2056, Fax: 416-952-0664, stuart.wason@osfi-bsif.gc.ca
Senior Director, Capital Division, Gilbert Ménard
613-990-8081, Fax: 613-991-6822, gilbert.menard@osfi-bsif.gc.ca
Senior Director, AML & Compliance, Nicolas Burbridge
416-973-6117, Fax: 416-954-3169, nicolas.burbridge@osfi-bsif.gc.ca
Senior Director, Legislation & Approvals, Patricia (Patty) A. Evanoff
613-990-9004, Fax: 613-998-6716, patty.evanoff@osfi-bsif.gc.ca
Managing Director, International Advisory Group, Arvind Baghel
416-973-6758, Fax: 416-952-1662, arvind.baghel@osfi-bsif.gc.ca
Senior Director, Accounting Policy, Karen F. Stothers
416-973-0744, Fax: 416-952-1662, karen.stothers@osfi-bsif.gc.ca
Director, Research, Gerald Goldstein
613-990-8911, Fax: 613-991-6822, gerald.goldstein@osfi-bsif.gc.ca
General Counsel, Legal Services, Alain Prévost
613-990-7787, Fax: 613-952-5031, alain.prevost@osfi-bsif.gc.ca

Supervision Sector / Secteur de la surveillance

Other Communication: Toronto Fax: 416/973-1168; Ottawa Fax: 613/993-6782
Assistant Superintendent, Ted F. Price
416-973-4385, Fax: 416-973-1168, ted.price@osfi-bsif.gc.ca
Senior Director, Financial Institutions Group, Karen Badgerow-Croteau
416-952-3909, Fax: 416-954-5015, karen.badgerow-croteau@osfi-bsif.gc.ca
Senior Director, Regulatory & Supervisory Practices Division, Bruce J. Rutherford
416-973-4378, Fax: 416-973-8994, bruce.rutherford@osfi-bsif.gc.ca
Managing Director, Operational Risk & Capital Assessment Services, Abhilash D. Bhachech
416-973-6654, Fax: 416-952-1663, abhilash.bhachech@osfi-bsif.gc.ca
Senior Director, Property & Casualty Insurance Group, Penny M. Lee
416-952-0557, Fax: 416-954-6478, penny.lee@osfi-bsif.gc.ca
Managing Director, Strategic Initiatives, Pamela H. Hopkins
416-973-6657, Fax: 416-973-1168, pamela.hopkins@osfi-bsif.gc.ca
Director, Supervision, Maria Moutafis
416-973-3699, Fax: 416-973-8994, maria.moutafis@osfi-bsif.gc.ca
Managing Director, Capital Markets/Risk Assessment, Douglas Sannuto
416-973-1671, Fax: 416-954-3170, douglas.sannuto@osfi-bsif.gc.ca

Fisheries & Oceans Canada (DFO) / Pêches et Océans Canada (MPO)

200 Kent St., Ottawa, ON K1A 0E6
613-993-0999 Fax: 613-990-1866
info@dfo-mpo.gc.ca
www.dfo-mpo.gc.ca
TTY: 800-465-7735

The Department of Fisheries & Oceans (DFO), on behalf of the Government of Canada, is responsible for policies & programs in support of Canada's economic, ecological & scientific interests in the oceans & freshwater fish habitat; for the conservation & sustainable utilization of Canada's fisheries resources in marine & inland waters; & for safe, effective & environmentally sound marine services responsive to the needs of Canadians in a global economy. The Department's mandate is extremely broad & covers management & protection of the marine & fisheries resources inside the 200-mile exclusive economic zone; management & protection of freshwater fisheries resources; marine safety along the world's longest coastline; facilitation of marine transportation; protection of the marine environment; support to other federal government institutions & objectives, as the government's civilian marine service; & research to support government priorities such as climate change & biodiversity. Because of its broad mandate, DFO does not operate alone. Federal & provincial governments share jurisdiction in a number of areas related to the Department's mandate. A $28-million investment over two years for the first phase of the Oceans Action Plan was announced in Feb ruary, 2005. The Plan is designed to develop ocean resources while protecting marine ecosystems, through sustainable development, integrated management plans, & marine protected areas.

Acts Administered:
Atlantic Fisheries Restructuring Act
Canada Shipping Act
Pleasure Craft Sewage Pollution Prevention Regulations
Coastal Fisheries Protection Act
Department of Fisheries & Oceans Act
Fisheries Act
Aboriginal Communal Fishing Licences Regulations
Alberta Fishery Regulations, 1998
Alice Arm Tailings Deposit Regulations
Atlantic Fishery Regulations
British Columbia Gravel Removal Order
British Columbia Logging Order
British Columbia Sport Fishing Regulations
Fish Health Protection Regulations
Fish Toxicant Regulations
Fishery (General) Regulations
Foreign Vessel Fishing Regulations
Management of Contaminated Fisheries Regulations
Manitoba Fishery Regulations
Marine Mammal Regulations
Maritime Provinces Fishery Regulations
Newfoundland & Labrador Fishery Regulations
Northwest Territories Fishery Regulations
Ontario Fishery Regulations
Pacific Fishery Management Area Regulations
Pacific Fishery Regulations
Potato Processing Plant Liquid Effluent Regulations
Provincial Regulations
Pulp & Paper Effluent Regulations
Quebec Fishery Regulations
Saskatchewan Fishery Regulations
Yukon Territory Fishery Regulations
Fisheries Development Act
Fisheries Improvement Loans Act
Fisheries & Oceans Canada Orders
Fishing & Recreational Harbours Act
Freshwater Fish Marketing Act
Great Lakes Fisheries Convention Act
Navigable Waters Protection Act
Oceans Act
Basic Head Marine Protected Area Regulations
Confederation Bridge Area Provincial (PEI) Laws Application Regulations
Eastport Marine Protected Area Regulations
Endeavour Hydrothermal Vents Marine Protected Areas Regulations
Fishing Zones of Canada (Zones 1, 2 & 3) Order
Fishing Zones of Canada (Zones 4 & 5) Order
Fishing Zones of Canada (Zone 6) Order
Gilbert Bay Marine Protected Area Regulations
Gully Marine Protected Area Regulations
Territorial Sea Geographical Coordinates (Area 7) Order
Territorial Sea Geographical Coordinated Order
Species at Risk Act

Minister, Fisheries & Oceans, Hon. Keith Ashfield
613-992-3474, Fax: 613-992-1974, Shea.G@parl.gc.ca; Min@dfo-mpo.gc.ca, Other Communications: Fisheries & Oceans, Phone: 613-992-3474
Deputy Minister, Claire Dansereau
613-993-2200, Fax: 613-993-2194
Executive Advisor to the Deputy Minister, Blair Hodgson
613-993-9226, Fax: 613-993-2194, blair.hodgson@dfo-mpo.gc.ca
Assistant Deputy Minister, Special Envoy for Asia-Pacific, France Pégeot
613-993-1808, Fax: 604-666-8959
Chief Financial Officer, Roch Huppé
613-990-0023
Director General, Communications, Susan Gardner-Barclay
613-990-0219, Fax: 613-941-0219
Executive Director & Acting Senior General Counsel, Lynn Lovett
613-993-0966
Parliamentary Secretary to the Minister of Fisheries & Oceans, Randy Kamp
613-992-3474, Fax: 613-947-4615, Kamp.R@parl.gc.ca

Executive Administrator, Budgeting, Planning & Resource Management, Dianne Payette
613-993-2735

Associated Agencies, Boards & Commissions:
• Fisheries Resource Conservation Council (FRCC) / Le Conseil pour la conservation des ressources halieutiques (CCRH)
PO Box 2001 D
Ottawa, ON K1P 5W3
613-998-0433 Fax: 613-998-1146
info@frcc-ccrh.ca
www.frcc.ca
Created in 1993 to form a partnership between scientific & academic expertise, & all sectors of the fishing industry. Council members make public recommendations to the Minister of Fisheries & Oceans on conservation measures for the Atlantic fishery.
• Freshwater Fish Marketing Corporation / Office de commercialisation du poisson d'eau douce
119 Plessis Rd.
Winnipeg, MB R2C 3L4
sandi.cain@freshwaterfish.com

Canadian Coast Guard (CCG) / Garde côtière canadienne
Centennial Towers, #6S018, 200 Kent St., Ottawa, ON K1A 0E6
613-993-0999 Fax: 613-990-1866
info@dfo-mpo.gc.ca
www.ccg-gcc.gc.ca
TTY: 613-941-6517
The Canadian Coast Guard provides the following maritime programs & services: search & rescue; marine communications & traffic services, including radio communications & radio navigational aids services; marine navigation services, a program which establishes & maintains navigational aids to assist vessels in safe navigation; enrvironmental response program, which works to minimize impacts of marine pollution incidents & to provide humanitarian aid in disasters; aids to navigation, such as the Differential Global Positioning System (DGPS) & Notices to Mariners (NOTMAR); icebreaking services; & client relations & international affairs.
Commissioner, Marc Grégoire
613-998-1571, Fax: 613-990-2780
Assistant Commissioner, Gary Sidock
613-990-9172, Fax: 613-993-3421
Acting Deputy Commissioner, Michel Vermette
613-994-9220, Fax: 613-949-6816
Special Advisor to the Commissioner, David G. Faulkner
613-993-1628, Fax: 613-993-5333
Director General, Fleet, Mario Pelletier
613-990-9172, Fax: 613-993-3421
Director General, Integrated Business Management Directorate, Denis C. Sing
613-998-1440, Fax: 613-998-3480
Director General, Maritime Services, Jacqueline Gonçalves
613-993-7728

Corporate Services & Human Resources / Services généraux
200 Kent St., Ottawa, ON K1A 0E6
Assistant Deputy Minister, Michaela Huard
613-993-8726, Fax: 613-993-3246
Director General, Human Resources, Bhagwant Sandhu
613-990-0013
Director, Human Resources, Marie LeBlanc
506-851-6973, Fax: 506-851-2605
Director, Finance & Assets Management, Robert C. Richard
506-851-2029, Fax: 506-851-2599
Director General, Real Property, Safety & Security, Krishna Sahay
613-993-9291, Fax: 613-991-0061

Ecosystems & Fisheries Management / Gestion des écosystèmes et des pêches
200 Kent St., Ottawa, ON K1A 0E6
Responsible for the management & development of all federal fisheries & habitat in Canada. The division conserves, protects, develops & enhances fishery resources & habitats, encompassing the Atlantic & Pacific sectors, adjacent provinces, & the 200-mile offshore zone. Also manages Canadian parts of trans-boundary rivers.
Assistant Deputy Minister, David Bevan
613-998-1796, Fax: 613-998-0499
Director General, Fisheries & Aboriginal Policy, Nadia Bouffard
613-998-3111
Director General, Conservation & Protection, Paul Steele
613-998-9537
Director General, International Affairs Directorate, Guy Beaupré
613-991-4315, Fax: 613-993-5995

Oceans & Science / Océans et science
200 Kent St., Ottawa, ON K1A 0E6
Services include: oceans sciences (ocean's physical properties, behaviour of organic & inorganic materials & their impact on fish & ecosystems, pollutants); regulation, enforcement & management of fisheries resources & habitat that are exploited for aboriginal, commercial & recreational purposes. The Marine Protected Areas Policy & the National Framework for Establishing & Managing Marine Protected Areas represents DFO's approach to establishing & maintaining MPOs in Canada.
Assistant Deputy Minister, Siddika Mithani
613-993-5123
Director General, Oceans Directorate, Wayne Moore
613-990-0001, Fax: 613-990-0313

Policy / Politiques
200 Kent St., Ottawa, ON K1A 0E6
Provides leadership in recommending, developing & monitoring policy frameworks that advance DFO's initiatives, support DFO programs, & are responsive to the changing needs of DFO clients. Provides strategic advice on departmental programs, develops long-term planning priorities for the department & coordinates cross-sectoral activities in support of government goals & departmental objectives.
Senior Assistant Deputy Minister, France Pégeot
613-993-1808
Assistant Deputy Minister, Mitch Bloom
613-993-1798
Manager, Economics & Analysis, Patrick Mahaux
604-666-6570

Science Sector / Secteur des sciences
200 Kent St., Ottawa, ON K1A 0E6
Services provided by the science sector include the following: research & data gathering; provision of information & advice in the fields of fisheries sciences (fish, invertebrates, marine mammals & plants, & ecosystems), oceans sciences (ocean's physical properties, behaviour of organic & inorganic materials & their impact on fish & ecosystems, pollutants), & hydrography (bathymetric, tide & current systems); & regulation, enforcement & management of fisheries resources & habitat that are exploited for aboriginal, commercial & recreational purposes. The sector assesses major stocks of exploited species of anadromous & marine fish, invertebrates, mammals & plants in Canada's Atlantic, Pacific, Arctic & marine waters, as well as freshwater fish in the Yukon & Northwest Territories. Research is conducted in the following areas: the biology & population of fish stocks, in order to provide scientific information & advice to fishery managers; the effects of changes in the ocean environment on the recruitment & distribution of fish populations; & studies to improve the productivity of aquaculture.
Assistant Deputy Minister, Siddika Mithani
613-990-5123, Fax: 613-990-5113
Director General, Canadian Hydrography Service, Savithri Narayanan
613-995-4413
Director General, Ecosystem Science, David Gillis
613-990-0271
Director General, Strategic & Regulatory Science, Wayne Moore
613-990-0001, Fax: 613-990-0313

Regional Directors:

Central & Arctic
#703, 201 Front St., Sarnia, ON N7T 8B1
519-383-1810 Fax: 519-464-5128
Regional Director, Bob Lambe
519-383-1810, Fax: 519-464-5128

Gulf
PO Box 5030, Moncton, NB E1C 9B6
506-851-7747 Fax: 506-851-2435
Regional Director General, Jim Jones
506-851-7750

Maritimes
176 Portland St., Halifax, NS B2Y 4T3
902-426-2581 Fax: 902-426-2479
Regional Director General, Faith Scattolon
902-426-2581

Newfoundland & Labrador
PO Box 5667 Whitehills, St. John's, NL A1C 5X1
709-772-4423 Fax: 709-772-4880
Regional Director General, Wayne Follett
709-772-4417, Fax: 709-772-6306

Pacific
#200, 401 Burrard St., Vancouver, BC V6C 3S4
604-666-0384 Fax: 604-666-8956
Regional Director General, Paul Sprout
604-666-6098, Fax: 604-666-8756

Québec
104, rue Dalhousie, Québec, QC G1K 7Y7
418-648-7747 Fax: 418-648-4758
Regional Director General, Marc Demonceaux

Research Facilities:

Bayfield Institute
867 Lakeshore Rd., PO Box 5050, Burlington, ON L7R 4A6
905-336-6240
Comprises fisheries research, habitat management, hydrographic surveys & chart production & ships support. Together with the Freshwater Institute in Winnipeg, it provides the federal Fisheries & Oceans science programs for the Central & Arctic Region. Multiple partnerships with a variety of external stakeholders allow the Institute to be recognized internationally as a site of leading research in freshwater science.
District Manager, Ron DesJardine
705-750-4017

Bedford Institute of Oceanography (BIO) / L'institut océanographique de Bedford
1 Challenger Dr., PO Box 1006, Dartmouth, NS B2Y 4A2
902-426-3492 Fax: 902-426-8484
www.bio.gc.ca
Administered by Fisheries & Oceans, Bedford Institute of Oceanography (BIO) is Canada's largest centre for ocean research. Scientists, engineers & technicians primarily from Fisheries & Oceans, & Natural Resources Canada, (smaller components are from National Defense & Environment Canada) perform targeted research & provide advice on Atlantic marine environments. Programs include: fisheries research, ocean sciences & management, habitat ecology, marine chemistry, Canadian Hydrographic Service (producing navigation charts for the Atlantic & Arctic areas), marine environmental regional & resources geoscience, & seabird research & management. BIO based staff also conduct joint projects, such as sea floor mapping & exploration, & provide scientific response to marine environmental emergencies. Also located at Bedford is the Canadian Shark Research Laboratory & the Otolith Research Laboratory.
Regional Science Director, Dr. Michael Sinclair
sinclairm@mar.dfo-mpo.gc.ca

Freshwater Institute / Institut des eaux douces
501 University Cres., Winnipeg, MB R3T 2N6
204-983-5000 Fax: 204-983-6285
Main areas of research are: fish habitats; limnology emphasizing mechanisms & processes of biological production & decomposition in lakes; studies related to energy development use, acidification, radionuclide & heavy metal pollution. Arctic research emphasizes commercially important fish & marine mammals & associated ecosystems, & the effects of hydroelectric developments & toxic chemical pollution on aquatic ecosystems. The Institute supports a major field camp at the Experimental Lakes Area. Activities include freshwater & arctic science, science oceans initiative, fish habitat management, fisheries management, small craft harbours, corporate services, communications & regional senior management. The federal fish inspection program, recently transferred to the new Canadian Food Inspection Agency (CFIA), continues to operate out of the FWI.
Administrative Assistant, Judy Fredette
204-983-5118

Gulf Fisheries Centre / Centre de poissonerie du gulfe
343, av Université, 5th Fl., Moncton, NB E1C 9B6
506-851-3886 Fax: 506-851-7732
Regional Director General, Serge Thériault
506-851-7750, Fax: 506-851-2224

Institut Maurice-Lamontagne / Maurice Lamontagne Institute
850, rte de le Mer, CP 1000, Mont-Joli, QC G5H 3Z4
418-775-0555 Fax: 418-775-0730
www.qc.dfo.ca/iml/en/intro.htm
Provides extensive research on: fisheries, fish habitat, oceanography, hydrography; development of marine renewable resources in the fields of fisheries, ocean industry development, commercial shipping & recreational boating. Main area of focus centres on the Gulf of St. Lawrence & estuary, Saguenay Fjord, Canadian Arctic, & the James, Hudson & Ungava Bays. Also performs the following research: environmental chemistry research on the distribution, transport & fate of contaminants in sediments, water & the food chain; ecotoxicology research & field assessments for biomarkers, fish pathology & embryotoxicity; molecular toxicology research for biomarkers, fish reproduction & steroid hormones; bioremediation study on the microbial degradation of petroleum oil hydrocarbons & microbial bioassays. Projects include the temporal & spatial monitoring of organic & inorganic contaminants in fish, shellfish & sediments of the St. Lawrence gulf & estuary. Also studying the effects of pulp & paper effluents & mercury & municipal effluents on the reproduction of fish.
Regional Director, Regional Science Branch, Ariane Plourde

Centre for Aquaculture & Environmental Research
4160 Marine Dr., West Vancouver, BC V7V 1N6
604-666-7453 Fax: 604-666-3497
The Center for Aquaculture & Environmental Research (CAER) is a specialized centre for aquaculture and coastal research co-founded by Fisheries and Oceans Canada and the University of British Columbia.
Regional Director, Science Branch, Laura Richards
250-729-8369, Fax: 250-756-7053

Institute of Ocean Sciences (IOS) / Institut des sciences de la mer (ISM)
9860 West Saanich Rd., PO Box 6000, Sidney, BC V8L 4B2
250-363-6517 Fax: 250-363-6390
Science divisions at IOS include: Canadian Hydrographic Service, Marine Environment & Habitat Science, Ocean Science & Productivity. Other departments & organizations at the IOS facility include: GSC Pacific - Sidney Pacific Geoscience Centre, Canadian Wildlife Service, Canadian Coast Guard, North Pacific Marine Science Organization (PICES). Science Division also includes Pacific Biological Station, West Vancouver Laboratory. Cultus Lake Laboratory.
Director, Denis D'Amours
250-363-6347

Pacific Biological Station (PBS) / La station de biologie du Pacifique
3190 Hammond Bay Rd., Nanaimo, BC V9T 6N7
250-756-7000 Fax: 250-756-7053
Research at PBS responds to stock assessment, aquaculture, marine environment & habitat science, & ocean science & productivity priorities.
Regional Director, Science Branch, Laura Richards
250-729-8369

St. Andrews Biological Station / La Station biologique de St. Andrews
531 Brandy Cove Rd., St Andrews, NB E5B 2L9
506-529-8854 Fax: 506-529-5862
XMARSABS@mar.dfo-mpo.gc.ca
www.mar.dfo-mpo.gc.ca/sabs
Chemical & ecological studies on the interaction between oceanography & fisheries/aquaculture & the aquatic environment. Stock assessments & associated research on commercially important groundfish, pelagic finfish, invertebrate species in the Bay of Fundy & other areas of Atlantic Canada. Research in support of the existing salmon aquaculture industry & research on other species with potential for aquaculture in Atlantic Canada. Major environmental research projects include: risk assessment of organic chemicals to fisheries; biochemical indicators of health of aquatic animals; aquatic toxicity of marine phytotoxins; molluscan toxins, techniques & improvements; phytotoxin research; aquaculture ecology research; effectiveness of acid rain control programs; effects of aquaculture in the coastal environment.
Section Head, Lara Cooper
506-529-5951, Fax: 902-529-5862

Foreign Affairs & International Trade Canada (FAIT) / Affaires étrangères et Commerce international Canada (AECT)

125 Sussex Dr., Ottawa, ON K1A 0G2
613-944-4000 Fax: 613-996-9709
800-267-8376
enqserv@international.gc.ca
www.international.gc.ca
TTY: 613-944-4000
Other Communication: Media Relations: 613-995-1874
FAIT works to ensure that its policies, programmes & operations reflect sustainable development criteria & to make a difference in sustainable development terms in the international arena. The Department defines its intent in a 3-year SD strategy which is tabled in Parliament. Annual progress reports are also tabled in Parliament. The current strategy, Agenda 2006, covers the 2004-2006 period. FAIT strives to defend & advance Canada's international interests in environmental protection & sustainable development in bilateral, multilateral & regional fora including issues relating to climate change, trade & environment, sustainable forest management, hazardous & toxic substances, desertification, human settlements, biological diversity, biosafety, genetic resources for food & agriculture, air & marine pollution, whaling, & non-Canada-USA freshwater. To achieve progress in this area of responsibility, FAIT's Environmental & Sustainable Development Bureau works with the major international environmental & sustainable development organizations. It also recommends & oversees funding where appropriate. Domestically, the Bureau works toward agreement & productive partnerships with other government departments, agencies & non-governmental environmental, no nuclear energy, developmental & business organizations. It prepares & monitors implementation of the Department's Sustainable Development Strategy & provides advice & assistance in the areas of environmental assessment & the greening of departmental operations both in Canada & at the 157 missions abroad. FAIT established an environmental management system (EMS), based on the International Organization for Standardization's (ISO) 14000 series, in a commitment to incorporate best environmental management practices into its operations. A database of international environmental treaties to which Canada is a party may be searched at www.treaty-accord.gc.ca

Acts Administered:
Asia-Pacific Foundation of Canada Act
Bretton Woods Agreements Act
Canadian Commercial Corporation Act
Canadian Institute for International Peace & Security Act
Comprehensive Nuclear Test-Ban Treaty Implementation Act
Cultural Property Export & Import Act
Department of Foreign Affairs & International Trade Act
Diplomatic & Consular Privileges & Immunities Act
Export Development Act
Export & Import Permits Act
Food & Agriculture Organization of the United Nations Act
Forgiveness of Certain Official Development Assistance Debts Act
Fort-Falls Bridge Authority Act
Geneva Conventions Act
High Commissioner of the United Kingdom Act
International Boundary Waters Treaty Act
International Development (Financial Institutions) Continuing Assistance Act
International Development Research Centre Act
Meat Import Act
North American Free Trade Agreement Implementation Act
Northern Pipeline Act
Privileges & Immunities (International Organizations) Act
Privileges & Immunities (North Atlantic Treaty Organization) Act
Prohibition of International Air Services Act
Rainy Lake Watershed Emergency Control Act
Roosevelt-Campobello International Park Commission Act
Skagit River Valley Treaty Implementation Act
State Immunity Act
United Nations Act

Minister, Foreign Affairs, Hon. John Baird
613-995-1851
Minister, International Trade, Hon. Edward Fast
613-992-7332
Minister of State of Foreign Affairs, Diane Ablonczy
613-994-2300

Foreign Affairs / Affaires étrangères
Deputy Minister, Morris Rosenberg
613-944-4491
Associate Deputy Minister, Gerald Cossette
613-994-2771
Parliamentary Secretary to the Minister of Foreign Affairs, Deepak Obhrai
613-947-4566, Fax: 613-947-4569

Global Issues / Enjeux mondiaux
Assistant Deputy Minister, Keith Christie
613-944-2273, Fax: 613-944-1315
Director General, International Organizations Bureau, David J. Angell
613-944-0928, Fax: 613-944-0722
Director General, Human Security & Human Rights, Adèle Dion
613-944-0325, Fax: 613-944-1121
Director General, Environment, Energy & Sustainable Development Bureau, Sheila Riordon
613-944-0886
Director General, Economic Policy Bureau, John C. Sloan
613-992-7825

International Security Branch & Political Director / Sécurité international et directeur politique
Assistant Deputy Minister, Colleen Swords
613-944-4228, Fax: 613-944-1180
Senior Coordinator, International Crime & Terrorism, Mark Gwozdecky
613-944-2906, Fax: 613-944-4827
Director General, Secretariat for the Stabilization & Reconstruction Task Force, Robert Derouin
613-995-6689
Director, Global Partnership Program, Troy Lulashnyk
613-944-3311, Fax: 613-944-1130
Director General, Security & Intelligence, Paul Meyer
613-992-7400, Fax: 613-996-1724
Director General, International Security Bureau, Donald Sinclair
613-992-3402
Director, Non-Proliferation, Arms Control & Disarmament, André-François Giroux
613-944-0324, Fax: 613-944-1835
Director, Nuclear & Chemical Disarmament Implementation Agency, James A. Junke
613-996-6901, Fax: 613-944-3105
Director, Defence & Security Relations Division, Shelley Whiting
613-992-7921
Director, Global & Security Policy, Janice Attree-Smith
613-944-7646, Fax: 613-944-2104
Director, Peacekeeping & Peace Operations Group, Michael N. Kaduck
613-992-5457, Fax: 613-944-2128
Senior Coordinator, Mine Action & Small Arms Team, Earl Turcotte
613-995-9282, Fax: 613-944-2501

Communications Bureau
125 Sussex Dr., Ottawa, ON K1A 0G2
613-944-0404 Fax: 613-944-0811
Director General, Communications Bureau, Debora Brown
613-944-2482
Director General, Communications Bureau, André-Marc Lanteigne
613-944-5400
Director, Communications Services, Kyle M. Nunas
613-995-0780, Fax: 613-944-0453
Director, Strategic Communications, Christopher Wallace
613-994-1714, Fax: 613-944-0453

Office of Protocol / Bureau du Protocole
125 Sussex Dr., Ottawa, ON K1A 0G2
613-996-8683 Fax: 613-943-1075
Chief of Protocol, Margaret Huber
613-992-2344
Deputy Chief of Protocol & Director, Diplomatic Corps Services, Isabelle Martin
613-995-5185, Fax: 613-943-1075

Strategic Policy & Planning
125 Sussex Dr., Ottawa, ON K1A 0G2
613-944-2696 Fax: 613-944-0285
Assistant Deputy Minister, Carmen Sylvain
613-944-3022

Associated Agencies, Boards & Commissions:
- Canadian International Development Agency / Agence canadienne de développement international
- Canadian International Grains Institute / Institut international du Canada pour le grain
- International Joint Commission (Canadian Section) / Commission mixte internationale

Passport Canada
Le 70 Crémazie, 70 Crémazie St., Gatineau, QC K1A 0G3
Fax: 819-953-5856
800-567-6868
www.pptc.gc.ca
Other Communication: TTY: 1-866-255-7655
CEO, Christine Desloges
819-994-3530, Fax: 819-994-7150
Information Officer, Denis Bertrand
819-953-1087
Information Officer, Patrice Brière
819-956-4981
Information Officer, Claire Delisle
819-934-3263
Information Officer, Anne Dubeau
819-934-9991
Information Officer, Mouland Nait-Yahia
819-934-6985
Information Officer, Trina Picard
819-934-6981
Information Officer, Jennifer Proulx
819-934-6354

Passport Canada Offices:

Brampton
#401, 40 Gillingham Dr., Brampton, ON

Calgary
Harry Hays Bldg., #150, 220 - 4th Ave. SE, Calgary, AB

Calgary South
14331 Macleod Trail SW, Calgary, AB

Edmonton
Canada Place Building, #126, 9700 Jasper Ave., Edmonton, AB

Fredericton
Frederick Square, #430, 77 Westmorland St., Fredericton, NB

Gatineau
Place du Centre, Commercial Level 2, 200 Promenade du Portage, Gatineau, QC

Halifax
Maritime Centre, #1508, 1505 Barrington St., Halifax, NS

Hamilton
Standard Life Bldg., #330, 120 King St. West, Hamilton, ON

Consular, Security & Emergency Management Branch
125 Sussex Dr., Ottawa, ON K1A 0G2
Fax: 613-943-3797
Assistant Deputy Minister, Blair M. James
613-943-3770, Fax: 613-947-0366

International Platform (ACM) Branch
125 Sussex Dr., Ottawa, ON K1A 0G2
Assistant Deputy Minister, Denis Kingsley
613-944-1115, Fax: 613-944-3362

Chief Audit Executive Bureau
125 Sussex Dr., Ottawa, ON K1A 0G2
Chief Audit Executive, Yves Vaillancourt
613-943-4743, Fax: 613-947-9374

Kelowna
#110, 1835 Gordon Dr., Kelowna, BC

Kitchener
40 Weber St. East, Kitchener, ON

Laval
#500, 3, place Laval, Laval, QC

London
#201, 400 York St., 2nd Fl., London, ON

Mississauga
Central Parkway Mall, #116, 377 Burnhamthorpe Rd. East, 2nd Fl., Mississauga, ON

Montréal
Complexe Guy Favreau, Tour Ouest, #103, 200, boul René-Lévesque ouest, Montréal, QC

North York
Joseph Shepard Bldg., #380, 4900 Yonge St., North York, ON

Ottawa
Level C, East Tower, C.D. Howe Bldg., 240 Sparks St., Ottawa, ON

Pointe Claire
Fairview Pointe-Claire Shopping Center, 6815, rte Transcanadienne, Pointe-Claire, QC

Québec
Tour Cominar, Place de la Cité, #200, 2640, boul Laurier, 2e étage, Québec, QC

Regina
#500, 1870 Albert St., Regina, SK

Richmond
#310, 5611 Cooney Rd., Richmond, BC

Saguenay
Immeuble St-Michel, #408, 3885, boul Harvey, Saguenay, QC

St. Catharines
Landmark Bldg., #600, 43 Church St., St Catharines, ON

St. John's
TD Place, #802, 140 Water St., St. John's, NL

Saint-Laurent
#100, 2089 boul Marcel-Laurin, Saint-Laurent, QC

Saskatoon
Federal Bldg., #405, 101 - 22 St. East, Saskatoon, SK

Scarborough
#210, 200 Town Centre Crt., Scarborough, ON

Surrey
10153 King George Blvd., Surrey, BC

Thunder Bay
979 Alloy Dr., 2nd Fl., Thunder Bay, ON

Toronto
#300, 74 Victoria St., Toronto, ON

Vancouver
Sinclair Centre, #200, 757 West Hastings St., Vancouver, BC

Victoria - Bay Centre
1150 Douglas St., 4th Fl., Victoria, BC

Whitby
Whitby Mall, 1615 Dundas St. East, Whitby, ON

Windsor
CIBC Building, #503, 100 Ouellette Ave., Windsor, ON

Regional Director, Christine Penney

Winnipeg
#400, 433 Main St., Winnipeg, MB

Central - HRM, East Hants, West Hants
Bedford Commons, #115, 30 Damascus Rd., Bedford, NS B4A 0C1
902-424-7773 Fax: 902-424-0597

Eastern - Port Hawkesbury, Sydney
295 Charlotte St., Sydney, NS B1P 6H7
902-563-2100 Fax: 902-563-2387

Regional Director, Roger Munroe
902-563-2100, Fax: 902-563-2387

Eastern - Richmond Co., Southern Inverness, Mulgrave, Auld's Cove
#12, 218 MacSween St., Port Hawkesbury, NS B9A 2J9
902-625-0791 Fax: 902-625-3722

District Manager, Terry MacPherson

Northern - Amherst, Antigosh, Truro, Pictou
#3, 36 Inglis Place, 2nd Fl., PO Box 824, Truro, NS B2N 5G6
902-667-6205 Fax: 902-667-6214

Northern - Antigosh, Guysborough Counties
#205, 155 Main St., Antigosh, NS B2N 2B6
902-667-6205 Fax: 902-667-6214

District Manager, Paul Keats

Northern - Colchester County
902-667-6205 Fax: 902-667-6214

District Manager, Wayne Faulkner

Northern - Cumberland County
71 East Victoria St., Amherst, NS B4H 1X7
902-667-6205 Fax: 902-667-6214

District Manager, Brad Skinner

Northern - Colchester County
20 Pumphouse Rd., RR3, New Glasgow, NS B2H 5C6
902-396-4194 Fax: 902-396-4765

District Manager, Penny McLeod

Western - Bridgewater, Kentville, Yarmouth
136 Exhibition St., Kentville, NS B4N 4E5
902-679-6088 Fax: 902-679-6186

Regional Director, Adrian Fuller
District Manager, Jennifer Lonergan

Western - Digby, Yarmouth & Shelburne Counties
13 First St., Yarmouth, NS B5A 1S9
902-742-8985 Fax: 902-742-7796

Western - Lunenberg & Queens Counties
60 Logan Rd., Bridgewater, NS B4V 3J8
902-543-4685 Fax: 902-527-5480

District Manager, Kristen Martell

Canada Post Receiving Agents:

Acton
53 Bower St., Acton, ON L7J 1E0
519-853-0410

Ancaster
27 Legend Court, Ancaster, ON L9K 1J0
866-607-6301

Anjou
7200 rue Joseph-Renaud, Anjou, QC H1K 3W0
866-607-6310

Aurora
20 Wellington St. East, Aurora, ON L4G 1H0
866-607-6301

Barrie
150 Collier St., Barrie, ON L4M 1G0
866-607-6301

Belleville
Station Main, 21 College St. West, #D, Belleville, ON K8N 3B0
613-968-3599

Boucherville
131 rue Jacques-Ménard, Boucherville, QC J4B 5B0
450-655-5782

Bracebridge
98 Manitoba St., Bracebridge, ON P1L 1A0
705-645-9955

Bradford
50 Barrie St., PO Box L3Z 1A0, Bradford, ON
905-775-3002

Brantford
58 Dalhousie St., Brantford, ON N3T 2J0
866-607-6301

Brossard
10 Place du Commerce, Brossard, QC J4W 4T0
866-607-6301

Cap Rouge
#122, 1100 de la Chaudiere Blvd., Cap-Rouge, QC G1Y 1C0
418-651-4194

Charlottetown
135 Kent St., Charlottetown, PE C1A 1M0
902-628-4400

Chatham
120 Wellington St. West, Chatham, ON N7M 4V0
519-352-1310

Georgetown
112 Guelph St., Georgetown, ON L7G 3Z0
905-877-1917

Guelph
88 Wyndham St. North, Guelph, ON N1H 4E0
519-822-3537

Kanata
145 Roland Michener Dr., Kanata, ON K2T 1G0
905-607-6301

Kelowna
Banks Centre Retail Post Office, 2453 Hwy. 97 North, Kelowna, BC V1X 4J0
866-607-6301

Kingston
120 Clarence St., Kingston, ON K7L 1X0
613-530-2260

Kirkland
16997 Aut. Transcanadienne, Kirkland, QC H9H 5J0
866-607-6301

Lasalle
7565 Newman Blvd., Lasalle, QC H8N 2X0
866-607-6301

Lévis
4870 de la Rive-Sud boul, Lévis, QC G6V 3P0
866-607-6301

Markham
21 Main St. North, Markham, ON L3P 1X0
866-607-6301

Midland
525 Dominion Ave., Midland, ON L4R 1P0
705-526-5571

Moncton
281 St. George St., Moncton, NB E1C 1H0
506-857-7258

North Bay
101 Worthington Ave., North Bay, ON P1B 1H0
866-607-6301

Oakville
193 Church St., Oakville, ON L6J 1N0
866-607-6301

Orangeville
216 Broadway Ave., Orangeville, ON L9W 1L0
519-941-1160

Orillia
25 Peter St. North, Orillia, ON L3V 4Y0
705-327-2918

Ottawa
1424 Sanford Fleming Ave., Ottawa, ON K1G 1C0
866-607-6301

Ottawa - Riverside Dr.
2701 Riverside Dr., Ottawa, ON K1A 0B1
613-734-4338

Owen Sound
901 3rd Ave. East, Owen Sound, ON N4K 2K0
519-371-5028

Peterborough
150 King St., Peterborough, ON K9J 2R0
705-743-7705

Pickering
1740 Kingston Rd., Pickering, ON L1V 1C0
866-607-6301

Pointe-Claire
15 Donegani Ave., Pointe-Claire, QC H9R 2V0
866-607-6301

Prince George
1323 - 5th Ave., Prince George, BC V2L 3L0
866-607-6301

Québec - Galleries de la Capitale
#119, 5401, boul Des Galleries, Québec, QC G2K 1A0
866-607-6301

Québec - Haute-Ville
5, rue Dufort, Québec, QC G1R 2J0
866-607-6301

Québec
Succ. Québec Centre, 710 rue Bouvier, #145, Québec, QC G2J 1C0
866-607-6301

Rimouski
136 St-Germain St. West, Rimouski, QC G5L 4B0
418-725-7378

Saint Bruno
50 de la Rabastalière St. West, Saint Bruno, QC J3V 1Y0
450-441-1583

Saint John
125 Rothesay Ave., Saint John, NB E2L 2B0
866-607-6301

Sarnia
105 Christina St. South, Sarnia, ON N7T 2M0
519-344-1644

Sault-Sainte-Marie
451 Queen St. East, Sault Ste Marie, ON P6A 1Z0
866-607-6301

Sherbrooke
50 Place de la Cité, Sherbrooke, QC H1H 4G0
819-823-9449

Stratford
75 Waterloo St. South, Stratford, ON N5A 4A0
866-607-6301

Sudbury - Lasalle Blvd.
1776 Lasalle Blvd., Sudbury, ON P3A 2A0
866-607-6301

Sudbury - Lisgar St.
1 Lisgar St., Sudbury, ON P3E 3L0
866-607-6301

Summerside
57 Central St., Summerside, PE C1N 3K0
902-436-5852

Sydney
269 Charlotte St., Sydney, NS B1P 1T0
866-607-6301

Toronto
2384 Yonge St., Toronto, ON M4P 2E0
866-607-6301

Trois-Rivières
1285 Notre Dame St., Trois-Rivières, QC G9A 4X0
819-691-4215

Uxbridge
67 Brock St. West, Uxbridge, ON L9P 1A0
905-852-7231

Woodstock
433 Norwich Ave., Woodstock, ON N4S 3W0
866-607-6301

Yarmouth
15 Willow St., Yarmouth, NS B5A 1T0
902-742-4221

Abbotsford
32525 Simon Ave., Abbotsford, BC
TTY: 800-926-9105

Ajax
274 Mackenzie Ave., Ajax, ON
TTY: 800-926-9105

Amherst
#202, 26-28 Prince Arthur St., Amherst, NS
TTY: 800-926-9105

Asbestos
#204, 309 Chase St., Asbestos, QC
TTY: 800-926-9105

Service Canada Receiving Agents:

Baie Comeau
#204, Laflèche Blvd. ouest, 2e étage, Baie-Comeau, QC
TTY: 800-926-9105

Barrie
48 Owen St., Barrie, ON
TTY: 800-926-9105

Bedford
1597 Bedford Hwy., 2nd Fl., Bedford, NS
TTY: 800-926-9105

Bracebridge
Federal Building, 98 Manitoba St., 2nd Fl., Bracebridge, ON
TTY: 800-926-9105

Brandon
#100, 1039 Princess Ave., Brandon, MB

Bridgewater
77 Dufferin St., Bridgewater, NS
TTY: 800-926-9105

Brockville
The Fuller Building, 14 Courthouse Ave., Brockville', ON
TTY: 800-926-9105

Brooks
#608, 2 St. West, Brooks, AB
TTY: 800-926-9105

Brossard
2501 Lapinere Blvd., Brossard, QC
TTY: 800-926-9105

Burnaby
#100, 3480 Gilmore Way, Burnaby, BC
TTY: 800-926-9105

Calgary (East)
Marlborough Mall, #1502, 515 Marlborough Way NE, Calgary, AB
TTY: 800-926-9105

Calgary (North)
One Executive Place, 1816 Crowchild Trail NW, Calgary, AB
TTY: 800-926-9105

Calgary (South)
Fisher Park Place II, #100, 6712 Fisher St. SE, Calgary, AB
TTY: 800-926-9105

Campbellton
157 Water St., Campbellton, NB
TTY: 800-926-9105

Cambridge Bay
PO Box 2010, Cambridge Bay, NU

Campbellton
157 Water St., Campbellton, NB

Canmore
Canmore Gateway Shops, #113, 802 Bow Valley Trail, Building C, Canmore, AB
TTY: 800-926-9105

Charlottetown
Jean Canfield Government of Canada Building, 191 University Ave., Charlottetown, PE
TTY: 800-926-9105

Chibougamau
623, 3e rue, Chibougamau, QC
TTY: 800-926-9105

Chicoutimi
100 Lafontaine Ave., Chicoutimi, QC
TTY: 800-926-9105

Chilliwack
45860 Cheam Ave., Chilliwack, BC
TTY: 800-926-9105

Coaticook
#300, 14 Adams St., Coaticook, QC
TTY: 800-926-9105

Collingwood
44 Hurontario St., Collingwood, ON
TTY: 800-926-9105

Coquitlam
#100, 2963 Glen Drive, Coquitlam, BC
TTY: 800-926-9105

Corner Brook
1 Regent Sq., Corner Brook, NL

Cornwall
#100, 111 Water St. East, Cornwall, ON
TTY: 800-926-9105

Courtenay
130-19th St., Courtenay, BC
TTY: 800-926-9105

Cowansville
224 South St., 2nd Fl., Cowansville, QC
TTY: 800-926-9105

Cranbrook
1113 Baker St., Cranbrook, BC
TTY: 800-926-9105

Drummondville
1525 Saint-Joseph Blvd., Drummondville, QC
TTY: 800-926-9105

Edmonton Meadowlark
Meadowlark Shopping Centre, #120, 15710 87th Ave. NW, Edmonton, AB

Edmonton Millbourne
148 Millbourne Market Mall, 38 Ave. & Millwoods Rd., Edmonton, AB

Edmonton North
Northgate Centre, #2000, 9499 137th Ave. NW, Edmonton, AB
TTY: 800-926-9105

Edmundston
Federal Building, 22 Emmerson St., Edmundston, NB
TTY: 800-926-9105

Edson
4905 4th Ave., Edson, AB
TTY: 800-926-9105

Elliot Lake
Algo Centre, 151 Ontario Ave., Upper Mall, Elliot Lake, ON
TTY: 800-926-9105

Espanola
#200, 721 Centre St., Espanola, ON
TTY: 800-926-9105

Estevan
1314 3rd St., Estevan, SK
TTY: 800-926-9105

Flin Flon
111 Main St., Flin Flon, MB

Fort Frances
301 Scott St., Fort Frances, ON
TTY: 800-926-9105

Fort McMurray
Provincial Bldg., Main Fl., 9915 Franklin Ave., Fort McMurray, AB

Fort Simpson
9606 - 100 St., Fort Simpson, NT

Fort Smith
136 McDougal Rd., Fort Smith, NT

Gander
1 Markham Pl., Gander, NL

Gaspé
Frederica-Giroux Building, 98 de la Reine St., Gaspé, QC
TTY: 800-926-9105

Georgetown
232 Guelph St., Georgetown, ON
TTY: 800-926-9105

Glace Bay
Senator's Place, #100, 633 Main St., Glace Bay, NS
TTY: 800-926-9105

Grand Falls (Grand-Sault)
#100, 441 Madawaska Rd., Grand Falls (Grand-Sault), NB
TTY: 800-926-9105

Grand Prairie
Town Centre Mall, #100, 9845 99th Ave., Grand Prairie, AB
TTY: 800-926-9105

Happy Valley
23 Broomfield St., Jau Valley-Goose Bay, NL

Hawkesbury
134 Main St. East, Hawkesbury, ON
TTY: 800-926-9105

Hay River
#204, 41 Capital Dr., Hay River, NT

Inuvik
170 McKenzie Rd., Inuvik, NT

Iqaluit
#300, Iqaluit House, Iqaluit, NU

Kamloops
317 Seymour St., Kamloops, BC
TTY: 800-926-9105

Kapuskasing
8 Queen St., Kapuskasing, ON
TTY: 800-926-9105

Kelowna
471 Queensway Ave., Kelowna, BC
TTY: 800-926-9105

Kentville
Federal Building, 495 Main St., 2nd Fl., Kentville, NS
TTY: 800-926-9105

Kenora
308 Second St., Kenora, ON
TTY: 800-926-9105

Labrador City
500 Vanier Ave., Labrador City, NL

Langley
#202, 8747 204th St., Langley, BC
TTY: 800-926-9105

7655 Newman Blvd.
7655 Newman Blvd., Lasalle, QC
TTY: 800-926-9105

La Tuque
290, rue St-Joseph, La Tuque, QC
TTY: 800-926-9105

Lethbridge
Crowsnest Trail Plaza, #101, 920 2A Ave. North, Lethbridge, AB

Lloydminster
5016 48th St., Lloydminster, AB
TTY: 800-926-9105

Longueuil
#100, 1195 Du Tremblay Rd., Longueuil, QC
TTY: 800-926-9105

Magog
100A, 1700 Sherbrooke St., Magog, QC
TTY: 800-926-9105

Maple Ridge
22325 Lougheed Hwy., Maple Ridge, BC
TTY: 800-926-9105

Marystown
#130, 140 Ville Marie Dr., Marystown, NL

Medicine Hat
78 8th St. NW, Medicine Hat, AB

Melfort
104 McKendry Plaza, Melfort, SK
TTY: 800-926-9105

Miramichi
150 Pleasant St., Miramichi, NB
TTY: 800-926-9105

Moncton
Heritage Court, #310, 95 Foundry St., Moncton, NB
TTY: 800-926-9105

Montague
541 Main St., Montague, PE
TTY: 800-926-9105

Montréal
5455 Chauvreau St., Montréal, QC
TTY: 800-926-9105

Moose Jaw
Victoria Place, #501, 111 Fairford St. E., Moose Jaw, SK
TTY: 800-926-9105

Morden
158 Stephen St., Morden, MB

Nanaimo
#201, 60 Front St., Nanaimo, BC
TTY: 800-926-9105

Nelson
Kutenai Building, 333 Victoria St., Nelson, BC
TTY: 800-926-9105

New Liskeard
290 Armstrong St. North, New Liskeard, ON
TTY: 800-926-9105

Newmarket
1-18183 Yonge St., East Gwillimbury, Newmarket, ON
TTY: 800-926-9105

New Westminster
#201, 620 Royal Ave., New Westminster, BC
TTY: 800-926-9105

North Vancouver
#100, 221 West Esplanade, North Vancouver, BC
TTY: 800-926-9105

North Battleford
9800 Territorial Dr., North Battleford, SK
TTY: 800-926-9105

Notre-Dame-de-Lourdes
51 Rodgers St., Notre Dame de Lourdes, MB

Oakville
#B5, 117 Cross Ave., Oakville, ON
TTY: 800-926-9105

Orangeville
#102, 210 Broadway Ave., Orangeville, ON
TTY: 800-926-9105

Oshawa
Midtown Mall, #C6, 200 John St. West, Oshawa, ON
TTY: 800-926-9105

Ottawa (East)
2339 Ogilvie Rd., Ottawa, ON
TTY: 800-926-9105

Ottawa (West)
Lincoln Heights Galleria, 2525 Carling Ave., Ottawa, ON
TTY: 800-926-9105

Owen Sound
Heritage Place Shopping Centre, 1350 16th St. East, Owen Sound, ON
TTY: 800-926-9105

Parry Sound
74 James St., Parry Sound, ON
TTY: 800-926-9105

The Pas
Government of Canada Building, 305 4th St. West, The Pas, MB

Pembroke
141 Lake St., Pembroke, ON
TTY: 800-926-9105

Penticton
#101, 386 Ellis St., Penticton, BC
TTY: 800-926-9105

Peterborough
#101, 185 King St., Peterborough, ON
TTY: 800-926-9105

Placentia
Dalfens Mall, 61 Blockhouse Rd., Placentia, NL

Powell River
7061 Duncan St., Powell River, BC
TTY: 800-926-9105

Prince George
1363-4th Ave., Prince George, BC
TTY: 800-926-9105

Rankin Inlet
PO Box 97, Rankin Inlet, NU

Red Deer
First Red Deer Place, 4911 51st St., 2nd Fl., Red Deer, AB
TTY: 800-926-9105

Regina
1783 Hamilton St., Regina, SK
TTY: 800-926-9105

Repentigny
#54, 155 Notre-Dame St., Repentigny, QC
TTY: 800-926-9105

Richmond Hill
35 Beresford Dr., Richmond Hill, ON
TTY: 800-926-9105

Rouyn-Noranda
Réal Caouette Building, #300, 151 du Lac Avenue, Rouyn-Noranda, QC
TTY: 800-926-9105

Saint-Hyacinthe
Galerie St-Hyacinthe Shopping Mall, #2550, 3225 Cusson Ave., 2nd Fl., Saint-Hyacinthe, QC
TTY: 800-926-9105

Saint John
1 Agar Place, Saint John, NB
TTY: 800-926-9105

Saint-Quentin
193 Canada St., Saint-Quentin, NB
TTY: 800-926-9105

Salmon Arm
191 Shuswap St. NW, Salmon Arm, BC
TTY: 800-926-9105

Sault-Sainte-Marie
Sault-Sainte-Marie, ON
TTY: 800-926-9105

St. Anthony
Viking Mall, 1 Goose Cove Rd., St. Anthony, NL

St. Stephen
Canada Post Building, 93 Milltown Blvd., St. Stephen, NB
TTY: 800-926-9105

Sept-Iles
701 Laure Blvd., 3rd Fl., Sept-Iles, QC
TTY: 800-926-9105

Sherbrooke
124 Wellington St. North, Sherbrooke, QC
TTY: 800-926-9105

Souris
IGA Mall, 173 Main St., 2nd Fl., Souris, PE
TTY: 800-926-9105

Steinbach
321 Main St., Steinbach, MB
TTY: 800-926-9105

Summerside
Government of Canada Building, 294 Church St., Summerside, PE
TTY: 800-926-9105

Terrace
4630 Lazelle Ave., Terrace, BC

Thetford Mines
#500, 250 Frontenac Blvd. West, Thetford Mines, QC
TTY: 800-926-9105

Thompson
#118, 3 Station Rd., Thompson, MB

Timmins
120 Cedar St. South, Timmins, ON
TTY: 800-926-9105

Toronto (Centre)
Arthur Meighen, 25 St. Clair Ave. East, Toronto, ON
TTY: 800-926-9105

Toronto (Lakeside)
Dufferin Mall, #0001, 900 Dufferin St., Toronto, ON
TTY: 800-926-9105

Toronto (Lawrence Square)
Lawrence Square Mall, #103-105, 700 Lawrence Ave. West, Toronto, ON
TTY: 800-926-9105

Trois-Rivières
Le Bourg du Fleuve, 55 Des Forges St., Trois-Rivières, QC
TTY: 800-926-9105

Val d'Or
400 Central Ave., Val-d'Or, QC
TTY: 800-926-9105

Valleyfield
#100, 73 Maden St., Valleyfield, QC
TTY: 800-926-9105

Vancouver
Harry Stevens Building, 125 10th Ave. East, Vancouver, BC
TTY: 800-926-9105

Verdun
4110 Wellington St., 2nd Fl., Montréal, QC
TTY: 800-926-9105

Victoria
595 Pandora Ave., Victoria, BC
TTY: 800-926-9105

Whitehorse
#125, 300 Main St., Whitehorse, YT
TTY: 800-926-9105

Woodstock
Canada Post Building, 680 Main St. East, Woodstock, NB
TTY: 800-926-9105

Yellowknife
5101 - 50th Ave., Yellowknife, NT
TTY: 800-926-9105

Yorkton
214 Smith St. East, Yorkton, SK

International Trade Canada (ITCan) / Commerce international Canada
125 Sussex Dr., Ottawa, ON K1A 0G2
613-944-4000

International Trade Canada works to position Canada as a business leader for the 21st century. ITCan helps large & small Canadian companies expand & succeed internationally, promotes Canada as a dynamic place to do business, & negotiates & administers trade agreements.

Deputy Minister, Louis Lévesque
613-944-5000, Fax: 613-944-8493, Other Communications: Secure Phone: 613-944-5000; Secure Fax: 613-944-0204
Acting Assistant Deputy Minister & Chief Financial Officer, Robert Dufresne
613-943-4811
Assistant Deputy Minister, Human Resources, Susan Gregson
613-996-5369, Fax: 613-944-2411
Legal Adviser, Alan Kessel
613-995-8901, Fax: 613-944-0845
Inspector General, Angela Bogdan
613-944-1931
Director General, Corporate Secretariat, Roxanne Dubé
613-944-2336, Fax: 613-943-6584

Global Operations
125 Sussex Dr,, Ottawa, ON K1A 0G2
613-944-2697 Fax: 613-996-1667

Assistant Deputy Minister, Americas, Jon Allen
613-944-6183, Fax: 613-944-0561
Assistant to the Deputy Minister, Sophie Gauthier
613-944-5547
Assistant Deputy Minister, Asia, Peter McGovern
613-944-2695, Fax: 613-944-2679
Assistant Deputy Minister, Europe, Eurasia & Africa, Jillian Stirk
613-996-5095, Fax: 613-944-1471
Assistant Deputy Minister, Afghanistan, Middle East & Maghreb, Gordon Venner
613-943-3660
Director General, Trade Commissioner Service - Operations, Louise Leger
613-944-1678

Director, Middle East, Maghred & Africa Commercial Relations Division, James K. Hill
613-944-2589

International Business Development, Investment & Innovation
111 Sussex Dr., Ottawa, ON K1N 1J1
Fax: 613-944-3178
Assistant Deputy Minister, Ian Burney
613-944-3122, Fax: 613-944-3178
Director General, International Trade Strategy & Portfolio Bureau, Robert Clark
613-992-7979
Director General, Global Business Opportunities, Peter MacArthur
613-996-1745
Director General, Invest in Canada, Danielle Thibault
613-996-2213, Fax: 613-944-3312

Trade Policy & Negotiations / Politique commercial et negociations
111 Sussex Dr., Ottawa, ON K1N 1J1
613-996-5677 Fax: 613-996-1667
Director General, Matthew Kronby
613-943-2803, Fax: 613-944-0027
Chief Air Negotiator & Director General, Robert Ready
613-944-1116, Fax: 613-944-0023
General Counsel, Trade Law Bureau, Tom J. Zuijdwijk
613-992-7785, Fax: 613-944-0027
Director, Investment & Services Law Division, Sylvie T. Tabet
613-944-0027, Fax: 613-944-1590
Director, Market Access & Trade Remedies Law Division, Cynthia A. Westaway
613-944-3046, Fax: 613-944-0027

Trade Law Bureau
125 Sussex Dr., Ottawa, ON K1A 0G2
613-943-2804 Fax: 613-944-0027
Assistant Deputy Minister, Don Stephenson
613-992-0293, Fax: 613-996-1667
Director General, North America Trade Policy Bureau, Laurent Cardinal
613-944-0462, Fax: 613-944-0231, Other Communications: Secure Phone: 613-944-0462
Director General, Trade Negotiations Bureau, Anne McCaskill
613-944-2002, Secure Fax: 613-944-0757
Director, Dennis G. Seebach
613-944-3159
Deputy Director, Regional / Bilateral Services Trade Policy, Colin Barker
613-996-7168
Deputy Director, Regional / Bilateral Services Trade Policy, Vincent Sacchetti
613-994-1484
Chief Trade Negotiator, Canadian-European Union, Steve Verheul
613-944-5880, Fax: 613-947-7483

Americas Strategy
125 Sussex Dr., Ottawa, ON K1A 0G2
Assistant Deputy Minister, Latin America & Caribbean, Alex Bugailiskis
613-944-1909
Special Advisor, Randolph Harwood
613-996-1427

International Trade Centres:

Calgary
#400, 639 - 5 Ave. SW, Calgary, AB T2P 0M9
403-292-4529 Fax: 403-292-4578
itc-calgary@ic.gc.ca
www.tradecommissioner.gc.ca/alta
Trade Commissioner, Barry Schlinker
403-292-4509, Fax: 403-292-4578

Charlottetown
191 University Ave., Charlottetown, PE C1A 4L2
902-566-7382 Fax: 902-566-7450
itc-charlottetown@ic.gc.ca
www.tradeteampei.com
Senior Trade Commissioner, Bernard Postma
902-566-7426, Fax: 613-566-6859

Edmonton
Canada Place, #725, 9700 Jasper Ave., Edmonton, AB T5J 4C3
780-495-2944 Fax: 780-495-4507
edmtn@international.gc.ca
www.tradecommissioner.gc.ca/alta
Director & Senior Trade Commissioner, PNR, Anthony Knill
780-495-3329
Senior Trade Commissioner, Tara Scheurwater
780-495-4415

Halifax
1791 Barrington St., 11th Fl., Halifax, NS B3J 3L1
902-426-7540 Fax: 902-426-5218
itc-halifax@ic.gc.ca
www.tradecommisioner.gc.ca/ns
Senior Trade Commissioner, Christine Smith
902-426-6660, Other Communications: Secure Fax: 902-426-5218

Montréal
#8750, 800, rue de la Gauchetiere ouest, Montréal, QC H3B 2G2
514-283-6328 Fax: 514-283-8794
mntrl@international.gc.ca
www.tradecommissioner.gc.ca/qc
Acting Deputy Director & Trade Commissioner, Michel Lamarre
514-283-6328, Fax: 514-283-8794
Director, Marcel Lebleu
613-996-3024

New Brunswick
#104, 1045 Main St., Moncton, NB E1C 1H1
506-851-6452 Fax: 506-851-6429
800-332-3801
itc-moncton@ic.gc.ca
www.ttnb.ca
Director & Senior Trade Commissioner, Michelyne Paulin
506-851-6440, Fax: 506-851-6429

Regina
#320, 1801 Hamilton St., Regina, SK S4P 3N9
306-780-5264 Fax: 306-780-8797
itc-regina@ic.gc.ca
www.canadabusiness.ca
Senior Trade Commissioner, Mona M. Taylor
306-780-6124, Fax: 306-780-8797

Saskatoon
Princeton Tower, 123 - 2nd Ave. South, 7th Fl., Saskatoon, SK S7K 7E6
306-975-5315 Fax: 306-975-5334
itc-saskatoon@ic.gc.ca
www.canadabusiness.ca
Trade Commissioner, Meghan Cross
306-975-4336, Fax: 306-975-5334

St. John's
John Cabot Bldg., Phase II, 10 Barter's HIll, 10th Fl., PO Box 8950, St. John's, NL A1B 3R9
709-772-5511 Fax: 709-772-2373
itc-stjohns@ic.gc.ca
www.canadabusiness.ca/eng/
Senior Trade Commissioner, Anthony McLevey
709-772-4910, Fax: 613-772-2373

Toronto
Yonge-Richmond Centre, 151 Yonge St., 4th Fl., Toronto, ON M5C 2W7
416-973-5053 Fax: 416-973-8161
itc-toronto@ic.gc.ca
www.tradecommisioner.gc.ca/ont
Director & Senior Trade Commissioner, Jim Feir
416-954-6326, Fax: 416-973-8161

Vancouver
#2000, 300 West Georgia St., Vancouver, BC V6B 6E1
604-666-0434 Fax: 604-666-0954
vncvr@international.gc.ca
www.bctradeevents.com
Regional Director & Senior Trade Commissioner, Dr. Anna Biolik
604-666-8888

Winnipeg
400 St. Mary Ave., 4th Fl., Winnipeg, MB R3C 4K5
204-983-4540 Fax: 204-983-3182
itc-winnipeg@ic.gc.ca
www.gov.mb.ca/trade/index.html
Johnson Qi
204-983-2594

Freshwater Fish Marketing Corporation / Office de commercialisation du poisson d'eau douce

1199 Plessis Rd., Winnipeg, MB R2C 3L4
204-983-6601 Fax: 204-983-6497
sandi.cain@freshwaterfish.com
www.freshwaterfish.com
The Corporation is a buyer, processor & marketer of freshwater fish, harvested from over 400 lakes in Manitoba, Saskatchewan, Alberta, the Northwest Territories & Northwestern Ontario. Reports to the government through the Minister of Fisheries & Oceans.
President/CEO, John Wood
CFO, Stan Lazar

Great Lakes Pilotage Authority / Administration de pilotage des Grands Lacs

202 Pitt St., 2nd fl., PO Box 95, Cornwall, ON K6H 5R9
613-933-2991 Fax: 613-932-3793
administration@glpa-apgl.com
www.glpa-apgl.com
The Authority provides pilotage services in the waters of the St. Lawrence River commencing at the northern entrance of St. Lambert Lock, the Great Lakes area & the Port of Churchill, Manitoba. Reports to government through the Minister of Transport.
CEO, Robert Lemire, C.A.
rlemire@glpa-apgl.com
Secretary/Treasurer, Réjean Ménard
rmenard@glpa-apgl.com
Administrative Asst., Nancy McAteer
nmcateer@glpa-apgl.com

Regional Offices:

Head Office & Cornwall Dispatch
202 Pitt St., 2nd Fl., Cornwall, ON K6H 5R79
613-933-2991 Fax: 613-932-3793

Thorold Office
Lock 7, Welland Canal, Thorold, ON
905-688-3399 Fax: 905-688-5599

Health Canada / Santé Canada

Tunney's Pasture, Ottawa, ON K1A 0K9
613-957-2991 Fax: 613-941-5366
866-225-0709
info@hc-sc.gc.ca
www.hc-sc.gc.ca
Other Communication: Office of the Access to Information: 613-954-8744
In partnership with provincial & territorial governments, Health Canada (HC) develops health policy, enforces health regulations, promotes disease prevention, & enhances healthy living for all Canadians. HC ensures that health services are available & accessible to First Nations & Inuit communities. It works closely with other federal departments, agencies & health stakeholders to reduce health & safety risks to Canadians. Through its Health Intelligence Network, HC works with other levels of government & the health care system in the surveillance, prevention, control & research of disease outbreaks across Canada & around the world. It also monitors health & safety risks related to the sale & use of drugs, food, chemicals, pesticides, medical devices & certain consumer products. HC negotiates agreements regarding hazardous materials in the workplace, performs medical assessments for pilots & air traffic controllers, & conducts environmental health assessments.
Acts Administered:
Assisted Human Reproduction Act
Canada Health Act
Canada Medical Act
Canadian Centre on Substance Abuse Act
Canadian Institutes of Health Research Act
Controlled Drug Substances Act
Department of Health Act
Financial Administration Act
Fitness & Amateur Sport Act
Food & Drugs Act (Agriculture & Agri-Food Canada)
Hazardous Materials Information Review Act (Human Resources & Skills Development)
Appeal Board Procedures Regulations
Hazardous Material Information Review Regulations
Hazardous Products Act
Consumer Chemicals & Containers Regulations
Controlled Products Regulations
Hazardous Products Regulations (Cellulose Insulation, Charcoal, Crocidolite Asbestos, Liquid Coating Materials, etc.)
Ingredient Disclosure List
Medical Research Council Act
Patent Act
Pest Control Products Act, 2002
Pesticide Residue Compensation Act
Quarantine Act
Queen Elizabeth II Canadian Research Fund Act
Radiation Emitting Devices Act
Tobacco Act
Minister, Health, Hon. Leona Aglukkaq
613-957-0200, Fax: 613-952-1154, aglukkaq.l@parl.gc.ca; minister_ministre@hc-sc.gc.ca
Director, Policy, Leah Canning, 2011-07-15
613-957-0200
Director, Parliamentary Affairs, Andrea Paine, 20110715
613-957-0200
Director, Communications, Tim Vail, 20110715
613-957-0200, Fax: 613-952-1154
Director Of Operations & CanNor, Rossana Whissell, 20110715
613-957-0200

Chief of Staff, Scott Tessier, 20110715
613-957-0200

Associated Agencies, Boards & Commissions:
• Canadian Institutes of Health Research / Instituts de recherche en santé du Canada
• Hazardous Materials Information Review Commission (HMIRC) / Conseil de contrôle des renseignements relatifs aux matières dangereuses
427 Laurier Ave. West, 7th Fl.
Ottawa, ON K1A 1M3
613-993-4331 Fax: 613-993-4686
hmirc-ccrmd@hc-sc.gc.ca
www.hmirc-ccrmd.gc.ca
The HMIRC is an administrative agency charged with carrying out a multi-faceted mandate under the authority of the Hazardous Materials Information Review Act, & provincial & territorial occupational health & safety acts. The mandate includes: formally registering claims for trade-secret exemptions & issuing registry numbers; adjudicating & issuing decisions on the validity of claims for exemption using prescribed regulatory criteria; making decisions on the compliance of material safety data sheets (MSDSs) & labels within the Workplace Hazardous Materials Information System (WHMIS) requirements; & convening independent, tripartite boards to hear appeals from claimants or affected parties on decisions & orders issued by HMIRC. Clients consist of a number of WHMIS stakeholders: suppliers & employers in the chemical industry who wish to protect their trade secrets from being disclosed on MSDSs or labels; employers who rely on supplier MSDS information to prepare their own workplace MSDSs & training programs; & labour organizations representing all workers who are exposed to these products.
• Pest Management Regulatory Agency (PMRA) / Agence de réglementation de la lutte antiparasitaire (ARLA)
2720 Riverside Dr.
Ottawa, ON K1A 0K9
613-736-3401 Fax: 613-736-3798
www.hc-sc.gc.ca/cps-spc/pest/index-eng.php
Other Communication: Pesticides Information: 1-800-267-6315
The PMRA determines if proposed pesticides can be used safely when label directions are followed & will be effective for their intended use. If there is reasonable certainty from scientific evaluation that no harm to human health, future generations or the environment will result from exposure to or use of a pesticide, its registration for use in Canada will be approved. Once the pesticides are on the market, the PMRA monitors their use through a series of education, compliance & enforcement programs. Pesticides are also reviewed every fifteen years or sooner as new information is discovered & as science evolves. Companies are also required to report any incident they receive about their products, just as the public is encouraged to report any incidents to these companies or through the Incident Reporting Program. The PMRA administers the Pest Control Products Act on behalf of the Minister of Health.
• Public Health Agency of Canada / Agence de santé publique du Canada
130 Colonnade Rd.
Ottawa, ON K1A 0K9
www.phac-aspc.gc.ca
Other Communication: Alberta/NWT: 780-495-2754; Atlantic: 902-426-2700; BC/Yukon: 604-666-2729; Manitoba/Saskatchewan: 204-789-2000; Ontario/Nunavut: 416-973-0003; Quebec: 514-283-2858
Promotes & protects the health & safety of all Canadians. Its activities focus on preventing chronic diseases, including cancer & heart disease, preventing injuries, & responding to public health emergencies & infectious disease outbreaks.

Audit & Accountability Bureau (AAB) / Bureau de la vérification et de la responsabilisation (BVR)
613-946-0361 Fax: 613-941-7319
aab-bvr@hc-sc.gc.ca
TTY: 800-267-1245
The AAB provides independent & objective advice & assurance to the Deputy Minister, on the effectiveness of risk management, controls & governance processes.

Chief Financial Officer Branch (CFOB) / Direction générale du contrôleur ministériel (DGCM)
613-957-3889 Fax: 613-952-9660
DPED_DEPM@hc-sc.gc.ca
Other Communication: Management Accountability Division: mcs-sfcm@hc-sc.gc.ca
The CFOB is the departmental focal point of accountability to ensure rigorous stewardship of resources & managing for results. The CFO provides the Minister, Deputy Minister, Associate Deputy Minister & the Departmental Executive with strategic advice on efficiency of expenditures & value-for-money, as well as anticipating & promoting future trends. The CFO reports directly to the Deputy Minister & is a key member of Health Canada's Senior Management Board. The CFO is also the lead executive with Central Agencies for overall financial management, with a functional reporting relationship to the Comptroller General of Canada.
Chief Financial Officer, Jamie Tibbetts, 20110715
613-952-3985, Fax: 613-952-7580,
jamie.tibbetts@hc-sc.gc.ca
Executive Asst. to the ADM, Kateri Beauregard, 20110715
613-952-3984, Fax: 613-952-7580,
kateri.beauregard@hc-sc.gc.ca
Coordinator, Correspondence, Cabinet Affairs & Parliament Relations, Jean Burns, 20110715
613-952-1299, Fax: 613-952-7580, jean.burns@hc-sc.gc.ca
Manager, Correspondence, Cabinet Affairs & Parliament Relations, Roxanne Fraser, 20110715
613-946-6363, Fax: 613-952-7580,
roxanne.fraser@hc-sc.gc.ca
Senior Advisor, Cheryl Larabie, 20110715
613-952-3986, Fax: 613-952-7580,
cheryl.larabie@hc-sc.gc.ca
Special Advisor, Gregory Wright, 20110715
613-952-3987, gregory.wright@hc-sc.gc.ca

Corporate Services Branch (CSB) / Direction générale aux services de gestion
The CSB provides corporate support & services across the Department in the following areas: human resources management; official languages; real property & facilities management; occupational health, safety emergency & security management; information technology & information management; executive correspondence; & access to information & privacy requests/issues.
Asst. Deputy Minister, Kin Choi
613-946-3209, Fax: 613-946-3236, kin.choi@hc-sc.gc.ca
Director, Health Club, Health Club Santé
613-954-5788, Fax: 613-954-3961,
health.club.sante@hc-sc.gc.ca
Director General, Facilities & Security Directorate, Gary Lacey
613-692-6190, Fax: 613-946-0807, gary.lacey@hc-sc.gc.ca
Director, Policy, Planning & Information, Sandi Wright
613-946-3208, Fax: 613-946-0807, sandi.wright@hc-sc.gc.ca
Director General, Human Resources, Gerard Etienne
613-957-3236, Fax: 613-941-1814,
gerard.etienne@hc-sc.gc.ca
Advisor, Human Resources, Leonce Philoctete
613-946-3756, Fax: 613-946-3804,
leonce.philoctete@hc-sc.gc.ca
Senior Business Analyst, Information Services Business Management, Steve Morphy
613-595-1657, Fax: 613-595-1657,
steve.morphy@hc-sc.gc.ca
Project Officer, Information Services Business Management, Manon Allard
613-451-2038, Fax: 613-595-0726,
manon.allard@hc-sc.gc.ca
Acting Director General, Planning, Integration & Management Services, Brenda Baxter
613-946-8132, Fax: 613-957-1587,
brenda.baxter@hc-sc.gc.ca
Project Officer, Planning, Integration & Management Services, Suzane-Renee Collette
613-957-7818, suzane-renee.collette@hc-sc.gc.ca
Executive Director, Solutions Centre, Christiana Cavazzoni
613-595-1371, Fax: 613-595-1822,
christiana.cavazzoni@hc-sc.gc.ca
Team Lead, Solutions Centre, Andrew Nice
613-668-2790, andrew.nice@hc-sc.gc.ca

Deputy Minister's Office / Bureau de la Sous-Ministre
Deputy Minister, Glenda Yeates, 20110718
613-957-0212, Fax: 613-952-8422,
glenda.yeates@hc-sc.gc.ca
Director, Robert Ianiro, 20110718
613-941-2526, robert.ianiro@hc-sc.gc.ca
Assoc. Deputy Minister, Associate Deputy Minister's Office, Anne-Marie Robinson, 20110718
613-954-5904, Fax: 613-952-8422,
anne-marie.robinson@hc-sc.gc.ca
Director General, Associate Deputy Minister's Office, Sony Perron, 20110718
613-941-2567, sony.perron@hc-sc.gc.ca

First Nations & Inuit Health Branch (FNIHB) / Direction générale de la santé des Premières nations et des Inuits (DGSPNI)
Assists First Nations & Inuit communities & people to address health inequalities & diseases threats through health surveillance & population health interventions. Ensures the availability of, or access to, health services for First Nations & Inuit people. Devolves control & management of community-based health services to First Nations & Inuit communities & organizations. The Environmental Health Division addresses conditions in the environment that could affect the health of community members, such as drinking water quality, mould, food safety, facilities inspections, transportation of dangerous goods. The Environmental Research Division conducts, coordinates & funds contaminants-related research, coordinates the replacement or upgrading of diesel-fuel tanks & remediation of fuel oil-contaminated sites, lab services for testing of PCBs & mercury, drinking water-related research & testing.
Asst. Deputy Minister, Michel Roy
613-957-7701, Fax: 613-957-1118, michel.roy@hc-sc.gc.ca
Senior Director General, Debbie L. Reid
613-952-3135, Fax: 613-957-1118, debbie.l.reid@hc-sc.gc.ca
Acting Director, Policy & Operations, Lori Brooks
613-941-4400, lori.brooks@hc-sc.gc.ca
Director General, Business Planning & Management Directorate, Stephane Hardy
613-946-8853, Fax: 613-948-4307,
stephane.hardy@hc-sc.gc.ca
Director General, Community Programs, Kathy Langlois
613-952-9616, Fax: 613-941-3170,
kathy.langlois@hc-sc.gc.ca
Acting Director General, Non-Insured Health Benefits, Scott Doidge
613-954-8825, Fax: 613-954-5265, scott.doidge@hc-sc.gc.ca
Executive Director, Office of Community Medicine, Dr. RoseMarie Ramsingh
613-941-5358, Fax: 613-952-6407,
rosemarie.ramsingh@hc-sc.gc.ca
Acting Executive Director, Office of Nursing Services, Dorothy Laplante
613-946-0442, Fax: 613-957-9986,
dorothy.laplante@hc-sc.gc.ca
Chief Dental Officer, Office of the Chief Dental Officer, Peter Cooney, 20110718
613-941-4748, Fax: 613-957-3687,
peter.cooney@hc-sc.gc.ca
Director, Primary Health Care & Public Health, Shelagh Jane Woods, 20110718
613-941-1956, Fax: 613-941-8904,
shelagh.jane.woods@hc-sc.gc.ca
Director, Environmental Public Health, Primary Health Care & Public Health, Ivy Chan, 20110718
613-948-7773, Fax: 613-952-8639, ivy.chan@hc-sc.gc.ca
Director, Environmental Health Research, Primary Health Care & Public Health, Roy Kwiatkowski
613-952-2828, Fax: 613-954-0692,
roy.kwiatkowski@hc-sc.gc.ca
Director General, Strategic Policy, Planning & Analysis, Valerie Gideon, 20110718
613-957-3402, valerie.gideon@hc-sc.gc.ca
Director, Strategic Relations, Strategic Policy, Planning & Analysis, Paul McKinstry, 20110718
204-983-0989, Fax: 204-983-0079,
paul.mckinstry@hc-sc.gc.ca

Health Canada Regulations / Section de la réglementation
Fax: 613-954-4627
General Counsel & Director, Claude Lesage, 20110718
613-952-9645, Fax: 613-954-4627,
claude.lesage@hc-sc.gc.ca
Senior Counsel, Wendy Gordon, 20110718
613-954-4761, Fax: 613-954-4627,
wendy.gordon@hc-sc.gc.ca

Health Products & Food Branch (HPFB) / Direction générale des produits de santé et des aliments (DGPSA)
HPFB's mandate is to take an integrated approach to the management of risks & benefits related to health products & food by minimizing health factors to Canadians while maximizing the safety provided by the regulatory system for health products & food; & to promote conditions that enable Canadians to make healthy choices & provide information so that they can make informed decisions about their health. The Environmental Impact Initiative develops strategy & policy in response to the Canadian Environmental Protection Act requirement that all new substances for use in Canada must be assessed for direct & indirect impact on human health & the environment.
Asst. Deputy Minister, Paul Glover
613-957-1804, Fax: 613-957-3954, paul.glover@hc-sc.gc.ca
Assoc. Asst. Deputy Minister, Catherine MacLeod
613-957-6817, Fax: 613-957-3954,
catherine.macleod@hc-sc.gc.ca
Director General, Biologics & Genetic Therapies Directorate, Elwyn Griffiths
613-957-8065, Fax: 613-957-1679,
elwyn.griffiths@hc-sc.gc.ca
Director General, Food Directorate, Dr. Samuel Godefroy
613-957-1821, Fax: 613-954-4674,
samuel.godefroy@hc-sc.gc.ca
Director General, Marketed Health Products Directorate, Dr. Chris Turner
613-941-8889, Fax: 613-952-7738, chris.turner@hc-sc.gc.ca
Director General, Natural Health Products, Scott Sawler
613-952-2558, Fax: 613-948-6810, scott.sawler@hc-sc.gc.ca
Director General, Office of Consumer & Public Involvement, Lucie Desforges, 20110718
613-948-8431, lucie.desforges@hc-sc.gc.ca
Director General, Office of Nutrition Policy & Promotion, Dr. Hasan Hutchinson
613-957-8330, Fax: 613-946-8073,
hasan.hutchinson@hc-sc.gc.ca

Director General, Policy, Planning & International Affairs Directorate, Kendal Weber
613-952-8149, Fax: 613-954-9981, kendal.weber@hc-sc.gc.ca
Director General, Therapeutic Products Directorate, Dr. Supriya Sharma
613-957-6466, Fax: 613-952-7756, supriya.sharma@hc-sc.gc.ca
Director General, Veterinary Drugs Directorate, Daniel Chaput
613-954-1873, Fax: 613-954-5694, daniel.chaput@hc-sc.gc.ca

Health Environments & Consumer Safety (HECSB) / Direction générale, santé environnementale et sécurité des consommateurs (DGSESC)

The HECSB mission is to help Canadians to maintain & improve their health by promoting healthy & safe living, working & recreational environments & by reducing the harm caused by tobacco, alcohol, controlled substances, environmental contaminants, & unsafe consumer & industrial products.

Asst. Deputy Minister, Hilary Geller, 20110718
613-946-6701, Fax: 613-946-6666, hilary.geller@hc-sc.gc.ca
Director General, Consumer Product Safety, Athana Mentzelopoulos, 20110718
613-960-4725, Fax: 613-946-1100, athana.mentzelopoulos@hc-sc.gc.ca
Director General, Controlled Substances & Tobacco, Cathy A. Sabiston, 20110718
613-941-1977, Fax: 613-946-6460, cathy.a.sabiston@hc-sc.gc.ca
Director General, Environmental & Radiation Health Sciences, Beth Pieterson, 20110718
613-954-3859, beth.pieterson@hc-sc.gc.ca
Director, Planning & Administrative Services, Policy, Planning & Integration, Wendy Kiernan, 20110718
613-941-3137, Fax: 613-941-8632, wendy.kiernan@hc-sc.gc.ca
Director, Planning & Administrative Services, Safe Environments, Karen Lloyd, 20110718
613-954-0291, Fax: 613-952-2206, karen.lloyd@hc-sc.gc.ca

Legal Services / Services juridiques

www.hc-sc.gc.ca/ahc-asc/branch-dirgen/ls-sj/index-eng.php
Senior General Counsel; Head, Legal Services, Irit Weiser, 20110718
613-957-3766, Fax: 613-954-9485, irit.weiser@hc-sc.gc.ca
Director, Planning & Operations, Steven Blake, 20110718
613-941-5343, steven.blake@hc-sc.gc.ca

Pest Management Regulatory Agency (PMRA) / Agence de réglementation de la lutte antiparasitaire (ARLA)

The PMRA is responsible for pesticide regulation in Canada. Created in 1995, this branch of Health Canada consolidates the resources & responsibilities for pest management regulation. Pesticides are stringently regulated in Canada to ensure they pose minimal risk to human health & the environment. Health Canada also promotes & verifies compliance with the Act & enforces situations of non compliance warranting action.

Executive Director, Richard Aucoin, 20110718
613-736-3701, Fax: 613-736-3707, richard.aucoin@hc-sc.gc.ca
Director General, Compliance, Lab Services & Regional Operations, Dr. Martin Tomkin, 20110718
613-736-3484, Fax: 613-736-3540, martin.tomkin@hc-sc.gc.ca
Director General, Environmental Assessment, Mary Mitchell, 20110718
613-736-3715, mary.mitchell@hc-sc.gc.ca
Director General, Health Evaluation, Dr. Peter Chan, PhD, 20110718
613-736-3510, Fax: 613-736-3909, peter.chan@hc-sc.gc.ca
Director General, Policy, Communications & Regulatory Affairs, Trish MacQuarrie, 20110718
613-736-3660, Fax: 613-736-3659, trish.macquarrie@hc-sc.gc.ca
Director General, Re-evaluation Management, Margherita Conti, 20110718
613-736-3485, Fax: 613-736-9840, margherita.conti@hc-sc.gc.ca
Director, Strategic Planning, Financial & Business Operations, Anne Lapierre, 20110718
613-736-3411, anne.lapierre@hc-sc.gc.ca
Director General, Value & Sustainability Assessment, John Worgan, 20110718
613-736-3780, Fax: 613-736-3770, john.worgan@hc-sc.gc.ca

Public Affairs, Consultation & Communications (PACCB) / Direction générale des affaires publiques, de la consultation et des communications (DGAPCC)

The PACCB integrates national & regional perspectives into all of its policies & strategies, communications & consultation functions. The Branch plays a key role in delivering Health Canada's commitment to transparency. Through PACCB, Health Canada will continue to improve communications & the flow of information to & from stakeholders, clients, partners, media & the Canadian public.

Asst. Deputy Minister, Anne Lamar, 20110718
613-960-2176, Fax: 613-960-2183, anne.lamar@hc-sc.gc.ca
Director General, Consultations, Planning & Coordination, Aruna Sadana, 20110718
613-960-6043, Fax: 613-960-6063, aruna.sadana@hc-sc.gc.ca
Director General, Marketing & Communications Services, Jane Hazel, 20110718
613-957-0215, Fax: 613-948-8092, jane.hazel@hc-sc.gc.ca
Director General, Strategic Communications, Charles Mojsej, 20110718
613-948-8916, Fax: 613-957-1729, charles.mojsej@hc-sc.gc.ca

Regions & Programs Branch / Direction générale des régions et des programmes

Asst. Deputy Minister, Michel C. Doré, 20110718
613-941-8081, Fax: 613-948-0082, michel.c.dore@hc-sc.gc.ca
Director, Colleen Ryan, 20110718
613-952-2074, Fax: 613-941-7360, colleen.ryan@hc-sc.gc.ca
Director General, Branch Management Services, Nicholas Trudel, 20110718
613-954-0681, Fax: 613-941-7360, nicholas.trudel@hc-sc.gc.ca
Director General, Emergency Preparedness & Occupational Health, Anthony Sangster, 20110718
613-957-7669, Fax: 613-954-5822, anthony.sangster@hc-sc.gc.ca
Acting Senior Director General, Programs, Debbie Beresford-Green, 20110718
613-952-3579, Fax: 613-941-7360, debbie.beresford-green@hc-sc.gc.ca

Strategic Policy Branch (SPB) / Direction générale de la politique stratégique (DGPS)

The SPB plays a lead role in health policy, communications & consultations. The SPB's objective is to promote national coordination & development of a strong, shared knowledge base to address health & health care priorities for all Canadians. They also aim to facilitate successful health system adaptation to changes in technology, society, industry & the environment, such that Canadians will continue to be protected from health risks, have access to quality health care, & gain positive health benefits from information & innovation.

Assoc. Asst. Deputy Minister, Abby Hoffman, 20110718
613-946-1791, Fax: 613-954-0336, abby.hoffman@hc-sc.gc.ca
Director General, Applied Research & Analysis, Sylvain Paradis, 20110718
613-946-8030, sylvain.paradis@hc-sc.gc.ca
Director, Canada Health Act Division, Gigi Mandy, 20110718
613-954-8685, Fax: 613-952-8542, gigi.mandy@hc-sc.gc.ca
Acting Director, Federal/Provincial Relations, Noel Kivimaki, 20110718
613-946-8860, Fax: 613-954-3580, noel.kivimaki@hc-sc.gc.ca
Acting Director General, Health Care Policy, Gavin Brown, 20110718
613-957-8994, Fax: 613-648-4663, gavin.brown@hc-sc.gc.ca
Director General, International Affairs, Bersabel Ephrem, 20110718
613-941-3335, Fax: 613-952-7417, bersabel.ephrem@hc-sc.gc.ca
Director General, Legislative & Regulatory Policy, Regi Mathew, 20110718
613-960-7353, regi.mathew@hc-sc.gc.ca
Executive Director, Office of Nursing Policy, Sandra MacDonald-Rencz, 20110718
613-941-4314, Fax: 613-946-3166, sandra.macdonald-rencz@hc-sc.gc.ca
Acting Executive Director, Office of Pharmaceuticals Management Strategies, Jean Pruneau, 20110718
613-941-8218, Fax: 613-941-5258, jean.pruneau@hc-sc.gc.ca
Director, Policy Coordination & Planning, Phyllis Colvin, 20110718
613-957-3085, phyllis.colvin@hc-sc.gc.ca
Director General, Science Policy, Dr. Pierre Charest, 20110718
613-941-3003, Fax: 613-941-3007, pierre.charest@hc-sc.gc.ca

Regional Offices:

Alberta
9700 Jasper Ave., Edmonton, AB T5J 4C3
780-495-6815 Fax: 780-495-5551
Regional Director General, Arthur J. Murphy
780-495-6737, arthur.j.murphy@hc-sc.gc.ca

Atlantic
#1525, 1505 Barrington St., Halifax, NS B3J 3Y6
902-426-2038 Fax: 902-426-3768
Regional Director General, Simon d'Entremont
902-426-4097, Fax: 902-426-6659, simon.dentremont@hc-sc.gc.ca

British Columbia
Winch Bldg., #410, 757 West Hastings St., Vancouver, BC V6C 1A1
604-666-2083 Fax: 604-666-2258
Regional Director General, Catherine Lappe
604-775-7003, catherine.lappe@hc-sc.gc.ca

Manitoba Region
#450, 391 York Ave., Winnipeg, MB R3C 4W1
204-983-2508 Fax: 204-983-3972
Regional Director General, Laurette Burch
204-984-4363, Fax: 204-983-5325, laurette.burch@hc-sc.gc.ca

Northern Region
#1400, 60 Queen St., PO Box 3914A, Ottawa, ON K1A 0K9
613-946-8081 Fax: 613-948-2428
Other Communication: General inquiries: 866-509-1769
Regional Director General, Cathy Praamsma
613-946-8104, Fax: 613-948-2428, cathy.praamsma@hc-sc.gc.ca

Ontario
180 Queen St. West, Toronto, ON M5V 3L7
416-973-4389 Fax: 416-973-1423
866-999-7612
Acting Regional Director General, Lucy Butts
416-954-3592, Fax: 416-954-3599, lucy.butts@hc-sc.gc.ca

Québec
Guy-Favreau Complexe, Tour Est, 200, boul René-Lévesque ouest, 2e étage, Montréal, QC H2Z 1X4
450-646-1353 Fax: 514-283-6739
800-561-3350
Regional Director General, Marie-France Bérard
514-283-2856, Fax: 514-283-0910, marie-france.berard@hc-sc.gc.ca

Saskatchewan
2045 Broad St., Regina, SK S4P 3T7
Regional Director General, Alexander Campbell, 20110718
306-780-3115, alexander.campbell@hc-sc.gc.ca

Human Resources & Skills Development Canada (HRSDC) / Ressources humaines et Développement des compétences Canada (RHDCC)

140 Promenade du Portage, Gatineau, QC K1A 0J9
www.hrsdc.gc.ca
Other Communication: Media enquiries: 819-994-5559

HRSDC works to build a competitive country & to support Canadians in making choices to live productively. The following are key responsibilities of the federal department: developing policies to assist Canadaians to use their talents, skills & resources to participate in learning, work, & their community; creating programs to support initiative to help citizens in life transitions; improving outcomes for people through services offered by Service Canada & other partners; & establishing a healthy work environment.

Acts Administered:
Canada Labour Code
Aviation Occupational Safety & Health Regulations
Canada Occupational Health & Safety Regulations
Coal Mines (CBDC) Occupational Safety & Health Regulations
Coal Mining Safety Commission Regulations
Marine Occupational Safety & Health Regulations
Oil & Gas Occupational Safety & Health Regulations
On Board Trains Occupational Safety & Health Regulations
Canada Pension Plan
Canada Student Financial Assistance Act
Canada Student Loans Act
Canadian Centre for Occupational Health & Safety Act
Corporations & Labour Unions Returns Act
Department of Human Resources Development Act
Employment Equity Act
Employment Insurance Act
Fair Wages & Hours of Labour Act
Family Orders & Agreements Enforcement Assistance Act
Federal-Provincial Fiscal Arrangements Act
Government Annuities Act
Government Employees Compensation Act
Labour Adjustment Benefits Act
Merchant Seamen Compensation Act
Non-smokers' Health Act (Transport Canada)
Old Age Security Act
Status of the Artist Act
Unemployment Assistance Act
Vocational Rehabilitation of Disabled Persons Act
Wages Liability Act

Minister, Human Resources & Skills Development, Hon. Diane Finley, B.A., M.B.A.
819-994-2482, Fax: 819-994-0448, diane.finley@hrsdc-rhdcc.gc.ca
Minister, Labour, Hon. Lisa Raitt
819-953-5646, Fax: 819-994-5168, lisa.raitt@hrsdc-rhdcc.gc.ca

Parliamentary Secretary to the Minister of Human Resources & Skills Development Canada & to the Minister of Labour, Dr. Kellie Leitch
613-992-4224, Fax: 613-992-2164

Deputy Minister, Human Resources & Skills Development Canada, Ian Shugart
819-994-4514, Fax: 819-953-5603,
ian.shugart@hrsdc-rhdcc.gc.ca

Associated Agencies, Boards & Commissions:

• Canada Employment Insurance Commission (CEIC) / Commission de l'assurance-emploi du Canada (CAEC)
140, Promenade du Portage, Phase IV
Gatineau, QC K1A 0J9
800-206-7218
www.ei-ae.gc.ca
Manages the Employment Insurance Program.

• Canada Industrial Relations Board / Conseil canadien des relations industrielles

• Canadian Centre for Occupational Health & Safety / Centre canadien d'hygiène et de sécurité au travail

• Canadian Council of Directors of Apprenticeship / Conseil canadien des directeurs de l'apprentissage
140 Promenade du Portage, 5th Fl, Phase IV
Gatineau, QC K1A 0J9
819-953-7443 Fax: 819-994-0202
redseal-sceaurouge@hrsdc-rhdcc.gc.ca
www.red-seal.ca
A national body responsible for the certification of skilled workers, in the regulated trade, under the Interprovincial Standards (Red Seal) Program. This program is designed to facilitate the mobility of workers employed in the apprenticeable occupations in Canada through the establishment of common standards for certification. The apprenticeship program is generally administered by provincial & territorial departments responsible for education, labour & training (under the direction of the provincial & territorial Director of Apprenticeship) with authority delegated from the legislation in each province & territory. Through the program, apprentices who have completed their training & certified journeymen are able to obtain a Red Seal endorsement on their Certificate of Qualification by successfully completing an Interprovincial Standards Examination. The program encourages standardization of provincial & territorial apprenticeship training & certification programs. The Red Seal allows qualified trade persons to practice the trade in any province or territory in Canada where the trade is designated without having to write further examinations.

• Merchant Seamen Compensation Board / Commission d'indemnisation des marins marchands du Canada
Secretary, Merchant Seamen Compensation Board
Phase II, Place du Portage, 10th Fl.
Ottawa, ON K1A 0J2
819-953-8001 Fax: 819-994-5368
The Merchant Seamen Compensation Board consists of three members who are appointed by the Governor in Council pursuant to the Merchant Seamen Compensation Act . The Board reports to the federal Minister of Labour who has the overall responsibility for the Act. The Board hears & decides claims arising under the Act. The Act provides benefits to merchant seamen who are injured or disabled as a result of their work. Employers are liable to pay benefits awarded & the administrative expenses of the Board. They must maintain insurance against the risk of claims & report all accidents to the Board.

• Office of the Commissioner of Review Tribunals / Bureau du Commissaire des tribunaux de revision
PO Box 8250 T
Ottawa, ON K1G 5S5
613-954-1313 Fax: 613-946-1588 800-363-0076
info@ocrt-bctr.gc.ca
www.ocrt-bctr.gc.ca
Review Tribunals were created to provide a body independent from government to make determinations about eligibility for persons claiming CPP & OAS benefits that had previously been denied.

• Pension Appeals Board / Commission d'appel des pensions
PO Box 8567 T
Ottawa, ON K1G 3H9
613-995-0612 Fax: 613-995-6834 888-640-8001
info@pab-cap.gc.ca
www.pab-cap.gc.ca
The Pension Appeals Board is the final opportunity for appeal under the Canada Pension Plan. Responsible for the hearing of appeals which arise from the decisions of the Review Tribunals of the Office of the Commissioner.

Chief Financial Officer's Office / Bureau de l'agent principal des finances

Chief Financial Officer, Alfred Tsang, 20110720
819-994-5898, Fax: 613-997-0699,
alfred.tsang@hrsdc-rhdcc.gc.ca

Director General, Corporate Accounting & Reporting, Patrick Amyot, 20110720
819-953-0033, Fax: 819-997-6149,
patrick.amyot@hrsdc-rhdcc.gc.ca

Senior Director General, Enabling Services, Victor Abele, 20110720
819-994-5159, Fax: 819-994-3378,
victor.abele@hrsdc-rhdcc.gc.ca

Director General, Internal Control & Business Services, Eddy G. Reitberger, 20110720
819-934-8434, Fax: 819-953-0177,
eddy.reitberger@hrsdc-rhdcc.gc.ca

Senior Director General, Investment, Asset & Procurement, Jane Cochran, 20110720
819-934-1749, Fax: 819-994-1114,
jane.cochran@hrsdc-rhdcc.gc.ca

Senior Director, Strategic Planning & Coordination, Petr Sops, 20110720
819-994-2682, Fax: 819-997-0699,
peter.sops@hrsdc-rhdcc.gc.ca

Human Resources Services Branch / Direction générale des services des ressources humaines

Human Resources Services provides human resource services and technical expertise to HRSDC including succession planning, career development, orientation and training; compensation and benefits; classification and staffing; organizational renewal design and development; labour relations; occupational health and safety; and employment equity and official languages.

Asst. Deputy Minister, Gina Rallis, 20110720
819-997-5564, Fax: 819-934-6620,
gina.rallis@hrsdc-rhdcc.gc.ca

Director General, Centres of Expertise, Sylvain Dufour, 20110720
819-953-1220, Fax: 819-953-1346,
sylvain.dufour@hrsdc-rhdcc.gc.ca

Director General, Operations Service Centre, Marilyn Dingwall, 20110720
819-994-4015, Fax: 819-953-1271,
marilyn.dingwall@hrsdc-rhdcc.gc.ca

Acting Director General, Strategy, Accountability & Policy Frameworks, Jason Dorey, 20110720
819-997-5816, Fax: 819-994-7930,
jason.dorey@hrsdc-rhdcc.gc.ca

Director General, Transformation & Change Leadership Office, Jacqueline Hilton, 20110720
613-990-4661, jacqueline.hilton@hrsdc-rhdcc.gc.ca

Director General, Transformation & Change Leadership Office, Anne Duguay, 20110720
819-953-1273, Fax: 819-994-7930,
anne.duguay@hrsdc-rhdcc.gc.ca

Innovation, Information & Technology Branch / Direction générale d'innovation, information et technologie

Innovation, Information & Technology provides information & technology services to HRSDC including business applications that support & streamline work processes, access data, & process millions of benefit-related transactions to address Canadians' needs. It is also responsible for the provision & management of telephony & data networks, applications & data stores, & new processes & technologies.

Director, Business Management Services, Gaétan Ouellette, 20110720
819-994-7850, Fax: 819-994-9706,
gaetan.ouellette@hrsdc-rhdcc.gc.ca

Acting Director, Chief Solutions Office, Kathleen Webster, 20110720
819-953-0254, Fax: 819-997-8888,
kathleen.c.webster@hrsdc-rhdcc.gc.ca

Chief Technology Officer, Senior Director General, Patrice Rondeau, 20110720
819-934-3289, Fax: 819-956-2010,
patrice.rondeau@hrsdc-rhdcc.gc.ca

Director General, Chief, Strategy Architecture, Lorne Sundby, 20110720
780-495-2358, Fax: 780-495-4250,
lorne.sundby@hrsdc-rhdcc.gc.ca

National Headquarters:

Income Security & Social Development Branch / Direction générale de la sécurité du revenu et du développement social

Income Security & Social Development is the focal point for social policy & programs designed to ensure that children, families, seniors, people with disabilities, the homeless & those at risk of homelessness, communities & others who are facing social challenges have the support, knowledge, & information they need to maintain their well-being & facilitate their participation in society.

Senior Asst. Deputy Minister, Income Security & Social Development Branch, Jacques Paquette, 20110720
613-957-3111, Fax: 613-957-1185,
jacques.paquette@hrsdc-rhdcc.gc.ca

Director General, Canada Pension Plan Directorate, Mary Pichette, 20110720
613-946-3005, Fax: 613-954-2578,
mary.pichette@hrsdc-rhdcc.gc.ca

Director General, Community Development & Partnerships Directorate, John Walker, 20110720
613-941-1180, Fax: 613-946-3024,
john.walker@hrsdc-rhdcc.gc.ca

Director General, Office for Disability Issues, Nancy Milroy-Swainson, 20110720
819-994-1941, Fax: 819-994-8634,
nancy.milroyswainson@hrsdc-rhdcc.gc.ca

Director General, Seniors & Pensions Policy Secretariat, Dominique La Salle, 20110720
613-957-1626, Fax: 613-946-8871,
dominique.lasalle@hrsdc-rhdcc.gc.ca

Director General, Strategic Integration, Planning & Accountability, Ouassim Meguellati, 20110720
613-954-0885, Fax: 613-952-4655,
ouassim.meguellati@hrsdc-rhdcc.gc.ca

Director General, Homelessness Partnering Secretariat, Barbara Lawless, 20110720
819-997-5464, Fax: 819-994-4211,
barbara.lawless@hrsdc-rhdcc.gc.ca

Labour Program / Programme du travail

The Labour Program promotes safe, healthy, cooperative & productive workplaces. They develop, administer & enforce workplace legislation & regulations, such as the Canada Labour Code, which covers industrial relations, health and safety & employment standards, & the Employment Equity Act, which promotes workplace equality by removing the barriers faced by women, Aboriginal peoples, persons with disabilities & visible minorities while on the job. These laws cover federally regulated workers & employers.

Deputy Minister, Hélène Gosselin
819-934-3320, Fax: 819-934-7066,
helene.gosselin@labour-travail.gc.ca

Asst. Deputy Minister, Marie-Geneviève Mounier
819-997-1493, Fax: 819-953-5685,
mg.mounier@labour-travail.gc.ca

Director General, Federal Mediation & Conciliation Service, Guy Baron
819-994-1118, Fax: 819-997-1693,
guy.baron@labour-travail.gc.ca

Director General, International & Intergovernmental Labour Affairs, Debra Young
819-953-7405, Fax: 819-953-0227,
debra.young@labour-travail.gc.ca

Director General, Program Development & Guidance Directorate, Caroline Cyr
819-934-3331, Fax: 819-953-8883,
caroline.cyr@labour-travail.gc.ca

Director General, Regional Operations & Compliance Directorate, Danica Shimbashi
819-997-0252, Fax: 613-956-7521,
danica.shimbashi@labour-travail.gc.ca

Director General, Strategic Policy, Analysis & Workplace, Anthony J. Giles
819-997-4621, Fax: 819-994-0165,
anthony.giles@labour-travail.gc.ca

Senior Director, Labour Standards & Workplace Equity, Jan Michaels
819-934-5745, Fax: 819-997-3701,
jan.michaels@labour-travail.gc.ca

Director, Occupational Health & Safety Tribunal Canada, Marie-Claude Turgeon
613-957-4105, Fax: 613-954-6404,
marieclaude.turgeon@ohstc-tsstc.gc.ca

Laboratory Manager, Technical Services, Ian Fraser
613-993-5141, Fax: 613-990-7709,
ian.fraser@labour-travail.gc.ca

Learning Branch / Apprentissage

The Learning branch helps Canadians attend college, university & trade schools by providing advice, loans, assistance, grants to students, by encouraging individuals & organizations to save for a child's post-secondary education, & by assisting children from low-income families through grants. It is responsible for programs & services related to learning, including student financial assistance, savings incentives for post-secondary education, & literacy.

Asst. Deputy Minister, Kathryn McDade
819-953-3712, Fax: 819-953-7427,
kathryn.mcdade@hrsdc-rhdcc.gc.ca

Director General, Canada Education Savings Program, David Swol
819-953-1530, Fax: 819-953-6500,
david.swol@hrsdc-rhdcc.gc.ca

Director General, Canada Student Loans Directorate, Marc LeBrun
819-997-6684, Fax: 819-953-4226,
marc.l.lebrun@hrsdc-rhdcc.gc.ca

Director General, Program Policy Planning, Danièle Besner
819-953-1966, Fax: 819-994-1868,
daniele.besner@hrsdc-rhdcc.gc.ca

Legal Services / Services juridiques
Legal Services provides legal services to support the core operations & key initiatives of HRSDC. The services provided include: legal advice on program statutes & policies administered by the Department, policy advice for developing policy & legislative or regulatory proposals, & representing the Department before boards, tribunals & courts.
Director, Anne Mongeon, 20110720
819-997-7383, Fax: 819-997-7547,
anne.mongeon@hrsdc-rhdcc.gc.ca
Director, Dispute Resolution, Peter R. Seguin, 20110720
819-994-2989, Fax: 819-953-7317,
peter.seguin@hrsdc-rhdcc.gc.ca
Senior Counsel & Group Head, Carol MacLean, 20110720
819-997-2440, Fax: 819-997-7547,
carol.mclean@hrsdc-rhdcc.gc.ca
Deputy Head & General Counsel, Stephen Sharzer, 20110720
819-953-8302, Fax: 819-953-7317,
stephen.sharzer@hrsdc-rhdcc.gc.ca

Program Operations / Opérations des programmes
Program Operations handles the operation & coordination of the Grant & Contributions programs across the Department.
Asst. Deputy Minister, Program Operations Branch, Joanne Lamothe, 20110720
819-934-7067, Fax: 819-934-7614,
joanne.lamothe@hrsdc-rhdcc.gc.ca
Director General, Aboriginal Program Operations, Marie-France Lamarche, 20110720
819-997-7583, Fax: 819-934-6339,
mariefrance.lamarche@hrsdc-rhdcc.gc.ca
Director General, Labour Market & Social Development Program Operations, Nancy Gardiner, 20110720
819-953-4662, Fax: 819-953-9354,
nancy.gardiner@hrsdc-rhdcc.gc.ca
Director General, Program Operations Management & Accountability, Kenneth Kerr, 20110720
819-997-1551, Fax: 819-994-7580,
kenneth.kerr@hrsdc-rhdcc.gc.ca

Public Affairs & Stakeholder Relations - ADMO / Affaires publiques et Relations avec les intervenants - BSMA
Public Affairs & Stakeholder Relations informs Canadians about HRSDC's mandate, policies & programs. It also supports departmental activities in engaging & communicating with stakeholders & citizens.
Asst. Deputy Minister, Peter Larose, 20110720
819-934-5760, Fax: 819-934-5751,
peter.larose@hrsdc-rhdcc.gc.ca
Director, Ministerial Communications Services, Brian Laghi, 20110720
819-934-5582, Fax: 819-994-6609,
brian.laghi@hrsdc-rhdcc.gc.ca
Director General, Program Communications, Public Affairs & Stakeholder Relations, Barry Frewer, 20110720
819-994-1361, Fax: 819-934-5751,
barry.frewer@hrsdc-rhdcc.gc.ca
Director General, Strategic Communications & Stakeholders Relations, Benoit Trottier, 20110720
819-953-1308, Fax: 819-953-3981,
benoit.trottier@hrsdc-rhdcc.gc.ca
Senior Director, Strategic Planning & Management Services, Anne Schroder, 20110720
819-997-2192, Fax: 819-934-5751,
anne.schroder@hrsdc-rhdcc.gc.ca

Skills & Employment / Direction générale des compétences et de l'emploi
Skills & Employment provides programs & initiatives that promote skills development, labour market participation & inclusiveness, as well as ensuring labour market efficiency. Specifically, these programs seek to address the employment & skills needs of those facing employment barriers, & contribute to life long learning & building a skilled inclusive labour force. Other programs that support an efficient labour market include the labour market integration of recent immigrants, the entry of temporary foreign workers, the mobility of workers across Canada & the dissemination of labour market information. This branch is also responsible for programs that provide temporary income support to eligible unemployed workers.
Senior Asst. Deputy Minister, Frank Vermaeten, 20110720
819-997-9236, Fax: 819-934-4040,
frank.vermaeten@hrsdc-rhdcc.gc.ca
Assoc. Asst. Deputy Minister, Louis Beauséjour, 20110720
819-997-9427, Fax: 819-934-4040,
louis.beausejour@hrsdc-rhdcc.gc.ca
Director, Aboriginal Affairs, Alfred M. Linklater, 20110720
819-934-6640, Fax: 819-994-3297,
alfred.linklater@hrsdc-rhdcc.gc.ca
Director General, Active Employment Measures, John Atherton, 20110720
819-994-4553, Fax: 819-934-7107,
john.atherton@hrsdc-rhdcc.gc.ca
Director General, Branch Management & Integrity, Dr. Joe Dragon, 20110720
819-956-9033, Fax: 819-953-1947,
joe.dragon@hrsdc-rhdcc.gc.ca
Director General, Employment Insurance Policy, Mireille Laroche, 20110720
819-997-8622, Fax: 819-934-6631,
mireille.laroche@hrsdc-rhdcc.gc.ca
Acting Director General, Federal/Provincial/Territorial Partnerships, Michel C. Caron, 20110720
819-997-5136, Fax: 819-934-7818,
michel.caron@hrsdc-rhdcc.gc.ca
Director General, Labour Market Integration, Jean-François LaRue, 20110720
819-997-9217, Fax: 819-934-6630,
jeanfrancois.larue@hrsdc-rhdcc.gc.ca
Director General, Office of Literacy & Essential Skills, Silvano Tocchi, 20110720
819-953-6967, Fax: 819-997-6777,
silvano.tocchi@hrsdc-rhdcc.gc.ca
Director General, Office of Literacy & Essential Skills, Silvano Tocchi, 20110720
819-953-6967, Fax: 819-997-6777,
silvano.tocchi@hrsdc-rhdcc.gc.ca
Acting Director General, Program Policy, Planning & Coordination, Alexis Conrad, 20110720
819-997-0037, Fax: 819-934-5333,
alexis.conrad@hrsdc-rhdcc.gc.ca
Director General, Temporary Foreign Workers, Andrew Kenyon, 20110720
819-994-1021, Fax: 819-997-5979,
andrew.kenyon@hrsdc-rhdcc.gc.ca
Director General, Workplace Partnerships, Martin Green, 20110720
819-994-3713, Fax: 819-953-3512,
martin.green@hrsdc-rhdcc.gc.ca

Strategic Policy & Research / Direction générale de la politique stratégique et de la recherche
Strategic Policy & Research leads on integrating human resources and social development issues in strategic policy, evaluation, & knowledge & research dissemination. It also leads on emerging & long-term policy development, corporate planning, & central agency, intergovernmental & international relations.
Senior Asst. Deputy Minister, David McGovern, 20110720
819-953-3729, Fax: 819-997-7329,
david.mcgovern@hrsdc-rhdcc.gc.ca
Assoc. Asst. Deputy Minister, Allen Sutherland, 20110720
819-994-6013, Fax: 819-997-7329,
allen.sutherland@hrsdc-rhdcc.gc.ca
Director General, Corporate Planning & Accountability, Bobby Mathesonnd, 20110720
819-994-2098, Fax: 819-994-2374,
bobby.matheson@hrsdc-rhdcc.gc.ca
Director General, Intergovernmental Relations, David Whillans, 20110720
819-994-4538, Fax: 819-953-4701,
david.whillans@hrsdc-rhdcc.gc.ca
Director General, Knowledge & Data Management, Christian Dea, 20110720
819-934-7655, Fax: 819-953-1947,
christian.dea@hrsdc-rhdcc.gc.ca
Director, Labour Market Policy, Christina Norris, 20110720
819-956-6983, Fax: 819-953-0519,
christina.norris@hrsdc-rhdcc.gc.ca
Director General, Learning Policy Directorate, Mark Hopkins, 20110720
819-953-8005, Fax: 819-997-5433,
mark.hopkins@hrsdc-rhdcc.gc.ca
Acting Director General, Policy Research Directorate, Jeff Frank, 20110720
819-953-6892, Fax: 819-953-8868,
jeff.frank@hrsdc-rhdcc.gc.ca
Director, Resource Management Directorate, Kata Kitaljevich, 20110720
819-953-2368, Fax: 819-953-4962,
kata.kitaljevich@hrsdc-rhdcc.gc.ca
Acting Director General, Social Policy, François Weldon, 20110720
819-994-3184, Fax: 819-953-9119,
francois.weldon@hrsdc-rhdcc.gc.ca
Acting Director General, Strategy & Integration, David Bailey, 20110720
819-953-4416, Fax: 819-953-0519,
david.bailey@hrsdc-rhdcc.gc.ca

Service Canada
140, Promenade du Portage, Gatineau, QC K1A 0J9
800-622-6232
www.servicecanada.gc.ca
TTY: 800-926-9105
Service Canada was created in 2005 to improve the delivery of government programs & services to Canadians, by making access to them faster, easier, & more convenient. Service Canada offers single-window access to a wide range of Government of Canada programs & services for citizens through more than 600 points of service located across the country, call centres, & the Internet.
Senior Assist. Deputy Minister, Carolina Giliberti
819-934-1504, Fax: 819-934-1505,
carolina.giliberti@servicecanada.gc.ca
Head, Service Delivery, Robin Flaherty
613-990-9105, Fax: 613-941-1827,
robin.flaherty@servicecanada.gc.ca
Director General, Citizen Service Strategy, Zahra Pourjafar-Ziaei
613-957-6727, Fax: 613-957-4400,
zahra.pourjafarziaei@servicecanada.gc.ca
Director General, Business Transformation, Mary O'Neill
819-956-7659, Fax: 819-997-9194,
mary.o'neill@servicecanada.gc.ca
Director, Web Strategies & Product Management, Minh Doan
613-957-6220, Fax: 613-957-6767,
minh.doan@servicecanada.gc.ca

Service Canada Centres:
800-622-6232
Other Communication: CPP/OAS: 800-277-9914; Record of Employment: 800-367-5693; Telephone Info Service: 800-206-7218; Telephone Reporting Service: 800-531-7555

Regional Offices:

Alberta:
Brooks
Cassils Plaza, 608 - 2 St. West, Brooks, AB T1R 1A8
Calgary Centre
#270, 220 - 4 Ave. SE, Calgary, AB T2G 4X3
Calgary East
#1502, 515 Marlborough Way NE, Calgary, AB T2A 7E7
Calgary North
One Executive Place, 1816 Crowchild Trail NW, PO Box 65037 North Hill, Calgary, AB T2N 4T6
Calgary South
Fisher Park Place II, #100, 6712 Fisher St. SE, Calgary, AB T2H 1X3
Camrose
Federal Bldg., 4901 - 50 Ave., Camrose, AB T4V 0S2
Canmore
Bldg. C, #113, 802 Bow Valley Trail, Canmore, AB T1W 1N6
Edmonton Canada Place
Canada Place, 9700 Jasper Ave., Main Fl., Edmonton, AB T5J 4C1
Edmonton Meadowlark
#120, 15710 - 87 Ave. NW, Edmonton, AB T5R 5W9
Edmonton Millbourne
148 Millbourne Market Mall, 38 Ave. & Millwoods Rd., Edmonton, AB T6K 3L6
Edmonton North
#2000, 9499 - 137 Ave. NW, Edmonton, AB T5E 5R8
780-495-3904
800-622-6232
Edson
4905 - 4 Ave., Edson, AB T7E
Fort McMurray
Provincial Bldg., 9915 Franklin Ave., Main Fl., Fort McMurray, AB T9H 2K4
Grande Prairie
Towne Centre Mall, #100, 9845 - 99 Ave., Grande Prairie, AB T8V 0R3
Lethbridge
Crowsnest Trail Plaza, 101, 920 - 2A Ave. North, Lethbridge, AB T1H 0E3
Lloydminster
5016 - 48 St., Lloydminster, AB T9V 0H8
Medicine Hat
Northside Centre, 78 - 8 St. NW, Medicine Hat, AB T1A 6P1
Red Deer
First Red Deer Place, 4911 - 51 St., 2nd Fl., Lethbridge, AB T4N 6A4
Slave Lake
Sawridge Plaza, 100 Main St. South, Slave Lake, AB T0G 2A3
St Paul
5126 - 50 Ave., St Paul, AB T0A 3A0

British Columbia:
Abbotsford
100, 32525 Simon Ave., Abbotsford, BC V2T 6T6
Burnaby
#100, 3480 Gilmore Way, Burnaby, BC V5G 4Y1
Campbell River
#101, 950 Alder St., Campbell River, BC V9W 2P8
Chilliwack
9345 Main St., Chilliwack, BC V2P 4M3
Comox Valley
130 - 19 St., Courtenay, BC V9N 8S1
Coquitlam
#100, 2963 Glen Dr., Coquitlam, BC V3B 2P7
Cowichan
211 Jubilee St., Duncan, BC V9L 1W8
Cranbrook
1113 Baker St., Cranbrook, BC V1C 1A7

Dawson Creek
#103, 1508 - 102 Ave., Dawson Creek, BC V1G 2E2
Kamloops
317 Seymour St., 1st Fl., Kamloops, BC V2C 2E8
Kelowna
#106, 471 Queensway Ave., Kelowna, BC V1Y 6S5
Langley
#102, 8747 - 204 St., Langley, BC V1M 2Y5
Nanaimo
#201, 60 Front St., Nanaimo, BC V9R 5H7
Nelson
Kutenai Bldg., 333 Victoria St., Main Fl., Nelson, BC V1L 4K3
New Westminster
#201, 620 Royal Ave., New Westminster, BC V3M 1J2
North Shore
#100, 221 West Esplanade, North Vancouver, BC V7M 3N7
Penticton
#100, 386 Ellis St., Penticton, BC V2A 8C9
Port Alberni
A, 4805 Mar St., Port Alberni, BC V9Y 8J5
Powell River
A, 7061 Duncan St., Powell River, BC V8A 1W1
Prince George
1363 - 4 Ave., Prince George, BC V2L 3J6
Prince Rupert
#100, 215 - 3 St., Prince Rupert, BC V8J 3J9
Quesnel
283 Reid St. East, Quesnel, BC V2J 2A8
Richmond
#350, 5611 Cooney Rd., Richmond, BC V6X 3K5
Ridge Meadows
22325 Loughheed Hwy., Maple Ridge, BC V2X 8T1
Salmon Arm
191 Shuswap St. NW, 1st Fl., Salmon Arm, BC
Sinclair Centre
#415, 757 Hastings St. West, Vancouver, BC V6B 1N9
Smithers
1020 Murray St., Smithers, BC V0J 2N3
Squamish
1440 Winnipeg St., Squamish, BC V8B 0J2
Surrey North
13889 - 104 Ave., Surrey, BC V3T 1W7
Surrey
7404 King George Hwy., Surrey, BC V3W 0L4
Terrace
4630 Lazelle Ave., Terrace, BC V8G 1S6
Trail
#101, 1101 Dewdney Ave., Trail, BC V1R 4A5
Vancouver East
1420 Kingsway, Vancouver, BC V5N 2R5
Vancouver
125 - 10 Ave. East, Vancouver, BC V5T 1Z3
Vanderhoof
189 Stewart St. East, Vanderhoof, BC
Vernon
3202 - 31 St., Vernon, BC V1T 5J1
Victoria
595 Pandora Ave., Victoria, BC V8W 1N6
Williams Lake
79 - 4 Ave. South, Williams Lake, BC V2G 1H2

Manitoba:
Aboriginal Single Window
Aboriginal Centre, #100, 181 Higgins Ave., Winnipeg, MB R3B 3G1
Brandon
Government of Canada Building, 1039 Princess Ave., Brandon, MB R7A 6E2
Churchill
1 Mantayo Seepee Meskanow, Churchill, MB
Dauphin
135 - 2 Ave. NE, Dauphin, MB R7N 0Z6
Flin Flon
Government of Canada Bldg., 111 Main St., Flin Flon, MB R8A 1J9
Morden
Government of Canada Bldg., 158 Stephen St., Morden, MB R6M 1T3
Notre-Dame-des-Lourdes
51 Rodgers St., Notre Dame de Lourdes, QC R0G 1M0
Portage la Prairie
Government of Canada Bldg., 1016 Saskatchewan Ave. East, Portage la Prairie, MB R1N 3V2
Saint-Pierre-Jolys
427 Sabourin St., Saint-Pierre-Jolys, MB R0A 1V0
Selkirk
Government of Canada Bldg., 237 Manitoba Ave., Main Fl., Selkirk, MB R1A 2M8
Steinbach
Steinbach, 321 Main St., Main Fl., Steinbach, MB R5G 1Z2
Swan River
#1, 355 Kelsey Trail, Swan River, MB R0L 1Z0
The Pas
Government of Canada Bldg., 305 - 4 St. West, The Pas, MB
Thompson
North Centre Mall, #118, 3 Station Rd., Thompson, MB R8N 0N3
Winnipeg Centre
Stanley Knowles Bldg., 391 York Ave., Winnipeg, MB R3C 1T9
Winnipeg La Verendrye
#100, 614 des Meurons St., Winnipeg, MB R2H 2R1
Winnipeg North-East
Kildonan Village Mall, 1122 Henderson Hwy., Winnipeg, MB R2G 1L1
Winnipeg South-West
Westwood Centre, 3338 Portage Ave., Winnipeg, MB R3K 0Z1
Winnipeg St. Vital
1001 St. Mary's Rd., Winnipeg, MB R2M 3S4

New Brunswick:
Bathurst
Nicolas Denys Bldg., 120 Harbourview Blvd., 1st Fl., Bathurst, NB E2A 1R6
Campbellton
Campbellton City Center Mall, #111, 157 Water St., Campbellton, NB E3N 3L3
Caraquet
Bellevue Place, 20E St. Pierre Blvd. West, Caraquet, NB E1W 1B6
Dalhousie
Darlington Mall, 110 Plaza Blvd., Dalhousie, NB E8C 2A3
Edmundston
Federal Bldg., 22 Emmerson St., Edmundston, NB E3V 1R7
Fredericton
Federal Bldg., 633 Queen St., Fredericton, NB E3B 5G4
Grande Falls
#100, 441 Madawaska Rd., Grand Falls, NB E3Y 1A3
Miramichi
Roach Bldg., 150 Pleasant St., Miramichi, NB E1V 1Y1
Moncton
Heritage Court, #310, 95 Foundry St., Moncton, NB E1C 8R5
Richibucto
Cartier Place, 25 Cartier Blvd., Richibucto, NB E4W 3W7
Sackville
East Main Plaza, 170 Main St., Sackville, NB E4L 4S2
Saint John
1 Agar Place, 1st Fl., Saint John, NB E2L 5G4
Saint Quentin
193 Canada St., Saint-Quentin, NB E8A 1G9
Shediac
Centre-Ville Mall, 342 Main St., Shediac, NB E4P 2E7
Shippagan
196A J.D. Gauthier Blvd., 1st Fl., Shippagan, NB E8S 1P3
Shippagan
Post Office Bldg., 93 Milltown Blvd., St. Stephen, NB E3L 3E2
Sussex
Mapleton Place, 10 Gateway St., Sussex, NB E4E 3E5
Tracadie-Sheila
Le Rond Point Shopping Center, #17, 3409 Principale St., Tracadie-Sheila, NB E1X 1A4
Woodstock
Post Office Bldg., 680 Main St., Woodstock, NB E7M 5Z7

Newfoundland & Labrador:
Clarenville
Park Place, 50 Manitoba Dr., Clarenville, NL A5A 1K5
Corner Brook
Joseph R. Smallwood Bldg., 1 Regent Sq., Corner Brook, NL A2H 491
Gander
McCurdy Complex, 1 Markham Place, 3rd Fl., Gander, NL A1V 1W7
Grand Falls-Windsor
Bailey Bldg., #100, 4A Bayley St., Grand Falls, NL A2A 2Y3
Happy Valley
23 Broomfield St., Happy Valley-Goose Bay, NL A0P 1E0
Harbour Grace
Babb Bldg., 33-35 Harvey St., Harbour Grace, NL A0A 2M0
Labrador City
Labrador Mall, 500 Vanier Ave., Labrador City, NL A2V 2W7
Marystown
Jerrett Bldg., #130, 140 Ville Marie Dr., Marystown, NL A0E 1L0
Placentia
Dalfens Mall, 61 Blockhouse Rd., Placentia, NL A0B 2Y0
Port Aux Basques
#4, 10 High St., Channel-Port aux Basques, NL A0M 1C0
Rocky Harbour
Budgeon Bldg., 118 Pond Rd., Rocky Harbour, NL A0K 4N0
Springdale
Wells Bldg., 130 Main St., Springdale, NL A0J 1T0
St. Anthony
Viking Mall, 1 Goose Cove Rd., St. Anthony, NL A0K 4S0
St. John's
Bldg. 223, Pleasantville, 223 Churchill Ave., St. John's, NL A1B 3P3
Stephenville
133 Carolina Ave., Stephenville, NL A2N 2S5

Northwest Territories:
Fort Simpson
Federal Bldg., 9606 - 100 St., Fort Simpson, NT X0E 0N0
867-695-2238 Fax: 867-695-2229
Fort Smith
Federal Bldg., 149 McDougal Rd., Fort Smith, NT X0E 0P0
867-872-2747
Hay River
#204, 41 Capital Dr., Hay River, NT X0E 1G2
867-874-6739 Fax: 867-874-6100
Inuvik
85 Kingmingya Rd., Inuvik, NT X0E 0T0
867-777-2122 Fax: 867-777-4369
Yellowknife
Greenstone Bldg., 5101 - 50 Ave., Main Fl., Yellowknife, NT X1A 3Z4
867-766-8300 Fax: 867-873-3621

Nova Scotia:
Amherst
#202, 26-28 Prince Arthur St., Amherst, NS B4H 1V6
Fax: 902-661-6637
Antigonish
Federal Bldg., 325 Main St., 2nd Fl., Antigonish, NS B2G 2C3
Fax: 902-863-7053
Bedford
Royal Bank Bldg., 1597 Bedford Hwy., 2nd Fl., Bedford, NS B4A 1E8
Fax: 902-426-5552
Bridgewater
Dawson B. Dauphinee Bldg., 77 Dufferin St., Bridgewater, NS B4V 2G1
Fax: 902-527-5624
Dartmouth
Royal Bank Bldg., 46 Portland St., 5th Fl., Dartmouth, NS B2Y 1H2
Fax: 902-426-7301
Digby
Maud Lewis Provincial Bldg., 84 Warwick St., Digby, NS B0V 1A0
Fax: 902-245-6226
Glace Bay
Senator's Place, #201, 633 Main St., Glace Bay, NS B1A 6J3
Fax: 902-842-2655
Guysborough
Chedabucto Centre, 9996 Hwy. 16, Guysborough, NS B0H 1N0
Fax: 902-533-2891
Halifax
Mumford Towers, Tower II, 7001 Mumford Rd., Halifax, NS B3L 4T8
Fax: 902-426-7690
Inverness
15926 Central Ave., Inverness, NS B0E 1X0
Fax: 902-258-3036
Kentville
Federal Bldg., 495 Main St., 2nd Fl., Kentville, NS B4N 3W5
Fax: 902-679-5786
New Glasgow
340 East River Rd., New Glasgow, NS B2H 3P7
Fax: 902-755-7869
North Sydney
105 King St., Main Fl., North Sydney, NS B2A 3S1
Fax: 902-794-5724
Port Hawkesbury
Shediac Shopping Centre, #8, 811 Reeves St., Port Hawkesbury, NS B9A 2S4
Fax: 902-625-4137
Shelburne
Loyalist Plaza, 218 Water St., Shelburne, NS B0T 1W0
Fax: 902-875-3505
Sydney
Commerce Tower, 15 Dorchester St., 1st Fl., Sydney, NS B1P 5Y9
Fax: 902-564-7104
Truro
#8, 60 Lorne St., Truro, NS B2N 3K3
Fax: 902-893-0075
Windsor
80 Water St., Windsor, NS B0P 1L0
Fax: 902-798-5816
Yarmouth
Canada Post Offive Bldg., 13 Willow St., 2nd Fl., Yarmouth, NS B5A 1T8
Fax: 902-742-0815

Ontario:
Ajax
#200, 274 Mackenzie Ave., Ajax, ON L1S 1P7
Arnprior
Heritage Square, #1 & 2, 75 Elgin St. West, Arnprior, ON K7S 3T9

Bancroft
Fairway Plaza, 5 Fairway Blvd., Bancroft, ON K0L 1C0
Barrie
48 Owen St., 1st Fl., Barrie, ON L4M 1G6
Belleville
Business Bldg., 1 North Front St., 2nd Fl., Belleville, ON K8P 3A7
Bracebridge
Federal Bldg., 98 Manitoba St., 2nd Fl., Bracebridge, ON P1L 1S1
Brampton
18 Corporation Dr., Brampton, ON L6S 6B2
Brantford
58 Dalhousie St., 2nd Fl., Brantford, ON N3T 2J2
Brockville
Thomas Fuller Bldg., 14 Court House Ave., 1st Fl., Brockville, ON K6V 3X3
Burlington
Burlington Resource Centre, 440 Elizaebth St., Burlington, ON L7R 2M1
Cambridge
350 Conestoga Blvd., #C2, Cambridge, ON N1R 7L7
Carleton Place
46 Lansdowne Ave., Carleton Place, ON K7C 3S9
Chatham-Kent
Federal Bldg., 120 Wellington St. West, Chatham, ON N7M 4V9
Cobourg
Fleming Bldg., #103, 1005 Elgin St. West, Cobourg, ON K9A 5J4
Collingwood
44 Huronontario St., Collingwood, ON L9Y 2L6
Cornwall
#100, 111 Water St. East, Cornwall, ON K6H 6S2
Dryden
41C Duke St., Dryden, ON P8N 1E6
Elliot Lake
Algo Centre, Upper Mall, 151 Ontario Ave., Elliot Lake, ON P5A 2T2
Espanola
#2, 721 Centre St., Espanola, ON P5E 1H7
Fort Frances
301 Scott St., Fort Frances, ON P9A 1H1
Gananoque
5 Charles St. South, Gananoque, ON K7G 1V9
Georgetown
232 Guelph St., 1st Fl., Georgetown, ON L7G 4B1
Geraldton
208 Beamish Ave. West, Geraldton, ON P0T 1M0
Goderich
52 East St., Goderich, ON N7A 1N3
Guelph
259 Woodlawn Rd. West, Suite C, Guelph, ON N1H 8J1
Hamilton - East
2255 Barton St. East, Hamilton, ON L8H 7T4
Hamilton - Main
1550 Upper James St., 1st Fl., Hamilton, ON L9B 1K3
Hawkesbury
134 Main St. East, Hawkesbury, ON K6A 1A3
Kapuskasing
8 Queen St., Kapuskasing, ON P5N 1G7
Kenora
Kenora Market Square, #201, 308 2 St. South, Kenora, ON P9N 1G3
Kingston
299 Concession St., Kingston, ON K7L 5H5
Kirkland Lake
10 Government Rd. East, Kirkland Lake, ON P2N 1A2
Kitchener
409 Weber St. West, Kitchener, ON N2H 4B1
Leamington
Leamington Mall, 215 Talbot St. East, Leamington, ON N8H 3X5
Lindsay
65 Kent St. West, Lindsay, ON K9V 2Y3
Listowel
210 Main St. East, Listowel, ON N4W 2B7
London
Dominion Public Bldg., 457 Richmond St., London, ON N6A 3E3
Malton
#5, 6877 Goreway Dr., Malton, ON L4V 1L9
Marathon
#105, 52 Peninsula Rd., Marathon, ON P0T 2E0
Markham
#14, 5051 Hwy. 7 East, Markham, ON L3T 7T1
Midland
Huronia Mall, 9225 Hwy. 93, Midland, ON L4R 4K4
Milton
Trafalgar Square, 310 Main St. East, Milton, ON L9T 1P4
Mississauga - East
2525 Dixie Rd., Mississauga, ON L4Y 2A1
Mississauga - West
3085A Glen Erin Dr., Mississauga, ON L5L 1J3

Napanee
Murphy's Plaza, 2 Dairy Ave., Napanee, ON K7R 3T1
New Liskeard
280 Armstrong St. North, New Liskeard, ON P0J 1P0
Newmarket
#1, 18183 Yonge St. East, East Gwillimbury, ON L3Y 4V8
Niagara Falls
Customs Bldg., 5853 Peer St., Niagara Falls, ON L2G 1X4
North Bay
Canada Place, #102, 107 Shirreff Ave., North Bay, ON P1B 7K8
Oakville
117 Cross Ave., #5B, Oakville, ON L6J 2W7
Orangeville
#102, 210 Broadway, Orangeville, ON L9W 5G4
Orillia
#101, 50 Andrew St. South, Orillia, ON L3V 7T5
Oshawa
Midtown Mall, 200 John St. West, Unit C6, Oshawa, ON L1J 2B4
Ottawa - Centre
L'Esplanade Laurier, 300 Laurier Ave. West, 2nd Fl., Ottawa, ON K2P 1W5
Ottawa - East
Beacon Hill Shopping Centre, 2339 Ogilvie Rd., Ottawa, ON K1A 0J6
Ottawa Government
110 Laurier Ave. West, Ottawa, ON K1P 1J1
Ottawa - West
Lincoln Fields Galleria, 2525 Carling Ave., 1st Fl., Ottawa, ON K2B 7Z2
Owen Sound
Heritage Place Shopping Centre, 1350 - 16 St. East, Owen Sound, ON N4K 6N7
Parry Sound
74 James St., 2nd Fl., Parry Sound, ON P2A 1T8

Saint John
1 Agar Place, PO Box 7000, Saint John, NB E2L 4V4
Fax: 506-636-3808
800-206-7218

Pembroke
141 Lake St., Pembroke, ON K8A 5L8
Perth
The Factory, 40 Sunset Blvd., Perth, ON K7H 2Y4
Peterborough
Jackson Square, #101, 185 King St., Peterborough, ON K9J 2R8
Picton
229 Main St., Picton, ON K0K 2T0
Prescott
292 Centre St., Prescott, ON K0E 1T0
613-925-2808 Fax: 613-925-3846
ontario.inquiry@hrsdc-rhdcc.gc.ca

Renfrew
350 Raglan St. South, Renfrew, ON K7V 1R6
Richmond Hill
35 Beresford Dr., Richmond Hill, ON L4B 4M3
Sarnia
529 Exmouth St., Sarnia, ON N7T 7S5
Sault Ste Marie
22 Bay St., 1st Fl., Sault Ste Marie, ON P6A 5S2
Simcoe
5 Queensway East, Simcoe, ON N3Y 5K2
Smiths Falls
#115, 91 Cornelia St. West, Smiths Falls, ON K7A 5L3
St Catherines
Henley Square Plaza, 395 Ontario St., Unit E & F, St Catharines, ON L2N 7N6
St Thomas
#34, 1010 Talbot St., St Thomas, ON N5P 4N2
Stratford
#2, 61 Lorne Ave., Ground Fl., Stratford, ON N5A 6S4
Sturgeon Falls
#2, 186 Main St., Sturgeon Falls, ON P2B 1N9
Sudbury
Federal Bldg., 19 Lisgar St., Main Fl., Sudbury, ON P3E 6L1
Thunder Bay
975 Alloy Dr., Thunder Bay, ON P7B 6N5
Tillsonburg
96 Tillson Ave., Tillsonburg, ON N4G 3A1
Timmins
120 Cedar St. South, 1st Fl., Timmins, ON P4N 1G2
Toronto - Centre
Arthur Meighen Bldg., 25 St. Clair Ave. East, 1st Fl., Toronto, ON M4T 3A4
Toronto - City Hall
City Hall, 100 Queen St. West, 1st Fl., Toronto, ON M5H 2N2
Toronto - Dufferin Mall
Dufferin Mall, #0001, 900 Dufferin St., Toronto, ON M6H 4B1
Toronto - Etobicoke
5343 Dundas St. West, Toronto, ON M9B 6K6
Toronto - Gerrard Square
Gerrard Square Mall, 1000 Gerrard St. East, #DD10/11, 2nd Fl., Toronto, ON M4M 1Z3

Toronto - Lawrence Square
Lawrence Square Mall, #103-105, 700 Lawrence Ave. West, Toronto, ON M6B 4L4
Toronto - Malvern
Malvern Town Centre Mall, 31 Tapscott Rd., Toronto, ON M1B 3G7
Toronto - North
3737 Chesswood Dr., Toronto, ON M3J 2P6
Toronto - Scarborough
Canada Centre, 200 Town Centre Ct., 1st Fl., Toronto, ON M1P 4X9
Toronto - Willowdale
Joseph Shepard Bldg., 4900 Yonge St., 1st Fl., Toronto, ON M2N 6B1
Trenton
50 Dundas St. West, Trenton, ON K8V 6R5
Walkerton
200 McNab St., Walkerton, ON N0G 2V0
Wallaceburg
Municipal Service Centre, 786 Dufferin Ave., 2nd Fl., Wallaceburg, ON N8A 2V3
Welland
250 Thorold Rd. West, Welland, ON L3C 3W3
905-988-2700 Fax: 905-735-7036

Windsor
#103, 400 City Hall Sq. East, Windsor, ON N9A 7K6
Woodstock
#101, 959 Dundas St., Woodstock, ON N4S 1H2

Prince Edward Island:
Charlottetown
Jean Canfield Goverment of Canada Bldg., 191 University Ave., Charlottetown, PE C1A 2A1
Fax: 902-368-0178

Montague
491 Main St., Montague, PE C0A 1R0
Fax: 902-838-3439

O'Leary
371 Main St., O'Leary, PE C0B 1V0
Fax: 902-859-1286

Souris
Save Easy Mall, 173 Main St., 2nd Fl., Souris, PE C0A 2B0
Fax: 902-687-3722

Summerside
Government of Canada Bldg., 294 Church St., Summerside, PE C1N 3H8
Fax: 902-432-6808

Quebec:
Alma
Jacques-Gagnon Complex, #105, 100, rue St-Joseph sud, Alma, QC G8B 6S9
Amos
101 - 1re av est, Amos, QC J9T 1H4
Fax: 819-732-7997

Asbestos
#204, 309, rue Chassé, Asbestos, QC J1T 2B3
Fax: 819-879-2501

Baie-Comeau
Centre commercial Laflèche, #204, 625, boul Laflèche ouest, Baie-Comeau, QC G5C 1C5
Fax: 418-295-1313

Beauport (Québec)
Centre commercial Les Promenades Beauport, #265, 3333, rue du Carrefour, 2e étage, Québec, QC G1C 7E1
Fax: 418-681-4810

Bécancour
#200, 1580, boul Port-Royal, 1e étage, Bécancour, QC G9H 1X6
Fax: 819-233-4398

Brossard
2501, boul Lapinière, Brossard, QC J4Z 3P1
Fax: 450-445-5760

Buckingham (Gatineau)
101, rue MacLaren est, 2e étage, Gatineau, QC J8L 2X1
Fax: 819-953-0267

Campbell's Bay
2, rue John, Campbell's Bay, QC J0X 1K0
Fax: 819-648-5102

Cap-aux-Meules
#200, 380, chemin Principal, Cap-aux-Meules, QC G4T 1J7
Fax: 418-986-2764

Causapscal
8, rue St-Jacques nord, Causapscal, QC G0J 1J0
Fax: 418-756-6002

Chandler
#201, 75 boul René-Lévesque est, Chandler, QC G0C 1K0
Fax: 418-689-4900

Chibougamau
623 - 3e Rue, Chibougamau, QC G8P 3A2
Fax: 418-748-6730

Chicoutimi
98, rue Racine est, Chicoutimi, QC G7H 1R7

Chisasibi
Complexe administratif, Chisasibi, QC
819-855-2675 Fax: 819-855-2109

Châteauguay
#101, 245, boul St-Jean Baptiste, Châteauguay, QC J6K 3C3
Fax: 450-691-4247

Coaticook
#300, 14, rue Adams, Coaticook, QC J1A 2B4
Fax: 819-849-4196

Cowansville
224, rue du Sud, 2e étage, Cowansville, QC J2K 1M7
Fax: 450-263-8838

Côte-des-Neiges (Montréal)
Carré Décarie, #3015, 6900, boul Décarie, 3e étage, Cote-St-Luc, QC H3X 2K5
Fax: 514-496-1335

Dolbeau
1500, rue des Érables, Dolbeau-Mistassini, QC G8L 1C4

Donnacona
#110, 100, rte 138, Donnacona, QC G3M 1C1
Fax: 418-681-4810

Drummondville
Édifice Surprenant, 1525, boul St-Joseph, Drummondville, QC J2C 2E9
Fax: 819-478-8137

Forestville
Centre Forestville, #800, 25, rte 138 est, Forestville, QC G0T 1E0
Fax: 418-587-4956

Gaspé
Édifice Frédérica-Giroux, 98, rue de la Reine, 1e étage, Gaspé, QC G4X 1E5
Fax: 418-368-2785

Gatineau
#150, 85, rue Bellehumeur, Gatineau, QC J8T 8B7
Fax: 819-561-2726

Granby
#201, 35, rue Dufferin, Granby, QC J2G 4W6
Fax: 450-378-5719

Hull-Aylmer (Gatineau)
920, boul St-Joseph, Gatineau, QC J8Z 1S9
Fax: 819-953-0267

Joliette
Comlexe Joliette, #100, 46, rue Gauthier sud, Joliette, QC J6E 4J4
Fax: 450-756-2579

Jonquière
#102, 3750, boul du Royaume, Ville de Saguenay, QC G7X 0A4

La Malbaie
541, rue St-Étienne, La Malbaie, QC G5A 1J3
Fax: 418-681-4810

La Pocatière
Les Cours Painchaud, #103, 708, 4e av, La Pocatière, QC G0R 1Z0
Fax: 418-856-3688

La Sarre
Centre commercial Carrefour La Sarre, #30, 255 - 3e rue est, La Sarre, QC J9Z 3N7
Fax: 819-333-3612

La Tuque
Centre commercial Carrefour La Tuque, 290, rue St-Joseph, La Tuque, QC G9X 1L1
Fax: 819-523-6028

Lac Mégantic
#201, 5200, rue Frontenac, 2e étage, Lac-Mégantic, QC G6B 2E7
Fax: 819-583-0944

Lasalle (Montréal)
7655, boul Newman, Lasalle, QC H8N 1X7
Fax: 514-363-9059

Laval
1041, boul des Laurentides, Laval, QC H7G 2W2
Fax: 450-682-3856

Lévis
Place Lévis, #175, 50 rte du Président-Kennedy, Lévis, QC G6V 6C7
Fax: 418-834-2551

Longueuil
#100, 1195, ch Du Tremblay, Longueuil, QC J4N 1A2
Fax: 450-448-7506

Louisville
507, rue Marcel, Louisville, QC J5V 1T7
Fax: 819-228-3848

Magog
1700, rue Sherbrooke, #100A, Magog, QC J1X 5B6
Fax: 819-843-5427

Maniwaki
Galeries Maniwaki, #220, 100, rue Principale sud, Maniwaki, QC J9E 1Z9
Fax: 819-449-7087

Matane
Les Galeries du Vieux Port, #220, 750, av du Phare ouest, Matane, QC G4W 1V4
Fax: 418-562-9200

Mercier (Montréal)
5455 rue Chauveau, 1e étage, Montréal, QC H1N 1G8
Fax: 514-355-8914

Mont-Laurier
431, rue de la Madone, 1e étage, Mont-Laurier, QC J9L 1S2
Fax: 819-623-7113

Montmagny
37, av Sainte-Brigitte sud, Montmagny, QC G5V 2Y3
Fax: 418-834-2551

Montréal (Centre-ville)
Complexe Guy-Favreau, #034, 200, boul René-Lévesque ouest, Montréal, QC H2Z 1X4
Fax: 514-496-5951

New Richmond
Carrefour Baie-des-Chaleurs, 122, boul Perron ouest, 2e étage, New Richmond, QC G0C 2B0
Fax: 418-392-4346

Nunavik
5207, ch de l'Aéroport, Kuujjuaq, QC J0M 1C0
866-351-6278 Fax: 866-534-5860

Pointe-Claire (Montréal)
#100, 181, boul Hymus, Pointe-Claire, QC H9R 1E9
Fax: 514-496-1335

Pointe-aux-Trembles (Montréal)
13313, rue Sherbrooke est, Montréal, QC H1A 1C2
Fax: 514-642-7640

Québec (Centre-ville)
330, rue de la Gare-du-Palais, Québec, QC G1K 7R1
Fax: 418-681-4810

Repentigny
Place Repentigny, #54, 155, rue Notre-Dame, Repentigny, QC J6A 7G5
Fax: 450-585-2180

Rimouski
Édifice Boisé Langevin, #201, 287, rue Pierre-Saindon, Rimouski, QC G5L 9A7
Fax: 418-722-3369

Rivière-du-Loup
298, boul Armand-Thériault, 2e étage, Rivière-du-Loup, QC G5R 4Y4
Fax: 418-862-1923

Roberval
Plaza Roberval, #202, 755, boul Saint-Joseph, Roberval, QC G8H 2L5

Rouyn-Noranda
Édifice Réal-Caouette, #300, 151, av du Lac, Rouyn-Noranda, QC J9X 6Z4
Fax: 819-762-4605

Saint-Eustache
250, boul Arthur-Sauvé, Saint-Eustache, QC J7R 2H9
Fax: 450-473-9020

Saint-Georges
11400 - 1re av est, 2e étage, Saint-Georges, QC G5Y 6R1
Fax: 418-335-3715

Saint-Hyacinthe
Galeries St-Hyacinthe, #2500, 3225, av Cusson, 2e étage, Saint-Hyacinthe, QC J2S 0H7
Fax: 450-773-8276

Saint-Jean-sur-Richelieu
#106, 320, boul du Séminaire nord, Saint-Jean-sur-Richelieu, QC J3B 5L1
Fax: 450-348-5303

Saint-Jérôme
#100, 339, boul Jean-Paul-Hogue, Saint-Jérôme, QC J7Z 7A5
Fax: 866-613-5613

Saint-Léonard (Montréal)
#500, 6020, rue Jean-Talon est, Saint-Léonard, QC H1S 3B1
Fax: 514-355-8914

Sainte-Agathe-des-Monts
118, rue Principale est, 2e étage, Sainte-Agathe-des-Monts, QC J8C 1L1
Fax: 819-326-6205

Sainte-Anne-des-Monts
230, 1ére av ouest, Sainte-Anne-des-Monts, QC G4V 1E2
Fax: 418-763-7414

Sainte-Foy (Québec)
Édifice Saint-Mathieu, #200, 3175, ch des Quatre-Bourgeois, 2e étage, Québec, QC G1X 2Z7
Fax: 418-681-4810

Sainte-Thérèse
#110, 100, boul Ducharme, Sainte-Thérèse, QC J7E 1X2
Fax: 450-430-5885

Senneterre
761 - 10e av, Senneterre, QC J0Y 2M0
Fax: 819-737-8872

Sept-Îles
701, boul Laure, 3e étage, Sept-Îles, QC G4R 1X8
Fax: 418-962-8301

Shawinigan
444 - 5e rue, Shawinigan, QC G9N 1E6
Fax: 819-536-7063

Sherbrooke
124, rue Wellington nord, Sherbrooke, QC J1H 5X8
Fax: 819-564-5769

Sorel-Tracy
101, rue Augusta, Sorel, QC J3P 1A7
Fax: 450-743-8338

Terrebonne
835, montée Masson, Terrebonne, QC J6W 2P4
Fax: 450-471-2417

Thetford Mines
#500, 350, boul Frontenac ouest, Thetford Mines, QC G6G 6K2
Fax: 418-335-3715

Trois-Rivières
Édifice Bourg du Fleuve, 55, rue des Forges, Trois-Rivières, QC G9A 2G6
Fax: 819-379-3085

Val-d'Or
400, av Centrale, Val-d'Or, QC J9P 1P4
Fax: 819-825-0726

Valleyfield
#100, 73, rue Maden, Salaberry-de-Valleyfield, QC J6S 3V4
Fax: 450-373-2356

Vaudreuil-Dorion
2555, rue Dutrisac, Vaudreuil-Dorion, QC J7V 7E6
Fax: 450-424-0506

Verdun
4110, rue Wellington, 2e étage, Montréal, QC H4G 2P4
Fax: 514-496-6986

Victoriaville
84, boul Labbé sud, Victoriaville, QC G6P 0E4
Fax: 819-758-7809

Ville-Marie
18, rue Notre-Dame-de-Lourdes, Ville-Marie, QC J9V 1X7
Fax: 819-629-3496

Villeray (Montréal)
#300, 1415, rue Jarry est, 3e étage, Montréal, QC H2E 3B4
514-723-7273 Fax: 514-723-6249

Saskatchewan:

Estevan
1314 - 3 St., Estevan, SK S4A 1E9

La Ronge
1016 La Ronge Ave., La Ronge, SK S0J 1L0

Melfort
McKendry Plaza, 104 McKendry Ave. West, Melfort, SK S0E 1A0

Moose Jaw
Victoria Place, #501, 111 Fairford St. East, Moose Jaw, SK S6H 0B8

North Battleford
Territorial Place, #15, 9800 Territorial Dr., North Battleford, SK S9A 3N6

Prince Albert
1288 Central Ave., Prince Albert, SK S6V 3B3

Regina
Alvin Hamilton Bldg., 1783 Hamilton St., Regina, SK S4P 4B4

Saskatoon
Federal Bldg., 101 - 22 St. East, Saskatoon, SK S7K 0E1

Swift Current
Chinook Bldg., 250 Central Ave. North, Swift Current, SK S9H 0L2

Weyburn
City Centre Mall, 110 Souris Ave., Main Fl., Weyburn, SK S4H 2Z8

Yorkton
Imperial Plaza, 214 Smith St. East, Yorkton, SK S3N 3S6

Yukon:

Whitehorse
Elijah Smith Bldg., #125, 300 Main St., Whitehorse, YK Y1A 2B5

Immigration & Refugee Board of Canada (IRB) / Commission de l'immigration et du statut de réfugié du Canada (CISR)

Canada Bldg, 344 Slater St., 12th Fl., Ottawa, ON K1A 0K1
613-995-6486 Fax: 613-943-1550
contact@irb-cisr.gc.ca
www.irb-cisr.gc.ca

The IRB is an independent administrative tribunal that reports to Parliament through the Minister of Citizenship & Immigration Canada (CIC). The Board's mission, on behalf of Canadians, is to make well-reasoned decisions on immigration & refugee matters efficiently, fairly, & in accordance with the law. As Canada's largest federal tribunal, the IRB consists of three divisions. The Refugee Protection Division decides claims for refugee protection made by persons in Canada. The Immigration Division conducts detention reviews & immigration inquiries for certain categories of people believed to be inadmissable, or removable from, Canada. The Immigration Appeal Division hears appeals of sponsorship applications refused by officials of Citizenship & Immigration Canada; appeals from certain removal orders made against permanent residents, refugees & other protected persons, & holders of permanent resident visas; appeals by permanent residents who have been found outside Canada not to have fulfilled their residency obligation; & appeals by CIC from decisions of the Immigration Division at admissability hearings.

Chair, Brian Goodman
613-996-4752, Fax: 613-947-5338, brian.goodman@irb-cisr.gc.ca
Executive Director, Simon Coakeley
613-947-1040, simon.coakeley@irb-cisr.gc.ca
Deputy Chairperson, Immigration Appeal Division, Shari Stein
613-995-7289, shari.stein@irb-cisr.gc.ca
Deputy Chairperson, Refugee Protection Division, Ken Sandhu
613-947-6711, ken.sandhu@irb-cisr.gc.ca
Director General, Corporate Planning & Services Branch, Serge Gascon
613-947-6679, serge.gascon@irb-cisr.gc.ca
Director General, Human Resources & Professional Development Branch, Diane Lacelle
613-995-0805, diane.lacelle@irb-cisr.gc.ca
Director General, Immigration Division, Susan Bibeau
613-947-6922, susan.bibeau@irb-cisr.gc.ca
Deputy Director General, Operations Branch, Thomas Vulpe
613-947-7184, thomas.vulpe@irb-cisr.gc.ca
Director General, Strategic Communication & Partnerships, Kevin White
613-995-3513, kevin.white@irb-cisr.gc.ca
Senior General Counsel, Legal Services, Sylvia Cox-Duquette
613-943-2310, Fax: 613-947-2607, sylvia.cox-duquette@irb-cisr.gc.ca
Director, Communications, Aarin Masson
613-996-1329, aarin.masson@irb-cisr.gc.ca
Communications Officer, Christopher Slaney
613-943-3940, christopher.slaney@irb-cisr.gc.ca

Treaty Negotiation Offices:

Vancouver
Comprehensive Claims Branch, #600, 1168 Melville St., Vancouver, BC V6E 4S3
604-775-7114 Fax: 604-666-2546

Victoria
#309, 1230 Government St., Victoria, BC V8W 2Z4
250-363-6910 Fax: 250-363-6911

Industry Canada / Industrie Canada

C.D. Howe Building, 235 Queen St., Ottawa, ON K1A 0H5
613-954-5031 Fax: 613-954-2340
800-328-6189
info@ic.gc.ca
www.ic.gc.ca
TTY: 866-694-8389

The mission of Industry Canada is to help make Canadians more productive & competitive in a global, knowledge-based economy. The department's policies, programs & services assist in the creation of an economy that provides more & better-paying jobs for Canadians; supports stronger business growth through sustained improvements in productivity; & gives consumers, businesses & investors confidence that the marketplace is fair, efficient & competitive. To reach its clients, Industry Canada collaborates extensively with partners at all levels of government & the private sector.

Acts Administered:
Agreement on Internal Trade Implementation Act
Agricultural & Rural Development Act
Atlantic Fisheries Restructuring Act
Bankruptcy & Insolvency Act
Bell Canada Act
Bills of Exchange Act
Boards of Trade Act
British Columbia Telephone Company Act
Budget Implementation Act, 1997
Business Development Bank of Canada Act
Canada Business Corporations Act
Canada Co-operative Associations Act
Canada Corporations Act
Canada Small Business Financing Act
Canadian Space Agency Act
Canadian Tourism Commission Act
Civil International Space Station Agreement Act
Companies' Creditors Arrangement Act
Competition Act
Competition Tribunal Act
Consumer Packaging & Labelling Act
Copyright Act
Corporations & Labour Unions Returns Act
Department of Industry Act
Electricity & Gas Inspection Act
Employment Support Act
Government Corporations Operations Act
Industrial & Regional Development Act
Industrial Design Act
Integrated Circuit Topography Act
Investment Canada Act
National Research Council Act
Natural Sciences & Engineering Research Council Act
Patent Act
Pension Fund Societies Act
Personal Information Protection & Electronic Dociuments Act
Precious Metals Marking Act
Public Documents Act
Public Officers Act
Public Servants Inventions Act
Radiocommunication Act
Regional Development Incentives Act
Seals Act
Small Business Loans Act
Social Sciences & Humanities Research Council Act
Special Areas Act
Standards Council of Canada Act
Statistics Act
Telecommunications Act
Teleglobe Canada Reorganization & Divestiture Act
Telesat Canada Reorganization & Divestiture Act
Textile Labelling Act
Timber Marking Act
Trade-marks Act
Trade Unions Act
Weights & Measures Act
Winding-up & Restructuring Act

Minister, Industry; Minister, State (Agriculture), Hon. Christian Paradis
613-995-9001, minister.industry@ic.gc.ca
Deputy Minister, Richard Dicerni
613-992-4292, Fax: 613-954-3272, richard.dicerni@ic.gc.ca
Sr. Associate Deputy Minister, Simon Kennedy
613-943-7164, Fax: 613-954-2137

Associated Agencies, Boards & Commissions:

• Canadian Tourism Commission (CTC) / Commission canadienne du tourisme (CCT)
#1400, 1055 Dunsmuir St.
PO Box 49230
Vancouver, BC V7X 1L2
604-638-8300
en-corporate.canada.travel
CTC is a unique partnership between tourism business & associations, provincial & territorial governments, & the Government of Canada. The CTC's Board of Directors is a decision-making body composed of 26 members with a wide variety of skills & knowledge, representing all regions of the country. The CTC's mission is to sustain a vibrant & profitable Canadian tourism industry.

• Communications Research Centre Canada (CRC) / Centre de recherches sur les communications
3701 Carling Ave.
PO Box 11490 H
Ottawa, ON K2H 8S2
613-991-3313 Fax: 613-998-5355
info@crc.gc.ca
www.crc.gc.ca
Dedicated to advanced communications research & development for over 50 years. Key research areas include radio science, terrestrial wireless systems, satellite communications broadcasting & broadband network technologies. CRC has a long history of technology transfer. CRC operates an Innovation Centre, a technology incubator for small & medium-sized high-tech start-ups, which provides increased access to CRC's technologies, research expertise & unique laboratories & facilities.

• Competition Tribunal / Tribunal de la concurrence
Thomas D'Arcy McGee Bldg.
#600, 90 Sparks St.
Ottawa, ON K1P 5B4
613-957-3172 Fax: 613-957-3170
tribunal@ct-tc.gc.ca
www.ct-tc.gc.ca
Hears & decides all applications made under Parts V11.1 & VIII of the Competition Act.

• Electronic Commerce Branch / Direction générale du commerce électronique
300 Slater St.
Ottawa, ON K1A 0C8
613-954-5031 Fax: 613-954-2340 800-328-6189 TTY: 866-694-8389
www.ic.gc.ca/eic/site/ecic-ceac.nsf/eng/h_gv00002.html
Coordinates the development & implementation of a national electronic commerce strategy. It is responsible for both domestic & international aspects of electronic commerce. The Canadian Electronic Commerce Strategy was announced in September 1998. The Strategy, which was developed in collaboration with provincial & territorial governments, industry & consumer groups, among others, establishes a framework, goals, timetable, & implementation plan for electronic commerce domestically. The Strategy involves coordinating strategic elements that fall within the federal government's responsibilities, including the policy development areas of encryption & privacy.

• Enterprise Cape Breton Corporation (ECBC) / Société d'expansion du Cap-Breton
Silicon Island
70 Crescent St.
Sydney, NS B1S 2Z7
902-564-3600 Fax: 902-564-3825 800-705-3926
information@ecbc-secb.gc.ca
www.ecbc-secb.gc.ca
Crown corporation established pursuant to Part II of the Government Organization Act, Atlantic Canada, 1987, with a jurisdictional mandate which includes all of Cape Breton Island & a portion of mainland Nova Scotia in & around the Town of Mulgrave. The Corporation is charged with the responsibility for promoting & assisting the financing & development of industry in the region, providing employment outside the coal-producing sector & broadening the base of the local economy.

• Standards Council of Canada / Conseil canadien des normes
#200, 270 Albert Street
Ottawa, ON K1P 6N7
613-238-3222 Fax: 613-569-7808
info@scc.ca
www.scc.ca
The Standards Council of Canada (SCC) works to promote the development & use of national & international standards and reports to Parliament through the Minister of Industry. It consists of 15 members and a staff of 90.

Audit & Evaluation Branch (AEB) / Direction générale de la vérification et de l'évaluation (DGVE)
613-943-7047 Fax: 613-995-8568
Director General, Audit & Evaluation, Susan Hart, CAE
613-954-5084, Fax: 613-954-5070

Canadian Intellectual Property Office (CIPO) / Office de la propriété intellectuelle du Canada (OPIC)
Place du Portage I, #C-229, 50 Victoria Street, Gatineau, QC K1A 0C9
866-997-1936 Fax: 819-953-7620
cipo.contact@ic.gc.ca
www.cipo.ic.gc.ca
TTY: 866-442-2476
Other Communication: International calls: 819-934-0544

Communications & Marketing Branch (CMB) / Direction générale des communications et du marketing (DGCM)
Director General, Brian Spurling
613-947-2597, Fax: 613-954-6436

Competition Bureau / Bureau de la concurrence
Place du Portage, Phase I, 50 Victoria Street, Ottawa, ON K1A 0C9
819-997-4282 Fax: 819-997-0324
800-348-5358
www.competitionbureau.gc.ca
TTY: 800-642-3844
The Competition Bureau is the organization responsible for the enforcement of the Competition Act, the Consumer Packaging & Labelling Act except as it relates to food, the Precious Metals Marking Act & the Textile Labelling Act. The Competition Bureau ensures compliance by the business community with legislation administered by the Bureau, & oversees the development of policy & dissemination of information aimed at ensuring optimal compliance levels.
Commissioner of Competition, Melanie Aitken
819-997-3304, Fax: 819-953-5013
Deputy Commissioner, Vicky Eatrides
819-997-5222, Fax: 819-953-5013

Industry Sector / Secteur de l'industrie
613-954-3395 Fax: 613-941-1134
Industry Sector (IS) assists Canadian industry & businesses compete, expand & create jobs in the knowledge-based economy. IS contributes to Industry Canada's strategic objectives, trade, investment, innovation, connectedness & marketplace. It facilitates delivery of industrial, related policy analyses & strategies to promote global competitiveness of Canadian industry. IS provides a broad range of services, information resources, sector policies & strategies to support business growth. IS provides Canadian businesses with timely information products, business tools, research, strategic analyses, data & information resources.
Sr. Assistant Deputy Minister, Ron Parker
613-954-3798, Fax: 613-941-1134

Aerospace, Defence & Marine Branch / Aérospatiale, defense et la marine
613-954-3786 Fax: 613-998-6703
Director General, Brian Gear
613-941-8123, Fax: 613-998-6703
Senior Policy Advisor, Katie Durling
613-960-9403, Fax: 613-998-6703

Automotive & Transportation Industries Branch / Direction générale des industries de l'automobile et des transports
613-952-0441 Fax: 613-952-8088
Director General, Alison Tait
613-954-2949, Fax: 613-941-2379

Life Science Industries Branch / Sciences de la vie
613-946-3144 Fax: 613-946-3144
Director General, Leah Clark
613-954-5258, Fax: 613-952-5822

Manufacturing & Resource Processing Industries Branch / Industries de la fabrication et de la transformation des ressources naturelles
613-954-2892 Fax: 613-941-8048
strategis.gc.ca/rpib
Director General, Tim Elliot
613-954-2990, Fax: 613-941-8048
Director, Forestry & Energy Industries Directorate, Jyotsna Dalvi
613-941-2274, Fax: 613-941-8048
Director, Manufacturing Sector Benchmarking & Collaborative Research Directorate, Patrick Hurens
613-952-1710, Fax: 613-954-3107
Director, Resource Manufacturing Industries Directorate, Daniel Charrette
613-954-2703, Fax: 613-954-3107

Regional Operations / Opérations régionales
613-941-3095 Fax: 613-954-4883
Asst. Deputy Minister, Mitch Davies
613-954-3405, Fax: 613-954-4883
Senior Advisor to the Asst. Deputy Minister, Diane St-Gelais
613-954-3407, Fax: 613-954-4883

Small Business, Tourism & Marketplace Services / Services axés sur le marché, le tourisme et la petite entreprise
613-995-9305 Fax: 613-941-1938
Asst. Deputy Minister, Marie-Josée Thivierge
613-995-9605, Fax: 613-948-9088

Chief Informatics Office / Bureau principal de l'informatique
613-954-3570 Fax: 613-941-1938

Corporations Canada
365 Laurier Avenue West, Ottawa, ON K1A 0C8
613-941-4550 Fax: 613-941-0601

Information Management Branch / Direction générale de la gestion de l'information
613-954-3749 Fax: 613-990-4848

Investment Review & Strategic Planning Branch / Direction générale de l'examen des investissements et de la planification stratégique
613-954-1887 Fax: 613-996-2515
investcan.ic.gc.ca

Measurement Canada / Mesures Canada
151 Tunney's Pasture Driveway, Ottawa, ON K1A 0C9
613-952-0652 Fax: 613-957-1265
mc.ic.gc.ca

Office of the Superintendent of Bankruptcy / Bureau du surintendant des faillites
155 Queen Street, Ottawa, ON K1A 0H5
613-941-1000 Fax: 613-941-2862
osb-bsf.ic.gc.ca

Small Business & Tourism Branch / Direction générale de la petite entreprise et du tourisme
613-954-5479 Fax: 613-946-1035

Spectrum, Information Technologies & Telecommunications / Spectre, technologies de l'information et télécommunications
Journal Tower North, 300 Slater St., 20th Fl., Ottawa, ON K1A 0C8
613-998-0368 Fax: 613-952-1203
Contributes to the Industry Canada mandate by fostering the early development & use of information & communications technologies, infrastructures & services. The sector uses its policy & regulatory rule-making powers, & marketplace & industry sectoral development services to ensure Canada has a world-class telecommunications & information infrastructure; promote the international competitiveness of Canadian information technologies by all sectors of the Canadian economy; & ensure effective & efficient use of the radio frequency spectrum.
Sr. Assistant Deputy Minister, Helen McDonald
613-998-0368, Fax: 613-952-1203
Assistant Deputy Minister, Susan Bincoletto
613-998-0368, Fax: 613-952-1203

Office of the Information Commissioner of Canada / Commissariat à l'information du Canada

Place de Ville, Tower B, 112 Kent St., 7th Fl., Ottawa, ON K1A 1H3
613-995-2410 Fax: 613-947-7294
800-267-0441
general@oic-ci.gc.ca
www.oic-ci.gc.ca
TTY: 613-947-0388
The Office of the Information Commissioner of Canada was established in 1983. It investigates complaints from people and organizations who believe they have been denied rights under the Access of Information Act, Canada's freedom of information legislation.
An independent ombudsperson appointed by Parliament, the Information Commissioner has strong investigative powers. The Information Commissioner mediates between government institutions & dissatisfied applicants, & may refer cases to the Federal Court for resolution.
Acts Administered:
Access to Information Act
Information Commissioner, Suzanne Legault
613-995-9976, Fax: 613-995-1501
Social Media: www.facebook.com/OICCANADA
Assistant Information Commissioner, Complaints Resolution & Compliance, Andrea J. Neill
613-995-2665, Fax: 613-947-7294
Interim Director General, Corporate Services Branch, Layla Michaud
613-995-2864, Fax: 613-995-1501
General Counsel, Legal Services, Emily McCarthy
613-947-1834, Fax: 613-947-5252

Infrastructure Canada

#1100, 180 Kent Street, Ottawa, ON K1P 0B6
613-948-1148 Fax: 613-946-9888
800-622-6232
info@infc.gc.ca
www.infc.gc.ca
TTY: 800-465-7735
Infrastructure Canada is part of the Ministry of Transport, Infrastructure & Communities (TIC). It works to develop a strong infrastructure across Canada through programs such as the Building Canada Plan and the Gas Tax Fund, which will result in cleaner air and water and reduced greenhouse gas emissions.
Minister, Transport, Infrastructure & Communities, Hon. Denis Lebel
613-991-0700, Fax: 613-995-0327, mintc@tc.gc.ca
Parliamentary Secretary, Brian Jean
613-992-1154, Fax: 613-992-4603, Jean.B@parl.gc.ca
Associate Deputy Minister, John Forster
613-948-8157, Fax: 613-948-2963, john.forster@infc.gc.ca

Corporate Services Branch / Direction générale des services ministériels
The Corporate Services Branch works to support corporate functions such as procurement, human resources, finance, security, planning & administration, internal audit & evaluation and IT.
Assistant Deputy Minister, David Miller
613-948-9161, Fax: 613-960-6348, david.miller@infc.gc.ca

Policy & Communications Branch / Politiques et communications
The branch conducts research, both independently & with partners, on infrastructure issues for potential federal action. Policy & Communications also shares knowledge to further understanding of infrastructure issues affecting cities & communities. Policy advice is also offered to the Minister.
Assistant Deputy Minister, Taki Sarantakis
613-946-5188, Fax: 613-960-9648, taki.sarantakis@infc.gc.ca
Director General, Communications Directorate, Jennifer Dawson
613-948-2940, Fax: 613-948-2940,
jennifer.dawson@infc.gc.ca
Director General, Policy & Priorities Directorate, Samantha Tattersall
613-948-7237, Fax: 613-948-9393,
samantha.tattersall@infc.gc.ca

Office of Intergovernmental Affairs (IGA) / Affaires intergouvernementales

c/o Privy Council Office, #1000, 85 Slater St., Ottawa, ON K1A 0A3
613-957-5153 Fax: 613-957-5043
info@pco-bcp.gc.ca
www.pco-bcp.gc.ca/aia
TTY: 613-957-5741
The federal government office is responsible for the management of federal-provincial-territorial relations.
The office supports & advises the Prime Minister & the Minister of Intergovernmental Affairs about issues related to federal-provincial-territorial relations, such as communications, policies, & parliamentary affairs. Fiscal federalism, the evolution of the federation, & Canadian unity are key areas for the IGA.
Minister, Intergovernmental Affairs; President, Queen's Privy Council for Canada, Hon. Peter Penashue, P.C.
613-996-4630, Fax: 613-996-7132,
peter.penashue@parl.gc.ca
Social Media: www.twitter.com/PeterPenashue,
www.facebook.com/peterpenashue
Deputy Minister; Associate Secretary to the Cabinet, Janice Charette, B.Comm. (Hons.)
613-957-5466
Parliamentary Secretary to the Prime Minister & to the Minister, Intergovernmental Affairs, Dean del Mastro, B. Comm. (Hons.)
613-995-6411, Fax: 613-996-9800,
dean.delmastro@parl.gc.ca; delmad1@parl.gc.ca
Social Media: www.twitter.com/mpdeandelmastro,
www.facebook.com/deandelmastro

International Development Research Centre (IDRC) / Centre de recherches pour le développement international (CRDI)

150 Kent St., PO Box 8500, Ottawa, ON K1G 3H9
613-236-6163 Fax: 613-238-7230
info@idrc.ca
www.idrc.ca
Helps scientists in developing countries identify long-term, practical solutions to pressing development problems. Support is given directly to scientists working in universities, private enterprise, government & non-profit-making organizations. Priority is given to research aimed at achieving equitable & sustainable development. One of the three program areas of focus is Environmental & Natural Resource Management. Initiatives in this area include a rural poverty & environment program initiative, an urban poverty & environment program, ecosystem approaches to human health, an international model forest network, biodiversity & regional water demand initiative.
Chair, Barbara McDougall
613-236-6163, Fax: 613-565-8212, bmcdougall@idrc.ca
President, David M. Malone
613-236-6163, Fax: 613-235-6391, dmalone@idrc.ca
Vice-President, Resources & CFO, Sylvain Dufour
613-236-6163, Fax: 613-236-7293, sdufour@idrc.ca
Vice-President, Programs & Partnership Branch, Rohinton Medhora
613-236-6163, Fax: 613-567-7748, rmedhora@idrc.ca
Director, Communications Division, Angela Prokopiak
613-236-6163, Fax: 613-563-2476, aprokopiak@idrc.ca
Director, Environmental & Natural Resource Management, Jean Lebel
613-236-6163, Fax: 613-567-7748, jlebel@idrc.ca
Chief, Public Affairs & Parliamentary Relations, VACANT
613-236-6163, Fax: 613-238-7230

Regional Offices:
Eastern & Southern Africa
IDRC, Liasion House, 2nd Floor, State House Avenue, Nairobi, 62084 00200 Kenya
vngugi@idrc.ca
www.idrc.ca/esaro
Other Communication: Tel: 254-20-2713160; Fax: 254-20-2711063
Latin America & the Caribbean
Avenida Brasil 2655, Montevideo, 11300 Uruguay
lacroinf@idrc.ca
www.idrc.ca/lacro
Other Communication: Tel: 598-2-709-0042; Fax: 598-2-708-6776
Middle East & North Africa
8 Ahmed Nessim St., 8th fl., PO Box 14, Giza, Cairo
skamel@idrc.ca
www.idrc.ca/cairo
Other Communication: Tel: 20-2-336-7051; Fax: 20-2-336-7056
South Asia & China
IDRC, 208 Jor Bagh, New Delhi, 110 003 India
saro@idrc.ca
www.idrc.ca/saro
Other Communication: Tel: 91-11-2461-9411; Fax: 91-11-2462-2707
Southeast & East Asia
IDRC, Tanglin, #02-55 - 22 Cross St., Singapore, 048421 Singapore
asro@idrc.ca
www.idrc.ca/asro
Other Communication: Tel: 65-6438-7877; Fax: 65-6438-4844
West & Central Africa
CRDI, CD Annexe, BP 11007, Peytavin, Dakar
waro@idrc.ca
www.idrc.ca/waro
Other Communication: Tel: 221-33-864-0000; Fax: 221-33-825-3255

International Joint Commission (IJC) / Commission mixte internationale (CMI)

234 Laurier Ave. West, 22nd Fl., Ottawa, ON K1P 6K6
613-947-1420 Fax: 613-993-5583
beckhoffb@ottawa.ijc.org
www.ijc.org
Other Communication: Great Lakes Water Quality Information: 519-257-6700

Established by the Boundary Waters Treaty of 1909 & is responsible for approving (by Order of Approval) certain works in boundary waters which affect levels & flows on both sides of the Canada-US border. The commission provides recommendations on matters along the common boundary which have been referred to the Commission by the governments. Also monitors & assesses the Great Lakes Water Quality Agreement (GLWQA) & is responsible for reviewing & commenting on Remedial Action Plans (RAPs) in coordination with eight US states & the province of Ontario.

Chair, Joseph Comuzzi
Commissioner, Lyall D. Knott
Commissioner, Pierre Trépanier

Great Lakes Regional Office
100 Ouellette Ave., 8th fl., Windsor, ON N9A 6T3
519-257-6733 Fax: 519-257-6740
nevinj@windsor.ijc.org
Other Communication: Information: 519-257-6700
Director, Great Lakes Regional Office, Dr. Saad Y. Jasim
519-257-6715, jasims@windsor.ijc.org

United States Section / Section des États-Unis
#615, 2000 L Street, Northwest, Washington, DC 20440 USA
202-736-9024 Fax: 202-643-2007
bevacquaf@washington.ijc.org
Chair, Lana Pollack
Commissioner, Dereth Glance
Commissioner, Rich Moy
Public Information Officer, Frank Bevacqua
202-736-9024, bevacquaf@washington.ijc.org

Justice Canada

East Memorial Bldg., 284 Wellington St., Ottawa, ON K1A 0H8
613-957-4222 Fax: 613-954-0811
webadmin@justice.gc.ca
www.justice.gc.ca
TTY: 613-992-4556
Other Communication: Media Relations Phone: 613-957-4207; Access to Information and Privacy Phone: 613-952-8361

The Department ensures that the Canadian justice system is fair, accessible & efficient. Responsibilities are as follows: provision of policy & program advice & direction by the development of the legal content of bills, regulations, & guidelines; prosecution of federal offences throughout Canada; litigation of civil cases by or on behalf of the federal Crown; & provision of legal advice to federal law enforcement agencies & other government departments.

Acts Administered:
Annulment of Marriages (Ontario) Act
Anti-Terroism Act
Canada Evidence Act
Canada Prize Act
Canada-United Kingdom Civil & Commercial Judgments Convention Act
Canadian Bill of Rights
Canadian Human Rights Act
Commercial Arbitration Act
Contraventions Act
Controlled Drugs & Substance Act
Crown Liability & Proceedings Act
Department of Justice Act
Divorce Act
Escheats Act
Extradition Act
Family Orders Agreements Enforcement Assistance Act
Federal Courts Act
Firearms Act
Foreign Enlistment Act
Foreign Extraterritorial Measures Act
Fugitive Offenders Act
Identification of Criminals Act
International Sale of Goods Contracts Convention Act
Interpretation Act
Judges Act
Law Commission of Canada Act
Marriage (Prohibited Degrees) Act
Mutual Legal Assistance in Criminal Matters Act
Official Languages Act
Postal Services Interruption Relief Act
Revised Statutes of Canada, 1985 Act
Security Offences Act
State Immunity Act
Statute Revision Act
Statutory Instruments Act
Supreme Court Act
Tax Court of Canada Act
United Nations Foreign Arbitral Awards Convention Act
Youth Criminal Justice Act

Minister of Justice shares responsibility to Parliament for the following Acts:
Access to Information Act (President of the Treasury Board)
Bills of Lading Act (Minister of Transport)
Criminal Code (Solicitor General & Minister of Agriculture & Agri-Foods)
Garnishment, Attachment Pension Diversion Act (Minister of National Defense, Minister of Finance & Minister of Public Works & Government Services)
Privacy Act (President of the Treasury Board)

Minister, Justice; Attorney General of Canada, Hon. Robert Douglas Nicholson
613-992-4621, Fax: 613-992-7910, Nicholson.R@parl.gc.ca
Parliamentary Secretary to the Minister of Justice, Anita McGuire
613-995-4621, Fax: 613-990-7255, anita.mcguire@parl.gc.ca
Deputy Minister & Deputy Attorney General, Miles J. Kirvan
613-957-4998
Associate Deputy Minister, Yves Côté
613-941-4073, Fax: 613-941-4074
Chief Audit Executive, Steve Samuels
613-991-8200, Fax: 613-998-4030
Head Integration, Barbara Ritzen
780-495-4074, Fax: 780-495-5835, Other Communications: Alternate telephone: 613-960-3420
Executive Director & General Counsel, Canadian Heritage, Legal Services, Marc Tremblay
819-997-2729, Fax: 819-997-2801

Aboriginal Affairs Portfolio / Portfeuille des affaires autochtones
Fax: 613-954-4737
Asst. Deputy Attorney General, Pamela McCurry
613-946-6633, Fax: 613-954-4737
Deputy Asst. Deputy Attorney General, Michael Hudson
604-775-5173, Fax: 604-775-5152, Other Communications: Alt. Phone: 613-946-1385
Senior General Counsel, Indian & Northern Affairs Canada, Legal Services Unit, Andrew Saranchuk
819-994-4141
Senior Counsel, Aboriginal Law & Strategic Initiatives, Danielle Dussault
613-941-2240
General Counsel, Indian & Northern Affairs Canada - Legal Services Unit, Margaret McIntosh
819-953-0856
Senior General Counsel, Resolution, Geoffrey Bickert
613-946-3839, Fax: 613-946-6896

Business & Regulatory Law Portfolio / Portefeuille du droit des affaires et du droit réglementaire
Fax: 613-946-9988
Asst. Deputy Minister, Pierre Legault
613-947-4944, Fax: 613-946-9988
General Counsel & Executive Director, Competition Bureau, Rhona Einbinder-Miller
819-997-9210, Fax: 819-953-9267
General Counsel, Transport Legal Services, Isabelle Jacques
613-993-4558, Fax: 613-990-5777

Central Agencies Group / Groupes centraux
Fax: 613-995-7223
Asst. Deputy Minister & Counsel to the Dept. of Finance, Sandra Hassan
613-996-4667, Fax: 613-995-7223
Senior General Counsel, Treasury Board, Michel LeFrançois
613-952-3379, Fax: 613-954-5806
Senior Counsel, Yvonne Milosevic
613-943-0418, Fax: 613-995-7223
General Counsel, Public Service Commission, Gaston Arseneault
613-995-0445, Fax: 613-995-0198
General Counsel, Office of the Superintendent of Financial Institutions, Alain Prévost
613-990-7787

Civil Litigation Division / Division du contentieux des affaires civiles
Asst. Deputy Attorney General, Simon Fothergill
613-957-4840, Fax: 613-941-1972
Director General & Senior General Counsel, Alain Préfontaine
613-946-3815, Fax: 613-954-1920

Communications Branch
284 Wellington St., Ottawa, ON K1A 0H8
Fax: 613-941-2329
Director General, Suesan Saville
613-957-9596, Fax: 613-941-2329
Information Officer, Valerie Laforce
613-957-4223, Fax: 613-954-0811
Director, Creative Services & Outreach, Dorothy Love
613-954-6327, Fax: 613-948-2983
Manager, Public & Media Relations, Christian Girouard
613-941-7326, Fax: 613-954-0811

Corporate Services / Services à la gestion
Fax: 613-957-8382
Asst. Deputy Minister, Joel A. Oliver
613-941-7890, Fax: 613-957-6377
Director General, Human Resources & Professional Development, Joan Pratt
613-941-1867, Fax: 613-954-1867
Chief Information Officer, Paul N. Wagner
613-941-5202, Fax: 613-941-5201

Federal Prosecution Service / Service fédéral des poursuites
Asst. Deputy Attorney General, Daniel Bellemare, Q.C.
613-957-4756, Fax: 613-954-2958
Senior General Counsel & Director, Strategic Operations Section, George Dolhai
613-941-2653
Senior General Counsel & Director, Criminal Law Section, Clare Barry
613-946-3822

Legislative Services Branch / Division des services législatifs
Chief Legislative Counsel, John Mark Keyes
613-954-5786, Fax: 613-952-4080
Chief Legislative Editor, Legislative Revising & Editing Services, Ingrid Ludchen
613-957-8497, Fax: 613-957-7866
Deputy Chief Legislative Counsel, Philippe Hallée
613-941-4178, Fax: 613-941-1193

Policy Sector / Secteur des politiques
Senior Asst. Deputy Minister, Donald K. Piragoff
613-957-4730, Fax: 613-957-9949
Director, Business Management, Senior Assistant Deputy Minister's Office, Paul Roy
613-954-3890, Fax: 613-957-9949
Senior Counsel & Director, Senior Assistant Deputy Minister's Office, Phaedra Glushek
613-941-8826, Fax: 613-941-2279
Senior General Counsel & Director General, Criminal Law Policy, Catherine Kane
613-957-4690, Fax: 613-952-1110
Director & General Counsel, Cabinet & Leg, Criminal Law Policy, Carole Morency
613-941-4044, Fax: 613-941-9310
Senior General Counsel, Family, Children & Youth Section, Elissa Lieff
613-957-1200, Fax: 613-952-5740
General Counsel & Director General, Youth Justice & Strategic Initiatives, Gillian Blackell
613-954-3233, Fax: 613-954-3275
Director General, International Legal Programs, Serge Lortie
613-954-7585, Fax: 613-948-8910
Director General, Policy Integration & Coordination Section, Stan E. Lipinski
613-941-2267, Fax: 613-957-4019
Director & General Counsel, Security, Terrorism & Governance, Criminal Law Policy, Doug Breithaupt
613-957-4743, Fax: 613-941-9310
General Counsel, Sentencing Reform, Criminal Law Policy, David Daubney
613-957-4755
Director, Programs & Corporate Affairs, Youth & Strategic Initiatives Section, Hana Hruska
613-957-3140, Fax: 613-954-3348
Senior Counsel, Youth & Strategic Initiatives Section, Paula Kingston
613-954-3187, Fax: 613-954-3275
Director, International Relations Group, Michelle Douglas
613-957-4959, Fax: 613-948-8910
Director & Senior Counsel, International Legal Programs, Aly N. Alibhai
613-952-4032, Fax: 613-948-8910
Senior Counsel Coordinator, Family Law Policy, Claire Farid
613-957-2788, Fax: 613-952-9600

Programs Branch / Direction générale des programmes
Director General, Office of the Director General, Barbara Merriam
613-957-4344, Fax: 613-954-4893
Director, Legal Aid, Bonny Wong-Fortin
613-952-5759, Fax: 613-954-9423
Director, Policy Implementation, Elizabeth Hendy
613-941-1085, Fax: 613-941-5446
Director, Aboriginal Justice Directorate, Karolyn Lui
613-946-6903, Fax: 613-957-4697
Senior Financial Advisor, Grants and Contribution Financial Services, Marc Bénard
613-941-4194, Fax: 613-941-2269
Director, Innovations, Analysis and Integration Directorate, Marc Rozon
613-954-2884, Fax: 613-941-5446

Public Law Sector / Secteur du Droit public
Asst. Deputy Minister, Carolyn P. Kobernick
613-957-4939, Fax: 613-957-1403
Senior General Counsel, Constitutional & Administrative Law Section, Ann Chaplin
613-948-2992, Fax: 613-941-1937
General Counsel & Director, Official Languages Law Group, Marie Tremblay
613-941-4037, Fax: 613-952-0677
General Counsel & Director, Information Law & Privacy, Denis Kratchanov
613-957-4624, Fax: 613-941-2002
Deputy Director General & General Counsel, Human Rights Law Section, Jodie van Dieen
613-952-4131, Fax: 613-952-4137
Director & General Counsel, International Private Law Section, Kathryn Sabo
613-957-4967, Fax: 613-957-3854

Public Safety, Defence & Immigration Portfolio / Sécurité Publique, défense & immigration
Asst. Deputy Attorney General, Daniel Therrien
613-952-4774, Fax: 613-957-7840
Director & General Counsel, Crimes Against Humanity & War Crimes, Terry Beitner
613-954-2351, Fax: 613-952-7370

Tax Law Services / Services du droit fiscal
Asst. Deputy Attorney General, Michelline van Erum
613-957-4811, Fax: 613-941-1221
Senior General Counsel, Canada Revenue Agency, Charles McNab
613-957-2358
Senior General Counsel, Canada Revenue Agency, Jean-Marc Raymond
613-954-5881
Senior General Counsel, Tax Law Services, Gordon Bourgard
613-952-9810, Fax: 613-946-7449
Senior Regional Director, Ted K. Tax
Senior Regional Director, Barbara Burns
604-666-0016
Senior Regional Director, Terance McAuley

Laurentian Pilotage Authority Canada / Administration de pilotage des Laurentides Canada

#1501, 555, boul René-Lévesque ouest, Montréal, QC H2Z 1B1
514-283-6320 Fax: 514-496-2409
administration@apl.gc.ca
www.pilotagestlaurent.gc.ca

The Authority provides pilotage services in the province of Québec, north of St-Lambert Lock. Reports to government through the Minister of Transport.

Chief Executive Officer, Réjean Lanteigne
514-283-6320
Director, Administrative Services, Claude Lambert
514-283-6320
Director, Dispatch Services, Sylvia Masson
514-283-6320
Director, Operations, Denys Pouliot
514-283-6320
Secretary & Legal Advisor, Mario St-Pierre
514-283-6320

Library & Archives Canada / Bibliothèque et archives Canada

395 Wellington St., Ottawa, ON K1A 0N4
613-996-5115 Fax: 613-995-6274
866-578-7777
reference@lac-bac.ca
www.collectionscanada.gc.ca
TTY: 613-992-6969
Other Communication: Genealogy Reference: 613/996-7458

The mandate of Library and Archives Canada is: To preserve the documentary heritage of Canada for the benefit of present and future generations; To be a source of enduring knowledge accessible to all, contributing to the cultural, social and economic advancement of Canada; To facilitate in Canada cooperation among communities involved in the acquisition, preservation and diffusion of knowledge; and To serve as the continuing memory of the government of Canada and its institutions.

Librarian & Archivist of Canada, Daniel J. Caron
819-934-5800, Fax: 819-934-5888, danielj.caron@lac-bac.gc.ca
Asst. Deputy Minister, Acquisitions Sector, Jean-Stéphen Piché
819-934-5790, Fax: 819-934-4422, jean-stephen.piche@bac-lac.gc.ca
Asst. Deputy Minister, Collections Management Sector, Doug Rimmer
819-934-4618, Fax: 819-934-5262, doug.rimmer@bac-lac.gc.ca
Acting Asst. Deputy Minister, Resource Discovery Sector, Cecilia Muir
613-992-7059, Fax: 613-992-5315, cecilia.muir@bac-lac.gc.ca
Senior Director General, General Stakeholder Relations, Sean Berrigan
819-934-5858, Fax: 819-934-5839, sean.berrigan@lac-bac.gc.ca
Executive Director, Friends of Library & Archives Canada, Georgia Ellis
613-943-1544, Fax: 613-943-2343, georgia.ellis@lac-bac.gc.ca
Director, Partnerships & Public Programs, Mireille Miniggio
613-947-4470, Fax: 613-995-0179, mireille.miniggio@bac-lac.gc.ca
Director General, Analogue Preservation Branch, Robert McIntosh
819-953-7701, Fax: 819-953-0070, robert.mcintosh@bac-lac.gc.ca
Director, Political & Social Division, Peter DeLottinville
819-934-7394, Fax: 819-934-7393, peter.delottinville@bac-lac.gc.ca

Library of Parliament / Bibliothèque du Parlement

Parliamentary Bldgs., 111 Wellington St., Ottawa, ON K1A 0A9
613-992-4793 Fax: 613-943-6383
866-599-4999
TTY: 613-995-2266
Other Communication: Visitors Information: 613/996-0896

The Library of Parliament provides Parliament with information, documentation, research & analysis; maintains collections to support parliamentarians in their work & provides information about Canada's Parliament to the public.

Parliamentary Librarian, William R. Young
613-992-3122, Fax: 613-943-6383
Director General, Corporate Services, Lynn Potter
613-992-6826
Director General, Learning & Access Services, Dianne Brydon
613-996-0238
Director General, Economic & Fiscal Analysis, Mostafa Askari
613-992-8045
Director General, Expenditure & Revenue Analysis, Sahir Khan
613-992-8044
Parliamentary Budget Officer, Kevin Page
613-992-8026
Senior Director, International Affairs, Trade & Finance, James Kalwarowsky
613-995-2728
Senior Director, Legal & Legislative Affairs, Kristen Douglas
613-995-3476
Senior Director, Reference & Strategic Analysis, Joseph Jackson
613-995-6363
Senior Director, Social Affairs, Yvan Gervais
613-995-7383

Marine Atlantic Inc. / Marine Atlantique

Baine Johnston Centre, #302, 10 Fort William Place, St. John's, NL A1C 1K4
709-772-8957 Fax: 709-772-8956
800-341-7981
info@marine-atlantic.ca
www.marine-atlantic.ca

A federal Crown corporation with a mandate to provide a passenger & commercial marine transportation ferry service between the Island of Newfoundland & the mainland of Canada.

Chair, Robert Crosbie
President/CEO, Wayne Follett
Communications Officer, Tara Laing
709-772-8974, tlaing@marine-atlantic.ca
Director, Marine Services, John Lochhead
Director, Human Resources, Rhona Green
902-794-5754, Fax: 902-794-5764
Senior Technical Manager, Anthony de Hoog
Chief Information Officer, Murray Hupman
709-695-4287

National Advisory Council on Aging / Conseil consultatif national sur le troisième âge

Jeanne Mance Bldg., 8th Fl., Postal Locator 1908 A1, Ottawa, ON K1A 0K9
613-957-1968 Fax: 613-957-7627

The Council advises the Minister of Health on issues related to the aging of the Canadian population & the quality of life of seniors. It reviews the needs & problems of seniors & recommends remedial action, liaises with other groups interested in aging, encourages public discussion & publishes & disseminates information on aging.

Interim Chair, Robert Dorie
NACA Coordinator, Marjolaine Thompson
613-957-2872, Fax: 613-957-1176

National Arts Centre (NAC) / Centre national des Arts (CNA)

53 Elgin St., PO Box 1534 B, Ottawa, ON K1P 5W1
613-947-7000 Fax: 613-996-9578
info@nac-cna.ca
www.nac-cna.ca
TTY: 613-947-7100

Dedicated to the development & promotion of the performing arts, the NAC co-produces & presents a wide range of theatre, music & dance productions. Reports to government through the Minister of Canadian Heritage.

Chair, Julia E. Foster
613-947-7000
President/CEO, Peter Herrndorf
613-947-7000, Fax: 613-238-4556, pherrndo@nac-cna.ca
Senior Director, Operations, Gilles Landry
613-947-7000, Fax: 613-947-4512, glandry@nac-cna.ca
CEO, NAC Foundation, Jayne Watson
613-947-7000, Fax: 613-947-8786, jwatson@nac-cna.ca
Chief Financial Officer, Daniel Senyk
613-947-7000, Fax: 613-943-1399, dsenyk@nac-cna.ca
Director, Communications, Public Affairs, Rosemary Thompson
613-947-7000, Fax: 613-996-9578, rthompson@nac-cna.ca
Music Director, NACO, Pinchas Zukerman
613-947-7000, Fax: 613-943-1400, pzukerman@nac-cna.ca
Artistic Director, English Theatre, Peter Hinton
613-947-7000, Fax: 613-943-1401, phinton@nac-cna.ca
Artistic Director, French Theatre, Wajdi Mouawad
613-947-7000, wmouawad@nac-cna.ca
Producer, Dance, Cathy Levy
613-947-7000, clevy@nac-cna.ca
Producer, Producer, Variety & Community Programming, Simone Deneau
613-947-7000, sdeneau@nac-cna.ca
Producer, New Media, Maurizio Ortolani
613-947-7000, Fax: 613-943-1399

National Battlefields Commission / Commission des champs de bataille nationaux

390, av de Bernières, Québec, QC G1R 2L7
418-648-3506 Fax: 418-648-3638
information@ccbn-nbc.gc.ca
www.ccbn-nbc.gc.ca

Established to preserve, administer & enhance the Plains of Abraham, the battlefields park in Québec City (Plains of Abraham & des Braves Park). Reports to government through the Minister of Canadian Heritage.

Communications Officer, Joanne Laurin
418-649-6251, Fax: 418-648-3809
Executive Secretary, Nathalie Marcotte
418-648-3506, Fax: 418-648-3638
Historian & Archivist, Hélène Quimper
418-648-2589, Fax: 418-648-3638

National Capital Commission (NCC) / Commission de la capitale nationale (CCN)

#202, 40 Elgin St., Ottawa, ON K1P 1C7
613-239-5555 Fax: 613-239-5063
800-704-8227
info@ncc-ccn.ca
www.canadascapital.gc.ca
TTY: 866-661-3530

Responsible for the planning, development & preservation of the National Capital Region. Maintains a "greenbelt" which includes historical bogs & swamps & a 40-hectare farm circa 1875. Responsible for the operation of Gatineau Park.

CEO, Marie Lemay
613-239-5194, Fax: 613-239-5039
Senior Vice-President, Capital Experience, Communications & Marketing, Guy Laflamme
613-239-5474, Fax: 613-239-5188
Vice-President, Environment, Capital Lands & Parks, Michelle Comeau
613-239-5209, Fax: 613-239-5337
Vice-President, Capital Planning, François Lapointe
613-239-5579, Fax: 613-239-5302
Vice-President, Real Estate Mangement, Design & Construction, Roland Morin
613-239-5589, Fax: 613-239-5302
Vice-President, Public & Corporate Affairs, Diane Dupuis
613-239-5363, Fax: 613-239-5749
Director, Audit & Corporate Ethics, Jennifer Wall
613-239-5629, Fax: 613-239-5695
General Counsel & Commission Secretary, Legal Services, Mark Dehler
613-239-5102, Fax: 613-239-5404

Vice-President, F&P & Chief Financial Officer, Finance & Procurement Branch, Pierre Désautels
613-239-5086, Fax: 613-239-5007
Director, Corporate Planning, Louise Mignault
613-239-5734, Fax: 613-239-5039

National Defence Canada / Défense nationale

Major-General George R. Pearkes Bldg., 101 Colonel By Dr., Ottawa, ON K1A 0K2
613-995-2534 Fax: 613-992-4739
800-856-8488
www.forces.gc.ca
TTY: 800-467-9877
Other Communication: Access to Information: 613-992-0996; Media Inquiries: 613-996-2353

The Minister of National Defence is responsible for the Department of National Defence (DND), the Canadian Forces (CF), & related organizations. Canadian Forces members protect Canada, defend North America, & contribute to international peace & security. The work of DND & CF includes the following: assisting civil authorities to protect national interests, to handle national emergencies & to maintain an adequate level of emergency preparedness throughout Canada; protecting Canadian approaches to the continent; promoting Arctic security; pursuing opportunities for Canada-U.S.A. defence co-operation; participating in multilateral operations through international organizations, such as the United Nations (UN) & the North Atlantic Treaty Organization (NATO); supporting humanitarian relief efforts; assisting in the restoration of conflict-devastated places; & participating in confidence-building measures, like arms-control programs.

Acts Administered:
Aeronautics Act, with respect to any matter relating to defence
Army Benevolent Act
Canadian Forces Superannuation Act
Defence Services Pension Continuation Act
Emergencies Act
Emergency Preparedness Act
Garnishment, Attachment & Pension Diversion Act, with respect to members & former members of the Canadian Forces
National Defence Act
Pension Benefits Division Act, with respect to members & former members of the Canadian Forces
Visiting Forces Act
In addition, the DND administers, under the general direction of the Chief Electoral Officer, the Special Voting Rules (Schedule II to the Canada Elections Act) as they relate to Canadian Forces electors.

Minister, National Defence, Hon. Peter Gordon MacKay
613-992-6022, Fax: 613-992-2337, MacKay.P@parl.gc.ca; Mackay.P@forces.gc.ca
Parliamentary Secretary to the Minister of National Defence, Laurie Hawn
613-992-4524, Fax: 613-943-0044, Hawn.L@parl.gc.ca
Deputy Minister, Robert Fonberg
613-992-4258, Fax: 613-995-2028
Chief of the Defence Staff, Gen. Walt Natynczyk
613-992-5054, Fax: 613-995-8578
Vice-Chief of Defence Staff, V.-Adm. Bruce Donaldson
613-992-6052, Fax: 613-992-3945, Other Communications: Secure Telephone: 613-995-0016
Assistant Deputy Minister, Finance & Corporate Services, Kevin Lindsey
613-992-5669, Fax: 613-992-9693
Assistant Deputy Minister, Information Management, John Turner
613-995-2017, Fax: 613-995-2189
Assistant Deputy Minister, Infrastructure & Environment, J. Scott Stevenson
613-945-7545, Fax: 613-995-6653
Assistant Deputy Minister, Human Resources - Civilian, Cynthia Binnington
613-992-7447, Fax: 613-995-8938
Assistant Deputy Minister, Materiel, Dan Ross
613-992-6622, Fax: 613-945-0949
Assistant Deputy Minister, Policy, Jill Sinclair
613-992-3458, Fax: 613-995-2876
Assistant Deputy Minister, Public Affairs, Josée Touchette
613-995-0383, Fax: 613-995-2610
Assistant Deputy Minister, Science & Technology; CEO, Defence R&D Canada, Dr. Robert S. Walker
613-996-2020, Fax: 613-995-3402
Associate Deputy Minister, National Defence, Matthew King
613-992-0275, Fax: 613-945-7011
Chief, Review Services, Greg Jarvis
613-992-7975, Fax: 613-992-0528
Director General, International Security Policy, Michael Grant
613-992-2769, Fax: 613-992-3990
Judge Advocate General, B.Gen. Ken Watkin
613-992-3019, Fax: 613-992-5078
Ombudsman, Pierre Daigle
613-996-2089, Fax: 613-996-3280, Other Communications: Secure Fax: 613-996-9562
Director, Defence Force Planning, Col Carl Wohlgemuth
613-996-2776, Fax: 613-992-5484
Director, General Safety, Sylvie Chateauvert
613-996-3551, Fax: 613-992-1512
Director General, Policy Planning, Michael Margolian
613-992-0799, Fax: 613-995-0446
Director General, Policy Coordination, Nada Vrany
613-995-8332, Fax: 613-995-2876
Director, Military Personnel Research & Analysis, Susan Truscott
613-992-6162, Fax: 613-995-5785
Director General, Health Services, BGen Hilary Jaeger
613-945-6827, Fax: 613-990-1345
Director, Civillian Employment Policies, Elaine Coldwell
613-971-0525, Fax: 613-971-0300
Director, Diversity & Well-Being, Lorraine MacIver
613-944-7002, Fax: 613-944-7055

Associated Agencies, Boards & Commissions:
• Communications Security Establishment / Centre de la sécurité des telecommunications
1500 Bronson Avenue
PO Box 9703 Terminal
Ottawa, ON K1A 0K2
613-991-7600 Fax: 613-991-8514
www.cse-cst.gc.ca
The Communications Security Establishment is Canada's national cryptologic agency, providing the Government of Canada with two key services: foreign signals intelligence in support of defence & foreign policy, & the protection of electronic information & communication.
• Office of the Communications Security Establishment Commissioner / Bureau du Commissaire du Centre de la sécurité des télécommunications
PO Box 1984 B
Ottawa, ON K1P 5R5
613-992-3044
csec-ccst.gc.ca
The Commissioner reviews the activities of the Communications Security Establishment for compliance with the law; advises the Minister of National Defence & the Attorney General of Canada of any CSE activity not in compliance with the law; receives complaints about CSE activities; carries out specific duties under the public interest provisions of the Security of Information Act.
• Military Police Complaints Commission / Commission d'examen des plaintes concernant la police militaire
270 Albert St., 10th Fl.
Ottawa, ON K1P 5G8
613-947-5625 Fax: 613-947-5713 800-632-0566
commission@mpcc-cppm.gc.ca
Other Communication: Toll Free Fax: 1-877-947-5713
Quasi-judicial, independent civilian agency examines complaints arising from either the conduct of military police members in the exercise of policing duties or functions or from interference in or obstruction of their police investigations.

Commands / Commandes
Chief of the Air Staff, Air Command, L.Gen. Angus Watt
613-995-9141, Fax: 613-995-8687, Other Communications: Secure Telephone: 613-996-5355
Chief of the Land Staff, Land Force Command, L.Gen. Andrew Leslie
613-945-0442, Fax: 613-945-0445
Chief of Maritime Staff, Maritime Command, V.Adm. Dean McFadden
613-945-0540, Fax: 613-945-7243
Commander, Canadian Operational Support Command, M.Gen. Daniel Benjamin
Commander, Canadian Expeditory Forces Command, L.Gen. Michel Gauthier
Commander, Canadian Special Forces Operations Command, Col. David Barr
Commander, Canadian Command, L.Gen. Walter Semianiw

Operations Groups:

Land Force Atlantic Area (Headquarters)
Halifax, NS
902-427-7631
Commander, B.Gen. Robert I. Stack

Land Force Central Area (Headquarters)
Toronto, ON
416-633-6200
Commander, B.Gen. Fred Lewis

Land Force Western Area (Headquarters)
Edmonton, AB
780-973-4011
Commander, B.Gen Paul Wynnyk

Maritime Forces Atlantic (Headquarters)
Halifax, NS
902-427-6355
Commander, Rear Adm. Dave Gardam

Maritime Forces Pacific (Headquarters)
Victoria, BC
250-363-2800
Commander, R.Adm. Nigel S. Greenwood

Secteur du Québec de la Force terrestre
Montréal, QC
514-252-2777
Commander, B.Gen. Simon Hébert

Canadian Forces Base (CFB) & Detachments:

BFC Bagotville
Alouette, QC G0C 1A0

CFB Borden
Borden, ON L0M 1C0

CFB Cold Lake
Cold Lake, AB T9M 2C6

CFB Comox
Lazo, BC V0R 2K0

CFB Edmonton
PO Box 10500, Edmonton, AB T5J 4J5

CFB Esquimalt
FMO, Victoria, BC V9A 7N2

CFB Gagetown
Oromocto, NB E2V 4J5

CFB Gander
PO Box 6000, Gander, NL A1V 1X1

CFB Goose Bay
Goose Airport, Happy Valley-Goose Bay, NL A0P 1S0

CFB Greenwood
Greenwood, NS B0P 1N0

CFB Halifax
Halifax, NS B3K 5X5

CFB Kingston
Vimy Post Office, Kingston, ON K7K 7B4

BFC Montréal
Richelain, QC J0J 1R0

CFB Moose Jaw
PO Box 5000, Moose Jaw, SK S6H 7Z8

CFB North Bay
Hornell Heights, ON P0H 1P0

CFB Petawawa
Petawawa, ON K8H 2X3

CFB Shilo
Shilo, MB R0K 2A0

CFB Suffield
PO Box 6000, Medicine Hat, AB T1A 8K8

CFB Trenton
Astra, ON K0K 3W0

BFC Valcartier
Courcelette, QC G0A 4Z0

CFB Winnipeg
Westwin, MB R3J 3Y5

Canadian Forces Stations:

CFS Alert
Belleville, ON K8N 5W6

CFS Leitrim
Ottawa, ON K1A 0K5

CFS Masset
PO Box 2000, Masset, BC V0T 1M0

CFS St. John's
PO Box 2028, St. John's, NL A1C 6B5

Canadian Defence Academy:

Canadian Forces College
Toronto, ON
416-482-6800
Commandant, B.Gen. D.C. Hilton

Canadian Land Forces Command & Staff College
Kingston, ON
613-451-5818
Commandant, Col. BWG McPherson

Royal Military College
Kingston, ON
613-541-6000
Commandant, Commodore William S. Truelove

Regional Public Affairs Office (National Defense):

Operational Research
Director, Operational Research (Corporate, Air & Maritime), John Evans
613-992-5026, Fax: 613-992-3342
Director, Operational Research (Joint & Land), Robert Dickinson
613-992-6866, Fax: 613-992-3342
Director, Military Personnel Operational Research & Analysis, Kelly Farley
613-996-1280, Fax: 613-995-2701
Director, DRDC CORA Director Corporate Services, Edward Pitula
613-992-5209, Fax: 613-992-3342
Chief Scientist, DRDC CORA Director Corporate Services, Mr. Paul Comeau
613-996-6502, Fax: 613-992-3342

Calgary
#418, 100 - 4th Ave. SW, Calgary, AB T2P 3N2
403-974-2822

Science & Technology:
Assistant Deputy Minister, Dr. Robert Walker
613-996-2020, Fax: 613-995-3402
Director General, Science and Technology Operations, Rick Williams
613-992-5776, Fax: 613-995-3402
Director, Science and Technology (Air), Joseph Templin
613-992-4338, Fax: 613-996-5177
Director, Science and Technology (Land), Michel Szymaczak
613-996-2608, Fax: 613-996-5177
Director, Science and Technology (Maritime), Keith Hendy
613-992-7695, Fax: 613-996-7063
Director, Science and Technology (Human Performance), Kurtis Simpson
613-947-7810, Fax: 613-990-1205
Director, Military Personnel Research and Analysis, Susan Truscott
613-992-6162, Fax: 613-995-5785
Director General, Defence Research and Development Canada - Ottawa, Maria Rey
613-998-2303, Fax: 613-993-6095
Director General, Defence Research and Development Canada - Toronto, René Larose
416-635-2030, Fax: 416-635-2011
Director General, Defence Research and Development Canada - Centre for Security Science, Dr. Anthony Ashley
613-944-8195, Fax: 613-995-0002

Halifax
#209, 6080 Young Street, PO Box 99000 Forces, Halifax, NS B3K 5X5
902-427-7452

Québec
Tour Ouest, Guy-Favreau Complex, #911, 200, boul Réné-Lévesque, Montréal, QC H2Z 1X4
514-283-5272

Toronto
4900 Yonge St., 6th Fl., Toronto, ON M2N 6B7
416-635-4406
888-564-8625

Vancouver
#201, 1090 West Pender, Vancouver, BC V6E 2N7
604-666-0199

Materiel:

National Energy Board (NEB) / Office national de l'énergie (ONE)

444 - 7 Ave. SW, Calgary, AB T2P 0X8
403-292-4800 Fax: 403-292-5503
800-899-1265
info@neb-one.gc.ca
www.neb-one.gc.ca
TTY: 800-632-1663
Other Communication: Toll-free fax: 877-288-8803

Federal regulatory tribunal whose powers include: authorizing oil, natural gas & electricity exploration; certifying interprovincial & international pipelines & designated power lines; & setting tolls & tariffs for oil & gas pipelines under federal jurisdiction. The NEB reviews Canadian supply of all major commodities, with emphasis on electricity, oil, natural gas, & oil & natural gas by-products. It also reviews the demand for Canadian energy in Canada & in export markets. In addition to its regulatory role, the NEB is responsible for advising the government on the development & use of energy resources. Its responsibilities include regulating exploration, development & production of oil & gas on frontier lands in a manner that promotes worker safety, environmental protection & resource conservation. The NEB is responsible for environmental matters relating to the construction & operation of facilities & programs within its jurisdiction. Its environmental activities are carried out in three phases: The first phase involves evaluating the potential environmental effects of proposed projects. In the second phase, the environment is protected through monitoring & enforcement of terms & conditions attached to project approval. The third phase include s ongoing monitoring of operations to ensure that cleanup, restoration & maintenance of sites & rights of way are conducted to acceptable standards. The Board also verifies that emergency response plans are in place & that it or the operator can respond immediately to any incidents

Acts Administered:
Canada Oil & Gas Operations Act
Canada Petroleum Resources Act
Canada Transportation Act
Canadian Environmental Assessment Act
Energy Administration Act
National Energy Board Act
Northern Pipeline Act

Chair/CEO, Gaétan Caron
403-299-2724, Fax: 403-299-5503,
gaetan.caron@neb-one.gc.ca

National Farm Products Council (NFPC) / Conseil national des produits agricoles (CNPA)

Canada Bldg., 344 Slater St., 10th Fl., Ottawa, ON K1R 7Y3
613-995-6752 Fax: 613-995-2097
fpcc-cpac@agr.gc.ca
http: //fpcc-cpac.gc.ca
TTY: 613-943-3707

Their mission is to oversee the national supply management agencies for poultry and eggs and national promotion research agencies to ensure an efficient system that works in the balanced interest of stakeholders, from producers to consumers. Reports to Government through the Minister of Agriculture & Agri-food.

Chair, Laurent Pellerin
613-995-2298, Fax: 613-995-2097, laurent.pellerin@agr.gc.ca
Executive Director, Claude Janelle
613-995-0682, Fax: 613-995-0682, claude.janelle@agr.gc.ca
Director, Corporate & Regulatory Affairs, Marc Chamaillard
613-995-4116, marc.chamaillard@agr.gc.ca
Director, Policy & Program Operations, Christine Kwasse
613-995-5553, christine.kwasse@agr.gc.ca
Communication Officer, Chantal Lafontaine
613-995-9148, chantal.lafontaine@agr.gc.ca

National Film Board of Canada (NFB) / Office national du film du Canada

3155, rue Côte de Liesse, CP 1600 Centre-ville, Saint-Laurent, QC H4N 2N4
514-283-9000 Fax: 514-283-7564
800-267-7710
www.nfb.ca

The Board is mandated to initiate & promote the production & distribution of films in the national interest, with the primary object of interpreting Canada to Canadians & to other nations. Reports to government through the Minister of Canadian Heritage.

Government Film Commissioner & Chair, Tom Perlmutter
514-283-9245
Director General, Accessibility & Digital Enterprises, Deborah Drisdell
514-283-9246
Director General, Marketing & Communications, Nathalie Courville
514-283-9246
Director General, English Program Branch, Cindy Witten
514-283-9501
Director General, Finance, Operations & Technology, Luisa Frate
514-283-9051
Director General, French Program Branch, Monique Simard
514-283-9285
Director, Human Resources, Robert Paquette
514-283-9108
Director, Technical Innovation & Resources, Joanne Carrière
514-283-9258
Director, Administration, Luisa Frate
514-283-9051

Regional Centres:

Edmonton
#100, 10815 - 104 Ave., Edmonton, AB T5J 4N6
780-495-3013 Fax: 780-495-6412
Executive Producer, David Christensen
780-495-3015

Halifax
#201 - 5475 Spring Garden Rd., Halifax, NS B3J 1G2
902-426-6000 Fax: 902-426-8901
Executive Producer, Kent Martin
902-426-7351

Moncton
#100, 95 Foundry St., Moncton, NB E1C 5H7
Fax: 506-851-2246
866-663-8331
Executive Producer, Jacques Turgeon
506-851-6105

Montréal
1564, rue St-Denis, Montréal, QC H2X 3K2
514-496-6887 Fax: 514-283-2816
cinerobotheque@nfb.ca

Québec
#368, 901 Cap Diamant, Québec, QC G1K 4K1
418-649-6377 Fax: 418-649-6379

Toronto
150 John St., Toronto, ON M5V 3C3
416-973-0904 Fax: 416-973-9640
ontarioinfo@nfb.ca

Toronto (French Program)
150 John St., Toronto, ON M5V 3C3
416-973-5382 Fax: 416-973-2594

Vancouver
#250, 351 Abbott St., Vancouver, BC V6B 0G6
604-666-3838 Fax: 604-666-1569
Executive Producer, Tracey Friesen
604-666-3411

Winnipeg
#300, 136 Market Ave., Winnipeg, MB R3B 0P4
204-983-3160 Fax: 204-983-0742
Executive Producer, Derek Mazur
204-983-7985

Offices Abroad:

France
5, rue de Constantine, Paris, 75007 France
Other Communication: 33-1-44-18-35-40; Fax: 33-1-47-05-75-89

USA
#4820, 350 Fifth Ave., New York, NY 10118 USA
514-283-9700 Fax: 514-495-2573
Head, North American Sales, Heather Wyer

National Gallery of Canada (NGC) / Musée des Beaux-Arts du Canada (MBAC)

380 Sussex Dr., PO Box 427 A, Ottawa, ON K1N 9N4
613-990-1985 Fax: 613-993-4385
800-319-2787
info@gallery.ca; info@beaux-arts.ca
www.national.gallery.ca
TTY: 613-990-0777
Other Communication: Bookstore: 613-990-1970

The permanent collection of the National Gallery comprises paintings, sculpture, prints & drawings, photographs, film & video art from the Canadian, European, American & Asian schools. Special exhibitions as well as permanent installations of the gallery's collections are on display. The gallery also sends its exhibitions on tour across the country & participates in international exhibitions. Services provided to the public include lectures, talks, tours, films, workshops, concerts & a bookstore.

Chair, Michael J. Audain
Vice-Chair, Michael J. Tims
Director/CEO, Marc Mayer
613-990-1927
Chief Curator & Deputy Director, David Franklin
613-990-0497, dfrankli@gallery.ca
Deputy Director, Administration & Finance, David Baxter
613-991-0040
Deputy Director, Exhibitions & Installations, Karen Colby-Stothart
613-998-4917
Director, Corporate Secretariat & Ministerial Liaison, Matthew Symonds
613-990-9232
Director, Human Resources Services, Michelle Miner
613-993-2856
Curator, Canadian Art, Charles Hill
613-990-0486, chill@gallery.ca
Curator, Contemporary Art, Josée Drouin-Brisebois
613-990-7645
Curator, European & American Art, Dr. Graham Larkin
613-990-8580
Curator, Indigenous Art, Greg Hill
613-949-0327
Curator, Photographs Collection, Ann Thomas
613-990-1961, athomas@gallery.ca
Associate Curator, Prints & Drawings, Sonia Couturier
613-990-8981
Senior Media & Public Relations Officer, Josée (Britanie) Mallet
613-990-6835

National Joint Council (NJC) / Conseil national mixte (CNM)

C.D. Howe Bldg., 240 Sparks St. West, 7th Fl., PO Box 1525 B, Ottawa, ON K1P 5V2
613-990-1805 Fax: 613-990-7071
email.courrier@njc-cnm.gc.ca
www.njc-cnm.gc.ca

Provides a forum for consultation on labour issues between the Government of Canada & the bargaining agents for its employees.

General Secretary, Barry Fennessy
613-990-1807, Barry.Fennessy@njc-cnm.gc.ca
Manager, NJC Operations, Nicole Paré
613-990-1806, Fax: 613-990-7071,
nicole.pare@njc-cnm.gc.ca
Committee Advisor, Jennifer Murphy
613-990-1725, Fax: 613-990-7071,
jennifer.murphy@njc-cnm.gc.ca

National Parole Board / Commission nationale des libérations conditionnelles

410 Laurier Ave. West, Ottawa, ON K1A 0R1
613-954-7474 Fax: 613-995-4380
800-874-2652
info@npb-cnlc.gc.ca
www.npb-cnlc.gc.ca
Other Communication: Communications Inquiries Phone: 613-954-6549; Pardons - Requests for Application Kit Toll Free: 1-800-874-2652; Victims Information Line Toll Free: 1-866-789-4636

Part of the criminal justice system, the National Parole Board makes independent, conditional release & pardon decisions & clemency recommendations. The Board also works to facilitate integration of offenders as law-abiding citizens.

Acts Administered:
Corrections & Conditional Release Act
Criminal Code
Criminal Records Act

Chair, Harvey Cenaiko
613-941-1154, Fax: 613-941-9426
Executive Vice-Chair, Marie-France Pelletier
613-954-6120
Executive Director, Shelley Trevethan
613-954-1153
Manager, Appeal Division, Denise Leblanc
613-954-5940
Director, Communications, Caroline Douglas
613-954-6547
Senior Counsel, Legal Services, Gertrude Lavigne
613-954-7451

Regional Offices:

Atlantic
1045 Main St., 1st Fl., Moncton, NB E1C 1H1
506-851-6345 Fax: 506-851-6926
Regional Director General, Brian Chase
506-851-6492
Vice-Chairperson, Louis-Philippe McGraw
506-851-6490

Ontario
516 O'Connor Dr., Kingston, ON K7P 1N3
613-634-3857 Fax: 613-634-3861
Regional Director General, Denise Preston
613-634-3857
Vice-Chairperson, Fred Tufnell

Pacific
1925 McCallum Road, 2nd Floor, Abbotsford, BC V2S 3N2
604-870-2468 Fax: 604-870-2498
Regional Director General, Harold Massey
Vice-Chairperson, Kelly-Ann Speck
604-870-2479

Prairies - Saskatoon
101 - 22 St. East, 6th Fl., Saskatoon, SK S7K 0E1
306-975-4228 Fax: 306-975-5892
Regional Director General, Michelle Van De Bogart
780-442-6770

Prairies - Edmonton
Scotia Place, Scotia 2, #401, 10060 Jasper Avenue, 4th Floor, Edmonton, AB T5J 3R8
780-495-3404 Fax: 780-495-3475
Regional Director General, Michelle Van De Bogart

Québec
Complexe Guy-Favreau, Tour ouest, #1001, 200, boul René-Lévesque ouest, Montréal, QC H2Z 1X4
514-283-4584 Fax: 514-283-5484
Regional Director, Jean-Marc Trudeau
514-283-4584
Vice-Chairperson, Denis Couillard
514-283-4584

National Research Council Canada (NRC) / Conseil national de recherches Canada (CNRC)

Bldg. M-58, 1200 Montreal Rd., Ottawa, ON K1A 0R6
613-993-9101 Fax: 613-952-7928
877-672-2672
info@nrc-cnrc.ca
www.nrc-cnrc.ca
TTY: 613-952-9907
Other Communication: IRAP Information: 613-993-1790; CISTI Information: 613-993-1600

NRC is Canada's principal public science & technology agency. It performs, supports & promotes scientific & industrial research for economic & social benefits, research & development in the national interest. Contributions are made to the national science & technology infrastructure & the development of a highly skilled workforce is fostered. Activities focus on strengthening industrial partnerships to bolster competitiveness in key information & telecommunications technologies. The Canada Institute for Scientific & Technical Information (CISTI), a component of NRC, provides access to hundreds of national/international databases, more than 50,000 journals, millions of books, technical reports & conference proceedings. Provides: customized literature searches; current awareness services; access to scientific, technical & medical databases; & referrals to experts. CISTI has an integrated online catalog accessible via the Internet. It publishes 14 international research journals including "Environmental Reviews". The NRC Industrial Research Assistance Program (IRAP) is Canada's national technology transfer & diffusion network helping Canadian firms develop world-class technology they cannot generate on their own. Advisory services involve assisting firms to: define technical needs; identify technical opportunities; obtain technical information & assistance; solve process & production problems; access or acquire technology & expertise from Canadian or foreign firms; & access financial assistance where appropriate. Technical & financial assistance is provided for R&D projects & for adapting existing technologies, with emphasis on advancing unproven technologies to the point of performance testing

President, Dr. John R. McDougall
613-993-2024, Fax: 613-957-8850
Vice-President, Research, Life Sciences, Dr. Roman Szumski
613-993-9244, Fax: 613-954-2066
Vice-President, Research, Physical Sciences, Dr. Danial D. Wayner
613-998-5404, Fax: 613-949-1314
Vice-President, Technology & Industry Support, Patricia Mortimer
613-998-3664, Fax: 613-998-3839
Vice-President, Engineering, Dr. Ian Potter
613-949-5955, Fax: 613-949-5987
Acting Vice-President, Corporate Management & CFO, Shane Brunas
613-991-3773, Fax: 613-991-3774
Acting Secretary General, Robert G. James
613-998-4579, Fax: 613-991-0398
Director General, Canada Institute for Scientific & Technical Information, Pam Bjornson
613-993-2341, Fax: 613-952-9112
Director General, Industrial Research Assistance Program (IRAP), Dr. Tony Rahilly
613-993-0695, Fax: 613-954-0501

IRAP Regional Offices:

Alberta & Northwest Territories
250 Karl Clark Rd., Edmonton, AB T6N 1E4
780-495-6509 Fax: 780-495-6510
Director, Dr. Kashmir Gill
780-495-2136, Fax: 780-495-6510,
kashmir.gill@nrc-cnrc.gc.ca

Atlantic/Nunavut Region
1411 Oxford St., Halifax, NS B3H 3Z1
902-426-3138 Fax: 902-426-1624
Executive Director, Bradley C. Goodyear
902-426-1055, Fax: 902-426-1624

Pacific Region
#650 - 1185 West Georgia St., Vancouver, BC V6E 4E6
604-221-3100 Fax: 604-221-3101
Executive Director, Christopher Ryan
604-221-3163, Fax: 604-221-3101,
christopher.ryan@nrc-cnrc.gc.ca

Newfoundland & Labrador
Kerwin Place & Arctic Ave., Memorial University, PO Box 12093, St. John's, NL A1B 3T5
709-772-5228 Fax: 709-772-5067
Director, David W. Rideout
709-772-2838, Fax: 709-772-5067,
dave.rideout@nrc-cnrc.gc.ca

New Brunswick
PO Box 5678 W, Fredericton, NB E3B 5G4
506-452-3831 Fax: 506-452-3827
877-994-4727
Executive Director, David Healey

Ontario
#903 55 St. Clair Ave. E, Toronto, ON M4T 1M2
416-973-4484 Fax: 416-973-4303
Executive Director, Dr. Sam Stevens
416-973-4483, Fax: 416-952-2996, r.stevens@nrc-cnrc.gc.ca

Québec
#P-101, 75, boul de Montagne, Boucherville, QC J4B 6Y4
450-641-5300 Fax: 450-641-5301
Executive Director, Bogdan Ciobanu
450-641-5305, Fax: 450-641-5301,
bogdan.ciobanu@cnrc-nrc.gc.ca

Saskatchewan & Manitoba
435 Ellice Ave., Winnipeg, MB R3B 1X6
204-983-0092 Fax: 204-983-8835
Director, Vivian Sullivan
204-984-6477, Fax: 204-983-8835,
vivian.sullivan@nrc-cnrc.gc.ca

Biotechnology Research Institute (BRI) / Institut de recherche en biotechnologie (IRB)
6100, av Royalmount, Montréal, QC H4P 2R2
514-496-6100 Fax: 514-496-1928
bri-info@cnrc-nrc.gc.ca
www.nrc-cnrc.gc.ca/eng/ibp/bri.html

Prevention & pollution control, including technology & process development, identification & behaviour of pollutants, monitoirng & ecotoxicological risk evaluation; green technologies & sustainable development. BRI scientists have unique expertise in the biotreatment of contaminated soils, groundwater, sediments, air, & industrial wastewater. The Sector works closely with industry on the R&D of innovative environmental technologies. BRI is also a founding member of the Montreal Centre of Excellence in Brownfields Rehabilitation (MCEBR), a joint initiative between government & industry to carry out research, development, & demonstration projects associated with soil decontamination & site rehabilitation.

Director General, Dr. Michel Desrochers
514-496-6101, Fax: 514-496-6388

Herzberg Institute of Astrophysics (HIA) / Institut Herzberg d'astrophysique (IHA)
5071 West Saanich Rd., Victoria, BC V9E 2E7
250-363-0001 Fax: 250-363-0045
hia-www@nrc-cnrc.gc.ca
www.nrc-cnrc.gc.ca/eng/ibp/hia.html

Operation & maintenance of astronomical observatories as national facilities available to all interested scientists. Conducts research programs in the fields of astronomy, space science & studies solar activity measurements of trace elements in the atmosphere.

Director General, Dr. Greg Fahlman
250-363-0040, Fax: 250-363-8483,
Gregory.Fahlman@nrc-cnrc.gc.ca
Director, Dominion Astrophysical Observatory, James E. Hesser
250-363-0007, Fax: 250-363-6970,
James.Hesser@nrc-cnrc.gc.ca
Director, Dominion Radio Astrophysical Observatory, Dr. Sean Dougherty
250-497-2359, Fax: 250-497-2355,
sean.dougherty@nrc-cnrc.gc.ca
Director Operations, Central Services, Susanna Gibson
250-363-0567, Fax: 250-363-0063,
susanna.gibson@nrc-cnrc.gc.ca

Industrial Materials Institute (IMI) / Institut des matériaux industriels
75, boul de Mortagne, Boucherville, QC J4B 6Y4
450-641-5000 Fax: 450-641-5101
Imi-Info@cnrc-nrc.gc.ca
www.nrc-cnrc.gc.ca/imi-imi

Materials processing technologies for the metal, polymer, aerospace & automotive sectors; virtual fabrication; advanced instrumentation & materials; envionmental technologies.

Director General, Dr. Blaise Champagne, Eng., Ph.D.
450-641-5050, Fax: 450-641-5101,
Blaise.Champagne@cnrc-nrc.gc.ca
Acting Director, Aluminium Technology Centre, Bernard Arsenault
418-545-5546, Fax: 418-545-5543,
Bernard.Arsenault@cnrc-nrc.gc.ca
Director, Modelling & Diagnostics, Jean F. Bussière
450-641-5252, Fax: 450-641-5106,
Jean.Bussiere@cnrc-nrc.gc.ca
Director, London - Center for Automotive Materials & Manufacturing (CAMM), Sylvain Pelletier
450-641-5239, Fax: 450-641-5105,
Sylvain.Pelletier@imi.cnrc-nrc.gc.ca

Institute for Aerospace Research (NRC) / Institut de recherche aérospatiale (IAR)
1200 Montreal Rd., Ottawa, ON K1A 0R6
613-990-0765 Fax: 613-952-7214
www.nrc-cnrc.gc.ca/iar-ira

Development & use of national aeronautical facilities; advanced design & manufacture; transportation & safety; aerospace & the environment; international programs & strategic intelligence.
Director General, Jerzy P. Komorowski
613-993-0141, jerzy.komorowski@nrc-cnrc.gc.ca
Director, Aerodynamics Laboratory, Dr. Steven J. Zan
613-993-2423, Fax: 613-957-4309
Director, Aerospace Manufacturing Technology Centre, Pierre Dicaire
514-283-9139, Fax: 514-283-9484
Director, Flight Research Laboratory, Stewart W. Baillie
613-998-3071, Fax: 613-952-1704
Director, Gas Turbine Laboratory, Dr. Ibrahim A. Yimer
613-991-1139
Director, Operations, Andrew B. Sullivan
613-993-9447
Director, Structures, Materials & Performance Laboratory, Dr. Prakash Patnaik
613-991-6915, Fax: 613-990-7444
Communications Officer, Sheila Noble
613-991-5738, sheila.noble@nrc-cnrc.gc.ca

Institute for Biodiagnostics / Institut du biodiagnostic
435 Ellice Ave., Winnipeg, MB R3B 1Y6
204-983-7692 Fax: 204-984-7217
Neela.Mitra@nrc-cnrc.gc.ca
www.nrc-cnrc.gc.ca/ibd-ibd
Director General, Dr. Ian Smith
204-983-7526, Fax: 204-984-6978, Ian.Smith@nrc-cnrc.gc.ca
Director, Business & Corporate Services, Paul Wiebe
204-984-6223, Fax: 204-983-3154, Paul.Wiebe@nrc-cnrc.gc.ca
Director, Research, Roxanne Deslauriers
204-984-5146, Fax: 204-984-6978, Roxanne.Deslauriers@nrc-cnrc.gc.ca
Communications Officer, Valerie McPherson
204-984-4890, Fax: 204-983-3154, Valerie.McPherson@nrc-cnrc.gc.ca

Institute for Biological Sciences (IBS) / Institut des sciences biologiques
Bldg. M-54, 1200 Montreal Rd., Ottawa, ON K1A 0R6
613-993-5812 Fax: 613-957-7867
www.nrc-cnrc.gc.ca/ibs-isb
Research in molecular genetics, immunochemistry, microbiology, biochemistry, neurobiology including cell signaling, transduction, in vivo & in vitro models for therapeutics evaluation.
Director General, Dr. James Richards
613-993-7506, Fax: 613-957-7867, James.Richards@nrc-cnrc.gc.ca
Director, Business Development & Research Services, Scott Ferguson
613-990-5948, Fax: 613-952-5136, Scott.Ferguson@nrc-cnrc.gc.ca
Director, Immunobiology Program, Jean-Robert Brisson
613-990-3244, Fax: 613-941-1327, Jean-Robert.Brisson@nrc-cnrc.gc.ca

Institute for Chemical Process & Environmental Technology (ICPET) / Institut de technologie des procédés chimiques et de l'environnement
Bldg. M-12, 1200 Montreal Rd., Ottawa, ON K1A 0R6
613-993-4041 Fax: 613-957-8231
www.nrc-cnrc.gc.ca/icpet-itpce
Focuses expertise in the areas of process & materials chemistry, process technology & related environmental technology. Supports environmentally responsible manufacturing in the fuel cell, oil sands & bioproducts sectors. Aids manufacturing & industrial clients in optimizing their process operations & reducing the impact of their operations on the environment. Promotes business opportunities in collaborative research, technology licensing & fee-for-service arrangements.
Director General, Dr. Janusz Lusztyk
Janusz.Lusztyk@nrc-cnrc.gc.ca
Director, Commercialization, Kanu Sikka
613-990-4624, Fax: 613-991-2384, Kanu.Sikka@nrc-cnrc.gc.ca
Director, Research, Kevin A. Jonasson
613-993-6570, Fax: 613-991-2384, kevin.jonasson@nrc-cnrc.gc.ca

Institute for Fuel Cell Innovation (IFCI) / Institut d'innovation en piles à combustible
4250 Wesbrook Mall, Vancouver, BC V6T 1W5
604-221-3000 Fax: 604-221-3001
info.itci-iipac@nrc-cnrc.gc.ca
www.nrc-cnrc.gc.ca/ifci-iipc
Strategic research aimed at advancing fuel cell science & technology & facilitating the commercialization of hydrogen & fuel cell systems.
Director General, Maja Veljkovic
604-221-3024, Fax: 604-221-3002, Maja.Veljkovic@nrc-cnrc.gc.ca
Director, Operations, David Semczyszyn
604-221-3013, David.Semczyszyn@nrc-cnrc.gc.ca
Director, Science & Technology, Dr. Dave Ghosh
604-221-3040, Dave.Ghosh@nrc-cnrc.gc.ca

Institute for Information Technology (IIT) / Institut de technologie de l'information
Bldg. M-50, 1200 Montreal Rd., Ottawa, ON K1A 0R6
613-991-3373 Fax: 613-952-0074
877-672-2672
www.nrc-cnrc.gc.ca/iit-iti
Director General, Christian Couturier
506-444-0555, Fax: 506-444-6187, christian.couturier@nrc-cnrc.gc.ca
Director, Commercialization & Strategy, Dr. Andrew Reddick
506-444-0540, Fax: 506-452-3814, andrew.reddick@nrc-cnrc.gc.ca
Acting Director, Research Programs, NCR, Charles-Antoine Gauthier
613-993-8551, Fax: 613-952-7998, Charles-Antoine.Gauthier@nrc-cnrc.gc.ca

Institute for Marine Biosciences (IMB) / Institut des biosciences marines (IBM)
1411 Oxford St., Halifax, NS B3H 3Z1
902-426-8332 Fax: 902-426-9413
communications.imb@nrc-cnrc.gc.ca
www.nrc-cnrc.gc.ca/imb-ibm
Aquatic animal health & nutrition; natural toxins; mass spectrometry & proteomics; cell & molecular biology.
Director General, Dr. Joan C. Kean-Howie
902-426-8278, Fax: 902-426-8514, Joan.Kean-Howie@nrc-cnrc.gc.ca
Director, Corporate & Business Relations, Denise LeBlanc MacDonald
902-426-2496, Denise.LeBlancMacDonald@nrc-cnrc.gc.ca
Director, Research, Aleksander Patrzykat
902-426-4080, Aleksander.Patrzykat@nrc-cnrc.gc.ca

Institute for Microstructural Sciences (IMS) / Institut des sciences des microstructures
Bldg. M-50, 1200 Montreal Rd., Ottawa, ON K1A 0R6
613-949-9660 Fax: 613-957-8734
ims.info@nrc-cnrc.gc.ca
www.nrc-cnrc.gc.ca/ims-ism
Director General, Marie D'Iorio
613-993-4597, Fax: 613-957-8734, Marie.D'iorio@nrc-cnrc.gc.ca
Director, Applications Technologies, Sylvain Charbonneau
613-998-9414, Sylvain.Charbonneau@nrc-cnrc.gc.ca
Director, Materials Technologies, Thomas E. Jackman
613-993-6711, Thomas.Jackman@nrc-cnrc.gc.ca
Director, Research Support Operations, Cheryl Lambert
613-991-4650, Cheryl.Lambert@nrc-cnrc.gc.ca

Institute for National Measurement Standards / Institut des étalons nationaux de mesure
Bldg. M-36, 1500 Montreal Rd., Ottawa, ON K1A 0R6
613-998-7018 Fax: 613-954-1473
alexandra.shaw@nrc-cnrc.gc.ca
www.nrc-cnrc.gc.ca/inms-ienm
Canada's national metrology institute (NMI), charged with the responsibility to investigate & determine standards & methods of measurement.
Director General, Dr. James W. McLaren
613-993-7319, Fax: 613-952-5113, James.McLaren@nrc-cnrc.gc.ca

Institute for Nutrisciences & Health / Institut des sciences nutritionelles et de la santé
550 University Ave., Charlottetown, PE C1A 4P3
902-566-7000 Fax: 902-569-4289
inh@nrc-cnrc.gc.ca
www.nrc-cnrc.gc.ca/inh-isns
Director General, Research, Dr. Joan C. Kean-Howie
902-426-8278, Fax: 902-426-8514

Institute for Ocean Technology (IOT) / Institut des technologies océaniques (ITO)
Kerwin Pl. & Arctic Ave., PO Box 12093, St. John's, NL A1B 3T5
709-772-4939 Fax: 709-772-2462
Noel.Murphy@nrc-cnrc.gc.ca
www.nrc-cnrc.gc.ca/iot-ito
Ocean technology research in the areas of offshore engineering, marine vessel design, underwater vehicles, propulsion, electronic navigation, ice-vessel & ice structure interaction. Provides assistance to Canadian ocean technology companies & Canadian government departments. Research services performed in the following areas: tanker offloading & stationkeeping, offshore platform efficiency, navigation safety, all aspects of ocean technology. The Ocean Technology Enterprise Centre assists in the growth & development of new ventures in ocean technology. The centre helps new & established enterprises to develop their concepts & technologies in a supportive environment, with access to IOT facilities & expertise.
Director General, Dr. F. Mary Williams
709-772-2469, Fax: 709-772-3101, f.williams@nrc-cnrc.gc.ca
Director, Facilities, Carl J. Harris
709-772-2326, Fax: 709-772-2462, Carl.Harris@nrc-cnrc.gc.ca
Director, Research, Dr. Bruce Parsons
709-772-2326, Fax: 709-772-2462, bruce.parsons@nrc-cnrc.gc.ca
Communications Coordinator, Derek J. Yetman
709-772-6001, Fax: 709-772-2462, Derek.Yetman@nrc-cnrc.gc.ca

Institute for Research in Construction (IRC) / Institut de recherche en construction
Bldg. M-24, 1500 Montreal Rd., Ottawa, ON K1A 0R6
613-993-2607 Fax: 613-952-7673
Irc.Client-Services@nrc-cnrc.gc.ca
www.nrc-cnrc.gc.ca/irc-irc
Research areas include building envelope & structure, indoor environment, urban infrastructure, fire research, sustainable built environment & climate change. A special initiative is the National Guide to Sustainable Municipal Infrastructure, in partnership with the Federation of Canadian Municipalities, Infrastructure Canada & the Canadian Public Works Association, a collection of best practices for core infrastructure.
Director General, Morad R. Atif
613-993-2443, Fax: 613-941-0822, Morad.Atif@nrc-cnrc.gc.ca

London - Centre for Automotive Materials & Manufacturing (CAMM) / Centre des matériaux et fabrication pour l'automobile
800 Collip Circle, London, ON N6G 4X8
519-430-7166 Fax: 519-430-7064
John.Lyons@nrc-cnrc.gc.ca
www.nrc-cnrc.gc.ca/eng/facilities/imi/camm.html
The Centre for Automotive Materials and Manufacturing serves as the national headquarters for the National Research Council's automotive-related capabilities and facilities across Canada. Their purpose is to lead in the development of scalable, sustainable manufacturing technologies for green vehicles. CAMM research is focused on laser materials processing, electrolytic, physical and chemical vapor deposition technologies and composites in manufacturing.
Director, Dr. Sylvain Pelletier
450-641-5239, Fax: 450-641-5105, Sylvain.Pelletier@imi.cnrc-nrc.gc.ca

National Institute of Nanotechnology / Institut national de nanotechnologie
Bldg. NINT, University of Alberta, 11421 Saskatchewan Dr., Edmonton, AB T6G 2M9
780-641-1600 Fax: 780-641-1601
nintinfo@nrc.gc.ca
www.nrc-cnrc.gc.ca/nint-innt
Multi-disciplined research in physics, chemistry, engineering, biology, informatics, pharmacy & medicine, with applications in medicine & biotechnology, energy & environment, computing & telecommunications.
Director General, Dr. Nils O. Petersen
780-641-1610, Nils.Petersen@nrc-cnrc.gc.ca
Director, Business Development & External Relations, Richard Brommeland
780-641-1620, Richard.Brommeland@nrc-cnrc.gc.ca
Director, Research Programs, Dr. Christopher J. Haugen
780-641-1615, Chris.Haugen@nrc-cnrc.gc.ca
Research Officer, Nano Ethical, Environmental, Economic, Legal & Societal Issues (NEEELS), Michael D. Lounsbury
780-492-1684, Fax: 780-492-3325, ml37@ualberta.ca

Plant Biotechnology Institute (PBI) / Institut de biotechnologie des plantes (IBP)
110 Gymnasium Pl., Saskatoon, SK S7N 0W9
306-975-5248 Fax: 306-975-4839
pbi-info@nrc-cnrc.gc.ca
www.nrc-cnrc.gc.ca/pbi-ibp
Canada's national laboratory for advanced research in new exploitable methods for genetic alteration of plants & for biochemical control of plant development in agriculture. Engineering projects include cell & molecular biology of higher plants. Technical services include: DNA synthesis & sequencing, bio-nuclear magnetic resonance spectroscopy, mass spectroscopy, advanced training services, & expert consultancy.
Director General, Jerome Konecsni
306-975-5575, Fax: 306-975-4191, Jerome.Konecsni@nrc-cnrc.gc.ca
Director, Business & Corporate Services, Jeffrey P. Parker
306-975-5568, Fax: 306-975-4839, Jeff.Parker@nrc-cnrc.gc.ca
Director, Research, Suzanne R. Abrams
306-975-5569, Fax: 306-975-4191, Sue.Abrams@nrc-cnrc.gc.ca

Steacie Institute for Molecular Sciences / Institut Steacie des sciences moléculaires
100 Sussex Dr., Ottawa, ON K1A 0R6
613-993-1212 Fax: 613-954-5242
Huguette.Morin-Dumais@nrc-cnrc.gc.ca
www.nrc-cnrc.gc.ca/sims-issm
NRC-SIMS conducts cutting-edge interdisciplinary research in selected areas of molecular sciences that have the potential to stimulate entirely new or emerging sectors of the Canadian economy. Strategic molecular sciences research fields for NRC-SIMS include: nanoscience, chemical biology, diagnostics, laser science, molecular interfaces, advanced materials, and their related technologies.
Acting Director General, Dr. James B. Webb
613-990-0915, James.Webb@nrc-cnrc.gc.ca

Technology Centres:

Canadian Hydraulics Centre (CHC) / Centre canadien d'hydraulique (CCH)
1200 Montreal Rd., Ottawa, ON K1A 0R6
613-993-9381 Fax: 613-952-7679
info.chc@nrc-cnrc.gc.ca
www.nrc-cnrc.gc.ca/chc-chc
One of North America's largest hydraulic engineering laboratories, with expertise & experience in physical & numerical modeling, analysis & field studies to solve a wide range of hydraulic engineering problems. Specializations include: coastal engineering; marine structures; cold regions; environmental hydraulics; laboratory technologies; numerical models. Environmental hydraulics services include: coastal ecosystem management; river & watershed management; flood management & dam break; chemical & oil spill migration; water quality & pollutant transport; sediment transport, including shoreline erosion & dredged spoil disposal; aquaculture management; environmental information & simulation systems.
Acting General Manager, Eric Magel
613-993-2417, Fax: 613-952-7679
Group Leader, Coastal Engineering, Andrew M. Cornett
613-993-6690, Andrew.Cornett@nrc-cnrc.gc.ca

Centre for Surface Transportation Technology (CSTT) / Centre de technologie des transports de surface (CTTS)
2320 Lester Rd., Ottawa, ON K1V 1S2
613-998-9639 Fax: 613-957-0831
inquiries.cstt@nrc-cnrc.gc.ca
www.nrc-cnrc.gc.ca/cstt-ctts
Road & rail vehicle performance technology, studies & rail tribology; climatic engineering.
Director General, Paul Treboutat
613-998-9635, Paul.Treboutat@nrc-cnrc.gc.ca
Director, Rail Division, Harold M. Kohn
613-991-5522, Harold.Kohn@nrc-cnrc.gc.ca
Director, Road Vehicles & Military Systems Division, Michael S. Halasz
613-998-8015, Michael.Halasz@nrc-cnrc.gc.ca

National Round Table on the Environment & Economy (NRTEE) / Table ronde nationale sur l'environnement et l'économie (TRNEE)

#200, 344 Slater St., Ottawa, ON K1R 7Y3
613-992-7189 Fax: 613-992-7385
admin@nrtee-trnee.ca
www.nrtee-trnee.ca
The National Round Table on the Environment & the Economy is an independent agency of the federal government committed to providing decision makers & opinion leaders with reliable information & objective views on the current state of the debate on the environment & the economy. Working with stakeholders across Canada, the NRTEE carries out its mandate by identifying key issues with both environmental & economic implications, fully exploring these implications, & suggesting action designed to balance economic prosperity with environmental preservation. A multistakeholder approach, combined with impartiality & neutrality, are the hallmarks of the NRTEE's activities. By creating an atmosphere in which all points of view can be expressed freely & debated openly, the NRTEE has established a process whereby stakeholders themselves define the environment/economy interface within issues, determine areas of consensus & identify the reasons for disagreement in other areas. The NRTEE's programs focus on the following areas: energy & climate change; capital markets & sustainability; climate change adaptation
President & CEO, David McLaughlin
613-943-0399, mclaughlind@nrtee-trnee.ca
Manager, Human Resources & Administrative Services, Hélène Sutton
613-992-7181
Director, Corporate Services, Jim McLachlan
613-947-4507, mclachlanj@nrtee-trnee.ca
Director, Policy & Research, René Drolet
613-996-4501, droletr@nrtee-trnee.ca

National Search & Rescue Secretariat / Secrétariat national de recherches et sauvetage

#400, 275 Slater St., Ottawa, ON K1A 0K2
613-992-0054 Fax: 613-996-3746
800-727-9414
inquiry@nss.gc.ca
www.nss.gc.ca
Provides a central managerial role in the overall coordination of search & rescue. It addresses program & policy issues related to the National Search & Rescue Program, & advises the Lead Minister for search & rescue.
Executive Director, Géraldine Underdown
613-992-0054, Fax: 613-996-3746
Communications Officer, Kim Fauteux
613-992-3472, Fax: 613-996-3746

Natural Resources Canada (NRCan) / Ressources naturelles Canada (RNCan)

580 Booth St., Ottawa, ON K1A 0E4
613-995-0947 Fax: 613-992-7211
www.nrcan-rncan.gc.ca/com/
TTY: 613-996-4397
Other Communication: Emergency Operations Centre: 613/995-5555, 943-0000
Advances development of Canada's economy by contributing to the development & use of Canada's mineral & energy resources in a manner consistent with federal environmental & social objectives; advances knowledge of the Canadian landmass through scientific & science-related activities.
Acts Administered:
Arctic Waters Pollution Prevention Act
Arctic Waters Experimental Pollution Regulations
Order Exempting the United States Coast Guard Icebreaker \Healy\" from the Application of the Arctic Shipping Pollution Prevention Regulations"
Canada Foundation for Sustainable Development Technology Act
Canada-Newfoundland Atlantic Accord Implementation Act
Canada-Newfoundland Oil & Gas Spills & Debris Liability Regulations
Newfoundland Offshore Area Oil & Gas Operations Regulations
Newfoundland Offshore Area Petroleum Diving Regulations
Newfoundland Offshore Area Petroleum Geophysical Operations Regulations
Newfoundland Offshore Area Petroleum Production & Conservation Regulations
Newfoundland Offshore Area Registration Regulations
Newfoundland Offshore Certificate of Fitness Regulations
Newfoundland Offshore Petroleum Drilling Regulations
Newfoundland Offshore Petroleum Installations Regulations
Canada-Nova Scotia Offshore Petroleum Resources Accord Implementation Act
Canada-Nova Scotia Oil & Gas Spills & Debris Liability Regulations
Nova Scotia Offshore Area Certificate of Fitness Regulations
Nova Scotia Offshore Area Petroleum Diving Regulations
Nova Scotia Offshore Area Petroleum Drilling Regulations
Nova Scotia Offshore Area Petroleum Geophysical Operations Regulations
Nova Scotia Offshore Area Petroleum Installations Regulations
Nova Scotia Offshore Area Petroleum Production & Conservation Regulations
Nova Scotia Resources (Ventures) Ltd. Drilling Assistance Regulations
Canada Oil & Gas Operations Act (Indian Affairs & Northern Development)
Canada Oil & Gas Certificate of Fitness Regulations
Canada Oil & Gas Diving Regulations
Canada Oil & Gas Drilling Regulations
Canada Oil & Gas Geophysical Operations Regulations
Canada Oil & Gas Installations Regulations
Canada Oil & Gas Operations Regulations
Canada Oil & Gas Production & Conservation Regulations
Nova Scotia Offshore Area Production & Conservation Regulations
Oil & Gas Spills & Debris Liability Regulations
Canada Petroleum Resources Act
Canadian Ownership & Control Determination Act
Co-operative Energy Act
Department of Natural Resources Act
Report on the State of Canada's Forests Regulations
Energy Administration Act
Energy Efficiency Act
Energy Monitoring Act
Energy Supplies Emergency Act
Explosives Act
Forestry Act
Gros Morne Forestry Timber Regulations
Timber Regulations
Hibernia Development Project Act
International Boundary Commission Act
Lands Surveys Act
Lands Surveyors Act
Motor Vehicle Fuel Consumption Standards Act
National Energy Board Act
National Energy Board Coast Recovery Regulations
National Energy Board Electricity Regulations
National Energy Board Export & Import Reporting Regulations
National Energy Board Pipeline Crossing Regulations, I & II
National Energy Board Processing Plant Regulations
National Energy Board Rules of Practice & Procedure
National Energy Board Substituted Service Regulations
Onshore Pipeline Regulations
Pipeline Arbitration Committee Procedure Rules
Power Line Crossing Regulations
Northern Pipeline Act
Uranium Mines (Ontario) Occupational Health & Safety Regulations
Nuclear Energy Control Act
Nuclear Fuel Waste Act, 2002
Nuclear Liability Act
Nuclear Safety & Control Act
Canadian Nuclear Safety Commission Rules of Procedure
Class I Nuclear Facilities Regulations
Class II Nuclear Facilities & Prescribed Equipment Regulations
General Nuclear Safety & Control Regulations
Nuclear Non-Proliferation Import & Export Control Regulations
Nuclear Security Regulations
Nuclear Substances & Radiation Devices Regulations
Packaging & Transport of Nuclear Substances Regulations
Radiation Protection Regulations
Uranium Mines & Mills Regulations
Uranium Mines (Ontario) Occupational Health & Safety Regulations
Oil Substitution & Conservation Act
Administration of Acts with respect to Changes in Provincial Boundaries
Alberta Act
Alberta/BC Boundary Act, 1974
Alberta/NWT Boundary Act, 1958
British Columbia 1857, 1866
BC-Yukon-NWT Boundary Act, 1967
Keewatin Act
Manitoba Boundaries Extension Act, 1912
Manitoba-NWT Boundary Act, 1966
Manitoba/Saskatchewan Boundary Act, 1966
New Brunswick, 1851
Newfoundland, 1949
Northwest Territories, 1905
Nova Scotia, 1851
Nunavut, 1993
Ontario, 1889
Ontario Boundaries Extension Act, 1912
Ontario-Manitoba Boundary Act
Prince Edward Island, 1873
Québec Boundaries Extension Act, 1912
Saskatchewan, 1905
Saskatchewan/NWT Boundary Act, 1966
Yukon, 1898
Acts Administered in Part by Natural Resources Canada
Arctic Waters Pollution Prevention Act (Transport Canada/Indian & Northern Affairs)
Arctic Shipping Pollution Prevention Regulations
Arctic Waters Pollution Prevention Regulations
Canada Lands Survey Act (Indian & Northern Affairs)
Canada Lands Surveys Examination Regulation
Canada-Newfoundland Oil & Gas Spills & Debris Liability Regulations
Land Survey Tariff Regulations
Newfoundland & Labrador Offshore Area Line Regulations
Newfoundland Offshore Area Oil & Gas Operations Regulations
Newfoundland Offshore Area Petroleum Diving Regulations
Newfoundland Offshore Area Petroleum Geophysical Operations Regulations
Newfoundland Offshore Area Petroleum Production & Conservation Regulations
Newfoundland Offshore Area Registration Regulations
Newfoundland Offshore Petroleum Drilling Regulations
Newfoundland Offshore Petroleum Installations Regulations
Newfoundland Offshore Petroleum Resource Revenue Fund Regulations
Nova Scotia Resources (Ventures) Limited Drilling Assistance Regulations
Shipping Safety Control Zones Order
Canada Petroleum Resources Act (Indian & Northern Affairs)
Environmental Studies Research Fund Regions Regulations
Frontier Lands Petroleum Royalty Regulations
Frontier Lands Registration Regulations
Lancaster Sound Designated Area Regulations
Orders Prohibiting the Issuance of Interests at Lapierre House Historic Site (Yukon) & Rampart House (Yukon)
Cape Breton Development Corporation Act
National Energy Board Act (Transport Canada)
Resources & Technical Surveys Act (Fisheries & Oceans/Environment)

Minister, Natural Resources, Hon. Joe Oliver
613-996-2007, Fax: 613-996-4516,
Minister.Ministre@NRCan-RNCan.gc.ca
Director of Parliamentary Affairs, Johnues Penner
613-996-2007, Fax: 613-943-0662,
john.penner@NRCan-RNCan.gc.ca
Deputy Minister, Serge Dupont
613-992-3280, Fax: 613-992-3828,
Serge.Dupont@NRCan-RNCan.gc.ca
Associate Deputy Minister, Karen Ellis
613-996-9753, Fax: 613-992-3828,
Karen.Ellis@NRCan-RNCan.gc.ca
Assistant Deputy Minister, Johanne Mongeon
613-992-3457, Fax: 613-992-3828,
Johanne.Mongeon@NRCan-RNCan.gc.ca
Chief Scientist, Geoff Munro
613-947-1435, Fax: 613-944-4747,
geoff.Munro@NRCan-RNCan.gc.ca
Director General, External Relations, Mark Pearson
613-996-6055, Fax: 613-996-0478,
Mark.Pearson@NRCan-RNCan.gc.ca
Chief Audit Executive, Joe Freamo
613-996-4940, Fax: 613-992-8799,
Joe.Freamo@NRCan-RNCan.gc.ca
Director General, Corporate Renewal Office, Sylvie Letellier
613-947-7403, Fax: 613-992-8922,
Sylvie.Letellier@NRCan-RNCan.gc.ca

Associated Agencies, Boards & Commissions:
• National Energy Board

Canadian Forest Service (CFS) / Service canadien des forêts
613-995-0947 Fax: 613-947-1208
cfs-scf@nrcan.gc.ca
http: //cfs.nrcan.gc.ca
TTY: 613-996-4397

Promotes the sustainable development of Canada's forests & competitiveness of the Canadian forest sector for the well-being of present & future generations of Canadians. It focuses on forest science & technology, & related national policy coordination. The CFS maintains five research centres across the country that share responsibility for research in the areas of biodiversity; biotechnology; climate change; ecology & ecosytems; entomology; forest conditions, monitoring & reporting; forest fires; forest & landscape management; pathology; silviculture & regeneration; & socioeconomics.

CFS Regional Offices:

Atlantic Forestry Centre / Centre de foresterie de l'Atlantique
1350 Regent St. South, PO Box 4000, Fredericton, NB E3B 5P7
506-452-3500 Fax: 506-452-3525
http: //cfs.nrcan.gc.ca/regions/afc

Responsible for the overall Canadian Forest Service operations & programs in the Atlantic region. Liaises & negotiates with provincial government, industry officials, & other sector-related senior management on behalf of the CFS in the region.
Regional Director General, John E. Richards
506-452-3508, JohnE.Richards@NRCan-RNCan.gc.ca
Director, Forest Production & Protection, Derek MacFarlane
506-452-3680, Derek.MacFarlane@NRCan-RNCan.gc.ca
Director, Science, Bruce Pendrel
506-452-3505, Bruce.Pendrel@NRCan-RNCan.gc.ca

Canadian Wood Fibre Centre (CWFC) / Centre canadien sur la fibre de bois (CCFB)
580 Booth Street, 8th Floor, Ottawa, ON K1A 0E4
613-947-9001 Fax: 613-947-8863
http: //cfs.nrcan.gc.ca/subsite/cwfc

The Canadian Wood Fibre Centre (CWFC) brings together forest sector researchers to develop solutions for the Canadian forest sector's wood fibre related industries in an environmentally responsible manner. Its mission is to create innovative knowledge to expand the economic opportunities for the forest sector to benefit from Canadian wood fibre.
Executive Director, George Alexande Bruemmer
613-947-7331, Fax: 613-947-8863,
GoergeAlexande.bruemmer@NRCan-RNCan.gc.ca

Great Lakes Forestry Centre / Centre de foresterie des Grands Lacs
1219 Queen St. East, PO Box 490, Sault Ste Marie, ON P6A 2E5
705-949-9461 Fax: 705-541-5700
http: //cfs.nrcan.gc.ca/regions/glfc

Responsibilities include: forest research & regional forestry activities in Ontario; provides the primary federal focus for forestry in Ontario; emphasis on boreal mixed wood forest management & environmental impacts of pollutants & forestry practices; efforts also directed at the reduction of losses from insects, disease & fire; ecosystem dynamics & classification; nutrient problems & impacts from forestry practices; acid rain impacts (carbon dioxide/nitrogen oxide interactions).
Director General, Theodore Van Lunen
705-541-5555, Theodore.VanLunen@NRCan-RNCan.gc.ca

Laurentian Forestry Centre / Centre de foresterie des Laurentides
1055, rue du PEPS, CP 10380 Sainte-Foy, Québec, QC G1V 4C7
418-648-3335 Fax: 418-648-5849
lucie.labrecque@RNCan-NRCan-gc.ca
http: //scf.rncan.gc.ca/regions/cfl

Responsibilities include: increasing scientific & technical knowledge in the area of forest biology which includes biodiversity, tree biotechnology & advanced genetics, pest management methods, & in the area of forest ecosystem which cover forest ecosystem processes, effects of forestry practices, landscape management & climate change.
Director General, Jacinthe Leclerc
418-648-3957, Jacinthe.Leclerc@RNCan-NRCan.gc.ca
Director, Forest Biology Program, Lise Caron
418-648-7616, Fax: 418-649-6956,
Lise.Caron@RNCan-NRCan.gc.ca
Research Director, Forest Ecosystems, Vincent Roy
418-648-3770, Fax: 418-649-6956,
Vincent.Roy@RNCan-NRCan.gc.ca
Director, Planning & Development, Normand Laflamme
418-648-2528, Fax: 418-648-2529,
Normand.Laflamme@RNCan-NRCan.gc.ca

Northern Forestry Centre / Centre de foresterie du Nord
5320 - 122 St., Edmonton, AB T6H 3S5
780-435-7210 Fax: 780-435-7359
http: //cfs.nrcan.gc.ca/regions/nofc

Responsibilities include: socio-economics & forest sociology; fire ecology, environment, & advanced fire management & prediction systems; climate change & forest interactions; carbon budget modeling; forest health, insect, & disease monitoring & management systems; remote sensing applications & landscape level classification systems; ecosystems productivity; biodiversity. Regional coordination of national programs relating to Model Forests & First Nation Forestry. Responsible for the direction of forestry programs in the provinces of Alberta, Saskatchewan, Manitoba & the NWT, including R&D, & four federal-provincial partnership agreements in forestry.
Director General, Timothy Sheldan
780-435-7202, Fax: 780-435-7396,
Timothy.Sheldan@NRCan-RNCan.gc.ca

Pacific Forestry Centre / Centre de foresterie du Pacifique
506 West Burnside Rd., Victoria, BC V8Z 1M5
250-363-0600 Fax: 250-363-0775
http: //cfs.nrcan.gc.ca/regions/pfc

Responsibilities include: forest management of federal lands; first nations programs; first nations land claims resource analysis; economic analysis of the regional forest sector (value-added, labour costs, & industrial sustainability); national strategic planning for the forestry practices & landscape management networks; science & technology programs in both forest biology (ecosystems processes, climate change, pest management, & tree biotechnology). Advises the CFS ADM on all forestry matters relating to the Pacific & Yukon region. The Mountain Pine Beetle Action Plan 2005-2010 set out strategies for confronting the infestation.
Director General, Kami Ramcharan
250-363-0608, Fax: 250-363-6088,
Kami.Ramcharan@NRCan-RNCan.gc.ca

Corporate Management & Services Sector / Secteur de la gestion et des services intégrés
613-995-4243 Fax: 613-922-8922

Asst. Deputy Minister/CFO, Bill Merklinger
613-995-4252, Fax: 613-992-8922,
Bill.Merklinger@NRCan-RNCan.gc.ca
Director General, Financial Management Branch, Thérèse Roy
613-943-8763, Fax: 613-996-2151,
Therese.Roy@NRCan-RNCan.gc.ca
Director General, Human Resources & Security Management Branch, Kiran Hanspal
613-996-4008, Fax: 613-995-0025,
kiran.hanspal@NRCan-RNCan.gc.ca
Director, Security, Safety & Emergency Management, Guy Morin
613-943-0594, Fax: 613-943-0336,
guy.morin@NRCan-RNCan.gc.ca

Earth Sciences Sector / Secteur des sciences de la Terre
http: //ess.nrcan.gc.ca/index_e.php

Provides Canadians with timely & reliable geomatics & geoscience knowledge, products & services of the highest standards & in the most cost-effective manner possible. The Earth Sciences Sector is a predominantly science- and technology-based sector & includes the Geological Survey of Canada, Geomatics Canada, & the Polar Continental Shelf Project. These groups are major contributors to the comprehensive geoscience knowledge base of Canada & provide surveying, mapping, remote sensing, & digital information services describing the Canadian landmass.
Asst. Deputy Minister, Brian Gray
613-992-9983, Fax: 613-995-1509,
brian.gray@NRCan-RNCan.gc.ca
Chief Geologist, Nunavut Geoscience Office, Paul Budkewitsch
867-975-4412, Fax: 867-979-0708,
paul.budkewitsch@NRCan-RNCan.gc.ca
Director General, Coordination & Strategic Issues Branch, Marian Campbell Jarvis
613-992-5032,
Marian.CampbellJarvis@NRCan-RNCan.gc.ca
Director General, Mapping Information Branch, Prashant Shukle
613-947-0467, Fax: 613-994-6749,
Prashant.Shukle@NRCan-RNCan.gc.ca
Director, Planning & Operations Division, Fram Engineer
613-996-1169, Fax: 613-947-8768,
Fram.Engineer@NRCan-RNCan.gc.ca

Geological Survey of Canada (GSC) / Commission géologique du Canada
601 Booth St., Ottawa, ON K1A 0E8
613-996-3919 Fax: 613-943-8742
esic@nrcan.gc.ca
http: //gsc.nrcan.gc.ca
Other Communication: Bookstore: 613-995-4342

Geoscientific information & research, geoscience surveys, sustainable development of Canada's resources, environmental protection, technology innovation.
Director General, Central & Northern Canada Branch, Dr. David Boerner
613-995-4314, Fax: 613-996-6575,
David.Boerner@NRCan-RNCan.gc.ca
Program Officer, Atlantic & Western Branch, Dan Richardson
613-996-9151, Fax: 613-996-6575,
dan.richardson@NRCan-RNCan.gc.ca

Energy Policy Sector / Secteur de la politique énergétique
613-996-7432 Fax: 613-992-1405
www.nrcan-rncan.gc.ca/eneene/polpol/index-eng.php

Develops & promotes economic, regulatory & voluntary approaches to encourage sustainable development of energy resources to meet domestic needs & export markets. Advises the government on federal energy policies, strategies, emergency plans & activities; promotes efficient energy use.
Asst. Deputy Minister, Mark Corey
613-947-2751, Mark.Corey@NRCan-RNCan.gc.ca
Director General, Energy Policy Branch, Nada Vrany
613-995-2821, Fax: 613-996-5943,
Nada.Vrany@NRCan-RNCan.gc.ca
Director General, Petroleum Resources Branch, Jeff Labonte
613-992-8609, Fax: 613-992-8738,
Jeff.Labonte@NRCan-RNCan.gc.ca

Innovation & Energy Technology Sector / Secteur de l'innovation et de la technologie énergétique
Asst. Deputy Minister, Geoff Munro
613-947-1435, Fax: 613-944-4747,
Geoff.Munro@NRCan-RNCan.gc.ca
Deputy Director General, Operations, Philippe Dauphin
613-943-4195, Fax: 613-995-7868,
Philippe.Dauphin@NRCan-RNCan.gc.ca
Director General, Devon Research Centre, Dr. Hassan Hamza
780-987-8617, Fax: 780-987-8690,
Hassan.Hamza@NRCan-RNCan.gc.ca
Director General, Ottawa Research Centre, John Marrone
613-996-8201, Fax: 613-947-2318,
John.Marrone@NRCan-RNCan.gc.ca
Director General, Strategic Science-Technology Branch, Martin Aubé
613-996-8109, Fax: 613-947-1016,
Martin.Aube@NRCan-RNCan.gc.ca
Director General, Varennes Research Centre, Gilles Jean
450-652-6639, Fax: 450-652-5994,
Gilles.Jean@RNCan-NRCan.gc.ca

Minerals & Metals Sector (MMS) / Secteur des minéraux et des métaux
613-947-6580
info-mms@nrcan-rncan.gc.ca
www.nrcan-rncan.gc.ca/mms-smm
TTY: 613-996-4397

MMS is the federal government's primary source of scientific & technological knowledge, & policy advice, on Canada's mineral & metal resources & on explosives regulation & technology. In addition to housing three scientific research institutions, MMS has the government lead in promoting sustainable development & responsible use of Canada's mineral & metal resources. The Sector is a leader in the generation & dissemination of knowledge on the Canadian minerals & metals industry, & collaborates with & provides research services to governmental, institutional & industrial clients for the development of new technology with economic, environmental & social benefits to Canadians.
Asst. Deputy Minister, Anil Arora
613-992-2490, Fax: 613-996-7425,
Anil.Arora@NRCan-RNCan.gc.ca

Director General, CANMET Materials Technology Laboratory, Dr. Jennifer Jackman
613-995-8248, Fax: 613-992-8735, Jennifer.Jackman@NRCan-RNCan.gc.ca
Director General, Explosives Safety & Security Branch, Patrick O'Neill
613-948-5181, Fax: 613-948-5195, patrick.o'neill@nrcan-rncan.gc.ca
Director General, Minerals, Metals & Materials Knowledge Branch, Christiane Villemure
613-996-5525, Fax: 613-943-8453, Christiane.Villemure@NRCan-RNCan.gc.ca
Director General, Minerals, Metals & Materials Policy Branch, Ginny Flood
613-996-5309, Fax: 613-952-7501, Ginny.Flood@NRCan-RNCan.gc.ca
Chief, Health & Safety, CANMET Mining & Mineral Sciences Laboratories, Katrina Nicholson
613-996-0826, Fax: 613-943-0575, Katrina.Nicholson@NRCan-RNCan.gc.ca

Canada Centre for Remote Sensing - Geomatics Canada (CCRSO) / Centre canadien de télédétection (CCT)
588 Booth St., Ottawa, ON K1A 0Y7
613-995-0947 Fax: 613-947-1382
http: //ccrs.nrcan.gc.ca
TTY: 613-996-4397

Remote sensing data for Canada; development of remote sensing technology & applications in conjunction with the private sector, & in support of environmental monitoring; development of the Canadian geospatial data infrastructure for distribution of remote sensing & other geographical databases, in partnership with other departments; development of GIS applications.

Director General, Douglas Bancroft
613-947-1358, Fax: 613-947-1382, Douglas.Bancroft@NRCan-RNCan.gc.ca
Director, Business, Policy & Planning, Gordon Deecker
613-947-1280, Fax: 613-947-1408, Gordon.Deecker@NRCan-RNCan.gc.ca
Director, Data Acquisition Division, Caroline Cloutier
613-995-0802, Fax: 613-947-1408, Caroline.Cloutier@NRCan-RNCan.gc.ca
Director, Earth Observation & GeoSolutions Divison, E. Paola de Rose
613-947-1350, Fax: 613-947-1385, E.Paola.deRose@NRCan-RNCan.gc.ca
Director, Geodetic Survey Division, Denis Hains
613-995-4282, Fax: 613-995-3215, Denis.Hains@NRCan-RNCan.gc.ca

Mapping Information Branch / Direction de l'information cartographique
615 Booth St., Ottawa, ON K1A 0E9
613-995-4945 Fax: 613-995-8737
Other Communication: Canada Map Office: 1-800-465-6277 or 613/952-7009; Help Desk: 613/996-5916

Director General, Prashant Shukle
613-947-0467, Fax: 613-994-6749, Prashant.Shukle@NRCan-RNCan.gc.ca
Senior Policy Advisor, Wendy Ripmeester
613-947-3736, Fax: 613-947-5977, wendy.ripmeester@nrcan-rncan.gc.ca
Director, Centre for Topographic Information - Ottawa, Douglas O'Brien
613-947-1287, Fax: 613-947-7948, Douglas.O'Brien@NRCan-RNCan.gc.ca
Project Manager, Centre for Topographic Information - Ottawa, Sylvain Lemay
613-992-3743, Fax: 613-995-4438, sylvain.lemay@nrcan-rncan.gc.ca
Director, Centre for Topographic Information - Sherbrooke, Eric Loubier
819-564-5600, Fax: 819-564-5698, Eric.Loubier@RNCan-NRCan.gc.ca
Project Manager, Centre for Topographic Information - Sherbrooke, Denis Genest
819-564-5600, Fax: 819-564-5698, denis.genest@nrcan-rncan.gc.ca
Director, Data Dissemination Division, Ann Martin
613-947-5849, Fax: 613-944-6749, Ann.Martin@NRCan-RNCan.gc.ca
Director, GeoConnections Division, Yvan Désy
613-947-0112, Fax: 613-947-2410, Yvan.Desy@NRCan-RNCan.gc.ca
Chair, Geographical Names Board of Canada, Bruce Amos
Fax: 613-943-8282, geonames@nrcan.gc.ca, Other Communications: URL: geonames.nrcan.gc.ca
Director General, Tom Wallace
613-996-3027

Natural Sciences & Engineering Research Council of Canada (NSERC) / Conseil des recherches en sciences naturelles et en génie du Canada (CRSNG)

Constitution Square, Tower II, 350 Albert St., Ottawa, ON K1A 1H5
613-995-4273 Fax: 613-943-1624
marie-josee.duval@nserc-crsng.gc.ca
www.nserc.gc.ca

Science & Engineering Research Canada (NSERC) is a federal agency whose role is to make investments in people, discovery & innovation for the benefit of all Canadians. With an annual budget of more than $860 million, it supports more than 20,000 university students & postdoctoral fellows in their advanced studies. NSERC promotes discovery by funding more than 10,000 university professors every year & helps make innovation happen by encouraging more than 500 Canadian companies to participate & invest in university research projects.

President, Dr. Suzanne Fortier
613-995-5840, suzanne.fortier@nserc-crsng.gc.ca
Vice-President, Research Grants & Scholarships Directorate, Isabelle Blain
613-995-5833, isabelle.blain@nserc-crsng.gc.ca
Vice-President, Research Partnerships Programs Directorate, Janet Walden
616-139-9215, Fax: 613-947-6371, janet.walden@nserc-crsng.gc.ca
Director, Communications Division, Jacqueline Couture
613-995-5993, Jacqueline.Couture@nserc-crsng.gc.ca
Vice-President, Common Administrative Services Directorate, Jaime Pitfield
613-995-3914, Fax: 613-991-0969, Jaime.Pitfield@nserc-crsng.gc.ca
Vice-President, Common Administrative Services, Michel Cavallin
Director, Finance & Awards Administration Division, Dominique Osterrath
613-996-8269, dominique.osterrath@nserc-crsng.gc.ca

North American Free Trade Agreement (NAFTA) Secretariat / Secrétariat de l'ALÉNA

Canadian Section, #705, 90 Sparks St., Ottawa, ON K1P 5B4
613-992-9388 Fax: 613-992-9392
webmaster@nafta-alena.gc.ca
www.nafta-alena.gc.ca

The NAFTA Secretariat, comprised of a Canadian Section, a United States Section and a Mexican Section, is responsible for the administration of the dispute settlement provisions of the North American Free Trade Agreement. The Canadian Section also carries responsibility for similar provisions under the Canada-Chile, Canada-Israel and Canada-Costa Rica free trade agreements.

Canadian Secretary, Marie-Josée, Langlois
613-992-9380, marie.josee.langlois@nafta-alena.gc.ca
Registrar/Acting Deputy Secretary, Feleke Bogale
613-992-9384, Fax: 613-992-9392, feleke.bogale@nafta-alena.gc.ca
Records & Information Management Officer, Marie-France Meunier
613-992-2303, Fax: 613-992-9392, mariefrance.meunier@nafta-alena.gc.ca

Northern Pipeline Agency Canada (NPAC) / Administration du pipe-line du Nord Canada (APNC)

580 Booth St., Ottawa, ON K1A 0E4
613-992-9612 Fax: 613-995-1913

Established to carry out federal responsibilities in relation to the planning & construction of the Canadian portion of the Alaska Natural Gas Transportation System.

Commissioner, Serge Dupont
613-992-3280, Fax: 613-992-3828
Assistant Commissioner & Comptroller, Christopher Cuddy
613-995-4297, Fax: 613-996-5354
Administrator, Carole Matte
613-992-1150, Fax: 613-996-5354

Office of the Commissioner of Official Languages / Commissariat aux langues officielles

344 Slater St., 3rd fl., Ottawa, ON K1A 0T8
613-996-6368 Fax: 613-993-5082
877-996-6368
www.ocol-clo.gc.ca
TTY: 800-880-1990

Responsible for ensuring the equality of English & French in Parliament, within the Government of Canada, the federal administration, & the institutions subject to the Official Languages Act; the preservation & development of official language communities in Canada; & the equality of English & French in Canadian society.

Acts Administered:
Official Languages Act

Commissioner of Official Languages, Graham Fraser
613-995-7488, Fax: 613-943-2255
Director, Audits, Nycole Lafond
613-943-1159, Fax: 613-943-0451
Director, Finance & Procurement, Colette M. Lagacé
613-995-0412, Fax: 613-993-5082
Director, Human Resources, Mario Séguin
613-943-0390, Fax: 613-944-5477
Director, Information Management & Technology, JoHanne Verrier
613-943-0220, Fax: 613-947-4751
Director, Investigations, Carole Beauvais
613-943-1161, Fax: 613-943-0451
Director & General Counsel, Legal Affairs, Johane Tremblay
613-995-9069, Fax: 613-996-9671
Director, Operational Integration Initiative, Corita Harty
613-992-9874, Fax: 613-995-1161
Director, Policy & Research, Johanne Lapointe
613-943-0429, Fax: 613-995-1161
Director, Strategic Communications & Production, Robin Cantin
613-995-9356, Fax: 613-995-1161
Director, Strategic Performance Measurement, Pierre Coulombe
613-995-0815, Fax: 613-943-0451

Pacific Pilotage Authority Canada / Administration de pilotage du Pacifique Canada

#1000, 1130 Pender St. West, Vancouver, BC V6E 4A4
604-666-6771 Fax: 604-666-1647
info@ppa.gc.ca
www.ppa.gc.ca
Other Communication: Vancouver Dispatch: 604-666-6776, Fax: 604-666-6093; Victoria Dispatch: 250-363-3878, Fax: 250-363-3293

Operates pilotage services in Canadian waters in & around British Columbia. Reports to government through the Minister of Transportation.

President/CEO, Capt. Kevin Obermeyer
Chair, David K. Gardiner
Director, Finance, Bruce Chadwick
Director, Operations, Capt. Brian Young

Parks Canada / Parcs Canada

25 Eddy St., Gatineau, QC K1A 0M5
613-860-1251
888-773-8888
information@pc.gc.ca
www.pc.gc.ca
TTY: 866-787-6221

Responsible for the protection, management, operation & maintenance of national parks, historic sites, canals & other significant examples of Canada's natural & cultural heritage, for the benefit, understanding & enjoyment of Canadians. Administers one of the largest park systems in the world. Working towards establishing parks in each of 39 distinct natural regions. In addition to the national parks, national historic sites & national marine conservation areas, Parks Canada coordinates other heritage programs, including federal heritage buildings, heritage railway stations, grave sites of Canadian Prime Ministers, heritage rivers, archaeology programs, international programs.

Minister of Environment; Minister Responsable, Hon. Peter Kent
613-992-0253, Fax: 613-992-0887, kentp@parl.gc.ca
Chief Executive Officer, Alan Latourelle
819-997-9525, Fax: 819-953-9745
Chief Audit & Evaluation Executive, Office of Internal Audit & Evaluation, Brian Evans
819-997-9928, Fax: 819-997-5285, Other Communications: Alt. Phone: 613-889-1675
Ombudsman, Luc Martin
819-934-7000, Fax: 819-210-3645
Director General, National Parks, Ron Hallman
819-994-2657, Fax: 819-994-5140
Director General, National Historic Sites, Larry S. Ostola
819-994-1808, Fax: 819-934-1526
Communications Advisor, Joanne Huppé
819-953-8699, Fax: 819-953-5523, Other Communications: Alt. Phone: 613-799-6269

Associated Agencies, Boards & Commissions:
• Historic Sites & Monuments Board of Canada / Commission des lieux et monuments historiques du Canada
Terrasses de la Chaudière
25 Eddy St.
Gatineau, QC K1A 0M5
Fax: 819-934-1115 855-283-8730
hsmbc-clmhc@pc.gc.ca
www.pc.gc.ca/clmhc-hsmbc/
A seventeen-member advisory board which reports to the Minister of Environment & recommends whether persons, places or events are of national historic &/or architectural significance,

& therefore warrant commemoration. The board also makes recommendations concerning the designation of heritage railway stations.

Canal Offices:

Carillon
230, rue du Barrage, Saint-André-d'Argenteuil, QC J0V 1X0
450-537-3534 Fax: 450-658-2428
parkscanada-que@pc.gc.ca
www.pc.gc.ca/canalcarillon

Chambly
1899, boul Périgny, Chambly, QC J3L 4C3
450-658-6525 Fax: 450-658-2428
parkscanada-que@pc.gc.ca
www.pc.gc.ca/canalchambly
Other Communication: Lock #9 (Saint-Jean), Phone: 450-348-3392

Lachine
200, boul René-Lévesque ouest, tour Ouest, 6e étage, Montréal, QC H2Z 1X4
514-283-6054 Fax: 514-496-1263
parcscanada-que@pc.gc.ca
www.pc.gc.ca/canallachine

Rideau
34 Beckwith St. South, Smiths Falls, ON K7A 2A8
613-283-5170 Fax: 613-283-0677
RideauCanal-info@pc.gc.ca
www.pc.gc.ca/eng/lhn-nhs/on/rideau/index.aspx

Sainte-Anne-de-Bellevue
170, rue Sainte-Anne, Sainte-Anne, QC H9X 1N1
514-457-5546 Fax: 450-658-2428
parkscanada-que@pc.gc.ca
www.pc.gc.ca/canalsteanne

Saint-Ours
2930, ch des Patriotes, Saint-Ours, QC J0G 1P0
450-785-2212 Fax: 450-658-2428
www.pc.gc.ca/canalstours

St. Peters
PO Box 8, St Peters, NS B0E 3B0
902-733-2280 Fax: 902-733-2362
information@pc.gc.ca
www.pc.gc.ca/stpeterscanal

Sault Ste Marie
1 Canal Dr., Sault Ste Marie, ON P6A 6W4
705-941-6262 Fax: 705-941-6206
info-saultcanal@pc.gc.ca
www.pc.gc.ca/eng/lhn-nhs/on/ssmarie/index.aspx

Trent-Severn Waterway
PO Box 567, Peterborough, ON K9J 6Z6
705-750-4900 Fax: 705-742-9644
888-773-7777
Ont.Trentsevern@pc.gc.ca
www.pc.gc.ca/trentsevern
TTY: 705-750-4949

Atlantic National Parks/National Historic Sites:

Alexander Graham Bell Historic Site of Canada
PO Box 159, Baddeck, NS B0E 1B0
902-295-2069 Fax: 902-295-3496
information@pc.gc.ca
www.pc.gc.ca/eng/lhn-nhs/ns/grahambell/index.aspx

Ardgowan National Historic Site of Canada
2 Palmer's Lane, Charlottetown, PE C1A 5V8
902-566-7050 Fax: 902-566-7226
www.pc.gc.ca/eng/lhn-nhs/pe/ardgowan/index.aspx

Bank Fishery National Heritage Exhibit
PO Box 9080 A, Halifax, NS B3K 5M7
902-426-5080 Fax: 902-426-4228
information@pc.gc.ca
www.pc.gc.ca/lhn-nhs/ns/bank/index.aspx

Boishébert & Beaubears Shipbuilding National Historic Sites of Canada
186, route 117, Kouchibouguac National Park, NB E4X 2P1
506-876-2443 Fax: 506-876-4802
kouch.info@pc.gc.ca
www.pc.gc.ca/lhn-nhs/nb/boishebert/index.aspx
TTY: 506-876-4205

Canso Islands National Historic Site of Canada
PO Box 159, Baddeck, NS B0E 1B0
902-295-2069 Fax: 902-295-3496
information@pc.gc.ca
www.pc.gc.ca/lhn-nhs/ns/canso/index.aspx

Cape Breton Highlands National Park of Canada
Ingonish Beach, NS B0C 1L0
902-224-2306 Fax: 902-285-2866
information@pc.gc.ca
www.pc.gc.ca/pn-np/ns/cbreton/index.aspx

Cape Spear National Historic Site of Canada
PO Box 1268, St. John's, NL A1C 5M9
709-772-5367 Fax: 709-772-6302
cape.spear@pc.gc.ca
www.pc.gc.ca/lhn-nhs/nl/spear/index.aspx

Carleton Martello Tower National Historic Site of Canada
454 Whipple St., Saint John, NB E2M 2R3
506-636-4011 Fax: 506-636-4574
info.martello@pc.gc.ca
www.pc.gc.ca/lhn-nhs/nb/carleton/index.aspx
TTY: 506-887-6015

Castle Hill National Historic Site of Canada
PO Box 10, Jerseyside, Placentia Bay, NL A0B 2G0
709-227-2401 Fax: 709-227-2452
castle.hill@pc.gc.ca
www.pc.gc.ca/lhn-nhs/nl/castlehill/index.aspx
Other Communication: Off-season: 709-772-5367, Fax: 709-772-6302

Fort Amherst/Port-La-Joye National Historic Site of Canada
2 Palmers Lane, Charlottetown, PE C1A 5V8
902-566-7626 Fax: 902-566-8295
www.pc.gc.ca/lhn-nhs/pe/amherst/index.aspx
Other Communication: July 1-August 31 Phone: 902-675-2220

Fort Anne National Historic Site of Canada
PO Box 9, Annapolis Royal, NS B0S 1A0
902-532-2397 Fax: 902-532-2232
information@pc.gc.ca
www.pc.gc.ca/lhn-nhs/ns/fortanne/index.aspx
Other Communication: Off-season: 902-532-2321

Fort Beauséjour National Historic Site of Canada
111 Fort Beauséjour Rd., Aulac, NB E4L 2W5
506-364-5080 Fax: 506-536-4399
fort.beausejour@pc.gc.ca
www.pc.gc.ca/lhn-nhs/nb/beausejour/index.aspx

Fort Edward National Historic Site of Canada
PO Box 9, Annapolis Royal, NS B0S 1A0
902-532-2321 Fax: 902-532-2232
www.pc.gc.ca/lhn-nhs/ns/edward/index.aspx
Other Communication: July & August: 902-798-4706

Fort McNab National Historic Site of Canada
PO Box 9080 A, Halifax, NS B3K 5M7
902-426-5080 Fax: 902-426-4228
halifax.citadel@pc.gc.ca
www.pc.gc.ca/lhn-nhs/ns/mcnab/index.aspx

Fortress of Louisbourg National Historic Site
259 Park Service Rd., Louisbourg, NS B1C 2L2
902-733-2280 Fax: 902-733-2362
information@pc.gc.ca
www.pc.gc.ca/lhn-nhs/ns/louisbourg/index.aspx
TTY: 902-733-3607

Fundy National Park of Canada
PO Box 1001, Alma, NB E4H 1B4
506-887-6000 Fax: 506-887-6008
fundy.info@pc.gc.ca
www.pc.gc.ca/pn-np/nb/fundy/index.aspx
TTY: 506-887-6015

Grand Pré National Historic Site of Canada
PO Box 150, Grand Pré, NS B0P 1M0
902-542-3631 Fax: 902-542-1691
866-542-3631
grandpre.info@pc.gc.ca; contact@grand-pre.com
www.pc.gc.ca/lhn-nhs/ns/grandpre/index.aspx;
www.grand-pre.com
TTY: 902-532-7472

Georges Island National Historic Site of Canada
PO Box 9080 A, Halifax, NS B3K 5M7
902-426-5080 Fax: 902-426-4228
georges.island@pc.gc.ca
www.pc.gc.ca/lhn-nhs/ns/georges/index.aspx

Green Gables Heritage Place
2 Palmer's Lane, Charlottetown, PE C1A 5V6
902-963-7874
greengables.info@pc.gc.ca
www.pc.gc.ca/lhn-nhs/pe/greengables/index.aspx

Gros Morne National Park of Canada
PO Box 130, Rocky Harbour, NL A0K 4N0
709-458-2417 Fax: 709-458-2059
grosmorne.info@pc.gc.ca
www.pc.gc.ca/pn-np/nl/grosmorne/index.aspx
TTY: 709-772-4564

Halifax Citadel National Historic Site of Canada
PO Box 9080 A, Halifax, NS B3K 5M7
902-426-5080 Fax: 902-426-4228
halifax.citadel@pc.gc.ca
www.pc.gc.ca/lhn-nhs/ns/halifax/index.aspx

Hawthorne Cottage National Historic Site of Canada
PO Box 5542, St. John's, NL A1C 5W4
709-753-9262 Fax: 709-753-0879
info@historicsites.ca
www.pc.gc.ca/lhn-nhs/nl/hawthorne/index.aspx
Other Communication: Off-season: 709-528-4004

Kejimkujik National Park of Canada
PO Box 236, Maitland Bridge, NS B0T 1B0
902-682-2772 Fax: 902-682-3367
kejimkujik.info@pc.gc.ca
www.pc.gc.ca/pn-np/ns/kejimkujik/index_e.asp

Kouchibouguac National Park of Canada
186, Route 117, Kouchibouguac National Park, NB E4X 2P1
506-876-2443 Fax: 506-876-4802
kouch.info@pc.gc.ca
www.pc.gc.ca/pn-np/nb/kouchibouguac/index.aspx
TTY: 506-876-4205

L'Anse aux Meadows National Historic Site of Canada
PO Box 70, St-Lunaire-Griquet, NL A0K 2X0
709-458-2417 Fax: 709-623-2028
viking.lam@pc.gc.ca
www.pc.gc.ca/lhn-nhs/nl/meadows/index.aspx

Marconi National Historic Site of Canada
PO Box 159, Baddeck, NS B0E 1B0
902-295-2069 Fax: 902-295-3496
information@pc.gc.ca
www.pc.gc.ca/lhn-nhs/ns/marconi/index.aspx

Monument Lefebvre National Historic Site of Canada
480 rue Centrale, Memramcook, NB E4K 3S6
506-758-9808 Fax: 506-758-9813
monument@nbnet.nb.ca
www.pc.gc.ca/lhn-nhs/nb/lefebvre/index.aspx

Port-au-Choix National Historic Site of Canada
PO Box 140, Port au Choix, NL A0K 4C0
709-458-2417 Fax: 709-861-3827
pac-historic-site@pc.gc.ca
www.pc.gc.ca/lhn-nhs/nl/portauchoix/index.aspx
Other Communication: Seasonal: 709-861-3522

Port Royal National Historic Site of Canada
PO Box 9, Annapolis Royal, NS B0S 1A0
902-532-2898 Fax: 902-532-2232
information@pc.gc.ca
www.pc.gc.ca/lhn-nhs/ns/portroyal/index.aspx
Other Communication: Off-season: 902-532-2232

Prince Edward Island National Park of Canada
2 Palmers Lane, Charlottetown, PE C1A 5V8
902-672-6350 Fax: 902-672-6370
pnipe.peinp@pc.gc.ca
www.pc.gc.ca/pn-np/pe/pei-ipe/index.aspx
TTY: 902-566-7061

Prince of Wales Tower National Historic Site
PO Box 9080 A, Halifax, NS B3K 5M7
902-426-5080 Fax: 902-426-4228
halifax.citadel@pc.gc.ca
www.pc.gc.ca/lhn-nhs/ns/prince/index.aspx

Province House National Historic Site of Canada
2 Palmer's Lane, Charlottetown, PE C1A 5V8
902-566-7626 Fax: 902-566-8295
information@pc.gc.ca
www.pc.gc.ca/lhn-nhs/pe/provincehouse/index.aspx

Red Bay National Historic Site of Canada
PO Box 103, Red Bay, NL A0K 4K0
709-920-2142 Fax: 709-458-2144
redbay.info@pc.gc.ca
www.pc.gc.ca/lhn-nhs/nl/redbay/index.aspx
Other Communication: Summer: 709-920-2051; Alt. Phone: 709-458-2417

Ryan Premises National Historic Site
PO Box 1451, Bonavista, NL A0C 1B0
709-468-1600 Fax: 709-468-1604
ryan.premises@pc.gc.ca
www.pc.gc.ca/lhn-nhs/nl/ryan/index.aspx

St. Andrews Blockhouse National Historic Site of Canada
454 Whipple St., Saint John, NB E2M 2R3
506-636-4011 Fax: 506-636-4574
fundy.info@pc.gc.ca
www.pc.gc.ca/lhn-nhs/nb/standrews/index.aspx
TTY: 506-887-6015
Other Communication: Summer: 506-529-4270

St. Peters Canada National Historic Site of Canada
PO Box 8, St Peters, NS B0E 3B0
902-733-2280 Fax: 902-733-2362
information@pc.gc.ca
www.pc.gc.ca/lhn-nhs/ns/stpeters/index.aspx

Signal Hill National Historic Site of Canada
PO Box 1268, St. John's, NL A1C 5M9
709-772-5367 Fax: 709-772-6302
signal.hill@pc.gc.ca
www.pc.gc.ca/lhn-nhs/nl/signalhill/index.aspx

Terra Nova National Park of Canada
General Delivery, Glovertown, NL A0G 2L0
709-533-2801 Fax: 709-533-2706
info.tnnp@pc.gc.ca
www.pc.gc.ca/pn-np/nl/terranova/index.aspx

York Redoubt National Historic Site of Canada
PO Box 9080 A, Halifax, NS B3K 5M7
902-426-5080 Fax: 902-426-4228
halifax.citadel@pc.gc.ca
www.pc.gc.ca/lhn-nhs/ns/york/index.aspx

Ontario National Parks/National Historic Sites:

Battle of the Windmill National Historic Site of Canada
370 Vankoughnet St., PO Box 479, Prescott, ON K0E 1T0
613-925-2896 Fax: 613-925-1536
ont.wellington@pc.gc.ca
www.pc.gc.ca/lhn-nhs/on/windmill/index.aspx

Bellevue House National Historic Site of Canada
35 Centre St., Kingston, ON K7L 4E5
613-545-8666 Fax: 613-545-8721
bellevue.house@pc.gc.ca
www.pc.gc.ca/lhn-nhs/on/bellevue/index.aspx
TTY: 613-545-8668

Bethune Memorial House National Historic Site of Canada
235 John St. North, Gravenhurst, ON P1P 1G4
705-687-4261 Fax: 705-687-4935
ont-bethune@pc.gc.ca
www.pc.gc.ca/lhn-nhs/on/bethune/index.aspx

Bois Blanc Island Lighthouse National Historic Site of Canada
c/o Fort Malden N.H.S., 100 Laird Ave., PO Box 38, Amherstburg, ON N9V 2Z2
519-736-5416 Fax: 519-736-6603
ont.fort-malden@pc.gc.ca
www.pc.gc.ca/lhn-nhs/on/boisblanc/index.aspx

Bruce Peninsula National Park
PO Box 189, Tobermory, ON N0H 2R0
519-596-2233 Fax: 519-596-2298
bruce-fathomfive@pc.gc.ca
www.pc.gc.ca/pn-np/on/bruce/index.aspx

Butler's Barracks c/o Fort George National Historic Site
25 Eddy St., Gatineau, QB K1A 0M5
905-468-6614 Fax: 905-468-4638
ont-niagara@pc.gc.ca
www.pc.gc.ca/lhn-nhs/on/fortgeorge/index.aspx

Fort George National Historic Site of Canada
25 Eddy St., Gatineau, QB K1A 0M5
905-468-6614 Fax: 905-468-4638
ont-niagara@pc.gc.ca
www.pc.gc.ca/lhn-nhs/on/fortgeorge/index.aspx

Fathom Five National Marine Park of Canada
PO Box 189, Tobermory, ON N0H 2R0
519-596-2233 Fax: 519-596-2298
bruce-fathomfive@pc.gc.ca
www.pc.gc.ca/eng/amnc-nmca/on/fathomfive/index.aspx

Fort Malden National Historic Site
100 Laird Ave., PO Box 38, Amherstburg, ON N9V 2Z2
519-736-5416 Fax: 519-736-6603
ont.fort-malden@pc.gc.ca
www.pc.gc.ca/eng/lhn-nhs/on/malden/index.aspx

Fort Mississauga National Historic Site of Canada
26 Queen St., PO Box 787, Niagara on the Lake, ON L0S 1J0
905-468-6614 Fax: 905-468-4638
www.friendsoffortgeorge.ca

Fort St. Joseph National Historic Site of Canada
PO Box 220, Richards Landing, ON P0R 1J0
705-246-2664 Fax: 705-246-1796
fortstjoseph-info@pc.gc.ca
www.pc.gc.ca/lhn-nhs/on/stjoseph.aspx

Fort Wellington National Historic Site of Canada
PO Box 479, Prescott, ON K0E 1T0
613-925-2896 Fax: 613-925-1536
ont-wellington@pc.gc.ca
www.pc.gc.ca/lhn-nhs/on/wellington.aspx
TTY: 613-925-2896

Georgian Bay Islands National Park of Canada
901 Wye Valley Rd., PO Box 9, Midland, ON L4R 4K6
705-526-9804 Fax: 705-526-5939
info.gbi@pc.gc.ca
www.pc.gc.ca/eng/pn-np/on/georg/index.aspx

Inverarden House National Historic Site of Canada
370 Vankoughnet St., PO Box 479, Prescott, ON K0E 1T0
613-925-2896 Fax: 613-925-1536
ont-wellington@pc.gc.ca
www.pc.gc.ca/lhn-nhs/on/inverarden/index.aspx

Kingston Martello Towers
35 Centre St., Kingston, ON K7L 4E5
613-545-8666 Fax: 613-545-8721
www.pc.gc.ca/lhn-nhs/on/bellevue/index.aspx
TTY: 613-545-8668

Laurier House National Historic Site of Canada
335 Laurier Ave. East, Ottawa, ON K1A 6R4
613-992-8142 Fax: 613-947-4851
laurier-house@pc.gc.ca
www.pc.gc.ca/lhn-nhs/on/laurier.aspx

Point Clark Lighthouse National Historic Site of Canada
c/o Woodside National Historic Site, 528 Wellington St. North, Kitchener, ON N2H 5L5
519-571-5684 Fax: 519-571-5286
ont-woodside@pc.gc.ca
www.pc.gc.ca/lhn-nhs/on/clark.aspx

Point Pelee National Park of Canada
407 Monarch Lane, RR#1, Leamington, ON N8H 3V4
519-322-2365 Fax: 519-322-1277
pelee.info@pc.gc.ca
www.pc.gc.ca/fra/pn-np/on/pelee.aspx

Pukaskwa National Park of Canada
PO Box 212, Heron Bay, ON P0T 1R0
807-229-0801 Fax: 807-229-2097
ont-pukaskwa@pc.gc.ca
www.pc.gc.ca/pn-np/on/pukaskwa.aspx

Queenston Heights & Brock's Monument
26 Queen St., PO Box 787, Niagara on the Lake, ON L0S 1J0
905-468-4257 Fax: 905-468-4638
ont-niagara@pc.gc.ca
www.pc.gc.ca/lhn-nhs/on/queenston/index.aspx

St. Lawrence Islands National Park of Canada
2 County Rd. 5, RR#3, Mallorytown Landing, ON K0E 1R0
613-923-5261 Fax: 613-923-1021
ont-sli@pc.gc.ca
www.pc.gc.ca/pn-np/on/lawren/index.aspx

Sir John Johnson National Historic Site of Canada
c/o Fort Wellington National Historic Site, 370 Vanhoughnet St., PO Box 479, Prescott, ON K0E 1T0
613-925-2896 Fax: 613-925-1536
ont.wellington@pc.gc.ca; sirjohnjohnson@sympatico.ca
www.pc.gc.ca/lhn-nhs/on/johnjohnson/index.aspx

Woodside National Historic Site of Canada
528 Wellington St. North, Kitchener, ON N2H 5L5
519-571-5684 Fax: 519-571-5686
ont-woodside@pc.gc.ca
www.pc.gc.ca/lhn-nhs/on/woodside/index.aspx

Quebec National Parks/National Historic Sites:

Artillery Park National Historic Site of Canada
2, rue d'Auteuil, CP 10 B, Québec, QC G1K 7A1
418-648-7016 Fax: 418-648-2506
parkscanada-que@pc.gc.ca
www.pc.gc.ca/lhn-nhs/qc/artiller.aspx

Carillon Barracks National Historic Site of Canada
1899, boul. Périgny, Chambly, QC J3L 4C3
450-658-0681 Fax: 450-658-2428
parkscanada-que@pc.gc.ca
www.pc.gc.ca/lhn-nhs/qc/carillon/index.aspx

Cartier-Brébeuf National Historic Site of Canada
175, rue de l'Espinay, CP 10 B, Québec, QC G1K 7A1
418-648-4038 Fax: 418-948-9181
parkscanada-que@pc.gc.ca
www.pc.gc.ca/lhn-nhs/qc/cartierbrebeuf.aspx

Battle of the Châteauguay National Historic Site of Canada
2371, ch de la Rivière Châteauguay nord, CP 250, Howick, QC J0S 1G0
450-829-2003 Fax: 450-829-3325
parkscanada-que@pc.gc.ca
www.pc.gc.ca/lhn-nhs/qc/chateauguay/index.aspx

Battle of the Restigouche National Historic Site of Canada
Route 132, CP 359, Pointe-à-la-Croix, QC G0C 1L0
418-788-5676 Fax: 418-788-5895
parkscanada-que@pc.gc.ca
www.pc.gc.ca/lhn-nhs/qc/ristigouche.aspx

Forges du Saint-Maurice National Historic Site of Canada
10000, boul des Forges, Trois-Rivières, QC G9C 1B1
819-378-5116 Fax: 819-378-0887
parkscanada-que@pc.gc.ca
www.pc.gc.ca/lhn-nhs/qc/saintmaurice.aspx

Coteau-du-Lac National Historic Site of Canada
308 A, ch du Fleuve, Coteau-du-Lac, QC J0P 1B0
450-763-5631 Fax: 450-763-1654
parkscanada-que@pc.gc.ca
www.pc.gc.ca/lhn-nhs/qc/coteaudulac.aspx

Forillon National Park of Canada
122, boul Gaspé, Gaspé, QC G4X 1A9
418-368-5505 Fax: 418-368-6837
parkscanada-que@pc.gc.ca
www.pc.gc.ca/pn-np/qc/forillon.aspx

Fort Chambly National Historic Site of Canada
2, rue de Richelieu, Chambly, QC J3L 2B9
450-658-1585 Fax: 450-658-7216
parkscanada-que@pc.gc.ca
www.pc.gc.ca/lhn-nhs/qc/fortchambly/index.aspx

Fort Lennox National Historic Site of Canada
1 - 61e av, St-Paul-de-l'Ile-aux-Noix, QC J0J 1G0
450-291-5700 Fax: 450-291-4389
parkscanada-que@pc.gc.ca
www.pc.gc.ca/lhn-nhs/qc/lennox.aspx

Fort Témiscamingue National Historic Site of Canada
830, ch du Vieux-Fort, Duhamel ouest, QC J9V 1N7
819-629-3222 Fax: 819-629-2977
fort.temiscaminque@pc.gc.ca
www.pc.gc.ca/fra/lhn-nhs/qc/temiscamingue.aspx

Fortifications of Québec National Historic Site of Canada
2, rue d'Auteuil, PO Box 10 B, Québec, QC G1K 7A1
418-648-7016 Fax: 418-648-2506
www.pc.gc.ca/lhn-nhs/qc/fortifications/index.aspx

Grosse Ile & the Irish Memorial National Historic Site of Canada
2 rue D'Auteuil, CP 10 B, Québec, QC G1K 7A1
418-234-8841 Fax: 866-790-8991
parkscanada-que@pc.gc.ca
www.pc.gc.ca/lhn-nhs/qc/grosseile/index.aspx

La Mauricie National Park of Canada
702, 5e rue, CP 160 Bureau-Chef, Shawinigan, QC G9N 6T9
819-538-3232 Fax: 819-536-3661
parkscanada-que@pc.gc.ca
www.pc.gc.ca/fra/pn-np/qc/mauricie.aspx

Lévis Forts National Historic Site of Canada
41, ch du Gouvernement, CP 10 B, Québec, QC G1K 7A1
418-835-5182 Fax: 418-948-9119
parkscanada-que@pc.gc.ca
www.pc.gc.ca/lhn-nhs/qc/levis/index.aspx

Louis S. St-Laurent National Historic Site of Canada
6790, rte Louis-St-Laurent, Compton, QC J0B 1L0
819-835-5448 Fax: 819-835-9101
parkscanada-que@pc.gc.ca
www.pc.gc.ca/fra/lhn-nhs/qc/stlaurent.aspx

Manoir Papineau National Historic Site of Canada
500, rue Notre-Dame, Montebello, QC J0V 1L0
819-423-6965 Fax: 819-423-6455
parkscanada-que@pc.gc.ca
www.pc.gc.ca/fra/lhn-nhs/qc/manoirpapineau/index.aspx

Mingan Archipelago National Park Reserve of Canada
1340, rue de la Digue, CP 1180, Havre-Saint-Pierre, QC G0G 1P0
418-538-3331 Fax: 418-538-3595
parkscanada-que@pc.gc.ca
www.pc.gc.ca/pn-np/qc/mingan.aspx
Other Communication: Information and/or Reservation: 418-538-3285; 418-949-2126

Pointe-au-Père Lighthouse National Historic Site of Canada
1034, rue du Phare, Pointe-au-Père, QC G5M 1L8
418-724-6214 Fax: 418-721-0815
parkscanada-que@pc.gc.ca
www.pc.gc.ca/lhn-nhs/qc/pointaupere/index.aspx

Saguenay St. Lawrence Marine Park of Canada
182, rte de l'Église, CP 220, Tadoussac, QC G0T 2A0
418-235-4703 Fax: 418-235-4686
parkscanada-que@pc.gc.ca
www.pc.gc.ca/amnc-nmca/qc/saguenay/default.aspx

Sir George-Étienne Cartier National Historic Site of Canada
458, rue Notre-Dame est, Montréal, QC H2Y 1C8
514-283-2282 Fax: 514-283-5560
cartier.maison@pc.gc.ca
www.pc.gc.ca/lhn-nhs/qc/etiennecartier.aspx

Sir Wilfrid Laurier National Historic Site of Canada
#945, 12e av, St-Lin-Laurentides, QC J5M 2W4
450-439-3702 Fax: 450-439-5721
parkscanada-que@pc.gc.ca
www.pc.gc.ca/fra/lhn-nhs/qc/wilfridlaurier.aspx

The Fur Trade at Lachine National Historic Site of Canada
1255, boul Saint-Joseph, Lachine, QC H8S 2M2
514-637-7433 Fax: 514-637-5325
parkscanada-que@pc.gc.ca
www.pc.gc.ca/lhn-nhs/qc/lachine/index.aspx
Other Communication: Winter, Phone: 514-283-6054; Fax: 514-496-1263

Western & Northern Canada National Parks/National Historic Sites:

Aulavik National Park of Canada
PO Box 29, Sachs Harbour, NT X0E 0Z0
867-690-3904 Fax: 867-690-4808
inuvik.info@pc.gc.ca
pc.gc.ca/pn-np/nt/aulavik/index_e.asp

Auyuittuq National Park of Canada
PO Box 353, Pangnirtung, NU X0A 0R0
867-473-2500 Fax: 867-473-8612
nunavut.info@pc.gc.ca
www.pc.gc.ca/pn-np/nu/auyuittuq/index_e.asp

Banff National Park of Canada
PO Box 900, Banff, AB T1L 1K2
403-762-1550 Fax: 403-762-1551
banff.vrc@pc.gc.ca
www.pc.gc.ca/pn-np/ab/banff/index_e.asp

Banff Park Museum National Historic Site of Canada
PO Box 900, Banff, AB T1L 1K2
403-762-1558 Fax: 403-762-1565
banff.vrc@pch.gc.ca
www.pc.gc.ca/lhn-nhs/ab/banff/index_E.asp

Bar U Ranch National Historic Site of Canada
PO Box 168, Longview, AB T0L 1H0
403-395-2212 Fax: 403-395-2331
BarU.Info@pc.gc.ca
www.pc.gc.ca/lhn-nhs/ab/baru/index_e.asp

Batoche National Historic Site of Canada
RR#1 Box 1040, Wakaw, SK S0K 4P0
306-423-6227 Fax: 306-423-5400
batoche@pc.gc.ca
www.pc.gc.ca/eng/lhn-nhs/sk/batoche/index.aspx
TTY: 306-423-5540

Cave & Basin National Historic Site of Canada
PO Box 900, Banff, AB T1L 1K2
403-762-1566 Fax: 403-762-1565
banff.vrc@pc.gc.ca
www.pc.gc.ca/lhn-nhs/ab/caveandbasin/index_e.asp

Chilkoot Trail National Historic Site of Canada
#205, 300 Main St., Whitehorse, YT Y1A 2B5
867-667-3910 Fax: 867-393-6701
800-661-0486
whitehorse.info@pc.gc.ca
www.pc.gc.ca/lhn-nhs/yt/chilkoot/index_e.asp

Dawson Historical Complex National Historic Site of Canada
PO Box 390, Dawson City, YT Y0B 1G0
867-993-7200 Fax: 867-993-7203
dawson.info@pc.gc.ca
www.pc.gc.ca/lhn-nhs/yt/dawson/index_E.asp

Dredge No. 4 National Historic Site of Canada
PO Box 390, Dawson City, YT Y0B 1G0
867-993-7200 Fax: 867-993-7203
dawson.info@pc.gc.ca
www.pc.gc.ca/lhn-nhs/yt/klondike.aspx

Elk Island National Park of Canada
RR#1, Site 4, Fort Saskatchewan, AB T8L 2N7
780-992-5790 Fax: 780-992-2951
elk.island@pc.gc.ca
www.pc.gc.ca/pn-np/ab/elkisland/index_e.asp
Other Communication: Administration: 780-992-2950

Fisgard Lighthouse National Historic Site of Canada
603 Fort Rodd Hill Rd., Victoria, BC V9C 2W8
250-478-5849 Fax: 250-478-2816
fort.rodd@pc.gc.ca
www.pc.gc.ca/lhn-nhs/bc/fisgard/index_e.asp

Fort Battleford National Historic Site of Canada
PO Box 70, Battleford, SK S0M 0E0
306-937-2621 Fax: 306-937-3370
battleford-info@pc.gc.ca
www.pc.gc.ca/lhn-nhs/sk/battleford/index_e.asp
TTY: 306-937-3199

Fort Langley National Historic Site of Canada
23433 Mavis Ave., PO Box 129, Fort Langley, BC V1M 2R5
604-513-4777 Fax: 604-513-4798
fort.langley@pc.gc.ca
www.pc.gc.ca/lhn-nhs/bc/langley/index_e.asp

Fort Rodd Hill National Historic Site of Canada
603 Fort Rodd Hill Rd., Victoria, BC V9C 2W8
250-478-5849 Fax: 250-478-2816
fort.rodd@pc.gc.ca
www.pc.gc.ca/lhn-nhs/bc/fortroddhill/index_e.asp

Fort St. James National Historic Site of Canada
PO Box 1148, Fort St James, BC V0J 1P0
250-996-7191 Fax: 250-996-8566
stjames@pc.gc.ca
www.pc.gc.ca/lhn-nhs/bc/stjames/index_e.asp

Fort Walsh National Historic Site of Canada
PO Box 278, Maple Creek, SK S0N 1N0
306-662-3590 Fax: 306-662-2711
fort.walsh@pc.gc.ca
www.pc.gc.ca/lhn-nhs/sk/walsh/index_e.asp
TTY: 306-662-3124
Other Communication: Administration: 306-662-2645

Gitwangak Battle Hill National Historic Site of Canada
PO Box 37, Queen Charlotte, BC V0T 1S0
250-559-8818 Fax: 250-559-8366
gwaii.haanas@pc.gc.ca
www.pc.gc.ca/lhn-nhs/bc/kitwanga/index_E.asp
TTY: 250-559-8139

Glacier National Park of Canada
PO Box 350, Revelstoke, BC V0E 2S0
250-837-7500 Fax: 250-837-7536
revglacier.reception@pc.gc.ca
www.pc.gc.ca/pn-np/bc/glacier/index_e.asp

Grasslands National Park of Canada
PO Box 150, Val Marie, SK S0N 2T0
Fax: 306-298-2042
877-345-2257
grasslands.info@pc.gc.ca
www.pc.gc.ca/pn-np/sk/grasslands/index_e.asp

Gulf Islands National Park Reserve of Canada
2220 Harbour Rd., Sidney, BC V8L 2P6
250-654-4000 Fax: 250-654-4014
866-944-1744
gulf.islands@pc.gc.ca
www.pc.gc.ca/pn-np/bc/gulf/index_E.asp

Gulf of Georgia Cannery National Historic Site of Canada
12138 Fourth Ave., Richmond, BC V7E 3J1
604-664-9009 Fax: 604-664-9008
gog.info@pc.gc.ca
www.pc.gc.ca/lhn-nhs/bc/georgia/index_e.asp

Gwaii Haanas National Park Reserve & Haida Heritage Site of Canada
60 Second Beach Rd., PO Box 37, Queen Charlotte, BC V0T 1S0
250-559-8818 Fax: 250-559-8366
877-559-8818
gwaii.haanas@pc.gc.ca
www.pc.gc.ca/pn-np/bc/gwaiihaanas/index_e.asp

Ivvavik National Park of Canada
PO Box 1840, Inuvik, NT X0E 0T0
867-777-8800 Fax: 867-777-8820
inuvik.info@pc.gc.ca
www.pc.gc.ca/pn-np/yt/ivvavik/index_e.asp

Jasper National Park of Canada
PO Box 10, Jasper, AB T0E 1E0
780-852-6176 Fax: 780-852-6152
pnj.jnp@pc.gc.ca
www.pc.gc.ca/pn-np/ab/jasper/index_e.asp

Kluane National Park & Reserve of Canada
PO Box 5495, Haines Junction, YT Y0B 1L0
867-634-7250 Fax: 867-634-7208
kluane.info@pc.gc.ca
www.pc.gc.ca/pn-np/yt/kluane/index_e.asp

Kootenay National Park of Canada
PO Box 220, Radium Hot Springs, BC V0A 1M0
250-347-9505 Fax: 250-347-9980
kootenay.info@pc.gc.ca
www.pc.gc.ca/pn-np/bc/kootenay/index_e.asp

Lower Fort Garry National Historic Site of Canada
5925 Highway 9, St. Andrews, MB R1A 4A8
204-785-6050 Fax: 204-482-5887
lfg.info@pc.gc.ca
www.pc.gc.ca/lhn-nhs/mb/fortgarry/index_e.asp

Motherwell Homestead National Historic Site of Canada
PO Box 70, Abernethy, SK S0A 0A0
306-333-2116 Fax: 306-333-2210
Motherwell.Homestead@pc.gc.ca
www.pc.gc.ca/lhn-nhs/sk/motherwell/index_e.asp

Mount Revelstoke National Park of Canada
PO Box 350, Revelstoke, BC V0E 2S0
250-837-7500 Fax: 250-837-7536
revglacier.reception@pc.gc.ca
www.pc.gc.ca/pn-np/bc/revelstoke/index_e.asp
TTY: 866-787-6221

Nahanni National Park Reserve of Canada
10002 - 100 Street, PO Box 348, Fort Simpson, NT X0E 0N0
867-695-7750 Fax: 867-695-2446
nahanni.info@pc.gc.ca
www.pc.gc.ca/pn-np/nt/nahanni/index_e.asp

Pacific Rim National Park Reserve of Canada
2185 Ocean Terrace Rd., PO Box 280, Ucluelet, BC V0R 3A0
250-726-3500 Fax: 250-726-3520
pacrim.info@pc.gc.ca
www.pc.gc.ca/pn-np/bc/pacificrim/index_e.asp

Prince Albert National Park of Canada
PO Box 100, Waskesiu Lake, SK S0J 2Y0
306-663-4522
panp.info@pc.gc.ca
www.pc.gc.ca/pn-np/sk/princealbert/index_e.asp

Prince of Wales Fort National Historic Site of Canada
PO Box 127, Churchill, MB R0B 0E0
204-675-8863 Fax: 204-675-2026
mannorth.nhs@pc.gc.ca
www.pc.gc.ca/lhn-nhs/mb/prince/index_e.asp

Quttinirpaaq National Park of Canada
PO Box 278, Iqaluit, NU X0A 0H0
867-975-4673 Fax: 867-975-4674
nunavut.info@pc.gc.ca
www.pc.gc.ca/pn-np/nu/quttinirpaaq/index_e.asp

Riding Mountain National Park of Canada
Wasagaming, MB R0J 2H0
204-848-7275 Fax: 204-848-2596
rmnp.info@pc.gc.ca
www.pc.gc.ca/pn-np/mb/riding/index_e.asp

Riel House National Historic Site of Canada
330 River Rd. (St. Vidal), PO Box 73, Winnipeg, MB R2N 3X9
204-257-1783 Fax: 204-983-2221
riel.info@pc.gc.ca
www.pc.gc.ca/lhn-nhs/mb/riel/index_E.asp
TTY: 866-787-6221
Other Communication: Winter: 204-983-6757

Rocky Mountain House National Historic Site of Canada
Site 127, Comp 6, RR#4, Rocky Mountain House, AB T4T 2A4
403-845-2412 Fax: 403-845-5320
rocky.info@pc.gc.ca
www.pc.gc.ca/lhn-nhs/ab/rockymountain/index_E.asp

Sirmilik National Park of Canada
PO Box 300, Pond Inlet, NU X0A 0S0
867-899-8092 Fax: 867-899-8104
sirmilik.info@pc.gc.ca
www.pc.gc.ca/pn-np/nu/sirmilik/index_E.asp

SS Keno National Historic Site of Canada
PO Box 390, Dawson City, YT Y0B 1G0
867-993-7200 Fax: 867-993-7203
dawson.info@pc.gc.ca
www.pc.gc.ca/lhn-nhs/yt/sskeno/index_e.asp

SS Klondike National Historic Site of Canada
#205, 300 Main St., Whitehorse, YT Y1A 2B5
Fax: 867-393-6701
800-661-0486
whitehorse.info@pc.gc.ca
www.pc.gc.ca/lhn-nhs/yt/ssklondike/index_E.asp
Other Communication: Summer: 867-667-4511

St. Andrews Rectory National Historic Site of Canada
374, chemin River, St. Andrews, MB R1A 2Y1
204-785-6050 Fax: 204-482-5887
lfg.info@pc.gc.ca
www.pc.gc.ca/lhn-nhs/mb/standrews/contact_e.asp

The Forks National Historic Site of Canada
401-25 Forks Market Rd., Winnipeg, MB R3C 4S8
204-983-6757 Fax: 204-983-2221
forks.fourche@pc.gc.ca
www.pc.gc.ca/lhn-nhs/mb/forks/index_e.asp

Tuktut Nogait National Park of Canada
PO Box 91, Paulatuk, NT X0E 1N0
867-580-3233 Fax: 867-580-3234
inuvik.info@pc.gc.ca
www.pc.gc.ca/pn-np/nt/tuktutnogait/index_e.asp

Ukkusiksalik National Park of Canada
PO Box 220, Repulse Bay, NU X0C 0H0
867-462-4500 Fax: 867-462-4095
ukkusiksalik.info@pc.gc.ca
www.pc.gc.ca/pn-np/nu/ukkusiksalik/index_E.asp

Wapusk National Park of Canada
Churchill Office, PO Box 127, Churchill, MB R0B 0E0
204-675-8863 Fax: 204-675-2026
wapusk.np@pc.gc.ca
www.pc.gc.ca/pn-np/mb/wapusk/index_e.asp

Vuntut National Park of Canada
PO Box 19, Old Crow, YT Y0B 1N0
867-667-3910 Fax: 867-393-6701
vuntut.info@pc.gc.ca
www.pc.gc.ca/pn-np/yt/vuntut/index_E.asp

Waterton Lakes National Park of Canada
PO Box 200, Waterton Park, AB T0K 2M0
403-859-5133 Fax: 403-859-5152
waterton.info@pc.gc.ca
www.pc.gc.ca/pn-np/ab/waterton/index_E.asp

York Factory National Historic Site of Canada
PO Box 127, Churchill, MB R0B 0E0
204-675-8863 Fax: 204-675-2026
888-773-8888
mannorth.nhs@pc.gc.ca
www.pc.gc.ca/lhn-nhs/mb/yorkfactory/index_E.asp
TTY: 866-787-6221

Wood Buffalo National Park of Canada
PO Box 750, Fort Smith, NT X0E 0P0
867-872-7900 Fax: 867-872-3910
wbnp.info@pc.gc.ca
www.pc.gc.ca/pn-np/nt/woodbuffalo/index_e.asp
TTY: 867-872-7961
Other Communication: 24 Hour Hotline: 867-872-7962

Yoho National Park of Canada
PO Box 99, Field, BC V0A 1G0
250-343-6783 Fax: 250-343-6012
yoho.info@pc.gc.ca
www.pc.gc.ca/pn-np/bc/yoho/index_E.asp

Patented Medicine Prices Review Board / Conseil d'examen du prix des médicaments brevetés

Standard Life Centre, #1400, 333 Laurier Ave. West, PO Box L40, Ottawa, ON K1P 1C1
613-954-8299 Fax: 613-952-7626
877-861-2350
pmprb@pmprb-cepmb.gc.ca
www.pmprb-cepmb.gc.ca
TTY: 613-957-4373

The Patented Medicine Prices Review Board (PMPRB) is an independent quasi-judicial body established by Parliament in 1987 under the Patent Act (Act). The PMPRB is responsible for regulating the prices that patentees charge, the "factory-gate" price, for prescription and non-prescription patented drugs sold in Canada, to wholesalers, hospitals or pharmacies, for human and veterinary use to ensure that they are not excessive. The PMPRB regulates the price of each patented drug product, including each strength of each dosage form of each patented medicine sold in Canada.

Chair, Mary Catherine Lindberg
613-952-3300
Vice-Chair, Mitchell Levine
613-960-4570, Fax: 613-952-7626
Executive Director, Michelle Boudreau
613-957-3656, Fax: 613-952-7626, Other Communications: Executive Assistant, Phone: 613-952-7617
Director, Board Secretariat & Communications, Sylvie Dupont
613-954-8299, Fax: 613-952-7626
Director, Corporate Services, Marian Eagen
613-952-3304, Fax: 613-952-7626
Director, Policy & Economic Analysis Branch, Gregory Gillespie
613-952-3305, Fax: 613-952-7626
Acting Director, Policy & Economic Analysis Branch, Karen Reynolds
613-941-0023, Fax: 613-952-7626
Director, Regulatory Affairs & Outreach, Ginette Tognet
613-954-8297, Fax: 613-952-7626

Privacy Commissioner of Canada / Commissariat à la protection de la vie privée du Canada

Tower B, Place de Ville, 112 Kent St., 3rd Fl., Ottawa, ON K1A 1H3
613-947-1698 Fax: 613-947-6850
800-282-1376
www.privcom.gc.ca
TTY: 613-992-9190

The Privacy Commissioner of Canada is an Officer of Parliament mandated to protect & promote privacy rights. She works independently from Government, reporting directly to the House of Commons & the Senate. The Privacy Commissioner oversees two federal privacy laws: the Privacy Act, which covers the federal government, & the new Personal Information Protection & Electronic Documents (PIPEDA) Act, which covers the collection use & disclosure of personal information in the course of commercial activities, except in provinces which have not, by then, enacted legislation that is deemed to be substantially similar to the federal law. The Privacy Commissioner's powers include: investigating complaints & conducting audits under both federal privacy laws; publishing information about personal information handling practices in the public & private sectors; conducting research into privacy issues; & promoting awareness & understanding of privacy issues in Canada.

Privacy Commissioner, Jennifer Stoddart
613-947-6000, Fax: 613-947-6850, Other Communications: Executive Assistant, Phone: 613-947-6000
Asst. Privacy Commissioner, Chantal Bernier
613-995-6402, Fax: 613-995-1139, Other Communications: Executive Assistant, Phone: 613-995-6402

Public Safety Canada / Sécurité publique Canada

269 Laurier Ave. West, Ottawa, ON K1A 0P8
613-944-4875 Fax: 613-954-5186
800-830-3118
communications@ps.gc.ca
www.publicsafety.gc.ca; www.securitepublique.gc.ca
TTY: 866-865-5667
Other Communication: National Crime Prevention Centre Toll Free: 1-877-302-6272; E-mail: prevention@ps.gc.ca; National Office for Victims Toll-Free: 866-525-0554; Media: 613-991-0657

Public Safety Canada works to keep Canadians safe in cases of natural disasters, crime, & terrorism. Policies are developed, & programs & services are delivered in the following areas: emergency management, including information about emergency preparedness; national security, which features the administration of the Government Operations Centre to monitor potential threats to the national interest; law enforcement, including the contribution of funds for policing services in First Nations & Inuit communities; federal corrections effectiveness, efficiency & accountability, with the development of federal policy & legislation; & crime prevention, such as work with other governments, businesses, & volunteer groups to support projects to reduce offences.

Acts Administered:
Canadian Security Intelligence Act
Corrections & Conditional Release Act
Criminal Records Act
Customs Act
Department of the Solicitor General Act
DNA Identification Act
Emergency Preparedness Act
Firearms Act
Prisons & Reformatories Act
Royal Canadian Mounted Police Act
Royal Canadian Mounted Police Pension Continuation Act
Transfer of Offenders Act
Witness Protection Program Act

Minister, Public Safety, Hon. Vic Toews
613-992-3128, Fax: 613-995-1049, Toews.V@parl.gc.ca, Other Communications: Public Safety & Emergency Preparedness: 613-991-2924
Deputy Minister, William V. Baker
613-991-2895
Inspector General, Canadian Security Intelligence Service (CSIS), Ian Blackie
613-993-7431
Senior Counsel / Strategic Policy Advisor, Mary-Anne Kirvan
613-954-1067
Deputy Executive Director & Senior Counsel, Legal Services, Caroline Fobes
613-949-9724
Parliamentary Secretary to the Minister of Public Safety, Dave MacKenzie
613-991-2924

Associated Agencies, Boards & Commissions:
• Canada Firearms Program (CAFC) / Centre des armes à feu Canada
Ottawa, ON K1A 0R2
Fax: 613-825-0297 800-731-4000
cfp-pcaf@rcmp-grc.gc.ca
www.rcmp.gc.ca/cfp
The Canada Firearms Centre oversees the administration of the Firearms Act and the Canadian Firearms Program (CFP).
• Canadian Security Intelligence Service (CSIS) / Service canadien du renseignement de sécurité (SCRS)
• Commission for Public Complaints Against the Royal Canadian Mounted Police / Commission des plaintes du public contre la Gendarmerie royale du Canada
National Intake Office
PO Box 88689
Surrey, BC V3W 0X1
Fax: 613-952-8045 800-665-6878 TTY: 866-432-5837
org@cpc-cpp.gc.ca
www.cpc-cpp.gc.ca
The Commission is responsible for the receipt of complaints from the public about the conduct of members of the RCMP. It is also responsible for the review of complaints when complainants are not satisfied with the disposition of their complaints by the RCMP. The Commission can inquire into complaints by means of public hearings & the chair of the Commission can investigate complaints. Annually, the chair reports to Parliament through the Minister of Public Safety & Emergency Preparedness Canada.
• Correctional Service of Canada / Service correctionnel Canada
• National Parole Board
• Royal Canadian Mounted Police
• Royal Canadian Mounted Police External Review Committee / Comité externe d'examen de la Gendarmerie royale du Canada
PO Box 1159 B
Ottawa, ON K1P 5R2
613-998-2134 Fax: 613-990-8969
org@erc-cee.gc.ca
www.erc-cee.gc.ca
The RCMP External Review Committee is an independent agency reporting to Parliament through the Minister of Public Safety Canada. It aims to independently and impartially promote fair and equitable labour relations within the RCMP, in accordance with applicable principles of law. To this end the Committee conducts an independent review of appeals in disciplinary and discharge and demotion matters, as well as certain categories of grievances that can be referred to it pursuant to s. 33 of the RCMP Act and s. 36 of the RCMP Regulations.

Regional Offices:

Community Safety & Partnerships Branch / Sécurité de la population et des partenariats
340 Laurier Ave. West, Ottawa, ON K1A 0P8
The Community Safety & Partnerships Branch consist of the Aboriginal Policing Directorate, the Corrections & Criminal Justice Directorate, & the National Crime Prevention Centre.
Assistant Deputy Minister, Shawn Tupper
613-993-4325
Director General, Corrections Directorate, Mary Campbell
613-991-2952
Director General, Aboriginal Policing Directorate, Mary Donaghy
613-990-2666
Executive Director, National Crime Prevention Centre, Wayne Stryde
613-957-9639
Senior Director, Operations, Claude Turgeon
613-990-8434

Corporate Management Branch / Secteur de la gestion ministérielle
340 Laurier Ave. West, Ottawa, ON K1A 0P8
Assistant Deputy Minister, Elisabeth Nadeau
613-990-2615
Chief Information Officer, Rosanna Di Paola
613-944-4878
Comptroller, Hélène Filion
613-998-0053
Director General, Corporate Services, René Bolduc
613-990-6101
Director General, Human Resources, Denis Desharnais
613-990-3496

Emergency Management & National Security Branch / Secteur de la gestion des urgences et de la sécurité nationale
340 Laurier Ave. West, Ottawa, ON K1A 0P8
The Emergency Management & National Security Branch consists of the following directorates & secretariat: Coordination Directorate; Emergency Management Policy Directorate; National Security Policy Directorate; Operations Directorate; Preparedness & Recovery Directorate; & the Cyber Security Strategy Secretariat.
Assistant Deputy Minister, Lynda Clairmont
613-990-4976
Assistant Deputy Minister, Gina Wilson
613-990-2743
Associate Assistant Deputy Minister, Daniel Lavoie
613-990-2743
Director General, National Security Policy, John Davies
613-991-1970

Director General, Regional Operations Directorate, Jamie Deacon
613-991-1699
Director General, National Cyber Security, Robert Dick
613-990-2661
Director General, Preparedness & Recovery, Robert Lesser
613-944-4853
Director General, National Security Operations, Michael MacDonald
613-993-4595
Director General, Operations, Greg Matte
613-991-3576
Director General, Operations, Continuity of Government, Preparedness & Recovery, Richard Moreau
613-990-7016
Senior Director, Public Service Renewal, Kevin Phillips
613-947-6492
Executive Director, Canadian Emergency Management College, Gary Donovan
613-949-5000
Associate Director General, Operations, Craig Oldham
613-991-7728
Senior Analyst, National Cyber Security, Tom Campbell
613-990-3577

Law Enforcement & Policing Branch / Secteur de la Police, et de l'application de la loi
340 Laurier Ave. West, Ottawa, ON K1A 0P8
The Policing, Law Enforcement & Interoperability Branch includes the following directorates: Law Enforcement & Border Strategies; Policing Policy; & Public Safety Interoperability.
Assistant Deputy Minister, Richard Wex
613-990-2703
Director General, Office of the Assistant Deputy Minister, Law Enforcement & Policing, Richard Clair
613-990-3969
Director General, Law Enforcement & Border Strategies Directorate, Barry MacKillop
613-991-4281
Acting Director General, Police Services Agreements, Scott Merrithew
613-949-1823, Fax: 613-990-9751
Director General, Police Services Agreements, Marty Muldoon
613-949-3097
Director General, Policing Policy Directorate, Mark Potter
613-991-1632

Strategic Policy Branch / Secteur de politiques stratégiques
340 Laurier Ave. West, Ottawa, ON K1A 0P8
Assistant Deputy Minister, Paul MacKinnon
613-949-6435
Director General, Cabinet, Parliamentary & Executive Services, Randall Koops
613-949-0477
Director General, Evaluation, Denis Gorman
613-990-2646
Director General, Intergovernmental Affairs & Citizen Engagement Directorate, Patrick Boucher
613-949-6553
Director General, Border Policy & International Affairs, Barbara Motzney
613-949-7260
Director General, Strategic Policy, Planning & Research, Robert Mundie
613-991-2824

Public Service Commission (PSC) / Commission de la fonction publique (CFP)

West Tower, 300 Laurier Ave. West, Ottawa, ON K1A 0M7
613-992-9562 Fax: 613-992-9352
infocom@psc-cfp.gc.ca
www.psc-cfp.gc.ca
TTY: 800-532-9397
An independent agency that reports directly to Parliament. For administrative purposes, the Minister of Canadian Heritage speaks on its behalf in the House of Commons, but has no jurisdiction over it. The commission is also responsible for safeguarding the values of a professional Public Service: competence, non-partisanship & representatives.
Acts Administered:
Canadian Human Rights Act
Canadian Charter of Rights & Freedoms
Employment Equity Act
Official Languages Act
Public Service Employment Act
Public Service Modernization Act
President, Maria Barrados
613-992-2788, Fax: 613-996-4337
Commissioner, Manon Vennat
613-943-8709
Senior Vice-President, Policy, Hélène Laurendeau
613-995-6135, Fax: 613-995-0221
Vice-President, Investigations, Denis Bilodeau
613-992-5418, Fax: 613-995-6985
Vice-President, Corporate Management Branch, Richard Charlebois
613-992-2425, Fax: 613-992-7519
Vice-President, Audit, Evaluation & Studies, Elizabeth Murphy-Walsh
613-947-0219, Fax: 613-995-6044
Vice-President, Staffing & Assessment Services, Gerry Thom
613-992-0894, Fax: 613-992-9905
Director General, Corporate Management Practices & Evaluation, Marvin Bedward
613-992-1225, Fax: 613-995-3795
Director General; Chief Information Officer, Information Technology Services, Hachem Ben Essalah
613-992-1981, Fax: 613-992-5948
Director General, Human Resources Management, Judith Flynn-Bédard
613-992-1225, Fax: 613-995-3795
Director General, Communications & Parliamentary Affairs, Andrew McGillivary
613-992-5428, Fax: 613-943-7723
Director General, Finance & Administration, Rafid Warsalee
613-992-0847, Fax: 613-947-9747

Regional Offices:

Alberta & NWT
Canada Place, #830, 9700 Jasper Ave., Edmonton, AB T5J 4G3
780-495-6134 Fax: 780-495-3145
TTY: 780-495-3130

Atlantic
Maritime Centre, 1505 Barrington St., 17th Fl., Halifax, NS B3J 3Y6
Fax: 888-457-5333
800-645-5605
TTY: 902-426-6246
Other Communication: Information: 1-877-998-7979

BC & Yukon
#210, 757 West Hastings St., Vancouver, BC V6C 3M2
Fax: 866-280-6356
800-645-5605
TTY: 604-666-6868

Central & Southern Ontario
Dominion Public Bldg., 1 Front St. West, 6th Fl., Toronto, ON M5J 2X5
416-973-3131 Fax: 888-515-4447
TTY: 416-973-2269

Central Prairies & Nunavut
320 Donald St., 1st Fl., Winnipeg, MB R3B 2H3
204-983-2486 Fax: 204-983-8188
TTY: 204-983-6066

National Capital & Eastern Ontario
66 Slater St., 4th Fl., Ottawa, ON K1A 0M7
Fax: 613-996-8048
800-645-5605
TTY: 613-996-1205

Québec
Complexe Guy-Favreau, Tour Est, 200, boul René-Lévesque ouest, 8e étage, Montréal, QC H2Z 1X4
Fax: 866-667-4936
800-645-5605
TTY: 514-283-2467
Director General, Hervé Déry
613-992-5354, Fax: 613-995-0221
Director, Strategic Policy, Policy Research & Library, Margaret Hill
613-947-2578, Fax: 613-992-9610
Director General, Equity & Diversity, Paula Green
613-943-8262, Fax: 613-992-9977
Director General, Policy Development, Jennifer Miles
613-947-0716, Fax: 613-943-2481
Director General, Political Activities, Kathy Nakamura
613-995-1125, Fax: 613-995-7699

Public Service Staffing Tribunal (PSSRB) / Tribunal de la dotation de la fonction publique

240 Sparks St., 6th Fl., Ottawa, ON K1A 0A5
613-949-6516 Fax: 613-949-6551
866-637-4491
info@psst-tdfp.gc.ca
www.psst-tdfp.gc.ca
TTY: 866-389-6901
Established under the Public Service Employment Act, the Tribunal deals with complaints related to internal appointments & lay offs in the federal public service. The Tribunal conducts hearings & provides mediation services in order to resolve complaints.
Acts Administered:
Public Service Employment Act
Chair/CEO, Guy Giguère
613-949-5435, Fax: 613-949-5514
Vice-Chair, John Mooney
613-949-5510, Fax: 613-949-5514
Executive Director & General Counsel, Josée Dubois
613-949-5511, Fax: 613-949-5514
Director, Human Resources & Corporate Services, Julie Brunet
613-949-9753, Fax: 613-949-5514
Director, Planning, Communications & Information Management, Diane Champagne
613-949-5513, Fax: 613-949-6551,
diane.champagne@psst-tdfp.gc.ca
Director, Registry, Operations & Policy, Christine Landry
613-949-6518, Fax: 613-949-6551,
christine.landry@psst-tdfp.gc.ca
Director, Dispute Resolution, Serge Roy
613-949-6518, Fax: 613-949-6551,
serge.roy@psst-tdfp.gc.ca

Public Works & Government Services Canada (PWGSC) / Travaux publics et services gouvernementaux

Place du Portage, Phase III, 11, rue Laurier, Ottawa, ON K1A 0S5
questions@tpsgc-pwgsc.gc.ca
www.tpsgc-pwgsc.gc.ca
TTY: 800-926-9105
Primary department responsible for purchasing goods & services for the Government of Canada. Purchases a variety of goods & services, construction, architectural, engineering & maintenance services & provides leasing services related to federal government works & facilities. Also maintains source lists of potential suppliers for some products. Ensures that the government's operational requirements are met in a cost-effective & timely manner, while taking into account the government's objectives including environmental considerations. As builders & caretakers of buildings, the department protects the environment by reducing solid waste, greening the construction & operation of buildings, conserving energy & water, improving fleet management, minimizing the effects of operations on climate change, & increasing environmental protection & conservation.
Acts Administered:
Anti-Personnel Mines Convention Implementation Act
Bridges Act
Canadian Arsenals Limited Divestiture Authorization Act
Defence Production Act
Dry Docks Subsidies Act
Expropriation Act
Federal District Commission to have acquired certain lands, An Act to Confirm the Authority of
Garnishment, Attachment & Pension Diversion Act
Government Property Traffic Act
Ottawa River, Act Respecting Certain Works
Pension Benefits Division Act
Public Works & Government Services Act
Seized Property Management Act
Statutes Act
Surplus Crown Assets Act
Translation Bureau Act
Minister, Public Works & Government Services; Minister for Status of Women, Hon. Rona Ambrose
819-997-5421, Fax: 819-956-8382,
Rona.Ambrose@tpsgc-pwgsc.gc.ca
Parliamentary Secretary, Jacques Gourde
613-992-2639, Fax: 613-992-1018, Gourdj@parl.gc.ca
Deputy Minister, François Guimont
819-956-1706, Fax: 819-956-8280,
francois.guimont@tpsgc-pwgsc.gc.ca
Assoc. Deputy Minister, Andrew Treusch
819-956-4472, Fax: 819-956-8280,
Andrew.Treusch@tpsgc-pwgsc.gc.ca
Asst. Deputy Minister, Human Resources, Diane Lorenzato
819-956-7548, Fax: 819-934-2523,
diane.lorenzato@tpsgc-pwgsc.gc.ca
Asst. Deputy Minister, Departmental Oversight, Barbara Glover
819-997-1094, Fax: 819-956-9949,
barbara.glover@tpsgc-pwgsc.gc.ca
Senior General Counsel/Executive Director, Sarah Paquet
819-956-0993, Fax: 819-953-3974,
sarah.paquet@tpsgc-pwgsc.gc.ca
Chief Financial Officer, Finance Branch, Alex Lakroni
819-956-7226, Fax: 819-956-5060,
alex.lakroni@tpsgc-pwgsc.gc.ca

Associated Agencies, Boards & Commissions:
• Canadian Wheat Board / Commission canadienne du blé
• Defence Construction Canada / Construction de Défense Canada

Acquisitions Branch / Direction générale des approvisionnements
Provides departments & agencies with expert assistance at each stage of the supply cycle & offers tools that simplify & accelerate

the acquisition of goods & services. It ensures that the government exercises due diligence & maintains the integrity of the procurement process. It is a primary service provider offering client departments a broad base of procurement solutions aimed at securing best value for their procurement dollar.
Asst. Deputy Minister, Tom Ring
819-956-1711, Fax: 819-953-1058,
tom.ring@tpsgc-pwgsc.gc.ca
Director General, Washington Sector, Martine Belanger
202-682-7609, Fax: 202-682-7613,
martine.belanger@pwgsc-tpsgc.gc.ca
Director General, Commercial Acquisitions & Supply Management Sector, Claire Caloren
819-956-6098, Fax: 819-956-4491,
claire.caloren@tpsgc-pwgsc.gc.ca
Acting Director General, Business Management Sector, Susan Daly
819-956-8166, Fax: 819-956-8303,
susan.daly@tpsgc-pwgsc.gc.ca
Director General, Services & Specialized Acquisitions Management Sector, Vicki L. Ghadban
819-956-1649, Fax: 819-956-4944,
vicki.ghadban@tpsgc-pwgsc.gc.ca
Director General, Marine Sector, Scott Leslie
613-943-3338, Fax: 613-944-7870,
scott.leslie@tpsgc-pwgsc.gc.ca
Director General, Services & Technology Acquisition Management Sector, Normand Masse
819-956-3937, Fax: 819-956-2675,
normand.masse@tpsgc-pwgsc.gc.ca
Director General, Office of Small & Medium Enterprises, Shereen Benzvy Miller
819-956-8416, Fax: 819-956-6859,
shereen.miller@tpsgc-pwgsc.gc.ca
Acting Director General, Defence & Major Projects Sector, Johanne Provencher
819-956-0010, Fax: 819-956-9110,
johanne.provencher@tpsgc-pwgsc.gc.ca
Director General, Policy, Risk, Integrity & Strategic Management Sector, Alain Vauclair
819-956-0299, Fax: 819-956-0355,
alain.vauclair@tpsgc-pwgsc.gc.ca

Audit Services Canada / Services de vérification Canada
Tower B, Place de Ville, 112 Kent St., Ottawa, ON K1A 0S5
613-996-0188
Chief Executive Officer, André Auger
613-996-2279, Fax: 613-947-2436,
andre.auger@tpsgc-pwgsc.gc.ca
Acting Director, NCR Operations, Daren Penteluke
613-992-6947, Fax: 613-947-2436,
daren.penteluke@tpsgc-pwgsc.gc.ca
Acting Regional Director, Ontario, Jerry Jeremiah
416-973-4196, Fax: 416-954-1729,
jerry.jeremiah@pwgsc-tpsgc.gc.ca
Regional Director, Pacific & Western, Badrudin Moosa
604-666-8228, Fax: 604-666-7330,
Badrudin.Moosa@pwgsc-tpsgc.gc.ca
Acting Regional Director, Atlantic, Montague J. Onyett
902-426-0521, Fax: 902-426-5419,
montague.onyett@pwgsc-tpsgc.gc.ca

Accounting, Banking & Compensation Branch / Direction générale de la comptabilité, gestion bancaire et rémunération
Responsible for managing the operations of the federal treasury, including issuing Receiver General payments for major government programs as well as maintaining the Accounts of Canada & producing the Government's financial statements. Responsible for providing government-wide accounting & reporting services. Directs the management & delivery of the administration of the public service pension & group insurance plans & maintains accounts for the various pension funds. Focuses in the financial management & control framework for the Department.
Asst. Deputy Minister, Accounting, Banking & Compensation, Renée Jolicoeur
819-934-0497, Fax: 819-934-0932,
renee.jolicoeur@tpsgc-pwgsc.gc.ca
Director General, Central Accounting & Reporting, Kim Croucher
819-956-2875, Fax: 819-956-8400,
kim.croucher@tpsgc-pwgsc.gc.ca
Director General, Compensation, Carrie Roussin
819-956-0481, Fax: 819-956-3000,
carrie.roussin@tpsgc-pwgsc.gc.ca

Information Technology Services Branch / Services d'infotechnologie
Provides common telecommunications & informatics services to government departments, agencies & organizations, to facilitate universal access to information throughout the federal government. Focussing on network & computer services, telecommunications, & application development, ITS is a key player in government-wide initiatives such as the Secure Channel, IM/IT community renewal, & Government-On-Line (GoL).
Acting Chief Executive Officer, Maurice Chénier
819-956-4614, Fax: 819-956-5189,
maurice.chenier@tpsgc-pwgsc.gc.ca
Chief Technology Officer, Jirka V. Danek
819-956-1166, Fax: 613-249-7220,
jirka.danek@tpsgc-pwgsc.gc.ca
Acting Chief Operating Officer, John Rath-Wilson
819-956-2632, Fax: 819-956-5189,
john.rath-wilson@tpsgc-pwgsc.gc.ca
Director General, Strategic Planning & Enterprise Architecture, François Audet
819-956-4745, Fax: 819-956-4261,
francois.audet@tpsgc-pwgsc.gc.ca
Director General, Application Management & IT Operational Services, Douglas Gauen
819-956-2354, Fax: 819-956-2960,
doug.gauen@tpsgc-pwgsc.gc.ca
Director General, Client Engagement, Paul Hession
819-956-0226, paul.hession@tpsgc-pwgsc.gc.ca
Director General, Project Delivery Office, Claude Lareau
819-956-8283, Fax: 819-956-6476,
claude.lareau@tpsgc-pwgsc.gc.ca
Director General, Service Transitions & Major Projects, Imran Mirza
819-956-6807, Fax: 819-956-4986,
imran.mirza@tpsgc-pwgsc.gc.ca
Director General, Government of Canada Marketplace, Christine Payant
819-956-3105, Fax: 819-956-4986,
christine.payant@tpsgc-pwgsc.gc.ca
Director General, Business Planning & Management Services, Roderick Raphael
819-956-9507, Fax: 819-956-4986,
roderick.raphael@tpsgc-pwgsc.gc.ca
Director General, Service Management & Delivery, Pankaj Sehgal
819-956-8510, pankaj.sehgal@tpsgc-pwgsc.gc.ca

MERX
PO Box 11684 Centre-ville, Montreal, QC H3C 6H4
Fax: 888-235-5800
merx@merx.com
www.merx.com
Other Communication: Suppliers Support: 1-800-964-MERX (6379); Buyers Support: 1-888-738-3005 (Ottawa: 613/737-3796)
The federal government's Government Electronic Tendering Service (GETS) contracts MERX to advertise government procurement opportunities online. Architectural & engineering consulting services, or services related to real property above $84,000 are advertised on MERX; below $84,000, they are handled through SELECT. Construction opportunities above $100,000 are advertised through MERX; below are handled through SELECT. MERX is used for printing services valued at $10,000 or above, & most goods & services valued at $25,000 or above. Below this level PWGSC uses a variety of bid solicitation methods: T-buys (purchasing by telephone when the product or service is required quickly and can easily be identified over the phone); RFQ (Request for Quotation); an Invitation to Tender (ITT) is used for straightforward requirements above $25,000 & where the lowest price will determine the awarding of the contract; RFP (Request for Proposal) for more complex requirements above $25,000; RFSO (Request for Standing Offer); RFSA (Request for Supply Arrangement); Sole-sourcing, subject to trade agreements & government contracting regulations. For products, individual departments have authority to buy up to $5,000 directly from suppliers; above $5,000, the department must go to PWGSC. Departments have authority to purchase nearly all their services; for program delivery services, departments may buy directly from suppliers up to $400,000 competitively or up to $100,000 without competition; they may also buy competitively up to $2 million when they advertise their requirements through MERX. Subscribers to MERX have access to an opportunity matching service, may view historical opportunities, review contract awards & international opportunities

Real Property Branch / Biens immobiliers
Fax: 613-736-2789
Manages office space & other general-purpose property; acts as custodian for $7.6 billion of real property holdings; administers 2,000 lease contracts; provides working space for 241,000 public servants in 1,810 locations across Canada; provides professional & technical services to government departments & agencies. Government buildings are 34 per cent more energy efficient & 24 per cent more greenhouse gas efficient than in 1990. Green Leases address key environmental standards such as proper management of wastewater, indoor air quality, recycling, energy efficient lighting fixtures, greenhouse gas reduction. Works with other departments on the remediation of contaminated sites & is the federal lead in the cleanup of the Sydney Tar Ponds in Nova Scotia.
Asst. Deputy Minister, John McBain
819-956-3189, Fax: 819-956-7130,
john.mcbain@tpsgc-pwgsc.gc.ca
Director General, Accommodation, Portfolio Management & Real Estate Services, Anne Auger
819-956-6304, Fax: 819-956-4347,
anne.auger@tpsgc-pwgsc.gc.ca
Director General, AFD Sector, Mark Campbell
819-775-7217, Fax: 819-775-7279,
mark.campbell@tpsgc-pwgsc.gc.ca
Director General, Special Initiatives Sector, Ralph Collins
613-947-9335, Fax: 613-947-9300,
ralph.collins@tpsgc-pwgsc.gc.ca
Director General, Professional & Technical Service Management, Anna Cullinan
819-956-2039, Anna.Cullinan@tpsgc-pwgsc.gc.ca
Director General, National Capital Area Operations Sector, Rick DeBenetti
819-956-2469, Fax: 819-956-2720,
rick.debenetti@tpsgc-pwgsc.gc.ca
Director General, CRA Portfolio, Bill Doering
613-954-8330, Fax: 613-949-1284,
bill.doering@tpsgc-pwgsc.gc.ca
Acting Director General, Client Consultancy & Real Property Solutions, Peter Marella
613-960-6713, Fax: 613-960-6399,
peter.marella@tpsgc-pwgsc.gc.ca
Director General, Strategic Planning, Administration & Renewal Sector, Diane Orange
819-956-6443, Fax: 819-956-7154,
Diane.Orange@tpsgc-pwgsc.gc.ca
Acting Director General, NCA Portfolio Management, Claude Séguin
819-956-6363, Fax: 819-956-0603,
claude.seguin@tpsgc-pwgsc.gc.ca
Director General, Program Management Sector, Stephen Twiss
819-956-6452, Fax: 819-934-0980,
stephen.twiss@tpsgc-pwgsc.gc.ca
Director General, Major Crown Projects, Jean Vézina
819-956-4935, Fax: 819-956-7384,
jean.vezina@tpsgc-pwgsc.gc.ca

Translation Bureau / Bureau de traduction
Richelieu Bldg., 975 St-Joseph Blvd., 5th Fl., Gatineau, QC K1A 0S5
819-934-0496 Fax: 819-997-9227
Chief Executive Officer, Donna Achimov
819-997-8825, Fax: 819-997-9227,
donna.achimov@tpsgc-pwgsc.gc.ca, Other Communications: Alternate Phone: 613-240-2552
Vice-President, Professional Services, Donald Barabé
819-994-1391, Fax: 819-934-0770,
donald.barabe@tpsgc-pwgsc.gc.ca
Vice-President, Corporate Services, Gisèle Côté
819-994-5221, gisele.cote@tpsgc-pwgsc.gc.ca
Vice-President, Client Services, Anne Nicholls
819-997-6339, Fax: 819-997-8917,
anne.nicholls@tpsgc-pwgsc.gc.ca
Director, Terminology Standardization, Gabriel Huard
819-997-6843, Fax: 819-953-8443,
gabriel.huard@tpsgc-pwgsc.gc.ca
Director, Interpretation & Parliamentary Translation, Alain Wood
613-992-0294, Fax: 613-996-8794, wooda@parl.gc.ca
Director General, George Butts
819-956-0867
Senior Director, Major Projects Services, Monty Mukerji
819-934-0960

Royal Canadian Mint / Monnaie royale canadienne

320 Sussex Dr., Ottawa, ON K1A 0G8
613-993-3500 Fax: 613-993-4092
800-267-1871
www.rcmint.ca
TTY: 613-949-7731
The RCM has two plants located in Ottawa & Winnipeg. Foreign & domestic circulating coinage is manufactured in Winnipeg. The Ottawa facility is responsible for the production of foreign & domestic numismatic products, precious metals & the refining of gold. Reports to government through Public Works & Government Services.
Vice-Chairman of the Board of Directors, James B. Love
President/CEO, Ian E. Bennett
613-993-1716
Vice-President, General Counsel & Corporate Secretary, Corporate & Legal Affairs, Marguerite F. Nadeau
613-993-1732
Vice-President/CFO, Finance & Administration, J. Marc Brûlé
613-993-5384

Royal Canadian Mounted Police (RCMP) / Gendarmerie royale du Canada (GRC)

1200 Vanier Pkwy., Ottawa, ON K1A 0R2
613-993-7267 Fax: 613-993-0260
www.rcmp-grc.gc.ca

In 1873 the North West Mounted Police was constituted to provide Police protection in the unsettled portions of the North West. In 1904 the title Royal was given to the Force. In 1920 The Dominion Police was amalgamated with this Force & the name changed to Royal Canadian Mounted Police. The headquarters was moved from Regina to Ottawa & the Force may be called upon to perform duties in any portion of the Dominion. In 1928 the RCMP absorbed the Saskatchewan Provincial Police & in 1932 the Provincial Police Forces of Alberta, Manitoba, New Brunswick, Nova Scotia & PEI were absorbed in like manner.

Acts Administered:
Canadian Peacekeeping Service Medal Act
Controlled Drugs & Substances Act
Criminal Code
Criminal Records Act
DNA Identification Act
Employment Equity Act
Excise Act
Export & Import Permits Act
Firearms Act
Foreign Missions & International Organizations Act
National Defence Act
Royal Canadian Mounted Police Act
Royal Canadian Mounted Police Pension Continuation Act
Royal Canadian Mounted Police Superannuation Act
Security Offences Act
Witness Protection Program Act

Commissioner, William J.S. Elliott
613-993-0400
Director General, National Headquarters, Claude Bisson
613-993-3627, Fax: 613-998-9444, Other Communications: Alternate Telephone: 613-794-5050
Deputy Commissioner, Atlantic Region, Steve Graham
902-496-5042
Deputy Commissioner, Contract & Aboriginal Policing, Doug Lang
Deputy Commissioner, North Western Region, Gerry B. Braun
306-780-6816
Deputy Commissioner, Pacific Region, Gary Bass
604-264-2003
CFAO, Alain Séguin
Deputy Commissioner, National Police Service, Joseph Buckle
613-993-1736
Deputy Commissioner, Operations & Integration, Tim Killam
613-993-3724
Deputy Commissioner, Special Advisor, Bill Sweeney
613-949-4760, Fax: 613-993-1941
Deputy Commissioner, Federal Policing, Raf Souccar
613-993-0403
Deputy Commissioner, Chief Human Resources Officer, Allen Nause
613-843-4634, Fax: 613-825-4790
Chief Financial & Administrative Officer, Corporate Management & Comptrollership, Alain P. Séguin
613-993-3193, Fax: 613-993-3770
Director, Executive Services & Ministerial Liaison, Kathryn McElhone
613-843-4611, Fax: 613-825-1949
Director General, Internal Audit, Denise Nesrallah
613-843-5453
Director, Professional Practice & Administration, Ian Christie
613-843-5495
Director, Access to Information & Privacy Branch, Supt. Yves Marineau
613-993-5162, Fax: 613-993-5080
Director General, National Communication Services, Supt. Tim Cogan
613-991-9164, Fax: 613-993-0953
Executive Director, Public Affairs, Sheila Bird
613-993-3113, Fax: 613-993-3936,
sheila.bird@rcmp-grc.gc.ca
Director, Adjudications, Supt. John Reid
613-991-0753
Director, Staff Relations Representative Program Office, Greg Nixon
613-843-5616

RCMP Divisions & Commanding Officers:

A Division
155 McArthur Ave., Ottawa, ON K1A 0R4
613-993-8860 Fax: 613-993-5870
Acting Commanding Officer, A/Commr. Allen Nause
613-993-8860, Fax: 613-993-5870

B Division
PO Box 9700 B, St. John's, NL A1A 3T5
709-772-5465
Commanding Officer, Assistant Commissioner, A/Commr. Bill Smith

C Division
4225, boul Dorchester ouest, Westmount, QC H3Z 1V5
514-939-8300 Fax: 514-283-2169
800-771-5401
Commanding Officer, A/Commr. François Deschênes

D Division
1091 Portage Ave., PO Box 5650, Winnipeg, MB R3C 3K2
204-983-5420
Commanding Officer, Bill Robinson

E Division
657 West 37 St., Vancouver, BC V5Z 1K6
604-264-3111 Fax: 604-264-3196
Commanding Officer, A/Commr. Peter Hourihan

F Division
6101 Dewdney Ave. West, PO Box 2500, Regina, SK S4P 3K7
306-780-5477 Fax: 306-780-5410
Commanding Officer, Russ Mirasty

G Division
Henry Larsen Bldg., 5010 - 49th Ave., PO Box 5010, Yellowknife, NT X1A 2R3
867-669-5100
Commanding Officer, Chief Superintendent, Tom Middleton

H Division
3139 Oxford St., PO Box 2286, Halifax, NS B3J 3E1
902-426-3940 Fax: 902-426-2481
Commanding Officer, DL Bishop
902-426-3940

J Division
1445 Regent St., PO Box 3900, Fredericton, NB E3B 4Z8
506-452-3400
Commanding Officer, Wayne Lang

K Division
11140 - 109 St., Edmonton, AB T5G 2T4
780-945-5444 Fax: 780-945-5601
Commanding Officer, R.R. (Rod) Knecht

L Division
450 University Ave., PO Box 1360, Charlottetown, PE C1A 7N1
902-566-7112 Fax: 902-566-7235
Commanding Officer, Tracy Hardy

M Division
4100 - 4th Ave., Whitehorse, YT Y1A 1H5
867-667-5551 Fax: 867-393-6791
Commanding Officer, Peter Clark

O Division
130 Dufferin Ave., 5th Fl., PO Box 3240 B, London, ON N6A 4K3
519-640-7267 Fax: 519-640-7255
TTY: 519-640-7495
Commanding Officer, Norm Mazerolle

V Division
PO Box 500 B, Iqaluit, NU X0A 0H0
867-975-4409
Commanding Officer, C/Supt. Steve McVarnock

Training Facilities:

Canadian Police College / École de police canadienne
PO Box 8900, Ottawa, ON K1G 3J2
613-993-9500 Fax: 613-990-9738
cpc-ccp@rcmp-grc.gc.ca
www.cpc.gc.ca
Director General & Chief Superintendent, Cal Corley
613-998-0883

RCMP Training Academy / Académie d'entrainement
6101 Dewdney Ave., Regina, SK S4P 3J7
306-780-5002 Fax: 306-780-7940
Officer in Charge, Centralized Training, Robert Castonguay

St. Lawrence Seaway Management Corporation (SLSMC) / Corporation de Gestion de la Voie Maritime du Saint-Laurent (CGVMSL)

202 Pitt St., Cornwall, ON K6J 3P7
613-932-5170 Fax: 613-932-7286
marketing@seaway.ca
www.greatlakes-seaway.com
Other Communication: billing@seaway.ca (Statistics & Research)

A not-for-profit corporation responsible for the safe & efficient movement of marine traffic through Canadian Seaway facilities. It shares operations with its American counterpart, the Saint Lawrence Seaway Development Corporation, in operating & maintaining 15 locks between Montréal & Lake Erie.

President/CEO, Terence F. Bowles

Regional Offices:

Maisonneuve
151, rue Ecluse, Saint-Lambert, QC J4R 2V6
Vice-President, A. Juster

Niagara
508 Glendale Ave., St Catharines, ON L2R 6V8
Vice-President, M. Drolet

Security Intelligence Review Committee (SIRC) / Comité de Surveillance des activités de renseignement de sécurité (CSARS)

Jackson Bldg., 122 Bank St., 4th Fl., PO Box 2430 D, Ottawa, ON K1P 5W5
613-990-8441 Fax: 613-990-5230
ellardm@sirc-csars.gc.ca
www.sirc-csars.gc.ca

Has as its mandate, under the Canadian Security Intelligence Service Act, to carry out the independent & external review of the Canadian Security Intelligence Service (CSIS) & to investigate complaints about CSIS activities. It is also required to investigate complaints from individuals who have had their employment prospects affected by the denial of a security clearance, & complaints referred to it by the Human Rights Commission. It is required to investigate reports made to it by the Minister of Citizenship & Immigration, & the Solicitor General of Canada, which relate to national security or to an individual's involvement in organized crime. The Committee is required to report annually to Parliament through the Minister of Public Safety & Emergency Preparedness on these matters.

Acts Administered:
Canadian Security Intelligence Service Act

Chair, Hon. Arthur Porter
613-991-9111, Fax: 613-990-5230
Executive Director, Susan Pollak
613-991-9111, Fax: 613-990-5230
Deputy Executive Director, Lori Biesenthal
613-991-9112, Fax: 613-990-5230

Social Sciences & Humanities Research Council of Canada (SSHRC) / Conseil de recherches en sciences humaines du Canada (CRSH)

Constitution Sq., 350 Albert St., PO Box 1610 B, Ottawa, ON K1P 6G4
613-992-0691 Fax: 613-992-1787
info@sshrc.ca
www.sshrc-crsh.gc.ca

The key national research agency investing in the knowledge & skills Canada needs to build the quality of its social, cultural & economic life. SSHRC supports university-based research & training in the human sciences. It funds basic, applied & collaborative research, student training, research partnerships, knowledge transfer & the communication of research findings in all disciplines of the social sciences & humanities. Grants & fellowships are awarded through national competitions adjudicated by eminent researchers & scholars.

President, Chad Gaffield
613-995-5488, Chad.Gaffield@sshrc-crsh.gc.ca
Executive Vice-President, Carmen Charette
613-947-3275, carmen.charette@sshrc-crsh.gc.ca
Vice-President, Research Capacity Directorate, Brent Herbert-Copley
613-995-5457, Brent.Herbert-Copley@sshrc-crsh.gc.ca
Vice-President, Common Administrative Services, Jaime Pitfield
613-995-3914, Fax: 613-991-0969,
Jaime.Pitfield@sshrc-crsh.gc.ca
Vice-President, Partnerships, Research Directorate, Gisèle Yasmeen
613-947-6938, gisele.yasmeen@sshrc-crsh.gc.ca

Specific Claims Tribunal Canada (SCT) / Tribunal des revendications particulières Canada (TRP)

#400, 427 Laurier Ave. West, PO Box 31, Ottawa, ON K1R 7Y2
613-947-0751 Fax: 613-943-0586
info@sct-trp.ca
www.sct-trp.ca

Created in 2008 as part of the federal government's Justice at Last policy. The Tribunal is an independent group of six federal judges who can make binding rulings on monetary damage claims filed by First Nations groups against the Crown.

Chairperson, Hon. Harry Slade
Justice, Hon. Patrick Smith
Justice, Hon. Johanne Mainville

Standards Council of Canada (SCC) / Conseil canadien des normes (CCN)

#200, 270 Albert St., Ottawa, ON K1P 6N7
613-238-3222 Fax: 613-569-7808
info@scc.ca
www.scc.ca

Federal Crown corporation with the mandate to promote efficient & effective standardization. The organization reports to Parliament through the Minister of Industry & oversees Canada's National Standards System. The National Standards System comprises organizations & individuals involved in voluntary standards development, promotion & implementation. In addition, more than 400 organizations have been accredited by the Standards Council, including environmental management systems (EMS) registration organizations that perform registrations to ISO 14000 series standards. The Council offers accreditation to registration bodies for specialized environmental management systems in industry-specific areas, including sustainable forestry management (CAN/CSZ809-02). Manages the Program for the Accreditation of Laboratories - Canada (PALCAN) which seeks to identify & accredit competent testing laboratories. Initial assessment is made & regular follow-up audits are performed; accredited organizations are included in the Standards Council directory of accredited testing organizations. Users of testing services can eliminate or reduce their need to establish the competence of a prospective lab. In cooperation with the Canadian Association of Environmental Analy tical Laboratories (CAEAL), SCC operates an accreditation program for environmental analytical laboratories. SCC's website provides free access to a wide variety of standards information, including searchable databases containing information on Canadian, foreign & international standards, regulations & SCC-accredited organizations. More speacialized information is available through SCC's information & Research Service. Other accreditation programs include ones for registrars of ISO 14000 environmental management systems; environmental auditor certifiers & auditor training course providers.

Chair, Hugh Krentz
613-238-3222, Fax: 613-569-7808
Executive Director, John Walter
613-238-3222, Fax: 613-569-7808, jwalter@scc.ca
Manager, Communications, Pilar Castro
613-238-3222, Fax: 613-569-7808, pcastro@scc.ca

Statistics Canada / Statistique Canada

R.H. Coats Bldg., Tunney's Pasture, 150 Tunney's Pasture Driveway, Ottawa, ON K1A 0T6
613-951-8116 Fax: 877-287-4369
800-263-1136
infostats@statcan.ca
www.statcan.ca
TTY: 800-363-7629

Agency of the federal government, headed by the Chief Statistician of Canada which reports to Parliament through the Minister of Industry. As Canada's central statistical agency, it has a mandate to collect, compile, analyse, abstract & publish statistical information relating to the commercial, industrial, financial, social, economic & general activities & condition of the people of Canada; coordinates activities with its federal & provincial partners in the national statistical system to avoid duplication of effort & to ensure the consistency & usefulness of statistics. The agency profiles & measures both social & economic changes in Canada. It presents a comprehensive picture of the national economy through statistics on manufacturing, agriculture, retail sales, services, prices, productivity changes, trade, transportation, employment & unemployment, & aggregate measures such as gross domestic product. It also presents a comprehensive picture of social conditions through statistics on demography, health, areas.

Acts Administered:
Corporations Returns Act
Statistics Act

Chief Statistician of Canada, Wayne Smith
613-951-9757, Fax: 613-951-3880,
Wayne.Smith@statcan.gc.ca

Calgary
Discovery Place, #201, 3553-31 St. NW, Edmonton, AB T2L 2K7
780-495-3027 Fax: 780-495-5318

Statistics Canada Regional Reference Centres/Centres de Référence Régionaux:

Edmonton
Park Square, 10001 Bellamy Hill, Edmonton, AB T5J 3B6
780-495-3027 Fax: 780-495-5318

Halifax
1770 Market St., 3rd Fl., Halifax, NS B3J 3M3

Montréal
Tour Est, Complexe Guy-Favreau, 200, boul René-Lévesque ouest, 4e étage, Montréal, QC H2Z 1X4

Ottawa
R.H. Coats Bldg., Lobby, Holland Ave., Ottawa, ON K1A 0T6

Regina
Avord Tower, 2001 Victoria Ave., 9th Fl., Regina, SK S4P 0R7

Toronto
Arthur Meighen Bldg., 25 St. Clair Ave. East, 10th Fl., Toronto, ON M4T 1M4

Vancouver
Library Square Tower, #600, 300 West Georgia St., Vancouver, BC V6B 6C7

Winnipeg
Via Rail Bldg., #200, 123 Main St., Winnipeg, MB R3C 4V9

Status of Women Canada (SWC) / Condition féminine Canada

123 Slater St., 10th Fl., Ottawa, ON K1P 1H9
613-995-7835 Fax: 613-947-0761
866-902-2719
infonational@swc-cfc.gc.ca
www.swc-cfc.gc.ca
TTY: 613-996-1322

The federal government agency promotes gender equality, & the participation of women in the economic, social, cultural, & political life in Canada. Status of Women Canada focuses its work in the following areas: improvement of women's economic autonomy & well-being; elimination of systemic violence against women & children; & the advancement of women's human rights. To achieve results, SWC works with & supports research organizations, equality-seeking organizations, the non-governmental, voluntary & private sectors, & international organizations.

Minister, Public Works & Government Services; Minister for Status of Women, Hon. Rona Ambrose
613-956-4000, Fax: 613-995-1761,
minister-ministre@swc-cfc.gc.ca
Parliamentary Secretary for Status of Women, Susan Truppe
613-992-0805, Fax: 613-992-9613
Coordinator/Head of Agency, Suzanne Clement
613-995-7838, Fax: 613-943-0449,
suzanne.clement@swc-cfc.gc.ca
Director General, Policy, Sébastien Goupil
613-995-4761, Fax: 613-947-0530,
sebastien.goupil@swc-cfc.gc.ca
Director, Women's Program, Linda Savoie
613-947-0355, Fax: 613-947-0761,
linda.savoie@swc-cfc.gc.ca
Director General, Communications & Strategic Planning Directorate, Nanci-Jean Waugh
613-995-7839, Fax: 613-943-2386,
nanci-jean.waugh@swc-cfc.gc.ca

Telefilm Canada / Téléfilm Canada

#500, 360, rue Saint-Jacques, Montréal, QC H2Y 1P5
514-283-6363 Fax: 514-283-2365
800-567-0890
info@telefilm.gc.ca
www.telefilm.gc.ca

Telefilm Canada is a Crown corporation reporting to Parliament through the Department of Canadian Heritage. Headquartered in Montréal, Telefilm provides services to the Canadian audiovisual industry by means of four regional offices located in Vancouver, Toronto, Montréal and Halifax. Dedicated to the development and promotion of the Canadian audiovisual industry.

Chair, Michel Roy
Executive Director, Carolle Brabant
Director, Communications, Denise Arab
Director, Business Affairs & Certification, Dave Forget, 20110721
Director, National & International Business Development, Sheila de La Varende, 20110721
Director, Public & Government Affairs, Jean-Claude Mahé
Director, Legal Services & Access to Information; Corporate Secretary, Stéphane Odesse, 20110721
Director, Administration & Corporate Services, Denis Pion, 20110721
Director, Projects Financing, Michel Pradier, 20110721

Offices in Canada:

Atlantic Region
1717 Barrington St., 4th Fl., Halifax, NS B3J 2A4
902-426-8425 Fax: 902-426-4445
800-565-1773
hal@telefilm.gc.ca

Ontario & Nunavut
#100, 474 Bathurst St., Toronto, ON M5T 2S6
416-973-6436 Fax: 416-973-8606

Western Region
#410, 609 Granville St., Vancouver, BC V7Y 1G5
604-666-1566 Fax: 604-666-7754

Transport Canada (TC) / Transports Canada

Place de Ville, 330 Sparks St., Tower C, Ottawa, ON K1A 0N5
613-990-2309 Fax: 613-954-4731
866-995-9737
www.tc.gc.ca
TTY: 888-675-6863

Using EMS 14000 standards, Transport Canada incorporates environmental considerations in all decision-making to fulfill the department's sustainable development strategy. Working with airports & airlines to minimize environmental effects of de-icing fluids; working with Environment Canada & industry to more effectively manage road salt; participating with ICAO's Committee on Aviation Environmental Protection (CAEP) concerning aircraft emissions, noise & land use planning. Ongoing contaminated sites management program. The Moving on Sustainable Transportation (MOST) Program supports projects that educate, raise awareness & provide tools to understand, promote & encourage sustainable transportation, such as neighbourhood transit passes, idle-free workplaces, school walking routes. Development of strategies to reduce greenhouse gas emissions from freight transportation; information on fuel consumption. Urban Transportation Showcase Program aims to reduce greenhouse gas emissions through showcasing demonstrations in communities across Canada (www.tc.gc.ca/ programs/environment/utsp/menu.htm).

Acts Administered:
Aeronautics Act
Air Canada Public Participation Act
Airport Transfer (Miscellaneous Matters) Act
Arctic Waters Pollution Prevention Act (Indian & Northern Affairs)
Bills of Landing Act
Blue Water Bridge Authority Act
Bridges Act
Buffalo & Fort Erie Public Bridge Company Act
Canada Marine Act
Canada Post Corporation Act
Canada Shipping Act, 2001 (Fisheries & Oceans)
Canada Strategic Infrastructure Fund Act
Canada Transportation Act
Canadian Air Transport Security Authority Act
Canadian National Montréal Terminals Act
Carriage by Air Act
Civil Air Navigation Services Commercialization Act
CN Commercialization Act
Coasting Trade Act
Department of Transport Act
Government Property Traffic Act
Harbour Commissions Act
International Bridges & Tunnels Act
International Interests in Mobile Equipment (aircraft equipment) Act
Marine Insurance Act
Marine Liability Act
Marine Transportation Security Act
Montréal Port Wardens Act
Motor Vehicle Fuel Consumption Standards Act
Motor Vehicle Safety Act
Motor Vehicle Transport Act
National Energy Board Act
Navigable Waters Projection Act
Northern Transportation Company Ltd. Disposal Authorization Act
Northumberland Strait Crossing Act
Pilotage Act
Pre-clearance Act
Québec Habor, Port Wardens Act
Railway Relocation & Crossing Act
Railway Safety Act
Safe Containers Convention Act
Transportation Appeal Tribunal of Canada Act
Transportation of Dangerous Goods Act, 1992
United States Wreckers Act

Minister, Transport, Infrastructure, & Communities, Hon. Denis Lebel
613-991-0700, Fax: 613-995-0327, mintc@tc.gc.ca
Deputy Minister, Yaprak Baltacioglu
613-990-4507, Fax: 613-991-0851,
yaprak.baltacioglu@tc.gc.ca
Director General, Communications & Marketing, Dan Dugas
613-990-6138, Fax: 613-991-6719, dan.dugas@tc.gc.ca
Parliamentary Secretary to the Minister of Transport, Infrastructure, & Communities, Pierre Poilievre
613-992-2772, Fax: 613-992-1209,
pierre.poilievre@parl.gc.ca
Executive Director, Henry K. Schultz
613-990-5768, Fax: 613-990-5777, henry.schultz@tc.gc.ca

Associated Agencies, Boards & Commissions:

• Atlantic Pilotage Authority Canada / Administration de pilotage de l'Atlantique Canada
• Canada Lands Company / Société Immobilière du Canada
• Canada Mortgage & Housing Corporation / Société canadienne d'hypothèques et de logement
• Canada Post Corporation / Société canadienne des postes
• Canadian Air Transport Security Authority (CATSA) / Administration canadienne de la sûreté du transport aérien (ACSTA)
99 Bank St., 13th Fl.
Ottawa, ON K1P 6B9
Fax: 613-990-1295 888-294-2202 TTY: 613-949-5534
www.catsa-acsta.gc.ca
CATSA secures critical elements of the air transportation system - from passenger screening to baggage screening - & encourages Canadians to Pack Smart for the benefit of all air travellers.
• Canadian Transportation Agency / Office des transports du Canada
• Federal Bridge Corporation Limited (FBCL) / Société des ponts fédéraux Limitée
#1210, 55 Metcalfe St.
Ottawa, ON K1P 6L5
613-993-6880 Fax: 613-993-6945
info@federalbridge.ca
www.federalbridge.ca
The FBCL was incorporated in 1998 to assume the non-navigational management responsibilities of the St. Lawrence Seaway Authority, including the Jacques Cartier & Champlain Bridges Incorporated, & in a joint venture with its U.S. partner, the Seaway International Bridge Corporation, Ltd. At the same time, the FBCL assumed responsibility for the management of the Canadian portion of the Thousand Islands International Bridge. In 2000, the FBCL acquired the Canadian half of the Sault Ste. Marie International Bridge.
• Great Lakes Pilotage Authority / Administration de pilotage des Grands Lacs
• Laurentian Pilotage Authority / Administration de pilotage des Laurentides Canada
• Marine Atlantic Inc. / Marine Atlantique
• Pacific Pilotage Authority / Administration de Pilotage du Pacifique Canada
• Royal Canadian Mint / Monnaie royale canadienne
• Transportation Appeal Tribunal of Canada / Anciennement le Tribunal de l'aviation civile
#1201, 333 Laurier Ave. West, 12th Fl.
Ottawa, ON K1A 0N5
613-990-6906 Fax: 613-990-9153
info@tatc.gc.ca
www.tatc.gc.ca
The Tribunal provides an independent review process for anyone who has been given notice of an administrative or enforcement action taken by the Minister of Transport, railway safety inspectors or the Canadian Transportation Agency under various federal transportation Acts.
• Transportation Safety Board of Canada / Bureau de la sécurité des transports du Canada
• VIA Rail Canada Inc.

Corporate Services / Services généraux
Corporate Services is part of the Department's administration business line & is responsible for providing services & functional expertise in the areas of finance & administration, technology & information management, human resources & access to information, Crown corporation portfolio coordination, internal audit & evaluation services.
Director General, Special Projects, Evelyn Marcoux, 20110721
613-998-6772, evelyn.marcoux@tc.gc.ca
Director General, Finance & Administration, Deloranda Munro
613-993-4307, Fax: 613-991-4410,
deloranda.munro@tc.gc.ca
Director General, Human Resources, Linda Brouillette
613-991-6317, Fax: 613-990-1880, linda.brouillette@tc.gc.ca
Director General, Technology & Information Management Services, Chris Molinski
613-998-6465, Fax: 613-990-2469, chris.molinski@tc.gc.ca
Director General, Crown Corporation Governance, April Nakatsu
613-991-2998, Fax: 613-991-4277, april.nakatsu@tc.gc.ca

Policy Group / Groupe de politiques
Responsible for setting policies relating to rail, marine, highways & borders, motor carrier, air, airports & accessible transportation, as well as setting departmental strategic policy & coordinating intergovernmental relations; assessing the performance of the overall transportation systems & its components, & developing supporting databases, forecasts & economic analysis; administering the management agreement with the St. Lawrence Seaway Management Corporation; & supporting rail passenger services through payments to VIA Rail & three regional railways, & ferry services through payments to Marine Atlantic & to provincial & private operators & border infrastructure improvements.
Asst. Deputy Minister, Kristine Burr
613-998-1880, Fax: 613-991-1440, kristine.burr@tc.gc.ca
Senior Policy Advisor, Félix Meunier
613-998-1877, Fax: 613-991-6445
Director General, Air Policy, Brigita Gravitis-Beck
613-993-0054, brigita.gravitis-beck@tc.gc.ca
Director General, International & Intergovernmental Relations, Arlene Turner
613-991-6500, Fax: 613-991-6422, arlene.turner@tc.gc.ca
Director General, Economic Analysis, Richard Thivierge
613-998-1881, Fax: 613-957-3280, richard.thivierge@tc.gc.ca
Director General, Marine Policy, Tim Meisner
613-991-3536, Fax: 613-998-1845, tim.meisner@tc.gc.ca
Director General, Surface Transportation Policy, Annette Gibbons
613-998-2689, Fax: 613-998-2686, annette.gibbons@tc.gc.ca
Director General, Strategic Policy, Sandra LaFortune
613-998-0402, Fax: 613-990-1719, sandra.lafortune@tc.gc.ca

Programs Group / Groupe des programmes
www.tc.gc.ca/eng/programs-menu.htm
Responsible for the transfer of ports, harbours & airports to communities & other interests; the oversight & lease management of divested facilities; the operation of facilities not yet divested; & real property management. Responsible for environmental programs & policies, including environmental management system, sustainable development strategies, environmental assessment & national environmental issues in transportation, such as climate change.
Asst. Deputy Minister, Mary Komarynsky
613-990-3001, Fax: 613-998-5008,
mary.komarynsky@tc.gc.ca
Director, Program Management, Airport & Port Programs, Michèle Bergevin
613-991-3025, Fax: 613-990-8889
Acting Director, Operations & Special Projects, Airport & Port Programs, Jason Tom, 20110721
613-990-0505, jason.tom@tc.gc.ca
Senior Director, Authorities Management & Real Property, Airport & Port Programs, Marc Brazeau, 20110721
613-990-1340, Fax: 613-990-8889, marc.brazeau@tc.gc.ca
Director General, Environmental Affairs, Catherine Higgens
613-991-5995, Fax: 613-993-8674,
catherine.higgens@tc.gc.ca
Director, Strategic Planning & Integration, Aline M. M. MacDougall
613-949-4157, Fax: 613-990-1427,
aline.macdougall@tc.gc.ca
Director General, Surface Infrastructure Programs, Jane Weldon
613-998-8137, Fax: 613-990-9639, jane.weldon@tc.gc.ca

Safety & Security Group / Groupe de sécurité et sûreté
The ADM, Safety & Security, directs the development of transportation safety & security legislation, regulations & national standards; is responsible for the uniform implementation of monitoring, testing, inspection, research & development, & subsidy programs in the aviation, marine, rail & road modes of transport; oversees the delivery of aircraft services to government & other transportation bodies; & is responsible for development & enforcement of regulations & standards under federal jurisdiction, to protect public safety in the transportation of dangerous goods, & to prevent unlawful interference in the aviation, marine & railways modes of transport, as well as ensuring that the department is prepared to respond to transportation & transportation-related emergencies.
Asst. Deputy Minister, Gerard A. McDonald
613-990-3838, Fax: 613-990-2947,
gerard.mcdonald@tc.gc.ca
Assoc. Asst. Deputy Minister, Laureen E. Kinney
613-949-2394, Fax: 613-990-2947, laureen.kinney@tc.gc.ca
Director General, Aircraft Services, Michel Gaudreau
613-998-3316, Fax: 613-991-0365,
michel.gaudreau@tc.gc.ca
Director General, Civil Aviation, Martin J. Eley
613-990-1322, martin.eley@tc.gc.ca
Director General, Marine Safety, Donald Roussel
613-998-0610, Fax: 613-954-1032, donald.roussel@tc.gc.ca
Director General, Marine Security, Fulvio Fracassi
613-991-4173, Fax: 613-993-1714, fulvio.fracassi@tc.gc.ca
Contact, Rail & Urban Transit Security
616-990-2015, sims-stti@tc.gc.ca
Director General, Rail Safety, Luc Bourdon
613-998-2984, Fax: 613-990-7767, luc.bourdon@tc.gc.ca
Director General, Road Safety & Motor Vehicle Regulation, Kash Ram
613-993-6735, Fax: 613-990-2914, kash.ram@tc.gc.ca
Director General, Security Program Support, Angelo Boccanfuso
613-990-1787, Fax: 613-998-8238,
angelo.boccanfuso@tc.gc.ca
Director General, Strategies & Integration, Melanie Tod
613-949-0864, Fax: 613-990-5058, melanie.tod@tc.gc.ca
Director General, Transportation of Dangerous Goods, Marie-France Dagenais
613-990-1147, Fax: 613-990-2917,
marie-france.dagenais@tc.gc.ca

Regional Offices:

Atlantic
Heritage Court, 95 Foundry St., 6th Fl., Moncton, NB E1C 5H7
506-851-7131 Fax: 506-851-2563

Ontario
#300, 4900 Yonge St., Toronto, ON M2N 6A5
416-952-0215 Fax: 416-952-0196

Pacific
#620, 800 Burrard St., Vancouver, BC V6Z 2J8
604-666-5575 Fax: 604-666-4839

Prairie & Northern
344 Edmonton St., 1st Fl., Winnipeg, MB R3C 0P6
204-983-4341 Fax: 204-984-2069

Québec
700, Leigh Capréol, 2e étage, Dorval, QC H4Y 1G7
514-633-3580 Fax: 514-633-3585

Transportation Safety Board of Canada / Bureau de la sécurité des transports du Canada

200 Promenade du Portage, 4th Fl., Ottawa, ON K1A 1K8
819-994-3741 Fax: 819-997-2239
800-387-3557
www.tsb.gc.ca
TTY: 819-953-7287

The Board is an independent agency reporting to Parliament through the President of the Queen's Privy Council. The formal name for the Board is the Canadian Transportation Accident Investigation & Safety Board. Its sole aim is the advancement of transportation safety in the marine, rail, pipeline & air modes of transport. The TSB conducts independent investigations into selected transportation occurences in order to make findings as to their causes & contributing factors; identifies safety deficiences, & makes recommendations designed to prevent further occurences. Because the Board is independent, its transportation accident investigations are completely separate from the regulatory agencies responsible for transportation. In making findings & recommendations it is not the function of the Board to assign fault or determine civil liability.
Acts Administered:
Access to Information Act
Canadian Transportation Accident Investigation & Safety Board Act
Privacy Act
Chair, Wendy A. Tadros
819-994-8000, Fax: 819-994-9759,
Wendy.Tadros@tsb.gc.ca, Other Communications: Executive Assistant, Phone: 819-994-8002
Chief Operating Officer, Jean L. Laporte
819-994-8004, Fax: 819-994-9759,
Jean.Laporte@bst-tsb.gc.ca
Director, Investigations, Air, Mark Clitsome
819-994-3813, Fax: 819-953-9586
Director, Investigations, Rail/Pipeline, Kirby Jang
819-953-6470, Fax: 819-953-7876, Kirby.jang@bst-tsb.gc.ca, Other Communications: Administrative Assistant, Phone: 819-953-1646
Director, Investigations, Marine, Marc-André Poisson
819-953-1398, Marc-Andre.Poisson@bst-tsb.gc.ca
Manager, Communications Products & Services, Publishing & Linquistic Services, Jacynthe Dubé
819-934-1762, Fax: 819-953-1733,
Jacynthe.Dube@bst-tsb.gc.ca
Acting Manager, Publishing & Linguistic Services, Chantal Laflamme
819-994-8032, Fax: 819-953-1733,
chantal.laflamme@bst-tsb.gc.ca

Treasury Board of Canada / Conseil du Trésor du Canada

140 O'Connor St., Ottawa, ON K1A 0R5
613-957-2400 Fax: 613-941-4000
877-636-0656
www.tbs-sct.gc.ca
TTY: 613-957-9090

The Treasury Board is a Cabinet Committee of government headed by the President of the Treasury Board. The committee constituting the Treasury Board includes, in addition to the President, the Minister of Finance & four other ministers appointed by the Governor-in-Council. The main role of the Treasury Board is the management of the government's financial, personnel & administrative responsibilities. The Treasury Board derives its authority primarily from the Financial Administration Act & is supported by the Treasury Board Secretariat.
Acts Administered:
Alternative Fuels Act
Federal Real Property & Federal Immovables Act

Minister, FedNor; President, Treasury Board, Hon. Tony Clement
613-944-7740, Fax: 613-992-5092
Parliamentary Secretary to the President of the Treasury Board, Andrew Saxton
613-995-1225, Fax: 613-992-7319, Saxton.A@parl.gc.ca
Secretary, Michelle d'Auray
613-952-1777, Fax: 613-952-6596
Comptroller General, James Ralston
613-957-7820, Fax: 613-952-0354
Associate Secretary, Alister Smith
613-941-1843, Fax: 613-952-6596
Assistant Deputy Minister, Compensation & Labour Relations, Marc-Arthur Hyppolite
613-952-3000, Fax: 613-952-8100
Assistant Deputy Minister, Executive Policies & Talent Management Sector, Yazmine Laroche
613-992-9160, Fax: 613-996-2228
Assistant Deputy Minister, Governance Planning & Policy Sector, Ross MacLeod
613-952-1173, Fax: 613-941-9450

Associated Agencies, Boards & Commissions:

• Public Sector Pension Investment Board / Office d'investissement des régimes de pensions du secteur public
#200, 440 Laurier Ave. West
Ottawa, ON K1R 7X6
613-782-3095 Fax: 613-782-6864
info@investpsp.ca
www.investpsp.ca
Crown corporation established by Parliament by the Public Sector Pension Investment Board Act (September 1999). The mandate of PSP Investments is to manage employer & employee contributions made after April 1, 2000 to the federal Public Service, the Canadian Forces & the Royal Canadian Mounted Police pension funds.

• Canada Public Service Agency (CPSA) / Agence de la fonction publique du Canada (AFPC)
122 Bank St.
Ottawa, ON K1A 0R5
Created in 2003 to put in place a new human resources management regime in the public service of Canada. Formerly the Public Service Human Resources Management Agency of Canada (PSHRMAC).

• Public Service Labour Relations Board / Commission des relations de travail dans la fonction publique
CD Howe Building
240 Sparks St., 6th Fl.
PO Box 1525 B
Ottawa, ON K1P 5V2
613-990-1800 Fax: 613-990-1849 866-931-3454
mail.courrier@pslrb-crtfp.gc.ca
www.pslrb-crtfp.gc.ca
Independent, quasi-judicial statutory tribunal responsible for administering the collective bargaining & grievance adjudication systems in the federal Public & Parliamentary Service. Also provides mediation & conflict resolution services, compensation analysis & research services.

Office of the Registrar of Lobbyists
255 Albert St., 10th Fl., Ottawa, ON K1A 0R5
613-957-2760 Fax: 613-957-3078
QuestionsLobbying@ocl-cal.gc.ca
www.ocl-cal.gc.ca

Registrar, Michael Nelson

Veterans Affairs Canada / Anciens combattants Canada

161 Grafton St., PO Box 7700, Charlottetown, PE C1A 8M9
902-566-8888
866-522-2111
information@vac-acc.gc.ca
www.vac-acc.gc.ca
Other Communication: Toll-Free French: 1-866-522-2022

Provides pensions for disability or death, economic support in the form of allowances, and health care benefits and services to veterans and members of the Canadian Armed Forces, members and ex-members of the RCMP, and their dependents.

Acts Administered:
Canadian Forces Members & Veterans Re-establishment & Compensation Act
Children of Deceased Veterans Education Assistance Act
Civilian War-related Benefits Act
Department of Veterans Affairs Act
Pension Act
Returned Soldiers' Insurance Act
Soldier Settlement Act
Special Operators War Service Benefits Act
Supervisors War Service Benefits Act
Veterans Review & Appeal Board Act
Veterans Benefit Act
Veterans Insurance Act
Veterans' Land Act
War Services Grants Act
War Veterans Allowance Act
Women's Royal Naval Services & the South African Military Nursing Service (Benefits) Act
Related Acts
Aeronautics Act, section 9
Halifax Relief Commission Pension Continuation Act
Indian Soldier Settlement Act
Royal Canadian Mounted Police Pension Continuation Act (in Part)
Royal Canadian Mounted Police Superannuation Act (in Part)

Minister, Veterans Affairs, Hon. Steven Blaney
613-992-7434, Fax: 613-995-6856, steven.blaney@parl.gc.ca
Parliamentary Secretary to the Minister of Veterans Affairs, Eve Adams
613-995-7784, Fax: 613-996-9817, Eve.Adams@parl.gc.ca
Deputy Minister, Suzanne Tining
902-566-8666, Fax: 902-566-7868
Assoc. Deputy Minister, Mary Chaput
902-370-4784, Fax: 902-370-4818
Chief of Staff, Frédérik Boisvert
613-996-4649, Fax: 613-996-0287
Director, Communications, Codie Taylor
613-996-4649, Fax: 613-996-0287

Associated Agencies, Boards & Commissions:

• Veterans Review & Appeal Board / Tribunal des anciens combattants (révision et appel)
Daniel J. MacDonald Bldg.
161 Grafton St.
PO Box 9900
Charlottetown, PE C1A 8V7
902-566-8751 Fax: 902-566-7850 800-450-8006
vrab_tacra@vac-acc.gc.ca
www.vrab-tacra.gc.ca
Other Communication: Ligne sans frais: 1-877-368-0859
The Board is an independent Board with full and exclusive jurisdiction to hear appeals from the decisions of the Minister of Veterans Affairs. The Board may affirm, vary or reverse the Minister's decisions, or refer decisions back to the Minister for reconsideration. The Board is completely independent from the Department of Veterans Affairs.

Audit & Evaluation Division / Direction générale de la vérification et de l'évaluation
Director General, Don Love
902-566-8018, Fax: 902-566-8343

Bureau of Pensions Advocates, Head Office / Bureau de services juridiques des pensions
Executive Director/Chief Pensions Advocate, Brian McKenna
902-566-8916, Fax: 902-566-7804, Other Communications: Alt Phone: 604-666-3627
Director, Legal Operations, Mark Belliveau
902-566-8021, Fax: 902-566-7804
Director, Strategic Planning & Management Support Directorate, Sue Lemaistre
902-566-6923, Fax: 902-368-0450

Corporate Services / Coordination des politiques
Asst. Deputy Minister, Heather Parry
902-566-8047, Fax: 902-566-8521
Director General, Corporate Planning Division, Murielle Belliveau
902-368-0510, Fax: 902-368-0437
Director General, Finance Division, André Joannette
902-566-8320, Fax: 902-368-0411
Director General, Information Technology & Information Management Division, John Walker
902-566-8236, Fax: 902-566-8351
Director, Information Management Services Directorate, Anne Murtha
902-566-7060, Fax: 902-368-0496

Federal Healthcare Partnership Secretariat / Secrétariat de partenariat fédéral pour les soins de santé
Chief Information Officer, LCol James Kirkland
613-947-3808, Fax: 613-992-8747
Director, Research, Analysis & Negotiations, Pierre de Montigny
613-947-4014, Fax: 613-992-8747

Human Resources Division / Direction générale des ressources humaines
Director General, Anthony Saez
902-566-8408, Fax: 902-566-8425
Senior Director, HR Services Directorate, Donna MacDonald
902-566-8373, Fax: 902-566-8425
Regional Director, Human Resources Charlottetown Division, Cheryl Gotell
902-370-4725, Fax: 902-566-7924
Director, Strategic Business Initiatives, Strategic Business Initiatives and HR Systems, Judy Gallant-MacIsaac
902-370-4475, Fax: 902-566-8425
Director, Corporate Labour Relations, Workplace Management Directorate, Pierre Lapointe
902-566-8375, Fax: 902-370-4768
Director, Workplace Management Directorate, Louise Wallis
902-368-0957, Fax: 902-566-8534

Legal Services Unit / Direction juridique
General Counsel, Alix Jenkins
902-566-8798, Fax: 902-566-8793
Senior Counsel, Neil Robinson
902-566-8992, Fax: 902-566-8793
Administrative & Financial Officer, Vanessa Kelly
902-566-8799, Fax: 902-566-8793

Policy, Communications & Commemoration / Politiques, communications et commémoration
Asst. Deputy Minister, James Gilbert
902-566-8100, Fax: 902-566-8780
Director General, Policy & Research Division, Bernard Butler
902-566-7438, Fax: 902-370-4727
Director General, Canada Remembers Division, Derek Sullivan
902-566-8026, Fax: 902-566-7056
Director General, Communications Division, Peter Yendall
613-996-0484, Fax: 613-996-9969, Other Communications: Executive Assistant, Phone: 613-996-2340

Service Delivery Branch / Prestation des services
Asst. Deputy Minister, Keith Hillier
902-626-2723, Fax: 902-566-8172
Director General, Centralized Operations Division, Nancy McRae
902-566-8644, Fax: 902-566-8337

Ste-Anne's Hospital / Hôpital Sainte-Anne
305 boul des Anciens-Combattants, Sainte-Anne-de-Bellevue, QC H9X 1Y9
514-457-3440
800-361-9287
steanne@vac-acc.gc.ca
The Hospital provides Veterans with long-term or respite care in addition to offering support services, through its day centre, to clients who still reside in the community and to Veterans and other clients who require mental health services or short-term hospitalization, through the National Centre for Operational Stress Injuries (NCOSI).
Executive Director, Rachel Corneille-Gravel
514-457-8400, Fax: 514-457-5741

Veterans Ombudsman

Veterans Ombudsman (Charlottetown) / Ombudsman des vétérans (Charlottetown)
134 Kent St., PO Box 7700, Charlottetown, PE C1A 8M9
Fax: 888-566-7582
877-330-4343

Director, Early Intervention, Michel Guay
902-626-2663, Fax: 902-566-7582
Acting Director, Corporate Services & Liaison, Wilma Hanscome
902-626-2913, Fax: 902-566-7582
Senior Projects Officer, Paulette McNally
902-566-8577, Fax: 902-626-2950

Veterans Ombudsman (Ottawa) / Ombudsman des vétérans (Ottawa)
PO Box 18 B, Ottawa, ON K1P 6C3
Fax: 888-566-7582
877-330-4343

Veterans Ombudsman, Guy Parent
613-944-2940, Fax: 613-944-2939, Other Communications: Executive Assistant, Phone: 613-943-3076
Director, Research & Investigation, Pierre Guénette
613-943-3027, Fax: 613-944-2939
Director, Communications Operations, Lynda Leblanc
613-944-2941, Fax: 613-944-2939
Director, Operations, Gary Walbourne
613-944-2943, Fax: 613-944-2939, Other Communications: Executive Assistant, Phone: 613-943-3028
Legal Advisor, Diane Guilmet-Harris
613-944-2942, Fax: 613-944-2939

Regional Offices:

Atlantic Region
40 Alderney Dr., 3rd Fl., Dartmouth, NS B2Y 2N5
902-426-0629 Fax: 902-426-7447
866-522-2122
Other Communication: Toll-Free French: 866-522-2022
Director General, Krista Locke
902-426-6305, Fax: 902-426-0555

Ontario Region
Bag Service 4000, 145 Government Rd. West, Kirkland Lake, ON P2N 2E8
705-567-9571 Fax: 705-567-7565
866-522-2122
Other Communication: Toll-Free French: 866-522-2022
Regional Director General, Dan Fenety
705-568-4132

Québec Region
Place Bonaventure, #6505, 800, rue de la Gauchetière Ouest, Montréal, QC H5A 1L8
514-496-6412 Fax: 514-283-2102
866-522-2122
Other Communication: Toll-Free French: 866-522-2022

Regional Director General, Charlotte Bastien
514-496-6412, Fax: 514-496-7303

Western Region (Vancouver)
#900, 605 Robson St., PO Box 5600, Vancouver, BC V6B 5G4
604-666-2675 Fax: 604-666-8839
866-522-2122
Other Communication: Toll-Free French: 866-522-2022
Regional Director General, Gisèle Toupin
604-666-2675, Fax: 604-666-8839

Western Region (Winnipeg)
#610, 234 Donald St., PO Box 6050, Winnipeg, MB R3C 4G5
204-983-5316 Fax: 204-983-6286
Regional Director General, Gisèle Toupin
204-983-5316, Fax: 204-983-6286

Via Rail Canada Inc.

#500, 3, Place Ville-Marie, Montréal, QC H3B 2C9
514-871-6000 Fax: 514-871-6104
888-842-7245
www.viarail.ca
TTY: 800-268-9503

The Corporation manages Canada's national passenger rail network. Reports to government through the Minister of Transport.
Chair, Paul G. Smith
President/Chief Executive Officer, Marc Laliberté
Chief Operating Officer, John Marginson
Chief Customer Experience Officer, Denis Pinsonneault
Chief Financial & Administration Officer, Robert St-Jean
Chief People Officer, Laurent F. Caron
Chief Marketing & Sales Officer, Steve Del Bosco
Chief Information Officer, Yves Bourbonnais
Senior Director, Safety, Security & Risk Management, Jean Tierney
General Counsel & Secretary, Yves Desjardins-Siciliano

Western Economic Diversification Canada (WD) / Diversification de l'économie de l'Ouest Canada (DEO)

Canada Place, #1500, 9700 Jasper Ave. NW, Edmonton, AB T5J 4H7
780-495-4164 Fax: 780-495-4557
888-338-9378
www.wd-deo.gc.ca
TTY: 877-303-3388

Responsible for promoting economic growth & diversification in the West. By investing in innovation, fostering entrepreneurship & using partnerships to enhance community sustainability, WD is helping to create a more prosperous future for western Canadians.Invests in R&D & commercialization in environmental technologies as a focus area for innovation strategies.
Minister of State (Western Economic Diversification), Hon. Lynne Yelich
613-952-2768, Fax: 613-952-1155, lynne.yelich@parl.gc.ca
Deputy Minister, Daniel Watson
780-495-5772, Fax: 780-495-6222, Other Communications: Ottawa: 613-952-9382
Executive Director, Finance & Corporate Management, Jim Saunderson
780-495-4301, Fax: 780-495-7618, Other Communications: Administrative Assistant, Phone: 780-495-5791
Director General, Planning & Programs, Nadean Langlois
780-495-4973, Fax: 780-495-6876
Director General, Audit, Evaluation & Disclosure, Donald MacDonald
780-495-8437, Fax: 780-495-6223
Director General, Finance & Management Accountability, Cathy Matthews
780-495-6336, Fax: 780-495-4434

Regional Offices:

Regional Offices:

Alberta (Edmonton)
Canada Place, #1500, 9700 Jasper Ave. Northwest, Edmonton, AB T5J 4H7
780-495-4164 Fax: 780-495-4557
888-338-9378
TTY: 877-303-3388
Asst. Deputy Minister, Doug Maley
780-495-4168, Fax: 780-495-6222, Other Communications: Executive Assistant, Phone: 780-495-4960
Director General, Operations, David Woynorowski
780-495-4970, Fax: 780-495-4557
Director, Policy, Planning & External Relations, Neil Kirkpatrick
780-495-6796, Fax: 780-495-4557

British Columbia (Vancouver)
Price Waterhouse Bldg., #700, 333 Seymour St., Vancouver, BC V6B 5G9
604-666-6256 Fax: 604-666-2353
888-338-9378
TTY: 877-303-3388
Asst. Deputy Minister, Gerry Salembier
604-666-6366, Fax: 604-666-1510
Director General, Naina Sloan
604-666-7011, Fax: 604-666-2353
Director, Innovation & Competitiveness, Tammy Schulz
604-666-1889, Fax: 604-666-2353
Director, Policy, Planning & Performance Integration, Martin Sutherland
604-666-4766, Fax: 604-666-2353

Calgary
#300, 639 - 5 Ave. SW, Calgary, AB T2P 0M9
403-292-5458 Fax: 403-292-5487
888-338-9378
TTY: 877-303-3388
Director, Tracy Sletto
403-292-4426, Fax: 403-292-5487

Manitoba (Winnipeg)
The Cargill Bldg., #620, 240 Graham Ave., Winnipeg, MB R3C 0J7
204-983-4472 Fax: 204-983-3852
888-338-9378
TTY: 877-303-3388
Asst. Deputy Minister, Marilyn Kapitany
204-983-5715, Fax: 204-983-0966, Other Communications: Executive Assistant, Phone: 204-983-4467
Executive Director, Manitoba Federal Council Secretariat, Cynthia Foreman
204-984-6815, Fax: 204-984-0105
Director General, Operations, Derryl Millar
204-983-4531, Fax: 204-983-1280
Director, Policy, Planning & External Relations, Tim Hibbard
204-983-0689, Fax: 204-984-0360
Associate Director, Infrastructure Secretariat, Ivan Didiuk
204-945-5557, Fax: 204-948-2035

Ottawa
#500, 141 Laurier Ave. West, Ottawa, ON K1P 5J3
613-952-2768 Fax: 613-952-9384
TTY: 877-303-3388
Asst. Deputy Minister, James Meddings
613-952-7096, Fax: 613-954-1044
Director, Francesco Del Bianco
613-954-9640, Fax: 613-952-3434
Director, Consultation, Marketing & Communications, Peter G. Wallace
613-952-7101, Fax: 613-952-6775

Saskatchewan (Saskatoon)
S.J. Cohen Bldg., #601, 119 - 4 Ave. South, PO Box 2025, Saskatoon, SK S7K 3S7
306-975-4373 Fax: 306-975-5484
888-338-9378
TTY: 877-303-3388
Asst. Deputy Minister, Sharon Lee Smith
306-975-5858, Fax: 306-975-5484
Executive Director, Saskatchewan Federal Council, Rhonda Laing
306-975-5944, Fax: 306-975-5484
Director General, Operations, Doug Zolinsky
306-975-6988, Fax: 306-975-5484

Government of Alberta

Seat of Government: PO Box 1333, Edmonton, AB T5J 2N2
780-427-2711 Fax: 780-422-2852
-310-0000
www.alberta.ca
TTY: 800-232-7215
Other Communication: TDD / TTY: 427-9999 (in Edmonton) o
Alberta was proclaimed as a province on September 1, 1905. The province has an elected Legislative Assembly, consisting of 83 members. The Premier & the Cabinet exercise executive power. The representative of the Crown is the Lieutenant Governor, who is appointed by the Governor General.

Office of the Lieutenant Governor

Office of the Lieutenant Governor of AB, Legislature Bldg., 10800 - 97 Ave., 3rd Fl., Edmonton, AB T5K 2B6
780-427-7243 Fax: 780-422-5134
ltgov@gov.ab.ca
www.lieutenantgovernor.ab.ca

The representative of the Crown in Alberta is the Lieutenant Governor, who is appointed by the Governor General, with the advice of the Prime Minister of Canada.
Lieutenant Governor, Hon. Donald S. Ethell, OC, OMM, AOE, MSC, CD, LLD
Note: The Queen's representative in Alberta is a retired Colonel.
Private Secretary to the Lieutenant Governor, Barb Walline
780-427-7243, Fax: 780-422-5134, barb.walline@gov.ab.ca
Communications Officer, Janet Resta
780-427-9222, Fax: 780-422-5134, janet.resta@gov.ab.ca

Office of the Premier

Office of the Premier, Legislature Building, #307, 10800 - 97 Ave., Edmonton, AB T5K 2B6
780-427-2251 Fax: 780-427-1349
-310-0000
www.premier.alberta.ca

The head of government in Alberta is the Premier. The Premier of the province is the leader of the political party that has the most seats in the Legislative Assembly. The Premier is head of the Executive Council, which works to put government policy into practice.
The Office of the Premier is led by the Chief of Staff. The following services are provided by the Office of the Premier: the provision of support to the Premier; issues management; the provision of strategic advice; correspondence; & scheduling.
Premier; President, Executive Council; Chair, Agenda & Priorities Committee, Hon. Alison Redford, QC
premier@gov.ab.ca
Chief of Staff, Ron Glen
780-427-2251, Fax: 780-427-1349, ron.glen@gov.ab.ca
Deputy Chief of Staff, Carol Haley
780-427-2251, Fax: 780-427-1349, carol.haley@gov.ab.ca
Deputy Chief of Staff, Operations & Legislative Affairs, George Samoil
780-427-2251, Fax: 780-427-1349, george.samoil@gov.ab.ca
Director, Scheduling, Raeanne Peers
780-427-2251, Fax: 780-427-1349, raeanne.peers@gov.ab.ca

Executive Council

Legislature Building, 10800 - 97 Ave., Edmonton, AB T5K 2B6
780-427-2711
-310-0000

The Executive Council consists of the Premier & cabinet ministers. Cabinet ministers are selected by the Premier from elected members of the Premier's party.
The Cabinet carries out the following functions: approving Orders in Council; ratifying policy matters; & acting as the final authority on issues related to the operation of the government.
The following is a list of members of the Executive Council, presented in order of precedence:
Premier; President, Executive Council; Chair, Agenda & Priorities Committee, Hon. Alison Redford, QC, Calgary-Elbow
780-427-2251, Fax: 780-427-1349, premier@gov.ab.ca
Deputy Premier; President, Treasury Board & Enterprise, Hon. Doug Horner, Spruce Grove-Sturgeon-St. Albert
780-415-4855, Fax: 780-415-4853
Social Media: www.twitter.com/hornerforab, www.facebook.com/DougHornerForAlberta www.linkedin.com/pub/doug-horner/30/310/206
Minister, Human Services; Government House Leader, Hon. David Hancock, QC, Edmonton-Whitemud
780-643-6210, Fax: 780-643-6214, dave.hancock@gov.ab.ca
Social Media: www.twitter.com/DaveHancockMLA
Minister, Energy, Hon. Ted Morton, Foothills-Rocky View
780-427-3740, Fax: 780-422-0195, minister.energy@gov.ab.ca
Social Media: www.facebook.com/TedMortonMLA
Minister, Justice; Attorney General; Deputy Government House Leader, Hon. Verlyn Olson, QC, Wetaskiwin-Camrose
780-427-2339, Fax: 780-422-6621, Other Communications: Justice Info Line: 780-427-2745
Social Media: www.facebook.com/verlynolsonmla
Note: Web Site, Justice & Attorney General: www.justice.alberta.ca
Minister, Health & Wellness, Hon. Fred Horne, Edmonton-Rutherford
780-427-3665, Fax: 780-415-0961, health.minister@gov.ab.ca
Social Media: www.facebook.com/pages/Fred-Horne/19085763782
Minister, Finance, Hon. Ronald Liepert, Calgary-West
780-427-8809, Fax: 780-427-5543, min.finance@gov.ab.ca
Social Media: www.facebook.com/ronliepertmla
Minister, Education, Hon. Thomas Lukaszuk, Edmonton-Castle Downs
780-427-5010, Fax: 780-427-5018
Social Media: www.twitter.com/lukaszukmla, www.facebook.com/Thomas-A-Lukaszuk/662272836
Minister, Environment & Water, Hon. Diana McQueen, Drayton Valley-Calmar
780-427-2391, Fax: 780-422-6259
Social Media: www.twitter.com/mcqueenmla, www.facebook.com/dianamcqueenmla
Minister, Public Security; Solicitor General; Deputy Government House Leader, Hon. Jonathan Denis, QC,

Calgary-Egmont
780-415-9406, Fax: 780-415-9566
Social Media: www.twitter.com/MinisterJono,
www.facebook.com/jonathandenismla

Minister, Intergovernmental, International, & Aboriginal Relations, Hon. Cal Dallas, Red Deer-South
780-643-6225, Fax: 780-643-6228
Social Media: www.facebook.com/caldallasmla

Minister, Agriculture & Rural Development, Hon. Evan Berger, Livingstone-Macleod
780-427-2137, Fax: 780-422-6035
Social Media:
www.facebook.com/pages/Evan-Berger-MLA/356351270299
www.linkedin.com/pub/evan-berger/29/6ba/96

Minister, Sustainable Resource Development, Hon. Frank Oberle, Peace River
780-415-4815, Fax: 780-415-4818

Minister, Seniors, Hon. George VanderBurg, Whitecourt-Ste. Anne
780-415-9550, Fax: 780-415-9411
Social Media:
www.facebook.com/George-VanderBurg/195871217330

Minister, Transportatiom, Hon. Ray Danyluk, Lac La Biche-St. Paul
780-427-2080, Fax: 780-422-2722
Social Media: www.facebook.com/raydanylukmla

Minister, Infrastructure, Hon. Jeff Johnson, Athabasca-Redwater
780-427-5041, Fax: 780-422-2002
Social Media:
www.facebook.com/pages/Jeff-Johnson/194208238162

Minister, Municipal Affairs, Hon. Doug Griffiths, Battle River-Wainwright
780-427-3744, Fax: 780-422-9550
Social Media: www.twitter.com/griffmla,
www.facebook.com/Griffs4ABsFuture?sk=app_53267368995

Minister, Advanced Education & Technology, Hon. Greg Weadick, Lethbridge-West
780-427-2025, Fax: 780-427-5582, Other Communications: Advanced Education & Technology, Phone: 780-422-5400
Social Media:
www.facebook.com/pages/Greg-Weadick/193042929182
Note: Web Site, Advanced Education & Technology:
www.advancededucation.gov.ab.ca/ministry/about/minister.aspx

Minister, Tourism, Parks, & Recreation, Hon. Jack Hayden, Drumheller-Stettler
780-427-4928, Fax: 780-427-0188
Social Media:
www.facebook.com/pages/Jack-Hayden/188272707966

Minister, Culture & Community Services, Hon. Heather Klimchuk, Edmonton-Glenora
780-422-3559, Fax: 780-427-7729
Social Media:
www.facebook.com/pages/Heather-Klimchuk/187574883149

Minister, Service Alberta, Hon. Manmeet Bhullar, Calgary-Montrose
780-422-6880, Fax: 780-422-2496
Social Media: www.twitter.com/manmeetsbhullar,
www.facebook.com/manmeetbhullarmla

Deputy Minister's Office
Executive Branch, Legislature Building, #305, 10800 - 97th Ave., Edmonton, AB T5K 2B6

The Executive Council Office is led by the Deputy Minister of the Executive Council.

Deputy Minister, Executive Council, Brian Manning
780-422-4910, Fax: 780-422-1882, brian.manning@gov.ab.ca

Deputy Minister, Premier's Council for Economic Strategy, Bob Fessenden
780-427-5524, Fax: 780-427-5498,
bob.fessenden@gov.ab.ca

Assistant Deputy Minister, Premier's Council for Economic Strategy, Ray Bassett
780-643-1469, Fax: 780-427-5498, ray.bassett@gov.ab.ca

Assistant Deputy Minister, Economic Policy, Matthew Machielse
780-422-7050, Fax: 780-427-0305,
matthew.machielse@gov.ab.ca

Deputy Chief, Policy Coordination, Roxanna Benoit
780-427-9229, Fax: 780-427-0305,
roxanna.benoit@gov.ab.ca

Executive Director, Strategic Planning & Policy Excellence, Bryce Stewart
780-422-5353, bryce.stewart@gov.ab.ca

Deputy Secretary to Cabinet, Dwight Dibben
780-420-2251, Fax: 780-422-1917

Protocol
Executive Branch, Legislature Annex, 9718 - 107 St., 11th Fl., Edmonton, AB T5K 1E4

Chief, Protocol, Betty Anne Spinks
780-422-2236, Fax: 780-422-0786,
bettyanne.spinks@gov.ab.ca

Deputy Chief, Protocol, Norm Davies
780-422-1845, Fax: 780-422-0786, norm.davies@gov.ab.ca

Manager, Government House, Gino Gadowsky
780-427-2281, Fax: 780-422-6508,
gino.gadowsky@gov.ab.ca

Coordinator, Government House, Christine Taylor
780-427-2281, Fax: 780-422-6508,
christine.taylor@gov.ab.ca

Public Affairs Bureau
Park Plaza, 10611 - 98 Ave., Edmonton, AB T5K 2P7
780-427-2754 Fax: 780-422-4168

Managing Director, Public Affairs Bureau, Lee Funke
780-644-5655, Fax: 780-427-1010, lee.funke@gov.ab.ca

Executive Director, Corporate Communications, Terry Willock
780-422-2787, Fax: 780-415-9485, terry.willock@gov.ab.ca

Director, Cross Ministry Initiatives, David Sands
780-644-3024, Fax: 780-415-9485, david.sands@gov.ab.ca

Senior Manager, Communications, Joanne Rosnau
780-644-8106, Fax: 780-427-1010, joanne.rosnau@gov.ab.ca

Cabinet Policy Committees
The following are Alberta's cabinet policy committees: Community Services; The Economy; Health; Public Safety & Services; & Resources & the Environment.

Chair, Community Services Committee, Art Johnston
780-415-9526, Fax: 780-427-1234

Chair, The Economy Committee, Kyle Fawcett
780-427-7984, Fax: 780-427-5441

Chair, Health Committee, Tony Vandermeer
780-422-5468, Fax: 780-427-4974

Chair, Public Safety & Services Committee, Dr. Neil Brwon
780-415-8368, Fax: 780-427-1234

Chair, Resources & the Environment Committee, George VanderBurg
780-415-9473, Fax: 780-427-5441

Legislative Assembly of Alberta

Legislature Annex, 9718 - 107 St., Edmonton, AB T5K 1E4
780-427-2826 Fax: 780-427-1623
laocommunications@assembly.ab.ca
www.assembly.ab.ca
Other Communication: Reference information: library.requests@assembly.ab.ca; Visitor Services Office: visitorinfo@assembly.ab.ca

The Legislative Assembly of Alberta is elected by voters. It consists of government members & opposition members.
The Legislative Assembly Office carries out the following main responsibilities: supporting the Speaker of the Legislative Assembly; supporting members; recording proceedings & maintaining records of the Legislative Assembly; educating the public; & providing services to external clients.
The Legislative Assembly Office is organized by services such as the following: management & communication services; house & committee services; legal services; human resource services; financial management & administrative services; visitor, ceremonial, & security services; library services; public information & reporting services; & information technology services.

Clerk, Dr. David McNeil
780-427-2478, Fax: 780-427-5688,
david.mcneil@assembly.ab.ca
Note: The Clerk acts as the Chief Executive Officer of the Legislative Assembly Office. In the Chamber, the Clerk advises the Speaker aboutprocedure. He also calls out the daily order of business.

Sergeant-at-Arms; Director, Visitor, Ceremonial & Security Services, Brian Hodgson
780-427-6048, Fax: 780-415-5829,
brian.hodgson@assembly.ab.ca
Note: The following duties are performed: management of visitors' services forthe Legislative Assembly; provision of security services; & the execution of ceremonial functions for the Legislative Assembly.

Senior Financial Officer; Director, Financial Management & Administrative Services, Scott Ellis
780-427-1566, Fax: 780-415-1714,
scott.ellis@assembly.ab.ca
Note: Financial Management & Administrative Services is responsiblefor financial processing, reporting, & control.

Director, Human Resources, Information Technology & Broadcast Services, Cheryl Scarlett
780-427-1368, Fax: 780-427-6436,
cheryl.scarlett@assembly.ab.ca
Note: Customized human resource management services are provided tosupport the operation of the Legislative Assembly of Alberta.

Legislature Librarian, Valerie Footz
780-427-0202, Fax: 780-427-6016, val.footz@assembly.ab.ca
Note: The Legislature Library provides services to Members of the Legislative Assembly of Alberta, Members' staff, LegislativeAssembly Office staff, & the general public.

Managing Editor, Hansard, Liz Sim
780-427-1875, Fax: 780-427-1623, liz.sim@assembly.ab.ca
Note: Hansard is the official report of the debates of a Legislature or a Parliament & its committees. It is named after the Hansardfamily, the printers who published the first official record of the British parliamentary debates in the 19th century.

Auditor General, Merwan Saher
780-422-6195, Fax: 780-422-9555
Note: Web Site: www.oag.ab.ca

Chief Electoral Officer, Brian O. Fjeldheim
780-427-1035, Fax: 780-422-2900,
brian.fjeldheim@elections.ab.ca
Note: Web Site: www.elections.ab.ca

Ethics Commissioner, Neil R. Wilkinson
780-422-2273, Fax: 780-422-2261,
generalinfo@ethicscommissioner.ab.ca
Note: Web Site: www.ethicscommissioner.ab.ca

Information & Privacy Commissioner, Frank Work
780-422-6860, Fax: 780-422-5682, fwork@oipc.ab.ca;
generalinfo@oipc.ab.ca
Note: WebSite: www.oipc.ab.ca

Director, Corporate Services, Ombudsman Alberta, Suzanne Richford
780-415-2510, Fax: 780-427-2759
Note: Web Site: www.ombudsman.ab.ca

Office of the Speaker
Legislative Branch, Legislature Building, 10800 - 97th Ave., Edmonton, AB T5K 2B6

The Speaker of the Alberta Legislative Assembly maintains orderly debate in the Chamber. He cannot engage in debate in the Assembly. As head of the Legislative Assembly Office, the Speaker also plays a role in the maintenance of records of the Assembly & the provision of services to members.

Speaker, Hon. Ken Kowalski
780-427-2464, Fax: 780-422-9553,
ken.kowalski@assembly.ab.ca
Social Media: www.facebook.com/ken.kowalski

Executive Assistant, Bev Alenius
780-427-2464, Fax: 780-422-9553,
bev.alenius@assembly.ab.ca

Government Members' Caucus Office
Legislative Branch, Legislature Building, #132, 10800 - 97th Ave., Edmonton, AB T5K 2B6
780-427-1800
support@mypcmla.ca
www.mypcmla.ca

Alberta's Progressive Conservatives hold the most seats in the Legislature & are the governing party in Alberta. Government Caucus is led by a whip, who sets agendas & chairs meetings.

Whip; Member, Legislative Assembly, Robin Campbell

Director, Caucus, Paul Bajcer
780-427-1198, Fax: 780-415-0968,
paul.bajcer@assembly.ab.ca

Director, Research & Communications, Jonathan Koehli
780-427-8256, Fax: 780-422-5266,
jonathan.koehli@assembly.ab.ca

Liberal Opposition Caucus Office
Legislature Annex, 9718 - 107 St., 2nd Fl., Edmonton, AB T5K 1E4
780-427-2292 Fax: 780-427-3697
liberal.correspondence@assembly.ab.ca
www.albertaliberalcaucus.com

Led by party leader, Dr. Raj Sherman, the Liberal Party occupies nine seats in the Legislative Assembly.

Leader, Alberta Liberal Official Opposition, Dr. Raj Sherman
780-415-0976, Fax: 780-638-4313
Social Media: www.twitter.com/RajShermanMLA,
www.facebook.com/rajshermanmla
Note: Web Site: www.electraj.ca

Chief, Staff, Rick Miller
780-442-7229, Fax: 780-427-3697,
rick.miller@assembly.ab.ca

Director, Southern Alberta Liberal Caucus Office, Denis Lapointe
403-233-8250, Fax: 403-233-8269,
denis.lapointe@assembly.ab.ca

Director, Communications, Brian Leadbetter
780-862-5661, Fax: 780-427-3697,
liberal.communications@assembly.ab.ca

Senior Research Analyst, Avril McCalla
780-427-2292, Fax: 780-427-3697,
avril.mccalla@assembly.ab.ca

Wildrose Alliance Party of Alberta Office
Legislature Annex, #502A, 9718 - 107 St., Edmonton, AB T5K 1E4
780-415-0975 Fax: 780-638-3506
www.wildrose.ca

The Wildrose Alliance Party of Alberta, led by Danielle Smith, occupies four seats in the Legislative Assembly.

Leader, Wildrose Alliance Party, Danielle Smith
403-769-0999, 888-262-1888, Fax: 866-620-4791,
rob.anderson@assembly.ab.ca
Social Media: www.twitter.com/ElectDanielle,
www.facebook.com/ElectDaniellewww.linkedin.com/in/electdanielle

Director, Communications, Brock Harrison
780-643-4032, Fax: 780-638-3506,
brock.harrison@assembly.ab.ca
Coordinator, Operations, Shannon Stubbs
780-638-4000, Fax: 780-638-3506,
shannon.stubbs@assembly.ab.ca

New Democratic Party Caucus Office
#501, 9718 - 107 St., Edmonton, AB T5K 1E4
780-415-1800 Fax: 780-415-0701
nd@assembly.ab.ca
www.ndpopposition.ab.ca
The New Democratic Party has two seats in the Legislative Assembly.
Leader, New Democratic Party Opposition, Brian Mason, Edmonton-Highlands-Norwood
780-415-1800, Fax: 780-415-0701,
brian.mason@assembly.ab.ca
Social Media: www.twitter.com/bmasonNDP, www.facebook.com/Brian-Mason/26993021019
Note: Web Site: www.brianmason.ca
Chief, Staff, Jim Gurnett
780-415-4634, Fax: 780-415-0701,
jim.gurnett@assembly.ab.ca
Director, Research, Sarah Hoffman
780-415-2028, sarah.hoffman@assembly.ab.ca
Officer, Administration, John Ashton
780-415-0944, Fax: 780-415-0701,
john.ashton@assembly.ab.ca
Officer, Communications, Richard Liebrecht
780-644-8669, Fax: 780-415-0701,
richard.liebrecht@assembly.ab.ca

Independent Office
Legislative Branch, Legislature Annex, #714, 9718 - 107 St., Edmonton, AB T5K 1E4
There is one independent member in Alberta's Legislative Assembly.
Independent Member, Legislative Assembly, Raj Sherman
780-415-0976, Fax: 780-422-1671
Chief, Staff, Jonathan Huckabay
780-638-4249, Fax: 780-638-4313,
jonathan.huckabay@assembly.ab.ca

Alberta Party Office
Legislative Branch, Legislature Annex, #401, 9718 - 107 St., Edmonton, AB T5K 1E4
The Alberta Party has on member in the Legislative Assembly.
Member, Legislative Assembly, Dave Taylor
780-427-2298, Fax: 780-638-3958
Research Assistant, Evan Galbraith
780-638-3956, Fax: 780-638-3958,
evan.galbraith@assembly.ab.ca
Office Assistant, Jacquie Lycka
780-427-2298, Fax: 780-638-3958,
jacquie.lycka@assembly.ab.ca

Committees of the Legislative Assemby of Alberta
Legislative Branch, Legislature Annex, #801, 9718 - 107 St., Edmonton, AB T5K 1E4
committees@assembly.ab.ca
Committees of the Legislative Assembly of Alberta include select special committees, special standing committees, policy field committees, & standing committees.
Current select special committees include the Select Special Information & Privacy Commissioner Search Committee & the Select Special Ombudsman Search Committee.
There is one special standing committee, the Special Standing Committee on Members' Services.
Policy field committees include the following: Standing Committee on Community Services; Standing Committee on Health; Satnding Committee on Public Safety & Services; Standing Committee on Resources & Environment; & the Standing Committee on the Economy.
Current standing committees are as follows: Standing Committee on Legislative Offices; Standing Committee on Private Bills; Standing Committee on Privileges & Elections, Standing Orders & Printing; Standing Committee on Public Accounts; & the Standing Committee on the Alberta Heritage Savings Trust Fund.
Chair, Select Special Information & Privacy Commissioner Search Committee, Leonard Mitzel, Cypress-Medicine Hat, Progressive Conservative
780-415-9590, Fax: 780-422-0351
Chair, Select Special Ombudsman Search Committee, Leonard Mitzel, Cypress-Medicine Hat, Progressive Conservative
780-415-9590, Fax: 780-422-0351
Chair, Special Standing Committee on Members' Services, Hon. Ken Kowalski, Barrhead-Morinville-Westlock, Progressive Conservative
780-427-2464, Fax: 780-422-9553,
ken.kowalski@assembly.ab.ca
Social Media: www.facebook.com/ken.kowalski
Chair, Standing Committee on the Alberta Heritage Savings Trust Fund, Janis Tarchuk, Banff-Cochrane, Progressive Conservative
780-415-0993, Fax: 780-427-1835
Chair, Standing Committee on Community Services, Arno Doerksen, Strathmore-Brooks, Progressive Conservative
780-415-6125, Fax: 780-415-0951
Chair, Standing Committee on the Economy, Naresh Bhardwaj, Edmonton-Ellerslie, Progressive Conservative
780-644-3845, Fax: 780-422-1671
Chair, Standing Committee on Health, Barry McFarland, Little Bow, Progressive Conservative
780-427-0879, Fax: 780-422-0351
Chair, Standing Committee on Legislative Offices, Leonard Mitzel, Cypress-Medicine Hat, Progressive Conservative
780-415-9590, Fax: 780-422-0351
Chair, Standing Committee on Private Bills, Dr. Neil Brown, QC, Calgary-Nose Hill, Progressive Conservative
780-415-8368, Fax: 780-427-1234
Chair, Standing Committee on Privileges & Elections, Standing Orders & Printing, Raymond Prins, Lacombe-Ponoka, Progressive Conservative
780-422-3353, Fax: 780-422-0351
Chair, Standing Committee on Public Accounts, Hugh MacDonald, Edmonton-Gold Bar
780-427-2292, Fax: 780-427-3697,
hugh.macdonald@assembly.ab.ca
Chair, Standing Committee on Public Safety & Services, Wayne Drysdale, Grande Prairie-Wapiti, Progressive Conservative
780-415-0107, Fax: 780-422-1671
Chair, Standing Committee on Resources & Environment, Raymond Prins, Lacombe-Ponoka, Progressive Conservative
780-422-3353, Fax: 780-422-0351

Twenty-seventh Legislature - Alberta

Legislature Bldg., 10800 - 97 Ave., Edmonton, AB T5K 2B6
780-427-2826
laocommunications@assembly.ab.ca
www.assembly.ab.ca
Other Communication: Reference Information, E-mail: library.requests@assembly.ab.ca
Last General Election, March 3, 2008.
Party Leaders:
Progressive Conservative Party: Hon. Alison Redford, Premier-Designate;
Liberal Party: Dr. Raj Sherman;
Wildrose Alliance Party: Danielle Smith;
New Democratic Party: Brian Mason;
Alberta Party: Glenn Taylor.
Party Standings:
Progressive Conservative Party 67;
Liberal Party 9;
Wildrose Alliance Party 4;
New Democratic Party 2;
Alberta Party 1;
Total 83.
Indemnities, Salaries, & Allowances:
MLA indemnity $52,092, plus $26,046 MLA tax free allowance.
In addition to this are the following indemnities & allowances:
Premier $81,312;
Speaker $63,912;
Ministers with portfolio $63,912;
Ministers without portfolio $28,392;
Leader of the Official Opposition $63,912;
Deputy Speaker & Chair, Committees $31,968;
Deputy Chair of Committees $15,984;
Leader of a recognized opposition parties $28,392.
The following are special members' allowances:
Official Opposition House Leader: $13,596;
Third Party House Leader (recognized opposition party): $10,872;
Chief Government Whip: $10,872;
Assistant Government Whip: $8,136;
Chief Opposition Whip: $8,136;
Assistant Opposition Whip: $6,792;
Third Party Whip: $6,792
Member, Legislative Assembly, Cindy Ady, Calgary-Shaw, Progressive Conservative
780-415-9472, Fax: 780-422-0351,
calgary.shaw@assembly.ab.ca; TPR.minister@gov.ab.ca, Other Communications: Constituency Phone: 403-256-8969; Fax: 403-256-8970
Social Media: www.twitter.com/CindyAdy_MLA, www.facebook.com/cindyadymla
Note: Web Site: www.cindyady.com
Member, Legislative Assembly, Ken Allred, St. Albert, Progressive Conservative
780-427-1148, Fax: 780-415-0951,
st.albert@assembly.ab.ca, Other Communications: Constituency Phone: 780-459-9113; Fax: 780-460-9815
Social Media: www.facebook.com/pages/Ken-Allred/216274214051?ref=ts
Note: Web Site: allred.mypcmla.ca
Member, Legislative Assembly, Moe Amery, Calgary-East, Progressive Conservative
780-422-5382, Fax: 780-427-1835,
calgary.east@assembly.ab.ca, Other Communications: Constituency Phone: 403-216-5450; Fax: 403-216-5452
Social Media: www.facebook.com/people/Moe-Amery/783777229
Note: Web Sites: www.moeamery.com; amery.mypcmla.ca
Member, Legislative Assembly; House Leader Wildrose Alliance Party of Alberta, Rob Anderson, Airdrie-Chestermere, Wildrose Alliance Party of Alberta
780-415-0975, 888-948-8741, Fax: 780-368-3506,
airdrie.chestermere@assembly.ab.ca, Other Communications: Constituency Phone: 403-948-8741;Fax: 403-948-8744
Social Media: www.twitter.com/randersonmla, www.facebook.com/pages/Rob-Anderson/199265040654?ref=mf
Note: Web Site: www.robanderson.ca
Member, Legislative Assembly, Carl Benito, Edmonton-Mill Woods, Progressive Conservative
780-422-9299, Fax: 780-422-1671,
edmonton.millwoods@assembly.ab.ca, Other Communications: Constituency Phone: 780-414-1000; Fax: 780-414-1278
Social Media: www.twitter.com/MLACarlBenito, www.facebook.com/pages/Carl-Benito/200550876439?ref=ts
Note: Web Site: benito.mypcmla.ca
Member, Legislative Assembly; Minister, Agriculture & Rural Development, Hon. Evan Berger, Livingstone-Macleod, Progressive Conservative
780-427-2137, 800-565-0962, Fax: 780-422-6035,
livingstone.macleod@assembly.ab.ca, Other Communications: Constituency Phone: 403-553-2400;Fax: 403-553-2133
Social Media: www.facebook.com/pages/Evan-Berger-MLA/356351270299
www.linkedin.com/pub/evan-berger/29/6ba/96
Note: Web Site: berger.mypcmla.ca
Member, Legislative Assembly, Naresh Bhardwaj, Edmonton-Ellerslie, Progressive Conservative
780-644-3845, Fax: 780-422-1671,
edmonton.ellerslie@assembly.ab.ca, Other Communications: Constituency Phone: 780-414-2000; Fax: 780-414-6383
Social Media: www.twitter.com/MLA_NBhardwaj, www.facebook.com/nareshbhardwajmla
Note: Web Site: bhardwaj.mypcmla.ca
Member, Legislative Assembly, Hon. Manmeet S. Bhullar, Calgary-Montrose, Progressive Conservative
780-422-6880, Fax: 780-422-2496,
calgary.montrose@assembly.ab.ca, Other Communications: Constituency Phone: 403-248-4487; Fax: 403-248-4487
Social Media: www.twitter.com/manmeetsbhullar, www.facebook.com/manmeetbhullarmla
Note: Web Site: bhullar.mypcmla.ca
Member, Legislative Assembly, Hon. Lindsay Blackett, Calgary-North West, Progressive Conservative
780-427-7216, Fax: 780-422-1671,
calgary.northwest@assembly.ab.ca; CCS.Minister@gov.ab.ca, Other Communications: Constituency Phone: 403-216-5444; Fax: 403-216-5442
Social Media: www.twitter.com/LindsayBlackett, www.facebook.com/lindsayblackett
Note: Web Site: www.lindsayblackett.com
Member, Legislative Assembly, Laurie Blakeman, Edmonton-Centre, Liberal
780-427-2292, Fax: 780-427-3697,
edmonton.centre@assembly.ab.ca, Other Communications: Constituency Phone: 780-414-0743; Fax: 780-414-0772
Social Media: www.facebook.com/laurieblakeman
Note: Web Site: www.laurieblakeman.com
Member, Legislative Assembly, Guy Boutilier, Fort McMurray-Wood Buffalo, Wildrose Alliance Party of Alberta
780-427-1865, Fax: 780-638-3277,
gboutilier@assembly.ab.ca;fortmcmurray.woodbuffalo@assembly.ab.ca, Other Communications: Constituency Phone: 780-790-6014; Fax: 780-791-3683
Social Media: www.facebook.com/gboutilier
Member, Legislative Assembly, Dr. Neil Brown, Q.C., Calgary-Nose Hill, Progressive Conservative
780-415-8368, Fax: 780-427-1234,
calgary.nosehill@assembly.ab.ca, Other Communications: Constituency Phone: 403-215-7710; Fax: 403-216-5410
Social Media: www.facebook.com/DrNeilBrown
Note: Web Site: www.myclients.ca
Member, Legislative Assembly, Pearl Calahasen, Lesser Slave Lake, Progressive Conservative
780-427-5285, 866-625-0648, Fax: 780-415-0951,
lesser.slavelake@assembly.ab.ca, Other Communications: Constituency Phone: 780-523-3171; Fax: 780-523-5150
Social Media: www.facebook.com/pearlcalahasen
Note: Web Site: calahasen.mypcmla.ca
Member, Legislative Assembly, Robin Campbell, West Yellowhead, Progressive Conservative
780-427-1879, 800-661-6517, Fax: 780-415-0968,
west.yellowhead@assembly.ab.ca, Other Communications: Constituency Phone: 780-865-9796; Fax: 780-865-9760

Social Media: www.facebook.com/robincampbellmla
Note: Web Site: campbell.mypcmla.ca
Member, Legislative Assembly, Wayne Cao, Calgary-Fort, Progressive Conservative
780-415-0984, Fax: 780-427-1835,
calgary.fort@assembly.ab.ca, Other Communications: Constituency Phone: 403-216-5454; Fax: 403-216-5455
Note: Web Site: www.waynecao.ca
Member, Legislative Assembly, Harry B. Chase, Calgary-Varsity, Liberal
780-427-2292, Fax: 780-427-3697,
calgary.varsity@assembly.ab.ca, Other Communications: Constituency Phone: 403-216-5436; Fax: 403-216-5438
Social Media: www.twitter.com/chasemla, www.facebook.com/harrychase
Note: Web Site: www.HarryChaseMLA.com
Member, Legislative Assembly; Minister, Intergovernmental, International, & Aboriginal Relations, Hon. Cal Dallas, Red Deer-South, Progressive Conservative
780-643-6225, Fax: 780-643-6228,
reddeer.south@assembly.ab.ca, Other Communications: Constituency Phone: 403-340-3565; Fax: 403-346-9260
Social Media: www.facebook.com/caldallasmla
Note: Web Site: dallas.mypcmla.ca
Member, Legislative Assembly; Minister, Transportation, Hon. Ray Danyluk, Lac La Biche-St. Paul, Progressive Conservative
780-427-2080, 866-674-6999, Fax: 780-422-2722,
laclabiche.stpaul@assembly.ab.ca, Other Communications: Constituency Phone: 780-645-6999; Fax: 780-645-5787
Social Media: www.facebook.com/raydanylukmla
Note: Web Site: danyluk.mypcmla.ca
Member, Legislative Assembly, Alana DeLong, Calgary-Bow, Progressive Conservative
780-415-9459, Fax: 780-427-1835,
calgary.bow@assembly.ab.ca, Other Communications: Constituency Phone: 403-216-5400; Fax: 403-216-5402
Social Media: www.twitter.com/alanadelong, www.facebook.com/pages/Alana-DeLong/17735737239?ref=ts
Note: Web Site: www.alanadelong.com
Member, Legislative Assembly; Minister, Public Security; Solicitor General; Deputy Government HouseLeader, Hon. Jonathan Denis, Q.C., Calgary-Egmont, Progressive Conservative
780-415-9406, Fax: 780-415-9566,
calgary.egmont@assembly.ab.ca, Other Communications: Constituency Phone: 403-640-1363; Fax: 403-640-2970
Social Media: www.twitter.com/MinisterJono, www.facebook.com/jonathandenismla
Note: Web Site: www.denismla.ca
Member, Legislative Assembly, Hon. Jeff Johnson, Athabasca-Redwater, Progressive Conservative
780-427-5041, Fax: 780-422-2002,
athabasca.redwater@assembly.ab.ca, Other Communications: Constituency Phone: 780-675-3232; Fax: 780-675-2396
Social Media:
www.facebook.com/pages/Jeff-Johnson/194208238162
Note: Web Site: johnson.mypcmla.ca
Member, Legislative Assembly, Arno Doerksen, Strathmore-Brooks, Progressive Conservative
780-415-6125, Fax: 780-415-0951,
strathmore.brooks@assembly.ab.ca, Other Communications: Constituency Phone: 403-362-6969; Fax: 403-362-5923
Note: Web Site: www.arnodoerksen.ca
Member, Legislative Assembly, Wayne Drysdale, Grande Prairie-Wapiti, Progressive Conservative
780-415-0107, Fax: 780-427-1671,
grandeprairie.wapiti@assembly.ab.ca, Other Communications: Constituency Phone: 780-538-1800; Fax: 780-538-1802
Social Media: www.facebook.com/waynedrysdalemla
Note: Web Site: drysdale.mypcmla.ca
Member, Legislative Assembly, Doug Elniski, Edmonton-Calder, Progressive Conservative
780-427-0858, Fax: 780-415-0951,
edmonton.calder@assembly.ab.ca, Other Communications: Constituency Phone: 780-451-2345; Fax: 780-451-2344
Social Media: www.twitter.com/dougelniski
Note: Web Sites: www.dougelniski.com; elniski.mypcmla.ca
Member, Legislative Assembly, Hon. Iris Evans, Sherwood Park, Progressive Conservative
780-422-0279, Fax: 780-422-0351,
iris.evans@assembly.ab.ca;
sherwood.park@assembly.ab.ca, Other Communications: Constituency Phone: 780-417-4747; Fax: 780-417-4748
Note: Web Site: www.irisevans.com
Member, Legislative Assembly, Kyle Fawcett, Calgary-North Hill, Progressive Conservative
780-427-7984, Fax: 780-427-5441,
calgary.northhill@assembly.ab.ca, Other Communications: Constituency Phone: 403-216-5430; Fax: 403-216-5432
Social Media: www.twitter.com/kyleMLA,
www.facebook.com/pages/Kyle-Fawcett/201067916433
Note: Web Site: www.kylefawcett.ca
Member, Legislative Assembly, Heather Forsyth, Calgary-Fish Creek, Wildrose Alliance Party of Alberta
780-415-0058, Fax: 780-638-3506,
calgary.fishcreek@assembly.ab.ca, Other Communications: Constituency Phone: 403-278-4444; Fax: 403-278-7875
Social Media: www.twitter.com/HeatherMLA, www.facebook.com/profile.php?id=1420582509
Note: Web Site: www.heatherforsyth.com
Member, Legislative Assembly, Yvonne Fritz, Calgary-Cross, Progressive Conservative
780-422-5375, Fax: 780-422-0351,
calgary.cross@assembly.ab.ca, Other Communications: Constituency Phone: 403-280-4022; Fax: 403-280-3877
Social Media: www.facebook.com/yvonnefritzmla
Note: Web Site: fritz.mypcmla.ca
Member, Legislative Assembly, Hector Goudreau, Dunvegan-Central Peace, Progressive Conservative
780-643-6452, 866-835-4988, Fax: 780-643-6452,
dunvegan.centralpeace@assembly.ab.ca, Other Communications: Phone, Falher: 780-837-3846; Fairview: 780-835-7211
Social Media:
www.facebook.com/pages/Hector-Goudreau/195236593554
Note: Web Site: www.goudreau.mypcmla.ca
Member, Legislative Assembly; Minister, Municipal Affairs, Hon. Doug Griffiths, Battle River-Wainwright, Progressive Conservative
780-427-3744, 855-464-7433, Fax: 780-422-9550,
battleriver.wainwright@assembly.ab.ca;
info@betteralberta.ca, Other Communications: Constituency Phone: 780-842-6177; Fax: 780-842-3171
Social Media: www.twitter.com/griffmla, www.facebook.com/Griffs4ABsFuture?sk=app_53267368995
Note: Web Site: www.douggriffiths.ca
Member, Legislative Assembly, Hon. George Groeneveld, Highwood, Progressive Conservative
780-422-7199, Fax: 780-427-1835,
highwood@assembly.ab.ca, Other Communications: Constituency Phone: 403-652-7100; Fax: 403-652-7757
Social Media:
www.facebook.com/pages/George-Groeneveld/208335376173
Note: Web Site: groeneveld.mypcmla.ca
Member, Legislative Assembly; Minister, Human Services; Government House Leader, Hon. David Hancock, QC, Edmonton-Whitemud, Progressive Conservative
780-643-6210, Fax: 780-643-6214,
edmonton.whitemud@assembly.ab.ca;
dave.hancock@gov.ab.ca, Other Communications: Constituency Phone: 780-413-5970; Fax: 780-413-5971
Social Media: www.twitter.com/DaveHancockMLA
Note: Web Site: www.davehancock.ca
Member, Legislative Assembly; Minister, Tourism, Parks, & Recreation, Hon. Jack Hayden, Drumheller-Stettler, Progressive Conservative
780-427-4928, Fax: 780-427-0188,
drumheller.stettler@assembly.ab.ca, Other Communications: Constituency Phone: 403-742-4284; Fax: 403-742-4295
Social Media:
www.facebook.com/pages/Jack-Hayden/188272707966
Note: Web Site: hayden.mypcmla.ca
Member, Legislative Assembly, Kent Hehr, Calgary-Buffalo, Liberal
780-427-2292, Fax: 780-427-3697,
calgary.buffalo@assembly.ab.ca, Other Communications: Constituency Phone: 403-244-7737; Fax: 403-541-9106
Note: Web Site: www.kenthehrmla.com
Member, Legislative Assembly; Deputy Leader, Wildrose Alliance Party of Alberta, Paul Hinman, Calgary-Glenmore, Wildrose Alliance Party of Alberta
780-638-3504, Fax: 780-638-3506,
calgary.glenmore@assembly.ab.ca, Other Communications: Constituency Phone: 403-216-5421;Fax: 403-216-5423
Social Media: www.twitter.com/PaulHinmanMLA, www.facebook.com/PaulHinmanMLA
Note: Web Site: www.paulhinman.ca
Member, Legislative Assembly, Len Webber, Calgary-Foothills, Progressive Conservative
780-415-9575, Fax: 780-415-0951,
calgary.foothills@assembly.ab.ca, Other Communications: Constituency Phone: 403-288-4453; Fax: 403-247-9863
Social Media: www.facebook.com/lenwebbermla
Note: Web Site: webber.mypcmla.ca
Member, Legislative Assembly; Minister, Health & Wellness, Hon. Fred Horne, Edmonton-Rutherford, Progressive Conservative
780-427-3665, Fax: 780-415-0961,
edmonton.rutherford@assembly.ab.ca, Other Communications: Constituency Phone: 780-414-1311; Fax: 780-414-1314
Social Media:
www.facebook.com/pages/Fred-Horne/190857637827
Note: Web Site: horne.mypcmla.ca
Member, Legislative Assembly; Deputy Premier; President of Treasury Board & Enterprise, Hon. Doug Horner, Spruce Grove-Sturgeon-St. Albert, Progressive Conservative
780-415-4855, Fax: 780-415-4853,
sprucegrovesturgeon.stalbert@assembly.ab.ca, Other Communications: ConstituencyPhone: 780-962-6606; Fax: 780-962-1568
Social Media: www.twitter.com/hornerforab, www.facebook.com/DougHornerForAlbertawww.linkedin.com/pub/doug-horner/30/310/206
Member, Legislative Assembly, Mary Anne Jablonski, Red Deer-North, Progressive Conservative
780-422-3882, Fax: 780-422-1671,
reddeer.north@assembly.ab.ca, Other Communications: Constituency Phone: 403-342-2263; Fax: 403-340-3185
Social Media: www.twitter.com/majablonski, www.facebook.com/pages/Mary-Anne-Jablonski/232935739198
Note: Web Site: jablonski.mypcmla.ca
Member, Legislative Assembly, Broyce Jacobs, Cardston-Taber-Warner, Progressive Conservative
780-422-0685, Fax: 780-427-1835,
cardston.taberwarner@assembly.ab.ca, Other Communications: Constituency Phone: 403-223-0001; Fax: 403-223-0002
Social Media:
www.facebook.com/pages/Broyce-Jacobs/247856901561
Note: Web Site: jacobs.mypcmla.ca
Member, Legislative Assembly, Art Johnston, Calgary-Hays, Progressive Conservative
780-415-9526, Fax: 780-427-1234,
calgary.hays@assembly.ab.ca, Other Communications: Constituency Phone: 403-215-4380; Fax: 403-215-4383
Social Media: www.facebook.com/artjohnstonmla
Note: Web Site: johnston.mypcmla.ca
Member, Legislative Assembly, Darshan Kang, Calgary-McCall, Liberal
780-427-2292, Fax: 780-427-3697,
calgary.mccall@assembly.ab.ca, Other Communications: Constituency Phone: 403-216-5424; Fax: 403-216-5426
Social Media: www.twitter.com/darshankang
Note: Web Site: www.constituency.dkang.ca
Member, Legislative Assembly; Minister, Culture & Community Services, Hon. Heather Klimchuk, Edmonton-Glenora, Progressive Conservative
780-780-4223, Fax: 780-427-7729,
edmonton.glenora@assembly.ab.ca, Other Communications: Constituency Phone: 780-455-7979;Fax: 780-455-2197
Social Media:
www.facebook.com/pages/Heather-Klimchuk/187574883149
Member, Legislative Assembly, Mel Knight, Grande Prairie-Smoky, Progressive Conservative
780-415-9470, Fax: 780-415-0951,
grandeprairie.smoky@assembly.ab.ca, Other Communications: Constituency Phone: 780-513-1233; Fax: 780-513-1247
Social Media: www.facebook.com/mlamelknight
Member, Legislative Assembly; Speaker, Hon. Ken Kowalski, Barrhead-Morinville-Westlock, Progressive Conservative
780-427-2464, Fax: 780-427-9553,
barrheadmorinvillewestlock@assembly.ab.ca, Other Communications: Constituency Phone: 780-674-3225; Fax: 780-674-6183
Social Media: www.facebook.com/ken.kowalski
Note: Web Site: kowalski.mypcmla.ca
Member, Legislative Assembly, Genia Leskiw, Bonnyville-Cold Lake, Progressive Conservative
780-415-0995, Fax: 780-415-0951,
bonnyville.coldlake@assembly.ab.ca; genia@genialeskiw.ca, Other Communications: Constituency Phone: 780-826-5658; Fax: 780-826-2165
Social Media: www.facebook.com/genia.leskiw1?ref
Note: Web Site: www.genialeskiw.ca
Member, Legislative Assembly; Minister, Finance, Hon. Ronald Liepert, Calgary-West, Progressive Conservative
780-427-8809, Fax: 780-427-5543,
calgary.west@assembly.ab.ca, Other Communications: Constituency Phone: 403-216-5439; 403-216-5441
Social Media: www.facebook.com/ronliepertmla
Note: Web Sites: liepert.mypcmla.ca; www.ronliepert.com
Member, Legislative Assembly, Hon. Fred Lindsay, Stony Plain, Progressive Conservative
780-422-2140, Fax: 780-427-1835,
stony.plain@assembly.ab.ca, Other Communications: Constituency Phone: 780-963-1444; Fax: 780-963-1730
Social Media:
www.facebook.com/pages/Fred-Lindsay/194808369751
Note: Web Site: lindsay.mypcmla.ca
Member, Legislative Assembly; Minister, Education, Hon. Thomas Lukaszuk, Edmonton-Castle Downs, Progressive Conservative
780-427-5010, Fax: 780-427-5018,

edmonton.castledowns@assembly.ab.ca, Other Communications: Constituency Phone: 780-414-0705; Fax: 780-414-0707
Social Media: www.twitter.com/lukaszukmla, www.facebook.com/Thomas-A-Lukaszuk/662272836
Note: Web Site: www.thomasmla.com (Personal Web Site)

Member, Legislative Assembly, Ty Lund, Rocky Mountain House, Progressive Conservative
780-422-5012, Fax: 780-427-1835, rocky.mountainhouse@assembly.ab.ca, Other Communications: Constituency Phone: 403-845-5154; Fax: 403-845-5525
Social Media: www.facebook.com/pages/Ty-Lund/196437102901
Note: Web Site: lund.mypcmla.ca

Member, Legislative Assembly, Hugh MacDonald, Edmonton-Gold Bar, Liberal
780-427-2292, Fax: 780-427-3697, hugh.macdonald@assembly.ab.ca; edmonton.goldbar@assembly.ab.ca, Other Communications: Constituency Phone: 780-414-1015; Fax: 780-414-1017
Social Media: www.twitter.com/leadliberals
Note: Web Site: www.hughmacdonald.com

Member, Legislative Assembly, Richard Marz, Olds-Didsbury-Three Hills, Progressive Conservative
780-415-0994, Fax: 780-415-0951, richard.marz@assembly.ab.ca, Other Communications: Constituency Phone: 403-556-3132; Fax: 403-556-3120
Social Media: www.facebook.com/richardmarzmla
Note: Web Site: marz.mypcmla.ca

Member, Legislative Assembly; Leader, New Democratic Party Opposition, Brian Mason, Edmonton-Highlands-Norwood, New Democratic Party
780-415-1800, Fax: 780-415-0701, edmonton.highlandsnorwood@assembly.ab.ca, Other Communications: Constituency Phone: 780-414-0682;Fax: 780-414-0684
Social Media: www.twitter.com/bmasonNDP, www.facebook.com/Brian-Mason/26993021019
Note: Web Site: www.brianmason.ca

Member, Legislative Assembly, Barry McFarland, Little Bow, Progressive Conservative
780-427-0879, 800-563-0917, Fax: 780-422-0351, little.bow@assembly.ab.ca, Other Communications: Constituency Phone: 403-643-2077; Fax: 403-643-2024
Note: Web Site: mcfarland.mypcmla.ca

Members, Legislative Assembly of Alberta

Member, Legislative Assembly; Minister, Environment & Water, Hon. Diana McQueen, Drayton Valley-Calmar, Progressive Conservative
780-427-2391, 800-542-7307, Fax: 780-422-6259, draytonvalley.calmar@assembly.ab.ca, Other Communications: Constituency Phone: 780-542-3355; Fax: 780-542-3331
Social Media: www.twitter.com/mcqueenmla, www.facebook.com/dianamcqueenmla
Note: Web Site: mcqueen.mypcmla.ca

Member, Legislative Assembly, Leonard Mitzel, Cypress-Medicine Hat, Progressive Conservative
780-415-9590, 866-339-2191, Fax: 780-422-0351, cypress.medicinehat@assembly.ab.ca, Other Communications: Constituency Phone: 403-528-2191; Fax: 403-528-2278
Social Media: www.twitter.com/lenmitzelmla, www.facebook.com/Leonard-Mitzel/23667497333
Note: Web Site: mitzel.mypcmla.ca

Member, Legislative Assembly; Minister, Energy, Hon. Ted Morton, Foothills-Rockyview, Progressive Conservative
780-427-3740, 866-843-4314, Fax: 780-422-0195, foothills.rockyview@assembly.ab.ca, Other Communications: Constituency Phone: 403-216-2221; Fax: 403-216-2225
Social Media: www.facebook.com/TedMortonMLA
Note: Web Site: www.tedmorton.ca

Member, Legislative Assembly, Rachel Notley, Edmonton-Strathcona, New Democratic Party
780-415-1800, Fax: 780-415-0701, edmonton.strathcona@assembly.ab.ca, Other Communications: Constituency Phone: 780-414-0702; Fax: 780-414-0703
Social Media: www.twitter.com/RachelNotley, www.facebook.com/people/Rachel-Notley/667840570
Note: Web Site: www.ndpopposition.ab.ca/rachelnotley

Member, Legislative Assembly; Minister, Sustainable Resource Development, Hon. Frank Oberle, Peace River, Progressive Conservative
780-415-4815, Fax: 780-415-4818, peace.river@assembly.ab.ca, Other Communications: Constituency Phone: 780-624-5400; Fax: 780-624-5464
Note: Web Site: oberle.mypcmla.ca

Member, Legislative Assembly; Minister, Justice; Attorney General; Deputy Government House Leader, Hon. Verlyn Olson, QC, Wetaskiwin-Camrose, Progressive Conservative
780-427-2339, Fax: 780-422-6621, wetaskiwin.camrose@assembly.ab.ca, Other Communications: Constituency Phone: 780-672-0000; Fax: 780-672-6945
Social Media: www.facebook.com/verlynolsonmla
Note: Web Sites: www.verlynolson.ca (Personal Web Site); www.justice.alberta.ca (Justice & Attorney General)

Member, Legislative Assembly, Luke Ouellette, Innisfail-Sylvan Lake, Progressive Conservative
780-422-5566, 888-655-2535, Fax: 780-415-0951, innisfail.sylvanlake@assembly.ab.ca, Other Communications: Constituency Phone: 403-227-1500; Fax: 403-227-5350
Social Media: www.facebook.com/pages/Luke-Ouellette/108363929210366
Note: Web Site: ouellette.mypcmla.ca

Member, Legislative Assembly, Bridget A. Pastoor, Lethbridge-East, Liberal
780-427-2292, Fax: 780-427-3697, lethbridge.east@assembly.ab.ca, Other Communications: Constituency Phone: 403-320-1011; Fax: 403-328-6613
Social Media: www.facebook.com/Bridget-A-Pastoor/145454248806541
Note: Web Site: www.albertaliberal.com/team.php?MLA=16084

Member, Legislative Assembly, Raymond Prins, Lacombe-Pomoka, Progressive Conservative
780-422-3353, 800-565-6432, Fax: 780-422-0351, lacombe.ponoka@assembly.ab.ca, Other Communications: Constituency Phone: 403-782-7725; Fax: 403-782-3307
Social Media: www.facebook.com/rayprinsmla
Note: Web Site: prins.mypcmla.ca

Member, Legislative Assembly, Dave Quest, Strathcona, Progressive Conservative
780-415-0990, Fax: 780-422-0351, strathcona@assembly.ab.ca, Other Communications: Constituency Phone: 416-416-2492; Fax: 780-416-7093
Social Media: www.twitter.com/davequestMLA, www.facebook.com/DaveQuestMLA
Note: Web Site: www.davequest.ca

Member, Legislative Assembly; Premier; President, Executive Council; Chair, Agenda & Priorities Committee, Hon. Alison Redford, QC, Calgary-Elbow, Progressive Conservative
780-427-3840, Fax: 780-422-1671, calgary.elbow@assembly.ab.ca, Other Communications: Constituency Phone: 403-252-0346; Fax: 403-252-0520
Note: Web Site: www.alisonredford.ca

Member, Legislative Assembly, Rob Renner, Medicine Hat, Progressive Conservative
780-422-5381, Fax: 780-422-1671, medicine.hat@assembly.ab.ca, Other Communications: Constituency Phone: 403-527-5622; Fax: 403-527-5112
Social Media: www.facebook.com/robrennermla
Note: Web Site: www.robrenner..ca

Member, Legislative Assembly, Dave Rodney, Calgary-Lougheed, Progressive Conservative
780-415-1325, Fax: 780-422-1671, calgary.lougheed@assembly.ab.ca, Other Communications: Constituency Phone: 403-238-1212; Fax: 403-251-5453
Social Media: www.facebook.com/Dave-Rodney/1079178864
Note: Web Site: www.daverodney.ca

Member, Legislative Assembly, George Rogers, Leduc-Beaumont-Devon, Progressive Conservative
780-422-2229, Fax: 780-422-0351, leduc.beaumontdevon@assembly.ab.ca, Other Communications: Constituency Phone: 780-986-4652; Fax: 780-986-5228
Social Media: www.twitter.com/rogersofleduc, www.facebook.com/George-Rogers/215811019107
Note: Web Site: rogers.mypcmla.ca

Member, Legislative Assembly, Peter Sandhu, Edmonton-Manning, Progressive Conservative
780-427-2729, Fax: 780-415-0951, edmonton.manning@assembly.ab.ca, Other Communications: Constituency Phone: 780-414-0714; Fax: 780-414-0716
Social Media: www.twitter.com/PeterSandhuMLA, www.facebook.com/petersandhumla
Note: Web Site: sandhu.mypcmla.ca

Member, Legislative Assembly, Janice Sarich, Edmonton-Decore, Progressive Conservative
780-415-9462, Fax: 780-415-0951, edmonton.decore@assembly.ab.ca, Other Communications: Constituency Phone: 780-414-1328; Fax: 780-414-1330
Social Media: www.twitter.com/JaniceSarichMLA, www.facebook.com/janicesarich
Note: Web Site: sarich.mypcmla.ca

Member, Legislative Assembly; Leader, Alberta Liberal Official Opposition, Dr. Raj Sherman, Edmonton-Meadowlark, Liberal
780-415-0976, Fax: 780-638-4313, edmonton.meadowlark@assembly.ab.ca, Other Communications: Constituency Phone: 780-414-0711;Fax: 780-414-0713
Social Media: www.twitter.com/RajShermanMLA, www.facebook.com/rajshermanmla
Note: Web Site: www.electraj.ca

Member, Legislative Assembly, Lloyd Snelgrove, Vermillion-Lloydminster, Progressive Conservative
780-415-9425, 800-567-7644, Fax: 780-422-1671, vermilion.lloydminster@assembly.ab.ca, Other Communications: Constituency Phone: 780-853-4202; Fax: 780-853-5770
Social Media: www.facebook.com/Lloyd-Snelgrove/200565175811

Member, Legislative Assembly, Hon. Edward "Ed" Michael Stelmach, Fort Saskatchewan-Vegreville, Progressive Conservative
780-427-2251, Fax: 780-427-1349, fortsaskatchewan.vegreville@assembly.ab.ca, Other Communications: Constituency Phone: 780-632-6840; Fax: 780-632-6888
Note: Web Site: www.stelmach.ca

Member, Legislative Assembly, Dr. David Swann, Calgary-Mountain View, Liberal
780-427-2292, Fax: 780-427-3697, calgary.mountainview@assembly.ab.ca, Other Communications: Constituency Phone: 403-216-5445; Fax: 403-216-5447
Social Media: www.twitter.com/davidswann, www.facebook.com/David-Swann/515014295
Note: Web Site: www.davidswann.ca

Member, Legislative Assembly, Dr. Kevin Taft, Edmonton-Riverview, Liberal
780-427-2292, Fax: 780-427-3697, edmonton.riverview@assembly.ab.ca, Other Communications: Constituency Phone: 780-414-0719; Fax: 780-414-0721
Note: Web Site: www.liberalopposition.com/index.php/site/MLAs/kevin_taft

Member, Legislative Assembly, Janis Tarchuk, Banff-Cochrane, Progressive Conservative
780-415-0993, 866-760-8281, Fax: 780-427-1835, banff.cochrane@assembly.ab.ca, Other Communications: Constituency Phone: 403-760-8281; Fax: 403-760-5009
Social Media: www.facebook.com/Janis-Tarchuk/193914609355
Note: Web Site: tarchuk.mypcmla.ca

Member, Legislative Assembly, Dave Taylor, Calgary-Currie, Alberta Party
780-427-2298, Fax: 403-638-3958, calgary.currie@assembly.ab.ca, Other Communications: Constituency Phone: 403-246-4794; Fax: 403-686-1543
Social Media: www.twitter.com/calgarycurrie, www.facebook.com/DaveTaylorMLA
Note: Web Site: www.davetaylormla.com

Member, Legislative Assembly; Minister, Seniors, Hon. George VanderBurg, Whitecourt-Ste. Anne, Progressive Conservative
780-415-9550, 800-786-7136, Fax: 780-415-9411, whitecourt.steanne@assembly.ab.ca, Other Communications: Constituency Phone: 780-786-1997; Fax: 780-786-1995
Social Media: www.facebook.com/George-VanderBurg/195871217330
Note: Web Site: vanderburg.mypcmla.ca

Member, Legislative Assembly, Tony Vandermeer, Edmonton-Beverly-Clareview, Progressive Conservative
780-422-5468, Fax: 780-427-4974, edmonton.beverlyclareview@assembly.ab.ca, Other Communications: Constituency Phone: 780-476-6467; Fax: 780-476-6473
Social Media: www.facebook.com/Tony-Vandermeer/194266109825
Note: Web Site: vandermeer.mypcmla.ca

Member, Legislative Assembly; Minister, Advanced Education & Technology, Hon. Greg Weadick, Lethbridge-West, Progressive Conservative
780-427-2025, Fax: 780-427-5582, lethbridge.west@assembly.ab.ca, Other Communications: Constituency Phone: 403-329-4644; Fax: 403-329-4289
Social Media: www.facebook.com/Greg-Weadick/193042929182
Note: Web Sites: www.gregweadick.com; weadick.mypcmla.ca (Personal Web Sites); www.advancededucation.gov.ab.ca/ministry/about/minister.aspx (AdvancedEducation & Technology)

Member, Legislative Assembly, Teresa Woo-Paw, Calgary-Mackay, Progressive Conservative
780-415-9479, Fax: 780-422-1671, calgary.mackay@assembly.ab.ca, Other Communications: Constituency Phone: 403-274-1931; Fax: 403-275-8421
Social Media: www.facebook.com/teresawoopawmla
Note: Web Sites: woo-paw.mypcmla.ca

Member, Legislative Assembly, David H. Xiao, Edmonton-McClung, Progressive Conservative
780-422-1992, Fax: 780-415-0951, edmonton.mcclung@assembly.ab.ca, Other Communications: Constituency Phone: 780-408-1860; Fax: 780-408-1864
Social Media: www.facebook.com/davidxiaomla
Note: Web Site: xiao.mypcmla.ca

Member, Legislative Assembly, Gene Zwozdesky, Edmonton-Mill Creek, Progressive Conservative
780-643-6241, Fax: 780-415-0961, edmonton.millcreek@assembly.ab.ca, Other Communications: Constituency Phone: 780-466-3737; Fax: 780-468-3359
Social Media: www.facebook.com/genezwozdeskymla
Note: Web Site: zwozdesky.mypcmla.ca

Alberta Government Departments & Agencies

Alberta Aboriginal Relations

Deputy Minister's Office, Commerce Place, 10155 - 102 St., 19th Fl., Edmonton, AB T5J 4G8
780-427-8407
www.aboriginal.alberta.ca
TTY: 800-232-7215
Other Communication: Toll-Free TDD/TTY throughout Alberta: 1-800-232-7215

Aboriginal Relations works with Aboriginal communities & other partners to enhance social & economic opportunities for Alberta's Aboriginal people.
Under Premier Redford, Aboriginal Relations became the responsibility of the new Ministry of Intergovernmental, International, & Aboriginal Relations.

Acts Administered:
Constitution of Alberta Amendment Act, 1990
Métis Settlements Act, 1990
Métis Settlements Land Protection Act, 1990
Métis Settlements Accord Implementation Act

Minister, Intergovernmental, International, & Aboriginal Relations, Hon. Cal Dallas
780-643-6225, Fax: 780-643-6338
Social Media: www.facebook.com/caldallasmla
Deputy Minister, Maria David-Evans
780-415-0900, Fax: 780-415-6144, maria.david-evans@gov.ab.ca
Director, Communications, Marie Iwanow
780-644-6829, Fax: 780-415-9548, marie.iwanow@gov.ab.ca
Manager, Ministerial Correspondence Unit, Ellen Anderson
780-643-1736, Fax: 780-415-6144, ellen.anderson@gov.ab.ca

Associated Agencies, Boards & Commissions:
• Métis Settlements Appeal Tribunal
14605 - 134 St.
Edmonton, AB T5L 4S9
780-422-1541 Fax: 780-422-0019 800-661-8864
www.msat.gov.ab.ca
Quasi-judicial body set up to hear evidence & make decisions to settle disputes about membership, land dealings, surface rights & any other matters where the parties involved agree to let the Tribunal resolve the issue.

Consultation & Land Claims
Commerce Place, 10155 - 102 St., 20th Fl., Edmonton, AB T5J 4G8
780-643-1731
Assistant Deputy Minister, Stan Rutwind, Q.C.
780-643-1731, Fax: 780-427-0401, stan.rutwind@gov.ab.ca
Executive Director, Aboriginal Consultation, Cole Pederson
780-427-8441, Fax: 780-427-0401, cole.pederson@gov.ab.ca
Director, Land Claims, Steven Andres
780-427-6084, Fax: 780-427-0401, steven.andres@gov.ab.ca
Director, Aboriginal Consultation, Cory Enns
780-644-1055, Fax: 780-427-0401, cory.enns@gov.ab.ca

First Nations & Metis Relations
Commerce Place, 10155 - 102 St., 19th Fl., Edmonton, AB T5J 4G8
Assistant Deputy Minister, Donavon Young
780-422-5925, Fax: 780-427-4019, donavon.young@gov.ab.ca
Executive Director, Métis Relations, Thomas Droege
780-427-9431, Fax: 780-427-4019, thomas.droege@gov.ab.ca
Executive Director, First Nations Relations, Cynthia Dunnigan
780-415-6141, Fax: 780-427-1760, cynthia.dunnigan@gov.ab.ca
Director, First Nations Development Fund, Peter Croseen
780-415-6142, Fax: 780-427-0401, peter.crossen@gov.ab.ca
Director, Aboriginal Economic Partnerships, Lanny Der
780-644-1057, Fax: 780-427-1760, lanny.der@gov.ab.ca
Director, Aboriginal Community Initiatives, Bronwyn Shoush
780-427-3060, Fax: 780-427-4019, bronwyn.shoush@gov.ab.ca
Registrar, Metis Settlements Land Registry, Lisa Chartrand
780-415-0168, Fax: 780-427-3656, lisa.chartrand@gov.ab.ca

Métis Settlements Appeal Tribunal (MSAT)
14605 - 134 Ave. NW, Edmonton, AB T5L 4S9
780-422-1541 Fax: 780-422-0019
800-661-8864
Chair, Don Cunningham
780-422-4978, Fax: 780-422-0019, don.cunningham@gov.ab.ca
Tribunal Secretary & Director, Metis Settlements Appeal Tribunal, Harold Robinson
780-422-5152, Fax: 780-422-0019, harold.robinson@gov.ab.ca

Métis Settlements Ombudsman Office
#203, 10525 - 170 St., Edmonton, AB T5P 4W2
780-427-9828 Fax: 780-427-9962
866-427-6813
Ombudsman, Metis Settlements Ombudsman Office, Harley Johnson
780-427-9463, Fax: 780-427-9962, harley.johnson@gov.ab.ca
Senior Manager, Metis Settlements Ombudsman Office, Linda Lewis
680-644-1004, Fax: 780-427-9962, linda.lewis@gov.ab.ca

Policy & Planning
Commerce Place, 10155 - 102 St., 20th Fl., Edmonton, AB T5J 4G8
Executive Director, Policy & Planning, Cameron Henry
780-427-2008, Fax: 780-427-0401, cameron.henry@gov.ab.ca
Director, Corporate Planning & Research, Ellen Tian
780-422-4061, Fax: 780-427-1760, ellen.tian@gov.ab.ca

Alberta Advanced Education & Technology

Legislature Bldg., #324, 10800 - 97 Ave., Edmonton, AB T5K 2B6
780-422-5400
-310-0000
www.advancededucation.gov.ab.ca

The key responsibilities of Advanced Education & Technology include apprenticeship & industry training, adult learning, & technology.
The following are some specific activities: developing program standards; counselling apprentices & employers; certifying apprentices & ocuupational trainees; licensing & certifying education providers; funding research, science & education providers; offering student financial assistance; & facilitating technology development & commercialization.

Acts Administered:
Access to the Future Act
Alberta Enterprise Corporation Act
Alberta Research & Innovation Act
Apprenticeship & Industry Training Act
Post-secondary Learning Act (PSLA)
Private Vocational Training Act
Student Support Legislation (various)
Advanced Education & Technology Grants Regulation

Minister, Advanced Education & Technology, Hon. Greg Weadick
780-427-2025, Fax: 780-427-5582
Social Media: www.facebook.com/Greg-Weadick/193042929182
Deputy Minister, Annette Trimbee
780-415-4744, Fax: 780-422-1801, annette.trimbee@gov.ab.ca
Executive Director & Senior Financial Officer, Corporate Services, Darrell Dancause
780-427-1897, Fax: 780-415-9823, darrell.dancause@gov.ab.ca
Executive Director, Human Resources, Dianna Wilk
780-422-5324, Fax: 780-427-3316, dianna.wilk@gov.ab.ca
Director, Communications, Kim Capstick
780-422-1562, Fax: 780-427-0821, kim.capstick@gov.ab.ca .ca

Associated Agencies, Boards & Commissions:
• Access Advisory Council
Sterling Place
9940 - 106 St., 4th Fl.
Edmonton, AB
780-644-3183
The council is appointed by the Minister of Advanced Education & Technology. The role of the council is to offer advice regarding the Access to the Future Fund.
• Alberta Apprenticeship & Industry Training Board
Commerce Place
10155 - 102nd St., 10th Fl.
Edmonton, AB T5J 4L5
780-427-8765 Fax: 780-422-7376 -310-0000 TTY: 780-427-9999
www.tradesecrets.gov.ab.ca
Other Communication: TTY Toll-Free: 1-800-232-7215
Board members are appointed by the Lieutenant Governor in Council, upon recommendation of the Minister of Advanced Education & Technology. The mission of the board is to maintain high quality training & certification standards in the apprenticeship & industry training system. The board offers recommendations to the Minister about the needs of the labour market in Alberta & the training & certification of persons in designated trades & occupations.
• Alberta Council on Admissions & Transfer (ACAT)
Commerce Place
10155 - 102 St., 11th Fl.
Edmonton, AB T5J 4L5
780-422-9021 Fax: 780-422-3688 -310-0000 TTY: 780-427-9999
acat@gov.ab.ca
www.acat.gov.ab.ca
Other Communication: TTY Toll-Free: 1-800-232-7215
The independent body advocates for learners by working to ensure transferability of educational courses & programs to benefit students. The role of the council is to develop policies & procedures to facilitate transfer agreements among post-secondary institutions.
• Alberta Enterprise Corporation Board
Alberta Enterprise Corporation
#1100, 10830 Jasper Ave.
Edmonton, AB T5J 2B3
780-392-3901
The Alberta Enterprise Corporation Board was established in 2008 through the Alberta Enterprise Corporation Act. The Alberta Enterprise Fund is the corporation's fund that targets technology venture capital funds.
• Alberta Innvoates - Bio Solutions (AI Bio)
Phipps McKinnon Bldg.
10020 - 101A Ave.
Edmonton, AB T5J 3G2
780-427-1956 Fax: 780-427-3252 877-828-0444
bio@albertainnovates.ca
www.albertainnovates.ca/bio
Other Communication: General inquiries related to research & innovation organizations throughout Alberta, Phone: 877-828-0444
Alberta Innovates Bio Solutions was established in 2010 under the Alberta Research & Innovation Act. It is part of the Alberta Innovates system, which reports to the Minister of Alberta Advanced Education & Technology. Investments are made in research & innovation to benefit Alberta's forestry, agriculture, & food sectors.
• Alberta Innovates - Energy & Environmental Solutions
AMEC Place
#2540, 801 - 6th Ave. SW
Calgary, AB T2P 3W2
403-297-7089
ees@albertainnovates.ca
www.albertainnovates.ca/energy/introduction
The Alberta energy & environmental research organization works to develop innovative methods for the conversion of natural resources into environmentally responsible, market-ready energy.
• Alberta Innovates - Health Solutions (AIHS)
#1500, 10104 - 103 Ave.
Edmonton, AB T5J 4A7
780-423-5727 Fax: 780-429-3509 877-423-5727
health@albertainnovates.ca
www.ahfmr.ab.ca
Alberta Innovates - Health Solutions supports research & innovation for the improvement of Albertans' health & well-being. The organization also works to create health related social & economic benefits.
• Alberta Innovates - Technology Futures
250 Karl Clark Rd.
Edmonton, AB T6N 1E4
780-450-5111 Fax: 780-450-5333
referral@albertainnovates.ca
www.albertatechfutures.ca
As part of the research & innovation system in Alberta, the organization works to build healthy, sustainable businesses. Technology Futures offers technical services, program funding, as well as regionally accessible commercialization support.
• Alberta Research & Innvoation Authority (ARIA)
Phipps-McKinnon Bldg.
#500, 101A Ave.
Edmonton, AB T5J 3G2
780-427-1488 Fax: 780-427-0979
aria@albertainnovates.ca
www.albertainnovates.ca/research/introduction
The advisory body offers recommendations to the Government of Alberta about research, emerging technologies, & policy direction.
• Campus Alberta Quality Council (CAQC)
Commerce Place
10155 - 102 St., 11th Fl.
Edmonton, AB T5J 4L5
780-427-8921 Fax: 780-427-4185
caqc@gov.ab.ca
www.caqc.gov.ab.ca
The arms-length quality assurance agency makes recommendations to the Minister of Advanced Education & Technology on applications from post-secondary institutions that want to offer new degree programs. All degree programs, except for degrees in divinity, offered by resident institutions & non-resident institutions in Alberta must be approved by the Minister.

• Student Financial Assistance Appeal Committee
Students Finance
PO Box 28000 Main
Edmonton, AB T5J 4R4
780-427-3722 800-222-6485
The committees in Edmonton & Calgary hear appeals from students who were not provided the entire amount of financial assistance requested, or who had their application for assistance refused. The committees make a recommendation to the Minister, who make a decision on the appeal.
• Students Finance Board

Established in 1953, the Students Finance Board advises the Minister of Advanced Education & Technology about student financial assistance, including scholarships.

Advanced Technology Industries Division
Phipps-McKinnon Bldg., 10020 - 101A Ave., 5th Fl., Edmonton, AB T5J 3G2
Branches & sections in this division include the following: Emerging Technology Industries; Information & Technology Management; Innovation Client Services; & Technology Industry Development.
Assistant Deputy Minister, Mel Wong
780-427-2084, Fax: 780-427-5924, mel.wong@gov.ab.ca
Executive Director & Chief Information Officer, Information & Technology Management Section, Leslie Sim-Kaiser
780-415-0813, Fax: 780-422-0880, leslie.sim-kaiser@gov.ab.ca
Executive Director, Technology Industry Development Section, Robert Lai
780-427-7722, Fax: 780-427-5924, robert.lai@gov.ab.ca
Branch Head, Emerging Technology Industries Branch, Ryan Leskiw
780-644-2587, Fax: 780-427-5924, ryan.leskiw@gov.ab.ca
Branch Head, Innovation Client Services Branch, Alex Umnikov
780-427-6620, Fax: 780-427-5924, alex.umnikov@gov.ab.ca

Community, Learner & Industry Connections Division
Phipps-McKinnon Bldg., 10020 - 101A Ave., 5th Fl., Edmonton, AB T5J 3G2
Units of the Community Learner & Industry Connections Division include Apprenticeship & Industry Training & Learner Assistance.
Assistant Deputy Minister, Darlene Bouwsema
780-422-1185, Fax: 780-422-2420, darlene.bouwsema@gov.ab.ca
Executive Director, Learner Assistance, Schubert Kwan
780-422-4498, Fax: 780-422-4517, schubert.kwan@gov.ab.ca, Other Communications: Learner Assistance, Main Phone: 780-422-0555
Director, Program, Policy & Systens Support, Trudy Dupre
780-422-1208, Fax: 780-422-4517, trudy.dupre@gov.ab.ca
Director, Financial Operations & Control Services, John Koehn
780-422-5109, Fax: 780-422-4517, john.koehn@gov.ab.ca
Director, Learner Funding, Launa Lebeau
780-427-9820, Fax: 780-422-4516, launa.lebeau@gov.ab.ca
Manager, Administration, Apprenticeship & Industry Training, Carl Hamilton
780-638-4449, Fax: 780-422-7376, carl.hamilton@gov.ab.ca, Other Communications: General Apprentice Inquiries, Phone: 780-427-8517

Post Secondary & Community Education Division
Commerce Place, 10155 - 102 St., 7th Fl., Edmonton, AB T5J 4L5
Campus Alberta Partnerships, Post-secondary Investments & Outcomes, & Strategic Directions make up the Post-secondary & Community Education Division.
Assistant Deputy Minister, Connie Harrison
780-427-5607, Fax: 780-427-9430, connie.harrison@gov.ab.ca
Executive Director, Campus Alberta Partnerships, Dan Rizzoli
780-415-2966, Fax: 780-427-0423, dan.rizzoli@gov.ab.ca
Executive Director, Post-secondary Investments & Outcomes, Gerry Waisman
780-427-9667, Fax: 780-427-4185, gerry.waisman@gov.ab.ca

Research & Innovation Division
Phipps-McKinnon Bldg., 10020 - 101A Ave., 5th Fl., Edmonton, AB T5J 3G2
The Research & Innovation Division consists of Cross Ministry Initiatives, Innovation Planning & Accountability, Alberta Research & Innovation Authority, Innovation Policy, & Alberta Innovates.
Assistant Deputy Minister, Dr. Ronald Dyck
780-427-4497, Fax: 780-427-0979, ron.dyck@gov.ab.ca
Executive Director, Innovation Planning & Accountability, Lisa Bowes
780-422-3117, Fax: 780-427-1430, lisa.bowes@gov.ab.ca
Executive Director, Cross Ministry Initiatives, Daphne Cheel
780-422-0054, Fax: 780-427-3252, daphne.cheel@gov.ab.ca
Director, Innovation Policy, Sandra Duxbury
780-427-4498, Fax: 780-427-5924, sandra.duxbury@gov.ab.ca

Alberta Agriculture & Rural Development

J.G. O'Donoghue Bldg., #100A, 7000 - 113th St., Edmonton, AB T6H 5T6
780-427-2727
-310-3276
duke@gov.ab.ca
www.agric.gov.ab.ca
Alberta's Agriculture & Rural Development is engaged in the following key activities: facilitating sustainable industry growth, enhancing rural sustainability, & strengthening business risk management.
Acts Administered:
Agricultural Operations Practices Act
Agricultural Pests Act
Agricultural Service Board Act
Agricultural Societies Act
Agriculture Financial Services Act
Agriculture Satutes Repeal Act, 2008
Alberta Wheat & Barley Test Market Act
Animal Health Act
Animal Keepers Act
Animal Protection Act
Bee Act
Crop Liens Priorities Act
Crop Payments Act
Dairy Industry Act
Farm Implement Act
Farm Implement Dealerships Act
Feeder Associations Guarantee Act
Fuel Tax Act
Fur Farms Act
Gas Distribution Act
Government Accountability Act
Government Organization Act
Heating Oil & Propane Rebate Act
Horned Cattle Purchases Repeal Act
Irrigation Districts Act
Line Fence Act
Livestock Identification & Commerce Act
Livestock Industry Diversification Act
Livestock & Livestock Products Act
Marketing of Agricultural Products Act
Meat Inspection Act
Rural Electrification Loan Act
Rural Electrification Long-term Financing Act
Rural Utilities Act
Soil Conservation Act
Stray Animals Act
Vegetable Sales (Alberta) Repeal Act
Weed Control Act
Wheat Board Money Trust Act
Women's Institute Act
Minister, Agriculture & Rural Development, Hon. Evan Berger
780-427-2137, Fax: 780-422-6035
Social Media:
www.facebook.com/pages/Evan-Berger-MLA/356351270299
www.linkedin.com/pub/evan-berger/29/6ba/96
Deputy Minister, John Knapp
780-427-2145, Fax: 780-415-6002, john.knapp@gov.ab.ca
Parliamentary Assistant, Bryce Jacobs, MLA
780-422-0685, Fax: 780-427-1835
Director, Communications Branch, Cathy Housdorff
780-422-7683, Fax: 780-638-4477, cathy.housdorff@gov.ab.ca

Associated Agencies, Boards & Commissions:
• Agricultural Products Marketing Council
JG O'Donoghue Bldg.
7000 - 113 St., 3rd Fl.
Edmonton, AB T6H 5T6
780-427-2164 Fax: 780-422-9690
The Alberta Agricultural Products Marketing Council supports legislation & regulations & offers policy advice to the Minister of Agriculture & Rural Development & industry organizations.
• Alberta Grains Council (AGC)
JG O'Donoghue Bldg.
7000 - 113 St., 3rd Fl.
Edmonton, AB T6H 5T6
780-427-7329 Fax: 780-422-9690
www1.agric.gov.ab.ca/$department/deptdocs.nsf/all/agc2620
The Alberta Grains Council makes recommendations to the Minister of Agriculture & Rural Affairs about issues in the grain industry.
• Alberta Livestock & Meat Agency (ALMA)
Ellwood Office Park South
#101, 1003 Ellwood Rd. SW
Edmonton, AB T6X 0B3
780-638-1699 Fax: 780-638-6495
info@almaltd.ca
www.alma.alberta.ca
The provincial government agency was established to advance the Alberta Livestock & Meat Strategy. The goal of the Alberta Livestock & Meat Agency is to develop a profitable & competitive Alberta livestock & meat industry, by offering information & investment opportunities to the industry & the Government of Alberta.
• Irrigation Council
Provincial Bldg.
200 - 5 Ave. South, 3rd Fl.
Lethbridge, AB T1J 4L1
403-381-5176 Fax: 403-382-4406
www1.agric.gov.ab.ca/$department/deptdocs.nsf/all/irc9432
The Irrigation Council was established under Section 50 of the Irrigation Districts Act. The provincial agency reports to the Minister of Agriculture & Rural Development.
• Office of the Farmers' Advocate
JG O'Donoghue Bldg.
7000 - 113 St.
Edmonton, AB T6H 5T6
-310-3276
www1.agric.gov.ab.ca/$department/deptdocs.nsf/all/ofa2621
The Farmers' Advocate Office offers rural consumer protection, rural opportunities, & fair process for rural Albertans. The Office supports programs to settle disputes or offer appeals privately.

Economics & Competitiveness Division
JG O'Donoghue Bldg., 7000 - 113 St., 3rd Fl., Edmonton, AB T6H 5T6
780-422-3771 Fax: 780-427-5220
Director, Economics & Competitiveness Division, Don Brown
780-644-5634, Fax: 780-427-5220, don.brown@gov.ab.ca
Branch Head, Competitiveness & Market Analysis Branch, Darren Chase
780-422-4056, Fax: 780-427-5220, darren.chase@gov.ab.ca
Branch Head, Statistics & Data Development Branch, Reynold Jaipaul
780-427-5376, Fax: 780-427-5220, reynold.jaipaul@gov.ab.ca
Branch Head, Economics Branch, Diane McCann-Hiltz
780-422-6081, Fax: 780-427-5220, diane.mccann-hiltz@gov.ab.ca

Environmental Stewardship Division
JG O'Donoghue Bldg., 7000 - 113 St., 3rd Fl., Edmonton, AB T6H 5T6
Executive Director, Environmental Stewardship Division, Brenda Brindle
780-427-0674, Fax: 780-422-9745, brenda.brindle@gov.ab.ca
Branch Head, Technology & Innovation Branch, Rick Atkins
403-329-1212, Fax: 403-328-5562, rick.atkins@gov.ab.ca
Branch Head, Agri-Environmental Management Branch, Sandi Jones
403-556-4278, Fax: 403-556-7545, sandi.jones@gov.ab.ca

Financial & Business Planning Services Division
JG O'Donoghue Bldg., 7000 - 113 St., 2nd Fl., Edmonton, AB T6H 5T6
780-427-2151 Fax: 780-422-6529
Senior Financial Officer, Jim Carter
780-427-2162, Fax: 780-422-6529, jim.carter@gov.ab.ca
Senior Writer & Supervisor, Correspondence Unit, Jared Schapansky
780-644-1206, Fax: 780-422-6529, jared.schapansky@gov.ab.ca

Food Processing Division
Development Centre, 6309 - 45 St., Leduc, AB T9E 7C5
780-986-4793 Fax: 780-986-5138
Executive Director, Ken Gossen
780-980-4860, Fax: 780-986-5138, ken.gossen@gov.ab.ca
Senior Manager, Programs, Karen Erin
780-980-4864, Fax: 780-986-5138, karen.erin@gov.ab.ca
Senior Manager, Operations, Robert Gibson
780-980-4866, Fax: 780-980-4250, robert.gibson@gov.ab.ca

Food Safety & Animal Health Division
Agriculture & Rural Development, OS Longman Bldg., 6909 - 116 St., Edmonton, AB T6H 4P2
780-427-6159
Executive Director, Food Safety & Animal Health Division, Greg Orriss
780-427-6159, Fax: 780-427-1437, greg.orriss@gov.ab.ca

Human Resource Services & Facilities Management Services
JG O'Donoghue Bldg., 7000 -113 St., Edmonton, AB T6H 5T6
780-427-2111 Fax: 780-427-3398
resumes@agric.gov.ab.ca
Executive Director, Heather K.M. Behman
780-427-2430, Fax: 780-427-3398, heather.behman@gov.ab.ca
Director, Human Resource Consulting Services, Helene Vegh
780-427-2967, Fax: 780-427-3398, helene.vegh@gov.ab.ca
Coordinator, Facilities Management Unit, Rose Alwood
780-422-4915, Fax: 780-427-4227, rose.alwood@gov.ab.ca

Industry Development & Food Safety Sector
JG O'Donoghue Bldg., 7000 - 113 St., Edmonton, AB T6H 5T6

Assistant Deputy Minister, Jason Krips
780-427-2439, Fax: 780-422-6317, jason.krips@gov.ab.ca

Information Management Division
JG O'Donoghue Bldg, 7000 - 113 St., 1st Fl., Edmonton, AB T6H 5T6
780-427-2727 Fax: 780-427-2861
Director, Information Management, Gerard Vaillancourt
780-422-6796, Fax: 780-427-2861, gerard.vaillancourt@gov.ab.ca
Administrator & Program Coordinator, Information Management, Lillian Chan
780-422-6796, Fax: 780-427-2861, gerard.vaillancourt@gov.ab.ca

Information Technology Division
JG O'Donoghue Bldg., 7000 - 113 St., 2nd Fl., Edmonton, AB T6H 5T6
Executive Director, Information Technology, Rob Pungor
780-422-6660, Fax: 780-422-4004, rob.pungor@gov.ab.ca
Manager, Technology Solutions, Dean Pratt
780-422-2142, Fax: 780-422-4004, dean.pratt@gov.ab.ca
Manager, Infrastructure, Al Schachtel
780-422-6777, Fax: 780-422-4004, al.schachtel@gov.ab.ca

Irrigation & Farm Water Division
Agriculture Centre, #100, 5401 - 1 Ave. South, Lethbridge, AB T1J 4V6
Executive Director, Irrigation & Farm Water Division, Brent Paterson
403-381-5143, Fax: 403-381-5903, brent.paterson@gov.ab.ca
Branch Head, Irrigation Secretariat, Roger Hohm
403-381-5176, Fax: 403-382-4406, roger.hohm@gov.ab.ca
Branch Head, Rural Water Branch, Marshall Eliason
780-427-4615, Fax: 780-422-9745, marshall.eliason@gov.ab.ca

Office of the Chief Provincial Veterinarian
OS Longman Bldg., 6909 - 116 St., Edmonton, T6H 4P2
780-427-3448 Fax: 780-415-0810
Chief Provincial Veterinarian, Dr. Gerald Hauer
780-415-9503, Fax: 780-415-0810, gerald.hauer@gov.ab.ca
Program Veterinarian, Dr. Hernan Ortegon
780-644-2148, Fax: 780-427-1437, hernan.ortegon@gov.ab.ca
Branch Head, Animal Health Branch, Ken Manninen
780-422-0808, Fax: 780-427-1437, ken.manninen@gov.ab.ca
Unit Leader, Livestock Welfare, Michelle Follensbee
780-644-3072, Fax: 780-415-0810, michelle.follensbee@gov.ab.ca

Policy & Environment Sector
JG O'Donoghue Bldg., 7000 - 113 St., 3rd Fl., Edmonton, AB T6H 5T6
Assistant Deputy Minister, Colin Jeffares
780-427-1957, Fax: 780-422-6317, colin.jeffares@gov.ab.ca

Policy, Strategy, & Intergovernmental Affairs Division
JG O'Donoghue Bldg., 7000 - 113 St., 2nd Fl., Edmonton, AB T6H 5T6
780-422-9167 Fax: 780-427-5921
Director, Strategy & Intergovernmental Affairs Division, Andre Tremblay
780-415-9755, Fax: 780-427-5921, andre.tremblay@gov.ab.ca
Manager, International Relations & Marketing Branch, Annalisa Baer
780-427-4148, Fax: 780-427-5921, annalisa.baer@gov.ab.ca
Branch Head, Policy Coordination & Research Branch, Dr. Shiferaw Adilu
780-422-7196, Fax: 780-427-5921, shiferaw.adilu@gov.ab.ca
Branch Head, Strategy & Program Delivery Branch, Linda Hawk
780-427-4463, Fax: 780-427-5921, linda.hawk@gov.ab.ca
Branch Head, Domestic & International Trade Policy Branch, Peter Kuperis
780-415-8608, Fax: 780-427-5921, peter.kuperis@gov.ab.ca
Branch Head, Growing Forward Coordination & Program Policy Branch, Wendy McCormick
403-340-5306, Fax: 403-340-4896, wendy.mccormick@gov.ab.ca

Regulatory Services Division
JG O'Donoghue Bldg., 7000 - 113 St., 3rd Fl., Edmonton, AB T6H 5T6
780-422-7197 Fax: 780-422-4513
Executive Director, Regulatory Services Division, Cliff Munroe
780-422-7249, Fax: 780-422-4513, cliff.munroe@gov.ab.ca
Branch Head, Meat Inspection Branch, Jake Kotowich
780-644-2371, Fax: 780-422-4513, jake.kotowich@gov.ab.ca
Branch Head, Inspection & Investigation Branch, Floyd Mullaney
403-340-5320, Fax: 403-340-5870, floyd.mullaney@gov.ab.ca

Research & Innovation Division
JG O'Donoghue Bldg., 7000 - 113 St., 3rd Fl., Edmonton, AB T6H 5T6
780-679-5172 Fax: 780-679-5175
Director, Research & Innovation, Connie Phillips
780-644-8124, Fax: 780-427-1057, connie.phillips@gov.ab.ca
Branch Head, Livestock Research Branch, Wesley Johnson
780-415-0828, Fax: 780-427-1057, wesley.johnson@gov.ab.ca
Branch Head, Bio-Industrial Opportunities Branch, Hong Qi
780-644-8128, Fax: 780-638-3586, hong.qi@gov.ab.ca
Senior Manager, Pest Surveillance Branch, Paul Laflamme
780-422-4911, Fax: 780-427-1057, paul.laflamme@gov.ab.ca
Centre Administrator, Food & Bio-Industrial Crops Branch, Anna Moeller
403-362-1302, Fax: 403-362-1306, anna.moeller@gov.ab.ca

Rural Development Division
JG O'Donoghue Bldg., 7000 - 113 St., Edmonton, AB T6H 5T6
780-427-2409 Fax: 780-427-4227
Executive Director, Rural Development, Ron Popek
780-422-1858, Fax: 780-427-4227, ron.popek@gov.ab.ca
Senior Manager, Rural Initiatives & Research Unit, Robert Hornbrook
780-427-4218, Fax: 780-427-4227, robert.hornbrook@gov.ab.ca

Rural Extension & Industry Development Division
Provincial Building, 4709 - 44 Ave., Stony Plain, AB T7Z 1N4
780-968-3557 Fax: 780-963-4709
Executive Director, Rural Extension & Industry Development Division, Jo-Ann Hall
780-968-3512, Fax: 780-963-4709, jo-ann.hall@gov.ab.ca
Branch Head, Crop Business Development Branch, James Calpas
403-340-5329, Fax: 403-340-4896, james.calpas@gov.ab.ca
Branch Head, Agriculture Grant Programs Branch, Murray Greer
780-980-4722, Fax: 780-980-4237, murray.greer@gov.ab.ca
Branch Head, Alberta Ag-Info Centre, Ross Hutchison
403-742-7542, Fax: 403-742-7527, ross.hutchison@gov.ab.ca
Branch Head, Local / Domestic Market Expansion Branch, Shauna Johnston
780-968-3553, Fax: 780-968-3554, shauna.johnston@gov.ab.ca
Branch Head, Livestock Business Development Branch, Carlyon Rod
780-349-4466, Fax: 780-349-5240, rod.carlyon@gov.ab.ca
Branch Head, Ag-Industry Extension Branch, Barb Shackel-Hardman
780-968-3550, Fax: 780-968-3554, barb.shackel.hardman@gov.ab.ca
Branch Head, 4-H & Agriculture Education Branch, Marguerite Stark
403-948-8510, Fax: 780-948-2069, marguerite.stark@gov.ab.ca
Branch Head, Processing Industry Business Development Branch, Lynn Stegman
403-340-7010, Fax: 403-340-4896, lynn.stegman@gov.ab.ca

Rural, Regulatory, Information & Technology
JG O'Donoghue Bldg., 7000 - 113 St., 3rd Fl., Edmonton, AB T6H 5T6
Assistant Deputy Minister, Rural, Regulatory, Information, & Technology, Jamie Curran
780-422-6166, Fax: 780-422-6317, jamie.curran@gov.ab.ca

Rural Utilities Division
JG O'Donoghue Bldg., 7000 - 113 St., 2nd Fl., Edmonton, AB T6H 5T6
780-427-0125 Fax: 780-422-1613
Director, Rural Utilities, Terry Holmes
780-427-0134, Fax: 780-422-1613
Branch Head, Rural Electric & Information Systems Branch, Tom Kee
780-427-0944, Fax: 780-422-1613
Branch Head, Safety & Technical Services Branch, Bruce Partington
780-427-0111, Fax: 780-422-1613

Traceability Division
JG O'Donoghue Bldg., 7000 - 113 St., 3rd Fl., Edmonton, T6H 5T6
780-643-1572 Fax: 780-422-3655
Executive Director, Traceability Division, John Brown
780-427-2799, Fax: 780-422-3655, john.brown@gov.ab.ca
Coordinator, Traceability Education, Kelly Gordon
780-638-3148, Fax: 780-422-3655, kelly.gordon@gov.ab.ca
Branch Head, Beef, Forage & Horse, Kirsty Piquette
780-427-7366
Branch Head, Livestock Products, Gordon Cover
403-340-5323, Fax: 403-340-4896, gordon.cove@gov.ab.ca
Branch Head, Pork, Poultry & Dairy, Gordon Cove
403-340-5322

Alberta Office of the Auditor General

9925 - 109 St., 8th Fl., Edmonton, AB T5K 2J8
780-427-4222 Fax: 780-422-9555
info@oag.ab.ca
www.oag.ab.ca

The Auditor General of Alberta is the independent auditor of all Government of Alberta ministries, departments, regulated funds, & agencies. Audits identify areas where improvement is required for the use of public resources & provide recommendations to improve practices.

Auditor General, Merwan Saher, CA
780-422-6195, Fax: 780-422-9555
Senior Financial Officer, Jeff Olson, CMA, MBA
780-422-6517, Fax: 780-427-5080, jolson@oag.ab.ca
General Counsel, Kerry Langford, LLB
780-422-6359, Fax: 780-422-9555, klangford@oag.ab.ca
Director, Human Resources, Jacquie M. Pylypiuk, CA, CHRP
780-422-6370, Fax: 780-427-5080, jpylypiuk@oag.ab.ca
Manager, Communications, Lori Trudgeon
780-422-6655, Fax: 780-422-9555, ltrudgeon@oag.ab.ca

Alberta Children & Youth Services

Communications, Sterling Place, 9940 - 106 St., 12th Fl., Edmonton, AB T5K 2N2
780-422-3004 Fax: 780-422-3071
-310-0000
cs.communications@gov.ab.ca
www.child.alberta.ca
Other Communication: Child Care Information Line: 1-866-714-5437; Family Violence Information Line, Toll-Free: 310-1818; Alberta Supports Ctr: 780-644-9992; Media Inquiries: 780-427-4801

A range of programs & services for children & families is offered. These programs & services are delivered by local offices in the Child & Family Services Authorities plus the eighteen Delegated First Nation Agencies.
Under Oremier Redford, children & youth services became the responsibility of the new Ministry of Human Services.

Acts Administered:
Child Care Licensing Act
Child, Youth, & Family Enhancement Act
Drug-endangered Children Act
Family & Community Support Services Act
Family Support for Children with Disabilities Act
Protection Against Family Violence Act
Protection of Sexually Exploited Children Act
Social Care Facilities Licensing Act
Social Care Facilities Review Committee Act

Minister, Humann Services; Government House Leader, Hon. David Hancock, QC
780-643-6210, Fax: 780-643-6214, dave.hancock@gov.ab.ca
Social Media: www.twitter.com/DaveHancockMLA
Deputy Minister, Steve MacDonald
780-427-6448, Fax: 780-422-9044, steve.macdonald@gov.ab.ca
Executive Director, Human Resources, Lawona Power
780-408-8492, Fax: 780-644-5052, lawona.power@gov.ab.ca
Executive Director, Family Violence Prevention, Bullying, & Youth Strategies, Susan Taylor
780-415-8907, Fax: 780-427-2039, susan.taylor@gov.ab.ca
Director, Communications, John Tuckwell
780-415-6490, Fax: 780-422-3071, john.tuckwell@gov.ab.ca

Office of the Child & Youth Advocate
Peace Hills Trust Tower, 10011 - 109 St., 8th Fl., Edmonton, AB T5J 3S8
780-422-6056 Fax: 780-644-8833
800-661-3446
Child & Youth Advocate (Alberta), Del Graff
780-644-8281, Fax: 780-644-8833, del.graff@gov.ab.ca
Manager, Legal Representation for Children & Youth Service, Terri Davies
780-415-8936, Fax: 780-644-7227, terri.davies@gov.ab.ca
Director, Community Partnerships & Youth Strategies, Ken Dropko
780-644-2485, Fax: 780-644-2671, ken.dropko@gov.ab.ca
Director, Research Innovation, Tim Moorhouse
780-422-3305, Fax: 780-415-5841, tim.moorhouse@gov.ab.ca
Director, Youth Strategies, Darren Joslin
780-422-5680, Fax: 780-422-5036, darren.joslin@gov.ab.ca

Aboriginal Policy & Initiatives Division
Sterling Place, 9940 - 106 St., Edmonton, AB T5K 2N2
Assistant Deputy Minister, Catherine Twinn
780-643-1157, Fax: 780-422-5415, catherine.twinn@gov.ab.ca
Director, Intergovernmental Initiatives, Mary Berube
780-422-4781, Fax: 780-422-6642, mary.berube@gov.ab.ca
Director, Business Strategies, Bree Claude
780-638-4115, Fax: 780-644-2646, bree.claude@gov.ab.ca
Director, Governance Services, Mary Jane Graham
780-422-5873, Fax: 780-644-6880, maryjane.graham@gov.ab.ca

Child Intervention Program Quality & Supports Division
Sterling Place, 9940 - 106 St., Edmonton, AB T5K 2N2
780-422-0305 Fax: 780-422-5415

Assistant Deputy Minister, Mark Hattori
780-415-1548, Fax: 780-422-5415, mark.hattori@gov.ab.ca
Director, Field Operations Support, Fred Anderson
780-644-6990, Fax: 780-422-5415, fred.anderson@gov.ab.ca
Director, Service Analysis, Maureen Mooney
780-422-5674, Fax: 780-422-5415,
maureen.mooney@gov.ab.ca
Director, Child, Youth, & Family Enhancement Act, David Wilson
780-422-4441, Fax: 780-422-5415, david.wilson@gov.ab.ca

Community Strategies & Support Division
Sterling Place, 9940 - 106 St., 10th Fl., Edmonton, AB T5K 2N2
780-427-6428 Fax: 780-422-9045

Assistant Deputy Minister, Karen Ferguson
780-427-6428, Fax: 780-422-9045,
karen.ferguson@gov.ab.ca
Director, Community Partnerships, Ken Dropko
780-644-2485, Fax: 780-644-2671, ken.dropko@gov.ab.ca
Director, Family Support for Children with Disabilities (FSCD), Laura Alcock
780-427-5869, Fax: 780-415-0651, laura.alcock@gov.ab.ca
Director, Child Development, Lynn Jerchel
780-422-4538, Fax: 780-427-1258, lynn.jerchel@gov.ab.ca

Ministry Support Services Division
Sterling Place, 9940 - 106 St., 12th Fl., Edmonton, AB T5K 2N2
780-415-6047 Fax: 780-422-6642

Assistant Deputy Minister, Gord Johnston
780-415-6594, Fax: 780-422-6642, gord.johnston@gov.ab.ca
Executive Director & Chief Information Officer, Information Strategies, Lorie Baddock
780-643-1727, Fax: 780-422-0562, lorie.baddock@gov.ab.ca
Director, Collaborative Policy & Analysis, Stephen Gauk
780-422-7960, Fax: 780-415-5841, stephen.gauk@gov.ab.ca
Senior Manager, Legal Services, Chris Welligan
780-427-7212, Fax: 780-422-0912, chris.welligan@gov.ab.ca
Manager, Administrative & Facility Services, Frances Cearns
780-427-7639, Fax: 780-644-4884,
frances.cearns@gov.ab.ca
Senior Financial Officer, Financial Strategies, Shehnaz Hutchinson
780-415-8911, Fax: 780-427-4067,
shehnaz.hutchinson@gov.ab.ca

Child & Family Services Regional Authorities
Services for Alberta's families & children are delivered from ten Child & Family Services Authorities located in regions throughout the province.
Region #1, Southwest Alberta, Chief Executive Officer, Lonnie Slezina
403-381-5570, Fax: 403-381-5791, lonnie.slezina@gov.ab.ca, Other Communications: Region #1 Main Phone: 403-381-5543
Note: Web Site: www.southwestalbertacfsa.gov.ab.ca
Region #2, Southeast Alberta, Chief Executive Officer, Bryan Heninger
403-529-3756, Fax: 403-528-5244,
bryan.heninger@gov.ab.ca, Other Communications: Region #2 Main Phone: 403-529-3753
Region #3, Calgary & Area, Chief Executive Officer, Bonnie Johnston
403-297-6100, Fax: 403-297-7214,
bonnie.johnston@gov.ab.ca
Region #4, Central Alberta, Chief Executive Officer, David Tunney
403-341-8655, Fax: 403-755-6184, david.tunney@gov.ab.ca, Other Communications: Region #4 Main Phone: 403-341-8642
Note: Web Site: www.centralalbertacfsa.gov.ab.ca
Region #5, East Central Alberta, Chief Executive Officer, Brian Holden
780-662-7055, Fax: 780-662-3854, brian.holden@gov.ab.ca, Other Communications: Region #5 Main Phone: 780-385-7160
Note: Web Site: www.eastcentralalbertacfsa.gov.ab.ca
Region #6, Edmonton & Area, Chief Executive Officer, Carole Anne Patenaude
780-415-2291, Fax: 780-422-6864,
caroleanne.patenaude@gov.ab.ca, Other Communications: Region #6 Main Phone: 780-427-2250
Note: Web Site: www.edmontonandareacfsa.gov.ab.ca
Region #7, North Central Alberta, Chief Executive Officer, Dr. David Rideout
780-305-2435, Fax: 780-305-2444, david.rideout@gov.ab.ca, Other Communications: Region #7 Main Phone: 780-305-2440
Region #8, Northwest Alberta, Chief Executive Officer, Rick Flette
780-538-5248, Fax: 780-538-5137, rick.flette@gov.ab.ca, Other Communications: Region #8 Main Phone: 780-538-5122
Region #9, Northeast Alberta, Chief Executive Officer, Ron Benson
780-743-7462, Fax: 780-743-7474, ron.benson@gov.ab.ca
Region #10, Métis Settlement, Chief Executive Officer, Lillian Parenteau
780-415-6170, Fax: 780-415-0177,
lillian.parenteau@gov.ab.ca, Other Communications: Region #10 Main Phone: 780-427-1033

Alberta Culture & Community Services

Communications Branch, Standard Life Centre, 10405 Jasper Ave., 7th Fl., Edmonton, AB T5J 4R7
780-427-6530
800-232-7215
ccs.Communications@gov.ab.ca
www.culture.alberta.ca
TTY: 780-427-9999

Alberta's Culture & Community Services supports arts & cultural industries throughout Alberta. Financial assistance is provided to the non-profit sector, film, the arts, & heritage.
The Ministry also supports human rights legislation to protect Albertans from discrimination.
The following agencies, boards, & commissions report directly to the Minister: Alberta Foundation for the Arts, Alberta Historical Resources Foundation, Alberta Human Rights Commission, Government House Foundation, Historic Resources Fund, & Human Rights Education & Multiculturalism Fund.
Acts Administered:
Alberta Foundation for the Arts Act
Emblems of Alberta Act
Film & Video Classification Act
First Nations Sacred Ceremonial Objects Repatriation Act
Foreign Cultural Property Immunity Act
Government House Act
Government Organization Act
Historical Resources Act
Holocaust Memorial Day & Genocide Remembrance Act
Alberta Human Rights Act
Queen Elizabeth II Golden Jubilee Recognition Act
Recreation Development Act
Minister, Culture & Community Services, Hon. Heather Klimchuk
780-422-3559, Fax: 780-427-7729
Social Media:
www.facebook.com/pages/Heather-Klimchuk/187574883149

Associated Agencies, Boards & Commissions:
• Alberta Foundation for the Arts (AFA)
10708 - 105 Ave.
Edmonton, AB T5H 0A1
780-427-9968 -310-0000
www.affta.ab.ca
The Foundation supports the development of arts throughout Alberta. It works to maintain & expand the AFA art collection for Albertans.
• Alberta Historical Resources Foundation (AHRF)
Old St. Stephen's College
8820 - 112 St.
Edmonton, AB T6G 2P8
780-431-2300 Fax: 780-427-5598
www.culture.alberta.ca/ahrf
Established through the Historical Resources Act, The Alberta Historical Resource Foundation raises awareness of Alberta's heritage.
• Alberta Human Rights Commission
Northern Regional Office, Standard Life Centre
#800, 10405 Jasper Ave.
Edmonton, AB T5J 4R7
780-427-7661 Fax: 780-427-6013 800-232-7215 TTY: 780-427-1597
humanrights@gov.ab.ca;
educationcommunityservices@gov.ab.ca
www.albertahumanrights.ab.ca
Other Communication: Education & Community Services, Phone: 403-297-8407
The Alberta Human Rights Act established the Alberta Human Rights Commission. In accordance with the Alberta Human Rights Act, the Commission works to foster equality & to reduce discrimination.
The address of the Alberta Human Rights Commission's Southern Regional Office is as follows: #310, 525 - 11th Ave. SW., Calgary, AB T2R 0C9. The confidential inquiry line for the Southern Regional Office is 403-297-6571. TTY service is also available for persons who are deaf or hard of hearing. The TTY number in Calgary is 403-297-5639. The fax number for the Southern Regional Office ix 403-297-6567.
• Government House Foundation
12845 - 102 Ave. NW
Edmonton, AB T5N 0M6
780-427-2281 Fax: 780-422-6508
governmenthouseinfo@gov.ab.ca
Established in 1976, the Government House Foundation consist of a board of up to 12 directors. The Lieutenant Governor appoints the directors who are responsible to the Minister of Culture & Community Spirit.
The board of directors is engaged in the following activities: advising the Minister of Culture & Community Spirit about the preservation of Government House, raising public awareness of the architectural development of Government House, & soliciting property for display in Government House.
• Historic Resources Fund
c/o Culture & Community Spirit, Old St. Stephen's College
8820 - 112 St.
Edmonton, AB T6G 2P8
780-431-2300 Fax: 780-427-5598
Under the authority of the Historical Resources Act, the Historic Resource Fund carries out its purpose to protect, enhance, display, & promote the historic resources of Alberta. It funds programs that are designated by the Lieutenant Governor.
• Human Rights Education & Multiculturalism Fund (HREM Fund)
Human Rights & Citizenship Branch, Standard Life Centre
#800, 10405 Jasper Ave.
Edmonton, AB T5J 4R7
780-427-4001 Fax: 780-422-3563 800-232-7215 TTY: 780-427-1597
educationcommunityservices@gov.ab.ca
www.culture.alberta.ca/hremf
Other Communication: TTY service in Calgary: 403-297-5639
Under the authority of the Alberta Human Rights Act, Chapter A-25.5, Revised Statutes of Alberta 2000, the Human Rights Education & Multiculturalism Fund carries out its purpose. The Fund promotes understanding of the racial & cultural composition of Alberta. Information is provided to Albertans about their responsibilities & rights under the Alberta Human Rights Act.
The Human Rights Education & Multiculturalism Fund does not have any employees. The Fund is administered by the staff of the Department of Culture & Community Spirit. An annua allocation is received from the Alberta Lottery Fund to support equality, fairness, & inclusion in the community.

Culture, Community, & Voluntary Services Division
Standard Life Centre, 9th Fl., 10405 Jasper Ave., 9th Fl., Edmonton, AB T5J 4R7
Assistant Deputy Minister, Culture, Community, & Voluntary Services Division, Tom Thackeray
780-415-5852, Fax: 780-422-2891, tom.thackeray@gov.ab.ca
Alberta Film Commissioner, Alberta Film, Jeff Brinton
780-422-8581, Fax: 780-422-8582, jeff.brinton@gov.ab.ca, Other Communications: Alberta Film, Toll-Free Phone: 1-888-813-1738
Executive Director, Arts Branch, Jeffrey Anderson
780-415-0283, Fax: 780-422-9132,
jeffrey.anderson@gov.ab.ca
Executive Director, Community Engagement & Inclusion Branch, Carol Moerth
780-415-4874, Fax: 780-427-4155, carol.moerth@gov.ab.ca
Director, Voluntary Sector Services Branch, Pat Blakney
780-422-1724, Fax: 780-427-4155, pat.blakney@gov.ab.ca
Director, Community Development Branch, Dianne Johnson
780-963-2281, Fax: 780-415-8594,
dianne.johnson@gov.ab.ca
Legal Counsel, Human Rights & Citizenship Branch, Janice Ashcroft
403-297-7419, Fax: 403-297-6567,
janice.ashcroft@gov.ab.ca

Heritage Division
Old St. Stephen's College, 8820 - 112 St., Edmonton, AB T6G 2P8
Assistant Deputy Minister, David Link
780-431-2313, Fax: 780-427-5598, david.link@gov.ab.ca
Executive Director & Provincial Archivist, Provincial Archives of Alberta, Leslie Latta-Guthrie
780-427-0058, Fax: 780-427-4646,
leslie.latta-guthrie@gov.ab.ca, Other Communications: Provincial Archives of Alberta, Phone: 780-427-1750
Executive Director, Royal Tyrrell Museum of Palaeontology, Andy Neuman
403-820-6201, Fax: 403-823-7131,
andrew.neuman@gov.ab.ca
Executive Director, Royal Alberta Museum, Chris Robinson
780-453-9168, Fax: 780-454-6629, chris.robinson@gov.ab.ca
Executive Director, Historic Sites & Museums, Catherine Whalley
780-431-2306, Fax: 780-427-5598,
catherine.whalley@gov.ab.ca
Director, Policy & Program Coordination, Marilyn Kimura
780-431-2314, Fax: 780-427-5598,
marilyn.kimura@gov.ab.ca

Hong Kong
Alberta Government Office, Admiralty Centre, Tower Two, #1004, 18 Harcourt Rd., Hong Kong
www.alberta.org.hk
Other Communication: International Number: 011-852-2528-4729; International Fax: 011-852-2529-8115
Trade Director, Alberta Hong Kong Office, Chris Liu
chris.liu@alberta.org.hk
Trade Director, Christopher Liu
chris.liu@alberta.org.hk, Other Communications: International Number: 011-852-2528-4729

Alberta Education

Commerce Place, 10155 - 102 St., 7th Fl., Edmonton, AB T5J 4L5
780-427-7219 Fax: 780-427-0591
-310-0000
www.education.alberta.ca
Other Communication: Media Inquiries, Phone: 780-422-4495
From Early Childhood Services (ECS) to Grade 12, Alberta Education supports students, parents, teachers & administrators. The Ministry is engaged in the following activities: developing & evaluating curriculum; setting standards; assessing outcomes; supporting the education of special needs, Aboriginal, & francophone students; developing & certifying teachers; funding & supporting school boards; overseeing educational policies & regulations; & managing the Alberta Initiative for School Improvement (AISI).
Acts Administered:
Alberta School Boards Association Act
Financial Administration Act
Freedom of Information & Protection of Privacy Act
Government Accountability Act
Government Organization Act
Northland School Division Act
Remembrance Day Act
School Act & Regulations
Teachers' Pension Plans Act & Regulations
Teaching Profession Act & Regulations
Minister, Education, Hon. Thomas Lukaszuk
780-427-5010, Fax: 780-427-5018
Social Media: www.twitter.com/lukaszukml, www.facebook.com/Thomas-A-Lukaszuk/662272836
Deputy Minister, Keray Henke
780-427-3659, Fax: 780-427-7733, keray.henke@gov.ab.ca
Director, Communications, Kathy Telfer
780-427-5423, Fax: 780-427-0591, kathy.telfer@gov.ab.ca
Parliamentary Assistant, Janice Sarich
780-415-9462, Fax: 780-415-0951, keray.henke@gov.ab.ca

Associated Agencies, Boards & Commissions:
• Council on Alberta Teaching Standards (COATS)
10044 - 108 St.
Edmonton, AB T5J 5E6
780-427-2045 Fax: 780-422-4199
www.teachingquality.ab.ca
Established by a Ministerial Order in 1985, the Council on Alberta Teaching Standards offers recommendations related to teaching to the Minister. Advice is provided on matters such as teacher certification, teacher preparation, & practice review.

Education Program Standards & Assessment Division
Commerce Place, 10155 - 102 St., 7th Fl., Edmonton, AB T5J 4L5
Assistant Deputy Minister, Ellen Hambrook
780-427-7484, Fax: 780-422-1400, ellen.hambrook@gov.ab.ca
Executive Director, French & International Education Services Sector, Gilbert Guimont
780-422-7793, Fax: 780-422-1947, gilbert.guimont@gov.ab.ca
Executive Director, Division Planning & Standards Sector, Paul Lamoureux
780-422-3183, Fax: 780-422-9735, paul.lamoureux@gov.ab.ca
Executive Director, Learner Assessment Sector, John Rymer
780-427-0010, Fax: 780-422-4200, john.rymer@gov.ab.ca
Communications Coordinator, Curriculum Sector, Wendy Narang
780-422-5631, Fax: 780-422-3745, wendy.narang@gov.ab.ca

Learning Supports & Information Management Division
Commerce Place, 10155 - 102 St., 7th Fl., Edmonton, AB T5J 4L5
Assistant Deputy Minister, Dean Lindquist
780-415-6092, Fax: 780-415-8938, dean.lindquist@gov.ab.ca
Executive Director, Learning & Program Resources Sector, Rick Baker
780-427-5277, Fax: 780-422-0130, rick.baker@gov.ab.ca
Executive Director, Capital Planning Sector, Laura Cameron
780-427-0289, Fax: 780-644-2284, laura.cameron@gov.ab.ca
Executive Director, FNMI & Field Services Sector, Rick Hayes
780-427-5378, Fax: 780-422-9682, rick.hayes@gov.ab.ca
Executive Director, Information & Technology Management Sector, Aziza Jivraj
780-427-3880, Fax: 780-422-0880, aziza.jivraj@gov.ab.ca
Executive Director, Program Delivery Sector, Lorraine Stewart
780-422-6554, Fax: 780-643-1188, lorraine.stewart@gov.ab.ca
Director, School Technology Sector, Bette Gray
780-427-1509, Fax: 780-415-1091, bette.gray@gov.ab.ca

People & Research Division
Commerce Place, 10155 - 102 St., Edmonton, AB T5J 4L5
Assistant Deputy Minister, Carol McLean
780-644-3578, Fax: 780-638-3272, carol.mclean@gov.ab.ca
Director, Teacher Relations Branch, Doug Aitkenhead
780-643-1277, Fax: 780-638-4197, doug.aitkenhead@gov.ab.ca
Director & Team Lead, Strategic Planning, Workplace Planning & Development Branch, Mark Bevan
780-644-3579, Fax: 780-644-3591, mark.bevan@gov.ab.ca
Director, Human Resources Branch, Doug German
780-644-7503, Fax: 780-422-5362, doug.german@gov.ab.ca
Director, School Research & Improvement Branch, Dr. Dianna Millard
780-427-7882, Fax: 780-415-2481, dianna.millard@gov.ab.ca
Director & Registrar, Professional Standards Branch, Marc Prefontaine
780-427-2045, Fax: 780-422-4199, marc.prefontaine@gov.ab.ca

Strategic Services Division
Commerce Place, 10155 - 102 St., 7th Fl., Edmonton, AB T5J 4L5
Assistant Deputy Minister, Michael Walter
780-427-3663, Fax: 780-422-0408, michael.walter@gov.ab.ca
Executive Director, Policy & Planning, Don Napier
780-427-9998, Fax: 780-422-5126, don.napier@gov.ab.ca
Executive Director, Strategic Financial Services Sector, Gene Williams
780-415-1489, Fax: 780-422-6996, gene.williams@gov.ab.ca
Director, Strategic Business Services Sector, Hank Koning
780-422-3279, Fax: 780-415-6546, hank.koning@gov.ab.ca

Alberta Office of the Chief Electoral Officer / Elections Alberta (OOCEO)

11510 Kingsway Ave., 1st Fl., Edmonton, AB T5G 2Y5
780-427-7191 Fax: 780-422-2900
info@electionsalberta.ab.ca
www.electionsalberta.ab.ca
The Office of the Chief Electoral Officer is engaged in the following activities: administering impartial, open, & fair elections; offering necessary information to political participants & voters; providing a high standard of customer service; training election officials; & adopting best practices & new technologies.
Acts Administered:
Election Act
Election Finances & Contributions Disclosure Act
Senatorial Selection Act
Chief Electoral Officer, O. Brian Fjeldheim
780-427-1035, Fax: 780-422-2900, brian.fjeldheim@elections.ab.ca
Deputy Chief Electoral Officer, Lori McKee-Jeske
780-427-6860, Fax: 780-422-2900, lori.mckeejeske@elections.ab.ca
Director, Information Technology & Geomatics, Keila Johnston
780-643-1105, Fax: 780-422-2900, keila.johnston@elections.ab.ca
Director, Election Finances, CJ Rhamey
780-427-1036, Fax: 780-422-2900, cj.rhamey@elections.ab.ca
Director, Election Operations & Communications, Drew Westwater
780-427-1038, Fax: 780-422-2900, drew.westwater@elections.ab.ca

Alberta Employment & Immigration

Minister's Office, Legislature Building, #418, 10800 - 97 Ave., Edmonton, AB T5K 2B6
780-644-5135
866-644-5135
eii.communications@gov.ab.ca
www.employment.alberta.ca
Employment & Immigration has the following key responsibilities: promoting labour force development; training Albertans to find employment; helping Albertans in need, with benefits & child support services; ensuring safe, healthy, & fair workplaces; assisting the Government of Alberta with immigration & interprovincial labour mobility policy; & supportitng the integration of new Albertans.
Under Premier Redford, Employment & Immigration became the responsibility of the new Ministry of Human Services.
Acts Administered:
Administrative Procedures Act
Adult Interdependent Relationships Act
Agrologists Act
Architects Act
Consulting Engineers of Alberta Act
Dower Act
Energy Resources Conservation Act
Engineering, Geological & Geophysical Professions Act
Expropriation Act
Family Law Act
Financial Administration Act
Income & Employment Supports Act
Interjurisdictional Support Orders Act
Interpretation Act
Land Agents Licensing Act
Land Surveyors Act
Land Titles Act
Maintenance Enforcement Act
Métis Settlements Act
Métis Settlements Land Protection Act
Occupational Health & Safety Act
Professional & Occupational Associations Registration Act
Regulated Accounting Profession Act
Regulated Forestry Profession Act
Surface Rights Act
Surveys Act
Veterinary Profession Act
Minister, Human Services; Government House Leader, Hon. David Hancock, QC
780-643-6210, Fax: 780-643-6214, dave.hancock@gov.ab.ca
Social Media: www.twitter.com/DaveHancockMLA
Director, Communications, Janice Schroeder
780-427-5649, Fax: 780-427-5988, janice.schroeder@gov.ab.ca
Parliamentary Assistant, Teresa Woo-Paw
780-415-9479, Fax: 780-442-2167
Deputy Minister, Shirley Howe
780-427-8305, Fax: 780-422-9205, shirley.howe@gov.ab.ca

Associated Agencies, Boards & Commissions:
• Alberta Labour Relations Board (ALRB)
Labour Building
10808 - 99 Ave., 5th Fl.
Edmonton, AB T5K 0G5
780-422-5926 Fax: 780-422-0970 800-463-2572
alrbinfo@lab.gov.ab.ca
www.alrb.gov.ab.ca
The independent & impartial tribunal is involved in the application & interpretation of labour lawa in Alberta. The Alberta Labour Relations Board administers the Labour Relations Code to handle disputes between trade unions & employers.
• Alberta Workers' Compensation Board (WCB)
9912 - 107 St.
Edmonton, AB T5K 2S5
780-498-3999 Fax: 780-427-5863 866-922-9221 TTY: 780-498-7895
www.wcb.ab.ca
Other Communication: Calgary, Phone: 403-517-6000; Toll-Free Phone, outside Alberta: 1-800-661-9608; Claims, Toll-Free Fax: 1-800-661-1993
The independent organization manages workers' compensation insurance, based on legislation. The Alberta Workers' Compensation Board compensates injured workers for costs such as lost income & health care.
• Appeals Commission for Alberta Workers' Compensation
Energy Square Building
#901, 10109 - 106th St.
Edmonton, AB T5J 3L7
780-412-8700 Fax: 780-412-8701
webmaster1@appealscommission.ab.ca
www.appealscommission.ab.ca
Other Communication: Phone, Calgary: 403-508-8800
The Appeals Commission for Alberta Workers' Compensation strives to offer an independent, fair, & timely appeals process. The Commission works to operate consistently with legislation & policy.
• Occupational Health & Safety Council (OHSC)
Labour Building
10808 - 99 Ave., 9th Fl.
Edmonton, AB T5K 0G5
780-415-8690 866-415-8690
Under the Occupational Health & Safety Act, the Occupational Health & Safety Council advises the Minister about matters related to the health & safety of Alberta's workers. Nine members serve on the Council, including the chair & representatives from employers, employees, & the public.

Delivery Services Division
Labour Building, 10808 - 99 Ave., 10th Fl., Edmonton, AB T5K 0G5
780-415-2946 Fax: 780-427-7548
Assistant Deputy Minister, Ken Shewchuk
780-415-2583, Fax: 780-427-7548, ken.shewchuk@gov.ab.ca
Executive Director, Centrally Delivered Services, Chuck Conroy
780-644-1911, Fax: 780-415-1667, chuck.conroy@gov.ab.ca

Regional Director, Calgary Region, Caroline Fairbrother
403-297-5334, Fax: 403-297-5988,
caroline.fairbrother@gov.ab.ca
Regional Director, Central Region, Clay Buchanan
403-340-7001, Fax: 403-340-7057
Regional Director, Edmonton Region, Elvin Collins
780-422-6993, Fax: 780-422-5125, elvin.collins@gov.ab.ca
Regional Director, Northeast Region, Bev Parker
780-623-5102, Fax: 780-623-5355, bev.parker@gov.ab.ca
Regional Director, Northwest Region, Nancy Schneider
780-324-3239, Fax: 780-324-3235,
nancy.schneider@gov.ab.ca
Regional Director, South Region, Noelle Becker
403-345-7979, Fax: 403-345-4915, noelle.becker@gov.ab.ca

Immigration Division
Labour Building, 10808 - 99 Ave., 9th Fl., Edmonton, AB T5K 0G5
780-638-3531 Fax: 780-422-2889
The Immigration Division oversees immigration policies & programs in Alberta.
Assistant Deputy Minister, Maryann Everett
780-422-9493, Fax: 780-422-2889,
maryann.everett@gov.ab.ca
Executive Director, Immigration Policy & Programs, Percy Cummings
780-415-8945, Fax: 780-643-0905,
percy.cummings@gov.ab.ca
Director, Strategic Marketing, Danielle Comeau
780-427-0528, Fax: 780-644-3329,
danielle.comeau@gov.ab.ca
Director, Alberta Immigrant Nominee Program, Brad Trefan
780-427-6496, Fax: 780-427-6560, brad.trefan@gov.ab.ca

Strategic Corporate Services Division
Labour Building, 10808 - 99 Ave., 10th Fl., Edmonton, AB T5K 0G5
780-427-6765 Fax: 780-427-5971
The Strategic Services & Information Division consists of Data Development & Evaluation, Human Resources, & Finance, Organizational Planning, & Administration.
Assistant Deputy Minister, Alex Stewart
780-427-6765, Fax: 780-427-5971, alex.stewart@gov.ab.ca a
Executive Director & Senior Financial Officer, Finance, Organizational Planning, & Administration, Shelley Engstom
780-427-0034, Fax: 780-422-2861,
shelley.engstrom@gov.ab.ca
Executive Director, Data Development & Evaluation, Yvonne McFadzen
780-427-9644, Fax: 780-422-5070,
yvonne.mcfadzen@gov.ab.ca
Executive Director, Human Resources, Rick Nisbet
780-427-7274, Fax: 780-427-3937, rick.nisbet@gov.ab.ca
Director, Appeals Secretariat, Kevin Young
780-422-9079, Fax: 780-422-1088, kevin.young@gov.ab.ca

Workforce Supports Division
Labour Building, 10808 - 99 Ave., 10th Fl., Edmonton, AB T5K 0G5
780-722-0010
The Workforce Supports Division features the following components: Alberta Works Programs, Business Innovations, & Labour Force Development.
Assistant Deputy Minister, Shannon Marchand
780-422-0194, Fax: 780-422-1651,
shannon.marchand@gov.ab.ca
Executive Director, Labour Force Development, Marilynn Boehm
780-422-1851, Fax: 780-422-6400,
marilynn.boehm@gov.ab.ca
Executive Director, Alberta Works Programs, Mic Farrell
780-427-0158, Fax: 780-422-0032, mic.farrell@gov.ab.ca
Director, Business Innovations, Brian Payne
780-427-6678, Fax: 780-422-6768, brian.payne@gov.ab.ca

Workplace Standards Delivery Division
Labour Building, 10808 - 99 Ave., 9th Fl., Edmonton, AB T5K 0G5
780-415-9533
Other Communication: Employment Standards Inquiries, Toll-Free Phone: 1-877-427-3731
The Division includes occupational health & saftety & employment standards program delivery.
Assistant Deputy Minister, Andrew Sharman
780-643-1391, Fax: 780-422-0014,
andrew.sharman@gov.ab.ca
Executive Director, Occupational Health & Safety, Brent McEwan
780-415-0603, Fax: 780-644-1508, brent.mcewan@gov.ab.ca
Executive Director, Employment Standards, Eric Reitsma
780-422-5932, Fax: 780-644-5424, eric.reitsma@gov.ab.ca

Workplace Standards Policy Division
Labour Building, 10808 - 99 Ave., 8th Fl., Edmonton, AB T5K 0G5
780-415-9057 Fax: 780-644-2100
Assistant Deputy Minister, Workplace Standards Policy Division, Dan Kennedy
780-415-0458, Fax: 780-644-2100, dan.kennedy@gov.ab.ca
Executive Director, Workplace Policy, Legislation, & Program Development, Tim Thompson
780-415-0527, Fax: 780-422-0014, tim.thompson@gov.ab.ca
Director, Occupational Health & Safety Program Development & Research, Sharon Chadwick
780-422-8185, Fax: 780-422-0014,
sharon.l.chadwick@gov.ab.ca
Director, Labour Mediation Services, Bertha Greenstein
780-415-0530, Fax: 780-427-6327,
bertha.greenstein@gov.ab.ca
Director, Occupational Health & Safety Policy & Legislation, Yan Lau
780-415-0595, Fax: 780-422-0014, yan.lau@gov.ab.ca
Director, Professions & Occupations & Land Agent Licensing, Adrian Pritchard
780-422-3740, Fax: 780-423-7173,
adrian.pritchard@gov.ab.ca
Director, Labour Relations Policy & Legislation, Myles Morris
780-643-0609, Fax: 780-638-4366, myles.morris@gov.ab.ca

Alberta Energy

North Petroleum Plaza, 9945 - 108 St., Edmonton, AB T5K 2G6
780-427-8050 Fax: 780-422-0698
-310-0000
Library.Energy@gov.ab.ca
www.energy.gov.ab.ca
TTY: 780-427-9999
Other Communication: Calgary, Phone: 403-297-8955; TTY Toll-Free: 1-800-232-7215; Library Services, Phone: 780-415-0351

Alberta Energy is responsible for the development of Alberta's non-renewable resources & renewable energy. Non-renewable resources include natural gas, conventional oil & oil sands, coal, & minerals. Renewable resources include wind, solar, geothermal, & hydro.
Other responsbilities of Alberta Energy are as follows: establishing & administering fiscal & royalty systems; granting the right to explore & develop resources; promoting energy conservation; & encouraging investment to create economic prosperity.

Acts Administered:
Alberta Corporate Tax Act
Alberta Utilities Commission Act
Security Management Regulation
Coal Conservation Act
Coal Sales Act
Electric Utilities Act
Flare Gas Generation Regulation
Independent Power & Small Power Regulation
Energy Resources Conservation Act
Freehold Mineral Rights Tax Act
Gas Resources Preservation Act
Gas Utilities Act
Hydro & Electric Energy Act
Mines & Minerals Act
Ammonite Shell Regulations
CO2 Projects Royalty Credit Regulation
Exploration Regulation
Gas Processing Efficiency Assistance Regulation
Innovative Energy Technologies Regulation
Metallic & Industrial Minerals Exploration Regulation
Metallic & Industrial Minerals Regulation
Mineral Rights Compensation Regulation
Oil Sands Tenure Regulation
Natural Gas Marketing Act
Natural Gas Price Protection Act
Oil & Gas Conservation Act
Oil Sands Conservation Act
Petroleum Marketing Act
Pipeline Act
Public Utilities Act
Small Power Research & Development Act
Turner Valley Unit Operations Act
Water, Gas & Electric Companies Act

Minister, Energy, Hon. Ted Morton
780-427-3740, Fax: 780-422-0195,
minister.energy@gov.ab.ca
Social Media: www.facebook.com/TedMortonMLA
Deputy Minister, Peter Watson
780-415-8434, Fax: 780-427-7737, peter.watson@gov.ab.ca
Executive Director, Human Rsources, Dave Prince
780-427-6294, Fax: 780-422-4299, david.prince@gov.ab.ca
Director, Communications, Jay O'Neill
780-422-3667, Fax: 780-422-0698, jay.o'neill@gov.ab.ca
Parliamentary Assistant, Diana McQueen
780-415-9466, Fax: 780-415-0951

Associated Agencies, Boards & Commissions:

• Alberta Utilities Commission (AUC)
Fifth Avenue Place
425 - 1st St. SW, 4th Fl.
Calgary, AB T2P 3L8
403-592-8845 Fax: 403-592-4406 -310-0000
info@auc.ab.ca; utilitiesconcerns@auc.ab.ca
www.auc.ab.ca
Other Communication: Edmonton Office, Phone: 780-427-4901; Edmonton Office, Fax: 780-427-6970
The Alberta Utilities Commission was established by the Government of Alberta as a quasi-judicial independent agency. It is responsible for regulating the utilities sector & the electricity & natural gas markets in Alberta to ensure that the delivery of utility service is responsible, fair, & in the public interest.
• Energy Resources Conservation Board (ERCB)
#1000, 250 - 5 Ave. SW
Calgary, AB T2P 0R4
403-297-8311 Fax: 403-297-7336 855-297-8311
inquiries@ercb.ca; infoservices@ercb.ca; ADR@ercb.ca
www.ercb.ca
Other Communication: Appropriate Dispute Resolution Program, Phone: 403-297-6252; ERCB Applications Help Line, Phone: 403-297-4369; E-mail: Directive56.Help@ercb.ca
As an independent, quasi-judicial agency of the Government of Alberta, the Energy Resources Conservation Board is responsible for regulating the safe & responsible development of energy resources in Alberta. The province's energy resources include coal, natural gas, oil, & oil sands.

Clean Energy Division
Centre West Building, 10035 - 108 St., Edmonton, AB T5J 3E1
Assistant Deputy Minister, Clean Energy Division, John Donner
780-638-4141, Fax: 780-638-4134, john.donner@gov.ab.ca
Project Coordinator Manager, Regulatory Enhancement Project, Anoushka Fernandes
780-427-2364, Fax: 780-427-7737,
anoushka.m.fernandes@gov.ab.ca
Director, Business Planning & Performance, Sandra Stemmer
780-643-1438, Fax: 780-422-0800,
sandra.stemmer@gov.ab.ca
Director, Strategic Energy Secretariat, Katherine Braun
780-427-7738, Fax: 780-427-7737,
katherine.braun@gov.ab.ca

Electricity, Alternative Energy, & Carbon Capture & Storage Division
Petroleum Plaza NT, 9945 - 108 St., 6th Fl., Edmonton, AB T5K 2G6
Assistant Deputy Minister, Tim Grant
780-644-2384, Fax: 780-427-7737, tim.grant@gov.ab.ca
Executive Director, Carbon Capture & Storage Development / Energy Efficiency & Conservation Branch, Sandra Locke
780-644-7126, Fax: 780-638-3031, sandra.locke@gov.ab.ca
Executive Director, Infrastructure & Alternative Energy Branch, Ian McKay
780-422-8726, Fax: 780-427-8065, ian.mckay@gov.ab.ca
Executive Director, Electricity Markets Branch, Kathryn Wood
780-644-1232, Fax: 780-427-8065, kathryn.wood@gov.ab.ca

Oil Sands Strategy & Operations
Petroleum Plaza NT, 9945 - 108 St., 6th Fl., Edmonton, AB T5K 2G6
Chief, Oil Sands Strategy & Operations, David Morhart
780-422-1781, Fax: 780-422-0692, david.morhart@gov.ab.ca
Executive Director, Value Added & Strategy Integration, Anne Denman
780-422-9212, Fax: 780-427-8065, anne.denman@gov.ab.ca
Branch Head, External Relations & Advocacy, Lyn Bilida
780-415-6187, Fax: 780-644-3234, lyn.bilida@gov.ab.ca
Branch Head, Operations, Steve Tkalcic
780-422-9121, Fax: 780-422-0692, steve.tkalcic@gov.ab.ca
Branch Head, Business Design & Evaluation, Larry Ziegenhagel
780-427-6384, Fax: 780-422-0692,
larry.ziegenhagel@gov.ab.ca

Regulatory Enhancement Project Implementation
Petroleum Plaza NT, 9945 - 108 St., 10th Fl., Edmonton, AB T5K 2G6
Assistant Deputy Minister, John Buie
780-427-2159, Fax: 780-644-1784, john.buie@gov.ab.ca
Executive Advisor, Robert Burwood
780-427-4300, Fax: 780-644-1784,
robert.burwood@gov.ab.ca
Executive Advisor, Charleen Schmidt
780-427-2368, Fax: 780-644-1784,
charleen.schmidt@gov.ab.ca

Resource Development Policy Division
Petroleum Plaza NT, 9945 - 108 St., Edmonton, AB T5K 2G6
Assistant Deputy Minister, Resource Development Policy Division, Jennifer Steber
780-427-6370, Fax: 780-427-7737, jennifer.steber@gov.ab.ca
Executive Director, Resource Development, Sharla Rauschning
780-427-6230, Fax: 780-644-3604,
sharla.rauschning@gov.ab.ca

Branch Head, Environment & Resource Services, Audrey Murray
780-427-6383, Fax: 780-422-3044, audrey.murray@gov.ab.ca
Associate Branch Head, Economics & Markets, Matthew Foss
780-422-5059, Fax: 780-422-9677, matthew.foss@gov.ab.ca
Branch Administrator, Aboriginal Relations / Single Aboriginal Affairs Branch, Tiffany Bailey
780-427-5110, Fax: 780-644-1271, tiffany.bailey@gov.ab.ca

Revenue & Operations Division
Petroleum Plaza NT, 9945 - 108 St., 10th Fl., Edmonton, AB T5K 2G6
Assistant Deputy Minister, Revenue & Operations Division, Rhonda Wehrhahn
780-422-9430, Fax: 780-422-1123, rhonda.wehrhahn@gov.ab.ca
Branch Head, Tenure, Brenda Allbright
780-422-9393, Fax: 780-422-1123, brenda.allbright@gov.ab.ca
Branch Head, Petroleum Registry of Alberta (Edmonton / Calgary), Wally Goeres
780-415-2079, Fax: 780-422-0229, wally.goeres@gov.ab.ca
Branch Head, Compliance & Assurance, Larry McGuinness
403-297-6742, Fax: 403-297-5199, larry.mcguinness@gov.ab.ca
Branch Head, Royalty Operations, Salim Merali
780-422-9124, Fax: 780-427-0865, salim.merali@gov.ab.ca
Branch Head, Petroleum Marketing & Valuation, & Site Services, Gale Robins
403-297-5460, gale.robins@gov.ab.ca
Branch Head, Coal & Mineral Development, Gary V. White
780-415-0349, Fax: 780-422-5447, gary.v.white@gov.ab.ca

Strategic Initiatives Division
Petroleum Plaza NT, 9945 - 108 St., 10th Fl., Edmonton, AB T5K 2G6
Assistant Deputy Minister, Mike Ekelund
780-422-0813, Fax: 780-427-7737, mike.ekelund@gov.ab.ca
Director, Strategic Initiatives, Menzie McEachern
780-638-4045, Fax: 780-427-7737, menzie.mceachern@gov.ab.ca

Strategic Services Division
Petroleum Plaza NT, 9945 - 108 St., 10th Fl., Edmonton, AB T5K 2G6
Assistant Deputy Minister, Strategic Services Division, Jeff Kucharski
780-638-3136, Fax: 780-427-7737, jeff.kucharski@gov.ab.ca
Director, Business Planning & Performance, Sandra Stemmer
780-643-1438, Fax: 780-422-0800, sandra.stemmer@gov.ab.ca
Branch Head, Finance & Business Services, Douglas Borland
780-427-6223, Fax: 780-422-4281, douglas.borland@gov.ab.ca
Branch Head, FOIP & Records Management Branch, Marlene Bruyere
780-644-3778, Fax: 780-644-3786, marlene.bruyere@gov.ab.ca
Branch Head, Information Management & Technology Services, Carol Anne Pasutto
780-415-2083, Fax: 780-427-5696, carolanne.pasutto@gov.ab.ca

Associated Agencies, Boards & Commissions:
• Alberta Environmental Appeals Board
Peace Hills Trust Tower
#306, 10011 - 109 St.
Edmonton, AB T5J 3S8
780-427-6207 Fax: 780-427-4693
www.eab.gov.ab.ca
The Environmental Appeals Board strives to offer fair, impartial, & efficient resolutions to matters in order to advance the protection & enhancement of the environment in Alberta.
• Alberta Recycling Management Authority (ARMA)
Scotia Tower 1
#1310, 10060 Jasper Ave.
PO Box 189
Edmonton, AB T5J 2J1
780-990-1111 Fax: 780-990-1122 888-999-8762
info@albertarecycling.ca
www.albertarecycling.ca
Other Communication: Toll-Free Fax: 1-866-990-1122; Electronics Recycling: electronics@albertarecycling.ca; Tire Recycling: tires@albertarecycling.ca; Paint: paint@albertarecycling.ca
Reporting to the Minister of Environment, the not-for-profit association manages tire, paint, & electronics recycling programs throughout Alberta.
• Alberta Used Oil Management Association (AUOMA)
Empire Building
#1008, 10080 Jasper Ave.
Edmonton, AB T5J 1V9
780-414-1510 Fax: 780-414-1519 866-414-1510
reception@usedoilrecycling.ca
www.usedoilrecycling.com/en/ab
Other Communication: Info Line (for information about the nearest Alberta Eco Centre / Collection Facility): 1-888-922-2298
The not-for-profit association encourages Albertans to return used oil, filters, & containers to collection facilities so they can be disposed of properly. The program is funded by an Environmental Handling Charge, & a Return Incentive is paid to private sector collectors.
• Beverage Container Management Board (BCMB)
#750, 10707 - 100 Ave.
Edmonton, AB T5J 3M1
780-424-3193 Fax: 780-428-4620 888-424-7671
www.bcmb.ab.ca
The Beverage Container Management Board is an alliance of the Alberta Government, municipalities, beverage manufacturers, environmental organizations, & the public. It was established in 1997 as a management board, under the Beverage Container Recycling Regulation pursuant to Section 175 of the Environmental Protection & Enhancement Act.
The Beverage Container Management Board oversees the collection & recycling of beverage containers throughout Alberta. Its policy parameters are established by the Minister of Environment. Funding is through a levy based on the returns of beverage containers.
• Environmental Response Centre
Twin Atria Bldg.
4999 - 98 Ave., 1st Fl.
Edmonton, AB T6B 2X3
780-427-2700
Other Communication: Environment Hotline (for reporting an environmental emergency or filing a complaint): 1-800-222-6514
Complaints about contraventions of the Environmental Protection & Enhancement Act are investigated.

Alberta Environment & Water (AE)

South Tower, Petroleum Plaza, 9915 - 108 St., 10th Fl., Edmonton, AB T5K 2G8
780-427-2700 Fax: 780-422-4086
-310-0000
env.infocent@gov.ab.ca
www.environment.alberta.ca
TTY: 780-427-9999
Other Communication: 24-hour Environment Hotline (to report an environmental emergency or file a complaint): 1-800-222-6514; Media Enquiries, Phone: 780-427-6267; TTY: 1-800-232-7215
Alberta Environment & Water works as a partner to protect & enhance the natural environment of Alberta.
The Minister of Environment & Water is repsonsible for the Environmental Appeals Board, & oversees the following agencies & boards: Alberta Recycling Management Authority, Alberta Used Oil Management Association, & the Beverage Container Management Board.
Acts Administered:
Climate Change & Emissions Management Act
Environmental Protection & Enhancement Act
Water Act
Minister, Environment & Water, Hon. Diana McQueen
780-427-2391, Fax: 780-422-6259
Social Media: www.twitter.com/mcqueenmla, www.facebook.com/dianamcqueenmla
Deputy Minister, Jim Ellis
780-427-6236, Fax: 780-427-0923, jim.ellis@gov.ab.ca
Director, Communications, Mark Cooper
780-427-2848, Fax: 780-427-1874, mark.cooper@gov.ab.ca

Clean Energy Division
Centre West Building, 10035 - 108 St., 8th Fl., Edmonton, AB T5J 3E1
Assistant Deputy Minister, John Donner
780-638-4141, Fax: 780-638-4134, john.donner@gov.ab.ca
Section Head, National / International Policy, Nicole Spears
780-427-4208, Fax: 780-415-1718, nicole.spears@gov.ab.ca

Corporate Division
Petroleum Plaza ST, 9915 - 108 St., 10th Fl, Edmonton, AB T5K 2G8
Assistant Deputy Minister, Al Sanderson
780-643-0890, Fax: 780-644-8469, al.sanderson@gov.ab.ca
Chief Information Officer, Office of the CIO & Information Management & Technology Branch, Roger Burns, Chief Information Officer
780-644-5065, roger.burns@gov.ab.ca
Executive Director & Senior Financial Officer, Finance & Administration Branch, Mike Dalrymple
780-427-9148, Fax: 780-427-0923, mike.dalrymple@gov.ab.ca
Director, Human Resources, George Murphy
780-427-8472, Fax: 780-644-7832, george.murphy@gov.ab.ca
Director, Corporate Performance, Larry Williams
780-644-1094, Fax: 780-638-4312, larry.williams@gov.ab.ca

Monitoring & Science Division
Petroleum Plaza ST, 9915 - 108 St., 10th Fl., Edmonton, AB T5K 2G8
Assistant Deputy Minister, Bob Barraclough
780-427-0029, Fax: 780-422-4192, bob.barraclough@gov.ab.ca
Director, Science, Evaluation & Reporting Branch, Albert Poulette
780-644-3771, Fax: 780-427-6334, albert.poulette@gov.ab.ca
Director, Data Monitoring & Validation Branch, Bob Stone
780-415-9356, Fax: 780-422-8606, bob.stone@gov.ab.ca

Operations Division
Petroleum Plaza ST, 9915 - 108 St., Edmonton, AB T5K 2G8
780-427-1335 Fax: 780-427-1335
Assistant Deputy Minister, Rick Brown
780-427-1335, Fax: 780-422-5141, rick.brown@gov.ab.ca
Director, Environmental Support & Emergency Response Team, Greg Carter
780-415-0989, Fax: 780-427-2278, greg.carter@gov.ab.ca
Director, Regional Integration Branch, Luke Pantin
780-427-2010, Fax: 780-427-2278, luke.pantin@gov.ab.ca
Team Leader, Environmental Assessment, Environmental Impact Assessmnet Group, Corinne Kristensen
780-427-9116, Fax: 780-427-9102, corinne.kristensen@gov.ab.ca
Environmental Investigation Liaison, Hanneke Brooymans
780-644-8355, Fax: 780-422-4086, hanneke.brooymans@gov.ab.ca

Policy Division
Petroleum Plaza ST, 9915 - 108 St., Edmonton, AB T5K 2G8
780-415-8183 Fax: 780-415-6492
Assistant Deputy Minister, Ernie Hui
780-415-8183, Fax: 780-415-6492, ernie.hui@gov.ab.ca
Director, Policy & Legislation Innovation Branch, Keith Leggat
780-427-2234, Fax: 780-422-4192, keith.leggat@gov.ab.ca
Director, Clean Energy Policy Branch, Roger Ramcharita
780-644-5290, Fax: 780-415-1718, roger.ramcharita@gov.ab.ca
Director, Water Policy Branch, Andy Ridge
780-638-4198, Fax: 780-442-4192, andy.ridge@gov.ab.ca
Director, Air, Land, & Waste Policy Branch, Kem Singh
780-427-7012, Fax: 780-422-4192, kem.singh@gov.ab.ca
Office Coordinator, Climate Change Secretariat, Eleanor Thibeau
780-644-6999, Fax: 780-415-1718, eleanor.thibeau@gov.ab.ca

Strategy Division
Petroleum Plaza ST, 9915 - 108 St., 10th Fl., Edmonton, AB T5K 2G8
Assistant Deputy Minister, Bev Yee
780-427-6247, Fax: 780-427-1014, bev.yee@gov.ab.ca
Director, System Management, Tom Davis
780-644-3205, Fax: 780-422-5120, tom.davis@gov.ab.ca
Director, Transboundary Water Policy, Robert Harrison
780-427-9288, Fax: 780-638-3187, robert.harrison@gov.ab.ca
Branch Head, Strategy Development & Foresight, Stephanie Clarke
780-422-1874, Fax: 780-644-7571, stephanie.clarke@gov.ab.ca
Section Head, Aboriginal Relations, Norman Calliou
780-422-7898, Fax: 780-421-0028, norman.calliou@gov.ab.ca

Alberta Office of the Ethics Commissioner

#1250, 9925 - 109 St. NW, Edmonton, AB T5K 2J8
780-422-2273 Fax: 780-422-2261
generalinfo@ethicscommissioner.ab.ca
www.ethicscommissioner.ab.ca
Established in 1992, the Office of the Ethics Commissioner for the Province of Alberta is engaged in the promotion of public confidence in the ethics of each Member of the Legislative Assembly.
Acts Administered:
Alberta Conflicts of Interest Act
Alberta Ethics Commissioner, Neil R. Wilkinson
780-422-2273, Fax: 780-422-2261, generalinfo@ethicscommissioner.ab.ca
Chief Administrative Officer, Office of the Ethics Commissioner, Glen Resler
780-422-4974, Fax: 780-422-2261, gresler@ethicscommissioner.ab.ca
Registrar, Lobbyists Act, & General Counsel, Brad Odsen, QC
780-644-3879, Fax: 780-422-2261, bodsen@ethicscommissioner.ab.ca

Alberta Finance

Terrace Building, #426, 9515 - 107 St., Edmonton, AB T5K 2C3
780-427-3035 Fax: 780-427-1147
tra.revenue@gov.ab.ca
www.finance.alberta.ca
Other Communication: Tax & Revenue Administration: 780-427-3044

Alberta Finance offers financial, economic, & fiscal policy advice to government. The Ministry also provides tax & regulatory administration to support strong government finances & to ensure that Alberta has a productive & competitive economy.

Acts Administered:
Alberta Capital Finance Authority Act
Alberta Competitiveness Act
Alberta Corporate Tax Act
Alberta Economic Development Authority Act
Alberta Heritage Savings Trust Fund Act
Alberta Income Tax Act
Alberta Investment Management Corporation (AIMCo) Act
Alberta Personal Income Tax Act
Alberta Stock Exchange Restructuring Act
Alberta Taxpayer Protection Act
Alberta Treasury Branches Act
Appropriation Act
Civil Service Garnishee Act
Credit Union Act
Electric Utilities Act
Employment Pension Plans Act
Farm Credit Stability Act
Financial Administration Act
Financial Consumers Act
Financial Sector Statutes Amendment Act, 2003
Fiscal Responsibility Act
Fuel Tax Act
Government Accountability Act
Government Fees & Charges Review Act
Government Organization Act
Hospitals Act
Income Trusts Liability Act
Insurance Act
Loan & Trust Corporations Act
Members of the Legislative Assembly Pension Plan Act
Municipal Debentures Act
Northern Alberta Development Council Act
Office of Statistics & Information Act
Pension Fund Act
Public Sector Pension Plans Act
Securities Act
Securities Transfer Act
Securities Transfer Act
Teachers' Pension Plans Act
Tobacco Tax Act
Tourism Levy Act
Unclaimed Personal Property & Vested Property Act

Minister, Finance, Hon. Ronald Liepert
780-427-8809, Fax: 780-427-5543, min.finance@gov.ab.ca
Social Media: www.facebook.com/ronliepertmla
Deputy Minister, Tim Wiles
780-427-4106, Fax: 780-427-0178, tim.wiles@gov.ab.ca
Executive Director, Human Resource Services, Rodney Yaremchuk
780-415-9109, Fax: 780-422-0421, rodney.yaremchuk@gov.ab.ca
Director, Communications, Robyn Cochrane
780-415-1541, Fax: 780-427-1147, robyn.cochrane@gov.ab.ca
Parliamentary Assistant, Cal Dallas
780-415-8673, Fax: 780-422-1671

Associated Agencies, Boards & Commissions:

• Alberta Automobile Insurance Rate Board
Canadian Western Bank Place
#2440, 10303 Jasper Ave.
Edmonton, AB T5J 3N6
780-427-5428 Fax: 780-638-4254 -310-0000
airb@gov.ab.ca
www.airb.alberta.ca
The Automobile Insurance Rate Board is engaged in the following activities: setting premiums for basic coverage; monitoring premiums for optional coverage; & reviewing & approving rating programs for new insurers.

• Alberta Capital Finance Authority (ACFA)
Canadian Western Bank Place
#2450, 10303 Jasper Ave.
Edmonton, AB T5J 3N6
780-427-9711 Fax: 780-422-2175
webacfa@gov.ab.ca
www.acfa.gov.ab.ca
Other Communication: Rate Information Line: 780-422-2632
Established in 1956, the Alberta Capital Finance Authority is a non-profit corporation that acts under the authority of the Alberta Capital Finance Authority Act (Alberta). Flexible funding for capital projects is provided by the provincial authority to Alberta's municipalities, school boards, & other local entities, at interest rates based on the cost of its borrowings.

• Alberta Investment Management Corporation (AIMCo)
1100 - 10830 Jasper Ave.
Edmonton, AB T5J 2B3
780-392-3600
inquiries@aimco.alberta.ca
www.aimco.alberta.ca
Other Communication: Toronto Office, Phone: 416-304-1160; Media Inquiries, Phone: 403-538-5645
Established as a Crown corporation in 2008, the Alberta Investment Management Corporation provides investment management services for a group of Alberta public sector funds.

• Alberta Pensions Services Corporation (APS)
5103 Windermere Blvd. SW
Edmonton, AB T6W 0S9
780-427-2782 800-661-8198
memberservices@apsc.ca; employerservices@apsc.ca; pay@apsc.ca
www.apsc.ca
Alberta Pensions Services Corporation was incorporated in 1995, under the Business Corporations Act of Alberta. The Crown Corporation administers seven statutory pension plans & two supplementary retirement plans.

• Alberta Securities Commission (ASC)
#600, 250 - 5th St. SW
Calgary, AB T2P 0R4
403-297-6454 Fax: 403-297-6156 877-355-0585
inquiries@asc.ca; media@asc.ca; complaints@asc.ca
www.albertasecurities.com
Other Communication: Commission Proceedings, E-mail: registrar@asc.ca; Investor Education, E-mail: checkfirst@asc.ca; Records & File Requests, E-mail: records.requests@asc.ca
The Alberta Securities Commission is a regulatory agency that is responsible for the administration of the Alberta Securities Act. The capital market in Alberta is regulated by the Alberta Securities Commission to protect investors.
The Alberta Securities Commission also works as a member of the Canadian Securities Administrators to coordinate & improve the regulation of Canada's capital markets.

• Alberta Teachers' Retirement Fund (ATRF)
Barnett House
11010 - 142 St. NW
Edmonton, AB T5N 2R1
780-451-4166 Fax: 780-452-3547 800-661-9582
info@atrf.com; member@atrf.com; pensioner@atrf.com
www.atrf.com
Other Communication: Employer Inquiries, E-mail: helpdesk@atrf.com
Established under the Teachers' Pension Plans Act, the Alberta Teachers' Retirement Fund has administered a pension plan for teachers employed in Alberta's school jurisdictions & charter schools since 1939.
The independent corporation also administers the Private School Teachers' Pension Plan for teachers at Alberta's private schools that have joined the plan.

• ATB Financial
9888 Jasper Ave.
Edmonton, AB T5J 1P1
403-245-8110 800-332-8383
www.atb.com
Other Communication: Privacy, Phone: 1-866-858-4175; Online Banking, Phone: 1-866-282-4932; Lost or stolen ATB Financail products, Phone: 1-800-224-3979
Established in 1938, ATB Financial has been a provincial Crown corporation since 1997. As the largest Alberta-based financial institution, ATB Financial serves people across Alberta through 165 branches, 131 agencies, & a Customer Contact Centre.

• Credit Union Deposit Guarantee Corporation (CUDGC)
#2000, 10104 - 103 St.
Edmonton, AB T5J 0H8
780-428-6680 Fax: 780-428-7571 800-661-0351
mail@cudgc.ab.ca
www.cudgc.ab.ca
Established untder the Alberta Credit Union Act, the Credit Union Deposit Guarantee Corporation is a provincial corporation. The Corporation is administered by a Board of Directors, who are appointed by the Lieutenant Governor in Council of Alberta. The Credit Union Deposit Guarantee Corporation guarantees deposits held with Alberta's credit unions & works to ensure that credit unions employ sound business practices.

• Locked-in Account Advisory Committee (LAAC)
Financial Hardship Unlocking
PO Box 982
Edmonton, AB T5J 2L8
780-427-8322
fhu@gov.ab.ca; employment.pensions@gov.ab.ca
The Locked-in Account Advisory Committee was created under the Government Organization Act. The advisory agency is accountable to the Minister of Finance & Enterprise.
The Committee provides guidance regarding applicants to the Superintendent of Pensions who request acccess to locked-in accounts.

• Northern Alberta Development Council (NADC)
Peace River Office, Provincial Building
#206, 9621 - 96 Ave.
PO Box 900-14
Peace River, AB T8S 1T4
780-624-6274 Fax: 780-624-6184 -310-0000
nadc.council@gov.ab.ca
www.nadc.gov.ab.ca
Other Communication: Bursary Information, E-mail: nadc.bursary@gov.ab.ca
The Northern Alberta Development Council focuses on the advancement of the northern economy. The Council is engaged in projects involving tourism, transportation, educational initiatives, value-added agriculture, & inter-jurisdictional projects.

Enterprise Division
Commerce Place, 10155 - 102 St., 6th Fl., Edmonton, AB T5J 4L6
Assistant Deputy Minister, Justin Riemer
780-427-6302, Fax: 780-422-0626, justin.riemer@gov.ab.ca
Executive Director, Industry Development, Kirsty Piquette
780-427-6987, Fax: 780-422-2091, kirsty.piquette@gov.ab.ca
Executive Director, Economic Development, Duane Pyear
780-427-0850, Fax: 780-422-0061, duane.pyear@gov.ab.ca
Executive Director, Regional Development, Diane Simsovic
780-427-6656, Fax: 780-422-5804, diane.simsovic@gov.ab.ca

Financial Sector Regulation & Policy (FSRP)
Terrace Building, 9515 - 107 St., 4th Fl., Edmonton, AB T5K 2C3
Asst. Deputy Minister, Financial Sector Regulation & Policy & Superintendent, Financial Institutions, Insurance, & Pensions, Mark Prefontaine
780-427-9722, Fax: 780-427-1636, mark.prefontaine@gov.ab.ca
Executive Director, Pension Policy, Ellen Nygaard
780-415-0513, Fax: 780-644-7771, ellen.nygaard@gov.ab.ca
Director, Public Sector Pension Policy, Lorna Mathews
780-427-8896, Fax: 780-644-7771, lorna.mathews@gov.ab.ca
Administrator, Financial Hardship Unlocking Program, James Skitsko
780-643-1656, Fax: 780-422-4283, james.skitsko@gov.ab.ca

Office of Budget & Fiscal Planning
Terrace Building, 9515 - 107 St., 4th Fl., Edmonton, AB T5K 2C3
Assistant Deputy Minister, Stephen LeClair
780-427-8417, Fax: 780-427-1296, stephen.leclair@gov.ab.ca
Chief Economist & Executive Director, Economics, Demography, & Public Finance, Katherine White
780-643-0980, Fax: 780-426-3951, katherine.white@gov.ab.ca
Executive Director, Tax Policy, Nancy Cuelenaere
780-427-8893, Fax: 780-426-4564, nancy.cuelenaere@gov.ab.ca
Executive Director, Budget Planning & Integration, James Forrest
780-427-8752, Fax: 780-426-4564, james.forrest@gov.ab.ca

Regulatory Review Secretariat
Terrace Building, 9515 - 107 St., 5th Fl., Edmonton, AB T5K 2C3
Director, Regulatory Review Secretariat, Mark Minenko
780-422-1736, Fax: 780-415-4860, mark.minenko@gov.ab.ca
Manager, Regulatory Review, Meenakshi Joshi
780-422-9341, Fax: 780-415-4860, meenakshi.joshi@gov.ab.ca
Manager, Regulatory Review Strategic Support, Keren Perla
780-422-3498, Fax: 780-415-4860, keren.perla@gov.ab.ca

Strategic & Business Services
Terrace Building, 9515 - 107 St., 4th Fl., Edmonton, AB T5K 2C3
780-427-3052
Assistant Deputy Minister, Darwin Bozek
780-415-9718, Fax: 780-427-1296, darwin.bozek@gov.ab.ca
Executive Director, Financial Services, Richard Isaak
780-415-9149, Fax: 780-422-2163, richard.isaak@gov.ab.ca
Director, Administrative & Information Services, Roger Mariner
780-415-9180, Fax: 780-422-7235, roger.mariner@gov.ab.ca
Director, Corporate Planning Services, Dave Olson
780-644-2614, Fax: 780-638-3128, dave.olson@gov.ab.ca
Director, Corporate Technology Services, Glen Sustrik
780-427-5741, Fax: 780-415-6416, glen.sustrik@gov.ab.ca

Tax & Revenue Administration
Sir Frederick W. Haultain Building, 9811 - 109 St., 2nd Fl., Edmonton, AB T5K 2L5
780-427-3044
Assistant Deputy Minister, Ian Ayton
780-427-9403, Fax: 780-422-0899, ian.ayton@gov.ab.ca
Executive Director, Audit, Melissa Banks
780-644-4212, Fax: 780-422-2090, melissa.banks@gov.ab.ca

Executive Director, Revenue Operations, Kent Heine
780-644-4257, Fax: 780-644-4921, kent.heine@gov.ab.ca
Executive Director, Tax Services, Angelina Leung
780-644-4064, Fax: 780-427-5074,
angelina.leung@gov.ab.ca
Executive Director, Business Technology Management, Patrick Marshall
780-644-4164, Fax: 780-644-5016,
patrick.marshall@gov.ab.ca
Director, Strategic & Client Services, Irene Chan
780-644-4171, Fax: 780-422-0899, irene.chan@gov.ab.ca

Treasury & Risk Management
Terrace Building, 9515 - 107 St., 3rd Fl., Edmonton, AB T5K 2C3
Assistant Deputy Minister, Treasury & Risk Management, Rod Matheson
780-415-0752, Fax: 780-427-2435, rod.matheson@gov.ab.ca
Executive Director, Risk Management & Insurance, Mark Day
780-644-4045, Fax: 780-422-5271, mark.day@gov.ab.ca
Executive Director, Capital Markets, Lowell Epp
780-422-4052, Fax: 780-427-2435, lowell.epp@gov.ab.ca
Executive Director, Financial Institutions Policy, James Flett
780-415-9233, Fax: 780-644-7759, james.flett@gov.ab.ca
Director, Banking & Cash Forecasting, David Hinman
780-415-9184, Fax: 780-427-0780, david.hinman@gov.ab.ca
Director, Capital Markets Policy, Marsha Manolescu
780-415-9243, Fax: 780-644-7759,
marsha.manolescu@gov.ab.ca

Alberta Health & Wellness

PO Box 1360 Main, Edmonton, AB T5J 2N3
780-427-7164 Fax: 780-427-1171
-310-0000
www.health.alberta.ca
TTY: 800-232-7215

Alberta Health & Wellness is involved in the following activities: establishing legislation, policy, & standards; supporting the health system; allocating resources; & administering provincial programs.

Acts Administered:
ABC Benefits Corporation Act
Alberta Cancer Prevention Legacy Act
Alberta Evidence Act
Alberta Health Act
Alberta Health Care Insurance Act
Charitable Donation of Food Act
Emergency Health Services Act
Emergency Medical Aid Act
Government Organization Act
Health Care Protection Act
Health Disciplines Act
Health Facilities Review Committee Act
Health Governance Transition Act
Health Information Act
Health Insurance Premiums Act
Health Professions Act
Hospitals Act
Human Tissue & Organ Donation Act
Mandatory Testing & Disclosure Act
Mental Health Act
M.S.I. Foundation Act
Nursing Homes Act
Opticians Act
Pharmacy & Drug Act
Physical Therapy Profession Act
Podiatry Act
Prevention of Youth Tobacco Use Act
Protection of Children Abusing Drugs Act
Provincial Health Authorities of Alberta Act
Public Health Act
Regional Health Authorities Act
Tobacco Reduction Act

Minister, Health & Wellness, Hon. Fred Horne
780-427-3665, Fax: 780-415-0961,
health.minister@gov.ab.ca
Social Media:
www.facebook.com/pages/Fred-Horne/19085763782
Deputy Minister, Jay Ramotar
780-422-0747, Fax: 780-427-1016, jay.ramotar@gov.ab.ca
Mental Health Patient Advocate, Fay Orr
780-422-1812, Fax: 780-422-0695, fay.orr@gov.ab.ca
Executive Director, Human Resources, F.W. (Rick) Brick
780-427-1060, Fax: 780-422-1700, rick.brick@gov.ab.ca
Director, Communications, Andy Weiler
780-427-5344, Fax: 780-427-1171, andy.weiler@gov.ab.ca

Associated Agencies, Boards & Commissions:
• Alberta Health Services (AHS)
Corporate Office, North Tower, Seventh Street Plaza
10030 - 107th St. NW, 14th Fl.
Edmonton, AB T5J 3E4
780-342-2000 Fax: 780-342-2060 888-342-2471
ahsb.admin@albertahealthservices.ca
www.albertahealthservices.ca
Other Communication: Board Office, Phone: 866-943-1120; Fax: 403-943-1124
Alberta Health Services was established in 2008, and became operational in 2009. The provincial health authority plans & delivers health services throughout Alberta.
• Health Quality Council of Alberta (HQCA)
#210, 811 - 14 St. NW
Calgary, AB T2N 2A4
403-297-8162 Fax: 403-297-8258
info@hqca.ca
www.hqca.ca
Other Communication: Edmonton Office, Phone: 780-429-3008, Fax: 780-429-0985
The Health Quality Council of Alberta is legislated under the Regional Health Authorities Act. The Council's responsibilities are set forth in the Health Quality Council of Alberta Regulation. The independent organization strives to improve the health service quality, patient safety, & performance of the health system in Alberta.
• Office of the Chief Medical Officer of Health (OCMOH)
Telus Plaza NT
10025 Jasper Ave., 24th Fl.
Edmonton, AB T5J 1S6
780-427-5263
The Office of the Chief Medical Officer of Health offers guidelines to Alberta Health Services about public health policy. The Office also provides information to the public about communicable diseases & public health programs.
The Chief Medical Officer of Health works under the authority of the Public Health Act to promote & protect the health of the people of Alberta.

Community & Population Health Division
Telus Plaza NT, 10025 Jasper Ave., 24th Fl., Edmonton, AB T5J 1S6
Assistant Deputy Minister, Margaret King
780-415-2783, Fax: 780-422-3671, margaret.king@gov.ab.ca
Executive Director, Health Protection, Dawn Friesen
780-415-2818, Fax: 780-427-1470, dawn.friesen@gov.ab.ca
Executive Director, Public Health Strategic Policy & Planning Branch, Neil MacDonald
780-415-2759, Fax: 780-422-5474,
neil.macdonald@gov.ab.ca
Executive Director, Surveillance & Assessment, Kathy Ness
780-422-2561, Fax: 780-427-1470, kathy.ness@gov.ab.ca
Executive Director, Community Health, Silvia Vajushi
780-422-1344, Fax: 780-422-6663, silvia.vajushi@gov.ab.ca

Corporate Support Division
Telus Plaza NT, 10025 Jasper Ave., 19th Fl., Edmonton, AB T5J 1S6
Assistant Deputy Minister, Martin Chamberlain
780-422-1045, Fax: 780-422-3674,
martin.chamberlain@gov.ab.ca
Director, Corporate Services, Stephen Arthur
780-415-0201, Fax: 780-427-1643,
stephen.arthur@gov.ab.ca
Executive Director, Health Care Insurance Plan Administration, Donna Manuel
780-644-3149, Fax: 780-644-1445, donna.manuel@gov.ab.ca
Executive Director, Compliance Monitoring & Risk Management Branch, Lorraine McKay
780-415-1424, Fax: 780-643-1527,
lorraine.mckay@gov.ab.ca
Legislative Counsel, Denise C. Gagnon
780-415-0230, Fax: 780-422-2512,
denise.gagnon@gov.ab.ca

Financial Accountability Division
Telus Plaza NT, 10025 Jasper Ave., 16th Fl., Edmonton, AB T5J 1S6
Assistant Deputy Minister, David Breakwell
780-415-1599, Fax: 780-422-3672,
david.breakwell@gov.ab.ca
Executive Director, Health Facilities Planning, Wayne Campbell
780-638-3546, Fax: 780-415-6442,
wayne.campbell@gov.ab.ca
Executive Director, Planning, Measuring & Reporting Branch, John Quince
780-415-1505, Fax: 780-422-2880, john.quince@gov.ab.ca
Executive Director, Financial Planning & Reporting Branches, Charlene Wong
780-427-7100, Fax: 780-422-3672,
charlene.wong@gov.ab.ca

Health Information Technology & Systems Division
Telus Plaza NT, 10025 Jasper Ave., 21st Fl., Edmonton, AB T5J 1S6
Assistant Deputy Minister & Chief Information Officer, Health Information Technology & Systems Division, Mark Brisson
780-427-1572, Fax: 780-422-5176, mark.brisson@gov.ab.ca
Executive Director, EHR Delivery Services, Susan Anderson
780-415-2492, Fax: 780-415-2289,
susan.anderson@gov.ab.ca
Executive Director, Information & Analysis, Tapan Chowdhury
780-427-4938, Fax: 780-427-1577,
tapan.chowdhury@gov.ab.ca
Executive Director, Information Systems Delivery Branch, Chris Kearney
780-415-2704, Fax: 780-415-2289, chris.kearney@gov.ab.ca
Executive Director, Information Management Branch, Sue Kessler
780-415-2788, Fax: 780-422-6663, sue.kessler@gov.ab.ca
Executive Director, Information Technology, Blaine Steward
780-415-1562, Fax: 780-644-3091,
blaine.steward@gov.ab.ca

Health Policy & Service Standards Division
Telus Plaza NT, 10025 Jasper Ave., 18th Fl., Edmonton, AB T5J 1S6
Assistant Deputy Minister, Susan A. Williams
780-644-3086, Fax: 780-415-0570,
susan.williams@gov.ab.ca
Executive Director, Clinical Advisory & Research Branch, Joan Berezanski
780-422-9325, Fax: 780-422-4482,
joan.berezanski@gov.ab.ca
Executive Director, Health Policy & Service Standards Development, Tyler James
780-422-9678, Fax: 780-422-1515, tyler.james@gov.ab.ca
Executive Director, Strategic Health & Intergovernmental Policy, Line Porfon
780-415-2762, Fax: 780-422-1515, line.porfon@gov.ab.ca

Health Workforce Division
Telus Plaza NT, 10025 Jasper Ave., 10th Fl., Edmonton, AB T5J 1S6
Assistant Deputy Minister, Glenn Monteith
780-427-1912, Fax: 780-415-8455,
glenn.monteith@gov.ab.ca
Executive Director, Labour Relations Branch, Deb Kaweski
780-415-0212, Fax: 780-415-1094, deb.kaweski@gov.ab.ca
Executive Director, Innovative Compensation, Yolanda Lackie
780-427-0380, Fax: 780-422-5208, yolanda.lackie@gov.ab.ca
Executive Director, Pharmaceutical Funding & Guidance, Steve Long
780-427-8019, Fax: 780-422-3646, steve.long@gov.ab.ca
Executive Director, Workforce Policy & Planning Branch, Linda Mattern
780-422-2720, Fax: 780-415-1094, linda.mattern@gov.ab.ca

Alberta Housing & Urban Affairs

44 Capital Blvd., 10044 - 108 St., 3rd Fl., Edmonton, AB T5J 5E6
780-422-0122
-310-0000
housing@gov.ab.ca
www.housing.alberta.ca
TTY: 800-232-7215

Housing & Urban Affairs strives to ensure safe, affordable, & sustainable housing for Albertans.
Under Premier Redford Housing & Urban Affairs became part of the new Ministry of Municipal Affairs.

Acts Administered:
Alberta Housing Act
Government Organization Act
Social Care Facilities Licensing Act

Minister, Municipal Affairs, Hon. Doug Griffiths
780-427-3744, Fax: 780-422-9550
Social Media: www.twitter.com/griffmla,
www.facebook.com/Griffs4ABsFuture?sk=app_53267368995
Deputy Minister, Marcia Nelson
780-644-5253, Fax: 780-644-5240, marcia.nelson@gov.ab.ca
Director, Communications, Dan Laville
780-643-1327, Fax: 780-644-5796, dan.laville@gov.ab.ca

Associated Agencies, Boards & Commissions:
• Gunn Centre
PO Box 130
Gunn, AB T0E 1A0
780-967-2221 Fax: 780-967-3494
Since 1941, the Gunn Centre has offered services to disadvantaged men. The Centre provides temporary accommodation & support services to help men reestablish their lives.

Homeless Support & Land Development
44 Capital Boulevard, 10044 - 108 St. 3rd Fl., Edmonton, AB T5J 5E6
780-427-4093 Fax: 780-422-8462
Assistant Deputy Minister, Lana Lougheed
780-643-0766, Fax: 780-644-8462, lana.lougheed@gov.ab.ca

Executive Director, Homeless Support & Alberta Secretariat for Action on Homelessness, Stephen Manley
403-297-7461, Fax: 403-297-6138, stephen.manley@gov.ab.ca
Director, Homeless Cross Ministry Initiatives, Barry Bezuko
780-643-0757, Fax: 780-415-9345, barry.bezuko@gov.ab.ca
Director, Land Management, Larry Laverty
780-644-5780, Fax: 780-415-9345, larry.laverty@gov.ab.ca

Housing Development & Operations
44 Capital Boulevard, 10044 - 108 St. 3rd Fl., Edmonton, AB T5J 5E6
780-643-1020 Fax: 780-422-8462
Assistant Deputy Minister, Mike Leathwood
780-643-1020, Fax: 780-422-8462, mike.leathwood@gov.ab.ca
Executive Director, Housing Development, Don Squire
780-427-5786, Fax: 780-422-5124, don.squire@gov.ab.ca
Director, Financial Monitoring & Contract Administration, Philip Henke
780-422-8157, Fax: 780-422-5124, philip.henke@gov.ab.ca
Administrator, Rent Supplement Program, Karen Butkowski
780-422-8202, Fax: 780-422-8551, karen.butkowski@gov.ab.ca

Strategic Services
44 Capital Boulevard, 10044 - 108 St. 3rd Fl., Edmonton, AB T5J 5E6
780-638-3736
Assistant Deputy Minister, Bruce McDonald
780-422-3188, Fax: 780-422-5124, bruce.mcdonald@gov.ab.ca
Chief Information Officer & Executive Director, Information Management & Technology, Dean Lussier
780-427-1751, Fax: 780-427-0418, dean.lussier@gov.ab.ca
Executive Director & Senior Financial Officer, Finance & Administrative Services, Robert Lee
780-643-1324, Fax: 780-427-0418, robert.lee@gov.ab.ca
Executive Director, Policy & Urban Affairs, Lora Pillipow
780-422-2816, Fax: 780-422-5124, lora.pillipow@gov.ab.ca
Director, Strategic Planning & Legislative Program Services, Cynthia Evans
780-422-8306, Fax: 780-422-5124, cynthia.evans@gov.ab.ca
Director, Strategic Policy & Urban Affairs, Patti Giberson
780-644-2609, Fax: 780-422-5124, patti.giberson@gov.ab.ca
Advisor, Privacy & Information, Holly Simpson
780-638-2979, Fax: 780-427-0418, holly.simpson@gov.ab.ca

Alberta Office of the Information & Privacy Commissioner

Office of the Information & Privacy Commissioner (Edmonton), #410, 9925 - 109 St., 4th Fl., Edmonton, AB T5K 2J8
780-422-6860 Fax: 780-422-5682
888-878-4044
generalinfo@oipc.ab.ca
www.oipc.ab.ca
Other Communication: Calgary Office, Phone: 403-297-2728, Fax: 403-297-2711

The Information & Privacy Commissioner has offices in Calgary & Edmonton. In Calgary, issues related to the Personal Information Protection Act are addressed. The Edmonton office handles issues under the Freedom of Information & Protection of Privacy Act & the Health Information Act.

Information & Privacy Commissioner, Frank Work
780-422-6860, Fax: 780-422-5682, fwork@oipc.ab.ca
Assistant Commissioner, Freedom of Information & Protection of Privacy Act Team (FOIP), Marilyn Mun
780-422-7617, Fax: 780-422-5682, mmun@oipc.ab.ca
Director, Legal Services, Sharon Ashmore
780-422-6860, Fax: 780-422-5682, sashmore@oipc.ab.ca
Director, Human Resources & Finance, Donna Check
780-422-9037, Fax: 780-644-6997, dcheck@oipc.ab.ca
Director, Adjudication Team, Christina Gauk
780-422-6860, Fax: 780-422-5682, cgauk@oipc.ab.ca
Director, Health Information Act Team, Brian Hamilton
780-415-6676, Fax: 780-422-5682, bhamilton@oipc.ab.ca
Director, Personal Information Protection Act Team (PIPA) - Calgary Office, Diane McLeod-McKay
403-297-6452, Fax: 403-297-2711, dmcleod-mckay@oipc.ab.ca
Director, Communications, Wayne Wood
780-644-4015, Fax: 780-422-5682, wwood@oipc.ab.ca

Alberta Infrastructure

Infrastructure Building, 6950 - 113 St., Edmonton, AB T6H 5V7
780-415-0507 Fax: 780-427-2187
-310-0000
Infra.Contact.Us.m@gov.ab.ca
www.infrastructure.alberta.ca

The Ministry supports the provision of well designed, high quality public infrastructure for the people of Aberta.

Acts Administered:
Builders' Lien Act
Government Organization Act (section 3 of schedule 1; section 4 (2) (f) & (g) & 9 of schedule 5; sections 4 to 8 of schedule 5; sections 1, 4, 5, 6-10, & 11-13 of schedule 11)
Hospitals Act (sections 28 (1) (a), 42, & 43 (h) to (j))
Land Assembly Project Area Act
Mental Health Act (section 53 (1) (c))
Nursing Homes Act (sections 6, 11, 23 (g) & (j), & 24 (l))
Post-secondary Learning Act (sections 66 (2) & (3), 67, 72 (3) & (4), 73, 80, 99 (1) (a) & (2) to (6))
Public Works Act
School Act (part 7, sections 195-206 & section 274)
Water, Gas & Electric Companies Act (section 4)
Deputy Minister, Barry Day
780-427-3835, Fax: 780-422-6565, barry.day@gov.ab.ca
Executive Director, Human Resources Branch, Dana Thompson
780-422-4623, Fax: 780-422-5138, dana.thompson@gov.ab.ca
Director, Human Resources Consulting Services, Linda Flynn
780-427-7371, Fax: 780-422-5138, linda.flynn@gov.ab.ca
Director, Communications, Bart Johnson
780-644-8596, Fax: 780-427-2187, bart.johnson@gov.ab.ca

Capital Projects Division
Infrastructure Building, 6950 - 113 St., 2nd Fl., Edmonton, AB T6H 5V7
780-427-3700
Assistant Deputy Minister, Diane Dagleish
780-422-7436, Fax: 780-422-7599, diane.dalgleish@gov.ab.ca
Executive Director, Health Facilities Branch, Brian Fedor
780-422-0616, Fax: 780-638-4158, brian.fedor@gov.ab.ca
Executive Director, Technical Services Branch, Tom O'Neill
780-422-7447, Fax: 780-422-7479, tom.o'neill@gov.ab.ca
Executive Director, Project Delivery Branch, Kent Phillips
780-422-0770, Fax: 780-422-9749, kent.phillips@gov.ab.ca
Executive Director, Learning Facilities & Alternative Procurement Branch, Guy A. Smith
780-422-7459, Fax: 780-427-5816, guy.smith@gov.ab.ca
Executive Director, Project Services Branch, Brian Soutar
780-422-7461, Fax: 780-422-9594, brian.soutar@gov.ab.ca
Director, Divisional Coordination Branch, Tania Arruda
780-638-4159, Fax: 780-422-7599, tania.arruda@gov.ab.ca

Policy & Corporate Services Division
Twin Atria Building, 4999 - 98 Ave., 3rd Fl., Edmonton, AB T6B 2X3
Assistant Deputy Minister, Alan Humphries
780-415-1386, Fax: 780-422-1070, alan.humphries@gov.ab.ca
Executive Director, Strategic Policy Branch, Arthur Arruda
780-415-8730, Fax: 780-644-1100, arthur.arruda@gov.ab.ca
Executive Director & Chief Information Officer, Information Management Branch, Ken Bainey
780-644-5114, Fax: 780-644-7028, ken.bainey@gov.ab.ca
Executive Director & Senior Financial Officer, Finance Branch, Rod Skura
780-644-1713, Fax: 780-643-0803, rod.skura@gov.ab.ca
Director, Strategic & Business Planning, Darcy Kolodnicki
780-427-8427, Fax: 780-644-1100, darcy.kolodnicki@gov.ab.ca
Director, Legislative Planning & FOIP, Nancy Mark
780-427-8469, Fax: 780-638-3497, nancy.mark@gov.ab.ca

Properties Division
Infrastructure Building, 6950 - 113 St., 3rd Fl., Edmonton, AB T6H 5V7
780-427-3881 Fax: 780-422-1389
Assistant Deputy Minister, John Enns
780-427-3875, Fax: 780-422-1389, john.enns@gov.ab.ca
Executive Director, Reality Services Branch, Dave Bentley
780-422-7489, Fax: 780-415-1641, dave.bentley@gov.ab.ca
Executive Director, Property Development Branch, Rod Dushnicky
780-422-3597, Fax: 780-422-5832, rod.dushnicky@gov.ab.ca
Executive Director, Property Management Branch - North Region, Ken Grey
780-427-9225, Fax: 780-422-0284, ken.grey@gov.ab.ca
Executive Director, Property Management Branch - South Region, George Tribe
780-427-2710, Fax: 780-422-0284, george.tribe@gov.ab.ca
Manager, Corporate Asset Management Program, Ali Ahmed-Hameed
780-644-3976, Fax: 780-427-2229, ali.ahmed-hameed@gov.ab.ca
Branch Administrator, Divisional Coordination Branch, Heidi Horne
780-422-8930, Fax: 780-422-9043, heidi.horne@gov.ab.ca

Alberta International, Intergovernmental, & Aboriginal Relations (IIR)

Commerce Place, 10155 - 102 St., 12th Fl., Edmonton, AB T5J 4G8
780-422-1510 Fax: 780-427-0699
-310-0000
www.international.alberta.ca

The ministry coordinates the province's regional, national, & global relationships. Alberta's International & Intergovernmental Relations also strives to facilitate trade & to attract investment. Another responsibility of the ministry is the management of Alberta's international offices in Beijing, Hong Kong, London, Mexico City, Munich, Seoul, Shanghai, Taipei, Tokyo, & Washington, D.C.

Acts Administered:
Constitutional Referendum Act
Government Organization Act
International Trade & Investment Agreements Implementation Act
Senatorial Selection Act
Minister, Intergovernmental, International, & Aboriginal Relations, Hon. Cal Dallas
780-643-6225, Fax: 780-643-6228
Social Media: www.facebook.com/caldallasmla
Deputy Minister, Paul Whittaker
780-427-6644, Fax: 780-423-6654, paul.whittaker@gov.ab.ca
Director, Communications, Mike Deising
780-422-2524, Fax: 780-422-2635, mike.deising@gov.ab.ca

Corporate Services
Commerce Place, 10155 - 102 St., 12th Fl., Edmonton, AB T5J 4G8
780-427-6543 Fax: 780-427-0939
Assistant Deputy Minister, Lorne Harvey
780-422-2429, Fax: 780-427-0939, lorne.harvey@gov.ab.ca
Executive Director, Human Resource Services, Georgina Riddell
780-422-1341, Fax: 780-427-1272, georgina.riddell@gov.ab.ca
Executive Director, Finance & Administration, Howard Wong
780-427-0939, Fax: 780-427-0939, howard.wong@gov.ab.ca
Director, Corporate Planning, Danielle Figura
780-644-1160, Fax: 780-644-4939, danielle.figura@gov.ab.ca
Director, FOIP, Gerry Kushlyk
780-427-9658, Fax: 780-644-4939, gerry.kushlyk@gov.ab.ca
Director, IMIT, Carol Lawrence
780-427-0269, Fax: 780-427-4625, carol.lawrence@gov.ab.ca

Intergovernmental Relations
Commerce Place, 10155 - 102 St., 12th Fl., Edmonton, AB T5J 4G8
780-427-6706 Fax: 780-427-0939
Assistant Deputy Minister, Garry Pocock
780-422-0453, Fax: 780-427-0939, garry.pocock@gov.ab.ca
Executive Director, Federal / Provincial Relations, Bruce Tait
780-422-1127, Fax: 780-427-0939, bruce.tait@gov.ab.ca
Executive Director, Social & Economic Policy, Gordon Vincent
780-415-6548, Fax: 780-427-0939, gordon.vincent@gov.ab.ca
Director, Federalism, Constitutional Federal / Provincial Relations, Heather Edwards
780-644-1223, Fax: 780-427-0939, heather.edwards@gov.ab.ca
Director, Economics & Resources, Randy Fischer
780-422-0959, Fax: 780-427-0939, randy.fischer@gov.ab.ca
Director, Social Policy, Don Kwas
780-422-0487, Fax: 780-427-0939, don.kwas@gov.ab.ca

International Relations
Commerce Place, 10155 - 102 St., 4h Fl., Edmonton, AB T5J 4L6
780-427-6543 Fax: 780-427-0699
Assistant Deputy Minister, John Cotton
780-422-2789, Fax: 780-427-0392, john.cotton@gov.ab.ca ca
Executive Director, US & International Offices, Chris Heseltine
403-297-6377, Fax: 403-297-6168, chris.heseltine@gov.ab.ca
Executive Director, Southern Hemisphere, Greg Jardine
780-427-6368, Fax: 780-422-9127, greg.jardine@gov.ab.ca
Executive Director, North Asia & Business Planning, Yvette Ng
780-422-2305, Fax: 780-427-0699, yvette.ng@gov.ab.ca
Executive Director, Advocacy, US Relations, & Mission Planning, Marvin Schneider
780-422-2332, Fax: 780-422-5486, marvin.schneider@gov.ab.ca

Alberta Justice & Attorney General

Communications, Bowker Building, 9833 - 109 St., 3rd Fl., Edmonton, AB T5K 2E8
780-427-2745
-310-0000
www.justice.alberta.ca

The mission of Alberta Justice & Attorney General is to provide a fair & safe province. Its core businesses are as follows:

promoting safe communities for the people of Alberta; facilitating access to justice; & providing legal & strategic services to government.

Acts Administered:

Administration of Estates Act
Administrative Procedures & Jurisdiction Act
Adult Interdependent Relationships Act
Age of Majority Act
Alberta Evidence Act (except section 9)
Alberta Personal Property Bill of Rights
Arbitration Act
Civil Enforcement Act
Class Proceedings Act
Commissioners for Oaths Act
Conflicts of Interest Act
Contributory Negligence Act
Court of Appeal Act
Court of Queen's Bench Act
Criminal Notoriety Act
Dangerous Dogs Act
Daylight Saving Time Act
Defamation Act
Dependants Relief Act
Devolution of Real Property Act
Expropriation Act (except sections 25 to 28 & 72)
Extra-provincial Enforcement of Custody Orders Act
Factors Act
Family Law Act
Fatal Accidents Act
Fatality Inquiries Act
Fraudulent Preferences Act
Frustrated Contracts Act
Government Organization Act, Schedule 9
Guarantees Acknowledgment Act
Innkeepers Act
Interjurisdictional Support Orders Act
International Child Abduction Act
International Commercial Arbitration Act
International Conventions Implementation Act
Interpretation Act
Interprovincial Subpoena Act
Intestate Succession Act
Judgement Interest Act
Judicature Act
Jury Act
Justice of the Peace Act
Landlord's Rights on Bankruptcy Act
Languages Act / Loi Linguistique
Legal Profession Act
Legitimacy Act
Limitations Act
Lobbyists Act
Maintenance Enforcement Act
Married Women's Act
Masters & Servants Act
Maternal Tort Liability Act
Matrimonial Property Act
Minors' Property Act
Motor Vehicle Accident Claims Act
Notaries Public Act
Oaths of Office Act
Occupiers' Liability Act
Perpetuities Act
Personal Property Security Act (Part 5 only)
Petty Trespass Act
Powers of Attorney Act
Proceedings Against the Crown Act
Provincial Court Act
Provincial Offences Procedure Act
Public Inquiries Act
Public Trustee Act
Queen's Counsel Act
Reciprocal Enforcement of Judgements Act
Recording of Evidence Act
Regulations Act
Road Building Machinery Equipment Act
Sale of Goods Act
Statute Revision Act
Survival of Actions Act
Survivorship Act
Tort-Feasors Act
Trespass to Premises Act
Trustee Act
Unconscionable Transactions Act
Victims Restitution & Compensation Payment Act
Warehouse Receipts Act
Wills Act
Young Justice Act

Minister, Justice; Attorney General; Deputy Government House Leader, Hon. Verlyn Olson
780-427-2339, Fax: 780-422-6621
Social Media: www.facebook.com/verlynolsonmla

Deputy Minister & Deputy Attorney General, Ray Bodnarek, Q.C.
780-427-5032, Fax: 780-422-9639, ray.bodnarek@gov.ab.ca

Executive Director, Human Resources, Lynn Cook
780-427-0441, Fax: 780-422-5575, lynn.cook@gov.ab.ca

Director, Issues Management, Sarah Dafoe
780-427-5032, Fax: 780-422-9639, sarah.dafoe@gov.ab.ca

Director, Communications, Jody Korchinski
780-427-6154, Fax: 780-422-7363, jody.korchinski@gov.ab.ca

Associated Agencies, Boards & Commissions:

• Alberta Review Board
Oxford Tower
10235 - 101 St., 11th Fl.
Edmonton, AB T5J 3E9
The Alberta Review Board is composed of nine members who are appointed by the lieutenant governor in council.
The Board is responsible for making or reviewing dispositions about any accused person for whom one of the following verdicts is rendered: "unfit to stand trial" or "not criminally responsible because of mental disorder". The Alberta Review Board also determines whether a person is subject to a detention order, a conditional discharge, or an absolute discharge.

• Fatality Review Board
4070 Bowness Rd. NW
Calgary, AB T3B 3R7
403-297-8123 Fax: 403-297-3429
The lieutenant governor in council appoints the members of the Fatality Review Board. The board consists of the chief medical examiner, a physician, a lawyer, & a layperson.
The Fatality Review Board reviews deaths investigated by the Office of the Chief Medical Examiner & makes recommendations to the Minister of Justice & Attorney General about whether or not a public fatality inquiry should take place in order to prevent similar deaths in the future.

• Judicial Council
Law Courts, Provincial Court of Alberta
1A Sir Winston Churchill Sq., 6th Fl.
Edmonton, AB T5J 0R2
780-427-6330 Fax: 780-427-2077
The Judical Council consists of six members. Two members of the council are appointed by the Minister of Justice, while the four other members are designated under the Judicature Act.
The role of the Judicial Council is to screen individuals to determine if they qualify for appointment to the Provincial Court of Alberta.

• Notaries Public Review Committee

780-427-5069
The Notaries Public Review Committee is made up of a member of the ministry, a member of the Law Society of Alberta, & a member of the business community. Each member is appointed by a ministerial order under the Government Organization Act.
The responsibility of the committee is to advise the Minister of Justice about appointments of lay notaries public.

• Provincial Court Nominating Committee
780-422-9625 Fax: 780-422-6613
Members of the Provincial Court Nominating Committee are appointed by the Minister of Justice. The committee makes recommendations to the Minister of Justice about appointments to the Provincial Court of Alberta.

• Rules of Court Committee
780-427-4995 Fax: 780-422-6613
The Rules of Court Committee consists of the following members: the Chief Justice of Alberta or designate; the Chief Justice of the Court of Queen's Bench or designate; the Chief Judge of the Provincial Court of Alberta or designate; two members appointed by the Minister of Justice on recommendation of the Law Society of Alberta; & one member appointed by the Minister of Justice.
Recommendations are made by the committee to the Minister of Justice about amendments to the Rules of Court made under the Court of Queen's Bench Act, the Judicature Act, or any other act.

Corporate Services Division

Bowker Building, 9833 - 109 St., 2nd Fl., Edmonton, AB T5K 2E8

Assistant Deputy Minister, Bruce M. Perry
780-427-3301, Fax: 780-422-9639, bruce.m.perry@gov.ab.ca
Executive Director, JIMS Program Support Office, Stepheen Bull
780-644-8414, Fax: 780-644-8424, stephen.bull@gov.ab.ca
Executive Director & Chief Information Officer, Barry Chatwin
780-415-6067, Fax: 780-427-6002, barry.chatwin@gov.ab.ca
Executive Director & Senior Financial Officer, Shawkat Sabur
780-427-4997, Fax: 780-422-1648, shawkat.sabur@gov.ab.ca
Director, Planning & Reporting Services, Mark Ham
780-422-2640, Fax: 780-422-2829, mark.ham@gov.ab.ca
Director, Business Services, Don Smallwood
780-427-6675, Fax: 780-427-9630, don.smallwood@gov.ab.ca

Court Services Division

Bowker Building, 9833 - 109 St., 2nd Fl., Edmonton, AB T5K 2E8

780-427-4992 Fax: 780-422-6613

Assistant Deputy Minister, Vicki Brandt
780-427-9620, Fax: 780-422-9639, vicki.brandt@gov.ab.ca
Registrar, Court of Appeal, Sue Stushnoff
780-422-7710, Fax: 780-422-7710, sue.stushnoff@gov.ab.ca
Executive Director, Edmonton Court Operations, Lorna Ross
780-422-2426, Fax: 780-422-9585, lorna.ross@gov.ab.ca
Executive Director, Regional Court Operations, Ed Towers
780-986-6903, Fax: 780-986-2429, ed.towers@gov.ab.ca
Executive Director, Planning & Business Services, Lynn Varty
780-644-8105, Fax: 780-422-9369, lynn.varty@gov.ab.ca
Director, Judicial Administration, Court of Queen's Bench, Bonita Dueck
403-297-4661, Fax: 403-297-8625, bonita.dueck@gov.ab.ca
Director, Court Technology Services, Faye Morrison
780-427-3430, Fax: 780-422-2962, faye.morrison@gov.ab.ca
Director, Alberta Law Libraries, Sonia Poulin
780-422-1011, Fax: 780-427-0397, sonia.poulin@gov.ab.ca
Senior Manager, Provincial Court, Hage Basem
403-297-3681, Fax: 403-592-4896, basem.hage@gov.ab.ca
Regional Manager, Regional Family Justice Services & the Provincial Court Civil Claims Mediation Program, Yogesh Gupta
780-980-4202, Fax: 780-980-3552, yogesh.gupta@gov.ab.ca
District Manager, South Regional Court Operations, Clara Finan
403-381-5453, Fax: 403-381-5762, clara.finan@gov.ab.ca
District Manager, Central Regional Court Operations, Ursula Owre
780-980-3550, Fax: 780-980-3551, ursula.owre@gov.ab.ca
District Manager, North Regional Court Operations, Wendy Smith
780-538-5360, Fax: 780-538-5454, wendy.smith@gov.ab.ca
Business Manager, Regional Family Justice Services, Joan Thember
780-980-7579, Fax: 780-980-3552, joan.thember@gov.ab.ca
Project Manager, Calgary Court Operations, Charles Hanna
403-297-3866, Fax: 403-297-7152, charles.hanna@gov.ab.ca
Project Manager, Regional Court Operations, Wendy Komarnisky
780-992-6832, Fax: 780-992-6831, wendy.komarnisky@gov.ab.ca
Project Manager, Edmonton Court Operations, Tracey Switzer
780-422-5210, Fax: 780-422-9585, tracey.switzer@gov.ab.ca
Manager, Provincial Court (Traffic & Civil), Linda Hawryluk
403-427-5913, Fax: 780-427-5791, linda.hawryluk@gov.ab.ca
Manager, Provincial Court (Family & Youth), Lisa Lindquist
403-297-3926, Fax: 403-297-3461, lisa.lindquist@gov.ab.ca
Manager, Transcript Management Service, Debra Watt
403-297-7392, Fax: 403-297-7034, debra.watt@gov.ab.ca

Criminal Justice Division

Bowker Building, 9833 - 109 St., 2nd Fl., Edmonton, AB T5K 2E8

Assistant Deputy Minister, Gregory Lepp, Q.C.
780-427-5046, Fax: 780-422-9639, greg.lepp@gov.ab.ca
Executive Director, Special Prosecutions (Edmonton), Sheila Brown, Q.C.
780-422-0640, Fax: 780-422-1217, sheila.brown@gov.ab.ca
Executive Director, Office of the ADM, Peter Teasdale, Q.C.
780-427-5050, Fax: 780-988-7639, peter.teasdale@gov.ab.ca
Executive Director, Appeals, Education, & Prosecution Policy Branch, Eric Tolppanen
403-297-6005, Fax: 403-297-3453, eric.tolppanen@gov.ab.ca
Chief Crown Prosecutor, Regulatory Prosecutions, Brian Caruk
780-644-2016, Fax: 780-644-2034, brian.caruk@gov.ab.ca

Justice Services Division

Bowker Building, 9833 - 109 St., Edmonton, AB T5K 2E8

Assistant Deputy Minister, Kim Armstrong
780-638-4616, Fax: 780-422-9639, kim.armstrong@gov.ab.ca
Executive Director, Maintenance Enforcement Program, Esther de Vos
780-401-7500, Fax: 780-401-7575, esther.devos@gov.ab.ca
Executive Director, Claims & Recoveries, Tracy Wyrstiuk
780-422-2610, Fax: 780-415-2200, tracy.wyrstiuk@gov.ab.ca
Chief Medical Examiner, Graeme Dowling
780-427-4987, Fax: 780-422-1265, graeme.dowling@gov.ab.ca
Chief Toxicologist, Graham Jones
780-427-4987, Fax: 780-422-1265, graham.jones@gov.ab.ca
Public Trustee, Cindy Bentz
780-422-3141, Fax: 780-422-9136, cindy.bentz@gov.ab.ca

Legal Services Division

Bowker Building, 9833 - 109 St., 2nd Fl., Edmonton, AB T5K 2E8

780-422-0500

Assistant Deputy Minister, Grant Sprague, Q.C.
780-415-2388, Fax: 780-422-9639, grant.sprague@gov.ab.ca
Executive Director, Corporate Legal Services, R. Neil Dunne
780-422-8787, Fax: 780-425-0307, r.neil.dunne@gov.ab.ca

Executive Director, Departmental Legal Services Delivery, Government Client Services Branch, Barbara Mason
780-427-9618, Fax: 780-425-0310, barb.mason@gov.ab.ca
Executive Director, Organizational Learning Office, Lorne Merryweather, Q.C.
780-422-9501, Fax: 780-427-1230, lorne.merryweather@gov.ab.ca
Executive Director, Constitutional Law, Nolan Steed, Q.C.
780-422-9653, Fax: 780-425-0307, nolan.steed@gov.ab.ca
Executive Director, Social Enhancement, Rita Sumka
780-422-3715, Fax: 780-427-5914, rita.sumka@gov.ab.ca
Chief Legislative Counsel, Peter Pagano, Q.C.
780-427-0303, Fax: 780-422-7366, peter.pagano@gov.ab.ca
Director, Divisional Planning & Management Branch, Ken Caron
780-422-8855, Fax: 780-425-0307, ken.caron@gov.ab.ca
Director, Legislative Reform, Averie McNary
780-422-8838, Fax: 780-422-8838, averie.mcnary@gov.ab.ca
Director & Corporate Counsel, Health Law, Denise Perret
780-422-8989, Fax: 780-422-2512, denise.perret@gov.ab.ca
Director, Environmental Law, Darin Stepaniuk
780-427-6121, Fax: 780-427-4343, darin.stepaniuk@gov.ab.ca
Director, Children & Youth Services, Susan Wismer
780-427-7207, Fax: 780-422-0912, susan.wismer@gov.ab.ca
Branch Head, Energy Law, Bruce Laycock
780-422-8085, Fax: 780-427-1871, bruce.laycock@gov.ab.ca

Safe Communities & Strategic Policy
Lethbridge Tower, 10707 - 100 Ave., Edmonton, AB T5J 3M1
780-644-5595 Fax: 780-644-5609
Assistant Deputy Minister, Kurt Sandstrom, Q.C.
780-422-4160, Fax: 780-422-6613, kurt.sandstrom@gov.ab.ca
Executive Director, Strategic Policy, Jeanette Fedorak
780-422-9760, Fax: 780-644-5609, jeanette.fedorak@gov.ab.ca
Director, Alberta Gang Reduction Strategy, Darren Caul
780-643-1347, Fax: 780-644-5609, darren.caul@gov.ab.ca
Director, Legislative Initiatives, Kelly Hillier
780-638-3744, Fax: 780-644-5609, kelly.hillier@gov.ab.ca
Director, Safe Communities, Gerald Lamoureux
780-644-5626, Fax: 780-638-2870, gerald.lamoureux@gov.ab.ca
Director, Long Term Framework, Marleen Poon
780-644-5733, Fax: 780-638-2870, marleen.poon@gov.ab.ca
Co-Manager, Safe Communities Innovation Fund, Doug Darwish
780-643-1346, Fax: 780-638-2870, doug.darwish@gov.ab.ca
Co-Manager, Safe Communities Innovation Fund, Bev Sochatsky
780-643-1345, Fax: 780-638-2870, bev.sochatsky@gov.ab.ca

Alberta Municipal Affairs

Communications Branch, Commerce Place, 10155 - 102 St., 18th Fl., Edmonton, AB T5J 4L4
780-427-2732 Fax: 780-422-1419
comments@gov.ab.ca
www.municipalaffairs.alberta.ca

Alberta's Ministry of Municipal Affairs is engaged in the following activities: assisting Alberta's municipalities in the provicsion of well-managed, accountable local government; managing municipal & library system boards; & administering a safety system for the construction & maintenance of equipment & buildings.

Acts Administered:
City of Lloydminster Act
Emergency Management Act
Government Organization Act
Libraries Act
Local Authorities Election Act
Municipal Government Act
Parks Towns Act
Public Highways Development Act
Safety Codes Act
Special Areas Act

Minister, Hon. Hector Goudreau
780-427-3744, Fax: 780-422-9550
Deputy Minister, Ray Gilmour
780-427-4826, Fax: 780-422-9561, ray.gilmour@gov.ab.ca
Executive Director, Human Resource Services, Sandra Kraatz
780-422-8681, Fax: 780-422-0214, sandra.kraatz@gov.ab.ca
Executive Director, Francophone Secretariat, Denis Tardif
780-415-3348, Fax: 780-422-7533, denis.tardif@gov.ab.ca
Director, Communications, Donna Babchishin
780-415-4758, Fax: 780-422-1419, donna.babchishin@gov.ab.ca
Director & Solicitor, Legal Services, Bill Nugent, Q.C.
780-422-8795, Fax: 780-427-0996, bill.nugent@gov.ab.ca

Associated Agencies, Boards & Commissions:

• Alberta Emergency Management Agency (AEMA)
c/o Alberta Municipal Affairs, Communications Branch
10155 - 102 St., 18th Fl.
Edmonton, AB T5J 4L4
780-422-9000 Fax: 780-644-1044 -310-0000
aema@gov.ab.ca
www.aema.alberta.ca
Other Communication: Alberta Emergency Management Agency Response Readiness Centre, Phone: 1-866-618-2362
The Alberta Emergency Management Agency coordinates organizations, such as government, municipalities, & first responders, which are involved in the prevention, preparedness, & response to emergencies.

• Capital Region Board
Bell Tower
#1405, 10104 - 103 Ave.
Edmonton, AB T5J 0H8
780-638-6000 Fax: 780-638-6009
www.capitalregionboard.ab.ca
The Government of Alberta established the Capital Region Board in 2008. The Board consists of members from twenty-four participating municipalities. They serve on the following committees: land use; transit; Geographic Information Services; housing; & governance.
The following are the municipalities of the Capital Region Board: Town of Beaumont; Town of Bon Accord; Town of Bruderheim; Town of Calmar; Town of Devon; City of Edmonton; City of Fort Saskatchewan; Town of Gibbons; Lamont County; Town of Lamont; City of Leduc; Leduc County; Town of Legal; Town of Morinville; Parkland County; Town of Redwater; City of St. Albert; City of Spruce Grove; Town of Stony Plain; Strathcona County; Sturgeon County; Village of Thorsby; Village of Wabamun; & the Village of Warburg.

• Municipal Government Board (MGB)
Commerce Place
10155 - 102 St., 15th Fl.
Edmonton, AB T5J 4L4
780-427-4864 Fax: 780-427-0986 -310-0000
mgbmail@gov.ab.ca
www.municipalaffairs.alberta.ca
Operating as an independent & impartial body, the Municipal Government Board decides upon certain appeals & disputes from the Municipal Government Act. Examples of issues dealt with by the Municipal Government Board are as follows: disputes between municipalities; annexation matters; linear property assessment complaints; & appeals about equalized assessment & subdivisions.

• Safety Codes Council (SCC)
#1000, 10665 Jasper Ave. NW
Edmonton, AB T5J 3S9
780-413-0099 Fax: 780-424-5134 888-413-0099
sccinfo@safetycodes.ab.ca
www.safetycodes.ab.ca
Other Communication: Toll-Free Fax: 1-888-424-5134
The Safety Codes Council is a corporation that supports the Ministry of Municipal Affairs' administration of the Safety Codes Act. The Council has the following business units: Accreditation & Appeals; Administration; Certification & Policy; Electronic Business Solutions; & Training.

• Special Areas Board
Special Areas Board Administration
212 - 2nd Ave. West
PO Box 820
Hanna, AB T0J 1P0
403-854-5600 Fax: 403-854-5527
specarea@telus.net
www.specialareas.ab.ca
Other Communication: Hanna, Phone: 403-854-5625; Oyen, Phone: 403-664-3618, Fax: 403-664-3320; Consort, Phone: 403-577-3523, Fax: 403-577-2446; Youngstown, Phone: 403-779-3733
The Special Areas Board is responsible for the management of public land in Alberta's three Special Areas. The Board also provides municipal services to eastern Alberta's dryland region. The following are examples of programs & services offered by the Special Areas Board: protective & emergency services; construction & maintenance of local roads; provision of water services; management of public land; operation & maintenance of Special Areas recreational parks & community pastures; conservation programming; agricultural development; & economic development programs.

Corporate Strategic Services Division
Commerce Place, 10155 - 102 St., 18th Fl., Edmonton, AB T5J 4L4
Assistant Deputy Minister, Anthony Lemphers
780-415-9099, Fax: 780-422-4923, anthony.lemphers@gov.ab.ca
Executive Director & Senior Financial Officer, Financial Services, Dan Balderston
780-644-8098, Fax: 780-422-5840, dan.balderston@gov.ab.ca
Executive Director, Corporate Planning & Policy, Indira Breitkreuz
780-422-7317, Fax: 780-422-4923, indira.breitkreuz@gov.ab.ca
Director, Information Technology, Heather Cox
780-427-6097, Fax: 780-422-0776, heather.cox@gov.ab.ca
Director, Public Library Services, Diana Davidson
780-415-0284, Fax: 780-415-8594, diana.davidson@gov.ab.ca
Director, Information Management, Legislative & Administrative Services, Wilma Sisk
780-422-8834, Fax: 780-643-1090, wilma.sisk@gov.ab.ca

Local Government Services Division
Commerce Place, 10155 - 102 St., 17th Fl., Edmonton, AB T5J 4L4
Assistant Deputy Minister, Michael Merritt
780-427-9660, Fax: 780-427-0453, michael.merritt@gov.ab.ca
Executive Director, Municipal Services Branch, Gary Sandberg
780-422-8034, Fax: 780-420-1016, gary.sandberg@gov.ab.ca
Executive Director, Assessment Services Branch, Steve White
780-422-1377, Fax: 780-422-3110, steve.white@gov.ab.ca
Director, Legislative Projects, Ronald Cust
780-422-8322, Fax: 780-644-4941, ron.cust@gov.ab.ca

Public Safety Division
Commerce Place, 10155 - 102 St., 16th Fl., Edmonton, AB T5J 4L4
Assistant Deputy Minister, Ivan Moore
780-638-3245, Fax: 780-427-2538, ivan.moore@gov.ab.ca
Executive Director, Safety Services Branch, Chris Tye
780-644-5691, Fax: 780-427-8686, safety.services@gov.ab.ca
Director, Legislation & Strategic Projects, Joan Armstrong
780-427-2279, Fax: 780-427-2538, joan.armstrong@gov.ab.ca
Director, Risk Management & Finance, Diane McLean
780-427-6133, Fax: 780-427-2538, diane.mclean@gov.ab.ca
Director, Safety Assurance Services, Alex Morrison
780-644-1010, Fax: 403-297-4174, safety.services@gov.ab.ca
Director, Codes & Standards, James Orr
780-644-1010, Fax: 780-427-8686, safety.services@gov.ab.ca
Director, Field Technical Services, Randy Paulson
780-644-1010, Fax: 780-427-8686, safety.services@gov.ab.ca
Manager, Operational Support Services, Don Rebus
780-644-1010, Fax: 780-427-8686, safety.services@gov.ab.ca

Alberta Office of the Ombudsman

Canadian Western Bank Building, #2800, 10303 Jasper Ave. NW, 28th Fl., Edmonton, AB T5J 5C3
780-427-2756 Fax: 780-427-2759
888-455-2756
info@ombudsman.ab.ca
www.ombudsman.ab.ca

As an Officer of the Legislative Assembly of Alberta, the Alberta Ombudsman reports directly to the Legislative Assembly. The Ombudsman carries out his role under the authority of Alberta's Ombudsman Act.
The Alberta Ombudsman operates independently from the Alberta government to investigate & respond to written complaints about unfair treatment from Alberta government authorities, designated professional organizations. The Ombudsman also handles the patient concerns resolution process of Alberta Health Services.

Ombudsman, Peter Hourihan
Director, Corporate Services, Suzanne Richford
780-415-2510, Fax: 780-427-2759
Team Leader & Senior Investigator, Ombudsman Alberta, Edmonton Office, Diann Bowes
780-427-2756, Fax: 780-427-2759
Team Leader & Senior Investigator, Ombudsman Alberta, Calgary Office, Joanne Roper
403-297-6185, Fax: 403-297-5121

Alberta Public Affairs Bureau (PAB)

Park Plaza, 10611 - 98 Ave., 6th Fl., Edmonton, AB T5K 2P7
780-427-2754 Fax: 780-422-4168
-310-0000
www.publicaffairs.alberta.ca

Communications are provided by the Public Affairs Bureau to support Alberta's government ministries. The Public Affairs Bureau provides information about government policies & programs to Albertans. The Bureau is also responsible for coordinating communications during public emergencies.

Managing Director, Lee Funke
780-644-5655, Fax: 780-427-1010, lee.funke@gov.ab.ca
Senior Manager, Communications, Joanne Rosnau
780-644-8106, Fax: 780-427-1010, joanne.rosnau@gov.ab.ca

Officer, Public Affairs, Chelsey Chapman
780-644-5300, Fax: 780-427-1010,
chelsey.chapman@gov.ab.ca

Alberta Seniors

Communications, Standard Life Centre, 10405 Jasper Ave., 3rd Fl., Edmonton, AB T5J 4R7
780-415-9950 Fax: 780-644-1227
866-477-8589
seniors.communications@gov.ab.ca
www.seniors.alberta.ca
Other Communication: Alberta Supports Contact Centre, Phone: 780-644-9992, Toll-Free Phone: 1-877-644-9992, Fax: 780-422-5954

The main responsibility of Alberta's Ministry of Seniors is the development & delivery of programs & services to Albertans. The Ministry is divided into the following divisions: Community Support Programs & Strategic Planning; Seniors Services; & Disability Supports.
The Community Support Programs & Strategic Planning Division oversees the following programs & services: the provision of direct guardianship services for dependent adults; the administration of the Protection for Persons in Care Act; monitoring the quality of services for the Persons with Developmental Disabilities program; monitoring accommodation standards for long-term care & supportive living facilities; & administration of the Seniors Lodge, Senior Self-Contained, & Unique Homes programs.
The Senior Services Division oversees programs such as the Alberta Seniors Benefit, the Special Needs Assistance for Seniors program, dental & optical programs, & the Education Property Tax Assistance program. The Division also provides information through the Seniors Information Line, Seniors Information Services Offices, & publications such as the annual "Senior Programs & Services Information Guide".
The Disability Supports Division administers the Alberta Aids to Daily Living program, as well as the Assured Income for the Severely Handicapped program. Community supports are also provided to persons with special needs, through programs such as the Fetal Alcohol Spectrum Disorder initiative & the Alberta Brain Injury initiative.

Acts Administered:
Alberta Housing Act (jointly with other Ministries)
Assured Income for the Severely Handicapped Act
Blind Persons' Rights Act
Dependent Adults Act
Government Organization Act (jointly with other Ministries)
Personal Directives Act
Persons with Developmental Disabilities Community Governance Act
Premier's Council on the Status of Persons with Disabilities Act
Protection for Persons in Care Act
Seniors Advisory Council for Alberta Act
Seniors Benefit Act
Service Dogs Act
Supportive Living Accommodation Licensing Act

Minister, Seniors, Hon. George VanderBurg
780-415-9550, Fax: 780-415-9411
Social Media:
www.facebook.com/George-VanderBurg/195871217330
Deputy Minister, Robert Bhatia
780-415-1357, Fax: 780-415-1686, robert.bhatia@gov.ab.ca
Executive Director, Human Resource Services, Dawn White
780-415-8964, Fax: 780-415-2003, dawn.white@gov.ab.ca
Director, Communications, Michael Shields
780-644-1108, Fax: 780-644-1227,
michael.shields@gov.ab.ca

Associated Agencies, Boards & Commissions:
• Persons with Developmental Disabilities Community Boards
c/o PDD Program Branch, Peace Hills Trust Tower
10011 - 109 St., 4th Fl.
Edmonton, AB T5J 3S8
780-427-1177 Fax: 780-427-1220 800-310-0000
PDDinfo@gov.ab.ca
www.seniors.alberta.ca/pdd
Six Persons with Developmental Disabilities Community Boards were established by the Persons with Developmental Disabilities Community Governance Act. The boards deliver supports to adults with developmental disabilities. The following services are funded by the program: community living supports for persons in their home environment; employment supports to educate & train individuals; community access supports; & specialized community supports.
• Premier's Council on the Status of Persons with Disabilities
HSBC Building
10055 - 106 St., 11th Fl.
Edmonton, AB T5J 1G3
780-422-1095 800-272-8841
pcspd@gov.ab.ca
www.seniors.alberta.ca/PremiersCouncil
Established in 1988, the mandate for the Premier's Council on the Status of Persons with Disabilities is outlined in the Premier's Council on the Status of Persons with Disabilities Act. The Premier's Council consists of up to fifteen volunteer members who communicate the concerns of Alberta's disability community to the provincial government.
• Seniors Advisory Council for Alberta
Standard Life Centre
#600, 10405 Jasper Ave., 6th Fl.
Edmonton, AB T5J 4R7
780-422-2321 Fax: 780-422-8762 -310-0000
saca@gov.ab.ca
www.seniors.alberta.ca/services_resources/advisory_council
The Seniors Advisory Council for Alberta consults with senior citizens & seniors' organizations in communities throughout Alberta. The Council then informs the Government of Alberta, through the Minister of Seniors & Community Supports, about the issues that affect Alberta's seniors.
The Seniors Advisory Council for Alberta is also engaged in planning the Seniors' Week celebration each years, supporting workshops for frontline workers & seniors, & participating in research projects.

Alberta Supports Initiative Division
Standard Life Centre, 10405 Jasper Ave., 4th Fl., Edmonton, AB T5J 4R7
Assistant Deputy Minister, Michele Kirchner
780-427-5634, Fax: 780-638-2821,
michele.kirchner@gov.ab.ca
Executive Director, Alberta Supports Implementation Office, Carolann Regular
780-643-1308, Fax: 780-638-2821,
carolann.regular@gov.ab.ca

Community Support Programs & Strategic Planning Division
Standard Life Centre, 10405 Jasper Ave., 3rd Fl., Edmonton, T5J 4R7
780-415-2466 Fax: 780-427-1689
Assistant Deputy Minister, Brenda Lee Doyle
780-427-2593, Fax: 780-427-1689,
brendalee.doyle@gov.ab.ca
Executive Director, Persons with Developmental Disabilities Program, Jim Menzies
780-427-1216, Fax: 780-427-1220, jim.menzies@gov.ab.ca
Director, Protection for Persons in Care, Edith Baraniecki
780-427-0552, Fax: 780-415-8611,
edith.baraniecki@gov.ab.ca
Executive Co-Lead, Persons with Developmental Disabilities Implementation Team, Ruth Hofer
780-427-7200, Fax: 780-427-1220, ruth.hofer@gov.ab.ca
Manager, Strategic Support & Issues Management, Lois Flynn
780-415-9498, Fax: 780-427-1689, lois.flynn@gov.ab.ca
Public Guardian Representative, Office of the Public Guardian, Lincoln Mar
780-638-3501, Fax: 780-422-6051, lincoln.mar@gov.ab.ca

Disability Supports Division
Milner Building, 10040 - 104 St., 12th Fl., Edmonton, AB T5J 0Z2
Assistant Deputy Minister, Donna Ludvigsen
780-427-1245, Fax: 780-427-5148,
donna.ludvigsen@gov.ab.ca
Executive Director, Delivery Services, Dale Beesley
780-644-4731, Fax: 780-644-3299, dale.beesley@gov.ab.ca
Executive Director, Policy, Innovation, & Partnerships, Helen Stacey
780-644-9910, Fax: 780-644-2315, helen.stacey@gov.ab.ca
Director, Health Related Supports, Marianne Baird
780-422-6985, Fax: 780-422-0968,
marianne.baird@gov.ab.ca
Manager, Financial Services, Jackie Lee
780-644-5179, Fax: 780-644-3299, jackie.lee@gov.ab.ca
Manager, Divisional Coordination & Issues Management Unit, Rosa Spadavecchia
780-427-2065, Fax: 780-427-5148,
rosa.spadavecchia@gov.ab.ca

Seniors Services Division
Standard Life Centre, 10405 Jasper Ave., 6th Fl., Edmonton, AB T5J 4R7
Assistant Deputy Minister, Chi Loo
780-422-3179, Fax: 780-644-7602, chi.loo@gov.ab.ca
Director, Seniors Financial Assistance Branch, John Cabral
780-422-7270, Fax: 780-644-1602, john.cabral@gov.ab.ca
Director, Seniors Policy & Planning, Sarah Carr
780-644-2975, Fax: 780-644-7602, sarah.carr@gov.ab.ca
Director, Client & Information Services Branch, Denine Ritchie
780-415-0845, Fax: 780-422-8762, denine.ritchie@gov.ab.ca

Strategic Services Division
Standard Life Centre, 10405 Jasper Ave., 2nd Fl., Edmonton, AB T5J 4R7
Assistant Deputy Minister & Senior Financial Officer, Carol Ann Kushlyk
780-422-8550, Fax: 780-644-2524,
carolann.kushlyk@gov.ab.ca
Executive Director & CIO, Corporate Services Branch, Kevin Molcak
780-644-1125, Fax: 780-427-9376, kevin.molcak@gov.ab.ca
Executive Director, Supportive Living & Long Term Care Branch, Marjory Sutherland
780-422-8219, Fax: 780-644-5499,
marjory.sutherland@gov.ab.ca
Director, Financial Planning & Reporting, Financial Planning Branch, Bill Cruikshank
780-644-1858, Fax: 780-644-2524, bill.cruikshank@gov.ab.ca
Director, Financial Services & Accountability Branch, Mahmud Dhala
780-427-2190, Fax: 780-644-2524,
mahmud.dhala@gov.ab.ca
Senior Manager, Corporate Planning, Policy, & Research Branch, Glen Hughes
780-427-1985, Fax: 780-427-1689, glen.hughes@gov.ab.ca

Alberta Service Alberta

Government of Alberta, PO Box 1333, Edmonton, AB T5J 2N2
780-427-4088
-310-0000
service.alberta@gov.ab.ca
www.servicealberta.ca
Other Communication: Consumer Information, E-mail: cs@gov.ab.ca; Corporate Registry, E-mail: cr@gov.ab.ca; Land Titles, E-mail: lto@gov.ab.ca; Landlords & Tenants, E-mail: rta@gov.ab.ca

The Ministry of Service Alberta offers information, services, & products to Albertans. The following are examples of the ministry's services: delivery of shared services to ministries, such as printing documents & technical support; management of the government's vehicle fleet; administration of the Freedom of Information & Protection of Privacy legislation; provision of licensing & registry services; & enforcement of high standards of consumer protection.

Acts Administered:
Agricultural & Recreational Land Ownership Act
Builders' Lien Act
Business Corporations Act
Cemeteries Act
Cemetery Companies Act
Change of Name Act
Charitable Fundraising Act
Companies Act
Condominium Property Act
Cooperatives Act
Debtors' Assistance Act
Dower Act
Electronic Transactions Act
Fair Trading Act
Franchises Act
Freedom of Information & Protection of Privacy Act
Funeral Services Act
Garage Keepers' Lien Act
Government Organization Act
Land Titles Act
Law of Property Act
Marriage Act
Mobile Home Sites Tenancies Act
Motor Vehicle Accident Claims Act
Partnership Act
Personal Information Protection Act
Personal Property Security Act
Possessory Liens Act
Queen's Printer Act
Real Estate Act
Religious Societies' Land Act
Residential Tenancies Act
Societies Act
Surveys Act
Traffic Safety Act
Vital Statistics Act
Warehousemen's Lien Act
Woodmen's Lien Act

Minister, Service Alberta, Hon. Manmeet Bhullar
780-422-6880, Fax: 780-422-2496
Social Media: www.twitter.com/manmeetsbhullar,
www.facebook.com/manmeetbhullarmla
Deputy Minister, Paul Pellis
780-427-1990, Fax: 780-427-4999, paul.pellis@gov.ab.ca
Executive Director, Human Resource Services, Gerry Jacubo
780-427-8352, Fax: 780-427-4999, gerry.jacubo@gov.ab.ca
Director, Communications, Sharon Lopatka
780-422-8049, Fax: 780-422-9816,
sharon.lopatka@gov.ab.ca

Associated Agencies, Boards & Commissions:

• Alberta Funeral Services Regulatory Board (AFSRB)
11810 Kingsway Ave.
Edmonton, AB T5G 0X5
780-452-6130 Fax: 780-452-6085 800-563-4652
office@afsrb.ab.ca; complaints@afsrb.ab.ca;
education@afsrb.ab.ca
www.afsrb.ab.ca
In 1992, the Alberta Funeral Services Regulatory Board was established under the Licensing of Trades & Businesses Act & the Funeral Services Business Licensing Regulation.
The Board provides the following services: establishing educational standards; licensing pre-need salespeople, funeral directors, embalmers, funeral businesses, & crematories; monitoring performance standards; & investigating consumer complaints.
• Alberta Motor Vehicle Industry Council (AMVIC)
#303, 9945 - 50 St.
Edmonton, AB T6A 0L4
780-466-1140 Fax: 780-462-0633
www.amvic.org
Other Communication: Investigations, Toll-Free Phone: 1-877-279-8200; Licensing, Toll-Free Phone: 1-877-979-8100
The Alberta Motor Vehicle Industry Council is responsible for the administration & enforcement of automotive industry regulations, under Alberta's Fair Trading Act.
• Money Mentors
Quikcard Centre
#175, 17010 - 102rd Ave.
Edmonton, AB T5S 1K7
Fax: 780-423-2791 888-294-0076
info@moneymentors.ca
www.moneymentors.ca
Formerly known as Credit Counselling Services of Alberta, Money Mentors is a not-for-profit credit counselling & money coaching organization. It serves Albertans by educating them about personal money management & offering alternatives for those who encounter financial difficulties.
• Real Estate Council of Alberta (RECA)
#350, 4954 Richard Rd. SW
Calgary, AB T3E 6L1
403-228-2954 Fax: 403-228-3065 888-425-2754
info@reca.ca
www.reca.ca
Operating under the Real Estate Act of Alberta, the Real Estate Council of Alberta is responsible for the regulation of professionals in the real estate, real estate appraisal, & mortgage broker industries. The Council is made up of the following committees: Audit, Finance, Governance, Hearings, & the Education Ad Hoc Committee.

Business Services
Telus Plaza South, 10020 - 100 St., 29th Fl., Edmonton, AB T5J 0N3
-310-0000
Other Communication: Consumer Contact Centre, Phone: 1-877-427-4088
Assistant Deputy Minister, Steve Burford
780-644-4527, Fax: 780-422-0956, steve.burford@gov.ab.ca
Executive Director, Procurement Services, Bill Moulton
780-427-4120, Fax: 780-422-9672, bill.moulton@gov.ab.ca
Executive Director, Client Services, Dianne Sutherland
780-644-2316, Fax: 780-415-6091, dianne.sutherland@gov.ab.ca
Director, Business Operations, Derek Thomson
780-643-1464, Fax: 780-415-2722, derek.thomson@gov.ab.ca

Consumer Services
Telus Plaza South, 10020 - 100 St., 29th Fl., Edmonton, AB T5J 0N3
-310-0000
Other Communication: Consumer Contact Centre, Phone: 1-877-427-4088
Consumer Services administers & enforces consumer protection legislation, in support of a fair & effective marketplace for Albertans. The Office of the Utilities Consumer Advocate is also the responsibility of Consumer Services. It ensures that consumers have the information & protection required for the electricity & natural gas markets in Alberta.
Assistant Deputy Minister, Brian Fischer
780-427-2214, Fax: 780-644-1015, brian.fischer@gov.ab.ca
Executive Director, Shared Network Services, Dennis Mudryk
780-427-6005, Fax: 780-638-5947, dennis.mudryk@gov.ab.ca
Executive Director, Consumer Services Programs, Rob Phillips
780-422-8177, Fax: 780-427-3033, rob.phillips@gov.ab.ca
Director, Information Technology, Kim Smadis
780-415-6010, Fax: 780-427-2959, kim.smadis@gov.ab.ca
Manager, Regulatory Operations, Office of the Utilities Consumer Advocate, Barry Shymanski
780-644-5477, Fax: 780-644-5129, barry.shymanski@gov.ab.ca

Enterprise Services
Telus Plaza South, 10020 - 100 St., 29th Fl., Edmonton, AB T5J 0N3
Enterprise Services oversees information & communication technology infrastructure services to government departments, plus some agencies, boards, & commissions. The Alberta government's Chief Information Officer Council also receives secretariat support from Enterprise Services.
Assistant Deputy Minister, Kate Rozmahel
780-644-4529, Fax: 780-422-0956, kate.rozmahel@gov.ab.ca
Executive Director, Office of the Corporate Chief Information Officer & ICT Service Delivery & Support, Ron Boehm
780-644-2536, Fax: 780-422-0956, ron.boehm@gov.ab.ca
Executive Director, Corporate Architecture & Planning, Rob Godin
780-644-4541, Fax: 780-427-0238, rob.godin@gov.ab.ca
Executive Director, Enterprise Technology Infrastructure Services, Dale Huhtala
780-427-2295, dale.huhtala@gov.ab.ca
Executive Director, Strategic Infrastructure Projects, Andrew Mak
780-644-2014, andrew.mak@gov.ab.ca
Manager, Financial Management, Monika Kossowska
780-644-3051, monika.kossowska@gov.ab.ca

Information Services
Telus Plaza South, 10020 - 100 St., 29th Fl., Edmonton, AB T5J 0N3
Assistant Deputy Minister, Ray Keroack
780-427-0057, Fax: 780-422-0956, ray.keroack@gov.ab.ca
Executive Director, Service Delivery, Frank Buckreus
780-427-0254, Fax: 780-422-8287, frank.buckreus@gov.ab.ca
Executive Director, Records & Information Management Branch, Laurel Franck
780-422-0267, Fax: 780-422-0818, laurel.frank@gov.ab.ca
Director, Audit & Investigation Branch, Brian Breakey
780-422-8008, Fax: 780-644-3536, brian.breakey@gov.ab.ca
Director, Policy & Governance, Cheryl Naundorf
780-427-6369, Fax: 780-427-1120, cheryl.naundorf@gov.ab.ca
Director, FOIP & Legislative Services, Di Nugent
780-422-7840, Fax: 780-427-1120, di.nugent@gov.ab.ca
Manager, Library Services, Linda R. Scott
780-415-8344, Fax: 780-427-8287, linda.r.scott@gov.ab.ca

Registry Services
Telus Plaza South, 10020 - 100 St., 29th Fl., Edmonton, AB T5J 0N3
Registries Services is responsible for ensuring that Albertans have access to registry information & services for motor vehicles, personal property, vital statistics, licensing, & businesses & non-profit groups. Land title services are provided under the Torrens Land Registration System. The Special Investigations Unit of Registries Services offers court certificates, facial recognition analysis, & support to the Ministries of Infrastructure & Transportation.
Assistant Deputy Minister, Janet Skinner
780-427-4095, Fax: 780-644-1015, janet.skinner@gov.ab.ca
Executive Director, Motor Vehicles & Agent Support, Doug Morrison
780-415-2847, Fax: 780-644-1040, doug.morrison@gov.ab.ca
Executive Director, Land Titles, Vital Statistics, & Corporate Registry, Les Speakman
780-427-0108, Fax: 780-422-3105, les.speakman@gov.ab.ca

Strategic Planning & Financial Services
Commerce Place, 10155 - 102 St., 13th Fl., Edmonton, AB T5J 4G8
780-422-8545
Executive Director & Senior Financial Officer, Strategic Planning & Financial Services, Althea Hutchinson
780-415-8975, Fax: 780-427-0307, althea.hutchinson@gov.ab.ca
Director, Planning & Performance Measurement, Chrenan Borradaile
780-427-0282, Fax: 780-427-0307, chrenan.borradaile@gov.ab.ca
Director, Financial Reporting & Policy, Rene Mella
780-427-1882, Fax: 780-427-0307, rene.mella@gov.ab.ca
Director, Shared Services Administration, Maureen Towle
780-427-1790, Fax: 780-427-4999, maureen.towle@gov.ab.ca
Manager, Financial Planning & Analysis, Jennifer Gleave
780-422-8167, Fax: 780-427-0307, jennifer.gleave@gov.ab.ca

Alberta Solicitor General & Public Security

Communications, John E. Browntree Building, 10365 - 97 St., 9th Fl., Edmonton, AB T5J 3W7
780-427-3441 Fax: 780-427-2789
-310-0000
www.solgps.alberta.ca
The Alberta Ministry of the Solicitor General & Public Security works to provide safe communities throughout the province by handling the following responsibilities: supporting crime prevention; ensuring effective policing; providing effective correctional services; & supporting victims of crime.
Acts Administered:
Corrections Act
Gaming & Liquor Act
Government Organization Act
Horse Racing Alberta Act
Peace Officer Act
Police Act
Private Investigators & Security Guards Act
Victims of Crime Act
Solicitor General & Minister, Public Security, Hon. Jonathan Denis, QC
780-415-9406, Fax: 780-415-9566
Social Media: www.twitter.com/MinisterJono, www.facebook.com/jonathandenismla
Deputy Solicitor General & Deputy Minister, Public Security, Brad Pickering
780-427-3841, Fax: 780-427-0727, brad.pickering@gov.ab.ca
Executive Director, Human Resource Services, Brigitte Fulgham
780-427-7602, Fax: 780-644-1395, brigitte.fulgham@gov.ab.ca
Director, Communications, Ryan Cromb
780-427-6153, Fax: 780-427-0771, ryan.cromb@gov.ab.ca

Associated Agencies, Boards & Commissions:
• Appeal Tribunal, Horse Racing
#720, 9707 - 110 St.
Edmonton, AB T5K 2L9
780-415-5432 888-553-7223
reception@thehorses.com
The Appeal Tribunal is an independent body that was established by the Horse Racing Alberta Act. Members of the Tribunal are appointed by the Solicitor General & Minister of Public Security. They adjudicate appeals by racing participants, who appeal the decisions of judges & stewards.
• Alberta Gaming & Liquor Commission (AGLC)
50 Corriveau Ave.
St. Albert, AB T8N 3T5
780-447-8600 Fax: 780-447-8916 800-272-8876
www.aglc.ca
Other Communication: Media, Phone: 780-447-8740
The Alberta Gaming & Liquor Commission operates as a crown commercial enterprise. As an agent of the Government of Alberta, it is responsible for the administration of the Gaming & Liquor Act, Regulation, & related policy.
Key activities of the Commission include ensuring that the gaming & liquor industries conduct their business with integrity, & maximizing the economic benefits of these industries.
• Criminal Injuries Review Board (CIRB)
#1502, 10025 - 102A Ave.
Edmonton, AB T5J 2Z2
780-427-7330 Fax: 780-427-7347
Established in 1997, the Criminal Injuries Review Board operates as an autonomous body, in accordance with the Victims of Crime Act. Members of the Board are appointed by the Lieutenant Governor in Council, as recommended by the Minister. They review the decisions of the Director of Victims of Crime Financial Benefits Program, or his or her designate.
• Law Enforcement Review Board (LERB)
City Centre Place
#1502, 10025 - 102A Ave.
Edmonton, AB T5J 2Z2
780-422-9376 Fax: 780-422-4782
lerb@gov.ab.ca
Established under Alberta's Police Act, the Law Enforcement Review Board conducts its business as an independent, quasi-judicial organization. Members of the Board are appointed by the Lieutenant Governor in Council as recommended by the Minister. They are charged with the responsibility of reviewing public complaints about the conduct of police officers & appeals by police officers.
• Victims of Crime Programs Committee
John E. Brownlee Building
10365 - 97 St., 10th Fl.
Edmonton, AB T5J 3W7
780-427-3460 Fax: 780-422-4213
Established under the Victims of Crime Act, the Victims of Crime Programs Committee consists of five members who have been appointed by the Solicitor General & Minister of Public Security. The Committee evaluates grant applications from programs. Recommendations are then made to the Minister for final approval.

Corporate Services Division
John E. Brownlee Building, 10365 - 97 St., 9th Fl., Edmonton, AB T5J 3W7
Assistant Deputy Minister, Jim Bauer
780-422-1033, Fax: 780-644-2537, jim.bauer@gov.ab.ca
Chief Information Officer & Executive Director, Information Technology Branch, Ayaaz Janmohamed

780-644-3171, Fax: 780-415-2887, ayaaz.janmohamed@gov.ab.ca
Executive Director, Planning & Policy Branch, Rae-Ann Lajeunesse
780-644-3010, Fax: 780-644-2763, rae-ann.lajeunesse@gov.ab.ca
Executive Director, Financial & Business Services Branch, Michael Michalski
780-427-7516, Fax: 780-427-2789, michael.michalski@gov.ab.ca
Director, Alberta Solicitor General & Public Security Staff College, Clarke Curtis
780-644-1778, Fax: 780-422-2854, curtis.clarke@gov.ab.ca

Correctional Services Division
John E. Brownlee Building, 10365 - 97 St., 10th Fl., Edmonton, AB T5J 3W7
780-427-3441 Fax: 780-427-5905
Assistant Deputy Minister, Bruce V. Anderson
780-427-3440, Fax: 780-427-5905, bruce.v.anderson@gov.ab.ca
Executive Director, Young Offender Branch, Judith Barlow
780-644-8080, Fax: 780-422-0732, judith.barlow@gov.ab.ca
Executive Director, Strategic Services Branch, Jim Cook
780-427-4568, Fax: 780-427-1903, jim.cook@gov.ab.ca
Executive Director, Community Corrections & Release Program Branch, Brent Doney
780-422-5757, Fax: 780-422-3098, brent.doney@gov.ab.ca
Executive Director, Adult Centre Operations Branch, Terry Garnett
780-427-3644, Fax: 780-427-1904, terry.garnett@gov.ab.ca
Executive Director, Project New Edmonton Remand Centre, Mike Tholenaer
780-422-1831, Fax: 780-427-1903, mike.tholenaer@gov.ab.ca
Co-Manager, Security Standards, Audits & Investigations Unit, Emery Ewanyshyn
403-297-6488, Fax: 403-297-2623, emery.ewanyshyn@gov.ab.ca
Co-Manager, Security Standards, Audits & Investigations Unit, Elaine MacDonald
780-427-3125, Fax: 780-422-0732, elaine.macdonald@gov.ab.ca

Public Security Division
John E. Brownlee Building, 10365 - 97 St., 10th Fl., Edmonton, AB T5J 3W7
780-427-7952 Fax: 780-427-1194
bill.meade@gov.ab.ca
Assistant Deputy Minister, Bill Meade
780-427-7952, Fax: 780-427-1194, bill.meade@gov.ab.ca
Executive Director, Sheriffs & Security Operations Branch, Vince Caleffi
780-422-3500, Fax: 780-422-3365, vince.caleffi@gov.ab.ca
Executive Director, Policy & Program Development Branch, Kathy Collins
780-427-7051, Fax: 780-422-4213, kathy.collins@gov.ab.ca
Executive Director, Alberta Serious Incident Response Team (ASIRT), Clif Purvis
780-644-1487, Fax: 780-644-1497, clif.purvis@gov.ab.ca

Alberta Sustainable Resource Development (SRD)

Information Centre, Great West Life Building, 9920 - 108 St., Main Fl., Edmonton, AB T5K 2M4
780-944-0313 Fax: 780-427-4407
877-944-0313
srd.infocent@gov.ab.ca
www.srd.alberta.ca
The Alberta Ministry of Sustainable Resource Development promotes the responsible use of natural resources in the province. Best practices in science, management, & stewardship are encouraged.
Acts Administered:
Boundary Surveys Act
Environmental Protection & Enhancement Act (sections 30 to 34, in common with the Minister of Environment & sections 37 (d) to (j), in common with the Minister of Community Development & the Minister of Environment)
Expropriation Act (sections 25 to 28 & 72)
Fisheries (Alberta) Act
Forest & Prairie Protection Act
Forest Reserves Act
Forests Act
Government Organization Act (sections 4 (2) (f) & (g) of Schedule 5, in common with the Minister of Environment & the Minister of Infrastructure)
Mines & Minerals Act (aections 108 (g), (h), & (j), in common with the Minister of Energy)
Natural Resources Conservation Board Act (in common with the Minister of Environment)
Public Lands Act
Surface Rights Act
Surveys Act
Wildlife Act

Minister, Sustainable Resource Development, Hon. Frank Oberle
780-415-4815, Fax: 780-415-4818
Deputy Minister, Eric McGhan
780-427-1799, Fax: 780-415-9669, eric.mcghan@gov.ab.ca
Executive Director, Human Resource Services, Mike Boyle
780-644-1398, Fax: 780-427-2513, mike.boyle@gov.ab.ca
Executive Director, Regulatory Enhancement Project, Cynthia Farmer
780-644-1750, Fax: 780-415-9669, cynthia.farmer@gov.ab.ca
Director, Communications, Carol Chawrun
780-427-8122, Fax: 780-422-6339, carol.chawrun@gov.ab.ca
Parliamentary Assistant, Evan Berger
780-427-3001, Fax: 780-415-0951

Associated Agencies, Boards & Commissions:
• Disabled Hunter Review Committee
c/o Fish & Wildlife Div,, Sustainable Resource Development
9915 - 108 St., 11th Fl.
Edmonton, AB T5K 2G8
-310-0000
The Disabled Hunter Review Committee is engaged in hearing appeals & reviewing applications by persons who received a negative decision when attempting to obtain a licences or permit for hunting. Depending upon the number of applications, the Committee holds hearings annually.
• Land Compensation Board (LCB)
1229 - 91 St. SW
Edmonton, AB T6X 1E9
srb.lcb@gov.ab.ca
www.landcompensation.gov.ab.ca
The Land Compensation Board listens to disputes & delivers a decision, within it legislated mandate, about the compensation for landowners or tenants when land is taken by an authority for public works projects. Applications to the Board can be made through forms found in the Expropriation Act Rules of Procedure & Practice.
• Natural Resources Conservation Board (NRCB)
Sterling Place
9940 - 106 St.
Edmonton, AB T5K 2N2
780-422-1977 Fax: 780-427-0607 866-383-6722
info@nrcb.gov.ab.ca
www.nrcb.gov.ab.ca
Established in 1991 by the Government of Alberta, the Natural Resources Conservation Board carries out its responsibilities under the Natural Resources Conservation Board Act. The quasi-judicial agency, which is accountable to the Minister of Sustainable Resource Development, reviews non-energy natural resource projects. The Board considers environmental, economic, & social effects in deciding if a project is in the public interest.
In accordance with the Agricultural Operation Practices Act, the Natural Resources Conservation Board also has regulatory authority for confined feeding operations in Alberta. Its work in this area includes administering policies, fulfilling applications, & conducting board reviews.
• Surface Rights Board (SRB)
1229 - 91 St. SW
Edmonton, AB T6X 1E9
780-427-2444 Fax: 780-427-5798 -310-0000
srb.lcb@gov.ab.ca
www.surfacerights.gov.ab.ca
The Surface Rights Board holds hearings on disputes related to energt activities & land access. The hearing usually involves a panel of three members of the Surface Rights Board. Members of the Board are appointed by an Order in Counsel, according to the Surface Rights Act. Affected parties may also participate in the hearings, which are open to the public.
The Board delivers decisions, within its legislated mandate, about compensation to landowners, surrounding issues such as oil & gas & power line activity. In determining compensation, the Board considers factors such as the value of the land, loss of use, inconvenience, nuisance, & noise, & adverse effects on remaining land.
• Wildfire Costs Assessment Committee
c/o Office of the Farmer's Advocate, JG O'Donoghue Building
7000 - 113 St., 3rd Fl.
Edmonton, AB T6H 5T6
The Wildfire Costs Assessment Committee is administered by the Farmers' Advocate Office. When a party is deemed responsible for starting a wildfire, the Committee evaluates that party's ability to pay the cost of fighting the fire.
• Wildlife Predator & Shot Livestock Compensation Committee
c/o Fish & Wildlife Div., Sustainable Resource Development
9920 - 108 St., 3rd Fl.
Edmonton, AB T5K 2M4
The reimbursement paid to a livestock producer, when an animal has been injured by a wildlife predator, or shot, is determined by the Predator & Shot Livestock Compensation Committee of Alberta. Compensation provided to the livestock owner is based upon a schedule for losses or injury to specified livestock.

Corporate Services Division
Petroleum Plaza ST, 9915 - 108 St., 11th Fl., Edmonton, AB T5K 2G8
780-422-8600
Fish & Wildlife Management ensures Albertans benefit economically, environmentally & socially from the province's fish & wildlife resources. Goals are to provide a balanced approach to fish & wildlife management through a fish & wildlife policy, legislative & regulatory framework that maximizes the benefits received from these resources, sustains the recreational enjoyment of fish & wildlife resources with appropriate allocation & licensing decisions, mitigates & reduces negative interactions between wildlife & humans & partner with Aboriginal communities to sustain traditional uses of fish & wildlife resources. Management plans are up-to-date for all game species & species at risk. Sustainable fishing has improved the viability of the commercial fishing industry, along with habitat maintenance, restoration, the system of stocking fish & appropriate management information.
Assistant Deputy Minister, Wendy Boje
780-415-2634, Fax: 780-422-6068, wendy.boje@gov.ab.ca
Executive Director & Senior Financial Officer, Finance & Administration Branch, Greg Kliparchuk
780-638-3199, Fax: 780-427-2512, greg.kliparchuk@gov.ab.ca
Executive Director, Resource Information Management Branch & GeoDiscover Alberta Program, Barry Liam
780-644-2657, Fax: 780-427-7434, barry.liam@gov.ab.ca
Executive Director, Corporate Business Support Branch, Scott Milligan
780-422-0672, Fax: 780-644-4682, scott.milligan@gov.ab.ca
Director, Information Communication Technology Branch, Joe Vance
780-644-8619, Fax: 780-427-7434, joe.vance@gov.ab.ca

Fish & Wildlife Division
Petroleum Plaza ST, 9915 - 108 St., 11th Fl., Edmonton, AB T5K 2G8
Assistant Deputy Minister, Rick Blackwood
780-427-1139, Fax: 780-427-8884, rick.blackwood@gov.ab.ca
Executive Director, Wildlife Management, Ron Bjorge
780-427-9503, Fax: 780-422-9557, ron.bjorge@gov.ab.ca
Executive Director, Enforcement Field Services, Deryl Empson
780-422-0044, Fax: 780-422-9560, deryl.empson@gov.ab.ca
Director, Fisheries Management Branch, Travis Ripley
780-427-7763, Fax: 780-422-9559, travis.ripley@gov.ab.ca

Forestry Division
Petroleum Plaza ST, 9915 - 108 St. 11th Fl., Edmonton, AB T5K 2G8
Assistant Deputy Minister, Bruce Mayer
780-427-3542, Fax: 780-422-6068, bruce.mayer@gov.ab.ca
Executive Director, Wildfire Management Branch, Hugh Boyd
780-442-7781, Fax: 780-415-1509, hugh.boyd@gov.ab.ca
Executive Director, Forest Management Branch, Darren Tapp
780-427-5324, Fax: 780-427-0085, darren.tapp@gov.ab.ca
Executive Director, Forest Industry Development Branch, Dan Wilkinson
780-427-6372, Fax: 780-644-5728, dan.wilkinson@gov.ab.ca
Director, Wildfire Operations Section, John Brewer
780-427-7925, Fax: 780-422-7230, john.brewer@gov.ab.ca

Land Use Secretariat
Centre West Building, 10035 - 108 St., Edmonton, AB T5J 3E1
780-644-7972 Fax: 780-644-1034
luf@gov.ab.ca
The Land Use Secretariat is a leader in the implementation of Alberta's Land-use Framework. The Secretariat assists regional advisory councils in offering advice to government about developing regional plans.
Executive Director, Regional Planning, Crystal Damer
780-644-5014, Fax: 780-644-1034, crystal.damer@gov.ab.ca
Commissioner, Stewardship, Morris Seiferling
780-644-7978, Fax: 780-644-1034, morris.seiferling@gov.ab.ca
Coordinator, Budget & Projects, Ursula Hung
780-427-9195, Fax: 780-644-1034, ursula.hung@gov.ab.ca
Officer, Public Affairs, Deleen Schoff
780-415-9547, Fax: 780-644-1034, deleen.schoff@gov.ab.ca

Lands Division
Petroleum Plaza ST, 9915 - 108 St., 11th Fl., Edmonton, AB T5K 2G8
780-415-1396 Fax: 780-422-6068
Assistant Deputy Minister, Glenn Selland
780-427-7061, Fax: 780-422-6068, glenn.selland@gov.ab.ca
Executive Director, Rangeland Management Branch, Keith Lyseng
780-427-3595, Fax: 780-422-0454, keith.lyseng@gov.ab.ca
Executive Director, Land Management Branch, Jeff Reynolds
780-644-1752, Fax: 780-427-1185, jeff.reynolds@gov.ab.ca
Director, Land Dispositions Branch, Val Hoover
780-427-3464, Fax: 780-422-2545, val.hoover@gov.ab.ca

Director, Project Management Branch, Gordon McClure
780-427-4743, Fax: 780-644-1142,
gordon.mcclure@gov.ab.ca
Lead, Regional Planning, Sustainable Resource Development Land Use Framework Integration Team, Darryl Johnson
403-562-3210, Fax: 403-562-7143, darryl.johnson@gov.ab.ca
Senior Manager, Fish & Wildlife Integration, Hugh Norris
780-644-8327, Fax: 780-638-3493, hugh.norris@gov.ab.ca
Senior Manager, Forestry Integration, Stephen Wills
780-422-5430, Fax: 780-638-3493, stephen.wills@gov.ab.ca

Alberta Tourism, Parks, & Recreation

Communications Branch, Commerce Place, 10155 - 102 St., 6th Fl., Edmonton, AB T5J 4L6
780-644-5589
TPR.Communications@gov.ab.ca
www.tpr.alberta.ca
TTY: 780-427-9999
Other Communication: TTT/TDY Toll-Free: 1-800-232-7215

Alberta's Ministry of Tourism, Parks, & Recreation was established in 2008.

The Ministry works to develop the tourism industry in Alberta by facilitating the profitability & sustainability of both existing & new tourism operations, positioning land for tourism, creating a positive policy environment, assisting with regulatory processes, & promoting tourism investment.

The Ministry of Tourism, Parks, & Recreation is also responsible for Alberta's network of parks & protected areas. These areas offer Albertans & tourists opportunities to appreciate the province's natural heritage & to participate in educational & recreational activities.

Promoting recreation & sports for healthy living & athletic excellence is another goal of the Ministry of Tourism, Parks, & Recreation. The government ministry works with recreation & sport associations & provides funding for recreation facilities across the province to achieve this goal.

Acts Administered:
Alberta Sport, Recreation, Parks, & Wildlife Foundation Act
Government Organization Act
Provincial Parks Act
Provincial Parks Amendment Act
Recreation Development Act
Travel Alberta Act
Wilderness Areas, Ecological Reserves, Natural Areas, & Heritage Rangelands Act
Willmore Wilderness Park Act

Minister, Hon. Jack Hayden
780-427-4928, Fax: 780-427-0188
Social Media:
www.facebook.com/pages/Jack-Hayden/188272707966
Deputy Minister, Bill Werry
780-644-5139, Fax: 780-644-5145, bill.werry@gov.ab.ca
Director, Communications, Anne Douglas
780-427-8761, Fax: 780-644-5586, anne.douglas@gov.ab.ca

Associated Agencies, Boards & Commissions:
• Alberta Sport, Recreation, Parks, & Wildlife Foundation (ASRPWF)
Standard Life Centre
#903, 10405 Jasper Ave., 9th Fl.
Edmonton, AB T5J 4R7
780-415-1167 Fax: 780-415-0308 -310-0000
www.cd.gov.ab.ca/asrpwf
Supported by the Alberta Lottery Fund, the Alberta Sport, Recreation, Parks, & Wildlife Foundation reports to the Minister of Alberta Tourism, Parks, & Recreation. The Foundation's objectives are provided in the Alberta, Sport, Recreation, Parks, & Wildlife Foundation Act.
The Alberta Sport, Recreation, Parks, & Wildlife Foundation develops partnerships with sport, recreation, active living, & parks & wildlife programs, in order to encourage & enhance athletic excellence, active lifestyles, & the conservation of natural areas. The Foundation funds a variety of organizations throughout Alberta, such as Alberta Active Living agencies, the Percy Page Centre, sport & recreation associations, & sport development centres.
• Travel Alberta
2500
Edmonton, AB T5J 2Z4
780-427-4321 800-252-3782
travelinfo@TravelAlberta.com
www.travelalberta.com
Travel Alberta is a marketing organization that is engaged in the following activities: promotion of Alberta as a tourist destination; administration of the Tourism Information System; management of the Travel Alberta Contact / Distribution Centre; & the operation of a network of Visitor Information Centres.

Parks Division
Oxbridge Place, 9820 - 106 St., 2nd Fl., Edmonton, AB T5K 2J6
780-427-3582 Fax: 780-427-5980
866-427-3582

Assistant Deputy Minister, Graham Statt
780-644-4948, Fax: 780-427-5980, graham.statt@gov.ab.ca
Executive Director, Program Coordination, Parks & Protected Areas Program, Steve Donelon
403-678-5500, Fax: 403-678-5505, steve.donelon@gov.ab.ca
Director, Policy & Strategic Support, Brian Kelly
780-427-9382, Fax: 780-427-5980, brian.kelly@gov.ab.ca
Director, Land Management, Archie Landals
780-427-9470, Fax: 780-427-5980, archie.landals@gov.ab.ca
Director, Parks Finance Section, Dale Schinkel
780-427-8224, Fax: 780-427-5980, dale.schinkel@gov.ab.ca
Director, Operations, Learning, & Stewardship, Mark Storie
780-427-9383, Fax: 780-427-5980, mark.storie@gov.ab.ca

Recreation & Sport Development Division
Standard Life Centre, 10405 Jasper Ave., 9th Fl., Edmonton, AB T5J 4R7

Assistant Deputy Minister, Tim Moorhouse
780-422-3305, Fax: 780-415-0308,
tim.moorhouse@gov.ab.ca
Executive Director, Recreation & Sport Development Division, Lloyd Bentz
780-415-0263, Fax: 780-415-0308, lloyd.bentz@gov.ab.ca
Director, Alberta Games & Marketing Branch, Dennis Allen
403-297-2729, Fax: 403-297-6669, dennis.allen@gov.ab.ca
Director, Sport Development Branch, Roger Kramers
780-415-0272, Fax: 780-427-5140, roger.kramers@gov.ab.ca
Director, Recreation Services Branch, Bernie MacDonald
780-415-0268, Fax: 780-427-5140,
bernie.macdonald@gov.ab.ca

Special Projects Division
Commerce Place, 10155 - 102 St., 6th Fl., Edmonton, AB T5J 4L6

Assistant Deputy Minister, Bob Scott
780-415-0892, Fax: 780-427-0778, bob.scott@gov.ab.ca

Strategic Corporate Services Division
Commerce Place, 10155 - 102 St., 6th Fl., Edmonton, AB T5J 4L6
780-415-0257

Chief Information Officer & Executive Director, Information Management & Technology Services, Mark Diner
780-427-1075, Fax: 780-644-1286, mark.diner@gov.ab.ca
Executive Director & Senior Financial Officer, Financial Services Branch, Cameron Steenveld
780-644-2714, Fax: 780-644-5586,
cameron.steenveld@gov.ab.ca

Tourism Division
Commerce Place, 10155 - 102 St., 6th Fl., Edmonton, AB T5J 4L6
780-427-3164

Assistant Deputy Minister, Reegan McCullough
780-643-1997, Fax: 780-427-6454,
reegan.mccullough@gov.ab.ca
Director, Tourism Services Branch, Elizabeth Kuhnel
780-427-6743, Fax: 780-415-0896,
elizabeth.kuhnel@gov.ab.ca
Director, Tourism Business Development, Ressearch, & Investment Branch, Moe Rehemtulla
780-427-6689, Fax: 780-427-6454,
moe.rehemtulla@gov.ab.ca
Manager, Contact Centre & Tourism Information System, Robin Luini
780-427-4965, Fax: 780-415-0896, robin.luini@gov.ab.ca
Manager, Visitor Information Centres & Support Services, Noel Ma
780-427-6512, Fax: 780-415-0896, noel.ma@gov.ab.ca
Manager, Tourism Research, Sid Nieuwenhuis
780-422-1058, Fax: 780-422-1759,
sid.nieuwenhuis@gov.ab.ca
Tourism Product Development Planner, Tourism Product Development Branch, Paul Radchenko
780-415-8743, Fax: 780-427-0778,
paul.radchenko@gov.ab.ca

Alberta Transportation

Twin Atria Building, 4999 - 98 Jasper Ave., 2nd Fl., Edmonton, AB T6B 2X3
780-427-2731
-310-0000
Trans.Contact.Us.m@gov.ab.ca
www.transportation.alberta.ca

Alberta's Ministry of Transportation consists of the Department of Transportation & the Transportation Safety Board. The Ministry strives to provide a safe & sustainable transportation system & water management infrastructure throughout the province.

Key activities of the Department are as follows: leading the planning, construction & preservation of highways across Alberta; offering information & education about transportation safety services & enforcement programs; designing, building, & maintaining the water management infrastructure in the province; managing grant programs to assist municipalities; & representing Alberta at all levels of government to ensure regulatory harmonization.

Acts Administered:
Dangerous Goods Transportation & Handling Act
Government Organization Act (jointly with other ministries)
Highways Development & Protection Act
Provincial Parks Act (jointly with other ministries)
Railway (Alberta) Act
Regional Airports Authorities Act
Traffic Safety Act
Water Act (jointly with other ministries)
Water, Gas, & Electric Companies Act (jointly with other ministries)

Associated Agencies, Boards & Commissions:
• Transportation Safety Board
North Office, Twin Atria Building
4999 - 98 Ave., Main Fl.
Edmonton, AB T6B 2X3
780-427-7178 Fax: 780-422-9739 -310-0000
www.atsb.alberta.ca
The Alberta Transportation Safety Board reports to the Minister of Transportation, through the Chair. The Board's members are chosen through a public recruitment process.
The Board hears appeals about licence suspensions & vehicle seizures. Its decisions are made in accordance with the Traffic Safety Act & the Railway (Alberta) Act.

Policy & Corporate Services Division
Twin Atria Building, 4999 - 98 Ave., 3rd Fl., Edmonton, AB T6B 2X3

The Policy & Corporate Services Division provides the following services: strategic policy, legislative planning, FOIP, finance, & information management.

Executive Director, Strategic Policy Branch, Arthur Arruda
780-415-8730, Fax: 780-422-1070, arthur.arruda@gov.ab.ca
Executive Director & Senior Financial Officer, Finance Branch, Winnie Yiu-Young
780-427-1440, Fax: 780-415-1219,
winnie.yiu-young@gov.ab.ca
Director, Transportation Development & Coordination, Jeff Paruk
780-415-2562, Fax: 780-422-1070, jeff.paruk@gov.ab.ca
Project Manager, Records & Information Management Initiative, Dennis Mitchell
780-427-3900, Fax: 780-427-6905,
dennis.mitchell@gov.ab.ca

Transportation & Civil Engineering Division
Twin Atria Building, 4999 - 98 Ave., 2nd Fl., Edmonton, AB T6B 2X3
780-422-2184 Fax: 780-415-1268

The Transportation & Civil Engineering Division carries out the following functions: planning & delivering highway construction & rehabilitation projects & special projects throughout the province; managing highway maintenance activities; constructing & upgrading management facilities; & managing grant programs, such as the Canada-Alberta Municipal Rural Infrastructure Fund.

Assistant Deputy Minister, Bruno Zutautas
780-422-2184, Fax: 780-415-1268,
bruno.zutautas@gov.ab.ca
Executive Director, Planning Branch, Jim Der
780-415-1300, Fax: 780-422-2027, jim.der@gov.ab.ca
Executive Director, Technical Standards Branch, Moh Lali
780-415-1083, Fax: 780-422-2027, moh.lali@gov.ab.ca
Executive Director, Major Capital Projects Branch, Tom Loo
780-415-4876, Fax: 780-415-0475, tom.loo@gov.ab.ca
Executive Director, Program Management Branch, Ranjit Tharmalingam
780-422-7672, Fax: 780-427-0783,
ranjit.tharmalingam@gov.ab.ca
Executive Director, Divisional Services, Gordon Zack
780-427-4548, Fax: 780-415-1268, gordon.zack@gov.ab.ca
Director & Chair, Strategic Planning, Louise Nelson
780-427-2595, Fax: 780-422-1070, louise.nelson@gov.ab.ca

Transportation Safety Services Division
Twin Atria Building, 4999 - 98 Ave., Main Fl., Edmonton, AB T6B 2X3
780-427-8901 Fax: 780-415-0782
800-666-5036

The Transportation Safety Services Division is responsible for the following services: monitoring the motor carrier industry & provincial railways; driver licensing & driver's licence enforcement; driver, vehicle, & road safety programs; impaired driving intervention programs; & dangerous goods control.

Assistant Deputy Minister, Shaun Hammond
780-415-1146, Fax: 780-415-0782,
shaun.hammond@gov.ab.ca
Chief Transport Officer, Commercial Vehicle Enforcement Branch, Steve Callahan
403-340-5225, Fax: 403-340-5074,
steve.callahan@gov.ab.ca
Executive Director, Office of Traffic Safety, Jeanette Espie
780-427-6588, Fax: 780-422-3682, jeanette.espie@gov.ab.ca
Executive Director, Driver Programs, Mitch Fuhr
780-644-4576, Fax: 780-427-0833, mitch.fuhr@gov.ab.ca
Director, Transport Engineering, Kim Durdle
403-340-5189, Fax: 403-340-5092, kim.durdle@gov.ab.ca

Director, Dangerous Goods, Vehicle, & Rail Safety Branch, Terry Wallace
780-427-7508, Fax: 780-422-9193, terry.wallace@gov.ab.ca

Alberta Treasury Board

Oxbridge Place, 9820 - 106 St., 5th Fl., Edmonton, AB T5K 2J6
780-415-4519
-310-000
www.treasuryboard.alberta.ca

Alberta's Ministry of Treasury Board manages government spending by carrying out the following responsibilities: leading the provincial government's capital planning process; providing advice & analysis on costs & capital spending; identifying alternatives for financing capital projects; & ensuring accounting standards & financial reporting.

Acts Administered:
Appropriation Act (2000 - 2009)
Appropriation (Interim Supply) Act (2001 - 2009)
Appropriation (Supplementary Supply) Act (2000 - 2009)
Financial Administration Act (sections 4 to 9 & part 3)
Fiscal Responsibility Act
Government Accountability Act
Public Service Act

Corporate Human Resources (CHR)
Peace Hills Trust Tower, 10011 - 109 St., Edmonton, AB T5J 3S8
780-408-8400
-310-0000
www.chr.alberta.ca

Corporate Human Resources offers advice to the Alberta provincial government about human resource administration. The following are some of the tasks performed by Corporate Human Resources: providing a corporate executive search program; coordinating job postings; delivering information about benefits, workplace health, labour relations, & other issues; advancing employee engagement; & offering learning opportunities to provincial government employees.

Public Service Commissioner, Dale Silver
780-408-8450, Fax: 780-422-5428, dale.silver@gov.ab.ca
Executive Director, Workforce Development, John Kelly
780-644-5083, Fax: 780-422-0835, john.kelly@gov.ab.ca
Executive Director, Labour Relations & Workplace Health, Lenore Neudorf
780-408-8430, Fax: 780-427-5131, lenore.neudorf@gov.ab.ca
Executive Director, Compensation, Job Evaluation, & Benefits, Debra Smith
780-408-8477, Fax: 780-422-3034, debra.smith@gov.ab.ca
Director, Human Resources, Liz Kennedy
780-408-8443, Fax: 780-644-4599, liz.kennedy@gov.ab.ca
Director, Executive Search, Trish Mills
780-408-8372, Fax: 780-422-0468, trish.mills@gov.ab.ca
Assistant Commissioner, Workforce Development & Engagement, Heather Caltagirone
780-408-8462, Fax: 780-422-0835, heather.caltagirone@gov.ab.ca
Assistant Commissioner, Attraction & Technology & Human Resource Community Development, Lori Cooper
780-644-7520, Fax: 780-644-1698, lori.cooper@gov.ab.ca
Assistant Commissioner, Labour & Employment Practices, Mary Anne Wilkinson
780-408-8478, Fax: 780-422-3034, maryanne.wilkinson@gov.ab.ca
Assistant Director, Communications, Marilyn Carlyle-Helms
780-408-8457, Fax: 780-644-4599, marilyn.carlyle-helms@gov.ab.ca

Corporate Internal Audit Services
Oxbridge Place, 9820 - 106th St., 4th Fl., Edmonton, AB T5K 2J6
780-644-7185

Corporate Internal Audit Services works with Alberta's government ministries to identify areas for improvement. Following the performance of internal audits, recommendations are provided to better operations & fiscal management.

Chief Internal Auditor, Dan Stadlwieser
780-644-4736, Fax: 780-644-4761, dan.stadlwieser@gov.ab.ca
Executive Director, Internal Audit Operations, Kathleen Gora
780-644-5271, Fax: 780-644-4761, kathleen.gora@gov.ab.ca
Director, Enterprise Audits, Enterprise Audits & Professional Practice, Nimal Chellappah
780-422-0065, Fax: 780-644-4761, nimal.chellappah@gov.ab.ca
Director, Professional Practice, Enterprise Audits & Professional Practice, Jonn Robertson
780-644-3438, Fax: 780-644-4761, jonn.robertson@gov.ab.ca

Office of the Controller
Oxbridge Place, 9820 - 106 St., 4th Fl., Edmonton, AB T5K 2J6

The Office of the Controller handles the following responsibilities: overseeing financial management & control policies; ensuring government accounting standards; reporting financial information; & planning.

Controller, Doug Lynkowski
780-427-3076, Fax: 780-422-2164, doug.lynkowski@gov.ab.ca
Executive Director, Business Process Reengineering Office, Nilam Jetha
780-643-0772, Fax: 780-422-2164, nilam.jetha@gov.ab.ca
Executive Director, Agency Governance Secretariat, Anita Lunden
780-643-1465, Fax: 780-422-2164, anita.lunden@gov.ab.ca
Executive Director, Performance Planning & Reporting, Murray Lyle
780-427-7784, Fax: 780-422-2164, murray.lyle@gov.ab.ca
Executive Director, Financial Accounting & Standards, Gisele Simard
780-415-9253, Fax: 780-422-2164, gisele.simard@gov.ab.ca
Director, Business Planning, Juliette Blair
780-422-5439, Fax: 780-427-2852, juliette.blair@gov.ab.ca

Oil Sands Sustainable Development Secretariat
Oxbridge Place, 9820 - 106 St., 3rd Fl., Edmonton, AB T5K 2J6

The Oil Sands Sustainable Development Secretariat works with governments & stakeholders to provide an integrated policy approach & to share information about Alberta's oil sands regions. The Secretariat also considers the economic, environmental, & social impacts of the oil sands, by leading the implementation of a strategy entitled, Responsible Actions: A Plan for Alberta's Oil Sands.

Spending Management & Planning
Oxbridge Place, 9820 - 106 St., 5th Fl., Edmonton, AB T5K 2J6

The Spending Management & Planning division works with Alberta Finance to monitor the fiscal activities of Alberta's ministries. The division offers recommendations about the budgeting, spending proposals, & spending of the provincial ministries.

Assistant Deputy Minister, Aaron Neumeyer
780-644-8078, Fax: 780-644-3907, aaron.neumeyer@gov.ab.ca
Executive Director, SMP 1, Larry Bailer
780-427-8701, Fax: 780-644-3907, larry.bailer@gov.ab.ca
Executive Director, SMP 2, Darren Hedley
780-415-4733, Fax: 780-644-3907, darren.hedley@gov.ab.ca
Executive Director, SMP 3, Greg Findlay
780-415-9258, Fax: 780-644-3907, greg.findlay@gov.ab.ca
Executive Director, SMP 4, Dale Fulford
780-427-8736, Fax: 780-644-3907, dale.fulford@gov.ab.ca
Director, Coordination & Integration, Wallace Currie
780-427-8702, Fax: 780-644-3907, wallace.currie@gov.ab.ca

Strategic Capital Planning
Oxbridge Place, 9820 - 106 St., 5th Fl., Edmonton, AB T5K 2J6

The Strategic Capital Planning division is responsible for the development & management of the Capital Plan. Advice & analysis are provided about planning & capital spending. Strategic Capital Planning also has responsibility for the Air Transportation Service. The Service serves government departments, boards, & agencies by providing air travel services.

Assistant Deputy Minister, Neill McQuay
780-415-1076, Fax: 780-440-8719, neill.mcquay@gov.ab.ca
Executive Director, Capital Planning & Spending, Tim Cartmell
780-427-8898, Fax: 780-644-3906, tim.cartmell@gov.ab.ca
Executive Director, Alternative Capital Financing, Faye McCann
780-644-8774, Fax: 780-644-3906, faye.mccann@gov.ab.ca
Director, Air Transportation Service, Rob Madden
780-427-7341, Fax: 780-422-1232, rob.madden@gov.ab.ca

Government of British Columbia

Seat of Government: Parliament Bldgs., Victoria, BC V8V 1X4
EnquiryBC@gov.bc.ca
www.gov.bc.ca

The Province of British Columbia entered Confederation on July 20, 1871. It has an area of 924,815.43 km2. According to Statistics Canada, the population of the province in 2010 was 4,551,853.

Office of the Lieutenant Governor

Government House, 1401 Rockland Ave., Victoria, BC V8S 1V9
250-387-2080 Fax: 250-387-2078
ghinfo@gov.bc.ca
www.ltgov.bc.ca

Lieutenant Governor, British Columbia, Hon. Steven L. Point, OBC
Private Secretary to the Lieutenant Governor & Executive Director, Government House, Herb A. LeRoy
250-387-2083, Fax: 250-387-2078

Director, Operations & Management Services, Jerymy Brownridge
250-387-2087

Office of the Premier

West Annex, Parliament Bldgs., PO Box 9041 Prov Govt, Victoria, BC V8W 9E1
250-387-1715 Fax: 250-387-0087
premier@gov.bc.ca
www.gov.bc.ca/premier

Premier, Hon. Christy Clark
Deputy Minister to the Premier, Cabinet Secretary & Head of the Public Service, John Dyble, QC
250-256-2209, Fax: 250-356-7258
Chief of Staff, Mike McDonald
Deputy Chief of Staff, Operations, Kim Kaakstad
Director, Communications, Shane Mills
Communications Officer & Deputy Press Secretary, Rebecca Scott

Executive Council

Parliament Bldgs., Victoria, BC V8V 1X4
www.gov.bc.ca/premier/cabinet_ministers

Premier, Hon. Christy Clark
250-387-1715, Fax: 250-387-0087, premier@gov.bc.ca
Minister, Finance & Deputy Premier, Hon. Kevin Falcon
250-387-3751, Fax: 250-387-5594, kevin.falcon.mla@leg.bc.ca
Minister, Aboriginal Relations & Reconciliation, Hon. Mary Polak
250-953-4844, Fax: 250-953-4856, mary.polak.mla@leg.bc.ca
Minister, Advanced Education, Hon. Naomi Yamamoto
250-356-0179, Fax: 250-952-0260, naomi.yamamoto.mla@leg.bc.ca
Minister, Agriculture, Hon. Don McRae
250-387-1023, Fax: 250-387-1522, don.mcrae.mla@leg.bc.ca
Attorney General, Hon. Barry Penner, Q.C.
250-387-1866, Fax: 250-387-6411, barry.penner.mla@leg.bc.ca; AG.Minister@gov.bc.ca
Minister, Children & Family Development, Hon. Mary McNeil
250-387-9699, Fax: 250-387-9722, mary.mcneil.mla@leg.bc.ca
Minister, Community, Sport & Cultural Development, Hon. Ida Chong
250-387-2283, Fax: 250-387-4312, ida.chong.mla@leg.bc.ca
Minister, Education, Hon. George Abbott
250-387-1977, Fax: 250-387-3200, george.abbott.mla@leg.bc.ca
Minister, Energy, Mines & Petroleum Resources; Minister Responsible for Housing, Hon. Rich Coleman
250-387-5896, Fax: 250-356-2965, rich.coleman.mla@leg.bc.ca
Minister, Environment, Hon. Terry Lake
250-387-1187, Fax: 250-387-1356, terry.lake.mla@leg.bc.ca
Minister, Forests, Lands & Natural Resource Operations, Hon. Steve Thomson
250-387-6240, Fax: 250-387-1040, steve.thomson.mla@leg.bc.ca
Minister, Health, Hon. Michael de Jong, QC
250-953-3547, Fax: 250-356-9587, mike.dejong.mla@leg.bc.ca
Minister, Jobs, Tourism & Innovation, Hon. Pat Bell
250-356-2771, Fax: 250-356-3000, pat.bell.mla@leg.bc.ca
Minister, Labour, Citizens' Services & Open Government, Hon. Stephanie Cadieux
250-952-7623, Fax: 250-952-7628, stephanie.cadieux.mla@leg.bc.ca
Minister, Public Safety & Solicitor General, Hon. Shirley Bond
250-356-7717, Fax: 250-356-8270, shirley.bond.mla@leg.bc.ca
Minister, Social Development; Minister Responsible for Multiculturalism, Hon. Harry Bloy
250-356-7750, Fax: 250-356-7292, harry.bloy.mla@leg.bc.ca
Minister, Transportation & Infrastructure, Hon. Blair Lekstrom
250-387-1978, Fax: 250-356-2290, blair.lekstrom.mla@leg.bc.ca
Speaker, Hon. Bill Barisoff
250-387-3952, 866-387-3952, Fax: 250-387-2813, bill.barisoff.mla@leg.bc.ca

Cabinet Operations
PO Box 9487 Prov Govt, Victoria, BC V8W 9W6
Fax: 250-387-7392

Deputy Cabinet Secretary, Elizabeth MacMillan
250-387-6020, Fax: 250-387-7392
Acting Executive Director, Cabinet Committees, Charlotte Powell
250-952-6748, Fax: 250-387-7392
Executive Director, Cabinet Committees, Carol Anne Rolf
250-952-7979, Fax: 250-387-7392
Director, Cabinet Operations, Rozlynne Mitchell
250-387-7380, Fax: 250-387-7392

Legislative Assembly & Independent Offices

Clerk's Office, #221, Parliament Bldgs., Victoria, BC V8V 1X4
250-387-3785 Fax: 250-387-0942
ClerkHouse@leg.bc.ca
www.leg.bc.ca

Clerk, E. George MacMinn, Q.C.
250-387-3785, Fax: 250-387-0942
Speaker, Legislative Assembly, Hon. Bill Barisoff
250-387-3952, Fax: 250-387-2813
Deputy Speaker, Legislative Assembly, Linda Reid
250-953-4887, Fax: 250-356-0596
Sergeant-at-Arms, Gary Lenz
250-356-6966
Legislative Comptroller, Dan Arbic
250-356-8588, Fax: 250-356-7517, Comptroller@leg.bc.ca
Acting Director, Hansard Production, Rob Sutherland
250-387-0944, Fax: 250-356-5681, Hansard.Services@leg.bc.ca
Director, Legislative Library Administration Office, Peter Gourlay
250-387-6508, Fax: 250-356-1373, Other Communications: URL: www.llbc.leg.bc.ca
Auditor General, John Doyle
250-419-6100, Fax: 250-387-1230, Other Communications: URL: www.bcauditor.com
Conflict of Interest Commissioner, Paul D.K. Fraser
250-356-9283, Fax: 250-356-6580, conflictofinterest@coibc.ca, Other Communications: URL: www.coibc.ca
Information & Privacy Commissioner, Elizabeth Denham
250-387-5629, Fax: 250-387-1696, info@oipc.bc.ca, Other Communications: URL: www.oipc.bc.ca
Merit Commissioner, Fiona Spencer
250-953-4208, Fax: 250-953-4160, merit@meritcomm.bc.ca, Other Communications: www.meritcomm.bc.ca
Police Complaint Commissioner, Stan T. Lowe
250-356-7458, Fax: 250-356-6503, info@opcc.bc.ca
Ombudsperson, Kim Carter
250-356-1559, Fax: 250-387-0198, info@opcc.bc.ca
Acting Chief Electoral Officer, Elections British Columbia, Craig James
250-387-5305, Fax: 250-387-3578, ElectionsBC@elections.bc.ca
Representative for Children & Youth, Mary Ellen Turpel-Lafond
250-356-6710, Fax: 250-356-0837, rcy@rcybc.ca

Government Caucus Office (Liberal)
East Annex, Parliament Bldgs., Victoria, BC V8V 1X4
250-356-6171 Fax: 250-356-6176
premier@gov.bc.ca
www.governmentcaucus.bc.ca

Leader, Hon. Christy Clark, Liberal
250-387-1715, Fax: 250-387-0087
Executive Director, Michael Morton
250-387-2950, Fax: 250-387-9066
Director, Research, Blair Phelps
250-387-8943, Fax: 250-356-0329
Director, Communications, Stephen Harris
250-208-7052, Fax: 250-387-7957
Senior Manager, Administration & Project Development, Christie Pruden
250-356-6134, Fax: 250-387-9066

Office of the Opposition (New Democrat)
#201, Parliament Bldgs., Victoria, BC V8V 1X4
250-387-3655 Fax: 250-387-4680
ndp@leg.bc.ca

Leader, Adrian Dix
250-387-3655, Fax: 250-387-4680, Adrian.Dix.MLA@leg.bc.ca
Executive Director, Mary O'Donoghue
250-387-3655, Fax: 250-387-4680
Director, Research, AnneMarie Delorey
250-387-3655, Fax: 250-387-4680

Legislative Committees
#224, Parliament Bldgs., Victoria, BC V8V 1X4
250-356-2933 Fax: 250-356-8172
ClerkComm@leg.bc.ca

At the beginning of each session, Select Standing Committees are established by the Legislative Assembly in British Columbia. The following nine Select Standing Committees have been established: Aboriginal Affairs; Children & Youth; Crown Corporations; Education; Finance & Government Services; Health; Legislative Initiatives; Parliamentary Reform, Ethical Conduct, Standing Orders, & Private Bills; & Public Accounts.
Clerk Assistant & Acting Clerk of Committees, Kate Ryan-Lloyd
250-356-2895, Fax: 250-356-8172

Thirty-ninth Legislature - British Columbia

Parliament Bldgs., Victoria, BC V8V 1X4
250-387-3785 Fax: 250-387-0942
ClerkHouse@leg.bc.ca
www.leg.bc.ca

Last General Election: May 12, 2009. Next General Election: May 14, 2013. Party Standings (July 2008): Liberal (Lib.) 49; New Democratic Party (NDP) 34; Independent 2; Total 85. Salaries, Indemnities & Allowances: (2009): Basic Compensation $101,859 for members. Each person who holds a salaried position receives an annual salary, determined as the amount of basic compensation for that year multiplied by the following values: Premier .90; Member of the Executive Council with portfolio .50; Member of the Executive Council without portfolio .35; Parliamentary Secretary .15; Speaker .50; Deputy Speaker .35; Leader of the Official Opposition .50; Leader of a recognized political party other than the government or the Official Opposition .25; Government Whip .20; Official Opposition Whip .20; Party Whip of a recognized political party other than the government or the Official Opposition .10; Official Opposition House Leader .20; House Leader of a recognized political party other than the government or the Official Opposition .10; Government Caucus Chair .20; Official Opposition Caucus Chair .20; Caucus Chair of a recognized political party other than the government or the Official Opposition .10; Chair of Select Standing or Special Committees .15. The following is a list of each MLA, the MLA's constitueny, party affiliation, & contact information:

Members

Hon. George Abbott, Shuswap, Liberal
250-387-1977, 877-771-7557, Fax: 250-387-3200, george.abbott.mla@leg.bc.ca, Other Communications: Constituency Phone: 250-833-7414, Fax: 250-833-7422
Robin Austin, Skeena, New Democratic Party
250-387-3655, Fax: 250-387-4680, robin.austin.mla@leg.bc.ca, Other Communications: Terrace Constituency Phone: 250-638-7906
Harry Bains, Surrey-Newton, New Democratic Party
250-387-3655, Fax: 250-387-4680, harry.bains.mla@leg.bc.ca, Other Communications: Constituency Phone: 604-597-8248, Fax: 604-597-8882
Hon. Bill Barisoff, Penticton, Liberal
250-387-3952, 866-387-3952, Fax: 250-387-2813, bill.barisoff.mla@leg.bc.ca, Other Communications: Constituency Phone: 250-487-4400, Fax: 250-487-4405
Donna Barnett, Cariboo-Chilcotin, Liberal
250-387-3820, Fax: 250-387-9066, donna.barnett.mla@leg.bc.ca, Other Communications: 100 Mile House Constituency Phone: 250-395-3916
Hon. Patrick Bell, Prince George-Mackenzie, Liberal
250-356-2771, Fax: 250-356-3000, pat.bell.mla@leg.bc.ca, Other Communications: Prince George Constituency Phone: 250-612-4194
Hon. Bill Bennett, East Kootenay, Liberal
250-356-1748, 866-417-6022, Fax: 250-952-7263, bill.bennett.mla@leg.bc.ca, Other Communications: Constituency Phone: 250-417-6022
Dawn Black, New Westminster, New Democratic Party
250-387-3655, Fax: 250-387-4680, dawn.black.mla@leg.bc.ca, Other Communications: Constituency Phone: 604-775-2101, Fax: 604-775-2121
Hon. Iain Black, Port Moody-Coquitlam, Liberal
250-356-1656, Fax: 250-952-7263, iain.black.mla@leg.bc.ca, Other Communications: Constituency Phone: 604-949-1226, Fax: 604-949-1281
Hon. Harry Bloy, Burnaby-Lougheed, Liberal
250-356-7750, Fax: 250-356-7292, harry.bloy.mla@leg.bc.ca, Other Communications: Constituency Phone: 604-664-0847, Fax: 604-664-0815
Hon. Shirley Bond, Prince George-Valemount, Liberal
250-356-7717, Fax: 250-356-8270, shirley.bond.mla@leg.bc.ca, Other Communications: Constituency Phone: 250-612-4181, Fax: 250 612-4188
Jagrup Brar, Surrey-Fleetwood, New Democratic Party
250-387-3655, Fax: 250-387-4680, jagrup.brar.mla@leg.bc.ca, Other Communications: Constituency Phone: 604-501-8227, Fax: 604-501-8233
Hon. Stephanie Cadieux, Surrey-Panorama, Liberal
250-952-7623, Fax: 250-952-7628, stephanie.cadieux.mla@leg.bc.ca, Other Communications: Constituency Phone: 604-574-5662, Fax: 604-574-5691
Ron Cantelon, Parksville-Qualicum, Liberal
250-387-2203, Fax: 250-387-9066, ron.cantelon.mla@leg.bc.ca, Other Communications: Constituency Phone: 250-951-6018, Fax: 250-951-6020
Spencer Chandra Herbert, Vancouver-WestEnd, New Democratic Party
250-387-3655, Fax: 250-387-4680, s.chandraherbert.mla@leg.bc.ca, Other Communications: Constituency Phone: 604-660-7307, Fax: 604-660-7300
Hon. Ida Chong, Oak Bay-Gordon Head, Liberal
250-387-2283, Fax: 250-387-4312, ida.chong.mla@leg.bc.ca, Other Communications: Gordon Head Constituency Phone: 250-472-8528
Raj Chouhan, Burnaby-Edmonds, New Democratic Party
250-387-3655, Fax: 250-387-4680, raj.chouhan.mla@leg.bc.ca, Other Communications: Constituency Phone: 604-660-7301, Fax: 250-387-4680
Hon. Christy Clark, Vancouver-Point Grey, Liberal
250-387-1715, Fax: 250-387-0087, premier@gov.bc.ca; christy@christyclark.ca, Other Communications: Constituency Phone: 604-775-1003, Fax: 250-387-0087
Murray Coell, Saanich North & theIslands, Liberal
250-387-8381, 866-655-5711, Fax: 250-387-9066, murray.coell.mla@leg.bc.ca, Other Communications: Constituency Phone: 250-655-5711, Fax: 250-655-5710
Hon. Rich Coleman, Fort Langley-Aldergrove, Liberal
250-387-5896, Fax: 250-356-2965, rich.coleman.mla@leg.bc.ca, Other Communications: Constituency Phone: 604-882-3151, Fax: 604-882-3154
Katrine Conroy, West Kootenay, New Democratic Party
250-387-3655, 888-755-0556, Fax: 250-387-4680, katrine.conroy.mla@leg.bc.ca, Other Communications: Constituency Phone: 250-304-2783, Fax: 250-304-2655
Gary Earl Coons, North Coast, New Democratic Party
250-387-3655, 866-624-7734, Fax: 250-387-4680, gary.coons.mla@leg.bc.ca, Other Communications: Constituency Phone: 250-624-7734, Fax: 250-624-7737
Kathy Corrigan, Burnaby-Deer Lake, New Democratic Party
250-387-3655, Fax: 250-387-4680, kathy.corrigan.mla@leg.bc.ca, Other Communications: Constituency Phone: 604-775-2414, Fax: 604-775-2550
Marc Dalton, Maple Ridge-Mission, Liberal
250-953-4769, 877-899-3215, Fax: 250-387-9100, marc.dalton.mla@leg.bc.ca, Other Communications: Maple Ridge Constituency Phone: 604-476-4530
Hon. Michael de Jong, QC, Abbotsford West, Liberal
250-953-3547, Fax: 250-356-9587, mike.dejong.mla@leg.bc.ca, Other Communications: Constituency Phone: 604-870-5486, Fax: 604-870-5444
Adrian Dix, Vancouver-Kingsway, New Democratic Party
250-387-3655, Fax: 250-387-4680, adrian.dix.mla@leg.bc.ca, Other Communications: Constituency Phone: 604-660-0314, Fax: 604-660-1131
Doug Donaldson, Stikine, New Democratic Party
250-387-3655, Fax: 250-387-4680, doug.donaldson.mla@leg.bc.ca, Other Communications: Hazelton Constituency Phone: 250-842-6338
Mable Elmore, Vancouver-Kensington, New Democratic Party
250-387-3655, Fax: 250-387-4680, mable.elmore.mla@leg.bc.ca, Other Communications: Constituency Phone: 604-775-1033, Fax: 604-775-1330
Hon. Kevin Falcon, Surrey-Cloverdale, Liberal
250-387-3751, Fax: 250-387-5594, kevin.falcon.mla@leg.bc.ca, Other Communications: Constituency Phone: 604-576-3792, Fax: 604-576-3797
Mike Farnworth, Port Coquitlam, New Democratic Party
250-387-3655, Fax: 250-387-4680, mike.farnworth.mla@leg.bc.ca, Other Communications: Constituency Phone: 604-927-2088, Fax: 604-927-2090
Rob Fleming, Victoria-Swan Lake, New Democratic Party
250-387-3655, Fax: 250-387-4680, rob.fleming.mla@leg.bc.ca, Other Communications: Constituency Phone: 250-360-2023, Fax: 250-360-2027
Eric Foster, Vernon-Monashee, Liberal
250-356-9574, Fax: 250-356-0596, eric.foster.mla@leg.bc.ca, Other Communications: Constituency Phone: 250-503-3600, Fax: 250-503-3603
Scott Fraser, Alberni-Pacific Rim, New Democratic Party
250-387-3655, 866-870-4190, Fax: 250-387-4680, scott.fraser.mla@leg.bc.ca, Other Communications: Port Alberni Constituency Phone: 250-720-4515
Guy Gentner, Delta North, New Democratic Party
250-387-3655, Fax: 250-387-4680, guy.gentner.mla@leg.bc.ca, Other Communications: Constituency Phone: 604-597-1488, Fax: 604-597-1466
Sue Hammell, Surrey-Green Timbers, New Democratic Party
250-387-3655, Fax: 250-387-4680, sue.hammell.mla@leg.bc.ca, Other Communications: Constituency Phone: 604-590-5868, Fax: 604-590-5873
Hon. Colin Hansen, Vancouver-Quilchena, Liberal
250-952-7270, Fax: 250-387-9100, colin.hansen.mla@leg.bc.ca, Other Communications: Constituency Phone: 604-664-0748, Fax: 604-664-0750
Randy Hawes, Abbotsford-Mission, Liberal
250-952-7275, 866-370-6203, Fax: 250-387-9100, randy.hawes.mla@leg.bc.ca, Other Communications: Mission Constituency Phone: 604-820-6203
Dave S. Hayer, Surrey-Tynehead, Liberal
250-387-8076, Fax: 250-387-9100, dave.hayer.mla@leg.bc.ca, Other Communications: Constituency Phone: 604-586-3747, Fax: 604-584-4741
Kash Heed, Vancouver-Fraserview, Liberal
250-356-0963, Fax: 250-387-9066, kash.heed.mla@leg.bc.ca, Other Communications: Constituency Phone: 604-775-2246, Fax: 604-775-2422

Hon. Gordon Hogg, Surrey-White Rock, Liberal
250-952-7638, Fax: 250-387-9066,
gordon.hogg.mla@leg.bc.ca, Other Communications: Constituency Phone: 604-542-3930, Fax: 604-542-3933
John Horgan, Juan de Fuca, New Democratic Party
250-387-3655, Fax: 250-387-4680,
john.horgan.mla@leg.bc.ca, Other Communications: Constituency Phone: 250-391-2801, Fax: 250-391-2804
Douglas Horne, Coquitlam-BurkeMountain, Liberal
250-953-4611, 800-691-9158, Fax: 250-387-9100,
douglas.horne.mla@leg.bc.ca, Other Communications: Constituency Phone: 604-949-1424, Fax: 604-949-1481
Rob Howard, Richmond Centre, Liberal
250-952-7616, Fax: 250-387-9100,
rob.howard.mla@leg.bc.ca, Other Communications: Constituency Phone: 604-775-0754
Vicki Huntington, Delta South, Independent
250-952-7594, Fax: 250-952-7598,
vicki.huntington.mla@leg.bc.ca, Other Communications: Constituency Phone: 604-940-7924
Carole James, Victoria-Beacon Hill, New Democratic Party
250-387-3655, Fax: 250-387-4680,
carole.james.mla@leg.bc.ca, Other Communications: Constituency Phone: 250-952-4211, Fax: 250-952-4586
Maurine Karagianis, Esquimalt-RoyalRoads, New Democratic Party
250-387-3655, Fax: 250-387-4680,
maurine.karagianis.mla@leg.bc.ca, Other Communications: Constituency Phone: 250-479-8326, Fax: 259-479-5003
Leonard Krog, Nanaimo, New Democratic Party
250-387-3655, Fax: 250-387-4680,
leonard.krog.mla@leg.bc.ca, Other Communications: Constituency Phone: 250-714-0630, Fax: 250-714-0859
Hon. Kevin Krueger, Kamloops-SouthThompson, Liberal
250-952-7269, Fax: 250-952-7263,
kevin.krueger.mla@leg.bc.ca, Other Communications: Constituency Phone: 250-314-6031, Fax: 250-314-6040
Jenny Wai Ching Kwan, Vancouver-MountPleasant, New Democratic Party
250-387-3655, Fax: 250-387-4680,
jenny.kwan.mla@leg.bc.ca, Other Communications: Constituency Phone: 604-775-0790, Fax: 604-775-0881
Hon. Terry Lake, Kamloops-North Thompson, Liberal
250-387-1187, Fax: 250-387-1356, terry.lake.mla@leg.bc.ca, Other Communications: Constituency Phone: 250-554-5413, Fax: 250-554-5417
Harry Lali, Fraser-Nicola, New Democratic Party
250-387-3655, 877-378-4802, Fax: 250-384-4680,
harry.lali.mla@leg.bc.ca, Other Communications: Constituency Phone: 250-378-4802, Fax: 250-378-4852
Richard T. Lee, Burnaby North, Liberal
250-356-3052, Fax: 250-387-9100,
richard.lee.mla@leg.bc.ca, Other Communications: Constituency Phone: 604 775-0778, Fax: 604-775-0833
Hon. Blair Lekstrom, Peace RiverSouth, Liberal
250-387-1978, 877-784-1330, Fax: 250-356-2290,
blair.lekstrom.mla@leg.bc.ca, Other Communications: Constituency Phone: 250-784-1330, Fax: 250-784-1333
John Les, Chilliwack, Liberal
250-356-6171, 866-424-8350, Fax: 250-387-3698,
john.les.mla@leg.bc.ca, Other Communications: Constituency Phone: 604-702-5214
Norm Letnick, Kelowna-LakeCountry, Liberal
250-953-5144, 866-765-8516, Fax: 250-387-9100,
norm.letnick.mla@leg.bc.ca, Other Communications: Constituency Phone: 205-765-8516, Fax: 250-765-7283
Margaret MacDiarmid, Vancouver-Fairview, Liberal
250-952-7271, Fax: 250-387-3698,
margaret.macdiarmid.mla@leg.bc.ca, Other Communications: Constituency Phone: 604-660-7061, Fax: 604-660-7065
Norm Macdonald, ColumbiaRiver-Revelstoke, New Democratic Party
250-387-3655, 866-870-4188, Fax: 250-387-4680,
norm.macdonald.mla@leg.bc.ca, Other Communications: Constituency Phone: 250-344-4816, Fax: 250-344-4815
Joan McIntyre, West Vancouver-Sea toSky, Liberal
250-953-4613, Fax: 250-387-9100,
joan.mcintyre.mla@leg.bc.ca, Other Communications: Constituency Phone: 604-981-0045, Fax: 604-981-0060
Hon. Mary McNeil, Vancouver-False Creek, Liberal
250-387-9699, Fax: 250-387-9722,
mary.mcneil.mla@leg.bc.ca, Other Communications: Constituency Phone: 604-775-2601, Fax: 604-775-2607
Hon. Don McRae, Comox Valley, Liberal
250-387-1023, Fax: 250-387-1522,
don.mcrae.mla@leg.bc.ca, Other Communications: Constituency Phone: 250-703-2422, Fax: 250-703-2425
Michelle Mungall, Nelson-Creston, New Democratic Party
250-387-3655, 877-388-4498, Fax: 250-387-4680,
wally.oppal.mla@leg.bc.ca, Other Communications: Constituency Phone: 250-354-5944, Fax: 250-354-5937
Hon. Barry Penner, Chilliwack-Hope, Liberal
250-387-1866, 866-553-5537, Fax: 250-387-6411,
barry.penner.mla@leg.bc.ca, Other Communications: Constituency Phone: 604-858-6202, Fax: 604-858-6254
Pat Pimm, Peace River North, Liberal
250-952-6784, 877-332-0101, Fax: 250-387-9100,
pat.pimm.mla@leg.bc.ca, Other Communications: Constituency Phone: 250-263-0101, Fax: 250-263-0104
Hon. Mary Polak, Langley, Liberal
250-953-4844, Fax: 250-953-4856,
mary.polak.mla@leg.bc.ca, Other Communications: Constituency Phone: 604-514-8206, Fax: 604-514-0195
Lana Popham, Saanich South, New Democratic Party
250-387-3655, Fax: 250-387-4680,
lana.popham.mla@leg.bc.ca, Other Communications: Constituency Phone: 250-479-4154, Fax: 250-479-4176
Bruce Ralston, Surrey-Whalley, New Democratic Party
250-387-3655, Fax: 250-387-4680,
bruce.ralston.mla@leg.bc.ca, Other Communications: Constituency Phone: 604-586-2740, Fax: 604-586-2800
Linda Reid, Richmond East, Liberal
250-953-4887, Fax: 250-356-0596, linda.reid.mla@leg.bc.ca, Other Communications: Constituency Phone: 604-775-0891, Fax: 604-775-0999
Bill Routley, Cowichan Valley, New Democratic Party
250-387-3655, 877-715-0127, Fax: 250-387-4680,
bill.routley.mla@leg.bc.ca, Other Communications: Constituency Phone: 250-715-0127, Fax: 250-715-0139
Doug Routley, Nanaimo-North Cowichan, New Democratic Party
250-387-3655, Fax: 250-387-4680,
douglas.routley.mla@leg.bc.ca, Other Communications: Ladysmith Constituency Phone: 250-245-9375
John Rustad, Nechako Lakes, Liberal
250-953-4892, 877-964-5650, Fax: 250-387-9066,
john.rustad.mla@leg.bc.ca, Other Communications: Vanderhoof Constituency Phone: 250-567-6820
Michael Sather, Maple Ridge-Pitt Meadows, New Democratic Party
250-387-3655, Fax: 250-387-4680,
michael.sather.mla@leg.bc.ca, Other Communications: Constituency Phone: 604-476-9823, Fax: 604-476-9820
Nicholas Simons, PowellRiver-Sunshine Coast, New Democratic Party
250-387-3655, 866-373-0792, Fax: 250-387-4680,
nicholas.simons.mla@leg.bc.ca, Other Communications: Powell River Constituency Office Phone: 604-485-1249
Bob Simpson, Cariboo North, Independent
250-387-8347, 866-991-0296, Fax: 250-387-8338,
bob.simpson.mla@leg.bc.ca, Other Communications: Quesnel Constituency Phone: 250-991-0296
Shane Simpson, Vancouver-Hastings, New Democratic Party
250-387-3655, Fax: 250-387-4680,
shane.simpson.mla@leg.bc.ca, Other Communications: Constituency Phone: 604-775-2277, Fax: 604-775-2352
John Slater, Boundary-Similkameen, Liberal
250-953-4869, 877-652-4304, Fax: 250-387-9100,
john.slater.mla@leg.bc.ca, Other Communications: Constituency Phone: 250-495-2042, Fax: 250-495-2077
Ben Stewart, Westside-Kelowna, Liberal
250-952-7280, Fax: 250-356-0596,
ben.stewart.mla@leg.bc.ca, Other Communications: Constituency Phone: 250-768-8426, Fax: 250-768-8436
Moira Stilwell, Vancouver-Langara, Liberal
250-952-7653, Fax: 250-387-9066,
moira.stilwell.mla@leg.bc.ca, Other Communications: Constituency Phone: 604-660-8380, Fax: 604-660-8383
Ralph Sultan, West Vancouver-Capilano, Liberal
250-356-9495, Fax: 250-387-9066,
ralph.sultan.mla@leg.bc.ca, Other Communications: Constituency Phone: 604-981-0050, Fax: 604-981-0055
Hon. Steve Thomson, Kelowna-Mission, Liberal
250-387-6240, Fax: 250-387-1040,
steve.thomson.mla@leg.bc.ca, Other Communications: Constituency Phone: 250-712-3620, Fax: 250-712-3626
Diane Thorne, Coquitlam-Maillardville, New Democratic Party
250-387-3655, Fax: 250-387-4680,
diane.thorne.mla@leg.bc.ca, Other Communications: Constituency Phone: 604-933-2001, Fax: 604-933-2022
Jane Thornthwaite, NorthVancouver-Seymour, Liberal
250-387-2796, Fax: 250-387-9100,
jane.thornthwaite.mla@leg.bc.ca, Other Communications: Constituency Phone: 604-983-9852, Fax: 604-983-9978
Claire Trevena, North Island, New Democratic Party
250-387-3655, 866-387-5100, Fax: 250-387-4680,
claire.trevena.mla@leg.bc.ca, Other Communications: Campbell River Constituency Phone: 250-287-5100
John van Dongen, Abbotsford South, Liberal
250-387-8950, Fax: 250-952-7263,
john.vandongen.mla@leg.bc.ca, Other Communications: Constituency Phone: 604-870-5945, Fax: 604-870-5950
Hon. Naomi Yamamoto, NorthVancouver-Lonsdale, Liberal
250-356-0179, Fax: 250-952-0260,
naomi.yamamoto.mla@leg.bc.ca, Other Communications: Constituency Phone: 604-981-0033, Fax: 604-981-0044
John Yap, Richmond-Steveston, Liberal
250-356-1631, Fax: 250-952-7263, john.yap.mla@leg.bc.ca, Other Communications: Constituency Phone: 604-241-8452, Fax: 604-241-8493

British Columbia Government Departments & Agencies

Ministry of Aboriginal Relations & Reconciliation

2957 Jutland Rd., PO Box 9100 Prov Govt, Victoria, BC V8W 9B1

250-387-6121
800-663-7867
abrinfo@gov.bc.ca
www.gov.bc.ca/arr
Other Communication: Vancouver Phone: 604-660-2421; Toll Free Phone Information: 1-800-880-1022

The Ministry's activities include negotiating treaties & other agreements & improving the lives of Aboriginal people.

Minister, Aboriginal Relations & Reconciliation, Hon. Mary Polak
250-953-4844, Fax: 250-953-4856, ABR.Minister@gov.bc.ca: mary.polak.mla@leg.bc.ca
Deputy Minister, Steve Munro
250-356-1394, Fax: 250-387-6073
Assistant Deputy Minister, Corporate Services Division, Tara Faganello
250-387-5258
Director, Workforce Strategies Branch, Ingrid Fee
250-952-4930, Fax: 250-952-4925, Ingrid.Fee@gov.bc.ca, Other Communications: Cell Phone: 250-415-7794
Director, Communications, Maria Wilkie
250-953-3211, Fax: 250-356-2213, maria.wilkie@gov.bc.ca

Associated Agencies, Boards & Commissions:
• British Columbia Treaty Commission (BCTC)
#700, 1111 Melville St.
Vancouver, BC V6E 3V6
604-482-9200 Fax: 604-482-9222 800-665-8330
info@bctreaty.net
www.bctreaty.net
The independent & neutral body facilitates treaty negotiations among the governments of Canada, British Columbia, & First Nations in BC.
• Native Economic Development Advisory Board
c/o Director, Economic Initiatives
PO Box 9100 Prov Govt
Victoria, BC V8W 9B1
250-387-2536 Fax: 250-356-9467
www.gov.bc.ca/arr/economic/fcf/nedab.html
Supporting sustainable Aboriginal economic development throughout British Columbia is the role of the Native Economic Development Advisory Board.

Fiscal Negotiations Team
Chief Negotiator, Rob Draeseke
250-356-8768, Fax: 250-356-5213, Rob.Draeseke@gov.bc.ca
Fiscal Negotiator, Heidi Reinebeck
250-356-5484, Fax: 250-387-5213, Heidi.Reinebeck@gov.bc.ca, Other Communications: Cell Phone: 250-896-5390
Director, Cost-sharing & Financial Mandates, Elisabeth Ellis
250-356-9070, Fax: 250-356-6073, Elisabeth.Ellis@gov.bc.ca, Other Communications: Cell Phone: 250-886-6192
Director, Fiscal Arrangements & Climate Change, Michael Matsubuchi
250-387-6387, Fax: 250-356-5312, Michael.Matsubuchi@gov.bc.ca, Other Communications: Cell Phone: 250-744-7454
Acting Director, Cost-sharing & Financial, Badema Karabegovic
250-953-3506, Fax: 250-387-6073, Badema.Karabegovic@gov.bc.ca

Negotiations & Regional Operations Division
Assistant Deputy Minister, Charles Porter
250-953-3541, Fax: 250-387-6073
Divisional Coordinator, Shawna Hill
250-953-3542, Fax: 250-387-6073, Shawna.Hill@gov.bc.ca
Chief Negotiator, Beedle Team, Tom Ethier
250-387-0024, Fax: 250-387-0887, Tom.Ethier@gov.bc.ca, Other Communications: Alternate Phone: 250-361-7372
Chief Negotiator, Lofthouse Team, Heinz Dyck
250-356-6599, Fax: 250-356-6159, Heinz.Dyck@gov.bc.ca
Chief Negotiator, Lofthouse Team, Mark Lofthouse
250-356-8769, Fax: 250-387-0887, Mark.Lofthouse@gov.bc.ca, Other Communications: Cell Phone: 250-480-8899
Executive Director, Negotiations & Regional Operations, Trish Balcaen
250-953-3954, Trish.Balcaen@gov.bc.ca

Partnerships & Community Renewal Division
Assistant Deputy Minister, Arlene Paton
250-356-8750, Fax: 250-387-6073, Arlene.Paton@gov.bc.ca

Divisional Coordinator, Janice Rashbrook
250-356-0213, Fax: 250-387-6073,
Janice.Rashbrook@gov.bc.ca
Chief Negotiator, Negotiations & Community Renewal Branch, Roger Graham
250-356-6599, Fax: 250-356-0366,
Roger.Graham@gov.bc.ca, Other Communications: Cell Phone: 250-812-8244
Executive Director, Intergovernmental & Community Relations, Ken Armour
250-387-2161, Fax: 250-356-9467, Ken.Armour@gov.bc.ca
Executive Director, Implementation & Legislation, Lloyd Roberts
250-952-4482, Fax: 250-952-4485,
Lloyd.Roberts@gov.bc.ca, Other Communications: Cell Phone: 250-380-8568

Strategic Initiatives Division
Assistant Deputy Minister, Julian C. Paine
250-387-6838, Fax: 250-387-6073, Other Communications: Cell Phone: 250-387-6838
Chief Negotiator, Glenn Ricketts
250-953-4004, Fax: 250-356-0366,
Glenn.Ricketts@gov.bc.ca, Other Communications: Cell Phone: 250-889-1695
Executive Director, Cross Government Initiatives, Lynn Beak
250-356-7214, Fax: 250-356-0366, Lynn.Beak@gov.bc.ca, Other Communications: Cell Phone: 250-920-6286
Executive Director, Strategic Policy & Planning Branch, Jaclynn Hunter
250-356-5267, Fax: 250-356-0366,
Jaclynn.Hunter@gov.bc.ca
Executive Director, Special Projects, Giovanni Puggioni
250-952-0530, Fax: 250-356-0366,
Giovanni.Puggioni@gov.bc.ca

Ministry of Advanced Education

PO Box 9059 Prov Govt, Victoria, BC V8W 9E2
250-952-6508 Fax: 250-356-6942
ALMD.WEBMASTER@gov.bc.ca
www.gov.bc.ca/aved/

The Ministry of Advanced Education strives to lead & support an excellent & accessible post-secondary education system, & to ensure an integrated approach to research & innovation.

Acts Administered:
Accountants (Certified General) Act
Accountants (Chartered) Act
Accountants (Management) Act
Applied Science Technologists & Technicians Act
Architects Act
Architects (Landscape) Act
College & Institute Act
Degree Authorization Act
Engineers & Geoscientists Act
Knowledge Network Corporation Act
Ministry of International Business & Immigration Act
Music Teachers (Registered) Act
Open Learning Agency Act
Private Career Training Institutions Act
Public Education Flexibility & Choice Act, Part I
Public Education Labour Relations Act
Public Sector Pension Plans Act (except as it relates to the Investment Management Corporation)
Public Service Act
Public Service Benefit Plan Act
Public Service Labour Relations Act
Royal Roads University Act
Thompson Rivers University Act
University Act
University Foundations Act
Workers Compensation Act, Section 3 (6)

Minister, Advanced Education, Hon. Naomi Yamamoto
250-356-0179, Fax: 250-952-0260,
naomi.yamamoto.mla@leg.bc.ca; AVED@gov.bc.ca
Deputy Minister, Cheryl Wenezenki-Yolland
250-356-5173, Fax: 250-356-5468,
ALMD.DeputyMinister@gov.bc.ca

Associated Agencies, Boards & Commissions:
• Degree Quality Assessment Board
Degree Quality Assessment Board Secretariat
PO Box 9177 Prov Govt
Victoria, BC V8W 9H8
250-387-5163
DQABsecretariat@gov.bc.ca
www.aved.gov.bc.ca/degree-authorization/board/welcome.htm
The Degree Quality Assessment Board reviews applications from British Columbia public post-secondary institutions, & private & out-of-province public post-secondary institutions. Applications concern new degree programs & exempt status, & the use of the word "university". Recommendations are then made to the Minister of Advanced Education & Labour Market Development.
• Industry Training Authority (ITA)
#1223, 13351 Commerce Pkwy.
Richmond, BC V6V 2X7
604-214-8700 Fax: 604-214-8701 866-660-6011
info@itabc.ca; customerservice@itabc.ca
www.itabc.ca
Other Communication: Customer Service: 778-328-8700
British Columbia's Industry Training Authority is a provincial government agency which oversees the province's training & apprenticeship system. The ITA works with industry, employers, training providers, trainees, & apprentices.
• Leading Edge Endowment Fund Board (LEEF)
1188 West Georgia St., 9th Fl.
Vancouver, BC V6E 4A2
604-438-3220
contact@leefbc.ca
www.leefbc.ca
To encourage social & economic development in British Columbia, the provincial government established the Leading Edge Endowment Fund in 2002. The Fund establishes Leadership Research Chairs at the province's public, post-secondary institutions, & Regional Innovation Chairs through colleges, university-colleges, & institutes.
• Private Career Training Institutions Agency
#300, 5172 Kingsway
Burnaby, BC V5H 2E8
604-660-4400 Fax: 604-660-3312 800-661-7441
info@pctia.bc.ca
www.pctia.bc.ca
The Private Career Training Institutions Agency is the regulatory agency for private training institutions in British Columbia. The Agency works in accordance with the Private Career Training Institutions Act, Regulations & Bylaws.

Students, Institutions & Programs Division
PO Box 9191 Prov Govt, Victoria, BC V8W 9E6
Fax: 250-356-5468
Acting Assistant Deputy Minister, Mark Gillis
250-952-0698, Fax: 250-356-5468, Mark.Gillis@gov.bc.ca
Executive Director, Research Universities & Health Programs Branch, Susan B. Brown
250-387-6193, Fax: 250-356-8851,
AVED.ResearchUniversities&HlthProgBr@gov.bc.ca
Executive Director, Teaching Universities, Institutes & Aboriginal Programs Branch, Deborah Hull
250-356-8382, Fax: 250-356-5962, MSUUAPB@gov.bc.ca
Executive Director, Governance & Quality Assurance Branch, Tony Loughran
250-356-7254
Executive Director, Colleges & Skills Development Branch, Dawn Minty
250-387-8871, Fax: 250-952-6110,
RESD.Agencies&QualityAssuranceBr@gov.bc.ca
Executive Director, StudentAid BC, Victoria Thibeau
250-387-3605, Fax: 250-356-5468,
Victoria.Thibeau@gov.bc.ca

Decision Support & Accountability Division
PO Box 9324 Prov Govt, Victoria, BC V8W 9N3
250-952-0606 Fax: 250-356-5468
Assistant Deputy Minister, Corporate Services, Brian Hansen
Chief Information Officer, Technology & Business Solutions Branch, Suzanne Manahan
250-952-0729, Fax: 250-952-0739
Executive Director, Open Government, Allan Pollock
250-356-7210, Allan.Pollock@gov.bc.ca
Executive Director, Policy Planning & Intergovernmental Relations, Jacqui Stewart
250-387-5029, Fax: 250-387-1377,
AVED.PolicyPlanning&IntergovRelationsBr@gov.bc.ca
Executive Director, Post Secondary Funding & Corporate Finance Branch, Joseph Thompson
250-387-8820, Fax: 250-356-7922,
Joe.Thompson@gov.bc.ca
Executive Director, Talent Strategies Branch, Lori Wiedeman
250-356-1777, Fax: 250-356-5468,
Lori.Wiedeman@gov.bc.ca
Director, Research & Analysis, Patty Beatty-Guenter
250-387-1105, Fax: 250-952-0606,
AVED.PolicyPlanning&IntergovRelationsBr@gov.bc.ca
Director, Projects & Planning, Kursti Calder
250-387-8874, Fax: 250-952-0606,
AVED.PolicyPlanning&IntergovRelationsBr@gov.bc.ca
Director, Corporate Policy, Kate Cotie
250-387-6197, Fax: 250-952-0606,
AVED.PolicyPlanning&IntergovRelationsBr@gov.bc.ca
Director, Post Secondary Finance, Colin Fowler
250-387-6142, Fax: 250-952-6103, Colin.Fowler@gov.bc.ca
Director, Financial Operations, Jennifer Ingram-Kum
250-356-1409, Fax: 250-387-6360,
Jennifer.IngramKum@gov.bc.ca
Director, Capital Unit, Catherine Nickerson
250-356-7896, Fax: 250-356-7922,
Catherine.Nickerson@gov.bc.ca
Director, Corporate Policy, Vincent Portal
250-356-6356, Fax: 250-952-0606,
AVED.PolicyPlanning&IntergovRelationsBr@gov.bc.ca
Director, Corporate Finance, Donna Porter
250-356-6819, Fax: 250-387-6360, Donna.Porter@gov.bc.ca
Director, Workforce Planning & Analysis, Kathy Philps
250-387-5600, Fax: 250-356-5468, Kathy.Philps@gov.bc.ca

Ministry of Agriculture

PO Box 9120 Prov Govt, Victoria, BC V8W 9E2
250-387-5121 Fax: 250-387-1522
www.gov.bc.ca/agri

The mission of the Ministry is to provide a business climate for a competitive & profitable industry that supplies safe, high quality food for consumers & the export market.

Acts Administered:
Agri-Food Choice & Quality Act
Organic Agricultural Products Certification Regulation
Agricultural Land Commission Act
Agricultural Produce Grading Act
Agrologists Act
Animal Disease Control Act
Bee Act
Farm Income Insurance Act
Farm Practices Protection (Right to Farm) Act
Farmers & Womens Institutes Act
Farming & Fishing Industries Development Act
Fish Inspection Act
Fisheries Act
Food Products Standards Act
Fur Farm Act
Game Farm Act
Insurance for Crops Act
Livestock Act
Livestock Identification Act
Livestock Lien Act
Local Government Act (in part)
Ministry of Agriculture & Food Act
Milk Industry Act (In Part)
Ministry of Forestry & Range Act
Natural Products Marketing (BC) Act
Plant Protection Act
Prevention of Cruelty to Animals Act
Range Act (In Part)
Seed Potato Act
Veterinarians Act
Veterinary Drugs Act

Minister, Agriculture, Hon. Don McRae
250-387-1023, Fax: 250-387-1522, AGR.Minister@gov.bc.ca;
don.mcrae.mla@leg.bc.ca
Deputy Minister, Wes Shoemaker
250-356-1800, Fax: 250-356-8392
Operations, Project & Administrative Coordinator, Naomi Boulay
250-387-7184, Fax: 250-356-8392, Naomi.Boulay@gov.bc.ca

Associated Agencies, Boards & Commissions:
• Agricultural Land Commission (ALC)
#133, 4940 Canada Way
Burnaby, BC V5G 4K6
604-660-7000 Fax: 604-660-7033
ALCBurnaby@Victoria1.gov.bc.ca
www.alc.gov.bc.ca
The independent Crown agency strives to preserve agricultural land in British Columbia. The Provincial Agricultural Land Commission also works to encourage & enable farm businesses throughout the province. The Commission's chief responsibility is the administration of the Agricultural Land Commission Act.
• British Columbia Broiler Hatching Egg Commission (BCBHEC)
#180, 32160 South Fraser Way
Abbotsford, BC V2T 1W5
604-850-1854 Fax: 604-850-1683
info@bcbhec.com
www.bcbhec.com
The British Columbia Broiler Hatching Egg Commission was formed in 1988 under the British Columbia Natural Products Marketing Act, & seeks to promote a better understanding of the broiler hatching egg industry.
• British Columbia Chicken Marketing Board (BCCMB)
#101, 32450 Simon Ave.
Abbotsford, BC V2T 4J2
604-859-2868 Fax: 604-859-2811
info@bcchicken.ca
www.bcchicken.ca
The purpose of the BC Chicken Marketing Board is to monitor & regulate the production of chicken in British Columbia. The Board works closely with hatcheries, growers, truckers & processors, & carries out field inspections, to accomplish this.
• British Columbia Cranberry Marketing Commission (BCCMC)
c/o #71, 4001 Old Clayburn Rd.
Abbotsford, BC V3S 1C5
604-302-1046
cranberries@telus.net
www.bccranberries.com

Since 1968 the BCCMC has administered the British Columbia Cranberry Marketing Scheme, established under the Natural Products Marketing (BC) Act. The Commission reports to the British Columbia Farm Industry Review Board.
• British Columbia Egg Marketing Board (BCEMB)
#250, 32160 South Fraser Way
Abbotsford, BC V2T 1W5
604-556-3348 Fax: 604-556-3410
bcemb@bcegg.com
www.bcegg.com
The BCEMB was established in 1967 in order to better regulate the price of eggs.
• British Columbia Farm Industry Review Board (BCFIRB)
780 Blanshard St.
PO Box 9129 Prov Govt
Victoria, BC V8W 9B5
250-356-8945 Fax: 250-356-5131
firb@gov.bc.ca
www.firb.gov.bc.ca
The British Columbia Farm Industry Review Board is a statutory appeal body. It is engaged in the general supervision of marketing boards & commodity boards which operate in the agricultural & aquaculture sectors.
• British Columbia Hog Marketing Commission (BCHMC)
PO Box 8000-280
Abbotsford, BC V2S 6H1
604-897-9252 Fax: 604-677-6058
dianned@bcpork.ca
www.bcpork.ca
The Commission seeks to promote BC-grown pork through the use of its logo on all BC pork products.
• British Columbia Milk Marketing Board (BCMMB)
#200, 32160 South Fraser Way
Abbotsford, BC V2T 1W5
604-556-3444 Fax: 604-556-7717
info@milk-bc.com
http: //bcmilkmarketing.worldsecuresystems.com/
The Board is reponsible for promoting, controlling & regulating the production, transportation, packing, storing & marketing of all BC milk products.
• British Columbia Turkey Marketing Board (BCTMB)
#106, 19329 Enterprise Way
Surrey, BC V3S 6J8
604-534-5644 Fax: 604-534-3651
info@bcturkey.com
www.bcturkey.com
Established in 1966, the Board oversees the licensing of turkey farmers and processors; prices for live turkeys; maintaining of a quota system; & promoting turkey products, under the authority of the Natural Products Marketing (BC) Act.
• British Columbia Vegetable Marketing Commission (BCVMC)
#207, 15252 32nd Ave.
Surrey, BC V3S 0R7
604-542-9734 Fax: 603-542-9753
info@bcveg.com
The Commission is responsible for promoting controlled marketing for BC vegetable producers, under the authority of the Natural Products Marketing (BC) Act.
• Muskwa-Kechika Advisory Board (M-KAB)
coordinator@muskwa-kechika.com
www.muskwa-kechika.com
The Board oversees the preservation of the Muskwa-Kechika Management Area, & ensures that activities carried out within the area meet the standards set by the Muskwa-Kechika Management Plan.

Agriculture Science & Policy
PO Box 9120 Prov Govt, Victoria, BC V8W 9B4
250-356-1816 Fax: 250-356-7279
Assistant Deputy Minister, Vacant
Director, Innovation & Governance Branch, Sean Darling
250-356-5338, Fax: 250-356-5367, Sean.Darling@gov.bc.ca
Director/Chief Veterinary Officer, Plant & Animal Health Branch, Abbotsford, Paul Kitching
604-556-3038, Fax: 604-556-3010, Paul.Kitching@gov.bc.ca
Director, Policy & Industry Competitiveness, Grant Thompson
250-356-8299, Fax: 250-387-0357, Grant.Thompson@gov.bc.ca
Assistant Director, Policy & Industry Competitiveness, Gavin Last
250-356-7640, Fax: 250-387-0357, Gavin.Last@gov.bc.ca

Animal Health Center
604-556-3003 Fax: 604-556-3010
Avian Pathologist, Dr. Victoria Bowes
604-556-3041, Victoria.Bowes@gov.bc.ca
Veterinary Pathologist, Dr. Ann Britton
604-556-3039, Ann.P.Britton@gov.bc.ca
Fish Pathologist, Dr. Gary Marty
604-556-3123, Gary.Marty@gov.bc.ca
Veterinary Pathologist, Dr. Stephen Raverty
604-556-3026, Stephen.Raverty@gov.bc.ca
Veterinary Virologist, Dr. John Robinson
604-556-3036, John.H.Robinson@gov.bc.ca
Microbiologist/Supervisor, Dr. Sean Byrne
604-556-3025, Sean.Byrne@gov.bc.ca
Poultry Health Veterinarian, Dr. William Cox
604-556-3150, William.Cox@gov.bc.ca

Strategic Industry Partnerships Division
PO Box 9120 Prov Govt, Victoria, BC V8W 9B4
250-356-1122 Fax: 250-356-7279
Assistant Deputy Minister, Grant Parnell
250-356-1802, Grant.Parnell@gov.bc.ca
Director, Head Office, Gary Falk
250-861-7232, Fax: 250-861-7490, Gary.Falk@gov.bc.ca
Director, Sustainable Agriculture Management, Land Program Services, Ken Nickel
604-556-3103, Fax: 604-556-3030, Ken.Nickel@gov.bc.ca
Director, Food Protection Branch, Jim Russell
250-897-7561, Fax: 250-334-1410, Jim.Russell@gov.bc.ca
Assistant Director, Sustainable Agriculture Management, Leslie S. MacDonald
604-556-3074, Fax: 604-556-3030, Leslie.MacDonald@gov.bc.ca
Agrologist, Head Office, Phil Croteau
250-861-7419, Fax: 250-861-7490, Phil.Croteau@gov.bc.ca

Ministry of the Attorney General

PO Box 9044 Prov Govt, Victoria, BC V8W 9E2
250-387-1866 Fax: 250-387-6411
www.gov.bc.ca/ag
The Ministry of the Attorney General strives to improve British Columbia's justice system, so that citizens have access to quality justice services.
Acts Administered:
Adult Guardianship Act
Age of Majority Act
Attorney General Act
Civil Rights Protection Act
Class Proceedings Act
Commercial Arbitration Act
Commissioner on Resources & Environment Act
Company Act
Conflict of Laws Rules for Trusts Act
Constitution Act
Constitutional Amendment Approval Act
Constitutional Question Act
County Boundary Act
Court Agent Act
Court of Appeal Act
Court Order Enforcement Act
Court Order Interest Act
Court Rules Act
Crown Counsel Act
Crown Franchise Act
Crown Proceeding Act
Debtor Assistance Act
Disciplinary Authority Protection Act
Election Act
Electoral Boundaries Commission Act
Electoral Districts Act
Enforcement of Canadian Judgments Act
Escheat Act
Estate Administration Act
Estates of Missing Persons Act
Evidence Act
Expropriation Act
Family Compensation Act
Family Maintenance Enforcement Act
Family Relations Act
Federal Courts Jurisdiction Act
Financial Disclosure Act
Foreign Arbitral Awards Act
Foreign Money Claims Act
Foresters Act s. 9 (2)
Fraudulent Conveyance Act
Fraudulent Preference Act
Frustrated Contract Act
Good Samaritan Act
Holocaust Memorial Day Act
Human Rights Code
Indian Cut-off Lands Dispute
Infants Act
Inquiry Act
Insurance Corporation Divisions 1 & 2 Act
Interjurisdictional Support Order Act
International Commerical Arbitration Act
International Sale of Goods Act
International Trusts Act
Interpretation Act
Judicial Review Procedure Act
Jury Act
Justice Administration Act
Law & Equity Act
Law Reform Commission Act
Legal Profession Act
Legal Services Society Act
Libel & Slander Act
Limitation Act
Lobbyists Registration Act
Members' Conflict of Interest Act
Ministry of Consumer & Corporate Affairs Act
Ministry of Provincial Secretary & Government Services Act
Negligence Act
Nisga'a Final Agreement
Notaries Act
Occupiers Liability Act
Offence Act
Office for Children & Youth Act
Ombudsman Act
Partition of Property Act
Patients Property Act
Perpetuity Act
Power of Appointment Act
Power of Attorney Act
Privacy Act
Probate Recognition Act
Property Law Act
Provincial Court Act
Public Guardian & Trustee Act
Queen's Counsel Act
Recall & Initiative Act
Referendum Act
Regulations Act
Representation Agreement Act
Representative for Children & Youth Act
Sechelt Indian Government District Enabling Act
Sheriff Act
Small Claims Act
Statute Revision Act
Statute Uniformity Act
Subpoena (Interprovincial) Act
Supreme Court Act
Survivorship & Presumption of Death Act
Treaty Commission Act
Trespass Act
Trust & Settlement Variation Act
Trustee Act
Trustee (Church Property) Act
Wills Act
Wills Variation Act
Young Offenders (British Columbia) Act
Attorney General, Hon. Barry Penner
250-387-1866, Fax: 250-387-6411, barry.penner.mla@leg.bc.ca; AG.Minister@gov.bc.ca
Deputy Attorney General, David Loukidelis
250-356-0149, Fax: 250-387-6224
Assistant Deputy Attorney General, Legal Services, Richard Fyfe, Q.C.
250-356-9260
Assistant Deputy Attorney General, Criminal Justice, Robert Gillen, Q.C.
250-387-5174
Assistant Deputy Minister, Management Services, Tara Faganello
250-387-5258, Tara.Faganello@gov.bc.ca
Assistant Deputy Minister, Justice Services, Jerry McHale, Q.C.
250-356-6582
Assistant Deputy Minister, Court Services, Rob Wood
250-356-1527
Executive Director, Organizational Development Team Office, Julie Spiteri
250-387-6917, Fax: 250-356-6323, Julie.Spiteri@gov.bc.ca
Executive Director, Facilities Services Division, Betty Chen-Mack
250-356-7159, Fax: 250-356-9528, Betty.ChenMack@gov.bc.ca
Director, Investigation & Standards Office, Sydney Swift
250-387-5948, Fax: 250-356-9875
Deputy Director, Investigation & Standards Office, Jim Shalkowsky
250-387-5948, Fax: 250-356-9875

Associated Agencies, Boards & Commissions:
• British Columbia Ferry Commission
PO Box 35119 Hillside
Victoria, BC V8T 5G2
250-590-2770
info@bcferrycommission.com
www.bcferrycommission.com
The British Columbia Ferry Commission was established under the Coastal Ferry Act. The fares & service levels of the province's ferry operator, British Columbia Ferry Services Inc., are regulated by the Commission.
• British Columbia Human Rights Tribunal
#1170, 605 Robson St.
Vancouver, BC V6B 5J3
604-775-2000 Fax: 604-775-2020 888-440-8844 TTY: 604-775-2021
BCHumanRightsTribunal@gov.bc.ca
www.bchrt.bc.ca

The independent, quasi-judicial body was established by the British Columbia Human Rights Code. The British Columbia Human Rights Tribunal is engaged in accepting, screening, mediating, & adjudicating human rights complaints.
• British Columbia Law Institute (BCLI)
University of British Columbia
1822 East Mall
Vancouver, BC V6T 1Z1
604-822-0142 Fax: 604-822-0144
bcli@bcli.org
www.bcli.org
The Institute was created in 1997 under the Provincial Society Act, & is tasked with promoting clarity in modern law; improvement in the administration of justice; & scholarly legal research.
• British Columbia Review Board
#1020, 510 Burrard St.
Vancouver, BC V6C 3A8
604-660-8789 Fax: 604-660-8809 877-305-2277
www.bcrb.bc.ca
The British Columbia Review Board was created in accordance with the Criminal Code of Canada. The Board is an independent tribunal, with responsibility for holding hearings to establish & review dispositions. The dispositions involve persons who have been charged with criminal offenses & received verdicts of not criminally responsible on account of mental disorder, or unfit to stand trial on account of mental disorder.
• Elections British Columbia
• Judicial Council of British Columbia
Pacific Centre
#602, 700 West Georgia St.
PO Box 10287
Vancouver, BC V7Y 1E8
604-660-2864 Fax: 604-660-1108
info@provincialcourt.bc.ca
www.provincialcourt.bc.ca/judicialcouncil
As designated by the Provincial Court Act, the Judicial Council of British Columbia consists of nine members. The process of the Judicial Council is governed by a Procedure Bylaw. The overall goal of the Council is the improvement of the quality of judicial service in the province.
• Justice Education Society (JES)
#260, 800 Hornby St.
Vancouver, BC V6Z 2C3
604-660-9870 Fax: 604-775-3476
info@justiceeducation.ca
www.justiceeducation.ca
Formerly the Law Courts Education Society, renamed in 2009, the Justice Education Society seeks to promote the understanding of, and access to, Canada's justice system for all groups of people, but especially youth, Aboriginals, ethnic & immigrant communities, deaf people, those with learning disabilities, & other groups as required.
• Legal Services Society (LSS)
#400, 510 Burrard St.
Vancouver, BC V6C 3A8
604-601-6000
www.lss.bc.ca
Other Communication: Call Centre: 1-866-577-2525; 604-408-2172 (Greater Vancouver); Media inquiries: 604-601-6004
The Legal Services Society was established by the Legal Services Society Act. The non-profit Society provides legal information, advice, & representation services to assist British Columbians in the resolution of their legal issues. Regional centres & local agents' offices are located throughout the province.
• Office of the Representative for Children & Youth (RCY)
#201, 546 Yates St.
Victoria, BC V8W 1K8
250-356-6710 Fax: 250-356-0837 800-476-3933
rcy@rcybc.ca
www.rcybc.ca
Other Communication: Northern Office - Prince George: 250-561-4626; Lower Mainland Office - Burnaby: 604-775-3213
Acting in accordance with British Columbia's Representative for Children and Youth Act, the Representative for Children & Youth is responsible for advocacy, monitoring, & investigation.
• Public Guardian & Trustee of British Columbia (PGT)
#700, 808 West Hastings St.
Vancouver, BC V6C 3L3
604-660-4444 Fax: 604-660-0374 800-663-7867
mail@trustee.bc.ca
www.trustee.bc.ca
Other Communication: Communications & Media Relations: 604-660-4474; Child & Youth Svs.: 604-775-3480; Estate & Personal Trust Svs.: 604-660-4444
The Public Guardian & Trustee of British Columbia was established under the Public Guardian and Trustee Act. The corporation offers the following programs: Child & Youth Services; Services to Adults; & Estate & Personal Trust Services.

Court Services Branch
PO Box 9249 Prov Govt, Victoria, BC V8W 9J2
250-356-1550 Fax: 250-356-8152
Executive Director, Corporate Support, Brenda Miller
250-356-1525, Fax: 250-387-4743
Acting Director, Court Reform, Business Transformation & Corporate Planning, Kashmiro Cheema
250-356-1826, Fax: 250-356-8152, Kashmiro.Cheema@gov.bc.ca
Executive Director, Business Transformation & Corporate Planning, Trish Shwart
250-356-6428, Fax: 250-356-8152, Trish.Shwart@gov.bc.ca
Director, Planning, Communications & Training, Business Transformation & Corporate Planning, Vacant
250-356-6680, Fax: 250-356-8152
Director, Service Transformation, Business Transformation & Corporate Planning, Alanna Valentine
250-356-9534, Fax: 250-356-8152, Alanna.Valentine@gov.bc.ca
Director, Financial Management & Administration, Ted Stevens
250-356-9469, Fax: 250-356-8152, Ted.Stevens@gov.bc.ca
Director, Strategic Information & Business Applications, Dan Chiddell
250-356-1565, Fax: 250-356-8152, Dan.Chiddell@gov.bc.ca

Criminal Justice Branch
1001 Douglas St., 9th Fl., PO Box 9276 Prov Govt, Victoria, BC V8W 9J7
250-387-3840 Fax: 250-387-0090
http: //www.ag.gov.bc.ca/prosecution-service/
Assistant Deputy Attorney General, Robert W.G. Gillen, Q.C.
250-387-3840, Fax: 250-387-0090

Finance & Administration Division
PO Box 9256 Prov Govt, Victoria, BC V8W 9J4
250-387-5505 Fax: 250-356-8739
Chief Financial Officer, David Hoadley
250-356-5393, Fax: 250-356-8739, David.Hoadley@gov.bc.ca
Director, Financial Planning & Analysis, Paul Cumberland
250-356-5499, Fax: 250-356-8739, Paul.Cumberland@gov.bc.ca
Director, Special Projects, Financial Planning & Analysis Division, Rod Seginson
250-356-7068, Fax: 250-356-8739, Rod.Seginson@gov.bc.ca
Director, Accounting, Budgeting & Reporting, William Skrlac
250-356-7077, Fax: 250-356-9185, William.Skrlac@gov.bc.ca

Information Technology Services Division
PO Box 9262 Prov Govt, Victoria, BC V8W 9J4
250-356-8972 Fax: 250-356-8739
Acting Executive Director/Chief Information Officer, Frank D'Argis
250-387-5258, Fax: 250-356-8739
Chief Technology Officer, Operations, Evan Schlaak
250-356-6061, Fax: 250-356-7699, Evan.Schlaak@gov.bc.ca
Chief Enterprise Architect, Stuart F. Cayzer
250-387-1111, Fax: 250-356-7699, Stuart.Cayzer@gov.bc.ca
Acting Director, Enterprise Architecture, Chris Mah
250-952-0591, Fax: 250-356-7699, Chris.Mah@gov.bc.ca
Director, Client Services, IM/IT Client Services, Larry Bjelde
250-356-9285, Fax: 250-356-7699, Larry.Bjelde@gov.bc.ca
Director, Technical Support Services, Ross Harris
250-415-3197, Fax: 250-356-7699, Ross.Harris@gov.bc.ca
Director, Application & Infrastructure Services, Carol Barnsley
250-356-1164, Fax: 250-356-7699, Carol.Barnsley@gov.bc.ca

Justice Service Branch
PO Box 9222 Prov Govt, Victoria, BC V8W 9J1
Provincial Executive Director, Family Justice Services, Irene Robertson
250-387-5903, Fax: 250-356-1279
Executive Director, Maintenance Enforcement & Locate Services, Christopher Beresford
604-660-2528, Fax: 604-660-1346, Chris.Beresford@gov.bc.ca
Executive Director, Civil Policy & Legislation Office, Nancy Carter
250-356-6182, Fax: 250-387-4525, Nancy.Carter@gov.bc.ca
Executive Director, Criminal Justice & Legal Access Policy Division, James Deitch
250-387-2109, Fax: 250-356-6552
Executive Director, Administrative Justice, Dianne Flood
250-387-0116, Fax: 250-387-0079
Executive Director, Dispute Resolution Office, David Merner
250-514-5507, Fax: 250-387-1189, David.Merner@gov.bc.ca
Director, Integrated Criminal Justice, Criminal Justice & Legal Access Policy Division, Allan Castle
250-356-6518, Fax: 250-356-6552, Allan.Castle@gov.bc.ca
Director, Criminal Justice Transformation Projects, Criminal Justice & Legal Access Policy Division, Judy Klima
250-387-0801, Fax: 250-356-6552, Judy.Klima@gov.bc.ca
Director, FPT Criminal Justice, Criminal Justice & Legal Access Policy Division, Jacquelyn Nelson
250-387-5004, Fax: 250-356-6552, Jacquelyn.Nelson@gov.bc.ca
Deputy Director, Maintenance Enforcement & Locate Services, Ringo Dosanjh
604-660-3746, Fax: 604-660-3728, Ringo.Dosanjh@gov.bc.ca
Director, Strategic Projects, Dispute Resolution Office, Kate Kimberley
250-356-6180, Fax: 250-387-1189

Legal Services Branch
PO Box 9280 Prov Govt, Victoria, BC V8W 9J7
Assistant Deputy Attorney General, Richard Fyfe, Q.C.
250-356-9260, Fax: 250-356-5111, Richard.Fyfe@gov.bc.ca
Acting Chief Legislative Counsel, Kenneth Downing, Q.C.
Fax: 250-356-5758, Ken.Downing@gov.bc.ca
Acting Director, Library & Research Services, Craig Huggins
250-356-8490, Fax: 250-387-5758, Craig.Huggins@gov.bc.ca
Director, Strategic & Business Initiatives, Patricia J. Kimmitt-Huxley
250-952-7540, Fax: 250-952-7555, Patricia.KimmittHuxley@gov.bc.ca
Director, Business Operations, Aaron Plater
250-952-7550, Fax: 250-952-7555, Aaron.Plater@gov.bc.ca
Director, Finance & Human Resources, Kyle Pollner
250-952-7554, Fax: 250-952-7555, Kyle.Pollner@gov.bc.ca
Supervising Counsel, Barristers Division - Aboriginal Litigation, Elizabeth Argall
250-356-5365, Fax: 250-387-0343, Elizabeth.Argall@gov.bc.ca
Supervising Counsel, Barristers Division - Civil Litigation, Gordon Houston
250-356-6175, Fax: 250-953-4348, Gordon.Houston@gov.bc.ca
Supervising Counsel, Barristers Division - Constitutional & Administrative Law, Craig Jones
250-387-3129, Fax: 250-356-9154, Craig.Jones@gov.bc.ca, Other Communications: Alternate Phone: 604-660-5476
Acting Supervising Solicitor, Solicitors Division - Resource, Environmental & Land Law, Christopher Jones
250-356-0464, Fax: 250-387-6597, Christopher.H.Jones@gov.bc.ca
Supervising Solicitor, Solicitors Division - Finance, Commercial & Transportation, Lauren Knoblauch
250-356-5744, Fax: 250-387-1010, Lauren.Knoblauch@gov.bc.ca
Supervising Solicitor, Solicitors Division - Justice, Education Law Group, Jean Morgan
250-356-8465, Fax: 250-356-9254, Jean.Morgan@gov.bc.ca
Supervising Solicitor, Solicitors Division - Aboriginal Law Group, Geoff Moyse
250-356-8937, Fax: 250-356-8939, Geoff.Moyse@gov.bc.ca
Supervising Solicitor, Solicitors Division - Revenue, Taxation, Jeff Pottinger
250-356-8845, Fax: 250-387-0700, Jeff.Pottinger@gov.bc.ca
Supervising Solicitor, Solicitors Division - Health & Social Services, Fiona St. Clair
250-356-8444, Fax: 250-356-8992, Fiona.StClair@gov.bc.ca

Office of the Auditor General

PO Box 9036 Prov Govt, Victoria, BC V8W 9A2
250-419-6100 Fax: 250-387-1230
www.bcauditor.com
The chief responsibility of the Office of the Auditor General is auditing most of the British Columbia provincial government, with its ministries, Crown corporations, & other organizations.
Auditor General, John Doyle, MAcc, CA
Executive Director, Michael Macdonell, MBA, CA
250-419-6109, mmacdonell@bcauditor.com

Financial Audit
Assistant Auditor General, Bill Gilhooly, BEcon, CA
250-419-6102, bgilhooly@bcauditor.com
Assistant Auditor General, Russ Jones, MBA, CA
250-419-6103, rjones@bcauditor.com
Executive Director, Peter Bourne, CA, CIA
250-419-6141, pbourne@bcauditor.com, Other Communications: Alternate Phone: 250-387-5600
Executive Director, Lisa Moore, CA
250-419-6188, lmoore@bcauditor.com
Executive Director, Jason Reid, BCcomm, CA
250-419-6204, jreid@bcauditor.com
Director, Ada Chiang
250-419-6144, achiang@bcauditor.com
Director, Bob Faulkner
250-419-6152, bfaulkner@bcauditor.com
Director, IT Audit, Pam Hamilton
250-419-6164, phamilton@bcauditor.com
Director, David K. Lau
250-419-6118, dlau@bcauditor.com
Director, Jamie Orr
250-419-6195, jorr@bcauditor.com

Performance Audit
Assistant Auditor General, Governance, Accountability & Education, Malcolm Gaston, CMA, CPFA
250-419-6105, mgaston@bcauditor.com
Assistant Auditor General, Sustainability & Environment, Morris Sydor, MBA, CA
250-419-6106, msydor@bcauditor.com
Director, Tara Anderson
250-419-6134, tanderson@bcauditor.com
Director, Sheila Dodds
250-419-6149, sdodds@bcauditor.com
Director, Mike McStravick
250-419-6185, mmcstravick@bcauditor.com
Director, Paul Nyquist
250-419-6194, pnyquist@bcauditor.com

Standards & Quality
Assistant Auditor General, Professsional Practices & Quality Assurance, Beverly Romeo-Beehler
250-419-6107, barombee@bcauditor.com
Executive Director, Professsional Practices & Quality Assurance, Brian Jones
250-419-6171, bjones@bcauditor.com
Director, Finance & Human Capital, Marc LeFebvre
250-419-6120, mlefebvre@bcauditor.com

British Columbia Centre for Disease Control (BCCDC)

655 West 12th Ave., Vancouver, BC V5Z 4R4
604-707-2400 Fax: 604-707-2401
admininfo@bccdc.ca
www.bccdc.ca
The BCCDC is both a provincial & national leader in public health as it detects, treats, & prevents diseases in its patients. Not only does it offer direct services for people with diseases & health concerns, but it also provides analytical & policy support to health authorities at all levels of government.

Ministry of Children & Family Development

PO Box 9770 Prov Govt, Victoria, BC V8W 9S5
250-387-7027
877-387-7027
MCF.CorrespondenceManagement@gov.bc.ca
www.mcf.gov.bc.ca
Other Communication: Helpline for Children: 310-1234; Emergencies outside office hours: 604-660-4927 (Vancouver); 604-660-8180 (Lower Mainland); 1-800-663-9122 (remainder of province)
The Ministry works toward the goal of healthy children & families living in safe & inclusive communities.
Acts Administered:
Adoption Act
Child Care BC Act
Child Care Subsidy Act
Child, Family & Community Service Act
Community Living Authority Act
Community Services Interim Authorities Act
Health & Social Services Delivery Act
Human Resource Facility Act
Social Workers Act
Youth Justice Act
Minister, Hon. Mary McNeil
250-387-9699, Fax: 250-387-9722, MCF.Minister@gov.bc.ca; mary.mcneil.mla@leg.bc.ca
Deputy Minister, Stephen Brown
250-387-2000, MCF.DeputyMinistersOffice@gov.bc.ca
Senior Director, Executive Operations, Debbie Godfrey
250-387-3717, mcf.deputyministersoffice@gov.bc.ca
Director, Executive Operations, Jason Gabitous
250-356-9541, mcf.deputyministersoffice@gov.bc.ca
Director, Transformation Support, Executive Operations, Frances Sasvari
250-387-2749, Fax: 250-356-5049
Acting Director, Executive Operations, Breanna Viala
250-356-9541, Fax: 250-356-2920
Director, Intergovernmental Relations, Executive Operations, Jo-Anne Will
250-952-6311, Fax: 250-952-6320

Associated Agencies, Boards & Commissions:
• British Columbia College of Social Workers (BCCSW)
#302, 1765 West 8th Ave.
Vancouver, BC V6J 5C6
604-737-4916 Fax: 604-737-6809
info@bccsw.ca
www.bccollegeofsocialworkers.ca
The regulatory body for the practice of social work in British Columbia is the Board of Registration for Social Workers in BC. The Board's responsibility is establishing & supporting high standards for Registered Social Workers in the province.

Aboriginal Policy & Service Support Team
PO Box 9721 Prov Govt, Victoria, BC V8W 9S2
250-387-5275 Fax: 250-356-6534
Assistant Deputy Minister, Debra Foxcroft
250-387-3810, Fax: 250-356-6534
Director/Project Director, Aboriginal Policy & Legislation/Jordan's Principle Implementation Team, Dena Carroll
250-356-5581, Fax: 250-387-1732, Other Communications: Team Phone: 250-356-9791, Fax: 250-387-1732
Acting First Nations Director, Aboriginal Services, Ray Bronson
250-387-0726, Fax: 250-387-1732
Director, Operations, Aboriginal Services, Rob Parenteau
250-387-7073, Fax: 250-387-1732
Executive Coordinator, Lisa Marshman
250-953-3450, Fax: 250-387-1732

Integrated Quality Assurance
PO Box 9721 Prov Govt, Victoria, BC V8W 9S2
250-356-9808 Fax: 250-356-6534
Assistant Deputy Minister, Sandra Griffin
Senior Director, Practice Support, Karen Blackman
250-387-7416, Fax: 250-387-8000
Senior Director, Practice Support, Joan Easton
250-387-7814, Fax: 250-387-7618
Director, Advocacy, Kathy Berggren-Clive
604-775-2165, Fax: 604-660-4007
Provincial Director, Adoptions, Anne Clayton
250-387-2281, Fax: 250-387-7914

Office of the Chief Operating Officer
PO Box 9721 Prov Govt, Victoria, BC V8W 9S2
250-387-3006 Fax: 250-356-6534
Assistant Deputy Minister, Integrated Policy & Legislation, Randi Mjolsness
250-387-7090, Fax: 250-356-2481
Chief Operating Officer, Derek Sturko
250-387-3006, Fax: 250-356-6534
Chief Information Officer, Information Management & Technology, Martin P. Wright
250-356-0463, Fax: 250-387-7421, Craig.Wilkinson@gov.bc.ca
Executive Financial Officer, Financial Services, Craig Wilkinson
250-356-2954, Fax: 250-356-2899, Craig.Wilkinson@gov.bc.ca
Executive Director, Strategic Policy & Operations, Integrated Policy & Legislation, Jennifer Erickson
250-387-7418
Executive Director, Accountability, Tessa Graham
250-953-3446, Fax: 250-356-6534
Executive Director, Legislation & Litigation, Integrated Policy & Legislation, Michael Turanski
250-387-6434, Fax: 250-356-8182, Keva.Glynn@gov.bc.ca
Senior Director, Early Years Policy, Integrated Policy & Legislation, Keva Glynn
250-387-9714, Fax: 250-356-0399, Keva.Glynn@gov.bc.ca
Senior Director, Children & Youth with Special Needs Provincial Operations, Integrated Policy & Legislation, Arif Lalani
250-387-7762, Fax: 250-356-0399
Senior Director, Child, Youth & Family Policy, Integrated Policy & Legislation, Sandy Wiens
250-387-1551, Fax: 250-356-0399
Director, Child Welfare Policy, Integrated Policy & Legislation, Mona Herring
250-356-2777, Fax: 250-356-2995
Director, Child & Youth Mental Health Policy, Integrated Policy & Legislation, Deborah Saari
250-356-5201, Fax: 250-356-0580
Director, Children & Youth with Special Needs, Integrated Policy & Legislation, Aleksandra Stevanovic
250-387-1828, Fax: 250-356-0399
Director, CYSN Services Transfer & Cross-Ministry Youth Transitions Framework, Integrated Policy & Legislation, Frank Van Zandwijk
250-356-2857, Fax: 250-953-4234
Director, Legislation, Leah Bailey
250-387-0372, Fax: 250-356-8182
Director, Infrastructure & Administrative Services, Information Management & Technology Branch, Dwayne Quesnel
250-387-7697, Fax: 250-387-2481
Director, Information Management & Governance, Information Management & Technology Branch, Ken Reimer
250-356-2831, Fax: 250-387-7726
Director, Client Services & Projects, Information Management & Technology Branch, Steve Wilson
250-356-9043, Fax: 250-387-7726

Provincial Services
PO Box 9717 Prov Govt, Victoria, BC V8W 9S1
250-387-0978 Fax: 250-356-2079
Senior Executive Director, Alan Markwart
Executive Director, Youth Custody Services, Barry Lynden
604-356-1970, Fax: 604-356-2079
Assistant Executive Director, Youth Custody Service, Rick Faoro
778-452-2065, Fax: 778-452-2076
Director, Case Management, Victoria Youth Custody Service, Jeff Haas
250-708-2218, Fax: 250-704-0283, Jeff.Haas@gov.bc.ca
Director, Victoria Youth Custody Service, Phil Hawley
250-708-2206, Fax: 250-704-0283, Jeff.Haas@gov.bc.ca
Acting Director, Operations, Victoria Youth Custody Service, Mike Macphee
250-708-2225, Fax: 250-704-0283, Mike.MacPhee@gov.bc.ca
Director, Programs, Victoria Youth Custody Service, Blade Tickner
250-708-2219, Fax: 250-704-0283, Blade.Tickner@gov.bc.ca
Director, Operations, Prince George Youth Custody Service, Jim Arnold
250-649-3852, Fax: 250-649-3878
Director, Victoria Youth Custody Service, Kim Fogtmann
250-562-5393, Fax: 250-649-3878
Director, Programs, Prince George Youth Custody Service, Shawn Young
250-562-5393, Fax: 250-565-6930
Director, Staffing Support Services, Burnaby Youth Custody Service, Doug Charmichael
Fax: 604-660-5994
Director, Operations, Burnaby Youth Custody Service, Andrew Cronkhite
604-419-1618, Fax: 604-660-5994
Director, Case Management, Burnaby Youth Custody Service, Anita McDonnell
604-419-1613, Fax: 604-660-5994
Director, Youth Justice Policy & Program Support, Chris Zatylny
250-387-1335, Fax: 250-356-2079
Provincial Director, Youth Forensic Psychiatric Services, Andre Picard
778-452-2202, Fax: 778-452-2201
Provincial Clinical Director, Youth Forensic Psychiatric Services, Dr. Kulwant Riar
778-452-2205, Fax: 778-452-2201
Director, Maples Adolescent Treatment Centre, Ken Moore
604-660-5811, Fax: 604-660-5814

Strategic Human Resource & Sectoral Relations
PO Box 9757 Prov Govt, Victoria, BC V8W 9S3
250-356-6883 Fax: 250-952-6880
Executive Director, Patrick Doyle
250-356-7103
Director, Strategic Human Resources Projects & Recruitment, Cheryl Howarth
250-387-7659
Acting Director, Human Resources Services, Tim Osborne
250-387-2466
Director, Sectoral Relations, Brian Scofield
250-953-3833
Acting Director, Learning & Development, Annemarie Travers
250-387-7665

Regional Offices:
Fraser & Vancouver Coastal Regions
604-660-2433 Fax: 604-660-1090
Assistant Deputy Minister, Beverly Dicks
Fax: 604-660-4005
Regional Executive Director, Fraser Regional Office, Barbara Walsh
604-586-4121, Fax: 604-596-4151
Regional Executive Director, Vancouver Coastal Regional Office, Dennis Padmore
604-660-2433, Fax: 604-660-1090
Executive Director, Practice, Fraser Regional Office, Bruce McNeill
604-586-4123, Fax: 604-586-4153
Director, Support to Operations, Fraser Regional Office, Donna Mathiasen
604-586-4109, Fax: 604-596-4151
Director, Practice, Fraser Regional Office, Amarjit Sahota
604-586-2628, Fax: 604-586-4153
Director, Aboriginal Service Change, Fraser Regional Office, Virge Silveira
604-586-4132, Fax: 604-586-4153
Director, Quality Assurance Practice, Fraser Regional Office, Susan Waldron
604-586-4100, Fax: 604-586-4153
Acting Director, Operations, Vancouver Coastal Regional Office, Holden Chu
604-660-2141, Fax: 604-660-5346, Meena.Sanghera@gov.bc.ca
Director, Financial Management & Administration, Vancouver Coastal Regional Office, Philip Dong
604-660-2433, Fax: 604-660-1090
Director, Practice, Vancouver Coastal Regional Office, Sheila Robinson
604-660-5673, Fax: 604-660-5072, Meena.Sanghera@gov.bc.ca
Interior Region
PO Box 9767 Prov Govt, Victoria, BC V8W 9S5
Fax: 250-387-7756
Assistant Deputy Minister, Doug Hughes
Regional Executive Director, Nancy McComb
250-354-6465, Fax: 250-354-6530

Director, Support to Practice, Karen Wallace
250-953-3835
Executive Coordinator, Faye McClinton
250-387-1068
North Region
250-565-4367 Fax: 250-565-4427
Assistant Deputy Minister, Peter Cunningham
Acting Regional Executive Director, Shirley Reimer
Executive Director, Practice/Director, Child Welfare, Robert Watts
250-565-4312
Director, Corporate Services, Sue Risby
250-565-4315
Deputy Director, Child Welfare, Joanne White
250-992-4158
Vancouver Island
PO Box 9767 Prov Govt, Victoria, BC V8W 9S5
250-387-7744 Fax: 250-387-7756
Assistant Deputy Minister, Chuck Eamer
Regional Executive Director, Mark Armitage
250-390-5458, Fax: 250-390-5477
Executive Director, Child Care Programs & Services Branch, Lenora Angel
250-952-6089, Fax: 250-953-3327, Lenora.Angel@gov.bc.ca
Director, Child Care Subsidy Service Centre - Operations, Doug Bell
888-338-6622, Fax: 250-387-0699
Director, Child Care Programs & Services, Andrew Morgan
250-356-5391
Director, Operations/Office Manager, Regional Finance & Administration, Susan Rivers
250-390-6018, Fax: 250-952-4282
Director, Program Support, Daniel Sobhana
250-952-0893
Director, Child Welfare, Director CF and Community Services, Thomas Weber
250-334-5820, Fax: 250-334-5844
Assistant Director, Child Care Subsidy Service Centre - Operations, Tim Anderson
888-338-6622, Fax: 250-387-0699

Columbia Power Corporation (CPC)

#200, 445 - 13th Ave., Castlegar, BC V1N 1G1
250-304-6060 Fax: 250-304-6083
cpc.info@columbiapower.org
www.columbiapower.org
Columbia Power Corporation was established under the Company Act in 1994. A Crown corporation, it is wholly owned & controlled by the Province of British Columbia. On a joint venture basis with the Columbia Basin Trust, Columbia Power Corporation undertakes power project investments as the agent of the Province of British Columbia. Some power projects include the following: Arrow Lakes Generating Station, Brilliant Expansion Project, & Waneta Expansion Project.
Chair, Lee Doney
Vice-Chair, Tim Stanley
President/Chief Executive Officer, Jane Bird
Chief Technical Officer, Victor Jmaeff
Vice-President, Capital Projects, Giulio Ambrosone
Vice-President, Human Resources & Corporate Services, Debbie Martin
Corporate Secretary, Don Rose

Ministry of Community, Sport & Cultural Development

PO Box 9056 Prov Govt, Victoria, BC V8W 9E2
250-387-2283 Fax: 250-387-4312
www.gov.bc.ca/cscd
The Ministry of Community, Sport and Cultural Development supports healthier, greener, & more inclusive communities in British Columbia.
Acts Administered:
Assessment Act
Assessment Authority Act
Capital Region Water Supply & Sooke Hills Protection
Columbia Basin Trust Act
Community Charter Act
Islands Trust Act
Land Title Act (in part)
Local Government Act
Local Government Grants Act
Local Services Act
Manufactured Home Tax Act
Ministry of Municipal Affairs Act
Municipal Aid Act
Municipal Finance Authority Act
North Island-Coast Development Initiative Act
Northern Development Initiative Trust Act
Ports Property Tax Act
Resort Associations Act
Resort Municipality of Whistler Act
Sechelt Indian Government District Enabling Act
Southern Interior Development Initiative Trust Act
Tourist Accommodation (Assessment Relief) Act
University Endowment Land Act
Vancouver Charter Act
Minister, Hon. Ida Chong
250-387-2283, Fax: 250-387-4312, ida.chong.mla@leg.bc.ca; CSCD.minister@gov.bc.ca
Deputy Minister, Don Fast
250-387-4104, Fax: 250-387-7973, Don.Fast@gov.bc.ca
Director, Executive Operations, Tom Brown
250-356-9037, Fax: 250-387-7973, Tom.Brown@gov.bc.ca
Manager, Strategic Information & Correspondence Branch, Sylvia Hawkins
250-356-9772, Fax: 250-953-3709, Sylvia.Hawkins@gov.bc.ca

Associated Agencies, Boards & Commissions:
• British Columbia Assessment Authority (BCAA)
#400, 3450 Uptown Blvd.
Victoria, BC V8Z 0B9
250-595-6211 Fax: 250-595-6222
info@bcassessment.ca
www.bcassessment.bc.ca
The British Columbia Assessment Authority is an independent, provincial Crown corporation. Governed by a Board of Directors, the role of BC Assessment is the production of annual property assessments for each property owner in British Columbia. Area offices are located across the province.
• BC Games Society
#200, 990 Fort St.
Victoria, BC V8V 3K2
250-387-1375 Fax: 250-387-4489
info@bcgames.org
www.bcgames.org
The BC Games Society is incorporated under the Societies Act. With responsibility to British Columbia's Minister of Healthy Living & Sport, the Crown Agency works with its partners to provide event management leadership. The Society strives to create development opportunities for athletes, coaches, & officials, sport organizations, & host communities.
• Board of Examiners
250-387-4085 Fax: 250-387-7972
www.cscd.gov.bc.ca/lgd/gov_structure/board_examiners/index.htm
• Columbia Basin Trust (CBT)
Southwest Basin
#300, 445 - 13 Ave.
Castlegar, BC V1N 1G1
250-365-6633 800-505-8998
cbt@cbt.org
www.cbt.org
Other Communication: Northwest Basin: 250-265-9936; Southeast Basin: 250-426-8810; Northeast Basin: 250-344-7065
The Columbia Basin Trust manages its assets to benefit the economy, environment, & social well-being of the region. The Trust works to establish collaborative partnerships to achieve improved self-sufficiency.
• Islands Trust
#200, 1627 Fort St.
Victoria, BC V8R 1H8
250-405-5151 Fax: 250-405-5155
information@islandstrust.bc.ca
www.islandstrust.bc.ca
Other Communication: Northern Office: 250-247-2063; Salt Spring Office: 250-537-9144
The Islands Trust area covers the following islands & waters between the British Columbia mainland & southern Vancouver Island: Bowen, Denman, Gabriola, Galiano, Gambier, Hornby, Lasqueti, Mayne, North Pender, Salt Spring, Saturna, South Pender, & Thetis. The Trust is a federation of independent local governments. The federation plans land use & regulates development to preserve & protect the area and its environment.
• Northern Development Initiative Trust
#301, 1268 Fifth Ave.
Prince George, BC V2L 3L2
250-561-2525 Fax: 250-561-2563
info@northerndevelopment.bc.ca
http: //northerndevelopment.bc.ca
The Northern Trust consists of a Board of Directors which makes funding decisions for programs of the Trust. According to provincial legislation, investments can be made in the following areas: agriculture, economic development, energy, forestry, mining, Olympic opportunities; pine beetle recovery, small business, tourism, & transportation.
• Property Assessment Appeal Board (PAAB)
#10, 10551 Shellbridge Way
Richmond, BC V6X 2W9
604-775-1740 Fax: 604-775-1742 888-775-1740
office@paab.bc.ca
www.assessmentappeal.bc.ca
Other Communication: Toll-Free Fax: 1-888-775-1742
The Board assists with assessment appeals for all types of properties, dealing with issues such as market value, classification, and qualification for tax exemption.
• Southern Interior Development Initiative Trust
#204, 3131 29th St.
Vernon, BC V1T 5A8
250-545-6829 Fax: 250-545-6896
admin@sidit-bc.ca
www.sidit-bc.ca
The government of British Columbia enacted legislation in 2006 to establish the Southern Interior Development Initiative Trust. The mission of the Trust is to grow & diversify the economy of the Southern Interior of British Columbia through investments in economic development projects that will benefit the area.

Arts, Culture & Sport

PO Box 9490 Prov Govt, Victoria, BC V8W 9N7
250-356-6914 Fax: 250-387-7973
Assistant Deputy Minister, David Galbraith
250-356-7139, Fax: 250-387-7973, David.Galbraith@gov.bc.ca
Executive Director, Arts & Culture Branch, Andrea Henning
250-356-6614, Fax: 250-387-4099, Andrea.Henning@gov.bc.ca
Executive Director, Sport Branch, Margo Ross
250-356-7168, Fax: 250-356-2842, Margo.Ross@gov.bc.ca
Executive Director, Special Projects, Vacant
250-356-9382, Fax: 250-356-7074
Executive Director, BC Arts Council, Gillian Wood
250-356-1725, Fax: 250-387-4099, Gillian.Wood@gov.bc.ca
Director, Business Development, Liz Lilly
250-356-7096, Fax: 250-387-4099, Liz.Lilly@gov.bc.ca
Acting Director, Sport Branch, Sharon White
250-387-5651, Fax: 250-356-2842, Sharon.D.White@gov.bc.ca
Director, Sport Branch, Doug Wrean
250-356-0364, Fax: 250-356-2842, Doug.Wrean@gov.bc.ca
Senior Financial Officer, Robert Easton
250-356-9416, Fax: 250-387-7973, Robert.Easton@gov.bc.ca
BC Film Commissioner, Susan Croome
604-660-3235, Fax: 604-660-4790, susanc@bcfilmcommission.com

Local Government

PO Box 9490 Prov Govt, Victoria, BC V8W 9N7
250-356-6575 Fax: 250-387-7973
www.cd.gov.bc.ca/lgd
Working with a great range of partners, the Local Government Department develops communities that can manage change & offer affordable services to residents of British Columbia. The Department's programs include the following: developing local government legislation; facilitating partnerships with local governments & First Nations; fostering positive inter-governmental relations to facilitate community & regional planning; offering financial support; & providing information & advice.
Assistant Deputy Minister/Inspector of Municipalities, Mike Furey
250-356-6575, Fax: 250-387-7973
Executive Director, Local Government Infrastructure & Finance, Glen Brown
250-387-4067, Fax: 250-356-1873, Glen.T.Brown@gov.bc.ca
Executive Director, Intergovernmental Relations & Planning, Lois-Leah Goodwin
250-356-1128, Fax: 250-387-6212, LoisLeah.Goodwin@gov.bc.ca
Executive Director, Local Government Policy & Research, Nicola Marotz
250-356-6257, Fax: 250-387-6212, Nicola.Marotz@gov.bc.ca
Executive Director, Governance & Structure, Gary Paget
250-953-4129, Fax: 250-387-7972, Gary.Paget@gov.bc.ca
Director, Structure, Governance & Structure, Marijke Edmondson
250-387-4058, Fax: 250-387-7972, Marijke.Edmondson@gov.bc.ca
Director, Advisory Services, Governance & Structure, Don Sutherland
250-387-4025, Fax: 250-387-7972, Don.Sutherland@gov.bc.ca
Director, Regional Initiatives, Governance & Structure, Derek Trimmer
250-356-9621, Fax: 250-387-7972, Derek.Trimmer@gov.bc.ca
Director, Commuity Relations, Governance & Structure, Cathy Watson
250-387-4057, Fax: 250-387-7972, Cathy.Watson@gov.bc.ca
Director, Intergovernmental Relations, Intergovernmental Relations & Planning Division, Rejan Farley
250-387-4046, Fax: 250-387-6212, Rejan.Farley@gov.bc.ca
Director, Planning Programs, Intergovernmental Relations & Planning Division, Meggin Messenger
250-387-4045, Fax: 250-387-6212, Meggin.Messenger@gov.bc.ca
Director, Infrastructure, Local Government Infrastructure & Finance, Liam Edwards
250-356-0218, Fax: 250-356-1873, Liam.Edwards@gov.bc.ca
Director, Local Government Finance, Local Government Infrastructure & Finance, Talitha Soldera

250-387-4063, Fax: 250-356-1873,
Talitha.Soldera@gov.bc.ca
Director, Legislation, Local Government Policy & Research, Meagan Gergley
250-387-4052, Fax: 250-387-6212,
Meagan.Gergley@gov.bc.ca

Management Services
PO Box 9842 Prov Govt, Victoria, BC V8W 9T2
250-387-8705 Fax: 250-387-7973
Assistant Deputy Minister, Shauna Brouwer
250-387-9180, Fax: 250-387-7973,
Shauna.Brouwer@gov.bc.ca
Executive Director/Chief Information Officer, Information Systems, Debbie Fritz
250-356-0803, Fax: 250-387-1590, Debbie.Fritz@gov.bc.ca
Executive Director, Strategic Human Resources & Corporate Policy & Planning, Kim Russell
Fax: 250-387-1407
Director/Chief Financial Officer, Finance & Administrative Services, Jim MacAulay
250-387-9179, Fax: 250-387-1590, Jim.MacAulay@gov.bc.ca
Director, Policy & Planning, Strategic Human Resources & Corporate Policy & Planning, Shannon Mullen
250-953-4334, Fax: 250-387-1407,
Shannon.Mullen@gov.bc.ca
Director, Strategic Human Resources, Strategic Human Resources & Corporate Policy & Planning, Vacant
250-356-2036, Fax: 250-387-1407

Office of the Conflict of Interest Commissioner

#101, 431 Menzies St., Victoria, BC V8V 1X4
250-356-0750 Fax: 250-356-6580
conflictofinterest@coibc.ca
www.gov.bc.ca/oci

The Conflict of Interest Commissioner is an independent Officer of the Legislative Assembly. The following roles are carried out by the Commissioner: Advising Members of the Legislative Assembly; Meeting with Members of the Legislative Assembly for review of disclosure of Members' interests, & obligations imposed by the Members' Conflict of Interest Act; & Undertaking investigations into alleged contraventions of the Act or the Constitution Act, section 25.

Acts Administered:
Members' Conflict of Interest Act
Commissioner, Paul D. K. Fraser, Q.C.
250-356-9283
Executive Coordinator, Daphene Thompson

Ministry of Education

PO Box 9146 Prov Govt, Victoria, BC V8W 9H1
250-387-1977 Fax: 250-387-3200
888-879-1166
www.bced.gov.bc.ca
Other Communication: Media Inquiries Phone: 250-356-5963; Fax: 250-356-5945

The Ministry's mission is the provision of high quality education for students in British Columbia from kindergarten to grade 12.

Acts Administered:
Independent School Act
School Act
Teaching Profession Act
Library Act
Minister, Hon. George Abbott
250-387-1977, Fax: 250-387-3200, Minister.Educ@gov.bc.ca; george.abbott.mla@leg.bc.ca
Deputy Minister, James Gorman
250-356-1234, Fax: 250-356-6007, dm.Education@gov.bc.ca
Superintendent, Liaison, Sherri Mohoruk
250-514-2543, Fax: 604-660-2124,
Sherri.Mohoruk@gov.bc.ca, Other Communications: URL: www.bced.gov.bc.ca/departments/liaison
Planning Manager, Care Team, Kim Kennedy
250-356-1904
Planning Manager, Care Team, Claire Miller
250-356-8064

Associated Agencies, Boards & Commissions:
• British Columbia College of Teachers
#400, 2025 West Broadway
Vancouver, BC V6J 1Z6
604-731-8170 Fax: 604-731-9142 800-555-3684
www.bcct.ca
The College was created in 1987 by the Teaching Profession Act to impose standards of quality and education on its members. Its duties include: assessing applicants for admission into the College; issuing certificates of qualification; reviewing certificate holders; and administering disciplinary action when necessary.
• BC Council on Admissions & Transfer
#709, 555 Seymour St.
Vancouver, BC V6B 3H6
604-412-7700 Fax: 604-683-0576
info@bccat.ca
www.bccat.ca

Achievement Division
PO Box 9187 Prov Govt, Victoria, BC V8W 9H3
250-356-2332 Fax: 250-356-0407
Superintendent, Achievement, Rick Davis
250-558-8722, Fax: 250-356-0407
Superintendent, Achievement, Alison Sidow
250-217-7002, Fax: 250-356-0407
Project Director, Sector Leadership Development, Cathy Elliott
604-649-0035, Fax: 604-356-0407
Director, Gerald Morton
250-356-2558, Fax: 250-356-0407, Gerald.Morton@gov.bc.ca
Manager, Data & Reporting, Brent Munro
250-508-4532, Fax: 250-356-0407,
Brent.D.Munro@gov.bc.ca

Business, Technology & Online Services Division
PO Box 9132 Prov Govt, Victoria, BC V8W 9B5
250-356-6068 Fax: 250-387-0044
EDUC.ADMO.Knowledge.Management@gov.bc.ca
Assistant Deputy Minister, Renate Butterfield
250-356-6068
Director, Common Business Initiatives, Andrew Macauley
250-387-0170, Fax: 250-953-4908, Other Communications: Alternate Phone: 250-387-0363
Director, Business Integration, Beverley Shaw
250-356-9546, Fax: 250-356-0277, Bev.Shaw@gov.bc.ca, Other Communications: Alternate Phone: 250-387-0363
Director, Strategic Initiatives, Information & Technology Management Branch, Hwee Boon Teo
250-356-1693, Fax: 250-356-8267,
EDUC.InformationManagement@gov.bc.ca

Governance & Independent Schools Division
PO Box 9146 Prov Govt, Victoria, BC V8W 9H1
250-356-1404 Fax: 250-953-4908
EDUC.GovernanceDepartment@gov.bc.ca
Responsibilities include legislation for & governance of the public school system, homeschooling, independent schools, & offshore schools.
Executive Director, Claire Avison
250-356-6760, Fax: 250-953-4908,
EDUC.GovernanceDepartment@gov.bc.ca
Executive Director & Inspector, Independent Schools, International Education, Ed Vanderboom
250-387-3711, Fax: 250-953-4908,
EDUC.IndependentSchoolsOffice@gov.bc.ca, Other Communications: URL: www.bced.gov.bc.ca/independentschools
Director, Governance & Legislation, Dave Duerksen
250-356-1404, Fax: 250-953-4908,
EDUC.GovernanceDepartment@gov.bc.ca, Other Communications: URL: www.bced.gov.bc.ca/legislation
Acting Deputy Inspector, Theo Vandeweg
250-387-3711, Fax: 250-953-4908,
EDUC.IndependentSchoolsOffice@gov.bc.ca

Learning Services Division
PO Box 9887 Prov Govt, Victoria, BC V8W 9T6
250-387-2046 Fax: 250-356-6007
Superintendent of Achievement, Rod Allen
250-213-3000, Fax: 250-356-6007
Executive Director, Diversity, Equity & Early Learning, Susan E. Kennedy
250-356-2337, Fax: 250-356-6161,
EDUC.EarlyLearning@gov.bc.ca
Field Director, Aboriginal Education, Ted Cadwallader
250-888-7739, Fax: 250-356-1742,
Ted.Cadwallader@gov.bc.ca
Director, Aboriginal Education, Trish Rosborough
250-356-1891, Fax: 250-356-1742, Other Communications: Cell Phone: 250-217-5748
Director, Diversity, Equity & Early Learning, Carolyn Henson
250-356-7561, Fax: 250-356-8322,
EDUC.DiversityandEquity@gov.bc.ca
Director, Student Assessment Branch, Nancy Walt
250-356-0519, Fax: 250-356-8334, EDUC.SAPE@gov.bc.ca, Other Communications: Cell Phone: 250-217-4978

Open Government Services Division
PO Box 9161 Prov Govt, Victoria, BC V8W 9H3
250-387-6399 Fax: 250-356-6007
EDUCADMO@Victoria1.gov.bc.ca
www.bced.gov.bc.ca/departments/partnerships_plan/
Assistant Deputy Minister, Paige MacFarlane
250-387-6399, EDUCADMO@Victoria1.gov.bc.ca
Director, Corporate Accountability & IGR, Caroline Ponsford
250-387-6282, Fax: 250-387-0044,
IGR.Education@gov.bc.ca
Special Advisor, Council of Ministers of Education, Canada, Jane Gardiner
250-356-7685, Fax: 250-387-0044,
IGR.Education@gov.bc.ca

Resource Management Division
PO Box 9151 Prov Govt, Victoria, BC V8W 9H1
250-356-2588 Fax: 250-356-8332
www.bced.gov.bc.ca/departments/resource_man/
Assistant Deputy Minister, Keith F. Miller
250-356-2588, Fax: 250-387-1451
Chief Financial Officer, Pat Brown
250-356-2470, Fax: 250-387-9695,
EDUC.FinanceAdministrativeServices@gov.bc.ca
Director, School District Financial Reporting, Ian Aaron
250-356-2585, Fax: 250-387-1451
Director, Funding & Compliance, Reg Bawa
250-356-2531, Fax: 250-387-1451
Director, Accounting, Budgeting & Reporting, Finance & Administrative Services Branch, Brian Fraser
250-356-2474, Fax: 250-387-9695,
EDUC.FinanceAdministrativeServices@gov.bc.ca
Director, Capital Management, Doug Stewart
250-356-7814, Fax: 250-387-1451

Elections British Columbia

PO Box 9275 Prov Govt, Victoria, BC V8W 9J6
250-387-5305 Fax: 250-387-3578
800-661-8683
electionsbc@elections.bc.ca
www.elections.bc.ca
TTY: 888-456-5448
Other Communication: Toll-free Fax: 1-866-466-0665

Elections British Columbia is a non-partisan, independent Office of the Legislature. Its responsibility is the administration of the electoral process in the province, including provincial general elections, by-elections, provincial referendums, & recall & initiative petitions & votes.

Acting Chief Electoral Officer, Craig James
250-387-5305
Assistant Chief Electoral Officer, Electoral Operations, Anton Boegman
250-387-5305, Anton.Boegman@elections.bc.ca
Assistant Chief Electoral Officer, Funding & Disclosure, M. Nola Western
250-387-4141, Nola.Western@elections.bc.ca
Director, Information Technology, Bob Jasperse
250-387-4139, Bob.Jasperse@elections.bc.ca
Director, Voter Registration & Boundaries, Peter Gzowski
250-387-7258, Peter.Gzowski@elections.bc.ca

Ministry of Energy & Mines

PO Box 9053 Prov Govt, Victoria, BC V8W 9E2
250-387-5896 Fax: 250-356-2965
www.gov.bc.ca/ener/

The development of sustainable & competitive energy & mineral resource sectors in British Columbia is the focus of the Ministry.

Acts Administered:
BC Hydro Public Power Legacy & Heritage Contract
Coal Act
Coalbed Gas Act, 2003
Columbia Basin Trust Act
Energy Efficiency Act
Energy Efficiency Standards Regulation
Gas Utility Act
Geothermal Resources Act
Hydro & Power Authority Act
Hydro Power Measures Act
Mineral Land Tax Act
Mineral Tax Act
Mineral Tenure Act
Mines Act
Mine Reclamation Fund Regulation
Mines Regulation
Workplace Hazardous Materials Information System Regulation (Mines)
Mining Right of Way Act
Mining Tax Act
Ministry of Energy & Mines Act
Natural Gas Price Act
Oil & Gas Commission Act
Petroleum & Natural Gas Act
Petroleum & Natural Gas (Vancouver Island Railway Lands) Act
Utilities Commission Act
Vancouver Island Natural Gas Pipeline Act
West Kootenay Power & Light Company, Ltd. Act
Clean Energy Act
Greenhouse Gas Reduction (Renewable and Low Carbon Fuel Requirements) Act
Safety Authority Act
Safety Standards Act
Fort Nelson Indian Reserve Minerals Revenue Sharing Act
Indian Reserve Mineral Resource Act
Assistance to Shelter Act
Building Officials' Association Act
Commercial Tenancy Act
Homeowner Protection Act
Manufactured Home Park Tenancy Act

Power for Jobs Development Act
Rent Distress Act
Residential Tenancy Act
Shelter Aid for Elderly Renters Act
Special Accounts Appropriation & Control Act (in part)
Strata Property Act
Minister, Hon. Rich Coleman
250-387-5896, Fax: 250-356-2965, EMH.Minister@gov.bc.ca; rich.coleman.mla@leg.bc.ca
Deputy Minister, Steve Carr
250-952-0504, Fax: 250-952-0269, Steve.Carr@gov.bc.ca
Director, Deputy Minister's Office, Simon Coley
250-952-0105, Fax: 250-952-0269, Simon.Coley@gov.bc.ca

Associated Agencies, Boards & Commissions:
• Assayers Certification Board of Examiners (ACBE)
PO Box 9333 Prov Govt
Victoria, BC V8W 9N3
250-952-0396
The Board of Examiners administers the Assayers Certification Program, invigilate the examinations, grade papers, and recommend candidates for qualification to the Responsible Minister. The Board operates under the Ministry of Energy & Mines Act.
• Building Code Appeal Board (BCAB)
c/o Building & Safety Standards Branch
PO Box 9844 Prov Govt
Victoria, BC V8W 1A4
250-387-3133 Fax: 250-387-8164
Building.Safety@gov.bc.ca
www.housing.gov.bc.ca/bcab
• Homeowner Protection Office (HPO)
c/o BC Housing
#650, 4789 Kingway
Burnaby, BC V5H 0A3
604-646-7050 Fax: 604-646-7051 800-407-7757
hpo@hpo.bc.ca
www.hpo.bc.ca
The Homeowner Protection Office seeks to protect buyers of new homes, to regulate the quality of residential construction, and to support residential construction research and education in British Columbia.
• Oil & Gas Commission (OGC)
#100, 10003 - 110 Ave.
Fort St John, BC V1J 6M7
250-794-5200 Fax: 250-794-5375
www.bcogc.ca
Other Communication: Incident Reporting: 1-800-663-3456; Victoria: 250-419-4400; Dawson Creek: 250-795-2140
The Oil & Gas Commission was enacted under the Oil & Gas Commission Act, The Commission regulates British Columbia's oil & gas activities & pipelines.
• Surface Rights Board
#10, 10551 Shellbridge Way
Richmond, BC V6X 2W9
604-775-1740 Fax: 604-775-1742 888-775-1740
office@surfacerightsboard.bc.ca
www.surfacerightsboard.bc.ca
The Surface Rights Board is an independent, quasi-judicial organization which was established under the authority of the Petroleum & Natural Gas Act. The Board functions under the following acts: the Geothermal Resources Act, the Mineral Tenure Act, the Mining Right of Way Act, & the Coal Act. It assists in resolving disputes between companies & landowners concerning petroleum or natural gas resources.

Electricity & Alternative Energy
PO Box 9314 Prov Govt, Victoria, BC V8W 9N1
250-387-2814 Fax: 250-952-0258
Assistant Deputy Minister, Les MacLaren
250-952-0204, Fax: 250-952-0926, Les.MacLaren@gov.bc.ca
Executive Director, ICE Fund, Dan Green
250-952-0279, Fax: 250-952-0351, Dan.Green@gov.bc.ca
Acting Executive Director, Electricity Transmission & Inter-jurisdictional Branch, Derek Griffin
250-952-0265, Fax: 250-952-0258
Executive Director, Electricity Generation & Regulation Branch, Vacant
Executive Director, Alternative Energy/Renewable Energy Development Branch, Paul Wieringa
250-952-0651, Fax: 250-952-0657
Director, Electricity Transmission & Inter-jurisdictional Branch, Scott Barillaro
250-952-0267, Fax: 250-952-0258, Scott.Barillaro@gov.bc.ca
Director, Electricity Generation & Regulation Branch, Sue Bonnyman
250-953-3365, Fax: 250-952-0258, Sue.Bonnyman@gov.bc.ca
Director, Renewable Energy Development Branch, Janice Larson
250-952-0706, Fax: 250-952-0258, Janice.Larson@gov.bc.ca
Director, Energy Efficiency Branch, Andrew Pape-Salmon
250-952-0819, Fax: 250-952-0258, Andrew.PapeSalmon@gov.bc.ca
Director, ICE Fund, Liz Wouters
250-387-2883, Fax: 250-952-0351, Liz.Wouters@gov.bc.ca

Mines & Mineral Resources
PO Box 9319 Prov Govt, Victoria, BC V8W 9N3
Acting Assistant Deputy Minister, Anne Currie
250-952-0470, Fax: 250-952-0491, Anne.Currie@gov.bc.ca
Chief Inspector, Mines, Al Hoffman
250-952-0494, Fax: 250-952-0491, Al.Hoffman@gov.bc.ca
Chief Geologist & Director, British Columbia Geological Survey, Dave Lefebvre
250-952-0374, Fax: 250-952-0381, Dave.Lefebure@gov.bc.ca
Deputy Chief Gold Commissioner & Director, Mineral Titles (Vancouver), Ed Collazzi
604-660-2814, Fax: 604-660-2653, Ed.Collazzi@gov.bc.ca
Acting Director, Mineral Development Office, Kirk Hancock
250-952-0433, Fax: 604-775-0313, Kirk.Hancock@gov.bc.ca, Other Communications: Alternate Phone: 604-660-3332
Director, Resource Information Section, Larry Jones
250-952-0386, Fax: 250-952-0381, Larry.Jones@gov.bc.ca
Director, Cordilleran Geoscience, Stephen Rowins
250-952-0454, Fax: 250-952-0381, Stephen.Rowins@gov.bc.ca
Director, Mining Operations (Kamloops), Joe Seguin
250-828-4448, Fax: 250-828-4154, Joe.Seguin@gov.bc.ca
Regional Director, Mining Operations (Victoria), Ed Taje
250-952-0732, Fax: 250-952-0491, Eddy.Taje@gov.bc.ca

Office of Housing & Construction Standards
PO Box 9319 Prov Govt, Victoria, BC V8W 9N3
Fax: 250-952-0269
Assistant Deputy Minister, Jeff Vasey
250-387-2001, Fax: 250-387-8164, Jeff.Vasey@gov.bc.ca
Acting Executive Director, Building & Safety Standards Branch, Trudy Rotgans
250-387-3754, Fax: 250-387-8164, Trudy.Rotgans@gov.bc.ca
Executive Director, Housing Policy Branch, Gregory Steves
250-387-3087, Fax: 250-356-8182, Gregory.Steves@gov.bc.ca
Director, Crown Agency Liaison, Simon Clews
250-387-1018, Fax: 250-356-8182, Simon.Clews@gov.bc.ca

Oil & Gas
PO Box 9323 Prov Govt, Victoria, BC V8W 9N3
Fax: 250-952-0926
Assistant Deputy Minister, Graeme McLaren
250-952-0115, Fax: 250-952-0926, Graeme.McLaren@gov.bc.ca
Executive Director, GeoScience & Natural Gas Development Branch, Richard Bader
250-356-1307, Fax: 250-953-3770, Richard.Bader@gov.bc.ca
Executive Director, Major Initiatives, Linda Beltrano
250-356-1183, Fax: 250-952-0255
Executive Director, Royalty Policy Branch, Ines Piccinino
250-356-9825, Fax: 250-952-0271, Ines.Piccinino@gov.bc.ca
Director, O&G Business Practices, Olga Klimko
250-953-3766, Fax: 250-952-0255, Olga.Klimko@gov.bc.ca
Director, Royalty & Policy, Aaron Nelson
250-953-3740, Fax: 250-953-3770, Aaron.Nelson@gov.bc.ca
Director, Infrastructure & Development Section, Stephen Pal
250-953-3738, Fax: 250-953-3770, Stephen.Pal@gov.bc.ca
Acting Director, Major Initiatives Branch, Michelle Schwabe
250-387-1585, Fax: 250-953-3770, Michelle.Schwabe@gov.bc.ca
Director, Economic Development, Ingrid Strauss
250-952-0185, Fax: 250-952-0255, Ingrid.Strauss@gov.bc.ca

Titles & Corporate Relations
PO Box 9315 Prov Govt, Victoria, BC V8W 9N1
Fax: 250-356-5092
Acting Assistant Deputy Minister, Laurel Nash
250-356-9569, Fax: 250-356-5092, Laurel.Nash@gov.bc.ca
Executive Director, Corporate Policy, Planning & Legislation, Karen Koncohrada
250-952-0274, Fax: 250-952-0637, Karen.Koncohrada@gov.bc.ca
Acting Executive Director/Director, Titles Branch/Resource Development, May Mah-Paulson
250-952-0335, Fax: 250-952-0291, May.Mah-Paulson@gov.bc.ca
Acting Director, Policy & Planning, Kelly Finck
250-952-0709, Fax: 250-952-0331, Kelly.Finck@gov.bc.ca
Director, Division Operation & Revenue Systems Branch, Debbie Fischer
250-952-0336, Fax: 250-952-0331, Debbie.Fischer@gov.bc.ca
Acting Director, Corporate Policy & Legislation, Barbara Thomson
250-952-0533, Fax: 250-952-0637, Barbara.Thomson@gov.bc.ca
Acting Director, Resource Development/Policy & Planning, Garth Thoroughgood
250-952-6382, Fax: 250-952-0331, Garth.Thoroughgood@gov.bc.ca

Ministry of Environment

PO Box 9339 Prov Govt, Victoria, BC V8W 9M1
250-387-1161 Fax: 250-387-5669
envmail@gov.bc.ca
www.gov.bc.ca/env
Other Communication: Environmental Emergencies: 1-800-663-3456; Report All Poachers & Polluters (RAPP): 1-877-952-7277
The Ministry provides sustainable environmental management to work towards a healthy, clean, & naturally diverse environment.
Acts Administered:
Agriculture Land Commission Act
Assessment Authority Act
Boundary Act
Budget Measures Implementation Act, 2000
Commercial River Rafting Safety Act
Creston Valley Wildlife Act
Discharge of Firearms Regulation
Summit Creek Campground & Recreation Area Regulations
Dike Maintenance Act
Drainage, Ditch & Dike Act
Ground Water Protection Regulations
Ecological Reserve Act
Application of Park Legislation to Ecological Reserves Regulation
Ecological Reserve Regulations
Emergency Program Act
Compensation & Disaster Financial Assistance Regulation
Emergency Program Management Regulation
Local Authority Emergency Management Regulation
Environment & Land Use Act (Sustainable Resource Management)
Environmental Assessment Act
Concurrent Approval Regulation
Public Consultation Policy Regulation
Transition Regulation
Environmental Management Act
Agricultural Waste Control Regulation
Antisapstain Chemical Waste Control Regulation
Asphalt Plant Regulation
Cleaner Gasoline Regulation
Code of Practice for the Discharge of Produced Water from Coalbed Gas Operations
Conservation Officer Service Authority Regulation
Contaminated Sites Regulation
Environmental Appeal Board Procedure Regulation
Environmental Data Quality Assurance Regulation
Environmental Impact Assessment Regulation
Finfish Aquaculture Waste Control Regulation
Gasoline Vapour Control Regulation
Hazardous Waste Regulation
Land-based Finfish Waste Control Regulation
Motor Vehicle Emissions Control Warranty Regulation
Municipal Sewage Regulation
Mushroom Composting Pollution Prevention Regulation
Oil & Gas Waste Regulation
Open Burning Smoke Control Regulation
Organic Matter Recycling Regulation
Ozone Depleting Substances & Other Halocarbons Regulation
Permit Fees Regulation
Petroleum Storage & Distribution Facilities Storm Water Regulation
Placer Mining Waste Control Regulation
Pulp Mill & Pulp & Paper Mill Liquid Effluent Control Regulation
Recycling Regulation
Solid Fuel Burning Domestic Appliance Regulation
Spill Cost Recovery Regulation
Spill Reporting Regulation
Storage of Recyclable Material Regulation
Sulphur Content of Fuel Regulation
Waste Discharge Regulation
Wood Residue Burner & Incinerator Regulation
Fish Protection Act
Riparian Areas Regulation
Sensitive Streams Designation & Licensing Regulation
Financial Administration Act
Flood Hazard Statutes Amendment Act, 2003
Forest & Range Practices Act
Forest Land Reserve Act
Hunting & Fishing Heritage Act
Industrial Operation Compensation Act
Integrated Pest Management Act
Land Act
Ministry of Environment Act
Park Act
Parks & Protected Areas Statutes Amendment Act, 2004
Pesticide Control Act
Protected Areas of British Columbia Act
Skagit Environmental Enhancement Act
Sustainable Environment Fund Act
Waste Management Act
Water, Land & Air Protection Statutes Amendment Act, 2003
Water Act

Water Protection Act
Water Utility Act
Wildlife Act
Angling & Scientific Collection Regulation
Closed Areas Regulation
Designation & Exemption Regulation
Designation of Officers Regulation
Freshwater Fish Regulation
Hunter Safety Training Regulation
Hunting Licensing Regulation
Hunting Regulation
Limited Entry Hunting Regulation
Management Unit Regulation
Motor Vehicle Prohibition Regulation
Permit Regulation
Public Access Prohibition Regulation
Tofino Mudflats Wildlife Management Area Regulation
Wildlife Act Commercial Activities Regulation
Wildlife Act General Regulation

Minister, Hon. Terry Lake
250-387-1187, Fax: 250-387-1356, env.minister@gov.bc.ca; terry.lake.mla@leg.bc.ca

Deputy Minister, Cairine MacDonald
250-387-5429, Fax: 250-387-6003

Associated Agencies, Boards & Commissions:
• British Columbia Environmental Assessment Office
• Environmental Appeal Board (EAB)
747 Fort St., 4th Fl.
PO Box 9425 Prov Govt
Victoria, BC V8W 3E9
250-387-3464 Fax: 250-356-9923
eabinfo@gov.bc.ca
www.eab.gov.bc.ca
The Environmental Appeal Board is an independent agency which was created under the Environment Management Act. The Board hears appeals from administrative decisions under the following acts: the Environmental Management Act, the Health Act, the Integrated Pest Management Act, the Water Act, & the Wildlife Act. Notices of appeal are reviewed & evaluated to determine if an alternative dispute resolution is possible.
• Fraser Basin Council (FBC)
Central Office
470 Granville St., 1st Fl.
Vancouver, BC V6C 1V5
604-488-5350 Fax: 604-488-5351
info@fraserbasin.bc.ca
www.fraserbasin.bc.ca
Other Communication: Thompson: 250-314-9660; Upper Fraser: 250-612-0252; Fraser Valley: 604-826-1661; Cariboo-Chilcotin: 250-392-1400; Greater Vancouver Sea to Sky: 604-488-5365
The Fraser Basin Council is a not-for-profit, non-partisan organization. The Council works to advance sustainability throughout the Fraser River Basin.

Climate Action Secretariat
PO Box 9486 Prov Govt, Victoria, BC V8W 9W6
Fax: 250-356-7286
climateactionsecretariat@gov.bc.ca
www.env.gov.bc.ca/cas//index.html

Head, James Mack
250-387-9456, Fax: 250-356-7286
Chief Negotiator/Executive Director, Business Development, Tim Lesiuk
250-387-9216, Fax: 250-356-7286, Other Communications: Cell Phone: 250-216-5893
Executive Director, Climate Policy, Lee Thiessen
250-356-7917, Fax: 250-356-7286
Director, Carbon Neutral Government & Outreach, Colleen Sparks
250-356-1810, Fax: 250-356-7286, Colleen.Sparks@gov.bc.ca
Director, Business Partnerhsips, Vacant
250-953-4883, Fax: 250-356-7286
Lead Negotiator/Director, Business Development, Jessica Verhagen
604-660-0788, Fax: 250-356-7286, Jessica.Verhagen@gov.bc.ca

Compliance Division - Enforcement Program / Conservation Officer Service
PO Box 9376 Prov Govt, Victoria, BC V8W 9M1
250-356-9234 Fax: 250-356-9197
conservation.officer.service@gov.bc.ca
www.env.gov.bc.ca/cos/
Other Communication: Wildlife conflict: 1-877-952-7277

Chief Conservation Officer, Enforcement Program/Conservation Officer Service, Ed Illi
250-356-9100, Fax: 250-356-9197, Ed.Illi@gov.bc.ca
Executive Director, Enforcement Program/Conservation Officer Service, Tom D. Clark
250-356-9443, Fax: 250-953-3414, Tom.D.Clark@gov.bc.ca, Other Communications: Cell Phone: 250-893-0990
Chief Superintendent, Program Governance, Lance Sundquist
250-751-3119, Fax: 250-751-7383, Lance.Sundquist@gov.bc.ca, Other Communications: Alternate Phone: 250-356-9121
Chief Superintendent, Program Governance, Barry Farynuk
250-354-6336, Fax: 250-354-6277, Barry.Farynuk@gov.bc.ca

Environmental Protection Division
PO Box 9339, Victoria, BC V8W 9M1
250-387-1288 Fax: 250-387-5669
www.env.gov.bc.ca/epd/

Assistant Deputy Minister, Jim Standen
250-387-1288, Fax: 250-387-5669, Jim.Standen@gov.bc.ca
Director, Environmental Management, Jim Hofweber
250-387-9971, Fax: 250-387-8897, Jim.Hofweber@gov.bc.ca
Director, Air Protection Branch, Glen Okrainetz
250-953-3417, Fax: 250-952-1713, Glen.Okrainetz@gov.bc.ca
Director, Environmental Standards Branch, David Ranson
250-387-9933, Fax: 250-356-7197, David.Ranson@gov.bc.ca
Deputy Director, Regional Operations, Christa Zacharias-Homer
250-356-8174, Fax: 250-356-5496, Christa.ZachariasHomer@gov.bc.ca
Regional Manager, Thompson Regional Office, Rick Adams
250-371-6299, Fax: 250-828-4000, Rick.P.Adams@gov.bc.ca
Regional Manager, Vancouver Island Regional Office, Randy Alexander
250-751-3176, Fax: 250-751-3103, Randy.Alexander@gov.bc.ca
Regional Manager, Lower Mainland Regional Office, Jonn Braman
604-582-5284, Fax: 604-584-9751
Regional Manager, Omineca Regional Office, Dean Cherkas
250-565-6443, Fax: 250-565-6629, Dean.Cherkas@gov.bc.ca
Regional Manager, Kootenay & Okanagan Regional Office, Robyn Roome
250-354-6362, Fax: 250-354-6332, Robyn.Roome@gov.bc.ca
Regional Manager, Skeena Regional Office, Ian Sharpe
250-847-7251, Fax: 250-847-7591, Ian.Sharpe@gov.bc.ca
Section Head, Cariboo Regional Office, Douglas Hill
250-398-4542, Fax: 250-398-4214

Environmental Stewardship Division
PO Box 9339 Prov Govt, Victoria, BC V8W 9M1
250-356-0121 Fax: 250-387-5669

Director, Regional Operations, Brian J. Clark
250-356-0874, Fax: 250-356-9299, Brian.J.Clark@gov.bc.ca
Manager, First Nations Relations, Bryan Williams
250-751-3155, Fax: 250-751-3208
Manager, Strategic Initiatives, Chris Tunnoch
604-942-2224, Fax: 604-924-2244, Chris.Tunnoch@gov.bc.ca
Regional Manager, Vancouver Island Regional Office, Don Cadden
250-751-3211, Fax: 250-751-3208, Don.Cadden@gov.bc.ca
Regional Manager, Thompson Regional Office, Jeff Leahy
250-371-6304, Fax: 250-828-4000, Jeff.Leahy@gov.bc.ca
Regional Manager, Peace Regional Office, Vacant
250-787-3426, Fax: 250-787-3490
Acting Regional Manager, Omineca Regional Office, Ted Zimmerman
250-614-9904, Fax: 250-565-6940, Ted.Zimmerman@gov.bc.ca
Section Head, Skeena Regional Office, Larry Boudreau
250-847-7655, Fax: 250-847-7728, Larry.Boudreau@gov.bc.ca
Section Head, Kootenay Regional Office, Glenn Campbell
250-489-8595, Fax: 250-489-8506, Glenn.Campbell@gov.bc.ca
Section Head, Cariboo Regional Office, Murray Carruthers
250-398-4924, Fax: 250-398-4214, Murray.Carruthers@gov.bc.ca
Section Head, Lower Mainland Regional Office, Vicki Haberl
604-898-3678, Fax: 604-898-4171, Vicki.Haberl@gov.bc.ca
Section Head, Okanagan Regional Office, Dave Richmond
250-490-8259, Fax: 250-490-2231, Dave.Richmond@gov.bc.ca

Environmental Sustainability & Strategic Policy Division
PO Box 9335 Prov Govt, Victoria, BC V8W 9M1
250-387-9666 Fax: 250-387-8894

Assistant Deputy Minister, Mark Zacharias
250-356-0121, Fax: 250-387-5669
Executive Director, Strategic Policy Branch, Anthony J. Danks
250-387-8483, Fax: 250-387-8894, Anthony.Danks@gov.bc.ca
Director, Ecosystems Branch, Kaaren Lewis
250-387-9731, Fax: 250-356-5104, Kaaren.Lewis@gov.bc.ca
Director, Knowledge Management Branch, Fern Schultz
250-387-6722, Fax: 250-356-1202, Fern.Schultz@gov.bc.ca
Director, Water Protection & Sustainability Branch, Lynn Kriwoken
250-387-9446, Fax: 250-356-1202, Lynn.Kriwoken@gov.bc.ca

Parks & Protected Areas Division
PO Box 9339 Prov Govt, Victoria, BC V8W 9M9
Fax: 250-953-3414

Assistant Deputy Minister, Lori Halls
250-387-9997, Fax: 250-953-3414
Director, Parks Planning & Management Branch, Brian Bawtinheimer
250-387-4355, Fax: 250-387-5757, Brian.Bawtinheimer@gov.bc.ca
Director, Visitor Services Branch, Christine Houghton
250-356-9241, Fax: 250-387-5757, Christine.Houghton@gov.bc.ca

Water Stewardship Division
PO Box 9339 Prov Govt, Victoria, BC V8W 9M1
Fax: 250-387-6003

Regional Manager, Thompson & Cariboo Regional Offices, Vacant
250-371-6200, Fax: 250-828-4000, Other Communications: Cariboo Fax: 250-398-4836
Regional Manager, Vancouver Island Regional Office, Larry Barr
250-751-7105, Fax: 250-751-7079, Larry.Barr@gov.bc.ca
Regional Manager, Lower Mainland Regional Office, Julia Berardinucci
604-582-5353, Fax: 604-582-5235, Julia.Berardinucci@gov.bc.ca
Regional Manager, Omineca, Peace, & Skeena Regional Offices, Norm Bilodeau
250-565-6424, Fax: 250-565-6629, Normand.Bilodeau@gov.bc.ca

British Columbia Environmental Assessment Office

836 Yates St., 1st Fl., PO Box 9426 Prov Govt, Victoria, BC V8W 9V1
250-356-7479 Fax: 250-356-6448
eaoinfo@gov.bc.ca
www.eao.gov.bc.ca

Operating independently, the Environmental Assessment Office (EAO) coordinates the assessment of proposed projects in British Columbia. The Office acts under the requirements of the Environmental Assessment Act. Working with the public, government agencies, & First Nations, the Environmental Assessment Office ensures that projects are developed in a sustainable manner.

Acting Executive Director, John Mazure
250-356-7475, Fax: 250-356-7477, John.Mazure@gov.bc.ca
Acting Executive Project Assessment Director, Kathy Eichenberger
250-387-2307, Fax: 250-387-2208, Kathy.Eichenberger@gov.bc.ca
Director, Strategy & Quality Assurance, Michelle Carr
250-387-6748, Fax: 250-356-6448, Michelle.Carr@gov.bc.ca
Director, Business Operations, Terri Starkes
250-356-5770, Fax: 250-356-7477, Terri.Starkes@gov.bc.ca
Project Assessment Director, Coal & Aggregates Mining Projects, Karen L. Christie
250-387-9675, Fax: 250-356-6448, Karen.L.Christie@gov.bc.ca
Project Assessment Director, Food Processing & Waste Management Projects, Chris Hamilton
250-387-1032, Fax: 250-387-2208, Chris.Hamilton@gov.bc.ca
Project Assessment Director, Power & Industrial Projects, Brian Murphy
250-387-2402, Fax: 250-387-2208, Brian.Murphy@gov.bc.ca
Project Assessment Director, Metal Mining & Transportation Projects, Shelley Murphy
250-387-1447, Shelley.Murphy@gov.bc.ca
Project Assessment Director, Destination Resorts & Oil & Gas Projects, Archie Riddell
250-952-6507, Fax: 250-387-2208, David.Riddell@gov.bc.ca

British Columbia Ferry Services Inc.

#500, 1321 Blanshard St., Victoria, BC V8W 0B7
250-381-1401
888-223-3779
www.bcferries.com
Other Communication: Outside North America Phone: 250-386-3431

BC Ferries operates as the primary provider of coastal ferry service in British Columbia. The fleet covers 25 routes.

Acts Administered:
Coastal Ferry Act

Chair, Donald P. Hayes
President/Chief Executive Officer, David L. Hahn
Executive Vice-President & Chief Financial Officer, Rob Clarke
Executive Vice-President & Chief Operating Officer, Mike Corrigan
Executive Vice-President, Human Resources & Corporate Development, Glen N. Schwartz

Ministry of Finance

PO Box 9417 Prov Govt, Victoria, BC V8W 9V1
250-387-3751 Fax: 250-387-5594
Fin.Minister@gov.bc.ca
www.gov.bc.ca/fin
Other Communication: Media Phone: 250-356-9872; Fax: 250-356-2822

The goal of the Ministry of Finance is the provision of strong fiscal management & a balanced budget. It develops fiscal policies & regulatory frameworks to maintain a vibrant provincial economy.

Acts Administered:
Auditor General Act
Balanced Budget & Ministerial Accountability Act
BC Railway Act
Bonding Act
Budget Transparency & Accountability Act
Business Corporations Act
Business Number Act
Capital Financing Authority Repeal & Debt Restructuring Act
Community Services Labour Relations Act
Constitution Act, ss. 25-27
Cooperative Association Act
Credit Union Incorporation Act
Creditor Assistance Act
Financial Administration Act
Financial Information Act
Financial Institutions Act
Industrial Development Act
Insurance Act
Insurance (Captive Company) Act
Insurance (Marine) Act
International Financial Business Act
Manufactured Home Act
Ministerial Accountability Bases (2004, 2004-2005) Acts
Ministry of Consumer & Corporate Affairs Act, ss. 3-4
Ministry of Intergovernmental Relations Act, s. 3
Miscellaneous Registrations Act, 1992
Mortgage Brokers Act
Mutual Fire Insurance Companies Act
Pacific North Coast Native Cooperative Act
Partnership Act
Pension Agreement Act
Pension Benefits Standards Act
Pension Fund Societies Act
Personal Property Security Act
Ports Property Tax Act
Probate Fee Act
Public Education Support Staff Collective Bargaining Assistance Act
Public Works Agreement Act
Real Estate Development Marketing Act
Real Estate Services Act
Repairers Lien Act
Securities (Forged Transfer) Act
Society Act
Strata Property Act
Tugboat Worker's Lien Act
Unclaimed Property Act
Warehouse Lien Act
Warehouse Receipt Act
Woodworker Lien Act

Minister, Finance & Deputy Premier, Hon. Kevin Falcon
250-387-3751, Fax: 250-387-5594, Fin.Minister@gov.bc.ca; kevin.falcon.mla@leg.bc.ca
Deputy Minister, Peter Milburn
250-387-3184, Fax: 250-387-1655
Director, Strategic Initiatives, Doug Foster
250-387-9022, Fax: 250-387-1655, Doug.Foster@gov.bc.ca

Associated Agencies, Boards & Commissions:
• Auditor Certification Board
PO Box 9431 Prov Govt
Victoria, BC V8W 9V3
250-356-8658 Fax: 250-356-9422
Kelly.Fitzsimonds@gov.bc.ca
The Auditor Certification Board is authorized under the Business Corporations Act. The Board receives applications from individuals who apply to becertified as auditors. Persons with the necessary qualifications are then certified.
• British Columbia Securities Commission
Pacific Centre
701 West Georgia St., 12th Fl.
PO Box 10142
Vancouver, BC V7Y 1L2
604-899-6500 Fax: 604-899-6506 800-373-6393
inquiries@bcsc.bc.ca
www.bcsc.bc.ca
The British Columbia Securities Commission is an independent provincial government agency. Through administration of the Securities Act, the Commission regulates securities trading in British Columbia.
• Crown Agencies Resource Office (CARO)
PO Box 9469 Prov Govt
Victoria, BC V8V 9V8
250-387-8770 Fax: 250-387-9061
CAS@gov.bc.ca
www.gov.bc.ca/caro
Implementation of the governance framework for British Columbia's Crown agencies is the role of the Crown Agencies Secretariat. The Secretariat advises Ministries & Crown agencies on the requirements of the Crown Agency Accountability System. It also maintains the Crown Agency Registry.
• Financial Institutions Commission (FICOM)
#1200, 13450 - 102 Ave.
Surrey, BC V3T 5X3
604-953-5300 Fax: 604-953-5301 866-206-3030
FICOM@ficombc.ca; HR@ficombc.ca
www.fic.gov.bc.ca
Other Communication: Complaints & inquiries: 604-953-5200
The Financial Institutions Commission is a regulatory agency of British Columbia's Ministry of Finance. The Commission's responsibility is the administration of statutes that regulate the financial services, pension, & real estate sectors in the province.
• Insurance Council of British Columbia
#300, 1040 West Georgia St.
PO Box 7
Vancouver, BC V6E 4H1
604-688-0321 Fax: 604-662-7767 877-688-0321
www.insurancecouncilofbc.com
The Insurance Council of British Columbia reports to the province's Minister of Finance. The Council has the following responsibilities: Licensing insurance agents, salespersons, & adjusters; Regulating insurance licensees; & Investigating & disciplining licensees.
• Real Estate Council of British Columbia
#900, 750 West Pender St.
Vancouver, BC V6C 2T8
604-683-9664 Fax: 604-683-9017 877-683-9664
info@recbc.ca
www.recbc.ca
The Real Estate Council of British Columbia is a regulatory agency with the following responsibilities under the requirements of the Real Estate Services Act: Licensing individuals & brokerages involved in real estate sales, rental & strata property management; Enforcing licensing qualifications & licensee conduct; & Investigating complaints against licensees & imposing discipline.

Corporate & Ministry Support Services
PO Box 9415 Prov Govt, Victoria, BC V8W 9V1
Assistant Deputy Minister, Deborah Fayad
250-387-8139, Fax: 250-387-8586, Deborah.Fayad@gov.bc.ca, Other Communications: Cell Phone: 250-589-2480
Chief Information Officer & Executive Director, Information Management, Michael Carpenter
250-387-3485, Fax: 250-356-1494, Michael.Carpenter@gov.bc.ca
Executive Director, Strategic Human Resources, Elaine Jones
250-387-2984, Fax: 250-356-7326, Elaine.F.Jones@gov.bc.ca
Executive Director & Chief Financial Officer, Financial Services & Administration, Steve Klak
250-356-1387, Fax: 250-356-7326, Steve.Klak@gov.bc.ca
Executive Director, Performance Management & Corporate Priorities Branch, Donna Selbee
250-387-4733, Fax: 250-356-7326, Donna.Selbee@gov.bc.ca
Director, Facilities Management, Shelly Akam
250-387-8125, Fax: 250-387-8586, Shelly.Akam@gov.bc.ca, Other Communications: Cell Phone: 250-588-3614
Director, Divisional Operations Branch, Heather L. Clark
250-356-9606, Fax: 250-387-8586, Heather.L.Clark@gov.bc.ca, Other Communications: Cell Phone: 250-216-4149
Director, Strategic Human Resources Branch, Bert Elliott
250-387-9504, Fax: 250-356-7326, Bert.Elliott@gov.bc.ca
Director, Operational Support, Tim Furmek
250-387-8962, Fax: 250-356-1494, Tim.Furmek@gov.bc.ca
Director, Business & Client Services, Mike Holt
250-953-3950, Fax: 250-356-1494, Mike.Holt@gov.bc.ca
Director, Financial Services, Kanwaljeet Kuckreja
250-387-3867, Fax: 250-356-7326, Kanwaljeet.Kuckreja@gov.bc.ca
Director, Financial Management & Reporting, Martha Okot Thomas
250-356-0403, Martha.Thomas@gov.bc.ca
Director, Financial Planning, Philip Twyford
250-387-9530, Fax: 250-356-7326, Philip.Twyford@gov.bc.ca

Deputy Secretary to Treasury Board
PO Box 9469 Prov Govt, Victoria, BC V8W 9V8
Assistant Deputy Minister/Deputy Secretary to Treasury Board, Sabine Feulgen
250-356-5427, Fax: 250-387-9054, Sabine.Feulgen@gov.bc.ca
Executive Director, SUCH Ministries, Gord Enemark
250-356-5032, Fax: 250-387-9054, Gord.Enemark@gov.bc.ca
Executive Director, Estimates & Reporting, Don Epp
250-387-9008, Fax: 250-387-0300, Don.Epp@gov.bc.ca
Executive Director, Performance Budgeting Office, David Fairbotham
250-387-8773, Fax: 250-387-9061, David.Fairbotham@gov.bc.ca
Executive Director, Social Policy, Kerri Harrison
250-387-9041, Fax: 250-387-9054, Kerri.Harrison@gov.bc.ca
Executive Director, Fiscal Planning, Dave Riley
250-387-9030, Fax: 250-387-0300, Dave.Riley@gov.bc.ca
Executive Director, Economic Development Policy, Marie Ty
250-952-6200, Fax: 250-387-9054, Marie.Ty@gov.bc.ca
Director, Performance Budgeting Office, Rebecca John
250-387-9034, Fax: 250-387-9054, Rebecca.John@gov.bc.ca
Manager, TB Operations, Jennifer Mitchell
250-387-9070, Fax: 250-356-7624, Jennifer.Michell@gov.bc.ca

Economics & Policy Division
Fax: 250-952-0137
Assistant Deputy Minister, Heather Wood
250-356-9911, Fax: 250-952-0137
Acting Executive Director, Financial & Corporate Sector Policy Branch, Marcus Gill
250-387-9090, Fax: 250-387-9093, Marcus.Gill@gov.bc.ca
Executive Director & Chief Economist, Economic Forecasting & Policy Analysis, Llew Hamdi
250-387-0368, Fax: 250-387-0300, Llew.Hamdi@gov.bc.ca
Executive Director, Intergovernmental Fiscal Relations, Rory Molnar
250-387-4174, Fax: 250-387-9061, Rory.Molnar@gov.bc.ca
Executive Director, Tax Policy Branch, Glen Armstrong
250-387-9011, Fax: 250-387-9061, Rory.Molnar@gov.bc.ca
Director, Intergovernmental Fiscal Relations, Patrick Ewing
250-952-0936, Fax: 250-387-9093, Patrick.Ewing@gov.bc.ca
Director, Financial & Corporate Sector Policy Branch, Mary Kimpton
250-387-9077, Fax: 250-387-9093, Mary.Kimpton@gov.bc.ca
Director, Intergovernmental Fiscal Relations, Russell Mellett
604-775-0703, Fax: 250-387-9061, Russell.Mellett@gov.bc.ca
Director, Intergovernmental Fiscal Relations, Grant Smith
250-387-1510, Fax: 250-387-9061, Grant.H.Smith@gov.bc.ca
Director, Intergovernmental Fiscal Relations, Brad Underwood
250-356-0513, Fax: 250-387-9061, Brad.Underwood@gov.bc.ca

Office of the Comptroller General
PO Box 9413 Prov Govt, Victoria, BC V8W 9V1
250-387-6692 Fax: 250-356-2001
Comptroller.General@gov.bc.ca
www.fin.gov.bc.ca/ocg.htm
Acting Comptroller General, Stuart Newton
Stuart.Newton@gov.bc.ca
Acting Executive Director, Internal Audit & Advisory Services, Chris Brown
250-387-9237, Fax: 250-356-2001, Chris.Brown@gov.bc.ca
Executive Director, Financial Management, George Farkas
250-387-0279, Fax: 250-356-6164, George.Farkas@gov.bc.ca, Other Communications: Alternate Phone: 250-213-1713
Executive Director, Financial Reporting & Advisory Services, Carl Fischer
250-356-9272, Fax: 250-356-8388, Carl.Fischer@gov.bc.ca
Executive Director, Corporate Compliance & Controls Monitoring & Legal Encumbrance, Chris Johnson
250-356-7434, Fax: 250-356-0560, Chris.Johnson@gov.bc.ca
Executive Director, Internal Audit & Advisory Services, Marg Sorensen
250-387-8172, Fax: 250-356-2001, Marg.Sorensen@gov.bc.ca

Provincial Treasury
PO Box 9414 Prov Govt, Victoria, BC V8V 9V1
250-387-4541 Fax: 250-356-3041
www.fin.gov.bc.ca/pt.htm
The Provincial Treasury consist of the following branches: Banking / Cash Management; Corporate Operations; Corporate & Project Finance; Debt Management; Information Systems; Risk Management; & BC Registry Services.
Assistant Deputy Minister, Jim Hopkins
250-387-5729, Fax: 250-356-3041, Jim.Hopkins@gov.bc.ca
Chief Security Officer, Risk Mitigation & Government Security, Shaun Fynes
250-387-0522, Fax: 250-356-6222, Shaun.Fynes@gov.bc.ca
Executive Director, Risk Management, Phil Grewar
250-387-0521, Fax: 250-356-6222, Phil.Grewar@gov.bc.ca
Executive Director, Debt Management, Darshi Klear
250-387-8815, Fax: 250-387-3024
Director, Information Systems, Tom Caldwell
250-356-5473, Fax: 250-387-6577, Tom.Caldwell@gov.bc.ca

Director, Client Services - Core Government & Crowns, Glen Frederick
250-356-8915, Fax: 250-356-6222, Glen.Frederick@gov.bc.ca
Director, Client Services - Education, Andrew Green
250-952-0785, Fax: 250-356-6222, Andrew.Green@gov.bc.ca
Director, Underwriting & Analysis, Laura Hughs
250-387-0519, Fax: 250-356-6222, Laura.Hughes@gov.bc.ca
Director, Client Services - Health Care, Linda Irvine
250-952-0849, Fax: 250-953-3050, Linda.Irvine@gov.bc.ca
Director, Banking/Cash Management, Nicholas Krischanowsky
250-387-7105, Nick.Krischanowsky@gov.bc.ca
Director, Claims & Litigation Management, Kim Oldham
250-952-0837, Fax: 250-356-0661, Kim.Oldham@gov.bc.ca
Director, Corporate & Project Finance, Matthew O'Rae
250-356-9370, Fax: 250-387-3024
Manager, Corporate Operations, Ida Stephenson
250-387-7124, Fax: 250-387-6577, Ida.Stephenson@gov.bc.ca

Revenue Programs Division
Fax: 250-387-3000
Assistant Deputy Minister, Elan Symes
250-387-0665, Elan.Symes@gov.bc.ca
Executive Director, Consumer Taxation Programs Branch, Jordan Goss
250-387-0611
Executive Director, Income Taxation Branch, Paula Harper
250-387-3968, Fax: 250-356-9243
Executive Director, Property Taxation Branch, Tara Richards
250-387-0532, Fax: 250-387-2210, Tara.Richards@gov.bc.ca
Acting Executive Director, Mineral, Oil & Gas Revenue Branch, Andrew Ritonja
250-356-0670, Fax: 250-952-0191, Andrew.Ritonja@gov.bc.ca
Director, Real Property Taxation, Art Chambers
250-356-9565, Fax: 250-387-2210, Art.Chambers@gov.bc.ca
Director, Audit & Compliance, Hilary Harley
250-387-0602, Fax: 250-953-3094, Hilary.Harley@gov.bc.ca
Director, Property Tax Services & Tax Deferment, Lori Kirk
250-387-5469, Fax: 250-386-5347, Lori.Kirk@gov.bc.ca
Director, Investigations Unit, Carson Kong
604-586-4172, Fax: 604-586-4172, Carson.Kong@gov.bc.ca
Director, Income Tax Advisory & Intergovernmental Relations, Jeffery Krasnick
250-953-3091, Fax: 250-356-9243, Jeffrey.Krasnick@gov.bc.ca
Director, Income Tax Programs, Steve Pleva
250-387-1201, Fax: 250-356-9243, Steve.Pleva@gov.bc.ca
Audit Director, Audit (Victoria), Carol O'Brien
250-387-9667, Fax: 250-356-0434, Carol.OBrien@gov.bc.ca

Revenue Services
Fax: 250-952-0113
Assistant Deputy Minister, Janet Baltes
250-387-1158, Fax: 250-952-0113, Janet.Baltes@gov.bc.ca
Executive Director, Revenue Solutions Branch, Pat Parkinson
250-356-9670, Fax: 250-356-1709, Pat.Parkinson@gov.bc.ca
Executive Director, Tax Appeals & Administrative Services Branch, Wayne Sparanese
250-387-0662, Wayne.Sparanese@gov.bc.ca
Acting Director, Integrated Services, Gina Curran
250-387-1199, Fax: 250-356-1706, Gina.Curran@gov.bc.ca
Director, Compliance & Customer Care, Gregg Danderfer
250-356-2522, Fax: 250-356-1706, Gregg.Danderfer@gov.bc.ca
Director, Student Loans Management Team, Steven Emery
250-387-1182, Fax: 250-356-1706, Steven.Emery@gov.bc.ca
Director, Performance & Reporting, Darrell Eng
250-356-2517, Fax: 250-356-1706, Darrell.Eng@gov.bc.ca
Director, Receivables Management Office, Dennis Forbes
250-356-8031, Fax: 250-356-5604, Dennis.Forbes@gov.bc.ca
Director, Appeals, Kinsburh Healey
250-387-5881, Fax: 250-387-5883, Kinsburh.Healey@gov.bc.ca
Acting Director, Appeals, Renny Lubberts
250-356-2758, Fax: 250-387-5883, Renny.Lubberts@gov.bc.ca
Director, ASD Contracts, David Sherwood
250-387-3864, Fax: 250-356-1706, David.Sherwood@gov.bc.ca, Other Communications: Cell Phone: 250-888-6480
Director, Client Portfolio, Elaine Smith
250-356-1564, Fax: 250-356-1706, Elaine.Smith@gov.bc.ca
Director, Appeals, Hilary Vance
250-952-0708, Fax: 250-387-5883, Hilary.Vance@gov.bc.ca
Manager, Corporate Operations, Leona Frenette
250-387-4175, Fax: 250-952-0113, Leona.Frenette@gov.bc.ca

Ministry of Forests, Lands & Natural Resource Operations

PO Box 9049 Prov Govt, Victoria, BC V8W 9E2
250-387-4809 Fax: 250-387-1040
www.gov.bc.ca/for
Other Communication: Report Wildfires Toll Free: 1-800-663-5555; Media Phone: 250-356-5261

The Ministry of Forests, Mines and Lands supports the sustainable development of forest, mineral and land resources. The Ministry is committed to a globally competitive resource sector that can provide enormous benefits for workers, communities and future generations.

Acts Administered:
Forest Act
Administrative Review & Appeal Procedure (Forest Act/Forest practices Code of BC Act) Regulation
Advertising, Deposits, Disposition & Extension Regulation
Allowable Annual Cut Administration Regulation
Allowable Annual Cut Partition Regulation
Annual Rent Regulation
BC Timber Sales Business Areas Regulation
BC Timber Sales Regulation
Christmas Tree Regulation
Community Tenures Regulation
Cut Control Regulation
Cutting Permit Postponement Regulation
Effective Director Regulation
Forest Accounts Receivable Interest Regulation
Forest Regions & Districts Regulation
Forest Revenue Audit Regulation
Free Use Permit Regulation
Innovative Forestry Practices Regulation
Interest Rate Under Various Statutes Regulation
Log Salvage Regulation (Vancouver District)
Manufactured Forest Products Regulation
Minimum Stumpage Rate Regulation
Performance Based Harvesting Regulation
Scaling Regulation
Special Forest Products Regulation
Timber Definition Regulation
Timber Harvesting Contract & Subcontract Regulation
Timber Marking & Transportation Regulation
Transfer Regulation
Tree Farm Licence Area-based Allowable Annual Cut Trial Program Regulation
Tree Farm Licence Management Plan
Woodlot Licence Regulation
Forestry Licence to Cut Regulation
Forest Practices Code of British Columbia Act
Provincial Forest Use Regulation
Forest & Range Practices Act
Administrative Orders & Remedies Regulation
Administrative Review & Appeal Procedure Regulation
Forest Planning & Practices Regulation
Forest Practices Board Regulation
Forest Recreation Regulation
Forest Service Road Use Regulation
Fort St. John Pilot Project Regulation
Invasive Plants Regulation
Range Planning & Practices Regulation
Security for Forest & Range Practice Liabilities Regulation
Stillwater Pilot Project Regulation
Woodlot Licence Planning & Practices Regulation
Government Actions Regulation
Transition Regulation
Forest Stand Management Fund Act
Foresters Act
Forestry Revitalization Act, 2003
Manufactured Forest Products Regulation
Ministry of Forests Act
Protected Areas Forests Compensation Act
Range Act
Safety Authority Act
Safety Standards Act
Timber Licences Settlement Act
Timber Sale Licence Replacement (Sliammon First Nation) Act
Wildfire Act, 2004
Wood First Act
Carrier Lumber Ltd. Forest Licence Compensation Act

Minister, Hon. Steve Thomson
250-387-6240, Fax: 250-387-1040, FLNR.Minister@gov.bc.ca; steve.thomson.mla@leg.bc.ca
Deputy Minister, Doug Konkin
250-952-6500, Fax: 250-387-3291, Doug.Konkin@gov.bc.ca
Director, Communications, Dave Crebo
250-356-6998, Fax: 250-953-3862, David.Crebo@gov.bc.ca
Director, Executive Operations, Karen McRae
250-356-2700, Fax: 250-387-3291, Karen.McRae@gov.bc.ca

Associated Agencies, Boards & Commissions:
• Forest Appeals Commission (FAC)
747 Fort St., 4th Fl.
PO Box 9425 Prov Govt
Victoria, BC V8W 9V1
250-387-3464 Fax: 250-356-9923
facinfo@gov.bc.ca
www.fac.gov.bc.ca
Established in 1996 under the Forest Practices Code of British Columbia Act, the Forest Appeals Commission is an independent agency which now continues under the Forest & Range Practices Act. The Commission hears appeals from administrative decisions made under the following statutes: Forest Act, Forest & Range Practices Act, Forest Practices Code of British Columbia Act, Private Managed Forest Land Act, Range Act, & the Wildfire Act.
• Forest Practices Board (FPB)
1675 Douglas St., 3rd Fl.
PO Box 9905 Prov Govt
Victoria, BC V8W 9R1
250-213-4700 Fax: 250-213-4725 800-994-5899
fpboard@gov.bc.ca
www.fpb.gov.bc.ca
Other Communication: Toll-Free Fax: 1-877-708-4607
British Columbia's Forest Practices Board is responsible for reporting to the government & public about compliance with the Forest & Range Practices Act. The Board engages in the following activities: Investigation of public complaints; Undertaking special investigations; Auditing forest practices of government, government enforcement of the Forest & Range Practices Act, & licence holders on public lands; Participation in appeals; & Provision of reports & recommendations.
• Forestry Innovation Investment Ltd. (FII)
#1200, 1130 West Pender St.
Vancouver, BC V6E 4A4
604-685-7507 Fax: 604-685-5373
info@bcfii.ca
www.bcfii.ca
British Columbia's Forestry Innovation Investment strives to support a prosperous & environmentally sustainable forest economy in the province. The role of the organization includes the following activities: Promotion of British Columbia's forest practices & wood products to international markets; Working in partnership with the forestry sector, the Government of British Columbia, & the Government of Canada; & Assisting the forestry sector with issues such as Mountain Pine Beetle outbreak.
• Timber Export Advisory Committee
PO Box 9514 Prov Govt
Victoria, BC V8W 9C2
250-387-8916 Fax: 250-387-5050

Corporate Initiatives
PO Box 9352 Prov Govt, Victoria, BC V8W 9M1
Acting Executive Director, Christine Gelowitz
250-387-8885, Fax: 250-356-5797, Christine.Gelowitz@gov.bc.ca
Acting Director, Strategic Initiatives, Gail P. Brewer
250-356-5299, Fax: 250-953-3481
Director, Legislation, Richard Grieve
250-387-8606, Fax: 250-356-7903, Richard.Grieve@gov.bc.ca
Acting Director, Natural Resource Authorization, Brian Westgate
250-953-4205, Brian.Westgate@gov.bc.ca
Senior Manager, Strategic Planning & Policy, Melissa Friesen
250-356-7278, Fax: 250-953-3603, Melissa.Friesen@gov.bc.ca

Integrated Resource Operations Division
PO Box 9352 Prov Govt, Victoria, BC V8W 9M1
250-356-1874 Fax: 250-387-2335
Assistant Deputy Minister, Gary Townsend
250-356-1874, Fax: 250-387-2335
Executive Director, Field Operations, Jim Maxwell
250-387-1236, Fax: 250-953-3687, Jim.Maxwell@gov.bc.ca
Executive Director, GeoBC & Compliance & Enforcement, Francesca Wheler
250-387-3745
Director, Range, Invasive Plants & Ecosystem Restoration, David Borth
250-371-3827, Fax: 250-828-4987, David.Borth@gov.bc.ca, Other Communications: Alternate Phone: 250-371-3836
Acting Director, Compliance & Enforcement, Kevin Edquist
250-387-8372, Fax: 250-387-2569, Kevin.Edquist@gov.bc.ca
Director, Recreation Sites & Trails BC, Bill Marshall
250-953-3678, Bill.Marshall@gov.bc.ca
Director, Wildfire Management Headquarters, Brian Simpson
250-356-1068, Fax: 250-387-5685, Brian.Simpson@gov.bc.ca
Manager, Regional Service Delivery, GeoBC, Janet Adams
250-387-9338, Fax: 250-356-5797, Janet.Adams@gov.bc.ca

Major Projects, First Nations & Community Opportunities Division
PO Box 9352 Prov Govt, Victoria, BC V8W 9M1
Fax: 250-387-2335

Assistant Deputy Minister, Peter Walters
250-356-7723, Fax: 250-387-2335
Executive Director, Major Projects Branch, Jennifer C. Davis
250-387-0738, Fax: 250-387-2335,
Jennifer.C.Davis@gov.bc.ca
Executive Director, Resort Development, Norman Lee
250-952-0478, Fax: 250-356-2842,
Norman.K.Lee@gov.bc.ca
Director, Archeology Branch, Justine Batten
250-953-3355, Fax: 250-953-3340, Justine.Batten@gov.bc.ca
Director, Crown Land Opportunities & Restoration, Ron Bronstein
250-387-1544, Fax: 250-356-6791, Ron.Bronstein@gov.bc.ca
Director, Heritage Branch, Jennifer Iredale
250-356-1431, Fax: 250-356-2842,
Jennifer.Iredale@gov.bc.ca
Director, First Nation Relations Branche, Darrell A. Robb
250-387-6719, Fax: 250-356-6076, Darrell.Robb@gov.bc.ca

Regional Operations Offices:

Coast
2100 Labieux Rd., Nanaimo, BC V9T 6E9
250-751-7001 Fax: 250-751-7190
Forests.CoastRegionOffice@gov.bc.ca
www.for.gov.bc.ca/rco

Assistant Deputy Minister, Jody Shimkus
250-387-9773, Fax: 250-356-2150, Jody.Shimkus@gov.bc.ca
Regional Executive Director, Coast, Brian J. Clark
250-356-0874, Fax: 250-356-9299, Brian.J.Clark@gov.bc.ca
Regional Executive Director, West Coast, Sharon Hadway
250-751-7161, Fax: 250-751-7196,
Sharon.Hadway@gov.bc.ca
Regional Executive Director, South Coast, Heather MacKnight
604-586-2892, Fax: 604-586-4434,
Heather.MacKnight@gov.bc.ca
Director, Resource Management (West Coast), Larry Barr
250-751-7105, Fax: 250-741-5686, Larry.Barr@gov.bc.ca
Director, Pricing/Tenures/Mines, Denis Collins
250-751-7121, Fax: 250-751-7196, Denis.Collins@gov.bc.ca
Director, Authorizations, Myles Mana
250-751-7308, Fax: 250-751-7081, Myles.Mana@gov.bc.ca
Director, Resource Management (South Coast), Jennifer McGuire
604-582-5370, Fax: 604-930-7119,
Jennifer.Mcguire@gov.bc.ca
Manager, Business Innovation & Information, Angus Carnie
250-387-3874, Fax: 250-387-5757, Angus.Carnie@gov.bc.ca
Manager, Permit & Authorization Service Bureau, Yvonne Foxall
250-387-3787, Fax: 250-387-1814, Yvonne.Foxall@gov.bc.ca
Manager, Wildlife Management, Ian Hatter
250-387-9792, Fax: 250-387-0239, Ian.Hatter@gov.bc.ca
Manager, Private Land & Wildlife, Jeff Morgan
250-371-6347, Fax: 250-828-4000
Manager, Fish & Wildlife Recovery, Chris Ritchie
250-614-9910, Fax: 250-565-6940, Chris.Ritchie@gov.bc.ca
Manager, Fisheries Management, Andrew Wilson
250-387-9788, Fax: 250-387-0239,
Andrew.Wilson@gov.bc.ca
Manager, Habitat Management, Andy Witt
250-356-2353, Fax: 250-356-5104, Andy.Witt@gov.bc.ca

North Area
1011 - 4 Ave., 5th Fl., Prince George, BC V2L 3H9
250-565-6100
www.for.gov.bc.ca/rni

Assistant Deputy Minister, Kevin Kriese
250-952-0596
Executive Director, Nick Crisp
250-356-7275, Fax: 250-356-5450, Nick.Crisp@gov.bc.ca
Executive Director, Site C, Norm Marcy
250-387-1780, Norman.Marcy@gov.bc.ca
Executive Director, Butch Morningstar
250-387-0844, Fax: 250-952-0491,
Butch.Morningstar@gov.bc.ca, Other Communications: Cell Phone: 250-847-0856
Regional Executive Director, Northeast, Dale Morgan
250-784-1200, Dale.Morgan@gov.bc.ca
Regional Executive Director, Skeena, Eamon O'Donoghue
250-847-7495, Fax: 250-847-7347,
Eamon.ODonoghue@gov.bc.ca
Regional Executive Director, Omineca, Bill Warner
250-565-6102, Fax: 250-565-6671, Bill.Warner@gov.bc.ca
Director, Authorizations (Prince George), Joyce Beaudry
250-565-4131, Fax: 250-565-6671,
Joyce.Beaudry@gov.bc.ca
Director, Resource Management (Omenica), Normand Bilodeau
250-565-6424
Director, Major Projects (Northeast), Todd Bondaroff
250-784-1245, Fax: 250-787-3219,
Todd.Bondaroff@gov.bc.ca
Director, Pricing & Tenures (Omineca), Heather Cullen
250-565-6102, Fax: 250-565-6671,
Heather.Cullen@gov.bc.ca
Director, Resource Management (Skeena), Loren Kelly
250-847-7653, Fax: 250-847-7603, Loren.Kelly@gov.bc.ca
Director, Authorizations (Skeena), Bobby Love
250-847-7517, Fax: 250-847-7347, Bobby.Love@gov.bc.ca
Director, Resource Authorizations (Northeast), Karrilyn Vince
250-787-3534, Fax: 250-787-3219, Karrilyn.Vince@gov.bc.ca
District Manager, Resource Operations (Vanderhoof/Fort St. James), Lynda Currie
250-996-5241, Fax: 250-996-5290, Lynda.Currie@gov.bc.ca
District Manager, Resource Operations (Mackenzie), Dave Francis
250-997-2203, Fax: 250-997-2203, Dave.Francis@gov.bc.ca
District Manager, Resource Operations (Dawson Creek), Robert Kopecky
250-784-1205, Fax: 250-784-1203
District Manager, Resource Operations (Fort Nelson), Steve Lindsey
250-774-5520, Fax: 250-774-3704, Steve.Lindsey@gov.bc.ca
District Manager, Resource Operations (Prince George), Greg Rawling
250-614-7400, Fax: 250-614-7435, Greg.Rawling@gov.bc.ca
District Manager, Kalum, Barry Dobbin
250-638-5100, Fax: 250-638-5176, Barry.Dobbin@gov.bc.ca
District Manager, Skeena Stikine, Jane Lloyd-Smith
250-847-6305, Fax: 250-847-6353,
Jane.LloydSmith@gov.bc.ca
District Manager, Nadina, Josh Pressey
250-692-2224, Fax: 250-692-7461, Josh.Pressey@gov.bc.ca

South
441 Columbia St., Kamloops, BC V2C 2T3
250-828-4131 Fax: 250-828-4154
www.for.gov.bc.ca/rsi

Acting Assistant Deputy Minister, Rick Manwaring
250-828-4292
Acting Executive Director, Madeline Maley
250-828-4114, Other Communications: Alternate Phone: 250-371-3747
Regional Executive Director, Thompson Okanagan, Kevin Dickenson
250-828-4445, Fax: 250-828-4442,
Kevin.Dickenson@gov.bc.ca
Regional Executive Director, Cariboo, Gerry MacDougall
Gerry.MacDougall@gov.bc.ca
Regional Executive Director, Kootenay Boundary, Tony Wideski
250-426-1741, Fax: 250-426-1767, Tony.Wideski@gov.bc.ca
Director, Resource Management (Kootenay), Tom G. Bell
250-354-6345, Fax: 250-354-6332, Tom.Bell@gov.bc.ca
Director, Resource Authorizations (Kamloops), Peter Lishman
250-828-4239, Fax: 250-828-4442,
Peter.Lishman@gov.bc.ca
Director, Resource Management (Kamloops), Dan Peterson
250-828-4124, Fax: 250-828-4154, Dan.Peterson@gov.bc.ca
Director, Pricing & Tenures (Kamloops), Jim Schafthuizen
250-828-4625, Fax: 250-828-4154,
Jim.Schafthuizen@gov.bc.ca
Director, Resource Management (Cariboo), Rodger Stewart
250-398-4549, Fax: 250-398-4214,
Rodger.Stewart@gov.bc.ca, Other Communications: Cell Phone: 250-305-8536
Director, Resource Operations (Cariboo), Ken Vanderburgh
250-398-4225, Fax: 250-398-4836,
Ken.Vanderburgh@gov.bc.ca
District Manager, Natural Resource Operations (100 Mile House), Patrick Byrne
250-395-7804, Fax: 250-395-7810, Pat.Byrne@gov.bc.ca
District Manager, Natural Resource Operations (Quensel), Steve Dodge
250-992-4465, Fax: 250-992-4403, Steve.Dodge@gov.bc.ca
Acting District Manager, Natural Resource Operations (Kamloops), Jennifer Fraser
250-371-6503, Jennifer.Fraser@gov.bc.ca
District Manager, Natural Resource Operations (Kamloops), Dave Hails
250-558-1729, Fax: 250-549-5485, Dave.Hails@gov.bc.ca
District Manager, Natural Resource Operations (Cascades), Charles van Hemmen
250-378-8402, Fax: 250-378-8481,
Charles.vanHemmen@gov.bc.ca, Other Communications: Cell Phone: 250-315-3773
District Manager, Natural Resource Operations (Central Cariboo/Chilcotin), Mike Pedersen
250-398-4355, Fax: 250-398-4790,
Mike.Pedersen@gov.bc.ca, Other Communications: Alternate Phone: 250-398-4345

Resource Stewardship Division
PO Box 9525 Prov Govt, Victoria, BC V8W 9C3
250-387-1296 Fax: 250-953-3687

Chief Forester, Jim Snetsinger
250-387-1296, Fax: 250-953-3687,
Jim.Snetsinger@gov.bc.ca
Acting Deputy Chief Forester, Susanna Laaksonen-Craig
250-387-1296, Fax: 250-953-3687,
Susanna.LaaksonenCraig@gov.bc.ca
Chief Financial Officer, Water Allocation & Safety, Ron Simmons
250-387-6308, Fax: 250-953-5124, Ron.Simmons@gov.bc.ca
Director, Tree Improvement Branch, Brian Barber
250-356-0888, Fax: 250-356-8124, Brian.Barber@gov.bc.ca, Other Communications: URL: www.for.gov.bc.ca/hti/
Director & Comptroller, Water Rights, Water Management, Glen Davidson, P.Eng
250-387-6949, Fax: 250-356-0605,
Glen.Davidson@gov.bc.ca
Director, Resource Management Objectives, Allan Lidstone
250-387-8372, Fax: 250-387-2410, Allan.Lidstone@gov.bc.ca
Director, Forest Analysis & Inventory Branch, Albert Nussbaum
250-356-5958, Fax: 250-953-3838,
Forests.ForestAnalysisBranchOffice@gov.bc.ca
Director, Resource Practices Branch, Jim D. Sutherland
250-398-4527, Fax: 250-387-2136,
Jim.D.Sutherland@gov.bc.ca, Other Communications: Alternate Phone: 250-387-0088
Director, Regional Operations, Water Stewardship, Brian Symonds
250-490-8255, Fax: 250-490-2231,
Brian.Symonds@gov.bc.ca
Director, Operations, Keith Thomas
250-952-0193, Fax: 250-953-3687, Keith.Thomas@gov.bc.ca
Assistant Deputy Minister, Dave Peterson
250-387-1057, Fax: 250-356-6791
Executive Director, Tenures, Duncan Williams
250-387-1810, Fax: 250-356-2150,
Duncan.Williams@gov.bc.ca
Director, Compensation & Business Analysis Branch, Peter Jacobsen
250-387-8643, Fax: 250-356-7903,
Peter.Jacobsen@gov.bc.ca, Other Communications: Cell Phone: 250-415-6638
Director, Forest Tenures Branch, Doug Stewart
250-387-8729, Fax: 250-387-6445,
Doug.B.Stewart@gov.bc.ca
Director, Land Tenures Branch, Ward Trotter
250-356-2166, Fax: 250-356-6791, Ward.Trotter@gov.bc.ca
Branch Coordinator, Competitiveness & Innovation Branch, Judith Elkins
250-356-7880, Fax: 250-356-7903, Judith.Elkins@gov.bc.ca

Timber Operations & Pricing Division
PO Box 9525 Prov Govt, Victoria, BC V8W 9C3
Fax: 250-953-3687

Assistant Deputy Minister, Tom Jensen
250-387-3656, Fax: 250-953-3687, Tom.Jensen@gov.bc.ca
Chief Engineer, Brian Chow
250-953-4370, Fax: 250-953-3687, Brian.Chow@gov.bc.ca
Executive Director, Field Operations, Mike Falkiner
250-387-8309, Fax: 250-953-3687, Mike.Falkiner@gov.bc.ca
Executive Director, Timber Operations & Pricing, Diane Medves
250-356-9287, Fax: 250-953-3687,
Diane.Medves@gov.bc.ca, Other Communications: Alternate Phone: 250-751-7196
Director, Resource Worker Safety, Tom Jackson
250-956-5105, Fax: 250-956-5045, Tom.Jackson@gov.bc.ca
Director, Timber Pricing Branch, Murray Stech
250-356-9807, Fax: 250-387-5670, Murray.Stech@gov.bc.ca
Director, Engineering Branch, Peter Wyatt
250-387-1295, Fax: 250-953-3687, Peter.Wyatt@gov.bc.ca

Corporate Services for the Natural Resources Sector

Finance, Client Services, Facilities, Infrastructure & Strategic Services
PO Box 9339 Prov Govt, Victoria, BC V8W 9M1
250-387-9878 Fax: 250-953-3414

Assistant Deputy Minister/Executive Financial Officer, Agriculture & Environment, Denise Bragg
250-387-9878, Fax: 250-953-3414, Denise.Bragg@gov.bc.ca
Chief Financial Officer, Aboriginal Relations & Reconciliation/Energy & Mines, Ranbir Parmar
250-387-1421, Fax: 250-387-1574,
Ranbir.Parmar@gov.bc.ca
Chief Financial Officer, Agriculture & Environment, Anne Minnings
250-356-9220, Fax: 250-356-9239,
Anne.Minnings@gov.bc.ca
Chief Financial Officer/Executive Director, Forests, Lands and Natural Resource Operations, Terry Gelinas
250-952-0174, Fax: 250-952-0161, Terry.Gelinas@gov.bc.ca
Executive Director, Client Services Branch, Trish Dohan
250-356-9221, Fax: 250-356-9239, Trish.Dohan@gov.bc.ca
Executive Director, Strategic & Operational Services Branch, Jeanne Sedun
250-387-7564, Jeanne.Sedun@gov.bc.ca
Director, Financial Planning & Reporting (Aboriginal Relations/Energy & Mines), Mary Myers
250-356-6624, Fax: 250-387-8818, Mary.Myers@gov.bc.ca
Director, Financial Policy & Compliance (Aboriginal Relations/Energy & Mines), Diane Ross
250-387-8800, Fax: 250-387-8864, Diane.Ross@gov.bc.ca
Director, Financial Planning & Reporting (Agriculture/Environment), Michael Lord
250-356-6132, Fax: 250-356-1769, Michael.Lord@gov.bc.ca

Director, Financial Operations (Agriculture/Environment), Sandra Winter
250-356-9227, Fax: 250-356-9239, Sandra.Winter@gov.bc.ca
Acting Director, Revenue (Forests), Cathy Gauthier
250-387-1589, Fax: 250-356-9239
Director, Financial Planning, Systems & Reporting (Forests), Barb Searle
250-387-1575, Michael.Lord@gov.bc.ca
Director, Fleet & Assets, Kevin Doran
250-387-3442, Fax: 250-387-1574, Kevin.Doran@gov.bc.ca
Director, Infrasturcture, Policy & Records, Diane St. Hilair
250-952-4944, Diane.StHilair@gov.bc.ca
Director, Corporate Security, Tina St. Hilaire
250-356-7641, Tina.St.Hilaire@gov.bc.ca

Information Management/Information Technology
PO Box 9352 Prov Govt, Victoria, BC V8W 9M1
250-953-4745 Fax: 250-953-3603
Assistant Deputy Minister/Executive Financial Officer (Forests), Craig Sutherland
250-953-4745, Fax: 250-356-5797, Craig.Sutherland@gov.bc.ca
Chief Information Officer/Executive Director, Information Management Branch, Doug Say
250-356-5216, Fax: 250-356-9836, Doug.Say@gov.bc.ca
Director, Business Service Desk, Mike Kelley
250-953-4201, Fax: 250-356-5797, Mike.Kelley@gov.bc.ca
Director, Business Applications, Bonnie Laine Farrell
250-356-2890, Fax: 250-387-5132, Bonnie.LaineFarrell@gov.bc.ca
Director, Client Business Solutions, Denise Rossander
250-356-7695, Fax: 250-356-9836, Denise.Rossander@gov.bc.ca, Other Communications: Cell Phone: 250-213-5206
Director, Information Security, Fary Eriksson
250-387-1373, Fax: 250-953-3752, Fary.Eriksson@gov.bc.ca
Director, Infrastructure Management, Terry Gunning
250-387-9975, Fax: 250-356-9836, Terry.Gunning@gov.bc.ca
Director, Middle Tier & Database Administration, Colleen Coccola
250-356-0603, Fax: 250-356-9836, Colleen.Coccola@gov.bc.ca
Director, Technology & Communication Services, Dave Rejminiak
250-387-6358, Fax: 250-387-5132, Dave.Rejminiak@gov.bc.ca

People & Workplace Strategies
PO Box 9339 Prov Govt, Victoria, BC V8W 9M1
250-356-8794 Fax: 250-953-3414
Assistant Deputy Minister/Executive Financial Officer (Agriculture & Energy & Mines), Neilane Mayhew
250-356-8794, Fax: 250-953-3414
Executive Director, Mike R. Hykaway
250-952-6626, Fax: 250-387-9086, Mike.Hykaway@gov.bc.ca
Director, Ingrid Fee
250-952-4930, Fax: 250-952-4925, Ingrid.Fee@gov.bc.ca
Director, Sonja Martins
250-387-9299, Fax: 250-387-3522, Sonja.Martins@gov.bc.ca

Ministry of Health

1515 Blanshard St., Victoria, BC V8W 3C8
250-952-1742 Fax: 250-356-9587
800-465-4911
hlth.health@gov.bc.ca
www.gov.bc.ca/health
Other Communication: Media Relations Phone: 250-952-1887; Fax: 250-952-1883

The Ministry of Health is responsible for guiding & enhancing British Columbia's health system. The goal of the Ministry is to improve health care & ensure that citizens of the province have access to the care they require, when they need it.

Acts Administered:
Access to Abortion Services Act
Anatomy Act
BC Benefits (Income Assistance) Act
Community Care Facility Act
Continuing Care Act
Drinking Water Protection Act
Forensic Psychiatry Act
Health Act
Health Authorities Act
Health Care (Consent) & Care Facility (Admission) Act
Emergebcy & Health Services Act
Emergency & Health Services regulation
Health Special Account Act
Health Planning Statutes Amendment Act, 2002
Hospital Act
Hospital District Act
Hospital Insurance Act
Human Tissue Gift Act
Marriage Act
Food Safety Act
Mental Health Act
Milk Industry Act
Ministry of Health Act
Name Act
Tobacco Sales Act
Vital Statistics Act
Wills Act (Part II)

Minister, Hon. Michael de Jong, Q.C.
250-953-3547, Fax: 250-356-9587, hlth.minister@gov.bc.ca; mike.dejong.mla@leg.bc.ca
Deputy Minister, Graham Whitmarsh
250-952-1590, Fax: 250-952-1909, hlth.dmoffice@gov.bc.ca
Provincial Health Officer, Dr. Perry Kendall
250-952-1330, Fax: 250-952-1362, Perry.Kendall@gov.bc.ca
Deputy Provincial Health Officer, Dr. Eric Young
250-952-1329, Fax: 250-952-1362
Director, Executive Operations, Julie Turner
250-952-1410, Fax: 250-952-1909, hlth.dmoffice@gov.bc.ca
Director, Patient Care Quality Review Boards Secretariat, Thomas Guerrero
Fax: 250-952-2428

Associated Agencies, Boards & Commissions:

• British Columbia Ambulance Service (BCAS)
PO Box 9600 Prov Govt
Victoria, BC V8W 9P1
250-953-3298 Fax: 250-953-3119
www.bcas.ca/
The BCAS operates under the Emergency Health Services Commission, legislated by the Emergency & Health Services Act.

• Emergency & Health Services Commission (EHSC)
2261 Keating Cross Rd.
Saanichton, BC V8M 2A5
250-953-3298 Fax: 250-953-3119
www.health.gov.bc.ca/ehsc/
Governed by the Emergency & Health Services Act, the EHCS allows British Columbia residents and health care professionals to access pre-hospital emergency services, as well as non-emergency health & information services (HealthLink BC).

• Hospital Appeal Board (HAB)
747 Fort St., 4th Fl.
PO Box 9425 Prov Govt
Victoria, BC V8W 9V1
250-387-3464 Fax: 250-356-9923 800-663-7867
hab@gov.bc.ca
www.hab.gov.bc.ca
The Hospital Appeal Board of British Columbia is an independent, quasi-judicial administrative appeal tribunal, which was created by the Hospital Act. The Board provides an appeal process for medical practitioners. The role of the Board is to review hospital board of management decisions concerning hospital privileges. Board members are appointed by British Columbia's Minister of Health.

• Medical Services Commission (MSC)
1515 Blanshard St., 3rd Fl.
Victoria, BC V8W 3C8
250-952-3073 Fax: 250-952-3131
www.health.gov.bc.ca/msp/legislation/msc.html
The Medical Services Commission is a statutory body made up of nine members. In accordance with the Medicare Protection Act & Regulations, the Commission acts on behalf of the Government of British Columbia to manage the Medical Services Plan. The Commission works to ensure British Columbia residents have access to medical care, & to manage the provision & payment of medical services.

• Mental Health Review Board (MHRB)
Dogwood Building
2601 Lougheed Hwy.
Coquitlam, BC V3C 4J2
604-524-7220 Fax: 604-524-7216

Office of the Chief Administrative Officer
250-952-1164 Fax: 250-952-1909
Chief Administrative Officer, John Bethel
250-952-2404, Fax: 250-952-1390
Acting Executive Director, Labour Relations Unit, Ted Patterson
250-952-1026, Fax: 250-952-1034, Ted.Patterson@gov.bc.ca
Director, Regulatory Services, Emergency Medical Assistants Licensing Board, Julie Brown
250-952-2613, Fax: 250-952-1222, emalb@victoria1.gov.bc.ca
Director/Registrar, Emergency Medical Assistants Licensing Board, Judy Thompson
250-952-1203, Fax: 250-952-1222, emalb@victoria1.gov.bc.ca
Director, Strategic & Corporate Services Branch, Vacant
250-952-1798, Fax: 250-952-1390
Manager, Corporate Services & Program Operations Standards, Anne Stearn
250-952-2636, Fax: 250-952-1909

Medical Services & Health Human Resources Division
250-952-3465 Fax: 250-952-3131
Assistant Deputy Minister, Sheila Taylor
250-952-3465, Fax: 250-952-3131, Sheila.Taylor@gov.bc.ca
Executive Director, Laboratory, Diagnostic & Blood Services Branch, Jane Crickmore
250-952-1323, Fax: 250-952-3133, Jane.Crickmore@gov.bc.ca
Executive Director, Physician Human Resource Management, Rod Frechette
250-952-3146, Fax: 250-952-3486, Rod.Frechette@gov.bc.ca
Executive Director, Medical Servcies Branch, Nichola Manning
250-952-1204, Fax: 250-952-3133
Executive Director, Health Human Resources Planning (Physicians), Libby Posgate
250-952-1107, Fax: 250-952-2125, Libby.Posgate@gov.bc.ca
Executive Director, Health Human Resources Planning (Nursing and Allied), Sharon Stewart
250-952-3656, Fax: 250-952-2125, Sharon.Stewart@gov.bc.ca
Executive Director, Primary Health Care, Valerie Tregillus
250-952-2961, Fax: 250-952-1417, Valerie.Tregillus@gov.bc.ca

Health Sector Information Management/Information Technology
250-952-2563 Fax: 250-952-1827
Assistant Deputy Minister, Linsday Kislock
250-952-2160, Fax: 250-952-2109
Executive Director, Business Management Office, Carolyn Bell
250-952-6202, Fax: 250-952-6084
Executive Director, Corporate Management & Operations, Darcy Goodwin
250-952-1432, Fax: 250-952-1186, Darcy.Goodwin@gov.bc.ca
Executive Director, eHealth Privacy, Security & Legislation, Deb McGinnis
250-952-2663, Fax: 250-952-3492
Executive Director, Public Health Systems, Kelly Moran
250-356-2434, Fax: 250-356-2530, Kelly.Moran@gov.bc.ca
Chief Data Steward/Executive Director, Strategic Policy, Information Management & Data Stewardship, Chris Norman
250-952-1822, Fax: 250-952-2202, Chris.Norman@gov.bc.ca
Executive Director, Integrated Health Information Technology Branch, Paul Shrimpton
250-356-2401, Fax: 250-356-2530

Pharmaceutical Services
250-952-1464 Fax: 250-952-1584
Assistant Deputy Minister, Bob Nakagawa
250-952-1464, Fax: 250-952-1584
Acting Executive Director, Business Management & Supplier Relations, Dennis Chan
604-660-5422, Fax: 604-660-2108
Executive Director, Drug Intelligence, Eric Lun
250-952-2272, Fax: 250-952-2216
Executive Director, Drug Use Optimization, Suzanne Taylor
604-660-1217, Fax: 604-660-2108, Suzanne.Taylor@gov.bc.ca
Executive Director, Policy, Outcomes Evaluation & Research, Darlene Therrien
250-952-1149, Fax: 250-952-1391, Darlene.Therrien@gov.bc.ca

Office of the Chief Operating Officer
Fax: 250-952-1909
Chief Operating Officer, Michael MacDougall
250-952-1764, Fax: 250-952-1909, Michael.MacDougall@gov.bc.ca
Executive Director, Intergovernmental Relations, Mariana Diacu
250-952-1304, Fax: 250-952-2516
Executive Director, Organizational Development & Engagement, Dale Samsonoff
250-952-1175, Fax: 250-952-2125
Acting Executive Director, Emergency Management Unit, Chris Smith
250-952-1456, Fax: 250-952-2467
Executive Project Director, Nikki Sieben
250-952-1170, Fax: 250-952-1909
Acting Director, Planning & Programs, Kirsten Brown
250-952-3214, Fax: 250-952-2467
Director, Operational Readiness, Dave Burgess
604-418-1634, Fax: 604-586-4334
Director, Intergovernmental Relations, Gayle Downey
250-952-1645, Fax: 250-952-2516
Director, Strategic Initiatives, Sandra Maxson
250-952-1685, Fax: 250-952-1909

Planning & Innovation Division
Fax: 250-952-1909
Assistant Deputy Minister, Elaine McKnight
250-952-2563, Fax: 250-952-1827, Elaine.McKnight@gov.bc.ca
Executive Director, Management Information Branch, Nick Grant
250-952-1116, Fax: 250-952-2002, Nick.Grant@gov.bc.ca
Executive Director, Legislation & Professional Regulation, Christine Massey
250-952-2281, Fax: 250-952-2205, HLTH.LPRAdmin@gov.bc.ca

Acting Executive Director, Financial Analysis Branch, Ted Patterson
250-952-1435, Fax: 250-952-2605, Glynis.Soper@gov.bc.ca
Executive Director, Modeling and Analysis Branch, Ian Rongve
250-952-1343, Fax: 250-952-3676, Ian.Rongve@gov.bc.ca
Executive Director, Strategic Management Planning, Anne Sandbu
250-952-1438, Fax: 250-952-2605, Anne.Sandbu@gov.bc.ca
Executive Director, Business Intelligence Branch, Glynis Soper
250-952-2406, Fax: 250-952-2605, Glynis.Soper@gov.bc.ca
Executive Director, Research, Knowledge Translation & Library Services Branch, Elisabeth Wagner
250-952-2282, Fax: 250-952-2516

Population & Public Health
250-952-1731 Fax: 250-952-1021
Acting Assistant Deputy Minister, Laurie Woodland
Acting Executive Director, Seniors' Healthy Living Secretariat, Silas Brownsey
250-356-1474, Fax: 250-387-1407, Silas.Brownsey@gov.bc.ca
Acting Executive Director, Healthy Women, Children & Youth Secretariat, Joan Geber
250-952-3678, Fax: 250-952-1570
Executive Director, Business Operations & Surveillance, Tom Gregory
250-952-1467, Fax: 250-952-1713
Acting Executive Director, Chronic Disease/Injury Prevention & Built Environment, Matt Herman
250-952-2847, Fax: 250-952-1570
Acting Executive Director, Health Protection, Tim Lambert
250-952-1987, Fax: 250-952-1713
Executive Director, Aboriginal Healthy Living, Shannon McDonald
250-952-2811, Fax: 250-952-1570
Acting Executive Director, Communicable Disease Prevention, Harm Reduction & Mental Health Promotion, Warren O'Briain
250-952-2481, Fax: 250-952-1570
Acting Executive Director, Health Promotion Supports & Engagement, Kate Fagan Taylor
250-356-9814, Fax: 250-387-8720, Kate.Fagan.Taylor@gov.bc.ca

Financial & Corporate Services
250-952-2067 Fax: 250-952-1573
Assistant Deputy Minister, Manjit Sidhu
250-952-2066, Fax: 250-952-1573
Chief Financial Officer/Executive Director, Finance & Decision Support, Hilary Woodward
250-952-2016, Fax: 250-952-2089
Executive Director, Capital Services, Kevin Brewster
250-952-1102, Fax: 250-952-2873
Executive Director, Regional Grants - Decision Support, Gordon Cross
250-952-1120, Fax: 250-952-1420
Director, Health Authority Funding, Rhonda Beveridge
250-952-1054, Fax: 250-952-1420
Director, Health Authority Funding, Blair Boland
250-952-2250, Fax: 250-952-1420
Director, Accounting Operations Branch, Ted Boomer
250-952-2053, Fax: 250-952-2090
Director, Decision Support - MSD, Betty-Anne Brazier
250-952-2048, Fax: 250-952-0989
Director, Health Authority Funding, Harry Hitchman
250-952-3673, Fax: 250-952-1420
Director, Finance, Decision Support - Pharmaceutical Services, Vitali Kozubenko
250-952-1953, Fax: 250-952-2089
Director, Capital Services, Shelley Moen
250-952-1518, Fax: 250-952-2873, Shelley.Moen@gov.bc.ca
Director, Financial Verification, Maria Perri
250-952-1011, Fax: 250-952-1573
Director, Capital Services, Cathy Sleeva
250-952-1510, Fax: 250-952-2873, Cathy.Sleeva@gov.bc.ca
Director, Decision Support - Health Sector Information Management/Information Technology, Glen Stusek
250-952-2100, Fax: 250-952-0989
Acting Director, Audit & Investigations Branch, Marie Thelisma
250-952-1665, Fax: 250-952-2089
Director, Capital Services, Scarlette Verjinschi
250-952-1494, Fax: 250-952-2873, Cathy.Sleeva@gov.bc.ca
Director, Capital Finance, Bonnie Wong
250-952-1646, Fax: 250-952-0989
Director, Finance & Funding, Mark Taylor
250-952-1177, Fax: 250-952-1420

Health Authorities Division
250-952-1049 Fax: 250-952-1052
Assistant Deputy Minister, Heather Davidson
Assisted Living Registrar, Susan Adams
604-714-3378, Fax: 604-733-5996, info@alregistrar.bc.ca

Health Authority Relations & Corporate Services
250-952-1382 Fax: 250-952-1689
For a certificate of a registration or record: $25 per copy. For each search for one registration or record for each three-year period or fraction thereof over which the search is conducted: $25.
Executive Director, Teri Collins
250-952-2871, Fax: 250-952-1052
Director, Planning & Divisional Support, Kim Grantham
250-952-2175, Fax: 250-952-1052
Director, Health Authority Relations, Valerie Stevens
250-952-1990, Fax: 250-952-1689

Hospital & Provincial Services Branch
250-952-1178 Fax: 250-952-1052
Executive Director, Effie Henry
250-952-1514, Fax: 250-952-1282
Director, Priority Projects-Surgical Services, Minjeet (Margi) Bhalla
250-952-1040, Fax: 250-952-1282
Director, Acute Program, Tricia Braidwood-Looney
250-952-1012, Fax: 250-952-1282
Director, Diagnostic Imaging & Piority Projects, Kirk Eaton
250-952-1599, Fax: 250-952-1052
Director, Performance Accountability, Provincial Health Services Authority, Alex Scheiber
250-952-3595, Fax: 250-952-1282
Director, Program Monitoring Hospital Service, Nancy South
250-952-3593, Fax: 250-952-1282

Home, Community & Integrated Care
250-952-3594 Fax: 250-952-1282
Executive Director, Leigh Ann Seller
250-952-1274, Fax: 250-952-1282
Director, Community Care Licensing, Sue Bedford
250-952-1442, Fax: 250-952-1713
Director, Service Redesign & Caregiving & Health-care Facilities, Katie Hill
250-952-1564, Fax: 250-952-1282
Director, Program Monitoring, Ramani Kumar
250-952-2011, Fax: 250-952-1282
Manager, Service Redesign Policy & Planning, Karen Archibald
250-952-2784, Fax: 250-952-1282
Manager, Program Monitoring, Shana Hall
250-952-1159, Fax: 250-952-1282
Manager, Residential Services, Brenda Higham
250-952-1188, Fax: 250-952-1282
Manager, End-of-Life Care & Special Populations, Pauline James
250-952-1536, Fax: 250-952-1282

Clinical Care & Patient Safety
250-952-1975 Fax: 250-952-1014
Executive Director, Brenda Canitz
250-952-2738, Fax: 250-952-1014
Director, Patient Safety, Brian G. Sagar
250-952-2753, Fax: 250-952-1014
Director, Clinical Innovation, Marc Woons
250-952-1950, Fax: 250-952-1014
Manager, Heather Davidson
250-952-3540, Fax: 250-952-1014

Mental Health & Substance Abuse
250-952-1608 Fax: 250-952-1689
Executive Director, Ann Marr
250-952-3519, Fax: 250-952-1689
Director, Program Monitoring, Ross Hayward
250-952-3638, Fax: 250-952-1689
Director, Mental Health, Gerrit van der Leer
250-952-1610, Fax: 250-952-1689
Director, Mental Health & Substance Abuse, Anita Snell
250-952-1270, Fax: 250-952-1689

HealthLink BC
PO Box 9600 Prov Govt, Victoria, BC V8W 9P1
604-215-8110 Fax: 250-952-6509
healthlinkbc@healthlinkbc.ca
www.HealthLinkBC.ca
Other Communication: HealthLink BC hotline: 8-1-1; TTY: 7-1-1
HealthLink BC allows residents of British Columbia to access health care information by phone or online, and incorporates the following previously existing services: BC HealthGuide, BC HealthFiles, BC NurseLine & Pharmacist service, & Dial-a-Dietitian.
Executive Lead, Bob Bell
250-356-0685, Fax: 250-952-6509, Other Communications: Alternate Phone: 250-356-0767
Executive Director, Clinical Practice & Integrated Knowledge Management, Alyse Capron
604-215-5191
Executive Director, Information Management, Simon Hall
250-356-3015, Fax: 250-952-6509, Simon.Hall@gov.bc.ca
Executive Director, Navigation Services, Michele Lane
604-215-5156, Fax: 604-215-8105
Executive Director, Business Development, Mark MacKinnon
250-952-6293, Fax: 250-952-6509
Executive Director, Operations, Marie Root
604-215-5118, Fax: 250-952-6509
Executive Director, Planning & Business Support, Dave Van Swieten
250-952-6294, Fax: 250-952-6509
Director, Change Management & Business Transformation, Lake Apted
250-952-6144, Fax: 250-952-6509
Director, Clinical Infomatics/Decision Support, Lee Ashbourne
250-953-4299, Fax: 250-952-6509
Director, Business Development, Kevin Brown
250-952-6281, Fax: 250-952-6509
Director, Business Development, Collette Christney
250-356-0339, Fax: 250-952-6509
Director, Marketing & Communications Services, Kate Jobling
250-953-3234
Director, Dietitian Services, Barbara Leslie
604-215-5138
Director, Business Development, Janice Linton
250-952-6280, Fax: 250-952-6509
Director, Information Technology & Telecom Ops & Architecture, John Martin
604-215-5128
Director, Quality Management & Professional Management, Peter Quick
604-215-5197
Director, Nursing Services, Kim Schmidt
604-215-5103
Director, Project Management Office, Irina Sladecek
250-356-0225, Fax: 250-952-6509
Manager, Directory Services, Adriana Poveda
604-215-7171, Fax: 250-953-0481, chard.support@gov.bc.ca

British Columbia Hydro

333 Dunsmuir St., Vancouver, BC V6B 5R3
604-224-9376
800-224-9376
www.bchydro.com
BC Hydro is a provincial Crown corporation. It reports to the Minister of Energy & Mines, & is regulated by the British Columbia Utilities Commission. BC Hydro is engaged in the generation & distribution of electricity throughout British Columbia. It strives to provide these services in an environmentally & socially responsible manner. As of 2010, BC Hydro and BC Transmission Corporation have been combined into one entity under the Clean Energy Act.
Chair, Dan Doyle
President/Chief Executive Officer, David Cobb
Deputy CEO/Executive Vice-President, Bev Van Ruyven
Chief Financial Officer/Executive Vice-President, Finance, Charles Reid
Executive Vice-President, Generation, Chris O'Riley
Executive Vice-President, Transmission & Distribution, Greg Reimer
Executive Vice-President, Site C, Susan Yurkovich
Senior Vice-President/General Counsel, Ray Aledguer
Chief Human Resources Officer/Senior Vice-President, Debbie Nagle
Senior Vice-President, Communications, Renee Smith-Valade

Associated Agencies, Boards & Commissions:
• Powerex Corp.
#1400, 666 Burrard St.
Vancouver, BC V6C 2X8
604-891-5000 Fax: 604-891-6060 800-220-4907
Brian.Moghadam@powerex.com
www.powerex.com
A wholly-owned subsidiary of BC Hydro, Powerex Corp. markets wholesale energy products & services to utilities, power pools, industrials, & power marketers in North America, particularly western Canada, the western United States.
• Powertech Labs Inc.
12388 - 88 Ave.
Surrey, BC V8W 7R7
604-590-7500 Fax: 604-590-6611
www.powertechlabs.com
A wholly owned subsidiary of BC Hydro, Powertech Labs offers environmental, mechanical, electrical, metallurgical, civil, chemical, gas technologies, & structural engineering to deal with technical problems with power equipment & systems.

Office of the Information & Privacy Commissioner for British Columbia (OIPC)

947 Fort St., 4th Fl., PO Box 9038 Prov Govt, Victoria, BC V8W 9A4
250-387-5629 Fax: 250-387-1696
800-663-7867
info@oipc.bc.ca
www.oipc.bc.ca
Other Communication: Vancouver Phone: 604-660-2421
Operating independently from the government, the Office of the Information & Privacy Commissioner is responsible for monitoring & enforcing the following acts in British Columbia: Freedom of Information & Protection of Privacy Act; & Personal Information Protection Act.
Commissioner, Elizabeth Denham

Assistant Commissioner, Investigation & Mediation, Catherine Tully
Assistant Commissioner, Policy & Adjudication, LeRoy Brower
Communications & Research officer, Maria Dupuis
250-387-5629, Fax: 250-387-1696, info@oipc.bc.ca
Senior Investigator, Jim Burrows
Senior Investigator, Patrick Egan
Registrar of Inquiries, Cindy Hamilton

Intergovernmental Relations Secretariat (IGRS)

PO Box 9333 Prov Govt, Victoria, BC V8W 9N3
250-387-0752 Fax: 250-387-1920
igrs@gov.bc.ca
www.igrs.gov.bc.ca

The mission of IGRS is to ensure that the province's relations with provincial governments, the federal government, & international governments advance British Columbia's interests.

Associate Deputy Minister, Pierrette Maranda
Pierrette.Maranda@gov.bc.ca
Executive Director, Federalism & Canadian Intergovernmental Policy, Paul Craven
250-356-2272, Fax: 250-387-1920, Paul.Craven@gov.bc.ca
Executive Director, US Relations & Partnerships, Bryant Fairley
250-387-1134, Fax: 250-387-1920, Bryant.Fairley@gov.bc.ca
Advisor/Executive Director, Economic Policy & Asia Pacific Relations, Donald Haney
250-387-5628, Fax: 250-387-1920, Donald.Haney@gov.bc.ca
Chief of Protocol/Executive Director, Marc-André Ouellette
250-387-4304, Fax: 250-356-2814, igrs@gov.bc.ca
Executive Director, Strategic Policy & Planning, Sukumar Periwal
250-387-0761, Fax: 250-387-1920,
Sukumar.Periwal@gov.bc.ca
Director, Communications, Nina Chiarelli
250-387-0793, Fax: 250-387-1920, igrs@gov.bc.ca

Insurance Corporation of British Columbia (ICBC)

151 West Esplanade, North Vancouver, BC V7M 3H9
604-661-2800
800-663-3051
www.icbc.com
Other Communication: New Claims, Lower Mainland Phone: 604-520-8222; Elsewhere in BC, Toll Free: 1-800-910-4222; TIPS Lower Mainland, Phone: 604-661-6844; TIPS BC Line: 1-800-661-6844

A provincial Crown corporation, The Insurance Corporation of British Columbia was established in 1973. The main responsibilities of the Insurance Corporation of British Columbia are as follows: Provision of universal auto insurance to motorists in British Columbia; Registration & licensing of vehicles; & Driver licensing.

Chair, Nancy McKinstry
President/Chief Executive Officer, Jon Schubert
Chief Financial Officer, Geri Prior
Chief Information Officer, Ward Chapin
Senior Vice-President, Insurance, Mark Blucher
Senior Vice-President, Claims, Craig Horton
Senior Vice-President, Corporate Affairs, Donnie Wing
Vice-President, Business Transformation, Sheila Eddin
Vice-President, Driver Licensing, Fred Hess
Vice-President, Human Resources & Corporate Law, Len Posyniak
Vice-President, Strategic Marketing, Jeff Schulz

Ministry of Jobs, Tourism, & Innovation

PO Box 9071 Prov Govt, Victoria, BC V8W 9E9
250-356-2771 Fax: 250-356-3000
JTI.Minister@gov.bc.ca
www.gov.bc.ca/jti/

The ministry combines the power of tourism, investment attraction and export market development to market British Columbia as never before and to fully realize this province's potential as Canada's Pacific Gateway. By bringing together synergistic elements from the former Ministry of Tourism, Culture and the Arts and the former Ministry of Small Business, Technology and Economic Development, the ministry is attracting new visitors, more investment and new customers for B.C. products in all of the province's traditional markets, as well as opening up new tourism, trade and investment opportunities in Asia, particularly in Japan, China, Korea and India.

Acts Administered:
British Columbia Enterprise Corporation Act
British Columbia Innovation Council Act
Builders Lien Act
Employee Investment Act
International Financial Activity Act (except Parts 3, 4, & 5, & Part 6, as it pertains to Parts 3, 4, & 5)
Ministry of International Business & Immigration Act (except as the act relates to immigrant recruitment & labour market development, & programs respecting immigrant & refugee settlement)
Small Business Venture Capital Act
Special Accounts Appropriation & Control Act (s. 9.5)
Trade, Investment, & Labour Mobility Agreement Implementation Act
Heritage Conservation Act
Hotel Guest Registration Act
Hotel Keepers Act
Ministry of Intergovernmental Relations Act
Provincial Symbols & Honours Act
Tourism Act
Trade, Investment & Labour Mobility Agreement Implementation Act
Vancouver Tourism Levy Enabling Act
Wood First Act

Minister, Hon. Pat Bell
250-356-2771, Fax: 250-356-3000, JTI.Minister@gov.bc.ca; pat.bell.mla@leg.bc.ca
Deputy Minister, Dana Hayden
250-952-0103, Fax: 250-356-1195, Dana.Hayden@gov.bc.ca
Executive Director, Strategic Initiatives, Softwood Lumber Agreement, Vera Sit
250-952-7358, Fax: 250-387-6445, Vera.Sit@gov.bc.ca
Director, Executive Operations, Maureen Yelovatz
250-952-0104, Fax: 250-356-1195

Associated Agencies, Boards & Commissions:

• Asia Pacific Foundation of Canada (APFC) / Fondation Asie Pacifique du Canada (FAPC)
#220, 890 West Pender St.
Vancouver, BC V6C 1J9
604-684-5986 Fax: 604-681-1370
info@asiapacific.ca; researchgrants@asiapacific.ca
www.asiapacific.ca
Other Communication: Media: communications@asiapacific.ca; News Servce: news@asiapacific.ca
The Asia Pacific Foundation of Canada is an independent think tank on Canadian-Asian relations. The Foundation's research grants program supports research & discussion on Canada's relations with Asia. The grants fund research, graduate & media fellowships, conferences, & special initiatives.

• Asia Pacific Trade Council
Robson Square, c/o Asia Pacific Business Centre
#288, 800 Hornby St.
Vancouver, BC V6Z 2C5
604-660-9727 888-880-2742
www.britishcolumbia.ca/AboutUs/AsiaPacificTradeCouncil
The Asia Pacific Trade Council advises the Premier of British Columbia on investment & trade opportunities with the Asia Pacific Region.

• British Columbia Innovation Council (BCIC)
1188 West Georgia St., 9th Fl.
Vancouver, BC V6E 4A2
604-683-2724 Fax: 604-683-6567 800-665-7222
info@bcic.ca
www.bcic.ca
The British Columbia Innovation Council strives to advance innovation & commercialization by focusing on the following strategies: developing, recruiting & retaining science & technology professionals; fostering innovation & entrepreneurship; & bringing innovation to commercial success by establishing partnerships.

• British Columbia Progress Board
1188 West Georgia St., 9th Fl.
Vancouver, BC V6E 4A2
604-775-1664
ideas@bcprogressboard.com
www.bcprogressboard.com
The BC Progress Board has the following responsibilities: Determining if the province is improving its competitiveness & quality of life; & Making recommendations to the Premier to enhance the province's economy & social well-being.

• International Financial Centre British Columbia (IFC BC)
Park Place
#1170, 666 Burrard St.
Vancouver, BC V6C 2X8
604-683-6626 Fax: 604-683-6646
info@ifcvancouver.com
www.ifcbc.com
The International Financial Centre British Columbia is a non-profit society which was established by the Federal Government. IFC BC promotes investment in British Columbia & the advantageous tax treatment available to corporations through the International Financial Activity Act (IFAA).

• Premier's Technology Council
604-775-2122 Fax: 604-775-2129
premiers.technologycouncil@gov.bc.ca
www.gov.bc.ca/premier/technology_council
The 23 member Premier's Technology Council advises the Premier on all technology-related issues that affect British Columbia & its residents.

• Small Business BC
#82, 601 West Cordova St.
Vancouver, BC V6B 1G1
604-775-5525 Fax: 604-775-5520 800-667-2272 TTY: 800-457-8466
askus@smallbusinessbc.ca
www.smallbusinessbc.ca
Small Business BC is a not-for-profit society, which was founded by British Columbia's Ministry of Small Business & Revenue & Western Economic Diversification Canada. The organization is a resource centre for business information & services in the province. The following are some of the services offered by Small Business BC: Business Bookstore, Library, & Information Services; Business Registration; Business Plan Advisory Services; Seminars; eBusiness Connection, Market Research Services; & Export Coaching.

Competitiveness & Innovation

PO Box 9327 Prov Govt, Victoria, BC V8W 9N3
Fax: 250-952-0137

Acting Assistant Deputy Minister, Jane Burnes
250-889-1054, Fax: 250-952-0137, Jane.Burnes@gov.bc.ca
Executive Director, Small Business Branch, Simone Decosse
250-387-0661, Simone.Decosse@gov.bc.ca
Acting Executive Director, Research & Innovation, Melanie Friesen
250-356-1894, Fax: 250-387-3725,
Melanie.Friesen@gov.bc.ca
Director, Economic Analysis, Dr. Linda ChaseWilde
250-952-0338, Fax: 250-952-0675,
Linda.ChaseWilde@gov.bc.ca
Director, Knowledge Transfer & Commercialization, Tim Ewanchuk
250-356-1593, Fax: 250-387-3725,
Tim.Ewanchuk@gov.bc.ca
Director, Division Operations, Jennifer Meadows
250-952-0710, Fax: 250-952-0137,
Jennifer.Meadows@gov.bc.ca
Director, Small Business Programs, Darryl Soper
250-356-7532, Fax: 250-952-0113,
Darryl.L.Soper@gov.bc.ca
Director, Research & Knowledge Development, Claudia Trudeau
250-387-6157, Fax: 250-387-3725,
Claudia.Trudeau@gov.bc.ca
Manager, Land Use Initiatives, Alison Coyne
250-356-0807, Fax: 250-952-0137, Alison.Coyne@gov.bc.ca

Investment Capital Branch

PO Box 9800 Prov Govt, Victoria, BC V8W 9V1
Fax: 250-952-0371

Vice-President/Executive Director, Investments/Venture Capital Programs, Todd Tessler
250-952-0612, Fax: 250-952-0371, Todd.Tessier@gov.bc.ca
Senior Portfolio Manager, Venture Capital Programs, Melanie Achtemichuk
604-660-6812, Fax: 604-660-6812,
Melanie.Achtemichuk@gov.bc.ca
Senior Portfolio Manager, Venture Capital Programs, Matthew Brown
250-952-0631, Fax: 250-952-0371,
Matthew.J.Brown@gov.bc.ca
Senior Portfolio Manager, International Business Activities, Lina Duong-Aihara
250-952-0420, Fax: 250-952-0371,
Lina.Duong-Aihara@gov.bc.ca
Senior Portfolio Manager, Venture Capital Programs, Ian Wong
250-952-6396, Fax: 250-952-0371, Ian.Wong@gov.bc.ca

Straightforward BC

PO Box 9822 Prov Govt, Victoria, BC V8W 9N3
Fax: 250-952-0113

Executive Director, Simone Decosse
250-387-0661, Fax: 250-952-0113
Acting Director, Strategic Planning & Partnership, Jennifer Gorman
250-387-8469, Fax: 250-952-0113
Director, Regulatory Reform, Heather Holley
250-387-8469, Fax: 250-952-0113,
Heather.Holley@gov.bc.ca
Senior Advisor, Regulatory Reform, Melanie Iwanow
250-952-0157, Fax: 250-952-0113,
Melanie.Iwanow@gov.bc.ca
Senior Advisor, Regulatory Reform, Carmen Ross
250-356-8098, Fax: 250-952-0113, Carmen.Ross@gov.bc.ca

Economic Development Division

Assistant Deputy Minister, Sandra Carroll
250-952-0601, Sandra.Carroll@gov.bc.ca
Chief Strategy Officer, Wood First & Wood Inovation & Design Centre, Joan Elangovan
250-952-6529, Fax: 250-356-1195,
Joan.Elangovan@gov.bc.ca
Executive Director, Economic Development, Steve Anderson
250-952-0644, Fax: 250-952-0351,
Steve.Anderson@gov.bc.ca

Executive Director, Pine Beetle Epidemic Response Branch, Gord Borgstrom
250-371-3741, Fax: 250-371-3735, Gordon.Borgstrom@gov.bc.ca
Executive Director, RuralBC Secretariat Strategic Initiatives Branch, Greg Goodwin
250-953-3008, Fax: 250-387-7972, Greg.Goodwin@gov.bc.ca
Executive Director, Economic Initiatives Branch, Dean Sekyer
250-952-0409, Fax: 250-952-0646, Dean.Sekyer@gov.bc.ca
Executive Director, Community Development Trust, Tracey Thompson
250-387-3130, Fax: 250-387-4425, Tracey.Thompson@gov.bc.ca
Director, Pine Beetle Epidemic Response Branch (Fort St. James), Jim Burck
250-996-5200, Fax: 250-387-1590, Jim.Burck@gov.bc.ca
Director, Pine Beetle Epidemic Response Branch (Williams Lake), Hugh Flinton
250-398-4224, Fax: 250-371-3735, Hugh.Flinton@gov.bc.ca
Director, Economic Initiatives, Chris Gilmore
250-952-0139, Fax: 250-952-0351, Christopher.Gilmore@gov.bc.ca
Director, Pine Beetle Epidemic Response Branch (Kamloops), Marc Imus
250-371-3937, Fax: 250-371-3735, Marc.Imus@gov.bc.ca
Director, Strategic Policy & Corporate Planning, Debra Larusson
250-952-0225, Fax: 250-889-3114, Debra.Larusson@gov.bc.ca
Director, Industrial Initiatives, Gary Schick
250-952-0643, Fax: 250-952-0646, Gary.Schick@gov.bc.ca
Director, Business Analysis, Sylvia Selig
250-387-7555, Fax: 250-952-0351, Sylvia.Selig@gov.bc.ca

International Trade & Investment Attraction Division
604-775-2100 Fax: 604-660-6835

Assistant Deputy Minister, Shom Sen
604-775-0005, Fax: 604-660-6832, Shom.Sen@gov.bc.ca
Executive Director, International Partnerships & Programs, Chris Carter
604-660-5896, Fax: 604-660-6835, Chris.Carter@gov.bc.ca
Executive Director/Practice Lead, International Relations & Business Development/Global Industry Practices, Marcus Ewert-Jones
604-775-2145, Fax: 604-775-2197, Marcus.Johns@gov.bc.ca
Acting Executive Director, Investor Services, Michael Track
604-775-2202, Fax: 604-775-2197, Michael.Track@gov.bc.ca
Executive Director, Trade Initiatives, Don D. White
250-952-0708, Don.D.White@gov.bc.ca
Director, Internal Trade, Gail Greenwood
250-387-7575, Fax: 250-952-0137, Gail.Greenwood@gov.bc.ca
Director, BC Business Services & Olympic Legacy, Brian Krieger
604-660-0220, Fax: 604-775-2197, Brian.Krieger@gov.bc.ca
Director, Special Projects, Christine Little
250-953-3479, Christine.Little@gov.bc.ca
Director, International Operations & Logistics, Gregory Matisz
605-660-5899, Fax: 604-660-2520, Gregory.Matisz@gov.bc.ca
Director, Trade Policy, Robert Musgrave
250-952-0711, Fax: 250-952-0716, Robert.Musgrave@gov.bc.ca
Director, International Trade, Janel Quiring
250-356-5867, Fax: 250-952-0351, Janel.Quiring@gov.bc.ca
Director, International Marketing Secretariat, Nancy Taylor
250-953-3397, Fax: 250-952-0716, Nancy.Taylor@gov.bc.ca
Director, Special Projects, Gloria Yang-Mason
604-660-5895, Fax: 604-660-6935, Gloria.Yang-Mason@gov.bc.ca

Labour Market & Immigration Division
PO Box 9213, Vancouver, BC V8W 9J1
250-953-3585 Fax: 250-356-0033

Assistant Deputy Minister, Shannon Baskerville
Shannon.Baskerville@gov.bc.ca
Acting Executive Director, Policy & Stakeholder Relations Branch, Sohee Ahn
250-952-6567, Fax: 250-387-0878, Sohee.Ahn@gov.bc.ca
Executive Director, Economic Immigration Programs Branch, Ian Mellor
604-775-2183, Fax: 604-660-4092, Ian.Mellor@gov.bc.ca
Executive Director, Labour Market Programs Branch, Melanie J. Stewart
250-387-3661, Fax: 250-387-4788, Melanie.J.Stewart@gov.bc.ca
Executive Director, Immigrant Integration Branch, Deb Zehr
250-356-1125, Fax: 250-356-0033, Deb.Zehr@gov.bc.ca
Director, Senior Relations, Dudley Alison
604-775-0694, Fax: 604-775-0670, Alison.Dudley@gov.bc.ca
Director, Immigration Policy, Francois Bertrand
604-660-3463, Fax: 604-660-4092, Francois.Bertrand@gov.bc.ca
Director, Client Engagement, Asha Bhat
250-387-3679, Fax: 250-356-0033, Asha.Bhat@gov.bc.ca
Director, Strategic Occupations, Michael Chew
604-775-2215, Fax: 604-660-4092, Michael.Chew@gov.bc.ca
Director, Labour Market Policy & Intergovernmental Relations, Suzanne Ferguson
250-387-7587, Fax: 250-387-4788, Suzanne.Ferguson@gov.bc.ca
Director, Skills For Growth, Keith Godin
250-387-5631, Fax: 250-387-4789, Keith.Godin@gov.bc.ca
Director, Partnerships & Productivity Unit, Nicola Lemmer
250-952-7584, Fax: 250-387-4788, Nicola.Lemmer@gov.bc.ca
Director, Program Management & Evaluation, Ben Pollard
604-775-0293, Fax: 604-775-0670, Ben.Pollard@gov.bc.ca
Director, Settlement Policy Unit, Catherine Poole
250-953-3292, Fax: 250-356-0033, Catherine.Poole@gov.bc.ca
Director, Business Immigration, S.P. Poon
604-775-2216, Fax: 604-660-4092, SP.Poon@gov.bc.ca
Director, Labour Market Agreement, Deb Rhymer
250-952-0642, Fax: 250-387-4789, Deborah.Rhymer@gov.bc.ca
Director, Labour Market Information Services, Brenda Scott
250-387-3517, Fax: 250-387-4788, Brenda.Scott@gov.bc.ca
Director, Program & Regional Operations, Lucy Swib
604-775-0458, Fax: 604-775-0670, Lucy.Swib@gov.bc.ca
Director, Industry Training Programs, Bev Verboven
250-356-9827, Fax: 250-387-4789, Bev.Verboven@gov.bc.ca
Director, Labour Market & Immigration Forecasting Unit, Kerry Young
250-387-5790, Fax: 250-387-4788, Kerry.Young@gov.bc.ca

Tourism Division
510 Burrard St., 12th Fl., Vancouver, BC V6C 3A8
Fax: 604-660-3383

Assistant Deputy Minister, Grant Mackay
604-660-6319, Fax: 604-660-3383, Grant.Mackay@gov.bc.ca
Director, Tourism Strategy, Policy & Research, Heather Brazier
250-952-6024, Fax: 250-356-8246, Heather.Brazier@gov.bc.ca
Director, Partnership Marketing, Peter Harrison
250-387-8578, Fax: 250-356-8246, Peter.Harrison@gov.bc.ca, Other Communications: URL: www.HelloBC.com
Director, Marketing (Overseas), Reg Krake
604-660-3769, Fax: 604-660-3383
Director, Industry Relations, Ray LeBlond
604-660-3233, Fax: 604-660-3383, Ray.LeBlond@gov.bc.ca
Director, Sector Development & City Destinations, Richard Lewis
604-660-3701, Fax: 604-660-3383, Richard.Lewis@gov.bc.ca
Director, Marketing Communications, Kathleen Lorentsen
604-660-4257, Fax: 604-660-3383, Kathleen.Lorentsen@gov.bc.ca
Director, Tourism Product Management, Margaret McCormick
604-660-4705, Fax: 604-660-3688, Margaret.McCormick@gov.bc.ca
Director, Marketing (North America), Carol Nelson
604-660-3755, Fax: 604-660-3383, Carol.Nelson@gov.bc.ca
Director, Visitor Services, Ninette Ollgaard
250-356-0453, Fax: 250-356-8246, Ninette.Ollgaard@gov.bc.ca
Director, Research, Planning & Evaluation, Richard Porges
250-356-9936, Fax: 250-356-8246, Richard.Porges@gov.bc.ca
Director, eMarketing, Vacant
Fax: 250-356-8246

Management Services Division
PO Box 9842 Prov Govt, Victoria, BC V8W 9T2
250-387-8705 Fax: 250-387-7973

Assistant Deputy Minister, Shauna Brouwer
250-387-9180, Fax: 250-387-7973, Shauna.Brouwer@gov.bc.ca
Chief Information Officer/Executive Director, Debbie Fritz
250-356-0803, Fax: 250-387-1590, Debbie.Fritz@gov.bc.ca
Executive Director, Strategic Human Resources & Corporate Policy & Planning, Kim Russell
250-387-8976, Fax: 250-387-8772, Kim.Russell@gov.bc.ca
Chief Financial Officer/Director, Finance & Administrative Services, Murray Jacobs
250-356-6950, Fax: 250-387-7973, Murray.Jacobs@gov.bc.ca
Director, Corporate Policy & Planning, Shannon Mullen
250-953-4334, Fax: 250-387-1407, Shannon.Mullen@gov.bc.ca
Director, Strategic Human Resources Branch, Vacant
250-356-2036, Fax: 250-387-1407

Ministry of Labour, Citizens' Services & Open Government

PO Box 9056 Prov Govt, Victoria, BC V8W 9K4
250-952-7623 Fax: 250-387-4312
800-663-7867
LCTZ.Minister@gov.bc.ca
www.gov.bc.ca/citz
Other Communication: Victoria: 2150-387-6121; Vancouver: 604-660-2421; Outside BC: 604-660-2421

Responsibilities of the Ministry of Labour include the following: Labour relations; Employment standards; Workers' Compensation Act; Occupational health & safety; Chief Information Officer; Information & privacy; Alternative Service Delivery Secretariat; Queen's Printer; Solutions BC; BC Stats; BC Internet Services; BC Online; Enquiry BC; BC Bid; Enquiry BC; & Canada-BC Business Service Centre.

Acts Administered:
BC Online Act
Business Number Act (s. 10.1)
Community Services Labour Relations Act
Document Disposal Act
Electronic Transactions Act
Employment Standards Act
Fire & Police Services Collective Bargaining Act
Fire Department Act
Fishing Collective Bargaining Act
Freedom of Information and Protection of Privacy Act
Labour Relations Code
Legislative Assembly Management Committee Act
Legislative Assembly Privilege Act
Legislative Library Act
Legislative Procedure Review Act
Members' Remuneration & Pensions Act
Ministry of Labour Act (except in relation to gas safety, electrical safety, elevating devices, boiler & pressure vessel safety)
Ministry of Provincial Secretary & Government Services Act (ss. 1, 2 (4) & 4)
Personal Information Protection Act
Procurement Services Act
Public Agency Accommodation Act
Queen's Printer Act
Statistics Act
Workers' Compensation Act

Minister, Hon. Stephanie Cadieux
stephanie.cadieux.mla@leg.bc.ca
Ministerial Assistant, Labour, Spencer Sproule
250-952-7623, Fax: 250-387-4312

Associated Agencies, Boards & Commissions:
• British Columbia Labour Relations Board
Oceanic Plaza
#600, 1066 West Hastings St.
Vancouver, BC V6E 3X1
604-660-1300 Fax: 604-660-1892
information@lrb.bc.ca
www.lrb.bc.ca
The British Columbia Labour Relations Board is an independent, administrative tribunal. The Board is responsible for mediating & adjudicating employment & labour relations matters related to unionized workplaces.
• Employment Standards Tribunal
Oceanic Plaza
#650, 1066 West Hastings St.
Vancouver, BC V6E 3X1
604-775-3512 Fax: 604-775-3372
registrar.est@bcest.bc.ca
www.bcest.bc.ca
Established under the Employment Standards Act, the Employment Standards Tribunal operates as an administrative tribunal. The responsibility of the Tribunal is to provide an independent appeal of Determinations made by the Director of Employment Standards.
• Workers' Compensation Appeal Tribunal (WCAT)
#150, 4600 Jacombs Rd.
Richmond, BC V6V 3B1
604-664-7800 Fax: 604-664-7898 800-663-2782
www.wcat.bc.ca
The Workers' Compensation Appeal Tribunal of British Columbia is an independent appeal tribunal, which was established by the Workers Compensation Amendment Act (No. 2), 2002. The Tribunal decides appeals from workers & employers from decisions of the Workers' Compensation Board (WorkSafeBC).
• Workers' Compensation Board

Citizens' Services & Open Government including Shared Services BC
PO Box 9440 Prov Govt, Victoria, BC V8W 9V3
250-387-8842 Fax: 250-387-8561

Deputy Minister, Kim Henderson
250-387-8852, Fax: 250-387-8561
Assistant to the Deputy Minister, Diane R. Taylor
250-387-8852, Fax: 250-387-8561, Diane.R.Taylor@gov.bc.ca

Business & Workforce Transformation
PO Box 9029 Prov Govt, Victoria, BC V8V 1T7
250-953-3470 Fax: 250-356-7391
Assistant Deputy Minister, Kevin Jardine
250-953-3470, Fax: 250-356-7391, Kevin.Jardine@gov.bc.ca
Executive Director, Public Service Initiative, Rueben Bronee
250-953-3460, Fax: 250-356-7391, Rueben.Bronee@gov.bc.ca
Executive Director, Workforce Strategies, Anne Horan
250-217-6129, Fax: 250-356-7391, Anne.Horan@gov.bc.ca
Executive Director, Citizen Engagement, David Hume
250-589-9043, Fax: 250-356-7391, David.Hume@gov.bc.ca
Director, Design & Web Strategy, Dominique Bohn
250-507-4791, Fax: 250-356-7391, Dominique.Bohn@gov.bc.ca
Director, Enterprise Data Services, Elaine Dawson
250-952-7957, Fax: 250-387-2144, Elaine.Dawson@gov.bc.ca
Director, Corporate Communications, Robin Farr
250-588-3126, Fax: 250-356-7391, Robin.Farr@gov.bc.ca
Acting Director, Internet Strategy, Alex MacLennan
250-507-6361, Fax: 250-387-2144, Alex.MacLennan@gov.bc.ca
Director, Project & Resource Management, Fran Morrison
250-952-6812, Fax: 250-387-2144, Fran.Morrison@gov.bc.ca
Director, Online Technical Services, Walter Moser
250-953-3979, Fax: 250-387-2144, Walter.Moser@gov.bc.ca
Director, IA & User Research, Blair Neufeld
250-953-3938, Fax: 250-387-2144, Blair.Neufeld@gov.bc.ca
Director, Financial Operations, Jack Taekema
250-953-5103, Fax: 250-387-2144, Jack.Taekema@gov.bc.ca
Director, Capacity Building, Tanya Twynstra
250-507-2163, Fax: 250-356-7391, Tanya.Twynstra@gov.bc.ca
Director, Design Strategy, David Wrate
250-588-9231, Fax: 250-356-7391, David.Wrate@gov.bc.ca

Shared Services BC, Chief Operating Office
PO Box 9412 Prov Govt, Victoria, BC V8W 9V1
250-952-6861 Fax: 250-387-5693
www.sharedservicesbc.gov.bc.ca/
Chief Operating Officer, Bert Phipps
250-952-6861, Fax: 250-387-5693, Bert.Phipps@gov.bc.ca
Executive Director, Strategic Partnerships & Planning Office, Tracey Collins
250-387-4488, Fax: 250-387-5693, Tracey.Colins@gov.bc.ca
Director, Change Management, Bruce Deacon
250-952-6437, Fax: 250-387-5693, Bruce.Deacon@gov.bc.ca
Director, Executive Operations, Vanessa Ginger
250-953-3945, Fax: 250-387-5693, Vanessa.Ginger@gov.bc.ca

Integrated Workplace Solutions Division
250-387-8280 Fax: 250-387-9651
Assistant Deputy Minister, Sarf Ahmed
250-953-4338, Fax: 250-387-9651, Sarf.Ahmed@gov.bc.ca
Executive Director, Facilities Contract Management, Patricia A. Marsh
250-952-4130, Fax: 250-952-8407, Patricia.A.Marsh@gov.bc.ca
Executive Director, Client Services (Ministries), Shirley Mitrou
250-952-8443, Fax: 250-952-8293
Executive Director, Client Services (Broader Public Sector), Bobbi Plecas
250-952-5407, Fax: 250-952-8293, Bobbi.Plecas@gov.bc.ca
Director, Real Estate Services, Jim Baker
250-952-8381, Fax: 250-952-8285, Jim.Baker@gov.bc.ca
Director, Integrated Planning & Project Office, David Bellows
250-952-8305, David.Bellows@gov.bc.ca
Director, Central Agencies/Business & Economy, Brian Clark
250-952-8783, Fax: 250-952-8293, Brian.W.Clark@gov.bc.ca, Other Communications: Cell Phone: 250-216-7874
Director, Client Relations (Social), Quinn Daly
250-952-4923, Fax: 250-952-8293, Quinn.Daly@gov.bc.ca
Director, Financial Planning & Reporting, Darlene Ell
250-952-8826
Director, Client Relations, Peter Gill
250-889-8552, Fax: 250-952-8293, Peter.Gill@gov.bc.ca
Director, Project Services, Robb Gillis
250-952-4830, Fax: 250-952-8707, Robert.Gillis@gov.bc.ca, Other Communications: Cell Phone: 250-361-6552
Director, Property Services, Patrick Gribbon
250-952-8452, Fax: 250-952-8407, Patrick.Gribbon@gov.bc.ca, Other Communications: Cell Phone: 250-812-8483
Director, Client Communications & Engagement, Sandra Hamel
250-952-7801, Fax: 250-952-8293, Sandra.Hamel@gov.bc.ca
Director, Client Relations (Health/Education), Lisa Koorbatoff
250-415-3133, Fax: 250-952-8293, Lisa.Koorbatoff@gov.bc.ca
Director, Contract Governance, Karen Liversedge
250-952-8867, Fax: 250-952-8407, Karen.Liversedge@gov.bc.ca
Director, Workplace Strategies & Planning, Robert Macdonald
250-952-8315, Fax: 250-952-8293, Robert.Macdonald@gov.bc.ca
Director, Leasing Services, John Marsh
250-952-8412, Fax: 250-952-8288, David.Bellows@gov.bc.ca, Other Communications: Alternate Phone: 250-360-7556
Director, Environmental Stewardship & Technical Value, Michael Masson
250-952-8633, Fax: 250-952-8297, Michael.Masson@gov.bc.ca
Director, Real Estate Strategy, Lorraine McMillan
250-952-8321, Fax: 250-952-8289, Lorraine.McMillan@gov.bc.ca
Director, Client Relations, Kwabena Owusu-Nyamekye
250-213-7210, Fax: 250-952-8293, Kwabena.OwusuNyamekye@gov.bc.ca
Director, Client Relations (Natural Resources), Wendy Robinson
250-952-8793, Fax: 250-952-8293, Wendy.Robinson@gov.bc.ca
Director, Real Estate Strategy, Doug Shepherd
250-952-8451, Fax: 250-952-8289, Doug.Shepherd@gov.bc.ca
Director, Workplace Development Services, Jim Thompson
250-952-8587, Fax: 250-952-8286, Jim.Thompson@gov.bc.ca
Director, Client Relations (Justice), Annette Wesley
250-952-5576, Fax: 250-952-8293, Annette.Wesley@gov.bc.ca

Logistics & Business Services Division
PO Box 9412 Prov Govt, Victoria, BC V8X 4S8
250-952-7983 Fax: 250-387-5633
www.pss.gov.bc.ca/
Assistant Deputy Minister, Vacant
250-952-7983, Fax: 250-387-5693
Executive Director, Supply Services, Laurie Barker
250-356-5849, Fax: 250-356-6036
Executive Director, Strategic Information Management, Mark Tatchell
250-217-8816, Fax: 250-387-9843, Mark.Tatchell@gov.bc.ca
Executive Director, Information Access Operations, Kathleen Ward
250-387-9807, Fax: 250-387-9843, Kathleen.Ward@gov.bc.ca
Acting Director, Procurement, Pelle Agerup
250-516-5340, Fax: 250-356-6601, Pelle.Agerup@gov.bc.ca
Director, Business Services & Resource Management, Judy Brachman
250-387-5104, Fax: 250-387-5693, Judy.Brachman@gov.bc.ca
Director, Information Technology Procurement Services, Diane Brodie
250-387-3836, Fax: 250-356-0303, Diane.Brodie@gov.bc.ca
Director, Strategic Pricing & Business Improvement/Store Front Services, Stan Hartfelder
250-387-6904, Fax: 250-356-6036, Stan.Hartfelder@gov.bc.ca
Director, Product Distribution Centre, Gary Heuer
604-927-2296, Fax: 604-660-0699, Gary.Heuer@gov.bc.ca
Acting Director, Strategic Acquistions & Technology Procurement/Purchasing Services Branch, Duncan McLelland
250-387-7312, Fax: 250-387-7309, SATP@gov.bc.ca; Duncan.McLelland@gov.bc.ca; purchasing@gov.bc.ca, Other Communications: Purchasing Fax: 250-387-7310
Director, BC Mail Plus, Don Swagar
250-952-5110, Fax: 250-952-5117, Don.Swagar@gov.bc.ca
Director, Staff Administration, Elizabeth Vander Beesen
250-387-1430, Fax: 250-387-9843, Elizabeth.vanderBeesen@gov.bc.ca
Director, Distribution Centre Victoria/Asset Investment Recovery, Leslie Walden
250-952-4561, Fax: 250-952-4442, DCVCustomerSer@gov.bc.ca, Other Communications: Asset Fax: 2150-952-4224
Director, Access & Records Service Delivery, Brad Williams
250-356-7343, Fax: 250-952-8293, Brad.Williams@gov.bc.ca
Director, Records Management Operations, Alexander Wright
250-588-4057, Fax: 250-387-9843, Alexander.Wright@gov.bc.ca

Technology Solutions Division
PO Box 9412 Prov Govt, Victoria, BC V8W 9V1
250-387-4779 Fax: 250-387-5693
Assistant Deputy Minister, Valerie St. John
250-387-2703, Fax: 250-387-5693, Valerie.St.John@gov.bc.ca
Acting Executive Director, Network Services Branch, Dan Ehle
250-387-4828, Dan.Ehle@gov.bc.ca
Acting Executive Director, Identity Management Service Division, Kevena Bamford
250-952-0482, Fax: 250-387-5693, Kevena.Bamford@gov.bc.ca
Executive Director, Planning, Reporting & Optimization, Sue Goldsmith
250-387-4821, Fax: 250-387-8419, Sue.Goldsmith@gov.bc.ca
Executive Director, Information Technology Alliance Management Office, Brad Kocurek
250-387-6196, Fax: 250-387-9451, Brad.Kocurek@gov.bc.ca
Executive Director, Division Support Services Branch, Wency Lum
250-387-0675, Wency.Lum@gov.bc.ca
Executive Director, Strategic Hosting Solutions Branch, Darren Stadel
250-387-8878, Darren.Stadel@gov.bc.ca
Executive Director, Corporate Application Services, Corinne Timmermann
250-387-8083, Fax: 250-356-0066, Corinne.Timmermann@gov.bc.ca
Associate Executive Director, Network Services, Howard Randell
250-953-3978, Fax: 250-387-3623, Howard.Randell@gov.bc.ca
Senior Director, Corporate Accounting, Ian Armstrong
250-356-9116, Fax: 250-953-3352, Ian.Armstrong@gov.bc.ca, Other Communications: Alternate Phone: 250-507-1072
Senior Director, Strategic Office - Deal Operations, Janine Love
250-952-6988, Fax: 250-387-2676, Janine.Love@gov.bc.ca
Director, Transformation Services, Gary Armstrong
250-952-6071, Gary.Armstrong@gov.bc.ca, Other Communications: Cell Phone: 250-514-1761
Director, Network Operations, Colin Coughlin
250-387-4347, Fax: 250-387-8419
Acting Director, Technology Stewardship, Tim Gagne
250-387-4670, Tim.G.Gagne@gov.bc.ca
Director, Service Management, Michael Gergel
250-387-3663, Fax: 250-387-9451, Michael.Gergel@gov.bc.ca
Director, Information Technology Project Management, Kadriye Graham
250-387-3890, Kadriye.Graham@gov.bc.ca
Director, Tchnical Stewardship, Chris Hauff
250-387-3341, Fax: 250-387-8419, Chris.Hauff@gov.bc.ca
Director, Service Management, Michael P. Hayes
250-952-6154, Fax: 250-387-9451, Michael.P.Hayes@gov.bc.ca
Director, Communication Services, Rosemarie Hayes
250-952-6964, Fax: 250-387-8419, Rosemarie.Hayes@gov.bc.ca
Director, Messaging, Authentication & Collaboration, Lynda Hoel
250-356-9101, Fax: 250-387-2907, Lynda.Hoel@gov.bc.ca
Director, Business Management, Leanne Howes
250-952-6026, Fax: 250-387-9451, Leanne.Howes@gov.bc.ca
Director, Carbon Measurement & Reporting Branch, Orest Maslany
250-952-8402, Fax: 250-952-6045, Orest.Maslany@gov.bc.ca, Other Communications: Cell Phone: 250-888-2780
Director, Business Management, Lisa Perkins
250-415-9269, Fax: 250-387-2676, Lisa.Perkins@gov.bc.ca
Director, Network Services Branch, Brian Severinsen
250-387-4817, Fax: 250-387-8419, Brian.Severinsen@gov.bc.ca
Director, Technical Stewardship, Michael Swift
250-415-6061, Fax: 250-387-8419, Michael.Swift@gov.bc.ca
Director, Service Management, Kate Weber
250-387-8135, Fax: 250-387-8419, Kate.Weber@gov.bc.ca
Director, Change Management, Jody Weeks
250-356-1098, Fax: 250-387-9451, Jody.Weeks@gov.bc.ca
Director, Enterprise Wide Application Services, Terry Whitney
250-952-6442, Terry.Whitney@gov.bc.ca

Chief Information Office
PO Box 9412 Prov Govt, Victoria, BC V8W 9V1
250-356-7970 Fax: 250-387-1940
www.cio.gov.bc.ca/
Assistant Deputy Minister, Strategic Partnerships, C.J. Ritchie
250-356-1789, Fax: 250-387-1940, CJ.Ritchie@gov.bc.ca
Chief Information Officer, Dave Nikolejsin
250-387-8509, Fax: 250-387-1940, Dave.Nikolejsin@gov.bc.ca
Executive Director, Architecture & Standards, Ian Bailey
250-387-8053, Fax: 250-952-6250, Ian.Bailey@gov.bc.ca
Executive Director, Community & External Initiatives (Network BC), Wilf R. Bangert
250-387-9637, Fax: 250-952-0254, Wilf.R.Bangert@gov.bc.ca
Executive Director, Strategic Initiatives Branch, Gary Cooney
250-387-5975, Fax: 250-953-3555, Gary.Cooney@gov.bc.ca
Executive Director, Information Security, Stu Hackett
250-387-5127, Fax: 250-387-3240, Stu.Hackett@gov.bc.ca
Executive Director, Integration Infrastructure Program, Don Henckelman
604-761-5380, Don.Henkelman@gov.bc.ca
Executive Director, Knowledge & Information Services, Charmaine Lowe
250-356-2507, Fax: 250-356-1182

Executive Director, Finance, Matt Mannix
250-356-8321, Fax: 250-387-1940, Matt.Mannix@gov.bc.ca
Executive Director, Regulatory Affairs, Roman Mateyko
250-356-1789, Fax: 250-387-1940, Roman.Mateyko@gov.bc.ca
Executive Director, Cross Government Information Management/Information Technology Initiatives, Peter Watkins
250-387-2184, Fax: 250-387-5693, Peter.Watkins@gov.bc.ca
Director, Chief Information Office, Danielle Burton
250-415-1476, Fax: 250-387-1940, Danielle.Burton@gov.bc.ca
Director, Business Engagement, Kieran Harrop
250-387-9191, Fax: 250-953-3555, Kieran.Harrop@gov.bc.ca
Director, Strategic Vendor Management, Mike Kishimoto
604-505-8998, Fax: 250-356-6601, Mike.Kishimoto@gov.bc.ca, Other Communications: Cell Phone: 604-505-8998
Director, Technical Architecture Standards, Lloyd Loisel
250-387-1534, Fax: 250-952-6250, Lloyd.Loisel@gov.bc.ca
Acting Director, Intellectual Property Program, Pamela Ness
250-356-0827, Fax: 250-387-1940, Pamela.Ness@gov.bc.ca
Director, Evidence Informed Decision Support, Dawn Nickel
250-356-0378, Fax: 250-356-1182, Dawn.Nickel@gov.bc.ca
Director, Information Security Investigations & Forensics, Margaret Patton
250-387-5931, Fax: 250-387-3240, Margaret.Patton@gov.bc.ca
Director, Legislation & Strategic Privacy Practices, Sharon Plater
250-356-0322, Fax: 250-356-1182, Sharon.Plater@gov.bc.ca
Director, Application Architecture & Standards, Derek Rutherford
250-356-7915, Fax: 250-952-6250, Derek.Rutherford@gov.bc.ca
Director, Strategic Vendor Management, Sandra Tanaka
250-356-0310, Fax: 250-387-7309, Sandra.Tanaka@gov.bc.ca
Director, Privacy Investigations, Wendy Taylor
250-952-6161, Fax: 250-387-3240, Wendy.Taylor@gov.bc.ca
Director, Strategic Initiative Support & Advisory Services, Rob Todd
250-387-8823, Fax: 250-387-3240, Rob.Todd@gov.bc.ca
Acting Director, Information Architecture & Standards, Patricia Wiebe
250-387-6818, Fax: 250-952-6250, Patricia.Wiebe@gov.bc.ca
Director, Strategic Information Management/Information Technology Management, Ashley Whitworth
250-953-3839, Fax: 250-953-3555, Ashley.Whitworth@gov.bc.ca

Corporate Services Division
Fax: 250-952-4347
Assistant Deputy Minister/Executive Financial Officer, Brad Gundy
250-952-4347, Brad.Grundy@gov.bc.ca
Ministry Information Security Officer, Garry Mierzuak
250-952-8681, Garry.Mierzuak@gov.bc.ca
Executive Director, Planning, Performance & Communications, Deborah Ainsworth
250-952-4273, Fax: 250-952-4272, Deborah.Ainsworth@gov.bc.ca
Executive Director/Acting Chief Financial Officer, Budgeting & Financial Analysis Branch/Governance & Financial Reporting, Teri Lavine
250-516-6812, Fax: 250-952-8389, Teri.Lavine@gov.bc.ca
Executive Director, Information Management Branch, Bobbi Sadler
250-952-4836, Bobbi.Sadler@gov.bc.ca
Director, Pricing & Recovery Management, Nicole Andersen
250-952-8835, Nicole.Andersen@gov.bc.ca
Director, Corporate Planning, Heidi Bergstrom
250-952-4040, Fax: 250-952-4272, Heidi.Bergstrom@gov.bc.ca
Director, Strategic Projects, Ken Brandt
250-952-8593, Ken.Brandt@gov.bc.ca, Other Communications: Cell Phone: 250-380-8161
Director, People & Organizational Performance, Sarah Francis
250-952-4369, Fax: 250-952-4272, Sarah.Francis@gov.bc.ca
Director, Facilities & Projects, Laurie Gowans
250-952-8540, Laurie.Gowans@gov.bc.ca
Director, Financial Policy, Reporting & Operations, Sandra Hall
250-952-8557, Fax: 250-952-8389, Sandra.Hall@gov.bc.ca
Director, Financial Risk & Assurance, Belinda Lucoe
250-952-8854, Belinda.Lucoe@gov.bc.ca
Director, Strategic Internal Communications, Anne McKinnon
250-356-5313, Fax: 250-387-9190, Anne.McKinnon@gov.bc.ca
Director, Applications, Integration & Technical Services, Shelley Mendez
250-952-5412, Shelley.Mendez@gov.bc.ca
Director, Capital Planning & Reporting, Wendy Turcotte
250-952-8282, Wendy.Turcotte@gov.bc.ca
Director, Budgets & Corporate Reporting, Jim Weir
250-952-8542, Fax: 250-952-8687, Jim.Weir@gov.bc.ca

Service BC
PO Box 9804 Prov Govt, Victoria, BC V8W 9W1
250-387-9170 Fax: 250-387-5633
www.servicebc.gov.bc.ca/

Service BC provides frontline government services & information. Citizens in British Columbia are assisted in accessing services they need. These programs & services are available in person, by phone, & online. Service BC Centres are located in 59 places throughout British Columbia. The following are examples of services offered by Service BC: Doing business in B.C.; Education; Employment & labour standards; Exploring B.C.; Fees & payments; Health; Land & property; Legal services; License & registration; Life events; Living in B.C.; Reports& publications; & Taxation.
Assistant Deputy Minister, Bette-Jo Hughes
250-387-9170, Fax: 250-387-5633
Executive Director, BC Stats, Angelo Cocco
250-356-2119, Fax: 250-387-0380, Angelo.Cocco@gov.bc.ca
Executive Director, Regional Operations, Ron Hinshaw
250-356-2031, Fax: 250-387-5633, Ron.Hinshaw@gov.bc.ca
Executive Director, BC OnLine Partnership Office, Sue Park
250-387-6683, Fax: 250-952-6115, Sue.Park@gov.bc.ca
Director, Financial Operations, Tavish Annis
250-387-0390, Fax: 250-387-5633, Tavish.Annis@gov.bc.ca
Director, Service Delivery & OneStop Business Registry, Patty Ballam
250-356-8657, Fax: 250-356-9422, Patty.Ballam@gov.bc.ca, Other Communications: Cell Phone: 250-415-3772
Director, Operations & Client Services, Brad Boquist
250-356-2039, Fax: 250-387-5633, Brad.Boquist@gov.bc.ca
Director, Application Management & Corporate Services, Catherine Clarke
250-953-4748, Fax: 250-356-9422, Catherine.Clarke@gov.bc.ca
Director, Operations, BC OnLine, Allan Crawshaw
250-953-8277, Fax: 250-953-8222, Allan.CRAWSHAW@accessbc.com
Director, Data Services, Paul Gosh
250-387-9221, Fax: 250-387-0380, Paul.Gosh@gov.bc.ca
Director, Non-Profit Partnerships, Colleen McCormick
250-356-7302, Fax: 250-387-5633, Colleen.McCormick@gov.bc.ca
Director, Surveys & Analysis, Martin Monkman
250-356-0025, Fax: 250-387-0380, Martin.Monkman@gov.bc.ca
Director, Labour & Social Statistics, Cathy Stock
250-953-3703, Fax: 250-387-0380, Cathy.Stock@gov.bc.ca
Director, Demographic Analysis, Jackie Storen
250-216-2291, Fax: 250-387-0380, Jackie.Storen@gov.bc.ca
Regional Director, Interior Northeast, Deborah Lipscombe
250-828-4545, Fax: 250-828-4542, Deborah.Lipscombe@gov.bc.ca
Regional Director, Northwest, Perry Slump
250-565-4488, Fax: 250-565-6638, Perry.Slump@gov.bc.ca

Government Communications & Public Engagement
PO Box 9409 Prov Govt, Victoria, BC V8W 9V1
250-387-1337 Fax: 250-387-3534
www.gov.bc.ca/gcpe/

Deputy Minister, Neil Sweeney
250-356-7398, Fax: 250-356-2872, Neil.Sweeney@gov.bc.ca
Assistant Deputy Minister, Strategic Planning & Public Engagement, John Paul Fraser
250-356-8527, Fax: 250-356-2872, JohnPaul.Fraser@gov.bc.ca
Executive Director, Communications Support Services, Primrose Carson
250-356-7823, Fax: 250-387-6070, Primrose.Carson@gov.bc.ca
Executive Director, Operations & Human Resources, Denise Champion
250-953-4685, Fax: 250-387-3534, Denise.Champion@gov.bc.ca
Director, Systems Solutions & Architecture, Stephen Bamford
250-387-1863, Fax: 250-387-6687, Stephen.Bamford@gov.bc.ca

Communications Division
PO Box 9409 Prov Govt, Victoria, BC V8W 9V1
250-387-1337 Fax: 250-387-6070

Assistant Deputy Minister, Communications & Media Relations, Kelly Gleeson
250-356-8608, Fax: 250-356-2872, Kelly.Gleeson@gov.bc.ca
Manager, Media Relations, Karen Murry
250-387-0779, Fax: 250-356-6070, Karen.Murry@gov.bc.ca

Labour, Deputy Minister's Office
PO Box 9594 Prov Govt, Victoria, BC V8W 9K4
250-387-3914 Fax: 250-356-5186

Deputy Minister, Robert Lapper
250-387-3914, Fax: 250-356-5186, SDL.DeputyMinister@gems3.gov.bc.ca
Assistant Deputy Minister, Industrial Relations, Trevor Hughes
250-356-1346, Fax: 250-356-5186, Trevor.Hughes@gov.bc.ca, Other Communications: Alt Phone: 604-660-5157; Cell Phone: 250-508-4273
Assistant Deputy Minister, Labour Programs, Barbara J. Walman
250-387-3672, Fax: 250-356-5186, Barbara.Walman@gov.bc.ca
Executive Director, Policy & Legislation, John Blakely
250-356-9987, Fax: 250-356-5335, John.Blakely@gov.bc.ca
Executive Director, Employment Standards Branch (Victoria Headquarters), Pat Cullinane
250-387-3300, Fax: 250-356-1886, SDL.EmploymentStandards@gov.bc.ca
Executive Director, Workers' Advisers Office, Ramona Soares
604-713-0364, Fax: 604-713-0311, wao@wao-bc.org
Director, Labour Policy & Legislation, Michael A. Tanner
250-356-7264, Fax: 250-356-5335, Michael.Tanner@gov.bc.ca

Office of the Ombudsperson

947 Fort St., 2nd Fl., PO Box 9039 Prov Govt, Victoria, BC V8W 9A5
250-387-5855 Fax: 250-387-0198
800-567-3247
systems@bcombudsperson.ca (Information technology inquiries)
www.ombudsman.bc.ca

Complaints about the services of public agencies are submitted to the Office of the Ombudsperson. The responsibility of the Office of the Ombudsperson is to investigate impartially these inquiries about the practices of public agencies within its jurisdiction. The Office determines if public agencies acted fairly in accordance with relevant legislation & policies.
Ombudsperson, Kim Carter
250-356-1559
Executive Director, Corporate Services, Shelley Forrester
250-356-7761
Executive Director, Investigations, Linda Carlson
250-387-0189
Executive Director, Intake & Systemic Investigations, Bruce Ronayne
250-387-0196

British Columbia Pavilion Corporation (PavCo)

#850, 999 West Hastings St., PO Box 16, Vancouver, BC V6C 2W2
604-482-2200 Fax: 604-484-5154
info@bcpavco.com
www.bcpavco.com

PavCo is a Crown Corporation of the Ministry of Jobs, Tourism & Innovation, and is responsible for operating BC Place & the Vancouver Convention Centre.
Chair, David R. Podmore
President/Chief Executive Officer, Warren Buckley
Chief Financial Officer/Corporate Secretary, John Harding

BC Place
777 Pacific Blvd., Vancouver, BC V6B 4Y8
604-669-2300 Fax: 604-661-3412
stadium@bcpavco.com
www.bcplace.com

General Manager, Howard Crosley
Director, Construction, Brian Griffin
Director, Business Development, Graham Ramsay
Director, Operations Division, Harvey Repp

Vancouver Convention Centre
1055 Canada Pl., Vancouver, BC V6C 0C3
604-689-8232 Fax: 604-647-7232
info@vancouverconventioncentre.com
www.vancouverconventioncentre.com

General Manager, Ken Cretney
Vice-President, Sales & Marketing, Claire Smith
Vice-President, Operations, Catherine Wong

British Columbia Provincial Emergency Program (PEP)

Block A, #200, 2261 Keating Cross Rd., Saanichton, BC V8M 2A5
250-952-4913 Fax: 250-952-4888
888-257-4777
www.pep.bc.ca
Other Communication: Emergency Coordination Centre: 1-800-663-3456; Recovery & Funding Programs Phone: 250-952-5505

The Provincial Emergency Program (PEP) is a division of the Ministry of Public Safety & Solicitor General, Emergency Management BC. PEP works with local governments to provide the following training & support services for emergencies: Awareness & education to lessen the effects of emergencies; Promotion of preparedness for disasters, through planning & exercises; Coordination & assistance in response to emergencies; & Development & implementation of recovery measures.
Minister, Public Safety & Solicitor General, Hon. Shirley Bond
250-356-7717, Fax: 250-356-8270, SG.Minister@gov.bc.ca; shirley.bond.mla@leg.bc.ca

Executive Director, Strategic Planning, Policy & Legislation, Cam Filmer
250-952-4881, Cam.Filmer@gov.bc.ca
Executive Director, Strategic Planning, Policy & Legislation, Cam Filmer
250-952-4881, Cam.Filmer@gov.bc.ca
Executive Director, Emergency Coordination, Chris Duffy
250-952-4544, Chris.Duffy@gov.bc.ca
Director, Integrated Planning, Aja Norgaard
250-952-4854, Aja.Norgaard@gov.bc.ca
Senior Regional Manager/Assistant Director, Operations, Ralph Mohrmann
250-952-4895, Ralph.Mohrmann@gov.bc.ca

Ministry of Public Safety & Solicitor General

PO Box 9290 Prov Govt, Victoria, BC V8W 9J7
250-387-6121
800-663-7867
pssgwebfeedback@gov.bc.ca
www.gov.bc.ca/pssg
Other Communication: B.C. Coroners Service: 604-660-7745; Provincial Emergency Program: 250-952-4913

The goal of the Ministry of Public Safety & Solicitor General is the maintenance & enhancement of public safety in communities across British Columbia. The following are the key responsibilities of the Ministry: Crime prevention programs; Police & correctional services; Criminal record check & protection order registry; Victim assistance; Provincial emergency management; Emergency social services; Consumer services; & Gaming enforcement.

Acts Administered:
Attorney General Act (ss. 2 (e), 5 & 6, as they relate to the powers, duties, & functions of the Minister of Public Safety & the Solicitor General)
BC Neurotrauma Fund Contribution Act
Business Practices & Consumer Protection Act
Business Practices & Consumer Protection Authority Act
Civil Forfeiture Act
Commercial Transport Act (ss. 2, 6, 7, 10, 13; & ss. 1, 4, 5, 8, 9, 11, 12 & 14, as they relate to affairs of the Insurance Corporation of British Columbia)
Coroners Act
Correction Act
Cremation, Interment & Funeral Services Act
Crime Victim Assistance Act
Criminal Injury Compensation Act
Criminal Records Review Act
Emergency Communications Corporations Act
Emergency Program Act
Fire Services Act (as it relates to the portfolio of the minister)
Firearm Act
Fireworks Act
Flood Relief Act
Food Donor Encouragement Act
Guide Animal Act
Insurance Corporation Act (Part 1)
Insurance (Vehicle) Act
Ministry of Consumer & Corporate Affairs Act (ss. 3 & 4 (a), in relation to consumer affairs; s. 4 (b)- (d))
Motion Picture Act
Motor Dealer Act
Motor Vehicle Act
Parental Responsibility Act
Police Act
Sale of Goods Act
Senior Citizen Automobile Insurance Grant Act
Sex Offender Registry Act (not in force)
Special Accounts Appropriation & Control Act (ss. 7 & 10 (2) (a) & (b))
Victims of Crime Act

Minister/Solicitor General, Hon. Shirley Bond
250-356-7717, Fax: 250-356-8270, SG.Minister@gov.bc.ca; shirley.bond.mla@leg.bc.ca
Deputy Solicitor General, Lori Wanamaker
250-356-0149, Fax: 250-387-6224, Lori.Wanamaker@gov.bc.ca
Executive Director, Civil Forteiture Office, Rob Kroeker
250-387-5091, Fax: 250-356-1092, Rob.Kroeker@gov.bc.ca
Executive Director, Corporate Policy & Planning Office, Toby Louie
250-356-6389, Fax: 250-387-2631, Toby.Louie@gov.bc.ca
Executive Director, Office to Combat Trafficking in Persons, Robin E. Pike
250-953-4969, Fax: 250-953-4756
Executive Director, Strategic Human Resources Office, Julie Spiteri
250-387-6917, Fax: 250-356-6323, Julie.Spiteri@gov.bc.ca
Executive Director, Strategic Information Management, Mark Tatchell
250-387-2036, Fax: 250-356-7747, Mark.Tatchell@gov.bc.ca
Director, Planning, Shelley Eisler
250-387-5918, Fax: 250-387-2631, Shelley.Eisler@gov.bc.ca
Director, Crystal Meth Secretariat, Kjerstine Holmes
250-387-2170, Fax: 250-356-7747, Kjerstine.Holmes@gov.bc.ca
Director, Corporate Initiatives, Lisa Howie
250-387-4774, Fax: 250-387-2631, Lisa.Howie@gov.bc.ca
Director, Policy & Legislation, Anne Preyde
250-356-2932, Fax: 250-387-2631, Anne.Preyde@gov.bc.ca

Associated Agencies, Boards & Commissions:

• British Columbia Lottery Corporation
74 West Seymour St.
Kamloops, BC V2C 1E2
250-828-5500 Fax: 250-828-5631 866-815-0222
www.bclc.com
Other Communication: Vancouver Phone: 604-215-0649

• British Columbia Office of the Police Complaint Commissioner
#501, 947 Fort St.
PO Box 9895 Prov Govt
Victoria, BC V8W 9T8
250-356-7458 Fax: 250-356-6503 877-999-8707
info@opcc.bc.ca
www.opcc.bc.ca
Established under the Police Act, the British Columbia Office of the Police Complaint Commissioner is an independent agency. The responsibility of the agency is overseeing complaints against municipal police & ensuring that these complaints are dealt with in a fair & impartial manner. The Office reports directly to the Legislature.

• British Columbia Pension Corporation
2995 Jutland Rd.
PO Box 9460
Victoria, BC V8W 9V8
250-387-1002 Fax: 250-953-0429 800-663-8823
PensionCorp@pensionsbc.ca; Retired.Members@pensionsbc.ca
www.pensionsbc.ca
Other Communication: College Pension Plan: 250-953-4324; Municipal Pension Plan: 250-953-3000; Public Service Pension Plan: 250-953-3033; Teachers' Pension Plan: 250-953-3022
The British Columbia Pension Corporation is a Crown corporation, which was established by The Public Sector Pension Plans Act. The Pension Corporation serves as the plan administrator for the following pension plans: College (CPP@pensionsbc.ca); Municipal (MPP@pensionsbc.ca); Public Service (PSPP@pensionsbc.ca); Teachers' (TPP@pensionsbc.ca); & the Workers' Compensation Board (WCB@pensionsbc.ca). The Corporation also continues to administer the Members of the Legislative Assembly Pension Plan.

• Commercial Appeals Commission
604-660-2987 Fax: 604-660-3372

• Consumer Protection BC
PO Box 9244 Prov Govt
Victoria, BC V8W 9J2
888-564-9963
www.consumerprotectionbc.ca/
Consumer Protection BC is a not-for-profit corporation established in 2004 to promote a fair marketplace for BC consumers and businesses.

• Coroners Service of British Columbia
Metrotower II
#800, 4720 Kingsway
Burnaby, BC V5H 4N2
604-660-7745 Fax: 604-660-7766
BC.CorSer@gov.bc.ca
www.pssg.gov.bc.ca/coroners
Governed by the Coroners Act, the Coroners Service of British Columbia investigates all unnatural, unexplained, unattended, or sudden & unexpected deaths. Based on its fact-finding, the agency recommends public safety improvements in order to prevent similar deaths.

• Criminal Injury Compensation Program (Workers' Compensation Board) / CICP
PO Box 5350
Vancouver, BC V6B 5L5
604-244-6400 Fax: 604-244-6480

• Public Sector Employers' Council Secretariat (PSEC)
#210, 880 Douglas St.
PO Box 9400 Prov Govt
Victoria, BC V8V 9V1
250-387-0842 Fax: 250-387-6258
www.aved.gov.bc.ca/psec
The coordination of the management of labour relations policies & practices in the public sector is the principal responsibility of the Public Sector Employers' Council. The Council consists of the following members: Eight Ministers or Deputy Ministers; Commissioner of the BC Public Service Agency; & Representatives from six public sector employers' associations. The Public Sector Employers' Council Secretariat carries out the work of the Council.

Corrections Branch

PO Box 9278 Prov Govt, Victoria, BC V8W 9J7
250-387-5059 Fax: 250-387-5698
www.pssg.gov.bc.ca/corrections
Other Communication: Adult Custody Phone: 250-387-5098; Community Corrections & Corporate Programs Phone: 250-356-7930

The Corrections Branch consists of the Adult Custody Division & the Community Corrections & Corporate Programs Division. The Adult Custody Division operates correctional centres for persons awaiting trial or serving a provincial custody sentence. The Community Corrections & Corporate Programs Division operates over fifty community corrections offices throughout British Columbia.

Assistant Deputy Minister, Corrections, Brent Merchant
250-387-5363, Fax: 250-387-5698
Provincial Director, Adult Custody Division, Pete Coulson
250-387-5959, Fax: 250-952-6883, Peter.Coulson@gov.bc.ca
Provincial Director, Community Corrections & Corporate Programs Division, Michelia Cameron
250-387-5930, Fax: 250-952-6883, Micheila.Cameron@gov.bc.ca
Deputy Provincial Director, Community Corrections & Corporate Programs Headquarters, Elenore Clark
250-387-5936, Fax: 250-387-5039, Elenore.Clark@gov.bc.ca
Acting Deputy Provincial Director, Operations, Debbie Hawboldt
250-356-5868, Fax: 250-952-6883, Debbie.Hawboldt@gov.bc.ca
Deputy Provincial Director, Capital Projects, Tedd Howard
250-514-8851, Fax: 250-952-6883, Tedd.Howard@gov.bc.ca
Deputy Provincial Director, Community Corrections & Corporate Programs Headquarters, Bill Small
250-387-6040, Fax: 250-387-5039, Bill.Small@gov.bc.ca

Emergency Management BC

PO Box 9223 Prov Govt, Victoria, BC V8W 9J1
250-953-4002 Fax: 250-953-4081
BC.CorSer@gov.bc.ca (Coroner); OFC@gov.bc.ca (Fire Commissioner)
www.pssg.gov.bc.ca/coroners; www.pssg.gov.bc.ca/firecom
Other Communication: Office of the Chief Coroner: 604-660-7745; Office of the Fire Commissioner Phone: 250-356-9000, Toll Free: 1-888-988-9488; Provincial Emergency Program: 250-952-4913

Emergency Management BC oversees the Coroners Service of British Columbia, the Office of the Fire Commissioner, & the Provincial Emergency Program (www.pep.bc.ca). B.C. Coroners Service investigates all unexpected, unnatural, unexplained, & unattended deaths in the province. Improvements to public safety & recommendations to prevent similar deaths are made by the Coroners Service. The Office of the Fire Commissioner administers & enforces fire safety legislation, trains local assistants to the fire commissioner, certifies fire fighters, provides public fire safety education, advises local governments, responds to major fires, & investigates fires. The Provincial Emergency Program provides training & support to local governments.

Fire & Emergency Management Commissioner, Becky Denlinger
250-953-4083, Fax: 250-387-4872, Becky.Denlinger@gov.bc.ca
Executive Officer, Cameron Lewis
250-953-4036, Fax: 250-953-4081, Cameron.Lewis@gov.bc.ca
Executive Director, Corporate Services, David Curtis
250-953-4034, Fax: 250-953-4081, David.Curtis@gov.bc.ca
Director, Flood Protection Program, Carol Loski
250-953-4003, Fax: 250-953-4081

BC Coroners Service

Metrotower II, #800, 4720 Kingsway, Burnaby, BC V5H 4N2
604-660-7745 Fax: 604-660-7766
BC.CorSer@gov.bc.ca
www.pssg.gov.bc.ca/coroners/

Chief Coroner, Lisa Lapointe
604-660-7745, Fax: 604-660-7766
Deputy Chief Coroner, Norm Leibel
604-660-7745, Fax: 604-660-7766, Norm.Leibel@gov.bc.ca
Executive Director, Kellie Kilpatrick
604-660-2556, Fax: 604-660-2640, Kellie.Kilpatrick@gov.bc.ca
Executive Director, Medical Services, Dr. Karla Pederson
604-660-7745, Fax: 604-660-7766
Director, Legal Services & Inquests, Rodrick MacKenzie
604-660-7745, Fax: 604-660-7766, Rodrick.MacKenzie@gov.bc.ca

Office of the Fire Commissioner

PO Box 9201 Prov Govt, Victoria, BC V8W 9J1
250-952-4913 Fax: 250-952-4888
888-988-9488
OFC@gov.bc.ca
www.pssg.gov.bc.ca/firecom/index.htm

Deputy Fire Commissioner, Community Support, Dave Ferguson
250-952-4919, Fax: 250-952-4888, Dave.Ferguson@gov.bc.ca

Assistant Fire Commissioner, Investigations, Rob Owens
250-952-4913, Fax: 250-952-4888, Rob.Owens@gov.bc.ca

Provincial Emergency Program
PO Box 9201 Prov Govt, Victoria, BC V8W 9J1
250-952-4913 Fax: 250-952-4888
800-663-3456
www.pep.bc.ca

Executive Director, Emergency Coordination, Chris Duffy
250-952-4544, Fax: 250-952-4888, Chris.Duffy@gov.bc.ca
Executive Director, Strategic Planning, Policy & Legislation, Cam Filmer
250-952-4881, Fax: 250-952-4888, Cam.Filmer@gov.bc.ca
Director, Integrated Public Safety Unit, Heather Lyle
604-586-4358, Fax: 604-586-4334, Heather.Lyle@gov.bc.ca
Director, Integrated Planning, Aja Norgaard
250-952-4854, Fax: 250-952-4888, Aja.Norgaard@gov.bc.ca
Senior Regional Manager/Assistant Director, Northwest & Vancouver Island Regions, Ralph Mohrmann
250-952-4895, Fax: 250-952-4888, Ralph.Mohrmann@gov.bc.ca, Other Communications: Vancouver Fax: 250-952-4304
Director, Financial Planning & Analysis Division, Rob Seginson
250-356-7068, Fax: 250-356-9185, Rod.Seginson@gov.bc.ca
Director, Accounting, Budgeting & Reporting, William Skrlac
250-356-7077, Fax: 250-356-9185, William.Skrlac@gov.bc.ca
Manager, Procurement, Betty-Ann Atherton
250-356-5060, Fax: 250-356-8731, BettyAnn.Atherton@gov.bc.ca
Manager, Financial Operations, Brent Morrison
250-387-6890, Fax: 250-356-8739, Brent.Morrison@gov.bc.ca

Gaming Policy & Enforcement
PO Box 9311 Prov Govt, Victoria, BC V8W 9N1
250-387-1301 Fax: 250-387-1818
www.hsd.gov.bc.ca/gaming

Assistant Deputy Minister, Douglas S. Scott
250-953-4482, Fax: 250-387-1818, Douglas.S.Scott@gov.bc.ca
Executive Director, Policy, Responsible Gambling & Business Services Division, Sue Birge
250-387-3211, Fax: 250-356-1910, Sue.Birge@gov.bc.ca
Executive Director, Licensing & Grants, Ursula Cowland
250-356-2975, Fax: 250-356-8149, Ursula.Cowland@gov.bc.ca
Executive Director, Racing, Samuel Hawkins
604-660-7405, Fax: 604-660-7414, Samuel.Hawkins@gov.bc.ca
Executive Director, Internal Compliance & Risk Management, Bill McCrea
250-356-1109, Fax: 250-387-1818, Bill.McCrea@gov.bc.ca
Executive Director, Registration & Certification Division, Rick Saville
250-356-0981, Fax: 250-952-5225, Rick.Saville@gov.bc.ca
Executive Director, Audit & Compliance Division, Terri Van Sleuwen
604-660-0274, Fax: 604-660-0267, Terri.VanSleuwen@gov.bc.ca
Executive Director, Investigations & Regional Operations Division, Larry Vander Graaf
604-660-0276, Fax: 604-660-0267, Larry.VanderGraaf@gov.bc.ca
Director, Personnel Registration, Garth Baillie
250-356-0983, Fax: 250-952-5225, Garth.Baillie@gov.bc.ca
Director, Casino Investigations, Derek Dickson
604-660-0299, Fax: 604-660-2030, Derek.Dickson@gov.bc.ca
Director, Licensing, Kathy Elder
250-356-6479, Fax: 250-356-8149, Kathy.Elder@gov.bc.ca
Director, Charitable Gaming Audit, Anna Fitzgerald
604-660-0269, Fax: 604-660-0267, Anna.Fitzgerald@gov.bc.ca
Director, Forensic Investigations, Al Giesbrecht
250-356-5550, Fax: 250-356-0782, Al.Giesbrecht@gov.bc.ca
Director, Responsible Gambling Strategy, David Horricks
250-953-3078, Fax: 250-356-1910, David.Horricks@gov.bc.ca
Director, Grants, Ron C. Johnson
250-356-2967, Fax: 250-356-8149, Ron.Johnson@gov.bc.ca
Director, Commercial Gaming Audit (Lottery), Karen Kraan
604-775-1103, Fax: 604-660-0267, Karen.Kraan@gov.bc.ca
Director, Certification & Game Integrity, Steve Lefler
250-356-6166, Fax: 250-356-0782, Stephen.Lefler@gov.bc.ca
Director, Lotteries Registration, Len Meilleur
250-356-6320, Fax: 250-356-0782, Len.Meilleur@gov.bc.ca
Director, Corporate Registration, Ron Merchant
250-356-0989, Fax: 250-356-5225, Ron.Merchant@gov.bc.ca
Director, Lottery Investigations, William Mulcahy
604-660-0278, Fax: 604-660-0267, William.Mulcahy@gov.bc.ca
Director, Commercial Gaming Audit (Casino/Bingo), David Pyatt
604-775-1198, Fax: 604-660-0267, David.Pyatt@gov.bc.ca
Director, Business Services, Susan Quesnel
250-356-9150, Fax: 250-356-1910, Susan.Quesnel@gov.bc.ca
Director, Race Operations, Doug Scott
604-328-1671, Fax: 604-660-7414, Douglas.F.Scott@gov.bc.ca

Information Technology Services Division
PO Box 9262 Prov Govt, Victoria, BC V8W 9J4
250-356-8787 Fax: 250-356-7699

Acting Executive Director & Chief Information Officer, Frank D'Argis
250-387-5258, Fax: 250-356-7699
Acting Director, Application & Infrastructure Services, Carol Barnsley
250-356-1164, Fax: 250-356-7699, Carol.Barnsley@gov.bc.ca
Director, Client Services, Larry Bjelde
250-356-9285, Fax: 250-356-7699, Larry.Bjelde@gov.bc.ca
Director, Strategic Management, Ross Harris
250-415-3197, Fax: 250-356-7699, Ross.Harris@gov.bc.ca
Director, Technical Operations & Information Technology Shared Services, Evan Schlaak
250-356-6061, Fax: 250-356-7699, Evan.Schlaak@gov.bc.ca

Liquor Control & Licensing Branch
PO Box 9292 Prov Govt, Victoria, BC V8W 9J8
250-952-5787 Fax: 250-952-7066
www.pssg.gov.bc.ca/lclb

Assistant Deputy Minister/General Manager, Karen Ayers
250-952-5791, Fax: 259-852-7066, Karen.Ayers@gov.bc.ca
Registrar, Elizabeth Barker
250-952-5793, Fax: 250-952-7066, Elizabeth.Barker@gov.bc.ca
Deputy General Manager, Licensing, Cheryl Caldwell
250-952-7046, Fax: 250-952-7060, Cheryl.Caldwell@gov.bc.ca
Deputy General Manager, Compliance & Enforcement Division, Bruce Edmundson
250-952-7037, Fax: 250-952-7059, Bruce.Edmundson@gov.bc.ca
Director, Policy, Planning & Communications, Barry Bieller
250-952-5755, Fax: 250-952-7066, Barry.Bieller@gov.bc.ca
Director, Management Services, Jan Evans
250-952-7031, Fax: 250-952-7066, Jan.L.Evans@gov.bc.ca

Liquor Distribution Branch
3200 East Broadway, Vancouver, BC V5M 1Z6
604-252-3000 Fax: 604-252-3026

General Manager, Jay Chambers
604-252-3021, Fax: 603-252-3026, Jay.Chambers@bcldb.com
Chief Financial Officer, Roger Bissoondatt
604-252-3151, Fax: 604-252-3175, Roger.Bissoondatt@bcldb.com
Executive Director, Information Services, Don Farley
604-252-3264, Fax: 604-252-3283, Don.Farley@bcldb.com
Executive Director, Human Resources, Michael Procopio
604-252-3243, Fax: 604-252-3200, Michael.Procopio@bcldb.com
Executive Director, Retail Services, Kelly Wilson
604-252-3103, Fax: 604-252-3127, Kelly.Wilson@bcldb.com
Director, Store Operations, Gary Branham
604-252-3109, Fax: 604-252-3127, Gary.Branham@bcldb.com
Director, Recruitment & Compensation, Terry Dobrozdravich
604-252-2977, Fax: 604-252-3274, Terry.Dobrozdravich@bcldb.com
Acting Director, Employee Relations & Occupational Health & Safety, Rita Ferrara
604-252-2948, Fax: 604-252-3274, Rita.Ferrara@bcldb.com
Director, Regulatory Division, Mark Fukuhara
604-252-3226, Fax: 604-252-3350, Mark.Fukuhara@bcldb.com
Director, Corporate Policy, Gord Hall
604-252-3035, Fax: 604-252-3026, Gord.Hall@bcldb.com
Acting Director, Information Technology Architecture & Planning, Rob James
604-252-3073, Rob.James@bcldb.com
Acting Director, Technical Services, Peter Kho
604-252-3046, Peter.Kho@bcldb.com
Director, Financial Planning & Reporting, Elaine Low
604-252-3158, Elaine.Low@bcldb.com
Director, Wholesale Business, Donna Mohn
604-252-3098, Fax: 604-252-3106, Donna.Mohn@bcldb.com
Director, Corporate Security/Emergency Management, Donna Morse
604-252-3051, Fax: 604-252-3450, Donna.Morse@bcldb.com
Acting Director, Corporate Projects, Amin Nanji
604-252-3408, Amin.Nanji@bcldb.com
Director, Marketing, Paulette Parry
604-252-3238, Fax: 604-252-3127, Paulette.Parry@bcldb.com
Director, Internal Audit, Patrick Seeley
604-252-3222, Patrick.Seeley@bcldb.com
Director, Finance Administration, Al Shariff
604-252-3354, Al.Shariff@bcldb.com
Acting Director, Application Services, Martin Straith
604-252-2901, Martin.Straith@bcldb.com
Director, Revenue Division, Norman Thompson
604-252-2998, Norman.Thompson@bcldb.com
Director, Real Estate, Bob Tougas
604-252-3133, Fax: 604-252-3141, Bob.Tougas@bcldb.com
Director, Distribution, Don Wilcox
604-252-3129, Fax: 604-252-3390, Don.Wilcox@bcldb.com

Management Services Branch
PO Box 9256 Prov Govt, Victoria, BC V8W 9J4
250-387-5258 Fax: 250-387-0081

Assistant Deputy Minister, Tara Faganello
250-387-5258, Fax: 250-387-0081, Tara.Faganello@gov.bc.ca
Acting Director, Risk Management, Anne McKeachie
250-356-8921, Fax: 250-356-8736, Anne.McKeachie@gov.bc.ca

Office of the Superintendent of Motor Vehicles (OSMV)
PO Box 9254 Prov Govt, Victoria, BC V8W 9J2
250-387-7747 Fax: 250-387-4891
OSMV.Mailbox@gov.bc.ca
www.pssg.gov.bc.ca/osmv

The Office of the Superintendent of Motor Vehicles is responsible for regulating drivers in British Columbia. The following services are provided: Establishment & maintenance of standards for driving behaviour & medical fitness; Provision of an independent method of appeal of certain Insurance Corporation of British Columbia decisions; Scheduling & hearing evidence related to proposals by the Insurance Corporation of British Columbia concerning licences, driving training schools, & AirCare Certified repair facilities; & Reviewing driving prohibitions & vehicle impoundments imposed by police.

Superintendent, Motor Vehicles, Steve Martin
250-387-5692, Fax: 250-356-5577
Director, Hearings & Fair Practices, Stephanie Melvin
250-953-3818, Fax: 250-356-5577, Stephanie.Melvin@gov.bc.ca
Director, Management Services, Deidre Moran
250-356-9482, Fax: 250-356-5568
Director, Policy & Research, Dana Tadla
250-356-0097, Fax: 250-356-5568

Policing & Security Programs Branch
PO Box 9285, Victoria, BC V8W 9J7
250-387-1100 Fax: 250-356-7747
sgpcsb@gov.bc.ca; victimservices@gov.bc.ca
www.pssg.gov.bc.ca/victimservices
Other Communication: Victim Services Phone: 604-660-5199; VictimLINK: 1-800-563-0808

Assistant Deputy Minister/Director, Policing & Community Safety Branch/Police Services, Clayton J.D. Pecknold
250-387-1100, Fax: 250-356-7747, Clayton.Pecknold@gov.bc.ca
Executive Director, Security Programs Division, Sam MacLeod
250-356-1501, Fax: 250-387-5367, Sam.MacLeod@gov.bc.ca; SGSPDSEC@gov.bc.ca
Deputy Director, Security Services & Screening, Fraser Marshall
250-356-0267, Fax: 250-387-5687, Fraser.Marshall@gov.bc.ca
Director, Management Services, Perry Clark
250-356-8146, Fax: 250-356-7747, sgpcsb@gov.bc.ca
Director, Crime Research & Analysis, Kjerstine Holmes
250-387-2170, Fax: 250-356-7747, Kjerstine.Holmes@gov.bc.ca
Director, Policy & Legislation, Katherine Kirby
250-387-6950, Fax: 250-356-7747, Katherine.Kirby@gov.bc.ca

BC Public Service Agency

#4, 810 Blanshard St., PO Box 9404 Prov Govt, Victoria, BC V8W 9V1
250-387-0518 Fax: 250-356-7074
www.bcpublicserviceagency.gov.bc.ca/

The provision of human resource management services is the responsibility of the British Columbia Service Agency. The services are provided to persons & organizations working in the provinces's public sector.

Head, British Columbia Public Service Agency, Lynda Tarras
250-387-2166, Fax: 250-356-7074, Lynda.Tarras@gov.bc.ca
Assistant Deputy Minister, Talent Management, Deborah Bowman
250-387-0428, Fax: 250-356-7074, Deborah.Bowman@gov.bc.ca
Assistant Deputy Minister, Employee Relations, Doug Caul
250-356-7448, Fax: 250-356-7074, Doug.Caul@gov.bc.ca
Assistant Deputy Minister, Client Services, Laurie Duncan
250-356-6830, Fax: 250-356-7074, Laurie.Duncan@gov.bc.ca
Executive Director, Executive Account Management, Lorne DeLarge

250-356-0708, Fax: 250-356-7074,
Lorne.DeLarge@gov.bc.ca
Executive Director, Business Performance Division, Marguerite Vickery
250-356-5431, Fax: 250-356-7074,
Marguerite.Vickery@gov.bc.ca

Ministry of Social Development

PO Box 9058 Prov Govt, Victoria, BC V8W 9E1
250-356-7750 Fax: 250-356-7292
SD.Minister@gov.bc.ca
www.gov.bc.ca/hsd/

The Ministry of Social Development (& Responsible for Multiculturalism) focusses on British Columbian customers by transforming service delivery; using effective outcome-based practices; & collaborating with other ministries, as well as with business, community & service organizations.

Acts Administered:
Child in the Home of a Relative Program Transition Regulation
Community Living Authority Act
Community Living Authority Regulation
Employment & Assistance Act
Employment & Assistance Regulations
Employment & Assistance For Persons with Disabilities Act
Employment & Assistance for Persons with Disabilities Regulations
Multiculturalism Act
Minister, Social Development, Hon. Harry Bloy
250-356-7750, Fax: 250-356-7292, SD.Minister@gov.bc.ca; harry.bloy.mla@leg.bc.ca
Deputy Minister, Mark Sieben
250-387-3471, Fax: 250-387-5775
Director, Disability Services Division, Rachael Ross
250-356-8987, Fax: 250-356-2734, Rachael.Ross@gov.bc.ca
Advocate for Service Quality, Jane Holland
604-775-1238, Fax: 604-660-1505

Associated Agencies, Boards & Commissions:
• Employment & Assistance Appeal Tribunal
PO Box 9994 Prov Govt
Victoria, BC V8W 9R7
250-356-6374 Fax: 250-356-9687 866-557-0035
eaat@gov.bc.ca
www.gov.bc.ca/eaat/

Employment & Labour Market Services Division
PO Box 9762 Prov Govt, Victoria, BC V8W 1A4
250-356-0050 Fax: 250-953-3928
Assistant Deputy Minister, Allison Bond
250-953-3924, Fax: 250-953-3928
Executive Director, Employment Program Management & Development, Sergei Bouslov
250-356-8128, Fax: 250-387-2069
Executive Director, Service Delivery, Tami Currie
250-387-9625, Fax: 250-356-2734, Tami.Currie@gov.bc.ca
Director, Multiculturalism Unit, Meharoona Ghani
604-660-5140, Fax: 604-775-0670
Director, Employment & Labour Market Programming, Anne A. Hill
250-387-2098, Fax: 250-387-2069, Anne.A.Hill@gov.bc.ca
Director, Stakeholder Relationships, Rachel Holmes
250-953-3917, Fax: 250-953-3928,
Rachel.Holmes@gov.bc.ca
Acting Director, Planning & Reporting, Tiffany Ma
250-953-4514, Fax: 250-953-3928, Tiffany.Ma@gov.bc.ca
Director, Disabilities & Specialized Employment, Sandy Rodgers
604-775-2065, Fax: 604-775-2075,
Sandy.Rodgers@gov.bc.ca
Executive Project Director, ICM Branch, Dexter Ratcliff
250-216-8721
Project Director, Social Integration, Bernard Achampong
250-953-4538, Fax: 250-953-3928,
Bernard.Achampong@gov.bc.ca
Project Director, Business Transformation, Linda Bradford
250-953-3917, Fax: 250-387-2089,
Linda.Bradford@gov.bc.ca

Integrated Case Management
PO Box 9436 Prov Govt, Victoria, BC V8W 9W3
250-356-6633
Assistant Deputy Minister, Jill Kot
250-356-6633, Fax: 250-356-1053
Executive Director, Kathleen Asher
250-356-2688, Fax: 250-356-1053
Executive Director, Robert O'Neill
250-356-9253, Fax: 250-356-5405
Executive Director, Wayne Powell
250-387-2223, Fax: 250-387-9737
Director, Vendor Management, Brad Boquist
250-387-1568
Director, Solution Alignment, Marcin Zaranski
250-387-5129

Management Services Division
PO Box 9940 Prov Govt, Victoria, BC V8W 9R2
250-387-3159 Fax: 250-387-2418
Assistant Deputy Minister/Executive Financial Officer, Wes Boyd
250-387-3159, Fax: 250-387-2418, Wes.Boyd@gov.bc.ca
Executive Director/Chief Financial Officer, Financial & Administrative Services Branch, Len Dawes
250-356-7047, Fax: 250-356-5994, Len.Dawes@gov.bc.ca
Executive Director/Chief Information Officer, Information Management Branch, Jeff Gauthier
250-387-3112, Fax: 250-387-6439, Jeff.Gauthier@gov.bc.ca
Executive Director, Engagement & Workforce Development, David Glockzin
250-387-7667, Fax: 250-387-4264,
David.Glockzin@gov.bc.ca
Acting Director, Business Services, Shelley Burnham
250-356-8988, Fax: 250-356-1612,
Shelley.Burnham@gov.bc.ca
Director, Financial Accounting & Reporting, Rob Byers
250-387-2132, Fax: 250-356-1051, Rob.Byers@gov.bc.ca
Director, Infrastructure Services, Claudia Lang
250-356-5103, Fax: 250-387-6439, Claudia.Lang@gov.bc.ca
Director, Facilities & Workplace Solutions, Joyce Metcalfe
250-217-4971, Fax: 250-356-5994,
Joyce.Metcalfe@gov.bc.ca
Director, Budget Management & Assurance, Cindy Petrowski
250-387-1623, Fax: 250-356-5994,
Cindy.Petrowski@gov.bc.ca
Director, Application Services, Jay Prill
250-356-7661, Fax: 250-387-6439, Jay.Prill@gov.bc.ca
Director, Corporate Planning & Performance, Kashi Tanaka
250-387-9075

Policy & Research Division
PO Box 9936 Prov Govt, Victoria, BC V8W 9R2
250-356-5065 Fax: 250-387-5775
Assistant Deputy Minister, Molly Harrington
250-356-5065, Fax: 250-387-2418
Executive Director, Employment & Income Assistance Branch, Robert Bruce
250-387-1486, Fax: 250-387-8164, Robert.Bruce@gov.bc.ca
Executive Director, Employment & Income Assistance Branch, Mark Medgyesi
250-953-3923, Fax: 250-387-8164,
Mark.Medgyesi@gov.bc.ca
Executive Director, Disability Services Branch, Harb Sihota
250-356-0923, Fax: 250-387-8164, Harb.Sihota@gov.bc.ca
Executive Director, Ministry of Social Development-Ministry of Children & Family Development Legislation & Litigation Branch, Michael Turnaski
250-387-6434, Fax: 250-356-8182,
Michael.Turanski@gov.bc.ca, Other Communications: Cell Phone: 250-588-9677
Executive Director, Provincial Services, Debi Upton
250-356-8506, Fax: 250-387-8261
Director, Legislation, Leah M. Bailey
250-387-0372, Fax: 250-356-8182, Leah.Bailey@gov.bc.ca
Director, Employment & Income Assistance Branch, Alison Bath
250-356-5002, Fax: 250-387-8164, Alison.Bath@gov.bc.ca
Director, Health Assistance Branch, Paul Beardmore
250-356-1746, Fax: 250-356-7290,
Paul.Beardmore@gov.bc.ca
Director, Disability Services Branch, Ian Brethour
250-387-3764, Fax: 250-387-8164
Director, Disability Services Branch, Odette Dantzer
250-356-2249, Fax: 250-387-8164
Director, Evaluation, Performance Management & Intergovernmental Relations, Linda DeBenedictis
250-387-4622, Fax: 250-387-8164,
Linda.DeBenedictis@gov.bc.ca

Regional Services Division
PO Box 9934 Prov Govt, Victoria, BC V8W 9R2
250-387-6905 Fax: 250-387-2418
Assistant Deputy Minister, Sharon Moysey
250-387-6905, Fax: 250-387-2418
Executive Director, Fraser Regional Office, Patricia Boyle
604-586-2959, Fax: 604-586-2681, Off300@gov.bc.ca
Executive Director, Regional Operations, Janice Nakamura
250-356-2220, Fax: 250-952-6450
Executive Director, Prevention & Loss Management Services, Kim Saastad
250-356-8200, Fax: 250-356-1615
Executive Director, Vancouver Coastal Regional Office, Nancy Shewchuk
604-660-3224, Fax: 604-660-2503
Executive Director, Interior Regional Office, Bruce Smith
888-939-9278, Fax: 250-828-4614, Bruce.Smith@gov.bc.ca, Other Communications: Alternate Phone: 250-828-4600
Director, Policy Interpretation & Stakeholder Relations Liaison Branch, Judy D'Gal
250-387-9271, Fax: 250-952-6450
Director, Project Management & Implementation Branch, Raymond Fieltsch
250-387-3865, Fax: 250-952-6450,
Raymond.Fieltsch@gov.bc.ca
Prevention & Loss Management Services
PO Box 9930 Prov Govt, Victoria, BC V8W 9R2
250-356-8200 Fax: 250-356-1615

British Columbia Transmission Corporation

Four Bentall Centre, #1100, 1055 Dunsmuir St., PO Box 49260, Vancouver, BC V7X 1V5
604-699-7539
Interconnections@bchydro.com (transmission interconnections)
http: //transmission.bchydro.com/home

As of 2010, the British Columbia Transmission Corporation is now part of BC Hydro under the Clean Energy Act. Its main activities still include the planning, operation, & maintenance of British Columbia's publicly-owned electrical transmission system.

Ministry of Transportation & Infrastructure

PO Box 9850 Prov Govt, Victoria, BC V8W 9T5
250-387-3198 Fax: 250-356-7706
tran.webmaster@gov.bc.ca
www.gov.bc.ca/tran

In carrying out its mission to move people & goods safely in British Columbia, the Ministry of Transportation & Infrastructure is responsible for the following: Transportation planning & policy; Highway construction & maintenance; Commercial vehicle safety & inspections; Infrastructure grants; & Port & airport development.

Acts Administered:
British Columbia Rail Benefits (First Nations) Trust Act
British Columbia Railway Act
British Columbia Transit Act
Coastal Ferry Act (Parts 1-3; & ss. 71, & 74-77)
Commercial Transport Act (s. 3; ss. 1, 4, 5, 8, 9, 11, & 12, as they relate to highway infrastructure & weigh scales; & ss. 1, 4, 5, 8, 9, 11, 12, & 14, as they relate to Commercial Vehicle Safety & Enforcement)
Industrial Roads Act
Land Title Act (s. 77.2)
Motor Vehicle Act (ss. 116.1, 118.94-118.992, 119-125.1, 126-135.1, 136-148.1, 149-169.1, 170-182, 185-209, 212-212.2, 213, 214, 216-218, 219, 223, 237, 239-240; ss. 1, 75-76, 78, 83, 83.1, 183 & 210; ss. 1, 66, 73, 75-76, 78,82-83, 210, 211, 220, 238)
Passenger Transportation Act
Public Works Agreement Act
Railway Act (ss. 1-5, 14-27, 30, 32, 34-63, 135, 136, 138, 161, 180, 183, 185 (1), (2) & (5)- (10), 186, 187, 197 (1)- (6), 198, 204-207, 225, 229-232, 253, 255-257, & 282)
Railway Safety Act
Significant Projects Streamlining Act
South Coast British Columbia Transportation Authority Act
Transport of Dangerous Goods Act
Transportation Act
Transportation Investment Act
Minister, Hon. Blair Lekstrom
250-387-1978, Fax: 250-356-2290,
Minister.Transportation@gov.bc.ca;
blair.lekstrom.mla@leg.bc.ca
Deputy Minister, Grant Main
250-387-3280, Fax: 250-387-6431,
DeputyMinister.Transportation.gov.bc.ca;
Grant.Main@gov.bc.ca
Chief Operating Officer, Dave Byng
250-387-7671, Fax: 250-387-6431, Dave.Byng@gov.bc.ca
Executive Director, Pacific Gateway Branch, Lisa Gow
250-387-2672, Fax: 250-387-5812, Lisa.Gow@gov.bc.ca, Other Communications: Cell Phone: 250-514-6826
Executive Project Director, Pacific Gateway Branch, Shelagh Ryan-McNee
250-387-4568, Fax: 250-387-5812,
Shelagh.RyanMcNee@gov.bc.ca
Acting Director, Strategic Outreach & Business Engagement, Kathryn LeSueur
250-356-0745, Fax: 250-387-5812,
Kathryn.Lesueur@gov.bc.ca
Director, Strategic Human Resources, Nancy Merston
250-387-7823, Fax: 250-387-5334,
Nancy.Merston@gov.bc.ca

Associated Agencies, Boards & Commissions:
• British Columbia Ferry Services Inc.
• British Columbia Railway Company
#600, 221 West Esplanade
North Vancouver, BC V7M 3J3
604-678-4735 Fax: 604-678-4736
westerhouts@bcrco.com
www.bcrco.com

• British Columbia Transit
520 Gorge Rd. East
Victoria, BC V8W 2P3
250-385-2551 Fax: 250-995-5639
www.bctransit.com
Other Communication: Community transit information: transitinfo@bctransit.com; Media: pr@bctransit.com
A provincial crown agency, BC Transit coordinates the delivery of public transportation in British Columbia, outside the Greater Vancouver Regional District. The corporation's specific role, in accordance with the BC Transit Act, is the planning, acquisition, construction, operation, & maintenance of public passenger transportation systems & rail systems.
• Passenger Transportation Board
#202, 940 Blanshard St.
PO Box 9850 Prov Govt
Victoria, BC V8W 9T5
250-953-3777 Fax: 250-953-3788
ptboard@gov.bc.ca
www.ptboard.bc.ca
The Passenger Transportation Board carries out its responsibilities in accordance with the Passenger Transportation Act. The independent tribunal makes decisions regarding the operation of passenger directed vehicles and inter-city buses in British Columbia.

Finance & Management Services Department
PO Box 9850, Victoria, BC V8W 9T5
250-387-3100 Fax: 250-387-6431
Assistant Deputy Minister, Finance & Management Services, Nancy Bain
250-387-3100, Fax: 250-387-6431, Nancy.Bain@gov.bc.ca
Chief Financial Officer, Financial Management, Dave Stewart
250-387-7505, Fax: 250-356-7706, Dave.Stewart@gov.bc.ca, Other Communications: Cell Phone: 250-818-5806
Executive Director, Crown Agencies, Carol Bishop
250-387-1936, Fax: 250-356-7706, Carol.Bishop@gov.bc.ca, Other Communications: Cell Phone: 250-888-1251
Executive Director/Chief Information Officer, Information Management Branch, Debbie Fritz
250-387-3580, Fax: 250-356-7184, Debbie.Fritz@gov.bc.ca
Director, Reporting & Analysis, Gail Silvestrini
250-387-3104, Fax: 250-387-7645, Gail.Silvestrini@gov.bc.ca
Director, Finance (British Columbia Transportation Finance Authority), Gary So
250-387-7873, Fax: 250-387-7645, Gary.So@gov.bc.ca

Highways Department
PO Box 9850, Victoria, BC V8W 9T5
250-387-3260 Fax: 250-387-6431
Assistant Deputy Minister, Mike Proudfoot
250-387-3260, Fax: 250-387-6431, Dave.Duncan@gov.bc.ca
Chief Engineer, Dirk Nyland
250-387-2310, Fax: 250-387-7735, Dirk.Nyland@gov.bc.ca, Other Communications: Cell Phone: 250-812-6645
Executive Director, Highway Operations, Shanna Mason
250-387-0159, Fax: 250-387-6431, Shanna.Mason@gov.bc.ca, Other Communications: Cell Phone: 250-889-3707
Director, Provincial Field Services, Keith Callander
250-828-4151, Fax: 250-828-4277, Keith.Callander@gov.bc.ca, Other Communications: Cell Phone: 604-880-2336
Director, Construction & Maintenance, Rodney Chapman
250-387-7626, Fax: 250-356-8143, Rodney.Chapman@gov.bc.ca, Other Communications: Cell Phone: 250-213-7499
Director, Rehabilitation & Maintenance, Reg Fredrickson
250-387-7627, Fax: 250-356-7276, Reg.Fredrickson@gov.bc.ca, Other Communications: Cell Phone: 250-480-9729
Director, Social Media Branch, Russel Lolacher
250-356-9682, Fax: 250-356-8767, Russel.Lolacher@gov.bc.ca, Other Communications: Cell Phone: 778-679-2482
Director, Commercial Vehicle Safety & Enforcement Branch, Brian Murray
250-953-4024, Fax: 250-952-0578, Brian.Murray@gov.bc.ca, Other Communications: Cell Phone: 778-888-8436
Director, Business Management Branch, Sandra Toth Nacey
250-356-9768, Fax: 250-256-8767, Sandra.TothNacey@gov.bc.ca, Other Communications: Cell Phone: 778-679-2483
Director, Engineering Systems, Al Szczawinski
250-387-7777, Fax: 250-387-8081, Al.Szczawinski@gov.bc.ca

Partnerships Department
PO Box 9850 Prov Govt, Victoria, BC V8W 9T5
250-356-1403 Fax: 250-387-6431
Acting Assistant Deputy Minister, Kirsten Pedersen
Kirsten.Pedersen@gov.bc.ca
Executive Director, Partnerships, Vacant
Director, Properties & Land Management Branch, Svein Haugen
250-356-7904, Fax: 250-356-6970, Svein.Haugen@gov.bc.ca
Director, Transit Branch, Jim Hester
250-387-6024, Fax: 250-387-5012, Jim.Hester@gov.bc.ca
Director, Real Esate, Richard Myhill Jones
604-678-4703, Fax: 604-678-4702, Richard.MyhillJones@gov.bc.ca
Director, Procurement & Operations, Bruce McAllister
250-356-7108, Fax: 250-356-6970, Bruce.McAllister@gov.bc.ca
Director, Partnership & Project Development, Bob Steele
250-356-2051, Fax: 250-356-2112, Bob.Steele@gov.bc.ca

Transportation Policy & Programs Department
PO Box 9850 Prov Govt, Victoria, BC V8W 9T5
250-387-5062 Fax: 250-387-6431
Assistant Deputy Minister, Jacquie Dawes
250-387-5062, Fax: 250-387-6431, Jacquie.Dawes@gov.bc.ca
Registrar/Director, Passenger Transportation Branch, Dawn Major
604-453-4278, Dawn.Major@gov.bc.ca, Other Communications: Cell Phone: 604-992-9140
Acting Director, Transportation Policy Branch, Greg Gilks
250-387-0882, Fax: 250-356-0897, Greg.Gilks@gov.bc.ca

Infrasturcture Department
PO Box 9850 Prov Govt, Victoria, BC V8W 9T5
250-387-6742 Fax: 250-387-6431
Assistant Deputy Minister, Kevin Richter
250-387-6742, Fax: 250-387-6431, Kevin.Richter@gov.bc.ca
Executive Director, Planning & Programming Branch, David Marr
250-356-2100, Fax: 250-356-0897, David.Marr@gov.bc.ca
Acting Executive Project Director, Evergreen Line Project, Jon Buckle
604-927-4452, Fax: 604-927-4453, Jon.Buckle@gov.bc.ca
Director, Marine Branch, Krik Handrahan
250-952-0678, Fax: 250-356-0897, Kirk.Handrahan@gov.bc.ca
Director, Infrastructure Development, Renee Mounteney
250-953-3689, Fax: 250-356-0897, Renee.Mounteney@gov.bc.ca, Other Communications: Cell Phone: 250-208-8876

British Columbia Utilities Commission

900 Howe St., 6th Fl., PO Box 250, Vancouver, BC V6Z 2N3
604-660-4700 Fax: 604-660-1102
800-663-1385
commission.secretary@bcuc.com
www.bcuc.com
The British Columbia Utilities Commission is an independent regulatory agency of the Provincial Government of British Columbia. The Commission's regulates the province's natural gas & electricity utilities. Other activities of the Utilities Commission include the regulation of universal compulsory automobile insurance & intra-provincial pipelines.
Acts Administered:
Utilities Commission Act
Chair/Chief Executive Officer, Len Kelsey
604-660-4757, len.kelsey@bcuc.com
Commission Secretary, Erica Hamilton
604-660-4727, Erica.Hamilton@bcuc.com
Acting Commission Secretary, Alanna Gillis
604-660-4727, alanna.gillis@bcuc.com
Director, Strategic Services, Doug Chong
604-660-4737, doug.chong@bcuc.com
Director, Rates & Finance, Philip W. Nakoneshny
604-660-4736, philip.nakoneshny@bcuc.com
Director, Emerging Technologies & Innovation, Mark Thomas
604-660-4726, mark.thomas@bcuc.com
Director, Engineering & Energy Markets, Brian Williston
604-660-4773, brian.williston@bcuc.com

British Columbia Vital Statistics Agency

PO Box 9657 Prov Govt, Victoria, BC V8W 9P3
250-952-2681 Fax: 250-952-9097
VSOFFCEO@gov.bc.ca
www.vs.gov.bc.ca
The Vital Statistics Agency operates under the Ministry of Health, and offers the following services: Birth registration; marriage certificates; death certificates; wills; name changes; and geneaology.
Chief Executive Officer, Jack Shewchuk
250-952-9039, Fax: 250-952-9097, Jack.Shewchuk@gov.bc.ca
Director, Bruce Klette
250-952-9040, Fax: 250-952-9097, Bruce.Klette@gov.bc.ca

Workers' Compensation Board of British Columbia

PO Box 5350 Terminal, Vancouver, BC V6B 5L5
604-276-3100 Fax: 604-276-3247
888-621-7233
www.worksafebc.com
Other Communication: Head Office Physical Address: 6951 Westminster Hwy., Richmond, BC; Claims: 604-231-8888, Fax: 604-233-9777; Employer services/Assessments: 604-244-6181
The Workers' Compensation Board of British Columbia, or WorkSafeBC, assists workers & employers in British Columbia by promoting health & safety in workplaces. WorkSafeBC's key repsonsiblities are as follows: Consultation with & education of employers & workers; Monitoring compliance with the Occupational Health & Safety Regulation; & Provision of return-to-work compensation, rehabilitation, health care benefits, & other services for parties affected by work-related injuries or diseases.
Chair, George Morfitt
President/Chief Executive Officer, David Anderson
Chief Financial Officer/Senior Vice-President, Finance Division, Steve Barnett
Senior Vice-President, Corporate Affairs, Roberta Ellis
Senior Vice-President, Operations, Diana Miles
Vice-President, Human Resources & Facilities, Pamela Cohen
Vice-President, Claims Services, Ian Munroe
Vice-President, Prevention Services, Betty Pirs
Vice-President, Industry Services & Sustainability, Donna Wilson
General Counsel & Secretary, Ed Bates

Government of Manitoba

Seat of Government: Legislative Building, Rm. 237, Winnipeg, MB R3C 0V8
204-945-3636 Fax: 204-948-2507
clerkla@leg.gov.mb.ca
www.gov.mb.ca
The Province of Manitoba entered Confederation July 15, 1870. It has an area of 647,797 km2, & the StatsCan census population in 2008 was 1,196,291.

Office of the Lieutenant Governor

Legislative Building, #235, 450 Broadway Ave., Winnipeg, MB R3C 0V8
204-945-2753 Fax: 204-945-4329
ltgov@leg.gov.mb.ca
www.lg.gov.mb.ca
Lieutenant Governor, Hon. Philip S. Lee, C.M., O.M.
Chief of Staff/ Private Secretary, Phyllis Fraser
204-945-2752, phyllis.fraser@leg.gov.mb.ca
Scheduling Coordinator, Elaine Embury
204-945-2753, elaine.embury@leg.gov.mb.ca
Government House Event Coordinator, Lisa Vermette
204-945-2753, lisa.vermette@leg.gov.mb.ca

Office of the Premier

Legislative Building, #204, 450 Broadway Ave., Winnipeg, MB R3C 0V8
204-945-3714 Fax: 204-949-1484
premier@leg.gov.mb.ca
www.gov.mb.ca
Premier, Hon. Greg Selinger
204-945-3714, Fax: 204-949-1484
Deputy Premier, Hon. Rosann Wowchuk
204-945-3952, Fax: 204-945-6057
Clerk of the Executive Council & Cabinet Secretary, Paul Vogt
204-945-5640, Fax: 204-945-8390
Chief of Staff, Michael Balagus
204-945-8753
Administrative Officer, Sonia Stubler
204-945-1494
Press Secretary to Cabinet, Rachel Morgan
204-945-1494

Manitoba Government Office - Ottawa
#908, 130 Albert St., Ottawa, ON K1P 5G4
613-233-4228 Fax: 613-233-3509
Reports to the Clerk of the Executive Council on Federal-Provincial issues & to the Minister of Intergovernmental Affairs & Trade on business & procurement issues.
Senior Representative, Jim Stewart

Executive Council

Legislative Building, 450 Broadway Ave., Winnipeg, MB R3C 0V8
www.gov.mb.ca/minister
Premier & President, Executive Council; Minister, Federal-Provincial Relations; Minister responsible for Francophone affairs, Hon. Greg Selinger
204-945-3714, Fax: 204-949-1484, premier@leg.gov.mb.ca

Minister, Infrastructure & Transportation; Minister responsible for Emergency Measures, Hon. Steve Ashton
204-945-3723, Fax: 204-945-7610, minmit@leg.gov.mb.ca
Minister, Conservation, Innovation, Energy & Mines, Hon. David Walter Chomiak
204-945-5356, Fax: 204-948-2692, miniem@leg.gov.mb.ca
Note: Chomiak is also Keeper of The Great Seal & the Minister charged with the administrationof the Manitoba Gaming Control Act.
Deputy Premier; Minister, Finance; Minister responsible for the Civil Service; Minister responsible for the Manitoba Securities Commission, Hon. Rosann Wowchuk
204-945-3952, Fax: 204-945-6057, minfin@leg.gov.mb.ca
Minister, Family Services & Consumer Affairs, Hon. Gord Mackintosh
204-945-4173, Fax: 204-945-5149, minfam@leg.gov.mb.ca
Deputy Premier; Minister, Aboriginal & Northern Affairs; Minister responsible for sport, Aboriginal Education & East Side Road Authority, Hon. Eric Robinson
204-945-3719, Fax: 204-945-8374, minna@leg.gov.mb.ca
Minister, Advanced Education & Literacy; Minister responsible for International Education, Hon. Diane McGifford
204-945-0825, Fax: 204-948-2216, minaed@leg.gov.mb.ca
Minister, Local Government, Hon. Ron Lemieux
204-945-3788, Fax: 204-945-1383, minlg@leg.gov.mb.ca
Minister, Agriculture, Food & Rural Initiatives, Finance, Hon. Stan Struthers
204-945-3722, Fax: 204-945-3470, minagr@leg.gov.mb.ca
Minister, Education, Hon. Nancy Allan
204-945-3720, Fax: 204-945-1291, minedu@leg.gov.mb.ca
Note: Gregory Selinger is also the Minister Responsible for the Civil Service Commission & Manitoba Hydro.
Minister, Healthy Living, Youth & Seniors; Minister responsible for Healthy Child Manitoba, Mental Health & Recreation, Hon. Jim Rondeau
204-945-1373, Fax: 204-945-2703, Minhliv@leg.gov.mb.ca
Minister, Entrepreneurship, Training & Trade, Hon. Peter Bjornson
204-945-0067, Fax: 204-945-4882, minett@leg.gov.mb.ca
Minister, Water Stewardship, Hon. Christine Melnick
204-945-1133, Fax: 204-948-2684, minwsd@leg.gov.mb.ca
Minister, Health, Hon. Theresa Oswald
204-945-3731, Fax: 204-945-0441, minhlt@leg.gov.mb.ca
Minister, Housing & Community Development; Minister responsible, Neighbourhoods Alive!, Community Places & Co-operative Development, Hon. Kerri Irvin-Ross
204-945-6190, Fax: 204-945-1491, minhcd@leg.gov.mb.ca
Attorney General; Minister, Justice; Minister responsible for Constitutional Affairs, Hon. Andrew Swan
204-945-3728, Fax: 204-945-2517, minjus@leg.gov.mb.ca
Minister, Labour & Immigration; Minister responsible for the Status of Women & Persons with Disabilities, Hon. Jennifer Howard
204-945-4079, Fax: 204-945-8312, minlab@leg.gov.mb.ca
Minister, Culture, Heritage & Tourism, Hon. Flor Marcelino
204-945-3729, Fax: 204-945-5223, mincht@leg.gov.mb.ca
Government House Leader; Minister, Minister of Advanced Education & Literacy, Hon. Erin Selby
204-945-0825, Fax: 204-948-2216, minaed@leg.gov.mb.ca

Cabinet Office
Legislative Assistant to the Premier, Bidhu Jha
204-945-6021, bjha@leg.gov.mb.ca
Legislative Assistant, Agriculture, Food & Rural Initiatives, Thomas Nevakshonoff
204-945-4966, tnevakshonoff@leg.gov.mb.ca
Legislative Assistant, Brandon & Western Manitoba, Drew Caldwell
Legislative Assistant, Culture, Heritage, Tourism & Sport, Flor Marcelino
Legislative Assistant, Family Services & Housing, Doug Martindale
204-945-2645, dmartindale@leg.gov.mb.ca
Legislative Assistant, Labour & Immigration, Justice, Marilyn Brick

Cabinet Committees
Community & Economic Development Committee Treasury Board Committee

Legislative Assembly

c/o Clerk's Office, Legislative Bldg., #237, 450 Broadway, Winnipeg, MB R3C 0V8
204-945-3636 Fax: 204-948-2507
clerkla@leg.gov.mb.ca
www.gov.mb.ca/legislature
Clerk of the Legislative Assembly, Patricia Chaychuk
204-945-3636, clerk@leg.gov.mb.ca
Speaker of the House, Hon. Daryl Reid
204-945-3706, speaker@leg.gov.mb.ca
Chief Electoral Officer, Vacant
204-945-3225, 866-628-6837, Fax: 204-945-6011, election@elections.mb.ca
Ombudsman, Irene Hamilton
204-982-9130, 800-665-0531, Fax: 204-942-7803, ombudsma@ombudsman.mb.ca
Commissioner, Conflict of Interest, Ron Perozzo
204-948-1018, Fax: 204-945-4585
Children's Advocate, Ms. Billie Schibler
204-988-7440, 800-263-7146, Fax: 204-988-7472, bschibler@childrensadvocate.mb.ca
Manager, Investigation, Access and Privacy, Nancy Love
204-982-9130, nancy.love@gov.mb.ca
Auditor General, Carol Bellringer
204-945-3790, carol.bellringer@gov.mb.ca
ADM/Chief Financial Officer, Mala Sachdeva
204-945-2540, mala.sachdeva@gov.mb.ca
Journals Clerk, Claude Michaud
204-945-6331

Government Caucus Office (New Democratic Party)
Legislative Bldg., #234, 450 Broadway Ave., Winnipeg, MB R3C 0V8
204-945-3710 Fax: 204-948-2005
www.ndpcaucus.mb.ca
Premier & Leader, Hon. Greg Selinger
204-945-3714, Fax: 204-949-1484, premier@leg.gov.mb.ca
Deputy Premier, Hon. Rosann Wowchuk
204-945-3722, Fax: 204-945-3470
Government House Leader, Hon. David Walter Chomiak
204-945-3728, Fax: 204-945-2517

Progressive Conservative Caucus Office
Legislative Building, #227, 450 Broadway Ave., Winnipeg, MB R3C 0V8
204-945-3709 Fax: 204-945-1284
800-282-8069
pccaucus@leg.gov.mb.ca
www.manpc.mb.ca
Leader of the Opposition, Hugh McFadyen
204-945-3593, Fax: 204-945-1299, hugh.mcfadyen@leg.gov.mb.ca
Communications Officer, Liz Peters
204-945-5519, Fax: 204-945-5921, liz.peters@leg.gov.mb.ca

Office of the Liberal Party of Canada in Manitoba
635 Broadway Ave., Winnipeg, MB R3C 0X1
204-988-9380 Fax: 204-284-1492
manager@manitobaliberals.ca
mlp.manitobaliberals.ca
Leader, Hon. Jon Gerrard
204-945-5194, Fax: 204-948-3220, jon.gerrard@leg.gov.mb.ca

Legislative Committees
Legislative Building, #249, 450 Broadway Ave., Winnipeg, MB R3C 0V8
Fax: 204-945-0038
Contact, Committee Clerks, Rick Yarish
204-945-4729, rick.yarish@leg.gov.mb.ca

Fortieth Legislature - Manitoba

Legislative Building, 450 Broadway Ave., Winnipeg, MB R3C 0V8
204-945-3636 Fax: 204-948-2507
clerkla@leg.gov.mb.ca
www.gov.mb.ca/legislature

Last General Election: Oct 04, 2011. Legal Duration: 5 Years. Party Standings (October 2011): New Democratic Party (NDP) - 37; Progressive Conservative (PC) - 19; Liberal (Lib.) - 1; Total - 57. Salaries, Indemnities & Allowances (April 2008): Members' basic annual indemnity - $83,722. In addition to this annual indemnity are the following annual salaries: Premier - $68,425; Cabinet Ministers (with portfolio) - $44,942; Cabiniet Ministers (without portfolio) - $39,837; Leader of the Official Opposition - $44,942; Leader of a Recognized Opposition Party - $39,837; Speaker - $44,942; Deputy Speaker - $8,852; Government House Leader - $8,852; House Leader of the Official Opposition - $6,323; House Leader of a Recognized Opposition Party - $5,060; Government Whip - $6,323; Whip of the Official Opposition - $5,060; Whip of a Recognized Opposition Party - $3,796; Caucus Chair - $5,450; Permanent Chairperson, Standing or Special Committees - $3,796. The following is a list of members of the legislative assembly, with their constituency, party affiliation, & contact information

Members
Hon. Nancy Allan, MLA, St. Vital, New Democratic Party
204-945-3720, Fax: 204-945-1291, minedu@leg.gov.mb.ca
Rob Altemeyer, MLA, Wolseley, New Democratic Party
204-945-5985, Fax: 204-948-2005, rob.altemeyer@leg.gov.mb.ca
Hon. Steve Ashton, Thompson, New Democratic Party
204-945-3723, Fax: 204-945-7610, minmit@leg.gov.mb.ca
Hon. Peter Bjornson, Gimli, New Democratic Party
204-945-3720, Fax: 204-945-1291, minett@leg.gov.mb.ca
Sharon Blady, Kirkfield Park, New Democratic Party
204-945-0932, Fax: 204-948-2005, sharon.blady@leg.gov.mb.ca
Hon. Jim Maloway, Elmwood, New Democratic Party
204-945-3710, jim.maloway@leg.gov.mb.ca
Reg Helwer, Brandon West, Progressive Conservative
204-945-8165, Fax: 204-942-6613, reg.helwer@leg.gov.mb.ca
Erna Braun, Rossmere, New Democratic Party
204-945-7349, Fax: 204-948-2005, erna.braun@leg.gov.mb.ca
Dave Gaudreau, St. Norbert, New Democratic Party
204-945-5479, Fax: 204-948-2005, dave.gaudreau@leg.gov.mb.ca
Stuart Briese, Ste. Rose, Progressive Conservative
204-945-4698, Fax: 204-948-2092, stuart.briese@leg.gov.mb.ca
Drew Caldwell, Brandon East, New Democratic Party
204-945-3081, Fax: 204-948-2005, drew.caldwell@leg.gov.mb.ca
Hon. David Walter Chomiak, Kildonan, New Democratic Party
204-945-5356, Fax: 204-948-2692, miniem@leg.gov.mb.ca
Cliff Cullen, Turtle Mountain, Progressive Conservative
204-945-5083, Fax: 204-945-5921, cliff.cullen@leg.gov.mb.ca
Len Derkach, Russell, Progressive Conservative
204-945-4812, Fax: 204-948-2092, len.derkach@leg.gov.mb.ca
Gregory Dewar, Selkirk, New Democratic Party
204-945-0143, Fax: 204-948-2005, greg.dewar@leg.gov.mb.ca
Myrna Driedger, Charleswood, Progressive Conservative
204-945-3280, Fax: 204-945-5921, myrna.driedger@leg.gov.mb.ca
Peter George Dyck, Pembina, Progressive Conservative
204-945-4469, Fax: 204-948-2092, peter.dyck@leg.gov.mb.ca
Ralph Eichler, Lakeside, Progressive Conservative
204-945-0541, Fax: 204-948-2092, ralph.eichler@leg.gov.mb.ca
Ian Wishart, Portage la Prairie, Progressive Conservative
204-945-8088, Fax: 204-942-6613, ian.wishart@leg.gov.mb.ca
Hon. Jon Gerrard, River Heights, Liberal
204-945-5194, Fax: 204-948-3220, jon.gerrard@leg.gov.mb.ca
Kelvin Goertzen, Steinbach, Progressive Conservative
204-945-0231, Fax: 204-942-6613, kelvin.goertzen@leg.gov.mb.ca
Cliff Graydon, Emerson, Progressive Conservative
204-945-5639, Fax: 204-942-6613, cliff.graydon@leg.gov.mb.ca
Wayne Ewasko, Lac du Bonnet, Progressive Conservative
204-945-8989, Fax: 204-945-6613, wayne.ewasko@leg.gov.mb.ca
Hon. Kevin Chief, Point Douglas, New Democratic Party
204-945-3710, kevin.chief@leg.gov.mb.ca
Hon. Jennifer Howard, Fort Rouge, New Democratic Party
204-945-4079, Fax: 204-945-8312, minlab@leg.gov.mb.ca
Hon. James Allum, Fort Garry, New Democratic Party
204-945-3710, james.allum@leg.gov.mb.ca
Clarence Petterson, Flin Flon, New Democratic Party
204-945-3710, clarence.pettersen@leg.gov.mb.ca
Bidhu Jha, Radisson, New Democratic Party
204-945-6021, Fax: 204-948-2005, bidhu.jha@leg.gov.mb.ca
Deanne Crothers, St. James, New Democratic Party
204-945-3710, deanne.crothers@leg.gov.mb.ca
Kevin Lamourex, Inkster, Liberal
204-945-5194, Fax: 204-948-3220, kevin.lamoureux@leg.gov.mb.ca
Hon. Dennis Smook, La Verendrye, Progressive Conservative
204-945-4339, Fax: 204-942-6613, dennis.smook@leg.gov.mb.ca
Hon. Gord Mackintosh, St. Johns, New Democratic Party
204-945-4173, Fax: 204-945-5149, minfam@leg.gov.mb.ca
Larry Maguire, Arthur-Virden, Progressive Conservative
204-945-4975, Fax: 204-948-2092, larry.maguire@leg.gov.mb.ca
Hon. Flor Marcelino, Wellington, New Democratic Party
204-945-3729, Fax: 204-945-5229, mincht@leg.gov.mb.ca
Melanie Wight, Burrows, New Democratic Party
204-945-3710, melanie.wight@leg.gov.mb.ca
Hugh McFadyen, Fort Whyte, Progressive Conservative
204-945-3593, Fax: 204-945-1299, hugh.mcfadyen@leg.gov.mb.ca
Hon. Diane McGifford, Lord Roberts, New Democratic Party
204-945-0825, Fax: 204-948-2216, minaed@leg.gov.mb.ca
Hon. Christine Melnick, Riel, New Democratic Party
204-945-1133, Fax: 204-948-2684, minwsd@leg.gov.mb.ca
Bonnie Mitchelson, River East, Progressive Conservative
204-945-0008, Fax: 204-942-6613, bonnie.mitchelson@leg.gov.mb.ca
Thomas G. Nevakshonoff, Interlake, New Democratic Party
204-945-4966, Fax: 204-948-2005, tom.nevakshonoff@leg.gov.mb.ca
Hon. Theresa Oswald, Seine River, New Democratic Party
204-945-3731, Fax: 204-945-0441, minhlt@leg.gov.mb.ca

Blaine Pedersen, Carman, Progressive Conservative
204-945-7909, Fax: 204-948-2092,
blaine.pedersen@leg.gov.mb.ca
Daryl Gary Reid, Transcona, New Democratic Party
204-945-0774, Fax: 204-948-2005, daryl.reid@leg.gov.mb.ca
Hon. Eric Robinson, Rupertsland, New Democratic Party
204-945-3719, Fax: 204-945-8374, minna@leg.gov.mb.ca
Hon. Jim Rondeau, Assiniboia, New Democratic Party
204-945-1373, Fax: 204-948-2703, minhliv@leg.gov.mb.ca
Leanne Rowat, Minnedosa, Progressive Conservative
204-945-0258, Fax: 204-942-6613,
leanne.rowat@leg.gov.mb.ca
Mohinder Saran, The Maples, New Democratic Party
204-945-3153, Fax: 204-948-2005,
mohinder.saran@leg.gov.mb.ca
Ron Schuler, Springfield, Progressive Conservative
204-945-4321, Fax: 204-942-6613,
ron.schuler@leg.gov.mb.ca
Erin Selby, Southdale, New Democratic Party
204-945-1190, Fax: 204-948-2005, erin.selby@leg.gov.mb.ca
Hon. Gregory F. Selinger, St. Boniface, New Democratic Party
204-945-3417, Fax: 204-949-1484, premier@leg.gov.mb.ca
Heather Stefanson, Tuxedo, Progressive Conservative
204-945-0827, Fax: 204-945-5921,
heather.stefanson@leg.gov.mb.ca
Hon. Stan Struthers, Dauphin-Roblin, New Democratic Party
204-945-3722, Fax: 204-945-3470, minagr@leg.gov.mb.ca
Hon. Andrew Swan, Minto, New Democratic Party
204-945-3728, Fax: 204-945-2517, minjus@leg.gov.mb.ca
Mavis Taillieu, Morris, Progressive Conservative
204-945-3525, Fax: 204-942-6613,
mavis.taillieu@leg.gov.mb.ca
Frank Whitehead, The Pas, New Democratic Party
204-945-1696, Fax: 204-945-2005,
frank.whitehead@leg.gov.mb.ca
Matt Wiebe, Concordia, New Democratic Party
204-945-6244, Fax: 204-948-2005,
matt.wiebe@leg.gov.mb.ca
Hon. Ron Kostyshyn, Swan River, New Democratic Party
204-945-3710, ron.kostyshyn@leg.gov.mb.ca

Associated Agencies, Boards & Commissions:
• Progressive Conservative Party
Legislative Bldg
#227, 450 Broadway
Winnipeg, MB R3C 0V8
204-945-3709 Fax: 204-945-1284 800-282-8069
pccaucus@leg.gov.mb.ca
www.manpc.mb.ca
• New Democratic Party
Legislative Bldg
#234, 450 Broadway
Winnipeg, MB R3C 0V8
204-945-3710 Fax: 204-948-2005
www.ndpcaucus.mb.ca/newCaucus
• Liberal Party
Legislative Bldg
#169, 450 Broadway
Winnipeg, MB R3C 0V8
204-945-5194 Fax: 204-948-3220
jgerrard@leg.gov.mb.ca

Manitoba Government Departments & Agencies

Manitoba Aboriginal & Northern Affairs

Legislative Bldg, 344-450 Broadway, Winnipeg, MB R3C 0V8
204-945-3719 Fax: 204-945-8374
anaweb@gov.mb.ca
www.gov.mb.ca/ana/

To improve the quality of life & opportunities for Aboriginal & Northern people. To facilitate better services, opportunities & results for Manitoba's Aboriginal & northern people. Goals are: to support the mental, emotional, physical & spiritual health of northern communities & Aboriginal people; to resolve outstanding provincial obligations to Aboriginal/northern communities; to foster self-determination, accountability & sustainable growth; to strengthen the participation of Aboriginal & northern people in Manitoba's economy

Acts Administered:
Manitoba Floodway and East Side Road Authority Act
Northern Affairs Act
Planning Act
Minister, Hon. Eric Robinson
204-945-3719, Fax: 204-954-8374, minna@leg.gov.mb.ca
Deputy Minister, Harvey Bostrom
204-945-0565, Fax: 204-945-1256, dmna@leg.gov.mb.ca
Director, Finance & Administrative Services, Justin Nedd
204-677-6609, Fax: 204-677-6753
Executive Director, Local Government Development Division, Freda Albert
204-677-6795
Director, Policy and Strategic Initiatives, Eleanor Brokington
204-945-0572

Director, Agreements Management, Dave Hicks
204-945-2506

Associated Agencies, Boards & Commissions:
• Communities Economic Development Fund
#100, 23 Station Rd.
Thompson, MB R8N 0N6
204-778-4138 Fax: 204-778-4313 800-561-4315
www.cedf.mb.ca

Aboriginal Affairs Secretariat
#200, 500 Portage Ave., Winnipeg, MB R3C 3X1
204-945-2510 Fax: 204-945-3689

Executive Director, Joe Morriseau
204-945-3689, Fax: 204-945-3689, jmorrissea@gov.mb.ca

Agreements Management
#200, 500 Portage Ave., Winnipeg, MB R3C 3X1
204-945-8337 Fax: 204-945-3689

Director, David Hicks
204-945-2506, Fax: 204-945-3689, dhicks@gov.mb.ca

Local Government Development Division
59 Elizabeth Dr., PO Box 33, Thompson, MB R8N 1X4
204-677-6794 Fax: 204-677-6525

Provides support to 50 northern & remote communities, including public works, environmental services, infrastructure development. Promotes cooperative, community-driven sustainable development
Executive Director, Freda Albert
204-677-6795, falbert@gov.mb.ca
Director, Program Planning & Development, Jeff Gordon
204-945-1713, jgordon@gov.mb.ca

Regional Offices:

Dauphin
Provincial Bldg., 27 Second Ave. SW, PO Box 15, Dauphin, MB R7N 3E5
204-622-2110 Fax: 204-622-2305
Regional Director, Karen Barker
kbarker@gov.mb.ca

Thompson
59 Elizabeth Dr., PO Box 27, Thompson, MB R8N 1X4
204-677-6786 Fax: 204-677-6525
Regional Director, Jean Merasty
jmerasty@gov.mb.ca

Manitoba Advanced Education & Literacy

Legislative Building, #162, 450 Broadway Ave., Winnipeg, MB R3C 0V8
204-945-0825 Fax: 204-948-2216
minaed@leg.gov.mb.ca
www.edu.gov.mb.ca

Acts Administered:
Adult Learning Centres Act
Adult Literacy Act
Advanced Education Administration Act
Brandon University Act
Colleges Act
Council on Post-Secondary Education Act
Degree Granting Act
Private Vocational Institutions Act
Student Aid Act
University College of the North Act
University of Manitoba Act
University of Winnipeg Act
Minister, Hon. Erin Selby
204-945-0825, Fax: 204-948-2216, minaed@leg.gov.mb.ca
Deputy Minister, Heather Reichert
204-945-1648, Fax: 204-945-8330, dmedu@leg.gov.mb.ca
Director, Human Resources, Robert Berube
204-945-6892
Manager, Pay & Benefits, Peggy Fontaine
204-945-6890
Director, Financial and Administrative Sevices, Claude Fortier
204-945-1117

Associated Agencies, Boards & Commissions:
• Council on Post-Secondary Education
#608, 330 Portage Ave.
Winnipeg, MB R3C 0C4
204-945-1833 Fax: 204-945-1841
info@copse.mb.ca
www.copse.mb.ca

Council on Post-Secondary Education
#608, 330 Portage Ave., Winnipeg, MB R3C 0C4
204-945-1833 Fax: 204-945-1841
info@copse.mb.ca
www.copse.mb.ca

Deputy Minister, Adult Learning and Literacy, Lynette Plett
204-945-4399, Fax: 204-948-1008
Manager, Policy Development & Analysis, Dan Smith
204-945-4720

Chief Financial Officer, Carlos Matias
204-945-1839
Director, Institutional Relations, Josh Watt
204-945-8597

College Expansion Initiative Branch
#401, 1181 Portage Ave., Winnipeg, MB R3G 0T3
204-945-5150 Fax: 204-948-2676
www.copse.mb.ca/en/cei/

Manager, College Relations, COPSE, Ray Karasevich
ray.karasevich@gov.mb.ca

Aboriginal Education Directorate
Director, Helen Robinson-Settee
204-945-4763
Program Manager & Evaluation Consultant, Dino Altieri
204-945-6181

Manitoba Agriculture, Food & Rural Initiatives

Legislative Bldg., 165-450 Broadway, Winnipeg, MB R3C 0V8
204-945-3722 Fax: 204-945-3470
minagr@leg.gov.mb.ca
www.gov.mb.ca/agriculture/

Acts Administered:
Agricultural Producers' Organization Funding Act
Manitoba Agricultural Services Corporation Act
Agricultural Societies Act
Department of Agriculture, Food and Rural Initiatives Act
Agrologists Act
Animal Care Act
Animal Diseases Act
Animal Liability Act
Cattle Producers Association Act
Coarse Grain Marketing Control Act
Community development Bonds Act
Crown Lands Act, (in part) Sections 6, 7, 10, 12 (1), 14, 16, 17, 18, 21, 23, 24 to 28 both inclusive
Dairy Act
Family Farm Protection Act
Farm Income Assurance Plans Act
Farm Lands Ownership Act
Farm Machinery & Equipment Act
Farm Practices Protection Act
Food Safety Act
Fruit & Vegetable Sales Act
Horse Racing Commission Act
Income Tax Act
Land Rehabilitation Act
Livestock Industry Diversification Act
Livestock & Livestock Products Act
Milk Prices Review Act
Natural Products Marketing Act
Noxious Weeds Act
Organic Agricultural Products Act
Pesticides & Fertilizers Control Act
Plant Pests and Diseases Act
Property Tax and Insulation Assistance Act
Seed & Fodder Relief Act
Veterinary Medical Act
Veterinary Science Scholarship Fund Act
Veterinary Services Act
Wildlife Act, (in part) Section 89 (e)
Women's Institute Act
Minister, Hon. Stan Struthers
204-945-3722, Fax: 204-945-3470, minagr@leg.gov.mb.ca
Deputy Minister, Barry Todd
204-945-3734, Fax: 204-948-2095, dmagr@leg.gov.mb.ca
Executive Director, Strategic Planning, Maurice Bouvier
204-792-5406
Chief Veterinary Officer, Food Safety Knowledge Centre, Wayne Lees
204-945-7685
Director, Crops Knowledge Centre, Mike Kagan
204-745-5653
Director, Land Use Planning Knowledge Centre, Robert Fleming
204-867-6551

Associated Agencies, Boards & Commissions:
• Agricultural Societies
1129 Queens Ave.
Brandon, MB R7A 1L9
204-726-6195 Fax: 204-726-6260
Promotes improvement in agriculture & development of Manitoba agricultural products. Provide organizational assistance to rural & urban people.
• Farm Lands Ownership Board
#812, Norquay Bldg.
401 York Ave.
Winnipeg, MB R3C 0P8
204-945-3149 Fax: 204-945-1489 800-282-8069
robert.mckenzie@gov.mb.ca
www.web2gov.mb.ca/agriculture/programs/

• Farm Machinery Board
Norquay Bldg.
#812, 401 York Ave.
Winnipeg, MB R3C 0P8
204-945-3856 Fax: 204-948-2844
randy.ozunko@gov.mb.ca
www.web2.gov.mb.ca/agriculture/programs/
• Food Development Centre
810 Phillips St.
PO Box 1240
Portage la Prairie, MB R1N 3J9
204-239-3150 Fax: 204-239-3180 800-870-1044
www.gov.mb.ca/agriculture/fdc
The Food Development Centre (FDC) is a Special Operating Agency of Manitoba Agriculture, Food and Rural Initiatives (MAFRI). Its mandate is to assist the agri-food industry in the development and commercialization of conventional and functional foods and natural health products.
• Manitoba Agricultural Services Corporation (MASC)
#100, 1525 First St. South
Brandon, MB R7A 7A1
204-726-6850 Fax: 204-726-6849
mailbox@masc.mb.ca
www.masc.mb.ca
Formerly the Manitoba Agricultural Credit Corporation & the Manitoba Crop Insurance Corporation. Manitoba Agricultural Services Corporation (MASC) fully supports the province's producers and rural communities, through innovative and targeted risk management and financial programs. MASC is represented across Manitoba by 19 insurance offices and 16 lending offices, with corporate offices located in Portage la Prairie and Brandon.
• Manitoba Farm Mediation Board
c/o Boards, Commissions & Legislation Branch
#812, 401 York Ave.
Winnipeg, MB R3C 0P8
204-945-0357 Fax: 204-945-1489
robert.mckenzie@gov.mb.ca
www.web2.gov.mb.ca/agriculture/programs/
Mediates options to legal action by creditors when farmers cannot meet their obligations.
• Farm Practices Protection Board
c/o Boards, Commissions & Legislation Branch
#812, 401 York Ave.
Winnipeg, MB R3C 0P8
204-945-0630 Fax: 204-948-2844
www.web2.gov.mb.ca/agriculture/programs/
• Farm Products Marketing Council
c/o Boards, Commissions & Legislation Branch
#812, 401 York Ave.
Winnipeg, MB R3C 0P8
204-945-4495 Fax: 204-948-2844
gordon.mackenzie@gov.mb.ca
www.web2.gov.mb.ca/agriculture/programs/
• Manitoba Horse Racing Commission
c/o Boards, Commissions & Legislation Branch
#812, 401 York Ave.
Winnipeg, MB R3C 0P8
204-945-4495 Fax: 204-948-2844
gordon.mackenzie@gov.mb.ca
www.web2.gov.mb.ca/agriculture/programs/
Governs, directs, controls, & regulates horse racing & the operation of all race tracks in Manitoba.
• Manitoba Milk Prices Review Commission
c/o Boards, Commissions & Legislation Branch
#812, 401 York Ave.
Winnipeg, MB R3C 0P8
204-945-3854 Fax: 204-948-2844
randy.ozunko@gov.mb.ca
www.web2.gov.mb.ca/agriculture/programs/

Agri-Food & Rural Development Division
Asst. Deputy Minister, Gerald Huebner
204-945-3735
Executive Director, Strategic Planning Directorate, Mona Cornock
204-726-7192
Director, Food Commercialization & Marketing Knowledge Centre, Randy Stoyko
204-795-2437
Director, GO Teams, Gerald Huebner
204-797-4522, Fax: 204-886-3657

Growing Opportunities (GO) Offices:

North Interlake
317 River Rd., PO Box 2000, Arborg, MB R0C 0A0
Fax: 204-376-3311
GO Team Manager, Susan Nicoll
204-641-1454

South Interlake
77 Main St., PO Box 70, Teulon, MB R0C 3B0
Fax: 204-886-3657
GO Team Manager, Wray Whitmore

Red River
67 - 2 St. NE, PO Box 969, Altona, MB R0G 0B0
Fax: 204-324-2803
GO Team Leader, Jacquie Cherewayko

Central Plains
Morris Ave., PO Box 532, Gladstone, MB R0J 0T0
204-871-4219
GO Team Leader, Dennis Beernaert

Pembina
279 Carlton St., PO Box 189, Somerset, MB R0G 2L0
GO Team Leader, Shane Dobson

Southwest
247 Wellington St., PO Box 850, Virden, MB R0M 2C0
Fax: 204-748-4775
GO Team Manager, John Corbey
204-851-2442

South Parkland
221 Elm St., Hwy 21 N, PO Box 50, Hamiota, MB R0M 0T0
GO Team Manager, Gwenda Skayman

Valleys North
120 - 6th Ave. North, PO Box 370, Swan River, MB R0L 1Z0
Fax: 204-734-5271
GO Team Manager, Allen Muggaberg

Eastman
20 First St. South, PO Box 50, Beausejour, MB R0E 0C0
204-268-6099 Fax: 204-268-6060
GO Team Manager, Shaunda Rossington

North Parkland
27 - Second Ave. SW, Dauphin, MB R7N 3E5
Fax: 204-734-5271
GO Team Manager, Debra Watson

Agri-Industry Development & Innovation Division
Asst. Deputy Minister, Allan Preston
204-945-3736
Acting Director, Agri-Environment, Leloni Scott
204-745-5658
Director, Agri-Food Innovation & Adaptation, Daryl Domitruk
204-745-0214
Director, Crops, Mike Kagan
204-745-5653
Director, Food Safety & Chief Veterinary Office, Dr. John Taylor
204-945-7690, Fax: 204-945-4327
Acting Director, Land Use Planning & Manager, Agricultural Crown Lands, Robert Fleming
204-867-6551

Regional Agricultural Services Division
Acting Asst. Deputy Minister, Dory Gingera-Beauchemin
204-945-3735
Director, Agricultural Crown Lands Branch, Dennis Hodgson
204-867-3419, Fax: 204-867-5696

Office of the Auditor General

#500, 330 Portage Ave., Winnipeg, MB R3C 0C4
204-945-3790 Fax: 204-945-2169
oag.contact@oag.mb.ca
www.oag.mb.ca

Established under The Auditor General Act, the Office of the Auditor General is an independent office of the Legislative Assembly. Through audit of management practices & accountability reports, the Office contributes to effective governance & public trust
Auditor General, Carol Bellringer, FCA, MBA
cbellringer@aog.mb.ca
Deputy Auditor General, Mala Sachdeva, CA
204-945-2686
Executive Director, Strategic Initiatives, Norman Ricard, CA
204-945-2782
Executive Director, Quality Assurance & Professional Practice, Greg MacBeth, CA
204-945-6883
Director, Special Audits, Jack Buckwold, BA, B. Comm.
204-945-1620

Manitoba Civil Service Commission

#935, 155 Carlton St., Winnipeg, MB R3C 3H8
204-945-2332 Fax: 204-945-1486
800-282-8069
cschrp@gov.mb.ca
www.gov.mb.ca/csc/

Acts Administered:
The Civil Service Act
Employment Standards Code
Freedom of Information & Protection of Privacy Act
Labour Relations Act
Manitoba Act
Personal Health Information Act
Minister responsible, Hon. Gregory F. Selinger
204-945-3952, Fax: 204-945-6057, minfin@leg.gov.mb.ca
Deputy Minister & Commissioner, Debra Woodgate

Associated Agencies, Boards & Commissions:
• Civil Service Commission Board
#935, 155 Carlton St.
Winnipeg, MB R3C 3H8
204-945-1435 Fax: 204-945-1486

Manitoba Entrepreneurship,Training & Trade

#1000, 259 Portage Ave, Winnipeg, MB R3B 3P4
204-945-2475 Fax: 204-945-3977
minctt@leg.gov.mb.ca
www.gov.mb.ca

Mission is to support the growth of business in the province, meet provincial labour demands, increase training opportunities, and expand global trade relations
Acts Administered:
Biofuels Act
Crocus Investment Fund
Design Institute Act
Development Corporations Act
Economic Innovation & Technology Council Act
Electronic Commerce & Information Act (except part 5)
Energy Act
Gas Allocation Act
Gas Pipe Line Act
Greater Winnipeg Gas Distribution Act (S.M. 1988-89, C.40)
Income Tax Act (S. 7.5 & 7.10)
Labour-Sponsored Venture Capital Corporations Act
Manitoba Health Research Council Act
Mines & Minerals Act
Mining & Metallurgy Compensation Act
Oil & Gas Act
Drilling & Production Regulation
Oil & Gas Production Tax Act
Statistics Act
Surface Rights Act
Sustainable Development Act
Minister, Hon. Peter Bjornson
204-945-0067, Fax: 204-945-4882, minett@leg.gov.mb.ca
Deputy Minister, Hugh Eliasson
204-945-4076, Fax: 204-945-1561, dmett@leg.gov.mb.ca
Director, Policy, Planning & Coordination, Alan Barber
204-945-8714, abarber@gov.mb.ca
Director, Financial & Administration Services, Craig Halwachs
204-945-3675, chalwachs@gov.mb.ca
Director, Industry Development Financial Services, Jim Kilgour
204-945-7626, jkilgour@gov.mb.ca
Senior Manager, Industry Consulting & Marketing Support, David Sprange
204-945-7938, dsprange@gov.mb.ca
Executive Director, Industry & Workforce Development, B. Knight

Associated Agencies, Boards & Commissions:
• Apprenticeship and Certification Board
#1010, 401 York Ave
Winnipeg, MB R3C 0P8
204-945-3337 Fax: 204-948-2346 877-978-7233
The Board is an advisory body which makes recommendations regarding the designation and regulation of trades and which approves apprenticeship training standards.
• Convention Centre Corporation Board of Directors
375 York Ave
Winnipeg, MB R3C 3J3
204-956-1720 Fax: 204-943-0310 800-565-7776
audra@wcc.mb.ca
The Board manages and administers the affairs of the corporation.

Community & Economic Development Committee of Cabinet Secretariat
#648, 155 Carlton St., Winnipeg, MB R3C 3H8
204-945-8221 Fax: 204-945-8229
Director, Anna Rothney
204-945-3036
Administrative Officer, Colleen Davies
204-945-4346, codavies@gov.mb.ca

Business Services Division - Financial Services
To encourage & facilitate entrepreneurial & employment opportunities within the Province through the establishment of new businesses or the expansion/retention of existing Manitoba businesses. The Branch promotes increased access to capital for industry by serving as a principal source of financial advice & assistance for businesses to expand or locate in Manitoba. The Branch develops & administers a number of third party delivered pools of risk capital
Executive Director, Jim Kilgour
204-945-7626
Librarian, Small Business Development, Peggy Neal
204-984-0779

Manitoba Bureau of Statistics
#824, 155 Carlton St., Winnipeg, MB R3C 3H9
204-945-2406 Fax: 204-945-0695
Chief Statistician, Wilf Falk
204-945-2988, wfalk@mbs.gov.mb.ca

Premier's Economic Advisory Council
#648, 155 Carlton St., Winnipeg, MB R3C 3N8
204-945-6133 Fax: 204-945-8229
Executive Coordinator, Alissa Brandt
204-945-5297

Small Business Development
#250, 240 Graham Ave., PO Box 2609, Winnipeg, MB R3C 4B3
204-984-2272 Fax: 204-983-3852
manitoba@cbsc.ic.gc.ca
www.cbsc.org/manitoba
Director, Tony Romeo
204-945-2019
Manager, Western Regional Office, Bonnie Nay
204-726-6253

Manitoba Conservation

200 Saulteaux Cres., Winnipeg, MB R3J 3W3
204-945-6784
800-214-6497
mincon@leg.gov.mb.ca
www.gov.mb.ca/conservation

Manitoba Conservation protects, conserves, manages & sustains development of forest, fisheries, wildlife, water, energy & Crown & Park land resources, protects environmental integrity & ensures a high level of environmental quality. The department is the lead agency for providing outdoor recreational opportunities for Manitobans & visitors. The department is a contributor to the economic development & wellbeing of the province, through resource-based harvesting operations & in co-operation with other departments responsible for agriculture & tourism. Providing for domestic use & protecting people & property from floods, wildfires & adverse effects of other natural occurrences, are also major roles. The department administers legislation & regulations protecting the environment & public health, participates in approval, licensing & appeals for industrial development activities, administers waste reduction & pollution prevention activities & monitors environmental quality

Acts Administered:
Climate Change and Emissions Reductions Act
Contaminated Sites Remediation Act
Crown Lands Act
Dangerous Goods Handling & Transportation Act
Dangerous Goods Handling & Transportation Fees Regulation
Dangerous Goods Handling & Transportation Regulation
Environmental Accident Reporting Regulation
Generator Registration & Carrier Licensing Regulation
Manifest Regulation
PCB Storage Site Regulation
Special Waste (Shredder Residue) Regulation
Storage & Handling of Petroleum Products & Allied Products Regulation
East Side Traditional Lands Planning and Special Protected Areas Act
Ecological Reserves Act
Ecological Reserves Designation Regulation
Endangered Species Act
Environment Act
Burning of Crop Residue & Non-Crop Herbage Regulation
Campgrounds Regulation
Classes of Development Regulation
Disposal of Whey Regulation
Environment Act Fees Regulation
Environmental Assessment Hearing Costs Recovery Regulation
Incinerators Regulation
Inco Ltd. & Hudson Bay Mining & Smelting Co., Ltd. Smelting Complex Regulation
Joint Environmental Assessment Regulation
Litter Regulation
Livestock Manure & Mortalities Management Regulation
Onsite Wastewater Management Systems Regulation
Participant Assistance Regulation
Peat Smoke Control Regulation
Pesticides Regulation
Rockwood Sensitive Area Regulation
Waste Disposal Grounds Regulation
Wastewater Management Systems Regulations
Water & Wastewater Facility Operators Regulation
Forest Act
Ground Water & Water Well Act
Well Drilling Regulation
High Level Radioactive Waste Act
International Peace Garden Act
Manitoba Hazardous Waste Management Corporation Act
Manitoba Natural Resources Transfer Act
Manitoba Natural Resources Transfer Act, Amendment Act
Manitoba Natural Resources Transfer Act, Amendment Act, 1963
Ozone Depleting Substances Act
Provincial Parks Act
Plant Pests & Diseases Act
Polar Bear Protection Act, 2003
Public Health Act
Protection of Water Resources Regulation
Sanitary Areas Regulation
Water Supplies Regulation
Water Works, Sewage & Sewage Disposal Regulations
Resource Tourism Operators Act
Surveys Act (Part II)
Sustainable Development Act
Waste Reduction & Prevention Act
Multi-Material Stewardship (Interim Measures) Regulation
Tire Stewardship Regulation
Used Oil, Oil Filters & Containers Stewardship Regulation
Water Commission Act
Wildlife Act
Designation of Wild Animals Regulation
Designation of Wildlife Lands Regulation
Threatened, Endangered & Extirpated Species Regulation
Water Resources Conservation & Protection Act
Water Rights Act
Wild Rice Act

Minister, Hon. Dave Chomiak
204-945-5356, Fax: 204-948-2692, mincon@leg.gov.mb.ca
Deputy Minister, Fred Meier
204-945-3785, Fax: 204-948-2403, dmcon@leg.gov.mb.ca
Assistant Deputy Minister, Administration and Finance, Bruce Gray
204-945-7006
Coordinator, Conservation Library Services, Wendy Barber
204-945-7126
Director, Conservation Programs, Wayne Leeman
204-945-0011

Associated Agencies, Boards & Commissions:
• Clean Environment Commission
#305, 155 Carlton St.
Winnipeg, MB R3C 3H8
204-945-0594 Fax: 204-945-0090
www.cecmanitoba.ca/
Arm's-length provincial agency that holds public hearings on the subject of the regulation of a broad range of private industry, municipal or provincial government operations. Investigates environmental matters or considers proposed abatement projects with public hearings. Reports to the Minister with advice & recommendations & acts as a mediator between two or more parties to an environmental dispute.
• Ecological Reserves Advisory Committee
c/o Manitoba Conservation, Parks & Natural Areas Branch
200 Saulteaux Cres.
Winnipeg, MB R3J 3W3
204-945-4148 Fax: 204-945-0012
hhernandez@gov.mb.ca
• Endangered Species Advisory Committee
200 Saulteaux Cres.
PO Box 24
Winnipeg, MB R3J 3W3
204-945-7465 Fax: 204-945-3077
• Lake of the Woods Control Board
c/o Executive Engineer
Ottawa, ON K1A 0H3
Fax: 819-953-4666 800-661-5922
secretariat@lwcb.ca
www.lwcb.ca

Conservation Programs Division
Manages Manitoba's natural resources, parks, lands, forests, fish, wildlife, & the environment. Implements the principles of sustainable development.
Asst. Deputy Minister, Fred Meier
204-945-7008, Fax: 204-945-3125
Director, Forestry, John Dojack
204-945-7998
Director, Lands & Geomatics, Harley Jonasson
204-945-8288
Director, Parks & Natural Areas, Barry J. Bentham
204-945-4413
Director, Survey Services, Wayne Leeman
204-945-0011
Director, Wildlife & Ecosystem Protection, Jack Dubois
204-945-7761
Director, Pollution Prevention, Laurie Streich
204-945-7482
Manager, Habitat Management & Ecosystem Monitoring, Floyd Phillips
204-945-7003

Environmental Stewardship Division
The Branch co-ordinates & integrates departmental policy, natural resource allocation & crown land-use planning, environmental impact assessment, legislative interpretation & co-management in accordance with principles of sustainable development. The Branch monitors cross-boundary water projects, administers licensing of resource-based tourism facilities, represents the department in issues related to internal & international trade agreements, co-ordinates settlements & litigation arising out of hydro-electric & water-control projects & Treaty Land Entitlement.
Asst. Deputy Minister, Serge Scrafield
204-945-7107, Fax: 204-945-5229
Director, Environmental Assessment & Licensing, Tracey Braun
204-945-7071
Director, Aboriginal Relations, Ron Missyabit
204-945-7088, Fax: 204-945-5229
Director, Sustainable Resource & Policy Management, Tammy Gibson
204-945-6658

Manitoba Round Table for Sustainable Development (MRTSD)
#160, 123 Main St., Winnipeg, MB R3C 1A5
204-945-1671 Fax: 204-948-2357
mrtsd@gov.mb.ca
Advisory body to the provincial government that provides advice & support to decision makers toward making responsible resource, land use, environment, social & economic development decisions for the province
Chair, Hon. Stan Struthers

Regional Operations Division
Operates six regional offices in rural Manitoba & co-ordinated from Headquarters operations in Winnipeg. The Division co-ordinates the delivery of programs & services at the community level
Asst. Deputy Minister, Bruce Bremner
204-945-4842

Regional Offices:

Eastern
Provincial Hwy #502, CP 4000, Lac du Bonnet, MB R0E 1A0
204-345-1431 Fax: 204-345-1440
Regional Director, Bruce Bremner

Central (Gimli)
75 - 7th Ave., PO Box 6000, Gimli, MB R0C 1B0
204-642-6070 Fax: 204-642-6108
Regional Director, Brian Gillespie

Northeastern
59 Elizabeth Dr., PO Box 28, Thompson, MB R8N 1X4
204-677-6648 Fax: 204-677-6359
Regional Director, Steve Kearney

Northwestern
3rd St. & Ross Ave., PO Box 2550, The Pas, MB R9A 1M4
204-627-8215 Fax: 204-623-1773

Central (Winnipeg)
#160, 123 Main St., Winnipeg, MB R3C 1A5
204-945-7100 Fax: 204-948-2338

Western
1129 Queens Ave., Brandon, MB R7A 1L9
204-726-6441 Fax: 204-726-6567
Regional Director, Bruce Wright

Manitoba Culture, Heritage, Tourism & Sport

Legislative Building, #118, 450 Broadway Ave., Winnipeg, MB R3C 0V8
204-945-3729 Fax: 204-945-5223
mincht@leg.gov.mb.ca
www.gov.mb.ca/chc

Committed to the development & implementation of programs & services which promote & enhance the well-being, identity & creativity of Manitobans & which contribute to Manitoba's continued economic growth & steadily rising quality of life. Working with its partners in the community & with government, the Department raises the national & international profile of the talents & abilities of our people, encourages healthy active living, promotes pride of place, creates jobs & attracts & maintains investment in our province

Acts Administered:
Amusements Act (except Part II)
Arts Council Act
Le Centre Culturel Franco-Manitobain Act
Coat of Arms, Emblems & The Manitoba Tartan Act
Foreign Cultural Objects Immunity from Seizure Act
Freedom of Information & Protection of Privacy Act
Heritage Manitoba Act
Heritage Resources Act
Income Tax Act
Legislative Library Act
Legislative Library Act
Manitoba Museum Act
Public Libraries Act
Public Printing Act
Travel Manitoba Act

Minister, Hon. Florfina Marcelino
204-945-3729, Fax: 204-945-5223, mincht@leg.gov.mb.ca
Deputy Minister, Sandra Hardy
204-945-4136, Fax: 204-948-3102, dmcht@leg.gov.mb.ca
Executive Director, Administration & Finance Division, David Paton
204-945-2233, Fax: 204-945-5760, dpaton@chc.gov.mb.ca

Associated Agencies, Boards & Commissions:
• Le Centre Culturel franco-manitobain/Franco-Manitoban Cultural Centre
340, boul Provencher
St Boniface, MB R2H 0G7
204-233-8972 Fax: 204-233-3324
ccfm@ccfm.mb.ca
www.ccfm.mb.ca
• Heritage Grants Advisory Council
213 Notre Dame Ave., 3rd Fl.
Winnipeg, MB R3B 1N3
204-945-2213 Fax: 204-948-2086
• Manitoba Arts Council
#525, 93 Lombard Ave.
Winnipeg, MB R3B 3B1
204-945-2237 Fax: 204-945-5925 866-994-2787
info@artscouncil.mb.ca
www.artscouncil.mb.ca
An arms-length agency of the provincial government dedicated to artistic excellence. It offers a broad-based granting program for professional artists & arts organizations. It promotes, preserves, supports & advocates for the arts as essential to the quality of life of all the people of Manitoba.
• Manitoba Centennial Centre Corporation
555 Main St.
Winnipeg, MB R3B 1C3
204-956-1360 Fax: 204-944-1390
• Manitoba Film Classification Board
#216, 301 Weston St.
Winnipeg, MB R3E 3H4
204-945-8962 Fax: 204-945-0890 866-612-2399
mfcb@gov.mb.ca
www.gov.mb.ca/filmclassification
• Manitoba Heritage Council
213 Notre Dame Ave., Main Fl.
Winnipeg, MB R3B 1N3
204-945-2118 Fax: 204-948-2384
hrb@gov.mb.ca
Protects, interprets & promotes the heritage resources of the province; offers advice & recommendations on places & events which should be protected by the department; protection of significant buildings & sites.
• Manitoba Museum / Musée du Manitoba
190 Rupert Ave.
Winnipeg, MB R3B 0N2
204-956-2830 Fax: 204-942-3679
info@manitobamuseum.mb.ca
www.manitobamuseum.mb.ca
Other Communication: Info Line: |204/943-3139
• Manitoba Film & Sound Recording Development Corporation
#410, 93 Lombard Ave.
Winnipeg, MB R3B 3B1
204-947-2040 Fax: 204-956-5261
carole@mbfilmsound.mb.ca
www.mbfilmsound.mb.ca
Pomotes the province's film & sound recording artists & industries.

Administration & Finance Division
Fax: 204-945-5760
Executive Director, David Paton
204-945-2233
Acting Director & Facilities Consultant, Community Places Program, Mark Ranson
204-945-1374
Director, Amalgamated Human Resources, Melanie Schade
204-945-3001

Communications Services Manitoba
155 Carlton St., 10th Fl., Winnipeg, MB R3C 3H8
204-945-3765 Fax: 204-948-2147
Asst. Deputy Minister, Cindy Stevens
204-945-4271, Fax: 204-948-2219
Director, Advertising & Program Promotion, Michelle Wallace
204-945-5164, Fax: 204-948-2147
Director, Public Affairs, Debbie MacKenzie
204-945-4971, Fax: 204-948-2147
Director, Creative Services, Cam McCullough
204-945-8830, Fax: 204-948-2147
Manager, Internet & Business Services, Mike Baudic
204-945-4392, Fax: 204-948-2219
Director, News Media Services, Stu Fawcett
204-945-3746
Manager, Production & Media Procurement, Heather A. Coleman
204-945-7121, Fax: 204-945-1366
Supervisor, Statutory Publications, Keith Holness
204-945-3101, Fax: 204-945-7172, statpub@gov.mb.ca

Culture, Heritage & Recreation Programs Division
Acting Asst. Deputy Minister, Ann Hultgren-Ryan
204-945-4078, Fax: 204-948-2739
Director, Arts Branch, Craig Walls
204-945-4579, Fax: 204-945-1684
Director, Historic Resources, Donna Dul
204-945-4389, Fax: 204-948-2384
Acting Director, Public Library Services, Trevor Surgenor
204-726-6864, Fax: 204-726-6868
Director, Recreation & Regional Services, Annette Willborn
204-945-4396, Fax: 204-945-1684

Provincial Services Division
#100, 200 Vaughan St., Winnipeg, MB R3C 1T5
Executive Director & Legislative Librarian, Legislative Library, Sue Bishop
204-945-4245
Director, Translation Services, Melanie Cwikla
204-945-3096

Sport Secretariat
213 Notre Dame Ave., Winnipeg, MB R3B 1N3
204-945-0216 Fax: 204-945-1675
diane.meldrum@gov.mb.ca
www.gov.mb.ca/chc/sport/
Acting Executive Director, Terry Welsh
204-945-2449

Tourism Secretariat & Travel Manitoba
155 Carlton St., 7th Fl., Winnipeg, MB R3C 3H8
800-665-0040
www.travelmanitoba.com
Acting Executive Director, Tourism Manitoba, Terry Welsh
204-945-2449

Manitoba Development Corporation (MDC)

#555, 155 Carlton St., Winnipeg, MB R3C 3H8
204-945-7626 Fax: 204-945-1193
General Manager, Jim Kilgour

Manitoba Education, Citizenship & Youth

#168, Legislative Bldg., 450 Broadway, Winnipeg, MB R3C 0V8
204-945-3720 Fax: 204-945-1291
minedu@leg.gov.mb.ca
www.edu.gov.mb.ca

Acts Administered:
Blind & Deaf Persons' Maintenance & Education Act
Education Administration Act
Property Tax and Insualtion Assistance Act (Part III.2)
Public Schools Act
Public Schools Finance Board Act
Teachers' Pension Act
Teachers' Society Act
Minister, Hon. Nancy Allan
204-945-3720, Fax: 204-945-1291, minedu@leg.gov.mb.ca
Deputy Minister, Gerald Farthing
204-945-1648, Fax: 204-945-8330, dmedu@leg.gov.mb.ca
Executive Director, Public Schools Finance, Rick Dedi
204-945-5534

Associated Agencies, Boards & Commissions:
• Public Schools Finance Board
#506, 1181 Portage Ave.
Winnipeg, MB R3G 0T3
204-945-6628 Fax: 204-948-2001
• Teachers' Retirement Allowances Fund Board
#330 Johnston Terminal
35 Forks Market Rd.
Winnipeg, MB R3C 4S8
204-949-0048 Fax: 204-944-0361

Division du Bureau de l'éducation française / French Language Education Office
#509, 1181 av Portage, Winnipeg, MB R3C 0T3
204-945-6916 Fax: 204-945-1625
Sous-ministre adjoint, Jean-Vianney Auclair
204-945-6928, Fax: 204-948-2994
Directeur (par intérim), Programmes, Jacques Dorge
204-945-6022, Fax: 204-945-1625
Directrice, Services de soutien en éducation, Florence Girouard
204-945-8797
Directeur, Programmes de langues officielles et services administratifs, Kassy Assie
204-945-6029, Fax: 204-945-1625
Directrice, Ressources éducatives françaises, Lynette Chartier
204-945-1342

Education Administration Services / Services Administratifs de l'Éducation
#507, 1181 av Portage, Winnipeg, MB R3C 0T3
204-945-6897 Fax: 204-945-2154
Director, David Yeo
204-945-8664
Program Coordinator, Professional Certification and Student Records, Allan Tataryn
204-773-2998
Senior Field Officer, Pupil Transportation, Chris Hagen
204-945-6898

MB4Youth Division
#310, 800 Portage Ave., Winnipeg, MB R3G 0N4
204-945-3556 Fax: 204-945-5726
mb4youth@gov.mb.ca
www.edu.gov.mb.ca/youth/
Executive Director, Veronica Dyck
204-945-0371
Executive Director, Partners for Careers, Roberta Hewson
204-945-0447

School Programs Division
#5, 1567 Dublin Ave, Winnipeg, MB R3E 3J5
204-945-7934 Fax: 204-945-8303
Asst. Deputy Minister, Aileen Najduch
204-945-7935
Director, Instruction, Curriculum & Assessment, Daryl Gervais
204-945-0294
Director, Program & Student Services, Joanna Blais
204-945-7911, Fax: 204-945-7914
Financial Coordinator, Yvonne Pennings
204-945-3546
Coordinator, Assessment, Ken Clark
204-945-3666
Coordinator, Development, Carole Bilyk
204-945-1773
Coordinator, Distance Learning, Susan Lee
204-325-1717
Coordinator, Financial and Administration Unit, Joanne Prins
204-945-7821
Coordinator, Learning Support and Technology, Cheryl Prokopanko
204-945-6435
Coordinator, Instructional Resources, John Tooth
204-945-7833
Coordinator, Deaf and Hard of Hearing Services, Karen Priestley
204-945-2051
Chief Operating Officer, Manitoba Text Book Bureau, Brenda McKinny
204-483-5035
Coordinator, Early Childhood Education, Wenda Dickens
204-945-1095
Coordinator, Media Production Services, Ani Granson
204-945-5266

Shared Services
510 Selkirk Ave., Winnipeg, MB R2W 2M7
Director, Aboriginal Education Directorate, Helen Robinson-Settee
204-945-4763, Fax: 204-948-2010
Executive Financal Officer, Claude Fortier
204-945-1117, Fax: 204-948-2851
Director, Amalgamated Human Resources, Robert (Butch) Berube
204-945-6892, Fax: 204-948-2193
Director, Systems & Technology Services, John Frazer
204-945-5843, Fax: 204-948-2542

Elections Manitoba

#120, 200 Vaughan St., Winnipeg, MB R3C 1T5
204-945-3225 Fax: 204-945-6011
866-628-6837
election@elections.mb.ca
www.electionsmanitoba.ca
Independent from government, Elections Manitoba conducts fair elections. It ensures that political financing laws are followed, & increases public awareness of the electoral process
Chief Electoral Officer, Richard D. Balasko
204-945-3225
Deputy Chief Electoral Officer, Scott Gordon
204-945-7156
Manager, Elections Finances, Shipra Verma, CA
204-945-1283
Analyst, Financial Compliance, Maggie Anderson
416-945-7559
Officer, Communications & Community Relations, Amanda Jeninga
204-945-3804

Manitoba Family Services & Housing

#219, 114 Garry St., Winnipeg, MB R3C 4V6
204-945-3242 Fax: 204-945-2156
minfam@leg.gov.mb.ca
www.gov.mb.ca/fs
Supports citizens in need to achieve fuller participation in society & greater self-suffiency & independence. Helps keep children, families & communities safe & secure & promotes healthy citizen

development & well-being. Mission is accomplished through: provision of financial support; provision of services & supports that assist individuals improve their attachment to the labour market; provision of supports & services for adults & children with disabilities; provision of child protection & related services; assistance to people facing family violence or family disruption; provision of services & supports to promote the healthy development & well-being of children & families; assistance to Manitobans to access safe, appropriate & affordable housing; fostering community capacity & engaging the broader community to participate in & contribute to decision-making; & respectful & appropriate delivery of programs & services

Acts Administered:
The Adoption Act
The Child & Family Services Act
The Child & Family Services Authorities Act
The Community Child Day Care Standards Act
The Elderly & Infirm Persons' Housing Act
The Employment & Income Assistance Act
The Elderly and Infirm Person's Housing Act
The Intercountry Adoption (Hague Convention) Act
The Parents' Maintenance Act (s. 10)
The Social Services Administration Act
The Social Services Appeal Board Act
The Vulnerable Persons Living with a Mental Disability Act

Minister, Hon. Gord Mackintosh
204-945-4173, Fax: 204-945-5149, minfam@leg.gov.mb.ca
Deputy Minister, Martin Billinkoff
204-945-6700, Fax: 204-948-1896, dmfam@leg.gov.mb.ca
Executive Director, Policy & Planning, Jan Forster
204-945-3231, Fax: 204-945-2156
Administrative Assistant, Financial & Administrative Services, Lana Harrison
204-945-8119, Fax: 204-945-2760

Associated Agencies, Boards & Commissions:
• Disabilities Issues Office
#630, 240 Graham Ave.
Winnipeg, MB R3C 0J7
204-945-7613 Fax: 204-948-2896 TTY: 204-948-2901
dio@gov.mb.ca
• Manitoba Housing Authority - Public Housing
#2100, 185 Smith St.
Winnipeg, MB R3C 3G4
204-945-4663 Fax: 204-948-2013 800-661-4663
www.gov.mb.ca/fs/housing/mha.html
• Manitoba Housing & Renewal Corporation
280 Broadway
Winnipeg, MB R3C 0R8
204-945-4895 Fax: 204-945-5710
www.gov.mb.ca/fs/org/eih/mhrc.html
• Social Services Appeal Board
175 Hargrave St., 7th Fl.
Winnipeg, MB R3C 3R8
204-945-3003 Fax: 204-945-1736 800-282-8069 TTY: 204-948-2037
www.gov.mb.ca/fs/ssab/index.html

Administration & Finance Division
Acting Asst. Deputy Minister, Sheila Lebredt
204-945-5943
Acting Director, Information Technology, Munna Zaman
204-945-4807, Fax: 204-948-2394
Director, Integrated Service Delivery, Debbie Besant
204-945-4998, Fax: 204-948-4656
Director & Chief Negotiator, Agency Accountability & Support Unit, Gord Greasley
204-945-7927, Fax: 204-948-4656

Child & Family Services Division
Acting Asst. Deputy Minister, Carolyn Loeppky
204-945-3257, Fax: 204-948-2669
Acting Executive Director, Child Protection, Josie Hill
204-945-4575, Fax: 204-945-6717
Acting Executive Director, Strategic Initiatives & Program Support, Tammy Mattern
204-945-8300
Acting Director, Child Care, Lois Speirs
204-945-2668, Fax: 204-948-2630
Acting Director, Family Violence Prevention, Paulette Fortier
204-945-7245

Community Service Delivery Division
Asst. Deputy Minister, Peter Dubienski
204-945-2204
Executive Director, Rural & Northern Services, Debbie Besant
204-945-4998
Executive Director, Winnipeg Services, Gerry Schmidt
204-945-2685, Fax: 204-945-0082
Executive Director, Service Delivery Support, Janet Wikstrom
204-945-1268, Fax: 204-948-3267
Director, Provincial Services, Pat Sanderson
204-945-6554, Fax: 204-945-3930
Acting CEO, Winnipeg Child & Family Services, Darlene MacDonald
204-944-4570, Fax: 204-944-4395

Employment, Income & Housing Division
#201, 280 Broadway Ave., Winnipeg, MB R3C 0R8
Asst. Deputy Minister, Joy Cramer
204-945-5600, Fax: 204-948-2736
Executive Director, Employment & Income Assistance Programs, Charlene Paquin
204-945-6374
Director, Corporate Services, Henry Bos
204-945-4703, Fax: 204-945-4710

Services for Persons with Disabilities
Asst. Deputy Minister, Gisela Rempel
204-945-2692, Fax: 204-948-2153
Executive Director, Disability Programs & EIA, Wes Henderson
204-945-6541, Fax: 204-945-5668
Acting Director, Children's Programs, Tracy Moore
204-945-3255, Fax: 204-945-5668
Acting Director, Strategic Initiatives & Program Support, Joy Goertzen
204-945-2326, Fax: 204-945-5668
Acting Director, Supported Living, Ralf Margraf
204-945-3589, Fax: 204-945-5668
Acting Vulnerable Persons' Commissioner, JoAnne Reinsch
204-945-0564, Fax: 204-948-2603

Manitoba Finance

#109, Legislative Bldg., Winnipeg, MB R3C 0V8
204-945-3754 Fax: 204-945-8316
minfin@leg.gov.mb.ca
www.gov.mb.ca/finance/

Established in 1969 under authority of the Financial Administration Act. Responsible for central accounting, payroll & financial reporting services for the government, consumer & corporate affairs & central financial control of cost-shared agreements. The ministry manages government borrowing programs & is responsible for federal-provincial relations.

Acts Administered:
Business Names Registration Act
Business Practices Act
Cemeteries Act
The title to Certain Lands Act (R.S.M. 1990, c.259).
Change of Name Act
Charities Endorsement Act
Commodity Futures Act
Condominium Act
Consumer Protection Act
Cooperatives Act
Corporations Act
Corporation Capital Tax Act
Credit Unions & Caisses Populaires Act
Electronic Commerce & Information Act
Embalmers & Funeral Directors Act
Energy Rate Stabilization Act
Financial Administration Act
Fire Insurance Reserve Fund Act
Fiscal Stabilization Fund Act
Gasoline Tax Act
Health & Post Secondary Education Tax Levy Act
Hospital Capital Financing Authority Act
Housing & Renewal Corporation Act
Hudson's Bay Company Land Register Act
Income Tax Act
Insurance Act
Insurance Corporations Tax Act
Landlord & Tenant Act
Life Leases Act
Manitoba Investment Pool Authority Act
Manitoba Evidence Act (Part II & III)
Manitoba Investment Pool Authority Act
Marriage Act
Mining Claim Tax Act
Mining Tax Act
Mortgage Act (Part III)
Mortgage Dealers Act
Motive Fuel Tax Act
Pari-Mutuel Levy Act
Partnership Act
Personal Investigations Act
Personal Property Security Act
Prearranged Funeral Services Act
Professional Home Economists Act
Property Tax & Insulation Assistance Act
Public Health Act
Bedding, Upholstered & Stuffed Articles Regulation
Public Officers Act
Public Utilities Board Act
Real Estate Brokers Act
Real Property Act
Registry Act
Religious Societies' Lands Act
Residential Tenancies Act
Retail Sales Tax Act
Revenue Act
Succession Duty Act
Securities Act
Special Survey Act
Suitors' Moneys Act
Surveys Act (Part I)
Provincial-Municipal Tax Sharing Act
Tobacco Tax Act
Trade Practises Inquiry Act
Vital Statistics Act

Minister, Hon. Stan Struthers
204-945-3722, Fax: 204-945-3470, minfin@leg.gov.mb.ca
Deputy Minister, Diane, Gray
204-945-5343, dmfin@leg.gov.mb.ca
Secretary, Treasury Board Secretariat, Tannis Mindell
204-945-1100
Assoc. Secretary, Treasury Board, David Woodbury
204-945-1524

Associated Agencies, Boards & Commissions:
• Automobile Injury Compensation Appeal Commission
#301, 428 Portage Ave..
Winnipeg, MB R3C 0E2
204-945-4155 Fax: 204-948-2402
autoinjury@gov.mb.ca
www.gov.mb.ca/cca/autom
• Claimant Adviser Office
#200, 330 Portage Ave.
Winnipeg, MB R3C 0C4
204-945-7413 Fax: 204-948-3157
• Credit Union Deposit Guarantee Corporation
#390, 200 Graham Ave.
Winnipeg, MB R3C 4L5
204-942-8480 Fax: 204-947-1723 800-697-4447
mail@cudgc.com
www.cudgc.com
• Crown Corporations Council / Conseil des corporations de la Couronne
#1130, 444 St. Mary Ave.
Winnipeg, MB R3C 3T1
204-949-5270 Fax: 204-949-5283
crowncc@mts.net
www.crowncc.mb.ca
• Manitoba Securities Commission
#500, 400 St. Mary Ave.
Winnipeg, MB R3C 4K5
204-945-2548 Fax: 204-945-0330 800-655-5244
securities@gov.mb.ca
www.msc.gov.mb.ca
The Manitoba Securities Commission is an independent agency of the Government of Manitoba that protects investors and promotes fair and efficient capital markets throughout the province.
• Public Utilities Board
#400, 330 Portage Ave.
Winnipeg, MB R3C 0C4
204-945-2638 Fax: 204-945-2643 866-854-3698
publicutilities@gov.mb.ca
www.pub.gov.mb.ca
Regulate the rates charged by Manitoba Hydro (electrical utility), Manitoba Public Insurance (auto insurance), some gas or propane utilities (Centra Gas, Stittco, Swan Valley Gas Corp.) and all water and sewer utilities outside Winnipeg.
• Residential Tenancies Commission
#1650, 155 Carlton St.
Winnipeg, MB R3C 3H8
204-945-2028 Fax: 204-945-5453 800-782-8403
rtc@gov.mb.ca
www.gov.mb.ca/finance/cca/residtc
Landlords and tenants may appeal orders and decisions issued by the Residential Tenancies Branch. The commission hears these appeals. Appeals are heard by a panel of three consisting of one landlord and one tenant representative and either the chief commissioner or a deputy commissioner as the neutral chairperson.

Administration & Finance Division
Executive Financial Officer, Erroll Kavanagh
204-945-4319
Director, Amalgamated Human Resources, Melanie Schade
204-945-3001
Director, Insurance & Risk Management, John Rislahti
204-945-2482

Comptroller Division
#715, 401 York Ave., Winnipeg, MB R3C 0P8
204-945-4920 Fax: 204-945-2394
Provides central accounting, payroll & financial reporting services, & central financial control of cost-shared agreements for the government. The division develops government-wide financial systems, policies & procedures, & provides policy advice for financial & management systems. The division coordinates, develops & maintains departmental data processing systems, & provides direction to the government on the effective use of information systems technology
Provincial Comptroller, Betty-Anne Pratt
204-945-4919

Director, Internal Audit & Consulting Services, Jane Holatko
204-945-8110
Director, Disbursements & Accounting, Terry Patrick
204-945-1343

Consumer & Corporate Affairs Division
Asst. Deputy Minister, Alexandra Morton, Q.C.
204-945-3742, Fax: 204-945-4009
Director, Research & Planning, Ian Anderson
204-945-7892
Director, Consumers' Bureau, Nancy Anderson
204-945-4062
Acting Director, Residential Tenancies Branch, Laura Gowerluk
204-945-0377, Fax: 204-945-6273
Director, Claimant Advisor Office, Bob Sample
204-945-8171

Federal-Provincial Relations & Research Division
#910, 386 Broadway, Winnipeg, MB R3C 3R6
204-945-3757 Fax: 204-945-5051
Provides research & analytical support for national/provincial fiscal & economic matters & inter-governmental financial relations. Also administers fiscal arrangements & tax collection agreements with the federal government & tax credit programs with federal & municipal governments
Asst. Deputy Minister, Heather Wood
204-945-4120, Fax: 204-945-5051
Director, Economic & Fiscal Analysis, Jim Hrichishen
204-945-1468
Acting Director, Intergovernmental Finance, René Perreault
204-945-1478
Director, Taxation Analysis Branch, Stephen Watson
204-945-1473

Taxation Division
#101, 401 York Ave., Winnipeg, MB R3C 0P8
204-945-6444 Fax: 204-948-2360

Treasury Division
Created as a separate entity in 1976, to address the need for placing greater emphasis on the management of substantial amounts of money, debt & investments. Currency & interest rate risk management programs have been developed due to the increase in volumes & dollar values. The division assists with the arrangement of financing for municipalities, schools & hospitals
Asst. Deputy Minister, Gary Gibson
204-945-1184
Director, Capital Markets, Deborah Deen
204-945-6637
Director, Treasury & Banking Operations, Scott Wiebe
204-945-6677

Companies Office
#1010, 405 Broadway, Winnipeg, MB R3C 3L6
204-945-2500 Fax: 204-945-1459
companies@gov.mb.ca
companiesoffice.gov.mb.ca
Chief Operating Officer, Myron Pawlowsky
204-945-4206

Financial Institutions Regulation Branch
#1115, 405 Broadway, Winnipeg, MB R3C 3L6
204-945-2542 Fax: 204-948-2268
Superintendent, Financial Institutions, Jim Scalena
204-945-3911
Deputy Superintendent, Lofgren Ken
204-945-6111
Deputy Superintendent, Insurance, Scott Moore
204-945-1150

Property Registry
Acting Director, Grant Kernested
204-945-1946

Vital Statistics
254 Portage Ave., Winnipeg, MB R3C 0B8
204-945-3701 Fax: 204-948-3128
800-282-8063
vitalstats@gov.mb.ca
www.gov.mb.ca/cca/vital
Other Communication: Fax Certificate Requests: 204/948-3128
Provincial agency responsible for the issuance of birth, death, change of name & marriage certificates. Written or faxed requests must be submitted.

Manitoba Health & Healthy Living

#100, 300 Carlton St., Winnipeg, MB R3B 3M9
204-786-7191
minhlt@leg.gov.mb.ca
www.gov.mb.ca/health/index.html
Responsible for the overall quality of the health system in the province, for maintaining the health system, & for ensuring that the health needs of Manitobans are met. Services are provided through regional delivery systems, hospitals & other health care facilities. The Department also makes insured benefits claims payments for residents of Manitoba related to the cost of medical, hospital, personal care, pharmacare & other health services. To lead the way to quality health care, built with creativity, compassion, confidence, trust & respect; empower Manitobans through knowledge, choices & access to the best possible health resources; & build partnerships & alliances for healthy & supportive communities. To foster innovation in the health care system. This is accomplished through: developing mechanisms to assess & monitor quality of care, utilization & cost effectiveness; fostering behaviours & environments which promote health; & promoting responsiveness & flexibility of delivery systems, & alternative & less expensive services.

Acts Administered:
Anatomy Act
Cancer Care Manitoba Act
Chiropractic Act
Dental Association Act
Dental Health Services Act
Dental Health Workers Act
Denturists Act
Department of Health Act
District Health & Social Services Act
Elderly & Infirm Persons' Housing Act (with respect to elderly persons housing units as defined in the Act)
Emergency Medical Response and Stretcher Transportation Act
Health Services Act
Health Services Insurance Act
Hearing Aid Act
Hospitals Act
Human Tissue Act
Licensed Practical Nurses Act
Medical Act
Manitoba Medical Association Dues Act
Mental Health Act (except parts 9 & 10 & clauses 125 (1) (i) & (j)
Medical Laboratory Technologists Act
Midwifery Act
Naturopathic Act
Occupational Therapists Act
Opticians Act
Optometry Act
Personal Health Information Act
Pharmaceutical Act
Physiotherapists Act
Podiatrists Act
Prescription Drugs Cost Assistance Act
Private Hospitals Act
Protection for Persons in Care Act
Psychologists Registration Act
Public Health Act
Atmospheric Pollution Regulation
Collection & Disposal of Wastes Regulation
Fumigation & Pest Control Regulation
Protection of Water Sources Regulation
Sanitation Regulation
Water Supplies Regulation
Water Works, Sewerage & Sewage Disposal Regulation
X-Ray Safety Regulation
Regional Health Authorities Act
Registered Dieticians Act
Registered Nurses Act
Registered Psychiatric Nurses Act
Registered Respiratory Therapists Act
Sanitorium Board of Manitoba Act
Tobacco Damages and Health Care Cost Recovery Act (not yet proclaimed)

Minister, Hon. Theresa Oswald
204-945-3731, Fax: 204-945-0441, minhlt@leg.gov.mb.ca
Deputy Minister, Arlene Wilgosh
204-945-3771, Fax: 204-945-4564, dmhlt@leg.gov.mb.ca
Chief Medical Officer of Health, Dr. Joel Kettner
204-788-6766, Fax: 204-948-2204
Provincial Director, Patient Access, Dr. Luis Oppenheimer
Administrative Secretary, Betty Rubin
204-786-7191, Fax: 204-774-1325, brubin@gov.mb.ca

Associated Agencies, Boards & Commissions:
• Appeal Panel for Home Care
#4012, 300 Carlton St.
Winnipeg, MB R3B 3M9
204-788-6788 Fax: 204-948-2024 800-491-4993
appeals@gov.mb.ca
• Manitoba Drug Standards & Therapeutics Committee
#1014, 300 Carlton St.
Winnipeg, MB R3B 3M9
204-786-7317 Fax: 204-942-2030
• Manitoba Health Appeal Board
#4011, 300 Carlton St.
Winnipeg, MB R3B 3M9
204-788-6704 Fax: 204-948-2024 866-744-3257
Quasi-judicial body responsible for making decisions on appeals under The Health Services Insurance Act, The Ambulance Services Act & The Mental Health Act.
• Addictions Foundation of Manitoba (AFM) / Fondation manitobaine de lutte contre les dépendances
1031 Portage Ave.
Winnipeg, MB R3G 0R8
204-944-6200 Fax: 204-786-7768
library@afm.mb.ca
www.afm.mb.ca
• Manitoba Seniors & Health Aging Secretariat

Corporate & Provincial Program Support
Fax: 204-775-3712
Asst. Deputy Minister, Kim Sharman
204-788-6439
Acting Director, Operations, Provincial Drug Programs, Jeannine Ste. Marie
204-786-7333, Fax: 204-786-6634
Director, Corporate Services, Valdine Berry
204-788-6749, Fax: 204-945-4559
Manager, Protection for Persons in Care, Paul Lamoureux
204-788-6347
Director, Information Systems - Technical Services & Operations, Cliff Greenhalgh
204-786-7234
Coordinator, French Language Services, Robert V. Loiselle
204-788-6698, Fax: 204-772-2943

Finance
Chief Financial Officer & Asst. Deputy Minister, Karen Herd
204-788-2525, Fax: 204-775-3412
Acting Executive Director, Nardia Maharaj
204-786-7138
Executive Director, Accountability Support, Lorraine E. Dacombe Dewar
204-786-7266
Acting Director, Health Information Management, Deborah Malazdrewicz
204-786-7149, Fax: 204-944-1911
Acting Director, Regional Financial Support, Rhonda Hogg
204-786-7140
Controller, Tony Messner
204-786-7135, Fax: 204-774-1325

Primary Care & Healthy Living
300 Carlton St., 2nd Floor, Winnipeg, MB R3B 3M9
Mission is to encourage the prevention of illness & injury, coordinate access to health care, & strengthen existing primary health care services with new initiatives
Asst. Deputy Minister, Marie O'Neill
204-786-6656, Fax: 204-948-2366
Acting Director, Chronic Disease Management, Kristin Anderson
204-788-6746
Executive Director, Mental Health & Addictions, Yvonne Block
204-786-7281
Executive Director, Aboriginal Health & Northern Nursing Stations, Rose Neufeld
204-788-6649, Fax: 204-945-4559
Executive Director, Primary Health Care, Barbara Wasilewski
204-786-7176
Acting Director, Emergency Medical Services, Brenda Gregory
204-945-0711

Public Health
300 Carlton St., 4th Fl., Winnipeg, MB R3B 3M9
204-788-6701 Fax: 204-948-2040
Mission is to assure conditions in which people can be healthy, by applying scientific & medical knowledge to systematically identify & analyze the health of groups & populations, & by assisting communities to organize, implement & monitor efforts aimed at the prevention & control of disease & promotion of health. The Environmental Health Unit of the Public Health Branch responds to biological, chemical or social health threats to the public. The Unit manages several programs including Environmental Health, Food Protection, Tobacco Reduction & Dental/Oral Health
Chief Provincial Public Health Officer, Dr. Joel Kettner
204-788-6766

Manitoba Healthy Child Office

#219, 114 Garry St., Winnipeg, MB R3C 1G1
204-945-2266
888-848-0140
healthychild@gov.mb.ca
Office provides leadership & encourages actions that address health concerns & reduces the need for medical care for children

Acts Administered:
The Addictions Foundation Act
The Non-Smokers Health Protection Act
Manitoba Prenatal Benefit Regulation

Minister, Hon. Kerri Irvin-Ross
204-945-1373, Fax: 204-948-2703
Chief Executive Officer, Healthy Child Manitoba, Jan Sanderson
204-945-6707, Fax: 204-948-2585
Director, Programs, Susan Tessler
204-945-1275

Manitoba Human Rights Commission

175 Hargrave St., 7th Fl., Winnipeg, MB R3C 3R8
204-945-3007 Fax: 204-945-1292
888-884-8681
hrc@gov.mb.ca
www.gov.mb.ca/hrc/
TTY: 204-945-3442

Executive Director, Dianna Scarth
204-945-3020

Manitoba Hydro

PO Box 815 Main, Winnipeg, MB R3C 2P4
204-474-3311 Fax: 204-475-0069
publicaffairs@hydro.mb.ca
www.hydro.mb.ca

Manitoba Hydro (MH) is a major energy utility. One of the largest electricity & natural gas utilities in Canada, it serves 521,600 electric customers throughout Manitoba & 261,150 gas customers in various communities throughout southern Manitoba. Virtually all electricity generated by the provincial Crown Corporation is from self-renewing water power. MH is the major distributor of natural gas in the province. Developing & implementing an environmental management system consistent with ISO standards. Actively pursuing a vairety or projects & programs aimed at reducing GHG & vehicle emissions, recycling, conserving energy, digging out contaminated soils, partnering with NGOs

Minister responsible, Hon. Dave Chomiak
204-945-5356, Fax: 204-948-2692, miniem@leg.gov.mb.ca
President/CEO, Bob B. Brennan
204-474-3600
Chair, Victor H. Schroeder, Q.C.
Vice-President, Customer Service & Marketing, Gerry W. Rose
Vice-President, Finance & Administration & CFO, Vince A. Warden
Vice-President, Power Supply, Ken R. Adams
Vice-President, Transmission & Distribution, Al M. Snyder
General Counsel & Corporate Secretary, Ken M. Tennenhouse

Manitoba Infrastructure & Transportation

Legislative Building, #203, 450 Broadway Ave., Winnipeg, MB R3C 0V8
204-945-3723 Fax: 204-945-7610
www.gov.mb.ca/mit/

Acts Administered:
CentrePort Canada Act
Crown Lands Act
Drivers & Vehicles Act
Government Air Services Act
Government House Act
Government Purchases Act
Highway Traffic Act
Highways Protection Act
Highways & Transportation Act
Highways & Transportation Construction Contracts Disbursement Act
Land Acquisition Act
Manitoba Floodway Authority Act
Manitoba Water Services Board Act
Off-Road Vehicles Act
Provincial Parks Act
Provincial Railways Act
Public Works Act
Taxicab Act
Trans-Canada Highway Act
Water Resources Administration Act
Wild Rice Act
Minister, Hon. Steve Ashton
204-945-3723, Fax: 204-945-7610, mininfratran@leg.gov.mb.ca
Deputy Minister, Andrew Horosko
204-945-3768, Fax: 204-945-4766, dminfratran@leg.gov.mb.ca

Associated Agencies, Boards & Commissions:
• Lake Winnipeg Stewardship Board
PO Box 305
Gimli, MB R0C 1B0
204-642-4899
www.lakewinnipeg.org
Established in 2003 to assist the government of Manitoba to achieve the main commitments in the Lake Winnipeg Action Plan of reducing phosphorus & nitrogen in the lake to pre-1970 levels. The Lake Winnipeg Stewardship Board's Interim Report (Jan. 2005), contained 32 sets of recommendations & was followed by public discussions.
• Highway Traffic Board/Motor Transport Board
#200, 301 Weston St.
Winnipeg, MB R3E 3H4
204-945-8912 Fax: 204-783-6529
• Manitoba Floodway Authority (MFA)
#200, 155 Carlton St.
Winnipeg, MB R3C 3H8
204-945-4900 Fax: 204-948-2462 866-356-6355
floodway@gov.mb.ca
Separate, independent, publicly accountable provincial agency that will manage the expansion & maintenance of the Red River Floodway on behalf of Manitobans.
• Manitoba Habitat Heritage Corporation
#200, 1555 St. James St.
Winnipeg, MB R3H 1B5
204-784-4350 Fax: 204-784-7359
mhhc@mhhc.mb.ca
www.mhhc.mb.ca
• License Suspension Appeal Board/Medical Review Committee
#200, 301 Weston St.
Winnipeg, MB R3E 3H4
204-945-7350 Fax: 204-948-2682
• Manitoba Water Services Board
PO Box 22080
Brandon, MB R7A 6Y9
204-726-6076 Fax: 204-726-6290
www.gov.mb.ca/waterstewardship/mwsb/
Assists rural residents outside Winnipeg in developing safe & sustainable water &/or sewerage facilities.
• Manitoba Land Value Appraisal Commission
800 Portage Ave.
Winnipeg, MB R3G 0N4
204-945-2941 Fax: 204-948-2235
• Taxicab Board
#200, 301 Weston St.
Winnipeg, MB R3E 3H4
Fax: 204-948-2315

Canada-Manitoba Infrastructure Secretariat
204-945-4074 Fax: 204-945-2035
800-268-4883
infra@gov.mb.ca

Government Services
Legislative Bldg., #332, 450 Broadway, Winnipeg, MB R3C 0V8

Accommodation Services
1700 Portage Ave., Winnipeg, MB R3J 0E1
Asst. Deputy Minister, Chris Hauch
204-945-7535, Fax: 204-945-2546
Director, Corporate Accommodation Planning, Hilary Oakman
204-945-7965
Director, Project Services, Pat Landry
204-945-6615
Director, Operations, Rod Berscheid
204-945-7528
Director, Security Branch, Gary Walker
204-945-7608

Supply & Services Division
270 Osborne St. North, Winnipeg, MB R3C 1V7
Asst. Deputy Minister, Tracey Danowski
204-945-6340, Fax: 204-948-2509
COO, Fleet Vehicles Agency, Al Franchuk
204-945-0275
Director, Procurement Services, David Ash
204-945-6380, Fax: 204-945-1455
COO, Materials Distribution Agency, David Bishop
204-945-6043, Fax: 204-948-3273

Transportation
Legislative Bldg., #209, 450 Broadway, Winnipeg, MB R3C 0V8
Deputy Minister, Andrew Horosko
204-945-3768, Fax: 204-945-4766

Construction & Maintenance Branch
#1610, 215 Garry St., Winnipeg, MB R3C 3Z1
Fax: 204-945-3841
Other Communication: Highway Condition Information: 204/945-3705, 1-877-627-6237
Executive Director, Ron Weatherburn
204-945-3775
Director, Mechanical Equipment Services, Mike Knight
204-945-8567, Fax: 204-948-3274

Administrative Services Division
215 Garry St., 17th Fl., Winnipeg, MB R3C 3Z1
Fax: 204-945-5115
Asst. Deputy Minister, Paul Rochon
204-945-3887
Acting Director, Financial Services, Ian Hasanally
204-945-3883
Director, Information Technology Services, Dan Buhler
204-945-4512
Director, Amalgamated Human Resources, Jennifer Morris
204-945-5846, Fax: 204-948-3382

Engineering & Operations Division
215 Garry St., 16th Fl., Winnipeg, MB R3C 3Z1
Fax: 204-945-3841
Asst. Deputy Minister, Lance Vigfusson
204-945-3733
Director, Northern Airports & Marine, Mary Bartman
204-945-3421

Highway Engineering Branch
Executive Director, Walter Burdz
204-945-3772
Director, Highway Planning & Design, Eric Christiansen
204-945-0236
Director, Materials Engineering, Said Kass
204-945-2279
Director, Traffic Engineering, Glenn Cuthbertson
204-945-0329

Transportation Policy Division
215 Garry St., 15th Fl., Winnipeg, MB R3C 3Z1
Fax: 204-945-5539
Asst. Deputy Minister, John Spacek
204-945-1025
Director, Corporate Policy & Legislation Branch, Lawrence Mercer
204-945-1894
Director, Transportation Policy & Service Development, Richard Danis
204-945-0800
Director, Transportation Systems Planning & Development, Amar Chadha
204-945-2269

Manitoba Intergovernmental Affairs

#301, 450 Broadway Ave., Winnipeg, MB R3C 0V8
Fax: 204-945-1383
mnia@leg.gov.mb.ca
www.gov.mb.ca/ia/

Mission is to improve the economic, social & environmental wellbeing of Manitoba communities & citizens. The Department serves individuals, local governments, community organizations & businesses; & establishes a legislative, financial, planning & policy framework that supports democratic, accountable, effective & financially efficient local government, & the sustainable development of our communities. Programs are aimed at meeting particular needs for training, on-going advice, technical analysis & funding related to community revitalization & development, infrastructure development, land management, business support & local governance. The Department functions as an advocate of community needs, a catalyst & co-ordinator of action, promotes & participates in partnerships with private sector & non-government organizations & intergovernmental alliances

Acts Administered:
Capital Region Partnership Act
City of Winnipeg Charter
Convention Centre Corporation Act
An Act respecting Debts Owing by Municipalities to School Districts
Emergency Measures Act
Emergency 911 Public Safety Answering Point Act
Liquor Control Act
Local Authorities Election Act
Local Government Districts Act
Manitoba Lotteries Corporation Act
Manitoba Trade & Investment Corporation Act
Municipal Act
Municipal Affairs Administration Act
Municipal Assessment Act
Municipal Board Act
Municipal Councils & School Boards Elections Act
Municipal Revenue (Grants & Taxation) (Part 2)
Official Time Act
Planning Act (in part)
Northern Manitoba Planning & Bylaws Regulation
Provincial Land Use Policies Regulation
Subdivision Regulation
Soldiers' Taxation Relief Act
Regional Waste Management Authorities Act
Unconditional Grants Act
Minister, Hon. Steve Ashton
204-945-3788, Fax: 204-945-1383, minia@leg.gov.mb.ca
Deputy Minister, Intergovernmental Affairs, Linda McFadyen
204-945-4309, Fax: 204-945-5255, dmnia@leg.gov.mb.ca
Director, Administration & Finance, Craig Halwachs
Director, Amalgamated Human Resources, Craig McGregor

Associated Agencies, Boards & Commissions:
• Manitoba Liquor Control Commission
1555 Buffalo Pl.
PO Box 1023
Winnipeg, MB R3C 2X1
204-284-2501 Fax: 204-475-7666
info@mlcc.mb.ca
www.mlcc.mb.ca

• Manitoba Municipal Board
#1144, 363 Broadway
Winnipeg, MB R3C 3N9
204-945-2941 Fax: 204-948-2235

Provincial-Municipal Support Services
#508, 800 Portage Ave., Winnipeg, MB R3G 0N4
Asst. Deputy Minister, Laurie Davidson
204-945-2565, Fax: 204-948-2107
Acting Director, Municipal Finance & Advisory Services, Denise Carlyle
204-945-1944, Fax: 204-948-2780
Provincial Municipal Assessor, Assessment Branch, Mark Boreskie
204-945-2604, Fax: 204-945-1994
Director, Information Systems, Larry Phillips
204-945-2585, Fax: 204-945-1994

Community Land Use Planning Services
#604, 800 Portage Ave., Winnipeg, MB R3G 0N4
Asst. Deputy Minister, Vacant
Director, Community Planning Services, David Neufeld
204-945-2192, Fax: 204-945-5059
Director, Provincial Planning Services, Michael Teillet
204-945-2592, Fax: 204-945-5059

Emergency Measures Organization (EMO)
405 Broadway Ave., 15th Floor, Winnipeg, MB R3C 3L6
204-945-4772 Fax: 204-945-4929
888-267-8298
emo@gov.mb.ca
www.manitobaemo.ca
Coordinates emergency response, municipal emergency planning & training, & disaster recovery programs
Executive Director, Chuck Sanderson
204-945-5228, Fax: 204-945-4929

Urban Strategic Initiatives
#607, 800 Portage Ave., Winnipeg, MB R3G 0N4
Fax: 204-948-3512
Asst. Deputy Minister, Vacant
Director, Programs & Policy, Jon Gunn
204-945-3864
Director, Winnipeg Partnership Agreement, Vacant
204-984-1806, Fax: 204-983-3844
Coordinator, Neighbourhoods Alive!, Bob Dilay
204-945-3379, Fax: 204-945-5059

Manitoba Justice

Legislative Building, #104, 405 Broadway Ave., Winnipeg, MB R3C 3L6
204-945-3728 Fax: 204-945-2517
minjus@gov.mb.ca
www.gov.mb.ca/justice/index.html
Promotes a safe, just & peaceful society supported by a justice system that is fair, effective, trusted & understood by: providing a fair & effective prosecution service; managing offenders in an environment that promotes public safety & rehabilitation; providing mechanisms for timely & peaceful resolution of civil & criminal matters; providing legal advice & services to government; providing programs which assist in protecting & enforcing individual & collective rights; providing support & assistance to victims of crime; & promoting effective policing & crime prevention initiatives
Acts Administered:
Canada-United Kingdom Judgements Enforcement Act
Constitutional Questions Act
Correctional Services Act
Court of Appeal Act
Court of Queens' Bench Act
Court Security Act
Crime Prevention Foundation Act
Crown Attorneys Act
Child Custody Enforcement Act
Department of Justice Act
Discriminatory Business Practices Act
Domestic Violence & Stalking Prevention, Protection & Compensation Act
Enforcement of Judgements Conventions Act
Escheats Act
Executive Government Organization Act (subsection 12 (2), only, as Keeper of the Great Seal)
Expropriation Act
Fatality Inquiries Act
Fortified Buildings Act
Helen Betty Osborne Memorial Foundation Act
Human Rights Code
Inter-jurisdictional Support Orders Act
International Commercial Arbitration Act
International Sale of Goods Act
Interprovincial Subpoena Act
Intoxicated Persons Detention Act
Jury Act
Law Enforcement Review Act
Law Fees & Probate Charge Act
Law Reform Commission Act
Legal Aid Services Society of Manitoba Act
Mental Health Act Part 10 & clauses 125 (1) (i) & (j)
Minors Intoxicating Substances Control Act
Privacy Act
Private Investigators & Security Guards Act
Proceedings Against the Crown Act
Provincial Police Act
Public Trustee Act
Reciprocal Enforcement of Judgement Act
Regulations Act
Safer Communities & Neighbourhood Act
Sheriffs Act
Summary Convictions Act
Transboundary Pollution Reciprocal Access Act
Uniform Law Conference Commissioners Act
Vacant Property Act
Victims' Bill of Rights
Minister & Attorney General, Hon. Andrew Swan
204-945-3728, Fax: 204-945-2517, minjus@leg.gov.mb.ca
Deputy Minister & Deputy Attorney General, Ron Perozzo, Q.C.
204-945-3739, Fax: 204-945-4133, dmjus@leg.gov.mb.ca
Associated Agencies, Boards & Commissions:
• Compensation for Victims of Crime
1410 - 405 Broadway
Winnipeg, MB R3C 3L6
204-945-0899 Fax: 204-948-3071 800-262-9344
www.gov.mb.ca/justice/victims/index.html
The Compensation for Victims of Crime Program provides compensation for personal injury or death resulting from certain crimes occurring within Manitoba.
• Law Enforcement Review Agency (LERA)
#420, 155 Carlton St.
Winnipeg, MB R3C 3H8
204-945-8667 Fax: 204-948-1014 800-282-8069
lera@gov.mb.ca
www.gov.mb.ca/justice/lera
The mission of the Law Enforcement Review Agency (LERA) is to deliver a judicious, timely, impartial, client-oriented service to the public and to the police services and police officers within its jurisdiction.
• Law Reform Commission
#432, 405 Broadway
Winnipeg, MB R3C 3L6
204-945-2896 Fax: 204-948-2184
lawreform@gov.mb.ca
www.gov.mb.ca/justice/mlrc
The Manitoba Law Reform Commission is an independent agency of the Government of Manitoba established by The Law Reform Commission Act, C.C.S.M. c. L95. The Commission's duties are to inquire into and consider any matter relating to law in Manitoba with a view to making recommendations for the improvement, modernization and reform of law.
• Legal Aid Manitoba
402 - 294 Portage Ave.
Winnipeg, MB R3C 0B9
204-985-8500 Fax: 204-944-8582 800-261-2960
info@legalaid.mb.ca
www.legalaid.mb.ca
Legal Aid Manitoba works to ensure people with low incomes have the protections guaranteed in Canada by the The Charter of Rights and Freedoms, enacted as part of The Constitution Act in 1982.
• Manitoba Gaming Control Commission
#800, 215 Garry St.
Winnipeg, MB R3C 3P3
204-954-9400 Fax: 204-954-9450 800-782-0363
information@mgcc.mb.ca
www.mgcc.mb.ca
Other Communication: Toll Free Fax: 1-866-999-6688
To regulate and control gaming activity in Manitoba by protecting the public interest, being proactive and responsive to Manitoba's evolving gaming environment and working in consultation with our clients, stakeholders and partners to establish fair, balanced and responsible gaming practices.
• Manitoba Human Rights Commission
• Office of the Chief Medical Examiner
#210, 1 Wesley Ave.
Winnipeg, MB R3C 4C6
204-945-2088 Fax: 204-945-2442 800-282-9069
www.gov.mb.ca/justice/about/chief.html
The Chief Medical Examiner's Office investigates deaths where the cause is not readily known or when the death is a result of violence.
• Office of the Public Trustee
#500, 155 Carlton St.
Winnipeg, MB R3C 5R9
204-945-2700 Fax: 204-948-2251
publictrustee@gov.mb.ca
www.gov.mb.ca/publictrustee/index.html
The Public Trustee of Manitoba is a provincial government Special Operating Agency that manages and protects the affairs of Manitobans who are unable to do so themselves and have no one else willing or able to act. This includes mentally incompetent and vulnerable adults, deceased estates, and children.
• Manitoba Review Board
408 York Ave., 2nd Fl.
Winnipeg, MB R3C 0P9
204-945-4438 Fax: 204-945-5751

Civil Justice Division
Acting Director, Civil Legal Services, Lynn Romeo
204-945-2846
Director, Constitutional Law, Heather Leonoff
204-945-0679
Director, Family Law, Joan A. MacPhail, Q.C.
204-945-0268, Fax: 204-948-2004

Corrections Division
#810, 405 Broadway Ave., Winnipeg, MB R3C 3L6
204-945-7291
Asst. Deputy Minister, Greg Graceffo
204-945-7291, Fax: 204-945-5537
Executive Director, Adult Custody, Reg Forester
204-945-7283, Fax: 204-945-5537
Acting Executive Director, Youth Correctional Services, Carolyn Brock
204-945-6063, Fax: 204-948-2166
Acting Director, Adult Probation Services, Bob Dojack
204-945-4639, Fax: 204-948-2166

Courts Division
405 Broadway, 2nd Fl., Winnipeg, MB R3C 3L6
Asst. Deputy Minister, Jeff Schnoor
204-945-3027
Acting Executive Director, Judicial Services, Lavonne Ross
204-945-0413
Executive Director, Regional Courts, Vacant
204-726-6561
Executive Director, Winnipeg Courts & Acting Director, Court Services, Debra Baker
204-945-5883, Other Communications: Court Services: 204/945-1579

Criminal Justice Division
Asst. Deputy Minister, Mike Horn
204-945-2887
Director, Aboriginal & Community Law Enforcement, Al Brolly
204-945-5556
Director, Victim Services, Vacant
204-945-4589

Legislative Counsel Division
#410, 405 Broadway Ave., Winnipeg, MB R3C 3L6
204-945-5758
Legislative Counsel & Asst. Deputy Minister, Valerie Perry
204-945-1727
Director, Legal Translation, Michel Nantel
204-945-4597

Prosecutions Division
#510, 405 Broadway Ave., Winnipeg, MB R3C 3L6
204-945-2852
Asst. Deputy Attorney General, Vacant
204-945-2873
Director, Regional Prosecutions & Legal Education, Brian Kaplan
204-945-2860
Director, Specialized Prosecutions & Appeals, Don Slough
204-945-2868
Director, Winnipeg Prosecutions, Jacqueline St.Hill
204-945-3228
Director, Policy Development & Analysis, Jeff Schnoor
204-945-2900
Director, Business Operations, Carol Abbott
204-945-3417

Manitoba Labour & Immigration

Legislative Building, 317, 450 Broadway Ave., Winnipeg, MB R3C 0V8
204-945-4079 Fax: 204-945-8312
minlab@leg.gov.mb.ca
www.gov.mb.ca/labour
Acts Administered:
Amusements Act (Part II)
Architects Act
Architects & Engineers Scope of Practice Dispute Settlement Act
Buildings & Mobile Homes Act
Construction Industry Wages Act
Department of Labour & Immigration Act
Electricians' Licence Act
Elevator Act
Employment Services Act
Employment Standards Code
Engineering & Geoscientific Professions Act
Fair Registration Practices in Regulated Professions Act
Firefighters & Paramedics Arbitration Act
Fires Prevention & Emergency Response Act
Gas & Oil Burner Act

Holocaust Memorial Day Act
Labour Relations Act
Manitoba Ethnocultural Advisory & Advocacy Council Act
Manitoba Immigration Council Act
Manitoba Multiculturalism Act
Manitoba Women's Advisory Council Act
Pay Equity Act
Pension Benefits Act
Power Engineers Act
Remembrance Day Act
Retail Business Holiday Closing Act
Steam & Pressure Plants Act
Worker Recruitment and Protection Act
Workplace Safety & Health Act
Construction Industry Safety Regulation
Fibrosis & Silicosis Regulation
Forestry, Logging & Log Hauling Regulation
Hearing Conservation & Noise Control Regulation
Operation of Mines Regulation
Sanitary & Hygienic Welfare Regulation
Workplace Hazardous Materials Information System Regulation
Workplace Health Hazard Regulation
Workplace Safety & Health Committee Regulation
Workplace Safety Regulation
Minimum Wage & Working Conditions Regulation

Minister, Hon. Jennifer Juliette Howard
204-945-4079, Fax: 204-945-8312, minlab@leg.gov.mb.ca
Deputy Minister, Jeff Parr
204-945-3782, Fax: 204-948-2203, dmlab@leg.gov.mb.ca
Director, Amalgamated Human Resources, Robert (Butch) Berube
204-945-6892

Associated Agencies, Boards & Commissions:

• Advisory Council on Workplace Safety & Health
#200, 401 York Ave.
Winnipeg, MB R3C 0P8
204-945-3446 Fax: 204-945-4556
www.gov.mb.ca/labour/safety/council.html
The Advisory Council on Workplace Safety & Health was established in 1977 under the authority of the Workplace Safety & Health Act. The council reports directly to the Minister of Labour & Immigration. The council advises & makes recommendations to the Minister of Labour & Immigration concerning general workplace safety & health issues, protection of workers in specific situations & appointment of consultants & advisors.

• Manitoba Civil Service Commission
#935, 155 Carlton St.
Winnipeg, MB R3C 3H8
204-945-2332 Fax: 204-945-1486
cschrp@gov.mb.ca
www.gov.mb.ca/csc/

• Manitoba Ethnocultural Advisory & Advocacy Council
215 Notre Dame Ave. 4th Fl.
Winnipeg, MB R3B 1N3
204-945-2339 Fax: 204-948-2323 800-665-8332
meaac@gov.mb.ca
www.gov.mb.ca/labour/immigrate/multiculturalism/5.html

• Manitoba Labour Board
A.A. Heaps Bldg.
#402, 258 Portage Ave.
Winnipeg, MB R3C 0B6
204-945-3783 Fax: 204-945-1296
mlb@gov.mb.ca
www.gov.mb.ca/labour/labbrd

• Manitoba Minimum Wage Board
614 - 401 York Ave.
Winnipeg, MB R3C 0P8
204-945-4889 Fax: 204-948-2085
mw@gov.mb.ca
www.gov.mb.ca/labour/labmgt/resbr/wages/minwagbd.html

• Manitoba Women's Advisory Council
#301, 155 Carlton St.
Winnipeg, MB R3C 3H8
204-945-6281 Fax: 204-945-6511 800-282-8069
001women@gov.mb.ca

• Multiculturalism Secretariat
213 Notre Dame Ave., 4th Fl.
Winnipeg, MB R3B 1N3
204-945-1156 Fax: 204-948-2323

• Office of the Fire Commissioner
#508, 401 York Ave.
Winnipeg, MB R3C 0P8
204-945-3322 Fax: 204-948-2089 800-282-8069
firecomm@gov.mb.ca
www.firecomm.gov.mb.ca/

• Pension Commission of Manitoba
#1004, 401 York Ave.
Winnipeg, MB R3C 0P8
204-945-2740 Fax: 204-948-2375
pensions@gov.mb.ca
www.gov.mb.ca/labour/pension/index.html

Employment Standards Division
204-945-3352 Fax: 204-948-3046
800-821-4307
employmentstandards@gov.mb.ca
Executive Director, Dave Dyson
204-945-3354, Fax: 204-948-3046

Immigration & Multiculturalism Division
213 Notre Dame Ave., 5th Floor, Winnipeg, MB R3B 1N3
204-945-6300 Fax: 204-948-2148
immigratemanitoba@gov.mb.ca
www.immigrationmanitoba.com
Asst. Deputy Minister, Gerald L. Clement
204-945-8174, Fax: 204-948-2882
Director, Adult Language Training Branch, Margaret Pidlaski
204-945-7415, Fax: 204-948-2148
Acting Director, Immigration Promotion & Recruitment, Ben Rempel
204-945-4984, Fax: 204-948-2256
Director, Settlement & Labour Market Services Branch, Ximena Munoz
204-945-5978, Fax: 204-948-2148

Status of Women
#409, 401 York Ave., Winnipeg, MB R3C 0P8
204-945-3476 Fax: 204-945-0013
800-263-0234
mwd@gov.mb.ca
Executive Director, Yvonne Spyropoulos
204-945-5812

Workplace Safety & Health Division
#200, 401 York Ave., Winnipeg, MB R3C 0P8
204-945-3446 Fax: 204-948-2209
wshcompl@gov.mb.ca
www.gov.mb.ca/labour/safety/index.html
Operates a 24-hour response service to accidents & complaints; monitors & evaluates workplace areas for chemical, physical, biological & ergonomic factors; participates in worker education & training programs for workers, employers & other interested parties on matters relating to maintaining a safe & healthy workplace
Asst. Deputy Minister, Don Hurst
204-945-3605
Director, Inspection Services, Bryan Zirk
204-945-8429, bzirk@gov.mb.ca
Acting Director, Mining Safety Unit, Bill Comaskey
204-677-6821, bcomaskey@gov.mb.ca
Chief Occupational Medical Officer, Dr. Ted Redekop
204-945-3608, tredekop@gov.mb.ca

Manitoba Lotteries Corporation

830 Empress St., Winnipeg, MB R3G 3H3
204-957-2500 Fax: 204-957-3991
800-265-2912
communications@casinosofwinnipeg.com
www.mlc.mb.ca
President/CEO, Winston Hodgins
Communications Coordinator, Lindsay Sprange
204-957-3930

Manitoba News Media Services

#29, Legislative Bldg., 450 Broadway, Winnipeg, MB R3C 0V8
204-945-3746 Fax: 204-945-3988
nmservices@leg.gov.mb.ca
Provides news releases, television & radio news items.
Supervisor, Stu Fawcett
204-945-4097, Fax: 204-945-3988, sfawcett@leg.gov.mb.ca

Manitoba Government Inquiry
204-945-3744 Fax: 204-945-4261
866-626-4862
mgi@gov.mb.ca
TTY: 204-945-4796
Answers queries regarding Manitoba's provincial government departments & agencies.
Supervisor, Aggie Hasselfield
204-945-2424, ahasselfield@gov.mb.ca

Statutory Publications
#20, 200 Vaughan St., Winnipeg, MB R3C 1T5
204-945-3101 Fax: 204-945-7172
800-321-1203
statpub@gov.mb.ca
www.gov.mb.ca/chc/statpub/
Sale & distribution of Manitoba statutes, regulations & a wide variety of other government publications & forms
Supervisor, Keith Holness
204-945-3101, Fax: 204-945-7172, kholness@gov.mb.ca

Manitoba Office of the Ombudsman

750 - 500 Portage Ave., Winnipeg, MB R3C 3X1
204-982-9130 Fax: 204-942-7803
800-665-0531
ombudsma@ombudsman.mb.ca
www.ombudsman.mb.ca
The Ombudsman, an independent & non-partisan Officer of the Legislative Assembly, investigates complaints from persons who feel they have been unfairly dealt with by government departments or agencies
Manitoba Ombudsman, Irene Hamilton

Manitoba Public Insurance

#B100, 234 Donald St., PO Box 6300, Winnipeg, MB R3C 4A4
204-985-7000 Fax: 204-985-3525
800-665-2410
www.mpi.mb.ca
TTY: 204-985-8832
Administers Manitoba's Public Automobile Insurance Program & sells extension auto coverage on a competitive basis.
Minister responsible, Hon. Andrew Swan
204-945-3728, Fax: 204-945-2517, minjus@leg.gov.mb.ca
President/CEO, Marilyn McLaren
Vice-President, Claims Operations & Safety Operations, Ted Hlynsky
Vice-President, Community & Corporate Relations, MaryAnn Kempe
Vice-President, Finance & CFO, Don Palmer
Vice-President, Service Operations, Christine Martin
Vice-President, Strategy & Innovation & Chief Information Officer, Dan Guimond
General Counsel & Corporate Secretary, Kathy Kalinowsky

Manitoba Science, Technology, Energy & Mines

#333, 450 Broadway, Winnipeg, MB R3C 0V8
www.gov.mb.ca/stem/index.html

Acts Administered:
Gaming Control Act
Manitoba Hydro Act
Minister, Dave Chomiak
204-945-5356, Fax: 204-948-2692, minstem@leg.gov.mb.ca
Deputy Minister, John Clarkson
204-945-2771, Fax: 204-948-2747, dmstem@leg.gov.mb.ca

Associated Agencies, Boards & Commissions:

• Industrial Technology Centre
#200, 78 Innovation Dr.
Winnipeg, MB R3T 6C2
www.itc.mb.ca

• Mining Board
#360, 1395 Ellice Ave.
Winnipeg, MB R3G 3P2
204-489-0018
Arbitration of disputes between surface rights holders & mineral rights holders with respect to accessing of minerals other than oil & gas.

• Surface Rights Board
#360, 1395 Ellice Ave.
Winnipeg, MB R3G 3P2
204-945-0731 Fax: 204-948-2578 800-282-8069
bmiskimmin@gov.mb.ca
Arbitrates disputes relating to right of entry or compensation for surface rights used by holders of oil & gas rights.

• Manitoba Education, Research & Learning Information Networks (MERLIN)
#100 - 135 Innovation Dr., University of Manitoba
Winnipeg, MB R3T 6A8
204-474-7800 Fax: 204-474-7830 800-430-6404
www.merlin.mb.ca

• Manitoba Health Research Council
#P216, 770 Bannatyne Ave.
Winnipeg, MB R3E 0W3
204-775-1096 Fax: 204-786-5401
info@mhrc.mb.ca
mhrc.mb.ca

Energy Development Initiative
The Initiative's focus is on: Agri-Energy, Biofuels, Geothermal systems, Wind Energy, Green Building & Energy Efficiency, Hydrogen, as well as hybrid-electric vehicles, solar energy, ethanol fuels
Asst. Deputy Minister, Energy Development Initiative, Garry Hastings
204-945-1454, Fax: 204-943-0031
Director, Energy Economic Development, Jim Crone
204-945-1874, Fax: 204-943-0031, jcrone@gov.mb.ca
Director, Energy Policy, Shaun Loney
204-945-5804, Fax: 204-943-0031, sloney@gov.mb.ca

Energy Climate Change & Green Strategy Initiatives Branch
#1202 - 155 Carlton St., Winnipeg, MB R3C 3H8
204-945-7382 Fax: 204-948-3739
ccinfo@gov.mb.ca
www.manitoba.ca

The Branch promotes awareness, programs & funding for climate change initiatives, facilitates partnerships between government & community to develop green initiatives that result in environmental, economic & social benefits, advances climate change mitigation & adaptation research, & develops regional partnerships for climate change action
Acting Executive Director, Andrea Merredew
204-945-2245

Mineral Resources Division
#360, 1395 Ellice Ave., Winnipeg, MB R3G 3P2
Fax: 204-945-8427
Promotes wise land management & environmentally sustainable economic development in the province based on Manitoba's mineral & petroleum resources; fosters & enhances business development opportunities in mineral & petroleum economic development through promotion & marketing activities; provides authoritative documentation of the province's mineral & petroleum endowment & development potential; administers the delivery of mineral & petroleum industry support programs; administers legislation governing the disposition of mineral rights, oil & gas rights, exploration, development & production of Manitoba's mineral & petroleum resources
Assistant Deputy Minister, John Fox
204-945-4317, Fax: 204-945-1406, jfox@gov.mb.ca

Manitoba Geological Survey
#360, 1394 Ellice Ave., Winnipeg, MB R3G 3P2
Fax: 204-945-1406
800-223-5215
minesinfo@gov.mb.ca
Generates technical information on the geology of Manitoba in order to encourage & guide mineral exploration in the province & to provide a database for developing mineral policy & for determining effective land-use policies.
Director, Ric Syme
204-945-6556, rsyme@gov.mb.ca

Mineral Policy & Business Development
Manager, Gary Ostry
204-945-6564, Fax: 204-945-8427, gostry@gov.mb.ca
MEAP Coordinator, Minerals Policy & Business Development, Linda Rogoski
204-945-6586, Fax: 204-945-8427, lrogoski@gov.mb.ca

Regional Geological Survey Offices:

Mines Branch
#360, 1395 Ellice Ave., Winnipeg, MB R3G 3P2
Fax: 204-948-2578
The Mines Branch administers legislation governing the disposition of mineral rights (permits, claims & leases), exploration, development, & production of the province's non-fuel mineral resources & the rehabilitation of mines & quarries.
Director, Ernie Armitt
204-945-6505, earmitt@gov.mb.ca

Regional Office:

Petroleum
#360, 1395 Ellice Ave., Winnipeg, MB R3G 3P2
204-945-6577 Fax: 204-945-0586
Administers provisions under The Oil & Gas Act & The Oil & Gas Production Tax Act relating to exploration, development, production & transportation of oil & gas. The Branch develops, recommends, implements & administers policies & legislation, to provide for the sustainable development of Manitoba's oil & gas resources. The Branch deals with matters relating to well spacing, production allowables, pool designations, salt water disposal, enhanced recovery projects & unitization. The Branch publishes several reports each year, providing the public, industry & government with information on the petroleum industry in Manitoba
Director, Keith Lowdon
klowdon@gov.mb.ca

District Offices:

Virden
Petroleum Inspection, 227 King St., Virden, MB R0M 2C0
204-748-4260 Fax: 204-748-2208

Waskada
Petroleum Inspection, 23 Railway Ave., Waskada, MB R0M 2E0
204-673-2472 Fax: 204-673-2767

ICT Services Manitoba
#300 - 259 Portage Ave., Winnipeg, MB R3B 2A9
800-665-0204
www.gov.mb.ca/est/KnowledgeEnterprises

Knowledge Enterprises Branch
259 Portage Ave., Winnipeg, MB R3B 3P4
204-945-6298 Fax: 204-945-3977
Director, Doug McCartney
204-945-6298, Fax: 204-945-3977, Douglas.McCartney@gov.mb.ca

Project Manager, ICT/Investment Promotion/Branch Communications, Cindy Hodges
204-945-6657, Cindy.Hodges@gov.mb.ca

Manitoba Seniors & Healthy Aging Secretariat

#822, 155 Carlton St., Winnipeg, MB R3C 3H8
204-945-6565 Fax: 204-948-2514
800-665-6565
seniors@gov.mb.ca
www.gov.mb.ca/shas
Minister responsible, Hon. Jim Rondeau
204-945-1373
Acting Executive Director, Patti Chiappetta
204-945-1825
Associated Agencies, Boards & Commissions:
• Manitoba Council on Aging
#822, 155 Carlton St.
Winnipeg, MB R3C 3H8
204-945-6565 Fax: 204-948-2514 800-665-6565

Manitoba Telecom Services Inc. (MTS)

333 Main St., PO Box 6666, Winnipeg, MB R3C 3V6
204-941-4111 Fax: 204-772-6391
www.mts.mb.ca/
Chair, Thomas E. Stefanson
CEO, Pierre Blouin
President, Enterprise Solutions, John A. MacDonald
President, Consumer Markets, Kelvin Shepherd, P.Eng.
CFO, Wayne S. Demkey, CA

Manitoba Treasury Board Secretariat

#200, 386 Broadway, Winnipeg, MB R3C 3R6
204-945-4150 Fax: 204-948-4878
The Treasury Board Secretariat provides financial and analytical support and advice to the Minister of Finance and Treasury Board.
Minister responsible, Hon. Rosann Wowchuk
204-945-3952, Fax: 204-945-6057, minfin@leg.gov.mb.ca
Secretary to the Treasury Board, Tannis Mindell
204-945-1100
Asst. Deputy Minister, Labour Relations, Richard (Rick) Stevenson
204-945-2136
Asst. Deputy Minister, Fiscal Management & Capital Planning, Barb Dryden
204-945-1096

Manitoba Water Stewardship

200 Saulteaux Cres., PO Box 11, Winnipeg, MB R3J 3W3
204-945-6398
800-282-8069
wsd@gov.mb.ca
www.gov.mb.ca/waterstewardship/index.html
Provides leadership in environmental stewardship for the benefit of current & future generations of Manitobans, so that the social, economic & inherent environmental value of water is protected & realized, Manitoba's water & fish resources are managed sustainably, & people are safe from water hazards. Comprised of the former Water Branch, Fisheries Branch, & Office of Drinking Water from Manitoba Conservation, the Manitoba Water Services Board, & the Conservation Districts Program from the Department of Intergovernmental Affairs
Acts Administered:
Conservation Agreements Act
Conservation Agreement Forms Regulation
Eligible Conservation Agencies Regulation
Conservation Districts Act
Drinking Water Safety Act, 2004
Dyking Authority Act
Fisheries Act
Fishermen's Assistance & Polluter's Liability Act
Floodway Authority Act
Ground Water & Water Well Act
Lake of the Woods Control Board Act
Manitoba Natural Resources Transfer Act
Natural Resources Agreement Act
Public Health Act
Water Power Act
Water Commission Act
Water Resources Administration Act
Water Resources Conservation Act
Water Rights Act
Water Supply Commissions Act
Minister, Hon. Christine Melnick
204-945-1133, Fax: 204-948-2684, minwsd@leg.gov.mb.ca
Deputy Minister, Don Norquay
204-945-0982, Fax: 204-948-2519, dmwsd@leg.gov.mb.ca
Executive Director, Regulatory & Operational Services, Steven Topping
204-945-7488, Fax: 204-945-7419
Associated Agencies, Boards & Commissions:

• Manitoba Conservation Districts Commission
Secretariat c/o Planning & Coordination Branch
123 Main St.
PO Box 20000
Neepawa, MB R0J 1H0
204-476-7033 Fax: 204-476-7539
whildebran@gov.mb.ca
The Conservation Districts Program has been delivering a comprehensive, sustainable approach to water & soil management for over 25 years. Conservation Districts are established under the authority of The Conservation District Act. There are 16 Conservation Districts covering approximately 60% of Agro-Manitoba. Individual district boundaries may vary depending on the needs of the people. Districts are usually based on the drainage basin or watershed of the major river in the area.

Ecological Services Division
Asst. Deputy Minister, Dwight Williamson
204-945-7030
Director, Fisheries Branch, Joe O'Connor
204-945-7814, Fax: 204-945-2308
Director, Planning & Coordination, Rhonda McDougal
204-945-8271
Director, Water Science & Management Branch, Nicole Armstrong
204-945-3991

Office of Drinking Water
1007 Century St., Winnipeg, MB R3H 0W4
204-945-5762 Fax: 204-945-1365
Coordinates the activities of the province's drinking water program; provides guidance, technical expertise, information & education materials; ensures water suppliers provide safe, adequate & aesthetically pleasing water
Manager, P.Eng. Don Rocan
204-945-7010

Manitoba Workers' Compensation Board

333 Broadway Ave., Winnipeg, MB R3C 4W3
204-954-4321 Fax: 204-954-4999
800-362-3340
wcb@wcb.mb.ca
www.wcb.mb.ca
President/CEO, Doug Sexsmith
CFO, Harold Dueck
Vice President, Prevention, Assessments & Customer Service, Alice Sayant
Vice President, Rehabilitation & Compensation Services, Dave Scott
General Counsel & Corporate Secretary, Lori Ferguson Sain
Associate Vice President, Human Resources & Administration, Rob Campbell
Director, Communications/SAFE Work, Warren Preece

Government of New Brunswick

Seat of Government: PO Box 6000, Fredericton, NB E3B 5H1
www.gnb.ca
The Province of New Brunswick entered Confederation July 1, 1867. It has an area of 71,355.12 km2. The Statistics Canada census population in 2006 was 730,000.

Office of the Lieutenant-Governor / Bureau du Lieutenant gouverneur

Old Government House, 51 Woodstock Rd., PO Box 6000, Fredericton, NB E3B 5H1
506-453-2505 Fax: 506-444-5280
www.gnb.ca/lg
Lieutenant-Governor, Hon. Nicholas Graydon
506-453-2505, Fax: 506-444-5280, ltgov@gnb.ca
Principal Secretary, Office of the Lieutenant-Governor, Tim Richardson
tim.richardson@gnb.ca

Office of the Premier / Cabinet du Premier ministre

Centennial Bldg., 670 King St., PO Box 6000, Fredericton, NB E3B 5H1
506-453-2144 Fax: 506-453-7407
premier@gnb.ca
www.gnb.ca/premier
Premier; President, Executive Council; Minister, Intergovernmental Affairs; Minister Responsible, Premier's Council on the Status of Disabled Persons; Minister Responsible, Aboriginal Affairs Secretariat, Citizens'Engagement, Hon. David Alward
david.alward@gnb.ca; Premier@gnb.ca
Chief of Staff, Nancy McKay
nancy.mckay@gnb.ca
Correspondence Manager, Correspondence, Linda Landry-Guimond
506-453-2144, Fax: 506-453-7407, linda.laundry-guimond@gnb.ca

Press Secretary, Communications, Jesse Robichaud
jesse.robichaud@gnb.ca

Executive Council / Conseil exécutif

Centennial Bldg., 670 King St., PO Box 6000, Fredericton, NB E3B 5H1
506-453-2144 Fax: 506-453-7407
david.alward@gnb.ca

Premier; President, Executive Council; Minister, Intergovernmental Affairs; Minister Responsible, Premier's Council on the Status of Disabled Persons; Minister Responsible, Aboriginal Affairs Secretariat, Citizens'Engagement, Hon. David Alward
506-453-2144, Fax: 506-453-7407, Premier@gnb.ca; david.alward@gnb.ca
Minister, Economic Development; Minister Responsible, Regional Development Corporation; Minister Responsible, Francophonie;, Minister Responsible, Northern New Brunswick Initiative, Hon. Paul Robichaud
506-453-5898, Fax: 506-453-6389, paul.robichaud@gnb.ca
Minister, Justice & Consumer Affairs & Attorney General, Hon. Marie-Claude Blais
506-453-3132, Fax: 506-453-3651, Marie-Claude.Blais@gnb.ca
Minister, Public Safety, Hon. Robert Trevors
506-453-7414, Fax: 506-453-3870, Robert.Trevors@gnb.ca
Minister, Finance; Minister, Office of Human Resources; Minister Responsible, NB Liquor Corporation, Minister Responsible, NB Lotteries & Gaming Corporation; Minister Responsible, NB Investment Management Corporation, Hon. Blaine Higgs
506-444-2627, Fax: 506-457-4989, Blaine.Higgs@gnb.ca
Minister, Transportation & Infrastructure; Minister Responsible, Supply & Services, Hon. Claude Williams
506-457-7345, Fax: 506-453-7987, Claude.Williams@gnb.ca
Minister, Natural Resources, Hon. Bruce Northrup
506-453-2510, Fax: 506-444-5839, bruce.northrup@gnb.ca
Minister, Energy; Minister Responsible, Efficiency NB, Hon. Craig Leonard
506-658-3179, Fax: 506-658-3191, Craig.Leonard@gnb.ca
Minister, Agriculture, Aquaculture & Fisheries, Hon. Michael Olscamp
506-453-2662, Fax: 506-453-3402, Mike.Olscamp@gnb.ca
Minister, Health, Hon. Madeleine Dubé
506-457-4800, Fax: 506-453-5442, Madeleine.Dubé@gnb.ca
Minister, Wellness, Culture, & Sport; Minister, Tourism & Parks, Hon. Trevor Holder
506-453-3009, Fax: 506-457-4984, trevor.holder@gnb.ca
Minister, Social Development; Minister Responsible, Senior & Healthy Aging Secretariat; Minister Responsible, Housing;, Minister Responsible, Community Non-Profit Organizations Secretariat, Hon. Sue Stultz
506-453-2001, Fax: 506-453-2164, sue.stultz@gnb.ca
Minister, Post-Secondary Education, Training, & Labour, Hon. Martine Coulombe
506-453-2342, Fax: 506-453-3038, martine.coulombe@gnb.ca
Minister, Education Early Childhood Development; Minister Responsible, NB Provincial Capital Commission, Hon. Jody Carr
506-453-2523, Fax: 506-457-4960, jody.carr@gnb.ca
Minister, Environment; Minister Responsible, Status of Women; Minister Responsible, Communications NB, Hon. Margaret-Ann Blaney
506-453-8126, Fax: 506-453-7977, margaret-ann.blaney@gnb.ca
Minister, Local Government; Minister Responsible, Service New Brunswick, Hon. Bruce Fitch
506-453-2807, Fax: 506-453-3988, Bruce.Fitch@gnb.ca

Executive Council Office
Centennial Bldg, #273, 670 King St., PO Box 6000, Fredericton, NB E3B 5H1
506-444-4417 Fax: 506-453-2266
www.gnb.ca/0012/index-e.asp

The Executive Council Office is responsible for the provision of secretariat & administrative services to the following: the Executive Council; Ministers with policy coordination responsibilities; & the Priorities Committee.

Premier; President, Executive Council; Minister, Intergovernmental Affairs; Minister Responsible, Aboriginal Affairs,, Premier's Council on the Status of Disabled Persons; Minister Responsble, Citizen'sEngagement, Hon. David Alward
506-453-2144, Fax: 506-453-7407, david.alward@gnb.ca
Deputy Minister; Clerk of the Executive Council; Secretary to Cabinet, Byron James
506-444-4417, Fax: 506-453-2266, byron.james@gnb.ca
Deputy Minister, Strategic Initiatives, Dallas McCready
506-453-2144, Fax: 506-453-7407, dallas.mccready@gnb.ca
Assistant Deputy Minister, Women's Issues, Norma Dubé
506-453-2975, Fax: 506-453-7977, Norma.Dube@gnb.ca
Assistant Deputy Minister, Assistant Secretary, Patricia MacKenzie
506-453-2314, Fax: 506-453-2266, patricia.mackenzie@gnb.ca
Policy Advisor, Policy & Priorities, Raj Venugopal
506-444-5126, Fax: 506-453-2266, raj.venugopal@gnb.ca

Legislative Assembly of New Brunswick / Assemblée législative

Centre Block, Legislative Bldg., 706 Queen St., PO Box 6000, Fredericton, NB E3B 5H1
506-453-2506 Fax: 506-453-7154
wwwleg@gnb.ca
www.gnb.ca/legis/index-e.asp

The Office of the Legislative Assembly is responsible for the following services: Assisting Members of the Legislative Assembly, their staff, & the public; Recording the proceedings of the Legislative Assembly; Maintaining the records of the Legislative Assembly; & Providing information services on behalf of the Legislative Assembly.

Speaker of the Legislative Assembly, Hon. Dale Graham
506-453-2907, Fax: 506-453-7154, dale.graham@gnb.ca
Deputy Speaker, Claude Landry
506-453-7494, Fax: 506-453-3461, claude.landry@gnb.ca
Clerk of the Legislative Assembly, Loredana Catalli Sonier
506-453-2506, Fax: 506-453-7154, l.catalli.sonier@gnb.ca
Director, Finance & Human Resources, Peter Wolters
506-453-2506, Fax: 506-444-3331, peter.wolters@gnb.ca
Sergeant-at-Arms, Daniel Bussières
506-453-2527, Fax: 506-453-7154, dan.bussieres@gnb.ca
Director, Finance & Human Resources, Peter Wolters
506-453-2506, Fax: 506-444-3331, peter.wolters@gnb.ca
Commissioner, Office of the Conflict of Interest, Hon. Patrick A.A. Ryan, Q.C.
506-457-7890, Fax: 506-444-5224, coi@gnb.ca
Official Reporter, Hansard Office, Linda Fahey
506-453-8352, Fax: 506-453-3199, linda.fahey@gnb.ca
Legislative Librarian, Kenda Clark-Gorey
506-453-8346, Fax: 506-444-5889, kenda.clark.gorey@gnb.ca
Manager, Debates Translation, Aurella Losier-Vienneau
506-453-6270, Fax: 506-453-3126, aurella.losier.vienneau@gnb.ca
Officer, Special Projects, Valmond LeBlanc
506-472-0214, Fax: 506-472-4724, vall2@rogers.com

Government Caucus Office (Liberal)
West Block, Departmental Bldg., 96 Saint John St., PO Box 6000, Fredericton, NB E3B 5H1
506-453-2548 Fax: 506-453-3956
denise.scott@gnb.ca

Leader of the Government (Premier); President, Executive Council; Minister, Intergovernmental Affairs; Minister Responsible, Premier's Council on the Status of Disabled Persons; Minister Responsible, Office ofSelf-Sufficiency, Hon. Alward David
506-453-2144, Fax: 506-453-7407, david.alward@gnb.ca
House Leader (Government), Hon. Paul Robichaud
506-453-7494, Fax: 506-453-3461, paul.robichaud@gnb.ca
Whip (Government), Brian MacDonald
506-453-7494, Fax: 506-453-3461, brian.t.macdonald@gnb.ca
Caucus Chair (Government), John Betts
506-453-7494, Fax: 506-453-3461, johnw.betts@gnb.ca
Chief of Staff (Office of the Government Members), Philip Chiasson
506-453-7494, Fax: 506-453-3461, philip.chiasson@gnb.ca
Director, Communications (Office of the Government Members), Heidi Cyr
506-453-7494, Fax: 506-453-3461, heidi.cyr@gnb.ca

Office of the Official Opposition (Progressive Conservative) / Bureau de l'opposition officielle
East Block, Old Education Bldg., 710 Queen St., PO Box 6000, Fredericton, NB E3B 5H1
506-453-7494 Fax: 506-453-3461
pcmemb@gnb.ca@gnb.ca

Leader of the Official Opposition, Victor Boudreau
506-453-2548, Fax: 506-453-3956, victor.boudreau@gnb.ca
Whip (Official Opposition), Denis Landry
506-453-2548, Fax: 506-453-3956, denis.landry@gnb.ca
Caucus Chair (Official Opposition), Roger Melanson
506-453-2548, Fax: 506-453-3956, roger.l.melanson@gnb.ca
Director, Communications (Official Opposition), Carl Davies
506-453-2548, Fax: 504-453-3956, carl.davies@gnb.ca
Chief of Staff, Official Opposition, Greg Byrne
506-453-2548, Fax: 504-453-3956, greg.byrne@gnb.ca
Press Secretary, Official Opposition, Hillary Casey
506-453-2548, Fax: 504-453-3956, hillary.casey@gnb.ca

Standing Committees of the House / Comités se pertenant de la chambre
The following are the Standing Committees of the Legislative Assembly of New Brunswick: Crown Corporations; Estimates; Health Care, Law Amendments; Legislative Administration; Legislative Officers; Private Bills; Privileges; Procedure; & Public Accounts.

Select Committees of the House / Comités Spéciaux
The following are the Select Committees of the Legislative Assembly of New Brunswick: Point Lepreau and Revision of the Official Languages Act.

Fifty-seventh Legislature - New Brunswick

Legislative Assembly of New Brunswick, 706 Queen St., PO Box 6000, Fredericton, NB E3B 5H1
506-453-2506 Fax: 506-453-7154
www.gnb.ca/legis/index-e.asp

Last General Election, September 27, 2010. Maximum Duration, 5 years. Party Standings (July 2011): Liberal (Lib.) 13; Progressive Conservatives (PC) 42; Total 55. Members' Salaries, Indemnities, & Allowances (2010): Members' annual indemnity $85,000. Additional Members' Salaries, Indemnities, & Allowances: Premier $79,000; Ministers $52,614; Leader of the Opposition $55,300; Leader of Registered Political Party $19,750; Speaker $52,614; Deputy Speaker $26,307; Government Whip $26,307; Official Opposition Whip $19,730; Government House Leader $26,307; Opposition House Leader $19,730. The following list of Members of the Legislative Assembly includes the following information: Constituency & population; Party affiliation; & Contact information.

Members
Hon. Hédard Albert, Caraquet,Electoral District 6, Liberal
506-444-2517, Fax: 506-453-6668, hedard.albert@gnb.ca, Other Communications: Constituency Phone: 506-726-2929; Fax: 506-726-2966
David Alward, Woodstock, Electoral District49, Progressive Conservative
506-453-7494, Fax: 506-453-3461, david.alward@gnb.ca, Other Communications: Constituency Phone: 506-325-4990; Fax: 506-325-4991
Hon. Donald Arseneault, Dalhousie-Restigouche East, Electoral District 2, Liberal
506-453-2510, Fax: 506-444-5839, donald.arseneault@gnb.ca, Other Communications: Constituency Phone: 506-685-5252; Fax: 506-685-5255
John W. Betts, Moncton-Crescent, ElectoralDistrict 24, Progressive Conservative
506-453-7494, Fax: 506-453-3461, johnw.betts@gnb.ca, Other Communications: Constituency Phone: 506-869-6579; Fax: 506-869-6614
Margaret-Ann Blaney, Rothesay,Electoral District 32, Progressive Conservative
506-453-7494, Fax: 506-453-3461, margaret-ann.blaney@gnb.ca, Other Communications: Constituency Phone: 506-848-6646; Fax: 506-848-6648
Greg Davis, Campbellton-Restigouche Centre,Electoral District 1, Liberal
506-453-7494, Fax: 506-453-3461, greg.davis@gnb.ca, Other Communications: Constituency Phone: 506-789-6272; Fax: 506-453-3461
Hon. Victor E. Boudreau, Shediac-Cap-Pelé,Electoral District 17, Liberal
506-444-2627, Fax: 506-457-4989, victor.boudreau@gnb.ca, Other Communications: Constituency Phone: 506-533-3450; Fax: 506-533-3452
Jake Stewart, Southwest-Miramichi, ElectoralDistrict 13, Liberal
506-453-7494, Fax: 506-453-3461, jake.stewart@gnb.ca, Other Communications: Constituency Phone: 506-843-7729; Fax: 506-843-7726
Troy Lifford, Fredericton-Nashwaaksis, Electoral District 42, Liberal
506-453-7494, Fax: 506-453-3461, troy.lifford@gnb.ca, Other Communications: Constituency Phone: 506-449-3902; 506-449-0433
Hon. Craig Leonard, Fredericton-Lincoln,Electoral District 44, Liberal
506-462-5188, Fax: 506-453-7195, craig.leonard@gnb.ca, Other Communications: Constituency Phone: 506-453-5723 Fax: 506-453-6057
Jody Carr, Oromocto, Electoral District 40, Progressive Conservative
506-453-7494, Fax: 506-453-3461, jody.carr@gnb.ca, Other Communications: Constituency Phone: 506-357-4141; Fax: 506-357-4147
Chris Collins, Moncton East, Electoral District21, Liberal
506-453-2548, Fax: 506-453-3956, chris.collins@gnb.ca, Other Communications: Constituency Phone: 506-453-2548; Fax: 506-856-2596
Carl Killen, Saint John Harbour, Electoral District34, Liberal
506-453-7494, Fax: 506-453-3461, carl.killen@gnb.ca, Other Communications: Constituency Phone: 506-642-9774; 506-642-9794
Hon. Rick Doucet, Charlotte-The Isles,Electoral District 38, Liberal
506-444-6734, Fax: 506-444-5477, rick.doucet@gnb.ca, Other Communications: Constituency Phone: 506-755-4200; Fax: 506-755-4207
Madeleine Dubé, Edmundston-Saint-Basile,Electoral District 54, Progressive Conservative
506-453-7494, Fax: 506-453-3461, madeleine.dube@gnb.ca,

Other Communications: Constituency Phone: 506-735-2528; Fax: 506-735-2583
Hon. Bruce Fitch, Riverview, ElectoralDistrict 26, Progressive Conservative
506-453-7494, Fax: 506-453-3461, bruce.fitch@gnb.ca, Other Communications: Constituency Phone: 506-869-6117; Fax: 506-869-6114
Hon. Robert Trevors, Miramichi Centre, Electoral District 12, Liberal
506-453-7414, Fax: 506-453-3870, robert.trevors@gnb.ca; robert.trevors.mla@bellaliant.com, Other Communications: Constituency Phone: 506-624-2144; Fax: 506-624-2151
Bill Fraser, Miramichi-Bay du Vin, ElectoralDistrict 11, Liberal
506-453-2548, Fax: 506-453-3956, bill.fraser@gnb.ca, Other Communications: Constituency Phone: 506-624-5516; Fax: 506-624-5517
Dale Graham, Carleton, Electoral District50, Progressive Conservative
506-453-7494, Fax: 506-453-3461, dale.graham@gnb.ca, Other Communications: Constituency Phone: 506-276-4016; Fax: 506-276-4020
Hon. Shawn M. Graham, Kent,Electoral District 15, Liberal
506-453-2144, Fax: 506-453-7407, Premier@gnb.ca; Shawn.Graham@gnb.ca, Other Communications: Constituency Phone: 506-523-7980; Fax: 506-523-7982
Hon. Roland Haché, Nigadoo-Chaleur, ElectoralDistrict 3, Liberal
506-444-5136, Fax: 506-453-3377, roland.hache@gnb.ca, Other Communications: Constituency Phone: 506-542-2424; Fax: 506-542-2425
Bev Harrison, Hampton-Kings, ElectoralDistrict 29, Progressive Conservative
506-453-7494, Fax: 506-453-3461, bev.harrison@gnb.ca, Other Communications: Constituency Phone: 506-832-6464; Fax: 506-832-6466
Trevor Holder, Saint John Portland,Electoral District 35, Progressive Conservative
506-453-7494, Fax: 506-453-3461, trevor.holder@gnb.ca, Other Communications: Constituency Phone: 506-657-2335; Fax: 506-642-2588
Curtis Malloch, Charlotte-Campobello,Electoral District 39, Progressive Conservative
506-453-7494, Fax: 506-453-3461, curtis.malloch@gnb.ca, Other Communications: Constituency Phone: 506-466-7688; 506-466-2191
Glenn Savoie, Saint John-Fundy,Electoral District 31, Liberal
506-453-7494, Fax: 506-453-3461, glensavoie@bellaliant.com, Other Communications: Constituency Phone: 506-658-6333; Fax: 506-658-5982
Jim Parrott, Fundy-RiverValley, Electoral District 37, Liberal
506-453-7494, Fax: 506-453-3461, jim.parrott@gnb.ca, Other Communications: Constituency Phone: 506-757-2088; Fax: 506-757-1009
Wes Mclean, Victoria-Tobique, Electoral District51, Liberal
506-453-7494, Fax: 506-453-3461, Other Communications: Constituency Phone: 506-273-2460; Fax: 506-453-3461
Brian Kenny, Bathurst, Electoral District4, Liberal
506-453-2548, Fax: 506-453-3956, brian.kenny@gnb.ca, Other Communications: Constituency Phone: 506-549-5355; Fax: 506-549-5261
Pam Lynch, Fredericton-Fort Nashwaak,Electoral District 43, Liberal
506-453-7494, Fax: 506-453-3461, pam.lynch@gnb.ca, Other Communications: Constituency Phone: 506-444-3322; Fax: 506-444-3384
Claude Landry, Tracadie-Sheila,Electoral District 9, Progressive Conservative
506-453-7494, Fax: 506-453-3461, claude.landry@gnb.ca, Other Communications: Constituency Phone: 506-395-9162; Fax: 506-393-7794
Hon. Denis Landry, Centre-Péninsule-Saint-Saveur, Electoral District 8, Liberal
506-457-7345, Fax: 506-453-7987, dlandry@nbnet.nb.ca, Other Communications: Constituency Phone: 506-764-2530; Fax: 506-764-2535
Ryan Riordon, Nepisiguit, Electoral District5, Liberal
506-453-7494, Fax: 506-453-3461, ryan.riordon@gnb.ca, Other Communications: Constituency Phone: 506-547-2355, Fax: 506-547-2353
Dorothy Shephard, Saint John Lancaster,Electoral District 36, Liberal
506-453-7494, Fax: 506-453-3461, dorothy.shephard@gnb.ca, Other Communications: Constituency Phone: 506-643-2900; Fax: 506-658-9885
Bernard LeBlanc, Memramcook-Lakeville-Dieppe, Electoral District 19, Liberal
506-453-2548, Fax: 506-453-3956, bernard.leblanc@gnb.ca, Other Communications: Constituency Phone: 506-758-4088; Fax: 506-758-4089
Roger Melason, Dieppe Centre-Lewisville,Electoral District 20, Progressive Conservative
506-453-2548, Fax: 506-453-3956, roger.l.melason@gnb.ca, Other Communications: Constituency Phone: 506-869-7000; Fax: 506-869-7007
Hon. Sue Stultz, Moncton West, ElectoralDistrict 22, Liberal
506-453-2001, Fax: 506-453-2164, sue.stultz@gnb.ca, Other Communications: Constituency Phone: 506-869-6164; Fax: 506-869-6553
Kirk MacDonald, YorkNorth, Electoral District 48, Progressive Conservative
506-453-7494, Fax: 506-453-3461, kirk.macdonald@gnb.ca, Other Communications: Constituency Phone: 506-363-4949; Fax: 506-363-4998
Glen Tait, Saint John East, Electoral District 33, Liberal
506-453-7494, Fax: 506-453-3461, glen.tait@gnb.ca, Other Communications: Constituency Phone: 506-643-3200; 506-643-3201
Ross Wetmore, Grand Lake-Gagetown, ElectoralDistrict 41, Liberal
506-453-7494, Fax: 506-453-3461, ross.wetmore@gnb.ca, Other Communications: Constituency Phone: 506-488-3577, Fax: 506-488-3511
Brian MacDonald, Fredericton-Silverwood, Electoral District 45, Liberal
506-453-7494, Fax: 506-453-2548, brian.t.macdonald@gnb.ca, Other Communications: Constituency Phone: 506-453-8461; Fax: 506-453-6057
Hon. Martine Coulombe, Restigouche-La-Vallée, Electoral District 53, Progressive Conservative
506-453-2342, Fax: 506-453-3038, martine.coulombe@gnb.ca, Other Communications: Constituency Phone: 506-235-6111; Fax: 506-235-6133
Hon. Marie-Claude Blais, Moncton North,Electoral District 23, Liberal
506-462-5100, Fax: 506-453-3651, marie-claude.blais@gnb.ca, Other Communications: Constituency Phone: 506-869-7050; Fax: 869-7096
Bruce Northrup, Kings East, Electoral District 28, Progressive Conservative
506-453-7494, Fax: 506-453-3461, bruce.northrup@gnb.ca, Other Communications: Constituency Phone: 506-432-2686; Fax: 506-432-2647
Mike Olscamp, Tantramar, Electoral District18, Progressive Conservative
506-453-7494, Fax: 506-453-3461, mike.olscamp@gnb.ca, Other Communications: Constituency Phone: 506-364-4774; Fax: 506-364-4775
Danny Soucy, Grand Falls-Drummond-Saint-André,Electoral District 52, Liberal
506-453-7494, Fax: 506-453-3461, danny.soucy@gnb.ca, Other Communications: Constituency Phone: 506-473-7740; 506-473-7745
Bernard LeBlanc, Rogersville-Kouchibouguac, Electoral District 14, Progressive Conservative
506-453-2548, Fax: 506-453-3956, bernard.leblanc@gnb.ca, Other Communications: Constituency Phone: 506-876-3592; Fax: 506-876-3590
Serge Robichaud, Miramichi Bay-Neguac,Electoral District 10, Liberal
506-453-7494, Fax: 506-453-3461, serge.j.robichaud@gnb.ca, Other Communications: Constituency Phone: 506-776-4005; Fax: 506-776-4006
Paul Robichaud, Lamèque-Shippagan-Miscou, Electoral District 7, Progressive Conservative
506-453-7494, Fax: 506-453-3461, paul.robichaud@gnb.ca, Other Communications: Constituency Phone: 506-336-3388; Fax: 506-336-3387
Hon. Blaine Higgs, Quispamsis, Electoral District30, Liberal
506-453-2451, Fax: 506-457-4989, blaine.higgs@gnb.ca, Other Communications: Constituency Phone: 506-848-5429; Fax: 506-848-5422
Wayne Steeves, Albert, Electoral District27, Progressive Conservative
506-453-7494, Fax: 506-453-3461, wayne.steeves@gnb.ca, Other Communications: Constituency Phone: 506-856-3006; Fax: 506-856-3000
Sherry Wilson, Petitcodiac, ElectoralDistrict 25, Liberal
506-453-7494, Fax: 506-453-3461, sherry.wilson@gnb.ca, Other Communications: Constituency Phone: 506-372-3301; Fax: 506-372-3304
Carl Urquhart, York, Electoral District47, Progressive Conservative
506-453-7494, Fax: 506-453-3461, carl.urquhart@gnb.ca, Other Communications: Constituency Phone: 506-457-7878; Fax: 506-457-7865
Yvon Bonenfant, Madawaska-les-Lacs,Electoral District 55, Progressive Conservative
506-453-7494, Fax: 506-453-3461, yvon.bonenfant@gnb.ca, Other Communications: Constituency Phone: 506-737-4420; Fax: 506-737-4436
Claude Williams, Kent South,Electoral District 16, Progressive Conservative
506-453-7494, Fax: 506-453-3461, claude.williams@gnb.ca, Other Communications: Constituency Phone: 506-525-4025; Fax: 506-525-4034
Jack Carr, New Maryland-SunburyWest, Electoral District 46
506-453-7494, Fax: 506-453-3461, jack.carr@gnb.ca, Other Communications: Constituency Phone: 506-368-2938, Fax: 506-368-2939

New Brunswick Government Departments & Agencies / Ministères et organismes du gouvernement du Nouveau-Brunswick

Aboriginal Affairs Secretariat / Secrétariat des affaires autochtones

Kings Place, #237, 440 King St., PO Box 6000, Fredericton, NB E3B 5H1
506-462-5177 Fax: 506-444-5142
www.gnb.ca/0016/index-e.asp

The Aboriginal Affairs Secretariat strives to enhance the Government of New Brunswick's relationship with Mi'kmaq & Maliseet communities & Aboriginal organizations. The Secretariat works with provincial departments in the areas of policies & intergovernmental processes related to Aboriginal people, dialogue between Aboriginal representatives & the government, the provision of information on programs & services, & increasing cross-cultural awareness.

Minister, Intergovernmental Affairs, Responsible for the Aboriginal Affairs Secretariat, Council on the Status of Disabled, Citizens'Engagement, Hon. David Alward
506-462-5177, Fax: 506-444-5142, david.alward@gnb.ca
Deputy Minister, Aboriginal Affairs Secretariat, Patrick Francis
506-462-5177, Patrick.Francis@gnb.ca
Director, Aboriginal Affairs Secretariat, Susi Derrah
506-462-5177, Fax: 506-444-5142, susi.derrah@gnb.ca
Relations Development Officer, Communications, Ryan Francis
506-444-4194, Fax: 506-444-5142, ryan.francis@gnb.ca
Officer, Legislature/Program, Lisa Rivett
506-462-5177, Fax: 506-444-5142, lisa.rivett@gnb.ca

Department of Agriculture, Aquaculture & Fisheries / Agriculture, Aquaculture et Pêches

Agricultural Research Station (Experimental Farm), PO Box 6000, Fredericton, NB E3B 5H1
506-453-2666 Fax: 506-453-7170
DAAF-MAAP@gnb.ca
www.gnb.ca/aquaculture

Acts Administered:
Agricultural Associations Act
Agricultural Commodity Price Stabilization Act
Agricultural Development Act
Agricultural Insurance Act
Agricultural Land Protection & Development Act
Agricultural Operation Practices Act
Agricultural Producers Registration and Farm Organizations Funding
Apiary Inspection Act
Aquaculture Act
Diseases of Animals Act
Farm Credit Corporation Assistance Act
Farm Improvement Assistance Loans Act
Farm Machinery Loans Act
Farm Income Assurance Act
Fish & Wildlife Act (in part)
Fisheries and Aquaculture Development Act
Inshore Fisheries Representation Act
Livestock Incentives Act
Livestock Operations Act
Marshland Reclamation Act
Mining Act
Natural Products Act
New Brunswick Grain Act
Plant Health Act
Potato Disease Eradication Act
Poultry Health Protection Act
Real Property Tax Act
Seafood Processing Act
Sheep Protection Act
Women's Institute & Institut féminin Act

Minister, Agriculture, Aquaculture & Fisheries, Hon. Michael Olscamp
506-453-2662, Fax: 506-453-3402, Mike.Olscamp@gnb.ca
Deputy Minister, Jean-Marc Dupuis
506-453-2450, Fax: 506-444-5022, jean-marc.dupuis@gnb.ca
Director, Communications, Gisèle Regimbal
506-444-4218, Fax: 506-444-5022, Gisele.Regimbal@gnb.ca
Director, Policy & Planning, Shirley Stuible
506-453-3451, Fax: 506-453-5210, shirley.stuible@gnb.ca

Associated Agencies, Boards & Commissions:
• New Brunswick Farm Products Commission / Commission des produits de ferme du Nouveau-Brunswick
c/o Department of Agriculture, Aquaculture & Fisheries
PO Box 6000
Fredericton, NB E3B 5H1
506-453-3647 Fax: 506-444-5969

Products Act. ment/administrative support to the Commission in the monitoring of commodity boards under the provisions of the Natural Products Act.

Agriculture & Bio-Economy Division / Agriculture et Bioéconomie
DAAF-MAAP@gnb.ca
www.gnb.ca/agriculture
To encourage the development of a prosperous, globally competitive & sustainable agriculture & agri-food business using the latest technologies to produce & market innovative & safe food as well as other bio-products.
Asst. Deputy Minister, Kevin McKendy
506-453-2366, Fax: 506-444-5022, kevin.mckendy@gnb.ca
Executive Director, Livestock Development, Michael Maloney
506-453-2457, michael.maloney@gnb.ca
Director, Crop Development, Kevin McCully
506-453-3481, kevin.mccully@gnb.ca
Director, Agricultural Financial Programs, Cathy Larochelle
506-444-2728, cathy.larochelle@gnb.ca
Director, Land & Environment, Sandi McGeachy
506-453-2109, sandi.mcgeachy@gnb.ca
Director, Regional Agri-Business Development, Gerry Chevrier
506-453-2172, gerald.chevrier@gnb.ca
Manager, Veterinary Laboratory & Pathology Services, James Goltz
506-453-5488, jim.goltz@gnb.ca
Manager, Food Safety & Quality, Clinton McLean
506-453-6735, clint.mclean@gnb.ca
Regional Offices:

Bathurst Agriculture Building, 1425 King Avenue, Bathurst, NB E2A 1S7
506-547-2088 Fax: 506-547-2064
DAAF-MAAP@gnb.ca
Regional Manager, Jean Marc Clavette

Bon Accord Elite Seed Potato Centre, 790 Kincardine Road, Bon Accord, NB E7H 2K8
506-273-4741 Fax: 506-273-4742
DAAF-MAAP@gnb.ca
Regional Manager, Pelkey Shaun

36 Court Street, Edmundston, NB E3V 1S3
506-735-2060 Fax: 506-735-2754
DAAF-MAAP@gnb.ca
Regional Manager, Charles Mallet

Chatham Town Centre, 1780 Water Street, Miramichi, NB E1N 1B6
506-778-6030 Fax: 506-778-6679
DAAF-MAAP@gnb.ca
Regional Manager, Scott McFarlane

PO Box 5001, Moncton, NB E1C 8R3
506-856-2277 Fax: 506-856-2092
DAAF-MAAP@gnb.ca
Regional Manager, Claude Robichaud

PO Box 5001, Grand Falls, NB E3Z 1G1
506-473-7755 Fax: 506-473-6641
DAAF-MAAP@gnb.ca
Specialist, Jacques Lavoie

#A, 366 Canada Street, Saint-Quentin, NB E8A 1H8
506-235-6050 Fax: 506-235-6055
DAA-MAA@gnb.ca
Regional Manager, André Clavet

Fisheries Division / Pêches
DAAF-MAAP@gnb.ca
www.gnb.ca/agriculture
Asst. Deputy Minister, Perron Sadie
506-457-6964, Fax: 506-444-5022, sadie.perron@gnb.ca
Executive Director, Fisheries Management & Operations, Yvon Chiasson
506-453-8432, Fax: 506-462-5929, yvon.chiasson@gnb.ca
Director, Business Development, Louis Arsenault
506-743-7222, louis.arsenault@gnb.ca
Director, Licensing & Technical Services, Ghislain Chiasson
506-453-2252, ghislain.chiasson@gnb.ca

107 Mount Pleasant Road, PO Box 1037, ST. George, NB E5C 3S9
506-755-4000 Fax: 506-755-4001
Regional Director, Kimberly Watson

PO Box 5305, Sussex, NB E4E 7H7
506-432-2150 Fax: 506-432-2044
DAA-MAA@gnb.ca
Regional Manager, David Taylor

Place Tracadie, 3518-1 Principale Street, Tracadie-Sheila, NB E1X 1C9
506-394-4128 Fax: 506-394-4128
DAA-MAA@gnb.ca
Coordinator, Denis Prince

Potato Development Centre, 39 Barker Lane, Wicklow, NB E7L 3S4
506-392-5100 Fax: 506-392-5089
888-622-4742
DAA-MAA@gnb.ca
Regional Manager, Brian Duplessis

26 Acadie Street, Bouctouche, NB E4S 2T2
506-743-7222 Fax: 506-743-7229
DAAF-MAAP@gnb.ca
Regional Director, Louis Arsenault

22 St-Pierre Boulevard East, Caraquet, NB E1W 1B6
506-726-2400 Fax: 506-726-2419
MDP-DOF@gnb.ca
Regional Director, Mario Gaudet

104 Aquarium Street, Shippagan, NB E8S 1H9
506-336-3751 Fax: 506-336-3057
DAA-MAA@gnb.ca
Regional Director, Christian Noris

Department of the Attorney General / Procureur général

Centennial Bldg., #412, 670 King St., PO Box 6000, Fredericton, NB E3B 5H1
506-453-3132 Fax: 506-453-3651
justice.comments@gnb.ca
www.gnb.ca/0062/index-e.asp
The Attorney General carries out responsibilities regarding criminal law enforcement, the provision of legal advice & representation to the Government, & the preparation of legislation & regulations.
Minister, Attorney General, Hon. Marie-Claude Blais
506-453-3132, Fax: 506-453-3651, marie-claude.blais@gnb.ca
Deputy Attorney General, Judith Keating
506-453-3132, Fax: 506-453-3651, judith.keating@gnb.ca

Legal Services
Centennial Bldg., #445, 670 King St., PO Box 6000, Fredericton, NB E3B 5H1
506-453-2222 Fax: 506-453-3275
Assistant Deputy Attorney General, Legal Services, Guy Daigle
506-453-222, guy.daigle@gnb.ca
Director, Commercial, Corporate, & Property Law Group, John Logan
506-453-2222, john.logan@gnb.ca
Director, Employment & Administrative Law Group, Andrea M. Folster
506-453-2222, andrea.folster@gnb.ca
Director, Government Services Group, Diane Audet Leger
506-453-2222, diane.audet-leger@gnb.ca
Executive Director, Litigation Group, Nancy E. Forbes
506-453-2222, nancy.forbes@gnb.ca

Legislative Services
Centennial Bldg., #418, 670 King St., PO Box 6000, Fredericton, NB E3B 5H1
506-453-2855 Fax: 506-457-7342
Assistant Deputy Attorney General, Legislative Services, Judith Keating, Q.C.
506-453-2544, Judith.Keating@gnb.ca
Registrar of Regulations, Legislative Drafting, Susan Burns
506-453-2569, Susan.Burns@gnb.ca
Solicitor, Law Reform, Tim Rattenbury
506-453-2569, Tim.Rattenbury@gnb.ca
Revisor, Jurilinguist, Statute Revision, Jacqueline Arseneau
506-444-5645, jacqueline.arseneau@gnb.ca
Solicitor & Queen's Printer, Queen's Printer, Elizabeth Strange
506-453-2520, Fax: 506-457-7899, Elizabeth.Strange@gnb.ca

Public Prosecutions
HSBC Place, 520 King St., 6th Fl., PO Box 6000, Fredericton, NB E3B 5H1
506-453-2784 Fax: 506-453-5364
Assistant Deputy Attorney General, Public Prosecutions, Glen Abbott, Q.C.
Director, Specialized Prosecutions, Jeffrey Mockler
Executive Director, Family & Youth Justice, Catherine A. Berryman
506-856-2310, Fax: 506-856-2625

Support Services
Centennial Bldg., #412, 670 King St., PO Box 6000, Fredericton, NB E3B 5H1
506-453-3132 Fax: 506-453-3651
general.comments@gnb.ca
Director, Information Management Technology, Michael Hennessey
506-453-2719, mike.hennessey@gnb.ca
Senior Policy Advisor, Policy & Planning, James Burns
506-453-6526, jim.burns@gnb.ca
Human Resources Advisor, Angela Bryden
506-444-4459, angela.bryden@gnb.ca
Manager, Applications Delivery, Lachlan Macquarrie-Mcleod
506-444-5855, lachlan.macquarrie-mcleod@gnb.ca

Office of the Auditor General / Bureau du Vérificateur général

HSBC Place, 520 King St., 6th Fl., Fredericton, NB E3B 6G3
506-453-2243 Fax: 506-453-3067
www.gnb.ca/OAG-BVG/Index.htm
The role of the Office of the Auditor General is the promotion of accountability. On behalf of the Legislative Assembly, the Office of the Auditor General audits the accounts of the province & certain Crown agencies. Objective information is provided to the citizens of New Brunswick through the Legislative Assembly.
Auditor General, Kim MacPherson, C.A.
506-453-2465, Kim.MacPherson@gnb.ca
Deputy Auditor General, Kenneth Robinson, C.A.
506-453-6751, ken.robinson@gnb.ca
Director, Value-for-money Audit, Brent White, C.A.
506-453-6752, brent.white@gnb.ca
Director, Financial Audit, Paul Jewett, C.A.
506-453-6754, paul.jewett@gnb.ca

Department of Business New Brunswick / Entreprises Nouveau-Brunswick

Centennial Bldg., 670 King St., PO Box 6000, Fredericton, NB E3B 5H1
506-453-3707 Fax: 506-453-3993
investnb@gnb.ca
www.gnb.ca/0398/index-e.asp
The Department of Business New Brunswick provides the following serices: Business expansion & innovation; Export development; Investment, for the establishment of new business in the province; & Services & support to the film & television industry in New Brunswick.
Acts Administered:
Agricultural Associations Act
Economic Development Act
Farm Credit Corporation Assistance Act
Farm Improvement Assistance Loans Act
Farm Machinary Loans Act
Fisheries Development Act
Industrial Relations Act
Livestock Incentives Act
Youth Assistance Act
Minister Responsible, Business New Brunswick, Hon. Paul Robichaud
506-453-5898, Fax: 506-453-6389, paul.robichaud@gnb.ca
Deputy Minister, Bill Levesque
506-453-5897, Fax: 506-453-6389, bill.levesque@gnb.ca
Director, Human Resource Services, Karen Tucker
506-457-6710, Fax: 506-444-5440, karen.tucker@gnb.ca
Director, Communications, Marie-Josée Groulx
506-444-3465, Fax: 506-453-3993, marie-josee.groulx@gnb.ca

Associated Agencies, Boards & Commissions:
• New Brunswick Industrial Development Board / Conseil de développement industriel du Nouveau-Brunswick
Business New Brunswick, Centennial Bldg.
670 King St.
PO Box 6000
Fredericton, NB E3B 5H1
506-453-4200 Fax: 506-444-4182

Business Financial Support & Corporate Services
Centennial Bldg., #571, 670 King St., PO Box 6000, Fredericton, NB E3B 5H1
506-453-2794 Fax: 506-444-4277
Helps companies be more successful by offering financial assistance and capital investment to new and existing entrepreneurs that want to grow and create sustainable employment in New Brunswick.
Assistant Deputy Minister, Sadie Perron
506-453-7499, sadie.perron@gnb.ca
Executive Director, Business Financial Support, John Rosengren
506-453-3929, john.rosengren@gnb.ca
Executive Director, Financial Administration, Barbara Yerxa
506-444-5197, Fax: 506-453-5428, Barbara.YERXA@gnb.ca

Executive Director, Policy & Planning, Shannon Sanford
506-444-5854, shannon.sanford@gnb.ca
Manager, Financial Programs, Kevin Kearns
506-444-5888, Fax: 506-453-7904, Kevin.kearns@gnb.ca

Communications
Centennial Bldg., 670 King St., 5th Fl., PO Box 6000, Fredericton, NB E3B 5H1
506-453-3707 Fax: 506-453-3993
Spreads the word about Business New Brunswick's efforts to help attract investment, retain and expand businesses and develop key economic clusters.
Director, Marie-Josée Groulx
506-444-3465, marie-josee.groulx@gnb.ca

Investment, Export & Business Development
Centennial Bldg., 670 King St., 5th Fl., PO Box 6000, Fredericton, NB E3B 5H1
506-453-2875 Fax: 506-444-4277
They get the word out among international corporate leaders that New Brunswick is the place to be in business, attracting new investment and jobs with specific focus on knowledge-based industries, value-added natural resources, bio-technologies and advanced manufacturing. Their export and trade staff members help companies be more profitable by exporting their products to new and existing markets, providing counseling, trade assistance and specialized services to export-ready businesses and existing exporters.
Assistant Deputy Minister, Jeff Trail
506-444-5775, jeff.trail@gnb.ca
Executive Director, Industry Services, Roger Y. Cyr
506-453-2402, Fax: 506-457-7282, roger.cyr@gnb.ca
Executive Director, Knowledge Industries & Innovation, Joanne Walker
506-457-4921, Fax: 506-444-4182, joanne.walker@gnb.ca
Director, Export Development, Michel Albert
506-444-5053, Fax: 506-453-3783, michel.albert@gnb.ca
Director, Investment, Joel Richardson
506-457-7545, joel.richardson@gnb.ca
Manager, Marketing, Monique Arsenault
506-444-2135, Fax: 506-444-4586, monique.arsenault@gnb.ca

Northern Development / Développement des entreprises
Harbourview Place, 275 Main St., Bathurst, NB E2A 1A9
506-547-2227 Fax: 506-547-2269
Assistant Deputy Minister, Roger Robichaud
roger.robichaud@gnb.ca
Director, Rick Lloyd
rick.lloyd@gnb.ca
Director, Denis Roy
denis.roy2@gnb.ca

Special Initiatives / Initiatives spéciales
Centennial Building, PO Box 6000, Fredericton, NB E3B 5H1
506-453-3707 Fax: 506-453-5428
Executive Director, Gary Jochelman
506-444-4238, gary.jochelman@gnb.ca
Director, Office of Red Tape Reduction, Wendy L. Betts
506-444-4167, Wendy.Betts@gnb.ca ca

Communications New Brunswick / Communications Nouveau-Brunswick

Wilcom Bldg., 225 King St., 2nd Fl., PO Box 6000, Fredericton, NB E3B 5H1
506-453-2240 Fax: 506-453-5329
www.gnb.ca/cnb
Communications New Brunswick provides a great range of communications services to government departments & agencies.
Minister, Environment New Brunswick; Minister Responsible, Status of Women New Brunswick; Minister Responsible, Communications New Brunswick, Hon. Margaret-Ann Blaney
506-444-5136, margaret-ann.blaney@gnb.ca
Deputy Minister, Tim Porter
506-453-6191, tim.porte@gnb.ca
Director, Rob Macleod
506-453-2425, rob.macleod@gnb.ca
Managing Director, Strategic Relations & Special Projects, Shawn Hearn
506-453-2203, shawn.hearn@gnb.ca
Managing Director, Corporate Communications, Chris Connor
506-457-4999, chris.connor@gnb.ca
Director, Web Services, Bonnie Buckingham Landry
506-453-3020, Bonnie.Buckingham-Landry@gnb.ca

Office of the Comptroller / Bureau du Contrôleur

Centennial Bldg., 670 King St., Fredericton, NB E3B 1G1
506-453-2565 Fax: 506-453-2917
wwwooc@gnb.ca
www.gnb.ca/0087/index-e.asp
Provide leadership in accounting and internal auditing services to their clients and encourage the effective management of the resources of the Province.
Comptroller, Janet Gallagher
506-453-2565, janet.gallagher@gnb.ca
Director, Accounting Services, Karen Cunningham
506-453-8975, karen.cunningham@gnb.ca
Director, Audit & Consulting Services, Stephen Thompson, C.M.A.
506-444-4560, steve.t.thompson@gnb.ca

Premier's Council on the Status of Disabled Persons / Conseil du Premier ministre sur la condition des personnes handicapées

Kings Place, #648, 440 King St., Fredericton, NB E3B 5H8
506-444-3000 Fax: 506-444-3001
800-442-4412
pcsdp@gnb.ca
www.gnb.ca/0048
The role of the Premier's Council on the Status of Disabled Persons is to provide advice to the provincial government of New Brunswick & the public about issues of interest & concern that affect the status of persons with disabilities.
Premier; President, Executive Council; Minister, Intergovernmental Affairs; Minister Responsible, Premier's Council on the Status of Disabled Persons; Minister Responsible, Citizens' Engagement, Hon. David Alward
506-453-2144, Fax: 506-453-7407, david.alward@gnb.ca
Chairperson, Michelle Horncastle
506-444-3000, Fax: 506-444-3001, pcsdp@gnb.ca, TTY: 506-444-3000
Executive Director, Christyne Allain
506-444-3004, Fax: 506-444-3001, pcsdp@gnb.ca

Department of Education / Education

Place 2000, 250 King St., PO Box 6000, Fredericton, NB E3B 5H1
506-453-3678 Fax: 506-453-3325
edcommunication@gnb.ca
http: //www.gnb.ca/education
The Department of Education, which oversees public schools in New Brunswick, consists of an Anglophone Sector & a Francophone Sector. The English Educational Services Division is responsible for curriculum development, student services, e-learning, & student evaluation & assessment. The Francophone Educational Services Division oversees curriculum development & implementation, special education, psychology, guidance counselling, professional development, & assessment & evaluation.
Acts Administered:
Education Act
Minister, Education & Early Childhood Development, Hon. Jody Carr
506-453-2523, Fax: 506-457-4960, jody.carr@gnb.ca
Sous-ministre, Doucet Roger
506-453-2409, Fax: 506-457-4810, roger.doucet@gnb.ca
Deputy Minister, Wendy McLeod-MacKnight
506-453-2529, Fax: 506-457-4810, wendy.mcleodmacknight@gnb.ca
Director, Communications, Christina Winsor
506-444-2455, Fax: 506-444-5529, christina.winsor@gnb.ca
Officer, Communications, Johanne Leblanc
506-444-2455, Fax: 506-444-5529, johanne.leblanc@gnb.ca
Project Executive, Special Project Team, Amanda Harpelle
506-453-6723, Fax: 506-444-5523, amanda.harpelle@gnb.ca

Corporate Services / Services Généraux
Place 2000, 250 King St., 4th Fl., PO Box 6000, Fredericton, NB E3B 5H1
506-453-2085 Fax: 506-457-4810
edcommunication@gnb.ca
http: //www.gnb.ca/education
Assistant Deputy Minister, Michel Thériault
506-453-2085, Fax: 506-457-4810, michel.theriault@gnb.ca
Director, Educational Facilities & Pupil Transportation, Ron J. White
506-453-2242, Fax: 506-444-5529, mailto: ron.white@gnb.ca
Director, Finance & Services, Luc Paulin
506-444-4963, Fax: 506-453-3325, luc.paulin@gnb.ca
Director, Human Resources, Valmond Guimond
506-444-4914, Fax: 506-444-4761, Valmond.Guimond@gnb.ca
Director, Information System Services, Louise Ouellette
506-453-7158, Louise.Ouellette@gnb.ca

Educational Services (Anglophone) / Division des services éducatifs
Place 2000, 250 King St., PO Box 6000, Fredericton, NB E3B 5H1
506-453-3326 Fax: 506-457-4810
edcommunication@gnb.ca
http: //www.gnb.ca/education
Assistant Deputy Minister, Zoë Watson
506-453-3326, Fax: 506-457-4810, zoe.watson@gnb.ca
Director, Student Services, Brian kelly
506-453-2816, Fax: 506-457-7835, brian.kelly@gnb.ca
Director, Assessment & Evaluation, Sandra Mazerall
506-453-2744, Fax: 506-457-6906, sandra.mazerall@gnb.ca
Director, Professional Learning Services, Inga Boehler
506-453-3696, Fax: 506-457-7835, inga.boehler@gnb.ca
Manager, District Education Councils, Stacey Brown
506-453-2618, stacey.brown@gnb.ca
Director, Strategic Partnerships, Dawn Weatherbie
506-453-2771, Fax: 506-457-7835, dawn.weatherbie@gnb.ca
Director, Curriculum Development & Implementation K-12, Darlene Whitehouse-Sheehan
506-453-2155, Fax: 506-457-7835, darlene.whitehouse-sheehan@gnb.ca

Policy & Planning
Place 2000, 250 King St., 4th Fl., PO Box 6000, Fredericton, NB E3B 5H1
506-453-3090 Fax: 506-453-3111
edcommunication@gnb.ca
http: //www.gnb.ca/education
Executive Director, Policy & Planning, Lise Bellefleur
506-453-8299, Fax: 506-453-3111, lise.bellefleur@gnb.ca
Director, Corporate Data Management and Analysis Branch, Monica LeBlanc
506-453-6124, Fax: 506-453-3111, monica.leblanc@gnb.ca

Secteur des services Éducatifs francophones / Educational Services Section
Place 2000, 250 King St., 4th Fl., Fredericton, NB E3B 9M9
506-453-2086 Fax: 506-457-4810
Assistant Deputy Minister, Guy Léveillé
506-453-2086, Fax: 506-457-4810, guy.leveille@gnb.ca
Director, École communautaire, du leadership et de la technologie, Alain Poitras
506-444-2575, Fax: 506-444-2969, alain.poitras@gnb.ca
Director, Programmes d'études et de l'apprentissage, Marcel Lavoie
506-453-2743, Fax: 506-457-7835, Marcel.Lavoie@gnb.ca
Manager, Conseils d'éducation de district, Rachel Dion
506-453-3037, Fax: 506-453-7942, rachel.dion@gnb.ca
Director, Services aux élèves, Gina St-Laurent
506-453-5876, Fax: 506-457-7835, gina.st-laurent@gnb.ca
Director, Mesure at évaluation, Robert Laurie
506-453-2157, Fax: 506-462-2201, robert.laurie@gnb.ca

Office of the Chief Electoral Officer / Bureau de la directrice générale des élections

PO Box 6000, Fredericton, NB E3B 5H1
506-453-2218 Fax: 506-457-4926
800-308-2922
www.gnb.ca/elections
Chief Electoral Officer, Michael Quinn
506-453-2218, michael.quinn@electionsnb.ca
Director, Operations, Craig Astle
506-453-2218, Fax: 506-457-4926, craig.astle@electionsnb.ca
Manager, Voter Information Systems, Ronald Armitage
506-453-2218, Fax: 506-457-4926, ron.armitage@electionsnb.ca
Manager, Policy & Development, Peggy Scott
506-453-2218, Fax: 506-457-4926, peggy.scott@electionsnb.ca
Supervisor, Finance & Human Resources, Theresa Comeau
506-453-2218, Fax: 506-453-6121, theresa.comeau@electionsnb.ca

Department of Energy / Énergie

Brunswick Square, #100M, 1 Germain St., Saint John, NB E2L 4V1
506-658-3180 Fax: 506-658-3191
DOEweb@gnb.ca
www.gnb.ca/energy
The New Brunswick Department of Energy is responsible for the following: Ensuring a reliable & cost effective energy supply; Promoting economic efficiency in energy systems; Encouraging economic development opportunities; Protecting & improving the environment; & Ensuring an effective regulatory regime.
Acts Administered:
Electricity Act
Energy Efficiency Act
Energy Efficiency & Conservation Agency of New Brunswick Act
Gas Distribution, 1999 Act
Petroleum Products Pricing Act
Pipeline, 2005 Act
Minister, Energy; Minister Responsible, New Brunswick Efficiency & Conservation Agency, Hon. Craig Leonard
506-658-3179, Fax: 506-658-3191, craig.leonard@gnb.ca
Deputy Minster, Douglas Holt
506-658-3179, doug.holt@gnb.ca

Associated Agencies, Boards & Commissions:

• Efficiency NB / Efficacité NB
#101, 33 Charlotte St.
Saint John, NB E2L 2H3
506-643-7826 Fax: 506-643-7835 866-643-8833
www.efficiencynb.ca
Efficiency NB is engaged in the following activities: Promoting energy efficiency measures throughout New Brunswick; Encouraging the development of an energy efficiency services industry; Implementing & offering programs related to energy efficiency; & Increasing awareness of the relation between energy efficiency measures & a reliable energy supply for the province.

Alternative Energy & Market Development
Brunswick Square, #M100, 1 Germain St., Saint John, NB E2L 4V1
506-658-3180 Fax: 506-658-3191
DOEweb@gnb.ca
www.gnb.ca/energy

Assistant Deputy Minister, Alternative Energy & Market Development, Neil Jacobsen
506-658-3132, Fax: 506-658-3191, neil.jacobsen@gnb.ca
Director, Electricity, Stephen Waycott
506-658-3126, Stephen.Waycott@gnb.ca
Director, Pipeline, Petroleum, & Natural Gas, Patrick Ervin
506-658-3124, patrick.ervin@gnb.ca
Policy Advisor, Renewable Energy and Emerging Technologies, Heather Quinn
506-658-3186, heather.quinn@gnb.ca
Policy Advisor, Alternative Energy and Market Development, David Sollows
506-658-3180, david.sollows@gnb.ca
Coordinator, Corporate Services, Education & Awareness, Bonnie Doyle
506-658-2410, bonnie.doyle@gnb.ca
Senior Consultant, Corporate Services, Education & Awareness, David Duplisea
506-658-3158, David.Duplisea@gnb.ca

Policy Development & Planning
Brunswick Square, #100M, 1 Germain St., Saint John, NB E2L 4V1
506-658-3180 Fax: 506-658-3191
Doeweb@gnb.ca
www.gnb.ca/energy

Executive Director, Policy Development & Planning, Shelley Rinehart
506-658-3123, shelley.rinehart@gnb.ca
Policy Advisor, Laura Delong
506-658-3184, laura.delong@gnb.ca
Senior Advisor, David Duplisea
506-658-3158, david.duplisea@gnb.ca

Associated Agencies, Boards & Commissions:
• New Brunswick Round Table on Environment & Economy / Table Ronde sur Environnement & Economie
20 McGloin St.
PO Box 6000
Fredericton, NB E3B 5H1
506-453-3703 Fax: 506-453-3876
Mandate is to monitor/report on New Brunswick's progress towards implementing the elements of its Plan for Action & to act as a catalyst for change towards sustainable development within the Province.

Department of the Environment / Environnement

Marysville Place, 20 McGloin St., PO Box 6000, Fredericton, NB E3B 5H1
506-453-2690 Fax: 506-457-7800
env-info@gnb.ca
www.gnb.ca/0009/index-e.asp

Other Communication: To report oil, pesticide, chemical spills, & other environmental emergencies, Toll-Free: 1-800-565-1633.
The Department of the Environment carries out the following responsibilities: Provision of integrated stewardship; Ensuring enforcement of environmental legislation & regulations; & Consultation with municipal governments & Local Service Districts.
Acts Administered:
Beverage Containers Act
Clean Air Act
Clean Environment Act
Clean Water Act
Community Planning Act
Environmental Trust Fund Act (except administration of fund)
Gas Distribution, 1999 Act (subsection 18 (2), paragraph 32 (1) (a), & subsection 39 (1))
Mining Act (subsection 68 (2))
Pesticides Control Act
Topsoil Preservation Act
Unsightly Premises Act
Minister, Hon. Margarett-Ann Blaney
506-444-5136, Fax: 506-453-3377, margaret-ann.blaney@gnb.ca
Deputy Minister, Perry Haines
506-453-3256, Fax: 506-453-3377, perry.haines@gnb.ca
Executive Director, Corporate Initiatives, K. Bradford Marshall
506-453-3700, Fax: 506-453-3676, Brad.Marshall@gnb.ca
Assistant Deputy Minister, Corporate Services, Community Funding & Technical Services, Allan Roy
506-453-6285, allan.roy@gnb.ca
Director, Public Affairs, Vicky Deschênes
506-453-3700, Fax: 506-453-3843, Vicky.Deschenes@gnb.ca
Executive Director, Policy & Strategic Initiatives, Elizabeth Hayward
506-453-8788, Fax: 506-453-3676, elizabeth.hayeard@gnb.ca
Director, Legislative Renewal & Legal Affairs, Denyse Smart
506-453-3700, Fax: 506-453-3676, denyse.smart@gnb.ca
Director, Inter-governmental Affairs, Stephanie Whalen
506-453-3700, Fax: 506-453-3676, stephanie.whalen@gnb.ca

Environmental Management / Gestion de l'environnement
Marysville Place, 20 McGloin St., PO Box 6000, Fredericton, NB E3B 5H1
506-444-5119 Fax: 506-457-7333
env-info@gnb.ca
www.gnb.ca/0009/index-e.asp

The main responsibility of the Environmental Management Division is initiatives to control pollutants, promote pollution prevention. & protect the environment. The Division acts as a major regulatory arm of the Department.
Assistant Deputy Minister, Mike Cormier
506-444-5119, mike.cormier@gnb.ca
Executive Director, State of the Environment, David Schellenberg
506-457-4844, dave.schellenberg@gnb.ca
Director, Sustainable Development, Planning & Impact Evaluation, Paul Vanderlaan
506-444-4599, paul.vanderlann@gnb.ca
Director, Impact Management, Gregory Shanks
506-453-7945, Fax: 506-453-2390, greg.shanks@gnb.ca
Director, Operational Continuous Improvement, Organizational Development Branch, Colleen Mullin
506-444-5119, Fax: 506-457-7333, colleen.mullin@gnb.ca
Director, Greg Shanks
506-453-7945, greg.shanks@gnb.ca

Regional Environmental Services

Bathurst Regional Office
#202, 159 Main St., Bathurst, NB E2A 1A6
506-547-2092 Fax: 506-547-7655
env-info@gnb.ca
www.gnb.ca/0009/index-e.asp

Regional Director, Paul Fournier
506-547-2092, Paul.Fournier@gnb.ca

Fredericton Regional Office
Priestman Centre, 565 Priestman St., PO Box 6000, Fredericton, NB E3B 5H1
506-444-5149 Fax: 506-453-2893
env-info@gnb.ca
www.gnb.ca/0009/index-e.asp

Regional Director, Serge Gagnon
506-444-5149, Serge.Gagnon@gnb.ca

Grand Falls Regional Office
#200, 65 Broadway Blvd., PO Box 5001, Grand Falls, NB E3Z 1G1
506-473-7744 Fax: 506-475-2510
env-info@gnb.ca
www.gnb.ca/0009/index-e.asp

Regional Director, Richard Keeley
506-473-7744, Richard.Keeley@gnb.ca

Miramichi Regional Office
Industrial Park, 316 Dalton Ave., Miramichi, NB E1V 3N9
506-778-6032 Fax: 506-778-6796
env-info@gnb.ca
www.gnb.ca/0009/index-e.asp

Regional Director, Denis Daigle
506-778-6032, Denis.Daigle@gnb.ca

Moncton Regional Office
Provincial Bldg., 428 Collishaw St., PO Box 5001, Moncton, NB E1C 8R3
506-856-2374 Fax: 506-856-2370
env-info@gnb.ca
www.gnb.ca/0009/index-e.asp

Regional Director, Laurie Collette
506-856-2374, Laurie.Collette@gnb.ca

Saint John Regional Office
8 Castle St., PO Box 5001, Saint John, NB E2L 4Y9
506-658-2558 Fax: 506-658-3046
env-info@gnb.ca
www.gnb.ca/0009/index-e.asp

Regional Director, Susan M. Atkinson
506-658-2558, susanm.atkinson@gnb.ca

Sciences & Planning / Science et planification
Marysville Place, 20 McGloin St., 2nd Fl., PO Box 6000, Fredericton, NB E3B 5H1
506-453-2862 Fax: 506-453-2265

Scientific assessment, monitoring functions, & planning for sustainability are the major activities of the Sciences & Planning Division.
Assistant Deputy Minister, Sciences & Planning, Diane Kent Gillis
diane.kentgillis@gnb.ca
Executive Director, Environmental Services, David Schellenberg
506-444-2654, Fax: 506-444-2734, dave.schellenberg@gnb.ca
Director, Science & Reporting, Daryl Pupek
506-457-4844, Darryl.Pupek@gnb.ca
Director, Sustainable Planning, Kim Hughes
506-457-4846, Fax: 506-457-7823, Kim.Hughes@gnb.ca
Director, Climate Change Secretariat, Dean Mundee
506-457-4844, Dean.Mundee@gnb.ca

Department of Finance / Finances

670 King St., PO Box 6000, Fredericton, NB E3B 5H1
506-453-2451 Fax: 506-457-4989
wwwfin@gnb.ca
www.gnb.ca/0024/index-e.asp

The Department of Finance manages the public finances of New Brunswick.
Acts Administered:
Appropriation Act
Arts Development Trust Fund
Beaverbrook Art Gallery Act (Section 9)
Beaverbrook Auditorium Act (Section 7)
Environmental Trust Fund (administration of fund)
Fees Act
Financial Administration Act (expect provisions assigned to the Office of the Comptroller or to the Board of Management)
Financial Corporation Capital Tax Act
Fiscal Responsibility and Balanced Budget Act
Fiscal Stabilization Fund
Fishermen's Disaster Fund Act (functions vested in Provincial Secretary-Treasurer)
Fredericton-Moncton Highway Financing Act
Gasoline & Motive Fuel Tax Act
Harmonized Sales Tax Act
Health Care Funding Guarantee Act
Income Tax Act
Loan Act
Metallic Minerals Act
Mining Act
Municipal Assistance Act (except Section 5, 9 & 10)
Municipalities Act (subsection 19 (8) & paragraphs 87.1 (b) & (2) (b)
New Brunswick Income Tax Act
Northumberland Strait Crossing Act
Oil and Natural Gas Act
Pari-Mutuel Tax Act
Petrolium Act (part13, except S.88)
Provincial Loans Act
Quarrible Substances Act
Real Property Tax Act (except Sections 4 & subsection 5 (10))
Real Property Transfer Tax Act
Retirement Plan Benificiaries Act
Revenue Administration Act
Small Business Investment Tax Credit Act
Social Services & Education Tax Act
Special Appropriations Act
Sport Development Trust Fund Act (administration of fund)
Statistics Act
Taxpayers Protection Act
Tobacco Tax Act
Tuition Tax Cash Back Credit Act
Statutes under the Jurisdiction of the Minister of Finance in the Minister's Capacity as Chairman of the Board of Management
Auditor General Act (subsections 4 (3) & 16 (1) & Section 17
Crown Construction Contracts Act
Expenditure Management Act, 1991
Expenditure Management Act, 1992
Financial Administration Act (responsibilties pursuant to subsection 2 (2) & Section 6
Member's Pension Act
Members Superannuation Act
Ombudsman Act (pension provision, subsection 2 (4))
Provincial Court Act (pension provisions)
Provincial Court Judges' Pension Act
Public Service Labour Relations Act (61)
Public Service Superannuation Act
Special Retirement Program Act
Teachers' Pension Act
Statutes under the Jurisdiction of the Minister of Finance & Administered by the Office of the Comptroller
Financial Administration Act (responsibilities pursuant to subsection 2 (1))
Statutes under the Jurisdiction of the Minister of Finance & Administered by a Board, Commission or Corporation

Gaming Control Act (part 2)
Maritime Provinces Harness Racing Commission Act
New Brunswick Investment Management Corporation Act
New Brunswick Liquor Corporation Act
New Brunswick Municipal Finance Corporation Act
Minister, Hon. Blaine Higgs
506-444-2627, Fax: 506-457-4989, Blaine.Higgs@gnb.ca
Deputy Minister, Michael Ferguson, C.A.
506-453-2534, Fax: 506-457-4989, mike.ferguson@gnb.ca
Director, Communications Services, Marc Belliveau
506-453-2451, Fax: 506-457-4989, Marc.Belliveau@gnb.ca
Director, Financial Services, Brenda Waye
506-453-2286, Fax: 506-462-5056, brenda.waye@gnb.ca
Director, Policy & Planning, Ann Deveau
506-444-4498, Fax: 506-444-4724, Ann.DEVEAU@gnb.ca
Director, Fiscal Policy & Economics, George Richardson
506-453-6917, Fax: 506-453-2281,
George.RICHARDSON@gnb.ca
Director, Board of Management Operations, Kelly Barr, C.G.A.
506-453-6006, Fax: 506-444-4499, Kelly.barr@gnb.ca
Director, Budget & Expenditure Monitoring, Ben Mersereau
506-453-8019, Fax: 506-444-4499, ben.mersereau@gnb.ca

Associated Agencies, Boards & Commissions:
• New Brunswick Lotteries & Gaming Corporation
Centennial Bldg.
670 King St.
PO Box 6000
Fredericton, NB E3B 5H1
506-444-3468 Fax: 506-444-5818
www.gnb.ca/0162/gaming/nblgc_welcome-e.asp
The name of the Lotteries Commission of New Brunswick, which was established as a Crown corporation under the Lotteries Act, was changed to the New Brunswick Lotteries & Gaming Corporation.
• New Brunswick Electric Finance Corporation / Corporation financière de l'électricité du N.-B.
#376, 670 King St.
PO Box 6000
Fredericton, NB E3B 5H1
506-453-3952 Fax: 506-453-2053
• New Brunswick Investment Management Corporation (NBIMC) / Société de gestion des placements du Nouveau-Brunswick
York Tower
#581, 440 King St.
Fredericton, NB E3B 5H8
506-444-5800 Fax: 506-444-5025
comments@nbimc.com
www.nbimc.com
The New Brunswick Investment Management Corporation assists in the development of the financial services industry & capital markets in the province of New Brunswick.
• New Brunswick Municipal Finance Corporation / Corporation de Financement des municipalités du Nouveau-Brunswick
#376, 670 King St.
PO Box 6000
Fredericton, NB E3B 5H1
506-453-3952 Fax: 506-453-2053

Budget & Financial Management / Gestion financière et budgétaire
Centennial Bldg., #250, 670 King St., PO Box 6000, Fredericton, NB E3B 5H1
506-453-2808 Fax: 506-444-4499
The Budget & Financial Management Division has the following responsibilities: Implementation of multi-year expenditure plans; Development & monitoring of budgets; & Offering options for the government to consider.
Assistant Secretary, Board of Management, Keith MacNevin
506-453-2808, Keith.MacNevin@gnb.ca
Director, Board of Management Operations, Kelly Barr
506-453-6006, Kelly.barr@gnb.ca
Director, Budget & Expenditure Monitoring, Ben Mersereau
506-453-8019, ben.mersereau@gnb.ca

Finance & Administration / Finances et administration
Centennial Bldg., #375, 670 King St., PO Box 6000, Fredericton, NB E3B 5H1
506-453-2451 Fax: 506-444-4724
This division uses a shared services model to provide a blend of corporate services to about 600 clients who work for 10 departments and 22 agencies, boards and commissions. The corporate services include financial services, information technology services and human resources services.
Director, Financial Services, Brenda Waye
506-453-2286, Fax: 506-462-5056, brenda.waye@gnb.ca
Director, Human Resources Services, Peter Trask
506-444-5099, peter.trask@gnb.ca
Director, Information Management & Technology, Pam Gagnon
506-453-3310, Fax: 506-444-3471, Pam.Gagnon@gnb.ca
Director, Policy & Planning, Ann Deveau
506-444-4498, Ann.Deveau@gnb.ca

Fiscal Policy / Politiques fiscales
Centennial Bldg., #245, 670 King St., PO Box 6000, Fredericton, NB E3B 5H1
506-453-2096 Fax: 506-453-2281
The Fiscal Policy Division provides the following services: Advice & analysis in the areas of fiscal & budget policy, federal-provincial fiscal relations, & the economy; Statistical services for the government; & Forecasting & monitoring of government revenues & the economy.
Assistant Deputy Minister, Fiscal Policy, Peter Kieley
506-453-6921, Fax: 506-453-2281, Peter.Kieley@gnb.ca
Director, Fiscal Policy & Economics, George Richardson
506-453-6917, George.Richardson@gnb.ca

Revenue & Taxation / Revenu et Impôt
Centennial Bldg., #671, 670 King St., PO Box 3000, Fredericton, NB E3B 5G5
506-444-2826 Fax: 506-444-4920
Provision of effective, efficient and fair administration of assigned revenue acts. In addition, provides policy and administration support to the Lotteries Commission.
Assistant Deputy Minister, James Turgeon
506-444-2826, James.Turgeon@gnb.ca
Provincial Tax Commissioner, Richard McCullough
506-444-2826, Rick.McCullough@gnb.ca
Executive Director, Tax Policy, George McAllister
506-444-4065, Fax: 506-444-5818,
George.Mcallister@gnb.ca
Director, Audit & Investigation Services, Diane Robichaud-Cormier
506-856-2202, Fax: 506-869-6057,
Diane.Robichaud-Cormier@gnb.ca
Director, Property Assessment & Tax System Renewal, Riva Dayle
506-457-4887, Fax: 506-444-4920, Dayle.Riva@gnb.ca

Treasury / Trésorerie
Centennial Bldg., #376, 670 King St., PO Box 6000, Fredericton, NB E3B 5H1
506-453-3952 Fax: 506-453-2053
The Treasury Division is responsible for financing the Province's cash requirements, cash management, administration of outstanding debt, investment management and administration of pension, sinking and special purpose trust funds, financial policy analysis and advice and Crown corporation and municipal financing.
Assistant Deputy Minister, Leonard Lee-White
Leonard.lee-white@gnb.ca
Managing Director, Capital Markets, Richard Luton
506-444-4161, Richard.Luton@gnb.ca
Managing Director, Banking & Cash Management, Catherine Mosher
506-453-2503, Catherine.MOSHER@gnb.ca

Department of Health / Santé

PO Box 5100, Fredericton, NB E3B 5G8
506-457-4800 Fax: 506-453-5243
dh-ms@dh-ms.ca
www.gnb.ca/0051/index-e.asp
To work with New Brunswickers in achieving well-being by promoting self-sufficiency & personal responsibility, & providing approved services as required. The development & delivery of health programs & services to New Brunswick residents is supported by a range of internal department functions such as administration, planning & evaluation, & program support. Provides the continuum of services to prevent illness & disability. The department's education & awareness raising initiatives promote the health & well-being of New Brunswickers of all ages so that they can achieve their best potential while enjoying an independent & healthy lifestyle for as long as possible.
Acts Administered:
Ambulance Services Act
Anatomy Act
Automated Defibrillator Act
Cemetery Companies Act
Clean Air (Paragraph 8 (2a) & Subsection 4)
Clean Water Act (in part)
Health Services Act
Hospital Act (except section 21)
Hospital Services Act
Human Tissues Gift Act
Insurance Act
Liquor Control Act
Medical Consent of Minors Act
Medical Services Payment Act
Mental Health Act
Mental Health Services Act
Motor Vehicle Act (in part)
Municipalities Act
Personal Health Information Privacy and Access Act
Pesticides Control Act (in part)
Prescription Drug Payment Act
Public Health
Regional Health Authorities Act
Smoke-Free Places Act, 2004
Tobacco Damages and Health Care Costs Recovery
Tobacco Sales Act
Minister, Hon. Madeleine Dubé
506-457-4800, Madeleine.Dubé@gnb.ca
Deputy Minister, Donald Ferguson
506-475-4800, don.j.ferguson@gnb.ca
Director, Communications, Tracey Burkhardt
506-453-2536, tracey.burkhardt@gnb.ca
Administrative Support, Kathy Densmore
506-453-2536, Fax: 506-444-4697, kathy.densmore@gnb.ca
Associate Deputy Minister, Francophone Services, Lyne St-Pierre-Ellis
506-457-4800, Fax: 506-444-4697,
lyne.st-pierre-ellis@gnb.ca
Director, Medicare-Insured Services & Physician Remuneration, Michel Léger
506-444-3633, Fax: 506-444-4697, michel.leger@gnb.ca
Executive Director, Pharmaceutical Services, Jardine Leanne
506-453-3884, Fax: 506-444-4697, leanne.jardine@gnb.ca
Director, Human Resources Branch, Joanne Stone
506-444-2521, Fax: 506-444-4697, joanne.stone@gnb.ca
Executive Director, E-Health, Cheryl Hansen
506-444-6782, Fax: 506-444-4697, cheryl.hansen@gnb.ca
Executive Director, Financial Services, Renée LaForest
506-453-3759, Fax: 506-444-4697, dh-ms@gnb.ca
Assistant Deputy Minister, Corporate Services, Tom Maston
506-453-2775, Fax: 506-444-4697, Tom.Maston@gnb.ca
Director, Information Technology Services, Dawn O'Donnell
506-453-2279, Fax: 506-444-4697, dawn.o'donnell@gnb.ca
Director, Health Emergency Management Services, Joanne Rosevear
506-453-2220, Fax: 506-444-4697,
Joanne.Rosevear@gnb.ca
Director, Hospital Clinical Services, Francine Bordage
506-453-2283, Fax: 506-444-4697,
Francine.Bordage@gnb.ca
Director, Hospital Operations, Kathy Perrin
506-453-2283, Fax: 506-444-4697, Kathy.Perrin@gnb.ca

Addiction & Mental Health Services Division / Services de traitement des dépendances et de santé mentale
506-444-4442
Asst. Deputy Minister, Kenneth Ross
506-457-4800, ken.ross@gnb.ca
Executive Director, Addiction & Mental Health Services, Barbara Whitenect
506-444-4442, Barbara.Whitenect@gnb.ca
Director, Adult Services, Sylvie Martin
506-444-5241, sylvie.martin@gnb.ca
Director, Child & Youth Services, Yvette Doiron
506-444-4442, yvette.doiron-brun@gnb.ca
Director, Primary Health Care, Bronwyn Davies
506-453-7926, bronwyn.davies@gnb.ca
Director, Extra-Mural Program, Jean Bustard
506-453-4303, jean.bustard@gnb.ca

Public Health & Medical Services / Santé publique et services médicaux
Public Health services are delivered through the province's seven health regions, under the management of Regional Directors. A Chief Medical Officer of Health & a Deputy Chief Medical Officer of Health oversee the development of policy & regulations, & provide medical operational support to the regional Medical Officers of Health. Public Health Services support healthy growth & development, foster healthy lifestyles, control communicable diseases, & protect the public from adverse health consequences of exposure to chemical, physical & biological agents.
Chief Medical Officer, Dr. Eilish Cleary
506-444-2112, Eilish.Cleary@gnb.ca
Deputy Chief Medical Officer Of Health, Dr. Denis Allard
506-856-2814, Denis.Allard@gnb.ca
Epidemiologist, Communicable Disease Control, Jastej Dhaliwal
506-444-3044, Jastej.Dhaliwal@gnb.ca

Office of Human Resources / Bureaux des ressources humaines

Centennial Bldg, #345, 670 King St., PO Box 6000, Fredericton, NB E3B 5H1
506-453-2264 Fax: 506-453-7195
www.gnb.ca/0163/index-e.asp
The Office of Human Resources has responsibility for the policies which govern the following human resources issues: Recruitment; Compensation; & Staff development for the provision of quality public services.
Acts Administered:
Civil Services Act (staffing responsibilities)
Public Interest Disclosure Act
Minister, Office of Human Resources, Hon. Blaine Higgs
506-462-5092, Fax: 506-453-7195, blaine.higgs@gnb.ca
Deputy Minister, Brian Durelle
506-453-3036, Fax: 506-453-7195, Brian.Durelle@gnb.ca

Director, Communications, Brendan Langille
506-444-4594, brendan.langille@gnb.ca

Pensions & Employee Benefits
York Tower, Kings Place, #680, 440 King St., PO Box 6000, Fredericton, NB E3B 5H8
506-453-2296 Fax: 506-457-7388
800-561-4012
www.gnb.ca/0163/pension/pension-e.asp
Assistant Deputy Minister, Pensions & Employee Benefits, Gaudet Mark
506-453-2296, Fax: 506-457-7388, Mark.Gaudet@gnb.ca
Manager, Benefit Services, Kim Fraser
506-453-2296, Fax: 506-457-7388, kim.fraser@gnb.ca
Manager, Committee Support & Development, Carolyn Roberts
506-453-2296, Fax: 506-457-7388, carolyn.roberts@gnb.ca
Manager, Finance & Administration, Marilyn Mcconnell
506-453-2296, marilyn.mcconnell@gnb.ca
Manager, Applications & System Management, Michael Mclaughlin
506-453-2296, Michael.Mclaughlin@gnb.ca
Manager, Data Services, Raymond David
506-453-2296, raymond.david@gnb.ca

Employee Relations Services
Centennial Bldg., #360, 670 King St., PO Box 6000, Fredericton, NB E3B 5H1
506-453-2115 Fax: 506-444-5786
Assistant Deputy Minister, Dorine P. Pirie
506-457-6739, Dorine.Pirie@gnb.ca
Director, Compensation, Classification & Corporate Research, Lori Anne Mccracken
506-457-7216, LoriAnne.Mccracken@gnb.ca
Director, Labor Relations, Frédéric Finn
506-453-8006, Frederic.Finn@gnb.ca

Human Resource Strategy & Programs
Centennial Bldg., #344, 670 King St., PO Box 6000, Fredericton, NB E3B 5H1
506-453-2264 Fax: 506-453-2124
Acting Director, HR Strategy & Development Branch, Jennifer Wilkins
506-453-2141, Fax: 506-453-2124, Jennifer.Wilkins@gnb.ca
Director, HR Programs & Official Languages, Janique Robichaud-Savoie
506-453-6088, Janique.Robichaud@gnb.ca

New Brunswick Human Rights Commission / Commission des droits de la personne

PO Box 6000, Fredericton, NB E3B 5H1
506-453-2301 Fax: 506-453-2653
888-471-2233
hrc.cdp@gnb.ca
TTY: 506-453-2911

The Human Rights Commission is a provincial government agency. It promotes equality and investigates and tries to settle complaints of discrimination and harassment. The Commission also works to prevent discrimination by promoting human rights and offering educational opportunities to employers, service providers and the general public.
Chairperson, Randy Dickinson
506-453-2301, hrc.cdp@gnb.ca
Director, Jill Peters
506-453-2301, jill.peters@gnb.ca
Legal Counsel, Sarina Mckinnon
506-453-2301, sarina.mckinnon@gnb.ca
Lawyer, Chantal Gauthier
506-453-2301, chantal.gauthier@gnb.ca

Department of Intergovernmental Affairs / Affaires intergouvernementales et relations internationales

Centennial Bldg., #274, 670 King St., PO Box 6000, Fredericton, NB E3B 5H1
506-444-5418 Fax: 506-453-2995
iga@gnb.ca
www.gnb.ca/0056/index-e.asp

New Brunswick's Department of Intergovernmental Affairs manages relations with governments, communities, & organizations. The North American Division, the International Relations & Francophonie Division, & the Trade Policy Division conduct operations with a strategic & corporate approach.
Acts Administered:
Maritime Economic Cooperation Act
Order of New Brunswick Act
Minister, Hon. David Alward
506-453-2144, Fax: 506-453-7407, iga@gnb.ca
Acting Deputy Minister, Jocelyne Mills
506-444-5179, Fax: 506-457-6507, jocelyne.mills@gnb.ca
Director, Craig Chouinard
506-444-2519, Fax: 506-457-6507, craig.chouinard@gnb.ca

International Relations & la Francophonie / Relations internationales et La Francophonie
Centennial Bldg., #118, 670 King St., PO Box 6000, Fredericton, NB E3B 5H1
506-453-3078 Fax: 506-453-2995
Assistant Deputy Minister, Mirelle Cyr
506-453-3078, Mirelle.Cyr@gnb.ca
Director, Canadian Francophonie & Official Languages, Line Pinet
506-444-4948, Fax: 506-444-5612, line.pinet@gnb.ca
Director, International Relations & Multilateral Francophonie, Danielle Mingay
506-444-4948, Fax: 506-444-5612, danielle.mingay@gnb.ca
Chief of Protocol, Office of the Protocol, Anne Reynolds
506-453-2671, Anne.Reynolds@gnb.ca

North American Relations Division / Division des relations nord-américaines
Centennial Bldg., #274, 670 King St., PO Box 6000, Fredericton, NB E3B 5H1
506-444-6775 Fax: 506-453-2995
Director, Phyllis Mockler-Caissie
506-444-2481, Phyllis.Mockler-Caissie@gnb.ca
Senior Policy Advisor, Dave Dell
506-444-6760, dave.dell@gnb.ca

Trade Policy
Centennial Bldg., #175, 670 King St., PO Box 6000, Fredericton, NB E3B 5H1
506-444-5094 Fax: 506-444-5299
Executive Director, Elaine Campbell
506-444-5788, elaine.campbell@gnb.ca
Senior Policy Advisor, Andrew David Hashey
506-444-4250, Andrew.Hashey@gnb.ca

Department of Justice & Consumer Affairs / Justice et la consommation

Centennial Bldg., 670 King St., PO Box 6000, Fredericton, NB E3B 5H1
506-462-5100 Fax: 506-453-3651
justice.comments@gnb.ca
www.gnb.ca/0062/index-e.asp

Promoting the impartial administration of justice, & ensuring protection of the public interest are the chief responsibilities of New Brunswick's Department of Justice & Consumer Affairs. The province's Public Legal Education & Information Service is funded by Justice Canada.
Acts Administered:
Auctioneers Licence Act
Collection Agencies Act
Commissioners for Taking Affidavits Act
Consumer Product Warranty and Liability Act
Co-operative Associations Act
Cost of Credit Disclosure Act
Court Security Act
Credit Unions Act
Creditors Relief Act
Direct Sellers Act
Family Services Act (Part VII)
Federal Courts Jurisdiction Act
Franchises Act
Gift Cards Act
Innkeepers Act
Insurance Act
Jury Act
Landlord & Tenant Act
Legal Aid Act
Loan & Trust Companies Act
Nursing Homes Pension Plans Act
Pension Benefits Act
Pre-arranged Funeral Services Act
Premium Tax Act
Probate Court Act
Provincial Court Act
Real Estate Agents Act
Recording of Evidence Act
Securities Transfer Act
Sheriffs Act
Special Insurance Companies Act (subject to proclamation)
Support Enforcement Act
Trustees Act
Minister, Justice & Consumer Affairs & Attorney General, Hon. Marie-Claude Blais
506-453-2583, Fax: 506-453-2237, Marie-Claude.Blais@gnb.ca
Acting Deputy Minister, Justice & Consumer Affairs, Judith Keating, Q.C.
506-453-2208, Judith.Keating@gnb.ca
Director, Financial Services, Bart Myers
506-453-2719, Fax: 506-453-8718, Bart.MYERS@gnb.ca
Executive Director, Public Legal Education & Information Service, Deborah Doherty
506-453-5369, Fax: 506-462-5193
Senior Policy Advisor, Policy & Planning, James Burns
506-453-6526, jim.burns@gnb.ca
Director, Communications, Paul Harpelle
506-462-5100, Paul.Harpelle@gnb.ca

Associated Agencies, Boards & Commissions:
• New Brunswick Credit Union Deposit Insurance Corp. / Société d'assurance-dépôts des caisses populaires du Nouveau-Brunswick
PO Box 6000
Fredericton, NB E3B 5H1
506-457-4852 Fax: 506-453-7474
www.assurance-nb.ca/index-e.asp
The New Brunswick Credit Union Deposit Insurance Corporation is a Crown corporation that provides deposit insurance to members of New Brunswick's credit unions and caisses populaires.
• New Brunswick Expropriations Advisory Office / Bureau sur l'expropriation
Phoenix Square Bldg.
371 Queen St.
Fredericton, NB E3B 1B1
506-453-7771 Fax: 506-453-9600
• New Brunswick Insurance Board / Commission des assurances du N.-B.
Saint John Mercantile Centre
#600, 55 Union St.
Saint John, NB E2L 5B7
506-643-7710 Fax: 506-652-5011
info@nbib-canb.org
www.nbib-canb.org
The New Brunswick Insurance Board regulates automobile insurance rates. The Board is also responsible for approving rates for all products being sold in New Brunswick as of January 2005.
• New Brunswick Real Estate Association / Association des agents immobiliers du Nouveau-Brunswick
#1, 22 Durelle St.
Fredericton, NB E3C 1N8
506-459-8055 Fax: 506-459-8057 800-762-1677
info@nbrea.ca
www.nbrea.ca
The New Brunswick Real Estate Association serves and regulates its members through education, professional and ethical standards, and promotion of public awareness for the benefit of REALTORS and the public they serve.
• New Brunswick Securities Commission / Commission des valeurs mobilières du N.-B.
#300, 85 Charlotte St.
Saint John, NB E2L 2J2
506-658-3060 Fax: 506-658-3059 866-933-2222
information@nbsc-cvmnb.ca
www.nbsc-cvmnb.ca/nbsc
The New Brunswick Securities Commission (NBSC) is the Crown Corporation established by the Province of New Brunswick in 2004 to regulate the securities industry and ensure the efficiency and integrity of capital markets in New Brunswick.

Court Services / Services à la court
506-453-2933 Fax: 506-453-3651
Asst. Deputy Minister, Marilyn Born
506-453-2933, marilyn.born@gnb.ca
Director, Program Support Services Branch, Anne McKay
506-453-8498, Fax: 506-453-2234, Anne.MCKAY@gnb.ca

Regional Court Services/Services aux tribunal regionaux:

Bathurst
Regional Director, Grégoire Boudreau
506-547-2150, Fax: 506-547-2966

Fredericton
Regional Director, Dominique Laundry
506-453-2015, Fax: 506-453-7921

Miramichi
Regional Director, Matthew Cripps
506-627-4023, Fax: 506-627-4069

Moncton
Regional Director, David Léger
506-856-2415, Fax: 506-869-6168

Saint John
Regional Director, Tom Bishop
506-658-2400, Fax: 506-658-3762

Justice Services / Services judiciaires
506-453-2458 Fax: 506-453-3651
Asst. Deputy Minister, Suzanne Bonnell-Burley
506-453-2458, Suzanne.BONNELL-BURLEY@gnb.ca
Registrar, Credit Unions, Cooperatives & Trust Companies & Examinations, Claire Gagnon
506-453-2315, Fax: 506-453-7474, Claire.GAGNON@gnb.ca
Manager, Insurance, Nola Carr, C.A.
506-453-2512, Fax: 506-453-7435, nola.carr@gnb.ca
Director, Consumer Affairs, Dianne Kelly
506-453-2659, Fax: 506-444-4494, Dianne.Kelly@gnb.ca

New Brunswick Liquor Corporation (Alcool NB Liquor) / Société des alcools du Nouveau-Brunswick

170 Wilsey Rd., PO Box 20787, Fredericton, NB E3B 5B8
506-452-6826 Fax: 506-462-2024
info@anbl.com
www.nbliquor.com
Other Communication: Public Affairs Phone: 506-452-6453
The Crown corporation manufactures, buys, imports, & sells liquor of every kind.
Minister, Hon. Blaine Higgs
506-453-2451, Fax: 506-457-4989, info@anbl.com
Chairperson, Ron Lindala
506-452-6826, ron.lindala@anbl.com
President/CEO, Daniel Allain
506-452-6522, daniel.allain@anbl.com
Senior Vice-President, Richard A. Smith
506-452-6826, rick.smith@anbl.com
Vice-President/CFO, Chris Evans
506-452-6460, chris.evans@anbl.com
Vice-President, Supply Chain/ Products & Marketing, Mike O'Brien
506-452-6505, mike.o'brien@anbl.com
Vice-President, Customer Service & Retail Operations, Brad Cameron
506-452-6511, brad.cameron@anbl.com

Department of Local Government / Gouvernementaux locales

Marysville Place, 20 McGloin St., PO Box 6000, Fredericton, NB E3B 5H1
506-453-2807 Fax: 506-453-3988
www.gnb.ca/0370/index-e.asp
The Department of Local Government oversees the following areas: Assessment & planning appeals; Local governance & regional collaboration for New Brunswick; Local Service Districts; Municipalities (cities, towns, & villages) & rural communities, including municipal capital borrowing, orientation, & restructuring; Registration of dogs & dog kennels in unincorporated areas; Resource manuals for local government in New Brunswick; & grants.
Acts Administered:
Agricultural Land Protection & Development Act (subsection 10 (2) & section 11)
Assessment & Planning Appeal Board Act
Business Improvement Areas Act
Cemetery Companies Act (paragraph 5 (1) (c))
Control of Municipalities Act
Days of Rest Act
Edmundston, 1998 Act
Evidence Act (sections 88, 89, & 90)
Highway Act (sections 58 - 62.1)
Metric Conversion Act
Municipal Assistance Act
Municipal Capital Borrowing Act
Municipal Debentures Act
Municipalities Act (except subsection 19 (8), 125 (1), & 188 (3))
Municipal Thoroughfare Easements Act
New Brunswick Municipal Finance Corporation Act (section 14 & subsection 16 (4))
Police Act (paragraph 17.05 (2) (b), subsections 17.06 (3), & (4), paragraph 17.2 (3) (b), & subsections 17.4 (3) & (4))
Real Property Tax (section 4 & subsection 5.1 (10))
Service New Brunswick Act (paragraph 15.1 (3) (b))
Society for the Prevention of Cruelty to Animals Act
To comply with the Request of the City of Saint John on Taxation of the LNG Terminal
Unsightly Premises Act
Minister, Local Government, Hon. Bruce Fitch
506-453-2807, Bruce.Fitch@gnb.ca
Deputy Minister, Sylvie Levesque-Finn
506-444-3356, Sylvie.Levesque-Finn@gnb.ca

Associated Agencies, Boards & Commissions:
• Assessment & Planning Appeal Board / Commission d'appel en matière d'évaluation et d'urbanisme
#201, 435 King St.
PO Box 6000
Fredericton, NB E3B 5H1
506-453-2126 Fax: 506-444-4881

Corporate Services, Community Funding & Technical Services
Marysville Place, 20 McGloin St., PO Box 6000, Fredericton, NB E3B 5H1
506-453-2154 Fax: 506-457-4933
Assistant Deputy Minister, Alan Roy
506-453-6254, alan.roy@gnb.ca
Director, Community Infrastructure, André Chenard
506-457-4947, Andre.Chenard@gnb.ca
Director, Information & Technology Management, Laurie Robichaud
506-453-2020, Laurie.Robichaud@gnb.ca
Director, Corporate Finance, Yvonne Samson
506-453-2020, Yvonne.Samson@gnb.ca
Director, Human Resources & Administration, Mary Ellen Somerville
506-453-2020, MaryEllen.Somerville@gnb.ca
Acting Director, Program & Engineering Services, André Chenard
506-444-2654, Andre.Chenard@gnb.ca
Manager, Compliance & Reporting, Greg Mignault
506-453-2020, Greg.Mignault@gnb.ca
Manager, Operations & Technical Support, Bradley Tozer
506-453-2020, Bradley.Tozer@gnb.ca
Manager, Systems Development, Todd Trask
506-453-2020, todd.trask@gnb.ca
Manager, Budget & Revenue, Julie Warren-Mccaul
506-453-2020, julie.warren-mccaul@gnb.ca

Policy & Strategic Initiatives
Marysville Place, 20 McGloin St., 2nd Fl., PO Box 6000, Fredericton, NB E3B 5H1
506-453-3700 Fax: 506-457-7128
Executive Director, Policy & Strategic Initiatives, Elizabeth Hayward
506-453-8788, bebo.hayward@gnb.ca
Director, Strategic Planning & Policy Development, Kim Hughes
506-453-3700, Fax: 506-453-7128, Kim.Hughes@gnb.ca
Director, Local Government Policy Branch, Christy Shaw
506-453-3700, Fax: 506-457-4933, Christy.Shaw@gnb.ca
Director, Legislative Renewal & Legal Affairs, Denyse Smart
506-453-3700, denise.smart@gnb.ca
Director, Inter-Governmental Affairs, Stephanie Whalen
506-453-3700, Stephanie.Whalen@gnb.ca
Director, Stakeholder Education & Engagement, Michelle Daigle
506-453-3700, Michelle.Daigle@gnb.ca

Assessment & Planning Appeal Board
City Centre, PO Box 6000, Fredericton, NB E3B 5H1
506-453-2126 Fax: 506-444-4881
Chairperson, Scott MacGregor
506-453-2126, scott.macgregor@gnb.ca
Administrative Assistant, Kathy Malcolm
506-453-2126, kathy.malcolm@gnb.ca

Department of Natural Resources / Ressources naturelles

Hugh John Flemming Forestry Centre, PO Box 6000, Fredericton, NB E3B 5H1
506-453-3826 Fax: 506-444-4367
dnrweb@gnb.ca
www.gnb.ca/naturalresources
Manages all natural resources within the province including fish & wildlife, timber, minerals, Crown lands & water resources. Responsible for the development, protection, allocation & utilization of resources in a way that is considered economically, environmentally & socially acceptable.
Acts Administered:
Act Respecting Angling Lease Number 7
Bituminous Shale Act
Conservation Easements Act
Crown Grant Restrictions Act
Crown Lands & Forests Act
Leasing Regulation
Endangered Species Act
Fish & Wildlife Act
Forest Fires Act
Grants Act
Kouchibouguac National Park, An Act to Implement Recommendation 16 of the Report of the Special Inquiry on
Mining Act (in part)
National Parks Act
Natural Products Act (in part)
Off-Road Vehicle Act
Oil & Natural Gas Act
Ownership of Minerals Act
Parks Act
Petroleum Act (except most of Part 13)
Protected Natural Areas Act, 2003
Quarriable Substances Act
Scalers Act
Territorial Divisions Act
Transportation of Primary Forest Products Act
Underground Storage Act
Acts administered by an Associated Agency, Board, Commission or Corporation
Forest Products Act
Maritime Forestry Complex Coporation Act
Roosevelt Campobello International Park Act
St. Croix International Waterway Commission Act
Minister, Hon. Bruce Northrup
506-453-2510, bruce.nortrup@gnb.ca
Deputy Minister, Phil Lepage
506-453-2501, Fax: 506-453-2930, Phil.Lepage@gnb.ca
Director, Communications, Steven Benteau
506-453-2614, Fax: 506-457-4881, Steve.Benteau@gnb.ca
Executive Secretary, Ginette Delfrate
506-453-2501, Fax: 506-457-4881, Ginette.Delfrate@gnb.ca

Associated Agencies, Boards & Commissions:
• Board of Examiners under the Scaler's Act / Bureau des examinateurs (Loi sur les mesureurs)
1350 Regent St. South
PO Box 6000
Fredericton, NB E3B 5H1
506-453-2441 Fax: 506-453-6689
• Forest Protection Limited / Protection des Forêts
2502 Hwy. 102
Lincoln, NB E3B 7E6
506-446-6930 Fax: 506-446-6934
info@forestprotectionlimited.com
www.forestprotectionlimited.com
Forest Protection Limited (FPL) is a non-profit aerial forest protection company whose mandate is to protect forests through assistance to the Forest Management Branch, for fire protection, fire fighting assistance & aerial surveys.
• New Brunswick Forest Products Commission / Commission des produits forestiers du Nouveau-Brunswick
PO Box 6000
Fredericton, NB E3B 5H1
506-453-2196 Fax: 506-457-4966
www.gnb.ca/0078/fpc/index.asp
The New Brunswick Forest Products Commission is an independent Commission overseeing the marketing relationships involving forest industries (pulp mills & sawmills), forest products marketing boards (private woodlot owners & producers) & the provincial government.

Corporate Services Division / Services Généraux Division
Hugh John Flemming Forestry Centre, 3rd Fl, PO Box 6000, Fredericton, NB E3B 5H1
506-453-2178 Fax: 506-453-2930
Assistant Deputy Minister, Corporate Services, Janet Higgins
506-453-2501, Fax: 506-453-2930, Janet.Higgins@gnb.ca
Director, Policy and Strategic Initiatives, Lesley Chenier-Aussant
506-444-4688, lesley.chenier-aussant@gnb.ca
Director, Human Resource Services, Kathleen Good Waite
506-453-2197, Kathleen.GoodWaite@gnb.ca
Director, Financial Services, Jean-Guy Leblanc
506-453-3826, JeanGuy.LeBlanc@gnb.ca
Assistant Director, Employee Relations, Barb Macintosh
506-453-3863, Barb.Macintosh@gnb.ca
Director, Information Services and Systems, Doris Wu
506-457-4922, Doris.Wu@gnb.ca

Lands, Minerals & Petroleum Division / Terres, Minéraux et Pétrole Division
Hugh John Flemming Forestry Centre, PO Box 6000, Fredericton, NB E3B 5H1
506-453-2684 Fax: 506-453-2930
dnrweb@gnb.ca
http: //www.gnb.ca/0078/minerals/index-e.asp
Asst. Deputy Minister, Samuel McEwan
506-453-2684, Sam.McEwan@gnb.ca
Director, Crown Lands, Peter Macnutt
506-453-6656, Peter.MacNutt@gnb.ca
Director, Geological Surveys Branch, Leslie Fyffe
506-444-5005, Les.Fyffe@gnb.ca
Acting Director, Minerals & Petroleum Development, Endresen Keith
506-444-2683, keith.endresen@gnb.ca

Renewable Resources / Ressources renouvelables
Hugh John Flemming Forestry Centre, Suite 310, Fl 3rd, PO Box 6000, Fredericton, NB E3B 5H1
506-453-2684 Fax: 506-453-2684
dnrweb@gnb.ca
www.gnb.ca/naturalresources
Asst. Deputy Minister, Paul Orser
506-453-2684, Paul.Orser@gnb.ca
Director, Fish & Wildlife, Michael Sullivan
506-453-7114, Mike.Sullivan@gnb.ca
Director, Forest Management, Thomas MacFarlane
506-453-6673, Tom.MacFarlane@gnb.ca
Executive Director, Regional Operations & Support Services, Julius Tarjan
506-453-2684, Julius.Tarjan@gnb.ca

Office of the Ombudsman / Bureau de l'ombudsman

767 Brunswick St., PO Box 6000, Fredericton, NB E3B 5H1
506-453-2789 Fax: 506-453-5599
800-465-1100
nbombud@gnb.ca
http: //www.gnb.ca/ombudsman
Ombudsman, François Levert
506-453-2789, Fax: 506-453-5599, Francois.Levert@gnb.ca
Executive Director, Steve Gilliland
506-453-2789, Fax: 506-453-5599, Steve.Gilliland@gnb.ca
Executive Secretary, Julie Dickison
506-453-2789, Fax: 506-453-5599, Julie.Dickison@gnb.ca

New Brunswick Police Commission (NBPC) / Commission de police du Nouveau-Brunswick

Fredericton City Centre, #202, 435 King St., Fredericton, NB E3B 1E5
506-453-2069 Fax: 506-457-3542
nbpc@gnb.ca
http: //www.gnb.ca/0075/index-e.asp

The Commission investigates & determines complaints alleging misconduct by municipal & regional police officers; investigates any matter relating to any aspect of policing in any area of the province; determines the adequacy of municipal, regional & RCMP police forces within the province.

Chair, Peter Seheult
506-453-2069, Fax: 506-457-3542
Vice-Chair, Donald R. Butler
506-453-2069, Fax: 506-457-3542
Executive Director, Pierre Beaudoin
506-453-2069, Fax: 506-457-3542, Pierre.Beaudoin@gnb.ca

Population Growth Secretariat

Centennial Bldg., 670 King St., PO Box 6000, Fredericton, NB E3B 5H1
506-453-3981 Fax: 506-444-6729
immigration@gnb.ca
www.gnb.ca/3100/index-e.asp

The Population Growth Secretariat consists of the Immigration Division & the Population Support Division. Issues such as settlement & multiculturalism, retention, & repatriation are handled by the Secretariat.

Minister, Business New Brunswick; Minister Responsible, Service New Brunswick; Minister Responsible, Population Growth Secretariat; Minister Responsible, Communications New Brunswick, Minister Responsible, Red Tape Reduction, Hon. Greg Byrne
506-453-5898, Fax: 506-453-5893, greg.byrne@gnb.ca
Assistant Deputy Minister, Picot Nicole
506-444-5663, Fax: 506-453-3899, nicole.picot@gnb.ca
Director, Settlement and Multiculturalism, Ashraf Ghanem
506-457-7644, Fax: 506-453-3899, ashraf.ghanem@gnb.ca
Director, Repatriation and Attraction, Ryan Jacobson
506-457-7646, Fax: 506-453-3899, ryan.jacobson@gnb.ca
Acting Director, Retention, Phillippe Ouellette
506-457-7645, Fax: 506-453-3899,
phillippe.ouellette@gnb.ca
Manager, Immigration, Tammy Caseley
506-444-5072, Fax: 506-444-6729, tammy.caseley@gnb.ca
Manager, Federal/Provincial/Territorial Relations and Research, Stephanie Eardley
506-457-7642, Fax: 506-453-3899,
stephanie.eardley@gnb.ca

Department of Post-Secondary Education, Training & Labour / Éducation postsecondaire, Formation et Travail

Chestnut Complex, 470 York St., PO Box 6000, Fredericton, NB E3B 5H1
506-453-2597 Fax: 506-453-3618
dpetlinfo@gnb.ca
www.gnb.ca/0105/index-e.asp

Formerly the Department of Training & Employment.

Acts Administered:
Adult Education & Training Act
Apprenticeship & Occupational Certification Act
Degree Granting Act
Employment Development Act
Employment Standards Act
Fisheries Bargaining Act
Human Rights Act
Industrial Relations Act
Labour & Employment Board Act
Labour Market Research Act
Maritime Provinces Higher Education Commission Act
New Brunswick Community Colleges Act
New Brunswick Public Libraries Act
Post Secondary Student Financial Assistance
Private Occupational Training Act
Silicosis Compensation Act

Minister, Hon. Martine Coulombe
506-453-2342, Fax: 506-453-3038,
martine.coloumbe@gnb.ca
Deputy Minister, Marc Léger
506-453-2343, Fax: 506-453-3038, Marc.Leger@gnb.ca
Director, Communications, Marie-Josée Groulx
506-444-3465, Fax: 506-444-4314,
marie-josee.groulx@gnb.ca
Media Relations Coordinator, Sheri Strickland
506-453-8617, Fax: 506-444-4314, sheri.strickland@gnb.ca

Associated Agencies, Boards & Commissions:
• Apprenticeship & Occupational Certification Board / Direction de l'apprentissage et de la certification professionnelle
PO Box 6000
Fredericton, NB E3B 5H1
506-453-2260 Fax: 506-453-5317
• Ministerial Advisory Committee on Multiculturalism / Comité consultatif ministériel sur le multiculturalisme
PO Box 6000
Fredericton, NB E3B 5H1
• New Brunswick Human Rights Commission / Commission des droits de la personne
• Workplace Health, Safety & Compensation Commission (WHSCC) / Commission de la santé, de la sécurité et de l'indemnisation des accidents au travail
• Workplace Health, Safety & Compensation Commission of New Brunswick (WHSC) / Commission de la santé, de la sécurité et de l'indemnisation des accidents au travail

Labour & Planning / Travail et Planification
Asst. Deputy Minister, Gérin Girouard
506-453-8202, Fax: 506-444-4314, gerin.girouard@gnb.ca
Deputy Director, Employment Standards, Giselle Goguen
506-453-3089, giselle.goguen@gnb.ca
Director, Policy & Planning, Dianne Nason
506-444-2071, dianne.nason@gnb.ca
Director, Industrial Relations & Employment Standards, Paula Ultican
506-453-3902, paula.ultican@gnb.ca

Post-Secondary Education / Éducation Postsecondaire
Asst. Deputy Minister/CEO, Yves Pelletier
506-457-4891, yves.pelletier
Director, College Admissions Service, Doris Adams
506-789-2016, doris.adams@gnb.ca
Director, Student Financial Services, Michael Barnett
506-453-3790, michael.barnett@gnb.ca
Assistant Director, Portfolio Management, David Belmore
506-444-5060, David.Belmore@gnb.ca
Director, University Relations, René Boudreau
506-452-5135, rene.boudreau@gnb.ca
Executive Director, College Support Service, Daniel Fraser
506-453-8230, daniel.fraser@gnb.ca

New Brunswick Power Group of Companies (NBPC) / Énergie NB

515 King St., PO Box 2000, Fredericton, NB E3B 4X1
506-458-4444 Fax: 506-458-4000
questions@nbpower.com
www.nbpower.com

NB Power will be restructured to form a holding company with four subsidiary companies, NB Power Generation, NB Power Nuclear, NB Power Transmission & NB Power Distribution & Customer Service. NB Power is legislated to provide electric power to the province of NB. It is the largest electric utility in Atlantic Canada. Economic generation is from hydro, oil, nuclear, coal & Orimulsion powered facilities. NB Power is developing a comprehensive station environmental management system & is moving towards ISO 14001 certification.The Corporate Environmental Policy applies to all aspects of NB Power's activities. These include the generation of electricity from various energy sources, including nuclear, oil, coal, Orimulsion (193), & hydro, the transmission & distribution of electricity to customers. It also includes those activities that support the generation, transmission & distribution of electricity, including management of land, raw materials, & by-products.

Acts Administered:
Electricity Act
Energy Efficiency Act
Energy Efficiency and Conservation Agency of New Brunswick Act
Gas Distribution, 1999 Act
Petroleum Products Pricing Act
Pipeline, 2005 Act

Minister, Hon. Craig Leonard
506-658-3179, Craig.Leonard@gnb.ca
Acting Deputy Minister, Douglas Holt
506-658-3179, doug.holt@gnb.ca
Communications Director, Jim Hennessy
506-658-3179, jim.hennessy@gnb.ca
Director, Elecricity, Stephen Waycott
506-658-3126, Stephen.Waycott@gnb.ca
Director, Pipeline, Petroleum & Natural Gas, Patrick Ervin
506-658-3124, patrick.ervin@gnb.ca
Director, Renewable Energy & Emerging Technologies, Bill Breckenridge
506-658-3144, bill.breckenridge@gnb.ca
Executive Director, Shelly Rinehart
506-658-3123, shelley.rinehart@gnb.ca

Department of Public Safety / Sécurité publique

364 Argyle St., PO Box 6000, Fredericton, NB E3B 5H1
506-453-3992 Fax: 506-453-3870
DPS-MSP.Information@gnb.ca
www.gnb.ca/0276/index-e.asp

Provides leadership in the areas of public order & community safety. Provides fair, accessible, community-focused, & coordinated public safety programs & services. Ensures effective inspection & enforcement of designated public safety programs & services. Acts in partnership with communities to prevent crime, assist victims, & create opportunities for offenders to change. Coordinates & cooperates with the federal government in the administration of correctional services & law enforcement in New Brunswick.

Acts Administered:
Boiler & Pressure Vessel Act
Coroners Act
Corrections Act
Cross Border Policing Act
Custody & Detention of Young Persons Act
Electrical Installation & Inspection Act
Elevators & Lifts Act
Emergency 911 Act
Emergency Measures Act
Film & Video Act
Fire Prevention Act
Gaming Control (except Part 2)
Industrial Relations (subsection 1 (8.11))
Intoxicated Persons Detention Act
Liquor Control Act
Motor Vehicle Act
New Brunswick Building Code Act
Plumbing Installation & Inspection Act
Police Act (Parts I,I1 and IV)
Private Investigators & Security Services Act
Restricted Beverage Act
Salvage Dealers Licensing Act
Transportation of Dangerous Goods Act
Victim Services Act

Minister, Hon. Robert Trevors
506-453-7414, Robert.Trevors@gnb.ca
Deputy Minister, Dale Wilson
506-453-7412, Dale.Wilson@gnb.ca
Director, Communications & Public Awareness, Deborah Nobes
506-444-3323, Deborah.Nobes@gnb.ca
Director, Financial Services, Deborah Carpenter
506-453-5446, Fax: 506-444-4743,
Deborah.Carpenter@gnb.ca
Director, Human Resources, Andrew Currie
506-453-3903, Fax: 506-453-7481, andrew.currie@gnb.ca
Director, Information Technology, Virender Ambwani
506-444-4433, Fax: 506-453-3321, vic.ambwani@gnb.ca
Executive Director, Jerome Connors
506-453-5975, Jerome.Connors@gnb.ca

Associated Agencies, Boards & Commissions:
• New Brunswick Emergency Measures Organization (EMO) / Organisation des mesures d'urgence (OMU)
Victoria Health Centre
65 Brunswick Ave.
Fredericton, NB E3B 1G5
506-453-2133 Fax: 506-453-5513 800-561-4034
emo@gnb.ca
www.gnb.ca/cnb/emo-omu/index-e.asp
Coordinates preparedness for emergencies by provincial government departments & municipal governments. NB EMO works at both provincial & municipal levels to ensure that communities are protcted by emergency plans. Coordinates provincial response operations during emergencies & administers disaster financial assistance programs.

Safety Services / Direction des services de sécurité
Provides leadership in the areas of law enforcement & community safety in order to preserve & enhance the quality of life in New Brunswick.
Asst. Deputy Minister, Michael Cameau
506-453-7142, Fax: 506-453-3870, michael.cameau@gnb.ca
Executive Director, Michael Johnston
506-453-7472, Mike.Johnston@gnb.ca
Director, Agency Services, Denis Deveau
506-453-2336, Denis.Deveau@gnb.ca
Director, Gaming Control, Brian Fillmore
506-453-3992
Director, Licensing & Registration, Darlene Harnish
506-453-7472, Darlene.Harnish@gnb.ca
Director, Gaming Control, Chris O'Connell
506-453-4332, Chris.O'Connell@gnb.ca
Deputy Registrar, Drivers & Vehicles, Susan Mccracken
506-453-2410
Inspector, Technical Inspections Services, Michel LaBlanc
506-453-2336
Inspector, Motor Vehicle Inspection Program, Guy Imbeault
506-547-5403, Guy.Imbeault@gnb.ca
Chief Fire Inspector, Fire Inspection Program, Kenneth Harris
506-453-8292, Ken.Harris@gnb.ca
Inspector, Motor Vehicle Inspection Program, Greg Bonnar
506-444-4814
Chief Inspector, Plumbing Inspection Program, William Fallow
506-453-2336, william.fallow@gnb.ca

Chief Coroner, Coroner Services, Gregory J. Forestell
506-453-3604, Greg.Forestell@gnb.ca
Deputy Fire Marshal, Benoit Laroche

Regional Development Corporation (RDC) / Société d'aménagement régional (SAR)

RDC Bldg., 836 Churchill Row, PO Box 428, Fredericton, NB E3B 5R4
506-453-2277 Fax: 506-453-7988
www2.gnb.ca/content/gnb/en/departments/regional_development.html

The Regional Development Corporation is a Crown corporation which carries out its mandate in accordance with the Regional Development Corporation Act. The following are responsibilities of the Corporation; Administration & management of development agreements between the Province of New Brunswick & the federal government; Assistance in the establishment & development of enterprises & institutions; Assistance to municipalities in the planning & development of projects to benefit the public; Assistance in the development of tourism & recreational facilities; Planning, coordinating, & guiding regional development; & Performing duties assigned by the Lieutenant-Governor-in-Council.

Minister Responsible, Hon. Paul Robichaud
506-453-5898, Fax: 506-453-6389, paul.robichaud@gnb.ca
President, Denis Caron
506-453-8542, denis.caron@gnb.ca
Acting Vice-President, Financial Services, Ann Marie Wood-Seems
506-453-8526, annmarie.wood-seems@gnb.ca
Vice-President, Development & Special Initiatives, Serge Doucet
506-457-4912, serge.doucet@gnb.ca
Corporate Secretary, Bruce Macfarlane
506-444-4606, bruce.macfarlane@gnb.ca

New Brunswick Research & Productivity Council (RPC) / Conseil de la recherche et de la productivité du Nouveau-Brunswick (RPC)

921 College Hill Rd., Fredericton, NB E3B 6Z9
506-452-1212 Fax: 506-452-1395
info@rpc.ca
www.rpc.ca

RPC's vision is to excel in technological innovation, enabling its partners in business & industry to create wealth & high quality employment opportunities in New Brunswick; to steadily improve its capacity to develop & apply new technology in partnership with firms in the private sector, & to provide an expanding range of high quality technical services to clients in the global marketplace. RPC is registered to the ISO 9001: 2000 International Standard.

Executive Director, Eric Cook, P.Eng.
506-452-0585, eric.cook@rpc.ca
CFO, Stephen A. Fox
506-452-1380, stephen.fox@rpc.ca
Head, Physical Metallurgy, John Aikens
506-460-5766, john.aikens@rpc.ca
Head, Food, Fisheries & Aquaculture, Dr. Rachael Ritchie
506-452-1365, rachael.ritchie@rpc.ca
Head, Inorganic Analytical Services, Ross Kean
506-452-1399, ross.kean@rpc.ca
Head, Mechanical Systems & Diagnostics, John Aikens
506-460-5766, john.aikens@rpc.ca
Manager, Organic Analytical Services, Bruce Phillips
506-452-1369, bruce.phillips@rpc.ca
Manager, High Res Section, Dr. John Macaulay
506-452-1369, john.macaulay@rpc.ca
Manager, Process Technology, Ross Gilders
506-460-5672, ross.gilders@rpc.ca
Manager, Air Quality Services, Thelma Green
506-452-0586, thelma.green@rpc.ca
Coordinator, Susi Chamberlain
506-452-1244, susi.chamberlain@rpc.ca
Executive Assistant, Linda Horsman
506-452-1363, Fax: 506-452-1386, linda.horsman@rpc.ca

Service New Brunswick (SNB) / Services Nouveau-Brunswick (SNB)

Westmorland Place, #200, 82 Westmorland St., PO Box 1998, Fredericton, NB E3B 5G4
506-457-3581 Fax: 506-457-7520
888-762-8600
snb@snb.ca
www.snb.ca
Other Communication: Technical Assistance: 1-888-832-2762; SNB TeleServices outside the province: 506-684-7901

Service New Brunswick provides authoritative information to the public about federal, provincial, & municipal government services. The Crown corporation, which is owned by the Province of New Brunswick, operates the following services: New Brunswick's Land Registry; New Brunswick's Personal Property Registry; New Brunswick's Corporate Affairs Registry; & New Brunswick's Property Assessment & Taxation System.

Acts Administered:
Air Space Act
Assessment Act
Boundaries Confirmation Act
Business Corporation Act
Common Business Identifier Act
Companies Act
Condominium Property Act
Corporations Act
Foreign Resident Corporations Act
Land Titles Act
Limited Partnership Act
Partnership Act
Partnerships & Business Names Registration Act
Personal Property Security Act
Registry Act
Residential Property Tax Relief Act
Service New Brunswick Act
Special Corporate Continuance Act
Standard Forms of Conveyances Act
Surveys Act
Winding-Up Act

Minister Responsible, Hon. Bruce Fitch
506-453-2807, Fax: 506-453-3988, bruce.fitch@gnb.ca
Chair, Derek Pleadwell
506-444-2897, Fax: 506-457-7520, derek.pleadwell@snb.ca
President, Sylvie Levesque-Finn
506-444-2897, sylvie.levesque-finn@snb.ca
Corporate Legal Counsel, Corporate Counsel Directorate, Claude Poirier
506-869-6389, Fax: 506-869-6523, claude.poirier@snb.ca
Vice-President, Technology & Business Development, Carol MacDonald
506-444-2322, Fax: 506-453-5384, carol.macdonald@snb.ca
Vice-President, Corporate Services, Dan Rae
506-457-4805, Fax: 506-444-5239, dan.rae@snb.ca
Vice-President, Operations, Bernard Arseneau
506-457-3582, Fax: 506-457-7520, bernard.arseneau@snb.ca
Executive Director, Strategy, Policy & Innovation, Judy Ross, C.A.
506-444-4103, Fax: 506-453-5384, judy.ross@snb.ca
Director, Communications, Brand & Customer Experience, Brent Staeben
506-453-6775, Fax: 506-453-5384, brent.staeben@snb.ca
Director, Human Resources, Donat Theriault
506-453-3912, Fax: 506-453-3043, donat.theriault@snb.ca

New Brunswick Advisory Council on the Status of Women / Conseil consultatif sur la condition de la femme au Nouveau-Brunswick

236 King St., Fredericton, NB E3B 1E2
506-444-4101 Fax: 506-444-4318
800-332-3087
acswcccf@gnb.ca
www.acswcccf.nb.ca

Chair, Elsie Hambrook
acswcccf@gnb.ca
Executive Director, Rosella Melanson
rosella.melanson@gnb.ca

Department of Social Development / Développement social

Sartain MacDonald Bldg., 551 King St., PO Box 6000, Fredericton, NB E3B 5H1
506-453-2001 Fax: 506-453-7478
sd-ds@gnb.ca
www.gnb.ca/socialdevelopment

The Department of Social Development oversees services to the following citizens of New Brunswick: Seniors & persons with disabilities who need long-term care & nursing home services; Children who require assistance to prepare for school; Abused & neglected children & adults; Families in need of affordable day care; & Persons in need of affordable housing & social assistance.

Acts Administered:
Charitable Donation of Food Act
Economic and Social Inclusion Act
Education Act (section 19)
Employment Standards Act (subsection 44.02 (6))
Essential Services in Nursing Homes
Family Income Security Act
Family Services Act (except Part VII)
Hospital Act (section 21)
Intercountry Adoption Act
Nursing Homes Act
Reciprocal Enforcement of Maintenance Orders Act (section 10)
Vocational Rehabilitation of Disabled Persons Act

Minister, Hon. Sue Schultz
506-453-2001, Fax: 506-453-2164, sue.stultz@gnb.ca
Deputy Minister, Edith Doucet
506-453-2590, Fax: 506-453-2164, Edith.Doucet@gnb.ca
Director, Communications, Jason Humphrey
506-444-2416, Fax: 506-453-6555, jason.humphrey@gnb.ca
Director, Human Resources Services, Manon Daigle
506-444-6715, Fax: 250-453-6555, manon.daigle@gnb.ca

Associated Agencies, Boards & Commissions:
- Family Income Security Appeal Board / Commission d'appel sur la sécurité du revenu familial
PO Box 6000
Fredericton, NB E3B 5H1
506-525-4007 Fax: 506-525-4008
- New Brunswick Advisory Council on Seniors / Conseil consultatif des ainés du N.-B.
#620, 440 King St.
Fredericton, NB E3B 5H8
506-444-5757 Fax: 506-446-784 888-762-5411

Planning & Corporate Services / Planification et services corporatif

Sartain MacDonald Bldg., 551 King St., 4th Fl., PO Box 6000, Fredericton, NB E3B 5H1
506-453-2181 Fax: 506-453-3829

Assistant Deputy Minister, Jack Brown
506-453-2181, Fax: 506-453-3829, Jack.Brown@gnb.ca
Director, Finance & Administration, Paulette Boudreau-Clark
506-457-6735, Fax: 506-453-2128, paulette.boudreau-clark@gnb.ca
Director, Information Technology Services, Carol LaChapelle
506-453-2033, Fax: 506-453-2841, carol.lachapelle@gnb.ca
Director, Policy, Legislation & Intergovernmental Relations, Bill MacKenzie
506-457-4803, Fax: 506-462-5150, Bill.MacKenzie@gnb.ca
Acting Director, Integrated Planning, Reporting & Accountabilities, Janet P. Thomas
506-444-3380, Fax: 506-462-5150, Janet.Thomas@gnb.ca

Program Delivery / Délivrance des programmes

Sartain MacDonald Bldg., 551 King St., 4th Fl., PO Box 6000, Fredericton, NB E3B 5H1
506-453-2379 Fax: 506-453-2164

Assistant Deputy Minister, Social Development, Hon. Geraldine Poirier-Baiani
506-453-2379, Fax: 506-453-2164, geraldine.poirier-baiani@gnb.ca
Minister Responsible, Community Non-Profit Organizations, Hon. Sue Stultz
506-453-2001, Fax: 506-444-2978, info.nonprofitsector@gnb.ca
Director, Operational Support, Charles Boulay
506-444-4828, Fax: 506-453-2152, Charles.Boulay@gnb.ca

Program Design & Quality Management / Division de la conception des programmes et de gestion de la qualité

Sartain MacDonald Bldg., #4007, 551 King St., PO Box 6000, Fredericton, NB E3B 5H1
506-453-2181 Fax: 506-453-3829

Assistant Deputy Minister, Lisa Doucette
506-453-2181, Fax: 506-453-2164, Lisa.Doucette@gnb.ca
Acting Director, Adults with Disabilities & Senior Services & Nursing Homes Services, André Lepine
416-457-6856, Fax: 506-453-2869, andre.lepine@gnb.ca
Director, Child & Youth Services, Claude Savoie
506-453-3622, claude.savoie@gnb.ca
Director, Community & Individual Development, Amélie Deschenês
506-453-7450, Amélie.Deschenês@gnb.ca
Manager, Nursing Homes Services, Rose-Marie St-Pierre
506-453-2376, RoseMarie.St-Pierre@gnb.ca
Manager, Community & Human Resources Development, John Otteson
506-444-2333, John.Otteson@gnb.ca
Manager, Long Term Care & Disability Support, Joan Mccarthy
506-462-5155, Joan.Mccarthy@gnb.ca
Manager, Clinical Auditing & Child Welfare Training, Wendy Chisholm-Spragg
506-457-6797, Wendy.Chisholm-Spragg@gnb.ca

Department of Supply & Services / Approvisionnement et services

PO Box 6000, Fredericton, NB E3B 5H1
506-453-3742 Fax: 506-444-4400
Reception.Marysville@gnb.ca
www.gnb.ca/0099/index-e.asp

Provides effective & efficient services within government. Among the varied & diverse services the department provides are: the procurement of goods & services; printing & postal services; translation services; records management; the construction & operation of government-owned buildings; & information technology management.

Acts Administered:
Archives Act
New Brunswick Internal Services Agency Act
Public Purchasing Act

Public Works Act
Right to Information and Protection of Privacy Act
Minister, Hon. Claude Williams
506-453-6100, Fax: 506-462-5049, claude.williams@gnb.ca
Deputy Minister, Louise Lemon
506-453-2504, Louise.LEMON@gnb.ca
Executive Director, Corporate Services, Eric Beaulieu
506-453-3742, eric.beaulieu@gnb.ca
Director, Technology Support, Christine Colborne
506-453-3742, Christine.Colborne@gnb.ca
Director, Human Resources & Administration, Ray Butler
506-453-3742, ray.butler@gnb.ca
Director, Finance & Administration, Lise Chiasson
506-453-3742, Fax: 506-462-2006, lise.chiasson@gnb.ca

Buildings Group / Direction générale des bâtiments
Asst. Deputy Minister, Robert Martin
506-453-2228, bob.martin@gnb.ca
Executive Director, Design & Construction, Bob Daigle
506-453-6118, bob.daigle@gnb.ca
Director, Property Management, Leah Essensa
506-453-2221, Leah.Essensa@gnb.ca
Executive Director, Special Projects Development, Gibson Scott
506-325-4520, Scott.Gibson@gnb.ca
Executive Director, Facilities Management, Gary Lynch
506-444-4527, Gary.Lynch@gnb.ca
Director, Planning & Project Development, Pam Barteaux
506-443-2362, Pam.Barteaux@gnb.ca
Director, Construction Services, Vincent MacDonald
506-453-8389, Vincent.Macdonald@gnb.ca

Services / Direction générale des services
www.gov.nb.ca/supply/sgs/index.htm (Purchasing)
Asst. Deputy Minister, Byard Smith
506-453-2245, byard.smith@gnb.ca
Acting Director, Procurement, Janice York
506-453-8880, janice.york@gnb.ca
Director, Provincial Archives of New Brunswick, Marion Beyea
506-453-2122, Marion.Beyea@gnb.ca
Director, Translation Bureau, Jo-Ann Leblanc
506-453-2920, Fax: 506-459-7911, jo-ann.leblanc@gnb.ca
Manager, Translation Services, Pascale Bergeron
506-453-2920, pascale.bergeron@gnb.ca

Department of Tourism & Parks / Tourisme et Parcs

Centennial Bldg., 670 King St., Fredericton, NB E3B 1G1
506-444-5205 Fax: 506-457-4984
taponlinedirectory@gnb.ca
www.gnb.ca/0397/index-e.asp
To increase the profile and performance of the tourism industry in New Brunswick and to ensure that provincial parks are an integral part of this effort.
Acts Administered:
Kings Landing Corporation Act
Municipalities Act (subsection 188 (3))
Off-Road Vehicle Act (sections 7.2 (1), 7.2 (3), 7.2 (5), 7.3 and 7.5 (1))
Parks Act
Tourism Development Act
Tourism Development,2008 Act
Minister, Hon. Trevor Holder
506-453-3009, trevor.holder@gnb.ca
Deputy Minister, Carolyn Mackay
506-453-3261, carolyn.mackay@gnb.ca
Director, Communications, Jane Matthews-Clark
506-444-4454, jane.matthews-clark@gnb.ca
Director, Information Technology Services, Doug Waugh
506-457-7324, doug.waugh@gnb.ca
Manager, Financial Services, Jo-Anne Lang
506-444-5813, jo-anne.lang@gnb.ca
Manager, Human Resource Services, Barbara Legacy
506-453-2198, barbara.legacy@gnb.ca
Acting Director, Strategic Planning & Policy, Shannon Ferris
506-462-5053, shannon.ferris@gnb.ca

Marketing, Development & Operations / Marketing, dévelopment et opérations
506-444-5205 Fax: 506-444-5760
taponlinedirectory@gnb.ca
http: //www.gnb.ca/0397/index-e.asp
Assistant Deputy Minister, Kelly Cain
506-444-4118, kelly.cain@gnb.ca
Executive Director, Kings Landing, Alain Boisvert
506-363-4957, alain.boisvert@gnb.ca
Director, Marketing, Kim Matthews
506-453-4284, kim.matthews@gnb.ca
Director, Content Development, Susan Morell
506-453-5896, Fax: 506-363-4989, susan.morell@gnb.ca
Director, Tourism Operations, Alain Basque
506-453-2170, alain.basque@gnb.ca
Director, Sales, Partnerships & Business Development, Cindy Creamer Rouse
506-444-4097, cindy.creamer-rouse@gnb.ca

Regional Operations Branch:

The Anchorage
136 Anchorage Road, Grand Manan, NB E5G 2H4
506-662-7022 Fax: 506-662-7035
Acting Manager, Lenora Lomax
506-662-7022, lenora.lomax@gnb.ca

De la république
35 Principale Street, Saint-Jacques, NB E7B 1V6
506-735-2525 Fax: 506-737-4445
Manager, Jocelyne St.Onge
506-735-2702, jocelyne.st-onge@gnb.ca

Herring Cove
136 Herring Cove Road, Welshpool, NB E5E 1B8
506-752-7010 Fax: 506-752-7012
Supervisor, Boland Tinker
506-752-7010

Mactaquac
1256 Route 105, Mactaquac, NB E6I 1B5
506-363-4747 Fax: 506-363-4900
Director, Neill Sandwith
506-363-4905, neil.sandwith@gnb.ca

Miscou
104 Aquarium Street, Shippagan, NB E8S 1H9
506-444-6752 Fax: 506-453-2854
Maintenance Supervisor, Donald Mallet
506-340-0451, taponlinedirectory@gnb.ca

Mount Carleton
7612 Route 385, PO Box 1424, Saint-Quentin, NB E8A 1A2
506-235-0793 Fax: 506-235-0795
Manager, Louis Comeau
506-235-0793, mt.carleton@gnb.ca

Murray Beach
1679 Route 955, Little Shemogue, Murray Corner, NB E4M 4A9
506-444-5205 Fax: 506-538-2107
Supervisor, Micheal Banks
506-538-2628

New River Beach
78 New River Beach Road, New River Beach, NB E5J 1G7
506-755-4042 Fax: 506-755-4063
Acting Manager, Lenora Lemax
506-755-4042, lenora.lemax@gnb.ca

Parlee Beach
45 Parlee Beach Road, Pointe-du-Chêne, NB E4P 8V5
506-533-3363 Fax: 506-533-3312
Manager, Marcel Richard
506-533-3363, marcel.richard@gnb.ca

Sugarloaf
596 Val d'Amour Road, Atholville, NB E3N 4C9
506-759-2366 Fax: 506-789-2099
Manager, Greg Dion
506-789-2366, grg.dion@gnb.ca

Department of Transportation / Transports

Kings Pl., 440 King St., PO Box 6000, Fredericton, NB E3B 5H8
506-453-3939 Fax: 506-453-2900
Transportation.Web@gnb.ca
www.gnb.ca/0113/index-e.asp
To ensure the effective development & implementation of an integrated transportation approach for New Brunswick (roads, airports, ports & other infrastructure), to support New Brunswick's economic & social goals; develop & maintain safe & efficient network of highways & roads; & maintain the long-term integrity of our transportation infrastructure including roads, ports & airports through effective planning, maintenance & oversight.
Acts Administered:
Gas Distribution,1999 Act (subsections 18 (2) and 39 (1))
Highway Act
Motor Carrier Act (except licensing of motor carriers)
New Brunswick Highway Corporation Act
New Brunswick Transportation Authority Act
Public Landings Act
Shortline Railways Act
Telephone Companies Act (Chief Highway Engineer under subsection 5 (3))
Minister, Hon. Claude Williams
506-457-7345, Fax: 506-453-7987, claude.williams@gnb.ca
Deputy Minister, Jean Castonguay
506-453-2549, Fax: 506-453-7987, Jean.Castonguay@gnb.ca
Director, Communications, Sarah Ketcheson
506-453-5634, Fax: 506-457-4968, sarah.ketcheson@gnb.ca
Associated Agencies, Boards & Commissions:
• NB Board of Commissioners of Public Utilities / Commission des entreprises de service public du N.-B.
#1400, 15 Market Sq.
PO Box 5001
Saint John, NB E2L 4Y9
506-658-2504 Fax: 506-643-7300 866-766-2782
general@pub.nb.ca
www.pub.nb.ca
• New Brunswick Transportation Authority / Régie des transports du Nouveau-Brunswick
Kings Place
440 King St.
PO Box 6000
Fredericton, NB E3B 5H1
506-453-3939 Fax: 506-453-2900
Crown corporation responsible for the promotion, operation & development of transportation terminals in New Brunswick. Encourages the development of transport terminal-related services.

Assistant Deputy Minister & Chief Engineer Office / Sous-ministre adjoint et ingénieur en chef
Assistant Deputy Minister, Chief Engineer, Dale Forster
506-453-3939, dale.forster@gnb.ca
Acting Assistant Deputy Minister, Engineering Services, Kim Daley
506-453-3939, kim.daley@gnb.ca
Executive Director, Operations, David Cogswell
506-453-3939, david.cogswell@gnb.ca
Director, Maintenance & Traffic, Kevin Maclean
506-444-2134, kevin.maclean@gnb.ca
Director, Construction, Carol Macquarrie
506-453-5714, carol.macquarrie@gnb.ca
Director, Design, Robert Sharpe
506-453-3939, robert.sharpe@gnb.ca

Corporate Services & Fleet Management / Services généraux et gestion de flotte
Asst. Deputy Minister, Kim Daley
506-453-3939, kim.daley@gnb.ca
Director, Information Management & Technology, Colleen Boldon
506-453-4498, colleen.boldon@gnb.ca
Director, Financial & Administrative Services, Charlotte Valley
506-453-3389, charlotte.valley@gnb.ca
Director, Human Resources, Myrna Belyea-Tracy
506-444-5531, myrna.belyea-tracy@gnb.ca

Policy, Strategic Development & Intergovernmental Relations / Politiques, développement et relations intergouvernementales
Asst. Deputy Minister, Margaret Grant-McGivney
506-453-3939, margaret.grant-mcgivney@gnb.ca
Director, Transportation Policy, Kelly Rodgers-Sturgeon
506-444-4356, kelly.rodgers-sturgeon@gnb.ca
Senior Policy Advisor, Strategic Development, John Weatherhead
506-444-3185, john.weatherhead@gnb.ca

Department of Wellness, Culture & Sport / Mieux-être, Culture et Sport

Place 2000, 250 King St., 4th Fl., PO Box 6000, Fredericton, NB E3B 5H1
506-453-2909 Fax: 506-453-6548
www.gnb.ca/0131/index-e.asp
The Department of Wellness, Culture, & Sport is repsonsible for arts development, heritage, wellness, & sport, recreation, & active living.
Acts Administered:
Arts Development Trust Fund Act (except administration of fund)
Assessment Act (s. 15.3)
Historic Sites Protection Act
Municipal Heritage Preservation Act
Sport Development Trust Fund Act (except administration of fund)
Youth Assistance Act (section 11)
Minister, Hon. Trevor Holder
506-453-3009, trevor.holder@gnb.ca
Deputy Minister, Carolyn Mackay
506-453-3261, Fax: 506-453-6668, carolyn.mackay@gnb.ca
Director, Communications, Jane Matthews-Clark
506-444-4454, Fax: 506-453-6668, WCScommunication@gnb.ca
Director, Policy & Planning, Shannon Ferris
506-453-2928, Fax: 506-453-6548, shannon.ferris@gnb.ca
Associated Agencies, Boards & Commissions:
• New Brunswick Arts Board / Conseil des arts Nouveau-Brunswick
61 Carleton St.
Fredericton, NB E3B 3T2
506-444-4444 Fax: 506-444-5543
1-866-460-2787
www.artsnb.ca

Arts funding agency with a legislated mandate to facilitate and promote the creation of art in New Brunswick as well as administer funding programs for professional artists in the province.
• New Brunswick Film / Film Nouveau-Brunswick
Place 2000
250 King St., 4th Fl.
PO Box 6000
Fredericton, NB E1B 5H1
506-453-2555 Fax: 506-453-2416
nbfilm@gnb.ca
www.nbfilm.ca
Responsible for fostering New Brunswick's film, television & new media industry.

Arts Development
Place 2000, 250 King St., Fredericton, NB E3B 9M9
506-453-2555 Fax: 506-453-2416
Director, Arts Development, Nathalie Dubois
506-453-2729, Fax: 506-453-2416, nathalie.dubois@gnb.ca
Coordinator, Art Bank Services, Caroline Walker
506-444-5303, Fax: 506-453-2416, Caroline.Walker@gnb.ca
Consultant, Programs, Desmond Maillet
506-453-2657, desmond.maillet@gnb.ca

Heritage
Place 2000, 250 King St., 4th Fl., PO Box 6000, Fredericton, NB E3B 5H1
506-453-2324 Fax: 506-453-2416
Acting Director, Heritage, William Hicks
506-444-5320, Fax: 506-453-2416, bill.hicks@gnb.ca
Manager, Archaeological Services, Albert M. Ferguson
506-453-2756, Fax: 506-457-4880, albert.ferguson@gnb.ca
Manager, Museum Services, Guy Tremblay
506-444-5892, Fax: 506-453-2416, Guy.Tremblay@gnb.ca
Manager, Toponymy, Gilles Bourque
506-453-8125, Fax: 506-453-2416, Gilles.Bourque@gnb.ca
Project Manager, Heritage Education, Cynthia Wallace-Casey
506-453-2915, Fax: 506-453-2416, Cynthia.Wallace-Casey@gnb.ca
Project Executive, Historic Places, Lawren Campbell
506-457-7843, Fax: 506-453-2416, lawren.campbell@gnb.ca

New Brunswick Museum
277 Douglas Ave., Saint John, NB E2K 1E5
506-643-2300 Fax: 506-643-2360
nbmuseum@nbm-mnb.ca
www.gnb.ca/0131/index-e.asp
Chief Executive Officer, New Brunswick Museum, Jane Fullerton
506-643-2346, Jane.Fullerton@nbm-mnb.ca
Head Curator, Natural Science, Donald McAlpine
506-643-2345, Fax: 506-643-2360, donald.mcalpine@nbm-mnb.ca
Manager, Library & Archives, Felicity Osepchook
506-643-2324, Fax: 506-643-2360, Felicity.Osepchook@nbm-mnb.ca
Manager, Interpretation Services, Rose Poirier
506-643-2339, Fax: 506-643-6081, rose.poirier@nbm-mnb.ca
Manager, Temporary Exhibitions, Regina Mantin
506-643-2330, Fax: 506-643-6081, regina.mantin@nbm-mnb.ca
Controller, Administration, Lane Atkinson
506-643-2356, Fax: 506-643-6081, lane.atkinson@nbm-mnb.ca

Wellness, Sport, & Community Development
Place 2000, 250 King St., 4th Fl., PO Box 6000, Fredericton, NB E3B 5H1
506-444-2451 Fax: 506-453-6548
Assistant Deputy Minister, Wellness, Sport, & Community Development, Jane Garbutt
506-444-2451, Fax: 506-453-6548, jane.garbutt@gnb.ca
Director, Sport & Recreation, Roger H. Duval
506-457-4950, Fax: 506-453-6548, roger.duval@gnb.ca
Acting Director, Regional Operations & Community Development, Michelle Bourgoin
506-453-2928, Fax: 506-453-6548, michelle.bourgoin@gnb.ca
Director, Wellness, Michelle Bourgoin
506-453-5526, Fax: 506-444-5722, michelle.bourgoin@gnb.ca

Workplace Health, Safety & Compensation Commission of New Brunswick (WHSCC) / La commission de la santé, de la sécurité et de l'indemnisation des accidents au travail du Nouveau-Brunswick

1 Portland St., PO Box 160, Saint John, NB E2L 3X9
506-632-2200
800-222-9775
communications@ws-ts.nb.ca
www.whscc.nb.ca
The Workplace Health, Safety & Compensation Commission (WHSCC) of New Brunswick is a crown corporation charged with overseeing the implementation & application of the New Brunswick Occupational Health & Safety Act, the Workers' Compensation Act of New Brunswick, & the Workplace Health, Safety & Compensation Commission Act of New Brunswick on behalf of the workers & employers of this province. The Commission administers no-fault workplace accident & disability insurance & comprehensive accident prevention health & safety initiatives for employers & their workers, funded solely through premiums paid by employers.
Acts Administered:
Firefighters' Compensation Act
Occupational Health & Safety Act
Workers' Compensation Act
Workplace Health, Safety & Compensation Commission Act
Chair, Sharon Tucker
President/CEO, Peter Murphy
Chair, Appeals Tribunal, Ronald Gaffney
Member Representing Workers, Danny King
Member Representing Workers, Maureen Wallace
Member Representing Workers, Michéle Caron
Member Representing Employers, David Ellis
Member Representing Employers, Marty Martell

New Brunswick Advisory Council on Youth (NBACY) / Conseil consultatif de la jeunesse du Nouveau-Brunswick (CCJNB)

Frederick Square, #130, 77 Westmorland St., PO Box 6000, Fredericton, NB E3B 5H1
506-453-3271 Fax: 506-444-4413
888-830-5588
nbacy-ccjnb@gnb.ca
www.gnb.ca
The Lieutenant Governor in Council appoints thirteen young people from all regions of New Brunswick, & from both official language groups, to a two-year term on the New Brunswick Advisory Council on Youth. Representative of youth, the Council on Youth voices the concerns, interests, needs, & perspectives of persons between fifteen & twenty-four years of age. The provincial body presents its recommendations to government.
Chair, Kara Hachey
Kara.Hachey@gnb.ca
Executive Director, Ivan Corbett
Ivan.Corbett@gnb.ca
Director, Communications, Brendan Languille
506-444-5070

Government of Newfoundland & Labrador

Seat of Government: Confederation Bldg., St. John's, NL A1B 4J6
info@gov.nl.ca
www.gov.nl.ca
The Province of Newfoundland & Labrador entered Confederation March 31, 1949. It has an area of 370,494.89 km2, & the StatsCan census population in 2006 was 505,469.

Office of the Lieutenant Governor

Government House, Military Rd., PO Box 5517, St. John's, NL A1C 5W4
709-729-4494 Fax: 709-729-2234
governmenthouse@gov.nl.ca
www.govhouse.nl.ca
Lieutenant Governor, The Hon. John C. Crosbie
709-729-4494, Fax: 709-729-2234
Private Secretary, Gary Cake
709-729-4494, Fax: 709-729-2234, gcake@gov.nl.ca

Office of the Premier

East Block, Confederation Bldg., 8th F., PO Box 8700, St. John's, NL A1B 4J6
709-729-3570 Fax: 709-729-5875
premier@gov.nl.ca
www.premier.gov.nl.ca
Premier, Hon. Kathy Dunderdale
709-729-3570, Fax: 709-729-5875, premier@gov.nl.ca
Chief of Staff, Brian Taylor
709-729-3966
Executive Assistant to the Premier, Maria Afonso
709-729-3565, Fax: 709-729-5875, MariaAfonso@gov.nl.ca
Director, Communications, Glenda Power
709-729-3960

Executive Council

c/o Communications Branch, East Block, Confederation Bldg., 10th Fl., St. John's, NL A1B 4J6
709-729-5645
info@gov.nl.ca
www.exec.gov.nl.ca/exec/
Premier, Hon. Kathy Dunderdale
709-729-3570, Fax: 709-729-5875, premier@gov.nl.ca
Minister, Transportation & Works; Responsible for Newfoundland & Labrador Housing Corporation, Hon. Thomas J. Hedderson
709-729-3679, Fax: 709-729-4285, thedderson@gov.nl.ca
Minister, Fisheries & Aquaculture; Deputy House Government Leader, Hon. Darin King
709-729-3705, Fax: 709-729-0360, DarinKingMHA@gov.nl.ca
Minister, Justice, Attorney General, Hon. Felix Collins
709-729-2869, Fax: 709-729-0469, felixcollins@gov.nl.ca
Minister, Municipal Affairs; Responsible for Fire & Emergency Services; Registrar General, Hon. Kevin O'Brien
709-729-3046, Fax: 709-729-0943, kevinobrien@gov.nl.ca
Minister, Education, Hon. Clyde Jackman
709-729-5040, Fax: 709-729-0414, clydejackman@gov.nl.ca
Minister, Environment & Conservation; Responsible for Labour Relations Agency, Multi-Materials Stewardship Board, & Office of Climate Change, Energy Efficiency & Emissions Trading, Hon. Terry French
709-729-2577, Fax: 709-729-0112, terryfrench@gov.nl.ca
Minister, Intergovernmental & Aboriginal Affairs; Responsible for Labrador Affairs, Hon. Nick McGrath
709-729-3400
Minister, Advanced Education & Skills; Responsible for Persons with Disabilities & Youth Engagement, Hon. Joan Burke
709-729-5040, Fax: 709-729-0414, joanburke@gov.nl.ca, Other Communications: Toll Free: 1-866-838-5620
Minister, Natural Resources; Government House Leader; Responsible for Forestry & Agrifoods Agency, Hon. Jerome P. Kennedy
709-729-2920, Fax: 709-729-0059, JeromeKennedy@gov.nl.ca
Minister, Health & Community Services; Responsible for Aging & Seniors, & Francophone Affairs, Hon. Susan Sullivan
709-729-3124, Fax: 709-729-0121, SusanSullivan@gov.nl.ca
Minister, Child, Youth & Family Services; Responsible for Status of Women, Hon. Charlene Johnson
709-729-0173, Fax: 709-729-1049, charlenejohnson@gov.nl.ca
Minister, Tourism, Culture & Recreation, Hon. Derrick Dalley
709-729-0659, Fax: 709-729-0662, DerrickDalley@gov.nl.ca
Minister, Finance; President, Treasury Board; Responsible for Public Secretariat, Public Service Commission, & Newfoundland & Labrador LiquorCorporation, Hon. Tom Marshall, Q.C.
709-729-3775, Fax: 709-729-2232, tommarshall@gov.nl.ca
Minister, Service Newfoundland & Labrador; Responsible for Government Purchasing Agency, Office of the CIO, & Workplace Health, Safety & CompensationCommission, Hon. Paul Davis
709-729-6670, Fax: 709-729-1503, padavis@gov.nl.ca
Minister, Innovation, Business & Rural Development; Responsible for Rural Secretariat, & Research Development Corporation, Hon. Keith Hutchings
709-729-4728, Fax: 709-729-0654, keithhutchings@gov.nl.ca
Document Control Officer, Patricia Oliver
709-729-6598, Fax: 709-729-5218, poliver@gov.nl.ca

Cabinet Committees
Cabinet Committee on Routine Matters & Appointments; Economic Policy Committee Planning & Priorities Committee; Social Policy Committee; Treasury Board Committee

Cabinet Secretariat
Fax: 709-729-5218
Clerk, Executive Council & Secretary to the Cabinet, Robert Thompson
709-729-2853, Fax: 709-729-5218, rthompson@gov.nl.ca
Deputy Clerk, Executive Council & Associate Secretary to the Cabinet, Julia Mullaley
709-729-2844, Fax: 709-729-5218
Assistant Secretary, Economic Policy, Dennis Hogan
709-729-2845, Fax: 709-729-5218
Assistant Secretary, Social Policy, Colleen Janes
709-729-2850, Fax: 709-729-5218, cjanes@gov.nl.ca
Executive Director, Planning & Co-ordination, Paula Burt
709-729-4340, Fax: 709-729-5218, paulaburt@gov.nl.ca

Office of the Chief Information Officer (OCIO)
40 Higgins Line, PO Box 8700, St. John's, NL A1B 4J6
709-729-4000 Fax: 709-729-6767
ocio@gov.nl.ca
The OCIO provides a professional Information Technology & Information Management capability aligned to support the business of government and the citizens of Newfoundland and Labrador.
Minister Responsible, Hon. Paul Davis
709-729-6670, Fax: 709-729-1503, padavis@gov.nl.ca
Chief Information Officer, Ellen MacDonald
709-729-2617, Fax: 709-729-1464
Executive Director, Application Services, Craig Slaney
709-729-5694, craigslaney@gov.nl.ca
Executive Director, Corporate Operations & Client Services, Jean Tilley
709-729-4110, Fax: 709-729-6767, jeantilley@gov.nl.ca

Executive Director, Information Management, Shelley Smith
709-729-6260, ssmith@gov.nl.ca
Executive Director, Operations, Randy Mouland
709-729-5227, randymouland@gov.nl.ca
Executive Director, Solution Delivery, Colin Tibbo
709-729-3617, colint@gov.nl.ca

Rural Secretariat
PO Box 8700, St. John's, NL A1B 4J6
709-729-7380 Fax: 709-729-1673
ruralinfo@gov.nl.ca
www.exec.gov.nl.ca/rural

The Rural Secretariat is a unique and innovative provincial government entity that strives to advance the sustainability of rural Newfoundland & Labrador communities & regions. It does this by: supporting the development of citizen-based policy advice; engaging citizens in the future of their province; & by supporting collaboration between & among rural stakeholders including governments.
Minister Responsible, Hon. Keith Hutchings
709-729-4728, Fax: 709-729-0654, keithhutchings@gov.nl.ca
Asst. Deputy Minister, Dr. Bruce Gilbert
709-729-1611, brucegilbert@gov.nl.ca

Women's Policy Office
Minister Responsible, Hon. Susan Sullivan
709-729-5040, Fax: 709-729-0414, ssullivan@gov.nl.ca
Asst. Deputy Minister, Heather MacLellan
709-729-5098, Fax: 709-729-2331, hmaclellan@gov.nl.ca

House of Assembly

c/o Clerk's Office, Confederation Bldg., PO Box 8700, St. John's, NL A1B 4J6
709-729-3405 Fax: 709-729-4820
www.gov.nl.ca/hoa
Other Communication: Legislative Library: 709-729-3604

Clerk, William MacKenzie
709-729-3405, Fax: 709-729-4820, ClerkHOA@gov.nl.ca; williammackenzie@gov.nl.ca
Speaker, Hon. Roger Fitzgerald
709-729-3404, Fax: 709-729-4820, rfitzgerald@gov.nl.ca
Citizens' Representative, Barry Fleming
709-729-7647, Fax: 709-729-7696, citrep@gov.nl.ca
Sergeant-at-Arms, Elizabeth Gallagher
709-729-3630, egallagher@gov.nl.ca
Director, Information Management (Legislative Library), Kimberley Hammond
709-729-5646, Fax: 709-729-0234, Kimberleyhammond@gov.nl.ca
Information & Privacy Commissioner, Ed Ring
709-729-6309, 877-729-6309, Fax: 709-729-6500, commissioner@oipc.nl.ca
Child & Youth Advocate, Carol A. Chafe
709-753-3888, 877-753-3888, Fax: 709-753-3988, office@ocya.nl.ca

Government Caucus Office (PC)
PO Box 8700, St. John's, NL A1B 4J6

Office of the Official Opposition (Lib.)
Confederation Building, East Block, 5th fl., PO Box 8700, St. John's, NL A1B 4J6
Leader, Kevin Aylward
709-729-6925, 800-286-9118, Fax: 709-729-5202, kevinaylward@gov.nl.ca
Opposition House Leader, Kelvin Parsons
709-729-0434, 800-518-9479, Fax: 709-729-5202, kparsons@gov.nl.ca

Office of the New Democratic Party (NDP)
PO Box 8700, St. John's, NL A1B 4J6
709-729-0270 Fax: 709-576-1443
ndpinfo@gov.nl.ca

Leader, Lorraine Michael
709-739-9661, lorrainemichael@nl.ndp.ca

House Committees
Clerk of Committees, Elizabeth Murphy
709-729-3434, Fax: 709-729-4820, emurphy@gov.nl.ca

Forty-seventh House of Assembly - Newfoundland & Labrador

PO Box 8700, St. John's, NL A1B 4J6
709-729-3405
ClerkHOA@gov.nl.ca
Other Communication: Tours: 709-729-3630

Last General Election, October 11, 2011. Maximum Duration, 4 years Party Standings (October 2011): Progressive Conservative (PC) 37 Liberal (Lib.) 6 New Democratic Party (NDP) 5 Total 48; Salaries, Indemnities & Allowances (December 2009): Members' sessional indemnity $95,357. In addition to this are the following: Ministers; Speaker; Leader of the Opposition $54,072; Government Whip & Opposition Whip $13,517; Chair of Committees (Deputy Speaker) $27,033, Deputy Chair of Committees $13,517; Opposition House Leader $27,033

Following is: constituency (population of constituency at 2011 election) member, party affiliation, telephone & fax number & email address. (Address for all is Confederation Bldg., PO Box 8700, St. John's NL A1B 4J6.)

Members
Hon. Nick McGrath, Labrador West, Progressive Conservative
709-729-3400
George Murphy, St. John's East, NDP
709-729-0270
Hon. Joan Burke, St. George's-Stephenville East, Progressive Conservative
709-729-5040, 866-838-5620, Fax: 709-729-0414, Joanburke@gov.nl.ca
Glenn Littlejohn, Port De Grave, Progressive Conservative
709-729-3400
Kevin Parsons, Cape St. Francis, Progressive Conservative
709-729-6979, Fax: 709-729-5774, KevinParsons@gov.nl.ca
Hon. Felix Collins, Placentia & St. Mary's, Progressive Conservative
709-729-6926, 877-898-0898, Fax: 709-729-2076, felixcollins@gov.nl.ca
Tony Cornect, Port au Port, Progressive Conservative
709-729-3138, 800-809-0360, Fax: 709-729-1082, tonycornect@gov.nl.ca
Hon. Derrick Dalley, The Isles of Notre Dame, Progressive Conservative
709-729-1191, Fax: 709-729-5774, derrickdalley@gov.nl.ca
Paul Lane, Mount Pearl South, Progressive Conservative
709-729-3400
John Dinn, Kilbride, Progressive Conservative
709-729-3758, Fax: 709-729-1082, johndinn@gov.nl.ca
Hon. Kathy Dunderdale, Virginia Waters, Progressive Conservative
709-729-4715, Fax: 709-729-2076, KathyDunderdale@gov.nl.ca
Glenn Little, Bonavista South, Progressive Conservative
709-729-3400
Clayton Forsey, Exploits, Progressive Conservative
709-729-6594, 888-554-7799, Fax: 709-729-1503, ClaytonForsey@gov.nl.ca
Hon. Terry French, Conception Bay South, Progressive Conservative
709-729-5907, Fax: 709-729-6996, Terryfrench@gov.nl.ca
Eli Cross, Bonavista North, Progressive Conservative
709-729-3400
Hon. Tom Hedderson, Harbour Main, Progressive Conservative
709-729-7032, 877-787-0707, Fax: 709-729-3686, thedderson@gov.nl.ca
Keith Russel, Lake Melville, Progressive Conservative
709-729-3400
Hon. Susan Sullivan, Grand Falls-Windsor-Green Bay South, Progressive Conservative
709-729-4729, 888-610-4440, Fax: 709-729-0654, susansullivan@gov.nl.ca
Hon. Keith Hutchings, Ferryland, Progressive Conservative
709-729-1390, Fax: 709-729-5774, keithhutchings@gov.nl.ca
Hon. Clyde Jackman, Burin-Placentia West, Progressive Conservative
709-729-0657, 800-423-3301, Fax: 709-729-0662, clydejackman@gov.nl.ca
Hon. Charlene Johnson, Trinity-Bay De Verde, Progressive Conservative
709-729-2574, Fax: 709-729-0112, charlenejohnson@gov.nl.ca
Yvonne Jones, Cartwright-L'Anse au Clair, Liberal
709-729-6925, 800-286-9118, Fax: 709-729-5202, yvonnejones@gov.nl.ca
Dwight Ball, Humber Valley, Liberal
709-729-3391
Hon. Jerome Kennedy, Q.C., Carbonear-Harbour Grace, Progressive Conservative
709-729-2869, Fax: 709-729-0469, jeromekennedy@gov.nl.ca
Steve Kent, Mount Pearl North, Progressive Conservative
709-729-1526, Fax: 709-729-1503, SteveKent@gov.nl.ca
Hon. Darin T. King, Ph.D, Grand Bank, Progressive Conservative
709-729-0340, Fax: 709-729-0414, darinking@gov.nl.ca
Eddie Joyce, Bay of Islands, Liberal
709-729-3391
Hon. Paul Davis, Topsail, Progressive Conservative
709-729-6670, Fax: 709-729-1503, padavis@gov.nl.ca
Hon. Tom Marshall, Humber East, Progressive Conservative
709-729-2858, Fax: 709-729-6791, tommarshall@gov.nl.ca, Other Communications: URL: www.tommarshall.ca
Lorraine Michael, Signal Hill-Quidi Vidi, NDP
709-729-0270, Fax: 709-576-1443, lorrainemichael@gov.nl.ca
Hon. Kevin O'Brien, Gander, Progressive Conservative
709-729-4712, 800-813-6850, Fax: 709-729-4754, kevinobrien@gov.nl.ca
Sandy Collins, Terra Nova, Progressive Conservative
709-467-1018, 800-670-2850, Fax: 709-729-5774, sandycollins@gov.nl.ca
Tom Osborne, St. John's South, Progressive Conservative
709-729-4882, Fax: 709-729-0469, TOsborne@gov.nl.ca
Dan Crummell, St. John's West, Progressive Conservative
709-729-3400
Andrew Parsons, Burgeo & La Poile, Liberal
709-729-3391
Calvin Peach, Bellevue, Progressive Conservative
709-729-1546, Fax: 709-729-1503, CalvinPeach@gov.nl.ca
Tracy Perry, Fortune Bay-Cape La Hune, Progressive Conservative
709-538-3112, Fax: 709-538-3079, TraceyPerry@gov.nl.ca
Randy Edmunds, Torngat Mountains, Liberal
709-729-3391
Kevin Pollard, Baie Verte-Springdale, Liberal
709-532-2243, 800-598-1806, Fax: 709-532-2239, KevinPollard@gov.nl.ca
Dale Kirby, St. John's North, NDP
709-729-0270
Gerry Rogers, St. John's Centre, NDP
709-729-0270
Christopher Mitchelmore, The Straits & White Bay North, NDP
709-729-0270
Wade Verge, Lewisporte, Progressive Conservative
709-729-3399, 877-585-0515, Fax: 709-729-1082, wadeverge@gov.nl.ca
David Brazil, Conception Bay East & Bell Island, Progressive Conservative
709-729-0334, Fax: 709-729-1503, davidbrazil@gov.nl.ca
Vaughn Granter, Humber West, Progressive Conservative
709-729-3400, Fax: 709-729-5774, vaughngranter@gov.nl.ca
Ross Wiseman, Trinity North, Progressive Conservative
709-729-3124, 800-514-9073, Fax: 709-729-0121, rosswiseman@gov.nl.ca
Jim Bennett, St. Barbe, Liberal
709-729-3391
Clerk, William MacKenzie
709-729-3405, clerkHOA@gov.nl.ca

Newfoundland & Labrador Government Departments & Agencies

Office of the Auditor General

PO Box 8700, St. John's, NL A1B 4J6
709-729-2695 Fax: 709-729-5970
oagmail@oag.nl.ca
www.ag.gov.nl.ca

The Auditor General's fundamental role is to bring an independent audit and reporting process to bear upon the manner in which Government and its various entities discharge their responsibilities, report on their planned programs and their use of public resources.

Department of Business

Confederation Bldg., East Block, 6th Fl., PO Box 8700, St. John's, NL A1B 4J6
709-729-3254 Fax: 709-729-3306
business@gov.nl.ca
www.nlbusiness.ca

New Department announced Spring 2006. As of October 2011, this Department will be merged into Innovation to create the new Department of Innovation, Business & Rural Development.
Minister, Hon. Keith Hutchings
709-729-4728, Fax: 709-729-0654, keithhutchings@gov.nl.ca
Deputy Minister, Ray Dillon
709-729-3451, Fax: 709-729-3306, raydillon@gov.nl.ca
Acting Director, Strategic Policy & Planning, Beulah Bouzane
709-729-5936, bbouzane@gov.nl.ca
Director, Communications, Carol Ann Carter
709-729-7628, carolanncarter@gov.nl.ca
Acting Director, Brand Development, Susan Clarke
709-729-0075, Fax: 709-729-3306, susanclarke@gov.nl.ca
Director, Regulatory Reform Initiative, Gerard Griffin
709-729-1002, gerardgriffin@gov.nl.ca
Director, Business Strategy, Jim House
709-729-7484, jameshouse@gov.nl.ca
Director, Business Analysis, Harman Khurana
709-729-3198, harmankhurana@gov.nl.ca
Director, Business Investment, Darin Steeves
709-729-3206, darinsteeves@gov.nl.ca

Department of Child, Youth & Family Services

PO Box 8700, St. John's, NL A1B 4J6
709-729-0760
www.gov.nl.ca/cyfs
Other Communication: Adoption Services Phone: 709-752-4406; Youth Corrections Program: 709-729-2794

Acts Administered:
Adoption Act
Child Care Services Act
Children & Youth Care & Protection Act
Young Persons Offences Act

Youth Criminal Justice Act
Minister, Hon. Charlene Johnson
709-729-0173, charlenejohnson@gov.nl.ca
Deputy Minister, Sheree MacDonald
709-729-0583, smacdonald@gov.nl.ca
Assistant Deputy Minister, Policy & Program, Lori Ann Companion
709-729-0088, loriannecompanion@gov.nl.ca
Assistant Deputy Minister, Corporate Services, Genevieve Dooling
709-729-0656, gdooling@gov.nl.ca
Assistant Deputy Minister, Services Delivery & Regional Operations, Genevieve Dooling
709-729-0656, gdooling@gov.nl.ca
Director, Communications, Michelle Hunt
709-729-5148, michellehunt@gov.nl.ca

Department of Education

West Block, Confederation Bldg., 100 Prince Philip Dr., 3rd Fl., PO Box 8700, St. John's, NL A1B 4J6
709-729-5097 Fax: 709-729-5896
education@gov.nl.ca
www.ed.gov.nl.ca

Responsible for the K-12 & post-secondary school system, literacy & library services; comprises four executive branches: Primary, Elementary & Secondary Education, Corporate Services Branch; Post-Secondary Branch; International Education & Planning Branch; Literacy School Services; reporting to the department through their various boards are the Provincial Information & Library Resources Board, the Literacy Development Council, 4 geographical school boards & a francophone school board. In October 2011, a separate Department called Advanced Education & Skills was created by Premier Kathy Dunderdale.

Acts Administered:
Apprenticeship & Certification Act
College Act
Degree Granting Act
Memorial University Act
Memorial University Foundation Act
Memorial University Pensions Act
Private Training Institutions Act
Public Libraries Act
School Boards' Association Act
Schools Act, 1997
Student Financial Assistance Act
Teacher Training Act
Teachers' Association Act
Minister, Hon. Clyde Jackman
709-729-5040, 866-838-5620, Fax: 709-729-0414, clydejackman@gov.nl.ca
Deputy Minister, Darren Pike
709-729-5086, darrenpike@gov.nl.ca
Assistant Deputy Minister, Advanced Studies, Bruce Belbin
709-729-3026, brucebelbin@gov.nl.ca
Acting Assistant Deputy Minister, Infrastructure, Ingrid E. Clarke
709-729-2496
Assistant Deputy Minister, Corporate Services, Ramona Cole
709-729-3025, ramonacole@gov.nl.ca
Assistant Deputy Minister, Primary, Elementary & Secondary Education, Janet Vivian-Walsh
709-729-5720, janetvivianwalsh@gov.nl.ca
Director, Communications, Heather May
709-729-0048, heathermay@gov.nl.ca

Associated Agencies, Boards & Commissions:
• Provincial Information & Library Resources Board
48 St. George's Ave
Stephenville, NL A2H 1K9
709-643-0900 Fax: 709-643-0925
www.nlpl.ca
To establish & operate those public libraries in the province that it considers necessary & provide support to ensure that library materials, information & programs are available to meet the needs of the public.

Advanced Studies Branch
Assistant Deputy Minister, Bruce Belbin
709-729-3026, brucebelbin@gov.nl.ca
Director, Adult Learning & Literacy, Candice Ennis-Williams
709-729-1738, candiceennis-williams@gov.nl.ca
Director, Institutional & Industrial Education, Cliff Mercer
709-729-2350, cliffordmercer@gov.nl.ca
Director, Student Loan Corporation of Newfoundland & Labrador, Julie Moore
709-729-6465, juliemoore@gov.nl.ca
Director, Student Financial Services, David Pike
709-729-3576, davidpike@gov.nl.ca

Corporate Services Branch
Assistant Deputy Minister, Ramona Cole
709-729-3025, rcole@gov.nl.ca
Acting Assistant Deputy Minister, Infrastructure, Ingrid Clarke
709-729-3025, ingridclarke@gov.nl.ca
Director, Information Management & Special Projects, Brian Evans
709-729-1841, brianevans@gov.nl.ca
Director, Financial Services, Don Stapleton
709-729-0837, Fax: 709-729-1330, donjstapleton@gov.nl.ca
Director, Policy, Planning & Accountability, Renee Williams
709-729-7425, reneewilliams@gov.nl.ca

Primary, Elementary & Secondary Education
Assistant Deputy Minister, Janet Vivian-Walsh
709-729-5720, Fax: 709-729-0987, janetvivianwalsh@gov.nl.ca
Director, Program Development, Bradley Clarke
709-729-3004, bradclarke@gov.nl.ca
Director, Student Support Services, Dan Goodyear
709-729-3023, dangoodyear@gov.nl.ca
Director, School Services, Bob Gardiner
709-729-3034, obgardiner@gov.nl.ca
Director, Early Childhood Learning, Paula Hennessey
709-729-5128, paulahennessey@gov.nl.ca
Director, Centre for Distance Learning & Innovation, Jim Tuff
709-729-7614, 866-836-3559, jimtuff@gov.nl.ca
Director, Evaluation & Research Division, Ron Smith
709-729-3000, ronsmith@gov.nl.ca

Office of the Chief Electoral Officer

39 Hallett Cr., St. John's, NL A1B 4C4
709-729-0712 Fax: 709-729-0679
877-729-7987
enl@gov.nl.ca
www.gov.nl.ca/elections

Chief Electoral Officer, Victor Powers
702-729-6068, vpowers@gov.nl.ca
Assistant Chief Electoral Officer & Director, Election Finance, Bruce Chaulk
709-729-4116, brucechaulk@gov.nl.ca
Director, Elections Operations & Special Ballot Administrator, Isabel Collins
709-729-0713, icollins@gov.nl.ca

Department of Environment & Conservation

Confederation Bldg., West Block, 4th Fl., PO Box 8700, St. John's, NL A1B 4J6
709-729-2664 Fax: 709-729-6639
800-563-6181
info@gov.nl.ca
www.env.gov.nl.ca

To protect, conserve & enhance the Province's environment through the management of water resources, the environmental assessment of undertakings & the control & management of substances & activities that may pollute the environment. The Department is actively working towards reducing the number of landfill sites & implementing the Provincial Waste Management Strategy.The strategy will divert 50 percent of materials from landfill sites, phase out municipal solid waste incinerators by 2008 & prohibit such facilities from being built in the future.

Acts Administered:
Dangerous Goods Transportation Act
Endangered Species Act
Environmental Assesment Act, 2000
Species Status Advisory Committee Regulations
Environmental Protection Act
Air Pollution Control Regulations, 2004
Environmental Assessment Regulations, 2003
Gasoline Volatility Control Regulations, 2003
Halocarbon Regulations
Heating Oil Storage Tank System Regulations
Ozone Depleting Substances Regulations, 2003
Pesticides Control Regulations, 2003
Storage & Handling of Gasoline & Associated Products Regulations, 2003
Storage of PCB Waste Regulations, 2003
Used Oil Control Regulations
Waste Management Regulations, 2003
Waste Material Disposal Areas Regulations
Geographical Names Board Act
Land Surveyors Act
Lands Act
National Park Lands Act
Provincial Parks Act
Water Resources Act
Environmental Control Water & Sewage Regulations
Notices of Protected Water Supplies, Watershed Areas, Wellhead Protected Water Supplies
Water Power Rental Regulations, 2003
Well Drilling Regulations, 2003
Wild Life Act
Wild Life Park Order
Wild Life Park Regulations
Wild Life Regulations
Wild Life Reserve Regulations
Wilderness & Ecological Reserves Act
Minister, Hon. Terry French
709-729-2577, Fax: 709-729-0112, terryfrench@gov.nl.ca
Deputy Minister, Bill Parrott
709-729-2572, Fax: 709-729-0112, wparrott@gov.nl.ca
Director, Communications, Melony O'Neil
709-729-2575, moneill@gov.nl.ca
Director, Policy & Planning, John Drover
709-729-1090, jdrover@gov.nl.ca

Associated Agencies, Boards & Commissions:
• Multi-Materials Stewardship Board (MMSB)
PO Box 8131 A
St. John's, NL A1B 3M9
709-753-0948 Fax: 709-753-0974 800-901-6672
inquiries@mmsb.nl.ca
www.mmsb.nf.ca

Environment Branch
Other Communication: Spill Reporting (24 hours): 709-772-2083; Environmental Assessment: 1-800-563-6181
Assistant Deputy Minister, Martin Goebel
709-729-2559, Fax: 709-729-7413, mgoebel@gov.nl.ca
Director, Environmental Assessment Division, Bas Cleary
709-729-0673, Fax: 709-729-5518, clearyb@gov.nl.ca
Director, Policy & Planning, John Drover, P. Eng
709-729-1090, Fax: 709-729-5818, jdrover@gov.nl.ca
Director, Water Resources, Hassen Khan
709-729-2535, Fax: 709-729-0320, hkhan@gov.nl.ca
Director, Pollution Prevention, Derrick Maddocks
709-729-5782

Lands Branch
Director, Surveys & Mapping Division, Allan Chafe
709-729-0602, achafe@gov.nl.ca
Director, Lands Management Division, Reginald Garland
709-729-3844, rgarland@gov.nl.ca
Director, Crown Lands Administration Division, Peter Howe
709-729-3174, phowe@gov.nl.ca

Natural Heritage
Assistant Deputy Minister, Ross Firth
709-637-2135, Fax: 709-637-2180, rossfirth@gov.nl.ca
Director, Wildlife Division, John Blake
709-637-2008, Fax: 709-637-2180, johnblake@gov.nl.ca
Director, Parks & Natural Areas, Sian French
709-637-4520, Fax: 709-635-4541, sianfrench@gov.nl.ca

Sustainable Development & Strategic Science Branch
Executive Director, Policy & Legislation, Shane P. Mahoney
709-729-2542, Fax: 709-729-7677, shanemahoney@gov.nl.ca
Director, Science, Monitoring & Data Synthesis, Rob Otto
709-637-6200, Fax: 709-639-7591, rotto@gov.nl.ca

Department of Finance

Confederation Bldg., PO Box 8700, St. John's, NL A1B 4J6
709-729-6165 Fax: 709-729-2070
finance@gov.nl.ca
www.fin.gov.nl.ca

Acts Administered:
Department of Finance Act
Financial Administration Act
Income Tax Act
Government Money Purchase Pension Plan Act
Industrial Development Corporation Act
Liquor Corporation Act
Loan Act
Loan & Guarantee Act, 1957
Local Authority Guarantee Act, 2005
Members of the House of Assembly Retiring Allowances Act
Municipal Financing Corporation Act
Pensions Funding Act
Public Service Pensions Act, 1991
School Tax Authorities Winding Up Act
Statistics Agency Act
Tax Agreement Act
Taxation of Utilities & Cable Television Companies Act
Teachers' Pensions Act
Tobacco Tax Act
Uniformed Services Pensions Act
Revenue Administration Act
Crown Guarantee & Loan Act
Crown Royalties Act
Government-Corner Brook Pump & Paper Limited Agreements Act
Labour-Sponsored Venture Capital Tax Credit Act
Liquor Corporation Act
Lotteries Act
Medication Association Agreement Act
Offshore Area Corporate Income Tax Act
Pension Contributions Reduction Act
Portability of Pensions Act
Provincial Court Judges' Pension Plan Act
Service Charges Act
Stock Savings Tax Credit Act
Supply Act
Venture Capital Act
War Service Pensions Act

Minister & President, Treasury Board, Hon. Tom Marshall, Q.C.
709-729-3775, Fax: 709-729-2232, financeminister@gov.nl.ca; tommarshall@gov.nl.ca
Deputy Minister, Terry Paddon
709-729-2946, tpaddon@gov.nl.ca
Comptroller General, Finance, Ron Williams
709-729-4866, rwilliams@gov.nl.ca
Director, Communications, Luke Joyce
709-729-6830, Fax: 709-729-2232, lukejoyce@gov.nl.ca
Director, Policy, Planning, Accountability & Information Management, K. Gail Boland
709-729-2950, Fax: 709-729-2070, gailboland@gov.nl.ca

Associated Agencies, Boards & Commissions:
• C.A. Pippy Park Commission
Mount Scio House
15 Mount Scio Rd.
St. John's, NL A1B 3T2
709-737-3655 Fax: 709-737-3303
info@pippypark.com
www.pippypark.com
C.A. Pippy Park was established by an Act of the Newfoundland Legislature in 1968. The Act created the C.A. Pippy Park Commission, a semi-autonomous Crown Corporation under the laws of the Province of Newfoundland and Labrador. The Commission currently reports to the Minister of Finance.
• Newfoundland & Labrador Municipal Financing Corporation (NMFC)
Confederation Bldg.
PO Box 8700
St. John's, NL A1B 4J6
709-729-6686 Fax: 709-729-2095
Newfoundland and Labrador Municipal Financing Corporation is a Crown Corporation established to consolidate the long-term borrowing programs of all municipalities in one central agency.
• Newfoundland & Labrador Liquor Corporation
90 Kenmount Rd.
PO Box 8750 A
St. John's, NL A1B 3V1
709-724-1100 Fax: 709-754-0321
info@nfliquor.com
www.nfliquor.com
The Newfoundland Labrador Liquor Corporation (NLC) is a provincial crown corporation responsible for managing the importation, sale and distribution of beverage alcohol within the province.

Economics & Statistics
Assistant Deputy Minister, Alton Hollett
709-729-3255, ahollett@gov.nl.ca
Director, Economic Research & Analysis, Rod Forsey
709-729-0864, rforsey@gov.nl.ca
Director, Newfoundland & Labrador Statistics Agency, Robert Reid
709-729-0158, Fax: 709-729-0393, robertr@gov.nl.ca

Financial Planning & Benefits Administration
Assistant Deputy Minister, Laurie Skinner
709-729-4039, laurieskinner@gov.nl.ca
Director, Insurance, James Doody
709-729-7471, jamesdoody@gov.nl.ca
Director, Budgeting, Glenn Grandy
709-729-1054, Fax: 709-729-2156, glenngrandy@gov.nl.ca
Director, Pensions Administration, Maureen McCarthy
709-729-5983, Fax: 709-729-6790, mccarthym@gov.nl.ca

Office of the Comptroller General
Comptroller General, Ronald Williams, C.A.
709-729-5926, Fax: 709-729-7627, rwilliams@gov.nl.ca
Director, Government Accounting, Ann Marie Miller, C.M.A.
709-729-2341, Fax: 709-729-7627, millera@gov.nl.ca
Director, Professional Services & Internal Audit, David Hill
709-729-0702, Fax: 709-729-7144, davehill@gov.nl.ca

Taxation & Fiscal Policy Branch
Assistant Deputy Minister, Bob Constantine
709-729-2944, rconstantine@gov.nl.ca
Director, Fiscal Policy, Chris Butt
709-729-6714, cbutt@gov.nl.ca
Director, Tax Policy, Jay Griffin
709-729-6847, jgriffin@gov.nl.ca
Director, Project Analysis, Brian Hurley
709-729-3664, bhurley@gov.nl.ca
Director, Debt Management, Paul Myrden
709-729-6848
Director, Tax Administration, Cathy M. Whalen
709-729-6307, Fax: 709-729-2277, cathywhalen@gov.nl.ca

Newfoundland & Labrador Fire & Emergency Services

25 Hallett Cres., PO Box 8700, St. John's, NL A1B 4J6
709-729-3703 Fax: 709-729-3757
www.gov.nl.ca/fes
Other Communication: Fire Service Phone: 709-729-1608; Fax: 709-729-2524

The Provincial Emergency Measures Program is responsible for the development & maintenance of provincial emergency preparedness, response & recovery measures with a view to mitigating the human suffering & loss of property caused by actual or imminent emergencies & disasters. Using its legislative support, The Emergency Measures Act, it has the responsibility to co-ordinate &/or manage an emergency situation. It is the only agency that is authorized to control & coordinate the activities of all Police, Fire, Health, Social Services, & other services in the area, either municipal or provincial, & to engage civilian personnel to assist in these services. Programs & Services provided include Emergency Response, Planning & Operations, Training & Education, Joint Emergency Preparedness, Disaster Financial Assistance Arrangements, Emergency Air Services & Emergency Response.

Acts Administered:
Emergency Services Act
Fire Prevention Act, 1991
Firefighters Protection Act
Municipalities Act (sections 204 & 405)
Minister Responsible, Kevin O'Brien
709-729-3046, Fax: 709-729-0943, kevinobrien@gov.nl.ca
Director, Fred Hollett
709-729-3703

Department of Fisheries & Aquaculture

Petten Bldg., 30 Strawberry Marsh Rd., PO Box 8700, St. John's, NL A1B 4J6
709-729-3723 Fax: 709-729-6082
fisheries@gov.nl.ca
www.fishaq.gov.nl.ca
Other Communication: Aquaculture Phone: 709-292-4100; Fax: 709-292-4113; Email: aquaculture@gov.nl.ca

Contributes to economic & community growth in the province by encouraging sustainable growth & development of the harvesting, processing, & distribution sectors; includes providing support for the marketing of fish & aquaculture products produced in Newfoundland & Labrador for domestic & export markets. Responsible for: setting & enforcing standards for the processing & sale of fish products in the province; licensing fish processing establishments; undertaking developmental initiatives in the harvesting, processing, & marketing sectors of the fishing industry; developing, promoting & licensing of aquaculture facilities; developing & maintaining strategic fisheries infrastructure; articulating policies & providing advice for the management & development of fisheries & aquaculture; providing statistical information.

Acts Administered:
Aquaculture Act
Fish Inspection Act
Fish Processing Licensing Board Act
Fisheries Act
Fishing Industry Collective Bargaining Act
Professional Fish Harvesters Act
Minister, Hon. Darin King
709-729-3705, Fax: 709-729-0360, DarinKingMHA@gov.nl.ca
Deputy Minister, Alastair O'Rielly
709-729-3707, Fax: 790-729-4219, aorielly@gov.nl.ca
Director, Communications, Jason Card
709-729-3733, jasoncard@gov.nl.ca
Manager, Finance & Budgeting, Barry Aylward
709-729-4764, Fax: 709-729-2092, baylward@gov.nl.ca

Associated Agencies, Boards & Commissions:
• Fish Processing Licensing Board
c/o Fish Processing Licensing Board Secretariat
30 Strawberry Marsh Rd.
St. John's, NL A1B 4J6
fplbsecretariat@gov.nl.ca
• Professional Fish Harvesters Certification Board (PFHCB)
368 Hamilton Ave.
PO Box 8541
St. John's, NL A1B 3P2
709-722-8170 Fax: 709-722-8201
pfh@pfhcb.com
www.pfhcb.com

Aquaculture Branch
Fax: 709-729-0360
The Branch is responsible for licensing & aquaculture development.
Assistant Deputy Minister, Brian Meaney
709-729-3710, Fax: 709-729-1882, bmeaney@gov.nl.ca
Director & Provincial Aquaculture Veterinarian, Dr. Daryl Whelan
709-729-6872, Fax: 709-729-1882, darylswhelan@gov.nl.ca

Fisheries Branch
Fax: 709-729-6082
Assistant Deputy Minister, Shawn Robinson
709-729-3723, Fax: 709-729-6082
Director, Licensing & Quality Assurance, Ian Burford
709-729-3736, Fax: 709-729-5995, iburford@gov.nl.ca
Director, Innovation & Development, Mark Rumboldt
709-729-3749, Fax: 709-729-1884, mrumboldt@gov.nl.ca
Director, Compliance & Enforcement, Milly Meaney
709-729-3717, Fax: 709-729-1881, mmeaney@gov.nl.ca

Policy Development & Planning Branch
Provides policy & program planning services to the Department. Through the Sustainable Fisheries & Oceans Policy Division participates in oceans policy & governance issues, in addition to the resource assessment & management process of the federal Department of Fisheries & Oceans, including local, national, & international bodies responsible for fisheries conservation & management.
Assistant Deputy Minister, David Lewis
709-729-3713, Fax: 709-729-0360, davidlewis@gov.nl.ca
Director, Sustainable Fisheries & Oceans Policy, Tom Dooley
709-729-0335, Fax: 709-729-6082
Director, Fishing Industry Renewal & Adjustment, Paul Martin
709-729-1073, Fax: 709-729-6082, pdmartin@gov.nl.ca
Director, Planning Services, Wandalee Wiseman
709-729-3765, Fax: 709-729-6082, wandaleewiseman@gov.nl.ca

Regional Offices:

Avalon & Eastern
709-832-2860 Fax: 709-832-1669
Regional Director, Rex Matthews
709-832-2860, Fax: 709-832-1669, rmatthews@gov.nl.ca

Northern
709-896-3412 Fax: 709-896-3483
Regional Director, Craig Taylor
709-896-3412, Fax: 709-896-3483, craigtaylor@gov.nl.ca

Western/Central
709-861-3537 Fax: 709-861-3556
Regional Director, Wilson Goosney
709-861-3537, Fax: 709-637-2908

Department of Government Services

PO Box 8700, St. John's, NL A1B 4J6
709-729-4834
gsinfo@gov.nl.ca
www.gs.gov.nl.ca

Departmental responsibilities include: motor vehicle registration, government service centres, consumer protection, trade practices, vital statistics, lotteries, registries, building accessibility, residential tenancies services, regulation of financial institutions, occupational health & safety, Office of the Queen's Printer, Government Purchasing Agency, permits, licences, approvals & inspections for public health & safety. As of October 2011 this Department has been rebranded Service Newfoundland & Labrador.

Acts Administered:
Accident & Sickness Insurance Act
Architects Act
Automobile Insurance Act
Buildings Accessibility Act
Business Electronic Filing Act
Certified General Accountants Act
Certified Management Accountants Act
Change of Name Act
Chartered Accountants Act
Collections Act
Consumer Protection & Business Practices Act
Condominium Act
Co-operatives Act
Conveyancing Act
Corporations Act
Credit Union Act
Criminal Code
Electronic Commerce Act
Embalmers & Funeral Directors Act
Engineers & Geoscientists Act
Fire Insurance Act
Income Tax Savings Plan Act
Insurance Adjusters, Agents & Brokers Act
Insurance Companies Act
Insurance Contracts Act
Life Insurance Act
Limited Partnership Act
Mechanics' Lien Act
Mortgage Brokers Act
Occupational Health & Safety Act
Asbestos Abatement Regulations
Asbestos Exposure Code Regulations
Mines Safety of Workers Regulations
Occupational Health & Safety Electrical & Fisheries Advisory Committees Regulations

Occupational Health & Safety Regulations
Workplace Hazardous Materials Information System (WHMIS) Regulations
Pension Benefits Act, 1997
Pension Plans Designation of Beneficiaries Act
Perpetuities & Accumulations Act
Personal Property Security Act
Prepaid Funeral Services Act
Printing Services Act
Private Investigation & Security Services Act
Public Accountancy Act
Public Safety Act
Radiation Health & Safety Act
Real Estate Trading Act
Registration of Deeds Act, 2009
Residential Tenancies Act, 2000
Sale of Goods Act
Securities Act
Security Interest Registration Act
Solemnization of Marriage Act
Trustee Act
Vital Statistics Act
Warehouse Receipts Act
Warehouser's Lien Act
Workplace Health, Safety & Compensation Act
Acts Shared in Part with Other Ministries
Adoption Act (jointly with Health & Community Services)
Building Standards Act (jointly with Municipal Affairs)
Child Care Services Act (jointly with Health & Community Services)
Child, Youth & Family Services Act (jointly with Health & Community Services)
Children's Law Act (jointly with Justice)
Communicable Diseases Act (jointly with Health & Community Services)
Dangerous Goods Transportation Act (jointly with Justice)
Environmental Protection Act (jointly with Environment & Conservation)
Fire Prevention Act, 1991 (jointly with Municipal Affairs)
Food & Drug Act (jointly with Health & Community Services)
Fraudulent Conveyances Act (jointly with Justice)
Health & Community Services Act (jointly with Health & Community Services)
Highway Traffic Act (jointly with Transportation & Works)
Meat Inspection Act (jointly with Natural Resources)
Motor Carrier Act (jointly with Transportation & Works)
Motorized Snow Vehicles & All-Terrain Vehicles Act (jointly with Natural Resources)
Tobacco Control Act (jointly with Health & Community Services)
Urban & Rural Planning Act (jointly with Municipal Affairs)
Water Resources Act (jointly with Environment & Conservation)
Minister, Hon. Paul Davis
709-729-6670, Fax: 709-729-1503, padavis@gov.nl.ca
Deputy Minister, David Norman
709-729-4752, Fax: 709-729-4754, davidnorman@gov.nl.ca
Director, Policy & Strategic Planning, Elizabeth Day
709-729-6470, Fax: 709-729-4754, elizabethday@gov.nl.ca
Director, Audit, Information & Training, Joseph Day
709-729-5429, dayj@gov.nl.ca
Director, Communications, Hugh Donnan
709-729-4860, Fax: 709-729-4754, hughdonnan@gov.nl.ca
Director, Procurement & Development, Patricia Hearn
709-729-3344, hearnp@gov.nl.ca
Director, Government Purchasing, Policy & Administration, Wayne Hendry
709-729-3347, Fax: 709-729-5817, hendryw@gov.nl.ca
Manager, Organizational Development, Leona O'Neill
709-729-0683, Fax: 709-729-6661, leonaoneill@gov.nl.ca

Associated Agencies, Boards & Commissions:
• Credit Union Deposit Guarantee Corporation
PO Box 340
Marystown, NL A0E 2M0
709-279-0170 Fax: 709-279-0177 877-279-0170
www.cudgcnl.com
The Credit Union Deposit Guarantee Corporation guarantees deposits up to $250,000 per account type: demand accounts, registered retirement savings plans, registered retirement income fund, trust accounts, and joint accounts. Established in 1991 under the Co-operative Societies Act, replacing the Newfoundland and Labrador Stabilization fund, which was enacted in 1983.
• Government Purchasing Agency
30 Strawberry Marsh Rd.
St. John's, NL A1B 4R4
709-729-3348 Fax: 709-729-5817
tenders@gov.nl.ca

Consumer & Commercial Affairs Branch
Promotes economic development by assisting businesses & protecting consumers. The branch is responsible for regulating the insurance industry, the securities industries, the trust & loan industry, the credit union industry, the real estate industry, collection agencies, mortgage brokers, automobile dealers, charitable gaming, private investigation agencies, & landlord-tenant relations.
Assistant Deputy Minister, Julian McCarthy
709-729-2570, Fax: 709-729-4151, jmccarth@gov.nl.ca
Assistant Deputy Minister, Winston Morris
709-729-2571, Fax: 709-729-4754, winstonmorris@gov.nl.ca
Director, Commercial Registrations Division, Dean Doyle
709-729-4043, Fax: 709-729-0232
Director, Consumer Affairs Division, Gerry Burke
709-729-2618, Fax: 709-729-6998
Director, Financial Services Regulation, Doug Connolly, C.A.
709-729-4909, Fax: 709-729-3205, connolly@gov.nl.ca
Deputy Registrar, Commercial Registrations, Trudy Wade
709-729-3300, Fax: 709-729-0232, twade@gov.nl.ca
Deputy Registrar, Commercial Registry, Lorraine Vokey
709-729-5724, Fax: 709-729-0232, lvokey@gov.nl.ca

Government Services Branch
Provides a one-stop service to the public & business community for a wide range of government regulatory & information functions. The Branch processes various permits, licences, & approvals, carries out inspections & investigations on behalf of various departments & conducts highway enforcement of the motor carrier industry. Also administers the Highway Traffic Act & registers vital events such as births, marriages, deaths & name changes. Through the Office of the Queen's Printer publishes, distributes & sells the Newfoundland & Labrador Consolidated Statutes, Regulations, the Newfoundland & Labrador Gazette & selected publications. Operates printing & micrographic services for all government departments.
Assistant Deputy Minster, Donna Kelland
709-729-3056, Fax: 709-729-4151, dkelland@gov.nl.ca
Director, Program & Support Services Division, Rick Curran
709-729-4875
Director, Engineering & Inspections, Dennis Eastman
709-729-2747, Fax: 709-729-2071, deastman@gov.nl.ca

Office of the Queen's Printer
Queen's Printer-Earl Tucker, Ground Fl., Confederation Blg., PO Box 8700, St. John's, NL A1B 4J6
709-729-3649 Fax: 709-729-1900
queensprinter@gov.nl.ca
Provides a retail outlet for purchase of government legislation & various government reports. Publishes Hansard, Bills, Statutes & Regulations for the House of Assembly. Publishes weekly The Newfoundland & Labrador Gazette which contains government & public legal notices as well as subordinate legislation. Provides subscription & mail-out services for some of these publications. Provides ISBN numbers for government publications.
Queen's Printer, William E. Parsons
709-729-3210, Fax: 709-729-1900, williamparsons@gov.nl.ca

Vital Statistics Division
5 Mews Pl., PO Box 8700, St. John's, NL A1B 4J6
709-729-3308 Fax: 709-729-0946
vstats@gov.nl.ca
Registers births, marriages & deaths in the province. In addition, the division registers adoptions & legal name changes & certifies clergy who are authorized to solemnize marriages. From this division, the public may obtain a birth, marriage, death, or change of name certificate, or a marriage licence. Vital Statistics services are also available from GSC offices.
Registrar, Ken Mullaly
709-729-3311, kmullaly@gov.nl.ca

Occupational Health & Safety Branch
Other Communication: Accident Reporting Line: 709-729-4444 (24 hours); Toll Free for Occupational Health & Safety: 1-800-563-5471 (in Nfld. & Lab.)
Maintains & improves health & safety standards in the workplace through the administration of the Occupational Health & Safety Act & Regulations, The Mines Safety of Workers Regulations, the Radiation Health & Safety Act & Regulations &, other associated regulations, codes of practice & specified standards. The Division is supported by inspections officers, industrial hygienists, engineers & radiation specialists to per form various multi-disciplinary activities such as: investigating workplace accidents & statistics; conducting compliance inspections & detailed audits of workplaces; hygiene assessments of various physical, chemical, biological & ergonomic agents in the workplace in order to protect worker health; evaluating & inspecting radiation control measures in workplaces & enforcing occupational health & safety Legislation.
Assistant Deputy Minister, Kim Dunphy
709-729-5544, Fax: 709-729-4151, kdunphy@gov.nl.ca
Director, Reg Bennett
709-729-7454, Fax: 709-729-3445, regbennett@gov.nl.ca

Regional Offices:

Eastern Office
15 Dundee Ave., Mount Pearl, NL A1N 4R6
709-729-2706 Fax: 709-729-3445

Corner Brook
Fortis Towers, 4 Herald Ave., 2nd fl., Corner Brook, NL
709-637-2946 Fax: 709-637-2928

Grand Falls-Windsor
7 High St., Grand Falls-Windsor, NL
709-292-4400 Fax: 709-292-4430

Labrador City
Provincial Court Bldg., Wabush, NL
709-282-2680 Fax: 709-282-2688

Department of Health & Community Services (HCS)
West Block, Confederation Bldg., PO Box 8700, St. John's, NL A1B 4J6
709-729-5021 Fax: 709-729-5824
healthinfo@gov.nl.ca
www.health.gov.nl.ca
Provides a leadership role in health & community service programs & policy development for the Province. This involves working in partnership with a number of key stakeholders including regional boards, community organizations, professional associations, post-secondary educational institutions, unions, consumer & other government departments.
Acts Administered:
Adoption Act
Centre for Health Information Act
Child Care Services Act
Chiropractors Act, 2009
Communicable Diseases Act
Dental Act
Denturists Act
Dieticians Act
Dispensing Opticians Act
Emergency Medical Aid Act
Food & Drug Act
Health & Community Services Act
Health Care Association Act
Hearing Aid Practitioners
Hospital Insurance Agreement Act
Human Tissue Act
Licensed Practical Nurses Act
Massage Therapy Act
Medical Act, 2011
Medical Care Insurance Act, 1999
Mental Health Care & Treatment Act
Neglected Adults Welfare Act
Occupational Therapists Act
Optometry Act
Pharmacy Act
Physiotherapy Act
Psychologists Act
Registered Nurses Act
Self-managed Home Support Services Act
Smoke-free Environment Act
Social Workers Act
Tobacco Control Act
Young Persons Offences Act
Youth Criminal Justice Act (Canada)
Adult Protection Act
Health Professions Act
Health Research Ethics Authority Act
Personal Health Information Act
Pharmaceutical Services Act
Regional Health Authorities Act
Minister, Hon. Susan Sullivan
709-729-3124, 800-514-9073, Fax: 709-729-0121, SusanSullivan@gov.nl.ca
Deputy Minister, Bruce Cooper
709-729-3125, Fax: 709-729-0121
Assistant Deputy Minister, Professional Services, Colleen Janes
709-729-1716, Fax: 709-729-5218, cjanes@gov.nl.ca
Assistant Deputy Minister, Tracy King
709-729-3103, Fax: 709-729-0121, tracyking@gov.nl.ca
Assistant Deputy Minister, Denise Tubrett
709-729-0580, Fax: 709-729-0640, dtubrett@gov.nl.ca
Assistant Deputy Minister, Regional Health Operations, Tony Wakeham
709-729-3127, tonywakeham@gov.nl.ca
Chief Nurse, Anita Ludlow
709-729-2039, anitaludlow@gov.nl.ca
Director, Communications, Jennifer Tulk
709-729-1377, Fax: 709-699-6524, jennifertulk@gov.nl.ca

Associated Agencies, Boards & Commissions:
• Newfoundland & Labrador Centre for Health Information
70 O'Leary Ave.
St. John's, NL A1B 2C7
709-752-6000 Fax: 709-752-6011
• Newfoundland & Labrador Health Boards Associations
Beothuck Bldg.
20 Crosbie Pl., 2nd Fl.
St. John's, NL A1B 3Y8
709-364-7701 Fax: 709-364-6460
www.nlhba.nl.ca

Public Health & Wellness Branch
Chief Medical Officer of Health, Public Health Division, Dr. Faith Stratton
709-729-3430
Director, Health Emergency Management, Dennis Davis
709-729-3912
Director, Environmental Public Health, Darryl Johnson
709-729-3422, Fax: 709-729-0730, djohnson@gov.nl.ca
Director, Health Promotion & Wellness, Eleanor Swanson
709-729-5023

Newfoundland & Labrador Housing Corporation (NLHC)

Sir Brian Dunfield Bldg., 2 Canada Dr., PO Box 220, St. John's, NL A1C 5J2
709-724-3000 Fax: 709-724-3250
www.nlhc.nl.ca

Minister Responsible, Hon. Thomas J. Hedderson
709-729-3679, Fax: 709-729-4285, thedderson@gov.nl.ca
Chair & Chief Executive Officer, Len Simms
709-724-3054, lensimms@nlhc.nl.ca
Manager, Communications, Jenny Bowring
709-724-3055, jmbowring@nlhc.nl.ca
Corporate Secretary, Janette Loveless
709-724-3067, Fax: 709-724-3250, jmloveless@nlhc.nl.ca

Department of Human Resources, Labour & Employment

Confederation Bldg., PO Box 8700, St. John's, NL A1B 4J6
709-729-2480 Fax: 709-729-6996
hreweb@gov.nl.ca
www.hrle.gov.nl.ca/hrle

Acts Administered:
Fishing Industry Collective Bargaining Act
Income & Employment Support Act
Interns & Residents Collective Bargaining Act
Labour Relations Act
Labour Standards Act
Public Service Collective Bargaining Act
Shops' Closing Act
Teachers' Collective Bargaining Act
Workplace Health, Safety & Compensation Act
Minister, Hon. Darin King
709-729-3580, Fax: 709-729-6996, darinking@gov.nl.ca
Deputy Minister, Baxter Rose
709-729-3582, Fax: 709-729-6996
Director, Communications, Bradley Power
709-729-0753, Fax: 709-729-6996, bradleypower@gov.nl.ca

Associated Agencies, Boards & Commissions:
• Income & Employment Support Appeal Board
Confederation Bldg.
PO Box 8700
St. John's, NL A1B 4J6
709-729-2479 Fax: 709-729-5139
• Labour Relations Board
Beothuck Bldg.
20 Crosbie Pl., 5th Fl.
PO Box 8700
St. John's, NL A1B 4J6
709-729-2707 Fax: 709-729-5738
lrb@gov.nl.ca
www.hrle.gov.nl.ca/lrb
• Standing Fish Price Setting Panel
Beothuck Bldg.
20 Crosbie Pl., 3rd Fl.
PO Box 8700
St. John's, NL A1B 4J6
709-729-2711 Fax: 709-729-5905
• Workplace Health, Safety & Compensation Commission

Corporate Services
Assistant Deputy Minister, Jim Strong
709-729-3594, Fax: 709-729-5139, jstrong@gov.nl.ca
Director, Finance & General Operations, Ken Curtis
709-729-3530, Fax: 709-729-4379, kcurtis@gov.nl.ca
Acting Director, Policy, Planning & Evaluation, Alicia Sutton
709-729-0494, aliciasutton@gov.nl.ca

Income, Employment & Youth Services
Assistant Deputy Minister, Marilyn Field
709-729-5151, Fax: 709-729-5139, marilynfield@gov.nl.ca
Acting Director, Income Support, Valerie Gregory
709-729-5135, valeriegregory@gov.nl.ca
Acting Director, Poverty Reduction Strategy, Donna O'Brien
709-729-6053, Fax: 709-729-5139, donnaobrien@gov.nl.ca

Labour Market Development & Client Services
Assistant Deputy Minister, Roxie Wheaton
709-729-2320, roxiewheaton@gov.nl.ca
Senior Director, Labour Market Services, Pamela Toope
709-729-6516, pamtoope@gov.nl.ca

Labour Relations Agency
Other Communication: Labour Standards: 1-877-563-1063
Minister Responsible, Hon. Terry French
709-729-2577, Fax: 709-729-0112, terryfrench@gov.nl.ca
Assistant Deputy Minister, Policy & Planning, Thomas Graham
709-729-1760, Fax: 709-729-5905
Chief Executive Officer, Rachelle Cochrane
709-729-2715, Fax: 709-729-1759
Director, Policy & Planning, Dan Mackenzie
709-729-5551, Fax: 709-729-5905, danm@gov.nl.ca
Director, Labour Relations, Yvonne Scott
709-729-0707, Fax: 709-729-5905, YScott@gov.nl.ca

Newfoundland & Labrador Human Rights Commission

PO Box 8700, St. John's, NL A1B 4J6
709-729-2709 Fax: 709-729-0790
800-563-5808
humanrights@mail.gov.nl.ca
www.justice.gov.nl.ca/hrc

Vice Chair, Stephanie Newell, Q.C.

Newfoundland & Labrador Hydro

Hydro Place, Columbus Dr., PO Box 12400, St. John's, NL A1B 4K7
709-737-1400 Fax: 709-737-1800
hydro@nlh.nl.ca
www.nlh.nl.ca

Crown corporation, owned by the Province of Newfoundland & Labrador. Hydro generates, transmits & distributes electrical power & energy to utility, residential & industrial customers throughout the province. Hydro is the parent company of the Hydro Group of Companies (Hydro Group), comprising Newfoundland & Labrador Hydro, Churchill Falls (Labrador) Corporation Limited (CF (L)Co), Lower Churchill Development Corporation Limited (LCDC), Gull Island Power Company Limited (GIPCo), & Twin Falls Power Corporation Limited (TwinCo). The Hydro Group's installed generating capacity is the fourth largest of all utility companies in Canada, consisting of ten hydroelectric plants, including the Churchill Falls hydraulic plant, which is the largest underground powerhouse in the world with a rated capacity of 5,428 megawatts (MW) of power, one oil-fired plant, four gas turbines & 26 diesel plants.
President & Chief Executive Officer, Ed Martin
Vice-President, Finance & Chief Financial Officer, Derrick Sturge
Vice-President, Human Resources & Organzational Effectiveness, Gerard McDonald
Vice-President, Regulated Operations, Jim Haynes

Churchill Falls (Labrador) Corporation Limited
Hydro Place, 500 Columbus Dr., PO Box 12500, St. John's, NL A1B 4K7
709-737-1859 Fax: 709-737-1816
Churchill Falls (Labrador) Corporation operates a hydroelectric generating plant & transmission facilities.
President & Chief Executive Officer, Ed Martin
Vice-President, Finance & Chief Financial Officer, Derrick Sturge

Gull Island Power Co. Ltd.
President & Chief Executive Officer, Ed Martin
Vice-President, Regulated Operations, Jim Haynes
Vice-President, Finance & Chief Financial Officer, Derrick Sturge

Lower Churchill Development Corporation Ltd.
Member, Board of Directors, Jim Haynes
Vice-President, Finance & Chief Financial Officer, Derrick Sturge

Twin Falls Power Corporation
PO Box 12500, St. John's, NL A1B 3T5
Twin Falls Power Corporation has developed a hydroelectric generating plant on the Unknown River in Labrador. The plant has been inoperative since 1974.
President, James R. Haynes
Vice-President, Finance & Cheif Financial Officer, Derrick Sturge

Department of Innovation, Trade & Rural Development

West Block, Confederation Bldg., PO Box 8700, St. John's, NL A1B 4J6
709-729-7000 Fax: 709-729-0654
intrd@gov.nl.ca
www.intrd.gov.nl.ca

The department has a number of initiatives to assist businesses in the province or to open in the province. As of October 2011, this Department is known as Innovation, Business & Rural Development.
Acts Administered:
Business Investment Corporation Act
Economic Diversification & Growth Enterprises (EDGE) Act
Research & Development Council Act
Minister, Hon. Keith Hutchings
709-729-4728, Fax: 709-729-0654, keithhutchings@gov.nl.ca
Deputy Minister, Brent Meade
709-729-4731, Fax: 709-729-0654, bmeade@gov.nl.ca
Director, Communications, Scott Barfoot
709-729-4570, Fax: 709-729-4880, ScottBarfoot@gov.nl.ca
Director, Policy & Strategic Planning, Sheila Fudge
709-729-7019, Fax: 709-729-4880, sfudge@gov.nl.ca
Director, Trade & Export Development, Linda Spurrell
709-729-7483, Fax: 709-729-5124, lspurrell@gov.nl.ca

Associated Agencies, Boards & Commissions:
• Ireland Business Partnership
PO Box 8700
St. John's, NL A1B 4J6
709-729-1684 Fax: 709-729-7234
ibp@gov.nl.ca
www.ibp.nl.ca
A joint public-private partnership with the Government of Ireland to promote business opportunities & educational & cultural exchanges with Newfoundland & Labrador.

Innovation
Assistant Deputy Minister, Jackie Collins
709-729-7102, Fax: 709-729-7234, jackiecollins@gov.nl.ca
Director, Innovation, Research & Technology, Sharon Tiller
709-729-7068, stiller@gov.nl.ca
Director, Information Management, Ruth Parsons
709-729-1940, Fax: 709-729-5124, ruthparsons@gov.nl.ca

Regional Development
Assistant Deputy Minister, Rita Malone
709-637-2977, Fax: 709-639-7713, rmalone@gov.nl.ca
Director, Regional Economic Development, John Wickham
709-729-7260, Fax: 709-729-5124, jwickham@gov.nl.ca

Regional Offices:

Avalon
28 Pippy Place, St. John's, NL A1B 3X4
Fax: 709-729-7135
Acting Regional Director, Jim Antsey
709-729-7124, Fax: 709-729-7135, jkantsey@gov.nl.ca

Central
McCurdy Complex, Markham Place, PO Box 2222, Gander, NL A1V 2N9
Fax: 709-256-1490
Regional Director, Percy Farwell
709-256-1483, pfarwell@gov.nl.ca

Eastern
211B Memorial Drive, Clarenville, NL A5A 1R3
Fax: 709-466-1306
Acting Regional Director, Denis Sullivan
709-466-4171, Fax: 709-466-1306, sullivan@gov.nl.ca

Labrador
2 Hillcrest Rd., PO Box 3014 B, Happy Valley-Goose Bay, NL A0P 1E0
709-896-2400 Fax: 709-896-0234
Regional Director, Reg Kean
709-896-0306, rkean@gov.nl.ca

Western
PO Box 2006, Corner Brook, NL A2H 6J8
Fax: 709-639-7713
Acting Regional Director, John Davis
709-637-2981, jdavis@gov.nl.ca

Strategic Industries & Business Development Branch
Assistant Deputy Minister, Peter W. Au
709-729-4711, Fax: 709-729-4858, peterau@gov.nl.ca
Director, Strategic Industries Development, Kirk Tilley
709-729-7080, Fax: 709-729-5124, ktilley@gov.nl.ca
Acting Director, Business Analysis, Ken Thompson
709-729-5622, Fax: 709-729-5124, kthompson@gov.nl.ca

Trade & Export Development Branch
Specializes in assisting provincial businesses develop an export plan to enter new markets, find export business partners & research national & international market opportunities.
Assistant Deputy Minister, Judith Hearn
709-729-0882, Fax: 709-729-7234, judithhearn@gov.nl.ca
Director, Linda Spurrell
709-729-7483, Fax: 709-729-5124, lspurrel@gov.nl.ca
Director, Strategic Partnership, Derek Staubitzer
709-729-7043, Fax: 709-729-5124, derekstaubitzer@gov.nl.ca

Intergovernmental Affairs Secretariat

Confederation Bldg., East Block, 7th Fl., PO Box 8700, St. John's, NL A1B 4J6
709-729-3164 Fax: 709-729-5038
iga@gov.nl.ca
www.exec.gov.nl.ca/exec/igas/index.html

As of October 2011, this Secretariat will be expanded into the full Department of Intergovernmental & Aboriginal Affairs.
Acts Administered:
Intergovernmental Affairs Act
Minister, Hon. Nick McGrath
709-729-3400

Deputy Minister, Sean Dutton
709-729-2134, sdutton@gov.nl.ca
Assistant Deputy Minister, Paul Scott
709-729-3164, paulscott@gov.nl.ca
Communications Specialist, Lesley Clarke
709-729-6026, lesleyclarke@gov.nl.ca
Acting Director, Social & Economic Policy, Cameron Bodnar
709-729-1341, Fax: 709-729-5038, cameronbodnar@gov.nl.ca
Acting Director, Resource & Fiscal Policy, John Cowan
709-729-6267, Fax: 709-729-1330, jcowan@gov.nl.ca

Department of Justice

Confederation Bldg., East Block, 4th Fl., PO Box 8700, St. John's, NL A1B 4J6
709-729-2869 Fax: 709-729-0469
justice@gov.nl.ca
www.justice.gov.nl.ca

The Department of Justice ensures the impartial administration of justice and the protection of the public interest through the dual offices of the Attorney General and Minister of Justice.

Acts Administered:
Adult Corrections Act
Advance Health Care Directives Act
Age of Majority Act
Agreement for Policing the Province Act
Apportionment Act
Arbitration Act
Bankers' Books Act
Blind Persons' Rights Act
Canada & United Kingdom Reciprocal Recognition & Enforcement of Judgments Act
Chattels Real Act
Children's Law Act (jointly with Government Services & Lands)
Commissioners for Oaths Act
Contributory Negligence Act
Criminal Code
Defamation Act
Detention of Intoxicated Persons Act
Electoral Boundaries Act
Enduring Powers of Attorney Act
Evidence Act
Exhumation Act
Family Law Act
Family Relief Act
Fatal Accidents Act
Fatalities Investigations Act
Federal Courts Jurisdiction Act
Fraudulent Conveyances Act (jointly with Government Services & Lands)
Frustrated Contracts Act
Human Rights Act, 2010
International Commercial Arbitration Act
International Sale of Goods Act
International Trusts Act
Interpretation Act
Interprovincial Subpoena Act
Intestate Succession Act
Judgement Enforcement Act
Judgment Interest Act
Judicature Act
Jury Act, 1991
Justices Act
Justices & Public Authorities Protection Act
Law Society Act, 1999
Leaseholds in St. John's Act
Legal Aid Act
Limitations Act
Mentally Disabled Persons' Estates Act
Notaries Public Act
Oaths Act
Oaths of Office Act
Partnership Act
Petty Trespass Act
Presumption of Death Act
Prisons Act
Prisons & Reformatories Act (Canada)
Privacy Act
Proceedings Against the Crown Act
Proof of Death Members of Armed Forces Act
Provincial Court Act, 1991
Provincial Offences Act
Public Inquiries Act
Public Investigations Evidence Act
Public Trustee Act, 2009
Public Utilities Acquisition of Lands Act
Public Utilities Act
Queen's Counsel Act
Quieting of Titles Act
Reciprocal Enforcement of Judgments Act
Recording of Evidence Act
Revised Statutes, 1990 Act
Royal Newfoundland Constabulary Act, 1992
Sheriff's Act, 1991
Small Claims Act
Statutes Act
Statutes Amendment Act, 1992
Statutes & Subordinate Legislation Act
Support Orders Enforcement Act (jointly with Social Services)
Survival of Actions Act
Survivorship Act
Tobacco Health Care Costs Recovery Act
Victims of Crime Services Act
Wills Act
Youth Criminal Justice Act (Canada) & Young Persons Offences Act (jointly with Social Services)
Access to Information & Protection of Privacy Act
Apology Act
Correctional Services Act
Corrections & Conditional Release Act (Canada)
Enforcement of Canadian Judgments Act
Family Violence Protection Act
Gunshot & Stab Wound Reporting Act
Interjurisdictional Support Orders Act
International Interests in Mobile Aircraft Equipment Act
Lobbyist Registration Act
Safer Communities & Neighbourhoods Act
Settlement of International Investment Disputes Act
Court Security Act, 2010

Minister, Hon. Felix Collins
709-729-2869, Fax: 709-729-0469, felixcollins@gov.nl.ca
Deputy Minister, Donald Burrage, Q.C.
709-729-2872, Fax: 709-729-0469, donburrage@gov.nl.ca
Assistant Deputy Minister, Donna Ballard, Q.C.
709-729-0288, Fax: 709-729-2129, dballard@gov.nl.ca
Executive Director, Human Rights Commission, Carey Majid
709-729-2709, careymajid@gov.nl.ca
Director, Quality Management & Support Services, Dan Chafe
709-729-1078, Fax: 709-729-5100
Director, Communications, Vanessa Colman-Sadd
709-729-6985, Fax: 709-729-0469, vanessacolmansadd@gov.nl.ca
Director, Legal Information Services, Sean Dawe
709-729-2861, Fax: 709-729-1370, seand@gov.nl.ca
Director, Policy & Strategic Planning, Jackie Lake-Kavanagh
709-729-0543, Fax: 709-729-3949, jackiekavanagh@gov.nl.ca
Director, Fines Administration, Susan Roberts
709-729-0250, Fax: 709-729-0595
Director, Court Services, Pamela Ryder-Lahey
709-729-2081, Fax: 709-729-2161

Associated Agencies, Boards & Commissions:
• Human Rights Commission
• Newfoundland & Labrador Board of Commissioners of Public Utilities
• Newfoundland & Labrador Legal Aid Commission
#300, 251 Empire Ave.
PO Box 399 C
St. John's, NL A1C 5J9
709-753-7863 Fax: 709-753-6226 800-563-9911
nlac@legalaid.nl.ca
The Legal Aid Commission ensures that persons with limited financial means have access to legal counsel.
• Royal Newfoundland Constabulary Public Complaints Commission
Bally Rou Place
#E-160, 280 Torbay Rd.
St. John's, NL A1A 3W8
709-729-0950 Fax: 709-729-1302
rnccomplaintscommission@gov.nl.ca
www.justice.gov.nl.ca/rncpcc
The Royal Newfoundland Constabulary Public Complaints Commission is an independent review authority established under Statute to hear and investigate complaints against members of the Royal Newfoundland Constabulary and, when appropriate, to conduct public hearings in respect of particular complaints.

Courts & Legal Services

Assistant Deputy Minister, Donna Ballard
709-729-0288, Fax: 709-729-2129, dballard@gov.nl.ca
Director, Legal Information Services, Sean Dawe
709-729-2861, Fax: 709-729-1370, seand@gov.nl.ca

Public Safety & Enforcement

Assistant Deputy Minister, Paul Noble
709-729-7357, Fax: 709-729-2129, pauln@gov.nl.ca
Superintendent, Prisons, Graham Rogerson
709-729-2978, Fax: 709-729-4312, grahamrogerson@gov.nl.ca
Chief, Royal Newfoundland Constabulary, R.P. Johnston
709-729-8155

Senior Legislative Counsel

Assistant Deputy Minister & Chief Legislative Counsel, Kimberly Hawley-George
709-729-4766, Fax: 709-729-2129, kimhawle@gov.nl.ca

Department of Labrador & Aboriginal Affairs

Confederation Bldg., East Block, 6th Fl., PO Box 8700, St. John's, NL A1B 4J6
709-729-4776 Fax: 709-729-4900
877-788-8822
laa@gov.nl.ca
www.laa.gov.nl.ca

Responsible for coordinating government's activities related to Labrador Affairs & Aboriginal Affairs, including developing policy & programs, managing federal-provincial agreements, negotiating land claims, public information & all matters of significant public interest in Labrador.The principal tasks of the Department in the field of Aboriginal Affairs are policy development for Aboriginal issues, negotiating land claims treaties & self-government agreements, implementing & managing land claims agreements once achieved & providing public information & education in matters related to land claims.The principal tasks of the Department in the field of Labrador Affairs are developing policies & programs related to significant issues of Government interest in Labrador, managing Federal-Provincial Agreements related to the development of Labrador & managing Federal-Provincial Agreements for the Innu & Inuit communities of Labrador. As of October 2011, this Department will become Intergovernmental & Aboriginal Affairs.

Acts Administered:
Labrador Inuit Land Claims Agreement Act

Minister & Minister Responsible, Labrador Affairs, Hon. Nick McGrath
709-729-3400
Acting Deputy Minister, Sean Dutton
709-896-1780, Fax: 709-896-0045, sdutton@gov.nl.ca
Assistant Deputy Minister, Labrador Affairs, Ron Bowles
709-896-1780, Fax: 709-896-0045, rabowles@gov.nl.ca
Assistant Deputy Minister, Aboriginal Affairs, Aubrey Gover
709-896-4776, Fax: 709-896-4900, aubreygover@gov.nl.ca
Director, Policy & Planning, Brian Harvey
709-729-1487, Fax: 709-729-4900, brianharvey@gov.nl.ca
Director, Communications, John Tompkins
709-729-1780, Fax: 709-729-0045, jtompkins@gov.nl.ca
Director, Aboriginal Planning Lead, Gale Warren
709-737-1249, gwarren@gov.nl.ca
Director, Labrador Affairs, Michelle Watkins
709-896-1780, Fax: 709-896-0045, michellewatkins@gov.nl.ca
Senior Negotiator, Inuit Land Claims, Ruby Carter
709-729-0137, Fax: 709-729-4900, rcarter@gov.nl.ca

Department of Municipal Affairs

West Block, Main Fl., Confederation Bldg., PO Box 8700, St. John's, NL A1B 4J6
709-729-3046 Fax: 709-729-0943
mainfo@gov.nl.ca
www.ma.gov.nl.ca

Works with municipalities to ensure communities are properly managed & planned to ensure residents have a high standard of living in a clean, healthy & safe environment. The department is responsible for community-related activities such as the Office of the Fire Commissioner, the Emergency Measures Organization, Engineering & Land Use Planning.

Acts Administered:
Assessment Act, 2006
Avian Emblem Act
Building Standards Act
City of Corner Brook Act
City of Mount Pearl Act
City of St. John's Act
Coat of Arms Act
Commemoration Day Act
Crown Corporations Local Taxation Act
Emergency Services Act
Evacuated Communities Act
Family Homes Expropriation Act
Firefighters' Protection Act
Fire Prevention Act, 1991
Floral Emblem Act
Housing Act
Labrador Act
Mineral Emblem Act
Municipal Affairs Act
Municipal Elections Act
Municipalities Act, 1999
Provincial Anthem Act
Provincial Flag Act
Remembrance Day Act
St. John's Centennial Foundation Act
St. John's Municipal Council Parks Act
Standard Time Act
Taxation of Utilities & Cable Television Companies Act
Urban & Rural Planning Act, 2000
City of St. John's Municipal Taxation Act
Fire Protection Services Act
Municipal Authorities Amendment Act, 1991

Minister, Hon. Kevin O'Brien
709-729-3046, Fax: 709-729-0943, kevinobrien@gov.nl.ca
Deputy Minister, Sandra Barnes
709-729-3049, Fax: 709-729-0943, sbarnes@gov.nl.ca
Assistant Deputy Minister, Employment Support, Rick Healey
709-729-3016, Fax: 709-729-0943, rhealey@gov.nl.ca
Assistant Deputy Minister, Municipal Engineering & Planning, Cluney Mercer
709-729-3051, Fax: 709-729-0477, mercercg@gov.nl.ca
Assistant Deputy Minister, Municipal Support & Policy, Paul C. Smith
709-729-3066, Fax: 709-729-4475, smithp@gov.nl.ca
Director, Local Governance, Chad M. Blundon
709-729-5519, Fax: 709-729-4475, chadblundon@gov.nl.ca
Director, Financial & General Operations, Scott Jones
709-729-5292, Fax: 709-729-5535, scottjones@gov.nl.ca
Director, Communications, Ken Morrissey
709-729-1983, Fax: 709-729-0943, kenmorrissey@gov.nl.ca
Director, Fire & Emergency Services, Pam Rodgers
709-729-6794, Fax: 709-729-5609, prodgers@gov.nl.ca

Associated Agencies, Boards & Commissions:
• Burin Peninsula Waste Management Corporation
PO Box 510
Burin Bay Arm, NL A0E 1G0
709-891-1717 Fax: 709-891-1727
info@burinpenwaste.com
burinpenwaste.com
• Eastern Waste Management Commission
#200, 120 Lemarchant Rd.
St. John's, NL A1C 2H2
709-579-7960 Fax: 709-579-5392
info@easternwaste.ca
easternwaste.ca
• Green Bay Waste Authority
PO Box 116
South Brook, NL A0J 1S0
709-657-2233 Fax: 709-657-2133 877-657-2233
info@greenbaywaste.com
greenbaywaste.com
• Northern Peninsula Regional Service Board
PO Box 130
St. Anthony, NL
709-454-3110 Fax: 709-454-3818
nprsb@nf.aibn.com
norpenwaste.com

Department of Natural Resources

Natural Resources Bldg., 50 Elizabeth Ave., 7th Fl., PO Box 8700, St. John's, NL A1B 4J6
709-729-2920 Fax: 709-729-0059
www.nr.gov.nl.ca

Responsible for the management of the province's mineral, energy, land, forest & wildlife resources in a manner that will ensure optimum benefits for the people of the province.

Acts Administered:
Abitibi-Consolidated Rights & Assets Act
Agrologists Act
Animal Health & Protection Act
Animal Protection Act
Canada-Newfoundland & Labrador Atlantic Accord Implementation Newfoundland & Labrador Act
Canada-Newfoundland & Labrador Oil & Gas Spills & Debris Liability Newfoundland & Labrador Regulations
Offshore Area Oil & Gas Operations Regulations
Offshore Area Petroleum Diving Newfoundland & Labrador Regulations
Churchill Falls (Labrador) Corporation Limited (Lease) Act, 1961
Crop Insurance Act
Dog Act
Donation of Food Act (jointly with Department of Health & Community Services)
Electrical Power Control Act, 1994
Abitibi-Consolidated Inc. & Abitibi Partner Exemption Order, 2002
Corner Brook Pulp & Paper Limited Exemption Order
Granite Canal Hydroelectric Project Exemption Order
Labrador Hydro Project Exemption Order
Newfoundland & Labrador Hydro-Abitibi Consolidated Inc. Exemption Order
Newfoundland & Labrador Hydro-Abitibi Consolidated Inc. Stephensville Operations Exemption Order
Newfoundland & Labrador Hydro-Corner Brook Pulp & Paper Limited Exemption Order
Water Management Regulations
Endangered Species Act (jointly with Department of Environment and Conservation)
Energy Corporation Act
Energy Corporation of Newfoundland & Labrador Water Rights Act
Farm Practices Protection Act
Farm Products Corporation Act
Food & Drug Act
Forest Protection Act
Forestry Act
Cutting of Timber Regulations
Directed Sale of Timber Regulations
Forest Fire Offence & Penalty Regulation
Forest Fire Regulations
Forest Fires Liability & Compensation Regulations
Forest Land Management & Taxation Regulations
Forest Management Districts Proclamation
Mill Regulations
Timber Royalty Regulations
Timber Scaling Regulations
Health & Community Services Act (jointly with Department of Health & Community Services)
Heritage Animals Act
Designation of Inspectors Order
Newfoundland Pony Designation Order
Hydro Corporation Act, 2007
Labrador Inuit Land Claims Agreement Act
Livestock Act
Livestock Regulations
Livestock Health Act
Livestock Health Regulations
Livestock Insurance Act
Livestock Owners Compensation Order
Lower Churchill Development Act
Meat Inspection Act
Meat Inspection Regulations
Mineral Act
Copper-in-Concentrate Exemption Order, 2009
Description of Lands Open for Staking in respect of which the Mineral Claims Recorder shall Issue only Map Staked Licenses Order
Mineral Act Baie Verte Area Exemption Regulations
Mineral Regulations
Nickel-in-Concentrate Exemption Order, 2009
Voisey's Bay Nickel Company Limited Primary Production Order
Voisey's Bay Nickel Company Limited Matte Plant Exemption Order
Mineral Holdings Impost Act
Mineral Holdings Impost Regulations
Mining Act
Mining Regulations
Small Scale Operations Regulations
Miscellaneous Financial Provisions Act, 1975
Motorized Snow Vehicles & All-Terrain Vehicles Act (jointly with Government Services)
Motorized Snow Vehicles & All-Terrain Vehicles Regulations
Natural Products Marketing Act
Agricultural Products Marketing Board Appeal Regulations
Agricultural Products Marketing Board Order
Assessment of Over-Marketing Regulations, 2009
Berry Regulations
Chicken Farmers of Newfoundland & Labrador Licensing Regulations
Chicken Farmers of Newfoundland & Labrador Quota Regulations
Chicken Farmers of Newfoundland & Labrador Marketing Board Regulations
Consolidated Chicken Farmers of Newfoundland & Labrador Order
Newfoundland & Labrador Chicken Marketing Scheme
Egg Regulations
Egg Scheme, 2000
Milk Regulations, 1998
Milk Scheme, 1998
Plebiscite Regulations
Newfoundland & Labrador Power Commission (Water Power) Act
Petroleum & Natural Gas Act
Oil Royalty Regulations
Petroleum Drilling Regulations
Petroleum Regulations
Port au Port Peninsula Petroleum & Natural Gas Development Area Order
Royalty Regulations, 2003
Plant Protection Act
Control of Nurseries & Dealers in Nursery Stock Regulations
Plant Quarantine Regulations
Seed Potato Regulations
Poultry & Poultry Products Act
Egg Grading & Inspection Regulations
Quarry Materials Act, 1998
Quarry Leases Rental Order
Quarry Materials Regulations
Revenue Administration Act
Undeveloped Minerals Areas Act
Undeveloped Minerals Areas Order
Vegetable Grading Act
Veterinary Medical Act, 2004
Wilderness & Ecological Reserves Act (jointly with Environment and Conservation)

Minister, Hon. Jerome P. Kennedy
709-729-2920, Fax: 709-729-0059, JeromeKennedy@gov.nl.ca
Deputy Minister, Diana Dalton
709-729-2766, Fax: 709-729-0059, dianadalton@gov.nl.ca
Assistant Deputy Minister, Keith Deering
709-729-2269, Fax: 709-637-2461, keithdeering@gov.nl.ca
Director, Communications, Heather Maclean
709-729-5282, Fax: 709-729-0059, heathermaclean@gov.nl.ca
Director, Strategic Planning & Policy Coordination, Tanya Noseworthy
709-729-1466, tanyanoseworthy@gov.nl.ca
Director, Mineral Lands, Kenneth Andrews
709-729-6425, Fax: 709-729-6782, kenandrews@gov.nl.ca
Director, Animal Health & Provincial Veterinarian, Dr. Hugh Whitney
709-729-6879, Fax: 709-729-0055, hughwhitney@gov.nl.ca

Associated Agencies, Boards & Commissions:
• Canada-Newfoundland Offshore Petroleum Board
TD Place
140 Water St., 5th Fl.
St. John's, NL A1C 6H6
709-778-1400 Fax: 709-778-1473
information@cnlopb.nl.ca
www.cnlopb.nl.ca
Other Communication: Core Storage & Research Centre, Phone: 709-778-1500, Email: csrc@cnlopb.nl.na
The Canada-Newfoundland Offshore Petroleum Board manages the petroleum resources in the Newfoundland offshore area on behalf of the Government of Canada & the Government of Newfoundland & Labrador. The Board's authority is derived from the legislation implementing the 1985 Atlantic Accord between the two governments.The Environmental Affairs department ensures that offshore oil & gas industrial activities proceed in an environmentally acceptable manner & evaluates the effect of the offshore environment upon the safety of offshore activities & by ensuring protection of the environment during the conduct of these activities. Working in close consultation with the Operations & Safety department, Environmental Affairs assesses the effects of environmental conditions, such as winds, waves & ice conditions, in the Newfoundland offshore area upon the safety of operations. Environmental Affairs reviews operators' plans for collecting the weather, oceanographic & ice data that they are required to measure at offshore

Agrifoods Development
Provincial Agriculture Bldg., Brookfield Rd., PO Box 8700, St. John's, NL A1B 4J6
709-729-6588 Fax: 709-729-2674
To contribute to economic & rural development throughout the province by promoting the continued development, expansion & diversification of competitive & sustainable primary & value-added agrifood businesses.
Assistant Deputy Minister, Keith Deering
709-729-3787, Fax: 709-729-0973, keithdeering@gov.nl.ca
Director, Animal Health Division & Provincial Veterinarian, Dr. Hugh Whitney
709-729-6879, Fax: 709-729-0055, hughwhitney@gov.nl.ca
Director, Agriculture Business Development Division, Cindy MacDonald
709-637-2077
Director, Production & Marketing Division, Dave Jennings
709-637-2046, davejennings@gov.nl.ca
Director, Land Resource Stewardship, Carey Richard
709-637-2081, Fax: 709-637-2586, rcarey@gov.nl.ca

Energy Branch
Associate Deputy Minister, Charles Bown
709-729-2349, Fax: 709-729-2871, cbown@gov.nl.ca
Director, Electricity & Alternative Energy, Walter Parsons
709-729-6760, Fax: 709-729-2508, walterparsons@gov.nl.ca
Assistant Deputy Minister, Petroleum Development, Wes Foote
709-729-2206, Fax: 709-729-2508, wesfoote@gov.nl.ca
Director, Energy Economics, Wayne Andrews
709-729-5899, wayneandrews@gov.nl.ca

Forestry Services
Fortis Bldg., PO Box 2006, Corner Brook, NL A2H 6J8
709-637-2284 Fax: 709-634-4378
Manages & conserves the Province's ecosystems, under the principles of sustainable development, using an ecologically based management philosophy, & sound environmental practices. This is achieved through the implementation of forest management programs, such as silviculture, access road construction, forest fire suppression, insect control, management planning, tree nursery operations, inventory, dealing with wildlife in residential areas, collisions or similar situations, & public relations. In addition the Department is responsible for issuing permits under various legislation as well as the enforcement of forestry & wildlife regulations in such areas as hunting & timber harvesting.

Forestry Branch (Newfoundland Forest Service) (NFS)
Fortis Bldg., PO Box 2006, Corner Brook, NL A2H 6J8
709-637-2349 Fax: 709-637-2403
Assistant Deputy Minister, James Evans
709-637-2339, Fax: 709-637-2461
Director, Forest Engineering & Industry Services, Eric Young
709-637-2350, Fax: 709-637-2403, emyoung@gov.nl.ca
Director, Forest Ecosystem Management, Ivan Downton
709-634-2284, idownton@gov.nl.ca
Director, Legislation & Compliance, Hubert Smith
709-637-2041, Fax: 709-637-2083, hubertsmith@gov.nl.ca

Mines Branch
Promotes & facilitates the sustainable development of the province's mineral & energy resources through its resource assessment, management & development activities for the overall benefit of the citizens of Newfoundland & Labrador.
Asst. Deputy Minister, David Liverman
709-729-2768, Fax: 709-729-2871, dliverman@gov.nl.ca
Director, Mineral Lands Division, Kenneth Andrews
709-729-6425, Fax: 709-729-6782, kenandrews@gov.nl.ca
Acting Director, Mineral Development, Alex Smith
709-729-6379, Fax: 709-729-3493
Asst. Deputy Minister, Industrial Benefits, Brian Condon
709-729-1644, Fax: 709-729-0868, bcondon@gov.nl.ca

Geological Survey
709-729-4014 Fax: 709-729-4270
Director, Lawson Dickson
709-729-2453, wldickson@gov.nl.ca

Eastern
PO Box 2222, Gander, NL A1V 5T4
709-256-1450 Fax: 709-256-1459
Regional Ecosystem Director, David Fong
709-256-1451

Labrador
PO Box 3014 B, Happy Valley-Goose Bay, NL A0P 1E0
709-896-3405
Other Communication: Fax: 709-896-3747 (Forestry); 896-0188 (Wildlife)
Regional Ecosystem Director, Carroll Colin
709-896-9377, Fax: 709-896-3747, colincarroll@gov.nl.ca

Western
Massey Drive Bldg., PO Box 2006, Corner Brook, NL A2H 6J8
709-637-2409 Fax: 709-639-1377
Regional Ecosystem Director, Perry Benoit
709-637-2692

Newfoundland & Labrador Public Service Commission

2 Canada Dr., 3rd Fl., PO Box 8700, St. John's, NL A1B 4J6
709-729-5810 Fax: 709-729-6234
www.gov.nl.ca/psc

Acts Administered:
Public Service Commission Act
Minister Responsible, Hon. Tom Marshall, Q.C.
709-729-3775, Fax: 709-729-2232, tommarshall@gov.nl.ca
Chair & Chief Executive Officer, Ed Walsh
709-729-2650, Fax: 709-729-3178, ewalsh@gov.nl.ca
Vice-Chair, Vacant
709-729-2651
Commissioner, Ann Chafe
709-729-2659, Fax: 709-729-3178, annchafe@gov.nl.ca

Public Service Secretariat

Confederation Bldg., Main Fl., East Block, PO Box 8700, St. John's, NL A1B 4J6
709-729-6479 Fax: 709-729-2156
Minister Responsible, Hon. Tom Marshall, Q.C.
709-729-3775, Fax: 709-729-2232, tommarshall@gov.nl.ca
Deputy Minister, Brenda Caul
709-729-2633, Fax: 709-729-1746, bcaul@gov.nl.ca
Director, Communications - Finance, Mark King
709-729-6830, Fax: 709-729-2232, markking@gov.nl.ca

Human Resources
Assistant Deputy Minister, Chantelle McDonald Newhook
709-729-3106, cnewhook@gov.nl.ca
Acting Director, Strategic Initiatives, Jeff Butt
709-729-2223, jeffkbutt@gov.nl.ca
Director, Policy & Planning, Marie Wells
709-729-7350, mwells@gov.nl.ca

Labour Relations
Assistant Deputy Minister, Geoff Williams
709-729-3559, Fax: 709-729-1746, geoffwilliams@gov.nl.ca
Executive Director, Employee Relations, Brian Miller
709-729-1585, Fax: 709-729-6842, brianmiller@gov.nl.ca
Director, Organizational Management & Design, Tony Cuomo
709-729-3387, Fax: 709-729-2156, tcuomo@gov.nl.ca
Director, Classification & Compensation, Terry Kennedy
709-729-7284, Fax: 709-729-7455, kennedyt@gov.nl.ca

Newfoundland & Labrador Board of Commissioners of Public Utilities

PO Box 21040, St. John's, NL A1A 5B2
709-726-8600 Fax: 709-726-9604
866-782-0006
ito@pub.nf.ca
www.pub.nf.ca
Regulates electrical utilities in Newfoundland & Labrador.
Acts Administered:
Access to Information and Protection of Privacy Act
Automobile Insurance Act
Electric Power Control Act
Expropriation Act
Hydro Corporation Act
Insurance Companies Act
Motor Carrier Act
Petroleum Products Act
Public Utilities Act
Public Utilities Acquisition of Lands Act
Chair & CEO, Andy Wells
709-726-1133, awells@pub.nl.ca
Vice-Chair, Darlene Whalen
709-726-0955, dwhalen@pub.nl.ca
Director, Corporate Services & Board Secretary, G. Cheryl Blundon
709-726-8600, Fax: 709-726-9604, cblundon@pub.nl.ca
Director, Regulatory & Advisory Services, Robert Byrne
709-726-0742, rbyrne@pub.nl.ca

Newfoundland & Labrador Research & Development Corporation (RDC)

187 Kenmount Rd., PO Box 13067 A, St. John's, NL A1B 3V8
709-758-0913 Fax: 709-758-0927
info@researchnl.com
www.researchnl.com
The RDC is a provincial Crown corporation established in 2008 to improve Newfoundland & Labrador's research & development capabilities.
Minister Responsible, Hon. Keith Hutchings
709-729-4728, Fax: 709-729-0654, keithhutchings@gov.nl.ca
Chair, Jackie Sheppard
Chief Executive Officer, Glenn Janes
Director, Business Development, Steve Mercer
709-758-0984, stevemercer@researchnl.com
Manager, Marketing & Communications, Jeff Green
709-758-0973, jeffsgreen@researchnl.com
Executive Assistant, Brenda Baird
709-758-0912, Fax: 709-758-0927, brendabaird@researchnl.com

Provincial Advisory Council on the Status of Women

#103, 15 Hallett Cres., St. John's, NL A1B 4C4
709-753-7270 Fax: 709-753-2606
877-753-7270
info@pacsw.ca
www.pacsw.com
Minister Responsible, Hon. Charlene Johnson
709-729-0173, Fax: 709-729-1049, charlenejohnson@gov.nl.ca
President/CEO, Linda Ross
709-753-7270, lindaross@pacsw.ca
Director, Communications, Danielle Finney
daniellefinney@pacsw.ca
Office Manager, Sandy Abbott
709-753-7270, Fax: 709-753-2606, sandyabbot@pacsw.ca

Department of Tourism, Culture & Recreation

Confederation Bldg., West Block, 2nd Fl., PO Box 8700, St. John's, NL A1B 4J6
709-729-0862 Fax: 709-729-0870
tcrinfo@gov.nl.ca
www.tcr.gov.nl.ca
Ensures the development of provincial vacation & business travel markets. The department conserves, preserves & protects natural & cultural resources & promotes the resources for economic benefit, sport & recreation in the province. It also protects, preserves & develops the historic resources of the province. Programs promote the development of travel & tourism & assist in transforming the province's natural & cultural attractions into opportunities for employment & revenue generation.
Acts Administered:
Arts Council Act
Books Preservation of Copies Act
Boxing Authority Act
Colonial Buildings Act
Cruiseship Authority Act
Grand Concourse Authority Act
Historic Resources Act
Inkeepers Act
Newspapers & Books Act
Rooms Act
Tourist Establishments Act
Minister, Hon. Derrick Dalley
709-729-0659, 877-787-0707, Fax: 709-729-0662, DerrickDalley@gov.nl.ca
Deputy Minister, Rick Hayward
709-729-3555, Fax: 709-729-0662
Director, Communications, Diana Quinton
709-729-0928, Fax: 709-729-0662, DianaQuinton@gov.nl.ca
Director, Human Resources, Gerry Crocker
709-729-5292, gcrocker@gov.nl.ca
Director, Tourism Marketing, Carmela Murphy
709-729-2831, Fax: 709-729-0057, carmelamurphy@gov.nl.ca
Director, Strategic Planning & Policy, Janet Miller-Pitt
709-729-5623, Fax: 709-729-0870, jpitt@gov.nl.ca

Associated Agencies, Boards & Commissions:
• Newfoundland & Labrador Film Development Corporation
12 King's Bridge Rd.
St. John's, NL A1C 3K3
709-738-3456 Fax: 709-739-1680 877-738-3456
info@nlfdc.ca
www.nlfdc.ca

Culture & Recreation
The department administers archeology permits, the Art Procurement Program, the Heritage Foundation of Newfoundland & Labrador, provides grants to artists, arts organizations, museums & archives through the Newfoundland & Labrador Arts Council, provides grants to assists the Newfoundland & Labrador Film Development Corporation & administers provincial historic sites.
Asst. Deputy Minister, Mark Jones
709-729-3609, Fax: 709-729-0870
Director, Culture, Recreation & Sport, Jim Tee
709-729-5241, Fax: 709-729-5293
Director, Art Gallery of Newfoundland & Labrador, Shauna McCabe
709-757-8042, Fax: 709-757-8041
Director, Arts & Culture Centres, Doreen McCarthy
709-729-3453
Manager, Cultural Affairs, Elizabeth A. Channing
709-729-3905, Fax: 709-729-5952
Director, Newfoundland Museum, Penney Houlden
709-757-8022, Fax: 709-757-8021
CEO, The Rooms, Dean Brinton
709-757-8012, Fax: 709-757-8017

Tourism
Asst. Deputy Minister, Mary Taylor-Ash
709-729-2821, Fax: 709-729-5293, mtaylorash@gov.nl.ca
Director, Tourism Product Development, Juanita Keel-Ryan
709-729-1708, Fax: 709-729-0474, jkeelryan@gov.nl.ca
Director, Tourism Marketing Division, Carmela Murphy
709-729-2831, Fax: 709-729-0057
Manager, Labrador Regional Office, Rose Dyson
709-896-8480

Department of Transportation & Works

Confederation Bldg., West Block, 6th Fl., PO Box 8700, St. John's, NL A1B 4J6
709-729-3679 Fax: 709-729-4285
twminister@gov.nl.ca
www.tw.gov.nl.ca
To provide a safe, efficient & sustainable transportation system & to provide landlord services & support services such as leasing & mail services for all government departments. The department liaises with other agencies & the federal government to ensure the overall public works & transportation needs & interest of the province are fully provided & protected.
Acts Administered:
Expropriation Act
Highway Traffic Act
Local Road Boards Act
Motor Carrier Act
Rail Service Act
Transportation & Works Act
Minister, Hon. Thomas J. Hedderson
709-729-3679, 866-996-5670, Fax: 709-729-4285, thedderson@gov.nl.ca
Deputy Minister, Jamie Chippett
709-729-3676, Fax: 709-729-4285
Director, Communications, Roger Scaplen
709-729-3015, Fax: 709-729-4285, rogerscaplen@gov.nl.ca
Legal Advisor, David Jones
709-729-1966, Fax: 709-729-6934, georgehoran@gov.nl.ca
Social Media: davidj@gov.nl.ca

Road & Air Transportation
Assistant Deputy Minister, Gary Goose
709-729-3796, Fax: 709-729-0283, gosseg@gov.nl.ca
Director, Highway Design & Construction, Brandon MacDonald
709-729-0648, Fax: 709-729-0283
Senior Engineer, Highway Design, Bill Skanes
709-729-5962, Fax: 709-729-0283

Chief Operating Officer, Marine Services, Tom Prim
709-429-3278, Fax: 709-729-6934

Strategic & Corporate Services
709-729-3019 Fax: 709-729-4658
Assistant Deputy Minister, Weldon Moores
709-729-6882, Fax: 709-729-3418, wmoores@gov.nl.ca

Works Branch
709-729-3019 Fax: 709-729-4658
Asst. Deputy Minister, Gerald Antle
709-729-5672, Fax: 709-729-5934, antleg@gov.nl.ca
Director, Design & Construction, Gunar Leja
709-729-1969, Fax: 709-729-0646, lejag@gov.nl.ca
Director, Engineering Support Services, Keith Noel
709-729-5786, Fax: 709-729-5934, noelka@gov.nl.ca
Director, Realty Services, Martin Balodis
709-729-3690, Fax: 709-729-0984

Newfoundland & Labrador Workplace Health, Safety & Compensation Commission

146 - 148 Forest Rd., PO Box 9000, St. John's, NL A1A 3B8
709-778-1000 Fax: 709-738-1714
800-563-9000
general.inquiries@whscc.nl.ca
www.whscc.nf.ca
Other Communication: Grand Falls toll-free: 800-563-3448; Corner Brook toll-free: 800-563-2772

Utilizing skilled, professional employees, in partnership with workplace parties, the commission facilitates safe & healthy workplaces by assisting employers & workers to prevent accidents, & manage workplace injuries/illnesses & return-to-work processes. Operating as the administrator of the workers' compensation insurance program, the commission provides a reasonable level of benefits to injured workers & their dependents based on reasonable assessment rates for employers, while maintaining or exceeding service level performance when compared to other jurisdictions in Canada.

Minister Responsible, Hon. Paul Davis
709-729-6670, Fax: 709-729-1503, padavis@gov.nl.ca
Chair, Ralph Tucker
CEO, Leslie Galway

Government of the Northwest Territories

Seat of Government: PO Box 1320, Yellowknife, NT X1A 2L9
www.gov.nt.ca

The Northwest Territories was reconstituted September 1, 1905. It has an area of 1,140,834.90 km2, & the StatsCan population in 2006 was 41,464. On April 1, 1999, the Northwest Territories was divided into two new territories: Nunavut Territories and the as yet unnamed territory (known as the Northwest Territories). The Northwest Territories is governed by a fully elected Legislative Assembly of 19 members elected for a four-year term. Government is by consensus rather than party politics. The Legislature elects the Premier & a seven-member Executive Council, which is charged with the operation of government & the establishment of program & spending priorities. The Commissioner of the Northwest Territories is appointed by the Federal Government, & serves a role similar to that of a Lieutenant Governor in provincial jurisdictions.

Department of the Executive
PO Box 1320, Yellowknife, NT X1A 2L9
executive@gov.nt.ca
Minister, Hon. Bob McLeod
867-669-2311, Fax: 867-873-0385, bob_mcleod@gov.nt.ca

Cabinet Secretariat
867-873-7817 Fax: 867-873-0279
Secretary to Cabinet, Dave Ramsden
867-873-7100, dave_ramsden@gov.nt.ca
Deputy Secretary to Cabinet, Alan Cash
867-873-7652, Fax: 867-873-0279, alan_cash@gov.nt.ca
Asst. Deputy Minister, Executive Operations, David Stewart
867-873-7823, david_stewart@gov.nt.ca
Director, Corporate Services, Cathy Myres
867-873-7148, cathy_myres@gov.nt.ca
Advisor, Status of Women, Gail Cyr
867-920-3106, gail_cyr@gov.nt.ca
Chief of Protocol, Carmen Moore
867-873-7167, carmen_moore@gov.nt.ca
Territorial Statistician, Bureau of Statistics, Angelo Cocco
867-873-7147, angelo_cocco@gov.nt.ca

Office of the Commissioner

#803 Northwest Tower, PO Box 1320, Yellowknife, NT X1A 2L9
867-873-7400 Fax: 867-873-0223
888-270-3318
commissioner@gov.nt.ca
www.commissioner.gov.nt.ca

Commissioner, Hon. George Tuccaro
867-873-7400, Fax: 867-873-0223, george_tuccaro@gov.nt.ca
Assistant to the Commissioner, Phila Fyten
867-873-7332, phila_fyten@gov.nt.ca

Office of the Premier

Legislative Assembly Bldg., PO Box 1320, Yellowknife, NT X1A 2L9
867-669-2311 Fax: 867-873-0385
premier@gov.nt.ca
www.premier.gov.nt.ca

Premier, Hon. Bob McLeod
867-669-2311, Fax: 867-873-0385, bob_mcleod@gov.nt.ca
Communications Officer, Vacant
867-669-2302
Press Secretary, Drew Williams
867-669-2304, drew_williams@gov.nt.ca
Executive Assistant, Stephen Dunbar
867-669-2307, stephen_dunbar@gov.nt.ca

Executive Council

PO Box 1320, Yellowknife, NT X1A 2L9
executive@gov.nt.ca
www.executive.gov.nt.ca
Other Communication: Protocol: executive_protocol@gov.nt.ca; Corporate Communications: executive_communications@gov.nt.ca; Corporate Services: executive_services@gov.nt.ca

Coordination & advisory functions are performed for the Government of the Northwest Territories.

Premier-elect, Hon. Bob McLeod
867-669-2311, Fax: 867-873-0385, bob_mcleod@gov.nt.ca
Minister, Portfolio Undecided, Hon. Glen Abernethy
867-669-2223, Fax: 867-873-0276, glen_abernethy@gov.nt.ca
Minister, Portfolio Undecided, Hon. Tom Beaulieu
867-669-2223, Fax: 867-873-0276, tom_beaulieu@gov.nt.ca
Minister, Portfolio Undecided, Hon. Jackson Lafferty
867-669-2399, Fax: 867-873-0274, jackson_lafferty@gov.nt.ca
Minister, Portfolio Undecided, Hon. Robert C. McLeod
867-669-2223, Fax: 867-873-0276, robert_c_mcleod@gov.nt.ca
Minister, Portfolio Undecided, Hon. J. Michael Miltenberger
867-669-2355, Fax: 867-873-0596, michael_miltenberger@gov.nt.ca
Note: The Honourable J. Michael Miltenberger is also the Minister Responsible for the NorthwestTerritories Housing Corporation.
Minister, Portfolio Undecided, Hon. David Ramsay
867-669-2223, Fax: 867-873-0276, david_ramsay@gov.nt.ca

Intergovernmental Affairs - Ottawa
613-234-6525 Fax: 613-234-9667
Contact, Rose McConville
rose_mcconville@gov.nt.ca

Legislation & House Planning
Legislative Coordinator, Kevin O'Keefe
867-669-2239, Fax: 867-873-0139, kevin_o'keefe@gov.nt.ca

Legislative Assembly

c/o Clerk's Office, PO Box 1320, Yellowknife, NT X1A 2L9
867-669-2299 Fax: 867-920-4735
800-661-0784
www.assembly.gov.nt.ca

Clerk, Tim Mercer
867-669-2299, tim_mercer@gov.nt.ca
Speaker-elect, Hon. Jackie Jacobson
867-669-2200, 800-661-0784, jackie_jacobson@gov.nt.ca
Deputy Clerk, Doug Schauerte
867-669-2277, doug_schauerte@gov.nt.ca
Director, Corporate Services, Darrin Ouellette
867-669-2334, Fax: 867-920-4735, darrin_ouellette@gov.nt.ca
Director, Research Services, Colette Langlois
867-669-2212, colette_langlois@gov.nt.ca
Legislative Librarian, Vera Raschke
867-669-2203, Fax: 867-873-0207, vera_raschke@gov.nt.ca
Acting Public Affairs & Communications Advisor, Jessica Fournier
867-669-2230, jessica_fournier@gov.nt.ca.ca

Elections NWT/Plebiscite Office
YK Centre East, #7, 4915-48th St., 3rd Fl., Yellowknife, NT X1A 3S4
867-920-6999 Fax: 867-873-0366
800-661-0796
electionsnwt@gov.nt.ca
www.electionsnwt.com
Other Communication: Toll-Free Fax: 1-800-661-0872
Chief Electoral Officer, David M. Brock
867-920-6999, david_brock@gov.nt.ca

Office of the Languages Commissioner
Laing Bldg., 5003 - 49 St., Yellowknife, NT X1A 2P4
867-873-7034 Fax: 867-873-0357
800-661-0889
langcom@gov.nt.ca
www.nwtlanguagescommissioner.ca
Languages Commissioner, Sarah Jerome
876-678-2200, Fax: 867-678-2201, sarah_jerome@gov.nt.ca
Information & Privacy Commissioner, Elaine Keenan-Bengts
867-669-0976, Fax: 867-920-2511, atippcom@theedge.ca
Conflict of Interest Commissioner, Gerald Gerrand
867-669-2298, Fax: 867-873-0276

Standing Committees of the Legislature
www.assembly.gov.nt.ca/_live/pages/wpPages/Committees.aspx
Priorities & Planning; Economic Development & Infrastructure; Rules & Procedures; Government Operations; Social Programs

Seventeenth Legislature - Northwest Territories

PO Box 1320, Yellowknife, NT X1A 2L9
867-669-2200 Fax: 867-920-4735
800-661-0784

Last General Election: October 3, 2011. Maximum Duration: Four years. Salaries, Indemnities & Allowances (April 1, 2007): Members of the Legislative Assembly are entitled to a basic indemnity of $90,199. Members are entitled to a non-taxable annual expense allowance of $6,988 for a Ministers or fors Members living within commuting distance of the capital. Members, who are not Ministers, & who do not live within commuting distance of the capital, are entitled to $10,797 annually. Up to $27,840 annually is paid to Members for accommodation, when their residence is not within 80 km of Yellowknife, & when they are attending sittings of the Legislature & performing constituency duties in Yellowknife. Members will be deducted $127 for each morning or afternoon that they fail to attend the sitting of the Legislature. Members are also provided with a set operating budget to defray the expenses of working on behalf of their constituents. In addition are the following remunerations: Premier $68,602; Minister $48,275; Speaker $39,260; Deputy Speaker $6,352; Deputy Chairperson of Committee of the Whole $3,812; Chairperson of a Standing Committee $5,628. The following is a list of members of the Legislative Assembly. The address in Yellowknife to reach all MLA s is as follows: PO Box 1320, Yellowknife, NT, X1A 2L9.

Members
Hon. Glen Abernethy, Yellowknife - Great Slave
867-669-2290, Fax: 867-873-0276, glen_abernethy@gov.nt.ca
Hon. Tom Beaulieu, Tu Nedhe
867-669-2287, Fax: 867-873-0276, tom_beaulieu@gov.nt.ca, Other Communications: Additional Phone: 867-444-8463
Wendy Bisaro, Yellowknife - Frame Lake
867-669-2274, Fax: 867-873-0276, wendy_bisaro@gov.nt.ca
Frederick Blake Jr., Mackenzie Delta
867-669-2223, Fax: 867-873-0274, frederick_blake@gov.nt.ca
Robert Bouchard, Hay River North
867-669-2223, Fax: 867-873-0276, robert_bouchard@gov.nt.ca
Bob Bromley, Yellowknife - Weledeh
867-669-2272, Fax: 867-873-0276, bob_bromley@gov.nt.ca
Daryl Dolynny, Yellowknife - Range Lake
867-669-2223, Fax: 867-873-0270, daryl_dolynny@gov.nt.ca
Jane Groenewegen, Hay River South
867-874-6141, Fax: 867-874-6143, jane_groenewegen@gov.nt.ca, Other Communications: Yellowknife Phone: 867-669-2292; Fax: 867-873-0276
Robert Hawkins, Yellowknife Centre
867-669-2265, Fax: 867-873-0276, robert_hawkins@gov.nt.ca
Hon. Jackie Jacobson, Nunakput
867-669-2276, Fax: 867-873-0276, jackie_jacobson@gov.nt.ca
Hon. Jackson Lafferty, Monfwi
867-669-2399, Fax: 867-873-0169, jackson_lafferty@gov.nt.ca
Hon. Bob McLeod, Yellowknife South
867-669-2388, Fax: 867-873-0169, bob_mcleod@gov.nt.ca
Hon. Robert C. McLeod, Inuvik Twin Lakes
867-669-2279, Fax: 867-873-0276, robert_mcleod@gov.nt.ca, Other Communications: Additional Phone: 867-678-0319
Kevin A. Menicoche, Nahendeh
867-695-3780, Fax: 867-695-3781, kevin_menicoche@gov.nt.ca, Other Communications: Yellowknife Phone: 867-669-2294; Fax: 867-873-0276
Hon. J. Michael Miltenberger, Thebacha
867-872-5511, Fax: 867-872-5642, michael_miltenberger@gov.nt.ca, Other Communications: Minister's Office: 867-669-2355; Fax: 867-873-0169
Alfred Moses, Inuvik Boot Lake
867-669-2223, Fax: 867-873-0276, alfred_moses@gov.nt.ca
Michael Nadli, Deh Cho
867-669-2223, Fax: 867-873-0276, michael_nadli@gov.nt.ca

Hon. David Ramsay, Kam Lake
867-669-2296, Fax: 867-873-0276, david_ramsay@gov.nt.ca
Norman Yakeleya, Sahtu
867-669-2366, Fax: 867-873-0169, norman_yakeleya@gov.nt.ca

Northwest Territories Government Departments & Agencies

Department of Aboriginal Affairs & Intergovernmental Relations

4910 - 52nd St., PO Box 1320, Yellowknife, NT X1A 2L9
867-873-7143 Fax: 867-873-0233
877-838-8194
nancy_gardiner@gov.nt.ca
www.daair.gov.nt.ca

The Department of Aboriginal Affairs & Intergovernmental Relations is charged with the following responsibilities: to negotiate, implement, & monitor land, resource & self-government agreements; to manage governmental relationships with Aboriginal, federal, provincial, & territorial governments, & with circumpolar countries; to provide advice on federal-provincial-territorial-Aboriginal relations; & to contribute to the political & constitutional development of the Northwest Territories.

Acts Administered:
National Aboriginal Day Act
Tlicho Community Government Act
Tlicho Community Services Agency Act
Tlicho Land Claims & Self-Government Agreement Act

Minister,
867-669-2311, Fax: 867-873-0385
Deputy Minister, Gabriela Sparling
867-873-7143, Fax: 867-873-0233, gabriela_sparling@gov.nt.ca
Director, Implementation, Scott Alexander
867-873-7149, Fax: 867-873-0540, scott_alexander@gov.nt.ca
Director, Intergovernmental Relations, Andy Bevan
867-920-8701, Fax: 867-873-0233, andy_bevan@gov.nt.ca
Director, Policy, Legislation & Communications, Richard Robertson
867-920-3141, Fax: 867-873-0540, richard_robertson@gov.nt.ca
Director, Negotiations, Fred Talen
867-873-7388, Fax: 867-873-0593, fred_talen@gov.nt.ca

Aurora Research Institute (ARI)

191 MacKenzie Rd., PO Box 1450, Inuvik, NT X0E 0T0
867-777-3298 Fax: 867-777-4264
webmaster@nwtresearch.com
www.nwtresearch.com
Other Communication: Twitter: twitter.com/nwtresearch

A division of Aurora College that is dedicated to excellence, leadership & innovations in Northern education & research. Administers the research licencing provisions of the Northwest Territories Scientists Act & provides year round logistical assistance for researchers.

Director, Pippa Seccombe
867-777-3298, pseccombe-hett@auroracollege.nt.ca

Northwest Territories Business Development & Investment Corporation (BDIC)

#701, 5201 - 50th Ave., Yellowknife, NT X1A 3S9
867-920-6455 Fax: 867-765-0652
www.bdic.ca

The BDIC provides access to business financing, support, & development assistance to communities throughout the Northwest Territories. Their focus is the small and mid-sized business sector.

Chair, Darrell Beaulieu
Chief Executive Officer, Pawan Chugh
867-920-3348
Director, Policy, Planning & Operations, Ron Chiasson
867-920-3355
Director, Finance & Subsidiaries, Leonard Kwong
867-920-3339

Department of Education, Culture & Employment (ECE)

PO Box 1320, Yellowknife, NT X1A 2L9
867-669-2399 Fax: 867-873-0431
866-606-5627
www.ece.gov.nt.ca
Other Communication: Jobs North Phone: 867-873-7690; Fax: 867-873-0636; Email: jobsnorth@gov.nt.ca

The Ministry's responsibilities cover the following areas: Early Childhood; Kindergarten to Grade 12; Adult & Post-Secondary Education; Career Development & Employment; Apprenticeship & Occupational Certification; Culture, Heritage & Languages; Income Security; & Labour Services.

Acts Administered:
Apprenticeship, Trade & Occupations Certification Act
Archives Act
Aurora College Act
Child Day Care Act
Education Act
Employment Standards Act
Historical Resources Act
Occupational Training Agreements Act
Official Languages Act
Public Libraries Act
Scientists Act
Senior Citizens Benefits Act
Social Assistance Act
Student Financial Assistance Act

Minister,
867-669-2399, Fax: 867-873-0274
Deputy Minister, Dan Daniels
867-920-6240, Fax: 867-873-0338, dan_daniels@gov.nt.ca
Director, Culture & Heritage, Barb Cameron
867-873-7551, barb_cameron@gov.nt.ca
Director, Official Languages, Albert Canadien
867-920-6484, albert_canadien@gov.nt.ca
Director, Strategic & Business Services, Paul Devitt
867-873-7739, paul_devitt@gov.nt.ca
Director, Education Operations & Development, Janet Grinsted
867-873-7673, janet_grinsted@gov.nt.ca
Director, Advanced Education, Laurie Morton
867-873-7552, laurie_morton@gov.nt.ca
Director, Income Security Programs, Jolene Saturnio
867-920-8921, jolene_saturnio@gov.nt.ca
Director, Early Childhood & School Services, Vacant
867-920-3491
Directeur General, Commission scolaire francophone, Philippe Brulot
867-873-6555, philippe_brulot@gov.nt.ca
Supervisor, Student Financial Assistance, Nicole Beauchamp
867-920-6236, nicole_beauchamp@gov.nt.ca

Associated Agencies, Boards & Commissions:
• Northwest Territories Apprenticeship, Trade & Occupations Certification Board
PO Box 1320
Yellowknife, NT X1A 2L9
867-873-7357 Fax: 867-873-0200
• NWT Arts Council
PO Box 1320 Main
Yellowknife, NT X1A 2L9
867-920-6370 Fax: 867-873-0205
pwnhc.learnnet.nt.ca/artscouncil/

Advanced Education & Income Security
Assistant Deputy Minister, Gloria Iatridis
867-873-7252, Fax: 867-873-0338, gloria_iatridis@gov.nt.ca
Director, Advanced Education, Laurie Morton
867-873-7552, Fax: 867-873-0200, laurie_morton@gov.nt.ca
Manager, Income Security Programs, Lois Walbourne
867-873-7746, Fax: 867-873-0443, lois_walbourne@gov.nt.ca

Education & Culture
867-920-8061 Fax: 867-873-0155
Asst. Deputy Minister, Roy Erasmus
867-920-8061, Fax: 867-873-0338, roy_erasmus@gov.nt.ca
Director, Culture & Heritage, Barb Cameron
867-873-7551, barb_cameron@gov.nt.ca
Director, Early Childhood & School Services, Vacant
867-920-3491, Fax: 867-873-0109
Territorial Archaeologist, Tom Andrews
867-873-7688, tom_andrews@gov.nt.ca
Territorial Archivist, Ian Moir
867-873-7177, ian_moir@gov.nt.ca
Territorial Librarian, Alison Hopkins
867-874-6531, Fax: 867-874-3321, alison_hopkins@gov.nt.ca

Department of Environment & Natural Resources (ENR)

PO Box 1320, Yellowknife, NT X1A 2L9
www.enr.gov.nt.ca

Operations cover a broad spectrum of activities directed at promoting a healthy environment that supports traditional lifestyles within a modern economy. The wise use & protection of natural resources are encouraged. The Department's activities are carried out through the following divisions: Environmental Protection, Forest Management, Policy, Legislation & Communications, Protected Areas Strategy, Informatics, & Wildlife.

Acts Administered:
Environmental Protection Act
Asphalt Paving Industry Emission Regulations
Spill Contingency Planning & Reporting Regulations
Used Oil & Waste Fuel Management Regulations
Environmental Rights Act
Forest Management Act
Forest Protection Act
Natural Resources Conservation Trust Act
Pesticide Act
Waste Reduction & Recovery Act
Beverage Container Regulations
Water Resources Agreement Act
Wildlife Act
Certification & Disposal of Wildlife Regulations
Critical Wildlife Areas Regulations
Sale of Wildlife Regulations
Trapping Regulations
Wildlife Export Regulations
Wildlife General Regulations
Wildlife Management Areas & Zones Regulations
Wildlife Preserves Regulations
Wildlife Sanctuaries Regulations
Species At Risk NWT Act (Not in force)

Minister,
867-669-2355, Fax: 867-873-0596
Deputy Minister, Gary Bohnet
867-873-7401, gary_bohnet@gov.nt.ca
Director, Environment, Ray Case
867-873-7654, Fax: 867-873-0221, ray_case@gov.nt.ca
Director, Policy & Strategic Planning, Doris Eggers
867-920-8046, Fax: 867-873-0114, doris_eggers@gov.nt.ca
Director, Shared Services, Finance & Administration, Nancy Magrum
867-920-8649, Fax: 867-920-2756, nancy_magrum@gov.nt.ca
Director, Forest Management, William Mawdsley
867-872-7725, Fax: 867-872-3019, william_mawdsley@gov.nt.ca
Director, Land & Water, Mary Tapsell
867-920-8069, Fax: 867-873-4229, mary_tapsell@gov.nt.ca
Director, Shared Services & Informatics, Rick Wind
867-920-3327, Fax: 867-920-2756, rick_wind@gov.nt.ca
Acting Director, Wildlife, Lynda Yonge
867-920-8675, Fax: 867-873-0293, lynda_yonge@gov.nt.ca

Regional Offices:

Deh Cho
Milton Bldg., 2nd Fl., PO Box 240, Fort Simpson, NT X0E 0N0
867-695-7450 Fax: 867-695-2381
Regional Superintendent, Carl Lafferty
867-695-7451, carl_lafferty@gov.nt.ca

Inuvik
Semmler Bldg., 2nd Fl., Bag Service #1, Inuvik, NT X0E 0T0
Fax: 867-678-6699
Regional Superintendent, Stephen Charlie
867-678-6690, stephen_charlie@gov.nt.ca

North Slave
PO Box 2668, Yellowknife, NT X1A 2P9
867-873-7184 Fax: 867-873-6230
Regional Superintendent, Fred Mandeville
867-920-6114, fred_mandeville@gov.nt.ca

Sahtu
PO Box 130, Norman Wells, NT X0E 0V0
867-587-3500 Fax: 867-587-3516
Regional Superintendent, Keith Hickling
867-587-3508, keith_hickling@gov.nt.ca

Fort Smith (South Slave)
Sweetgrass Bldg., PO Box 390, Fort Smith, NT X0E 0P0
867-872-6400 Fax: 867-872-4250
Regional Superintendent, Jack Bird
867-872-6401, jack_bird@gov.nt.ca

Department of Finance

Arthur Laing Building, 5th Fl., 5003 - 49th St., PO Box 1320, Yellowknife, NT X1A 2L9
867-873-7117 Fax: 867-873-0414
www.fin.gov.nt.ca

The government of the Northwest Territories has a budget of over $700,000,000 (including federal government transfers of over $500,000,000). The Department of Finance obtains the financial resources to carry on the functions of government & for intergovernmental fiscal negotiations & arrangements.

Acts Administered:
Borrowing Authorization Act
Central Trust Company Act
Certified General Accountants' Association Act
Financial Agreement Act
Income Tax Act
Income Tax Collection Agreement Questions Act
Institute of Chartered Accountants Act
Insurance Act
Liquor Act
Loan Authorization Act
Northwest Territories Energy Corporation Ltd. Loan Guarantee Act
Payroll Tax Act, 1993

Petroleum Products Tax Act
Property & Assessment Taxation Act (jointly with Department of Municipal & Community Affairs)
Public Utilities Income Tax Rebates Act
Risk Capital Investment Tax Credit Act
Society of Management Accountants Act
Tobacco Tax Act
Appropriation Act
Financial Administration Act
Forgiveness of Debts Act
Northern Employee Benefits Services Pension Plan Protection Act
Retirement Plan Beneficiaries Act
Revolving Funds Act
Supplementary Appropriation Act
Union of Northern Workers Act
Write-Off of Assets & Debts Act
Minister,
867-669-2355, Fax: 867-873-0596
Acting Deputy Minister, Sandy Kalgutkar
867-873-7117, Fax: 867-873-0414,
sandy_kalgutkar@gov.nt.ca

Associated Agencies, Boards & Commissions:
• Northwest Territories Liquor Commission
#201, 31 Capital Dr.
Hay River, NT X0E 1G2
867-874-2100 Fax: 867-874-2180
• Northwest Territories Liquor Licensing Board
#210, 31 Capital Dr.
Hay River, NT X0E 1G2
867-874-2906 Fax: 867-874-6011
delilah_st-arneault@gov.nt.ca
• Northwest Territories Liquor Licensing & Enforcement
#210, 31 Capital Dr.
Hay River, NT X0E 1G2
867-874-2906 Fax: 867-874-6011

Financial Services
867-873-7148 Fax: 867-873-0110
betty_low@gov.nt.ca (Secretary)
Executive Director, Shared Services, Thomas Beard
867-873-7158, thomas_beard@gov.nt.ca
Manager, Contracts, Ilona Legler
867-873-7932, ilona_legler@gov.nt.ca
Manager, Financial Services, James Ssenyange
867-873-7416, james_ssenyange@gov.nt.ca

Fiscal Policy
867-920-6436 Fax: 867-873-0128
Responsible for developing policies & providing research, analysis & recommendations on the fiscal policies of government. The Division also administers the Formula Financing Agreement with Canada & is responsible for intergovernmental fiscal relations.
Director, Kelly Bluck
867-920-6436, kelly_bluck@gov.nt.ca

Treasury
867-873-7308 Fax: 867-873-0325
Treasury is responsible for managing the government's cash position; conducting banking, borrowing & investment activities; protecting the government's activities & assets from risk of loss by means of appropriate insurance coverage & risk management activities; & regulating insurance companies, agents, brokers & adjusters operating in the NWT.
Director & Superintendent, Insurance, Doug Doak
867-920-3423, doug_doak@gov.nt.ca

Financial Management Board Secretariat (FMBS)

c/o Secretary of the FMB / Comptroller General, 5003 - 49 St., PO Box 1320, Yellowknife, NT X1A 2L9
Coordinating & promoting the efficient use of the Government's financial & information resources are the chief responsibilities of the Financial Management Board Secretariat. The central agency, that supports the Minister of Finance, provides leadership in functions related to governmental business planning, information management, & program & service evaluation. The FMBS also supports sustainable resource development, self-government development, & the improvement of programs & services.
Minister Responsible,
867-669-2355, Fax: 867-873-0385
Comptroller General, Warren StGermaine
867-920-6196, Fax: 867-873-0296,
warren_stgermaine@gov.nt.ca
Manager, Budget Development, Chuck Gibson
867-873-7883, chuck_gibson@gov.nt.ca
Deputy Secretary, Sandy Kalgutkar
867-920-6196, sandy_kalgutkar@gov.nt.ca

Vital Statistics
Bag #9, Inuvik, NT X0E 0T0
867-777-7400 Fax: 867-777-3197
800-661-0830
hsa@gov.nt.ca
Birth certificates: $10
Registrar General, Jenetta Day
867-777-7422, jenetta_day@gov.nt.ca

Regional & Community Boards:

Deh Cho
PO Box 246, Fort Simpson, NT X0E 0N0
867-695-3815 Fax: 867-695-2920

Tlicho
Bag #5, Behchoko, NT X0E 0Y0
867-392-3000 Fax: 867-392-3001

Fort Smith
PO Box 1080, Fort Smith, NT X0E 0P0
867-872-6200 Fax: 867-872-6275

Hay River
3 Gaetz Dr., Hay River, NT X0E 0R8
867-874-7100 Fax: 867-874-7118

Beaufort-Delta
Bag #2, 285 Mackenzie Rd., Inuvik, NT X0E 0T0
867-777-8000 Fax: 867-777-8062

Sahtu
PO Box 340, Norman Wells, NT X0E 0V0
867-587-3650 Fax: 867-587-3436

Stanton
PO Box 10, Yellowknife, NT X1A 2N1
867-669-4224 Fax: 867-669-4128
www.srhb.org

Yellowknife
Jan Stirling Bldg., 4702 Franklin Ave., PO Box 608, Yellowknife, NT X1A 2N5
867-873-7276 Fax: 867-920-7025
yhssa@gov.nt.ca
www.yhssa.org

Department of Health & Social Services

Centre Square Tower, PO Box 1320, Yellowknife, NT X1A 2L9
Fax: 867-873-0266
www.hlthss.gov.nt.ca
The Department of Health & Social Services is mandated to provide a broad range of health & social programs & services to the residents of the NWT. Seven regional Health & Social Services Authorities plan, manage & deliver a full spectrum of community & facility-based services for health care & social services. Community health programs include daily sick clinics, public health clinics, home care, school health programs & educational programs. Visiting physicians & specialists routinely visit the communities.
Acts Administered:
Aboriginal Custom Adoption Recognition Act
Adoption Act
Change of Name Act
Child & Family Services Act
Dental Auxiliaries Act
Dental Mechanics Act
Dental Profession Act
Emergency Medical Aid Act
Guardianship & Trusteeship Act (jointly with Deptartment of Justice)
Hospital Insurance & Health & Social Services Administration Act
Human Tissue Act
Intercountry Adoption (Hague Convention) Act
Licensed Practical Nurses Act
Marriage Act
Medical Care Act
Medical Profession Act
Mental Health Act
Midwifery Profession Act
Nursing Profession Act
Ophthalmic Medical Assistants Act
Optometry Act
Personal Directives Act
Pharmacy Act
Psychologists Act
Public Health Act
Communicable Diseases Regulation
General Sanitation Regulations
Meat Inspection Regulations
Public Sewerage Systems Regulation
Public Water Supply Regulations
Tobacco Control Act
Veterinary Profession Act
Vital Statistics Act
Minister,
867-669-2344, Fax: 867-873-0481
Acting Deputy Minister, Debbie DeLancey
867-920-6173, Fax: 867-873-0266,
debbie_delancey@gov.nt.ca
Assistant Deputy Minister, Operational Support Branch, Dana Heide
867-873-7737, Fax: 867-873-0266, dana_heide@gov.nt.ca
Director, Innovation, Reform & Legislation, Denise Canuel
867-920-3283, Fax: 867-873-0204, denise_canuel@gov.nt.ca
Director, Corporate Planning, Reporting & Evaluation, Lisa Cardinal
867-873-7908, Fax: 867-873-0484, lisa_cardinal@gov.nt.ca
Director, Children & Family Services, Simone Fournel
867-873-7046, Fax: 867-873-7706,
simone_fournel@gov.nt.ca
Director, Finance & Infrastructure Planning, Jeannie Mathison
867-873-7367, jeannie_mathison@gov.nt.ca
Director, Health Services Administration, Nick Saturnino
867-777-7400, 800-661-0830, Fax: 867-777-3197,
nick_saturnino@gov.nt.ca
Director, Population Health, Wanda White
867-873-7403, wanda_white@gov.nt.ca
Chief Public Health Officer, Lorne Clearsky
867-920-8646, lorne_clearsky@gov.nt.ca
Chief Information Officer, Information Services, Michele Herriot
867-920-8907, Fax: 867-873-0280,
michele_herriot@gov.nt.ca
Public Guardian, Beatrice Raddi
867-920-8025, Fax: 867-873-0248, beatrice_raddi@gov.nt.ca
Comptroller, Financial Services, Kim Weir
867-920-3003, kim_weir@gov.nt.ca
Communications Officer, Dorothy Westerman
867-920-3373, Fax: 867-873-0204,
dorothy_westerman@gov.nt.ca
Director, Andre Corriveau
867-920-3231, andre_corriveau@gov.nt.ca

Northwest Territories Housing Corporation

Scotia Centre, 5102 50th Ave., PO Box 2100, Yellowknife, NT X1A 2P6
867-873-7853 Fax: 867-873-9426
www.nwthc.gov.nt.ca
Other Communication: Official Languages Coordination Phone: 867-873-7899; Fax: 867-669-7901
The mandate of the Northwest Territories Housing Corporation is to ensure, where necessary, a sufficient supply of affordable, adequate & suitable housing to meet the needs of residents. To accomplish this mandate, the corporation works with citizens, communities, Local Housing Organizations, aboriginal organizations, the business community, non-government organizations, & other governments. Through Housing Choices, the following four programs are available: Providing Assistance for Territorial Homeownership (PATH); Contributing Assistance for Repairs and Enhancements (CARE); Homeowner Entry Level Program (HELP); & Solutions to Educate People (STEP).
Minister Responsible,
867-669-2377, Fax: 867-873-0596
President, Jeff Polakoff
867-873-7853, Fax: 867-873-9426, jeff_polakoff@gov.nt.ca
Vice President, Finance & Infrastructure Services, Jeff Anderson
867-873-7873, Fax: 867-920-8024, jeff_anderson@gov.nt.ca
Vice-President, Programs & District Operations, Franklin Carpenter
867-873-7858, Fax: 867-669-7901,
franklin_carpenter@gov.nt.ca
Director, Infrastructure Services, Scott Reid
867-873-7875, Fax: 867-669-7010, scott_reid@gov.nt.ca

Department of Human Resources

PO Box 1320, Yellowknife, NT X1A 2L9
867-920-3409 Fax: 867-873-0306
866-475-8162
www.hr.gov.nt.ca
Other Communication: Yellowknife Recruitment Office Phone: 867-920-8900; Fax: 867-873-0282; Email: jobsyk@gov.nt.ca; Current Employment Opportunities: www.hr.gov.nt.ca/employment
The Department services the people of the Northwest Territories & supports the development of employees in the northern public service. Services are provided through the following divisions: Management & Recruitment Services; Corporate Human Resource Services; Human Resource Strategy & Policy; & Employee Services.
Acts Administered:
Teachers' Association Act
Public Service Act
Minister,
867-669-2388, Fax: 867-873-0306
Deputy Minister, Tom R. Williams
867-873-7187, Fax: 867-873-0667, tom_r_williams@gov.nt.ca
Associate Deputy Minister, Sheila Bassi-Kellett
867-873-7187, Fax: 867-873-0667,
sheila_bassi-kellett@gov.nt.ca

Director, Corporate Human Resources, Sharilyn Alexander
867-873-7852, sharilyn_alexander@gov.nt.ca
Director, Strategy & Policy, Michelle Beard
867-873-7786, michelle_beard@gov.nt.ca
Acting Director, Management & Recruitment Services, Ross Thomas
867-920-8717, ross_thomas@gov.nt.ca
Director, Employee Services, Alison Welch
867-873-7906, Fax: 867-873-0167, alison_welch@gov.nt.ca
Manager, Finance & Corporate Support, Roxanne Campbell
867-920-8948, roxanne_campbell@gov.nt.ca
Manager, Labour Relations, Vacant
867-920-6158

Department of Industry, Tourism & Investment (ITI)

PO Box 1320, Yellowknife, NT X1A 2L9

Fax: 867-873-0306
info@iti.ca
www.iti.gov.nt.ca

The Department of Industry, Tourism & Investment promotes & supports economic prosperity & community self-reliance in the Northwest Territories by providing programs & services. Programs & services are available through the following departmental divisions: Diamonds; Energy Planning; Industrial Initiatives; Informatics; Investment & Economic Analysis; Mackenzie Valley Pipeline Office; Minerals, Oil & Gas; Policy, Legislation & Communications; & Tourism & Parks.

Acts Administered:
Agricultural Products Marketing Act
Business Development & Investment Corporation Act
Co-operative Associations Act (jointly with Department of Justice)
Credit Union Act
Freshwater Fish Marketing Act
Herd & Fencing Act
Territorial Parks Act

Minister,
867-669-2388, Fax: 867-873-0306
Deputy Minister, Peter Vician
867-920-8048, Fax: 867-873-0563, peter_vician@gov.nt.ca
Assistant Deputy Minister, Programs & Operations, Vacant
867-873-7115
Director, Minerals, Oil & Gas, Deborah Archibald
867-920-3222, deborah_archibald@gov.nt.ca
Director, Planning & Coordination, Mackenzie Valley Pipeline Office, Tim Coleman
867-874-5405, tim_coleman@gov.nt.ca
Director, Shared Services, Finance & Administration, Nancy Magrum
867-920-8649, Fax: 867-920-2756, nancy_magrum@gov.nt.ca
Director, Energy Planning, Dave Nightingale
867-920-3274, dave_nightingale@gov.nt.ca
Director, Policy, Legislation & Communications, Sonya Saunders
867-873-7005, Fax: 867-873-0645, sonya_saunders@gov.nt.ca
Director, Investment & Economic Analysis, Kevin Todd
867-873-7361, Fax: 867-873-0101, kevin_todd@gov.nt.ca
Director, Shared Services, Informatics, Rick Wind
867-920-3327, Fax: 867-920-2756, rick_wind@gov.nt.ca
Director, Tourism & Parks, Richard Zieba
867-873-7903, Fax: 867-873-0163, richard_zieba@gov.nt.ca
Chief Geologist, Northwest Territories Geoscience Office, Scott Cairns
867-669-2479, scott_cairns@gov.nt.ca

Department of Justice

Courthouse, 4903 - 49th St., 6th Fl., PO Box 1320, Yellowknife, NT X1A 2L9

867-920-6197
www.justice.gov.nt.ca
Other Communication: Access to Information and Protection of Privacy Phone: 867-920-6418

The following are some of the services offered by the Department of Justice: Aboriginal Rights Court Challenges Program; Access to Information & Protection of Privacy; Commissioner for Oaths/Notary Public; Coroner; Corporate Registries; Land Titles Office; Legal Aid; Maintenance Enforcement; Mental Disorder Review Board; Personal Property Registry; Public Trustee; Rental Office; Securities Registry; Victim Services; Witness Expense Assistance Program; & Youth Justice.

Acts Administered:
Access to Information & Protection of Privacy Act (jointly with Legislative Assembly)
Adoption of the French Version of Statutes & Statutory Instruments Act
Age of Majority Act
Arbitration Act
Business Corporations Act
Children's Law Act
Choses In Action Act
Commercial Tenancies Act
Condominium Act
Conflict of Interest Act
Contributory Negligence Act
Coroners Act
Corrections Act
Court Security Act
Creditors Relief Act
Defamation Act
Department of Justice Act
Dependants Relief Act
Devolution of Real Property Act
Donation of Food Act
Engineering & Geoscience Professions Act
Evidence Act
Exemptions Act
Expropriation Act
Factors Act
Family Law Act
Fatal Accidents Act
Fine Option Act
Frustrated Contracts Act
Garage Keepers Lien Act
Hotel Keepers Act
Interjurisdictional Support Orders Act
International Child Abduction Act
International Commercial Arbitration Act
International Interests in Mobile Aircraft Equipment Act
International Sale of Goods Act
Interpretation Act
Interprovincial Subpoenas Act
Intestate Succession Act
Judicature Act
Jury Act
Justices of the Peace Act
Land Titles Act
Legal Profession Act
Legal Questions Act
Legal Services Act
Limitation of Actions Act
Maintenance Orders Enforcement Act
Married Women's Property Act
Mechanics Lien Act
Miners Lien Act
Partnership Act
Perpetuities Act
Personal Property Security Act
Powers of Attorney Act
Presumption of Death Act
Professional Corporations Act
Protection Against Family Violence Act
Public Inquiries Act
Public Printing Act
Public Service Garnishee Act
Public Trustee Act
Reciprocal Enforcement of Judgments Act
Reciprocal Enforcement of Judgments (Canada-UK) Act
Religious Societies Land Act
Residential Tenancies Act
Retirement Plan Beneficiaries Act (jointly with Department of Finance)
Royal Canadian Mounted Police Agreements Act
Sale of Goods Act
Securities Act
Securities Transfer Act
Seizures Act
Settlement of International Investment Disputes Act
Societies Act
Statute Revision Act
Statutory Instruments Act
Summary Conviction Procedures Act
Survivorship Act
Tenants in Common Act
Territorial Court Act
Trustee Act
Variation of Trusts Act
Victims of Crime Act
Warehouse Keepers Lien Act
Wills Act
Youth Justice Act

Minister,
867-669-2399, Fax: 867-873-0274
Deputy Minister, Bronwyn Watters
867-920-6197, Fax: 867-873-0307, brownyn_watters@gov.nt.ca
Acting Assistant Deputy Minister & Attorney General, Mark Aitken
867-920-6197, mark_aitken@gov.nt.ca
Assistant Deputy Minister & Solicitor General, Sylvia Haener
sylvia_haener@gov.nt.ca
Chief Coroner, Coroner's Office, Cathy Menard
867-973-7448, Fax: 867-873-0426, cathy_menard@gov.nt.ca
Chief Information Officer, Norm Embleton
867-920-6100, Fax: 867-873-0197, norm_embleton@gov.nt.ca
Public Trustee, Public Trustee's Office, Brian Asmundson
867-873-7464, 866-535-0423, Fax: 867-873-0184, larry_pontus@gov.nt.ca
Executive Director, Legal Services Board, Lucy Austin
867-873-7450, Fax: 867-873-5320, lucy_austin@gov.nt.ca
Director, Legislation Division, Mark Aitken
867-873-7462, Fax: 867-873-0234, mark_aitken@gov.nt.ca
Director, Corrections Services, Greg Debogorski
867-920-8922, Fax: 867-873-0299, greg_debogorski@gov.nt.ca
Director, Court Services, Anne Mould
867-920-8852, Fax: 867-873-0307, anne_mould@gov.nt.ca
Director, Community Justice & Community Policing, Shirley KemeysJones
867-873-7002, Fax: 867-873-0199, shirley_kemeysjones@gov.nt.ca
Director, Legal Registries, Gary MacDougall
867-873-7490, Fax: 867-873-0243, gary.macdougall@gov.nt.ca
Director, Finance, Kim Schofield
867-873-7641, Fax: 867-873-0173, kim_schofield@gov.nt.ca
Director, Policy & Planning, Laura Seddon
867-920-3225, Fax: 867-873-0659, laura_seddon@gov.nt.ca
Director, Legal Division, Brad Patzer
867-920-3248, Fax: 867-873-0234, brad_patzer@gov.nt.ca
Registrar, Land Titles, Tom Hall
867-920-8986, Fax: 867-873-0243, tom_hall@gov.nt.ca
Registrar, Corporate Registries, Donald MacDougall
867-920-8984, Fax: 867-873-0243, donald_macdougall@gov.nt.ca
Administrator, Commissioner for Oaths / Notary Public, Cindy Pettes
867-920-8985, Fax: 867-873-0243, cindy_pettes@gov.nt.ca

Associated Agencies, Boards & Commissions:
• Judicial Council
PO Box 550
Yellowknife, NT X1A 2N4
867-873-7105 Fax: 867-873-0287
• Legal Services Board of the Northwest Territories
PO Box 1320
Yellowknife, NT X1A 2L9
867-873-7450 Fax: 867-873-5320
• Victims Assistance Committee
c/o Community Justice Division
PO Box 1320
Yellowknife, NT X1A 2L9
867-920-6911 Fax: 867-873-0199

Associated Agencies, Boards & Commissions:
• Assessment Appeal Tribunal of the Northwest Territories
#400, 5201 - 50th Ave.
PO Box 1320
Yellowknife, NT X1A 2L9
867-873-7125 Fax: 867-873-0609
• Territorial Board of Revision
#400, 5201 - 50th Ave.
PO Box 1320
Yellowknife, NT X1A 2L9
867-873-7125 Fax: 867-873-0609

Department of Municipal & Community Affairs

PO Box 1320, Yellowknife, NT X1A 2L9

867-873-7118 Fax: 867-873-0309
www.maca.gov.nt.ca

Supports capable, accountable & self-directed community governments providing a safe, sustainable & healthy environment for community residents. Works with community governments & other partners in supporting community residents as they organize & manage democratic, responsible & accountable community governments. The Department assists municipalities with administrative services & infrastructure project management, provides expertise in engineering to communities & arranges for debentures on behalf of communities which are undertaking public works programs. Advisory services are supplied to community councils for the planning, development & administration of public lands within municipal boundaries. Technical expertise is provided for mapping, surveying & air photography & zoning by-law administration.

Acts Administered:
Area Development Act
Civil Emergency Measures Act
Commissioner's Land Act
Community Employees Benefits Act
Consumer Protection Act
Curfew Act
Dog Act
Film Classification Act
Fire Prevention Act
Hamlets Act
Home Owner's Property Tax Rebate Act

Local Authorities Elections Act
Lotteries Act
Pawnbrokers & Second-Hand Dealers Act
Planning Act
Property Assessment & Taxation Act (jointly with Department of Finance)
Real Estate Agent's Licensing Act
Senior Citizens' & Disabled Persons' Property Tax Relief Act
Settlements Act
Western Canada Lotteries Act
Business Licence Act
Charter Communities Act
Cities, Towns & Villages Act
Hamlets Act
Tlicho Community Government Act

Minister,
867-669-2344, Fax: 867-873-0431
Deputy Minister, Mike Aumond
867-873-7118, Fax: 867-873-0309, mike_aumond@gov.nt.ca
Assistant Deputy Minister, Regional Operations, Eleanor Young
867-873-7118, Fax: 867-873-0309, eleanor_young@gov.nt.ca
Director, Corporate Affairs, Laura Gareau
867-873-7613, laura_gareau@gov.nt.ca
Acting Director, Community Operations, David Kravitz
867-873-7571, david_kravitz@gov.nt.ca
Director, Sport, Recreation & Youth, Ian Legaree
867-873-7245, Fax: 867-920-6467, ian_legaree@gov.nt.ca
Director, Public Safety, Alan McIntosh
867-873-7565, alan_mcintosh@gov.nt.ca
Project Coordinator, Public Safety, Eric Bussey
867-873-7334, eric_bussey@gov.nt.ca
Fire Marshal, Stephen Moss
867-873-7469, Fax: 867-873-0260, stephen_moss@gov.nt.ca
Records Coordinator, Corporate Affairs, Terry Kungl
867-873-7474, terry_kungl@gov.nt.ca

Lands Administration
867-873-7569 Fax: 867-920-6156

Responsible for the administration of Commissioner's lands in & around the communities of the Northwest Territories. Commissioner's lands make up about 2 percent of all land in the North. The Federal Government administers about 97 percent & municipal corporations administer the remaining 1 percent. Under the Lands Program, MACA is in the process of transferring certain lands from the Commissioner to municipalities. Land administration is being decentralized from MACA headquarters to regional offices or to the communities. As authority for land devolves, MACA will take on a training & advisory role, teaching & advising communities how to look after their own lands. The division supplies information & advice regarding land leases, surrenders, transfers, & mortgage registration for Commissioner's land & notifications.

Director, Beverly Chamberlain
867-920-6284, beverly_chamberlain@gov.nt.ca
Manager, Lands Policy, Michelle Chappell
867-920-6318, michelle_chappell@gov.nt.ca

School of Community Government
#500, 5201 - 50th Ave., Yellowknife, NT X1A 3S9
867-920-3159 Fax: 867-873-0584
877-531-9194

Director, Dan Schofield
867-873-7755, Fax: 867-873-0584, dan_schofield@gov.nt.ca

Northwest Territories Power Corporation

4 Capital Dr., Hay River, NT X0E 1G2
867-874-5200 Fax: 867-874-5251
info@ntpc.com
www.ntpc.com
Other Communication: Fort Simpson: 800-288-4784; Fort Smith: 800-661-0855; Inuvik: 800-661-0856; Yellowknife: 800-661-0854

Made up of 28 separate power systems, the NWT Power Corporation serves approximately 42,000 people in communities across the Northwest Territories. Facilities include hydro-electric, diesel & natural gas generation plants, transmission systems, & several isolated electrical distribution systems. The Corporation works to provide environmentally sound, safe, reliable, cost-effective energy & related services in the territories.

Minister Responsible,
867-669-2311, Fax: 867-873-0169
Chair, Brendan Bell
Acting President/Chief Executive Officer & Chief Operating Officer, Emanuel DaRosa
Chief Financial Officer, Judith Goucher

Public Utilities Board of the Northwest Territories (PUB)

#203, 62 Woodland Dr., PO Box 4211, Hay River, NT X0E 1G1
867-874-3944 Fax: 867-874-3639
www.nwtpublicutilitiesboard.ca

The independent, quasi-judicial agency of the Government of the Northwest Territories is responsible for the regulation of public utilities in the territory. Its authority is from the Public Utilities Act. Issues are handled by an application & decision process.

Minister Responsible,
867-669-2388, Fax: 867-873-0431
Chair, Joe Acorn
Board Secretary, Louise-Ann Larocque
louise-ann_larocque@gov.nt.ca

Department of Public Works & Services

PO Box 1320, Yellowknife, NT X1A 2L9
www.pws.gov.nt.ca

Designs, constructs, maintains & operates territorial buildings; implements energy efficiency projects; provides essential petroleum products to the public where they are not available from the private sector; provides data systems & communication services to government departments.

Acts Administered:
Architects Act
Boilers & Pressure Vessels Act
Electrical Protection Act
Gas Protection Act
Purchasing Management Association Act

Minister,
867-669-2377, Fax: 867-873-0169
Deputy Minister, Paul Guy
867-873-7114, Fax: 867-873-0226, paul_guy@gov.nt.ca
Director, Design & Technical Services, Sukhi Cheema
867-920-8088, sukhi_cheema@gov.nt.ca
Director, Technology Service Centre (TSC), Laurie Gault
867-873-7836, Fax: 867-873-0135, laurie_gault@gov.nt.ca
Director, Corporate Services, Steve Lewis
867-920-8672, Fax: 867-873-0212, steve_lewis@gov.nt.ca
Director, Infrastructure, Operations & Accommodations, Brian Nagel
867-920-6465, brian_nagel@gov.nt.ca
Director, Petroleum Products Division, John Vandenberg
867-920-8693, Fax: 867-873-0100, john_vandenberg@gov.nt.ca
Executive Secretary, Marvia Rivet
867-873-7114, Fax: 867-873-0226, marvia_rivet@gov.nt.ca

Status of Women Council of the Northwest Territories

PO Box 1320, Yellowknife, NT X1A 2L9
867-920-6177 Fax: 867-873-0285
888-234-4485
council@statusofwomen.nt.ca
www.statusofwomen.nt.ca

To work towards the equality of women through advice to the government; research; public education; advocacy on behalf of women; & workshops & other support for the development of women's groups, & other groups working on issues of concern to women.

Minister Responsible,
867-669-2344, Fax: 867-873-0481
President, Therese Dolly Simon
Vice-President, Su-Ellen Kolback
Executive Director, Lorraine Phaneuf
lorraine@statusofwomen.nt.ca

Department of Transportation

Lahm Ridge Bldg., 4501 50 Ave., PO Box 1320, Yellowknife, NT X1A 2L9
867-920-3460 Fax: 867-873-0363
www.dot.gov.nt.ca

Acts Administered:
All-Terrain Vehicles Act
Deh Cho Bridge Act
Motor Vehicles Act
Public Airports Act
Public Highways Act
Transportation of Dangerous Goods Act, 1990
Transportation of Dangerous Goods Regulations

Minister,
867-669-2377, Fax: 867-873-0388
Deputy Minister, Russell Neudorf
867-920-3460, Fax: 867-873-0363, russell_neudorf@gov.nt.ca
Assistant Deputy Minister, Daniel Auger
867-920-3461, Fax: 867-873-0363, daniel_auger@gov.nt.ca
Director, Corporate Services, Jim Martin
867-920-3459, Fax: 867-873-0283, jim_martin@gov.nt.ca
Director, Planning, Policy & Environment Division, Jayleen Robertson
867-920-3366, Fax: 867-920-2565, jayleen_robertson@gov.nt.ca
Director, Mackenzie Valley Highway, Jim Stevens
867-920-6247, jim_stevens@gov.nt.ca

Airports
YK Centre, 4922 - 28th St., 4th fl., PO Box 1320, Yellowknife, NT X1A 2L9
867-873-7725 Fax: 867-873-0297

Director, Delia Chesworth
867-873-7561, delia_chesworth@gov.nt.ca
Assistant Director, Airport Facilities, Vacant
867-873-7845
Assistant Director, Programs & Standards, Ben Webber
867-873-7822, Fax: 867-873-0297, ben_webber@gov.nt.ca

Highways & Marine
4510 - 50 Ave., 2nd fl., PO Box 1320, Yellowknife, NT X1A 2L9
867-920-8771 Fax: 867-873-0288

Director, Kevin McLeod
867-873-7800, Fax: 867-873-0288, kevin_mcleod@gov.nt.ca
Head, Structures, Ann Lanteigne
867-920-8010, ann_lanteigne@gov.nt.ca

Road Licensing & Safety
4510 - 50 Ave., 1st fl., PO Box 1320, Yellowknife, NT X1A 2L9
867-873-7972 Fax: 867-873-0120

Acting Director, Michael Conway
867-920-3068, Fax: 867-873-0120, michael_conway@gov.nt.ca

Northwest Territories Water Board

125 Mackenzie Rd., PO Box 2531, Yellowknife, NT X0E 0T0
867-678-2942 Fax: 867-678-2943
info@nwtwb.com
www.nwtwb.com

Responsible for the development, maintenance & conservation of water resources; administers licences for utilizing water or disposing of wastes into water under the Northwest Territories Waters Act; has federal/territorial jurisdiction.

Chair, Eddie T. Dillon
Executive Director, Mike Harlow
867-678-8609, harlowm@nwtwb.com
Office & Finance Administrator, Freda Wilson
867-678-2942, wilsonf@nwtwb.com

Northwest Territories & Nunavut Workers' Safety & Compensation Commission (WCB)

Centre Square Tower, 5022 - 49th St., 5th Fl., PO Box 8888, Yellowknife, NT X1A 2R3
867-920-3888 Fax: 867-873-4596
800-661-0792
www.wscc.nt.ca
Other Communication: Toll Free Fax: 1-866-277-3677; Incident/Accident Line: 1-800-661-0792

The Workers' Safety & Compensation Commission is engaged in the following activities: ensuring compensation & pensions are awarded to injured workers or their dependents; assessubg enokiters sufficiently & fairly to meet obligations; maintaining balance in providing benefits to injured workers, while keeping costs to employers as low as possible; & promoting safe workplaces through education & enforcement.

Acts Administered:
Explosives Use Act
Mine Health & Safety Act
Environmental Tobacco Smoke Worksite Regulations
Safety Act
Asbestos Safety Regulations
Mine Health & Safety Regulations
Work Site Hazardous Materials Information System Regulations
Summary Convictions Procedures Act
Workers' Compensation Act

Minister Responsible, Northwest Territories,
867-669-2355, Fax: 867-873-0596
President/Chief Executive Officer, Dave Grundy
867-669-4442
Vice-President, Revenue & Financial Services, Gloria Badari
867-920-3824
Vice-President, Prevention Services, Cara Benoit
867-669-4407
Vice-President, Client & Central Services, Kim Collins Riffel
867-920-3821
Vice-President, Nunavut Operations, Derek Dinham
902-979-8507
Vice-President, Corporate Communications & Policy Services, Edith Johnston-Ryder
867-669-4431
Chief Information Officer, Harmeet Jagpal
867-669-4446
General Counsel, Amy Groothuis
867-920-3813

Government of Nova Scotia

Seat of Government: Province House, 1726 Hollis St., Halifax, NS B3J 2T3
www.gov.ns.ca

The Province of Nova Scotia entered Confederation July 1, 1867. It has an area of 52,917,46 km2, & the StatsCan census population in 2006 was 913,462.

Office of the Lieutenant Governor

Government House, 1451 Barrington St., Halifax, NS B3J 1Z2
902-424-7001 Fax: 902-424-0537
lgoffice@gov.ns.ca
www.lt.gov.ns.ca

The primary responsibility of the Lieutenant Governor is to act as the Crown's representative & Chief Executive Officer of the Province of Nova Scotia. The Lieutenant Governor, therefore, is apolitical.

Lieutenant Governor, Hon. Mayann Francis
Fax: 902-424-1790
Note: http://www.facebook.com/pages/Office-of-the-Lieutenant-Governor-of-Nova-Scotia/138942176151803

Private Secretary, Dr. Christopher McCreery
902-424-7050, mccreecp@gov.ns.ca
Note: http://www.facebook.com/pages/Office-of-the-Lieutenant-Governor-of-Nova-Scotia/138942176151803

Office of the Premier

One Government Place, 1700 Granville St., 7th Fl., PO Box 726, Halifax, NS B3J 2T3
902-424-6600 Fax: 902-424-7648
800-267-1993
premier@gov.ns.ca
www.premier.gov.ns.ca

Premier, Hon. Darrell Dexter
premier@gov.ns.ca

Deputy Premier, Frank Corbett
902-862-9550, Fax: 902-862-9501, corbetf@gov.ns.ca

Chief of Staff, Dan O'Connor
oconnoda@gov.ns.ca

Director, Communications, Shawn Fuller
902-240-7575, fullersz@gov.ns.ca

Director, Strategic Operations, Shawna Martin
martinsl@gov.ns.ca

Principal Secretary to the Premier, Matt Hebb
hebbmg@gov.ns.ca

Manager, Administration, Operations, Events Management, Military/ Protocol Liasion & Special Projects, Jo Anne Fisher
fisherjc@gov.ns.ca

Executive Council

One Government Place, 1700 Granville St., 5th Fl., PO Box 2125, Halifax, NS B3J 3B7
902-424-5970 Fax: 902-424-0667
execounc@gov.ns.ca
www.gov.ns.ca/exec_council
TTY: 866-206-6844
Other Communication: 902-424-6611 (General Inquiries)

The ECO is non-departmental in function & purpose. It serves the Executive Council (Cabinet) & its committees, the exectuve teams of Treasury Board Office & the Office of Policy & Priorities, as well as departments, agencies, boards, & commissions. The office aims to ensure that the business of the Cabinet and its committees is conducted in a timely, efficient way & that proper collective information is provided. The ECO works to improve agenda management for the Cabinet its committees, by developing policies & procedures for more efficient & effective operations of the decision-making process.

Premier & President, Executive Council, Minister, Policy & Priorities; Minister, Intergovernmental Affairs; Minister, Aboriginal Affairs; Min. responsible for Military Relations, Hon. Darrell Dexter
902-424-6600, 800-261-1933, Fax: 902-424-7648, premier@gov.ns.ca

Deputy Premier & Deputy President, Minister, Public Service Commission; Minister, Communications Nova Scotia; Minister, Information Management; Chair of TreasuryBoard, Hon. Frank Corbett
902-424-5465, Fax: 902-424-0555, min_psc@gov.ns.ca

Minister, Fisheries & Aquaculture & Minister, Environment, Hon. Sterling Belliveau
902-424-3736, Fax: 902-424-1599, min_env@gov.ns.ca; min_dfa@gov.ns.ca

Minister, Transportation & Infrastructure Renewal; Minister responsible for the Sydney Tar Ponds Agency, Minister responsible for the Sydney Steel Corporation Act; Member of Treasury Board Committee, Hon. Bill Estabrooks
902-424-5875, Fax: 902-424-0171, tirmin@gov.ns.ca

Minister, Education; Minister responsible for Youth; Member of Treasury Board Committee, Hon. Ramona Jennex
902-424-4236, Fax: 902-424-0680, educmin@gov.ns.ca

Attorney General & Minister, Justice; Provincial Secretary, responsible for Human Rights Act, Regulations Act, Workers' Compensation Act (Part II), Retail Business Uniform Closing Day Act, &Elections, Hon. Ross Landry
902-424-4044, Fax: 902-424-0510, justmin@gov.ns.ca

Minister, Labour & Advanced; Minister, Immigration; & Minister, Voluntary Sector, responsible for the Advisory Council on the Status of Women Act, Apprenticeship & Trades Qualifications Act, Workers Compensation Act, Hon. Marilyn More
902-424-6647, Fax: 902-424-0575, min_lae@gov.ns.ca

Minister, Economic & Rural Development & Tourism; Minister, African Nova Scotian Affairs, Minister responsible for the Gateway Initiative, Nova Scotia Business Incorporated, & Innovation Corporation Act, Hon. Percy Paris
902-424-5790, Fax: 902-424-0514, econmin@gov.ns.ca

Minister, Natural Resources; Minister, Energy, Hon. Charlie Parker
902-424-4037, Fax: 902-424-0594, min_dnr@gov.ns.ca; energyminister@gov.ns.ca

Minister, Community Services & Minister, Seniors; Minister responsible, Disabled Persons' Commission Act; Chair of the Senior Citizens'Secretariat, Hon. Denise Peterson-Rafuse
902-424-4304, Fax: 902-428-0618, petersdj@gov.ns.ca

Minister, Health & Wellness; Minister, Gaelic Affairs, Hon. Maureen MacDonald
902-424-3377, Fax: 902-424-0559, health.minister@gov.ns.ca

Minister, Agriculture; Minister, Service Nova Scotia & Municipal Relations; Minister responsible, Residential Tenancies Act, Minister responsible for the Maritime Provinces Harness Racing Commission Act; Minister responsible forPart II of the Gaming Control Act, Hon. John MacDonell
902-424-4388, Fax: 902-424-0699, min_dag@gov.ns.ca
Note: Member of Treasury Board Committee

Minister, Finance; Minister, Acadian Affairs; Minister responsible for the Securities Act, Insurance Act, Liquor Control Act, Credit Union Act, Utility & Review Board Act, Nova Scotia Liquor Control Corporation; Member of TreasuryBoard Committee, Hon. Graham Steele
902-424-5720, Fax: 902-424-0635, financeminister@gov.ns.ca

Minister, Communities, Culture, & Heritage; Minister responsible for the Heritage Property Act & Gaming Control Act (Part 1), Hon. David Wilson
902-424-4889, Fax: 902-424-4872, min_cch@gov.ns.ca

Council Order Clerk, Ann T. Broughm-Veinotte
902-424-5152

Legislative House of Assembly

c/o Clerk's Office, Province House, 1st Fl., PO Box 1617, Halifax, NS B3J 2Y3
902-424-5978 Fax: 902-424-0632
www.gov.ns.ca/legi/house.htm
Other Communication: 902-424-0526 (Fax, Office of the Speaker)

Chief Clerk, Neil R. Ferguson
fergusnr@gov.ns.ca

Speaker, Gordie Gosse
902-564-9161, Fax: 902-564-9975, gordiegosse@ns.aliantzinc.ca

Sergeant-at-Arms, Kenneth Greenham
902-424-4603, greenhkh@gov.ns.ca

Legislative Librarian, Margaret Murphy
902-424-5932, Fax: 902-424-0220, leglib@gov.ns.ca

Editor, Hansard, Robert Kinsman
902-424-5706, Fax: 902-424-0593, publications@gov.ns.ca
Note: www.nslegislature.ca/index.php/people/offices/hansard-reporting-services/

Assistant Clerk, Annette M. Boucher
902-424-6187

Director, Administration, Deborah Lusby
902-424-4479, Fax: 902-424-2404, lusbyda@gov.ns.ca

Director, Legislative TV, Jim MacInnes
902-424-3875, Fax: 902-424-0604, macinnjt@gov.ns.ca

Chief Legislative Counsel, Gordon D. Hebb
902-424-8941, Fax: 902-424-0547, legc.office@gov.ns.ca

Government Caucus Office (NDP)

Centennial Bldg., #1001, 1660 Hollis St., Halifax, NS B3J 1V7
902-424-4134 Fax: 902-424-0504
888-247-0448
ndpcaucus@gov.ns.ca
www.ndpcaucus.ns.ca

Caucus Chair, Vicki Conrad
902-354-5203, 888-354-5203, Fax: 902-354-5247, vconrad@ns.aliantzinc.ca

Office of the Official Opposition (Liberal)

Bank of Montreal Building, #1402, 5151 George St., PO Box 741, Halifax, NS B3J 2T3
902-424-8637 Fax: 902-424-0539
877-778-1917
info@nsliberalcaucus.ca, lco@gov.ns.ca
www.nsliberalcaucus.ca

Caucus Chair, Kelly Regan
902-407-3777, kelly@kellyregan.ca

Chief of Staff, Kirby McVicar
mcvicaks@gov.ns.ca

Director, Communications, Kyley Harris
902-223-2387, harriskz@gov.ns.ca

Director, Outreach, Glennie Langille
langilgj@gov.ns.ca

Director, Research, Tracey Preeper
preepetk@gov.ns.ca

Office of the Progressive Conservative Party

#801, 1660 Hollis St., Halifax, NS B3J 1V7
902-424-9470 Fax: 902-423-2465
pcmlas@gov.ns.ca
www.pccaucus.ns.ca

Leader, Jamie Baillie
jaimiebaillie@gov.ns.ca, Other Communications: www.jaimiebailliemla.ca
Social Media: www.twitter.com/JamieBaillie
Note: www.chrisdentremont.blogspot.com

Caucus Chair, Keith Bain
902-674-0089, Fax: 902-674-0191, keithbainmla@ns.sympatico.ca

Chief of Staff, Ted Larsen
902-424-2731, larsentc@gov.ns.ca

Standing Committees of the House

Committees Office, 1740 Granville St., 3rd Fl., PO Box 2630 M, Halifax, NS B3J 3N5
902-424-4432 Fax: 902-424-0513
legcomm@gov.ns.ca
www.nslegislature.ca/index.php/committees/

Legislative committees are appointed by the Nova Scotia House of Assembly & are comprised of Members of the House. The committee system allows for detailed examination of matters in a manner which would not be possible in the larger House & also allows members of the public to have direct input into the parliamentary process by making submissions & attending public hearings.

Clerk, Legislative Committees, Darlene Henry

Sixty-first Assembly - Nova Scotia

Province House, PO Box 1617, Halifax, NS B3J 2Y3
902-424-5978 Fax: 902-424-0632

Last General Election, June 9, 2009. Maximum Duration, 5 years. Party Standings (June 2009): New Democratic Party (NDP) 31 Liberal (Lib.) 11 Progressive Conservatives (PC) 10, Total: 52; Salaries, Indemnities & Allowances: MLA 86,619.01 total; Premier 109,484.76; Ministers $47,608.72; Leader of a recognized Opposition Party $23,804.36; Speaker $47,608.72; Deputy Speaker $23,804.36. Following is: constituency (number of eligible voters at 2009 election) member, party affiliation. (Address for all is c/o House of Assembly, Province House, Halifax NS B3J 2Y3.) Refer to Cabinet List, Government Caucus Office, the Office of the Official Opposition & of the Progressive Conservative Party, for phone & fax numbers.

Members

Keith Bain, Victoria-The Lakes, Progressive Conservative
Sterling Belliveau, Shelburne, New Democratic Party
Pam Birdsall, Lunenburg, New Democratic Party
Jim Boudreau, Guysborough-Sheet Harbour, New Democratic Party
Gary Burrill, Colchester-Musquodoboit Valley, New Democratic Party
Hon. Karen Casey, Colchester North, Progressive Conservative
Keith Colwell, Preston, Liberal
Vicki Conrad, Queens, New Democratic Party
Frank Corbett, Cape Breton Centre, New Democratic Party
Hon. Chris A. d'Entremont, Argyle, Progressive Conservative
Darrell Dexter, Cole Harbour, New Democratic Party
Howard Epstein, Halifax Chebucto, New Democratic Party
Bill Estabrooks, Timberlea-Prospect, New Democratic Party
Wayne J. Gaudet, Clare, Liberal
Leo Glavine, Kings West, Liberal
Gordie Gosse, Cape Breton Nova, New Democratic Party
Ramona Jennex, Kings South, New Democratic Party
Becky Kent, Cole-Harbour-Eastern Passage, New Democratic Party
Ross Landry, Pictou Centre, New Democratic Party
Manning MacDonald, Cape Breton South, Liberal
Maureen MacDonald, Halifax Needham, New Democratic Party
John MacDonell, Hants East, New Democratic Party
Clarrie MacKinnon, Pictou East, New Democratic Party
Alfie MacLeod, Cape Breton West, Progressive Conservative
Stephen McNeil, Annapolis, Liberal

Marilyn More, Dartmouth South-Portland Valley, New Democratic Party
Jim Morton, Kings North, New Democratic Party
Eddie Orrell, Cape Breton North, Progressive Conservative
Percy Paris, Waverley-Fall River-Beaverbank, New Democratic Party
Charlie Parker, Pictou West, New Democratic Party
Chuck Porter, Hants West, Progressive Conservative
Denise Peterson-Rafuse, Chester-St. Margaret's, New Democratic Party
Chuck Porter, Hants West, Progressive Conservative
Sidney Prest, Eastern Shore, New Democratic Party
Leonard Preyra, Halifax Citadel, New Democratic Party
Gary Ramey, Lunenberg West, New Democratic Party
Michèle Raymond, Halifax Atlantic, New Democratic Party
Kelly Regan, Bedford-Birch Cove, Liberal
Michael Samson, Richmond, Liberal
Brian Skabar, Cumberland North, Progressive Conservative
Graham Steele, Halifax Fairview, New Democratic Party
Harold Theriault, Jr., Digby-Annapolis, Liberal
Diana Whalen, Halifax Clayton Park, Liberal
Mat Whynott, Hammonds Plains - Upper Sackville, New Democratic Party
David Wilson, Sackville-Cobequid, New Democratic Party
Andrew Younger, Dartmouth East, Liberal
Lenore Zann, Truro-Bible Hill, New Democratic Party

Nova Scotia Government Departments & Agencies

Office of Aboriginal Affairs

5251 Duke St., 5th Fl., PO Box 1617, Halifax, NS B3J 1P3
902-424-7409 Fax: 902-424-0728
oaa@gov.ns.ca
www.gov.ns.ca/abor/

The Office undertakes activities that increase the level of pubic awareness of Aboriginal people and the issues they face. It also works collaboratively with Aboriginal communities and organizations and other levels of government to coordinate Aboriginal and tri-partite initiatives, develop strategies, and build and maintain a sustainable foundation for Aboriginal-Government relations.

Minister, Hon. Darrell Dexter
902-424-7648, 800-267-1993, Fax: 902-424-7648, premier@gov.ns.ca
Deputy Minister, Judith Sullivan-Corney
902-424-3219, Fax: 902-424-4166, corneyjm@gov.ns.ca
Director, Consultation, Jay Hartling
902-424-4214, hartlij@gov.ns.ca
Director, Negotiations, Tom Soehl
902-424-4224, Fax: 902-424-4225, soehlto@gov.ns.ca
Director, Policy, Ernest Walker
902-424-4931, Fax: 902-424-4225

Office of Acadian Affairs

Dennis Building, 1740 Granville St., 7th Fl., PO Box 682, Halifax, NS B3J 2T7
902-424-1267 Fax: 902-428-0124
866-382-5811
bonjour@gov.ns.ca
www.gov.ns.ca/acadian/e

The mission of the Office of Acadian Affairs is to offer advice & support to departments, offices, agencies, & Crown corporations so they can develop & adapt policies, programs, & services that reflect the needs of the Acadian & francophone community of Nova Scotia.

Minister, Hon. Graham Steele
finamin@gov.ns.ca
Deputy Minister & Chief Executive Officer, Vaughne Madden
902-424-3821, maddenve@gov.ns.ca

Department of Agriculture

1741 Brunswick St., 3rd Fl., PO Box 2223, Halifax, NS B3J 3C4
902-424-4560 Fax: 902-424-4671
www.gov.ns.ca/nsaf

The Department of Agriculture has a legislated mandate to support & develop the agriculture & food industries, recognizing that these sectors are economic engines of Nova Scotia's rural communities. Fosters prosperous & sustainable agriculture & food industries through the delivery of quality public services for the betterment of rural communities in Nova Scotia.

Acts Administered:
Agriculture & Marketing Act
Agriculture & Rural Credit Act
Agriculture Marshland Conservation Act
Animal Protection Act
Health Protection Act (Food Regulations & Milk Production, Transportation & Pasteurization Regulations only)
Marsh Land Use Regulations: Bishop-Beckwith, Dentiballis, Dugau/Ryerson, Grand Pré, Lower Truro, Masstown, Victoria Diamond Jubilee, Wellington
Non-Agricultural Use Land Exemption Regulations
Agrologists Act
Animal Cruelty Prevention Act
Animal Health & Protection Act
Animal Health & Protection Regulations
Baby Chick Protection Act
Bee Industry Act
Cattle Pest Control Act
Crop & Livestock Insurance Act
Dairy Industry Act
Farm Practices Act
Farm Registration Act
Federations & Agriculture Act
Fences & Detention of Stray Livestock Act
Health Act (Food Safety, Inspection & Regulations)
Imitation Dairy Products Act
Livestock Brands Act
Livestock Health Services Act
Livestock Health Services Regulations
Margarine Act
Maritime Provinces Harness Racing Commission Act
Meat Inspection Act
Natural Products Act
Potato Industry Act
Provincial Berry Act
Sheep Protection Act
Veterinary Medical Act
Weed Control Act
Wildlife Act
Women's Institute of Nova Scotia Act

Minister, Hon. John MacDonnell
902-424-4388, Fax: 902-424-0699, min_dag@gov.ns.ca
Deputy Minister, Paul LaFleche
902-424-0300, Fax: 902-424-0698, laflecpt@gov.ns.ca
Executive Director, Industry Development & Business Services, Linda MacDonald
902-424-8870, macdonald@gov.ns.ca
Acting Director, Policy & Planning, Mike Chisholm
902-424-8860, chishomg@gov.ns.ca
Director, Communications, Celeste Sulliman
902-424-0192, Fax: 902-424-3948, sullimcc@gov.ns.ca
Executive Secretary, Yvelle Poirier
902-424-4388, ypoirier@gov.ns.ca

Associated Agencies, Boards & Commissions:

• Nova Scotia Crop & Livestock Insurance Commission
MacRae Library Building
137 College Rd.
PO Box 1092
Truro, NS B2N 5G9
902-424-4560 Fax: 902-895-4622
nsclic@gov.ns.ca
www.gov.ns.ca/agri/ci
Under the Crop & Livestock Insurance Act, the Commission is responsible for administering the program under the direction, supervision, & control of the Minister of Agriculture.

• Nova Scotia Farm Loan Board
PO Box 550
Truro, NS B2N 5E3
902-893-6506 Fax: 902-895-7693
flb@gov.ns.ca
www.gov.ns.ca/agri/farmlb/
Other Communication: Kentville location: Phone: 902-679-6009, Fax: 902-679-4997
The Nova Scotia Farm Loan Board operates as a Corporation of the Crown & supports the development of sustainable agriculture & agri-rural business in Nova Scotia through responsible lending.

• Nova Scotia Farm Practices Board
PO Box 550
Truro, NS B2N 5E3
902-893-7314
www.gov.ns.ca/agri/legislaton/fpb.shtml
The Farm Practices Board provides a structure to hear complaints & decide on normal farm practices. The Board provides a mechanism for resolving issues between farmers & their neighbours regarding odour, noise, dust, vibration, light, smoke or other disturbance resulting from a farming activity.

• Nova Scotia Natural Products Marketing Council
179 College Rd.
PO Box 550
Truro, NS B2N 5E3
902-893-6306 Fax: 902-893-7579
www.gov.ns.ca/agri/npmc/
The Council, an agency of the NS Government, is responsible for the administration of the Natural Products Act & the Dairy Industry Act. Ten marketing boards are established under the Natural Products Act & the Dairy Farmers of Nova Scotia is established under the Dairy Industry Act. These boards are producer elected & the Council delegates or regulates authority to them specific to their farm product. The Council is a regulatory & supervisory body, a major role of which is to balance industry interests with teh broader public interest.

Legislation & Compliance Services
www.gov.ns.ca/agri/department/divisions/legcom.shtml
Licenses meat processing, retail food outlets & restaurants, fur & game farms, oversees activities related to food & consumer safety, as well as on-farm quality evaluation. Responsible for monitoring & enforcing compliance with departmental regulations.
Executive Director, Leo Muise
902-424-0337, muiselj@gov.ns.ca

Nova Scotia Agricultural College (NSAC)
PO Box 550, Truro, NS B2N 5E3
902-893-6600
webmaster@snac.ca
www.nsac.ca
Licenses meat processing, retail food outlets & restaurants, fur & game farms, oversees activities related to food & consumer safety, as well as on-farm quality evaluation. Responsible for monitoring & enforcing compliance with departmental regulations.
Co-President, Bernie MacDonald
902-893-6034, Fax: 902-893-4601, bmacdonald@nsac.ca
Co-President, Leslie MacLaren
902-893-6030

Office of the Auditor General

#302, 1888 Brunswick St., Halifax, NS B3J 3J8
902-424-5907 Fax: 902-424-4350
www.oag-ns.ca

The mission of the Auditor General is to make a significant contribution to enhanced accountability & performance in the provincial sector. The Auditor General serves the public interest as the House of Assembly's primary source of assurance on government performance.

Auditor General, Jacques R. Lapointe, B.A., C.A., C.I.A., C.G.A.P.
902-424-4046, lapoinjr@gov.ns.ca
Deputy Auditor General, Alan D. Horgan, C.A.
902-424-3945, horganad@gov.ns.ca
Asst. Auditor General, Evangeline Colman-Sadd, C.A.
902-424-4347, colmansa@gov.ns.ca
Asst. Auditor General, Ann T. McDonald, C.A.
902-424-4970, mcdonaat@gov.ns.ca
Asst. Auditor General, Terry M. Spicer, C.M.A.
902-424-8565, spicert@gov.ns.ca

Communications Nova Scotia

1723 Hollis St., 3rd Fl., PO Box 608, Halifax, NS B3J 2R7
902-424-7690 Fax: 902-424-0515
www.gov.ns.ca/cns/
Other Communication: Queen's Printer: 902-424-4481

Communications Nova Scotia strives to help Nova Scotians understand what their government is doing & why. They provide a complete range of professional communications services to provincial government departments, agencies, boards & commissions.

Minister, Hon. Frank Corbett
corbetfr@gov.ns.ca
Deputy Minister, Gregory P. Keefe
902-424-8940, Fax: 902-428-3191, keefeg@gov.ns.ca
Associate Deputy Minister, Tracey Taweel
902-424-3839, taweelt@gov.ns.ca
Director, Production, Diane Leblanc
902-424-2077
Director, Communications, Tom Peck
902-424-1593
Director, Communications, Catherine Shaw
902-424-8787
Director, Communications, Celeste Sulliman
902-424-7957
Director, Communications, Kristen Tynes MacEachern
902-424-4038
Director, Communications, Webster Natalie Joy
902-424-7280
Director, Communications, Valerie Bellafontaine
902-424-7942
Director, Communications, Carla Burns
902-424-2876
Director, Communications, Daniel Davis
902-424-8978
Director, Communications, Michelle Robin Lucas
902-424-3731
Director, Communications, Catherine MacIsaac
902-424-6283
Director, Communications, Susan McKeage
902-424-7942
Director, Communications, Ross McLaren
902-424-4536
Director, Communications, Janet Lynn McNeil
902-424-7420

Department of Communities, Culture & Heritage

World Trade & Convention Centre, 1800 Argyle St., 6th Fl., PO Box 456, Halifax, NS B3J 3N8
902-424-4510 Fax: 902-424-0710
culture@gov.ns.ca
www.gov.ns.ca/tch

The Department of Communities, Culture & Heritage is responsible for contributing to the well-being & prosperity of Nova Scotia's diverse & creative communities through the promotion, development, preservation & celebration of culture, heritage, identity & languages, and by providing leadership, expertise, & innovation to stakeholders.

Acts Administered:
Art Council Act
Art Gallery of Nova Scotia Act
Cemeteries Protection Act
Cultural Foundation Act
Government Records Act
Heritage Property Act
Libraries Act
Multiculturalism Act
Nova Scotia Museum Act
Nova Scotia Tartan Act
Order of Nova Scotia Act
Peggy's Cove Commission Act
Public Archives Act
Schooner Bluenose Foundation Act
Sherbrooke Restoration Commission Act
Special Places Protection Act (Ecological Site Designations: Abraham Lake, Bornish Hill, Duncans Cove, Great Barren & Quinan Lakes, Indian Man Lake, MacFarlane Woods, Panuke Lake, Ponhook Lake, Quinns Meadow, River Inhabitants,Roman Valley
Tourist Accommodations Act

Minister, Hon. David Wilson
902-424-4889, Fax: 902-424-4872, min_cch@gov.ns.ca
Deputy Minister, Laura Lee Langley
902-424-4938, Fax: 902-424-4872, langley@gov.ns.ca
Director, Communications, Michael Noonan
902-424-1593, Fax: 902-424-4872, noonanmg@gov.ns.ca

Associated Agencies, Boards & Commissions:
• Nova Scotia Tourism Partnership Council
World Trade & Convention Centre
#603, 1800 Argyle St.
Halifax, NS B3J 3N8
902-424-0048 Fax: 902-424-0723
www.gov.ns.ca/econ/tourism/nstpc/
The Council is an industry & government partnership that shares in planning & decision making for tourism marketing, research & product development in Nova Scotia.

NS Archives
6016 University Ave., Halifax, NS B3H 1W4
902-424-6060 Fax: 902-424-0628
nsarm@gov.ns.ca
www.gov.ns.ca/nsarm/
Other Communication: www.facebook.com/novascotiaarchvies; www.twitter.com/NS_Archives
As a documentary heritage institution for the province, the NS Archives serves as the permanent repository for the archival records of the government of Nova Scotia; acquires & preserves provincially significant archival records from the private sector; delivers a range of professional, client-centred reference services; develops & maintains two websites; & provides strategic support & financial assistance to strengthen the provincial archival community.
Provincial Archivist, Vacant
Director, Public Services, Lois Yorke
902-424-6068, yorkelk@gov.ns.ca
Director, Archives Management, Margaret Campbell
902-424-6076, campbemj@gov.ns.ca
Director, Records Management, Thomas Parker
902-424-3012, parkertg@gov.ns.ca

Culture Division
#601, 1800 Argyle St., PO Box 456, Halifax, NS B3J 2R5
902-424-4510 Fax: 902-424-0710
culture@gov.ns.ca
www.gov.ns.ca/tch/culture_mandate.asp
Responsible for Nova Scotia museums which administer the Special Places Protection Act; preserves ecological sites in the province.
Interim Executive Director, Culture Division, Marcel Philip McKenough
902-424-6393

Heritage Division
1747 Summer St., Halifax, NS B3H 3A6
902-424-7344 Fax: 902-424-0560
800-632-1114
heritage@gov.ns.ca
www.gov.ns.ca/tch/heritage_mandate.asp
The mission of Heritage Division is to protect, enhance, & celebrate heritage for all Nova Scotians & for future generations.
Executive Director, Heritage Division, Bill Greenlaw
902-424-4986, greenlbe@gov.ns.ca

Department of Community Services

Nelson Place, 5675 Spring Garden Rd., 8th Fl., PO Box 696, Halifax, NS B3J 2T7
902-424-4304 Fax: 902-428-0618
www.gov.ns.ca/coms
The Department of Community Services is committed to a sustainable social service system that promotes the independence, self-reliance, & security of the people it serves.

Acts Administered:
Adoption Information Act
Children & Family Services Act
Day Care Act
Disabled Persons' Commission Act
Employment Support & Income Assistance Act
Homes for Special Care Act
Housing Act
Housing Development Corporation Act
Intercountry Adoption Act
North Queens Nursing Home Act
Protection for Persons in Care Act
Senior Citizens' Financial Aid Act
Senior Citizens' Secretariat Act
Senior Citizens' Social Services Act
Social Assistance Act

Minister, Hon. Denise Peterson-Rafuse
petersdj@gov.ns.ca
Deputy Minister, Robert Wood
902-424-4325, Fax: 902-424-3287, woodrj@gov.ns.ca
Executive Director, Finance & Administration, George Hudson
902-424-2750
Acting Director, Communications, Kirsten Tynes
902-424-6283, Fax: 902-424-3287, tyneska@gov.ns.ca

Associated Agencies, Boards & Commissions:
• Nova Scotia Disabled Persons Commission (NSDPC)
Dartmouth Professional Center
#104, 277 Pleasant St.
Dartmouth, NS B2Y 4B7
902-424-8280 Fax: 902-424-0592 800-565-8280
www.gov.ns.ca/disa
The NSDPC gives people with disabilities a way to participate in the provincial government policy-making process. Its mission is to champion the social & economic inclusion of citizens with disabilities.

Affordable Housing & Repairs
www.gov.ns.ca/coms/housing/index.html
The provincial government offers a number of programs to help lower income households maintain, acquire or rent safe, adequate & ffordable housing.
Director, Housing, Neil MacDonald
902-424-2409

Children, Youth & Families
Fax: 902-424-0708
Executive Director, George Savoury
902-424-8256
Director, Services for Persons with Disabilities, Lorna McPherson
902-424-3387
Director, Child Welfare, Victoria Wood
902-424-5653

Employment Support & Income Assistance
Fax: 902-424-0721
The Employment Support & Income Assistance (ESIA) program helps by giving money for living costs, or providing other kinds of help, when individuals are unable to support themselves or their family.
Director, Income Assistance, Janet Rathbun
902-424-6104
Director, Employment Support Services, Mike Townsend
902-424-4329

Services for Persons with Disabilities
The SPD Program serves children, youth & adults with intellectual disabilities, long-term mental illness, & physical disabilities in a range of community-based, residential & vocational/day programs.
Director, Lorna McPherson
902-424-3787

Regional Offices:

Eastern
#25, 360 Prince St., Sydney, NS B1P 5L1
902-563-3302 Fax: 902-563-5693
Regional Administrator, Cyril Leblanc
902-563-2125

Eastern
295 Charlotte St., Sydney, NS B1P 1C6
902-563-2093 Fax: 902-563-1648
Controller, Winston Musgrave

Central
664 Prince St., 2nd Fl., Truro, NS B2N 1G6
902-893-5896 Fax: 902-893-1648
Controller, Dominic Fewer

Western
151 Exhibition St., Kentville, NS B4N 4E5
902-679-6100 Fax: 902-679-6322
Controller, Vern Fraser

Central
McDonald Bldg., 2131 Gottingen St., PO Box 2623, Halifax, NS B3J 3E4
902-424-5074 Fax: 902-424-5115
Regional Administrator, Lynn Brogan
902-424-2681

Northern
161 Terra Cotta Drive, New Glasgow, NS B2H 6B6
902-755-7023 Fax: 902-752-5088
Regional Administrator, Geraldine MacDonald
902-863-7569

Western
#202, 10 Webster St., Kentville, NS B4N 1H7
902-679-6715 Fax: 902-679-6127
Regional Administrator, Phil Warren
902-863-6716

Council of Atlantic Premiers (CAP)

Council Secretariat, #1006, 5161 George St., PO Box 2044, Halifax, NS B3J 2Z1
902-424-7590 Fax: 902-424-8976
info@cap-cpma.ca
www.cap-cpma.ca
The Premiers of New Brunswick, Newfoundland & Labrador, Nova Scotia & Prince Edward Island constitute the Council. It was established by memorandum of understanding to: promote unity of purpose among their respective Governments; ensure maximum coordination of the activities of the Governments & their agencies; & establish a framework for joint action & undertakings. The Council meets up to four times annually to discuss matters of mutual interest or concern to the four Atlantic governments. A Secretariat acts as the focal point for coordinating the efforts of the four Governments in identifying potential benefits that could result from a regional approach to policy formulation & program development.
Secretary to Council, Don Osmond
902-424-7600
Chief Financial Officer, Rod Casey
902-424-5078
Director, Federal/Provincial Relations, Charles Ayles
902-424-8577, cayles@cap-cmpa.ca

Associated Agencies, Boards & Commissions:
• Council of Atlantic Ministers of Education & Training
PO Box 2044
Halifax, NS B3J 2Z1
902-424-5352 Fax: 902-424-8976
camet_camef@cap-cpma.ca
www.camet-camef.ca
• Maritime Provinces Higher Education Commission (MPHEC) / Commission de l'engseignement supérieur des Provinces Maritimes (CESPM)
#401, 82 Westmorland
Fredericton, PE E3B 5H1
506-453-2844 Fax: 506-453-2106
mphec@mphec.ca
www.mphec.ca
As an Agency of the Council of Atlantic Premiers that provides advice to Ministers responsible for Post-Secondary Education in the Maritimes, the Commission assists institutions & governments in enhancing a post-secondary learning environment that reflects quality, accessibility, mobility, relevance, accountability, scholarship & research.
• Maritime Provinces Harness Racing Commission
5 Gerald McCarville Dr.
PO Box 128
Kensington, PE C0B 1M0
902-836-5500 Fax: 902-836-5320
www.mphrc.ca
The Commission governs, regulates, & supervises harness racing in all of its forms relevant & related to pari-mutuel betting.

Department of Economic & Rural Development

Centennial Building, #600, 1660 Hollis St., PO Box 2311, Halifax, NS B3J 1V7
902-424-0377 Fax: 902-424-0500
comm@gov.ns.ca
www.gov.ns.ca/econ/
The office assists with knowledge management, trade policy, special projects, government relations regarding economic development issues, labour advice, regarding the work force of the future, information on the business climate & assistance on strategic infrastructure. It provides assistance with strategic

management & rural development regarding the business climate, & services such as the Rural Development Branch, Rural Development Service Locations & Co-operatives Branch, dealing with trade policy negotiations & agreements.

Acts Administered:
Business Development Corporation Act
Cooperation Associations Act
Economic Renewal Agency Act
Industry Closing Act
Industrial Development Act
Industrial Estates Limited Act
Industrial Loan Act
Industrial Property Act
Innovation Corporation Act
Nova Scotia Business Incorporated Act
Nova Scotia Film Development Corporation Act
Regional Community Development Act
Research Foundation Corporation Act
Small Business Development Act
Sydney Steel Corporation Act
Tourist Accommodations Act
Trade Development Authority Act
Venture Corporation Act
Venture Corporation Act - Regulations
Voluntary Planning Act

Minister, Hon. Percy Paris
902-424-5790, Fax: 902-424-0514, econmin@gov.ns.ca
Deputy Minister, Ian Thompson
902-424-2901, Fax: 902-424-0619, thompsia@gov.ns.ca
Executive Director, Tourism Division, John Somers
902-424-4554, somersjh@gov.ns.ca
Director, Program Managment, Elizabeth D. Beck
902-424-4641
Director, Robert Edwin Book
902-424-7577
Director, Procurement, Rick Draper
902-424-4557
Acting Director, Communications, Jennifer Gavin
902-424-4998, Fax: 902-424-7008
Director, Economic Strategies & Initiatives, Bruce Hennebury
902-424-5757, hennebub@gov.ns.ca
Director, Decision Support, Liliani Kumaranayake
902-424-4641
Director, Development Initiatives, Marvyn C. Robar
902-424-3973

Associated Agencies, Boards & Commissions:
• Canada-Nova Scotia Offshore Petroleum Board
TD Centre
1791 Barrington St., 6th Fl.
Halifax, NS B3J 3K9
902-422-5588 Fax: 902-422-1799
postmaster@cnsopb.ns.ca
www.cnsopb.ns.ca
The Canada-Nova Scotia Offshore Petroleum Board (CNSOPB) is responsible for protection of the environment during all phases of offshore petroleum activities, from initial exploration to abandonment. The Board is a Federal Authority under the Canadian Environmental Assessment Act. The environmental assessment process starts at the Call for Bids stage. At this stage, a strategic or broad environmental assessment is conducted which identifies environmental concerns or issues. All subsequent projects, including seismic programs & exploratory wells, must undergo an environmental assessment prior to approval by the CNSOPB. The Board also uses class screenings or generic assessments to streamline the regulatory process. These more in-depth environmental assessments, usually jointly funded by a number of petroleum companies, provide more detailed overviews of potential environmental effects, research priorities & mitigation measure than can be accomplished in a single project-specific environmental assessment.
• InNOVACorp
#1400, 1801 Hollis St.
Halifax, NS B3J 3N4
902-424-8670 Fax: 902-424-4679 800-565-7051
communications@innovacorp.ca
www.innovacorp.ns.ca
Other Communication: www.twitter.com/innovacorp
A network of business resources for the early stage technology entrepreneur. Key services include research & development support, business advice, investment & partnership advice. Focuses on two main growth sectors: life sciences & information technology.
• Nova Scotia Business Inc. (NSBI)
World Trade & Convention Centre
#701, 1800 Argyle St.
PO Box 2374
Halifax, NS B3J 3N8
902-424-6650 Fax: 902-424-5739 800-260-6682
info@nsbi.ca
www.novascotiabusiness.com
Other Communication: www.twitter.com/nsbi; www.facebook.com/novscotiabusiness
NSBI is the first point of contact for local companies that want to grow in Nova Scotia, and for international companies that have heard about the province and want to know more.
• Film Nova Scotia
Collins Bank Bldg.
1869 Upper Water St., 3rd Fl.
Halifax, NS B3J 1S9
902-424-7177 Fax: 902-424-0617 888-360-2111
www.film.ns.ca
Created in 1990 under the Film Development Corporation Act, Film Nova Scotia is a Provincial Crown Corporation reporting to the Minister of Economic and Rural Development. A Board of Directors, appointed by the Governor in Council, directs the Corporation's activities.
• Trade Centre Limited
1800 Argyle St.
PO Box 955
Halifax, NS B3J 2V9
902-421-8686 Fax: 902-422-2922
www.tradecentrelimited.com
Trade Centre Limited creates economic benefits by bringing people together in Halifax & Nova Scotia.
• Waterfront Development Corporation Ltd.
1751 Lower Water St., 2nd Fl.
Halifax, NS B3J 1S5
902-422-6591 Fax: 902-422-7582
info@wdcl.ca
www.my-waterfront.ca/about-wdcl
Other Communication: www.facebook.com/pages/my-waterfront/139091936107397; www.twitter.com/my_waterfront
Coordinates the commercial & recreational development of the downtown waterfront of Halifax & Dartmouth.

Regional/Service Offices:

Amherst
35 Church St., Amherst, NS B4H 4A1
902-667-3233 Fax: 902-667-2270

Antigonish
#4, 149 Church St., Antigonish, NS B2G 2E2
902-863-7539 Fax: 902-863-7477

Bridgewater
220 North St., Bridgewater, NS B4V 2V6
902-530-3117 Fax: 902-543-1156

Cape Breton
#207, 275 Charlotte St., Sydney, NS B1P 1C6
902-563-2070 Fax: 902-563-0500

Capital Region
Centennial Building, #600, 1660 Hollis St., PO Box 2311, Halifax, NS B3J 1V7
902-424-4319 Fax: 902-424-1263
800-565-2009

Kentville
#103, 35 Webster St., Kentville, NS B4N 1H4
902-679-6116 Fax: 902-679-6094

Northeastern Region
#3-80 Walker St., Truro, NS B2N 4A7
902-893-6212 Fax: 902-893-6108

Southwestern Shore/Valley
Pier One Complex, 103 Water St., Yarmouth, NS B5A 4P4
902-742-8404 Fax: 902-742-0019

Department of Education

Trade Mart Bldg., #402-2021 Brunswick St., PO Box 578, Halifax, NS B3J 2S9
902-424-5168 Fax: 902-424-0680
www.ednet.ns.ca
Other Communication: www.twitter.com/nseducation

The mission of the Department of Education is to provide excellence in education & training for personal fulfillment & for a productive, prosperous society.

Acts Administered:
Acadia University Act
Agriculture & Marketing Act, as it pertains to the Agreements of the Nova Scotia Agricultural College Regulations
Apprenticeship & Trades Qualifications Act
Atlantic Provinces Special Education Act
Atlantic School of Theology Act
Barbers Act
Community Colleges Act
Cosmetology Act
Dalhousie College & University Act
Dalhousie-Technical University Amalgamation Act
Degree Granting Act
Education Act
Education Assistance Act
Hospital Education Assistance Act
Libraries Act
Maritime Provinces Higher Education (Nova Scotia) Act
Mi'kmaq Education Act
Mount Saint Vincent University Act
Nova Scotia College of Art & Design Act
Nova Scotia School Boards Association Act
Nova Scotia Teachers College Foundation Act
Private Career Colleges Regulations Act
Registered Barbers Act
Saint Mary's University Act
School Loan Fund Act
Southwestern Nova Scotia Community College Act
St. Francis Xavier University Act
Student Aid Act
Teachers' Collective Bargaining Act
Teaching Profession Act
Universities Assistance Act
Université Saint-Anne Act
University Foundations Act
University College of Cape Breton Act
University Kings College Act
Youth Secretariat Act

Minister, Hon. Ramona Jennex
902-424-4236, Fax: 902-424-0680, educmin@gov.ns.ca
Deputy Minister, Rosalind C. Penfound
902-424-5643, repenfou@gov.ns.ca
Director, Communication, Peter McLaughlin
mclaughpx@gov.ns.ca

Associated Agencies, Boards & Commissions:
• Nova Scotia Advisory Board on Colleges & Universities
2021 Brunswick St.
PO Box 2086 M
Halifax, NS B3J 3B7
Fax: 902-424-0651

Acadian & French Language Services
902-424-3927 Fax: 902-424-3937
www.ednet.ns.ca/afls.shtml
Other Communication: www.dsalf.ednet.ns.ca
The Acadian & French Language Services Branch monitors & approves curriculum development for French first language education, collaborates with other branches of the department to ensure common services are available in French for first language schools, coordinates activities related to federal-provincial funding agreements for French minority language education and French language instruction, & coordinates & manages implementation of national official language programs in Nova Scotia.
Senior Executive Director, Acadian & French Language Programs, Gilles LeBlanc
902-424-6097, leblangg@gov.ns.ca
Director, French Programs, Margelaine Holding
902-424-6626, holdingms@gov.ns.ca
Director, Services to Francophones, Ronald Boudreau
902-424-0538, Fax: 902-424-6546, boudrere@gov.ns.ca

Corporate Policy
902-424-5294 Fax: 902-424-0519
www.ednet.ns.ca/corporatepolicy.shtml
Other Communication: 902-424-4684 (Freedom of Information & Protection of Privacy Review Office)
Corporate Policy is responsible for providing assistance & support in policy, planning, legislation, research, coordination, & information & publishing services to all areas of the department. It also coordinates departmental accountability processes including the departmental business plan & support to school board planning processes.
Officer, Freedom of Information & Protection of Privacy Review, Dulcie McCallum
902-424-8277, mccalld@gov.ns.ca
Director, Policy & Planning, Shannon Delbridge
902-424-5242, delbrisd@gov.ns.ca

Corporate Services
www.ednet.ns.ca/corporateservices.shtml
This branch comprises Financial Management, Education Funding & Accountability, Facilities Management, Information Technology Services, Statistics & Data Management, & Teacher Certification. It is responsible for the delivery of business & support services to the Department of Education, including financial management & controllership responsibilities, provision of facilities planning & capital projects, coordination of pupil transportation with boards, information technology, and province-wide delivery of data communications.
Chief Operating Officer, Frank Dunn
902-423-7635, Fax: 902-424-1866, dunnfm@gov.ns.ca
Director, Financial Management, Ben McIntyre
902-424-5698, Fax: 902-424-1866, mcintybr@gov.ns.ca
Director, Grants & Audits, Joe MacEachern
902-424-3956, Fax: 902-424-1866, maceacj@gov.ns.ca
Director, Information Technology Services, John Fahie
902-424-2823, Fax: 902-424-0874, fahiejw@gov.ns.ca
Assistant Director, Facilities Management, Charles Ritchey
902-424-7499, Fax: 902-424-0732, ritcheyc@gov.ns.ca

Public Schools
www.ednet.ns.ca/publicschools.shtml

The Public Schools Branch designs, develops, implements, & evaluates programs, courses, services, related policies & resources including student & teaching resources to support implementation, for the public school system, correspondence studies, & on-line learning.
Senior Executive Director, Alan Lowe
902-424-5829, lowead@gov.ns.ca
Executive Director, English Program Services, Ann Blackwood
902-424-5475
Director, Mi'Kmaq Liasion Office, Candy Palmater
902-424-8625

Elections Nova Scotia

#6-7037 Mumford Rd., PO Box 2246, Halifax, NS B3J 2J1
902-424-8584 Fax: 902-424-6622
800-565-1504
elections@gov.ns.ca
www.electionsnovascotia.ns.ca
TTY: 866-774-7074

Elections Nova Scotia is independent of any political affiliation, including the government in power. It ensures that every election, by-election, & liquor plebiscite is held in a fair & impartial manner (according to the Elections Act and other relevant laws) & that all political parties & candidates act within the rules.
Chief Electoral Officer, Christine McCulloch
mccullca@gov.ns.ca
Director, Communications, Dana Doiron
902-424-3275, doriondp@gov.ns.ca

Nova Scotia Emergency Management Office (EMO)

PO Box 2581, Halifax, NS B3J 3N5
902-424-5620 Fax: 902-424-5376
866-424-5620
emo@gov.ns.ca
www.gov.ns.ca/emo

Coordinating agency of the Nova Scotia Government with the responsibility of assisting municipalities to plan & prepare for emergencies; responsible for the implementation of the province-wide 911 service. Coordinates emergency efforts of provincial & federal departments & agencies, as well as private health & social services, to provide assistance to disaster areas; sponsors the Ground Search & Rescue Program; maintains a professional planner at all offices. Coordinates all emergency preparedness training for municipal staff at the Emergency Preparedness College (Arnprior, ON) & through the Joint Emergency Preparedness Program (JEPP), which provides a federal government cost-sharing formula for emergency equipment for first-response agencies.
Acts Administered:
Emergency Management Act
Emergency 911 Act
Minister Responsible, Hon. Ross Landry
902-424-4044, Fax: 902-424-0510, justmin@gov.ns.ca
Chief Executive Officer & Deputy Minister, Marian Tyson
tysonmf@gov.ns.ca
Director, Emergency Services, Michael Myette
902-424-6206
Director, Emergency Services, Michelle Perry
902-424-0284, perrymx@gov.ns.ca

Department of Energy

Bank of Montreal Bldg., #400, 5151 George St., PO Box 2664, Halifax, NS B3J 3P7
902-424-4575 Fax: 902-424-0528
energyinfo@gov.ns.ca
www.gov.ns.ca/energy

To serve as the government's focal point in the development of the province's energy resources, as outlined in the Energy Strategy. Responsible for a wide range of initiatives in the following areas: energy transportation & utilization policy & analysis; resource assessment & royalties; climate change; business & technology; communications & public education.
Acts Administered:
Canada-Nova Scotia Offshore Petroleum Resources Accord Implementation (Nova Scotia) Act
Canada-Newfoundland Labrador Offshore Area Regulations
Nova Scotia Offshore Area Certificate of Fitness Regulations
Nova Scotia Offshore Area Oil & Gas Spills & Debris Liability Regulations
Nova Scotia Offshore Area Petroleum Diving Regulations
Nova Scotia Offshore Area Petroleum Drilling Regulations
Nova Scotia Offshore Area Petroleum Geophysical Operations Regulations
Nova Scotia Offshore Area Petroleum Installations Regulations
Nova Scotia Offshore Petroleum Production & Conservation Regulations
Sable Offshore Energy Project Regulations
Electricity Act
Energy-Efficient Appliances Act
Energy Resources Conservation Act
Gas Plant Facility Regulations
Onshore Petroleum Geophysical Exploration Regulations
Gas Distribution Act
Natural Gas Transmission Pipeline Assessment Regulations
Offshore Petroleum Royalty Act
Petroleum Resources Act
Onshore Petroleum Drilling Regulations
Onshore Petroleum Geophysical Exploration Regulations
Petroleum Resources Removal Permit Act
Pipeline Act
Land Acquisition Regulations
Pipeline Benefits Plan Regulations
Pipeline Regulations
Sable Offshore Energy Project Regulations
Underground Hydrocarbons Storage Act
Minister, Hon. Charlie Parker
902-424-7793, Fax: 902-424-3265, energyminister@gov.ns.ca
Deputy Minister, Murray Coolican
902-424-4450, Fax: 902-424-3265, coolicm@gov.ns.ca
Executive Secretary to the Minister, Diane Bernard
902-424-7793, Fax: 902-424-3265, bernardm@gov.ns.ca

Associated Agencies, Boards & Commissions:
• Utility & Review Board (UARB)
Summit Place
1601 Lower Water St., 3rd Fl.
PO Box 1692 M
Halifax, NS B3J 3S3
902-424-4448 Fax: 902-424-3919
uarb.board@gov.ns.ca
www.nsuarb.ca
The Nova Scotia Utility & Review Board is an independent quasi-judicial body which has both regulatory adjudicative jurisdiction flowing from the Utility and Review Board Act.

Business & Technology
http://www.gov.ns.ca/energy/what-we-do.asp#business-technology
Director, Charles Bernard MacDonald
902-424-2704

Communications & Public Education
http: //www.gov.ns.ca/energy/what-we-do.asp#communications
Director, Communications, Nancy Watson
902-424-1195, watsonnm@gov.ns.ca

Energy Fiscal Affairs
902-424-6673
http: //www.gov.ns.ca/energy/what-we-do.asp#energy-fiscal
Director, Energy Markets, Reginald Scott McCoombs
Director, Chris Spencer

Energy Markets
http: //www.gov.ns.ca/energy/what-we-do.asp#energy-markets

Resource Assessment
http://www.gov.ns.ca/energy/what-we-do.asp#resource-assessment

Strategic Policy, Planning & Services
http: //www.gov.ns.ca/energy/what-we-do.asp#spps

Department of Environment

5151 Terminal Rd., 5th Fl., PO Box 442, Halifax, NS B3J 2P8
902-424-3600 Fax: 902-424-0503
877-936-8476
www.gov.ns.ca/nse

Major program responsibilities for Nova Scotia Environment are environmental & natural areas management, environmental monitoring & compliance, & climate change. Pollution prevention, the NS Youth Conservation Corps., solid waste reduction & recycling, & environmental trade & innovation are all part of the new Nova Scotia Environment.
Acts Administered:
Anti-idling Act
Court & Administrative Reform Act (Department of Justice)
Environment Act
Environmental Goals & Sustainable Prosperity Act
Health Protection Act
Non-essential Pesticides Control Act
Off-highway Vehicles Act
Special Places Protection Act
Wilderness Areas Protection Act
Minister, Hon. Sterling Belliveau
902-424-3736, Fax: 902-424-1599, min_env@gov.ns.ca
Deputy Minister, Sara Jane Snook
902-424-8150, Fax: 902-424-1599, snooksj@gov.ns.ca
Executive Secretary, Virginia Messervey
902-424-3736, messerv@gov.ns.ca
Acting Director, Jason Hollett
902-424-0784, holletjn@gov.ns.ca

Communications
www.gov.ns.ca/nse/dept/division.communications.asp
The Communications Division provides strategic communications planning & advice for the department. It is responsible for all external communications functions carried out for the department, including issues management, advertising, & media relations, & shares responsibility within the department for internal communications.
Director, Karen White
whitekl@gov.ns.ca

Environmental Monitoring & Compliance
902-424-2547 Fax: 902-424-0569
877-936-8476
emc@gov.ns.ca
www.gov.ns.ca/nse/dept/division.emc.asp
The Environmental Monitoring Compliance Division is responsible for the majority of field operations relating to environmental protection.
Executive Director, Regional & District Offices, Darlene Fenton
902-424-2547, 877-936-8476, Fax: 902-424-0569

Environment & Sustainable Prosperity Partnerships
www.gov.ns.ca/nse/dept/division.espp.asp
The Division aims to provide leadership & coordination of community engagement activities in Environment (and more broadly) is responsible for delivery of major environmental service contracts with the private sector.

Environmental Science & Program Management
www.gov.ns.ca/nse/dept/division.espm.asp
The Environmental Science & Program Management Division promotes sustainable management & protection of the environment through both regulatory & non-regulatory means, including developing & implementing plans, standards, guidelines, & policies for the management & protection of Nova Scotia's air, water & terrestrial resources including protected areas, & by providing regionally-based regulatory approval, inspection, monitoring & enforcement.

Policy & Corporate Services
www.gov.ns.ca/nse/dept/division.pcs.asp
Founded in 2009, this division combines former divisions (Competitiveness & Compliance, Environmental Assessment, Information & Business Services, & Policy).
Director, Scott Nicholson
nicholsw@gov.ns.ca
Librarian, Natalie MacPherson
902-424-8474, macphend@gov.ns.ca
Executive Director, Policy & Corporate Services, Chris Daly
902-424-4936

Department of Finance

Provincial Bldg., 1723 Hollis St., 7th Fl., PO Box 187, Halifax, NS B3J 2N3
902-424-5554 Fax: 902-424-0635
FinanceWeb@gov.ns.ca
www.gov.ns.ca/fina
Other Communication: www.twitter.com/NSFinance

The Department of Finance's vision is to provide financial leadership that strengthens Nova Scotia; & their mission is to provide corporate financial services & manage the province's financial affairs & policies in the interests of Nova Scotians.
Acts Administered:
Corporation Capital Tax Act
Credit Union Act
Equity Tax Credit Act
Finance Act
Gaming Control Act - Part I
Halifax-Dartmouth Bridge Commission Act
Home Ownership Savings Plan (Nova Scotia) Act
Homeowners' Incentive Act
Income Tax Act
Insurance Act
Insurance Premiums Tax Act
Members' Retiring Allowances Act
NS Power Privatization Act
Public Sector Compensation Disclosure Act
Public Sector Unpaid Leave Act
Public Service Superannuation Act
Public Sector Unpaid Leave Act
Revenue Act
Sales Tax Act
Securities Act
Sydney Steel Corporation Sale Act
Tax Collection Agreement (1961) Act
Trust & Loan Companies Act
Teachers' Pension Act
Utility & Review Board Act
Minister, Hon. Graham Steele
902-424-5720, financeminister@gov.ns.ca
Deputy Minister, Margaret MacDonald
902-424-5744, macdonmf@gov.ns.ca
Associate Deputy Minister, Bryon Rafuse
902-424-4168, rafusebg@gov.ns.ca
Executive Secretary to the Deputy Minister, Barbara Alison MacIsaac
902-424-5553, macisaab@gov.ns.ca

Associated Agencies, Boards & Commissions:

• Nova Scotia Utility & Review Board (NSUARB)
Summit Place
1601 Lower Water St., 3rd Fl.
Halifax, NS B3J 3P6
902-424-4448 Fax: 902-424-3919
uarb.board@gov.ns.ca
www.nsuarb.ca
The Nova Scotia Utility & Review Board (NSUARB) is an independent quasi-judicial body which has both regulatory & adjudicative jurisdiction flowing from the Utility & Review Board Act. It reports to the Legislature through the Minister of Finance.

Capital Markets Administration
http://www.gov.ns.ca/finance/en/home/aboutfinance/divisions.aspx
The Capital Markets Administration division provides all post trade settlement & accounting functions for the Nova Scotia Pension Agency investment & the Province's debt portfolio activities.
Director, Vicki Dimick

Communications
http://www.gov.ns.ca/finance/en/home/aboutfinance/divisions.aspx
The Communications division promotes the Department of Finance's programs & policies to the public, primarily Nova Scotians.
Director, Michelle Lucas
902-424-8787, lucasms@gov.ns.ca

Corporate Information Systems (CIS)
http://www.gov.ns.ca/finance/en/home/aboutfinance/divisions.aspx
CIS provides ongoing support for the SAP systems within provincial departments & agencies, school boards, regional housing authorities & six municipalities within Nova Scotia.
Director, Steve Feindel
902-424-2939, feindesj@gov.ns.ca

Finance Corporate Services Unit (CSU)
The Finance CSU supplies support in all aspects of financial management to other government departments.
Director, Joyce McDonald
902-424-7395, mcdonajm@gov.ns.ca

Financial Institutions
902-424-6331 Fax: 902-424-1298
The Financial Institutions Division regulates the operations of credit unions, trust & loan companies & insurance companies, agents, brokers & adjusters in the Province. The Division also provides a complaint & enquiry service to the public relating to financial institutions & the insurance industry & collects & verifies the insurance premiums tax.
Director, Doug Murphy
902-424-7552, murphydh@gov.ns.ca
Manager, Audit & Examination, William Ngu
902-424-2787

Fiscal & Economic Policy Branch
www.gov.ns.ca/finance/en/home/aboutfinance/divisions.aspx
Executive Director, Michael DeCoste
902-424-2421
Director, Economic & Statistics, Thomas Storring
902-424-2410, storrith@gov.ns.ca
Director, Taxation & Fiscal Policy, Paul Davies
902-424-4655, Fax: 902-424-0590, daviespb@gov.ns.ca

Government Accounting
http://www.gov.ns.ca/finance/en/home/aboutfinance/divisions.aspx
Director, Financial Accounting, Suzanne Wile
902-424-7021, wilesm@gov.ns.ca

Information Management
http://www.gov.ns.ca/finance/en/home/aboutfinance/divisions.aspx
Promotes the coordinated & consistent management of records & information throughout their life cycle. IM supports informed decision making, access to information & protection of privacy, & due diligence through good record keeping.
Manager, Angela Smith
902-424-7932, ajsmith@gov.ns.ca

Internal Audit Centre
http://www.gov.ns.ca/finance/en/home/aboutfinance/divisions.aspx
Internal Audit strives to improve the effectiveness of risk management, control, & governance processes. It examines & evaluates internal controls to determine if they're adequate & effective. Compliance issues are regularly addressed & operational reviews assess efficiency & performance.
Executive Director, Ted Doane
DOANEET@gov.ns.ca

Liability Management & Treasury Services
http://www.gov.ns.ca/finance/en/home/aboutfinance/divisions.aspx
Responsible for ensuring effective money management, maximizing return on investments & minimizing debt servicing costs within risk tolerances acceptable to government.
Executive Director, Peter Urbanc
902-424-2435, urbancpv@gov.ns.ca

Middle Office Compliance & Reporting
http://www.gov.ns.ca/finance/en/home/aboutfinance/divisions.aspx
Ensures that the investment & debt management activities are compliant with legislature as well as Finance's objectives & policy limits by guaranteeing that best-in-class practices/policies/processes are in place to adequately control activities, such as monitoring & reporting ongoing investment & debt activities to management & Governance Committees.
Director, Vicki Dimick
dimickvc@gov.ns.ca

Payroll Services
http://www.gov.ns.ca/finance/en/home/aboutfinance/divisions.aspx
Provides payroll services for employees of the Province, the regional school boards, & selective crown corporations, agencies & boards, as well as for retirees of the province & teachers superannuation plans.
Director, Blair McNaughton
MCNAUGBN@gov.ns.ca

Policy & Planning
www.gov.ns.ca/finance/en/home/aboutfinance/divisions.aspx
Works in cooperation with the Treasury & Policy Board to develop corporate fiscal & economic policies, & supports coordinated information flows into & out of the department & intra & inter-departmental collaboration.
Executive Director, Diana Eisenhauer
eisendi@gov.ns.ca

Department of Fisheries & Aquaculture

1741 Brunswick St., 3rd Fl., PO Box 2223, Halifax, NS B3J 3C4
902-424-4560 Fax: 902-424-4671
www.gov.ns.ca/fish
The Department of Fisheries & Aquaculture's mission is to foster prosperous and sustainable fisheries, aquaculture and food industries through the delivery of quality public services for the betterment of coastal communities and of all Nova Scotians.
Acts Administered:
Fisheries & Coastal Resources Act
Fisheries Organizations Support Act
Wildlife Act (Fishing Regulations only)
Minister, Hon. Sterling Belliveau
902-637-3200, Fax: 902-637-3530, min_dfa@gov.ns.ca,
Other Communications: 902-875-9090 (Shelburne office)
Deputy Minister & Chief Executive Officer, Paul LaFleche
902-424-0300, laflecpt@gov.ns.ca
Associate Deputy Minister, Gregory Roach
902-424-0348, Fax: 902-424-1766, roachg@gov.ns.ca
Director, Communications, Celeste Sulliman
902-424-0192, sullimcc@gov.ns.ca

Associated Agencies, Boards & Commissions:
• Fisheries & Aquaculture Loan Board
1741 Brunswick St., 3rd Fl.
PO Box 2223
Halifax, NS B3J 3C4
902-424-0318 Fax: 902-424-3502
www.gov.ns.ca/nsaf/loanboards/fishlb/

Nova Scotia Pension Agency
Purdy's Landing, #400, 1949 Upper Water St., PO Box 371, Halifax, NS B3J 3N3
PensionsInfo@gov.ns.ca
Other Communication: www.novascotiapension.ca
Chief Executive Officer, Steven R. Wolff
902-424-3746, wolffsr@gov.ns.ca
Director, Investments, Elizabeth Vandenburg
902-424-2715, Fax: 902-424-4539, vandenbe@gov.ns.ca
Director, Pensions Operations, Kim Blinn
902-424-8415, blinnkm@gov.ns.ca

Marine Division
Manager, Innovations & Field Services, Bruce Osborne
902-424-0352, osbornbd@gov.ns.ca

Aquaculture Division
Director, Marshall Giles
902-424-3664, gilesm@gov.ns.ca

Inland Fisheries Division
Director, Murray Hill
902-485-7021, macleand@gov.ns.ca

Department of Health & Wellness

Joseph Howe Bldg., 1690 Hollis St., 4th Fl., PO Box 488, Halifax, NS B3J 2R8
902-424-5818 Fax: 902-424-0730
800-387-6665
DoHweb@gov.ns.ca
www.gov.ns.ca/health
TTY: 800-670-8888
Other Communication: TeleHealth Network: 1-800-889-5949
Mission: Working together to empower individuals, families, partners, and communities to promote, improve, and maintain the health of Nova Scotians through a proactive and sustainable health care system.
Acts Administered:
Chiropractic Act
Cobequid Multi-Service Centre Act
Dental Act
Dental Hygienists Act
Dental Technicians Act
Denturist Act
Department of Health Promotion & Protection Act
Disabled Persons Commissions Act
Dispensing Opticians Act
Drug Dependency Act
Fair Drug Pricing Act
Health Act
Health Authorities Act
Health Protection Act
Health Research Foundation Act
Health Services & Insurance Act
Homemakers' Services Act
Homes for Special Care Act
Hospitals Act
Involuntary Psychiatric Treatment Act
Licensed Practical Nurses Act
Mandatory Testing & Disclosure Act
Medical Act
Medical Professional Corporations Act
Medical Laboratory Technology Act
Medical Radiation Technologists Act
Midwifery Act
Municipal Hospitals Loan Act
Occupational Therapists Act
Optometry Act
Part I - Gaming Control Act
Pharmacy Act
Physiotherapy Act
Prescription Monitoring Act
Protection for Persons in Care Act
Psychologists Act
Registered Nurses' Act
Registered Nurses Association Act
Registered Therapists Act
Safer Needles in Healthcare Workplaces Act
Smoke-free Places Act
Social Assistance Act
Tanning Beds Act
Tobacco Access Act
Minister, Hon. Maureen MacDonald
902-424-3377, Fax: 902-424-0559,
health.minister@gov.ns.ca
Deputy Minister, Kevin McNamara
902-424-7570, Fax: 902-424-4570, mcnamakd@gov.ns.ca
Associate Deputy Minister, Frances Martin
902-424-2080, martinfr@gov.ns.ca
Chief Financial Officer, Linda Ruth Penny
902-424-4840
Executive Director, Strategic Financial Operations, Abram James Almeda
902-424-4476
Executive Director, Health System Workforce, Carmelle d'Entremont
902-424-8686
Executive Director, Policy & Planning, Tracey Williams
902-424-7931
Senior Director, Labour Relations, Richard Anderson
902-424-7730
Senior Director, Janet Braunstein
902-424-5187
Senior Director, Sport & Research, Farida Gabbani
902-424-7554
Chief Medical Director, Carman Giacomantonio
902-473-6177
Senior Director, Physical Activity, Sport & Recreation, Farida Gabbani
902-424-7554, gabbanfg@gov.ns.ca
Senior Director, Legislative Policy, Dennis Holland
902-424-3351
Director, Communications, Sherri Aikenhead
902-424-5579, sherri.aikenhead@gov.ns.ca
Director, Policy & Planning, Tracey Barbrick
902-424-7337

Director, Acute & Tertiary Care, Lewis Bedford
902-424-5497
Director, Health Intergovernmental Affairs, Vijay Bhashyakarla
902-424-2842
Director, Heather Jane Christian
902-424-5869
Director, Carolyn Davison
902-424-7218, davisocj@gov.ns.ca
Director, Technical Operations, Anthony Eden
902-424-4429
Director, Health Services, Kevin Elliott
902-424-6869
Director, Acute Care, Katherine Fraser
902-424-4878
Director, Active & Healthy Living, Rick Gilbert
902-424-2772, Fax: 902-424-0520, gilberrf@gov.ns.ca
Director, Fin. & Admin. Internal Support, Gary Glessing
902-424-6138
Director, Primary Health Care, Lisa Ruth Grandy
902-424-4617
Director, Long Term Care, Dean Hirtle
902-424-1797
Director, Chronic Disease & Injury Prevention, Nancy Hoddinott
902-424-5840
Director, Lindsay Marja Hugenholtz
902-490-3200
Director, Health Economics, Michael Joyce
902-427-6879
Director, Health Privacy Office, Maria Lasheras
902-424-8214
Director, Insured Services, Harold McCarthy
902-424-7538
Director, Karen McDuff
902-424-2635
Director, Environmental Health, Gary O'Toole
902-424-1262
Director, AIDS Commission, Michelle Proctor-Simms
902-424-4741
Director, Standards & Policy, Susan Stevens
902-424-6857
Director, Emergency Managment Centre, Russell Stuart
902-424-0000

Associated Agencies, Boards & Commissions:
• Nova Scotia Advisory Commission on AIDS
Dennis Bldg.
1740 Granville St., 6th Fl.
Halifax, NS B3J 1X5
902-424-5730 Fax: 902-424-4727
AIDS@gov.ns.ca
www.gov.ns.ca/aids/
• Seniors' Secretariat
Dennis Bldg.
1740 Granville St., 4th Fl.
PO Box 2065
Halifax, NS B3J 2Z1
902-424-0065 Fax: 902-424-0561 800-670-0065
seniors@gov.ns.ca
www.gov.ns.ca/seniors/

Nova Scotia Human Rights Commission

Joseph Howe Bldg., 1690 Hollis St., 6th Fl., Halifax, NS B3J 3C4
902-424-4111 Fax: 902-424-0596
hrcinquiries@gov.ns.ca
www.humanrights.gov.ns.ca
TTY: 902-424-3139

Acts Administered:
Human Rights Act
Minister, Justice, Hon. Ross Landry
902-424-4044, Fax: 902-424-0510, justmin@gov.ns.ca
Director & CEO, Vacant

Regional Offices:

Digby
84 Warwick St., PO Box 1029, Digby, NS B0V 1A0
902-245-4791 Fax: 902-245-7103

Office of Immigration

#110A, 1741 Brunswick St., PO Box 1535, Halifax, NS B3J 2Y3
902-424-5230 Fax: 902-424-7936
immigration@gov.ns.ca
www.novascotiaimmigration.com

Mission: Working together to empower individuals, families, partners, and communities to promote, improve, and maintain the health of Nova Scotians through a proactive and sustainable health care system.
Minister, Hon. Marilyn More
902-424-7627, Fax: 902-428-3178, min_immigration@gov.ns.ca
Deputy Minister, Hon. Judith Ferguson
902-424-3603, fergusjf@gov.ns.ca
Director, Communications, Tom Peck
902-423-3742, peckto@gov.ns.ca

Communications
902-424-7640 Fax: 902-424-0692
Director, Donna Chislett
902-424-3313, Fax: 902-424-0510, chisledp@gov.ns.ca
Director, Ross McLaren
902-424-3313, Fax: 902-424-0510, MCLARENR@gov.ns.ca

Sydney
Provincial Bldg., 360 Prince St., Sydney, NS B1P 5L1
902-563-2140 Fax: 902-563-5613

Correctional Services
902-424-7640 Fax: 902-424-0692
Executive Director, Corrections, Diana MacKinnon
902-424-5661
Director, David Bungay
902-563-2362
Director, David William Horner
902-424-6437
Director, Sean Kelly
902-424-5342

Department of Intergovernmental Affairs

Duke Tower, 5251 Duke St., 5th Fl., PO Box 1617, Halifax, NS B3J 2Y3
Fax: 902-424-0728
iga@gov.ns.ca
http: //gov.ns.ca/iga

Provides leadership in the development of corporate strategies for Nova Scotia's relations with governments & organizations.
Minister, Hon. Darrell Dexter
902-424-6600, 800-267-1993, Fax: 902-424-7648, premier@gov.ns.ca
Deputy Minister, Judith Sullivan-Corney
902-424-3219, corneyjm@gov.ns.ca
Associate Deputy Minister, Scott Logan
902-424-2094, logansm@gov.ns.ca
Director, Regional Relations, Darryl C. Eisan
902-424-4535, dceisan@gov.ns.ca
Director, Strategic Policy, Norma MacIsaac
902-424-7662, macisanj@gov.ns.ca
Director, Economic Policy & Analysis, André Moore
902-424-7728, mooreac@gov.ns.ca
Director, Environmental & Social Affairs, Albert Walzak
902-424-7748, walzakag@gov.ns.ca

Court Services
902-424-7640 Fax: 902-424-0692
Director, William Clancey
902-424-6414
Director, Shauna Lee Wilson
902-563-3545

Finance & Administration
902-424-7640 Fax: 902-424-0692
Director, Finance, Lisa MacKinnon
902-424-6530

Department of Justice

5151 Terminal Rd., 4th Fl., PO Box 7, Halifax, NS B3J 2L6
902-424-4030 Fax: 902-424-0510
justweb@gov.ns.ca
www.gov.ns.ca/just/

Acts Administered:
Age of Majority Act
Alimony Act
Alternative Penalty Act
Apportionment Act
Arbitration Act
Architects Act
Assignments & Preferences Act
Barristers & Solicitors Act
Beneficiaries Designation Act
Bills of Lading Act
Canada & the United Kingdom Reciprocal Recognition & Enforcement of Judgments Act
Canadian Forces Reservists Protection Act
Cape Breton Barristers' Society Act
Change of Name Act
Child Abduction Act
Collection Act
Communications & Information Act
Compensation for Victims of Crime Act
Constables Act
Constables' Protection Act
Constitutional Questions Act
Contributory Negligence Act
Controverted Elections Act
Conveyancing Act
Corrections Act
Costs & Fees Act
Corporations Miscellaneous Provisions Act
Correctional Services Act
Court & Administrative Reform
Court for Divorce & Matrimonial Causes Act
Court Houses & Lockup Houses Act
Court Officials Act
Court Security Act
Creditors' Relief Act
Defamation Act
Demise of the Crown Act
Descent of Property Act
Divorce Act
Domestic Violence Act
Engineering Profession Act
Elections Act
Enforcement of Canadian Judges & Decrees Act
Escheats Act
Estate Actions Act
Estreats Act
Evidence Act
Expropriation Act
Family Court Act
Family Maintenance Act
Family Orders Information Release Act
Fatal Injuries Act
Fatality Investigations Act
Federal/Provincial Power Act
Flea Markets Regulation Act
Floral Emblem Act
Forcible Entry & Detainer Act
Freedom of Information & Protection of Privacy Act
Guardianship Act
Gunshot Wounds Act
House of Assembly Act
Human Rights Act
Incompetent Persons Act
Indigent Debtors Act
Inebriates' Guardianship Act
Interest on Judgements Act
Interior Designers Act
Interjurisdictional Act
International Commercial Arbitration Act
Interpretation Act
Interprovincial Subpoena Act
Intestate Succession Act
Judicature Act
Judicial Disqualifications Removal Act
Juries Act
Justices of the Peace Act
Land Actions Venue Act
Law Reform Commission Act
Legal Aid Act
Liberty of the Subject Act
Lieutenant Governor & Great Seal Act
Limitation of Actions Act
Lobbyists' Registration Act
Maintenance Enforcement Act
Maintenance & Custody Act
Maintenance Orders Enforcement Act
Married Women's Deed Act
Married Women's Property Act
Matrimonial Property Act
Mechanics' Lien Act
Medal of Bravery Act
Members & Public Employees Disclosure Act
Municipal Conflict of Interest Act
Night Courts Act
Notaries & Commissioners Act
Nova Scotia Tartan Act
Occupiers Liability Act
Official Tree Act
Ombudsman Act
Overholding Tenants Act
Partition Act
Payment into Court Act
Personal Directives Act
Personal Information International Disclosure Protection Act
Pledging of Service Emblems Act
Police Act
Police Services Act
Powers of Attorney Act
Presumption of Death Act
Private Investigators & Private Guards Act
Probate Act
Proceedings Against the Crown Act
Protection of Property Act
Provincial Bird Act
Provincial Court Act
Provincial Dog Act
Public Inquiries Act
Public Prosecutions Act
Public Service Act
Public Subscriptions Act

Public Trustee Act
Quieting Titles Act
Real Property Act
Real Property Transfer Validation Act
Reciprocal Enforcement of Judgment Orders Act
Reciprocal Enforcement of Judgments Orders
Regulations Act
Religious & Charitable Corporations Property Act
Religious Congregations & Societies Act
Remembrance Day Act
Remission of Penalties Act
Residential Tenancies Act
Retail Business Uniform Closing Day Act
Safer Communities & Neighbours Act
Sale of Goods Act
Sale of Land under Execution Act
Salvage Yards Licensing Act
Securities Act
Small Claims Court Act
Solemnization of Marriage Act
Sureties Act
Statute Revision Act
Summary Proceedings Act
Supreme & Exchequer Courts of Canada Act
Survival of Actions Act
Survivorship Act
Taxing Masters Act
Tenancies & Distress for Rent Act
Testators' Family Maintenance Act
Ticket of Leave Act
Time Definition Act
Tortfeasors Act
Trustee Act
Unclaimed Articles Act
Uniform Law Act
Utility & Review Board Act
Variation of Trusts Act
Vendors & Purchasers Act
Victims' Rights & Services Act
Volunteer Services Act
Warehouse Receipts Act
Warehousemen's Lien Act
Wills Act
Woodmen's Lien Act
Workers' Compensation Act
Young Persons Summary Proceedings Act
Youth Criminal Justice Act
Youth Justice Act

Minister & Attorney General, Hon. Ross Landry
902-424-4044, Fax: 902-424-0510, justmin@gov.ns.ca
Deputy Minister, Marian F. Tyson, Q.C.
902-424-4223, tysonmf@gov.ns.ca
Executive Director, Public Safety & Security, Robert Purcell
902-424-7795, purcelrf@gov.ns.ca
Director, Strategic Policy, Laurie Alexander
Director, Regional & Canada US Relations, Daryl Eisan
Director, Crime Prevention, Patricia Gorham
902-424-3306
Director, Victim Services, John Joyce-Robinson
902-424-3309
Director, Contracts, Edward Kirby
902-424-3178
Director, Emergency Programs, Andrew Lathem
000-424-5620
Director, Economic Policy & Analysis, Andre Moore
Director, Emergency Services, Michael Myette
902-424-6206
Director, Information Technology, Charles Purcell
902-424-6349
Director, Social & Environmental Affairs, Albert Walzak
902-563-5648

Associated Agencies, Boards & Commissions:
• Human Rights Commission
Joseph Howe Building
1690 Hollis St., 6th Fl.
PO Box 2221
Halifax, NS B3J 3C4
902-424-4111 Fax: 902-424-0596 877-269-7699 TTY: 877-424-3139
hrcinquiries@gov.ns.ca
www.humanrights.gov.ns.ca/
• Nova Scotia Legal Aid Commission
#102, 137 Chain Lake Dr.
Halifax, NS B3S 1B3
902-420-6573 Fax: 902-420-3471
nsla.exec@ns.sympatico.ca
• Office of the Chief Medical Examiner
Halifax Insurance Bldg.
#701, 5670 Spring Garden Rd.
Halifax, NS B3J 1H7
902-424-2722 Fax: 902-424-0607
www.gov.ns.ca/just/CME.asp
• Nova Scotia Police Commission
#300, 1601 Lower Water St.
PO Box 1573
Halifax, NS B3J 2Y3
902-424-3246 Fax: 902-424-3919
uarb.polcom@gov.ns.ca
www.gov.ns.ca/just/polcomm.htm
• Public Trustee Office
#405, 5670 Spring Garden Rd.
PO Box 685
Halifax, NS B3J 2T3
902-424-7760 Fax: 902-424-0616
PublicTrusteeHCD@gov.ns.ca (Health Care Decisions Division)
www.gov.ns.ca/just/pto/
• Workers' Compensation Appeals Tribunal
#1002, 5670 Spring Garden Rd.
Halifax, NS B3J 1H6
902-424-2250 Fax: 902-424-2321 800-274-8281
www.gov.ns.ca/wcat/

Maintenance Enforcement Program
902-424-7640 Fax: 902-424-0692
Director, Judith Crump
902-424-3641

Department of Labour & Advanced Education

5151 Terminal Rd., 6th Fl., PO Box 697, Halifax, NS B3J 2T8
902-424-5301 Fax: 902-424-0575
www.gov.ns.ca/lwd

The Department of Labour & Workforce Development focuses on labour issues, employment rights & responsibilities, adult learning, apprenticeship training & trade qualification, skill development, public & workplace safety, industry regulation, licensing & pensions.

Acts Administered:
Amusement Devices Safety Act
Apprenticeship & Trades Qualifications Act
Building Code Act
Court & Administrative Reform Act (Labour Relations Board Orders Regulations only)
Degree Granting Act
Electrical Installation & Inspection Act
Elevators & Lifts Act
Fire Safety Act
Labour Standards Code
Occupational Health & Safety Act
Pay Equity Act
Pension Benefits Act
Private Career Colleges Regulation Act
Registered Barbers Act
Retail Business Designated Day Closing Act
Retail Business Uniform Closing Day Act
Student Aid Act
Teachers' Collective Bargaining Act
Technical Safety Act
Theatres & Amusements Act
Trade Union Act
Universities Assistance Act
University Foundations Act
Voluntary Fire Services Act
Voluntary Protection Act
Voluntary Services Act
Workers' Compensation Act

Minister, Hon. Marilyn More
902-424-6647, Fax: 902-424-0575, min_lae@gov.ns.ca
Deputy Minister, Judith Ferguson
902-424-4148, fergusjf@gov.ns.ca
Associate Deputy Minister, Jeff Conrad
902-424-6270, conradja@gov.ns.ca
Director, Communications, Karen Stone
902-424-2107, Fax: 902-424-0644, stonekk@gov.ns.ca

Associated Agencies, Boards & Commissions:
• Nova Scotia Apprenticeship Board
2021 Brunswick St.
PO Box 578
Halifax, NS B3J 2S9
902-424-0872 Fax: 902-424-0488 800-494-5651
bedgoomm@gov.ns.ca
www.gov.ns.ca/lae/Apprenticeshipboard
Other Communication: 902-424-5651 (Registration & Renewals)
The Nova Scotia Apprenticeship Board is the voice of industry to the Minister of Labour & Advanced Education. The primary role of the board is to consult with industry on apprenticeship matters & to make recommendations to the Minister. In particular, the Board reviews current trade regulations & recommends proposed trades for designation & compulsory certification.
• Crane Operators Appeal Board
5151 Terminal Rd., 7th Fl.
PO Box 697
Halifax, NS B3J 2T8
902-424-8595 Fax: 902-424-0217
fernanfs@gov.ns.ca
www.gov.ns.ca/lae/coab
The Crane Operators Appeal Board was created pursuant to the Crane Operators & Power Engineers Act, which came into force on September 1, 2001. It is an independent adjudicative tribunal charged with considering appeals filed under Part I of the Act.
• Elevators & Lifts Appeal Board
5151 Terminal Rd., 7th Fl.
PO Box 697
Halifax, NS B3J 2T8
902-424-8595 Fax: 902-424-0217
www.gov.ns.ca/lae/elab
The Crane Operators Appeal Board was created pursuant to the Crane Operators & Power Engineers Act, which came into force on September 1, 2001. It is an independent adjudicative tribunal charged with considering appeals filed under Part I of the Act.
• Occupational Health & Safety Advisory Council
PO Box 697
Halifax, NS B3J 2T8
902-424-2484 Fax: 902-424-5640
www.gov.ns.ca/lae/abct/ohsadvisory.asp
The Crane Operators Appeal Board was created pursuant to the Crane Operators & Power Engineers Act, which came into force on September 1, 2001. It is an independent adjudicative tribunal charged with considering appeals filed under Part I of the Act.
• Pay Equity Commission
5151 Terminal Rd., 6th Fl.
PO Box 697
Halifax, NS B3J 2T8
902-424-2385 Fax: 902-424-0575
www.gov.ns.ca/lwd/payequity
The Pay Equity Commission is responsible for administrating the Pay Equity Act. In addition to monitoring the pay equity process, the Commission has the power to resolve disputes when employers and employees cannot agree, conducts research, maintains statistics, and advises the Minister of Labour on matters relating to pay equity.
• Power Engineers & Operators Appeal Committee
5151 Terminal Rd., 7th Fl.
PO Box 697
Halifax, NS B3J 2T8
902-424-8595 Fax: 902-424-0217
www.gov.ns.ca/lae/peoac/
The Workers' Advisers Program is a legal clinic that is funded by the provincial government offering services to injured workers. Our purpose is to provide legal assistance when an injured worker has been denied Workers' Compensation Board benefits.
• Workers' Advisers Program
#502, 5670 Spring Garden Rd.
PO Box 1063
Halifax, NS B3J 2X1
902-424-5050 Fax: 902-424-0530 800-774-4712
www.gov.ns.ca/lwd/wap
The Workers' Advisers Program is a legal clinic that is funded by the provincial government offering services to injured workers. Our purpose is to provide legal assistance when an injured worker has been denied Workers' Compensation Board benefits.

Advanced Education
Brunswick Place, 2021 Brunswick St., 4th Fl., PO Box 578, Halifax, NS B3J 2S9
www.gov.ns.ca/lae/divisions/
Consists of Post-Secondary Disability Services, Private Career Colleges, Student Assistance, & Universities & Colleges.
Executive Director, Student Assistance
902-424-5636

Alcohol & Gaming
780 Windmill Rd., 2nd Fl., PO Box 545, Dartmouth, NS B2Y 3Y8
Fax: 902-424-6160
877-565-0556
www.gov.ns.ca/lae/divisions/
Consists of Post-Secondary Disability Services, Private Career Colleges, Student Assistance, & Universities & Colleges.

Labour Services Branch
www.gov.ns.ca/lae/divisions/
Consists of Conciliation & Labour Tribunals, Labour Standards, Pension Regulation, & Workers' Advisers Program.
Executive Director, Labour Services, Barbara Jones-Gordon
902-424-2385
Director, Labour Services, William Grant
902-424-3549, grantwa@gov.ns.ca
Director, Labour Standards, Evelyn Hartley
902-424-3345
Director, Labour Standards, J. Anne Partridge
902-424-2219

Policy, Planning & Professional Services Branch
www.gov.ns.ca/lae/policy/
Other Communication:
www.gov.ns.ca/lae/ProfessionalServices.asp
Consists of Federal/Provincial Relations & Research, Policy & Planning, & Professional Services
Executive Director, Marjorie Davison
902-424-5191

Director, Professional Services, Stewart Sampson
902-424-8055

Safety Branch
www.gov.ns.ca/lae/publicsafety/
Other Communication: www.gov.ns.ca/lae/ohs/
Consists of Building, Fire & Technical Safety/Office of the Fire Marshall, & Occupational Health & Safety.
Executive Director, James LeBlanc
902-424-8477
Regional Director, David Clark
902-752-2641
Director & Fire Marshal, Harold James Pothier
902-538-4112
Director, Technical Safety, David Wigmore
902-424-5434

Skills & Learning Branch
www.gov.ns.ca/lae/divisions/
Consists of Adult Education, Apprenticeship Training, Employment Nova Scotia, & Skill Development.
Director, Apprenticeship, Joseph Rudderham
902-424-3206

Volunteerism
www.gov.ns.ca/lae/volunteerism/

Policy & Information Management
902-424-7640 Fax: 902-424-0692
Executive Director, Judith McPhee
902-424-4632

Nova Scotia Liquor Corporation

Bayers Lake Business Park, 93 Chain Lake Dr., Halifax, NS B3S 1A3
902-450-6752
800-567-5874
www.mynslc.com
Other Communication: www.facebook.com/theNSLC?ref=td; www.twitter.com/theNSLC
Minister Responsible, Hon. Graham Steele
graham@grahamsteele.ca
Chair, Sherry Porter
902-420-5243, sherry.porter@thenslc.com
President & Chief Executive Officer, Bret Mitchell
902-450-5802, bret.mitchell@thenslc.com

Department of Natural Resources

Founder's Square, 1701 Hollis St., 3rd Fl., PO Box 698, Halifax, NS B3J 2T9
902-424-5935 Fax: 902-424-0594
800-565-2224
www.gov.ns.ca/natr
Responsible for the administration & management of provincial Crown lands, development of mineral & energy resources, protection & sustainable development of forest resources & operation & maintenance of parks system, & promoting the conservation & sustainable use of wildlife populations, habitat & ecosystems.Initiatives include: a State of the Forest report; working with other departments on State of the Environment report; leading the development of a provincial climate change strategy; implementing recovery plans for endangered & threatened wildlife species; & developing strategic land use plans for Crown lands using an integrated resource management planning process.
Acts Administered:
Act to Confer Certain Powers Upon the Lieutenant Governor in Council & to amend the Mines Act
Angling Act
Beaches Act
Blueberry Association Act
Bowater Mersey Agreement Act
Conservation Easements Act
Endangered Species Act
Expropriation Act
Forests Act
Christmas Tree Grading Regulations
Christmas Tree Levy Regulations
Dutch Elm Disease Regulations
Forest Fire Protection Regulations
Forest Sustainability Regulations
Registration & Statistical Returns Regulations
Timber Loan Board Regulations
Wildlife Habitat & Watercourses Protection Regulations
Gypsum Mining Income Tax Act
Indian Lands Act
Halifax Power & Pulp Company Limited Agreement Act, 1962
Land Holdings Disclosure Act
Land Surveyors Act
Mineral Resources Act
Mines Act
Nova Scotia Federation of Anglers & Hunters Act
Off Highway Vehicles Act
Primary Forest Products Marketing Act
Provincial Parks Act
Private Ways Act
Scalers Act
Scott Maritimes Limited Agreement (1965) Act
Special Places Protection Act (jointly with Tourism, Culture & Heritage)
Stora Forest Industries Agreement Act
Trails Act
Treasure Trove Act
Wildlife Act
General Wildlife Regulations
Minister, Hon. Charlie Parker
902-424-4037, Fax: 902-424-0594, min_dnr@gov.ns.ca
Deputy Minister, Rick Williams
902-424-7751, Fax: 902-428-2137, williarm@gov.ns.ca
Director, Communications, Dan Davis
902-424-2354, Fax: 902-424-7735, davisds@gov.ns.ca

Associated Agencies, Boards & Commissions:
• Crown Land Information Management Centre
Founders Square
#501, 1701 Hollis St.
PO Box 698
Halifax, NS B3J 2T9
902-424-3171
• NS Primary Forest Products Marketing Board
#804, 45 Alderney Dr.
Dartmouth, NS B2Y 2N6
902-424-7598 Fax: 902-424-6965
www.gov.ns.ca/pfpmb/

Land Services Branch
www.gov.ns.ca/natr/thedepartment/landservices.asp
The Land Services Branch management oversees, coordinates & approves all activities within the Branch relating to the administration of Crown land. The Branch provides advice on legislative revisions & advises & drafts policies relating to the administration of Crown land.
Executive Director, Gretchen Pohlkamp
902-424-4267, pohlkagg@gov.ns.ca
Director, Land Administration, Arlene D'Eon
902-424-6335
Director, Eli Elias
902-424-1190
Director, Surveys, Bruce Albert MacQuarrie
902-424-3144

Minerals Resources Branch
Fax: 902-424-7735
www.gov.ns.ca/natr/meb/
Implements policies & programs dealing with the exploration, development, management & efficient use of energy & mineral resources, promotes scientific studies of the geology of the province for use by government, industry & the public, provides a mineral rights tenure system to establish legal rights to minerals for exploration & development. Promotes concepts of environmental responsibility & sustainability.
Executive Director, Mines & Minerals, Michael MacDonald
902-424-2523
Director, Mines & Energy Development, Alan Davison
902-424-5618

Planning Secretariat
Provides planning & policy coordination support to the Department, ensures that policies & plans developed in the Department are coordinated, supports the integrated management of natural resources. Also provides a range of administrative, planning, research, information management, information distribution, graphics, cartographic, communication, & occupational health & safety-related services.
Executive Director, Patricia Bernadette MacNeil
902-424-4988, macneipb@gov.ns.ca
Director, Robert Naylor
902-424-8119

Regional Services Branch
Delivers departmental programs & services through a field office network, responsible for forest protection & planning, forest nurseries, research & development, enforcement, coordination of the hunter safety program, regional geological services, Crown land surveys, operation & maintenance of provincial parks, resource conservation, forest fire prevention & monitoring of forest insects & diseases.
Executive Director, Brian Stanley Gilbert
902-424-3949, giberbs@gov.ns.ca
Director, Enforcement Division, John Mombourquette
902-424-5254, jamombou@gov.ns.ca

Renewable Resources
The Land Services Branch management oversees, coordinates & approves all activities within the Branch relating to the administration of Crown land. The Branch provides advice on legislative revisions & advises & drafts policies relating to the administration of Crown land & provides on all matters respecting Crown land administration.
Executive Director, Julie Towers
902-679-6139
Director, Resource Management, Daniel Lewis Eidt
902-494-7594
Director, Forestry, Jonathan Kierstead
902-893-5673
Director, Program Development, Peter MacQuarrie
902-424-7708, gpmacqua@gov.ns.ca
Director, Wildlife, Robert Petrie
902-679-4366

Regional Offices:

Central
626 College Rd., Bible Hill, NS B2N 2R2
902-893-5620 Fax: 902-893-5613
Regional Director, J. Allan Eddy
902-893-5627

Eastern
300 Mountain Rd., Sydney, NS B1L 1A9
902-563-3370 Fax: 902-567-2535
Regional Director, Donald Feldman
902-533-3370

Western
Provincial Bldg., 99 High St., Bridgewater, NS B4V 1V8
902-543-8167 Fax: 902-543-6157
Regional Director, Gerald Joudrey
902-543-0622, gtjoudre@gov.ns.ca
Director, Ross Wickwire
902-758-7019, Fax: 902-758-3355, wickwira@gov.ns.ca

Office of the Ombudsman

#700, 5670 Spring Garden Rd., PO Box 2152, Halifax, NS B3J 3B7
902-424-6780 Fax: 902-424-6675
800-670-1111
ombudsman@gov.ns.ca
www.gov.ns.ca/ombu
Ombudsman, Dwight Bishop
Office Manager, Lois Smith
902-424-5401, Fax: 902-424-6675
Executive Director, Janet Anne McKinnon
902-424-8898, Fax: 902-424-6675

Office of Policy & Priorities

1700 Granville St., 3rd Fl., 1 Government Place, Halifax, NS B3J 2Y3
902-424-7751 Fax: 902-428-2137
PPenquiries@gov.ns.ca
On July 9, 2009, a new government committee was established to provide policy direction to government. It is responsible for all affairs & matters pertaining to identification, prioritization, & development of government policy issues, plans & strategies.
Minister, Hon. Darrell Dexter
premier@gov.ns.ca
Deputy Minister, Rick Williams, EdD
willarm@gov.ns.ca

Public Service Commission

1800 Argyle St., 5th Fl., PO Box 943, Halifax, NS B3J 2V9
902-424-7660
www.gov.ns.ca/psc
Minister, Human Resources, Hon. Frank Corbett
902-424-5465, min_psc@gov.ns.ca
Deputy Minister, Kelliann Dean
902-424-6617, deankm@gov.ns.ca
Executive Director, Employee Relations, Gordon MacLean
902-424-7644, macleang@gov.ns.ca
Director, Communications, Sue McKeage
902-424-7280, mckeagsm@gov.ns.ca

Department of Seniors

1740 Granville St., PO Box 2065, Halifax, NS B3J 2Z1
902-424-0065 Fax: 902-424-0561
800-670-0065
seniors@gov.ns.ca
www.gov.ns.ca/seniors
The agency advocates for improved legislation, policies & programs for women, & provides research & policy advice to government on ways in which public policies & programs could better serve women.
Minister, Hon. Denise Peterson-Rafuse
petersdj@gov.ns.ca
Deputy Minister, Kelliann Dean
902-424-6617, deankm@gov.ns.ca
Chief Executive Officer, Valerie White
902-424-6322, whitevj@gov.ns.ca
Director, Programs, Wendy Aird
902-424-4649
Director, Corporate Strategy & Policy, Faizal Nanji
902-424-7921
Director, Communications, Natalie Webster
902-424-7957

Nova Scotia Securities Commission

Joseph Howe Building, 1690 Hollis St., 2nd Fl., PO Box 458, Halifax, NS B3J 3J9
902-424-7768 Fax: 902-424-4625
855-424-2499
www.gov.ns.ca/nssc/

Coordinates the workers' compensation system to assist injured workers & their employers by providing timely medical & rehabilitative support to help injured workers return to work. Also, to provide appropriate compensation for work-related injuries & illnesses.

Chairman, H. Leslie O'Brien, Q.C.
902-424-7079, obrienhl@gov.ns.ca
Vice Chair, Sarah P. Bradley
902-424-7768
Executive Director, Securities, J. William Slatterly
slattejw@gov.ns.ca
Director, Policy & Market Regulation, Shirley Lee
leesp@gov.ns.ca
Director, Corporate Finance, Kevin G. Redden
reddenkg@gov.ns.ca

Department of Service Nova Scotia & Municipal Relations

1505 Barrington St., PO Box 216, Halifax, NS B3J 3K5
902-424-5200 Fax: 902-424-0581
800-670-4357
askus@gov.ns.ca
www.gov.ns.ca/snsmr
TTY: 877-404-0720
Other Communication: Nova Scotia Business Registry: 1-800-670-4357

Provides leadership in the achievement of effective local government, assessment services, business licensing & registration, vehicle registration & driver licensing, taxation & revenue collection, vital statistics & an integrated land information management system to meet the needs of local & provincial agencies & residents of Nova Scotia.

Acts Administered:
Assessment Act
Business Electronic Filing Act
Cemetery & Funeral Services Act
Chartered Accountants Act
Change of Name Act
Collection Agencies Act
Communications & Information Act
Companies Act
Condominium Act
Consumer Creditors' Conduct Act
Consumer Protection Act
Consumer Reporting Act
Consumer Services Act
Corporations Registration Act
Direct Sellers' Regulation Act
Embalmers & Funeral Directors Act
Land Registration Act
Liquor Control Act
Limited Partnerships Act
Lobbyists' Registration Act
Marketable Titles Act
Mortgage Brokers' & Lenders' Registration Act
Motor Vehicle Act
Municipal Conflict of Interest Act
Municipal Elections Act
Municipal Finance Corporation Act
Municipal Fiscal Year Act
Municipal Government Act
Municipal Government Act Resource Binder
Municipal Grants Act
Municipal Housing Corporations Act
Municipal Loan & Building Fund Act
Off-Highway Vehicles Act
Oil Refineries & L.N.G. Plants Municipal Taxation Act
Part II of the Gaming Control Act
Part IV of the Revenue Act for administrative purposes
Part X of the Bankruptcy & Insolvency Act
Partnership Act
Partnerships & Business Names Registration Act
Personal Property Security Act
Petroleum Products Pricing Act
Private Investment Holding Companies Act
Private Investment Holding Companies Act
Property Valuation Services Corporation Act
Public Accountants Act
Real Estate Trading Act
Registry Act
Rental Property Conversion Act
Residential Tenancies Act
Rent Review Act
Rural Fire District Act
Sales Tax Act
Societies Act
Solemnization of Marriage Act
Unconscionable Transactions Relief Act
Vital Statistics Act
Wind Turbine Facilities Municipal Taxation Act

Minister, Hon. John MacDonnell
902-424-5550, Fax: 902-424-0581, snsmrmin@gov.ns.ca
Deputy Minister, Kevin Malloy
902-424-4100, Fax: 902-424-0581, keefeg@gov.ns.ca
Executive Director, Strategic & Transition Planning, Cheryl Burgess
902-424-5604, Fax: 902-424-0581
Executive Director, Human Resources Services & Client Support, Sharalyn Young
902-424-0944, Fax: 902-424-0581
Director, Human Resources, Kimberley Aselstine
902-424-3930, Fax: 902-424-0581
Director, Compensation & Benefits, John Campbell
902-424-2824, Fax: 902-424-0581
Director, Audit & Evaluation, Katharine Cox-Brown
902-424-8383, Fax: 902-424-0581
Director, Human Resources, Isabel Hache
902-424-7840, Fax: 902-424-0581
Director, Human Resources, Catherine Francis Martin
902-424-2751, Fax: 902-424-0581
Director, Communications, Penny McCormick
902-424-6336, Fax: 902-424-0581
Director, Recruitment Services, Jocelyn Pletz
902-722-1327, Fax: 902-424-0581
Director, Human Resources, Dale Rushton
902-424-6498, Fax: 902-424-0581
Director, Human Resources, Leslie Shanahan
902-424-8861, Fax: 902-424-0581
Director, Human Resources, Marica Mary Smythe
902-424-3443, Fax: 902-424-0581
Director, Staff Relations, Cynthia Yazbek
902-424-4588, Fax: 902-424-0581

Associated Agencies, Boards & Commissions:
• Nova Scotia Municipal Finance Corporation
Maritime Centre
1505 Barrington St., 10th Fl. South
PO Box 850 M
Halifax, NS B3J 2V2
902-424-4590 Fax: 902-424-0525
www.gov.ns.ca/nsmfc
NSMFC issues pooled debentures that provide low-cost, long-term capital financing for municipal capital projects. The NSMFC issues in capital markets twice a year, generally in the spring & fall. On occasion the NSMFC will do a single issue, provided the size is large enough.

Capped Assessment Program
Fax: 902-424-0587
www.gov.ns.ca/snsmr/muns/cap.asp

Program Management & Corporate Services
Acting Executive Director, Cameron MacNeil
902-424-4417

Co-operatives Branch
#3, 80 Walker St., Truro, NS B2N 4A7
902-893-6190 Fax: 902-893-6108
nscoop@gov.ns.ca
Inspector, Lynda C. H. Russell

Tax Commission
Maritime Centre, 1505 Barrington St., 8th St., PO Box 1003, Halifax, NS B3J 2X1
902-424-6300 Fax: 902-424-7434
800-565-4357
www.gov.ns.ca/snsmr/taxcomm/

Integrated Service Delivery
Fax: 902-424-5510
Executive Director, Service Delivery, Nancy MacLellan
902-424-5181

Nova Scotia Geomatics Centre
160 Willow St., Amherst, NS B4H 3W5
902-667-7231 Fax: 902-667-6008
800-798-0706
geoinfo@gov.ns.ca
www.gov.ns.ca/snsmr/land/
Manager, Robert Neil Caldwell
902-667-6287

Registry of Deeds
PO Box 2205, Halifax, NS B3J 3C4
Fax: 902-424-5872
www.gov.ns.ca/snsmr/property/default.asp?mn=282.46.1064
Registrar, L. Nellie Anderson
902-667-6540
Registrar, Shelley Archibald
902-893-5869
Registrar, Elaine Marie Deion
902-837-3500
Registrar, C. Darlene Dixon
902-485-7176
Registrar, Elaine Howatt
902-742-0776
Registrar, Marian MacPherson
902-863-2677
Registrar, Joan Plunkett
902-543-5095
Registrar, Mary Elizabeth Shaw
902-226-2818
Registrar, Peggy Zwicker
902-354-5715

Registry of Joint Stock Companies
Maritime Centre, 1505 Barrington St., 9th Fl., Halifax, NS B3J 2Y4
902-424-7770 Fax: 902-424-4633
800-225-8227
joint-stock@gov.ns.ca
www.gov.ns.ca/snsmr/rjsc
Registrar, Hayley Clarke
902-424-7742, clarkehe@gov.ns.ca

Registry of Motor Vehicles
1505 Barrington St., 8th Fl. North, PO Box 2734, Halifax, NS
902-424-7801 Fax: 902-424-0772
800-898-7668
www.gov.ns.ca/snsmr/rmv/
Registrar & Director, Paul Arsenault
902-424-7801

Vital Statistics
Joseph Howe Bldg., 1690 Hollis St., Ground Floor, PO Box 157, Halifax, NS B3J 2M9
902-424-4071 Fax: 902-424-0678
877-848-2578
vstat@gov.ns.ca
www.gov.ns.ca/snsmr/access/vitalstats.asp

Service Delivery
Maritime Centre, 1505 Barrington St., 8th Fl. North, PO Box 2734, Halifax, NS B3J 3P7
Executive Director, Graham Poole
902-424-4597

Access Nova Scotia Centres:

Bridgewater
80 Logan Rd., Bridgewater, NS B4V 3J8

Antigonish
Antigosh Mall Annex, #3, 149 Church St., Antigonish, NS B2G 2E2
800-670-4357

Dartmouth
Super Store Mall, 650 Portland St., Dartmouth, NS B2W 6A3

Halifax
Bayers Lake Business Park, 300 Horseshoe Lake Drive, Halifax, NS B3S 0B7

Port Hawkesbury
Provincial Building, #22, 218 MacSween St., Port Hawkesbury, NS B9A 2J9

Kentville
5 Shylah Drive, Kentville, NS B4N 0H2

Municipal Services Division
Fax: 902-424-0821
www.gov.ns.ca/snsmr/muns/http: //www.gov.ns.ca/snsmr/muns/
Executive Director, Nathan Gorall
902-424-2499
Acting Director, Advisory Services, Mark Peck
902-424-7917
Director, Policy & Finance, Jeff Shute
902-424-6161
Acting Director, Planning, Dave Smith
902-424-7918
Director, Grants & Programs, Aileen Waller-Hebb
902-424-7414
Director, Strategy & Sector Relations, Brant Wishart
902-424-7418

Sydney
Moxam Centre, 380 King's Rd., Sydney, NS B1S 1A8

Truro
#3, 80 Walker St., Truro, NS B2N 4A7

Yarmouth
Provincial Bldg., #127, 10 Starrs Rd., Yarmouth, NS B5A 2T1
902-742-8565 Fax: 902-742-6244
info@yarmouth-town.com
www.yarmouth-town.com

Nova Scotia Advisory Council on the Status of Women

1700 Granville St., PO Box 943, Halifax, NS B3J 2V9
902-424-7660
women@gov.ns.ca
www.women.gov.ns.ca

The agency advocates for improved legislation, policies & programs for women, & provides research & policy advice to government on ways in which public policies & programs could better serve women.
Minister Responsible, Hon. Marilyn More
902-424-8662, Fax: 902-424-0573
Executive Director, Stephanie MacInnis-Langley
902-424-7548

Department of Transportation & Infrastructure Renewal

Johnston Bldg., 1672 Granville St., 2nd Fl., PO Box 186, Halifax, NS B3J 2N2
902-424-2297 Fax: 902-424-0532
tpwpaff@gov.ns.ca
http: //gov.ns.ca/tran
TTY: 888-432-3233

Provides a transportation network for the safe & efficient movement of people & goods; serves the building, property & accommodation needs of government departments & agencies; employs professional, dedicated people & offers a high level of customer service.
Acts Administered:
Dangerous Goods Transportation Act
Dangerous Goods Transportation Regulations
Ferries Act
Highway 104: Western Alignment Act
Motor Carrier Act
Motor Vehicle Act
Off-Highway Vehicles Act
Public Highways Act
Railways Act
Surplus Crown Property Disposal Act
Minister, Hon. Bill Estabrooks
902-424-5875, Fax: 902-424-0171, tirmin@gov.ns.ca
Deputy Minister, David Darrow
902-424-4036, Fax: 902-424-2014, ddarrow@gov.ns.ca
Director, Public Affairs & Communications, Cathy MacIsaac
902-424-8978, Fax: 902-424-0532, macisacl@gov.ns.ca

Associated Agencies, Boards & Commissions:
• Sydney Tar Ponds Agency
1 Inglis St.
PO Box 1028 A
Sydney, NS B1P 6J7
902-567-1035 Fax: 902-567-1032
www.tarpondscleanup.ca

Highway Operations

www.gov.ns.ca/tran/highways

This division provides for provincial highway & bridge maintenance, as well as the operation of the Department's fleet management & a strategic planning section. District Services provides general services on primary & secondary roads & works with private sector contractors to provide the public with enhanced road systems.
Executive Director, Highway Engineering & Construction, Kevin Caines
902-424-5687
Executive Director, Highway Maintenance & Operations, Charles Joseph MacDonald
902-295-2700

Public Works

www.gov.ns.ca/tran/works/

This division provides technical expertise & services required by the Department's highway, building & property divisions. The Highway Engineering Services section provides delivery of highway planning, geometric & structural design, traffic engineering, capital program maintenance & asset management business functions. The Engineering & Design section provides engineering, architectural, environmental & technical services & project management services for projects that are related to maintaining & constructing highway & building infrastructure. The Building Services & Operations section oversees the management, operation, maintenance & renovation of government buildings, infrastructure & properties, as well as the provision of trade & contract services in both leased & owned premises.
Acting Director, Building Services & Operations, Neil Whyte
902-424-2281

Nova Scotia Treasury & Policy Board

1700 Granville St., 5th Fl., PO Box 1617, Halifax, NS B3J 2Y3
902-424-8910 Fax: 902-424-7638
TBenquiries@gov.ns.ca
www.gov.ns.ca/tpb

On July 9, 2009, a new government committee was established to provide policy direction to the government. Treasury & Policy Board was separated into a Policy & Priorities Committee & a stand-alone Treasury Board.
President, Executive Council, Hon. Darrell E. Dexter
902-424-6600, Fax: 902-424-7648, premier@gov.ns.ca
Deputy Minister, Treasury Board, Gregory P. Keefe
keefeg@gov.ns.ca
Chair, Treasury Board, Hon. Frank Corbett
902-424-8910, Fax: 902-424-7638

Nova Scotia Utility & Review Board

Summit Place, 1601 Lower Water St., 3rd Fl., PO Box 1692 M, Halifax, NS B3J 3S3
902-424-4448 Fax: 902-424-3919
uarb.board@gov.ns.ca
www.nsuarb.ca

The Board has a very broad mandate encompassing a number of Acts. Operations fall into two categories, regulatory & adjudicative. The regulatory category includes the regulation of public utilities, licensing of public passenger carriers, monitoring of automobile insurance rates, the approval of Halifax-Dartmouth bridge fares, & the regulation of natural gas distribution & pipelines. The Board conducts hearings relating to gaming control, liquor control & film classification. The adjudicative category includes appeals or applications relating to property assessments, expropriation compensation claims, planning & subdivisions, heritage properties, criminal injury compensation claims, municipal boundaries, municipal & school board electoral boundaries, as well as gasoline, diesel oil & tobacco taxes. The Board receives its authority from the Public Inquiries Act & the Utility & Review Board Act.
Acts Administered:
Assessment Act
Electrical Installation & Inspection Act
Education Act
Energy & Mineral Resources Conservation Act
Expropriation Act
Fire Safety Act
Gaming Control Act (Part II)
Gas Distribution Act
Halifax-Dartmouth Bridge Commission Act
Liquor Control Act
Motor Carrier Act (public passenger only)
Motor Vehicle Transport Act of Canada, 1987 (Federal)
Municipal Government Act
Nova Scotia Power Finance Corporation Act
Nova Scotia Power Privatization Act
Petroleum Products Pricing Act
Petroleum Resources Removal Permit Act
Pipeline Act
Public Utilities Act
Railways Act
Revenue Act
Theatres & Amusement Act
Underground Hydrocarbons Storage Act
Utility & Review Board Act
Victims' Rights & Services Act
Chair, Peter W. Gurnham, Q.C.
uarb.board@gov.ns.ca
Administrator, Paul G. Allen
902-424-4448, uarb.paul@gov.ns.ca

Workers' Compensation Board of Nova Scotia

5668 South St., PO Box 1150, Halifax, NS B3J 2Y2
902-491-8999 Fax: 902-491-8002
800-870-3331
info@wcb.gov.ns.ca
www.wcb.ns.ca

Coordinates the workers' compensation system to assist injured workers & their employers by providing timely medical & rehabilitative support to help injured workers return to work. Also, to provide appropriate compensation for work-related injuries & illnesses.
Chair, Elaine Sibson
CEO, Nancy MacCready-Williams
902-491-8300
Deputy Chair, Chris Power

Government of the Nunavut Territory

Seat of Government: PO Box 1200, Iqaluit, NU X0A 0H0
888-252-9869
info@gov.nu.ca
www.gov.nu.ca

On April 1, 1999, Nunavut Territory was created as part of the Nunavut Land Claims Agreement signed in 1993. It has area of 1,932,254.97 km2, & the StatsCan population in 2010 was 32,220. Nunavut Territory is governed by a fully elected Legislative Assembly of 19 members elected for a five-year term. Government is by consensus rather than party politics. The Legislature elects the Premier & a seven-member Executive Council, which is charged with the operation of government & the establishment of program & spending priorities. Nunavut Territory acts under the same conditions as other territories in Canada. For an explanation of the difference between provinces & territories please see the Yukon Territory listing. The Commissioner of Nunavut Territory is appointed by the Federal Government, & serves a role similar to that of the Lieutenant Governor in provincial jurisdictions.

Office of the Commissioner

PO Box 2379, Iqaluit, NU X0A 0H0
867-975-5120 Fax: 867-975-5123
nunavutcommissioner@gov.nu.ca
www.gov.nu.ca/commissioner

Commissioner, Hon. Edna Ekhivalak Elias
Asst. to the Commissioner, Marie Fortier
867-975-5120, Fax: 867-975-5123, mfortier@gov.nu.ca

Office of the Premier

Legislative Assembly Bldg., 2nd Fl., PO Box 2410, Iqaluit, NU X0A 0H0
867-975-5050 Fax: 867-975-5051
www.gov.nu.ca

Premier, Hon. Eva Aariak
867-975-5050, Fax: 867-975-5051, premier@gov.nu.ca
Principal Secretary, Joe Kunuk
867-975-5050, Fax: 867-975-5051, jkunuk@gov.nu.ca
Executive Assistant, Madeleine Allakariallak
mallakariallak@gov.nu.ca

Executive Council

Legislative Bldg., 2nd Fl., Box 2410, Iqaluit, NU X0A 0H0
867-975-5090 Fax: 867-975-5095

Premier & Minister, Executive & Intergovernmental Affairs; Status of Women; Immigration; Aboriginal Affairs; Education, Hon. Eva Aariak
867-975-5050, Fax: 867-975-5051, premier@gov.nu.ca
Deputy Premier & Minister, Economic Development & Transportation; Nunavut Business Credit Corporation; Nunavut Development Dorporation; Mines, Hon. Peter Taptuna
867-975-5076, Fax: 867-975-5016
Minister, Health & Social Services & Minister; Nunavut Housing Corporation; Homelessness; Workers' Safety & Compensation Commission, Hon. Tagak Curley
867-975-5005, Fax: 867-975-5095
Government House Leader & Minister, Community & Government Services; Energy; Qulliq Energy Corporation, Hon. Lorne Kusuqak
867-975-5003, Fax: 867-975-5095
Minister, Finance; Justice; Public Agencies Council; Labour Standards Board; Liquor Licensing Board, Hon. Keith Peterson
867-975-5007, Fax: 867-975-5095
Minister, Environment; Nunavut Arctic College; Human Resources, Hon. Daniel Shewchuk
867-975-5001, Fax: 867-975-5044
Minister, Culture, Language, Elders & Youth; Languages; Utility Rates Review Council, Hon. James Arreak
867-924-6423, Fax: 867-924-6429
Executive Secretary, Dorcas Nattaq-Hamioui
867-975-5050, Fax: 867-975-5051,
dnattaq-hamioui@gov.nu.ca

Legislative Assembly

926 Federal Rd., PO Box 1200, Iqaluit, NU X0A 0H0
867-975-5000 Fax: 867-975-5190
877-334-7266
leginfo@assembly.nu.ca
www.assembly.nu.ca

Clerk of the Assembly, John Quirke
867-975-5100, jquirke@assembly.nu.ca
Speaker, Hon. Hunter Tootoo
867-975-5023, Fax: 867-975-5095, htootoo@assembly.nu.ca
Deputy Clerk, Nancy Tupik
867-975-5115, ntupik@assembly.nu.ca
Legislative Librarian, Yvonne Earle
867-975-5134, yearle@assembly.nu.ca

Second Legislature - Nunavut

PO Box 1200, Iqaluit, NU X0A 0H0
www.assembly.nu.ca

Last General Election: Oct. 27, 2008. Maximum Duration, five years. Following is: constituency, member, phone & fax number. Address for all is care of the Legislative Assembly of Nunavut, PO Box 1200, Iqaluit NU X0A 0H0.
Fred Schell, South Baffin (Cape Dorset, Kimmirut)
867-897-8753, Fax: 867-897-8645, fschell@assembly.nu.ca, Other Communications: Legislature Phone: 867-975-5031
Hon. Daniel Shewchuk, Arviat
867-857-4485, Fax: 867-857-4486, daniel.shewchuk@gov.nu.ca, Other Communications: Legislature Phone: 867-975-5024
Hon. James Arreak, Uqqummiut (Clyde River, Qikiqtarjuak)
867-924-6423, Fax: 867-924-6429, jarreak@assembly.nu.ca, Other Communications: Legislature Phone: 867-975-5019

Ron Elliot, Quttiktuq (Arctic Bay, Resolute, Grise Fiord)
867-439-8050, Fax: 867-439-8051, relliott@assembly.nu.ca, Other Communications: Legislature Phone: 867-975-5015
Hon. Lorne Kusugak, Rankin Inlet South (Whale Cove)
867-645-4866, Fax: 867-645-4865, lorne.kusugak@gov.nu.ca, Other Communications: Legislature Phone: 867-975-5020
Hon. Tagak Curley, Rankin Inlet North
867-645-4900, Fax: 867-645-4981, tagak.curley@gov.nu.ca, Other Communications: Legislature Phone: 867-975-5026
Hon. Peter Taptuna, Kugluktuk
867-982-4232, Fax: 867-982-5733, ptaptuna@gov.nu.ca, Other Communications: Legislature Phone: 867-975-5075
Allan Rumbolt, Hudson Bay (Sanikiluaq)
867-266-8518, Fax: 867-266-8315, arumbolt@assembly.nu.ca, Other Communications: Legislature Phone: 867-975-5032
Vacant, Pangnirtung
867-473-8220, Fax: 867-473-8227, Other Communications: Legislature Phone: 867-975-5047
John Ningark, Akulliq (Kugaaruk, Repulse Bay)
867-462-4363, Fax: 867-462-4364, jningark@assembly.nu.ca, Other Communications: Legislature Phone: 867-975-5014
Johnny Ningeongan, Nanulik
867-925-9890, Fax: 867-925-9891, jningeongan@assembly.nu.ca, Other Communications: Legislature Phone: 867-975-5021
Vacant, Iqaluit West
867-975-5017, Fax: 867-975-5112, Other Communications: Legislature Phone: 867-975-5017
Hon. Keith Peterson, Cambridge Bay
867-983-3777, Fax: 867-983-3778, keith.peterson@gov.nu.ca, Other Communications: Legislature Phone: 867-975-5028
Hon. Eva Aariak, Iqaluit East
867-979-0410, Fax: 867-979-0415, eva.aariak@gov.nu.ca, Other Communications: Legislature Phone: 867-975-5050
Moses Aupaluktuq, Baker Lake
867-793-4949, Fax: 867-793-4950, maupaluktuq@assembly.nu.ca, Other Communications: Legislature Phone: 867-975-5030
Louis Tapardjuk, Amittuq (Igloolik, Hall Beach)
867-934-4070, Fax: 867-934-4071, ltapardjuk@assembly.nu.ca, Other Communications: Legislature Phone: 867-975-5070
Hon. Hunter Tootoo, Iqaluit Centre
867-979-2210, Fax: 867-979-2211, htootoo@assembly.nu.ca, Other Communications: Legislature Phone: 867-975-5023
Vacant, Tununiq (Pond Inlet)
867-899-8999, Fax: 867-899-8713, Other Communications: Legislature Phone: 867-975-5035
Deputy Clerk, Nancy Tupik
867-975-5115, ntupik@assembly.nu.ca

Nunavut Territory Government Departments & Agencies

Department of Community & Government Services

W.G. Brown Bldg., 4th Fl., PO Box 1000 700, Iqaluit, NU X0A 0H0
867-975-5400 Fax: 867-975-5305
Other Communication: 867-975-5306

To support the development, provision & maintenance of programs & services which affect the communities in all areas of municipal responsibility & transportation.

Acts Administered:
Area Development Act
Resolute Bay Development Area Regulations
Strathcona Sound Development Area Regulations
Boilers & Pressure Vessels Act
Business Licenses Act
Cities, Towns & Villages Act
Iqaluit By-Law Exemption Order
Town of Iqaluit Continuation Order
Emergency Measures Act
Commissioner's Land Act
Commissioner's Airport Lands Regulations
Commissioner's Land Regulations
Community Employees' Benefits Program Transfer Act
Conflict of Interest Act
Consumer Protection Act
Dog Act
Electrical Protection Act
Film Classification Act
Fire Prevention Act
Fire Prevention Regulations
Fireworks Regulations
Propane Cylinder Storage
Gas Protection Act
Hamlets Act
Home Owners Property Tax Rebate Act
Local Authorities Elections Act
Lotteries Act
Pawnbrokers & Second-Hand Dealers Act
Planning Act
Property Assessment & Taxation Act
Real Estate Agents Licencing Act
Religious Societies Lands Act
Residential Tenancies Act
Senior Citizens & Disabled Persons Property Tax Relief Act
Settlements Act
Technical Standards & Safety Act

Minister, Hon. Lorne Kusugak
867-975-5003, Fax: 867-975-5095
Deputy Minister (interim), Shawn Maley
867-645-8101, Fax: 867-645-8141
Asst. Deputy Minister, Lorne Levy
867-975-5306, Fax: 867-975-5305, smaley@gov.nu.ca
Director, Policy & Procedures, Lucy Magee
867-975-5309, Fax: 867-975-5351, lmagee@gov.nu.ca
Director, Financial Services, Alma Power
867-975-5333, apower@gov.nu.ca
Director, Protection Services, Ed Zebedee
867-975-5319, Fax: 867-975-5453, ezebedee@gov.nu.ca
Senior Consumer Affairs Officer, Leah Aupaluktuq
867-793-3303, Fax: 867-793-3321
Administrative Officer, Dorothy Kaludjak
867-975-5306, Fax: 867-975-5305, dkaludjak@gov.nu.ca

Regional Offices:
Kitikmeot
PO Box 200, Cambridge Bay, NU X0B 0C0
Regional Director, Kevin Niptanatiak
867-983-4138, Fax: 867-983-4026
Qikiqtaaluk
PO Box 330, Cape Dorset, NU X0A 0C0
Regional Director, Timoon Toonoo
867-897-3607, ttoonoo@gov.nu.ca
Kivalliq
PO Box 490, Rankin Inlet, NU X0C 0G0
Regional Director, Ralph Ruediger
867-645-8153, Fax: 867-645-8197

Department of Culture, Language, Elders & Youth (CLEY)

PO Box 1000 800, Iqaluit, NU X0A 0H0
867-975-5500 Fax: 867-975-5504
866-934-2035
www.cley.gov.nu.ca

Responsible for the protection, preservation & promotion of Inuit languages. Cultural initiatives & departmental goals are reached in coordination with & in support of elder & youth groups. CLEY acts in respect to issues concerning women & people with disabilities. The government is dedicated to preserving & promoting elements that make up the Inuit identity.

Acts Administered:
Archives Act
Historical Resources Act
Official Languages Act

Minister, Hon. James Arreak
867-975-5019, Fax: 867-975-5114, jarreak@assembly.nu.ca
Deputy Minister, Simon Awa
867-975-5501, simon.awa@gov.nu.ca
Asst. Deputy Minister, Naullaq Arnaquq
867-975-5532, Fax: 867-975-5504, narnaquq@gov.nu.ca
Director, Elders & Youth, Joanna Quassa
867-934-2032, jquassa@gov.nu.ca
Director, Culture & Heritage, Dr. Douglas Stenton
867-975-5524, dstenton1@gov.nu.ca
Director, Corporate Services, Nikki Nweze
867-975-5514, nnweze@gov.nu.ca
Director, Inuit Quajimajatuqangit, Shuvinai Mike
867-975-5525, Fax: 867-975-5504, smike@gov.nu.ca
Director, Official Languages, Rhoda Cunningham
867-975-5507, rcunningham@gov.nu.ca
Director, Policy & Planning, Jodi Durdie
867-975-5505, jdurdle@gov.nu.ca
Director, Sports & Recreation, Kyle Seeley
867-793-3301, kseeley@gov.nu.ca
Director, Inuit Uqausinginnik Taiguusiliuqtiit, Eileen Kilabuk-Weber
867-975-5527, ekilabuk-weber@gov.nu.ca
Director, Piqqusilirivvik, Jonathan Palluq
867-899-7392, jpalluq@gov.nu.ca

Department of Economic Development & Transportation

Bldg. 1104 A, Inuksugait Plaza, PO Box 1000 1500, Iqaluit, NU X0A 0H0
867-975-7800 Fax: 867-975-7870
888-975-5999
edt@gov.nu.ca
www.edt.gov.nu.ca

Acts Administered:
All-Terrain Vehicles Act
All-Terrain Vehicles Regulations
Special All-Terrain Vehicles Fees Regulations
Special All-Terrain Vehicles Helmet Regulations
Economic Development Agreements Act
Motor Vehicles Act
Carrier Fitness Regulations
Exemption of Motor Vehicles Act Regulations
Hours of Service Regulations
Large Vehicle Control Regulations
Motor Vehicle Equipment Regulations
School Bus Regulations
Seasonal Highway Regulations
Nunavut Development Corporation
Public Highways Act
Highway Designation & Classification Regulations
Highway Signs Regulations
Transportation of Dangerous Goods Act
Transportation of Dangerous Goods Regulations
Travel & Tourism Act
Guide Exemption Regulations
Outfitter Regulations
Tourist Establishment Regulations
Travel Development Area Regulations

Minister, Hon. Peter Taptuna
867-975-5076, Fax: 867-975-5016
Deputy Minister, Robert Long
867-975-7829, rlong@gov.nu.ca
Director, Transportation Policy & Planning, John Hawkins
867-975-7826, jhawkins@gov.nu.ca
Director, Policy, Planning & Communications, Matthew Bowler
867-975-7808, mbowler@gov.nu.ca
Director, Finance & Administration, Tanya Winmill
867-975-7816, twinmill@gov.nu.ca
Manager, Communications, Matthew Illaszewicz
867-975-7818, Fax: 867-975-7870

Associated Agencies, Boards & Commissions:
• Nunavut Business Credit Corporation
Parnaivak Bldg.
#100
PO Box 2548
Iqaluit, NU X0A 0H0
867-975-7891 Fax: 867-975-7897 800-758-0038
credit@nbcc.nu.ca
www.nbcc.nu.ca

Economic Development
Asst. Deputy Minister, Gordon MacKay
867-975-7822, gmackay@gov.nu.ca
Director, Community Operations, Kitikmeot, Vacant
Director, Community Operations, Kivalliq, Laura MacKenzie
867-645-8458, lmackenzie@gov.nu.ca
Director, Community Operations, Qikiqtaaluk, Rhoda Katsak
867-899-7339, rkatsak@gov.nu.ca
Director, Minerals & Petroleum Resources, Eric Prosh
867-975-7827, eprosh@gov.nu.ca
Director, Tourism & Cultural Industries, Vacant

Transportation
Asst. Deputy Minister, Methusalah Kunuk
867-975-7832, Fax: 867-975-7880, mkunuk@gov.nu.ca
Director, Iqaluit International Airport, John Graham
867-979-5224, jgraham@gov.nu.ca
Director, Motor Vehicles, Lorna Gee
867-360-4614, lgee@gov.nu.ca
Director, Nunavut Airports, Shawn Maley
867-645-8203, smaley@gov.nu.ca
Director, Transportation Policy & Planning, John Hawkins
867-975-7826, jhawkins@gov.nu.ca

Community Operations:

Kitikmeot
PO Box 316, Kugluktuk, NU X0B 0E0
867-982-7453
Director, Vacant
867-982-7459, Fax: 867-982-3204

Kivalliq
PO Box 2, Rankin Inlet, NU X0C 0G0
867-645-8450
Director, Laura MacKenzie
867-645-8458, Fax: 867-645-8455

Qikiqtaaluk
#1045, PO Box 389, Pond Inlet, NU X0A 0S0
867-899-7338
888-899-7338
Director, Rhoda Katsak
867-899-7339, Fax: 867-899-7348

Department of Education

Sivummut Bldg., 2nd Fl., PO Box 1000 910, Iqaluit, NU X0A 0H0
867-975-5600 Fax: 867-975-5605
www.edu.gov.nu.ca

Acts Administered:
Apprenticeship, Trade & Occupation Certification Act
Child Care Act
Education Act
Federation of Nunavut Teachers Act
Library Act (CLEY)
Occupational Training Agreement Act
Official Languages Act (CLEY)
Public Colleges Act
Scientists & Education Act (CLEY)
Senior Citizens Benefits Act
Social Assistance Act
Student Financial Assistance Act
Minister, Hon. Eva Aariak
867-975-5050, Fax: 867-975-5051
Deputy Minister, Kathy Okpik
867-975-5601, Fax: 867-975-5635
Director, Corporate Services, Murray Horn
867-975-5616, Fax: 867-975-5605, mhorn@gov.nu.ca
Director, Policy & Planning, Brad Chambers
867-975-5606, bchambers@gov.nu.ca

Adult Learning, Career & Early Childhood Services
Fax: 867-857-3090
Asst. Deputy Minister, Irene Tanuyak
867-975-5604, Fax: 867-975-5635, itanuyak@gov.nu.ca
Director, Income Support, Sandy Teiman
867-975-5685, Fax: 867-975-5690, steiman@gov.nu.ca
Director, Adult Learning & Post-Secondary Services, Edward Duru
867-857-3056, eduru@gov.nu.ca

Curriculum & School Services
Asst. Deputy Minister, Peter Geikie
867-975-5604, Fax: 867-975-5635
Director, Curriculum Development, Cathy McGregor
867-975-5641, Fax: 867-975-5635, cmcgregor@gov.nu.ca
Director, French, Leonie Aissaoui
867-975-5627, laissaoui@gov.nu.ca

Regional Offices:
867-983-7214 Fax: 867-983-2004
Cambridge Bay
867-983-4031 Fax: 867-983-7309
Director, Career & Early Childhood, Brenda Jancke
867-983-4030, Fax: 867-983-4191, bjancke@gov.nu.ca
Kivalliq
867-645-5040 Fax: 867-645-2148

Nunavut Emergency Management

PO Box 1000 700, Iqaluit, NU X0A 0H0
867-975-5403 Fax: 867-979-4221
800-693-1666
cgs.gov.nu.ca/en/nunavut-emergency-management
Other Communication: 867-979-6262
Manager, Emergency Services, Glen Higgins
867-975-5403, Fax: 867-979-4221, ghiggins@gov.nu.ca
Deputy Fire Marshall, Robert Prima
867-645-8127, rprima@gov.nu.ca

Department of Environment

PO Box 1000 1300, Iqaluit, NU X0A 0H0
867-975-7700 Fax: 867-975-7742
environment@gov.nu.ca
Acts Administered:
Environmental Protection Act
Asphalt Paving Industry Emission Regulations
Spill Contingency Planning & Reporting
Used Oil & Waste Fuel Management
Environmental Rights Act
Flood Damage Reduction Agreements Act
Forest Management Act
Forest Management Regulations
Forest Protection Act
Freshwater Fish Marketing Act
Establishing Freshwater Fish Marketing Corporation Regulations
Herd & Fencing Act
Pesticides Act
Territorial Parks Act
Community Parks Order
Heritage Parks, Natural Environment Parks & Recreation Parks Regulations
Natural Environment Recreation Park Order
Historic Parks Order
Outdoor Recreation Parks Order
Territorial Parks Regulations
Wayside Parks Order
Travel & Tourism Act
Outfitter Regulations
Tourist Establishment Regulations
Waste Reduction & Recovery Act
Travel Development Area Regulation
Water Resources Agreements Act
Wildlife Act
Big Game Hunting Regulations
Birds of Prey Regulations
Certification & Disposal of Wildlife Regulations
Critical Wildlife Areas Regulations
Dempster Highway Special Management Area Regulations
Nuisance Bison Control Regulations
Polar Bear Defence Kill Regulations
Sale of Wildlife Regulations
Small Game Hunting Regulations
Trapping Regulations
Wildlife Business Regulations
Wildlife Export Regulations
Wildlife General Regulations
Wildlife Licenses & Permits Regulations
Wildlife Management Barren Ground Caribou Area Regulation
Wildlife Management Grizzly Bear Area Regulations
Wildlife Management Muskox Areas Regulations
Wildlife Management Outfitter Area Regulations
Wildlife Management Polar Bear Areas Regulations
Wildlife Management Units Regulations
Wildlife Management Wood Bison Area Regulations
Wildlife Management Zones Regulations
Wildlife Preserves Regulations
Wildlife Regions Regulations
Wildlife Sanctuaries Regulations
Minister, Hon. Daniel Shewchuk
867-975-5001, Fax: 867-975-5044
Deputy Minister, David Akeeagok
867-975-7705, dakeeagok@gov.nu.ca
Asst. Deputy Minister, Earle Baddaloo
867-975-7705, Fax: 867-975-7740, ebaddaloo@gov.nu.ca
Director, Corporate Services, Camilius Egeni
867-975-7708, Fax: 867-975-7740, cegeni@gov.nu.ca
Director, Environmental Protection, Rob Eno
867-975-7729, Fax: 867-975-7739, cegeni@gov.nu.ca
Director, Parks & Conservation Areas, David Monteith
867-975-7723, Fax: 867-975-7739, dmonteith@gov.nu.ca
Director, Policy, Planning & Legislation, Steve Pinksen
867-975-7718, Fax: 867-975-7740, spinksen@gov.nu.ca
Director, Fisheries & Sealing, Wayne Lynch
867-975-7750, Fax: 867-975-7742, cegeni@gov.nu.ca
Executive Secretary, Lena Hughes
867-975-7705, Fax: 867-975-7740, lhughes@gov.nu.ca

Regional Offices:
Baffin
PO Box 569, Pond Inlet, NU X0A 0S0
Regional Wildlife Manager, Alex Millar
867-899-8034, Fax: 867-889-8050, amillar@gov.nu.ca
Kitikmeot
PO Box 377, Kugluktuk, NU X0B 0E0
Kivalliq
PO Box 120, Arviat, NU X0C 0E0

Department of Executive & Intergovernmental Affairs

1084 Aeroplex bldg., PO Box 1000 200, Iqaluit, NU X0A 0H0
867-975-6000 Fax: 867-975-6099
www.eia.gov.nu.ca
The department provides advice & administrative support to Cabinet & the government, works to ensure that the Nunavut Land Claims Agreement & Nunavut's relationships with other governments in Canada & the circumpolar world are used to support common goals. The department compiles & communicates information & evaluates government programs & data.The Intergovernmental Affairs Division is responsible for the management & development of government strategies, policies & initiatives relating to federal, provincial, territorial, circumpolar & aboriginal affairs. This office participates in preparations for Intergovernmental activities such as the Western & Annual Premiers Conferences, First Ministers meetings & the Social Union Framework Agreement, the Arctic Council, the Nunavut Implementation Panel & the Clyde River Protocol.
Acts Administered:
Nunavut Power Corporation Assets Transfer Confirmation Act
Public Utilities Act
Public Utilities Regulations
Minister, Hon. Eva Aariak
867-975-5050, Fax: 867-975-5051
Deputy Minister of Executive, Daniel Vandermeulen
867-975-6011, Fax: 867-975-6095, dvandermeuleneia@gov.nu.ca
Deputy Minister, Intervovernmental Affairs, Aluki Rojas
867-975-6034, Fax: 867-975-6091, arojas@gov.nu.ca
Asst. Deputy Minister, Intergovernmental Affairs - Ottawa Liason, Robert Carson
613-233-9890, Fax: 613-233-2543
Asst. Deputy Minister, Policy, Planning & Evaluation, Paul Suvega
867-975-6009, Fax: 867-975-6089
Director, Aboriginal & Circumpolar Affairs, Letia Obed
867-975-6036, Fax: 867-975-6091, lobed@gov.nu.ca
Director, Policy, Planning & Evaluation, Rachel Mark
867-975-6029, Fax: 867-975-6029, rmark@gov.nu.ca
Director, Corporate Services, David Pealow
867-975-6002, dpealow@gov.nu.ca
Director, Communications, Pam Coulter
867-975-6049, pcoulter2@gov.nu.ca
Director, Statistics, Ron McMahon
867-473-2693, Fax: 867-473-2626, rmcmahon@gov.nu.ca

Department of Finance

Bldg. 1079, 1st Fl., PO Box 1000 330, Iqaluit, NU X0A 0H0
867-975-5800 Fax: 867-975-5805
www.finance.gov.nu.ca
The Department of Finance is committed to provide direction and leadership to ensure fiscal responsibility and to create a secure base for Nunavut's economic growth, while promoting and maintaining public confidence in the prudence, propriety and integrity of government financial operations and respecting the principles of Inuit Qaujimajatuqangit (IQ).
Acts Administered:
Explosives Use Act
Mine Health & Safety Act
Safety Act
Environmental Tobacco Smoke Work Site Reguations
Technical Standards & Safety Act
Worker's Compensation Act
Minister, Hon. Keith Peterson
867-975-5070
Deputy Minister, Peter Ma
867-975-5803, Fax: 867-975-5805, pma@gov.nu.ca
Comptroller General, Jeff Chown
867-975-5833, Fax: 867-975-5896, jchown@gov.nu.ca
Asst. Deputy Minister, Chris D'Arcy
867-975-6865, Fax: 867-975-5805
Director, Finance, Kerry Angidlik
867-645-8515, kangidlik@gov.nu.ca
Director, Corporate Services, Scott Mariott
867-975-6803, Fax: 867-975-6868, smarriott@gov.nu.ca
Director, Accounting Policy, Vacant
Acting Director, Expenditure Management, Jeff Chown
867-975-5835, Fax: 867-975-6825, jchown@gov.nu.ca
Acting Manager, Taxation, Daniel Young
867-975-5812, Fax: 867-975-5845, dyoung1@gov.nu.ca
Director, Compensation & Benefits, Nasim Bhanji
867-975-5847, Fax: 867-975-5863, nbhanji@gov.nu.ca
Asst. Comptroller General,
867-975-5866, Fax: 867-975-5896
Acting Chief Internal Auditor, Grace Wilk
867-975-6848, Fax: 867-975-6842, gwilk@gov.nu.ca

Associated Agencies, Boards & Commissions:
• Nunavut Liquor Licensing Board
Bag 002
Rankin Inlet, NU X0C 0G0
Fax: 867-645-3327

Regional Offices:
867-983-4043 Fax: 867-983-4041
Kitikmeot
Director, Regional Financial Services, Sandra Peterson
867-983-4042, speterson@gov.nu.ca
Kivalliq
Director, Regional Financial Services, Kerry Angidlik
867-645-8515, Fax: 867-645-8511, kangidlik@gov.nu.ca
Qikiqtaaluk
867-934-2056 Fax: 867-934-8677
Director, Regional Financial Services, Vacant

Department of Health & Social Services

PO Box 1000 1000, Iqaluit, NU X0A 0H0
867-975-5700 Fax: 867-975-5705
www.hss.gov.nu.ca
The Environmental Health Specialist provides recommendations & direction, consultation, development of standards, monitoring, maintenance & evaluation of all environmental health programs within Nunavut. Reviews the Public Health Act & Regulations & environmental health standards & policies & makes recommendations for revisions. Guides the regional environmental health officers in development & implementation of programs & policies in prevention of diseases caused by environmental factors, including food, water, waste disposal, housing & the sanitation of public places, including schools, day cares & other institutional facilities. Guides the Regional Environmental Health Officers in water & food-borne related illness investigations & food recalls. Guides the regions in the monitoring of drinking water supplies. Assists with development of health education & promotional materials & activities related to environmental health.
Acts Administered:
Boards of Management Dissolution Act
Disease Registries Act
Reportable Diseases Order
Public Health Act
Camp Sanitation Regulations
Communicable Diseases Regulations
General Sanitation Exemption Regulations

General Sanitation Regulations
Meat Inspection Regulations
Public Sewerage Systems Regulations
Public Water Supply Regulations
Tourist Accomodation Health Regulations
Tobacco Control Act
Minister, Hon. Tagak Curley
867-975-5005, Fax: 867-975-5095
Deputy Minister, Peter Ma
pma@gov.nu.ca
Chief Medical Officer of Health, Dr. Geraldine Osborne
867-975-5774, gosborne@gov.nu.ca
Director, Finance, Ramanath Kamath
867-975-5736, rkamath@gov.nu.ca
Asst. Deputy Minister, Operations, Monita O'Connor
867-975-5704, mo'connor@gov.nu.ca
Executive Director, Corporate Services, Debora Voth
867-975-5742, dvoth@gov.nu.ca
Executive Director, Population Health, Gogi Greeley
867-975-5709, ggreeley@gov.nu.ca
Acting Director, Communications, Yasmine Pepa
867-975-5714, Fax: 867-975-5705
Director, Health & Social Services, Virginia Turner
867-473-2629, Fax: 867-473-2657, vturner@gov.nu.ca
Acting Director, Medical Affairs & Telehealth, Dr. William MacDonald
867-979-7601, Fax: 876-979-7346, wmacdonald2@gov.nu.ca
Director, Health Information, Martin Joy
867-975-5903, mjoy@gov.nu.ca
Manager, Public Health, Kristine Hutchinson
867-975-4805, khutchinson@gov.nu.ca
Home Care Coordinator, Tracy Palm
867-266-8965, tpalm@gov.nu.ca

Nunavut Housing Corporation

PO Box 480, Arviat, NU X0C 0E0
867-857-3000 Fax: 867-857-3040
www.nunavuthousing.ca

Minister Responsible, Hon. Tagak Curley
867-975-5005, Fax: 867-975-5095
President, Alain Barriault
867-975-7200, Fax: 867-979-4194, abarriault@gov.nu.ca
Vice-President, Jamie Flaherty
867-975-7200, Fax: 867-979-4194, jflahertynhc@gov.nu.ca
Manager, Rental Programs, Don Moors
867-857-3006, Fax: 867-857-3040, dmoors@gov.nu.ca
Executive Director, Corporate Services & CFO, Lori Kimball
867-975-7200, Fax: 867-979-4194, dmoors@gov.nu.ca

Department of Human Resources

PO Box 1000 400, Iqaluit, NU X0A 1H0
Fax: 867-975-6216
888-668-9993
gnhr@gov.nu.ca

Minister, Hon. Daniel Shewchuk
867-975-5001, Fax: 867-975-5044
Deputy Minister, Louise Wasson
867-975-6213, Fax: 867-975-6216, louise.wasson@gov.nu.ca
Asst. Deputy Minister, Tiffany Gautier
867-975-6204, Fax: 867-975-6216, tgauthier@gov.nu.ca
Executive Secretary, Lizzie Ryan
867-975-6213, Fax: 867-975-6216, lryan1@gov.nu.ca
Acting Director, Corporate Services, David Kolot
867-975-6203, Fax: 867-975-6266, dkolot@gov.nu.ca
Director, Employee Relations, Deborah Evans
867-975-6257, Fax: 867-975-6241, devans@gov.nu.ca
Acting Director, Inuit Employee Planning, Steven Lonsdale
867-975-6272, Fax: 867-975-6280, slonsdale@gov.nu.ca
Director, Job Evaluation & Organization Design, Diane Stenton
867-975-6208, Fax: 867-975-6215, dstenton@gov.nu.ca
Director, Policy & Planning Division, David Kolot
867-975-6203, Fax: 867-975-6216, dkolot@gov.nu.ca
Director, Training & Development, Sheyla Kolola
867-975-6283, Fax: 867-975-6245, skolola@gov.nu.ca
Director, Staffing, Vacant
867-975-6223, Fax: 867-975-6220

Regional Offices:
Cambridge Bay
PO Box 2375, Cambridge Bay, NU X0B 0C0
867-983-4058 Fax: 867-983-4061
866-667-6624

Director, Community Operations, Alice Lafrance
867-983-4060, Fax: 867-983-4061, alafrance@gov.nu.ca
Qikigtaaluk
PO Box 233, Igloolik, NU X0A 0L0
Fax: 867-934-2027
800-682-9033

Director, Community Operations, Kaylan Jambunathan
867-934-2024, Fax: 867-934-2027, kjambunathan@gov.nu.ca
Rankin Inlet
PO Box 930, Rankin Inlet, NU X0C 0G0
Fax: 867-645-8097
800-933-3072

Director, Community Operations, Jacqueline Curley
867-645-8064, Fax: 867-645-8097, jcurley@gov.nu.ca

Department of Justice

Sivummut, 1st Fl., PO Box 1000 500, Iqaluit, NU X0A 0H0
867-975-6170 Fax: 867-975-6195
justice@gov.nu.ca
www.justice.gov.nu.ca

Acts Administered:
Engineers, Geologists & Geophysicists Act
Expropriation Act
Land Titles Act
Minister, Hon. Keith Peterson
867-975-5007, Fax: 867-975-5095
Deputy Minister, Janet Slaughter
867-975-6180, Fax: 867-975-6195, janet.slaughter@gov.nu.ca
Asst. Deputy Minister, Rebekah Williams
867-975-6180, Fax: 867-975-6195, rwilliams@gov.nu.ca
Director, Legal & Constitutional Law, Norman Tarnow
867-975-6332, Fax: 867-975-6151, ntarnow@gov.nu.ca
Director, Corporate Services, Edward Dingle
867-975-6181, Fax: 867-975-6188, edingle@gov.nu.ca

Associated Agencies, Boards & Commissions:
• Baffin Correctional Centre
1550 Federal Rd.
PO Box 368
Iqaluit, NU X0A 0H0
867-979-8100 Fax: 867-979-4646
• Office of the Chief Coroner
PO Box 1000 590
Iqaluit, NU X0A 0H0
• Legal Services Board of Nunavut
PO Box 125
Gjoa Haven, NU X0A 0H0
Fax: 867-360-6112
• Young Offenders
1548 Federal Rd.
PO Box 1439
Iqaluit, NU X0A 0H0
867-979-4452 Fax: 867-979-5506

Community Justice & Corrections
Director, Alan Hartley
867-975-6176, Fax: 867-975-6160, ahartley@gov.nu.ca
Director, Corrections, Doug Strader
867-975-6501, Fax: 867-975-6515, dstrader@gov.nu.ca
Manager, Community Corrections, Vacant

Court Services
866-286-0546

Director, Lou Hall
867-975-6131, Fax: 867-975-6511, lhall@gov.nu.ca
Sheriff, Chris Kennedy
867-975-6119, Fax: 867-975-6168, ckennedy@gov.nu.ca

Legal & Constitutional Division
867-975-6321 Fax: 867-975-6349

Director, Norman M. Tarnow
867-975-6332, Fax: 867-975-6349, ntarnow@gov.nu.ca
Legal Counsel, Adrienne Silk
867-975-6172, asilk@gov.nu.ca
Legal Counsel, Erin George
867-975-6354, egeorge@gov.nu.ca
Public Trustee, Esmeralda Bautista
867-975-6311, Fax: 867-975-6343, ebautista@gov.nu.ca

Legislation Division
867-975-6330 Fax: 867-975-6189

Director & Registrar, Regulations, Susan Hardy
867-975-6334, shardy@gov.nu.ca
Manager, Legal Translation - Inuktitut & Inuinnaqtun, Betty Brewster
867-975-6164, bbrewster@gov.nu.ca
Manager, Legal Translation - French, Vacant
867-975-6336

Nunavut Legal Registries Division
Brown Bldg., 1st Fl., PO Box 1000 570, Iqaluit, NU X0A 0H0
Fax: 867-975-6594

Director, Louis Arki
867-975-6587, larki@gov.nu.ca
Registrar, Land Titles, Vacant
867-975-6590
Deputy Registrar, Securities & Corporate Registry, Tammy Heffernan
867-975-6597, theffernan@gov.nu.ca

Policy & Planning Division
Fax: 867-975-6151

Director, Richard Paton
867-975-6335, Fax: 867-975-6151, rpaton@gov.nu.ca

Ottawa Office

#1209, 350 Sparks St., Ottawa, ON K1R 7S8
613-233-9890 Fax: 613-233-2543

Minister, Hon. Eva Aariak
867-975-5050, Fax: 867-975-5051
Asst. Deputy Minister, Intergovernmental Affairs, Robert Carson
613-233-9890, Fax: 613-233-2543, rcarson@gov.nu.ca
Senior Legal Advisor, Vacant
613-233-9890
Acting Office Manager, Carmel Murphy
613-233-9890, cmurphy@gov.nu.ca

Northwest Territories & Nunavut Workers' Compensation Board

For a detailed listing please see Northwest Territories.

Government of Ontario

Seat of Government: Queen's Park, Toronto, ON M7A 1A2
416-326-1234
800-267-8097
www.gov.on.ca
TTY: 800-268-7095

The Province of Ontario entered Confederation July 1, 1867. It has an area of 907,573.82 km2, & the StatsCan census population in 2006 was 12,160,282.

Office of the Lieutenant Governor

Room 131, Legislative Bldg., Queen's Park, Toronto, ON M7A 1A1
416-325-7780 Fax: 416-325-7787
ltgov@gov.on.ca
www.lt.gov.on.ca

Represents Her Majesty The Queen in Ontario. The Office coordinates, supports & promotes the activities of the Lieutenant Governor. In his constitutional role, the Lieutenant Governor swears-in the Executive Council, outlines the Government's plans in the Speech from the Throne, provides the Royal Assent needed for bills to become laws, approves orders-in-council & appointments recommended by Cabinet, & prorogues or dissolves each session of Parliament. In his community role, he represents the people of Ontario & acts as the Province's official host, welcoming world leaders & diplomats. He hosts or attends hundreds of community events throughout Ontario & presents honours & awards to outstanding Ontarians. His Honour has focused on three themes: reducing the stigma of mental illness, fighting racism, & supporting aboriginal youth. His Honour is also a champion for people living with disabilities.
Lieutenant Governor, Hon. David C. Onley, O.Ont.
416-325-7780, Fax: 416-325-7787, ltgov@gov.on.ca
Chief of Staff, Nanda Casucci-Bryne
416-325-7781, nanda.casuccibyrne@ontario.ca
Chief Aide-de-Camp, A.G. (Sandy) Cameron
416-325-7780, ltgov@gov.on.ca
Chief Steward, Robert Adams
416-325-7794, robert.adams@ontario.ca

Office of the Premier

Legislative Bldg., #281, 1 Queen's Park Cres. South, Toronto, ON M7A 1A1
416-325-1941 Fax: 416-325-3745
www.premier.gov.on.ca
TTY: 800-387-5559

Premier, Hon. Dalton McGuinty
416-325-1941, Fax: 416-325-3745, dmcguinty.mpp.co@liberal.ola.org
Chief of Staff, Chris Morley
416-325-2228, Fax: 416-325-9895
Press Secretary, Jane Almeida
416-314-8975, Fax: 416-325-0803
Director & Executive Assistant, Tracey Sobers
416-325-2228, Fax: 416-325-9895
Executive Director, Communications, Aaron Lazarus
416-325-5972, Fax: 416-325-0803
Director, Caucus Relations, Rod MacDonald
416-325-2491, Fax: 416-314-5189
Director, Issues Management & Legislative Affairs, Alicia Johnston
416-325-8510, Fax: 416-325-0246
Deputy Chief of Staff, Operations, Dave Gene
416-325-2486, Fax: 416-325-6749
Executive Director, Policy & Research, Alex Johnston
416-314-2598, Fax: 416-314-3853
Special Assistant to the Chief of Staff, Wendy Wai
416-325-1619, Fax: 416-325-9895

Executive Council

Whitney Block, Queen's Park, 99 Wellesley St. West, 6th Fl., Toronto, ON M7A 1A1
416-325-5721 Fax: 416-314-1551

Premier & President, Council, Hon. Dalton McGuinty
416-325-1941, Fax: 416-325-3745, premier@gov.on.ca; dmcguinty.mpp.co@liberal.ola.org, TTY: 416-325-7702
Social Media: www.twitter.com/Dalton_McGuinty, www.facebook.com/PremierMcGuinty

Minister, Nothern Development, Mines & Forestry; Chair of Cabinet, Hon. Rick Bartolucci
416-327-0633, Fax: 416-327-0665, rbartolucci.mpp.co@liberal.ola.org
Social Media: www.twitter.com/rickbartolucci, www.facebook.com/rick.bartolucci

Minister, Energy, Hon. Chris Bentley
416-327-6758, Fax: 416-327-6754, cbentley.mpp.co@liberal.ola.org
Social Media: www.twitter.com/Chris_Bentley

Minister, Consumer Services, Hon. Margarett Best
416-327-8300, Fax: 416-326-1947, mbest.mpp.co@liberal.ola.org
Social Media: www.facebook.com/people/Margarett-Best/772159453www.linkedin.com/pub/christina-bisanz/2/7a4/599

Minister, Environment, Hon. James J. Bradley
416-314-6790, Fax: 416-314-6748, jbradley.mpp.co@liberal.ola.org
Social Media: www.facebook.com/votebradley

Minister, Education; Responsible for Women's Issues, Hon. Laurel Broten
416-325-2600, Fax: 416-325-2608, lbroten.mpp.co@liberal.ola.org

Minister, Tourism & Culture, Hon. Michael Chan
416-326-9326, Fax: 416-314-7854, mchan.mpp.co@liberal.ola.org
Social Media: www.facebook.com/group.php?gid=2401349051

Minister, Infrastructure, Hon. Bob Chiarelli
416-325-5270, Fax: 416-325-8860, bchiarelli.mpp.co@liberal.ola.org
Social Media: www.Bob_Chiarelli, www.facebook.com/BobChiarelliMPP

Minister, Transportation, Hon. Bob Chiarelli
416-327-9200, Fax: 416-327-9188, bchiarelli.mpp.co@liberal.ola.org
Social Media: www.Bob_Chiarelli, www.facebook.com/BobChiarelliMPP

Minister, Economic Development & Innovation, Hon. Brad Duguid
416-325-6900, Fax: 416-325-6918, bduguid.mpp.co@liberal.ola.org
Social Media: www.twitter.com/VoteBradDuguid, www.facebook.com/VoteBradDuguid www.linkedin.com/pub/brad-duguid/3/b01/6a3

Minister, Finance; Deputy Premier; Chair, Management Board of the Cabinet, Hon. Dwight Duncan
416-325-0400, Fax: 416-325-0374, dduncan.mpp.co@liberal.ola.org
Social Media: www.twitter.com/DwightDuncan, www.facebook.com/dwight1?sk=wallwww.linkedin.com/pub/dwight-duncan/31/774/8b1

Minister, Natural Resources, Hon. Michael Gravelle
416-314-2301, Fax: 416-325-5316, mgravelle.mpp.co@liberal.ola.org

Minister, Children & Youth Services, Hon. Eric Hoskins
416-212-7432, Fax: 416-212-7431, ehoskins.mpp.co@liberal.ola.org
Social Media: www.twitter.com/DrEricHoskins, www.facebook.com/drerichoskins

Minister, Labour; Responsible for Seniors' Secretariat, Hon. Linda Jeffrey
416-326-7600, Fax: 416-326-1449, ljeffrey.mpp.co@liberal.ola.org
Social Media: www.twitter.com/LindaJeffrey

Minister, Health & Long-Term Care, Hon. Deborah Matthews
416-327-4300, Fax: 416-327-3679, dmatthews.mpp.co@liberal.ola.org
Social Media: www.twitter.com/Deb_Matthews

Minister, Agriculture, Food & Rural Affairs, Hon. Ted McMeekin
416-326-3074, Fax: 416-326-3083, tmcmeekin.mpp.co@liberal.ola.org
Social Media: www.twitter.com/TedMcMeekin

Minister, Community Safety & Correctional Services; Responsible for Francophone Affairs, Hon. Madeleine Meilleur
416-325-0408, Fax: 416-325-6067, mmeilleur.mpp.co@liberal.ola.org
Social Media: www.facebook.com/group.php?gid=5634816945&v=info

Minister, Community & Social Services; Government House Leader, Hon. John Milloy
416-325-5225, Fax: 416-325-3347, jmilloy.mpp.co@liberal.ola.org
Social Media: www.twitter.com/John_Milloy

Minister, Training, Colleges & Universities, Hon. Glen Murray
416-326-1600, Fax: 416-326-1656, gmurray.mpp.co@liberal.ola.org
Social Media: www.twitter.com/Glen4TC, www.facebook.com/GlenMurrayMPP www.linkedin.com/in/glenmurraympp

Minister, Citizenship & Immigration, Hon. Charles Sousa
416-325-6200, Fax: 416-325-6195, csousa.mpp.co@liberal.ola.org
Social Media: www.twitter.com/SousaCharles, www.facebook.com/people/Charles-Sousa/541270855 www.linkedin.com/in/charlessousa

Minister, Government Services, Hon. Harinder S. Takhar
416-327-2333, Fax: 416-327-3790, htakhar.mpp.co@liberal.ola.org
Social Media: www.twitter.com/harindertakhar, www.facebook.com/HarinderTakharMPP www.linkedin.com/pub/hon-harinder-takhar/34/a2a/58

Minister, Aboriginal Affairs, Hon. Kathleen Wynne
416-325-5110, Fax: 416-314-2701, kwynne.mpp.co@liberal.ola.org
Social Media: www.twitter.com/Kathleen_Wynne, www.facebook.com/kwynnemppwww.linkedin.com/in/kathleenwynne

Minister, Municipal Affairs & Housing, Hon. Kathleen Wynne
416-585-7000, Fax: 416-585-6470, kwynne.mpp.co@liberal.ola.org
Social Media: www.twitter.com/Kathleen_Wynne, www.facebook.com/kwynnempp www.linkedin.com/in/kathleenwynne

Cabinet Office
Whitney Block, 99 Wellesley St. West, 6th Fl., Toronto, ON M7A 1A1
416-325-7635 Fax: 416-325-3004
TTY: 416-314-5721

Secretary of the Cabinet & Head of the Ontario Public Service, Shelly Jamieson
416-325-7641, Fax: 416-314-8980, shelly.jamieson@ontario.ca

Deputy Minister, Communications & Associate Secretary of Cabinet, Lynn Betzner
416-325-9698, Fax: 416-325-1979, lynn.betzner@ontario.ca

Deputy Minister, Intergovernmental Affairs; Francophone Affairs & Associate Secretary of the Cabinet, Paul Genest
416-314-9710, Fax: 416-325-4787, paul.genest@ontario.ca

Deputy Minister, Policy & Delivery & Associate Secretary of Cabinet, Giles Gherson
416-325-3759, Fax: 416-325-7631, giles.gherson@ontario.ca

Assistant Deputy Minister, Corporate Planning & Services, Linda Jackson
416-314-0817, Fax: 416-325-2388, linda.jackson@ontario.ca

Legislative Assembly

c/o Clerk's Office, #104, Legislative Bldg., Queen's Park, Toronto, ON M7A 1A2
416-325-7500 Fax: 416-325-7489
assemblyinternet@ontla.ola.org
www.ontla.on.ca
TTY: 416-325-9426
Other Communication: Hansard Email: hansard@ontla.ola.org

Acts Administered:
Election Act
Election Finances Act
Fewer Politicians Act, 1996
Freedom of Information & Protection of Privacy Act
Legislative Assembly Act
Legislative Assembly Retirement Allowances Act
Members' Integrity Act
Ombudsman Act

Speaker, Hon. Steve Peters
416-325-7435, Fax: 416-325-7483, speters.mpp.co@liberal.ola.org

Clerk, Deborah Deller
416-325-7341, Fax: 416-325-7344, debbie_deller@ontla.ola.org

Executive Director, Administrative Services, Sylvia Nemanic
416-325-3568, Fax: 416-314-5995, sylvia_nemanic@ontla.ola.org

Deputy Clerk & Executive Director, Legislative Services, Todd Decker
416-325-3502, Fax: 416-325-5848, todd_decker@ontla.ola.org

Executive Director & Legislative Librarian, Information & Technology Services, Vicki Whitmell
416-325-3939, Fax: 416-325-3909, vicki_whitmell@ontla.ola.org, Other Communications: Reference Inquiries: 416-325-3900

Sergeant-at-Arms & Executive Director, Precinct Properties Division, Dennis M. Clark
416-325-7446, Fax: 416-325-7154, dennis_clark@ontla.ola.org

Executive Assistant to the Clerk, Zina Decker
416-325-7343, Fax: 416-325-7344, zina_decker@ontla.ola.org

Government Members Services
#124, North Wing, Legislative Bldg., Queen's Park, 111 Wellesley St. West, Toronto, ON M7A 1A8
416-325-7200 Fax: 416-325-3810

Government House Leader, Hon. John Milloy
416-325-5225, Fax: 416-325-3347, jmilloy.mpp.co@liberal.ola.org

Chief Government Whip, Jeff Leal
416-325-0534

Chair, Management Board of the Cabinet, Hon. Dwight Duncan
416-325-0400, Fax: 416-325-0374, dduncan.mpp.co@liberal.ola.org

Office of the Opposition (PC)
Legis. Bldg., North Wing, #381, Queen's Park, Toronto, ON M7A 1A8
416-325-0445 Fax: 416-325-0491
www.ontariopc.com
TTY: 416-325-5771

Leader, Tim Hudak
416-325-0445, Fax: 416-325-0491

Deputy Leader, Christine Elliott
416-325-1331, Fax: 416-325-1423

Opposition House Leader, John Yakabuski
416-325-2170, Fax: 416-325-2196, john.yakabuski@pc.ola.org

Deputy House Leader, Ted Arnott
416-325-3880, Fax: 416-325-6649

Chief Opposition Whip, Norm Miller
416-325-7736, Fax: 416-325-7739, norm.miller@pc.ola.org

Opposition Caucus Chair, Toby Barrett
416-325-8404, Fax: 416-325-8408

New Democratic Party
Legislative Bldg., #113, Queen's Park, Toronto, ON M7A 1A5
416-325-7116 Fax: 416-325-8222
www.ontariondp.com
TTY: 416-325-6564

Leader, Andrea Horwath
416-325-8300, Fax: 416-325-8222

Standing Committees of the Legislative Assembly:

Estimates Committee
Clerk, Valerie Quioc Lim
416-325-7352, valerie_quioc@ontla.ola.org

Finance & Economic Affairs Committee
Clerk, Valerie Quioc Lim
416-325-7352, valerie_quioc@ontla.ola.org

General Government Committee
Clerk, Sylwia Przezdziecki
416-325-3515, sylwia_przezdziecki@ontla.ola.org

Government Agencies
Clerk, Trevor Day
416-325-3509, trevor_day@ontla.ola.org

Justice Policy Committee
Clerk, William Short
416-325-3883, william_short@ontla.ola.org

Legislative Assembly Committee
Clerk, Trevor Day
416-325-3509, trevor_day@ontla.ola.org

Public Accounts Committee
Clerk, William Short
416-325-3883, william_short@ontla.ola.org

Regulations & Private Bills Committee
Clerk, Tamara Pomanski
416-325-3506, tamara_pomanski@ontla.ola.org

Social Policy
Clerk, Katch Koch
416-325-3526, katch_koch@ontla.ola.org

Fortieth Parliament - Ontario

Clerk's Office, Legislative Bldg., Queen's Park, Toronto, ON M7A 1A2
416-325-7500 Fax: 416-325-7489
www.ontla.on.ca
TTY: 416-325-9426

Last General Election, October 6, 2011. Maximum Duration, 5 years. Party Standings (October 2011): Liberal (Lib.) 53; Progressive Conservative (PC) 37; New Democratic Party (NDP) 17; Total 107; Salaries, Indemnities & Allowances (April 1, 2005): Each Member is entitled to an annual base salary of $86,860. Additional salary is paid to the following office holders: Premier $68,880; Cabinet Ministers $36,742 (with portfolio); Cabinet Ministers $16,677 (without portfolio); Leader of the Official

Opposition $47,947; Leaders of Parties with recognized membership of 8 or more in the Assembly $31,009; Speaker $27,100; Parliamentary Assistants $12,421; Deputy Speaker & Chair of the Committee of the Whole House $12,855. The following is: member, constituency, population, total eligible voters, party affiliation & contact information:

Laura Albanese, YorkSouth-Weston, Liberal
416-243-7984, Fax: 416-243-0327, lalbanese.mpp.co@liberal.ola.org, Other Communications: Queen's Park Phone: 416-325-1800; Fax: 416-325-1802
Social Media: www.twitter.com/Laura_Albanese, www.facebook.com/pages/Laura-Albanese-MPP/313504007063
Note: Total Eligible Voters (2011): 66,984

Teresa Armstrong, London-Fanshawe, NDP
519-451-0099
Social Media: www.twitter.com/Teresa_NDP
Note: Total Eligible Voters (2011): 73,487

Ted Arnott, Wellington-Halton Hills, Progressive Conservative
519-787-5247, 800-265-2366, Fax: 519-787-5249, ted.arnottco@pc.ola.org; ted.arnott@pc.ola.org, Other Communications: Queen's Park Phone: 416-325-3880; Fax: 416-325-6649
Social Media: www.facebook.com/ted.arnott.ont
Note: Total Eligible Voters (2011): 81,006

Robert (Bob) Bailey, Sarnia-Lambton, Progressive Conservative
519-337-0051, Fax: 519-337-3246, bob.bailey@pc.ola.org; bob.baileyco@pc.ola.org, Other Communications: Queen's Park Phone: 416-325-1715; Fax: 416-325-1852
Social Media: www.twitter.com/BobBaileyPC
Note: Total Eligible Voters (2011): 77,443

Bas Balkissoon, Scarborough-Rouge River, Liberal
416-325-3804, Fax: 416-212-4174, bbalkissoon.mpp.co@liberal.ola.org, Other Communications: Queen's Park Phone: 416-212-3066; Fax: 416-325-3862
Social Media: www.twitter.com/basbalkissoon, www.facebook.com/pages/Bas-Balkissoon/191306360704
Note: Total Eligible Voters (2011): 82,788

Toby Barrett, Haldimand-Norfolk, Progressive Conservative
519-428-0446, Fax: 519-428-0835, toby.barrett@pc.ola.org, Other Communications: Queen's Park Phone: 416-325-8404; Fax: 416-325-8408
Social Media: www.twitter.com/tobybarretmpp
Note: TotalEligible Voters (2011): 76,176

Hon. Rick Bartolucci, Sudbury, Liberal
705-675-1914, Fax: 705-675-1456, rbartolucci.mpp.co@liberal.ola.org, Other Communications: Queen's Park Phone: 416-585-7000; Fax: 416-585-6470
Social Media: www.twitter.com/rickbartolucci, www.facebook.com/rick.bartolucci
Note: Total Eligible Voters (2011): 63,501

Hon. Christopher Bentley, London West, Liberal
519-657-3120, 800-518-7901, Fax: 519-657-0368, cbentley.mpp@liberal.ola.org; cbentley.mpp.co@liberal.ola.org, Other Communications: Queen's Park Phone: 416-326-2220; Fax: 416-326-4007, TTY: 416-326-4012
Social Media: www.twitter.com/Chris_Bentley
Note: Total Eligible Voters (2011): 91,404

Lorenzo Berardinetti, Scarborough Southwest, Liberal
416-261-9525, Fax: 416-261-0381, lberardinetti.mpp@liberal.ola.org, Other Communications: Queen's Park Phone: 416-325-1008; Fax: 416-325-1219
Social Media: www.twitter.com/LBerardinetti, www.facebook.com/berardinetti
Note: Total Eligible Voters (2007): 67,617

Hon. Margarett Best, Scarborough-Guildwood, Liberal
416-281-2787, Fax: 416-281-2360, mbest.mpp.co@liberal.ola.org; mbest.mpp@liberal.ola.org, Other Communications: Queen's Park Phone: 416-326-8500; Fax: 416-326-8520
Social Media: www.facebook.com/people/Margarett-Best/772159453www.linkedin.com/pub/christina-bisanz/2/7a4/599
Note: Total Eligible Voters (2011): 66,009

Christina Bisanz, Newmarket-Aurora, Liberal
905-726-8122
Social Media: www.twitter.com/ChristinaBisanz, www.facebook.com/votebisanz
Note: Total Eligible Voters (2011): 89,777

Gilles Bisson, Timmins-James Bay, New Democratic Party
705-268-6400, 800-461-9878, Fax: 705-266-9125, gbisson@ndp.on.ca, Other Communications: Queen's Park Phone: 416-325-7122; Fax: 416-325-7111
Social Media: www.twitter.com/bissongilles, www.facebook.com/pages/Gilles-Bisson/104067992963846www.linkedin.com/pub/gilles-bisson/32/42b/363
Note: Total Eligible Voters (2011): 48,660

Hon. James J. Bradley, St. Catharines, Liberal
905-935-0018, Fax: 905-935-0191, jbradley.mpp.co@liberal.ola.org; jbradley.mpp@liberal.ola.org, Other Communications: Queen's Park Phone: 416-585-7000; Fax: 416-585-6470
Social Media: www.facebook.com/votebradley
Note: Total Eligible Voters (2011): 83,148

Hon. Laurel C. Broten, Etobicoke-Lakeshore, Liberal
416-259-2249, Fax: 416-259-3704, lbroten.mpp@liberal.ola.org; lbroten.mpp.co@liberal.ola.org, Other Communications: Queen's Park Phone: 416-212-7432; Fax: 416-212-7431
Note: Total Eligible Voters (2011): 84,167

Sarah Campbell, Kenora-Rainy River, New Democratic Party
807-467-2415, 800-465-8501, Fax: 807-467-2641, Other Communications: Queen's Park Phone: 416-325-2750; Fax: 416-325-1645
Social Media: www.twitter.com/Sarah4NWO, www.facebook.com/sarah4nwo
Note: TotalEligible Voters (2011): 45,113

Donna H. Cansfield, Etobicoke Centre, Liberal
416-234-2800, Fax: 416-234-2276, dcansfield.mpp@liberal.ola.org; dcansfield.mpp.co@liberal.ola.org, Other Communications: Queen's Park Phone: 416-585-7007; Fax: 416-585-4035
Social Media: www.twitter.com/DCansfield, www.facebook.com/DonnaCansfieldwww.linkedin.com/pub/donna-cansfield/39/3a0/735
Note: Total Eligible Voters (2011): 79,230

Hon. Michael Chan, Markham-Unionville, Liberal
905-305-1935, Fax: 905-305-1938, mchan.mpp@liberal.ola.org; mchan.mpp.co@liberal.ola.org, Other Communications: Queen's Park Phone: 416-326-9326; Fax: 416-326-9338
Social Media: www.facebook.com/group.php?gid=2401349051
Note: Total Eligible Voters (2011): 90,392

Hon. Bob Chiarelli, OttawaWest-Nepean, Liberal
613-721-8075, Fax: 613-721-5756, bchiarelli.mpp.co@liberal.ola.org, Other Communications: Queen's Park Phone: 416-325-8841; Fax: 416-325-8860
Social Media: www.Bob_Chiarelli, www.facebook.com/BobChiarelliMPP
Note: Total Eligible Voters (2011): 81,111

Ted Chudleigh, Halton, Progressive Conservative
905-878-1729, Fax: 905-878-5144, ted.chudleigh@pc.ola.org, Other Communications: Queen's Park Phone: 416-325-5747; Fax: 416-325-5750
Social Media: www.twitter.com/TChudleigh2011
Note: Total EligibleVoters (2011): 124,958

Steve Clark, Leeds-Grenville, Progressive Conservative
613-342-9522, 800-267-4408, Fax: 613-342-2501, steve.clark@pc.ola.org, Other Communications: Queen's Park Phone: 416-325-1522; Fax: 416-325-1493
Social Media: www.twitter.com/steveclarkelib, www.facebook.com/VoteSteveClarke
Note: Total Eligible Voters (2011): 74,309

Mike Colle, Eglinton-Lawrence, Liberal
416-781-2395, Fax: 416-781-4116, mcolle.mpp@liberal.ola.org; mcolle.mpp.co@liberal.ola.org, Other Communications: Queen's Park Phone: 416-325-4091; Fax: 416-325-4136
Social Media: www.twitter.com/mikecolleMPPwww.linkedin.com/pub/mike-colle-mpp/15/55a/748
Note: Total Eligible Voters (2011): 71,670

Michael Coteau, Don Valley East, Liberal
416-494-6856, Fax: 416-494-9937, Other Communications: Queen's Park Phone: 416-325-3290; Fax: 416-325-3204
Social Media: www.twitter.com/coteau, www.facebook.com/michaelcoteau
Note: Total Eligible Voters (2011): 67,718

Grant Crack, Glengarry-Prescott-Russell, Liberal
613-446-4010, 800-355-9666, Fax: 613-446-6605, Other Communications: Queen's Park Phone: 416-325-7289; Fax: 416-325-2827
Social Media: www.twitter.com/GrantCrack
Note: TotalEligible Voters (2011): 82,717

Kim Craitor, Niagara Falls, Liberal
905-357-0681, Fax: 905-357-9456, kcraitor.mpp@liberal.ola.org; kcraitor.mpp.co@liberal.ola.org, Other Communications: Queen's Park Phone: 416-325-3715; Fax: 416-212-7155
Social Media: www.facebook.com/people/Kim-Craitor-Mpp/100002625582257www.linkedin.com/pub/kim-craitor/30/291/771
Note: Total Eligible Voters (2011): 93,555

Dipika Damerla, Mississauga-East-Cooksville, Liberal
Social Media: www.twitter.com/DipikaDamerla, www.facebook.com/DipikaDamerla.MEC?sk=wall&filter=2
Note: Total Eligible Voters (2011): 82,167

Bob Delaney, Mississauga-Streetsville, Liberal
905-569-1643, Fax: 905-569-6416, bdelaney.mpp@liberal.ola.org; bdelaney.mpp.co@liberal.ola.org, Other Communications: Queen's Park Phone: 416-325-0161; Fax: 416-325-0186
Social Media: www.facebook.com/BobDelaneyMPPwww.linkedin.com/in/bobdelaneympp
Note: Total Eligible Voters (2011): 85,309

Vic Dhillon, Brampton West, Liberal
905-796-8669, Fax: 905-796-8069, vdhillon.mpp@liberal.ola.org; vdhillon.mpp.co@liberal.ola.org, Other Communications: Queen's Park Phone: 416-325-0241; Fax: 416-325-0272
Social Media: www.twitter.com/dhillonvic, www.facebook.com/dhillonvic
Note: Total Eligible Voters (2011): 111,992

Joe Dickson, Ajax-Pickering, Liberal
905-427-2060, Fax: 905-427-6976, jdickson.mpp@liberal.ola.org, Other Communications: Queen's Park Phone: 416-325-1182; Fax: 416-325-1191
Social Media: www.twitter.com/votejoedickson
Note: Total Eligible Voters (2011): 89,921

Cheri DiNovo, Parkdale-High Park, New Democratic Party
416-763-5630, Fax: 416-763-5640, dinovoc-qp@ndp.on.ca; dinovoc-co@ndp.on.ca, Other Communications: Queen's Park phone: 416-325-0244; Fax: 416-325-0305
Social Media: www.twitter.com/cheridinovo, www.facebook.com/CheriDiNovoParkdaleHighParkwww.linkedin.com/pub/cheri-dinovo/12/715/157
Note: Total Eligible Voters (2011): 72,892

Hon. Brad Duguid, Scarborough Centre, Liberal
416-615-2183, Fax: 416-615-2011, bduguid.mpp@liberal.ola.org; bduguid.mpp.co@liberal.ola.org, Other Communications: Queen's Park Phone: 416-327-6758; Fax: 416-327-6754
Social Media: www.twitter.com/VoteBradDuguid, www.facebook.com/VoteBradDuguidwww.linkedin.com/pub/brad-duguid/3/b01/6a3
Note: Total Eligible Voters (2011): 69,170

Hon. Dwight Duncan, Windsor-Tecumseh, Liberal
519-251-5199, Fax: 519-251-5299, dduncan.mpp@liberal.ola.org; dduncan.mpp.co@liberal.ola.org, Other Communications: Queen's Park Phone: 416-325-0400; Fax: 416-325-0374
Social Media: www.twitter.com/DwightDuncan, www.facebook.com/dwight1?sk=wallwww.linkedin.com/pub/dwight-duncan/31/774/8b1
Note: Total Eligible Voters (2011): 82,525

Garfield Dunlop, Simcoe North, Progressive Conservative
705-326-3246, 800-304-7341, Fax: 705-326-9579, garfield.dunlop@pc.ola.org; garfield.dunlopco@pc.ola.org, Other Communications: Queen's Park Phone: 416-325-3855; Fax: 416-325-9035
Social Media: www.twitter.com/Garfield_Dunlop, www.facebook.com/pages/Garfield-Dunlop/119367071443387
Note: Total Eligible Voters (2011): 88,943

Christine Elliott, Whitby-Oshawa, Progressive Conservative
905-430-1141, Fax: 905-430-1840, christine.elliott@pc.ola.org, Other Communications: Queen's Park Phone: 416-325-1331; Fax: 416-325-1423
Social Media: www.twitter.com/votechristine
Note: Total Eligible Voters (2011): 101,282

Vic Fedeli, Nipissing, Liberal
705-474-8340, Fax: 705-474-9747, Other Communications: Queen's Park Phone: 416-325-7754; Fax: 416-325-7755
Social Media: www.twitter.com/victorfedeli, www.facebook.com/pages/Vic-Fedeli/195238410500602?sk=wallwww.linkedin.com/in/victorfedeli
Note: Total Eligible Voters (2011): 58,099

Kevin Daniel Flynn, Oakville, Liberal
905-827-5141, Fax: 905-827-3786, kflynn.mpp@liberal.ola.org; kflynn.mpp.co@liberal.ola.org, Other Communications: Queen's Park Phone: 416-325-7215; Fax: 416-325-9295
Social Media: www.twitter.com/OakvilleMPPwww.linkedin.com/pub/kevin-flynn/1b/73a/9b1
Note: Total Eligible Voters (2007): 81,551

Cindy Forster, Welland, New Democratic Party
905-732-6884, Fax: 905-732-9782, Other Communications: Queen's Park Phone: 416-325-7106
Social Media: www.facebook.com/CindyForsterNDP
Note: Total Eligible Voters (2011): 83,160

France Gélinas, Nickel Belt, New Democratic Party
705-969-3621, Fax: 705-969-3538, fgelinas-co@ndp.on.ca; fgelinas-qp@ndp.on.ca, Other Communications: Queen's Park Phone: 416-325-9203; Fax: 416-325-9185
Social Media: www.twitter.com/NickelBelt
Note: Total Eligible Voters (2011): 60,565

Hon. John Gerretsen, Kingston & the Islands, Liberal
613-547-2385, Fax: 613-547-5001, jgerretsen.mpp@liberal.ola.org; jgerretsen.mpp.co@liberal.ola.org, Other Communications: Queen's Park Phone: 416-327-8300; Fax: 416-326-1947
Note: Total Eligible Voters (2011): 92,518

Hon. Michael Gravelle, Thunder Bay-Superior North, Liberal
807-345-3647, 888-516-5555, Fax: 807-345-2922, mgravelle.mpp@liberal.ola.org, Other Communications:

Queen's Park Phone: 416-327-0633; Fax: 416-327-0665
Note: Total Eligible Voters (2011): 52,924
Ernie Hardeman, Oxford, Progressive Conservative
519-537-5222, 800-265-4046, Fax: 519-537-3577, ernie.hardeman@pc.ola.org; ernie.hardemanco@pc.ola.org, Other Communications: Queen's Park Phone: 416-325-1239; Fax: 416-325-1259
Social Media: www.facebook.com/people/Ernie-Hardeman/505534292www.linkedin.com/pub/ernie-hardeman/2b/18a/37a
Note: Total Eligible Voters (2011): 74,799
Michael Harris, Kitchener-Conestoga, Progressive Conservative
519-954-3276, Fax: 519-748-9876, info@michaelharrispc.ca
Social Media: www.twitter.com/Michaelharrispc, www.facebook.com/group.php?gid=2418112067
Note: Total Eligible Voters (2011): 85,748
Randy Hillier, Lanark-Frontenac-Lennox &Addington, Progressive Conservative
613-267-8293, Fax: 613-267-7398, randy.hillierco@pc.ola.org, Other Communications: Queen's Park Phone: 416-325-2244; Fax: 416-325-2166
Social Media: www.twitter.com/randyhillier, www.facebook.com/pages/Randy-Hillier-MPP/178772728799738www.linkedin.com/pub/randy-hillier/34/496/41b
Note: Total Eligible Voters (2011): 86,592
Andrea Horwath, Hamilton Centre, New Democratic Party
905-544-9644, Fax: 905-544-5152, ahorwath-qp@ndp.on.ca; ahorwath-co@ndp.on.ca, Other Communications: Queen's Park Phone: 416-325-2777; Fax: 416-325-2770
Social Media: www.twitter.com/andreahorwath, www.facebook.com/AndreaHorwathONDP
Note: Total Eligible Voters (2011): 76,790
Hon. Eric Hoskins, St.Paul's, Liberal
416-656-0943, Fax: 416-656-0875, ehoskins.mpp.co@liberal.ola.org, Other Communications: Queen's Park Phone: 416-325-6200; Fax: 416-325-6195
Social Media: www.twitter.com/DrEricHoskins, www.facebook.com/drerichoskins
Note: Total Eligible Voters (2011): 82,424
Tim Hudak, NiagaraWest-Glanbrook, Progressive Conservative
905-563-1755, 800-665-3697, Fax: 905-563-1317, tim.hudakco@pc.ola.org, Other Communications: Queen's Park Phone: 416-325-8454; Fax: 416-325-0998
Social Media: www.twitter.com/timhudak, www.facebook.com/timhudakwww.linkedin.com/in/timhudak
Note: Total Eligible Voters (2011): 86,714
Rod Jackson, Barrie, Progressive Conservative
705-881-1519
Social Media: www.twitter.com/RodneyJackson, www.facebook.com/pages/Elect-Rod-Jackson/168359439854698?sk=wall
Note: Total Eligible Voters (2011): 92,791
Helena Jaczek, OakRidges-Markham, Liberal
905-294-4931, 866-531-9551, Fax: 905-294-0014, hjaczek.mpp@liberal.ola.org, Other Communications: Queen's Park Phone: 416-325-0737; Fax: 416-325-4112
Social Media: www.twitter.com/helenajaczek, www.facebook.com/helenajaczekwww.linkedin.com/pub/helena-jaczek/4/6a5/b77
Note: Total Eligible Voters (2011): 147,426
Hon. Linda Jeffrey, Brampton-Springdale, Liberal
905-495-8030, Fax: 905-495-1041, ljeffrey.mpp@liberal.ola.org; ljeffrey.mpp.co@liberal.ola.org, Other Communications: Queen's Park Phone: 416-314-2301; Fax: 416-325-5316
Social Media: www.twitter.com/LindaJeffrey
Note: Total Eligible Voters (2011): 85,029
Sylvia Jones, Dufferin-Caledon, Progressive Conservative
519-941-7751, Fax: 519-941-3246, sylvia.jones@pc.ola.org; sylvia.jonesco@pc.ola.org, Other Communications: Queen's Park Phone: 416-325-1898; Fax: 416-325-1936
Social Media: www.twitter.com/SylviaJonesMPP, www.facebook.com/group.php?gid=336959233065
Note: Total Eligible Voters (2011): 78,039
Monte Kwinter, York Centre, Liberal
416-630-0080, Fax: 416-630-8828, mkwinter.mpp@liberal.ola.org; mkwinter.mpp.co@liberal.ola.org, Other Communications: Queen's Park Phone: 416-325-0036; Fax: 416-325-0316
Social Media: www.twitter.com/MonteKwinter, www.facebook.com/ReElectMonteKwinter
Note: Total Eligible Voters (2011): 71,448
Jeff Leal, Peterborough, Liberal
705-742-3777, Fax: 705-742-1822, jleal.mpp@liberal.ola.org; jleal.mpp.co@liberal.ola.org, Other Communications: Queen's Park Phone: 416-325-0534; Fax: 416-325-0570
Social Media: www.twitter.com/reelectjeffleal
Note: Total Eligible Voters (2011): 89,444
Rob Leone, Cambridge, Progressive Conservative
519-623-5852, Fax: 519-623-3250, Other Communications: Queen's Park Phone: 416-325-8451; Fax: 416-325-8413
Social Media: www.twitter.com/robleone
Note: Total Eligible Voters (2011): 89,584
Dave Levac, Brant, Liberal
519-759-0361, Fax: 519-759-6439, dlevac.mpp@liberal.ola.org; dlevac.mpp.co@liberal.ola.org, Other Communications: Queen's Park Phone: 416-325-4140
Note: Total Eligible Voters (2011): 93,195
Tracy MacCharles, Pickering-Scarborough East, Liberal
905-492-8683, Other Communications: Queen's Park Phone: 416-325-3581; Fax: 416-325-3453
Social Media: www.twitter.com/votemaccharles, www.facebook.com/votemaccharles
Note: Total Eligible Voters (2011): 77,112
Jack MacLaren, Carleton-MississippiMills, Progressive Conservative
513-599-3000, 800-267-1020, Fax: 613-599-8183, Other Communications: Queen's Park Phone: 416-314-7900; Fax: 416-314-7966
Social Media: www.twitter.com/jackmaclaren, www.facebook.com/pages/Jack-MacLaren/181470968553829?sk=info
Note: Total Eligible Voters (2011): 101,434
Lisa MacLeod, Nepean-Carleton, Progressive Conservative
613-823-2116, Fax: 613-823-8284, lisa.macleod@pc.ola.org, Other Communications: Queen's Park Phone: 416-325-6351; Fax: 416-325-6364
Social Media: www.facebook.com/LisaMacLeodMPPwww.linkedin.com/pub/lisa-macleod/13/675/163
Note: Total Eligible Voters (2011): 107,776
Amrit Mangat, Mississauga-Brampton South, Liberal
905-696-0367, Fax: 905-696-7545, amangat.mpp.co@liberal.ola.org, Other Communications: Queen's Park Phone: 416-325-1050; Fax: 416-325-1138
Social Media: www.twitter.com/amrit_mangat, www.facebook.com/pages/Amrit-Mangat/265148843495306?v=info
Note: Total Eligible Voters (2011): 91,127
Michael Mantha, Algoma-Manitoulin, New Democratic Party
705-848-0431, mikemantha@ontariondp.ca
Social Media: www.facebook.com/MikeManthaONDP
Note: Total Eligible Voters (2011): 49,675
Rosario Marchese, Trinity-Spadina, New Democratic Party
416-603-9664, Fax: 416-603-1241, rmarchese-co@ndp.on.ca, Other Communications: Queen's Park Phone: 416-325-9092; Fax: 416-325-4976
Social Media: www.twitter.com/RMarcheseMPP, www.facebook.com/RosarioMarcheseMPP
Note: TotalEligible Voters (2011): 101,970
Hon. Deborah Matthews, London North Centre, Liberal
519-432-7339, Fax: 519-432-0613, dmatthews.mpp@liberal.ola.org; dmatthews.mpp.co@liberal.ola.org, Other Communications: Queen's Park Phone: 416-327-4300; Fax: 416-327-3679
Social Media: www.twitter.com/Deb_Matthews
Note: Total Eligible Voters (2011): 88,192
Bill Mauro, ThunderBay-Atikokan, Liberal
807-623-9237, Fax: 807-623-4983, bmauro.mpp.co@liberal.ola.org, Other Communications: Queen's Park Phone: 416-327-6611; Fax: 416-327-6618
Social Media: www.twitter.com/billmurompp www.linkedin.com/pub/bill-mauro/1a/447/6a8
Note: Total Eligible Voters (2011): 56,381
Jim McDonell, Stormont-Dundas-South Glengarry, Progressive Conservative
613-933-7447, jimmcdonellcampaign@gmail.com
Note: Total Eligible Voters (2011): 75,097
Hon. Dalton McGuinty, OttawaSouth, Liberal
613-736-9573, Fax: 613-736-7374, dmcguinty.mpp.co@liberal.ola.org, Other Communications: Queen's Park Phone: 416-325-1941; Fax: 416-325-3745
Social Media: www.twitter.com/Dalton_McGuinty, www.facebook.com/PremierMcGuinty
Note: Total Eligible Voters (2007): 85,876
Jane McKenna, Burlington, Progressive Conservative
905-639-7924, Fax: 905-639-3284, Other Communications: Queen's Park Phone: 416-325-5362; Fax: 416-325-5357
Social Media: www.twitter.com/VoteJaneMcKenna
Note: Total Eligible Voters (2011): 89,511
Hon. Ted McMeekin, Ancaster-Dundas-Flamborough-Westdale, Liberal
905-690-6552, 888-566-6614, Fax: 905-690-6562, tmcmeekin.mpp@liberal.ola.org; tmcmeekin.mpp.co@liberal.ola.org, Other Communications: Queen's Park Phone: 416-326-1600; Fax: 416-326-2807
Social Media: www.twitter.com/TedMcMeekin
Note: Total Eligible Voters (2011): 85,812
Monte McNaughton, Lambton-Kent-Middlesex, Progressive Conservative
519-205-8875
Social Media: www.twitter.com/MonteMcNaughton/
Note: Total Eligible Voters (2011): 76,717
Phil McNeely, Ottawa-Orléans, Liberal
613-834-8679, Fax: 613-834-7647, pmcneely.mpp@liberal.ola.org; pmcneely.mpp.co@liberal.ola.org, Other Communications: Queen's Park Phone: 416-325-0505; Fax: 416-325-0532
Social Media: www.twitter.com/PhilMcNeelyMPP
Note: Total Eligible Voters (2011): 86,668
Hon. Madeleine Meilleur, Ottawa-Vanier, Liberal
613-744-4484, 800-628-7507, Fax: 613-744-0889, mmeilleur.mpp.co@liberal.ola.org; ofa@ofa.gov.on.ca, Other Communications: Queen's Park Phone: 416-325-5225; Fax: 416-325-5191
Social Media: www.facebook.com/group.php?gid=5634816945&v=info
Note: Total Eligible Voters (2011): 79,161
Norm Miller, ParrySound-Muskoka, Progressive Conservative
705-746-4266, 888-701-1176, Fax: 705-746-1578, norm.millerco@pc.ola.org, Other Communications: Queen's Park Phone: 416-325-1012; Fax: 416-325-1153
Social Media: www.twitter.com/normmillermpp
Note: Total Eligible Voters (2011): 67,209
Paul Miller, HamiltonEast-Stoney Creek, New Democratic Party
905-545-0114, Fax: 905-545-9024, pmiller-co@ndp.on.ca; pmiller-qp@ndp.on.ca, Other Communications: Queen's Park Phone: 416-325-0707; Fax: 416-325-0853
Note: Total Eligible Voters (2011): 85,024
Rob Milligan, Northumberland-Quinte West, Progressive Conservative
905-372-5433, rrmilligan@hotmail.ca
Social Media: www.twitter.com/RobMilligan, www.facebook.com/pages/Rob-Milligan/210851462262701
Note: Total Eligible Voters (2011): 90,640
Hon. John Milloy, Kitchener Centre, Liberal
519-579-5460, Fax: 519-579-2121, jmilloy.mpp@liberal.ola.org; jmilloy.mpp.co@liberal.ola.org, Other Communications: Queen's Park Phone: 416-326-1600; Fax: 416-326-1656
Social Media: www.twitter.com/John_Milloy
Note: Total Eligible Voters (2011): 78,709
Reza Moridi, Richmond Hill, Liberal
905-884-8080, Fax: 905-884-1040, rmoridi.mpp@liberal.ola.org, Other Communications: Queen's Park Phone: 416-326-5968; Fax: 416-326-5834
Social Media: www.twitter.com/rezamoridi, www.facebook.com/rmoridiwww.linkedin.com/pub/reza-moridi-mpp/6/673/bb4
Note: TotalEligible Voters (2011): 89,189
Julia Munro, York-Simcoe, Progressive Conservative
905-478-2572, 866-206-1373, Fax: 905-478-8470, julia.munro@pc.ola.org; julia.munroco@pc.ola.org, Other Communications: Queen's Park Phone: 416-325-3392; Fax: 416-325-3466
Social Media: www.twitter.com/juliamunropc, www.facebook.com/juliamunropc
Note: Total Eligible Voters (2011): 88,916
Hon. Glen R. Murray, TorontoCentre, Liberal
416-972-7683, Fax: 416-972-7686, gmurray.mpp.co@liberal.ola.org, Other Communications: Queen's Park Phone: 416-325-5744; Fax: 416-325-5754
Social Media: www.twitter.com/Glen4TC, www.facebook.com/GlenMurrayMPPwww.linkedin.com/in/glenmurraympp
Note: Total Eligible Voters (2011): 90,342
Taras Natyshak, Essex, New Democratic Party
519-776-4957, 866-660-1460
Social Media: www.twitter.com/Taras4EssexMPP, www.facebook.com/TarasNatyshakMPP
Note: Total Eligible Voters (2011): 87,986
Yasir Naqvi, Ottawa Centre, Liberal
613-722-6414, Fax: 613-722-6703, ynaqvi.mpp@liberal.ola.org, Other Communications: Queen's Park Phone: 416-327-4394; Fax: 416-314-9369
Social Media: www.twitter.com/Yasir_Naqvi, www.facebook.com/YasirNaqviMPPwww.linkedin.com/in/yasirnaqvimpp
Note: TotalEligible Voters (2011): 90,251
Rick Nicholls, Chatham-Kent-Essex, Progressive Conservative
Social Media: www.twitter.com/RickNicholls, www.facebook.com/RickNichollsPCofCKEX?sk=wallwww.linkedin.com/pub/rick-nicholls/10/280/b05
Note: Total Eligible Voters (2011): 72,821
David Orazietti, Sault Ste. Marie, Liberal
705-949-6959, Fax: 705-946-6269, dorazietti.mpp@liberal.ola.org; dorazietti.mpp.co@liberal.ola.org, Other Communications: Queen's Park Phone: 416-314-6467; Fax: 416-314-6470
Social Media: www.twitter.com/DavidOrazietti, www.facebook.com/davidorazietti?v=info
Note: Total Eligible Voters (2011): 58,054
John O'Toole, Durham, Progressive Conservative
905-697-1501, 800-661-2433, Fax: 905-697-1506, john.otoole@pc.ola.org; john.otooleco@pc.ola.org, Other Communications: Queen's Park Phone: 416-325-6745; Fax: 416-325-6255
Note: Total Eligible Voters (2011): 90,170
Jerry J. Ouellette, Oshawa, Progressive Conservative
905-723-2411, Fax: 905-723-1054, jerry.ouellette@pc.ola.org; jerry.ouelletteco@pc.ola.org, Other Communications:

Queen's Park Phone: 416-325-2147; Fax: 416-325-2169
Social Media:
www.linkedin.com/pub/jerry-ouellette/27/12b/751
Note: Total Eligible Voters (2011): 88,127

Randy Pettapiece, Perth-Wellington, Progressive Conservative
Social Media: www.twitter.com/randypettapiece, www.facebook.com/pages/Randy-Pettapiece/116053045144846
Note: Total Eligible Voters (2011): 70,491

Teresa Piruzza, Windsor West, Liberal
519-977-7191, Fax: 519-977-7029, Other Communications: Queen's Park Phone: 416-325-6900; Fax: 416-325-6918
Social Media: www.twitter.com/VotePiruzza, www.facebook.com/VotePiruzza?sk=wall&filter=2www.linkedin.com/pub/teresa-piruzza/21/461/486
Note: Total Eligible Voters (2011): 81,133

Michael Prue, Beaches-EastYork, New Democratic Party
416-690-1032, Fax: 416-690-8420, mprue-qp@ndp.on.ca; mprue-co@ndp.on.ca, Other Communications: Queen's Park Phone: 416-325-1303; Fax: 416-325-1367
Note: Total Eligible Voters (2011): 72,502

Shafiq Qaadri, Etobicoke North, Liberal
416-745-2859, Fax: 416-745-4601, sqaadri.mpp@liberal.ola.org; sqaadri.mpp.co@liberal.ola.org, Other Communications: Queen's Park Phone: 416-325-6679; Fax: 416-325-6691
Social Media: www.linkedin.com/in/doctorqca
Note: Total Eligible Voters (2011): 61,447

Liz Sandals, Guelph, Liberal
519-836-4190, Fax: 519-836-4191, lsandals.mpp@liberal.ola.org; lsandals.mpp.co@liberal.ola.org, Other Communications: Queen's Park Phone: 416-327-1322; Fax: 416-325-3862
Note: Total Eligible Voters (2011): 90,445

Jonah Schein, Davenport, New Democratic Party
416-531-7495, jonah@jonahschein.ca
Social Media: www.twitter.com/jonahschein, www.facebook.com/votejonahschein
Note: Total Eligible Voters (2011): 65,471

Laurie Scott, Haliburton-Kawartha Lakes-Brock, Liberal
705-880-5674
Social Media: www.twitter.com/LaurieScott_PC, www.facebook.com/pages/Laurie-Scott/199126813450886?v=info
Note: Total Eligible Voters (2011): 87,272

Mario Sergio, York West, Liberal
416-743-7272, Fax: 416-743-3292, msergio.mpp@liberal.ola.org, Other Communications: Queen's Park Phone: 416-325-4925; Fax: 416-325-4926
Social Media: www.linkedin.com/pub/mario-sergio/18/b65/28
Note: TotalEligible Voters (2011): 56,389

Peter Shurman, Thornhill, Progressive Conservative
905-731-8462, Fax: 905-731-2984, peter.shurman@pc.ola.org; peter.shurmanco@pc.ola.org, Other Communications: Queen's Park Phone: 416-325-1415; Fax: 416-325-3810
Social Media: www.twitter.com/shurmanator, www.facebook.com/pages/Peter-Shurman/136034076479824
Note: Total Eligible Voters (2011): 97,154

Jagmeet Singh, Bramalea-Gore-Malton, Liberal
905-456-7125, contact@jagmeetsingh.ca
Social Media: www.twitter.com/JagmeetSingh, www.facebook.com/jagmeetndp?sk=pe
Note: Total Eligible Voters (2011): 102,788

Todd Smith, Prince Edward-Hastings, Progressive Conservative
Social Media: www.twitter.com/toddsmithpc
Note: Total Eligible Voters (2011): 85,229

Greg Sorbara, Vaughan, Liberal
905-851-0440, Fax: 905-851-0210, gsorbara.mpp@liberal.ola.org; gsorbara.mpp.co@liberal.ola.org, Other Communications: Queen's Park Phone: 416-212-1022; Fax: 416-212-1025
Social Media: www.twitter.com/greg_sorbara
Note: Total Eligible Voters (2011): 118,226

Hon. Charles Sousa, Mississauga South, Liberal
905-274-8228, Fax: 905-274-8552, csousa.mpp@liberal.ola.org; csousa.mpp.co@liberal.ola.org, Other Communications: Queen's Park Phone: 416-327-6611; Fax: 416-327-6618
Social Media: www.twitter.com/SousaCharles, www.facebook.com/people/Charles-Sousa/541270855www.linkedin.com/in/charlessousa
Note: Total Eligible Voters (2011): 77,313

Peter Tabuns, Toronto-Danforth, New Democratic Party
416-461-0223, Fax: 416-461-9542, tabunsp-qp@ndp.on.ca; tabunsp-co@ndp.on.ca, Other Communications: Queen's Park Phone: 416-325-3250; Fax: 416-325-3252
Note: Total Eligible Voters (2011): 74,040

Hon. Harinder S. Takhar, Mississauga-Erindale, Liberal
905-828-8989, Fax: 905-828-8670, htakhar.mpp@liberal.ola.org; htakhar.mpp.co@liberal.ola.org, Other Communications: Queen's Park Phone: 416-327-2333; Fax: 416-327-3790
Social Media: www.twitter.com/harindertakhar, www.facebook.com/HarinderTakharMPPwww.linkedin.com/pub/hon-harinder-takhar/34/a2a/58
Note: Total Eligible Voters (2011): 100,987

Monique Taylor, Hamilton Mountain, New Democratic Party
905-546-0606, moniquetaylor@ontariondp.ca
Social Media: www.twitter.com/MoniqueONDP, www.facebook.com/group.php?gid=151616944893613
Note: Total Eligible Voters (2011): 88,751

Lisa Thompson, Huron-Bruce, Liberal
Note: Total Eligible Voters (2011): 74,490

John Vanthof, Timiskaming-Cochrane, New Democratic Party
705-647-3940
Social Media: www.facebook.com/JohnVanthof
Note: Total Eligible Voters (2011): 48,331

Bill Walker, Bruce-Grey-Owen Sound, Progressive Conservative
519-371-2421, 800-461-2664, Fax: 519-371-0953, Other Communications: Queen's Park Phone: 416-325-6242; Fax: 416-325-6248
Social Media: www.twitter.votebillwalker, www.facebook.com/pages/Bill-Walker/231771823522746?sk=photos
Note: TotalEligible Voters (2011): 73,364

Jim Wilson, Simcoe-Grey, Progressive Conservative
705-446-1090, 800-268-7542, Fax: 705-446-3397, jim.wilson@pc.ola.org; jim.wilsonco@pc.ola.org, Other Communications: Queen's Park Phone: 416-325-2069; Fax: 416-325-2079
Social Media: www.twitter.com/jwilsonmpp
Note: Total Eligible Voters (2011): 95,479

Elizabeth Witmer, Kitchener-Waterloo, Progressive Conservative
519-725-3477, Fax: 519-725-3667, elizabeth.witmer@pc.ola.org; elizabeth.witmerco@pc.ola.org, Other Communications: Queen's Park Phone: 416-325-1306; Fax: 416-325-1329
Social Media: www.twitter.com/WitmerMPP
Note: Total Eligible Voters (2011): 93,939

Soo Wong, Scarborough-Agincourt, Liberal
416-297-6568, Fax: 416-297-4962, Other Communications: Queen's Park Phone: 416-325-3628; Fax: 416-314-7421
Social Media: www.twitter.com/votesoo
Note: Total EligibleVoters (2011): 72,337

Hon. Kathleen Wynne, Don Valley West, Liberal
416-425-6777, Fax: 416-425-0350, kwynne.mpp@liberal.ola.org; kwynne.mpp.co@liberal.ola.org, Other Communications: Queen's Park Phone: 416-327-9200; Fax: 416-327-9188
Social Media: www.twitter.com/Kathleen_Wynne, www.facebook.com/kwynnemppwww.linkedin.com/in/kathleenwynne
Note: Total Eligible Voters (2011): 79,468

John Yakabuski, Renfrew-Nipissing-Pembroke, Progressive Conservative
613-735-6627, Fax: 613-735-6692, john.yakabuski@pc.ola.org; john.yakabuskico@pc.ola.org1, Other Communications: Queen's Park Phone: 416-325-2170; Fax: 416-325-2196
Social Media: www.twitter.com/JYakabuskiMPP
Note: Total Eligible Voters (2011): 72,051

Jeff Yurek, Elgin-Middlesex-London, Progressive Conservative
519-631-0280, votejeff@yurek.com
Social Media: www.twitter.com/jeffreyyurek
Note: Total Eligible Voters (2011): 79,624

David Zimmer, Willowdale, Liberal
416-733-7878, Fax: 416-733-7709, dzimmer.mpp@liberal.ola.org; dzimmer.mpp.co@liberal.ola.org, Other Communications: Queen's Park Phone: 416-327-4516; Fax: 416-325-4175
Social Media:
www.facebook.com/group.php?gid=81031428325
Note: Total Eligible Voters (2011): 93,529

Ontario Government Departments & Agencies

Ontario Ministry of Aboriginal Affairs / Ministère des Affaires autochtones

160 Bloor St. East, 4th & 9th Fl., Toronto, ON M7A 2E6
416-326-4740 Fax: 416-326-4017
www.aboriginalaffairs.gov.on.ca

The Ministry operates with the following units: Office of the Deputy Minister of Aboriginal Affairs; Office of the Assistant Deputy Minister of Aboriginal Affairs; Policy & Relationships Branch; Ipperwash Response Team; Negotiations Branch; Legal Services Branch; Communications Branch; & the Business Services Unit.

Acts Administered:
English & Wabigoon River Systems Mercury Contamination Settlement Agreement Act

Minister, Hon. Kathleen Wynne
416-325-5110, Fax: 416-314-2701, kwynne.mpp.co@liberal.ola.org
Deputy Minister, Lori Sterling
416-314-1141, Fax: 416-314-1165, lori.sterling@ontario.ca
Acting Chief Administrative Officer, David Lynch
416-314-1939, Fax: 416-326-4017, david.lynch@ontario.ca

Aboriginal Relations & Ministry Partnership Division
416-326-4740 Fax: 416-314-2102
Assistant Deputy Minister, Deborah Richardson
416-325-0304, deborah.richardson@ontario.ca
Director, Resource & Economic Development, Pam Wheaton
416-326-4053, pam.wheaton@ontario.ca
Director, Social & Education, Anita Tiefenbach
416-325-7032, anita.tiefenbach@ontario.ca

Business & Financial Services Branch
416-326-4740 Fax: 416-212-1644
Corporate functions are provided by the branch. Functions include the following: business planning; financial control & budgeting; & facilities & assets management
Manager, Glenn Wetherall
519-826-4769, glenn.wetherall@ontario.ca

Communications Services Branch
441-632-5110 Fax: 416-326-4779
The team factitlate coordination of response to the Ipperwash Inquiry Report & researches & analyzes the implementation of the inquiry recommendations.
Director, Greg Coleman
416-314-5383, greg.coleman@ontario.ca

Legal Services Branch
416-326-4740 Fax: 416-326-4017
Director, Grant Wedge
416-326-2372, Grant.Wedge@ontario.ca

Negotiations Branch
416-326-4740 Fax: 416-326-2361
The branch carries out the following responsibilities: researching & conducting land claim negotiations; managing & coordinating negotiations; representing the province for federally-led governance negotiations; & implementing settlements.
Assistant Deputy Minister, Doug Carr
416-326-4741, doug.carr@ontario.ca
Director, David Didluck
416-326-2839, Fax: 416-326-4017, David.didluck@ontario.ca

Policy & Planning Branch
416-326-4743
The branch is engaged in the following key activities: developing & coordinating government-wide Aboriginal policy; providing corporate planning & policy advice on Aboriginal matters; & developing & maintaining positive relationships with Aboriginal leaders.
Assistant Deputy Minister, Bryan Kozman
416-212-2302, bryan.cozman@ontario.ca
Director, Jonathan Lebi
416-314-1607, jonathan.lebi@ontario.ca

Ontario Ministry of Agriculture, Food & Rural Affairs (OMAFRA)

Ontario Government Bldg., 1 Stone Rd. West, Guelph, ON N1G 4Y2
519-826-3100
888-466-2372
www.omafra.gov.on.ca

The ministry works in partnership with an industry that employs over 640,000 people & contributes over $25 billion annually to the provincial economy. The ministry plays a key role in bringing a strong agricultural & rural perspective to provincial policies. The ministry works with other ministries to resolve local economic issues & assists rural communities in retaining & attracting business. Staff at the ministry's Guelph headquarters & across the province provide a wide range of agri-food & rural economic development programs & services to clients.

Acts Administered:
AgriCorp Act
Agricultural Employees Protection Act 2002
Agricultural & Horticultural Organizations Act
Agricultural Research Institute of Ontario Act
Agricultural Lands Regulations
Agricultural Tile Drainage Installation Act
Animals for Research Act
Beef Cattle Marketing Act
Bees Act
Crop Insurance Act (Ontario)
Drainage Act
Farm Products Container Act
Farm Products Marketing Act
Farm Implements Act
Farm Products Grades & Sales Act
Farm Products Payments Act
Farm Registration & Farm Organizations Funding Act
Farming & Food Production Protection Act
Food Safety & Quality Act, 2001
Grains Act
Livestock & Livestock Products Act
Livestock Community Sales Act
Livestock Identification Act
Livestock Medicines Act
Protection of Livestock & Poultry from Dogs Act

Milk Act
Ministry of Agriculture, Food & Rural Affairs Act
Nutrient Management Act, 2002
Ontario Food Terminal Act
Plant Diseases Act
Pounds Act
Tile Drainage Act
Veterinarians Act
Weed Control Act
Animal Health Act
Commodity Board Members Act
Commodity Boards & Marketing Agencies Act
Ministry of Energy Act (sections dealing with the Ontario Ethanol Growth Fund program)
Nutrient Management Act (in part)
Ontario Agriculture Week Act

Minister, Hon. Ted McMeekin
416-326-3074, Fax: 416-326-3083, tmcmeekin.mpp.co@liberal.ola.org
Deputy Minister, John Burke
416-326-3101, john.burke@ontario.ca
Director, Communications, Diane Gumbs
416-326-5196, diane.gumbs@ontario.ca
Director, Legal Services, Michael Brady
519-826-3378, Fax: 519-826-3385, michael.p.brady@ontario.ca
Parliamentary Assistant, Maria Van Bommel
416-326-6160, Fax: 416-326-3106, mvanbommel.mpp.co@liberal.ola.org

Associated Agencies, Boards & Commissions:

• AGRICORP
1 Stone Rd. West, 3rd Fl.
PO Box 3660 Central
Guelph, ON N1H 8M4
Fax: 519-826-4118 888-247-4999
cac@agricorp.com
www.agricorp.com
Responsible for delivering government & non-government priority products & services that assist Ontario's agri-food industry in managing risks. Since its inception, AGRICORP has developed a reputation for innovation, excellent customer service & reliable, cost-effective delivery

• Agricultural Research Institute of Ontario (ARIO)
1 Stone Rd. West, 2nd Fl.
Guelph, ON N1G 4Y2
519-826-4199 Fax: 519-826-4211
The role of ARIO is to enquire into programs of research with respect to agriculture, veterinary medicine & consumer studies, select & recommend areas of research for the betterment of agriculture, veterinary medicine & consumer studies, & stimulate interest in research as a means of developing a high degree of efficiency in the production & marketing of agricultural products in Ontario.

• Agriculture, Food & Rural Affairs Tribunal
1 Stone Rd. West, 2nd Fl.
Guelph, ON N1G 4Y2
519-826-3433 Fax: 519-826-4232
appeals.tribunal@omafra.gov.on.ca

• College of Veterinarians of Ontario
2106 Gordon St.
Guelph, ON N1L 1G6
519-824-5600 Fax: 519-824-6497 800-424-2856
inquiries@cvo.org
www.cvo.org

• Board of Negotiation
1 Stone Rd. West
Guelph, ON N1G 4Y2

• Grain Financial Protection Board
1 Stone Rd. West, 1st Fl. Northeast
PO Box 3660 Central
Guelph, ON N1H 8M4
519-826-3949 Fax: 519-826-3367

• Livestock Financial Protection Board
1 Stone Rd. West, 5th Fl. Northwest
Guelph, ON N1G 4Y2
519-826-3886 Fax: 519-826-4375

• Livestock Medicines Advisory Committee
1 Stone Rd. West, 3rd Fl. Northeast
Guelph, ON N1G 4Y2
519-826-4110 Fax: 519-826-3254

• Normal Farm Practices Protection Board
1 Stone Rd. West, 3rd Fl.
Guelph, ON N1G 4Y2
Fax: 519-826-3259 877-424-1300

• Ontario Farm Products Marketing Commission
1 Stone Rd. West, 5th Fl. Southwest
Guelph, ON N1G 4Y2
519-826-4220 Fax: 519-826-3400

• Ontario Food Terminal Board
165 The Queensway
Toronto, ON M8Y 1H8
416-259-5479 Fax: 416-259-4303
www.oftb.com

• Rural Economic Development (RED) Panel
1 Stone Rd. West, 4th Fl.
Guelph, ON N1G 4Y2
Fax: 519-826-4336 888-588-4111
red.omafra@ontario.ca
www.ontario.ca/rural

Food Safety & Environment Division
519-826-4304 Fax: 519-826-4416

Asst. Deputy Minister, Dr. Dave Hope
519-826-4301, Fax: 519-826-4416, dave.hope@ontario.ca
Director, Animal Health & Welfare, Dr. Jim Richardson
519-826-3577, Fax: 519-826-4375, jim.richardson@ontario.ca
Director, Food Inspection Branch, Gavin Downing
519-826-4366, Fax: 519-826-4375, gavin.downing@ontario.ca
Acting Director, Food Safety Programs, Gwen McBride
519-826-3112, Fax: 519-826-4466, gwen.mcbride@ontario.ca
Director, Environmental Management, Clarence Haverson
519-826-4975, Fax: 519-826-6611, clarence.haverson@ontario.ca

Office of the Chief Information officer, Land & Resources I&IT Cluster

Chief Information Officer, Robert Hollis
416-314-1528, robert.hollis@ontario.ca
Manager, Business & Financial Management, Glenn Wetherall
519-826-4769, glenn.wetherall@ontario.ca
Head, Service Management, Uwe Helmer
519-826-5160, uwe.helmer@ontario.ca
Head, Strategy Information & Program Management, Doug Green
519-826-3236, doug.greeen@ontario.ca

Policy & Programs Division
519-826-4020 Fax: 519-826-3492

Responsible for the ministry's policy processes, the administration & delivery of several farm business risk management programs & the management of the ministry's strategic partnership with AGRICORP.

Asst. Deputy Minister, Dave Antle
519-826-4151, Fax: 519-826-3492, dave.antle@ontario.ca
Director, Farm Finance, Tracy Dallaire
519-826-3244, Fax: 519-826-3170, tracy.dallaire@ontario.ca
Director, Food Safety & Environmental Policy Branch, Rena Hubers
519-826-3241, Fax: 519-826-3492, rena.hubers@ontario.ca
Director, Strategic Policy, George McCaw
519-826-4002, george.mccaw@ontario.ca

Research & Corporate Services Division
1 Stone Road W., 2nd Fl. Northwest, Guelph, ON N1G 4Y2
519-826-4551 Fax: 519-826-3390

Asst. Deputy Minister, Karen D. Chan
519-826-6599, Fax: 519-826-3390, karen.chan@ontario.ca
Director, Financial Management, Lee-Ann Walker
519-826-3336, Fax: 519-826-4130, leeann.walker@ontario.ca
Director, Business Services Branch, Shelly Gibson
519-826-4698, shelley.gibson@ontario.ca
Director, Research & Innovation, Dr. Michael Toombs
519-826-4172, Fax: 519-826-4211, michael.toombs@ontario.ca
Manager, French Language Services, Louise Gagnon
416-212-4274, louise.gagnon@ontario.ca
Director, Internal Audit Services, Nancy Lavoie
905-704-2870, Fax: 705-755-1599, nancy.lavoie@ontario.ca

Economic Development Division
1 Stone Road W., 2nd Fl., Guelph, ON N1G 4Y2
519-826-6636 Fax: 519-826-4328

Asst Deputy Minister, Bonnie Winchester
519-826-3528, bonnie.winchester@ontario.ca
Director, Agriculture Development Branch, Aileen MacNeil
519-826-6588, aileen.macneil@ontario.ca
Director, Business Development, George Borovilos
519-826-4452, Fax: 519-826-4336, george.borovilos@ontario.ca
Director, Rural Community Development, Martin Bohl
519-826-3419, Fax: 519-826-4336, martin.bohl@ontario.ca

Ontario Ministry of the Attorney General

McMurtry-Scott Bldg., 720 Bay St., 11th Fl., Toronto, ON M5G 2K1

416-326-2220 Fax: 416-326-4007
800-518-7901
www.attorneygeneral.jus.gov.on.ca
TTY: 416-326-4012

Justice services are delivered to Ontarians by the Ministry of the Attorney General. The Ministry is engaged in the following activities: supporting victims of crime; providing justice support services to vulnerable people in the province; ensuring the availability of effective & efficient criminal, civil & family courts, plus related justice services; prosecuting crime; & giving legal advice & services to government.

Acts Administered:

Absconding Debtors Act
Absentees Act
Accumulations Act
Administration of Justice Act
Age of Majority & Accountability Act
Aliens' Real Property Act
Arbitration Act
Architects Act
Assessment Review Board Act
Bail Act
Barristers Act
Blind Persons' Rights Act
Bulk Sales Act
Business Records Protection Act
Chartered Accountants Act
Charities Accounting Act
Children's Law Reform Act
Class Proceedings Act
Commercial Mediation Act
Commissioners for Taking Affidavits Act
Compensation for Victims of Crime Act
Construction Lien Act
Conveyancing & Law of Property Act
Costs of Distress Act
Courts of Justice Act
Crown Administration of Estates Act
Crown Agency Act
Crown Attorneys Act
Crown Witnesses Act
Declarations of Death Act
Disorderly Houses Act
Dog Owners' Liability Act
Electronic Commerce Act
Employers & Employees Act
Enforcement of Judgement Conventions Act
Escheats Act
Estates Act
Estates Administration Act
Evidence Act
Execution Act
Expropriations Act
Family Law Act
Fines & Forfeitures Act
Fraudulent Conveyances Act
Frustrated Contracts Act
Habeas Corpus Act
Hospitals & Charitable Institutions Inquiries Act
International Commercial Arbitration Act
International Sale of Goods Act
Inter-Provincial Summonses Act
Judicial Review Procedure Act
Juries Act
Justices of the Peace Act
Law Society Act
Legal Aid Services Act
Libel & Slander Act
Limitations Act
Mercantile Law Amendment Act
Ministry of the Attorney General Act
Mortgages Act
Negligence Act
Notaries Act
Occupiers' Liability Act
Ombudsman Act
Parental Responsibility Act
Partition Act
Pawnbrokers Act
Perpetuities Act
Police Services Act (s. 113)
Powers of Attorney Act
Proceedings Against the Crown Act
Professional Engineers Act
Property & Civil Rights Act
Provincial Offences Act
Public Authorities' Protection Act
Public Guardian & Trustee Act
Public Officers Act
Reciprocal Enforcement of Judgements Act
Reciprocal Enforcement of Judgements (U.K.) Act
Religious Freedom Act
Religious Organizations' Lands Act
Safe Streets Act
Sale of Goods Act
Settled Estates Act
Short Forms of Leases Act
Solicitors Act
Statute of Frauds
Statutory Powers Procedure Act
Substitute Decisions Act
Succession Law Reform Act
Ticket Speculation Act
Time Act
Transboundary Pollution Reciprocal Access Act
Trespass to Property Act
Trustee Act

Unconscionable Transactions Relief Act
Variation of Trusts Act
Vendors & Purchasers Act
Victims Bill of Rights Act
Wages Act
Warehouse Receipts Act
Alcohol & Gaming Regulation & Public Protection Act (Part I)
Apology Act
Certified General Accountants Act
Certified Management Accountants Act
Child & Family Services Act (sec. 162-174)
Civil Remedies Act
Donation of Food Act
Education Act (sec. 57)
Election Act
Election Finances Act
Electoral System Referendum Act
Environmental Review Tribunal Act
Executive Council Act
Gaming Control Act
Good Samaritan Act
Human Rights Code
Interjurisdictional Support Orders
International Interests in Mobile Equipment Act (Aircraft Equipment)
Legislation Act
Legislative Assembly Act
Lieutenant Governor Act
Liquor Licence Act
Members' Integrity Act
Ontario Association of Former Parliamentarians Act
Ontario Heritage Act
Ontario Municipal Board Act
Ontario Works Act (Part IV)
Prohibiting Profiting from Recounting Crimes Act
Public Accounting Act
Real Property Limitations Act
Representation Act
Rescuing Children from Sexual Exploitation Act (Parts III & IV)
Residential Tenancies Act (in part)
Revised Statutes Confirmation & Corrections Act
Settlement of International Investment Disputes Act
Tobacco Damages & Health Care Costs Recovery

Attorney General, Hon. John Gerretsen
416-326-2220, 800-518-7901, Fax: 416-326-4007, jgerretsen.mpp.co@liberal.ola.org, TTY: 416-326-4012

Deputy Attorney General, Murray Segal
416-326-2640, Fax: 416-326-4018, Murray.Segal@ontario.ca

Acting Director, Communications, Marianne Summers
416-326-2604, Fax: 416-326-4007, marianne.summers@ontario.ca

Parliamentary Assistant, David Zimmer
416-327-4516, Fax: 416-325-4175, dzimmer.mpp@liberal.ola.org; dzimmer.mpp.co@liberal.ola.org

Associated Agencies, Boards & Commissions:

• Alcohol & Gaming Commission of Ontario
90 Sheppard Ave. East
Toronto, ON M2N 0A4
416-326-8700 Fax: 416-326-5555 800-522-2876
www.agco.on.ca

• Assessment Review Board
Eaton Tower
#1500, 655 Bay St.
Toronto, ON M5G 1E5
416-212-6349 Fax: 416-314-3717 866-448-2248 TTY: 877-849-2066
assessment.review.board@ontario.ca
www.arb.gov.on.ca

• Chief Inquiry Officer - Expropriations Act
McMurtry-Scott Bldg.
720 Bay St., 8th Fl.
Toronto, ON M7A 2S9
416-314-2226

• Criminal Injuries Compensation Board
439 University Ave., 4th Fl.
Toronto, ON M5G 1Y8
416-326-2900 Fax: 416-326-2883 800-372-7463
info.cicb@ontario.ca
www.cicb.gov.on.ca
Other Communication: Victim Support Line: 1-888-579-2888

• Human Rights Tribunal of Ontario
655 Bay St., 14th Fl.
Toronto, ON M7A 2A3
416-326-1312 Fax: 416-326-2027 866-598-0322 TTY: 416-326-2027
hrto.tdpo@ontario.ca
www.hrto.ca
Other Communication: Toll-Free TTY: 1-866-607-1240

• Judicial Appointments Advisory Committee
McMurtry-Scott Bldg.
720 Bay St., 3rd Fl.
Toronto, ON M7A 2S9
416-326-4060 Fax: 416-212-7316

• Legal Aid Ontario
#404, 375 University Ave.
Toronto, ON M5G 2G1
416-979-1446 Fax: 416-979-8669 800-668-8258 TTY: 416-598-8867
info@lao.on.ca
www.legalaid.on.ca
Other Communication: Toll-Free TTY: 1-866-641-8867

• Office for Victims of Crime
700 Bay St., 3rd Fl.
Toronto, ON M5G 1Z6
416-326-1682 Fax: 416-326-4497 887-435-7661 TTY: 416-325-9341

• Office of the Independent Police Review Director
655 Bay St., 10th Fl.
Toronto, ON M7A 2T4
416-246-7071 Fax: 416-327-8332 877-411-4773 TTY: 877-414-4773
www.oiprd.on.ca
Other Communication: Toll-Free Fax: 877-415-4773

• Ontario Human Rights Commission

• Ontario Municipal Board & Board of Negotiation
655 Bay St., 15th Fl.
Toronto, ON M5G 1E5
416-326-6800 Fax: 416-326-5370 866-887-8820
www.omb.gov.on.ca

• Social Justice Tribunals Ontario
40 Dundas St. West
Toronto, ON M7A 0A9
416-212-8000 Fax: 416-212-8024

Corporate Services Management Division

Asst. Deputy Attorney General & Chief Admin. Officer, Dante Pontone
416-326-9844, dante.pontone@ontario.ca
Director, Business & Fiscal Planning, Maureen Buckley
416-326-4020, Fax: 416-326-4019, maureen.buckley@ontario.ca
Director, Human Resources Branch, Barbara Ross
416-326-3283, Fax: 416-326-2298, barbara.ross@ontario.ca
Director, Facilities Management, Judy Stamp
416-326-4033, Fax: 416-326-4029, judy.stamp@ontario.ca
Director, Diversity & Inclusiveness, Tom Fagan
416-314-3590, tom.fagan@ontario.ca
Director, Ontario Internal Audit, Justice Audit Service, David Horie
705-329-6747, david.horie@ontario.ca

Court Services Division

Asst. Deputy Attorney General, Lynne Wagner
416-326-2609, Fax: 416-326-2652, lynne.wagner@ontario.ca
Head, Business Solutions, Chris Walpole
416-326-4267, Fax: 416-212-4981, chris.walpole@ontario.ca
Director, Family Policy & Programs, Anne Marie Predko
416-326-7867, annemarie.predko@ontario.ca
Acting Director, Corporate Planning, Sheila Bristo
416-314-4608, Fax: 416-326-1011, sheila.bristo@ontario.ca
Director, Criminal/POA Policy & Programs Branch, Diana Hunt
416-326-2531, Fax: 416-326-1869, diana.hunt@ontario.ca

Regional Court Services Offices:

Central East
#201, 1091 Gorham St., Newmarket, ON L3Y 8X7
905-836-5621 Fax: 905-836-5620
Acting Director, Court Operations, Sarina Kashak
905-836-5484, Fax: 905-836-5620, sarina.kashak@ontario.ca

Central West
#518B, 45 Main St. East, Hamilton, ON L8N 2B7
905-645-5333 Fax: 905-645-5375
Director, Court Operations, Joanne Spriet
905-645-5333, Fax: 905-645-5375, joanne.spriet@ontario.ca

East
#100 - 343 Preston St., Ottawa, ON K1S 1N4
613-239-1551 Fax: 613-239-1273
Director, Court Operations, Viviane Carpentier
613-239-1597, viviane.carpentier@ontario.ca

Northeast
501, 159 Cedar St., Sudbury, ON P3E 6A5
705-564-7675 Fax: 705-564-7664
Director, Court Operations, Robert Gordon
807-343-2701, robert.gordon@ontario.ca

Northwest
277 Camelot St., Thunder Bay, ON P7A 4B3
807-343-2747 Fax: 807-345-6383
Director, Court Operations, Robert Gordon
807-343-2701, Fax: 807-345-6383, robert.gordon@ontario.ca

Toronto
#1601, 700 Bay St., Toronto, ON M5G 1Z6
416-326-4249 Fax: 416-326-2073
Regional Director, Lynn Norris
416-326-4250, Fax: 416-326-2073, lynn.norris@ontario.ca

West
80 Dundas St., Unit D, London, ON N6A 6A4
519-660-3090 Fax: 519-660-3098
Director, Court Operations, Paul Langlois
519-660-3094, paul.langlois@ontario.ca

Criminal Law Division
McMurty-Scott Bldg., 720 Bay St., 6th fl., Toronto, ON M5G 2K1
416-326-4656 Fax: 416-326-2063
Asst. Deputy Attorney General, Criminal Law, John D. Ayre
416-326-2616, Fax: 416-326-2063, john.ayre@ontario.ca
Director, Criminal Law Policy Branch, Mary Nethery
416-325-8663, mary.nethery@ontario.ca
Deputy Director, Crown Law Office - Criminal, John Corelli
416-326-2618, john.corelli@ontario.ca
Deputy Director, Crown Law Office - Criminal, Rosella Cornaviera
416-326-4616, rosella.cornaviera@ontario.ca
Deputy Director, Crown Law Office - Criminal, David Finley
416-326-4587, david.finley@ontario.ca
Deputy Director, Crown Law Office - Criminal, Howard Leibovich
416-326-2002, howard.leibovich@ontario.ca
Deputy Director, Crown Law Office - Criminal, Susan Reid
416-326-2682, susan.reid@ontario.ca
Director, Divisional Planning & Administration, Stephanie Crawford
416-326-2099, Fax: 416-326-2423, stephanie.crowford@ontario.ca
Acting Director, Law & Technology, Alexander Smith
416-212-1166, alexander.smith@ontario.ca

Legal Services Division
McMurty-Scott Bldg., 720 Bay St., 6th fl., Toronto, ON M5G 2K1
416-326-0891 Fax: 416-326-6996
Acting Asst. Deputy Attorney General, Malliha Wilson
416-326-2505, Fax: 416-326-6996, malliha.wilson@ontario.ca
Director, Constitutional Law, Michel Y. Hélie
416-326-4454, Fax: 416-326-4015, michel.helie@ontario.ca
Director, Crown Law Office-Civil, Craig Slater
416-326-4100, Fax: 416-326-4181, craig.slater@ontario.ca
Director, Legal Services Program Support Branch, Paula Konstantinidis
416-326-4173, Fax: 416-314-7926, paula.konstantinidis@ontario.ca

Civil Remedies for Illicit Activities
77 Wellesley St. West, PO Box 333, Toronto, ON M7A 1N3
416-212-0556 Fax: 416-314-3714
Legal Director, Jeff Simser
416-326-4188, Fax: 416-314-3714, jeff.simser@ontario.ca

Legislative Counsel
Whitney Block, #3600, 99 Wellesley St. West, Toronto, ON M7A 1A2
416-326-2841 Fax: 416-326-2806
Chief Legislative Counsel, Mark Spakowski
416-326-2740, mark.spakowski@ontario.ca
Assoc. Chief Legislative Counsel, Cornelia Schuh
416-326-2741, cornelia.schuch@ontario.ca
Director, French Legislative Services, Gerard Hernando
416-326-2793, gerard.hernando@ontario.ca

Policy & Adjudicative Tribunals Division
McMurtry-Scott Bldg, 720 Bay St, 11th Fl., Toronto, ON M7A 2S9
416-326-2500 Fax: 416-326-2699
Asst. Deputy Attorney General, Mark Leach
416-326-2711, mark.leach@ontario.ca
Director, Corporate Policy & Agency Relations Branch, Martha Otton
416-326-4932, martha.otton@ontario.ca
Director, Justice Policy Development Branch, Andrea Storm
416-326-2482, andrea.storm@ontario.ca
Director, Special Investigations Unit, Ian Scott
416-622-0748, ian.scott@ontario.ca

Victims & Vulnerable Persons Division
18 King St. E, 7th Fl., Toronto, ON M5C 1C4
416-325-3265 Fax: 416-212-1091
Asst. Deputy Minister, Irwin Glasberg
416-326-0190, irwin.glasberg@ontario.ca
Director, Programs & Community Development, Linda D. Haldenby
416-326-2428, Fax: 416-212-1091, linda.d.haldenby@ontario.ca
Director, Policy & Program Development, Patricia Bishop
416-325-3695, Fax: 416-212-1091, patricia.bishop@ontario.ca

Office of the Auditor General

Atrium on Bay, #1530, 20 Dundas St. West, PO Box 105, Toronto, ON M5G 2C2
416-327-2381 Fax: 416-327-9862
comments@auditor.on.ca
www.auditor.on.ca
TTY: 416-327-6123

Auditor General, Jim R. McCarter
416-327-1326, jim.mccarter@auditor.on.ca
Deputy Auditor General, Gary Peall
416-327-1658, gary.peall@auditor.on.ca
Director, Crown Agencies (2) Portfolio, Laura Bell
416-327-2377, laura.bell@auditor.on.ca
Director, Community, Social Services & Revenue Portfolio, Walter Bordne
416-327-1329, walter.bordne@auditor.on.ca
Director, Public Accounts, Finance, Environment & Natural Resources Portfolio, Gus Chagani
416-327-2395, gus.chagani@auditor.on.ca
Director, Education & Training Portfolio, Gerard Fitzmaurice
416-327-1371, gerard.fitzmaurice@auditor.on.ca
Director, Health & Long-term Care Providers Portfolio, Susan Klein
416-327-1668, susan.klein@auditor.on.ca
Director, Justice & Regulatory Portfolio, Vince Mazzone
416-327-1669, vince.mazzone@auditor.on.ca
Director, Crown Agencies (1) Portfolio, John McDowell
416-327-1656, john.mcdowell@auditor.on.ca
Manager, Transportation, Infrastructure & Municipal Affairs Portfolio, Kim Cho
416-327-3059, kim.cho@auditor.on.ca

Ontario Ministry of Children & Youth Services

56 Wellesley St. West, 14th Fl., Toronto, ON M5S 2G3
Fax: 416-325-5191
866-821-7770
www.children.gov.on.ca
TTY: 800-387-5559

Working collaboratively with community partners, as well as the Ministries of Education, Health & Long-Term Care, Community & Social Services, Citizenship & Immigration, Culture, & Tourism & Recreation to integrate a number of Ontario's children & youth programs & services. By bringing these programs under one roof, this government is making children a top priority to give them the best start in life, to prepare youth to become productive adults, & to make it easier for families to get the services they need at all stages of a child's development.

Acts Administered:
Child & Family Services Act
Day Nurseries Act
Health Protection and Promotion Act
Intercountry Adoption Act, 1998
Ministry of Community and Social Services Act
Ministry of Correctional Services Act
Rescuing Children from Sexual Exploitation Act
British Home Child Day Act
Ontario Child Benefit Equivalent Act
Poverty Reduction Act
Provincial Advocate for Children & Youth Act

Minister, Hon. Eric Hoskins
416-212-7432, Fax: 416-212-7431, ehoskins.mpp.co@liberal.ola.org
Deputy Minister, George Zegarak
416-212-2280, george.zegarak@ontario.ca
Provincial Advocate, Office of The Provincial Advocate for Children & Youth, Irwin Elman
416-325-5989, Fax: 416-325-5681, irwin.elman@provincialadvocate.on.ca, Other Communications: URL: www.provincialadvocate.on.ca
Director, Communications & Marketing Branch, Jean-Claude Camus
416-326-3512, Fax: 416-325-5191, jean-claude.camus@ontario.ca
Director, Legal Services Branch, Diane Zimnica
416-314-5173, Fax: 416-327-0568, diane.zimnica@ontario.ca
Chief Information Officer, Children, Youth & Social Services, Corbin Kerr
416-326-4330, Fax: 416-325-0266, corbin.kerr@ontario.ca

Business Planning & Corporate Services
Asst. Deputy Minister, Lorraine Graham-Watson
416-325-5588, lorraine.graham-watson@ontario.ca
Director, Capital & Accommodation Services, Angela James
416-325-4600, angela.james@ontario.ca
Director, Emergency Management Program, Linda MacQueen
416-327-3950, linda.macqueen@ontario.ca
Director, Financial Planning & Business Management, Martin Thumm
416-325-5139, martin.thumm@ontario.ca
Director, Human Resources, Frank Caccia
416-327-4753, frank.caccia@ontario.ca
Director, Internal Audit Services, David W. Johnston
416-585-6550, david.w.johnston@ontario.ca

Policy Development & Program Design
56 Wellesley St. W, 14th Fl., Toronto, ON M5S 2S3
416-327-4865 Fax: 416-314-1862
Assistant Deputy Minister, Aryeh Gitterman
416-212-1961, Fax: 416-314-1862, aryeh.gitterman@ontario.ca
Senior Adviser, Pamela Loring
416-314-5857, Fax: 416-314-1862, pamela.loring@ontario.ca
Director, Specialized Services & Supports Branch, Louise Paul
416-325-5331, Fax: 416-325-8330, louise.paul@ontario.ca
Director, Children & Youth at Risk, Marian Mlakar
416-212-5205, Fax: 416-212-2021, marian.mlakar@ontario.ca
Director, Child Welfare Secretariat, Jennifer Morris
416-325-3560, jennifer.morris@ontario.ca

Service Delivery Division
Asst. Deputy Minister, Nancy Matthews
416-212-3141, nancy.matthews@ontario.ca
Director, Client Services, Greg Douglas
416-327-2531, greg.douglas@ontario.ca
Director, Resource Management, Sally Johnson
416-325-5510, sally.johnson@ontario.ca

Strategic Policy & Planning Division
56 Wellesley St., 14th Fl., Toronto, ON M5S 2S3
416-327-9460 Fax: 416-314-1862
Asst. Deputy Minister, Darryl Sturtevant
416-327-9481, Fax: 416-314-1862, darryl.sturtevant@ontario.ca
Director, Early Learning & Child Development Branch, Julie Mathien
416-325-5874, Fax: 416-326-0478
Director, Research & Outcome Measurement, Anne Premi
416-325-5944, Fax: 416-327-0570, anne.premi@ontario.ca
Director, Strategic Planning, Rachel Simeon
416-314-1489, Fax: 416-326-3140, rachel.simeon@ontario.ca

Youth Justice Services
56 Wellesley St. W, 14th fl., Toronto, ON M5S 2S3
416-314-3502 Fax: 416-327-0478
Asst. Deputy Minister, JoAnn Miller-Reid
416-327-9910, joann.miller-reid@ontario.ca
Director, Operational Support, John Scarfo
416-212-7609, Fax: 416-327-2418, john.scarfo@ontario.ca
Director, Planning & Program Development, Trish Moloughney
416-212-7610, trish.moloughney@ontario
Director, Information Management Unit, Cindy Cowper
705-494-3117, cindy.cowper@ontario.ca

Regional Offices:

Toronto
477 Mount Pleasant Rd., 3rd Fl., Toronto, ON M7A 1G1
416-325-0500 Fax: 416-325-0541
416-325-3600

Central East
#1, 17310 Yonge St., Newmarket, ON L3Y 7R8
905-868-8900

Central West
#200, 6733 Mississauga Rd., Mississauga, ON L5N 6J5
905-567-7177 Fax: 905-567-3215
877-832-2818

Eastern
347 Preston St., Ottawa, ON K1S 2T7
613-234-1188 Fax: 613-787-5252
800-267-5111

Hamilton Niagara
Ellen Fairclough Bldg., 119 King St., Hamilton, ON L8P 4Y7
905-521-7280 Fax: 905-546-8277
TTY: 905-546-8276

North East
621 Main St., North Bay, ON P1B 2V6
705-474-3540 Fax: 705-474-5815
800-461-6977
TTY: 705-474-7665

Northern
#1002, 199 Larch St., Sudbury, ON P3E 5P9
705-564-6699 Fax: 705-564-3099
800-265-1222

South East
11 Beechgrove Lane, Kingston, ON K7M 9A6
613-545-0539 Fax: 613-536-7272
800-646-3209
TTY: 613-536-7304

South West
#203, 217 York St., PO Box 5217, London, ON N6A 5R1
519-438-5111 Fax: 519-672-9510
800-265-4197
TTY: 519-663-5276

Ontario Ministry of Citizenship & Immigration

400 University Ave., 6th Fl., Toronto, ON M7A 2R9
416-327-2422 Fax: 416-314-4965
800-267-7329
www.citizenship.gov.on.ca
TTY: 416-326-0148
Other Communication: Information URL: ontarioimmigration.ca

Acts Administered:
Ontario Human Rights Code
Fair Access to Regulated Professions Act
Holocaust Memorial Day Act
Holodomor Memorial Day Act
Ministry of Citizenship & Culture Act (in part)
Remembrance Day Observance Act
Vimy Ridge Day Act

Minister, Hon. Charles Sousa
416-325-6200, Fax: 416-325-6195, csousa.mpp.co@liberal.ola.org, TTY: 888-335-6611
Deputy Minister, Chisanga Puta-Chekwe
416-325-6220, chisanga.puta-chekwe@ontario.ca
Director, Communications, Deborah Swain
416-314-7606, Fax: 416-314-4965, deborah.swain@ontario.ca

Associated Agencies, Boards & Commissions:
• Office of the Fairness Commissioner
#1201, 595 Bay St.
Toronto, ON M7A 2B4
416-325-9380 Fax: 416-326-6081 877-727-5365
ofc@ontario.ca

Citizenship & Immigration Division
400 University Ave., 3rd Fl., Toronto, ON M7A 2R9
416-314-7541 Fax: 416-314-7599
Asst. Deputy Minister, Marsha Barnes
416-325-6278, marsha.barnes@ontario.ca
Director, Immigration Programs, Catherine Finley
416-212-4290, Fax: 416-314-7307, catherine.finley@ontario.ca
Director, Immigration Policy, Alice Young
416-326-8595, Fax: 416-314-7307, alice.young@ontario.ca

Office of the Chief Information Officer
Mowat Block, 900 Bay St. 3rd FL, Toronto, ON M7A 1L2
416-325-4598
Assistant Deputy Minister, Soussan Tabari
416-326-8216, tabari.soussan@ontario.ca
Information Technology Service Management, Joanne Hiscock
416-327-1087, joanne.hiscock@ontario.ca
Strategic Planning & Business Relationship Management, Lolita Singh
416-326-7942, lolita.singh@ontario.ca
Technology & Business Solutions, Sanaul Haque
416-585-6746, sanaul.haque@ontario.ca

Regional & Corporate Services Division
400 University Ave., 2nd fl., Toronto, ON M7A 2R9
416-314-7311 Fax: 416-314-7313
Asst. Deputy Minister & Chief Administration Officer, Robert Montgomery
416-314-7311, Fax: 416-314-7313, robert.m.montgomery@ontario.ca
Chief Information Officer, French Language Services, Education & Community Services Cluster, Dominique Guillaumant
416-326-9749, dominique.guillaumant@ontario.ca
Director, Human Resources, Cindy Lam
416-212-2783, Fax: 416-325-6371, cindy.lam@ontario.ca
Director, Regional Services, Brian Lemiere
416-314-6680, Fax: 416-314-6686, brian.lemire@ontario.ca

Central Area Regional Offices:

Bracebridge
15 Dominion St., Bracebridge, ON P1L 2E7
705-646-0641 Fax: 705-646-0544

Hamilton
119 King St. West, 14th Fl., Hamilton, ON L8P 4Y7
905-521-7459 Fax: 905-521-7398
877-998-9927
Regional Advisor, Lorraine Hogan
905-521-7459, lorraine.hogan@ontario.ca

Huntsville
207 Main St. West, Huntsville, ON P1H 1Z9
705-789-4448 Fax: 705-789-9533
Regional Advisor, Larry Curley
705-789-4448, larry.curley@ontario.ca

Midhurst
2284 Nursery Rd., Midhurst, ON L0L 1X0
Fax: 705-739-6697
877-395-4105

Toronto
180 Dundas St. West, 5th Fl., Toronto, ON
416-314-6044 Fax: 416-314-2024
877-395-4105

Regional Advisor, Freba Shahsamand
416-314-1990, freba.shahsamand@ontario.ca
Regional Advisor, Roya Alaei
416-212-6504, roya.alaei@ontario.ca
Regional Advisor, Carol Law
416-325-6542, carol.law@ontario.ca

Northern Area Regional Offices:

Dryden
Ontario Government Bldg., 479 Government Rd., PO Box 3000, Dryden, ON P8N 3B3
Fax: 807-223-8502
800-525-8785

Regional Advisor, Natasha Lovenuk Markham
807-223-8682, natasha.lovenukmarkham@ontario.ca

Kenora
810 Robertson St., Kenora, ON P9N 4J4
807-468-2540 Fax: 807-468-2788
800-465-1108

North Bay
447 McKeown Ave., North Bay, ON P1B 9S9
705-494-4182 Fax: 705-494-4069
800-461-9563

Sault Ste. Marie
Roberta Bondar Place, #200, 70 Foster Dr., Sault Ste Marie, ON P6A 6V8
705-945-5885 Fax: 705-945-5931
800-461-7284

Sioux Lookout
62 Queen St., PO Box 267, Sioux Lookout, ON P8T 1A3
Fax: 807-737-3419
800-529-6619

Sudbury
Ontario Government Bldg., #401, 199 Larch St., Sudbury, ON P3E 5P9
705-564-3035 Fax: 705-564-3043
800-461-4004

Thunder Bay
#334, 435 James St. South, Thunder Bay, ON P7E 6S7
807-475-1683 Fax: 807-475-1297
800-465-6861

Regional Advisor, Marlene Wright
807-475-1658, marlene.wright@ontario.ca

Timmins
Ontario Government Complex, Hwy. 101 East, PO Box 3085, South Porcupine, ON P0N 1H0
705-235-1550 Fax: 705-235-1553
800-305-4442

Southeast Area Regional Offices:

Kingston
Ontario Government Bldg., Beechgrove Complex, 51 Heakes Lane, Kingston, ON K7M 9B1
613-531-5580 Fax: 613-531-5585
800-293-7543

Ottawa
347 Preston St., 4th Fl., Ottawa, ON K1S 3J4
613-742-3360 Fax: 613-742-5300
800-267-9340

Manager, Valerie Andrews
613-742-3366, valerie.andrews@ontario.ca

Peterborough
Robinson Pl., South Tower, 300 Water St., 2nd Fl., Peterborough, ON K9J 8M5
705-755-2624 Fax: 705-755-2631
800-461-7629

Southwest Area Regional Offices:

Kitchener
#405, 30 Duke St. West, Kitchener, ON N2H 3W5
519-578-3600 Fax: 519-578-1632
800-265-2189

Regional Advisor, Sonja Erstic
519-571-6117, sonja.erstic@ontario.ca

London
659 Exeter Rd., 2nd Fl., London, ON N6A 1L3
Fax: 519-873-4061
800-265-4730

St Catharines
301 St Paul St., 9th Fl., St Catharines, ON L2R 7R4
Fax: 905-704-3955
800-263-2441

Walkerton
Bldg. 3, 220 Trillum Crt., Walkerton, ON N0G 2V0
Fax: 519-881-0525
800-265-5520

Windsor
221 Mill St., Windsor, ON N9C 2R1
Fax: 519-973-1414
800-265-1330

Ontario Ministry of Community & Social Services (MCSS)

Hepburn Block, 80 Grosvenor St., 6th Fl., Toronto, ON M7A 1E9
416-325-5666 Fax: 416-325-5172
888-789-4199
www.mcss.gov.on.ca
TTY: 800-387-5559
Other Communication: Welfare Fraud Hotline: |1-800-394-7867

Acts Administered:
Child & Family Services Act
District Social Services Administration Boards Act
Indian Welfare Services Act
Ministry of Community & Social Services Act
Ontario Disability Support Program Act, 1997
Ontario Works Act, 1997
Social Work & Social Service Work Act, 1998
Soldiers' Aid Commission Act
Accessibility for Ontarians with Disabilities Act
Deaf-Blind Awareness Month Act
Family Responsibility & Support Arrears Enforcement Act
Ontarians with Disabilities Act
Services & Supports to Promote the Social Inclusion of Persons with Developmental Disabilities Act

Minister & Government House Leader, Hon. John Milloy
416-325-5225, Fax: 416-325-3347,
jmilloy.mpp.co@liberal.ola.org
Deputy Minister, Marguerite Rappolt
416-325-5225, Fax: 416-325-5240,
marguerite.rappolt@ontario.ca
Director, Communications & Marketing, Karin Dillabough
416-325-5203, karin.dillabough@ontario.ca
Director, Legal Services, Diane Zimnica
416-314-5173, diane.zimnica@ontario.ca
Chief Information Officer, Children, Youth & Social Services Cluster, Corbin Kerr
416-326-4330, Fax: 416-325-0266, corbin.kerr@ontario.ca
Assistant Deputy Minister, Family Responsibility Office, Bohodar Rubashewsky
416-240-2477, bohar.rubashewsky@ontario.ca

Associated Agencies, Boards & Commissions:
• Social Benefits Tribunal
1075 Bay St., 7th Fl.
Toronto, ON M5S 2B1
416-326-0978 Fax: 416-325-5135 800-753-3895 TTY: 416-325-3408
www.sbt.gov.on.ca
Other Communication: Toll-Free TTY: 1-800-268-7095

Accessibility Directorate of Ontario
#601, 777 Bay St., Toronto, ON M7A 2J4
416-326-0207 Fax: 416-325-5615
866-515-2025
TTY: 800-268-7095

Asst. Deputy Minister, Ellen Waxman
416-325-5247, Fax: 416-326-9725
Director, Outreach & Compliance, Alfred Spencer
416-314-7289, Fax: 416-326-9725,
alfred.spencer@ontario.ca
Director, Standards, Policy & Coordination, Brenda Lewis
416-325-5586, Fax: 416-327-9725, brenda.lewis@ontario.ca

Business Planning & Corporate Services Division
Hepburn Block, 80 Grosvenor St., 6th Fl., Toronto, ON M7A 1E9
416-325-5595 Fax: 416-325-5615

Asst. Deputy Minister, Lorraine Graham-Watson
416-325-5588, Fax: 416-325-5615,
lorraine.graham-watson@ontario.ca
Director, Capital & Accommodation Services, Angela James
416-325-4600, Fax: 416-325-5397, angela.james@ontario.ca
Director, Financial Planning & Business Management Branch, Martin Thumm
416-325-5139, martin.thumm@ontario.ca
Director, Human Resources, Frank Caccia
416-327-4753, Fax: 416-325-0561, frank.caccia@ontario.ca

Operations Division
Hepburn Block, 80 Grosvenor St., 6th Fl., Toronto, ON M7A 1E9
416-325-5581 Fax: 416-325-5432
Other Communication: Client Information & Support Services: 416/325-5766; 1-800-665-6129

Asst. Deputy Minister, David Zuccato
416-325-5579, Fax: 416-325-5432, david.zuccato@ontario.ca
Director, Controllership & Accountability, Sandy Henderson
416-325-4401, sandy.henderson@ontario.ca
Director, Developmental Services Implementation Project Office, Linda Henry
416-438-5111, linda.henry@ontario.ca
Director, ODSP Modernization Team, Susan Waring
416-326-3302, susan.waring@ontario.ca
Director, Services & Supports Branch, Nancy Lytle
416-325-5446, nancy.lytle@ontario.ca

Regional Offices:

Central East
#1, 17310 Yonge St., Newmarket, ON L3Y 7R8
905-868-8900 Fax: 905-895-4330
877-669-6658
TTY: 905-715-7759

Regional Director, Claudine Cousins
905-952-1871, claudine.cousins@ontario.ca

Central West
#200, 6733 Mississauga Rd., Mississauga, ON L5N 6J5
905-567-7177 Fax: 905-567-3215
877-832-2818
TTY: 905-567-3219
Other Communication: French Phone: 905-567-7177

Regional Director, Vince Tedesco
905-567-7177, vince.tedesco@ontario.ca

Eastern
347 Preston St., 2nd & 3rd fl., Ottawa, ON K1S 3H8
613-234-1188 Fax: 613-787-3990
800-267-5111

Regional Director, Suzanne Gagnon
613-787-3962, suzanne.gagnon@ontario.ca

Hamilton Niagara
Ellen Fairclough bldg., 119 King St. West, 7th Fl., Hamilton, ON L8P 4Y7
905-521-7280 Fax: 905-546-8277
TTY: 866-221-2229

Regional Director, Sandra Datars Bere
905-521-7844

Northern
#1002, 199 Larch St., Sudbury, ON P3E 5P9
705-564-6699 Fax: 705-564-3099
800-265-1222

Regional Director, June Kelloway-Tarrant
807-223-2241

North East
621 Main St. West, North Bay, ON P1B 2V6
705-474-3540 Fax: 705-474-5815
800-461-6977
TTY: 705-474-7665

Regional Director, Monique Legault
705-474-3540, monique.legault@ontario.ca

South East
11 Beechgrove Lane, Kingston, ON K7M 9A6
613-545-0539 Fax: 613-536-7272
800-646-3209
TTY: 613-536-7304

Executive Assistant/Project Manager, Mary-Anne Baun
613-536-7262, mary-anne.baun@ontario.ca

South West
#203, 217 York St., PO Box 5217, London, ON N6A 5R1
519-483-5111 Fax: 519-672-9510
800-265-4197
TTY: 519-663-5276

Regional Director, Peter Steckenreiter
519-438-5111

Toronto
477 Mount Pleasant Rd., 3rd Fl., Toronto, ON M7A 1G1
416-325-0500 Fax: 416-325-0541
TTY: 416-325-3600

Regional Director, Richard K. Jackson
416-325-0536, Fax: 416-325-0541,
richard.k.jackson@ontario.ca

Social Policy Development Division
Hepburn Block, 80 Grosvenor St, 6th fl., Toronto, ON M7A 1E9
416-325-5421 Fax: 416-325-9408

Asst. Deputy Minister, David Carter-Whitney
416-325-3592, Fax: 416-325-9408,
david.carter-whitney@ontario.ca
Director, Community & Developmental Services, Carol Latimer
416-325-5359, Fax: 416-325-8865, carol.latimer@ontario.ca
Director, Planning & Strategic Policy, Erin Hannah
416-325-5550, erin.hannah@ontario.ca
Director, Ontario Disabilities Support Program, Patti Redmond
416-314-1122, Fax: 416-326-1735, patti.redmond@ontario.ca
Acting Director, Ontario Works, Tanya Vrooman
416-325-1107, tanya.vrooman@ontario.ca
Director, Policy Research & Analysis, Peter Amenta
416-212-6274, Fax: 416-325-8764, peter.amenta@ontario.ca

Ontario Ministry of Community Safety & Correctional Services

George Drew Bldg., 25 Grosvenor St., 18th Fl., Toronto, ON M7A 1Y6
416-326-5000 Fax: 416-326-0498
866-517-0571
mcscs.feedback@ontario.ca
www.mcscs.jus.gov.on.ca
TTY: 416-326-5511
Other Communication: TTY Toll Free: 1-866-517-0572

The Ministry ensures that communities across the province are protected by safe, effective & accountable law enforcement and public safety systems. General responsibilities of the ministry are as follows: correctional services; public safety & security; & policing services.

Acts Administered:
Ammunition Regulation Act, 1994
Anatomy Act
Christopher's Law (Sex Offender Registry), 2000
Coroners Act
Emergency Management & Civil Protection Act
Fire Protection & Prevention Act, 1997
Firefighters' Memorial Day Act
Imitation Firearms Regulation Act
Mandatory Blood Testing Act
Mandatory Gunshot Wounds Reporting Act
Ministry of Correctional Services Act
Ministry of the Solicitor General Act
Ontario Society for the Prevention of Cruelty to Animals Act
Police Services Act
Private Security & Investigative Services Act, 2005
Public Works Protection Act
Interprovincial Policing Act, 2009

Minister, Hon. Madeleine Meilleur
416-325-0408, Fax: 416-325-6067, mmeilleur.mpp.co@liberal.ola.org
Deputy Minister, Community Safety, Ian Davidson
416-326-5060, ian.davidson@ontario.ca
Deputy Minister, Correctional Services, Jay Hope
416-327-9734, jay.hope@ontario.ca
Acting Director, Communications, Debbie Conrad
416-326-5004, Fax: 416-326-3200, debbie.conrad@ontario.ca
Parliamentary Assistant, Correctional Services, Mario Sergio
416-325-4925, mario.sergio@ontario.ca

Associated Agencies, Boards & Commissions:

• Animal Care Review Board
77 Grenville St., 8th Fl.
Toronto, ON M5S 1B3
416-314-3509 Fax: 416-314-3518

• Death Investigation Oversight Council
George Drew Bldg.
25 Grosvenor St., 1st Fl.
Toronto, ON M7A 1Y6
416-212-4041
dioc@ontario.ca
www.dioc.gov.on.ca

• Fire Safety Commission
Place Nouveau Bldg.
5775 Yonge St., 7th Fl.
Toronto, ON M2M 4J1
416-325-3100 Fax: 416-314-1217

• Ontario Civilian Police Commission (OCPC)
250 Dundas St. West, 6th Fl.
Toronto, ON M7A 2T3
416-314-3004 Fax: 416-314-0198 888-515-5005
www.ocpc.ca
Other Communication: Complaints (GTA): 416-326-1189; Toll-Free Fax: 1-888-311-7555

• Ontario Parole Board
#1803, 415 Yonge St.
Toronto, ON M5B 2E7
416-325-4480 Fax: 416-325-4485 888-579-2888
www.operb.gov.on.ca

• Ontario Police Arbitration Commission
George Drew Bldg.
25 Grosvenor St., 1st Fl.
Toronto, ON M7A 1Y6
416-314-3520 Fax: 416-314-3522
www.policearbitration.on.ca

Community Safety
416-314-3000 Fax: 416-314-4037
Commissioner for Community Safety, Dan Hefkey
416-212-7656, dan.hefkey@ontario.ca

Emergency Management Ontario
77 Wellesley St. W, PO Box 222, Toronto, ON M7A 1N3
416-314-3723 Fax: 416-314-3758
Assistant Deputy Minister & Chief, Allison J Stuart
416-314-6186, Fax: 416-314-3758, allison.j.stuart@ontario.ca
Deputy Chief, Program Development, Michael Morton
416-212-3472, Fax: 416-314-3758, michael.j.morton@ontario.ca
Deputy Chief, Program Delivery, Joy McLeod
416-314-8610, joy.mcleod@ontario.ca
Director, Support Programs, Barney Owens
416-314-2393, barney.owens@ontario.ca
Deputy Chief, Operations & Analysis, Tom Kontra
416-314-8595, tom.kontra@ontario.ca

Ontario Provincial Police (OPP)
Lincoln M. Alexander Bldg., 777 Memorial Ave., Orillia, ON L3V 7V3
705-329-6111
888-310-1122
www.opp.ca
TTY: 888-310-1133
Other Communication: Crime Stoppers: 1-800-222-8477
Commissioner, Chris D. Lewis
705-329-6199, Fax: 705-329-6195, chris.d.lewis@ontario.ca
Deputy Commissioner & Provincial Commander, Traffic Safety & Operational Support, Larry Beechey
705-329-7500, Fax: 705-329-6317, larry.beechey@ontario.ca
Provincial Commander, Corporate Services, Gwen M. Strachan
705-329-7500, Fax: 705-329-6317

Public Safety Division
George Drew bldg, 25 Grosvenor St., 12th fl., Toronto, ON M7A 2H3
416-314-3000 Fax: 416-314-4037
Asst. Deputy Minister, Glen Murray
416-325-3454, Fax: 416-314-4037, glenn.murray@ontario.ca
Police Support Services, Stephen Waldie
416-325-3132, stephen.waldie@ontario.ca
Director, Centre of Forensic Sciences, Dr. Anthony Tessarolo
416-314-3224, Fax: 416-314-3225, anthony.tessarolo@ontario.ca
Acting Director, External Relations Branch, Fay Patey
416-314-3015, fay.patey@ontario.ca
Director, Lisa Kool
416-326-0817, lisa.kool@ontario.ca

Corporate Services Division
George Drew bldg., 25 Grosvenor St., 13th fl., Toronto, ON M7A 1Y6
416-325-3445 Fax: 416-325-3465
Asst. Deputy Minister & Chief Administration Officer, Allan Gunn
416-325-9208, Fax: 416-326-3149, allan.gunn@ontario.ca
Director, Business & Financial Planning, Shawn Lawson
416-326-1016, Fax: 416-325-3465, shawn.lawson@ontario.ca
Acting Director, Facilities, Peter Kaftarian
416-314-6683, Fax: 416-327-1470, peter.kaftarian@ontario.ca
Director, Human Resources, Jane Albright
416-212-3555, Fax: 416-314-5559, jane.albright@ontario.ca

Correctional Services
Asst. Deputy Minister, Adult Community Corrections, Marg Welch
519-661-1773, marg.welch@ontario.ca
Asst. Deputy Minister, Adult Institutional Services, Steven F. Small
416-327-9992, Fax: 416-314-6669, steve.small@ontario.ca
Director, Management & Operational Support, Lynn Kenn
416-327-9918, Fax: 416-314-5987, lynn.kenn@ontario.ca
Director, Strategic & Operational Initiatives, Wendy Love
416-327-2329, Fax: 416-314-5987, wendy.love@ontario.ca

Justice Technology Services Division
#300, 21 College St, Toronto, ON M5G 2B3
416-326-6950 Fax: 416-326-1104
Asst. Deputy Minister & Chief Information Officer, John DiMarco
416-326-6954, Fax: 416-326-1104, john.dimarco@ontario.ca
Manager, I&IT Security, Gregory Wilson
416-212-0602, gregory.wilson@ontario.ca
Head, Court Business Solutions Branch, Chris Walpole
416-326-4267, chris.walpole@ontario.ca
Head, Technology Solutions, Sandy Mannering
705-494-3226, sandy.mannering@ontario.ca

Ontario Ministry of Consumer Services

Mowat Block, 900 Bay St., 6th Fl., Toronto, ON M7A 1L2
416-327-8300 Fax: 416-326-1947
866-665-0662
infomcs@ontario.ca
www.sse.gov.on.ca
TTY: 877-666-6545
Other Communication: Consumer Protection Branch Phone: 416-326-8800; Fax: 416-326-8665; TTY: 416-229-6086; Email: consumer@ontario.ca

The Ministry seeks to educate, protect & serve consumers in Ontario by maintaining a fair, safe & informed marketplace; providing modern information services; & regulating practices that serve the interests of Ontarians.

Acts Administered:
Apportionment Act
Arthur Wishart Act (Franchise Disclosure)
Assignments & Preferences Act
Athletics Control Act
Bailiffs Act
Business Corporations Act (in part)
Business Names Act (in part)
Business Regulation Reform Act (in part)
Cemeteries Act (Revised)
Collection Agencies Act
Collision Repair Standards Act
Condominium Act (in part)
Consumer Protection Act
Consumer Reporting Act
Corporations Act (in part)
Corporations Information Act (in part)
Debt Collectors Act
Discriminatory Business Practices Act
Electricity Act (in part)
Electronic Registration Act (in part)
Extra-Provincial Corporations Act (in part)
Factors Act
Film Classification Act
Funeral, Burial & Cremation Services Act
Funeral Directors & Establishments Act
Horse Riding Safety Act
Limited Partnerships Act
Ministry of Consumer & Business Services Act
Motor Vehicle Dealers Act, 2002
Not-for-Profit Corporations Act (in part)
Ontario New Home Warranties Plan Act
Paperback & Periodical Distributors Act
Partnerships Act
Payday Loans Act
Personal Property Security Act
Real Estate & Business Brokers Act
Repair & Storage Liens Act (in part)
Residential Complex Sales Representation Act
Retail Business Holidays Act
Safety & Consumer Statutes Administration Act
Securities Transfer Act
Technical Standards & Safety Act
Travel Industry Act
Vinters Quality Alliance Act
Wine Content & Labelling Act

Minister, Hon. Margarett Best
416-327-8300, Fax: 416-326-1947, mbest.mpp.co@liberal.ola.org
Deputy Minister, George Ross
416-327-8342, Fax: 416-314-7167, george.ross@ontario.ca
Director, Legal Services, James Girling
416-212-4273, james.girling@ontario.ca
Director, Communications, Cindy Greeniaus
416-326-7208, Fax: 416-326-7445, cindy.greeniaus@ontario.ca
Director, Internal Audit, Culture & Innovation Audit Service, Charles Meehan
416-325-5983, Fax: 416-326-1712, charles.meehan@ontario.ca
Parliamentary Assistant, Jim Brownell
416-325-5300, jbrownell.mpp.co@liberal.ola.org

Associated Agencies, Boards & Commissions:

• Ontario Film Review Board
#101B, 4950 Yonge St.
Toronto, ON M1N 6K1
416-314-2626 Fax: 416-314-3632
www.ofrb.gov.on.ca

Corporate Services Division
Hearst Block, 900 Bay St., 7th Fl., Toronto, ON M7A 2E1
416-325-6486 Fax: 416-325-6392
Assistant Deputy Minister & Chief Administrative Officer, David Clifford
416-325-6600, david.clifford@ontario.ca
Director, Business Planning & Finance, Robert Burns
416-327-1137, Fax: 416-327-4236, robert.burns@ontario.ca
Director, Strategic Human Resources Business Unit, Dan Keating
416-325-6598, Fax: 416-325-6715, dan.keating@ontario.ca
Director, Service Management & Facilities, Isolina Kuzminski
416-325-9366, Fax: 416-325-1118, isolina.kuzminski@ontario.ca

Policy & Consumer Protection Services Division
College Park, 777 Bay St., 5th Fl., Toronto, ON M7A 2J3
416-326-8578 Fax: 416-325-6192
Assistant Deputy Minister, Frank Denton
416-326-2826, frank.denton@ontario.ca
Director, Consumer Policy & Liaison, David Brezer
416-326-8868, david.brezer@ontario.ca
Director, Consumer Protection, Barbara Duckitt
416-326-8598, barbara.duckitt@ontario.ca
Director, Public Safety, Nicole Stewart
416-326-8877, nicole.stewart@ontario.ca

Ontario Ministry of Economic Development & Innovation

Hearst Block, 900 Bay St., 8th Fl., Toronto, ON M7A 2E1
416-325-6666 Fax: 416-325-6688
866-668-4249
info@edt.gov.on.ca
www.ontariocanada.com/ontcan/1medt/en/home_en.jsp
TTY: 416-325-4402

Promotes economic development & job creation in Ontario by creating a climate for business to prosper & eliminate red tape as well as stimulating trade. This Ministry markets the province as a desirable place to live, work, invest & raise a family. It works with its private sector partners to ensure that its core responsibilities of employment & business development, investment & trade continue to help Ontario businesses compete globally; contribute to a highly-skilled, well-educated workforce; & generate prosperity for all Ontarians. In Northern Ontario, the Ministry is represented by the Northern Development Division of the Ministry of Northern Development & Mines.

Acts Administered:
Development Corporations Act
Dissolution of Inactive Corporations Act
Idea Corporation Act
Ministry of Industry, Trade & Technology Act
Research Foundation Act

Minister, Hon. Brad Duguid
416-325-6900, Fax: 416-325-6918,
bduguid.mpp.co@liberal.ola.org
Parliamentary Assistant, Monte Kwinter
416-630-0080, mkwinter.mpp.co@liberal.ola.org
Director, Communications Branch, Dino Rocca
416-325-8058, dino.rocca@ontario.ca

Corporate Services Division
Hearst Block, 900 Bay St., 7th fl., Toronto, ON M7A 2E1
416-325-6486 Fax: 416-325-6392
Assistant Deputy Minister & Chief Executive Officer, David Clifford
416-325-6600, david.clifford@ontario.ca

Economic Development Division
Hearst Block, 900 Bay St., 7th fl., Toronto, ON M7A 2E1
Fax: 416-325-2102
Assistant Deputy Minister, Mahmood Nanji
416-325-3668

International Trade & Marketing Division
Hearst Block, 900 Bay St., 5th fl., Toronto, ON M7A 2E1
416-325-9802 Fax: 416-325-5617
Assistant Deputy Minister, Cameron Sinclair
416-325-9801, cameron.sinclair@ontario.ca

Investment Division
Hearst Block, 900 Bay St., 5th fl., Toronto, ON M7A 2E1
416-212-0864 Fax: 416-212-3658
Assistant Deputy Minister, Tony LaMantia
416-325-6623, tony.lamantia@ontario.ca

Ontario-Open for Business
#700-375 University Ave., Toronto, ON M5G 2J5
416-326-7206 Fax: 416-212-3288
Assistant Deputy Minister, Morah Fenning
416-212-3283, morah.fenning@ontario.ca

Small & Medium Enterprise Division
56 Wellesley St. W., Toronto, ON M7A 2E7
Fax: 416-326-5154
Assistant Deputy Minister, Keith West
416-212-7793, keith.west@ontario.ca

Strategic Policy Division
Hearst Block, 900 Bay St., 3rd Fl., Toronto, ON M7A 2E7
416-212-6653 Fax: 416-326-6393
Assistant Deputy Minister, Maurice Bitran
416-212-6510, maurice.bitran@ontario.ca

Ontario Ministry of Education

Mowat Block, 900 Bay St., 22nd. Fl., Toronto, ON M7A 1L2
416-325-2929 Fax: 416-325-2934
800-387-5514
info@edu.gov.on.ca
www.edu.gov.on.ca
TTY: 500-263-2892

Acts Administered:
Education Act
Education Quality & Accountability Office Act, 1996
Fairness for Parents & Employees Act (Teachers' Withdrawal of Services), 1997
Ontario College of Teachers Act, 1996
Ontario Institute for Studies in Education Repeal Act, 1996
Ontario School Trustees' Council Act
Provincial Schools Negotiations Act
School Trust Conveyances Act
Teachers' Pension Act
Teaching Profession Act
Day Nurseries Act
Early Childhood Educators Act
Ministry of Community & Social Services Act
Ontario Educational Communications Authority Act
Ontario French-Language Educational Communications Authority Act
Ottawa-Carleton French-Language School Board Transferred Employees Act
Sabrina's Law

Minister, Hon. Laurel Broten
613-325-2600, Fax: 416-325-2608,
ldombrowsky.mpp.co@liberal.ola.org
Deputy Minister, Kevin Costante
416-325-2600, kevin.costante@ontario.ca
Chief Information Officer, Soussan Tabari
416-326-8216, Fax: 416-325-8371,
soussan.tabari@ontario.ca
Director, Communications, Murray Leaning
416-325-2742, Fax: 416-212-4158,
murray.leaning@ontario.ca

Associated Agencies, Boards & Commissions:
• Education Quality & Accountability Office (EQAO)
#1200, 2 Carlton St.
Toronto, ON M5B 2M9
416-314-0146 Fax: 416-325-2956 888-327-7377
www.eqao.com
• Languages of Instruction Commission of Ontario
Mowat Block
900 Bay St., 8th Fl.
Toronto, ON M7A 1L2
416-314-3500 Fax: 416-325-2979
• Minister's Advisory Council on Special Education
900 Bay St., 18th Fl.
Toronto, ON M7A 1L2
416-314-2333 Fax: 416-314-0637 877-699-5431
macse@ontario.ca
www.edu.gov.on.ca/eng/general/abcs/acse/acse_eng.html
• Ontario Educational Communications Authority (TVO)
2180 Yonge St.
PO Box 200 Q
Toronto, ON M4T 2T1
416-484-2600 800-613-0513
www.tvo.org
• Provincial Schools Authority
255 Ontario St. South
Milton, ON L9T 2M5
905-878-2851 TTY: 905-878-8405

Corporate Management & Services Division
Mowat Block, #342, 900 Bay St., Toronto, ON M7A 1L2
416-325-2772 Fax: 416-325-2778
Chief Administrative Officer & Assistant Deputy Minister, David Fulford
416-325-2773, david.fulford@ontario.ca
Director, Legal Services, John Calcott
416-325-2399, Fax: 416-325-2410, john.calcott@ontario.ca
Director, Strategic Human Resources Branch, Sandra Diprospero
416-325-4511, Fax: 416-327-9043,
sandra.diprospero@ontario.ca
Director, Corporate Finance & Services Branch, Dasha Hubschmann
416-325-1822, Fax: 416-325-1835,
dasha.hubschmann@ontario.ca
Director, Internal Audit Services, Warren McCay
416-212-4814, Fax: 416-325-1120, warren.mccay@ontario.ca

Early Learning Division
Mowat Block, 900 Bay St., 24th Fl., Toronto, ON M7A 1L2
416-212-4714 Fax: 416-314-7836
Assistant Deputy Minister, Jim Grieve
416-314-9393, jim.grieve@ontario.ca
Director, Early Learning & Child Care Policy & Program Branch, Rupert Gordon
416-314-8241, rupert.gordon@ontario.ca
Director, Early Learning & Child Care Implementation Branch, Pam Musson
416-314-8192, pam.musson@ontario.ca
Director, Child Care Quality Assurance & Licensing Branch, Jill Vienneau
416-314-2190, jill.vienneau@ontario.ca

Elementary/Secondary Business & Finance Division
Mowat Block, 900 Bay St., 20th fl., Toronto, ON M7A 1L2
416-325-6127 Fax: 416-325-9560
Assistant Deputy Minister, Gabriel Sékaly
416-325-6127, Fax: 416-325-9560, gabriel.sekaly@ontario.ca
Director, Financial Analysis & Accountability Branch, Andrew Davis
416-314-3711, Fax: 416-325-2007, andrew.davis@ontario.ca
Director, School Business Support Branch, Cheri Hayward
416-327-7503, Fax: 416-212-3990, cheri.hayward@ontario.ca
Acting Director, Capital Policy Branch, Grant Osborn
416-325-1705, Fax: 416-326-9959, grant.osborn@ontario.ca
Director, Education Finance Branch, Didem Proulx
416-327-9060, Fax: 416-325-6370, didem.proulx@ontario.ca
Director, Capital Programs Branch, Nancy Whynot
416-325-4030, Fax: 416-325-4024, nancy.whynot@ontario.ca

French Language, Aboriginal Learning & Research Division
Mowat Block, 900 Bay St., 22nd fl., Toronto, ON M7A 1L2
416-325-2132 Fax: 416-327-1182
Assistant Deputy Minister, Raymond Theberge
416-325-2132, Fax: 416-327-1182,
raymond.theberge@ontario.ca
Director, Aboriginal Education Office, Alayne Bigwin
416-325-8561, alayne.bigwin@ontario.ca
Director, Education Statistics & Analysis Branch, Taddesse Haile
416-325-9122, taddesse.haile@ontario.ca
Acting Director, Education Research & Evaluation Strategy Branch, Doris McWhorter
416-314-3819, doris.mcwhorter@ontario.ca
Director, French Language Education Policy & Programs, Ginette Plourde
416-327-9072, Fax: 416-325-2156,
ginette.plourde@ontario.ca
Director, Field Services, Kathy Verduyn
416-325-2588, kathy.verduyn@ontario.ca

Instruction & Leadership Development Division
Mowat Block, 900 Bay St., 13th fl., Toronto, ON M7A 1L2
416-314-3664 Fax: 416-325-7019
Assistant Deputy Minister, Barry Pervin
416-325-2411, Fax: 416-325-7019, barry.pervin@ontario.ca
Director, Teaching Policy & Standards, Paul Anthony
416-325-7744, Fax: 416-326-1113, paul.anthony@ontario.ca
Director, Learning Environment Branch, Marg Connor
416-325-7645, Fax: 416-325-2664, marg.connor@ontario.ca
Director, Leadership Development Branch, Bruce Drewett
416-325-1079, Fax: 416-325-7019, bruce.drewett@ontario.ca
Director, Inclusive Education Branch, Ruth Flynn
416-326-7597, Fax: 416-325-7019, ruth.flynn@ontario.ca
Director, Labour Relations & Governance Branch, Margot Trevelyan
416-325-2826, Fax: 416-325-7247,
margot.trevelyan@ontario.ca

Learning & Curriculum Division
Mowat Block, 900 Bay st., 22nd fl., Toronto, ON M7A 1L2
416-325-2135 Fax: 416-327-1182
Assistant Deputy Minister, Grant Clarke
416-314-5788, Fax: 416-327-1182, grant.clarke@ontario.ca
Director, Curriculum & Assessment Policy Branch, Sue Durst
416-325-2576, Fax: 416-325-2575, sue.durst@ontario.ca
Director, Special Education Policy & Programs Branch, Barry Finlay
416-325-2889, Fax: 416-314-0637, barry.finlay@ontario.ca
Director, Provincial Schools Branch, Nancy Sanders
905-878-2851, Fax: 905-878-1354,
nancy.sanders@ontario.ca

Student Achievement Division
Mowat Block, 900 Bay St., 10th Fl., Toronto, ON M7A 1L2
Chief Student Achievement Officer of Ontario & Assistant Deputy Minister, Mary Jean Gallagher
416-325-9964, maryjean.gallagher@ontario.ca
Senior Executive Officer, Literacy & Numeracy Secretariat, Roderick Benns
416-325-9389, roderick.benns@ontario.ca
Director, Student Success/Learning to 18 Implementation, Training & Evaluation Branch, David Euale
416-326-9369, david.euale@ontario.ca
Director, Student Success/Learning to 18 Strategic Policy Branch, Richard Franz
416-314-1410, richard.franz@ontario.ca

Elections Ontario

51 Rolark Dr., Toronto, ON M1R 3B1
416-326-6300 Fax: 416-326-6200
888-668-8683
info@elections.on.ca
www.elections.on.ca
TTY: 866-479-1118
Other Communication: Election Finances 416-325-9401 or 866-566-9066; Fax: 416-325-9466

Acts Administered:
Election Act
Elections Finance Act

Chief Electoral Officer, Greg Essensa
416-326-6383, Fax: 416-326-6201,
greg.essensa@elections.on.ca
Deputy Chief Electoral Officer, Loren A. Wells
416-326-6387, Fax: 416-326-6201,
loren.wells@elections.on.ca
Chief Operating Officer, Michael Stockfish
416-325-9450, Fax: 416-326-6201,
michael.stockfish@elections.on.ca

Communications
Lalitha Flach
416-326-5688, lalitha.flach@elections.on.ca

Corporate Services
Director, Lisa Forte
416-326-4394, lisa.forte@elections.on.ca

Election Finances
Director, Jonathan Batty
416-212-3367, jonathan.batty@elections.on.ca

Electoral Event Services
Director, Barbara McEwan
416-326-1971, barbara.mcewan@elections.on.ca

Technology Services
Andrew Herd
416-326-1972, andrew.herd@elections.on.ca

Ontario Ministry of Energy

Hearst Block, 900 Bay St., 4th Fl., Toronto, ON M7A 2E1
416-327-6758 Fax: 416-325-8440
888-668-4636
write2us@ontario.ca
www.energy.gov.on.ca
TTY: 800-239-4224

The Ministry of Energy's responsibility is to ensure that Ontario's electricity system functions at the highest level of reliability & productivity. The electricity system lies at the heart of the economy & way of life & by ensuring the system remains reliable, efficient & secure, the ministry is making sure Ontario remains one of the best places in the world in which to live, work, invest & raise a family. The Ministry of Energy is also focused on promoting ingenuity & innovation in the energy sector. By encouraging the development of new ideas & technologies it is helping to make Ontario a world leader in the global energy market. Protecting the environment is also a top priority for the Ministry. Developing renewable sources of energy, cleaner forms of fuel, as well as fostering a conservation culture, are all cornerstones of the Ministry's vision for Ontario's electricity future.

Acts Administered:
Hydro One Inc. Directors & Officers Act, 2002
Ministry of Energy Act, 2011
Ontario Energy Board Act
Power Corporation Act
Toronto District Heating Corporation Act, 1980
Toronto District Heating Corporation Act, 1998
Electricity Act
Energy Consumer Protection Act
Green Energy Act
Ontario Clean Energy Benefit Act

Minister, Hon. Chris Bentley
416-327-6758, Fax: 416-327-6754,
bduguid.mpp.co@liberal.ola.org
Deputy Minister, David Lindsay
416-327-6734, david.lindsay@ontario.ca
Director, Legal Services Branch, Halyna Perun
416-325-6681, Fax: 416-325-1781,
halyna.perun2@ontario.ca
Director, Communications Branch, Rula Sharkawi
416-327-6541, Fax: 416-326-3947, rula.sharkawi@ontario.ca

Associated Agencies, Boards & Commissions:
- Hydro One Inc.
- Independent Electricity System Operator
- Ontario Energy Board
#2700, 2300 Yonge St.
Toronto, ON M4P 1E4
416-481-1967 Fax: 416-440-7656 888-632-6273
www.ontarioenergyboard.ca
- Ontario Power Authority
#1600, 120 Adelaide St. West
Toronto, ON M5H 1T1
416-967-7474 Fax: 416-967-1947 800-797-9604
info@powerauthority.on.ca
www.powerauthority.on.ca
- Ontario Power Generation

Corporate Development Division
880 Bay St., 5th Fl., Toronto, ON M7A 2C1
416-327-7106 Fax: 416-314-3354

Provides a structure to identify strategic issues, to coordinate policy & program development; & to coordinate & integrate action by the Ministry & other governments.

Assistant Deputy Minister & Interim Chief Administrative Officer, John Whitehead
416-325-6544, john.whitehead@ontario.ca
Director, Service Management Branch, Betty Morgan
416-314-3309, Fax: 416-314-3354, betty.morgan@ontario.ca
Acting Director, Business & Resource Planning, Lourdes Valenton
416-327-7227, Fax: 416-314-3354,
lourdes.valenton@ontario.ca

Energy Supply, Transmission & Distribution Policy
880 Bay St., 3rd Fl., Toronto, ON M7A 2C1
416-327-7353 Fax: 416-314-6224

Assistant Deputy Minister, Rick Jennings
416-314-6190, Fax: 416-314-6224, rick.jennings@ontario.ca
Director, Energy Supply - Nuclear Branch, Cedric Jobe
416-325-6545, Fax: 416-212-1117, cedric.jobe@ontario.ca
Director, Energy Supply & Competition, Garry McKeever
416-325-8627, Fax: 416-325-7023,
garry.mckeever@ontario.ca
Director, Transmission & Distribution Policy, Jonathan Norman
416-326-1759, Fax: 416-325-7023,
jonathan.norman@ontario.ca

Regulatory Affairs & Strategic Policy
Mowat Block, 900 Bay St., 5th Fl., Toronto, ON M7A 2E3
416-325-6559 Fax: 416-325-7041

Provides strategic policy coordination & development for the ministry as well as policy analysis & advice related to energy conservation & efficiency, demand management, & conservation.

Assistant Deputy Minister, John Whitehead
416-325-6559, Fax: 416-325-7041,
john.whitehead@ontario.ca
Director, Planning & Agency Relations Branch, Alex Killoch
416-326-5572, Fax: 416-325-7041, alex.killoch@ontario.ca
Director, Strategic Policy & Research Branch, Kaili Sermat-Harding
416-327-5555, kaili.sermat-harding@ontario.ca

Renewables & Energy Efficiency
880 Bay St., 6th Fl., Toronto, ON M7A 2C1
416-314-6216 Fax: 416-325-3438

The branch provides analysis, advice & policy development on issues relating to energy efficiency, demand management & conservation as well as administering the Energy Efficiency Act.

Ontario Ministry of Environment (MOE)

135 St. Clair Ave. West, Toronto, ON M4V 1P5
416-325-4000 Fax: 416-325-3159
800-565-4923
www.ene.gov.on.ca
TTY: 800-515-2759
Other Communication: Pollution Hotline: 1-866-MOE-TIPS (1-866-663-8477); Spills or Emergencies: 1-800-268-6060; Public Information: 1-800-565-4923

The ministry is responsible for protecting clean & safe air, land & water to ensure healthy communities, ecological protection & sustainable development for present & future generations of Ontarians. Using stringent regulations, targeted enforcement & a variety of innovative programs & initiatives, the ministry continues to address environmental issues that have local, regional &/or global effects. The ministry has built a strong foundation of clear laws, stringent regulations, tough standards & rigorous permits & approvals. The ministry monitors pollution & restoration trends in an effort to determine the effectiveness of its activities & to assess risks to human health & the environment. This information is used to develop & implement environmental legislation, regulations, standards, policies, guidelines & programs to enhance environmental protection.

Acts Administered:
Adams Mine Lake Act, 2004
Environmental Assessment Act
Designations & Exemptions
Electricity Projects Regulation
Environmental Assessment General Regulations
Environmental Bill of Rights Act
Environmental Protection Act
Air Contaminants from Ferrous Foundries Regulation
Air Pollution - Local Quality Regulations
Airborne Contaminant Discharge Monitoring & Reporting Regulations
Ambient Air Quality Criteria Regulations
Boilers Regulation
Certificates of Approval Exemptions Air Regulation
Classes of Contaminants Exemption Regulations
Classification & Exemption of Spills Regulations
Containers Regulation
Deep Well Disposal Regulation
Designation of Waste Regulation
Discharge of Sewage from Pleasure Boats Regulation
Disposable Containers for Milk Regulations
Disposable Paper Containers for Milk Regulations
Dry Cleaners Regulations
Effluent Monitoring & Effluent Limits Regulations (organic chemicals, inorganic chemicals, iron & steel manufacturers, electric power generation, petroleum sector, metal mining sector, industrial minerals sector, metal castingsector, pulp & paper sector
Emissions Trading Regulation
Ethanol in Gasoline
Exemption Regulations
Gasoline Volatility Regulation
General Waste Management Regulation
Ground Source Heat Pumps Regulation
Halon Fire Extinguishing Equipment Regulation
Hot Mix Asphalt Facilities Regulation
Industrial, Commercial & Institutional Source Separation Programs Regulation
Industry Emissions - Nitrogen Oxides & Sulphur Dioxide
Lakeview Generating Station Regulations
Lambton Industry Meteorology Alert Regulation
Land Disposal Restrictions
Landfilling Sites Regulation
Marinas Regulation
Mobil PCB Destruction Facilities Regulation
Motor Vehicles Regulation
Municipal Sewage & Water & Roads Class Environmental Assessment Project Regulation
Municipalities, Secured Creditors, Receivers, Trustees in Bankruptcy & Fiduciaries, Pt.XV.2 of the Act Regulations, 2002
Ontario Power Generation Regulations
Ozone Depleting Substances Regulation
Packaging Audits & Packaging Reduction Work Plans Regulation
Records of Site Condition, Pt.XV.1 of the Act Regulations, 2004
Recovery of Gasoline Vapour in Bulk Transfers Regulation
Recycling & Composting of Municipal Waste Regulation
Refillable Containers for Carbonated Soft Drink Regulation
Refrigerants Regulation
Reporting Requirements, Sulphur Levels in Gasoline Regulations
Sewage System Regulations & Exemptions
Solvents Regulation
Spills Regulation
Sterilants Regulation
Sulphur Content of Fuels Regulation
Transitional Provisions Relating to the Repeal of Pt.VIII of the Act Regulations
Waste Audits & Waste Reduction Workplans Regulation
Waste Disposal Sites & Waste Management Systems Subject to Approval under the Environmental Assessment Act Regulations
Waste Management (PCBs) Regulation
Environmental Review Tribunal Act, 2000
Ministry of the Environment Act
Ontario Water Resources Act
Additional Charges Regulation
Licensing of Sewage Works Operators Regulations
Municipal Sewage & Water & Roads Class Environmental Assessment Projects Regulation
Secured Creditors, Receivers, Trustees in Bankruptcy Regulations, 2002
Sewage Works Subject to Approval under the Environmental Assessment Act Regulations
Transitional Provisions Relating to the Repeal of Pt.VIII of the Environmental Protection Act Regulations
Water Taking & Transfer Regulation
Wells Regulation
Pesticides Act
Safe Drinking Water Act, 2002
Certification of Drinking-Water System Operators & Water Quality Analysts
Compliance & Enforcement
Definitions of \Deficiency\" & \"Municipal Drinking-Water System\" Regulations
Definitions of Words & Expressions Used in the Act Regulations, 2003
Drinking-Water Systems Regulations, 2003
Drinking-Water Testing Services Regulations, 2003
Non-Residential & Non-Municipal Seasonal Residential Systems that do not Service Designated Facilities
Ontario Drinking-Water Quality Standards Regulations, 2003
Schools, Private Schools & Day Nurseries Regulations, 2003
Sustainable Water & Sewage Systems Act, 2002
Waste Diversion Act, 2002
Blue Box Waste Regulations, 2002
Used Oil Material Regulations, 2003
Used Tires Regulations, 2003
Waste Electrical & Electronic Equipment
Capital Investment Plan Act
Clean Water Act
Consolidated Hearings Act
Lake Simcoe Protection Act
Municipal Water & Sewage Transfer Act
Nutrient Management Act
Toxins Reduction Act
Water Opportunities Act

Minister, Hon. James J. Bradley
416-314-6790, Fax: 416-314-6748,
jbradley.mpp.co@liberal.ola.org
Deputy Minister, Gail Beggs
416-314-6753, Fax: 416-314-6791
Chief Information Officer, Robert Hollis
416-314-1528, Fax: 705-755-1599, robert.hollis@ontario.ca
Acting Director, Communications Branch, Michelle Garrett
416-314-6695, Fax: 416-314-6711,
michelle.garrett@ontario.ca

Associated Agencies, Boards & Commissions:
• Office of Consolidated Hearings
#1500, 655 Bay St.
Toronto, ON M5G 1E5
416-212-6349 Fax: 416-314-4506
Under the Consolidated Hearings Act, the Environmental Assessment Board holds public hearings in conjunction with the Ontario Municipal Board. This occurs when a proposal requires more than one tribunal hearing under more than one of the acts set out in the schedule to the Consolidated Hearings Act, 1981. The hearings registrar must receive written notice from the person proposing the undertaking, specifying the nature of the undertaking, required hearings & governing acts. The matter is then referred to the chairs of the two boards, who establish a joint board for the hearing. The board's decision can be varied or rescinded only by the Lieutenant-Governor-in-Council or, on a question of law, may be appealed to the Divisional Court.
• Advisory Council on Drinking Water Quality & Testing Standards
40 St. Clair Ave. West, 3rd Fl.
Toronto, ON M4V 1M2
416-212-7779 Fax: 416-212-7595
• Environmental Review Tribunal
#1500, 655 Bay St.
Toronto, ON M5G 1E5
416-212-6349 Fax: 416-314-4506 866-448-2248 TTY: 800-855-1155
erttribunalsecretary@ontario.ca
www.ert.gov.on.ca
The Environmental Review Tribunal's primary role is adjudicating applications & appeals under various environmental & planning statutes. The Tribunal hears applications & appeals under the Environmental Assessment Act, the Environmental Protection Act, the Ontario Water Resources Act, & the Pesticides Act, & leave to appeal applications under the Environmental Bill of Rights, 1993. The Environmental Review Tribunal also functions as the Office of Consolidated Hearings to hear applications made under the Consolidated Hearings Act & as the Niagara Escarpment Hearing Office to hear development permit appeals & Niagara Escarpment Plan amendment applications under the Niagara Escarpment Planning & Development Act.
• Ontario Clean Water Agency (OCWA)
1 Yonge St., 17th Fl.
Toronto, ON M5E 1E5
416-314-5600 Fax: 416-314-8300 800-667-6292
www.ocwa.com
The Ontario Clean Water Agency (OCWA) was established as a Provincial Crown Agency in November 1993 & is committed to providing safe & reliable clean water services. The Agency is an established leader in the operation, maintenance & management of water & wastewater treatment facilities & their associated distribution & collection systems. OCWA operates hundreds of water & wastewater facilities, ranging in size from small wells & pumping stations to large-scale urban water & wastewater systems.
• Pesticides Advisory Committee
135 St. Clair Ave. West, 15th Fl.
Toronto, ON M4V 1P5
416-314-9230 Fax: 416-314-9237
www.opac.gov.on.ca
This committee advises the Minister of the Environment on matters pertaining to pesticides. It annually reviews the Pesticides Act & regulations, & government publications respecting pesticides & control of pests. The committee also recommends classifications for all new pesticide products prior to their marketing & use in Ontario, & publishes an annual report, which is available upon request. For other ministry publications on pests & pest control & information on pesticide licensing, contact the Standards Development Branch, Pesticides Section.
• Walkerton Clean Water Centre
20 Ontario Rd.
PO Box 160
Walkerton, ON N0G 2V0
519-881-2003 Fax: 519-881-4947 866-515-0550
inquiry@wcwc.ca
www.wcwc.ca
The vision of the Walkerton Clean Water Centre is to create a world-class intitute dedicated to safe & secure drinking water for the people of Ontario. Established by Ontario Regulation 304/04 as a crown agency of the Ministry of the Environment in October 2004, & governed by a 12-member board of directors, the Centre's work will complement & support that of the Ministry with a focus on ensuring that training, education & information is available & accessible to owners, operators & operating authorities of Ontario's drinking water systems, particularly in rural & remote communities.

Corporate Management Division
135 St. Clair Ave. West, 14th Fl., Toronto, ON M4V 1P5
416-314-6426 Fax: 416-314-6425
Assistant Deputy Minister & Chief Administrative Officer, Debra Sikora
416-314-6424, debra.sikora@ontario.ca
Director, Business & Fiscal Planning, Rob W. Campbell
416-314-7370, Fax: 416-314-7858, rob.w.campbell@ontario.ca
Director, Strategic Human Resources Branch, Jacques LeGris
416-314-9305, Fax: 416-314-9313, jacques.legris@ontario.ca
Director, Information Management & Access Branch, Jim Lewis
416-314-3856, Fax: 416-314-6872, jim.d.lewis@ontario.ca
Director, Legal Services Branch, Rand Roszell
416-212-0853, Fax: 416-314-6579, rand.roszell@ontario.ca
Director, Transition Officer, Becky Taylor
416-314-5606, Fax: 416-325-7962, becky.taylor@ontario.ca

Drinking Water Management Division
135 St. Clair Ave. West, Toronto, ON M4V 1P5
416-314-4475 Fax: 416-314-6935
The Drinking Water Management Division, led by the Chief Drinking Water Inspector, has lead responsibility for program & operational activities related to the protection & provision of safe drinking water in Ontario.
Assistant Deputy Minister & Chief Drinking Water Inspector, John Stager
416-314-4463, john.stager@ontario.ca
Director, Safe Drinking Water Branch, Paul Neiweglowski
416-314-1977, Fax: 416-212-7576, paul.nieweglowski@ontario.ca
Director, Drinking Water Programs Branch, Orna Salamon
416-212-2355, Fax: 416-314-9477, orna.salamon@ontario.ca
Director, Source Protection Programs Branch, Ian R. Smith
416-212-6459, Fax: 416-212-2757, ian.r.smith@ontario.ca

Environmental Programs Division
135 St. Clair Ave. West, 14th Fl., Toronto, ON M4V 1P5
416-326-7203 Fax: 416-327-8777
Assistant Deputy Minister, George Rocoski
416-314-9530, Fax: 416-327-8777, george.rocoski@ontario.ca
Director, Aboriginal Affairs Branch/Lake Simcoe Project, Mary Hennessy
416-327-6953, Fax: 416-326-8114, mary.hennessy@ontario.ca
Director, Program Planning & Implementation Branch/Toxics Reduction Project, Kevin Perry
416-327-9730, Fax: 416-325-8475, kevin.perry@ontario.ca
Director, Modernization of Approvals Project, Marcia Wallace
416-327-9466, Fax: 416-325-7962, marcia.wallace@ontario.ca
Director, Environmental Innovations Branch, Douglas S. Wright
416-325-8068, Fax: 416-314-7919, douglas.wright@ontario.ca

Environmental Sciences & Standards Division
135 St. Clair Ave. West, 14th Fl., Toronto, ON M4V 1P5
416-314-6357 Fax: 416-314-6358
The Environmental Sciences & Standards Division (ESSD) provides the best available science & technology to support decisions about the natural environment, & implements those decisions by developing & managing programs & partnerships, setting scientifically credible standards, monitoring the environment & providing valuable analytical & scientific expertise. Programs such as Drive Clean, that improve the environment & increase public awareness, are central to the ministry's efforts to strengthen environmental protection.
Assistant Deputy Minister, Deb Stark
416-314-6310, deb.stark@ontario.ca
Director, Drive Clean Office, Dale Henry
416-327-5543, Fax: 416-314-4160, dale.henry@ontario.ca
Director, Standards Development, Steve Klose
416-314-1501, Fax: 416-327-2936, steve.klose@ontario.ca
Director, Environmental Monitoring & Reporting Branch, John Mayes
416-235-6160, Fax: 416-235-5770, john.mayes@ontario.ca
Director, Laboratory Services, Joseph Odumeru
416-235-5747, Fax: 416-235-5744, joseph.odumeru@ontario.ca

Central District Offices:
District Manager, Dave Fumerton
905-427-5626

Eastern District Offices:

Northern District Offices:

Southwestern District Offices:

West Central District Offices:

Integrated Environmental Policy Division
77 Wellesley St. West, 11th Fl., Toronto, ON M7A 2T5
416-314-6338 Fax: 416-314-6346
Integrated Environmental Planning Division is responsible for integrating the overall policy development & planning functions of the Ministry. This involves integrating & synthesizing all information, data & perspectives on the many aspects of the Ministry's mandate. The division consults extensively on developing policies, strategies & programs that support the Ministry's core business of conservation & environmental protection.
Assistant Deputy Minister, Paul Evans
416-314-6352, Fax: 416-314-6346, paul.evans@ontario.ca
Director, Land & Water Policy, Sharon Bailey
416-314-7020, Fax: 416-314-7200, sharon.bailey@ontario.ca
Director, Environmental Intergovernmental Affairs Branch, Brian Nixon
416-212-1340, brian.nixon2@ontario.ca
Acting Director, Strategic Policy, Debbie Ramsay
416-327-9743, Fax: 416-325-8181, debbie.ramsay@ontario.ca
Director, Air Policy & Climate Change, Adam Redish
416-314-5148, Fax: 416-314-4128, adam.redish@ontario.ca
Director, Waste Management Policy, Greg Sones
416-326-1825, Fax: 416-325-4233, greg.sones@ontario.ca
Director, Air Policy Instruments & Programs Design Branch, Jim Whitestone
416-314-8562, jim.whitestone@ontario.ca

Operations Division
135 St. Clair Ave. West, 8th Fl., Toronto, ON M4V 1P5
416-314-6378 Fax: 416-314-6396
The Operations Division is the operations & program delivery arm of the ministry. It is responsible for delivering programs to protect air quality, to protect surface & ground water quality & quantity, to ensure appropriate management of wastes, to ensure an adequate quality of drinking water & to control the use of pesticides. In addition, the division is responsible for administering the ministry's approvals & licensing programs as well as an investigative & enforcement program to ensure compliance with environmental laws. The division has a province-wide network of regional, district & area offices.
Assistant Deputy Minister, Kevin French
416-314-6366, Fax: 416-314-6396, kevin.french@ontario.ca
Director, Sector Compliance, Andy Dominski
416-314-4241, Fax: 416-314-4464, andy.dominski@ontario.ca
Director, Environmental Approvals Access & Service Integration, Doris Dumais
416-314-8171, Fax: 416-314-8452, doris.dumais@ontario.ca
Director, Investigations & Enforcement Branch, Lisa Feldman
416-326-3444, Fax: 416-326-5256, lisa.feldman@ontario.ca
Director, Environmental Approvals, Agatha Garcia-Wright
416-314-7288, Fax: 416-314-8452, agatha.garciawright@ontario.ca
Director, Operations Integration, Jim O'Mara
416-314-3994, james.omara@ontario.ca
Director, Central Regional Office, Dolly Goyette
416-314-3920, 800-810-8048, Fax: 416-325-6345, dolly.goyette@ontario.ca
Director, Eastern Regional Office, Hollee Kew
613-548-6901, Fax: 613-548-6911, hollee.kew@ontario.ca
Director, Northern Regional Office, John P. Taylor
807-475-1690, Fax: 807-475-1754, john.p.taylor@ontario.ca
Director, Southwestern Regional Office, Franca Dignem
519-873-5001, 800-265-7672, Fax: 519-873-5020, franca.dignem@ontario.ca
Director, West Central Regional Office, Bill Bardswick
905-521-7652, 800-668-4557, Fax: 905-521-7820, bill.bardswick@ontario.ca

Environmental Commissioner of Ontario (ECO)

#605, 1075 Bay St., Toronto, ON M5S 2B1
416-325-3377 Fax: 416-325-3370
800-701-6454
commissioner@eco.on.ca
www.eco.on.ca
An independent officer of the Legislative Assembly of Ontario, the Environmental Commissioner of Ontario promotes the values, goals & purposes of the Environmental Bill of Rights (EBR) to improve the quality of Ontario's natural environment. The ECO monitors & reports on the application of the EBR, provides public education to facilitate Ontario residents' participation in the EBR & reviews government accountability for environmental decision-making.
Commissioner, Gord Miller
Director, Operations, Peter Lapp
416-325-3369, peter.lapp@eco.on.ca

Ontario Ministry of Finance

Frost Bldg. South, 7 Queen's Park Cres., 7th Fl., Toronto, ON M7A 1Y7
Fax: 866-888-3850
800-263-7965
financecommunications.fin@ontario.ca
www.fin.gov.on.ca
TTY: 800-263-7776
Other Communication: Toll Free (French): 1-800-668-5821
The Ministry of Finance recommends taxation, fiscal & economic policies. Other responsibilities include the management of provincial finances & the development & allocation of Ontario's budget.
Acts Administered:
Assessment Act
Auditor General Act

Automobile Insurance Rate Stabilization Act, 2003
Capital Investment Plan Act, 1993
Community Small Business Investment Funds Act
Compulsory Automobile Insurance Act
Co-operative Corporations Act
Corporations Tax Act
Credit Unions and Caisses Populaires Act, 1994
Crown Foundations Act, 1996
Education Act (in part)
Employer Health Tax Act
Estate Administration Tax Act, 1998
Financial Administration Act
Financial Services Commission of Ontario Act, 1997
Fiscal Transparency and Accountability Act, 2004
Fuel Tax Act
Gasoline Tax Act
Highway Traffic Act (only specific provisions)
Income Tax Act
Insurance Act
Land Transfer Tax Act
Loan & Trust Corporations Act
Marine Insurance Act
Mining Tax Act
Ministry of Revenue Act
Mortgage Brokerages, Lenders & Administrators Act, 2006
Motor Vehicle Accident Claims Act
MPPs Pension Act, 1996
Municipal Property Assessment Corporation Act, 1997
Ontario Guaranteed Annual Income Act 1996
Ontario Loan Act, 2005, S.O. 2005, c. 28, Sched. K
Ontario Loan Act, 2006, S.O. 2006, c. 9, Sched. J
Pension Benefits Act 1990
Prepaid Hospital & Medical Services Act
Province of Ontario Savings Office Act
Province of Ontario Savings Office Privatization Act, 2002
Provincial Land Tax Act, 1990
Provincial Land Tax Act, 2006
Public Sector Salary Disclosure Act, 1996
Race Tracks Tax Act
Registered Insurance Brokers Act
Retail Sales Tax Act
SkyDome Act (Bus Parking), 2002
Small Business Development Corporations Act, 2009
Social Contract Act, 1993
Statistics Act
Supply Act, 2007
Tax Incentive Zones Act (Pilot Projects), 2002
Tax Increment Financing Act, 2006
Taxpayer Protection Act, 1999
Tobacco Tax Act
Unclaimed Intangible Property Act
Canadian Public Accountability Board Act (Ontario)
Commercial Concentration Tax Act
Commodity Futures Act
Interim Appropriation for 2011-2012 Act
Investing in Ontario Act
Liquor Control Act
Ontario Loan Act, 2007, S.O. 2007, c. 7, Sched. 29
Ontario Loan Act, 2008, S.O. 2008, c. 7, Sched. P
Ontario Loan Act, 2009, S.O. 2009, c. 18, Sched. 21
Ontario Loan Act, 2009 (No. 2), S.O. 2009, c. 34, Sched. O
Ontario Loan Act, 2010, S.O. 2010, c. 1, Schedule 22
Ontario Loan Act, 2011, S.O. 2011, c. 9, Schedule 33
Public Sector Compensation Restraint to Protect Public Services Act
Racing Commission Act
Securities Act
Succession Duty Act Supplementary Provisions Act, 1980
Supplementary Interim Appropriation Act, 2011
Supply Act, 2008
Supply Act, 2009
Supply Act, 2010
Supply Act, 2011
Taxation Act, 2007
Toronto Stock Exchange Act
Trust Beneficiaries' Liability Act

Minister, Hon. Dwight Duncan
416-325-0400, Fax: 416-325-0374, dduncan.mpp.co@liberal.ola.org

Deputy Minister, Peter Wallace
416-325-1592, Fax: 416-325-1595, peter.wallace@ontario.ca

Director, Legal Services, James D. Sinclair
416-325-1450, Fax: 416-325-1460, james.sinclair@ontario.ca

Director, Communications, Dianne Lone
416-212-1440, Fax: 416-325-0339, dianne.lone@ontario.ca

Associated Agencies, Boards & Commissions:

• Deposit Insurance Corporation of Ontario
#700, 4711 Yonge St.
Toronto, ON M2N 6K8
416-325-9444 Fax: 416-325-9722 800-268-6653
www.dico.com
The Deposit Insurance Corporation of Ontario provides deposit insurance, to the extent provided under the Credit Unions and Caisses Populaires Act, on deposits of members of credit unions and caisses populaires.

• Financial Services Commission of Ontario (FSCO)
New York City Ctr.
5160 Yonge St., 17th Fl.
PO Box 85
Toronto, ON M2N 6L9
416-250-7250 Fax: 416-590-7070 800-668-0128 TTY: 800-387-0584
www.fsco.gov.on.ca
Regulates insurance, pensions plans, credit unions, caisses populaires, mortgage brokers, cooperative corporations & loan & trust companies in Ontario. FSCO provides regulatory services that protect financial services consumers & pension plan beneficiaries & support a healthy & competitive financial services industry.

• Liquor Control Board of Ontario (LCBO)
55 Lake Shore Blvd. East
Toronto, ON M5E 1A4
416-365-5900 Fax: 416-864-2476 800-668-5226
infoline@lcbo.com
www.lcbo.com
The Liquor Control Board of Ontario (LCBO) is a provincial Crown corporation in Ontario, Canada established in 1927 by Lieutenant Governor William Donald Ross, on the advice of his Premier, Howard Ferguson, to sell liquor, wine, and beer through a chain of retail stores.

• Ontario Electricity Financial Corporation (OEFC)
#1400, 1 Dundas St. West
Toronto, ON M7A 1Y7
416-325-8000 Fax: 416-325-8005
www.oefc.on.ca

• Ontario Financing Authority (OFA)
#1400, 1 Dundas St. West
Toronto, ON M7A 1Y7
416-325-8000 Fax: 416-325-8005
www.ofina.on.ca
The Ontario Financing Authority (OFA) is an agency of the Province of Ontario that manages the Province's debt and borrowing program. The OFA is governed by a Board of Directors that reports to the Minister of Finance.

• Ontario Lottery & Gaming Corporation (OLG)
Roberta Bondar Pl.
#800, 70 Foster Dr.
Sault Ste Marie, ON P6A 6V2
705-946-6464 Fax: 416-224-7000 800-387-0098 TTY: 800-563-5357
www.olg.ca
Created on April 1, 2000 under the Ontario Lottery and Gaming Corporation Act, 1999, the Ontario Lottery and Gaming Corporation (OLG) is a provincial agency operating and managing province-wide lotteries, casinos and slots facilities at horse racing tracks.

• Ontario Racing Commission (ORC)
#400, 10 Carlson Crt.
Toronto, ON M9W 6L2
416-213-0520 Fax: 416-213-7827
inquiry@ontarioracingcommission.ca
www.ontarioracingcommission.ca

• Ontario Securities Commission (OSC) / Commission des valeurs mobilières de l'Ontario
#1903, 20 Queen St. West
PO Box 55
Toronto, ON M5H 3S8
416-597-0681 Fax: 416-593-8241
www.osc.gov.on.ca
The mandate of the Ontario Securities Commission (OSC) is to protect investors while fostering capital formation and the efficiency and integrity of Ontario's and Canada's capital markets.

• Stadium Corporation of Ontario Ltd.
33 King St. West, 6th Fl.
Oshawa, ON L1H 8H5
416-314-5158 Fax: 905-433-6688
The corporation continues to exist to comply with legal commitments by the Province of Ontario as part of the sale of SkyDome. The agency is currently commercially active as it addresses obligations to provide a permanent solution to SkyDome bus parking. The agency has real estate assets in the form of a bus parking facility.

Corporate & Quality Service Division
Michael Starr Bldg., 33 King St. West, 6th Fl., Toronto, ON L1H 8H5
905-433-6844 Fax: 905-433-6688

Other Communication: Freedom of Information & Protection of Privacy: 416-325-8370, Toll Free: 1-800-263-7965, Ligne sans frais: 1-800-668-5821

Assistant Deputy Minister & Chief Administrative Officer, Helmut Zisser
416-314-5158, helmut.zisser@ontario.ca
Director, Corporate Planning & Finance Branch, Linda Gibney
905-433-5637, Fax: 905-433-5124, linda.gibney@ontario.ca
Director, Business Services Branch, Paula Reid
905-440-4263, paula.reid@ontario.ca
Director, Strategic Human Resources Services Branch, Allyson Thompson
905-433-5482, allyson.thompson@ontario.ca

Office of Economic Policy
Frost Bldg. North, 95 Grosvenor St., 5th Fl., Toronto, ON M7A 1Z1
416-325-0840 Fax: 416-325-9224

Assistant Deputy Minister & Chief Economist, Patrick Deutscher
416-325-0850, Fax: 416-325-9224, pat.deutscher@ontario.ca
Director, Industrial & Financial Policy Branch, Alvaro del Castillo
416-325-0928, Fax: 416-325-1187, alvaro.delcastillo@ontario.ca
Director, Labour & Demographic Analysis Branch, Ambaye Kidane
416-325-0801, Fax: 416-325-0841, ambaye.kidane@ontario.ca
Director, Economic & Revenue Forecasting & Analysis, Brian Lewis
416-325-0754, Fax: 416-325-0796, brian.Lewis@ontario.ca

Office of Taxation, Agencies & Pensions
Frost Bldg. South, 7 Queen's Park Cres., 7th Fl., Toronto, ON M7A 1Y7
416-325-0400 Fax: 416-325-0290

Assistant Deputy Minister, Steve Orsini
416-327-0223, steve.f.orsini@ontario.ca
Assistant Deputy Minister, Pension, Income Security & Research Division, Leslie Cooke
416-212-5983, Fax: 416-327-0160, leslie.cooke@ontario.ca
Assistant Deputy Minister, Revenue Agencies Oversight Division, Barry Goodwin
416-325-2880, barry.goodwin@ontario.ca
Assistant Deputy Minister, Taxation Policy Division, Sriram Subrahmanyan
416-327-7294, sriram.subrahmanyan@ontario.ca
Director, Alcohol & Fees Policy Branch, Barbara Hewett
416-314-4288, barbara.hewett@ontario.ca
Director, Gaming Policy Branch, Steen Hume
416-325-2070, steen.hume@ontario.ca
Director, Corporate & Commodity Taxation Branch, Ann Langleben
416-327-0222, ann.langleben@ontario.ca
Director, Pension Policy Branch, Bruce Macnaughton
416-327-0140, bruce.macnaughton@ontario.ca
Director, Personal Tax Policy & Design Branch, Kostas Plainos
416-327-0246, kostas.plainos@ontario.ca
Director, Strategic Quantitative Research Branch, Charles Whitfield
416-327-0143, charles.whitfield@ontario.ca

Office of the Budget & Treasury Board
Frost Bldg. South, 95 Grosvenor St., 4th Fl., Toronto, ON M7A 1Z1
416-325-7620 Fax: 416-212-7767

Associate Deputy Minister, Greg Orencsak
416-325-4569, greg.orencsak@ontario.ca
Assistant Deputy Minister, BPS Supply Chain Secretariat, Peggy Mooney
416-314-1869, peggy.mooney@ontario.ca, Other Communications: URL: www.fin.gov.on.ca/bpssupplychain
Assistant Deputy Minister & Acting Provincial Controller, Murray Lindo
416-325-8017, Fax: 416-325-2029, murray.lindo@ontario.ca
Director, Health & Demand Forecasting Branch, Jay Coghill
416-325-8244, jay.coghill@ontario.ca
Director, Education, Justice & Quantitative Management Branch, Maria Duran-Schneider
416-212-9693, Fax: 416-327-9115, maria.duran-schneider@ontario.ca
Director, General Government, Planning & Resources Branch, Joshua Paul
416-327-0206, joshua.paul@ontario.ca
Director, Social Policy & Fiscal Framework Branch, Tim Schuurman
416-327-0173, tim.schuurman@ontario.ca

Provincial-Local Finance Division
College Park, 777 Bay St., 10th Fl., Toronto, ON M5G 2C8
416-327-0264 Fax: 416-325-7644

Assistant Deputy Minister, Allan Doheny
416-327-9592, allan.doheny@ontario.ca
Acting Director, Property Tax Analysis & Municipal Funding Policy, Chris Broughton
416-314-3801, Fax: 416-314-3853, chris.broughton@ontario.ca
Director, Provincial Local Initiatives, Helen Harper
416-314-2286, Fax: 416-314-3853, helen.harper@ontario.ca
Director, Property Tax Legislation & Assessment Policy, Diane Ross
416-327-0266, Fax: 416-314-7670, diane.ross@ontario.ca

Secretariat to Commission on the Reform of Ontario's Public Services
Frost Bldg. South, 7 Queen's Park Cres., 1st Fl., Toronto, ON M7A 1YA
416-326-9847 Fax: 416-212-7767
Assistant Deputy Minister & Executive Lead, Scott Thompson
416-327-2060, d.scott.thompson@ontario.ca
Director, Craig Fowler
416-326-2381, craig.fowler@ontario.ca

Office of Francophone Affairs

#200, 777 Bay St., Toronto, ON M7A 0A2
416-325-4949 Fax: 416-325-4980
800-268-7507
ofa@ontario.ca
www.ofa.gov.on.ca
TTY: 416-325-0017
A central agency that assists the Government of Ontario in its delivery of services in French, & in the development of policies & programs that meet the needs of the province's francophones.
Acts Administered:
French Language Services Act
Minister Responsible, Hon. Madeleine Meilleur
416-744-4484, Fax: 416-325-4980, mmeilleur.mpp.co@liberal.ola.org
Deputy Minister, Paul Genest
416-314-9710, Fax: 416-325-5240, paul.genest@ontario.ca
Assistant Deputy Minister, Daniel Cayen
416-325-4936, daniel.cayen@ontario.ca
Acting Director, Policy & Ministry Services, Éric Mézin
416-325-4943, eric.mezin@ontario.ca
Director, Strategic Communications Branch, Charles Jean Sucsan
416-325-4968, charlesjean.sucsan@ontario.ca

Ontario Ministry of Government Services (MGS)

Whitney Block, #4320, 99 Wellesley St. West, 4th Fl., Toronto, ON M7A 1W3
416-326-1234 Fax: 416-327-3790
800-268-1142
www.mgs.gov.on.ca
TTY: 416-326-8566
Other Communication: Consumer Protection, Phone: 416-326-8800; Toll Free: 1-800-889-9768
MGS is responsible for the delivery of government services, the government workforce, procurement & technology resources. The ministry is engaged in the following main activities: providing government information to individuals & businesses, including distribution through Publications Ontario; protecting consumers through information about frauds & scams & mediating complaints about businesses; & issuing birth, death & marriage certificates, & managing Land Registry Offices throughout the province.
Acts Administered:
Adjudicative Tribunals Accountability, Governance & Appointments Act
Archives & Recordkeeping Act
Boundaries Act
Business Corporations Act
Business Names Act
Business Regulation Reform Act
Cabinet Ministers' & Opposition Leaders' Expenses Review & Accountability Act
Change of Name Act
Condominium Act, 2011
Corporations Act
Corporations Information Act
Electronic Land Registration Services Act
Electronic Registration Act
Extra-Provincial Corporations Act
Flag Act
Floral Emblem Act
Freedom of Information & Protection of Privacy Act
Government Advertising Act
Land Registration Reform Act
Land Titles Act
Licence Appeal Tribunal Act
Limited Partnerships Act
Lobbyists Registration Act
Marriage Act
Ministry of Government Services Act
Municipal Freedom of Information & Protection of Privacy Act
Official Notices Publication Act
Ontario Provincial Police Collective Bargaining Act
Ontario Public Service Employees' Union Pension Act
Partnerships Act
Personal Property Security Act
Public Sector Expenses Review Act
Public Service of Ontario Act
Public Service Pension Act
Registry Act
Repair & Storage Liens Act
Residential Complex Sales Representation Act
Vital Statistics Act
Broader Public Sector Accountability Act
Highway Traffic Act
Not-for-Profit Corporations Act, 2010
Minister, Hon. Harinder S. Takhar
416-327-2333, Fax: 416-327-3790, htakhar.mpp.co@liberal.ola.org
Deputy Minister, MGS, Associate Secretary of the Cabinet & Secretary of Mgmt Board of Cabinet, Ron McKerlie
416-325-1607, Fax: 416-325-1612, ron.mckerlie@ontario.ca
Parliamentary Assistant, Bill Mauro
416-327-6611, Fax: 416-325-4136, bmauro.mpp.co@liberal.ola.org
Assistant Deputy Minister, Labour Relations Secretariat, Tim Hadwen
416-326-4195, Fax: 416-326-5265
Assistant Deputy Minister, Ontario Public Service Green Office, Neil Sentance
416-327-3536, neil.sentance@ontario.ca
Chief Officer, Diversity & Accessibility, Shamira Madhany
416-314-6989, shamira.madhany@ontario.ca
Director, Operations, Deborah E. Brown
416-325-1609, Fax: 416-325-1612, deborah.e.brown@ontario.ca
Director, Legal Services, Sean Kearney
416-327-6396, Fax: 416-326-6383, sean.kearney@ontario.ca
Acting Director, Communications, Sevaun Palvetzian
416-325-1376, Fax: 416-327-2817, sevaun.palvetzian@ontario.ca

Associated Agencies, Boards & Commissions:
- Advertising Review Board
Macdonald Block
#M2-56, 900 Bay St., 2nd Fl.
Toronto, ON M7A 1N3
416-327-2183 Fax: 416-327-2179
- Conflict of Interest Commissioner
#1802, 2 Bloor St. East
Toronto, ON M4W 3J6
416-325-1571 Fax: 416-325-4330
- Licence Appeal Tribunal (LAT)
20 Dundas St. West, 5th Fl.
Toronto, ON M5G 2C2
416-314-4260 Fax: 416-314-4270 800-255-2214
www.lat.gov.on.ca
Other Communication: Toll Free Fax: 1-800-720-5292
The LAT hears appeals when a decision or order to suspend or a proposal is made to cancel or to refuse to grant or renew a registration, certificate or a licence, or when a claim for compensation has been denied.
- Ontario Pension Board
Sun Life Bldg.
#2200, 200 King St. West
Toronto, ON M5H 3X6
416-364-8558 Fax: 416-364-7578 800-668-6203
office.services@opb.on.ca
www.opb.on.ca
- OPSEU Pension Trust
#1200, 1 Adelaide St. East
Toronto, ON M5C 3A7
416-681-6161 Fax: 416-681-6175 800-637-0024
www.optrust.com
- Provincial Judges Pension Board
c/o Ontario Pension Board
#1100, 1 Adelaide St. East
Toronto, ON M5C 2X6
416-327-8395 Fax: 416-366-0199
- Public Service Commission
Whitney Block
99 Wellesley St. West, 5th Fl.
Toronto, ON M7A 1W4
416-325-1750

Corporate Services Division
College Park, 777 Bay St., 5th Fl., Toronto, ON M7A 2J3
416-314-5187 Fax: 416-327-2866
Assistant Deputy Minister & Chief Administrative Officer, Karen Hughes
416-325-3311, karen.hughes@ontario.ca
Director, Business Planning & Financial Management Branch, Lillian Duda
416-212-3124, lillian.duda@ontario.ca
Director, Service Management & service Delivery Branch, Karl Cunningham
416-326-8896, karl.cunningham@ontario.ca
Director, Enterprise Services Strategic Business Unit, Tracey McConnell
416-327-3821, tracey.mcconnell@ontario.ca

Enterprise Services Cluster
Ferguson Block, 77 Wellesley St. West, 8th Fl., Toronto, ON M7A 1N3
416-326-2700 Fax: 416-326-3347
Chief Information Officer, Enterprise Services Cluster, Ron Huxter
416-327-1476, ron.huxter@ontario.ca
Head, Enterprise HR Systems Branch, John Deans
416-327-9210, john.deans@ontario.ca
Head, Enterprise Financial Systems, Tricia Ireland
416-326-9624, tricia.ireland@ontario.ca
Head, Information Technology Source, Fred Pitt
416-327-5010, fred.pitt@ontario.ca
Head, Technology & Applied Architecture, John Van den Hoven
416-326-9477, john.vandenhoven@ontario.ca
Head, Business & Application Modernization, Russ Whitehead
416-327-3431, russ.whitehead@ontario.ca

HR Ontario
Whitney Block, #5320, 99 Wellesley St. West, Toronto, ON M7A 1N3
416-212-2057 Fax: 416-325-6317
Associate Deputy Minister, Angela Coke
416-325-5065, angela.coke@ontario.ca
Assistant Deputy Minister, HR Management & Corporate Policy Division, Catherine D. Brown
416-327-9223, catherine.brown@ontario.ca
Assistant Deputy Minister, Employee Relations Division, David Logan
416-325-1476, david.logan@ontario.ca
Assistant Deputy Minister, HR Service Delivery Division, Debbie Moretta
416-325-7612, debbie.moretta@ontario.ca
Assistant Deputy Minister, Centre for Leadership & Learning, Kerry Pond
416-325-1777, kerry.pond@ontario.ca
Assistant Deputy Minister, Centre for Organizational Excellence, Leslie Slater
416-325-1737, leslie.slater@ontario.ca
Director, Strategic Business Performance Branch, Lisa Sherin
416-326-8774, lisa.sherin@ontario.ca

Information, Privacy & Archives Division
134 Ian Macdonald Blvd., Toronto, ON M7A 2C5
416-327-1600 Fax: 416-327-1999
800-668-9933
www.archives.gov.on.ca
Acting Chief Privacy Officer & Archivist of Ontario, Angela Forest
416-327-1602, Fax: 416-327-1992, angela.forest@ontario.ca
Director, Mary Anne Henderson
416-327-1577, Fax: 416-327-1999, maryanne.henderson@ontario.ca

Office of the Corporate Chief Information Officer (OCCIO)
Ferguson Block, 77 Wellesley St. West, 5th Fl., Toronto, ON M7A 1N3
416-327-3442 Fax: 416-327-3264
Corporate Chief Information & Information Technology Officer, David Nicholl
416-327-9696, david.nicholl@ontario.ca
Corporate Chief, Infrastructure Technology Services, Marty Gallas
416-326-7224, marty.gallas@ontario.ca
Corporate Chief Strategist, Samantha Liscio
416-212-1624, Fax: 416-314-7710, samantha.liscio@ontario.ca
Acting Head, I&IT Strategy, Policy & Planning Branch, Linda Haldenby
416-314-2060, linda.haldenby@ontario.ca
Head, Corporate Security, Peter Macaulay
416-327-0413, Fax: 416-327-3262, peter.macaulay@ontario.ca

Ontario Shared Services
700 University Ave., 6th Fl., Toronto, ON M7A 2S4
416-326-9300
866-979-9300
Associate Deputy Minister, Lois Bain
416-212-7550, lois.bain@ontario.ca
Assistant Deputy Minister, Strategy & Enterprise Services, Glen Medeiros
416-212-6569, Fax: 416-327-4246
Assistant Deputy Minister, Enterprise Financial Services, Roman Zydownyk
416-212-3713, Fax: 416-212-3715, roman.zydownyk@ontario.ca
Assistant Deputy Minister, Pay & Benefits Services Division, Riet Verheggen
416-212-6731, Fax: 416-325-1165, riet.verheggen@ontario.ca

Supply Chain Management
413-212-0967 Fax: 416-327-3573
www.ontario.ca/supplychain
Develops & implements an integrated corporate procurement strategy to: leverage & optimize government procurement of goods & services; identify and implement procurement process improvements; enhance procurement controllership; provide strategic advice on large scale procurements; develop innovative

policy frameworks to support service delivery through third party service providers.
Assistant Deputy Minister, Marian Macdonald
416-327-7508, Fax: 416-327-3573, marian.macdonald@ontario.ca
Director, Procurement Policy & Planning Branch, Susan Hoyle-Howieson
416-327-8765, Fax: 416-327-3573, susan.hoyle-howieson@ontario.ca
Director, Enterprise Procurement Branch, Wes Lapish
416-327-3518, Fax: 416-327-3573, wes.lapish@ontario.ca
Director, Procurement Strategies & Enablement Branch, Ben Sopel
416-325-7553, Fax: 416-327-3573, ben.sopel@ontario.ca

ServiceOntario
College Park, 777 Bay St., 15th fl., Toronto, ON M7A 2J3
416-326-1234 Fax: 416-326-1313
800-267-8097
www.serviceontario.ca
TTY: 800-268-7095
Deputy Minister & Chief Executive Officer, Bob Stark
416-326-7102, bob.stark@ontario.ca
Assistant Deputy Minister, Business Improvement, Bev Hawton
416-326-6062, bev.hawton@ontario.ca
Assistant Deputy Minister, Business Development Division, Frank D'Onofrio
416-314-3709, Fax: 416-326-0277, frank.d'onofrio@ontario.ca
Assistant Deputy Minister, Central Services Division, Sam Erry
416-314-4877, sam.erry@ontario.ca
Assistant Deputy Minister, Customer Care Division, Helga Iliadis
416-326-2784, helga.iliadis@ontario.ca
Assistant Deputy Minister, Service Delivery Strategy Division, Richard Steele
416-325-8804, richard.steele@ontario.ca

Land Registrars:

Algoma
420 Queen St. East, Sault Ste Marie, ON P6A 1Z7
705-253-8887 Fax: 705-253-9245

Brant
Court House, 80 Wellington St., Brantford, ON N3T 2L9
519-752-8321 Fax: 519-752-0273

Bruce
203 Cayley St., PO Box 1690, Walkerton, ON N0G 2V0
519-881-2259 Fax: 519-881-2322

Cochrane
143 - 4th Ave., PO Box 580, Cochrane, ON P0L 1C0
705-272-5791 Fax: 705-272-2951
877-817-6636

Dufferin
#7, 41 Briadway Ave., Orangeville, ON L9W 1J7
519-941-1481 Fax: 519-941-6444

Dundas
8 Fifth St., PO Box 645, Morrisburg, ON K0C 1X0
613-543-2583 Fax: 613-543-4541

Durham
590 Rossland Rd. East, Whitby, ON L1N 9G5
416-665-4007 Fax: 416-665-5247

Elgin
#36, 1010 Talbot St., St Thomas, ON N5P 4N2
519-631-3015 Fax: 519-631-8182

Essex
#100, 949 McDougall St., Windsor, ON N9A 1L9
519-971-9980 Fax: 519-971-9937

Frontenac
1 Court St., Kingston, ON K7L 2N4
613-548-6767 Fax: 613-548-6766

Glengarry
63 Kenyon St. West, Alexandria, ON K0C 1A0
613-525-1315 Fax: 613-525-0509

Grenville
499 Centre St., PO Box 1660, Prescott, ON K0E 1T0
613-925-3177 Fax: 613-925-0302

Grey
East Court Plaza, #1-2, 1555 - 16th St. East, Owen Sound, ON N4K 5N3
519-376-1637 Fax: 519-376-1639

Haldimand
10 Echo St. West, PO Box 310, Cayuga, ON N0A 1E0
905-772-3531 Fax: 905-772-0105

Haliburton
12 Newcastle St., PO Box 270, Minden, ON K0M 2K0
705-286-1391 Fax: 705-286-4324

Halton
2800 Highpoint Dr., 2nd Fl., Milton, ON L9T 6P4
905-864-3500 Fax: 905-864-3549

Hastings
#109, 199 Front St., Belleville, ON K8N 5H5
613-968-4597 Fax: 613-968-3606
Land Registrar, David Faires
613-968-4597

Huron
38 North St., Goderich, ON N7A 2T4
519-524-9562 Fax: 519-524-2482

Kenora
220 Main St. South, Kenora, ON P9N 1T2
807-468-2794 Fax: 807-468-2796

Kent
40 William St. North, Chatham, ON N7M 4L2
519-352-5520 Fax: 519-352-3222

Lambton
#102, 700 North Christina St., Sarnia, ON N7V 3C2
519-337-2393 Fax: 519-337-8371

Lanark
2 Industrial Dr., PO Box 1180, Almonte, ON K0A 1A0
613-256-1496 Fax: 613-256-0940

Leeds
7 King St. West, Brockville, ON K6V 3P7
613-345-5751 Fax: 613-345-7390

Lennox
#2, 7 Snow Rd., Napanee, ON K7R 0A2
613-354-3751 Fax: 613-354-1474

Manitoulin
Courthouse, 27 Phipps St., PO Box 619, Gore Bay, ON P0P 1H0
705-282-2442 Fax: 705-282-2131

Middlesex
100 Dundas St., London, ON N6A 5B6
519-675-7600 Fax: 519-675-7611

Muskoka
15 Dominion St. North, Bracebridge, ON P1L 2E7
705-645-4415 Fax: 705-645-7826

Niagara North & South
59 Church St., St. Catharines, ON L2R 3C3
905-684-6351 Fax: 905-684-5874

Nipissing
360 Plouffe St., North Bay, ON P1B 9L5
705-474-2270 Fax: 705-495-8511

Norfolk
Court House, #201, 50 Frederick Hobson VC Dr., Simcoe, ON N3Y 4K8
519-426-2216 Fax: 519-426-9627

Northumberland
Fleming Bldg., #105, 1005 Elgin St. West, Cobourg, ON K9A 5J4
705-372-3813 Fax: 905-372-4758

Ottawa-Carleton
Court House, 161 Elgin St., 4th Fl., Ottawa, ON K2P 2K1
613-239-1230 Fax: 613-239-1422

Oxford
75 Graham St., Woodstock, ON N4S 6J8
519-537-6287 Fax: 519-537-3107

Parry Sound
28 Miller St., Parry Sound, ON P2A 1T1
705-746-5816 Fax: 705-746-6517

Peel
7765 Hurontario St., 1st Fl., Brampton, ON L6W 4S8
905-874-4008 Fax: 905-874-4012

Perth
5 Huron St., Stratford, ON N5A 5S4
519-271-3343 Fax: 519-271-2550

Peterborough
Robinson Pl. North Tower, 300 Water St., 1st Fl., PO Box 7000, Peterborough, ON K9J 8M5
705-755-1342 Fax: 705-755-1343

Prescott
499 Centre St., PO Box 1660, Prescott, ON K0E 1T0
613-925-3177 Fax: 613-925-0302

Prince Edward
1 Pitt St., PO Box 1310, Picton, ON K0K 2T0
613-476-3219 Fax: 613-476-7908

Rainy River
353 Church St., Fort Frances, ON P9A 1C9
807-274-5451 Fax: 807-274-1704

Renfrew
400 Pembroke St. East, Pembroke, ON K8A 3K8
613-732-8331 Fax: 613-732-0297

Russell
1122 Concession St., PO Box 10, Russell, ON K4R 1C8
613-445-2138 Fax: 613-445-0614

Simcoe
Court House, 114 Worsley St., Barrie, ON L4M 1M1
705-725-7232 Fax: 705-725-7246

Stormont
#2, 720 14th St. West, Cornwall, ON K6J 5T9
613-932-4522 Fax: 613-932-4524

Sudbury
#300, 199 Larch St., Sudbury, ON P3E 5P9
705-675-4300 Fax: 705-675-4148

Thunder Bay
189 Red River Rd., 2nd Fl., Thunder Bay, ON P7B 1A2
807-343-7436 Fax: 807-343-7439

Timiskaming
375 Main St., PO Box 159, Haileybury, ON P0J 1K0
705-672-3332 Fax: 705-672-3906

Toronto (Metropolitan Registry)
Atrium on Bay, #420, 20 Dundas St. West, PO Box 117, Toronto, ON M5G 2C2
416-314-4430 Fax: 416-314-4453

Toronto (Metropolitan Land Titles)
#420, 20 Dundas St. West, PO Box 117, Toronto, ON M5G 2C2
416-314-4430 Fax: 416-314-4453

Victoria
322 Kent St. West, Lindsay, ON K9V 4T7
705-324-4912 Fax: 705-324-6290

Waterloo
30 Duke St. West, 2nd Fl., Kitchener, ON N2H 3W5
519-571-6043 Fax: 519-571-6067

Wellington
1 Stone Rd. West, Guelph, ON N1G 4Y2
519-826-3372 Fax: 519-826-3373
Land Registrar, Donna Trevors
519-826-3372, Fax: 519-826-3373, donna.trevors@ontario.ca

Wentworth
119 King St. West, 4th Fl., Hamilton, ON L8P 4Y7
905-521-7561 Fax: 905-521-7505

York Region
50 Bloomington Rd. West, Aurora, ON L4G 0L8
905-713-7798 Fax: 905-713-7799

Ontario Ministry of Health & Long-Term Care

Hepburn Block, 80 Grosvenor St., 10th Fl, Toronto, ON M7A 2C4
416-327-4327
800-268-1153
www.health.gov.on.ca
Other Communication: TTY: 1-800-387-5559

The ministry is responsible for administering the health care system & providing services to the Ontario public through such programs as health insurance, drug benefits, assistive devices, care for the mentally ill, long-term care, home care, community & public health, & health promotion & disease prevention. It also regulates hospitals & nursing homes, operates psychiatric hospitals & medical laboratories, & co-ordinates emergency health services.

Acts Administered:
Alcoholism & Drug Addiction Research Foundation Act
Ambulance Act
Audiology & Speech-Language Pathology Act
Cancer Act
Chiropody Act, 2009
Chiropractic Act
Community Care Access Corporations Act
Dental Hygiene Act, 1991
Dental Technology Act, 1991
Dentistry Act, 1991
Denturism Act, 1991
Dietetics Act, 1991
Drug & Pharmacies Regulation Act
Drug Interchangeability & Dispensing Fee Act
Drugless Practitioners Act
Elderly Persons Centres Act
Health Care Consent Act
Health Facilities Special Orders Act
Health Insurance Act
Health Protection & Promotion Act
Homemakers & Nurses Services Act
Homes for Special Care Act
Trillium Gift of Life Network Act
Immunization of School Pupils Act
Independent Health Facilities Act
Laboratory & Specimen Collection Centres Licensing Act
Massage Therapy Act
Mental Health Act

Midwifery Act, 1991
Ministry of Community & Social Services Act (sections 11.1 & 12 re: long-term care programs & services only)
Ministry of Health & Long-Term Care Act
Nursing Act
Occupational Therapy Act
Ontario Drug Benefit Act
Ontario Medical Association Dues Act, 1991
Ontario Mental Health Foundation Act
Opticianry Act, 1991
Optometry Act, 1991
Pharmacy Act, 1991
Physiotherapy Act, 1991
Private Hospitals Act
Psychology Act, 1991
Public Hospitals Act
Regulated Health Professions Act, 1991
Respiratory Therapy Act, 1991
Brain Tumour Awareness Month Act, 2001
Broader Public Sector Accountability Act, 2010
Chase McEachern Act (Heart Defibrillator Civil Liability), 2007
Commitment to the Future of Medicare Act, 2004
Excellent Care for All Act, 2010
Fluoridation Act
Healing Arts Radiation Protection Act
Homeopathy Act, 2007
Home Care & Community Services Act, 1994
Katelyn Bedard Bone Marrow Awareness Month Act, 2010
Kinesiology Act
Local Health System Integration Act, 2006
Long-Term Care Homes Act, 2007
Medical Laboratory Technology Act
Medical Radiation Technology Act
Medicine Act
Ministry of Health & Long-Term Care Appeal & Review Boards Act
Narcotics Safety & Awareness Act
Natruopathy Act
Ontario Agency for Health Protection & Promotion Act, 2007
Patient Restraints Minimization Act
Personal Health Information Protection Act
Psychotherapy Act
Quality of Care Information Protection Act
Traditional Chinese Medicine Act
University Health Network Act
University of Ottawa Heart Institute Act

Minister, Hon. Deborah Matthews
416-327-4300, Fax: 416-327-2679, dmatthews.mpp.co@liberal.ola.org
Deputy Minister, Saäd Rafi
416-327-4496, Fax: 416-326-1570, saad.rafi@ontario.ca
Parliamentary Assistant, Dr. Kuldip Kular
416-325-0235, kkular.mpp.co@liberal.ola.org
Associate Deputy Minister, David Hallett
416-327-2605, david.hallett@ontario.ca
Director, Legal Services, Janice B. Crawford
416-327-8565, janice.b.crawford@ontario.ca

Associated Agencies, Boards & Commissions:

• Cancer Care Ontario
620 University Ave., 15th Fl.
Toronto, ON M5G 2L7
416-971-9800 Fax: 416-971-6888
www.cancercare.on.ca

• Consent & Capacity Board
151 Bloor St. West, 10th Fl.
Toronto, ON M5S 2T5
416-327-4142 Fax: 416-924-8873 866-777-7391 TTY: 877-301-0889
www.ccboard.on.ca
Other Communication: Toll-Free Fax: 1-866-777-7273
Hears appeals relating to involuntary placement in a psychiatric facility, capacity to make personal care & financial decisions & access to personal records from a psychiatric facility.

• eHealth Ontario
College Park
#701, 777 Bay St.
Toronto, ON M5G 2C8
416-586-6535 Fax: 416-586-4363 888-411-7742 TTY: 855-645-3390
info@ehealthontario.on.ca
www.ehealthontario.on.ca

• Health Boards Secretariat
151 Bloor St. West, 9th Fl.
Toronto, ON M5S 2T5
416-327-8512 Fax: 416-327-8524 866-282-2179

• Health Quality Ontario
#702, 130 Bloor St. West
Toronto, ON M5S 1N5
416-323-6868
www.ohqc.ca

• Medical Eligibility Committee
370 Select Dr.
PO Box 168
Kingston, ON K7M 8T4
613-548-6405
Deals with the eligibility of insured services as well as other matters assigned to it by the act or the regulation or by the minister; makes recommendations to the general manager with respect to these decisions.

• Ontario Mental Health Foundation
441 Jarvis St., 2nd Fl.
Toronto, ON M4Y 2G8
416-920-7721 Fax: 416-920-0026
grants@omhf.on.ca
www.omhf.on.ca

• Ontario Review Board
151 Bloor St. West, 10th Fl.
Toronto, ON M5S 2T5
416-327-8866 Fax: 416-327-8867
www.orb.on.ca

• Public Health Ontario
#300, 480 University Ave.
Toronto, ON M5G 1V2
647-260-7100 Fax: 647-260-7600
www.oahpp.ca

• Trillium Gift of Life Network
#900, 522 University Ave.
Toronto, ON M5G 1W7
416-363-4001 Fax: 416-363-4002 800-263-2833
www.giftoflife.on.ca

Chief Medical Officer of Health
Hepburn Block, 80 Grosvenor St., 11th Fl., Toronto, ON M7A 1R3
416-212-3831 Fax: 416-325-8412

Chief Medical Officer of Health, Dr. Arlene King
416-212-3831, Fax: 416-325-8412, arlene.king@ontario.ca
Associate Chief Medical Officer of Health, Protection & Prevention, Dr. David Williams
416-326-0392, david.williams@ontario.ca
Associate Chief Medical Officer of Health, Transition, Dr. Robin Williams
416-325-7672, dr.robin.williams@ontario.ca
Executive Director, Public Health, Roselle Martino
416-327-9555, Fax: 416-325-8412, roselle.martino@ontario.ca
Acting Director, Emergency Management, Tiffany Jay
416-212-5229, Fax: 416-212-4466, tiffany.jay@ontario.ca
Director, Operational Effectiveness, Becky Taylor
416-326-2783, Fax: 416-314-7078, becky.taylor@ontario.ca

Corporate Services Division
Hepburn Block, 80 Grosvenor St., 11th Fl., Toronto, ON M7A 1R3
416-327-4266 Fax: 416-314-5915

Assistant Deputy Minister & Chief Administrative Officer, Ruth Hawkins
416-327-4387, Fax: 416-314-5915, ruth.hawkins@ontario.ca
Director, HR Ontario Strategic Business Unit, Lori Aselstine
416-327-8747, Fax: 416-327-7580, lori.aselstine@ontario.ca
Director, Health Audit Service Team, Ken Flynn
416-327-7786, Fax: 416-327-7809, ken.flynn@ontario.ca
Director, Supply Chain & Facilities Branch, Paul Latremouille
416-327-0782, Fax: 416-327-7312, paul.latremouille@ontario.ca
Director, Fiscal Oversight & Performance Branch, Michael Parzei
416-327-8674, michael.parzei@ontario.ca
Director, Corporate Management Branch, Michele Sanborn
416-326-5725, Fax: 416-327-2714, michele.sanborn@ontario.ca
Director, Accounting Policy & Financial Reporting, Joy Stevenson
416-327-7350, Fax: 416-327-7364, joy.stevenson@ontario.ca
Director, Financial Management Branch, Pier Faltico
416-212-0723, Fax: 416-212-0683, pier.falotico@ontario.ca

Direct Services Division
56 Wellesley St. West, 2nd Fl., Toronto, ON M5S 2S3
416-314-5915

Assistant Deputy Minister, Patricia Li
416-327-4845, Fax: 416-314-5915, patricia.li@ontario.ca
Director, Emergency Health Services (Land & Air), Malcolm Bates
416-327-7909, Fax: 416-327-7879, malcolm.bates@ontario.ca
Director, Psychiatric Patient Advocate Office, Vahe Kehyayan
416-327-7007, Fax: 416-327-7008, vahe.kehyayan@ontario.ca
Director, Assistive Devices Program, Susan Picarello
416-212-5906, Fax: 416-327-8192, susan.picarello@ontario.ca
Director, Registration & Claims Branch, Dianne Wylie
613-548-6454, Fax: 416-548-6320, dianne.wylie@ontario.ca

Health Human Resources Strategy Division
Macdonald Block, #M2-61, 900 Bay St., 2nd Fl., Toronto, ON M7A 1R3
416-212-6115 Fax: 416-314-3751

Acting Assistant Deputy Minister, Suzanne McGurn
416-212-7688, Fax: 416-314-3751, suzanne.mcgurn@ontario.ca
Provincial Chief Nursing Officer, Debra Bournes
416-212-4835, Fax: 416-327-1878, debra.bournes@ontario.ca
Director, Health Sector Labour Market Policy, John Amodeo
416-212-0873, Fax: 416-325-9827, john.amodeo@ontario.ca
Director, Health Human Resources Policy, Jeff Goodyear
416-327-7482, Fax: 416-327-9429, jeff.goodyear@ontario.ca
Director, Health Professionals Regulatory Policy & Programs Branch, Marilyn Wang
416-327-8888, Fax: 416-327-8879, marilyn.wang@ontario.ca

Health Services Information & Information Technology Cluster
56 Wellesley St. West, 10th Fl., Toronto, ON M5S 2S3
416-314-4243 Fax: 416-314-0289

Chief Information Officer, Lorelle Taylor
416-314-1276, Fax: 416-314-0289, lorelle.taylor@ontario.ca
Director, Business & Financial Services Branch, Raj Sharda
416-327-6962, Fax: 416-314-4182, raj.sharda@ontario.ca
Head, Business Consulting & Governance Branch, Joan Berry
416-326-7133, Fax: 416-314-0289, joan.berry@ontario.ca
Acting Head, I&IT Strategy & Architecture Branch, Kevan Malden
613-548-6395, Fax: 613-548-6587, kevan.malden@ontario.ca
Head, Technology management & Solutions Integration, Shelley Woods
613-548-6688, Fax: 416-327-4429, shelley.woods@ontario.ca

Health System Accountability & Performance Division
Hepburn Block, 80 Grosvenor St., 5th Fl., Toronto, ON M7A 1R3
416-212-1859

Assistant Deputy Minister, Alexander Bezzina
416-212-1134, Fax: 416-212-1859, alexander.bezzina@ontario.ca
Provincial Lead, Critical Care & Trauma, Dr. Bernard Lawless
416-340-4800, Fax: 416-212-1859, lawlessb@smh.toronto.on.ca
Director, Implementation Branch, Melissa Farrell
416-327-7135, melissa.farrell@ontario.ca
Acting Director, Performance Improvement & Compliance Branch, Rachel E. Kampus
416-212-2362, rachel.e.kampus@ontario.ca
Director, LHIN Liaison Branch, Kathryn McCulloch
416-314-1864, kathryn.mcculloch@ontario.ca

Health System Information Management & Investment Division
1075 Bay St., 13th Fl., Toronto, ON M5S 2B1
416-212-1852 Fax: 416-327-8835

Assistant Deputy Minister, Don Young
416-327-8854, don.young@ontario.ca
Director, Health Capital Investment Branch, James Alberding
416-314-0402, james.alberding@ontario.ca
Director, Health Analytics Branch, Sten Ardal
416-327-6483, sten.ardal@ontario.ca
Director, Information Management Strategy & Policy Branch, Alison Blair
416-212-4433, alison.blair@ontario.ca
Director, Special Projects, Aileen Chan
416-325-2311, aileen.chan@ontario.ca
Director, E-Health Liaison Branch, Greg Hein
416-325-9075, greg.hein@ontario.ca
Director, Health System Funding Policy, Christina Hoy
416-326-5707, christina.hoy@ontario.ca
Director, Health Data Branch, Jeanette Munshaw
416-212-9163, jeanette.munshaw@ontario.ca
Director, Knowledge Management Branch, Ann-Marie Strapp
416-327-8453, ann-marie.strapp@ontario.ca

Health System Strategy & Policy Division
Hepburn Block, 80 Grosvenor St., 8th Fl., Toronto, ON M7A 1R3
416-327-8295 Fax: 416-327-5109

Assistant Deputy Minister, Dr. Vasanthi Srinivasan
416-327-7261, Fax: 416-327-5109, vasanthi.srinivasan@ontario.ca
Senior Medical Scientific & Health Technology Advisor, Dr. Leslie Levin
416-314-0249, les.levin@ontario.ca
Director, Community & Population Health Branch, Sheree Davis
416-327-8319, Fax: 416-314-8275, sheree.davis@ontario.ca
Acting Director, System Policy & Strategy Branch, Sylvia Moustacalis
416-212-4366, sylvia.moustacalis@ontario.ca
Director, Policy Care Standards Branch, Susan Paetkau
416-327-8533, susan.paetkau@ontario.ca

Acting Director, Planning, Research & Analysis Branch, Alison Paprica
416-327-0951, Fax: 416-327-3200, alison.paprica@ontario.ca
Director, Strategic Alignment Branch, Richard Prial
416-327-1535, Fax: 416-212-7144, richard.prial@ontario.ca
Manager, Intergovernmental Relations Unit, Louis Dimitracopoulos
416-327-8850, louis.dimitracopoulos@ontario.ca

Negotiations & Accountability Management Division
Hepburn Block, 80 Grosvenor St., 5th Fl., Toronto, ON M7A 1R3
416-212-7012 Fax: 416-327-5186
Assistant Deputy Minister, Susan Fitzpatrick
416-212-7012, susan.fitzpatrick@ontario.ca
Director, Health Quality Branch, L. Miin Alikhan
416-325-2658, miin.alikhan@ontario.ca
Acting Director, Negotiations, David Clarke
613-212-4904, david.w.clarke@ontario.ca
Director, Primary Health Care, Mary Fleming
613-650-5430, mary.fleming@ontario.ca
Director, Diagnostic Services & Planning Branch, Sandy Nuttall
416-212-4576, sandy.nuttall@ontario.ca
Director, Provincial Programs Branch, Kathryn Pagonis
416-326-3834, kathryn.pagonis@ontario.ca
Director, Health Services Branch, Pauline Ryan
613-536-3031, pauline.ryan@ontario.ca

Ontario Public Drug Programs Division
Hepburn Block, 80 Grosvenor St., 9th Fl., Toronto, ON M7A 1R3
416-212-4724 Fax: 416-327-5219
Assistant Deputy Minister & Executive Officer, Diane MacArthur
416-327-0902, diane.mcarthur@ontario.ca
Director, Drug Program Services, Brent Fraser
416-327-8315, brent.fraser@ontario.ca
Director, Exceptional Access Program Branch, Lana Sheinbaum
416-327-8118, lana.sheinbaum@ontario.ca

Ontario Ministry of Health Promotion & Sport

College Park, 777 Bay Street, 18th Fl., Toronto, ON M7A 1S5
416-326-8475 Fax: 416-326-4864
info@mhp.gov.on.ca
www.mhp.gov.on.ca
TTY: 866-263-1410
Other Communication: Sport & Recreation Inquiries: 416-314-7440; Chronic Disease Inquiries: 416-327-7384; Smoke-Free Ontario Cessation & Prevention Inquiries: 416-327-7384

Formed in 2005, the Ministry assists people in Ontario to lead healthier lives. To accomplish this goal, the Ministry works with partners, stakeholders & all levels of government to deliver programs which promote healthy choices & lifestyles. As of October 2011, the Ministry will be folded into Health & Long-Term Care.

Acts Administered:
Community Recreation Centres Act
Health Protection & Promotion Act (sec. 7)
Ministry of Health and Long-Term Care Act
Ministry of Tourism & Recreation Act
Smoke-Free Ontario Act

Minister, Hon. Deborah Matthews
416-326-8500, Fax: 416-326-8520, dmatthews.mpp.co@liberal.ola.org
Deputy Minister, Judith Wright
416-326-8481, Fax: 416-326-8409, judith.wright@ontario.ca
Assistant Deputy Minister, Pan/Parapan Am Games, Tim Casey
416-326-4832, Fax: 416-326-8409, tim.casey@ontario.ca
Parliamentary Assistant, Jean-Marc Lalonde
416-325-7289, Fax: 416-325-9006, jmlalonde.mpp.rockland@liberal.ola.org
Chief Medical Officer of Health, Public Health Division, Dr. Arlene King
416-212-3831, Fax: 416-325-8412, arlene.king@ontario.ca
Chief Information Officer, Health Services I&IT Cluster, Lorelle Taylor
416-314-1279, Fax: 416-314-0289, lorelle.taylor@ontario.ca
Director, Communications, Garth Cramer
416-326-4863, Fax: 416-326-4864, garth.cramer@ontario.ca
Director, Legal Services, Janice B. Crawford
416-327-8565, Fax: 416-327-8605, janice.b.crawford@ontario.ca
Acting Manager, Planning & Operations, Emergency Management Unit, Clint Shingler
416-327-8865, clint.shingler@ontario.ca

Sport, Public Health & Community Programs
416-326-4371 Fax: 416-326-4366
Assistant Deputy Minister, Steve Harlow
416-212-7397, steve.harlow@ontario.ca
Director, Sport, Recreation & Community Programs Branch, Rick Beaver
416-314-7696, rick.beaver@ontario.ca
Director, Standards, Programs & Community Development, Laura Pisko
416-327-7745, Fax: 416-314-5497, laura.pisko@ontario.ca

Strategic Policy Division
Assistant Deputy Minister, Kate Manson-Smith
416-326-4790, kate.manson-smith@ontario.ca
Acting Director, Olha Dobush
416-325-5817, olha.dobush@ontario.ca
Director, Domenica Ozarko
416-326-4355, domenica.ozarko@ontario.ca

Health Promotion
416-326-4371 Fax: 416-326-4366
Acting Assistant Deputy Minister, Mary Beth Valentine
416-326-4790, marybeth.valentine@ontario.ca
Director, Chronic Desease Prevention & Health Promotion Branch, Pegeen Walsh
416-327-7445, Fax: 416-314-5497, pegeen.walsh@ontario.ca
Director, Sport & Recreation Branch, Janie Romoff
416-314-7185, janie.romoff@ontario.ca

Ontario Human Rights Commission

180 Dundas St. West, 7th Fl., Toronto, ON M7A 2R9
416-326-9511 Fax: 416-314-4494
800-387-9080
www.ohrc.on.ca
TTY: 800-308-5561

Chief Commissioner, Barbara Hall
416-314-4536
Chief Administrative Officer, Karen Pereira
416-314-4480, Fax: 416-314-4494, karen.pereira@ohrc.on.ca
Executive Director, Nancy Austin
416-326-0567, Fax: 416-325-2004, nancy.austin@ohrc.on.ca
Acting Director, Policy, Education, Monitoring & Outreach, Shaheen Azmi
416-314-4532, Fax: 416-314-4533, shaheen.azmi@ohrc.on.ca

Hydro One Inc.

North Tower, 483 Bay St., Toronto, ON M5G 2P5
416-345-5000
877-955-1155
customercommunications@HydroOne.com
www.HydroOne.com

President & Chief Executive Officer, Laura Formusa
Chief Financial Officer & Executive Vice-President, Corporate Support, Sandy Struthers
Chief Risk Officer & Senior Vice-President, John Fraser
Chief Investment & Pension Officer & Senior Vice-President, Robert Cultraro
Executive Vice-President, Operations, Peter Gregg
Executive Vice-President, Strategy, Carmine Marcello
Senior Vice-President, Customer Operations & President/Chief Executive Officer, Hydro One Remotes Inc., Myles D'Arcey
Senior Vice-President, Engineering & Project Delivery, Nairn McQueen
Senior Vice-President, Grid Operations, Wayne Smith
Vice-President, Health, Safety & Environment, John Macnamara
President & Chief Executive Officer, Hydro One Telecom Inc., Paul Marchant
President & Chief Executive Officer, Hydro One Brampton Inc., Remy Fernandes
General Counsel, Joe Agostino

Independent Electricity System Operator (IESO)

PO Box 4474 A, Toronto, ON M5W 4E5
905-403-6900 Fax: 905-403-6921
888-448-7777
customer.relations@ieso.ca
www.ieso.ca

President & Chief Executive Officer, Paul Murphy
paul.murphy@ieso.ca
Vice-President, Resource Integration, Bruce Campbell
416-506-2829, bruce.campbell@ieso.ca
Vice-President, Finance, Ted Leonard
ted.leonard@ieso.ca
Vice-President, Organizational Development, Bill Limbrick
bill.limbrick@ieso.ca
Vice-President, Operations, Kim Warren
kim.warren@ieso.ca
Vice-President, Corporate Relations, Terry Young
terry.young@ieso.ca
General Counsel & Corporate Secretary, Human Resources, Roy Stewart
roy.stewart@ieso.ca

Information & Privacy Commissioner of Ontario

#1400, 2 Bloor St. East, Toronto, ON M4W 1A8
416-326-3333 Fax: 416-325-9195
800-387-0073
info@ipc.on.ca
www.ipc.on.ca
TTY: 416-325-7539

The IPC is the oversight body for Ontario's three provincial freedom of information & protection of privacy statues, & is responsible for resolving appeals when government organizations refuse to grant access to information; investigating privacy complaints related to government-held information; ensuring government compliance with the acts; conducting research on access & privacy issues & providing advice on proposed government legislation & programs; educating the public on Ontario's access, privacy & personal health information laws & access & privacy issues; investigating complaints related to personal health information; reviewing policies & procedures, & ensuring compliance with the Personal Health Information Protection Act.

Acts Administered:
Freedom of Information & Protection of Privacy Act
Municipal Freedom of Information & Protection of Privacy Act
Personal Health Information Protection Act

Commissioner, Ann Cavoukian
416-326-3333, commissioner@ipc.on.ca
Assistant Commissioner, Privacy, Ken Anderson
416-326-3942, ken.anderson@ipc.on.ca
Assistant Commissioner, Access, Brian Beamish
416-326-3333, brian.beamish@ipc.on.ca
Director, Policy, Michelle Chibba
416-326-3966, michelle.chibba@ipc.on.ca
Registrar, Tribunal Services, Robert Binstock
416-326-0008, robert.binstock@ipc.on.ca

Ontario Ministry of Infrastructure

Mowat Block, 900 Bay St., 5th Fl., Toronto, ON M7A 1C2
888-668-4636
www.moi.gov.on.ca
TTY: 800-239-4224

Acts Administered:
Electricity Act
Green Energy Act
Ministry of Infrastructure Act, 2011
Ontario Infrastructure & Lands Corporation Act
Places to Grow Act
Toronto Waterfront Revitalization Corporation Act

Minister, Hon. Bob Chiarelli
416-325-5270, Fax: 416-325-8860, bchiarelli.mpp.co@liberal.ola.org
Deputy Minister, Drew Fagan
416-212-0646, Fax: 416-212-0641
Assistant Deputy Minister, Corporate Development Division/Regulatory Affairs & Strategic Policy, John Whitehead
416-325-6544, Fax: 416-314-3354, john.whitehead@ontario.ca
Provincial Development Facilitator, Paula Dill
416-325-9764, Fax: 416-325-0209, paula.dill@ontario.ca
Acting Director, Legal Services, Halyna Perun
416-325-6681, Fax: 416-325-1781, halyna.perun2@ontario.ca
Director, Communications Branch, Rula Sharkawi
416-327-6541, Fax: 416-326-3947, rula.sharkawi@ontario.ca

Associated Agencies, Boards & Commissions:
• Infrastructure Ontario
College Park
777 Bay St., 6th Fl.
Toronto, ON M5G 2C8
416-327-6008 Fax: 416-326-9291
info@infrastructureontario.ca
www.infrastructureontario.ca
Management of complex infrastructure projects identified in the government's mulit-year capital plan as alternative financing & procurement projects.
• Ontario Realty Corporation
#2000, 1 Dundas St. West
Toronto, ON M5G 2L5
416-327-3937 Fax: 416-327-1906 877-863-9672
feedback@ontariorealty.ca
www.ontariorealty.ca
Other Communication: Accounts Payable Fax: 416-327-1834
The Ontario Realty Corporation manages one of the largest real estate portfolios in Canada, consisting of approximately 6,000 buildings and structures and over 80,000 acres of land across the province. The portfolio includes a wide variety of properties ranging from detention centres to office space, courthouses and heritage buildings.

• Waterfront Toronto
#1310, 20 Bay St.
Toronto, ON M5J 2N8
416-241-1344 Fax: 416-214-4591
info@waterfrontoronto.ca
www.waterfrontoronto.ca

Infrastructure Policy & Planning Division
Frost Bldg. South, 7 Queen's Park Cres., 6th Fl., Toronto, ON M7A 1Y7
416-325-9411 Fax: 416-325-8851
Assistant Deputy Minister, Chris Giannekos
416-325-5621, chris.giannekos@ontario.ca
Director, Infrastructure Planning & Budgeting, Adrian Franko
416-325-3307, adrian.franko@ontario.ca
Director, Infrastructure Implementation Secretariat, Heather Fraser
416-326-3340, heather.fraser@ontario.ca
Director, Infrastructure Economics & Finance Branch, John Gerritsen
416-325-6801, john.gerritsen@ontario.ca
Director, Infrastructure Partnerships Branch, Joe Iannace
416-325-3359, joe.iannace@ontario.ca
Director, Infrastructure Policy Branch, Kelly Shields
416-325-3349, kelly.shields@ontario.ca

Ontario Growth Secretariat
College Park, #425, 777 Bay St., Toronto, ON M5G 2E5
416-325-1210 Fax: 416-325-7405
866-479-9781
Assistant Deputy Minister, Victor Severino
416-325-5803, victor.severino@ontario.ca
Director, Growth Policy, Planning & Analysis Branch, Tija Dirks
416-325-1546, Fax: 416-325-7403, tija.dirks@ontario.ca
Director, Partnerships & Consultation Branch, Hannah Evans
416-325-5799, Fax: 416-325-7403, hannah.evans@ontario.ca

Strategic Real Estate Asset Management
College Park, 777 Bay St., 4th Fl., Toronto, ON M5G 2E5
416-327-5596 Fax: 416-325-4920
Assistant Deputy Minister, Victoria Vidal-Ribas
416-314-4835, victoria.vidal-ribas@ontario.ca
Acting Director, Accommodation & Property Management Policy Branch, Maggie Allan
416-212-1167, maggie.allan@ontario.ca
Director, Policy & Planning Branch, Barbara Ko
416-327-2840, barbara.ko@ontario.ca
Director, Real Estate Policy Branch, Bruce Singbush
416-326-1766, bruce.singbush2@ontario.ca

Office of the Integrity Commissioner

#2101, 2 Bloor St. East, Toronto, ON M4W 1A8
416-314-8983 Fax: 416-314-8987
integrity.mail@oico.on.ca
www.oico.on.ca

The Commissioner administers the Member's Integrity Act, 1994 as it applies to members of the Legislative Assembly & Executive Council in Ontario, including the filing of Public Disclosure Statements, & the right to conduct an inquiry if there are reasonable & probable grounds to believe that the Act has been contravened. The Commissioner also has responsiblity under the MPP Compensation Reform Act (Arm's Length Process), 2001 & the Accountability for Expenses Act (Cabinet Ministers & Opposition Leaders), 2002
Commissioner, Lynn Morrison
416-314-8983, lynn.morrison@oico.on.ca
Office Assistant, Janelle King
416-314-8983, janelle.king@oico.on.ca

Lobbyists Registration Office
#2101, 2 Bloor St. E., Toronto, ON M4W 1A8
416-327-4053 Fax: 416-327-4017
lobbyist.mail@oico.on.ca
lobbyist.oico.on.ca
Under the Lobbyists Registration Act, 1998, the Registrar is responsible for administering the lobbyist registration process, ensuring paid lobbyists report their lobbying of public office holders by filing a return; & ensuring public accessibility to the information contained in the lobbyist's registry.
Registrar, Lynn Morrison
416-327-4053, lynn.morrison@oico.on.ca

Ontario Ministry of Intergovernmental Affairs

77 Wellesley St. West, Toronto, ON M7A 1N3
416-325-4800 Fax: 416-325-4787
www.ontario.ca/en/your_government/ONT06_023584
Acts Administered:
Ministry of Intergovernmental Affairs Act
Minister & Premier, Hon. Dalton McGuinty
416-325-7754, Fax: 416-325-7755, dmcguinty.mpp.co@liberal.ola.org
Deputy Minister, Paul Genest
416-314-9710, paul.genest@ontario.ca
Assistant Deputy Minister, Economics & Justice, Craig McFadyen
416-325-4603, craig.mcfadyen@ontario.ca
Assistant Deputy Minister, Health, Social, Environment & National Institutions, Ernie Bartucci
416-325-4804, ernie.bartucci@ontario.ca
Assistant Deputy Minister & Chief of Protocol, Office of International Relations & Protocol, Mary Shenstone
416-325-8545, mary.shenstone@ontario.ca

Ontario Ministry of Labour

400 University Ave., 14th Fl., Toronto, ON M7A 1T7
416-326-7160
800-531-5551
www.labour.gov.on.ca
TTY: 866-567-8893

Advances safe, fair & harmonious workplace practices that are essential to the social & economic well-being of the people of Ontario. Through the ministry's key areas of occupational health & safety, employment rights & responsibilities, labour relations & internal administration, the ministry's mandate is to set, communicate & enforce workplace standards while encouraging greater workplace self-reliance. A range of specialized agencies, boards & commissions assist the ministry in its work.
Acts Administered:
Ambulance Services Collective Bargaining Act
Crown Employees Collective Bargaining Act, 2011
Employment Standards Act, 2011
Fire Protection & Prevention Act
Hospital Labour Disputes Arbitration Act
Labour Relations Act
Ministry of Labour Act
Occupational Health & Safety Act
Control of Exposure to Biological or Chemical Agents Regulations
Designated Substance Regulations (Various)
Workplace Hazardous Materials Information System (WHMIS) Regulations
Pay Equity Act
Public Sector Dispute Resolution Act
Public Sector Labour Relations Transitions Act
Rights of Labour Act
Workplace Safety & Insurance Act
Back to School Act (Hamilton-Wentworth District School Board), 2000
Back to School Act (Simcoe Muskoka Catholic District School Board), 2002
Back to School (Toronto & Windsor), 2001
Back to School Act (Toronto Catholic Elementary) & Education & Provincial Schools Negotiations Amendment Act, 2003
City of Toronto Labour Disputes Resolution Act
Employment Protection for Foreign Nationals Act (Live-in Caregivers & Others), 2009
Fairness for Parents & Employees Act (Teachers' Withdrawal of Services), 1997
Regulatory Modernization Act, 2007
SARS Assistance & Recovery Strategy Act, 2003
Toronto Public Transit Service Resumption Act, 2008
Toronto Transit Commission Labour Disputes Resolution Act, 2011
York University Labour Disputes Resolution Act, 2009
Minister, Hon. Linda Jeffrey
416-326-7600, Fax: 416-326-1449, ljeffrey.mpp.co@liberal.ola.org
Deputy Minister, Cynthia Morton
416-326-7576, Fax: 416-326-0507, www.labour.gov.on.ca
Chief Information Officer, Ken Kawall
416-327-1955, Fax: 416-327-3755, ken.kawall@ontario.ca
Chief Prevention Officer, George Gritziotis
416-314-6342, george.gritziotis@ontario.ca
Director, Legal Services, Bridget Lynett
416-326-7953, Fax: 416-326-7985, bridget.lynett@ontario.ca
Director, Health & Safety Review Project Secretariat, John Vander Doelen
416-325-9280, Fax: 416-325-9286, john.vanderdoelen@ontario.ca
Director, Communications & Marketing, Tom Zach
416-326-7404, Fax: 416-314-5809, tom.zach@ontario.ca

Associated Agencies, Boards & Commissions:
• Office of the Employer Advisor
#704, 151 Bloor St. West.
Toronto, ON M5S 1S4
416-327-0020 Fax: 416-327-0726 800-387-0774
www.employeradviser.ca
Advise & represent employers with fewer than 100 employees in relation to worker's compensation issues at no cost to the employer.
• Office of the Worker Advisor
#1300, 123 Edward St.
Toronto, ON M5G 1E2
416-325-8570 Fax: 416-325-4830 800-435-8980
www.owa.gov.on.ca
• Ontario Labour Relations Board (OLRB)
505 University Ave., 2nd Fl.
Toronto, ON M5G 2P1
416-326-7500 Fax: 416-326-7531 877-339-3335 TTY: 416-212-7036
www.olrb.gov.on.ca
• Pay Equity Commission
#300, 180 Dundas St. West
Toronto, ON M7A 2S6
416-314-1896 Fax: 416-314-8741 800-387-8813
www.payequity.gov.on.ca
• Workplace Safety & Insurance Appeals Tribunal
505 University Ave., 7th Fl.
Toronto, ON M5G 2P2
416-314-8800 Fax: 416-326-5164 888-618-8846 TTY: 416-314-1787
www.wsiat.on.ca
• Workplace Safety & Insurance Board

Internal Administrative Services Division
416-326-7586 Fax: 416-326-5809
Assistant Deputy Minister & Chief Administrative Officer, Len Marino
416-326-7305, Fax: 416-326-5809, len.marino@ontario.ca
Director, Finance & Administration, Susan Flanagan
416-326-7271, Fax: 416-326-9069, susan.flanagan@ontario.ca
Director, Strategic Business Unit, Marcelina Galvan
416-326-7215, marcelina.galvan@ontario.ca

Operations Division
416-326-7606 Fax: 416-212-4455
Assistant Deputy Minister, Sophie Dennis
416-326-7665, sophie.dennis@ontario.ca
Acting Director, Employment Practices, Stephen Grier
416-326-7004, Fax: 416-326-7061, stephen.grier@ontario.ca
Director, Divisional Learning Unit, Don Hall
905-577-1238, don.hall@ontario.ca
Director, Occupational Health & Safety, Renu Kulendran
416-326-7866, Fax: 416-326-7242, renu.kulendran@ontario.ca

Regional Offices:

Central East
#1600, 5001 Yonge St., Toronto, ON M7A 0A3
647-777-5005 Fax: 647-777-5010
Regional Director, Ken Fox
647-777-5112, ken.fox@ontario.ca

Central West
#400, 1290 Central Pkwy. West, Mississauga, ON L5C 4R3
416-235-5330 Fax: 416-235-5355
877-202-0008
TTY: 866-567-8893
Regional Director, Jody Young
905-615-6543, jody.young@ontario.ca

Eastern
Preston Sq., 347 Preston St., 4th Fl., Ottawa, ON K1S 3J4
613-228-8050 Fax: 613-727-2900
Regional Director, Sandra Lawson
613-727-2844, Fax: 613-727-2900, sandra.lawson@ontario.ca

Northern
#301, 159 Cedar St., Sudbury, ON P3E 6A5
705-564-7400 Fax: 705-670-7435
800-461-6325
TTY: 866-567-8893
Regional Director, Peter Augruso
705-564-7433, peter.augruso@ontario.ca

Western
119 King St. West, 13th Fl., Hamilton, ON L8P 4Y7
905-577-6221 Fax: 905-577-1200
800-263-6906
Regional Director, Filomena Savoia
905-577-1238, filomena.savoia@ontario.ca

Policy, Program Development & Dispute Resolution Services
416-326-7558 Fax: 416-326-7599
The Division provides the Minister & senior officials with information, analysis & advice to assist in the development, adoption & implementation of policies, programs & legislation related to the workplace. The division includes policy & information co-ordination.
Assistant Deputy Minister, Kevin J. Wilson
416-326-7555, Fax: 416-326-7599, kevin.j.wilson@ontario.ca
Acting Director, Corporate Policy Branch, Janis Bartley
416-327-0001, janis.bartley@ontario.ca
Acting Director, Employment & Labour Policy & Program Development Branch, Careen Jones
416-326-0809, Fax: 416-314-5855, careen.jones@ontario.ca
Acting Director, Jobs Protection Office, Bob Onyschuk
613-260-8363, Fax: 613-260-8369, bob.onyschuk@ontario.ca

Acting Director, Health & Safety Policy & Program Development Branch, Maria Papoutsis
416-326-7628, Fax: 416-314-7650, maria.papoutsis@ontario.ca
Director, Dispute Resolution Services, Reg Pearson
416-326-7322, Fax: 416-314-8755, reg.pearson@ontario.ca

Ontario Ministry of Municipal Affairs & Housing

College Park, 777 Bay St., 17th Fl., Toronto, ON M5G 2E5
416-585-7041 Fax: 416-585-6470
866-220-2290
mininfo@ontario.ca
www.mah.gov.on.ca
TTY: 866-220-2290
Other Communication: TTY: 416-585-6991

Responsible for providing provincial leadership in defining the framework for governance, finances & management for the local government systems; as well as leadership in the development & administration of the legislative & policy framework for land use planning. It is also responsible for providing the operational, policy & accountability framework for local government to fund & administer social housing; policy & program instruments to create a competitive marketplace for rental housing; & the regulatory framework for buildings.

Acts Administered:
Barrie-Innisfil Boundary Adjustment Act, 2009
Building Code Act
City of Greater Sudbury Act
City of Hamilton Act
City of Kawartha Lakes Act
City of Ottawa Act
City of Toronto Act, 2006
Commercial Tenancies Act
Development Charges Act
Elderly Person's Housing Aid Act
Geographic Township of Creighton-Davies Act
Greenbelt Act
Housing Development Act
Ministry of Municipal Affairs & Housing Act
Municipal Act
Municipal Affairs Act
Municipal Arbitrations Act
Municipal Conflict of Interest Act
Municipal Corporations Quieting Orders Act
Municipal Elections Act
Municipal Extra-Territorial Tax Act
Municipal Franchises Act
Municipal Tax Assistance Act
Oak Ridges Moraine Conservation Act
Oak Ridges Moraine Protection Act, 2001
Designation of the Oak Ridges Moraine Area
Municipalities that are Required to Prepare & Adopt Official Plan Amendments
Oak Ridges Moraine Conservation Plan
Ontario Mortgage & Housing Corporation Act
Ontario Municipal Employees Retirement System Act, 2006
Planning Act
Public Utilities Act
Road Access Act
Shoreline Property Assistance Act
Social Housing Reform Act
Statute Labour Act
Tax Sales Confirmation Act
Toronto Islands Residential Community Stewardship Act
Town of Haldimand Act
Town of Moosonee Act
Town of Norfolk Act
Housing Services Act, 2011
Line Fences Act
OC Transpo Payments Act
Ontario Planning & Development Act
Regional Municipality of Peel Act, 2005
Residential Tenancies Act, 2006
Territorial Division Act

Minister, Hon. Kathleen Wynne
416-585-7000, minister.mah@ontario.ca; kwynne.mpp.co@liberal.ola.org
Deputy Minister, William Forward
416-585-7100, william.forward@ontario.ca
Chief Information Officer & Assistant Deputy Minister, Soussan Tabari
416-326-8216, Fax: 416-325-8371, soussan.tabari@ontario.ca
Director, Communications, Jodi Melnychuk
416-585-6900, jodi.melnychuk@ontario.ca
Executive Assistant, Communications Branch, Lina Minniti
416-585-7105, Fax: 416-585-6227, lina.minniti@ontario.ca

Associated Agencies, Boards & Commissions:
• Building Code Commission (BCC)
777 Bay St., 2nd Fl.
Toronto, ON M5G 2E5
416-585-6666 Fax: 416-585-7531
www.mah.gov.on.ca/Page7394.aspx
Works with the municipal & building sectors & consumer groups to improve & streamline the building regulatory system. This leads to efficient development & more construction jobs, while protecting public safety. The Branch administers the Building Code Act (BCA) & the Ontario Building Code (OBC), which govern the construction of new buildings & the renovation & maintenance of existing buildings. It provides enforcement officials & other building code users with advice & information so that they can apply building code requirements more consistently.
• Building Materials Evaluation Commission (BMEC)
777 Bay St., 2nd Fl.
Toronto, ON M5G 2E5
416-585-4234 Fax: 416-585-7531
www.mah.gov.on.ca/Page8295.aspx

Business Management Division
416-585-7209 Fax: 416-585-6191

Assistant Deputy Minister, Pam Skinner
416-585-6670, Fax: 416-585-6191, pam.skinner@ontario.ca
Director, Controllership & Financial Planning, Jim Cassimatis
416-585-7693, Fax: 416-585-7328, jim.cassimatis@ontario.ca
Director, Legal Services, Joanne Davies
416-585-6551, Fax: 416-585-4003, joanne.davies@ontario.ca
Director, Information Technology Service Management, Joanne Hiscock
416-327-1087, Fax: 416-327-1093, joanne.hiscock@ontario.ca
Director, Human Resources Strategies Branch, Diane Phillipson
416-585-6742, Fax: 416-585-7259, diane.phillipson@ontario.ca
Director, Corporate Planning, Karen Rodman
416-585-7321, Fax: 416-585-7643, karen.rodman@ontario.ca

Housing Division
416-585-6238 Fax: 416-585-6800

Assistant Deputy Minister, Janet Hope
416-585-6755, janet.hope@ontario.ca
Director, Housing Programs Branch, Rob Cressman
416-585-7021, rob.cressman@ontario.ca
Director, Housing Funding & Risk Management Branch, Keith Extrance
416-585-7524, keith.extance@ontario.ca
Director, Housing Policy, Melissa Thomson
416-585-6400, Fax: 416-585-7607, melissa.thomson@ontario.ca

Local Government & Planning Policy Division
416-585-6320 Fax: 416-585-6463

Assistant Deputy Minister, Dana Richardson
416-585-6320, Fax: 416-585-6463, dana.richardson@ontario.ca
Director, Provincial Planning Policy Branch, Audrey Bennett
416-585-6072, Fax: 416-585-6870, audrey.bennett@ontario.ca
Director, Municipal Finance Policy Branch, Trevor Bingler
416-585-6951, Fax: 416-585-6315, trevor.bingler@ontario.ca
Director, Intergovernmental Relations & Partnerships Branch, Diane McArthur-Rodgers
416-585-6047, Fax: 416-585-7638, diane.mcarthur-rodgers@ontario.ca
Director, Local Government Policy Branch, Ralph Walton
416-585-7260, Fax: 416-585-7638, ralph.walton@ontario.ca

Municipal Services Division
Fax: 416-585-6445

Assistant Deputy Minister, Elizabeth Harding
416-585-6427, Fax: 416-585-6445, Liz.Harding@ontario.ca
Acting Director, Building & Development Branch, Denise K. Evans
416-585-6656, Fax: 416-585-7531, denise.k.evans@ontario.ca
Acting Director, Municipal Programs & Education Branch, Donna Simmonds
416-585-7226, Fax: 416-585-7292, donna.simmonds@ontario.ca

Municipal Services Offices:

Central
777 Bay St., 2nd Fl., Toronto, ON M5G 2E5
416-585-6226 Fax: 416-585-6882
800-668-0230
Regional Director, Larry Clay
416-585-7264, Fax: 416-585-6882, larry.clay@ontario.ca

Eastern
Rockwood House, 8 Estate Lane, Postal Bag 2500, Kingston, ON K7M 9A8
613-545-2100 Fax: 613-548-6822
800-267-9438
Regional Director, Vincent Fabilli
613-545-2133, Fax: 613-548-6822, vincent.fabiilli@ontario.ca

Northeastern
#401, 159 Cedar St., Sudbury, ON P3E 6A5
705-564-0120 Fax: 705-564-6863
800-461-1193
Regional Director, Lynn Buckham
705-564-6858, Fax: 705-564-6863, lynn.buckham@ontario.ca

Northwestern
#223, 435 James St. South, Thunder Bay, ON P7E 6S7
807-475-1651 Fax: 807-475-1196
800-465-5027
Acting Regional Director, Lynn Buckingham
807-475-1187, Fax: 807-475-1196, lynn.buckham@ontario.ca

Western
659 Exeter Rd., 2nd Fl., London, ON N6E 1L3
519-873-4020 Fax: 519-873-4018
800-265-4736
Regional Director, Micheline Riopelle
519-873-4037, Fax: 519-873-4018, micheline.riopelle@ontario.ca

Ontario Ministry of Natural Resources (MNR)

Whitney Block, #6630, 99 Wellesley St. West, 6th Fl., Toronto, ON M7A 1W3
800-667-1940
www.mnr.gov.on.ca

The MNR manages & protects natural resources in the province for wise use. Working with environmental organizations, private industries, fish & game associations, researchers, & other government agencies, the MNR is responsible for the following areas: science & information resources; forest management; fish & wildlife management; land & waters management; Ontario Parks; aviation & forest fire management; & geographic information.

Acts Administered:
Aggregate Resources Act
Algonquin Forestry Authority Act
An Act for the Settlement of certain Questions between the Governments of Canada & Ontario respecting Indian Reserve Lands
An Act to Confirm the title of the Government of Canada to certain Lands & Indian Lands
Arboreal Emblem Act
Beds of Navigable Waters Act
Conservation Authorities Act
Conservation Land Act
Conservation Bodies Land Regulation
Crown Forest Sustainability Act
Endangered Species Act, 2007
Endangered Species Regulation
Fish & Wildlife Conservation Act
Possession, Buying & Selling of Wildlife
Wildlife in Captivity
Wildlife Management Units
Wildlife Schedules
Forest Fires Prevention Act
Forestry Act
Forestry Workers Lien for Wages Act
Freshwater Fish Marketing Act (Ontario)
Gas & Oil Leases Act
Heritage Hunting & Fishing Act, 2002
Indian Lands Act
Industrial & Mining Lands Compensation Act
Kawartha Highlands Signature Site Park Act
Lake of the Woods Control Board Act
Lakes & Rivers Improvement Act
Mineral Emblem Act
Mining Act
Ministry of Natural Resources Act
Niagara Escarpment Planning & Development Act
North Georgian Bay Recreational Reserve Act
Oil, Gas & Salt Resources Act
Ontario Geographic Names Board Act
Ottawa River Water Powers Act
Designation of Parks
Guides in Quetico Provincial Park
Mining in Provincial Parks
Public Lands Act
Surveys Act
Wild Rice Harvesting Act
Wilderness Areas Act
Avian Emblem Act
Duffins Rouge Agricultural Preserve Act, 2005
Far North Act
Fish Inspection Act
Fisheries Loans Act
Indian Lands Agreement (1986) Confirmation Act, 2010
Professional Foresters Act
Provincial Parks & Conservation Reserves Act
Seine River Diversion Act
Surveyors Act

Minister, Hon. Michael Gravelle
416-314-2301, Fax: 416-325-5316, minister.mnr@ontario.ca; mgravelle.mpp.co@liberal.ola.org
Deputy Minister, David O'Toole
416-314-2150, Fax: 416-314-2159, david.o'toole@ontario.ca
Chief Information Officer, Robert Hollis
416-314-1528, Fax: 416-314-6901, robert.hollis@ontario.ca

Commissioner, Mining & Lands, Linda Kamerman
416-314-2322, Fax: 416-314-2327,
linda.kamerman@ontario.ca
Director, Legal Services, Anne Marie Gutierrez
416-314-2025, Fax: 416-314-2030,
annemarie.gutierrez@ontario.ca
Director, Ontario Resources & Labour Audit Service Team, Ray Masse
416-314-9208, Fax: 416-314-9220, ray.masse2@ontario.ca
Director, Communications, John Whytock
416-314-2119, Fax: 416-314-2102, john.whytock@ontario.ca
Parliamentary Assistant, David Orazietti
416-314-6467, Fax: 416-314-6470,
dorazietti.mpp.co@liberal.ola.org

Associated Agencies, Boards & Commissions:
• Academic & Experience Requirements Committee of the Association of Ontario Land Surveyors (AERC)
1043 McNicoll Ave.
Toronto, ON M1W 3W6
416-491-9020 Fax: 416-491-2576
• Algonquin Forestry Authority - Huntsville
222 Main St. West
Huntsville, ON P1H 1Y1
705-789-9647 Fax: 705-789-3353
info@algonquinforestry.on.ca
www.algonquinforestry.on.ca
Ensures the viability of the local forest industry while preserving the soil & water resources, fish & wildlife habitat & recreational areas in the park.
• Algonquin Forestry Authority - Pembroke
Victoria Centre
84 Isabella St., 2nd Fl.
Pembroke, ON K8A 5S5
613-735-0173 Fax: 613-735-4192
info@algonquinforestry.on.ca
www.algonquinforestry.on.ca
• Association of Ontario Land Surveyors
1043 McNicoll Ave.
Toronto, ON M1W 3W6
416-491-9020 Fax: 416-491-2576
• Ontario Fish & Wildlife Heritage Commission
Robinson Pl.
300 Water St.
PO Box 7000
Peterborough, ON K9J 8M5
705-755-1905 Fax: 705-755-1900
• Ontario Geographic Names Board
Robinson Place
300 Water St., 2nd Fl.
PO Box 7000
Peterborough, ON K9J 8M5
705-755-2134
The Board investigates the background of geographic names & recommends names to be used on maps.
• Ontario Moose & Bear Allocation Advisory Committee
PO Box 964
Sioux Lookout, ON P8T 1B3
807-737-2615 Fax: 807-737-4173
An independent advisory committee to allocate moose & bear hunting opportunities provided by the Ministry of Natural Resources within the tourism industry in a manner which is ecologically sustainable & supports the economic viability of the industry in general & specific tourist establishments.
• Ottawa River Regulation Planning Board / Commission de planification de la régularisation de la rivière des Outaouais
351 St Joseph Blvd.
Hull, QC J8Y 3Z5
613-994-7079 800-778-1246
secretariat@ottawariver.ca
www.ottawariver.ca
Established under the terms of a Canada-Ontario-Québec Agreement, it is responsible for the preparation & continuing review of policies, guidelines & criteria for the integrated management of the principal reservoirs of the Ottawa River Basin in order to reduce flood damages along the river, its tributaries & in the Montréal area; it is also responsible for the operation & coordination of inflow forecasting, flow routing & optimization models that will reduce flood damages while having the least possible impact on users of the basin.
• Rabies Advisory Committee
Trent University Science Complex
PO Box 4840
Peterborough, ON K9J 8N8
705-755-2270
Established in 1979 it advises the Minister on the development of suitable vaccines against rabies & an effective system for vaccinating wild animals.
• Shibogama Interim Planning Board
PO Box 105
Wunnumin, ON P0V 2Z0
807-442-2559 Fax: 807-442-2627
Advises the province on land use & resource development in an 11,131-square-kilometre area south of Big Trout Lake in northwestern Ontario.
• Windigo Interim Planning Board
PO Box 299
Sioux Lookout, ON P8T 1A3
807-737-1585 Fax: 807-737-3133
Advises the province on land use & resource development in two areas totalling 15,959 square kilometres south of Big Trout Lake.

Niagara Escarpment Commission (NEC)
232 Guelph St., Georgetown, ON L7G 4B1
905-877-5191 Fax: 905-873-7452
Responsible for implementing the Niagara Escarpment Planning & Development Act, which is designed to maintain the escarpment & surrounding area as a continuous natural environment & to ensure that all new development in the escarpment area is compatible with provincial goals of environmental protection & conservation. The commission is also the main source of information on the Niagara Escarpment & the Niagara Escarpment Plan.
Chair, Don Scott
905-877-5594, Fax: 905-873-7452, don.scott@ontario.ca
Director, Mark Frawley
905-877-4810, Fax: 905-873-7452, mark.frawley@ontario.ca

Corporate Management Division
416-314-1900 Fax: 416-314-1994
Assistant Deputy Minister, David Lynch
416-314-1939, Fax: 416-314-1994, david.lynch@ontario.ca, Other Communications: Alternate Phone: 705-755-2700
Director, Corporate Finance & Controllership Branch, Brian Baker
705-755-1857, brian.baker@ontario.ca
Director, Services & Infrastructure Management Branch, Larry Davis
705-755-2532, Fax: 705-755-2508, larry.davis@ontario.ca
Director, Strategic Human Resources Business Branch, Pat Freistatter
705-755-3131, pat.freistatter@ontario.ca

Provincial Services Division
416-326-9504
Field Services Division is the ministry's local presence in communities across the province, delivering integrated programs on resource management through 3 regions & 25 districts. The division delivers programs on provincial enforcement, native affairs, fisheries, forests & provincial lands, in addition to resources such as finance, facilities & engineering infrastructure, equipment & vehicles.
Assistant Deputy Minister, Tracey Mill
416-326-9502, tracey.mill@ontario.ca
Acting Director, Ontario Parks, Bruce Bateman
705-755-1702, Fax: 705-755-1701,
bruce.bateman@ontario.ca
Director, Enforcement Branch, Lois Deacon
705-755-1750, Fax: 705-755-1757, lois.deacon@ontario.ca
Director, Fish & Wildlife Services Branch, Mike Morencie
519-873-4609, Fax: 705-755-1901,
mike.morencie@ontario.ca
Director, Aviation, Forest Fire & Emergency Services Branch, Al Tithecott
705-945-5937, al.tithecott@ontario.ca

Regional Operations Division
Fax: 416-314-2629
800-667-1940
Assistant Deputy Minister, David de Launay
416-314-2621, david.delaunay@ontario.ca
Director, Far North Branch, Dianne Corbett
705-235-1284, Fax: 705-235-1106,
dianne.corbett@ontario.ca
Director, Integration Branch, Dan Marinigh
705-755-1620, Fax: 705-755-1201, dan.marinigh@ontario.ca

Regional Offices:

Northeast Region
Ontario Government Complex, 5520 Hwy. 101 East, PO Box 3020, South Porcupine, ON P0N 1H0
705-235-1157 Fax: 705-235-1246
Regional Director, Ginette Brindle
705-235-1153, Fax: 705-235-1226, ginette.brindle@ontario.ca

Northwest Region
Ontario Government Bldg., #221A, 435 James St. South, Thunder Bay, ON P7E 6S8
807-475-1261 Fax: 807-473-3023
Regional Director, Allan Willcocks
807-475-1264, allan.willcocks@ontario.ca
District Manager, Kim Groenendyk
807-887-5013, kim.groenendyk@ontario.ca

Southern Region
Robinson Place, South Tower, 300 Water St., 4th Fl. South, PO Box 7000, Peterborough, ON K9J 8M5
705-755-2000 Fax: 705-755-3233
Regional Director, Carrie Hayward
705-755-3235, carrie.hayward@ontario.ca

Policy Division
Fax: 416-314-1994
800-667-1940
Provides assistance, advice & direction to ministry staff at all levels, on a variety of compliance & law enforcement matters. The branch is responsible for the development, coordination & delivery of an Integrated Provincial Compliance Program which focuses on the promotion, monitoring & enforcement aspects of compliance.
Assistant Deputy Minister, Rosalyn Lawrence
416-314-6131, rosalyn.lawrence@ontario.ca
Director, Aboriginal Branch, Karan Aquino
705-755-1996, Fax: 705-755-1372, karan.aquino@ontario.ca
Director, Biodiversity Branch & Renewable Energy Program, Eric Boysen
705-755-5999, Fax: 705-755-2901, eric.boysen@ontario.ca
Director, Strategic Policy & Economics Branch, Craig Brown
416-314-1923, Fax: 416-314-1948, craig.brown@ontario.ca
Director, Natural Heritage, Lands & Protected Spaces Branch, Ray Pichette
705-755-1241, Fax: 705-755-1971, ray.pichette@ontario.ca
Director, Species at Risk Branch, Marc Rondeau
416-314-1819, Fax: 705-755-5483, marc.rondeau@ontario.ca
Director, Forests Branch, Chris M. Walsh
705-945-6653, Fax: 705-945-6667, chris.m.walsh@ontario.ca

Science & Information Resources Division
Roberta Bondar Pl., #400, 70 Foster Dr., Sault Ste Marie, ON P6A 6V5
705-755-2000 Fax: 705-755-2802
800-667-1940
The division leads the development & application of scientific knowledge, information management systems & information technologies in support of the Ministry mandate. The division is responsible for ensuring operational decision-making requirements of the Ministry are supported by sound science & reliable data, by providing accurate, relevant & timely information to manage resources in an ecologically sustainable manner.
Assistant Deputy Minister, Frank Kennedy
705-945-6703, Fax: 705-755-2802, frank.kennedy@ontario.ca
Acting Director, Science & Information Branch, Cameron Mack
705-755-1909, Fax: 705-945-6527,
cameron.mack@ontario.ca
Director, Geographic Information Branch, Brian Maloney
705-755-2204, Fax: 705-755-1640,
brian.j.maloney@ontario.ca
Director, Applied Research & Development Branch, Anne Neary
705-755-2807, Fax: 705-755-2802, anne.neary@ontario.ca

Niagara Falls Bridge Commission

PO Box 395, Niagara Falls, ON L2E 6T8
905-354-5641 Fax: 905-353-6644
Chair, Patrick Brown
Vice-Chair, Michael Goodale
Secretary, Ernest Smith
Treasurer, Thomas Pryce

Ontario Ministry of Northern Development, Mines & Forestry

99 Wellesley St. West, Toronto, ON M7A 1W3
416-327-0633 Fax: 416-327-0651
www.mndmf.gov.on.ca
TTY: 866-349-1388
Other Communication: Sudbury Phone: 705-670-5755; Fax: 705-670-5818
The Ministry of Northern Development & Mines is the only regional ministry within the government & plays a central role in northern affairs. MNDM supports the mineral industry by providing it with valuable information about the province's geology. It also delivers & administers Ontario's Mining Act to improve the investment climate for mineral development. The ministry has a two-fold mandate, to promote northern economic development & support mineral sector competitiveness. The ministry is developing an initiative to help Ontario's Far North communities attract environmentally sound development, work with First Nation communities, partner ministries, the federal government, the mineral sector & private sector stakeholders to create opportunities for residents to help First Nation communities become more self-reliant. The ministry works with the Northern Ontario Heritage Fund Corporation & with the Ontario Northland Transportation Commission to bring much-needed service improvements to the northeast.
Acts Administered:
Mining Act
Ministry of Northern Development, Mines & Forestry Act
Northern Services Boards Act
Ontario Northland Transportation Commission Act
Forestry Workers Lien for Wages Act
Northern Ontario Grow Bonds Corporation Act
Northern Ontario Grow Bonds Corporation Repeal Act, 2011
Northern Ontario Heritage Fund Act
Northern Forest Tenure Modernization Act, 2011
Professional Geoscientists Act

Minister, Hon. Rick Bartolucci
416-327-0633, Fax: 416-327-0665, ndmminister@ontario.ca; rbartolucci.mpp.co@liberal.ola.org
Deputy Minister, David O'Toole
416-212-2701, david.o'toole@ontario.ca
Assistant Deputy Minister, Ring of Fire Secretariat, Christine Kaszycki
705-670-5877, 888-415-9845, Fax: 705-670-5818, christine.kaszycki@ontario.ca
Director, Corporate Policy Secretariat, Alison Drummond
416-327-0302, Fax: 416-327-0634, alison.drummond@ontario.ca
Director, Legal Services, Andrew Macdonald
416-327-0640, Fax: 416-327-0646, andrew.macdonald@ontario.ca
Director, Communications Branch, Fadia Mishrigi
416-327-0687, Fax: 416-327-0664, fadia.mishrigi@ontario.ca

Associated Agencies, Boards & Commissions:
• Ontario Northland
555 Oak St. East
North Bay, ON P1B 8L3
705-472-4500 Fax: 705-472-4267 800-363-7512
info@ontarionorthland.ca
www.ontarionorthland.ca
• Owen Sound Transportation Company Ltd.
717875, Hwy. 6
Owen Sound, ON N4K 5N7
519-376-8740 800-265-3163
www.ontarioferries.com

Corporate Management Division
#704, 159 Cedar St., Sudbury, ON P3E 6A5
705-564-7443 Fax: 705-564-7447
Assistant Deputy Minister & Chief Adminstrative Officer, Don Ignacy
705-564-7443, Fax: 705-564-7447, don.ignacy@ontario.ca
Director, Human Resources Business Unit, Cleo Degagne
705-564-7445, Fax: 705-564-7942, cleo.degagne@ontario.ca

Forestry Division
Roberta Bondar Pl., #201, 70 Foster Dr., Sault Ste. Marie, ON P6A 6V5
Fax: 705-945-5977
800-667-1940
Assistant Deputy Minister, Bill Thornton
705-945-6660, bill.thornton@ontario.ca
Acting Director, Industry Relations Branch, David Hayhurst
705-945-5733, david.hayhurst@ontario.ca
Director, Forest Sector Competitiveness Secretariat, Kathleen McFadden
705-945-6767, kathleen.mcfadden@ontario.ca

Mines & Minerals Division
Willet Green Miller Centre, 933 Ramsey Lake Rd., Sudbury, ON P3E 6B5
705-670-5755 Fax: 705-670-5818
888-415-9845
The Mines & Minerals Division works to generate new wealth & benefits for the residents of Ontario by providing basic geological information gathering & interpretation in support of Ontario's exploration, mine development & mining sectors & the administration of Ontario's Mining Act in a fair & consistent fashion. Collects, analyzes & publishes valuable information about the state of the mining & mineral industries, as well as specific information about the location & quality of mineral deposits. The field staff throughout the province provide consultative services to the industry through all phases of the mining sequence, & include resident geologists, mining recorders & mineral development officers.
Assistant Deputy Minister, Ray Mantha
705-670-5755, Fax: 705-670-5818, ray.mantha@ontario.ca
Director, Mineral Development & Lands Branch, Cindy Blancher-Smith
705-670-5787, Fax: 705-670-5803, cindy.blancher-smith@ontario.ca
Director & Chief Gemmologist, Diamond Sector Unit, Ron Gashinski
705-670-5609, Fax: 705-670-5818, ron.gashinski@ontario.ca
Director, Aboriginal Relations Unit, Bernie Hughes
705-670-5743, Fax: 705-670-5818, bernie.hughes@ontario.ca
Director, Mining Act Modernization, Robert Merwin
705-670-5627, Fax: 416-327-0634, robert.merwin@ontario.ca
Director, Executive Projects Office, Indira Singh
807-475-1687, Fax: 705-475-1120, indira.singh1@ontario.ca

Northern Development Division
Roberta Bondar Place, #200, 70 Foster Dr., Sault Ste Marie, ON P6A 6V8
705-945-5900 Fax: 705-945-5931
800-461-2287
Other Communication: Delivery of Government Services: 705-945-5904
Responsible for promoting business, industrial, community & regional economic development & diversification; improving access to social & health services for northerners; planning & coordinating an integrated transportation system to meet private & commercial transportation needs at local, regional & provincial levels; coordinating the policies & programs of other ministries to ensure the special needs of northerners are addressed by government.
Assistant Deputy Minister, Cal McDonald
705-564-7569, Fax: 705-945-5932, cal.mcdonald@ontario.ca
Executive Director, Northern Ontario Heritage Fund Corporation, Bruce Strapp
705-945-6734, Fax: 705-564-7447, bruce.strapp@ontario.ca
Director, Strategic Development Branch, Faye Johnson
705-945-5903, Fax: 705-564-7597, faye.johnson@ontario.ca
Director, Regional Economic Development, Helen Mulc
705-564-7134, Fax: 705-564-7582, helen.mulc@ontario.ca

Area Offices:

Kenora
#104, 810 Robertson St., Kenora, ON P9N 4J2
807-468-2937 Fax: 807-468-2930
Manager, Christine Hansen
807-468-2938, christine.hansen@ontario.ca

North Bay
#203, 447 McKeown Ave., North Bay, ON P1B 9S9
705-494-4045 Fax: 705-494-4069
Manager, Moe Dorie
705-494-4176, moe.dorie@ontario.ca

Sault Ste. Marie
Roberta Bondar Place, #200, 70 Foster Dr., Sault Ste Marie, ON P6A 6V8
705-945-5914 Fax: 705-945-5931
Manager, Denis Rochon
705-356-3004, denis.rochon@ontario.ca

Sudbury
#601, 159 Cedar St., Sudbury, ON P3E 6A5
705-564-7517 Fax: 705-564-7583
Manager, Murray Morello
705-564-7519, murray.morello@ontario.ca

Thunder Bay
#332, 435 James St. South, Thunder Bay, ON P7E 6L3
807-475-1648 Fax: 807-475-1589
Manager, Dale Willis
807-475-1573, dale.willis@ontario.ca

Timmins
5520 Hwy. 101 East, PO Box 3060, South Porcupine, ON P0N 1H0
705-235-1664 Fax: 705-235-1660
Manager, Brian Pountney
705-235-1654, brian.pountney@ontario.ca

Office of the Ombudsman

Bell Trinity Sq., South Tower, 483 Bay St., 10th Fl., Toronto, ON M5G 2C9
416-586-3300 Fax: 416-586-3485
800-263-1830
info@ombudsman.on.ca
www.ombudsman.on.ca
TTY: 866-411-4211
Other Communication: Ligne sans frais: 1-800-387-2620 (Français)
An impartial body independent of government that investigates & resolves complaints about the administrative actions & decisions of provincial government organizations such as ministries, boards, agencies, commissions & tribunals. The Ombudsman is an Officer of the provincial Legislature & has jurisdiction over all provincial government organizations as an office of last resort. All available complaint & appeal procedures whenever possible should be used before the Ombudsman conducts an investigation. The Ombudsman decides cases based on independent investigations & works to find solutions that are acceptable to everyone involved. Services are free & confidential & are available in English, French or any other language.
Acts Administered:
Ombudsman Act
Ombudsman, André Marin
416-586-3300
Manager, Communications & Media Relations, Linda Williamson
416-586-3426, Fax: 416-586-3485

Ontario Power Generation

700 University Ave., Toronto, ON M5G 1X6
416-592-2555
877-592-2555
webmaster@opg.com
www.opg.com
Other Communication: Media Relations Email: media@opg.com; Investor Relations Email: investor.relations@opg.com
Mandate is to meet Ontario's requirements for electricity so as to result in the greatest overall benefit to the community & the lowest cost to the consumer, while operating in a safe & environmentally responsible manner. Assets include 3 nuclear generating stations, 5 fossil generating stations, 64 hydroelectric stations, 3 wind generating stations.
Chair, Hon. Jake Epp
President & Chief Executive Officer, Tom Mitchell
Chief Financial Officer, Donn Hanbridge
Senior Vice-President, Business Services & Information Technology, Robert Boguski
Executive Vice-President, Corporate Affairs, Bruce Boland
Executive Vice-President, Hydro, John Murphy
Senior Vice-President, Human Resources & Chief Ethics Officer, Barb Keenan
Senior Vice-President, Law & General Counsel, David Brennan
Chief Nuclear Officer, Wayne Robbins
Manager, Media Relations,
416-592-4008, media@opg.com, Other Communications: Toll-free Ontario: 877/592-4008

Ontario Ministry of Research & Innovation

Ferguson Block, 56 Wellesley St. West, 7th Fl., Toronto, ON M7A 2E7
416-325-5181 Fax: 416-325-3877
866-446-5216
www.mri.gov.on.ca
TTY: 416-325-9275
The Ministry of Research & Innovation works collaboratively across all government ministries to ensure improved coordination & alignment of research, commercialization & innovation activities & to foster a culture of innovation. The Ministry of Research & Innovation is also committed to engaging all external partners, including the private sector, education & research communities in supporting & delivering on the research & innovation agenda. As of October 2011, the Ministry will be folded into Economic Development.
Acts Administered:
Ontario Capital Growth Corporation Act
Water Opportunities Act
Minister, Hon. Brad Duguid
bduguid.mpp.co@liberal.ola.org
Deputy Minister, George Ross
416-325-7517, Fax: 416-325-5927, george.ross@ontario.ca

Associated Agencies, Boards & Commissions:
• Ontario Capital Growth Corporation
#1701, 393 University Ave.
Toronto, ON M5G 1E6
416-325-6874 Fax: 416-212-0794 877-422-5818
www.ocgc.gov.on.ca
The OCGC was established by the Ontario Capital Growth Corporation Act, 2008. The Corporation's main focus is the management of the Government of Ontario's interests in the Ontario Venture Capital Fund LP and the Ontario Emerging Technologies Fund.

Corporate Services Division
Hearst Block, 900 Bay St., 7th Fl., Toronto, ON M7A 2E1
416-325-6486 Fax: 416-325-6392
Assistant Deputy Minister & Chief Administrative Officer, David Clifford
416-325-6600, Fax: 416-325-6392, david.clifford@ontario.ca
Director, Business Planning & Finance, Robert Burns
416-327-1137, robert.burns@ontario.ca
Director, Strategic Human Resources Business Unit, Dan Keating
416-325-6598, dan.keating@ontario.ca
Director, Service Management & Facilities Branch, Isolina Kuzminski
416-325-9366, isolina.kuzminski@ontario.ca

Innovation & Commercialization Division
416-314-1163 Fax: 416-314-4344
Assistant Deputy Minister, Brad Graham
416-314-8219, brad.graham@ontario.ca
Director, Commercialization Branch, George Cadete
416-314-0670, Fax: 416-314-0680, george.cadete@ontario.ca
Acting Director, Access to Capital & Business Development Branch, Marie Larose
416-327-4430, marie.larose@ontario.ca
Manager, Business Services, Stephen Cox
416-314-8211, stephen.cox@ontario.ca

Science & Research Division
416-325-5181 Fax: 416-327-9573
Other Communication: Reception Fax: 416-325-3877
Acting Assistant Deputy Minister, Bill Mantel
416-327-2889, bill.mantel@ontario.ca
Director, Research Branch, Allison Barr
416-212-6990, allison.barr@ontario.ca
Acting Director, Strategic Planning & Policy Branch, Ryan Lock
416-326-6237, ryan.lock@ontario.ca
Manager, Health Science & Innovation, Dr. Walter Kushnir
416-326-9243, walter.kushnir@ontario.ca

Ontario Ministry of Revenue

Frost Bldg. South, 7 Queen's Park Cres., 6th Fl., Toronto, ON M7A 1Y7
Fax: 866-888-3850
866-668-8297
www.rev.gov.on.ca
TTY: 800-263-7776

The Ministry of Revenue administers Ontario's major tax statutes & tax assistance programs. Taxpayer education & customer service are provided, as well as enforcement activities for non-compliance. As of October 2011 the Ministry will be folded into Finance.

Acts Administered:
Commercial Concentration Tax Act
Community Small Business Investment Funds Act
Corporations Tax Act
Employer Health Tax Act
Fuel Tax Act
Gasoline Tax Act
Highway Traffic Act (only specific provisions)
Income Tax Act (Ontario)
Land Transfer Tax Act
Mining Tax Act
Ontario Guaranteed Annual Income Act
Ontario Home Ownership Savings Plan Act
Provincial Land Tax Act
Provincial Land Tax Act, 2006
Race Tracks Tax Act
Retail Sales Tax Act
Small Business Development Corporations Act
Succession Duty Legislation Repeal Act, 2009
Tobacco Tax Act
Alcohol & Gaming Regulation & Public Protection Act
Estate Administration Tax Act
Ministry of Revenue Act
Ontario Clean Energy Benefit Act
Taxation Act

Minister, Hon. Dwight Duncan
416-325-2338, dduncan.mpp.co@liberal.ola.org
Deputy Minister, Steve Orsini
905-436-4674, steve.f.orsini@ontario.ca
Assistant Deputy Minister, Tax Administration Policy & Partnerships, Terry Hewak
905-433-5614, terry.hewak@ontario.ca
Assistant Deputy Minister, Tax Program Strategies, Peter Rzadki
905-429-4769, peter.rzadki@ontario.ca
Director, Finance & Revenue Autdit Service Team, Linda Lim
416-325-8323, Fax: 416-325-5096, linda.lim@ontario.ca
Director, Communications & Corporate Affairs Branch, Dianne Lone
416-212-1440, dianne.lone@ontario.ca
Director, Legal Services, James D. Sinclair
416-325-1457, Fax: 416-325-1460, james.sinclair@ontario.ca
Director, Ont-Taxes Project, Sue Tilley
905-433-6377, Fax: 905-433-6305, sue.tilley@ontario.ca

Central Agencies Information & Information Technology Cluster
33 King St. West, 5th Fl., Oshawa, ON L1H 8H5
905-433-6797 Fax: 905-433-5708

The Central Agencies Information and Information Technology Cluster (CA) supports the Ministry of Finance, Ministry of Revenue, Cabinet Office, and Ministry of Energy and Infrastructure.
Chief Information Officer, Jim Hamilton
416-433-6890, jim.hamilton@ontario.ca

Corporate & Quality Service Division
Michael Starr Bldg., 33 King St. West, 6th Fl., Oshawa, ON L1H 8H5
Fax: 905-433-6688

Assistant Deputy Minister & Chief Administrative Officer, Helmut Zisser
416-314-5158, helmut.zisser@ontario.ca
Director, Corporate Planning & Finance, Linda Gibney
905-433-5637, Fax: 905-433-5124, linda.gibney@ontario.ca
Director, Business Services Branch, Paula Reid
905-440-4263, paula.reid@ontario.ca
Acting Director, Strategic Human Resources Branch, Allyson Thompson
905-433-5482, allyson.thompson@ontario.ca

Compliance Programs Division
1550 Bayly St., Pickering, ON L1W 3W1
866-668-8297

Assistant Deputy Minister, John Andersen
905-837-5236, john.andersen@ontario.ca
Director, Investigations & Inspection Branch, Peter Deschamps
905-837-5234, peter.deschamps@ontario.ca
Director, Audit Branch, Scott Nixon
613-842-3590, scott.nixon@ontario.ca
Director, Collections Branch, Christine Primeau
905-433-5640, christine.primeau@ontario.ca
Acting Director, RST Audit, Dev Ram
905-615-5840, dev.ram@ontario.ca

Program Delivery Division
Michael Starr Bldg., 33 King St. West, 3rd Fl., Oshawa, ON L1H 8H5
905-440-2410 Fax: 905-433-5247

Assistant Deputy Minister, Marion Crane
905-435-3545, marion.crane@ontario.ca
Acting Director, Client Accounts & Services Branch, Denise Paulin
905-433-6556, denise.paulin@ontario.ca
Acting Director, Records & Operations Customer Service Branch, Steve Bridcut
905-433-5880, steve.bridcut@ontario.ca
Senior Manager, Operations, Terry O'Brien
905-433-6822, terry.o'brien@ontario.ca

Strategic Partnerships & Program Policy Division
Michael Starr Bldg., 33 King St. West, 6th Fl., Oshawa, ON L1H 8Z5
Fax: 905-433-6686

Assistant Deputy Minister, Bob Laramy
905-433-6219, bob.laramy@ontario.ca
Director, Objections & Appeals, Tom Abi-Rashed
905-435-2040, 866-668-8297, tom.abi-rashed@ontario.ca
Director, Strategic Planning & Performance Management, Nancy Crabbe
905-433-6307, nancy.crabbe@ontario.ca
Director, Advisory Services & Program Policy, Richard Gruchala
905-433-6156, richard.gruchala@ontario.ca
Director, Strategic Partnerships Branch, Pieta Settimi
905-433-4942, pieta.settimi@ontario.ca

Ontario Ministry of Tourism & Culture

Hearst Block, 900 Bay St., 9th Fl., Toronto, ON M7A 2E1
416-326-9326 Fax: 416-314-7854
800-668-2746
www.mtc.gov.on.ca
TTY: 416-325-5807
Other Communication: Ontario Travel Information: 1-800-668-2746; Toll-Free TTY: 1-866-700-0040

Acts Administered:
Historical Parks Act
Ontario Place Corporation Act
St. Lawrence Parks Commission Act
Ministry of Tourism & Recreation Act
AGO Act
Arts Council Act
George R. Gardiner Museum of Ceramic Art Act
Hummingbird Performing Arts Centre Corporation Act
McMichael Canadian Art Collection Act
Metropolitan Toronto Convention Centre Act
Ontario Heritage Act
Public Libraries Act
Royal Ontario Museum Act
Science North Act
Asian Heritage Act
Celebration of Portuguese Heritage Act
Centennial Centre of Science & Technology Act
Dutch Heritage Month Act
Emancipation Day Act
Foreign Cultural Objects Immunity from Seizure Act
German Pioneers Day Act
Hotel Registration of Guests Act
Innkeepers Act
Irish Heritage Day Act
Italian Heritage Month Act
Ministry of Citizenship & Culture Act
Niagara Parks Act
Ontario Wine Week Act
Ottawa Convention Centre Corporation Act
South Asian Heritage Act
Status of Ontario Artists Act
Tartan Act
Ukrainian Heritage Day Act
United Empire Loyalists' Day Act

Minister, Hon. Michael Chan
416-326-9326, Fax: 416-314-7854, mchan.mpp.co@liberal.ola.org
Acting Deputy Minister, Steven Davidson
416-314-7846, steven.davidson@ontario.ca
Director, Communications, Jennifer E. Lang
416-212-3929, Fax: 416-325-5968, jennifer.lang@ontario.ca
Director, Internal Audit, Culture & Innovation Audit Service Team, Charles Meehan
416-325-5983, Fax: 416-326-1712, charles.meehan@ontario.ca

Associated Agencies, Boards & Commissions:
• Art Gallery of Ontario
317 Dundas St. West
Toronto, ON M5T 1G4
416-977-0414 Fax: 416-979-6669
www.ago.net
The St. Clair Parks Commission is committed to creating, maintaining & operating, in cooperation with other agencies, regional parks for people of the region & tourists; people-oriented outdoor recreation facilities; fiscal accountability; environmental accountability by action, example & education.
• Conservation Review Board
400 University Ave. 4th Fl.
Toronto, ON M7A 2R9
416-314-7137 Fax: 416-314-7175
conservation.review.board@ontario.ca
www.crb.gov.on.ca
• McMichael Canadian Art Collection
10365 Islington Ave.
Kelinburg, ON L0J 1C0
905-893-1121 Fax: 905-893-2588
www.mcmichael.com
• Metro Toronto Convention Centre Corporation
255 Front St. West
Toronto, ON M5V 2W6
416-585-8000 Fax: 416-585-8224
info@mtcc.com
www.mtcc.com
• Minister's Advisory Council for Arts & Culture
400 University Ave., 5th Fl.
Toronto, ON M7A 2R9
416-314-8321 Fax: 416-314-7091
macac@ontario.ca
• Niagara Parks Commission
Oak Hall Administration Bldg.
7400 Portage Rd. South
PO Box 150
Niagara Falls, ON L2E 6T2
905-356-2241 Fax: 905-354-6041 877-642-7275
www.niagaraparks.com
• Ontario Arts Council
151 Bloor St. West, 5th Fl.
Toronto, ON M5S 1T6
416-961-1660 Fax: 416-961-7796
www.arts.on.ca
• Ontario Heritage Trust (OHT)
10 Adelaide St. East
Toronto, ON M5C 1J3
416-325-5000 Fax: 416-325-5071
www.heritagetrust.on.ca
For more than three decades, the Ontario Heritage Trust has preserved, protected & promoted Ontario's rich & varied heritage. The Trust celebrates the people, places & events that have influenced & continue to shape our culture. As Ontario's lead heritage agency, the Trust's work extends to every corner of the province.
• Ontario Library Service - North / Service des bibliothèques de l'Ontario - Nord
334 Regent St.
Sudbury, ON P3C 4E2
705-675-6467 Fax: 705-675-2285 800-461-6348
www.olsn.ca
• Ontario Media Development Corporation (OMDC)
South Tower
#501, 175 Bloor St. East
Toronto, ON M4W 3R8
416-314-6858 Fax: 416-314-6876
mail@omdc.on.ca
www.omdc.on.ca
Formerly the Ontario Film Development Corporation (OFDC).
• Ontario Place Corporation
955 Lake Shore Blvd. West
Toronto, ON M6K 3B9
416-314-9900 Fax: 416-314-9992
www.ontarioplace.com
• Ontario Science Centre
770 Don Mills Rd.
Toronto, ON M3C 1T3
416-696-1000 Fax: 416-696-3124
www.ontariosciencecentre.ca
• Ontario Tourism Marketing Partnership Corporation
#900,10 Dundas St. East
Toronto, ON M7A 2A1
416-212-0757 Fax: 416-325-6004 800-668-2746
www.ontariotravel.net
• Ontario Trillium Foundation
800 Bay St., 5th Fl.
Toronto, ON M5S 3A9
416-963-4927 Fax: 416-963-8781 800-263-2887 TTY: 416-963-7905
trillium@trilliumfoundation.org
www.trilliumfoundation.org
The Ontario Trillium Foundation is an agency of the Ministry of Culture. Grants are provided to eligible not-for-profit & charitable organizations in the areas of arts & culture, sports and recreation, human & social services, & the environment.

• Ottawa Convention Centre
55 Colonel By Dr.
Ottawa, ON K1N 9J2
613-563-1984 Fax: 613-563-7646
www.ottawaconventioncentre.com
• Royal Botanical Gardens
680 Plains Rd. West
Burlington, ON L7T 4H4
905-527-1158 Fax: 905-577-0375 800-694-4769
www.rbg.ca
• Royal Ontario Museum (ROM)
100 Queen's Park Cres.
Toronto, ON M5S 2C6
416-586-5549 Fax: 416-586-5685
info@rom.on.ca
www.rom.on.ca
• Science North
100 Ramsey Lake Rd.
Sudbury, ON P3E 5S9
705-522-3701 Fax: 705-522-4954
www.sciencenorth.ca
• Southern Ontario Library Service
#902, 111 Peter St.
Toronto, ON M5V 2H1
416-961-1669 Fax: 416-961-5122 800-387-5765
www.sols.org
• St. Lawrence Parks Commission
RR#1
Morrisburg, ON K0C 1X0
613-543-3704 Fax: 613-543-2847 800-437-2233 TTY: 613-543-4181
www.parks.on.ca
The St. Lawrence Parks Commission is an Ontario provincial agency established in 1955 to provide recreation, tourism, cultural & educational opportunities for residents of Ontario & visitors to the province through the presentation & interpretation of historical attractions & the development & operation of parks, campgrounds, scenic parkways & recreational areas.

Culture Division
#1800, 401 Bay St., Toronto, ON M7A 0A7
416-314-7265 Fax: 416-314-7461
Acting Assistant Deputy Minister, Donna Ratchford
donna.ratchford@ontario.ca
Director, Programs & Services Branch, Peter Armstrong
416-314-7342, peter.armstrong@ontario.ca
Acting Director, Culture & Strategic Policy Branch, Suzanne Rowe Knight
416-314-7122, suzanne.roweknight@ontario.ca
Director, Agencies Branch, Nancy Rowland
416-327-4305

Office of the Chief Information Officer, Community Services I & IT Cluster
Assistant Deputy Minister & Chief Information Officer, Soussan Tabari
416-326-8216, soussan.tabari@ontario.ca
Director, Technology & Business Solutions, Sanaul Haque
416-585-6746, sanaul.haque@ontario.ca
Director, Information Technology Service Management, Joanne Hiscock
416-327-1087, joanne.hiscock@ontario.ca
Director, Strategic Planning & Business Relationship Management Branch, Lolita Singh
416-326-7942, lolita.singh@ontario.ca

Ontario Seniors' Secretariat
#601C, 777 Bay St., 6th Fl., Toronto, ON M7A 2J4
416-326-7076 Fax: 416-326-7078
www.ontarioseniors.ca
Minister Responsible, Hon. Sophia Aggelonitis
416-314-1675, saggelonitis.mpp.co@liberal.ola.org
Assistant Deputy Minister, Juanita Dobson
416-326-7069, Fax: 416-326-7079, juanita.dobson@ontario.ca
Director, Retirement Homes Project, Abby Katz Starr
416-325-2649, abby.katzstarr@ontario.ca
Manager, Policy Initiatives, Elizabeth Esteves
416-326-7064, elizabeth.esteves@ontario.ca
Manager, Public Education & Awareness, Diane Varga
416-326-7058, diane.varga@ontario.ca

Tourism Planning & Operations Division
Assistant Deputy Minister, Shirley Phillips
416-325-2861, shirley.phillips@ontario.ca
General Manager, Fort William Historical Park, Sergio Buonocore
807-473-2341, sergio.buonocore@ontario.ca, Other Communications: URL: www.fwhp.ca
General Manager, Huronia Historical Parks, Jan Gray
705-528-7690, jan.gray@ontario.ca, Other Communications: URL: www.hhp.on.ca
Director, Tourism Agencies Branch, Dean Hustwick
416-326-9579, dean.hustwick@ontario.ca

Tourism Policy & Development Division
416-326-9326 Fax: 416-325-6985
Assistant Deputy Minister, Richard McKinnell
416-325-6961, richard.mckinnell@ontario.ca
Director, War of 1812 Bicentennial Planning, Angela Faienza
416-212-5290, angela.faienza@ontario.ca
Director, Investment & Development Office, Michael Langford
416-314-7105, Fax: 416-327-2506, michael.langford@ontario.ca
Acting Director, Tourism Policy & Research, Diane Wise
416-325-6055, Fax: 416-314-7341, diane.wise@ontario.ca

Regional & Corporate Services Division
416-314-7311 Fax: 416-314-7313
Assistant Deputy Minister & Chief Administrative Officer, Robert M. Montgomery
robert.m.montgomery@ontario.ca
Acting Director, Legal Services, James Girling
416-314-7022, Fax: 416-314-7038, james.girling@ontario.ca
Director, Regional Services Branch, Brian Lemire
416-314-6680, Fax: 416-314-6686, brian.lemire@ontario.ca
Director, Corporate Resources Branch, Heather Taylor
416-325-6135, Fax: 416-314-4968, heather.taylor@ontario.ca

Regional Offices:
Central Region
400 University Ave., 4th Fl., Toronto, ON M7A 2R9
416-314-6044 Fax: 416-314-2024
877-395-4105
Manager, Tom Chrzan
416-314-6682, tom.chrzan@ontario.ca
East Region
347 Preston St., 4th Fl., Ottawa, ON K1S 3J4
613-742-3360 Fax: 613-742-5300
800-267-9340
Manager, Valerie Andrews
613-742-3366, valerie.andrews@ontario.ca
North Region
#334, 435 James St. South, Thunder Bay, ON P7E 6S7
807-475-1683 Fax: 807-475-1297
800-465-6861
Manager, Elaine Lynch
807-475-1635, elaine.lynch@ontario.ca
West Region
#405, 30 Duke St. West, Kitchener, ON N2H 3W5
Fax: 519-578-1632
800-265-2189
Manager, George Potter
519-571-6050, george.potter@ontario.ca

Ontario Ministry of Training, Colleges & Universities

Mowat Block, 900 Bay St., 14th Fl., Toronto, ON M7A 1L2
416-325-2929 Fax: 416-325-6348
800-387-5514
information.met@ontario.ca
www.tcu.gov.on.ca
TTY: 800-263-2892

Acts Administered:
Apprenticeship & Certification Act, 1998
Colleges Collective Bargaining Act, 2008
Ministry of Training, Colleges & Universities Act
Ontario Colleges of Applied Arts & Technology Act, 2002
Post-secondary Education Choice & Excellence Act, 2000
Private Career Colleges Act, 2005
Trades Qualification & Apprenticeship Act
University Foundations Act, 1992
Algoma University Act
Education Act (in part)
Higher Education Quality Council of Ontario Act
Ontario College of Art & Design University Act
Ontario College of Trades & Apprenticeship Act
Ontario Labour Mobility Act
University Expropriation Powers Act
University of Ontario Institute of Technology Act
Minister, Hon. Glen Murray
416-326-1600, Fax: 416-326-1656, gmurray.mpp.co@liberal.ola.org
Deputy Minister, Deborah Newman
416-314-9244, Fax: 416-314-7117, deborah.newman@ontario.ca
Chief Information Officer/Assistant Deputy Minister, Soussan Tabari
416-326-8216, Fax: 416-325-8371, soussan.tabari@ontario.ca
Director, Communications, Heather Wright
416-325-2944, Fax: 416-212-4158, heather.wright@ontario.ca
Team Lead, Change Management Office, Charmaine Charles
416-325-9231, charmaine.charles@ontario.ca
Manager, Brian Fleming Research & Learning Library, Simon Loban
416-325-2654, Fax: 416-325-4235, simon.loban@ontario.ca

Associated Agencies, Boards & Commissions:
• Ontario Graduate Scholarship Program Selection Board
189 Red River Rd., 4th Fl.
PO Box 4500
Thunder Bay, ON P7B 6G9
807-343-7257 Fax: 807-343-7278 800-465-3957
www.osap.gov.on.ca
Provides advice & recommendations to the minister concerning the policies & administration of the Ontario Graduate Scholarship program & selects successful candidates for funding under the program.
• Ontario Student Assistance Appeal Board
Mowat Block
900 Bay St., 7th Fl.
Toronto, ON M7A 1L2
416-314-0714 Fax: 416-325-3096
• Post-secondary Education Quality Assessment Board
#1511, 2 Carlton St.
Toronto, ON M5B 1J3
416-212-1230 Fax: 416-212-6620
peqab.ca

Corporate Management & Services Division
Mowat Block, #342 - 900 Bay St., Toronto, ON M7A 1L2
416-325-2772 Fax: 416-325-2778
Assistant Deputy Minister/Chief Administrative Officer, David Fulford
416-325-2773, david.fulford@ontario.ca
Director, Legal Services, John Calcott
416-325-2399, Fax: 416-325-2410, john.calcott@ontario.ca
Director, Strategic Human Resources, Sandra Diprospero
416-325-4511, Fax: 416-327-9043, sandra.diprospero@ontario.ca
Director, Internal Audit Services, Education Audit Service Team, Warren McCay
416-212-4814, Fax: 416-325-1120, warren.mccay@ontario.ca
Director, Corporate Coordination, Russell Riddell
416-326-6662, Fax: 416-314-0558, russell.riddell@ontario.ca

Employment & Training Division
Fax: 416-325-2995
888-562-4769
Assistant Deputy Minister, Laurie LeBlanc
416-325-2989, laurie.leblanc@ontario.ca
Director, Service Standards & Accountability Branch, Todd Kilpatrick
416-325-2751, todd.kilpatrick@ontario.ca
Director, Business & Systems Management Branch, Robert Lowry
416-325-4056, Fax: 416-314-0499, robert.lowry@ontario.ca
Director, Service Delivery Branch, Barbara Simmons
416-314-4268, Fax: 416-325-6162, barbara.simmons@ontario.ca
Director, Strategic Oversight Office, Andrew Tang
416-212-6222, andrew.tang@ontario.ca

Post-secondary Education Division
416-325-2199 Fax: 416-326-3256
Assistant Deputy Minister, Nancy Naylor
416-325-2116, nancy.naylor@ontario.ca
Director, Post-secondary Accountability Branch, Martin Hicks
416-325-1815, martin.hicks@ontario.ca
Acting Director, Post-secondary Finance & Information Management Branch, Jeff Lennon
416-325-1952, jeff.lennon@ontario.ca
Director, Student Financial Assistance Branch, Noah Morris
416-325-2853, Fax: 416-325-3096, noah.morris@ontario.ca
Director, Private Career Colleges Branch, Allan Scott
416-314-9474, allan.scott@ontario.ca

Strategic Policy & Programs Division
Assistant Deputy Minister, Marie-Lison Fougère
416-212-5420, marie-lison.fougere@ontario.ca
Director, Programs Branch, Virginia Hatchette
416-326-5849, virginia.hatchette@ontario.ca
Director, Research & Planning Branch, Chris Monahan
416-325-4034, chris.monahan@ontario.ca
Director, Strategic Policy & Initiatives Branch, Ellen Passmore
416-326-6023, ellen.passmore@ontario.ca

Ontario Ministry of Transportation (MTO)

Ferguson Block, 77 Wellesley St. West, 3rd Fl., Toronto, ON M7A 1Z8
416-235-4686 Fax: 905-704-2001
800-268-4686
www.mto.gov.on.ca
TTY: 905-704-2426
Other Communication: TTY Toll Free: 1-866-471-8929; Driver and Vehicle Licensing: 1-800-387-3445; Road Test Booking: 1-888-570-6110
The Ministry performs the following functions: planning, designing & building highways; performing environmental assessments; rehabilitating existing highways to increase their efficiency & safety; performing ongoing highway maintenance; developing standards, operational guidelines & policies relating to highways; & researching & introducing new technologies for

more effective highway management. MTO commits to providing & promoting transportation services in a way that sustains a healthful environment through the Ministry's Statement of Environmental Values. The Ministry applies & integrates environmental concerns, along with prevailing social, economic, scientific & other considerations when conducting its business activities.

Acts Administered:
Airports Act
Bluewater Bridge Act
Bridges Act
Capital Investment Plan Act
Dangerous Goods Transportation Act
Highway 407 Act
Highway 407 East Completion Act
Highway Memorials for Fallen Police Officers Act
Highway Traffic Act
Improving Customer Service for Road Users Act
Local Roads Boards Act
Ministry of Transportation Act
Motor Vehicle Transportation Act
Motorized Snow Vehicles Act
Northern Transportation Commission Act
Off-Road Vehicles Act
Ontario Highway Transport Board Act
Ontario Transportation Development Corporation Act
Photo Card Act
Public Service Works on Highways Act
Public Transportation & Highway Improvement Act
Public Vehicles Act
Railways Act
Rainbow Bridge Act
Shortline Railways Act
Statute Labour Act (part)
Toll Bridges Act
Toronto Area Transit Operating Authority Act
Township of Pelee Act
Urban Transportation Development Corporation Ltd. Act

Minister, Hon. Bob Chiarelli
416-327-9200, Fax: 416-327-9188,
bchiarelli.mpp.co@liberal.ola.org
Deputy Minister, Carol Layton
416-327-9162, carol.layton@ontario.ca
Director, Communications, Kimberley Bates
416-327-2117, Fax: 416-327-2591,
kimberley.bates@ontario.ca
Director, Legal Services, Mary Gersht
416-235-4406, Fax: 416-235-4924, mary.gersht@ontario.ca
Parliamentary Assistant, Amrit Mangat
416-327-0806

Associated Agencies, Boards & Commissions:
• Metrolinx
#600, 20 Bay St.
Toronto, ON M5J 2W3
416-869-3200 Fax: 416-869-3525 888-438-6646 TTY:
800-387-3652
www.gotransit.com
• Ontario Highway Transport Board
151 Bloor St. West, 10th Fl.
Toronto, ON M5S 2T5
416-326-6732 Fax: 416-326-6738
ohtb@mto.gov.on.ca
www.ohtb.gov.on.ca

Corporate Services Division
Garden City Tower, 301 St. Paul St., 6th Fl., St Catharines, ON L2R 7R4
905-704-2693 Fax: 905-704-2445
Assistant Deputy Minister, Mike Goodale
905-704-2701, mike.goodale@ontario.ca
Director, Strategic Human Resources, Alan Hogan
905-704-2688, alan.hogan@ontario.ca
Director, Finance, Jill Hughes
905-704-2702, jill.hughes@ontario.ca
Director, Facilities & Business Services, Lesley Spinney
905-704-2727, lesley.spinney@ontario.ca

Labour & Transportation I&IT Cluster
400 University Ave., 9th Fl., Toronto, ON M7A 1T7
416-327-3754 Fax: 416-327-3755
Chief Information Officer, Ken Kawall
416-327-1955, Fax: 416-327-3755, ken.kawall@ontario.ca
Director, Strategic & Resources Planning, Michael Anderson
416-327-5314, michael.anderson@ontario.ca
Director, Highways & Economics Solutions Branch, Howard Bertrand
905-704-2488, howard.bertrand@ontario.ca
Director, Service Management, Dani Danyluk
905-704-2834, dani.danyluk@ontario.ca
Director, Road User Safety Solutions Branch, Bob Stephens
416-235-5209, Fax: 416-235-5658, bob.stephens@ontario.ca

Policy & Planning Division
Ferguson Block, 77 Wesley St., 3rd Fl., Toronto, ON M7A 1Z8
416-327-8521 Fax: 416-327-8746
Assistant Deputy Minister, Scott Thompson
416-327-6521, scott.thompson@ontario.ca
Director, Transportation Planning, Pat Boeckner
905-585-7238, Fax: 905-704-2445, pat.boeckner@ontario.ca
Director, Transportation Policy, Linda McAusland
416-585-7177, Fax: 905-704-2445,
linda.mcausland@ontario.ca
Director, Transit Policy, Andrew Posluns
416-585-7347, Fax: 905-704-2445,
andrew.posluns@ontario.ca
Director, Strategic Policy & Transportation, Economics, David Ward
416-212-1893, Fax: 905-704-2445, david.ward@ontario.ca

Provincial Highways Management Division
Ferguson Block, 77 Wellesley St. West, 3rd Fl., Toronto, ON M7A 1Z8
416-327-9044 Fax: 416-327-9226
Assistant Deputy Minister, Gerry Chaput
416-327-9044, Fax: 416-327-9226, gerry.chaput@ontario.ca
Acting Executive Director, Asset Management & Director, Highway Standards Branch, Steve Cripps
905-704-2299, Fax: 905-704-2562, steve.cripps@ontario.ca
Acting Director, Investment Strategies Branch, Dino Bagnariol
905-704-2044, Fax: 905-704-2626, dino.bagnariol@ontario.ca
Director, Contract Management & Operations Branch, Paul M. Leocoarer
905-704-2601, Fax: 905-704-2030, paul.lecoarer@ontario.ca
Director, Windsor Border Initiatives Implementation Group (BIIG), Fausto Natarelli
416-326-6876, Fax: 416-326-7056,
fausto.natarelli@ontario.ca
Manager, Division Services Office, Cindy Lucas
905-704-2473, cindy.lucas@ontario.ca

Regional Offices:

Central
Atrium Tower, 1201 Wilson Ave., Downsview, ON M3M 1J8
416-235-5412 Fax: 416-235-5266
Regional Director, Lou Politano
416-235-5400, Fax: 416-235-5266, lou.politano@ontario.ca

Eastern
1355 John Counter Blvd., PO Box 4000, Kingston, ON K7L 5A3
613-545-4711 Fax: 613-545-4786
800-267-0295
Regional Director, Kathryn Moore
613-545-4600, kathryn.moore@ontario.ca

Northeastern
Ontario Government Bldg., 447 McKeown Ave., 1st Fl., North Bay, ON P1B 9S9
705-472-7900 Fax: 705-497-5422
800-461-9547
Regional Director, Eric Doige
705-497-5500, eric.doige@ontario.ca

Northwestern
615 James St. South, Thunder Bay, ON P7E 6P6
807-473-2000 Fax: 807-473-2157
800-465-5034
Regional Director, Ian Smith
807-473-2050, Fax: 807-473-2165, ian.smitht@ontario.ca

Western
659 Exeter Rd., 4th Fl., London, ON N6E 1L3
519-873-4335 Fax: 519-873-4236
800-265-6072
Regional Director, Ann Baldwin
519-873-4333, Fax: 519-873-4236, ann.baldwin@ontario.ca

Road User Safety Division
Bldg A, #191, 1201 Wilson Ave., Downsview, ON M3M 1J8
416-235-2999 Fax: 416-235-4153
The division sets safety standards, develops policies, legislation & regulation, & educates road users about road user safety. Responsibilities include evaluating the effectiveness of safety measures, inspecting, monitoring & enforcing compliance with standards, testing, licenses & drivers, & registering vehicles. Through public education, legislation & enforcement, the government strives to ensure all motorists take responsibility for their driving behaviour. The Assistant Deputy Minister, Road User Safety, is responsible for the co-ordination of all Road User Safety activities for the province & acts as the Registrar of Motor Vehicles for Ontario.
Assistant Deputy Minister, Rob Fleming
416-235-4453, Fax: 416-235-4153, rob.fleming@ontario.ca
Director, Licencing Services, Paul Brown
416-235-4392, Fax: 416-235-5139, paul.h.brown@ontario.ca
Director, RUS Modernization Project, Linda Dunstall
416-235-4628, linda.dunstall@ontario.ca
Director, Regional Operations, Tony Foster
416-235-3526, tony.foster@ontario.ca
Director, Safety Policy & Education, Heidi Francis
416-235-4050, Fax: 416-235-5139, heidi.francis@ontario.ca
Director, Program Development & Evaluation, Paul Harbottle
416-235-4199, paul.harbottle@ontario.ca
Director, Carrier Safety & Enforcement, Peter Hurst
416-235-2501, paul.harbottle@ontario.ca
Director, Service Delivery Partnerships, Kim Lambert
416-235-5312, kim.lambert@ontario.ca
Director, Oranizational Development, Shelley Unterlander
416-235-4769, shelley.unterlander@ontario.ca

Ontario Women's Directorate (OWD)

777 Bay St., 6th Fl., Toronto, ON M7A 2J4
416-314-0300 Fax: 416-314-0247
866-510-5902
owd@ontario.ca
www.citizenship.gov.on.ca/owd
TTY: 416-314-0258
A division of the Ministry of Citizenship and Immigration, the OWD focuses upon the following issues related to women: social, economic & justice-related concerns. The main activities of the OWD are preventing violence against women & promoting women's economic independence.
Minister Responsible, Hon. Laurel Broten
416-212-7432, Fax: 416-212-7431,
lbroten.mpp.co@liberal.ola.org
Executive Director, Susan Seaby
416-314-1850, Fax: 416-314-0247, susan.seaby@ontario.ca
Manager, Stakeholder Relations & Policy Development, Suzanne Hastie
416-314-1783, Fax: 416-314-0255,
suzanne.hastie@ontario.ca
Parliamentary Assistant, Leeanna Pendergast
416-325-1270, Fax: 416-326-3951,
lpendergast.mpp@liberal.ola.org

Workplace Safety & Insurance Board

200 Front St. West, Ground Fl., Toronto, ON M5V 3J1
416-344-1000 Fax: 416-344-4684
800-387-0750
www.wsib.on.ca
TTY: 800-387-0050
Chair, Hon. Steven W. Mahoney, P.C.
416-344-4451
President & Chief Executive Officer, David Marshall
416-344-4009
Chief Prevention & Corporate Strategy Officer, Tom Beegan
416-344-4446, tom_beegan@wsib.on.ca
Acting Chief Financial Officer, Dan Hogg
416-344-6147, dan_hogg@wsib.on.ca
Chief Operating Officer, John Slinger
416-344-4450, john_slinger@wsib.on.ca
Chief Corporate Services Officer, Tom Teahen
416-344-6129, tom_teahen@wsib.on.ca
Chief Strategy Officer, Susanna Zagar
416-344-6188, susanna_zagar@wsib.on.ca
General Counsel & Vice-President, Legal Services & Secretary to the Board, Brenda Abrams
416-344-4880, brenda_abrams@wsib.on.ca
Vice-President, Health Services, Donna Bain
416-344-5610, donna_bain@wsib.on.ca
Vice-President, Investment Division & Chief Investment Officer, John Denham
416-344-4095, john_denham@wsib.on.ca
Vice-President, Business Technology Services & Chief Information Officer, John Hill
416-344-4024, john_hill@wsib.on.ca
Vice-President & Chief Actuary, Actuarial Services, Rob Hinrichs
416-344-5300, rob_hinrichs@wsib.on.ca
Vice-President, Communications & Public Affairs, Moira McIntyre
416-344-4374, Fax: 416-344-4366,
moira_mcintyre@wsib.on.ca
Board Auditor, Internal Audit, Roman W. Kosmyna
416-344-4537, roman_kosmyna@wsib.on.ca

Government of Prince Edward Island

Seat of Government: Island Information Service, PO Box 2000, Charlottetown, PE C1A 7N8
902-368-4000
island@gov.pe.ca
www.gov.pe.ca
Other Communication: Tourism Information, Toll-Free Phone: 1-800-463-4734
The Province of Prince Edward Island entered Confederation on July 1, 1873. It has an area of 5,683.91 km2, with a population of 135,851, according to the 2006 national census.

Office of the Lieutenant Governor

Government House, PO Box 846, Charlottetown, PE C1A 7L9
902-368-5480 Fax: 902-368-5481
www.gov.pe.ca/olg

The Honourable H. Frank Lewis was sworn in as the 41st Lieutenant Governor of Prince Edward Island by the Chief Justice of the Supreme Court of Prince Edward Island at Province House on August 15, 2011.

Lieutenant Governor, Hon. H. Frank Lewis
902-368-5480, Fax: 902-368-5481, hflewis@gov.pe.ca
Executive Assistant, Cindy Cheverie
ccheverie@gov.pe.ca
Administrative Assistant, Krista Rodd
klrodd@gov.pe.ca

Office of the Premier

Shaw Bldg., 95 Rochford St. South, 5th Fl., PO Box 2000, Charlottetown, PE C1A 7N8
902-368-4501 Fax: 902-368-6118
www.gov.pe.ca/premier

Honourable Robert W.J. Ghiz is the thirty-first Premier of Prince Edward Island. In the October 2011 provincial election, he secured his second majority government.

Premier, Prince Edward Island; President, Executive Council; Minister Responsible, Intergovernmental Affairs; Minister Responsible, Acadian & Francophone Affairs; Leader, Liberal Party of Prince Edward Island, Hon. RobertW.J. Ghiz
902-368-4400, Fax: 902-386-4416, premier@gov.pe.ca; robert.ghiz@liberal.pe.ca
Social Media:
www.facebook.com/pages/Robert-Ghiz-PEI-Premier/117411911662012
Deputy Premier, Prince Edward Island; Minister, Agriculture, Hon. George T. Webster
902-368-4820, Fax: 902-368-4846, gtwebster@gov.pe.ca; george.webster@liberal.pe.ca
Chief of Staff, Allan V. Campbell
902-368-4400, Fax: 902-368-4416, avcampbell@gov.pe.ca
Director, Communications & Legislative Affairs, Geoff Townsend
902-368-4400, gatownsend@gov.pe.ca
Executive Assistant, Ian "Tex" MacDonald
902-368-4400, Fax: 902-368-4416, ilmacdonald@gov.pe.ca

Executive Council

Shaw Bldg., 5th Fl., PO Box 2000, Charlottetown, PE C1A 7N8
902-368-4502 Fax: 902-368-6118
www.gov.pe.ca/ec

The Executive Council of Prince Edward Island is made up of Ministers of the Crown. The role of the Executive Council is to decide upon the policy & direction that the government will take & to advise the Lieutenant Governor. Consisting of Ministers of the Crown, the Executive Council advises the Lieutenant Governor on the policy & direction which the government will take.

President, Executive Council; Premier, Prince Edward Island; Minister Responsible, Intergovernmental Affairs; Minister Responsible, Acadian & Francophone Affairs; Leader, Liberal Party of Prince Edward Island, Hon. RobertW.J. Ghiz
902-368-4400, Fax: 902-368-4416, premier@gov.pe.ca; robert.ghiz@liberal.pe.ca
Social Media:
www.facebook.com/pages/Robert-Ghiz-PEI-Premier/117411911662012
Note: Web Site: www.gov.pe.ca/premier (Office of the Premier)
Minister, Agriculture; Deputy Premier, Prince Edward Island, Hon. George T. Webster
902-368-4820, Fax: 902-368-4846, gtwebster@gov.pe.ca; george.webster@liberal.pe.ca, Other Communications: Department Phone: 902-368-4880; Fax: 902-368-4857
Note: Web Site: www.gov.pe.ca/agriculture (Department of Agriculture)
Minister, Fisheries, Aquaculture, & Rural Development, Hon. Ron W. MacKinley
902-368-5120, 877-407-0187, Fax: 902-368-5385, rwmackinley@gov.pe.ca; ron.mackinley@liberal.pe.ca, Other Communications: Department Phone: 902-838-0910; Fax: 902-838-0975
Social Media:
www.facebook.com/pages/Ron-MacKinley/60342728811
Note: Web Site: www.gov.pe.ca/fard (Department of Fisheries, Aquaculture, & Rural Development)
Minister, Health & Wellness; Minister Responsible, Aboriginal Affairs, Hon. Doug W. Currie
902-368-5152, Fax: 902-368-4910, dwcurrie@gov.pe.ca; doug.currie@liberal.pe.ca, Other Communications: Department Phone: 902-368-6414; Fax: 902-368-4121
Social Media: www.twitter.com/DougCurrie, www.facebook.com/doug.w.currie
Note: Web Sites: www.gov.pe.ca/health (Department of Health & Wellness); www.dougcurrie.ca (PersonalWebsite)
Minister, Finance & Municipal Affairs, Hon. Wesley J. Sheridan
902-368-4050, Fax: 902-368-6575, wjsheridan@gov.pe.ca; wes.sheridan@liberal.pe.ca, Other Communications: Department Phone: 902-368-4000; Fax: 902-368-5544
Social Media:
www.facebook.com/profile.php?id=100002547484282&ref=ts
Note: Web Site: www.gov.pe.ca/finance (Department of Finance & Municipal Affairs)
Minister, Community Services, Seniors, & Labour; Minister Responsible, Status of Women, Hon. Valerie E. Docherty
902-368-4330, 866-594-3777, Fax: 902-368-4348, vedocherty@assembly.pe.ca; valerie.docherty@liberal.pe.ca, Other Communications: Department Phone: 902-620-3777;Fax: 902-368-4740
Social Media:
www.facebook.com/profile.php?id=100002087193589
Note: Web Site: www.gov.pe.ca/sss (Department of Community Services, Seniors, & Labour)
Minister, Environment, Energy, & Forestry, Hon. Janice A. Sherry
902-368-4930, Fax: 902-368-4974, jasherry@gov.pe.ca; janice.sherry@liberal.pe.ca, Other Communications: Department Phone: 902-368-5000; Fax: 902-368-5830
Social Media:
www.facebook.com/people/Janice-Sherry/100002079465746
Note: Web Site: www.gov.pe.ca/eef (Department of Environment, Energy, & Forestry)
Minister, Transportation & Infrastructure Renewal, Hon. Robert S. Vessey
902-368-4801, Fax: 902-368-5277, rsvessey@gov.pe.ca; robert.vessey@liberal.pe.ca, Other Communications: Department Phone: 902-368-5100; Fax: 902-368-5395
Note: Web Site: www.gov.pe.ca/tir (Department of Transportation & Infrastructure Renewal)
Minister, Tourism & Culture, Hon. Robert L. Henderson
902-368-5540, Fax: 902-368-5277, rlhenderson@assembly.pe.ca; robert.henderson@liberal.pe.ca
Social Media:
www.facebook.com/profile.php?id=100001965683516
Note: Web Site: www.gov.pe.ca/tourism (Department of Tourism & Culture)
Minister, Education & Early Childhood Development; Minister, Justice & Public Safety; Attorney General, Hon. J. Alan McIsaac
902-368-4330, Fax: 902-368-4348, jamcisaac@assembly.pe.ca; alan.mcisaac@liberal.pe.ca, Other Communications: Department Phone: 902-438-4130; Fax: 902-438-4062
Social Media:
www.facebook.com/profile.php?id=100001892659368
Note: Web Sites: www.gov.pe.ca/eecd (Department of Education & Early Childhood Development);www.gov.pe.ca/jps (Department of Justice & Public Safety)
Minister, Innovation & Advanced Learning, Hon. Allen F. Roach
allen.roach@liberal.pe.ca, Other Communications: Department Phone: 902-368-4240; Fax: 902-368-4242
Social Media:
www.facebook.com/profile.php?id=100002417155344
Note: Web Site: www.gov.pe.ca/ia (Department of Innovation & Advanced Learning)

Executive Council Office

Shaw Bldg., 5th Fl., PO Box 2000, Charlottetown, PE C1A 7N8
902-368-4000
www.gov.pe.ca/eco

It is the responsibility of the Executive Council Office to provide administrative services & advice to the Executive Council. Advice & support are also offered to the government's departments & agencies.
The Executive Council Office supports the Acadian & Francophone Community. A key activitiy is the assistance given to departments & agencies in planning & delivering French language programs & services.
Another important activity of the Executive Council Office is the provision of research & analysis on intergovernmental affairs. Advice is given related to social & economic policies.
The Executive Office is also involved in the coordination of traditional ceremonial or legal requirements, such as the swearing into office of Members of Cabinet or the Lieutenant Governor.

Premier, Prince Edward Island; President, Executive Council; Minister Responsible, Intergovernmental Affairs; Minister Responsible, Acadian & Francophone Affairs; Leader, Liberal Party of Prince Edward Island, Hon. RobertW.J. Ghiz
902-368-4400, Fax: 902-368-4416, premier@gov.pe.ca; robert.ghiz@liberal.pe.ca
Social Media:
www.facebook.com/pages/Robert-Ghiz-PEI-Premier/117411911662012
Note: Web Site: www.gov.pe.ca/premier (Office of the Premier)
Clerk of the Executive Council; Secretary to Cabinet, Rory Beck
902-368-4502, Fax: 902-368-6118, rbeck@gov.pe.ca
Chief, Protocol & Events, Mary Ellen E. Moerike
902-368-4501, Fax: 902-368-6118, memoerike@gov.pe.ca
Deputy Minister, Intergovernmental Affairs, Sandy Stewart
902-368-4502, Fax: 902-368-6118, swstewart@gov.pe.ca
Assistant Deputy Minister, Acadian & Francophone Affairs, Aubrey Cormier
902-368-6337, Fax: 902-368-6118, arcormier@gov.pe.ca
Director, Acadian & Francophone Affairs, Diane Arsenault
902-368-4872, Fax: 902-368-4857, dianearsenault@gov.pe.ca
Director, Intergovernmental Affairs, Rochelle Gallant
902-368-4415, Fax: 902-368-6118, rgallant@gov.pe.ca

Operations Committee

Shaw Bldg., 5th Fl., PO Box 2000, Charlottetown, PE C1A 7N8
902-368-4305 Fax: 902-368-6118

The Operations Committee coordinates the legislative development process. All proposed legislation, regulations, & amendments to regulations are reviewed & analyzed prior to submission to the Executive Council for approval.
Secretary, Operations Committee, Matt McGuire
902-368-4407, Fax: 902-368-6118, mdmcguire@gov.pe.ca

Policy Board Committee

Shaw Bldg., 5th Fl., PO Box 2000, Charlottetown, PE C1A 7N8
902-368-4502 Fax: 902-368-6118
Secretary to the Policy Board, Wendy MacDonald
902-620-3457, Fax: 902-368-6118, wimacdonald@gov.pe.ca

Treasury Board Committee

Shaw Bldg., 95 Rochford St. South, 3rd Fl., PO Box 2000, Charlottetown, PE C1A 7N8
The Executive Council Act established the Treasury Board as a committee of the Executive Council. The Board advises the Executive Council about budgetary & financial matters & the mamagement of the Public Service.
Secretary to the Treasury Board, Doug Clow, CA
902-368-4052, Fax: 902-368-6575, dmclow@gov.pe.ca
Treasury Officer, Margaret Simpson
902-368-4140, Fax: 902-368-4077

Legislative Assembly

Province House, 165 Richmond St., 1st Fl., PO Box 2000, Charlottetown, PE C1A 7N8
902-368-5970 Fax: 902-368-5175
877-315-5518
legislativelibrary@assembly.pe.ca
www.assembly.pe.ca

The Legislative Assembly of Prince Edward Island consists of the lawmakers & the offices & officials who support their work.
Director, Security & Sergeant-at-Arms, W/O Al J. McDonald
902-368-5976, Fax: 902-368-5175, ajmcdonald@assembly.pe.ca
Committee Clerk, Melissa M. Keefe
902-620-3764, Fax: 902-368-5175, mmkeefe@assembly.pe.ca

Office of the Clerk

Province House, 165 Richmond St., 1st Fl., PO Box 2000, Charlottetown, PE C1A 7N8
902-368-5970 Fax: 902-368-5175

The Clerk of the Legislative Assembly is responsible for providing administrative support to the Speaker, the House, & its members. Decisions of the House are recorded by the Clerk & published in the Journals of the Legislative Assembly of Prince Edward Island.
Clerk of the Legislative Assembly, Charles MacKay
902-368-5970, Fax: 902-368-5175, chmackay@assembly.pe.ca
Clerk of Committees & Clerk Assistant, Marian Johnston
902-368-5972, Fax: 902-368-5175, majohnston@assembly.pe.ca
Administrative Officer, Cheryl Stead
902-368-5970, Fax: 902-368-5175, chstead@assembly.pe.ca

Office of the Conflict of Interest Commissioner

Province House, 165 Richmond St., 1st Fl., PO Box 2000, Charlottetown, PE C1A 7N8
902-368-5970 Fax: 902-368-5175

The Conflict of Interest Commissioner is an independent officer of the Legislative Assembly who administers the Conflict of Interest Act. To enhance public confidence in the Legislative Assembly, the Conflict of Interest Act ensures that Ministers & Members reconcile their private & public interests & conduct their responsibilities with integrity.
Commisioner, Conflict of Interest, Neil Robinson
anrobinson@assembly.pe.ca

Government Members' Office (Liberal)
Coles Bldg., 175 Richmond St., 2nd Fl., PO Box 2890, Charlottetown, PE C1A 8C5
902-368-4330 Fax: 902-368-4348
Administrative support to government backbenchers is provided by the Government Members' Office.
Premier, Prince Edward Island; Leader, Liberal Party of Prince Edward Island; President, Executive Council; Minister Responsible, Intergovernmental Affairs; Minister Responsible, Acadian & Francophone Affairs, Hon. RobertW.J. Ghiz
902-368-4400, Fax: 902-368-4416, premier@gov.pe.ca; robert.ghiz@liberal.pe.ca
Social Media:
www.facebook.com/pages/Robert-Ghiz-PEI-Premier/1174119 11662012
Note: Web Site: www.gov.pe.ca/premier (Office of the Premier)
Government House Leader; Member, Legislative Assembly, Sonny Gallant
902-368-4330, Fax: 902-368-4348, sjgallant@assembly.pe.ca; sonny.gallant@liberal.pe.ca
Social Media:
www.facebook.com/people/Sonny-Gallant/100001793535144
Office Manager, Hazel Gallant
902-368-4341, Fax: 902-368-4348, hggallant@assembly.pe.ca
Researcher, Kathy Paugh
902-368-4330, Fax: 902-368-4348, kjpaugh@gov.pe.ca

Hansard Office
J. Angus MacLean Bldg., 94 Great George St., 2nd Fl., PO Box 774, Charlottetown, PE C1A 7L3
902-368-5371 Fax: 902-368-5175
The published daily debates of Members in the House & in committees are known as Hansard. Staff of the Hansard Office transcribes, publishes, & indexes the debates.

Office of the Information & Privacy Commissioner
J. Angus MacLean Bldg., 180 Richmond St., 2nd Fl., PO Box 2000, Charlottetown, PE C1A 7K7
902-368-4099 Fax: 902-368-5947
The Information & Privacy Commissioner is appointed by the Legislature for a five year term. The Commissioner, who is an independent officer of the Legislative Assembly, reports annually to the Speaker of the Legislative Assembly about the work of the Office.
The Commissioner accepts Requests for Review from persons who are not satisfied with responses as a result of access to information requests made under the Freedom of Information & Protection of Privacy Act. Upon conclusion of a review, the order of the Information & Privacy Commissioner is final. Applicants, the public body, or a third party may only apply to the Supreme Court of Prince Edward Island for judicial review.
The Commissioner also conducts investigations related to privacy complaints.
Commissioner, Information & Privacy, Maria C. MacDonald
902-368-4099, Fax: 902-368-5947, mariamacdonald@gov.pe.ca

Legislative Library & Research Service
Coles Bldg., 175 Richmond St., 1st Fl., PO Box 2000, Charlottetown, PE C1A 7N8
902-620-3765 Fax: 902-620-3975
Opened in 2008, the Legislative Library supports members, committees, & house officers in their work. Non-partisan reports are provided by the research service.
Research Librarian, Laura Morrell
902-620-3765, Fax: 902-368-5175, lemorrell@assembly.pe.ca
Research Officer, Ryan Reddin
902-620-3766, Fax: 902-368-5175, rmreddin@assembly.pe.ca

Office of the Official Opposition (Progressive Conservative)
Coles Bldg., 175 Richmond St., 3rd Fl., PO Box 338, Charlottetown, PE C1A 7K7
902-368-4360 Fax: 902-368-4377
The Official Opposition raises concerns of Islanders & hold the government accountable for its policies & promises.
Leader, Official Opposition, Hon. Olive Crane
902-368-4360, Fax: 902-368-4377, omcrane@assembly.pe.ca
Advisor, Communications & Research, Iris Phillips
902-368-4358, Fax: 902-368-4377, iephillips@assembly.pe.ca
Researcher, Andrew Halliday
902-368-7554, Fax: 902-368-4377, amhalliday@assembly.pe.ca
Press Secretary, Sheryl MacAulay
semacaulay@assembly.pe.ca

Office of the Speaker
Province House, 165 Richmond St., 1st Fl., PO Box 2000, Charlottetown, PE C1A 7N8
902-368-4310 Fax: 902-368-4473
At the beginning of each new General Assembly, a Speaker of the Legislative Assembly is elected by secret ballot. The following Members of the Legislative Assembly are ineligible to be the Speaker: the Premier, the Leader of the Opposition & leaders of other political parties in the Assembly, & Members of the Executive Council.
Administrative Assistant, Speaker's Office, Barbara O'Donnell
902-368-4310, Fax: 902-368-4473, baodonnell@assembly.pe.ca

Sixty-fourth General Assembly - Prince Edward Island

Province House, 165 Richmond St., 1st Fl., PO Box 2000, Charlottetown, PE C1A 7N8
902-368-5970 Fax: 902-368-5175
877-315-5518
www.assembly.pe.ca
Last Provincial General Election: October 3, 2011.
Next Provincial General Election (scheduled under the province's fixed-date legislation): October 2015.
Party Standings (October 2011):
Liberal: 22;
Progressive Conservative 5;
Total: 27.
Salaries, Indemnities & Allowances (April 2010):
A Member of the Legislative Assembly's salary is $65,344.
In addition to this basic salary for each Member of the Legislative Assembly are the following additional salaries:
Premier $71,094 (total $136,438);
Ministers $45,688 (total $111,032);
Speaker $38,474 (total $103,818);
Deputy Speaker $19,237 (total $84,581);
Leader of the Opposition $45,688 (total $111,032);
Government House Leader $12,337 (total $77,681);
Opposition House Leader $4,339 (total $69,683);
Government Whip & Opposition Whip $3,659 (total $69,003);
Non-Ministerial Members of Executive Council Committees $5,996 (total $71,340);
Leader of a Third Party $16,764 (total $82,108).
The following is a list of Members of the Legislative Assembly, with their electoral district number & name, party affiliation, & contact information. The general address for all Members of the Legislative Assembly is as follows: PO Box 2000, Charlottetown PE, C1A 7N8.
Member, Legislative Assembly, James Aylward, District #6 - Stratford - Kinlock, Progressive Conservative
902-368-4360, jamesaylward@peipcparty.ca
Member, Legislative Assembly, Hon. Carolyn Bertram, District #18 - Rustico - Emerald, Liberal
902-368-5250, Fax: 902-368-4121, cibertram@gov.pe.ca; carolyn.bertram@liberal.pe.ca, Other Communications: Constituency Phone: 902-963-2700 or902-964-2015
Member, Legislative Assembly, Paula Biggar, District #23 - Tyne Valley - Linkletter, Liberal
902-368-4330, Fax: 902-368-4348, pjbiggar@assembly.pe.ca; paula.biggar@liberal.pe.ca, Other Communications: Constituency Phone: 902-831-2686 or 902-436-5066
Social Media: www.twitter.com/pjbiggar, www.facebook.com/paula.biggarwww.linkedin.com/pub/paula-biggar/17/13a/392
Member, Legislative Assembly, Hon. Richard Brown, District #12 - Charlottetown - Victoria Park, Liberal
902-368-6410, Fax: 902-368-6488, rebrown@gov.pe.ca; richard.brown@liberal.pe.ca, Other Communications: Constituency Phone: 902-566-4560
Social Media: www.facebook.com/profile.php?id=712491160
Member, Legislative Assembly, Hon. Kathleen Casey, District #14 - Charlottetown - Lewis Point, Liberal
902-368-4310, Fax: 902-368-4473, kmcasey@assembly.pe.ca; kathleen.casey@liberal.pe.ca, Other Communications: Constituency Phone: 902-566-5036
Social Media:
www.facebook.com/profile.php?id=100001926175864www.linkedin.com/pub/kathleen-casey/9/a84/134
Member, Legislative Assembly; Leader, Opposition, Hon. Olive Crane, District #7 - Morell - Mermaid, Progressive Conservative
902-368-4360, Fax: 902-368-4377, omcrane@assembly.pe.ca; olivecrane@peipcparty.ca
Social Media: www.twitter.com/olivecrane, www.facebook.com/OliveCranewww.linkedin.com/pub/olive-crane/2a/abb/58
Member, Legislative Assembly; Minister, Health & Wellness; Minister Responsible, Aboriginal Affairs, Hon. Doug W. Currie, District #11 - Charlottetown - Parkdale, Liberal
902-368-5152, Fax: 902-368-4910, dwcurrie@gov.pe.ca;doug.currie@liberal.pe.ca, Other Communications: Constituency Phone: 902-566-4160
Social Media: www.twitter.com/DougCurrie, www.facebook.com/doug.w.currie
Note: Web Sites: www.dougcurrie.ca (Personal Website); www.gov.pe.ca/health (Department of Health & Wellness)
Member, Legislative Assembly; Minister, Community Services, Seniors. & Labour; Minister Responsible, Status of Women, Hon. Valerie E. Docherty, District #17 - Kellys Cross - Cumberland, Liberal
902-368-4330, Fax: 902-368-4348, vedocherty@assembly.pe.ca; valerie.docherty@liberal.pe.ca, Other Communications: Constituency Phone: 902-675-4215
Social Media:
www.facebook.com/profile.php?id=100002087193589
Note: Web Site: www.gov.pe.ca/sss (Department ofCommunity Services, Seniors, & Labour)
Member, Legislative Assembly, Bush Dumville, District #15 - West Royalty - Springvale, Liberal
902-368-4330, Fax: 902-368-4348, sfdumville@assembly.pe.ca; bush.dumville@liberal.pe.ca, Other Communications: Constituency Phone: 902-566-5150
Social Media:
www.facebook.com/profile.php?id=100002345233840
Member, Legislative Assembly; Government House Leader, Sonny Gallant, District #24 - Evangeline - Miscouche, Liberal
902-368-4330, Fax: 902-368-4348, sjgallant@assembly.pe.ca; sonny.gallant@liberal.pe.ca, Other Communications: Constituency Phone: 902-854-3214
Social Media:
www.facebook.com/people/Sonny-Gallant/100001793535144
Member, Legislative Assembly; Premier, Prince Edward Island; President, Executive Council; Minister Responsible, Intergovernmental Affairs; Minister Responsible, Acadian &Francophone Affairs; Leader, Liberal Party of Prince Edward Island, Hon. Robert W.J. Ghiz, District #13 - Charlottetown - Brighton, Liberal
902-368-4400, Fax: 902-368-4416, premier@gov.pe.ca; robert.ghiz@liberal.pe.ca, Other Communications: Constituency Phone: 902-566-4832
Social Media:
www.facebook.com/pages/Robert-Ghiz-PEI-Premier/1174119 11662012
Note: Web Site: www.gov.pe.ca/premier (Office of the Premier)
Member, Legislative Assembly, Hon. Gerard Greenan, District #22 - Summerside - St. Eleanors, Liberal
902-368-4330, Fax: 902-368-4348, lggreenan@assembly.pe.ca; gerard.greenan@liberal.pe.ca, Other Communications: Constituency Phone: 902-436-4788
Social Media: www.twitter.com/gerardgreenan, www.facebook.com/gerardgreenan
Member, Legislative Assembly; Minister, Tourism & Culture, Hon. Robert L. Henderson, District #25 - O'Leary - Inverness, Liberal
902-368-4330, Fax: 902-368-4348, rlhenderson@assembly.pe.ca; robert.henderson@liberal.pe.ca, Other Communications: Constituency Phone: 902-859-2955
Social Media:
www.facebook.com/profile.php?id=100001965683516
Note: Web Site: www.gov.pe.ca/tourism (Department of Tourism & Culture)
Member, Legislative Assembly, Colin LaVie, District #1 - Souris - Elmira, Progressive Conservative
902-368-4360, colinlavie@peipcparty.ca
Social Media:
www.facebook.com/profile.php?id=100002620587903
Member, Legislative Assembly; Minister of Fisheries, Aquaculture, & Rural Development, Hon. Ron W. MacKinley, District #16 - Cornwall - Meadowbank, Liberal
902-368-5120, Fax: 902-368-5385, rwmackinley@gov.pe.ca;ron.mackinley@liberal.pe.ca, Other Communications: Constituency Phone: 902-566-6600
Social Media:
www.facebook.com/pages/Ron-MacKinley/60342728811
Note: Web Site: www.gov.pe.ca/fard (Department of Fisheries, Aquaculture, & RuralDevelopment)
Member, Legislative Assembly, Charles McGeoghegan, District #4 - Belfast - Murray River, Liberal
902-368-4330, Fax: 902-368-4348, cemcgeoghegan@assembly.pe.ca; charlie.mcgeoghegan@liberal.pe.ca, Other Communications: Constituency Phone: 902-962-4020
Social Media:
www.facebook.com/profile.php?id=100002798127012
Member, Legislative Assembly; Minister, Education & Early Childhood Development; Minister, Justice & Public Safety; Attorney General, Hon. J. Alan McIsaac, District #5 - Vernon River - Stratford, Liberal
902-368-4330, Fax: 902-368-4348, jamcisaac@assembly.pe.ca; alan.mcisaac@liberal.pe.ca, Other Communications: Constituency Phone: 902-569-2200
Social Media:
www.facebook.com/profile.php?id=100001892659368
Note: Web Sites: www.gov.pe.ca/eecd (Department of Education & Early Childhood Development); www.gov.pe.ca/jps (Department of Justice & Public Safety)
Member, Legislative Assembly, Robert Mitchell, District #10 - Charlottetown - Sherwood, Liberal

902-368-4330, Fax: 902-368-4348, rjmitchell@gov.pe.ca; robert.mitchell@liberal.pe.ca, Other Communications: Constituency Phone: 902-566-3973
Social Media: www.facebook.com/profile.php?id=625801979
Member, Legislative Assembly, Pat Murphy, District #26 - Alberton - Roseville, Liberal
902-368-4330, Fax: 902-368-4348, pwmurphy@assembly.pe.ca; pat.murphy@liberal.pe.ca, Other Communications: Constituency Phone: 902-853-4393
Social Media: www.facebook.com/pwmurphy
Member, Legislative Assembly, Steven Myers, District #2 - Georgetown - St. Peters, Progressive Conservative
902-368-4360, stevenmyers@peipcparty.ca
Member, Legislative Assembly, Hal Perry, District #27 - Tignish - Palmer Road, Progressive Conservative
902-368-4360, halperry@peipcparty.ca
Member, Legislative Assembly; Minister, Innovation & Advanced Learning, Hon. Allen F. Roach, District#3 - Montague - Kilmur, Liberal
allen.roach@liberal.pe.ca, Other Communications: Constituency Phone: 902-838-5406
Social Media: www.facebook.com/profile.php?id=100002417155344
Note: Web Site: www.gov.pe.ca/ia (Department of Innovation & Advanced Learning)
Member, Legislative Assembly; Minister, Finance & Municipal Affairs, Hon. Wesley J. Sheridan, District #20 - Kensington - Malpeque, Liberal
902-368-4050, Fax: 902-368-6575, wjsheridan@gov.pe.ca; wes.sheridan@liberal.pe.ca, Other Communications: Constituency Phone: 902-836-7000
Social Media: www.facebook.com/profile.php?id=100002547484282&ref=ts
Note: Web Site: www.gov.pe.ca/finance (Department of Finance & Municipal Affairs)
Member, Legislative Assembly; Minister, Environment, Energy, & Forestry, Hon. Janice A. Sherry, District #21 - Summerside - Wilmot, Liberal
902-368-4930, Fax: 902-368-4974, jasherry@gov.pe.ca; janice.sherry@liberal.pe.ca, Other Communications: Constituency Phone: 902-436-2588
Social Media: www.facebook.com/people/Janice-Sherry/100002079465746
Note: Web Site: www.gov.pe.ca/eef (Department of Environment, Energy, & Forestry)
Member, Legislative Assembly; Minister, Transportation & Infrastructure Renewal, Hon. Robert S. Vessey, District #9 - York - Oyster Bed, Liberal
902-368-4801, Fax: 902-368-5277, rsvessey@gov.pe.ca;robert.vessey@liberal.pe.ca, Other Communications: Constituency Phone: 902-672-2774
Note: Web Site: www.gov.pe.ca/tir (Department of Transportation & InfrastructureRenewal)
Member, Legislative Assembly, Buck Watts, District #8 - Tracadie - Hillsborough Park, Liberal
902-368-4330, Fax: 902-368-4348, fdwatts@assembly.pe.ca; buck.watts@liberal.pe.ca, Other Communications: Constituency Phone: 902-566-6551
Social Media: www.facebook.com/profile.php?id=100002411296559
Member, Legislative Assembly; Deputy Premier, Prince Edward Island; Minister, Agriculture, Hon. George T. Webster, District #19 - Borden - Kinkora, Liberal
902-368-4820, Fax: 902-368-4846, gtwebster@gov.pe.ca;george.webster@liberal.pe.ca, Other Communications: Constituency Phone: 902-887-3185
Note: Web Site: www.gov.pe.ca/agriculture (Department of Agriculture)

Prince Edward Island Government Departments & Agencies

Prince Edward Island Department of Agriculture

Jones Bldg., 11 Kent St., PO Box 2000, Charlottetown, PE C1A 7N8
902-368-4880 Fax: 902-368-4857
www.gov.pe.ca/agriculture

Prince Edward Island's Department of Agriculture provides programs & services to farmers. Programs are developed within the context of the Sustainable Resource Policy, which protects the province's land, water, & air.
The following are some examples of program categories: AgriFlexibility; Buy PEI;, Crop Production; Food Safety, Biosecurity, & Traceability; Forestry; Innovation & Applied Research; Laboratory Services; Livestock; Organic; & Training.

Acts Administered:
Agricultural Crop Rotation Act
Agricultural Insurance Act
Agricultural Products Standards Act
Agrologists Act
Animal Health & Protection Act
Artificial Insemination Act
Companion Animal Protection Act
Dairy Industry Act
Dairy Producers Act
Dog Act
Environmental Protection Act
Farm Machinery Dealers & Vendors Act
Farm Practices Act
Farm Registration & Farm Organization Funding Act
Fire Prevention Act
Forest Management Act
Gasoline Tax Act
Grain Elevators Corporation Act
Lands Protection Act, P.E.I.
Livestock Community Auction Sales Act
Natural Areas Protection Act
Natural Products Marketing Act
Occupational Health & Safety Act
PEI Farm Safety Code of Practice
Pesticides Control Act
Planning Act
Plant Health Act
Public Forest Council Act
Real Property Assessment Act
Real Property Tax Act
Revenue Tax Axt
Smoke Free Places Act
Stray Livestock Act
Veterinary Profession Act
Weed Control Act
Women's Institute Act

Minister, Agriculture; Deputy Premier, Prince Edward Island, Hon. George T. Webster
902-368-4820, Fax: 902-368-4846, gtwebster@gov.pe.ca; george.webster@liberal.pe.ca, Other Communications: Department Phone: 902-368-4880; Fax: 902-368-4857
Deputy Minister, Brian Douglas
902-368-4830, Fax: 902-368-4846, bwdouglas@gov.pe.ca
Communications Officer, Alf Blanchard
902-368-4888, Fax: 902-368-4857, ahblanchard@gov.pe.ca

Associated Agencies, Boards & Commissions:
• Agricultural Insurance Corporation
29 Indigo Cres.
PO Box 1600
Charlottetown, PE C1A 7N3
902-368-4842 Fax: 902-368-6677
www.gov.pe.ca/growingforward
Production insurance is administered by the Prince Edward Island Agricultural Insurance Corporation. It provides production risk protection to producers who may sustain crop losses due to natural hazards.
Programs administered by the Corporation are as follows: AgriStability, AgriInvest, AgriInsurance, & AgriRecovery.
• Farm Practices Review Board
The Farm Practices Review Board is responsible for reviewing concerns from the public about farm practices.
• Grain Elevators Corporation
7 Gerald McCarville Dr.
PO Box 250
Kensington, PE C0B 1M0
902-836-8935 Fax: 902-836-8926
www.peigec.com
The Prince Edward Island Grain Elevators Corporation is a leader in the province's cereal & protein sector.
For growers who want the pooled return, the Corporation operates grain marketing pools. Producers may also sell part of their crop to the Corporation at daily market prices.
Grain & products marketed throughout Prince Edward Island & Atlantic Canada.
• Marketing Council

Agriculture Policy & Regulatory Division
Jones Bldg., 11 Kent St., 5th Fl., Charlottetown, PE C1A 7N8
The Agriculture Policy & Regulatory Division oversees areas such as the following: research; administration of industry development programs; community pastures; on-farm food safety; food quality; marketing legislation; domestic & foreign trade; traceability; foreign animal disease; & emergency preparedness.
Director, Agriculture Policy & Regulatory Division, Shane Murphy
902-620-3084, srmurphy@gov.pe.ca
Manager, Agriculture Regulatory Programs, Brian Matheson
902-368-5087, Fax: 902-368-4857, bgmatheson@gov.pe.ca

Agriculture Resource Division
Research Station, University Ave., PO Box 1600, Charlottetown, PE C1A 7N3
902-368-4145 Fax: 902-368-5661
The Agriculture Resource Division delivers sustainable resource & farm extension programs & services.
Director, Agriculture Resource Division, Tracy Wood
902-368-5645, Fax: 902-368-5661, tmwood@gov.pe.ca
Manager, Agriculture Information, Sandra MacKinnon
902-368-5647, Fax: 902-368-5729, sjmackinnon@gov.pe.ca
Manager, Agriculture Innovation, Lynda MacSwain
902-368-4815, Fax: 902-368-5729, lemacswain@gov.pe.ca
Manager, Sustainable Agriculture Resources, Barry Thompson
902-368-6366, Fax: 902-368-5661, blthompson@gov.pe.ca

Corporate & Financial Services Division
Jones Bldg., 11 Kent St., 5th Fl., PO Box 2000, Charlottetown, PE C1A 7N8
902-368-4880 Fax: 902-368-4857
Financial, administrative, & human resources services are provided by the Corporate & Financial Services Division.
Director, Corporate & Financial Services, Jerry Gavin
902-368-5741, Fax: 902-368-4857, jpgavin@gov.pe.ca
Manager, Human Resources, Tory Kennedy
902-368-6694, Fax: 902-368-4857, tkkennedy@gov.pe.ca
Coordinator, Records Management, Diana MacGillivray
902-368-4840, Fax: 902-368-4857, dxmacgillivray@gov.pe.ca

Prince Edward Island Analytical Laboratories
Research Station, University Ave., PO Box 1600, Charlottetown, PE C1A 7N3
902-368-4190
Prince Edward Island Analytical Laboratories include the Dairy Laboratory, the Soil, Feed, & Water Chemistry Testing Laboratory, & the Water Microbiology Laboratory.
The Dairy Laboratory works in support of the Prince Edward Island Dairy Industry Act & Regulations. It also provides services to VALACTA in Prince Edward Island, Nova Scotia, & New Brunswick.
The Soil, Feed, & Water Chemistry Testing Laboratory provides analytical information for farmers & the public.
Manager, Prince Edward Island Laboratories, Anna Marie MacFarlane
902-368-4190, Fax: 902-368-4486, ammacfarlane@gov.pe.ca
Officer, Quality Assurance, Marlene MacNeill
902-894-0318, Fax: 902-569-7778, mcmacneill@gov.pe.ca
Supervisor, Soil, Feed, & Water Chemistry Testing Laboratory, Lori C. Connolly-Brine
902-368-5671, Fax: 902-368-6299, lcconnolly@gov.pe.ca
Supervisor, Dairy Laboratory & Water Microbiology Laboratory; Mass Spectrometry Technologist, April M. Driscoll
902-314-2811, amdriscoll@gov.pe.ca
Diagnostician, Plant Disease, Marleen Clark
902-836-8922, Fax: 902-836-8921, mmclark@gov.pe.ca

Office of the Auditor General

Shaw Bldg., 105 Rochford St. North, 2nd Fl., Charlottetown, PE C1A 7N8
902-368-4520 Fax: 902-368-4598
www.assembly.pe.ca
Accountability & best practices in government operations are promoted by the Office of the Auditor General. Independent audits & examinations are conducted by the Office of the Auditor General for the Legislative Assembly of Prince Edward Island.
Auditor General, Colin P. Younker, CA
902-368-4520, Fax: 902-368-4598, cpyounker@gov.pe.ca
Audit Director, B. Jane MacAdam, CA
902-368-4524, Fax: 902-368-4598, bjmacadam@gov.pe.ca
Audit Director, Scott Messervey, CA, MPA
902-368-4518, Fax: 902-368-4598, dsmesservey@gov.pe.ca

Prince Edward Island Department of Community Services, Seniors, & Labour

Jones Bldg., 11 Kent St., 2nd Fl., PO Box 2000, Charlottetown, PE C1A 7N8
902-620-3777 Fax: 902-368-4740
866-594-3777
www.gov.pe.ca/sss
The Department of Community Services, Seniors, & Labour strives to develop healthy & self-reliant individuals & to support vulnerable members of the province. Programs & services are offered to promote social & economic prosperity & the creation of work environments that contribute to a safe, healthy, & engaged workforce.

Acts Administered:
Adoption Act
Advisory Council on the Status of Women Act
Blind Workers' Compensation Act
Child Protection Act
Employment Standards Act
Family & Child Services Act (Repealed)
Health Authorities' Employees Act (Repealed)
Housing Corporation Act
Labour Act
North American Labour Cooperation Agreement Implementation Act
Occupational Health & Safety Act
Pay Equity Act
Rehabilitation of Disabled Persons Act
Social Assistance Act
Social Work Act
Youth Employment Act

Minister, Community Services, Seniors & Labour; Minister Responsible, Status of Women, Hon. Valerie E. Docherty
902-368-4330, 866-594-3777, Fax: 902-368-4348, vedocherty@assembly.pe.ca; valerie.docherty@liberal.pe.ca

Social Media:
www.facebook.com/profile.php?id=100002087193589
Deputy Minister, Sharon Cameron
902-368-6520, Fax: 902-368-4740, secameron@gov.pe.ca
Communications Officer, Amber Nicholson
902-620-3409, Fax: 902-894-0242, amnicholson@gov.pe.ca

Associated Agencies, Boards & Commissions:
• Advisory Council on the Status of Women
Sherwood Business Centre
161 St. Peter's Rd., Main Level
PO Box 2000
Charlottetown, PE C1A 7N8
902-368-4510 Fax: 902-368-3269
peistatusofwomen@eastlink.ca
www.gov.pe.ca/acsw
The Prince Edward Island Advisory Council on the Status of Women consists of nine members. Members are appointed by government to serve on the government advisory agency. The Council advises the Minister Responsible for the Status of Women & works to support equality & the participation of women in economic, political, legal, & cultural activities.
• Employment Standards Board
Sherwood Business Centre
161 St. Peters Rd., 2nd Fl.
Charlottetown, PE C1A 7N8
www.gov.pe.ca/sss
The Employment Standards Board listens to appeals from employers regarding alleged violations of the Employment Standards Act. The Employment Standards Board is also responsible for presenting recommendations about the Minimum Wage Order to the Lieutenant Governor in Council.
• Labour Relations Board
Sherwood Business Centre
161 St. Peters Rd., 2nd Fl.
PO Box 2000
Charlottetown, PE C1A 7N8
902-368-5550 Fax: 902-368-5476 800-333-4362
www.gov.pe.ca/sss
The Labour Relations Board works to resolve applications received from labour or management, in accordance with Prince Edward Island's Labour Act.
• Workers Compensation Appeal Tribunal (WCAT)
161 St. Peters Rd., 1st Fl.
PO Box 2000
Charlottetown, PE C1A 7N8
Established under Prince Edward Island's Worker's Compensation Act, the Workers Compensation Appeal Tribunal operates as an independent quasi-judicial administrative tribunal. Workers or employers who are dissatisfied with a decision made by the Internal Reconsideration Officer can appeal it through the Workers Compensation Appeal Tribunal. The appeal body is the last level of appeal for workers' compensation matters.
The Office of the Workers Compensation Appeal Tribunal Coordinator is responsible for administrative duties related to the tribunal. The coordinator attends all hearings, but is not part of the decision making process.

Child & Family Services Division
Jones Bldg., 11 Kent St., 2nd Fl., PO Box 2000, Charlottetown, PE C1A 7N8
902-368-5294
The Child & Family Services Division offers a wide range of programs & services to care for Prince Edward Island's children & families. Examples of programs include child protection, foster care, & adoption services.
Director, Child & Family Services, Rona Brown
902-368-5396, Fax: 902-368-4258, rmbrown@gov.pe.ca
Provincial Coordinator, Child Protection, Maureen G. MacEwen
902-368-6161, Fax: 902-620-3362, mgmacewen@gov.pe.ca
Coordinator, Prevention & Residential Services, Child Protection & Youth Services, Barry L. Chandler
902-368-6180, Fax: 902-620-3362, blchandler@gov.pe.ca
Coordinator, Family Violence Prevention & Community Development, Premier's Action Committee on Family Violence Prevention, Dr. Wendy Verhoek-Oftedahl
902-368-6712, Fax: 902-368-6169,
wverhoekoftedahl@gov.pe.ca

Corporate & Financial Services Division
Jones Bldg., 11 Kent St., 2nd Fl., PO Box 2000, Charlottetown, PE C1A 7N8
Fax: 902-894-0242
The Corporate & Financial Services Division is responsible for the following areas: finance, administration, human resources, communications, French language services, intergovernmental & external relations, records information management, & emergency social services.
Director, Corporate & Financial Services, W. Lorne Clow
902-368-6109, Fax: 902-894-0242, wlclow@gov.pe.ca
Manager, Financial Services & Audit, Sonya L. Cobb
902-620-3408, Fax: 902-894-0242, slcobb@gov.pe.ca
Manager, Human Resources, Luanne M. Gallant
902-368-5529, Fax: 902-894-0242, lmgallant@gov.pe.ca
Coordinator, Federal, Provincial, Territorial, & Corporate Relations, Jennifer Burgess
902-368-5199, Fax: 902-894-0242, jmburgess@gov.pe.ca

Interministerial Women's Secretariat
Sullivan Bldg., 16 Fitzroy St., 1st Fl., PO Box 2000, Charlottetown, PE C1A 7N8
902-368-6494 Fax: 902-569-7798
The role of the Interministerial Women's Secretariat is to assist the Minister Responsible for the Status of Women to protect & promote gender equality.
Minister Responsible, Status of Women; Minister, Community Services, Seniors, & Labour, Hon. Valerie E. Docherty
902-368-4330, Fax: 902-368-4348,
vedocherty@assembly.pe.ca; valerie.docherty@liberal.pe.ca
Social Media:
www.facebook.com/profile.php?id=100002087193589
Director, Interministerial Women's Secretariat, Michelle Harris-Genge
902-368-5557, Fax: 902-569-7798,
mdharris-genge@gov.pe.ca

Labour & Industrial Relations & Seniors Division
Sherwood Business Centre, 161 St. Peters Rd., 2nd Fl., PO Box 2000, Charlottetown, PE C1A 7N8
902-368-5550 Fax: 902-368-5476
800-333-4362
The Labour & Industrial Relations & Seniors Division consists of the following areas: Senior's Secretariat; Office of the Employer Advisor; Employment Standards Branch; Worker Advisor Program; & the Industrial Relations Branch.
The Senior's Secretariat strives to improve the quality of life for seniors in Prince Edward Island, by providing advice & information.
The Office of the Employer Advisor helps employers in the administration of the Occupational Health & Safety Act & the Workers Compensation Act.
The Employment Standards Act is administered by the Employment Standards Branch. Information provided by the branch includes employee entitlements to wages, statutory holidays, vacation pay, overtime pay, maternity & parental leave, & notice of termination.
Injured workers find assistance through the Worker Advisor Program. It provides information about benefits, according to Prince Edward Island's Workers Compensation Act.
Prince Edward Island's unionized workforce may look to the Industrial Relations Branch for services, such as the development of labour & management relations, conciliation & mediation services, & third party assistance.
Director, Labour & Industrial Relations & Seniors; Chief Conciliation Officer, Industrial Relations Branch, Faye M. Martin
902-569-0545, 866-770-0588, Fax: 902-894-0242,
fmmartin@gov.pe.ca
Chief Labour Standards Officer, Employment Standards Branch, Robert Yeo
902-368-5552, 800-333-4362, Fax: 902-368-5476,
rgyeo@gov.pe.ca
Manager, Worker Advisor Program, Maureen Peters
902-368-5587, 800-658-1806, Fax: 902-368-6576,
mapeters@gov.pe.ca
Senior's Policy Advisor, Senior's Secretariat, Catherine A. Freeze
902-620-3785, 866-770-0588, Fax: 902-894-0242,
cafreeze@gov.pe.ca
Employer Advisor, Office of the Employer Advisor, Patricia McPhail
902-368-6132, Fax: 902-368-4382, phmcphail@gov.pe.ca

Social Programs & Housing Division
Jones Bldg., 11 Kent St., 2nd Fl., PO Box 2000, Charlottetown, PE C1A 7N8
The Social Programs & Housing Division provides services related to social assistance, disability support, & housing.
Director, Social Programs & Housing, Bob D. Creed
902-368-6446, Fax: 902-620-3553, bdcreed@gov.pe.ca
Coordinator, Provincial Housing, Bill Fleming
902-368-5779, Fax: 902-894-5471, bhfleming@ihis.org
Coordinator, Social Assistance & Disability Support Programs (East), Rhea M. Jenkins
902-368-5904, Fax: 902-368-6443, rmjenkins@ihis.org
Coordinator, Social Assistance & Disability Support Programs (West), Pat W. MacDonald
902-888-8149, Fax: 902-888-8398, pwmacdonald@ihis.org

Prince Edward Island Department of Education & Early Childhood Development

Holman Centre, #101, 250 Water St., Summerside, PE C1N 1B6
902-438-4130 Fax: 902-438-4062
www.gov.pe.ca/education
Other Communication: Charlottetown Phone: 902-368-4600
Prince Edward Island's Department of Education & Early Childhood Development offers programs & services for children from birth to the conclusion of twelfth grade.

Acts Administered:
Child Care Facilities Act
Island Regulatory & Appeals Commission Act
School Act
Teachers' Superannuation Act
Minister, Education & Early Childhood Development; Minister, Justice & Public Safety; Attorney General, Hon. J. Alan McIsaac
902-368-4330, Fax: 902-368-4348,
jamcisaac@assembly.pe.ca; alan.mcisaac@liberal.pe.ca
Social Media:
www.facebook.com/profile.php?id=100001892659368
Deputy Minister, Dr. Alex (Sandy) MacDonald
902-438-4876, Fax: 902-438-4150, agmacdonald@edupe.ca
Coordinator, Communications, Rebecca Bruce
902-368-6449, Fax: 902-368-4663, rebruce@gov.pe.ca

Associated Agencies, Boards & Commissions:
• Children's Secretariat
c/o Sarah Henry, Education & Early Childhood Development
161 St. Peters Rd.
PO Box 2000
Charlottetown, PE C1A 7N8
Prince Edward Island's Children's Secretariat consists of government & community representatives. They strive to improve outcomes for children to age eight, in areas such as healthy child development & public education.
• Eastern School District
PO Box 8600
Charlottetown, PE C1A 8V7
902-368-6990 Fax: 902-368-6960
www.edu.pe.ca/esd
The Eastern School District consists of 36 schools. Education is offered to students from kindergarten to grade 12.
• French Language School Board / La Commission scolaire de langue française de l'îlw-du-Prince-Édouard
1596, rte 124
Abram-Village, PE C0B 2E0
902-854-2975 Fax: 902-854-2981
cslf@edu.pe.ca
www.edu.pe.ca/cslf
Prince Edward Island's French Language School Board administers six schools.
• Prince Edward Island Athletic Association (PEISAA)
#101, 250 Water St.
Summerside, PE C1N 1B6
902-438-4846 Fax: 902-438-4884
www.peisaa.pe.ca
The Prince Edward Island Athletic Association was established as the governing body for all school sports in the province. The association is a member of the Canadian School Sport Federation & is affiliated with the National Federation of State High School Athletic Associations.
• Western School Board of Prince Edward Island
Summerside Office
272 MacEwen Dr.
Summerside, PE C1N 2P7
902-888-8400 Fax: 902-888-8449
www.edu.pe.ca/wsb
Other Communication: Elmsdale Office, Phone: 902-853-8602, Fax: 902-853-8679
The Western School Board oversees twenty-one schools situated in the western region of Prince Edward Island.

Administration & Corporate Services Division
#101. 250 Water St., Summerside, PE C1N 1B6
902-438-4819 Fax: 902-438-4874
The Administration & Corporate Services Division oversees the following areas: finance & school board operations; program evaluation & student assessment; research & corporate services; technology in education; human resources; & the Office of the Registrar.
Senior Director, Administration & Corporate Services, Terry Keefe
902-438-4880, Fax: 902-438-4874, tekeefe@gov.pe.ca
Director, Finance & School Board Operations, Gordon MacFadyen
902-438-4882, Fax: 902-438-4874, gsmacfadyen@gov.pe.ca
Manager, Research & Corporate Services, Robin Phillips
902-438-4837, Fax: 902-438-4874
Manager, Human Resources, Tanya Tynski
902-438-4881, Fax: 902-438-4874, tmtynski@gov.pe.ca
Manager, Program Evaluation & Student Assessment, Cindy Wood
902-438-4904, Fax: 902-438-4889, clwood@gov.pe.ca
Registrar & Coordinator, International Education, Nancy Desrosiers
902-438-4827, Fax: 902-438-4062, ndesrosiers@gov.pe.ca
Coordinator, Information Management, Mark DeMone
902-438-4839, Fax: 902-438-4874, mxdemone@gov.pe.ca
Coordinator, Education Technology, Edward MacLean
902-438-4834, Fax: 902-438-4874, edmaclean@gov.pe.ca

Learning & Early Childhood Development Division
Holman Centre, 250 Water St., Summerside, PE C1N 1B6
902-438-4816 Fax: 902-438-4874
The Public Education Branch is responsible for the following services: early childhood development & kindergarten; child & student services; & English & French programs.
Senior Director, Learning & Early Childhood Development, Imelda Arsenault
902-438-4879, Fax: 902-438-4150, imarsenault@edu.pe.ca
Director, French Programs, Guy Albert
902-438-4155, Fax: 902-438-4884, gcalbert@edu.pe.ca
Director, Child & Student Services, Glenn Edison
902-438-4886, Fax: 902-438-4884, ggedison@edu.pe.ca
Director, English Programs, Kathy McDonald
902-438-4870, Fax: 902-438-4062, kmmcdonald@edu.pe.ca
Manager, Early Childhood Development & Kindergarten, Carolyn Simpson
902-438-4883, Fax: 902-438-4884, cesimpson@edu.pe.ca
Coordinator, Elementary Education, Sheila Barnes
902-438-4800, Fax: 902-438-4062, sebarnes@edu.pe.ca
Coordinator, Autism, Marlene Breitenbach
902-569-7792, Fax: 902-368-4622, mmbreitenbach@edu.pe.ca
Coordinator, Student Services, Sterling Carruthers
902-438-4134, Fax: 902-438-4062, sdcarruthers@edu.pe.ca
Coordinator, Healthy Child Development, Sarah Henry
902-438-4843, Fax: 902-438-4874, skhenry@edu.pe.ca
Coordinator, Secondary Education, Mike Leslie
902-438-4801, Fax: 902-438-4062, mjleslie@edu.pe.ca
Coordinator, Professional Development, Leona McIsaac-Moran
902-438-4858, Fax: 902-438-4884, lmmoran@edu.pe.ca
Coordinator, Special Education, Peter Meggs
902-438-4850, Fax: 902-438-4884, pcmeggs@edu.pe.ca
Coordinator, Community Information, Melanie Melanson
902-438-4842, Fax: 902-438-4874, mdmelanson@edu.pe.ca
Administrator, English as an Additional Language, Janet Perry-Payne
902-620-3735, Fax: 902-620-3737, jlpayne@edu.pe.ca

Elections Prince Edward Island

J. Angus MacLean Bldg., 94 Great George St., 1st Fl., PO Box 774, Charlottetown, PE C1A 7L3
902-368-5895 Fax: 902-368-6500
888-234-8783
www.electionspei.ca
Elections Prince Edward Island provides information to electors & candidates. Guided by the Canadian Charter of Rights & Freedoms, Elections Prince Edward Island works to ensure that electors & candidates have the opportunity to exercise their democratic right.
Chief Electoral Officer, Lowell Croken
902-368-5898, Fax: 902-368-6500, ljcroken@gov.pe.ca
Deputy Chief Electoral Officer, Norma E. Palmer-Bowers
902-368-5895, Fax: 902-368-6500, nepalmer@gov.pe.ca
Manager, Election Operations, Judy Richard
902-620-3709, Fax: 902-368-6500, jgrichard@gov.pe.ca

Prince Edward Island Department of Environment, Energy, & Forestry

Jones Bldg., 11 Kent St., 4th Fl., PO Box 2000, Charlottetown, PE C1A 7N8
902-368-5000 Fax: 902-368-5830
www.gov.pe.ca/eef
Staff members of the Department of Environment, Energy, & Forestry work to achieve the following goals: to preserve the province's natural environment; to encourage sustainable development; & to cultivate Prince Edward Island's energy resources.
The mission of the department is carried out by establishing standards, ensuring compliance to protect the environment, & promoting energy development from sustainable local resources.
Acts Administered:
Agriculture Crop Rotation Act
Amusement Devices Act
Automobile Junk Yards Act
Beverage Containers Act
Boilers & Pressure Vessels Act
Electrical Inspection Act
Elevators & Lifts Act
Energy Corporation Act
Environmental Protection Act
Forest Management Act
Institute of Man & Resources Act
Lightning Rod Act
Mineral Resources Act
Natural Areas Protection Act
Oil & Natural Gas Act
Pesticides Control Act
Power Engineers Act
Provincial Building Code Act
Public Forest Council Act
Renewable Energy Act
Unsightly Property Act
Wildlife Conservation Act
Minister, Environment, Energy, & Forestry, Hon. Janice A. Sherry
902-368-6410, Fax: 902-368-6488, jasherry@gov.pe.ca; janice.sherry@liberal.pe.ca
Social Media: www.facebook.com/people/Janice-Sherry/100002079465746
Deputy Minister, John MacQuarrie
902-368-5340, Fax: 902-368-6488, jamacquarrie@gov.pe.ca
Officer, Communications, Kim Devine
902-368-5286, Fax: 902-368-5830, kmdevine@gov.pe.ca

Associated Agencies, Boards & Commissions:
• Environmental Advisory Council
PO Box 2000
Charlottetown, PE C1A 7N8
The Environmental Advisory Council advises the Minister responsible for the environment about environmental concerns. Members of the council are appointed by the Lieutenant Governor in Council.
• Prince Edward Island Energy Corporation
Jones Bldg.
11 Kent St., 4th Fl.
PO Box 2000
Charlottetown, PE C1A 7N8
The Prince Edward Island Energy Corporation promotes the development, generation, transmission, & distribution of energy in an economic & efficient manner.
• Public Forest Council (PFC)
c/o PEI Department of Environment, Energy, & Forestry
Forestry Division
PO Box 2000
Charlottetown, PE C1A 7N8
Fax: 902-368-4713
publicforest@gov.pe.ca
www.gov.pe.ca/eef/PFC
The Public Forest Council is made up of six private sector members & three public sector members, who are appointed by the Lieutenant Governor in Council. Council members foster discussion about the potential for provincial woodlands. The council is especially interested in non-traditional, non-consumptive uses of public forests.
• Species at Risk Advisory Committee
The Species at Risk Advisory Committee performs the following tasks: assessing the province's wildlife resources; advising the Minister of Environment, Energy, & Forestry about the species that should be listed at risk; analyzing the effects of land use on wildlife & their habitat; & making recommendations about the conservation of wildlife & its habitat.

Administrative Services Division
Jones Bldg., 11 Kent St., 4th Fl., PO Box 2000, Charlottetown, PE C1A 7N8
902-368-5000 Fax: 902-368-5830
Administrative services, human resources, & finances are the responsibilities of this division.
Director, Administrative Services, Mary Kinsman
902-368-5032, Fax: 902-368-5830, makinsman@gov.pe.ca

Energy & Minerals Division
Jones Bldg., 4th Fl., Charlottetown, PE C1A 7N8
902-894-0288 Fax: 902-894-0290
The Energy & Minerals Division is engaged in the following activities: developing & managing energy policies & programs; overseeing the development of mineral resources; & supporting gas exploration.
Director, Energy & Minerals, Wayne MacQuarrie
902-894-0289, Fax: 902-894-0290, dwmacquarrie@gov.pe.ca
Manager, Office Of Energy Efficiency, Mike Proud
902-620-3792, Fax: 902-620-3796, mpproud@gov.pe.ca
Officer, Sustainable Operations Program, George Meggison
902-620-3793, Fax: 902-620-3796, gemeggison@gov.pe.ca

Environment Division
Jones Bldg., 11 Kent St., 4th Fl., PO Box 2000, Charlottetown, PE C1A 7N8
902-368-5044 Fax: 902-368-5830
866-368-5044
The Environment Division oversees programs that protect the province's environement, including the following elements: groundwater; inland surface water & coastal estuaries; drinking water; the ozone layer; & air quality.
The division is also involved in waste management activities, such as the handling of litter, beverage containers, hazardous wastes, used oil, petroleum storage tanks, lead-acid batteries, tires, & derelict vehicles.
Director, Environment, Jim Young, P.Eng
902-368-5034, Fax: 902-368-5830, jjyoung@gov.pe.ca
Manager, Air & Hazardous Materials, Todd Fraser
902-368-5037, Fax: 902-368-5830, ktfraser@gov.pe.ca
Manager, Administrative & Customer Services, Roxanne Larter
902-368-5561, Fax: 902-368-5526, rmkarter@gov.pe.ca
Manager, Prince Edward Island Analytical Laboratories, Anna Marie MacFarlane
902-268-4190, Fax: 902-368-4486, ammacfarlane@gov.pe.ca
Manager, Inspection Services, Glenda MacKinnon-Peters, P.Eng.
902-368-4874, Fax: 902-368-5526, gcmackinnon-peters@gov.pe.ca
Manager, Watershed & Subdivision Planning, Bruce Raymond
902-368-5054, Fax: 902-368-5830, bgraymond@gov.pe.ca
Manager, Drinking Water, Land, & Systems Protection, George Somers
902-368-5046, Fax: 902-368-5830, ghsomers@gov.pe.ca
Manager, Environmental Impact Assessment & Land Management, Greg Wilson
902-368-5274, Fax: 902-368-5830, gbwilson@gov.pe.ca
Chief, Safety Standards, Alan Robison
902-368-4892, Fax: 902-368-5526, amrobison@gov.pe.ca
Chief Engineer, Building Standards, Garth Simmons
902-569-7746, Fax: 902-368-5830, gssimmons@gov.pe.ca
Chief Officer, Boiler & Pressure Vessel, Plumbing & Propane Inspection, Steve Townsend
902-368-5567, Fax: 902-368-5526, srtownsend@gov.pe.ca
Coordinator, Pesticide Monitoring & Control, Thane Clarke
902-368-5599, Fax: 902-368-5830, ktclarke@gov.pe.ca
Coordinator, Watershed & ALUS, Shawn Hill
902-620-3725, Fax: 902-368-5830, sjhill@gov.pe.ca
Coordinator, Emergency Response, Land & Systems Protection, Debbie Johnston
902-368-5059, Fax: 902-368-5830
Coordinator, Climate Change, Erin Taylor
902-368-6111, Fax: 902-368-5830, eotaylor@gov.pe.ca

Forests, Fish, & Wildlife Division
J. Frank Gaudet Tree Nursery, 183 Upton Rd., PO Box 2000, Charlottetown, PE C1A 7N8
902-368-4700 Fax: 902-368-4713
The Forests, Fish, & Wildlife Division oversees the following programs & services: the provincial forests; the private forest program; production development; resource inventory & modelling; & wildlife & fish.
Director, Forests, Fish, & Wildlife, Kate E. MacQuarrie
902-368-4705, Fax: 902-368-4713, kemacquarrie@gov.pe.ca
Senior Manager, Forests, Fish, & Wildlife, Dan McAskill
902-368-6730, Fax: 902-368-4713, jdmcaskill@gov.pe.ca
Manager, Private Forests, Brian Brown
902-368-6431, Fax: 902-368-4713
Manager, Production Development, Bill Butler
902-368-4711, Fax: 902-368-4713, wabutler@gov.pe.ca
Manager, Public Lands, Jon Hutchinson
902-368-4707, Fax: 902-368-4713, pjhutchinson@gov.pe.ca
Manager, Fish & Wildlife, Gerald MacDougall
902-368-5111, Fax: 902-368-4713, dgmacdougall@gov.pe.ca
Inventory Forester, Resource Inventory & Modelling, Mike Montigny
902-368-4709, mmontigny@gov.pe.ca

Investigation & Enforcement Division
PO Box 2000, Charlottetown, PE C1A 7N8
902-368-4808 Fax: 902-368-5830
The Investigation & Enforcement Division employs conservation & intelligence officers & pesticide regulatory inspectors to carry out its work.
Manager, Investigation & Enforcement, Wade MacKinnon
902-368-5000, Fax: 902-368-5830, wjmackinnon@gov.pe.ca
Officer, Conservation, Roland Richard
902-854-7250, Fax: 902-854-7255, rjrichard@gov.pe.ca
Officer, Aboriginal Conservation, Aaron Waddell
902-859-8816, Fax: 902-859-8709, awwadell@gov.pe.ca
Officer, Intelligence, Locke Jones
902-368-5044, Fax: 902-368-5830, lfjones@gov.pe.ca

Prince Edward Island Department of Finance & Municipal Affairs

Shaw Bldg., 95 Rochford St. South, 2nd Fl., PO Box 2000, Charlottetown, PE C1A 7N8
902-368-4000 Fax: 902-368-5544
www.gov.pe.ca/finance
The Department of Finance & Municipal Affairs facilitates the management of the Government of Prince Edward Island's human & financial resources.
Acts Administered:
Charlottetown Area Municipalities Act
Civil Service Act
Civil Service Superannuation Act
Community Development Equity Tax Credit Act
Condominium Act
Deposit Receipt (Winding-up) Act
Environment Tax Act
Financial Administration Act
Financial Corporation Capital Tax Act
Gasoline Tax Act
Health Tax Act
Income Tax Act
Lands Protection Act, P.E.I.
Lotteries Commission Act
Maritime Provinces Harness Racing Commission Act
Municipal Boundaries Act

Municipal Debenture Guarantee Act
Municipalities Act
Northumberland Strait Crossing Act
Planning Act
Public Purchasing Act
Public Sector Pay Reduction Act
Queen's Printer Act
Real Property Assessment Act
Real Property Tax Act
Real Property Transfer Tax Act
Registry Act
Revenue Administration Act
Revenue Tax Act
Statistics Act
City of Summerside Act
Tobacco Tax Act

Minister, Finance & Municipal Affairs, Hon. Wesley J. Sheridan
902-368-4050, Fax: 902-368-6575, wjsheridan@gov.pe.ca; wes.sheridan@liberal.pe.ca
Social Media:
www.facebook.com/profile.php?id=100002547484282&ref=ts

Deputy Minister, Doug Clow, CA
902-368-4053, Fax: 902-368-6575, dmclow@gov.pe.ca

Officer, Communications, MacDonald-Donovan Jennifer
902-620-3679, Fax: 902-368-6575, jwmacdonald@gov.pe.ca

Associated Agencies, Boards & Commissions:

• Office of the Child & Youth Services Commissioner
Homan Bldg.
#101, 250 Water St.
Summerside, PE C1N 1B6
902-438-4872 Fax: 902-438-4874
www.gov.pe.ca/childandyouth
The Child & Youth Services Commissioner deals with issues that affect children & youth in Prince Edward Island. The following legislation in Prince Edward Island affects children & youth: Child Protection Act; Mental Health Act; School Act; & Youth Justice Act.

• Commission on the Land & Local Governance
Aubin Arsenault Bldg.
3 Brighton Rd.
Charlottetown, PE C1A 8T6
www.gov.pe.ca/landandlocalgovernance

• Public Service Commission (PSC)
Shaw Bldg. North
105 Rochford St., 1st Fl.
PO Box 2000
Charlottetown, PE C1A 7N8
902-368-4080 Fax: 902-368-4383
www.gov.pe.ca/psc
The independent & impartial agency coordinates human resources in the public sector of Prince Edward Island. All government departments & agencies, health authorities, & other public sector employers are served by Prince Edward Island's Public Service Commission. Examples of services include recruitment, selection, occupational health & safety, payroll & benefits administration, & the employee assistant program.

Communications Prince Edward Island

Shaw Bldg., 95-105 Rochford St., 5th Fl., Charlottetown, PE C1A 7N8
www.gov.pe.ca/finance

Communications PEI provides provincial government departments, agencies, & crown corporations with a variety of communication services, such as graphic design, video & radio production, photography services, & mail services.

Assistant Deputy Minister, Communications Prince Edward Island, Matt McGuire
902-368-4407, Fax: 902-368-6118, mdmcguire@gov.pe.ca
Director, Strategic & Corporate Communications, Patricia Devine
902-368-5513, pdevine@gov.pe.ca
Queen's Printer & Manager, Document Publishing Centre & PEI Mail, Mike Fagan
902-368-5192, Fax: 902-368-5168, ssccoles@gov.pe.ca
Manager, Strategic Marketing & Graphic Design, Sheri Coles
902-368-6326, Fax: 902-569-7543, ssccoles@gov.pe.ca
Manager, Communications, Jean Doherty
902-569-0548, jmdoherty@gov.pe.ca
Manager, Multimedia Services, Peter MacPhee
902-368-6322, Fax: 902-368-5641, pwmacphee@gov.pe.ca
Officer, Corporate Communications, Heather Robinson
902-620-3144, hrobinson@gov.pe.ca

Office of the Comptroller

Shaw Bldg., 95 Rochford St., 2nd Fl., PO Box 2000, Charlottetown, PE C1A 7N8
902-368-4201 Fax: 902-368-6661
www.gov.pe.ca/finance

The Office of the Comptroller carries out the following responsibilities: operating the government's corporate accounting system; providing advice related to financial management; administering the corporate procurement service for departments & agencies; managing a corporate fleet information system; & producing the province's public accounts.

Comptroller, Scott K. Stevens, BBA, CGA
902-368-4001, Fax: 902-368-6661, ksstevens@gov.pe.ca
Manager, Procurement Services, Ian K. Burge
902-368-4041, Fax: 902-368-5171, ikburge@gov.pe.ca
Manager, Accounting, Doug H. Carr, FCGA
902-368-4014, Fax: 902-368-6661, dhcarr@gov.pe.ca
Manager, Risk, Linus Kelly
902-368-6165, Fax: 902-368-6243, lmkelly@gov.pe.ca
Manager, Administration Services, Lane Pineau
902-569-7559, Fax: 902-368-6661, lepineau@gov.pe.ca
Administrator, Financial System Administration, Helen Clow
902-368-4012, Fax: 902-368-6661, nhclow@gov.pe.ca
Supervisor, Accounts Payable, Theresa A. DesRoches
902-368-4067, Fax: 902-368-6661, tadesroches@gov.pe.ca
Analyst, Budget, Alan Silliker, CA
902-569-7666, Fax: 902-368-4077, agsilliker@gov.pe.ca

Economics, Statistics, & Federal Fiscal Relations Division

Shaw Bldg., 95 Rochford St., 2nd Fl., PO Box 2000, Charlottetown, PE C1A 7N8
902-368-4030 Fax: 902-368-4034
www.gov.pe.ca/finance

The Economics, Statistics, & Federal Fiscal Relations Division is engaged in the following activities: offering economic policy, statistical, tax, & fiscal advice; providing a liaison with the federal government & the other provinces on fiscal arrangements; & responding to queries regarding statistical information.

Director, Economics, Statistics, & Federal Fiscal Relations, Nigel Burns
902-368-4181, Fax: 902-368-4034, ndburns@gov.pe.ca
Economist, Tax Policy, Brad Binns
902-368-4984, Fax: 902-368-4034, bjbinns@gov.pe.ca
Economist, Statistics, Colin Mosley
902-368-4035, Fax: 902-368-4034, cdmosley@gov.pe.ca
Economist, Fiscal, Meaghan A. Zwicker
902-368-4032, Fax: 902-368-4034, mazwicker@gov.pe.ca

Fiscal Management Division

Shaw Bldg., 95 Rochford St. South, 3rd Fl., PO Box 2000, Charlottetown, PE C1A 7N8
902-368-5802 Fax: 902-368-4077
www.gov.pe.ca/finance

The Fiscal Management Division has the following roles: administering pensions & benefits; offering administrative support & financial analysis to the Treasury Board, & ensuring that public funds are budgeted & monitored properly.

Executive Director, Budget Management, Jim Miles, CA
902-368-6278, Fax: 902-368-4077, jamiles@gov.pe.ca
Manager, Pensions & Benefits, Terry Hogan
902-368-4002, Fax: 902-620-3096, tmhogan@gov.pe.ca
Analyst, Budget, George W. Mason, CA, FCMA
902-620-3351, Fax: 902-368-4077, gwmason@gov.pe.ca
Officer, Treasury, Margaret Simpson
902-368-4140, Fax: 902-368-4077, mrmacewen@gov.pe.ca

Information Technology Shared Services Division

Shaw Bldg., 95-105 Rochford St., 2nd Fl., PO Box 2000, Charlottetown, PE C1A 7N8
902-368-6160 Fax: 902-368-6575
www.gov.pe.ca/finance

Information Technology Shared Services consists of the following sections: Client Services; Information Technology Infrastructure Support; Corporate, Operations, Finance & Policy Planning; Business Systems; & Enterprise Architecture Services.

Chief Operating Officer, Information Technology Shared Services, Elizabeth (Beth) Gaudet
902-368-6430, Fax: 902-368-6575, eagaudet@gov.pe.ca
Director, Enterprise Architecture Services, Scott Cudmore
902-569-7510, Fax: 902-569-7632, fscudmore@gov.pe.ca
Director, Corporate, Operations, Finance & Policy Planning, Randy Francis
902-569-7611, Fax: 902-620-3503, drfrancis@gov.pe.ca
Director, Infrastructure, Edmund Malone
902-368-4111, Fax: 902-368-4716, emmalone@gov.pe.ca
Director, Business Application Services, Carol A. Mayne
902-368-4126, Fax: 902-368-5444, camayne@gov.pe.ca

Municipal Affairs & Provincial Planning Division

3 Brighton Rd., PO Box 2000, Charlottetown, PE C1A 7N8
902-620-3558 Fax: 902-569-7545
www.gov.pe.ca/finance

Municipal Affairs acts as the liaison with municipalities & municipal interest groups on municipal matters. Consulting services are available regarding governance, administration, operations, & municipal land use planning.
Provincial Planning works in accordance with Prince Edward Island's Planning Act & Lands Protection Act related to land use & development in the province. Efforts are made to achieve sustainable development in the province.

Director, Municipal Affairs & Provincial Planning, Albert MacDonald
902-368-5582, Fax: 902-569-7545, afmacdonald@gov.pe.ca
Manager, Land Use & Local Governance, Implementation, Christine MacKinnon
902-368-5282, Fax: 902-569-7545, cgmackinnon@gov.pe.ca
Manager, Municipal Affairs, Samantha J. Murphy
902-368-5892, Fax: 902-569-7545, sjmurphy@gov.pe.ca
Manager, Provincial Planning, Jack Saunders
902-368-4220, Fax: 902-569-7545, mjsaunders@gov.pe.ca
Senior Provincial Planner, Dale McKeigan
902-620-3634, Fax: 902-569-7545, dfmckeigan@gov.pe.ca

Taxation & Property Records Division

Shaw Bldg., 95 Rochford St., 1st Fl., PO Box 2000, Charlottetown, PE C1A 7N8
902-368-4070 Fax: 902-368-6164
www.gov.pe.ca/finance

The role of the Taxation & Property Records Division is to ensure equity in the collection of provincial tax revenues & in the production of both provincial & municipal real property assessment rolls. Services are coordinated with federal, provincial, & municipal governments.

Provincial Tax Commissioner, Elizabeth (Beth) Gaudet
902-368-5686, Fax: 902-368-6584, eagaudet@gov.pe.ca
Manager, Corporate & Tax Administration Services, Lorne Bay, CA
902-368-5137, Fax: 902-368-6164, lwbay@gov.pe.ca

Prince Edward Island Department of Fisheries, Aquaculture, & Rural Development

548 Main St., PO Box 1180, Montague, PE C0A 1R0
902-838-0910 Fax: 902-838-0975
877-407-0187
www.gov.pe.ca/fard

The Department of Fisheries, Aquaculture, & Rural Development is guided by the following federal legislation: Aboriginal Communal Fishing Licences Regulations; Atlantic Fishery Regulations, 1985; Canada's Species at Risk Act; Federal Fisheries Act; Fishery Health Protection Regulations; Fishery (General) Regulations; Management of Contaminated Fisheries Regulations; Maritime Provinces Fishery Regulations; & the Navigable Waters Protection Act. The department carries out its mission through its divisions.
The Marine Fisheries & Seafood Services Division provides information to clients & advocates on behalf of the marine fisheries industry.
The Aquaculture Division offers assistance to the aquaculture & estuarial shellfish fisheries.
The Rural Development Division serves rural clients through community development & the delivery of employment programs.
Access PEI offers provincial government programs, services, & information to residents of Prince Edward Island. Examples of Access PEI's services include purchasing a fishing license or obtaining a drivers license.

Acts Administered:
Fish Inspection Act
Fisheries Act

Minister, Fisheries, Aquaculture, & Rural Developmen, Hon. Ron W. MacKinley
902-838-0976, 877-407-0187, Fax: 902-838-0972, rwmackinley@gov.pe.ca
Social Media:
www.facebook.com/pages/Ron-MacKinley/60342728811

Deputy Minister, Fisheries, Aquaculture, & Rural Development, Richard Gallant
902-838-0983, 877-407-0187, Fax: 902-838-0972, rkgallant@gov.pe.ca

Officer, Communications, Alf Blanchard
902-368-4888, Fax: 902-368-4857, ahblanchard@gov.pe.ca

Aquaculture Division

548 Main St., Montague, PE C0A 1R0
902-838-0828 Fax: 902-838-0975
877-407-0187

The Aquaculture Division delivers the following services: advice & information to the provinces's aquaculture industry; financial programs to assist in aquaculture development; & biological & technical services to the shellfish & finfish sectors on the Island.

Director, Aquaculture Division, Neil MacNair
902-838-0685, 877-407-0187, Fax: 902-838-0975, ngmacnair@gov.pe.ca
Aquaculture Biologist, Kim Gill
902-838-0859, Fax: 902-838-0975, klgill@gov.pe.ca
Aquaculture Biologist, Aaron Ramsay
902-838-0827, Fax: 902-838-0975, apramsay@gov.pe.ca
Mussel Technician, Brian Gillis
902-838-0895, Fax: 902-838-0975, blgillis@gov.pe.ca
Shellfish Technician, Gary Smith
902-838-5287, Fax: 902-838-0975, gbsmith@gov.pe.ca
Oyster Technician, Matt Smith
902-838-0890, Fax: 902-838-0975, mesmith@gov.pe.ca

Marine Fisheries & Seafood Services Division

548 Main St., PO Box 1180, Montague, PE C0A 1R0
902-838-0612 Fax: 902-838-0975
877-407-0187

The Marine Fisheries & Seafood Services Division is engaged in the following activities: advocating for Prince Edward Island's fishing industry; offering programs to support new technology &

value-added processing of seafood; supporting development of emerging species; undertaking biological research in support of major fish species; issuing licences for fish buying, fish peddling, & fish processing; managing & maintaining shellfish launching sites around the province; enforcing regulations under Prince Edward Island's Fish Inspection Act & Fisheries Act; overseeing the dead mammal removal program from the province's shore line; & compiling statistics about the fishing industry.

Director, Marine Fisheries & Seafood Service, Barry MacPhee
902-838-0625, 877-407-0187, Fax: 902-838-0975, jbmacphee@gov.pe.ca

Manager, Marine Fisheries, David MacEwen
902-838-0635, Fax: 902-838-0975, dgmacewen@gov.pe.ca

Manager, Seafood Services, David McGuire
902-838-0691, Fax: 902-838-0975, dpmcguire@gov.pe.ca

Lobster Biologist, Robert MacMillan
902-838-0699, Fax: 902-838-0975, rjmacmillan@gov.pe.ca

Fisheries Technician, Michelle Dixon
902-838-0819, Fax: 902-838-0975, madixon@gov.pe.ca

Officer, Program Statistics, Cheryl Campbell
902-838-0826, Fax: 902-838-0975, cherylcampbell@gov.pe.ca

Rural Development Division
548 Main St., PO Box 1180, Montague, PE C0A 1R0
902-838-0910 Fax: 902-838-0975

The responsibilities of the Rural Development Division are as follows: implementing action items in the Rural Action Plan; overseeing the delivery of the Island Community Fund; & ensuring the effectiveness of the Seasonal Hiring Centre & the Employment Development Agency.

Director, Rural Development, Brian Schmeisser
902-838-0662, Fax: 902-838-0975, beschmeisser@gov.pe.ca

Community Development Officer, Giselle Bernard
902-854-3680, Fax: 902-854-3099, gbbernard@gov.pe.ca

Community Development Officer, Eastern Kings, Chris Blaisdell
902-687-7083, Fax: 902-687-7091, cwblaisdell@gov.pe.ca

Community Development Officer, Southern Kings, Stephen Lewis
902-838-0618, Fax: 902-838-0975, sjlewis@gov.pe.ca

Community Development Officer, East Prince, Kellie Mulligan
902-887-3975, Fax: 902-887-2400, kamulligan@gov.pe.ca

Community Development Officer, Rural Queens, Nancy Murphy
902-894-0347, Fax: 902-368-5542, nkmurphy@gov.pe.ca

Community Development Officer, West Prince, Brenda Profit
902-853-0104, Fax: 902-853-3839, bfprofit@gov.pe.ca

Single Window Service / Access PEI
548 Main St., PO Box 1180, Montague, PE C0A 1R0
902-838-0910 Fax: 902-838-0975
www.gov.pe.ca/accesspei
TTY: 877-407-0187

Prince Edward Island Provincial Government services are available at government service centres, known as Access PEI locations. At the eight Access PEI centres across Prince Edward Island, citizens obtain information about the Provincial Government & its programs.

The Access PEI Centres are situated in the following places:
Alberton (902-853-8622);
Charlottetown (902-368-5200);
Montague (902-838-0600);
O'Leary (902-859-8800);
Souris' Johnny Ross Young Service Centre (902-687-7000);
Summerside (902-888-8000;
Tignish (902-882-7351); &
Wellington (902-854-7250).

Director, Access PEI / Single Window Service, Tim G. Garrity
902-838-0651, Fax: 902-838-0975, tggarrity@gov.pe.ca

Manager, Access PEI Summerside & PEI Wellington, Cindy Lou Andrews
902-888-8001, Fax: 902-888-8306, ckandrews@gov.pe.ca; accesspeisummerside@gov.pe.ca, Other Communications: Access PEI Wellington: accesspeiwellington@gov.pe.ca

Manager, Access PEI Montague & Access PEI Souris, Eleanor Avery
902-687-7050, Fax: 902-687-7091, emavery@gov.pe.ca; accesspeimontague@gov.pe.ca, Other Communications: Access PEI Souris, E-mail: accesspeisouris@gov.pe.ca

Manager, Access PEI Alberton, Access PEI O'Leary, & Access PEI Tignish, Martha Dawson
902-859-8801, Fax: 902-859-8709, accesspeialberton@gov.pe.ca; accesspeioleary@gov.pe.ca, Other Communications: Access PEI Tignish E-mail: accesspeitignish@gov.pe.ca

Manager, Access PEI Charlottetown, Paulette Gallant
902-368-6847, Fax: 902-569-7560, plgallant@gov.pe.ca; accesspeicharlottetown@gov.pe.ca, Other Communications: Access PEI Charlottetown, Fax: 902-569-7560

Prince Edward Island Department of Health & Wellness

105 Rochford St. North, 4th Fl., PO Box 2000, Charlottetown, PE C1A 7N8
902-368-6414 Fax: 902-368-4121
www.gov.pe.ca/health/index.php3

The Department of Health & Wellness carries out the following responsibilities: ensuring quality health care to the citizens of Prince Edward Island; providing leadership in policy, programs, & operations; maintaining & improving the health of citizens; playing a leadership role in innovation; coordinating the implementation of the Healthy Living Strategy; providing regulatory services to the health system; acting as a central contact for Aboriginal organizations; & promoting cooperation on governmental matters related to Aboriginal affairs.

Acts Administered:
Adult Protection Act
Archaeological Sites Protection Act (Repealed)
Archaeology Act
Change of Name Act (Repealed)
Change of Name Act
Chiropractic Act (Repealed)
Chiropractic Act
Community Care Facilities & Nursing Homes Act
Community Hospital Authorities Act (Repeal)
Consent to Treatment &d Health Care Directives Act
Dental Profession Act
Denturists Act
Dietitians Act
Dispensing Opticians Act
Donation of Food Act
Drug Cost Assistance Act
Health & Community Services Reorganization Act (Repeal)
Health Services Act (Repealed)
Health Services Act
Health & Community Services Act (Repealed)
Health Services Payment Act
Hospital & Diagnostic Services Insurance Act
Hospitals Act (Repealed)
Hospitals Act
Human Tissue Donation Act
Licensed Nursing Assistants Act (Repealed)
Licensed Practical Nurses Act
Long-Term Care Subsidization
Marriage Act
Medical Act
Mental Health Act (Repealed)
Mental Health Act
Nurses Act (repealed)
Occupational Therapists Act
Optometry Act
Pharmaceutical Information Act
Pharmacy Act
Physiotherapy Act
Premarital Health Examination Act (Repealed)
Provincial Health Number Act
Psychologists Act
Psychologists Act (Repealed)
Public Health Act
Registered Nurses Act
Smoke-free Places Act
Tobacco Sales & Access Act
Vital Statistics Act
Welfare Assistance Act (Renamed)
White Cane Act

Minister, Health & Wellness; Minister Responsible, Aboriginal Affairs, Hon. Doug W. Currie
902-368-5152, Fax: 902-368-4910, dwcurrie@gov.pe.ca; doug.currie@liberal.pe.ca
Social Media: www.twitter.com/DougCurrie, www.facebook.com/doug.w.currie

Deputy Minister, Tracey Cutcliffe
902-368-5290, Fax: 902-368-4121, tdcutcliffe@gov.pe.ca

Communications Officer, Laura Steeves
902-368-5610, Fax: 902-368-4224, lcsteeves@gov.pe.ca

Associated Agencies, Boards & Commissions:
• Prince Edward Island Pharmacy Board
Trans Canada Hwy.
PO Box 89
Crapaud, PE C0A 1J0
902-658-2780 Fax: 902-658-2198
peipharm@pei.aibn.com
www.napra.org
The Prince Edward Island Pharmacy Board regulates the practice of pharmacy in Prince Edward Island. Its goal is to promote high standards of pharmaceutical service for the welfare of the public.

Aboriginal Affairs Secretariat
Shaw Bldg., 105 Rochford St. North, 4th Fl., Charlottetown, PE
www.gov.pe.ca/aboriginalaffairs

The Aboriginal Affairs Secretariat coordinates & manages Aboriginal Affairs for the provincial government. Specific duties include developing policy, negotiating with the federal government & organizations representing the Mi'kmaq & other Aboriginal people, & managing federal-provincial agreements.

Director, Aboriginal Affairs Secretariat, Dr. Helen E. Kristmanson
902-368-5378, Fax: 902-368-4224, hekristmanson@gov.pe.ca

Policy Analyst, Andrew Ramsay
902-368-6583, Fax: 902-368-4224

Chief Health Office
Sullivan Bldg., 16 Fitzroy St., 2nd Fl., Charlottetown, PE C1A 7N8

The Chief Health Office administers & enforces the Public Health Act. The office also delivers services in the following areas: environmental health, epidemiology, reproductive care, & vital statistics.

Chief Health Officer, Dr. Heather G. Morrison
902-368-4996, Fax: 902-620-3354, hgmorrison@gov.pe.ca

Deputy Chief Health Officer, Dr. Lamont Sweet
902-368-4996, Fax: 902-620-3354, lesweet@ihis.org

Coordinator, Provincial Infection Control Program, Stacey L. Burns
902-368-4934, Fax: 902-620-3354, slburns@ihis.org

Coordinator, Communicable Disease & Immunization, Anne M. Neatby
902-368-6114, Fax: 902-620-3354, amneatbty@ihis.org

Coordinator, Infection Control Services, Corrine A. Rowswell
902-368-6190, Fax: 902-620-3354, carowswell@ihis.org

Manager, Environmental Health, Joe Bradley
902-368-4792, Fax: 902-368-6468, joebradley@ihis.org

Manager, Vital Statistics, Thelma A. Johnston
902-838-0884, Fax: 902-838-0883, tajohnston@ihis.org

Provincial Epidemiologist, Dr. Carolyn J. Sanford
902-368-4964, Fax: 902-620-3354, cjsanford@gov.pe.ca

Finance & Corporate Management Division
Shaw Bldg., 105 Rochford St. North, 4th Fl., PO Box 2000, Charlottetown, PE C1A 7N8

The Finance & Corporate Management Division supports the Department of Health & Wellness in the areas of finances, human resources, communications, & the administration of the Freedom of Information & Protection of Privacy Act.

Director, Finance & Corporate Management Division, Kevin Barnes, CA
902-368-4865, Fax: 902-368-4224, kcbarnes@gov.pe.ca

Manager, Financial Services & Administration, Barry Gosby
902-368-4897, Fax: 902-368-5335, bbgosby@gov.pe.ca

Manager, Human Resources, Michael Ready
902-569-0549, Fax: 902-368-4224, mcready@gov.pe.ca

Coordinator, Freedom of Information & Protection of Privacy Act; Communications Officer, Autumn Tremere
902-368-5610, Fax: 902-368-4224, agtremere@gov.pe.ca

Health System Planning & Development Division
Sullivan Bldg., 16 Fitzroy St., 3rd Fl., Charlottetown, PE C1A 7N8

The Health System Planning & Development Division supports the Department of Health & Wellness. It includes the Health Recruitment & Retention section.

Manager, Health Recruitment & Retention, Marney MacRae
902-620-3874, Fax: 902-620-3875, mjmacrae@gov.pe.ca

Coordinator, Physician Recruitment, Sheila MacLean
902-368-6302, Fax: 902-620-3875, smmaclean@gov.pe.ca

Consultant, Pharmacy, Roy Cairns
902-368-4907, Fax: 902-368-4905, brcairns@gov.pe.ca

Consultant, Dietetic Services, Diane M. Clow
902-368-6262, Fax: 902-569-7656, mdclow@ihis.org

Consultant, Community Care Facilities & Nursing Homes, Mary P. MacSwain
902-368-4953, Fax: 902-569-7656, mpmacswain@ihis.org

Legislative Specialist, Nichola M. Hewitt
902-368-6681, Fax: 902-620-3081, nmhewitt@gov.pe.ca

Planner & Policy Analyst, Shaun MacNeill
902-368-6117, Fax: 902-368-4224, smacneill@gov.pe.ca

Sport, Recreation, & Healthy Living Division
Shaw Bldg., 105 Rochford St. North, 4th Fl., PO Box 2000, Charlottetown, PE

The main role of the Sport, Recreation & Healthy Living Division is to encourage citizens of Prince Edward Island to be active. Sport, recreation, & other physical activities are promoted. Consultation services & grants are available for community, regional, & provincial groups.

Director, Sport, Recreation, & Healthy Living, John Morrison
902-894-0283, Fax: 902-368-4224, jwmorris@gov.pe.ca

Officer, Health Promotion & Chronic Disease Prevention, Laraine Poole
902-368-4926, Fax: 902-620-3081, lfpoole@gov.pe.ca

Coordinator, Central Region, Sport, Recreation, & Healthy Living, Francois R. Caron
902-432-2706, Fax: 902-888-8023, frcaron@gov.pe.ca

Coordinator, Eastern Region, Sport, Recreation, & Healthy Living, Neil A. Kinsman
902-687-7041, Fax: 902-368-4224, nakinsman@gov.pe.ca

Coordinator, Western Region, Sport, Recreation, & Healthy Living, Joanne P. Wallace
902-859-8861, Fax: 902-859-8709, jpwallace@gov.pe.ca

Health PEI

16 Garfield St., PO Box 2000, Charlottetown, PE C1A 7N8
902-368-6130 Fax: 902-368-6136
healthinput@gov.pe.ca
www.healthpei.ca

When the Health Services Act was proclaimed in 2010, Health PEI took on responsibility for the operation & delivery of health services in the province.
The main goals of Health PEI are to improve access to quality health care across Prince Edward Island & to develop more consistent standards & practices for health services

Chief Executive Officer, Keith Dewar
902-368-4935, Fax: 902-368-4974, kdewar@gov.pe.ca
Chair, Leo Steven
902-368-5810, Fax: 902-368-5835, lsteven@gov.pe.ca
Vice-Chair, Gordon MacKay
Manager, Communications, Brad Chatfield
902-368-6135, Fax: 902-368-4969, bpchatfield@gov.pe.ca

Community Hospitals & Primary Health Care Division
16 Garfield St., 1st Fl., Charlottetown, PE C1A 6A5
Executive Director, Community Hospitals & Primary Health Care, Deborah Bradley
902-368-6157, Fax: 902-569-0579, mdbradley@gov.pe.ca
Director, Primary Care Networks & Chronic Desease Prevention & Management, Marilyn A. Barrett
902-569-7640, Fax: 902-569-0579, mabarrett@gov.pe.ca
Director, Public Health, Kathy Jones
902-894-0247, Fax: 902-569-0579, kljones@gov.pe.ca
Director, Mental Health & Addictions, Margaret Kennedy
902-368-6197, Fax: 902-569-0579, mmkennedy@gov.pe.ca
Administrator, Community Hospitals East, Terry S. Campbell
902-687-7150, Fax: 902-687-7175, tscampbell@gov.pe.ca
Administrator, Community Hospitals West, Andrew MacDougall
902-368-5773, Fax: 902-368-6764, asmacdougall@gov.pe.ca

Corporate Development & Innovation Division
16 Garfield St., 2nd Fl., Charlottetown, PE C1A 6A5
Executive Director, Corporate Development & Innovation, Pamela Trainor
902-368-5804, Fax: 902-368-4969, pjtrainor@gov.pe.ca
Director, Quality & Access Management, Joanne Donahoe
902-368-5815, Fax: 902-368-4969, jmdonahoe@gov.pe.ca
Director, Human Resources, Glen Doyle
902-368-6257, Fax: 902-368-4969, grdoyle@gov.pe.ca
Director, Strategy & Performance, Una Hassenstein
902-368-4932, Fax: 902-368-4969, uehassenstein@gov.pe.ca

Financial Services Division
16 Garfield St., 1st Fl., Charlottetown, PE C1A 6A5
Executive Director, Financial Services, Denise Lewis Fleming
902-368-6125, Fax: 902-368-6136, dmlewis@gov.pe.ca
Director, Fiscal Planning, Analysis, & Audit, Kellie C. Hawes
902-569-0506, Fax: 902-368-6136, kchawes@ihis.org
Director, Materials Management, Deborah Steeves
902-894-2097, Fax: 902-894-2384, dasteeves@ihis.org
Comptroller, Accounting Services, Pat G. Ryan
902-368-4921, Fax: 902-368-6136, pgryan@gov.pe.ca

Health Information Management Division
16 Garfield St., 1st Fl., Charlottetown, PE C1A 6A5
The Health Information Management Division oversees the following areas: eHealth implementation; eHealth operations; eHealth strategy; health information; IM & IT planning; & privacy & information access.
Executive Director, Health Information Management, Liam Whitty
902-620-3165, Fax: 902-368-6136, lwhitty@gov.pe.ca
Project Manager, iEHR & eHealth Project Implementation, Brenda Campbell
902-368-6517, Fax: 902-620-3061, bccampbell@gov.pe.ca
Coordinator, Privacy & Information Access, Marina Fay
902-368-4942, Fax: 902-368-4969, mafay@ihis.org
Information Technology Architect, Jackie Irwin
902-620-3229, Fax: 902-368-6136, jrirwin@gov.pe.ca

Home-Based & Long-Term Care Division
16 Garfield St., 1st Fl., Charlottetown, PE C1A 6A5
Executive Director, Home-Based & Long-Term Care, Cecil Villard
902-894-0337, Fax: 902-368-6136, cfvillard@gov.pe.ca
Director, Home Care, Mary Sullivan
902-888-8005, Fax: 902-432-2610, mksullivan@gov.pe.ca
Administrator, Long Term Care, East, Jean Fallis
902-838-0643, Fax: 902-838-5294, njfallis@gov.pe.ca
Administrator, Long Term Care, East Prince, Gayle Lamont
902-888-8350, Fax: 902-888-8369, gdlamont@gov.pe.ca
Administrator, Long Term Care, Queens, Andrew MacDougall
902-368-5773, Fax: 902-368-6764, asmacdougall@gov.pe.ca
Administrator, Long Term Care, West Prince, John Martin
902-859-8734, Fax: 902-859-8774, jmartin@gov.pe.ca
Coordinator, Provincial Geriatric Services, Elaine Campbell
902-432-2861, Fax: 902-432-2859, eecampbell@ihis.org
Consultant, Seniors' Mental Health Services, Debye Macdonald Connolly
902-368-4602, Fax: 902-368-6136, damacdonald-connolly@ihis.org

Medical Affairs Division
16 Garfield St., 2nd Fl., Charlottetown, PE C1A 6A5
Executive Director, Medical Affairs, Dr. Richard Wedge
902-368-6261, Fax: 902-620-3072, rhwedge@gov.pe.ca
Manager, Physician Services, Johanne Irwin
902-368-6736, Fax: 902-620-3072, jcirwin@gov.pe.ca
PHC Medical Director, Summerside, Dr. Andre Celliers
acelliers@ihis.org
PHC Medical Director, West Prince, Dr. Gil Grimes
gcgrimes@gov.pe.ca
PHC Medical Director, Kings, Dr. David Hambly
jdhambly@ihis.org
PHC Medical Director, Queens, Dr. Alf Morais
902-569-7625, Fax: 902-620-3072, jamorais@ihis.org

Prince County Hospital (PCH)
65 Boates Ave., PO Box 3000, Summerside, PE C1N 2A9
902-438-4200 Fax: 902-438-4511
www.healthpei.ca/pch
Executive Director, Prince County Hospital, Arlene Gallant-Bernard
902-438-4514, Fax: 902-438-4381, algallant-bernard@gov.pe.ca
Director, Hospital Services, Cynthia Bryanton
902-438-4519, Fax: 902-438-4381, clbryanton@gov.pe.ca
Director, Administration & Support Services, Margie Kays
902-438-4530, Fax: 902-438-4381, mrkays@gov.pe.ca
Director, Medical Services, Dr. Wassim Salamoun
902-438-4518, Fax: 902-438-4381, wsalamoun@ihis.org
Director, Nursing Services, Brenda Worth
902-438-4516, Fax: 902-438-4381, baworth@gov.pe.ca

Provincial Clinical Services Division
16 Garfield St., 3rd Fl., Charlottetown, PE C1A 6A5
Executive Director, Provincial Clinical Services, Jamie MacDonald
902-894-2277, Fax: 902-894-2276, jamiemacdonald@ihis.org
Director, Provincial Diagnostic Imaging Services, Theresa Callaghan
902-894-2979, Fax: 902-894-2416, tkcallaghan@gov.pe.ca
Manager, Provincial Pharmacare Program, Faye E. Campbell
902-368-6338, Fax: 902-368-4905, fecampbell@ihis.org
Manager, Emergency Health Services, Alan Toombs
902-368-6719, Fax: 902-368-6136, altoombs@gov.pe.ca
Coordinator, Pharmaceutical Information Program, Kelly Drummond
902-620-3762, Fax: 902-368-4905, ktdrummond@gov.pe.ca

Queen Elizabeth Hospital
60 Riverside Dr., PO Box 6600, Charlottetown, PE C1A 8T5
902-894-2111 Fax: 902-894-2416
www.healthpei.ca/index.php3?number=1020318&lang=E
TTY: 902-894-2204
Executive Director, Rick Adams
902-894-2351, Fax: 902-894-2416, radams@gov.pe.ca
Director, Nursing Services, Marion H. Dowling
902-894-2356, Fax: 902-894-2926, mhdowling@gov.pe.ca
Director, Medical Services, Dr. Rosemary Henderson
902-894-2411, Fax: 902-894-2416, rfhenderson@gov.pe.ca
Director, Hospital Services, Kelley Rayner
902-894-2364, Fax: 902-894-0138, kjrayner@gov.pe.ca
Director, Support Services, David J. White
902-894-2353, Fax: 902-894-2416, jdwhite@gov.pe.ca

Prince Edward Island Human Rights Commission

53 Water St., PO Box 2000, Charlottetown, PE C1A 7N8
902-368-4180 Fax: 902-368-4236
800-237-5031
www.peihumanrights.ca

The Prince Edward Island Human Rights Act is administered & enforced by the Prince Edward Island Human Rights Commission.
The Commission receives, investigates, & settles & makes rulings on complaints. Other tasks of the Commission include the development of public information & educational programs & the provision of advice to the government about human rights issues.

Chair, Anne Nicholson
902-368-4180, Fax: 902-368-4236
Commissioner, Arthur Currie, Q.C.
902-368-4180, Fax: 902-368-4236
Commissioner, George Lyle
902-368-4180, Fax: 902-368-4236
Commissioner, John Rogers
902-368-4180, Fax: 902-368-4236
Commissioner, Lou Ann Thomson
902-368-4180, Fax: 902-368-4236
Executive Director, Greg Howard
902-368-4134, Fax: 902-368-4236, ghoward@peihumanrights.ca
Human Rights Officer, Wendy Baker
902-368-4180, Fax: 902-368-4236, wbaker@peihumanrights.ca
Administrative / Intake Officer, R. Lorraine Buell
902-368-4180, Fax: 902-368-4236, lbuell@peihumanrights.ca

Prince Edward Island Department of Innovation & Advanced Learning

Shaw Bldg., 105 Rochford St., 5th Fl., PO Box 2000, Charlottetown, PE C1A 7N8
902-368-4240 Fax: 902-368-4242
www.gov.pe.ca/ial

The role of Prince Edward Island's Department of Innovation & Advanced Learning is to manage the implementation of The Island Prosperity Strategy, A Focus for Change. This is the provincial government's economic strategy. It is the goal of the government to improve post-secondary opportunities for Islanders to ensure a strong workforce prepared for the present economy.

Acts Administered:
Apprenticeship & Trades Qualification Act
Area Industrial Commission Act
Business Development Inc. Act, P.E.I. (Repealed)
Employment Development Agency Act
Hairdressers Act
Holland College Act
Innovation PEI Act
Island Investment Development Act
Labour Mobility Act
Lending Agency Act
Maritime Economic Cooperation Act
Maritime Provinces Higher Education Commission Act (Repealed)
Maritime Provinces Higher Education Commission Act
Prince Edward Island Science & Technology Corporation Act (Repealed)
Private Training Schools Act
Student Financial Assistance Act
University Act

Minister, Innovation & Advanced Learning, Hon. Allen F. Roach
allen.roach@liberal.pe.ca
Social Media:
www.facebook.com/profile.php?id=100002417155344
Deputy Minister, Dr. Michael Mayne
902-368-4250, Fax: 902-368-4242, mbmayne@gov.pe.ca
Officer, Communications, Ron Ryder
902-620-3774, Fax: 902-368-4242, rrryder@gov.pe.ca

Associated Agencies, Boards & Commissions:
• Anne of Green Gables Licensing Authority Inc.
94 Euston
PO Box 910
Charlottetown, PE C1A 7L9
902-569-7787 Fax: 902-368-6301
kobaker@gov.pe.ca; aggla@bellnet.ca
Other Communication: Toronto Office, Phone: 416-971-7473
The Anne of Green Gables Licensing Authority Inc. controls the use of Anne of Green Gables & related trademarks, protects the integrity of Anne images, & preserves the legacy of L.M. Montgomery & her works. The authority is jointly owned by the Province of Prince Edward Island Ruth Macdonald & David Macdonald.
• BIO FOOD TECH
101 Belvedere Ave.
PO Box 2000
Charlottetown, PE C1A 7N8
902-368-5548 Fax: 902-368-5549 877-368-5548
biofoodtech@biofoodtech.ca
www.biofoodtech.ca
Formerly known as the PEI Food Technology Centre, BIO FOOD TECH operates as a contract research & analytical services company. It serves companies & entrepreneurs in the food & bioprocessing sectors.
• Charlottetown Area Development Corporation (CADC)
4 Pownal St.
PO Box 786
Charlottetown, PE C1A 7L9
902-892-5341 Fax: 902-368-1935
www.cadcpei.com
The Charlottetown Area Development Corporation operates as a self-financed entity that aims to attract private sector development to the Greater Charlottetown area. To carry out its work, the Charlottetown Area Development Corporation partners with the Province of Prince Edward Island, the City of Charlottetown, & the Town of Stratford.
• Charlottetown Civic Centre Management Inc.
46 Kensington Rd.
Charlottetown, PE C1A 5H7
902-629-6600 Fax: 902-629-6650
www.civiccentre.pe.ca

The Charlottetown Civic Centre is a multi-purpose facility.
• Innovation PEI
94 Euston St.
PO Box 910
Charlottetown, PE C1A 7L9
902-368-6300 Fax: 902-368-6301 800-563-3734
www.innovationpei.com
Innovation PEI strives to advance economic development in Prince Edward Island. It promotes small business development, business improvement, employment creation, research, innovation, market access, & trade. Through the Island Prosperity Strategy, Innovation PEI focuses upon the following sectors: renewable energy, aerospace, information technology, & bioscience.
• Island Investment Development Inc. (IIDI)
94 Euston St., 2nd Fl.
Charlottetown, PE C1A 7M8
902-620-3628 Fax: 902-368-5886
peinominee@gov.pe.ca
www.gov.pe.ca/immigration
The Island Investment Development Inc. is a crown corporation. Its business name is Immigration Services. The organization oversees the Prince Edward Island Provincial Nominee Program.
• Prince Edward Island Lending Agency
Homburg Financial Tower
98 Fitzroy St., 2nd Fl.
Charlottetown, PE C1A 1R7
902-368-6200 Fax: 902-368-6201
Assistance is provided by the Lending Agency to new & growing businesses. Loans are available for organizations with export potential in the following industries: agriculture, fisheries & aquaculture, tourism, manufacturing & processing, information technology, & small business.
• Summerside Regional Development Corporation Ltd. (SRDC)
268 Water St.
Summerside, PE C1N 1B6
902-436-2246 Fax: 902-436-9269
acroken@srdcpei.com
www.summersidewaterfront.com
Formerly known as the Summerside Waterfront Development Corporation, the Summerside Regional Development Corporation works to facilitate economic development in Summerside & the surrounding region. Shareholders of the corporation include the Province of Prince Edward Island, the City of Summerside, & the Greater Summerside Development Inc.

Finance & Administration Division
105 Rochford St., Charlottetown, PE C1A 7N8
902-368-5878 Fax: 902-368-7087
Responsibilities include financial management, administration, the Prince Edward Island Business Development Inc., & human resource management.
Director, Finance & Administration, Shannon Burke, CA
902-368-5875, Fax: 902-268-7087, slburke@gov.pe.ca
Controller, Jean Kimpton, CMA
902-894-0343, Fax: 902-368-6255, jakimpton@gov.pe.ca
Manager, Human Resources, Leah Eldershaw
902-368-5876, Fax: 902-368-7087, ljelders@gov.pe.ca
Coordinator, FOIPP; Officer, Human Resources, Camilla McAleer
902-368-5869, Fax: 902-368-5756, ccmcaleer@gov.pe.ca

Population Secretariat
Atlantic Technology Centre, 90 University Ave., Charlottetown, PE C1A 4K9
902-620-3656 Fax: 902-368-4252
populationsecretariat@gov.pe.ca
www.gov.pe.ca/ial/popsec
The Population Secretariat promotes Prince Edward Island as a welcoming place to live. The Secretariat works to attract immigrants & former Islanders, & to retain youth & immigrants.
Director, Population Secretariat, Jane Mallard
902-569-7556, Fax: 902-368-4252, jmallard@gov.pe.ca
Officer, Attraction & Promotion, Isabelle Dasylva-Gill
902-569-7539, Fax: 902-368-4252, idasylvagill@gov.pe.ca
Officer, Policy, Research, & Planning, Erin Docherty
902-368-5127, Fax: 902-368-4252, ecdocherty@gov.pe.ca
Officer, Settlement, Joey Jeffrey
902-368-4861, Fax: 902-368-4252, jajeffrey@gov.pe.ca
Officer, Retention, Ian G. Lane
902-368-5368, Fax: 902-368-4252, iglane@gov.pe.ca

Post-Secondary & Continuing Education
Atlantic Technology Centre, #212, 90 University Ave., 2nd Fl., Charlottetown, PE C1A 4K9
Director, Post-Secondary & Continuing Education, Susan A. MacKenzie
902-368-4615, Fax: 902-368-6144, samackenzie@gov.pe.ca
Manager, Student Financial Services, Patrick Davis
902-368-4229, Fax: 902-368-6144, pjdavis@gov.pe.ca
Manager, Apprenticeship Training, Susan LeFort
902-368-4625, Fax: 902-368-6144, sflefort@gov.pe.ca
Manager, Literacy Initiatives Secretariat; GED Chief Examiner; Administrator, Private Training Schools, Barbara Macnutt
902-368-6286, Fax: 902-368-6144, bemacnutt@edu.pe.ca
Senior Officer, Financial Awards, Don Currie
902-368-4604, Fax: 902-368-6144, dscurrie@gov.pe.ca

SkillsPEI
Atlantic Technology Centre, #212, 90 University Ave., Charlottetown, PE C1A 4K9
902-368-4260 Fax: 902-368-6340
877-491-4766
Skills PEI manages the delivery of training & skills development programs. The programming is funded by the Labour Market Agreement & the Canada-Prince Edward Island Labour Market Development Agreement. Examples of programs include Training PEI, Employ PEI, Self Employ PEI, Community Internship, Immigrant Work Experience, & Labour Market Partnerships. SkillsPEI offices are located across Prince Edward Island.
Director, SkillsPEI, Birt MacKinnon
902-368-4244, Fax: 902-368-6580, bwmackinnon@gov.pe.ca
Director, Special Projects, Scott MacDonald
902-368-6521, Fax: 902-368-6340, dsmacdonald@gov.pe.ca
Manager, Service Delivery, Kings & Queens County, Blair Aitken
902-368-4178, Fax: 902-368-6580, abaitken@gov.pe.ca
Manager, Service Delivery, Prince County, Mary Hunter
902-438-4110, Fax: 902-438-4096, mehunter@gov.pe.ca
Manager, Labour Mobility, Jeannie Pitts
902-368-5825, Fax: 902-368-6340, jpitts@gov.pe.ca
Coordinator, Provincial Employment, Heather Berrigan
902-368-5908, Fax: 902-368-5909, heberrigan@gov.pe.ca
Coordinator, Passport to Employment Program, Maitland MacIsaac
902-368-4466, Fax: 902-368-5909, mamacisaac@gov.pe.ca
Coordinator, Foreign Qualifications Recognition Project, Rebecca Murphy
902-620-3082, Fax: 902-368-6340, romurphy@gov.pe.ca

Prince Edward Island Department of Justice & Public Safety

Shaw Bldg., 95 Rochford St. South, 4th Fl., PO Box 2000, Charlottetown, PE C1A 7N8
www.gov.pe.ca/jps
The Department of Justice & Public Safety oversees programs & services in the areas of justice, public safety, & consumer & corporate services in order to foster respect for the law, access to justice, & safe communities.
Acts Administered:
Affidavits Act
Age of Majority Act
Ancient Burial Grounds Act
Appeals Act
Apportionment Act
Arbitration Act
Auctioneers Act
Bailable Proceedings Act
Business Practices Act
Canada-United Kingdom Judgments Recognition Act
Canadian Judgments (Enforcement) Act
Cemeteries Act
Charities Act
Child Status Act
Collection Agencies Act
Commorientes Act
Companies Act
Consumer Protection Act
Consumer Reporting Act
Contributory Negligence Act
Controverted Elections (Provincial) Act
Co-operative Associations Act
Coroners Act (Repealed)
Coroners Act
Correctional Services Act
Court Reporters Act
Court Security Act
Credit Unions Act
Crown Proceedings Act
Custody Jurisdiction & Enforcement Act
Defamation Act
Dependants of a Deceased Person Relief Act
Designation of Beneficiaries Under Benefit Plans Act
Direct Sellers Act
Electronic Commerce Act
Electronic Evidence Act
Emergency 911 Act
Emergency Measures Act (Repealed)
Emergency Measures Act
Emergency Measures Act
Escheats Act
Evidence Act
Extra-Provincial Corporations Registration Act
Factors Act
Family Law Act
Fatal Accidents Act
Films Act
PEI Firefighters Long Service Medal Act
PEI Firefighters Long Service Medal Act
Fire Prevention Act
Fire Prevention Act
Floral Hills Memorial Gardens Administration Act
Foreign Resident Corporations Act
Franchises Act
Frauds on Creditors Act
Freedom of Information & Protection of Privacy Act
Frustrated Contracts Act
Garage Keepers' Lien Act
Garnishee Act
Gift Cards
Gulf Trust Corporation Act
Habeas Corpus Act
Human Rights Act
Insurance Act
Intercountry Adoption (Hague Convention) Act
Interjurisdictional Support Orders Act
International Commercial Arbitration Act
International Sale of Goods Act
International Trusts Act
Interpretation Act
Interprovincial Subpoena Act
Investigation of Titles Act
Islander Day
Judgment & Execution Act
Judicature Act
Judicial Review Act
Jury Act
Landlord & Tenant Act
Legal Profession Act
Licensing Act (Repealed)
Limited Partnerships Act
Maintenance Enforcement Act
Mechanics' Lien Act
Occupiers' Liability Act
Partnership Act
Partnership Act
Perpetuities Act
Personal Property Security Act
Police Act (Repealed)
Police Act
Powers of Attorney Act
Prearranged Funeral Services Act
Premium Tax Act
Private Investigators & Security Guards Act
Probate Act
Probation Act
Provincial Administrator of Estates Act
Provincial Court Act
Public Accounting & Auditing Act (Repealed)
Public Accounting & Auditing Act
Public Trustee Act
Quieting Titles Act
Real Estate Trading Act
Real Property Act
Reciprocal Enforcement of Judgments Act
Reciprocal Enforcement of Maintenance Orders Act (Repealed)
Retail Business Holidays Act
Rural Community Fire Companies Act
Sale of Goods Act
Securities Act (Repealed)
Securities Act
Sheriffs Act
Statute of Frauds
Statute of Limitations
Store Hours Act
Summary Proceedings Act
Supreme Court Act (Repealed)
Supreme Court Reporters Act (Renamed)
Survival of Actions Act
Time in Public Offices Act (Repealed)
Time Uniformity Act
Transboundary Pollution (Reciprocal Access) Act
Trespass to Property Act
Truck Operators' Remuneration Act
Trust & Fiduciary Companies Act
Trustee Act
Unclaimed Articles Act
Unconscionable Transactions Relief Act
Uniformity Commissioners Act
Variation of Trusts Act
Vendors & Purchasers Act
Victims of Crime Act
Victims of Family Violence Act
Volunteers Liability Act
Warehousemen's Lien Act
Winding-up Act
Young Offenders (P.E.I.) Act (Renamed)
Youth Justice Act
Minister, Justice & Public Safety; Attorney General; Minister, Education & Early Childhood Development,

Hon. J. Alan McIsaac
902-368-4330, Fax: 902-368-4348,
jamcisaac@assembly.pe.ca; alan.mcisaac@liberal.pe.ca
Social Media:
www.facebook.com/profile.php?id=100001892659368
Deputy Minister, Shauna Sullivan Curley
902-368-5152, Fax: 902-368-4910, sscurley@gov.pe.ca
Contact, Media Queries, Joanne MacKinnon
902-368-5010, Fax: 902-368-5335, jymackinnon@gov.pe.ca

Associated Agencies, Boards & Commissions:
• Office of the Police Commissioner
114 Kent St.
PO Box 427
Charlottetown, PE C1A 7K7
902-368-7200 Fax: 902-368-1123 877-541-7204
www.policecommissioner.pe.ca
The Office of the Police Commissioner investigates & resolves complaints about the unprofessional conduct of police, other than the RCMP. Under the Police Act, a person who is 18 years of age & over, who has been directly affected by the conduct of municipal police officer, may make a complaint. The Office of the Police Commissioner also handles complaints about a chief of a municipal police service, a director or instructing officer at the Atlantic Police Academy, or a security police officer at the University of Prince Edward Island. The independent statutory office works to carry out its mission in a timely & impartial manner.
Persons must call the Office of the Police Commissioner to book an appointment.

Community & Correctional Services Division
109 Water St., Summerside, PE C1N 1A8
902-432-2847 Fax: 902-432-2851
www.gov.pe.ca/jps
The Community & Correctional Services Division provides community & custody programs to contribute to the rehabilitation of youth & adult offenders. The division also offers the following services: research; policy development; support services to the courts & victims of crime; crime prevention programs; & public education.
The work of the Community & Correctional Services Division is conducted by the following sections: Community Programs; Correctional Programs; Victim Services; & Clinical Services.
Director, Community & Correctional Services, John R. Picketts
902-432-2850, Fax: 902-432-2851, jrpicketts@gov.pe.ca
Provincial Manager, Community Services, Karen MacDonald
902-368-5295, Fax: 902-368-4579, kamacdonald@gov.pe.ca
Provincial Manager, Victim Services, Susan Maynard
902-368-4584, Fax: 902-368-4514, smaynard@gov.pe.ca
Provincial Manager, Correctional Programs, Donna Myers
902-569-7683, Fax: 902-569-7711, dfmyers@gov.pe.ca
Manager, Prince Edward Island Youth Centre, Shannon L. Ellis
902-888-8256, Fax: 902-888-8247, slellis@gov.pe.ca
Manager, Youth Justice Services (West), Paula Finkle
902-888-8254, Fax: 902-888-8214, plfinkle@gov.pe.ca
Manager, Clinical Services, Dr. Edward F. Hansen
902-569-7684, Fax: 902-368-5644, efhansen@gov.pe.ca
Manager, Provincial Correctional Centre, Kim Kempton
902-368-4885, Fax: 902-368-5834, kjkempton@gov.pe.ca
Manager, Youth Justice Services (East), Glenda L. Lutes
902-368-4578, Fax: 902-368-4579, gllutes@gov.pe.ca
Manager, Prince Correctional Centre, Gordon Roche
902-888-8209, Fax: 902-888-8464, gmroche@gov.pe.ca
Manager, Corporate Services, Denise M. Spenceley
902-569-7681, Fax: 902-569-7711, dmspenceley@gov.pe.ca
Manager, Probation Services, Gary Trainor
902-368-4697, Fax: 902-368-4579, gjtrainor@gov.pe.ca

Consumer, Corporate, & Insurance Division
Shaw Bldg., 95 Rochford St., 4th Fl., PO Box 2000, Charlottetown, PE C1A 7N8
902-368-4550 Fax: 902-368-5283
www.gov.pe.ca/jps
The Consumer, Corporate, & Insurance Division consists of the following sections: Consumer Affairs; Corporations; Securities; Firearms Office; & Insurance & Real Estate.
The Consumer Affairs section administers the Lottery Schemes Order. It also responds to complaints & inquiries from consumers.
The Corporations section handles the registration of partnerships & business names. It also oversees the incorporation of companies, non-profit corporations, co-operatives, & credit unions.
The Securities Act is administered & enforced by the Securities Division.
The Gun Control Program is administered by the Firearms Office, in accordance with the Criminal Code of Canada & the federal Firearms Act. The Firearms Office is also responsible for the administration of the Private Investigators & Security Guards Act.
Under the supervision of the Superintendent of Insurance, the Insurance & Real Estate section administers the Fire Prevention Act, the Insurance Act, the Premium Tax Act, & the Real Estate Trading Act.
Director, Consumer, Corporate, & insurance Division, Katharine Tummon
902-368-4542, Fax: 902-368-5283, kptummon@gov.pe.ca
Superintendent, Insurance, Robert Bradley
902-368-6478, Fax: 902-368-5283, rabradley@gov.pe.ca
Chief Firearms Officer, Firearms Office, Vivian Hayward
902-368-4585, Fax: 902-368-5198, vdhayward@gov.pe.ca
Compliance Officer, Insurance & Real Estate Section, Sandra Furlotte
902-368-4577, Fax: 902-368-5283, skfurlotte@gov.pe.ca
Corporations Officer, Corporation Section, Joan MacKay
902-368-4509, Fax: 902-368-5283, jmmakday@gov.pe.ca
Compliance Officer, Consumer Affairs Section, Linda Peters
902-368-5653, Fax: 902-368-5283, lmpeters@gov.pe.ca
Capital Markets Contact, Securities Section, Janice Callbeck
902-368-6288, Fax: 902-368-5283, jccallbeck@gov.pe.ca
Corporate Finance Contact, Securities Section, Lorraine Matheson
902-368-4569, Fax: 902-368-5283, lamatheson@gov.pe.ca

Crown Attorneys Office
197 Richmond St., Charlottetown, PE C1A 1J3
902-368-4595 Fax: 902-368-5812
www.gov.pe.ca/jps
It is the responsibility of the Crown Attoneys Office to prosecute criminal cases under provincial statutes & the Criminal Code of Canada.
Director, Crown Attorneys Office, Cyndria L. Wedge
902-368-5073, Fax: 902-368-5812, clwedge@gov.pe.ca
Senior Crown Attorney, Summerside Location, David P. O'Brien, QC
902-888-8047, Fax: 902-888-8224, dpobrien@gov.pe.ca
Senior Crown Attorney, Charlottetown Location, Gerald Quinn, QC
902-368-5076, Fax: 902-368-5812, gkquinn@gov.pe.ca

Legal Aid
40 Great George St., PO Box 2000, Charlottetown, PE C1A 7N8
www.gov.pe.ca/jps
The Legal Aid program in Prince Edward Island is staffed by lawyers who offer direct assistance to legal aid clients in the areas of family & criminal law. In order to be eligible for these legal services, potential clients are required to take a financial means test.
Funding of the family legal aid program is provided by the province of Prince Edward Island & the Prince Edward Island Law Foundation. Prince Edward Island & Canada fund the criminal legal aid program.
Director, Legal Aid, W. Kent Brown, Q.C.
902-368-6043, Fax: 902-368-6122, wkbrown@gov.pe.ca
Administrative Officer, Legal Aid, Jackie M. Hamm
902-368-6016, Fax: 902-368-6122, jmhamm@gov.pe.ca

Legal & Court Services Division
Shaw Bldg., 95 Rochford St., 4th Fl., Charlottetown, PE C1A 7N8
902-368-6522 Fax: 902-368-4563
www.gov.pe.ca/jps
The Legal & Court Services Division consists of the following sections: Office of the Public Trustee & Public Guardian; Court Services; Legal Services; Law Enforcement; & Family Law.
The Office of the Public Trustee & Public Guardian administers the Provincial Administrator of Estates Act & the Public Trustee Act.
The Court Services Section oversees court personnel & services, while the Legal Services Section handles legal services to the provincial government's departments & agencies.
The Law Enforcement Section is headed by the Commanding Officer of the RCMP, the Provincial Police Force. Police protection throughout the province is handled by the RCMP, except for the areas of Borden-Carleton, Charlottetown, Kensington, St. Eleanors, & Summerside which have municipal police forces.
The following programs & services are administered by the Family Law Section: Parent Education Program, Family Court Counsellors' Office, Child Support Guidelines Office, Administrative Recalculation Office, & the Maintenance Enforcement Program.
Director, Legal & Court Services, Barrie L. Grandy, QC
902-368-4554, Fax: 902-368-4563, blgrandy@gov.pe.ca
Public Trustee & Guardian, Office of the Public Trustee & Public Guardian, Denise Doiron
902-368-6590, Fax: 902-368-4969, dndoiron@gov.pe.ca
Deputy Public Trustee, Office of the Public Trustee & Public Guardian, Robert Landry
902-368-4561, Fax: 902-368-5283, rllandry@gov.pe.ca
Prothonotary & Registrar, Court Services Section, Charles P. Thompson, O.C.
902-368-6669, Fax: 902-368-0266, cpthompson@gov.pe.ca
Chief Superintendent & Commanding Officer, RCMP, Law Enforcement Section, Tracy Hardy
902-566-7132, Fax: 902-566-7235,
tracy.hardy@rcmp-grc.gc.ca
Chief Sheriff, Court Services Section, Ron Dowling
902-368-6055, Fax: 902-368-6571, rjdowling@gov.pe.ca
Chief Provincial Court Clerk, Court Services Section, Kevin Gotell
902-368-6693, Fax: 902-368-6210
Manager, Family Law Section, Loretta Coady MacAulay
902-368-4886, Fax: 902-368-6474, llmacaulay@gov.pe.ca
Manager, Legal Services Section, Terri MacPherson, Q.C.
902-368-5145, Fax: 902-368-4563, tamacpherson@gov.pe.ca
Manager, Court Services & Deputy Registrar, Court Services Section, Judy A. Turpin
902-368-6005, Fax: 902-368-6210, jaturpin@gov.pe.ca
Director, Maintenance Enforcement Program, Family Law Section, Norma Reardon
902-368-6499, Fax: 902-368-6934, nireardon@gov.pe.ca
Coordinator, Parent Education Program, Family Law Section, Gordon Ritchie
902-368-4333, 877-203-8828, Fax: 902-368-6934,
giritchie@gov.pe.ca
Coordinator, Family Court Counsellors' Office, Family Law Section, Ron Stanley
902-836-8924, Fax: 902-368-6934, rdstanley@gov.pe.ca
Trial Coordinator, Supreme Court of Prince Edward Island, Court Services Section, Shelley Young Brennan
902-368-6023, Fax: 902-368-6123, sdyoung@gov.pe.ca
Administrative Recalculation Officer, Family Law Section, Sharon Fortier
902-368-4109, Fax: 902-368-6934, safortier@gov.pe.ca
Child Support Guidelines Officer, Charlottetown Location, Family Law Section, Angelie C. Murnaghan
902-368-6658, Fax: 902-368-6934, acmurnaghan@gov.pe.ca
Child Support Guidelines Officer, Summerside Location, Family Law Section, Barbara Richard
902-888-8188, Fax: 902-888-8222, bmrichard@gov.pe.ca

Legislative Counsel
J. Angus MacLean Bldg., 180 Richmond St., PO Box 2000, Charlottetown, PE C1A 7N8
www.gov.pe.ca/jps
The Legislative Counsel is responsible for the following duties: drafting statutes & regulations; revising statutes, & producing loose-leaf updates of the consolidations of statutes & regulations.
Chief Legislative Counsel, Shawn Flynn
902-368-5284, Fax: 902-368-5176, sbflynn@gov.pe.ca
Legislative Counsel, Janet Counsel
902-368-4295, Fax: 902-368-5176, jmchristian@gov.pe.ca
Legislative Editor, Kent W. Walker
902-368-4269, Fax: 902-368-5176, kwwalker@gov.pe.ca

Policy & Administration Division
Shaw Bldg., 105 Rochford St., 4th Fl., PO Box 2000, Charlottetown, PE C1A 7N8
902-368-4865 Fax: 902-368-5335
www.gov.pe.ca/jps
The Policy & Administration Division provides financial administration & human resource management services for the Department of Justice & Public Safety.
Director, Policy & Administration, Kevin Barnes, CA
902-368-4865, Fax: 902-368-4224, kcbarnes@gov.pe.ca
Manager, Financial Administration, Barry Gosby
902-368-4897, Fax: 902-368-5335, bbgosby@gov.pe.ca
Manager, Human Resource Management, Michael Ready
902-569-0549, Fax: 902-368-4224, mcready@gov.pe.ca

Policy, Policing, & Crime Prevention Division
Shaw Bldg., 105 Rochford St., 4th Fl., Charlottetown, PE C1A 7N8
902-368-6620 Fax: 902-368-5335
www.gov.pe.ca/jps
The Policy, Policing, & Crime Prevention Division is comprised of the following sections: Justice Resource Service; Policing Services; & Access & Privacy Services.
The Justice Resource Service supports government & community organizations in justice issues, with a focus on community & social development.
The Police Act is administered by the Policing Services Section.
The Access & Privacy Services Section offers advice regarding the operation of the Freedom of Information & Protection of Privacy (FOIPP) Act & its regulations.
Director, Policy, Policing, & Crime Prevention, Erin Mitchell
902-368-6619, Fax: 902-368-5335, etmitchell@gov.pe.ca
Provincial Manager, Access & Privacy Services, Kathryn Dickson
902-569-0568, Fax: 902-368-4096, kedickson@gov.pe.ca
Manager, Policing Services, Gordon Garrison
902-368-4823, Fax: 902-368-5335, gagarrison@gov.pe.ca
Manager, Justice Resource Service, Jill Lightwood
902-368-4583, Fax: 902-368-4096, jlightwood@gov.pe.ca
Coordinator, Planning & Communications, Policy, Policing, & Crime Prevention, Joanne MacKinnon
902-368-5010, Fax: 902-368-5335, jymackinnon@gov.pe.ca

Office of Public Safety
National Bank Tower, #600, 134 Kent St., 6th Fl., PO Box 2000, Charlottetown, PE C1A 7N8
902-894-0385 Fax: 902-368-6362
www.gov.pe.ca/jps

The Office of Public Safety includes the following sections: 911 Administration Office; Emergency Measures Organization; Fire Marshal's Office; & the Office for Business Continuity Management Planning.

Director, Office of Public Safety, Aaron Campbell
902-894-0385, Fax: 902-368-6362, acampbell@gov.pe.ca
Provincial Coordinator, 911 Call Answer & Transfer Service, Pat J. Kelly
902-894-0299, Fax: 902-368-6362, pjkelly@gov.pe.ca
Provincial Emergency Management Coordinator, Emergency Measures Organization, Tanya Mullally
902-368-5980, Fax: 902-368-6362, tlmullally@gov.pe.ca
Coordinator, Civic Addressing, 911 Call Answer & Transfer Service, D. Steven Dickie
902-368-6361, Fax: 902-368-6362, dsdickie@gov.pe.ca
Fire Marshal, Fire Marshal's Office, David Rossiter
902-368-4869, Fax: 902-368-5526, derossiter@gov.pe.ca
Project Manager, Public Safety Radio, Office of Public Safety, Larry Avery
902-368-4073, Fax: 902-368-6362, jlavery@gov.pe.ca
Senior Planning & Policy Officer, Office of Public Safety, Connie McNeill
902-894-0374, Fax: 902-368-6362, cbmcneill@gov.pe.ca
Senior Business Continuity Planner, Office for Business Continuity Management Planning, Brian McFeely
902-438-4174, Fax: 902-432-2659, bcmcfeely@gov.pe.ca
Building Safety Inspector, Fire Marshal's Office, Robert Arsenault
902-368-4893, Fax: 902-368-5526, robarsenault@gov.pe.ca

Prince Edward Island Liquor Control Commission (PEILCC)

3 Garfield St., PO Box 967, Charlottetown, PE C1A 7M4
902-368-5710 Fax: 902-368-5735
www.peilcc.ca

Under the authority of the Liquor Control Act & Regulations, the Prince Edward Island Liquor Control Commission is responsible for managing the distribution of alcohol & regulating the sale & purchase of all alcoholic beverages. The crown corporation also administers the operation of nineteen retail liquor stores across the province. Licenses are issued by the commission for dining rooms, clubs, lounges, special premises, military canteens, & caterers & waiters.

Chief Executive Officer, Brooke MacMillan
902-368-5720, Fax: 902-368-5735, jbmacmillan@gov.pe.ca
Director, Sales & Marketing, Fred J. MacDonald
902-368-5715, Fax: 902-368-5735, fjmacdonald@gov.pe.ca
Director, Finance & Retail Operations, Wendy L. MacDonald, CA
902-368-5126, Fax: 902-368-5395, wlmacdonald@gov.pe.ca
Director, Licensing & Security, James C. MacLeod
902-368-5714, Fax: 902-368-5735, jcmacleod@gov.pe.ca
Director, Purchasing & Distribution, David Stewart
902-368-5721, Fax: 902-368-5735, dlstewart@gov.pe.ca

Prince Edward Island Regulatory & Appeals Commission (IRAC) / Commission de réglementation et d'appels

National Bank Tower, #501, 134 Kent St., PO Box 577, Charlottetown, PE C1A 7L1
902-892-3501 Fax: 902-566-4076
800-501-6268
info@irac.pe.ca
www.irac.pe.ca

Prince Edward Island's Regulatory & Appeals Commission was established in 1991, with the amalgamation of the Office of the Director of Residential Property, the Public Utilities Commission, & the Land Use Commission.

Operating under the authority of the Island Regulatory & Appeals Commission Act, the Regulatory & Appeals Commission works at arms-length from the provincial government to administer statutes dealing with economic regulation. The quasi-judicial tribunal also listens to appeals dealing with property & revenue sales tax, land use, & unsightly premises.

The Regulatory & Appeals Commission reports to the Legislative Assembly of Prince Edward Island through the Minister of Education & Early Childhood Development.

Acts Administered:
Electric Power Act
Environmental Protection Act
Insurance Act
Lands Protection Act
Petroleum Products Act
Renewable Energy Act
Water & Sewerage Act

Director, Land, Corporate & Appellate Services Division, Eileen Callaghan
mecallaghan@irac.pe.ca
Director, Residential Rental Property, Cathy Flanagan
cflanagan@irac.pe.ca
Director, Technical & Regulatory Services Division, Allison MacEwen
amacewen@irac.pe.ca

Prince Edward Island Department of Tourism & Culture

PO Box 2000, Charlottetown, PE C1A 7N8
902-368-5540 Fax: 902-368-5277
tpswitch@gov.pe.ca
www.gov.pe.ca/tourism

Prince Edward Island's Department of Tourism & Culture is engaged in the following activities: promoting tourism & special events; facilitating product development; managing infrastructure projects such as parks & golf courses; providing library services; promoting historic preservation & documentation; & encouraging cultural development.

Acts Administered:
Archives Act (Repealed)
Archives & Records Act
Confederation Birthplace Act (Repealed)
Fathers of Confederation Buildings Act
Heritage Places Protection Act
Highway Advertisements Act (Repealed)
Highway Signage Act
Liquor Control Act
Lucy Maud Montgomery Foundation Act
Museum Act
National Park Act
Public Libraries Act
Recreation Development Act
Tourism Industry Act
Tourism PEI Act
Tourism PEI Act
Trails Act

Minister, Tourism & Culture, Hon. Robert L. Henderson
902-368-5540, Fax: 902-368-5277,
rlhenderson@assembly.pe.ca;
robert.henderson@liberal.pe.ca
Social Media:
www.facebook.com/profile.php?id=100001965683516
Deputy Minister, Melissa MacEachern
902-368-5956, Fax: 902-368-5277,
mamaceachern@gov.pe.ca
Communications Officer, Mary Moszynski
902-368-5535, Fax: 902-894-0342, mamoszynski@gov.pe.ca

Associated Agencies, Boards & Commissions:

• Museum & Heritage Foundation
Beaconsfield Historic House
2 Kent St.
Charlottetown, PE C1A 1M6
902-368-6600 Fax: 902-368-6608
mhpei@gov.pe.ca
www.peimuseum.com; www.gov.pe.ca/peimhf
Governed by the Museum Act, the Prince Edward Island Museum & Heritage Foundation operates as a Schedule B Provincial Crown Corporation. The mandate of the registered charitable corporation is to collect, preserve, & interpret Prince Edward Island's human & natural heritage.
The following seven provincial museums & heritage sites across Prince Edward Island are administered by the organization for the benefit & enjoyment of the people of the province & tourists: Elmira Railway Museum; Basin Head Fisheries Museum; Orwell Corner Historic Village & Agricultural Museum; Beaconsfield Historic House; Eptek Art & Culture Centre; The Acadian Museum of Prince Edward Island; & Green Park Shipbuilding Museum & Yeo House. There are more than 90,000 artifacts in the Provincial Collection, which are the responsibility of the Foundation.

• Tourism Advisory Council of Prince Edward Island (TAC)
Shaw Bldg., 3rd Fl.
Rochford St.
PO Box 2000
Charlottetown, PE C1A 7N8
902-368-5907
www.peitac.com
An industry advisory board to the Minister of Tourism & Culture, Prince Edward Island's Tourism Advisory Council features nineteen members. Members include senior provincial & federal government members & industry stakeholders who discuss the challenges of the tourism industry.
The Tourism Advisory Council works to ensure growing revenues in the tourism industry. To achieve this goal, the council partners with the Tourism Industry Association of PEI, Tourism PEI, & the Atlantic Canada Opportunities Agency.
The Minister of Tourism & Culture receives advice from the council about research initiatives, product development, & marketing.

Corporate Services Division
PO Box 2000, Charlottetown, PE C1A 7N8

Activities of the Corporate Services Division include financial services, administration, human resources, insurance matters, records management, & the operation of provincial parks & golf courses.

Director, Corporate Services, Kevin Jenkins, CA
902-368-5874, Fax: 902-894-0342, wkjenkin@gov.pe.ca
General Manager, Provincial Golf Courses, Ryan Garrett
902-368-4238, Fax: 902-894-0342, ragarrett@gov.pe.ca
Manager, Provincial Parks, Shane Arbing
902-368-4404, Fax: 902-894-0342, sdarbing@gov.pe.ca
Manager, Financial Services, Beecher D. Gillis, CMA
902-368-5932, Fax: 902-894-0342, bdgillis@gov.pe.ca
Manager, Human Resources, Danny McLaughlin
902-368-5520, Fax: 902-368-0342, djmclaughlin@gov.pe.ca
Controller, Vicki Cotton, CA
902-368-6628, Fax: 902-894-0342, vlcotton@gov.pe.ca
Coordinator, Records Information, Lorianne McCormack
902-569-7597, lxmccormack@gov.pe.ca

Consumer Sales & Customer Relationship Management Division
PO Box 2000, Charlottetown, PE C1A 7N8
902-368-6316 Fax: 902-368-4438

The Consumer Sales & Customer Relationship Management Division is involved in the operation of Visitor Information & Call Centres, as well as the Central Reservation System & Integrated Tourism Solution Technology.

Director, Consumer Sales & Customer Relationship Management, Sebastian Manago
902-368-6316, Fax: 902-368-4438, srmanago@gov.pe.ca
Manager, Call Centre, Jennifer Bernard
902-437-8570, Fax: 902-437-8536, jfbernard@gov.pe.ca
Manager, Visitor Services, Heather Pollard
368-444-1570, Fax: 902-368-4438, hlpollard@gov.pe.ca

Culture, Heritage, & Libraries Division
Sullivan Bldg., 16 Fitzroy St., 1st Fl., PO Box 2000, Charlottetown, PE C1A 7N8
902-368-4787 Fax: 902-368-4663

The Culture, Heritage, & Libraries Division acts as a liaison between the Prince Edward Island provincial government & organizations that represent the library, heritage, & cultural sectors.

Director, Culture, Heritage, & Libraries, Harry Holman
902-368-4784, Fax: 902-368-4663, htholman@gov.pe.ca
Provincial Librarian, Kathleen Eaton
902-961-7316, Fax: 902-961-7322, keeaton@gov.pe.ca
Provincial Archivist, Jill MacMicken-Wilson
902-368-4351, Fax: 902-368-6327, jswilson@gov.pe.ca
Francophone Cultural Affairs Officer, Cecile Arsenault
902-854-7265, Fax: 902-854-7255, ccarsenault@gov.pe.ca
Heritage Officer, Charlotte Stewart
902-368-5940, Fax: 902-368-4663, clstewart@gov.pe.ca

Marketing Communications Division
Shaw Bldg., 95-105 Rochford St., 3rd Fl., PO Box 2000, Charlottetown, PE C1A 7N8

The role of the Marketing Communications Division is the promotion of Prince Edward Island as an excellent tourist destination.

Director, Marketing & Communications, Brenda Gallant
902-368-6066, Fax: 902-368-4438, bgallant@gov.pe.ca
Manager, Advertising & Publicity, Robert Ferguson
902-368-5522, Fax: 902-368-4438, mfergus@gov.pe.ca
Manager, Trade & Sales, Craig Sulis
902-368-5754, Fax: 902-368-4438, cdsulis@gov.pe.ca
Information Officer, Carol Johnston
902-368-4447, Fax: 902-368-4438, cajohnston@gov.pe.ca
Editorial & Marketing Officer, Alison MacDougall
902-368-6343, Fax: 902-368-4438, alimacdougall@gov.pe.ca
Coordinator, Publications, Paul Baglole
902-368-6334, Fax: 902-368-4438, pnbaglol@gov.pe.ca
Coordinator, Print & Photography; Marketing Officer, Interactive Media, Marc C. Dagenais
902-368-5882, Fax: 902-368-4438, mcdagenais@gov.pe.ca
Coordinator, Fulfilment, Harold McGuigan
902-368-4452, Fax: 902-368-4459, hjmcguig@gov.pe.ca

Strategy, Evaluation, & Industry Investment Division

The Strategy, Evaluation, & Industry Investment Division works with regional tourism associations to help them prosper. Overseeing the development of support programs is a key activity.

The division is also responsible for the management of regulatory affairs related to the Highway Signage Act & the Tourism Industry Act. Examples of these responsibilities include special event signage, on-premise signage, licensing, & occupancy reports.

Advocating for the interests of the tourism industry is another part of the mandate for The Strategy, Evaluation, & Industry Investment Division. The division has represented the tourism industry in areas such as the Atlantic Gateway Initiative & land use issues.

Director, Strategy, Evaluation, & Industry Investment Division, Chris K. Jones
902-368-6342, Fax: 902-368-4438, ckjones@gov.pe.ca
Manager, Evaluation, Measurement, & Business Intelligence Unit, Brian Dunn
902-368-4237, Fax: 902-368-4438, bjdunn@gov.pe.ca
Manager, Product Development, Investment, & Regulatory Affairs Unit, Janet Wood
902-368-5508, Fax: 902-368-4438, jewood@gov.pe.ca
Senior Research Analyst, Evaluation, Measurement, & Business Intelligence Unit, Sharon Chuu
902-368-6321, Fax: 902-368-4438, schuu@gov.pe.ca
Registrar, Signage, Product Development, Investment, & Regulatory Affairs Unit, Hubert MacIsaac
902-368-4398, Fax: 902-368-6568, hamacisaac@gov.pe.ca

Prince Edward Island Department of Transportation & Infrastructure Renewal

Jones Bldg., 11 Kent St., 3rd Fl., PO Box 2000, Charlottetown, PE C1A 7N8
902-368-5100 Fax: 902-368-5395
www.gov.pe.ca/tir

Prince Edward Island's Department of Transportation & Infrastructure Renewal maintains & enhances transportation systems & services throughout the province to ensure the safe & efficient movement of people, goods, & services.
The department also works to provide necessary infrastructure for the efficient operation of government. The department is therefore involved in crown land management & building construction & maintenance.

Acts Administered:
Architects Act
Crown Building Corporation Act
Dangerous Goods (Transportation) Act
Engineering Profession Act
Expropriation Act
Highway Traffic Act
Land Survey Act
Land Survey Act (Repealed)
Land Surveyors Act
Off-Highway Vehicle Act
Public Works Act
Roads Act
Closing of Roads Regulations
Highway Access Regulations
Public Utility Easement (Fees) Regulation
Vehicle Weights & Dimensions Regulations

Minister, Transportation & Infrastructure Renewal, Hon. Robert S. Vessey
902-368-4801, Fax: 902-368-5277, rsvessey@gov.pe.ca; robert.vessey@liberal.pe.ca
Deputy Minister, Steve MacLean, P. Eng
902-368-5130, Fax: 902-368-5385, scmaclean@gov.pe.ca
Communications Officer, Andrew Sprague
902-368-5112, Fax: 902-368-5385, asgsprague@gov.pe.ca

Associated Agencies, Boards & Commissions:
• Island Waste Management Corporation (IWMC)
110 Watts Ave.
Charlottetown, PE C1E 2C1
902-894-0330 Fax: 902-894-0331 888-280-8111
reception@iwmc.pe.ca; info@iwmc.pe.ca
www.iwmc.pe.ca
The Island Waste Management Corporation is a provincial Crown Corporation that was formed in 1999, according to the Environmental Act R.S.P.E.I. 1988, Cap. E-9. Conducting business throughout Prince Edward Island, the corporation administers & provides solid waste management services to both commercial & residential sectors.
One of the Island Waste Management Corporation's successful environmental programs is Waste Watch. Everyone in Prince Edward Island must separate waste into one of three categories: compost, marketable recyclable material, & waste. Waste Watch Drop-Off Centres also accept household hazardous waste free of charge.
In addition to operating the Waste Watch Drop-Off Centres, the Island Waste Management Corporation also operates or oversees the following facilities: Central Compost Facility, East Prince Waste Management Facility, & the Energy from Waste Facility.

Capital Projects Division

Jones Bldg., 11 Kent St., 3rd Fl., Charlottetown, PE C1A 7N8

The following sections make up the Capital Projects Division: Engineering Services; Highway Construction; Materials Lab; & Planning & Design. Staff take care of the design & construction of highways & building infrastructure.
Director, Capital Projects Division; Chief Engineer, Stephen J. Yeo, P.Eng.
902-368-5105, Fax: 902-368-5425, sjyeo@gov.pe.ca
Senior Manager, Materials Lab, Terry Kelly, P.Eng.
902-676-7979, Fax: 902-676-7994, jtkelly@gov.pe.ca
Manager, Design & Bridge Maintenance, Darrell Evans, P.Eng.
902-569-0578, Fax: 902-368-5395, djevans@gov.pe.ca
Manager, GIS-T, Dan MacDonald
902-368-5158, Fax: 902-368-5425, wdmacdonald@gov.pe.ca
Engineer, Traffic Operations, Alan Aitken, P.Eng.
902-368-5006, Fax: 902-368-5425, aaaitken@gov.pe.ca
Regional Engineer, Eastern Highway Construction, Matt Collins, P.Eng.
902-652-8998, Fax: 902-652-8981, mscollins@gov.pe.ca
Regional Engineer, Central Highway Construction, Mark Sherren, P.Eng.
902-368-6195, Fax: 902-368-5425, mesherren@gov.pe.ca

Finance & Human Resources Division

Jones Bldg., 11 Kent St., 2nd Fl., Charlottetown, PE C1A 7N8
902-368-5100 Fax: 902-368-5395

The fiscal matters & human resources issues of the Department of Transportation & Infrastructure Renewal are handled by the Finance & Human Resources Division.
Director, Finance & Human Resource Division, Wendy L. MacDonald, CA
902-368-5126, Fax: 902-368-5395, wlmacdonald@gov.pe.ca
Manager, Human Resources, Anne MacAulay
902-620-3356, Fax: 902-894-0368, ammacaulay@gov.pe.ca

Highway Maintenance Division

Park St. & Riverside Dr. Provincial Headquarters, PO Box 2000, Charlottetown, PE C1A 7N8
902-368-5090 Fax: 902-368-6244

The Highway Maintenance Division is responsible for the upkeep of the total povincial highway system.
Director, Highway Maintenance Division, Darren Chaisson, P.Eng
902-368-5103, Fax: 902-368-6244, ddchaisson@gov.pe.ca
Manager, Fleet, Mechanical Branch, Wilfred J. MacDonald
902-368-5222, Fax: 902-368-5994, wjmacdonald@gov.pe.ca
Manager, Inventory Control, Provincial Headquarters, Robert A. MacKinnon
902-368-4746, Fax: 902-368-6244, ramackinnon@gov.pe.ca
Superintendent, Western Highway Maintenance, Mike Berrigan
902-888-8282, Fax: 902-888-8291, mjberrigan@gov.pe.ca
Superintendent, Central Highway Maintenance, Gordie Lund
902-368-5172, Fax: 902-368-6244, gllund@gov.pe.ca
Superintendent, Eastern Highway Maintenance, Gerard F. Morrison
902-652-8971, Fax: 902-652-8978, gfmorrison@gov.pe.ca

Highway Safety Division

33 Riverside Dr., Charlottetown, PE C1A 9R9
902-368-5228 Fax: 902-368-5236

Safety issues from the province's highways are handled by the Highway Safety Division.
Director, Highway Safety Division, John B. MacDonald
902-368-5225, Fax: 902-368-5236, jbmacdonald@gov.pe.ca
Registrar, Motor Vehicles, Graham L. Miner
902-368-5223, Fax: 902-368-5236, glminer@gov.pe.ca
Coordinator, Safety, Doug J. MacEwen
902-368-5219, Fax: 902-368-5236, djmacewen@gov.pe.ca

Infrastructure Division

#303, 75 Fitzroy St., PO Box 2000, Charlottetown, PE C1A 7N8
902-620-3383
888-240-4411
cpei-infrastructure@gov.pe.ca
www.gov.pe.ca/tir

Infrastructure is a joint initiative between the Government of Prince Edward Island & the Government of Canada.
Provincial Manager, Infrastructure, Darlene Rhodenizer
902-368-6213, Fax: 902-620-3383, dlrhodenizer@gov.pe.ca
Federal Manager, Pat MacAulay
902-368-0987, 888-240-4411, Fax: 902-620-3383, pat.macaulay@acoa-apeca.gc.ca
Provincial Project Officer, John Arsenault
902-368-4882, Fax: 902-620-3383, jearsenault@gov.pe.ca
Federal Project Officer, Kandace McEntee
902-566-7097, 888-240-4411, Fax: 902-620-3383, kandace.mcentee@acoa-apeca.gc.ca

Land & Environment Division

Jones Bldg., 11 Kent St., 3rd Fl., PO Box 2000, Charlottetown, PE C1A 7N8
902-368-5221 Fax: 902-368-5395

The Land & Environment Division is responsible for provincial lands. Environmental services are also provided by the Land & Environment Division for projects related to transportation & public works. Staff members ensure compliance with provincial & federal environmental legislation & regulations during highway construction & maintenance projects.
Director, Land & Environment Division, Brian F. Thompson, P.Eng.
902-368-5185, Fax: 902-368-5395, bfthompson@gov.pe.ca
Chief Surveyor, David R.J. Morriwr, P.Eng, PEILS, CLS
902-368-5143, Fax: 902-620-3033, drjmorris@gov.pe.ca
Manager, Provincial Land, Leo J. Creamer
902-368-5134, Fax: 902-368-5395, jlcreamer@gov.pe.ca
Supervisor, Land Administration, Carol Craswell, BBA
902-368-6119, Fax: 902-368-5395, cmcraswell@gov.pe.ca
Supervisor, Provincial Roads, Sharon N. Slauenwhite, BA
902-368-6387, Fax: 902-368-5395, snslauenwhite@gov.pe.ca
Environmental Coordinator, Shelley Cole-Arbing
902-368-5095, Fax: 902-368-5395, slcole@gov.pe.ca

Public Works & Planning Division

Jones Bldg., 11 Kent St., 3rd Fl., Charlottetown, PE C1A 7N8
902-368-5100 Fax: 902-368-5395

The Public Works & Planning Division is engaged in the following activities: analyzing long term transportation requirements; planning & designing construction projects; implementing major projects; & maintaining buildings.
Director, Public Works & Planning, Alan Maynard, P.Eng.
902-368-5147, Fax: 902-569-0590, aemaynard@gov.pe.ca
Manager, Planning, Paul Godfrey, P.Eng.
902-368-4849, Fax: 902-569-0590, jpgodfrey@gov.pe.ca
Manager, Building Maintenance & Accommodation, Holly Hinds
902-368-4854, Fax: 902-368-5395, hahinds@gov.pe.ca
Manager, Building Construction Contract Administration, Kevin Kennedy
902-368-5148, Fax: 902-368-5395, kjkennedy@gov.pe.ca
Manager, Building Design & Construction, Tyler Richardson, P.Eng.
902-368-4249, Fax: 902-569-0590, ttrichardson@gov.pe.ca

Prince Edward Island Workers Compensation Board (WCB)

14 Weymouth St., PO Box 757, Charlottetown, PE C1A 7L7
902-368-5680 Fax: 902-368-5696
800-237-5049
www.wcb.pe.ca
Other Communication: Customer Liaison Service, Toll-Free Phone: 1-866-460-3074; Employer Services, Phone: 902-368-5705

The Workers Compensation Board of Prince Edward Island operates as an independent, non-profit organization. Prince Edward Island employers provide funding for the board. Both workers & employers are served by the Workers Compensation Board through the promotion of workplace health & safety & the provision of workplace injury & illness insurance.

Acts Administered:
Occupational Health & Safety Act
Workers Compensation Act

Chair, Nancy Guptill
Chief Executive Officer, Carol Anne Duffy
902-368-5688, caduffy@wcb.pe.ca
Director, Corporate Development, Bonnie Blakney
902-620-3478, blblakney@wcb.pe.ca
Director, Client Services, Mary Hughes Power
902-368-5687, mhpower@wcb.pe.ca
Director, Occupational Health & Safety, Bill Reid
902-368-5562, bkreid@wcb.pe.ca
Director, Corporate Services, Tammy Turner
902-368-4102, teturner@wcb.pe.ca
Manager, Case Management, Dawn Bradley
902-368-6044, dbradley@wcb.pe.ca
Manager, Employer Services, Greg MacCallum
902-368-5679, ggmaccallum@wcb.pe.ca
Manager, Information Technology Services, Darren MacDonald
902-368-5669, dpmacdonald@wcb.pe.ca
Manager, Intake & Entitlement, Kate Marshall
902-368-6358, kmarshall@wcb.pe.ca
Manager, Human Resources, Wendy McIsaac
902-894-0315, wlmcisaac@wcb.pe.ca
Manager, Facilities & Procurement, Chris Power
902-368-4091, cipower@wcb.pe.ca a
Manager, OHS, Ian Rodd
902-368-5575, ihrodd@wcb.pe.ca

Gouvernement du Québec / Government of Québec

Siege du gouvernement: Hôtel du Parlement, 1045, rue des Parlementaires, Québec, QC G1A 1A3
418-643-7239 Fax: 418-646-4271
866-337-8837
www.gouv.qc.ca; www.assnat.qc.ca

La Province de Québec est entrée dans la Confédération le 1ère juillet, 1867. Terre: 1,356,366.78 km2. Population: 7,866,108 (2010)

Cabinet du Lieutenant-gouverneur / Office of the Lieutenant Governor

Édifice André-Laurendeau, 1050, rue des Parlementaires R.C., Québec, QC G1A 1A1
418-643-5385 Fax: 418-644-4677
866-791-0766
www.lieutenant-gouverneur.qc.ca

Rôles constitutionnels et cérémoniels: le lieutenant-gouverneur a des pouvoirs constitutionnels d'un chef d'État et est le

fonctionnaire exécutif en chef de la province; il/elle donne une suite légale à la politique déterminée par le gouvernement en ce qui concerne la nomination du premier ministre, et les membres du Conseil exécutif, la convocation, la prorogation et la dissolution de l'Assemblée nationale, la ratification des décrets du gouvernement, et la nomination des juges des cours de la province; il/elle occupe le plus haut rang protocolaire du Québec et il/elle a préséance sur tous les membres de la famille royale, à l'exception de Sa Majesté qu'il/elle représente
Lieutenant-gouverneur, L'hon. Pierre Duchesne
Administrateur, France Thibault
418-649-3515

Cabinet du premier ministre / Office of the Premier

Édifice Honoré-Mercier, 835, boul René-Lévesque est, 3e étage, Québec, QC G1A 1B4
418-643-5321 Fax: 418-643-3924
www.premier-ministre.gouv.qc.ca
Other Communication: Alternative Phone: 514-873-3411; Alternative Fax: 514-873-6769
Premier ministre/Premier, L'hon. Jean Charest
Secrétaire général/Secretary General, Gérard Bibeau
418-643-7355
Attaché de presse, Hugo D'Amours
418-643-5321, communications-pm@mce.gouv.qc.ca

Ministère du Conseil exécutif / Executive Council

875, Grande Allée est, Québec, QC G1R 4Y8
418-646-3021 Fax: 418-528-9242
www.mce.gouv.qc.ca
Other Communication: Montréal: 514-873-7029
Premier ministre, Ministre responsable des dossiers jeunesse, L'hon. Jean Charest
418-643-5321, Fax: 418-643-3924
Vice-première ministre & Ministre, Ressources naturelles et de la Faune; Ministre responsable du Plan Nord, L'hon. Nathalie Normandeau
418-643-7295, Fax: 418-643-4318, ministre@mrnf.gouv.qc.ca
Ministre des Relations internationales, Ministre responsable de la Francophonie, L'hon. Monique Gagnon-Tremblay
418-649-2319, Fax: 418-643-4804, cabinet@mri.gouv.qc.ca
Ministre, Justice; Ministre responsable de la Réforme des institutions démcratiques; Ministre responsable de l'Accès à l'information, L'hon. Jean-Marc Fournier
ministre@justice.gouv.qc.ca
Ministre, Éducation, Loisir et Sport, L'hon. Line Beauchamp
418-644-0664, Fax: 418-646-7551,
line.beauchamp@mels.gouv.qc.ca
Présidente, Conseil du trésor; Ministre responsable de l'Administration gouvernementale; Ministre des Services gouvernementaux, L'hon. Michelle Courchesne
418-643-5926, Fax: 418-643-7824, cabinet@sct.gouv.qc.ca
Ministre, Agriculture, Pêcheries & Alimentation; Ministre resp. Affaires autochtones, L'hon. Pierre Corbeil
418-380-2525, Fax: 418-380-2184,
ministre.mapaq@mapaq.gouv.qc.ca
Ministre, Finances; Ministre du Revenu, L'hon. Raymond Bachand
418-643-5270, Fax: 418-646-1574,
ministre@finances.gouv.qc.ca
Ministre, Santé et Services Sociaux, L'hon. Dr Yves Bolduc
418-266-7171, Fax: 418-266-7197,
ministre@msss.gouv.qc.ca
Ministre, Emploi et Solidarité sociale, L'hon. Julie Boulet
418-643-4810, Fax: 418-643-2802,
ministre@mess.gouv.qc.ca
Ministre, Transports, L'hon. Sam Hamad
418-643-6980, Fax: 418-643-2033, ministre@mtq.gouv.qc.ca
Ministre, Affaires municipales, Régions & Occupation du territoire, L'hon. Laurent Lessard
418-691-2050, Fax: 418-643-1795,
ministre@mamrot.gouv.qc.ca
Ministre, Développement économique, Innovation & Exportation, L'hon. Clément Gignac
418-691-5650, Fax: 418-643-8553,
ministre@mdeie.gouv.qc.ca
Ministre, Sécurité publique; Leader parlementaire adjoint du gouvernement, L'hon. Robert Dutil
418-643-2112, Fax: 418-646-6168, ministre@msp.gouv.qc.ca
Ministre, Développement durable, Environnement et Parcs, L'hon. Pierre Arcand
418-521-3911, Fax: 418-643-4143,
ministre@mddep.gouv.qc.ca
Ministre, Culture, Communications et Condition féminine, L'hon. Christine St-Pierre
418-380-2310, Fax: 418-380-2311,
ministre@mcccf.gouv.qc.ca
Ministre, Famille et Aînés, L'hon. Yolande James
418-643-2181, Fax: 418-643-2640,
ministre.famille@mfa.gouv.qc.ca
Ministre, Immigration et Communautés culturelles, L'hon. Kathleen Weil
418-644-2128, Fax: 418-528-0829, cabinet@micc.gouv.qc.ca
Ministre, Travail, L'hon. Lise Thériault
418-643-5297, Fax: 418-644-0003,
ministre@travail.gouv.qc.ca
Ministre, Tourisme, L'hon. Nicole Ménard
418-528-8063, Fax: 418-528-8066,
ministre@tourisme.gouv.qc.ca
Ministre responsable des, Aînés, L'hon. Marguerite Blais
418-646-7757, Fax: 418-646-7769, m.blais@aines.gouv.qc.ca
Ministre responsable des, Affaires autochtones, L'hon. Geoffrey Kelley
418-646-9131, Fax: 418-646-9487,
ministre.autochtones@mce.gouv.qc.ca
Ministre responsable des, Affaires intergouvernementales canadiennes & Francophonie canadienne, L'hon. Pierre Moreau, 20110727
418-646-5950, Fax: 418-528-0981,
ministre.saic@mce.gouv.qc.ca
Ministre délégué aux, Transports, L'hon. Norman MacMillan
418-643-6980, Fax: 418-643-7606,
ministredelegue@mtq.gouv.qc.ca
Ministre déléguée aux, Services sociaux, L'hon. Dominique Vien
418-266-7181, Fax: 418-266-7197,
ministre.deleguee@msss.gouv.qc.ca
Ministre délégué aux, Ressources naturelles & Faune, L'hon. Serge Simard
418-643-7295, Fax: 418-643-4318,
ministredelegue@mrnf.gouv.qc.ca
Whip en chef, L'hon. Lucie Charlebois
418-643-6018, Fax: 418-643-5462, lcharlebois@assnat.qc.ca
Président du, Caucus du gouvernement, L'hon. Lawrence S. Bergman
418-528-1960, Fax: 418-643-0183,
lbergman-dmg@assnat.qc.ca

Cabinet du Conseil exécutif / Cabinet Office
Édifice Honoré-Mercier, #2.12A, 835, boul René-Lévesque est, Québec, QC G1A 1B4
418-643-7355 Fax: 418-528-9552
Secrétaire général, Gérard Bibeau
gerard.bibeau@mce.gouv.qc.ca

Comités ministériels / Cabinet Committees
Secrétariat général, Édifice Honoré-Mercier, #2.12A, 835, boul René-Lévesque est, Québec, QC G1A 1B4
418-643-7355 Fax: 418-528-9552
Répondante, Sylvie Banville
418-646-4495

L'Assemblée nationale / National Assembly

Hôtel du Parlement, 1045, rue des Parlementaires, Québec, QC G1A 1A3
418-643-7239 Fax: 418-646-4271
866-337-8837
responsable.contenu@assnat.qc.ca
www.assnat.qc.ca
Président de l'Assemblée nationale/Speaker of the National Assembly, Président de la Commission de l'Assemblée nationale, et la Sous-commission de la réforme parlementaire, Yvon Vallières
418-644-0675, Fax: 418-643-1734,
yvallieres-ricm@assnat.qc.ca
Première vice-présidente/First Vice-President, Fatima Houda-Pepin
418-643-2750, Fax: 418-643-2942,
fhoudapepin@assnat.qc.ca
Deuxième vice-président/Second Vice-President, François Ouimet
418-643-2810, Fax: 418-643-3688,
fouimet-marq@assnat.qc.ca
Troisième vice-président/Third Vice-President, François Gendron
418-644-1007, Fax: 418-644-1368, fgendron@assnat.qc.ca
Secrétaire général/Secretary General, Michel Bonsaint
418-643-2724, Fax: 418-643-5062,
sec.general@assnat.qc.ca
Whip en chef du gouvernement, Lucie Charlebois
418-643-6018, Fax: 418-643-5462, lcharlebois@assnat.qc.ca
Whip adjoint du gouvernement, Vincent Auclair
418-644-0877, Fax: 418-528-0421,
vauclair-vimo@assnat.qc.ca
Whip adjointe du gouvernement, Danielle St-Amand
418-528-0413, Fax: 418-646-8169,
dstamand-tri@assnat.qc.ca
Leader parlementaire du gouvernement, Jean-Marc Fournier
418-643-3804, Fax: 418-643-2514,
ministre@justice.gouv.qc.ca
Leader parlementaire adjoint du gouvernement, Robert Dutil
418-643-2112, Fax: 418-646-6168, ministre@msp.gouv.qc.ca
Leader parlementaire adjoint du gouvernement, Henri-François Gautrin
418-646-7497, Fax: 418-643-0241,
hfgautrin-verd@assnat.qc.ca

Cabinet du chef de l'opposition officielle / Office of the Official Opposition (ADQ)
Hôtel du Parlement, #2.89, 1045, rue des Parlementaires, Québec, QC G1A 1A4
Chef de l'opposition officielle/Leader of the Official Opposition, Pauline Marois
418-643-2743, Fax: 418-643-2957,
pauline.marois@assnat.qc.ca
Leader parlementaire de l'opposition officielle, Stéphane Bédard
418-643-1275, Fax: 418-643-1906, sbedard@assnat.qc.ca
Whip en chef de l'opposition officielle, Nicole Léger
418-643-2301, Fax: 418-643-3325, nleger-pat@assnat.qc.ca
Whip adjointe de l'opposition officielle, Marjolain Dufour
418-644-0809, Fax: 418-646-7811,
marjolaindufour-rele@assnat.qc.ca

Direction de l'Assemblée nationale du Québec / Directorate of the National Assembly of Québec
Directeur, Secrétariat du Bureau, Marc Painchaud
418-643-2724, Fax: 418-644-7124
Directeur général, Information & affaires institutionnelles, Frédéric Fortin
418-643-2383
Secrétaire générale adjointe, Administration & Information, Jacques Jobin
418-643-6000
Directrice, Secrétariat des commissions, François Arsenault
418-643-2722
Directeur, Gestion immobilière & ressources matérielles, Guy L. Huot
418-643-1828
Reponsable par intérim, Service des restaurant, Jacques Jobin
Directrice, Procédure & affaires parlementaires, Ariane Mignolet
418-528-0020
Directrice, Protocole et accueil, Dominique Drouin
418-643-4206
Directeur, Affaires juridiques et législatives, René Chrétien
418-528-0727, Fax: 418-641-2642
Directeur, Diffusion des débats, Martin-Philippe Côté
418-643-2890
Directeur, Communications, Jean Dumas
418-643-1992
Directeur, Relations interparlementaires et internationales, Dominic Toupin
418-643-7391
Directeur, Secrétariat de l'Assemblée, Jacques Gagnon
418-643-2793
Directeur, Ressources humaines, Serge Bouchard
418-644-5444
Directrice, Ressources financières et services de l'approvisionnement, Lyne Bergeron
418-643-3022
Directeur, Sécurité, Pierre Duchaine
418-644-2783
Directeur, Informatique & télécommunications, Claude Dugas
418-643-2725
Directrice, Bibliothèque, Hélène Galarneau
418-643-4408
Directrice, Traduction & édition des lois, Louise Auger
418-643-2840
Directrice, Éducation à la démocratie parlementaire, Isabelle Giguère
418-643-4101

Les Régions administratives au Québec - Les ministres responsables / Regional Parliamentary Assistants
Abitibi-Témiscamingue, L'hon. Pierre Corbeil
Bas-Saint-Laurent, L'hon. Nathalie Normandeau
Capitale-Nationale, L'hon. Sam Hamad
Centre-du-Québec, L'hon. Laurent Lessard
Chaudière-Appalaches, L'hon. Laurent Lessard
Côte-Nord, L'hon. Serge Simard
Estrie, L'hon. Monique Gagnon-Tremblay
Gaspésie-Iles-de-la-Madeleine, L'hon. Nathalie Normandeau
Laurentides, L'hon. Michelle Courchesne
Lanaudière, L'hon. Michelle Courchesne
Laval, L'hon. Michelle Courchesne
Mauricie, L'hon. Julie Boulet
Montérégie, L'hon. Nicole Ménard
Montréal, L'hon. Raymond Bachand
Nord-du-Québec, L'hon. Pierre Corbeil
Outaouais, L'hon. Norman MacMillan
Saguenay-Lac-Saint-Jean, L'hon. Serge Simard

Trente-neuvième assemblée nationale / Thirty-ninth National Assembly - Québec

Hôtel du Parlement, 1045, rue des Parlementaires, Québec, QC G1A 1A4
418-643-7239 Fax: 418-646-4271
866-337-8837
www.assnat.qc.ca
La dernière élection générale: le 8 décembre, 2008. Depuis le 21 juin 2011, la composition de l'Assemblée est la suivante: Parti Libéral du Québec (PLQ): 65; Parti québécois (PQ): 46; Action

démocratique du Québec (ADQ): 4; Québec solidaire: 1; Indépendants: 9; Total: 125. Salaires, indemnités, allocations: indemnité annuelle: $85,388 et une allocation de dépenses de $15,538. L'indemnité annuelle des membres de l'Assemblée nationale n'est pas majorée du 1er avril 2010 au 31 mars 2012. En plus, le Premier ministre reçot $89,657, les ministres $64,041, le Leader parlementaire du gouvernement et le Président $64,041, le Chef de l'Opposition officielle $64,041. Par la suite: membre, circonscription, allégeance politique, téléphone & télécopieur, courriel, (Adresse: Hôtel du Parlement, Québec, QC G1A 1A4)

Members

L'hon. Pierre Arcand, Mont-Royal, Liberal
418-521-3911, Fax: 418-643-4143, ministre@mddep.gouv.qc.ca

Vincent Auclair, Vimont, Liberal
418-644-0877, Fax: 418-528-0421, vauclair-vimo@assnat.qc.ca

Jean-Martin Aussant, Nicolet-Yamaska, 2008-09-10, Independent
418-646-7505, Fax: 418-643-3423, jmaussant-niya@assnat.qc.ca

Claude Bachand, Arthabaska, Liberal
418-644-1470, Fax: 418-646-7791, cbachand-arth@assnat.qc.ca

L'hon. Raymond Bachand, Outremont, Liberal
418-643-5270, Fax: 418-646-1574, ministre@finances.gouv.qc.ca

L'hon. Line Beauchamp, Bourassa-Sauvé, Liberal
418-644-0664, Fax: 418-646-7551, line.beauchamp@mels.gouv.qc.ca

Denise Beaudoin, Mirabel, Parti Quebecois
418-644-1543, Fax: 418-644-9697, denise.beaudoin-mira@assnat.qc.ca

Louise Beaudoin, Rosemont, Independent
418-644-1667, Fax: 418-643-8924, lbeaudoin-rose@assnat.qc.ca

Stéphane Bédard, Chicoutimi, Parti Quebecois
418-643-1275, Fax: 418-643-1906, sbedard@assnat.qc.ca

Stéphane Bergeron, Verchères, Parti Quebecois
418-644-9368, Fax: 418-646-6640, sbergeron-verc@assnat.qc.ca

L'hon. Lawrence S. Bergman, D'Arcy-McGee, Liberal
418-528-1960, Fax: 418-643-0183, lbergman-dmg@assnat.qc.ca

Daniel Bernard, Rouyn-Noranda-Témiscamingue, 2008-09-11, Liberal
418-644-0588, Fax: 418-528-0416, dbernard-rnt@assnat.qc.ca

Raymond Bernier, Montmorency, Liberal
418-644-9600, Fax: 418-646-7795, rbernier-mont@assnat.qc.ca

Pascal Bérubé, Matane, 2008-09-10, Parti Quebecois
418-644-0054, pberube@assnat.qc.ca

Stéphane Billette, Huntingdon, Liberal
418-644-5992, Fax: 418-646-8169, sbillette-hunt@assnat.qc.ca

L'hon. Marguerite Blais, Saint-Henri-Sainte-Anne, 2008-09-10, Liberal
418-646-7757, Fax: 418-646-7769, m.blais@aines.gouv.qc.ca

Yves-François Blanchet, Drummond, 2008-09-11, Parti Quebecois
418-644-1052, Fax: 418-643-1216, yfblanchet-drum@assnat.qc.ca

L'hon. Yves Bolduc, Jean-Talon, Liberal
418-266-7171, Fax: 418-266-7197, ministre@msss.gouv.qc.ca

François Bonnardel, Shefford, 2008-09-10, Action Democratique du Qc
418-528-0407, Fax: 418-528-9479, fbonnardel-shef@assnat.qc.ca

Etienne-Alexis Boucher, Johnson, 2008-09-10, Parti Quebecois
418-644-1541, Fax: 418-646-4098, eaboucher-john@assnat.qc.ca

Marie Bouillé, Iberville, 2008-09-11, Parti Quebecois
418-644-1475, Fax: 418-644-1085, mbouille-iber@assnat.qc.ca

L'hon. Julie Boulet, Laviolette, Liberal
418-643-4810, Fax: 418-643-2802, ministre@mess.gouv.qc.ca

Éric Caire, La Peltrie, 2008-09-10, Independent
418-644-0185, Fax: 418-528-6935, ecaire-lape@assnat.qc.ca

Marc Carrière, Chapleau, Liberal
418-528-0390, Fax: 418-528-5668, mcarriere-chap@assnat.qc.ca

Jacques Chagnon, Westmount-Saint-Louis, Liberal
418-643-2820, Fax: 418-643-3423, presidentcabinet@assnat.qc.ca

Noëlla Champagne, Champlain, Parti Quebecois
418-644-2499, Fax: 418-528-0427, nchampagne-chmp@assnat.qc.ca

Francine Charbonneau, Mille-Îles, Liberal
418-644-0866, Fax: 418-644-5990, fcharbonneau-miil@assnat.qc.ca

L'hon. Jean Charest, Sherbrooke, Liberal
418-643-5321, Fax: 418-646-1854, www.premier-ministre.gouv.qc.ca/premier-ministre/nous-joindre/

Benoit Charette, Deux-Montagnes, 2008-09-11, Independent
418-528-0765, Fax: 418-643-3423, bcharette-demo@assnat.qc.ca

L'hon. Lucie Charlebois, Soulanges, Liberal
418-643-6018, Fax: 418-643-5462, lcharlebois@assnat.qc.ca

Germain Chevarie, Îles-de-la-Madeleine, Liberal
418-644-1454, Fax: 418-644-5990, gchevarie-idlm@assnat.qc.ca

Alexandre Cloutier, Lac-Saint-Jean, 2008-09-10, Parti Quebecois
418-644-0901, Fax: 418-644-2062, acloutier-lsj@assnat.qc.ca

L'hon. Pierre Corbeil, Abitibi-Est, 2008-09-11, Liberal
418-380-2525, Fax: 418-380-2184, ministre.mapaq@mapaq.gouv.qc.ca

L'hon. Michelle Courchesne, Fabre, Liberal
418-643-5926, Fax: 418-643-7824, cabinet@sct.gouv.qc.ca

Claude Cousineau, Bertrand, Parti Quebecois
418-643-2769, Fax: 418-644-2121, ccousineau-berr@assnat.qc.ca

Pierre Curzi, Borduas, 2008-09-10, Independent
418-644-0752, Fax: 418-643-3423, pcurzi-bord@assnat.qc.ca

Jean D'Amour, Rivière-du-Loup, Liberal
418-528-2914, Fax: 418-644-5990, jdamour-rdl@assnat.qc.ca

Gérard Deltell, Chauveau, Action Democratique du Qc
418-644-9318, Fax: 418-528-9479, gdeltell-chau@assnat.qc.ca

Jean-Paul Diamond, Maskinongé, 2008-09-10, Liberal
418-644-0617, Fax: 418-646-8169, jpdiamond-mask@assnat.qc.ca

Danielle Doyer, Matapédia, Parti Quebecois
418-646-6147, Fax: 418-644-7851, ddoyer-matp@assnat.qc.ca

Bernard Drainville, Marie-Victorin, 2008-09-10, Parti Quebecois
418-643-5611, Fax: 418-646-7812, bdrainville-mavi@assnat.qc.ca

André Drolet, Jean-Lesage, 2008-09-11, Liberal
418-646-7635, Fax: 418-528-0425, adrolet-jele@assnat.qc.ca

Emmanuel Dubourg, Viau, 2008-09-10, Liberal
418-646-7648, Fax: 514-728-2759, edubourg-viau@assnat.qc.ca

Marjolain Dufour, René-Lévesque, Parti Quebecois
418-644-0809, Fax: 418-646-7811, marjolaindufour-rele@assnat.qc.ca

L'hon. Robert Dutil, Beauce-Sud, 2008-09-11, Liberal
418-643-2112, Fax: 418-646-6168, ministre@msp.gouv.qc.ca

Luc Ferland, Ungava, 2008-09-10, Parti Quebecois
418-644-1363, Fax: 418-528-0439, lferland-unga@assnat.qc.ca

L'hon. Jean-Marc Fournier, Saint-Laurent, Liberal
418-643-4210, Fax: 418-646-0027, ministre@justice.gouv.qc.ca

L'hon. Monique Gagnon-Tremblay, Saint-François, Liberal
418-649-2319, Fax: 418-643-4804, cabinet@mri.gouv.qc.ca

Maryse Gaudreault, Hull, 2008-09-10, Liberal
418-644-9954, Fax: 418-643-0595, mgaudreault-hull.assnat.qc.ca

Sylvain Gaudreault, Jonquière, 2008-09-10, Parti Quebecois
418-646-7647, Fax: 418-646-7801, sgaudreault-jonq@assnat.qc.ca

Henri-François Gautrin, Verdun, Liberal
418-646-7497, Fax: 418-643-0241, hfgautrin-verd@assnat.qc.ca

René Gauvreau, Groulx, 2008-09-11, Independent
418-644-0958, Fax: 418-643-3423, rgauvreau-grou@assnat.qc.ca

François Gendron, Abitibi-Ouest, Parti Quebecois
418-644-1007, Fax: 418-644-1368, fgendron@assnat.qc.ca

L'hon. Clément Gignac, Marguerite-Bourgeoys, Liberal
418-691-5650, Fax: 418-643-8553, ministre@mdeie.gouv.qc.ca

Nicolas Girard, Gouin, Parti Quebecois
418-644-1367, Fax: 418-644-6828, ngirard-goui@assnat.qc.ca

Johanne Gonthier, Mégantic-Compton, 2008-09-11, Liberal
418-644-0711, Fax: 418-646-0516, jgonthier-meco@assnat.qc.ca

Janvier Grondin, Beauce-Nord, Action Democratique du Qc
418-643-5016, Fax: 418-528-9479, jgrondin@assnat.qc.ca

L'hon. Sam Hamad, Louis-Hébert, Liberal
418-643-6980, Fax: 418-643-2033, ministre@mtq.gouv.qc.ca

Véronique Hivon, Joliette, 2008-09-10, Parti Quebecois
418-644-1598, Fax: 418-644-9697, vhivon-joli@assnat.qc.ca

Fatima Houda-Pepin, La Pinière, Liberal
418-643-2750, Fax: 418-643-2942, fhoudapepin@assnat.qc.ca

Patrick Huot, Vanier, Liberal
418-643-7719, Fax: 418-643-9164, phuot-vani@assnat.qc.ca

L'hon. Yolande James, Nelligan, Liberal
418-643-2181, Fax: 418-643-2640, ministre.famille@mfa.gouv.qc.ca

L'hon. Geoffrey Kelley, Jacques-Cartier, Liberal
418-646-7627, Fax: 418-643-0595, gkelley@assnat.qc.ca

Amir Khadir, Mercier, QS
418-644-1430, Fax: 418-643-0624, akhadir-merc@assnat.qc.ca

Maka Kotto, Bourget, 2008-09-11, Parti Quebecois
418-646-2128, Fax: 418-646-8166, mkotto-bour@assnat.qc.ca

Lisette Lapointe, Crémazie, 2008-09-11, Independent
418-643-2152, Fax: 418-643-3423, lisette.lapointe-crem@assnat.qc.ca

Charlotte L'Écuyer, Pontiac, Liberal
418-644-0679, Fax: 418-528-5668, clecuyer-pont@assnat.qc.ca

Guy Leclair, Beauharnois, Parti Quebecois
418-644-7844, Fax: 418-528-7410, guy.leclair-beau@assnat.qc.ca

Nicole Léger, Pointe-aux-Trembles, Parti Quebecois
418-643-2301, Fax: 418-643-3325, nleger-pat@assnat.qc.ca

Gilles Lehouillier, Lévis, 2008-09-11, Liberal
418-646-7673, Fax: 418-528-7447, glehouillier@assnat.qc.ca

Martin Lemay, Sainte-Marie-Saint-Jacques, Parti Quebecois
418-644-1632, Fax: 418-528-9534, mlemay-smsj@assnat.qc.ca

L'hon. Laurent Lessard, Frontenac, Liberal
418-691-2050, Fax: 418-643-1795, ministre@mamrot.gouv.qc.ca

L'hon. Norman MacMillan, Papineau, Liberal
418-643-6980, Fax: 418-643-7606, ministredelegue@mtq.gouv.qc.ca

Marie Malavoy, Taillon, Parti Quebecois
418-646-4283, Fax: 418-644-9697, mmalavoy-tail@assnat.qc.ca

Agnès Maltais, Taschereau, Parti Quebecois
418-644-1042, Fax: 418-646-4991, amaltais-tasc@assnat.qc.ca

Georges Mamelonet, Gaspé, Liberal
418-528-5818, Fax: 418-646-8169, gmamelonet-gasp@assnat.qc.ca

Nicolas Marceau, Rousseau, 2008-09-11, Parti Quebecois
418-644-1417, Fax: 418-646-7804, nmarceau-rous@assnat.qc.ca

Yvon Marcoux, Vaudreuil, Liberal
418-646-7623, Fax: 418-528-5668, ymarcoux-vaud@assnat.qc.ca

Pauline Marois, Charlevoix, Parti Quebecois
418-643-2743, Fax: 418-643-2957, pauline.marois@assnat.qc.ca

Pierre Marsan, Robert-Baldwin, Liberal
418-646-5554, Fax: 418-643-9127, pmarsan-roba@assnat.qc.ca

Michel Matte, Portneuf, 2008-09-10, Liberal
418-644-1473, Fax: 418-268-4348, mmatte@assnat.qc.ca

Scott McKay, L'Assomption, 2008-09-11, Parti Quebecois
418-528-5974, Fax: 418-528-0439, smckay-asso@assnat.qc.ca

L'hon. Nicole Ménard, Laporte, 2008-09-11, Liberal
418-528-8063, Fax: 418-528-8066, ministre@tourisme.gouv.qc.ca

L'hon. Pierre Moreau, Châteauguay, 2008-09-11, Liberal
418-646-5950, Fax: 418-528-0981, ministre.saic@mce.gouv.qc.ca

Norbert Morin, Montmagny-L'Islet, 2008-09-11, Liberal
418-644-0513, Fax: 418-644-8589, nmorin-mois@assnat.qc.ca

L'hon. Nathalie Normandeau, Bonaventure, Liberal
418-643-7295, Fax: 418-643-4318, ministre@mrnf.gouv.qc.ca

Martine Ouellet, Vachon, Parti Quebecois
418-644-0751, Fax: 418-646-7810, martineouellet@assnat.qc.ca

Guy Ouellette, Chomedey, 2008-09-11, Liberal
418-644-4050, Fax: 418-646-7385, gouellette-chom@assnat.qc.ca

François Ouimet, Marquette, Liberal
418-643-2810, Fax: 418-643-3688, fouimet-marq@assnat.qc.ca

Sylvain Pagé, Labelle, Parti Quebecois
418-528-1349, Fax: 418-528-7185, spage@assnat.qc.ca

L'hon. Alain Paquet, Laval-des-Rapides, Liberal
418-643-5270, Fax: 418-646-7147, ministre.delegue@finances.gouv.qc.ca

Pierre Paradis, Brome-Missisquoi, Liberal
418-644-0551, Fax: 418-646-6684, pparadis-brmi@assnat.qc.ca

Émilien Pelletier, Saint-Hyacinthe, 2008-09-11, Parti Quebecois
418-644-5283, Fax: 418-646-7815, epelletier-sahy@assnat.qc.ca

Irvin Pelletier, Rimouski, 2008-09-11, Parti Quebecois
418-644-1386, Fax: 418-644-7851, ipelletier-rimo@assnat.qc.ca

Marc Picard, Chutes-de-la-Chaudière, Independent
418-528-1694, Fax: 418-528-6935, mpicard-cdlc@assnat.qc.ca

Michel Pigeon, Charlesbourg, 2008-09-11, Liberal
418-644-9506, Fax: 418-643-9127,
mpigeon-chlb@assnat.qc.ca
Claude Pinard, Saint-Maurice, 2008-09-10, Parti Quebecois
418-528-1277, Fax: 418-528-0427,
cpinard-sama@assnat.qc.ca
Carole Poirier, Hochelaga-Maisonneuve, Parti Quebecois
418-644-1629, Fax: 418-646-7810, cpoirier@assnat.qc.ca
Daniel Ratthé, Blainville, 2008-09-11, Parti Quebecois
418-644-1444, Fax: 418-646-7804, dratthe-blai@assnat.qc.ca
François Rebello, La Prairie, 2008-09-11, Parti Quebecois
418-644-1489, Fax: 418-644-2062,
frebello-lapr@assnat.qc.ca
Pierre Reid, Orford, Liberal
418-644-3944, Fax: 418-646-0516, preid-orfo@assnat.qc.ca
Lorraine Richard, Duplessis, Parti Quebecois
418-643-2446, Fax: 418-644-3219,
lorrainerichard-dupl@assnat.qc.ca
Monique Richard, Margeurite-D'Youville, 2008-09-10, Parti Quebecois
418-644-0655, Fax: 418-644-3712,
mrichard-mayo@assnat.qc.ca
Gilles Robert, Prévost, 2008-09-10, Parti Quebecois
418-644-1504, Fax: 418-646-7804,
grobert-prev@assnat.qc.ca
Filomena Rotiroti, Jeanne-Mance-Viger, 2008-09-11, Liberal
418-646-5743, Fax: 418-644-5990, frotiroti-jmv@assnat.qc.ca
Sylvie Roy, Lotbinière, Action Democratique du Qc
418-644-1467, Fax: 418-528-9479, sylvieroy@assnat.qc.ca
André Simard, Kamouraska-Témiscouata, Parti Quebecois
418-643-6295, Fax: 418-646-7810,
andre.simard-kate@assnat.qc.ca
L'hon. Serge Simard, Dubuc, Liberal
418-643-7295, Fax: 418-528-0178,
ministredelegue@mrnf.gouv.qc.ca
Sylvain Simard, Richelieu, Parti Quebecois
418-644-1587, Fax: 418-644-1085,
ssimard-ricl@assnat.qc.ca
Gerry Sklavounos, Laurier-Dorion, 2008-09-11, Liberal
418-644-5987, Fax: 418-644-5977,
gsklavounos-lado@assnat.qc.ca
Danielle St-Amand, Trois-Rivières, 2008-09-11, Liberal
418-528-0413, Fax: 418-646-8169,
dstamand-trri@assnat.qc.ca
Bertrand St-Arnaud, Chambly, 2008-09-11, Parti Quebecois
418-646-7508, Fax: 418-643-0616,
bstarnaud-chmb@assnat.qc.ca
L'hon. Christine St-Pierre, Acadie, 2008-09-11, Liberal
418-380-2310, Fax: 418-380-2311,
ministre@mcccf.gouv.qc.ca
L'hon. Lise Thériault, Anjou, Liberal
418-643-5297, Fax: 418-644-0003,
ministre@travail.gouv.qc.ca
Tony Tomassi, LaFontaine, Independent
418-528-7413, Fax: 418-528-7415,
ttomassi-lafo@assnat.qc.ca
Mathieu Traversy, Terrebonne, 2008-09-11, Parti Quebecois
418-644-1616, Fax: 418-644-5976,
mtraversy-terr@assnat.qc.ca
Guillaume Tremblay, Masson, 2008-09-11, Parti Quebecois
418-643-5771, Fax: 418-528-2960,
gtremblay-mass@assnat.qc.ca
Denis Trottier, Roberval, Parti Quebecois
418-644-0707, Fax: 418-646-7801,
dtrottier-robe@assnat.qc.ca
Dave Turcotte, Saint-Jean, 2008-09-11, Parti Quebecois
418-644-1463, Fax: 418-646-7798,
dave.turcotte-saje@assnat.qc.ca
Stéphanie Vallée, Gatineau, 2008-09-11, Liberal
418-644-5980, Fax: 418-528-5668, svallee-gati@assnat.qc.ca
Yvon Vallières, Richmond, Liberal
418-644-0675, Fax: 418-643-1734,
yvallieres-ricm@assnat.qc.ca
L'hon. Dominique Vien, Bellechasse, 2008-09-10, Liberal
418-266-7181, Fax: 418-266-7199,
ministre.deleguee@msss.gouv.qc.ca
André Villeneuve, Berthier, 2008-09-10, Parti Quebecois
418-644-1399, Fax: 418-646-7801,
avilleneuve-berh@assnat.qc.ca
L'hon. Kathleen Weil, Notre-Dame-de-Grâce, Liberal
418-644-2128, Fax: 418-528-0829, cabinet@micc.gouv.qc.ca
David Whissell, Argenteuil, Liberal
418-528-6379, Fax: 418-643-5462,
dwhissell-arge@assnat.qc.ca
Directeur, Direction des communications, Jean Dumas
418-643-1992, communications@assnat.qc.ca

Ministères et organismes du gouvernement du Québec / Québec Government Departments & Agencies

Agences, Conseils et Commissions Associés/ Associated Agencies, Boards & Commission:

• Commission municipale du Québec / Québec Municipal Commission
Mezzanine, aile Chauveau
10, rue Pierre-Olivier-Chauveau
Québec, QC G1R 4J3
418-691-2014 Fax: 418-644-4676 866-353-6767
cmq@mamr.gouv.qc.ca
www.cmq.gouv.qc.ca
CMQ est un tribunal et un organisme administratif, d'enquête et de conseil, spécialisé en matière municipale.
• Régie du logement du Québec / Québec Rental Board
Pyramide Ouest
#2095, 5199, rue Sherbrooke est
Montréal, QC H1T 3X1
514-873-2245 Fax: 514-864-8077 800-683-2245
www.rdl.gouv.qc.ca
Other Communication: Montréal, Laval & Longueuil: 514-873-2245
• Société d'habitation du Québec / Housing Québec
Aile St-Amable
1054, rue Louis-Alexandre-Taschereau, 3e étage
Québec, QC G1R 5E7
418-643-4035 Fax: 418-643-2533 800-463-4315
www.habitation.gouv.qc.ca

Secrétariat aux affaires autochtones / Aboriginal Affairs

905, av Honoré-Mercier, 1er étage, Québec, QC G1R 5M6
418-643-3166 Fax: 418-646-4918
www.autochtones.gouv.qc.ca

Ministre responsable, L'hon. Geoffrey Kelley
418-646-9131, Fax: 418-646-9487,
ministre.autochtones@mce.gouv.qc.ca
Note: Ministre responsable des Affaires autochtones; Comité ministériel du développement social, éducatif etculturel

Secrétariat aux affaires intergouvernementales canadiennes / Canadian Intergovernmental Affairs Secretariat

875, Grande Allée est, 3e étage, Québec, QC G1R 4Y8
418-643-4011 Fax: 418-528-0052
www.saic.gouv.qc.ca

Ministre responsable, Pierre Moreau
418-646-5950, Fax: 418-528-0981,
ministre.saic@mce.gouv.qc.ca
Note: Ministre responsable des Affaires intergouvernementales canadiennes et de la Francophonie canadienne; et Ministreresponsable de la Réforme des institutions démocratiques et de l'Accès à l'information
Secrétaire général associé, aux Affaires intergouvernementales canadiennes, Yves Castonguay
418-646-9562
Secrétaire adjointe, Suzanne Lévesque
Secrétaire adjointe, à la Francophonie canadienne, Sylvie Lachance
418-643-4060
Directeur, des Affaires économiques, culturelles et sociales, Artur J. Pires
418-646-5914
Directeur, des Politiques institutionnelles et constitutionnelles, Michel Frédérick, 2008-09-12
418-528-0919
Directeur, de la Francophonie et des Bureaux du Québec au Canada, Yves Robertson
418-643-1645
Directeur, de la Réflexion stratégique, Simon Carmichael
418-646-2483
Responsable, Bureau du Secrétaire général associé/Responsable de l'accès à l'information, Mario Plamondon, 2008-09-12
418-646-5948

Bureaux du Quebec au Canada/Regional Offices:

Moncton
Bureau du Québec dans les Provinces atlantiques, #510, 777, rue Main, 5e étage, Moncton, NB E1C 1E9
506-857-9851 Fax: 506-857-9883
bqmoncton@mce.gouv.qc.ca
Chef de poste, Richard Barrette

Ottawa
Bureau du Québec à Ottawa, #300, 81 rue Metcalfe, 3e étage, Ottawa, ON K1P 6K7
613-238-5322 Fax: 613-563-9137
bqottawa@mce.gouv.qc.ca

Toronto
Bureau du Québec à Toronto, #1504, 20 rue Queen ouest, CP 13, Toronto, ON M5H 3S3
416-977-6060 Fax: 416-596-1407
bqtoronto@mce.gouv.qc.ca
Chef de poste, Paul-Arthur Huot

Vancouver
Antenne de Vancouver, #780, 789 rue Pender ouest, Vancouver, BC V6C 1H2
604-682-3500 Fax: 604-682-6670
vancouver@mce.gouv.qc.ca
Sous la responsabilité du Bureau du Québec à Toronto
Responsable, Paul-Arthur Huot

Ministère des Affaires municipales et Occupation du territoire / Municipal Affairs

Aile Chaveau, 10, rue Pierre-Olivier-Chauveau, 3e étage, Québec, QC G1R 4J3
418-691-2019 Fax: 418-643-7385
communications@mamrot.gouv.qc.ca
www.mamrot.gouv.qc.ca

A la charge de conseiller le gouvernement & d'assurer la coordination interministérielle dans ces domaines; a pour mission de favoriser la mise en place & le maintien d'un cadre de vie & de services municipaux de qualité pour des citoyens/citoyennes; le développement des régions & des milieux ruraux; & le progrès & le rayonnement de la métropole; intervient auprès des municipalités locales, régionales de comté, des communautés métropolitaines de Montréal & de Québec, & de l'administration régionale Kativik

Acts Administered:
Code municipal du Québec
Loi concernant la consultation des citoyens sur la réorganisation territoriale
Loi concernant la négociation d'ententes relatives à la réduction des coûts de main-d'oeuvre dans le secteur municipal
Loi concernant la réglementation municipale des édifices publics
Loi concernant la Ville de Schefferville
Loi concernant les droits sur les mutations immobilières
Loi instituant le fonds spécial de financement des activités locales
Loi modifiant de nouveau diverses dispositions législatives concernant le domaine municipal
Loi portant réforme de l'organisation territoriale municipale des régions métropolitaines de Montréal, de Québec et de l'Outaouais
Loi sur Immobilière SHQ
Loi sur l'aide municipale à la protection du public aux traverses de chemin de fer
Loi sur l'aménagement et l'urbanisme
Loi sur l'exercice de certaines compétences municipales dan certaines agglomérations
Loi sur l'expropriation
Loi sur l'instruction publique
Loi sur l'instruction publique pour les autochtones cris, inuits et naskapis
Loi sur l'interdiction de subventions municipales
Loi sur l'organisation territoriale municipale
Loi sur la Commission municipale
Loi sur la Communauté métropolitaine de Montréal
Loi sur la Communauté métropolitaine de Québec
Loi sur la conservation du patrimoine naturel
Loi sur la conservation et la mise en valeur de la faune
Loi sur la fiscalité municipale
Loi sur la police
Loi sur la qualité de l'environnement
Loi sur la Régie du logement
Loi sur la Société d'habitation du Québec
Loi sur la Société du Parc industriel et portuaire de Bécancour
Loi sur la Société Innovatech du grand Montréal
Loi sur la Société québécoise d'assainissement des eaux
Loi sur le développement de la région de la Baie-James
Loi sur le Ministère de l'Agriculture, des Pêcheries et de l'Alimentation
Loi sur le Ministère du Développement durable, de l'Environnement et des Parcs
Loi sur le régime de retraite des élus municipaux
Loi sur les abus préjudiciables à l'agriculture
Loi sur les compétences municipales
Loi sur les cités et villes
Loi sur les conseils intermunicipaux de transport dans la région de Montréal
Loi sur les cours municipales
Loi sur les dettes et les emprunts municipaux
Loi sur les élections et les référendums dans les municipalités
Loi sur les espèces menacées ou vulnérables
Loi sur les immeubles industriels municipaux
Loi sur les impôts
Loi sur les régimes de retraite des maires et des conseillers des municipalités
Loi sur les sociétés de transport en commun
Loi sur les sociétés d'économie mixte dans le secteur municipal
Loi sur le traitement des élus municipaux
Loi sur les travaux municipaux
Loi sur les villages cris et le village Naskapi
Loi sur les villages Nordiques et l'Administration régionale Kativik

Ministre, L'hon. Laurent Lessard
418-691-2050, Fax: 418-643-1795,
ministre@mamrot.gouv.qc.ca
Sous-ministre, Marc Lacroix
418-691-2040, Fax: 418-643-7708
Sous-ministre adjoint, (Politiques), Sylvain Boucher
418-691-2040
Sous-ministre adjoint, (Infrastructures & finances municipales), Jean Monfet
418-691-2007
Sous-ministre adjoint, (Métropole), Jerome Unterberg
514-873-8395

Territoires / Regions
Sous-ministre adjointe, Linda Morin
418-691-2040
Directeur général, Opération régionales & municipales de la géomatique & de la statistique, Dominique Jodoin
418-691-2088
Directrice (par intérim), Développement rural, Danielle Leduc
418-691-2078
Directrice (par intérim), Développement régional & Économie sociale, Mélissa Auclair
418-691-2016
Directeur du projet, Occupation des territoires, Yannick Routhier
418-691-2038

Directions régionales/Regional Offices:

Abitibi-Témiscamingue
#105, 170, av Principale, 1er étage, Rouyn-Noranda, QC J9X 4P7
819-763-3582 Fax: 819-763-3803
dr.abitibi-temis@mamrot.gouv.qc.ca
Directeur, Denis Moffet

Bas-Saint-Laurent
337, rue Moreault, 2e étage, Rimouski, QC G5L 1P4
418-727-3629 Fax: 418-727-3537
dr.bas-st-laur@mamrot.gouv.qc.ca
Directeur, Gilles Julien

Capitale-Nationale
Aile Chauveau, 10, rue Pierre-Olivier-Chauveau, 3e étage, Québec, QC G1R 4J3
418-691-2016 Fax: 418-643-2206
dr.capnat@mamrot.gouv.qc.a
Directeur, Stéphane Bouchard

Centre-du-Québec
#S-05, 62, rue Saint-Jean-Baptiste, Victoriaville, QC G6P 4E3
819-752-2453 Fax: 819-795-3673
Dr.Centre-Quebec@mamrot.gouv.qc.ca
Directeur, Gaétan Désilets

Centre-du-Québec
le Chauveau, 62, rue Saint-Jean-Baptiste, #S-05, Québec, QC G6P 4E3
819-752-2453 Fax: 819-795-3673
dr.centre-quebec@mamrot.gouv.qc.a
Directeur, Gaétan Désilets, 20110729

Chaudière-Appalaches
#102, 1100, boul Frontenac est, Thetford Mines, QC G6G 6H1
418-338-4624 Fax: 418-338-1908
dr.chaud-app@mamrot.gouv.qc.ca
Directrice, Danie Croteau

Côte-Nord
625, boul Laflèche, #RC-708, Baie-Comeau, QC G5C 1C5
418-295-4241 Fax: 418-295-4955
dr.cotenord@mamrot.gouv.qc.ca
Directeur, Jacques Tremblay

Estrie
#4.04, 200, rue Belvédère nord, Sherbrooke, QC J1H 4A9
819-820-3244 Fax: 819-820-3979
dr.estrie@mamrot.gouv.qc.ca
Directeur, Pierre Poulin

Gaspésie-Iles-de-la-Madeleine
#10B, 500, av Daigneault, Chandler, QC G0C 1K0
418-689-5024 Fax: 418-689-4823
dr.gaspe-ilesmad@mamrot.gouv.qc.ca
Directeur, Michel Gionest

Lanaudière
#3200, 40, rue Gauthier sud, Joliette, QC J6E 4J4
450-752-8080 Fax: 450-752-8087
dr.lanaudiere@mamrot.gouv.qc.ca
Directeur, Jean Ouellet

Laurentides
#210, 161, rue de la Gare, Saint-Jérôme, QC J7Z 2B9
450-569-7646 Fax: 450-569-3131
dr.laurentides@mamrot.gouv.qc.ca
Directeur, Jean Ouellet

Mauricie
#321, 100, rue Laviolette, 3e étage, Trois-Rivières, QC G9A 5S9
819-371-6653 Fax: 819-371-6953
dr.mauricie@mamrot.gouv.qc.ca
Directeur, Pierre Robert

Métropole
Tour-de-la-Bourse, #2.00, 800, rue du Square-Victoria, Montréal, QC H4Z 1B7
514-873-8246 Fax: 514-864-5912
courrier.dmaam@mamrot.gouv.qc.ca
Directrice, Lucie Tremblay, 20110729

Montérégie
#403, 201, place Charles-Le Moyne, Longueuil, QC J4K 2T5
450-928-5670 Fax: 450-928-5673
dr.monteregie@mamrot.gouv.qc.ca
Directeur, Robert Sabourin

Nord-du-Québec
#1, 215, 3e Rue, Chibougamau, QC G8P 1N3
418-748-7737 Fax: 418-748-7841
nord-du-quebec@mamrot.gouv.qc.ca
Directeur, Richard Leclerc

Outaouais
#9.300, 170, rue de l'Hôtel-de-Ville, Gatineau, QC J8X 4C2
819-772-3006 Fax: 819-772-3989
dr.outaouais@mamrot.gouv.qc.ca
Directeur (par intérim), Yannick Gignac

Saguenay-Lac-Saint-Jean
227, rue Racine est, #RC.03, Chicoutimi, QC G7H 7B4
418-698-3523 Fax: 418-698-3526
dr.sag-lac@mamrot.gouv.qc.ca
Directeur (par intérim), Gilles Gauthier

Infrastructures et finances municipales / Infrastructures & Municipal Financing
Sous-ministre adjoint (par intérim), Jean Monfet
418-691-2040
Directeur général, Finances municipales, Jean Monfet
418-691-2007
Directeur général, Infrastructures, Pierre Aubé
418-691-2005

Métropole / Metropolitan Regions
Sous-ministre adjoint, Jérôme Unterberg
514-873-8395
Directeur, Développement régional & métropolitain, VACANT
514-873-6992
Directrice métropolitaine, Aménagement et des affaires municipales, Lucie Tremblay
514-873-8246

Politiques / Policy
Sous-ministre adjoint (par intérim), Jérôme Unterberg
418-691-2040
Directrice générale, Urbanisme/Aménagement du territoire, Marie-Lise Côté
418-691-2015
Directeur, Évaluation foncière, Luc Sauvageau
418-691-2044
Directeur général, Fiscalité, Bernard Guay
418-691-2035
Directrice générale, Politiques, Jocelyn Savoie
418-691-2015

Services à la gestion / Administrative Services

Ministère de la Culture, des Communications & de la Condition féminine / Culture, Communications & the Status of Women

225, Grande Allée est, Québec, QC G1R 5G5
888-380-8882
www.mcccf.gouv.qc.ca

Acts Administered:
Charte de la langue française
Loi sur Bibliothèque et archives nationales du Québec
Loi sur la programmation éducative
Loi sur la Société de développement des entreprises culturelles
Loi sur la Société de la Place des Arts de Montréal
Loi sur la Société de télédiffusion du Québec
Loi sur la Société du Grand Théâtre de Québec
Loi sur le cinéma
Loi sur le Conseil des arts et des lettres du Québec
Loi sur le Conservatoire de musique et d'art dramatique du Québec
Loi sur le développement des entreprises québécoises dans le domaine du livre
Loi sur le ministère de la Culture et des Communications
Loi sur le Musée des beaux-arts de Montréal
Loi sur le statut professionnel des artistes des arts visuels, des métiers d'art et de la littérature et sur leurs contrats avec les diffuseurs
Loi sur le statut professionnel et les conditions d'engagement des artistes de la scène, du disque et du cinéma
Loi sur les archives
Loi sur les biens culturels
Loi sur les concours artistiques, littéraires et scientifiques
Loi sur les musées nationaux

Ministre, L'hon. Christine St-Pierre
418-380-2310, Fax: 418-380-2311,
ministre@mcccf.gouv.qc.ca
Sous-ministre, Sylvie Barcelo
418-380-2330, Fax: 418-380-2391,
sylvie.barcelo@mcccf.gouv.qc.ca
Sous-ministre adjoint, Action territoriale, Louis Vallée
418-380-2330, Fax: 418-380-2392,
louis.vallee@mcccf.gouv.qc.ca
Sous-ministre adjointe, Secrétariat à la condition féminine, Thérèse Mailloux
418-646-8395, Fax: 418-643-4991,
therese.mailloux@mcccf.gouv.qc.ca
Responsable, Planification stratégique, Jacques Laflamme
418-380-2362, Fax: 418-380-2345,
jacques.laflamme@mcccf.gouv.qc.ca
Responsable, Secrétariat à la diversité culturelle, Dave Atkinson
418-380-2372, Fax: 418-380-2340,
dave.atkinson@mcccf.gouv.qc.ca
Directrice, Communications & affaires publiques, Colette Duval
418-380-2363, Fax: 418-380-2364,
colette.duval@mcccf.gouv.qc.ca
Directeur, Affaires juridiques, Yves D. Dussault
418-643-3747, Fax: 418-646-6849,
yvesd.dussault@mels.gouv.qc.ca
Directeur général, Administration, VACANT
418-380-2355, Fax: 418-380-2394
Directeur, Ressources financières et matérielles, Geneviève Vézina
418-380-2301, Fax: 418-380-2302,
genevieve.vezina@mcccf.gouv.qc.ca
Directeur, Ressources humaines/Gestion immobilière, Marc Tremblay
418-380-2329, Fax: 418-380-2332,
marc.tremblay@mcccf.gouv.qc.ca
Directeur, Technologies de l'information, Louis Guilbault
418-380-2312, Fax: 418-380-2314,
louis.guilbault@mcccf.gouv.qc.ca
Directrice, Documentation/Communication interne, Monique Lachance
418-380-2358, Fax: 418-380-2364,
monique.lachance@mcccf.gouv.qc.ca

Directions régionales/Regional Offices:

Abitibi-Témiscamingue et Nord-du-Québec
#450, 19, rue Perreault ouest, Rouyn-Noranda, QC J9X 6N5
819-763-3517 Fax: 819-763-3382
dratnq@mcccf.gouv.qc.ca
Directrice, Monik Duhaime
monik.duhaime@mcccf.gouv.qc.ca

Bas-St-Laurent
337, rue Moreault, # RC-12, Rimouski, QC G5L 1P4
418-727-3650 Fax: 418-727-3824
drbsl@mcccf.gouv.qc.ca
Directeur (par intérim), Louis Landry

Capitale-Nationale
Bloc C, RC, 225, Grande-Allée est, Québec, QC G1R 5G5
418-380-2346 Fax: 418-380-2347
dcn@mcccf.gouv.qc.ca
Directeur, Martin Pineault
418-380-2346, martin.pineault@mcccf.gouv.qc.ca

Chaudière-Appalaches
51, rue du Mont-Marie, Lévis, QC G6V 0C3
418-838-9886 Fax: 418-838-1485
drca@mcccf.gouv.qc.ca
Directrice, Nicole Champagne
418-838-9886, nicole.champagne@mcccf.gouv.qc.ca

Côte-Nord
#1.806, 625, boul Laflèche, Baie-Comeau, QC G5C 1C5
418-295-4979 Fax: 418-295-4070
drcn@mcccf.gouv.qc.ca
Directrice, Françoise Aubry
francoise.aubry@mcccf.gouv.qc.ca

Estrie
#410, 225, rue Frontenac, Sherbrooke, QC J1H 1K1
819-820-3007 Fax: 819-820-3930
dre@mcccf.gouv.qc.ca
Directrice, Jocelyne Jacques
819-820-3012, jocelyne.jacques@mcccf.gouv.qc.ca

Gaspésie-Iles-de-la-Madeleine
146, av de Grand-Pré, Bonaventure, QC G0C 1E0
418-534-4431 Fax: 418-534-4564
drgim@mcccf.gouv.qc.ca

Directrice, Hélène Latérière
helene.lateriere@mcccf.gouv.qc.ca

Laval, Lanaudière et les Laurentides
#200, 300, rue Sicard, Sainte-Thérèse, QC J7E 3X5
450-430-3737 Fax: 450-430-2475
drlll@mcccf.gouv.qc.ca

Directeur, Gilbert Lepage
450-430-2271

Mauricie et Centre-du-Québec
#315, 100, rue Laviolette, Trois-Rivières, QC G9A 5S9
819-387-6001 Fax: 819-371-6984
drmcq@mcccf.gouv.qc.ca

Directrice, Hélène McGee
helene.mcgee@mcccf.gouv.qc.ca

Montérégie
#500, 2, boul Desaulniers, Saint-Lambert, QC J4P 1L2
450-671-1231 Fax: 450-671-3884
drmonter@mcccf.gouv.qc.ca

Directrice, Annie Goudreault
annie.goudreault@mcccf.gouv.qc.ca

Montréal
#600, 480, boul St-Laurent, Montréal, QC H2Y 3Y7
514-873-2255 Fax: 514-864-2448
dm@mcccf.gouv.qc.ca

Directrice, Brigitte Jacques
brigitte.jacques@mcccf.gouv.qc.ca

Outaouais
#4.140, 170, rue de l'Hôtel-de-Ville, 4e étage, Gatineau, QC J8X 4C2
819-772-3002 Fax: 819-772-3950
dro@mcccf.gouv.qc.ca

Directrice, Anne-Marie Gendron
819-772-3282, anne-marie.gendron@mcccf.gouv.qc.ca

Saguenay-Lac-Saint-Jean
202, rue Jacques-Cartier est, Chicoutimi, QC G7H 6R8
418-698-3500 Fax: 418-698-3522
drslstj@mcccf.gouv.qc.ca

Directeur, Réjean Goudreault
rejean.goudreault@mcccf.gouv.qc.ca

Action territoriale
Sous-ministre adjointe, Louis Vallée
418-380-2330, Fax: 418-380-2392,
louis.vallee@mcccf.gouv.qc.ca
Directeur, Affaires internationales & Relations intergouvernementales, Michel Lafleur
418-380-2335, Fax: 418-380-2340,
michel.lafleur@mcccf.gouv.qc.ca
Directeur générale, Interventions régionales, Jean Bissonnette
418-380-2348, Fax: 418-380-2349,
jean.bissonnette@mcccf.gouv.qc.ca

Bibliothèque et Archives nationales du Québec (BAnQ) / National Library & Archives of Québec
475, boul De Maisonneuve est, Montréal, QC H2L 5C4
514-873-1100 Fax: 514-873-9312
800-363-9028
www.banq.qc.ca

Président-directeur générale, Guy Berthiaume

Commission des biens culturels du Québec / Québec Cultural Property Commission
Bloc A-RC, 225, Grande Allée est, Québec, QC G1R 5G5
418-643-8378 Fax: 418-643-8591
info@cbcq.gouv.qc.ca
www.cbcq.gouv.qc.ca

Président, Yves Lefebvre
Vice-présidente, Ann Mundy

Conseil des arts et des lettres du Québec
79, boul René-Lévesque est, 3e étage, Québec, QC G1R 5N5
418-643-1707 Fax: 418-643-4558
800-897-1707
info@calq.gouv.qc.ca
www.calq.gouv.qc.ca

Président et Directeur général, Yvan Gauthier

Musée d'art contemporain de Montréal (MACM) / Montréal Museum of Contemporary Art
185, rue Ste-Catherine ouest, Montréal, QC H2X 3X5
514-847-6226 Fax: 514-847-6290
info@macm.org
www.macm.org

Directrice Générale, Paulette Gagnon

Musée de la civilisation / Museum of Civilisation
85, rue Dalhousie, CP 155 B, Québec, QC G1K 7A6
418-643-2158 Fax: 418-646-9705
866-710-8031
mcqweb@mcq.org
www.mcq.org

Présidente, Margaret Delisle
Directrice générale, Danielle Poiré

Musée national des beaux-arts du Québec
Parc des Champs-de-Bataille, 1, av Wolfe-Montcalm, Québec, QC G1R 5H3
418-643-2150 Fax: 418-646-3330
866-220-2150
webmestre@mnba.qc.ca
www.mnba.qc.ca

Directrice générale, Sylvie Desjardins
418-644-6460, sylvie.desjardins@mnba.qc.ca
Conseillère juridique, Louise Pradet-Jobin
418-644-6460, Fax: 418-644-1067, louise.jobin@mnba.qc.ca

Politiques, patrimoine, muséologie & communications / Policy, Heritage, Museology & Communication
Sous-ministre adjoint, France Dionne
418-380-2330, Fax: 418-380-2331,
france.dionne@mcccf.gouv.qc.ca
Directeur, Patrimoine, muséologie & immobilisations, René Bouchard
418-380-2352, Fax: 418-380-2336,
rene.bouchard@mcccf.gouv.qc.ca
Directeur général, Centre de conservation du Québec, Daniel Bastille, 20110802
418-643-7001, Fax: 418-646-5419,
daniel.bastille@mcccf.gouv.qc.ca
Directrice, Développement des services, Francine Lalonde, 20110802
418-380-2333, Fax: 418-380-2324,
francine.lalonde@mcccf.gouv.qc.ca
Directrice, Développement des services, Francine Lalonde, 20110802
418-380-2333, Fax: 418-380-2324,
francine.lalonde@mcccf.gouv.qc.ca
Directeur général, Politiques de culture & de communications, Daniel Cloutier
418-380-2365, Fax: 418-380-2340,
daniel.cloutier@mcccf.gouv.qc.ca
Directrice, Médias & télécommunications, Louise Gingras, 20110802
418-380-2307, Fax: 418-380-2316,
louise.gingras@mcccf.gouv.qc.ca
Directrice, Lectorat & politiques, Josée Blackburn, 20110802
418-380-2322, Fax: 418-380-2345,
josee.blackburn@mcccf.gouv.qc
Responsable, Secrétariat à la condition socioéconomique des artistes, Gaétan Patenaude, 20110802
418-380-2322, Fax: 418-380-2345,
gaetan.pateneaude@mcccf.gouv.qc.ca

Régie du cinéma / Film Board
#100, 390, rue Notre-Dame ouest, Montréal, QC H2Y 1T9
514-873-2371 Fax: 514-873-8874
800-463-2463
regieducinema@rcq.gouv.qc.ca
www.rcq.gouv.qc.ca

Présidente, France Boucher
Directeur, Planification & communications, Robert Arthur

Secrétariat à la Condition féminine / Status of Women Secretariat
#905, av Honoré-Mercier, 3e étage, Québec, QC G1R 5M6
418-643-9052 Fax: 418-643-4991
www.scf.gouv.qc.ca

Sous-ministre adjointe, Thérèse Mailloux
418-646-8395, Fax: 418-643-4991
Directrice, Coordination & administration, Gina Morency
418-644-4417, Fax: 418-643-4991

Secrétariat à la politique linguistique / French Language Board
225 Grande-Allée est, 4e étage, Québec, QC G1R 5G5
418-643-4248 Fax: 418-646-7832
info@spl.gouv.qc.ca
www.spl.gouv.qc.ca

Sous-ministre associé responsable de l'application de la politique linguistique, Jacques Gosselin

Société de développement des entreprises culturelles (SODEC) / Arts & Cultural Enterprise Development Commission
#800, 215, rue Saint-Jacques, Montréal, QC H2Y 1M6
514-841-2200 Fax: 514-841-8606
800-363-0401
info@sodec.gouv.qc.ca
www.sodec.gouv.qc.ca

Président, François Macerola
Directeur des affaires juridiques & Secrétaire, Jean Valois
Directrice générale, Contrôle & gestion financière, Carole Hamelin

Société de la Place des Arts de Montréal / Montréal Place des Arts Corporation
260, boul de Maisonneuve ouest, Montréal, QC H2X 1Y9
514-285-4200 Fax: 514-285-1968
info@pda.qc.ca
www.pda.qc.ca

Présidente-Directrice générale, Marie Lavigne

Société de télédiffusion du Québec (Télé-Québec) / Radio-Québec
1000, rue Fullum, Montréal, QC H2K 3L7
514-521-2424 Fax: 514-873-2601
800-361-4362
info@telequebec.tv
www.telequebec.tv

Présidente-directrice générale, Michèle Fortin

Société du Grand Théâtre de Québec / Grand Theatre of Québec
269, boul René-Lévesque est, Québec, QC G1R 2B3
418-643-8111
gtq@grandtheatre.qc.ca
www.grandtheatre.qc.ca

Président-directeur général, Marcel Dallaire

Ministère de l'Agriculture, des Pêcheries et de l'Alimentation (MAPAQ) / Agriculture, Fisheries & Food

200, ch Sainte-Foy, Québec, QC G1R 4X6
418-380-2110
888-222-6272
www.mapaq.gouv.qc.ca

Le Ministère influence et appuie l'essor de l'industrie bioalimentaire québécoise dans une perspective de développement durable; réalise des interventions en production, transformation, commercialisation & consommation des produits agricoles, marins & alimentaires; & joue un rôle important en matière de recherche & de développement, d'enseignement & de formation

Acts Administered:
Code municipal du Québec/Municipal Code of Québec (certain sections)
Loi sur l'acquisition de terres agricoles par des non-résidants/An Act governing the acquisition of farm land by non-residents
Loi sur les appellations réservées et les termes valorisants
Loi sur l'aquaculture commerciale/ An Act respecting commercial aquaculture
Loi sur l'assurance-prêts agricoles et forestiers/An Act respecting farm-loan insurance & forestry-loan insurance
Loi sur l'assurance-récolte/Crop Insurance Act
Loi sur l'assurance-stabilisation des revenus agricoles/An Act respecting farm income stabilization insurance
Loi sur l'école de laiterie et les écoles moyennes d'agriculture/An Act respecting the École de laiterie & intermediate agricultural schools
Loi sur la commercialisation des produits marins/An Act respecting the marketing of marine products
Loi sur la conservation et la mise en valeur de la faune/An Act respecting the conservation & development of wildlife
Loi sur la protection des animaux pur sang/Thoroughbred Cattle Act
Loi sur la protection des plantes/Plant Protection Act
Loi sur la protection sanitaire des animaux/Animal Health Protection Act
Loi sur la transformation des produits marins/The Marine Products Processing Act
Loi sur le financement de la pêche commerciale/Maritime Fisheries Credit Act
Loi sur le mérite national de la pêche et de l'aquaculture/Fishermen's Merit Act
Loi sur le Mérite national de la restauration et de l'alimentation/Restaurant Merit Act
Loi sur le ministère de l'Agriculture, des Pêcheries et de l'Alimentation/An Act respecting the Ministère de l'Agriculture, des Pêcheries et de l'Alimentation
Loi sur les abus préjudiciables à l'agriculture/Agricultural Abuses Act
Loi sur les cités et villes/Cities & Towns Act (certain sections)
Loi sur les pêcheries commerciales et la récolte commerciale de végétaux aquatiques
Loi sur les produits agricoles, les produits marins et les aliments/Farm, Food & Fishery Products Act
Loi sur les producteurs agricoles/Farm Producers Act
Loi sur les produits alimentaires/Food Products Act
Loi sur les races animales du Patrimoine agricole du Qu ébec
Loi sur les sociétés agricoles et laitières/An Act respecting farmers' & dairymen's associations
Loi sur les sociétés d'horticulture/Horticultural Societies Act
Loi sur les terres agricoles du domaine de l'État/An Act respecting agricultural lands in the domain of the state
Ordre national du mérite agricole/Agricultural Merit Act
La Charte de la ville de Québec/The Charter of the City of Québec (certain sections)
La Charte de la Ville de Sherbrooke/The Charter of the City of Sherbrooke (certain sections)
La Charte de la Ville de Trois-Rivières/The Charter of the City of Trois-Rivières (certain sections)

Ministre, Pierre Corbeil
418-380-2525, Fax: 418-380-2184,
ministre.mapaq@mapaq.gouv.qc.ca

Sous-ministre, Norman Johnston
418-380-2136, Fax: 418-380-2171
Sous-ministre associée, Transformation Alimentaire Québec, Dominique Fortin
418-380-2136, Fax: 418-380-2171
Sous-ministre adjoint & Directeur général, Politiques agroalimentaires, Bernard Verret
418-380-2136, Fax: 418-380-2171
Sous-ministre adjoint & Directeur général, Développement régional & développement durable, Michel Bonneau
418-380-2136, Fax: 418-380-2171
Sous-ministre adjointe & Directrice générale, Santé animale & inspection des aliments, Madeleine Fortin
418-380-2136, Fax: 418-380-2171
Sous-ministre adjoint & Directeur général, Pêches & aquaculture commerciales, Hélène Vincent
418-380-2136, Fax: 418-380-2171

Agences, Conseils et Commissions Associés/ Associated Agencies, Boards & Commission:

• Commission de protection du territoire agricole du Québec / Agricultural Land Preservation Commission
200, ch Ste-Foy, 2e étage
Québec, QC G1R 4X6
418-643-3314 Fax: 418-643-2261 800-667-5294
info@cptaq.gouv.qc.ca
www.cptaq.gouv.qc.ca
• La financière agricole de Québec
1400, boul de la Rive-Sud
Saint-Romuald, QC G6W 8K7
418-838-5602 Fax: 418-833-3871 800-749-3646
financiereagricole@fadq.qc.ca
www.financiereagricole.qc.ca
• Régie des marchés agricoles et alimentaires du Québec / Québec Agriculture & Food Marketing Board
201, boul Crémazie est, 5e étage
Montréal, QC H2M 1L3
514-873-4024 Fax: 514-873-3984
www.rmaaq.gouv.qc.ca

Pêches et aquaculture commerciales / Commercial Fishing & Aquaculture
Sous-ministre adjointe, Hélène Vincent
418-380-2136, Fax: 418-380-2171
Directeur, Analyses et politiques, Abdoul Aziz Niang
418-380-2100, Fax: 418-380-2182

Directions régionales/Regional Offices:

Côte-Nord
466, av Arnaud, Sept-îles, QC G4R 3B1
418-964-8521 Fax: 418-964-8744
drcn@mapag.gouv.qc.ca
Directeur régional, Alain Côté

Estuaire et eaux intérieures
460, boul Louis-Fréchette, RC, Nicolet, QC J3T 1Y2
819-293-5677 Fax: 819-293-8519
dreei@mapaq.gouv.qc.ca
Directeur régional, Denis Lacerte

Gaspésie
#205, 96, montée de Sandy Beach, Gaspé, QC G4X 2V6
418-368-7630 Fax: 418-360-8851
drg@mapaq.gouv.qc.ca
Directeur régional, Marcel Roussy

îles-de-la-Madeleine
Édifice Réjean-Richard, 101-125, ch du Parc, Cap-aux-Meules, QC G4T 1B3
418-986-2098 Fax: 418-986-4421
drim@mapaq.gouv.qc.ca
Directeur régional, Donald Arseneau

Transformation Alimentaire Québec
Sous-ministre associé, Dominique Fortin
418-380-2136, Fax: 418-380-2171
Directeur (par intérim), Amélioration de la compétitivité & analyses stratégiques, Denis Desrosiers, 20110803
Directrice, Développement des marchés intérieurs & affaires ministérielles, France St-Onge, 20110803
514-873-4147
Directeur (par intérim), Développement des marchés extérieurs & entreprises, Bernard Houle, 20110803
514-873-4147, bernard.houle@mapaq.gouv.qc.ca

Développement régional et développement durable / Regional Development/Sustainable Development
Sous-ministre adjoint, Michel Bonneau
Coordinateur, Opérations régionales, Sylvain Tremblay
Directeur, Soutien à l'enregistrement & remboursement des taxes, François Michaud
Directrice, Appui au développement des entreprises et de l'aménagement du territoire, Hélène Doddridge
Directeur, Agroenvironnement et développement durable, Michel Riendeau

Abitibi-Témiscamingue - Nord-du-Québec
#2.01, 180, boul Rideau, Rouyn-Noranda, QC J9X 1N9
819-763-3287 Fax: 819-763-3359
Directrice régionale, Line Charland

Montérégie - Secteur Est
#3300, 1355, rue Johnson ouest, Saint-Hyacinthe, QC J2S 8W7
450-778-6530 Fax: 450-778-6540
Directeur régional, Jean-Pierre Lessard

Capitale Nationale
#RC.22, 1685, boul Wilfrid-Hamel ouest, Québec, QC G1N 3Y7
418-643-0033 Fax: 418-644-8263
Directrice régionale, Suzanne Pilote

Saguenay-Lac-Saint-Jean
801, ch du Pont-Taché nord, Alma, QC G8B 5W2
418-662-6457 Fax: 418-668-8694
866-727-6584
Directeur régional, Sylvie Denis

Santé animale & inspection des aliments / Food
dgsaia@mapaq.gouv.qc.ca
Sous-ministre adjointe, Madeleine Fortin
418-380-2136, Fax: 418-380-2171
Directrice, Coordination administrative et Services à la clientèle, Michèle Lavoie
418-380-2100, Fax: 418-380-2169
Directrice, Laboratoire d'expertises et d'analyses alimentaires, Ginette Levesque
418-266-4440, Fax: 418-266-4438, dleaa@mapaq.gouv.qc.ca
Directeur, Inspection des viandes, Claude Rivard
418-380-2100, Fax: 418-380-2169

Directions régionales/Regional Offices:

Bas-Saint-Laurent - Gaspésie - Iles-de-la-Madeleine - Saguenay - Lac Saint Jean
#2, 1600, rue Bersimis, Chicoutimi, QC G7K 1H9
418-698-3530 Fax: 418-698-3533
Directrice régionale, Johanne Martel

Laurentides - Outaouais - Abitibi-Témiscamingue
Galeries de Buckingham, 999, rue Dollard, Gatineau, QC J8L 3E6
819-986-8985 Fax: 819-986-9793
Directrice régionale, Joanne Twigg

Mauricie - Centre-du-Québec - Estrie
#55, 5195, boul des Forges, Trois-Rivières, QC G8Y 4Z3
819-475-8506 Fax: 819-371-4907
Directeur régional, Guy Caron

Montréal - Laval - Lanaudière
201, boul Crémazie est, 2e étage, Montréal, QC H2M 1L4
514-873-8101 Fax: 514-873-9994
Directeur régional (par intérim), Guy Caron

Québec - Chaudière-Appalaches
#C RC.245, 2700, rue Einstein, Québec, QC G1P 3W8
418-643-6140 Fax: 418-644-6327
Directeur régional, Laurent Bolduc

Ministère du Développement durable, de l'Environnement et des Parcs / Sustainable Development, Environment & Parks

Édifice Marie-Guyart, 675, boul René-Lévesque est, 29e étage, Québec, QC G1R 5V7
418-521-3830 Fax: 418-646-5974
800-561-1616
info@mddep.gouv.qc.ca
www.mddep.gouv.qc.ca

A pour mission d'assurer la protection de l'environnement & des écosystèmes naturels; de promouvoir le développement durable & d'assurer à la population un environnement sain en harmonie avec le développement économique & le progrès social du Québec

Acts Administered:
Loi portant restrictions à l'élevage de porcs/Act to Impose Restrictions on Pig Farming, 2002
Loi portant sur la délimitation de la ligne des hautes eaux du Fleuve Saint-Laurent sur le territoire de la municipalité régionale de comté de la Côte-de-Beaupré/An Act to delimit the high water mark of the St. Lawrence River inthe territory of Municipa
Loi sur la conservation du patrimoine naturel/Natural Heritage Conservation Act
Loi sur la conservation et la mise en valeur de la faune/Act respecting the Conservation & Development of Wildlife (in part)
Loi sur la protection des arbres/Tree Protection Act
Loi sur la provocation artificielle de la pluie/Act respecting the artificial inducement of rain
Loi sur la qualité de l'environnement/Environment Quality Act
Agricultural Operations Regulation, 2002
Groundwater Catchment Regulation, 2002
Land Protection & Rehabilitation Regulation, 2003
Regulation respecting certain bodies for the protection of the environment and social milieu of the territory of James Bay and Northern Québec
Regulation respecting Compensation for Municipal Services Provided to Recover & Reclaim Residual Materials
Regulation respecting Environmental Impact Assessments & review applicable to part of Northeastern Québec
Regulation respecting Halocarbons
Regulation respecting Hazardous Materials
Regulation respecting Hot Mix Asphalt Plants
Regulation respecting Industrial Depollution Attestations
Regulation respecting Motor Vehicle Traffic in Certain Fragile Environments
Regulation respecting Permits & Certificates for the Sale & Use of Pesticides
Regulation respecting Pits & Quarries
Regulation respecting Prevention of Water Pollution in Livestock Operations
Regulation respecting Public Swimming & Wading Pools
Regulation respecting Pulp & Paper Mills
Regulation respecting Sanitary Conditions in Industrial or other Camps
Regulation respecting Snow Elimination Sites
Regulation respecting Solid Waste
Regulation respecting the Application of the Environment Quality Act
Regulation respecting the Artificial Inducement of Rain
Regulation respecting the Burial of Contaminated Soils
Regulation respecting the environmental and social impact assessment and review procedure applicable to the territory of James Bay and Northern Québec
Regulation respecting the environmental impact assessment and review applicable to a part of the northeastern Québec region
Regulation respecting the Liquid Effluents of Petroleum Refineries
Regulation respecting the Quality of Drinking Water
Regulation respecting the Quality of the Atmosphere
Regulation respecting the Recovery & Reclamation of Discarded Paint Containers & Paints
Regulation respecting the Recovery & Reclamation of Used Oils, Oil or Fluid Containers & Used Filters
Regulation respecting threatened or vulnerable plant species and their habitats
Regulation respecting Used Tire Storage
Regulation Respecting Waste Water Disposal Systems for Isolated Dwellings
Regulation respecting the Water Property in the Domain of the State, 2003
Regulation respecting Waterworks & Sewer Services
Rules of internal management of the James Bay Advisory Committee on the Environment
Rules of internal management of the Kativik Environmental Advisory Committee
Loi sur la sécurité des barrages/Dam Safety Act
Loi sur la Société des établissements de plein air du Québec
Loi sur la Société québécoise de récupération et de recyclage
Loi sur la vente et la distribution de bière et de boissons gazeuses dans des contenants à remplissage unique/Act respecting the Sale & Distribution of Beer & Soft Drinks in Non-returnable Containers
Loi sur le développement durable
Loi sur le ministère du Développement durable, de l'Environnement et des Parcs
Loi sur le parc de la Mauricie et ses environs
Loi sur le Parc Forillon et des environs
Loi sur le parc marin du Saguenay-Saint-Laurent
Loi sur le régime des eaux/Watercourses Act
Loi sur les espèces menacées ou vulnérables/Act respecting Threatened or Vulnerable Species
Loi sur les pesticides/Pesticides Act
Pesticides Management Code, 2003
Loi sur les parcs
Loi sur les villages cris et le village naskapi/The Cree Villages and the Naskapi Village Act
Loi visant la préservation des ressources en eau/Water Resources Preservation Act

Ministre, L'hon. Pierre Arcand
418-521-3911, Fax: 418-643-4143
Sous-ministre, Diane Jean
418-521-3861, Fax: 418-643-3619
Directrice, Affaires juridiques, Monique Rousseau
418-521-3816, Fax: 418-646-0908
Secrétaire générale et Directrice, Vérification interne, Caroline Drouin
418-521-3810, Fax: 418-646-4762
Directeur, Communications, Jérôme Thibaudeau
418-521-3823, Fax: 418-646-4852
Directeur du Cabinet, François Émond
418-521-3911
Sous-ministre adjointe, Services à la gestion & au milieu terrestre, Brigitte Portelance
Sous-ministre adjoint, Changements climatiques, à l'air & à l'eau, Charles Larochelle

Sous-ministre adjoint, Développement durable, Léopold Gaudreau
Sous-ministre adjoint, Expertise hydrique, analyse et évaluations environnementales, Jacques Dupoint
Sous-ministre adjoint, Analyse & expertise régionales/Centre de contrôle environnemental du Québec, Michel Rousseau

Agences, Conseils et Commissions Associés/ Associated Agencies, Boards & Commission:

• Bureau d'audiences publiques sur l'environnement (BAPE) / Environmental Public Hearing Board
Édifice Lomer-Gouin
#2.10, 575, rue Saint-Amable
Québec, QC G1R 6A6
418-643-7447 Fax: 418-643-9474 800-463-4732
communication@bape.gouv.qc.ca
www.bape.gouv.qc.ca
• Comité consultatif de l'environnement Kativik (CCEK) / Kativik Environmental Advisory Committee
CP 930
Kuujjuaq, QC J0M 1C0
819-964-2961 Fax: 819-964-0694
• Société des établissements en plein air du Québec (SÉPAQ)
Place de la Cité, Tour Cominar
#250, 2640, boul Laurier, 2e étage
Québec, QC G1V 5C2
418-890-6527 Fax: 418-528-6025 800-665-6527
inforeservation@sepaq.com
www.sepaq.com
• Société québécoise de récupération et de recyclage (RECYC-QUÉBEC)
#200, 420, boul Charest est
Québec, QC G1K 8M4
418-643-0394 Fax: 418-643-6507 866-523-8290
info@recyc-quebec.gouv.qc.ca
www.recyc-quebec.gouv.qc.ca
Other Communication: Infoline: 1-800-807-0678; Montréal: 514-351-7835

Analyse et expertise régionales / Regional Analysis & Expertise
Édifice Marie-Guyart, 675, boul René-Lévesque est, 30e étage, Québec, QC G1R 5V7
418-521-3861 Fax: 418-646-1800
La mission est d'assurer l'analyse & la délivrance d'autorisations environnementales & d'offrir une expertise professionnelle en matière d'environnement
Sous-ministre adjoint, Michel Rousseau
418-521-3861, Fax: 418-646-1800

Directions régionales/Regional Offices:

Baie-Comeau
20, boul Comeau, Baie-Comeau, QC G4Z 3A8
418-294-8888 Fax: 418-294-8018
cote-nord@mddep.gouv.qc.ca
Directeur, Alain Gaudreault

Gatineau
#7.340, 170, rue de l'Hôtel-de-Ville, Gatineau, QC J8X 4C2
819-772-3434 Fax: 819-772-3952
outaouais@mddep.gouv.qc.ca
Directeur, Marc Dubreuil

Laval
850, boul Vanier, Laval, QC H7C 2M7
450-661-2008 Fax: 450-661-2217
laval@mddep.gouv.qc.ca
Directeur, Pierre Robert

Longueuil
201, Place Charles-Le Moyne, 2e étage, Longueuil, QC J4K 2T5
450-928-7607 Fax: 450-928-7625
monteregie@mddep.gouv.qc.ca
Directeur adjoint, Pierre Paquin

Montréal
#3860, 5199, rue Sherbrooke est, Montréal, QC H1T 3X9
514-873-3636 Fax: 514-873-5662
montreal@mddep.gouv.qc.ca
Directeur, Pierre Robert

Nicolet
1579, boul Louis-Fréchette, Nicolet, QC J3T 2A5
819-293-4122 Fax: 819-293-8322
centre-du-quebec@mddep.gouv.qc.ca
Directeur, Luc St-Martin

Québec
#100, 1175, boul Lebourgneuf, Québec, QC G2K 0B7
418-644-8844 Fax: 418-646-1214
capitale-nationale@mddep.gouv.qc.ca
Directrice, Isabelle Olivier

Repentigny
100, boul Industriel, Repentigny, QC J6A 4X6
450-654-4355 Fax: 450-654-6131
lanaudiere@mddep.gouv.qc.ca
Directeur, Pierre Robert

Rimouski
212, av Belzile, Rimouski, QC G5L 3C3
418-727-3511 Fax: 418-727-3849
bas-saint-laurent@mddep.gouv.qc.ca
Directeur, Jean-Marie Dionne

Rouyn-Noranda
180, boul Rideau, 1er étage, Rouyn-Noranda, QC J9X 1N9
819-763-3333 Fax: 819-763-3202
abitibi-temiscamingue@mddep.gouv.qc.ca
Directrice, Édith van de Walle

Saguenay
3950, boul Harvey, 4e étage, Saguenay, QC G7X 8L6
418-695-7883 Fax: 418-695-7897
saguenay-lac-saint-jean@mddep.gouv.qc.ca
Directrice, Édith Tremblay

Sainte-Anne-des-Monts
124, 1re av ouest, Sainte-Anne-des-Monts, QC G4V 1C5
418-763-3301 Fax: 418-763-7810
gaspesie-iles-de-la-madeleine@mddep.gouv.qc.ca
Directeur, Jean-Marie Dionne

Sainte-Marie
#200, 675, rte Cameron, Sainte-Marie, QC G6E 3V7
418-386-8000 Fax: 418-386-8080
chaudiere-appalaches@mddep.gouv.qc.ca
Directrice, Isabelle Olivier

Sainte-Thérèse
#80, 300, rue Sicard, Sainte-Thérèse, QC J7E 3X5
450-433-2220 Fax: 450-433-1315
laurentides@mddep.gouv.qc.ca
Directeur, Pierre Robert

Sept-îles
818, boul Laure, Sept-îles, QC G4R 1Y8
418-964-8888 Fax: 418-964-8023
cote-nord@mddep.gouv.qc.ca
Directeur, Alain Gaudreault

Sherbrooke
770, rue Goretti, Sherbrooke, QC J1E 3H4
819-820-3882 Fax: 819-820-3958
estrie@mddep.gouv.qc.ca
Directeur, Pierre Paquin

Trois-Rivières
#102, 100, rue Laviolette, Trois-Rivières, QC G9A 5S9
819-371-6581 Fax: 819-371-6987
mauricie@mddep.gouv.qc.ca
Directeur, Luc St-Martin

Changements climatiques, de l'air et de l'eau / Climate Change
675, boul René-Lévesque est, 30e étage, Québec, QC G1R 5V7
418-521-3861 Fax: 418-643-9990
Sous-ministre adjoint, Charles Larochelle
418-521-3868, Fax: 418-646-4920
Directrice, Bureau des changements climatiques, Geneviève Moisan
Directrice, Relations intergouvernementales, Danielle Pronovost
Directeur, Politiques de l'eau, Marcel Gaucher
Directeur, Politiques de la qualité de l'atmosphère, Michel Goulet

Directions régionales/Regional Offices:

Baie-Comeau
20, boulevard Comeau, Baie-Comeau, QC G4Z 3A8
418-294-8888 Fax: 418-294-8018
cote-nord@mddep.gouv.qc.ca
Directrice, Nathalie Chouinard

Gatineau
 # 7.340, 170, rue de l'Hôtel-de-Ville, Gatineau, QC J8X 4C2
819-772-3434 Fax: 819-772-3952
outaouais@mddep.gouv.qc.ca
Directeur, Alexandre Iracà

Nicolet
1579, boul Louis-Fréchette, Nicolet, QC J3T 2A5
819-293-4122 Fax: 819-293-8322
centre-du-quebec@mddep.gouv.qc.ca
Directeur, Pierre Boucher

Rimouski
212, av Belzile, Rimouski, QC G5L 3C3
418-727-3511 Fax: 418-727-3849
bas-saint-laurent@mddep.gouv.qc.ca
Directeur, Jules Boulanger

Rouyn-Noranda
180, boul Rideau, 1er étage, Rouyn-Noranda, QC J9X 1N9
819-763-3333 Fax: 819-763-3202
abitibi-temiscamingue@mddep.gouv.qc.ca
Directrice (par intérim), Hélène Iracà

Saguenay
3950, boul Harvey, 4e étage, Saguenay, QC G7X 8L6
418-695-7883 Fax: 418-695-7897
saguenay-lac-saint-jean@mddep.gouv.qc.ca
Directeur, Daniel Labrecque

Sainte-Marie
#200, 675, rte Cameron, Sainte-Marie, QC G6E 3V7
418-386-8000 Fax: 418-386-8080
chaudiere-appalaches@mddep.gouv.qc.ca
Directeur, Jean-Marc Lachance

Sherbrooke
770, rue Goretti, Sherbrooke, QC J1E 3H4
819-820-3882 Fax: 819-820-3958
estrie@mddep.gouv.qc.ca
Directeur, Émile Grieco

Montréal
#3860, 5199, rue Sherbrooke est, Montréal, QC H1T 3X9
514-873-3636 Fax: 514-873-5662
montreal@mddep.gouv.qc.ca
Directrice (par intérim), Hélène Proteau

Développement durable / Sustainable Development
418-521-3861 Fax: 418-646-5883
Sous-ministre adjoint, Léopold Gaudreau
418-521-3861, Fax: 418-646-5883
Directrice, Suivi de l'état de l'environnement, Linda Tapin
418-521-3820, Fax: 418-643-9591
Directeur, Bureau de Coordination du développement durable, Luc Vézina
418-521-3848, Fax: 418-646-6169
Directeur, Patrimoine écologique et des parcs, Patrick Beauchesne
418-521-3907, Fax: 418-646-6169

Expertise hydrique, analyse & évaluations environnementales / Water Systems, Analysis & Environmental Assessment
418-521-3861 Fax: 418-643-7812
Sous-ministre adjoint, Jacques Dupont
418-521-3861, Fax: 418-643-7812
Directrice, Évaluations environnementales, Marie-Josée Lizotte
Directeur général, Centre d'expertise en analyse environnementale du Québec, Guy Chouinard
Directeur général, Centre d'expertise hydrique du Québec, Yvon Gosselin
Directeur (par intérim), Accréditation et Relations externes, Louis Martel

Services à la gestion & au milieu terrestre / Administrative Services & Earth Environment
418-521-3861 Fax: 418-643-9990
Sous-ministre adjoint, Brigitte Portelance
418-521-3861, Fax: 418-643-9990
Directeur, Matières résiduelles & lieux contaminés, Mario Bérubé
418-521-3950, Fax: 418-644-3386
Directeur, Secteur agricole & pesticides, Didier Bicchi
418-521-3950, Fax: 418-644-8562
Directeur, Ressources informationnelles & matérielles, Yvan Déry
418-521-3838, Fax: 418-643-8999
Directrice, Ressources humaines, Sylvie Beaulieu
418-521-3811, Fax: 418-646-6498
Directeur général, Planification, analyse économique & ressources financières, Frédéric Guay
418-521-3861, Fax: 418-643-0083

Ministère du Développement économique, de l'Innovation et de l'Exportation / Economic Development, Innovation & Export Trade

710, place D'Youville, 3e étage, Québec, QC G1R 4Y4
418-691-5950 Fax: 418-644-0118
866-680-1884
www.mdeie.gouv.qc.ca
A pour mission de soutenir le développement économique, l'innovation & l'exportation; d'offrir des services-conseils; de promouvoir l'image du Québec à l'étranger auprès des investisseurs
Acts Administered:
Loi favorisant l'augmentation du capital des petites et moyennes entreprises/An Act to promote the capitalization of small and medium-sized businesses
Loi sur Investissement Québec/An Act respecting Investissement Québec
Loi sur l'aide au développement des coopérative et des personnes morales sans but lucratif/An Act respecting assistance for the development of cooperatives and non-profit legal persons

Loi sur la Régie des installations olympiques
Loi sur la Société des alcools du Québec/An Act respecting the Société des alcools du Québec
Loi sur la Société du Centre des congrès de Québec
Loi sur la Société du Palais de Congrès de Montréal
Loi sur la Société du parc industriel et portuaire de Bécancour/ An Act respecting the Société du parc industriel et portuaire de Bécancour
Loi sur la Société Innovatech du Grand Montréal/An Act respecting the Société Innovatech du Grand Montréal
Loi sur la Société Innovatech du sud du Québec/An Act respecting the Société Innovatech du sud du Québec
Loi sur la Société Innovatech Québec et Chaudière-Appalaches/An Act respecting Société Innovatech Québec et Chaudière-Appalaches
Loi sur la Société Innovatech Régions ressources/An Act respecting Société Innovatech Régions ressources
Loi sur le Centre de recherche industriel du Québec/An Act respecting the Centre de recherche industrielle du Québec
Loi sur le ministère des Relations internationales/An Act respecting the Ministère des Relations internationales
Loi sur le ministère du Développement économique, de l'Innovation et de l'Esportation
Loi sur les concours artistiques, littéraires et scientifiques/An Act respecting artistic, literary and scientific competitions
Loi sur les coopératives/Cooperatives Act
Loi sur les heures et les jours d'admission dans les établissements commerciaux/An Act respecting hours and days of admission to commercial establishments
Loi sur les matériaux de rembourrage et les articles rembourrés/An Act respecting stuffing and upholstered and stuffed articles
Loi sur les sociétés de placement dans l'entreprise québécoise

Ministre, L'hon. Clément Gignac
418-691-5650, Fax: 418-643-8553
Sous-ministre, Christyne Tremblay
418-691-5656, Fax: 418-646-6497
Directeur général, Communications et services à la clientèle, Pierre Tessier
418-691-5653
Directrice générale, Services à la gestion, Carole Lafond
418-691-5963
Directeur, Vérification interne, Jacques St-Pierre
418-691-5698
Secrétaire générale, Linda Landry
418-691-5656, Fax: 418-646-6497

Agences, Conseils et Commissions Associés/ Associated Agencies, Boards & Commission:

• Centre de recherche industrielle du Québec (CRIQ) / Industrial Research Centre of Québec
333, rue Franquet
Québec, QC G1P 4C7
418-659-1550 Fax: 418-652-2251 800-667-2386
infocriq@criq.qc.ca
www.criq.qc.ca
Recherche industrielle appliquée; services de RD pour des entreprises

• Fonds québécois de la recherche sur la nature et les technologies / Québec Fund for Research on Nature and Technologies
#450, 140, Grande Allée est
Québec, QC G1R 5M8
418-643-8560 Fax: 418-643-1451
info@fqrnt.gouv.qc.ca
www.fqrnt.gouv.qc.ca

• Fonds québécois de la recherche sur la société et la culture / Québec Fund for Research on Society and Culture
#470, 140, Grande Allée est
Québec, QC G1R 5M8
418-643-7582 Fax: 418-644-5248
fqrsc@fqrsc.gouv.qc.ca
www.fqrsc.gouv.qc.ca

• Fonds de la recherche en santé du Québec / Québec Health Research Fund
#800, 500, rue Sherbrooke ouest
Montréal, QC H3A 3C6
514-873-2114 Fax: 514-873-8768
www.frsq.gouv.qc.ca

• Investissement Québec / Investment Québec
#500, 1200, rte de l'Église
Québec, QC G1V 5A3
418-643-5172 866-870-0437
www.investquebec.com

• Innovatech Québec
#410, 888, rue St-Jean
Québec, QC G1R 5H6
418-528-9770 Fax: 418-528-9783 866-605-1676
www.innovatechquebec.com

Services aux entreprises
Sous-ministre adjoint, Jean-Marc Sauvé
Directrice, Coordination régionale, Michèle Robert
418-528-0930, Fax: 418-528-8428
Directeur, Projet ACCORD, Xavier Fonteneau
Directrice, Programmes et mesures, Lise Mathieu
418-643-0060, Fax: 418-646-3609
Directeur, Développement des entreprises, Bertrand Verbruggen
514-499-2199
Directeur général, Affaires économiques métropolitaines, VACANT

Affaires économiques internationales / International Economic Affairs
Sous-ministre adjoint, Jean Séguin
514-499-2188, Fax: 514-873-4230
Directrice générale adjointe, Suzanne Éthier
514-499-2199
Directeur, Amérique latine et Antilles, Rafaël Sanchez
418-691-5698, Fax: 418-643-0825
Directrice, Amérique du Nord, Chantal Castonguay
514-499-2199
Directeur (par intérim), Asie-Pacifique, Afrique et Moyen-Orient, Alain Carrier
Directeur, Europe, Yves Lafortune
514-499-2185, Fax: 514-873-1540
Directeur, Promotion des investissements, Alain Proulx
514-499-2199

Secteurs stratégiques et des projets économiques / Strategic Sectors and Economic Projects
Sous-ministre adjoint, Mario Bouchard
418-691-5698
Directrice, Biens de consommation, Marie-Annick Drouin
418-691-5698
Directeur, Chimie, plasturgie, métallurgie et équipements, Clément Drolet
418-691-5976, Fax: 418-644-0519
Directrice, Coordination, Lisette Seyer
418-691-5698
Directrice, Développement des industries, Diane Hastie
418-691-5698
Directeur, Environnement et services aux entreprises, Gaétan Poiré
418-691-5698, Fax: 418-644-1687
Directeur, Équipements de transport, Martin Aubé
514-499-2199
Directrice, Santé et biotechnologies, Michèle Houpert
514-499-6534, Fax: 514-864-3755
Directrice, Technologies de l'information et des communications, Guylaine Leblanc
418-691-5957, Fax: 418-643-6947
Directeur, Commerce et construction, Pierre A. Forgues, 2008-09-16
514-499-2199

Services à la gestion / Administrative Services
Directrice générale, Carole Lafond
418-691-5963
Directeur, Ressources financières, Francis Mathieu
418-691-5698
Directrice, Ressources humaines, Nicole Lévesque
418-691-5698
Directeur, Ressources informationnelles, Guy Leclerc
418-691-5965

Politiques et sociétés d'État / Policy & Crown Corporations
Sous-ministre adjointe, Suzanne Lévesque
418-528-2931
Directeur, Analyse économique, Denise Lacroix
418-691-5698
Directrice, Politiques économiques, Christiane Morin
418-691-5698
Directeur (par intérim), Politique commerciale pour les accords internationaux, VACANT
Directrice, Coopératives, Lise Jacob
418-646-6145, Fax: 418-646-6145
Directrice (par intérim), Sociétés d'État & entrepreneuriat, Nathalie Perreault
450-834-4453
Directeur, Coordinationn et évaluation, François-Maxime Langlois
418-691-5698
Directeur (par intérim), Politique commerciale/Politique commerciale pour l'Amérique du Nord, Patrick Muzzi
418-643-4347, Fax: 418-691-5995

Recherche, innovation, science et société / Research, Innovation, Science & Society
Sous-ministre adjointe, Geneviève Tanguay
418-691-5973
Directrice, Collaborations internationales, Marie-Josée Blais
Directeur, Recherche universitaire & collégiale, Luc Castonguay
418-691-5973
Directeur, Financement des infrastructures de recherche, Gaston Beaudoin
418-691-5973
Directrice, Innovation & transfert, Monique LaRue
418-691-5973
Directrice, Science & société, Christian Desbiens
418-691-5973
Directeur (par intérim), Politiques & analyses, Mawana Pongo
418-691-5973
Directrice, Coordination & concertation, Marie-Odile Koch
418-691-5973

Directions régionales/Regional Offices:

Abitibi-Témiscamingue
#202, 170, av Principale, Rouyn-Noranda, QC J9X 4P7
819-763-3561 Fax: 819-763-3462
866-463-6642
Directeur, Yves Drolet

Bas-St-Laurent
#RC 04, 337, rue Moreault, Rimouski, QC G5L 1P4
418-727-3577 Fax: 418-727-3640
866-463-6642
Directeur (par intérim), Denis Goulet

Capitale-Nationale
900, place d'Youville, 3e étage, Québec, QC G1R 3P7
418-691-5824 Fax: 418-643-4099
866-463-6642
Directeur (par intérim), Jean-François Talbot

Centre-du-Québec
Édifice provincial, #1.03, 62, rue Saint-Jean-Baptiste, Victoriaville, QC G6P 4E3
819-752-9781 Fax: 819-758-4306
866-463-6642
Directeur, Vincent Bourassa

Chaudière-Appalaches
#1, 1055, boul Vachon nord, Sainte-Marie, QC G6E 1M4
418-386-8677 Fax: 418-386-8037
866-463-6642
Directeur, Roch Delagrave

Côte-Nord
#RC 711, 625, boul Laflèche, Baie-Comeau, QC G5C 1C5
418-589-4349 Fax: 418-295-4199
866-463-6642
Directeur, Jacques Chiasson

Estrie
#4.05, 200, rue Belvédère nord, Sherbrooke, QC J1H 4A9
819-820-3731 Fax: 819-820-3929
866-463-6642
Directeur, Robert Fortin

Gaspésie/Iles-de-la-Madeleine
#10-A, 500, av Daigneault, CP 1360, Chandler, QC G0C 1K0
418-689-1200 Fax: 418-689-4108
866-463-6642
Directeur, Roger Cyr

Lanaudière
#3300, 40, rue Gauthier sud, Joliette, QC J6E 4J4
450-752-8050 Fax: 450-752-8064
866-463-6642
Directeur, Daniel Boutin

Laurentides
#C-3.35, 85, rue de Martigny, Saint-Jérôme, QC J7Y 3R8
450-569-3031 Fax: 450-569-3039
866-463-6642
Directeur (par intérim), Serge Thériault

Laval
#RC 30, 705, ch du Trait-Carré, Laval, QC H7N 1B3
450-680-6175 Fax: 450-972-3090
866-463-6642
Directrice, Diane F. Bélanger

Mauricie
Édifice Capitanal, #114, 100, rue Laviolette, Trois-Rivières, QC G9A 5S9
819-371-6617 Fax: 819-371-6960
866-463-6642
Directeur (par intérim), Denis Hébert

Montérégie
#101, 201, place Charles-Le Moyne, Longueuil, QC J4K 2T5
450-928-7645 Fax: 450-928-7465
866-463-6642
Directeur, Jacques La Rue

Montréal
380, rue Saint-Antoine ouest, 5e étage, Montréal, QC H2Y 3X7
514-499-2550 Fax: 514-873-9913
866-463-6642
Directeur, Daniel Gagné

Nord-du-Québec
333, 3e rue, Chibougamau, QC G8P 1N4
418-748-6681 Fax: 418-748-6698
866-463-6642
Directeur, Joseph Molina

Outaouais
#7.200, 170, rue de l'Hôtel-de-Ville, Gatineau, QC J8X 4C2
819-772-3219 Fax: 819-772-3968
866-463-6642
Directeur, Jeffrey MacHan

Saguenay/Lac-Saint-Jean
#2.05, 3950, boul Harvey, 2e étage, Jonquière, QC G7X 8L6
418-695-7971 Fax: 418-695-7870
866-463-6642
Directeur, Joseph Molina

Commission des droits de la personne et des droits de la jeunesse / Commission for Human Rights & the Rights of Youth

360, rue St-Jacques, 2e étage, Montréal, QC H2Y 1P5
514-873-5146 Fax: 514-873-6032
800-361-6477
accueil@cdpdj.qc.ca
www.cdpdj.qc.ca

A pour mission d'assurer la promotion et la respect des droits et libertés affirmés par la Charte des droits et libertés de la personne, par la Loi sur la protection de la jeunesse, et par la Loi sur les jeunes contrevenants
Président, Gaétan Cousineau
Vice-présidente, Sylvie Godin

Ministère de l'Éducation, du Loisir et du Sport / Education, Leisure & Sports

1035, rue De La Chevrotière, 28e étage, Québec, QC G1R 5A5
418-643-7095 Fax: 418-646-6561
866-747-6626
www.mels.gouv.qc.ca

Acts Administered:
Charte de la langue française/Charter of the French language
Loi concernant le transfert de la propriété d'un immeuble à la Commission scolaire de Montréal et modifiant la Loi sur l'instruction publique/Act respecting the transfer of the ownership of an immovable to the Commission scolairede Montréal & amending t
Loi concernant les conditions d'utilisation d'immeubles de la Commission des écoles protestantes du Grand Montréal par la Commission des écoles catholiques de Montréal/Act respecting conditions governing the use of immovables ofthe Protestant School Boa
Loi du mérite scolaire/Scholastic Merit Act
Loi favorisant la conclusion d'ententes dans le secteur de l'éducation/Act to foster labour agreements in the education sector
Loi modifiant diverses dispositions législatives dans le secteur de l'éducation concernant la confessionnalité/Act to amend various legislative provisions respecting education as regards confessional matters
Loi sur l'accréditation et le financement des associations d'élèves ou d'étudiants/Act respecting the accreditation and financing of students' associations
Loi sur l'aide financière aux études/Act respecting financial assistance for education expenses
Loi sur l'École de laiterie et les écoles moyennes d'agriculture/Act respecting the École de laiterie and intermediate agricultural schools
Loi sur l'élection des premiers commissaires des commissions scolaires nouvelles et modifiant diverses dispositions législatives/Act respecting the election of the first commissioners of the new school boards and amending variouslegislative provisions
Loi sur l'enseignement privé/Act respecting private education
Loi sur l'Institut de tourisme et d'hôtellerie du Québec/Act respecting the Institut de tourisme et d'hôtellerie du Québec
Loi sur l'instruction publique/Education Act
Loi sur l'instruction publique pour les autochtones cris, inuits et naskapis/Education Act for Cree, Inuit and Naskapi Native Persons
Loi sur l'Université du Québec/Act respecting the Université du Québec
Loi sur la Commission d'évaluation de l'enseignement collégial/Act respecting the Commission d'évaluation de l'enseignement collégial
Loi sur le Conseil supérieur de l'éducation/Act respecting the Institut de tourisme et d'hôtellerie du Québec
Loi sur le ministère de l'Éducation, du Loisir et du Sport/Act respecting the Ministère de l'Éducation, du Loisir et du Sport
Loi sur les collèges d'enseignement général et professionnel/General and Vocational Colleges Act
Loi sur les élections scolaires/Act respecting school elections
Loi sur les établissements d'enseignement de niveau universitaire/Act respecting educational institutions at the university level
Loi sur les fondations universitaires/Act respecting university foundations
Loi sur les investissements universitaires/Univeristy Investments Act

Ministre, L'hon. Line Beauchamp
418-644-0664, Fax: 418-646-7551, line.beauchamp@mels.gouv.qc.ca
Sous-ministre, Louise Pagé
418-643-3810, Fax: 418-644-4591
Directeur, Secrétariat aux affaires religieuses, Roger Boisvert
418-643-7070, Fax: 418-644-7142
Directeur, Accès à l'information et plaintes, Paul Rémillard
418-646-5324
Directeur, Affaires juridiques, Yves D. Dussault
418-643-3747, Fax: 418-646-6849
Directrice, Secrétariat général, Anne Moore
418-643-3810
Directrice, Condition féminine, Raymonde Villemure
418-643-3810
Directeur, Vérification interne, Christian Boivin
418-643-8194
Directrice, Communications, Mireille Dubé
418-528-2265
Sous-ministre adjoint, Services à la communauté anglophone & Affaires autochtones, Leo La France
514-873-3788
Sous-ministre adjointe, Réseaux, Manuelle Oudar
418-643-3810
Sous-ministre adjointe, Formation professionnelle, technique & continue, Brigitte Guay
418-643-3810
Sous-ministre adjointe, Enseignement supérieur, Christiane Piché
Sous-ministre adjoint, Politiques, recherche et statistiques, Gilles Charland
418-643-3810
Sous-ministre adjoint, Services en soutien à la mission & aide financière aux études, Raymond Lesage
418-643-3810
Sous-ministre adjoint, Loisir et sport, Jean-Guy Ouellette
418-646-6018

Agences, Conseils et Commissions Associés/ Associated Agencies, Boards & Commission:

• Commission consultative de l'enseignement privé / Advisory Committee on Private Education
1035, rue de la Chevrotière, 14e étage
Québec, QC G1R 5A5
418-646-1249 Fax: 418-643-7752
commission.consultative@mels.gouv.qc.ca
Other Communication: Téléphone poste: 2503
• Commission de l'éducation en langue anglaise / Advisory Board on English Education
600, rue Fullum, 9e étage
Montréal, QC H2K 4L1
514-873-5656 Fax: 514-864-4181
cela-abee@mels.gouv.qc.ca
www.mels.gouv.qc.ca/cela/anglais.htm
• Commission d'évaluation de l'enseignement collégial / College Teachers Assessment Commission
800, place d'Youville, 18e étage
Québec, QC G1R 5P4
418-643-9938 Fax: 418-643-9019
info@ceec.gouv.qc.ca
www.ceec.gouv.qc.ca
• Comité-conseil sur les programmes d'études
1035, de la Chevrotière, 17e étage
Québec, QC G1R 5A5
418-646-0133 Fax: 418-643-0056
ccpe@mels.gouv.qc.ca
www.ccpe.gouv.qc.ca
• Conseil supérieur de l'éducation / Superior Council of Education
#180, 1175, av Lavigerie
Québec, QC G1V 5B2
418-643-3850 Fax: 418-644-2530
panorama@cse.gouv.qc.ca
www.cse.gouv.qc.ca

Direction générale des politiques, recherche et statistiques / Policy, Research & Statistics
Sous-ministre adjoint, Gilles Charland
Directrice, Politiques, Josée Bourdages
Directrice, Recherche, statistiques et information, Myriam Proulx
Directrice (par intérim), Service de la recherche et évaluation, Valérie Saysset
Directrice, Service de l'information décisionnelle et de la géomatique, Richard Bélanger

Aide financière aux études / Student Financial Aid
1035, rue De La Chevrotière, Québec, QC G1R 5A5
418-643-3750
877-643-3750
www.afe.gouv.qc.ca
Sous-ministre adjoint, Raymond Lesage
418-644-3810, Fax: 418-528-0779
Directrice, Services administratifs, Nicole Martel
Directeur, Service de planification & programmes, Robert Sasseville
418-643-6276
Directrice, Gestion des prêts, Suzanne Gingras
418-646-5115

Éducation préscolaire, enseignement primaire et secondaire et régions / Preschool, Elementary & Secondary School Education
Sous-ministre adjoint, Alain Veilleux
418-643-3810, Fax: 418-644-2131
Directrice, Services de soutien aux élèves, Denise Gosselin
418-266-0156
Directeur, Services à l'enseignement, Guy Dumais
418-643-3452
Directeur, Service aux communautés culturelles, Christian Rousseau
514-873-3744
Directrice, Programmes, Catherine Dupont
418-644-5240, Fax: 418-528-8023
Directrice, Adaptation scolaire, Anne Robitaille
418-646-7000, Fax: 418-644-5914
Directeur, Sanction des études, Jean-Guy Hamel
418-644-0905, Fax: 418-644-6909
Directrice, Évaluation, Linda Drouin
514-864-1896, Fax: 514-873-2571
Directeur (par intérim), Ressources didactiques, Guy Dumais
418-643-3452

Enseignement supérieur / Higher Education
Sous-ministre adjointe, Christiane Piché
418-643-3810, Fax: 418-646-1526
Directeur, Affaires universitaires et collégiales, Robert Poulin
418-643-6671
Directeur, Affaires étudiantes, Jean-François Noël
418-646-4133, Fax: 418-643-0622
Directeur, Enseignement collégial, Christian Ragusich
418-644-8976, Fax: 418-646-7447
Directrice, Équipement, Hélène Guenette
418-643-6524, Fax: 418-644-3090
Directeur, Financement et équipement, Pierre Boutet
418-646-4533, Fax: 418-644-3090
Directeur, Programmation budgétaire et financement, Jean Leroux
418-528-0074, Fax: 418-644-3090
Directrice, Soutien aux établissements, Ginette Dion
418-646-1534, Fax: 418-643-7100
Directeur, Systèmes et contrôle, Pierre Larochelle
418-643-2999, Fax: 418-643-8456

Régions / Regions
Directeur général, Régions, Guylaine Larose
418-643-7498, Fax: 418-646-8419
Abitibi-Témiscamingue/Nord-du-Québec
215, boul Rideau, 1er étage, Rouyn-Noranda, QC J9X 5Y6
819-763-3001 Fax: 819-763-3017
dr-08@mels.gouv.qc.ca
Directrice régionale par intérim, Louise Bilodeau
Bas-Saint-Laurent/Gaspésie/Iles-de-la-Madeleine
355, boul Saint-Germain ouest, 2e étage, Rimouski, QC G5L 0A5
418-727-3600 Fax: 418-727-3557
dr-01@mels.gouv.qc.ca
Directeur régional, Gérard Bédard
Capitale-Nationale/Chaudière-Appalaches
1020, rte de l'Église, 3e étage, Québec, QC G1V 3V9
418-643-7934 Fax: 418-643-0972
dr-03@mels.gouv.qc.ca
Directrice (par intérim), Suzanne Côté
Côte-Nord (Services adm. et gen.)
Édifice Paul-Provencher, #1.812, RC, 625, boul Laflèche, Baie-Comeau, QC G5C 1C5
418-295-4400 Fax: 418-295-4467
dr09-bc@mels.gouv.qc.ca
Directrice régionale, Lucy de Mendonça
Côte-Nord (Services éducatifs)
#201, 106, rue Napoléon, Sept-Iles, QC G4R 3L7
418-964-8420 Fax: 418-964-8504
dr09-si@mels.gouv.qc.ca
Directrice (par intérim), Suzanne Côté
Estrie
#3.05, 200, rue Belvédère nord, Sherbrooke, QC J1H 4A9
819-820-3382 Fax: 819-820-3947
dr-05@mels.gouv.qc.ca
Directeur régional, Roger Tremblay
Laval/Laurentides/Lanaudière
#200, 300, rue Sicard, Sainte-Thérèse, QC J7E 3X5
450-430-3611 Fax: 450-430-4005
dr-061@mels.gouv.qc.ca
Directrice régionale, Lauraine Langlois

Mauricie/Centre-du-Québec
Édifice Capitanal, #213, 100, rue Laviolette, Trois-Rivières, QC G9A 5S9
819-371-6711 Fax: 819-971-6075
dr-04@mels.gouv.qc.ca
Other Communication: Email: dr-17@mels.gouv.qc.ca
Directrice régionale, Carole Gaudet
Montérégie
Édifice Montval, 201, place Charles-Le Moyne, 6e étage, Longueuil, QC J4K 2T5
450-928-7438 Fax: 450-928-7451
dr-062@mels.gouv.qc.ca
Directrice régionale, Lise Langlois
Montréal
600, rue Fullum, 10e étage, Montréal, QC H2K 4L1
514-873-4630 Fax: 514-873-0620
dr-063@mels.gouv.qc.ca
Directeur régional, Francis Culée
Outaouais
170, rue de l'Hôtel-de-Ville, 4e étage, Gatineau, QC J8X 4C2
819-772-3382 Fax: 819-772-3955
dr-07@mels.gouv.qc.ca
Directrice régionale (par intérim), Dominique Vaillancourt
Saguenay/Lac-Saint-Jean
2220, rue St-David, Jonquière, QC G7X 0L3
418-695-7982 Fax: 418-695-7990
dr-02@mels.gouv.qc.ca
Directeur régional, Francis Paradis

Formation professionnelle et technique et formation continue / Professional & Technical Training & Continuing Education
Sous-ministre adjointe, Brigitte Guay
418-643-3810, Fax: 418-644-4591
Directeur, Éducation des adultes & action communautaire, VACANT
Directrice, Formation continue et soutien, Sonia Léveillé
418-646-1536
Directeur, Gestion sectorielle des ressources, Yves Bourassa
418-646-4225
Directrice, Planification et coordination sectorielles, Julie Lévesque
418-646-9477
Directrice, Programmes et la veille sectorielle, Nora Desrochers
418-646-4215

Réseaux / Networks
Sous-ministre adjointe, Manuelle Oudar
418-643-3810, Fax: 418-646-9220
Directeur, Financement et équipement, René Lepage
418-528-7406
Directrice, Enseignement privé, Lise Briand
418-646-3939
Directeur (par intérim), Relations du travail-personnel professionnel & soutien, Richard Du Chemin
418-646-9000
Directeur, Relations du travail, Éric Bergeron
418-646-9000
Directrice (par intérim), Relations du travail-personnel enseignant, Linda Boutin
418-646-9000
Directeur, Politiques et opérations budgétaires, Serge Dupéré
418-643-1497
Directeur, Équipement scolaire, Gilles Marchand
418-644-2525, Fax: 418-643-9224
Directrice, Conditions de travail du personnel d'encadrement, Françoise Dion
418-646-9000
Directrice, Opérations financières aux réseaux, Catherine Tremblay
418-643-5432
Responsable, Greffe des tribunaux d'arbitrage, Marc Pelletier
418-528-7693

Loisir et sport / Sport & Recreation
Sous-ministre adjoint, Jean-Guy Ouellette
418-646-6018, Fax: 418-644-9474
Directrice, Sport, loisir et activité physique, France Vigneault
418-646-6142
Directeur, Bureau des grands projets, Robert Bédard
418-646-6137

Services à la communauté anglophone, affaires autochtones & Plan Nord / Anglophone Services, Aboriginal Affairs & Northern Plan
Sous-ministre adjoint, Directeur, Politiques & projets, Leo La France
514-873-3788
Directrice, Production en langue anglaise, Liette Michaud
514-873-6073, Fax: 514-873-2687
Directeur, Production en langue anglaise, VACANT

Directeur général des Élections du Québec / Chief Electoral Officer of Québec

Édifice René-Lévesque, 3460, rue de La Pérade, Québec, QC G1X 3Y5
418-528-0422 Fax: 418-643-7291
888-353-2846
info@electionsquebec.qc.ca
www.electionsquebec.qc.ca
TTY: 418-646-0644

Acts Administered:
Loi électorale du Québec/Election Act
Loi sur la consultation populaire/Referendum Act
Loi sur les élections et les référendums dans les municipalités/An Act respecting Elections & Referendums in Municipalities
Loi sur les élections scolaires
Directeur général, Président de la commission de la représentation électorale, Jacques Drouin
418-646-3569
Adjoint au président, Secretaire, Denis Fontaine
418-646-6072

Ministère de l'Emploi et de la Solidarité sociale / Employment & Social Solidarity

425, rue St-Amable, 4e étage, Québec, QC G1R 4Z1
418-643-4721
888-643-4721
www.mess.gouv.qc.ca

Acts Administered:
Loi favorisant le développement et la reconnaissance des compétences de la main d'oeuvre/An Act to promote workforce skills development & recognition
Loi sur l'Office de la sécurité du revenu des chasseurs et piégeurs cris/An Act respecting income security for Cree hunters and trappers who are beneficiaries under the Agreement concerning James Bay and Northern Québec
Loi sur la formation et la qualification professionnelles de la main-d'ouvre/An Act respecting manpower vocational training and qualification
Loi sur le ministère de l'Emploi et de la Solidarité sociale et sur la Commission des partenaires du marché du travail/An Act respecting the ministère de l'Emploi et de la Solidarité sociale & the Commission des partenaires dumarché du travail
Loi sur le ministère du Conseil exécutif/An Act respecting the Ministère du Conseil exécutif
Loi sur le régime de rentes du Québec/An Act respecting the Québec Pension Plan
Loi sur l'aide aux personnes et aux familles/Individual & Family Assistance Regulation
Loi sur les régimes complémentaires de retraite/Supplemental Pension Plans Act
Loi sur les villages nordiques et l'Administration régionale Kativik/An Act respecting Northern villages and the Kativik Regional Government
Loi visant à lutter contre la pauvreté et l'exclusion sociale/An Act to combat poverty and social exclusion
Ministre, L'hon. Julie Boulet
418-643-4810, Fax: 418-643-2802,
ministre@mess.gouv.qc.ca
Sous-ministre, Dominique Savoie
418-643-4820, Fax: 418-643-1226
Directeur, Bureau de la sous-ministre, Patrick Grenier
418-646-0425, Fax: 418-643-1226
Directeur, Affaires juridiques, Daniel Morin
418-643-4998, Fax: 418-646-8559
Directrice (par intérim), Direction de la vérification interne et des enquêtes administratives, Michelle Coudé
418-646-0425, Fax: 418-644-3641
Directrice (par intérim), Ressources humaines, Sylvie Grenier
418-646-0425

Agences, Conseils et Commissions Associés/ Associated Agencies, Boards & Commission:

• Commission des partenaires du marché du travail / Labour Market Partnerships Commission
800, rue du Square-Victoria, 28e étage
CP 100
Montréal, QC H4Z 1B7
514-873-5252 Fax: 514-864-8005
partenaires@mess.gouv.qc.ca
www.cpmt.gouv.qc.ca
• Office de la sécurité du revenu des chasseurs et piégeurs cris / Cree Hunters & Trappers Income Security Board
Édifice Champlain
#1110, 2700, boul Laurier
Québec, QC G1V 4K5
418-643-7300 Fax: 418-643-6803 800-363-1560
courrier@osrcpc.ca
www.osrcpc.ca
• Régie des rentes du Québec / Québec Pension Board
CP 5200
Sainte-Foy, QC G1K 7S9
418-643-5185 800-463-5185
rrq@rrq.gouv.qc.ca
www.rrq.gouv.qc.ca

Affaires gouvernementales et relations avec les citoyens / Governmental Affairs & Citizen Relations
Sous-ministre adjoint, Jacques Duguay
418-646-0425
Directrice, Communications, Josée Tremblay
418-646-0425
Directrice, Bureau des renseignements et plaintes, Louise Proulx
418-646-0425
Directrice, Affaires canadiennes et internationales, Anne Racine
418-646-0425
Directeur, Révision et recours administratifs, Bertrand Olivier
418-646-0425

Centre de communication avec la clientèle / Client Call Centre
514-873-4000
877-767-8773
Centre d'appels dont la mission est de répondre rapidement aux questions sur les services de solidarité sociale

Emploi-Québec / Employment Québec
425, rue St-Amable, #RC 175, Québec, QC G1R 4Z1
418-643-4721
888-643-4721
www.emploiquebec.net
Sous-ministre associé, Bernard Matte
418-646-0425

Opérations / Operations
Sous-ministre adjointe, Ginette Sylvain
514-873-0800
Directeur général adjoint, Administration et des projets corporatifs, Michel Lalande
418-521-3816
Directeur, Coordination du développement des systèmes d'information, Beniamino Colombo
418-646-0425
Directrice, Budget et des services administratifs, Johanne Blanchette
514-873-0800
Directeur, Soutien et de la qualité des applications informatiques, Mario Godin
418-646-0425

Politiques & l'analyse stratégique / Policy & Strategic Analysis
Sous-ministre adjointe, Marie-Renée Roy
418-646-0425
Directeur général adjoint, Recherche, évaluation & statistique, Serge Hamel
418-646-0425
Directeur général adjoint, Politiques & prospective, Éric Théroux
418-646-0425
Directeur, Politiques d'emploi & de main-d'oeuvre, Daniel Doyon
418-646-0425

Ministère de la Famille et des Aînés / Family & Seniors

425, rue Saint-Amable, 1er étage, Québec, QC G1R 4Z1
877-216-6202
www.mfa.gouv.qc.ca

Acts Administered:
Loi favorisant l'établissement d'un régime de retraite à l'intention d'employés oeuvrant dans le domaine des services de garde à l'enfance/An Act to facilitate the establishment of a Pension Plan for employees working in ChildcareServices
Loi sur le ministère de la Famille, des Aînés et de la Condition féminine/An Act respecting the Ministère de la Famille, des Aînés et de la Condition féminine
Loi sur les services de garde éducatifs à l'enfance/Educational Childcare Act
Loi sur les prestations familiales/An Act respecting Family Benefits
Ministre, Famille, L'hon. Yolande James
418-643-2181, Fax: 418-643-2640,
ministre.famille@mfa.gouv.qc.ca
Ministre responsable, Aînés, L'hon. Marguerite Blais
418-646-7757, Fax: 418-646-7769
Sous-ministre, Line Bérubé
418-646-4680, Fax: 418-646-4903
Secretaire générale, Chantal Maltais
418-528-6689

Agences, Conseils et Commissions Associés/ Associated Agencies, Boards & Commission:

• Comité national d'éthique sur le vieillissement et les changements démographiques / National Ethics Committee on Aging & Demographic Changes
#700, 875, Grande Allée est, 5e étage
Québec, QC G1R 5W5
418-643-0098 Fax: 418-643-0082
jacques.vaillancourt@mfa.gouv.qc.ca
• Conseil du statut de la femme / Status of Women Council
#300, 800, place D'Youville, 3e étage
Québec, QC G1R 6E2
418-643-4326 Fax: 418-643-8926 800-463-2851
csf@csf.gouv.qc.ca
www.csf.gouv.qc.ca
• Curateur public du Québec / Québec Public Trustee
600, boul René-Lévesque ouest
Montréal, QC H3B 4W9
514-873-4074 Fax: 514-873-5033 800-363-9020
www.curateur.gouv.qc.ca

Ministère des Finances / Finance

Édifice Gérard-D.-Lévesque, 12, rue Saint-Louis, Québec, QC G1R 5L3
418-528-9323 Fax: 418-646-1631
info@finances.gouv.qc.ca
www.finances.gouv.qc.ca

Acts Administered:
Loi sur l'administration financière/Financial Administration Act
Loi sur l'assurance automobile
Loi sur l'assurance-dépôts
Loi sur les assurances
Loi sur l'Autorité des marchés financiers
Loi sur la Caisse de dépôt et placement du Québec
Loi sur les caisses d'entraide économique
Loi concernant certaines caisses d'entraide économique
Loi constituant Capital régional et coopératif Desjardins
Loi sur les centres financiers internationaux
Loi sur les compagnies
Loi sur les compagnies de télégraphe et de téléphone
Loi sur les compagnies minières
Loi sur les coopératives de services financiers
Loi sur le courtage immobilier
Loi sur les dépôts et consignations
Loi sur la distribution de produits et services financiers
Loi sur l'équilibre budgétaire
Loi sur l'exercice des activités de bourse au Québec par Nasdaq
Loi sur Financement-Québec
Loi constituant Fondaction, le Fonds de développement de la Confédération des syndicats nationaux pour la coopération et l'emploi
Loi constituant le Fonds de solidarité des travailleurs du Québec
Loi sur les frais de garantie relatifs aux emprunts des organismes gouvernementaux
Loi sur l'Institut de la statistique du Québec
Loi sur le ministère de l'Agriculture, des Pêcheries et de l'Alimentation
Loi sur le ministère des Finances
Loi sur le Mouvement Desjardins
Loi sur les pouvoirs spéciaux des personnes morales
Loi sur la réduction du capital-actions de personnes morales de droit public et leurs filiales
Loi sur la Régie de l'assurance maladie du Québec
Loi sur le remplacement de programmes conjoints par un abattement fiscal
Loi sur la Société de financement des infrastructures locales du Québec
Loi sur la Société des alcools du Québec
Loi sur la Société des loteries du Québec
Loi concernant la Société nationale du cheval de course
Loi sur les sociétés d'entraide économique
Loi sur les sociétés fiducie et les sociétés d'épargne
Loi concernant les subventions relatives au paiement en capital et intérêts des emprunts des organismes publics ou municipaux
Loi sur les valeurs mobilières
Ministre, L'hon. Raymond Bachand
418-643-5270, Fax: 418-646-1574
Sous-ministre, Gilles Paquin
418-643-5738, Fax: 418-528-5546
Sous-ministre associé, Financement, gestion de la dette & opérations financières, Bernard Turgeon
418-643-5738, Fax: 418-646-8611
Sous-ministre adjoint, Politiques économiques & fiscales, Carl Gauthier
418-691-2214, Fax: 418-646-6688
Sous-ministre adjoint, Politiques relatives aux institutions financières et au droit corporatif, Richard Boivin
418-646-7563, Fax: 418-646-7610
Sous-ministre adjointe, Droit fiscal & la fiscalité, Josée Morin
418-691-2261, Fax: 418-644-1666
Sous-ministre adjoint, Politique budgétaire et à l'économique, Luc Monty
418-528-7678
Contrôleur, Finances et comptabilité gouvernementale, Simon-Pierre Falardeau

Agences, Conseils et Commissions Associés/ Associated Agencies, Boards & Commission:

• Autorité des marchés financiers
Tour de la Bourse
800, Square Victoria, 22e étage
Montréal, QC H4Z 1G3
514-395-0337 Fax: 514-873-3090 877-525-0337
www.lautorite.qc.ca
• Caisse de dépôt et placement du Québec
1000, place Jean-Paul-Riopelle
Montréal, QC H2Z 2B3
514-842-3261 Fax: 514-842-4833 866-330-3936 TTY: 514-847-2190
info@lacaisse.com
www.lacaisse.com
• Institut de la statistique du Québec (BSQ) / Québec Statistics Office
200, ch Ste-Foy, 1er étage
Québec, QC G1R 5T4
418-691-2401 Fax: 418-643-4129 800-463-4090
direction@stat.gouv.qc.ca
www.stat.gouv.qc.ca
• Loto-Québec / Québec Lotteries
500, rue Sherbrooke ouest
Montréal, QC H3A 3G6
514-282-8000 Fax: 514-873-8999
lotoquebec.com
• Société des alcools du Québec (SAQ) / Québec Liquor Corporation
905, av De Lorimier
Montréal, QC H2K 3V9
514-873-2020 Fax: 514-873-6788 866-873-2020
info@saq.com
www.saq.com
• Investissement Québec (IQ)
#1500, 600, rue de la Gauchetière ouest
Montréal, QC H3B 4L8
514-873-4664 866-870-0437
www.investquebec.com

Droit fiscal et la fiscalité / Fiscal Law & Taxation
Sous-ministre adjointe, Josée Morin
418-691-2236, Fax: 418-644-5262
Directeur, Impôts des entreprises, Agathe Simard
Directrice, Impôts des particuliers, Lyse Gauthier
Directrice, Taxes, Lyne Dussault

Financement, gestion de dette et opérations financières / Financing, Debt Management & Financial Transactions
Sous-ministre adjoint, Bernard Turgeon
418-643-5738
Directeur général, Opérations bancaires et financières, François Tardif
Directeur général, Financement et gestion de la dette, Alain Bélanger
Directrice, Financement des organismes publics et de la documentation financière, Nathalie Parenteau
Directeur général, Prévisions financières et des relations avec les agences de crédit, Gino Ouellet
Directeur, Gestion de l'encaisse, Renaud Raymond
Directeur, Gestion des risques, Éric Deschênes
Directeur, Analyse et des prévisions du service de la dette, Jean-Charles Doucet
Directeur, Gestion des fonds et des paiements, Harold Garneau
Directrice, Gestion de la dette et de l'ingénierie financière, Marie-Pierre Hillinger
Directeur, Comptabilité et du bureau des dépôts et consignations, Michel Breault
Directrice, Produits d'épargne et du suivi des transactions financières, Isabelle Blackburn
Sous-ministre adjoint, Politiques fédérales-provinciales et financières, Patrick Déry
Directrice, Relations fédérales-provinciales, Marie-Claude Lavallée
Directeur, Projets spéciaux, Martin Guérard

Politique budgétaire et économique / Budgetary & Economic Policy
Sous-ministre adjoint, Luc Monty
Directeur général, Simon Bergeron
Directeur général, Analyse et de la prévision économiques, Marc Sirois
Directeur général, Organisation financière et du suivi des opérations budgétaires et non budgétaires, Jacques Caron
Directeur général, Politiques locales et autochtones et de l'optimisation des revenus, Marc Grandisson
Directeur, Économie québécoise et canadienne, Michel Dionne
Directeur, Analyse et de la prévision des dépenses et de la tarification, Richard Masse

Politiques économiques et fiscales / Economic & Fiscal Policy
Sous-ministre adjoint, Carl Gauthier
Directeur général, Politiques aux entreprises, Éric Ducharme
Directeur général, Politiques aux particuliers, Éric Fournier
Directeur, Développement économique, Brigitte Bazin
Directeur, Études économiques et fiscales et taxes de vente, David Bahan
Directeur, Mesures structurantes, Luc Bilodeau
Directeur, Politique sociale, Gilbert Fontaine
Directeur, Taxation des particuliers, Jean-Pierre Simard
Directeur, Taxation des entreprises, Bertrand Cayouette

Politiques relatives aux institutions financières et au droit corporatif / Policy Regarding Financial Institutions & Corporations
Sous-ministre adjoint, Richard Boivin
Directeur général, Pierre Rhéaume
Directeur, Encadrement du secteur financier, François Bouchard
Directeur, Développement du secteur financier et des personnes morales, Martin Landry

Commission de la fonction publique / Public Service Commission

800, place D'Youville, 7e étage, Québec, QC G1R 3P4
418-643-1425 Fax: 418-643-7264
800-432-0432
cfp@cfp.gouv.qc.ca
www.cfp.gouv.qc.ca
Présidente, Christiane Barbe

Hydro-Québec

75, boul René-Lévesque ouest, Montréal, QC H2Z 1A4
514-289-2211
www.hydroquebec.com
Président, Conseil d'administration, Michael Louis Turcotte
Président-directeur général, Thierry Vandal
Vice-présidente exécutive, Affaires corporatives & Secrétaire générale, Marie-José Nadeau
Vice-président exécutif, Technologie, Élie Saheb
Président, Hydro-Québec TransÉnergie, André Boulanger
Président, Hydro-Québec Production, Richard Cacchione
Président, Hydro-Québec Équipement & services partagés, Réal Laporte
Président-directeur général, Thierry Vandal

Subsidiaries/Filiales:

Société d'énergie de la Baie-James (SEBJ) / James Bay Energy
888, de Maisonneuve est, 6e étage, Montréal, QC H2L 5B2
514-286-2020
www.hydroquebec.com/sebj
Président-directeur général, Réal Laporte
Directeur, Projets de l'Eastmain, Normand Béchard

Ministère de l' Immigration et des Communautés culturelles / Immigration & Cultural Communities

Édifice Gérald-Godin, 360, rue McGill, Montréal, QC H2Y 2E9
514-864-9191 Fax: 514-864-2899
877-864-9191
www.immigration-quebec.gouv.qc.ca
TTY: 514-864-8158
Other Communication: Téléscripteur: 1-866-227-5968
Acts Administered:
Loi sur l'immigration au Québec/An act respecting immigration to Québec
Loi sur le ministère de l'Immigration et des Communautés culturelles/An act respecting the ministère de l'Immigration et des Communautés culturelles
Ministre, Kathleen Weil
418-644-2128, Fax: 418-528-0829, cabinet@micc.gouv.qc.ca
Sous-ministre, Marie-Claude Champoux
514-873-9450
Directeur, Affaires juridiques, Daniel Morin
514-873-7484
Directrice, Affaires publiques et communications, Hélène Saint-Pierre
514-873-8624, Fax: 514-873-7349
Secrétaire général & Directeur, Vérification interne, Younes Mihoubi
514-873-3464

Agences, Conseils et Commissions Associés/ Associated Agencies, Boards & Commission:

• Conseil des relations interculturelles (CRI)
#10.04, 500, boul René-Lévesque ouest
Montréal, QC H2Z 1W7
514-873-5634 Fax: 514-873-3469
info@conseilinterculturel.gouv.qc.ca
www.conseilinterculturel.gouv.qc.ca

Performance et francisation
Sous-ministre adjoint, Yvan Turcotte
514-873-5942
Directeur, Ressources financières et matérielles, Denis Lazure
514-873-1565

Directeur, Francisation, Jacques Leroux
514-864-3511
Directeur, Systèmes des l'information, François Mongrain
514-873-2396, Fax: 514-873-8180
Directrice, Ressources humaines, Dominique Laniel
514-873-7172

Immigration / Immigration
Sous-ministre adjoint, Robert Baril
514-873-0706, Fax: 514-873-0453
Directeur, Opérations, Éric Gervais
514-873-2446
Directrice, Politiques et programmes d'immigration, Marie-Josée Lemay
514-873-5914
Directeur, Prospection et promotion, Bernard Roy
514-873-5914
Directeur, Immigration économique - International, Owen-John Peate
514-873-2812
Directeur (par intérim), Immigration économique - Québec, Éric Gervais
514-864-1165
Directrice, Immigration familiale & humanitaire, Chantal Drolet
514-864-9305
Directrice, Courrier et encaissement, Michèle Langlois
514-864-9097

Intégration / Integration
Sous-ministre adjointe, Claire Deronzier
514-864-3404
Directeur, Planification, relations interculturelles et intégration, Martine Faille
514-873-6440, Fax: 514-864-4695
Directeur, Mobilité professionnelle et services aux entreprises, François Plourde
514-864-8352
Directrice, Intervention territoriale, Louise Boucher
418-646-1605

Immigration-Québec - Capitale-Nationale/Est-de-Québec
Édifice Bois-Fontaine, 930, ch Sainte-Foy, RC, Québec, QC G1S 2L4
418-643-1435 Fax: 418-646-7460
888-643-1435
direction.quebec@micc.gouv.qc.ca
www.immigration-quebec.gouv.qc.ca
Directeur régionale, Yvon Doyle
418-646-1605

Immigration-Québec - Estrie/Mauricie/Centre-du-Québec
202, rue Wellington nord, Sherbrooke, QC J1H 5C6
819-820-3606 Fax: 819-820-3213
888-879-4288
direction.estrie@micc.gouv.qc.ca
www.immigration-quebec.gouv.qc.ca
Directrice régionale, Chantal Lussier
819-820-3600

Immigration-Québec - Laval, Laurentides et Lanaudière
1438, boul Daniel-Johnson, Laval, QC H7N 4B5
450-687-1220 Fax: 450-687-7327
800-375-7426
direction.drlll@micc.gouv.qc.ca
www.immigration-quebec.gouv.qc.ca
Directeur régional, Serge Tétreault
450-687-9080

Immigration-Québec - Montérégie
2, boul Desaulniers, 3e étage, Saint-Lambert, QC J4P 1L2
450-466-4461 Fax: 450-466-4481
888-287-5819
direction.monteregie@micc.gouv.qc.ca
www.immigration-quebec.gouv.qc.ca
Directeur régional, Guy Gagnon
450-466-4025

Immigration-Québec - Outaouais/Abitibi-Témiscamingue/Nord-du-Québec
#100, 227, rue Montcalm, Gatineau, QC J8Y 3B9
819-246-3212 Fax: 819-246-3314
direction.outaouais@micc.gouv.qc.ca
www.immigration-quebec.gouv.qc.ca
Directrice régionale, Sylvie Proulx
819-246-3212

Ministère de la Justice / Justice

Édifice Louis-Philippe-Pigeon, 1200, rte de l'Église, Québec, QC G1V 4M1
418-643-5140
866-536-5140
informations@justice.gouv.qc.ca
www.justice.gouv.qc.ca

Acts Administered:
Charte des droits et libertés de la personne/Charter of Human Rights & Freedoms (in part)
Code civil du Québec/Civil Code of Québec
Code de la sécurité routière/Highway Safety Code (in part)
Code de procédure civile/Code of Civil Procedure
Code de procédure pénale/Code of Penal Procedure
Code des professions/Professional Code
Code du travail/Labour Code
Convention des Nations Unies sur les contrats de vente internationale de marchandises/An Act respecting the United Nations Convention on Contracts for the International Sale of Goods
Jugements rendus par la Cour suprême du Canada sur la langue des lois et d'autres actes de nature législative/An Act respecting the Judgements rendered in the Supreme Court of Canada on the language of statutes & other instrumentsof a legislative nature
Loi assurant l'application de l'entente sur l'entraide judiciaire entre la France et le Québec/An Act to secure the carrying out of the Entente between France & Québec respecting mutual aid in judicial matters
Loi concernant la loi constitutionnelle de 1982/An Act respecting Constitution Act, 1982
Loi concernant le cadre juridique des technologies de l'information/An Act to establish a Legal framework for information technology
Loi d'interprétation/Interpretation Act
Loi médicale/Medical Act
Loi sur l'acupuncture/An Act respecting Acupuncture
Loi sur l'aide aux victimes d'actes criminels/An Act respecting Assistance for victims of crime
Loi sur l'aide juridique/Legal Aid Act
Loi sur l'exécution réciproque d'ordonnances alimentaires/An Act respecting Reciprocal enforcement of maintenance orders
Loi sur l'indemnisation des victimes d'actes criminels/Crime Victims Compensation Act
Loi sur l'optométrie/Optometry Act
Loi sur la chiropratique/Chiropractic Act
Loi sur la denturologie/Denturologists Act
Loi sur la division territoriale/Territorial Division Act (in part)
Loi sur la justice administrative/An Act respecting Administrative Justice
Loi sur la liberté des cultes/Freedom of Worship Act
Loi sur la pharmacie/Pharmacy Act
Loi sur la podiatrie/Podiatry Act
Loi sur la presse/Press Act
Loi sur la protection de la jeunesse/Youth Protection Act (in part)
Loi sur la protection du consommateur/Consumer Protection Act
Loi sur la réforme du cadastre québécois/An Act to promote the Reform of the cadastre in Québec
Loi sur la Société québécoise d'information juridique/An Act respecting the Société québécoise d'information juridique
Loi sur la transparence et l'éthique en matière de lobbyisme/Lobbying transparency and Ethics Act
Loi sur le barreau/An Act respecting the Barreau
Loi sur le drapeau et les emblèmes du Québec/An Act respecting the Flag and emblems of Québec
Loi sur le ministère de la Justice/An Act respecting the Ministère de la Justice
Loi sur le notariat/Notarial Act
Loi sur le paiement de certaines amendes/An Act respecting the Payment of certain fines
Loi sur le paiement de certains témoins/An Act respecting Payment of certain Crown witnesses
Loi sur le recours collectif/An Act respecting the Class Action
Loi sur le recouvrement de certaines créances/An Act respecting the collection of certain debts
Loi sur le Recueil des lois et des règlements du Québec
Loi sur les agences des voyages/Travel Agents Act
Loi sur les agronomes/Agrologists Act
Loi sur les architectes/Architects Act
Loi sur les arpenteurs-géomètres/Land Surveyors Act
Loi sur les arrangements préalables de services funéraires et de sépulture/An Act respecting Prearranged funeral services and sepultures
Loi sur les aspects civils de l'enlèvement international et interprovincial d'enfants/An Act respecting Civil aspects of international and interprovincial child abduction
Loi sur les audioprothésistes/Hearing-aid Acousticians Act
Loi sur les chimistes professionnels/Professional Chemists Act
Loi sur les commissions d'enquête/An Act respecting Public inquiry commissions
Loi sur les comptables agréés/Chartered Accountants Act
Loi sur les cours municipales/An Act respecting the Municipal courts
Loi sur les dentistes/Dental Act
Loi sur les employés publics/Public Officers Act
Loi sur les huissiers de justice/Court Bailiffs Act
Loi sur les infirmières et infirmiers/Nurses Act
Loi sur les ingénieurs/Engineers Act
Loi sur les ingénieurs forestiers/Forest Engineers Act
Loi sur les journaux et autres publications/Newspaper Declaration Act
Loi sur les jurés/Jurors Act
Loi sur les maisons de désordre/Disorderly Houses Act
Loi sur les médecins vétérinaires/Veterinary Surgeons Act
Loi sur les opticiens d'ordonnance/Dispensing Opticians Act
Loi sur les privilèges des magistrats/Magistrate's Privileges Act
Loi sur les règlements/Regulations Act (in part)
Loi sur les renvois à la Cour d'appel/Court of Appeal Reference Act
Loi sur les sages-femmes/Midwives Act
Loi sur les salaires d'officiers de justice/An Act respecting the Salaries of officers of Justice
Loi sur les shérifs/Sheriffs' Act
Loi sur les sténographes/Stenographers' Act
Loi sur les substituts du procureur général/An Act respecting Attorney General's Prosecutors
Loi sur les technologues en radiologie/Radiology Technologists Act
Loi sur les tribunaux judiciaires/Courts of Justice Act
Loi visant à favoriser le civisme/An Act to promote Good citizenship

Ministre, L'hon. Jean-Marc Fournier
418-643-4210, Fax: 418-646-0027, ministre@justice.gouv.qc.ca
Sous-ministre, Denis Marsolais
418-643-4090
Directrice, Bureau du sous-ministre, Andrée Giguère
418-643-4090
Directeur, Communications, Jean Guay
Directrice, Vérification interne, Francine Asselin
418-643-8372

Agences, Conseils et Commissions Associés/ Associated Agencies, Boards & Commission:

• Commission des services juridiques / Legal Services Commission
Tour de l'Est
#1404, 2, Complexe Desjardins
Montréal, QC H5B 1B3
514-873-3562 Fax: 514-873-8762
info@csj.qc.ca
www.csj.qc.ca/
• Conseil de la justice administrative / Administrative Justice Council
#RC-01, 575, rue Saint-Amable
Québec, QC G1R 2G4
418-644-6279 Fax: 418-528-8471 888-848-2581
courrier@cja.gouv.qc.ca
www.cja.gouv.qc.ca
• Conseil de la magistrature
#5.12, 300, boul Jean-Lesage
Québec, QC G1K 8K6
418-644-2196 Fax: 418-528-1581
information@cm.gouv.qc.ca
www.cm.gouv.qc.ca
• Directeur de l'état civil / Vital Statistics
2535, boul Laurier
Québec, QC G1V 5C5
418-643-3900 Fax: 418-646-3255 800-567-3900
etatcivil@gouv.qc.ca
www.etatcivil.gouv.qc.ca
Other Communication: Montréal: 514/864-3900, Fax: 514/864-4563
• Fonds d'aide aux recours collectifs
#10.30, 1, rue Notre-Dame est
Montréal, QC H2Y 1B6
514-393-2087 Fax: 514-864-2998
farc@justice.gouv.qc.ca
• Office des professions du Québec / Occupations Board
• Société québécoise d'information juridique / Judicial Information Society of Québec
715, carré Victoria, 8e étage
Montréal, QC H2Y 2H7
514-842-8741 Fax: 514-844-8984 800-363-6718
info@soquij.qc.ca
www.soquij.qc.ca
• Tribunal administratif du Québec / Administrative Tribunal of Québec
575, rue Saint-Amable
Québec, QC G1R 5R4
418-643-3418 Fax: 418-643-5335
www.taq.gouv.qc.ca
Other Communication: EMail: tribunal.administratif@taq.gouv.qc.ca

Affaires juridiques et législatives / Judicial & Legislative Affairs
Sous-ministre associée, Dominique Langis
418-643-4228, Fax: 418-644-0420
Directrice générale adjointe, Anne Trotier
418-643-4228
Directrice général adjoint, Affaires économiques et territoriales, France Fradette
Directeur général associé, Affaires contentieuses, Jean-Yves Bernard
Directrice générale associée, Litige et Droit public, Judith Sauvé
Directeur, Réseaux et Affaires gouvernementales, Françios Bélanger

Services à l'organisation / Administrative Services
Sous-ministre associé, Fernand Archambault
418-643-4314
Directeur général associé, Personnel & administration, Gaëtan Tremblay
Directeur général associé, Ressources informationnelles, Michel Lapointe

Services de justice & Registres / Judicial Services & Registries
Sous-ministre associée (par intérim), France Lynch
418-644-7700, Fax: 418-528-9539
Directrice générale associée, Services judiciaires de la Métropole, Marcelle Beaulieu
Directrice générale associée, Services judiciaires de la Capitale-Nationale et des régions, Chantal Couturier
Directrice (par intérim), Soutien aux activités judiciaires, Francine Des Roches
Directeur, Gestion immobilière, Donald Tremblay
Directeur, Centre administratif et judiciaire, Riccardo Binotto
Directrice générale associée, Registres & la certification, Suzanne Potvin Plamondon
Directeur (par intérim), Soutien à la gestion, Patrice Blackburn

Office des professions du Québec / Occupations Board

800, place D'Youville, 10e étage, Québec, QC G1R 5Z3
418-643-6912 Fax: 418-643-0973
800-643-6912
courrier@opq.gouv.qc.ca
www.opq.gouv.qc.ca

Acts Administered:
Code des professions/Professional Code
Loi médicale/Medical Act
Loi sur l'acupuncture/An Act respecting Acupuncture
Loi sur l'optométrie/Optometry Act
Loi sur la chiropratique/Chiropractic Act
Loi sur la denturologie/Denturologists Act
Loi sur la pharmacie/Pharmacy Act
Loi sur la podiatrie/Podiatry Act
Loi sur le Barreau/An Act respecting the Barreau de Québec
Loi sur le notariat/Notarial Act
Loi sur les agronomes/Agrologists Act
Loi sur les architectes/Architects Act
Loi sur les arpenteurs-géomètres/Land Surveyors Act
Loi sur les audioprothésistes/Hearing-aid Acousticians Act
Loi sur les chimistes professionnels/Professional Chemists Act
Loi sur les comptables agrées/Chartered Accountants Act
Loi sur les dentistes/Dental Act
Loi sur les géologues/Geologists Act
Loi sur les infirmières et les infirmiers/Nurses Act
Loi sur les ingénieurs/Engineers Act
Loi sur les ingénieurs forestiers/Forest Engineers Act
Loi sur les médecins vétérinaires/Veterinary Surgeons Act
Loi sur les opticiens d'ordonnances/Dispensing Opticians Act
Loi sur les sages-femmes/Midwives Act
Loi sur les Technologues en imagerie médicale et en radio-oncologie/Act respecting medical imaging technologists & radiation oncology technologists
Président, Jean Paul Dutrisac
418-643-6912
Vice-présidente, Christiane Gagnon
Directeur, Affaires juridiques, Jean-François Paquet
Directrice, Recherche & analyse, Hélène Dubois
Directeur, Services administratifs, Jacques Laflamme

Le Protecteur du Citoyen / Ombudsman

#1.25, 525, boul René-Lévesque est, Québec, QC G1R 5Y4
418-643-2688 Fax: 418-643-8759
800-463-5070
protecteur@protecteurducitoyen.qc.ca
www.protecteurducitoyen.qc.ca
TTY: 866-410-0901
Protectrice du citoyen, Raymonde Saint-Germain
Vice-protecteur, Prévention & innovation, Marc-André Dowd
Directeur, Ressources humaines & l'administration, Marcel Domingue

Registraire des entreprises

787, boul Lebourgneuf, Québec, QC G2J 1C3
418-644-4545 Fax: 418-528-5703
877-644-4545
registre@servicesquebec.gouv.qc.ca
www.registreentreprises.gouv.qc.ca
TTY: 800-361-9596

Acts Administered:
Charte de la Ville de Québec/Charter of Ville de Québec
Code civil du Québec/Civil Code of Québec
Code de procédure civile/Civil Code of Québec
Code du travail/Labour Code
Code municipal du Québec/Municipal Code of Québec
Loi concernant les services de transport par taxi
Loi constituant Capital régional et cooperatif Desjardins
Loi constituant Fondaction, le Fonds de développement de la Confédération des syndicats nationaux pour la coopération et l'emploi
Loi constituant le Fonds de solidarité des travailleurs du Québec
Loi sur la constitution de certaines Églises/Québec Church Incorporation Act
Loi sur la liquidation des compagnies/Winding Up Act
Loi sur la publicité légale des entreprises/An Act respecting the Legal Publicity of enterprises
Loi sur le courtage immobilier
Loi sur le ministère de la Culture et des Communications
Loi sur le registraire des entreprises/An Act respecting the Entreprise registrar
Loi sur les assurances/Québec Act respecting insurance
Loi sur les cités et villes/Cities & Towns Act
Loi sur les clubs de chasse et de pêche/Québec Fish and Game Clubs Act
Loi sur les clubs de récréation/Québec Amusement Clubs Act
Loi sur les compagnies/Québec Companies Act
Loi sur les compagnies de cimetière/Québec Cemetery Companies Act
Loi sur les compagnies de cimetière catholiques romains/Québec Act respecting Roman Catholic cemetery corporations
Loi sur les compagnies de flottage/Québec Timber-Driving Companies Act
Loi sur les compagnies de gaz, d'eau et d'électricité/Québec Gas, Water and Electricity Companies Act
Loi sur les compagnies de télégraphe et de téléphone/Québec Telegraph and Telephone Companies Act
Loi sur les compagnies minières Québec/Québec Mining Companies Act
Loi sur les coopératives/Québec Cooperatives Act
Loi sur les coopératives de services financiers/Québec Act respecting financial services cooperatives
Loi sur les corporations religieuses/Québec Religious Corporations Act
Loi sur les Évêques catholiques romains/Québec Roman Catholic Bishops Act
Loi sur les fabriques/Québec Act respecting fabriques
Loi sur les pouvoirs spéciaux des personnes morales
Loi sur les services de santé et les services sociaux/Québec Act respecting health services & social services
Loi sur les services de santé et les services sociaux pour les autochtones cris/Act respecting health services & social services for Native persons
Loi sur les sociétés agricoles et laitières/Québec Act respecting farmers' and dairymen's associations
Loi sur les sociétés d'horticulture/Québec Horticultural Societies Act
Loi sur les sociétés de fiducie et les sociétés d'épargne/Québec Act respecting trust companies and savings companies
Loi sur les sociétés de transport en commun
Loi sur les sociétés préventives de cruauté envers les animaux/Québec Act respecting societies for the prevention of cruelty to animals
Loi sur les sociétés nationales de bienfaisance/Qué National Benefit Societies Act
Loi sur les syndicats professionnels/Québec Professional Syndicates Act
Ministre responsable, L'hon. Robert Dutil
418-652-6835, Fax: 418-643-7379

Ministère des Relations internationales / International Relations

Édifice Hector-Fabre, 525, boul Réne-Lévesque est, Québec, QC G1R 5R9
418-649-2300 Fax: 418-649-2656
www.mri.gouv.qc.ca

Acts Administered:
Loi sur l'immigration au Québec/An act respecting immigration to Québec
Loi sur le ministère de l'Immigration et des Communautés culturelles/An act respecting the ministère de l'Immigration et des Communautés culturelles
Ministre, L'hon. Monique Gagnon-Tremblay
418-649-2319, Fax: 418-643-4804
Sous-ministre, Marc Croteau
418-649-2335, Fax: 418-649-2667
Directeur, Communications & affaires publiques, Gilles Beaulé
418-649-2333
Directeur, Affaires bilatérales, Robert Keating
418-649-2335
Directrice, Politiques & affaires francophones & multilatérales, Marie-Claude Francoeur
418-649-2400
Directrice (par intérim), Protocole & missions, Marie-Claude Francoeur
418-649-2346, Fax: 418-649-2657
Directeur, Administration, Bernard Dubois
418-649-2666

Administration / Administration
Directeur général, Bernard Dubois
418-649-2666
Directeur, Ressources humaines, Carol Proulx
418-649-2339
Directeur, Ressources financières, Sylvain Berniere
418-649-2316
Directrice, Gestion immobilière, Marie Savard
418-649-2337
Directeur, Ressources informationnelles, David Beardsell
418-649-2326
Directeur, Technologies, Bruno Légaré
418-649-2400

Affaires bilatérales / Bilateral Affairs
Directeur, Robert Keating
418-649-2335

Amériques du Nord / North America
Directeur, Amérique du Nord, Jean Saintonge
418-649-2310

Bureaux à l'étranger/Offices Abroad:
Atlanta, GA, USA
Délégation du Québec à Atlanta, #3240, 191 Peachtree St. NE, Atlanta, GA 30303 USA
404-584-2995 Fax: 404-584-2089
qc.atlanta@mri.gouv.qc.ca
Chef de poste, Ginette Chenard
Boston, MA, USA
One Boston Place, #3850, 201 Washington St., Boston, MA 02108 USA
617-482-1193 Fax: 617-482-1195
qc.boston@mri.gouv.qc.ca
Chef de poste, Jean-Stéphane Bernard
Chicago, IL, USA
Délégation du Québec à Chicago, #3650, 444 N Michigan Ave., Chicago, IL 60611 USA
312-645-0932 Fax: 312-645-0542
qc.chicago@mri.gouv.qc.ca
Chef de poste, Marc T. Boucher
Los Angeles, CA, USA
Délégation du Québec à Los Angeles, #720, 10940 Wilshire Blvd., Los Angeles, CA 90024 USA
310-824-4173 Fax: 310-824-7759
qc.losangeles@mri.gouv.qc.ca
Chef de poste, Alain Houde
Mexico City, Mexico
Délégation générale du Québec, Avenida Taine 411, Colonia Bosques de Chapultepec, Mexico, DF 11580 Mexico
qc.mexico@mri.gouv.qc.ca
Other Communication: Téléphone: 52-55-1100-4330; Fax: 52-55-1100-4331
New York, NY, USA
Délégation générale du Québec, One Rockefeller Plaza, 26the Fl., New York, NY 10020-2102 USA
212-843-0950 Fax: 212-376-8983
qc.newyork@mri.gouv.qc.ca
Chef de poste, John Parisella
Washington, DC, USA
Bureau du Québec à Washington, #450, 805 15th St. NW, Washington, DC 20005 USA
202-659-8990 Fax: 202-659-5654
qc.washington@mri.gouv.qc.ca
Chef de poste (par intérim), Frédéric Bolduc

Asie-Pacifique, Amérique latine et Antilles / Asia-Pacific, Latin America & Antilles
Directeur général, Affaires bilatérales, Robert Keating
Directeur, Asie-Pacifique, Amérique latine et Antilles, Éric Marquis
418-649-2662

Bureaux à l'étranger/Offices Abroad:
Beijing, Chine
Ambassade du Canada, 19, Dongzhimenwai Dajie, Dist. de Chaoyang, Beijing, 100600 China
rene.milot@international.gc.ca
Other Communication: Tél: 86 10 5139 4445 poste 3600; Téléc: 86 10 6532 1304
Chef de poste, René Milot
Hong Kong, Chine
Bureau d'immigration, Exchange Square, Tower 1, 8, Connaught Pl., Central, 10th Fl., Hong Kong
biq.hkong@micc.gouv.qc.ca
Other Communication: Téléphone: 852-2810-7183; Télécopieur: 852 2845 3889
Mumbai, Inde
Bureau du Québec à Mumbai, Fort House, 221, Dr. D.N. Rd., 6e étage, Mumbai, MH 400 001 India
qc.mumbai@mri.gouv.qc.ca
Other Communication: Téléphone: 91-22-6749-4444; Télécopieur: 91-22-6749-4454

Sao Paulo, Brésil
Avenida Engenheiro Luis Carlos Berrini, 1511, CJ 151 e 152, 15e Andar, Sao Paolo, SP 04571-011 Brésil
qc.saopaulo@mri.gouv.qc.ca
Other Communication: Téléphone: 55-11-5505-0444; Télécopieur: 55-11-5505-0445
Chef de poste, Louis Hamann
Santiago, Las Condes, Chili
Antenne du Québec, Torre Norte, #904, Nueva Tajamar 481, Santiago
qc.santiago@mri.gouv.qc.ca
Other Communication: Téléphone: 56-2-350-4255
Séoul, Korea
Antenne du Québec, 5F, Leema Bldg., 146-1, Soosong-dong, Jongno-gu, Séoul, 110-755 Korea
qc.seoul@mri.gouv.qc.ca
Other Communication: Téléphone: 82-2-3703-7700; Télécopieur: 82-2-732-5175
Chef de poste, Chungyoll Yoo
Shanghai, Chine
a/s Consulat général du Canada, Shanghai Centre, #604, West Tower, 1376 Nanjing Xi Rd., Shanghai, 200040 Chine
qc.shanghai@mri.gouv.qc.ca
Other Communication: Téléphone: 86-21-3279-2800, poste 3600; Télécopieur: 86-21-3279-2801
Chef de poste, François Gaudreau
Taipei, Taïwan
Antenne du Québec, Quartier XinYi, 1, rue Song Zhi, 6e étage, Taipei, 11047 Taïwan
qc.taipei@mri.gouv.qc.ca
Other Communication: Téléphone: 886-2-8789-3556; Télécopieur: 886-2-8789-2898
Chef de poste, Michael Chen
Tokyo, Japon
Délégation générale du Québec, Shiroyama JT Trust Tower, 32e étage, 4-3-1 Toranomon, Minato-Ku, Tokyo, 105-6032 Japan
qc.tokyo@mri.gouv.qc.ca
Other Communication: Téléphone: 81-3-5733-4001; Télécopieur: 81-3-5472-6721
Chef de poste, Claude-Yves Charron

Europe, Afrique et Moyen-Orient / Europe, Africa & the Middle East
Directeur général, Affaires bilatérales, Robert Keating
418-649-2335
Directeur, France, Christian Deslauriers
418-649-2329, Fax: 418-649-2654
Directrice, Europe ouest & nord/Institutions européennes, Rita Poulin
418-649-2669, Fax: 418-649-2421
Directrice, Solidarité internationale/Haïti et Afrique subsaharienne, Marjolaine Ricard
418-649-2341
Directeur, Europe méditerranéenne et est/Maghreb et Moyen-Orient, Bernard Denault
418-649-2343

Bureaux à l'étranger/Offices Abroad:
Barcelone, Espagne
Bureau du Québec, Avinguda Diagonal, 420, 3er 1a, Barcelone, 08037 Espagne
qc.barcelone@mri.gouv.qc.ca
Other Communication: Téléphone: 34-93-476-42-5; Télécopieur: 34-93-476-47-74
Berlin, Allemagne
Bureau du Québec, Pariser Platz 6A, Berlin, 10117 Allemagne
qc.berlin@mri.gouv.qc.ca
Other Communication: Téléphone: 49-30-5900646-0; Télécopieur: 49-30-5900646-29
Chef de poste, Serge Vaillancourt
Bruxelles, Belgique
Délégation générale du Québec, 46, av des Arts, 7e étage, Bruxelles, 1000 Belgique
qc.bruxelles@mri.gouv.qc.ca
Other Communication: Téléphone: 32-2-512-00-36; Télécopieur: 32-2-514-26-41
Chef de poste, Christos Sirros
Londres, Angleterre
Délégation générale du Québec, 59 Pall Mall, Londres, SW1Y 5JH Royaume-Uni
qc.londres@mri.gouv.qc.ca
Other Communication: Téléphone: 44-207-766-5900; Télécopieur: 44-207-930-7938
Chef de poste, Pierre Boulanger
Milan, Italie
Antenne économique du Québec, #337, 1 via Manfredo Camperio, 3e étage, Milan, 20123 Italie
qc.milan@mri.gouv.qc.ca
Other Communication: Téléphone: 39-02-8052-210; Télécopieur: 39-02-72016399
Munich, Allemagne
Délégation générale du Québec, Karl-Scharnagl-Ring 6, Munich, 80539 Allemagne
qc.munich@mri.gouv.qc.ca
Other Communication: Téléphone: 49-89-2554931-0; Télécopieur: 49-89-21019473
Chef de poste, Charles Villiers
Paris, France
Délégation générale du Québec, 66, rue Pergolèse, Paris, 75116 France
qc.paris@mri.gouv.qc.ca
Other Communication: Téléphone: 33-1-40-67-85-00; Télécopieur: 33-1-40-67-85-19
Chef de poste, Michel Robitaille
Rome, Italie
Délégation du Québec, #5, 16 via Delle Quattro Fontane, 2e étage, Rome, 00184 Italie
qc.rome@mri.gouv.qc.ca
Other Communication: Téléphone: 39-06-4203-4501, poste 54301; Télécopieur: 39-06-4203-4502
Chef de poste, Amalia Daniela Renosto
Stockholm, Suède
Bureau d'Investissement Québec à Stockholm, Klarabergsgatan 23, 6e étage, CP 16129, Stockholm, 103 23 Suède
Other Communication: Téléphone: 46-8-453-30-37; Télécopieur: 46-8-453-30-16
Vienne, Autriche
Bureau d'immigration du Québec, Ambassade du Canada, Laurenzerberg 2, Vienne, A-1010 Autriche
biq.vienne@micc.gouv.qc.ca
Other Communication: Téléphone: 43-1-53-138-3005; Télécopieur: 43-1-53-138-3443
Chef de poste, Elena Voicu

Politiques et affaires francophones et multilatérales / Policy and Francophone and Multilateral Affairs
Directrice générale, Marie-Claude Francoeur
418-649-2335
Directeur, Planification et politiques, Roger Ménard
418-649-2305
Directeur adjoint, Analyses, Claude Trudelle
418-649-2428
Directeur, Organisations internationales, Daniel Lacroix
418-649-2320, Fax: 418-649-2403
Directeur, Engagements internationaux, Patrice Bachand
418-649-2411
Directrice, Francophonie, Régine Lavoie
418-649-2444
Directeur (par intérim), Ententes de reconnaissance des qualifications professionnelles, Patrice Bachand
418-649-2321

Ministère des Ressources naturelles et de la Faune / Natural Resources & Wildlife

880, ch Sainte-Foy, Québec, QC G1S 4X4
418-627-8600 Fax: 418-644-6513
866-248-6936
services.clientele@mrnf.gouv.qc.ca
www.mrnf.gouv.qc.ca

Acts Administered:
Loi approuvant la convention de la Baie-James et du nord québécois/An Act approving the Agreement concerning James Bay and Northern Québec
Loi approuvant la convention du nord-est québécois/An Act approving the Northeastern Québec Agreement
Loi assurant la mise en oeuvre de l'entente concernant une nouvelle relation entre le gouvernement du Québec et les Cris du Québec/An Act to ensure the implementation of the Agreement Concerning a New Relationship Between theGovernment of Québec and the
Loi concernant les droits sur les mines/Mining Duties Act
Loi de 1994 sur la convention concernant les oiseaux migrateurs
Loi favorisant la réforme du cadastre québécois/An Act to promote the reform of the cadastre in Québec
Loi favorisant le crédit forestier par les institutions privées/An Act to promote forest credit by private institutions
Loi sur les forêts/Forest Act
Loi sur Hydro-Québec/Hydro-Québec Act
Loi sur la conservation et la mise en valeur de la faune/Act respecting the conservation and development of wildlife
Regulation respecting aquaculture and the sale of fish
Lands in the Domain of the State Designated for Development of Wildlife Resources Regulation
Règlement sur les zones d'exploitation contrôlée de chasse et de pêche/Regulation respecting hunting & fishing controlled zones
Règlement sur l'application de dispositions législatives par les agents de protection de la faune/Regulation respecting enforcement of certain legislative & regulatory provisions respecting protection of environment by wildlifeprotection officers
Regulation respecting wildlife habitats
Regulation respecting wildlife sanctuaries
Loi sur la division territoriale/Territorial Division Act
Loi sur la Régie de l'énergie/An Act respecting the Régie de l'énergie
Loi sur la société de développement autochtone de la Baie James/An Act respecting the James Bay Native Development Corporation
Loi sur la société Eeyou de la Baie-James/An Act respecting the James Bay Eeyou Corporation
Loi sur la société nationale de l'amiante/An Act respecting the Société nationale de l'amiante
Loi sur le cadastre/Cadastre Act
Loi sur le crédit forestier/Forestry Credit Act
Loi sur le développement et l'organisation municipale de la région de la Baie-James/James Bay Region Development and Municipal Organization Act
Loi sur le ministère des ressources naturelles et de la faune/An Act respecting the Ministère des Ressources naturelles et de la Faune
Loi sur le mode de paiement des services d'électricité et de gaz dans certains immeubles/An Act respecting the mode of payment for electric and gas service in certain buildings
Loi sur le programme d'aide aux Inuits bénéficiaires de la convention de la Baie-James et du nord québécois pour leurs activités de chasse, de pêche et de piégeage/An Act respecting the support program for Inuit beneficiaries ofthe James Bay and Norther
Loi sur le régime des eaux/Watercourses Act
Règlement sur le domaine hydrique de l'État/Regulation respecting the water property in the domain of the State
Loi sur le régime des terres dans les territoires de la Baie-James et du Nouveau-Québec/An Act respecting the land regime in the James Bay and New Québec territories
Loi sur les arpentages/An Act respecting land survey
Loi sur les bureaux de la publicité des droits/An Act respecting registry offices
Loi sur les clubs de chasse et de pêche/Fish and Game Clubs Act
Loi sur les compagnies de flottage/Timber-Driving Companies Act
Loi sur les droits de chasse et de pêche dans les territoires de la Baie James et du Nouveau-Québec/An Act respecting hunting and fishing rights in the James Bay and New Québec territories
Loi sur les espèces menacées ou vulnérables/An Act respecting threatened or vulnerable species
Loi sur les mesurers de bois/Cullers Act
Loi sur les mines/Mining Act
Loi sur les Pêches
Règlement sur les produits pétroliers/Petroleum Products Regulation
Loi sur les systèmes municipaux et les systèmes privés d'électricité/An Act respecting municipal and private electric power systems
Loi sur les terres du domaine de l'état/An Act respecting the lands in the domain of the State
Loi sur les titres de propriété dans certains districts électoraux/An Act respecting land titles in certain electoral districts
Loi sur l'exportation de l'électricité/An Act respecting the exportation of electric power
Ministre, L'hon. Nathalie Normandeau
418-643-7295, Fax: 418-643-4318
Sous-ministre, Robert Sauvé
418-627-6370, Fax: 418-643-1443
Directeur général, Administration/Connaissance géographique, Ubald Gagné
418-627-6260, Fax: 418-646-2614
Sous-ministre associé, Opérations régionales, Pierre Grenier
418-627-6354, Fax: 418-646-0042

Agences, Conseils et Commissions Associés/ Associated Agencies, Boards & Commission:

• Agence de l'efficacité énergétique / Energy Efficiencies Agency
5700, 4e av ouest
Québec, QC G1H 6R1
418-627-6379 Fax: 418-643-5828 877-727-6655
efficaciteenergetique@mrnf.gouv.qc.ca
www.efficaciteenergetique.mrnf.gouv.qc.ca
Promotes the efficient use of all forms of energy, in all sectors of activity, for the benefit of the people of Québec. The Agency achieves this through demonstration projects, which highlight new technologies, new approaches or new applications that save energy; design, management & evaluation of energy efficient programs; information, training & educational materials; technical & organizational support for export of products & services; review, commentary on proposed amendments to applicable laws & regulations.
• Comité conjoint de chasse, de pêche et de piégeage / Hunting, Fishing & Trapping Joint Committee
#C220, 383 rue Saint-Jacques
Montréal, QC H2Y 1N9
514-284-2151 Fax: 514-284-0039
infohftcc@cccpp-hftcc.com
www.cccpp-hftcc.com

• Fondation de la faune du Québec / Québec Wildlife Foundation
Place Iberville II
#420, 1175, av Lavigerie
Québec, QC G1V 4P1
418-644-7926 Fax: 418-643-7655 877-639-0742
ffq@fondationdelafaune.qc.ca
www.fondationdelafaune.qc.ca
Non-profit organization whose mission is to enhance the value & promote the conservation of wildlife & its habitats.
• Hydro Québec
75, boul René-Lévesque ouest
Montréal, QC H2Z 1A4
514-385-7252 800-790-2424
www.hydroquebec.com
Other Communication: Residential Customer Service: 1-888-385-7252; TTY: 711; Persons with a visual impairment: 1-888-385-7252
• Régie de l'énergie / Energy Regulation Board
Tour de la Bourse
#2.55, 800, Place Victoria
Montréal, QC H4Z 1A2
514-873-2452 Fax: 514-873-2070 888-873-2452
secretariat@regie-energie.qc.ca
www.regie-energie.qc.ca
An economic regulation agency, its mission is to reconcile the public interest, consumer protection, & fair treatment of the electricity carrier & distributors.
• Société de développement de la Baie James (SDBJ) / James Bay Development Society
110, boul Matagami
CP 970
Matagami, QC J0Y 2A0
819-739-4717 Fax: 819-739-4329
mat@sdbj.gouv.qc.ca
www.sdbj.gouv.qc.ca
Developed in 1971, this organization uses its resources & vast knowledge of the territory, contributors, & development projects to promote & maintain activities in the James Bay area, with a perspective of integrated economic development & harmonious cohabitation with territorial residents.

Énergie / Energy
#B401, 5700, 4e av ouest, Québec, QC G1H 6R1
418-627-6377 Fax: 418-643-0701
Le gouvernement québécois prévoit le lancement des projets hydoélectriques représentant 4,500 MW, qui susciteront des investissements de l'ordre de 25m de dollars, et la création d'environ 70,000 emplois sur six ans. Il mise sur le développement du potentiel existant d'énergie éolienne, avec l'objectif de 4,000 MW d'ici 2015, et prend plusieurs moyens afin de renforcer la sécurité des approvisionnements en pétrole et gaz naturel
Sous-ministre associé, Mario Gosselin
Directrice générale, Électricité, Julie Grignon
418-627-6386
Directeur général, Hydrocarbures et Bioarburants, Alain Lefebvre
418-627-6385
Directeur (par intérim), Efficacité et innovation énergétiques, Mario Gosselin

Faune Québec / Wildlife Québec
RC-120, 880, ch Sainte-Foy, Québec, QC G1S 4X4
418-627-8652

Foncier Québec
5700, 4e av ouest, Québec, QC G1H 6R1
418-643-3582 Fax: 418-528-8721
866-226-0977
assistance.clientele@mrnf.registrefoncier.gouv.qc.ca
Sous-ministre associée, Louise Ouellet
418-627-6252, Fax: 418-643-3954
Directeur général, Arpentage et cadastre, Julien Arsenault
418-627-6267, Fax: 418-646-7405
Directrice générale, Registre Foncier, Marie-Claude Rioux
418-627-6264

Forêt Québec / Québec Forests
880, ch Ste-Foy, #RC 120, Québec, QC G1S 4X4
418-627-8652 Fax: 418-528-1278
foretquebec@mrnf.gouv.qc.ca
Sous-ministre associé, Richard Savard
Sous-ministre associé/Forestier en chef, Gérard Szaraz
Directrice générale, Connaissance et gestion de l'information forestière, Elisabeth Bossert
Directeur général, Attribution des bois et développement industriel, Pierre Marineau
Directeur (par intérim), Aménagement durable des forêts, Mario Gibeault
Directeur, Recherche forestière, Robert Jobidon
Directeur, Gestion de l'information forestière, Denis Robitaille
Directeur, Développement de l'industrie et des produits forestiers, André Denis
Directeur, Gestion des stocks ligneux, Réal Paris

Sous-ministre associé & Forestier en chef / Chief Forester
845, boul Saint-Joseph, Roberval, QC G8H 2L4
418-275-7770 Fax: 418-275-8884
bureau@forestierenchef.gouv.qc.ca
www.forestierenchef.gouv.qc.ca
Forestier en chef, Gérard Szaraz

Mines
Centre de service des Mines, 1685, boul Wilfrid Hamel ouest, 1er étage, Québec, QC G1N 3Y7
418-627-6278 Fax: 418-644-8960
800-363-7233
service.mines@mrnf.gouv.qc.ca
Sous-ministre associé, Mines, Jean-Sylvain Lebel
418-627-8652
Directeur général, Géologie Québec, Robert Marquis
819-354-4514
Directeur général, Développement de l'industrie minérale, Pierre Verpaelst
418-627-6292
Directrice générale, Gestion du milieu minier, Lucie Ste-Croix
418-627-6292

Territoire / Lands
#A313, 5700, 4e av ouest, Québec, QC G1H 6R1
418-627-6256 Fax: 418-528-2075
Le Ministère favorise une utilisation du territoire qui rejoint les préoccupations économiques, sociales & environnementales des Québécois
Sous-ministre associé (par intérim), Plan Nord et Territoire, Robert Sauvé
418-627-6370
Directeur général, Affaires stratégiques et territoire, André Auclair
418-627-6256
Directrice, Coordination du Plan Nord, Andrée Bélanger
418-627-6368
Directeur, Environnement et Coordination, Marcel Grenier
418-627-6256
Directeur, Affaires autochtones, François Dupuis
418-627-6254
Directeur, Politiques et Intégité du territoire, Mario Perron
418-627-6362

Bureaux de la protection de la faune/Regional Wildlife Proection Offices:

Abitibi-Témiscamingue
70, av Québec, Rouyn-Noranda, QC J9X 6R1
819-763-3388 Fax: 819-763-3186

Bas-Saint-Laurent
#207, 92, 2e rue ouest, Rimouski, QC G5L 8B3
418-727-3710 Fax: 418-727-3735

Capitale-Nationale-Chaudière-Appalaches
8400, av Sous-le-Vent, Charny, QC G6X 3S9
418-832-7222 Fax: 418-832-1827

Mauricie-Centre-du-Québec
#207, 100 rue Laviolette, Trois-Rivières, QC G9A 5S9
819-371-6151 Fax: 819-371-6978
866-821-4625

Côte-Nord
456, av Arnaud, 1er étage, Sept-îles, QC G4R 3B1
418-964-8300 Fax: 418-964-8506
cote-nord@mrnf.gouv.qc.ca

Estrie-Montréal-Montérégie
770, rue Goretti, Sherbrooke, QC J1E 3H4
819-820-3883 Fax: 819-820-3747

Gaspésie-Iles-de-la-Madeleine
124, 1re Avenue ouest, Sainte-Anne-des-Monts, QC G4V 1C5
418-763-3302 Fax: 418-764-2378

Laval-Lanaudière-Laurentides
#1.50B, 999, rue Nobel, Saint-Jérôme, QC J7Z 7A3
450-569-3113 Fax: 450-469-7568

Nord-du-Québec
1121, boul Industriel, CP 159, Lebel-sur-Quévillon, QC J0Y 1X0
819-755-4838 Fax: 819-755-3541
nord-du-quebec@mrnf.gouv.qc.ca

Outaouais
#RC 100, 16, impasse de la Gare-Talon, Gatineau, QC J8T 0B1
819-246-4827 Fax: 819-246-5049
outaouais@mrnf.gouv.qc.ca

Saguenay-Lac-Saint-Jean
3950, boul Harvey, 4e étage, Jonquière, QC G7X 8L6
418-695-8125 Fax: 418-695-8436
saguenay-lac-saint-jean@mrnf.gouv.qc.ca

Opérations régionales/Regional Operations:

Abitibi-Témiscamingue
70, av Québec, Rouyn-Noranda, QC J9X 6R1
819-763-3388 Fax: 819-763-3216
abitibi-temiscamingue@mrnf.gouv.qc.ca
Directeur général, Martin Gingras

Bas-Saint-Laurent
#207, 92, 2e Rue ouest, Rimouski, QC G5L 8B3
418-727-3710 Fax: 418-727-3735
bas-saint-laurent@mrnf.gouv.qc.ca
Directeur général (par intérim), Alain Lachapelle

Capitale-Nationale-Chaudières-Appalaches
#1.14, 1685, boul Wilfrid Hamel ouest, Québec, QC G1N 3Y7
418-643-4680 Fax: 418-644-8960
capitale-nationale@mrnf.gouv.qc.ca
Other Communication: chaudiere-appalaches@mrnf.gouv.qc.ca
Directrice générale, Line Drouin

Côte-Nord
#RC 702, 625, boul Laflèche, Baie-Comeau, QC G5C 1C5
418-295-4676 Fax: 418-295-4682
cote-nord.@mrnf.gouv.qc.ca
Directeur général, Normand Laprise

Gaspésie-Iles-de-la-Madeleine
195, boul Perron est, Caplan, QC G0C 1H0
418-388-2125 Fax: 418-388-2444
gaspesie-iles-de-la-madeleine@mrnf.gouv.qc.ca
Directeur général, Bernard Landry

Mauricie-Centre-du-Québec
#207, 100, rue Laviolette, Trois-Rivières, QC G9A 5S9
418-371-6151 Fax: 418-371-6978
866-821-4625
mauricie@mrnf.gouv.qc.ca
Other Communication: centreduquebec@mrnf.gouv.qc.ca
Directeur général, Alain Simard

Estrie-Montréal-Montérégie et Laval-Lanaudière-Laurentides
545, boul Crémazie est, 8e étage, Montréal, QC H2M 2V1
514-873-2140 Fax: 514-873-8983
estrie@mrnf.gouv.qc.ca
Other Communication: montreal@mrnf.gouv.qc.ca; monteregie@mrnf.gouv.qc.ca; laval@mrnf.gouv.qc.ca; lanaudiere@mrnf.gouv.qc.ca; laurentides@mrnf.gouv.qc.ca
Directeur général, André B. Lemay

Nord-du-Québec
1121, boul Industriel, CP 159, Lebel-sur-Quévillon, QC J0Y 1X0
819-755-4838 Fax: 819-755-3541
nord-du-quebec@mrnf.gouv.qc.ca
Directeur général, Guy Hétu

Outaouais
#RC 100, 16, impasse de la Gare-Talon, Gatineau, QC J8T 0B1
819-246-4827 Fax: 819-246-5049
outaouais@mrnf.gouv.qc.ca
Directeur général, Jean Benoît

Saguenay-Lac-Saint-Jean
3950, boul Harvey, 3e étage, Jonquière, QC G7X 8L6
418-695-8125 Fax: 418-695-8133
saguenay-lac-saint-jean@mrnf.gouv.qc.ca
Directeur général, Alain Thibeault

Revenu Québec / Revenue Québec

Direction des relations publiques/Communications, 3800, rue de Marly, Québec, QC G1X 4A5
418-652-6831 Fax: 418-646-0167
www.revenu.gouv.qc.ca

Acts Administered:
Loi concernant l'application de la Loi sur les impôts/Act respecting the application of the Taxation Act
Loi concernant l'impôt sur le tabac/Tobacco Tax Act
Loi concernant la taxe sur les carburants/Fuel Tax Act
Loi favorisant le développement et la reconnaissance des compétences de la main d'oeuvre/Act to promote workforce skills development and recognition (in part)
Loi facilitant le paiement des pensions alimentaires/Act to facilitate the payment of support
Loi sur la fiscalité municipale/Act respecting municipal taxation (in part)
Loi sur la Régie de l'assurance maladie du Québec (partiellement)/Act respecting the Régie de l'assurance-maladie du Québec (in part)
Loi sur la Société d'habitation du Québec (partiellement)/Act respecting the Société d'habitation du Québec (in part)
Loi sur la taxe d'accise (partiellement)/Excise Tax Act (in part)
Loi sur la taxe de vente du Québec/Act respecting the Québec Sales Tax
Loi sur le ministère du Revenu/Act respecting the Ministère du Revenu
Loi sur le Régime de rentes du Québec (partiellement)/Act respecting the Québec Pension Plan (in part)

Loi sur le remboursement d'impôts fonciers/Act respecting real estate tax refund
Loi sur l'aide aux personnes et aux familles (partiellement)/Individual and Family Assistance Act (in part)
Loi sur les centres financiers internationaux (partiellement)/Act respecting international financial centres (in part)
Loi sur les impôts/Taxation Act
Loi sur les licences/Licenses Act
Loi sur les normes du travail (partiellement)/Act respecting labour standards (in part)
Ministre, L'hon. Raymond Bachand
514-482-0199, Fax: 514-482-9985, cabinet@mrq.gouv.qc.ca
Président-directeur général, Jean St-Gelais
418-652-6833, Fax: 418-577-5030

Bureau de président-directeur général / Office of the President/Director General
Président-directeur général, Jean St-Gelais
418-652-6833, Fax: 418-577-5030
Directeur du Bureau & Secrétaire général, Sin-Bel Khuong
418-652-6834
Directeur, Registre des entreprises, Yves Bannon
Directrice, Traitement des plaintes, Diane Lelièvre
418-652-6159, Fax: 418-652-4036
Directeur, Vérification interne, enquêtes et évaluation, Pierre Gagné
418-652-6808, Fax: 418-652-4913
Directrice, Relations publiques et Communications, Michelle Rompré

Centre de perception fiscale et des biens non réclamés / Tax Collection
3800, rue de Marly, Secteur 6-4-3, Québec, QC G1X 4A5
Le rôle du Centre est de recouvrer les créances de la clientèle de Revenu Québec
Vice-président & Directeur général, Centre de perception fiscale et biens non réclamés, Françios T. Tremblay
418-577-0011, Fax: 418-646-8269
Directeur régional, Capitale-Nationale et autres régions, Marcel Turgeon
418-577-0313, Fax: 418-646-7057
Directrice régionale, Montérégie, Claire Garceau
450-466-6210, Fax: 450-928-8606
Directeur régional, Montréal, Lucien Larrivée
514-415-5012, Fax: 514-285-3820
Directeur régional, Outaouais, Alain Gamache
819-779-7321, Fax: 819-779-6085
Directeur régional, Laval-Laurentides-Lanaudière, Jacques Hébert
450-967-6466, Fax: 450-967-4761
Directeur, Services administratifs et techniques, Richard Demers
418-577-0033, Fax: 418-646-8269

Législation & enquêtes / Legislation & Investigations
3800, rue de Marly, Secteur 5-1-9, Québec, QC G1X 4A5
418-652-6844 Fax: 418-643-9381
Vice-président & Directeur général, Législation, enquêtes & Registraire des entreprises, André Legault
418-652-6844, Fax: 418-643-9381
Directeur (par intérim), Lois sur les impôts, Gaétan Lépine
418-652-6836, Fax: 418-643-2699
Directrice, Accès à l'information et protection des renseignements confidentiels, Danielle Corriveau
418-652-5772, Fax: 418-577-5233
Directrice, Services administratifs & informatiques, Ginette St-Laurent
418-652-6840, Fax: 418-652-6237
Directeur, Oppositions de Québec, Denis Morin
418-652-6268, Fax: 418-643-5025
Directrice, Oppositions de Montréal, Louise Haspect
514-287-8322, Fax: 514-873-9253
Directeur, Enquêtes, Pierre Bouchard
418-652-5195, Fax: 418-528-2049
Chef, Enquêtes et inspections de Québec, Guy Perrault
Directrice, Inspection & enquêtes informatiques, Luc Boulanger
514-287-4146, Fax: 514-285-5388
Directeur, Enquêtes et projets spéciaux, Daniel Caumartin
514-287-4146, Fax: 514-864-3669

Planification, administration et recherche / Planning, Administration & Research
3800, rue de Marly, Secteur 3-4-4, Québec, QC G1X 4A5
Vice-président & Directeur général, Daniel Prud'homme
418-652-4152, Fax: 418-528-6882
Directeur, Services administratifs et gestion des renseignements, Alain Gagnon
418-652-4764, Fax: 418-528-6882
Directrice, Ressources matérielles et immobilières, Renée Delisle
418-652-5549, Fax: 418-643-1347
Directeur, Planification stratégique & gestion des revenus, Éric Maranda
418-652-4839, Fax: 418-577-5015
Directrice, Planification et de la reddition de comptes, Valérie Dran
Directeur, Recherche et Innovation, Gilles Bernard
514-287-6707, Fax: 514-873-0758
Directrice, Études économiques, fiscales et statistiques, Sylvie Thomas
418-652-4556, Fax: 418-652-5730
Directeur, Bureau de la lutte contre l'évasion fiscale, Sami Jabbour
514-287-6707, Fax: 514-873-0758
Directrice générale, Ressources humaines, Line Paulin
418-652-5348, Fax: 418-646-1827
Directeur, Paie et avantages sociaux, Claude Hogue
418-652-4222, Fax: 418-652-0240
Directrice, Santé et mieux-être au travail, Danielle Rheault
418-652-6433, Fax: 418-646-9546

Traitement et des Technologies / Data Processing & Technologies
3800, rue de Marly, Secteur 6-2-9, Québec, QC G1X 4A5
Sous-ministre adjoint & directeur général, Jean-Marie Lévesque
418-652-4959, Fax: 418-577-5041
Directeur, Solutions informatiques pour les entreprises, Marco Beaulieu
418-652-5425, Fax: 418-577-5223
Directeur, Traitement massif, Hajib Amachi
Directeur, Solutions informatiques pour les particuliers, Denis Légaré
418-652-6738, Fax: 418-646-3461
Directeur, Solutions informatiques de perception & Administration, Daniel Forest

Particuliers / Individuals Directorate
Vice-président & Directrice générale, Particuliers, Hajib Amachi
418-652-6807, Fax: 418-652-5049
Directrice, Services à la clientèle des particuliers, Mary-Andrée Jobin
418-689-1400, Fax: 418-689-1420
Directeur régional, Services à la clientèle des particuliers - Centre et Sud du Québec, Normand Bilodeau
819-694-4811, Fax: 819-577-5069
Directrice régionale, Services à la clientèle des particuliers - Montréal, Michelle Page-Melançon
514-215-3719, Fax: 514-215-3575
Directeur régional (par intérim), Services à la clientèle des particuliers - Nord et Ouest du Québec, France Richard
819-779-6035, Fax: 819-772-3377
Directeur régional, Contrôle fiscal des particuliers - Capitale-Nationale et autres régions, Michel Lepage
418-725-6900, Fax: 418-727-3922
Directeur, Comptabilisation et non-production des déclarations de particuliers, Magdi Abdel-Malak
418-652-4726, Fax: 418-577-5047
Directrice, Cotisation des particuliers, Céline Goyette
418-652-5126, Fax: 418-646-1649
Directeur, Pensions alimentaires, Michel Stewart
418-652-6704, Fax: 418-646-8270

Registre des Entreprises / Businesses Directorate
Vice-président & Directeur général, André Legault
Directeur, Soutien opérationnel et Développement des compétences, Danny Pagé
514-287-2020, Fax: 514-864-7242
Directeur régional, Vérification des entreprises de Montréal, Pierre Leclerc
514-287-4187, Fax: 514-285-3875
Directrice régionale, Vérification des entreprises - Nord et Ouest du Québec, Camelia Attya
514-215-3600, Fax: 514-215-3670, Other Communications: Nord et Ouest: 450-972-2356, Fax: 450-972-2354
Directeur, Cotisation des entreprises, Gilbert Caccia
514-287-8126, Fax: 514-285-5374
Directrice régionale, Vérification des entreprises - Capitale-Nationale, Sud et Est du Québec, Sylvie Bégin
418-652-6811, Fax: 418-643-5050
Directeur principal, Services à la clientèle des entreprises, Denis Gendron
514-287-8055, Fax: 514-864-4364
Directeur, Bureau de Toronto, Jocelyn Hamel
416-977-6713, Fax: 416-977-9748

Ministère de la Santé et des Services sociaux / Health & Social Services

Direction des communications, 1075, ch Sainte-Foy, 16e étage, Québec, QC G1S 2M1
418-643-9395 Fax: 418-643-4768
regisseur.web@msss.gouv.qc.ca
www.msss.gouv.qc.ca

Acts Administered:
Loi assurant l'exercice des droits des personnes handicapées/An Act to secure the handicapped in the exercise of their rights
Loi assurant la mise en oeuvre de la Convention sur la protection des enfants et la coopération en matière d'adoption internationale et modifiant diverses dispositions législatives en matière d'adoption/An Act to implement theConvention on Protection of
Loi assurant le maintien des services essentiels dans le secteur de la santé et des services sociaux/An Act to ensure that essential services are maintained in the health and social services sector
Loi concernant les unités de négociation dans le secteur des affaires sociales/An Act respecting bargaining units in the social affairs sector
Loi sur Héma-Québec et sur le Comité d'hémovigilance/An Act respecting Héma-Québec and the haemovigilance committee
Loi sur l'administration publique/Public Administration Act
Loi sur l'assurance-hospitalisation/Hospital Insurance Act
Loi sur l'assurance-maladie/Health Insurance Act
Loi sur l'assurance-médicaments/An Act respecting prescription drug insurance
Loi sur l'équilibre budgétaire du réseau public de la santé et des services sociaux/An Act to provide for balanced budgets in the public health and social services network
Loi sur l'Institut national de Santé publique du Québec/An Act respecting the Institut national de Santé publique du Québec
Loi sur la protection de la jeunesse/Youth Protection Act
Loi sur la protection de la santé publique/Public Health Protection Act
Loi sur la protection des personnes dont l'état mental présente un danger pour elles-mêmes ou pour autrui/An Act respecting the protection of persons whose mental state presents a danger to themselves or to others
Loi sur la Régie de l'assurance-maladie du Québec/An Act respecting the Régie de l'assurance-maladie du Québec
Loi sur la santé publique/Public Health Act
Loi sur le Commissaire à la santé et au bien-être/An Act respecting the Health and Welfare Commissioner
Loi sur le Conseil médical du Québec/An Act respecting the Conseil médical du Québec
Loi sur le ministère de la Santé et des Services Sociaux/An Act respecting the Ministède la Santé des Services sociaux
Loi sur le Protecteur des usagers en matière de santé et de services sociaux/An Act respecting the Health and Social Services Ombudsman
Loi sur le tabac/Tobacco Act
Loi sur les activités cliniques et de recherche en matière de procréation assistée
Loi sur les agences de développement de réseaux locaux de services de santé et de services sociaux/An Act respecting local health and social services network development agencies
Loi sur les cimetières non-Catholiques/Non-Catholic Cemeteries Act
Loi sur les inhumations et les exhumations/Burial Act
Loi sur les laboratoires médicaux, la conservation des organes, des tissus, des gamètes et des embryons, les services ambulanciers et la disposition des cadavres/An Act respecting medical laboratories, organ, tissue, gamete andembryo conservation, and t
Loi sur les sages-femmes/Midwives Act
Loi sur les services de santé et les services sociaux/An Act respecting health services and social services
Loi sur les services de santé et les services sociaux pour les autochtones cris/An Act respecting health services and social services for Cree Native persons
Ministre, L'hon. Dr Yves Bolduc
418-266-7171, Fax: 418-266-7197, ministre@msss.gouv.qc.ca
Ministre déléguée, Services sociaux, L'hon. Dominique Vien
418-266-7181, Fax: 418-266-7199, Ministre.deleguee@msss.gouv.qc.ca
Sous-ministre, Jacques Cotton
418-266-8989, Fax: 418-266-8990
Sous-ministre adjoint, Planification, performance & qualité, Denis Lalumière
418-266-5990
Sous-ministre adjoint, Santé publique, Alain Poirier
418-266-6700
Sous-ministre adjoint, Services sociaux, Sylvain Gagnon
418-266-6800
Sous-ministre adjointe, Personnel réseau et ministériel, Édith Lapointe
418-266-8400
Sous-ministre associé, Coordination, financement, immobilisations et budget, Michel Fontaine
418-266-8850
Sous-ministre associée, Technologies de l'information, Lise Verreault
418-266-8770
Sous-ministre adjoint, Services de santé et médecine universitaire, Jean Rodrigue
418-266-6930

Agences, Conseils et Commissions Associés/ Associated Agencies, Boards & Commission:

• Agence d'évaluation des technologies et des modes d'intervention en santé (AETMIS) / Technology Assessment & Health Solutions Agency
#10.083, 2021, av Union
Montréal, QC H3A 2S9
514-873-2563 Fax: 514-873-1369
www.aetmis.gouv.qc.ca
• Bureau des projets Centres hospitaliers universitaires de Montréal, CHUM, CUSM et CHU Sainte-Justine / Project Office for the Modernization of Montréal's University Health Centres CHUM, MUHC and Sainte-Justine UHC
#10.049, 2021, rue Union
Montréal, QC H3A 2S9
514-864-9883 Fax: 514-873-7362
info.construction3chu@msss.gouv.qc.ca
www.construction3chu.msss.gouv.qc.ca
• Secrétariat à l'accès aux services en langue anglaise et aux communautés ethnoculturelles / English Language & Ethnocultural Communities Services Secretariat
#1.03, 201 boul Crémazie est, 1er étage
Montréal, QC H2M 1L2
514-873-5163 Fax: 514-873-9876
www.msss.gouv.qc.ca/ministere/saslacc
• Conseil du médicament / Medication Council
#100, 1195, av Lavigerie, 1er étage
Québec, QC G1V 4N3
418-644-8103 Fax: 418-644-8120
cdm@cdm.gouv.qc.ca
www.cdm.gouv.qc.ca
• Commissaire à la santé et du bien-être / Health & Welfare Commission
#700, 1020, rte de l'Église
Québec, QC G1V 3V9
418-643-3040 Fax: 418-644-0654
csbe@csbe.gouv.qc.ca
www.csbe.gouv.qc.ca
• Corporation d'hébergement du Québec / Long Term Care Facilities Corporation of Québec
2535, boul Laurier, 5e étage
Québec, QC G1V 4M3
418-644-3600 Fax: 418-644-3609
clientele.sante@siq.gouv.qc.ca
www.chq.gouv.qc.ca
• Institut national de santé publique du Québec / National Public Health Institute of Québec
945, av Wolfe
Québec, QC G1V 5B3
418-650-5115 Fax: 418-646-9328
info@inspq.qc.ca
www.inspq.qc.ca
Other Communication: Poste: 5336
• Office des personnes handicapées du Québec / Office for Handicapped Persons
309, rue Brock
Drummondville, QC J2B 1C5
Fax: 819-475-8753 800-567-1465 TTY: 800-567-1477
michael.magner@ophq.gouv.qc.ca
www.ophq.gouv.qc.ca
• Urgences-santé Québec / Emergency Health Services Québec
3232, rue Bélanger
Montréal, QC H1Y 3H5
514-723-5600
info@urgences-sante.qc.ca
www.urgences-sante.qc.ca
• Régie de l'assurance maladie du Québec / Québec Health Insurance Board
1125, Grande Allée ouest
Québec, QC G1S 1E7
418-646-4636
www.ramq.gouv.qc.ca

Planification, performance et qualité / Planning, Performance and Quality
Sous-ministre adjoint, Denis Lalumière
418-266-5990
Directrice, Qualité, Sylvie Bernier
418-266-7505
Directrice, Évaluation, Monique Savoie
418-266-7030
Directrice, Affaires intergouvernementales & coopération internationale, Patricia Caris
418-266-8740
Directrice, Études et des analyses, Harold Côté
418-266-7025
Directrice, Planification et orientations stratégiques, Andrée Quenneville, 2010-09-13
418-266-7088
Directrice, Recherche, innovation et transfert des connaissances, Manon St-Pierre
418-266-7056

Services de santé et médecine universitaire / Health Services & Academic Medicine
Sous-ministre adjoint, Services de santé et médecine universitaire, Jean Rodrigue
418-266-6930
Directrice, Main d'oeuvre médicale, Isabelle Savard
418-266-6975
Directeur (par intérim), Organisation des services médicaux et technologiques, Yves Jalbert
418-266-6946
Directrice, Services médicaux généraux, Jeannine Auger
418-266-5827
Directeur, Affaires universitaires, Louis R. Dufresne
418-266-7500
Directrice, Organisation des services de première ligne intégrés, Yolaine Galarneau
418-266-6976
Directeur, Santé mentale, André Delorme
418-266-6835
Directeur nationale, Urgences, services de traumatologie & services préhospitaliers d'urgence, Daniel Lefrançois
418-266-5811
Directeur, Biovigilance, Yves Jalbert
418-266-6946
Sous-ministre adjoint, Sylvain Gagnon, 2010-09-13
418-266-6800
Directrice, Secrétariat à l'adoption internationale, Luce de Bellefeuille, 2010-09-13
514-873-4747
Directeur, Personnes âgées en perte d'autonomie, Christian Gagné, 2010-09-13
418-266-6818
Directrice, Personnes handicapées/Programme dépendances, Rachel Ruest, 2010-09-13
418-266-6852
Directeur, Services sociaux généraux/Activités communautaires, Mario Frechette, 2010-09-13
418-266-6936
Directrice (par intérim), Jeunes et des familles, Natalie Rosebush, 2010-09-13
418-226-6840

Technologies de l'information / Information Technology
Sous-ministre associée, Technologies de l'information, Lise Verrault
418-266-8770
Directeur général adjoint, Projets, Éric Lefebvre
418-266-8770
Directeur, Relations d'affaires avec les clientèles, Clermont Saucier
418-266-6935
Directeur (par intérim), Relations avec les partenaires et les mandataires, Clermont Saucier
418-266-6935
Directrice, Sécurité des technologies de l'information, Sonia Roy
418-266-6935
Directeur, Service financiers & administratif, Philippe Moss
418-266-7118
Directeur, Soutien ministériel & infrastructures communes, Michel Rochette
418-266-2287

Santé publique / Public Health
Sous-ministre adjoint, Alain Poirier
418-266-6700, Fax: 418-266-6707
Directrice, Planification, évaluation et développement en santé publique, Lyne Jobin
418-266-6780
Directeur, Développement des individus et de l'environnement social, André Dontigny
418-266-6714
Directrice, Prévention des maladies chroniques et des traumatismes, Marie Rochette
418-266-6750
Directeur, Protection de la santé publique, Horacio Arruda
418-266-6720
Directrice (par intérim), Surveillance de l'état de santé, Lyne Jobin
418-266-6780

Commission de la santé et de la sécurité du travail du Québec (CSST) / Québec Occupational Health & Safety Commission

524, rue Bourdages, CP 1200 Terminus postal, Québec, QC G1K 7E2
418-266-4850 Fax: 418-266-4669
866-302-2778
www.csst.qc.ca
A pour mission de soutenir aux travailleurs & aux employeurs dans leurs démarches pour éliminer les dangers présents dans leur milieu de travail, inspecter des lieux de travail, & promouvoir la santé & sécurité du travail
Président & Chef de la direction, Luc Meunier
Vice-présidente, Partenariat et l'expertise-conseil, Claude Sicard
Vice-présidente, Administration, communications & relations publiques, Carole Théberge
Vice-président, Finances, André Beauchemin
Vice-président, Opérations, Paul Marceau

Ministère de la Sécurité publique / Ministry of Public Security

Tour des Laurentides, 2525, boul Laurier, 5e étage, Québec, QC G1V 2L2
418-643-2112 Fax: 418-646-6168
866-644-6826
www.securitepublique.gouv.qc.ca
A pour mission d'assurer la sécurité publique au Québec
Acts Administered:
Loi sur la police/Police Act
Loi sur la propriété des bicyclettes/Bicycle Ownership Act
Loi sur la recherche des causes et des circonstances des décès/An Act respecting the determination of the causes & circumstances of death
Loi sur la sécurité civile/Civil Protection Act
Loi sur la sécurité dans les sports/An Act respecting safety in sports
Loi sur la sécurité incendie/Fire Safety Act
Loi sur la Société des alcools du Québec/An Act respecting the Société des alcools du Québec (partially administered by MSP)
Loi sur la Société des loteries du Québec/An Act respecting the Société des loteries du Québec (partially administered by the MSP)
Loi sur le ministère de la Sécurité publique/An Act respecting the Ministère de la Sécurité publique
Loi sur le régime syndical applicable à la Sûreté du Québec/An Act respecting the Syndical Plan of the Sûreté du Québec
Loi sur le système correctionnel du Québec/An Act respecting the Québec correctional system
Loi sur les agences d'investigation ou de sécurité/An Act respecting detectives or security agencies
Loi sur les bombes lacrymogènes/Act respecting tear bombs
Loi sur les coffrets de sûreté/Safe-Deposit Boxes Act
Loi sur les courses/An Act respecting racing
Loi sur les explosifs/An Act respecting explosives
Loi sur les infractions en matière de boissons alcooliques/An Act respecting offences relating to Alcoholic Beverages
Loi sur les loteries, les concours publicitaires et les appareils d'amusement/An Act respecting lotteries, publicity, contests & amusement machines
Loi sur les permis d'alcool/An Act respecting liquor permits
Loi sur les services correctionnels/An Act respecting correctional services
Loi sur les villages nordiques et l'Administration régionale Kativik/An Act respecting Northern Villages & the Kativik Regional Government (partially administered by the MSP)
Ministre, L'hon. Robert Dutil
418-643-2112, Fax: 418-646-6168, ministre@msp.gouv.qc.ca
Note: www.securitepublique.gouv.qc.ca
Sous-ministre, Robert Lafrenière
418-643-3500, Fax: 418-643-0275
Directrice de cabinet, Isabelle Lessard
418-643-2112, Fax: 418-646-6168
Directeur, Vérification interne, enquêtes & inspection, Sylvain Ayotte
418-644-6777

Agences, Conseils et Commissions Associés/ Associated Agencies, Boards & Commission:
• Bureau du coroner / Office of the Coroner
Édifice le Delta 2
#390, 2875, boul Laurier
Québec, QC G1V 5B1
418-643-1845 Fax: 418-643-6174 866-312-7051
clientele.coroner@msp.gouv.qc.ca
www.coroner.gouv.qc.ca
• Comité de déontologie policière / Police Ethics Committee
Tour du Saint-Laurent
#A-200, 2525, boul Laurier, 2e étage
Québec, QC G1V 4Z6
418-646-1936 Fax: 418-528-0987
comite.deontologie@msp.gouv.qc.ca
www.deontologie-policiere.gouv.qc.ca
• Commissaire à la déontologie policière / Police Ethics Commissioner
#1-40, 1200, rte de l'Église
Québec, QC G1V 4Y9
418-643-7897 Fax: 418-528-9473 877-237-7897
deontologie-policiere.quebec@msp.gouv.qc.ca
www.deontologie-policiere.gouv.qc.ca

• Commissariat des incendies / Fire Commissioner
455, rue Dupont
Québec, QC G1K 6N2
418-529-5706 Fax: 418-529-9922
cdelage@notarius.net
www.securitepublique.gouv.qc.ca/securite-incendie.html
• Commission québecoise des libérations conditionnelles / Parole Board
#1.32A, 300, boul Jean-Lesage
Québec, QC G1K 8K6
418-646-8300 Fax: 418-643-7217
cqlc@msp.gouv.qc.ca
www.cqlc.gouv.qc.ca
• Direction générale de la Sûreté du Québec / Provincial Police
1701, rue Parthenais
Montréal, QC H2K 3S7
514-598-4141 Fax: 514-598-4242
www.surete.qc.ca
• École nationale de police du Québec / National Police School of Québec
350, rue Marguerite-d'Youville
Nicolet, QC J3T 1X4
819-293-8631 Fax: 819-293-8630
courriel@enpq.qc.ca
www.enpq.qc.ca
• École nationale des pompiers du Québec / Québec National Fire Fighters School
#3.08, 2800, boul Saint-Martin ouest
Laval, QC H7T 2S9
450-680-6800 Fax: 450-680-6818 866-680-3677
www.enpq.gouv.qc.ca
• Régie des alcools, des courses et des jeux / Liquor, Gaming & Racing Board
560, boul Charest est
Québec, QC G1K 3J3
418-643-7667 Fax: 418-643-5971 800-363-0320
www.racj.gouv.qc.ca

Affaires policières / Police Services
418-643-3500 Fax: 418-643-0275
Sous-ministre associé & directeur général, Martin Prud'homme
Directrice générale adjointe, Sylvie Tousignant
418-646-6777, Fax: 418-644-0132

Sécurité civile et Sécurité incendie / Public Safety & Fire Services
Sous-ministre associé & directeur général, Guy Laroche
418-643-3500, Fax: 418-643-0275
Directeur, Opérations, Éric Houde
418-646-6777, Fax: 418-646-5426
Directrice, Mobilisation, Hélène Chagnon
418-646-6777, Fax: 418-646-5427
Directeur, Gestion des risques, Martin Simard
418-643-3821, Fax: 418-644-4547
Directeur, Rétablissement, Denis Landry, 2008-09-19
418-646-6638, Fax: 418-646-6628

Directions régionales/Regional Offices:
Bas-Saint-Laurent, Gaspésie et Iles-de-la-Madeleine
#60, 70, rue Saint-Germain est, Rimouski, QC G5L 7J9
418-727-3589 Fax: 418-727-3643
securite.civile01@msp.gouv.qc.ca
Directrice, Guylaine Rousseau
Capitale-Nationale, Chaudière Appalaches et Nunavik
#200, 1122, Grande-Allée ouest, Québec, QC G1S 1E5
418-643-3244 Fax: 418-644-2080
securite.civile03@msp.gouv.qc.ca
Directrice, France-Sylvie Loisel
Estrie et Montérégie
165, rue Jacques-Cartier nord, Saint-Jean-sur-Richelieu, QC J3B 6S9
450-346-3200 Fax: 450-346-5856
securite.civile16@msp.gouv.qc.ca
Directeur, Yvan Leroux
Mauricie et Centre-du-Québec
4000, rue Louis-Pinard, Trois-Rivières, QC G8Y 4L9
819-371-6703 Fax: 819-371-6983
securite.civile04@msp.gouv.qc.ca
Directeur, Jacques Raymond
Montréal, Laval, Lanaudière et Laurentides
RC #23, 5100, rue Sherbrooke est, Montréal, QC H1V 3R9
514-873-1300 Fax: 514-864-8654
securite.civile06@msp.gouv.qc.ca
Other Communication: securite.civile13@msp.gouv.qc.ca; securite.civile14@msp.gouv.qc.ca; securite.civile15@msp.gouv.qc.ca
Directeur (par intérim), Éric Doneys
Outaouais, Abitibi-Témiscamingue et Nord-du-Québec
817, boul St-René ouest, Gatineau, QC J8T 8M3
819-772-3737 Fax: 819-772-3954
securite.civile07@msp.gouv.qc.ca
Directeur, Jacques Viger
Saguenay-Lac-Saint-Jean et Côte-Nord
RC #01, 3950, boul Harvey, Saguenay, QC G7X 8L6
418-695-7872 Fax: 418-695-7875
securite.civile02@msp.gouv.qc.ca

Directeur, Réal Delisle

Services correctionnels / Correctional Services
Sous-ministre associé/Directeur général, Gilles Martin
Directrice générale adjointe, Programmes et sécurité, Johanne Beausoleil
418-644-7887, Fax: 418-644-5645
Directeur, Administration, Robert Beaulieu
418-646-6777, Fax: 418-643-3426
Directrice, Recherche, Johanne Lévesque
418-646-6767, Fax: 418-646-6228
Directrice, Conseil à l'organisation, Marlène Langlois
418-646-6777, Fax: 418-644-5645

Directions régionales/Regional Offices:
Abitibi-Témiscamingue, Nord-du-Québec
851, 3e Rue est, Amos, QC J9T 2T4
819-444-5222 Fax: 819-444-5298
Directrice, Sylvie Messier
Bas-Saint-Laurent
200, rue des Négociants, Rimouski, QC G5M 1B6
418-727-3534 Fax: 418-727-3799
Directeur, Michel Levasseur
Côte-Nord
73, av Mance, Baie-Comeau, QC G4Z 1N1
418-294-8646 Fax: 418-294-8853
866-640-3026
Directrice (par intérim), Josée Morissette
Estrie
1055, rue Talbot, Sherbrooke, QC J1G 2P3
819-820-3100 Fax: 819-820-3964
Directrice, Kathleen Carroll
Gaspésie-Iles-de-la-Madeleine
#206, 484, Hôtel-de-Ville, Chandler, QC G0C 1K0
418-689-4947 Fax: 418-689-2478
Directrice, Suzanne Bourget
suzanne.bourget@msp.gouv.qc.ca
Mauricie-Centre-du-Québec
7 600, boul Parent, Trois-Rivières, QC G9A 5E1
819-372-1311 Fax: 819-371-6979
866-292-6281
Directeur (par intérim), Christian Thibeault
Montérégie
75, boul Poliquin, Sorel-Tracy, QC J3P 7Z5
450-742-0471 Fax: 450-742-8399
Directrice, Céline Jacques
Montréal
#11.87, 10, rue Saint-Antoine est, Montréal, QC H2Y 1A2
514-864-1800 Fax: 514-873-9362
Directeur, Pierre Couture
Outaouais
75, rue Saint-François, Gatineau, QC J9A 1B4
819-772-3065 Fax: 819-772-3076
866-466-7603
Directeur, Denis Germain
Saguenay-Lac-Saint-Jean
237, rue Price est, Saguenay, QC G7H 2E5
418-698-3841 Fax: 418-690-8560
Directrice, Josée Desjardins

Sûreté du Québec / Québec Provincial Police
Directeur général, Richard Deschesnes
514-598-4488

Ministère des Services gouvernementaux / Government Services

875, Grande Allée est, 4e étage - Secteur 500, Québec, QC G1R 5R8
418-643-1529 Fax: 418-643-9226
communication@sct.gouv.qc.ca
www.msg.gouv.qc.ca

A pour mission de faire progresser la modernisation de l'État, simplifier l'accès aux services gouvernementaux, regrouper des services pour l'Administration, et développer le gouvernement en ligne

Acts Administered:
Loi concernant le cadre juridique des technologies de l'information
Loi sur la Société immobilière du Québec
Loi sur le Centre de services partagés du Québec
Loi sur le fonds du service aérien gouvernemental
Loi sur le ministère des Services gouvernementaux
Loi sur le Service des achats du gouvernement
Loi sur Services Québec

Ministre, L'hon. Michelle Courchesne
418-643-5926, Fax: 418-643-7824, cabinet@sct.gouv.qc.ca
Secréraire, sous-ministre & dirigeant principal de l'information, Denys Jean
Directeur, Cabinet, Jean-Pascal Bernier
Directeur général, Service aérien gouvernemental, Lucien Tremblay
Directeur, Communications, Francine Tremblay

Agences, Conseils et Commissions Associés/ Associated Agencies, Boards & Commission:

• Services Québec
800, place D'Youville, 20e étage
Québec, QC G1R 3P4
418-646-4011 877-644-4545 TTY: 800-361-9596
www.gouv.qc.ca/portail/quebec/pgs/citoyens
Other Communication: Montréal: 514-644-4545
Services Québec est un guichet multiservices chargé d'offrir des services intégrés aux citoyens et aux entreprises
• Société immobilière du Québec (SIQ) / Québec Buildings Corp.
1075, rue de l'Amérique-Française, 1er étage
Québec, QC G1R 5P8
418-646-1766 Fax: 418-646-6911 877-747-9911
courrier@siq.gouv.qc.ca
www.siq.gouv.qc.ca
La Société immobilière du Québec (SIQ) a pour mission de mettre à la disposition des ministères et organismes publics des immeubles et de leur fournir des services de construction, d'exploitation et de gestion immobilière

Centre de services partagés / Shared Services Centre
875, Grande Allée est, 4e étag, Secteur 4.550, Québec, QC G1R 5W5
418-643-6080 Fax: 418-528-2733
renseignements@cspq.gouv.qc.ca
www.cspq.gouv.qc.ca
Président-directeur général, Claude Blouin
Vice-président, Ressources humaines, François Bérubé
Vice-président, Projets majeurs, Gordon Smith
Vice-président, Technologies de l'information, Michel Gauthier
Vice-président, Ressources matérielles et moyens de communication, Daniel Gilbert
Directrice générale, Information gouvernementale, Céline Roy
Directeur général, Solutions d'affaires en gestion intégrée des ressources, Denis Gagnon
Directeur général, Acquisitions, Lison Dubé
Directeur général, Services aux utilisateurs & opérations, Claude Morin
Directeur général (par intérim), Réseaux de télécommunications, Gordon Smith
Responsable, Services en région, Magali Demay
Responsable, Services de rémunération, Mylène Martel

Société immobilière du Québec
1075, rue de l'Amérique-Française, 1er étage, Québec, QC G1R 5P8
418-646-1766 Fax: 418-646-6911
courrier@siq.gouv.qc.ca
www.siq.gouv.qc.ca
A pour mission à loger les ministères & organismes publics au meilleur rapport qualité & prix. Créée en 1984, la SIQ a remplacé le Ministère des Travaux publics et de l'Approvisionnement
Président & Chef de la direction, Richard Verreault
Vice-président, Exploitation, Claude Dubé
Vice-président, Expertise et Gestion de projets-Clientèle ministères et organismes, Daniel Primeau

Services Québec

Bureau de la qualité, 800, place D'Youville, 20e étage, Québec, QC G1R 3P4
418-644-4545
877-644-4545
www.gouv.qc.ca/portail/quebec/servicesquebec/
TTY: 800-361-9596
Other Communication: Montréal: 514-644-4545
Présidente-Directrice, Guylaine Rioux
418-528-9328
Vice-présidente, Services à la clientèle, Guylaine Rioux
418-528-9328
Directrice, Affaires organisationnelles, Réjeanne Lachance
Directeur général, Services à l'organisation et communications, Yves Pepin
Directeur, État civil, Reno Bernier
Directrice, Services juridiques, Manon Godin

Les Publications du Québec
#500, 1000 rte de l'Église, Québec, QC G1V 3V9
418-643-5150 Fax: 418-643-6177
800-463-2100
publicationsduquebec@cspq.gouv.qc.ca
www.publicationsduquebec.gouv.qc.ca

Directions régionales/Regional Offices:
Abitibi-Témiscamingue-Nord-du-Québec
RC #01, 255, av Principale, Rouyn-Noranda, QC J9X 7G9
418-643-0599
Bas-Saint-Laurent
#195B, av Léonidas sud, Rimouski, QC G5L 1S7
418-727-3950
Capitale-Nationale
787, boul Lebourneuf, Québec, QC G2J 1C3
418-643-0599

Chaudière-Appalaches
44, rte du Président-Kennedy, Lévis, QC G6V 6C5
418-643-0599

Côte-Nord
280, av Arnaud, Sept-Iles, QC G4R 3A7
418-295-4047

Estrie
RC #02, 200, rue Belvédère nord, Sherbrooke, QC J1H 4A9
418-820-3164

Gaspésie-Iles-de-la-Madeleine
39-5, montée Sandy Beach, Gaspé, QC G4X 2W4
418-360-8086

Lanaudière
RC #20, 450, rue Saint-Louis, Joliette, QC J6E 2Y8
514-873-9670

Laurentides
Galeries des Laurentides, #1503C, 500, boul des Laurentides, Saint-Jérôme, QC J7Z 4M2
514-873-9670

Laval
1796, boul des Laurentides, Laval, QC H7M 2P6
514-873-9670

Mauricie
3225, boul Saint-Jean, Trois-Rivières, QC G9B 2M1
450-928-8798

Montérégie
#105, 174, boul Sainte-Foy, Longueuil, QC J4J 1W7
450-928-8798

Montréal
RC #10, 2050, rue De Bleury, Montréal, QC H3A 2J5
514-873-9670

Outaouais
RC #120, 170, rue de l'Hôtel-de-Ville, Gatineau, QC J8X 4C2
514-873-9670

Centre-du-Québec
RC #16, 270, rue Lindsay, Drummondville, QC J2B 1G3
450-928-8798

Saguenay-Lac-Saint-Jean
2655, boul du Royaume, Jonquière, QC G7S 4S9
418-695-8140

Ministère du Tourisme / Tourism Québec

#400, 900, boul René-Lévesque est, Québec, QC G1R 2B5
418-643-5959 Fax: 418-646-8723
800-482-2433
www.tourisme.gouv.qc.ca

Acts Administered:
Loi sur l'aide au développement touristique
Loi sur le ministère du Tourisme
Loi sur l'Institut de tourisme et d'hôtellerie du Québec
Loi sur les établissements d'hébergement touristique

Ministre, L'hon. Nicole Ménard
418-528-8063, Fax: 418-528-8066
Sous-ministre, Suzanne Giguère
418-643-9141, Fax: 418-643-2268
Directrice générale, Administrations, Clémence Verret
Directeur général, Développement, François Diguer
Sous-ministre adjoint, Marketing & clientèles touristiques, Georges Vacher

Agences, Conseils et Commissions Associés/ Associated Agencies, Boards & Commission:

• Palais des congrès de Montréal
159, rue Saint-Antoine ouest, 9é étage
Montréal, QC H2Z 1H2
514-871-8122 Fax: 514-871-9389 800-268-8122
info@congresmtl.com
congresmtl.com
• Société du Centre des congrès de Québec / Québec City Convention Centre
1000, boul René-Lévesque est
Québec, QC G1R 5T8
418-644-4000 Fax: 418-644-6455 888-679-4000
www.convention.qc.ca

Administration / Administration
Directrice générale, Clémence Verret
Directrice, Ressources humaines, Valérie Lévesque
Directeur, Ressources financières & matérielles, Sylvain Bergeron
Directeur, Ressources informationelles, Denis Archambault

Développement / Development
Directeur général, Développement, François Diguer
Directeur, Partenariat et intervention régionale, François Côté
Directeur, Croisières internationales, François Belzile
Directrice, Stratégies & développement des entreprises touristiques, Geneviève LeBlanc

Marketing et clientèles touristiques / Marketing & Tourism Consumers
Sous-ministre adjoint, Georges Vacher
514-864-1016, Fax: 514-864-6152
Directrice générale, Marketing, Sylvie Quenneville
Directeur général, Services à la clientèle touristique, Sylvain Lacombe
Directrice, Centre d'affaires électroniques, Michèle Morel
Directrice, Renseignements par téléphone et Internet, Nicole Desrochers

Ministère des Transports (MTQ) / Transportation

700, boul René-Lévesque est, 28e étage, Québec, QC G1R 5H1
418-643-6980 Fax: 418-643-2033
888-355-0511
communications@mtq.gouv.qc.ca
www.mtq.gouv.qc.ca
Other Communication: Au Québec: 5-1-1

Acts Administered:
Code de la sécurité routière/Highway Safety Code
Loi concernant la Compagnie de gestion de Matane inc./Act respecting the Compagnie de gestion de Matane Inc.
Loi concernant les partenariats en matière d'infrastructures de transport/Act respecting transport infrastructure partnerships
Loi concernant les propriétaires et exploitants de véhicules lourds/Act respecting owners and operators of heavy vehicles
Loi concernant les services de transport par taxi/Act respecting transportation services by taxi
Loi interdisant l'affichage publicitaire le long de certaines voies de circulation/Act to prohibit commercial advertising along certain thoroughfares
Loi sur l'Agence métropolitaine de transport/Act respecting the Agence métropolitaine de transport
Loi sur l'assurance automobile/Automobile Insurance Act
Loi sur l'expropriation/Expropriation Act
Loi sur la publicité au long des routes/Roadside Advertising Act
Loi sur la sécurité du transport terrestre guidé/Act to ensure safety in guided land transportation
Loi sur la Société de l'assurance automobile du Québec/Act respecting the Société de l'assurance automobile du Québec
Loi sur la Société des traversiers du Québec/Act respecting the Société des Traversiers du Québec
Loi sur la Société du port ferroviaire de Baie-Comeau-Hauterive/Act respecting the Société du port ferroviaire de Baie-Comeau-Hauterive
Loi sur la voirie/Act respecting roads
Loi sur le Ministère des Transports/Act respecting the Ministère des Transports
Loi sur les chemins de fer/Railway Act
Loi sur les conseils intermunicipaux de transport dans la région de Montréal/Act respecting intermunicipal boards of transport in the area of Montreal
Loi sur les sociétés de transport en commun/Act respecting public transit authorities
Loi sur les transports/Transport Act
Loi sur les transports instituant la Commission des transports du Québec/Transport Act established by the Commission des transports du Québec
Loi sur les véhicules hors route/Act respecting off-highway vehicles

Ministre, L'hon. Sam Hamad
418-643-6980, Fax: 418-643-2033
Ministre délégué, Norman MacMillan
418-643-6980, Fax: 418-643-2033
Sous-ministre, Michel Boivin
418-643-6740, Fax: 418-643-9836
Directeur général, Sous-ministre associé, Montréal & de l'Ouest, Jacques Filion
514-873-0234
Directeur général, Sous-ministre adjoint, Québec & de l'Est, André Caron
418-528-0808
Directrice générale, Sous-ministre Adjointe, Infrastructures & Technologies, Anne-Marie Leclerc
418-528-0808
Directrice générale, Services à la gestion, Josée Dupont
418-528-0808
Directeur général, Sous-minster adjoint, Politiques & sécurité en transport, André Meloche
418-528-0808

Agences, Conseils et Commissions Associés/ Associated Agencies, Boards & Commission:

• Commission des transports du Québec / Québec Transport Commission
200, ch Sainte-Foy, 7e étage
Québec, QC G1R 5V5
Fax: 418-644-8034 888-461-2433
courrier@ctq.gouv.qc.ca
www.ctq.gouv.qc.ca
• Société de l'assurance automobile du Québec
333, boul Jean-Lesage
CP 19600 Terminus
Québec, QC G1K 8J6
418-643-7620 Fax: 418-644-0339 800-361-7620 TTY: 800-565-7763
courrier@saaq.gouv.qc.ca
www.saaq.gouv.qc.ca
• Société du port ferroviaire Baie-Comeau-Hauterive / Baie-Comeau-Hauterive Railway Station
18, rte Maritime
Baie-Comeau, QC G4Z 2L6
418-296-6785 Fax: 418-296-2377
societeduport@globetrotter.net
www.sopor.ca
• Société des traversiers du Québec / Ferries Québec
250, rue Saint-Paul
Québec, QC G1K 9K9
418-643-2019 Fax: 418-643-7308 877-787-7483
stq@traversiers.gouv.qc.ca
www.traversiers.gouv.qc.ca

Infrastructures et technologies / Infrastructure & Technologies
Directrice générale, Sous-ministre adjointe, Anne-Marie Leclerc
418-528-0808
Directeur, Laboratoire des chaussées, Guy Tremblay
418-643-6618
Directeur, Structures, Daniel Bouchard
418-643-6906
Directeur, Soutien aux opérations, Éric Breton
418-643-9298
Directeur, Environnement et recherche, Christian Therrien
418-643-8326
Directeur, Parcs routiers, Claude Marquis
418-646-8301

Montréal et de l'Ouest / Montreal & the West
Directeur, Planification & coordination des ressources, Pierre Fernandez Galvan
514-864-1730

Directions régionales/Regional Offices:
Abitibi-Témiscamingue-Nord-du-Québec
80, av Québec, Rouyn-Noranda, QC J9X 6R1
819-763-3271 Fax: 819-763-3493
dat@mtq.gouv.qc.ca
Directeur régional, Yves Coutu
819-763-9237

Est-de-la-Montérégie
201, place Charles-Lemoyne, 5e étage, Longueuil, QC J4K 2T5
450-677-3413 Fax: 450-442-1317
dtem@mtq.gouv.qc.ca
Directrice régionale, Sylvie Laroche
450-677-8974

Estrie
#2.02, 200, rue Belvédère nord, Sherbrooke, QC J1H 4A9
819-820-3280 Fax: 819-820-3118
dte@mtq.gouv.qc.ca
Directeur régional, Louis Ferland
819-820-3280

Île-de-Montréal
500, boul René-Lévesque ouest, 12e étage, CP 5, Montréal, QC H2Z 1W7
514-873-7781 Fax: 514-864-3867
dtim@mtq.gouv.qc.ca
Directeur régional, Maroun Shaneen
514-873-7781

Laurentides-Lanaudière
222, rue Saint-Georges, 2e étage, Saint-Jérôme, QC J7Z 4Z9
450-569-3057 Fax: 450-569-3072
dll@mtq.gouv.qc.ca
Directeur régional (par intérim), Luc Cossette
450-569-3057

Laval-Mille-Îles
1725, boul Le Corbusier, Laval, QC H7S 2K7
450-680-6330 Fax: 450-973-4959
dtlmi@mtq.gouv.qc.ca
Directeur régional (par intérim), Fadi Moubayed
450-680-6333

Ouest-de-la-Montérégie
#200, 180, boul d'Anjou, Châteauguay, QC J6K 1C4
450-698-3400 Fax: 450-698-3452
dtom@mtq.gouv.qc.ca
Directrice régional, Joceline Béland
450-698-3400

Outaouais
#5.110, 170, rue de l'Hôtel-de-Ville, Gatineau, QC J8X 4C2
819-772-3849 Fax: 819-772-3338
dto@mtq.gouv.qc.ca
Directeur général (par intérim), Jacques Henry
819-772-3107

Politiques et sécurité en transport / Transportation Policy & Security
Directeur général, Sous-ministre adjoint, André Meloche
418-528-0808
Directeur, Transport routier des marchandises, Benoît Cayouette
418-528-0631
Directeur, Sécurité en transport, Claude Morin
418-643-1564
Directrice, Transport terrestre des personnes, France Dompierre
418-644-0324
Directrice (par intérim), Transport maritime, aérien et ferroviaire, Josée Hallé
418-643-1864

Québec et de l'Est / Québec & the East
Directrice (par intérim), Coordination, planification & ressources, Nathalie Gosselin
418-643-7726

Directions régionales/Regional Offices:
Bas-Saint-Laurent-Gaspésie-Iles-de-la-Madeleine
#101, 92, 2e rue ouest, Rimouski, QC G5L 8E6
418-727-3674 Fax: 418-727-3673
dtbgi@mtq.gouv.qc.ca
Directeur régional, Mario Bergeron
418-727-4131
Chaudière-Appalaches
1156, boul de la Rive-Sud, Saint-Romuald, QC G6W 5M6
418-839-5581 Fax: 418-834-7338
dtca@mtq.gouv.qc.ca
Directeur régional, Richard Charpentier
418-839-5581
Côte-Nord
#110, 625, boul Laflèche, Baie-Comeau, QC G5C 1C5
418-295-4765 Fax: 418-295-4766
cotenord@mtq.gouv.qc.ca
Directeur régional, Michel Bérubé
418-295-4778
Mauricie-Centre-du-Québec
100, rue Laviolette, 4e étage, Trois-Rivières, QC G9A 5S9
819-371-6896 Fax: 819-371-6136
dmcq@mtq.gouv.qc.ca
Directeur régional, Richard Dionne
819-371-6896
Capitale-Nationale
475, boul de l'Atrium, 2e étage, Québec, QC G1H 7H9
418-643-1911 Fax: 418-646-0003
dcnat@mtq.gouv.qc.ca
Directeur régional, Jean-François Saulnier
418-380-2003
Saguenay-Lac-Saint-Jean-Chibougamau
3950, boul Harvey, Jonquière, QC G7X 8L6
418-695-7916 Fax: 418-695-7926
dt.slsjc@mtq.gouv.qc.ca
Directeur régional, Donald Turgeon
418-695-7916

Services à la gestion / Administrative Services
Directrice (par intérim), Josée Dupont
418-528-0808
Directrice, Ressources humaines, Andrée Blanchet
418-646-4157
Directrice, Ressources financières, Danièle Cantin
418-646-9934
Directeur, Contrats et ressources matérielles, Marcel Carpentier
418-643-5473
Directrice, Technologies de l'information, Odile Béland
418-643-4431

Ministère du Travail / Labour

200, ch Sainte-Foy, 5e étage, Québec, QC G1R 5S1
418-644-4545 Fax: 418-528-0559
800-643-4817
www.travail.gouv.qc.ca

Acts Administered:
Code du travail/Labour Code
Loi assurant l'exercice des droits des personnes handicapées/Act to secure the handicapped in the exercise of their rights
Loi sur le ministère du Travail/Act respecting the Ministère du travail
Loi sur le régime de négociation des conventions collectives dans les secteurs public et parapublic/Act respecting the process of negotiating of the collective agreements in the public & parapublic sectors
Loi sur les décrets de convention collective/Act respecting Collective Agreement Decrees
Loi sur les relations du travail, la formation professionnelle et la gestion de la main-d'ouvre dans l'industrie de la construction/Act Respecting Labour Relations, Vocational Training, and Manpower Management in the ConstructionIndustry
Loi sur les syndicats professionnels/Professional Syndicates Act
Acts administered by Labour Agencies
Commission de l'équité salariale
Loi sur l'équité salariale/Pay Equity Act
Commission de la construction du Québec
Loi sur les relations du travail, la formation professionnelle et la gestion de la main-d'ouvre dans l'industrie de la construction/Act respecting labour relations vocational training & manpower management in the constructionindustry
Commission de la santé et de la sécurité du travail
Loi sur les accidents du travail et les maladies professionnelles/Act respecting accidents at work & professional illness or sickness
Loi sur l'indemnisation des victimes d'amiantose ou de silicose dans les mines et les carrières/Act respecting compensation - victims of asbestos or silicosis in mines & quarries
Loi sur la santé et la sécurité du travail/Occupational Health & Safety Act
Commission des lésions professionelles
Commission des normes du travail
Loi sur la fête nationale/National Holiday Act
Loi sur les normes du travail/Act respecting Labour Standards
Conseil consultatif du travail et de la main-d'oeuvre
Loi sur le bâtiment /Building Act
Loi sur le Conseil consultatif du travail et de la main-d'ouvre/Act respecting the Conseil consultatif du travail et de la main d'oeuvre
Loi sur les appareils sous pression/Act respecting pressure vessels
Régie du bâtiment du Québec
Loi sur l'économie de l'énergie dans le bâtiment/Act respecting the conservation of energy in buildings
Loi sur la distribution du gaz/Gas distribution Act
Loi sur la sécurité dans les édifices publics/Public Buildings Safety Act
Loi sur les mécaniciens de machines fixes/Master Pipe Mechanics Act
Ministre, L'hon. Lise Thériault
418-643-5297, Fax: 418-644-0003, ministre@travail.gouv.qc.ca
Sous-ministre, Jocelin Dumas
418-643-2902, Fax: 418-643-0735
Directeur, Communications, Gervais Fortier
418-646-2642
Directrice, Cabinet du ministre, Louise Bédard
418-643-5297

Agences, Conseils et Commissions Associés/ Associated Agencies, Boards & Commission:

• Commission de la construction du Québec / Québec Construction Commission
3530, rue Jean-Talon ouest
Montréal, QC H3R 2G3
514-341-7740 Fax: 514-341-6354 888-842-8282
www.ccq.org
• Commission de l'équité salariale / Pay Equity Commission
200, ch Ste-Foy, 4e étage
Québec, QC G1R 6A1
418-528-8765 Fax: 418-528-6999 888-528-8765
equite.salariale@ces.gouv.qc.ca
www.ces.gouv.qc.ca
• Commission des lésions professionnelles / Work-Related Injuries Commission
#700, 900, Place d'Youville
Québec, QC G1R 3P7
418-644-7777 Fax: 418-644-6443 800-463-1591
www.clp.gouv.qc.ca
Administrative tribunal that is the last recourse for employers or workers who contest a decision made by the Commission de la sant, et de la s,curit, du travail.
• Commission des normes du travail / Labour Standards Commission
Hall Est
400, boul Jean-Lesage, 7e étage
Québec, QC G1K 8W1
418-644-0817 Fax: 418-643-5132 800-563-9058
www.cnt.gouv.qc.ca
• Commission des relations du travail / Labour Relations Commission
900, boul René-Lévesque est, 5e étage
Québec, QC G1R 6C9
418-643-3208 Fax: 418-643-8946 866-864-3646
crtm@crt.gouv.qc.ca
www.crt.gouv.qc.ca
• Commission de la santé et de la sécurité du travail (CSST) / Occupational Health & Safety Commission
425, rue du Pont
CP 4900 Terminus
Québec, QC G1K 7S6
418-266-4000 Fax: 418-266-4015 888-999-2778
www.csst.qc.ca
Other Communication: Ile-de-Montréal: 514-906-3000; Address: Tour Sud, 1, complexe Desjardins, 31e étage, CP 3, Succursale Place-Desjardins, Montréal, QC, H5B 1H1
• Conseil consultatif du travail et de la main d'oeuvre / Advisory Council on Labour & Manpower
#9.400, 500, boul René-Lévesque ouest
Montréal, QC H2Z 1W7
514-873-2880 Fax: 514-873-1129
cctm@cctm.gouv.qc.ca
www.cctm.gouv.qc.ca
• Conseil des services essentiels du Québec / Essential Services Council
#9.100, 500, boul René-Lévesque ouest, 9e étage
CP 38
Montréal, QC H2Z 1W7
514-873-7246 Fax: 514-873-3839 800-337-7246
info@cses.gouv.qc.ca
www.cses.gouv.qc.ca
• Régie du bâtiment du Québec / Québec Construction Companies Board
545, boul Crémazie est, 4e étage
Montréal, QC H2M 2V2
514-873-0976 Fax: 514-864-2903 800-361-0761
crc@rbq.gouv.qc.ca
www.rbq.gouv.qc.ca

Politiques et recherche / Policy & Research
Sous-ministre adjoint, Normand Pelletier
Directeur, Politiques du travail, Steeve Audet
Directeur, Information sur le travail, Gilles Fleury
Directeur, Recherche et innovation en milieu de travail, Dalil Maschino

Relations du travail / Labour Relations
Sous-ministre adjointe, Suzanne Thérien
Directeur générale, Daniel Cholette
Directeur, Médiation-conciliation & prévention (Montréal), Julien Perron
Directeur, Médiation-conciliation, prévention & arbitrage (Québec), Jean Poirier
Directeur, Bureau d'évaluation médicale, Dr André Perron

Secrétariat du Conseil du trésor / Treasury Board

875, Grande Allée est, 5e étage, secteur 500, Québec, QC G1R 5R8
418-643-1529 Fax: 418-643-9226
866-552-5158
communication@sct.gouv.qc.ca
www.tresor.gouv.qc.ca
Ministre responsable de l'Administration gouvernementale & Présidente du Conseil du trésor, L'hon. Michelle Courchesne
418-643-5926, Fax: 418-643-7824, cabinet@sct.gouv.qc.ca
Secrétaire, Marc Lacroix
418-643-1977, Fax: 418-643-6494, communication@sct.gouv.qc.ca
Directrice-générale, Vérification interne, l'accès à l'information & la gestion documentaire, Hélène Caouette
418-646-6833, Fax: 418-528-6271
Greffière adjointe, Guylaine Bérubé
418-528-6108, Fax: 418-643-4877
Directrice, Affaires juridiques, Josée De Bellefeuille
418-528-6666
Directeur général (par intérim), Administration, Yvan Bouchard
418-644-2541
Directrice, Communications, Francine Tremblay
418-644-9067

Agences, Conseils et Commissions Associés/ Associated Agencies, Boards & Commission:

• Infrastructure Québec / Infrastructure
#408, 1050, boul René-Lévesque est
Québec, QC G1R 4X3
418-646-6097 Fax: 418-528-7155
communications@infra.gouv.qc.ca
www.infra.gouv.qc.ca
• Commission administrative des régimes de retraite et d'assurances (Québec) / Retirement & Insurance Planning Commission
475, rue Saint-Amable
Québec, QC G1R 5X3
418-643-4881 Fax: 418-644-3839 800-463-5533
www.carra.gouv.qc.ca
• Commission de la fonction publique (Québec) / Public Service Commission
800, Place d'Youville, 7e étage
Québec, QC G1R 3P4
418-643-1425 Fax: 418-643-7264 800-432-0432
cfp@cfp.gouv.qc.ca
www.cfp.gouv.qc.ca
The Commission works towards the following goals: to ensure equal access for all citizens to the public service; to ensure the competence of persons recruited & promoted; & to guarantee the fairness of decisions in human resources management.

Agences, conseils et commissions associés/Associated Agencies, Boards & Commissions:

Sous-secrétariat au personnel de la fonction publique
Secrétaire associé, Guy Mercier
418-528-6180
Directeur général (par intérim), Relations de travail, Rhéal St-Pierre, 2010-09-17
418-528-0202
Directeur, Relations professionnelles, Rhéal St-Pierre
418-528-6227
Directrice, Planification de la main-d'oeuvre & de l'information de gestion, Marie-Claude Corbeil-Gravel
418-528-6397
Directeur, Gestion de main-d'oeuvre, VACANT
Directeur, Classification & rémunération, secteur fonction publique, Jean-Olivier Ferron
418-528-6479
Directrice, Assurance traitement de la santé & sécurité du travail, Chantal Gagnon
418-643-0875
Directrice, Développement des persones et des organisations, Jocelyne Tremblay
418-528-6461

Sous-secrétariat aux marchés publics / Public Markets
418-643-1529 Fax: 418-643-9226
marches.publics@sct.gouv.qc.ca
Secrétaire associé, Alain Parenteau
418-643-9383, Fax: 418-528-6877
Directeur général, Bureau de gouvernance des grandes infrastructures publiques, Bernard Buteau, 2010-09-17
418-528-1098
Directeur général, Politiques de marchés publics, Marc Samson
418-643-0875
Directrice générale, Services à la gestion contractuelle, Julie Blackburn
418-528-6166
Directeur, Analyse & vérification aux contrats, Étienne Sabourin
418-528-2861
Directeur, Réglementation & politiques de gestion contractuelle, Robert Villeneuve
418-643-0875
Directrice, Formation sur les marchés publics, Pauline Larouche, 2010-09-17
418-646-6171
Directeur, Tarification & accords sur les marchés publics, Marc Sarra-Bournet, 2010-09-17
418-643-5838
Directrice, Services d'information à la gestion contractuelle, Doris Blanchet, 2010-09-17
418-528-6114

Sous-secrétariat aux politiques budgétaires et programmes / Budget Policies & Programs
Secrétaire associée, Clément D'Astous
418-643-0875
Directeur général, Politiques & opérations budgétaires, Jacques Fortin
418-528-6301, Fax: 418-643-4974
Directeur général, Programmes administratifs, sociaux & de santé, Jean-François Lachaine
418-528-6512
Directeur général, Programmes économiques, éducatifs & culturels, Yves Lessard
418-528-6252, Fax: 418-643-7288
Directrice, Programmes administratifs, Danielle Hubert
418-643-0875
Directeur, Programmes économiques, Lysane Montminy
418-643-0875
Directrice, Programmes éducatifs & culturels, Anne Boucher
418-528-6260
Directeur, Programmes sociaux & de santé, Serge Garon
418-643-0875
Directrice, Opérations de prévisions & de suivi des dépenses, Claire Rainville
418-528-6303, Fax: 418-643-4974
Directeur, Études & analyses en dépenses publiques, Carl Lessard, 2010-09-17
418-646-5333
Directeur (par intérim), Analyses des investissements en infrastructures & technologies de l'information, Jean Léveillé, 2010-09-17
418-643-0875

Sous-secrétariat aux politiques de rémunération & coordination intersectorielle des négociations
Secrétaire associée, Dominique Gauthier
418-643-0875
Directeur général, Régimes collectifs & actuariat, Jean-Marc Tardif, 2010-09-17
418-528-6431
Directeur général, Politiques de rémunération, Charles Duclos, 2010-09-17
418-528-6424
Directeur, Actuariat, Michel Groulx, 2010-09-17
418-644-3682
Directeur, Politiques de rémunération & conditions de travail, Bruno Côté, 2010-09-17
418-528-6411
Directeur, Coordination intersectorielle des négociations & organismes publics, Robert Lessard, 2010-09-17
418-644-2145
Directrice, Analyse & comparaison de marché en rémunération, Brigitte Dufort, 2010-09-17
418-528-6406

Vérificateur général du Québec / Auditor General

750, boulevard Charest est, 3e étage, Québec, QC G1K 9J6
418-691-5900 Fax: 418-644-4460
verificateur.general@vgq.gouv.qc.ca
www.vgq.gouv.qc.ca

Le Vérificateur général du Québec a pour mission de favoriser par la vérification le contrôle parlementaire sur les fonds et autres biens publics.
Vérificateur général, Renaud Lachance
418-691-5901

Government of Saskatchewan

Seat of Government: Regina, SK S4S 0B3
www.gov.sk.ca

The Province of Saskatchewan entered Confederation on September 1, 1905. It has an area of 588,276.09 km2, & the StatsCan census population in 2006 was 968,157.

Office of the Lieutenant Governor

Government House, 4607 Dewdney Ave., Regina, SK S4T 1B7
306-787-4070 Fax: 306-787-7716
lgo@ltgov.sk.ca
www.ltgov.sk.ca

Lieutenant Governor, Hon. Dr. Gordon L. Barnhart
Private Secretary, Heather Salloum
hsalloum@ltgov.sk.ca

Office of the Premier

Legislative Bldg., #226, 2405 Legislative Dr., Regina, SK S4S 0B3
306-787-9433 Fax: 306-787-0885
premier@gov.sk.ca
www.gov.sk.ca/premier

Premier, Hon. Brad Wall
premier@gov.sk.ca; bradw@bradwall.com, Other Communications: URL: www.bradwall.com
Deputy Minister to the Premier, Doug Moen
306-787-6338, Fax: 306-787-8338, doug.moen@gov.sk.ca
Cabinet Secretary & Clerk of the Executive Council, Rick Mantey
306-787-9630, Fax: 206-787-8299, rick.mantey@gov.sk.ca
Chief of Staff to the Premier, Joe Donlevy
306-787-0064, Fax: 306-787-0883, joe.donlevy@gov.sk.ca
Executive Director, Communications, Kathy Young
306-787-0425, Fax: 206-787-0883, Kathy.Young@gov.sk.ca
Director, Media Relations, Leanne Persicke
306-787-2127, Fax: 206-787-8233, leanne.persicke@gov.sk.ca

Intergovernmental Affairs
1919 Saskatchewan Dr., Regina, SK S4P 4H2
206-787-8003
webmaster2@gr.gov.sk.ca
www.gov.sk.ca/intergovernmental-affairs/
Associate Deputy Minister, Dylan Jones
306-787-4220, Fax: 306-787-0973, Dylan.Jones@gov.sk.ca
Executive Director, Canadian Intergovernmental Relations, Cammy Colpitts
306-787-7962, Fax: 306-787-7317, Cammy.Colpitts@gov.sk.ca
Executive Director, Trade Policy, Robert Donald
306-787-8910, Fax: 306-787-7317, Robert.Donald@gov.sk.ca
Executive Director, International Relations, Wes Jickling
306-787-7855, Fax: 306-787-7317, Wes.Jickling@gov.sk.ca
Director, Strategic Initiatives, Kari Harvey
306-787-0306, Fax: 306-787-0973, kari.harvey@gov.sk.ca
Director, China Unit, William Wang
306-798-7045, Fax: 306-787-7317, william.wang@gov.sk.ca

Executive Council

Legislative Bldg., 2405 Legislative Dr., Regina, SK S4S 0B3
306-787-7448
admin.ec@gov.sk.ca
www.gov.sk.ca/cabinet

Led by the Premier, the Cabinet, or Executive Council of Saskatchewan is a decision-making body. The Premier appoints each cabinet minister. Each minister has responsibility for a department or portfolio.

Premier & President, Executive Council, Hon. Brad Wall
306-787-9433, Fax: 306-787-0885, premier@gov.sk.ca; bradw@bradwall.com, Other Communications: URL: www.bradwall.com
Minister, Finance; Deputy Premier, Hon. Ken Krawetz
306-787-6060, Fax: 306-787-6055, minister.fin@gov.sk.ca
Minister, Energy & Resources; Minister Responsible, SaskTel, Hon. Bill Boyd
306-787-9124, Fax: 306-787-0395, minister.er@gov.sk.ca
Minister, Social Services; Minister Responsible, Status of Women; Minister Responsible, Public Service Commission, Hon. June Draude
306-787-3661, Fax: 306-787-0656, minister.cc@gov.sk.ca
Minister, Agriculture; Minister Responsible, Saskatchewan Crop Insurance Corporation, Hon. Bob Bjornerud
306-787-0338, Fax: 306-787-0630, minister.ag@gov.sk.ca
Minister, Health, Hon. Don McMorris
306-787-7345, Fax: 306-787-0237, minister.he@gov.sk.ca
Minister, Education; Provincial Secretary, Hon. Donna Harpauer
306-787-7360, Fax: 306-798-0263, minister.edu@gov.sk.ca
Minister, Justice; Attorney General; Labour Relations & Workplace Safety; Minister Responsible, Saskatchewan Workers' Compensation Board, Hon. Don Morgan, Q.C.
306-787-5353, Fax: 306-787-1232, minister.ju@gov.sk.ca
Minister, First Nations & Métis Relations; Minister Responsible, Northern Affairs; Minister Responsible, Saskatchewan Gaming Corporation, Hon. Ken Cheveldayoff
306-787-0605, Fax: 306-798-8050, minister.fnmr@gov.sk.ca
Minister, Advanced Education, Employment & Immigration; Minister Responsible, Innovation; Minister Responsible, Saskatchewan Power Corporation, Hon. Rob Norris
306-787-1117, Fax: 306-787-6946, minister.aeei@gov.sk.ca
Minister, Municipal Affairs, Hon. Darryl Hickie
306-787-6100, Fax: 306-787-0399, minister.ma@gov.sk.ca
Minister, Tourism, Parks, Culture & Sport; Minister Responsible, Provincial Capital Commission, Hon. Bill Hutchinson
306-787-0354, Fax: 306-798-0264, minister.tpcs@gov.sk.ca
Minister, Corrections, Public Safety & Policing, Hon. D.F. (Yogi) Huyghebaert
306-787-4377, Fax: 306-787-5331, minister.cpsp@gov.sk.ca
Minister, Environment; Minister Responsible, Saskatchewan Water Corporation; Minister Responsible, SaskEnergy Incorporated, Hon. Dustin Duncan
306-787-0393, Fax: 306-787-1669, minister.env@gov.sk.ca
Deputy Government House Leader; Minister, Enterprise; Minister Responsible, Trade, Hon. Jeremy Harrison
306-787-0804, Fax: 306-798-2009, Minister.ES@gov.sk.ca
Minister, Highways & Infrastructure; Minister Responsible, Saskatchewan Transportation Company/The Global Transportation Hub Authority, Hon. Jim Reiter
306-787-6447, Fax: 306-787-1736, minister.hi@gov.sk.ca
Minister Responsible, Crown Investments Corporation, Information Technology Office, Information Services Corporation, Saskatchewan Government Insurance, Hon. Tim McMillan
306-787-7339, Fax: 206-798-3140, minister.cc@gov.sk.ca
Minister, Government Services, Hon. Laura Ross
306-787-0942, Fax: 306-787-8677, minister.gs@gov.sk.ca

Deputy Minister's Office
Legislative Bldg., #135, 2405 Legislative Dr., Regina, SK S4S 0B3
306-787-6337 Fax: 306-787-8338
dmo.ec@gov.sk.ca
www.executive.gov.sk.ca/branch_info/dmo.htm
The Office of the Deputy Minister to the Premier has the following functions: to support the Premier; to provide executive leadership; to oversee financial & human resource needs of the department; to provide coordination between government departments, agencies, Crown corporations & Cabinet; & to coordinate appointments of senior executives for departments & certain agencies.
Deputy Minister to the Premier, Doug Moen
306-787-6338, Doug.Moen@gov.sk.ca
Co-ordinator, Executive Resourcing, Sheree Ruller
306-787-2059, Fax: 306-787-8337

Cabinet Secretariat
Legislative Bldg., #145, 2405 Legislative Dr., Regina, SK S4S 0B3
306-787-9636 Fax: 306-787-8299
cabsec.ec@gov.sk.ca
www.gov.sk.ca/executive-council/cabinet-secretariat
The Cabinet Secretariat is charged with the following responsibilities: to support the Premier in his role as President of Executive Council; to provide administrative support to the Cabinet & cabinet committees; to maintain public records of all orders in council & regulations; to give secretariat support for the Legislative Instruments Committee; & to maintain employment contracts of senior executives pursuant to The Crown Employment Contracts Act.

Cabinet Secretary & Clerk of the Executive Council, Rick Mantey
306-787-9630, Fax: 306-787-8299, rick.mantey@gov.sk.ca

Cabinet Planning Unit
Legislative Bldg., #37, 2405 Legislative Dr., Regina, SK S4S 0B3
306-787-7162 Fax: 306-787-0012
cpu.ec@gov.sk.ca
www.gov.sk.ca/executive-council/cabinet-planning

The Cabinet Planning Unit gives secretariat support & policy analysis to the Committee on Planning & Priorities, & to the Premier & members of Executive Council.

Associate Deputy Minister, Cabinet Planning, James Saunders
306-787-6339, Fax: 306-787-0012, James.Saunders@gov.sk.ca
Senior Policy Advisor, Nancy Cherney
306-787-1301, Fax: 306-787-0012, Nancy.Cherney@gov.sk.ca
Senior Policy Advisor, Nancy Martin
306-787-9727, Fax: 306-787-0012, nancy.martin@gov.sk.ca
Senior Policy Advisor, Gord Sisson
306-787-6308, Fax: 306-787-0012, Gord.Sisson@gov.sk.ca

Legislative Assembly

c/o Clerk's Office, Legislative Bldg., #123, 2405 Legislative Dr., Regina, SK S4S 0B3
306-787-2376 Fax: 306-787-1558
info@legassembly.sk.ca
www.legassembly.sk.ca
Other Communication: Visitor Services: visitorserv@legassembly.sk.ca; Library Reference Questions: reference@legassembly.sk.ca

Clerk, Greg Putz
306-787-2335, Fax: 306-787-0408, gputz@legassembly.sk.ca
Principal Clerk, Committees, Iris Lang
306-787-1743, Fax: 306-798-9650, ilang@legassembly.sk.ca
Speaker, Hon. Don Toth
306-787-2282, Fax: 306-787-2283, speaker@legassembly.sk.ca
Sergeant-at-Arms, Patrick Shaw
306-787-8798
Chief Technology Officer, Communication & Information Technology Systems, Darcy Hislop
306-787-8071, Fax: 306-789-4278, darcy@gov.sk.ca; dhislop@legassembly.sk.ca
Director, Financial & Administrative Services, Marilyn Borowski
306-787-2384, Fax: 306-798-0040, mborowski@legassembly.sk.ca
Director, Parliamentary Publications, Lenni Frohman
306-787-1924, Fax: 306-787-1556, lfrohman@legassembly.sk.ca
Director, Human Resource & Payroll Services, Linda Kaminski
306-787-2338, Fax: 306-787-1558, lkaminski@legassembly.sk.ca
Director, Visitor Services, Lorraine deMontigny
306-787-5357, Fax: 306-787-8217, ldemontigny@legassembly.sk.ca
Law Clerk & Parliamentary Counsel, Kenneth S. Ring, Q.C.
306-787-2298, Fax: 306-787-1246, kring@legassembly.sk.ca
Legislative Librarian, Melissa Bennett
306-787-2277, Fax: 306-787-1772, mbennett@legassembly.sk.ca

Opposition Caucus Office (New Democratic Party)
#265, Legislative Bldg., 2405 Legislative Dr., Regina, SK S4S 0B3
306-787-7388 Fax: 306-787-6247
caucus@ndpcaucus.sk.ca
www.ndpcaucus.sk.ca

Leader, Dwain Lingenfelter
306-525-4155, Fax: 306-525-4470
Caucus Chair, Judy Junor
306-787-0367, Fax: 306-787-6247, saskatooneastview@ndpcaucus.sk.ca
Chief of Staff, Stephen Moore
306-787-1907, Fax: 306-787-6247, smoore@ndpcaucus.sk.ca
Director, Human Resources & Administration, Cheryl Stecyk
306-787-7389, Fax: 306-787-6247, cstecyk@ndpcaucus.sk.ca
Director, Communications, Sandra Jackle
306-787-6349, Fax: 306-787-6247, sjackle@ndpcaucus.sk.ca

Government Caucus Office (Saskatchewan Party)
Legislative Bldg., #203, 2405 Legislative Dr., Regina, SK S4S 0B3
306-787-4300 Fax: 306-787-3174
info@skcaucus.com
www.skcaucus.com

Caucus Chair, Doreen Eagles
306-787-4300, Fax: 306-787-3174, doreen.eagles@gov.sk.ca
Chief of Staff, Gerald Proctor
306-787-4300, Fax: 306-787-3174, gproctor@skcaucus.com
Government Whip, Randy Weekes
206-787-1479, randy.weekes@gov.sk.ca
Deputy Government Whip, Andy Iwanchuk
306-787-6485

Crown Investments Corporation of Saskatchewan (CIC)

#400, 2400 College Ave., Regina, SK S4P 1C8
306-787-6851 Fax: 306-787-8125
www.cicorp.sk.ca

Acting as a financially self-sufficient holding company, Crown Investments Corporation of Saskatchewan oversees the operations of commercial Crown corporations. The main functions of the CIC are as follows: establishing the strategic direction for subsidiary Crown corporations; & through the Crown corporations, enhancing the province's long term economic growth & diversification.

Minister Responsible, Hon. Tim McMillan
306-787-7339, Fax: 306-798-3140, minister.cc@gov.sk.ca
President/Chief Executive Officer, Dick Carter
306-787-4553, dcarter@cicorp.sk.ca
Senior Vice-President & Chief Financial Officer, Blair Swystun
306-787-9085, bswystun@cicorp.sk.ca
Vice-President, Crown Sector Initiatives, Iain Harry
306-787-8647, iharry@cicorp.sk
Vice-President, Asset Management, Rae Haverstock
306-787-6773, rhaverstock@am.cicorp.sk.ca
Vice-President/General Counsel, Human Resources, Policy & Governance Division, Doug Kosloski
306-787-5892, dkosloski@cicorp.sk.ca
Executive Director, Human Resources Policy, Nancy Croll
306-787-1257, ncroll@cicorp.sk.ca
Executive Director, Policy Analysis, James Hoffman
306-787-0474, jhoffman@cicorp.sk.ca
Executive Director, Capital Pension & Benefits Administration, Ken Klein
306-787-5948, ken.klein@capitalpension.com
Executive Director, Communications, Mike Woods
306-787-5889, mwoods@cicorp.sk.ca

Provincial Auditor Saskatchewan

#1500, 1920 Broad St., Regina, SK S4P 3V2
306-787-6398 Fax: 306-787-6383
info@auditor.sk.ca
www.auditor.sk.ca

The Provincial Auditor is the auditor of public money managed by the Government of Saskatchewan. The Provincial Auditor Act gives the Provincial Auditor the responsibility, authority, and independence to audit and publicly report on all government organizations.

Provincial Auditor, Bonnie Lysyk
306-787-6366, Fax: 306-787-6383, lysyk@auditor.sk.ca
Deputy Provincial Auditor, Education, Ed Montgomery
306-787-6389, Fax: 306-787-6383, montgomery@auditor.sk.ca
Deputy Provincial Auditor, Finance & Crown Corporations, Judy Ferguson
306-787-6372, Fax: 306-787-6383, ferguson@auditor.sk.ca
Deputy Provincial Auditor, Gaming & Insurance, Mike Heffernan
306-787-6364, Fax: 306-787-6383, heffernan@auditor.sk.ca
Deputy Provincial Auditor, Health, Mobashar Ahmad
306-787-6387, Fax: 306-787-6383, ahmad@auditor.sk.ca
Administrative Services Manager, Deann Dickin
306-787-6377, Fax: 306-787-6383, dickin@auditor.sk.ca

Standing Committees of the Legislature
The following are the four Standing Policy Committees of the Saskatchewan Legislature: Standing Committee on Crown & Central Agencies; Standing Committee on Human Services; Standing Committee on the Economy; & Standing Committee on Intergovernmental Affairs & Justice.

Chair, Standing Committee on Crown & Central Agencies, Delbert Kirsch
Chair, Standing Committee on Intergovernmental Affairs & Justice, Warren Michelson
Chair, Standing Committee on Human Services, Greg Ottenbreit
Chair, Standing Committee on the Economy, Lyle Stewart

Twenty-sixth Legislature - Saskatchewan

#123, Legislative Bldg., 2405 Legislative Dr., Regina, SK S4S 0B3
306-787-2376 Fax: 306-787-1558
info@legassembly.sk.ca
www.legassembly.sk.ca
Other Communication: Library Reference Questions: reference@legassembly.sk.ca; Visitor Services: visitorserv@legassembly.sk.ca

Last General Election: Nov. 7, 2007; Maximum Duration: 4 Years; Next General Election: Nov. 7, 2011; Party Standings (Nov. 2007): Saskatchewan Party (SP): 38 seats, New Democratic Party (NDP): 20 seats, Total 58; Salaries, Indemnities & Allowances (April 2008): Member's indemnity: $84,409, Member's expense allowance: $0. In addition to this, are the following amounts: Premier $61,390, Deputy Premier: $49,114, Ministers: $42,975, Leader of the Opposition: $42,975, Speaker $42,975, Deputy Speaker $12,560. The following is a list of members, with their constituency, the population of the constituency, party affiliation, & contact information.

Members

Denis Allchurch, Rosthern-Shellbrook, Saskatchewan Party
306-883-3003, 877-580-8988, Fax: 306-883-3012, dallchurch@mla.legassembly.sk.ca, Other Communications: URL: www.denisallchurch.ca
Pat Atkinson, Saskatoon Nutana, New Democratic Party
306-664-6101, Fax: 306-665-5633, patkinson@mla.legassembly.sk.ca
Buckley Belanger, Athabasca, New Democratic Party
306-833-3200, 800-239-9820, Fax: 306-833-2622, bbelanger@mla.legassembly.sk.ca
Hon. Bob Bjornerud, Melville-Saltcoats, Saskatchewan Party
306-728-3882, Fax: 306-728-3883, bbjornerud@mla.legassembly.sk.ca; minister.ag@gov.sk.ca, Other Communications: URL: www.bobbjornerud.ca; Saltcoats: 306-744-2519
Hon. Bill Boyd, Kindersley, Saskatchewan Party
306-463-4480, Fax: 306-463-6873, bboyd@mla.legassembly.sk.ca; minister.er@gov.sk.ca, Other Communications: URL: www.billboyd.ca
Fred Bradshaw, Carrot River Valley, Saskatchewan Party
306-768-3977, Fax: 306-768-3979, fbradshaw@mla.legassembly.sk.ca, Other Communications: URL: www.fredbradshaw.ca
Greg P. Brkich, Arm River-Watrous, Saskatchewan Party
306-567-2843, 800-539-3979, Fax: 306-567-3259, gbrkich@mla.legassembly.sk.ca, Other Communications: URL: www.gregbrkich.ca
Cam Broten, Saskatoon Massey Place, New Democratic Party
306-384-7200, Fax: 306-384-4280, cbroten@mla.legassembly.sk.ca
Danielle Chartier, Saskatoon Riversdale, New Democratic Party
306-244-5167, Fax: 306-244-6070, dchartier@mla.legassembly.sk.ca
Hon. Ken Cheveldayoff, Saskatoon Silver Springs, Saskatchewan Party
306-651-7100, Fax: 306-651-6008, kcheveldayoff@mla.legassembly.sk.ca; minister.fnmr@gov.sk.ca, Other Communications: URL: www.cheveldayoff.com
Michael Chisholm, CutKnife-Turtleford, Saskatchewan Party
306-893-2619, Fax: 306-893-2660, mchisholm@mla.legassembly.sk.ca, Other Communications: URL: www.michaelchisholm.ca
Dan D'Autremont, Cannington, Saskatchewan Party
306-443-2420, Fax: 306-443-2269, ddautremont@mla.legassembly.sk.ca, Other Communications: URL: www.dandautremont.ca
Hon. June Draude, Kelvington-Wadena, Saskatchewan Party
306-338-3973, 800-234-4134, Fax: 306-338-3977, jdraude@mla.legassembly.sk.ca; minister.ss@gov.sk.ca, Other Communications: URL: www.junedraude.ca
Hon. Dustin Duncan, Weyburn-Big Muddy, Saskatchewan Party
306-842-4810, Fax: 306-842-4811, dduncan@mla.legassembly.sk.ca; minister.env@gov.sk.ca, Other Communications: URL: www.dduncan.ca
Doreen Eagles, Estevan, Saskatchewan Party
306-634-7311, Fax: 306-634-7332, deagles@mla.legassembly.sk.ca
Wayne Elhard, Cypress Hills, Saskatchewan Party
306-295-3688, 877-703-3374, Fax: 306-295-3699, welhard@mla.legassembly.sk.ca, Other Communications: URL: www.wayneelhard.ca
David Forbes, Saskatoon Centre, New Democratic Party
306-244-3555, Fax: 306-244-3602, dforbes@mla.legassembly.sk.ca, Other Communications: URL: dforbes.sasktelwebhosting.com
Darcy Furber, Prince Albert Northcote, New Democratic Party
306-763-4400, Fax: 306-763-1827, dfurber@mla.legassembly.sk.ca
Rod Gantefoer, Melfort, Saskatchewan Party
306-752-9500, 800-242-6796, Fax: 306-752-9005, rgantefoer@mla.legassembly.sk.ca, Other Communications: URL: www.melfortconstituency.ca
Hon. Donna Harpauer, Humboldt, Saskatchewan Party
306-682-5141, 800-682-9909, Fax: 306-682-5144, dharpauer@mla.legassembly.sk.ca; minister.edu@gov.sk.ca, Other Communications: URL: www.donnaharpauer.ca
Ron Harper, Regina Northeast, New Democratic Party
306-569-2233, Fax: 306-569-2303, rharper@mla.legassembly.sk.ca, Other Communications: URL: www.ronharper.ca
Jeremy Harrison, Meadow Lake, Saskatchewan Party
306-236-6669, 877-234-6669, Fax: 306-236-6744, jharrison@mla.legassembly.sk.ca
Glen Hart, Last Mountain-Touchwood, Saskatchewan Party
306-723-4421, 877-723-4488, Fax: 306-723-4654,

ghart@mla.legassembly.sk.ca, Other Communications: URL: www.glenhart.ca
Nancy Heppner, Martensville, Saskatchewan Party
306-975-0284, 866-639-4377, Fax: 306-975-0283, nheppner@mla.legassembly.sk.ca, Other Communications: URL: www.nancyheppner.com
Hon. Darryl Hickie, Prince AlbertCarlton, Saskatchewan Party
306-922-4676, Fax: 306-922-4674, dhickie@mla.legassembly.sk.ca; minister.ma@gov.sk.ca, Other Communications: URL: www.darrylhickie.ca
Deb Higgins, Moose Jaw Wakamow, New Democratic Party
306-694-1001, Fax: 306-691-0486, dhiggins@mla.legassembly.sk.ca
Hon. Bill Hutchinson, Regina South, Saskatchewan Party
306-205-2067, Fax: 306-205-2069, bhutchinson@mla.legassembly.sk.ca; minister.tpcs@gov.sk.ca
Hon. D.F. (Yogi) Huyghebaert, Wood River, Saskatchewan Party
306-642-4744, Fax: 306-642-4515, yhuyghebaert@mla.legassembly.sk.ca; minister.cpsp@gov.sk.ca, Other Communications: URL: www.mlawoodriver.ca; Alt Phone: 306-266-2100
Andy Iwanchuk, Saskatoon Fairview, New Democratic Party
306-651-3801, Fax: 306-651-3804, aiwanchuk@mla.legassembly.sk.ca
Judy Junor, Saskatoon Eastview, New Democratic Party
306-477-4233, Fax: 306-477-4236, jjunor@mla.legassembly.sk.ca, Other Communications: URL: www.judyjunor.ca
Delbert Kirsch, Batoche, Saskatchewan Party
306-256-3930, Fax: 306-256-3924, dkirsch@mla.legassembly.sk.ca
Hon. Ken Krawetz, Canora-Pelly, Saskatchewan Party
306-563-4425, 800-213-4279, Fax: 306-563-5752, kkrawetz@mla.legassembly.sk.ca; minister.fin@gov.sk.ca, Other Communications: URL: www.kenkrawetz.ca
Dwain Lingenfelter, Regina Douglas Park, New Democratic Party
306-525-4155, Fax: 306-525-4470, dlingenfelter@mla.legassembly.sk.ca
Warren McCall, Regina Elphinstone-Centre, New Democratic Party
306-352-2002, Fax: 306-352-2065, wmccall@mla.legassembly.sk.ca
Hon. Tim McMillan, Lloydminster, Saskatchewan Party
306-825-4477, Fax: 306-825-4473, tmcmillan@mla.legassembly.sk.ca; minister.cc@gov.sk.ca
Hon. Don McMorris, IndianHead-Milestone, Saskatchewan Party
306-771-2733, 877-337-3366, Fax: 306-771-2574, dmcmorris@mla.legassembly.sk.ca; minister.he@gov.sk.ca, Other Communications: URL: www.donmcmorris.ca
Warren Michelson, Moose Jaw North, Saskatchewan Party
306-692-8884, Fax: 306-692-8872, wmichelson@mla.legassembly.sk.ca
Hon. Don Morgan, SaskatoonSoutheast, Saskatchewan Party
306-955-4755, Fax: 306-955-4765, dmorgan@mla.legassembly.sk.ca; minister.ju@gov.sk.ca, Other Communications: URL: www.donmorgan.ca
Sandra Morin, Regina Walsh Acres, New Democratic Party
306-781-9102, Fax: 306-781-4227, smorin@mla.legassembly.sk.ca, Other Communications: URL: www.sandramorin.ca
John Nilson, Q.C., Regina Lakeview, New Democratic Party
306-751-7740, Fax: 306-585-2030, jnilson@mla.legassembly.sk.ca
Hon. Rob Norris, Saskatoon Greystone, Saskatchewan Party
306-933-7852, Fax: 306-933-7869, rnorris@mla.legassembly.sk.ca
Greg Ottenbreit, Yorkton, Saskatchewan Party
306-783-7275, Fax: 306-783-7273, gottenbreit@mla.legassembly.sk.ca, Other Communications: URL: www.gregottenbreit.ca
Frank Quennell, Q.C., Saskatoon Meewasin, New Democratic Party
306-651-3581, Fax: 306-651-4670, fquennell@mla.legassembly.sk.ca, Other Communications: URL: www.frankquennell.ca
Hon. Jim Reiter, Rosetown-Elrose, Saskatchewan Party
306-882-4105, Fax: 306-882-4108, jreiter@mla.legassembly.sk.ca; minister.hi@gov.sk.ca, Other Communications: URL: www.jimreiter.ca; Alt Phone: 306-867-8770
Hon. Laura Ross, Regina Qu'Appelle Valley, Saskatchewan Party
306-545-6333, Fax: 306-545-6112, lross@mla.legassembly.sk.ca; minister.gs@gov.sk.ca
Joceline Schriemer, Saskatoon Sutherland, Saskatchewan Party
306-244-5623, Fax: 306-244-5626, jschriemer@mla.legassembly.sk.ca, Other Communications: URL: www.jocelinemla.ca
Lyle Stewart, Thunder Creek, Saskatchewan Party
306-693-3229, Fax: 306-693-3251, lstewart@mla.legassembly.sk.ca, Other Communications: URL: www.lylestewart.ca
Len Taylor, The Battlefords, New Democratic Party
306-445-5454, Fax: 306-445-5617, ltaylor@mla.legassembly.sk.ca
Christine Tell, Regina Wascana Plains, Saskatchewan Party
306-205-2126, Fax: 306-205-2127, ctell@mla.legassembly.sk.ca
Hon. Donald J. Toth, Moosomin, Saskatchewan Party
306-435-3329, 888-255-8684, Fax: 306-435-3921, dtoth@mla.legassembly.sk.ca; speaker@legassembly.sk.ca, Other Communications: URL: www.dontoth.ca
Kim Trew, Regina Coronation Park, New Democratic Party
306-775-2444, Fax: 306-352-4999, ktrew@mla.legassembly.sk.ca
Doyle Vermette, Cumberland, New Democratic Party
306-425-2525, Fax: 306-425-2885, dvermette@mla.legassembly.sk.ca
Hon. Brad Wall, Swift Current, Saskatchewan Party
306-778-2429, Fax: 306-778-3614, bradw@bradwall.com; premier@gov.sk.ca, Other Communications: URL: www.bradwall.com
Randy Weekes, Biggar, Saskatchewan Party
306-948-4880, 877-948-4880, Fax: 306-948-4882, rweekes@mla.legassembly.sk.ca, Other Communications: URL: www.randyweekes.ca
Nadine Wilson, Saskatchewan Rivers, Saskatchewan Party
306-763-0615, Fax: 306-763-2503, nwilson@mla.legassembly.sk.ca
Trent Wotherspoon, Regina Rosemont, New Democratic Party
306-565-2444, Fax: 306-565-2952, twotherspoon@mla.legassembly.sk.ca
Gordon Wyant, Saskatoon Northwest, New Democratic Party
306-934-2847, Fax: 306-934-2867, gwyant@mla.legassembly.sk.ca
Kevin Yates, Regina Dewdney, New Democratic Party
306-569-0247, Fax: 306-569-0805, kyates@mla.legassembly.sk.ca, Other Communications: URL: www.kevinyates.ca

Saskatchewan Government Departments & Agencies

Saskatchewan Advanced Education, Employment & Immigration (AEEI)

1945 Hamilton St., Regina, SK S4P 2C8
306-787-9478
aeeinquiry@gov.sk.ca
www.aee.gov.sk.ca
Other Communication: SaskJobs: saskjobs@gov.sk.ca; General Educational Development: GED@sasked.gov.sk.ca

The Ministry strives to create a vital, educated & skilled workforce by focussing on the following areas: retaining educated & skilled workers in Saskatchewan; providing educational & training programs to develop a skilled workforce; & promoting the province's opportunities to attract educated & skilled workers from outside Saskatchewan & Canada. In November 2007, a new provincial government resulted in the reorganization of provincial government ministries. An expanded Ministry of Advanced Education, Employment & Labour was formed, & was subsequently changed to Advanced Education, Employment & Immigration.

Acts Administered:
Apprenticeship & Trade Certification Act
Post-Secondary Education & Skills Training Act
Private Vocational Schools Regulation Act
Regional Colleges Act
Saskatchewan Indian Institute of Technologies Act
Saskatchewan Institute of Applied Science & Technology Act
Student Assistance & Student Aid Fund Act
University of Regina Act
University of Saskatchewan Act

Minister, Advanced Education, Employment & Immigration; Minister Responsible, Innovation; Minister Responsible, Saskatechewan Power Corporation, Hon. Rob Norris
306-787-0341, Fax: 306-787-6946, minister.aeei@gov.sk.ca
Deputy Minister, Advanced Education, Employment & Immigration, Clare Isman
306-787-7071, Fax: 306-798-0975, Clare.Isman@gov.sk.ca
Assistant Deputy Minister, Rupen Pandya
306-787-6846, Fax: 306-798-0975, Rupen.Pandya@gov.sk.ca
Acting Assistant Deputy Minister, Immigration, Kirk Westgard
306-787-0370, Fax: 306-798-0975, Kirk.Westgard@gov.sk.ca
Executive Director, Marketing & Communications, Herman Hulshof
306-787-9715, Fax: 306-798-5021, Herman.Hulshof@gov.sk.ca
Director, Public Affairs, Rikki Bote
306-787-4156, Fax: 306-798-5021, Rikki.Bote@gov.sk.ca

Associated Agencies, Boards & Commissions:

• Saskatchewan Apprenticeship & Trade Certification Commission
2140 Hamilton St.
Regina, SK S4P 2E3
306-787-2444 Fax: 306-787-5105 877-363-0536
apprenticeship@gov.sk.ca
www.saskapprenticeship.ca

Advanced Education & Student Services
Assistant Deputy Minister, David Boehm
306-787-0835, Fax: 306-798-0975, david.boehm@gov.sk.ca
Executive Director, Program Innovation, Ted Amendt
306-787-5984, Fax: 306-787-7182, Ted.Amendt@gov.sk.ca
Executive Director, Student Financial Assistance, Tammy Bloor Cavers
306-787-2044, Fax: 306-787-7537, Tammy.BloorCavers@gov.sk.ca
Executive Director, Quality Assurance, Ann Lorenzen
306-787-2267, Fax: 306-798-3379, Ann.Lorenzen@gov.sk.ca
Executive Director, Public Institutions & Infrastructure, Dion McGrath
306-787-7974, Fax: 306-798-3159, Dion.McGrath@gov.sk.ca
Director, Public Institutions & Infrasturcture, Brent Brownlee
306-787-7027, Fax: 306-798-3159, Brent.Brownlee@gov.sk.ca
Director, Program Innovation, Tim Caleval
306-787-8131, Fax: 306-787-7182, Tim.Caleval@gov.sk.ca
Director, Public Institutions & Infrasturcture, Heather George
306-787-5900, Fax: 306-798-3159, Heather.George@gov.sk.ca
Director, Income Support, Rose-Ann Hamer
306-787-0692, Fax: 306-787-0760, Rose-Ann.Hamer@gov.sk.ca
Director, Private Vocational Schools, Darlene Heska-Willard
306-787-5457, Fax: 306-798-3379, Darlene.Heska-Willard@gov.sk.ca
Director, Business & Information Technology Services, Ron Kitchen
306-787-6231, Fax: 306-787-7537, ron.kitchen@gov.sk.ca
Director, Program Innovation, Jim Seiferling
306-787-0477, Fax: 306-787-7182, Jim.Seiferling@gov.sk.ca
Director, Strategic Initiatives, Kirk Wosminity
306-787-8064, Fax: 306-787-7537, Kirk.Wosminity@gov.sk.ca

Can-Sask Career & Employment Services
1945 Hamilton St., 8th Fl., Regina, SK S4P 2C8
306-787-0701 Fax: 306-798-5022
www.aeei.gov.sk.ca/career-employment/
Executive Director, Jan Morgan
306-787-1626, Fax: 306-798-5022, Jan.Morgan@gov.sk.ca
Director, Jan Kot
306-787-8458, Fax: 306-798-5022, Jan.Kot@gov.sk.ca
Regional Director, North West Region, Pat Bauer
306-446-7890, Fax: 306-446-8707, Pat.Bauer@gov.sk.ca
Regional Director, Centre Region, Chris Broten
306-933-5780, Fax: 306-933-7801, Chris.Broten@gov.sk.ca
Regional Director, South West Region, Dennis Schafer
306-787-2352, Fax: 306-798-0079, Dennis.Schafer@gov.sk.ca
Regional Director, South East Region, Darcy Smycniuk
306-786-5808, Fax: 306-786-1541, Darcy.Smycniuk@gov.sk.ca
Regional Director, North East Region, Penny Sommervill
306-953-2203, Fax: 306-953-2763, Penny.Sommervill@gov.sk.ca

Corporate Services
1945 Hamilton St., 14th Fl., Regina, SK S4P 2C8
306-787-3920 Fax: 306-787-7392
Executive Director, Karen Allen
306-787-5654, Fax: 306-787-7392, Karen.Allen@gov.sk.ca
Director, Financial Planning, Scott Giroux
306-787-3501, Fax: 306-787-7392, Scott.Giroux@gov.sk.ca
Director, Financial Operations, Candace Malowany
306-787-7384, Fax: 306-787-7392, Candace.Malowany@gov.sk.ca
Director, Audit Services Unit, Duane Rieger
306-787-1421, Fax: 306-798-0016, Duane.Rieger@gov.sk.ca
Director, Financial Planning & Business Systems, Brian Schwab
306-787-4209, Fax: 306-787-7392, Brian.Schwab@gov.sk.ca
Director, Support Services & Accommodations, Tim Selinger
306-798-5902, Fax: 306-798-0193, Tim.Selinger@gov.sk.ca

Immigration Services
1945 Hamilton St., 7th Fl., Regina, SK S4P 2C8
306-798-7467 Fax: 306-933-7901
immigration@gov.sk.ca
www.immigration.gov.sk.ca
Acting Director, Policy & Program Support, Eric Johansen
306-787-0254, Fax: 306-798-3405, Eric.Johansen@gov.sk.ca
Acting Director, Immigration Policy, Anne McRorie
306-798-5904, Fax: 306-798-0713, Anne.McRorie@gov.sk.ca
Director, Community Partnerships & Settlement, Giovanna Pirro
306-787-2890, Fax: 306-798-0713, Giovanna.Pirro@gov.sk.ca

Director, Program Integrity/Saskatchewan Immigrant Nominee Program, Kirk Westgard
306-787-0370, Fax: 306-798-0713, Kirk.Westgard@gov.sk.ca
Acting Office Manager, Thera Lovelace
306-787-2206, Fax: 306-798-0713, Thera.Lovelace@gov.sk.ca

Policy & Planning
1945 Hamilton St., 15th Fl., Regina, SK S4P 2C8
306-787-5663 Fax: 306-787-5870
Executive Director, Linda Smith
306-787-2984, Fax: 306-787-5870, Linda.Smith@gov.sk.ca; linda.smith@pnrha.ca, Other Communications: Alternate Email: linda.smith@hrha.sk.ca
Director, Strategic Policy, Karen Banks
306-787-4347, Fax: 306-787-5870, Karen.Banks@gov.sk.ca
Director, Economic/Labour Market Information & Analysis, Lorraine Beckman
306-787-5626, Fax: 306-787-5870, Lorraine.Beckman@gov.sk.ca
Director, Policy & Intergovernmental, Mary Didowycz
306-787-6224, Fax: 306-787-5870, Mary.Didowycz@gov.sk.ca
Director, Privacy Coordinator, Jan Gray
306-787-2638, Fax: 306-787-5870, Jan.Gray@gov.sk.ca

Saskatchewan Agriculture (AG)

Walter Scott Bldg., 3085 Albert St., Regina, SK S4S 0B1
866-457-2377
aginfo@gov.sk.ca
www.agriculture.gov.sk.ca

The Ministry's mandate is to foster, in partnership with individuals, communities, industry, & government, a commercially viable, self-sufficient, & sustainable agricultural sector in Saskatchewan. The Ministry addresses needs of individual farmers & ranchers, encourages & develops higher value production & processing, & promotes sustainable economic development in rural areas of the province. Some responsibilities are as follows: agri-business development through provision of agriculture-based business experts & technical support; agricultural research to promote development & diversification; corporate services to support the Information Technology Office & the Rural Economic Co-operative Development; crop development; financial programs; inspection & administration of regulations for food & crop protection, animal disease surveillance, environmental reviews, licenses, registrations, & complaint resolution; irrigation development; promotion of sustainable use of Crown land; livestock development; provision of food safety, quality, policy, regulatory, market & business development programs; policy analysis, strategies, & agricultural information services; & delivery of Saskatchewan Crop Insurance Corporation programs & services.

Acts Administered:
Agri-Food Act, 2004
Agri-Food Innovation Act
Agricultural Credit Corporation of Saskatchewan Act
Agricultural Equipment Dealerships Act
Agricultural Implements Act
Agricultural Operations Act
Agricultural Safety Net Act
Agricultural Societies Act
Agrologists Act, 1994
Animal Identification Act
Animal Products Act
Animal Protection Act, 1999
Apiaries Act
Cattle Marketing Deductions Act, 1998
Crop Insurance Act
Crop Payments Act
Department of Agriculture, Food & Rural Revitilization Act
Disease of Animals Act
Expropriation (Rehabilitation Projects) Act
Farm Financial Stability Act
Farmers' Counselling & Assistance Act
Farming Communities Land Act
Government Organization Act
Grain Charges Limitation Act
Horned Cattle Purchases Act
Irrigation Act
Land Bank Repeal & Temporary Provisions Act
Leafcutting Beekeepers Registration Act
Line Fence Act
Milk Control Act, 1992
On-farm Quality Assurance Programs Act
Pastures Act
Pest Control Act
Bacterial Ring Rot Control Regulations
Dutch Elm Disease Control Regulations
Pest Control Products (Saskatchewan) Act
Prairie Agricultural Machinery Institute Act, 1999
Provincial Lands Act
Sale or Lease of Certain Lands Act
Saskatchewan 4-H Foundation Act
Saskatchewan Farm Security Act
Saskatchewan Wetland Conservation Corporation Land Regulation
Soil Drifting Control Act
Stray Animals Act
Vegetable, Fruit & Honey Sales Act
Veterinarians Act, 1987
Veterinary Services Act
Weed Control Act

Minister, Hon. Bob Bjornerud
306-787-0338, Fax: 306-787-0630, minister.ag@gov.sk.ca
Deputy Minister, Alanna Koch
306-787-5170, Fax: 306-787-2393, alanna.koch@gov.sk.ca
Assistant Deputy Minister, Rick Burton
306-787-8077, Fax: 306-787-2393, rick.burton@gov.sk.ca
Assistant Deputy Minister, Nithi Govindasamy
306-787-5247, Fax: 306-787-2393, nithi.govindasamy@gov.sk.ca
Executive Director, Corporate Services, Raymond Arscott
306-787-5211, Fax: 306-787-0600, raymond.arscott@gov.sk.ca
Executive Director, Policy, Scott Brown
306-787-5961, Fax: 306-787-5134, Scott.Brown@gov.sk.ca
Director, Regional Services, Lee Auten
306-787-5018, Fax: 306-787-9623, lee.auten@gov.sk.ca
Director, Irrigation, John Babcock
306-787-8711, Fax: 306-787-9623, John.Babcock@gov.sk.ca
Director, Crops, Doug Billett
306-787-8061, Fax: 306-787-0428, doug.billett@gov.sk.ca
Acting Director, Lands, Wally Hoehn
306-787-1045, Fax: 306-787-5180, Wally.Hoehn@gov.sk.ca
Director, Agriculture Research, Abdul Jalil
306-787-5960, Fax: 306-787-2654, abdul.jalil@gov.sk.ca
Director, Livestock, Paul Johnson
306-787-6423, Fax: 306-787-1315, paul.johnson@gov.sk.ca; paul.johnson@saskatoonhealthregion.ca
Director, Communications, Donna Rehirchuk
306-787-5389, Fax: 306-787-0216, Donna.Rehirchuk@gov.sk.ca
Director, Financial Programs, Tom Schwartz
306-787-6395, Fax: 306-798-3042, tom.schwartz@gov.sk.ca

Associated Agencies, Boards & Commissions:
• Agri-Food Council
#302, 3085 Albert St.
Regina, SK S4S 0B1
306-787-5978 Fax: 306-787-5134
corey.ruud@gov.sk.ca
www.agriculture.gov.sk.ca/Agri-Food-Council
The Agri-Food Council is an independent board appointed by the provincial government. The Council is accountable to the Minister of Agriculture for the supervision of all agencies established under The Agri-Food Act, 2004.
• Agricultural Implements Board
#202, 3085 Albert St.
Regina, SK S4S 0B1
306-787-4693 Fax: 306-787-1315
• Farm Stress Unit
#125, 3085 Albert St.
Regina, SK S4S 0B1
306-787-5196 Fax: 306-798-3042 800-667-4442
• Farmland Security Board
#207, 3988 Albert St.
Regina, SK S4S 3R1
306-787-5047 Fax: 306-787-8599
• Prairie Agricultural Machinery Institute (PAMI)
Hwy 5 West
PO Box 1150
Humboldt, SK S0K 2A0
306-682-2555 Fax: 306-682-5080 800-567-7264
humboldt@pami.ca
www.pami.ca
PAMI works for the advancement of technology in agriculture through research and development.
• Saskatchewan Crop Insurance Corporation
484 Prince William Dr.
PO Box 3000
Melville, SK S0A 2P0
306-728-7200 Fax: 306-728-7202 888-935-0000
customer.service@scic.gov.sk.ca
www.saskcropinsurance.com
The provincial Crown Corporation provides responsive & flexible risk management tools. Crop insurance programs are as follows: Multi-Peril Insurance; Organic Insurance; Forage Insurance; & Weather Based Insurance.
• Saskatchewan Egg Producers (SEP)
496 Hoffer Dr.
PO Box 1263
Regina, SK S4P 3B8
306-924-1505 Fax: 306-924-1515
sep@saskegg.ca
www.saskegg.ca
• Saskatchewan Lands Appeal Board (SLAB)
#202, 3085 Albert St.
Regina, SK S4S 0B1
306-787-4693 Fax: 306-787-1315
Donald.Brooks@gov.sk.ca
• Saskatchewan Milk Marketing Board (SMMB)
444 McLeod St.
Regina, SK S4N 4Z3
306-949-6999 Fax: 306-949-2605
www.saskmilk.ca
• Saskatchewan Sheep Development Board
2213C Hanselman Crt.
Saskatoon, SK S7L 6A8
306-933-5200 Fax: 306-933-7182
sheepdb@sasktel.net; gordsheepdb@sasktel.net
www.sksheep.com
• Saskatchewan Turkey Producers Marketing Board
502 - 45th St. West, 2nd Fl.
Saskatoon, SK S7L 6H2
306-931-1050 Fax: 306-931-2825
saskaturkey@sasktel.net
The STP manages the supply management system in Saskatchewan & raises levies in order to submit their own levy to the Canadian Turkey Marketing Agency (CTMA). The STP negotiates the province's quota levels with the CTMA, negotiates price levels with local processors, & develops a long-term strategy for the turkey industry in Saskatchewan.

Saskatchewan Archives Board

University of Regina, 3303 Hillsdale St., PO Box 1665, Regina, SK S4P 3C6
306-787-4068 Fax: 306-787-1197
info.regina@archives.gov.sk.ca
www.saskarchives.com

The Saskatchewan Archives is a joint university-government agency, which was established under legislation. The Archives collects official records of the Government of Saskatchewan, as well as documentary material from local government & private sources.

Minister in charge, Hon. Bill Hutchinson
306-787-0354
Chair, Trevor Powell
306-585-0390
Provincial Archivist, Linda McIntyre
306-798-4018, lmcintyre@archives.gov.sk.ca
Chief Archivist/Production Coordinator, Reference Services Unit, Regina, Nadine Charabin
306-933-8321, ncharabin@archives.gov.sk.ca
Chief Archivist, Records Processing, Bruce Dawson
306-798-4015, bdawson@archives.gov.sk.ca
Chief Archivist, Appraisal, Acquisition & Collections Management, Trina Gillis
306-787-0452, tgillis@archives.gov.sk.ca
Acting Chief Archivist, Information Management, Anna Stoszek
306-787-0700, astoszek@archives.gov.sk.ca
Director, Archival Programs & Information Management, Lenora Toth
306-787-4741, ltoth@archives.gov.sk.ca

Saskatchewan Assessment Management Agency (SAMA)

#200, 2201 - 11th Ave., Regina, SK S4P 0J8
306-924-8000 Fax: 306-924-8070
800-667-7262
info.request@sama.sk.ca
www.sama.sk.ca

SAMA is an independent agency with responsibility to develop & maintain the province's assessment policies, standards & procedures, audit assessments, & review & confirm municipal assessment rolls & provide property valuation services to local governments (municipalities & school boards).

Chair, Neal Hardy
Chief Executive Officer, Irwin Blank
306-924-8046, Fax: 306-924-8060
Managing Director, Finance, George Dobni
306-924-8025, Fax: 306-924-8060
Managing Director, Assessment Services, Brad Korbo
306-924-8017, Fax: 306-924-8070
Managing Director, Administration, Betty Rogers
306-924-8032, Fax: 306-924-8060
Managing Director, Quality Assurance, Gordon Senz
306-924-8008, Fax: 306-924-8067
Managing Director, Technical Standards & Policy, Steve Suchan
306-924-8024, Fax: 306-924-8060

Saskatchewan Communications Network (SCN)

#313E, 2440 Broad St., Regina, SK S4P 0A5
306-779-2726 Fax: 306-545-8649
inquiries@scn.ca
www.scn.ca

The regional, public broadcaster delivers cultural, informational & educational programming through the following services: Broadcast Network, E Learning Network, & Technology Services. SCN also acts as an enabler for the regional film & television industry.
Chair, Wynne Young

Corporate Services Division
306-787-3984 Fax: 306-787-1032
Assistant Deputy Minister, Alan Syhlonyk
306-787-7348, Fax: 306-787-1032, Alan.Syhlonyk@gov.sk.ca
Executive Director, Enterprise Projects & Risk Management, Lorne Brown
306-787-3940, Fax: 306-798-2118, Lorne.Brown@gov.sk.ca
Executive Director, Status of Women Office, Pat Faulconbridge
306-787-7423, Fax: 306-787-2058, Pat.Faulconbridge@gov.sk.ca
Acting Executive Director, Strategic Policy, Glenda Francis
306-787-1338, Fax: 306-787-3650, glenda.francis@gov.sk.ca
Executive Director, Finance & Administration, Miriam Myers
306-787-8666, Fax: 306-787-6825, Miriam.Myers@gov.sk.ca
Director, Information Technology Services, Sharon Amorth
306-787-4173, Fax: 306-798-2118, Sharon.Amorth@gov.sk.ca
Director, Risk Management & Business Improvement, Maury Harvey
306-787-6097, Fax: 306-798-5550, maury.harvey@gov.sk.ca
Director, Enterprise Projects, Ron MacLeod
306-787-5241, Fax: 306-798-2118, ron.macleod@gov.sk.ca
Director, Financial Planning, Lori Mann
306-787-1911, Fax: 306-787-6825, lori.mann2@gov.sk.ca
Director, Child & Family Policy, Janet Mitchell
306-787-1533, Fax: 306-787-3650, Janet.Mitchell@gov.sk.ca
Director, Financial Services, Cathy Myres
306-787-3575, Fax: 306-787-1600, cathy.myres@gov.sk.ca; C.Myres@gov.sk.ca, Other Communications: Alternate phone: 306-787-1804
Director, Planning & Performance, Randy Passmore
306-798-2035, Fax: 306-787-3650, Randy.Passmore@gov.sk.ca
Director, Housing Finance, Rachel Ratch
306-787-4961, Fax: 306-787-8571
Director, Benefits Policy, Doug Scott
306-787-0626, Fax: 306-787-3650, Doug.Scott@gov.sk.ca
Director, Community-Based Organization Contract Management, Gail Stuermer
306-787-9105, Fax: 306-787-8203, Gail.Stuermer@gov.sk.ca
Director, Persons with Disabilities Policy, Tara Truemner
306-787-3621, Fax: 306-787-3650, Tara.Truemner@gov.sk.ca
Director, Accommodation Services, Dale Von Hagen
306-787-1383, Fax: 306-798-0077, Dale.VonHagen@gov.sk.ca
Director, Housing Policy, Shauna Wouters
306-787-6118, Fax: 306-787-3650, Shauna.Wouters@gov.sk.ca

Child & Family Services Division
306-787-7010 Fax: 306-787-1032
Assistant Deputy Minister, Louise Greenberg
306-787-4909, Fax: 306-787-1032, louise.greenberg@gov.sk.ca
Executive Director, Program & Service Design, Lynn Allan
306-798-4118, Fax: 306-787-0925, Lynn.Allan@gov.sk.ca
Executive Director, Child & Family Service Delivery, Andrea Brittin
306-787-3652, Fax: 306-787-0925, andrea.brittin@gov.sk.ca
Executive Director, Child & Family Community Services, Wayne Phaneuf
306-787-5481, Fax: 306-787-0925, Wayne.Phaneuf@gov.sk.ca
Director, Child & Family Community Services, Karen Wasylenka
306-787-5698, karen.wasylenka@gov.sk.ca

Income Assistance & Disability Services Division
306-787-1032
Assistant Deputy Minister, Bob Wihidal
306-787-7357, Fax: 306-787-1032, Bob.Wihlidal@gov.sk.ca
Executive Director, Income Assistance Service Delivery, Jeff Redekop
306-787-9013, Fax: 306-787-4450, Jeff.Redekop@gov.sk.ca
Executive Director, Community Living Service Delivery, Beverly Smith
306-787-1951, Fax: 306-787-4450, Beverly.Smith@gov.sk.ca
Executive Director, Linkin Enterprise, Lynn Tullach
306-787-1967, Fax: 306-787-1032, lynn.tulloch@gov.sk.ca
Executive Director, Program & Service Division, Gord Tweed
306-787-0015, Fax: 306-787-3650, gord.tweed@gov.sk.ca

Housing Division
306-787-4177 Fax: 306-798-3110
800-667-7567
www.socialservices.gov.sk.ca/housing
Assistant Deputy Minister, Don Allen
306-787-4174, Fax: 306-787-1032, Don.Allen@gov.sk.ca
Executive Director, Program & Service Design, Eileen Badiuk
306-787-7288, Fax: 306-798-3110, Eileen.Badiuk@gov.sk.ca
Executive Director, Housing Network, Dianne Baird
306-787-8569, Fax: 306-798-3110, Dianne.Baird@gov.sk.ca
Executive Director, Housing Development, Tim Gross
306-787-1008, Fax: 306-798-3110, Tim.Gross@gov.sk.ca

Saskatchewan Corrections, Public Safety & Policing (CPSP)

1874 Scarth St., Regina, SK S4P 4B3
306-787-7872
communicationsCPSP@gov.sk.ca
www.cpsp.gov.sk.ca
The Ministry of Corrections, Public Safety & Policing promotes safe communities in Saskatchewan. Adult correction & young offender programs & services are delivered that serve individuals in conflict with the law. Public safety is also addressed through the following programs & services: protection & emergency planning & communication; monitoring of building standards; fire prevention & disaster assistance programs; & licensing & inspections services.
Acts Administered:
Amusement Ride Safety Act
Boiler & Pressure Vessel Act, 1999
Correctional Services Act
Electrical Licensing Act
Emergency 911 System Act
Emergency Planning Act
Fire Prevention Act, 1992
Gas Licensing Act
Passenger & Freight Elevator Act
Uniform Building & Accessibility Standards Act
Youth Justice Administration Act
Minister, Hon. D.F. (Yogi) Huyghebaert
306-787-4377, Fax: 306-787-5331, minister.cpsp@gov.sk.ca
Deputy Minister, Alan Hilton
306-787-8065, Fax: 306-798-0270, Alan.Hilton@gov.sk.ca
Executive Director, Strategic Policy, Karen Lautsch
306-787-7344, Fax: 306-798-0270, karen.lautsch@gov.sk.ca
Director, Information Management, Cathy Drader
306-787-9512, Fax: 306-787-6979, Cathy.Drader@gov.sk.ca
Director, Communications, Judy Orthner
306-787-5883, Fax: 306-787-3874, judy.orthner@gov.sk.ca
Director, Communications (Justice & Attorney General), Linsay Rabyj
306-787-0775, Fax: 306-787-3874, Linsay.Rabyj@gov.sk.ca

Associated Agencies, Boards & Commissions:
• Saskatchewan Police College (SkPC)
217 College West Bldg., University of Regina
3737 Wascana Pkwy.
Regina, SK S4S 0A2
306-787-8870 Fax: 306-787-8876
www.uregina.ca/police
• Saskatchewan Police Commission
1850 - 1881 Scarth St.
Regina, SK S4P 4K9
306-787-6518 Fax: 306-787-0136
www.cpsp.gov.sk.ca/Saskatchewan-Police-Commission
The Commission promotes crime prevention, improved police relationships with communities, & effective policing throughout Saskatchewan by working closely with police services & Boards of Police Commissioners.

Corporate Services & Public Safety
306-787-8633 Fax: 306-798-0270
Assistant Deputy Minister, Mae Boa
306-787-8081, Fax: 306-798-0270, Mae.Boa@gov.sk.ca
Executive Director, Margaret Anderson
306-798-3283, Fax: 306-798-8882, Margaret.Anderson@gov.sk.ca
Director, Administrative Services, Rhonda Bobst
306-787-6107, Fax: 306-798-8882, Rhonda.Bobst@gov.sk.ca
Director, Financial Planning Services, Jeff Markewich
306-787-9415, Fax: 306-798-0270, jeff.markewich@gov.sk.ca
Director, Gas & Electrical Lighting, Nick Surtees
306-787-9076, Fax: 306-798-8882, Nick.Surtees@gov.sk.ca

Adult Corrections
306-787-8958 Fax: 306-787-0676
www.cpsp.gov.sk.ca/Corrections
Executive Director, Tammy Kirkland
306-787-3573, Fax: 306-787-0676, Tammy.Kirkland@gov.sk.ca
Director, Health Services, Syd Bolt
306-787-2676, Fax: 306-787-0676, Syd.Bolt@gov.sk.ca
Director, Policy & Planning, Fred Burch
306-787-3242, Fax: 306-787-0676, Fred.Burch@gov.sk.ca
Director, Strategic Business & Information Technology, Rick Davis
306-787-3640, Fax: 306-787-0676, Rick.Davis@gov.sk.ca
Director, Community Corrections, Carol Fiedelleck
306-787-3572, Fax: 306-787-0676, Carol.Fiedelleck@gov.sk.ca
Director, Security & Intelligence, Julien Hulet
306-798-8159, Fax: 306-787-0676, Julien.Hulet@gov.sk.ca
Director, Finance, John Igbokwe
306-787-3599, Fax: 306-787-0676, John.Igbokwe@gov.sk.ca
Director, Program Development & Therapeutic Services, Brian Rector
306-787-3892, Fax: 306-787-0676, Brian.Rector@gov.sk.ca
Director, Institutional Operations, Heather Scriver
306-787-3571, Fax: 306-787-0676, heather.scriver@gov.sk.ca
Director, Community Facilities, Dana Wilkins
306-798-0988, Fax: 306-787-0676, Dana.Wilkins@gov.sk.ca

Emergency Management & Fire Safety
#100, 1855 Victoria Ave., Regina, SK S4P 3T2
306-787-8568 Fax: 306-787-1694
www.cpsp.gov.sk.ca/ProtectionandEmergencyServices
Delivers emergency planning & preparedness services, including Sask 911 emergency calling, the Provincial Disaster Assistance Program (PDAP), building standards & the Office of the Fire Commissioner.
Executive Director, Tom Young
306-787-3316, Fax: 306-787-1694, tom.young@gov.sk.ca
Director, Financial Services, Deana Carter Keller
306-787-6068, Fax: 306-787-7107, Deana.CarterKeller@gov.sk.ca
Director, Strategic Planning, Legislative & Program Development, Kevin Roche
306-787-9567, Fax: 306-787-1694, Kevin.Roche@gov.sk.ca

Office of the Fire Commissioner
306-787-3774 Fax: 306-787-7107
866-757-5911
www.cpsp.gov.sk.ca/OFC
The Office of the Fire Commissioner provides communities, fire departments & emergency service organizations with information, education & leadership to enhance their capabilities to protect people, property & the environment from the devastation of fire. The Office includes the Fire Commissioner, Fire Prevention Officer supervisors in charge of regional services, technical services, programs & standards & Fire Prevention Officers who deliver programs to regions.
Fire Commissioner, Duane McKay
306-787-4516, Fax: 306-787-7107, duane.mckay@gov.sk.ca

Saskatchewan Emergency Management Organization (SaskEMO)
306-787-9563 Fax: 306-787-1694
infosafety@cps.gov.sk.ca
www.cpsp.gov.sk.ca/saskemo
Saskatchewan Emergency Management Organization (SaskEMO) maintains the Provincial Emergency Plan & related contingencies as part of their provincial preparedness program to deal with events that may affect government operations. SaskEMO also offers training & education for emergency measures officials, volunteer organizations & public service groups &, to support community preparedness, has municipal emergency measures advisors available 24 hours per day to advise & assist municipalities during local emergencies.
Acting Director, Mieka Torgrimson
306-787-9012, Fax: 306-798-2318, Mieka.Torgrimson@gov.sk.ca

Young Offender Programs
306-787-5699 Fax: 306-787-0676
www.cpsp.gov.sk.ca/yo
Executive Director, Bob Kary
306-787-4701, Fax: 306-787-0676, bob.kary@gov.sk.ca
Director, Custody Programs, Constance Hourie
306-787-9237, Fax: 306-787-0676, Constance.Hourie@gov.sk.ca
Director, Community Youth Services, Kim Gurnsey
306-787-1394, Fax: 306-787-0676, Kim.Gurnsey@gov.sk.ca
Director, Program Development & Therapeutic Services, Brian Rector
306-787-3892, Fax: 306-787-0676, brian.rector@gov.sk.ca
Director, Financial Services, Gaylene Weir
306-787-0721, Fax: 306-787-0676, Gaylene.Weir@gov.sk.ca

Regional Offices
Central Region
#903, 122 3rd Ave. North, Saskatoon, SK S7K 2H6
306-933-6052 Fax: 306-964-1103
Regional Director, Harry Smith
306-933-7438, Fax: 306-964-1103, Harry.Smith@gov.sk.ca
Director, Clinical Services, Dean Carey
306-933-7435, Fax: 306-964-1103, Dean.Carey@gov.sk.ca
Northeast Region
PO Box 3003, Prince Albert, SK S6V 6G1
306-953-2643 Fax: 306-953-2649
866-397-7826
Regional Director, Fraser Denton
306-953-2583, Fax: 306-953-2649
Regional Director, Jarrett Parker
306-953-3192, Fax: 306-953-2649, Jarrett.Parker@gov.sk.ca

South Region
2045 Broad St., 5th Fl., Regina, SK S4P 3T7
306-787-9137 Fax: 306-787-5559
Regional Director, Rick Bereti
306-787-3695, Fax: 306-787-5559, Rick.Bereti@gov.sk.ca
Director, Clinical Services, Jamie Smith
306-787-8643, Fax: 306-787-7546, Jamie.Smith@gov.sk.ca

Policing Services Division
1850 - 1881 Scarth St., Regina, SK S4P 4K9
306-787-6518 Fax: 306-787-0136
pisg@justice.gov.sk.ca
www.cpsp.gov.sk.ca/Police-Services-Division
Executive Director, Murray Sawatsky
306-787-6534, Murray.Sawatsky@gov.sk.ca
Director, Aboriginal Policing Service, Bernadette Aubichon
306-953-3466, Fax: 306-953-2537, bernadette.aubichon@gov.sk.ca
Director, Program & Finance, Terry Hawkes
306-787-1150, Fax: 306-787-0136, Terry.Hawkes@gov.sk.ca
Director, Strategic Policy Development, Richard Peach
306-787-9292, Fax: 306-787-0136, Richard.Peach@gov.sk.ca
Director, Financial Services, Trevor Wowk
306-787-8608, Fax: 306-787-0136
Director, David Horn
306-787-0400, Fax: 306-798-7700, David.Horn@gov.sk.ca
Director, Saskatchewan Witness Protection Program, Randy Koroluk
306-798-0262, Fax: 306-798-7700, Randy.Koroluk@gov.sk.ca
Director, Seizure of Criminal Property, Don Perron
306-798-8155, Fax: 306-798-7700, Don.Perron@gov.sk.ca
Senior Investigator, Safer Communities & Neighbourhoods Investigation Unit, Blair Ritchie
306-933-8373, Fax: 306-933-8392, Blair.Ritchie@gov.sk.ca

Custody Programs
306-787-1352 Fax: 306-798-0012

Saskatchewan Education (ED)

2220 College Ave., Regina, SK S4P 4V9
linquiry@gov.sk.ca
www.education.gov.sk.ca
The Ministry provides programs & services in the following key areas: early learning & child care, the prekindergarten to grade 12 education system, & the Provincial Library. In November 2007, a new provincial government resulted in the reorganization of provincial government ministries. The work of Saskatchewan Learning was merged into a newly named ministry. Ken Krawetz was named the Minister of Education.
Acts Administered:
Education Act
League of Educational Administrators, Directors & Superintendents Act
Public Libraries Act
Registered Music Teachers Act
Teachers' Dental Plan Act
Teachers' Federation Act
Teachers' Life Insurance (Government Contributory) Act
Teachers' Superannuation & Disability Benefits Act
Child Care Act (jointly with Social Services)
Government Organization Act
Libraries Co-operation Act
Minister, Education, Hon. Donna Harpauer
306-787-7360, Fax: 306-798-0263, minister.edu@gov.sk.ca
Chief of Staff, Raynelle Wilson
306-787-9125, Fax: 306-798-0263, Raynelle.Wilson@gov.sk.ca
Acting Deputy Minister, Cheryl Senecal
306-787-2471, Fax: 306-787-1300, cheryl.senecal@gov.sk.ca
Assistant Deputy Minister, Greg Miller
306-787-3222, Fax: 306-787-1300, greg.miller2@gov.sk.ca
Acting Assistant Deputy Minister, Ted Warawa
306-787-6056, Fax: 306-787-1300, ted.warawa@gov.sk.ca
Executive Director, Ministry Renewal Team, Jane Thurgood Sagal
306-787-6842
Executive Director, Communications, Jill Welke
306-787-5609, Fax: 306-798-2045, Jill.Welke@gov.sk.ca
Director, Finance, Corporate Services, Dawn Court
306-787-7206, Fax: 306-798-5042, Dawn.court@gov.sk.ca

Associated Agencies, Boards & Commissions:
• Teachers' Superannuation Commission
#129, 3085 Albert St.
Regina, SK S4S 0B1
306-787-6440 Fax: 306-787-1939 877-364-8202
mail@stsc.gov.sk.ca
www.stsc.gov.sk.ca

Saskatchewan Energy & Resources (ER)

#300, 2103 - 11th Ave., Regina, SK S4P 3Z8
306-787-2528
webmasterer@gov.sk.ca
www.er.gov.sk.ca
The Ministry encourages the growth & development of the provincial resource sector. The Ministry's two main roles are as follows: offering programs & services to individuals & businesses; & coordinating economic development activities with other departments & agencies. In November 2007, a new provincial government resulted in the reorganization of provincial government ministries. The work of Saskatchewan Industry & Resources was merged into a newly named ministry. Bill Boyd was named the Minister of Energy & Resources.
Acts Administered:
Crown Minerals Act
Department of Economic Development Act, 1993
Department of Energy & Mines Act
Ethanol Fuel Act, 2002
Ethanol Fuel (General) Regulations
Ethanol Fuel (Grant) Regulations
Mineral Resources Act, 1985
Seismic Exploration Regulations
Oil & Gas Conservation Act
Oil & Gas Conservation Regulations
Pipelines Act, 1998
Minister, Energy & Resources, Hon. Bill Boyd
306-787-9124, Fax: 306-787-0395, minister.er@gov.sk.ca
Deputy Minister, Energy & Resources, Kent Campbell
306-787-9580, Fax: 306-787-2159, kent.campbell@gov.sk.ca
Associate Deputy Minister, Forestry Development, Bob Ruggles
306-787-5122, Fax: 306-798-0599, Bob.Ruggles@gov.sk.ca; Bob.Ruggles3@gov.sk.ca
Director, Public Affairs, Bob Ellis
306-787-8983, Fax: 306-787-2198, robert.ellis@gov.sk.ca

Associated Agencies, Boards & Commissions:
• Saskatchewan Trade & Export Partnership (STEP)
#320, 1801 Hamilton St.
PO Box 1787
Regina, SK S4P 3C6
306-787-9210 Fax: 306-787-6666
inquire@sasktrade.sk.ca
www.sasktrade.sk.ca
Other Communication: Saskatchewan exports information: 1-888-976-7875
Works in partnership with provincial export companies & emerging export companies to maximize commercial success in foreign ventures. STEP provides marketing services using a team of trade professionals, innovative approaches & world-wide networks. By promoting & developing sales, contracts, projects & referrals, STEP increases exports to existing foreign markets & taps into new markets.
• Surface Rights Board of Arbitration
113 - 2nd Ave. East
PO Box 1597
Kindersley, SK S0L 1S0
306-463-5447 Fax: 306-463-5449
surfacerightsboard@gov.sk.ca
www.er.gov.sk.ca/surfacerights
Governed by The Surface Rights Acquisition and Compensation Act, the Surface Rights Board of Arbitration is a last resort when an occupant or landowner & an oil, gas or potash operator are unable to reach an agreement.

Enterprise Saskatchewan

#200, 3085 Albert St., Regina, SK S4S 0B1
306-787-4484 Fax: 306-798-0629
800-265-2001
webmaster@enterprisesask.ca; invest@enterprisesask.ca
www.enterprisesaskatchewan.ca
Enterprise Saskatchewan (ES) is a bold and innovative approach to creating sustainable economic growth in Saskatchewan. It is a special agency for co-ordinating the province's growth agenda, led by key economic development and community stakeholders with one ultimate goal: to ensure Saskatchewan has a competitive environment that will attract investment at every level. Enterprise Saskatchewan provides leadership as the central co-ordinating agency of the Government of Saskatchewan for economic development. In partnership with key stakeholders, Enterprise Saskatchewan advances a transformative sustainable economic growth agenda and develops a culture of innovation and entrepreneurship that encourages investment and population growth, creating prosperity for all Saskatchewan residents.
Acts Administered:
Economic & Co-operative Development Act
Regional Economic & Co-operative Development Act
Minister, Enterprise, Hon. Jeremy Harrison
306-787-0804, Fax: 306-798-2009, minister.es@gov.sk.ca
Chief Executive Officer, Chris Dekker
306-933-6744, Fax: 306-798-0629, chris.dekker@enterprisesask.ca, Other Communications: Alternate Phone: 306-787-7518
Chief Financial Officer, Denise Haas
306-787-2756, Fax: 306-798-0629, denise.haas@enterprisesask.ca
Vice-President, Sector Development, Tony Baumgartner
306-787-3435, Fax: 306-787-3989, tony.baumgartner@enterprisesask.ca
Vice-President, Regional Enterprise, Ernest Heapy
306-787-2561, Fax: 306-787-7559, ernest.heapy@enterprisesask.ca
Vice-President, Competitiveness & Strategy, Angela Schmidt
306-933-8223, Fax: 306-933-8244, angela.schmidt@enterprisesask.ca

Parks Service Division
3211 Albert St., 2nd Fl., Regina, SK S4S 5W6
306-787-7031 Fax: 306-787-7000
www.tpcs.gov.sk.ca/Parks/
Associate Deputy Minister, Lin Gallagher
306-798-3905, Fax: 306-787-7000, Lin.Gallagher@gov.sk.ca
Executive Director, Park Operations & Planning, Cindy MacDonald
306-787-0731, Fax: 306-787-7000, Cindy.MacDonald@gov.sk.ca
Director, Facilities, Bob Lalonde
306-787-2783, Fax: 306-787-4218, Bob.Lalonde@gov.sk.ca
Director, Park Management Services, Bob McEachern
306-787-2948, Fax: 306-787-7000, Bob.McEachern@gov.sk.ca

Elections Saskatchewan

1702 Park St., Regina, SK S4N 6B2
306-787-4000 Fax: 306-787-4052
877-958-8683
info@elections.sk.ca
www.elections.sk.ca
Other Communication: Toll-Free Fax: 1-866-678-4052
Acting Chief Electoral Officer, Dave Wilkie
306-787-4027, 877-958-8683, dwilkie@elections.sk.ca
Chief Operating Officer, Saundra Arberry
306-787-4061, 866-247-5404, sarberry@elections.sk.ca
Manager, Information Technology, Jeff Livingstone
306-787-9327, 866-250-2263, jlivingstone@elections.sk.ca
Manager, Election Finances, Brent Nadon
306-787-4017, 866-249-7186, bnadon@elections.sk.ca
Communications, Daniel Bodgon
306-787-7355, 855-220-7355, dbogdon@elections.sk.ca

Saskatchewan Environment (ENV)

3211 Albert St., 2nd Fl., Regina, SK S4S 5W6
306-787-2584 Fax: 306-787-9544
800-567-4224
Centre.Inquiry@gov.sk.ca
www.environment.gov.sk.ca
Other Communication: Parkwatch Line: 1-800-667-1788; Firewatch Line: 1-800-667-9660; Spill Control Centre: 1-800-667-7525; TIP (Turn in Poachers: 1-800-667-7561
Saskatchewan Environment protects & mananges the province's environmental & natural resources by offering the following programs & services: compliance & enforcement to protect the public's interests in the management of air, land, water & natural resources; protection & management of forest ecosystems; wildfire management; Green Strategy; environmental assessment; legislation, & policies to ensure that Crown land is used in ways that respect environmental, economic & social values; fishing & fisheries management; hunting management; licensing & guiding the trapping industry; protection of wildlife; recycling; waste management; & water resource & treatment plant operations management.
Acts Administered:
Clean Air Act
Clean Air Regulation
Conservation Easements Act
Potash Refining Air Emissions Regulations
Ecological Reserves Act
Assiniboine Slopes Provincial Ecological Reserves Regulations
Buffalograss Ecological Reserve Regulations
Provincial Ecological Reserves Regulation
Qu'Appelle Coulee Provincial Ecological Reserves Regulations
Representative Area Ecological Reserve Regulations
Environmental Assessment Act
Environmental Management & Protection Act, 2002
Environmental Spill Control Regulations
Halocarbon Control Regulations
Hazardous Substances & Dangerous Goods Regulations
Mineral Industry Environmental Protection Regulations
Municipal Refuse Management Regulations
Ozone-Depleting Substances Control Regulations
PCB Waste Storage Regulations
Reservoir Development Area Regulations
Scrap Tire Management Regulations
Used Oil Collection Regulations
Waste Electronic Equipment Regulations

Waste Paint Management Regulations
Water Regulations
Fisheries Act
Fisheries Regulations
Forest Resources Management Act
Dutch Elm Disease Regulations
Forest Resources Management Regulations
Indian Treaty Obligations Regulations
Surface Lease Agreement Regulations: Beaverlodge, Cigar Lake, Cluff Lake, Jolu Project, Key Lake, Konuto Project, McArthur River Operation, McClean Lake, Midwest Joint, Rabbit Lake
Wild Rice Regulations
Withdrawal of Land from Forests; Historical Interest Regulations
Grasslands National Park Act
Litter Control Act
Natural Resources Act
Commercial Activities Regulations
Commercial Fishing Production Incentive Regulations
Outfitter & Guide Regulations, 1996
Resource Protection & Development Services Regulations
Park Land Reserve Regulations
Parks Regulations
Recreation Site Regulations, 1991
Parks Act
Government Land Reserves Regulation
Historic Sites Regulations
Park Land Reserves Regulations
Prairie & Forest Fires Act, 1982
Provincial Lands Act
Crown Resource Lands Regulations, 1989
Provincial Lands Regulations
Surface Rights Regulations (Grasslands Park, Komis Project, Parks Lake Uranium Mining, Seabee)
Sale or Lease of Certain Lands Act
Saskatchewan Watershed Authority Act 2005
Drainage Control Regulations
Groundwater Regulations
Reservoir Development Area Regulations
State of the Environment Report Act
Water Appeal Board Act
Wildlife Act, 1998
Captive Wildlife Regulations
Dog Training Regulations
Open Seasons Game Regulations
Wild Species at Risk Regulations
Wildlife Landowner Assistance Regulations, 1991
Wildlife Management Zones & Special Areas Boundaries Regulations, 1990
Wildlife Regulations, 1981
Wildlife Habitat Protection Act
Treaty Land Entitlement Withdrawal Regulations
Wildlife Habitat Lands Designation Regulations
Wildlife Habitat Lands Disposition & Alteration Regulations
Forestry Professions Act

Minister, Hon. Dustin Duncan
306-787-0393, Fax: 306-787-1669, minister.env@gov.sk.ca
Deputy Minister, Liz Quarshie
306-787-2930, Fax: 306-787-2947, liz.quarshie@gov.sk.ca
Acting Executive Director, Strategic Planning & Performance Improvement, Greg Leake
306-787-5511, Fax: 306-787-2947, Greg.Leake@gov.sk.ca
Acting Director, Communications, Everett Dorma
306-787-2770, Fax: 306-787-3941, Everett.Dorma@gov.sk.ca

Associated Agencies, Boards & Commissions:

• Saskatchewan Conservation Data Centre
3211 Albert St.
Regina, SK S4S 5W6
306-787-9038 Fax: 306-787-9544
www.biodiversity.sk.ca
The SKCDC was formed as a co-operative venture between the province, The Nature Conservancy USA & The Nature Conservancy of Canada. The SKCDC gathers, interprets & distributes scientific information on the ecological status of provincial wild species & communities. The SKCDC is committed to conserving biological diversity; producing scientific reports & being the provincial clearinghouse for threatened & endangered species information.

• Saskatchewan Watershed Authority
111 Fairford St. East
Moose Jaw, SK S6H 7X9
306-694-3900 Fax: 306-694-3465
comm@swa.ca
www.swa.ca
The Saskatchewan Watershed Authority administers the following legislation and regulations: Conservation & Development Act; Saskatchewan Watershed Authority Act, 2005; Water Power Act; Watershed Associations Act; Conservation & Development Regulations; Drainage Control Regulations; Ground Water Regulations; & Reservoir Development Area Regulations.

• Water Appeal Board
#217, 3085 Albert St.
Regina, SK S4S 0B1
306-798-7462 Fax: 306-787-8558
www.gov.sk.ca/wb

Environmental Protection & Audit Division
3211 Albert St., 5th Fl., Regina, SK S4S 5W6
306-787-2947
Protects human health & ecosystem integrity.
Assistant Deputy Minister, Mark Wittrup
306-787-5419, Fax: 306-787-2947, mark.wittrup@gov.sk.ca
Chief Engineer, Technical Resources Branch, Kevin McCullum
306-787-2739, Fax: 306-787-2947, Kevin.McCullum@gov.sk.ca
Executive Director, Municipal Branch, Sam Ferris
306-787-6193, Fax: 306-787-0197, sam.ferris@gov.sk.ca
Executive Director, Industrial Branch, Wes Kotyk
306-933-6542, Fax: 306-933-8442, Wes.Kotyk@gov.sk.ca
Executive Director, Wildfire Management Branch, Steve Roberts
306-953-2206, Fax: 306-953-3575, Steve.Roberts@gov.sk.ca
Director, Environmental Assessment Branch, Tareq Al Zabet
306-787-1023, Fax: 306-787-0930, tareq.alzabet@gov.sk.ca
Acting Director, Wildfire Support Section, Daryl Jessop
306-953-3472, Fax: 306-953-3670, Daryl.Jessop@gov.sk.ca
Director, Wildfire Management Operations Section, Curtis Lee
306-953-3429, Fax: 306-953-3575, Curtis.Lee@gov.sk.ca
Director, Environmental Protection Services Section, Thon Phommavong
306-787-9986, Fax: 306-787-0197, Thon.Phommavong@gov.sk.ca
Director, Aviation Operations, Denis Renaud
306-425-4586, Fax: 306-425-4538, Denis.Renaud@gov.sk.ca

Environmental Support Division
3211 Albert St., 5th Fl., Regina, SK S4S 5W6
Fax: 306-787-2947
Acting Assistant Deputy Minister, Donna Johnson
306-787-5737, Fax: 306-787-2947, Donna.Johnson@gov.sk.ca
Chief Information Officer, Information Management & Geomatics Services, Kevin Saunderson
306-798-3901, Fax: 306-787-3913, Kevin.Saunderson@gov.sk.ca
Acting Executive Director, Finance & Administration, Laurel Welsh
306-787-2484, Fax: 306-787-8441, Laurel.Welsh@gov.sk.ca
Director, Climate Change, Kim Graybiel
306-787-0114, Fax: 306-787-0024, Kim.Graybiel@gov.sk.ca
Director, Financial Management, Susan Loewen
306-787-7609, Fax: 306-787-8441, Susan.Loewen@gov.sk.ca
Director, Aboriginal Affairs, Jennifer McKillop
306-787-9643, Fax: 306-787-0197, Jennifer.Mckillop@gov.sk.ca
Acting Director, Financial & Property Management, Zachery Solomon
306-798-3904, Fax: 306-787-8441, zachery.solomon@gov.sk.ca

Resource Management & Compliance Division
3211 Albert St., 5th fl., Regina, SK S4S 5W6
Fax: 306-787-2947
Assistant Deputy Minister, Kevin Murphy
306-787-8567, Fax: 306-787-2947, Kevin.Murphy@gov.sk.ca
Executive Director, Compliance & Field Services, Kevin Callele
306-787-3388, Fax: 306-787-3913, Kevin.Callele@gov.sk.ca
Executive Director, Fish & Wildlife, Lyle Saigeon
306-787-2309, Fax: 306-787-9544, Lyle.Saigeon@gov.sk.ca
Executive Director, Forest Service, Bob Wynes
306-953-2491, Fax: 306-953-2360, Bob.Wynes@gov.sk.ca
Director, Lands, Todd Olexson
306-953-2586, Fax: 306-953-2684, Todd.Olexson@gov.sk.ca
Director, Field Services, Brent Webster
306-446-7424, Fax: 306-446-7464, Brent.Webster@gov.sk.ca

Regional Operations
Beauval Compliance Area
Lavoie St., PO Box 280, Beauval, SK S0M 0G0
306-288-4710 Fax: 306-288-4717
Compliance Manager, Dennis Daigneault
306-288-4713, Fax: 306-288-4717, Dennis.Daigneault@gov.sk.ca
La Ronge Compliance Area
Mistasinihk Place, #1100 - 1328 La Ronge Ave., PO Box 5000, La Ronge, SK S0J 1L0
306-425-4234 Fax: 306-425-2580
Compliance Manager, Daryl Minster
306-425-4244, Fax: 306-425-2580, Daryl.Minter@gov.sk.ca
Meadow Lake Compliance Area
#1, 101 Railway Pl., Meadow Lake, SK S9X 1X6
306-236-7557 Fax: 306-236-7677
Acting Compliance Manager, Marc Painchaud
306-236-9833, Fax: 306-236-7677, Marc.Painchaud@gov.sk.ca
Prince Albert Compliance Area
800 Central Ave., PO Box 3003, Prince Albert, SK S6V 6G1
306-953-2322 Fax: 306-953-2321
Compliance Manager, Bill Zimmer
306-953-2945, Fax: 306-953-2999, Bill.Zimmer@gov.sk.ca
Saskatoon Compliance Area
112 Research Dr., Saskatoon, SK S7N 3R3
306-933-6240 Fax: 306-933-5773
Compliance Manager, Doug Robinson
306-933-7929, Fax: 306-933-5773, doug.robinson@gov.sk.ca
Swift Current Compliance Area
350 Cheadle St. West, PO Box 5000, Swift Current, SK S9H 4G3
306-778-8205 Fax: 306-778-8212
Compliance Manager, Bob Roberts
306-778-8644, Fax: 306-778-8212, bob.roberts@gov.sk.ca
Yorkton Compliance Area
120 Smith St. East, Yorkton, SK S3N 3V3
Fax: 306-786-5716
Compliance Manager, Phil Decker
306-786-1692, Fax: 306-786-5716, Phil.Decker@gov.sk.ca

Saskatchewan Finance (FI)

2350 Albert St., Regina, SK S4P 4A6
306-787-6768 Fax: 306-787-0241
communications@finance.gov.sk.ca
www.finance.gov.sk.ca
Other Communication: General Tax Inquiries: 1-800-667-6102
The Ministry of Finance manages the financing, revenue, & expenses of the provincial government. The following are some of the duties performed by the department: administering provincial taxes, grant, & refund programs; managing banking, investment, & public debt functions; providing financial & policy analysis; offering economic forecasting & economic & social statistics; producing the provincial budget; assisting the government in the management of public monies; & managing governmental pension & benefit plans.

Acts Administered:
Certified General Accountants Act, 1994
Certified Management Accountants Act (not yet proclaimed)
Certified Management Consultants Act
Chartered Accountants Act, 1986
Corporation Capital Tax Act
Federal-Provincial Agreements Act
Financial Administration Act, 1993
Fuel Tax Act, 2000
Home Energy Loan Act
Income Tax Act
Income Tax Act, 2000
Insurance Premiums Tax Act
Liquor Board Superannuation Act
Liquor Consumption Tax Act
Management Accountants Act
Members of the Legislative Assembly Benefits Act
Motor Vehicle Insurance Premiums Tax Act
Municipal Employees' Pension Act
Municipal Financing Corporation Act
Provincial Auditor Act
Provincial Sales Tax Act
Public Employees Pension Plan Act
Public Service Superannuation Act
Revenue & Financial Services Act
Saskatchewan Development Fund Act
Saskatchewan Pension Annuity Fund Act
Saskatchewan Pension Plan Act
Statistics Act
Superannuation (Supplementary Provisions) Act
Tabling of Documents Act, 1991
Tobacco Tax Act, 1998

Minister, Hon. Ken Krawetz
306-787-6060, Fax: 306-787-6055, minister.fin@gov.sk.ca
Deputy Minister, Karen Layng
306-787-6621, Fax: 306-787-7155, Karen.Layng@gov.sk.ca, Other Communications: Alternate Phone: 306-787-3102
Executive Director, Communications, Randy Burton
306-787-6578, Fax: 306-787-7155, Randy.Burton@gov.sk.ca
Executive Director, Personnel Policy Secretariat, Tor Veltheim
306-787-3101, Fax: 306-798-0386, tor.veltheim@gov.sk.ca; torv@saho.org
Director, Financial Services, Louise Usick
306-787-6530, Fax: 306-787-6576, Louise.Usick@gov.sk.ca

Associated Agencies, Boards & Commissions:

• Board of Revenue Commissioners
#480, 2151 Scarth St.
Regina, SK S4P 2H8
306-787-6221 Fax: 306-787-1610
www.gov.sk.ca/BRC
Any write-off or cancellation of monies owing to the Crown is subject to prior approval of the Board of Revenue Commissioners as delegated by the Treasury Board. The Board has the power to hear & determine appeals respecting taxes imposed or assessed pursuant to & by virtue of any taxing

enactment & respecting other monies claimed to be due & payable to the Crown where the right of taking appeal to the Board is given by any statute.

• Municipal Employees' Pension Commission
#1000, 1801 Hamilton St.
Regina, SK S4P 4W3
Fax: 306-787-8822
www.peba.gov.sk.ca/MEPP/mepp_commission.htm
The Municipal Employees' Pension Commission is responsible for the administration of the Municipal Employees' Pension Fund.

• Municipal Financing Corporation of Saskatchewan (MFC)
2350 Albert St., 6th Fl.
Regina, SK S4P 4A6
306-787-8150 Fax: 306-787-8493
www.gov.sk.ca/mfc
The MFC, established in 1969 under the authority of The Municipal Financing Corporation Act, makes capital funds available to the financing of sewer & water, school, hospital, & other vital municipal construction projects.

• Saskatchewan Development Fund Corporation
#400, 2400 College Ave.
Regina, SK S4P 1C8
306-787-1645 Fax: 306-787-8125
www.cicorp.sk.ca/funds/saskatchewan_development_fund_corp
The Saskatchewan Development Fund is a low risk investment fund that provides income & long-term investment growth to Saskatchewan residents. The Fund is administered by the Saskatchewan Development Fund Corporation. Since 1983, the Fund no longer sells new shares to the public.

• Saskatchewan Pension Plan
PO Box 5555
Kindersley, SK S0L 1S0
306-463-5410 Fax: 306-463-3500 800-667-7153
www.saskpension.com

Budget Analysis Division
306-787-6742

Associate Deputy Minister, Taxation & Intergovernmental Affairs Branch, Kirk McGregor
306-787-6731, Fax: 306-787-7003, kirk.mcgregor@gov.sk.ca
Assistant Deputy Minister, Treasury Board, Denise Macza
306-787-6780, Fax: 306-787-3982, Denise.Macza@gov.sk.ca
Executive Director, Economic & Fiscal Policy Branch, Joanne Brockman
306-787-6743, Fax: 306-787-1426, joanne.brockman@gov.sk.ca
Executive Director, Estimates, Al Dennett
306-787-6726, Fax: 306-787-3982, Al.Dennett@gov.sk.ca
Director, Performance Management Branch, Raelynn Douglas
306-787-7762, Fax: 306-787-3982, Raelynn.Douglas@gov.sk.ca

Provincial Comptroller's Division
306-787-6353 Fax: 306-787-9720

Provincial Comptroller, Terry Paton
306-787-9254, Fax: 306-787-9720, Terry.Paton@gov.sk.ca

Public Employees Benefits Agency
1000 - 1801 Hamilton St., Regina, SK S4P 4W3
306-787-2992 Fax: 306-787-8822
peba@peba.gov.sk.ca
www.peba.gov.sk.ca

Assistant Deputy Minister, Brian L. Smith
306-787-6757, Fax: 306-798-0065, brian.smith@peba.gov.sk.ca

Revenue Division
306-787-6645 Fax: 306-787-0776
800-667-6102

Assistant Deputy Minister, Margaret Johannsson
306-787-6685, Fax: 306-787-0241, margaret.johannsson@gov.sk.ca
Director, Provincial Sales Tax (PST) Branch, Rob Dobson
306-787-7785, Fax: 306-798-3045, rob.dobson@gov.sk.ca; rob.dobson2@gov.sk.ca
Director, Audit Branch, Brent Herbert
306-787-7784, Fax: 306-798-3045, Brent.Hebert@gov.sk.ca
Director, Revenue Programs Branch, Doug Lambert
306-787-4600, Fax: 306-787-0241, Doug.Lambert@gov.sk.ca
Director, Revenue Operations Branch, Kelly Laurans
306-787-7788, Fax: 306-787-6653, kelly.laurans@gov.sk.ca

Treasury & Debt Management Division
306-787-6752 Fax: 306-787-8493

Assistant Deputy Minister, Rae Haverstock
306-787-9473, Fax: 306-787-8493
Executive Director, Cash & Debt Management Branch, Jim Fallows
306-787-3923, Fax: 306-787-8493, jim.fallows@gov.sk.ca
Executive Director, Capital Markets Branch, Vacant
306-787-6753, Fax: 306-787-8493
Director, Liability & Risk Management, Carla Brown
306-787-9474, Fax: 306-787-8493, carla.brown@gov.sk.ca
Director, Investments, Doug Dorsch
306-787-3905, Fax: 306-787-8493, Doug.Dorsch@gov.sk.ca

Saskatchewan First Nations & Métis Relations (FNMR)

#1020, 1855 Victoria Ave., Regina, SK S4P 3T2
306-787-6250 Fax: 306-798-0083
www.fnmr.gov.sk.ca

Working with First Nations and Métis people, the Ministry carries out the following responsibilities: providing overall direction to the government's approach to issues concerning First Nations & Métis people; coordinating programs in other government departments; ensuring that Saskatchewan's commitments regarding lands & resources are fulfilled; & working in partnership with First Nations & Métis people on issues of education & economic participation.

Acts Administered:
Indian & Native Affairs Act
Métis Act
Saskatchewan Gaming Corporation Act, Part III
Treaty Land Entitlement Implementation Act
Government Organization Act (Department of First Nations & Métis Relations Regulations)

Minister, Hon. Ken Cheveldayoff
306-787-0605, Fax: 306-798-8050, minister.fnmr@gov.sk.ca
Deputy Minister, Ron Crowe
306-787-6253, Fax: 306-798-0083, ron.crowe@gov.sk.ca
Assistant Deputy Minister, James Froh
306-787-7405, Fax: 306-798-0083, James.Froh@gov.sk.ca
Executive Director, Strategic Initiatives, Seonaid MacPherson
306-787-8142, Fax: 306-798-0083, Seonaid.MacPherson@gov.sk.ca
Executive Director, Relationships & Policy, Giselle Marcotte
306-787-0998, Fax: 306-787-5832, Giselle.Marcotte@gov.sk.ca
Director, Relationships & Policy, Alethea Foster
306-787-5176, Fax: 306-787-5832, Alethea.Foster@gov.sk.ca
Director, Finance, Accountability & Corporate Services, Kerry Gray
306-787-2123, Fax: 306-798-0004, kerry.gray@gov.sk.ca
Acting Director, Communications, Cathe Offet
306-787-5701, Fax: 306-798-0083, Cathe.Offet@gov.sk.ca
Director, Gaming Trusts & Grants, Sam Swan
306-787-1695, Fax: 306-798-0004, Sam.Swan@gov.sk.ca

Lands & Consultation
306-787-5722 Fax: 306-787-6336

Manages & coordinates Saskatchewan's obligations under Treaty Land Entitlement. The Branch also performs a similar function with respect to Specific Claims.
Executive Director, Trisha Delormier-Hill
306-787-6681, Fax: 306-798-0004, trisha.delormier-hill@gov.sk.ca
Director, Susan Carani
306-787-9706, Fax: 306-798-0004, susan.carani@gov.sk.ca

Northern Affairs Division
306-425-4207 Fax: 306-425-4349
admin@sna.gov.sk.ca
www.fnmr.gov.sk.ca/northern

Assistant Deputy Minister, Toby Greschner
306-425-4203, Toby.Greschner@gov.sk.ca
Executive Director, Northern Regional Economic Development, Doug Howorko
306-798-5167, Fax: 306-787-6014, Doug.Howorko2@gov.sk.ca
Executive Director, Northern Social Development, Mark LaRocque
306-787-6400, Fax: 306-787-6014, Mark.LaRocque@gov.sk.ca
Executive Director, Northern Industry & Resource Development, Richard Turkheim
306-787-2143, Fax: 306-787-6014, Richard.Turkheim@gov.sk.ca

Saskatchewan Gaming Corporation (SaskGaming)

1880 Saskatchewan Dr., 3rd Fl., Regina, SK S4P 0B2
306-787-1590
www.casinoregina.com/corporate

SaskGaming was created by The Saskatchewan Gaming Corporation Act in 1994, in order to establish and operate casinos across the province.

Minister Responsible, Hon. Ken Cheveldayoff
306-787-0605, Fax: 306-798-8050, minister.fnmr@gov.sk.ca
President/Chief Executive Officer, Twyla Meredith
306-787-1291, Fax: 306-787-1444, twyla.meredith@saskgaming.com
Senior Vice-President, Finance & Administration, Tony Coppola
306-798-0998, Fax: 306-798-0824, tony.coppola@saskgaming.com
Senior Vice-President, Operations, Gerry Fischer
306-787-1483, Fax: 306-787-5880, gerry.fischer@saskgaming.com
Vice-President, Corporate Risk & Compliance, Bob Arlint
306-787-2353, Fax: 306-798-2308, bob.arlint@saskgaming.com
Vice-President, Marketing, Susan Flett
306-787-1356, Fax: 306-787-0639, susan.flett@saskgaming.com
Vice-President, Communications & Community Relations, Michelle Hunter
306-787-2263, Fax: 306-787-4880, michelle.hunter@saskgaming.com
Vice-President, Human Resources, Blaine Pilatzke
306-787-1401, Fax: 306-798-0449, blaine.pilatzke@saskgaming.com

Saskatchewan Government Insurance (SGI)

2260 - 11th Ave., Regina, SK S4P 0J9
306-751-1200 Fax: 306-787-7477
800-667-8015
sgiinquiries@sgi.sk.ca
www.sgi.sk.ca
Other Communication: Customer Service Centre: 1-800-667-9868

Operating in twenty claims centres in Saskatchewan communities, SGI sells property & casualty insurance products. One of SGI's operations is The Saskatchewan Auto Fund, the province's compulsory auto insurance program. The Auto Fund administers the driver's licensing & vehicle registration system.

Minister Responsible, Hon. Tim McMillan
306-787-7339, Fax: 306-798-3140, minister.cc@gov.sk.ca
Chair, Board of Directors, Warren Sproule
President/Chief Executive Officer, Andrew Cartmell
306-751-1717, Fax: 306-525-6040, acartmell@sgi.sk.ca
Chief Financial Officer, Jeff Stepan
306-775-6004, jstepan@sgi.sk.ca
Chief Internal Auditor, Kevin Taylor
306-751-1781, ktaylor@sgi.sk.ca
Vice-President, Auto Fund, Sherry Wolf
306-751-1646, swolf@sgi.sk.ca
Vice-President, Canadian Operations, John Dobie
306-751-1597, jdobie@sgi.sk.ca
Vice-President, Claims & Salvage, Earl Cameron
306-751-1705, ecameron@sgi.sk.ca
Vice-President, Product Management, Don Thompson
306-751-1585, dthompson@sgi.sk.ca
Vice-President, Systems & Facilities, Dwain Wells
306-775-6093, dwells@sgi.sk.ca
Vice-President, Underwriting, Randy Heise
306-751-1653, rheise@sgicanada.ca
Assistant Vice-President, Corporate Affairs & Planning, Barbara Cross
306-751-1652, Fax: 306-525-6040, bcross@sgi.sk.ca
Assistant Vice-President, Human Resources & Corporate Services, Tamara Erhardt
306-775-6994, Fax: 306-347-0089, terhardt@sgi.sk.ca
Assistant Vice-President, Marketing & Communications, Tim Kydd
306-775-6739, tkydd@sgi.sk.ca

Saskatchewan Government Services (GS)

1920 Rose St., Regina, SK S4P 0A9
306-787-6911 Fax: 306-787-1061
GSReception@gs.gov.sk.ca
www.gs.gov.sk.ca

The Ministry has the following main duties: to create & maintain effective partnerships with governments in Saskatchewan, Canada, & abroad; to promote the province's interests with other governments; to support local governance to meet the needs of municipal governments; to coordinate & manage matters related to Government House, French language services, official protocol, & provincial honours; & to provide administrative services to the Office of the Lieutenant Governor. In November 2007, a new provincial government resulted in the reorganization of provincial government ministries. Saskatchewan Government Relations established separate roles for the Provincial Secretary, Municipal Affairs, & Intergovernmental Affairs. Bill Hutchinson was named Minister of Municipal Affairs.

Acts Administered:
Architects Act, 1996
Interior Designers Act
Public Works & Services Act
Purchasing Act, 2004

Minister, Government Services, Hon. Laura Ross
306-787-0942, Fax: 306-787-8677, minister.gs@gov.sk.ca
Chief of Staff, Gary Hutchings
306-787-0326, Fax: 306-787-8677, Gary.Hutchings@gov.sk.ca
Deputy Minister, Ron Dedman
306-787-6520, Fax: 306-787-6547, ron.dedman@gov.sk.ca
Executive Director, Communications, Robin Campese
306-787-5959, Fax: 306-787-8582, robin.campese@gov.sk.ca

Accommodation Services Division
The Municipal Relations Division strengthens Saskatchewan communities by providing the legal framework, organizational support, financial assistance & other services for the operation of municipalities. Working in partnership with municipal organizations & other communities, the Division encourages cooperation, understanding & self-reliance.
Assistant Deputy Minister, Asset Management, Allen Mullen
306-787-8018, Fax: 306-798-0370, allen.mullen@gov.sk.cas
Assistant Deputy Minister, Facility Management, Richard Murray
306-787-9586, Fax: 306-798-0371, richard.murray@gov.sk.ca
Director, Sustainability & Energy Management, Howard Arndt
306-787-2033, Fax: 306-787-1980, Howard.Arndt@gov.sk.ca
Director, Pricing & Data Management Services, Garth Belanger
306-787-9680, Fax: 306-787-1980, garth.belanger@gov.sk.ca
Director, Real Estate Services, Alf Bernstein
306-787-6959, Fax: 306-787-1980, alf.bernstein@gov.sk.ca
Director, Infrastructure Support Services, Dave Bryanton
306-787-0959, Fax: 306-787-2019,
Dave.Bryanton@gov.sk.ca
Director, Project Delivery North, Ivan Francis
306-933-5676, Fax: 306-933-6999, ivan.francis@gov.sk.ca
Director, Capital & Infrastructure Management, Todd Godfrey
306-787-2253, Fax: 306-787-1980, todd.godfrey@gov.sk.ca
Director, Project Delivery South, Paul Nepper
306-787-0990, Fax: 306-798-0370, paul.nepper@gov.sk.ca
Director, Strategic Portfolio Management, Loreen Porter
306-787-4241, Fax: 306-787-1980, loreen.porter@gov.sk.ca

Commercial Services Division
306-787-8942 Fax: 306-787-1061
www.gs.gov.sk.ca/commercial/
Executive Director, Greg Lusk
306-787-7842, Fax: 306-787-1061, Greg.Lusk@gov.sk.ca
Acting Director, Telecommunications, Cindy Cullen
306-787-6899, Fax: 306-798-0371, cindy.cullen@gov.sk.ca
Director, Mail Services, Carol Halvorson
306-787-6866, Fax: 306-787-1873,
carol.halvorson@gov.sk.ca
Director, Executive Air Services, Chris Olsen
306-787-7717, Fax: 306-787-1424, chris.oleson@gov.sk.ca
Director, CVA Business Process & Systems Implementation, Paul Radigan
306-787-9046, Fax: 306-787-1061, paul.radigan@gov.sk.ca
Director, Air Ambulance Services, Lee Smith
306-933-6501, Fax: 306-933-5490, Lee.Smith@gov.sk.ca;
lee.smith2@gov.sk.ca

Corporate Support Services Division
306-787-6945 Fax: 306-798-0700
Assistant Deputy Minister, Debbie Koshman
306-787-1071, Fax: 306-798-0700,
debbie.koshman@gov.sk.ca
Director, Purchasing Branch, Rob Isbister
306-787-6005, Fax: 306-787-3023, rob.isbister@gov.sk.ca
Director, Internal Audit/Planning & Policy, Patrick Lumb
306-787-1139, Fax: 306-798-0700, patrick.lumb@gov.sk.ca
Director, Risk Management Services, Glynn Mitchell
306-787-9280, Fax: 306-798-0700, glynn.mitchell@gov.sk.ca
Director, Financial Services Branch, Shelley Reddekopp
306-787-4468, Fax: 306-798-0700,
shelley.reddekopp@gov.sk.ca

Saskatchewan Health (HE)

T.C. Douglas Bldg., 3475 Albert St., Regina, SK S4S 6X6
306-787-0146
800-667-7766
info@health.gov.sk.ca
www.health.gov.sk.ca
Other Communication: Family Health Benefits: 1-800-266-0695; HealthLine: 1-877-800-0002; Health Registration / Health Card: 1-800-667-7551; Prescription Drug Plan: 1-800-667-7581
Saskatchewan Health offers the following programs & services: continuing care to help people live independently; e-health & information systems for access to medical information; emergency services; health benefits; recruitment & retention of healthcare providers; promotion of mental health & treatment for mental illness & addictions; personal health services; prescription drug coverage; public health programs; privacy of health information; services for people with long term disabilities or illnesses; surgery & diagnostics initiatives; & vital statistics.
Acts Administered:
Ambulance Act
Cancer Agency Act
Change of Name Act, 1995
Chiropody Profession Act
Chiropractic Act, 1994
Dental Care Act
Dental Disciplines Act
Department of Health Act
Dietitians Act
Emergency Medical Aid Act
Health Districts Act
Health Facilities Licensing Act
Health Information Protection Act
Health Quality Control Act
Hearing Aid Act
Hearing Aid Sales & Services Act
Hospital Standards Act
Housing & Special-care Homes Act
Human Tissue Gift Act
Licensed Practical Nurses Act
Medical & Hospitalization Tax Repeal Act
Medical Laboratory Licensing Act, 1994
Medical Laboratory Technologists Act, 1994
Medical Profession Act, 1981
Medical Radiation Technologists Act, 1994
Mental Health Services Act
Midwifery Act
Mutual Medical & Hospital Benefit Associations Act
Naturopathy Act
Occupational Therapists Act, 1997
Opthalmic Dispensers Act
Optometry Act, 1985
Personal Care Homes Act
Pharmacy Act, 1996
Physical Therapists Act, 1998
Prescription Drugs Act
Psychologists Act
Public Health Act
Regional Health Services Act
Registered Nurses Act, 1988
Registered Psychiatric Nurses Act
Saskatchewan Health Research Foundation Act
Saskatchewan Medical Care Insurance Act
Speech Language Pathologists & Audiologists Act
Tobacco Control Act
Vital Statistics Act, 1995
White Cane Act
Youth Drug Detoxification & Stabilization Act
Fetal Alcohol Syndrome Awareness Day Act
Paramedics Act
Podiatry Act
Prostate Cancer Awareness Month Act
Residential Services Act
Respiratory Therapists Act
Senior Citizens' Heritage Program Act
Tobacco Damages & Health Care Costs Recovery Act
Minister, Hon. Don McMorris
306-787-7345, Fax: 306-787-0237, minister.he@gov.sk.ca
Deputy Minister, Dan Florizone
306-787-3041, Fax: 306-787-4533, dan.florizone@gov.sk.ca
Assistant Deputy Minister, Lauren Donnelly
306-787-0513, Fax: 306-787-4533,
lauren.donnelly@gov.sk.ca
Executive Director, Physician Leadership & Organizational Development, Brad Havervold
306-787-0716, Fax: 306-787-2974,
Bhavervold@health.gov.sk.ca
Executive Director, Saskatchewan Surgical Initiative, Mark Wyatt
306-787-3153, Fax: 306-798-3367, mark.wyatt@gov.sk.ca,
Other Communications:
www.health.gov.sk.ca/saskatchewan-surgical-initiative
Director, Patient Safety Unit, Valerie Phillips
306-787-3542, vphillips@health.gov.sk.ca

Associated Agencies, Boards & Commissions:
• Health Quality Council
241, 111 Research Dr.
Saskatoon, SK S7N 3R2
306-668-8810 Fax: 306-668-8820
info@hqc.sk.ca
www.hqc.sk.ca
• Saskatchewan Health Research Foundation
#253, 111 Research Dr.
Saskatoon, SK S7N 3R2
306-975-1680 Fax: 306-975-1688 800-975-1699
www.shrf.ca

Acute & Emergency Services
306-787-3204 Fax: 306-787-6113
www.health.gov.sk.ca/acute-emergency
Executive Director, Deborah Jordan
306-787-7854, Fax: 306-787-6113, djordan@health.gov.sk.ca
Acting Director, Research & Clinical Pathway Development, Gwendolyn Friedrich
306-787-3656, Fax: 306-787-6113,
gfriedrich@health.gov.sk.ca
Acting Director, Cancer Services & EMS, Jason Liggett
306-787-1101, Fax: 306-787-6113, jliggett@health.gov.sk.ca
Acting Director, Cancer Services & EMS, Patrick O'Byrne
306-787-3219, Fax: 306-787-6113,
pobyrne@health.gov.sk.ca

Communications Branch
306-787-3696 Fax: 306-787-8310
800-667-7766
www.health.gov.sk.ca/communications
Executive Director, Kimberly Kratzig
306-787-8433, Fax: 306-787-8310,
kimberly.kratzig@gov.sk.ca
Program Services, Joan Petrie
306-787-2743, Fax: 306-787-8310, joan.petrie@gov.sk.ca
Correspondence & Internal Communications, Karen Prokopetz
306-787-2036, Fax: 306-787-8310,
karen.prokopetz@gov.sk.ca
Regional Services, Lorri Thacyk
306-787-7296, Fax: 306-787-8310, lorri.thacyk@gov.sk.ca

Community Care Branch
306-787-7239 Fax: 306-787-7095
www.health.gov.sk.ca/community-care
Executive Director, Roger Carriere
306-787-6092, Fax: 306-787-7095,
rcarriere@health.gov.sk.ca
Director, Program Support Unit A, Linda Restau
306-787-7901, Fax: 306-787-7095, lrestau@health.gov.sk.ca
Director, Program Support Unit B, Heather Murray
306-787-3236, Fax: 306-787-7095
Director, Mental Health & Addictions, Kathy Willerth
306-787-5020, Fax: 306-787-7095,
kwillerth@health.gov.sk.ca

Drug Plan & Extended Benefits Branch
306-787-3317 Fax: 306-787-8679
www.health.gov.sk.ca/drugplan-extendedbenefits
Executive Director, Kevin Wilson
306-787-3301, Fax: 306-787-8679, kwilson@health.gov.sk.ca
Director, Business Unit, Morley Machin
306-787-3031, mmachin@health.gov.sk.ca
Director, Pharmaceutical Services, Tracey Smith
306-787-3305, Fax: 306-787-8679, tsmith@health.gov.sk.ca
Acting Director, Operations Unit, Susan Yee
306-787-9268, Fax: 306-787-8679, syee@health.gov.sk.ca

Financial Services Branch
306-787-4923 Fax: 306-787-0218
www.health.gov.sk.ca/financial-services
Executive Director, Ted Warawa
306-787-5006, Fax: 306-787-0218, ted.warawa@gov.sk.ca
Director, Financial Management & Internal Audit, Garth Herbert
306-787-7738, Fax: 306-787-0218,
gherbert@health.gov.sk.ca
Director, Regional Financial Services Unit, Jeannette Lowe
306-787-0050, Fax: 306-787-0218, jlowe@health.gov.sk.ca
Director, Budget & Financial Planning, Brenda Russell
306-787-5025, Fax: 306-787-0218, brussell@health.gov.sk.ca

Health Registration
Fax: 306-787-8951
800-667-7551
www.health.gov.sk.ca/health-registration
Vital Statistics Unit is responsible for the issuance of provincial birth, marriage & death certificates. Fee for each certificate is $20.00.
Director, Pat Cambridge
306-787-3249, Fax: 306-787-8951,
pcambridge@health.gov.sk.ca

Medical Services Branch
306-787-3475 Fax: 306-787-3761
800-667-7523
www.health.gov.sk.ca/medical-services
Executive Director, Shaylene Salazar
306-787-3423, Fax: 306-787-3761,
ssalazar@health.gov.sk.ca
Director, Professional Review & Quality Management, Perry Behl
306-787-3442, Fax: 306-787-3761, pbehl@health.gov.sk.ca
Director, Operations & Client Services, Lori St. Dennis
306-787-3425, Fax: 306-787-3761,
lstdennis@health.gov.sk.ca
Director, Management Services/Policy & Regional Programs, June Schultz
306-798-2655, Fax: 306-787-3761, jschultz@health.gov.sk.ca

Primary Health Services Branch
Fax: 306-787-0890
www.health.gov.sk.ca/primary-health-services
Executive Director, Donna Magnusson
306-787-0875, Fax: 306-787-0890,
dmagnusson@health.gov.sk.ca
Director, Margaret Baker
306-787-0670, Fax: 306-787-8697, mbaker@health.gov.sk.ca
Director, Fay Schuster
306-787-5058, Fax: 306-787-0890,
fschuster@health.gov.sk.ca
Director, Operations, Primary Health Care Redesign, Andrea Wagner
306-798-7491, Fax: 306-787-0890,
awagner1@health.gov.sk.ca

Population Health Branch
306-787-8847 Fax: 306-787-3237
www.health.gov.sk.ca/population-health

Chief Medical Health Officer, Dr. Moira McKinnon
306-787-4722, Fax: 306-787-3237
Deputy Chief Medical Health Officer, Dr. Saqib Shabab
306-787-4722, Fax: 306-787-3237
Chief Population Health Epidemiologist, Dr. Valerie Mann
306-787-4086, Fax: 306-787-3823, vmann@health.gov.sk.ca
Executive Director, Rick Trimp
306-787-8847, Fax: 306-787-3237, rtrimp@health.gov.sk.ca
Director, Health Promotion, Tami Denomie
306-787-7110, Fax: 306-787-3823,
tami.denomie@health.gov.sk.ca
Director, Epidemiology & Research, Winanne Downey
306-787-7625, Fax: 306-787-3237
Director, Corporate Services, Paul Leech
306-787-6544, Fax: 306-787-3237, pleech@health.gov.sk.ca
Director, Environmental Health, Tim Macaulay
306-787-7128, Fax: 306-787-3237,
tmacaulay@health.gov.sk.ca
Director, Disease Prevention, Jim Myres
306-787-1580, Fax: 306-787-3823,
jim.myres@health.gov.sk.ca

Risk & Relationship Management
306-787-3143 Fax: 306-787-2974
www.health.gov.sk.ca/risk-and-relationship-management
Other Communication: Alternate Phone: 306-787-3150
Acting Executive Director, Jacqueline Messer-Lepage
306-787-2137, Fax: 306-787-2974,
jmesserlepage@health.gov.sk.ca
Director, Intergovernmental, First Nations & Métis Relations, Melissa Cote
306-787-8197, Fax: 306-787-2974, mcote@health.gov.sk.ca
Director, Regional Planning & Support, Lori Hutchison Hunter
306-787-7954, Fax: 306-787-2974,
lhutchison@health.gov.sk.ca
Director, Operations, Health & Emergency Management, Garnet Matchett
306-787-3179, Fax: 306-798-3093,
gmatchett@health.gov.sk.ca
Director, Governance & Policy, David Smith
306-787-0297, Fax: 306-787-2974, David.Smith@gov.sk.ca; dsmith@health.gov.sk.ca, Other Communications: Alt Email: david.smith@saskatoonhealthregion.ca
Director, Health Information Policy & Legislation, Vacant
306-787-3155, Fax: 306-787-4534

Saskatchewan Disease Control Laboratory
5 Research Dr., Regina, SK S4S 0A4
306-787-3131 Fax: 306-787-1525
www.health.gov.sk.ca/lab
Executive Director, Rick Trimp
306-787-3129, Fax: 306-787-1525, rtrimp@health.gov.sk.ca
Medical Director, Dr. Greg Horsman
306-787-8316, Fax: 306-787-1525,
ghorsman@health.gov.sk.ca
Director, Environmental Services, Dr. Phillip Bailey
306-787-3140, Fax: 306-787-1525, pbailey@health.gov.sk.ca
Director, Immunoserology & Virology, Niki Coffin
306-798-4153, Fax: 306-787-1525, ncoffin@health.gov.sk.ca
Director, Screening & Reference Testing, Jeff Eichhorst
306-787-3284, Fax: 306-798-0955,
jeichhorst@health.gov.sk.ca
Director, Operations, Joyce Kirsch
306-787-9404, Fax: 306-787-1525,
joyce.kirsch@health.gov.sk.ca
Director, Bacteriology, Dr. Christine Turenne
306-798-4154, Fax: 306-787-1525,
cturenne@health.gov.sk.ca
Director, Administration, Debra Ulrich
306-787-3033, Fax: 306-787-1525, dulrich@health.gov.sk.ca

Strategy & Innovation Branch
306-787-0769 Fax: 306-787-2974
www.health.gov.sk.ca/strategic-planning-branch
Executive Director, Pauline M. Rousseau
306-787-3951, Fax: 306-787-2974
Director, Health System Quality & Efficiency Management, Trish Livingstone
306-787-3146, Fax: 306-787-2974,
tlivingstone@health.gov.sk.ca
Director, Capital Asset Planning, Richard Moen
306-787-3232, Fax: 306-787-2974, rmoen@health.gov.sk.ca
Director, Health System Planning, Kathleen Peterson
306-787-3163, Fax: 306-787-2974,
kpeterson@health.gov.sk.ca

Workforce Planning Branch
306-787-3152 Fax: 306-798-0023
www.health.gov.sk.ca/workforce-planning
Executive Director, Ron Knaus
306-787-6672, Fax: 306-798-0023, rknaus@health.gov.sk.ca
Chief Nursing Officer, Lynn Digney-Davis
306-787-7195, Fax: 306-798-0023,
ldigneydavis@health.gov.sk.ca
Director, Planning & Provincial Recruitment Projects, Andy Churko
306-787-3072, Fax: 306-798-0023,
achurko@health.gov.sk.ca
Director, Programs & Resource Development, Sandra Cripps
306-787-5693, Fax: 306-798-0023, scripps@health.gov.sk.ca

Saskatchewan Highways & Infrastructure (HI)

Victoria Tower, 1855 Victoria Ave., Regina, SK S4P 3T2
306-787-4800
communications@highways.gov.sk.ca
www.highways.gov.sk.ca
Other Communication: Hotline for Road Information: 306-933-8333 (North SK); 306-787-7623 (South SK); Toll Free: 888-335-7623; Website: roadinfo.telenium.ca/shwyw.html
The Ministry operates, preserves, & guides the development of the transportation system in Saskatchewan.
Acts Administered:
Dangerous Goods Transportation Act
Engineering & Geoscience Professions Act
Highway Traffic Act
Highways & Transportation Act, 1997
Railway Act
Sand & Gravel Act
Minister, Highways & Infrasturcture, Hon. Jim Reiter
306-787-6447, Fax: 306-787-1736, minister.hi@gov.sk.ca
Deputy Minister, Rob Penny
306-787-4949, Fax: 306-787-9777, Rob.Penny@gov.sk.ca
Executive Director, Communications, Rosann Semchuk
306-787-6815, Fax: 306-798-0438,
Rosann.semchuk@gov.sk.ca
Director, Communications, Doug Wakabayashi
306-787-4804, Fax: 306-798-0438,
doug.wakabayashi@gov.sk.ca

Associated Agencies, Boards & Commissions:
• Global Transportation Hub Authority
#350, 1777 Victoria Ave.
Regina, SK S4P 4K5
306-787-4842 Fax: 306-798-4600
www.gtha.ca
The Hub Authority was created in June 2009, & is the primary agency in charge of planning, developing, constructing & promoting the Global Transportation Hub - a transportation & logistics centre encompassing 2,000 acres of serviced land.
• Saskatchewan Grain Car Corporation
#1210, 1855 Victoria Ave.
Regina, SK S4P 3T2
306-787-1137 Fax: 306-798-0931
www.sgcc.gov.sk.ca
The SGCC works with farmers, community groups, shippers, & railroads to maximize the efficiency and effectiveness of transporting grain across the province.
• Saskatchewan Highway Traffic Board
1550 Saskatchewan Dr.
Regina, SK S4P 0E4
306-775-6674
contactus@highwaytrafficboard.sk.ca
www.highwaytrafficboard.sk.ca
The Highway Traffic Board's mandate is to establish & to administer legislation related to the safe & legal operations of private vehicles, the bus-truck industry & the short line rail industry in Saskatchewan, where specifically legislated to do so.

Corporate Services Division
306-787-4904
Assistant Deputy Minister, Jennifer Ehrmantraut
306-787-4859, Fax: 306-787-9777,
Jennifer.Ehrmantraut@gov.sk.ca, Other Communications: jennifer.ehrmantraut@saskatoonhealthregion.ca
Director, Financial Services Branch, Gary Diebel
306-787-4794, Fax: 306-787-8700, gary.diebel@gov.sk.ca
Director, Land Branch, Jeff Grigg
306-787-4885, Fax: 306-787-4100, Jeff.Grigg@gov.sk.ca
Director, Information Management Branch, Bryan Peacock
306-787-0764, Fax: 306-787-8700,
Bryan.Peacock@gov.sk.ca
Director, Corporate Support, Barbara Tofte
306-787-8721, Fax: 306-787-8700, Barbara.Tofte@gov.sk.ca

Operations Division
306-787-4901
Assistant Deputy Minister, Ted Stobbs
306-787-9287, Ted.Stobbs@gov.sk.ca
Director, Construction & Contracts, Richard Flaman
306-787-4943, Fax: 306-787-4836,
Richard.Flaman@gov.sk.ca
Director, Design & Traffic Engineering Standards, Sukhy Kent
306-787-4945, Fax: 306-787-4836, Sukhy.Kent@gov.sk.ca
Director, Preservation & Surfacing, Brent Marjerison
306-933-5208, Fax: 306-933-7090,
Brent.Marjerison@gov.sk.ca
Director, Materials & Testing, Bill Pacholka
306-787-4917, Fax: 306-787-4582, Bill.Pacholka@gov.sk.ca
Executive Director, Technical Standards Branch, Dave Stearns
306-787-2295, Fax: 306-787-4910

Planning & Policy Division
306-787-4904
Assistant Deputy Minister, George Stamatinos
306-787-5028, Fax: 306-787-9777,
george.stamatinos@gov.sk.ca
Executive Director, Systems Planning & Management, Miranda Carlberg
306-787-0825, Fax: 306-787-3963,
Miranda.Carlberg@gov.sk.ca
Executive Director, Strategic Planning & Policy, Harold Hugg
306-787-5311, Fax: 306-787-3963, Harold.Hugg@gov.sk.ca
Acting Director, Legislation & Administration, Miranda Carlberg
306-964-1210, Fax: 306-933-5188,
Miranda.Carlberg@gov.sk.ca
Director, Strategic Municipal Policy, Wayne Gienow
306-787-1355, Fax: 306-787-3963, wayne.gienow@gov.sk.ca
Acting Director, Transport Compliance Branch, Brian Johnson
306-933-5293, Fax: 306-933-5276, Brian.Johnson@gov.sk.ca
Director, Provincial Transportation Infrastructure, Andrew Liu
306-787-4784, Fax: 306-787-3963, Andrew.Liu@gov.sk.ca
Director, Strategic Business Planning, Cathy Lynn Borbely
306-787-4787, Fax: 306-787-3963,
CathyLynn.Borbely@gov.sk.ca
Director, Multimodal, Trade & Logistics, Michael Makowsky
306-787-7664, Fax: 306-787-3963,
Michael.Makowsky@gov.sk.ca
Acting Director, Rail Services, Ed Zsombor
306-787-5847, Fax: 306-787-3963, Ed.Zsombor@gov.sk.ca

Saskatchewan Human Rights Commission (SHRC)

Saskatoon Office, Sturdy Stone Bdg., #816, 122 - 3 Ave. North, 8th Fl., Saskatoon, SK S7K 2H6
306-933-5952 Fax: 306-933-7863
800-667-9249
shrc@gov.sk.ca
www.shrc.gov.sk.ca
TTY: 306-373-2119
The Saskatchewan Human Rights Commission promotes & protects individual dignity & equal rights by discouraging & eliminating discrimination. The Commission's guide is The Saskatchewan Human Rights Code. The following are the principle functions of the Commission: approving equity programs; educating people & promoting human rights laws in Saskatchewan; & investigating complaints of discrimination.
Minister Responsible, Hon. Don Morgan, Q.C.
306-787-5353, Fax: 306-787-1232, minister.ju@gov.sk.ca
Chief Commissioner, Hon. David M. Arnot
306-933-7796, Fax: 306-933-7863, David.Arnot@gov.sk.ca
Manager, Finance & Administration, Sue Lake
306-787-2704, Fax: 306-787-0454, Sue.Lake@gov.sk.ca
Manager, Operations, Rebecca McLellan
306-787-2394, Fax: 306-787-0454,
Rebecca.McLellan@gov.sk.ca
Manager, Human Resources, Brenda Rorke
306-933-8285, Fax: 306-933-7863, brenda.rorke@gov.sk.ca

Corporate & Financial Services
306-787-8178 Fax: 306-787-2198
Assistant Depty Minister, Twyla MacDougall
306-787-6717, Fax: 306-787-3872,
twyla.macdougall@gov.sk.ca
Director, Revenue Operations & Audit Services, Dale Amundson
306-787-5343, Fax: 306-798-2158,
dale.amundson@gov.sk.ca
Director, Planning, Evaluation & External Relations, Cam Pelzer
306-787-2378, Fax: 306-787-2198, Cam.Pelzer@gov.sk.ca
Director, Process Renewal & Infrastructure Management Enhancement (PRIME) Project, Jeff Ritter
306-787-0999, Fax: 306-787-3872, Jeff.Ritter@gov.sk.ca
Director, Administrative & Financial Services, Doreen Yurkoski
306-787-1612, Fax: 306-787-3872,
doreen.yurkoski@gov.sk.ca
Assistant Director, Revenue Operations, Glen Downton
306-787-2830, Fax: 306-787-0083, glen.downton@gov.sk.ca

Minerals, Lands & Policy
306-787-8178 Fax: 306-787-2198
Assistant Deputy Minister, Hal Sanders
306-787-3524, Fax: 306-787-2198, Hal.Sanders@gov.sk.ca
Executive Director, Lands & Development Services, Doug MacKnight
306-787-2082, Fax: 306-787-7338,
Doug.Macknight@gov.sk.ca
Executive Director, Energy Policy, Floyd Wist
306-787-2477, Fax: 306-787-2198, Floyd.Wist@gov.sk.ca
Executive Director, Major Projects, George Patterson
306-787-2560, Fax: 306-787-1284,
George.Patterson@gov.sk.ca
Director, Energy Economics, Mike Balfour
306-787-2479, Fax: 306-787-2198, Mike.Balfour@gov.sk.ca
Director, Regulatory Affairs, Jane Chapco
306-787-9637, Fax: 306-787-7338, Jane.Chapco@gov.sk.ca; jane.chapco2@gov.sk.ca

Director, Saskatchewan Geological Survey, Gary Delaney
306-787-1160, Fax: 306-787-1284, gary.delaney@gov.sk.ca
Director, Mines, Mike Detharet
306-787-2139, Fax: 306-798-0047, Mike.Detharet@gov.sk.ca
Director, Mineral Policy, Cory Hughes
306-787-3628, Fax: 306-787-2198, Cory.Hughes@gov.sk.ca
Director, Energy Development & Climate Change, Howard Loseth
306-787-3379, Fax: 306-787-2198, Howard.Loseth@gov.sk.ca
Acting Director, Petroleum Geology, Melinda Yurkowski
306-787-0650, Fax: 306-787-4608, melinda.yurkowski@gov.sk.ca

Petroleum & Natural Gas Division
306-787-2592 Fax: 306-787-2478
Assistant Deputy Minister, Ed Dancsok
306-787-2591, Fax: 306-787-2478, Ed.Dancsok@gov.sk.ca
Director, Petroleum Development, Todd Han
306-787-2221, Fax: 306-787-2478, todd.han@gov.sk.ca
Director, Petroleum Royalties, Mike Ferguson
306-787-2605, Fax: 306-787-2478, mike.ferguson@gov.sk.ca
Director, Petroleum Tenure Branch, Paul Mahnic
306-787-5385, Fax: 306-787-0620, Paul.Mahnic@gov.sk.ca
Director, Petroleum Statistics, Darwin Roske
306-787-2607, Fax: 306-787-8236, darwin.roske@gov.sk.ca
Director, Engineering Services Branch, Steve Rymes
306-787-2318, Fax: 306-787-2478, Steve.Rymes@gov.sk.ca

Information & Privacy Commissioner of Saskatchewan

#503, 1801 Hamilton St., Regina, SK S4P 4B4
306-787-8350 Fax: 306-798-1603
877-748-2298
webmaster@oipc.sk.ca
www.oipc.sk.ca

Commissioner, R. Gary Dickson, Q.C.
306-787-8350, Fax: 306-798-1603, gdickson@oipc.sk.ca

Information Services Corporation of Saskatchewan (ISC)

#300, 10 Research Dr., Regina, SK S4S 7J7
306-798-0641
866-275-4721
www.isc.ca

The ISC is a provincial Crown corporation responsible for the administration of land titles, vital statistics, survey, personal property & corporate registeries, & related geographic information.

Minister Responsible, Hon. Tim McMillan
306-787-7339, Fax: 306-798-3140, minister.cc@gov.sk.ca
President/Chief Executive Officer, Jeff Stusek
306-787-1364, Fax: 306-787-9220, jeff.stusek@isc.ca
Vice-President, Operations, Ken Budzak
306-787-9631, Fax: 306-787-9220, ken.budzak@isc.ca
Vice-President, Marketing & Business Development, Bryan Burnett
306-798-8755, Fax: 306-787-9220, bryan.burnett@isc.ca
Vice-President, Finance & Administration, Charlene Gavel
306-798-8760, Fax: 306-787-9220, charlene.gavel@isc.ca
Vice-President & General Counsel, Corporate Affairs, Kathy Hillman-Weir
306-787-7299, Fax: 306-798-4125, kathy.hillman-weir@isc.ca

Saskatchewan Information Technology Office (ITO)

2101 Scarth St., 8th Fl., Regina, SK S4P 2H9
306-787-4586 Fax: 306-787-5718
inquiries@ito.gov.sk.ca
www.ito.gov.sk.ca

The ITO serves as the primary IT services supplier for Saskatchewan government ministries and agencies. Its services include: help desk, hardware & software, application development, & IT security. The Office also sets standards & policies in IT infrastructure, support services, security, & telecommunications across the provincial government.

Acts Administered:
Canadian Information Processing Society of Saskatchewan Act, 2005
Information Technology Office Regulations, December 2004

Minister Responsible, Hon. Tim McMillan
306-787-7339, Fax: 306-798-3140, minister.cc@gov.sk.ca
Deputy Minister/Chief Information & Services Officer, Robert Guillaume
306-787-2210, Fax: 306-787-5718, robert.guillaume@gov.sk.ca
Assistant Deputy Minister/Chief Technology Officer, Vacant
306-787-6771, Fax: 306-787-5718
Assistant Deputy Minister, Corporate Services, Tim Kealey
306-787-9302, Fax: 306-787-5718, tim.kealey@gov.sk.ca
Assistant Deputy Minister, Operations, Phil Lambert
306-787-4718, Fax: 306-787-5718, phil.lambert@gov.sk.ca
Chief Architect, Application Architecture, Doug Quail
306-787-2540, Fax: 306-787-5718, doug.quail@gov.sk.ca
Executive Director, Supply Chain Management, Ken Esplen
306-787-8892, Fax: 306-798-0313, ken.esplen@gov.sk.ca
Acting Executive Director, Support Services, Kelly Fuessel
306-787-7894, Fax: 306-798-0355, kelly.fuessel@gov.sk.ca
Executive Director, Application Management, Joe Przepiorka
306-798-3286, Fax: 306-787-5454, joe.przepiorka@gov.sk.ca

Saskatchewan Justice & Attorney General (JU)

1874 Scarth St., Regina, SK S4P 4B3
306-787-8971
communications@justice.gov.sk.ca
www.justice.gov.sk.ca

Acts Administered:
Aboriginal Courtworkers Commission Act
Absconding Debtors Act
Administration of Estates Act
Adult Guardianship & Co-decision-making Act
Age of Majority Act
Agreements of Sale Cancellation Act
Alberta-Saskatchewan Boundary Act, 1939
Arbitration Act, 1992
Assignment of Wages Act
Attachments of Debts Act
Auctioneers Act
Builders' Lien Act
Business Corporations Act
Business Names Registration Act
Canada-United Kingdom Judgements Enforcement Act
Canadian Institute of Management (Saskatchewan Division) Act
Cemeteries Act, 1999
Charitable Fundraising Businesses Act
Children's Law Act, 1997
Choses in Action Act
Class Actions Act
Closing-out Sales Act
Collection Agents Act
Commercial Liens Act
Commissioners for Oaths Act
Companies Act
Companies Winding Up Act
Condominium Property Act, 1993
Constituency Boundaries Act, 1993
Constitutional Questions Act
Consumer & Commercial Affairs Act
Consumer Protection Act
Contributory Negligence Act
Co-operatives Act, 1996
Coroners Act, 1999
Cost of Credit Disclosure Act 2002
Court Jurisdiction & Proceedings Transfer Act
Court of Appeal Act, 2000
Court Officials Act, 1984
Court Reporting Act
Credit Reporting Act
Credit Union Act, 1985 (Mainly Repealed)
Credit Union Act, 1998
Creditors' Relief Act
Criminal Enterprise Suppression Act
Crown Employment Contracts Act
Crown Suits (Costs) Act
Department of Justice Act
Dependants' Relief Act, 1996
Direct Sellers Act
Distress Act
Electronic Information & Documents Act, 2000
Enforcement of Judgements Act, 2002
Enforcement of Foreign Judgements Act
Enforcement of Foreign Arbitral Awards Act, 1996
Enforcement of Canadian Judgements Conventions Act (NYP)
Enforcement of Maintenance Orders Act, 1997
Equality of Status of Married Persons Act
Escheats Act
Executions Act
Exemptions Act
Expropriation Act
Expropriation Procedure Act
Factors Act
Family Maintenance Act, 1997
Family Property Act
Fatal Accidents Act
Federal Courts Act
Film & Video Classification Act
Fraudulent Preferences Act
Freedom of Information & Protection of Privacy Act
Frustrated Contracts Act
Funeral & Cremation Services Act
Guarantee Companies Securities Act
Health Care Directives & Substitute Health Care Decision Makers Act
Home Owners' Protection Act
Homesteads Act, 1989
Hotel Keepers Act
Improvements Under Mistake of Title Act
Interjurisdictional Support Orders Act
International Child Abduction Act, 1996
International Commercial Arbitration Act
International Protection of Adults Act (NYP)
International Sale of Goods Act
Interpretation Act, 1995
Interprovincial Subpoena Act
Intestate Succession Act, 1996
Judges' Orders Enforcement Act
Judgments Extension Act
Jury Act, 1998
Justice of the Peace Act, 1988
Land Contracts (Actions) Act
Land Information Services Facilitation Act
Land Titles Act, 2000
Land Surveyors & Professional Surveyors Act
Land Surveys Act, 2000
Landlord & Tenant Act
Language Act
Law Reform Commission Act
Legal Aid Act
Legal Profession Act, 1990
Libel & Slander Act
Limitations Act
Limitation of Civil Rights Act
Local Authority Freedom of Information & Protection of Privacy Act
Lord's Day (Saskatchewan) Act
Mandatory Testing & Disclosure (Bodily Substances) Act
Marriage Act, 1995
Marriage Settlement Act
Members' Conflict of Interest Act
Mentally Disordered Persons Act
Mortgage Brokerages & Mortgage Administrators Act
Motor Dealers Act
Municipal Hail Insurance Act
Names of Homes Act
New Generation Co-operatives Act
Non-profit Corporations Act, 1995
Notaries Public Act
Ombudsman & Children's Advocate Act
Parents' Maintenance Act
Partnership Act
Pawned Property (Recording) Act
Penalties & Forfeitures Act
Pension Benefits Act, 1992
Personal Property Security Act, 1993
Powers of Attorney Act, 2002
Pre-judgement Interest Act
Privacy Act
Proceedings Against the Crown Act
Professional Corporations Act
Provincial Court Act, 1998
Provincial Mediation Board Act
Public Guardian & Trustee Act
Public Inquiries Act
Public Utilities Easements Act
Queen's Bench Act, 1998
Queen's Counsel Act
Queen's Printer Act
Real Estate Act
Reciprocal Enforcement of Judgments Act, 1996
Recovery of Possession of Land Act
Referendum & Plebiscite Act
Registered Plan (Retirement Income) Exemption Act
Regulations Act, 1995
Religious Societies Land Act
Residential Tenancies Act
Revised Statutes Act, 1979
Sale of Goods Act
Sales on Consignment Act
Saskatchewan Financial Services Commission Act
Saskatchewan Human Rights Code
Saskatchewan Insurance Act
Securities Act, 1988
Seizure of Criminal Property Act
Slot Machine Act
Small Claims Act, 1997
Summary Offences Procedure Act, 1990
Survival of Actions Act
Survivorship Act, 1993
Thresher Employees Act
Threshers' Lien Act
Trading Stamp Act
Traffic Safety Court of Saskatchewan Act, 1988
Trust & Loan Corporations Act, 1997
Trustee Act, 2009
Trusts Convention Implementation Act
Unconscionable Transactions Relief Act
Variation of Trusts Act
Victims of Crime Act, 1995
Victims of Domestic Violence Act
Wills Act, 1996
Woodmen's Lien Act
Change of Name Act, 1995

Court Security Act
Evidence Act
Gunshot & Stab Wounds Mandatory Reporting Act
Income Trust Liability Act
International Interests in Mobile Aircraft Equipment Act (NYP)
Missing Persons & Presumption of Death Act
Non-Profit Corporations Amendment Act, 2005
Payday Loans Act (NYP)
Securities Act, 1988
Settlement of International Investment Disputes Act
Statutes & Regulations Revision Act
Ticket Sales Act
Trespass to Property Act
Vital Statistics Act, 2009
Vital Statistics Administration Transfer Act

Minister & Attorney General, Hon. Don Morgan, Q.C.
306-787-5353, Fax: 306-787-1232, minister.ju@gov.sk.ca
Chief of Staff, Denise Batters, Q.C.
306-787-5353, Fax: 306-787-1232, denise.batters@gov.sk.ca
Deputy Minister & Deputy Attorney General, Gerald Tegart
306-787-5352, Fax: 306-787-3874, gerald.tegart@gov.sk.ca
Executive Director, Civil Law Division, Rick Hischebett
306-787-6642, Fax: 306-787-0581,
Rick.Hischebett@gov.sk.ca, Other Communications: URL: www.justice.gov.sk.ca/civillaw
Executive Director, Policy, Planning & Evaluation, Betty Ann Pottruff, Q.C.
306-787-8954, Fax: 306-787-9008,
bettyann.pottruff@gov.sk.ca
Executive Director, Corporate Services, Dave Tulloch
306-787-5472, Fax: 306-787-5830, dave.tulloch@gov.sk.ca; dave.tulloch3@gov.sk.ca
Director, Financial & Resource Planning, Mindy Gudmundson
306-787-5580, Fax: 306-787-5830,
mindy.gudmundson@gov.sk.ca
Director, Assurance & Financial Reporting, Brad Gurash
306-798-5112, Fax: 306-787-5830, brad.gurash2@gov.sk.ca
Director, Communications, Linsay Rabyj
306-787-0775, Fax: 306-787-3874, Linsay.Rabyj@gov.sk.ca

Associated Agencies, Boards & Commissions:

• Automobile Injury Appeal Commission
#504, 2400 College Ave.
Regina, SK S4P 1C8
306-798-5545 Fax: 306-798-5540 866-798-5544
aiac@gov.sk.ca
www.autoinjuryappeal.sk.ca

• Law Reform Commission of Saskatchewan
c/o University of Saskatchewan, College of Law
#209, 15 Campus Drive
Saskatoon, SK S7N 5A6
306-966-1625 Fax: 306-966-5900
director.research@sasklawreform.com
www.lawreformcommission.sk.ca
The Law Reform Commission of Saskatchewan was established by An Act to Establish a Law Reform Commission, proclaimed in force in November, 1973, and began functioning in February of 1974.

• Office of Residential Tenancies (ORT)
#120, 2151 Scarth St.
Regina, SK S4P 2H8
306-787-2699 Fax: 306-787-5574 888-215-2222
Other Communication: Toll-Free Fax: 1-888-867-7776

• Provincial Mediation Board
#120, 2151 Scarth St.
Regina, SK S4P 2H8
306-787-5387 Fax: 306-787-5574 877-787-5408
www.justice.gov.sk.ca/PMB
Other Communication: Toll-Free Fax: 1-888-867-7776
The Provincial Mediation Board provides budgeting advice and counselling to individuals with personal debt problems. It may be able to arrange repayment plans with creditors. The Board also deals with problems of debtors related to property tax arrears, eviction of commercial tenants and residential mortgage foreclosures.

• Public & Private Rights Board
#323, 3085 Albert St.
Regina, SK S4S 0B1
306-787-4071 Fax: 306-787-0088
www.justice.gov.sk.ca/publicandprivaterightsboard

• Saskatchewan Film & Video Classification Board
#500, 1919 Saskatchewan Dr.
Regina, SK S4P 4H2
306-787-5550 Fax: 306-787-9779 888-374-4636
www.justice.gov.sk.ca/filmandvideoclassification
On October 1, 1997, an agreement between the province of British Columbia and Saskatchewan came into effect, under which the British Columbia Film Classification Office will classify all new theatrical releases and adult videos on behalf of the Saskatchewan Film and Video Classification Board.

• Saskatchewan Financial Services Commission (SFSC)
#601, 1919 Saskatchewan Dr.
Regina, SK S4P 4H2
306-787-5645 Fax: 306-787-5899
www.sfsc.gov.sk.ca
The Saskatchewan Financial Services Commission (SFSC) protects consumer and public interests and supports economic well-being through responsive financial marketplace regulation. The SFSC enhances consumer protection through licensing, registration, audit, complaint handling and enforcement activities pursuant to various provincial statutes.

• Saskatchewan Human Rights Commission (SHRC)
#301, 1942 Hamilton St.
Regina, SK S4P 2C5
306-787-2530 Fax: 306-787-0454 800-667-8577 TTY: 306-787-8550
shrc@gov.sk.ca
www.shrc.gov.sk.ca

• Saskatchewan Legal Aid Commission
#502, 201 - 21 St. East
Saskatoon, SK S7K 0B8
306-933-5300 Fax: 306-933-6764 800-667-3764
www.legalaid.sk.ca
The Saskatchewan Legal Aid Commission provides legal services to persons and organizations for criminal and civil matters where those persons and organizations are financially unable to secure these services from their own resources. The organization has been in existence since 1974.

• Saskatchewan Public Complaints Commission
#300, 1919 Saskatchewan Dr.
Regina, SK S4P 4H2
306-787-6519 Fax: 306-787-6528 866-256-6194
www.publiccomplaintscommission.ca
The Public Complaints Commission (PCC) is a five-person, non-police body appointed by the government. It is responsible for ensuring that both the public and police receive a fair and thorough investigation of a complaint against the police or an investigation of a possible criminal offence by a police officer.

• Saskatchewan Review Board
#200, 520 Spadina Cres.
Saskatoon, SK S7K 2P3
306-933-5156 Fax: 306-933-5725
lfulawka@sasktel.net
www.justice.gov.sk.ca/saskatchewanreviewboard
The Saskatchewan Review Board was established under the Criminal Code of Canada to review decisions & orders regarding an accused person, where a verdict of not criminally responsible by reason of mental disorder or unfit to stand trial on account of mental disorder has been made.

Community Justice Division

306-787-5096 Fax: 306-787-0078
www.justice.gov.sk.ca/communityservicesdivision

Executive Director & Executive Director, Community Services, Jan Turner
306-787-5112, Fax: 306-787-0078, jan.turner@gov.sk.ca; jan.turner@saskatoonhealthregion.ca
Executive Director, Aboriginal Courtworker Program, Chris LaFontaine
306-787-6470, Fax: 306-787-0078,
chris.lafontaine@gov.sk.ca
Chief Coroner, R. Kent Stewart
306-787-5541, Fax: 306-787-5503, kent.stewart@gov.sk.ca; ocoroner@gov.sk.ca, Other Communications: URL: www.justice.gov.sk.ca/officeofthechiefcoroner
Director, Interpersonal Violence & Abuse Unit, Linda Selin
306-787-8657, Fax: 306-787-0078, Linda.Selin@gov.sk.ca
Director, Victims Services, Pat Thiele
306-787-6707, Fax: 306-787-0081, patrick.thiele@gov.sk.ca
Assistant Director, Aboriginal & Northern Justice Initiations Branch, Rhonda Hueser
306-953-2352, Fax: 306-953-2353,
Rhonda.Hueser@gov.sk.ca

Courts & Civil Justice Division

306-787-5359 Fax: 306-787-8737

Assistant Deputy Minister, Ken Acton
306-787-0991, Fax: 306-787-8737, ken.acton@gov.sk.ca
Executive Legal Officer & Registrar, Court of Appeal, Melanie Baldwin
306-787-5382, Fax: 306-787-5815,
lschwann@sasklawcourts.ca
Executive Director, Court Services, Linda Bogard
306-787-5680, Fax: 306-787-8737, linda.bogard@gov.sk.ca
Director, Dispute Resolution Office, Glen Gardner
306-787-5749, Fax: 306-787-0088, glen.gardner@gov.sk.ca
Director, Family Justice Services/Maintenance Enforcement Office, Lionel McNabb
306-787-1650, Fax: 306-787-1420, lionel.mcnabb@gov.sk.ca

Public Law Division

306-787-8389

Executive Director, Susan Amrud, Q.C.
306-787-8990, susan.amrud@gov.sk.ca
Chief Legislative Crown Counsel, Legislative Drafting, Ian Brown, Q.C.
306-787-9346, Fax: 306-787-9111, ian.brown@gov.sk.ca
Director, Aboriginal Law, Mitch McAdam
306-787-7846, Fax: 306-787-9111,
Mitch.McAdam@gov.sk.ca
Director, Constitutional Law Branch, Graeme G. Mitchell, Q.C.
306-787-8385, Fax: 306-787-9111,
graeme.mitchell@gov.sk.ca
Manager, Queen's Printer, Marilyn Lustig-McEwen
306-787-9345, 800-226-7302, Fax: 306-798-0835,
marilyn.lustig-mcewen@gov.sk.ca, Other Communications: URL: www.qp.gov.sk.ca

Public Prosecutions Division

306-787-5490 Fax: 306-787-8878
www.justice.gov.sk.ca/publicprosecutionsdivision

Executive Director, Daryl Rayner, Q.C.
306-787-5490, Fax: 306-787-8878
Director, Financial & Information Services, Shari Parisian
306-787-8943, Fax: 306-787-8878
Director, Appeals, Dean Sinclair
306-787-5490, Fax: 306-787-8878

Regulatory Services Division

306-787-8995 Fax: 306-787-5830

Assistant Deputy Minister, Rod Cook
306-787-7869, Fax: 306-787-5830, Rod.Crook@gov.sk.ca
Public Guardian & Trustee, Ronald J. Kruzeniski, Q.C.
306-787-5427, Fax: 306-787-5065, ron.kruzeniski@gov.sk.ca
Director, Information Management Branch, Cathy Drader
306-787-9512, Fax: 306-787-6979, Cathy.Drader@gov.sk.ca
Director, Consumer Protection Branch, Eric Greene
306-787-2952, Fax: 306-787-9779, Eric.Greene@gov.sk.ca, Other Communications: Alternate Phone: 306-787-8607
Executive Director, Access & Privacy Branch, Duane Mombourquette
306-787-6428, Fax: 306-798-4064,
Duane.Mombourquette@gov.sk.ca

Saskatchewan Labour Relations & Workplace Safety (LRWS)

#300, 1870 Albert St., Regina, SK S4P 4W1
306-787-7404
webmaster@lab.gov.sk.ca
www.lrws.gov.sk.ca

The Ministry is responsible for labour standards, labour support services, labour relations, mediation, occupational health & safety, & workers' advocacy.

Acts Administered:

Building Trades Protection Act
Construction Industry Labour Relations Act, 1992
Employment Agencies Act
Labour Standards Act
Occupational Health & Safety Act, 1993
Mines Regulation
Occupational Health & Safety Regulations, 1996
Radiation Health & Safety Act, 1985
Radiation Health & Safety Regulations
Trade Union Act
Worker's Compensation Act
Worker's Compensation Act Exclusion Regulations
Worker's Compensation General Regulations, 1985
Public Interest Discolsure Act
Public Service Essential Service Act

Minister & Attorney General, Hon. Don Morgan, Q.C.
306-787-5353, Fax: 306-787-1232, minister.ju@gov.sk.ca
Deputy Minister, Mike Carr
306-787-7424, Fax: 306-798-5190, mike.carr@gov.sk.ca
Executive Director, Corporate Services (Shared Services), Karen Allen
306-787-5654, Fax: 306-787-7392, karen.allen@gov.sk.ca
Executive Director, Central Services, Laurier Donais
306-787-8078, Fax: 306-798-5190, laurier.donais@gov.sk.ca
Executive Director, Labour Relations & Mediation, Doug Forseth
306-787-9106, Fax: 306-787-1064, doug.forseth@gov.sk.ca
Executive Director, Marketing & Communications (Shared Services), Herman Hulshof
306-787-9715, Fax: 306-798-5021,
herman.hulshof@gov.sk.ca

Associated Agencies, Boards & Commissions:

• Labour Relations Board
#1600, 1920 Broad St.
Regina, SK S4P 3V2
306-787-2406 Fax: 306-787-2664
www.sasklabourrelationsboard.com
An independent, quasi-judicial tribunal charged with the responsibility of adjudicating disputes that arise under The Trade Union Act, The Construction Industry Labour Relations Act, 1992 & The Health Labour Relations Reorganization Act

• Minimum Wage Board
#400, 1870 Albert St.
Regina, SK S4P 4W1
www.aeei.gov.sk.ca/minimum-wage-board-review-reporting
Makes recommendations respecting minimum employment standards including: the minimum wage, minimum age, maximum work periods, maximum rates for room & board & minimum rest periods.

• Office of the Worker's Advocate
#300, 1870 Albert St.
Regina, SK S4P 4W1
306-787-2456 Fax: 306-787-0249 877-787-2456
www.lrws.gov.sk.ca/wao
The Office of the Worker's Advocate provides free assistance to workers who are experiencing difficulties with workers' compensation claims. The Office offers information about the following programs & services: wage loss, benefits, survivor's benefits, medical aid, rehabilitation, & retraining. Working with advocacy groups & unions, The Office of the Worker's Advocate strives to improve service to injured workers. Workers' Compensation Board (WCB) decisions about claims can be reviewed & appealed.
• Saskatchewan Workers' Compensation Board
#200, 1881 Scarth St.
Regina, SK S4P 4L1
306-787-4370 Fax: 306-787-7582 800-667-7590 TTY: 888-844-7773
internet_clientsvc@wcbsask.com
www.wcbsask.com
Other Communication: Injury Reports: 1-800-787-9288; Employer Inquiries: reainquiry@wcbsask.com; Health Care Provider Inquiries: internet_healthcare@wcbsask.com; Appeal Fax: 306-787-1116

Labour Standards
306-787-2438 Fax: 306-787-4780
800-667-1783
www.lrws.gov.sk.ca/ls
Executive Director, Greg Tuer
306-787-2432, Fax: 306-787-4780, greg.tuer@gov.sk.ca
Director, Compliance and Investigations (Saskatoon), Glen McRorie
306-933-5087, Fax: 306-787-4780, glen.mcrorie@gov.sk.ca
Director, Legal & Education Services, Daniel Parrott
306-787-9454, Fax: 306-787-4780, daniel.parrott@gov.sk.ca

Occupational Health & Safety Division
306-787-4496 Fax: 306-787-2208
800-567-7233
www.lrws.gov.sk.ca/ohs
Executive Director, Glennis Bihun
306-787-4481, Fax: 306-787-2208, glennis.bihun@gov.sk.ca
Chief Mines Inspector, Mines Safety, Neil Crocker
306-933-5106, Fax: 306-933-7339, neil.crocker@gov.sk.ca
Director, Health Services, Rita Coshan
306-787-4539, Fax: 306-787-2208, rita.coshan@gov.sk.ca
Director, Safety Services, Jennifer Fabian
306-787-0486, Fax: 306-787-2208, jennifer.fabian@gov.sk.ca
Director, Radiation Safety, Wayne Tiefenbach
306-787-4538, Fax: 306-787-2208,
Wayne.Tiefenbach@gov.sk.ca

Early Years
306-787-2004 Fax: 306-787-0277
Executive Director, Lois Zelmer
306-787-0765, Fax: 306-787-0277, Lois.Zelmer@gov.sk.ca
Director, Early Childhood Education, Kathy Abernethy
306-787-6158, Fax: 306-787-0277,
Kathy.Abernethy@gov.sk.ca
Director, Early Learning & Child Care, Brenda Dougherty
306-787-3858, Fax: 306-787-0277,
Brenda.Dougherty@gov.sk.ca
Director, Regional Child Care Services, Cindy Jeanes
306-787-3750, Fax: 306-798-3146, Cindy.Jeanes@gov.sk.ca
Director, Early Childhood Development & Intregrated Services, Gail Russell
306-787-8301, Fax: 306-787-0277, Gail.Russell@gov.sk.ca

Information Management & Support
#128, 1621 Albert St., Regina, SK S4P 2S5
306-787-2494 Fax: 306-787-0035
Executive Director, Joylene Campbell
Joylene.Campbell@gov.sk.ca

Infrasturcture & Education Funding
306-787-3341 Fax: 306-787-5059
Executive Director, Vacant
306-787-6634, Fax: 306-787-5059
Director, Infrastructure, Mike Back
306-787-7856, Fax: 306-798-0787, Mike.Back@gov.sk.ca
Director, Education Funding, Clint Repski
306-787-4658, Fax: 306-787-5059, Clint.Repski@gov.sk.ca

Provincial Library & Literacy Office
409A Park St., Regina, SK S4N 5B2
306-787-2976 Fax: 306-787-2029
srp.adm@prov.lib.sk.ca
www.education.gov.sk.ca/Provincial-Library
Other Communication: Literacy Office:
www.education.gov.sk.ca/literacy
Provincial Librarian, Brett Waytuck
306-787-2972, Fax: 306-787-2029, Brett.Waytuck@gov.sk.ca
Director, Library Accountability & Administration, Barbara Bulat
306-787-6032, Fax: 306-787-2029, barbara.bulat@gov.sk.ca
Director, Public Library Planning, Stephanie Hall
306-787-3005, Fax: 306-787-2029, stephanie.hall@gov.sk.ca
Director, Literacy Office, Vacant
306-787-8020, Fax: 306-787-4345

Strategic Policy
306-787-6769 Fax: 306-798-2572
Executive Director, Rosanne Glass
306-787-3897, Fax: 306-798-2572,
Rosanne.Glass@gov.sk.ca;
rosanne.glass@saskatoonhealthregion.ca

Regional Offices:

Southern Region
1831 College Ave., 3rd Fl., Regina, SK S4P 4V5
Fax: 306-787-6139
Regional Director, Darlene Thompson
306-787-6075, Fax: 306-787-6139,
Darlene.Thompson@gov.sk.ca

Central Region
122 3rd Ave. North, 8th Fl., Saskatoon, SK S7K 2H6
Fax: 306-933-7469
Regional Director, Crandall Hrynkiw

Northern Region
Mistasinihk Place, #2200 1328 La Ronge Ave., PO Box 5000, La Ronge, SK S0J 1L0
306-425-4380 Fax: 306-425-4383
800-667-4380
Regional Director, Daryl Arnott
306-425-4382

Student Achievement & Supports
Executive Director, Simone Gareau
306-787-5632, Fax: 306-787-3164,
Simone.Gareau@gov.sk.ca
Director, Learning Program (French), Lucie Anderson
306-787-6089, Fax: 306-787-3164,
Lucie.Anderson@gov.sk.ca
Director, Assessment & Accountability, Michelle Belisle
306-787-6053, Fax: 306-787-9178, Other Communications: URL: www.education.gov.sk.ca/programs-services
Director, Learning Program (English), Gerry Craswell
306-787-5974, Fax: 306-787-2223,
Gerry.Craswell@gov.sk.ca
Director, Supports for Learning, Sharon Yuzdepski
306-787-6025, Fax: 306-787-2223,
Sharon.Yuzdepski@gov.sk.ca

Saskatchewan Liquor & Gaming Authority (SLGA)

2500 Victoria Ave., PO Box 5054, Regina, SK S4P 3M3
306-787-4213
inquiry@slga.gov.sk.ca
www.slga.gov.sk.ca
The Treasury Board Crown Corporation is responsible for the distribution, control, & regulation of liquor & most gaming across Saskatchewan.
Minister Responsible, Hon. Tim McMillan
306-787-7339, Fax: 306-798-3140, mminister.cc@gov.sk.ca
President/Chief Oxecutive Officer, Barry Lacey
306-787-1737, Fax: 306-787-8439, blacey@slga.gov.sk.ca
Director, Human Resources Branch, Leeann Pillipow-Kautz
306-798-8483, Fax: 306-787-7336

Saskatchewan Municipal Affairs (MA)

1855 Victoria St., Regina, SK S4P 3T2
306-787-8885
www.municipal.gov.sk.ca
The Ministry of Municipal Affairs seeks to strengthen Saskatchewan's system of municipal government through partnerships with municipal associations, municipal councils & administrators, community planners, & property assessment appraisers. The Ministry also collaborates with other provincial ministries & consults the federal government where necessary.
Acts Administered:
Assessment Appraisers Act
Assessment Management Agency Act
Border Areas Act
Cities Act
City of Lloydminster Act
Community Planning Profession Act
Controverted Municipal Elections Act
Cut Knife Reference Act
Department of Rural Development Act
Department of Urban Affairs Act
Flin Flon Extension of Boundaries Act, 1952
Local Government Election Act
Local Improvements Act, 1993
Municipal Board Act
Municipal Debentures Repayment Act
Municipal Development & Loan (Saskatchewan) Act
Municipal Expropriation Act
Municipal Industrial Development Corporations Act
Municipal Grants Act
Municipal Tax Sharing (Potash) Act
Municipalities Act
Municipality Improvements Assistance (Saskatchewan) Act
Northern Municipalities Act
Planning & Development Act, 1983
Rural Development Act
Rural Municipal Administrators Act
Subdivisions Act
Tax Enforcement Act
Time Act
Urban Municipal Administrators Act
Urban Municipality Act, 1984
Minister, Municipal Affairs, Hon. Darryl Hickie
306-787-6100, Fax: 306-787-0399, minister.ma@gov.sk.ca
Deputy Minister, Van Isman
306-787-1925, Fax: 306-787-1987, van.isman@gov.sk.ca
Assistant Deputy Minister, Keith Comstock
306-787-5765, Fax: 306-787-1987,
keith.comstock@gov.sk.ca
Executive Director, Policy Development, John Edwards
306-787-2665, Fax: 306-787-5822,
john.edwards2@gov.sk.ca
Executive Director, Strategy & Sector Relations, Sheldon Green
306-787-7883, Fax: 306-798-2568, sheldon.green@gov.sk.ca
Executive Director, Communications, Jeff Welke
306-787-6156, Fax: 306-787-4181, jeff.welke@gov.sk.ca
Director, Northern Municipal Services, Randy Braaten
306-425-4322, Fax: 306-425-2401, randy.braaten@gov.sk.ca
Director, Communications, Nicole Fellinger
306-787-2687, Fax: 306-787-4181, nicole.fellinger@gov.sk.ca

Associated Agencies, Boards & Commissions:
• Saskatchewan Municipal Board (SMB)
#480, 2151 Scarth St.
Regina, SK S4P 2H8
306-787-6221 Fax: 306-787-1610
info@smb.gov.sk.ca
www.smb.gov.sk.ca

Community Planning
306-787-9411 Fax: 306-798-0194
Executive Director, Ralph Leibel
306-787-7672, Fax: 306-798-0194, ralph.leibel@gov.sk.ca
Director, Community Planning (Regina), Barry Braitman
306-787-2893, Fax: 306-798-0194, barry.braitman@gov.sk.ca
Director, Community Planning (Saskatoon), Len Kowalko
306-933-6118, Fax: 306-933-7720, len.kowalko@gov.sk.ca

Grants Administration & Financial Management
306-787-8808 Fax: 306-787-3641
Executive Director/Director, New Deal Secretariat, Rintoul Kathy
306-787-8887, Other Communications: New Deal Secretariat: 306-787-9699
Director, Grants Administration, Kyle Toffan
306-787-7994, Fax: 306-787-3641, kyle.toffan@gov.sk.ca

Central Management Services
306-787-2136 Fax: 306-787-4161
Executive Director, Wanda Lamberti
306-787-1640, Fax: 306-787-4161,
Wanda.Lamberti@gov.sk.ca
Director, Financial Planning, Marj Abel
306-787-4172, Fax: 306-787-4161, Marj.Abel@gov.sk.ca
Director, Financial Services, Janie Markewich
306-787-6408, Fax: 306-787-4161

Ombudsman Saskatchewan

#150, 2401 Saskatchewan Dr., Regina, SK S4P 4H8
306-787-6211 Fax: 306-787-9090
800-667-7180
ombreg@ombudsman.sk.ca
www.ombudsman.sk.ca
Other Communication: Saskatoon e-mail:
ombsktn@ombudsman.sk.ca
The Ombudsman is an Officer of the Legislative Assembly with the authority to investigate complaints received from members of the public who believe the government administration has dealt with them unfairly. Government administration includes any department, branch, board, agency or commission responsible to the Crown & any public servant in Saskatchewan. The Ombudsman was established by the Ombudsman & Children's Advocate Act.
Ombudsman, Kevin Fenwick, Q.C.
Deputy Ombudsman, Regina Office, Janet Mirwaldt
306-787-6142, jmirwaldt@ombudsman.sk.ca
Deputy Ombudsman, Saskatoon Office, Joni Sereda
306-933-8165, Fax: 306-933-8406,
jsereda@ombudsman.sk.ca

Saskatchewan Opportunities Corporation (SOCO)

Innovation Place, #114, 14 Innovation Blvd., Saskatoon, SK S7N 2X8
306-933-6295 Fax: 306-933-8215
saskatoon@innovationplace.com
www.innovationplace.com/corporate.php

The Opportunities Corporation aims to support Saskatchewan's technology sector through the development and operation of research parks.

Minister Responsible, Hon. Rob Norris
306-787-0341, Fax: 306-787-6946, minister.aeei@gov.sk.ca
President/Chief Executive Officer, Doug Tastad
306-933-6258, Fax: 306-933-8215, tastad@innovationplace.com
Chief Financial Officer & Vice-President, Finance & Administration, Charlene Callander
306-787-8534, Fax: 306-787-8601, ccallander@innovationplace.com
Chief Operating Officer & Vice-President, Research Park Operations, Ken Loeppky
306-787-5706, Fax: 306-787-8601, kloeppky@innovationplace.com
Vice-President, Corporate Relations, Austin Beggs
306-933-7464, Fax: 306-933-8215, austin@innovationplace.com

Saskatchewan Power Corporation (SaskPower)

2025 Victoria Ave., Regina, SK S4P 0S1
306-566-3306 Fax: 800-757-6937
888-757-6937
www.saskpower.com
Other Communication: Media phone: 306-536-2886

A Crown Corporation which provides services to over 439,000 customers over 652,000 square kilometres of diverse terrain in Saskatchewan; operates 15 generating facilities including, four base-load thermal stations, seven hydroelectric stations, three gas-fired peaking stations, & the Cypress Wind Power facility; capacity of 3,655 megawatts. The SaskPower Environmental policy maintains a commitment to environmental responsibility. The policy includes compliance with relevant environmental legislation, regulations & corporate environmental committees; continual improvement of environmental management systems & prevention of pollution. SaskPower's management system is ISO 14001 registered.

Minister Responsible, Hon. Rob Norris
306-787-0341, Fax: 306-787-6946, minister.aeei@gov.sk.ca
President/Chief Executive Officer, NorthPoint Energy Solutions, Robert Watson
306-566-3103
Chief Information Officer & Vice-President, Corporate Information & Technology, Tom Kindred
306-566-2146, tkindred@saskpower.com
Chief Financial Officer & Vice-President, Corporate & Financial Services, Sandeep Kalra
306-566-2620, skalra@saskpower.com
Vice-President, Planning, Environment & Regulatory Affairs, Guy Bruce
306-566-2386, gbruce@saskpower.com
Vice-President, Corporate Relations, Kevin Doherty
306-566-3581, kdoherty@saskpower.com
Vice-President, Power Production, John Lebersback
306-566-3228, jlebersback@saskpower.com
Vice-President, Transmission & Distribution, Mike Marsh
306-566-3271, mmarsh@saskpower.com
Vice-President, Customer Services, Judy May
306-566-2161
Vice-President, Clean Coal Technology, Michael Monea
306-566-3132, mmonea@saskpower.com
Vice-President, Law, Land & Regulatory Affairs, Rachelle Verret Morphy
306-566-3139, rverretmor@saskpower.com

Office of the Provincial Capital Commission

4607 Dewdney Ave., Regina, SK S4T 1B7
306-787-9261
www.opcc.gov.sk.ca

The mandate of the Provincial Capital Commission is to promote, preserve & strengthen Saskatchewan heritage & culture through the promotion of tourism in the capital city.

Acts Administered:
Office of the Provincial Capital Commission Regulations
Air, Army, Sea & Navy League Cadets Recognition Day Act
Archives Act, 2004
Culture & Recreation Act (jointly with Tourism, Culture, Parks & Sport)
Heritage Property Act (jointly with Tourism, Culture, Parks & Sport)
Historic Properties Foundations Act
Government House Foundation Regulations
National Peacekeepers Recognition Day Act
Recognition of John George Diefenbaker Day Act
Saskatchewan Centre of the Arts Act, 2000
Saskatchewan Heritage Foundation Act (jointly with Tourism, Culture, Parks & Sport)
Tartan Day Act
Tommy Douglas Day Act
Wascana Centre Act

Minister Responsible, Hon. Bill Hutchinson
306-780-0354, Fax: 306-798-0264, minister.tpcs@gov.sk.ca
Chief Executive Officer, Harley Olsen
306-787-9461, Fax: 306-787-5714, harley.olsen@gov.sk.ca
Executive Director, Central Management Services, Wanda Lamberti
306-787-1640, Fax: 306-787-4161, wanda.lamberti@gov.sk.ca
Executive Director, Communications, Jeff Welke
306-787-6156, Fax: 306-787-4181, jeff.welke@gov.sk.ca
Director, Operations, Gwen Jacobson
306-787-6863, Fax: 306-787-5714, Gwen.Jacobson@gov.sk.ca
Director, Communications, Nicole Fellinger
306-787-2687, Fax: 306-787-4181, nicole.fellinger@gov.sk.ca
Director, Financial Planning, Marj Abel
306-787-4172, Fax: 306-787-4161, marj.abel@gov.sk.ca
Director, Financial Services, Janie Markewich
306-787-6408, Fax: 306-787-4161, janie.markewich@gov.sk.ca

Associated Agencies, Boards & Commissions:

• Conexus Arts Centre
200A Lakeshore Dr.
Regina, SK S4S 7L3
306-565-4500 Fax: 306-565-3274
cac.admin@conexusartscentre.ca
www.conexusartscentre.ca

• Government House
4607 Dewdney Ave.
Regina, SK S4T 1B7
306-787-5773 Fax: 306-787-5714
governmenthouse@gov.sk.ca

• Wascana Centre
Wascana Place
2900 Wascana Dr.
PO Box 7111
Regina, SK S4P 3S7
306-522-3661 Fax: 306-565-2742
wca@wascana.sk.ca
www.wascana.sk.ca

Office of the Provincial Secretary

Legislative Bldg., #348, 2405 Legislative Dr,, Regina, SK S4S 0B3
306-787-7360 Fax: 306-798-0263
www.ops.gov.sk.ca

The Office of the Provincial Secretary manages official protocol, provincial honours & awards, Government House, French-language services, & provides administrative services to the Office of the Lieutenant Governor.

Acts Administered:
Provincial Emblems & Honours Act
Provincial Secretary's Act
Recognition of Telemiracle Week Act

Provincial Secretary & Minister, Education, Hon. Donna Harpauer
306-787-7360, Fax: 306-798-0263, minister.edu@gov.sk.ca
Deputy Provincial Secretary, Van Isman
306-787-1925, Fax: 306-787-1987, van.isman@gov.sk.ca
Acting Chief of Protocol, Linda Spence
306-787-7315, Fax: 306-787-1269, linda.spence@gov.sk.ca
Registrar, Honours & Awards, Elisabeth Hugel
306-787-4195, Fax: 306-787-1269, elisabeth.hugel@gov.sk.ca
Executive Director, Central Management Services, Wanda Lamberti
306-787-1640, Fax: 306-787-4161, wanda.lamberti@gov.sk.ca
Executive Director, Francophone Affairs Branch/Direction des affaires francophones, Charles-Henri Warren
306-787-8035, Fax: 306-787-6352, charleshenri.warren@gov.sk.ca; fab-daf@gov.sk.ca, Other Communications: URL: www.ops.gov.sk.ca/fab-daf
Director, Financial Planning, Marj Abel
306-787-4172, Fax: 306-787-4161, marj.abel@gov.sk.ca
Director, Communications, Nicole Fellinger
306-787-2687, Fax: 306-787-4181, nicole.fellinger@gov.sk.ca
Executive Director, Communications, Jeff Welke
306-787-6156, Fax: 306-787-4181, jeff.welke@gov.sk.ca

Saskatchewan Public Service Commission (PSC)

2100 Broad St., Regina, SK S4P 1Y5
306-787-7853
866-319-5999
psc.webmaster@gov.sk.ca; inquiry@psc.gov.sk.ca
www.psc.gov.sk.ca

The independent agency provides leadership & policy direction for the human resource function in the public service. The PSC works with departments to deliver human resource services.

Acts Administered:
Financial Administration Act, 1993
Freedom of Information & Protection of Privacy Act
Health Information Protection Act
Government Organization Act
Labour Standards Act
Labour Standards Regulations, 1995
Occupational Health & Safety Act, 1993
Occupational Health & Safety Regulations, 1996
Public Employees Pension Plan Act
Public Service Act, 1998
Public Service Superannuation Act
Public Service Regulations, 1999
Trade Union Act
Superannuation (Supplementary Provisions) Act

Minister Responsible, Hon. June Draude
306-787-3661, Fax: 306-787-0656, minister.ss@gov.sk.ca
Chair, Don Wincherauk
306-787-7552, Fax: 306-798-5045, don.wincherauk@gov.sk.ca
Executive Director, Organizational Effectiveness, Ken Ludwig
306-787-7591, Fax: 306-787-4074, ken.ludwig@gov.sk.ca
Director, Communications, Shelley Banks
306-787-6479, Fax: 306-798-2251, shelley.banks@gov.sk.ca
Director, Corporate Services, Mike Pestill
306-787-8278, Fax: 306-787-7578, mike.pestill@gov.sk.ca

Corporate HR Management & Employee Relations
2350 Albert St., 2nd Fl., Regina, SK S4P 4A6
306-787-7611 Fax: 306-798-5045

Assistant Chair, Don Zerr
306-787-7606, Fax: 306-798-5045, don.zerr@gov.sk.ca

Human Resource Client Service & Support Division
2350 Albert St., 2nd Fl., Regina, SK S4P 4A6
Fax: 306-798-5045

Assistant Chair, Karen Aulie
306-787-4870, Fax: 306-798-5045, karen.aulie@gov.sk.ca

Regional Offices:

Estevan
#303, 1133 - 4th St., PO Box 5000, Estevan, SK S4A 0W6
306-637-4505 Fax: 306-637-4510
800-265-2001

Regional Enterprise Manager, Linda Mack
linda.mack@enterprisesask.ca

Moose Jaw
88 Saskatchewan St. East, Moose Jaw, SK S6H 0V4
306-694-3624 Fax: 306-694-3500
800-265-2001

Regional Enterprise Manager, Jim Dixon
jim.dixon@enterprisesask.ca

North Battleford
1202 - 101st St., North Battleford, SK S9A 1E9
306-446-7664 Fax: 306-446-7442
800-265-2001

Acting Regional Enterprise Manager, Christa Watson
christa.watson@enterprisesask.ca

Prince Albert
225 - 1061 Central Ave., Prince Albert, SK S6V 6G1
306-953-2275 Fax: 306-922-6499
800-265-2001

Regional Enterprise Manager, Warren McLeod
warren.mcleod@enterprisesask.ca

Swift Current
885 - 6th Ave. NE, Swift Current, SK S9H 2M9
306-778-8200 Fax: 306-778-8526
800-265-2001

Regional Enterprise Manager, Daniel Leiva
daniel.leiva@enterprisesask.ca

Yorkton
72 Smith St. West, Yorkton, SK S3N 2Y4
306-786-1416 Fax: 306-786-1417
800-265-2001

Regional Enterprise Manager, Joelene Kotzer-Mitschke
joelene.mitschke@enterprisesask.ca

Saskatchewan Research Council (SRC)

#125, 15 Innovation Blvd., Saskatoon, SK S7N 2X8
306-933-5400 Fax: 306-933-7446
info@src.sk.ca
www.src.sk.ca

Research activities include: gas emissions testing; indoor environment testing; groundwater pesticides testing; indoor air quality & source testing for rayon & asbestos; spray drift research; vegetation studies for range, forestry, conservation; aquatic monitoring & assessment methods; climate impact assessment for environmental economic & urban stormwater management; development of plant bioassays for assessing the effects of hazardous materials in aquatic ecosystems; radiochemistry, chromatographic analysis, water analysis; parenting verification centre for the Canadian livestock industry; develops the optimum engine & fuel system for natural gas operation; bioprocessing technology; emulsions research; studies to support mineral exploration; analyses various sample material used in mineral exploration; geoenvironmental research. SRC's Biofuels Test Centre opened in September, 2006.

President/Chief Executive Officer, Dr. Laurier Schramm
306-933-5402, schramm@src.sk.ca; presidentsoffice@src.sk.ca
Chief Financial Officer, Crystal Nett
306-933-8111, Fax: 306-933-7519, crystal.nett@src.sk.ca
Vice-President, Organizational Effectiveness, Toby Arnold
306-933-5479, Fax: 306-933-7896, arnold@src.sk.ca
Vice-President, Environment, Joe Muldoon
306-933-5439, Fax: 306-933-7299, muldoon@src.sk.ca
Vice-President, Mining & Minerals, Craig Murray
306-933-5482, Fax: 306-933-7446, murray@src.sk.ca
Vice-President, Business Ventures & Communications, Wanda Nyirfa
306-933-5400, Fax: 306-933-7519, advertising@src.sk.ca; media@src.sk.ca
Vice-President, Energy, Ernie S. Pappas
306-787-9351, Fax: 306-787-8811, pappas@src.sk.ca
Vice-President, Agriculture & Biotechnology, Phillip Stephan
306-933-8199, Fax: 306-933-7662, stephan@src.sk.ca

SaskEnergy Incorporated

1777 Victoria Ave., Regina, SK S4P 4K5
306-777-9225
800-567-8899
www.saskenergy.com
Other Communication: Emergency & safety Line: 1-888-700-0427; Line Locates: 1-866-828-4888

The provincial Crown corporation provides natural gas to residential, farm, commercial, & industrial customers in 92% of Saskatchewan's communities.

Acts Administered:
SaskEnergy Act

Minister Responsible, Hon. Dustin Duncan
306-787-0393, Fax: 306-787-1669, minister.env@gov.sk.ca
Chair, Rob Pletch
306-777-9901
President/Chief Executive Officer, Doug Kelln
306-777-9568, Fax: 306-777-9889, dkelln@saskenergy.com
Vice-President, General Counsel & Corporate Secretary, Mark Guillet
306-777-9427, Fax: 306-565-3332, mguillet@saskenergy.com
Executive Director, Corporate Affairs, Ron Podbielski
306-777-9432, Fax: 306-352-4438, rpodbielski@saskenergy.com

Saskatchewan Social Services (SS)

1920 Broad St., Regina, SK S4P 3V6
306-787-3700
866-221-5200
socialservicesinquiry@gov.sk.ca
www.socialservices.gov.sk.ca
TTY: 306-787-7283
Other Communication: Income Assistance: 306-798-0660; Media inquiries: 306-787-3686; Staus of Women Office: 306-787-7401

The Ministry works with citizens in the following areas: income support; child & family services; supports for persons with disabilities; affordable housing; economic independence; & active involvement in the labour market & the community. In November 2007, a new provincial government resulted in the reorganization of provincial government ministries. The work of Saskatchewan Community Resources was merged into a newly named ministry. Donna Harpauer was named the Minister of Social Services.

Acts Administered:
Adoption Act
Child Care Act
Child & Family Services Act
Department of Social Services Act
Donation of Food Act
Emergency Protection for Victims of Child Sexual Abuse & Exploitation Act
Intercountry Adoption (Hague Convention) Implementation Act
Rehabilitation Act
Residential Services Act
Saskatchewan Assistance Act
Saskatchewan Housing Corporation Act
Saskatchewan Income Plan Act
Social Workers Act
Condominium Property Act, 1993
Landlord & Tenant Act

Minister, Social Services, Hon. June Draude
306-787-3661, Fax: 306-787-0656, minister.ss@gov.sk.ca
Deputy Minister, Marian Zerr
306-787-3491, Fax: 306-787-1032, Marian.Zerr@gov.sk.ca
Executive Director, Communications, Trish Alcorn
306-787-0916, Fax: 306-787-8669, Trish.Alcorn@gov.sk.ca
Director, Child & Family Services (South Service Area), Janice Krumenacker
306-787-9109, Fax: 306-787-4940, janice.krumenacker@gov.sk.ca
Director, Child & Family Services (Centre Service Area), Garry Prediger
306-933-6075, Fax: 306-933-5665, Garry.Prediger@gov.sk.ca

Saskatchewan Tourism, Parks, Culture & Sport (TPCS)

1919 Saskatchewan Dr., 4th Fl., Regina, SK S4P 4H2
306-787-5729 Fax: 306-787-8560
info@cyr.gov.sk.ca
www.tpcs.gov.sk.ca

The Ministry enhances the province's cultural, artistic, recreational & social life by working cooperatively with diverse groups & communities as it strives to promote leadership, recognize accomplishments, & sustain excellence in the arts, culture & sport. It is dedicated to ensuring that Saskatchewan people, especially the young people, reach their fullest potential in provincial, national, & international communities. In November 2007, a new provincial government resulted in the reorganization of provincial government ministries. The work of Saskatchewan Culture, Youth & Recreation was merged into an expanded ministry.

Acts Administered:
Active Families Benefit Act
Archives Act, 2004
Arts Board Act, 1997
Arts Professions Act
Communications Network Corporations Act
Culture & Recreations Act, 1993
Doukhobors of Canada C.C.U.B. Trust Fund Act
Film Employment Tax Credit Act
Geographic Names Board Act
Grasslands National Park Act
Heritage Property Act
Holocaust Memorial Day Act
Interprovincial Lotteries Act, 1984
Jean-Louis Légaré Act
Meewasin Valley Authority Act
Multiculturalism Act
Parks Act
Regional Parks Act, 1979
Royal Saskatchewan Museum Act
Saskatchewan Centre of the Arts Act, 2000
Saskatchewan Gaming Corporation Act (part IV - Community Initiatives Fund)
Saskatchewan Heritage Foundation Act
Tartan Day Act
Tourism Authority Act
Wakamow Valley Authority Act
Wanuskewin Heritage Park Act, 1997
Wascana Centre Act
Western Development Museum Act

Minister, Tourism, Parks, Culture & Sport, Hon. Bill Hutchinson
306-787-0354, Fax: 306-798-0264, minister.tpcs@gov.sk.ca
Deputy Minister, Wynne Young
306-787-5050, Fax: 306-798-0033, Wynne.Young@gov.sk.ca
Executive Director, Tourism, Ken Dueck
306-787-7871, Fax: 306-798-3177, Ken.Dueck@gov.sk.ca
Executive Director, Culture & Heritage, Susan Hetu
306-787-0730, Fax: 306-798-3177, susan.hetu@gov.sk.ca
Executive Director, Sport, Recreation & Stewardship, Scott Langen
306-787-0685, Fax: 306-787-0069, Scott.Langen@gov.sk.ca
Executive Director, Policy, Planning & Evaluation, Leanne Thera
306-798-8762, Fax: 306-798-0033, Leanne.Thera@gov.sk.ca; L.Thera@gov.sk.ca
Director, Heritage Resources, Carlos Germann
306-787-5772, Fax: 306-787-0069, Carlos.Germann@gov.sk.ca
Director, Communications, Jennifer Johnson
306-787-0619, Fax: 306-798-0033, jennifer.johnson@gov.sk.ca
Director, Corporate Services, Melinda Leibel
306-787-5896, Fax: 306-798-0033, Melinda.Leibel@gov.sk.ca

Associated Agencies, Boards & Commissions:

• Saskatchewan Communications Network (SCN)
#313E, 2440 Broad St.
Regina, SK S4P 0A5
306-779-2726 Fax: 306-545-8649
inquiries@scn.ca
www.scn.ca

• Royal Saskatchewan Museum
2445 Albert St.
Regina, SK S4P 4W7
306-787-2815 Fax: 306-787-2820
rsminfo@gov.sk.ca
www.royalsaskmuseum.ca

• Saskatchewan Archives Board
University of Regina
3303 Hillsdale St.
PO Box 1665
Regina, SK S4P 3C6
306-787-4068 Fax: 306-787-1197
info.regina@archives.gov.sk.ca
www.saskarchives.com

• Sask Film
1831 College Ave.
Regina, SK S4P 4V5
306-798-9800 Fax: 306-798-7768 800-561-9933
www.saskfilm.com
Provides support, financial assistance & equity financing to the Saskatchewan film, television & new media industries through a variety of programs & services. Saskfilm administers the Saskatchewan Film Employment Tax Credit Program, & manages the Saskatchewan Production Studios.

• Saskatchewan Heritage Foundation
1919 Saskatchewan Dr., 9th Fl.
Regina, SK S4P 4H2
306-787-4188 Fax: 306-787-0069
www.tpcs.gov.sk.ca/SHF

• Saskatchewan Arts Board
1355 Broad St.
Regina, SK S4R 7V1
306-787-4056 Fax: 306-787-4199 800-667-7526
info@artsboard.sk.ca
www.artsboard.sk.ca

• Saskatchewan Science Centre
2903 Powerhouse Dr.
Regina, SK S4N 0A1
306-522-4629 800-667-6300
info@sasksciencecentre.com
www.sasksciencecentre.com
Other Communication: Administration: 306-791-7900; Media: 306-791-7917

• Tourism Saskatchewan
#189, 1621 Albert St.
Regina, SK S4P 2S5
306-787-9600 877-237-2273
www.sasktourism.com
Tourism Saskatchewan is a market-driven, industry-led partnership responsible for developing and promoting tourism in Saskatchewan.

• Wanuskewin Heritage Park
RR#4 Penner Rd.
Saskatoon, SK S7K 3J7
306-931-6767 Fax: 306-931-4522
roxanne.parker@wanuskewin.com
www.wanuskewin.com

• Western Development Museum
2935 Melville St.
Saskatoon, SK S7J 5A6
306-934-1400 Fax: 306-934-4467 800-363-6345
info@wdm.ca
www.wdm.ca

Saskatchewan Telecommunications (SaskTel)

2121 Saskatchewan Dr., 7th Fl., Regina, SK S4P 4C3
306-777-3737
800-727-5835
corporate.comments@sasktel.sk.ca
www.sasktel.com

The provincial Crown Corporation delivers full service telecommunications to the people of Saskatchewan. Services are as follows: competitive voice, data, dial-up, & high speed internet; entertainment & multimedia services; security; web hosting; text & messaging services; & cellular & wireless data services.

Minister Responsible, Hon. Bill Boyd
306-787-9124, Fax: 306-787-0395, minister.er@gov.sk.ca
Chair, Grant Kook
306-777-2201
President/Chief Executive Officer, Ron Styles
306-777-2200, ron.styles@sasktel.sk.ca
Chief Financial Officer, Mike Anderson
306-777-3185
Chief Technology Officer, Kym Wittal
306-777-4504
Chief Information Officer, John Hill
306-777-2327, john.hill@gov.sk.ca
Vice-President, Human Resources & Corporate Services, Doug Burnett
306-777-2283
Vice-President, Customer Service (Sales), Ken Keesey
306-931-5915

Senior Director, Corporate Communications, Darcee MacFarlane
306-777-4441
Vice-President, Corporate Counsel, Regulatory Affairs & Partnership Development, John Meldrum
306-777-2223
Vice-President, Marketing, Stacey Sandison
306-777-3670

Saskatchewan Transportation Company (STC)

1717 Saskatchewan Dr., Regina, SK S4P 2E2
306-787-3347 Fax: 306-787-1633
info@stcbus.com
www.stcbus.com

The STC was established in 1946 to provide safe, affordable & accessible freight and passenger bus service throughout Saskatchewan.

Minister Responsible, Hon. Jim Reiter
306-787-6447, Fax: 306-787-1736, minister.hi@gov.sk.ca
President/Chief Executive Officer, Shawn Grice
306-787-2116, Fax: 306-798-4754, sgrice@stcbus.com
Chief Operating Officer, Customer Services/Maintenance, Phil Bohay
306-787-7302, Fax: 306-787-1633, pbohay@stcbus.com
Acting Chief Financial Officer, Jason Sherwin
306-787-8189, Fax: 306-787-3429, jsherwin@stcbus.com

Corporate Support
Fax: 306-777-9561
Vice-President, Colleen Huber
306-777-9660, chuber@saskenergy.com

Distribution Utility
306-777-9994 Fax: 306-522-2217
Executive Vice-President, Dean Reeve
306-777-9402, Fax: 306-522-2217, dreeve@saskenergy.com
Executive Director, Distribution Customer Service, Randy Greggains
306-777-9233, Fax: 306-522-2217, rgreggains@saskenergy.com

Finance
Fax: 306-777-9070
Vice-President & Chief Financial Officer, Dennis Terry
306-777-9417, dterry@saskenergy.com

Gas Supply & Business Development
306-777-9354 Fax: 306-569-3522
Senior Vice-President, Daryl Posehn
306-777-9567, Fax: 306-569-3522, dposehn@saskenergy.com

Human Resources
Fax: 306-781-7050
Vice-President, Robert Haynes
306-777-9405, rhaynes@saskenergy.com

TransGas Limited
Fax: 306-352-8892
TransGas & its affiliates, Many Islands Pipelines Canada Limited, MIPCL, & Swan Valley Gas Corporation, SVGC, own & operate over 13,800 kilometres of gathering & transmission pipeline in Saskatchewan, operates storage facilities to ensure safe & reliable operation during the winter. TransGas transports natural gas for over 280 customers, producers & industrial & commercial customers. The TransGas pipeline system is connected to TransCanada pipelines, ATCO pipelines, & Havre pipeline, providing the Saskatchewan market access to Alberta & Montana gas supplies. TransGas' & MIPCL's interconnections with other transmission systems, Foothills Pipelines Ltd., TransCanada Pipelines Ltd., Swan Valley Gas & Williston Basin Interstate, provide access to Manitoba, eastern Canadian & United States markets for Saskatchewan, Alberta & United States-sourced gas supplies
Vice-President, Operations & Engineering, Phil Sandham
306-777-9603, psandham@transgas.com
Vice-President, Market Service & System Management, Debbie McKague
306-777-9595, Fax: 306-525-3422, dmckague@transgas.com
Executive Director, Pipeline & Facility Automation, Ron Carman
306-777-9652, Fax: 306-777-9191, rcarman@transgas.com
Executive Director, Transmission Operations, Myron Dressler
306-777-9006, mdressler@transgas.com
Executive Director, Engineering & Technology, Brian Torgunrud
306-777-9357, Fax: 306-525-1088, btorgunrud@transgas.com

Saskatchewan Water Corporation (SaskWater)

#200, 111 Fairford St. East, Moose Jaw, SK S6H 1C8
Fax: 306-694-3207
888-230-1111
comm@saskwater.com; customerservice@saskwater.com
www.saskwater.com
Other Communication: SaskWater Customer Emergencies: 1-800-667-5799

SaskWater, a provincial Crown corporation, is Saskatchewan's water utility service provider. Lines of business are as follows: supply of potable & non-potable water; treatment & management of wastewater; & certified operations & maintenance. SaskWater is responsible for designing, building, & operating transmission, regional, & stand-alone water supply & wastewater systems. All systems must meet regulatory requirements.

Acts Administered:
Saskatchewan Water Corporation Act, 2002

Minister Responsible, Hon. Dustin Duncan
306-787-0393, Fax: 306-787-1669, minister.env@gov.sk.ca
President, Doug Matthies
306-694-3903, Fax: 306-694-3207, doug.matthies@saskwater.com
Vice-President, Business Development & Corporate Services Division, Marie Alexander
306-694-3916, Fax: 306-694-3207, marie.alexander@saskwater.com
Vice-President, Operations & Engineering, Mart Cram
306-694-3909, Fax: 306-694-3207, mart.cram@saskwater.com

Saskatchewan Workers' Compensation Board

#200, 1881 Scarth St., Regina, SK S4P 4L1
306-787-4370 Fax: 306-787-4311
800-667-7590
internet_clientsvc@wcbsask.com
www.wcbsask.com
Other Communication: Injury Reports: 1-800-787-9288; Employer Inquiries: reainquiry@wcbsask.com; Health Care Provider Inquiries: internet_healthcare@wcbsask.com; Appeal Fax: 306-787-1116

The Saskatchewan's Workers' Compensation Board was created by the following provincial legislation in Saskatchewan: the Workers' Compensation Act 1979, General Regulations, & Exclusion Regulations. The Board is an independent body that administers a no-fault compensation system to protect employers and workers against the result of work injuries. The WCB provides financial protection, medical benefits. & rehabilitation services to injured workers & their dependents in cases of injury or death arising from, & in the course of, employment.

Minister Responsible, Hon. Don Morgan, Q.C.
306-787-5353, Fax: 306-787-1232, minister.ju@gov.sk.ca
Chairman, David Eberle
306-787-4379, Fax: 306-787-0213
Chief Executive Officer, Peter Federko
306-787-7398, Fax: 306-787-0213, pfederko@wcbsask.com
Vice-President, Human Resources & Team Support, Donna Kane
306-787-4440, Fax: 306-787-0213, dkane@wcbsask.com
Vice-President, Prevention, Finance & Information Technology, Gail Kruger
306-787-2475, Fax: 306-787-0213, gkruger@wcbsask.com
Vice-President, Operations, Graham Topp
306-787-4371, Fax: 306-787-7582, gtopp@wcbsask.com

Government of the Yukon Territory

Seat of Government: PO Box 2703, Whitehorse, YT Y1A 2C6
867-667-5811
800-661-0408
www.gov.yk.ca
TTY: 867-393-7460

The Yukon was created as a separate territory June 13, 1898. It has an area of 474,711.02 km2, & StatsCan's population estimate in 2010 was 34,500. A federally appointed commissioner (similar to a provincial lieutenant-governor) oversees federal interests in the territory, but the day-to-day operation of the government rests with the wholly elected executive council (cabinet). The territorial legislature has power to make acts on generally all matters of a local nature in the territory, including the imposition of local taxes, property & civil rights & the administration of justice, education & health & social services. Legislative powers vested in the provinces but not available to the territory include control of unoccupied Crown land, renewable & non-renewable resources (except wildlife & sport fisheries) & the power to amend the Yukon Act, a federal statute.

Office of the Commissioner

Closeleigh Manor, 1098 First Ave., Whitehorse, YT Y1A 0C1
867-667-5121 Fax: 867-393-6201
commissioner@gov.yk.ca
www.commissioner.gov.yk.ca

The Yukon Territory is governed by a commissioner appointed for a 5-year term by the federal government, a government leader, an executive council which functions as a cabinet, & a legislative assembly. The Yukon Act provides for the establishment of a commissioner & the elected legislative assembly.

Commissioner, Hon. Doug Phillips
Executive Assistant, Cathy Cheeseman
867-456-6548, cathy.cheeseman@gov.yk.ca

Office of the Premier

2071 Second Ave., PO Box 2703, Whitehorse, YT Y1A 1B2
867-667-8660 Fax: 867-393-6252
premier@gov.yk.ca
www.yukonpremier.ca

Darrell Pasloski was elected Leader of the Yukon Party on May 28, 2011. He was first sworn in as Premier on June 11, 2011. In the general election of October 11, 2011, The Honourable Darrell Pasloski was elected to the Yukon Legislative Assembly.

Premier, Yukon Territory; Leader, Yukon Party; Minister Responsible, Executive Council Office; Member, Legislative Assembly, Hon. Darrell Pasloski, Yukon Party
867-667-8660, Fax: 867-393-6252, premier@gov.yk.ca;darrell.pasloski@gov.yk.ca
Social Media: www.twitter.com/bsp82, www.facebook.com/TeamYukonca.linkedin.com/pub/darrell-pasloski/18/943/975
Principal Secretary & Chief of Staff, Gordon Steele
867-667-5842, gordon.steele@gov.yk.ca
Senior Cabinet Communications Advisor, Elaine Schiman
867-633-7961, elaine.schiman@gov.yk.ca
Director, John Gunter, 2011-11-01
867-667-5073, john.gunter@gov.yk.ca

Executive Council

#2071, 2nd Ave., Whitehorse, YT Y1A 2C6
867-667-5393 Fax: 867-393-6214
eco@gov.yk.ca

The Executive Council of Yukon Territory is selected by the Honourable Darrell Pasloski, Premier. Members of Yukon's cabinet are members of the Yukon Party, following its victory in the October 2011 general election.

Acts Administered:
Cabinet & Caucus Employees Act
Conflict of Interest Act
Cooperation in Governance Act
Corporate Governance Act
First Nations (Yukon) Self-Government Act
Flag Act
Floral Emblem Act
Government Organisation Act
Intergovernmental Agreements Act
Languages Act
Official Tree Act
Plebiscite Act
Public Inquiries Act
Raven Act
Statistics Act
Waters Act (jointly with Environment & Energy, Mines & Resources)
Yukon Act (Canada)
Yukon Environmental & Socio-Economic Assessment Act
Yukon Land Claim Final Agreements, An Act Approving
Yukon Tartan Act

Premier, Yukon Territory; Minister Responsible, Executive Council Office; Leader, Yukon Party; Member, Legislative Assembly, Hon. Darrell Pasloski
867-667-8660, Fax: 867-393-6252, premier@gov.yk.ca;darrell.pasloski@gov.yk.ca
Social Media: www.twitter.com/bsp82, www.facebook.com/TeamYukonca.linkedin.com/pub/darrell-pasloski/18/943/975
Minister, Finance,
867-393-7053, Fax: 867-393-6252
Minister, Tourism & Culture,
867-667-8641, Fax: 867-393-6252
Minister, Justice,
867-633-7973, Fax: 867-393-7400
Minister, Community Services,
867-667-8643, Fax: 867-393-7400
Minister, Health & Social Services,
867-667-8629, Fax: 867-393-6252
Minister, Economic Development,
867-668-8628, Fax: 867-393-7400
Minister, Energy, Mines & Resources,
867-667-8644, Fax: 867-393-7400
Minister, Environment,
867-667-5806, Fax: 867-393-6252
Minister, Education,
867-667-8644, Fax: 867-393-7400
Minister, Highways & Public Works,
867-667-8643, Fax: 867-393-7400

Executive Council Office
867-667-5393 Fax: 897-393-6252
Deputy Minister & Cabinet Secretary, Janet Moodie
867-667-5866, Fax: 867-393-6214, janet.moodie@gov.yk.ca
Assistant Deputy Minister, Governance Liaison/ Capacity Development, John Burdek
867-456-6840, Fax: 867-456-6833, john.burdek@gov.yk.ca

Assistant Deputy Minister, Corporate Services, Janet Mann
867-667-5866, janet.mann@gov.yk.ca
Assistant Deputy Minister, Land Claims & Implementation Secretariat/First Nations Relations, Karyn Armour
867-667-8566, Fax: 867-667-3599, karyn.armour@gov.yk.ca
Director, Intergovernmental Relations, Andrea Buckley
867-667-5744, Fax: 867-393-6202, andrea.buckley@gov.yk.ca
Director, Government Audit Services, John Gunter
867-667-5073, Fax: 867-456-6522, john.gunter@gov.yk.ca
Director, Implementation, Michael Hale
867-667-8797, Fax: 867-667-3599, michael.hale@gov.yk.ca
Director, Policy & Planning, Karen Hougen-Bell
867-667-8201, karen.hougen-bell@gov.yk.ca
Director, Policy, Administration & Communication, Al Jones
867-667-8523, Fax: 867-667-3599, al.jones@gov.yk.ca
Director, First Nation Relations, Cheryl McLean
867-667-5801, Fax: 867-667-3599, cheryl.mclean@gov.yk.ca
Director, Development Assessment, Diane Reed
867-393-6431, Fax: 867-667-3216, diane.reed@gov.yk.ca
Director, Bureau of Statistics, Vacant
867-667-5463, Fax: 867-393-6203
Senior Government Representative, Intergovernmental Relations Office, Harley Trudeau
613-234-3206, Fax: 613-563-9602, harley.trudeau@gov.yk.ca
Chief of Protocol, Pamela Bangart
867-667-5875, Fax: 867-563-9602, pamela.bangart@gov.yk.ca
Manager, Youth Directorate, Gord Kurzynski
867-667-8213, Fax: 867-393-6341, gord.kurzynski@gov.yk.ca
Manager, Yukon Water Board, Carola Scheu
867-456-3984, Fax: 867-456-3890, carola.scheu@gov.yk.ca

Government Inquiry Office
Yukon Government Administration Building, 2071 Second Ave., PO Box 2703, Whitehorse, YT Y1A 2C6
867-667-5811
information@gov.yk.ca
www.gov.yk.ca/contactus.html
TTY: 867-393-7460
Other Communication: Alternate Phone: 867-667-5812

Legislative Assembly

2071 Second Ave., PO Box 2703, Whitehorse, YT Y1A 2C6
867-667-5498 Fax: 867-393-6280
yla@gov.yk.ca
www.legassembly.gov.yk.ca

Acts Administered:
Cabinet & Caucus Employees Act
Child & Youth Advocate Act
Conflict of Interest (Members & Ministers) Act
Elections Act
Electoral District Boundaries Act
Legislative Assembly Act
Ombudsman Act
Yukon Day Act
Clerk, Floyd McCormick
867-667-5494, Fax: 867-393-6280, floyd.mccormick@gov.yk.ca
Speaker, Ted Staffen
867-667-8661, Fax: 867-393-7400, ted.staffen@gov.yk.ca
Sergeant-at-Arms, Rudy Courture
Deputy Speaker, Vacant
Deputy Clerk, Linda Kolody
867-667-5499, linda.kolody@gov.yk.ca
Receptionist/Finance Clerk, Dawn-Alena Brown
867-667-5498, dawn-alena.brown@gov.yk.ca

Government Caucus Office (Yukon Party)
2076 2nd Ave., PO Box 31113, Whitehorse, YT Y1A 5P7
867-668-6505 Fax: 867-456-3175
www.yukonpartyelection.com
In September 2009, Elizabeth Hanson became the leader of Yukon's New Democratic Party. After the New Democratic Party won six seats in the general election of October 11, 2011, Hanson became Leader of the Official Opposition.
Leader, Darrell Pasloski
darrell.paslowki@gov.yk.ca

Office of the Official Opposition (New Democratic Pary)
P.O. Box 31516, Whitehorse, YT Y1A 6K8
867-668-2203
www.yukonndp.ca
In September 2009, Elizabeth Hanson became the leader of Yukon's New Democratic Party. After the New Democratic Party won six seats in the general election of October 11, 2011, Hanson became Leader of the Official Opposition.
Leader, Official Opposition; Member, Legislative Assembly, Elizabeth Hanson, Whitehorse Centre, New Democratic Party
867-393-7050, Fax: 867-393-6499, elizabeth.hanson@yla.gov.yk.ca
Social Media: www.twitter.com/lizhansonndp, www.facebook.com/lizhansonMLAca.linkedin.com/pub/elizabeth-hanson/39/a51/4a4

Office of the Leader of the Third Party (Liberal Party)
Following the general election of October 2011, Darius Elias was named the interim leader of the Yukon Liberal party. He is the MLA for Vuntut Gwitchin, & one of two Liberals elected in the October 2011 election.
Interim Leader, Yukon Liberal Party; Member, Legislative Assembly, Darius Elias, Liberal
867-456-6710, Fax: 867-393-7444, darius.elias@yla.gov.yk.ca

Standing Committees of the Legislature
Members' Services Board; Rules, Elections & Privileges; Public Accounts; Statuatory Instruments; Appointments to Major Government Boards & Committees

Thirty-third Legislative Assembly - Yukon Territory

Yukon Legislative Assembly Office, 2071 Second Ave., PO Box 2703, Whitehorse, YT Y1A 2C6
867-667-5498
Last General Election: October 11, 2011. Percentage of eligible voters who cast a ballot in the October 2011 general election: 76.2% Party Standings (October 2011): Yukon Party 11; New Democratic Party 6; Liberal Party 2; Total Seats 19 Party Leaders: Yukon Party Hon. Darrell Pasloski, Premier; New Democratic Party Elizabeth Hanson, Official Opposition Leader Liberal Party Darius Elias, Third Party Leader Salaries, Indemnities, & Allowances (2011-2012): Members' indemnity $69,531, plus $13,171 expense allowances for both Whitehorse & rural members; Minister's salary $37,439; Premier's salary $16,046; Leader of the Official Opposition's salary $37,439; Leader of the Third Party's salary $16,046; Speaker's salary $26,743; Deputy Speaker's salary $10,697. Members of the 33rd Legislative Assembly are listed with their constituency, number of electors, party affiliation, & contact information. The address for all Members of the Yukon Legislative Assembly is as follows: PO Box 2703, Whitehorse, YT, Y1A 2C6.
Acts Administered:
Cabinet & Caucus Employees Act (jointly with Executive Council Office)
Child & Youth Advocate Act
Conflict of Interest (Members & Ministers) Act (jointly with Executive Council Office)
Elections Act
Electoral District Boundaries Act, 2002
Legislative Assembly Act
Legislative Assembly Retirement Allowances Act
Ombudsman Act
Yukon Day Act
Members:
Kevin Barr, Mount Lorne - Southern Lakes, New Democratic Party
867-393-7050, Fax: 867-393-6499, kevin.barr@yla.gov.yk.ca
Social Media: www.facebook.com/KevinBarrYNDP
Hon. Brad Cathers, Lake Laberge, Yukon Party
867-667-8625, Fax: 867-456-6741, brad.cathers@gov.yk.ca; brad@bradcathers.ca
Social Media: www.twitter.com/BradCathers, www.facebook.com/pages/Brad-Cathers-MLA/163755667012676
Currie Dixon, Copperbelt North, Yukon Party
867-667-5800, Fax: 867-393-6252, currie.dixon@gov.yk.ca
Social Media: www.twitter.com/curriedixon
Interim Leader, Yukon Liberal Party, Darius Elias, VuntutGwitchin, Liberal
867-456-6710, Fax: 867-393-7444, darius.elias@yla.gov.yk.ca
Doug Graham, Porter Creek North, Yukon Party
867-667-5800, Fax: 867-393-6252, doug.graham@gov.yk.ca
Leader, Official Opposition, Elizabeth (Liz) Hanson, Whitehorse Centre, New Democratic Party
867-393-7050, Fax: 867-393-6499, elizabeth.hanson@yla.gov.yk.ca
Social Media: www.twitter.com/lizhansonndp, www.facebook.com/lizhansonMLAca.linkedin.com/pub/elizabeth-hanson/39/a51/4a4
Stacey Hassard, Pelly-Nisutlin, Yukon Party
867-667-5800, Fax: 867-393-6252, stacey.hassard@gov.yk.ca
Wade Istchenko, Kluane, Yukon Party
867-667-5800, Fax: 867-393-6252, wade.istchenko@gov.yk.ca
Social Media: www.facebook.com/groups/219916094720643
Scott Kent, Riverdale North, Yukon Party
867-667-5800, Fax: 867-393-6252, scott.kent@gov.yk.ca; scott@yukonparty.ca
Social Media: www.facebook.com/pages/Scott-Kent-Riverdale-North/287536247929989
David Laxton, Porter Creek Centre, Yukon Party
867-667-5800, Fax: 867-393-6252, david.laxton@gov.yk.ca
Social Media: www.facebook.com/pages/David-Laxton/159369217480362
Patti McLeod, Watson Lake, Yukon Party
867-667-5800, Fax: 867-393-6252, patti.mcleod@gov.yk.ca
Social Media: www.facebook.com/pages/Patti-McLeod-for-MLA/223446187711079
Lois Moorcroft, Copperbelt South, New Democratic Party
867-393-7050, Fax: 867-393-6499, lois.moorcroft@yla.gov.yk.ca
Social Media: www.facebook.com/LoisMoorcroftNDP
Mike Nixon, Porter Creek South, Yukon Party
867-667-5800, Fax: 867-393-6252, mike.nixon@gov.yk.ca; mikenixon@yukonparty.ca
Social Media: www.twitter.com/nixon_mike, www.facebook.com/group.php?gid=264844376862257
Premier, Yukon Territory; Minister Responsible, Executive Council Office; Leader, Yukon Party, Hon. Darrell Pasloski, Mountainview, Yukon Party
867-393-7053, Fax: 867-393-6252, darrell.pasloski@gov.yk.ca; premier@gov.yk.ca, Other Communications: Premier's Office, Phone: 867-667-8660; Fax: 393-6252
Social Media: www.twitter.com/bsp82, www.facebook.com/TeamYukonca.linkedin.com/pub/darrell-pasloski/18/943/975
Sandy Silver, Klondike, Liberal
867-667-8941, Fax: 867-393-7444, sandy.silver@yla.gov.yk.ca
Jan Stick, Riverdale South, New Democratic Party
867-393-7050, Fax: 867-393-6499, jan.stick@yla.gov.yk.ca; Jan@YukonNDP.ca
Social Media: www.twitter.com/janstickndp, www.facebook.com/janstickYNDP
Deputy Premier, Yukon Territory, Hon. Elaine Taylor, Whitehorse West, Yukon Party
867-667-8641, Fax: 867-939-2652, elaine.taylor@gov.yk.ca;elainetaylor@yukonparty.ca
Social Media: www.facebook.com/pages/Elaine-Taylor/135880316425564
Jim Tredger, Mayo-Tatchun, New Democratic Party
867-393-7050, Fax: 867-393-6499, jim.tredger@yla.gov.yk.ca; Jim@YukonNDP.ca
Social Media: www.facebook.com/JimTredgerNDP
Kate White, Takhini-Kopper King, New Democratic Party
867-393-7050, Fax: 867-393-6499, kate.white@yla.gov.yk.ca; Kate@YukonNDP.ca
Social Media: www.twitter.com/MsKateWhite, www.facebook.com/KateWhiteNDP

Yukon Territory Government Departments & Agencies

Yukon Community Services

PO Box 2703, Whitehorse, YT Y1A 2C6
867-667-5811 Fax: 867-393-6295
800-661-0408
inquiry@gov.yk.ca
www.community.gov.yk.ca
TTY: 867-393-7460
The main purpose of the department is to serve Yukoners & their communities by providing access to services to strengthen communities. The department focuses on community affairs & municipal relations within government on behalf of Yukon communities & acts as a liaison between community groups & government departments.
Acts Administered:
Animal Protection Act (jointly with Energy, Mines & Resources)
Area Development Act
Assessment & Taxation Act
Boiler & Pressure Vessels Act
Builder's Lien Act
Building Standards Act
Business Corporations Act
Cemeteries & Burial Sites Act
Certified General Accountants Act
Certified Management Accountants Act
Chartered Accountants Act
Chiropractors Act
Choses in Action Act (jointly with Department of Justice)
Civil Emergency Measures Act
Consumers Protection Act
Cooperative Associations Act
Dawson Municipal Election (2006) Act
Dental Profession Act
Denturists Act
Dog Act
Electrical Protection Act
Elevator & Fixed Conveyances Act
Emergency Medical Aid Act
Employment Agencies Act
Employment Standards Act
Engineering Profession Act
Factors Act
Fire Prevention Act
First Nation Indemnification (Fire Management) Act
Forest Protection Act (jointly with Department of Energy, Mines & Resources)

Funeral Directors Act
Garage Keepers Lien Act
Gas Burning Devices Act
Gasoline Handling Act
Health Professions Act
Home Owner's Grant Act
Insurance Act
International Commercial Arbitration Act
International Sale of Goods Act
Landlord & Tenant Act
Licensed Practical Nurses Act
Lottery Licensing Act
Medical Profession Act
Miner's Lien Act
Motor Vehicles Act (jointly with Highways & Public Works)
Municipal Act
Municipal Finance & Community Grants Act
Municipal Loans Act
Noise Prevention Act
Optometrists Act
Partnership & Business Name Act
Pawnbrokers & Second-Hand Dealers Act
Personal Property Security Act
Pharmacists Act
Private Investigators & Security Guards Act
Public Libraries Act
Real Estate Agents Act
Recreation Act
Registered Nurses Profession Act
Sales of Goods Act
Seniors Property Tax Deferment Act
Societies Act
Subdivision Act
Trustee Act
Warehouse Keepers Lien Act
Warehouse Receipts Act
Whitehorse Streets & Lanes Ordinance
Yukon Foundation Act

Minister,
867-667-8643, Fax: 867-393-7400
Deputy Minister, Jeff O'Farrell
867-456-6512, Fax: 867-633-7957, jeff.o'farrell@gov.yk.ca
Director, Safety Resources, Michelle Christensen-Toews
867-456-6580, Fax: 867-393-6404, michelle.christensen-toews@gov.yk.ca
Director, Communications, Joanna Lilley
867-456-6580, Fax: 867-393-6404, joanna.lilley@gov.yk.ca
Director, Corporate Policy, Caitlin Kerwin
867-456-5524, Fax: 867-393-6404, caitlin.kerwin@gov.yk.ca
Director, Finance, Systems & Administration, Christine Mahar
867-667-5311, Fax: 867-393-6264, christine.mahar@gov.yk.ca
Director, Human Resources, Judy Tomlin
867-667-5667, Fax: 867-393-6933, judy.tomlin@gov.yk.ca

Associated Agencies, Boards & Commissions:

• Assessment Appeal Board
867-668-6598 Fax: 867-633-2640

• Driver Control Board
2130 Second Ave., 3rd Fl.
PO Box 2703
Whitehorse, YT Y1A 2C6
867-667-5111 Fax: 867-667-3609
dcb@gov.yk.ca
www.community.gov.yk.ca/dcb
Other Communication: 800-661-0408 (ext. 5111)

• Yukon Lottery Commission
312 Wood St.
Whitehorse, YT Y1A 2E6
867-633-7890 Fax: 867-668-7561
lotteriesyukon@gov.yk.ca
www.lotteriesyukon.com

Community Development

The branch assists, advises & organizes municipal & unincorporated communities, provides funding by administering the comprehensive municipal grants & grants in lieu of taxes, assesses properties, collects property taxes & administers the Rural Electrification & Telecommunication program & the Home Owner Grant program. The branch collaborates with communities for the planning, design, & construction of land development projects & includes residential, rural residential, commercial, industrial, & cottage lots. The branch is responsible for regulatory approvals & design, managing construction capital works projects, such as upgrading roads, water & sewage treatment facilities & solid waste disposal sites & assists communities in developing land use plans, working closely with the Yukon Municipal Board & the Association of Yukon Communities. The branch is responsible for the operation of Yukon Government owned facilities for water supply & distribution, sewage treatment & solid waste disposal.

Assistant Deputy Minister, Community Development, Paul Moore
867-667-3534, Fax: 867-393-6216, paul.moore@gov.yk.ca
Director, Property Assessment & Taxation, Kelly Eby
867-667-5234, Fax: 867-667-8276, kelly.eby@gov.yk.ca
Director, Public Libraries, Julie Ourom
867-667-5447, Fax: 867-393-6333, julie.ourom@gov.yk.ca
Director, Community Affairs, Christine Smith
867-667-8684, Fax: 867-393-6258, christine.smith@gov.yk.ca
Director, Sport & Recreation, Karen Thomson
867-667-5608, Fax: 867-393-6416, karen.thomson@gov.yk.ca

Emergency Measures Organization (EMO)
PO Box 2703, Whitehorse, YT Y1A 2C6
867-667-5220 Fax: 867-393-6266
800-661-0408
emo.yukon@gov.yk.ca
www.community.gov.yk.ca/emo/index.html

Responsible for coordinating the Territory's preparedness for, response to, & recovery from, major emergencies & disasters. EMO provides authority to ensure that contingency plans are in place to deal with foreseeable risks & hazards. The Yukon EMO is divided into 13 geographical preparedness areas, mirroring the RCMP detachment boundaries. Eight of these areas have incorporated Municipalities that have appointed a Municipal EMO Coordinator to chair the local Emergency Planning Committee. In the remaining areas, the Emergency Measures Branch appoints a co-ordinator.

Manager, Michael Templeton
867-667-5220, Fax: 867-393-6266
Finance/Admin. Assistant, Bridget Wondga
867-667-8894, Fax: 867-456-6589

Consumer Services & Information Development

Assistant Deputy Minister, Dan Boyd
867-667-5486, Fax: 867-393-6251, dan.boyd@gov.yk.ca
Director, Fiona Charbonneau
867-667-5257, fiona.charbonneau@gov.yk.ca
Director, Pat Molloy
867-667-5425, pat.molloy@gov.yk.ca
Director, Fred Pretorius
867-667-5225, fred.pretorius@gov.yk.ca
Director, Bill Wilcox
867-667-5259, bill.wilcox@gov.yk.ca

Fire Marshal's Office
PO Box 2703, Whitehorse, YT Y1A 2C6
867-667-5811 Fax: 867-393-6295
inquiry@gov.yk.ca
www.community.gov.yk.ca/fireprotection/index.html

The Fire Marshal's Office works to reduce the loss of life & property due to fire & is responsible for public education & fire fighter training, as well as for funding & administering volunteer fire departments in Yukon unincorporated communities. Staff carry out fire & life safety inspections on hotels, motels, public assembly buildings, schools, day care centers, homes for special care, restaurants, etc. throughout Yukon. The Office inspects & permits underground fuel storage tank installations.

Fire Marshal, Marty Dobbin
867-667-5217, Fax: 867-667-3165

Protective Services

Assistant Deputy Minister, Rick Smith
867-393-7409, rick.smith@gov.yk.ca
Fire Marshal & Director, Fire & Life Safety, Dennis Berry
867-667-5217, dennis.berry@gov.yk.ca
Director, Wildland Fire Management, Ken Colbert
867-456-3904, ken.colbert@gov.yk.ca
Fire Marshal & Director, Emergency Medical Services, Michael McKeage
867-456-6591, michael.mckeage@gov.yk.ca
Director, Emergency Measures Organization, Michael Templeton
867-667-5220, michael.templeton@gov.yk.ca

Yukon Development Corporation (YDC)

#2 Miles Canyon Rd., PO Box 5920, Whitehorse, YT Y1A 6S7
867-393-5337 Fax: 867-393-5401
www.ydc.yk.ca

The Yukon Development Corporation (YDC) assists with implementation of energy policies from the Department of Energy, Mines & Resources, by designing & delivering related energy programs. YDC facilitates the generation, production, transmission & distribution of energy in a manner consistent with sustainable development. YDC has investments in electricity & related energy infrastructure & acts as the primary vehicle for delivery of territorial energy programs & services. YDC owns two subsidiary corporations, Yukon Energy Corporation, YEC, & the Energy Solutions Centre Inc., ESC. YEC is the primary producer & transmitter of electrical energy in the territory & operates under the Yukon Utilities Board & the Public Utilities Act. ESC provides technical services, promotes efficiency & renewable energy technologies, co-ordinates & delivers federal & territorial energy programs to households, businesses, institutions, First Nation & public governments.

Acts Administered:
Yukon Development Corporation Act

Chief Executive Officer, David Morrison
867-393-5400, Fax: 867-393-5401, david.morrison@gov.yk.ca

Yukon Economic Development

PO Box 2703, Whitehorse, YT Y1A 2C6
867-393-7191 Fax: 867-393-6412
800-661-0408
ecdev@gov.yk.ca
www.economicdevelopment.gov.yk.ca

The Department works with the Yukon business community & with other governments to support business development, trade & investment opportunities, & partnerships for the development of the Yukon economy. It co-ordinates & facilitates the Yukon Government's economic development agenda. The Department is focused on creating a positive business climate in Yukon & is committed to First Nation business development in the territory. Economic Development markets Yukon as a great place to do business.

Minister,
867-667-8628, Fax: 867-393-7400
Deputy Minister, Harvey Brooks
867-393-7191, Fax: 867-667-3159, harvey.brooks@gov.yk.ca
Assistant Deputy Minister, Operations, Terry Hayden
867-456-3912, Fax: 867-667-3159, terry.hayden@gov.yk.ca
Director, Finance & Information Services, Karen Mason
867-667-5933, Fax: 867-393-7199, karen.mason@gov.yk.ca
Director, Policy, Planning & Research, Stephen Rose
867-667-8416, Fax: 867-393-6412, stephen.rose@gov.yk.ca
Executive Assistant to the Minister, Valerie Boxall
867-667-8628, Fax: 867-393-7400, valerie.boxall@gov.yk.ca
Executive Assistant to the Deputy Minister, Judith Voswinkel
867-393-7191, Fax: 867-667-3159, judith.voswinkel@gov.yk.ca

Business & Economic Research
Fax: 867-393-6412
economics@gov.yk.ca
www.economics.gov.yk.ca

Provides research, analysis & reports to support a broad understanding of the economy & the assessment of its impacts on Yukon's fiscal position, budgetary projections & financial decision making.

Clint Ireland
867-667-8011, clint.ireland@gov.yk.ca

Business & Industry Development
867-456-3920 Fax: 867-393-6944
investyukon@gov.yk.ca
www.economicdevelopment.gov.yk.ca/bidb.html
Other Communication: business.trade@gov.yk.ca

Director, Barbara Dunlop
867-667-3430, Fax: 867-393-6944, barbara.dunlop@gov.yk.ca

Regional Economic Development
red@gov.yk.ca

Director, Bert Perry
867-667-8853, bert.perry@gov.yk.ca

Film & Sound Commission
Closeleigh Manor, 101 Elliott St., PO Box 2703, Whitehorse, YT Y1A 2C6
867-667-5400 Fax: 867-393-7040
info@reelyukon.com
www.reelyukon.com
Other Communication: 800-661-0408, ext. 5400 (toll-free)

Film & Sound Commissioner, Vacant
867-667-8285, Fax: 867-393-7040

Yukon Education

PO Box 2703, Whitehorse, YT Y1A 2C6
867-667-5141 Fax: 867-393-6254
contact.education@gov.yk.ca
www.education.gov.yk.ca
Other Communication: 800-661-0408, ext. 5141 (toll-free)

The Yukon has 28 public schools (14 in Whitehorse, 14 in other communities) & two private schools. The public schools are administered directly by the Department of Education, although elected school council officials are gradually assuming more powers under the 1990 Education Act, & may evolve into school boards in the near future. In 1996, the Yukon Francophone School Board was created, becoming Yukon's first school board. Curriculum is largely based on that of British Columbia, with flexibility for locally developed courses, particularly from a First Nations perspective (approximately one-third of the Yukon's students are of First Nations ancestry). Instruction is English-based for the majority of students. French & Aboriginal languages are widely offered as second language instruction. French Immersion & French First Language education is offered in Whitehorse.

Acts Administered:
Apprentice Training Act
Canada Student Loans Act (federal)
Education Act

Labour Mobility Amendments Act
Occupational Training Act
School Trespass Act
Students' Financial Assistance Act
Teaching Profession Act
Trade Schools Regulation Act
Yukon College Act
Minister,
867-667-8644, Fax: 867-393-7400
Deputy Minister, Alison Conant
867-667-5126, alison.conant@gov.yk.ca

Advanced Education
867-667-5131 Fax: 867-667-8555
contact.education@gov.yk.ca
www.education.gov.yk.ca
Assistant Deputy Minister, Brent Slobodin
867-667-5129, brent.slobodin@gov.yk.ca
Director, Apprenticeship Training, Judy Thrower
867-667-5133, judy.thrower@gov.yk.ca
Director, Labour Market Programs & Services, Shawn Kitchen
867-667-5727, shawn.kitchen@gov.yk.ca

Education Support Services
Fax: 867-393-6254
www.education.gov.yk.ca/ess/index.html
Director, Finance & Administration, Cyndy Dekuysscher
867-667-5701, cyndy.dekuysscher@gov.yk.ca
Director, Human Resources, Val Jensen
867-667-5808, Fax: 867-667-5435, val.jensen@gov.yk.ca
Director, Policy, Planning & Evaluation, Ann MacDonald
867-667-8181, Fax: 867-456-6788,
ann.macdonald@gov.yk.ca

Public Schools Branch
1000 Lewes Blvd.
867-667-5068 Fax: 867-393-6339
www.education.gov.yk.ca/psb
Assistant Deputy Minister, Christie Whitley
867-667-5127, christie.whitley@gov.yk.ca
Coordinator, Francophone Partnerships, Yann Herry
867-667-8610, Fax: 867-393-6366, yann.henry@gov.yk.ca
Director, First Nations Programs & Partnerships, Edmund Schultz
867-393-6905, Fax: 867-456-6766,
edmund.schultz@gov.yk.ca
Director, Native Language Centre, John Ritter
867-668-8820, Fax: 867-668-8825, john.ritter@gov.yk.ca
Director, Programs & Services, Elizabeth Lemay
867-667-8238, Fax: 867-393-6339,
elizabeth.lemay@gov.yk.ca

Yukon Energy, Mines & Resources

PO Box 2703, Whitehorse, YT Y1A 2C6
867-667-3130 Fax: 867-456-3965
800-661-0408
emr@gov.yk.ca
www.emr.gov.yk.ca
TTY: 867-393-7460

The territory has extensive mineral deposits, oil & gas potential, with two producing gas wells, which rank among the top producing wells in Canada, forest reserves & local manufacturing of wood products, such as furniture, wood laminate stock & lumber. The territory has abundant & diverse energy resources due to the presence of fossil fuel reserves, numerous lakes & rivers, windy & mountainous terrain, broad forest cover & sunny conditions. The Yukon is one of the few places left in Canada where Crown land can be obtained for agricultural purposes.

Acts Administered:
Agricultural Products Acts
Agriculture Development Act
Animal Health Act (jointly with Environment)
Animal Protection Act (jointly with Community Services)
Area Development Act
Brands Act
Economic Development Act (jointly with Economic Development)
Energy Conservation Assistance Act
Forest Protection Act (jointly with Community Services)
Lands Act
Oil & Gas Act
Oil & Gas Disposition Regulations
Oil & Gas Drilling & Production Regulations
Oil & Gas Geoscience & Exploration Regulations
Oil & Gas Licence Administration Regulations
Placer Mining Act
Pounds Act
Quartz Mining Act
Subdivision Act
Territorial Lands (Yukon) Act
Waters Act (jointly with Environment & the Executive Council Office)
Minister,
867-667-8644, Fax: 867-393-7400
Deputy Minister, Angus Robertson
867-667-5417, Fax: 867-393-7167,
angus.robertson@gov.yk.ca
Executive Director, Yukon Placer Secretariat, Vacant
867-667-5802, Fax: 867-667-3632

Agriculture
867-667-5838 Fax: 867-393-6222
agriculture@gov.yk.ca
www.emr.gov.yk.ca/agriculture/index.html
Other Communication: 800-661-0408, ext. 5838 (toll-free)
Director, Tony Hill
tony.hill@gov.yk.ca

Assessment & Abandoned Mines
Assessment Centre, #2C, 4114 4th Ave., Whitehorse, YT Y1A 2C6
867-393-7098 Fax: 867-456-6780
yukonabandonedmines@gov.yk.ca
www.emr.gov.yk.ca
Other Communication: 800-661-0408, ext. 7098 (toll-free)
Director, Stephen Mead
867-393-6904, stephen.mead@gov.yk.ca

Client Services & Inspections
www.emr.gov.yk.ca/csi/index.html
Director, Robert Thomson
867-667-3136, Fax: 867-667-3199,
robert.thomson@gov.yk.ca

Energy Policy & Programs
867-667-5015 Fax: 867-667-8601
energy@gov.yk.ca
www.emr.gov.yk.ca/energy
Other Communication: 800-661-0408, ext. 5015 (toll-free)
Assistant Deputy Minister, Shirley Abercrombie
867-667-3187, Fax: 867-393-7421,
shirley.abercrombie@gov.yk.ca
Director, Communications, Mark Roberts
867-667-5307, Fax: 867-393-7421, mark.roberts@gov.yk.ca
Director, Corporate Services, Ross McLachlan
867-456-3960, Fax: 867-456-3965,
ross.mclachlan@gov.yk.ca
Director, Corporate Policy & Planning, John Spicer
867-393-7126, Fax: 867-393-7421, john.spicer@gov.yk.ca

Forestry
Mile 918 Alaska Hwy., PO Box 2703, Whitehorse, YT Y1A 2C6
867-456-3999 Fax: 867-667-3138
forestry@gov.yk.ca
www.emr.gov.yk.ca/forestry
Acting Director, Pat MacDonell
867-633-7917, patrick.macdonnell@gov.yk.ca

Human Resources
230-300 Main St., PO Box 2703, Whitehorse, YT Y1A 2C6
867-667-3007 Fax: 867-393-7422
www.emr.gov.yk.ca/hr
Other Communication: 800-661-0408, ext. 3007 (toll-free)
Director, Ingrid Fawcus
867-667-3549, ingrid.fawcus@gov.yk.ca

Land Services
#320, 300 Main St., Whitehorse, YT Y1A 2C6
867-667-5215
www.emr.gov.yk.ca/lands
Director, Land Planning, George Stetkiewicz
867-667-3530, Fax: 867-393-6340,
george.stetkiewicz@gov.yk.ca
Manager, Programs & Policy Support, Mike Draper
867-667-3185, Fax: 867-393-6340, mike.draper@gov.yk.ca
Manager, Land Use, Marg White
867-667-3173, Fax: 867-667-3214, marg.white@gov.yk.ca
Manager, Land Client Services, John Cole
867-667-5882, Fax: 867-667-3214, john.cole@gov.yk.ca

Library
Elijah Smith Building, #335, 300 Main St., Whitehorse, YT Y1A 2B5
867-667-3111 Fax: 867-456-3888
emrlibrary@gov.yk.ca
www.emr.gov.yk.ca/library
Manager, Aimee Ellis
867-667-3108, aimee.ellis@gov.yk.ca

Mining
#400, 211 Main St., Whitehorse, YT Y1A 2B2
867-633-7952 Fax: 867-456-3899
mining@gov.yk.ca
www.emr.gov.yk.ca/mining
Other Communication: 800-661-0408, ext. 7952 (toll-free)
Director, Mineral Resources, Bob Holmes
867-667-3126, robert.holmes@gov.yk.ca

Oil & Gas Mineral Resources
#300, 211 Main St., Whitehorse, YT Y1A 2B2
867-667-5087 Fax: 867-393-6262
oilandgas@gov.yk.ca
www.emr.gov.yk.ca/oilandgas
Other Communication: 800-661-0408, ext. 5087 (toll-free)
Director, Brian Love
867-667-3566, brian.love@gov.yk.ca

Yukon Geological Survey
Elijah Smith Building, #102-300 Main St., Whitehorse, YT
867-667-5097 Fax: 867-393-6262
oilandgas@gov.yk.ca
www.emr.gov.yk.ca/oilandgas
Other Communication: 800-661-0408, ext. 5087 (toll-free)
Also located at the Professional Building at 2099-2nd Ave.
Director, Carolyn Relf
867-667-8892, carolyn.relf@gov.yk.ca
Director, Dave Beckman
david.beckman@gov.yk.ca

Yukon Environment

PO Box 2703, Whitehorse, YT Y1A 2C6
867-667-5652 Fax: 867-393-7197
environment.yukon@gov.yk.ca
www.env.gov.yk.ca
Other Communication: 800-661-0408, ext. 5652 (toll-free)

The department is responsible for legislation, regulations licensing, management, policies, programs, services, education & information regarding the natural environment in three program areas: fish & wildlife, environmental protection & assessment & parks & protection areas. The department's branches educate resource users & the general public, develop & enforce policies, regulations, & legislation & assist other departments in the sustainable use & management of the territory's natural resources. The department supports land claims negotiations & assists in implementing land claims agreements. The department represents the Yukon government at national & global environmental forums on issues such as climate change & biodiversity conservation.Through the Environmental Awareness Fund the government provides funding to assist registered non-government organizations to promote environmental education or awareness, resource planning & sustainable development in the Yukon.

Acts Administered:
Animal Health Act (jointly with Energy, Mines & Resources)
Environment Act
Administrative Regulation
Air Emissions Regulations
Beverage Container Regulation
Contaminated Sites Regulations
Designated Materials
Ozone Depleting Substances & Other Halocarbons Regulation
Pesticides Regulations
Recycling Fund Regulation
Solid Waste Regulations
Special Waste Regulations
Spills Regulations
Storage Tank Regulations
Yukon Council on the Economy & the Environment Regulation
Activities Requiring Environmental Assessment (Inclusion List) Regulations
Comprehensive Study List Regulation
Coordination of Environmental Assessment Procedures & Requirement Regulations
Exclusion List Regulation
Law List Regulation
Mackenzie River Basin Agreement Act
Parks & Land Certainty Act
Campground Regulations
Coal River Springs Ecological Reserve
Establish Ni'iinlii Njik (Fishing Branch) Ecological Reserve
Establish Ni'iinlii Njik (Fishing Branch) Wilderness Preserve
Herschel Island Nature Preserve
Herschel Island Park Regulations
Tombstone Territorial Park Regulations
Waters Act (jointly with Energy, Mines & Resources & the Executive Council Office)
Waters Regulation
Wilderness Tourism Licensing Act
Wildlife Act
Concession & Compensation Review Board Regulations
Conservation Fund Regulations
Game Farm Regulations
Game Management Sub-zone Regulations
Outfitting Concession Area Boundary Regulations
Trapping Concession Area Boundary Regulations
Trapping Regulations
Wildlife Sanctuary Regulation
Yukon River Basin & Alsek River Basin Agreements Act
Minister,
867-667-5806, Fax: 867-393-6252
Deputy Minister, Kelvin Leary
867-667-5460, Fax: 867-393-6213, kelvin.leary@gov.yk.ca

Director, Policy & Planning, Vacant
867-667-3028, Fax: 867-393-6213

Associated Agencies, Boards & Commissions:

• Alsek Renewable Resource Council (ARRC)
PO Box 2077
Haines Junction, YT Y0B 1L0
867-634-2524 Fax: 867-634-2527
www.alsekrrc.ca/www.alsekrrc.ca
A voice for local community members in managing renewable resources, such as fish, wildlife and forests, ARRC was formed in 1995 with the signing of the Champagne & Aishihik First Nations (CAFN) Final Agreement.

• Carcross/ Tagish Renewable Resource Council
PO Box 70
Tagish, YT Y0B 1T0
867-399-4923 Fax: 867-399-4978
carcrosstagishrrc@gmail.com

• Carmacks Renewable Resource Council
PO Box 122
Carmacks, YT Y0B 1C0
867-863-6838 Fax: 867-863-6429
carmacksrrc@northwestel.net
Other Communication: www.yfwmb.ca/rrc/carmacks

• Dan Keyi Renewable Resource Council
PO Box 50
Burwash Landing, YT Y0B 1V0
867-841-5820 Fax: 867-841-5821
dankeyirrc@northwestel.net

• Dawson District Renewable Resource Council
PO Box 1380
Dawson City, YT Y0B 1G0
867-993-6976 Fax: 867-993-6093
dawsonrrc@northwestel.net
www.yfwmb.ca/rrc/dawson

• Laberge Renewable Resource Council
#202, 102 Copper Rd.
Whitehorse, YT Y1A 2Z6
labergerrc@northwestel.net

• Mayo District Renewable Resources Council
PO Box 249
Mayo, YT Y0B 1M0
867-996-2942 Fax: 867-996-2948
mayorrc@yknet.yk.ca

• North Yukon Renewable Resources Council
PO Box 80
Old Crow, YT Y0B 1N0
867-966-3034 Fax: 867-966-3036
vgrrc@yknet.yk.ca
www.yfwmb.ca/rrc/northyukon

• Selkirk Renewable Resources Council
PO Box 32
Pelly Crossing, YT Y0B 1P0
867-537-3937 Fax: 867-537-3939
selkirkrrc@yknet.yk.ca
www.yfwmb.ca/rrc/selkirk

• Teslin Renewable Resource Council
PO Box 186
Teslin, YT Y0A 1B0
867-390-2323 Fax: 867-390-2919
teslinrrc@northwestel.net
www.yfwmb.ca/rrc/teslin

• Yukon Fish & Wildlife Management Board
106 Main St., 2nd Fl.
Whitehorse, YT Y1A 5P7
867-667-3754 Fax: 867-393-6947
officemanager@yfwmb.ca
www.yfwmb.ca
The Board focuses its efforts on territorial policies, legislation & other measures to help guide management of fish & wildlife, conserve habitat & enhance the renewable resources economy. The Board influences management decisions through public education & by making recommendations to Yukon, Federal and First Nations governments. Recommendations & positions are based on the best technical, traditional & local information available.

• Yukon Land Use Planning Council
#201, 307 Jarvis St.
Whitehorse, YT Y1A 2H3
867-667-7397 Fax: 867-667-4624
ylupc@planyukon.ca
www.planyukon.ca/
The Yukon Land Use Planning Council assists government & Yukon First Nationsto co-ordinate efforts to conduct community based regional land use planning. This planning is necessary to resolve land use & resource conflicts. The plans ensure that use of lands & resources is consistent with social, cultural, economic & environmental values. These plans build upon traditional knowledge & experience of the residents of each region.

Climate Change Secretariat
867-456-5544 Fax: 867-456-5543
800-661-0408
ClimateChange@gov.yk.ca
Other Communication:
www.env.gov.yk.ca/monitoringenvironment/climate_change_secretariat.php
The Secretariat has the lead role in ensuring Yukon government actions support a healthy & resilient Yukon in a changing climate. It strives to identify needs, opportunities & priorities; promote & support action; & monitor & report on progress.
Director, Eric Schroff
867-633-7971, eric.schroff@gov.yk.ca

Conservation Officer Services
867-667-8005 Fax: 867-393-6206
800-661-0408
coservicesgov.yk.ca
www.env.gov.yk.ca/branches/conservation_officer_services.php
Other Communication: T.I.P. line: 800-661-0525
The Branch provides environmental education, environmental youth camps & projects, provides hunting, fishing & trapping licences, provides hunter & trapper education, resource management support, wildlife safety for the public & provides enforcement & compliance.
Director, John Russell
867-667-5786, Fax: 867-393-6206, john.russell@gov.yk.ca

Corporate Services
867-667-5652 Fax: 867-393-7197
800-661-0408
environmentyukon@gov.yk.ca
www.env.gov.yk.ca/branches/corporate_services.php
Provides support services to the Department of Environment.
Director, Mindy Crayford
867-667-8486, Fax: 867-393-7012, mindy.crayford@gov.yk.ca
Manager, Client Services, Dee Balsam
867-667-5797, Fax: 867-393-7197, dee.balsam@gov.yk.ca
Manager, Information Management & Technology, Beth Hawkings
867-667-8137, Fax: 867-393-7003, beth.hawkings@gov.yk.ca
Manager, Financial Services Branch, Darrell Branch
867-667-5160, Fax: 867-393-6219, darrell.branch@gov.yk.ca
Manager, Communications, Dennis Senger
867-667-5237, Fax: 867-393-6213, dennis.senger@gov.yk.ca

Environmental Programs
867-667-5683 Fax: 867-393-6213
800-661-0408
envprot@gov.yk.ca
www.env.gov.yk.ca/branches/environmental_programs.php
Formed in 1994, the Branch is responsible for development of regulations & standards under the Environment Act & programs associated with everyday waste management, contaminated sites, air quality & pesticides. The Branch is also responsible for monitoring & inspection of permits, spill cleanup & environmental assessments of development projects, recycling education & promotion, public education & awareness.
Director, Jon Bowen
867-667-8177, Fax: 867-393-6213, jon.bowen@gov.yk.ca

Fish & Wildlife
867-667-5715 Fax: 867-393-6405
800-661-0408
fish.wildlife@gov.yk.ca
www.env.gov.yk.ca/branches/fish_wildlife.php
The Branch maintains the ecosystem based on sound management of fish, wildlife & their habitats, preserves the sustainability of fish & wildlife populations, works with First Nations & community relations to preserve & enhance the ecosystem, develops management plans, provides policy & planning, collects, assesses & disseminates natural resource data & provides public education for resource users.
Director, Dan Lindsey
867-667-5715, Fax: 867-393-6405, dan.lindsey@gov.yk.ca

Parks
867-667-5648 Fax: 867-393-6223
800-661-0408
yukon.parks@gov.yk.ca
www.environmentyukon.gov.yk.ca/parks/parks.html
Director, Erik Val
867-667-5639, Fax: 867-393-6223, erik.val@gov.yk.ca

Water Resources
867-667-3171 Fax: 867-667-3195
800-661-0408
water.resources@gov.yk.ca
www.env.gov.yk.ca/monitoringenvironment/aboutwaterresources.php
Director, Kevin McDonnell
867-667-3145, Fax: 867-667-3195, kevin.mcdonnell@gov.yk.ca
Manager, Richard Janowicz
867-667-3223, richard.janowicz@gov.yk.ca
Manager, Collin Remillard
867-667-3227, collin.remillard@gov.yk.ca
Manager, Bob Truenelson
867-667-3217, bob.truenelson@gov.yk.ca

Yukon Finance

PO Box 2703, Whitehorse, YT Y1A 2C6
867-667-5343 Fax: 867-393-6217
fininfo@gov.yk.ca
www.finance.gov.yk.ca

Acts Administered:
Appropriation Acts
Banking Agency Guarantee Act
Faro Mine Loan Act
Financial Administration Act
Fireweed Fund Act
Fuel Oil Tax Act
Income Tax Act
Insurance Premium Tax Act
Interim Supply Appropriation Acts
Liquor Tax Act
Taxpayer Protection Act
Tobacco Tax Act
Yukon Development Corporation Loan Guarantee Act

Minister,
867-393-7053, Fax: 867-393-6252
Deputy Minister, David Hrycan
867-667-3571, Fax: 867-393-6217, david.hrycan@gov.yk.ca
Director, Finance & Administration, Bill Curtis
867-667-5276, Fax: 867-393-6217, bill.curtis@gov.yk.ca

Financial Operations & Taxation
Fax: 867-393-6217
Assistant Deputy Minister, Clarke Laprarie
867-667-5355, Fax: 867-393-6217, clarke.laprarie@gov.yk.ca
Comptroller, Miko Miyahara
867-667-5375, miko.miyahara@gov.yk.ca
Acting Director, Financial Systems, Alan Houston
867-667-5278, Fax: 867-393-6217, alan.houston@gov.yk.ca
Director, Investments & Debt Services, Elaine Carlyle
867-667-5346, elaine.carlyle@gov.yk.ca
Director, Taxation, Gerald Gagnon
867-667-3074, Fax: 867-456-6709

Fiscal Relations & Management Board Secretariat
Fax: 867-393-6355
Director, Budgets, Christina Frisch
867-667-5277, Fax: 867-393-6355
Director, Fiscal Relations, Tim Shoniker
867-667-5303, Fax: 867-393-6355
Director, Management Board Secretariat, Mary Rae Cafferty
867-667-3542, Fax: 867-393-6355, mary.cafferty@gov.yk.ca

Yukon Health & Social Services

PO Box 2703, Whitehorse, YT Y1A 2C6
867-667-3673 Fax: 867-667-3096
hss@gov.yk.ca
www.hss.gov.yk.ca
Committed to quality health & social services for Yukoners by helping individuals acquire the skills to live responsible, healthy & independent lives; & providing a range of accessible, affordable services that assist individuals, families & communities to reach their full potential.

Acts Administered:
Adult Protection & Decision-Making Act
Canadian Blood Agency/Canadian Blood Services Indemnification Act
Canadian Council for Donation & Transplantation Indemnifiction Act
Change of Name Act
Care Consent Act
Child Care Act
Child & Family Services Act
Children's Act
Decision Making, Support & Protection to Adults Act
Health Act
Health Care Insurance Plan Act
Hospital Act
Hospital Insurance Services Act
Intercountry Adoption (Hague Convention) Act
Marriage Act
Mental Health Act
Pioneer Utility Grant Act
Public Health & Safety Act
Regulations to Establish Butylnitrite as Regulated Matter
Rubbish Disposal
Sewage Disposal Systems Regulations
Rehabilitation Services Act
Seniors' Income Supplement Act
Smoke-Free Places Act
Social Assistance Act
Travel for Medical Treatment Act
Vital Statistics Act
Young Persons Offences Act

Youth Criminal Justice Act (Canada; jointly with Justice)
Yukon Family Services Association Rent Guarantee Act
Minister,
867-667-8629, Fax: 867-393-6252
Deputy Minister, Stuart Whitley
867-667-5770, Fax: 867-667-3096, stuart.whitley@gov.yk.ca

Associated Agencies, Boards & Commissions:
• Health & Social Service Council
This advisory body makes recommendations to the government relating to issues of health, social services, education & justice.
• Yukon Child Care Board
This advisory body makes recommendations to the Minister of Health & Social Services, on any issues that pertain to child care.

Continuing Care
307 Black St., Whitehorse, YT Y1A 2N1
867-667-5945
www.hss.gov.yk.ca/continuing.php
Other Communication: 800-661-0408, ext. 5945 (toll-free)
Provides residential, home care & regional therapy services for the citizens of the Yukon Territory.
Assistant Deputy Minister, Cathy Morton-Bielz
867-667-8922, Fax: 867-456-6545, cathy.morton-bielz@gov.yk.ca
Director, Nancy Kidd
867-667-8750, Fax: 867-456-6545, nancy.kidd@gov.yk.ca

Coporate Services
www.hss.gov.yk.ca/corporate.php
Plays a key role in ensuring that Yukon residents have accurate, up-to-date information about the territory's health & social programs, services & systems.
Assistant Deputy Minister, Birgitte Hunter
867-667-8309, Fax: 867-393-6457, birgitte.hunter@gov.yk.ca
Director, Brian Kitchen
867-667-5688, Fax: 867-667-3096, brian.kitchen@gov.yk.ca

Health Services
Financial Plaza, 204 Lambert St., 4th Fl., Whitehorse, YT Y1A 3T2
Fax: 867-393-6486
www.hss.gov.yk.ca/healthservices.php
Responsible for a variety of health care, disease prevention & treatment services which assist eligible Yukon residents in attaining maximum individual independence within their community.
Director, Insured Health & Hearing Services, Paul Gudaitis
867-667-5209, Fax: 867-393-6486
Director, Community Nursing, Joy Kajiwara
867-667-8324, Fax: 867-667-8338
Director, Community Health Programs, Cathy Stannard
867-667-8340, Fax: 867-456-6502, cathy.stannard@gov.yk.ca

Social Services
www.hss.gov.yk.ca/socialservices.php
Consists of Adult Community Services, Alcohol & Drug Services, Family & Children's Services, Regional Services, Senior Services, Seniors & Elder Abuse, Services for People With Disabilities, & Social Assistance.
Acting Director, Michele McDonnell
867-667-3705, Fax: 867-393-6926, michele.mcdonnell@gov.yk.ca
Supervisor, Dale Gordon
867-393-6913, Fax: 867-667-8471, dale.gordon@gov.yk.ca
Supervisor, Marg Render
867-667-5819, Fax: 867-667-5669, marg.render@gov.yk.ca
Supervisor, Adult Community Services & Employment Training Services, Vacant
867-667-5979, Fax: 867-393-6278
Manager, Community Audit Services Unit, Tim Brady
867-667-5691, Fax: 867-393-6278
Manager, Seniors' Services/ Adult Protection, Kelly Cooper
867-456-3948, Fax: 867-393-6926
Acting Manager, Program Management, Sandy Schmidt
867-667-5056, Fax: 867-667-8471

Yukon Highways & Public Works

PO Box 2703, Whitehorse, YT Y1A 2C6
867-393-7193 Fax: 867-393-6218
800-661-0408
hpw-info@gov.yk.ca
www.hpw.gov.yk.ca
TTY: 867-393-7460
The Department of Highways & Public Works is responsible for ensuring safe & efficient public highways, airstrips, buildings & information systems.
Acts Administered:
Access to Information & Protection of Privacy Act
Dangerous Goods Transportation Act
Highways Act
Languages Act
Motor Vehicles Act (jointly with Community Services)
Public Printing Act
Minister,
867-667-8643, Fax: 867-393-7400
Deputy Minister, Mike Johnson
867-667-3732, Fax: 867-393-6218, mike.johnson@gov.yk.ca
Director, Policy & Communications, Kendra Black
867-667-5436, Fax: 867-393-6218, kendra.black@gov.yk.ca
Director, Finance, Jacqueline McBride-Dickson
867-667-5410, Fax: 867-667-8231, jackie.mcbride-dixon@gov.yk.ca
Director, Human Resources, Carolyn MacDonald
867-667-5156, Fax: 867-667-3685, carolyn.macdonald@gov.yk.ca

Aviation
867-634-2450 Fax: 867-634-2131
aviation@gov.yk.ca
Other Communication: 800-661-0408, ext. 2450 (toll-free)

Corporate Services
867-667-5128
Other Communication: 800-661-0408, ext. 5128 (toll-free)
Assistant Deputy Minister, Leslie Anderson
867-667-5128, Fax: 867-393-6218, leslie.anderson@gov.yk.ca
Senior Advisor, Transporation Maintenance, Catherine Harwood
867-667-5761, Fax: 867-667-3648, catherine.harwood@gov.yk.ca

Information & Communications Technology
867-667-5397 Fax: 867-667-5304
Other Communication: 800-661-0408, ext. 5397 (toll-free)
Assistant Deputy Minister, Siegfried Fuchsbichler
867-667-3712, Fax: 867-667-5304, siegfried.fuchsbichler@gov.yk.ca
Deputy Chief Information Officer, Chris Bookless
867-456-6781, Fax: 867-667-5304, chris.bookless@gov.yk.ca
Director, David Downing
867-667-8329, david.downing@gov.yk.ca
Director, Technology Infrastructure & Operations, Shane Horsnell
867-667-5396, Fax: 867-393-6200, shane.horsnell@gov.yk.ca
Acting Director, Space Planning, Sheila Stockton
867-667-3064, Fax: 867-667-5349, sheila.stockton@gov.yk.ca
Director, Facilities Management, Lynn Standing
867-667-3589, Fax: 867-393-7039, lynn.standing@gov.yk.ca

Property Management Agency
867-667-5879 Fax: 867-667-5349
Other Communication: 800-661-0408, ext. 5879 (toll-free)
Manager, Finance & Administration, Faye Doiron
867-667-3706, faye.doiron@gov.yk.ca
Director, Facilities Management & Regional Services, Lynn Standing
867-667-3589, Fax: 867-393-7039, lynn.standing@gov.yk.ca

Community & Correctional Service
Prospector Building, 301 Jarvis St., PO Box 2703, Whitehorse, YK Y1A 2C6
867-393-7077 Fax: 867-393-6326
800-661-0408
justice@gov.yk.ca
Provides programs & services for victims & offenders, & has as its primary goal the safe integration of offenders into communities as law-abiding citizens.
Director, Tricia Ratel
867-667-8294, Fax: 867-393-6326, tricia.ratel@gov.yk.ca

Supply Services
867-667-5432 Fax: 867-667-2958
hpw-info@gov.yk.ca
Other Communication: 800-661-0408, ext. 5432 (toll-free)
Director, Carl Rumscheidt
867-667-5289, Fax: 867-667-2958, carl.rumscheidt@gov.yk.ca
Manager, Procurement Services, David Knight
867-393-6387, Fax: 867-667-2958, david.knight@gov.yk.ca
Manager, Queen's Printer, Jo Pond
867-667-3585, Fax: 867-393-6210, jo.pond@gov.yk.ca

Transportation
Other Communication: 800-661-0408, ext. 7193 (toll-free)
Assistant Deputy Minister, Allan Nixon
867-667-5196, Fax: 867-393-6218, allan.nixon@gov.yk.ca
Director, Transportation Maintenance, Don Hobbis
867-667-5761
Director, Transportation Engineering, Robin Walsh
867-633-7928, Fax: 867-393-6447
Director, Transport Services Branch, Vern Janz
867-667-5833, Fax: 867-667-5799

Yukon Housing Corporation

410H Jarvis St., PO Box 2703, Whitehorse, YT Y1A 2H5
867-667-5759 Fax: 867-667-3664
800-661-0408
ykhouse@housing.yk.ca
www.housing.yk.ca/
Links families, communities & the housing industry with programs & services that work to support the housing needs of Yukoners.
Acts Administered:
Government Employee Housing Plan Act
Housing Corporation Act
Housing Development Act
President, Ron Macmillan
867-667-5155, Fax: 867-393-6274, ron.macmillan@gov.yk.ca
Director, Systems & Administration, Mark Davey
867-667-8773, Fax: 867-393-6399, mark.davey@gov.yk.ca
Director, Capital Development, Mike Fraser
867-456-6190, Fax: 867-393-6441, mike.fraser@gov.yk.ca
Director, Policy & Communications, JoAnne Harach
867-456-6802, Fax: 867-393-6274, joanne.harach@gov.yk.ca
Director, Community & Industry Partnering, Allyn Lyon
867-667-3773, Fax: 867-393-6441, allyn.lyon@gov.yk.ca
Director, Program Delivery, Marc Perreault
867-393-7154, marc.perreault@gov.yk.ca
Director, Human Resources, Sue Richards
867-667-8272, Fax: 867-393-6933, sue.richards@gov.yk.ca

Yukon Justice

Andrew Philipsen Law Centre, 2134 Second Ave., PO Box 2703, Whitehorse, YT Y1A 2C6
867-667-3033 Fax: 867-393-5790
jus.msb@gov.yk.ca
www.justice.gov.yk.ca

Acts Administered:
Adult Protection & Decision-Making Act
Age of Majority Act
Arbitration Act
Auxiliary Police Act
Canadian Charter of Rights & Freedoms (Canada) Act
Choices in Action Act
Collection Act
Condominium Act
Conflict of Laws (Traffic Accidents) Act
Constitutional Questions Act
Consumers Protection Act
Continuing Consolidation of Statutes Act
Contributory Negligence Act
Coroners Act
Corrections Act
Court of Appeal Act
Creditor's Relief Act
Crime Prevention & Victim Services Trust Act
Decision Making, Support & Protection to Adults Act (jointly with Health & Social Services
Defamation Act
Department of Justice Act
Dependant's Relief Act
Devolution of Real Property Act
Distress Act
Electronic Evidence Act
Electronic Registration (Department of Public Statutes) Act
Enactment Republication Act
Enduring Power of Attorney Act
Estate Administration Act
Evidence Act
Executions Act
Exemptions Act
Expropriation Act
Family Property & Support Act
Family Violence Prevention Act
Fatal Accidents Act
Fine Option Act
Foreign Arbitral Awards Act
Fraudulent Preferences & Conveyances Act
Frustrated Contracts Act
Garnishee Act
Human Rights Act
Human Tissue Gift Act
Interjurisdictional Support Orders Act
International Child Abduction (Hague Convention) Act
Interpretation Act
Interprovincial Subpoena Act
Judicature Act
Jury Act
Land Titles Act
Legal Profession Act
Legal Services Society Act
Limitation of Actions Act
Lord's Day Act
Maintenance Enforcement Act
Maintenance & Custory Orders Enforcement Act
Married Women's Property Act

Mediation Board Act
Notaries Act
Perpetuities Act
Presumption of Death Act
Public Guardian & Trustee Act
Public Utilities Act
Reciprocal Enforcement of Judgements Act
Reciprocal Enforcement of Judgements UK Act
Reciprocal Enforcement of Maintenance Orders Act
Recording of Evidence Act
Regulations Act
Retirement Plan Beneficiaries Act
Safer Communities & Neighbours Act
Spousal Tort Immunity Abolition Act
Small Claims Court Act
Summary Convictions Act
Supreme Court Act
Survival of Actions Act
Survivorship Act
Tenants in Common Act
Territorial Court Act
Torture Prohibition Act
Variation of Trusts Act
Victims of Crime Act
Wills Act
Youth Criminal Justice Act (Canada) (jointly with Health & Social Services)

Minister,
867-633-7973, Fax: 867-393-7400
Deputy Minister, Dennis Cooley
867-667-5959, Fax: 867-393-5790, jus.dm@gov.yk.ca
Director, Finance, Systems & Administration, Luda Ayzenberg
867-667-5615, Fax: 867-667-5790, luda.ayzenberg@gov.yk.ca
Director, Policy & Communications, Dan Cable
867-667-3508, Fax: 867-677-5790, dan.cable@gov.yk.ca
Director, Human Resources, Brian Farrell
867-667-5105
Director, Planning & Intergovernmental Relations, Vacant
Executive Assistant to the Deputy Minister, Charmaine Hall
867-667-5959, Fax: 867-667-5790, charmaine.hall@gov.yk.ca
Executive Assistant to the Minister, Christopher Young
867-633-7973, Fax: 867-393-7400, christopher.young@gov.yk.ca

Associated Agencies, Boards & Commissions:

• Law Society of Yukon - Executive
#202, 302 Steele St.
Whitehorse, YT Y1A 2C5
867-668-4231 Fax: 867-667-7556
info@lawsocietyyukon.com
www.lawsocietyyukon.com
This regulatory society serves & protects the public interest in the administration of justice.

• Law Society of Yukon - Discipline Committee
#202, 302 Steele St.
Whitehorse, YT Y1A 3W8
867-668-4231 Fax: 867-667-7556
lsy@yknet.yk.ca
www.lawsocietyyukon.com
This adjudicative committee conducts inquiries/investigations into matters regarding the conduct of a member or a student-at-law.

• Yukon Human Rights Commission
#101, 9010 Quartz St.
Whitehorse, YT Y1A 2Z5
867-667-6226 Fax: 867-667-2662 800-661-0535
humanrights@yhrc.yk.ca
www.yhrc.yk.ca
The Commission administers the Human Rights Act, hears complaints & arranges for adjudication if required. Promotes & coordinates public education & research programs in the area of human rights.

• Yukon Human Rights Board of Adjudication
#202, 407 Black St.
Whitehorse, YT Y1A 2N2
867-667-5412 Fax: 867-633-6952
beyondwords@northwestel.net
As part of the human rights complaint process, the Commission may ask for a decision from the Human Rights Board of Adjudication, which is independent of the Yukon Human Rights Commission.

• Yukon Judicial Council
PO Box 31222
Whitehorse, YT Y1A 5P7
867-667-5438 Fax: 867-393-6400
courtservices@gov.yk.ca
www.yukoncourts.ca/courts/territorial/judicialcouncil.html
The Council makes recommendations respecting appointments of judges& justices, & deals with formal complaints respecting judges & justices. It makes recommendations respecting the efficiency, uniformity & quality of judicial services provided by the Territorial Court or the Justice of the Peace Court. It also performs other duties requested by the Minister.

• Yukon Law Foundation
PO Box 31789
Whitehorse, YT Y1A 6L3
867-668-4231 Fax: 867-667-7556
lsy@yknet.yk.ca
www.yukonlawfoundation.com

• Yukon Legal Services Society/Legal Aid
#203, 2131 - 2nd Ave.
Whitehorse, YT Y1A 1C3
867-667-5210 Fax: 867-667-8649 800-661-0408
legalaid@yknet.yk.ca
www.legalaid.yk.ca
Other Communication: 1-800-661-0408, extension 5210 (Yukon only); administration@legalaid.yk.ca

• Yukon Utilities Board
#19, 1114 - 1st Ave.
PO Box 31728
Whitehorse, YT Y1A 6L3
867-667-5058 Fax: 867-667-5059
yub@utilitiesboard.yk.ca
This regulatory board consists of three to five members appointed by the Government of Yukon. It receives its mandate from the Public Utilities Act & Regulations.

Community Justice & Public Safety Branch
Prospector Building, 301 Jarvis St., 2nd Fl., Whitehorse, YK Y1A 2C6
867-393-7077 Fax: 867-393-6326
cjps@gov.yk.ca

Assistant Deputy Minister, Robert Riches
867-393-7077, Fax: 867-393-6326, robert.riches@gov.yk.ca
Chief Coroner, Coroner's Service, Sharon Hanley
867-667-5317, Fax: 867-456-6826, sharon.hanley@gov.yk.ca
Director, Special Projects & Partnerships, Sandi Gleason
867-667-3656, Fax: 867-393-6326, sandi.gleason@gov.yk.ca

Court Services
867-667-5441

Legal & Regulatory Services
Andrew Philipsen Law Centre, 2130 Second Avenue, PO Box 2703, Whitehorse, YT Y1A 2C6
867-667-5764 Fax: 867-393-6379
legalservices@gov.yk.ca

Assistant Deputy Minister, Thomas Ullyett
867-667-3469, Fax: 867-393-6379, thomas.ullyett@gov.yk.ca

Yukon Liquor Corporation

9031 Quartz Rd., Whitehorse, YT Y1A 4P9
867-667-5245 Fax: 867-393-6306
yukon.liquor@gov.yk.ca
www.ylc.yk.ca

Acts Administered:
Liquor Act
Public Lotteries Act

President, Ron MacMillan
867-667-5155
Vice-President, Virginia Labelle
867-667-5708, virginia.labelle@gov.yk.ca
Director, Retail Sales & Territorial Agent Services, Allison Briden
867-667-8924, allison.briden@gov.yk.ca
Director, Finance, Systems & Administration, Mark Davey
867-667-8773, mark.davey@gov.yk.ca
Director, Purchasing & Distribution, Geoff Dixon
867-667-5244, geoff.dixon@gov.yk.ca
Director, Licensing & Social Responsibility, Terry Grabowski
867-667-8926, terry.grabowski@gov.yk.ca
Director, Policy & Communications, JoAnne Harach
867-456-6802, joanne.harach@gov.yk.ca
Director, Human Resources, Sue Richards
867-667-8272, sue.richards@gov.yk.ca

Yukon Ombudsman & Privacy Commissioner

#201, 211 Hawkins St., Whitehorse, YT Y1A 2C6
867-667-8468 Fax: 867-667-8469
info@ombudsman.yk.ca
www.ombudsman.yk.ca/ombudsman/
Other Communication: 800-661-0408, ext. 8468

Yukon Public Service Commission

Yukon Government Administration Building, #2071-2nd Ave., PO Box 2703, Whitehorse, YT Y1A 2C6
867-667-5653 Fax: 867-667-5755
800-661-0408
PSCWebsite@gov.yk.ca
www.psc.gov.yk.ca
TTY: 867-667-5864

This central agency has a mandate to provide human resource advice & support services to Yukon government departments & employees, to act as the employer on behalf of the Yukon government & to establish & maintain human resource legislation, policies & collective agreements.

Acts Administered:
Education Labour Relations Act
Public Sector Compensation Restraint Act
Public Servants Superannuation Act
Public Service Act
Public Service Group Insurance Benefit Plan Act
Public Service Labour Relations Act
Retirement Plan Beneficiaries Act
Territorial Court Judiciary Pension Plan Act

Commissioner, Catharine Read
867-667-5252, Fax: 867-393-6919, catharine.read@gov.yk.ca
Director, Corporate Human Resource Services, Martha Kenney
867-667-5250, Fax: 867-667-5755, martha.kenney@gov.yk.ca
Director, Finance & Administration, Bonnie Love
867-667-5861, Fax: 867-667-6705, bonnie.love@gov.yk.ca
Director, Employee Compensation, Terry Kinney
867-667-5251, Fax: 867-667-6705, terry.kinney@gov.yk.ca
Director, Policy, Planning & Communication, Deborah McNevin
867-667-3537, Fax: 867-667-6705, deborah.mcnevin@gov.yk.ca
Director, Staff Relations, Megan Slobodin
867-667-5201, Fax: 867-393-6919, megan.slobodin@gov.yk.ca
Director, Human Resource Management, Felix Vogt
867-667-8222, Fax: 867-667-6705, felix.vogt@gov.yk.ca

Staff Development
Hougen's Center, #3106, 3rd Avenue, 3rd Fl.
867-667-8198 Fax: 867-393-6920

Acting Director, Tracey Johnson
867-667-8267, tracey.johnson@gov.yk.ca

Yukon Tourism & Culture

100 Hanson St., Whitehorse, YT Y1A 2C6
867-667-5036 Fax: 867-667-3546
www.tc.gov.yk.ca/

The department focuses on business, tourism, cultural industries & technology/telecommunications to develop & promote economic capacity & entrepreneurial skills to stimulate economy. The department works with the Yukon's diverse arts communities to foster creativity & quality of life & with heritage interests to preserve & interpret heritage resources.

Acts Administered:
Archives Act
Arts Act
Arts Centre Act
Historical Resources Act
Hotels & Tourist Establishments Act
Scientists & Explorers Act

Minister,
867-667-8641, Fax: 867-393-6252
Deputy Minister, Joy Waters
867-667-5430, Fax: 867-667-8844

Corporate Services

Provides a range of central support services within the Department of Tourism & Culture. These include human resources, information technology, administration, information management, & finance.
Director, Lucy Coulthard
867-667-3009, lucy.coulthard@gov.yk.ca

Cultural Services
867-667-8589
800-661-0408
TTY: 867-393-6456

Dedicated to the preservation, development, interpretation of Yukon's heritage resources & to fostering the growth & mpact of the territory's visual, literary, & performing arts.
Territorial Archivist, Ian Burnett
867-667-5275, ian.burnett@gov.yk.ca
Yukon Archeologist, Ruth Gotthardt
867-667-5983, ruth.gotthardt@gov.yk.ca
Yukon Archeologist, Greg Hare
867-667-3771, greg.hare@gov.yk.ca
Acting Manager, Brian Groves
867-667-3582, brian.groves@gov.yk.ca
Manager, Heritage Resources, Jeff Hunston
867-667-5363, jeff.hunston@gov.yk.ca
Director, Cultural Services, Rick Lemaire
867-667-8592, rick.lemaire@gov.yk.ca
Manager, Historic Sites, Doug Olynyk
867-667-5295, doug.olynyk@gov.yk.ca
Manager, Arts, Laurel Parry
867-667-5264, laurel.parry@gov.yk.ca
Development Assessment Archeologist, Christian Thomas
867-456-6102, christian.thomas@gov.yk.ca
Acting Manager, Stacie Zaychuk
867-667-3516, stacie.zatchuk@gov.yk.ca

Yukon Paleontologist, Grant Zazula
867-667-8089, grant.zazula@gov.yk.ca

Policy & Communications

867-667-8304 Fax: 867-393-8844
800-661-0408

Provides legislative & policy support for Tourism & Culture & coordinates the communications efforts of the department.

Director, Jonathan Parker
867-667-3016, jonathan.parker@gov.yk.ca

Tourism & Culture

867-667-3053
800-661-0408

Engages in tourism marketing, product development, & research in order to bring the scenic natural beauty and rich & diverse cultural heritage of Yukon to the attention of potential visitors.

Supervisor, Digital Assets & Photography, Marten Berkman
867-667-5434, marten.berkman@gov.yk.ca
Manager, Product & Research Development, Robert Clark
867-667-5632, robert.clark@gov.yk.ca
Director, Pierre Germain
867-667-3087, pierre.germain@gov.yk.ca

Yukon Women's Directorate

#1, 404 Hason St., Whitehorse, YT Y1A 1Y8
867-667-3030 Fax: 867-393-6270
www.womensdirectorate.gov.yk.ca

Acts Administered:
Yukon Advisory Council on Women's Issues Act

Director, Shauna Curtin
867-667-5182, shauna.curtin@gov.yk.ca
Manager, Administration & Finance, Lorie Larose
867-667-3026, lorie.larose@gov.yk.ca

Yukon Workers' Compensation Health & Safety Board (YWCHSB)

401 Strickland St., Whitehorse, YT Y1A 5N8
867-667-5645 Fax: 867-393-6279
800-661-0443
worksafe@gov.yk.ca
wcb.yk.ca/

The Yukon Workers' Compensation Health & Safety Board (YWCHSB) administers workers' compensation & occupational health & safety in the Yukon.

Acts Administered:
Day of Mourning for Victims of Workplace Injuries Act
Occupational Health & Safety Act
Spousal Compensation Act
Workplace Hazardous Materials Information System (WHMIS) Regulations

President & Chief Executive Officer, Valerie Royle
867-667-8983, Fax: 867-393-6419, valerie.royle@gov.yk.ca
Vice President & Chief Financial Officer, Jim Stephens
867-667-8210, jim.stephens@gov.yk.ca
Director, Human Resources, Doug Heynen
867-667-8190, doug.heynen@gov.yk.ca
Director, Social Marketing & Communications, Mark Hill
867-667-8695, mark.hill@gov.yk.ca
Director, Occupational Health & Safety, Kurt Dieckmann
867-667-3726, kurt.dieckmann@gov.yk.ca
Director, Assessments, Clarence Timmons
867-667-5831, clarence.timmons@gov.yk.ca
Acting Director, Claimant Services, Michael McBride
867-667-8186, michael.mcbride@gov.yk.ca,

The Queen & Royal Family

The House of Windsor

In 1917 the late King George V, by Proclamation, changed the House name of the Royal Family from Saxe-Coburg-Gotha to the House of Windsor.

THE QUEEN. - Elizabeth the Second, (Elizabeth Alexandra Mary, of Windsor) by the Grace of God, of the United Kingdom, Canada and Her other Realms and Territories Queen; Head of the Commonwealth, Defender of the Faith, Succeeded to the throne February 6th, 1952 , and was crowned June 2nd, 1953, at Westminster Abbey. Her Majesty, the elder daughter of the late King George VI and Queen Elizabeth The Queen Mother, was born at 17 Bruton St., London, W.1, on April 21st, 1926, married November 20th, 1947, H.R.H. The Prince Philip, Duke of Edinburgh, K.G., K.T., O.M., G.B.E., A.C., Q.S.O.

THE CHILDREN of Queen Elizabeth and H.R.H. The Prince Philip, Duke of Edinburgh are:

H.R.H. Prince Charles Philip Arthur George, Prince of Wales and Earl of Chester, Duke of Cornwall and Duke of Rothesay, Earl of Carrick and Baron Renfrew, Lord of the Isles, and Great Steward of Scotland, K.G., K.T., G.C.B., O.M., A.K., Q.S.O., A.D.C., born November 14th, 1948. Married July 29th, 1981. Marriage dissolved 1996. The Lady Diana Spencer (died August 31st, 1997) and has issue. Prince William, Prince of Wales and Duke of Cambridge, born June 21st, 1982 (married April 29, 2011, Kate Middleton, H.R.H. Duchess of Cambridge) and Prince Henry of Wales, born September 15th, 1984. Prince Charles married April 9th, 2005 Mrs. Camilla Parker Bowles (H.R.H. The Duchess of Cornwall).

H.R.H. The Princess Royal, Anne Elizabeth Alice Louise, K.G., K.T., G.C.V.O., Q.S.O., born August 15th, 1950. Married 1st November 14th, 1973 Captain Mark Anthony Peter Phillips, C.V.O., A.D.C. and has issue. Peter Phillips born November 15th, 1977 and Zara Phillips born May 15th, 1981. Marriage dissolved 1992. Married 2nd December 12th, 1993 Commodore Timothy James Hamilton Laurence, M.V.O., R.N.

H.R.H. The Prince Andrew Albert Christian Edward, K.C.V.O., A.D.C., Duke of York, Earl of Inverness and Baron Killyleagh, born February 19th, 1960, married July 23rd, 1986 Miss Sarah Margaret Ferguson and has issue, Princess Beatrice of York, born August 8th, 1988, and Princess Eugenie of York, born March 23rd, 1990. Marriage dissolved 1996.

H.R.H. The Prince Edward Antony Richard Louis, K.C.V.O., Earl of Wessex, and Viscount Severn, born March 10th, 1964, married June 19, 1999 Miss Sophie Rhys-Jones.

THE LATE GEORGE VI. - George VI succeeded to the Throne December 11th, 1936; and was crowned at Westminster Abbey, May 12th, 1937. Second son of King George V and Queen Mary, he was born at York Cottage, Sandringham, on December 14th, 1895, married, April 26th, 1923, Lady Elizabeth Bowes-Lyon, daughter of the Earl and Countess of Strathmore and Kinghorne. As Heir Presumptive succeeded to the Throne on the abdication of Edward VIII.

QUEEN ELIZABETH, THE QUEEN MOTHER - born August 4th, 1900, daughter of the 14th Earl of Strathmore and Kinghorne; married, April 26th, 1923. Died March 30th, 2002.

THE ISSUE of the late King George VI and Queen Elizabeth are:

The reigning Sovereign, Elizabeth the Second (elder daughter).

The Princess Margaret (Rose), Countess of Snowdon, C.I., G.C.V.O., born August 21st, 1930, married Antony Charles Robert Armstrong-Jones, G.C.V.O., (since created Earl of Snowdon) May 6th, 1960, and has issue, Viscount Linley, born November 3rd, 1961 and the Lady Sarah Frances Elizabeth Armstrong-Jones, born May 1st, 1964. Marriage dissolved 1978. Died February 9th, 2002.

SUCCESSION-The order stands:

The Prince of Wales
Prince William of Wales
Prince Henry of Wales
The Duke of York
Princess Beatrice of York
Princess Eugenie of York
The Earl of Wessex
The Lady Louise Mountbatten-Windsor
The Princess Royal
Mr. Peter Phillips
Miss Zara Phillips
Viscount Linley
The Hon. Charles Armstrong-Jones
The Hon. Margarita Armstrong-Jones
The Lady Sarah Chatto
Master Samuel Chatto
Master Arthur Chatto
The Duke of Gloucester
Earl of Ulster
The Lady Davina Windsor
The Lady Rose Windsor
The Duke of Kent
The Lady Marina Charlotte Windsor
The Lady Amelia Windsor
The Lady Helen Taylor
Master Columbus Taylor
Master Cassius Taylor
Miss Eloise Taylor
The Lord Frederick Windsor
The Lady Gabriella Windsor
Princess Alexandra, The Hon. Lady Ogilvy
Mr. James Ogilvy
Master Alexander Ogilvy
Miss Flora Ogilvy
Mrs. Paul Mowatt
Master Christian Mowatt
Miss Zenouska Mowatt
The Earl of Harewood

NOTES

1. The Sucession is governed by the Act of Settlement 1701 (12 & 13 Will 3 c 2) which limits the succession to the Throne to the heirs, being Protestants, of Princess Sophia of Hanover, granddaughter of King James I. Section 6 (4) of the Legitimacy Act of 1959 (ôNothing in this Act affects the succession to the Throneö) is also relevant.
2. Earl of St. Andrews & Prince Michael of Kent were excluded from the succession to the Throne on marriage to Roman Catholics, & Lord Downpatrick & the Lord Nicholas Windsor on conversion to Roman Catholicism.

HER MAJESTY'S HOUSEHOLD

Lord Chamberlain, The Lord Luce, G.C.V.O.
Private Secretary to The Queen, The Rt. Hon. Sir Robin Janvrin, K.C.V.O., K.C.B.
The Lord Chamberlain has the general supervision of the Royal Household.

The Commonwealth

The Commonwealth is a voluntary association of 53 independent member countries representing 1.8 billion people around the world - in Africa, the Americas, Asia, the Caribbean, Europe & the Pacific. It promotes good governance, democracy, sustainable economic & social development, the rule of law & human rights. These & other principles are enshrined in the Harare Commonwealth Declaration of 1991.

There are three principal international organizations of the Commonwealth:

THE COMMONWEALTH SECRETARIAT

Marlborough House, Pall Mall, London SW1Y 5HX, +44 (0)20 7747 6500; Fax: +44 (0)20 7930 0827, Email: info@commonwealth.int, URL: www.thecommonwealth.org
Rt. Hon. Donald C. McKinnon (New Zealand), Commonwealth Secretary-General
Florence Mugasha, Commonwealth Deputy Secretary-General
Ransford Smith, Commonwealth Deputy Secretary-General
Winston Cox, Commonwealth Deputy Secretary-General (Development Co-operation)
Joel Kibazo, Official Spokesperson, Director, Communicaitons & Public Affairs
For information pertaining to the Commonwealth write to: The Director, Information Public Affairs Division, Commonwealth Secretariat, Marlborough House, Pall Mall, London SW1Y 5HX, U.K.

THE COMMONWEALTH FOUNDATION

Marlborough House, Pall Mall, London SW1Y 5HY, +44 (0)20 7830 3783; Fax: +44 (0)20 7839 8157, Email: geninfo@commonwealth.int, URL: www.commonwealthfoundation.com

THE COMMONWEALTH OF LEARNING (COL)

#1200-1055 West Hastings, Vancouver BC V6E 2E9, 604/775-8200; Fax: 604/775-8210, Email: info@col.org, URL: www.col.org
The Commonwealth of Learning's focus is in strengthening institutions in developing Commonwealth countries that are striving to provide affordable education to larger numbers of their citizens.

Member States

(showing capital, population (2003) & date of membership. Dates for Australia, Canada & New Zealand are those on which Dominion Status was acquired):

Antigua & Barbuda - St. John's; 73,000; Nov. 1, 1981
Australia - Canberra; 19,731,000; Jan. 1, 1901
- External territories: Norfolk Island, Coral Sea Islands Territory, Australian Antarctic Territory, Heard Island & McDonald Islands, Cocos (Keeling) Islands, Christmas Island, Territory of Ashmore & Cartier Islands

The Bahamas - Nassau; 340,000; July 10, 1973
Bangladesh - Dhaka; 143,736,000; Mar. 26, 1972
Barbados - Bridgetown; 270,000; Nov. 30, 1966
Belize - Belmopan; 256,000; Sept. 21, 1981
Botswana - Gaborone; 1,785,000; Sept. 30, 1966
Brunei Darussalam - Bandar Seri Begawan; 358,000; Feb. 23, 1984
Cameroon - Yaoundé; 16,018,000; May 20, 1995
Canada - Ottawa; 31,510,000; July 1, 1867
Cyprus - Nicosia; 802,000; Oct. 1, 1961
Dominica - Roseau; 79,000; Nov. 3, 1978
Fiji Islands - Suva; 839,000; Oct. 10, 1997 N.B. Fiji Islands was suspended from the councils of the Commonwealth in May 2000 following the overthrow of its democratically elected government.
The Gambia - Banjul; 1,426,000; Feb. 18, 1965
Ghana - Accra; 20,922,000; Mar. 6, 1957
Grenada - St. George's; 80,000; Feb. 7, 1974
Guyana - Georgetown; 765,000; Feb. 23, 1966
India - New Delhi; 1,065,426,000; Jan. 26, 1947
Jamaica - Kingston; 2,651,000; Aug. 6, 1962
Kenya - Nairobi; 31,987,000; Dec. 12, 1963
Kiribati - Tarawa; 88,000; July 12, 1979
Lesotho - Maseru; 1,802,000; Oct. 4, 1966
Malawi - Lilongwe; 12,105,000; July 6, 1964
Malaysia - Kuala Lumpur; 24,425,000; Aug. 31, 1957
Maldives - Malé; 318,000; July 26, 1982
Malta - Valletta; 394,000; Mar. 31, 1964
Mauritius - Port Louis; 1,221,000; Mar. 12, 1968
Mozambique - Maputo; 18,863,000; June 25, 1995
Namibia - Windhoek; 1,987,000; Mar. 21, 1990
Nauru - Nauru; 13,000; Jan. 31, 1968 [Special Member as of July 1, 2005]
New Zealand - Wellington; 3,875,000; Sept. 26, 1907 - Includes the territories of Tokelau & the Ross Dependency (Antarctic). Self-governing countries in free association with New Zealand: Cook Islands & Niue.
Nigeria - Abuja; 124,009,000; Oct. 1, 1960
Pakistan - Islamabad; 153,578,000; Mar. 23, 1989 (previously member 1947-1972; rejoined in 1989) N.B. Pakistan was suspended from participation in the councils of the Commonwealth in October1999 following a military coup.
Papua New Guinea - Port Moresby; 5,711,000; Sept. 16, 1975
St. Kitts & Nevis - Basseterre; 42,000; Sept. 19, 1983
St. Lucia - Castries; 149,000; Feb. 22, 1979
St. Vincent & The Grenadines - Kingstown; 120,000; Oct. 27, 1979
Samoa - Apia; 178,000; June 1, 1970
Seychelles - Victoria; 81,000; June 18, 1976
Sierra Leone - Freetown; 4,971,000; Apr. 27, 1961
Singapore - Singapore; 4,253,000; Aug. 9, 1965
Solomon Islands - Honiara; 477,000 (2001); July 7, 1978
South Africa - Pretoria; 45,026,000; 1931 - Left Commonwealth 1961, rejoined 1994
Sri Lanka - Colombo; 19,065,000; Feb. 4, 1948
Swaziland - Mbabane; 1,077,000; Sept. 6, 1968
Tonga - Nuku'alofa; 104,000; June 4, 1970
Trinidad & Tobago - Port of Spain; 1,303,000; Aug. 31, 1962
Tuvalu - Funafuti; 11,000; Oct. 1, 1978
Uganda - Kampala; 25,827,000; Oct. 9, 1962
United Kingdom- London; 59,251,000
- Overseas territories: Anguilla, Bermuda, British Antarctic Territory, British Indian Ocean Territory, British Virgin Islands, Cayman Islands, Falkland Islands, Gibraltar, Montserrat, Pitcairn, Henderson, Ducie & Oeno Islands, St. Helena & St. Helena Dependencies (Ascension & Tristan da Cunha), South Georgia & the South Sandwich Islands, & Turks & Caicos Islands

United Republic of Tanzania - Dar es Salaam; 36,977,000; Dec. 9, 1961
Vanuatu - Port Vila; 212,000; July 30, 1980
Zambia - Lusaka; 10,812,000; Oct. 24, 1964

La Francophonie

ORGANISATION INTERNATIONALE DE LA FRANCOPHONIE

Secrétariat général, 28, rue de Bourgogne, 75007 Paris, France 1- 44-11-12-50; Téléc: 1-44-11-12-80; URL: www.francophonie.org

Member States

(showing member name, population, national holiday):

Albanie (République d'), 3,100 M, 11 janvier et 28 novembre
Andorre (Principauté), 0,078 M, 8 septembre
Belgique (Royaume de), 10,400 M, 21 juillet
Bénin (République du), 8,400 M, 1er août
Bulgarie (République de), 7,700 M, 3 mars
Burkina Faso, 13,200 M, 11 décembre
Burundi (République du), 7,500 M, 1er juillet
Cambodge (Royaume du), 14,100 M, 7 janvier - 17 avril
Cameroun (République du), 16,300 M, 20 mai
Canada, 32,300 M, 1er juillet
Canada - Nouveau-Brunswick (Province du), 0,730 M, 15 août
Canada - Québec (Province du), 7,500 M, 24 juin
Cap-Vert (République du), 0,400 M, 5 juillet
Centrafricaine (République), 4 M, 1er décembre
Communauté française de Belgique (Wallonie-Bruxelles), 4 M, 27 septembre
Comores (Union des), 0,558 M, 6 juillet

Congo (République du), 4 M, 15 août
Congo (République démocratique du Congo), 57,500 M, 30 juin
Côte d'Ivoire (République de), 18,200 M, 7 août
Djibouti (République de), 0,632 M, 27 juin
Dominique (Commonwealth de la), 0,730 M, 3 novembre
Égypte (République arabe d'), 74,000 M, 23 juillet
France (République française), 62 M, 14 juillet
Gabon (République gabonaise), 1,400 M, 17 août
Grèce, 11,100 M, 25 mars
Guinée (République de), 9,400 M, 2 octobre
Guinée-Bissau (République de), 1,600 M, 24 septembre
Guinée-équatoriale (République de), 0,457 M, 12 octobre
Haïti (République d'), 8,500 M, 1er janvier
Laos (République démocratique populaire Lao), 5,900 M, 2 décembre
Liban (République libanaise), 3,600 M, 22 novembre
Luxembourg (Grand-Duché de), 0,438 M, 23 juin
Macédonie (ARY), 2 M, 8 septembre
Madagascar (République de), 18,600 M, 26 juin
Mali (République du), 13,500 M, 22 septembre
Maroc (Royaume du), 31,500 M, 30 juillet
Maurice (République de), 1,200 M, 12 mars
Mauritanie (République islamique de), 3,100 M, 28 novembre
Moldavie, 4,200 M, 27 août
Monaco (Principauté de), 0,032 M, 19 novembre
Niger (République du), 14 M, 18 décembre
Roumanie, 21,700 M, 1er décembre
Rwanda (République rwandaise), 9 M, 1er juillet
Sainte-Lucie, 0,156 M, 22 février
Sao Tomé et Principe (République démocratique de), 0,148 M, 12 juillet
Sénégal (République du), 11,700 M, 4 avril
Seychelles (République des), 0,081 M, 18 juin
Suisse (Confédération), 7,300 M, 1er août
Tchad (République du), 9,700 M, 11 janvier
Togo (République du), 6,100 M, 13 janvier et 27 avril
Tunisie (République tunisienne), 10,100 M, 20 mars
Vanuatu (République de), 0,197 M, 30 juillet
Vietnam (République socialiste du), 84,200 M, 2 septembre

Canadian Permanent Missions Abroad

Canadian Joint Delegation to NATO (North Atlantic Treaty Organization)
Léopold III Blvd., Brussels, 1110 Belgium
322-707-5041, Fax: 322-707-5057
natocanada@dfait-maeci.gc.ca
www.dfaitmaeci.gc.ca/foreign _policy/nato/canada_natoen.asp
Jean-Pierre Juneau, Ambassador & Permanent Representative of Canada
Vice-Admiral Glenn Davidson, Military Representative of Canada CMM, CD

Mission of Canada to the European Union, Brussels
2, av de Tervuren, Brussels, 1040 Belgium
322-741-06-60, Fax: 322-741-06-29
annie.bollaert@international.gc.ca
www.dfait-maeci.gc.ca/canada-europa/E U
Jeremy K.B. Kinsman, Ambassador
Kevin D. O'Shea, Deputy Head of Mission
Denis Robert, Counsellor & Sec. Head, Pol. Affairs, Foreign & Sec. Policy

NORAD (North American Aerospace Defense Command)
NORAD Public Affairs, Peterson AFB, #B-016, 250 Vandenberg, Colorado Springs, 80914-3808 USA
719-554-6889
noradpa@norad.mil
www.norad.mil
Timothy J. Keating, Commander, Adm. USN
Eric A. Findley, Deputy Commander-in-Chief, Lt. Gen. Cdn. Forces CMM, CD, Ph.D.

Organization for Economic Cooperation & Development
2, rue André Pascal, Paris, F-75775 France
331-45-24-82-00, Fax: 331-45-24-85-00
webmaster@oecd.org
www.oecd.org
Angel Gurria, Secretary-General

Permanent Mission of Canada to the Organization of American States
501 Pennsylvania Ave. NW, Washington, DC 20001 USA
202-682-1768, Fax: 202-682-7264
wshdc-prmoas@dfait-maeci.gc.ca
www.dfaitmaeci.gc.ca/latin-america/latina merica
Paul Durand, Permanent Representative of Canada

UN: Permanent Delegation of Canada to the UN Educational, Scientific & Cultural Organization
UNESCO, 1, rue Mollis, Paris, 75732 France
331-45-68-35-17, Fax: 331-43-06-87-27
pesco@international.gc.ca
www.dfait-maeci.gc.ca/canada_un/paris/
Yvon Charbonneau, Ambassador & Permanent Delegate

UN: Permanent Mission of Canada to the Food & Agriculture Organization (FAO)
FAO, Via Zara 30, Rome, 00198 Italy
39-06-854-441, Fax: 39-06-85444-2930
fao-hq@fao.org
www.fao.org
Robert R. Fowler, Permanent Representative
J. Melanson, Deputy Permanent Representative
K. McKinley, Alternate Permanent Representative

UN: Permanent Mission of Canada to the International Civil Aviation Organization
ICAO, #1535, 999, rue Université, Montréal, QC H3C 5J9 Canada
514-954-5800, Fax: 514-954-5809
icaohq@icao.int
www.icao.int

UN: Permanent Mission of Canada to the International Organizations in Vienna
Laurenzerberg 2, Vienna, A-1010 Austria
431-531-38-3000, Fax: 431-531-38-3915
vosce@international.gc.ca
www.international.gc.ca/world/embassies/mission-en.asp?MID=239
Ingrid Hall, Permanent Representative & Ambassador
LCol. A. Sevigny, Military Adviser

UN: Permanent Mission of Canada to the Office of the UN, The Conference on Disarmement
5, av de l'Ariana, Geneva, 1202 Switzerland
41-22-919-9200, Fax: 41-22-919-9233
genev@dfait-maeci.gc.ca
www.dfait-maeci.gc.ca/geneva
Hon. Don Stephenson, Permanent Representative & Ambassador
Paul Meyer, Alternate Permanent Representative & Ambassador

UN: Permanent Mission of Canada to the United Nations
One Dag Hammarskjold Plaza, 885 Second Ave., 14th Fl., New York, NY 10017 USA
212-848-1100, Fax: 212-848-1195
prmny@international.gc.ca
www.dfait-maeci.gc.ca/canada_un/new_york/about/
John McNee, Permanent Representative, Ambassador

UN: Permanent Mission of Canada to the United Nations Centre for Human Settlements (Habitat)
PO Box, Nairobi, 00621 Kenya
254-20-366-3000, Fax: 254-20-366-3900
nrobi@international.gc.ca
www.dfait-maeci.gc.ca/world/embassies/mission-en.asp?MID=92
James Wall, Permanent Representative
B. Liddar, Deputy Permanent Representative
L. Hindle, Second Secretary

UN: Permanent Mission of Canada to the United Nations Environment Program
PO Box, Nairobi, 00621 Kenya
254-20-366-3000, Fax: 254-20-366-3900
nrobi@international.gc.ca
www.unep.org
James Wall, Permanent Representative
B. Liddar, Deputy Permanent Representative

Diplomatic & Consular Representatives in Canada

Islamic State of Afghanistan
240 Argyle Ave., Ottawa, ON K2P 1B9
613-563-4223, Fax: 613-563-4962,
Seddiqullah Habibi, Second Secretary
His Excellency Jawed Ludin, Ambassador
Mehrabodin Masstan, Counsellor
Mirwais Salehi, Third Secretary

Republic of Albania
Embassy of Albania (to Canada), #302, 130 Albert St., Ottawa, ON K1P 5G4
613-236-4114, Fax: 613-236-0804,
embassyrepublicofalbania@on.aibn.com
His Excellency Besnik Konci, Ambassador
Fatbardha Kola, First Secretary

People's Democratic Republic of Algeria
Embassy of Algeria, 500 Wilbrod St., Ottawa, ON K1N 6N2
613-789-8505, Fax: 613-789-1406,
www.ambalgott.com
Redhouane Malek, Counsellor
Nadia Lamrani, First Secretary
Mohamed Reza Louzouaz, Attaché
Abbesed Benoussat, Minister-Counsellor
Alil Alaoui, Counsellor
His Excellency Smail Benamara, Ambassador

Argentina
Embassy of the Argentine Republic, 81 Metcalfe St., 7th Fl., Ottawa, ON K1P 6K7
613-236-2351, Fax: 613-235-2659,
embargentina@argentina-canada.net
www.argentina-canada.net
Maria Cristina Tosonotti, Counsellor
His Excellency Arturo G. Bothamley, Ambassador
Ricardo Fernando Fernandez, Minister
Luis Fernando Del Solar Dorrego, Counsellor

Commonwealth of Australia
Australian High Commission, #710, 50 O'Connor St., Ottawa, ON K1P 6L2
613-236-0841, Fax: 613-236-4376,
Lt.Col. Lyndon Anderson, Defence Advisor
Wendy Walsh, First Secretary
Caroline Jane Linke, First Secretary
Glenda Price, Second Secretary
Christine Florence França Pearce, First Secretary, Immigration
Jo-Anne Lorraine Hardie, First Secretary & Consul
His Excellency Justin Hugh Brown, High Commissioner
Martin Anthony Huber, Counsellor & Deputy High Commissioner

Republic of Austria
Embassy of Austria, 445 Wilbrod St., Ottawa, ON K1N 6M7
613-789-1444, Fax: 613-789-3431,
ottawa-ob@bmaa.gv.at
www.austro.org
Maria Unger, Third Secretary & Vice-Consul, Administrative Affairs
Sigurd Pacher, Minister-Counsellor
His Excellency Werner Brandstetter, Ambassador

Republic of Azerbaijan
Embassy of Azerbaijan (to Canada), #904, 275 Slater St., Ottawa, ON K1P 5H9
613-288-0497, Fax: 613-230-8089,
azerbaijan@azembassy.ca
www.azembassy.ca
Farid Shafiyev, Counsellor
Orkhan Hajiyev, Third Secretary & Consul, Legal Affairs
Jeyhun Shahverdiyev, Third Secretary, Economic & Political Affairs
His Excellency Fakhraddin Gurbanov, Ambassador

Commonwealth of The Bahamas
High Commission for the Commonwealth of The Bahamas, #1313, 50 O'Connor St., Ottawa, ON K1P 6L2
613-232-1724, Fax: 613-232-0097,
ottawa-mission@bahighco.com
www.bahamas.gov.bs
Donald M. McCartney, Counsellor & Consul
Kerry Bonamy, Second Secretary & Vice-Consul
His Excellency Michael Douglas Smith, High Commissioner

Kingdom of Bahrain
Embassy of Bahrain (to Canada), 3502 International Dr. NW, Washington, DC 20008 USA
202-342-0741, Fax: 202-362-2192,
Her Excellency Huda Ezra Ebrahim Nonoo, Ambassador

People's Republic of Bangladesh
Bangladesh High Commission, #1250, 340 Albert St., Ottawa, ON K1R 7Y6
613-236-0138, Fax: 613-567-3213,
bang@bellnet.ca
www.bdhc.org
Abu Saleb Md. Mamunur R. Khalili, Ckounsellor, Commercial
Syed Masud Mahmood Khundoker, Counsellor
Fawzia Nahar Islam, First Secretary
Mohammed Erfan Sharif, First Secretary
His Excellency A.M. Yakub Ali, High Commissioner

Barbados
High Commission for Barbados, #470, 55 Metcalfe St., Ottawa, ON K1P 6L5
613-236-9517, Fax: 613-230-4362,
ottawa@foreign.gov.bb
Estuko Anderson, Counsellor
His Excellency Edward E. Greaves, High Commissioner

Natalie Cox, First Secretary

Kingdom of Belgium
#820, 360 Albert St., Ottawa, ON K1R 7X7
613-236-7267, Fax: 613-236-7882,
ottawa@diplobel.org
www.diplomatie.be/ottawa
Robert S.J.G. Gernay, Minister-Counsellor
His Excellency Jean L.A. Lint, Ambassador

Belize
High Commission for Belize, 2535 Massachusetts Ave. NW, Washington, DC 20008 USA
202-332-9636, Fax: 202-332-6888,
hcbelize@bellnet.ca
Vacant, High Commissioner

Republic of Benin
Embassy of Benin, 58 Glebe Ave., Ottawa, ON K1S 2C3
613-233-4429, Fax: 613-233-8952,
ambaben2@on.aira.com
www.benin.ca
Awahou Labouda, Minister-Counsellor & Chargé d'Affaires
Laure Regina Vignon Codo, Second Counsellor
His Excellency Honoré Théodore Ahimakin, Ambassador

Bhutan
Royal Bhutanese Embassy, 763 United Nations Plaza, 1st Ave., New York, NY 10017 USA
212-682-2268, Fax: 212-661-0551,
His Excellency Lhatu Wangchuk, Ambassador
Tshering Gyaltshen Penjor, First Secretary

Republic of Bolivia
Embassy of Bolivia, #416, 130 Albert St., Ottawa, ON K1P 5G4
613-236-5730, Fax: 613-236-8237,
bolivianembassy@bellnet.ca
Virginia de la Quintana, Counsellor
Juan Garrett Kent, First Secretary
His Excellency Edgar Jose Torrez Mosqueira, Ambassador

Bosnia & Herzegovina
#805, 130 Albert St., Ottawa, ON K1P 5G4
613-236-0028, Fax: 613-236-1139,
embassyofbih@bellnet.ca
www.bhembassy.ca
His Excellency Mithat Pasic, Ambassador

Republic of Botswana
High Commission for Botswana (to Canada): c/o Republic of Botswana, 1531 - 1533 New Hampshire Ave. NW, Washington, DC 20036 USA
202-244-4990, Fax: 202-244-4164,
www.botswanaembassy.org
Herold Caspar Luke, Second Secretary
His Excellency Lapologang Lekoa, High Commissioner
Lt.Col. Jeremiah Therego, Defence Attaché

Federative Republic of Brazil
Embassy of Brazil, 450 Wilbrod St., Ottawa, ON K1N 6M8
613-237-1090, Fax: 613-237-6144,
mailbox@brasembottawa.org
www.brasembottawa.org
Ivanise de Melo Maciel, First Secretary
Celso de Tarso Pereira, First Secretary
Norberto Moretti, First Secretary
His Excellency Paolo Corderio de Andrade Pinto, Ambassador
Pedro Murilo Ortega Terra, Counsellor

Brunei Darussalam
High Commission of Brunei Darussalam, 395 Laurier Ave. East, Ottawa, ON K1N 6R4
613-234-5656, Fax: 613-234-4397,
bhco@bellnet.ca
Faizal Bahrin Haji Bakri, Second Secretary
Haji Mursidi Bin Haji Setia, Third Secretary
Her Excellency Rakiah Hj Abd Lamit, High Commissioner

Republic of Bulgaria
Embassy of the Republic of Bulgaria, 325 Stewart St., Ottawa, ON K1N 6K5
613-789-3215, Fax: 613-789-3524,
mailmn@storm.ca
Dimiter Dimitrov, Minister & Chargé d'Affaires
Galina Genova Bachvarova, Third Secretary
His Excellency Evgueni Stefanov Stoytchev, Ambassador

Burkina-Faso
Embassy of Burkina-Faso, 48 Range Rd., Ottawa, ON K1N 8J4
613-238-4796, Fax: 613-238-3812,
burkina.faso@sympatico.ca
Fatimata Diallo, Counsellor, Economic & Commercial Affairs
Charles Karosy Bamouni, First Counsellor
Her Excellency Juliette Bonkoungou Yameogo, Ambassador

Republic of Burundi
Embassy of Burundi, #815, 325 Dalhousie St., Ottawa, ON K1N 7G2
613-789-0414, Fax: 613-789-9537,
ambabucanada@infonet.ca
Pascal Kamo, First Counsellor
Her Excellency Appolonie Simbizi, Ambassador

Republic of Cameroon
Cameroon High Commission, 170 Clemow Ave., Ottawa, ON K1S 2B4
613-236-1522, Fax: 613-236-3885,
cameroun@rogers.com
His Excellency Solomon Azoh-Mbi Anu'A-Gheyle, High Commissioner
Jean Bosco Etoa Etoa, Counsellor, Cultural Affairs
Labarang Abdoullahi, First Secretary
Joseph Pipimae Ayafor, First Secretary, Administration & Consular Affairs

Republic of Cape Verde
Embassy of Cape Verde (to Canada), 3415 Massachusetts Ave. NW, Washington, DC 20007 USA
202-965-6820, Fax: 202-965-1207,
cveisabel@caboverdeus.net
www.virtualcapeverde.net
Maria Semedo, Second Secretary
Emanuel Duarte, Chargé d'Affaires
Her Excellency Maria de Fátima Lima de Veiga, Ambassador

Central African Republic
Embassy of Central African Republic (to Canada), 1618 - 22nd St. NW, Washington, DC 20008 USA
202-483-7800, Fax: 202-332-9893,
Vacant, Ambassador

Republic of Chad
Embassy of Chad (to Canada), 2002 R St. NW, Washington, DC 20009 USA
202-462-4009, Fax: 202-265-1937,
info@chadembassy.org
www.chadembassy-usa.org
His Excellency Adam Bechir Mahamoud, Ambassador

Republic of Chile
Embassy of Chile, #1413, 50 O'Connor St., Ottawa, ON K1P 6L2
613-235-4402, Fax: 613-235-1176,
echileca@chile.ca
www.chile.ca
Fidel Coloma Grimberg, First Secretary
Annemarie Duncker, Third Secretary & Consul
His Excellency Eugenio Luis Ortega Riquelme, Ambassador
Eduardo Tapia, Minister-Counsellor

People's Republic of China
Embassy of China, 515 St. Patrick St., Ottawa, ON K1N 5H3
613-789-3434, Fax: 613-789-1911,
www.chinaembassycanada.org
Yuansong Jiang, Counsellor & Consul General
Huikang Huang, Minister-Counsellor & Deputy Head of Mission
Shuyun Shi, Minister-Counsellor
Xuelun Yang, Counsellor
Lushan Sun, Counsellor
Yongyue Hyang, Counsellor
Weidong Zhang, Minister-Counsellor
Guosheng Liu, Minister-Counsellor
His Excellency Lijun Lan, Ambassador

Republic of Colombia
Embassy of Colombia, #1002, 360 Albert St., Ottawa, ON K1R 7X7
613-230-3760, Fax: 613-230-4416,
embajada@embajadacolombia.ca
www.embajadacolombia.ca
Rafael Arismendy, First Secretary, Consular Affairs
His Excellency Jaime Giron Duarte, Ambassador
Guillermo Mejia, Minister-Counsellor

Commonwealth of Dominica
See: Organization of the Eastern Caribbean Stat

Republic of the Congo
Embassy of the Congo (to Canada), 4891 Colorado Ave. NW, Washington, DC 20011 USA
202-726-5500, Fax: 202-726-1860,
Jean-Christophe Lingoua, First Secretary
Henri Blaise Gotienne, Minister-Counsellor
Albert Ondongo, Second Secretary
His Excellency Serge Mombouli, Ambassador

Republic of Costa Rica
Embassy of Costa Rica, #407, 325 Dalhousie St., Ottawa, ON K1N 7G2
613-562-2855, Fax: 613-562-2582,
Ana Matilde Rivera Figueroa, Counsellor
Lina Eugenia Ajoy Rojas, Minister-Counsellor & Consul General
Her Excellency Emilia Maria Alvarez Navarro, Ambassador

Republic of Côte d'Ivoire
Embassy of Côte d'Ivoire, 9 Marlborough Ave., Ottawa, ON K1N 8E6
613-236-9919, Fax: 613-563-8287,
info@canada.diplomatie.gouv.ci
www.canada.diplomatie.gouv.ci
Ibrahim Cissoko, Counsellor
Georges Aboua, First Counsellor, Economic Affairs
His Excellency Louis Leon Boguy Bony, Ambassador

Republic of Croatia / Hrvatska
Embassy of Croatia, 229 Chapel St., Ottawa, ON K1N 7Y6
613-562-7820, Fax: 613-562-7821,
croemb.ottawa@mvpei.hr
ca.mfa.hr
Vesela Mrden Korac, Ambassador

Republic of Cuba
Embassy of Cuba, 388 Main St., Ottawa, ON K1S 1E3
613-563-0141, Fax: 613-563-0068,
cuba@embacuba.ca
http://embacu.cubaminrex.cu/Default.aspx?tabid=73
Denia Bada Gonzalez, Counsellor
Ceferino H. Hernandez Palenzuela, Counsellor
Mary Carmen Arencibia Vazquez, Counsellor, Commercial
Antonio G. Castanon Perez, Counsellor, Economic Affairs
Her Excellency Teresita De Jesus Vicente Sotolongo, Ambassador

Republic of Cyprus
High Commission of the Repulic of Cyprus, 2211 R St. NW, Washington, DC 20008 USA
202-462-5772, Fax: 202-483-6710,
info@cyprusembassy.net
www.cyprusembassy.net
Other information: Phone, Press Office: 202-232-8993; Fax, Press Room: 202-234-1936
His Excellency Andreas S. Kakouris, High Commissioner
Mr. Solon Savva, Deputy High Commissioner
Mr. Nicholaos Manolis, First Secretary

Czech Republic
Embassy of the Czech Republic, 251 Cooper St., Ottawa, ON K2P 0G2
613-562-3875, Fax: 613-562-3878,
ottawa@embassy.mzv.cz
www.czechembassy.org
Stanislav Benes, Counsellor, Commercial
His Excellency Karel Zebrakovsky, Ambassador
Jan Buben, Third Secretary
Tomas Vacek, Councellor
Karel Hejc, First Secretary

Democratic Republic of Congo
18 Range Rd., Ottawa, ON K1N 8J3
613-230-6391, Fax: 613-230-1945,
Vacant, Ambassador
Louise Nzanga Ramazani, First Counsellor & Chargé d'Affaires

Kingdom of Denmark
Royal Danish Embassy, #450, 47 Clarence St., Ottawa, ON K1N 9K1
613-562-1811, Fax: 613-562-1812,
ottamb@um.dk
www.ambottawa.um.dk/en
Vacant, Ambassador
Jakob Henningsen, First Secretary & Chargé d'Affaires

Republic of Djibouti
c/o Embassy of the Republic of Djibouti, #515, 1156 - 15th St. NW, Washington, DC 20005 USA
202-331-0270, Fax: 202-331-0302,
usdjibouti@aol.com
Issa Bouraleh, First Secretary
His Excellency Roble Olhaye, Ambassador

Dominican Republic
#418, 130 Albert St., Ottawa, ON K1P 5G4
613-569-9893, Fax: 613-569-8673,
info@drembassy.org
www.drembassy.org
Angelica M. Florentino Morel, Counsellor
Luis Maria Kalaff Sanchez, Minister-Counsellor
Iris Joseline Pujol Rodriguez, First Secretary
His Excellency Jose Del Carmen Urena Almonte, Ambassador
Renso Antonio Herrera Franco, Minister-Counsellor

Republic of Ecuador
Embassy of Ecuador, #316, 50 O'Connor St., Ottawa, ON K1P 6L2
613-563-8206, Fax: 613-235-5776, mecuacan@rogers.com
Oscar Filipe Izquierdo Arboleda, First Secretary
Ruth Maria Duenas Monteeroa, Counsellor & Deputy Head of Mission
His Excellency Franklin Gustavo Chavez Pareja, Ambassador

Egypt
Embassy of the Arab Republic of Egypt, 454 Laurier Ave. East, Ottawa, ON K1N 6R3
613-234-4931, Fax: 613-234-9347, egyptemb@sympatico.ca
Amr Mahmoud Abbas Abdel Hadi, Minister & Deputy Head of Mission
Maha Gamil Ali Hamdy, First Secretary
His Excellency Shalem Elsayed Nasser, Ambassador
Hoda Aly Sayed El Mazriky, Counsellor, Press & Information

Republic of El Salvador
Embassy of El Salvador, 209 Kent St., Ottawa, ON K2P 1Z8
613-238-2939, Fax: 613-238-6940, embajada@elsalvador-ca.org
His Excellency Rafael Angel Alfaro Pineda, Ambassador
Mireya Carolina Calderon Tovar, Minister-Counsellor

Equatorial Guinea
242 East 51st St., New York, NY 10022 USA
212-223-2324, Fax: 212-223-2366,
His Excellency Lino-Sima Ekua Avomo, Ambassador

Eritrea
Embassy of Eritrea (to Canada), #610, 75 Albert St., Ottawa, ON K1P 5E7
613-234-3989, Fax: 613-234-6213,
Vacant, Ambassador

Embassy of the Republic of Estonia
Embassy of Estonia, #210, 260 Dalhousie St., Ottawa, ON K1N 7E4
613-789-4222, Fax: 613-789-9555, embassy.ottawa@mfa.ee
www.estemb.ca
Rasmus Lumi, Counsellor ja Chargé d'Affaires
His Excellency Jüri Luik, Ambassador (Washington)

Democratic Republic of Ethiopia
Embassy of Federal Democratic Republic of Ethiopia, #210, 151 Slater St., Ottawa, ON K1P 5H3
613-235-6637, Fax: 613-235-4638, infoethi@magi.com
Tebege Berhe Shook, Counsellor
Birtukan Ayano Dadi, First Secretary
His Excellency Getachew Hamussa Hailemariam, Ambassador
Almaz Amaha Tesfay, Minister-Counsellor

European Union
Delegation of the European Commission to Canada, #1900, 45 O'Connor St., Ottawa, ON K1P 1A4
613-238-6464, Fax: 613-238-5191, Delegation-Canada@ec.europa.eu
www.delcan.ec.europa.eu
Christopher John Otto Kendall, Counsellor
Eric Hayes, Ambassador & Head of Delegation
Anya Irmgard Oram, Counsellor

Federal Republic of Nigeria
Nigeria High Commission, 295 Metcalfe St., Ottawa, ON K2P 1R9
613-236-0521, Fax: 613-236-0529, chancery@nigeriahcottawa.com
www.nigeriahcottawa.com
Walter Iteky Ajogbor, Minister
Zhiri James Gana, Minister
Ahmed Adams, Minister
Sola Enikanolaiye, Minister
Eniola Otepola, Minister
Iyorwuese Hagher, High Commissioner

Fiji
Embassy of Fiji (to Canada), 200 M St. NW #240, Washington, DC 20036 USA
202-337-8320, Fax: 202-466-8325, info@fijiembassy.com
www.fijiembassydc.com
Sakiusa Rabuka, Counsellor
Penijamini R.T. Lomaloma, Acting High Commissioner

Republic of Finland
Embassy of Finland, #850, 55 Metcalfe St., Ottawa, ON K1P 6L5
613-288-2233, Fax: 613-288-2244, embassy@finland.ca
www.finland.ca
His Excellency Risto Piipponen, Ambassador
Matti Toumas Juhani Aaltola, Counsellor

French Republic
Embassy of France, 42 Sussex Dr., Ottawa, ON K1M 2C9
613-789-1795, Fax: 613-562-3735, politique@ambafrance-ca.org
www.ambafrance-ca.org
Xavier Barès, Counsellor, Cultural Affairs
Gilles Baudouin, Counsellor, Commerical & Economics
Jean-Baptiste Lesecq, Second Secretary, Economic & Commercial Affairs
His Excellency François Marie Delattre, Ambassador
Philippe Henri Albert Meunier, Minister-Counsellor

Gabonese Republic
Embassy of Gabon, PO Box 368 , 4 Range Rd., Ottawa, ON K1N 8J5
613-232-5301, Fax: 613-232-6916, ambgabon@sprint.ca
François Ebibi Mba, First Counsellor
Venance Mbingt Abdoulaye, Counsellor, Economic Affairs
His Excellency Andre William Anguile, Ambassador
Lucien Moubouyi, First Counsellor, Economic, Commercial & Consular Affaires

Republic of the Gambia
High Commission for Gambia (to Canada): c/o Gambia Embassy, #600, 1424 K St. NW, Washington, DC 20005 USA
202-785-1399, Fax: 202-785-1430, info@gambiaembassy.us
www.gambiaembassy.us
Pa Njagga Mendy, First Secretary
Tijan Masanneh Ceesay, First Secretary
His Excellency Dodou Bammy Jagne, High Commissioner

Embassy of the Federal Republic of Germany
Embassy of Germany, 1 Waverley St., Ottawa, ON K2P 0T8
613-232-1101, Fax: 613-594-9330, info@ottawa.diplo.de
www.ottawa.diplo.de
Embassy wants people excluded for the Embassy and Consulates General due to constant changes.
His Excellency Johann Georg Witschel, Ambassador

Republic of Ghana
High Commission for Ghana, 1 Clemow Ave., Ottawa, ON K1S 2A9
613-236-0871, Fax: 613-236-0874, ghanacom@ghanahighcommission-canada.com
www.ghc-ca.com
Kwadwo Tuntum Addo, Counsellor
Yaw Odei Osei, Deputy High Commissioner
Yaw Asa Yirenkyi, First Secretary
Francis Danti Kotia, Acting High Commissioner
Susan Hagan Annobil, Minister

Hellenic Republic
Embassy of Greece, 80 MacLaren St., Ottawa, ON K2P 0K6
613-238-6271, Fax: 613-238-5676, embassy@greekembassy.ca
www.greekembassy.ca
Theodosios Dimitrakopoulos, Press Counsellor, Press
His Excellency Nikolaos Matsis, Ambassador
Michael Votsis, First Secretary
Kostas Dikaros, Commercial Attaché

Grenada
See: Organization of the Eastern Caribbean Stat

Republic of Guatemala
Embassy of Guatemala, #1010, 130 Albert St., Ottawa, ON K1P 5G4
613-233-7237, Fax: 613-233-0135, embassy1@embaguate-canada.com
Sandra Refugio Cruz Ordonez, Third Secretary, Cultural & Tourism Affairs
Martha Aida Rogelia Argueta Molina, First Secretary
His Excellency Georges de la Roche Plihal, Ambassador

Republic of Guinea
Embassy of Guinea, 483 Wilbrod St., Ottawa, ON K1N 6N1
613-789-8444, Fax: 613-789-7560, ambaguineaott@sympatico.ca
Hawa Diakité, Counsellor & Chargé d'Affaires
Frederick Bangoura, Counsellor (Finance & Consular Affairs), Financial & Consular Affairs
Vacant, Ambassador
Aïssata Sow, Counsellor (Cultural Affairs), Cultural Affairs

Republic of Guinea-Bissau
Embassy of Guinea-Bissau (to Canada), 15929 Yukon Lane, Washington, DC 20855 USA
301-947-3958, Fax: 301-947-3958,
Vacant, Ambassador
Henrique Da Silva, Minister-Counsellor & Chargé d'Affaires

Republic of Guyana
Burnside Bldg., #309, 151 Slater St., Ottawa, ON K1P 5H3
613-235-7249, Fax: 613-235-1447, guyanahcott@rogers.com
His Excellency Rajnarine Singh, High Commissioner

Republic of Haiti
Embassy of Haiti, #1500, 130 Albert St., Ottawa, ON K1P 5G4
613-238-1628, Fax: 613-238-2986, bohio@sympatico.ca
Joseph Pierre Daniel Charles, Counsellor
Marie-Jose Justinvil, Counsellor
Marjorie Auguste, First Secretary
Margarete Lemaire, Counsellor
Marie Menos-Gissel, Minister-Counsellor & Chargé d'Affaires
Vacant, Ambassador

Republic of Honduras
Embassy of Honduras, #805, 151 Slater St., Ottawa, ON K1P 5H3
613-233-8900, Fax: 613-232-0193, embhonca@magma.ca
www.embassyhonduras.ca
Guillermo J. Vallagares Lainez, Counsellor & Chargé d'Affaires
Erich Roberto Bondy Reyes, First Secretary
Delia Beatriz Valle Marichal, Ambassador

Republic of Hungary
Embassy of the Republic Hungary, 299 Waverley St., Ottawa, ON K2P 0V9
613-230-2717, Fax: 613-230-7560, sysadmin@huembott.org
www.mfa.gov.hu/emb/ottawa
Laszlo Bakos, Attaché & Consul, Cultural Affairs
His Excellency Pal Vastagh, Ambassador
Ferenc Banyai, Counsellor

Republic of Iceland
Embassy of Iceland, #710, 360 Albert St., Ottawa, ON K1R 7X7
613-482-1944, Fax: 613-482-1945, www.iceland.org/ca
Her Excellency Sigridur Anna Thordardottir, Ambassador

Republic of India
High Commission of India, 10 Springfield Rd., Ottawa, ON K1M 1C9
613-744-3751, Fax: 613-744-0913, hicomind@hciottawa.ca
www.hciottawa.ca
Niraj Srivastava, Deputy High Commissioner
Narendra Kumar Sharma, Counsellor
Vinod Kumar Sachdeva, Minister
Chandra Ballabh Thapliyal, First Secretary
Ajay Kumar Sharma, First Secretary
Rani Malick, Second Secretary
Rakesh Kumar Malhotra, Second Secretary
R.R.P.N. Sahi, Minister, Consular Affairs
His Excellency Shashishekhar Madhukar Gavai, High Commissioner

Republic of Indonesia / Republik Indonesia
55 Parkdale Ave., Ottawa, ON K1Y 1E5
613-724-1100, Fax: 613-724-1105, info@indonesia-ottawa.org
www.indonesia-ottawa.org
Sadewo Joedo, Minister & Deputy Head of Mission
XXX Iswayudha, Minister-Counsellor, Public Affairs
His Excellency Djoko Hardono, Ambassador
Ronald Yosef Pariaman Manik, Minister-Counsellor, Economic Affairs

Islamic Republic of Iran
Embassy of the Islamic Republic of Iran, 245 Metcalfe St., Ottawa, ON K2P 2K2
613-235-4726, Fax: 613-238-5712, iranemb@salamiran.org
www.salamiran.org
Ataollah Mobarhani, First Counsellor
Seyed Mohammad Kazem Naeimi, First Counsellor
Seyed Javad Azhari, Counsellor, Science
Vacant, Ambassador
Bahram Ghasemi, Chargé d'Affaires

Republic of Iraq
Embassy of Iraq, 215 McLeod St., Ottawa, ON K2P 0Z8
613-236-9177, Fax: 613-236-9641,
media@iraqembassy.ca
www.iraqembassy.ca
His Excellency Howar M. Ziad, Ambassador

Republic of Ireland
Embassy of Ireland, #1105, 130 Albert St., Ottawa, ON K1P 5G4
613-233-6281, Fax: 613-233-5835,
embassyofireland@rogers.com
Karl Gardner, First Secretary
His Excellency Declan Michael Kelly, Ambassador

Islamic Federal Republic of the Comoros
c/o Permanent Mission of the Comoros to the UN, #418, 866 UN Plaza, New York, NY 10017 USA
212-750-1637, Fax: 212-750-1657,
comoros@un.int
www.un.int/comoros
Vacant, Ambassador

State of Israel
Embassy of Israel, #1005, 50 O'Connor St., Ottawa, ON K1P 6L2
613-567-6450, Fax: 613-567-8978,
info@ottawa.mfa.gov.il
www.ottawa.mfa.gov.il
Ofir Gendelman, Second Secretary
Amit Gil-Bayaz, Counsellor & Deputy Head of Mission
Her Excellency Miriam Ziv, Ambassador

Italian Republic
Embassy of Italy, 275 Slater St., 21st Fl., Ottawa, ON K1P 5H9
613-232-2401, Fax: 613-233-1484,
ambital@italyincanada.com
www.ambottawa.esteri.it/ambasciata_ottawa
Giulio Alaimo, Counsellor, Social Affairs
Spartaco Caldararo, First Secretary, Commercial Affairs
His Excellency Gabriele Sardo, Ambassador
Alessandro Cortese, Deputy Head of Mission & Minister Counsellor

Ivory Coast
See: Republic of Côte d'Ivoire

Jamaica
Jamaican High Commission, #800, 275 Slater St., Ottawa, ON K1P 5H9
613-233-9311, Fax: 613-233-0611,
hc@jhcottawa.ca
www.jhcottawa.ca
Her Excellency Ruby Violet Evadne Coye, High Commissioner
Lola Patrica Rodney Evering, Counsellor

Japan
Embassy of Japan, 255 Sussex Dr., Ottawa, ON K1N 9E6
613-241-8541, Fax: 613-241-2232,
www.ca.emb-japan.go.jp
Masataka Tarahara, Minister & Deputy Head of Mission
His Excellency Tsuneo Nishida, Ambassador
Yasushi Misawa, Minister

Hashemite Kingdom of Jordan
Embassy of Jordan, #701, 100 Bronson Ave., Ottawa, ON K1R 6G8
613-238-8090, Fax: 613-232-3341,
Jordon@on.aibn.com
www.embassyofjordan.ca
Ma'en A. Al-Khreasat, Third Secretary
His Excellency Nabil Ali Mohamed Barto, Ambassador

Republic of Kazakhstan
Embassy of the Republic of Kazakhstan, 56 Hawthorne Ave., Ottawa, ON K1S 0B1
613-788-3704, Fax: 613-788-3702,
kazak@intr.net
His Excellency Yerlan Abildayev, Ambassador
Samat Zhanabay, Second Secretary
Aigul Moldabekova, Second Secretary
Talgat Kaliyev, Counsellor & Deputy Chief of Mission
Mainyura Murzamadiyeva, Counsellor
Roman Vassilenko, First Secretary
Aibek Nurbalin, Third Secretary

Republic of Kenya
High Commission for Kenya, 415 Laurier Ave. East, Ottawa, ON K1N 6R4
613-563-1773, Fax: 613-233-6599,
kenyahighcommission@rogers.com
www.kenyahighcommission.ca
Michael Aor Oloo, First Secretary
His Excellency Simon Waynonyi Nabukwesi, High Commissioner
Christine Martha Wanjiru Mwangi, Counsellor & Deputy High Commissioner

Kingdom of Cambodia
327 East 58 St., New York, NY 10022 USA
212-336-0777, Fax: 212-759-7672,
cambodia@un.int
www.un.int/cambodia
His Excellency Kosal Sea, Ambassador

Kingdom of Tonga
High Commission for the Kingdom of Tonga, 250 East 51st St., New York, NY 10022 USA
917-369-1025, Fax: 917-369-1024,
Her Excellency Fekitamoeloa T.M. Utoikamanu, High Commissioner

Republic of Korea
Embassy of Korea, 150 Boteler St., Ottawa, ON K1N 5A6
613-244-5010, Fax: 613-244-5034,
Gi Soo Ryu, Minister-Counsellor
His Excellency Chan Ho Ha, Ambassador
Soontaik Hwang, Minister

Democratic People's Republic of Korea
Permanent Mission of Democratic People's Republic of Korea to the UN, 820 Second Ave., 13th Fl., New York, NY 10017 USA
212-972-3105, Fax: 212-972-3154,
His Excellency Son Ho Sin, Ambassador
Song Chol Sin, First Secretary

State of Kuwait
Embassy of Kuwait, 333 Sussex Dr., Ottawa, ON K1N 1J9
613-780-9999, Fax: 613-780-9905,
info@embassyofkuwait.com
www.embassyofkuwait.ca
Mohammad S.R.B. Al-Mutairi, Second Secretary
Mesaid Al-Kulaib, Third Secretary
His Excellency Musaed Rashed A. Al-Haroun, Ambassador
Yaqoub Yousef Eid Khalaf Al-Sanad, First Secretary

Kyrgyz Republic
Embassy of the Kyrgyz Republic, 2360 Masachussets. Ave. NW, Washington, DC 20008 USA
202-449-9822, Fax: 202-386-7550,
consul@kgembassy.org
www.kyrgyzembassy.org
Her Excellency Zamira Sydykova, Ambassador

Laos
The Embassy of the Lao People's Democratic Republic (to Canada), 2222 S St. NW, Washington, DC 20008 USA
202-332-6416, Fax: 202-332-4923,
laoemb@erols.com
www.laoembassy.com
Amphayvanh Chanthavong, Third Secretary
Khamphanthong Soutsady, Third Secretary
Chansamone Thonpraseuth, Second Secretary
Bounneme Chouanghom, First Secretary
Inphachanh Sisavath, First Secretary
Vanhtha Sengmeuang, Second Secretary
His Excellency Phiane Philakone, Ambassador
Phomma Sidsena, Counsellor & Deputy Chief of Mission

Embassy of the Republic of Latvia
Embassy of Latvia, #1200, 350 Sparks St., Ottawa, ON K1R 7S8
613-238-6014, Fax: 613-238-7044,
embassy.canada@mfa.gov.lv
www.ottawa.mfa.gov.lv
His Excellency Margers Krams, Ambassador

Lebanese Republic
Embassy of Lebanon, 640 Lyon St., Ottawa, ON K1S 3Z5
613-236-5825, Fax: 613-232-1609,
info@lebanonembassy.ca
www.lebanonembassy.ca
His Excellency Massoud Maalouf, Ambassador
Oussama Khachab, First Secretary

Kingdom of Lesotho
#1820, 130 Albert St., Ottawa, ON K1P 5G4
613-234-0770, Fax: 636-234-5665,
Lesotho.Ottawa@bellnet.ca
Her Excellency Motseoa Philadel Senyane, High Commissioner
Tumelo Ephraim Raboletsi, First Secretary
Lerato Makoele Agnes Khutlnag, Third Secretary

Republic of Liberia
Embassy of the Republic of Liberia, 5201, 16th St. NW, Washington, DC 20011 USA
202-723-0437, Fax: 202-723-0436,
His Excellency Charles A. Minor, Ambassador

Libya
Embassy of the Great Socialist People's Libyan Arab Jamahiriya, #1000, 81 Metcalfe, Ottawa, ON K1P 6K7
613-230-0919, Fax: 613-230-0683,
info@libya-canada.org
www.libya-canada.org/index-eng.html
Al Hussein A.M. Elzawawi, Counsellor & Chargé d'Affaires
Hasan M.A. Eilabidi, Counsellor, Finance
Sadegh M.O Bensadegh, Counsellor
Maatoug A.M. Embarak, Counsellor, Cultural Affairs
Vacant, Ambassador

Liechtenstein
See: Swiss Confederation

Embassy of the Republic of Lithuania
Embassy of Lithuania, #1600, 150 Metcalfe St., Ottawa, ON K2P 1P1
613-567-5458, Fax: 613-567-5315,
ottawa@lithuanianembassy.ca
www.lithuanianembassy.ca
Migle Jurgita Jankauskiene, Counsellor, 613-567-5458 ext.22, migle.jankuskiene@lithuanianembassy.ca
Ramune Zitikiene, First Secretary, 613-567-5458 ext.25, ramune.zitikiene@lithuanianembassy.ca
Her Excellency Ginte Damusis, Ambassador

Grand Duchy of Luxembourg
Embassy of Luxembourg (to Canada), 2200 Massachusetts Ave. NW, Washington, DC 20008 USA
202-265-4171, Fax: 202-328-8270,
Washington.Amb@mae.etat.lu
His Excellency Jean-Paul Ernest Senninger, Ambassador
Paul Schmidt, Deputy Head of Mission

Republic of Macedonia
Embassy of the Republic of Macedonia, #1006, 130 Albert St., Ottawa, ON K1P 5G4
613-234-3882, Fax: 613-233-1852,
emb.macedonia.ottawa@sympatico.ca
www3.sympatico.ca/emb.macedonia.ottawa /
His Excellency Sasko Nasevt, Ambassador
Slavica Dimovska, First Secretary & Chargé d'Affaires

Republic of Madagascar
Embassy of Madagascar, 3 Raymond St., Ottawa, ON K1R 1A3
613-537-0505, Fax: 613-537-2882,
ambamadcanada@bellnet.ca
www.madagascar-embassy.ca
His Excellency Simon Constant Horace, Ambassador

Republic of Malawi
High Commission for Malawi, #1000, 1029 Vermont Ave., Washington, DC 20005 USA
202-721-0270, Fax: 202-721-0288,
malawi.highcommission@bellnet.ca
Her Excellency Hawa Olga Ndilowe, High Commissioner

Malaysia
High Commission of Malaysia, 60 Boteler St., Ottawa, ON K1N 8Y7
613-241-5182, Fax: 613-241-5214,
mwottawa@kln.gov.my
His Excellency Selwyn Vijayarajan Das, High Commissioner
Mohamad Nizan bin Mohamed, Counsellor

Republic of Mali
Embassy of Mali, 50 Goulburn Ave., Ottawa, ON K1N 8C8
613-232-1501, Fax: 613-232-7429,
ambassadedumali@rogers.com
www.ambamalicanada.org
Mamadou Mandjou Berthe, Second Counsellor
Nene Fofana Kebe, First Secretary
His Excellency Mamadou Bandiougoi Diawara, Ambassador
Macki N'Diaye, First Counsellor

Republic of the Marshall Islands
2433 Massachusetts Ave. NW, Washington, DC 20008 USA
202-234-5414, Fax: 202-232-3236,
His Excellency Banny De Brum, Ambassador

Islamic Republic of Mauritania
Permanent Mission of the Islamic Republic of Mauritania, 116 East 38th St., New York, NY 10016 USA
212-252-0113, Fax: 212-252-0175,
Aicha Mint Mohamed Saleck, First Counsellor
Jiddou Ould Abderrahmane, First Counsellor
Youssouf Ould Mohamed Mahmoud, First Counsellor
His Excellency Abderrahim Oluld Hadrami, Ambassador

Republic of Mauritius
High Commission for Mauritius (to Canada): c/o Embassy of Mauritius, #441, 4301 Connecticut Ave. NW, Washington, DC 20008 USA
202-244-1491, Fax: 202-966-0983, mauritius.embassy@prodigy.net
His Excellency Keerteecoomar Ruhee, High Commissioner

United Mexican States
Embassy of Mexico, #1000 & #1030, 45 O'Connor St., Ottawa, ON K1P 1A4
613-233-8988, Fax: 613-235-9123, www.sre.gob.mx/canada
Carlos Jesus Pinera Gonzalez, Minister, Trade
His Excellency Francisco Javier Barrio Terrazas, Ambassador
Jose Ignacio Madrazo Bolivar, Minister & Deputy Head of Mission

Mongolia
Embassy of Mongolia, #503, 151 Slater St., Ottawa, ON K1P 5H3
613-569-3830, Fax: 613-569-3916, mail@mongolembassy.org
www.mongolembassy.org
Khaliun Dalantai, First Secretary & Consul
Narangua Puntsagnorov, First Secretary
His Excellency Gotov Dugerjav, Ambassador

Montenegro
Embassy of the Republic of Montenegro, 1610 New Hampshire Ave., Washington, DC
202-234-6108, Fax: 202-234-6109,
His Excellency Miodrag Vlahovic, Ambassador

Montserrat
See: Organization of the Eastern Caribbean Stat

Kingdom of Morocco
Embassy of Morocco, 38 Range Rd., Ottawa, ON K1N 8J4
613-236-7391, Fax: 613-236-6164, info@ambamaroc.ca
www.ambamaroc.ca
Salim Lhjomri, Counsellor
Mohamed Aziz Mouline, Counsellor
Fatima Bouziani, Counsellor
Mohamed Taieb Ben Faida, Counsellor
Her Excellency Nouzha Chekrouni, Ambassador
El Mostafa Benmegdoul, Minister

Republic of Mozambique
High Commission of the Republic of Mozambique to Canada, 1525 New Hampshire Ave. NW, Washington, DC 20036 USA
202-293-7146, Fax: 202-835-0245, mozambvisa@aol.com
www.embamoc-usa.org
His Excellency Armando A. Panguene, High Commissioner

Myanmar
Embassy of the Union of Myanmar, #902/903, 85 Range Rd., Ottawa, ON K1N 8J6
613-232-9990, Fax: 613-232-6999, meottawa@rogers.com
Aung Ba Kyu, Counsellor & Chargé d'Affaires
Wai Zin Tun, Second Secretary
Daw Ni Ni Shein, Second Secretary
Vacant, Ambassador

Republic of Namibia
High Commission for Namibia (to Canada), 1605 New Hampshire Ave. NW, Washington, DC 200092503 USA
202-986-0540, Fax: 202-986-0443, info@namibianembassyusa.org
www.namibianembassyusa.org
Selma Ashipala-Musavyi, Minister-Counsellor & Deputy Head of Mission
His Excellency Patrick Nandago, High Commissioner

Kingdom of Nepal
Royal Nepalese Embassy (to Canada): c/o Embassy of Nepal, 2131 Leroy Place NW, Washington, DC 20008 USA
202-667-4550, Fax: 202-667-5534, nepali@erols.com
Netra Bahadur Tandan, Third Secretary
Krishna C. Aryal, First Secretary
His Excellency Kedar Bhakta Shyestha, Ambassador

Kingdom of the Netherlands
Royal Netherlands Embassy, #2020, 350 Albert St., Ottawa, ON K1R 1A4
613-237-5031, Fax: 613-237-6471, nlgovott@netcom.ca
www.netherlandsembassy.ca
Saskia Elisabeth De Lang, Minister & Deputy Head of Mission
Hillebrand Dirk Knook, Counsellor, Commercial
His Excellency Wilhelm Julius Petrus Geerts, Ambassador

New Zealand
New Zealand High Commission, Clarica Centre, #727, 99 Bank St., Ottawa, ON K1P 6G3
613-238-5991, Fax: 613-238-5707, info@nzhcottawa.org
www.nzembassy.com/canada
Elizabeth Dixon, Second Secretary
Her Excellency Kathleen Janet Lackey, High Commissioner
Andrew Needs, Deputy High Commissioner
Barry Prior, Counsellor

Republic of Nicaragua
Embassy of Nicaragua, 1627 New Hamphire Ave. NW, Washington, DC 20009 USA
202-939-6570, Fax: 202-939-6545,
Vacant, Ambassador

Republic of Niger
Embassy of Niger, 38 Blackburn Ave., Ottawa, ON K1N 8A3
613-232-4291, Fax: 613-230-9808, ambanigeracanada@rogers.com
www.ambanigeracanada.ca
Fifi Mahamane Bachir, Counsellor
Her Excellency Nana Aicha Mouctari Foumakoye, Ambassador
Moumouni Saley Brah, Second Secretary, Financial Affairs

Kingdom of Norway
Royal Norwegian Embassy, #1300, 130 Albert St., Ottawa, ON K2P 1P1
613-238-6571, Fax: 613-238-2765, emb.ottawa@mfa.no
www.emb-norway.ca
Kristin Melsom, First Secretary
Vacant, Ambassador
Mr. Jo Sletbak, Minister-Counsellor & Chargé d'Affaires

Sultanate of Oman
Embassy of Oman (to Canada), 2535 Belmont Rd. NW, Washington, DC 20008 USA
202-387-1980, Fax: 202-745-4933, www.omani.info
Talib Issa Zahran Al Salmi, Attaché, Cultural Affairs & Education
Her Excellency Hunaina Sultan Ahmed Al Mughairy, Ambassador

Organization of the Eastern Caribbean States (OECS)
High Commission for the Countries of the Eastern Caribbean States, #700, 130 Albert St., Ottawa, ON K1P 5G4
613-236-8952, Fax: 613-236-3042, oesec@oecs.org
www.oecs.org
Includes: Antigua & Barbuda, Commonwealth of Dominica, Grenada, Montserrat, Saint Christopher (Saint Kitts) & Nevis, Saint Lucia, Saint Vincent & the Grenadines
Darius Pope, Third Secretary
Anita Joseph, First Secretary
His Excellency Brendon Browne, High Commissioner

Islamic Republic of Pakistan
High Commission for Pakistan, Burnside Bldg., 10 Range Rd., Ottawa, ON K1N 8J3
613-238-7881, Fax: 613-238-7296, parepottawa@rogers.com
Saqlain Asad, First Secretary
His Excellency Akbar Zeb, High Commissioner
Najm us Saqib, Counsellor

Republic of Panama
Embassy of Panama, #300, 130 Albert St., Ottawa, ON K1P 5G4
613-236-7177, Fax: 613-236-5775, info@embassyofpanama.ca
www.embassyofpanama.ca
Jorge E. Constantino Gonzalez, Minister-Counsellor
Carlos Diaz Vallarino, Counsellor, Economic Affairs
Vacant, Ambassador

Papua New Guinea
High Commission of Papua New Guinea (to Canada), #805, 1779 Massachusetts Ave. NW, Washington, DC 20036 USA
202-745-3680, Fax: 202-745-3679, info@pngembassy.org
www.pngembassy.org
His Excellency Evan Jeremy Paki, High Commissioner

Republic of Paraguay
Embassy of Paraguay, #501, 151 Slater St., Ottawa, ON K1P 5H3
613-567-1283, Fax: 613-567-1679, consularsection@embassyofparaguay.ca
www.embassyofparaguay.ca
Helena Concepci¢n Felip-Salazar, Counsellor
His Excellency Juan Esteban O. Aguirre Martinez, Ambassador
Victor Hugo Rondan Samaniego, First Secretary

Republic of Peru
Embassy of Peru, #1901, 130 Albert St., Ottawa, ON K1P 5G4
613-238-1777, Fax: 613-232-3062, emperuca@bellnet.ca
www.embassyofperu.ca
Pedro Buitron, Minister
His Excellency Jorge Juan Castaneda Mendez, Ambassador

Republic of the Philippines
Embassy of the Philippines, #606, 130 Albert St., Ottawa, ON K1P 5G4
613-233-1121, Fax: 613-233-4165, embassyofphilippines@rogers.com
Rhenita Rodriguez, Second Secretary & Vice-Consul
Shirley E. Banquicio, First Secretary & Consul
Eloy Luis Bello, Second Secretary & Vice-Consul
His Excellency Jose S. Brillantes, Ambassador
Joseph Gerard B. Angeles, Minister & Consul General

Republic of Poland
Embassy of Poland, 443 Daly Ave., Ottawa, ON K1N 6H3
613-789-0468, Fax: 613-789-1218, ottawa@ottawa.polemb.net
www.ottawa.polemb.net
Artur Antoni Michalski, Counsellor, Political Affairs
Grazyna Sosnowska-Sikorska, First Counsellor
His Excellency Piotr Ogrodzinski, Ambassador

Portuguese Republic
Embassy of Portugal, 645 Island Park Dr., Ottawa, ON K1Y 0B8
613-729-0883, Fax: 613-729-4236, embportugal@embportugal-ottawa.org
www.embportugal-ottawa.org
Other information: Consular Section: Tel: 613/729-2270
Carlos Alberto Gomes da Silva, Counsellor, Social & Cultural Affairs
Luis Miguel Santos Moura, Counsellor, Economic Affairs
His Excellency Pedro Luis Baptista Moitinho de Almeida, Ambassador
Maria Joao Boavida Urbano, Counsellor

Principality of Andorra
Two United Nations Plaza, 25th Fl., New York, NY 10017 USA
212-750-8064, Fax: 212-750-6630,
Jelena Pia Comella, Minister & Chargé d'Affaires
Vacant, Ambassador

State of Qatar
Embassy of Qatar (to Canada), 2555 M Street NW, Washington, DC 20037-1305 USA
202-274-1600, Fax: 202-237-0061, ingo@qatarembassy.net
www.qatarembassy.net
His Excellency Ali Fahad F.A. Al-Hajri, Ambassador

Republic of Angola
189 Laurier Ave. East, Ottawa, ON K1N 6P1
613-234-1152, Fax: 613-234-1179, info@embangola-can.org
www.embangola-can.org
Mayuma T. Afonso Do Nascimento, Attaché
Manuel Espirito Santo, Attaché
Mario Augusto, Attaché, Press
Sofia Silvério Pegado da Silva, Minister Counselor & Chargé d'Affaires
Emanuel Fontes Pereira, Third Secretary, Consular Affairs
Eliseu Prata Silas Nunulo, First Secretary, Economic Affairs
Vacant, Ambassador

Republic of Armenia
7 Delaware Ave., Ottawa, ON K2P 0Z2
613-234-3710, Fax: 613-234-3444, embottawa@rogers.com
www.armembassycanada.ca
Arman Akopian, Minister-Counsellor & Chargé d'Affaires
Mikhayil Vardanian, Counsellor
Lilit Davtyan, Second Secretary & Consul
Vacant, Ambassador

Republic of Belarus
#600, 130 Albert St., Ottawa, ON K1P 5G4
613-233-9994, Fax: 613-233-8500, belamb@igs.net
Pavel Pustovoy, Counsellor & Chargé d'Affaires
Uladzimir Matusevich, First Secretary & Consul
Vacant, Ambassador

Republic of Georgia
Embassy of Georgia, 2209 Massachusetts Ave., NW, Washington, DC 20008 USA
202-387-2390, Fax: 202-387-0864, embgeorgiausa@yahoo.com
Malkhaz Mikeladze, Minister & Chargé d'Affaires
Beka Dvali, Senior Counsellor & Consul
His Excellency Vasil Sikharulidze, Ambassador

Republic of Malta
High Commission for Malta (to Canada); c/o Embassy of Malta, 2017 Connecticut Ave. NW, Washington, DC 20008 USA
202-462-3611, Fax: 202-387-5470, maltaembassy.washington@gov.mt
www.gov.mt
Christine Pace, First Secretary & Chargé d'Affaires
His Excellency Mark Amthony Miceli-Farrugia, High Commissioner

Republic of Moldova
2101 S St. NW, Washington, DC 20008 USA
202-667-1130, Fax: 202-667-1204, moldova@dgsys.com
His Excellency Nicolae Chirtoaca, Ambassador

Republic of Turkmenistan
2207 Massachussets Ave. NW, Washington, DC 20008 USA
202-588-1500, Fax: 202-588-0697,
Vacant, Ambassador

Republic of Uzbekistan
1746 Massachusetts Ave. NW, Washington, DC 20036 USA
202-887-5300, Fax: 202-293-6804, uzbekembassy@covad.net
www.uzbekistan.org
Bakhtiyorkhon Abdullakhanov, Counsellor, Trade & Economic Affairs
Iamatulla Fayzullaev, First Secretary
His Excellency Abdulaziz Kamilov, Ambassador

Romania
Embassy of Romania, 655 Rideau St., Ottawa, ON K1N 6A3
613-789-3709, Fax: 613-789-4365, romania@romanian-embassy.com
www.ampli2de.com/embassy/ottawa_en.php
Aurelian Cretu, Minister-Counsellor, Consular Affairs
Dragos Viorel Radu Tigau, Counsellor & Deputy Head of Mission, Political Affairs
Petre Andrei, Counsellor, Economic Affairs
George Sorin Zaharia, First Secretary, Political Affairs
Danut Cristian Matei, Counsellor, Press & Cultural Affairs
Col. Marius Gabriel Safta, Defence, Military, Naval & Air Attaché
Her Excellency Elena Stefoi, Ambassador

Russian Federation
Embassy of the Russian Federation, 285 Charlotte St., Ottawa, ON K1N 8L5
613-235-4341, Fax: 613-236-6342, rusemb@intranet.ca
www.russianembassy.net
Alexander Komarov, Counsellor
Valery Chumakov, Counsellor
His Excellency Georgy Mamedov, Ambassador
Sergey Petrov, Minister-Counsellor
Nikolay Orekhov, Counsellor

Republic of Rwanda
121 Sherwood Dr., Ottawa, ON K1Y 3V1
613-569-5420, Fax: 613-569-5421, generalinfo@ambarwaottawa.ca
www.ambarwaottawa.ca
Déo Nkusi, First Counsellor
Her Excellency Edda Mukabagwiza, Ambassador

Saint Kitts & Nevis
See: Organization of the Eastern Caribbean Stat

Saint Lucia
See: Organization of the Eastern Caribbean Stat

Saint Vincent & the Grenadines
See: Organization of the Eastern Caribbean Stat

Samoa
#400J, 800 Second Ave., New York, NY 10017 USA
212-599-6196, Fax: 212-599-0797, samoa@un.int
His Excellency Ali'ioaiga Feturi Elisaia, High Commissioner

Democratic Republic of Sao Tomé & Principe
1211 Conneticut Ave., NW Suite 300, Washington, DC 20036 USA
202-775-2075, Fax: 202-775-2077,
Ovidio Manuel Barbosa Pequeno, Ambassador
Domingos Ferreira, First Secretary

Kingdom of Saudi Arabia
Royal Embassy of Saudi Arabia, 201 Sussex Dr., Ottawa, ON K1N 1K6
613-237-4100, Fax: 613-237-0567,
Fouad M.F. Shukrey, First Secretary
Abdullah Saleh Al Awwad, Counsellor & Chargé d'Affaires
Vacant, Ambassador

Republic of Senegal
Embassy of Senegal, 57 Marlborough Ave., Ottawa, ON K1N 8E8
613-238-6392, Fax: 613-238-2695, ambassn@sympatico.ca
Lamine Lo, Second Counsellor
Daouda Ba, First Counsellor
His Excellency Issakha Mbacke, Ambassador
Mamadou Saliou Diouf, Minister-Counsellor

Serbia
See: Serbia & Montenegro 17 Blackburn Ave., Ottawa, ON K1N 8A2 Canada 613-233-6289, Fax: 613-233-7850,
Mr. Djordje Ciklovan, Minister-Counsellor & Chargé d'Affaires
Vacant, Ambassador

Republic of Seychelles
High Commission for Seychelles (to Canada), #400C, 800 Second Ave., New York, NY 10017 USA
212-972-1785, Fax: 212-972-1786, seychelles@un.int
His Excellency Roland Jean Jumeau, High Commissioner

Republic of Sierra Leone
High Commission for Sierra Leone (to Canada), 1701 - 19th St. NW, Washington, DC 20009 USA
202-939-9261, Fax: 202-483-1793, slehoc@starpower.net
Hassan Mohamed Conteh, Minister-Counsellor
Sheku Mesali, First Secretary
His Excellency Bockari Kortu Stevens, High Commissioner

Republic of Singapore
c/o Permanent Mission of the Republic of Singapore to the UN, 231 East 51st St., New York, NY 10022 USA
212-826-0840, Fax: 212-826-2964,
His Excellency Yong Guan Koh, High Commissioner
Syed Muhammad Raziff Aljunied, Counsellor

Slovak Republic / Slovenská Republika
Embassy of the Slovak Republic, 50 Rideau Terrace, Ottawa, ON K1M 2A1
613-749-4442, Fax: 613-749-4989, slovakemb@sprint.ca
www.ottawa.mfa.sk
Viera Ruzekova, Counsellor
Ladislav Babcan, Third Secretary
Rastislav Puchala, Third Secretary, Consular Affairs
His Excellency Stanislav Opiela, Ambassador

Republic of Slovenia
Embassy of Slovenia, #2200, 150 Metcalfe St., Ottawa, ON K2P 1P1
613-565-5781, Fax: 613-565-5783, vot@gov.si
www.gov.si/mzz/dkp/vot/eng
His Excellency Tomaz Kunstelj, Ambassador
Boris Jelovsek, Counsellor
Barbara Susnik, First Secretary

Solomon Islands
High Commission c/o Permanent Mission to the U.N., #400L, 800 - 2 Ave., New York, NY 10017 USA
212-599-6192, Fax: 212-661-8925,
His Excellency Collin David Beck, High Commissioner

Republic of South Africa
High Commission for South Africa, 15 Sussex Dr., Ottawa, ON K1M 1M8
613-744-0330, Fax: 613-741-1639, rsafrica@sympatico.ca
www.southafrica-canada.ca
Christina Louisa Britz, First Secretary, Administration & Consular Affairs
Nowetu Ethel Luti, Counsellor & Chargé d'Affaires
Abraham Sokhaya Nkomo, High Commissioner

Kingdom of Spain
Embassy of Spain, 74 Stanley Ave., Ottawa, ON K1M 1P4
613-747-2252, 613-236-0409, Fax: 613-744-1224, Fax: 613-563-2849, embespca@mail.mae.es
Enrique Fanjul Martin, Counsellor, Economic & Commercial Affairs
Antonio Torres-Dulce Ruiz, Minister-Counsellor
His Excellency Eudaldo Mirapeix, Ambassador Baron of Abella

Democratic Socialist Republic of Sri Lanka
High Commission of the Democratic Socialist Republic of Sri Lanka, #1204, 333 Laurier Ave. West, Ottawa, ON K1P 1C1
613-233-8449, Fax: 613-238-8448, slhcit@rogers.com
www.srilankahcottawa.org
Susiri Kumararatne Raigala D.L., Minister, Commercial & Economics
His Excellency Dayananda Rupasoma Perera, High Commissioner

Republic of The Sudan
Embassy of The Sudan, 354 Stewart St., Ottawa, ON K1N 6K8
613-235-4000, Fax: 613-235-6880, sudanembassy-canada@rogers.com
www.sudanembassy.ca
Asim Mohamed Ali Mukhtar Ibrahim, Minister
His Excellency Dr. Faiza Hassan Taha Armousa, Ambassador
Adil Yousif Omer Banaga, Minister

Republic of Suriname
Embassy of Suriname (to Canada), Van Ness Center, #460, 4301 Connecticut Ave. NW, Washington, DC 20008 USA
202-244-7488, Fax: 202-244-5878, embsur@erols.com
His Excellency Jacques Ruben Constantijn Kross, Ambassador

Kingdom of Swaziland
High Commission for Swaziland, 1712 New Hampshire, Washington, DC 20009 USA
202-234-5002, Fax: 202-234-8254,
www.magma.ca/~mali/swaziland
His Excellency Ephraim Mandlenkosi M. Hlophe, High Commissioner

Embassy of Sweden
Embassy of Sweden, 377 Dalhousie St., Ottawa, ON K1N 9N8
613-244-8200, Fax: 613-241-2277, sweden.ottawa@foreign.ministry.se
www.swedishembassy.ca
Her Excellency Ingrid Iremark, Ambassador
Pontus Melander, Counsellor

Switzerland
Embassy of Switzerland, 5 Marlborough Ave., Ottawa, ON K1N 8E6
613-235-1837, Fax: 613-563-1394, vertretung@ott.rep.admin.ch
www.eda.admin.ch/canada
Claude Charles Wild, Minister
Jean Philippe Praz, First Secretary
His Excellency Werner Baumann, Ambassador

Syrian Arab Republic
Embassy of Syria (to Canada), 46 Cartier St., Ottawa, ON K2P 1J3
613-569-5556, Fax: 613-569-3800, syrianembassy@on.aibn.com
www.syrianembassy.ca
Bashar Safiey, Second Secretary
Mounzer Ahmad, Third Secretary
His Excellency Jamil Sakr, Ambassador

Tanzania
High Commission of the United Republic of Tanzania, 50 Range Rd., Ottawa, ON K1N 8J4
613-232-1500, Fax: 613-232-5184, tzottawa@synapse.net
Dora Msechu, Minister
Richard Tibandebage, Minister
His Excellency Peter Allan Kallaghe, High Commissioner

Kingdom of Thailand
Royal Thai Embassy, 180 Island Park Dr., Ottawa, ON K1Y 0A2
613-722-4444, Fax: 613-722-6624, thaiott@magma.ca
www.magma.ca/~thaiott/mainpage.htm
Ruengdej Mahasaranond, Minister & Chargé d'Affaires
Chatchai Viriyavejakul, First Secretary
Montri Kittiwangchai, Minister-Counsellor
Walaiporn Pitawanik, Second Secretary
Vacant, Ambassador

Republic of Togo
Embassy of Togo, 12 Range Rd., Ottawa, ON K1N 8J3
613-238-5916, Fax: 613-235-6425,
His Ecxellency Bawoumondom Amelete, Ambassador

Republic of Trinidad & Tobago
High Commission for Trinidad & Tobago, 200 First Ave., 3rd Fl., Ottawa, ON K1S 2G6
613-232-2418, Fax: 613-232-4349, ottawa@ttmissions.com
www.ttmissions.com
Her Excellency Camille Rosemarie Robinson-Regis, High Commissioner
Garth Andrew Lamsee, First Secretary

Republic of Tunisia
Embassy of Tunisia, 515 O'Connor St., Ottawa, ON K1S 3P8
613-237-0330, Fax: 613-237-7939, aottawa@comnet.ca
Slaheddine Ben Mahmoud, Minister-Counsellor
Mohamed Elloumi, Counsellor
His Excellency Mouldi Sakri, Ambassador

Republic of Turkey
Embassy of Turkey, 197 Wurtemburg St., Ottawa, ON K1N 8L9
613-789-4044, Fax: 613-789-3442, turkishottawa@mfa.gov.tr
turkishembassy.com
Other information: Commercial Section: 613/789-2090; Fax: 613/789-2306
Turgul Biltekin, First Secretary
Yonet Can Tezel, Counsellor
Gulcan Akoguz Karagoz, Counsellor, Commercial Affairs
His Excellency Merih Rafet Akgunay, Ambassador

Republic of Uganda
High Commission for Uganda, 231 Cobourg St., Ottawa, ON K1N 8J2
613-789-7797, Fax: 613-789-8909, uhc@ugandahighcommission.com
www.ugandahighcommission.com
Joseph Kiiza Kahigwa, Deputy High Commissioner
Berti Kawooya, Counsellor
His Excellency George Marino Abola, High Commissioner

Republic of Ukraine
Embassy of Ukraine, 310 Somerset St. West, Ottawa, ON K2P 0J9
613-230-2961, 613/230-8015, Fax: 613-230-2400, Fax: 613/230-2655, emb_ca@ukremb.ca
www.ukremb.ca
Mykola Kryzhanovskyi, Counsellor, Trade & Economic Affairs
Vadym Prystaiko, Counsellor & Chargé d'Affaires
His Excellency Ihor Ostash, Ambassador

United Arab Emirates
Embassy of the United Arab Emirates, World Exhange Plaza, #1800, 45 O'Connor St., Ottawa, ON K1P 1A4
613-565-7272, Fax: 613-565-8007, safara@uae-embassy.com
www.uae-embassy.com
His Excellency Mohamed Abdulla Alghafli, Ambassador

United Kingdom of Great Britain
British High Commission, 80 Elgin St., Ottawa, ON K1P 5K7
613-237-1530, Fax: 613-237-7980, generalenquiries@britainincanada.org
www.britishhighcommission.gov.uk
His Excellency Anthony Joyce Cary, High Commissioner
Julian Evans, Deputy High Commissioner
Martin Hill, Counsellor, Economic, Science & Trade
Clive Newell, Counsellor, Political Affairs

United States of America
Embassy of USA, PO Box 866 B, 490 Sussex Dr., Ottawa, ON K1P 5T1
613-238-5335, 613/238-5335, Fax: 613-688-3088, Fax: 613/688-3032,
Ambassador pending confirmation as of September 2009
Brian Flora, Minister-Counsellor, Political Affairs
Brian Jeffery Mohler, Minister-Counsellor, Economic Affairs
Thomas Lee Boam, Minister-Counsellor, Foreign Commercial Affairs
Timothy Edward Roddy, Minister-Counsellor
His Excellency David Jacobson, Ambassador
John S. Dickson, Minister

Oriental Republic of Uruguay
Embassy of Uruguay, #1905, 130 Albert St., Ottawa, ON K1P 5G4
613-234-2727, Fax: 613-233-4670, embassy@embassyofuruguay.ca
www.embassyofuruguay.ca
Eduardo Bouzout Vignoli, Minister-Counsellor
His Excellency Enrique Juanlo Delgado Genta, Ambassador

Holy See
Apostolic Nunciature, 724 Manor Ave., Rockcliffe Park, Ottawa, ON K1M 0E3
613-746-4914, Fax: 613-746-4786, apostolic.nunciature@rogers.com
Monsignor Michael F. Crotty, First Secretary
His Excellency The Most Re Luigi Ventura, Apostolic Nuncio

Republic of Venezuela
Embassy of Venezuela, 32 Range Rd., Ottawa, ON K1N 8J4
613-235-5151, Fax: 613-235-3205, info.canada@misionvenezuela.org
www.misionvenezuela.org
Vacant, Ambassador

Socialist Republic of Vietnam
Embassy of Vietnam, 470 Wilbrod St., Ottawa, ON K1N 6M8
613-236-0772, Fax: 613-236-2704, vietem@istar.ca
Ngoc Canh Pham, Counsellor, Commercial
Hoang Le Huy, Minister-Counsellor & Deputy Head of Mission
His Excellency Duc Hung Nguyen, Ambassador

Republic of Yemen
Embassy of the Republic of Yemen, 54 Chamberlain Ave., Ottawa, ON K1S 1V9
613-729-6627, Fax: 613-729-8915,
Farook Mohamed Saeed Shibani, Minister
His Excellency Khaled Mahfoudh Bahah, Ambassador

Republic of Zambia
High Commission for Zambia (to Canada), #205, 151 Slater St., Ottawa, ON K1B 5H3
613-232-4400, Fax: 613-232-4410, embzambia@aol.com
Lubasi Nyambe, First Secretary, Economic Affairs
His Excellency David Clifford Saviye, High Commissioner

Republic of Zimbabwe
Embassy for the Republic of Zimbabwe, 332 Somerset St. West, Ottawa, ON K2P 0J9
613-421-2824, Fax: 613-422-7403, zimembassy@bellnet.ca
www.zimbabweembassy.ca
Bornway Mwanyara Chiripanhura, Counsellor
Her Excellency Florence Zano Chideya, Ambassador
Makumbe Makambwa, Counsellor

Canadian Diplomatic & Consular Representatives Abroad

Islamic State of Afghanistan
Canadian Embassy, House 256, Street 15, Wazir-Akbar-Khan, Kabul, Afghanistan
93-0-799-742-800, Fax: 93-0-799-742-805, Kabul@international.gc.ca
www.canada-afghanistan.gc.ca
J. Goodings, First Secretary, Development
E. Baldwin-Jones, Counsellor, Political
K. Ursu, Consul
William Crosbie, Ambassador

Republic of Albania
See: Italian Republic

People's Democratic Republic of Algeria
Canadian Embassy, PO Box 48 , Alger-Gare, 16035 Algeria
011-213-7008-3000, Fax: 011-213-7008-3070, alger@international.gc.ca
www.international.gc.ca/world/embassies/algeri a/
E. Mercier, First Secretary & Consul
Kristine Randall, Second Secretary (Commercial & Development), Trade Commissio, Environmental Industries
P. Parisot, Ambassador
A. Dubois, Counsellor, Commercial

Principality of Andorra
See: Kingdom of Spain

People's Republic of Angola
See: Republic of Zimbabwe

Anguilla
See: Barbados

Antigua & Barbuda
See: Barbados

Argentine Republic
Canadian Embassy, Casilla de Correo 1598, Correa Central, Buenos Aires, C1000WAP Argentine
011-54-11-4808-1000, Fax: 011-54-11-4808-111, bairs-webmail@international.gc.ca
www.buenosaires.gc.ca
R. Miller, Counsellor, Commercial
T. Toung, Counsellor, Development
Paula Solari, Trade Commissioner, Environmental Industries
T. Martin, Ambassador
D. Graham, Counsellor

Republic of Armenia
See: Russian Federation

Aruba
See: Republic of Venezuela

Commonwealth of Australia
Canadian High Commission, Commonwealth Ave., Canberra, ACT 2600 Australia
61-2-6270-4000, Fax: 61-2-6270-3585, cnbra@international.gc.ca
www.canada.org.au
K. Madan, Counsellor, Commercial
Sarah Powles, Trade Commissioner
Ilsa Stuart-Muirk, Trade Commissioner
Michael Leir, High Commissioner
R. Cremonese, Deputy High Commissioner
D. Menzies-McVey, Counsellor, Political

Republic of Austria
Canadian Embassy, Laurenzerberg 2, Vienna, A-1010 Austria
43-1-531-38-3321, Fax: 43-1-531-38-3910, vienn@international.gc.ca
www.dfait-maeci.gc.ca/canadaeurope/austria
Roland Rossi, Trade Commissioner, Environmental Industries, roland.rossi@international.gc.ca
P. Hay, Counsellor, Commercial
Marie Gervais-Vidricaire, Ambassador
S. Coutts, Counsellor, Political
N. Smolynec, Counsellor, Immigration

Republic of Azerbaijan
See: Republic of Turkey

Commonwealth of the Bahamas
See: Jamaica

State of Bahrain
See: Kingdom of Saudi Arabia

People's Republic of Bangladesh
Canadian High Commission, GPO Box 569, Dhaka, 1212 Bangladesh
88-2-988-7091, Fax: 88-2-882-3043, dhaka@international.gc.ca
www.bangladesh.gc.ca
Mortoza Tarafder, Sr. Trade Commissioner, Environmental Industries, mortoza.tarafder@international.gc.ca
Robert McDougall, High Commissioner
J. Sebhatu, First Secretary, Development

Barbados
Canadian High Commission, PO Box 404 , Bridgetown, Barbados
246-429-3550, Fax: 246-429-3780, bdgtn@international.gc.ca
D. Holland, Counsellor
Tammy Griffith, Trade Commissioner, Environmental Industries
D. Smyl, Second Secretary, Administration
J. Desjardins, Counsellor, Commercial
Ruth Archibald, High Commissioner

Republic of Belarus
See: Republic of Poland

Kingdom of Belgium
Canadian Embassy, 2, av de Tervuren, Brussels, 1040 Belgium
32-2-741-0611, Fax: 32-2-741-0643, bru@international.gc.ca
www.ambassade-canada.be
A. Vary, Counsellor, Commercial
Fabienne De Kimpe, Trade Commissioner, Environmental Industries, fabienne.de-kimpe@international.gc.ca
F. LaRochelle, Counsellor
L. de Lorimier, Ambassador
L. Sustersich, Counsellor (Administration) & Consul

Belize
See: Republic of Guatemala

Republic of Benin
See: Republic of Ivory Coast

Bermuda
See: United States of America c/o New York City Office,

Republic of Bolivia
See: Republic of Peru

Bosnia & Herzegovina
See: Hungary
P. Paproski, Counsellor, Technical Assistance
B. Steen, First Secretary, Development
D. Kelly, Second Secretary & Consul
David Hutchings, Ambassador

Republic of Botswana
See: Republic of Zimbabwe

Federative Republic of Brazil
Canadian Embassy, SES-Av. das Naçes - Qd. 803 - Lote 16, Brasilia, D.F., 70410-900 Brazil
55-61-424-5400, Fax: 55-61-424-5490, brsla@international.gc.ca
www.canadainternational.gc.ca/brazil/
Jillian Senkiw, Third Secretary & Trade Commissioner, Environmental Industries, jillian.senkiw@international.gc.ca
K. McDonald, Minister-Counseller, Political
F. Lafond, Counsellor, Commercial
R. Beaulieu, Counsellor, Development
P. Hunt, Ambassador
R. Siwak, Counsellor (Administration) & Consul

British Virgin Islands
See: Barbados

Brunei Darussalam
Canadian High Commission, PO Box 2808 , Bandar Seri Begawan, BS8675 Brunei Darussalam
673-2-220-043, Fax: 673-2-220-040, bsbgn@international.gc.ca
www.dfait-maeci.gc.ca/brunei
Celestina Leong, Trade Commissioner, celestina.leong@international.gc.ca
Wendell Sanford, High Commissioner
Peter Chen, Trade Commissioner, peter.chen@international.gc.ca

Republic of Bulgaria
See: Republic of Romania c/o Republic of Romania, Consulate of Canada, 9, Moskovska str., Sofia, Bulgaria (011-359-2)969-9719, Fax: (011-359-2)981-6081, bucst-td@international.gc.ca
Magdalena Goranova, Trade Commissioner, Environmental Industries

Burkina-Faso
Canadian Embassy, PO Box 548, Ouagadugou 01, Kadiogo, Burkina-Faso
226-50-31-18-94, Fax: 226-50-31-19-00, ouaga@international.gc.ca
Jules Savaria, Ambassador

Republic of Burundi
See: Republic of Kenya

Kingdom of Cambodia
See: Thailand

Republic of Cameroon
Canadian High Commission, Immeuble SCI-TOM (formerly Stamatiades), PO Box 572 , Yaoundé, Cameroon
011-237-2223-2311, Fax: 011-237-2222-1090, yunde@international.gc.ca
Gillian Goodwin, Management Consular Officer
Jude Bijingsi, Trade Commissioner, Environmental Industries, jude.bijingsi@international.gc.ca
Jean Pierre Lavoie, High Commissioner
G. Mercier, Counsellor, Development

Republic of Cape Verde
See: Republic of Senegal

Cayman Islands
See: Jamaica

Central African Republic
See: Republic of Cameroon

Republic of Chad
See: Republic of Cameroon

Republic of Chile
Canadian Embassy, Cassilla 139, Correo 10, Santiago, Chile
56-2-652-3800, Fax: 56-2-652-3912, stago@international.gc.ca
www.chile.gc.ca
Margot Edwards, Trade Commissioner, Environmental Industries
J. Kimmell, Counsellor (Admimistration) & Consul
P. Furesz, Counsellor, Commercial
S. Fountain Smith, Ambassador
H. Laverdiere, Counsellor, Political/Economic
J. Jonk, Counsellor, Immigration

People's Republic of China
Canadian Embassy, 19 Dong Zhi Men Wai St., Chao Yang Dist., Beijing, 100600 China
011-86-10-5139-4000, Fax: 011-86-10-5139-4454, bejing@international.gc.ca
www.beijing.gc.ca
T. Khan, Counsellor, Development
S. Frank, Minister-Counsellor
K. Lewis, Minister, Commercial
Owen Teo, Senior Trade Commissioner, Environmental Industries
David Mulroney, Ambassador
J. Nankivell, Minister
M. Kruger, Minister-Counsellor

Republic of Colombia
Canadian Embassy, Apartado Aereo 110067, Bogota, Colombia
57-1-657-9800, Fax: 57-1-657-9912, bgota@international.gc.ca
www.bogota.gc.ca
G. Salesse, Counsellor
Claudia Paola Gutierrez Chaves, Trade Commissioner
J. Tabah, Counsellor, Development
G. des Rivières, Ambassador
W. Farrell, Counsellor, Immigration
David Smarth, Counsellor (Adminitration) & Consul

Islamic Federal Republic of the Comoros
See: United Republic of Tanzania

Democratic Republic of Congo
Canadian Embassy to the Democratic Republic of Congo, PO Box 8341 , Kinshasa, Democratic Republic of Congo
243-89895-0310, Fax: 243-81301-6515, knsha@international.gc.ca
www.dfait-maeci.gc.ca/world/embassies/drc/
J.C. Mailhot, Counsellor, Development
J. Crôteau, Counsellor & Consul
G. Goodwin, Counsellor (Administration) & Consul
S.A. Johnson, Ambassador

Republic of Costa Rica
Canadian Embassy, Apartado Postal 351-1007 Centro Colon, San José, Costa Rica
506-2242-4400, Fax: 506-2242-4410, sjcra@international.gc.ca
www.costarica.gc.ca
Adolfo Quesada, Trade Commissioner, Environmental Industries, adolfo.quesada@international.gc.ca
S. Veilleux, First Secretary, Commercial
Julia McNeill, Counsellor (Administration) & Consul

N. Reeder, Ambassador
S. Hughes, Counsellor

Republic of Croatia
Prilaz Gjure Dezelica #4, Zagreb, 10 000 Croatia
385-1-488-1200, Fax: 385-1-488-1230, zagrb@international.gc.ca
Synthia Dodig, Trade Commissioner, Environmental Industries, synthia.dodig@international.gc.ca
Claude Demers, First Secretary
Thomas Marr, Ambassador

Republic of Cuba
Canadian Embassy, Calle 30, No. 518, Esquina 7a, Miramar, Havana, Cuba
53-7-204-2516, Fax: 53-7-204-9772, havan@international.gc.ca
www.dfait-maeci.gc.ca/cuba
Francisco Rodriguez, Trade Commissioner, Environmental Industries
M. Schroeter, Second Secretary, Commercial
J.P. Juneau, Ambassador
S. Cridland, First Secretary

Republic of Cyprus
See: Republic of Romania c/o Republic of Romania, PO Box 22125 , Consulate of Canada c/o The Canadian Embassy, Nicosia, 1517 Cyprus (00-357-22 775-508, Fax: (00-357-22) 779-905, info@consulcanada.com.cy
Rhea Pelides, Trade Commissioner, Environmental Industries

Czech Republic
Canadian Embassy, Muchova 6, 160 00, Prague, 6 Czech Republic
420 272 101 800, Fax: 420 272 101 898, prgue@dfait-maeci.gc.ca
www.canada.cz
M. Kahle, First Secretary (Administration) & Consul
Lyne-Marie Tremblay, Counsellor, Trade Policy
Jitka Hoskova, Trade Commissioner, Environmental Industries, jitka.hoskova@international.gc.ca
Y. Saint-Hilaire, Counsellor, Political/Economic
Michael Calcott, Ambassador

Kingdom of Denmark
Canadian Embassy, Kr. Bernikows Gade 1, Copenhagen, DK-1105 Denmark
45-33-48-32-00, Fax: 45-33-48-32-20, copen@international.gc.ca
www.denmark.gc.ca
His Excellency P. Lundy, Ambassador
Suzanne Steensen, Trade Commissioner, Environmental Industries

Republic of Djibouti
The Embassy of Canada, Place Lagarde, Djibouti, 1188 Djibouti

Commonwealth of Dominica
See: Barbados

Dominican Republic
Canadian Embassy, PO Box 2054 , Santo Domingo, Dominican Republic
809-685-1136, Fax: 809-682-2691, sdmgo@international.gc.ca
www.santodomingo.gc.ca
Vacant, Ambassador
Regis Batista-Lemaire, Trade Commissioner, Environmental Industries, regis.barista@international.gc.ca
N. Larocque, First Secretary (Administration) & Consul
H. Guillot, Counsellor, Commercial

Republic of Ecuador
PO Box 17-11-6512 , Quito, Ecuador
593-2-2455-499, Fax: 593-2-2277-672, quito@international.gc.ca
www.ecuador.gc.ca
Ryan Kuffner, Trade Commissioner, Environmental Industries
A. Shisko, Ambassador
A.M. Alvarez Tello, First Secretary (Administration) & Consul

Arab Republic of Egypt
Canadian Embassy, PO Box 1667 , Cairo, Egypt
(011 20 2) 2791-8700, Fax: (011 20 2) 2791-8860, cairo@international.gc.ca
www.dfait-maeci.gc.ca/cairo
F. de Kerckhove, Ambassador
Christopher Hull, Counsellor, Political
J. Broadbent, Counsellor, Commercial
P. Paproski, Counsellor, Development
J. Loo, Counsellor & Consul, Administration

Republic of El Salvador
Canadian Embassy, Edificio Centro Financiero Gigante, Alameda Roosevelt y 63 Avenida Sur, Nivel Lobby 2, Loca, San Salvador, El Salvador
503-2279-4655, Fax: 503-2279-0765,
ssal@international.gc.ca
www.sansalvador.gc.ca
Romeo Calderon, Trade Commissioner, Environmental Industries, romeo.calderon@international.gc.ca
Claire A. Poulin, Ambassador

England
See: United Kingdom of Great Britain & Northern

Republic of Equatorial Guinea
See: Gabonese Republic

Eritrea
See: Republic of Kenya

Republic of Estonia
Office of the Canadian Embassy, Toom Kooli 13, 2nd Fl., Tallinn, 0100 Estonia
372-627-3311, Fax: 372-627-3312,
tallinn@canada.ee
www.canada.ee
S. Heatherington, Ambassador (located in Riga, Latvia)

Federal Democratic Republic of Ethiopia
Canadian Embassy, PO Box 1130 , Addis Ababa, Ethiopia
251-1-71-30-22, Fax: 251-1-71-30-33,
addis@international.gc.ca
I. Hentic, First Secretary, Development
Richard Le Bars, Second Secretary & Vice-Consul & Sr. Trade Commissioner, Environmental Industries, richard.lebars@international.gc.ca
Vacant, Ambassador

European Union
The Mission of Canada to the European Union, 2, av de Tervuren, Brussels, 1040 Belgium
322-741-0660, Fax: 322-741-0629,
breu@international.gc.ca
www.canadainternational.gc.ca/eu-ue
Jean Saint-Jacques, Minister-Counsellor & Deputy Head of Mission
Y. Mondy, First Secretary, Trade Policy
Ross Hornby, Ambassador & Head of Mission
T. Milanetti, Counsellor, Agriculture

Faroe Islands
See: Kingdom of Denmark

Fiji
See: New Zealand

Republic of Finland
Canadian Embassy, PO Box 779 , Helsinki, FIN-00101 Finland
358-9-228-530, Fax: 358-9-601-060,
hsnki@international.gc.ca
www.canada.fi
Aline Lemieux-Lewin, Attaché & Vice-Consul
Seppo Vihersaari, Trade Commissioner, Environmental Industries, seppo.vihersaari@international.gc.ca
Scott Fraser, Ambassador

French Republic
Canadian Embassy, 35 - 37, av Montaigne, Paris, 75008 France
33-1-44-43-29-00, Fax: 33-1-44-43-29-99,
paris@international.gc.ca
www.international.gc.ca/canada-europa/france
S. Scrimshaw, Minister
Michel Charland, Counsellor, Commercial
Musto Mitha, Trade Commissioner, Environmental Industries
M. Lortie, Ambassador
Richard Têtu, Minister-Counsellor, Political
André Dubois, Minister-Counsellor

Gabonese Republic
Canadian Embassy, PO Box 4037 , Libreville, Gabon
241-73-73-54, Fax: 241-73-73-88,
lbrve@international.gc.ca
François Coté, Trade Commissioner, Environmental Industries, francois.cote@international.gc.ca
Louis Guay, Ambassador

Republic of the Gambia
See: Republic of Senegal

Republic of Georgia
See: Republic of Turkey

Federal Republic of Germany
Canadian Embassy, Leipziger Platz 17, Berlin, 10117 Germany
41-30-20-312-0, Fax: 49-30-20-312-590,
brlin@international.gc.ca
www.dfait-maeci.gc.ca/canada-europa/germany
Dr. Steffen Preusser, Trade Commissioner, Environmental Industries, steffen.preusser@international.gc.ca
J. Kur, Minister-Counsellor, Commecial/Economic
P. Boehm, Ambassador
H. Childs-Adams, Minister

Republic of Ghana
Canadian High Commission, PO Box 1639 , 42 Independence Ave., Accra, Ghana
233-21-211521, Fax: 233-21-211523,
accra@international.gc.ca
www.dfait-maeci.gc.ca/accra
Joseph Abanyin, Commercial Officer
W. McKenzie, Counsellor, Commercial
J. Tieman, Second Secretary, Immigration
D. Schemmer, Ambassador

Hellenic Republic
Canadian Embassy, 4 Ioannou Ghennadiou St., Athens, 115 21 Greece
30-210-727-3400, Fax: 30-210-727-3480,
athns@international.gc.ca
www.dfait-maeci.gc.ca/canadaeuropa/greece/
Marguerita Niada, Trade Commissioner, Environmental Industries, marguerita.niada@international.gc.ca
D. Tessier, Counsellor, Political
G. Ptolemy, First Secretary (Administration) & Consul
C. Rego, Second Secretary (Administration) & Vice-Consul
B. Young, Counsellor, Commercial
R. Wielgosz, Ambassador

Greenland
See: Kingdom of Denmark

Grenada
See: Barbados

Saint Vincent & the Grenadines
See: Barbados

Republic of Guatemala
Canadian Embassy, PO Box 400 , Guatemala City, 1001 Guatemala
502-2363-4348, Fax: 502-2365-1210,
gtmla@international.gc.ca
www.guatemala.gc.ca
D. Carriere, Counsellor, Immigration
M. Guibeault, Counsellor, Political
M. Veilleux, First Secretary, Development
L. McKechnie, Ambassador
Christine Luttmann, Trade Commissioner, Environmental Industries

Republic of Guinea-Bissau
See: Republic of Senegal

Republic of Guyana
Canadian High Commission, PO Box 10880 , Georgetown, Guyana
592-227-2081, Fax: 592-225-8380,
grgtn@international.gc.ca
www.guyana.gc.ca
A. Gibbons, Second Secretary, Development
C. Munante, First Secretary (Administration) & Consul
Vacant, High Commissioner
Lyris Primo, Commercial Officer, lyris.primo@international.gc.ca

Republic of Haiti
PO Box 826 , Port-au-Prince, Haiti
509-2249-9000, Fax: 509-2249-9920,
prnce@international.gc.ca
www.port-au-prince.gc.ca
F. Montour, Counsellor, Development
G. Rivard, Ambassador
Svend Holm, Counsellor (Administration) & Consul

Republic of Honduras
Canadian Embassy, PO Box 3552 , Tegucigalpa, Honduras
504-232-4551, Fax: 504-239-7769,
tglpa@international.gc.ca
www.canadainternational.gc.ca/costa_rica
N. Reeder, Ambassador

Republic of Hungary
Canadian Embassy, Ganz U. 12-14, Budapest, 10 1027 Hungary
36-1-392-3360, Fax: 36-1-392-3390,
bpest@international.gc.ca
www.canadaeuropa.gc.ca/hungary
Zsuzsanna Matyus, Trade Commissioner, Environmental Industries, zsuzsanna.matyus@international.gc.ca
R. Martin-Nielsen, Counsellor
E. Yu, Counsellor & Consul, Administration
Micheal Danagher, Counsellor, Commercial
P. Guimond, Ambassador

Republic of Iceland
PO Box 1510 , Reykjavik, 121 Iceland
354-575-6500, Fax: 354-575-6501,
rkjvk@international.gc.ca
www.canada.is
Alan Bones, Ambassador
Kristbjorg Agustsdottir, Trade Commissioner, Environmental Industries, kristbjorg.agustsdottir@international.gc

Republic of India
Canadian High Commission, PO Box 5208 , New Delhi, 110021 India
91-11-4178-2000, Fax: 91-11-4178-2020,
delhi@international.gc.ca
www.india.gc.ca
Viney Gupta, Trade Commissioner, Environmental Industries, delhi.commerce@international.gc.ca
K. Macartney, Deputy High Commissioner
S. Tuckey, Counsellor
P. Beaudoin, Minister-Counsellor
Joseph Caron, High Commissioner
T. Kernighan, Counsellor

Republic of Indonesia
Canadian Embassy, PO Box 8324/JKS.MP, Jakarta, 12083 Indonesia
62-21-2550-7800, Fax: 62-21-2550-7811,
jkrta@international.gc.ca
www.jakarta.gc.ca
Dian Martosoebroto, Trade Commissioner, Environmental Industries
P. McCullagh, Counsellor
G. Shantz, Counsellor, Commercial/Economic
Mackenzie Clugston, Ambassador

Islamic Republic of Iran
Canadian Embassy, 57 Shahid Sarafraz St., Dr. Beheshti Ave., Tehran, 15868 Iran
98-21-8873-2623, Fax: 98-21-8873-3202,
teran@international.gc.ca
www.dfait-maeci.gc.ca/world/embassies/iran/
R. Cooper, Counsellor, Political
D. Horak, First Secretary
D. Horak, Counsellor
Vacant, Ambassador

Republic of Iraq
See: Hashemite Kingdom of Jordan Iraq
Vacant, Ambassador

Republic of Ireland
Canadian Embassy, 7-8 Wilton Terrace, Dublin 2, Ireland
353-1-234-4000, Fax: 353-1-234-4101,
dubln@international.gc.ca
www.canada.ie
Gerry Mongey, Trade Commissioner, Environmental Industries, gerry.mongey@international.gc.ca
M. Leroux, Counsellor & Consul
Aslin Unlusoy, Trade Commissioner
Richard Philippe, First Secretary, Commercial
P. Binns, Ambassador

State of Israel
Canadian Embassy, PO Box 9442 , 3 Nirim St., 4th Fl., Tel Aviv, 67060 Israel
011-972-3-636-3300, Fax: 011-972-3-636-3380,
taviv@international.gc.ca
www.dfait-maeci.gc.ca/telaviv/
Mona Ashkar, Trade Commissioner, Environmental Industries
L. Helfand, Minister-Counsellor
W. Bazette, Counsellor, Immigration
R. Wassill, Counsellor, Communications & Culture
Jon Allen, Ambassador

Italian Republic
Canadian Embassy, Villa Grazioli, Via Salaria 243, Rome, 00199 Italy
39-06-85444-1, Fax: 39-06-85444-3947,
rome@international.gc.ca
www.canada.it
Patrizia Giuliotti, Trade Commissioner, Environmental Industries
T. Guttman, Minister-Counsellor
Khawar Nasim, Senior Trade Commissioner
J. Fox, Ambassador

Republic of Ivory Coast
Canadian Embassy, Immeuble Trade Centre, 23, av Nogues, 6th & 7th Fls., Le Plateau, Abidjan, 01 Ivory Coast
225-20 30 07 00, Fax: 225-20 30 07 20,
abdjn@international.gc.ca
www.dfait-maeci.gc.ca/abidjan
Jean-Claude Diplo, Trade Commissioner, Environmental Services, jean-claude.diplo@international.gc.ca
L. Jouvarne, Counsellor & Consul
Marie-Isabelle Massip, Ambassador

Jamaica
Canadian High Commission, PO Box 1500 , Kingston, 10 Jamaica
876/926-1500-7, Fax: 876/511-3494,
kngtn-cs@international.gc.ca
www.kingston.gc.ca
Yasmin Chong, Trade Commissioner, Environmental Industries, yasmin.chong@international.gc.ca
C. Duggan, Counsellor, Political/Economic
R. Merifield, Counsellor, Commercial
Vacant, High Commissioner

Hashemite Kingdom of Jordan
Canadian Embassy, PO Box 815403 , Amman, 11180 Jordan
962-6-520-3300, Fax: 962-6-520-3390,
amman@international.gc.ca
www.amman.gc.ca
Wafa Herzallah, Trade Commissioner, Environmental Industries, wafa.herzallah@international.gc.ca
E. Madueno, First Secretary, Development
M. Huber, Ambassador
S. Pomel, Counsellor

Republic of Kazakhstan
Canadian Embassy, 34 Karasai Batir St., Almaty, 050010 Kazakhstan
73-27-250-11-51, Fax: 73-27-258-24-93,
almat@international.tc.ca
www.infoexport.gc.ca/kz
David Mallette, Trade Commissioner
Mark Opgenorth, First Secretary
Maxim Berdichevsky, First Secretary & Vice-Consul
Guillaume Legros, First Secretary, Development
Jan Sheltinga, Counsellor, Development
Margaret Skok, Ambassador

Republic of Kenya
Canadian High Commission, PO Box 1013, Nairobi, 00621 Kenya
254-20-366-3000, Fax: 254-20-366-3900,
nrobi@international.gc.ca
www.nairobi.gc.ca
Dominique Collinge, Counsellor, Immigration
Stephen Weaver, Counsellor, Development
Ross Hynes, High Commissioner
D. Burns, Counsellor

Republic of Kiribati
See: New Zealand

Republic of Korea
Canadian Embassy, 16-1 Jeong-dong, Jung-gu, Seoul, Korea
82-2-3783-6000, Fax: 82-2-3783-6239,
seoul@international.gc.ca
www.korea.gc.ca
Yon-Ho Choi, Trade Commissioner, Environmental Industries, yon-ho.cho@international.gc.ca
Duane McMullen, Minister-Counsellor, Commercial
Ted Lipman, Ambassador

State of Kuwait
Canadian Embassy, PO Box 25281, Safat, Kuwait City, 13113 Kuwait
965-2256-3025, Fax: 965-2256-0173,
kwait@international.gc.ca
www.infoexport.gc.ca/kw
Martin Barratt, Sr. Trade Commissioner, martin.barratt@international.gc.ca
Reif Henry, Ambassador
G. Sanderson, Counsellor (Commercial) & Consul)

Kyrgyz Republic
See: Republic of Kazakhstan

Republic of Latvia
Canadian Embassy, 20/22 Baznicas St., 6th Fl., Riga, LV-1010 Latvia
371-6781-3945, Fax: 371-6781-3960,
riga@international.gc.ca
www.balticstates.gc.ca
Irena Cirpuse, Trade Commissioner, Environmental Industries, irena.cirpuse@international.gc.ca
Scott Heatherington, Ambassador

Lebanese Republic
Canadian Embassy, 43 Autostrade Jal El Dib, Beirut, Lebanon
961-4-713-900, Fax: 961-4-710-595,
berut@international.gc.ca
www.dfait-maeci.gc.ca/beirut/
G. Menard, Counsellor, Immigration
Grace Dib, Trade Commissioner, Environmental Industries, grace.dib@international.gc.ca
Vacant, Ambassador
C. Miranda, First Secretary, Commercial
D. Joly, Counsellor

Kingdom of Lesotho
See: Republic of South Africa

Republic of Liberia
See: Republic of Ivory Coast

Socialist People's Libyan Arab Jamahiriya
PO Box 93392 , Al-Fateh Tower, 7th Fl., Tripoli, Libya
218-21-335-1633, Fax: 218-21-335-1630,
trpli@international.gc.ca
www.dfait-maeci.gc.ca/world/embassies/libya/
Hesham Ganem, Trade Commissioner, Environmental Industries, hesham.ganem@international.gc.ca
S. McCardell, Ambassador
M.A. Jacques, Second Secretary (Administration) & Consul

Principality Liechtenstein
See: Swiss Confederation

Republic of Lithuania
Office of the Canadian Embassy, Business Center 2000, Jogailos St. 4, 7th Fl., Vilnius, LT-01116 Lithuania
370-5249-0950, Fax: 370-5249-7865,
vilnius@canada.lt
www.balticstates.gc.ca
Scott Heatherington, Ambassador (located in Riga)
H. Massoud, Chargé d'Affaires

Grand Duchy of Luxembourg
See: Kingdom of Belgium

Macao
See: People's Republic of China

Democratic Republic of Madagascar
Embassy of Canada, PO Box 1022 , Dar es Salaam, Tanzania

Republic of Malawi
See: Republic of Zambia

Federation of Malaysia
Canadian High Commission, PO Box 10990 , Kuala Lumpur, Malaysia
60-3-2718-3333, Fax: 60-3-2718-3399,
klmpr@international.gc.ca
http://www.international.gc.ca/missions/malays ia-malaisie/
Mia Yen, Second Secretary (Commercial) & Trade Commissioner, Environmental Industries, mia.yen@international.gc.ca
René-François Désamoré, Counsellor, Commercial
David Collins, High Commissioner

Republic of Maldives
See: Democratic Socialist Republic of Sri Lanka

Republic of Mali
Canadian Embassy, PO Box 198 , Route de Koulikoro, Immeuble séméga, Bamako, Mali
223-2021-2236, Fax: 223-2021-4362,
bmako@international.gc.ca
www.bamako.gc.ca
S. Tremblay, First Secretary & Consul
Ernest Akpoue, Trade Commissioner, Environmental Industries, ernest.akpoue@international.gc.ca
S. Marchand, First Secretary, Cooperation
Virginie Saint-Louis, Ambassador

Republic of Malta
See: Italian Republic

Marshall Islands
See: Republic of the Philippines

Islamic Republic of Mauritania
See: Kingdom of Morocco

Republic of Mauritius
See: Republic of South Africa

United Mexican States
Canadian Embassy, Apartado Postal 105-05, Mexico City, 11580 Mexico
52-57-24-7900, Fax: 52-57-24-7980,
mxico@international.gc.ca
www.mexico.gc.ca
Other information: Emergency: 1-800-703-2900
Paula Caldwell, Senior Trade Commissioner, mexico.commerce@international.gc.ca
Rosalba Cruz, Trade Commissioner, Environmental Industries, mexico.commerce@international.gc.ca
G. Manuge, Minister-Counsellor, Commercial
Guillermo Rishchynski, Ambassador
J. Herran-Lima, Deputy Head of Mission & Minister-Counsellor

Federated States of Micronesia
See: Republic of The Philippines

Republic of Moldova
See: Republic of Romania

Principality of Monaco
See: French Republic

Mongolian People's Republic
The Canadian Embassy, 2nd Fl., 8 Zovkhis building, Seoul St., Ulaanbaatar, 210628 Mongolia
A. Biolik, Ambassador

Montenegro
See: Serbia & Montenegro

Montserrat
See: Barbados

Kingdom of Morocco
Canadian Embassy, PO Box 709 , Rabat-Agdal, Morocco
212-37-68-74-00, Fax: 212-37-68-74-30,
rabat@international.gc.ca
www.rabat.gc.ca
V. Saint-Louis, Counsellor, Political & Consul
G. Tassé, Counsellor, Commercial
R. Gaulin, First Secretary & Consul
Asmae Amrouche, Trade Commissioner, Environmental Industries
Vacant, Ambassador
M. Floyd, Counsellor, Immigration

Republic of Mozambique
Canadian High Commission, PO Box 1578 , 1138, Kenneth Kaunda Ave., Maputo, Mozambique
258-21-492-623, Fax: 258-21-492-667,
mputo@international.gc.ca
R. Kerr, First Secretary & Consul
Lurdes Magneli, Trade Commissioner, Environmental Industries
Philip Baker, High Commissioner
K. Neufeld, Counsellor, Development

Union of Myanmar
See: Kingdom of Thailand

Republic of Namibia
See: Republic of South Africa

Nauru
See: Commonwealth of Australia c/o Canberra,

Kingdom of Nepal
Canadian Embassy to Nepal, c/o Canadian Cooperation Office, PO Box 4574 , Kathmandu, Nepal
977-1-441-5193, Fax: 977-1-441-0422,
cco@canadanepal.org
Joseph Caron, Ambassador (located in New Delhi, India)

Kingdom of the Netherlands
Canadian Embassy, Sophialaan 7, The Hague, 2514 JP The Netherlands
31-70-311-1600, Fax: 31-70-311-1620,
hague@international.gc.ca
www.canada.nl

G. Martindale, Counsellor
Judith Baguley, Trade Commissioner, Environmental Industries
Y. Saint-Hilaire, Counsellor, Economic
Ann Adcock-Hart, Counsellor (Administration) & Consul
J. Wall, Ambassador
P. Leduc, Counsellor

Netherlands Antilles
See: Republic of Venezuela

New Caledonia
See: Commonwealth of Australia

New Zealand
Canadian High Commission, PO Box 8047 , 125 The Terrace, Wellington, 6143 New Zealand
64-4-473-9577, Fax: 64-4-471-2082, wlgtn@international.gc.ca
www.wellington.gc.ca
P. Deacon, Counsellor
Caroline Chrétien, High Commissioner

Republic of Nicaragua
c/o Canadian Embassy, Apartado Postal 25, Managua, Nicaragua
505-268-0433, Fax: 505-268-0437, mngua@international.gc.ca
www.nicaragua.gc.ca
N. Reeder, Ambassador (located in Costa Rica)

Republic of Niger
Canadian Embassy, PO Box 362 , Niamey, Niger
227-753-686, Fax: 227-753-107, niamy@international.gc.ca
Michèle Lévesque, Ambassador (located in Côte d'Ivoire)

Federal Republic of Nigeria
Canadian High Commission, 15 Bobo St., Maitama, Abuja, Nigeria
234-9-413-9910, Fax: 234-9-413-9911, abuja@international.gc.ca
www.dfait-maeci.gc.ca/nigeria/
K. Garner, First Secretary, Political
Sylvia Koleva, Trade Commissioner, Environmental Industries, sylvia.koleva@international.gc.ca
Denis Kingsley, High Commissioner
M.E. Havlik, Counsellor & Consul
J. Bracken, Counsellor, Development

Northern Ireland
See: United Kingdom of Great Britain & Northern

Northern Marianas
See: Commonwealth of Australia

Kingdom of Norway
Canadian Embassy, Wergelandsveien 7, Oslo, 0244 Norway
47-2299-5300, Fax: 47-2299-5301, oslo@international.gc.ca
www.canada.no
John Winterbourne, Trade Commissioner, Environmental Industries, john.winterbourne@international.gc.ca
Georges Lemieux, Councellor, Commercial
John Hannaford, Ambassador
G. Norman, Councellor, Political

Sultanate of Oman
See: Kingdom of Saudi Arabia c/o The Canadian Embassy, PO Box 94321 , Riyad, 11693 Saudi Arabia

Islamic Republic of Pakistan
Canadian High Commission, PO Box 1042 , Islamabad, 44000 Pakistan
92-51-208-6000, Fax: 92-51-227-9188, isbad@internationl.gc.ca
M. Samper, Counsellor, Development
M. Denton, Counsellor, Commercial
B. Marshall, First Secretary, Immigration
Randolph Mank, High Commissioner
K. Roberts, Counsellor

Republic of Panama
Apartado Postal 0832-2446, Estafata World Trade Centre, Panama City, Panama
011-507-264-9731, Fax: 011-507-263-8083, panam@international.gc.ca
www.panama.gc.ca
J. Herran-Lima, Ambassador Designate
Luis Cedeno, Trade Commissioner, Environmental Industries, luis.cedeno@international.gc.ca

Papua New Guinea
See: Commonwealth of Australia Australia

Republic of Paraguay

Republic of Peru
Canadian Embassy, Calle Bolognesi 228, Miraflores, Lima, Peru
511-319-3200, Fax: 511-446-4912, lima@international.gc.ca
E. Jager, First Secretary, Commercial
Alexandra Laverdure, Trade Commissioner, Environmental Industries, lima.commerce@international.gc.ca
M. Friesen, First Secretary
S. Roy, Counsellor (Administration) & Consul
J.B. Parenteau, First Secretary, Cooperation
Richard Lecoq, Ambassador

Republic of the Philippines
PO Box 2098, Makati Central Post Office, Makati City, 1200 Philippines
63-2-857-9000, Fax: 63-2-843-1082, manil@international.gc.ca
www.dfait-maeci.gc.ca/manila/
Ramon Yazon, Trade Commissioner, Environmental Industries, ramon.yazon@international.gc.ca
A. Dugas, Counsellor (Administration) & Consul
E.R. Zeisler, Counsellor, Commercial
T. Carroll, Counsellor, Development
S. Rheault Kihara, Counsellor, Political/Economic
R. Desjardins, Ambassador

Republic of Poland
Canadian Embassy, ul. Jana Matejiki 1/5, Warsaw, 00-481 Poland
48-22-584-3100, Fax: 48-22-584-3192, wsaw@international.gc.ca
www.canada.pl
B. St-Jean, Counsellor, Political, Cultural & Academic Relations
S. Flamand-Hubert, Counsellor (Administration) & Consul
Ewa Gawron-Dobroczynska, Trade Commissioner, Environmental Industries
David Preston, Ambassador
Roger Bélanger, Counsellor, Trade
C. Bailey, Counsellor, Immigration

Portuguese Republic
Canadian Embassy, Avenida da Liberdade, 196-200, 3rd Fl., Lisbon, 1269-121 Portugal
351-21-316-4600, Fax: 351-21-316-4691, lsbon@international.gc.ca
www.portugal.gc.ca
Lyne Boulet, First Secretary (Administration) & Consul
L. Levasseur, First Secretary, Commercial
Carlos Lindo da Silva, Trade Commissioner, Environmental Industries
Anne-Marie Bourcier, Ambassador
C. Sheck, Counsellor, Political

Principe
See: Gabonese Republic

Puerto Rico
See: United States of America

State of Qatar
See: State of Kuwait

Republic of Palau
See: Republic of the Philippines

Republic of Romania
Canadian Embassy, 1-3 Tuberozelor Str., Bucharest, 011411 Romania
40-21-307-5000, Fax: 40-21-307-5010, bucst@international.gc.ca
www.dfait-maeci.gc.ca/bucharest
Octavian Bonea, Trade Commissioner, Environmental Industries
C. Lord, Counsellor, Immigration
P. Beaulne, Ambassador
D. McGregor, Counsellor, Commercial

Russian Federation
Canadian Embassy, 23 Starokonyushenny Pereulok, Moscow, 119002 Russian Federation
7-495-925-6000, Fax: 7-495-925-6025, mosco@international.gc.ca
Lilya Panova, Trade Commissioner, Environmental Industries, lilya.panova@international.gc.ca
Ralph Lysyshyn, Ambassador
J. Kur, Minister-Counsellor, Commercial
J. Morrison, Minister-Counsellor

Rwandese Republic
Canadian Embassy, PO Box 1117 , Kigali, Rwanda
250-573-210, Fax: 250-572-719, kgali@international.gc.ca
J. Fournier, Second Secretary, Development & Vice-Consul
Jim Wall, Ambassador (located in Kenya)

Saint Kitts & Nevis
See: Barbados

Saint Lucia
See: Barbados

Samoa
See: New Zealand

Republic of San Marino
See: Italian Republic Italy

Kingdom of Saudi Arabia
Canadian Embassy, PO Box 94321 , Riyadh, 11693 Saudi Arabia
966-1-488-2288, Fax: 966-1-488-1997, ryadh@international.gc.ca
Ursula Holland, Counsellor, Political
Mazen El-Khatib, Trade Commissioner, Environmental Industries, mazen.el-khatib@international.gc.ca
C. Andeel, Counsellor (Administration) & Consul
P. MacKinnon, Ambassador
Andreas Weichert, Minister-Counsellor, Commercial

Scotland
See: United Kingdom of Great Britain & Northern

Republic of Senegal
Canadian Embassy, PO Box 3373 , Dakar, Senegal
221-33-889-4700, Fax: 221-33-889-4720, dakar@international.gc.ca
www.dakar.gc.ca
Aminata Ly Faye, Trade Commissioner, Environmental Industries, aminata.ly@international.gc.ca
L. Minville, First Secretary, Development
J.P. Bolduc, Ambassador

Serbia
See: Serbia & Montenegro

Serbia & Montenegro
Canadian Embassy, Kneza Milosa 75, Belgrade, 11000 Serbia & Montenegro
381-11-306-3000, Fax: 381-11-306-3042, bgrad@international.gc.ca
www.serbia.gc.ca
K. Sooley, Counsellor (Administration) & Consul
B. Steen, Counsellor, Development
John Morrison, Ambassador

Republic of Seychelles
See: United Republic of Tanzania

Republic of Sierra Leone
See: Republic of Ivory Coast

Republic of Singapore
Canadian High Commission, PO Box 845 , Singapore, 901645 Singapore
65 68545900, Fax: 65 68545930, spore@international.gc.ca
www.dfait-maeci.gc.ca/singapore/
Fumiko Kitano, Second Secretary (Commercial) & Trade Commissioner
R. Borowyk, Counsellor, Commercial
J. Gobeil, Counsellor, Administration
David Sevigny, High Commissioner

Slovak Republic
Embassy of Canada, Mostova 2, Bratislava, 811 02 Slovak Republic
421-259-204-031, Fax: 421-254-434-227, brtsv@international.gc.ca
www.ocanada.sk
Ambassador resides in Prague, Czech Republic
M. Calcott, Ambassador

Republic of Slovenia
See: Republic of Hungary

Solomon Islands
See: Commonwealth of Australia

Somali Democratic Republic
See: Republic of Kenya

Republic of South Africa
Canadian High Commission, Private Bag X13, Hatfield, Pretoria, 0028 South Africa
27-12-422-3000, Fax: 27-12-422-3052,
pret@international.gc.ca
www.canada.co.za

G. Rent, Second Secretary
Col. R. Hatton, Counsellor
Adèle Dion, High Commissioner
P. Jamieson, First Secretary, Immigration

Kingdom of Spain
Canadian Embassy, Apartado 587, Madrid, 28080 Spain
34-9-423-3250, Fax: 34-9-423-3251,
mdrid@international.gc.ca
www.spain.gc.ca

S. Savage, Minister-Counsellor
M. Lebleu, Counsellor, Commercial
C. Munante, Counsellor (Administration) & Consul
Amaya Jauregui, Trade Commissioner, Environmental Industries
Graham Shantz, Ambassador

Democratic Socialist Republic of Sri Lanka
Canadian High Commission, PO Box 1006 , Colombo, 7 Sri Lanka
94-11-522-6232, Fax: 94-11-522-6299,
clmbo@international.gc.ca

Sanjeeva Sellahewe, Trade Commissioner, Environmental Industries, sanjeeva.sellahewe@international.gc.ca
R. Bedlington, Chargé d'Affaires
Angela Bogdan, High Commissioner
C. Parker, Counsellor, Development

Republic of The Sudan
Canadian Embassy, 29 Africa Rd., Block 56, Khartouom, 10503 Sudan
249-156-550-500, Fax: 249-156-550-501,
KHRM@international.gc.ca

S. Hanson, Chargé d'Affaires

Republic of Suriname
See: Republic of Guyana

Kingdom of Swaziland
See: Republic of South Africa

Kingdom of Sweden
Canadian Embassy, PO Box 16129, Stockholm, 103 23 Sweden
46-8-453-3000, Fax: 46-8-453-3016,
stkhm@international.gc.ca
www.canadaeuropa.gc.ca/sweden

M.A. Jacques, First Secretary & Consul
M. Siewecke, Counsellor, Commercial
Inga-Lill Olsson, Trade Commissioner, Environmental Industries
A. Volkoff, Ambassador
P. Low-Bédard, Counsellor

Swiss Confederation
Canadian Embassy, Kirchenfeldstrasse 88, Bern, CH-3005 Switzerland
41-31-357-3200, Fax: 41-31-357-3210,
bern@international.gc.ca
www.switzerland.gc.ca

Werner Naef, Trade Commissioner, Environmental Industries, werner.naef@international.gc.ca
C. Schwenger, Counsellor & Consul
Roberta Santi, Ambassador

Syrian Arab Republic
Canadian Embassy, PO Box 3394 , Damascus, Syria
963-11-611-6692, Fax: 963-11-611-4000,
dmcus@international.gc.ca
www.international.gc.ca/syria

Nidal Bitar, Trade Commissioner, Environmental Industries, nidal.bitar@international.gc.ca
M. Dupuis, Counsellor, Immigration
Glenn Davidson, Ambassador
C. Hull, Counsellor
Stéphane Beaulieu, Counsellor (Commercial) & Sr. Trade Commissioner, stephane.beaulieu@international.gc.ca

Taiwan
Canadian Trade Office, 365 Fu Hsing North Rd., 13th Fl., Taipei, 10483 Taiwan
886-2-2544-3000, Fax: 886-2-2544-3592,
taipei@international.gc.ca
www.canada.org.tw

Karen Huang, Sr. Commercial Officer, Trade
Francis Huot, Deputy Director
Ron MacIntosh, Executive Director
Stephanie Berlet, Deputy Director, Investment Promotion
J. Reeve, Director, General Relations
Vanessa Chen, Commercial Officer, Environmental Industries, vanessa.chen@international.gc.ca
S. McLuckie, Director, Visa

Republic of Tajikistan
See: Republic of Kazakhstan

United Republic of Tanzania
Canadian High Commission, PO Box 1022 , Dar-es-Salaam, Tanzania
255-22-216-3300, Fax: 255-22-211-6897,
dslam@international.gc.ca
www.dfait-maeci.gc.ca/tanzania

Noel Amos, Trade Commissioner, Environmental Industries, noel.amos@international.gc.ca
J. Moore, Counsellor, Development
R. Orr, Counsellor, Development
Janet Sidall, High Commissioner
S. Potter, Counsellor, Development

Kingdom of Thailand
Canadian Embassy, PO Box 2090 , Bangkok, 10501 Thailand
66-2-636-0540, Fax: 66-2-636-0566,
bngkk@international.gc.ca
www.thailand.gc.ca

Orawan Chandrangsu, Trade Commissioner, Environmental Industries
D. Yasui, Counsellor, Development
D. Danch, Counsellor (Administration) & Consul
R. Hoffmann, Ambassador
G. Goldhawk, Counsellor, Commercial

Republic of Togo
See: Republic of Ghana

Kingdom of Tonga
See: New Zealand

Republic of Trinidad & Tobago
Canadian High Commission, PO Box 1246 , Port of Spain, Trinidad
868-622-6232, Fax: 868-628-2581,
pspan@international.gc.ca
www.trinidadandtobago.gc.ca

Michaeline Narcisse, Trade Commissioner, Environmental Industries, michaeline.narcisse@international.gc.ca
F. Fournier, Counsellor, Commercial
C. Guimond, Counsellor, Immigration
Karen L. McDonald, High Commissioner

Republic of Tunisia
Canadian Embassy, PO Box 31, Tunis, 1002 Tunisia
216-71-104-000, Fax: 216-71-104-191,
tunis@international.gc.ca
www.dfait-maeci.gc.ca/tunisia

Lassaad Bourguiba, Trade Commissioner, Environmental Industries, lassaad.bourguiba@international.gc.ca
Peter Stulken, Counsellor, Commercial, peter.stulken@international.gc.ca
Jean Se@nécal, Management/Consular Officer, jean.senedal@international.gc.ca
Ariel Delouya, Ambassador

Republic of Turkey
Canadian Embassy, Cinnah Caddesi 58, Cankaya, Ankara, 06690 Turkey
90-312-409-2700, Fax: 90-312-312-409-2810,
ankra@international.gc.ca
www.dfait-maeci.gc.ca/canadaeuropa/turkey/menu -en.asp

Akin Kosetorunu, Trade Commissioner, Environmental Industries, akin.kosetorunu@international.gc.ca
J. Davison, Counsellor
M. Ward, First Secretary, Commercial
M. Bailey, Ambassador
D. Vaughan, Counsellor, Immigration

Turkmenistan
See: Republic of Turkey

Turks & Caicos Islands
See: Jamaica

Republic of Tuvalu
See: New Zealand

Republic of Uganda
See: Republic of Kenya

Ukraine
Canadian Embassy, 31 Yaroslaviv Val, Kyiv, 1901 Ukraine
380-44-590-3100, Fax: 380-44-590-3109,
kyiv@international.gc.ca
www.kyiv.gc.ca

George Grushchenko, Trade Commissioner
Valerie Sorel, Mission Consular Officer
Doris Wong, Counsellor, CIDA/Development
Yury Mardak, Trade Commissioner, Environmental Industries, yury.mardak@international.gc.ca
Daniel Caron, Ambassador
Michael Bates, Counsellor, Political/Economic

United Arab Emirates
The Canadian Embassy, PO Box 6970 , Abu Dhabi, United Arab Emirates
971-2-694-0300, Fax: 971-2-694-0399,
abdbi@international.gc.ca
www.uae.gc.ca

Sara Hradecky, Ambassador
P. Bedard, Counsellor (Administration) & Consul
Imad Arafat, Trade Commissioner, Environmental Industries, imad.arafat@international.gc.ca
M. Lazaruk, Counsellor, Commercial

United Kingdom of Great Britain & Northern Ireland
Canadian High Commission, MacDonald House, One Grosvenor Sq., London, W1K 4AB United Kingdom
44-20-7258-6600, Fax: 44-20-7258-6384,
ldn@international.gc.ca
www.london.gc.ca

C. Boucher, Deputy High Commissioner
J. St-George, Minister, Commercial/Economic
A. Arnott, Minister-Counsellor, Immigration
Sushma Gera, Trade Commissioner, Environmental Industries
James Wright, High Commissioner
R. Fry, Minister-Counsellor, Political/Public Affairs

United States of America
Canadian Embassy, 501 Pennsylvannia Ave. NW, Washington, DC 20001 USA
202-682-1740, Fax: 202-682-7726,
wshdc@international.gc.ca
www.canadianembassy.org

His Excellency Gary Doer, Ambassador

Eastern Republic of Uruguay
Canadian Embassy, #102, Plaza Independencia 749, C.P. 11100, Montevideo, Uruguay
598-2-902-2030, Fax: 598-2-902-2029,
mvdeo@international.gc.ca
www.montevideo.gc.ca

C. Hardman, Second Secretary & Consul
Patricia Wilson, Trade Commissioner, Environmental Industries
A. Latulippe, Ambassador

Republic of Uzbekistan
See: Russian Federation

Republic of Vanuatu
See: Commonwealth of Australia

Holy See
Canadian Embassy, Via della Conciliazione 4/D, Rome, 00193 Italy
39-06-6830-7316, Fax: 39-06-6880-6283,
vatcn@international.gc.ca
www.dfait-maeci.gc.ca/canadaeuropa/holysee/

Jean Bourassa, Counsellor
Anne Leahy, Ambassador

Republic of Venezuela
Canadian Embassy, Apartado Postal 62302, Caracas, 1060A Venezuela
58-212-600-3000, Fax: 58-212-263-8326,
crcas@international.gc.ca
www.caracas.gc.ca

Guy Salesse, Trade Commissioner
Denise Keating, Counsellor (Administration) & Consul
Daniela Oyague, Trade Commissioner, Environmental Industries
Perry Calderwood, Ambassador

N. Morgan, First Secretary

Socialist Republic of Vietnam
Canadian Embassy, 31 Huong Vuong St., Hanoi, Vietnam
84-4-3734-5000, Fax: 84-4-3734-5049,
hanoi@international.gc.ca
www.vietnam.gc.ca
Dang-Anh Thu, Trade Commissioner, Environmental Industries, dang-anh.thu@international.gc.ca
M. Perras, Counsellor (Administration) & Consul
D. Horton, Ambassador
Pierre Delorme, Counsellor, Trade

Wales
See: United Kingdom of Great Britain & Northern

Republic of Yemen
See: Kingdom of Saudi Arabia

Republic of Zambia
Canadian High Commission, PO Box 31313 , Lusaka, 10101 Zambia
260-1-25-08-33, Fax: 260-1-25-41-76,
lsaka@international.gc.ca
www.international.gc.ca/world/embassies/zambia /
S. Landry, First Secretary & Consul
Solomon Milimbo, Trade Commissioner, Environmental Industries, solomon.milimbo@international.gc.ca
P.P. Perron, Acting High Commissioner
L. Rogers, First Secretary, Development

Republic of Zimbabwe
Canadian Embassy, PO Box 1430 , Harare, Zimbabwe
263-425-2181, Fax: 263-425-2186,
hrare@international.gc.ca
www.zimbabwe.gc.ca
N. Forfar, Second Secretary
M. Nyiramana, Counsellor, Development
Barbara Richardson, Ambassador
D. Langlois, Counsellor

Lobbyists

1323666 Ontario Inc
431 Roxborough Ave., Ottawa, ON K1M 0L3
Tel: 613-746-8849, *Fax:* 613-745-8950
Edmond Chiasson
echiasson@rogers.com

2037770 Ontario Inc
90 Shannon Rd, Mount Albert, ON L0G 1M0
Tel: 905-473-3418
Richard Ciano
rciano@campaignresearch.ca

2053891 Ontario Limited
 # 3, 49 Huron St., Collingwood, ON L9Y 1C5
Tel: 705-445-8540, *Fax:* 705-445-2681
Paul Bonwick
paul_bonwick@sympatico.ca

Alanco Inc
1550 Gordon St., Guelph, ON N1L 1C7
Tel: 519-546-3960
Frank Johansen
frank.johansen@alanco.ca

Apco Worldwide
#703 255 Albert St., Ottawa, ON K1P 6A9
Tel: 613-565-4242
Evan Zelikovitz
ezelikovitz@apcoworldwide.com

Asper Foundation
#1504, 201 Portage Ave., Winnipeg, MB R3B 3K6
Tel: 204-989-5538, *Fax:* 204-989-5536
Moses Levy
mlevy@aspergroup.com

Baker & Mckenzie LLP
#2100, 181 Bay St., P.O. Box 874, Toronto, ON M5J 2T3
Tel: 416-863-1221
Kevin Coon
kevin.b.coon@bakernet.com

Blake, Cassels & Graydon LLP
#2000, 45 O'connor St, Ottawa, ON K1P 1A4
Tel: 613-788-2200
Eric R. Elvidge

Borden Ladner Gervais LLP
Canterra Tower #1000, 400, 3rd Ave. SW, Calgary, AB T2P4H2
Tel: 403-232-9500, *Fax:* 403-266-1395
info@blgcanada.com
Ross D. Freeman

Borden Ladner Gervais LLP
#1200, 200 Burrard St., P.O. Box 48600, Vancouver, BC V7X 1T2
Tel: 604-687-5744, *Fax:* 604-687-1415
info@blgcanada.com
Bradley J. Freedman

Brown & Cohen Communications
321 Brooke Ave., Toronto, ON M5M 2L4
Tel: 416-484-1132x1
Howard Brown
howard@brown-cohen.com

Burrard Communications Inc
#200, 409 Granville St., Vancouver, BC
Tel: 604-619-1980, *Fax:* 604-689-0477
John Fraser
fraser@burrardcom.com

C & E Management Consulting
P.O. Box 972, Cheticamp, NS B0E 1H0
Tel: 902-224-1662
Chester Muise
chester.muise@ns.sympatico.ca

Campbell Strategies Inc.
95 Wellington St. West, Toronto, ON M5GJ 2N7
Tel: 416-368-7353
Paul Brown
paulb@campbellstrategies.com

Canadian Corporate Consultants Ltd
#1202, 10109- 106 St., Edmonton, AB T5J 3L7
Tel: 780-429-4488
Michael Fowler
cancorpavi@compusmart.ab.ca

Canadian Corporate Consultants Ltd
#250, 11331 Coppersmith Way, Richmond, BC V7A 5J9
Tel: 604-241-4420, *Fax:* 604-241-4419
Warren Stevenson
wstevenson@cancorp.com

Canadian Diamond Consultants Inc
2895 Old Montreal Road, Ottawa, ON K4C 1G2
Tel: 613-833-5499
c.d.c@rogers.com
Pierre Leblanc

Canwest Direction Ltd.
#1504, 201 Portage Ave., Winnipeg, MB R3B 8K6
Tel: 204-989-5525
Gail S. Asper
gasper@aspergroup.com

Capital Hill Group
#1540, 45 O'connor St., Ottawa, ON K1P 1A4
Tel: 613-235-0221, *Fax:* 613-235-9694
Sandra Graham

Capital Hill Group
#300, 66 Queen St., Ottawa, ON K1P 5C6
Tel: 613-235-0221, *Fax:* 613-235-9694
Steven Dover
sdover@capitalhill.ca

Capital Hill Group
1100 De La Gauchetiere Ouest, Bureau #C-23, Montreal, QC H3B 2S2
Tel: 514-844-5530x222
info@capitalhill.ca
Patrick Doyan

Carscallen Lockwood LLP
#1500, 407 - 2 St SW, Calgary, AB
Tel: 403-262-3775, *Fax:* 403-262- 295
Peter Hayvren

Cassels Brock & Blackwell LLP
Scotia Plaza #2100, 40 King St. West, Toronto, ON M5H 3C2
Tel: 416-869-5300
Terrance D. Hall
thall@casselsbrock.com

Cfn Consultants
#1502, 222 Queen St., Ottawa, ON K1P 5V9
Tel: 613-232-1576, *Fax:* 613-238-5519
Noel Bhumgara
nbhumgara@cfncon.com

Cg Management & Communications Inc
#200, 175 Commerce Valley Dr. West, Markham, ON L3T 7P6
Tel: 905-709-4424, *Fax:* 905-709-2664
Nancy Coldham
ekim@cggroup.com

Charles Milne & Company Inc
68 Bridle Path, Rr # 3, Guelph, ON N1H 6H9
Tel: 519-767-9062
Charles Milne
charles@sgci.com

Charman Broadcasting Policy Inc
47 Elke Dr, Nepean, ON K2J 2B9
Tel: 613-825-2770
Wayne Charman
wcharman@rogers.com

Chipeur Advocates
 # 2380, 440- 2 Ave. SW, Calgary, AB T2P 5E9
Tel: 403-537-6536
Gerald Chipeur
gerald@chipeur.com

Civica Inc
45 O'connor St., Ottawa, ON K1P 1A4
Tel: 613-232-0969, *Fax:* 613-447-2730
Christopher Wilson
cwilson@civica.ca

Civicworks Consulting Group Inc.
246 Sandringham Dr., Toronto, ON M3H 1G3
Tel: 416-587-7053
Bobby Walman
bobbywalman@rogers.com

Clean 16 Environmental Technologies Corp.
#6134, 2100 Bloor St. West, Toronto, ON M6S 5A5
Tel: 416-352-1973, *Fax:* 416-352-1973
info@clean16.com
Michael Marks

Cogitare
2294 Courtice Ave., Ottawa, ON K1H 7G8
Tel: 613-733-6165
Benoit Hubert
bhubert@cogiscene.com

Communication New Brunswick
Centennial Building, P.O. Box 6000, Fredericton, NB E3B 5H1
Tel: 506-444-2381
Maurice Robichaud
maurice_robichaud@gnb.ca

Connected Insight
123 Jefferson Ave., Toronto, ON M6K 3E4
Tel: 416-203-8222
Hal Dremin
hal@connectedinsight.ca

Consultations Delaney Inc.
101 Av Dresden, Mont Royal, Montreal, QC H3P 3K1
Tel: 514-733-7754
Franklin Delaney
delaneyf@sympatico.ca

Cordwood International Inc
25 Macnabb Pl., Ottawa, ON K1L 8J5
Tel: 613-741-1615, *Fax:* 613-741-9388
Ted Gibson
ted.gibson@sympatico.ca

Corporate Communications Limited
7051 Bayers Rd., Suite 400, Halifax, NS B3L 4V2
Tel: 902-421-1777, *Fax:* 902-453-5221
Kelly

Corporate Strategic Consulting
60 Bellbrook Cres., Dartmouth, NS B2W 6S2
Tel: 902-434-3998, *Fax:* 902-434-8933
Richard Mann
richie.mann@ns.sympatico.ca

Corporated Communications Limited
#202, 335 Maclaren St., Ottawa, ON K2P 0M5
Tel: 613-324-2928
Robert Frelich
rfrelich.ccl@cclgroup.ca

Counsel Public Affairs Inc
#1606, 95 St. Clair West, Toronto, ON M4V 1N6
Tel: 416-920-0716
Charles Beer
kmolyneux@counselpa.com

Crestview Public Affairs Inc
#1510, 85 Albert St., Ottawa, ON K1P 6A4
Tel: 613-232-0462
Mike Donison
donison.m@gmail.com

Current Consulting
454 St. John's Rd., Toronto, ON M6S 2L2
Tel: 416-767-3514
Terry Doner
terrydooner@alumni.uwaterloo.ca

Dai Inc.
 # 300, 67a Sparks St., Ottawa, ON K1P 5A5
Tel: 613-238-6317
Alex Taylor
ataylor@daigroup.ca

David Chown Consulting
P.O. Box 5095, Waverley, NS B2R 1S2
Tel: 902-860-1104, *Fax:* 902-860-2655
David Chown
david.chown@ns.sympatico.ca

Davies Ward Phillips & Vineberg LLP
#4400, 1 First Canadian Place, Toronto, ON M5X 1B1
Tel: 416-863-0900
Neal H. Armstrong
narmstrong@dwpv.com

Deloitte & Touche
100 Queen St., Ottawa, ON K1P 5T8
Tel: 613-751-5242, *Fax:* 613-236-2328
Mark Noonan

Deloitte & Touche
5140 Yonge St., Toronto, ON M2N 6L7
Tel: 416-601-6266
Robert Sacco
bsacco@deloitte.ca

Dennis A. Forbes & Associates
155 Rupert St,, Thunder Bay, ON P7B 3X2
Tel: 807-345-1250, *Fax:* 807-345-1250
Dennis Forbes
dennis@dennisforbes.com

Devon Government Relations
#903, 1200 Bay St., Toronto, ON M5R 2A5
Tel: 416-504-5151x340, *Fax:* 416-504-5655
Gillian Mcarthur
gmcarthur@devongroup.ca

Dickie & Lyman Lawyers LLP
#440, 55 Metcalfe St., Ottawa, ON K1P6L5
Tel: 613-235-0101, *Fax:* 613-238-0101
John Dickie

Directis Consulting Group Ltd.
#720, 999 Broadway West, Vancouver, BC V5Z 1K5
Tel: 604-730-2668
Susan Low
sue@directis.ca

Dlb Consulting Inc.
590 Queen St., Unit #310, Fredericton, NB E3B 7H9
Tel: 506-459-4546
Deborah L. Burns
dlbcons@rogers.com

Donald Partsch
1718 Des Sapins Gardens, Orleans, ON K1C 8E4
Tel: 613-837-3655
Donald Partsch
donald.partsch@sympatico.ca

Duboff Edwards Haight & Schachter
#1900, 155 Carlton St., Winnipeg, MB R3C 3H8
Tel: 204-942-3361
Paul Edwards
pedwards@dehslaw.com

Earnscliffe Bc Inc
#617, 1030 West Georgia St., Vancouver, BC V6E 2Y3
Tel: 604-678-2900
Mike Drummond
mdrummond@earnscliffe.ca

Earnscliffe Strategy Group Inc
#300, 46 Elgin St., Ottawa, ON K1P 5K6
Tel: 613-563-4455
Andre Albinati
andre@earnscliffe.ca

Economic Development Consultants
100 Macewan Park View, Calgary, AB T3K 4E7
Tel: 403-730-6101, *Fax:* 403-730-6102
Ronald Edwards
ron.edwards@shaw.ca

Emerson Communications Inc
12931 Land O'nod, Rr #3, North Augusta, ON K0G 1R0
Tel: 613-290-7905
Elisabeth Ostiguy
eostiguy@magma.ca

Environent
300 Dufferin Avenue,, London, ON N6B 1Z2
Tel: 519-661-2500x939
Grant H. London

Equinox Affairs Publiques
1155 Elmlea Dr., Gloucester, ON K1J 6W1
Tel: 877-640-7933
Mona Fortier
mona@equinoxinc.ca

Everson Public Affairs
13 Morris St., Ottawa, ON K1S 4A6
Tel: 613-233-0573
Jennifer Sexton
sexton@sympatico.ca

Everson Public Affairs
882 Rollin Rd., Rockland, ON K4K 1W7
Tel: 613-488-9916
Jim Everson
jeverson@magma.ca

Excalibur Communications
1653 Kathryn Dr., London, ON N6G 2R7
Tel: 519-439-1140
Mary Mclaughlin
mary@excaliburcommunications.ca

Felesky Flynn
Petro Canada Centre, #5000, 150- 6th Ave. SW, Calgary, AB T2P 3Y7
Tel: 403-260-3300, *Fax:* 403-263-9649
Sandra E. Jack
sjack@felesky.com

Fleishman-Hillard Canada
#1300, 100 Queen St., Ottawa, ON K1P 1J9
Tel: 613-238-2090x254
Kevin

Fleishman-Hillard Canada Inc
#1000, 1122 - 4th St. SW, Calgary, AB T2R 1M1
Tel: 403-266-4710x237
Bryan Thomas
bryan.thomas@fleishman.ca

Forrest C. Hume
1080 Howe St., Vancouver, BC V6Z 2T1
Tel: 604-488-1499, *Fax:* 604-488-1489
Forrest Clyde Hume
fchume@sprint.ca

Foxcreek Consulting Services
383 Windsor Backroad, Rr # 1, Martock, ON B0N 2T0
Tel: 902-497-1691
foxcreek@ns.sympatico.ca
John Houck

Francopol Inc.
1364 Ogden St., Ottawa, ON K1J 8C4
Tel: 613-796-5363
Jean-Claude Trottier
jctrottier@francopol.ca

Fraser Milner Casgrain LLP
Fifth Avenue Place, 237-4 Ave. SW 30th Fl., Calgary, AB T2P 4X7
Tel: 403-268-7000, *Fax:* 403-268-3100
Douglas J. Black
doug.black@fmclaw.com

Fraser Milner Casgrain LLP
#1420, 99 Bank St., Ottawa, ON K1P 1H4
Tel: 613-783-9600
Stephanie Ramsy

Fred Doucet Consulting International Inc
#372, 440 Laurier Ave. West, Ottawa, ON K1R 7X6
Tel: 613-782-2217
Fred Doucet
fdoucet@rogers.com

Fredrick D. & Associates Inc
#830, 167 Lombard Ave., Winnipeg, MB R3C 0B3
Tel: 204-453-8065
Fredrick D. Mantey
fmantey@fdanda.com

Freeman Mandel & Milne
1082 Staghorn Ct., Mississauga, ON L5C 3R2
Tel: 905-566-9461, *Fax:* 905-566-0137
Stephan Freeman
steve@mcfree.net

G. Decker Consulting Services
1168 Bordeau Grove, Orleans, ON K1C 2M7
Tel: 613-824-7672
Glen Decker
gdecker@magma.ca

Gerald Doucet Consulting Inc
6970 Armview Ave., Halifax, NS B3H 2M4
Tel: 941-758-9843
Gerald Doucet

Gilbert's LLP
49 Wellington St. East, Toronto, ON M5E1C9
Tel: 416-703-1100
Tim Gilbert
tim@gilbertslaw.ca

Global Public Affairs Inc
#1600, 800-6th Ave. SW, Calgary, AB T2P 3G3
Tel: 403-264-3800x3810, *Fax:* 403-264-3808
Lorraine Royer
lroyer@globalpublic.com

Global Public Affairs Inc
#901, 50 O'connor St., Ottawa, ON K1P 6L2
Tel: 613-782-2336
Kristin Anderson

Global Trade Resources
 # 609, 1009 Expo Blvd., Vancouver, BC V6Z 2V9
Tel: 604-306-7475
Irfan Rehmanji
irehamji@novuscom.net

Global Ventures
E3-296 Mill Rd., Toronto, ON M9C 4X8
Tel: 416-569-9306
Russi Surti
consultrussi@aol.com

Goodfellow Agricola Consultants Inc
2005- 6th Line R., Rr # 1, Dunrobin, ON K0A 1T0
Tel: 613-832-0865
Randal Goodfellow
randal@goodfellowagricola.com

Goodman, Soloman & Gold
#1500, 439 University Ave., Toronto, ON M5G 1Y8
Tel: 416-595-5555
Daniel Solomon

Goodmans LLP
#2400, 250 Yonge St., Toronto, ON M5B 2M6
Tel: 416-979-2211
Dina Graser
jjohnson@goodmans.ca

Gottlieb & Pearson
#510, 30 St. Clair Ave West., Toronto, ON M4V 3A1
Tel: 416-250-1550, *Fax:* 416-250-7889
toronto@gottliebpearson.com
Jesse I. Goldman

Gottlieb & Pearson
#1920, 2020 Rue University, Montreal, QC H3A 2A5
Tel: 514-288-1744
Michael Woods

Government Policy Research Associates Inc.
#107, 408 Queen St., Ottawa, ON K1R 5A7
Tel: 613-235-5360
Gordon A. Harrison
isa@intersectalliance.ca

Gowling Lafleur Henderson LLP
Scotia Centre, #1400, 700- 2nd St. SW, Calgary, AB T2P 4V5
Tel: 403-298-1000, *Fax:* 403-263-9193
John N. Iredale
john.iredale@gowlings.com

Gowling Lafleur Henderson LLP
#2600, 160 Elgin St., Ottawa, ON K1P 1C3
Tel: 613-233-1781
Henry S. Brown

Gr Strategies Inc.
#602, 134 Abbott St., Vancouver, BC V6B 2K4
Tel: 604-739-1950
Cynthia Grauer
cg@grstrategies.com

Grey, Clark, Shih & Associates
#901, 100 Sparks St., Ottawa, ON K1P 5B7
Tel: 613-238-7743, *Fax:* 613-238-0368
Peter J. Clark
jpclark@greyclark.com

Gribbis Enterprises Ltd.
20 Ellisson Way, Ottawa, ON K1G 4P6
Tel: 613-738-1632
Francis Gribben
jim.gribben@sympatico.ca

Griffels Accociates Limited
30 International Blvd., Toronto, ON M9W 5P3
Tel: 416-675-5950x5597
Stephen O'brien
stephen.obrien@giffels.com

Grosso Mccarthy Inc.
#1400, 10 Bay Street, Toronto, ON M5J 2R8
Tel: 416-362-6141, *Fax:* 416-840-6139
Francesca Grosso
fgrosso@grossomccarthy.com

Gs Government Consulting Services
26 Maple Stand Way, Ottawa, ON K2G 6P4
Tel: 613-823-8079
Gordon Shields
gshields@magma.ca

Hamilton Duncan Armstrong & Stewart LLP
#1450, 13410- 108th Ave., Surrey, BC V3T 5T3
Tel: 604-581-4677, *Fax:* 604-581-5947
S.L. Nicoll
sln@hdas.com

Harris & Company
Bentall 5, #1400, 550 Burrard St., Vancouver, BC V6C 2B5
Tel: 604-684-6633
Dean Crawford

Hazzard & Hore
#1002, 141 Adelaide St.West, Toronto, ON M5H 3L5
Tel: 416-868-0074, *Fax:* 416-868-1468
Edward J. Hore
edhore@hazzardandhore.com

Heenan Blaikie Sencrl-Srl/LLP
Bay Adelaide Centre, 333 Bay Street, Suite 2900, Toronto, ON M5H 2T4
Tel: 416-643-6828x242019, *Fax:* 416-360-8425
Paul Lalonde
plalonde@heenan.ca

High Park Advocacy Group
263 Roncesvalles Ave., Toronto, ON M6R 2L9
Tel: 416-535-2815
Julio Lagos
jlagos@highparkgroup.com

High Park Advocacy Group
303 Jane Street, Toronto, ON M6S 3Z3
Tel: 416-535-2815
Timothy Egan
tegan@highparkgroup.com

High Park Group
#421, 130 Albert St., Ottawa, ON K1G 5P4
Tel: 613-234-3039
Peter Naglik
pnaglik@highparkgroup.com

Hill & Knowlton
 # 540, 202- 6th Ave. SW, Calgary, AB T2P 2R9
Tel: 403-299-9380, *Fax:* 403-299-9389
Beth Halford
beth.halford@hillandknowlton.ca

Hill & Knowlton
#1100, 55 Metcalfe St., Ottawa, ON K1P 6L5
Tel: 613-238-4371
Matthew Behan

Hill & Knowlton
#700, 160 Bloor St. East, Toronto, ON M4W3P7
Tel: 416-413-1218
John Capobianco

Hillwatch Inc.
#200, 334 Maclaren St., Ottawa, ON K2P 0M6
Tel: 613-238-8700x1001
Scott Proudfoot
proudfoot@hillwatch.com

Humphreys Public Affairs Group Inc.
#1620, 130 Albert St., Ottawa, ON K1P 5G4
Tel: 613-230-3155, *Fax:* 613-236-2556
David L. Humphrey
dhumphreys@hpag.ca

Hydroplane Services Mergus Inc
2575 Conc. 2, Lefaivre, ON K0B 1J0
Tel: 613-676-2510
Jf Ferrary
jferrary@hotmail.com

Icf Consulting Canada Inc.
#808, 277 Wellington St. West, Toronto, ON M5V 3E4
Tel: 416-341-0990x3038
Errick Willis
ewillis@icfconsulting.com

Impact Public Affairs
#910, 50 O'Connor St., Ottawa, ON K1P 6L2
Tel: 613-233-8906
Cynthia Waldmeier

Implementation & Advisory Group Ltd
#1400, 10025- 106 St, Edmonton, AB T5J 1G4
Tel: 780-482-5577
Tg Keil
robin.bobocel@iag.ca

Inac Services Limited
232 Dublin St. North, Guelph, ON N1H 4P3
Tel: 519-766-1395, *Fax:* 519-766-1348
David Reynolds
dreynolds@inacservices.com

International Project & Protocol Services Inc
307 St. Clements Ave., Toronto, ON M4R 1H3
Tel: 416-481-7623
ipps@rogers.com
Frederick Keenan

Intervistas Consulting Inc.
#550, 1200 West 73rd Ave., Vancouver, BC V6P 6G5
Tel: 604-717-1800, *Fax:* 604-717-1880
Gerry Bruno
gerry_bruno@intervistas.com

Intervistas Consulting Inc.
#901, 50 O'Connor St., Ottawa, ON K1P 6L2
Tel: 613-783-3448
Sam Barone
sam_barone@intervistas.com

Ir Councel Inc.
417 Guildwood Pkwy, Toronto, ON M1E 1R3
Tel: 416-822-3130
Brian Smith
bsmith@ironline.ca

Irh & Associates
2388 Wyndale Cres., Ottawa, ON K1H 7A6
Tel: 613-737-4636
Louis Huneault
lhuneault@livingstonintl.com

J & L Associates
1863 Des Epinettes Ave., Orleans, ON K1C 6N5
Tel: 613-355-9545
Gordan Sharpe
gordonsharpe@aol.com

J. Robert Wood & Associates
#419, 1400 The Esplanade North, Pickering, ON L1V 6V2
Tel: 905-837-9425, *Fax:* 905-837-9168
John Wood
jrwood@rogers.com

Jack Soule Consulting
60 Riverside Dr., Kingston, ON K7L 4V1
Tel: 613-541-0013
Jack Soule
jack@soule.ca

John Moonen & Associates Ltd.
6475 Fox St., Vancouver, BC V7W 2C3
Tel: 604-921-6433, *Fax:* 604-921-6433
John Moonen
johnmoonen@telus.net

John Todd Holdings Ltd
#102, 10178- 117 St, Edmonton, AB T5K 2X9
Tel: 780-906-1759
John Todd
bremertodd@shaw.ca

Johnston & Buchan LLP
#1700, 275 Slater St., Ottawa, ON K1P 5H9
Tel: 613-236-3882, *Fax:* 613-230-6423
Stephen B. Acker
info@johnstonbuchan.com

Justenvironment
15 Timber Run Crt., Campbellville, ON L0P 1B0
Tel: 905-659-4732
Mark S. Rudolph
mrudolph@justenvironment.com

K.J. Chapman
#208, 10080 Jasper Ave Nw, Edmonton, AB T5J 1V9
Tel: 780-420-0505, *Fax:* 780-420-1256
Ken J. Chapman
ken@cambridgestrategies.com

Karta Strategy
#609, 45 Carlton St., Toronto, ON M5B 2H9
Tel: 416-506-0609
Kamal Chopra
kamalbir@rogers.com

Ketchum Communications Ltd.
3220 Mathers Ave., West Vancouver, BC V7T 2W6
Tel: 604-922-5204, *Fax:* 604-922-9774
Jess D. Ketchum
jketchum@direct.ca

Kirkby Law Office
#102, 1061 Central Ave., Prince Albert, SK S6V 4V4
Tel: 306-764-4673
Gordon Kirkby
kirkbylaw@sasktel.net

Kirkland Capital Corporation
#105, 120 Rosedale Valley Rd., Toronto, ON M4W 1P8
Tel: 416-921-9992
info@kirklandcapital.com
Ellis Kirkland

Kpmg
#2000, One Lombard Pl., Winnipeg, MB K3B 0X3
Tel: 204-957-2277, *Fax:* 204-989-8077
Allan Thordarson
athordarson@kpmg.ca

Kpmg
Commerce Court West, #3300, 199 Bay St., P.O. Box 31, Toronto, ON M5L 1B2
Tel: 416-777-3680
Derrold Norgaard

L. Power Consulting Inc
59 Hayward Ave., St. John's, NL A1C 3W6
Tel: 709-682-3543, *Fax:* 709-726-4849
Leo Power
leopower@nf.sympatico.ca

L.A. Lombardi & Co. Ltd.
#200, 66 West Beaver Creek, Richmond Hill, ON L4B 1G5
Tel: 416-924-9559x342
Len Lombardi

Lac Des Milles Lacs First Nation
Suite #328, 1100 Memorial Ave., Thunder Bay, ON P7B 4A3
Tel: 807-622-9835
Quentin Snider
quentinlaptop@tbaytel.net

Ledrew Laishley Reed LLP
#505, 3 Church Street, Toronto, ON M5E 1M2
Tel: 416-981-9460, *Fax:* 416-981-0060
Stephan Ledrew

Link Strategies Inc.
#910, 1 Toronto St., P.O. Box 28, Toronto, ON M5C 2V6
Tel: 416-368-0323
Kevin Gallagher
kgallagher@linkstrategies.ca

Macdonald Group
4 Swanwick Ave, Toronto, ON M4E1Z1
Tel: 416-937-6646
Jodi Macdonald
jmacdonald@bot.com

Macleod Dixon LLP
 # 3700, 400, Third Ave. SW, Calgary, AB T2P 4H2
Tel: 403-267-9404, *Fax:* 403-264-5973
Orville Pyrcz
orville.pyrcz@macleoddixon.com

Macpherson Leslie & Tyerman LLP
Hill Centre 1, #1500, 1874 Scarth St., Regina, SK S4P 4E9
Tel: 306-347-8000
Harold H. Mackay
hmackay@mlt.com

Marian D. Hebb
#404, 179 John St., Toronto, ON M5T 1X4
Tel: 416-971-6618, *Fax:* 416-971-4144
Marian D. Hebb
mhebb@sympatico.ca

Mary Granskou Consulting
#101 Clearview Ave., Ottawa, ON K1Y 2L1
Tel: 613-722-6800
Mary Granskou
granskou@magma.ca

Mccarthy Tetrault LLP
Toronto Dominion Bank Tower, #4700, P.O. Box 48, Stn Td Tower, Toronto, ON M5K 1E6
Tel: 416-362-1812
Barry Sookman

Mcilroy & Mcilroy Inc
#1410, 155 University Ave., Toronto, ON M5H 3B7
Tel: 416-777-0447
James P. Mcilroy

Mcinnes Cooper
Bank Of Montreal Bldg., #1600, 5151 George St., Halifax, NS B3J 2V1
Tel: 902-425-6500, *Fax:* 902-425-6350
George Cooper
george.cooper@mcinnescooper.com

Mckercher Mckercher & Whitmore LLP
374 Third Ave South, Saskatoon, SK S7K 1M5
Tel: 306-653-2000, *Fax:* 306-653-2669
Doug Richardson
d.richardson@mckercher.ca

Mcmahon Consulting
418 Cordova St., Winnipeg, MB R3N 1A6
Tel: 204-489-0756, *Fax:* 204-487-4724
Robert Mcmahon
mcmahon@mts.net

Miller Thomson LLP
Scotia Plaza, #5800, 40 King St. West, Toronto, ON M5H 3S1
Tel: 416-595-8500
S Freeman

Morrison Brown Sosnovitch
#910, 1 Toronto St., P.O. Box 28, Toronto, ON M5C 2V6
Tel: 416-368-0600
Libby Burnham
lburnham@businesslawyers.com

Mulholland Consulting
#401, 790 Bay St., Toronto, ON M5G 1N8
Tel: 416-596-2119
Elisabeth Mulholland
emulholland@rightplay.com

National Public Relations
#350, 355 Burrard St., Vancouver, BC V6C 2G8
Tel: 604-684-6655, *Fax:* 604-684-6981
Nicola Lambrechts
nlambrechts@national.ca

Navigator Ltd.
British Colonial Bldg., 8 Wellington St. East, 3rd Fl., Toronto, ON M5E 1C5
Tel: 416-640-1579
John Ratchford
jratchford@navltd.com

Nutrisphere
118 Grey Fox Dr., Carp, ON K0A 1L0
Tel: 613-256-4091, *Fax:* 613-256-4091
Helen Macdonald
helyn.mac@sympatico.ca

O.P. Mccarthy & Associates Inc
#4, 5700 Timberlea Blvd, Mississauga, ON L4W 5B9
Tel: 905-602-6488
Blair Gilmour
bgilmour@opmccarthy.com

On The Hill Consulting
611 Merkley Dr., Orleans, ON K4A 1SE
Tel: 613-875-1795
Richard Phillips
phillips@telus.blackberry.ca

Ontario Craft Brewers
75 Horner Avenue, Suite 1, Toronto, ON M8Z 4X5
Tel: 416-494-2766, *Fax:* 416-494-5586
John Hay
john.hay@sympatico.ca

P3 Strategic Alliance Inc
106 Starwood Rd, Nepean, ON K2G 1Z7
Tel: 888-791-7834
Craig Pitt
cpitt@rogers.com

Palliser Strategy
812b- 16th Ave. SW, Calgary, AB T2R 0S9
Tel: 403-209-5710
John Bethel
jbethel@palliserstrategy.com

Payne Group International Inc
145 Wakefield Cres., London, ON N5X 1Z6
Tel: 519-859-7442
Rhonda Payne
rpayne@pgi2.com

Perterson Consulting
136 Cedar St. South, Timmins, ON P4N 2G8
Tel: 705-264-5323, *Fax:* 705-268-0300
pcmanage@nt.net
Ken Peterson

Pinnacle Public Affairs
#1203, 275 Slater St., Ottawa, ON K1P 5H9
Tel: 613-594-8484
Titch Dharamsi
titch@pinnaclepublicaffairs.com

Policy Alliance Inc
2030 Merchants Gate, Oakville, ON L6M 2Z8
Tel: 905-842-5910
Terence Young
youngt.policyalliance@cogeco.ca

Policy Concepts
21 St. Clair Ave East, Toronto, ON M4T 1L9
Tel: 416-922-6156x24
George Boddington

Policy Insights Inc.
#402, 222 Queen St., Ottawa, ON K1P 5V9
Tel: 613-563-8078, *Fax:* 613-563-4284
admin@policyinsights.com
Mac Evans

Portland Group
#518, 1001 Bay St,, Toronto, ON M5S 3A6
Tel: 416-413-9206
Tom Robson
trobson@rogers.com

Pricewaterhouse Coopers
#3100, 111- 5th Ave SW, Calgary, AB T2P 5L3
Tel: 403-509-7500, *Fax:* 403-781-1825
Dale Meister
dale.s.meister@ca.pwc.com

Pricewaterhouse Coopers
Royal Trust Tower, #3000, 77 King St. West, P.O. Box 82, Toronto, ON M5K 1G8
Tel: 416-863-1133
Larry Chapman
larry.chapman@ca.pwc.com

Pricewaterhousecooper
#700, 250 Howe St., Vancouver, BC V6C 3S7
Tel: 604-806-7039, *Fax:* 604-806-7806
Tom Falconer
tom.falconer@ca.pwc.com

Pricewaterhousecoopers
#1900, 5700 Yonge Street, Toronto, ON M2M 4K7
Tel: 416-218-1491
Katherine Munro
kathy.m.munro@ca.pwc.com

Prime Strategies Group Inc
#220, 156 Front St. West, Toronto, ON M5J 2L6
Tel: 416-313-3031x229
Vic Gupta
vic@primestrat.com

Prismatic Group
#205, 3132 Parsons Rd, Edmonton, AB T6N 1L6
Tel: 780-495-0200
Bill Donahue
bill.donahue@prismatic.ca

Prospectus Associates Inc.
19 Foxberry Hill, Glen Haven, NS B3Z 2V7
Tel: 902-820-2115
Sean Kirby
kirby@prospectusassociates.com

Public Affairs Counsel
177 Powell Ave., Ottawa, ON K1S 2A2
Tel: 613-292-0326, *Fax:* 613-235-9790
Isabel Metcalfe
isabel.metcalfe@sympatico.ca

Public Affairs Strategy Group
#406, 350 Sparks St., Ottawa, ON K1R 7S8
Tel: 613-594-0202, *Fax:* 613-233-5880
info@deltamedia.ca
Lisa Grenier

Public Knowledge Canada
855 Explorer Lane, Ottawa, ON K1C 2S3
Tel: 613-834-8403
Garth Williams
garth.williams@publicknowledge.ca

Pwm Consulting
#344, 300 Earl Grey Dr., Kanata, ON K2T 1C1
Tel: 613-839-1555
Peter Maddocks
peterm@pwmconsulting.com

Quadra Consulting Group
26 Dalhousie St., Toronto, ON M5B 2A5
Tel: 416-364-0073
Peter Meyer
pmeyer@quadraconsultinggroup.com

Ra Mentor
6 Wyndholme Ave., Dartmouth, NS B2Y 1T3
Tel: 902-464-9628, *Fax:* 902-461-1350
Robert Mackay
rmackay1@ns.sympatico.ca

Ramm Consultants Inc
2944 Vivian Rd., Newmarket, ON L3Y 4W1
Tel: 905-715-7513
Terry Ramm
tramm@rammconsultants.com

Rawson Group Initiatives
#300, 222 Argyle Ave., Ottawa, ON K2P 1B9
Tel: 613-236-7960
Marion Lefebvre

Renald Remillard
, Winnipeg, MB R2H 1T2
Tel: 204-237-1818x436
Renald Remillard
rremillard@ustboniface.mb.ca

Ryk Oliver Corporation
1130 Castle Hill Cres., Ottawa, ON K2C 2A8
Tel: 613-723-2816, *Fax:* 613-723-5525
Robert Van Eyk
vaneyk@rogers.com

S.A. Murray Consulting Inc
#203, 1220 Yonge St., Toronto, ON M4T 1W1
Tel: 416-922-5152x233
Diane Douglas
smurray@samcitor.samci.com

Saija Enterprises Inc
96 Chatterson Dr., Ancaster, ON L9G 3X2
Tel: 905-648-5973
Niranjan Desai
nirudesail100@hotmail.com

Samdan Man
295 Woodbine Blvd. SW, Calgary, AB T2W 4K8
Tel: 403-238-8605
Robert Nault
samdan@shaw.ca

Saxony Canadian Consulting Corp.
1224 Rideau Bend Cres., Manotick, ON K4M 1A8
Tel: 613-692-2355
Roy Macrae
rfmacrae@yahoo.ca

Sj Consulting
Unit 208, 7165 Granville St., Vancouver, BC V6P 4X6
Tel: 877-753-2678, *Fax:* 877-753-2679
sjconsulting@telus.net
Stephen Eddy

Skorupinski Enterprises
2 Ararat Ct,, Nepean, ON K2H 8R9
Tel: 613-828-5969
Slawek Skorupinski
sskorupinski@rogers.com

Stikeman Elliott LLP
Commerce Court West, #5300, 199 Bay St., Toronto, ON M5L 1B9
Tel: 416-869-5500
Margaret Grottenhaler
mgrottenhaler@stikeman.com

Strategic Growth & Relations Management
11 Calgary St., St. John's, NL A1A 3W1
Tel: 709-743-2427
Greg Mercer
gregmercer@nl.rogers.com

Strategycorp Ottawa Inc
150 John St. 10th Floor, Toronto, ON M5V 3C3
Tel: 416-864-7112
Denise Cole

Sussex Strategy Group
#200, 440 Laurier West, Ottawa, ON K1R 7X6
Tel: 613-782-2320
Franco Iacono
fiacono@sussex-strategy.com

Sussex Strategy Group
55 University Ave, Suite 600, Toronto, ON M5J 2H7
Tel: 416-961-6611x104
Chris Benedetti
cbenedetti@sussex-strategy.com

Tanner & Guiney
#530, 2810 Matheson Blvd. East, Mississauga, ON L4W 4X7
Tel: 905-206-9740
David Guiney
djguiney@tannerandguiney.com

Technology Strategies Group Inc
#400, 1122- 4 St SW, Calgary, AB T2R 1M1
Tel: 403-245-2110, *Fax:* 403-265-8740
Receptionist
brett.bastable@tsgi.ca

Teeger Schiller Inc
304 Richview Ave., Toronto, ON M5P 3G5
Tel: 888-816-0222x102
Elliot Schiller
eschiller@teegerschiller.com

Temple Scott Associates Inc
#301, 250 The Esplanade, Toronto, ON M5A 1J2
Tel: 416-360-6183x233
Ian Anderson

The Strategy Project
38 Melgund Ave., Ottawa, ON K1S 2S2
Tel: 613-567-9592, *Fax:* 613-567-9561
Jim Thompson
jim@strategyproject.ca

Torys LLP
Toronto Dominion Centre, #3000, 79 Wellington St. West, P.O. Box 270, Toronto, ON M5K 1N2
Tel: 416-865-0040
Blaire W. Keefe
bkeefe@torys.com

True North Public Affairs
22 Crestwood Pl., Dartmouth, NS B2V 2P5
Tel: 902-440-2634
Cheryl Bidgood
cbidgood@ns.sympatico.ca

True North Public Affairs
#1302, 155 Queen St., Ottawa, ON K1P 6L1
Tel: 613-232-7777x221, *Fax:* 613-232-7667
Tristan Laflamme
tlaflamme@tnpa.ca

W.A. Macdonald Associates Inc.
Bce Place, #3720, 161 Bay St, P.O. Box 621, Toronto, ON M5J 2S1
Tel: 416-865-7091
William Macdonald

Waldrum & Associates
29 Honeysuckle Dr., Guelph, ON N1G 4X7
Tel: 613-822-6330
Alexander J. Waldrum
butch@thewaldrums.com

Welland & Associates
P.O. Box 504, Chester, NS B0J 1J0
Tel: 902-275-4792, *Fax:* 902-275-4414
welland@ns.sympatico.ca
Derek M. Wells

Western Policy Consultants Inc.
Pacific Centre #1450, 700 West Georgia St. P.O. Box 10015, Vancouver, BC V7Y 1A1
Tel: 604-684-2228
western@telus.net
Michael A. Bailey

William L. Lees & Associates Ltd.
491 Richmond St., Thunder Bay, ON P7A 1R2
Tel: 807-683-6946
William L. Lees
wllees@shaw.ca

SECTION 8
GOVERNMENT/MUNICIPAL

Listings in this section are arranged by province and are as current as possible at time of publication. For appointments made and results of elections held after publication, please refer to Canada's Information Resource Centre (CIRC), if your library subscribes to this online database. Each provincial section includes a district map, notes concerning local government structure and elections, and the following categories:

Counties & Municipal Districts

Major Municipalities

Other Municipalities

ALBERTA

The major legislation concerning municipal government in Alberta is the Municipal Government Act.

Municipal government in Alberta is rural, urban or specialized. Rural municipal governments are organized into Municipal Districts, with Specialized Municipalities created to meet the unique needs of a specific municipality. Elected councils are responsible for the welfare and interests of the municipalities. Two other rural categories are Improvement Districts and Special Areas, which are geographically large, sparsely populated areas for which the provincial government levies and collects all taxes and provides services.

Urban municipalities include Summer Villages, Villages, Towns and Cities. These are fully autonomous municipal units, each with an elected council. They are responsible for providing all municipal services within their corporate limits and for levying taxes and rates.

In addition to the above forms of municipal government there are eight Metis Settlements established under the Metis Settlements Act.

Types of Municipalities that may be formed:

- Municipal District: A majority of the buildings used as dwellings are on parcels of land with an area of at least 1,850 square metres and there is a population of 1,000 or more.
- Village: A majority of the buildings are on parcels of land smaller than 1,850 square metres and there is a population of 300 or more.
- Town: A majority of the buildings are on parcels of land smaller than 1,850 square metres and there is a population of 1,000 or more.
- City: A majority of the buildings are on parcels of land smaller than 1,850 square metres and there is a population of 10,000 or more.

Specialized Municipality: An area in which the Minister is satisfied that a type of municipality (as listed above) does not meet the needs of the proposed municipality; to provide for a form of local government that, in the opinion of the Minister, will provide for the orderly development of the municipality to a type of municipality (as listed above), or to another form of specialized municipality; an area in which the Minister is satisfied for any other reason that it is appropriate in the circumstances to form a specialized municipality.

Incorporation and changes in status are determined by the Lieutenant Governor in Council (Provincial Cabinet) on the recommendation of the Minister of Municipal Affairs. It is not necessary to change status by reason of population change. Elections are held in October. Terms of office are three years (2010, 2013, etc.).

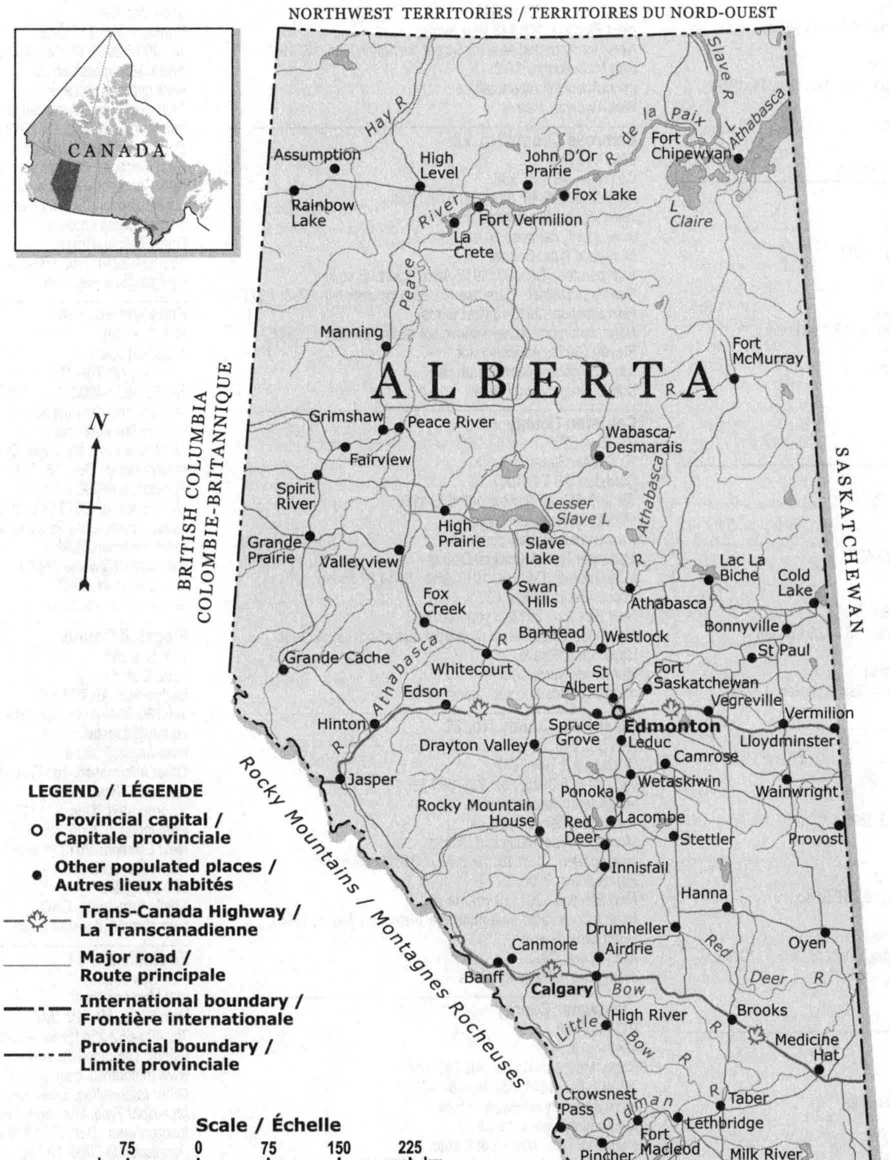

Reproduced with the permission of Natural Resources Canada 2011, courtesy of the Atlas of Canada.

Alberta

Counties & Municipal Districts in Alberta

Acadia No. 34
P.O. Box 30
Acadia Valley, AB T0J 0A0
Tel: 403-972-3808; *Fax:* 403-972-3833
md34@mdacadia.ab.ca
www.mdacadia.ab.ca
Municipal Type: Municipal District
Incorporated: Dec. 9, 1913 *Area:* 1,076.26 sq km
Population in 2006: 545
Next Election: 2013 (3 year terms)
Dwight Meers, Reeve
councillor.meers@mdacadia.ab.ca
Gary E. Peers, Municipal Administrator
cao@mdcadia.ab.ca

Athabasca County No. 12
3602 - 48 Ave.
Athabasca, AB T9S 1M8
Tel: 780-675-2273; *Fax:* 780-675-5512
info@athabascacounty.com
www.athabascacounty.com
Municipal Type: Municipal District
Incorporated: Dec. 18, 1913 *Area:* 6,126.43 sq km
Population in 2006: 7,587
Next Election: 2013 (3 year terms)
Note: Incorporated as a municipal district on Dec. 14, 1914.
David Yurdiga, Reeve
dyurdiga@athabascacounty.com
Gary Buchanan, CAO
gbuchanan@athabascacounty.com

Beaver County
P.O. Box 140
Ryley, AB T0B 4A0
Tel: 780-663-3730; *Fax:* 780-663-3602
administration@beaver.ab.ca
www.beaver.ab.ca
Municipal Type: Municipal District
Incorporated: Feb. 1, 1943 *Area:* 3,319.1 sq km
Population in 2006: 5,676
Next Election: 2013 (3 year terms)
Robert Young, Reeve
division1@mcsnet.ca
Bob Beck, CAO
bbeck@beaver.ab.ca

Big Lakes
P.O. Box 239
5305 -56 ST.
High Prairie, AB T0G 1E0
Tel: 780-523-5955; *Fax:* 780-523-4227
biglakes@mdbiglakes.ca
www.mdbiglakes.ca
Municipal Type: Municipal District
Incorporated: Dec. 18, 1913 *Area:* 13,892.91 sq km
Population in 2006: 5,805
Next Election: 2013 (3 year terms)
Note: Incorporated as a municipal district on Jan. 1, 1995.
Alvin Billings, Reeve

Bighorn No. 8
P.O. Box 310
2 Heart Mountain Drive
Exshaw, AB T0L 2C0
Tel: 403-673-3611; *Fax:* 403-673-3895
bighorn@mdbighorn.ca
www.mdbighorn.ca
Municipal Type: Municipal District
Incorporated: April 1, 1945 *Area:* 2,767.94 sq km
Population in 2006: 1,264
Next Election: 2013 (3 year terms)
Note: Incorporated as a municipal district on Jan. 1, 1988.
Dene Cooper, Reeve
Martin Buckley, CAO
martin.buckley@mdbighorn.ca

Birch Hills
P.O. Box 157
Wanham, AB T0H 3P0
Tel: 780-694-3793; *Fax:* 780-694-3788
irenec@birchhillscounty.com
www.birchhillscounty.com
Municipal Type: Municipal District
Incorporated: Dec. 18, 1913 *Area:* 2,856.69 sq km
Population in 2006: 1,470
Next Election: 2013 (3 year terms)
Warren Smith, Reeve
Irene Cooper, CAO

Bonnyville No. 87
P.O. Box 1010
4905 - 50 Ave.
Bonnyville, AB T9N 2J7
Tel: 780-826-3171; *Fax:* 780-826-4524
kkalinski@md.bonnyville.ab.ca
www.md.bonnyville.ab.ca
Municipal Type: Municipal District
Incorporated: Dec. 14, 1914 *Area:* 6,057.44 sq km
Population in 2006: 10,194
Next Election: 2013 (3 year terms)
Ryan Poole, CAO
rpoole@md.bonnyville.ab.ca
Ed Rondeau, Reeve

Brazeau County
P.O. Box 77
5516 Industrial Rd.
Drayton Valley, AB T7A 1R1
Tel: 780-542-7777; *Fax:* 780-542-7770
krobinson@brazeau.ab.ca
www.brazeau.ab.ca
Municipal Type: Municipal District
Incorporated: Dec. 18, 1913 *Area:* 3,015.83 sq km
Population in 2006: 7,040
Next Election: 2013 (3 year terms)
Note: Incorporated as a municipal district on Dec. 13, 1915.
Ron McCullough, CAO
rmccullough@brazeau.ab.ca
Wes Tweedle, Reeve

Camrose County No. 22
3755 - 43 Ave.
Camrose, AB T4V 3S8
Tel: 780-672-4446; *Fax:* 780-672-1008
county@county.camrose.ab.ca
www.county.camrose.ab.ca
Municipal Type: County
Incorporated: Dec. 23, 1912 *Area:* 3,331.98 sq km
County or District: Camrose No. 22; *Population in 2008:* 7,577
Next Election: 2013 (3 year terms)
Note: Incorporated as a municipal district on Jan. 1, 1944.
Steven Gerlitz, Administrator
sgerlitz@county.camrose.ab.ca
Don L. Gregorwich, Reeve

Cardston County
P.O. Box 580
1050 Main Street
Cardston, AB T0K 0K0
Tel: 403-653-4977; *Fax:* 403-653-1126
office@cardstoncounty.com
www.cardstoncounty.com
Municipal Type: Municipal District
Incorporated: Dec. 18, 1913 *Area:* 3,414.87 sq km
Population in 2006: 4,037
Next Election: 2013 (3 year terms)
Note: Incorporated as a municipal district on Jan. 1, 1946.
Lloyd Kearl, Reeve
Murray Millward, CAO
murray@cardstoncounty.com

Clear Hills County No. 21
P.O. Box 240
Worsley, AB T0H 3W0
Tel: 780-685-3925; *Fax:* 780-685-3960
info@clearhillscounty.ab.ca
www.clearhillscounty.ab.ca
Municipal Type: Municipal District
Incorporated: Dec. 18, 1913 *Area:* 15,112.69 sq km
Population in 2006: 2,714
Next Election: 2013 (3 year terms)
Note: Incorporated as a municipal district on Jan. 1, 1995.
Miron Croy, Reeve
Allan Rowe, CAO
allan@clearhillscounty.ab.ca

Clearwater County
P.O. Box 550
4340 - 47th Ave.
Rocky Mountain House, AB T4T 1A4
Tel: 403-845-4444; *Fax:* 403-845-7330
admin@county.clearwater.ab.ca
www.county.clearwater.ab.ca
Municipal Type: Municipal District
Incorporated: April 1, 1945 *Area:* 18,691.65 sq km
Population in 2006: 11,826
Next Election: 2013 (3 year terms)
Note: Incorporated as a municipal district on Jan. 1, 1985.
Ron Leaf, County Manager
rleaf@county.clearwater.ab.ca
Pat Alexander, Reeve
Joe Baker, Manager, Planning / West Country
jbaker@county.clearwater.ab.ca
Kim Nielsen, Manager, Agricultural Services
knielsen@county.clearwater.ab.ca
Marshall Morton, Manager, Public Works
mmorton@county.clearwater.ab.ca

Crowsnest Pass
P.O. Box 600
Blairmore, AB T0K 0E0
Tel: 403-562-8833; *Fax:* 403-563-5474
reception@crowsnestpass.com
www.town.crowsnestpass.ab.ca
Municipal Type: Regional Municipality
Incorporated: Jan. 1, 1979 *Area:* 373.07 sq km
Population in 2006: 5,749
Provincial Electoral District(s): Livingstone-Macleod
Federal Electoral District(s): Macleod
Next Election: 2013 (3 year terms)
Bruce Decoux, Mayor
Kevin Robins, CAO
cao@crowsnestpass.com

Cypress County
816 - 2nd Ave.
Dunmore, AB T1B 0K3
Tel: 403-526-2888; *Fax:* 403-526-8958
cypress@cypress.ab.ca
www.cypress.ab.ca
Municipal Type: Municipal District
Incorporated: Dec. 18, 1913 *Area:* 13,166.13 sq km
Population in 2006: 6,729
Next Election: 2013 (3 year terms)
Note: Incorporated as a municipal district on Jan. 1, 1985.
Lutz Perschon, County Manager
lutz@cypress.ab.ca
Darcy Geigle, Reeve
403-834-2244, Fax: 403-834-2270
dgeigle@xplornet.com

Fairview No. 136
P.O. Box 189
10957-91 Ave.
Fairview, AB T0H 1L0
Tel: 780-835-4903; *Fax:* 780-835-3131
mdinfo@medfairview.ab.ca
www.mdfairview.com
Municipal Type: Municipal District
Incorporated: Dec. 18, 1913 *Area:* 1,390.66 sq km
Population in 2006: 1,432
Next Election: 2013 (3 year terms)
Note: Incorporated as a municipal district on Dec. 9, 1914.
Ernie Newman, Reeve
fcseedplant@wispernet.ca
Ben Boettcher, CAO
ben@mdfairview.ab.ca

Flagstaff County
P.O. Box 358
4202-50th St.
Sedgewick, AB T0B 4C0
Tel: 780-384-4100; *Fax:* 780-384-3635
county@flagstaff.ab.ca
www.flagstaff.ab.ca
Other Information: Toll-Free: 1-877-387-4100
Municipal Type: County
Incorporated: Dec. 9, 1912 *Area:* 4,066.92 sq km
Population in 2006: 3,506
Next Election: 2013 (3 year terms)
Henry Hays, Reeve
780-888-2242
Shelly Armstrong, CAO
sarmstrong@flagstaff.ab.ca

Foothills No. 31
P.O. Box 5605
309 Macleod Trail
High River, AB T1V 1M7
Tel: 403-652-2341; *Fax:* 403-652-7880
mdfthlls@mdfoothills.com
www.mdfoothills.com
Other Information: Emergencies: 1-888-808-3722
Municipal Type: Municipal District
Incorporated: Dec. 23, 1912 *Area:* 3,643.6 sq km
Population in 2006: 19,736
Next Election: 2013 (3 year terms)
Note: Incorporated as a municipal district on Jan. 1, 1944.
Harry Riva Cambrin, Municipal Manager
hrc@mdfoothills.com

Roy McLean, Reeve
council@mdfoothills.com
Graham Clark, Fire Chief, Protective Services
graham.clark@mdfoothills.com
Tom Gillis, Director, Public Works & Engineering
tom.gillis@mdfoothills.com
Nasir Sheikh, Municipal Engineer
nasir.sheikh@mdfoothills.com
Judy Gordon, Coordinator, Planning & Development
judy.gordon@mdfoothills.com
Marilyn Gordon-Cooper, Contact, Property Tax & Utilities Department
marilyn.gordon-cooper@mdfoothills.com
Heather Hemingway, Contact, Environment Committee
heather.hemingway@mdfoothills.com
Ken McKay, Contact, Building Safety Codes & Bylaw Enforcement
ken.mckay@mdfoothills.com

Forty Mile County No. 8
P.O. Box 160
303 Main St.
Foremost, AB T0K 0X0
Tel: 403-867-3530; *Fax:* 403-867-2242
info@fortymile.ab.ca
www.40mile.ca
Municipal Type: County
Incorporated: Dec. 9, 1912 *Area:* 7,229.84 sq km
Population in 2006: 3,414
Next Election: 2013 (3 year terms)
Tom Thacker, Reeve
403-545-2477
Dale Brown, Administrator
dale@fortymile.ab.ca

Grande Prairie No. 1
10001 - 84 Ave.
Clairmont, AB T0H 0W0
Tel: 780-532-9722; *Fax:* 780-539-9880
info@countygp.ab.ca
www.countygp.ab.ca
Municipal Type: County
Incorporated: Dec. 9, 1912 *Area:* 5,883.92 sq km
Population in 2006: 17,970
Next Election: 2013 (3 year terms)
Note: Incorporated as a county on Jan. 1, 1951.
W.A. Rogan, County Administrator
brogan1@countygp.ab.ca
Everett McDonald, Reeve
John Simpson, Director, Planning
780-513-3950
plan@countygp.ab.ca
Everett Cooke, Fire Chief
780-567-5590
fire@countygp.ab.ca
Steve Madden, Manager, Environment
780-532-7393
Herb Pfau, Superintendent, Public Works
780-532-7393
pubwks@countygp.ab.ca

Greenview No. 16
P.O. Box 1079
Valleyview, AB T0H 3N0
Tel: 780-524-7600; *Fax:* 780-524-4307
mdg1@mdgreenview.ab.ca
www.mdgreenview.ab.ca
Municipal Type: Municipal District
Incorporated: Jan. 1, 1969 *Area:* 32,994.14 sq km
Population in 2006: 5,464
Next Election: 2013 (3 year terms)
Note: Incorporated as a municipal district on Jan. 1, 1994.
Tony Yelenik, Reeve
780-524-2269
Esecretary@mdgreenview.ab.ca
Jim Squire, CAO
Jim@mdgreenview.ab.ca

Jasper
P.O. Box 520
Jasper, AB T0E 1E0
Tel: 780-852-3356; *Fax:* 780-852-4019
j.cooper@town.jasper.ab.ca
www.jasper-alberta.com
Municipal Type: Regional Municipality
Incorporated: Aug. 31, 1995 *Area:* 925.52 sq km
Population in 2006: 4,265
Next Election: 2013 (3 year terms)
Note: Incorporated as a specialized municipality on July 20, 2001.
Richard Ireland, Mayor
rireland@town.jasper.ab.ca
George Krefting, Municipal Manager
gkrefting@town.jasper.ab.ca

Kneehill County
P.O. Box 400
Three Hills, AB T0M 2A0
Tel: 403-443-5541; *Fax:* 403-443-5115
office@kneehillcounty.com
www.kneehillcounty.com
Municipal Type: Municipal District
Incorporated: Dec. 9, 1912 *Area:* 3,380.04 sq km
Population in 2006: 5,218
Next Election: 2013 (3 year terms)
Carol Calhoun, Reeve
Kevin Miner, CAO
kevincao@kneehillcounty.com

Lac La Biche County
P.O. Box 1679
Lac La Biche, AB T0A 2C0
Tel: 780-623-1747; *Fax:* 780-623-2039
main.office@laclabichecounty.com
www.laclabichecounty.com
Other Information: Toll-Free: 1-877-806-5632
Municipal Type: County
Incorporated: Aug. 1, 2007
Provincial Electoral District(s): Lac La Biche-St. Paul
Federal Electoral District(s): Fort McMurray-Athabasca
Next Election: 2013 (3 year terms)
Note: The Town of Lac La Biche & Lakeland County amalgamated on August 1, 2007 to create Lac La Biche County.
Peter Kirylchuk, Mayor
780-623-7732, Fax: 780-623-7720
Lucien Cloutier, County Clerk
lucien.cloutier@laclabichecounty.com

Lac Ste. Anne County
P.O. Box 219
4928 Langston St.
Sangudo, AB T0E 2A0
Tel: 780-785-3411; *Fax:* 780-785-2359
lsac@gov.lacsteanne.ab.ca
www.gov.lacsteanne.ab.ca
Other Information: Toll-Free: 1-866-880-5722
Municipal Type: Municipal District
Incorporated: Jan. 1, 1944 *Area:* 2,842.46 sq km
Population in 2006: 9,516
Next Election: 2013 (3 year terms)
Lloyd Giebelhaus, Reeve
Len Szybunka, County Manager
lszybunka@gov.lacsteanne.ab.ca

Lacombe County
RR#3
Lacombe, AB T4L 2N3
Tel: 403-782-6601; *Fax:* 403-782-3820
info@lacombecounty.com
www.lacombecounty.com
Municipal Type: County
Incorporated: Jan. 1, 1944 *Area:* 2,777.26 sq km
County or District: Lacombe No. 14; *Population in 2008:* 10,507
Next Election: 2013 (3 year terms)
Note: Incorporated as a county on Jan. 1, 1961.
Terry Hager, County Commissioner
thager@lacombecounty.com
Terry Engen, Reeve
Keith Boras, Manager, Agriculture Services
kboras@lacombecounty.com
Dale Freitag, Manager, Planning Services
dfreitag@lacombecounty.com
Julian Veuger, County Constable, Disaster Services
jveuger@lacombecounty.com
Dale Freitaq, Planner & Development Officer
dfreitaq@lacombecounty.com
Dale Kary, Project Coordinator, Public Works
dkary@lacombecounty.com
Phil Lodermeier, Supervisor, Public Works
plodermeier@lacombecounty.com

Lamont County
Administration Bldg.
5303 - 50 Ave.
Lamont, AB T0B 2R0
Tel: 780-895-2233; *Fax:* 780-895-7404
countyinfo@lamontcounty.ca
www.lamontcounty.ca
Other Information: Toll-Free: 1-877-895-2233
Municipal Type: County
Incorporated: Dec. 23, 1912 *Area:* 2,400.78 sq km
County or District: Lamont No. 30; *Population in 2006:* 3,925
Next Election: 2013 (3 year terms)
Note: Incorporated as a county on Jan. 1, 1968.
Wayne Woldanski, Reeve
wayne.w@lamontcounty.ca
Allan Harvey, CAO
allan.h@tclamont.ca

Leduc County
#101, 1101 - 5 St.
Nisku, AB T9E 2X3
Tel: 780-955-3555; *Fax:* 780-955-3444
shaunaf@leduc-county.com
www.leduc-county.com
Other Information: Toll free: 1-800-379-9052
Municipal Type: County
Incorporated: Jan. 1, 1944 *Area:* 2,610.25 sq km
County or District: Leduc No. 25; *Population in 2006:* 12,730
Next Election: 2013 (3 year terms)
Note: Incorporated as a county on Jan. 1, 1964.
Doug Wright, County Manager
780-955-6400
dougw@leduc-county.com
John Whaley, Reeve
Michael MacLean, Director, Public Works & Engineering
780-955-6416
michael@leduc-county.com
Phil Newman, Director, Planning & Development
780-955-6413
phil@leduc-county.com
Dean Ohnysty, Director, Parks & Recreation
780-955-4535
dean@leduc-county.com
Garett Broadbent, Director, Agricultural Services
780-955-6404
garett@leduc-county.com
Bob Galloway, Chief, Fire
780-955-7099
bobg@leduc-county.com
Deryld Dublanko, Manager, Maintenance & Materials Supply
780-955-2469
deryld@leduc-county.com
Janis Fong, Manager, Public Works & Infrastructure
Des Mryglod, Manager, Engineering
Dave McPhee, Officer, Utilities
780-955-4541
dave@leduc-county.com

Lesser Slave River No. 124
P.O. Box 722
Slave Lake, AB T0G 2A0
Tel: 780-849-4888; *Fax:* 780-849-4939
md124@md124.ca
www.md124.ca
Municipal Type: Municipal District
Incorporated: Jan. 1, 1969 *Area:* 10,075.88 sq km
Population in 2006: 2,820
Next Election: 2013 (3 year terms)
Note: Incorporated as a municipal district on Jan. 1, 1995.
Denny Garratt, Reeve
denny1@telusplanet.net
Allan Winarski, CAO
allan.winarski@md124.ca

Lethbridge County
#100, 905 - 4 Ave. South
Lethbridge, AB T1J 4E4
Tel: 403-328-5525; *Fax:* 403-328-5602
mailbox@lethcounty.ca
www.county.lethbridge.ab.ca
Municipal Type: County
Incorporated: Jan. 1, 1954 *Area:* 2,839.28 sq km
County or District: Lethbridge No. 26; *Population in 2006:* 10,302
Next Election: 2013 (3 year terms)
Note: Incorporated as a county on Jan 1, 1964.
Lorne Hickey, Reeve
lhickey@lethcounty.ca
Dennis Shigematsu, County Manager
dshigematsu@lethcounty.ca

Mackenzie County
P.O. Box 640
4511 - 46 Ave.
Fort Vermilion, AB T0H 1N0
Tel: 780-927-3718; *Fax:* 780-927-4266
office@mackenziecounty.com
www.mackenziecounty.com
Other Information: Toll Free: 1-877-927-0677
Municipal Type: Regional Municipality
Incorporated: Jan. 1, 1995 *Area:* 80,484.42 sq km
Population in 2006: 10,002
Next Election: 2013 (3 year terms)
Note: Incorporated as a specialized municipality on June 23,

1999. Name changed from The Municipal District of Mackenzie No. 23 to Mackenzie County in 2007.
William (Bill) Kostiw, CAO
780-841-1801
bkostiw@mackenziecounty.com
Gregory Alan Newman, Reeve
780-927-3807
greg@mackenziecounty.com

Minburn County No. 27
P.O. Box 550
4909-50 St.
Vegreville, AB T9C 1R6
Tel: 780-632-2082; *Fax:* 780-632-6296
info@minburncounty.ab.ca
www.minburncounty.ab.ca
Municipal Type: County
Incorporated: Jan. 30, 1942 *Area:* 2,911.14 sq km
County or District: Minburn No. 27; *Population in 2006:* 3,319
Next Election: 2013 (3 year terms)
Note: Incorporated as a county on Jan. 1, 1965.
Eric Anderson, Reeve
David Marynowich, Manager

Mountain View County
P.O. Box 100
1408 Twp Rd. 320
Didsbury, AB T0M 0W0
Tel: 403-335-3311; *Fax:* 403-335-9207
info@mountainviewcounty.com
www.mountainviewcounty.com
Other Information: Toll Free Phone: 1-877-264-9754
Municipal Type: County
Incorporated: Dec. 9, 1912 *Area:* 3,804.43 sq km
Population in 2007: 12,570
Next Election: 2013 (3 year terms)
Note: Incorporated as a county on Jan. 1, 1961.
Doug Plamping, CAO
doug.plamping@mountainviewcounty.com
Albert Kemmere, Reeve
Steve McInnis, Director, Operational Services
steve.mcinnis@mountainviewcounty.com
Tony Martens, Director, Legislative & Community Services
tony.martens@mountainviewcounty.com
Jeff Holmes, Manager, Agriculture & Parks Services
jeff.holmes@mountainviewcounty.com

Newell County No. 4
P.O. Box 130
707 - 2nd Ave. East
Brooks, AB T1R 1B2
Tel: 403-362-3266; *Fax:* 403-362-8681
administration@countyofnewell.ab.ca
www.countyofnewell.ab.ca
Municipal Type: County
Incorporated: Feb. 10, 1948 *Area:* 5,903.47 sq km
Population in 2009: 7,101
Next Election: 2013 (3 year terms)
Note: Incorporated as a county on Jan. 1, 1953.
Kevin Stephenson, CAO
stephensonk@countyofnewell.ab.ca
Molly Douglass, Reeve

Northern Lights No. 22
P.O. Box 10
#600, 7th Ave. NW
Manning, AB T0H 2M0
Tel: 780-836-3348; *Fax:* 780-836-3663
info@mdnorth22.ab.ca, mdnorth22@mdnorth22.ab.ca
www.mdnorth22.ab.ca
Municipal Type: Municipal District
Incorporated: Dec. 18, 1913 *Area:* 20,745.45 sq km
Population in 2006: 3,772
Next Election: 2013 (3 year terms)
Note: Incorporated as a municipal district on April 1, 1995.
Edward Kamieniecki, Reeve
Theresa Van Oort, CAO
cao@mdnorth22.ab.ca

Northern Sunrise County
P.O. Box 1300
Peace River, AB T8S 1Y9
Tel: 780-624-0013; *Fax:* 780-624-0023
general@northernsunrise.net
www.northernsunrise.net
Municipal Type: Municipal District
Incorporated: Dec. 18, 1913 *Area:* 21,141.25 sq km
Population in 2006: 1,747
Next Election: 2013 (3 year terms)
Note: Incorporated as a municipal district on April 1, 1994.
Carolyn Kolebaba, Reeve
Bob Miles, CAO
ramiles@northernsunrise.net

Opportunity No. 17
P.O. Box 60
Wabasca, AB T0G 2K0
Tel: 780-891-3778; *Fax:* 780-891-4283
general_inquiries@mdopportunity.ab.ca
www.mdopportunity.ab.ca
Municipal Type: Municipal District
Incorporated: Dec. 18, 1913 *Area:* 29,140.78 sq km
Population in 2006: 2,847
Next Election: 2013 (3 year terms)
Note: Incorporated as a municipal district on Aug. 1, 1995.
Paul Sinclair, Reeve
Simon Cardinal, Manager
SCardinal@mdopportunity.ab.ca

Paintearth County No. 18
P.O. Box 509
Castor, AB T0C 0X0
Tel: 403-882-3211; *Fax:* 403-882-3560
glucas@countypaintearth.ca
www.countypaintearth.ca
Municipal Type: County
Incorporated: Dec. 8, 1913 *Area:* 3,287.24 sq km
County or District: Paintearth No. 18; *Population in 2006:* 2,126
Next Election: 2013 (3 year terms)
Note: Incorporated as a county on Jan. 1, 1962.
George Glazier, Reeve
gglazier@countypaintearth.ca
Tarolyn Peach, CAO
tpeach@countypaintearth.ca

Parkland County
53109A Sec Hwy. 779
Parkland County, AB T7Z 1R1
Tel: 780-968-8888; *Fax:* 780-968-8413
inquiries@parklandcounty.com
www.parklandcounty.com
Other Information: Toll Free: 1-888-880-0858
Municipal Type: County
Incorporated: March 1, 1918 *Area:* 2,392.61 sq km
Population in 2009: 30,089
Next Election: 2013 (3 year terms)
Note: Incorporated as a county on Jan. 1, 1969.
Pat Vincent, CAO
780-968-8411
pvincent@parklandcounty.com
Rodney Shaigec, Mayor
rshaigec@parklandcounty.com
Mark Cardinal, Manager, Agricultural Services
mcardinal@parklandcounty.com
Andy Haden, Manager, Planning & Development Services
ahaden@parklandcounty.com
Rob McGowan, Manager, Engineering Services
rmcgowan@parklandcounty.com
Daryl Phillips, Manager, Public Works
dphillips@parklandcounty.com
Ken Saulit, Manager, Protective Services
ksaulit@parklandcounty.com
Ken Van Buul, Manager, Recreation & Parks Services
kvanbuul@parklandcounty.com
Janette Szucs, Coordinator, Purchasing
jszucs@parklandcounty.com
Trent Tompkins, Coordinator, Solid Waste
ttompkins@parklandcounty.com
Kevin Bryant, Supervisor, Utilities & Waste Services
kbryant@parklandcounty.com
Brian Rimmer, Supervisor, Environmental Services
brimmer@parklandcounty.com
Grace Horsfield, Officer, Development
ghorsfield@parklandcounty.com

Peace No. 135
P.O. Box 34
Berwyn, AB T0H 0E0
Tel: 780-338-3845; *Fax:* 780-338-2222
mdpeace@wispernet.ca
www.mdpeace.com
Municipal Type: Municipal District
Incorporated: Dec. 11, 1916 *Area:* 851.92 sq km
Population in 2006: 1,487
Next Election: 2013 (3 year terms)
Veronica Bliska, Reeve
Lyle McKen, CAO
780-338-3845

Pincher Creek No. 9
P.O. Box 279
Pincher Creek, AB T0K 1W0
Tel: 403-627-3130; *Fax:* 403-627-5070
info@mdpinchercreek.ab.ca
www.mdpinchercreek.ab.ca
Municipal Type: Municipal District
Incorporated: Jan. 1, 1944 *Area:* 3,482.26 sq km
Population in 2006: 3,309
Next Election: 2013 (3 year terms)
Rodney Cyr, Reeve
bhammond@mdpinchercreek.ab.ca
Wendy Kay, CAO
wkay@mdpinchercreek.ab.ca

Ponoka County
4205 Hwy. 2A
Ponoka, AB T4J 1V9
Tel: 403-783-3333; *Fax:* 403-783-6965
ponokacounty@ponokacounty.com
www.ponokacounty.com
Municipal Type: County
Incorporated: Jan. 1, 1944 *Area:* 2,807.94 sq km
County or District: Ponoka No. 3; *Population in 2006:* 8,640
Next Election: 2013 (3 year terms)
Note: Incorporated as a county on July 1, 1999.
Charlie Cutforth, CAO
charliecutforth@ponokacounty.com
Gordon Svenningsen, Reeve

Provost No. 52
P.O. Box 300
Provost, AB T0B 3S0
Tel: 780-753-2434; *Fax:* 780-753-6432
mdprovost@mdprovost.ca
www.mdprovost.ca
Municipal Type: Municipal District
Incorporated: Dec. 9, 1912 *Area:* 3,625.2 sq km
Population in 2006: 2,547
Next Election: 2013 (3 year terms)
Allan Murray, Reeve
780-753-6531
Tyler Lawrason, Administrator
tlawrason@mdprovost.ca

Ranchland No. 66
P.O. Box 1060
Nanton, AB T0L 1R0
Tel: 403-646-3131; *Fax:* 403-646-3141
admin@ranchland66.com
www.mdranchland.ca
Municipal Type: Municipal District
Incorporated: Jan. 1, 1969 *Area:* 2,639.16 sq km
Population in 2006: 86
Next Election: 2013 (3 year terms)
Note: Incorporated as a municipal district on Jan. 1, 1995.
Harry Streeter, Reeve
Gregory Brkich, CAO
cao@ranchland66.com

Red Deer County
Red Deer County Centre
38106 Range Rd. 275
Red Deer County, AB T4S 2L9
Tel: 403-350-2150; *Fax:* 403-346-9840
info@rdcounty.ca
http://rdcounty.ca
Municipal Type: County
Incorporated: Jan. 1, 1944 *Area:* 4,002.58 sq km
Population in 2006: 19,108
Next Election: 2013 (3 year terms)
Note: Incorporated as a county on Jan. 1, 1963.
Curtis Herzberg, County Manager
cherzberg@reddeercounty.ab.ca
Jim Wood, Mayor
403-350-2152
Harry Harker, Director, Planning & Development
hharker@reddeercounty.ab.ca
Ric Henderson, Director, Community & Protective Services
rhenderson@reddeercounty.ab.ca
Frank Peck, Director, Operations Services
fpeck@reddeercounty.ab.ca
Cliff Fuller, Fire Chief
cfuller@reddeercounty.ab.ca
Don Bardonnex, Manager, Fire Services
dbardonnex@reddeercounty.ab.ca
Joe D'Onofrio, Manager, Land
jd'onofrio@reddeercounty.ab.ca
Linda Henrickson, Manager, Rural Planning
lhenrickson@reddeercounty.ab.ca
Johan van der Bank, Manager, Urban Planning
jvanderbank@reddeercounty.ab.ca

Marty Campbell, Coordinator, Engineering
mcampbell@reddeercounty.ab.ca
Jo-Ann Symington, Coordinator, Community Services
jsymington@reddeercounty.ab.ca
Andrew Treu, Coordinator, Environmental Services
atreu@reddeercounty.ab.ca
Donna Trottier, Coordinator, Conservation
Dawna Barnes, Specialist, Community Development
dbarnes@reddeercounty.ab.ca
Art Preachuk, Fieldman, Agricultural Services
apreachuk@reddeercounty.ab.ca

Rocky View No. 44
911 - 32 Ave. NE
Calgary, AB T2E 6X6
Tel: 403-230-1401; *Fax:* 403-277-5977
comments@rockyview.ca
www.rockyview.ca
Municipal Type: Municipal District
Incorporated: Feb. 1, 1943 *Area:* 4,014.89 sq km
Population in 2006: 34,171
Next Election: 2013 (3 year terms)
Robert Coon, CAO
rcoon@rockyview.ca
Lois Habberfield, Reeve
council@rockyview.ca
Brian Jobson, Director, Transportation Services
bjobson@gov.mdrockyview.ab.ca
Frank Misura, Manager, Development/Utility Services
Linda Ratzlaff, Coordinator, Policy Planning
403-520-8166
Tim Dietzler, Fieldman, Agriculture
403-520-1271

Saddle Hills County
P.O. Box 69
Spirit River, AB T0H 3G0
Tel: 780-864-3760; *Fax:* 780-864-3904
admin@saddlehills.ab.ca
www.saddlehills.ab.ca
Municipal Type: Municipal District
Incorporated: April 1, 1945 *Area:* 5,836.94 sq km
Population in 2006: 2,458
Next Election: 2013 (3 year terms)
Note: Incorporated as a municipal district on Jan. 1, 1995.
Tim Stone, Reeve
council@saddlehills.ab.ca
Dianne Nellis, CAO
dnellis@saddlehills.ab.ca

St. Paul County No. 19
5015 - 49 Ave.
St Paul, AB T0A 3A4
Tel: 780-645-3301; *Fax:* 780-645-3104
countysp@county.stpaul.ab.ca
www.county.stpaul.ab.ca
Municipal Type: Municipal District
Incorporated: Jan. 30, 1942 *Area:* 3,297.74 sq km
Population in 2006: 5,925
Next Election: 2013 (3 year terms)
Steve Upham, Reeve
Sheila Kitz, CAO
skitz@county.stpaul.ab.ca

Smoky Lake County
P.O. Box 310
Smoky Lake, AB T0A 3C0
Tel: 780-656-3730; *Fax:* 780-656-3768
county@smokylakecounty.ab.ca
www.smokylakecounty.ab.ca
Other Information: toll free: 888-656-3730
Municipal Type: Municipal District
Incorporated: May 3, 1922 *Area:* 3,412.81 sq km
Population in 2006: 3,357
Next Election: 2013 (3 year terms)
Dareld Cholak, Reeve
dcholak@smokylakecounty.ab.ca
Cory Ollikka, CAO
collika@smokylakecounty.ab.ca

Smoky River No. 130
P.O. Box 210
Falher, AB T0H 1M0
Tel: 780-837-2221; *Fax:* 780-837-2453
rtherriault@mdsmokyriver.com
www.mdsmokyriver.com
Municipal Type: Municipal District
Incorporated: Dec. 18, 1913 *Area:* 2,842.82 sq km
Population in 2006: 2,442
Next Election: 2013 (3 year terms)
Note: Incorporated as a municipal district on Jan. 1, 1952.
Robert Brochu, Reeve
Lucien G. Turcotte, CAO
lturcotte@mdsmokyriver.com

Spirit River No. 133
P.O. Box 389
Spirit River, AB T0H 3G0
Tel: 780-864-3500; *Fax:* 780-864-4303
mdsr133@mdspiritriver.ab.ca
www.mdspiritriver.ab.ca
Municipal Type: Municipal District
Incorporated: Dec. 18, 1913 *Area:* 684.14 sq km
Population in 2006: 662
Next Election: 2013 (3 year terms)
Note: Incorporated as a municipal district on Dec. 11, 1916.
Stanley W. Bzowy, Reeve
Kelly Hudson, CAO
mdsr133@mdspiritriver.ab.ca

Starland County
P.O. Box 249
Morrin, AB T0J 2B0
Tel: 403-772-3793; *Fax:* 403-772-3807
info@starlandcounty.com
www.starlandcounty.com
Municipal Type: Municipal District
Incorporated: Dec. 9, 1912 *Area:* 2,557.7 sq km
Population in 2006: 2,371
Next Election: 2013 (3 year terms)
J. Barrie Hoover, Reeve
bhoover@starlandcounty.com
Ross D. Rawlusyk, CAO
ross@starlandcounty.com

Stettler County No. 6
P.O. Box 1270
Stettler, AB T0C 2L0
Tel: 403-742-4441; *Fax:* 403-742-1277
info@stettlercounty.ca
www.stettler.net
Municipal Type: Municipal District
Incorporated: Dec. 9, 1912 *Area:* 4,008.72 sq km
Population in 2006: 5,216
Next Election: 2013 (3 year terms)
Wayne Nixon, Reeve
Tim Fox, CAO
tfox@stettlercounty.ca

Strathcona County
2001 Sherwood Dr.
Sherwood Park, AB T8A 3W7
Tel: 780-464-8111; *Fax:* 780-464-8050
info@strathcona.ab.ca
www.strathcona.ab.ca
Municipal Type: Regional Municipality
Incorporated: Jan. 1, 1962 *Area:* 1,179.43 sq km
Population in 2009: 87,998
Next Election: 2013 (3 year terms)
Note: Incorporated as a specialized municipality on Jan. 1, 1996.
Robyn W. Singleton, Q.C., Chief Commissioner
780-464-8100
singleton@strathcona.ab.ca
Linda Osinchuk, Mayor
Peter Vana, Associate Commissioner, Infrastructure & Planning Services
780-464-8188
vana@strathcona.ab.ca
Denise Exton, Associate Commissioner, Community Services
780-464-8291
exton@strathcona.ab.ca

Sturgeon County
9613 - 100 St.
Morinville, AB T8R 1L9
Tel: 780-939-4321; *Fax:* 780-939-3003
sturgeonmail@sturgeoncounty.ab.ca
www.sturgeoncounty.ab.ca
Other Information: Toll free: 1-866-939-9303
Municipal Type: Municipal District
Incorporated: Feb. 1, 1943 *Area:* 2,108.9 sq km
Population in 2008: 19,165
Next Election: 2013 (3 year terms)
Case Van Herk, County Commissioner
780-939-8345
cvanherk@sturgeoncounty.ab.ca
Donald Rigney, B.Sc., MBA, Mayor
780-921-3041, Fax: 780-921-3041
drigney@sturgeoncounty.ab.ca
Ian McKay, General Manager, Infrastructure Services
780-939-8337
imckay@sturgeoncounty.ab.ca
Peter Tarnawsky, General Manager, Public Services
780-939-8344
ptarnawsky@sturgeoncounty.ab.ca
Bart Clark, Manager, Protective Services
780-939-0600
bclark@sturgeoncounty.ab.ca
Collin Steffes, Manager, Planning & Development
780-939-8275
csteffes@sturgeoncounty.ab.ca
Roy Lidgren, Manager, Transportation Services
780-939-8250
rlidgern@sturgeoncounty.ab.ca
Quentin Bochar, Manager, Agriculture Services
780-939-8325
qbochar@sturgeoncounty.ab.ca
Mike Hittinger, Coordinator, Municipal Conservation
780-939-8339
nwaci@sturgeoncounty.ab.ca

Taber
4900B - 50 St.
Taber, AB T1G 1T2
Tel: 403-223-3541; *Fax:* 403-223-1799
dkrizsan@mdtaber.ab.ca
www.mdtaber.ab.ca
Municipal Type: Municipal District
Incorporated: April 1, 1945 *Area:* 4,204.38 sq km
Population in 2006: 6,280
Next Election: 2013 (3 year terms)
T. Brian Brewin, Reeve
Derrick Krizsan, Municipal Administrator

Thorhild County No. 7
P.O. Box 10
Thorhild, AB T0A 3J0
Tel: 780-398-3741; *Fax:* 780-398-3748
angela@thorhildcounty.com
www.thorhildcounty.com
Municipal Type: County
Incorporated: Jan. 1, 1955 *Area:* 1,998.38 sq km
County or District: Thorhild No. 7; *Population in 2006:* 3,042
Next Election: 2013 (3 year terms)
Charles Newell, Reeve
cnewell@mcsnet.ca
Angela Bilski, County Manager
angela@thorhildcounty.com

Two Hills County No. 21
P.O. Box 490
Two Hills, AB T0B 4K0
Tel: 780-657-3358; *Fax:* 780-657-3504
rjorgensen@thcounty.ab.ca
www.thcounty.ab.ca
Municipal Type: County
Incorporated: Jan. 1, 1944 *Area:* 2,630.95 sq km
County or District: Two Hills No. 21; *Population in 2006:* 2,801
Next Election: 2013 (3 year terms)
Note: Incorporated as a county on Jan. 1, 1963.
Allen Sayler, Reeve
asayler@thcounty.ab.ca
Robert Jorgensen, CAO
rjorgensen@thcounty.ab.ca

Vermilion River County
P.O. Box 69
4912 - 50 Ave.
Kitscoty, AB T0B 2P0
Tel: 780-846-2244; *Fax:* 780-846-2716
county24@telusplanet.net
www.vermilion-river.com
Municipal Type: Municipal District
Incorporated: Jan. 1, 1944 *Area:* 5,518.71 sq km
Population in 2008: 7,900
Next Election: 2013 (3 year terms)
Note: Name changed from Vermilion River No. 24 County on Sept. 13, 2006.
Rhonda King, County Administrator
780-846-3303
rking@county24.com
Richard Van Ee, Reeve
780-853-2730

Vulcan County
P.O. Box 180
Vulcan, AB T0L 2B0
Tel: 403-485-2241; *Fax:* 403-485-2920
administration@vulcancounty.ab.ca
www.vulcancounty.ab.ca
Municipal Type: County
Incorporated: April 1, 1945 *Area:* 5,430.06 sq km
County or District: Vulcan County; *Population in 2006:* 3,718

Next Election: 2013 (3 year terms)
Note: Incorporated as a county on Jan. 1, 1951.
David Schneider, Reeve
Leo Ludwig, County Administrator
cao@vulcancounty.ab.ca

Wainwright No. 61
717 - 14 Ave.
Wainwright, AB T9W 1B3
Tel: 780-842-4454; *Fax:* 780-842-2463
info@mdwainwright.ca
www.mdwainwright.ca
Municipal Type: Municipal District
Incorporated: Jan. 30, 1942 *Area:* 4,154.74 sq km
Population in 2006: 3,558
Next Election: 2013 (3 year terms)
Bob Barss, Reeve
Kelly Buchinski, Municipal Administrator
admin@mdwainwright.ca

Warner County No. 5
P.O. Box 90
Warner, AB T0K 2L0
Tel: 403-642-3635; *Fax:* 403-642-3631
county5@countyofwarner5.ab.ca
www.countyofwarner5.ab.ca
Municipal Type: Municipal District
Incorporated: Dec. 9, 1912 *Area:* 4,519.77 sq km
Population in 2006: 3,674
Next Election: 2013 (3 year terms)
Robert Jones, Reeve
div5_wa@countyofwarner5.ab.ca
Shawn Hathaway, CAO
administrator@countyofwarner5.ab.ca

Westlock County
10336 - 106 St.
Westlock, AB T7P 2G1
Tel: 780-349-3346; *Fax:* 780-349-2012
info@westlockcounty.com
www.westlockcounty.com
Municipal Type: Municipal District
Incorporated: Feb. 1, 1943 *Area:* 3,174.6 sq km
Population in 2006: 6,910
Next Election: 2013 (3 year terms)
Charles Navratil, Reeve
780-349-2818
Edward LeBlanc, CAO
eleblanc@westlockcounty.com

Wetaskiwin County No. 10
P.O. Box 6960
Wetaskiwin, AB T9A 2G5
Tel: 780-352-3321; *Fax:* 780-352-3486
fcoutney@county.wetaskiwin.ab.ca
www.county.wetaskiwin.ab.ca
Other Information: Toll Free: 1-800-661-4125
Municipal Type: County
Incorporated: Dec. 13, 1915 *Area:* 3,130.9 sq km
County or District: Wetaskiwin No. 10; *Population in 2006:* 10,535
Next Election: 2013 (3 year terms)
Note: Incorporated as a county on Jan. 1, 1958.
Frank Coutney, County Administrator
fcoutney@county.wetaskiwin.ab.ca
Garry Dearing, Reeve
Ken Carlson, Director, Disaster Services
780-361-6340
kcarlson@county.wetaskiwin.ab.ca
Dave Dextraze, Director, Public Works
780-361-6230
ddextraze@county.wetaskiwin.ab.ca
Steve Majek, Director, Agricultural Services
780-361-6226
smajek@county.wetaskiwin.ab.ca

Wheatland County
Hwy. 1, RR#1
Strathmore, AB T1P 1J6
Tel: 403-934-3321; *Fax:* 403-934-4889
admin@wheatlandcounty.ca
www.wheatlandcounty.ca
Municipal Type: County
Incorporated: April 1, 1945 *Area:* 4,550.92 sq km
Population in 2006: 8,164
Next Election: 2013 (3 year terms)
Note: Incorporated as a county on Jan. 1, 1961.
Ben Armstrong, Reeve
ben.armstrong@wheatlandcounty.ca
Jennifer Deak, County Manager
jennifer.deak@wheatlandcounty.ca

Willow Creek No. 26
P.O. Box 550
Claresholm, AB T0L 0T0
Tel: 403-625-3351; *Fax:* 403-625-3886
md26@mdwillowcreek.com
www.mdwillowcreek.com
Other Information: Toll free: 1-888-337-3351
Municipal Type: Municipal District
Incorporated: Jan. 1, 1944 *Area:* 4,560.22 sq km
Population in 2006: 5,337
Next Election: 2013 (3 year terms)
Henry Van Hierden, Reeve
403-553-2015
Cynthia Vizzutti, Administrator

Wood Buffalo
9909 Franklin Ave.
Fort McMurray, AB T9H 2K4
Tel: 780-743-7000; *Fax:* 780-743-7028
communications@woodbuffalo.ab.ca
www.woodbuffalo.ab.ca
Other Information: Toll Free: 1-800-973-9663
Municipal Type: Regional Municipality
Incorporated: April 1, 1995 *Area:* 63,342.89 sq km
Population in 2006: 51,496
Next Election: 2013 (3 year terms)
Kelly Kloss, Acting CAO
780-743-7023
kelly.kloss@woodbuffalo.ab.ca
Melissa Blake, Mayor
Wes Holodniuk, Manager, Operations & Maintenance
780-743-7931, Fax: 780-799-5909
wes.holodniuk@woodbuffalo.ab.ca
Salem Abushawashi, Superintendent, Fort Chipewyan
780-697-3600
salem.abushawashi@woodbuffalo.ab.ca
Guy Jette, Acting Superintendent, Operations & Facilities Maintenance
780-799-7486
guy.jette@woodbuffalo.ab.ca
Darcy Elder, Superintendent, Infrastructure
780-799-7475
darcy.elder@woodbuffalo.ab.ca
Michel Savard, Superintendent, Environment
780-799-7490
michel.savard@woodbuffalo.ab.ca
Dwayne Harvie, Project Engineer
780-743-7855
dwayne.harvie@woodbuffalo.ab.ca

Woodlands County
P.O. Box 60
Whitecourt, AB T7S 1N3
Tel: 780-778-8400; *Fax:* 780-778-8402
admin@woodlands.ab.ca
www.woodlands.ab.ca
Other Information: Toll free: 1-888-870-6315
Municipal Type: Municipal District
Incorporated: Jan. 1, 1969 *Area:* 7,668.11 sq km
Population in 2006: 4,158
Next Election: 2013 (3 year terms)
Note: Incorporated as a municipal district on Jan. 1, 1994.
Jim Rennie, Reeve
jim.rennie@woodlands.ab.ca
Luc Mercier, CAO
luc.mercier@woodlands.ab.ca

Yellowhead County
2716 - 1st Ave.
Edson, AB T7E 1N9
Tel: 780-723-4800; *Fax:* 780-723-5066
info@yellowheadcounty.ab.ca
www.yellowheadcounty.ab.ca
Other Information: Toll Free Phone: 1-800-665-6030
Municipal Type: Municipal District
Incorporated: Jan. 1, 1994 *Area:* 22,303.82 sq km
Population in 2006: 10,045
Next Election: 2013 (3 year terms)
Jack Ramme, CAO
jack.ramme@yellowheadcounty.ab.ca
Gerald Soroka, Mayor
gsoroka@yellowheadcounty.ab.ca

Major Municipalities in Alberta

Airdrie
400 Main St. SE
Airdrie, AB T4B 3C3
Tel: 403-948-8800; *Fax:* 403-948-6567
information.systems@airdrie.ca; www.airdrie.ca
Municipal Type: City
Incorporated: Sept. 10, 1909 *Area:* 33.10 sq km
Population in 2010: 39,822
Provincial Electoral District(s): Airdrie-Chestermere
Federal Electoral District(s): Wild Rose
Next Election: 2013 (3 year terms)
Note: Incorporated as a city on Jan. 1, 1985.
George Keene, City Manager
george.keen@airdrie.ca
Peter Brown, Mayor
mayor@airdrie.ca
Mark Locking, Director, Engineering & Public Works
Jeff Greene, City Planner & Team Leader
403-948-8848
planning.development@airdrie.ca
Dave Rimes, Leader, Parks
403-948-8402
parks@airdrie.ca
Mary Grace Curtis, Coordinator, Recycling & Composting
780-948-0246
environmental.services@airdrie.ca
Darryl Wolski, Coordinator, Solid Waste
403-948-0246
pubwrks@airdrie.ca

Emergency Services

Beaumont
5600 - 49 St.
Beaumont, AB T4X 1A1
Tel: 780-929-8782; *Fax:* 780-929-8729
admin@town.beaumont.ab.ca
www.town.beaumont.ab.ca
Municipal Type: City
Incorporated: Jan. 1, 1973 *Area:* 10.5 sq km
Population in 2010: 12,586
Provincial Electoral District(s): Leduc-Beaumont-Devon
Federal Electoral District(s): Edmonton-Mill Woods-Beaumont
Next Election: 2013 (3 year terms)
Note: Incorporated as a town on Jan 1, 1980.
Marc Landry, General Manager
marc.landry@town.beaumont.ab.ca
Camille Bérubé, Mayor

Brooks
P.O. Box 880
201 - 1 Ave. West
Brooks, AB T1R 0Z6
Tel: 403-362-3333; *Fax:* 403-362-4787
admin@brooks.ca
www.brooks.ca
Municipal Type: City
Incorporated: July 14, 1910 *Area:* 17.7 sq km
Population in 2007: 13,581
Provincial Electoral District(s): Strathmore-Brooks
Federal Electoral District(s): Medicine Hat
Next Election: 2013 (3 year terms)
Note: Incorporated as a city on Sept. 1, 2005.
Kevin Stephenson, City Manager
kstephenson@brooks.ca
Martin Shields, Mayor
mshields@brooks.ca
Neil Hollands, Director, Engineering & Property Services
nhollands@brooks.ca
Kevin Swanson, Director, Protective Services
403-362-2331
Terry Walsh, Director, Parks & Recreation
twalsh@brooks.ca
Maurice Landry, Manager, Development Services
mlandry@brooks.ca
Bill Prentice, Manager, Public Works
403-362-3146
bprentice@brooks.ca
Gord Shaw, Manager, Planning Services
gshaw@brooks.ca

Calgary
P.O. Box 2100 M
800 Macleod Trail SE
Calgary, AB T2P 2M5
Tel: 403-268-2489; *Fax:* 403-538-6111
www.calgary.ca
Other Information: TTY: 403-268-4889
Municipal Type: City
Incorporated: Nov. 7, 1884 *Area:* 726.5 sq km
Population in 2009: 1,230,248
Provincial Electoral District(s): Cal.-Bow; Cal.-Buffalo; Cal.-Cross; Cal.-Currie; Cal.-Egmont; Cal.-East; Cal.-Elbow; Cal.-Fish Creek; Cal.-Foothills; Cal.-Fort; Cal.-Glenmore; Cal.-Hays; Cal.-Lougheed; Cal.-McCall; Cal.-Mackay; Cal.-Montrose; Cal.-Mountain View; Cal.-North Hill; Cal.-Nose Hill; Cal.-Shaw; Cal.-Varsity; Cal.-West

Federal Electoral District(s): Calgary Centre; Calgary Centre-North; Calgary East; Calgary Northeast; Calgary-Nose Hill; Calgary Southeast; Calgary Southwest; Calgary West; Macleod; Wild Rose
Next Election: 2013 (3 year terms)
Note: Incorporated as a city on Jan. 1, 1894.
Diana L. Garner, City Clerk
403-268-5861, Fax: 403-268-2362
cityclerk@calgary.ca
Naheed K. Nenshi, Mayor
403-268-5622, Fax: 403-268-8130
themayor@calgary.ca
Dale Hodges, Aldermen, Ward(s): 1
403-268-2445, Fax: 403-268-8091
George McLauchlan, Director, Human Resources
403-268-2201, Fax: 403-268-4680
Frederick Gordon Lowe, Aldermen, Ward(s): 2
403-268-2430, Fax: 403-268-3823
Stuart Dalgleish, Director & City Assessor
403-268-4609, Fax: 403-268-8278
Jim Stevenson, Aldermen, Ward(s): 3
403-268-2430, Fax: 403-268-8091
J. Bernie Trahan, Director, Fleet Services
403-268-1122, Fax: 403-266-2496
btrahan@calgary.ca
Gael MacLeod, Aldermen, Ward(s): 4
403-268-2430, Fax: 403-268-8091
Anne Charlton, Director, Parks
403-268-3888
Ray Jones, Aldermen, Ward(s): 5
403-268-2430, Fax: 403-268-3823
John Hubbell, General Manager, Transportation
Richard Pootmans, Aldermen, Ward(s): 6
403-268-2430, Fax: 403-268-8091
Mary Axworthy, Director, Land Use Planning & Policy
Druh Farrell, Aldermen, Ward(s): 7
403-268-2475, Fax: 403-268-3823
David L. Day, Director, Environmental & Safety Management
403-268-3668
John Mar, Aldermen, Ward(s): 8
403-268-2430, Fax: 403-268-3823
Dave Griffiths, Director, Waste & Recycling Services
Gian-Carlo Carra, Aldermen, Ward(s): 9
403-268-2430, Fax: 403-268-8091
Allyn Humber, Director, Water Services
403-268-2702
waterworks@calgary.ca
Andre Chabot, Aldermen, Ward(s): 10
403-268-2430, Fax: 403-268-3823
Ian Norris, Director, Transportation Infrastructure
403-974-4876
Brian Pincott, Aldermen, Ward(s): 11
403-268-2430, Fax: 403-268-8091
Wolf Keller, Director, Water Resources
403-268-6752
Shane A. Keating, Aldermen, Ward(s): 12
403-268-2430, Fax: 403-268-4673
Jack Beaton, Chief of Police
403-206-5900
Diane Colley-Urquhart, Aldermen, Ward(s): 13
403-268-2430, Fax: 403-268-8091
W. Bruce Burrell, Fire Chief
403-287-4255, Fax: 403-243-1490
Linda Fox-Mellway, Aldermen, Ward(s): 14
403-268-2430, Fax: 403-268-3823
Tom Sampson, Deputy Chief, Calgary Emergency Management Agency
tom.sampson@calgary.ca
Owen Tobert, P.Eng., City Manager
owens.tobert@calgary.ca
David Watson, General Manager, Planning Development & Assessment
403-268-2601
david.watson@calgary.ca
Rob Pritchard, General Manager, Utilities & Environmental Protection
403-268-2042, Fax: 403-537-3023
Erika Hargesheimer, General Manager, Community & Protective Services
403-268-5636
Kathy Strong-Duffin, Manager, Environmental Policy & Strategic Initiatives
403-268-4699
kstrongd@calgary.ca
Kevan van Velzen, M.Sc., P.Biol., Manager, Environmental Assessment & Liabilities
403-250-6448
Richard Binder, Manager, Infrastructure & Program Development
richard.binder@calgary.ca

Camrose
City Hall
5204 - 50 Ave.
Camrose, AB T4V 0S8
Tel: 780-672-4426; *Fax:* 780-672-2469
admin@camrose.ca
www.camrose.ca
Municipal Type: City
Incorporated: May 4, 1905 *Area:* 31.14 sq km
Population in 2008: 16,543
Provincial Electoral District(s): Wetaskiwin-Camrose
Federal Electoral District(s): Crowfoot
Next Election: 2013 (3 year terms)
Note: Incorporated as a city on Jan. 1, 1955.
Marshall Chalmers, Mayor
admin@camrose.ca
Brian Hamblin, P.Eng., City Manager
bhamblin@camrose.ca
Damian Herle, Manager, Corporate & Protective Services
Diane Urkow, Manager, Financial Services
Jeremy Enarson, Acting City Engineer, Engineering Services
Chris Clarkson, Director, Parks
780-672-9195
Jim Kupka, Director, Public Works
780-672-5513
Darrell Kambeitz, Police Chief
Peter Krich, Fire Chief/Deputy Director, Emergency Management
Brenda Hisey, Director, Planning & Development
780-672-4428
Doug Delmage, Chief Building Inspector
780-672-4428

Canmore
902 - 7 Ave.
Canmore, AB T1W 3K1
Tel: 403-678-1500; *Fax:* 403-678-1524
info@canmore.ca
www.canmore.ca
Municipal Type: City
Incorporated: Jan. 1, 1965 *Area:* 68.9 sq km
Population in 2006: 12,039
Provincial Electoral District(s): Banff-Cochrane
Federal Electoral District(s): Wild Rose
Next Election: 2013 (3 year terms)
Note: Incorporated as a town on June 1, 1966.
Don Kochan, CAO
donkochan@canmore.ca
Ron Casey, Mayor
mayor@canmore.ca
Don Kochan, Director, Environmental Services
donkochan@canmore.ca
Doug Townsend, Manager, Facilities
403-678-1586
Kevin Van Vliet, Manager, Engineering
403-678-1545, Fax: 403-678-1534

Chestermere
105 Marina Rd.
Chestermere, AB T1X 1V7
Tel: 403-207-7050; *Fax:* 403-569-0512
town@chestermere.ca
www.chestermere.ca
Municipal Type: City
Incorporated: April 1, 1977 *Area:* 8.91 sq km
Population in 2010: 14,285
Provincial Electoral District(s): Airdrie-Chestermere
Federal Electoral District(s): Crowfoot
Next Election: 2013 (3 year terms)
Note: Incorporated as a town on March 1, 1993.
Terry Hurlbut, CAO
403-207-7070
thurlbut@chestermere.ca
Patricia Matthews, Mayor
403-207-7073
pmatthews@chestermere.ca
Patrick Bergen, Councillor
Heather Davies, Councillor
Stewart Hutchinson, Councillor
Kelsey Johnson, Councillor
Terry Leighton, Councillor
Christopher Steeves, Councillor

Cochrane
P.O. Box 10
101 Ranche House Rd.
Cochrane, AB T4C 2K8
Tel: 403-851-2505; *Fax:* 403-851-2581
cochrane@cochrane.ca
www.cochrane.ca
Municipal Type: City
Incorporated: June 17, 1903 *Area:* 30.03 sq km
Population in 2006: 13,760
Provincial Electoral District(s): Banff-Cochrane
Federal Electoral District(s): Wild Rose
Next Election: 2013 (3 year terms)
Note: Incorporated as a town on Feb. 15, 1971.
Julian deCocq, Clerk
julian.decocq@cochrane.ca
Truper McBride, Mayor
truper.mcbride@cochrane.ca
Jim Anderson, Director, Operational Services
403-851-2560
jim.anderson@cochrane.ca
Lori Leipnitz, Director, Corporate Services
403-851-2510
lori.leipnitz@cochrane.ca
Ian Smith, Director, Community & Protective Services
403-851-2530
ian.smith@cochrane.ca
Frank Wesseling, Director, Planning & Engineering
403-851-2570
frank.wesseling@cochrane.ca
Elise Harnick, Engineer, Subdivision & Development
403-851-2575
elise.harnick@cochrane.ca

Cold Lake
5513 - 48 Ave.
Cold Lake, AB T9M 1A1
Tel: 780-594-4494; *Fax:* 780-594-3480
city@coldlake.com
www.coldlake.com
Municipal Type: City
Incorporated: Dec. 31, 1953 *Area:* 59.3 sq km
Population in 2009: 13,924
Provincial Electoral District(s): Bonnyville-Cold Lake
Federal Electoral District(s): Westlock-St. Paul
Next Election: 2013 (3 year terms)
Note: Incorporated as a city on Oct. 1, 2000.
Gordon Frank, CAO
gfrank@coldlake.com
Craig Copeland, Mayor
Allan Weiss, Chief, Fire
780-594-4494
Carry Grant, Manager, Operations
780-594-3776
cgrant@coldlake.com
George McIntosh, Foreman, Utilities
780-639-3604
wtp@coldlake.com
John McLean, Foreman, Parks & Facilities
780-594-3776
parks@coldlake.com

RCMP Inquiries
Kevin Nagoya, Director of Public Works & Infrastructure

Public Works Shop

Edmonton
City Hall
1 Sir Winston Churchill Sq., 3rd Fl.
Edmonton, AB T5J 2R7
Fax: 780-496-8210
311@edmonton.ca
www.edmonton.ca
Other Information: Telephone: 311 in Edmonton; or 780-442-5311
Municipal Type: City
Incorporated: Jan. 9, 1892 *Area:* 684.37 sq km
Population in 2009: 782,439
Provincial Electoral District(s): Ed.-Beverly-Clareview; Ed.-Calder; Ed.-Castle Downs; Ed.-Centre; Ed.-Decore; Ed.-Ellerslie; Ed.-Glenora; Ed.-Gold Bar; Ed.-Highlands-Norwood; Ed.-Manning; Ed.-McClung; Ed.-Meadowlark; Ed.-Mill Creek; Ed.-Mill Woods; Ed.-Riverview; Ed.-Rutherford; Ed.-Strathcona; Ed.-Whitemud
Federal Electoral District(s): Edmonton Centre; Edmonton East; Edmonton-Leduc; Edmonton-Mill Woods-Beaumont; Edmonton-Sherwood Park; Edmonton-Spruce Grove; Edmonton-St. Albert; Edmonton-Strathcona
Next Election: 2013 (3 year terms)
Note: Incorporated as a city on Oct. 08, 1904.
Stephen Mandel, Mayor
780-496-8100, Fax: 780-496-8292
Simon Farbrother, City Manager
780-496-8231, Fax: 780-496-8220
simon.farbrother@edmonton.ca
David Edey, General Manager, Corporate Services
780-496-7201, Fax: 780-496-8854
david.edey@edmonton.ca

Linda Sloan, Councillor, Ward(s): 1
780-496-8122, Fax: 780-496-8113
linda.sloan@edmonton.ca
Kim Krushell, Councillor, Ward(s): 2
780-496-8128, Fax: 780-496-8113
kim.krushell@edmonton.ca
David Wiun, City Auditor
780-496-8315, Fax: 780-496-8062
david.wiun@edmonton.ca
Dave Loken, Councillor, Ward(s): 3
dave.loken@edmonton.ca
Mike Boyd, Police Chief
780-421-3333
Ed Gibbons, Councillor, Ward(s): 4
ed.gibbons@edmonton.ca
Dave Galea, Director, Office of Emergency Preparedness
780-944-6420, Fax: 780-496-3062
david.galea@edmonton.ca
Karen Leibovici, Councillor, Ward(s): 5
780-496-8120, Fax: 780-496-8113
karen.leibovici@edmonton.ca
Doug Costigan, Director, Asset Management & Public Works, Parks Branch
780-496-4956, Fax: 780-496-4978
doug.costigan@edmonton.ca
Jane Batty, Councillor, Ward(s): 6, Fax: 780-496-8113
jane.batty@edmonton.ca
John Hodgson, Manager, Drainage Services
780-496-5658, Fax: 780-496-3629
Tony Caterina, Councillor, Ward(s): 7
780-496-8333, Fax: 780-496-8113
tony.caterina@edmonton.ca
Gerald W. Goodall, Consultant, Corporate Services, Materials Management Branch
780-496-3729, Fax: 780-496-5015
gerry.goodall@edmonton.ca
Ben Henderson, Councillor, Ward(s): 8
780-496-8146, Fax: 780-496-8113
ben.henderson@edmonton.ca
Audra Jones, Director, Transportation Planning
780-496-1790, Fax: 780-496-4287
Bryan Anderson, Councillor, Ward(s): 9
780-496-8130, Fax: 780-496-8113
bryan.anderson@edmonton.ca
Gary Klassen, General Manager, Planning & Development
780-496-6050, Fax: 780-496-6916
gary.klassen@edmonton.ca
Don Iveson, Councillor, Ward(s): 10
780-496-8132, Fax: 780-496-8113
don.iveson@edmonton.ca
Bob Boutilier, General Manager, Transportation
780-496-2808, Fax: 780-496-2803
transportation@edmonton.ca
Kerry Diotte, Councillor, Ward(s): 11, Fax: 780-496-8113
kerry.diotte@edmonton.ca
Linda Cochrane, General Manager, Community Services
780-496-5804, Fax: 780-577-3525
linda.cochrane@edmonton.ca
Amarjeet Sohi, Councillor, Ward(s): 12
780-496-8148, Fax: 780-496-8113
amarjeet.sohi@edmonton.ca
Joyce Tustian, General Manager, Deputy City Manager's Office
780-442-6356, Fax: 780-496-8220
joyce.tustian@edmonton.ca
Mary Pat Barry, Manager, Deputy City Manager's Office, Communications Branch
780-496-8191, Fax: 780-496-4877
marypat.barry@edmonton.ca
Peter Muller, EMT-P, ABCP, Emergency Management Officer (Planning), Office of Emergency Preparedness
780-496-1530, Fax: 780-496-3062
peter.muller@edmonton.ca
Grant Pearsell, Director, Asset Management & Public Works, Parks Branch
780-496-6080, Fax: 780-496-5636
grant.pearsell@edmonton.ca
Garth Clyburn, Planner II, Planning & Development, Planning & Policy Branch
780-496-6209, Fax: 780-496-6299
garth.clyburn@edmonton.ca
Roy Neehall, Manager, Waste Management
780-496-5405, Fax: 780-496-5657

Fort Saskatchewan

10005 - 102 St.
Fort Saskatchewan, AB T8L 2C5
Tel: 780-992-6200; *Fax:* 780-998-4774
lrosen@fortsask.ca
www.fortsask.ca
Municipal Type: City
Incorporated: March 1, 1899 *Area:* 48.12 sq km
Population in 2009: 17,469
Provincial Electoral District(s): Fort Saskatchewan-Vegreville
Federal Electoral District(s): Edmonton-Sherwood Park
Next Election: 2013 (3 year terms)
Note: Incorporated as a city on July 1, 1985.
Lorna Rosen, City Manager
Gale Katchur, Mayor
John Rop, Treasurer
Scott Mack, Director, Planning
780-992-6573
smack@fortsask.ca
Todd Burge, Manager, Corporate Services
780-992-6255
tburge@fortsask.ca
Richard Hobson, Manager, Community & Protective Services
780-992-6205, Fax: 780-992-0192
rhobson@fortsask.ca
Dave Worman, Manager, Planning & Public Works
780-992-6207
dworman@fortsask.ca
Ken Lura, Superintendent, Public Works
780-992-6247
klura@fortsask.ca
Gale Katchur, Contact, Environmental Awareness Committee
gkatchur@fortsask.ca

Grande Prairie

P.O. Box 4000
10205 - 98 St.
Grande Prairie, AB T8V 6V3
Tel: 780-538-0300; *Fax:* 780-538-0746
www.cityofgp.com
Municipal Type: City
Incorporated: April 30, 1914 *Area:* 61.08 sq km
Population in 2006: 47,076
Provincial Electoral District(s): Grande Prairie-Smoky; Grande Prairie-Wapiti
Federal Electoral District(s): Peace River
Next Election: 2013 (3 year terms)
Note: Incorporated as a city on Jan. 1, 1958.
Bill Given, Mayor
bgiven@cityofgp.com
Greg Scerbak, City Manager
780-538-0312, Fax: 780-814-7560
gscerbak@cityofgp.com
Janette Ferguson, City Clerk
780-538-0314, Fax: 780-539-1056
jferguson@cityofgp.com
Frank Daskewech, Director, Public Works
780-538-0350, Fax: 780-538-4667
fdaskewech@cityofgp.com
Ken Anderson, Director, Financial Services
780-538-0302, Fax: 780-539-1056
kanderson@cityofgp.com
Josy Burrough, Manager, Parks
780-538-0476, Fax: 780-532-7588
jburrough@cityofgp.com
Michael MacIntyre, Planning Manager, Development Services
780-538-0440, Fax: 780-538-0746
mmacintyre@cityofgp.com
Valerie Norris-Kirk, Development Coordinator, Development Services
780-513-5236, Fax: 780-538-0746
vnorrisk@cityofgp.com
Uli Wolf, Solid Waste Services Supervisor, Aquatera Utilities Inc.
780-538-0360, Fax: 780-830-7060
uwolf@aquatera.ca
Amy Horne, Recycling Coordinator, Aquatera Utilities Inc.
780-538-0452, Fax: 780-830-7060
ahorne@aquatera.ca
Mark Simpson, Operations Coordinator, Aquatera Utilities Inc.
780-538-0442, Fax: 780-830-7430
msimpson@aquatera.ca
Dan Lemieux, Sr. Deputy Fire Chief
780-538-0398, Fax: 780-538-0395
dlemieux@cityofgp.com

High River

309B MacLeod Trail SW
High River, AB T1V 1Z5
Tel: 403-652-2110; *Fax:* 403-652-2396
info@highriver.ca
www.highriver.ca
Municipal Type: City
Incorporated: Dec. 5, 1901 *Area:* 14.27 sq km
Population in 2010: 11,788
Provincial Electoral District(s): Highwood
Federal Electoral District(s): Macleod
Next Election: 2013 (3 year terms)
Note: Incorporated as a town on Feb. 12, 1906.
Harry Harker, Town Manager
Emile Blokland, Mayor

Lacombe

5432 - 56 Ave.
Lacombe, AB T4L 1E9
Tel: 403-782-6666; *Fax:* 403-782-5655
webmaster@lacombe.ca
www.lacombe.ca
Municipal Type: City
Incorporated: July 28, 1896 *Area:* 18.24 sq km
Population in 2009: 11,733
Provincial Electoral District(s): Lacombe-Ponoka
Federal Electoral District(s): Wetaskiwin
Next Election: 2013 (3 year terms)
Note: Incorporated as a town on May 5, 1902.
Ken Kendall, CAO
kkendall@town.lacombe.ab.ca
Steve Christie, Mayor

Leduc

1 Alexandra Park
Leduc, AB T9E 4C4
Tel: 780-980-7177; *Fax:* 780-980-7127
info@leduc.ca
www.leduc.ca
Municipal Type: City
Incorporated: Dec. 15, 1899 *Area:* 36.97 sq km
Population in 2010: 23,293
Provincial Electoral District(s): Leduc-Beaumont-Devon
Federal Electoral District(s): Edmonton-Leduc
Next Election: 2013 (3 year terms)
Note: Incorporated as a city on Sept. 01, 1983.
Laura Knoblock, City Clerk
lknoblock@leduc.ca
Greg Krischke, Mayor
mayor@leduc.ca
Linda Kyluik, Treasurer
Paul Benedetto, City Manager
pbenedetto@leduc.ca
Kevin Cole, Director, Public Services
Doug Parrish, Director, Planning & Development
780-980-7124
dparrish@leduc.ca
Rick Sereda, Fire Chief & Director, Protective Services
Allan Yamashita, City Engineer & General Manager, Operations

Lethbridge

City Hall
910 - 4 Ave. South
Lethbridge, AB T1J 0P6
Tel: 403-329-7355; *Fax:* 403-320-7575
info@lethbridge.ca
www.lethbridge.ca
Municipal Type: City
Incorporated: Nov. 29, 1890 *Area:* 121.97 sq km
Population in 2010: 86,659
Provincial Electoral District(s): Lethbridge-East; Lethbridge-West
Federal Electoral District(s): Lethbridge
Next Election: 2013 (3 year terms)
Note: Incorporated as a city on May 9, 1906.
Dianne Nemeth, City Clerk
403-320-3821, Fax: 403-320-7575
dnemeth@lethbridge.ca
Rajko Dodic, Mayor
403-320-3823, Fax: 403-320-7575
mayor@lethbridge.ca
Bob Babki, Aldermen, Fax: 403-320-7575
Garth Sherwin, B.Comm., CA, City Manager
gsherwin@lethbridge.ca
Jeff Carlson, Aldermen
403-360-7550, Fax: 403-320-7575
aldermancarlson@gmail.com
Douglas Hudson, Q.C., City Solicitor
dhudson@lethbridge.ca
Faron Ellis, Aldermen, Fax: 403-320-7575
Brian Cornforth, Fire Chief
403-320-3800, Fax: 403-327-3503
astrandlund@lethbridge.ca
Liz Iwaskiw, Aldermen, Fax: 403-320-7575
Tom McKenzie, Police Chief
403-327-2210, Fax: 403-328-6999
Joe Mauro, Aldermen, Fax: 403-320-7575
Byron Buzunis, M.Eng., PMP, P.Eng., Urban Construction Manager
403-320-3975
Bridget Mearns, Aldermen, Fax: 403-320-7575
Kathy Hopkins, Director, Community Services
403-320-3015, Fax: 403-380-2512
khopkins@lethbridge.ca

Ryan Parker, Aldermen
403-380-4848, Fax: 403-320-7575
aldermanryanparker@gmail.com
Warren Andrews, Manager, Public Operations
wandrews@lethbridge.ca
Tom Wickersham, Aldermen
403-381-1521, Fax: 403-381-1571
thwicker@gmail.com
Kevin Viergutz, Manager, Transportation Operations
kviergutz@lethbridge.ab.ca
Bary Beck, Director, Corporate Initiatives
Jody Meli, Manager, Corporate & Community Relations
jmeli@lethbridge.ca
John King, Manager, Transit
403-320-3884, Fax: 403-380-3876
jking@lethbridge.ca
Craig Milley, Manager, Purchasing
403-320-3961
cmilley@lethbridge.ca
Kevin Theodore, Manager, Waste & Recycling
403-320-3088
ktheodore@lethbridge.ab.ca
Don Bulpitt, Manager, Water & Wastewater Operations
dbulpitt@lethbridge.ca
Kevin Jensen, Coordinator, Parks
403-330-5108
kjensen@lethbridge.ab.ca
George Kuhl, Senior Planner, Development Services
403-327-3926, Fax: 403-327-6571
gkuhl@lethbridge.ca

Lloydminster
City Hall
4420 - 50 Ave.
Lloydminster, AB T9V 0W2
Tel: 780-875-6184; *Fax:* 780-871-8345
jkeeley@lloydminster.ca
www.lloydminster.ca
Municipal Type: City
Incorporated: Nov. 25, 1903 *Area:* 24.19 sq km
Population in 2009: 26,502
Provincial Electoral District(s): Vermilion-Lloydminster
Federal Electoral District(s): Vegreville-Wainwright
Next Election: 2013 (3 year terms)
Note: Population figure represents both the Alberta & Saskatchewan populations. Incorporated as a city on Jan. 1, 1958.
Jeff Mulligan, Mayor
mayor@lloydminster.ca
Beth Kembel, City Clerk
780-871-8328
bkembel@lloydminster.ca
Glenn Carroll, City Manager
780-871-8326
gcarroll@lloydminster.ca
Diane Beecroft, Treasurer
780-875-6184
dbeecroft@lloydminster.ca
Adam Homes, Deputy CAO, Infrastructure Services
780-875-8332
ahomes@lloydminster.ca
Ken Coleman, Deputy CAO, Community Services
780-875-4529
kcoleman@lloydminster.ca
Don Newlin, Deputy CAO, Finance
780-871-8330
dnewlin@lloydminster.ca
Brent Stasiuk, Deputy CAO, Protective Services
780-874-9054
bstasiuk@lloydminster.ca

Medicine Hat
City Hall
580 - 1 St. SE
Medicine Hat, AB T1A 8E6
Tel: 403-529-8115; *Fax:* 403-529-8182
clerk@medicinehat.ca
www.medicinehat.ca
Municipal Type: City
Incorporated: May 31, 1894 *Area:* 112.01 sq km
Population in 2009: 61,097
Provincial Electoral District(s): Cypress-Medicine Hat; Medicine Hat
Federal Electoral District(s): Medicine Hat
Next Election: 2013 (3 year terms)
Note: Incorporated as a city on May 9, 1906.
Dave Leflar, City Clerk
403-529-8234, Fax: 403-529-8182
davlef@medicinehat.ca
Normand Boucher, Mayor
403-529-8181, Fax: 403-529-8182
mayor@medicinehat.ca; norbou@medicinehat.ca
Ted Clugston, Aldermen
403-526-8760
tedclu@medicinehat.ca
Gerry Labas, COO
403-529-8222
gerlab@medicinehat.ca
Wayne Craven, Aldermen, Fax: 403-529-8182
waycra@medicinehat.ca
John Hughes, City Solicitor
403-529-8350
johhug@medicinehat.ca
Robert C. Dumanowski, Aldermen
Andy McGrogan, Police Chief
403-529-8410, Fax: 403-529-8444
John Hamill, Aldermen
403-526-7196, Fax: 403-529-8282
johham@medicinehat.ca
Ron Robinson, Fire Chief
403-502-8006, Fax: 403-526-1352
Graham Kelly, Aldermen
403-527-1891, Fax: 403-528-2453
gldarops@shaw.ca
Albert Bizio, Commissioner, Public Services
403-529-8229
albbiz@medicinehat.ca
Les Pearson, Aldermen
lespea@medicinehat.ca
Don Knutson, Acting Commissioner, Corporate Services
403-529-8231
onknu@medicinehat.ca
Jeremy Thompson, Aldermen
403-504-5647, Fax: 403-526-1422
jertho@medicinehat.ca
John Komanchuk, Commissioner, Development & Infrastructure
403-529-8354
johjo@medicinehat.ca
Phil Turnbull, Aldermen
Dwight Brown, General Manager, Planning, Building & Development Services
Dale Descoteau, General Manager, Information & Computer Services
403-529-8108
daldes@medicinehat.ca
John Fedoruk, General Manager, Environmental Utilities
403-529-8176, Fax: 403-528-4955
eu@medicinehat.ca
Tony Klauwers, General Manager, Municipal Works
Grant MacKay, General Manager, Human Resources
403-529-8239
gramac@medicinehat.ca
Dave Panabaker, General Manager, Gas Utility
403-529-8288
davepan@medicinehat.ca
Ron Webb, General Manager, Community Development
403-529-8310
ronweb@medicinehat.ca
Les Wickenheiser, General Manager, Corporate Asset Management
403-529-8327
leswic@medicinehat.ca
Kendall Woodacre, General Manager, Electric Utility
403-502-8081
kenwoo@medicinehat.ca
R. Vizbar, General Manager, Parks & Outdoor Recreation
403-529-8312, Fax: 403-527-4798
parks@medicinehat.ca
Russ Smith, Manager, Environment Management
403-529-8188
russmi@medicinhat.ca
Frank Wetsch, Manager, Water & WasteWater Treatment
403-529-8227
S. Schentag, Coordinator, Recycling Development
403-502-8593
Ron Davis, Officer, Health & Safety
403-529-8359
rondav@medicine-hat.ca

Okotoks
P.O. Box 20 Main
5 Elizabeth St.
Okotoks, AB T1S 1K1
Tel: 403-938-4404; *Fax:* 403-938-7387
info@okotoks.ca
www.okotoks.ca
Municipal Type: City
Incorporated: Oct. 25, 1899 *Area:* 18.55 sq km
Population in 2010: 23,201
Provincial Electoral District(s): Highwood
Federal Electoral District(s): Macleod
Next Election: 2013 (3 year terms)
Note: Incorporated as a town on June 1, 1904.
Rick Quail, Municipal Manager
403-938-8900
municipalmanager@okotoks.ca
Bill Robertson, Mayor
mayor@okotoks.ca
Marley Oness, Municipal Engineer
403-938-8930
municipalengineer@okotoks.ca
Dave Robertson, Manager, Operations
403-938-8952
operations@okotoks.ca
Ken Thevenot, Fire Chief
403-938-4066
fire@okotoks.ca

Red Deer
City Hall
P.O. Box 5008
4914 - 48th Ave.
Red Deer, AB T4N 3T4
Tel: 403-342-8111; *Fax:* 403-346-6195
feedback@reddeer.ca
www.reddeer.ca
Municipal Type: City
Incorporated: May 31, 1894 *Area:* 69.23 sq km
Population in 2010: 90,084
Provincial Electoral District(s): Red Deer-North; Red Deer-South
Federal Electoral District(s): Red Deer
Next Election: 2013 (3 year terms)
Note: Incorporated as a city on March 25, 1913.
Craig Curtis, City Manager
403-342-8156, Fax: 403-342-8365
craig.curtis@reddeer.ca
Morris Flewwelling, Mayor
403-342-8154, Fax: 403-342-8365
mayor@reddeer.ca
Buck Buchanan, Councillor
403-343-6550, Fax: 403-346-6195
buck.buchanan@reddeer.ca
Lorraine Poth, Director, Corporate Services
lorraine.poth@reddeer.ca
Paul Harris, Councillor
Don Simpson, City Solicitor
Cindy Jefferies, Councillor
403-302-3706, Fax: 403-346-6195
cindy.jefferies@reddeer.ca
Brian Simpson, Superintendent, RCMP
rcmp@reddeer.ca
Lynne Mulder, Councillor
403-341-6418, Fax: 403-346-6195
lynne.mulder@reddeer.ca
Paul Goranson, Director, Development Services
403-342-8162, Fax: 403-342-8211
paul.goranson@reddeer.ca
Chris Stephan, Councillor
Colleen Jensen, Director, Community Services
403-342-8323, Fax: 403-342-8222
communityservices@reddeer.ca
Tara Veer, Councillor
403-358-3568, Fax: 403-340-7466
tara.veer@reddeer.ca
Scott Cameron, Manager, Social Planning
403-342-8100
communityservices@reddeer.ca
Frank Wong, Councillor
403-347-6514, Fax: 403-346-6195
frank.wong@reddeer.ca
Frank Colosimo, Manager, Public Works
403-342-8238, Fax: 403-343-7074
publicworks@reddeer.ca
Dianne Wyntjes, Councillor
Kevin Joll, Manager, Transit
403-342-8225, Fax: 403-342-8116
transit@reddeer.ca
Paul Meyette, Director, Planning Division
Rod Risling, Manager, Assessment & Taxation
assessment@reddeer.ca
Greg Scott, Manager, Recreation, Parks & Culture
403-342-8159, Fax: 403-342-8222
Dave Matthews, Supervisor, Planning & Technical Services
Tom Marstaller, Superintendent, Environmental Services
403-342-8238, Fax: 403-343-7074
publicworks@reddeer.ca

St. Albert
5 St. Anne St.
St. Albert, AB T8N 3Z9
Tel: 780-459-1500; *Fax:* 780-460-2394
stalbert@st-albert.net
www.stalbert.ca
Municipal Type: City
Incorporated: Dec. 7, 1899 *Area:* 35.04 sq km
Population in 2010: 60,138
Provincial Electoral District(s): Spruce Grove-Sturgeon-St. Albert; St. Albert
Federal Electoral District(s): Edmonton-St. Albert
Next Election: 2013 (3 year terms)
Note: Incorporated as a city on Jan. 1, 1977.
Bill Holtby, City Manager
780-459-1607, Fax: 780-459-1591
bholtby@st-albert.net
Nolan Crouse, Mayor
780-459-1606, Fax: 780-459-1591
mayor@st-albert.net
Len Bracko, Councillor
780-458-6478, Fax: 780-418-2961
len@bracko.ca
Gail Barrington-Moss, General Manager, Community & Protective Services
Wes Broadhead, Councillor
N. Jamieson, General Manager, Planning & Engineering Services
Cathy Heron, Councillor
D. Screpnek, General Manager, Corporate Services
Roger Lemieux, Councillor
780-460-7223, Fax: 780-651-6147
jrcl@shaw.ca
B. Treidler, General Manager, Business & Strategic Services
Cam MacKay, Councillor
C. Cundy, Director, Planning & Development
Malcolm Parker, Councillor
D. Irving, Manager, Planning
S. Laarhuis, Chief Legislative Officer
Tracy Young, Administrative Resources Coordinator, Fire & Emergency Medical Services
780-458-2020, Fax: 780-459-7636

Spruce Grove
315 Jespersen Ave.
Spruce Grove, AB T7X 3E8
Tel: 780-962-2611; *Fax:* 780-962-2526
info@sprucegrove.org
www.sprucegrove.org
Municipal Type: City
Incorporated: March 14, 1907 *Area:* 26.4 sq km
Population in 2010: 24,646
Provincial Electoral District(s): Spruce Grove-Sturgeon-St. Albert
Federal Electoral District(s): Edmonton-Spruce Grove
Next Election: 2013 (3 year terms)
Note: Incorporated as a city on March 1, 1986.
Doug Lagore, City Manager
dlagore@sprucegrove.org
Stuart Houston, Mayor
shouston@sprucegrove.org
Kathy Chan, Treasurer
Ken Luck, Director, FCSS & Recreation
Jackie Araujo, General Manager, Community Services
780-962-7617
David Hales, General Manager, Planning & Infrastructure
780-962-7622
Robert Kosterman, Chief, Fire
780-962-4496
Jeff Mustard, Superintendent, Engineering
780-962-7624
Paul Hanlan, Supervisor, Planning & Development
Jane Holmes, Coordinator, Sustainable Development

Stony Plain
4905 - 51 Ave.
Stony Plain, AB T7Z 1Y1
Tel: 780-963-2151; *Fax:* 780-963-2197
info@stonyplain.com
www.stonyplain.com
Municipal Type: City
Incorporated: March 14, 1907 *Area:* 35.61 sq km
Population in 2010: 14,177
Provincial Electoral District(s): Stony Plain
Federal Electoral District(s): Edmonton-Spruce Grove
Next Election: 2013 (3 year terms)
Note: Incorporated as a town on Dec. 10, 1908
Thomas Goulden, Manager
780-963-8584, Fax: 780-963-2197
t.goulden@stonyplain.com
Ken Lemke, Mayor
780-963-6310
k.lemke@stonyplain.com

Strathmore
680 Westchester Rd.
Strathmore, AB T1P 1J1
Tel: 403-934-3133; *Fax:* 403-934-4713
Lindan@strathmore.ca
www.strathmore.ca
Municipal Type: City
Incorporated: March 20, 1908 *Area:* 15.59 sq km
Population in 2010: 12,139
Provincial Electoral District(s): Strathmore-Brooks
Federal Electoral District(s): Crowfoot
Next Election: 2013 (3 year terms)
Note: Incorporated as a town on July 6, 1911.
Dwight Stanford, CAO
dwights@strathmore.ca
Steve Grajczyk, Mayor
council@strathmore.ca

Sylvan Lake
4926 - 50th Ave.
Sylvan Lake, AB T4S 1A1
Tel: 403-887-2141; *Fax:* 403-887-3660
tsl@sylvanlake.ca
www.sylvanlake.ca
Municipal Type: City
Incorporated: Dec. 30, 1912 *Area:* 10.83 sq km
Population in 2008: 11,115
Provincial Electoral District(s): Innisfail-Sylvan Lake
Federal Electoral District(s): Red Deer
Next Election: 2013 (3 year terms)
Note: Incorporated as a town on May 20, 1946.
Archie Grover, Acting CAO
403-887-2141
Susan Samson, Mayor
ssamson@sylvanlake.ca

Wetaskiwin
P.O. Box 6210
4705 - 50th Ave.
Wetaskiwin, AB T9A 2E9
Tel: 780-361-4400; *Fax:* 780-352-0930
reception@wetaskiwin.ca
www.wetaskiwin.ca
Other Information: Toll Free Phone: 1-800-989-6899
Municipal Type: City
Incorporated: Dec. 4, 1899 *Area:* 16.74 sq km
Population in 2009: 12,285
Provincial Electoral District(s): Wetaskiwin-Camrose
Federal Electoral District(s): Wetaskiwin
Next Election: 2013 (3 year terms)
Note: Incorporated as a city on May 9, 1906.
Ted Gillespie, City Manager
Bill Elliot, Mayor
mayor@wetaskiwin.ca
Merlin Klassen, Fire Chief
780-361-4429, Fax: 780-352-6261
fireservices@wetaskiwin.ca

Other Municipalities in Alberta

Acme
P.O. Box 299
Acme, AB T0M 0A0
Tel: 403-546-3783; *Fax:* 403-546-3014
clerk@acme.ca
www.acme.ca
Municipal Type: Village
Incorporated: July 7, 1910 *Area:* 2.47 sq km
Population in 2006: 656
Provincial Electoral District(s): Olds-Didsbury-Three Hills
Federal Electoral District(s): Crowfoot
Next Election: 2013 (3 year terms)
Bruce McLeod, Mayor
Sue Schmidt, Municipal Clerk
acme@airenet.com

Alberta Beach
P.O. Box 278
Alberta Beach, AB T0E 0A0
Tel: 780-924-3181; *Fax:* 780-924-3313
abofficea@albertabeach.com
www.albertabeach.com
Municipal Type: Village
Incorporated: Aug. 23, 1920 *Area:* 1.98 sq km
Population in 2006: 339
Provincial Electoral District(s): Whitecourt-Ste. Anne
Federal Electoral District(s): Yellowhead
Next Election: 2013 (3 year terms)
Note: Status changed to a village on Nov. 25, 1998.
Lou Hudon, Mayor
Dan Kanuka, Assessor
780-939-3310

Alix
P.O. Box 87
4849 - 50 St.
Alix, AB T0C 0B0
Tel: 403-747-2495; *Fax:* 403-747-3663
info@villageofalix.ca; cao@villageofalix.ca
www.villageofalix.ca
Municipal Type: Village
Incorporated: June 3, 1907 *Area:* 3.15 sq km
Population in 2006: 851
Provincial Electoral District(s): Lacombe-Ponoka
Federal Electoral District(s): Wetaskiwin
Next Election: 2013 (3 year terms)
Curtis Peterson, Mayor
403-747-2414
Lyle Wack, CAO

Alliance
P.O. Box 149
Alliance, AB T0B 0A0
Tel: 780-879-3911; *Fax:* 780-879-2235
info@villageofalliance.ca
www.villageofalliance.ca
Municipal Type: Village
Incorporated: Aug. 26, 1918 *Area:* 0.64 sq km
Population in 2006: 158
Provincial Electoral District(s): Battle River-Wainwright
Federal Electoral District(s): Vegreville-Wainwright
Next Election: 2013 (3 year terms)
Muriel Fankhanel, Mayor
Laura Towers, Administrator

Amisk
P.O. Box 72
Amisk, AB T0B 0B0
Tel: 780-856-3980; *Fax:* 780-856-3980
amiskvil@telusplanet.net
www.amisk.ca
Municipal Type: Village
Incorporated: Jan. 1, 1956 *Area:* 0.76 sq km
Population in 2006: 172
Provincial Electoral District(s): Battle River-Wainwright
Federal Electoral District(s): Vegreville-Wainwright
Next Election: 2013 (3 year terms)
Arnold Nordin, Mayor
Kathy Ferguson, Municipal Administrator

Andrew
P.O. Box 180
5021 - 50 St.
Andrew, AB T0B 0C0
Tel: 780-365-3687; *Fax:* 780-365-2061
pat@villageofandrew.net
www.villageofandrew.net
Municipal Type: Village
Incorporated: June 24, 1930 *Area:* 1.23 sq km
Population in 2006: 465
Provincial Electoral District(s): Fort Saskatchewan-Vegreville
Federal Electoral District(s): Vegreville-Wainwright
Next Election: 2013 (3 year terms)
Eldon Feniac, Mayor
edon@villageofandrew.net
Pat Skoreyko, CAO
pat@villageofandrew.net

Argentia Beach
P.O. Box 100
Ma-Me-O Beach, AB T0C 1X0
Tel: 780-586-2494; *Fax:* 780-586-3567
svadminoffice@xplornet.com
Municipal Type: Summer Village
Incorporated: Jan. 1, 1967 *Area:* 0.69 sq km
Population in 2006: 52
Provincial Electoral District(s): Drayton Valley-Calmar
Federal Electoral District(s): Wetaskiwin
Next Election: 2013 (3 year terms)
Denis Rowley, Mayor
Sylvia Roy, CAO
Jacques Thériault, Conseillers et Districts, Ward(s): la Pointe

Arrowwood
P.O. Box 36
22 Center St.
Arrowwood, AB T0L 0B0
Tel: 403-534-3821; *Fax:* 403-534-3821
vlgarrw@telusplanet.net
www.villageofarrowwood.ca
Municipal Type: Village
Incorporated: May 13, 1926 *Area:* 0.66 sq km
Population in 2006: 221
Provincial Electoral District(s): Little Bow
Federal Electoral District(s): Macleod
Next Election: 2013 (3 year terms)
Matt Crane, Mayor
Ted Oakes, Village Administrator

Athabasca
4705 - 49 Ave.
Athabasca, AB T9S 1B7
Tel: 780-675-2063; *Fax:* 780-675-4242
town@town.athabasca.ab.ca
www.town.athabasca.ab.ca
Municipal Type: Town
Incorporated: May 18, 1905 *Area:* 16.98 sq km
Population in 2006: 2,575
Provincial Electoral District(s): Athabasca-Redwater
Federal Electoral District(s): Fort McMurray-Athabasca
Next Election: 2013 (3 year terms)
Note: Incorporated as a town on Aug. 4, 1913.
Roger Morrill, Mayor
Doug Topinka, CAO

Banff
P.O. Box 1260
Banff, AB T1L 1A1
Tel: 403-762-1200; *Fax:* 403-762-1260
comments@banff.ca
www.banff.ca
Municipal Type: Town
Incorporated: Jan. 1, 1990 *Area:* 4.85 sq km
Population in 2007: 7,437
Provincial Electoral District(s): Banff-Cochrane
Federal Electoral District(s): Wild Rose
Next Election: 2013 (3 year terms)
Robert Earl, Town Manager
403-762-1203
robert.earl@banff.ca
Karen Sorensen, Mayor

Barnwell
P.O. Box 159
Barnwell, AB T0K 0B0
Tel: 403-223-4018; *Fax:* 403-223-2373
barnwell@platinum.ca
Municipal Type: Village
Incorporated: Jan. 1, 1980 *Area:* 0.9 sq km
Population in 2006: 613
Provincial Electoral District(s): Cardston-Taber-Warner
Federal Electoral District(s): Medicine Hat
Next Election: 2013 (3 year terms)
Delbert Bodnarek, Mayor
Wendy Bateman, Administrator

Barons
P.O. Box 129
Barons, AB T0L 0G0
Tel: 403-757-3633; *Fax:* 403-757-2599
barons@figment.ca
Municipal Type: Village
Incorporated: May 6, 1910 *Area:* 0.68 sq km
Population in 2006: 276
Provincial Electoral District(s): Little Bow
Federal Electoral District(s): Lethbridge
Next Election: 2013 (3 year terms)
Ronald Gorzitza, Mayor
Laurie Beck, CAO

Barrhead County No. 11
5306-49 Street
Barrhead, AB T7N 1N5
Tel: 780-674-3331; *Fax:* 780-674-2777
countybarrhead@phrd.ab.ca
www.barrhead.ca
Municipal Type: Town
Incorporated: Nov. 14, 1927 *Area:* 8.1 sq km
Population in 2006: 4,209
Provincial Electoral District(s): Barrhead-Morinville-Westlock
Federal Electoral District(s): Yellowhead
Next Election: 2013 (3 year terms)
Note: Proclaimed as a town on Nov. 26, 1946.
Bill Lee, Reeve
780-584-2323
Mark Oberg, County Manager
moberg@phrd.ab.ca

Barrhead
P.O. Box 4189
Barrhead, AB T7N 1A2
Tel: 780-674-3301; *Fax:* 780-674-5648
town@barrhead.ca
www.barrhead.ca
Municipal Type: Town
Incorporated: Nov. 14, 1927 *Area:* 8.1 sq km
Population in 2006: 4,209
Provincial Electoral District(s): Barrhead-Morinville-Westlock
Federal Electoral District(s): Yellowhead
Next Election: 2013 (3 year terms)
Note: Proclaimed as a town on Nov. 26, 1946.
Brian Schultz, Mayor
bdschultz@barrhead.ca
Martin Taylor, CAO
mtaylor@barrhead.ca

Bashaw
P.O. Box 510
Bashaw, AB T0B 0H0
Tel: 780-372-3911; *Fax:* 780-372-2335
admin@townofbashaw.com
www.townofbashaw.com
Municipal Type: Town
Incorporated: Aug. 18, 1911 *Area:* 2.84 sq km
Population in 2006: 796
Provincial Electoral District(s): Lacombe-Ponoka
Federal Electoral District(s): Crowfoot
Next Election: 2013 (3 year terms)
Note: Incorporated as a town on May 1, 1964.
Robert (Bob) Cammidge, Mayor
Rosemary Wittevrongel, CAO
rwittevrongel@townofbashaw.com

Bassano
P.O. Box 299
Bassano, AB T0J 0B0
Tel: 403-641-3788; *Fax:* 403-641-2585
townbass@telus.net
www.bassano.ca
Municipal Type: Town
Incorporated: Dec. 28, 1909 *Area:* 5.16 sq km
Population in 2006: 1,345
Provincial Electoral District(s): Strathmore-Brooks
Federal Electoral District(s): Medicine Hat
Next Election: 2013 (3 year terms)
Note: Incorporated as a town on Jan. 16, 1911.
Tom Rose, Mayor
Sabine Nasse, CAO
basscao@telus.net

Bawlf
P.O. Box 40
Bawlf, AB T0B 0J0
Tel: 780-373-3797; *Fax:* 780-373-3798
vilbawlf@syban.net
www.bawlf.com
Municipal Type: Village
Incorporated: Oct. 12, 1906 *Area:* 0.96 sq km
Population in 2006: 367
Provincial Electoral District(s): Battle River-Wainwright
Federal Electoral District(s): Crowfoot
Next Election: 2013 (3 year terms)
Gordon Blatz, Mayor
780-373-3733
gblatz@bawlf.com
Lynn Horbasenko, Village Manager
LHorbasenko@bawlf.com

Beaverlodge
P.O. Box 30
Beaverlodge, AB T0H 0C0
Tel: 780-354-2201; *Fax:* 780-354-2207
ivan@beaverlodge.ca
www.beaverlodge.ca
Municipal Type: Town
Incorporated: July 31, 1929 *Area:* 5.58 sq km
Population in 2006: 2,264
Provincial Electoral District(s): Grande Prairie-Wapiti
Federal Electoral District(s): Peace River
Next Election: 2013 (3 year terms)
Note: Incorporated as a town on Jan. 24, 1956.
Ivan Hegland, Town Manager
ivan@beaverlodge.ca
Leona Hanson, Mayor
leona@coaction.ca

Beiseker
P.O. Box 349
Beiseker, AB T0M 0G0
Tel: 403-947-3774; *Fax:* 403-947-2146
beiseker@beiseker.com
www.beiseker.com
Municipal Type: Village
Incorporated: Feb. 23, 1921 *Area:* 2.84 sq km
Population in 2006: 804
Provincial Electoral District(s): Airdrie-Chestermere
Federal Electoral District(s): Crowfoot
Next Election: 2013 (3 year terms)
Bruce T. Rowe, Mayor
Jo-Anne Lambert, CAO
gpeckham@beiseker.com

Bentley
P.O. Box 179
Bentley, AB T0C 0J0
Tel: 403-748-4044; *Fax:* 403-748-3213
vlgben@telusplanet.net
www.town.bentley.ab.ca
Municipal Type: Town
Incorporated: March 17, 1915 *Area:* 2.3 sq km
Population in 2006: 1,083
Provincial Electoral District(s): Rocky Mountain House
Federal Electoral District(s): Wetaskiwin
Next Election: 2013 (3 year terms)
Note: Incorporated as a town on Jan. 1, 2001.
Joan Dickau, Mayor
Elizabeth Smart, CAO
liz.bentley@telus.net

Berwyn
P.O. Box 250
Berwyn, AB T0H 0E0
Tel: 780-338-3922; *Fax:* 780-338-2224
vberwynadmin@sebernet.com
www.berwyn.govoffice.com
Municipal Type: Village
Incorporated: Nov. 28, 1936 *Area:* 1.66 sq km
Population in 2006: 516
Provincial Electoral District(s): Dunvegan-Central Peace
Federal Electoral District(s): Peace River
Next Election: 2013 (3 year terms)
Ron Longtin, Mayor
RonLongtin@wispernet.ca
Mike Rudkin, Municipal Administrator
vberwyn@serbernet.com

Betula Beach
P.O. Box 161
Seba Beach, AB T0E 2B0
Tel: 780-797-2455;
svbetula@telusplanet.net
Municipal Type: Summer Village
Incorporated: Jan. 1, 1960 *Area:* 0.18 sq km
Population in 2006: 15
Provincial Electoral District(s): Stony Plain
Federal Electoral District(s): Yellowhead
Next Election: 2013 (3 year terms)
Rob Dickie, Mayor
Linda Bolton, Administrator

Big Valley
P.O. Box 236
29 - 1 Ave. South
Big Valley, AB T0J 0G0
Tel: 403-876-2269; *Fax:* 403-876-2223
villagebigvalley@libs.prl.ab.ca; info@villagebigvalley.ca
www.villagebigvalley.ca
Municipal Type: Village
Incorporated: July 28, 1914 *Area:* 1.84 sq km
Population in 2006: 351
Provincial Electoral District(s): Drumheller-Stettler
Federal Electoral District(s): Crowfoot
Next Election: 2013 (3 year terms)
Rick Kargaard, Mayor
Corinne Feusi, CAO

Birch Cove
P.O. Box 7
#19, RR 1
Gunn, AB T0E 1A0
Tel: 780-446-1426;
devans@birchcove.ca
www.albertasummervillages.org
Municipal Type: Summer Village
Incorporated: Dec. 31, 1988 *Area:* 0.29 sq km
Population in 2006: 38
Provincial Electoral District(s): Whitecourt-Ste. Anne

Federal Electoral District(s): Yellowhead
Next Election: 2013 (3 year terms)
Steven Tymafichuk, Mayor
Dennis Evans, Administrator

Birchcliff
#104, 4505 - 50 Ave.
Sylvan Lake, AB T4S 1W2
Tel: 403-887-2822; *Fax:* 403-887-2897
fivesv@telusplanet.net
Municipal Type: Summer Village
Incorporated: Jan. 1, 1972 *Area:* 0.98 sq km
Population in 2006: 125
Provincial Electoral District(s): Rocky Mountain House
Federal Electoral District(s): Wetaskiwin
Next Election: 2013 (3 year terms)
Joyce Megson, Mayor
Myra Reiter, Administrator

Bittern Lake
P.O. Box 5
300 Rail Way Ave.
Bittern Lake, AB T0C 0L0
Tel: 780-672-7373; *Fax:* 780-672-2353
vobl@syban.net
www.villageofbitternlake.ca
Municipal Type: Village
Incorporated: Nov. 21, 1904 *Area:* 6.64 sq km
Population in 2006: 225
Provincial Electoral District(s): Wetaskiwin-Camrose
Federal Electoral District(s): Crowfoot
Next Election: 2013 (3 year terms)
Ken Feth, Mayor
Theresa Fuller, CAO

Black Diamond
P.O. Box 10
Black Diamond, AB T0L 0H0
Tel: 403-933-4348; *Fax:* 403-933-5865
info@town.blackdiamond.ab.ca
www.town.blackdiamond.ab.ca
Municipal Type: Town
Incorporated: May 8, 1929 *Area:* 3.21 sq km
Population in 2006: 1,900
Provincial Electoral District(s): Foothills-Rocky View
Federal Electoral District(s): Macleod
Next Election: 2013 (3 year terms)
Note: Incorporated as a town on Jan 1, 1956.
Sharlene Brown, Mayor
Leonard Smith, Town Manager

Blackfalds
P.O. Box 220
5018 Waghorn St.
Blackfalds, AB T0M 0J0
Tel: 403-885-4677; *Fax:* 403-885-4610
info@blackfalds.com
www.blackfalds.com
Municipal Type: Town
Incorporated: June 17, 1904 *Area:* 8.4 sq km
Population in 2006: 4,571
Provincial Electoral District(s): Lacombe-Ponoka
Federal Electoral District(s): Wetaskiwin
Next Election: 2013 (3 year terms)
Note: Incorporated as a town on April 1, 1980.
Melodie Stol, Mayor
melodie@blackfalds.com
Corinne Newman, CAO
corinne@blackfalds.com

Bon Accord
P.O. Box 779
5025-50 Ave
Bon Accord, AB T0A 0K0
Tel: 780-921-3550; *Fax:* 780-921-3585
townoffice@town.bonaccord.ab.ca
www.town.bonaccord.ab.ca
Municipal Type: Town
Incorporated: Jan. 1, 1964 *Area:* 2.11 sq km
Population in 2006: 1,534
Provincial Electoral District(s): Athabasca-Redwater
Federal Electoral District(s): Westlock-St. Paul
Next Election: 2013 (3 year terms)
Note: Incorporated as a town on Nov. 20, 1979.
Randy Boyd, Mayor
boyd@town.bonaccord.ab.ca
Vicky Zinyk, Town Manager
cao@town.bonaccord.ab.ca

Bondiss
724 Baptiste Dr.
West Baptiste, AB T9S 1R8
Tel: 780-675-9270; *Fax:* 780-675-9526
tomaszyk@mcsnet.ca
Municipal Type: Summer Village
Incorporated: Jan. 1, 1983 *Area:* 1.33 sq km
Population in 2006: 131
Provincial Electoral District(s): Athabasca-Redwater
Federal Electoral District(s): Fort McMurray-Athabasca
Next Election: 2013 (3 year terms)
Murray Olsen, Mayor
Edwin Tomaszyk, CAO
Marc Losier, Director, Design & Construction
city.operationalservices@bathurst.ca

Bonnyville
P.O. Box 1006
4917 - 49 Ave.
Bonnyville, AB T9N 2J7
Tel: 780-826-3496; *Fax:* 780-826-4806
admin@town.bonnyville.ab.ca
www.town.bonnyville.ab.ca
Other Information: Toll free: 1-866-826-3496
Municipal Type: Town
Incorporated: Sept. 19, 1929 *Area:* 14.1 sq km
Population in 2009: 6,470
Provincial Electoral District(s): Bonnyville-Cold Lake
Federal Electoral District(s): Westlock-St. Paul
Next Election: 2013 (3 year terms)
Note: Proclaimed as a town on Feb. 3, 1948.
Mark Power, CAO
mpower@town.bonnyville.ab.ca
Ernie Isley, Mayor

Bonnyville Beach
P.O. Box 6439
Bonnyville, AB T9N 2G9
Tel: 780-826-2925; *Fax:* 780-812-2904
svbbeach@mcsnet.ca
Municipal Type: Summer Village
Incorporated: Jan 1, 1958 *Area:* 0.38 sq km
Population in 2006: 97
Provincial Electoral District(s): Bonnyville-Cold Lake
Federal Electoral District(s): Westlock-St. Paul
Next Election: 2013 (3 year terms)
Chuck Dechene, Mayor
Lionel P. Tercier, Administrator
Robert Langlais, Fire Chief
506-548-0439
city.fire@bathurst.ca

Botha
P.O. Box 160
Botha, AB T0C 0N0
Tel: 403-742-5079; *Fax:* 403-742-6586
vlbotha@xplornet.com
Municipal Type: Village
Incorporated: Sept. 5, 1911 *Area:* 1.09 sq km
Population in 2006: 185
Provincial Electoral District(s): Drumheller-Stettler
Federal Electoral District(s): Crowfoot
Next Election: 2013 (3 year terms)
Josie Hunter, Mayor
Michelle Renschler, CAO

Bow Island
P.O. Box 100
Bow Island, AB T0K 0G0
Tel: 403-545-2522; *Fax:* 403-545-6642
townoffice@bowisland.com
www.bowisland.com
Municipal Type: Town
Incorporated: June 14, 1910 *Area:* 5.92 sq km
Population in 2006: 1,790
Provincial Electoral District(s): Cypress-Medicine Hat
Federal Electoral District(s): Medicine Hat
Next Election: 2013 (3 year terms)
Note: Incorporated as a town on Feb. 1, 1912.
Gordon Reynolds, Mayor
mayor@bowisland.com
Anna-Marie Bridge, Town Manager
anna-marie@bowisland.com

Bowden
P.O. Box 338
Bowden, AB T0M 0K0
Tel: 403-224-3395; *Fax:* 403-224-2244
admin@town.bowden.ab.ca
www.town.bowden.ab.ca
Municipal Type: Town
Incorporated: June 17, 1904 *Area:* 1.9 sq km
Population in 2006: 1,205
Provincial Electoral District(s): Innisfail-Sylvan Lake
Federal Electoral District(s): Red Deer
Next Election: 2013 (3 year terms)
Note: Incorporated as a town on Sept. 1, 1981.
Robb Stuart, Mayor
bowdenmayor@gmail.com
Lori Conkin, CAO
cao@town.bowden.ab.ca

Boyle
P.O. Box 9
Boyle, AB T0A 0M0
Tel: 780-689-3643; *Fax:* 780-689-3998
admin@villageofboyle.com
www.villageofboyle.com
Municipal Type: Village
Incorporated: Dec. 31, 1953 *Area:* 4.1 sq km
Population in 2006: 844
Provincial Electoral District(s): Athabasca-Redwater
Federal Electoral District(s): Fort McMurray-Athabasca
Next Election: 2013 (3 year terms)
Don Radmanovich, Mayor
Charlie Ashbey, CAO

Breton
P.O. Box 480
4916 - 50 Ave.
Breton, AB T0C 0P0
Tel: 780-696-3636; *Fax:* 780-696-3590
vbreton@telusplanet.net
www.village.breton.ab.ca
Municipal Type: Village
Incorporated: Jan. 1, 1957 *Area:* 1.73 sq km
Population in 2006: 550
Provincial Electoral District(s): Drayton Valley-Calmar
Federal Electoral District(s): Wetaskiwin
Next Election: 2013 (3 year terms)
Janet Young, Mayor

Bruderheim
P.O. Box 280
Bruderheim, AB T0B 0S0
Tel: 780-796-3731; *Fax:* 780-796-3037
info@bruderheim.ca
www.bruderheim.ca
Municipal Type: Town
Incorporated: May 29, 1908 *Area:* 4.23 sq km
Population in 2006: 1,215
Provincial Electoral District(s): Fort Saskatchewan-Vegreville
Federal Electoral District(s): Vegreville-Wainwright
Next Election: 2013 (3 year terms)
Note: Incorporated as a town on Sept. 17, 1980.
Karl Hauch, Mayor
Tim Duhamel, CAO
duhamel@strathcona.ab.ca

Burnstick Lake
P.O. Box 1555
Cochrane, AB T4C 1B5
Tel: 403-932-3866; *Fax:* 403-932-6652
rickbutler@pathcom.ca
www.burnsticklakesummervillage.ca
Municipal Type: Summer Village
Incorporated: Dec. 31, 1991 *Area:* 0.18 sq km
Population in 2006: 43
Provincial Electoral District(s): Rocky Mountain House
Federal Electoral District(s): Wild Rose
Next Election: 2013 (3 year terms)
Harold Esche, Mayor
Harold Northcott, Administrator

Calmar
P.O. Box 750
Calmar, AB T0C 0V0
Tel: 780-985-3604; *Fax:* 780-985-3039
info@calmar.ca
www.town.calmar.ab.ca
Municipal Type: Town
Incorporated: Jan. 1, 1949 *Area:* 4.34 sq km
Population in 2006: 1,959
Provincial Electoral District(s): Drayton Valley-Calmar
Federal Electoral District(s): Wetaskiwin
Next Election: 2013 (3 year terms)
Note: Incorporated as a town on Jan. 19, 1954.
Don Faulkner, Mayor
dfaulkner@calmar.ca
Kathy Rodberg, Town Manager
krodberg@calmar.ca

Carbon
P.O. Box 249
Carbon, AB T0M 0L0
Tel: 403-572-3244; *Fax:* 403-572-3778
admincarbon@wildroseinternet.ca
Municipal Type: Village
Incorporated: Nov. 18, 1912 *Area:* 2 sq km
Population in 2006: 570
Provincial Electoral District(s): Olds-Didsbury-Three Hills
Federal Electoral District(s): Crowfoot
Next Election: 2013 (3 year terms)
Valorie Reed, Mayor
Debra Grosfield, Municipal Administrator
caocarbon@wildroseinternet.ca

Cardston
P.O. Box 280
Cardston, AB T0K 0K0
Tel: 403-653-3366; *Fax:* 403-653-2499
info@cardston.ca
www.cardston.ca
Municipal Type: Town
Incorporated: Dec. 29, 1898 *Area:* 8.64 sq km
Population in 2006: 3,452
Provincial Electoral District(s): Cardston-Taber-Warner
Federal Electoral District(s): Lethbridge
Next Election: 2013 (3 year terms)
Note: Incorporated as a town on July 2, 1901.
Rick Schow, Mayor
Marian Carlson, Administrator
marian@cardston.ca

Carmangay
P.O. Box 130
Carmangay, AB T0L 0N0
Tel: 403-643-3595; *Fax:* 403-643-2007
villagec@telusplanet.net
Municipal Type: Village
Incorporated: Jan. 20, 1910 *Area:* 1.86 sq km
Population in 2006: 336
Provincial Electoral District(s): Little Bow
Federal Electoral District(s): Macleod
Next Election: 2013 (3 year terms)
Kim Nichols, Mayor
Carolyn Erb, Administrator

Caroline
P.O. Box 148
Caroline, AB T0M 0M0
Tel: 403-722-3781; *Fax:* 403-722-4050
administration@caroline.ca
www.caroline.ca
Municipal Type: Village
Incorporated: Dec. 31, 1951 *Area:* 1.98 sq km
Population in 2006: 515
Provincial Electoral District(s): Rocky Mountain House
Federal Electoral District(s): Wild Rose
Next Election: 2013 (3 year terms)
Laura Cudmore, Mayor
Brian Irmen, CAO
Mary Hughes, Technician, Solid Wastes Recycling
403-329-7367
mhughes@lethbridge.ca

Carstairs
P.O. Box 370
Carstairs, AB T0M 0N0
Tel: 403-337-3341; *Fax:* 403-337-3343
admin@town.carstairs.ab.ca
www.carstairs.ca
Municipal Type: Town
Incorporated: May 15, 1903 *Area:* 5 sq km
Population in 2006: 2,656
Provincial Electoral District(s): Olds-Didsbury-Three Hills
Federal Electoral District(s): Wild Rose
Next Election: 2013 (3 year terms)
Note: Incorporated as a town on Sept. 1, 1966.
Lance Colby, Mayor
Carl McDonnell, CAO
carlm@carstairs.ca

Castle Island
11318 - 10th Ave.
Edmonton, AB T6J 6S9
Tel: 780-431-9712; *Fax:* 780-431-0882
svoffice@telusplanet.net
Municipal Type: Summer Village
Incorporated: Jan. 1, 1955 *Area:* 0.05 sq km
Population in 2006: 22
Provincial Electoral District(s): Whitecourt-Ste. Anne
Federal Electoral District(s): Yellowhead
Next Election: 2013 (3 year terms)
Cornelia Helland, Mayor
Anita Blais, Administrator

Castor
P.O. Box 479
Castor, AB T0C 0X0
Tel: 403-882-3215; *Fax:* 403-882-2700
sandi@townofcastor.ca
www.castor.ca
Municipal Type: Town
Incorporated: Nov. 26, 1909 *Area:* 2.72 sq km
Population in 2006: 931
Provincial Electoral District(s): Battle River-Wainwright
Federal Electoral District(s): Crowfoot
Next Election: 2013 (3 year terms)
Note: Incorporated as a town on June 27, 1910.
Gerry DeVloo, Mayor
Michael Yakielashek, CAO

Cereal
P.O. Box 160
Cereal, AB T0J 2J0
Tel: 403-326-3823;
vofc@telusplanet.net
Municipal Type: Village
Incorporated: Aug. 19, 1914 *Area:* 0.95 sq km
Population in 2006: 126
Provincial Electoral District(s): Drumheller-Stettler
Federal Electoral District(s): Crowfoot
Next Election: 2013 (3 year terms)
Allen Buetter, Mayor
Mary Ann Salik, Administrator

Champion
P.O. Box 367
Champion, AB T0L 0R0
Tel: 403-897-3833; *Fax:* 403-897-2250
champvil@wildroseinternet.ca
Municipal Type: Village
Incorporated: May 27, 1911 *Area:* 0.88 sq km
Population in 2006: 364
Provincial Electoral District(s): Little Bow
Federal Electoral District(s): Macleod
Next Election: 2013 (3 year terms)
Richard Ellis, Mayor
Amy Rupp, Administrator

Chauvin
P.O. Box 160
Chauvin, AB T0B 0V0
Tel: 780-858-3881; *Fax:* 780-858-2125
vchauvin@cciwireless.ca
www.villagechauvin.ca
Municipal Type: Village
Incorporated: Dec. 30, 1912 *Area:* 2.32 sq km
Population in 2006: 308
Provincial Electoral District(s): Battle River-Wainwright
Federal Electoral District(s): Vegreville-Wainwright
Next Election: 2013 (3 year terms)
Christine Smith, Mayor
Shelly McMann, Municipal Administrator
vchauvin@wy-com.ca

Chipman
P.O. Box 176
4816-50 St.
Chipman, AB T0B 0W0
Tel: 780-363-3982; *Fax:* 780-363-2386
chipmanab@mcsnet.ca
www.chipmanab.ca
Municipal Type: Village
Incorporated: Oct. 21, 1913 *Area:* 0.62 sq km
Population in 2006: 238
Provincial Electoral District(s): Fort Saskatchewan-Vegreville
Federal Electoral District(s): Vegreville-Wainwright
Next Election: 2013 (3 year terms)
Jim Palmer, Mayor
Pat Tomkow, Village Clerk

Claresholm
P.O. Box 1000
221-45 Ave w
Claresholm, AB T0L 0T0
Tel: 403-625-3381; *Fax:* 403-625-3869
clares@telusplanet.net
www.townofclaresholm.com
Municipal Type: Town
Incorporated: May 30, 1903 *Area:* 8.3 sq km
Population in 2006: 3,700
Provincial Electoral District(s): Livingstone-Macleod
Federal Electoral District(s): Macleod
Next Election: 2013 (3 year terms)
Note: Incorporated as a town on Aug. 31, 1905.
David Moore, Mayor
david.moore@townofclaresholm.com
Kris Holbeck, CAO
kris.holbeck@townofclaresholm.com

Clive
P.O. Box 90
Clive, AB T0C 0Y0
Tel: 403-784-3366; *Fax:* 403-784-2012
cliveab@platinum.ca
www.clive.ca
Municipal Type: Village
Incorporated: Jan. 9, 1912 *Area:* 2.12 sq km
Population in 2006: 562
Provincial Electoral District(s): Lacombe-Ponoka
Federal Electoral District(s): Wetaskiwin
Next Election: 2013 (3 year terms)
Anita Gillard, Mayor
Karen Kane, CAO

Clyde
P.O. Box 190
Clyde, AB T0G 0P0
Tel: 780-348-5356; *Fax:* 780-348-5699
admin@villageofclyde.ca
www.villageofclyde.ca
Municipal Type: Village
Incorporated: Jan. 28, 1914 *Area:* 1.36 sq km
Population in 2006: 470
Provincial Electoral District(s): Barrhead-Morinville-Westlock
Federal Electoral District(s): Westlock-St. Paul
Next Election: 2013 (3 year terms)
Wayne Wilcox, Mayor
mayor@villageofclyde.ca
Melanie Beastall, CAO
cao@villageofclyde.ca

Coaldale
1920 - 17 St.
Coaldale, AB T1M 1M1
Tel: 403-345-1300; *Fax:* 403-345-1311
admin@coaldale.ca
www.coaldale.ca
Municipal Type: Town
Incorporated: Dec. 27, 1919 *Area:* 7.95 sq km
Population in 2009: 6,943
Provincial Electoral District(s): Little Bow
Federal Electoral District(s): Lethbridge
Next Election: 2013 (3 year terms)
Note: Incorporated as a town on Jan. 7, 1952.
Leo Ludwig, Town Manager
lludwig@coaldale.ca
Kim Craig, Mayor

Coalhurst
P.O. Box 456
Coalhurst, AB T0L 0V0
Tel: 403-381-3033; *Fax:* 403-381-2924
main@town.coalhurst.ab.ca
www.town.coalhurst.ab.ca
Municipal Type: Town
Incorporated: Dec. 17, 1913 *Area:* 1.64 sq km
Population in 2006: 1,523
Provincial Electoral District(s): Little Bow
Federal Electoral District(s): Lethbridge
Next Election: 2013 (3 year terms)
Note: Incorporated as a town on June 1, 1995.
Dennis Cassie, Mayor
cassiefamily@shaw.ca
R. Kim Hauta, CAO
rkhauta@town.coalhurst.ab.ca

Consort
P.O. Box 490
Consort, AB T0C 1B0
Tel: 403-577-3623; *Fax:* 403-577-2024
consort@xplornet.com
www.village.consort.ab.ca
Municipal Type: Village
Incorporated: Sept. 23, 1912 *Area:* 2.63 sq km
Population in 2006: 739
Provincial Electoral District(s): Drumheller-Stettler
Federal Electoral District(s): Crowfoot
Next Election: 2013 (3 year terms)
Wayne Walker, Mayor
wwalker@xplorenet.com
Monique Jeffrey, CAO
mjeffrey@netago.ca

Coronation
P.O. Box 219
Coronation, AB T0C 1C0
Tel: 403-578-3679; *Fax:* 403-578-3020
admin@town.coronation.ab.ca
www.town.coronation.ab.ca
Municipal Type: Town
Incorporated: Dec. 16, 1911 *Area:* 3.73 sq km
Population in 2006: 1,015
Provincial Electoral District(s): Battle River-Wainwright
Federal Electoral District(s): Crowfoot
Next Election: 2013 (3 year terms)
Note: Incorporated as a town on April 29, 1912.
Dawna Elliott, Mayor
Sandra Kulyk, Town Manager

Coutts
P.O. Box 236
Coutts, AB T0K 0N0
Tel: 403-344-3848; *Fax:* 403-344-4360
vilcoutt@telus.net
www.villagecoutts.ab.ca
Municipal Type: Village
Incorporated: Jan. 1, 1960 *Area:* 0.98 sq km
Population in 2006: 305
Provincial Electoral District(s): Cardston-Taber-Warner
Federal Electoral District(s): Lethbridge
Next Election: 2013 (3 year terms)
Thomas Butler, Mayor
Lori Rolfe, CAO

Cowley
P.O. Box 40
Cowley, AB T0K 0P0
Tel: 403-628-3808; *Fax:* 403-628-2807
vilocow@shaw.ca
Municipal Type: Village
Incorporated: Aug. 16, 1906 *Area:* 1.4 sq km
Population in 2006: 219
Provincial Electoral District(s): Livingstone-Macleod
Federal Electoral District(s): Macleod
Next Election: 2013 (3 year terms)
Garry Hackler, Mayor
Laurie Wilgosh, Administrator
wilgosh@shaw.ca

Cremona
P.O. Box 10
Cremona, AB T0M 0R0
Tel: 403-637-3762; *Fax:* 403-637-2101
admin@village.cremona.ab.ca
www.village.cremona.ab.ca
Municipal Type: Village
Incorporated: Jan. 1, 1955 *Area:* 0.68 sq km
Population in 2006: 463
Provincial Electoral District(s): Olds-Didsbury-Three Hills
Federal Electoral District(s): Wild Rose
Next Election: 2013 (3 year terms)
Leslie Abrams, Mayor
Terry Lofstrom, CAO

Crossfield
P.O. Box 500
Crossfield, AB T0M 0S0
Tel: 403-946-5565; *Fax:* 403-946-4523
town@crossfieldalberta.com
www.crossfieldalberta.com
Municipal Type: Town
Incorporated: June 3, 1907 *Area:* 4.8 sq km
Population in 2006: 2,648
Provincial Electoral District(s): Foothills-Rocky View
Federal Electoral District(s): Wild Rose
Next Election: 2013 (3 year terms)
Note: Incorporated as a town on Aug. 1, 1980.
Nathan Anderson, Mayor
Cheryl Skelly, CAO
cheryls@crossfieldalberta.com

Crystal Springs
256 Grandview, RR#1
Westerose, AB T0C 2V0
Tel: 780-586-3522; *Fax:* 780-586-2037
crystalsprings@xplornet.com
www.svcrystalsprings.ca
Municipal Type: Summer Village
Incorporated: Jan. 1, 1957 *Area:* 0.58 sq km
Population in 2006: 112
Provincial Electoral District(s): Drayton Valley-Calmar
Federal Electoral District(s): Wetaskiwin
Next Election: 2013 (3 year terms)
Walter Schlese, Mayor
780-586-2555
Sylvia Roy, CAO

Czar
P.O. Box 30
Czar, AB T0B 0Z0
Tel: 780-857-3740; *Fax:* 780-857-2353
villczar@xplornet.com
Municipal Type: Village
Incorporated: Nov. 12, 1917 *Area:* 1.18 sq km
Population in 2006: 175
Provincial Electoral District(s): Battle River-Wainwright
Federal Electoral District(s): Vegreville-Wainwright
Next Election: 2013 (3 year terms)
Angela Large, Mayor
Tricia Strang, Administrator

Daysland
P.O. Box 610
Daysland, AB T0B 1A0
Tel: 780-374-3767; *Fax:* 780-374-2455
daystown@telusplanet.net
www.daysland.com
Municipal Type: Town
Incorporated: April 23, 1906 *Area:* 1.75 sq km
Population in 2006: 818
Provincial Electoral District(s): Battle River-Wainwright
Federal Electoral District(s): Vegreville-Wainwright
Next Election: 2013 (3 year terms)
Note: Incorporated as a town on April 2, 1907.
Jim Martin, Mayor
Sari-Anne Doolaege, CAO

Delburne
P.O. Box 341
Delburne, AB T0M 0V0
Tel: 403-749-3606; *Fax:* 403-749-2800
village@delburne.ca
www.delburne.ca
Municipal Type: Village
Incorporated: Jan. 17, 1913 *Area:* 1.32 sq km
Population in 2006: 765
Provincial Electoral District(s): Innisfail-Sylvan Lake
Federal Electoral District(s): Red Deer
Next Election: 2013 (3 year terms)
Ray Reckseidler, Mayor
ray.reckseidler@delburne.ca
Karen Fegan, CAO
karen.fegan@delburne.ca

Delia
P.O. Box 206
218 Main Street
Delia, AB T0J 0W0
Tel: 403-364-3787; *Fax:* 403-364-2089
delia@netago.ca
Municipal Type: Village
Incorporated: July 20, 1914 *Area:* 1.31 sq km
Population in 2006: 207
Provincial Electoral District(s): Drumheller-Stettler
Federal Electoral District(s): Crowfoot
Next Election: 2013 (3 year terms)
Gordon Isaac, Mayor
Caroline Siverson, CAO
cao.delia@netago.ca

Devon
1 Columbia Ave. West
Devon, AB T9G 1A1
Tel: 780-987-8300; *Fax:* 780-987-4778
www.town.devon.ab.ca
Municipal Type: Town
Incorporated: Dec. 31, 1949 *Area:* 8.63 sq km
Population in 2009: 6,534
Provincial Electoral District(s): Leduc-Beaumont-Devon
Federal Electoral District(s): Edmonton-Leduc
Next Election: 2013 (3 year terms)
Note: Incorporated as a town on Feb. 24, 1950.
Tony Kulbisky, CAO
780-987-8301
Anita Marie Fisher, Mayor

Dewberry
P.O. Box 30
Dewberry, AB T0B 1G0
Tel: 780-847-3053; *Fax:* 780-847-3057
dewberry@hmsinet.ca; ecodew@hmsinet.ca
www.villageofdewberry.ca
Municipal Type: Village
Incorporated: Jan. 1, 1957 *Area:* 0.84 sq km
Population in 2006: 196
Provincial Electoral District(s): Vermilion-Lloydminster
Federal Electoral District(s): Vegreville-Wainwright
Next Election: 2013 (3 year terms)
Sherry Johnson, Acting Sec.-Treas.
Headley Dennill, Mayor

Didsbury
P.O. Box 790
Didsbury, AB T0M 0W0
Tel: 403-335-3391; *Fax:* 403-335-9794
iquiries@didsbury.ca
www.didsbury.ca
Municipal Type: Town
Incorporated: Dec. 24, 1901 *Area:* 5.47 sq km
Population in 2006: 4,275
Provincial Electoral District(s): Olds-Didsbury-Three Hills
Federal Electoral District(s): Wild Rose
Next Election: 2013 (3 year terms)
Note: Incorporated as a town on Sept. 27, 1906.
Brian Wittal, Mayor
bwittal@didsbury.ca
Roy Brown, CAO
rbrown@didsbury.ca

Donalda
P.O. Box 160
Donalda, AB T0B 1H0
Tel: 403-883-2345; *Fax:* 403-883-2022
vdonalda@telusplanet.net
www.village.donalda.ab.ca
Municipal Type: Village
Incorporated: Dec. 30, 1912 *Area:* 0.99 sq km
Population in 2006: 224
Provincial Electoral District(s): Drumheller-Stettler
Federal Electoral District(s): Crowfoot
Next Election: 2013 (3 year terms)
Bruce Gartisde, Mayor
Joan Kapiniak, CAO
cao@village.donalda.ab.ca

Donnelly
P.O. Box 200
Donnelly, AB T0H 1G0
Tel: 780-925-3835; *Fax:* 780-925-2100
vilofdon@serbernet.com
www.villageofdonelly.drackir.com
Municipal Type: Village
Incorporated: Jan. 1, 1956 *Area:* 1.04 sq km
Population in 2006: 293
Provincial Electoral District(s): Dunvegan-Central Peace
Federal Electoral District(s): Peace River
Next Election: 2013 (3 year terms)
Charles Doyle, Mayor
Rita Therriault, Administrator

Drayton Valley
P.O. Box 6837
5120 - 52nd St.
Drayton Valley, AB T7A 1A1
Tel: 780-514-2200; *Fax:* 780-542-5753
info@town.draytonvalley.ab.ca
www.town.draytonvalley.ab.ca
Municipal Type: Town
Incorporated: Jan. 1, 1956 *Area:* 12.27 sq km
Population in 2006: 6,893
Provincial Electoral District(s): Drayton Valley-Calmar
Federal Electoral District(s): Yellowhead
Next Election: 2013 (3 year terms)
Note: Incorporated as a town on June 1, 1956.
Manny Deol, Town Manager
mdeol@town.draytonvalley.ab.ca
Mohammed (Moe) Hamdon, Mayor
mayor@town.draytonvalley.ab.ca

Drumheller
703 - 2nd Ave. West
Drumheller, AB T0J 0Y3
Tel: 403-823-6300; *Fax:* 403-823-7739
rmroman@dinosaurvalley.com
www.dinosaurvalley.com
Municipal Type: Town
Incorporated: May 15, 1913 *Area:* 107.93 sq km
Population in 2006: 7,932
Provincial Electoral District(s): Drumheller-Stettler
Federal Electoral District(s): Crowfoot
Next Election: 2013 (3 year terms)
Note: Incorporated as a town on March 2, 1916.
Ray Romanetz, CAO
rmroman@dinosaurvalley.com
Terry Yemen, Mayor

Duchess
P.O. Box 158
Duchess, AB T0J 0Z0
Tel: 403-378-4452; *Fax:* 403-378-3860
administration@villageofduchess.com
www.villageofduchess.com
Municipal Type: Village
Incorporated: May 12, 1921 *Area:* 1.89 sq km
Population in 2006: 978
Provincial Electoral District(s): Strathmore-Brooks
Federal Electoral District(s): Medicine Hat
Next Election: 2013 (3 year terms)
Anthony Steidel, Mayor
Yvonne Cosh

Eckville
P.O. Box 578
Eckville, AB T0M 0X0
Tel: 403-746-2171; *Fax:* 403-746-2900
info@eckville.com
www.eckville.com
Municipal Type: Town
Incorporated: Nov. 3, 1921 *Area:* 1.58 sq km
Population in 2006: 951
Provincial Electoral District(s): Rocky Mountain House
Federal Electoral District(s): Wetaskiwin
Next Election: 2013 (3 year terms)
Note: Incorporated as a town on July 1, 1966.
Helen Posti, Mayor
Therese Kleeberger, Administrator
admin@eckville.com

Edberg
P.O. Box 160
Edberg, AB T0B 1J0
Tel: 780-877-3999; *Fax:* 780-877-2562
vledberg@syban.net
www.villageofedberg.com
Municipal Type: Village
Incorporated: Feb. 4, 1930 *Area:* 0.36 sq km
Population in 2006: 155
Provincial Electoral District(s): Lacombe-Ponoka
Federal Electoral District(s): Crowfoot
Next Election: 2013 (3 year terms)
Lorne Klevgaard, Mayor
Patrick Risk, CAO

Edgerton
P.O. Box 57
Edgerton, AB T0B 1K0
Tel: 780-755-3933; *Fax:* 780-755-3750
info@edgerton-oasis.ca
www.edgerton-oasis.ca
Municipal Type: Village
Incorporated: Sept. 11, 1917 *Area:* 1.22 sq km
Population in 2006: 373
Provincial Electoral District(s): Battle River-Wainwright
Federal Electoral District(s): Vegreville-Wainwright
Next Election: 2013 (3 year terms)
Barbara L. Sjoquist, Mayor
Al Gordon, CAO

Edson
P.O. Box 6300
605 - 50th St.
Edson, AB T7E 1T7
Tel: 780-723-4401; *Fax:* 780-723-8617
civiccentre@townofedson.ca
www.townofedson.ca
Municipal Type: Town
Incorporated: Jan. 9, 1911 *Area:* 29.54 sq km
Population in 2006: 8,098
Provincial Electoral District(s): West Yellowhead
Federal Electoral District(s): Yellowhead
Next Election: 2013 (3 year terms)
Note: Incorporated as a town on Sept. 21, 1911.
Clarence Joly, CAO
clarencej@townofedson.ca
Greg Pasychny, Mayor

Elk Point
P.O. Box 448
Elk Point, AB T0A 1A0
Tel: 780-724-3810; *Fax:* 780-724-2762
town@elkpoint.ca
www.elkpoint.ca
Municipal Type: Town
Incorporated: May 31, 1938 *Area:* 4.88 sq km
Population in 2006: 1,487
Provincial Electoral District(s): Lac La Biche-St. Paul
Federal Electoral District(s): Westlock-St. Paul
Next Election: 2013 (3 year terms)
Note: Incorporated as a town on Jan. 1, 1962.
Parrish Tung, Mayor
parrish.tung@elkpoint.ca
Myron J. Goyan, Manager
mjgoyan@elkpoint.ca

Elnora
P.O. Box 629
Elnora, AB T0M 0Y0
Tel: 403-773-3922; *Fax:* 403-773-3173
elnoravl@platinum.ca
www.villageofelnora.com
Municipal Type: Village
Incorporated: July 22, 1929 *Area:* 0.69 sq km
Population in 2006: 275
Provincial Electoral District(s): Innisfail-Sylvan Lake
Federal Electoral District(s): Red Deer
Next Election: 2013 (3 year terms)
Rob Aellen, Mayor
Michelle White, Administrator

Empress
P.O. Box 159
Empress, AB T0J 1E0
Tel: 403-565-3938; *Fax:* 403-565-2010
voe14@telus.net
www.villageofempress.com
Municipal Type: Village
Incorporated: Feb. 5, 1914 *Area:* 1.75 sq km
Population in 2006: 136
Provincial Electoral District(s): Drumheller-Stettler
Federal Electoral District(s): Medicine Hat
Next Election: 2013 (3 year terms)
Roderick L. Briggs, Mayor
Darran Dick, CAO
darran.dick@gov.ab.ca

Fairview
P.O. Box 730
10209 - 109 St.
Fairview, AB T0H 1L0
Tel: 780-835-5461; *Fax:* 780-835-3576
municipalsecretary@fairview.ca
www.fairview.ca
Municipal Type: Town
Incorporated: March 28, 1929 *Area:* 9.65 sq km
Population in 2006: 3,297
Provincial Electoral District(s): Dunvegan-Central Peace
Federal Electoral District(s): Peace River
Next Election: 2013 (3 year terms)
Note: Incorporated as a town on April 25, 1949.
Martin Taylor, CAO
cao@fairview.ca
Gordon MacLeod, Mayor
mayor@fairview.ca

Falher
P.O. Box 155
Falher, AB T0H 1M0
Tel: 780-837-2247; *Fax:* 780-837-2647
info@town.falher.ab.ca
www.town.falher.ab.ca
Municipal Type: Town
Incorporated: Sept. 05, 1923 *Area:* 2.87 sq km
Population in 2006: 941
Provincial Electoral District(s): Dunvegan-Central Peace
Federal Electoral District(s): Peace River
Next Election: 2013 (3 year terms)
Note: Incorporated as a town on Jan. 1, 1955.
Adele Parker, CAO
aparker@town.falher.ab.ca
Margaret Tardif, Mayor
mtardif@town.falher.ab.ca

Ferintosh
P.O. Box 160
Ferintosh, AB T0B 1M0
Tel: 780-877-3767; *Fax:* 780-877-2338
ferintosh@mailhub.ca
www.ferintosh.info
Municipal Type: Village
Incorporated: Jan. 9, 1911 *Area:* 0.62 sq km
Population in 2006: 153
Provincial Electoral District(s): Lacombe-Ponoka
Federal Electoral District(s): Crowfoot
Next Election: 2013 (3 year terms)
Marvin Jassman, Mayor
Patrick Risk, CAO

Foremost
P.O. Box 159
Foremost, AB T0K 0X0
Tel: 403-867-3733; *Fax:* 403-867-2031
vlg4most@telusplanet.net
www.foremostalberta.com
Municipal Type: Village
Incorporated: Dec. 31, 1950 *Area:* 1.74 sq km
Population in 2006: 524
Provincial Electoral District(s): Cypress-Medicine Hat
Federal Electoral District(s): Medicine Hat
Next Election: 2013 (3 year terms)
Kenneth R. Kultgen, Mayor
Kelly Calhoun, Municipal Administrator

Forestburg
P.O. Box 210
Forestburg, AB T0B 1N0
Tel: 780-582-3668; *Fax:* 780-582-2233
forestburg@persona.ca
www.forestburg.ca
Municipal Type: Village
Incorporated: Aug. 21, 1919 *Area:* 2.19 sq km
Population in 2006: 895
Provincial Electoral District(s): Battle River-Wainwright
Federal Electoral District(s): Vegreville-Wainwright
Next Election: 2013 (3 year terms)
Robert Frizzell, Mayor
Debra Moffatt, CAO

Fort Macleod
P.O. Box 1420
Fort MacLeod, AB T0L 0Z0
Tel: 403-553-4425; *Fax:* 403-553-2426
administration@fortmacleod.com
www.fortmacleod.com
Other Information: Toll free: 1-877-622-5366
Municipal Type: Town
Incorporated: Dec. 31, 1892 *Area:* 23.34 sq km
Population in 2006: 3,072
Provincial Electoral District(s): Livingstone-Macleod
Federal Electoral District(s): Macleod
Next Election: 2013 (3 year terms)
R. Shawn Patience, Mayor
mayor@fortmacleod.com
Barry Elliott, Municipal Manager
manager@fortmacleod.com

Fox Creek
P.O. Box 149
102 Kaybob Drive
Fox Creek, AB T0H 1P0
Tel: 780-622-3896; *Fax:* 780-622-4247
info@town.fox-creek.ab.ca
www.fox-creek.ca
Municipal Type: Town
Incorporated: July 19, 1967 *Area:* 11.54 sq km
Population in 2006: 2,278
Provincial Electoral District(s): Grande Prairie-Smoky
Federal Electoral District(s): Yellowhead
Next Election: 2013 (3 year terms)
Leora MacKinnon, Mayor
leora@foxcreek.ca
Ken Gwozdz, CAO
cao@foxcreek.ca

Gadsby
P.O. Box 80
Gadsby, AB T0C 1K0
Tel: 403-574-3793; *Fax:* 403-574-2369
vgadsby@telusplanet.net
Municipal Type: Village
Incorporated: May 6, 1910 *Area:* 0.82 sq km
Population in 2006: 35
Provincial Electoral District(s): Drumheller-Stettler
Federal Electoral District(s): Crowfoot
Next Election: 2013 (3 year terms)
Fred Entwisle, Mayor
Lavonne Smith, CAO

Galahad
P.O. Box 66
Galahad, AB T0B 1R0
Tel: 780-583-3741; *Fax:* 780-583-2230
office@villageofgalahad.net
www.villagofgalahad.ca
Municipal Type: Village
Incorporated: March 5, 1918 *Area:* 0.6 sq km
Population in 2006: 134
Provincial Electoral District(s): Battle River-Wainwright
Federal Electoral District(s): Vegreville-Wainwright
Next Election: 2013 (3 year terms)

Sheryl Fossen, Mayor
Brent Hoyland, Assistant CAO
gpoyser@flagstaff.ab.ca

Ghost Lake
P.O. Box 5754
High River, AB T1V 1P3
Tel: 403-652-4636; *Fax:* 403-206-7209
admin@ghostlake.ca
www.ghostlake.ca
Municipal Type: Summer Village
Incorporated: Dec. 31, 1953 *Area:* 0.63 sq km
Population in 2006: 78
Provincial Electoral District(s): Banff-Cochrane
Federal Electoral District(s): Wild Rose
Next Election: 2013 (3 year terms)
Richard Elvey, Mayor
403-881-2276
Sharon Plett, CAO

Gibbons
P.O. Box 68
4807 - 50 Ave.
Gibbons, AB T0A 1N0
Tel: 780-923-3331; *Fax:* 780-923-3691
town@gibbons.ca
www.gibbons.ca
Municipal Type: Town
Incorporated: Jan. 1, 1959 *Area:* 6.46 sq km
Population in 2007: 2,848
Provincial Electoral District(s): Athabasca-Redwater
Federal Electoral District(s): Westlock-St. Paul
Next Election: 2013 (3 year terms)
Note: Incorporated as a town on April 1, 1977.
Maisie Metrunec, Town Manager
mmetrunec@gibbons.ca
William H. Nimmo, Mayor
gov@gibbons.ca

Girouxville
P.O. Box 276
Girouxville, AB T0H 1S0
Tel: 780-323-4270; *Fax:* 780-323-4110
girouxvl@telusplanet.net
Municipal Type: Village
Incorporated: Dec. 31, 1951 *Area:* 0.58 sq km
Population in 2006: 282
Provincial Electoral District(s): Dunvegan-Central Peace
Federal Electoral District(s): Peace River
Next Election: 2013 (3 year terms)
Carmen Ewing, Mayor
Estelle Girard, Municipal Administrator

Glendon
P.O. Box 177
Glendon, AB T0A 1P0
Tel: 780-635-3807; *Fax:* 780-635-2100
glendon@mcsnet.ca
Municipal Type: Village
Incorporated: Jan. 1, 1956 *Area:* 1.98 sq km
Population in 2006: 421
Provincial Electoral District(s): Bonnyville-Cold Lake
Federal Electoral District(s): Westlock-St. Paul
Next Election: 2013 (3 year terms)
John Larry Lofstrand, Mayor
Paula Mack, CAO

Glenwood
Main Ave
Glenwood, AB T0k 2R0
Tel: 403-626-3233; *Fax:* 403-626-3234
admin@glenwood.ca
www.glenwood.ca
Municipal Type: Village
Incorporated: Jan. 1, 1961 *Area:* 1.46 sq km
Population in 2006: 280
Provincial Electoral District(s): Cardston-Taber-Warner
Federal Electoral District(s): Macleod
Next Election: 2013 (3 year terms)
Doral Lybbert, Mayor
Brad Salmon, CAO

Golden Days
605-2nd Ave.
MA-ME O Beach, AB T0k 1x0
Tel: 780-586-2494; *Fax:* 780-586-3567
svoffice@telusplanet.net
Municipal Type: Summer Village
Incorporated: Jan. 1, 1965 *Area:* 2.27 sq km
Population in 2006: 207
Provincial Electoral District(s): Drayton Valley-Calmar
Federal Electoral District(s): Wetaskiwin
Next Election: 2013 (3 year terms)
Randal Kay, Mayor
Sylvia Roy, Administrator

Grande Cache
P.O. Box 300
Grande Cache, AB T0E 0Y0
Tel: 780-827-3362; *Fax:* 780-827-2406
admin@grandecache.ca
www.grandecache.ca
Municipal Type: Town
Incorporated: Sept. 1, 1966 *Area:* 35.48 sq km
Population in 2006: 3,783
Provincial Electoral District(s): West Yellowhead
Federal Electoral District(s): Yellowhead
Next Election: 2013 (3 year terms)
Louise Krewusik, Mayor
Darren Ottaway, CAO
darren.ottaway@grandecache.ca

Grandview
P.O. Box 100
603 - 2nd Ave.
Ma-Me-O Beach, AB T0C 1X0
Tel: 780-586-2494; *Fax:* 780-586-3567
svadminoffice@xplornet.com
www.grandview.com
Municipal Type: Summer Village
Incorporated: Jan. 1, 1967 *Area:* 0.8 sq km
Population in 2006: 127
Provincial Electoral District(s): Drayton Valley-Calmar
Federal Electoral District(s): Wetaskiwin
Next Election: 2013 (3 year terms)
Don Davidson, Mayor
Sylvia Roy, CAO

Granum
P.O. Box 88
Granum, AB T0L 1A0
Tel: 403-687-3822; *Fax:* 403-687-2285
tmgr.townofgranum@shaw.ca
www.townofgranum.ca
Municipal Type: Town
Incorporated: July 12, 1904 *Area:* 1.87 sq km
Population in 2006: 415
Provincial Electoral District(s): Livingstone-Macleod
Federal Electoral District(s): Macleod
Next Election: 2013 (3 year terms)
Note: Incorporated as a town on Nov. 7, 1910.
Gerald Brown, Mayor
Interim Mayor
Larry Flexhaug, Municipal Administrator
cao.townofgranum@shaw.ca

Grimshaw
P.O. Box 377
Grimshaw, AB T0H 1W0
Tel: 780-332-4626; *Fax:* 780-332-1250
wjohnson@grimshaw.ca
www.grimshaw.ca
Municipal Type: Town
Incorporated: Feb. 18, 1930 *Area:* 7.21 sq km
Population in 2006: 2,537
Provincial Electoral District(s): Dunvegan-Central Peace
Federal Electoral District(s): Peace River
Next Election: 2013 (3 year terms)
Note: Incorporated as a town on Feb. 2, 1953.
Brian Allen, Mayor
Wendy Johnson, CAO
wjohnson@grimshaw.ca

Gull Lake
P.O. Box 5
RR#1, Site 2
Lacombe, AB T4L 2N1
Tel: 403-784-2966; *Fax:* 888-241-6027
admin@summervillageofgulllake.com
www.summervillageofgulllake.com
Municipal Type: Summer Village
Incorporated: Sept. 1, 1993 *Area:* 0.7 sq km
Population in 2006: 204
Provincial Electoral District(s): Rocky Mountain House
Federal Electoral District(s): Wetaskiwin
Next Election: 2013 (3 year terms)
Rick Assinger, Mayor
assinger@telus.net
Harold Northcott, CAO
admin@summervillageofgulllake.com

Half Moon Bay
#90B Hewlett Park Landing
Sylvan Lake, AB T4S 2J3
Tel: 403-887-2822; *Fax:* 403-887-2897
fivesv@telusplanet.net
Municipal Type: Summer Village
Incorporated: Jan. 1, 1978 *Area:* 0.17 sq km
Population in 2006: 32
Provincial Electoral District(s): Rocky Mountain House
Federal Electoral District(s): Wetaskiwin
Next Election: 2013 (3 year terms)
Edward (Ted) Hiscock, Mayor
Myra Reiter, Administrator

Halkirk
P.O. Box 126
Halkirk, AB T0C 1M0
Tel: 403-884-2464; *Fax:* 403-884-2113
halkirk@wildroseinternet.ca
Municipal Type: Village
Incorporated: Feb. 10, 1912 *Area:* 0.65 sq km
Population in 2006: 113
Provincial Electoral District(s): Battle River-Wainwright
Federal Electoral District(s): Crowfoot
Next Election: 2013 (3 year terms)
Dale Kent, Mayor
Doris Cordel, Village Administrator

Hanna
P.O. Box 430
Hanna, AB T0J 1P0
Tel: 403-854-4433; *Fax:* 403-854-2772
admin@hanna.ca
www.hanna.ca
Municipal Type: Town
Incorporated: Dec. 31, 1912 *Area:* 8.39 sq km
Population in 2006: 2,847
Provincial Electoral District(s): Drumheller-Stettler
Federal Electoral District(s): Crowfoot
Next Election: 2013 (3 year terms)
Note: Incorporated as a town on April 14, 1914.
Mark Nikota, Mayor
Geraldine Gervais, CAO
ggervais.cao@hanna.ca

Hardisty
P.O. Box 10
Hardisty, AB T0B 1V0
Tel: 780-888-3623; *Fax:* 780-888-2200
town.office@hardisty.ca
www.hardisty.ca
Municipal Type: Town
Incorporated: Dec. 11, 1906 *Area:* 5.48 sq km
Population in 2006: 760
Provincial Electoral District(s): Battle River-Wainwright
Federal Electoral District(s): Vegreville-Wainwright
Next Election: 2013 (3 year terms)
Note: Incorporated as a town on Nov. 9, 1910.
Kevin O'Grady, Mayor
Alan Parkin, CAO
alanparkin@hardisty.ca

Hay Lakes
P.O. Box 40
Hay Lakes, AB T0B 1W0
Tel: 780-878-3200; *Fax:* 780-878-3897
haylakes@syban.net
www.villageofhaylakes.com
Municipal Type: Village
Incorporated: April 17, 1928 *Area:* 0.58 sq km
Population in 2006: 362
Provincial Electoral District(s): Leduc-Beaumont-Devon
Federal Electoral District(s): Crowfoot
Next Election: 2013 (3 year terms)
Steve Nickoleff, Mayor
Heather Nadeau, Municipal Administrator

Heisler
P.O. Box 60
Heisler, AB T0B 2A0
Tel: 780-889-3774; *Fax:* 780-889-2280
administration@villageofheisler.ca
www.villageofheisler.ca
Municipal Type: Village
Incorporated: July 27, 1920 *Area:* 0.75 sq km
Population in 2006: 153
Provincial Electoral District(s): Battle River-Wainwright
Federal Electoral District(s): Vegreville-Wainwright
Next Election: 2013 (3 year terms)
Shean Maciborski, Mayor
Brenda Loesch, CAO

High Level
10511 - 103 St.
High Level, AB T0H 1Z0
Tel: 780-926-2201; *Fax:* 780-926-2899
town@highlevel.ca
www.highlevel.ca
Municipal Type: Town
Incorporated: June 1, 1965 *Area:* 31.99 sq km
Population in 2006: 3,887
Provincial Electoral District(s): Peace River
Federal Electoral District(s): Peace River
Next Election: 2013 (3 year terms)
Dean Krause, CAO
780-821-4001
dkrause@highlevel.ca
Peter Ernst, Mayor
780-926-4878
mayor@highlevel.ca

High Prairie
P.O. Box 179
High Prairie, AB T0G 1E0
Tel: 780-523-3388; *Fax:* 780-523-5930
reception@highprairie.ca
www.highprairie.ca
Municipal Type: Town
Incorporated: April 6, 1945 *Area:* 6.39 sq km
Population in 2006: 2,750
Provincial Electoral District(s): Lesser Slave Lake
Federal Electoral District(s): Fort McMurray-Athabasca
Next Election: 2013 (3 year terms)
Note: Incorporated as a town on Jan. 10, 1950.
Rick Dumont, Mayor
mayor@highprairie.ca
Christopher J. Parker, Town Manager
cao@highprairie.ca

Hill Spring
P.O. Box 40
Hill Spring, AB T0K 1E0
Tel: 403-626-3876; *Fax:* 403-626-2333
office@hillspring.ca
www.hillspring.ca
Municipal Type: Village
Incorporated: Jan. 1, 1961 *Area:* 1.11 sq km
Population in 2006: 192
Provincial Electoral District(s): Cardston-Taber-Warner
Federal Electoral District(s): Macleod
Next Election: 2013 (3 year terms)
Monte Christensen, Mayor
office@hillspring.ca
Kurtis Pratt, CAO
kurtispratt@raymond.ca

Hines Creek
P.O. Box 421
Hines Creek, AB T0H 2A0
Tel: 780-494-3690; *Fax:* 780-494-3605
stacey@hinescreek.com
www.hinescreek.com
Other Information: Other Phone: 780-494-3690
Municipal Type: Village
Incorporated: Dec. 31, 1951 *Area:* 4.37 sq km
Population in 2006: 430
Provincial Electoral District(s): Dunvegan-Central Peace
Federal Electoral District(s): Peace River
Next Election: 2013 (3 year terms)
Ashley Zavisha, Mayor
ashley@zavishamills.com
Leila Sumner, Municipal Manager
lsumner@hinescreek.com

Hinton
131 Civic Centre Rd., 2nd Fl.
Hinton, AB T7V 2E5
Tel: 780-865-6000; *Fax:* 780-865-5706
bkreiner@town.hinton.ab.ca
www.hinton.ca
Municipal Type: Town
Incorporated: Nov. 1, 1956 *Area:* 25.76 sq km
Population in 2009: 9,825
Provincial Electoral District(s): West Yellowhead
Federal Electoral District(s): Yellowhead
Next Election: 2013 (3 year terms)
Bernie Kreiner, Town Manager
bkreiner@hinton.ca
Glenn Taylor, Mayor
mayor@hinton.ca

Holden
P.O. Box 357
Holden, AB T0B 2C0
Tel: 780-688-3928; *Fax:* 780-688-2091
vholden@telusplanet.net
www.village.holden.ab.ca
Municipal Type: Village
Incorporated: April 14, 1909 *Area:* 1.7 sq km
Population in 2006: 398
Provincial Electoral District(s): Fort Saskatchewan-Vegreville
Federal Electoral District(s): Vegreville-Wainwright
Next Election: 2013 (3 year terms)
Christine Mackay, Mayor
Katherine Whiteside, CAO

Horseshoe Bay
P.O. Box 1053
5837 - 44 Ave.
St Paul, AB T0A 3A0
Tel: 780-724-4422; *Fax:* 780-724-4422
d_smereka@telus.net
www.svhorseshoebay.ca
Municipal Type: Summer Village
Incorporated: Jan. 1, 1985 *Area:* 1.04 sq km
Population in 2006: 214
Provincial Electoral District(s): Lac La Biche-St. Paul
Federal Electoral District(s): Westlock-St. Paul
Next Election: 2013 (3 year terms)
Gary Burns, Mayor
780-645-4609
g_burns@telus.net
Darlene Smereka, Administrator
dsmereka@county.stpaul.ab.ca

Hughenden
P.O. Box 26
Hughenden, AB T0B 2E0
Tel: 780-856-3830; *Fax:* 780-856-2034
hughenden@xplornet.com
Municipal Type: Village
Incorporated: Dec. 27, 1917 *Area:* 0.78 sq km
Population in 2006: 231
Provincial Electoral District(s): Battle River-Wainwright
Federal Electoral District(s): Vegreville-Wainwright
Next Election: 2013 (3 year terms)
Aaron Gramlich, Mayor
hughenden@xplorenet.com
Lawrence Komaranky, CAO
hughendencao@xplornet.com

Hussar
P.O. Box 100
Hussar, AB T0J 1S0
Tel: 403-787-3766; *Fax:* 403-787-2560
hussar@myipplus.net
Municipal Type: Village
Incorporated: April 20, 1928 *Area:* 1.05 sq km
Population in 2006: 187
Provincial Electoral District(s): Strathmore-Brooks
Federal Electoral District(s): Crowfoot
Next Election: 2013 (3 year terms)
Bruce Kaufman, Mayor
Tracy Anderson, CAO

Hythe
P.O. Box 219
Hythe, AB T0H 2C0
Tel: 780-356-3888; *Fax:* 780-356-2009
admin@hythe.ca
www.hythe.ca
Municipal Type: Village
Incorporated: Aug. 31, 1929 *Area:* 4.12 sq km
Population in 2006: 821
Provincial Electoral District(s): Grande Prairie-Wapiti
Federal Electoral District(s): Peace River
Next Election: 2013 (3 year terms)
Gary Burgess, Mayor
mayor@hythe.ca
Greg Gayton, Administrator

Innisfail
4943 - 53 St.
Innisfail, AB T4G 1A1
Tel: 403-227-3376; *Fax:* 403-227-4045
townhall@innisfail.ca
www.townofinnisfail.com
Municipal Type: Town
Incorporated: Dec. 15, 1899 *Area:* 13.02 sq km
Population in 2009: 7,883
Provincial Electoral District(s): Innisfail-Sylvan Lake
Federal Electoral District(s): Red Deer
Next Election: 2013 (3 year terms)
Note: Incorporated as a town on Nov. 20, 1903.
Helen Dietz, Town Manager
helen.dietz@innisfail.ca
Jim Romane, Mayor
mayor@innisfail.ca

Innisfree
P.O. Box 69
Innisfree, AB T0B 2G0
Tel: 780-592-3886; *Fax:* 780-592-3729
inisfree@telus.net
www.villageofinnisfree.com
Municipal Type: Village
Incorporated: March 11, 1911 *Area:* 1.27 sq km
Population in 2006: 233
Provincial Electoral District(s): Vermilion-Lloydminster
Federal Electoral District(s): Vegreville-Wainwright
Next Election: 2013 (3 year terms)
Ron Konieczny, Mayor
Lori Leibel, Municipal Administrator
lorileibel@telus.net

Irma
P.O. Box 419
Irma, AB T0B 2H0
Tel: 780-754-3665; *Fax:* 780-754-3668
jfenton@irma.ca
www.villageofirma.com
Municipal Type: Village
Incorporated: May 30, 1912 *Area:* 1.11 sq km
Population in 2006: 444
Provincial Electoral District(s): Battle River-Wainwright
Federal Electoral District(s): Vegreville-Wainwright
Next Election: 2013 (3 year terms)
Douglas Coubrough, Mayor
780-754-3077
Jackie Fenton, CAO
780-754-2160
Jackie@villageofirma.ca

Irricana
P.O. Box 100
Irricana, AB T0M 1B0
Tel: 403-935-4672; *Fax:* 403-935-4270
irricana@irricana.com
www.irricana.com
Municipal Type: Town
Incorporated: June 9, 1911 *Area:* 3.18 sq km
Population in 2006: 1,243
Provincial Electoral District(s): Airdrie-Chestermere
Federal Electoral District(s): Crowfoot
Next Election: 2013 (3 year terms)
Note: Incorporated as a town on June 9, 2005.
Joshua Taylor, Mayor
jtaylor@irricana.com
Alvin Melton, CAO
cao@irricana.com

Island Lake
10511-109 ST.
Westlock, AB T7P 1A9
Tel: 780-349-3651; *Fax:* 780-349-5194
gmbancroft@shaw.ca
www.myislandlakesouth.com
Municipal Type: Summer Village
Incorporated: Jan. 1, 1958 *Area:* 1.45 sq km
Population in 2006: 351
Provincial Electoral District(s): Athabasca-Redwater
Federal Electoral District(s): Fort McMurray-Athabasca
Next Election: 2013 (3 year terms)
Bob Yontz, Mayor
Marion Bancroft, CAO

Island Lake South
10511 - 109th St.
Westlock, AB T7P 1A9
Tel: 780-349-3651; *Fax:* 780-349-5194
gmbancroft@shaw.ca
www.myislandlakesouth.com
Municipal Type: Summer Village
Incorporated: Jan. 1, 1983 *Area:* 0.63 sq km
Population in 2006: 105
Provincial Electoral District(s): Athabasca-Redwater
Federal Electoral District(s): Fort McMurray-Athabasca
Next Election: 2013 (3 year terms)
Jim Sandmaier, Mayor
Garth Bancroft, Administrator

Itaska Beach
5515 - 44 Ave., #A
Wetaskiwin, AB T9A 0C8
Tel: 780-312-0928; *Fax:* 780-401-3161
cao@extremesolutions.org
www.itaska.ca
Municipal Type: Summer Village
Incorporated: June 30, 1953 *Area:* 0.28 sq km
Population in 2006: 35
Provincial Electoral District(s): Drayton Valley-Calmar
Federal Electoral District(s): Wetaskiwin
Next Election: 2013 (3 year terms)
Ralph Johnston, Mayor
rbjohns@telusplanet.net
June Boyda, CAO
cao@extremesolutions.org

Jarvis Bay
90B Hewlett Park Landing
Sylvan Lake, AB T4S 1W2
Tel: 403-887-2822; *Fax:* 403-887-2897
fivesv@telusplanet.net
Municipal Type: Summer Village
Incorporated: Jan. 1, 1986 *Area:* 0.55 sq km
Population in 2006: 183
Provincial Electoral District(s): Innisfail-Sylvan Lake
Federal Electoral District(s): Red Deer
Next Election: 2013 (3 year terms)
Bob Thomlinson, Mayor
Myra Reiter, Administrator

Kapasiwin
P.O. Box 9
Kapasiwin, AB T0E 2Y0
Tel: 780-892-2684;
gckapa@cruzinternet.com
www.kapasiwinalberta.com
Municipal Type: Summer Village
Incorporated: Oct. 25, 1913 *Area:* 0.31 sq km
Population in 2006: 39
Provincial Electoral District(s): Stony Plain
Federal Electoral District(s): Yellowhead
Next Election: 2013 (3 year terms)
Note: Incorporated as a summer village on Sept. 01, 1993.
Brent Baim, Mayor
George Jones, Administrator

Killam
P.O. Box 189
Killam, AB T0B 2L0
Tel: 780-385-3977; *Fax:* 780-385-2120
tkillam@telusplanet.net
www.town.killam.ab.ca
Municipal Type: Town
Incorporated: Dec. 29, 1906 *Area:* 4.53 sq km
Population in 2006: 1,019
Provincial Electoral District(s): Battle River-Wainwright
Federal Electoral District(s): Vegreville-Wainwright
Next Election: 2013 (3 year terms)
Note: Incorporated as a town on May 1, 1965.
H.L. (Bud) James, Mayor
bjames@town.killam.ab.ca
Kimberly Borgel, CAO
cao@town.killam.ab.ca

Kitscoty
P.O. Box 128
Kitscoty, AB T0B 2P0
Tel: 780-846-2221; *Fax:* 780-846-2213
kitscoty@ruralsurf.net
Municipal Type: Village
Incorporated: March 22, 1911 *Area:* 1.54 sq km
Population in 2006: 709
Provincial Electoral District(s): Vermilion-Lloydminster
Federal Electoral District(s): Vegreville-Wainwright
Next Election: 2013 (3 year terms)
Daryl Frank, Mayor
Harold Trew, CAO

Lakeview
P.O. Box 190
Seba Beach, AB T0E 2B0
Tel: 780-797-3863; *Fax:* 780-797-3800
svseba@telusplanet.net
Municipal Type: Summer Village
Incorporated: Oct. 25, 1913 *Area:* 0.33 sq km
Population in 2006: 36
Provincial Electoral District(s): Stony Plain
Federal Electoral District(s): Yellowhead
Next Election: 2013 (3 year terms)
Earle Robertson, Mayor
Susan H. Evans, CAO

Lamont
P.O. Box 330
Lamont, AB T0B 2R0
Tel: 780-895-2010; *Fax:* 780-895-2595
tom.m@tclamont.ca
www.lamont.ca
Municipal Type: Town
Incorporated: June 14, 1910 *Area:* 4.59 sq km
Population in 2006: 1,664
Provincial Electoral District(s): Fort Saskatchewan-Vegreville
Federal Electoral District(s): Vegreville-Wainwright
Next Election: 2013 (3 year terms)
Note: Incorporated as a town on May 31, 1968.
Denis Durand, Mayor
Tom Miller, CAO

Larkspur
10511-109 St.
Westlock, AB T2P 1A9
Tel: 780-349-3651; *Fax:* 780-349-5194
gmbancroft@shaw.ca
www.myislandlakesouth.com
Municipal Type: Summer Village
Incorporated: Jan. 1, 1985 *Area:* 0.22 sq km
Population in 2006: 56
Provincial Electoral District(s): Barrhead-Morinville-Westlock
Federal Electoral District(s): Westlock-St. Paul
Next Election: 2013 (3 year terms)
Frank Atkinson, Mayor
Marion Bankroft, CAO
gmbancroft@shaw.ca

Legal
P.O. Box 390
Legal, AB T0G 1L0
Tel: 780-961-3773; *Fax:* 780-961-4133
main@town.legal.ab.ca
www.town.legal.ab.ca
Municipal Type: Town
Incorporated: Feb. 20, 1914 *Area:* 2.55 sq km
Population in 2006: 1,192
Provincial Electoral District(s): Barrhead-Morinville-Westlock
Federal Electoral District(s): Westlock-St. Paul
Next Election: 2013 (3 year terms)
Note: Incorporated as a town on Jan. 1, 1998.
Albert St. Jean, Mayor
astjean@town.legal.ab.ca
Robert Proulx, Administrator
rproulx@town.legal.ab.ca

Linden
P.O. Box 213
Linden, AB T0M 1J0
Tel: 403-546-3888; *Fax:* 403-546-2112
cao@linden.ca
www.linden.ca
Municipal Type: Village
Incorporated: Jan. 1, 1964 *Area:* 2.56 sq km
Population in 2006: 660
Provincial Electoral District(s): Olds-Didsbury-Three Hills
Federal Electoral District(s): Crowfoot
Next Election: 2013 (3 year terms)
Darwin Moon, Mayor
Joanne Weller, Municipal Administrator

Lomond
P.O. Box 268
Lomond, AB T0L 1G0
Tel: 403-792-3611; *Fax:* 403-792-3300
voflom@keltech.ab.ca
Municipal Type: Village
Incorporated: Feb. 16, 1916 *Area:* 1.28 sq km
Population in 2006: 175
Provincial Electoral District(s): Little Bow
Federal Electoral District(s): Macleod
Next Election: 2013 (3 year terms)
Brad Koch, Mayor
bkoch@telusplanet.net
Tracy Doram, CAO

Longview
P.O. Box 147
Longview, AB T0L 1H0
Tel: 403-558-3922; *Fax:* 403-558-3743
info@village.longview.ab.ca
www.village.longview.ab.ca
Other Information: Other Email:
office-manager@village.longview.ab.ca
Municipal Type: Village
Incorporated: Jan. 1, 1964 *Area:* 1.09 sq km
Population in 2006: 300
Provincial Electoral District(s): Highwood
Federal Electoral District(s): Macleod
Next Election: 2013 (3 year terms)
Ivor McCorquindale, Mayor
mayor@village.longview.ab.ca
Leslie Fitzgerald, CAO
cao@village.longview.ab.ca

Lougheed
P.O. Box 5
Lougheed, AB T0B 2V0
Tel: 780-386-3970; *Fax:* 780-386-2136
villageoflougheed@xplorenet.com
www.villageoflougheed.com
Municipal Type: Village
Incorporated: Nov. 7, 1911 *Area:* 1.13 sq km
Population in 2006: 217
Provincial Electoral District(s): Battle River-Wainwright
Federal Electoral District(s): Vegreville-Wainwright
Next Election: 2013 (3 year terms)
Debra Smith, Mayor
lardebsm@xplorenet.com
Linda Felske, Acting CAO
lougheedassist@xplornet.com

Ma-Me-O Beach
P.O. Box 100
603 - 2 Ave.
Ma-Me-O Beach, AB T0C 1X0
Tel: 780-586-2494; *Fax:* 780-586-3567
information@svofficepl.com
www.svofficepl.com
Municipal Type: Summer Village
Incorporated: Dec. 31, 1948 *Area:* 0.65 sq km
Population in 2006: 155
Provincial Electoral District(s): Drayton Valley-Calmar
Federal Electoral District(s): Wetaskiwin
Next Election: 2013 (3 year terms)
Don Fleming, Mayor
780-437-4101
Sylvia Roy, Administrator
sylvia.roy@svofficepl.com

Magrath
P.O. Box 520
Magrath, AB T0K 1J0
Tel: 403-758-3212; *Fax:* 403-758-6333
wade@magrath.ca
www.townofmagrath.ca
Municipal Type: Town
Incorporated: Aug. 20, 1901 *Area:* 4.97 sq km
Population in 2006: 2,081
Provincial Electoral District(s): Cardston-Taber-Warner
Federal Electoral District(s): Lethbridge
Next Election: 2013 (3 year terms)
Note: Incorporated as a town on July 24, 1907.
Russ Barnett, Mayor
Wade Alston, CAO
wade@magrath.ca
Sunni-Jeanne Walker, Mayor
sonnij@telus.net
John Brodrick, CAO
jbrodrick@manning.ca

Manning
P.O. Box 125
Manning, AB T0H 2M0
Tel: 780-836-3606; *Fax:* 780-836-3570
info@manning.ca
www.manning.ca
Municipal Type: Town
Incorporated: Dec. 31, 1951 *Area:* 3.42 sq km
Population in 2006: 1,493
Provincial Electoral District(s): Peace River
Federal Electoral District(s): Peace River
Next Election: 2013 (3 year terms)
Note: Incorporated as a town on Jan. 1, 1957.

Mannville
P.O. Box 180
5127 - 50th St.
Mannville, AB T0B 2W0
Tel: 780-763-3500; *Fax:* 780-763-3643
info@mannville.com; cao@mannville.com
www.mannville.com
Municipal Type: Village
Incorporated: Dec. 29, 1906 *Area:* 2.15 sq km
Population in 2006: 782
Provincial Electoral District(s): Vermilion-Lloydminster
Federal Electoral District(s): Vegreville-Wainwright
Next Election: 2013 (3 year terms)
Al Good, Mayor
council@mannville.com

Marwayne
P.O. Box 113
Marwayne, AB T0B 2X0
Tel: 780-847-3962; *Fax:* 780-847-3324
marwayne@hmsinet.ca
www.village.marwayne.ab.ca
Municipal Type: Village
Incorporated: Dec. 31, 1952 *Area:* 1.15 sq km
Population in 2006: 516
Provincial Electoral District(s): Vermilion-Lloydminster
Federal Electoral District(s): Vegreville-Wainwright
Next Election: 2013 (3 year terms)
Jenelle Saskiw, Mayor
marwayne@hmsinet.ca
Joanne Horton, Administrative Officer
cao.marwayne@hmsinet.ca

Mayerthorpe
P.O. Box 420
Mayerthorpe, AB T0E 1N0
Tel: 780-786-2416; *Fax:* 780-786-4590
admin@mayerthorpe.ca
www.mayerthorpe.ca
Municipal Type: Town
Incorporated: March 5, 1927 *Area:* 4.78 sq km
Population in 2006: 1,474
Provincial Electoral District(s): Whitecourt-Ste. Anne
Federal Electoral District(s): Yellowhead
Next Election: 2013 (3 year terms)
Note: Incorporated as a town on March 20, 1961.
Doug McDermid, Mayor
Kim Connell, CAO
cao@mayerthorpe.ca

McLennan
P.O. Box 356
19 - 1st Ave. NW
McLennan, AB T0H 2L0
Tel: 780-324-3065; *Fax:* 780-324-2288
twnmcl@serbernet.com
www.townofmclennan.com
Municipal Type: Town
Incorporated: Feb. 1, 1944 *Area:* 3.58 sq km
Population in 2006: 824
Provincial Electoral District(s): Dunvegan-Central Peace
Federal Electoral District(s): Peace River
Next Election: 2013 (3 year terms)
Note: Incorporated as a town on Feb. 11, 1948.
Donald Regier, Mayor
Lorraine Willier, CAO

Mewatha Beach
10511 - 109th St.
Westlock, AB T7P 1A9
Tel: 780-349-3651; *Fax:* 780-349-5194
gmbancroft@shaw.ca
www.mymewathabeach.com
Municipal Type: Summer Village
Incorporated: Jan. 1, 1978 *Area:* 0.78 sq km
Population in 2006: 167
Provincial Electoral District(s): Athabasca-Redwater
Federal Electoral District(s): Fort McMurray-Athabasca
Next Election: 2013 (3 year terms)
Barry J. Walker, Mayor
Garth Bancroft, Administrator
gmbancroft@shaw.ca

Milk River
P.O. Box 270
Milk River, AB T0K 1M0
Tel: 403-647-3773; *Fax:* 403-647-3772
main@milkriver.ca
www.milkriver.ca
Municipal Type: Town
Incorporated: July 11, 1916 *Area:* 2.39 sq km
Population in 2006: 816
Provincial Electoral District(s): Cardston-Taber-Warner
Federal Electoral District(s): Lethbridge
Next Election: 2013 (3 year terms)
Note: Incorporated as a town on Feb. 7, 1956.
Terry Michaelis, Mayor
main@milkriver.ca
Mario Berthiaume, CAO
cao@milkriver.ca

Millet
P.O. Box 270
Millet, AB T0C 1Z0
Tel: 780-387-4554; *Fax:* 780-387-4459
millet@millet.ca
www.millet.ca
Municipal Type: Town
Incorporated: June 17, 1903 *Area:* 3.74 sq km
Population in 2006: 2,068
Provincial Electoral District(s): Wetaskiwin-Camrose
Federal Electoral District(s): Wetaskiwin
Next Election: 2013 (3 year terms)
Note: Incorporated as a town on Sept. 1, 1983.
Robert E. Lorenson, Mayor
Teri Pelletier, CAO
cao@millet.ca

Milo
P.O. Box 65
Milo, AB T0L 1L0
Tel: 403-599-3883; *Fax:* 403-599-2201
vilmilo@wildroseinternet.ca
www.villageofmilo.ca
Municipal Type: Village
Incorporated: May 7, 1931 *Area:* 0.48 sq km
Population in 2006: 100
Provincial Electoral District(s): Little Bow
Federal Electoral District(s): Macleod
Next Election: 2013 (3 year terms)
Rafael Zea, Mayor
Kwabena Oduro-Kontoh, Municipal Administrator
kodurokontoh@gmail.com

Minburn
P.O. Box 65
Minburn, AB T0B 3B0
Tel: 780-593-3939; *Fax:* 780-593-3944
vminburn@telus.net
Municipal Type: Village
Incorporated: June 24, 1919 *Area:* 0.73 sq km
Population in 2006: 65
Provincial Electoral District(s): Vermilion-Lloydminster
Federal Electoral District(s): Vegreville-Wainwright
Next Election: 2013 (3 year terms)
Nick W. Marusiak, Mayor
Karen McQuarrie, CAO

Morinville
10125 - 100 Ave.
Morinville, AB T8R 1L6
Tel: 780-939-4361; *Fax:* 780-939-5633
treaume@morinville.ca
www.morinville.ca
Municipal Type: Town
Incorporated: Aug. 24, 1901 *Area:* 11.34 sq km
Population in 2009: 7,636
Provincial Electoral District(s): Barrhead-Morinville-Westlock
Federal Electoral District(s): Westlock-St. Paul
Next Election: 2013 (3 year terms)
Note: Incorporated as a town on April 21, 1911.
R. Lloyd Bertschi, Mayor
mayor@morinville.ca
Debbie Oyarzun, CAO
doyarzun@morinville

Morrin
P.O. Box 149
Morrin, AB T0J 2B0
Tel: 403-772-3870; *Fax:* 403-772-2123
morrin@netago.ca
Municipal Type: Village
Incorporated: April 16, 1920 *Area:* 0.82 sq km
Population in 2006: 253
Provincial Electoral District(s): Drumheller-Stettler
Federal Electoral District(s): Crowfoot
Next Election: 2013 (3 year terms)
Suzanne Lacher, Mayor
Annette Plachner, CAO

Mundare
P.O. Box 348
5128 - 50 St.
Mundare, AB T0B 3H0
Tel: 780-764-3929; *Fax:* 780-764-2003
info@mundare.ca
www.mundare.ca
Municipal Type: Town
Incorporated: March 6, 1907 *Area:* 3 sq km
Population in 2006: 712
Provincial Electoral District(s): Fort Saskatchewan-Vegreville
Federal Electoral District(s): Vegreville-Wainwright
Next Election: 2013 (3 year terms)
Note: Incorporated as a town on Jan. 4, 1951.
Michael Saric, Mayor
msaric@mundare.ca
Colin Zyla, CAO
cao@mundare.ca

Munson
P.O. Box 10
Munson, AB T0J 2C0
Tel: 403-823-6987; *Fax:* 403-823-9883
munson@netago.ca
Municipal Type: Village
Incorporated: May 5, 1911 *Area:* 2.6 sq km
Population in 2006: 217
Provincial Electoral District(s): Drumheller-Stettler
Federal Electoral District(s): Crowfoot
Next Election: 2013 (3 year terms)
Scott Dudley, Mayor
Lyle Cawiezel, Administrator

Myrnam
P.O. Box 278
5007 - 50th St.
Myrnam, AB T0B 3K0
Tel: 780-366-3910; *Fax:* 780-366-2246
vmyrnam@mcsnet.ca
www.myrnam.info
Municipal Type: Village
Incorporated: Aug. 22, 1930 *Area:* 2.76 sq km
Population in 2006: 362
Provincial Electoral District(s): Lac la Biche-St. Paul
Federal Electoral District(s): Vegreville-Wainwright
Next Election: 2013 (3 year terms)
Edward Sosnowski, Mayor
Gary Dupuis, Administrator

Nakamun Park
13 Grandin Rd.
St Albert, AB T8N 3B2
Tel: 780-460-7226; *Fax:* 780-419-2476
hmarsh@telusplanet.net
www.svnakamun.com
Municipal Type: Summer Village
Incorporated: Jan. 1, 1966 *Area:* 0.41 sq km
Population in 2006: 88
Provincial Electoral District(s): Whitecourt-Ste. Anne
Federal Electoral District(s): Yellowhead
Next Election: 2013 (3 year terms)
Janice Baker, Mayor
780-482-2728
Hilda Marsh, CAO
hmarsh@telusplanet.net

Nampa
P.O. Box 69
Nampa, AB T0H 2R0
Tel: 780-322-3852; *Fax:* 780-322-2100
office@nampa.ca
www.nampa.ca
Municipal Type: Village
Incorporated: Jan. 1, 1958 *Area:* 1.86 sq km
Population in 2006: 360
Provincial Electoral District(s): Peace River
Federal Electoral District(s): Peace River
Next Election: 2013 (3 year terms)
Klaus Noruchat, Mayor
khn@serbernet.com
Ray Coad, CAO
cao@nampa.ca

Nanton
P.O. Box 609
Nanton, AB T0L 1R0
Tel: 403-646-2029; *Fax:* 403-646-2653
cao@nanton.ca
www.nanton.ca
Municipal Type: Town
Incorporated: June 22, 1903 *Area:* 4.25 sq km
Population in 2006: 2,055
Provincial Electoral District(s): Livingstone-Macleod
Federal Electoral District(s): Macleod
Next Election: 2013 (3 year terms)
Note: Incorporated as a town on Aug. 9, 1907.
John J. Blake, Mayor
Brad Mason, CAO
cao@town.nanton.ab.ca

New Norway
P.O. Box 60
New Norway, AB T0B 3L0
Tel: 780-855-3915; *Fax:* 780-855-3916
admin@villageofnewnorway.ca
www.villageofnewnorway.ca
Municipal Type: Village
Incorporated: May 6, 1910 *Area:* 1.12 sq km
Population in 2006: 323
Provincial Electoral District(s): Lacombe-Ponoka

Federal Electoral District(s): Crowfoot
Next Election: 2013 (3 year terms)
Tonya Ratushniak, Mayor
Dirk Bannister, CAO

Nobleford
P.O. Box 67
906 Highway Ave.
Nobleford, AB T0L 1S0
Tel: 403-824-3555; *Fax:* 403-824-3553
admin@village.nobleford.ab.ca
www.village.nobleford.ab.ca
Municipal Type: Village
Incorporated: Feb. 28, 1918 *Area:* 1.17 sq km
Population in 2006: 689
Provincial Electoral District(s): Little Bow
Federal Electoral District(s): Lethbridge
Next Election: 2013 (3 year terms)
Marguerite Wobicke, Mayor
Kirk Hofman, CAO
caohofman@village.nobleford.ab.ca

Norglenwold
90B Hewlett Park Landing
Sylvan Lake, AB T4S 2J3
Tel: 403-887-2822; *Fax:* 403-887-2897
fivesv@telusplanet.net
Municipal Type: Summer Village
Incorporated: Jan. 1, 1965 *Area:* 0.67 sq km
Population in 2006: 270
Provincial Electoral District(s): Innisfail-Sylvan Lake
Federal Electoral District(s): Red Deer
Next Election: 2013 (3 year terms)
Carol McMillan, Mayor
Myra Reiter, Administrator

Norris Beach
P.O. Box 100
Ma-Me-O Beach, AB T0C 1X0
Tel: 780-586-2494; *Fax:* 780-586-3567
information@svofficepl.com
www.svofficepl.com
Municipal Type: Summer Village
Incorporated: Dec. 31, 1988 *Area:* 0.16 sq km
Population in 2006: 40
Provincial Electoral District(s): Drayton Valley-Calmar
Federal Electoral District(s): Wetaskiwin
Next Election: 2013 (3 year terms)
Bruce Fowlie, Mayor
Sylvia Roy, Administrator
sylvia.roy@svofficepl.com

Olds
4512 - 46 St.
Olds, AB T4H 1R5
Tel: 403-556-6981; *Fax:* 403-556-6537
admin@olds.ca
www.olds.ca
Municipal Type: Town
Incorporated: May 26, 1896 *Area:* 11.05 sq km
Population in 2006: 7,248
Provincial Electoral District(s): Olds-Didsbury-Three Hills
Federal Electoral District(s): Wild Rose
Next Election: 2013 (3 year terms)
Note: Incorporated as a town on July 01, 1905.
Judy Dahl, Mayor
403-507-4114
mayor@olds.ca
Norman McInnis, CAO
mcInnis@olds.ca

Onoway
P.O. Box 540
Onoway, AB T0E 1V0
Tel: 780-967-5338; *Fax:* 780-967-3226
info@onoway.com
www.onoway.com
Municipal Type: Town
Incorporated: June 25, 1923 *Area:* 3.34 sq km
Population in 2006: 875
Provincial Electoral District(s): Whitecourt-Ste. Anne
Federal Electoral District(s): Yellowhead
Next Election: 2013 (3 year terms)
Note: Incorporated as a town on Sept. 1, 2005.
Dale Krasnow, Mayor
Wendy Wildman, Interim CAO
cao@onoway.com

Oyen
P.O. Box 360
Oyen, AB T0J 2J0
Tel: 403-664-3511; *Fax:* 403-664-3712
townoffice@townofoyen.com
www.townofoyen.com
Municipal Type: Town
Incorporated: Jan. 17, 1913 *Area:* 4.93 sq km
Population in 2006: 1,015
Provincial Electoral District(s): Drumheller-Stettler
Federal Electoral District(s): Crowfoot
Next Election: 2013 (3 year terms)
Note: Incorporated as a town on Sept. 1, 1965.
Paul Christianson, Mayor
Herman Minderlein, Administrator
cao@townofoyen.com

Paradise Valley
P.O. Box 24
Paradise Valley, AB T0B 3R0
Tel: 780-745-2287; *Fax:* 780-745-2287
villageofpv@mcsnet.ca
Municipal Type: Village
Incorporated: Jan. 1, 1964 *Area:* 0.57 sq km
Population in 2006: 183
Provincial Electoral District(s): Vermilion-Lloydminster
Federal Electoral District(s): Vegreville-Wainwright
Next Election: 2013 (3 year terms)
Curtis Schneider, Mayor
Connie Wilkinson, Municipal Administrator
villageofpv@mcsnet.ca

Parkland Beach
P.O. Box 130
Rimbey, AB T0C 2J0
Tel: 403-843-2055; *Fax:* 888-470-2762
admin@parklandbeachsv.ca
Municipal Type: Summer Village
Incorporated: Jan. 1, 1984 *Area:* 0.93 sq km
Population in 2006: 135
Provincial Electoral District(s): Lacombe-Ponoka
Federal Electoral District(s): Wetaskiwin
Next Election: 2013 (3 year terms)
Larry Scheible, Mayor
Marilee Yakunin, Chief Administrative Officer
admin@parklandbeachsv.ca

Peace River
P.O. Box 6600
9911 - 100 St.
Peace River, AB T8S 1S4
Tel: 780-624-2574; *Fax:* 780-624-4664
info@peaceriver.net
http://peaceriver.net
Municipal Type: Town
Incorporated: June 2, 1914 *Area:* 24.87 sq km
Population in 2006: 6,315
Provincial Electoral District(s): Peace River
Federal Electoral District(s): Peace River
Next Election: 2013 (3 year terms)
Note: Incorporated as a town on Dec. 1, 1919.
Norma MacQuarrie, CAO
nmacquarrie@peaceriver.net
Lorne Mann, Mayor
780-624-8384

Pelican Narrows
P.O. Box 7878
Bonnyville, AB T9N 2J2
Tel: 780-826-5907; *Fax:* 780-826-2804
plapointe@mcsnet.ca
Municipal Type: Summer Village
Incorporated: July 1, 1979 *Area:* 0.7 sq km
Population in 2006: 141
Provincial Electoral District(s): Bonnyville-Cold Lake
Federal Electoral District(s): Westlock-St.Paul
Next Election: 2013 (3 year terms)
Robert Hornseth, Mayor
Padey Lapointe, Administrator

Penhold
P.O. Box 10
1 Waskasoo Ave.
Penhold, AB T0M 1R0
Tel: 403-886-4567; *Fax:* 403-886-4039
community1@townofpenhold.ca
www.townofpenhold.ca
Municipal Type: Town
Incorporated: May 4, 1904 *Area:* 2.35 sq km
Population in 2006: 1,961
Provincial Electoral District(s): Innisfail-Sylvan Lake
Federal Electoral District(s): Red Deer
Next Election: 2013 (3 year terms)
Note: Incorporated as a town on Sept. 1, 1980.
Dennis Cooper, Mayor
Rick Binnendyk, Chief Administrative Officer
cao@townofpenhold.ca

Picture Butte
P.O. Box 670
Picture Butte, AB T0K 1V0
Tel: 403-732-4555; *Fax:* 403-732-4334
info@picturebutte.ca
www.picturebutte.ca
Municipal Type: Town
Incorporated: Feb. 4, 1943 *Area:* 2.9 sq km
Population in 2006: 1,592
Provincial Electoral District(s): Little Bow
Federal Electoral District(s): Lethbridge
Next Election: 2013 (3 year terms)
Note: Incorporated as a town on Jan. 1, 1960.
Terry Kerkhoff, Mayor
tkerkhoff@picturebutte.ca
Audrey Mortensen, Chief Administrative Officer
audrey@picturebutte.ca

Pincher Creek
P.O. Box 159
Pincher Creek, AB T0K 1W0
Tel: 403-627-3156; *Fax:* 403-627-4784
reception@pinchercreek.ca
www.pinchercreek.ca
Municipal Type: Town
Incorporated: Aug. 18, 1898 *Area:* 8.84 sq km
Population in 2006: 3,625
Provincial Electoral District(s): Livingstone-Macleod
Federal Electoral District(s): Macleod
Next Election: 2013 (3 year terms)
Note: Incorporated as a town on May 12, 1906.
Ernie Olsen, Mayor
Laurie Wilgosh, Chief Administrative Officer
laurie@pinchercreek.ca

Point Alison
4323 - 49A St.
Edmonton, AB T6L 6J5
Tel: 780-462-6372;
thomtom@telus.net
www.pointalison.com
Municipal Type: Summer Village
Incorporated: Dec. 31, 1950 *Area:* 0.16 sq km
Population in 2006: 15
Provincial Electoral District(s): Stony Plain
Federal Electoral District(s): Yellowhead
Next Election: 2013 (3 year terms)
C. Gordon Wilson, Mayor
Tom Thompson, Administrator
thomtom@telus.net

Ponoka
5102 - 48 Ave.
Ponoka, AB T4J 1P7
Tel: 403-783-4431; *Fax:* 403-783-6745
town@ponoka.org
www.ponoka.org
Municipal Type: Town
Incorporated: Oct. 19, 1900 *Area:* 13.05 sq km
Population in 2006: 6,576
Provincial Electoral District(s): Lacombe-Ponoka
Federal Electoral District(s): Wetaskiwin
Next Election: 2013 (3 year terms)
Note: Incorporated as a town on Oct. 15, 1904.
Larry L. Henkelman, Mayor
Brad Watson, Chief Administrative Officer
bwatson@ponoka.org

Poplar Bay
P.O. Box 100
Ma-Me-O Beach, AB T0C 1X0
Tel: 780-586-2494; *Fax:* 780-586-3567
information@svofficepl.com
www.svofficepl.com
Municipal Type: Summer Village
Incorporated: Jan. 1, 1967 *Area:* 0.76 sq km
Population in 2006: 84
Provincial Electoral District(s): Drayton Valley-Calmar
Federal Electoral District(s): Wetaskiwin
Next Election: 2013 (3 year terms)
Kevin D. Davies, Mayor
Sylvia Roy, Chief Administrative Officer
sylvia.roy@svofficepl.com

Provost
P.O. Box 449
Provost, AB T0B 3S0
Tel: 780-753-2261; *Fax:* 780-753-6889
info@townofprovost.ca
www.provost.ca
Municipal Type: Town
Incorporated: Jan. 20, 1910 *Area:* 4.93 sq km
Population in 2006: 2,072
Provincial Electoral District(s): Battle River-Wainwright
Federal Electoral District(s): Vegreville-Wainwright
Next Election: 2013 (3 year terms)
Note: Incorporated as a town on Dec. 29, 1952.
Kenneth E. (Ken) Knox, Mayor
Judy Larson, Administrator
administrator@townofprovost.ca

Rainbow Lake
P.O. Box 149
Rainbow Lake, AB T0H 2Y0
Tel: 780-956-3934; *Fax:* 780-956-3570
admin@rainbowlake.ca
www.rainbowlake.ca
Municipal Type: Town
Incorporated: Sept. 1, 1966 *Area:* 11.04 sq km
Population in 2006: 965
Provincial Electoral District(s): Peace River
Federal Electoral District(s): Peace River
Next Election: 2013 (3 year terms)
Rose Cretney, Mayor
Rosemary Offrey, Chief Administrative Officer
roffrey@rainbowlake.ca

Raymond
P.O. Box 629
15 Broadway St.
Raymond, AB T0K 2S0
Tel: 403-752-3322; *Fax:* 403-752-4379
contact@raymond.ca
www.raymond.ca
Municipal Type: Town
Incorporated: May 30, 1902 *Area:* 4.75 sq km
Population in 2006: 3,205
Provincial Electoral District(s): Cardston-Taber-Warner
Federal Electoral District(s): Lethbridge
Next Election: 2013 (3 year terms)
Note: Incorporated as a town on July 1, 1903.
George Bohne, Mayor
bohne@raymond.ca
J. Scott Barton, Chief Administrative Officer
scottbarton@raymond.ca

Redcliff
P.O. Box 40
Redcliff, AB T0J 2P0
Tel: 403-548-3618; *Fax:* 403-548-6623
redcliff@town.redcliff.ab.ca
www.town.redcliff.ab.ca
Municipal Type: Town
Incorporated: Oct. 29, 1910 *Area:* 10.51 sq km
Population in 2006: 5,096
Provincial Electoral District(s): Cypress-Medicine Hat
Federal Electoral District(s): Medicine Hat
Next Election: 2013 (3 year terms)
Note: Incorporated as a town on Aug. 5, 1912.
Robert Hazelaar, Mayor
mayor@town.redcliff.ab.ca
David Wolanski, Municipal Manager
davidw@town.redcliff.ab.ca

Redwater
P.O. Box 397
Redwater, AB T0A 2W0
Tel: 780-942-3519; *Fax:* 780-942-4321
www.redwater.ca
Municipal Type: Town
Incorporated: Dec. 31, 1949 *Area:* 7.95 sq km
Population in 2006: 2,192
Provincial Electoral District(s): Athabasca-Redwater
Federal Electoral District(s): Westlock-St. Paul
Next Election: 2013 (3 year terms)
Note: Incorporated as a town on Dec. 31, 1950.
Mel Smith, Mayor
mayor@redwater.ca
Deb Hamilton, Town Manager

Rimbey
P.O. Box 350, 4938 - 50th Ave.
Rimbey, AB T0C 2J0
Tel: 403-843-2113; *Fax:* 403-843-6599
rtown@rimbey.com
www.rimbey.com
Municipal Type: Town
Incorporated: June 13, 1919 *Area:* 11.34 sq km
Population in 2006: 2,252
Provincial Electoral District(s): Lacombe-Ponoka
Federal Electoral District(s): Wetaskiwin
Next Election: 2013 (3 year terms)
Note: Incorporated as a town on Dec. 13, 1948.
Sheldon Ibbotson, Mayor
mayor@rimbey.com
Tony Goode, Chief Administrative Officer
tony@rimbey.com

Rochon Sands
1 Hall St.
Rochon Sands, AB T0C 3B0
Tel: 403-742-4717; *Fax:* 403-742-4771
info@rochonsands.net
www.rochonsands.net
Municipal Type: Summer Village
Incorporated: May 17, 1929 *Area:* 2.32 sq km
Population in 2006: 66
Provincial Electoral District(s): Drumheller-Stettler
Federal Electoral District(s): Crowfoot
Next Election: 2013 (3 year terms)
Wayne Miller, Mayor
Alan Willis, Village Administrator
info@rochonsands.net

Rocky Mountain House
P.O. Box 1509
Rocky Mountain House, AB T4T 1B2
Tel: 403-845-2866; *Fax:* 403-845-3230
town@rockymtnhouse.com
www.rockymtnhouse.com
Municipal Type: Town
Incorporated: May 15, 1913 *Area:* 12.44 sq km
Population in 2006: 6,874
Provincial Electoral District(s): Rocky Mountain House
Federal Electoral District(s): Wetaskiwin
Next Election: 2013 (3 year terms)
Note: Incorporated as a town on Aug. 31, 1939.
Fred Nash, Mayor
Todd Becker, Town Manager
tbecker@rockymtnhouse.com

Rockyford
P.O. Box 294
Rockyford, AB T0J 2R0
Tel: 403-533-3950; *Fax:* 403-533-3744
loism_village@rockyford.ca
www.rockyford.ca
Municipal Type: Village
Incorporated: March 28, 1919 *Area:* 1.05 sq km
Population in 2006: 349
Provincial Electoral District(s): Strathmore-Brooks
Federal Electoral District(s): Crowfoot
Next Election: 2013 (3 year terms)
Darcy J. Burke, Mayor
dburke@rockyford.ca
Lois Mountjoy, Administrator

Rosalind
P.O. Box 181
Rosalind, AB T0B 3Y0
Tel: 780-375-3996; *Fax:* 780-375-3997
rosalindvillage@xplornet.com
www.villageofrosalind.ca
Municipal Type: Village
Incorporated: Jan. 1, 1966 *Area:* 0.59 sq km
Population in 2006: 190
Provincial Electoral District(s): Battle River-Wainwright
Federal Electoral District(s): Crowfoot
Next Election: 2013 (3 year terms)
James McTavish, Mayor
Nancy Friend, Chief Administrative Officer

Rosemary
P.O. Box 128
Rosemary, AB T0J 2W0
Tel: 403-378-4246; *Fax:* 403-378-3144
rosemary.admin@eidnet.org
www.myrosemary.org
Municipal Type: Village
Incorporated: Dec. 31, 1951 *Area:* 0.56 sq km
Population in 2006: 388
Provincial Electoral District(s): Strathmore-Brooks
Federal Electoral District(s): Medicine Hat
Next Election: 2013 (3 year terms)
Don L. Gibb, Mayor
dgibb@eidnet.org
Margaret Loewen, Chief Administrative Officer

Ross Haven
P.O. Box 7
Site 19, RR#1
Gunn, AB T0E 1A0
Tel: 780-967-1426; *Fax:* 780-702-6743
d.evans@xplornet.com
Municipal Type: Summer Village
Incorporated: Jan. 1, 1962 *Area:* 0.7 sq km
Population in 2006: 198
Provincial Electoral District(s): Whitecourt-Ste. Anne
Federal Electoral District(s): Yellowhead
Next Election: 2013 (3 year terms)
Kelly Demkiw, Mayor
Dennis Evans, Municipal Administrator

Rycroft
P.O. Box 360
Rycroft, AB T0H 3A0
Tel: 780-765-3652; *Fax:* 780-765-2002
rycroft@rycroft.ca
www.rycroft.ca
Municipal Type: Village
Incorporated: March 15, 1944 *Area:* 1.69 sq km
Population in 2006: 638
Provincial Electoral District(s): Dunvegan-Central Peace
Federal Electoral District(s): Peace River
Next Election: 2013 (3 year terms)
Whitney Burback, Mayor
wburback@rycroft.ca
Norma Maxwell, Interim Chief Administrative Officer
nmaxwell@rycroft.ca

Ryley
P.O. Box 230
Ryley, AB T0B 4A0
Tel: 780-663-3653; *Fax:* 780-663-3541
info@ryley.ca
www.ryley.ca
Municipal Type: Village
Incorporated: April 2, 1910 *Area:* 1.97 sq km
Population in 2006: 458
Provincial Electoral District(s): Fort Saskatchewan-Vegreville
Federal Electoral District(s): Vegreville-Wainwright
Next Election: 2013 (3 year terms)
Jorge Mendoza, Mayor
j.mendoza@ryley.ca
Emily House, Chief Administrative Officer
cao@ryley.ca

St. Paul
P.O. Box 1480
St. Paul, AB T0A 3A0
Tel: 780-645-4481; *Fax:* 780-645-5076
townhall@town.stpaul.ab.ca
www.town.stpaul.ab.ca
Municipal Type: Town
Incorporated: June 14, 1912 *Area:* 6.86 sq km
Population in 2006: 5,106
Provincial Electoral District(s): Lac La Biche-St. Paul
Federal Electoral District(s): Westlock-St. Paul
Next Election: 2013 (3 year terms)
Note: Incorporated as a town on Dec. 15, 1936.
Glenn Andersen, Mayor
glksand@gmail.com
Ronald O. Boisvert, Chief Administrative Officer
rboisvert@town.stpaul.ab.ca

Sandy Beach
P.O. Box 63
Site 1, RR#1
Onoway, AB T0E 1V0
Tel: 780-967-2873; *Fax:* 780-967-2813
svsandyb@xplornet.ca
Municipal Type: Summer Village
Incorporated: Jan. 1, 1956 *Area:* 2.43 sq km
Population in 2006: 239
Provincial Electoral District(s): Whitecourt-Ste. Anne
Federal Electoral District(s): Yellowhead
Next Election: 2013 (3 year terms)
Gordon Drybrough, Mayor
gordon@canniff.ca
Wendy Wildman, Chief Administrative Officer

Seba Beach
P.O. Box 190
Seba Beach, AB T0E 2B0
Tel: 780-797-3863; *Fax:* 780-797-3800
svseba@telusplanet.net
www.sebabeach.ca
Municipal Type: Summer Village
Incorporated: Aug. 2, 1920 *Area:* 0.66 sq km
Population in 2006: 203

Provincial Electoral District(s): Stony Plain
Federal Electoral District(s): Yellowhead
Next Election: 2013 (3 year terms)
Doug Thomas, Mayor
Susan H. Evans, Chief Administrative Officer

Sedgewick
P.O. Box 129
Sedgewick, AB T0B 4C0
Tel: 780-384-3504; *Fax:* 780-384-3545
sedgewick@persona.ca
www.sedgewick.ca
Municipal Type: Town
Incorporated: March 6, 1907 *Area:* 2.6 sq km
Population in 2006: 891
Provincial Electoral District(s): Battle River-Wainwright
Federal Electoral District(s): Vegreville-Wainwright
Next Election: 2013 (3 year terms)
Note: Incorporated as town on May 1, 1966.
Helen Marie Whitten, Mayor
sedgewick.mayor@eastlink.ca
Thelma Rogers, Chief Administrative Officer
sedgewick.cao@persona.ca

Sexsmith
9927 - 100 St.
Sexsmith, AB T0H 3C0
Tel: 780-568-3681; *Fax:* 780-568-2200
www.sexsmith.ca
Municipal Type: Town
Incorporated: April 12, 1929 *Area:* 3.43 sq km
Population in 2007: 2,255
Provincial Electoral District(s): Grande Prairie-Smoky
Federal Electoral District(s): Peace River
Next Election: 2013 (3 year terms)
Note: Incorporated as a town on Oct. 15, 1979.
Carolyn Gaunt, Town Manager
cagaunt@sexsmith.ca
Claude Lagace, Mayor

Silver Beach
P.O. Box 619
4917 Hankin St.
Thorsby, AB T0C 2P0
Tel: 780-789-3935; *Fax:* 780-789-3779
hwynne@village.thorsby.ab.ca
www.sbalberta.ca
Municipal Type: Summer Village
Incorporated: Dec. 31, 1953 *Area:* 0.66 sq km
Population in 2006: 47
Provincial Electoral District(s): Drayton Valley-Calmar
Federal Electoral District(s): Wetaskiwin
Next Election: 2013 (3 year terms)
Brad Clough, Mayor
Harold Wynne, Chief Administrative Officer

Silver Sands
P.O. Box 8
Alberta Beach, AB T0E 0A0
Tel: 780-924-3024; *Fax:* 780-924-3025
administration@wildwillowenterprises.com
www.wildwillowenterprises.com
Municipal Type: Summer Village
Incorporated: Jan. 1, 1969 *Area:* 2.35 sq km
Population in 2006: 173
Provincial Electoral District(s): Whitecourt-Ste. Anne
Federal Electoral District(s): Yellowhead
Next Election: 2013 (3 year terms)
Bernie Poulin, Mayor
bpoulin@xplornet.com
Wendy Wildman, Chief Administrative Officer

Slave Lake
P.O. Box 1030
Slave Lake, AB T0G 2A0
Tel: 780-849-8000; *Fax:* 780-849-2633
town@slavelake.ca
www.slavelake.ca
Municipal Type: Town
Incorporated: Jan. 1, 1961 *Area:* 14.18 sq km
Population in 2006: 6,703
Provincial Electoral District(s): Lesser Slave Lake
Federal Electoral District(s): Fort McMurray-Athabasca
Next Election: 2013 (3 year terms)
Note: Incorporated as a town on Aug. 2, 1965.
Karina Pillay-Kinnee, Mayor
karina@slavelake.ca
Brian Vance, Chief Administrative Officer
brian@slavelake.ca

Smoky Lake
P.O. Box 460
Smoky Lake, AB T0A 3C0
Tel: 780-656-3674; *Fax:* 780-656-3675
fcss@smokylake.ca
www.smokylake.ca
Municipal Type: Town
Incorporated: March 26, 1923 *Area:* 4.2 sq km
Population in 2006: 1,010
Provincial Electoral District(s): Athabasca-Redwater
Federal Electoral District(s): Westlock-St. Paul
Next Election: 2013 (3 year terms)
Note: Incorporated as a town on Feb. 1, 1962.
Hank Holowaychuk, Mayor
mayor@smokylake.ca
R. Dean Pickering, Chief Administrative Officer
cao@smokylake.ca

South Baptiste
724 Baptiste Dr.
West Baptiste, AB T9S 1R8
Tel: 780-675-9270; *Fax:* 780-675-9526
tomaszyk@mcsnet.ca
www.southbaptiste.com
Municipal Type: Summer Village
Incorporated: Jan. 1, 1983 *Area:* 1.05 sq km
Population in 2006: 69
Provincial Electoral District(s): Athabasca-Redwater
Federal Electoral District(s): Fort McMurray-Athabaska
Next Election: 2013 (3 year terms)
Steve Hamilton, Mayor
Edwin Tomaszyk, Chief Administrative Officer

South View
P.O. Box 8
Alberta Beach, AB T0E 0A0
Tel: 780-924-3024; *Fax:* 780-924-3025
administration@wildwillowenterprises.com
www.wildwillowenterprises.com
Municipal Type: Summer Village
Incorporated: Jan. 1, 1970 *Area:* 0.69 sq km
Population in 2006: 115
Provincial Electoral District(s): Whitecourt-Ste. Anne
Federal Electoral District(s): Yellowhead
Next Election: 2013 (3 year terms)
Sandra Benford, Mayor
Wendy Wildman, Chief Administrative Officer
administration@wildwillowenterprises.com

Spirit River
P.O. Box 130
Spirit River, AB T0H 3G0
Tel: 780-864-3998; *Fax:* 780-864-3433
clerk@townofspiritriver.ca
www.townofspiritriver.ca
Municipal Type: Town
Incorporated: June 13, 1916 *Area:* 2.81 sq km
Population in 2006: 1,148
Provincial Electoral District(s): Dunvegan-Central Peace
Federal Electoral District(s): Peace River
Next Election: 2013 (3 year terms)
Note: Incorporated as a town on Sept. 18, 1951.
Allan J. Georget, Mayor
ageorget@atb.com
Lloyd Johnston, Chief Administrative Officer
manager@townofspiritriver.ca

Spring Lake
990 Bauer Ave.
Spring Lake, AB T7Z 2S9
Tel: 780-963-4211; *Fax:* 780-963-4260
villageoffice@springlakealberta.com
www.springlakealberta.com
Municipal Type: Village
Incorporated: Jan. 1, 1959 *Area:* 2.12 sq km
Population in 2006: 501
Provincial Electoral District(s): Stoney Plain
Federal Electoral District(s): Edmonton-Spruce Grove
Next Election: 2013 (3 year terms)
Note: Incorporated as a village on Jan. 1, 1999.
Don Dobing, Mayor
Emily House, Chief Administrative Officer
emily@springlakealberta.com

Standard
P.O. Box 249
Standard, AB T0J 3G0
Tel: 403-644-3968; *Fax:* 403-644-2284
cao@standardab.ca
www.standardab.ca
Municipal Type: Village
Incorporated: April 29, 1922 *Area:* 2.34 sq km
Population in 2006: 380
Provincial Electoral District(s): Strathmore-Brooks
Federal Electoral District(s): Crowfoot
Next Election: 2013 (3 year terms)
Donald Cuthill, Mayor
dwcutts@standardab.ca
Leah Jensen, Chief Administrative Officer

Stavely
P.O. Box 249
Stavely, AB T0L 1Z0
Tel: 403-549-3761; *Fax:* 403-549-3743
stavely@platinum.ca
www.stavely.ca
Municipal Type: Town
Incorporated: Oct. 16, 1903 *Area:* 1.62 sq km
Population in 2006: 435
Provincial Electoral District(s): Livingstone-Macleod
Federal Electoral District(s): Macleod
Next Election: 2013 (3 year terms)
Note: Incorporated as a town on May 25, 1912.
Barry Johnson, Mayor
Sheryl Fath, Municipal Administrator

Stettler
P.O. Box 280
Stettler, AB T0C 2L0
Tel: 403-742-8305; *Fax:* 403-742-1404
townoffice@stettler.net
www.stettler.net
Municipal Type: Town
Incorporated: June 30, 1906 *Area:* 9.5 sq km
Population in 2006: 5,418
Provincial Electoral District(s): Drumheller-Stettler
Federal Electoral District(s): Crowfoot
Next Election: 2013 (3 year terms)
Note: Incorporated as a town on Nov. 23, 1906.
Dick Richards, Mayor
dick_richards@cooperators.ca
Robert Stoutenberg, Chief Administrative Officer
robs@stettler.net

Stirling
P.O. Box 360
229 Fourth Ave.
Stirling, AB T0K 2E0
Tel: 403-756-3379; *Fax:* 403-756-2262
stirl_ng@telus.net
Municipal Type: Village
Incorporated: Sept. 3, 1901 *Area:* 2.64 sq km
Population in 2006: 921
Provincial Electoral District(s): Cardston-Taber-Warner
Federal Electoral District(s): Lethbridge
Next Election: 2013 (3 year terms)
Jason Edwards, Mayor
J. Scott Barton, Chief Administrative Officer
scottbarton@raymond.ca

Strome
P.O. Box 179
5025 - 50th St.
Strome, AB T0B 4H0
Tel: 780-376-3558; *Fax:* 780-376-3557
strome@syban.net
www.villageofstrome.com
Municipal Type: Village
Incorporated: Feb. 3, 1910 *Area:* 0.92 sq km
Population in 2006: 252
Provincial Electoral District(s): Battle River-Wainwright
Federal Electoral District(s): Vegreville-Wainwright
Next Election: 2013 (3 year terms)
Bruce Curtis, Mayor
Connie Prendergast, Administrative Clerk

Sunbreaker Cove
90B Hewlett Park Landing
Sylvan Lake, AB T4S 2J3
Tel: 403-887-2822; *Fax:* 403-887-2897
fivesv@telusplanet.net
Municipal Type: Summer Village
Incorporated: Dec. 31, 1990 *Area:* 0.49 sq km
Population in 2006: 137
Provincial Electoral District(s): Rocky Mountain House
Federal Electoral District(s): Wetaskiwin
Next Election: 2013 (3 year terms)
Bill Carr, Mayor
Myra Reiter, Administrator
fivesv@telusplanet.net

Sundance Beach
P.O. Box 658
Thorsby, AB T0C 2P0
Tel: 780-789-3935; *Fax:* 780-789-3779
hwynne@thorsby.ca
Municipal Type: Summer Village
Incorporated: Jan. 1, 1970 *Area:* 0.42 sq km
Population in 2006: 102
Provincial Electoral District(s): Drayton Valley-Calmar
Federal Electoral District(s): Wetaskiwin
Next Election: 2013 (3 year terms)
Peter Pellatt, Mayor
Harold Wynne, Chief Administrative Officer

Sundre
P.O. Box 420
Sundre, AB T0M 1X0
Tel: 403-638-3551; *Fax:* 403-638-2100
townmail@sundre.com
www.sundre.com
Municipal Type: Town
Incorporated: Dec. 31, 1949 *Area:* 7.65 sq km
Population in 2006: 2,518
Provincial Electoral District(s): Rocky Mountain House
Federal Electoral District(s): Wild Rose
Next Election: 2013 (3 year terms)
Note: Incorporated as a town on Jan. 1, 1956.
Annette Clews, Mayor
annetteclews@gmail.com
Ryan Leuzinger, Interim Chief Administrative Officer
ryan.l@sundre.com

Sunrise Beach
P.O. Box 63
Site 1, RR#1
Onoway, AB T0E 1V0
Tel: 780-967-2873; *Fax:* 780-967-2813
svsandyb@xplornet.ca
Municipal Type: Summer Village
Incorporated: Dec. 31, 1988 *Area:* 1.72 sq km
Population in 2006: 170
Provincial Electoral District(s): Whitecourt-Ste. Anne
Federal Electoral District(s): Yellowhead
Next Election: 2013 (3 year terms)
Cindy MacDonald, Mayor
cindysvsunrisebeach@hotmail.com
Wendy Wildman, Chief Administrative Officer

Sunset Beach
724 Baptiste Dr.
West Baptiste, AB T9S 1R8
Tel: 780-675-3270; *Fax:* 780-675-9526
sunsetbeach@mcsnet.ca
Municipal Type: Summer Village
Incorporated: May 1, 1977 *Area:* 0.99 sq km
Population in 2006: 88
Provincial Electoral District(s): Athabasca-Redwater
Federal Electoral District(s): Fort McMurray-Athabasca
Next Election: 2013 (3 year terms)
Mark Lindskoog, Mayor
mlindskoog@nichollandakers.com
Edwin Tomaszyk, Chief Administrative Officer
tomaszyk@mcsnet.ca

Sunset Point
13 Grandin Rd.
St. Albert, AB T8N 3B2
Tel: 780-460-7226; *Fax:* 780-419-2476
hmarsh@telusplanet.net
Municipal Type: Summer Village
Incorporated: Jan. 1, 1959 *Area:* 1.11 sq km
Population in 2006: 242
Provincial Electoral District(s): Whitecourt-Ste. Anne
Federal Electoral District(s): Yellowhead
Next Election: 2013 (3 year terms)
Elizabeth Morrison, Mayor
Hilda Marsh, Chief Administrative Officer

Swan Hills
P.O. Box 149
Swan Hills, AB T0G 2C0
Tel: 780-333-4477; *Fax:* 780-333-4547
town@townofswanhills.com
www.townofswanhills.com
Municipal Type: Town
Incorporated: Sept. 1, 1959 *Area:* 25.44 sq km
Population in 2006: 1,645
Provincial Electoral District(s): Barrhead-Morinville-Westlock
Federal Electoral District(s): Yellowhead
Next Election: 2013 (3 year terms)
Mark Pickering, Mayor
mark.pickering@townofswanhills.com
Douglas Borg, Interim Chief Administrative Officer
doug.borg@townofswanhills.com

Taber
4900A - 50 St.
Taber, AB T1G 1T1
Tel: 403-223-5500; *Fax:* 403-223-5530
town@taber.ca
www.taber.ca
Municipal Type: Town
Incorporated: March 15, 1905 *Area:* 15.09 sq km
Population in 2008: 7,821
Provincial Electoral District(s): Cardston-Taber-Warner
Federal Electoral District(s): Medicine Hat
Next Election: 2013 (3 year terms)
Note: Incorporated as a town on July 1, 1907.
Gordon Frank, CAO
town@taber.ca
Ray Bryant, Mayor
mayor@taber.ca

Thorsby
P.O. Box 297
Thorsby, AB T0C 2P0
Tel: 780-789-3935; *Fax:* 780-789-3779
hwynne@thorsby.ca
www.village.thorsby.ab.ca
Municipal Type: Village
Incorporated: Dec. 31, 1949 *Area:* 2.92 sq km
Population in 2006: 945
Provincial Electoral District(s): Drayton Valley-Calmar
Federal Electoral District(s): Wetaskiwin
Next Election: 2013 (3 year terms)
Barry Rasch, Mayor
Harold Wynne, Chief Administrative Officer

Three Hills
P.O. Box 610
Three Hills, AB T0M 2A0
Tel: 403-443-5822; *Fax:* 403-443-2616
info@threehills.ca
www.threehills.ca
Municipal Type: Town
Incorporated: June 14, 1912 *Area:* 5.63 sq km
Population in 2006: 3,089
Provincial Electoral District(s): Olds-Didsbury-Three Hills
Federal Electoral District(s): Crowfoot
Next Election: 2013 (3 year terms)
Note: Incorporated as a town on Jan. 1, 1929.
Timothy J. Shearlaw, Mayor
Jack Ramsden, Town Manager
jramsden@threehills.ca

Tilley
P.O. Box 155
Tilley, AB T0J 3K0
Tel: 403-377-2203; *Fax:* 403-377-2234
village.tilley@eidnet.org
Municipal Type: Village
Incorporated: May 9, 1940 *Area:* 0.62 sq km
Population in 2006: 381
Provincial Electoral District(s): Strathmore-Brooks
Federal Electoral District(s): Medicine Hat
Next Election: 2013 (3 year terms)
John Timko, Mayor
john.timko@tyson.com
Jeannette Zahn, Chief Administrative Officer

Tofield
P.O. Box 30
Tofield, AB T0B 4J0
Tel: 780-662-3269; *Fax:* 780-662-3929
tofield@supernet.ab.ca
www.tofieldalberta.ca
Municipal Type: Town
Incorporated: Sept. 9, 1907 *Area:* 6.01 sq km
Population in 2006: 1,876
Provincial Electoral District(s): Fort Saskatchewan-Vegreville
Federal Electoral District(s): Vegreville-Wainwright
Next Election: 2013 (3 year terms)
Note: Incorporated as a town on Sept. 10, 1909.
Cindy Neufeld, CAO
cneufeld@tofieldalberta.ca
Nabil Chehayeb, Mayor

Trochu
P.O. Box 340
Trochu, AB T0M 2C0
Tel: 403-442-3085; *Fax:* 403-442-2528
secretary@town.trochu.ab.ca
www.town.trochu.ab.ca
Municipal Type: Town
Incorporated: May 5, 1911 *Area:* 2.82 sq km
Population in 2006: 1,005
Provincial Electoral District(s): Olds-Didsbury-Three Hills
Federal Electoral District(s): Crowfoot
Next Election: 2013 (3 year terms)
Note: Incorporated as a town on Aug. 1, 1962.
Barry Kletke, Mayor
Maureen Malaka, Chief Administrative Officer

Turner Valley
P.O. Box 330
Turner Valley, AB T0L 2A0
Tel: 403-933-4944; *Fax:* 403-933-5377
admin@turnervalley.ca
www.turnervalley.ca
Municipal Type: Town
Incorporated: Feb. 25, 1930 *Area:* 5.45 sq km
Population in 2006: 1,908
Provincial Electoral District(s): Foothills-Rocky View
Federal Electoral District(s): Macleod
Next Election: 2013 (3 year terms)
Note: Incorporated as a town on Sept.1, 1977.
Kelly Tuck, Mayor
kellyt@turnervalley.ca
Leslie Fitzgerald, Chief Administrative Officer
cao@turnervalley.ca

Two Hills
P.O. Box 630
Two Hills, AB T0B 4K0
Tel: 780-657-3395; *Fax:* 780-657-2158
info@townoftwohills.com
www.townofhills.com
Municipal Type: Town
Incorporated: June 4, 1929 *Area:* 3.31 sq km
Population in 2006: 1,047
Provincial Electoral District(s): Lac La Biche-St. Paul
Federal Electoral District(s): Vegreville-Wainwright
Next Election: 2013 (3 year terms)
Note: Incorporated as a town on Jan. 1, 1955.
Elaine Sorochan, Mayor
Elsie Howanyk, Chief Administrative Officer
cao@townoftwohills.com

Val Quentin
P.O. Box 7
Site 19, RR#1
Gunn, AB T0E 1A0
Tel: 780-446-1426;
d.evans@xplornet.com
Municipal Type: Summer Village
Incorporated: Jan. 1, 1966 *Area:* 0.3 sq km
Population in 2006: 181
Provincial Electoral District(s): Whitecourt-Ste. Anne
Federal Electoral District(s): Yellowhead
Next Election: 2013 (3 year terms)
Bob Lehman, Mayor
Dennis Evans, Chief Administrative Officer

Valleyview
P.O. Box 270
Valleyview, AB T0H 3N0
Tel: 780-524-5150; *Fax:* 780-524-2727
valvadmn@telusplanet.net
http://valleyview.govoffice.com
Municipal Type: Town
Incorporated: Jan. 1, 1955 *Area:* 4.57 sq km
Population in 2007: 1,884
Provincial Electoral District(s): Grande Prairie-Smoky
Federal Electoral District(s): Peace River
Next Election: 2013 (3 year terms)
Note: Incorporated as a town on Feb. 5, 1957.
Frank Besinger, Twon Manager
Vern Lymburner, Mayor

Vauxhall
P.O. Box 509
Vauxhall, AB T0K 2K0
Tel: 403-654-2174; *Fax:* 403-654-4110
cao@town.vauxhall.ab.ca
www.town.vauxhall.ab.ca
Municipal Type: Town
Incorporated: Dec. 31, 1949 *Area:* 2.88 sq km
Population in 2006: 1,069
Provincial Electoral District(s): Little Bow
Federal Electoral District(s): Medicine Hat
Next Election: 2013 (3 year terms)
Note: Incorporated as a town on Jan. 1, 1961.
Gordon Brown, Mayor
Barbara Miller, Chief Administrative Officer
bmiller@town.vauxhall.ab.ca

Vegreville
P.O. Box 640
Vegreville, AB T9C 1R7
Tel: 780-632-2606; *Fax:* 780-632-3088
vegtown@vegreville.com
www.vegreville.com
Municipal Type: Town
Incorporated: April 4, 1906 *Area:* 13.49 sq km
Population in 2006: 5,519
Provincial Electoral District(s): Fort Saskatchewan-Vegreville
Federal Electoral District(s): Vegreville-Wainwright
Next Election: 2013 (3 year terms)
Note: Incorporated as a town on Aug 15, 1906.
Richard N. Coleman, Mayor
Jody Quickstad, Town Manager
jquickstad@vegreville.com

Vermilion
5021 - 49th Ave.
Vermilion, AB T9X 1X1
Tel: 780-853-5358; *Fax:* 780-853-4910
townofvermilion@vermilion.ca
www.vermilion.ca
Municipal Type: Town
Incorporated: Feb. 17, 1906 *Area:* 13.69 sq km
Population in 2006: 4,036
Provincial Electoral District(s): Vermilion-Lloydminster
Federal Electoral District(s): Vegreville-Wainwright
Next Election: 2013 (3 year terms)
Note: Incorporated as a town on Aug. 27, 1906.
Bruce Marriott, Mayor
bgmarr@telusmail.net
Dion Pollard, Town Manager
dpollard@vermilion.ca

Veteran
P.O. Box 439
Veteran, AB T0C 2S0
Tel: 403-575-3954; *Fax:* 403-575-3954
veteran@veterancable.net
Municipal Type: Village
Incorporated: June 30, 1914 *Area:* 0.84 sq km
Population in 2006: 293
Provincial Electoral District(s): Drumheller-Stettler
Federal Electoral District(s): Crowfoot
Next Election: 2013 (3 year terms)
Pat Gorcak, Mayor
psgorcak@veterancable.net
Debbie Johnstone, Chief Administrative Officer

Viking
P.O. Box 369
Viking, AB T0B 4N0
Tel: 780-336-3466; *Fax:* 780-336-2660
www.town.viking.ab.ca
Municipal Type: Town
Incorporated: Feb. 5, 1909 *Area:* 3.76 sq km
Population in 2006: 1,085
Provincial Electoral District(s): Vermilion-Lloydminster
Federal Electoral District(s): Vegreville-Wainwright
Next Election: 2013 (3 year terms)
Note: Incorporated as a town on Nov. 10, 1952.
Marlene Grandinetti, Mayor
Rod Krips, Chief Administrative Officer
rod.krips@town.viking.ab.ca

Vilna
P.O. Box 10 Mainstreet
Vilna, AB T0A 3L0
Tel: 780-636-3964; *Fax:* 780-636-3022
info@historicvilna.ca
Municipal Type: Village
Incorporated: June 23, 1923 *Area:* 0.9 sq km
Population in 2006: 274
Provincial Electoral District(s): Lac La Biche-St. Paul
Federal Electoral District(s): Westlock-St. Paul
Next Election: 2013 (3 year terms)
Donald Romanko, Mayor
pdromanko@yahoo.com
Earla Wagar, Interim Chief Administrative Officer

Vulcan
P.O. Box 360
Vulcan, AB T0L 2B0
Tel: 403-485-2417; *Fax:* 403-485-2914
vulcan@townofvulcan.ca
www.town.vulcan.ab.ca
Municipal Type: Town
Incorporated: Dec. 23, 1912 *Area:* 6.58 sq km
Population in 2006: 1,940
Provincial Electoral District(s): Little Bow
Federal Electoral District(s): Macleod
Next Election: 2013 (3 year terms)
Note: Incorporated as a town on Jun 15, 1921.
Howard Dirks, Mayor
Alcide Cloutier, Chief Administrative Officer
acloutier@townofvulcan.ca

Wabamun
P.O. Box 240
5217 - 52 St.
Wabamun, AB T0E 2K0
Tel: 780-892-2699; *Fax:* 780-892-2669
admin@wabamun.ca
www.wabamun.ca
Municipal Type: Village
Incorporated: July 18, 1912 *Area:* 3.24 sq km
Population in 2006: 601
Provincial Electoral District(s): Stony Plain
Federal Electoral District(s): Yellowhead
Next Election: 2013 (3 year terms)
William F. Purdy, Mayor
Linda Hannah, Chief Administrator Officer
cao@wabamun.ca

Wainwright
1018 - 2 Ave.
Wainwright, AB T9W 1R1
Tel: 780-842-3381; *Fax:* 780-842-2898
info@wainwright.ca
www.wainwright.ca
Municipal Type: Town
Incorporated: March 25, 1909 *Area:* 8.55 sq km
Population in 2006: 5,426
Provincial Electoral District(s): Battle River-Wainwright
Federal Electoral District(s): Vegreville-Wainwright
Next Election: 2013 (3 year terms)
Note: Incorporated as town on July 14, 1910.
Norm Coleman, Mayor
Ray Poulin, Chief Administrative Officer
rpoulin@wainwright.ca

Waiparous
P.O. Box 19554
RPO South Cranston
Calgary, AB T3M 0N5
Tel: 403-652-4636; *Fax:* 403-206-7209
admin@waiparous.ca
www.waiparous.ca
Municipal Type: Summer Village
Incorporated: Jan. 1, 1986 *Area:* 0.41 sq km
Population in 2006: 49
Provincial Electoral District(s): Banff-Cochrane
Federal Electoral District(s): Wild Rose
Next Election: 2013 (3 year terms)
Shirley Begg, Mayor
403-932-2611
Sharon Plett, Administrator
403-554-5515, Fax: 403-206-7209

Warburg
P.O. Box 29
5212 - 50 Ave.
Warburg, AB T0C 2T0
Tel: 780-848-2841; *Fax:* 780-848-2296
villageofwarburg@wildroseinternet.ca
www.villageofwarburg.ab.ca
Municipal Type: Village
Incorporated: Dec. 31, 1953 *Area:* 2.08 sq km
Population in 2006: 621
Provincial Electoral District(s): Drayton Valley-Calmar
Federal Electoral District(s): Wetaskiwin
Next Election: 2013 (3 year terms)
Dawson Kohl, Mayor
Christine Pankewitz, Municipal Administrator

Warner
P.O. Box 88
Warner, AB T0K 2L0
Tel: 403-642-3877; *Fax:* 403-642-2011
vowarner@shockware.com
www.warner.ca
Municipal Type: Village
Incorporated: Nov. 12, 1908 *Area:* 1.15 sq km
Population in 2006: 307
Provincial Electoral District(s): Cardston-Taber-Warner
Federal Electoral District(s): Lethbridge
Next Election: 2013 (3 year terms)
Jon Hood, Mayor
Lisa C. Carroll, Chief Administrative Officer

Waskatenau
P.O. Box 99, 5008 - 51st St.
Waskatenau, AB T0A 3P0
Tel: 780-358-2208; *Fax:* 780-358-2208
info@waskatenau.ca
www.waskatenau.ca
Municipal Type: Village
Incorporated: May 19, 1932 *Area:* 0.6 sq km
Population in 2006: 278
Provincial Electoral District(s): Athabasca-Redwater
Federal Electoral District(s): Westlock-St. Paul
Next Election: 2013 (3 year terms)
Casey Caron, Mayor
Bernice Macyk, Chief Administrative Officer

Wembley
P.O. Box 89
Wembley, AB T0H 3S0
Tel: 780-766-2269; *Fax:* 780-766-2868
office@wembley.ca
www.wembley.ca
Municipal Type: Town
Incorporated: Jan. 3, 1928 *Area:* 3.63 sq km
Population in 2006: 1,443
Provincial Electoral District(s): Grande Prairie-Wapiti
Federal Electoral District(s): Peace River
Next Election: 2013 (3 year terms)
Note: Incorporated as a town on Aug. 1, 1980.
Chris Turnmire, Mayor
clturnmire@telus.net
Lori Parker, Chief Administrative Officer
admin@wembley.ca

West Baptiste
945 Baptiste Dr.
West Baptiste, AB T9S 1R8
Tel: 780-675-3900; *Fax:* 780-675-4174
viviandriver@mcsnet.ca
Municipal Type: Summer Village
Incorporated: Jan. 1, 1983 *Area:* 0.6 sq km
Population in 2006: 104
Provincial Electoral District(s): Athabasca-Redwater
Federal Electoral District(s): Fort McMurray-Athabasca
Next Election: 2013 (3 year terms)
Keith Wilson, Mayor
wilsonkd@shaw.ca
Vivian Driver, Administrator
viviandriver@mcsnet.ca

West Cove
P.O. Box 7
Site 19, RR#1
Gunn, AB T0E 1A0
Tel: 780-446-1426;
d.evans@xplornet.com
Municipal Type: Summer Village
Incorporated: Jan. 1, 1963 *Area:* 1.21 sq km
Population in 2006: 169
Provincial Electoral District(s): Whitecourt-Ste. Anne
Federal Electoral District(s): Yellowhead
Next Election: 2013 (3 year terms)
David Breton, Mayor
Dennis Evans, Municipal Administrator

Westlock
10003 - 106 St.
Westlock, AB T7P 2K3
Tel: 780-349-4444; *Fax:* 780-349-4436
info@westlock.ca
www.westlock.ca
Municipal Type: Town
Incorporated: March 13, 1916 *Area:* 9.64 sq km
Population in 2006: 5,008
Provincial Electoral District(s): Barrhead-Morinville-Westlock
Federal Electoral District(s): Westlock-St. Paul
Next Election: 2013 (3 year terms)
Note: Incorporated as a town on Jan. 7, 1947.
Bruce Lennon, Mayor
blennon@westlock.ca
Darrell Garceau, Town Manager
dgarceau@westlock.ca

Whispering Hills
10511 - 109 St.
Westlock, AB T7P 1A9
Tel: 780-349-3651; *Fax:* 780-349-5194
gmbancroft.@shaw.ca
www.mywhisperinghills.com
Municipal Type: Summer Village
Incorporated: Jan. 1, 1983 *Area:* 1.73 sq km
Population in 2006: 125
Provincial Electoral District(s): Athabasca-Redwater
Federal Electoral District(s): Fort McMurray-Athabasca
Next Election: 2013 (3 year terms)
Dennis Irving, Mayor

Garth Bancroft, Administrator

White Sands
P.O. Box 119
Stettler, AB T0C 2L0
Tel: 403-742-8305; *Fax:* 403-742-1404
townoffice@stettler.net
www.stettler.net
Municipal Type: Summer Village
Incorporated: Jan. 1, 1980 *Area:* 1.6 sq km
Population in 2006: 120
Provincial Electoral District(s): Drumheller-Stettler
Federal Electoral District(s): Crowfoot
Next Election: 2013 (3 year terms)
Lorne Thurston, Mayor
kathyandlorne@yahoo.ca
Greg Switenky, Chief Administrative Officer
403-742-8305
gswitenky@stettler.net

Whitecourt
P.O. Box 509
5004 - 52 Ave.
Whitecourt, AB T7S 1N6
Tel: 780-778-2273; *Fax:* 780-778-2062
administration@whitecourt.ca
www.whitecourt.ca
Municipal Type: Town
Incorporated: Jan. 1, 1959 *Area:* 26.14 sq km
Population in 2008: 9,202
Provincial Electoral District(s): Whitecourt-Ste. Anne
Federal Electoral District(s): Yellowhead
Next Election: 2013 (3 year terms)
Note: Incorporated as a town on Aug. 15, 1961.
Peter Smyl, CAO
petersmyl@whitecourt.ca
Trevor Thain, Mayor
780-778-0909
trevorthain@whitecourt.ca

Willingdon
P.O. Box 210
Willingdon, AB T0B 4R0
Tel: 780-367-2337; *Fax:* 780-367-2167
vilwil@rjvnet.ca
Municipal Type: Village
Incorporated: Aug. 31, 1928 *Area:* 0.97 sq km
Population in 2006: 295
Provincial Electoral District(s): Lac La Biche-St. Paul
Federal Electoral District(s): Vegreville-Wainwright
Next Election: 2013 (3 year terms)
Lillian Bezovie, Mayor
Elsie Howanyk, Chief Administrative Officer
cao@townoftwohills.com

Yellowstone
P.O. Box 8
Alberta Beach, AB T0E 0A0
Tel: 780-924-3024; *Fax:* 780-924-3025
administration@wildwillowenterprises.com
www.wildwillowenterprises.com
Municipal Type: Summer Village
Incorporated: Jan. 1, 1965 *Area:* 0.28 sq km
Population in 2006: 170
Provincial Electoral District(s): Whitecourt-Ste. Anne
Federal Electoral District(s): Yellowhead
Next Election: 2013 (3 year terms)
Alice Solesbury, Mayor
Wendy Wildman, Chief Administrative Officer

Youngstown
P.O. Box 99
Youngstown, AB T0J 3P0
Tel: 403-779-3873; *Fax:* 403-779-3875
ytown@xplornet.com
Municipal Type: Village
Incorporated: March 8, 1913 *Area:* 1 sq km
Population in 2006: 170
Provincial Electoral District(s): Drumheller-Stettler
Federal Electoral District(s): Crowfoot
Next Election: 2013 (3 year terms)
Robert Blagen, Mayor
Emma Garlock, Municipal Administrator

Improvement Districts

Improvement District No. 12 (Jasper National Park)
Municipal Services Branch
10155 - 102 St., 17th Fl.
Edmonton, AB T5J 4L4
Tel: 780-427-2225; *Fax:* 780-420-1016
lgsmail@gov.ab.ca
Municipal Type: Improvement Districts
Incorporated: April 1, 1945 *Area:* 10,181.58 sq. km
Population in 2006: 24
Faye Sheridan, ID Manager
faye.sheridan@gov.ab.ca

Improvement District No. 13 (Elk Island)
Municipal Services Branch
10155 - 102 St., 17th Fl.
Edmonton, AB T5J 4L4
Tel: 780-427-2225; *Fax:* 780-420-1016
lgsmail@gov.ab.ca
Municipal Type: Improvement Districts
Incorporated: April 1, 1958 *Area:* 165.28 sq. km
Population in 2006: 21
Faye Sheridan, ID Manager
faye.sheridan@gov.ab.ca

Improvement District No. 24 (Wood Buffalo)
Municipal Services Branch
10155 - 102 St., 17th Fl.
Edmonton, AB T5J 4L4
Tel: 780-427-2225; *Fax:* 780-420-1016
lgsmail@gov.ab.ca
Municipal Type: Improvement Districts
Incorporated: Jan. 1, 1967 *Area:* 165.28 sq km.
Population in 2006: 422
Faye Sheridan, ID Manager
faye.sheridan@gov.ab.ca
Faye Sheridan, ID Manager
faye.sheridan@gov.ab.ca

Improvement District No. 25 (Willmore Wilderness)
Municipal Services Branch
10155 - 102 St., 17th Fl.
Edmonton, AB T5J 4L4
Tel: 780-427-2225; *Fax:* 780-420-1016
lgsmail@gov.ab.ca
Municipal Type: Improvement Districts
Incorporated: Jan. 2, 1994 *Area:* 4,604.97 sq. km

Improvement District No. 4 (Waterton)
Municipal Services Branch
10155 - 102 St., 17th Fl.
Edmonton, AB T5J 4L4
Tel: 403-752-3322; *Fax:* 403-752-4379
lgsmail@gov.ab.ca
Municipal Type: Improvement Districts
Incorporated: Jan. 1, 1944 *Area:* 480.58 sq. km
Population in 2006: 160
Rick Reeves, Chairperson
J. Scott Barton, Chief Administrative Officer
scottbarton@raymond.ca

Improvement District No. 9 (Banff)
Municipal Services Branch
10155 - 102 St., 17th Fl.
Edmonton, AB T5J 4L4
Tel: 780-720-1994; *Fax:* 780-665-7369
lgsmail@gov.ab.ca
Municipal Type: Improvement Districts
Incorporated: April 1, 1945 *Area:* 6,782.26 sq. km
Population in 2006: 938
Rick Werner, Chairperson
rick.werner@skilouise.com
J. Scott Barton, Chief Administrative Officer
scottbarton@raymond.ca

Kananaskis Improvement District
P.O. Box 70
Kananaskis, AB T0L 2H0
Tel: 403-591-7774; *Fax:* 403-591-7123
tammi.pretty@gov.ab.ca
www.kananaskisid.ca
Municipal Type: Improvement Districts
Incorporated: April 1, 1945 *Area:* 4,210.72 sq km
Population in 2006: 429
Dan DeSantis, Chairperson
ddesantis@deltahotels.com
Shawn Polley, Chief Administrative Officer
shawn.polley@gov.ab.ca

Thorhild
P.O. Box 10
Thorhild, AB T0A 3J0
Tel: 780-398-3741; *Fax:* 780-398-3748
laurie@thorhildcounty.com
www.thorhildcounty.com
Municipal Type: Rural Municipality
Incorporated: Apr. 1, 2009 *Area:* 1.67 sq km
Population in 2006: 505
Provincial Electoral District(s): Athabasca-Redwater
Federal Electoral District(s): Westlock-St. Paul
Next Election: 2013 (3 year terms)
Charles Newell, Reeve
cnewell@mcsnet.ca
William Kostiw, Interim Chief Administrative Officer
bill@thorhildcounty.com

Metis Settlement in Alberta

Buffalo Lake
P.O. Box 16
Caslan, AB T0A 0R0
Tel: 780-689-2170; *Fax:* 780-689-2024
hbylan@buffalolakemetis.com
Municipal Type: Metis Settlement
Stan Delorme, Chairperson
Harold Blyan, Administrator
hblyan@buffalolakemetis.com

East Prairie
P.O. Box 1289
High Prairie, AB T0G 1E0
Tel: 780-523-2594; *Fax:* 780-523-2777
jhaggerty@eastprairiemetis.ca
Municipal Type: Metis Settlement
Robert L'Hirondelle, Chairperson
Harry Supernault, Administrator
hsupernault@eastprairiemetis.ca

Elizabeth
P.O. Box 420
Cold Lake, AB T9M 1P1
Tel: 780-594-5026; *Fax:* 780-594-5452
ems@jetnet.ab.ca
Municipal Type: Metis Settlement
Allan Wells, Chairperson
emscon@incentre.net
Jeanette Calliou, Administrator
emscouncil@jetnet.ab.ca

Fishing Lake
General Delivery
Sputinow, AB T0A 3G0
Tel: 780-943-2202; *Fax:* 780-943-2575
www.fishinglakems.ca
Municipal Type: Metis Settlement
Lorne Dustow, Chairperson
Margaret Daniels, Administrator

Gift Lake
P.O. Box 60
Gift Lake, AB T0G 1B0
Tel: 780-767-3794; *Fax:* 780-767-3888
glms@telus.net
Municipal Type: Metis Settlement
Hector Lamouche, Chairperson
Gerry Peardon, Administrator
gerrygl@telus.net

Kikino
General Delivery
Kikino, AB T0A 2B0
Tel: 780-623-7868; *Fax:* 780-623-7080
kiadmin@telus.net
Municipal Type: Metis Settlement
Floyd Thompson, Chairperson
Roger Littlechilds, Administrator
kikinoranch@mcsnet.ca

Paddle Prairie
P.O. Box 58
Paddle Prairie, AB T0H 2W0
Tel: 780-981-2227; *Fax:* 780-981-3737
reception@paddleprairie.com
Municipal Type: Metis Settlement
Greg Calliou, Chairperson
Darla Wanuch, Administrator
darla@paddleprairie.com

Peavine
P.O. Box 238
High Prairie, AB T0G 1E0
Tel: 780-523-2557; *Fax:* 780-523-2626
Municipal Type: Metis Settlement
Ken Noskey, Chairperson
ken.noskey@peavinemetis.com
Fahim Haque, Administrator
fahim.haque@peavinemetis.com

BRITISH COLUMBIA

Incorporated municipalities in British Columbia include Villages, Towns, Cities, and District Municipalities as well as one Indian Government District, a Resort Municipality, and an Island Municipality. Twenty-seven regional districts provide services to unincorporated areas and member municipalities.

Municipal elections in all municipalities are held on the third Saturday of November. Terms of office are three years (2011, 2014, etc.).

Legislation: The Local Government Act, excluding the City of Vancouver, which is regulated under the provisions of the Vancouver Charter.

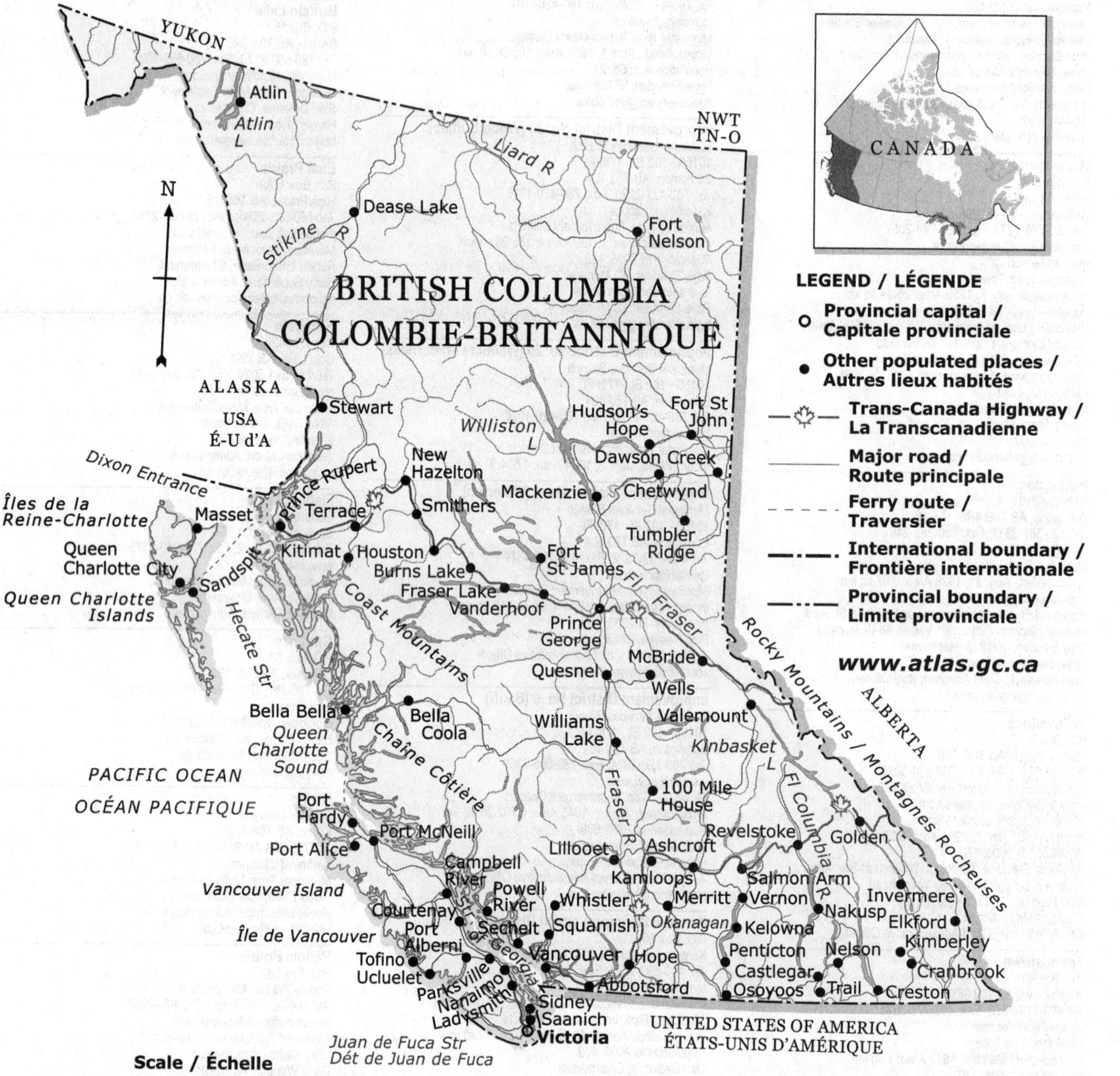

Reproduced with the permission of Natural Resources Canada 2011, courtesy of the Atlas of Canada.

British Columbia

Counties & Municipal Districts in British Columbia

Alberni-Clayoquot
3008 - 5 Ave.
Port Alberni, BC V9Y 2E3
Tel: 250-720-2700; *Fax:* 250-723-1327
mailbox@acrd.bc.ca
www.acrd.bc.ca
Municipal Type: Regional Districts
Incorporated: April 21, 1966 *Area:* 6,596.58 sq km
Population in 2006: 30,664
Next Election: Nov. 2011 (3 year terms)
Note: Member municipalities: Port Alberni; Tofino; Ucluelet.
Glenn Wong, Chair
250-724-4847, Fax: 250-724-4847
glwong@telus.net; chairperson@acrd.bc.ca
Russell Dyosn, Chief Administrative Officer
250-720-2705
rdyson@acrd.bc.ca
Wendy Thompson, Deputy Corporate Officer
250-720-2706
wendy.thomson@acrd.bc.ca
Teri Fong, Manager, Finance
250-720-2707
teri.fong@acrd.bc.ca
Mike Irg, Manager, Planning & Development
250-720-2710
mirg@acrd.bc.ca
Tracy Bond, Secretary
250-720-2700
tbond@acrd.bc.ca
John Thomas, Bamfield Water System
250-720-2718
Joe Daley, Millstream Water System
250-726-7351

Bulkley-Nechako
P.O. Box 820
37, 3rd Ave.
Burns Lake, BC V0J 1E0
Tel: 250-692-3195; *Fax:* 250-692-3305
inquiries@rdbn.bc.ca
www.rdbn.bc.ca
Other Information: Toll Free Phone: 1-800-320-3339
Municipal Type: Regional Districts
Incorporated: Feb. 1, 1966 *Area:* 73,440.95 sq km
Population in 2006: 38,243
Next Election: Nov. 2011 (3 year terms)
Note: Member municipalities: Smithers; Fort St. James; Housten; Vanderhoof; Burns Lake; Fraser Lake; Granisle; Telkwa.
Lance Hamblin, Chair
250-845-7849
chair@rdbn.bc.ca
Gail Chapman, Chief Administrative Officer
250-692-3195, Fax: 250-692-3305
gail.chapman@rdbn.bc.ca
Jason Llewellyn, Director, Planning
jason.llewellyn@rdbn.bc.ca
Janine Dougall, Director, Environmental Services
250-692-3195
janine.dougall@rdbn.bc.ca
Hans Berndorff, C.A., Administrator, Financial Services
hans.berndorff@rdbn.bc.ca
Richard Wainwright, C.A., Chief Building Inspector
richard.wainwright@rdbn.bc.ca
Corrine Swenson, C.A., Regional Strategic Development Analyst, Community Economic Development
richard.wainwright@rdbn.bc.ca
Rory McKenzie, Supervisor, Field Operations, Environmental Services
rory.mckenzie@rdbn.bc.ca

Capital Regional District
625 Fisgard St.
Victoria, BC V8W 1R7
Tel: 250-360-3000;
www.crd.bc.ca
Other Information: Mailing address: PO Box 1000, Victoria, BC V8W 2S6
Municipal Type: Regional Districts
Incorporated: Feb. 1, 1966 *Area:* 2,341.02 sq km
Population in 2006: 345,164
Next Election: Nov. 2011 (3 year terms)
Note: Member municipalities: Central Saanich; Colwood; Esquimalt; Highlands; Langford; Metchosin; North Saanich; Oak Bay; Saanich; Sidney; Sooke; Victoria; View Royal.
Geoff Young, Board Chair
250-385-5711, Fax: 250-361-0348
Diana Lokken, General Manager, Corporate Services
250-360-3010
Larissa Hutcheson, General Manager, Environmental Sustainability
250-360-3085
Jack Hull, General Manager, Integrated Water Services
250-474-9604
Robert Lapham, General Manager, Planning & Protective Services
250-360-3285
Andy Orr, Senior Manager, Corporate Communications
250-360-3229
Dan Telford, Senior Manager, Environmental Engineering
250-360-3064
Glenn Harris, Senior Manager, Environmental Protection
250-360-3090
Russ Smith, Senior Manager, Environmental Resource Management
250-360-3083
Tim Tanton, Senior Manager, Infrasturcture Engineering
250-474-9611
Maurice Rachwalski, Senior Manager, Health & Capital Planning Strategies
250-360-3114
Ian Hennigar, Senior Manager, Peninsula Recreation Commission/Panorama Recreation
250-655-2170
Margaret Misek-Evans, Senior Manager, Regional Planning
250-360-3244
Ted Robbins, Senior Manager, Water Management
250-360-3061
Stewart Irwin, Senior Manager, Water Quality
250-474-9603
Gordon Joyce, Senior Manager, Watershep Protection
250-474-9621

Cariboo
180 North 3rd Ave., #D
Williams Lake, BC V2G 2A4
Tel: 250-392-3351; *Fax:* 250-392-2812
mailbox@cariboord.bc.ca
www.cariboord.bc.ca
Other Information: Toll Free Phone: 1-800-665-1636
Municipal Type: Regional Districts
Incorporated: July 9, 1968 *Area:* 80,629.34 sq km
Population in 2006: 62,190
Next Election: Nov. 2011 (3 year terms)
Note: Member municipalities: 100 Mile House; Quesnel; Wells; Williams Lake.
Al Richmond, Chairperson
arichmond@cariboord.bc.ca
Janis Bell, Chief Administrative Officer
jbell@cariboord.bc.ca
Rick Hodgson, Deputy Chief Administrative Officer
rhodgson@cariboord.bc.ca
Alice Johnston, Corporate Officer
ajohnston@cariboord.bc.ca
Scott Reid, Chief Financial Officer
sreid@cariboord.bc.ca
Graham Barbour, Chief Building Official
gbarbour@cariboord.bc.ca
Mitch Minchau, Manager, Utilities/Solid Waste Management
mminchau@cariboord.bc.ca
Rick Brundrige, Manager, Planning Services
rbrundrige@cariboord.bc.ca
Darron Campbell, Manager, Community Services/Recreation/Airports
dcampbell@cariboord.bc.ca
Rowena Bastien, Manager, Protective Services
rbastien@cariboord.bc.ca

Central Coast
P.O. Box 186
626 Cliff St.
Bella Coola, BC V0T 1C0
Tel: 250-799-5291; *Fax:* 250-799-5750
info@ccrd-bc.ca
www.ccrd-bc.ca
Municipal Type: Regional Districts
Incorporated: July 16, 1968 *Area:* 24,556.35 sq km
Population in 2006: 3,189
Next Election: Nov. 2011 (3 year terms)
Brian Lande, Chair
Joy MacKay, Chief Administrative Officer
cao@ccrd-bc.ca
Donna Mikkelson, Chief Financial Officer
cfo@ccrd-bc.ca
Stephen Waugh, Emergency Program Coordinator
epc@ccrd-bc.ca

Central Kootenay
P.O. Box 590
202 Lakeside Dr.
Nelson, BC V1L 5R4
Tel: 250-352-6665; *Fax:* 250-352-9300
info@rdck.bc.ca
www.rdck.bc.ca
Other Information: Toll Free Phone: 1-800-268-7325
Municipal Type: Regional Districts
Incorporated: Nov. 30, 1965 *Area:* 22,130.72 sq km
Population in 2006: 55,883
Next Election: Nov. 2011 (3 year terms)
Note: Member municipalities: Castlegar; Creston; Kaslo; Nakusp; Nelson; New Denver; Salmo; Silverton; Slocan.
John Kettle, Chair
250-428-5560, Fax: 250-428-5567
jrkettlejgalt@ shaw.ca
Jim Gustafson, Chief Administrative Officer
250-352-8152
jgustafson@rdck.bc.ca
Grant Roeland, Chief Financial Officer
250-352-8150
groeland@rdck.bc.ca
Ann Fisher, Human Resources/Corporate Safety Officer
250-352-8193
afisher@rdck.bc.ca
Joe Chirico, General Manager, Community Services
250-352-8158
jchirico@rdck.bc.ca
Dawn Attorp, General Manager, Corporate Administration
250-352-8167
dattorp@rdck.bc.ca
Uli Wolf, General Manager, Environmental Services
250-352-8163
uwolf@rdck.bc.ca
David Oosthuizen, Manager, Information Technology Services
250-352-8188

Central Okanagan
1450 KLO Rd.
Kelowna, BC V1W 3Z4
Tel: 250-763-4918; *Fax:* 250-763-0606
info@cord.bc.ca
www.cord.bc.ca
Municipal Type: Regional Districts
Incorporated: Aug. 24, 1967 *Area:* 2,904.01 sq km
Population in 2006: 162,276
Next Election: Nov. 2011 (3 year terms)
Note: Member municipalities: Kelowna; West Kelowna; Lake Country; Peachland.
Robert Hobson, Chair
250-469-6224
rhobson@cord.bc.ca
Harold Reay, Chief Administrative Officer
Marilyn Rilkoff, Director, Administration & Finance
250-469-6242
finance@cord.bc.ca
Dan Plamondon, Director, Development Services
250-868-5227
planning@cord.bc.ca
Robert Fine, Director, Economic Development Commission
250-469-6280
info@investkelowna.com
Chris Radford, Director, Environmental Services
250-469-6241
engineer@cord.bc.ca
Murray Kopp, Director, Parks Services
Peter Rotheisler, Manager, Regional Waste Reduction Office
250-469-6250, Fax: 250-762-7011
recycle@cord.bc.ca
Cary Berger, Manager, Police Services
250-470-6212, Fax: 250-470-7011

Columbia-Shuswap
P.O. Box 978
781 Marine Park Dr. NE
Salmon Arm, BC V1E 4P1
Tel: 250-832-8194; *Fax:* 250-832-3375
enquiries@csrd.bc.ca
www.csrd.bc.ca
Other Information: Toll Free Phone: 1-888-248-2773
Municipal Type: Regional Districts
Incorporated: Nov. 30, 1965 *Area:* 29,003.97 sq km
Population in 2006: 50,141
Next Election: Nov. 2011 (3 year terms)
Note: Member municipalities: Golden; Revelstoke; Sicamous; Salmon Arm.
Ron Oszust, Chair
Charles Hamilton, Chief Administrative Officer
250-832-8194
admin@csrd.bc.ca, chamilton@csrd.bc.ca

Robyn Cyr, Economic development Officer/Film Commissioner
250-833-5928
rcyr@csrd.bc.ca
Gerald Christie, Manager, Development Services
250-833-5919
gchristie@csrd.bc.ca
Gary Holte, Manager, Environment & Engineering Services
250-833-5935
gholte@csrd.bc.ca
Peter Jarman, Manager, Finance & Information Technology
250-833-5908
pjarman@csrd.bc.ca
Jack Blair, Co-ordinator, Fire Services
250-833-5945
jblair@csrd.bc.ca
Hamish Kassa, Co-ordinator, Environment Services
250-833-5942
hkassa@csrd.bc.ca
Terry Langois, Co-ordinator, Water Systems
250-833-5941
tlanglois@csrd.bc.ca
Ben Van Nostrand, Co-ordinator, Waste Management
250-833-5940
bvannostrand@csrd.bc.ca

Comox Valley
600 Comox Rd.
Courtenay, BC V9N 3P6
Tel: 250-334-6000; *Fax:* 250-334-4358
administration@comoxvalleyrd.ca
www.comoxvalleyrd.ca
Other Information: Toll Free Phone: 1-800-331-6007
Municipal Type: Regional Districts
Incorporated: Aug. 19, 1965 *Area:* 20,013.48 sq km
Population in 2006: 101,595
Next Election: Nov. 2011 (3 year terms)
Note: Member municipalities: Comox; Courtenay; Cumberland.
Edwin Grieve, Chair
edwingrieve@shaw.ca
Debra Oakman, Chief Administrative Officer
Beth Dunlop, Corporate Financial Officer
James Warren, Corporate Legislative Officer
Ian Smith, General Manager, Community Services
Kevin Lorette, General Manager, Property Service Branch
Leigh Carter, General Manager, Public Affairs/Information Systems Branch
Will Hwang, Executive Manager, Human Resources
Geoff Garbutt, Manager, Strategic & Long Range Planning

Cowichan Valley
175 Ingram St.
Duncan, BC V9L 1N8
Tel: 250-746-2500;
cvrd@cvrd.bc.ca
www.cvrd.bc.ca
Other Information: Toll Free Phone: 1-800-665-3955
Municipal Type: Regional Districts
Incorporated: Sept. 26, 1967 *Area:* 3,473.12 sq km
Population in 2006: 79,929
Next Election: Nov. 2011 (3 year terms)
Note: Member municipalities: Duncan; Ladysmith; Lake Cowichan; North Cowichan.
Gerry Giles, Chair
chairperson@cvrd.bc.ca
Warren Jones, Chief Administrative Officer
250-746-2510
wjones@cvrd.bc.ca
Mark Kueber, General Manager, Corporate Services
250-746-2571
mkueber@cvrd.bc.ca
Brian Dennison, General Manager, Engineering & Environment
250-746-2532
bdennison@cvrd.bc.ca
Ron Austen, General Manager, Parks, Recreation & Culture
250-746-2635
rausten@cvrd.bc.ca
Tom R. Anderson, General Manager, Planning & Development
250-746-2601
tanderson@cvrd.bc.ca
Sybille Sanderson, Acting General Manager, Public Safety
250-746-2562
ssanderson@cvrd.bc.ca

East Kootenay
19 - 24 Ave. South
Cranbrook, BC V1C 3H8
Tel: 250-489-2791; *Fax:* 250-489-3498
info@rdek.bc.ca
www.rdek.bc.ca
Other Information: Toll Free Phone: 1-888-478-7335
Municipal Type: Regional Districts
Incorporated: Nov. 30, 1965 *Area:* 27,560.49 sq km
Population in 2006: 55,485
Next Election: Nov. 2011 (3 year terms)
Note: Member municipalities: Canal Flats; Cranbrook; Kimberley; Fernie; Sparwood; Elkford; Invermere; Radium Hot Springs.
Scott Manjak, Chair
Lee-Ann Crane, Chief Administrative Officer
lcrane@rdek.bc.ca
Shawn Tomlin, Chief Financial Officer
stomlin@rdek.bc.ca
Dan McNeill, Manager, Building & Protective Services
dmcneill@rdek.bc.ca
Loree Duczek, Manager, Communications
lduczek@rdek.bc.ca
Shannon Moskal, Manager, Community Services
smoskal@rdek.bc.ca
Brian Funke, Manager, Engineering Services
bfunke@rdek.bc.ca
Kevin Paterson, Manager, Environmental Services
kpaterson@rdek.bc.ca
Lori Engler, Manager, Human Resources
lengler@rdek.bc.ca
Andrew McLeod, Manager, Planning & Development Services
amcleod@rdek.bc.ca

Fraser Valley
#1, 45950 Cheam Ave.
Chilliwack, BC V2P 1N6
Tel: 604-702-5000; *Fax:* 604-792-9684
info@fvrd.bc.ca
www.fvrd.com
Other Information: Toll Free Phone: 1-800-528-0061
Municipal Type: Regional Districts
Incorporated: Dec. 12, 1995 *Area:* 13,361.74 sq km
Population in 2006: 257,031
Next Election: Nov. 2011 (3 year terms)
Note: Member municipalities: Abbotsford; Chilliwack; Hope; Kent; Mission; Harrison Hot Springs.
Patricia Ross, Chair
pross@fvrd.bc.ca
Gerald H. Kingston, Chief Administrative Officer
gkingston@fvrd.bc.ca
George Murray, General Manager, Finance
604-702-5033
gmurray@fvrd.bc.ca
Doug Joinson, Manager, Communications & Information Services
djoinson@fvrd.bc.ca
Mike Phelan, Manager, Finance
mphelan@fvrd.bc.ca
Tareq Islam, P.Eng., Director, Engineering
604-702-5026
tislam@fvrd.bc.ca
Lance Lilley, Planner, Watershed
llilley@fvrd.bc.ca

Fraser-Fort George
155 George St.
Prince George, BC V2L 1P8
Tel: 250-960-4400;
district@rdffg.bc.ca
www.rdffg.bc.ca
Other Information: Toll Free Phone: 1-800-667-1959
Municipal Type: Regional Districts
Incorporated: March 8, 1967 *Area:* 50,705.84 sq km
Population in 2006: 92,264
Next Election: Nov. 2011 (3 year terms)
Note: Member municipalities: McBride; Mackenzie; Prince George; Valemount.
Art Kaehn, Chair
akaehn@rdffg.bc.ca
Terry Burgess, Vice-Chair
tburgess@rdffg.bc.ca
Reneé McCloskey, Manager, External Relations
250-960-4453

Kitimat-Stikine
#300, 4545 Lazelle Ave.
Terrace, BC V8G 4E1
Tel: 250-615-6100; *Fax:* 250-635-9222
info@rdks.bc.ca
www.rdks.bc.ca
Other Information: Toll Free Phone: 1-800-663-3208
Municipal Type: Regional Districts
Incorporated: Sept. 14, 1967 *Area:* 91,917.88 sq km
Population in 2006: 37,999
Next Election: Nov. 2011 (3 year terms)
Note: Member municipalities: Kitimat; Terrace; Stewart; Hazelton; New Hazelton.
Harry Nyce, Board Chair
Robert Marcellin, Administrator
Verna Wickie, Treasurer
Lori Stark, Confidential Secretary to the Board
Andrew Webber, Manager, Planning & Economic Development
awebber@rdks.bc.ca
Roger Tooms, Manager, Works & Services
rtooms@rdks.bc.ca
Ken Newman, Planner
knewman@rdks.bc.ca
Ted Pellegrino, Planner
tpellegrino@rdks.bc.ca

Kootenay Boundary
#202, 843 Rossland Ave.
Trail, BC V1R 4S8
Tel: 250-368-9148; *Fax:* 250-368-3990
Other Information: Toll Free Phone: 1-800-355-7352 (BC only)
Municipal Type: Regional Districts
Incorporated: Feb. 22, 1966 *Area:* 8,095.63 sq km
Population in 2006: 30,742
Next Election: Nov. 2011 (3 year terms)
Note: Member municipalities: Fruitvale; Grand Forks; Greenwood; Midway; Montrose; Rossland; Trail; Warfield.
Marguerite Rotvold, Chair
rotvoldrdkb@shaw.ca
John MacLean, Chief Administrative Officer
jmaclean@rdkb.com
Sig Dreher, Chief Building & Plumbing Official
jmaclean@rdkb.com
Elaine Kumar, Director, Corporate Administration
ekumar@rdkb.com
Alan Stanley, Director, Environmental Services
astanley@rdkb.com
Gerry Gardner, Director, Finance
ggardner@rdkb.com
Mark Andison, Director, Planning & Development
mandison@rdkb.com
Dale Green, Manager, Information Services
dgreen@rdkb.com

Metro Vancouver
4330 Kingsway
Burnaby, BC V5H 4G8
Tel: 604-432-6200; *Fax:* 604-436-6901
icentre@metrovancouver.org
www.metrovancouver.org
Municipal Type: Regional Districts
Incorporated: June 29, 1967 *Area:* 2,877.36 sq km
Population in 2006: 2,116,581
Next Election: Nov. 2011 (3 year terms)
Note: Member municipalities: Anmore; Belcarra; Bowen Island; Burnaby; Coquitlam; Delta; Langley; Lions Bay; New Westminster; North Vancouver; Pitt Meadows; Port Coquitlam; Port Moody; Richmond; Surrey; Vancouver; West Vancouver; White Rock
Lois Jackson, Chair
Johnny Carline, Chief Administrative Officer/Commissioner
Delia Laglagaron, Deputy Chief Administrative Officer/Deputy Commissioner
Jim Rusnak, Chief Financial Officer
Heather Shoemaker, Manager, Corporate Relations
Greg Smith, Manager, Corporate Services
Tim Jervis, P.Eng., Manager, Engineering & Construction
Linda Shore, Manager, Human Resources
Malcolm Graham, Manager, Labour Relations
Doug Humphris, P.Eng., Manager, Operations & Maintenance
Tovio Allas, Manager, Policy & Planning
Don Littleford, Manager, Regional Housing
Mitch Sokalski, Acting Manager, Regional Parks

Mount Waddington
P.O. Box 729
2044 McNeill Rd.
Port McNeill, BC V0N 2R0
Tel: 250-956-3301; *Fax:* 250-956-3232
info@rdmw.bc.ca
www.rdmw.bc.ca
Other Information: Alternate Phone: 250-956-3161
Municipal Type: Regional Districts
Incorporated: June 13, 1966 *Area:* 20,288.19 sq km
Population in 2006: 11,651
Next Election: Nov. 2011 (3 year terms)
Note: Member municipalities: Alert Bay; Port Alice; Port Hardy; Port McNeill.
Al Huddlestan, Chair
chair@rdmw.bc.ca
Greg Fletcher, Administrator
Joe MacKenzie, Treasurer
Neil Smith, Manager, Economic Development/Parks
Patrick Donaghy, Manager, Operations
Jeff Long, Manager, Planning
Bonnie Danyk, Financial Clerk
Paddy Hinton, Supervisor, Parks

Nanaimo
6300 Hammond Bay Rd.
Nanaimo, BC V9T 6N2
Tel: 250-390-4111; *Fax:* 250-390-4163
corpsrv@rdn.bc.ca
www.rdn.bc.ca
Other Information: Toll Free Phone: 1-877-607-4111
Municipal Type: Regional Districts
Incorporated: Aug. 24, 1967 *Area:* 2,034.93 sq km
Population in 2006: 138,631
Next Election: Nov. 2011 (3 year terms)
Note: Member municipalities: Nanaimo; Lantzville; Parksville; Qualicum Beach.
Joseph Stanhope, Chair
jstanhope@shaw.ca
Carol Mason, Chief Administrative Officer
250-390-4111
Neil Connelly, General Manager, Community Services
250-390-6510
John Finnie, General Manager, Regional & Community Utilities
250-390-6560
Wendy Idema, Acting General Manager, Finance & Information Services
250-390-4111
widema@rdn.bc.ca
Tom Osborne, General Manager, Recreation & Parks Services
recparks@rdn.bc.ca
Paul Thorkelsson, General Manager, Development Services
250-390-6530
Dennis Trudeau, General Manager, Transportation & Solid Waste
250-390-6565

North Okanagan
9848 Aberdeen Rd.
Coldstream, BC V1B 2K9
Tel: 250-550-3700; *Fax:* 250-550-3701
info@nord.ca
www.nord.ca
Municipal Type: Regional Districts
Incorporated: Nov. 9, 1965 *Area:* 7,511.94 sq km
Population in 2006: 77,301
Next Election: Nov. 2011 (3 year terms)
Note: Member municipalities: Enderby; Armstrong; Spallumcheen; Vernon; Coldtream; Lumby.
Herman Halvorson, Chair
Christy Malden, Executive Assistant to the Administrator
250-550-3752
christy.malden@rdno.ca
David Sewell, Chief Financial Officer
250-550-3724
pat.luscombe@rdno.ca
Pat Luscombe, Chief Building Inspector
250-550-3724
pat.luscombe@rdno.ca
Leah Mellott, Acting General Manager, Corporate & Electoral Area Services
250-550-3722
leah.mellott@rdno.ca
Al McNiven, General Manager, Greater Vernon Parks, Recreation & Culture
250-550-3664
Ron Baker, Manager, Comunity Protective Services
doug.buchholz@rdno.ca
Nicole Kohnert, Regional Manager, Engineering Services
250-550-3674
nicole.kohnert@rdno.ca
Dale Danallanko, Manager, Recycling & Disposal Facilities Operations
250-550-3744
dale.danallanko@rdno.ca
Al Cotsworth, Manager, Utilities
250-550-3674
al.cotsworth@rdno.ca
Renee Clark, Manager, Water Quality
250-550-3747
renee.clark@rdno.ca
Greg Routley, Planner, Development Services
250-550-3734
greg.routley@rdno.ca
Marnie Skobalski, Planner, Development Services
250-550-3737
marnie.skobalski@rdno.ca

Northern Rockies
P.O. Box 399
5319 - 50th Ave. South
Fort Nelson, BC V0C 1R0
Tel: 250-774-2541; *Fax:* 250-774-6794
justask@northernrockies.ca
www.northernrockies.ca
Municipal Type: Regional Districts
Incorporated: Oct. 31, 1987 *Area:* 85,148.87 sq km
Population in 2006: 6,147
Next Election: Nov. 2011 (3 year terms)
Note: Member municipality: Fort Nelson.
Randy McLean, Chief Administrative Officer
250-774-2541
admin@northernrockies.ca
Doug Tofte, Community Resource & Planning Officer
Jaylene Arnold, Economic Development & Tourism Officer
Erin La Vale, Human Resources, Safety & Research Officer
Jack Stevenson, Director, Community Development & Planning
250-774-2541
ecdev@northernrockies.ca
Harvey Woodland, Director, Recreation
250-774-2541
rec@northernrockies.ca
Ross Coupé, Manager
Heather Cosman, Manager, Corporate
Danielle Morin, Manager, Recreation Program

Okanagan-Similkameen
101 Martin St.
Penticton, BC V2A 5J9
Tel: 250-492-0237;
info@rdos.bc.ca
www.rdos.bc.ca
Other Information: Toll Free Phone: 1-877-610-3737
Municipal Type: Regional Districts
Incorporated: March 4, 1966 *Area:* 10,412.64 sq km
Population in 2006: 79,475
Next Election: Nov. 2011 (3 year terms)
Note: Member municipalities: Penticton; Summerland; Oliver; Osoyoos; Princeton; Keremeos.
Dan Ashton, Chair
Bill Newell, Chief Administrative Officer
250-492-0237
info@rdos.bc.ca
Mark Woods, Manager, Community Services
250-490-4132
mwoods@rdos.bc.ca
Donna Butler, Manager, Development Services
250-490-4109
dbutler@rdos.bc.ca
Warren Everton, BA, CMA, Manager, Finance
250-490-4105
Patty Tracy, Manager, Human Resources
250-490-4138
pderkach@rdos.bc.ca
Tim Bouwmeester, Manager, Information Services
Doug French, P.Eng., Manager, Public Works
250-490-4103

Peace River
P.O. Box 810
1981 Alaska Ave.
Dawson Creek, BC V1G 4H8
Tel: 250-784-3200; *Fax:* 250-784-3201
prrd.dc@prrd.bc.ca
prrd.bc.ca
Other Information: Toll-Free Phone: 1-800-670-7773
Municipal Type: Regional Districts
Incorporated: Oct. 31, 1987 *Area:* 117,761.07 sq km
Population in 2006: 58,264
Next Election: Nov. 2011 (3 year terms)
Note: Member municipalities: Dawson Creek; Fort St. John; Chetwynd; Hudson's Hope; Tumbler Ridge; Pouce Coupe; Taylor.
Karen Goodings, Chair
Fred Banham, Chief Administrative Officer
250-784-3208
Kim French, Chief Financial Officer
250-784-3221
Faye Salisbury, Corporate Officer
250-784-3216
Bruce Simard, General Manager, Development Services
250-784-3204
Shannon Anderson, General Manager, Environmental Services
250-784-3203
Trish Morgan, Manager, Community Services
250-784-3218
Jeff Rahn, Manager, Solid Waste Services
250-784-3226

Powell River
5776 Marine Ave.
Powell River, BC V8A 2M4
Tel: 604-483-3231; *Fax:* 604-483-2229
administration@powellriverrd.bc.ca
www.powellriverrd.bc.ca
Municipal Type: Regional Districts
Incorporated: Dec. 19, 1967 *Area:* 5,092.05 sq km
Population in 2006: 19,599
Next Election: Nov. 2011 (3 year terms)
Note: Member municipality: Powell River.
Colin Palmer, Chair
Malcolm Fraser, Chief Administrative Officer
Sean McGinn, Manager, Community Services
Linda Greenan, Manager, Financial Services
Shawn Gullette, Foreman, Parks & Properties
Don Turner, Senior Planner

Skeena-Queen Charlotte
100 - 1st Ave. East
Prince Rupert, BC V8J 1A6
Tel: 250-624-2002; *Fax:* 250-627-8493
musgrave@sqcrd.bc.ca
www.sqcrd.bc.ca
Other Information: Toll Free Phone: 1-888-301-2002
Municipal Type: Regional Districts
Incorporated: Aug. 17, 1967 *Area:* 19,871.85 sq km
Population in 2006: 19,664
Next Election: Nov. 2011 (3 year terms)
Note: Member municipalities: Prince Rupert; Port Edward; Queen Charlotte; Port Clemens; Masset.
Barry Pages, Chair
250-626-3995, Fax: 250-626-5503
bpages@mhtv.ca
Joan Merrick, Chief Administrative Officer
Jennifer Robb, Treasurer

Squamish-Lillooet
P.O. Box 219
1350 Aster St.
Pemberton, BC V0N 2L0
Tel: 604-894-6371; *Fax:* 604-894-6526
info@slrd.bc.ca
www.slrd.bc.ca
Other Information: Toll Free Phone: 1-800-298-7753
Municipal Type: Regional Districts
Incorporated: Oct. 3, 1968 *Area:* 16,353.66 sq km
Population in 2006: 35,225
Next Election: Nov. 2011 (3 year terms)
Note: Member municipalities: Squamish; Whistler; Pemberton; Lillooet.
Susan Gimse, Chair
604-894-6371
sgimse@telus.net
Dennis Back, Chief Administrative Officer
604-894-6371
dback@slrd.bc.ca
Leslie Lloyd, Director, Administrative Services
604-894-6371
llloyd@slrd.bc.ca
Suzanne Lafrance, Director, Finance
604-894-6371
slafrance@slrd.bc.ca
Steven Olmstead, Manager, Planning & Development
604-894-6371
Janis Netzel, Director, Utilities & Environmental Services
604-894-6371
rdsouza@slrd.bc.ca

Strathcona
#301, 990 Cedar St.
Campbell River, BC V9W 7Z8
Tel: 250-830-6700; *Fax:* 250-830-6710
administration@strathconard.ca
www.strathconard.ca
Other Information: Toll Free Phone: 1-877-830-2990
Municipal Type: Regional Districts
Incorporated: Feb. 15, 2008 *Area:* 22,000 sq km
Population in 2006: 42,771
Next Election: Nov. 2011 (3 year terms)
Note: Member municipalities: Campbell River; Gold River; Sayward; Tahsis; Zeballos.
Craig Anderson, Chair
250-283-2202
dabear10@cablerocket.com
B. Reardon, Chief Administrative Officer
J. Rohne, Manager, Facilities
Y. Bienvenu, Manager, Facilities Services
D. Christenson, Manager, Financial Services
L. Parker, Manager, Operations
S. Bullock, Manager, Programs

Sunshine Coast
1975 Field Rd.
Sechelt, BC V0N 3A1
Tel: 604-885-6800; *Fax:* 604-885-7909
info@scrd.ca
www.scrd.ca
Other Information: Toll Free Phone: 1-800-687-5753

Municipal Type: Regional Districts
Incorporated: Jan. 4, 1967 *Area:* 3,778.08 sq km
Population in 2006: 27,759
Next Election: Nov. 2011 (3 year terms)
Note: Member municipalities: Sechelt; Gibsons.
Garry Nohr, Chair
John France, Chief Administrative Officer
Randy Brown, Manager, Human Resources
randy.brown@scrd.ca
Angie Legault, Manager, Legislative Services
David Rafael, Senior Planner
604-885-6804
david.rafael@scrd.ca

Thompson-Nicola
#300, 465 Victoria St.
Kamloops, BC V2C 2A9
Tel: 250-377-8673; *Fax:* 250-372-5048
admin@tnrd.bc.ca
www.tnrd.bc.ca
Other Information: Toll Free Phone: 1-877-377-8673
Municipal Type: Regional Districts
Incorporated: Nov. 24, 1967 *Area:* 44,475.73 sq km
Population in 2006: 122,286
Next Election: Nov. 2011 (3 year terms)
Note: Member municipalities: Ashcroft; Barriere; Cache Creek; Chase; Clearwater; Clinton; Kamloops; Logan Lake; Lytton; Merritt; Sun Peaks.
Peter Milobar, Chair
mayor@kamloops.ca
Greg Toma, Chief Administrative Officer
250-377-8673
gtoma@tnrd.bc.ca
Vicci Weller, Executive Director, Film Commission
250-377-7058
vweller@tnrd.bc.ca
Lyle Huntley, Clerk/Director, Corporate & Community Services
250-377-7052
lhuntley@tnrd.bc.ca
Regina Sadilkova, Director, Development Services
250-377-7060
rsadilkova@tnrd.bc.ca
Peter Hughes, Director, Environmental Services
phughes@tnrd.bc.ca
Sukh Gill, Director/Deputy Administrator, Finance & Information Technology
250-377-8673
sgill@tnrd.bc.ca
Kevin Kierans, Director, Libraries
250-374-8866
kevink@tnrdlib.bc.ca
Ron Popoff, Manager, Building Inspection Services
250-377-7062
rpopoff@tnrd.bc.ca
Don May, Manager, Environmental Health Services
250-377-7057
dmay@tnrd.bc.ca
Bob Finley, Manager, Planning Services
250-377-7062
bfinley@tnrd.bc.ca
Arden Bolton, Manager, Utility Services
250-377-7056
abolton@tnrd.bc.ca

Major Municipalities in British Columbia

Abbotsford
32315 South Fraser Way
Abbotsford, BC V2T 1W7
Tel: 604-853-2281; *Fax:* 604-853-1934
www.abbotsford.ca; twitter.com/City_Abbotsford
Other Information: Toll Free Phone: 1-866-853-2281
Municipal Type: City
Incorporated: Jan. 1, 1995 *Area:* 359.36 sq km
County or District: Fraser Valley; *Population in 2006:* 123,864
Provincial Electoral District(s): Abbotsford-Mission; Abbotsford South; Abbotsford West
Federal Electoral District(s): Abbotsford
Next Election: Nov. 2011 (3 year terms)
George Peary, Mayor
604-864-5500
mayor@abbotsford.ca
Bill Flitton, City Clerk
604-864-5603
bflitton@abbotsford.ca
Les Barkman, Councillor
lbarkman@abbotsford.ca
Patricia Soanes, General Manager, Finance & Corporate Services
604-864-5524, Fax: 604-853-7968
finance-info@abbotsford.ca
Simon Gibson, Councillor
sgibson@abbotsford.ca
Jay Teichroeb, General Manager, Economic Development/Development Services
604-864-5586
econdev@abbotsford.ca
Mohindar (Moe) Gill, Councillor
mgill@abbotsford.ca
Jim Gordon, P.Eng., General Manager, Engineering & Regional Utilities
604-864-5514
eng-info@abbotsford.ca
Lynne Harris, Councillor
lharris@abbotsford.ca
Mark Taylor, General Manager, Parks, Recreation & Culture
604-859-3134
prcoffice@abbotsford.ca
Dave Loewen, Councillor
dfloewen@abbotsford.ca
Don Beer, Fire Chief
604-853-3566
fire-info@abbotsford.ca
Bill MacGregor, Councillor
bmacgregor@abbotsford.ca
Bob Rich, Chief Constable, Abbotsford Police Department
604-859-5225, Fax: 604-859-4812
Patricia Ross, Councillor
pross@abbotsford.ca
Karen Sinclair, Director, Strategic Planning & Business Improvement
604-865-5640
ksinclair@abbotsford.ca
John Smith, Councillor
jgsmith@abbotsford.ca
Mike Pastro, General Manager, Airport
604-864-5651
mpastro@abbotsford.ca
Frank Pizzuto, City Manager
604-864-5501
fpizzuto@abbotsford.ca

Burnaby
4949 Canada Way
Burnaby, BC V5G 1M2
Tel: 604-294-7944;
postmaster@burnaby.ca
www.city.burnaby.bc.ca
Municipal Type: City
Incorporated: Sept. 22, 1892 *Area:* 89.12 sq km
County or District: Metro Vancouver; *Population in 2006:* 202,799
Provincial Electoral District(s): Burnaby-Edmonds; Burnaby North; Burnaby-Willingdon
Federal Electoral District(s): Burnaby-Douglas; Burnaby-New Westminster
Next Election: Nov. 2011 (3 year terms)
Derek Corrigan, Mayor
604-294-7340
Debbie R. Comis, City Clerk
604-294-7290, Fax: 604-294-7537
Pietro Calendino, Councillor
604-614-7379
pietro.calendino@burnaby.ca
Denise Jorgeonson, Director, Finance
604-294-7002, Fax: 604-294-7544
Richard Chang, Councillor
richard.chang@burnaby.ca
Basil Luksun, Director, Planning & Building
604-294-7400, Fax: 604-294-7220
Sav Dhaliwal, Councillor
604-420-8188, Fax: 604-420-8133
sav.dhaliwal@burnaby.ca
D. Ellenwood, Director, Parks, Recreation & Cultural Services
604-294-7450
parks@burnaby.ca
Dan Johnston, Councillor
778-228-6714
dan.johnston@burnaby.ca
Lambert Chu, Director, Engineering
604-294-7460
Colleen Jordan, Councillor
604-970-8117
cjordan@comsavings.com
Anne Kang, Councillor
604-346-6732, Fax: 604-439-1576
anne.kang@burnaby.ca
Robert H. Moncur, City Manager
604-294-7101
Paul McDonell, Councillor
paul.mcdonell@burnaby.ca
Chad Turpin, Deputy City Manager
Nick Volkow, Councillor
778-228-6713, Fax: 604-437-1169
nick.volkow@burnaby.ca
B.R. Rose, City Solicitor
Patrick Shek, P.Eng, Chief Building Inspector
Bob Cook, Fire Chief
604-294-7195

Campbell River
301 St. Ann's Rd.
Campbell River, BC V9W 4C7
Tel: 250-286-5700;
info@campbellriver.ca
www.campbellriver.ca
Municipal Type: City
Incorporated: June 24, 1947 *Area:* 143.48 sq km
County or District: Strathcona; *Population in 2006:* 29,572
Provincial Electoral District(s): North Island
Federal Electoral District(s): Vancouver Island North
Next Election: Nov. 2011 (3 year terms)
Charlie Cornfield, Mayor
250-285-5710
mayor.cornfield@campbellriver.ca
Andrew Adams, Councillor
councillor.adams@campbellriver.ca
Roy Grant, Councillor
councillor.grant@campbellriver.ca
Ryan Mennie, Councillor
councillor.mennie@campbellriver.ca
Claire Moglove, Councillor
councillor.moglove@campbellriver.ca
Ziggy Stewart, Councillor
councillor.stewart@campbellriver.ca
Mary Storry, Councillor
councillor.storry@campbellriver.ca
Peter Wipper, City Clerk
250-286-5707
peter.wipper@campbellriver.ca
Andy Laidlaw, City Manager
250-286-5740
andy.laidlaw@campbellriver.ca
Laura Ciarniello, General Manager, Corporate Services
250-286-5759
laura.ciarniello@campbellriver.ca
Dave Morris, General Manager, Facilities & Supply Management
250-286-5739
dave.morris@campbellriver.ca
Ron Neufeld, General Manager, Operations Services
250-286-5765
ron.neufeld@campbellriver.ca
Ross Milnthorp, General Manager, Parks, Recreation & Culture
250-286-5797
ross.milnthorp@campbellriver.ca
Andrew Bailey, Manager, Facilities - Property
250-286-5709
andrew.bailey@campbellriver.ca
Jason Hartley, Manager, Capital Works
250-286-5790
jason.hartley@campbellriver.ca
Ross Blackwell, Manager, Land Use
250-286-5748
ross.blackwell@campbellriver.ca
Drew Hadfield, Manager, Transportation
250-286-5783
drew.hadfield@campbellriver.ca
Warren Kalyn, Manager, Information Services
250-286-5716
warren.kalyn@campbellriver.ca
Jennifer Peters, Manager, Utilities
250-286-5730
jennifer.peters@campbellriver.ca
Amber Zirnhelt, Manager, Sustainability
250-286-5742
amber.zirnhelt@campbellriver.ca
Carrie Jacobs, RCMP Municipal Manager
250-286-5611
carrie.jacobs@campbellriver.ca
Dean Spry, Fire Chief
250-286-6266
dean.spry@campbellriver.ca

Chilliwack
8550 Young Rd
Chilliwack, BC V2P 8A4
Tel: 604-792-9311; *Fax:* 604-795-8443
www.chilliwack.com
Municipal Type: City
Incorporated: Jan. 1, 1980 *Area:* 260.19 sq km

County or District: Fraser Valley; *Population in 2006:* 69,217
Provincial Electoral District(s): Chilliwack-Kent, Chilliwack-Sumas
Federal Electoral District(s): Chilliwack-Fraser Canyon
Next Election: Nov. 2011 (3 year terms)
Sharon Gaetz, Mayor
604-793-2900, Fax: 604-792-2561
Robert Carnegie, Director, Corporate Services
604-793-2986, Fax: 604-793-2715
Sue Attrill, Councillor
Jerry Spencer, General Manager/Deputy Chief Administrative Officer, Community Development
604-792-9311, Fax: 604-795-8443
Ryan Mulligan, Manager, Civic Facilities
604-793-2704, Fax: 604-792-2583
Gillian Villeneuve, Manager, Development Planning
604-793-2779
Kathleen Fraser, Deputy Director, Finance
604-792-9311, Fax: 604-795-8443
Pat Clark, Councillor
David Blain, Director, Engineering
604-793-2907, Fax: 604-793-2285
Ken Huttema, Councillor
Glen MacPherson, Director, Public Works
604-792-2810, Fax: 604-793-2997
Stewart McLean, Councillor
Kurt Houlden, Director, Planning & Strategic Initiatives
604-793-2906
Gordon Pederson, Director, Parks, Recreation & Culture
604-793-2996, Fax: 604-793-8443
Chuck Stam, Councillor
Peter Monteith, Chief Administrative Officer
604-793-2903, Fax: 604-792-2561
Rick Ryall, Fire Chief
604-792-8713, Fax: 604-702-5087
Janet Demarcke, Manager, Environmental Services
604-792-2907, Fax: 604-795-8443
Erik Leidekker, Manager, Information Technology
604-793-2912, Fax: 604-793-1812
Rod Sanderson, Manager, Transportation & Drainage
604-793-2907
Karen Stanton, Manager, Long Range Planning
604-793-2906
Paul Whitehouse, Manager, Purchasing
604-793-2809, Fax: 604-795-2963

Colwood

3300 Wishart Rd.
Victoria, BC V9C 1R1
Tel: 250-478-5541; *Fax:* 250-478-7516
generalinquiry@colwood.ca
colwood.ca
Municipal Type: City
Incorporated: June 24, 1985 *Area:* 17.76 sq km
County or District: Capital; *Population in 2006:* 14,687
Provincial Electoral District(s): Esquimalt-Metchosin
Federal Electoral District(s): Esquimalt-Juan de Fuca
Next Election: Nov. 2011 (3 year terms)
David Saunders, Mayor
250-213-9407
mayor@colwood.bc.ca; mayorsaunders@telus.net
Judith Cullington, Councillor
250-391-8772
judith@cullington.ca
Cynthia Day, Councillor
250-474-5687
councillorday@shaw.ca
Gordie Logan, Councillor
250-478-3630
councillor@telus.net
Ernie Robertson, Councillor
250-857-9558
councillor-robertson@hotmail.com
Brian Tucknott, Councillor
250-474-8180
tucknott@shaw.ca
Shaun Wysiecki, Councillor
250-415-7535
shaun@shaunw.ca
Ross McPhee, Chief Administrative Officer
rmcphee@colwood.ca
Michael Baxter, Director, Engineering
mbaxter@colwood.ca
Jennifer Reed, Acting Director, Finance
jreed@colwood.ca
Dan Brazier, Manager, Public Works
250-474-4133, Fax: 250-474-6977
dbrazier@colwood.ca
Alan Haldenby, Director, Planning
ahaldenby@colwood.ca
Flo Pikula, Chief Building Inspector
fpikula@colwood.ca
Russ Cameron, Fire Chief
250-478-8321, Fax: 250-478-8032
rcameron@colwood.bc.ca

Comox

Town Hall
1809 Beaufort Ave.
Comox, BC V9M 1R9
Tel: 250-339-2202; *Fax:* 250-339-7110
town@comox.ca
www.comox.ca
Municipal Type: City
Incorporated: Jan. 14, 1946 *Area:* 15.16 sq km
County or District: Comox Valley; *Population in 2006:* 12,136
Provincial Electoral District(s): Comox Valley
Federal Electoral District(s): Vancouver Island North
Next Election: Nov. 2011 (3 year terms)
Paul Ives, Mayor
250-339-9109
pives@comox.ca
Russ Arnott, Councillor
250-339-2569
rarnott@comox.ca
Patti Fletcher, Councillor
250-339-6683
pfletcher@comox.ca
Ken Grant, Councillor
250-339-1355
kgrant@comox.ca
Tom Grant, Councillor
250-339-7761
tgrant@comox.ca
Hugh MacKinnon, Councillor
250-339-0661
hmackinnon@comox.ca
Marcia Turner, Councillor
250-339-0167
mturner@comox.ca
Gord Schreiner, Fire Chief
250-339-2432, Fax: 250-339-1988
Allan Fraser, Superintendent, Parks
250-339-2421
Marvin Kamenz, Municipal Planner
250-339-1118
Glenn Westendorp, Superintendent, Public Works
250-339-5410, Fax: 250-890-0698
Richard Kanigan, Chief Administrative Officer
Donald Jacquest, Director, Finance
Jim Stevenson, Director, Recreation
250-339-2255

Coquitlam

3000 Guildford Way
Coquitlam, BC V3B 7N2
Tel: 604-927-3000;
feedback@coquitlam.ca
www.coquitlam.ca
Municipal Type: City
Incorporated: July 25, 1891 *Area:* 121.69 sq km
County or District: Metro Vancouver; *Population in 2006:* 114,565
Provincial Electoral District(s): Coquitlam-Maillardville
Federal Electoral District(s): New Westminster-Coquitlam; Port Moody-Westwood-Port Coquitlam
Next Election: Nov. 2011 (3 year terms)
Richard Stewart, Mayor
604-927-3001
rstewart@coquitlam.ca
Jay Gilbert, City Clerk
604-927-3013
Brent Asmundson, Councillor
604-616-6331
basmundson@coquitlam.ca
Sheena Macleod, Treasurer & Manager, Financial Services
604-927-3031
Peter Steblin, City Manager
604-927-2006
managersoffice@coquitlam.ca
Barrie Lynch, Councillor
604-616-3335
blynch@coquitlam.ca
Lori MacKay, General Manager, Parks, Recreation & Culture Services
604-927-3538
prcs@coquitlam.ca
Doug Macdonell, Councillor
604-505-5574
dmacdonell@coquitlam.ca
Neal Nicholson, Councillor
604-218-1398
nnicholson@coquitlam.ca
Jim McIntyre, General Manager, Planning & Development
604-927-3400, Fax: 604-927-3405
planninganddevelopment@coquitlam.ca
Karen Basi, Manager, Emergency Programs
604-927-3481
Michelle Hunt, Manager, Corporate Planning
604-927-3531, Fax: 604-927-3015
Mae Reid, Councillor
604-464-0414
mreid@coquitlam.ca
Bill Susak, General Manager, Engineering & Public Works
604-927-2504, Fax: 604-927-3505
engineeringandpublicworks@coquitlam.ca
Linda Reimer, Councillor
604-617-1490
lreimer@coquitlam.ca
Selina Robinson, Councillor
604-729-0702
srobinson@coquitlam.ca
Ron Price, Manager, Human Resources
604-927-3070
Lou Sekora, Councillor
604-941-7916
lsekora@coquitlam.ca

Courtenay

830 Cliffe Ave.
Courtenay, BC V9N 2J7
Tel: 250-334-4441; *Fax:* 250-334-4241
info@courtenay.ca
www.courtenay.ca
Municipal Type: City
Incorporated: Jan. 1, 1915 *Area:* 26.68 sq km
County or District: Comox Valley; *Population in 2006:* 21,940
Provincial Electoral District(s): Comox Valley
Federal Electoral District(s): Vancouver Island North
Next Election: Nov. 2011 (3 year terms)
Greg Phelps, Mayor
250-703-4842
gphelps@courtenay.ca
Jon Ambler, Councillor
250-334-3458
jambler@courtenay.ca
Doug Hillan, Councillor
250-334-4441
dhillian@courtenay.ca
Larry Jangula, Councillor
250-338-1501
ljangula@courtenay.ca
Ronna-Rae Leonard, Councillor
250-334-4441
rleonard@courtenay.ca
Murray Presley, Councillor
250-338-1394
mpresley@courtenay.ca
Manno Theos, Councillor
250-334-4441
mtheos@courtenay.ca
Sandy Gray, City Administrator
sgray@courtenay.ca
Peter Crawford, Director, Planning Services
planning@courtenay.ca
Tillie Manthey, Director, Financial Services
finance@courtenay.ca
Lis Pedersen, Director, Human Resources
John Ward, Director, Corporate Services
Randy Wiwchar, Director, Community Services
Kevin Lagan, Director, Operational Services

Cranbrook

40 - 10th Ave. South
Cranbrook, BC V1C 2M8
Tel: 250-426-4211; *Fax:* 250-426-4026
info@cranbrook.ca
www.cranbrook.ca
Other Information: Toll Free Phone: 1-800-728-2726
Municipal Type: City
Incorporated: Nov. 1, 1905 *Area:* 25.14 sq km
County or District: East Kootenay; *Population in 2006:* 18,267
Provincial Electoral District(s): East Kootenay
Federal Electoral District(s): Kootenay-Columbia
Next Election: Nov. 2011 (3 year terms)
Scott Manjak, Mayor
Angus Davis, Councillor
Denise Pallesen, Councillor
Diana J. Scott, Councillor
Liz Schatschneider, Councillor
Bob Whetham, Councillor

Jim Wavrecan, Councillor
Roy Hales, Director, Corporate Services
hales@cranbrook.ca
Jamie Hodge, City Engineer
hodge@cranbrook.ca
Joe McGowan, Director, Public Works
mcgowan@cranbrook.ca
Chris Zettel, Corporate Communications Officer
zettel@cranbrook.ca
Wayne Price, Coordinator, Emergency Program
price@cranbrook.ca
Will Pearce, Chief Administrative Officer
pearce@cranbrook.ca
Marnie Dueck, Municipal Clerk
dueck@cranbrook.ca
Diane Butz, Director, Leisure Services
butz@crankbook.ca
Wayne Price, Director, Fire & Emergency Services
price@crankbook.ca
Wayne Staudt, CA, Director, Finance & Computer Services
staudt@crankbook.ca

Dawson Creek

P.O. Box 150
10105 - 12A St.
Dawson Creek, BC V1G 4G4
Tel: 250-784-3600; *Fax:* 250-782-3203
admin@dawsoncreek.ca
www.dawsoncreek.ca
Other Information: General Fax: 250-782-3352
Municipal Type: City
Incorporated: May 26, 1936 *Area:* 22.32 sq km
County or District: Peace River; *Population in 2006:* 10,994
Provincial Electoral District(s): Peace River South
Federal Electoral District(s): Prince George-Peace River
Next Election: Nov. 2011 (3 year terms)
Mike Bernier, Mayor
250-784-3616, Fax: 250-782-3203
mayorbernier@dawsoncreek.ca
Marilyn Belak, Councillor
250-782-3222
mbelak@dawsoncreek.ca
Theresa Gladue, Councillor
250-782-1752
tgladue@dawsoncreek.ca
Sue Kenny, Councillor
250-782-2511
skenny@dawsoncreek.ca
Terry McFadyen, Councillor
250-782-2237
tmcfadyen@dawsoncreek.ca
Bud Powell, Councillor
250-843-7354
bpowell@dawsoncreek.ca
Cheryl Shuman, Councillor
250-782-5323
cshuman@dawsoncreek.ca
Jim Chute, Chief Administrative Officer
250-784-3613
jchute@dawsoncreek.ca
Shelly Woolf, Chief Financial Officer
250-784-3611
swoolf@dawsoncreek.ca
Jim Chute, Director, Community Services
250-784-3605
breynard@dawsoncreek.ca
Brenda Ginter, Director, Corporate Administration
250-784-3614
bginter@dawsoncreek.ca
Kevin Henderson, Director, Infrastructure & Sustainable Development
250-784-3622
khenderson@dawsoncreek.ca
Greg Dobrowolski, Manager, Special Projects
250-784-3619
gdobrowolski@dawsoncreek.ca
Chante Patterson Elden, Manager, recreation Facilities
250-782-2229
celden@dawsoncreek.ca
Darcy Perrin, Manager, Parks Facilities
250-784-3632
rharmon@dawsoncreek.ca
Gordon (Shorty) Smith, Fire Chief
250-784-3635
shorty@dawsoncreek.ca

Fort St. John

10631 - 100 St.
Fort St John, BC V1J 3Z5
Tel: 250-787-8150; *Fax:* 250-787-8181
info@fortstjohn.ca
www.fortstjohn.ca
Municipal Type: City
Incorporated: Dec. 31, 1947 *Area:* 22.74 sq km
County or District: Peace River; *Population in 2006:* 17,402
Provincial Electoral District(s): Peace River North
Federal Electoral District(s): Prince George-Peace River
Next Election: Nov. 2011 (3 year terms)
Bruce Lantz, Mayor
250-787-8160
blantz@fortstjohn.ca
Lori Ackerman, Councillor
250-787-8458
lackerman@fortstjohn.ca
Trevor Bolin, Councillor
250-262-7334
tbolin@fortstjohn.ca
Bruce Christensen, Councillor
250-787-2202
bchristensen@forststjohn.ca
Dan Davies, Councillor
250-787-5847
ddavies@fortstjohn.ca
Larry Evans, Councillor
250-785-2416
levans@fortstjohn.ca
Don Irwin, Councillor
250-785-0704
dirwin@fortstjohn.ca
Dianne Hunter, City Manager
citymanager@fortstjohn.ca
Janet Prestley, Director, Legislative & Administrative Services
jprestley@fortstjohn.ca
Fred Burrows, Fire Chief
250-785-4333, Fax: 250-785-0080
fburrows@fortstjohn.ca
Don Demers, Director, Public Works & Utilities
ddemers@fortstjohn.ca
Sarah Cockerill, Director, Community Services
scockerill@fortstjohn.ca
Grace Fika, Director, Corporate Affairs & Human Resources
gfika@fortstjohn.ca
Jim Rogers, Director, Facilities & Protective Services
jrogers@forststjohn.ca
Laura Sanders, Director, Finance
lsanders@forststjohn.ca
Victor Shopland, Director, Infrastructure & Capital Works
vshopland@forststjohn.ca
Horacio Galanti, Director, Planning & Engineering
hgalanti@fortstjohn.ca

Kamloops

City Hall
7 Victoria St. West
Kamloops, BC V2C 1A2
Tel: 250-828-3311;
info@kamloops.ca
www.kamloops.ca
Municipal Type: City
Incorporated: Oct. 17, 1967 *Area:* 297.3 sq km
County or District: Thompson-Nicola; *Population in 2006:* 80,376
Provincial Electoral District(s): Kamloops; Kamloops-North Thompson
Federal Electoral District(s): Kamloops-Thompson-Cariboo
Next Election: Nov. 2011 (3 year terms)
Peter Milobar, Mayor
250-828-3495
mayor@kamloops.ca
Len Hrycan, Director, Community & Corporate Affairs
250-828-3455
legislate@kamloops.ca
Nancy Bepple, Councillor
250-828-3494
nbepple@kamloops.ca
Sally Edwards, Director, Finance & Information Technology
250-828-3413
finance@kamloops.ca
John De Cicco, Councillor
250-374-6042
jdecicco@kamloops.ca
Jim Harker, Councillor
250-318-8353
jharker@kamloops.ca
David Duckworth, Director, Public Works & Sustainability
250-828-3348
publicworks@kamloops.ca
Tina Lange, Councillor
250-372-0902
tlange@kamloops.ca
Byron McCorkell, Director, Parks, Recreation & Culture Services
250-828-3400
parks@kamloops.ca
David A. Trawin, Director, Development & Engineering Services
250-828-2561
devadmin@kamloops.ca
Marg Spina, Councillor
250-372-0440
mspina@kamloops.ca
Randy H. Diehl, Chief Administrative Officer
250-828-3498
rdiehl@kamloops.ca
Patricia Wallace, Councillor
250-828-3494
pwallace@kamloops.ca
Denis Walsh, Councillor
250-828-3494
dwalsh@kamloops.ca
Neill Moroz, Fire Chief, Fire & Rescue Services
250-372-5131, Fax: 250-372-1447
fireinfo@kamloops.ca

Kelowna

City Hall
1435 Water St.
Kelowna, BC V1Y 1J4
Tel: 250-469-8500; *Fax:* 250-862-3399
ask@kelowna.ca
www.kelowna.ca
Municipal Type: City
Incorporated: May 4, 1905 *Area:* 211.69 sq km
County or District: Central Okanagan; *Population in 2006:* 106,707
Provincial Electoral District(s): Kelowna-Mission; Kelowna-Lake Country; Westside-Kelowna
Federal Electoral District(s): Kelowna-Lake Country; Okanagan-Coquihalla
Next Election: Nov. 2011 (3 year terms)
Sharon Shepherd, Mayor
mayorandcouncil@kelowna.ca
Ronald Mattiussi, City Manager
Andre F. Blanleil, Councillor
ablanleil@andres1.com
Stephen Fleming, Clerk
cityclerk@kelowna.ca
Kevin Craig, Councillor
kcraig@kelowna.ca
John Vos, General Manager, Community Services
Robert Douglas Hobson, Councillor
robert.hobson@cord.bc.ca
Jim Paterson, General Manager, Community Sustainability
Charlie Hodge, Councillor
chodge@kelowna.ca
Paul Macklem, General Manager, Corporate Sustainability
Graeme James, Councillor
gjames@kelowna.ca
David Graham, Director, Strategic Initiatives
Keith Grayston, Director, Financial Services
Angela Reid-Nagy, Councillor
areid@kelowna.ca
Joe Creron, Director, Civic Operations
Michele Rule, Councillor
mrule@kelowna.ca
William J. Berry, Director, Design & Construction Services
Luke Stack, Councillor
lstack@kelowna.ca
Mo Bayat, Director, Development Services
Jim Gabriel, Director, Recreation & Cultural Services
Doug Gilchrist, Director, Real Estate & Building Services
Randy Cleveland, Director, Infrastructure Planning
Shelley Gambacort, Director, Land Use Management
Signe Bagh, Director, Policy & Planning
Ron W. Westlake, Director, Regional Services
Carla Stephens, Director, Community & Media Relations
Charlene Covington, Director, Human Resources
Rob Mayne, Director, Corporate Services
Steve Kinsey, Fire Chief

Langford

877 Goldstream Ave., 2nd Fl.
Victoria, BC V9B 2X8
Tel: 250-478-7882;
www.cityoflangford.ca
Municipal Type: City
Incorporated: Dec. 8, 1992 *Area:* 39.55 sq km
County or District: Capital; *Population in 2006:* 22,459
Provincial Electoral District(s): Malahat-Juan de Fuca

Federal Electoral District(s): Esquimalt-Juan de Fuca
Next Election: Nov. 2011 (3 year terms)
Stewart Young, Mayor
Denise Blackwell, Councillor
Winnie Sifert, Councillor
Lillian Szpak, Councillor
Matt Sahlstrom, Councillor
Lindy Kaercher, Deputy Clerk
Steve Ternent, Acting Administrator
John Manson, City Engineer
Matthew Baldwin, City Planner

Langley
20399 Douglas Cres.
Langley, BC V3A 4B3
Tel: 604-514-2800; *Fax:* 604-530-4371
www.city.langley.bc.ca
Municipal Type: City
Incorporated: March 15, 1955 *Area:* 10.22 sq km
County or District: Metro Vancouver; *Population in 2006:* 23,606
Provincial Electoral District(s): Langley
Federal Electoral District(s): Langley
Next Election: Nov. 2011 (3 year terms)
Peter Fassbender, Mayor
Jack Arnold, Councillor
Darrin W. Leite, Director, Corporate Services
Dave Hall, Councillor
Gerald Minchuk, Director, Development Services & Economic Development
Teri James, Councillor
Gary Vlieg, Director, Engineering, Parks & Environment
Gayle Martin, Councillor
Francis Cheung, Chief Administrative Officer
Patty Gilfillan, Chief Bylaw Enforcement Officer
Rudy Storteboom, Councillor
Rory Thompson, Fire Chief
Rosemary Wallace, Councillor
Kim Hilton, Director, Recreation, Culture & Community Services
Carolyn Bonnick, Manager/Corporate Officer, Legislative Services
Judy Hale, Manager, Human Resources

Nanaimo
455 Wallace St.
Nanaimo, BC V9R 5J6
Tel: 250-754-4251;
legislativeservices.office@nanaimo.ca
www.nanaimo.ca
Municipal Type: City
Incorporated: Dec. 24, 1874 *Area:* 89.3 sq km
County or District: Nanaimo; *Population in 2006:* 78,692
Provincial Electoral District(s): Nanaimo-Parksville; Nanaimo
Federal Electoral District(s): Nanaimo-Cowichan; Nanaimo-Alberni
Next Election: Nov. 2011 (3 year terms)
John Ruttan, Mayor
250-755-4400
john.ruttan@nanaimo.ca
Doug Holmes, Assistant City Manager/General Manager, Corporate Services
250-755-4488
doug.holmes@nanaimo.ca
William Leslie (Bill) Bestwick, Councillor
250-753-7065
bill.bestwick@nanaimo.ca
Brian Clemens, Director, Finance
250-755-4431
brian.clemens@nanaimo.ca
Ted Greves, Councillor
250-729-0714
ted.greves@nanaimo.ca
William James Holdom, Councillor
250-729-8983
bill.holdom@nanaimo.ca
Richard Harding, Director, Parks, Recreation & Culture
250-755-7516
richard.harding@nanaimo.ca
Diana Johnstone, Councillor
250-754-9996
diana.johnstone@nanaimo.ca
Tom Hickey, General Manager, Community Services
250-756-5301
tom.hickey@nanaimo.ca
Jim Kipp, Councillor
250-753-5212
jim.kipp@nanaimo.ca
Joan Harrison, Manager, Legislative Services
506-755-4489
joan.harrison@nanaimo.ca
Terry Hartley, Director, Human Resources
250-755-4427
terry.hartley@nanaimo.ca
Fred Pattje, Councillor
250-758-7575
fred.pattje@nanaimo.ca
Andrew Tucker, Director, Planning
250-755-4450
andrew.tucker@nanaimo.ca
Loyd John Sherry, Councillor
250-729-7323
loyd.sherry@nanaimo.ca
Alastair (Al) Kenning, City Manager
250-755-4401
alastair.kenning@nanaimo.ca
Mervin Wayne (Merv) Unger, Councillor
250-756-0399
merv.unger@nanaimo.ca
Ron Lambert, Fire Chief
250-755-4555
ron.lambert@nanaimo.ca
Ted Swabey, General Manager, Development Services
250-755-4451
ted.swabey@nanaimo.ca
Rick Kroeker, Manager, Occupational Health & Rehabilitation
250-755-4508
rick.kroeker@nanaimo.ca
Brian Denbigh, Manager, Roads & Traffic Services
250-756-5303
Kurtis Felker, Manager, Purchasing & Stores
250-756-5317
kurtis.felker@nanaimo.ca
John Elliot, Manager, Utilities
250-756-5305
john.elliot@nanaimo.ca
Gary Franssen, Manager, Sanitation, Recycling & Cemeteries
250-756-5307
gary.franssen@nanaimo.ca
Bob Prokopenko, Manager, Engineering Services
250-755-4495
bob.prokopenko@nanaimo.ca
Jeff Ritchie, Senior Manager, Parks
250-755-7503
jeff.ritchie@nanaimo.ca
Jeff Lott, Superintendent & Officer-in-Charge, Nanaimo RCMP Detachment
250-754-2345
jeff.lott@nanaimo.ca

New Westminster
511 Royal Ave.
New Westminster, BC V3L 1H9
Tel: 604-521-3711; *Fax:* 604-521-3895
postmaster@newwestcity.ca
www.city.new-westminster.bc.ca
Municipal Type: City
Incorporated: July 16, 1860 *Area:* 15.41 sq km
County or District: Metro Vancouver; *Population in 2006:* 58,549
Provincial Electoral District(s): New Westminster
Federal Electoral District(s): Burnaby-New Westminster; New Westminster-Coquitlam
Next Election: Nov. 2011 (3 year terms)
Wayne Wright, Mayor
604-527-4522, Fax: 604-527-4594
wwright@newwestcity.ca
Rick Page, Director, Legislative Services & Communications
rpage@newwestcity.ca
Jonathan Cote, Councillor
778-773-1364
jcote@newwestcity.ca
Gary Holowatiuk, Director, Finance & Information Technology
gholowatiuk@newwestcity.ca
Bill Harper, Councillor
778-227-4869
bharper@newwestcity.ca
Paul Daminato, City Administrator
pdaminato@newwestcity.ca
Jamie McEvoy, Councillor
604-522-9114
jmcevoy@newwestcity.ca
Dean Gibson, Director, Parks, Culture & Recreation
dgibson@newwestcity.ca
Betty McIntosh, Councillor
778-773-0546
bmcintosh@newwestcity.ca
Jim Lowrie, Director, Engineering Services
jlowrie@newwestcity.ca
Bob Osterman, Councillor
604-521-7603
bosterman@newwestcity.ca
Dave Jones, Police Chief, Police Services
djones@nwpolice.org
Tim Armstrong, Fire Chief, Fire & Rescue Services
tarmstrong@newwestcity.ca
Lorrie Williams, Councillor
604-521-3416, Fax: 604-523-3416
lwilliams@newwestcity.ca
Lisa Spitale, Director, Development Services
lspitale@newwestcity.ca
Joan Burgess, Director, Human Resources
jburgess@newwestcity.ca
Rod Carle, General Manager, Electric Utility
rcarle@newwestcity.ca

North Vancouver
141 - 14 St. West
North Vancouver, BC V7M 1H9
Tel: 604-985-7761; *Fax:* 604-985-9417
info@cnv.org
www.cnv.org
Municipal Type: City
Incorporated: May 13, 1907 *Area:* 11.85 sq km
County or District: Metro Vancouver; *Population in 2006:* 45,165
Provincial Electoral District(s): N. Vancouver-Lonsdale; N. Vancouver-Seymour; W. Vancouver-Capilano; W. Vancouver-Garibaldi
Federal Electoral District(s): North Vancouver
Next Election: Nov. 2011 (3 year terms)
Darrell R. Mussatto, Mayor
604-998-3280
dmussatto@cnv.org
Pam Bookham, Councillor
604-986-5560
pbookham@cnv.org
Rod Clark, Councillor
604-351-8166
rclark@cnv.org
Bob Fearnley, Councillor
604-808-1223
bfearnley@cnv.org
Guy Heywood, Councillor
604-988-5325
gheywood@cnv.org
Craig Keating, Councillor
604-984-7485, Fax: 604-904-7968
ckeating@cnv.org
Mary Trentadue, Councillor
604-715-7072
mtrentadue@cnv.org
Robyn Anderson, City Clerk
604-990-4233, Fax: 604-990-4202
randerson@cnv.org
Ken Tollstam, City Manager
604-990-4243, Fax: 604-985-5971
ktollstam@cnv.org
Isabel Gordon, Director, Finance
604-983-7387, Fax: 604-985-1573
igordon@cnv.org
Susan Ney, Acting Director, Human Resources
604-990-4241, Fax: 604-985-9149
sney@cnv.org
Barrie Penman, Fire Chief
604-904-5201, Fax: 604-980-8544
bpenman@cnv.org
Steven Ono, City Engineer
604-983-7336, Fax: 604-985-8439
sono@cnv.org
Emilie K. Adin, City Planner
604-982-3922, Fax: 604-985-0576
Francis Caouette, Director, Corporate Services
604-990-4221, Fax: 604-985-7492
fcaouette@cnv.org
Richard White, Director, Community Development
604-990-4215, Fax: 604-985-0576
rwhite@cnv.org
Percy Melville, Manager, Inspections
604-983-7375, Fax: 604-985-0576
pmelville@cnv.org
David Nelson, Manager, Information Technology
604-983-7318, Fax: 604-985-7492
dnelson@cnv.org
Connie Rabold, Manager, Communications
604-983-7383, Fax: 604-985-5971
crabold@cnv.org
Glenn Stainton, Manager, City Facilities
604-983-7305, Fax: 604-985-1573
gstainton@cnv.org
Wolfgang Beier, Manager, Purchasing
604-983-7392, Fax: 604-985-1573
wbeier@cnv.org

Navin Chad, Manager, Financial Planning
604-983-7320, Fax: 604-985-1573
nchand@cnv.org
Janice Irwin, Manager, Financial Services
604-983-7300, Fax: 604-985-1573
jirwin@cnv.org
Nikii Hoglund, Manager, Operations
604-983-7388, Fax: 604-987-5379
nhoglund@cnv.org
Mike Hunter, Manager, Environment & Parks
604-983-7335, Fax: 604-985-8439
mhunter@cnv.org

Parksville

P.O. Box 1390
100 Jensen Ave. East
Parksville, BC V9P 2H3
Tel: 250-248-6144; *Fax:* 250-248-6650
www.parksville.ca
Municipal Type: City
Incorporated: June 19, 1945 *Area:* 14.6 sq km
County or District: Nanaimo; *Population in 2006:* 10,993
Provincial Electoral District(s): Nanaimo-Parksville
Federal Electoral District(s): Nanaimo-Alberni
Next Election: Nov. 2011 (3 year terms)
Chris R. Burger, Acting Mayor
250-954-4661
cburger@parksville.ca
Al Greir, Councillor
250-248-1285
hockeypuck1@shaw.ca
Marc Lefebvre, Councillor
250-248-2292
janetmarc@shaw.ca
Teresa C. Patterson, Councillor
250-954-9488
tc.patterson@shaw.ca
Sue E. Powell, Councillor
250-951-1082
kfsue@shaw.ca
Carrie J. Powell-Davidson, Councillor
250-954-3758
cpowelldavidson@shaw.ca
Fred Manson, Chief Administrative Officer
250-954-4666
fmanson@city.parksville.bc.ca
Doug Banks, Fire Chief
250-954-4671
dbanks@parksville.ca
Gayle Jackson, Director, Community Planning
250-954-4656
gjackson@city.parksville.bc.ca
Lucy Butterworth, Director, Finance
250-954-3063
lbutterworth@parksville.ca
Robert Harary, Director, Engineering & Operations
250-951-2477
rharary@parksville.ca
Debbie Comis, Director, Administrative Services
250-954-3068
dcomis@parksville.ca

Penticton

171 Main St.
Penticton, BC V2A 5A9
Tel: 250-490-2400; *Fax:* 250-490-2402
www.penticton.ca
Municipal Type: City
Incorporated: Jan. 1, 1909 *Area:* 42.02 sq km
County or District: Okanagan-Similkameen; *Population in 2006:* 31,909
Provincial Electoral District(s): Penticton-Okanagan Valley
Federal Electoral District(s): Okanagan-Coquihalla
Next Election: Nov. 2011 (3 year terms)
Dan Ashton, Mayor
250-809-2540
Andrew Jakubeit, Councillor
250-809-2397
Garry Litke, Councillor
250-809-2021
Mike Pearce, Councillor
250-809-0425
Judy Sentes, Councillor
250-490-6446
John Vassilaki, Councillor
250-490-1034
Annette Antoniak, Chief Administrative Officer
250-490-2407
Cathy Ingram, Manager, Purchasing
250-490-2555
Anthony Haddad, Director, Development Services
250-490-2520
Berne Udala, Supervisor, Water Quality
250-490-2564
Douglas Leahy, Chief Financial Officer/Treasurer, Accounting & Finance
250-490-2413
Wayne Williams, Fire Chief
250-490-2309
Chuck Loewen, General Manager, Recreation
250-490-2445
Gillian Kenny, Manager, Human Resources
250-490-2470
Ken Kunka, Manager, Building & Permitting
250-490-2505
Dave Lieskovsky, Manager, Facilities
250-490-2433
Eric Livolsi, Manager, Electric Utility
250-490-2537
Peter Ord, Manager, Museum
250-490-2452
Len Robson, Manager, Public Works
250-490-2500
Kristin Wilkes, Manager, Information Technology
250-490-2499
Mitch Moroziuk, Director, Operations
250-490-2515
Brent Edge, Supervisor, Water
brent.edge@penticton.ca
Carolyn Stewart, Environmental Coordinator, Water Treatment Plant
250-490-2562

Pitt Meadows

Municipal Hall
12007 Harris Rd.
Pitt Meadows, BC V3Y 2B5
Tel: 604-465-5454; *Fax:* 604-465-2404
info@pittmeadows.bc.ca
www.pittmeadows.bc.ca
Municipal Type: City
Incorporated: April 25, 1914 *Area:* 85.38 sq km
County or District: Metro Vancouver; *Population in 2006:* 15,623
Provincial Electoral District(s): Maple Ridge-Pitt Meadows
Federal Electoral District(s): Pitt Meadows-Maple Ridge-Mission
Next Election: Nov. 2011 (3 year terms)
Note: Effective Jan. 1, 2007, Pitt Meadows' designation was changed from a district to a city.
Don MacLean, Mayor
604-465-2416
dmaclean@pittmeadows.bc.ca
John Becker, Councillor
jbecker@pittmeadows.bc.ca
Bruce Bell, Councillor
bbell@pittmeadows.bc.ca
Doug Bing, Councillor
dbing@pittmeadows.bc.ca
Tracy Miyashita, Councillor
tmiyashita@pittmeadows.bc.ca
Gwen O'Connell, Councillor
goconnell@pittmeadows.bc.ca
Deb Walters, Councillor
dwalters@pittmeadows.bc.ca
Laurie Darcus, Director, Corporate Services
604-465-2449
Lorna Jones, Director, Human Resources & Communications
604-465-2448
Jake Rudolph, Chief Administrative Officer
604-465-2413
Don Jolley, Fire Chief, Protective Services
604-465-2401
Dave Walsh, Superintendent, RCMP
604-463-6251
Kelly Swift, General Manager, Community Development, Parks & Recreation
604-467-7337
Kim Grout, Director, Operations & Development Services
604-465-2428

Port Alberni

4850 Argyle St.
Port Alberni, BC V9Y 1V8
Tel: 250-723-2146; *Fax:* 250-723-1003
citypa@portalberni.ca
www.portalberni.ca
Municipal Type: City
Incorporated: Oct. 28, 1967 *Area:* 19.92 sq km
County or District: Alberni-Clayoquot; *Population in 2006:* 17,548
Provincial Electoral District(s): Alberni-Qualicum
Federal Electoral District(s): Nanaimo-Alberni
Next Election: Nov. 2011 (3 year terms)
Ken McRae, Mayor
250-720-2822
ken_mcrae@portalberni.ca
Hira Chopra, Councillor
250-723-7629
citypa@portalberni.ca
John Douglas, Councillor
250-720-2822
jmdouglas56@hotmail.com
Jack McLeman, Councillor
250-723-5851
jmcln@shaw.ca
Cindy Solda, Councillor
250-723-7139
cindysolda@me.com
Kenn Whiteman, Councillor
250-723-7158
parider@shaw.ca
Davina Sparrow, City Clerk
250-720-2810
davina_sparrow@portalberni.ca
Cathy Rothwell, Director, Finance
250-720-2821
cathy_rothwell@portalberni.ca
Guy Cicon, City Engineer
250-720-2838
guy_cicon@port-alberni.ca
Ken Watson, City Manager
250-720-2824
ken_watson@portalberni.ca
Jean McIntosh, Director
250-720-2501
jean_mcintosh@portalberni.ca
Scott Smith, City Planner
250-720-2808
scott_smith@port-alberni.ca
Scott Kenny, Director, Parks & Recreation
250-720-2507
scott_kenny@portalberni.ca
Randy Fraser, Superintendent, Streets
250-720-2845
randy_fraser@portalberni.ca
Brian Mousley, Superintendent, Utilities
250-720-2849
brian_mousley@portalberni.ca
Tim Pley, Fire Chief
250-720-2540
tim_pley@portalberni.ca

Port Coquitlam

2580 Shaughnessy St.
Port Coquitlam, BC V3C 2A8
Tel: 604-927-5411; *Fax:* 604-927-5360
info@portcoquitlam.ca
www.portcoquitlam.ca
Municipal Type: City
Incorporated: March 7, 1913 *Area:* 28.85 sq km
County or District: Metro Vancouver; *Population in 2006:* 52,687
Provincial Electoral District(s): Port Coquitlam-Burke Mountain
Federal Electoral District(s): Port Moody-Westwood-Port Coquitlam
Next Election: Nov. 2011 (3 year terms)
Greg Moore, Mayor
604-927-5410, Fax: 604-927-5331
mooreg@portcoquitlam.ca
Susan Rauh, CMC, Corporate Officer/City Clerk
604-927-5421, Fax: 604-927-5402
corporateoffice@portcoquitlam.ca
Tony Chong, P. Eng., Chief Administrative Officer
604-927-5410, Fax: 604-927-5331
chongt@portcoquitlam.ca
Kathleen Vincent, Director, Legislative & Administrative Services
604-927-5335
vincentk@portcoquitlam.ca
Igor Zahynacz, P. Eng., Director, Engineering & Operations
604-927-5453
zahynaczi@portcoquitlam.ca
Sherry Carroll, Councillor
604-942-3260, Fax: 604-942-3268
carrolls@portcoquitlam.ca
Mike Forrest, Councillor
604-942-6289, Fax: 604-464-6280
forrestm@portcoquitlam.ca
Darrell Penner, Councillor
604-941-9823, Fax: 604-941-9887
pennerd@portcoquitlam.ca
Terry Hochstetter, Acting Fire Chief
604-927-5494
hochstettert@portcoquitlam.ca

Glenn Pollock, Councillor
604-771-4415, Fax: 604-942-6963
pollockg@portcoquitlam.ca
Brian North, Manager, Revenues & Collections
604-927-5426, Fax: 604-927-5401
northb@portcoquitlam.ca
Brad West, Councillor
604-313-9185, Fax: 604-927-5331
westb@portcoquitlam.ca
Michael Wright, Councillor
604-942-8897, Fax: 604-942-8744
wrightm@portcoquitlam.ca
Mindy Smith, Director, Corporate Services
604-927-5211, Fax: 604-927-5402
smithm@portcoquitlam.ca
Pardeep Purewal, Manager, Communications & Administrative Services
604-927-5335, Fax: 604-927-5331
purewalp@portcoquitlam.ca
Karen Laustrup, Manager, Purchasing
604-927-5430, Fax: 604-927-5408
laustrupk@portcoquitlam.ca
Robin Wishart, Manager, Information Services
604-927-5302, Fax: 604-927-5403
wishartr@portcoquitlam.ca

Port Moody
P.O. Box 36
100 Newport Dr.
Port Moody, BC V3H 3E1
Tel: 604-469-4500; *Fax:* 604-469-4550
info@cityofportmoody.com
www.cityofportmoody.com
Municipal Type: City
Incorporated: March 11, 1913 *Area:* 25.62 sq km
County or District: Metro Vancouver; *Population in 2006:* 27,512
Provincial Electoral District(s): Port Moody-Westwood
Federal Electoral District(s): Port Moody-Westwood-Port Coquitlam; New Westminster-Coquitlam
Next Election: Nov. 2011 (3 year terms)
Joe Trasolini, Mayor
604-469-4501
jtrasolini@portmoody.ca
Mike Clay, Councillor
604-469-4585
mclay@portmoody.ca
Diana Dilworth, Councillor
604-469-4516
ddilworth@portmoody.ca
Bob Elliot, Councillor
604-469-4586
belliott@portmoody.ca
Meghan Lahti, Councillor
604-469-4584
mlahti@portmoody.ca
Gerry Nuttall, Councillor
604-469-4517
gnuttall@portmoody.ca
Karen Rockwell, Councillor
604-469-4518
krockwell@portmoody.ca
Colleen Rohde, City Clerk/Acting City Manager
604-469-4519
citymanager@portmoody.ca
Paul Rockwood, Director, Corporate Services
Mary De Paoli, Manager, Planning
604-469-4540
planning@portmoody.ca
J. LaCroix, Manager, Recreation
Cory Day, City Engineer
Brad Parker, Chief Constable, Police Services
Remo Faedo, Fire Chief
pmfd.info@portmoody.ca
Ron Higo, Director, Community Services
Lynne Russell, Director, Library Services
Jim Weber, Acting Director, Development Services
Devin Jain, Manager, Cultural Services
D. Kidd, Manager, Operations
Angie Parnell, Manager, Human Resources
Julie Pavey, Manager, Parks & Environmental Services

Powell River
6910 Duncan St.
Powell River, BC V8A 1V4
Tel: 604-485-6291; *Fax:* 604-485-2913
info@cdpr.bc.ca
www.powellriver.ca
Municipal Type: City
Incorporated: Oct. 15, 1955 *Area:* 29.77 sq km
County or District: Powell River; *Population in 2006:* 12,957
Provincial Electoral District(s): Powell River-Sunshine Coast
Federal Electoral District(s): West Vancouver-Sunshine Coast-Sea to Sky Country
Next Election: Nov. 2011 (3 year terms)
Stewart Alsgard, Mayor
604-485-4489
salsgard@cdpr.bc.ca
Debbie Dee, Councillor
604-485-0342
ddee@cdpr.bc.ca
Dave Formosa, Councillor
604-485-6080
dformosa@cdpr.bc.ca
Maggie Hathaway, Councillor
604-485-1249
mhathaway@cdpr.bc.ca
Chris McNaughton, Councillor
604-483-9597
cmcnaughton@cdpr.bc.ca
Jim Palm, Councillor
604-483-3171
jpalm@cdpr.bc.ca
Aaron Pinch, Councillor
604-483-0888
apinch@cdpr.bc.ca
Marie Claxton, City Clerk
604-485-8601, Fax: 604-485-8628
Stan Westby, Chief Administrative Officer
604-485-8601, Fax: 604-485-8628
Dave Douglas, Director, Financial Services
604-485-8617, Fax: 604-485-8644
finance@cdpr.bc.ca
Bill Reid, Director, Parks, Recreation & Culture
604-485-2891, Fax: 604-485-2162
breid@cdpr.bc.ca
Lynda Sowerby, Manager, Accounting Services
604-485-8617, Fax: 604-485-8644
lsowerby@cdpr.bc.ca
Charlie Kregel, Chief Librarian, Fire & Emergency Services
604-485-8661, Fax: 604-485-5320
ckregel@powellriverlibrary.ca
Dan Ouellette, Fire Chief/Director, Fire & Emergency Services
604-485-4431
Tor Birtig, Manager, Operational Division
604-485-6291, Fax: 604-485-2913
tbirtig@cdpr.bc.ca
Mike Elvy, Manager, Arena & Sport
604-485-2891, Fax: 604-485-2162
parksrec@cdpr.bc.ca
Barb Mohan, Manager, Human Resources
604-485-8638, Fax: 604-485-2913
Regina Sadilkova, Manager, Development Services
604-485-8612, Fax: 604-485-2913
Vacant, City Engineer

Prince George
City Hall
1100 Patricia Blvd.
Prince George, BC V2L 3V9
Tel: 250-561-7600;
cityclerk@city.pg.bc.ca
princegeorge.ca
Municipal Type: City
Incorporated: March 6, 1915 *Area:* 316 sq km
County or District: Fraser-Fort George; *Population in 2006:* 70,981
Provincial Electoral District(s): Pr. George-Mt. Robson; Pr. George N.; Pr. George-Omineca
Federal Electoral District(s): Prince George-Peace River; Cariboo-Prince George
Next Election: Nov. 2011 (3 year terms)
Dan Rogers, Mayor
mayor@city.pg.bc.ca
Walter Babicz, Corporate Officer/Manager, Legislative Services
250-561-7605, Fax: 250-561-0283
Don Bassermann, Councillor
bassermann@shaw.ca
Sandra Stibrany, Manager, Financial Services
250-561-7677, Fax: 250-561-7724
Garth Frizzell, Councillor
250-613-2363
garthfrizzell@citynotice.ca
Derek Bates, City Manager
250-561-7607, Fax: 250-561-0183
Shari Green, Councillor
greeninpg@gmail.com
Dave Dyer, Chief Engineer
250-561-7663, Fax: 250-561-7721
Murry Krause, Councillor
murry.krause@cinhs.org
John Lane, Fire Chief
250-561-7667, Fax: 250-561-7703
Debora Munoz, Councillor
deboramunoz@shaw.ca
Colleen Van Mook, Director, Community Services
250-561-7675, Fax: 250-561-7718
Brian Skakun, Councillor
250-964-2489
bskakun@telus.net
Dan Milburn, Acting Director, Planning & Development Contracts
250-561-7614, Fax: 250-561-7721
Rob Whitwham, Director, Public Safety & Civic Facilities
250-561-7608, Fax: 250-561-0183
Cameron Stolz, Councillor
250-640-5299
cameron@cameronstolz.ca
Kathleen Soltis, Director, Corporate Services
250-561-7630, Fax: 250-561-7759
Dave Wilbur, Councillor
councillordavewilbur@shaw.ca
Scott Bone, Manager, Supply & Fleet Services
250-561-7511, Fax: 250-612-5603
Frank Blues, Asset Manager, Downtown Projects
250-561-7503, Fax: 250-561-7721
Dan Adamson, Manager, Environment
250-561-7698, Fax: 250-561-7721
Marco Fornari, Manager, Utilities
250-561-7573, Fax: 250-561-7519
Flavio Viola, Manager, Parks & Solid Waste Services
250-561-7575, Fax: 250-612-5612
Glenn Stanker, Engineer, Transportation
250-561-7757

Prince Rupert
424 - 3rd Ave. West
Prince Rupert, BC V8J 1L7
Tel: 250-627-0934; *Fax:* 250-627-0999
cityhall@princerupert.ca
www.princerupert.ca
Municipal Type: City
Incorporated: March 10, 1910 *Area:* 54.9 sq km
County or District: Skeena-Queen Charlotte; *Population in 2006:* 12,815
Provincial Electoral District(s): North Coast
Federal Electoral District(s): Skeena-Bulkley Valley
Next Election: Nov. 2011 (3 year terms)
Jack Mussallem, Mayor
250-627-0939
Anna Ashley, Councillor
Kathy Bedard, Councillor
250-628-3275
Gina Garon, Councillor
Sheila Gordon-Payne, Councillor
250-624-9530
Nelson Kinney, Councillor
250-624-9116
Joy Thorkelson, Councillor
250-624-6048
Gord Howie, City Manager
R. Grodecki, Corporate Administrator
Dan Rodin, Chief Financial Officer
250-627-0935, Fax: 250-627-0918
drodin@princerupert.ca
Bill Horne, General Manager, Engineering, Public Works & Development Services
bill.horne@princerupert.ca
Rudy Kelly, Director, Recreation & Community Services
rudy.kelly@princerupert.ca
Keith Cameron, Manager, Engineering Services
keith.cameron@princerupert.ca
Garin Gardiner, Manager, Operations
garin.gardiner@princerupert.ca
Calvin Grav, Manager, Aquatic
calvin.grav@princerupert.ca
Christine Yew, Manager, Budgets & Accounting
250-627-0921, Fax: 250-627-0918
cyew@princerupert.ca
Dave Mckenzie, Fire Chief
250-624-5115
dave.mckenzie@princerupert.ca
Z. Krekic, City Planner

Richmond
6911 No. 3 Rd.
Richmond, BC V6Y 2C1
Tel: 604-276-4000;
www.richmond.ca
Other Information: TTY: 604-276-4311
Municipal Type: City
Incorporated: Nov. 10, 1879 *Area:* 128.76 sq km
County or District: Metro Vancouver; *Population in 2006:* 174,461
Provincial Electoral District(s): Richmond-Centre; Richmond E.;

Richmond-Steveston
Federal Electoral District(s): Richmond; Delta-Richmond East
Next Election: Nov. 2011 (3 year terms)
Malcolm D. Brodie, Mayor
mayorandcouncillors@richmond.ca
David Weber, Director, City Clerk's Office
604-276-4007, Fax: 604-278-5139
Linda Barnes, Councillor
Cathryn Carlile, General Manager, Community Services
604-276-4068
cathryn.carlile@richmond.ca
Andrew Nazareth, General Manager, Business & Finance Services
604-276-4095
finance@richmond.ca
Derek Dang, Councillor
George Duncan, Chief Administrative Officer
604-276-4336, Fax: 604-276-4222
administratorsoffice@richmond.ca
Evelina Halsey-Brandt, Councillor
William (John) McGowan, Fire Chief
604-303-2719
fire@richmond.ca
Greg Halsey-Brandt, Councillor
Sherrdean Turley, N.C.O. in Charge of Strategic Communications
604-765-4779, Fax: 604-207-4716
Sue Halsey-Brandt, Councillor
Jerry Chong, Director, Finance
604-276-4064, Fax: 604-276-4162
Ken Johnston, Councillor
Allan Cameron, Director, Information Technology
604-276-4096
Bill McNulty, Councillor
Robert Gonzalez, P. Eng., General Manager, Engineering & Public Works
604-276-4150
robert.gonzalez@richmond.ca
Harold Steves, Councillor
Mike Pellant, Director, Human Resources
604-276-4105
hr@richmond.ca
Dave Semple, Director, Operations
604-244-1206
dave.semple@richmond.ca
Dave Semple, General Manager, Parks & Recreation
604-233-3350
dave.semple@richmond.ca
Phyllis Carlyle, General Manager, Law & Community Safety
604-276-4104
phyllis.carlyle@richmond.ca
Jeff Day, P.Eng., General Manager, Project Development & Facility Management
604-276-4019
jeff.day@richmond.ca
Joe Erceg, General Manager, Planning & Development
604-276-4214
planningdevelopment@richmond.ca
Mike Kirk, Deputy Chief Administrative Officer, Corporate Services
604-276-4147
corporateservices@richmond.ca
Jane Fernyhough, Director, Arts, Culture & Heritage Services
604-276-4288
jane.fernyhough@richmond.ca
Greg Buss, Chief Librarian
604-231-6418
greg.buss@rpl.richmond.bc.ca

Salmon Arm

P.O. Box 40
500 - 2nd Ave. NE
Salmon Arm, BC V1E 4N2
Tel: 250-803-4000; *Fax:* 250-803-4041
cityhall@salmonarm.ca
www.salmonarm.ca
Municipal Type: City
Incorporated: May 15, 1905 *Area:* 155.36 sq km
County or District: Columbia-Shuswap; *Population in 2006:* 16,012
Provincial Electoral District(s): Shuswap
Federal Electoral District(s): Okanagan-Shuswap
Next Election: Nov. 2011 (3 year terms)
Marty Bootsma, Mayor
250-803-4034
mbootsma@salmonarm.ca
Debbie Cannon, Councillor
dcannon@salmonarm.ca
Chad Eliason, Councillor
celiason@salmonarm.ca
Kevin Flynn, Councillor
kflynn@salmonarm.ca
Alan Harrison, Councillor
aharrison@salmonarm.ca
Ivan Idzan, Councillor
iidzan@salmonarm.ca
Ken Jamies, Councillor
kjamieson@salmonarm.ca
Carl Bannister, Chief Administrative Officer
cbannistser@salmonarm.ca
Brad Shirley, Fire Chief
250-803-4060
bshirley@salmonarm.ca
Dale McTaggart, Director, Engineering & Public Works
dmctaggart@salmonarm.ca
Corey Paiement, Director, Development Services
cpaiement@salmonarm.ca
Betty Hiebert, Manager, Financial Services
bhiebert@salmonarm.ca
Maurice Roy, Manager, Permits/Licensing
mroy@salmonarm.ca
John Rosenberg, Manager, Public Works
jrosenberg@salmonarm.ca
Donna Shultz, Manager, Human Resources
dshultz@salmonarm.ca
Monica Dalziel, Director, Corporate Services
mdalziel@salmonarm.ca

Sidney

Municipal Hall
2440 Sidney Ave.
Sidney, BC V8L 1Y7
Tel: 250-656-1184; *Fax:* 250-655-4508
www.sidney.ca
Municipal Type: City
Incorporated: Sept. 30, 1952 *Area:* 5.04 sq km
County or District: Capital; *Population in 2006:* 11,315
Provincial Electoral District(s): Saanich N. & the Islands
Federal Electoral District(s): Saanich-Gulf Islands
Next Election: Nov. 2011 (3 year terms)
Larry Cross, Mayor
250-656-4201
Jeannette Hughes, Councillor
250-656-0441
Mervyn Lougher-Goodey, Councillor
250-656-7303
Marilyn Loveless, Councillor
250-479-6898
Cliff McNeil-Smith, Councillor
250-655-9632
Kenny Podmore, Councillor
250-655-4631
Steve Price, Councillor
250-655-4077
Murray Clarke, Chief Administrative Officer/Corporate Administrator
250-656-1139
Randy Humble, Director, Development Services
250-655-5418
Valla Tinney, Director, Corporate Services
250-655-5409
Pete Harrison, Manager, Operations
250-656-1034
Andrew Hicik, Manager, Finance
250-655-5410
Peter Payerl, Manager, Information Technology
250-655-5422
Rob Hall, P.Eng., Director, Engineering & Works
250-656-4502
Wendy Taylor, Manager
250-656-1139
Dan Holder, Fire Chief
250-655-5421
Shari Holmes-Saltzman, Municipal Planner
250-655-5419
Jim Marshall, Senior Building Official
250-655-5412
Mike van der Linden, Manager, Engineering
250-655-5416

Surrey

14245 - 56th Ave.
Surrey, BC V3X 3A2
Tel: 604-591-4011; *Fax:* 604-591-8731
www.surrey.ca
Municipal Type: City
Incorporated: Nov. 10, 1879 *Area:* 317.19 sq km
County or District: Metro Vancouver; *Population in 2006:* 394,976
Provincial Electoral District(s): Surrey-Cloverdale; Surrey-Green Timbers; Surrey-Newton; Surrey-Panorama Ridge; Surrey-Tynehead; Surrey-Whalley; Surrey-White Rock
Federal Electoral District(s): Surrey North; South Surrey-White Rock-Cloverdale; Newton-North Delta; Fleetwood-Port Kells
Next Election: Nov. 2011 (3 year terms)
Dianne L. Watts, Mayor
604-591-4126, Fax: 604-591-5175
Jane Sullivan, City Clerk
604-591-4132
clerkswebmail@surrey.ca
Robert Bose, Councillor
604-591-4624
rjbose@surrey.ca
Vivienne Wilke, General Manager, Finance & Technology
604-591-4235, Fax: 604-591-3654
financeinquiry@surrey.ca
Tom Gill, Councillor
604-591-4634
tsgill@surrey.ca
Murray Dinwoodie, City Manager
604-591-4122, Fax: 604-591-4357
Linda Hepner, Councillor
604-591-4626
lmhepner@surrey.ca
Craig MacFarlane, City Solicitor
Marvin Hunt, Councillor
604-591-4635
jmhunt@surrey.ca
Len Garis, Fire Chief
604-541-4011
W. Fraser MacRae, Assistant Commissioner/Officer in Charge, RCMP Surrey Detachment
604-599-0502, Fax: 604-599-8894
Mary Martin, Councillor
604-591-4622
mmartin@surrey.ca
Laurie Cavan, General Manager, Parks, Recreation & Culture
604-598-5760, Fax: 604-598-5781
Barinder Rasode, Councillor
604-591-4011
bkrasode@surrey.ca
Vincent Lalonde, P.Eng., General Manager, Engineering
604-591-4314, Fax: 604-591-8693
H. Barbara Steele, Councillor
604-591-4623
hbsteele@surrey.ca
Jean Lamontagne, General Manager, Planning & Development
604-591-4441, Fax: 604-591-2507
Sheila McKinnon, Manager, Arts
604-591-5127
Judy Villeneuve, Councillor
604-591-4625
javilleneuve@surrey.ca
Shaun Greffard, General Manager, Investment & Intergovernmental Relations
604-591-4571, Fax: 604-594-3055
spgreffard@surrey.ca
Nicola Webb, General Manager, Human Resources
604-591-4846, Fax: 604-591-4517
Jeff Arason, P. Eng., Manager, Utilities
604-591-4367
Jamie Boan, P. Eng., Manager, Transportation
604-591-4514
Sam Chauhan, Manager, Operational Health & Safety
604-591-4658
Violet McGregor, CMA, C.P.P., Manager, Purchasing & Payments
604-591-4011
Gerry McKinnon, Manager, Operations
604-590-7211
Sam Lau, P. Eng., Acting Manager, Land Development
604-591-4276
Mary Ann Smith, Senior Economic Development Officer
604-591-4333
masmith@surrey.ca
Beth Barlow, Chief Librarian
604-598-7304
babarlow@surrey.ca

Terrace

3215 Eby St.
Terrace, BC V8G 2X8
Tel: 250-635-6311; *Fax:* 250-638-4777
cityhall@terrace.ca
www.terrace.ca
Municipal Type: City
Incorporated: Dec. 31, 1927 *Area:* 41.52 sq km
County or District: Kitimat-Stikine; *Population in 2006:* 11,320
Provincial Electoral District(s): Skeena
Federal Electoral District(s): Skeena-Bulkley Valley
Next Election: Nov. 2011 (3 year terms)

David Pernarowski, Mayor
dpernarowski@terrace.ca
Bruce Bidgood, Councillor
bbidgood@terrace.ca
Lynne Christiansen, Councillor
lchristiansen@terrace.ca
Brian Downie, Councillor
bdownie@terrace.ca
Carol Leclerc, Councillor
cleclerc@terrace.ca
Bruce Martindale, Councillor
bmartindale@terrace.ca
Brad Pollard, Councillor
bpollard@terrace.ca
Alisa Thompson, Interim Clerk
250-638-4721
athompson@terrace.ca
Heather Nunn, Interim Chief Administrative Officer
250-638-4722
hnunn@terrace.ca
Ron Bowles, Director, Finance
205-638-4725
rbowles@terrace.ca
Lisa Teggarty, Deputy Treasurer
rbowles@terrace.ca
David Block, City Planner
250-615-4028
dblock@terrace.ca
John Klie, Fire Chief
250-638-4742
jklie@terrace.ca
Dana Hart, Officer in Charge, RCMP Terrace Detachment
250-638-7400
Herb Dusdal, Director, Public Works
250-615-4030
hdusdal@terrace.ca
Brad Hansen, Manager, Information Systems Manager
250-638-4701
bhansen@terrace.ca
Marvin Kwiatkowski, Director, Development Services
250-615-4041
mkwiatkowski@terrace.ca
Lyle Marleau, Foreman, Environmental Health
250-635-6871
lmarleau@terrace.ca

Vancouver

453 West 12th Ave.
Vancouver, BC V5Y 1V4
Tel: 604-873-7000;
info@vancouver.ca
www.vancouver.ca
Other Information: Telephone locally: 311; TTY: 711
Municipal Type: City
Incorporated: November 15, 2008 *Area:* 114.71 sq km
County or District: Metro Vancouver; *Population in 2006:* 578,041
Provincial Electoral District(s): Vancouver Burrard; Vanc.-Fraserview; Vanc.-Hastings; Vanc.-Kensington; Vanc.-Kingsway; Vanc.-Langara; Vanc.-Mt. Pleasant; Vanc.-Point Grey; Vanc.-Quilchena; Vanc.-Fairview
Federal Electoral District(s): Vancouver Centre; Vancouver East; Vancouver-Kingsway; Vancouver Quadra; Vancouver South
Next Election: Nov. 2011 (3 year terms)
Gregor Robertson, Mayor
604-873-7621, Fax: 604-873-7685
gregor.robertson@vancouver.ca
Marg Coulson, City Clerk
Suzanne Anton, Councillor
604-873-7248, Fax: 604-873-7750
clranton@vancouver.ca
Ken Bayne, General Manager, Business Planning & Services
ken.bayne@vancouver.ca
David Cadman, Councillor
604-873-7244, Fax: 604-873-7750
clrcadman@vancouver.ca
Penny Ballem, City Manager
George Chow, Councillor
604-873-7245, Fax: 604-873-7750
clrchow@vancouver.ca
Jim Chu, Chief Constable, Vancouver Police Department
604-717-3321
Heather Deal, Councillor
604-873-7242, Fax: 604-873-7750
clrdeal@vancouver.ca
Garrick Bradshaw, Director, Facilities Design & Management
Kerry Jang, Councillor
604-873-7246, Fax: 604-873-7750
clrjang@vancouver.ca
Richard Newirth, Managing Director, Cultural Services
Raymond Louie, Councillor
604-873-7243, Fax: 604-873-7750
clrlouie@vancouver.ca
Frances J. Connell, Director, Legal Services
Geoff Meggs, Councillor
604-873-7249, Fax: 604-873-7750
clrmeggs@vancouver.ca
Kevin Wallinger, Director
Andrea Reimer, Councillor
604-873-7241, Fax: 604-873-7750
clrreimer@vancouver.ca
Peter Kuran, Acting General Manager, Board of Parks & Recreation
Tim Stevenson, Councillor
604-873-7247, Fax: 604-873-7750
clrstevenson@vancouver.ca
Annette Klein, Director, Operational Information & Planning
Ellen Woodsworth, Councillor
604-873-7240, Fax: 604-873-7750
clrwoodsworth@vancouver.ca
David McLellan, General Manager, Community Services
david.mclellan@vancouver.ca
John McKearney, General Manager & Fire Chief, Fire & Rescue Services
604-873-7000
vfrscommunications@vancouver.ca
Patrice Impey, General Manager & Chief Financial Officer, Financial Services Group
Peter Judd, General Manager, Engineering Services

Vernon

3400 - 30th St.
Vernon, BC V1T 5E6
Tel: 250-545-1361; *Fax:* 250-545-7876
admin@vernon.ca
www.vernon.ca
Municipal Type: City
Incorporated: Dec. 30, 1892 *Area:* 94.2 sq km
County or District: North Okanagan; *Population in 2006:* 35,944
Provincial Electoral District(s): Okanagan-Vernon
Federal Electoral District(s): Okanagan-Shuswap; Vancouver Island North
Next Election: Nov. 2011 (3 year terms)
Wayne Lippert, Mayor
mayor@vernon.ca
Buffy Baumbrough, B.Sc., Ph.D., Councillor
bbaumbrough@vernon.ca
Jack Gilroy, Councillor
jgilroy@vernon.ca
Shawn Lee, Councillor
slee@vernon.ca
Patrick Nicol, Councillor
pnicol@vernon.ca
Mary-Jo O'Keefe, Councillor
mokeefe@vernon.ca
Bob Spiers, Councillor
bspiers@vernon.ca
Patti Bridal, City Clerk & Manager, Corporate Services
Leon Gous, Chief Administrative Officer
250-550-3515
lgous@vernon.ca
James Rice, Manager, Public Works
jrice@vernon.ca
Tony Kopp, Manager, Utilities
250-549-6757
Kevin Bertles, Manager, Finance
Rob Dickinson, Manager, Engineering
Kim Flick, Manager, Planning, Development & Engineering Services
Shirley Koenig, Manager, Operations
Ed Stranks, Manager, Engineering Development
Keith Green, Fire Chief
250-550-3561
fire@vernon.ca

Victoria

1 Centennial Sq.
Victoria, BC V8W 1P6
Tel: 250-385-5711; *Fax:* 250-361-0214
publicsrv@victoria.ca
www.victoria.ca
Municipal Type: City
Incorporated: Aug. 2, 1862 *Area:* 19.68 sq km
County or District: Capital Regional District; *Population in 2006:* 78,057
Provincial Electoral District(s): Victoria-Beacon Hill; Victoria-Hillside; Oak Bay-Gordon Head. In Greater Victoria: Esquimalt-Metchosin; Saanich South; Saanich North & the Islands; and Malahat-Juan de Fuca
Federal Electoral District(s): Victoria
Next Election: Nov. 2011 (3 year terms)
Dean Fortin, Mayor
250-361-0200, Fax: 250-361-0348
Wael (Bill) Fanous, Director, Internal Audit & Risk Management
250-361-0524
Brenda Warner, Director, Finance
250-361-0597
Robert Woodland, Director, Legislative & Regulatory Services
250-361-0203
Marianne Alto, Councillor
250-361-0216
malto@victoria.ca
Gail Stephens, City Manager
250-361-0202
Kevin Greig, General Manager, Corporate Services
250-361-0247
Chris Coleman, Councillor
250-361-0223
ccoleman@victoria.ca
Doug Angrove, Fire Chief
250-920-3353
Lynn Hunter, Councillor
250-361-0218
lhunter@victoria.ca
Jamie Graham, Chief Constable
250-995-7217
Phillipe Lucas, Councillor
250-361-0217
plucas@victoria.ca
John Basey, City Solicitor
250-361-0588, Fax: 250-361-0348
John Luton, Councillor
250-361-0222
jluton@victoria.ca
Deborah Day, Director, Planning & Development
250-361-0511
Pamela Madoff, Councillor
250-361-0221
pmadoff@victoria.ca
Trina Harrison, Director, Human Resources
250-361-0229
Charlayne Thornton-Joe, Councillor
250-361-0219
cthornton-joe@victoria.ca
Peter Sparanese, General Manager, Operations
250-361-0292
Geoff Young, Councillor
250-361-0220
gyoung@victoria.ca
Jocelyn Jenkyns, General Manager, Victoria Conference Centre
250-361-1000
Dwayne Kalynchuk, Director, Engineering & Public Works
250-361-0522
Ed Robertson, Assistant Director, Public Works
250-361-0457
John Sturdy, Assistant Director, Utilities & Facilities
250-361-0531
Katie Josephson, Director, Communications
250-361-0210
Kate Friars, Director, Parks, Recreation & Community Development
250-361-0355
Scott Clark, Manager, Information Systems
250-361-0265
Rebecca Chow, Manager, Health & Safety
250-361-0574
Mark Hayden, Manager, Bylaw & Licensing Services
250-361-0592
Janice Schmidt, Manager, Corporate Planning & Policy
250-361-0543
Glen Oberg, Manager, Supply Management Services
250-361-0271
Pete Sparanese, Acting Director, Sustainability
250-361-0292
Don Schaffer, Manager, Legislative Services
250-361-0549

White Rock

15322 Buena Vista Ave.
White Rock, BC V4B 1Y6
Tel: 604-541-2100; *Fax:* 604-541-2118
whiterockcouncil@city.whiterock.bc.ca
www.city.whiterock.bc.ca
Municipal Type: City
Incorporated: April 15, 1957 *Area:* 5.16 sq km
County or District: Metro Vancouver; *Population in 2006:* 18,755
Provincial Electoral District(s): Surrey-White Rock
Federal Electoral District(s): South Surrey-White Rock-Cloverdale
Next Election: Nov. 2011 (3 year terms)
Catherine Ferguson, Mayor
cferguson@city.whiterock.bc.ca

Mary-Wade Anderson, Councillor
mwade-anderson@city.whiterock.bc.ca
Alan Campbell, Councillor
acampbell@city.whiterock.bc.ca
Helen Fathers, Councillor
hfathers@city.whiterock.bc.ca
Doug McLean, Councillor
dmclean@city.whiterock.bc.ca
Grant Meyer, Councillor
gmeyer@city.whiterock.bc.ca
Lynne Sinclair, Councillor
lsinclair@city.whiterock.bc.ca
Tracey Arthur, City Clerk
604-541-2212
tarthur@city.whiterock.bc.ca
Sandra Kurylo, Director, Financial Services
604-541-2111
skurylo@city.whiterock.bc.ca
Peggy Clark, Chief Administrative Officer
604-541-2133, Fax: 604-541-9348
pclark@city.whiterock.bc.ca
Phil Lemire, Fire Chief
604-541-2122
plemire@city.whiterock.bc.ca
Lesli Roseberry, White Rock RCMP Detachment Commander
604-541-5101
lesli.roseberry@rcmp-grc.gc.ca
Rob Thompson, Director, Municipal Operations
604-541-2181
rthompson@city.whiterock.bc.ca
Chris Zota, Manager, Information Technology
604-541-2113
czota@city.whiterock.bc.ca
Paul Stanton, Director, Development Services
604-541-2142
pstanton@city.whiterock.bc.ca
Sylvia Yee, Acting Director, Development Services
604-541-2173
syee@city.whiterock.bc.ca
Jacquie Johnstone, Director, Human Resources
604-541-2157
jjohnstone@city.whiterock.bc.ca

Williams Lake
450 Mart St.
Williams Lake, BC V2G 1N3
Tel: 250-392-2311; *Fax:* 250-392-4408
corporateservices@williamslake.ca
www.williamslake.ca
Municipal Type: City
Incorporated: March 15, 1929 *Area:* 33.11 sq km
County or District: Cariboo; *Population in 2006:* 10,744
Provincial Electoral District(s): Cariboo North; Cariboo South
Federal Electoral District(s): Cariboo-Prince George
Next Election: Nov. 2011 (3 year terms)
Kerry Cook, Mayor
250-392-2311
mayor@williamslake.ca
Tom Barr, Councillor
tbarr@williamslake.ca
Geoff Bourdon, Councillor
gbourdon@williamslake.ca
Natalie Hebert, Councillor
nhebert@williamslake.ca
Laurie Walters, Councillor
lwalters@williamslake.ca
Sue Zacharias, Councillor
szacharias@williamslake.ca
Brian Carruthers, Chief Administrative Officer
250-392-1763
bcarruthers@williamslake.ca
Geoff Goodall, General Manager, Planning & Operations
250-392-1766
ggoodall@williamslake.ca
Randy Isfeld, Director/Fire Chief, Protective Services
250-392-1779
risfeld@williamslake.ca
Geoff Goodall, Director, Development Services
250-392-1766
ggoodall@williamslake.ca
Patricia Higgins, Director, Financial Services
250-392-1762
phiggins@williamslake.ca
Geoff Paynton, Director, Community Services
250-392-1786
gpaynton@williamslake.ca
Kevin Goldfuss, Director, Municipal Services
250-392-1783
kgoldfuss@williamslake.ca
Cindy Bouchard, Manager, Legislative Services
cbouchard@williamslake.ca
Joe Engelberts, Manager, Water/Sewer Division
jengelberts@williamslake.ca

Other Municipalities in British Columbia

100 Mile House
P.O. Box 340
385 South Birch Ave.
100 Mile House, BC V0K 2E0
Tel: 250-395-2434; *Fax:* 250-395-3625
district@dist100milehouse.bc.ca
www.100milehouse.com
Municipal Type: District
Incorporated: July 27, 1965 *Area:* 51.34 sq km
County or District: Cariboo; *Population in 2006:* 1,885
Provincial Electoral District(s): Cariboo South
Federal Electoral District(s): Kamloops-Thomson-Cariboo
Next Election: Nov. 2011 (3 year terms)
Mitch Campsall, Mayor
mcampsall@dist100milehouse.bc.ca
Roy Scott, Chief Administrative Officer, Corporate Administration
rscott@dist100milehouse.bc.ca

Alert Bay
P.O. Box 2800
15 Maple Rd.
Alert Bay, BC V0N 1A0
Tel: 250-974-5213; *Fax:* 250-974-5470
officeclerk@alertbay.ca
www.alertbay.ca
Municipal Type: Village
Incorporated: Jan. 14, 1946 *Area:* 1.78 sq km
County or District: Mount Waddington; *Population in 2006:* 556
Provincial Electoral District(s): North Island
Federal Electoral District(s): Vancouver Island North
Next Election: Nov. 2011 (3 year terms)
Michael Berry, Mayor
Madeline McDonald, Chief Administrative Officer

Anmore
2697 Sunnyside Rd.
Anmore, BC V3H 3C8
Tel: 604-469-9877; *Fax:* 604-469-0537
village.hall@anmore.com
www.anmore.com
Municipal Type: Village
Incorporated: Dec. 7, 1987 *Area:* 27.42 sq km
County or District: Metro Vancouver; *Population in 2006:* 1,785
Provincial Electoral District(s): Port Moody-Westwood
Federal Electoral District(s): Port Moody-Westwood-Port Coquitlam
Next Election: Nov. 2011 (3 year terms)
Heather Anderson, Mayor
604-469-0929
heather.m.anderson@telus.net
Howard Carley, Chief Administrative Officer
howard.carley@anmore.com

Armstrong
P.O. Box 40
3570 Bridge St.
Armstrong, BC V0E 1B0
Tel: 250-546-3023; *Fax:* 250-546-3710
info@cityofarmstrong.bc.ca
www.cityofarmstrong.bc.ca
Municipal Type: Town
Incorporated: March 31, 1913 *Area:* 5.24 sq km
County or District: North Okanagan; *Population in 2006:* 4,241
Provincial Electoral District(s): Shuswap
Federal Electoral District(s): Okanagan-Shuswap
Next Election: Nov. 2011 (3 year terms)
Chris Pieper, Mayor
250-550-7239
mayor@cityofarmstrong.bc.ca; cpieper@telus.net
Patti Ferguson, Chief Administrative Officer

Ashcroft
P.O. Box 129
Ashcroft, BC V0K 1A0
Tel: 250-453-9161; *Fax:* 250-453-9664
admin@ashcroftbc.ca
www.ashcroftbc.ca
Other Information: Toll Free Phone: 1-877-453-9161
Municipal Type: Village
Incorporated: June 27, 1952 *Area:* 51.45 sq km
County or District: Thompson-Nicola; *Population in 2006:* 1,664
Provincial Electoral District(s): Cariboo South
Federal Electoral District(s): Chilliwack-Fraser Canyon
Next Election: Nov. 2011 (3 year terms)
Andy Anderson, Mayor
250-453-9161, Fax: 250-453-9664
council@ashcroftbc.ca
Michelle Allen, Chief Administrative Officer

Barriere
P.O. Box 219
4936 Barriere Town Rd.
Barriere, BC V0E 1E0
Tel: 250-672-9751; *Fax:* 250-672-9708
inquiry@districtofbarriere.com
www.districtofbarriere.com
Other Information: Toll Free Phone: 1-866-672-9751
Municipal Type: District
Incorporated: Dec. 4 2007 *Area:* 6.17 sq km
County or District: Thompson-Nicola; *Population in 2006:* 1,209
Provincial Electoral District(s): Lower North Thompson
Federal Electoral District(s): Kamloops-Thompson-Cariboo
Next Election: Nov. 2011 (3 year terms)
Mike Fennell, Mayor
250-319-9136
mfennell@districtofbarriere.com
Colleen Hannigan, Chief Administrative Officer
250-672-9751
channigan@districtofbarriere.com

Belcarra
4084 Bedwell Bay Rd.
Belcarra, BC V3H 4P8
Tel: 604-937-4100; *Fax:* 604-939-5034
belcarra@belcarra.ca
www.belcarra.ca
Municipal Type: Village
Incorporated: Aug. 22, 1979 *Area:* 5.46 sq km
County or District: Metro Vancouver; *Population in 2006:* 676
Provincial Electoral District(s): Port Moody-Westwood
Federal Electoral District(s): Port Moody-Westwood-Port Coquitlam
Next Election: Nov. 2011 (3 year terms)
Ralph E. Drew, Mayor
604-937-0143
rdrew@belcarra.ca
Lynda Floyd, Chief Administrative Officer
604-937-4101
lfloyd@belcarra.ca

Bowen Island
981 Artisan Lane
Bowen Island, BC V0N 1G0
Tel: 604-947-4255; *Fax:* 604-947-0193
bim@bimbc.ca
www.bimbc.ca
Municipal Type: Island Municipality
Incorporated: Dec. 4, 1999 *Area:* 49.94 sq km
County or District: Metro Vancouver; *Population in 2006:* 3,362
Provincial Electoral District(s): West Vancouver-Garibaldi
Federal Electoral District(s): West Vancouver-Sunshine Coast-Sea to Sky Country
Next Election: Nov. 2011 (3 year terms)
Bob Turner, Mayor
604-785-3096
bob.turner7@gmail.com
Brent Mahood, Chief Administrative Officer
bmahood@bimbc.ca

Burns Lake
P.O. Box 570
Burns Lake, BC V0J 1E0
Tel: 250-692-7587; *Fax:* 250-692-3059
village@burnslake.org
www.burnslake.org
Other Information: Fire Hall Phone: 250-692-3664
Municipal Type: Village
Incorporated: Dec. 6, 1923 *Area:* 7.17 sq km
County or District: Bulkley-Nechako; *Population in 2006:* 2,107
Provincial Electoral District(s): Bulkley Valley-Stikine
Federal Electoral District(s): Skeena-Bulkley Valley
Next Election: Nov. 2011 (3 year terms)
Bernice Magee, Mayor
Sheryl Worthing, Chief Administrative Officer

Cache Creek
P.O. Box 7
Cache Creek, BC V0K 1H0
Tel: 250-457-6237; *Fax:* 250-457-9192
admin@cachecreek.info
www.cachecreekvillage.com
Municipal Type: Village
Incorporated: Nov. 28, 1967 *Area:* 10.57 sq km
County or District: Thompson-Nicola; *Population in 2006:* 1,037
Provincial Electoral District(s): Cariboo South

Federal Electoral District(s): Chilliwack-Fraser Canyon
Next Election: Nov. 2011 (3 year terms)
John Ranta, Mayor
bigjohn4@telus.net
Leslie Lloyd, Chief Administrative Officer

Canal Flats
P.O. Box 159
8853 Grainger Rd.
Canal Flats, BC V0B 1B0
Tel: 250-349-5462; *Fax:* 250-349-5460
village@canalflats.ca
www.canalflats.com
Municipal Type: Village
Incorporated: June 29, 2004 *Area:* 10.84 sq km
County or District: East Kootenay; *Population in 2006:* 700
Provincial Electoral District(s): Columbia River-Revelstoke
Federal Electoral District(s): Kootenay-Columbia
Next Election: Nov. 2011 (3 year terms)
Bruce Woodbury, Mayor
250-349-5814
bwoodbury@gmail.com
Brian Woodward, Chief Administrative Officer

Castlegar
460 Columbia Ave.
Castlegar, BC V1N 1G7
Tel: 250-365-7227; *Fax:* 250-365-4810
www.castlegar.ca
Municipal Type: Town
Incorporated: Jan. 1, 1974 *Area:* 19.8 sq km
County or District: Central Kootenay; *Population in 2006:* 7,259
Provincial Electoral District(s): West Kootenay-Boundary
Federal Electoral District(s): British Columbia Southern Interior
Next Election: Nov. 2011 (3 year terms)
Lawrence Chernoff, Mayor
John Malcolm, Chief Administrative Officer

Central Saanich
1903 Mt. Newton Cross Rd.
Saanichton, BC V8M 2A9
Tel: 250-652-4444; *Fax:* 250-652-0135
www.centralsaanich.ca
Municipal Type: District
Incorporated: Dec. 12, 1950 *Area:* 41.42 sq km
County or District: Capital; *Population in 2006:* 15,745
Provincial Electoral District(s): Saanich North & the Islands
Federal Electoral District(s): Saanich-Gulf Islands
Next Election: Nov. 2011 (3 year terms)
Jack Mar, Mayor
250-652-8449
Alastair Bryson, Councillor
250-544-0668
John Garrison, Councillor
250-514-4217
Ron Kubek, Councillor
250-544-2929
Susan Mason, Councillor
250-652-0783
Adam Olsen, Councillor
778-426-1000
Terry Siklenka, Councillor
250-508-8313
Susan Brown, Municipal Clerk
Gary C. Nason, Administrator
Nirmal Bhattacharya, P.Eng., Municipal Engineer, Public Works & Operationss
Bruce Greig, Planner
Ron French, Fire Chief
250-544-4227

Chase
P.O. Box 440
826 Okanagan Ave.
Chase, BC V0E 1M0
Tel: 250-679-3238; *Fax:* 250-679-3070
chase@chasebc.ca
www.chasebc.ca
Municipal Type: Village
Incorporated: April 22, 1969 *Area:* 3.75 sq km
County or District: Thompson-Nicola; *Population in 2006:* 2,409
Provincial Electoral District(s): Kamloops-North Thompson
Federal Electoral District(s): Okanagan-Shuswap
Next Election: Nov. 2011 (3 year terms)
Harry Danyluk, Mayor
Martin Dalsin, Chief Administrative Officer
mdalsin@chasebc.ca

Chetwynd
P.O. Box 357
5400 North Access Rd.
Chetwynd, BC V0C 1J0
Tel: 250-401-4100; *Fax:* 250-401-4101
d-chet@gochetwynd.com
www.gochetwynd.com
Municipal Type: District
Incorporated: Sept. 25, 1962 *Area:* 64.32 sq km
County or District: Peace River; *Population in 2006:* 2,633
Provincial Electoral District(s): Peace River South
Federal Electoral District(s): Prince George-Peace River
Next Election: Nov. 2011 (3 year terms)
Evan Saugstad, Mayor
250-401-4102
esaugstad@gochetwynd.com
Doug Fleming, Chief Administrative Officer
250-401-4103
dfleming@gochetwynd.com

Clearwater
P.O. Box 157
132 Clearwater Station Rd.
Clearwater, BC V0E 1N0
Tel: 250-674-2257; *Fax:* 250-674-2173
admin@districtofclearwater.com
www.districtofclearwater.com
Municipal Type: District
Incorporated: Dec. 7 2007 *Area:* 60 sq km
County or District: Thompson-Nicola; *Population in 2006:* 4,960
Provincial Electoral District(s): Kamloops-North Thompson
Federal Electoral District(s): Kamloops-Thompson-Cariboo
Next Election: Nov. 2011 (3 year terms)
John Harwood, Mayor
Leslie Groulx, Interim Chief Administrative Officer
lgroulx@docbc.ca

Clinton
P.O. Box 309
1423 Cariboo Hwy.
Clinton, BC V0K 1K0
Tel: 250-459-2261; *Fax:* 250-459-2227
admin@village.clinton.bc.ca
www.village.clinton.bc.ca
Municipal Type: Village
Incorporated: July 16, 1963 *Area:* 4.36 sq km
County or District: Thompson-Nicola; *Population in 2006:* 578
Provincial Electoral District(s): Cariboo South
Federal Electoral District(s): Kamloops-Thompson-Cariboo
Next Election: Nov. 2011 (3 year terms)
Roland Stanke, Mayor
mayor@village.clinton.bc.ca
Heidi Frank, Chief Administrative Officer
250-459-2261
hfrank@village.clinton.bc.ca

Coldstream
9901 Kalamalka Rd.
Coldstream, BC V1B 1L6
Tel: 250-545-5304; *Fax:* 250-545-4733
info@districtofcoldstream.ca
www.districtofcoldstream.ca
Municipal Type: District
Incorporated: Dec. 21, 1906 *Area:* 67.25 sq km
County or District: North Okanagan; *Population in 2006:* 9,471
Provincial Electoral District(s): Okanagan-Vernon
Federal Electoral District(s): Okanagan-Shuswap
Next Election: Nov. 2011 (3 year terms)
Jim Garlick, Mayor
250-307-9490
Michael Stamhuis, Chief Administrative Officer
mstamhuis@district.coldstream.bc.ca

Creston
P.O. Box 1339
#238, 10th Ave. North
Creston, BC V0B 1G0
Tel: 250-428-2214; *Fax:* 250-428-9164
info@creston.ca
www.creston.ca
Municipal Type: Town
Incorporated: May 14, 1924 *Area:* 8.48 sq km
County or District: Central Kootenay; *Population in 2006:* 4,826
Provincial Electoral District(s): Nelson-Creston
Federal Electoral District(s): Kootenay-Columbia
Next Election: Nov. 2011 (3 year terms)
Ron Toyota, Mayor
ron.toyota@creston.ca
Lou Varela, Town Manager

Cumberland
P.O. Box 340
2673 Dunsmuir Ave.
Cumberland, BC V0R 1S0
Tel: 250-336-2291; *Fax:* 250-336-2321
www.cumberlandbc.net
Municipal Type: Village
Incorporated: Jan. 1, 1898 *Area:* 29.13 sq km
County or District: Comox Valley; *Population in 2006:* 2,762
Provincial Electoral District(s): Comox Valley
Federal Electoral District(s): Vancouver Island North
Next Election: Nov. 2011 (3 year terms)
Fred Bates, Mayor
fbates@shaw.ca
Dave Durrant, Chief Administrative Officer
ddurrant@cumberlandbc.net

Delta
4500 Clarence Taylor Cres.
Delta, BC V4K 3E2
Tel: 604-946-4141;
www.corp.delta.bc.ca
Municipal Type: District
Incorporated: Nov. 10, 1879 *Area:* 183.7 sq km
County or District: Metro Vancouver; *Population in 2006:* 96,723
Provincial Electoral District(s): Delta North; Delta South
Federal Electoral District(s): Delta-Richmond East; Newton-North Delta
Next Election: Nov. 2011 (3 year terms)
Lois E. Jackson, Mayor
604-946-3210, Fax: 604-946-6055
mayor@corp.delta.bc.ca
Robert Campbell, Councillor
604-948-0623
rcampbell@corp.delta.bc.ca
Scott Hamilton, Councillor
604-599-9261
shamilton@corp.delta.bc.ca
Heather King, Councillor
604-943-9607
hking@corp.delta.bc.ca
Bruce McDonald, Councillor
604-596-8345
bmcdonald@corp.delta.bc.ca
Anne Peterson, Councillor
604-578-7742
apeterson@corp.delta.bc.ca
Angila Bains, Municipal Clerk
604-946-3220, Fax: 604-946-3390
clerks@corp.delta.bc.ca
George Harvie, Chief Administrative Officer
604-946-3212, Fax: 604-946-3864
cao@corp.delta.bc.ca
Ken Kuntz, Director, Parks, Recreation & Culture
604-952-3000, Fax: 604-946-4693
park-rec@corp.delta.bc.ca
Steven Lan, Director, Engineering
604-946-3260, Fax: 604-946-7492
engineering@corp.delta.bc.ca
Thomas Leathem, Director, Community Planning & Development
604-946-3380
com-pln-dev@corp.delta.bc.ca
Sean McGill, Director, Human Resources & Corporate Planning
604-946-3246
human-resources@corp.delta.bc.ca
Karl Preuss, CA, Director, Finance
604-946-3230, Fax: 604-946-3962
finance@corp.delta.bc.ca
Mike Brotherston, Manager, Climate Action & Environment
604-946-3253
cae@corp.delta.bc.ca
Greg Vanstone, Municipal Solicitor
604-952-3138
legalservices@corp.delta.bc.ca
Dan Copeland, Fire Chief
604-946-8541, Fax: 604-946-0436
fire@corp.delta.bc.ca
Jim Cessford, Chief Constable
604-946-4411, Fax: 604-946-3729
officechiefconstable@deltapolice.ca

Duncan
200 Craig St.
Duncan, BC V9L 1W3
Tel: 250-746-6126; *Fax:* 250-746-6129
duncan@duncan.ca
www.duncan.ca
Municipal Type: Town
Incorporated: March 4, 1912 *Area:* 2.05 sq km
County or District: Cowichan Valley; *Population in 2006:* 4,986

Provincial Electoral District(s): Cowichan-Ladysmith
Federal Electoral District(s): Nanaimo-Cowichan
Next Election: Nov. 2011 (3 year terms)
Phil Kent, Mayor
250-709-0186
mayor@duncan.ca
Tom Ireland, Chief Administrative Officer
tireland@duncan.ca

Elkford
P.O. Box 340
Elkford, BC V0B 1H0
Tel: 250-865-4000; *Fax:* 250-865-4001
info@elkford.ca
www.elkford.ca
Municipal Type: District
Incorporated: July 16, 1971 *Area:* 101.59 sq km
County or District: East Kootenay; *Population in 2006:* 2,463
Provincial Electoral District(s): East Kootenay
Federal Electoral District(s): Kootenay-Columbia
Next Election: Nov. 2011 (3 year terms)
Dean McKerracher, Mayor
mayor@elkford.ca
Corien L. Speaker, Chief Administrative Officer
cspeaker@elkford.ca

Enderby
P.O. Box 400
619 Cliff Ave.
Enderby, BC V0E 1V0
Tel: 250-838-7230; *Fax:* 250-838-6007
enderbycity@sunwave.net
www.enderby.com; cityofenderby.com
Municipal Type: Village
Incorporated: March 1, 1905 *Area:* 4.23 sq km
County or District: North Okanagan; *Population in 2006:* 2,828
Provincial Electoral District(s): Shuswap
Federal Electoral District(s): Okanagan-Shuswap
Next Election: Nov. 2011 (3 year terms)
Dee Wejr, Mayor
jazzdee@telus.net
Barry Gagnon, Chief Administrative Officer
bgagnon@sunwave.net

Esquimalt
1229 Esquimalt Rd.
Victoria, BC V9A 3P1
Tel: 250-414-7100; *Fax:* 250-414-7111
www.esquimalt.ca
Municipal Type: Township
Incorporated: Sept. 1, 1912 *Area:* 7.04 sq km
County or District: Capital; *Population in 2006:* 16,840
Provincial Electoral District(s): Esquimalt-Metchosin
Federal Electoral District(s): Esquimalt-Juan de Fuca
Next Election: Nov. 2011 (3 year terms)
Barbara Desjardins, Mayor
250-883-1944
Meagan Brame, Councillor
250-285-0660
Randall Garrison, Councillor
250-590-3756
Alison Gaul, Councillor
250-383-1703
Lynda Hundleby, Councillor
250-383-3759
Don Linge, Councillor
250-888-5081
Bruce McIldoon, Councillor
250-382-6586
Laurie Hurst, Chief Administrative Officer
250-414-7133
Karen Blakely, Chief Financial Officer & Director, Financial Services
250-414-7141
Scott Hartman, Director, Parks & Recreation
250-412-8509
Jeff Miller, Director, Engineering & Public Works
250-414-7147
Barbara Snyder, Director, Development Services
250-414-7146
Wayne Martin, Manager, Public Works
Trevor Parkes, Senior Planner, Development Services
David Ward, Fire Chief
250-414-7125

Fernie
P.O. Box 190
#501, 3rd Ave.
Fernie, BC V0B 1M0
Tel: 250-423-6817; *Fax:* 250-423-3034
cityhall@fernie.ca
www.fernie.ca
Municipal Type: Town
Incorporated: July 28, 1904 *Area:* 16.05 sq km
County or District: East Kootenay; *Population in 2006:* 4,217
Provincial Electoral District(s): East Kootenay
Federal Electoral District(s): Kootenay-Columbia
Next Election: Nov. 2011 (3 year terms)
Cindy Corrigan, Mayor
cindy.corrigan@fernie.ca
Allan Chabot, Chief Administrative Officer
250-423-2225
allan.chabot@fernie.ca

Fort Nelson
P.O. Box 399
5319 - 50th Ave.
Fort Nelson, BC V0C 1R0
Tel: 250-774-2541;
justask@northernrockies.ca
www.northernrockies.ca
Municipal Type: Town
Incorporated: Oct. 31, 1987 *Area:* 13.26 sq km
County or District: Northern Rockies; *Population in 2006:* 4,514
Provincial Electoral District(s): Peace River North
Federal Electoral District(s): Prince George-Peace River
Next Election: Nov. 2011 (3 year terms)
Bill Streeper, Mayor
mayor@northernrockies.org
Randy McLean, Chief Administrative Officer
admin@northernrockies.ca

Fort St. James
P.O. Box 640
477 Stuart Dr. West
Fort St James, BC V0J 1P0
Tel: 250-996-8233; *Fax:* 250-996-2248
www.stuartnechako.ca/fort-st-james
Municipal Type: District
Incorporated: Dec. 19, 1952 *Area:* 22.1 sq km
County or District: Bulkley-Nechako; *Population in 2006:* 1,355
Provincial Electoral District(s): Prince George-Omineca
Federal Electoral District(s): Skeena-Buckley Valley
Next Election: Nov. 2011 (3 year terms)
Sandra Harwood, Mayor
mayor@fortstjames.ca
Kevin Crook, Chief Administrative Officer
cao@fortstjames.ca

Fraser Lake
P.O. Box 430
210 Carrier Cres.
Fraser Lake, BC V0J 1S0
Tel: 250-699-6257; *Fax:* 250-699-6469
village@fraserlake.ca
www.fraserlake.ca
Municipal Type: Village
Incorporated: Sept. 27, 1966 *Area:* 3.9 sq km
County or District: Bulkley-Nechako; *Population in 2006:* 1,113
Provincial Electoral District(s): Prince George-Omineca
Federal Electoral District(s): Skeena-Bulkley Valley
Next Election: Nov. 2011 (3 year terms)
Dwayne Lindstrom, Mayor
Clinton Mauthe, Director, Corporate Affairs

Fruitvale
P.O. Box 370
1947 beaver St.
Fruitvale, BC V0G 1L0
Tel: 250-367-7551; *Fax:* 250-367-9267
www.village.fruitvale.bc.ca
Municipal Type: Village
Incorporated: Nov. 4, 1952 *Area:* 36.86 sq km
County or District: Kootenay Boundary; *Population in 2006:* 1,952
Provincial Electoral District(s): West Kootenay-Boundary
Federal Electoral District(s): British Columbia Southern Interior
Next Election: Nov. 2011 (3 year terms)
Libby Nelson, Mayor
libbynelson@netidea.com
Lila Cresswell, Chief Administrative Officer

Gibsons
P.O. Box 340
474 South Fletcher Rd.
Gibsons, BC V0N 1V0
Tel: 604-886-2274; *Fax:* 604-886-9735
info@gibsons.ca
www.gibsons.ca
Municipal Type: Town
Incorporated: March 4, 1929 *Area:* 4.33 sq km
County or District: Sunshine Coast; *Population in 2006:* 4,182
Provincial Electoral District(s): Powell River-Sunshine Coast
Federal Electoral District(s): West Vancouver-Sunshine Coast-Sea to Sky Country
Next Election: Nov. 2011 (3 year terms)
Barry Janyk, Mayor
bjanyk@gibsons.ca
Wayne Waycheshen, Chief Administrative Officer
wwaycheshen@gibsons.ca

Gold River
P.O. Box 610
499 Muchalat Dr.
Gold River, BC V0P 1G0
Tel: 250-283-2202; *Fax:* 250-283-7500
villageofgoldriver@cablerocket.com
www.goldriver.ca
Municipal Type: Village
Incorporated: Aug. 26, 1965 *Area:* 10.51 sq km
County or District: Strathcona; *Population in 2006:* 1,362
Provincial Electoral District(s): North Island
Federal Electoral District(s): Vancouver Island North
Next Election: Nov. 2011 (3 year terms)
Craig Anderson, Mayor
250-283-7100
dabear10@cablerocket.com
Larry Plourde, Chief Administrative Officer
grlplourde@cablerocket.com

Golden
P.O. Box 350
Golden, BC V0A 1H0
Tel: 250-344-2271; *Fax:* 250-344-6577
enquiries@town.golden.bc.ca
www.town.golden.bc.ca
Municipal Type: Town
Incorporated: June 26, 1957 *Area:* 11.02 sq km
County or District: Columbia-Shuswap; *Population in 2006:* 3,811
Provincial Electoral District(s): Columbia River-Revelstoke
Federal Electoral District(s): Kootenay-Columbia
Next Election: Nov. 2011 (3 year terms)
Christina Benty, Mayor
christina.benty@golden.ca
Viv Thoss, Council Clerk
council.clerk@golden.ca
David Allen, Chief Administrative Officer
cao@town.golden.bc.ca

Grand Forks
P.O. Box 220
7217 - 4th St.
Grand Forks, BC V0H 1H0
Tel: 250-442-8266; *Fax:* 250-442-8000
info@city.grandforks.bc.ca
www.city.grandforks.bc.ca
Municipal Type: Town
Incorporated: April 15, 1897 *Area:* 10.44 sq km
County or District: Kootenay Boundary; *Population in 2006:* 4,036
Provincial Electoral District(s): West Kootenay-Boundary
Federal Electoral District(s): British Columbia Southern Interior
Next Election: Nov. 2011 (3 year terms)
Brian Taylor, Mayor
btaylor@grandforks.ca
Lynne Burch, Chief Administrative Officer
lburch@grandforks.ca

Granisle
P.O. Box 128
Granisle, BC V0J 1W0
Tel: 250-697-2248; *Fax:* 250-697-2306
www.granisle.net
Municipal Type: Village
Incorporated: June 29, 1971 *Area:* 40.21 sq km
County or District: Bulkley-Nechako; *Population in 2006:* 364
Provincial Electoral District(s): Bulkley Valley-Stikine
Federal Electoral District(s): Skeena-Buckley Valley
Next Election: Nov. 2011 (3 year terms)
Frederick J. Clarke, Mayor
fclarke@villageofgranisle.ca
Gilles Archambault, Chief Administrative Officer
250-697-2428

Greenwood
P.O. Box 129
202 Government Ave.
Greenwood, BC V0H 1J0
Tel: 250-445-6644; *Fax:* 250-445-6441
greenwoodcity@shaw.ca
www.greenwoodcity.com
Municipal Type: Village
Incorporated: July 12, 1897 *Area:* 2.52 sq km
County or District: Kootenay Boundary; *Population in 2006:* 625
Provincial Electoral District(s): West Kootenay-Boundary

Federal Electoral District(s): British Columbia Southern Interior
Next Election: Nov. 2011 (3 year terms)
Colleen Lang, Mayor
250-445-6558
langcolleen55@yahoo.ca
Gerald A. Henke, Administrator

Harrison Hot Springs
P.O. Box 160
495 Hot Springs Rd.
Harrison Hot Springs, BC V0M 1K0
Tel: 604-796-2171; *Fax:* 604-796-2192
info@harrisonhotsprings.ca
www.harrisonhotsprings.ca
Municipal Type: Village
Incorporated: May 27, 1949 *Area:* 5.47 sq km
County or District: Fraser Valley; *Population in 2006:* 1,573
Provincial Electoral District(s): Chilliwack-Kent
Federal Electoral District(s): Chilliwack-Fraser Canyon
Next Election: Nov. 2011 (3 year terms)
Ken Becotte, Mayor
mayor@harrisonhotsprings.ca
Ted Tisdale, Chief Administrative Officer
ttisdale@harrisonhotsprings.ca

Hazelton
P.O. Box 40
Hazelton, BC V0J 1Y0
Tel: 250-842-5991; *Fax:* 250-842-5152
info@village.hazelton.bc.ca
www.village.hazelton.bc.ca
Municipal Type: Village
Incorporated: Feb. 15, 1956 *Area:* 2.85 sq km
County or District: Kitimat-Stikine; *Population in 2006:* 293
Provincial Electoral District(s): Bulkley Valley-Stikine
Federal Electoral District(s): Skeena-Bulkley Valley
Next Election: Nov. 2011 (3 year terms)
Alice Maitland, Mayor
amaitland@village.hazelton.bc.ca
Kelly Mattson, Administrator
administrator@village.hazelton.bc.ca

Highlands
1980 Millstream Rd.
Victoria, BC V9B 6H1
Tel: 250-474-1773; *Fax:* 250-474-3677
www.highlands.bc.ca
Municipal Type: District
Incorporated: Dec. 7, 1993 *Area:* 37.87 sq km
County or District: Capital; *Population in 2006:* 1,903
Provincial Electoral District(s): Malahat-Juan de Fuca
Federal Electoral District(s): Esquimalt-Juan de Fuca
Next Election: Nov. 2011 (3 year terms)
Jane Mendum, Mayor
jmendum@highlands.ca
Christopher D. Coates, Administrator
ccoates@highlands.ca

Hope
325 Wallace St.
Hope, BC V0X 1L0
Tel: 604-869-5671; *Fax:* 604-869-2275
info@hope.ca
www.hope.ca
Municipal Type: District Municipality
Incorporated: April 6, 1929 *Area:* 41.42 sq km
County or District: Fraser Valley; *Population in 2006:* 6,185
Provincial Electoral District(s): Yale-Lillooet
Federal Electoral District(s): Chilliwack-Fraser Canyon
Next Election: Nov. 2011 (3 year terms)
Laurence (Laurie) French, Mayor
lfrench@hope.ca
Earl Rowe, Town Manager
erowe@hope.ca

Houston
P.O. Box 370
3367 - 12th St.
Houston, BC V0J 1Z0
Tel: 250-845-2238; *Fax:* 250-845-3429
doh@houston.ca
www.houston.ca
Municipal Type: District
Incorporated: March 4, 1957 *Area:* 72.83 sq km
County or District: Bulkley-Nechako; *Population in 2006:* 3,163
Provincial Electoral District(s): Bulkley Valley-Stikine
Federal Electoral District(s): Skeena-Buckley Valley
Next Election: Nov. 2011 (3 year terms)
Bill Holmberg, Mayor
bholmberg@finning.ca
Linda Poznikoff, Chief Administrative Officer
poznikoff@houston.ca

Hudson's Hope
P.O. Box 330
9904 Dudley Dr.
Hudson's Hope, BC V0C 1V0
Tel: 250-783-9901; *Fax:* 250-783-5741
www.hudsonshope.ca
Municipal Type: District
Incorporated: Nov. 16, 1965 *Area:* 869.43 sq km
County or District: Peace River; *Population in 2006:* 1,012
Provincial Electoral District(s): Peace River North
Federal Electoral District(s): Prince George-Peace River
Next Election: Nov. 2011 (3 year terms)
Karen Anderson, Mayor
mayor@hudsonshope.ca
Mike Carter, Acting Chief Administrative Officer/Director, Public Works
mike@hudsonshope.ca

Invermere
P.O. Box 339
914 - 8th Ave.
Invermere, BC V0A 1K0
Tel: 250-342-9281; *Fax:* 250-342-2934
info@invermere.net
www.invermere.net
Municipal Type: District
Incorporated: May 22, 1951 *Area:* 10.18 sq km
County or District: East Kootenay; *Population in 2006:* 3,002
Provincial Electoral District(s): Columbia River-Revelstoke
Federal Electoral District(s): Kootenay-Columbia
Next Election: Nov. 2011 (3 year terms)
Gerry Taft, Mayor
mayor@invermere.net
Christopher Prosser, Cheif Administrative Officer
cao@invermere.net

Kaslo
P.O. Box 576
312 Fourth St.
Kaslo, BC V0G 1M0
Tel: 250-353-2311; *Fax:* 250-353-7767
village@netidea.com
www.kaslo.ca
Municipal Type: Village
Incorporated: Aug. 14, 1893 *Area:* 2.8 sq km
County or District: Central Kootenay; *Population in 2006:* 1,072
Provincial Electoral District(s): Nelson-Creston
Federal Electoral District(s): British Columbia Southern Interior
Next Election: Nov. 2011 (3 year terms)
Greg Lay, Mayor
Rae Sawyer, Chief Administrative Officer
kasloclerk@netidea.com

Kent
P.O. Box 70
7170 Cheam Ave.
Agassiz, BC V0M 1A0
Tel: 604-796-2235; *Fax:* 604-796-9854
www.district.kent.bc.ca
Municipal Type: District
Incorporated: Jan. 1, 1895 *Area:* 166.51 sq km
County or District: Fraser Valley; *Population in 2006:* 4,738
Provincial Electoral District(s): Chilliwack-Kent
Federal Electoral District(s): Chilliwack-Fraser Canyon
Next Election: Nov. 2011 (3 year terms)
Lorne Fisher, Mayor
lfisher@district.kent.bc.ca
Wallace Mah, Chief Administrative Officer
wmah@district.kent.bc.ca

Keremeos
P.O. Box 160
702 - 4th St.
Keremeos, BC V0X 1N0
Tel: 250-499-2711; *Fax:* 250-499-5477
town@keremeos.ca
www.keremeos.ca
Municipal Type: Village
Incorporated: Oct. 30, 1956 *Area:* 2.11 sq km
County or District: Okanagan-Similkameen; *Population in 2006:* 1,289
Provincial Electoral District(s): Yale-Lillooet
Federal Electoral District(s): British Columbia Southern Interior
Next Election: Nov. 2011 (3 year terms)
Walter F. Despot, Mayor
250-499-5587
Joni Heinrich, Chief Administrative Officer
cao@keremeos.ca

Kimberley
340 Spokane St.
Kimberley, BC V1A 2E8
Tel: 250-427-5311; *Fax:* 250-427-5252
info@city.kimberley.bc.ca; operations@city.kimberley.bc.ca
www.city.kimberley.bc.ca
Municipal Type: Town
Incorporated: March 29, 1944 *Area:* 58.31 sq km
County or District: East Kootenay; *Population in 2006:* 6,139
Provincial Electoral District(s): Columbia River-Revelstoke
Federal Electoral District(s): Kootenay-Columbia
Next Election: Nov. 2011 (3 year terms)
James E. Ogilvie, Mayor
mayor@city.kimberley.bc.ca
Al Mulholland, Chief Administrative Officer
amulholland@city.kimberley.bc.ca
George Stratton, Chief Corporate Administrative Officer
gstratton@city.kimberley.bc.ca

Kitimat
270 City Centre
Kitimat, BC V8C 2H7
Tel: 250-632-8900; *Fax:* 250-632-4995
feedback@kitimat.ca
www.kitimat.ca
Municipal Type: District
Incorporated: March 31, 1953 *Area:* 242.63 sq km
County or District: Kitimat-Stikine; *Population in 2006:* 8,987
Provincial Electoral District(s): Skeena
Federal Electoral District(s): Skeena-Bulkley Valley
Next Election: Nov. 2011 (3 year terms)
Joanne Monaghan, Mayor
Walter McLellan, Municipal Clerk
250-632-8914
Ron Poole, Municipal Manager
250-632-8916
Steve Christiansen, Treasurer
250-632-8909

Ladysmith
Town Hall
P.O. Box 220 Main
410 Esplanade
Ladysmith, BC V9G 1A2
Tel: 250-245-6400; *Fax:* 250-245-6411
info@ladysmith.ca
www.ladysmith.ca
Municipal Type: Town
Incorporated: June 3, 1904 *Area:* 12.18 sq km
County or District: Cowichan Valley; *Population in 2006:* 7,538
Provincial Electoral District(s): Cowichan-Ladysmith
Federal Electoral District(s): Nanaimo-Cowichan
Next Election: Nov. 2011 (3 year terms)
Robert Hutchins, Mayor
rhutchins@ladysmith.ca
Ruth E. Malli, City Manager
rmalli@ladysmith.ca

Lake Country
10150 Bottom Wood Lake Rd.
Lake Country, BC V4V 2M1
Tel: 250-766-5650; *Fax:* 250-766-0116
admin@lakecountry.bc.ca; customerservice@lakecountry.bc.ca
www.lakecountry.bc.ca
Municipal Type: District
Incorporated: May 2, 1995 *Area:* 122.16 sq km
County or District: Central Okanagan; *Population in 2006:* 9,606
Provincial Electoral District(s): Kelowna-Lake Country
Federal Electoral District(s): Kelowna-Lake Country
Next Election: Nov. 2011 (3 year terms)
James Baker, Mayor
baker@lakecountry.bc.ca
Alberto De Feo, Chief Administrative Officer
250-766-6671

Lake Cowichan
P.O. Box 860
39 South Shore Rd.
Lake Cowichan, BC V0R 2G0
Tel: 250-749-6681; *Fax:* 250-749-3900
general@lakecowichan.ca
www.town.lakecowichan.bc.ca
Municipal Type: Town
Incorporated: Aug. 19, 1944 *Area:* 8.25 sq km
County or District: Cowichan Valley; *Population in 2006:* 2,948
Provincial Electoral District(s): Cowichan-Ladysmith
Federal Electoral District(s): Nanaimo-Cowichan
Next Election: Nov. 2011 (3 year terms)
Ross Forrest, Mayor
rforrest@town.lakecowichan.bc.ca
Joseph A. Fernandez, Chief Administrative Officer
jfernandez@lakecowichan.ca

Langley
20338 - 65 Ave.
Langley, BC V2Y 3J1
Tel: 604-534-3211;
info@tol.ca
www.tol.ca
Municipal Type: Township
Incorporated: April 26, 1873 *Area:* 306.93 sq km
County or District: Metro Vancouver; *Population in 2006:* 93,726
Provincial Electoral District(s): Fort Langely-Aldergrove
Federal Electoral District(s): Langley
Next Election: Nov. 2011 (3 year terms)
Rick Green, Mayor
rgreen@tol.ca
Bev Dornan, Councillor
bdornan@tol.ca
Steve Ferguson, Councillor
sferguson@tol.ca
Charlie Fox, Councillor
cfox@tol.ca
Mel Kositsky, Councillor
mkositsky@tol.ca
Bob Long, Councillor
blong@tol.ca
Kim Richter, Councillor
krichter@tol.ca
Grant Ward, Councillor
gward@tol.ca
Eric Britton, Township Clerk/Manager, Legislative Services
Mark Bakken, Administrator
604-533-6115
Ramin Sefi, Acting General Manager, Community Development
604-533-6034
cdinfo@tol.ca
Jason Winslade, General Manager, Corporate Administration & Community Services
Colin Wright, General Manager, Engineering
604-532-7300
enginfo@tol.ca
Christine Corfe, Director, Corporate Administration
604-533-6015, Fax: 604-533-6010
ccorfe@tol.bc.ca
Shannon Harvey-Renner, Director, Human Resources
604-533-6061
hrinfo@tol.ca
David Leavers, Director, Recreation, Culture & Parks
604-533-6068
prinfo@tol.ca
Hilary Tsikayi, Director, Finance
604-533-6022
fininfo@tol.ca
Doug Wade, Fire Chief
604-532-7500
fireinfo@tol.ca
Janice Armstrong, Superintendent, RCMP
604-532-3200
langleyrcmp@rcmp-grc.gc.ca

Lantzville
P.O. Box 100
7192 Lantzville Rd.
Lantzville, BC V0R 2H0
Tel: 250-390-4006; *Fax:* 250-390-5188
district@lantzville.ca
www.lantzville.ca
Municipal Type: District
Incorporated: June 25, 2003 *Area:* 27.87 sq km
County or District: Nanaimo; *Population in 2006:* 3,661
Provincial Electoral District(s): Nanaimo-Parksville
Federal Electoral District(s): Nanaimo-Alberni
Next Election: Nov. 2011 (3 year terms)
Colin Haime, Mayor
colinhaime@shaw.ca
Twyla Graff, Chief Administrative Officer
twyla@lantzville.ca

Lillooet
P.O. Box 610
615 Main St.
Lillooet, BC V0K 1V0
Tel: 250-256-4289; *Fax:* 250-256-4288
cityhall@lillooetbc.com
www.lillooetbc.com
Municipal Type: District
Incorporated: Dec. 31, 1946 *Area:* 27.83 sq km
County or District: Squamish-Lillooet; *Population in 2006:* 2,324
Provincial Electoral District(s): Yale-Lillooet
Federal Electoral District(s): Chilliwack-Fraser Canyon
Next Election: Nov. 2011 (3 year terms)
Dennis Bontron, Mayor
Grant Loyer, Chief Administrative Officer
gloyer@lillooetbc.com

Lions Bay
P.O. Box 141
400 Centre Rd.
Lions Bay, BC V0N 2E0
Tel: 604-921-9333; *Fax:* 604-921-6643
reception@lionsbay.ca
www.lionsbay.ca
Municipal Type: Village
Incorporated: Dec. 17, 1970 *Area:* 2.55 sq km
County or District: Metro Vancouver; *Population in 2006:* 1,328
Provincial Electoral District(s): West Vancouver-Garibaldi
Federal Electoral District(s): West Vancouver-Sunshine Coast-Sea to Sky Country
Next Election: Nov. 2011 (3 year terms)
Brenda Broughton, Mayor
mayor.broughton@lionsbay.ca
Rory Mandryk, Village Manager
admin@lionsbay.ca

Logan Lake
P.O. Box 190
1 Opal Dr.
Logan Lake, BC V0K 1W0
Tel: 250-523-6225; *Fax:* 250-523-6678
districtofloganlake@loganlake.ca
www.loganlake.ca
Municipal Type: District
Incorporated: Nov. 10, 1970 *Area:* 325.4 sq km
County or District: Thompson-Nicola; *Population in 2006:* 2,162
Provincial Electoral District(s): Yale-Lillooet
Federal Electoral District(s): Okanagan-Coquihalla
Next Election: Nov. 2011 (3 year terms)
Marlon Dosch, Mayor
mdosch@loganlake.ca
Wayne Vollrath, Chief Administrative Officer
wvollrath@loganlake.ca

Lumby
P.O. Box 430
1775 Glencaird St.
Lumby, BC V0E 2G0
Tel: 250-547-2171; *Fax:* 250-547-6894
info@lumby.ca
www.lumby.ca
Municipal Type: Village
Incorporated: Dec. 20, 1955 *Area:* 5.27 sq km
County or District: North Okanagan; *Population in 2006:* 1,634
Provincial Electoral District(s): Okanagan-Vernon
Federal Electoral District(s): Okanagan-Shuswap
Next Election: Nov. 2011 (3 year terms)
Lori Mindnich, Mayor
mayor@lumby.ca
Frank Kosa, Village Administrator
fkosa@lumby.ca

Lytton
P.O. Box 100
380 Main St.
Lytton, BC V0K 1Z0
Tel: 250-455-2355; *Fax:* 250-455-2142
hotspot@lytton.ca
www.lytton.ca
Municipal Type: Village
Incorporated: May 3, 1945 *Area:* 6.71 sq km
County or District: Thompson-Nicola; *Population in 2006:* 235
Provincial Electoral District(s): Yale-Lillooet
Federal Electoral District(s): Chilliwack-Fraser Canyon
Next Election: Nov. 2011 (3 year terms)
Jessoa Lightfoot, Mayor
jlightfoot@lytton.ca
Ian Hay, Administrator
ian@lytton.ca

Mackenzie
P.O. Box 340
1 Mackenzie Blvd.
Mackenzie, BC V0J 2C0
Tel: 250-997-3221; *Fax:* 250-997-5186
info@district.mackenzie.bc.ca
www.district.mackenzie.bc.ca
Municipal Type: District
Incorporated: May 19, 1966 *Area:* 159.09 sq km
County or District: Fraser-Fort George; *Population in 2006:* 4,539
Provincial Electoral District(s): Prince George North
Federal Electoral District(s): Prince George-Peace River
Next Election: Nov. 2011 (3 year terms)
Stephanie Killam, Mayor
Mark Fercho, Chief Administrative Officer
mark@district.mackenzie.bc.ca

Maple Ridge
11995 Haney Pl.
Maple Ridge, BC V2X 6A9
Tel: 604-463-5221; *Fax:* 604-467-7329
enquiries@mapleridge.ca
www.mapleridge.ca
Municipal Type: District
Incorporated: Sept. 12, 1874 *Area:* 265.79 sq km
County or District: Metro Vancouver; *Population in 2006:* 68,949
Provincial Electoral District(s): Maple Ridge-Pitt Meadows; Maple Ridge-Mission
Federal Electoral District(s): Pitt Meadows-Maple Ridge-Mission
Next Election: Nov. 2011 (3 year terms)
Ernie Daykin, Mayor
edaykin@mapleridge.ca
Cheryl Ashlie, Councillor
cashlie@mapleridge.ca
Judy Dueck, Councillor
jdueck@mapleridge.ca
Al Hogarth, Councillor
ahogarth@mapleridge.ca
Linda King, Councillor
lking@mapleridge.ca
Mike Morden, Councillor
mmorden@mapleridge.ca
Craig Speirs, Councillor
cspeirs@mapleridge.ca
Jim Rule, Chief Administrative Officer
604-463-5221
jrule@mapleridge.ca
John Bastaja, Chief Information Officer
604-467-7479
jbastaja@mapleridge.ca
Paul Gill, General Manager, Corporate & Financial Services
pgill@mapleridge.ca
Frank Quinn, General Manager, Public Works & Development Services
fquinn@mapleridge.ca
Kelly Swift, General Manager, Community Development, Parks & Recreation Services
kswift@mapleridge.ca
David Boag, Director, Parks & Facilities
604-467-7344
dboag@mapleridge.ca
Russ Carmichael, Director, Engineering Operations
604-467-7363
Liz Holitzki, Director, Licences, Permits & Bylaws
604-467-7370
lholitzki@mapleridge.ca
Wendy McCormick, Director, Recreation
604-467-7328
wmccormick@mapleridge.ca
Jane Pickering, Director, Planning
604-467-7471
jpickering@mapleridge.ca
Sue Wheeler, Director, Community Services
604-467-7308
swheeler@mapleridge.ca
Fred Armstrong, Manager, Corporate Communications
farmstrong@mapleridge.ca
Chuck Goddard, Manager, Development & Environmental Services
604-466-4336
cgoddard@mapleridge.org
Ceri Marlo, P.Eng., Manager, Legislative Services
604-467-7482
cmarlo@mapleridge.ca
Peter Grootendorst, Fire Chief
604-476-3056
pgrootendorst@mapleridge.ca
Dave Walsh, Superintendent, Police Services
604-463-6251

Masset
P.O. Box 68
Masset, BC V0T 1M0
Tel: 250-626-3995; *Fax:* 250-626-3968
vom@mhtv.ca
www.massetbc.com
Municipal Type: Village
Incorporated: May 11, 1961 *Area:* 19.45 sq km
County or District: Skeena-Queen Charlotte; *Population in 2006:* 940
Provincial Electoral District(s): North Coast
Federal Electoral District(s): Skeena-Bulkley Valley
Next Election: Nov. 2011 (3 year terms)
Barry Pages, Mayor
Trevor Jarvis, Chief Administrative Officer

McBride
P.O. Box 519
100 Robson Centre
McBride, BC V0J 2E0
Tel: 250-569-2229; *Fax:* 250-569-3276
www.mcbride.ca
Municipal Type: Village
Incorporated: April 7, 1932 *Area:* 4.43 sq km
County or District: Fraser-Fort George; *Population in 2006:* 660
Provincial Electoral District(s): Prince George-Mount Robson
Federal Electoral District(s): Prince George-Peace River
Next Election: Nov. 2011 (3 year terms)
Michael Frazier, Mayor
Eliana Clements, Chief Administrative Officer

Merritt
P.O. Box 189
2185 Voght St.
Merritt, BC V1K 1B8
Tel: 250-378-4224; *Fax:* 250-378-2600
info@merritt.ca
www.merritt.ca
Municipal Type: Town
Incorporated: April 1, 1911 *Area:* 24.94 sq km
County or District: Thompson-Nicola; *Population in 2006:* 6,998
Provincial Electoral District(s): Yale-Lillooet
Federal Electoral District(s): Okanagan-Coquihalla
Next Election: Nov. 2011 (3 year terms)
Susan Roline, Mayor
mayorroline@merritt.ca
Matt Noble, Chief Administrative Officer/Clerk
mnoble@merritt.ca

Metchosin
4450 Happy Valley Rd.
Victoria, BC V9C 3Z3
Tel: 250-474-3167; *Fax:* 250-474-6298
info@metchosin.ca
www.metchosin.ca
Municipal Type: District
Incorporated: Dec. 3, 1984 *Area:* 71.32 sq km
County or District: Capital; *Population in 2006:* 4,795
Provincial Electoral District(s): Esquimalt-Metchosin
Federal Electoral District(s): Esquimalt-Juan de Fuca
Next Election: Nov. 2011 (3 year terms)
John Ranns, Mayor
jranns@metchosin.ca
Rachel Parker, Clerk
rparker@metchosin.ca
Joe Martignago, Chief Administrative Officer
cao@metchosin.ca

Midway
P.O. Box 160
661 Eighth Ave.
Midway, BC V0H 1M0
Tel: 250-449-2222; *Fax:* 250-449-2258
midwaybc@shaw.ca
www.midwaybc.ca
Municipal Type: Village
Incorporated: May 25, 1967 *Area:* 12.16 sq km
County or District: Kootenay Boundary; *Population in 2006:* 621
Provincial Electoral District(s): West Kootenay-Boundary
Federal Electoral District(s): British Columbia Southern Interior
Next Election: Nov. 2011 (3 year terms)
Randy Kappes, Mayor
Jim Madder, Administrator
jfmadder@shaw.ca

Mission
P.O. Box 20
8645 Stave Lake St.
Mission, BC V2V 4L9
Tel: 604-820-3700; *Fax:* 604-820-3715
info@mission.ca
www.mission.ca
Municipal Type: District
Incorporated: June 2, 1892 *Area:* 225.78 sq km
County or District: Fraser Valley; *Population in 2006:* 34,505
Provincial Electoral District(s): Maple Ridge-Mission
Federal Electoral District(s): Pitt Meadows-Maple Ridge-Mission
Next Election: Nov. 2011 (3 year terms)
James Atebe, Mayor
jatebe@mission.ca; atebejm@gmail.com
Terry Gidda, Councillor
terrygidda3@gmail.com
Paul Horn, Councillor
bootstrapconsulting@telus.net
Danny Plecas, Councillor
dannyplecas@hotmail.com
Mike Scudder, Councillor
mscudder@mission.ca
Jenny Stevens, Councillor
jennystevens@shaw.ca
Heather Stewart, Councillor
heatherstewart@shaw.ca
Glenn Robertson, Chief Administrative Officer
604-820-3704
grobertson@mission.ca
Kim Allan, Director, Forest Management
604-820-3764
kallan@mission.ca
Ken Bjorgaard, Director, Finance
kbjorgaard@mission.ca
Rick Bomhof, Director, Engineering & Public Works
604-820-3739
rbomhof@mission.ca
Sharon Fletcher, Director, Planning
604-820-3730
sfletcher@mission.ca
Ray Herman, Director, Parks, Recreation & Culture
604-820-5355
rherman@mission.ca
Beverly Endersby, Manager, Inspection Services
604-820-3732
bendersby@mission.ca
Michael Giesbrecht, Manager, Purchasing & Stores
604-820-3756
mgiesbrecht@mission.ca
Ian Fitzpatrick, Fire Chief
604-820-5390
ifitzpatrick@mission.ca

Montrose
P.O. Box 510
565 - 11th Ave.
Montrose, BC V0G 1P0
Tel: 250-367-7234; *Fax:* 250-367-7288
montvill@telus.net
www.montrose.ca
Municipal Type: Village
Incorporated: June 22, 1956 *Area:* 1.53 sq km
County or District: Kootenay Boundary; *Population in 2006:* 1,012
Provincial Electoral District(s): West Kootenay-Boundary
Federal Electoral District(s): British Columbia Southern Interior
Next Election: Nov. 2011 (3 year terms)
Griff Welsh, Mayor
Kevin Chartres, Chief Administrative Officer

Nakusp
P.O. Box 280
91 - 1st St. NW
Nakusp, BC V0G 1R0
Tel: 250-265-3689; *Fax:* 250-265-3788
info@nakusp.com
www.nakusp.com
Municipal Type: Village
Incorporated: Nov. 24, 1964 *Area:* 8 sq km
County or District: Central Kootenay; *Population in 2006:* 1,524
Provincial Electoral District(s): Nelson-Creston
Federal Electoral District(s): Kootenay-Columbia
Next Election: Nov. 2011 (3 year terms)
Karen Hamling, Mayor
khamling@nakusp.com
Linda Tynan, Acting Chief Administrative Officer
ltynan@nakusp.com

Nelson
#101, 310 Ward St.
Nelson, BC V1L 5S4
Tel: 250-352-5511; *Fax:* 250-352-2131
www.nelson.ca
Municipal Type: Town
Incorporated: March 18, 1897 *Area:* 11.72 sq km
County or District: Central Kootenay; *Population in 2006:* 9,258
Provincial Electoral District(s): Nelson-Creston
Federal Electoral District(s): British Columbia Southern Interior
Next Election: Nov. 2011 (3 year terms)
John Dooley, Mayor
250-354-9615
Kevin Cormack, City Manager
250-352-8203

New Denver
P.O. Box 40
115 Slocan Ave.
New Denver, BC V0G 1S0
Tel: 250-358-2316; *Fax:* 250-358-7251
office@newdenver.ca
www.newdenver.ca
Municipal Type: Village
Incorporated: Jan. 12, 1929 *Area:* 1.1 sq km
County or District: Central Kootenay; *Population in 2006:* 512
Provincial Electoral District(s): Nelson-Creston
Federal Electoral District(s): British Columbia Southern Interior
Next Election: Nov. 2011 (3 year terms)
Gary Wright, Mayor
Carol Gordon, Chief Administrative Officer

New Hazelton
P.O. Box 340
3026 Bowser St.
New Hazelton, BC V0J 2J0
Tel: 250-842-6571; *Fax:* 250-842-6077
info@newhazelton.ca
www.newhazelton.ca
Municipal Type: District
Incorporated: Dec. 15, 1980 *Area:* 25.64 sq km
County or District: Kitimat-Stikine; *Population in 2006:* 627
Provincial Electoral District(s): Bulkley Valley-Stikine
Federal Electoral District(s): Skeena-Bulkley Valley
Next Election: Nov. 2011 (3 year terms)
Pieter Weeber, Mayor
250-842-6247
pweeber@newhazelton.ca
Donny van Dyk, Chief Administrative Officer
donny@newhazelton.ca

North Cowichan
P.O. Box 278
7030 Trans Canada Hwy.
Duncan, BC V9L 3X4
Tel: 250-746-3100; *Fax:* 250-746-3133
info@northcowichan.bc.ca
www.northcowichan.bc.ca
Municipal Type: District
Incorporated: June 18, 1873 *Area:* 193.66 sq km
County or District: Cowichan Valley; *Population in 2006:* 27,557
Provincial Electoral District(s): Cowichan-Ladysmith
Federal Electoral District(s): Nanaimo-Cowichan
Next Election: Nov. 2011 (3 year terms)
Tom Walker, Mayor
council@northcowichan.ca
Garrett Elliot, Councillor
Ruth Hartmann, Councillor
Dave Haywood, Councillor
John Koury, Councillor
George Seymour, Councillor
Al Siebring, Councillor
Dave Devana, Chief Administrative Officer
Mark O. Ruttan, Deputy Chief Administrative Officer/Director
ruttan@northcowichan.bc.ca
Bruce L. Oliphant, Chief Building Inspector
oliphant@northcowichan.ca
Mark Frame, Director, Finance
frame@northcowichan.bc.ca
Scott Mack, Director, Planning & Development
John Mackay, Director, Engineering
Ernie Mansueti, Director, Parks & Recreation
mansueti@northcowichan.bc.ca

North Saanich
1620 Mills Rd.
North Saanich, BC V8L 5S9
Tel: 250-656-0781; *Fax:* 250-656-3155
admin@northsaanich.ca
www.northsaanich.ca
Municipal Type: District
Incorporated: Aug. 19, 1965 *Area:* 37.14 sq km
County or District: Capital; *Population in 2006:* 10,823
Provincial Electoral District(s): Saanich North & the Islands
Federal Electoral District(s): Saanich-Gulf Islands
Next Election: Nov. 2011 (3 year terms)
Alice Finall, Mayor
250-656-6668
Dunstan Browne, Councillor
250-655-4811
Peter Chandler, Councillor
250-656-7226
Ruby Commandeur, Councillor
250-655-3368
Cairine Green, Councillor
778-433-8585
Craig Mearns, Councillor
250-656-1173
Anny Scoones, Councillor
778-440-4124
Rob Buchanan, Chief Administrative Officer
250-655-5452
rbuchan@northsaanich.ca
Curt Kingsley, Manager, Corporate Services
250-655-5453
ckingsley@northsaanich.ca

Mark Brodrick, Director, Planning & Community Services
250-655-5471
mbrodrick@northsaanich.ca
Patrick O'Reilly, Director, Infrastructure Services
250-655-5461
poreilly@northsaanich.ca
Patricia Roberts, Director, Financial Services
250-655-5495
proberts@northsaanich.ca
Gary Wilton, Director, Emergency Services
250-661-0223
gwilton@northsaanich.ca

North Vancouver
355 West Queens Rd.
North Vancouver, BC V7N 4N5
Tel: 604-990-2311;
infoweb@dnv.org
www.dnv.org
Municipal Type: District Municipality
Incorporated: Aug. 10, 1891 *Area:* 160.67 sq km
County or District: Metro Vancouver; *Population in 2006:* 82,562
Provincial Electoral District(s): N. Vancouver-Lonsdale; N. Vancouver-Seymour; W. Vancouver-Capilano; W. Vancouver-Garibaldi
Federal Electoral District(s): North Vancouver; West Vancouver-Sunshine Coast-Sea to Sky Country
Next Election: Nov. 2011 (3 year terms)
Richard Walton, Mayor
604-990-2208
rwalton@dnv.org; council@dnv.org
Roger Bassam, Councillor
rbassam@dnv.org
Robin Hicks, Councillor
rhicks@dnv.org
Mike Little, Councillor
mlittle@dnv.org
Doug Mackay-Dunn, Councillor
dmackay-dunn@dnv.org
Lisa Muri, Councillor
lmuri@dnv.org
Alan Nixon, Councillor
anixon@dnv.org
David Stuart, Chief Administrative Officer
604-990-2209
stuartd@dnv.org
Brian Bydwell, Director, Planning, Permits & Bylaws
604-990-2387
bydwellb@dnv.org
Nicole Deveaux, Director, Financial Services
604-990-2233
deveauxn@dnv.org
Jozsef Dioszeghy, P.Eng., Director, Environment, Parks & Engineering
604-990-3885
dioszeghyj@dnv.org
Ian Forsyth, Director, The Arts Office
604-980-3559
ian.forsyth@nvoca.ca
Gavin Joyce, Director, Corporate Services
604-990-2416
joyceg@dnv.org
Dorit Mason, Director, North Shore Emergency Management Office
604-983-7440
dmason@cnv.org
Heather Scoular, Director, Library Services
604-990-5800
scoularh@nvdpl.ca
Heather Turner, Director, Recreation
604-983-6306
turnerh@northvanrec.com
Allen Lynch, Manager, North Shore Recycling Program
604-984-9730
allen@nsrp.bc.ca
Doug Trussler, Fire Chief
604-990-3651
dtrussler@dnv.org
Tonia Enger, Superintendent, North Vancouver RCMP Detachment
604-985-1311

Health Department
Brian O'Connor, Medical Health Officer

Oak Bay
2167 Oak Bay Ave.
Victoria, BC V8R 1G2
Tel: 250-598-3311; *Fax:* 250-598-9108
obcouncil@oakbay.ca
www.oakbaybc.org
Municipal Type: District
Incorporated: July 2, 1906 *Area:* 10.38 sq km
County or District: Capital; *Population in 2006:* 17,908
Provincial Electoral District(s): Oak Bay-Gordon Head
Federal Electoral District(s): Victoria
Next Election: Nov. 2011 (3 year terms)
Christopher M. Causton, Mayor
Hazel Braithwaite, Councillor
Pam Copley, Councillor
John Herbert, Councillor
Nils Jensen, Councillor
Tara Ney, Councillor
Loranne Hilton, Clerk
Mark Brennan, Administrator
Patricia A. Walker, Treasurer & Collector
Lorna Curtis, Director, Parks & Recreation
250-592-7275
Dave Marshall, Director, Engineering Services
Roy Thomassen, Director, Building & Planning
Janet Barclay, Manager, Recreation Program Services
Lorne Middleton, Manager, Parks Services
250-592-7275
Phil Barnett, Superintendent, Public Works
250-598-4501
Gerry Adam, Fire Chief
250-592-9121
Derek Egan, Interim Chief Constable
250-592-2424
Police Services

Oliver
P.O. Box 638
35016 - 97th St.
Oliver, BC V0H 1T0
Tel: 250-485-6200; *Fax:* 250-498-4466
admin@oliver.ca
www.oliver.ca
Municipal Type: Town
Incorporated: Dec. 31, 1945 *Area:* 4.95 sq km
County or District: Okanagan-Similkameen; *Population in 2006:* 4,370
Provincial Electoral District(s): Penticton-Okanagan Valley
Federal Electoral District(s): British Columbia Southern Interior
Next Election: Nov. 2011 (3 year terms)
Pat Hampson, Mayor
250-485-6205, Fax: 250-498-4466
phampson@oliver.ca
Tom Szalay, Municipal Manager
tszalay@oliver.ca

Osoyoos
P.O. Box 3010
8707 Main St.
Osoyoos, BC V0H 1V0
Tel: 250-495-6515; *Fax:* 250-495-2400
tosoyoos@osoyoos.ca
www.osoyoos.ca
Municipal Type: Town
Incorporated: Jan. 14, 1946 *Area:* 8.76 sq km
County or District: Okanagan-Similkameen; *Population in 2006:* 4,752
Provincial Electoral District(s): Penticton-Okanagan Valley
Federal Electoral District(s): British Columbia Southern Interior
Next Election: Nov. 2011 (3 year terms)
Stu Wells, Mayor
swells@osoyoos.ca
Barry Romanko, Chief Administrative Officer
bromanko@osoyoos.ca

Peachland
5806 Beach Ave.
Peachland, BC V0H 1X7
Tel: 250-767-2647; *Fax:* 250-767-3433
ppalmer@peachland.ca
www.peachland.ca
Municipal Type: District
Incorporated: Jan. 1, 1909 *Area:* 15.98 sq km
County or District: Central Okanagan; *Population in 2006:* 4,883
Provincial Electoral District(s): Okanagan-Westside
Federal Electoral District(s): Okanagan-Coquihalla
Next Election: Nov. 2011 (3 year terms)
Keith Fielding, Mayor
250-767-2770
mayor@peachland.ca
Elsie Lemke, Chief Administrative Officer
elemke@peachland.ca

Pemberton
P.O. Box 100
7400 Prospect St.
Pemberton, BC V0N 2L0
Tel: 604-894-6135; *Fax:* 604-894-6136
www.pemberton.ca
Municipal Type: Village
Incorporated: July 20, 1956 *Area:* 4.45 sq km
County or District: Squamish-Lillooet; *Population in 2006:* 2,192
Provincial Electoral District(s): West Vancouver-Garibaldi
Federal Electoral District(s): Chilliwack-Fraser Canyon
Next Election: Nov. 2011 (3 year terms)
Jordan Sturdy, Mayor
jsturdy@pemberton.ca
Daniel Sailland, Chief Administrative Officer
dsailland@pemberton.ca

Port Alice
P.O. Box 130
1061 Marine Dr.
Port Alice, BC V0N 2N0
Tel: 250-284-3391; *Fax:* 250-284-3416
info@portalice.ca
www.portalice.ca
Municipal Type: Village
Incorporated: June 16, 1965 *Area:* 7.65 sq km
County or District: Mount Waddington; *Population in 2006:* 821
Provincial Electoral District(s): North Island
Federal Electoral District(s): Vancouver Island North
Next Election: Nov. 2011 (3 year terms)
Gail Neely, Mayor
Gail Lind, Chief Administrative Officer

Port Clements
P.O. Box 198
36 Cedar Ave. West
Port Clements, BC V0T 1R0
Tel: 250-557-4295; *Fax:* 250-557-4568
office@portclements.com
www.portclements.com
Municipal Type: Village
Incorporated: Dec. 31, 1975 *Area:* 13.59 sq km
County or District: Skeena-Queen Charlotte; *Population in 2006:* 440
Provincial Electoral District(s): North Coast
Federal Electoral District(s): Skeena-Bulkley Valley
Next Election: Nov. 2011 (3 year terms)
Cory Delves, Mayor
cdelves@portclements.com
Heather Nelson-Smith, Clerk/Treasurer
heather@portclements.com

Port Edward
P.O. Box 1100
770 Pacific Ave.
Port Edward, BC V0V 1G0
Tel: 250-628-3667; *Fax:* 250-628-9225
info@portedward.ca
www.portedward.ca
Municipal Type: District
Incorporated: June 29, 1966 *Area:* 168.12 sq km
County or District: Skeena-Queen Charlotte; *Population in 2006:* 577
Provincial Electoral District(s): North Coast
Federal Electoral District(s): Skeena-Bulkley Valley
Next Election: Nov. 2011 (3 year terms)
Dave MacDonald, Mayor
Ron Bedard, Chief Administrative Officer

Port Hardy
P.O. Box 68
7360 Columbia St.
Port Hardy, BC V0N 2P0
Tel: 250-949-6665; *Fax:* 250-949-7433
general@porthardy.ca
www.porthardy.ca
Municipal Type: District
Incorporated: May 5, 1966 *Area:* 40.81 sq km
County or District: Mount Waddington; *Population in 2006:* 3,822
Provincial Electoral District(s): North Island
Federal Electoral District(s): Vancouver Island North
Next Election: Nov. 2011 (3 year terms)
Bev Parnham, Mayor
mayor@porthardy.ca
Rick Davidge, Chief Administrative Officer
rickd@porthardy.ca
Deb Clipperton, Director, Financial Services
dclipperton@porthardy.ca
Gloria LeGal, Director, Corporate Services
gloria@porthardy.ca

Port McNeill
P.O. Box 728
1775 Grenville Pl.
Port McNeill, BC V0N 2R0
Tel: 250-956-3111; *Fax:* 250-956-4300
reception.portmcneill@telus.net
www.town.portmcneill.bc.ca
Municipal Type: Town
Incorporated: Feb. 18, 1966 *Area:* 7.74 sq km
County or District: Mount Waddington; *Population in 2006:* 2,623
Provincial Electoral District(s): North Island
Federal Electoral District(s): Vancouver Island North
Next Election: Nov. 2011 (3 year terms)
Gerry Furney, Mayor
mayor.portmcneill@telus.net
Albert Sweet, BA CA, Administrator/Treasurer/Collector
pmfinance@telus.net

Pouce Coupé
P.O. Box 190
5011 - 49 Ave.
Pouce Coupe, BC V0C 2C0
Tel: 250-786-5794; *Fax:* 250-786-5257
admin@poucecoupe.ca
www.poucecoupe.ca
Municipal Type: Village
Incorporated: Jan. 5, 1932 *Area:* 2.06 sq km
County or District: Peace River; *Population in 2006:* 739
Provincial Electoral District(s): Peace River South
Federal Electoral District(s): Prince George-Peace River
Next Election: Nov. 2011 (3 year terms)
Lyman Clark, Mayor
mayor@poucecoupe.ca
Karen P. Mellor, Chief Administrative Officer
cao@poucecoupe.ca

Princeton
P.O. Box 670
169 Bridge St.
Princeton, BC V0X 1W0
Tel: 250-295-3135; *Fax:* 250-295-3477
admin@princeton.ca
www.princeton.ca
Municipal Type: Town
Incorporated: Sept. 11, 1951 *Area:* 10.25 sq km
County or District: Okanagan-Similkameen; *Population in 2006:* 2,677
Provincial Electoral District(s): Yale-Lillooet
Federal Electoral District(s): British Columbia Southern Interior
Next Election: Nov. 2011 (3 year terms)
Randy McLean, Mayor
Patrick Robins, Chief Administrative Officer

Qualicum Beach
P.O. Box 130
#201, 660 Primrose St.
Qualicum Beach, BC V9K 1S7
Tel: 250-752-6921; *Fax:* 250-752-1243
qbtown@qualicumbeach.com
www.qualicumbeach.com
Municipal Type: Town
Incorporated: May 5, 1942 *Area:* 18 sq km
County or District: Nanaimo; *Population in 2006:* 8,502
Provincial Electoral District(s): Alberni-Qualicum
Federal Electoral District(s): Nanaimo-Alberni
Next Election: Nov. 2011 (3 year terms)
Teunis Westbroek, Mayor
mayor@qualicumbeach.com
Mark D. Brown, Chief Administrative Officer
markb@qualicumbeach.com

Queen Charlotte
P.O. Box 580
903A Oceanview Dr.
Queen Charlotte, BC V0T 1S0
Tel: 250-559-4765; *Fax:* 250-559-4742
office@queencharlotte.ca
www.queencharlotte.ca
Municipal Type: Village
Incorporated: Dec. 7, 2005 *Area:* 37.28 sq km
County or District: Skeena-Queen Charlotte; *Population in 2006:* 948
Provincial Electoral District(s): North Coast
Federal Electoral District(s): Skeena-Bulkley Valley
Next Election: Nov. 2011 (3 year terms)
Carol Kulesha, Mayor
250-559-4634
Bill Beamish, Chief Administrative Officer
250-559-4765

Quesnel
410 Kinchant St.
Quesnel, BC V2J 7J5
Tel: 250-992-2111; *Fax:* 250-992-2206
cityhall@quesnel.ca
www.quesnel.ca
Municipal Type: Town
Incorporated: March 21, 1928 *Area:* 35.34 sq km
County or District: Cariboo; *Population in 2006:* 9,326
Provincial Electoral District(s): Cariboo North
Federal Electoral District(s): Cariboo-Prince George
Next Election: Nov. 2011 (3 year terms)
Mary Sjostrom, Mayor
msjostrom@quesnel.ca
Michael Cave, Councillor
mikecave@shaw.ca
Peter Couldwell, Councillor
250-249-5364
Coralee Oakes, Councillor
coralee@quesnelbc.com
Ron Paull, Councillor
ronpaull@shaw.ca
Laurey Roodenburg, Councillor
l_roodenburg@yahoo.ca
Sushil Thepar, Councillor
thaparquesnel@gmail.com
John Stecyk, City Manager
jstecyk@quesnel.ca
Jeff Norburn, General Manager, Community Services
jnorburn@quesnel.ca
Kari Bolton, Director, Finance
kbolton@quesnel.ca
Ken Coombs, Acting Director, Public Works & Engineering
kcoombs@quesnel.ca
Tanya Turner, Planner
tturner@quesnel.ca
Chris Coben, Superintendent, Utilities
ccoben@quesnel.ca
Alec Darragh, Supervisor, Parks & Solid Waste
adarragh@quesnel.ca
Sylvian Gauthier, Fire Department
sgauthier@quesnel.ca

Radium Hot Springs
P.O. Box 340
Radium Hot Springs, BC V0A 1M0
Tel: 250-347-6455; *Fax:* 250-347-9068
www.radiumhotsprings.ca
Municipal Type: Village
Incorporated: Dec. 10, 1990 *Area:* 6.31 sq km
County or District: East Kootenay; *Population in 2006:* 735
Provincial Electoral District(s): Columbia River-Revelstoke
Federal Electoral District(s): Kootenay Columbia
Next Election: Nov. 2011 (3 year terms)
Dee Conklin, Mayor
mayor@radiumhotsprings.ca
Mark Read, Chief Administrative Officer/Clerk/Approving Officer
mark.read@radiumhotsprings.ca

Revelstoke
P.O. Box 170
216 Mackenzie Ave.
Revelstoke, BC V0E 2S0
Tel: 250-837-2161; *Fax:* 250-837-4930
www.cityofrevelstoke.com
Municipal Type: Town
Incorporated: March 1, 1899 *Area:* 31.9 sq km
County or District: Columbia-Shuswap; *Population in 2006:* 7,230
Provincial Electoral District(s): Columbia River-Revelstoke
Federal Electoral District(s): Kootenay-Columbia
Next Election: Nov. 2011 (3 year terms)
David Raven, Mayor
david.raven@revelstoke.ca
Tim Palmer, Chief Adminsitrative Officer/Director, Corporate Administration

Rossland
P.O. Box 1179
1899 Columbia Ave.
Rossland, BC V0G 1Y0
Tel: 250-362-7396; *Fax:* 250-362-5451
cityhall@rossland.ca
www.rossland.ca
Municipal Type: Town
Incorporated: March 18, 1897 *Area:* 57.97 sq km
County or District: Kootenay Boundary; *Population in 2006:* 3,278
Provincial Electoral District(s): West Kootenay-Boundary
Federal Electoral District(s): British Columbia Southern Interior
Next Election: Nov. 2011 (3 year terms)
Greg Granstrom, Mayor
250-362-5527
Victor Kumar, Chief Administrative Officer
250-362-2324

Saanich
770 Vernon Ave.
Victoria, BC V8X 2W7
Tel: 250-475-1775;
www.saanich.ca
Municipal Type: District Municipality
Incorporated: Dec. 12, 1950 *Area:* 103.44 sq km
County or District: Capital; *Population in 2006:* 108,265
Provincial Electoral District(s): Oak Bay-Gordon Head; Saanich N. & the Islands; Saanich S.
Federal Electoral District(s): Esquimalt-Juan de Fuca; Saanich-Gulf Islands; Victoria
Next Election: Nov. 2011 (3 year terms)
Frank Leonard, Mayor
250-475-5510
mayor@saanich.ca; council@saanich.ca
Susan Brice, Councillor
Judy Brownoff, Councillor
jbrownof@telus.net
Vic Derman, Councillor
Paul Gerrard, Councillor
Wayne Hunter, Councillor
Dean Murdock, Councillor
dean.murdock@telus.net
Vicki Sanders, Councillor
vicki_sanders@telus.net
Leif Wergeland, Councillor
wergeland@shaw.ca
Tim Wood, Administrator
250-475-5555, Fax: 250-475-5440
tim.wood@saanich.ca
Bonnie Cole, Director, Corporate Services
bonnie.cole@saanich.ca
Colin Doyle, Director, Engineering
250-475-5575, Fax: 250-475-5450
colin.doyle@saanich.ca
Doug Henderson, Director, Parks & Recreation
250-475-5421, Fax: 250-475-5411
doug.henderson@saanich.ca
Sharon Hvozdanski, Director, Planning
250-475-5470, Fax: 250-475-5430
sharon.hvozdanski@saanich.ca
Carrie M. MacPhee, Director, Legislative Services
carrie.macphee@saanich.ca
Paul Murray, Director, Finance
250-475-5521, Fax: 250-475-5429
paul.murray@saanich.ca
Donavon (Von) Bishop, Manager, Development & Municipal Facilities
von.bishop@saanich.ca
Dwayne Halldorson, Manager, Underground Services
250-475-5574, Fax: 250-475-5450
dwayne.halldorson@saanich.ca
Jim Hemstock, Manager, Transportation
250-475-5464, Fax: 250-475-5450
jim.hemstock@saanich.ca
Mike Ippen, Manager, Public Works
250-475-5494, Fax: 250-475-5487
mike.ippen@saanich.ca
Alan Keiser, Manager, Water Works
250-475-5494, Fax: 250-475-5487
alan.keiser@saanich.ca
Quenton Lehmann, Manager, Recreation
250-475-5452, Fax: 250-475-5411
quenton.lehmann@saanich.ca
Cory Manton, Manager, Forestry, Horticulture & Natural Areas
250-475-5488
cory.manton@saanich.ca
Dave McAra, Manager, Solid Waste Services
250-475-5432, Fax: 250-475-5590
david.mcara@saanich.ca
Adriane Pollard, Manager, Environmental Services
250-475-5494, Fax: 250-475-5430
adriane.pollard@saanich.ca
Anne Topp, Manager, Community Planning
250-475-5494, Fax: 250-457-5430
anne.topp@saanich.ca
Michael Burgess, Fire Chief
Mike Chadwick, Chief Constable
250-475-4321, Fax: 250-475-6138
community@saanichpolice.ca

Salmo
P.O. Box 1000
423 Davies Ave.
Salmo, BC V0G 1Z0
Tel: 250-357-9433; *Fax:* 250-357-9633
salvil@telus.net
salmo.ca
Municipal Type: Village
Incorporated: Oct. 30, 1946 *Area:* 2.38 sq km
County or District: Central Kootenay; *Population in 2006:* 1,007
Provincial Electoral District(s): Nelson-Creston
Federal Electoral District(s): British Columbia Southern Interior
Next Election: Nov. 2011 (3 year terms)
Ann Henderson, Mayor
Scott Sommerville, Chief Administrative Officer

Sayward
P.O. Box 29
601 Kelsey Way
Sayward, BC V0P 1R0
Tel: 250-282-5512; *Fax:* 250-282-5511
www.sayward.ca
Municipal Type: Village
Incorporated: June 27, 1968 *Area:* 4.72 sq km
County or District: Strathcona; *Population in 2006:* 341
Provincial Electoral District(s): North Island
Federal Electoral District(s): Vancouver Island North
Next Election: Nov. 2011 (3 year terms)
John MacDonald, Mayor
westie@saywardvalley.net
Colum McCready, Chief Administrative Officer/Chief Financial Officer
cao@saywardvalley.net

Sechelt
P.O. Box 129
5797 Cowrie St., 2nd Fl.
Sechelt, BC V0N 3A0
Tel: 604-885-1986; *Fax:* 604-885-7591
info@sechelt.ca
www.sechelt.ca
Municipal Type: District Municipality
Incorporated: Feb. 15, 1956 *Area:* 39.71 sq km
County or District: Sunshine Coast; *Population in 2006:* 8,454
Provincial Electoral District(s): Powell River-Sunshine Coast
Federal Electoral District(s): West Vancouver-Sunshine Coast-Sea to Sky Country
Next Election: Nov. 2011 (3 year terms)
Darren Inkster, Mayor
inkster@sechelt.ca
Warren Allan, Councillor
allan@sechelt.ca
Alice Janisch, Councillor
janisch@sechelt.ca
Ann Kershaw, Councillor
kershaw@sechelt.ca
Alice Lutes, Councillor
lutes@sechelt.ca
Fred Taylor, Councillor
taylor@sechelt.ca
Keith Thirkell, Councillor
thirkell@sechelt.ca
Rob Brenner, Chief Administrative Officer
rbremner@sechelt.ca

Sicamous
P.O. Box 219
446 Main St.
Sicamous, BC V0E 2V0
Tel: 250-836-2477; *Fax:* 250-836-4314
cityhall@sicamous.ca
www.sicamous.ca
Municipal Type: District
Incorporated: Dec. 4, 1989 *Area:* 14.68 sq km
County or District: Columbia-Shuswap; *Population in 2006:* 2,676
Provincial Electoral District(s): Shuswap
Federal Electoral District(s): Okanagan-Shuswap
Next Election: Nov. 2011 (3 year terms)
Malcolm MacLeod, Mayor
mayor@sicamous.ca
Alan Harris, Chief Administrative Officer
aharris@sicamous.ca

Silverton
P.O. Box 14
421 Lake Ave.
Silverton, BC V0G 2B0
Tel: 250-358-2472; *Fax:* 250-358-2321
administration@silverton.ca
www.silverton.ca
Municipal Type: Village
Incorporated: May 6, 1930 *Area:* 0.44 sq km
County or District: Central Kootenay; *Population in 2006:* 185
Provincial Electoral District(s): Nelson-Creston
Federal Electoral District(s): British Columbia Southern Interior
Next Election: Nov. 2011 (3 year terms)
John Everett, Mayor
mayor@silverton.ca
Elaine Rogers, Acting Chief Administrative Officer
cfo@silverton.ca

Slocan
P.O. Box 50
503 Slocan Ave.
Slocan, BC V0G 2C0
Tel: 250-355-2277; *Fax:* 250-355-2666
info@villageofslocan.ca
www.slocancity.com
Other Information: Toll Free Phone: 1-866-355-2023
Municipal Type: Village
Incorporated: June 1, 1901 *Area:* 0.75 sq km
County or District: Central Kootenay; *Population in 2006:* 314
Provincial Electoral District(s): Nelson-Creston
Federal Electoral District(s): British Columbia Southern Interior
Next Election: Nov. 2011 (3 year terms)
Madeline Perriere, Mayor
Jack Richardson, Chief Administrative Officer

Smithers
P.O. Box 879
1027 Aldous St.
Smithers, BC V0J 2N0
Tel: 250-847-1600; *Fax:* 250-847-1601
general@smithers.ca
www.smithers.ca
Municipal Type: Town
Incorporated: Oct. 6, 1921 *Area:* 15.69 sq km
County or District: Bulkley-Nechako; *Population in 2006:* 5,217
Provincial Electoral District(s): Bulkley Valley-Stikine
Federal Electoral District(s): Skeena-Bulkley Valley
Next Election: Nov. 2011 (3 year terms)
Cress Farrow, Mayor
Deborah Sargent, Chief Administrative Officer

Sooke
2205 Otter Point Rd.
Sooke, BC V9Z 1J2
Tel: 250-642-1634; *Fax:* 250-642-0541
info@sooke.ca
www.sooke.ca
Municipal Type: District
Incorporated: Dec. 7, 1999 *Area:* 50.01 sq km
County or District: Capital; *Population in 2006:* 9,704
Provincial Electoral District(s): Malahat-Juan de Fuca
Federal Electoral District(s): Esquimalt-Juan de Fuca
Next Election: Nov. 2011 (3 year terms)
Janet Evans, Mayor
jevans@sooke.ca
Evan Parliament, Chief Administrative Officer
eparliament@sooke.ca

Spallumcheen
4144 Spallumcheen Way
Spallumcheen, BC V0E 1B6
Tel: 250-546-3013; *Fax:* 250-546-8878
mail@spallumcheentwp.bc.ca
www.spallumcheentwp.bc.ca
Municipal Type: Township
Area: 254.9 sq km
County or District: North Okanagan; *Population in 2006:* 4,960
Provincial Electoral District(s): Shuswap
Federal Electoral District(s): Okanagan-Shuswap
Next Election: Nov. 2011 (3 year terms)
Will Hansma, Mayor
mayor@spallumcheentwp.bc.ca
Lynda Shykora, Chief Administrative Officer

Sparwood
P.O. Box 520
136 Spruce Ave.
Sparwood, BC V0B 2G0
Tel: 250-425-6271; *Fax:* 250-425-7277
sparwood@sparwood.bc.ca
www.sparwood.bc.ca
Municipal Type: District
Incorporated: Oct. 6, 1964 *Area:* 177.71 sq km
County or District: East Kootenay; *Population in 2006:* 3,618
Provincial Electoral District(s): East Kootenay
Federal Electoral District(s): Kootenay-Columbia
Next Election: Nov. 2011 (3 year terms)
Sharon Fraser, Acting Mayor
mfraser5@telus.net
Terry Melcer, Chief Administrative Officer/Director, Corporate Services
tmelcer@sparwood.bc.ca

Squamish
P.O. Box 310
37955 Second Ave.
Squamish, BC V0N 3G0
Tel: 604-892-5217; *Fax:* 604-892-1083
www.squamish.ca
Municipal Type: District
Incorporated: May 18, 1948 *Area:* 106.11 sq km
County or District: Squamish-Lillooet; *Population in 2006:* 14,949
Provincial Electoral District(s): West Vancouver-Garibaldi
Federal Electoral District(s): West Vancouver-Sunshine Coast-Sea to Sky Country
Next Election: Nov. 2011 (3 year terms)
Greg Gardner, Mayor
ggardner@squamish.ca
Bryan Raiser, Councillor
braiser@squamish.ca
Corinne Lonsdale, Councillor
clonsdale@squamish.ca
Doug Race, Councillor
drace@squamish.ca
Patricia Heintzman, Councillor
pheintzman@squamish.ca
Paul Lalli, Councillor
plalli@squamish.ca
Rob Kirkham, Councillor
rkirkham@squamish.ca
Kevin Ramsay, Chief Administrative Officer
604-892-5217
kramsay@squamish.ca
Mark Caulton, Acting Chief Operator, Waterworks
mcaulton@squamish.ca
Wayne Chadwick, Acting Chief Operator, Wastewater Treatment Plant
wchadwick@squamish.ca
Robin Arthurs, General Manager, Corporate Services
rarthurs@squamish.ca
Cameron Chalmers, General Manager, Community Services
604-815-5000
cchalmers@squamish.ca
Linda Glenday, General Manager, Protective & Support Services
lglenday@squamish.ca .
Joanne Greenless, General Manager, Financial Services
jgreenlees@squamish.ca
Chris Bishop, Acting Manager, Planning & Building
cbishop@squamish.ca
Bob Smith, Manager, Operations
bsmith@squamish.ca
Jim Lang, Coordinator, Emergency Program
jlang@squamish.ca
Russ Inouye, Acting Fire Chief
rinouye@squamish.ca

Stewart
P.O. Box 460
705 Brightwell St.
Stewart, BC V0T 1W0
Tel: 250-636-2251; *Fax:* 250-636-2417
info@districtofstewart.com
www.districtofstewart.com
Municipal Type: District
Incorporated: May 16, 1930 *Area:* 571.5 sq km
County or District: Kitimat-Stikine; *Population in 2006:* 496
Provincial Electoral District(s): North Coast
Federal Electoral District(s): Skeena-Bulkley Valley
Next Election: Nov. 2011 (3 year terms)
Angela Brand Danuser, Mayor
mayor@districtofstewart.com
Douglas Jay, Chief Administrative Officer

Summerland
P.O. Box 159
11321 Henry Ave.
Summerland, BC V0H 1Z0
Tel: 250-494-6451; *Fax:* 250-494-1415
info@summerland.ca
www.summerland.ca
Municipal Type: District
Incorporated: Dec. 21, 1906 *Area:* 73.88 sq km
County or District: Okanagan-Similkameen; *Population in 2006:* 10,828
Provincial Electoral District(s): Okanagan-Westside
Federal Electoral District(s): Okanagan-Coquihalla
Next Election: Nov. 2011 (3 year terms)
Janice Perrino, Mayor
Lloyd Christopherson, Councillor
Gordon Clark, Councillor

Sam Elia, Councillor
Bruce Hallquist, Councillor
Jim Kyluik, Councillor
Ken Roberge, Councillor
Don DeGagne, Chief Administrative Officer
ddegagne@summerland.ca
Don Darling, Director, Engineering & Public Works
ddarling@summerland.ca
Dale McDonald, Director, Parks & Recreation
dmacdonald@summerland.ca
Ian McIntosh, Director, Development Services
imcintosh@summerland.ca
Ken Ostraat, Director, Finance
kostraat@summerland.ca
Dave Hill, Superintendent, Public Works
dhill@summerland.ca
Scott Lee, Superintendent, Water Operations
slee@summerland.ca
Glenn Noble, Fire Chief
gnoble@summerland.ca

Tahsis
P.O. Box 219
Tahsis, BC V0P 1X0
Tel: 250-934-6344;
reception@villageoftahsis.com
www.villageoftahsis.com
Municipal Type: Village
Incorporated: June 17, 1970 *Area:* 5.73 sq km
County or District: Strathcona; *Population in 2006:* 366
Provincial Electoral District(s): North Island
Federal Electoral District(s): Vancouver Island North
Next Election: Nov. 2011 (3 year terms)
Corrine Dahling, Mayor
mayor@villageoftahsis.com
Harmony Nielsen, Corporate Officer, Corporate Administration
hnielsen@villageoftahsis.com

Taylor
P.O. Box 300
10007 - 100A St.
Taylor, BC V0C 2K0
Tel: 250-789-3392; *Fax:* 250-789-3543
www.districtoftaylor.com
Municipal Type: District
Incorporated: Aug. 23, 1958 *Area:* 16.61 sq km
County or District: Peace River; *Population in 2006:* 1,384
Provincial Electoral District(s): Peace River South
Federal Electoral District(s): Prince George-Peace River
Next Election: Nov. 2011 (3 year terms)
Fred S. Jarvis, Mayor
Charlette LcLeod, Administrator
cmcleod@districtoftaylor.com

Telkwa
P.O. Box 220
1704 Riverside St.
Telkwa, BC V0J 2X0
Tel: 250-846-5212; *Fax:* 250-846-9572
info@telkwa.com
www.telkwa.com
Municipal Type: Village
Incorporated: July 18, 1952 *Area:* 6.56 sq km
County or District: Bulkley-Nechako; *Population in 2006:* 1,295
Provincial Electoral District(s): Bulkley Valley-Stikine
Federal Electoral District(s): Skeena-Bulkley Valley
Next Election: Nov. 2011 (3 year terms)
Carman Graf, Mayor
Kim Martinsen, Chief Administrative Officer

Tofino
P.O. Box 9
121 Third St.
Tofino, BC V0R 2Z0
Tel: 250-725-3229; *Fax:* 250-725-3775
office@tofino.ca
www.tofino.ca
Municipal Type: District
Incorporated: Feb. 5, 1932 *Area:* 10.54 sq km
County or District: Alberni-Clayoquot; *Population in 2006:* 1,655
Provincial Electoral District(s): Alberni-Qualicum
Federal Electoral District(s): Nanaimo-Alberni
Next Election: Nov. 2011 (3 year terms)
John Fraser, Mayor
fraser@tofino.ca
Braden Smith, Chief Administrative Officer
bsmith@tofino.ca

Trail
1394 Pine Ave.
Trail, BC V1R 4E6
Tel: 250-364-1262; *Fax:* 250-364-0830
info@trail.ca
www.trail.ca
Municipal Type: Town
Incorporated: June 14, 1901 *Area:* 34.78 sq km
County or District: Kootenay Boundary; *Population in 2006:* 7,237
Provincial Electoral District(s): West Kootenay-Boundary
Federal Electoral District(s): British Columbia Southern Interior
Next Election: Nov. 2011 (3 year terms)
Dieter Bogs, Mayor
dbogs@trail.ca
Dave Perehudoff, Chief Administrative Officer/Financial Administrator
dperehudoff@trail.ca

Tumbler Ridge
P.O. Box 100
305 Founders St.
Tumbler Ridge, BC V0C 2W0
Tel: 250-242-4242; *Fax:* 250-242-3993
tradmin@dtr.ca
www.tumblerridge.ca
Municipal Type: District
Incorporated: April 9, 1981 *Area:* 1,574.45 sq km
County or District: Peace River; *Population in 2006:* 2,454
Provincial Electoral District(s): Peace River South
Federal Electoral District(s): Prince George-Peace River
Next Election: Nov. 2011 (3 year terms)
Larry White, Mayor
lwhite@dtr.ca
Barry Elliot, Chief Administrative Officer
250-242-4242

Ucluelet
P.O. Box 999
200 Main St.
Ucluelet, BC V0R 3A0
Tel: 250-726-7744; *Fax:* 250-726-7335
info@ucluelet.ca
www.ucluelet.ca
Municipal Type: District
Incorporated: Feb. 26, 1952 *Area:* 6.55 sq km
County or District: Alberni-Clayoquot; *Population in 2006:* 1,487
Provincial Electoral District(s): Alberni-Qualicum
Federal Electoral District(s): Nanaimo-Alberni
Next Election: Nov. 2011 (3 year terms)
Eric Russcher, Mayor
Andrew Yeates, Chief Administrative officer

Valemount
P.O. Box 168
735 Cranberry Lake Rd.
Valemount, BC V0E 2Z0
Tel: 250-566-4435; *Fax:* 250-566-4249
office@valemount.ca
www.valemount.ca
Municipal Type: Village
Incorporated: Dec. 13, 1962 *Area:* 4.96 sq km
County or District: Fraser-Fort George; *Population in 2006:* 1,018
Provincial Electoral District(s): Prince George-Mount Robson
Federal Electoral District(s): Kamloops-Thompson-Cariboo
Next Election: Nov. 2011 (3 year terms)
Bob Smith, Mayor
mayor@valemount.ca
Tom Dall, Chief Administrative Officer
cao@valemount.ca

Vanderhoof
P.O. Box 900
160 Connaught St.
Vanderhoof, BC V0J 3A0
Tel: 250-567-4711; *Fax:* 250-567-9169
info@district.vanderhoof.ca
www.vanderhoof.ca/district.html
Municipal Type: District
Incorporated: Jan. 22, 1926 *Area:* 54.85 sq km
County or District: Bulkley-Nechako; *Population in 2006:* 4,064
Provincial Electoral District(s): Prince George-Omineca
Federal Electoral District(s): Cariboo-Prince George
Next Election: Nov. 2011 (3 year terms)
Gerry Thiessen, Mayor
mayor@district.vanderhoof.ca
Joe Ukryn, Chief Administrative Officer
cao@district.vanderhoof.ca

View Royal
45 View Royal Ave.
Victoria, BC V9B 1A6
Tel: 250-479-6800; *Fax:* 250-727-9551
www.viewroyal.ca
Municipal Type: Town
Incorporated: Dec. 5, 1988 *Area:* 14.48 sq km
County or District: Capital; *Population in 2006:* 8,768
Provincial Electoral District(s): Esquimalt-Metchosin
Federal Electoral District(s): Esquimalt-Juan de Fuca
Next Election: Nov. 2011 (3 year terms)
Graham Hill, Mayor
mayorandcouncil@town.viewroyal.bc.ca
K. Anema, Chief Administrative Officer

Warfield
555 Schofield Hwy.
Trail, BC V1R 2G7
Tel: 250-368-8202; *Fax:* 250-368-9354
www.warfield.ca
Municipal Type: Village
Incorporated: Dec. 8, 1952 *Area:* 1.9 sq km
County or District: Kootenay Boundary; *Population in 2006:* 1,729
Provincial Electoral District(s): West Kootenay-Boundary
Federal Electoral District(s): British Columbia Southern Interior
Next Election: Nov. 2011 (3 year terms)
James Nelson, Mayor
Vince Morelli, CAO/Clerk/Treasurer

Wells
P.O. Box 219
Wells, BC V0K 2R0
Tel: 250-994-3330; *Fax:* 250-994-3331
wells@goldcity.net
www.district.wells.bc.ca
Municipal Type: District
Incorporated: June 29, 1998 *Area:* 159.15 sq km
County or District: Cariboo; *Population in 2006:* 236
Provincial Electoral District(s): Cariboo North
Federal Electoral District(s): Cariboo-Prince George
Next Election: Nov. 2011 (3 year terms)
Jay Vermette, Mayor
Sundance Topham, Chief Administrative Officer
administrator@district.wells.bc.ca

West Kelowna
2760 Cameron Rd.
West Kelowna, BC V1Z 2T6
Tel: 778-797-1000; *Fax:* 778-797-1001
info@districtofwestkelowna.ca
www.districtofwestkelowna.ca
Municipal Type: District
Incorporated: Dec. 6, 2007 *Area:* 121.4 sq km
County or District: Central Okanagan; *Population in 2007:* 28,793
Provincial Electoral District(s): Westside-Kelowna
Federal Electoral District(s): Okanagan-Coquihalla
Next Election: Nov. 2011

Council
Doug Findlater, Mayor
250-801-3814
doug.findlater@districtofwestkelowna.ca
David Knowles, Councillor
250-801-4479
david.knowles@districtofwestkelowna.ca
Gord Milsom, Councillor
250-801-4781
gord.milsom@districtofwestkelowna.ca
Rosalind Neis, Councillor
250-801-3795
rosalind.neis@districtofwestkelowna.ca
Duane Ophus, Councillor
250-801-5281
duane.ophus@districtofwestkelowna.ca
Bryden Winsby, Councillor
250-801-9557
bryden.winsby@districtofwestkelowna.ca
Carol Zanon, Councillor
250-801-5937
carol.zanon@districtofwestkelowna.ca

Council
Tracey Batten, City Clerk
778-797-2250
Jason Johnson, Chief Administrative Officer
778-797-2210
Jim Zaffino, Chief Financial Officer
778-797-8860
Nancy Henderson, Director, Planning
778-797-8830
Marnie Manders, Director

Gary O'Rourke, Director, Engineering
778-797-8840
Dave Slobodan, Director, Building & Regulatory Services
Linda Langston-Vicioso, Manager, Human Resources
778-797-8890
Lorne Raymond, Manager, Finance
Dallas Johnson, Senior Planner
Wayne Schnitzler, Fire Chief
250-769-1640, Fax: 250-769-4800
Duncan Dixon, Commander, RCMP West Kelowna Detachment
250-768-2880

West Vancouver
750 - 17 St.
West Vancouver, BC V7V 3T3
Tel: 604-925-7000; *Fax:* 604-925-5999
info@westvancouver.ca
www.westvancouver.ca
Municipal Type: District
Incorporated: March 15, 1912 *Area:* 87.13 sq km
County or District: Metro Vancouver; *Population in 2006:* 42,131
Provincial Electoral District(s): N. Vancouver-Lonsdale; W. Vancouver-Capilano; W. Vancouver-Garibaldi
Federal Electoral District(s): West Vancouver-Sunshine Coast-Sea to Sky Country
Next Election: Nov. 2011 (3 year terms)
Pamela Goldsmith-Jones, Mayor
pgoldsmith-jones@westvancouver.ca
Michael Evison, Councillor
mevison@westvancouver.ca
Michael Lewis, Councillor
mlewis@westvancouver.ca
Trish Panz, Councillor
tpanz@westvancouver.ca
Michael Smith, Councillor
msmith@westvancouver.ca
Bill Soporovich, Councillor
bsoprovich@westvancouver.ca; wsbs@shaw.ca
Shannon Walker, Councillor
shannonwalker@westvancouver.ca
Grant McRadu, Chief Administrative Officer
604-925-7008
gmcradu@westvancouver.ca
Jenny Benedict, Director, Library Services
604-925-7274
jbenedict@westvanlibrary.ca
Jessica Delaney, Director, Communications
604-925-4736
jdelaney@westvancouver.ca
Raymond Fung, Director, Engineering & Transportation
604-925-7159
rfung@westvancouver.ca
Nina Leemhuis, Director, Financial Services
604-925-7084
nleemhuis@westvancouver.ca
Anne Mooi, Director, Parks & Community Services
604-925-7235
amooi@westvancouver.ca
Bob Sokol, Director, Planning, Lands & Permits
604-925-7058
bsokol@westvancouver.ca
Allen Lynch, Manager, North Shore Recycling Program
604-984-9730, Fax: 604-984-3563
John McMahon, Acting Manager, Roads & Transportation
604-921-2197
jmcmahon@westvancouver.ca
Gareth Rowlands, Acting Manager, Transit
604-985-3500
growlands@westvancouver.ca
Jim Cook, Fire Chief
604-925-7370
jcook@westvancouver.ca

Whistler
4325 Blackcomb Way
Whistler, BC V0N 1B4
Tel: 604-932-5535; *Fax:* 604-935-8109
info@whistler.ca
www.whistler.ca
Municipal Type: Resort Municipality
Incorporated: Sept. 6, 1975 *Area:* 161.71 sq km
County or District: Squamish-Lillooet; *Population in 2006:* 9,248
Provincial Electoral District(s): West Vancouver-Garibaldi
Federal Electoral District(s): West Vancouver-Sunshine Coast-Sea to Sky Country
Next Election: Nov. 2011 (3 year terms)
Ken Melamed, Mayor
mayorsoffice@whistler.ca
Bill Barrett, Administrator
604-935-8105
bbarrett@whistler.ca

Zeballos
P.O. Box 127
Zeballos, BC V0P 2A0
Tel: 250-761-4229; *Fax:* 250-761-4331
adminzeb@recn.ca
www.zeballos.com
Municipal Type: Village
Incorporated: June 27, 1952 *Area:* 130 sq km
County or District: Strathcona; *Population in 2006:* 189
Provincial Electoral District(s): North Island
Federal Electoral District(s): Vancouver Island North
Next Election: Nov. 2011 (3 year terms)
Edward (Ted) Lewis, Mayor
Holli Bellavie, Chief Administrative Officer

Indian Government District in British Columbia

Sechelt
P.O. Box 740
5555 Sunshine Coast Hwy.
Sechelt, BC V0N 3A0
Tel: 604-885-2273;
rbaptiste@secheltnation.net
www.secheltnation.ca
Municipal Type: Metis Settlement
Incorporated: March 17, 1988 *Area:* 10.95 sq km
Population in 2006: 844
Next Election: Nov. 2011 (3 year terms)
Garry Feschuk, Chief
604-885-2273

MANITOBA

All municipalities in Manitoba (except Winnipeg, which is governed by the City of Winnipeg Act) come under authority of the Manitoba Municipal Act.

In Manitoba there are no counties or regional governments; there are only urban and rural municipalities. Incorporation of a new municipality requires a population of at least 1,000 residents and a population density of at least 400 residents per square kilometre for an urban municipality and a population density of less than 400 residents per square kilometre for a rural municipality. Urban municipalities may be called cities, towns, villages or urban municipalities. The population requirement for a city is at least 7,500 residents.

All municipal elections are held every four years (October 2010, October 2014, etc.).

Reproduced with the permission of Natural Resources Canada 2011, courtesy of the Atlas of Canada.

Manitoba

Major Municipalities in Manitoba

Brandon
410 - 9th St.
Brandon, MB R7A 6A2
Tel: 204-729-2186; *Fax:* 204-729-8244
cityclerk@brandon.ca
www.brandon.ca
Municipal Type: City
Incorporated: May 3, 1882 *Area:* 76.89 sq km
Population in 2006: 41,511
Provincial Electoral District(s): Brandon East; Brandon West
Federal Electoral District(s): Brandon-Souris
Next Election: Oct. 2014 (4 year terms)
Conrad R. Arvisais, City Clerk
204-729-2207, Fax: 204-729-0975
c.arvisais@brandon.ca
Shari Decter Hirst, Mayor
mayor@brandon.ca
Jeff Fawcett, Councillor, Ward(s): 1. Assiniboine
Grant McMillan, General Manager & City Treasurer, Corporate Services
204-729-2209
g.mcmillan@brandon.ca
Corey Roberts, Councillor, Ward(s): 2. Rosser
Brian MacRae, City Manager
204-729-2204, Fax: 204-729-0975
b.macrae@brandon.ca
Murray Blight, Councillor, Ward(s): 3. Victoria
Brian Kayes, Director, Emergency Coordination
best@brandon.ca
Jeff Harwood, Councillor, Ward(s): 4. University
Rick Bailey, Director, Public Works
r.bailey@brandon.ca
James McCrae, Councillor, Ward(s): 5. Meadows
Jeff Roziere, Director, Sanitation
204-573-6480
j.roziere@brandon.ca
Garth Rice, Councillor, Ward(s): 6. South Centre
Cathy Snelgrove, General Manager, Operations
204-729-2145, Fax: 204-729-2191
c.snelgrove@brandon.ca
Shawn Berry, Councillor, Ward(s): 7. Linden Lanes
Ted Snure, General Manager & City Engineer, Development Services
204-729-2214, Fax: 204-725-3235
t.snure@brandon.ca
Stephen Montague, Councillor, Ward(s): 8. Richmond
Ian Christiansen, Manager, Engineering Services & Water Resources
i.christiansen@brandon.ca
Len Isleifson, Councillor, Ward(s): 9. Riverview
Sandy Trudel, Officer, Economic Development
s.trudel@brandon.ca
Jan Chaboyer, Councillor, Ward(s): 10. Green Acres
Vivianne Lockerby, CPP, Supervisor, Purchasing
v.lockerby@brandon.ca
Brent Dane, Fire Chief
204-729-2404, Fax: 204-729-2153
b.dane@brandon.ca

Flin Flon
20 - 1st Ave.
Flin Flon, MB R8A 0T7
Tel: 204-684-7511; *Fax:* 204-681-7530
mkolt@city.flinflon.mb.ca
www.cityofflinflon.com
Municipal Type: City
Incorporated: Jan. 1, 1933 *Area:* 13.88 sq km
Population in 2006: 5,836
Provincial Electoral District(s): Flin Flon
Federal Electoral District(s): Churchill
Next Election: Oct. 2014 (4 year terms)
Note: Flin Flon straddles a provincial boundary. The population shown represents Manitoba (5,594) & Saskatchewan (242) figures.
George Fontaine, Mayor
Mark Kolt, Chief Administrative Officer

Portage La Prairie
97 Saskatchewan Ave. East
Portage la Prairie, MB R1N 0L8
Tel: 204-239-8337; *Fax:* 204-239-1532
swilliams@city-plap.com
www.city-plap.com
Municipal Type: City
Incorporated: Jan. 3, 1907 *Area:* 24.67 sq km
Population in 2006: 12,728
Provincial Electoral District(s): Portage la Prairie
Federal Electoral District(s): Portage-Lisgar
Next Election: Oct. 2014 (4 year terms)
Earl Porter, Mayor
eporter@city-plap.com
Brent Budz, Councillor
bbudz@city-plap.com
Liz Driedger, Councillor
ldriedger@city-plap.com
Ryan Espey, Councillor
respey@city-plap.com
Irvine Ferris, Councillor
iferris@city-plap.com
Brent Froese, Councillor
bfroese@city-plap.com
Diane Stasiuk, Councillor
dstasiuk@city-plap.com
Dale Lyle, City Manager
Kelly Braden, Director, Operations
204-239-8350, Fax: 204-857-7275
kbraden@city-plap.com
Kathy McGregor, Administrative Assistant, Economic & Community Development
kmcgregor@city-plap.com
Phil Carpenter, Chief, Fire & Emergency
204-239-8340, Fax: 204-239-5154
sharont@city-plap.com
Doug Campbell, Manager, Water Treatment
204-239-8373
dcampbell@city-plap.com
Dave Green, Manager, Parks
204-239-8325
dgreen@city-plap.com
Ian Milne, Manager, Engineering
204-239-8349
imilne@city-plap.com
Brian Taylor, Manager, Public Works
204-239-8352
btaylor@city-plap.com
Wayne Wall, Manager, Water Pollution Control Facility
204-239-8359
wwall@city-plap.com

Selkirk
200 Eaton Ave.
Selkirk, MB R1A 0W6
Tel: 204-785-4900; *Fax:* 204-482-5448
cityofselkirk@cityofselkirk.com
www.cityofselkirk.com
Municipal Type: City
Incorporated: June 5, 1882 *Area:* 24.87 sq km
Population in 2006: 9,515
Provincial Electoral District(s): Selkirk
Federal Electoral District(s): Selkirk-Interlake
Next Election: Oct. 2014 (4 year terms)
Larry Johannson, Mayor
Randy Borsa, Chief Administrative Officer

Steinbach
225 Reimer Ave.
Steinbach, MB R5G 2J1
Tel: 204-326-9877; *Fax:* 204-346-6235
info@steinbach.ca
www.steinbach.ca
Municipal Type: City
Incorporated: Jan. 3, 1946 *Area:* 25.57 sq km
Population in 2006: 11,066
Provincial Electoral District(s): Steinbach
Federal Electoral District(s): Provencher
Next Election: Oct. 2014 (4 year terms)
Chris Goertzen, Mayor
John Fehr, Councillor
Earl Funk, Councillor
Cari Penner, Councillor
Susan Penner, Councillor
Jac Siemens, Councillor
Michael Zwaagstra, Councillor
Jack Kehler, Chief Administrative Officer

Thompson
226 Mystery Lake Rd.
Thompson, MB R8N 1S6
Tel: 204-677-7910; *Fax:* 204-677-7981
rpatrick@city.thompson.mb.ca
www.thompson.ca
Municipal Type: City
Incorporated: Jan. 5, 1970 *Area:* 17.18 sq km
Population in 2006: 13,446
Provincial Electoral District(s): Thompson
Federal Electoral District(s): Churchill
Next Election: Oct. 2014 (4 year terms)
Tim Johnston, Mayor
204-677-7920, Fax: 204-677-7920
johnston@thompson.ca
Brad Evenson, Councillor
Erin Stewart, Councillor
Stella Locker, Councillor
Charlene Lafreniere, Councillor
Judy Kolada, Councillor
Dennis Fenske, Councillor
Penny Byer, Councillor
Luke Robinson, Councillor
Eric Stewart, Councillor
Randy Patrick, Chief Administrative Officer
Gary Ceppetelli, Director, Planning & Community Development
gceppetelli@city.thompson.mb.ca
Ian Thompson, Fire Chief
204-677-7915
fchief@city.thompson.mb.ca
Wayne Koversky, Director, Public Works
koversky@city.thompson.mb.ca
Mike Webb, Technician, Water & Sewer
mwebb@city.thompson.mb.ca
Ken Ament, Technician, Buildings & Roads
kament@city.thompson.mb.ca
Joyce Kopp, Agent, Purchasing
jkopp@city.thompson.mb.ca

Winkler
185 Main St.
Winkler, MB R6W 1B4
Tel: 204-325-9524; *Fax:* 204-325-5915
admin@cityofwinkler.ca
www.cityofwinkler.ca
Municipal Type: City
Incorporated: Jan. 6, 1954 *Area:* 17.01 sq km
Population in 2006: 9,106
Provincial Electoral District(s): Pembina
Federal Electoral District(s): Portage-Lisgar
Next Election: Oct. 2014 (4 year terms)
Martin Harder, Mayor
mayor@cityofwinkler.ca
Dave Burgess, Chief Administrative Officer

Winnipeg
City Hall
510 Main St.
Winnipeg, MB R3B 1B9
Tel: 204-986-6432; *Fax:* 204-947-3452
www.winnipeg.ca
Other Information: Phone or Fax: 311 for information on city services
Municipal Type: City
Incorporated: Nov. 8, 1873 *Area:* 464.01 sq km
Population in 2006: 633,451
Provincial Electoral District(s): Assibonia; Burrows; Charleswood; Concordia; Elmwood; Ft. Garry-Riverview; Ft. Rouge; Ft. Whyte; Inkster; Kildonan; Kirkfield Park; Logan; Minto; Point Douglas; Radisson; Riel; River East; River Heights; Rossmere; Seine River; Southdale; St. Boniface; St. James; St. Johns; St. Norbert; St. Vital; The Maples; Transcona; Tuxedo; Tyndall Park; Wollseley
Federal Electoral District(s): Charleswood-St. James-Assiniboia; Elmwood-Transcona; Kildonan-St. Paul; Saint Boniface; Winnipeg Centre; Winnipeg North; Winnipeg South; Winnipeg South Centre
Next Election: Oct. 2014 (4 year terms)
Richard Kachur, City Clerk
204-986-2428, Fax: 204-947-3452
Sam Katz, Mayor
204-986-2171, Fax: 204-949-0566
feedback@winnipeg.ca
Paula Havixbeck, Councillor, Ward(s): Charleswood-Tuxedo
Jo-Anne Ferrier, City Treasurer
Harvey Smith, Councillor, Ward(s): Daniel McIntyre
204-986-5951, Fax: 204-986-7000
Michael P. Ruta, Deputy CAO/CFO
Thomas Steen, Councillor, Ward(s): Elmwood-East Kildonan
Glen Laubenstein, Chief Administrative Officer
Jenny Gerbasi, Councillor, Ward(s): Fort Rouge-East Fort Garry
204-986-5878, Fax: 204-986-5636
Jim Brennan, Chief, Winnipeg Fire Paramedic Service
Ross Eadie, Councillor, Ward(s): Mynarski
Keith McCaskill, Chief of Police, Winnipeg Police Service
Jeff Browaty, Councillor, Ward(s): North Kildonan
204-986-5196, Fax: 204-986-3725
Linda Black, Director, Corporate Support Services
Devi Sharma, Councillor, Ward(s): Old Kildonan
Nelson Karpa, Director, Assessment & Taxation
Mike Pagtakhan, Councillor, Ward(s): Point Douglas
204-986-8401, Fax: 204-986-3531
Bill Larkin, Director, Public Works

John Orlikow, Councillor, Ward(s): River Heights-Fort Garry
204-986-5236, Fax: 204-986-3725
Barry MacBride, Director, Water & Waste
Daniel Vandal, Councillor, Ward(s): St. Boniface
204-986-5206, Fax: 204-986-3725
Deepak Joshi, Director, Planning, Property & Development
Grant Nordman, Councillor, Ward(s): St. Charles
204-986-5920, Fax: 204-986-7359
Dave Wardrop, Director, Winnipeg Transit
Scott Fielding, Councillor, Ward(s): St. James-Brooklands
204-986-5848, Fax: 204-986-4320
Clive Wightman, Director, Community Services
Justin Swandel, Councillor, Ward(s): St. Norbert
204-986-6824, Fax: 204-986-3725
Kelly Kjartanson, Manager, Environmental Standards
Gord Steeves, Councillor, Ward(s): St. Vital
204-986-5088, Fax: 204-986-3725
Dave Domke, Manager, Parks & Open Space
Russ Wyatt, Councillor, Ward(s): Transcona
204-986-8087, Fax: 204-986-4530
Brad Sacher, Manager, Transportation

Other Municipalities in Manitoba

Altona
P.O. Box 1630
111 Centre Ave. East
Altona, MB R0G 0B0
Tel: 204-324-6468; *Fax:* 204-324-1550
info@townofaltona.com
www.townofaltona.com
Municipal Type: Town
Incorporated: Jan. 1, 1956 *Area:* 9.39 sq km
Population in 2006: 3,709
Provincial Electoral District(s): Emerson
Federal Electoral District(s): Portage-Lisgar
Next Election: Oct. 2014 (4 year terms)
Melvin H. Klassen, Mayor
Russ Phillips, Chief Administrative Officer

Arborg
P.O. Box 159
337 River Rd.
Arborg, MB R0C 0A0
Tel: 204-376-2647; *Fax:* 204-376-5379
townofarborg@mymts.net
www.townofarborg.com
Municipal Type: Town
Incorporated: 1964 *Area:* 2.26 sq km
Population in 2006: 1,021
Provincial Electoral District(s): Interlake
Federal Electoral District(s): Selkirk-Interlake
Next Election: Oct. 2014 (4 year terms)
Randy Sigurdson, Mayor
Lorraine Bardarson, Chief Administrative Officer

Beausejour
P.O. Box 1427
639 Park Ave.
Beausejour, MB R0E 0C0
Tel: 204-268-7550; *Fax:* 204-268-3107
townoffice@townofbeausejour.com
www.townofbeausejour.com
Municipal Type: Town
Incorporated: Jan. 2, 1912 *Area:* 5.35 sq km
Population in 2006: 2,823
Provincial Electoral District(s): Lac du Bonnet
Federal Electoral District(s): Selkirk-Interlake
Next Election: Oct. 2014 (4 year terms)
Brad Saluk, Mayor
Jack Douglas, Chief Administrative Officer

Benito
P.O. Box 369
126 Main St.
Benito, MB R0L 0C0
Tel: 204-539-2634; *Fax:* 204-539-2221
benitov@mts.net
community.svcn.mb.ca/benito
Municipal Type: Village
Incorporated: Jan. 4, 1941 *Area:* 0.92 sq km
Population in 2006: 370
Provincial Electoral District(s): Swan River
Federal Electoral District(s): Dauphin-Swan River-Marquette
Next Election: Oct. 2014 (4 year terms)
Marion Meadows, Mayor
Patricia Ellingson, Chief Administrative Officer

Binscarth
P.O. Box 54
116 Russell St.
Binscarth, MB R0J 0G0
Tel: 204-532-2223; *Fax:* 204-532-2153
vilbins@mts.net
www.binscarth.mb.com
Municipal Type: Village
Incorporated: Jan. 2, 1917 *Area:* 1.52 sq km
Population in 2006: 395
Provincial Electoral District(s): Russell
Federal Electoral District(s): Dauphin-Swan River-Marquette
Next Election: Oct. 2014 (4 year terms)
Dale Sawchuk, Mayor
Sandra Birch, Chief Administrative Officer

Birtle
P.O. Box 70
678 Main St.
Birtle, MB R0M 0C0
Tel: 204-842-3234; *Fax:* 204-842-3496
cao@birtle.ca
www.town.birtle.mb.ca
Municipal Type: Town
Incorporated: Jan. 3, 1884 *Area:* 14.25 sq km
Population in 2006: 662
Provincial Electoral District(s): Russell
Federal Electoral District(s): Dauphin-Swan River-Marquette
Next Election: Oct. 2014 (4 year terms)
James Vinie, Mayor
Debbie Jensen, Chief Administrative Officer

Boissevain
P.O. Box 490
420 South Railway
Boissevain, MB R0K 0E0
Tel: 204-534-2433; *Fax:* 204-534-3710
boissevain@mts.net
www.boissevain.ca
Municipal Type: Town
Incorporated: 1906 *Area:* 2.77 sq km
Population in 2006: 1,497
Provincial Electoral District(s): Arthur-Virden
Federal Electoral District(s): Brandon-Souris
Next Election: Oct. 2014 (4 year terms)
M. Edward Anderson, Mayor
Lloyd Leganchuk, Chief Administrative Officer

Bowsman
P.O. Box 244
105 - 2nd St.
Bowsman, MB R0L 0H0
Tel: 204-238-4351; *Fax:* 204-238-4292
bowsman@mts.net
Municipal Type: Village
Incorporated: Jan. 7, 1949 *Area:* 2.63 sq km
Population in 2006: 315
Provincial Electoral District(s): Swan River
Federal Electoral District(s): Dauphin-Swan River-Marquette
Next Election: Oct. 2014 (4 year terms)
Leanne Hutman, Mayor
Patti Simpson, Chief Administrative Officer

Carberry
P.O. Box 130
316 - 4th Ave.
Carberry, MB R0K 0H0
Tel: 204-834-6600; *Fax:* 204-834-6604
town@townofcarberry.ca
www.townofcarberry.ca
Municipal Type: Town
Incorporated: Jan. 1, 1905 *Area:* 4.79 sq km
Population in 2006: 1,502
Provincial Electoral District(s): Turtle Mountain
Federal Electoral District(s): Brandon-Souris
Next Election: Oct. 2014 (4 year terms)
Wayne Blair, Mayor
Brent McMillan, Chief Administrative Officer

Carman
P.O. Box 160
12 - 2nd Ave. SW
Carman, MB R0G 0J0
Tel: 204-745-2443; *Fax:* 204-745-2903
info@townofcarman.com
www.townofcarman.com
Municipal Type: Town
Incorporated: Jan. 1, 1905 *Area:* 4.12 sq km
Population in 2006: 2,880
Provincial Electoral District(s): Carman
Federal Electoral District(s): Portage-Lisgar
Next Election: Oct. 2014 (4 year terms)
Bob Mitchell, Mayor
Cheryl Young, Chief Administrative Officer

Cartwright
P.O. Box 9
485 Curwen St.
Cartwright, MB R0K 0L0
Tel: 204-529-2363; *Fax:* 204-529-2288
colleen@cartwrightmb.ca
www.cartwrightmb.ca
Municipal Type: Village
Incorporated: Jan. 5, 1948 *Area:* 1.86 sq km
Population in 2006: 282
Provincial Electoral District(s): Turtle Mountain
Federal Electoral District(s): Brandon-Souris
Next Election: Oct. 2014 (4 year terms)
Bruce Leadbeater, Mayor
Colleen Mullin, Chief Administrative Officer

Churchill
P.O. Box 459
180 LaVerendrye Blvd.
Churchill, MB R0B 0E0
Tel: 204-675-8871; *Fax:* 204-675-2934
townofchurchill@churchill.ca
www.churchill.ca
Municipal Type: Town
Incorporated: Jan. 4, 1997 *Area:* 53.96 sq km
Population in 2006: 923
Provincial Electoral District(s): Rupertsland
Federal Electoral District(s): Churchill
Next Election: Oct. 2014 (4 year terms)
Michael Spence, Mayor
Albert Meijering, Chief Executive Officer

Crystal City
P.O. Box 310
26 South Railway Ave.
Crystal City, MB R0K 0N0
Tel: 204-873-2591; *Fax:* 204-873-2459
crystalcity@inetlink.ca
www.crystalcitymb.ca
Municipal Type: Village
Incorporated: Dec. 4, 1947 *Area:* 2.84 sq km
Population in 2006: 400
Provincial Electoral District(s): Turtle Mountain
Federal Electoral District(s): Portage-Lisgar
Next Election: Oct. 2014 (4 year terms)
William (Bill) McKitrick, Mayor
Alexis Gardiner, Chief Administrative Officer

Dauphin
100 Main St. South
Dauphin, MB R7N 1K3
Tel: 204-622-3200; *Fax:* 204-622-3290
info@dauphin.ca
www.dauphin.ca
Municipal Type: Town
Incorporated: Jan. 7, 1898 *Area:* 12.65 sq km
Population in 2006: 7,906
Provincial Electoral District(s): Dauphin-Roblin
Federal Electoral District(s): Dauphin-Swan River-Marquette
Next Election: Oct. 2014 (4 year terms)
Eric B. Irwin, Mayor
Brad D. Collett, Chief Administrative Officer

Deloraine
P.O. Box 510
102 Broadway St. South
Deloraine, MB R0M 0M0
Tel: 204-747-2655; *Fax:* 204-747-2927
deloraine@deloraine.org
www.deloraine.org
Municipal Type: Town
Incorporated: Jan. 6, 1904 *Area:* 2.25 sq km
Population in 2006: 977
Provincial Electoral District(s): Arthur-Virden
Federal Electoral District(s): Brandon-Souris
Next Election: Oct. 2014 (4 year terms)
Brian Franklin, Mayor
Debbie Adams, Chief Administrative Officer

Dunnottar
P.O. Box 321
44 Whytewold Rd.
Matlock, MB R0C 2B0
Tel: 204-389-4962; *Fax:* 204-389-4966
info@dunnottar.ca
www.dunnottar.ca
Municipal Type: Village
Area: 2.79 sq km
Population in 2006: 692

Provincial Electoral District(s): Interlake
Federal Electoral District(s): Selkirk-Interlake
Next Election: Oct. 2014 (4 year terms)
Richard Gamble, Mayor
Janice M. Thevenot, Chief Administrative Officer

Elkhorn
P.O. Box 280
10 Grange St.
Elkhorn, MB R0M 0N0
Tel: 204-845-2161; *Fax:* 204-845-2312
info@elkhorn.mb.ca
www.elkhorn.mb.ca
Municipal Type: Village
Incorporated: Jan. 2, 1906 *Area:* 2.73 sq km
Population in 2006: 461
Provincial Electoral District(s): Arthur-Virden
Federal Electoral District(s): Brandon-Souris
Next Election: Oct. 2014 (4 year terms)
Roland Gagnon, Mayor
Garth Mitchell, Chief Administrative Officer

Emerson
P.O. Box 340
104 Church St.
Emerson, MB R0A 0L0
Tel: 204-373-2002; *Fax:* 204-373-2486
info@townofemerson.com
www.townofemerson.com
Municipal Type: Town
Incorporated: Nov. 3, 1879 *Area:* 22.28 sq km
Population in 2006: 689
Provincial Electoral District(s): Emerson
Federal Electoral District(s): Provencher
Next Election: Oct. 2014 (4 year terms)
Wayne Arseny, Mayor
Jeannette Sabourin, Chief Administrative Officer

Erickson
P.O. Box 40
45 Main St.
Erickson, MB R0J 0P0
Tel: 204-636-2431; *Fax:* 204-636-2516
ericksonadmin@mts.net
www.townerickson.ca
Municipal Type: Town
Incorporated: Jan. 5, 1953 *Area:* 1.3 sq km
Population in 2006: 456
Provincial Electoral District(s): Russell
Federal Electoral District(s): Dauphin-Swan River-Marquette
Next Election: Oct. 2014 (4 year terms)
Val Soltys, Mayor
Kat Bridgeman, Chief Administrative Officer

Ethelbert
P.O. Box 185
5 - 2nd St.
Ethelbert, MB R0L 0T0
Tel: 204-742-3301; *Fax:* 204-742-3228
ethelbert@mts.net
Municipal Type: Village
Incorporated: Jan. 1, 1950 *Area:* 2.47 sq km
Population in 2006: 312
Provincial Electoral District(s): Swan River
Federal Electoral District(s): Dauphin-Swan River-Marquette
Next Election: Oct. 2014 (4 year terms)
Mercil (Mitch) Michaluk, Mayor
Libby Moroz, Chief Administrative Officer

Gilbert Plains
P.O. Box 39
114 Main St. North
Gilbert Plains, MB R0L 0X0
Tel: 204-548-2761; *Fax:* 204-548-2473
townofgp@mts.net
www.gilbertplains.com
Municipal Type: Town
Incorporated: July 1, 1906 *Area:* 2.66 sq km
Population in 2006: 760
Provincial Electoral District(s): Dauphin-Roblin
Federal Electoral District(s): Dauphin-Swan River-Marquette
Next Election: Oct. 2014 (4 year terms)
Lyle Smith, Mayor
Janice Lagoski, Chief Administrative Officer

Gillam
P.O. Box 100
323 Railway Ave.
Gillam, MB R0B 0L0
Tel: 204-652-3150; *Fax:* 204-652-3199
information@townofgillam.com
www.townofgillam.com
Municipal Type: Town
Area: 1,996.35 sq km
Population in 2006: 1,209
Provincial Electoral District(s): Rupertsland
Federal Electoral District(s): Churchill
Next Election: Oct. 2014 (4 year terms)
James Goymer, Mayor
Jackie Clayton, Chief Administrative Officer

Gladstone
P.O. Box 25
14 Dennis St.
Gladstone, MB R0J 0T0
Tel: 204-385-2332; *Fax:* 204-385-2391
info@gladstone.ca
www.gladstone.ca
Municipal Type: Town
Incorporated: Jan. 1, 1882 *Area:* 2.43 sq km
Population in 2006: 802
Provincial Electoral District(s): Ste. Rose
Federal Electoral District(s): Dauphin-Swan River-Marquette
Next Election: Oct. 2014 (4 year terms)
Eileen Clarke, Mayor
Louise E. Blair, Chief Administrative Officer

Glenboro
P.O. Box 190
618 Railway Ave.
Glenboro, MB R0K 0X0
Tel: 204-827-2083; *Fax:* 204-827-2123
gcdc@glenboro.com
www.glenboro.com
Municipal Type: Village
Incorporated: Jan. 1, 1950 *Area:* 2.68 sq km
Population in 2006: 633
Provincial Electoral District(s): Turtle Mountain
Federal Electoral District(s): Brandon-Souris
Next Election: Oct. 2014 (4 year terms)
Robert Jewsbury, Mayor
Eric Plaetinck, Chief Administrative Officer

Grand Rapids
P.O. Box 301
200 Grand Rapids Dr.
Grand Rapids, MB R0C 1E0
Tel: 204-639-2260; *Fax:* 204-639-2475
towngra@xplornet.ca
Municipal Type: Town
Incorporated: Jan. 2, 1962 *Area:* 85.95 sq km
Population in 2006: 336
Provincial Electoral District(s): Swan River
Federal Electoral District(s): Churchill
Next Election: Oct. 2014 (4 year terms)
John Morrisseau, Mayor
Karen Turner, Chief Administrative Officer

Grandview
P.O. Box 219
531 Main St.
Grandview, MB R0L 0Y0
Tel: 204-546-5250; *Fax:* 204-546-5269
townofgv@mts.net
www.grandviewmanitoba.net
Municipal Type: Town
Incorporated: Jan. 1, 1905 *Area:* 2.87 sq km
Population in 2006: 839
Provincial Electoral District(s): Dauphin-Roblin
Federal Electoral District(s): Dauphin-Swan River-Marquette
Next Election: Oct. 2014 (4 year terms)
Tom Bohun, Mayor
Sharon Dalgleish, Chief Administrative Officer

Gretna
P.O. Box 280
612 - 7th St.
Gretna, MB R0G 0V0
Tel: 204-327-5578; *Fax:* 204-327-5458
info@gretna.ca
www.gretna.ca
Municipal Type: Town
Incorporated: Jan. 6, 1886 *Area:* 2.79 sq km
Population in 2006: 574
Provincial Electoral District(s): Emerson
Federal Electoral District(s): Portage-Lisgar
Next Election: Oct. 2014 (4 year terms)
Mark Ratzlaff, Mayor
Michele Sawatzky, Chief Administrative Officer

Hamiota
P.O. Box 100
75 Maple Ave. East
Hamiota, MB R0M 0T0
Tel: 204-764-3050; *Fax:* 204-764-3055
info@hamiota.com
www.hamiota.com
Municipal Type: Town
Incorporated: 1907 *Area:* 3.38 sq km
Population in 2006: 823
Provincial Electoral District(s): Russell
Federal Electoral District(s): Dauphin-Swan River-Marquette
Next Election: Oct. 2014 (4 year terms)
Larry Oakden, Mayor
Tom Mollard, Chief Administrative Officer

Hartney
P.O. Box 339
209 Airdrie St.
Hartney, MB R0M 0X0
Tel: 204-858-2429; *Fax:* 204-858-2681
hartney@mts.net
Municipal Type: Town
Incorporated: Jan. 1, 1905 *Area:* 2.45 sq km
Population in 2006: 400
Provincial Electoral District(s): Arthur-Virden
Federal Electoral District(s): Brandon-Souris
Next Election: Oct. 2014 (4 year terms)
Lori Taylor, Mayor
Brad Coe, Chief Administrative Officer

Killarney - Turtle Mountain
P.O. Box 10
415 Broadway Ave.
Killarney, MB R0K 1G0
Tel: 204-523-7247; *Fax:* 204-523-4637
info@killarney.ca
www.killarney.ca
Municipal Type: Municipality
Incorporated: Jan. 1, 1882 *Area:* 925.13 sq km
Population in 2006: 3,299
Provincial Electoral District(s): Turtle Mountain
Federal Electoral District(s): Brandon-Souris
Next Election: Oct. 2014 (4 year terms)
Note: The municipalities of Killarney & Turtle Mountain amalgamated to form one entity effective Jan. 1, 2007.
Rick Pauls, Mayor
Jim Dowsett, Chief Administrative Officer

Lac du Bonnet
P.O. Box 339
84 - 2nd St.
Lac du Bonnet, MB R0E 1A0
Tel: 204-345-8693; *Fax:* 204-345-8694
townldb@mts.net
www.lacdubonnet.com
Municipal Type: Town
Incorporated: Jan. 4, 1947 *Area:* 2.25 sq km
Population in 2006: 1,009
Provincial Electoral District(s): Lac du Bonnet
Federal Electoral District(s): Provencher
Next Election: Oct. 2014 (4 year terms)
Bill Campbell, Mayor
Colleen L. Johnson, Chief Administrative Officer

Leaf Rapids
Town Centre Complex
P.O. Box 340
Leaf Rapids, MB R0B 1W0
Tel: 204-473-2436; *Fax:* 204-473-2566
administrator@townofleafrapids.ca
www.townofleafrapids.ca
Municipal Type: Town
Incorporated: Jan. 5, 1976 *Area:* 1,272.87 sq km
Population in 2006: 539
Provincial Electoral District(s): Flin Flon
Federal Electoral District(s): Churchill
Next Election: Oct. 2014 (4 year terms)
Geraldine Cockerill, Mayor
Pat Horsley, Chief Administrative Officer

Lynn Lake
P.O. Box 100
503 Sherritt Ave.
Lynn Lake, MB R0B 0W0
Tel: 204-356-2418; *Fax:* 204-356-8297
info@lynnlake.ca
www.lynnlake.ca
Municipal Type: Town
Incorporated: 1950 *Area:* 910.23 sq km
Population in 2006: 714
Provincial Electoral District(s): Flin Flon

Federal Electoral District(s): Churchill
Next Election: Oct. 2014 (4 year terms)
Sean Maher, Mayor
Floyd Buhler, Chief Administrative Officer

MacGregor
P.O. Box 190
27 Hampton St. East
MacGregor, MB R0H 0R0
Tel: 204-685-2211; *Fax:* 204-685-2616
office@macgregor.ca
www.macgregor.ca
Municipal Type: Town
Incorporated: Jan. 4, 1947 *Area:* 2.13 sq km
Population in 2006: 921
Provincial Electoral District(s): Turtle Mountain
Federal Electoral District(s): Portage-Lisgar
Next Election: Oct. 2014 (4 year terms)
William Wiebe, Mayor
Valorie Unrau, Chief Administrative Officer

Manitou
P.O. Box 280
261 Main St.
Manitou, MB R0G 1G0
Tel: 204-242-2515; *Fax:* 204-242-3281
manitou@goinet.ca
www.townofmanitou.ca
Municipal Type: Town
Incorporated: 1897 *Area:* 2.94 sq km
Population in 2006: 718
Provincial Electoral District(s): Pembina
Federal Electoral District(s): Portage-Lisgar
Next Election: Oct. 2014 (4 year terms)
Jake Goertzen, Mayor
Wes Unrau, Chief Administrative Officer

McCreary
P.O. Box 267
436 - 2nd Ave.
McCreary, MB R0J 1B0
Tel: 204-835-2341; *Fax:* 204-835-2658
mccreary@mts.net
www.exploremccreary.com
Municipal Type: Village
Incorporated: Jan. 4, 1964 *Area:* 1.7 sq km
Population in 2006: 487
Provincial Electoral District(s): Ste. Rose
Federal Electoral District(s): Dauphin-Swan River-Marquette
Next Election: Oct. 2014 (4 year terms)
Linda Cripps, Mayor
Wendy Turko, Chief Administrative Officer

Melita
P.O. Box 364
79 Main St.
Melita, MB R0M 1L0
Tel: 204-522-3413; *Fax:* 204-522-3587
tofmel@mts.net
www.melitamb.ca
Municipal Type: Town
Incorporated: Jan. 2, 1906 *Area:* 2.96 sq km
Population in 2006: 1,051
Provincial Electoral District(s): Arthur-Virden
Federal Electoral District(s): Brandon-Souris
Next Election: Oct. 2014 (4 year terms)
Robert Walker, Mayor
Julie Chase, Chief Administrative Officer

Minitonas
P.O. Box 9
311 Main St.
Minitonas, MB R0L 1G0
Tel: 204-525-4461; *Fax:* 204-525-4857
rmmin@minitonas.ca
minitonas.ca
Municipal Type: Town
Incorporated: Jan. 5, 1948 *Area:* 2.01 sq km
Population in 2006: 497
Provincial Electoral District(s): Swan River
Federal Electoral District(s): Dauphin-Swan River-Marquette
Next Election: Oct. 2014 (4 year terms)
Henry Barkowski, Mayor
Carolyn Gordon, Chief Administrative Officer

Minnedosa
P.O. Box 426
103 Main St. South
Minnedosa, MB R0J 1E0
Tel: 204-867-2727; *Fax:* 204-867-2686
minnedosa@mts.net
Municipal Type: Town
Incorporated: Jan. 5, 1948 *Area:* 15.26 sq km
Population in 2006: 2,474
Provincial Electoral District(s): Minnedosa
Federal Electoral District(s): Dauphin-Swan River-Marquette
Next Election: Oct. 2014 (4 year terms)
Ray Orr, Mayor
Ken Jenkins, Chief Administrative Officer

Morden
#100, 195 Stephen St.
Morden, MB R6M 1V3
Tel: 204-822-4434; *Fax:* 204-822-6494
tmorden@mordenmb.com
www.mordenmb.com
Municipal Type: Town
Incorporated: Jan. 1, 1882 *Area:* 16.39 sq km
Population in 2006: 6,571
Provincial Electoral District(s): Pembina
Federal Electoral District(s): Portage-Lisgar
Next Election: Oct. 2014 (4 year terms)
Ken Wiebe, Mayor
Ernie Epp, Chief Administrative Officer

Morris
P.O. Box 28
#1, 380 Stampede Grounds
Morris, MB R0G 1K0
Tel: 204-746-2531; *Fax:* 204-746-6009
tomorris@mts.net
www.town.morris.mb.ca
Municipal Type: Town
Incorporated: Jan. 2, 1883 *Area:* 6.1 sq km
Population in 2006: 1,643
Provincial Electoral District(s): Morris
Federal Electoral District(s): Provencher
Next Election: Oct. 2014 (4 year terms)
Gavin van der Linde, Mayor
Brigitte Doerksen, Chief Administrative Officer

Neepawa
P.O. Box 339
275 Hamilton St.
Neepawa, MB R0J 1H0
Tel: 204-476-7600; *Fax:* 204-476-7624
neepawa@wcgwave.ca
www.neepawa.ca
Municipal Type: Town
Incorporated: Jan. 2, 1883 *Area:* 17.57 sq km
Population in 2006: 3,298
Provincial Electoral District(s): Ste. Rose
Federal Electoral District(s): Dauphin-Swan River-Marquette
Next Election: Oct. 2014 (4 year terms)
Ron Forsman, Mayor
Allison Bardsley, Chief Administrative Officer

Niverville
P.O. Box 267
86 Main St.
Niverville, MB R0A 1E0
Tel: 204-388-4600; *Fax:* 204-388-6110
cao@whereyoubelong.ca
www.whereyoubelong.ca
Municipal Type: Town
Incorporated: Jan. 4, 1969 *Area:* 8.79 sq km
Population in 2006: 2,464
Provincial Electoral District(s): Steinbach
Federal Electoral District(s): Provencher
Next Election: Oct. 2014 (4 year terms)
Greg Fehr, Mayor
mayor@whereyoubelong.ca
G. Jim Buys, Chief Administrative Officer

Notre Dame de Lourdes
P.O. Box 89
55 Rodgers St.
Notre Dame de Lourdes, MB R0G 1M0
Tel: 204-248-7290; *Fax:* 204-248-7289
villagend@mts.net
www.notre-dame-de-lourdes.ca
Municipal Type: Village
Incorporated: Jan. 3, 1963 *Area:* 2.58 sq km
Population in 2006: 589
Provincial Electoral District(s): Carman
Federal Electoral District(s): Portage-Lisgar
Next Election: Oct. 2014 (4 year terms)
Denis Bibault, Mayor
Jean Gaultier, Chief Administrative Officer

Oak Lake
P.O. Box 100
293 - 2nd Ave. West
Oak Lake, MB R0M 1P0
Tel: 204-855-2423; *Fax:* 204-855-2836
cao_sifton@mymts.net
www.oaklakeandarea.com
Municipal Type: Town
Incorporated: Jan. 3, 1907 *Area:* 2.73 sq km
Population in 2006: 363
Provincial Electoral District(s): Arthur-Virden
Federal Electoral District(s): Brandon-Souris
Next Election: Oct. 2014 (4 year terms)
Jeffrey Sigurdson, Mayor
Mary Smith, Chief Administrative Officer

Pilot Mound
P.O. Box 39
219 Broadway Ave.
Pilot Mound, MB R0G 1P0
Tel: 204-825-2587; *Fax:* 204-825-2362
vlgpm@mts.net
www.pilotmound.com
Municipal Type: Town
Incorporated: May 4, 1904 *Area:* 2.7 sq km
Population in 2006: 630
Provincial Electoral District(s): Turtle Mountain
Federal Electoral District(s): Portage-Lisgar
Next Election: Oct. 2014 (4 year terms)
R. Brent Checkley, Mayor
Doris F. Heaver, Chief Administrative Officer

Plum Coulee
P.O. Box 36
253 Main Ave.
Plum Coulee, MB R0G 1R0
Tel: 204-829-3419; *Fax:* 204-829-3436
pcoulee@mts.net
www.townofplumcoulee.com
Municipal Type: Town
Incorporated: Jan. 6, 1901 *Area:* 2.48 sq km
Population in 2006: 770
Provincial Electoral District(s): Emerson
Federal Electoral District(s): Portage-Lisgar
Next Election: Oct. 2014 (4 year terms)
Archie Heinrichs, Mayor
Susan Stein, Chief Administrative Officer

Powerview - Pine Falls
P.O. Box 220
277B Main St.
Powerview, MB R0E 1P0
Tel: 204-367-8483; *Fax:* 204-367-4747
munclerk@mts.net
www.powerview-pinefalls.com
Municipal Type: Town
Incorporated: Jan. 2, 1951 *Area:* 5.05 sq km
Population in 2006: 1,294
Provincial Electoral District(s): Lac du Bonnet
Federal Electoral District(s): Provencher
Next Election: Oct. 2014 (4 year terms)
Gordon Watson, Mayor
Margaret Bonekamp, Chief Administrative Officer

Rapid City
P.O. Box 130
410 - 3rd Ave.
Rapid City, MB R0K 1W0
Tel: 204-826-2679; *Fax:* 204-826-2652
rapcity@mts.net
www.rapidcitymb.ca
Municipal Type: Town
Incorporated: Jan. 2, 1883 *Area:* 5.38 sq km
Population in 2006: 416
Provincial Electoral District(s): Minnedosa
Federal Electoral District(s): Dauphin-Swan River-Marquette
Next Election: Oct. 2014 (4 year terms)
Orest Woloski, Mayor
Kim Moyer, Chief Administrative Officer

Rivers
P.O. Box 520
670 - 2nd Ave.
Rivers, MB R0K 1X0
Tel: 204-328-5250; *Fax:* 204-328-5374
rivers@mts.net
www.townofrivers.mb.ca
Municipal Type: Town
Incorporated: Jan. 4, 1913 *Area:* 7.97 sq km
Population in 2006: 1,193
Provincial Electoral District(s): Minnedosa

Federal Electoral District(s): Brandon-Souris
Next Election: Oct. 2014 (4 year terms)
Todd Gill, Mayor
Dennis Higginson, Chief Administrative Officer

Riverton
P.O. Box 250
56 Laura Ave.
Riverton, MB R0C 2R0
Tel: 204-378-2281; *Fax:* 204-378-5616
vilofriv@mts.net
Municipal Type: Village
Incorporated: Jan. 2, 1951 *Area:* 1.11 sq km
Population in 2006: 537
Provincial Electoral District(s): Interlake
Federal Electoral District(s): Selkirk-Interlake
Next Election: Oct. 2014 (4 year terms)
Colin Bjarnason, Mayor
Nadine Eyjolfson, Chief Administrative Officer

Roblin
P.O. Box 730
125 - 1st Ave. NW
Roblin, MB R0L 1P0
Tel: 204-937-8333; *Fax:* 204-937-4382
toroblin@mts.net
www.roblinmanitoba.com
Municipal Type: Town
Incorporated: Jan. 4, 1913 *Area:* 3.79 sq km
Population in 2006: 1,672
Provincial Electoral District(s): Dauphin-Roblin
Federal Electoral District(s): Dauphin-Swan River-Marquette; Brandon-Souris
Next Election: Oct. 2014 (4 year terms)
Betty Nykyforak, Mayor
Twyla Ludwig, Chief Administrative Officer

Rossburn
P.O. Box 70
43 Main St. North
Rossburn, MB R0J 1V0
Tel: 204-859-2762; *Fax:* 204-859-2022
town.rsb@mts.net
www.town.rossburn.mb.ca
Municipal Type: Town
Incorporated: Jan. 4, 1913 *Area:* 3.43 sq km
Population in 2006: 546
Provincial Electoral District(s): Russell
Federal Electoral District(s): Dauphin-Swan River-Marquette
Next Election: Oct. 2014 (4 year terms)
Shirley Kalyniuk, Mayor
Kerry Lawless, Chief Administrative Officer

Russell
P.O. Box 10
178 Main St. North
Russell, MB R0J 1W0
Tel: 204-773-2253; *Fax:* 204-773-3370
town@russellmb.com
www.russellmb.com
Municipal Type: Town
Incorporated: Jan. 4, 1913 *Area:* 3.15 sq km
Population in 2006: 1,428
Provincial Electoral District(s): Russell
Federal Electoral District(s): Dauphin-Swan River-Marquette
Next Election: Oct. 2014 (4 year terms)
Chris Radford, Mayor
Wally R. Melnyk, Chief Administrative Officer

Ste. Anne
30 Dawson Rd., Unit B
Ste. Anne, MB R5H 1B5
Tel: 204-422-5293; *Fax:* 204-422-5459
town@steannemb.ca
www.steannemb.ca
Municipal Type: Town
Incorporated: Jan. 3, 1963 *Area:* 4.19 sq km
Population in 2006: 1,534
Provincial Electoral District(s): La Verendrye
Federal Electoral District(s): Provencher
Next Election: Oct. 2014 (4 year terms)
Bernard Vermette, Mayor
Nicole Champagne, Chief Administrative Officer

St. Claude
P.O. Box 249
12 - 1st St.
St Claude, MB R0G 1Z0
Tel: 204-379-2382; *Fax:* 204-379-2072
stclaude@mts.net
www.stclaude.ca
Municipal Type: Village
Incorporated: Jan. 3, 1963 *Area:* 1.8 sq km
Population in 2006: 588
Provincial Electoral District(s): Carman
Federal Electoral District(s): Portage-Lisgar
Next Election: Oct. 2014 (4 year terms)
Norman Carter, Mayor
204-379-2720
Simone Dupasquier, Chief Administrative Officer

St. Lazare
P.O. Box 100
100 Chartier Ave. West
St Lazare, MB R0M 1Y0
Tel: 204-683-2241; *Fax:* 204-683-2317
laz_ell@mts.net
stlazare-ellice.com
Municipal Type: Village
Incorporated: Jan. 1, 1950 *Area:* 2.91 sq km
Population in 2006: 265
Provincial Electoral District(s): Russell
Federal Electoral District(s): Dauphin-Swan River-Marquette
Next Election: Oct. 2014 (4 year terms)
Martin Dupont, Mayor
Richard W. Fouillard, Chief Administrative Officer

St. Pierre-Jolys
P.O. Box 218
555 Hébert St.
St. Pierre-Jolys, MB R0A 1V0
Tel: 204-433-7832; *Fax:* 204-433-7053
st-pierre-jolys@mts.net
www.stpierrejolys.com
Municipal Type: Village
Incorporated: Jan. 4, 1947 *Area:* 2.6 sq km
Population in 2006: 839
Provincial Electoral District(s): Morris
Federal Electoral District(s): Provencher
Next Election: Oct. 2014 (4 year terms)
Denis Fillion, Mayor
Rachelle Tessier, Chief Administrative Officer

Ste. Rose du Lac
P.O. Box 445
722 Central Ave.
Ste. Rose du Lac, MB R0L 1S0
Tel: 204-447-2229; *Fax:* 204-447-2875
sterose@mts.net
www.town.sterosedulac.mb.ca
Municipal Type: Town
Incorporated: Jan. 5, 1920 *Area:* 2.53 sq km
Population in 2006: 995
Provincial Electoral District(s): Ste. Rose
Federal Electoral District(s): Dauphin-Swan River-Marquette
Next Election: Oct. 2014 (4 year terms)
Rene L. Maillard, Mayor
Marlene M. Bouchard, Chief Administrative Officer

Snow Lake
P.O. Box 40
113 Elm St.
Snow Lake, MB R0B 1M0
Tel: 204-358-2551; *Fax:* 204-358-2112
snowlake@mts.net
www.snowlake.com
Municipal Type: Town
Incorporated: 1947 *Area:* 1,211.89 sq km
Population in 2006: 837
Provincial Electoral District(s): Flin Flon
Federal Electoral District(s): Churchill
Next Election: Oct. 2014 (4 year terms)
Clarence Fisher, Mayor
Jeff Precourt, Chief Administrative Officer

Somerset
P.O. Box 187
307 - 3rd St.
Somerset, MB R0G 2L0
Tel: 204-744-2171; *Fax:* 204-744-2618
somerset@mts.net
Municipal Type: Village
Incorporated: Jan. 2, 1962 *Area:* 2.45 sq km
Population in 2006: 432
Provincial Electoral District(s): Carman
Federal Electoral District(s): Portage-Lisgar
Next Election: Oct. 2014 (4 year terms)
Gilbert Mabon, Mayor
Linda Talbot, Chief Administrative Officer

Souris
P.O. Box 518
100 - 2nd St. South
Souris, MB R0K 2C0
Tel: 204-483-5200; *Fax:* 204-483-5203
tnsouris@mts.net
www.sourismanitoba.com
Municipal Type: Town
Incorporated: Jan. 6, 1904 *Area:* 3.64 sq km
Population in 2006: 1,772
Provincial Electoral District(s): Minnedosa
Federal Electoral District(s): Brandon-Souris
Next Election: Oct. 2014 (4 year terms)
Darryl Jackson, Mayor
Charlotte Parham, Chief Administrative Officer

Stonewall
P.O. Box 250
293 Main St.
Stonewall, MB R0C 2Z0
Tel: 204-467-7979; *Fax:* 204-467-7999
info@stonewall.ca
www.stonewall.ca
Municipal Type: Town
Incorporated: Jan. 4, 1908 *Area:* 6.02 sq km
Population in 2006: 4,376
Provincial Electoral District(s): Lakeside
Federal Electoral District(s): Selkirk-Interlake
Next Election: Oct. 2014 (4 year terms)
Ross Thompson, Mayor
Robert Potter, Chief Administrative Officer

Swan River
P.O. Box 879
135 - 5th Ave. North
Swan River, MB R0L 1Z0
Tel: 204-734-4586; *Fax:* 204-734-5166
main@townsr.ca
www.swanrivermanitoba.ca
Municipal Type: Town
Incorporated: Jan. 4, 1908 *Area:* 6.78 sq km
Population in 2006: 3,859
Provincial Electoral District(s): Swan River
Federal Electoral District(s): Dauphin-Swan River-Marquette
Next Election: Oct. 2014 (4 year terms)
Glen McKenzie, Mayor
Shirley Bateman, Chief Administrative Officer

Teulon
P.O. Box 69
44 - 4 Ave. SE
Teulon, MB R0C 3B0
Tel: 204-886-2314; *Fax:* 204-886-3918
teulon@mts.net
www.teulon.ca
Municipal Type: Town
Incorporated: Jan. 4, 1919 *Area:* 3.2 sq km
Population in 2006: 1,124
Provincial Electoral District(s): Lakeside
Federal Electoral District(s): Selkirk-Interlake
Next Election: Oct. 2014 (4 year terms)
Bert Campbell, Mayor
Grant MacAulay, Chief Administrative Officer

The Pas
P.O. Box 870
81 Edwards Ave.
The Pas, MB R9A 1K8
Tel: 204-627-1100; *Fax:* 204-623-5506
randis@townofthepas.ca
www.thepasarea.com
Municipal Type: Town
Incorporated: Jan. 2, 1912 *Area:* 47.83 sq km
Population in 2006: 5,589
Provincial Electoral District(s): The Pas
Federal Electoral District(s): Churchill
Next Election: Oct. 2014 (4 year terms)
Alan McLauchlan, Mayor
Randi Salamanowicz, Chief Administrative Officer

Treherne
P.O. Box 30
215 Broadway St.
Treherne, MB R0G 2V0
Tel: 204-723-2044; *Fax:* 204-723-2719
treherneinfo@mts.net
www.treherne.ca
Municipal Type: Town
Incorporated: Jan. 5, 1948 *Area:* 1.96 sq km
Population in 2006: 646
Provincial Electoral District(s): Carman

Federal Electoral District(s): Portage-Lisgar
Next Election: Oct. 2014 (4 year terms)
James Knockaert, Mayor
Jackie Jenkinson, Chief Administrative Officer

Virden
P.O. Box 310
236 Wellington St. West
Virden, MB R0M 2C0
Tel: 204-748-2440; *Fax:* 204-748-2501
virden_cao@mts.net
virden.cimnet.ca
Municipal Type: Town
Incorporated: Jan. 6, 1904 *Area:* 8.56 sq km
Population in 2006: 3,010
Provincial Electoral District(s): Arthur-Virden
Federal Electoral District(s): Brandon-Souris
Next Election: Oct. 2014 (4 year terms)
Jeff McConnell, Mayor
Rhonda Stewart, Chief Administrative Officer

Waskada
P.O. Box 40
33 Railway Ave.
Waskada, MB R0M 2E0
Tel: 204-673-2401; *Fax:* 204-673-2663
waskadan@mts.net
www.waskada.ca
Municipal Type: Village
Incorporated: Jan. 7, 1949 *Area:* 0.77 sq km
Population in 2006: 199
Provincial Electoral District(s): Arthur-Virden
Federal Electoral District(s): Brandon-Souris
Next Election: Oct. 2014 (4 year terms)
Gary Williams, Mayor
Diane Woodworth, Chief Administrative Officer

Wawanesa
P.O. Box 278
106 - 4th St.
Wawanesa, MB R0K 2G0
Tel: 204-824-2244; *Fax:* 204-824-2244
vwawa@mts.net
www.wawanesa.ca
Municipal Type: Village
Incorporated: Jan. 6, 1909 *Area:* 2.26 sq km
Population in 2006: 535
Provincial Electoral District(s): Minnedosa
Federal Electoral District(s): Brandon-Souris
Next Election: Oct. 2014 (4 year terms)
Bruce Gullett, Mayor
Leonard Plett, Chief Administrative Officer

Winnipeg Beach
P.O. Box 160
29 Robinson Ave.
Winnipeg Beach, MB R0C 3G0
Tel: 204-389-2698; *Fax:* 204-389-2019
info@winnipegbeach.ca
www.winnipegbeach.ca
Municipal Type: Town
Incorporated: Jan. 5, 1914 *Area:* 3.88 sq km
Population in 2006: 1,017
Provincial Electoral District(s): Gimli
Federal Electoral District(s): Selkirk-Interlake
Next Election: Oct. 2014 (4 year terms)
Tony Pimentel, Mayor
Doreen Steg, Chief Administrative Officer

Winnipegosis
P.O. Box 370
130 - 2nd St.
Winnipegosis, MB R0L 2G0
Tel: 204-656-4791; *Fax:* 204-656-4751
vofwinnipegosis@mts.net
www.winnipegosis.ca
Municipal Type: Village
Incorporated: Jan. 6, 1915 *Area:* 2.5 sq km
Population in 2006: 628
Provincial Electoral District(s): Swan River
Federal Electoral District(s): Dauphin-Swan River-Marquette
Next Election: Oct. 2014 (4 year terms)
Dan Brown, Mayor
Jackie Patterson, Chief Administrative Officer

Rural Municipality

Albert
P.O. Box 70
14 Morris St.
Tilston, MB R0M 2B0
Tel: 204-686-2271; *Fax:* 204-686-2335
rmalbert@xplornet.com
Municipal Type: Rural Municipality
Incorporated: Jan. 3, 1946 *Area:* 769.55 sq km
Population in 2006: 339
Provincial Electoral District(s): Arthur-Virden
Federal Electoral District(s): Brandon-Souris
Next Election: Oct. 2014 (4 year terms)
Tom Campbell, Reeve
Trudy Murray, Chief Administrative Officer

Alexander
P.O. Box 100
104058 Provincial Trunk Hwy. 11
St Georges, MB R0E 1V0
Tel: 204-367-6170; *Fax:* 204-367-2257
info@rmalexander.com
Municipal Type: Rural Municipality
Incorporated: Jan. 2, 1945 *Area:* 1,568.66 sq km
Population in 2006: 2,978
Provincial Electoral District(s): Lac du Bonnet; Selkirk
Federal Electoral District(s): Provencher; Brandon-Souris; Selkirk-Interlake
Next Election: Oct. 2014 (4 year terms)
Ed Arnold, Reeve
Scott Spicer, Chief Administrative Officer

Alonsa
P.O. Box 127
20 Railway Ave.
Alonsa, MB R0H 0A0
Tel: 204-767-2054; *Fax:* 204-767-2044
rmalonsa@inetlink.ca
Municipal Type: Rural Municipality
Area: 2,977.50 sq km
Population in 2006: 1,446
Provincial Electoral District(s): Ste. Rose
Federal Electoral District(s): Dauphin-Swan River-Marquette
Next Election: Oct. 2014 (4 year terms)
Stan Asham, Reeve
Pamela Sul, Chief Administrative Officer

Archie
P.O. Box 67
202 Qu'Appelle St.
McAuley, MB R0M 1H0
Tel: 204-722-2053; *Fax:* 204-722-2027
rmarchie@mts.net
Municipal Type: Rural Municipality
Incorporated: Jan. 2, 1883 *Area:* 577.68 sq km
Population in 2006: 330
Provincial Electoral District(s): Russell
Federal Electoral District(s): Dauphin-Swan River-Marquette
Next Election: Oct. 2014 (4 year terms)
Wendy Davidson, Reeve
Nicole Webb, Chief Administrative Officer

Argyle
P.O. Box 40
132 - 2nd St. North
Baldur, MB R0K 0B0
Tel: 204-535-2176; *Fax:* 204-535-2505
rmofargyle@inetbiz.ca
Municipal Type: Rural Municipality
Incorporated: Jan. 1, 1882 *Area:* 770.44 sq km
Population in 2006: 1,073
Provincial Electoral District(s): Turtle Mountain
Federal Electoral District(s): Brandon-Souris; Selkirk-Interlake
Next Election: Oct. 2014 (4 year terms)
Bob Conibear, Reeve
Janine Wiebe, Chief Administrative Officer

Armstrong
P.O. Box 69
55 Hwy. 17
Inwood, MB R0C 1P0
Tel: 204-278-3377; *Fax:* 204-278-3437
rmofarmstrong@highspeedcrow.ca
Municipal Type: Rural Municipality
Incorporated: Dec. 5, 1944 *Area:* 1,864.96 sq km
Population in 2006: 1,919
Provincial Electoral District(s): Interlake
Federal Electoral District(s): Selkirk-Interlake
Next Election: Oct. 2014 (4 year terms)
Garry Wasylowski, Reeve
Carole Oppermann, Chief Administrative Officer

Arthur
P.O. Box 429
138 Main St.
Melita, MB R0M 1L0
Tel: 204-522-3263; *Fax:* 204-522-8706
rmarthur@mts.net
Municipal Type: Rural Municipality
Area: 765.77 sq km
Population in 2006: 440
Provincial Electoral District(s): Arthur-Virden
Federal Electoral District(s): Brandon-Souris
Next Election: Oct. 2014 (4 year terms)
James Trewin, Reeve
Sandra Anderson, Chief Administrative Officer

Bifrost
P.O. Box 70
329 River Rd.
Arborg, MB R0C 0A0
Tel: 204-376-2391; *Fax:* 204-376-2742
bifrost@mts.net
Municipal Type: Rural Municipality
Incorporated: Jan. 4, 1908 *Area:* 1,642.58 sq km
Population in 2006: 2,972
Provincial Electoral District(s): Interlake
Federal Electoral District(s): Selkirk-Interlake
Next Election: Oct. 2014 (4 year terms)
Harold J. Foster, Reeve
R. Kim Dalton, Chief Administrative Officer

Birtle
P.O. Box 70
678 Main St.
Birtle, MB R0M 0C0
Tel: 204-842-3403; *Fax:* 204-842-3496
cao@birtle.ca
Municipal Type: Rural Municipality
Incorporated: Jan. 3, 1884 *Area:* 849.13 sq km
Population in 2006: 666
Provincial Electoral District(s): Russell
Federal Electoral District(s): Dauphin-Swan River-Marquette
Next Election: Oct. 2014 (4 year terms)
Roger Wilson, Reeve
Debbie Jensen, Chief Administrative Officer

Blanshard
P.O. Box 179
10 Cochrane St.
Oak River, MB R0K 1T0
Tel: 204-566-2146; *Fax:* 204-566-2126
blanshardrm@inetlink.ca
www.rmofblanshard.ca
Municipal Type: Rural Municipality
Incorporated: Jan. 3, 1884 *Area:* 578.98 sq km
Population in 2006: 586
Provincial Electoral District(s): Russell
Federal Electoral District(s): Dauphin-Swan River-Marquette
Next Election: Oct. 2014 (4 year terms)
Brent Fortune, Reeve
Diane Kuculym, Chief Administrative Officer

Brenda
P.O. Box 40
33 Railway Ave.
Waskada, MB R0M 2E0
Tel: 204-673-2401; *Fax:* 204-673-2663
waskadan@mts.net
Municipal Type: Rural Municipality
Area: 766 sq km
Population in 2006: 549
Provincial Electoral District(s): Arthur-Virden
Federal Electoral District(s): Brandon-Souris
Next Election: Oct. 2014 (4 year terms)
Duncan Stewart, Reeve
Diane Woodworth, Chief Administrative Officer

Brokenhead
P.O. Box 490
72013 Rd. 42 East
Beausejour, MB R0E 0C0
Tel: 204-268-6700; *Fax:* 204-268-1504
rmbroken@granite.mb.ca
www.granite.mb.ca/erdc/brokenhead/main.html
Municipal Type: Rural Municipality
Incorporated: Jan. 2, 1900 *Area:* 750.54 sq km
Population in 2006: 3,940
Provincial Electoral District(s): Lac du Bonnet
Federal Electoral District(s): Selkirk-Interlake
Next Election: Oct. 2014 (4 year terms)
Glen Dudek, Reeve
Christine Hutlet, Chief Administrative Officer

Cameron
P.O. Box 399
209 Airdrie St.
Hartney, MB R0M 0X0
Tel: 204-858-2590; *Fax:* 204-858-2681
hartney@mts.net
Municipal Type: Rural Municipality
Incorporated: Jan. 6, 1897 *Area:* 759.15 sq km
Population in 2006: 433
Provincial Electoral District(s): Arthur-Virden
Federal Electoral District(s): Brandon-Souris
Next Election: Oct. 2014 (4 year terms)
Wayne Drummond, Reeve
Brad Coe, Chief Administrative Officer

Cartier
P.O. Box 117
28 Provincial Rd. 248 South
Elie, MB R0H 0H0
Tel: 204-353-2214; *Fax:* 204-353-2335
anne@rm-cartier.mb.ca
www.rm-cartier.mb.ca
Municipal Type: Rural Municipality
Incorporated: Jan. 5, 1914 *Area:* 553.42 sq km
Population in 2006: 3,162
Provincial Electoral District(s): Morris
Federal Electoral District(s): Portage-Lisgar
Next Election: Oct. 2014 (4 year terms)
Roland Rasmussen, Reeve
Anne Burns, Chief Administrative Officer

Clanwilliam
P.O. Box 40
45 Main St.
Erickson, MB R0J 0P0
Tel: 204-636-2431; *Fax:* 204-636-2516
erikclan@mts.net
Municipal Type: Rural Municipality
Incorporated: Jan. 3, 1884 *Area:* 354.01 sq km
Population in 2006: 494
Provincial Electoral District(s): Russell
Federal Electoral District(s): Dauphin-Swan River-Marquette
Next Election: Oct. 2014 (4 year terms)
Victor Baraniuk, Reeve
Kat Bridgeman, Chief Administrative Officer

Coldwell
P.O. Box 90
35 Main St.
Lundar, MB R0C 1Y0
Tel: 204-762-5421; *Fax:* 204-762-5177
coldwell@mts.net
Municipal Type: Rural Municipality
Incorporated: Jan. 4, 1913 *Area:* 901.84 sq km
Population in 2006: 1,339
Provincial Electoral District(s): Lakeside
Federal Electoral District(s): Selkirk-Interlake
Next Election: Oct. 2014 (4 year terms)
Brian Sigfusson, Reeve
Nicole Christensen, Chief Administrative Officer

Cornwallis
P.O. Box 10 500
RR#5
Brandon, MB R7A 5Y5
Tel: 204-725-8686; *Fax:* 204-725-3659
info@gov.cornwallis.mb.ca
www.gov.cornwallis.mb.ca
Municipal Type: Rural Municipality
Incorporated: Jan. 3, 1884 *Area:* 500.82 sq km
Population in 2006: 4,058
Provincial Electoral District(s): Minnedosa
Federal Electoral District(s): Brandon-Souris
Next Election: Oct. 2014 (4 year terms)
Reg Atkinson, Reeve
Donna Anderson, Chief Administrative Officer

Daly
P.O. Box 538
645 - 2nd Ave.
Rivers, MB R0K 1X0
Tel: 204-328-7410; *Fax:* 204-328-4431
rmdaly@mts.net
www.townofrivers.mb.ca
Municipal Type: Rural Municipality
Area: 562.44 sq km
Population in 2006: 868
Provincial Electoral District(s): Minnedosa
Federal Electoral District(s): Brandon-Souris
Next Election: Oct. 2014 (4 year terms)
Evan Smith, Reeve
Lorne Green, Chief Administrative Officer

Dauphin
P.O. Box 574
Hwy. 20A East
Dauphin, MB R7N 2V4
Tel: 204-638-4531; *Fax:* 204-638-7598
rmofdphn@mts.net
Municipal Type: Rural Municipality
Area: 1,516.1 sq km
Population in 2006: 2,328
Provincial Electoral District(s): Dauphin-Roblin
Federal Electoral District(s): Dauphin-Swan River-Marquette
Next Election: Oct. 2014 (4 year terms)
Dennis Forbes, Reeve
Marlene Durston, Chief Administrative Officer

De Salaberry
P.O. Box 40
466 Sabourin St.
St Pierre Jolys, MB R0A 1V0
Tel: 204-433-7406; *Fax:* 204-433-7063
info@rmdesalaberry.mb.ca
www.rmdesalaberry.mb.ca
Municipal Type: Rural Municipality
Incorporated: Jan. 2, 1883 *Area:* 670.29 sq km
Population in 2006: 3,349
Provincial Electoral District(s): Morris
Federal Electoral District(s): Provencher
Next Election: Oct. 2014 (4 year terms)
Ron Musick, Reeve
Luc Lahaie, Chief Administrative Officer

Dufferin
P.O. Box 100
12 - 2nd Ave. SW
Carman, MB R0G 0J0
Tel: 204-745-2301; *Fax:* 204-745-6348
rmduff@mts.net
Municipal Type: Rural Municipality
Incorporated: Feb. 7, 1880 *Area:* 915.72 sq km
Population in 2006: 2,199
Provincial Electoral District(s): Carman
Federal Electoral District(s): Portage-Lisgar
Next Election: Oct. 2014 (4 year terms)
Shawn McCutcheon, Reeve
Sharla Murray, Chief Administrative Officer

East St. Paul
#1, 3021 Bird's Hill Rd.
East St Paul, MB R2E 1A7
Tel: 204-668-8112; *Fax:* 204-668-1987
administration.department@eaststpaul.com
www.eaststpaul.com
Municipal Type: Rural Municipality
Incorporated: May 2, 1916 *Area:* 42.1 sq km
Population in 2006: 8,733
Provincial Electoral District(s): Springfield
Federal Electoral District(s): Kildonan-St. Paul
Next Election: Oct. 2014 (4 year terms)
Jerome Mauws, Chief Administrative Officer
Lawrence Morris, Reeve

Edward
P.O. Box 100
58 Railway Ave.
Pierson, MB R0M 1S0
Tel: 204-634-2231; *Fax:* 204-634-2479
rmofedw@inethome.ca
Municipal Type: Rural Municipality
Incorporated: Jan. 1, 1905 *Area:* 769.14 sq km
Population in 2006: 621
Provincial Electoral District(s): Arthur-Virden
Federal Electoral District(s): Brandon-Souris
Next Election: Oct. 2014 (4 year terms)
Ralph Wang, Reeve
Audrey Bird, Chief Administrative Officer

Ellice
P.O. Box 100
100 Chartier Ave. West
St. Lazare, MB R0M 1Y0
Tel: 204-683-2241; *Fax:* 204-683-2317
laz_ell@mts.net
Municipal Type: Rural Municipality
Incorporated: Jan. 2, 1883 *Area:* 572.74 sq km
Population in 2006: 423
Provincial Electoral District(s): Russell
Federal Electoral District(s): Dauphin-Swan River-Marquette
Next Election: Oct. 2014 (4 year terms)
Guy Huberdeau, Reeve
Richard W. Fouillard, Chief Administrative Officer

Elton
Forest, MB R0K 0W0
Tel: 204-728-7834; *Fax:* 204-725-1865
elton@inetlink.ca
Municipal Type: Rural Municipality
Incorporated: Jan. 2, 1883 *Area:* 571.85 sq km
Population in 2006: 1,285
Provincial Electoral District(s): Minnedosa
Federal Electoral District(s): Brandon-Souris
Next Election: Oct. 2014 (4 year terms)
Jim Boyd, Reeve
Kathleen E.I. Steele, Chief Administrative Officer

Eriksdale
P.O. Box 10
10 Main St.
Eriksdale, MB R0C 0W0
Tel: 204-739-2666; *Fax:* 204-739-2073
admin@eriksdale.com
www.eriksdale.com
Municipal Type: Rural Municipality
Incorporated: Jan. 6, 1904 *Area:* 784.76 sq km
Population in 2006: 911
Provincial Electoral District(s): Interlake
Federal Electoral District(s): Selkirk-Interlake
Next Election: Oct. 2014 (4 year terms)
Arne Lindell, Reeve
Arlene Brandson Darknell, Chief Administrative Officer

Ethelbert
P.O. Box 115
5 Railway Ave. North
Ethelbert, MB R0L 0T0
Tel: 204-742-3212; *Fax:* 204-742-3642
rmethelbert@inetlink.ca
Municipal Type: Rural Municipality
Incorporated: Jan. 1, 1905 *Area:* 1,134.5 sq km
Population in 2006: 383
Provincial Electoral District(s): Swan River
Federal Electoral District(s): Dauphin-Swan River-Marquette
Next Election: Oct. 2014 (4 year terms)
Art Potoroka, Reeve
Loretta Woytkiewicz, Chief Administrative Officer

Fisher
P.O. Box 280
30 Tache St.
Fisher Branch, MB R0C 0Z0
Tel: 204-372-6393; *Fax:* 204-372-8470
rmoffisher@mts.net
Municipal Type: Rural Municipality
Incorporated: Jan. 2, 1945 *Area:* 1,481.35 sq km
Population in 2006: 1,944
Provincial Electoral District(s): Interlake
Federal Electoral District(s): Selkirk-Interlake
Next Election: Oct. 2014 (4 year terms)
Richard Hyde, Reeve
Linda Podaima, Chief Administrative Officer

Franklin
P.O. Box 66
115 Waddell Ave.
Dominion City, MB R0A 0H0
Tel: 204-427-2557; *Fax:* 204-427-2224
rmfrank@mts.net
Municipal Type: Rural Municipality
Area: 953.34 sq km
Population in 2006: 1,768
Provincial Electoral District(s): Emerson
Federal Electoral District(s): Dauphin-Swan River-Marquette; Provencher
Next Election: Oct. 2014 (4 year terms)
Greg Janzen, Reeve
Tracey French, Chief Administrative Officer

Gilbert Plains
P.O. Box 220
201 Main St. North
Gilbert Plains, MB R0L 0X0
Tel: 204-548-2326; *Fax:* 204-548-2564
rmofgilbertplains@mts.net
www.gilbertplains.com
Municipal Type: Rural Municipality
Incorporated: Jan. 3, 1901 *Area:* 1,048.14 sq km
Population in 2006: 834
Provincial Electoral District(s): Dauphin-Roblin
Federal Electoral District(s): Dauphin-Swan River-Marquette
Next Election: Oct. 2014 (4 year terms)
Gary Momotiuk, Reeve
Susan Boyachek, Chief Administrative Officer

Gimli
P.O. Box 1246
62 - 2nd St.
Gimli, MB R0C 1B0
Tel: 204-642-6650; *Fax:* 204-642-6660
gimli@rmgimli.com
www.gimli.ca
Municipal Type: Rural Municipality
Incorporated: Jan. 7, 1887 *Area:* 319.25 sq km
Population in 2006: 5,797
Provincial Electoral District(s): Gimli
Federal Electoral District(s): Selkirk-Interlake
Next Election: Oct. 2014 (4 year terms)
Lynn Greenberg, Reeve
Joann King, Chief Administrative Officer

Glenella
P.O. Box 10
50 Main St. North
Glenella, MB R0J 0V0
Tel: 204-352-4281; *Fax:* 204-352-4100
rmofglen@inetlink.ca
Municipal Type: Rural Municipality
Incorporated: Jan. 5, 1920 *Area:* 497.14 sq km
Population in 2006: 517
Provincial Electoral District(s): Ste. Rose
Federal Electoral District(s): Dauphin-Swan River-Marquette
Next Election: Oct. 2014 (4 year terms)
Derek Klassen, Reeve
Wendy Wutzke, Chief Administrative Officer

Glenwood
P.O. Box 487
100 - 2nd St. South
Souris, MB R0K 2C0
Tel: 204-483-2822; *Fax:* 204-483-2062
rmglenwood@mts.net
Municipal Type: Rural Municipality
Incorporated: 1883 *Area:* 577.58 sq km
Population in 2006: 640
Provincial Electoral District(s): Minnedosa
Federal Electoral District(s): Brandon-Souris
Next Election: Oct. 2014 (4 year terms)
M.E. (Sandy) Sanderson, Reeve
Lisa Greig, Chief Administrative Officer

Grahamdale
P.O. Box 160
23 Government Rd.
Moosehorn, MB R0C 2E0
Tel: 204-768-2858; *Fax:* 204-768-3374
info@grahamdale.ca
www.grahamdale.ca
Municipal Type: Rural Municipality
Incorporated: Jan. 2, 1945 *Area:* 2,384.62 sq km
Population in 2006: 1,416
Provincial Electoral District(s): Interlake
Federal Electoral District(s): Selkirk-Interlake
Next Election: Oct. 2014 (4 year terms)
Diane Price, Reeve
Shelly Schwitek, Chief Administrative Officer

Grandview
P.O. Box 340
531 Main St.
Grandview, MB R0L 0Y0
Tel: 204-546-5080; *Fax:* 204-546-5089
rmgra@inetlink.ca
www.rmofgrandview.ca
Municipal Type: Rural Municipality
Incorporated: Jan. 3, 1901 *Area:* 1,152.5 sq km
Population in 2006: 736
Provincial Electoral District(s): Dauphin-Roblin
Federal Electoral District(s): Dauphin-Swan River-Marquette
Next Election: Oct. 2014 (4 year terms)
Clifford Kutzan, Reeve
Sharon Storozuk, Chief Administrative Officer

Grey
P.O. Box 99
34 Main St. North
Elm Creek, MB R0G 0N0
Tel: 204-436-2014; *Fax:* 204-436-2543
rmofgrey@mts.net
www.rmofgrey.ca
Municipal Type: Rural Municipality
Incorporated: Jan. 2, 1906 *Area:* 958.49 sq km
Population in 2006: 2,004
Provincial Electoral District(s): Carman
Federal Electoral District(s): Portage-Lisgar
Next Election: Oct. 2014 (4 year terms)
Ted Tkachyk, Reeve
Kim Gibson, Chief Administrative Officer

Hamiota
P.O. Box 100
45 Maple Ave. East
Hamiota, MB R0M 0T0
Tel: 204-764-3050; *Fax:* 204-764-3055
info@hamiota.com
www.hamiota.com
Municipal Type: Rural Municipality
Incorporated: 1906 *Area:* 572.38 sq km
Population in 2006: 437
Provincial Electoral District(s): Russell
Federal Electoral District(s): Dauphin-Swan River-Marquette
Next Election: Oct. 2014 (4 year terms)
Randy Lints, Reeve
Tom Mollard, Chief Administrative Officer

Hanover
P.O. Box 1720
28 Westland Dr.
Steinbach, MB R5G 1N4
Tel: 204-326-4488; *Fax:* 204-326-4830
www.hanovermb.ca
Municipal Type: Rural Municipality
Incorporated: Jan. 7, 1881 *Area:* 740.31 sq km
Population in 2006: 11,871
Provincial Electoral District(s): Steinbach
Federal Electoral District(s): Provencher
Next Election: Oct. 2014 (4 year terms)
Stan Toews, Reeve
Douglas E. Cavers, Chief Administrative Officer

Harrison
P.O. Box 220
108 Main St.
Newdale, MB R0J 1J0
Tel: 204-849-2107; *Fax:* 204-849-2190
rmharris@inetbiz.ca
www.rmofharrison.com
Municipal Type: Rural Municipality
Incorporated: Jan. 2, 1883 *Area:* 476.73 sq km
Population in 2006: 812
Provincial Electoral District(s): Russell
Federal Electoral District(s): Dauphin-Swan River-Marquette
Next Election: Oct. 2014 (4 year terms)
Murray Davies, Reeve
Donna Memryk, Chief Administrative Officer

Headingley
#1, 126 Bridge Rd.
Headingley, MB R4H 1G9
Tel: 204-837-5766; *Fax:* 204-831-7207
dwhite@rmofheadingley.ca
www.rmofheadingley.ca
Municipal Type: Rural Municipality
Incorporated: Jan. 4, 1992 *Area:* 106.96 sq km
Population in 2006: 2,726
Provincial Electoral District(s): Morris
Federal Electoral District(s): Charleswood-St. James-Assiniboia
Next Election: Oct. 2014 (4 year terms)
Wilfred R. Taillieu, Reeve
Chris Fulsher, Chief Administrative Officer

Hillsburg
P.O. Box 1180
130 - 2nd Ave. NW
Roblin, MB R0L 1P0
Tel: 204-937-2155; *Fax:* 204-937-3317
rmhills@mts.net
Municipal Type: Rural Municipality
Incorporated: Jan. 2, 1912 *Area:* 656.76 sq km
Population in 2006: 484
Provincial Electoral District(s): Dauphin-Roblin
Federal Electoral District(s): Dauphin-Swan River-Marquette
Next Election: Oct. 2014 (4 year terms)
Robert Misko, Reeve
Robin Perchaluk, Chief Administrative Officer

Kelsey
P.O. Box 578
264 Fischer Ave.
The Pas, MB R9A 1K6
Tel: 204-623-7474; *Fax:* 204-623-4546
rmkelsey@mts.net
Municipal Type: Rural Municipality
Incorporated: Jan. 7, 1944 *Area:* 867.64 sq km
Population in 2006: 2,453
Provincial Electoral District(s): Flin Flon; The Pas
Federal Electoral District(s): Churchill
Next Election: Oct. 2014 (4 year terms)
Rod Berezowecki, Reeve
Jerry Hlady, Chief Administrative Officer

La Broquerie
P.O. Box 130
123 Simard St.
La Broquerie, MB R0A 0W0
Tel: 204-424-5251; *Fax:* 204-424-5193
labroquerie@rmlabroquerie.ca
www.labroquerie.com
Municipal Type: Rural Municipality
Incorporated: Jan. 2, 1883 *Area:* 578.2 sq km
Population in 2006: 3,659
Provincial Electoral District(s): Emerson
Federal Electoral District(s): Provencher
Next Election: Oct. 2014 (4 year terms)
Claude Lussier, Reeve
Roger Bouvier, Chief Administrative Officer

Lac du Bonnet
P.O. Box 100
4187 Provincial Trunk Hwy. 317
Lac du Bonnet, MB R0E 1A0
Tel: 204-345-2619; *Fax:* 204-345-6716
rmldb@mts.net
www.lacdubonnet.com
Municipal Type: Rural Municipality
Incorporated: Jan. 2, 1917 *Area:* 1,100.17 sq km
Population in 2006: 2,812
Provincial Electoral District(s): Lac du Bonnet
Federal Electoral District(s): Provencher
Next Election: Oct. 2014 (4 year terms)
Karl Gugenheimer, Reeve
Donna Tschetter, Chief Administrative Officer

Lakeview
P.O. Box 100
101 Main St.
Langruth, MB R0H 0N0
Tel: 204-445-2243; *Fax:* 204-445-2162
rmlakeview@mts.net
Municipal Type: Rural Municipality
Incorporated: Jan. 5, 1920 *Area:* 567.87 sq km
Population in 2006: 342
Provincial Electoral District(s): Ste. Rose
Federal Electoral District(s): Dauphin-Swan River-Marquette
Next Election: Oct. 2014 (4 year terms)
Philip Thordarson, Reeve
Ron Brown, Chief Administrative Officer

Langford
P.O. Box 280
275 Hamilton St.
Neepawa, MB R0J 1H0
Tel: 204-476-7600; *Fax:* 204-476-7624
langford@westman.wave.ca
Municipal Type: Rural Municipality
Area: 561.95 sq km
Population in 2006: 787
Provincial Electoral District(s): Ste. Rose
Federal Electoral District(s): Dauphin-Swan River-Marquette
Next Election: Oct. 2014 (4 year terms)
Kathy Jasienczyk, Reeve
Allison Bardsley, Chief Administrative Officer

Lansdowne
P.O. Box 141
302 Lansdowne Ave.
Arden, MB R0J 0B0
Tel: 204-368-2202; *Fax:* 204-368-2278
rmlansdowne@inetlink.ca
Municipal Type: Rural Municipality
Incorporated: Jan. 3, 1884 *Area:* 766.29 sq km
Population in 2006: 750
Provincial Electoral District(s): Ste. Rose
Federal Electoral District(s): Dauphin-Swan River-Marquette
Next Election: Oct. 2014 (4 year terms)
Richard Funk, Reeve
Tracey Winthrop-Meyers, Chief Administrative Officer

Lawrence
P.O. Box 220
714 Main St.
Rorketon, MB R0L 1R0
Tel: 204-732-2333; *Fax:* 204-732-2557
rmlaw@inetlink.ca
Municipal Type: Rural Municipality
Incorporated: Jan. 5, 1914 *Area:* 761.64 sq km
Population in 2006: 501
Provincial Electoral District(s): Dauphin-Roblin
Federal Electoral District(s): Dauphin-Swan River-Marquette
Next Election: Oct. 2014 (4 year terms)
Fred Taylor, Reeve

Vacant, Chief Administrative Officer

Lorne
P.O. Box 10
307 - 3rd St.
Somerset, MB R0G 2L0
Tel: 204-744-2133; *Fax:* 204-744-2349
rmlorne@inetlink.ca
Municipal Type: Rural Municipality
Incorporated: Jan. 5, 1880 *Area:* 906.82 sq km
Population in 2006: 2,003
Provincial Electoral District(s): Carman
Federal Electoral District(s): Portage-Lisgar
Next Election: Oct. 2014 (4 year terms)
Aurel Pantel, Reeve
Shannon Gaultier, Chief Administrative Officer

Louise
P.O. Box 310
26 South Railway Ave. East
Crystal City, MB R0K 0N0
Tel: 204-873-2591; *Fax:* 204-873-2459
rmlouise@inetlink.ca
Municipal Type: Rural Municipality
Incorporated: Jan. 5, 1880 *Area:* 932.67 sq km
Population in 2006: 819
Provincial Electoral District(s): Turtle Mountain
Federal Electoral District(s): Portage-Lisgar
Next Election: Oct. 2014 (4 year terms)
Kenneth S. Buchanan, Reeve
Alexis Gardiner, Chief Administrative Officer

Macdonald
P.O. Box 100
161 Mandan Dr.
Sanford, MB R0G 2J0
Tel: 204-736-2255; *Fax:* 204-736-4335
info@rmofmacdonald.com
rmofmacdonald.com
Municipal Type: Rural Municipality
Incorporated: Jan. 7, 1881 *Area:* 1,156.62 sq km
Population in 2006: 5,653
Provincial Electoral District(s): Morris
Federal Electoral District(s): Portage-Lisgar
Next Election: Oct. 2014 (4 year terms)
Rodney Burns, Reeve
W. Tom Raine, Chief Administrative Officer

McCreary
P.O. Box 338
432 - 1st Ave.
McCreary, MB R0J 1B0
Tel: 204-835-2309; *Fax:* 204-835-2649
rmmccreary@inetlink.ca
Municipal Type: Rural Municipality
Incorporated: Jan. 6, 1909 *Area:* 522.69 sq km
Population in 2006: 476
Provincial Electoral District(s): Ste. Rose
Federal Electoral District(s): Dauphin-Swan River-Marquette
Next Election: Oct. 2014 (4 year terms)
Larry McLauchlan, Reeve
Margaret I. Roncin, Chief Administrative Officer

Miniota
P.O. Box 70
111 Sarah Ave.
Miniota, MB R0M 1M0
Tel: 204-567-3683; *Fax:* 204-567-3807
miniota@mts.net
Municipal Type: Rural Municipality
Incorporated: 1900 *Area:* 832.75 sq km
Population in 2006: 904
Provincial Electoral District(s): Russell
Federal Electoral District(s): Dauphin-Swan River-Marquette
Next Election: Oct. 2014 (4 year terms)
Olive McKean, Reeve
Tina Collier, Chief Administrative Officer

Minitonas
P.O. Box 9
311 Main St.
Minitonas, MB R0L 1G0
Tel: 204-525-4461; *Fax:* 204-525-4857
rmmin@mts.net
Municipal Type: Rural Municipality
Incorporated: Jan. 3, 1901 *Area:* 1,197.67 sq km
Population in 2006: 1,105
Provincial Electoral District(s): Swan River
Federal Electoral District(s): Dauphin-Swan River-Marquette
Next Election: Oct. 2014 (4 year terms)
Michael McIntosh, Reeve
Carolyn Gordon, Chief Administrative Officer

Minto
P.O. Box 247
49 Main St. South
Minnedosa, MB R0J 1E0
Tel: 204-867-3865; *Fax:* 204-867-1937
rmminto@mts.net
Municipal Type: Rural Municipality
Incorporated: Jan. 5, 1903 *Area:* 363.65 sq km
Population in 2006: 667
Provincial Electoral District(s): Minnedosa
Federal Electoral District(s): Brandon-Souris; Dauphin-Swan River-Marquette
Next Election: Oct. 2014 (4 year terms)
Calvin Jacobson, Reeve
Aaren Robertson, Chief Administrative Officer

Montcalm
P.O. Box 300
46 - 1st St. East
Letellier, MB R0G 1C0
Tel: 204-737-2271; *Fax:* 204-737-2326
montcalm@mts.net
Municipal Type: Rural Municipality
Incorporated: Jan. 1, 1882 *Area:* 469.41 sq km
Population in 2006: 1,317
Provincial Electoral District(s): Emerson
Federal Electoral District(s): Provencher
Next Election: Oct. 2014 (4 year terms)
Roger Vermette, Reeve
Mitch Duval, Chief Administrative Officer

Morris
P.O. Box 518
207 Main St. North
Morris, MB R0G 1K0
Tel: 204-746-2642; *Fax:* 204-746-8801
rmmorris@mts.net
Municipal Type: Rural Municipality
Incorporated: Jan. 5, 1880 *Area:* 1,041.15 sq km
Population in 2006: 2,662
Provincial Electoral District(s): Morris
Federal Electoral District(s): Provencher
Next Election: Oct. 2014 (4 year terms)
Ralph Groening, Reeve
Michelle Robert, Chief Administrative Officer

Morton
P.O. Box 490
420 South Railway
Boissevain, MB R0K 0E0
Tel: 204-534-2433; *Fax:* 204-534-3710
boissevain@mts.net
Municipal Type: Rural Municipality
Area: 1,089.88 sq km
Population in 2006: 718
Provincial Electoral District(s): Arthur-Virden
Federal Electoral District(s): Brandon-Souris
Next Election: Oct. 2014 (4 year terms)
Robert J.D. McCallum, Reeve
Lloyd Leganchuk, Chief Administrative Officer

Mossey River
P.O. Box 80
100 - 2nd Ave. East
Fork River, MB R0L 0V0
Tel: 204-657-2331; *Fax:* 204-657-2202
rmmossey@inetlink.ca
Municipal Type: Rural Municipality
Incorporated: Jan. 2, 1906 *Area:* 1,123.06 sq km
Population in 2006: 614
Provincial Electoral District(s): Swan River
Federal Electoral District(s): Dauphin-Swan River-Mossey River
Next Election: Oct. 2014 (4 year terms)
Ron Kostyshyn, Reeve
Linda Rosteski, Chief Administrative Officer

Mountain
P.O. Box 155
200 Drury Ave.
Birch River, MB R0L 0E0
Tel: 204-236-4222; *Fax:* 204-236-4773
rmmountn@mts.net
Municipal Type: Rural Municipality
Area: 2607.69 sq km
Population in 2006: 1,336
Provincial Electoral District(s): Swan River
Federal Electoral District(s): Dauphin-Swan River-Marquette
Next Election: Oct. 2014 (4 year terms)
Robert Hanson, Reeve
Norman Bruce, Chief Administrative Officer

Mystery Lake
P.O. Box 189 Main
Airport Rd. South
Thompson, MB R8N 1N1
Tel: 204-677-4075; *Fax:* 204-778-7642
lgdmystlake@mymts.net
Municipal Type: Local Goverment District
Incorporated: Jan. 1, 1956 *Area:* 3,464.06 sq km
Population in 2006: 147
Next Election: Oct. 2014 (4 year terms)
Corinne Stewart, Resident Administrator & Acting Chief Administrative Officer

North Cypress
P.O. Box 130
316 - 4th Ave.
Carberry, MB R0K 0H0
Tel: 204-834-6600; *Fax:* 204-834-6604
north.cypress@rmofnorthcypress.ca
www.rmofnorthcypress.ca
Municipal Type: Rural Municipality
Incorporated: Jan. 1, 1882 *Area:* 1,199.92 sq km
Population in 2006: 1,902
Provincial Electoral District(s): Turtle Mountain
Federal Electoral District(s): Brandon-Souris
Next Election: Oct. 2014 (4 year terms)
Ralph Oliver, Reeve
Brent McMillan, Chief Administrative Officer

North Norfolk
P.O. Box 190
27 Hampton St. East
MacGregor, MB R0H 0R0
Tel: 204-685-2211; *Fax:* 204-685-2616
office@northnorfolk.ca
northnorfolk.ca
Municipal Type: Rural Municipality
Incorporated: Jan. 1, 1882 *Area:* 1,158.76 sq km
Population in 2006: 2,742
Provincial Electoral District(s): Turtle Mountain
Federal Electoral District(s): Portage-Lisgar
Next Election: Oct. 2014 (4 year terms)
Neil Christoffersen, Reeve
Valorie Unrau, Chief Administrative Officer

Oakland
P.O. Box 28
1 Main St.
Nesbitt, MB R0K 1P0
Tel: 204-824-2666; *Fax:* 204-824-2374
rm_of_oakland@hotmail.com
Municipal Type: Rural Municipality
Incorporated: Jan. 2, 1883 *Area:* 575.21 sq km
Population in 2006: 1,033
Provincial Electoral District(s): Minnedosa
Federal Electoral District(s): Brandon-Souris; Portage Lisgar
Next Election: Oct. 2014 (4 year terms)
David B. Inkster, Reeve
Marlene Biles, Chief Administrative Officer

Ochre River
P.O. Box 40
206 MacKenzie Ave.
Ochre River, MB R0L 1K0
Tel: 204-733-2423; *Fax:* 204-733-2259
rmochre@inetlink.ca
www.mts.net/~rmochre
Municipal Type: Rural Municipality
Incorporated: Jan. 3, 1901 *Area:* 535.59 sq km
Population in 2006: 929
Provincial Electoral District(s): Dauphin-Roblin
Federal Electoral District(s): Dauphin-Swan River-Marquette
Next Election: Oct. 2014 (4 year terms)
Clinton Cleave, Reeve
Pat Nichols, Chief Administrative Officer

Odanah
P.O. Box 1197
49 Main St. South
Minnedosa, MB R0J 1E0
Tel: 204-867-3282; *Fax:* 204-867-1937
rmminto@mts.net
Municipal Type: Rural Municipality
Incorporated: Jan. 2, 1883 *Area:* 380.25 sq km
Population in 2006: 540
Provincial Electoral District(s): Minnedosa
Federal Electoral District(s): Dauphin-Swan River-Marquette
Next Election: Oct. 2014 (4 year terms)
James A. Andersen, Reeve
Aaren Robertson, Chief Administrative Officer

Park
P.O. Box 190
43 Gateway St.
Onanole, MB R0J 1N0
Tel: 204-848-7614; *Fax:* 204-848-2082
admin@rmpark.org
www.rmpark.org
Municipal Type: Rural Municipality
Incorporated: Jan. 6, 1954 *Area:* 793.38 sq km
Population in 2006: 1,291
Provincial Electoral District(s): Dauphin-Roblin; Russell
Federal Electoral District(s): Dauphin-Swan River-Marquette
Next Election: Oct. 2014 (4 year terms)
Craig Atkinson, Reeve
Chad Davies, Chief Administrative Officer

Pembina
P.O. Box 189
315 Main St.
Manitou, MB R0G 1G0
Tel: 204-242-2838; *Fax:* 204-242-2798
admin@rmofpembina.com
www.rmofpembina.com
Municipal Type: Rural Municipality
Incorporated: Jan. 4, 1890 *Area:* 1,114.76 sq km
Population in 2006: 1,712
Provincial Electoral District(s): Pembina
Federal Electoral District(s): Portage-Lisgar
Next Election: Oct. 2014 (4 year terms)
Kim Taylor, Reeve
Judy D. Young, Chief Administrative Officer

Pinawa
P.O. Box 100
36 Burrows Rd.
Pinawa, MB R0E 1L0
Tel: 204-753-5100; *Fax:* 204-753-2770
info@pinawa.com
www.pinawa.com
Municipal Type: Local Goverment District
Incorporated: Jan. 3, 1963 *Area:* 128.47 sq km
Population in 2006: 1,450
Next Election: Oct. 2014 (4 year terms)
Blair Skinner, Mayor
Gary Hanna, Resident Administrator

Piney
P.O. Box 48
6092 Boundary St.
Vassar, MB R0A 2J0
Tel: 204-437-2284; *Fax:* 204-437-2556
martin_rmpiney@wiband.ca
www.rmofpiney.mb.ca
Municipal Type: Rural Municipality
Area: 2,433.77 sq km
Population in 2006: 1,755
Provincial Electoral District(s): Emerson
Federal Electoral District(s): Provencher
Next Election: Oct. 2014 (4 year terms)
Duane Boutang, Reeve
Martin Van Osch, Chief Administrative Officer

Pipestone
P.O. Box 99
401 - 3rd Ave.
Reston, MB R0M 1X0
Tel: 204-877-3327; *Fax:* 204-877-3999
admin@rmofpipestone.com
www.rmofpipestone.com
Municipal Type: Rural Municipality
Incorporated: Jan. 6, 1897 *Area:* 1,147.35 sq km
Population in 2006: 1,419
Provincial Electoral District(s): Arthur-Virden
Federal Electoral District(s): Brandon-Souris
Next Election: Oct. 2014 (4 year terms)
Ross Tycoles, Reeve
June Greggor, Chief Administrative Officer

Portage la Prairie
35 Tupper St. South
Portage la Prairie, MB R1N 1W7
Tel: 204-857-3821; *Fax:* 204-239-0069
info@rmofportage.ca
www.rmofportage.ca
Municipal Type: Rural Municipality
Incorporated: Jan. 4, 1879 *Area:* 1,964.32 sq km
Population in 2006: 6,793
Provincial Electoral District(s): Portage la Prairie; Carman
Federal Electoral District(s): Portage-Lisgar; Selkirk-Interlake
Next Election: Oct. 2014 (4 year terms)
Kam Blight, Reeve
Daryl Hrehirchuk, Chief Administrative Officer

Reynolds
P.O. Box 46
46044 Hwy. 11
Hadashville, MB R0E 0X0
Tel: 204-426-5305; *Fax:* 204-426-5552
rmreynol@mts.net
www.rmofreynolds.com
Municipal Type: Rural Municipality
Incorporated: Jan. 2, 1945 *Area:* 3,573.31 sq km
Population in 2006: 1,410
Provincial Electoral District(s): La Verendrye; Lac du Bonnet
Federal Electoral District(s): Provencher
Next Election: Oct. 2014 (4 year terms)
David Turchyn, Reeve
Holly Krysko, Chief Administrative Officer

Rhineland
P.O. Box 270
72 - 2nd St. NE
Altona, MB R0G 0B0
Tel: 204-324-5357; *Fax:* 204-324-1516
rhineland@mts.net
Municipal Type: Rural Municipality
Incorporated: Jan. 3, 1884 *Area:* 953.42 sq km
Population in 2006: 4,125
Provincial Electoral District(s): Emerson
Federal Electoral District(s): Portage-Lisgar
Next Election: Oct. 2014 (4 year terms)
Grant Heinrichs, Reeve
Michael Rempel, Chief Administrative Officer

Ritchot
352 Main St.
St. Adolphe, MB R5A 1B9
Tel: 204-883-2293; *Fax:* 204-883-2674
municipaloffice@ritchot.com
www.ritchot.com
Municipal Type: Rural Municipality
Incorporated: Jan. 4, 1890 *Area:* 333.53 sq km
Population in 2006: 5,051
Provincial Electoral District(s): La Verendrye; Morris
Federal Electoral District(s): Provencher; Winnipeg South
Next Election: Oct. 2014 (4 year terms)
Robert Stefaniuk, Mayor
Florence May, Chief Administrative Officer

Riverside
P.O. Box 126
110 Rea St.
Dunrea, MB R0K 0S0
Tel: 204-776-2113; *Fax:* 204-776-2228
riverside@mts.net
www.rmriverside.ca
Municipal Type: Rural Municipality
Area: 577.34 sq km
Population in 2006: 809
Provincial Electoral District(s): Turtle Mountain
Federal Electoral District(s): Brandon-Souris; Provencher; Kildonan-St. Paul
Next Election: Oct. 2014 (4 year terms)
Lonn Dunlop, Reeve
Lori Bessant, Chief Administrative Officer

Roblin
P.O. Box 9
485 Curwen St.
Cartwright, MB R0K 0L0
Tel: 204-529-2363; *Fax:* 204-529-2288
www.cartwrightroblin.ca
Municipal Type: Rural Municipality
Incorporated: Jan. 4, 1902 *Area:* 716.15 sq km
Population in 2006: 964
Provincial Electoral District(s): Turtle Mountain
Federal Electoral District(s): Brandon-Souris; Dauphin-Swan River-Marquette
Next Election: Oct. 2014 (4 year terms)
Tom Mowbray, Reeve
Colleen Mullin, Chief Administrative Officer

Rockwood
P.O. Box 902
285 Main St.
Stonewall, MB R0C 2Z0
Tel: 204-467-2272; *Fax:* 204-467-5329
info@rockwood.ca
www.rockwood.ca
Municipal Type: Rural Municipality
Incorporated: Jan. 7, 1881 *Area:* 1,199.76 sq km
Population in 2006: 7,692
Provincial Electoral District(s): Lakeside
Federal Electoral District(s): Selkirk-Interlake
Next Election: Oct. 2014 (4 year terms)
Jim Campbell, Reeve
L. Grant Thorsteinson, Chief Administrative Officer

Roland
P.O. Box 119
45 - 3rd St.
Roland, MB R0G 1T0
Tel: 204-343-2061; *Fax:* 204-343-2001
rmroland@pmcnet.ca
Municipal Type: Rural Municipality
Incorporated: Jan. 4, 1908 *Area:* 485.06 sq km
Population in 2006: 1,002
Provincial Electoral District(s): Carman
Federal Electoral District(s): Portage-Lisgar
Next Election: Oct. 2014 (4 year terms)
Brian Coates, Reeve
Kristi Olson, Chief Administrative Officer

Rosedale
P.O. Box 100
282 Hamilton St.
Neepawa, MB R0J 1H0
Tel: 204-476-5414; *Fax:* 204-476-5431
rosedale@mts.net
Municipal Type: Rural Municipality
Incorporated: Jan. 3, 1884 *Area:* 865.58 sq km
Population in 2006: 1,658
Provincial Electoral District(s): Ste. Rose
Federal Electoral District(s): Dauphin-Swan River-Marquette
Next Election: Oct. 2014 (4 year terms)
Edward Levandoski, Reeve
Karen McDonald, Chief Administrative Officer

Rossburn
P.O. Box 100
39 Main St. North
Rossburn, MB R0J 1V0
Tel: 204-859-2779; *Fax:* 204-859-2959
rsbrm@mts.net
Municipal Type: Rural Municipality
Incorporated: Jan. 3, 1884 *Area:* 679.29 sq km
Population in 2006: 514
Provincial Electoral District(s): Russell
Federal Electoral District(s): Dauphin-Swan River-Marquette
Next Election: Oct. 2014 (4 year terms)
Ed Mychasiw, Reeve
Marianne Choptuik, Chief Administrative Officer

Rosser
P.O. Box 131
Provincial Rd. 221
Rosser, MB R0H 1E0
Tel: 204-467-5711; *Fax:* 204-467-5958
info@rmofrosser.com
www.rmofrosser.com
Municipal Type: Rural Municipality
Incorporated: Jan. 1, 1893 *Area:* 441.43 sq km
Population in 2006: 1,364
Provincial Electoral District(s): Lakeside
Federal Electoral District(s): Selkirk-Interlake
Next Election: Oct. 2014 (4 year terms)
Frances Smee, Chief Administrative Officer
Beverley Wells, Reeve

Russell
P.O. Box 220
362 Main St. North
Russell, MB R0J 1W0
Tel: 204-773-2294; *Fax:* 204-773-3841
rmrussel@mts.net
Municipal Type: Rural Municipality
Incorporated: Jan. 1, 1882 *Area:* 567.83 sq km
Population in 2006: 487
Provincial Electoral District(s): Russell
Federal Electoral District(s): Dauphin-Swan River-Marquette
Next Election: Oct. 2014 (4 year terms)
Robert W. Muir, Reeve
Nicole Burdeniuk, Chief Administrative Officer

St. Andrews
P.O. Box 130
500 Railway Ave.
Clandeboye, MB R0C 0P0
Tel: 204-738-2264; *Fax:* 204-738-2500
info@rmofstandrews.com
www.rmofstandrews.com
Municipal Type: Rural Municipality
Incorporated: Jan. 5, 1880 *Area:* 752.7 sq km
Population in 2006: 11,359
Provincial Electoral District(s): Gimli
Federal Electoral District(s): Selkirk-Interlake
Next Election: Oct. 2014 (4 year terms)

Don Forfar, Reeve
Sue Sutherland, Chief Administrative Officer

Ste. Anne
141 Central Ave.
Ste. Anne, MB R5H 1C3
Tel: 204-422-5929; *Fax:* 204-422-9723
info@rmofsteanne.com
www.rmofsteanne.com
Municipal Type: Rural Municipality
Incorporated: Feb. 3, 1881 *Area:* 477.65 sq km
Population in 2006: 4,509
Provincial Electoral District(s): La Verendrye
Federal Electoral District(s): Provencher
Next Election: Oct. 2014 (4 year terms)
Art Bergmann, Reeve
A.T. (Loni) Eskildsen, Chief Administrative Officer

St. Clements
P.O. Box 2
1043 Kittson Rd.
East Selkirk, MB R0E 0M0
Tel: 204-482-3300; *Fax:* 204-482-3098
info@rmofstclements.com
www.rmofstclements.com
Municipal Type: Rural Municipality
Incorporated: July 7, 1883 *Area:* 728.67 sq km
Population in 2006: 9,706
Provincial Electoral District(s): Selkirk
Federal Electoral District(s): Selkirk-Interlake
Next Election: Oct. 2014 (4 year terms)
Steve Strang, Reeve
DJ Sigmundson, Chief Administrative Officer

St. François Xavier
1060 Hwy. 26
St François Xavier, MB R4L 1A5
Tel: 204-864-2092; *Fax:* 204-864-2390
info@rm-stfrancois.mb.ca
www.rm-stfrancois.mb.ca
Municipal Type: Rural Municipality
Incorporated: Jan. 5, 1880 *Area:* 204.55 sq km
Population in 2006: 1,087
Provincial Electoral District(s): Morris
Federal Electoral District(s): Portage-Lisgar
Next Election: Oct. 2014 (4 year terms)
Roger Poitras, Reeve
Robert Poirier, Chief Administrative Officer

St. Laurent
P.O. Box 220
436 St. Laurent Veterans Memorial Rd.
St Laurent, MB R0C 2S0
Tel: 204-646-2259; *Fax:* 204-646-2705
rmstlaur@mts.net
www.rmofstlaurent.ca
Municipal Type: Rural Municipality
Incorporated: Jan. 1, 1882 *Area:* 462.51 sq km
Population in 2006: 1,454
Provincial Electoral District(s): Lakeside
Federal Electoral District(s): Selkirk-Interlake
Next Election: Oct. 2014 (4 year terms)
Earl Zotter, Reeve
Diana Friesen, Chief Administrative Officer

Ste. Rose
P.O. Box 30
630 Central Ave.
Ste. Rose du Lac, MB R0L 1S0
Tel: 204-447-2633; *Fax:* 204-447-2278
rmstrose@mymts.net
www.sterose.ca
Municipal Type: Rural Municipality
Incorporated: Nov. 7, 1902 *Area:* 626.03 sq km
Population in 2006: 791
Provincial Electoral District(s): Ste. Rose
Federal Electoral District(s): Dauphin-Swan River-Marquette
Next Election: Oct. 2014 (4 year terms)
Maurice Maguet, Reeve
Michelle Denys, Chief Administrative Officer

Saskatchewan
P.O. Box 9
435 - 3rd Ave.
Rapid City, MB R0K 1W0
Tel: 204-826-2515; *Fax:* 204-826-2274
rmsk@mts.net
Municipal Type: Rural Municipality
Incorporated: Jan. 2, 1883 *Area:* 563.73 sq km
Population in 2006: 593
Provincial Electoral District(s): Minnedosa
Federal Electoral District(s): Dauphin-Swan River-Marquette
Next Election: Oct. 2014 (4 year terms)
Robert Sharpe, Reeve
Lois Sharpe, Chief Administrative Officer

Shell River
P.O. Box 998
213 - 2nd Ave. NW
Roblin, MB R0L 1P0
Tel: 204-937-4430; *Fax:* 204-937-8496
shellrvr@mts.net
www.rm.shellriver.mb.ca
Municipal Type: Rural Municipality
Incorporated: Jan. 3, 1884 *Area:* 735.12 sq km
Population in 2006: 931
Provincial Electoral District(s): Dauphin-Roblin
Federal Electoral District(s): Dauphin-Swan River-Marquette
Next Election: Oct. 2014 (4 year terms)
Albert Nabe, Reeve
Dione Cherneski, Chief Administrative Officer

Shellmouth - Boulton
P.O. Box 110
118 Main St.
Inglis, MB R0J 0X0
Tel: 204-564-2589; *Fax:* 204-564-2643
rmosb@mts.net
Municipal Type: Rural Municipality
Incorporated: Jan. 6, 1999 *Area:* 1,095.07 sq km
Population in 2006: 920
Provincial Electoral District(s): Russell
Federal Electoral District(s): Dauphin-Swan River-Marquette
Next Election: Oct. 2014 (4 year terms)
Alvin Zimmer, Reeve
Cindy Marzoff, Chief Administrative Officer

Shoal Lake
P.O. Box 278
306 Elm St.
Shoal Lake, MB R0J 1Z0
Tel: 204-759-2565; *Fax:* 204-759-2740
shoalake@goinet.ca
www.shoallake.ca
Municipal Type: Rural Municipality
Area: 568.18 sq km
Population in 2006: 555
Provincial Electoral District(s): Russell
Federal Electoral District(s): Dauphin-Swan River-Marquette
Next Election: Oct. 2014 (4 year terms)
Donald Yanick, Reeve
Nadine Gapka, Chief Administrative Officer

Sifton
P.O. Box 100
293 - 2nd Ave. West
Oak Lake, MB R0M 1P0
Tel: 204-855-2423; *Fax:* 204-855-2836
cao_sifton@mts.net
Municipal Type: Rural Municipality
Incorporated: Jan. 3, 1884 *Area:* 768.11 sq km
Population in 2006: 796
Provincial Electoral District(s): Arthur-Virden
Federal Electoral District(s): Brandon-Souris; Dauphin-Swan River-Marquette
Next Election: Oct. 2014 (4 year terms)
Rick Plaisier, Reeve
Mary Smith, Chief Administrative Officer

Siglunes
P.O. Box 370
38 Main St.
Ashern, MB R0C 0E0
Tel: 204-768-2641; *Fax:* 204-768-2301
siglunes@mts.net
Municipal Type: Rural Municipality
Incorporated: Jan. 2, 1917 *Area:* 837.42 sq km
Population in 2006: 1,480
Provincial Electoral District(s): Interlake
Federal Electoral District(s): Selkirk-Interlake
Next Election: Oct. 2014 (4 year terms)
Barry Zacharias, Reeve
William Hildebrand, Chief Administrative Officer

Silver Creek
P.O. Box 130
307 Main St.
Angusville, MB R0J 0A0
Tel: 204-773-2449; *Fax:* 204-773-3101
silcreek@mts.net
Municipal Type: Rural Municipality
Incorporated: Jan. 3, 1884 *Area:* 525.46 sq km
Population in 2006: 483
Provincial Electoral District(s): Russell
Federal Electoral District(s): Dauphin-Swan River-Marquette
Next Election: Oct. 2014 (4 year terms)
Fred Dunn, Reeve
Cheryl Mernyk, Chief Administrative Officer

South Cypress
P.O. Box 219
618 Railway Ave.
Glenboro, MB R0K 0X0
Tel: 204-827-2252; *Fax:* 204-827-2123
caormsc@mts.net
Municipal Type: Rural Municipality
Incorporated: Jan. 7, 1881 *Area:* 1,095.08 sq km
Population in 2006: 834
Provincial Electoral District(s): Turtle Mountain
Federal Electoral District(s): Brandon-Souris
Next Election: Oct. 2014 (4 year terms)
Earl E. Malyon, Reeve
Eric C. Plaetinck, Chief Administrative Officer

South Norfolk
P.O. Box 30
180 Broadway St.
Treherne, MB R0G 2V0
Tel: 204-723-2044; *Fax:* 204-723-2719
treherne@mts.net
Municipal Type: Rural Municipality
Area: 726.76 sq km
Population in 2006: 1,170
Provincial Electoral District(s): Carman
Federal Electoral District(s): Portage-Lisgar
Next Election: Oct. 2014 (4 year terms)
Craig Spencer, Reeve
Jackie Jenkinson, Chief Administrative Officer

Springfield
P.O. Box 219
628 Main St.
Oakbank, MB R0E 1J0
Tel: 204-444-3321; *Fax:* 204-444-2137
ltetrault@rmofspringfield.ca
www.rmofspringfield.ca
Municipal Type: Rural Municipality
Incorporated: Jan. 4, 1873 *Area:* 1,100.81 sq km
Population in 2006: 12,990
Provincial Electoral District(s): Springfield
Federal Electoral District(s): Provencher; Selkirk-Interlake
Next Election: Oct. 2014 (4 year terms)
Jim McCarthy, Reeve
Laurent Tétrault, Chief Administrative Officer

Stanley
#100, 379 Stephen St.
Morden, MB R6M 1V1
Tel: 204-822-6251; *Fax:* 204-822-3596
info@rmofstanley.ca
www.rmofstanley.ca
Municipal Type: Rural Municipality
Incorporated: Nov. 7, 1890 *Area:* 835.59 sq km
Population in 2006: 6,367
Provincial Electoral District(s): Pembina
Federal Electoral District(s): Portage-Lisgar
Next Election: Oct. 2014 (4 year terms)
Art Petkau, Reeve
Rick Klippenstein, Chief Administrative Officer

Strathclair
P.O. Box 160
127 Veterans Way
Strathclair, MB R0J 2C0
Tel: 204-365-2196; *Fax:* 204-365-2056
strathrm@inetbiz.ca
Municipal Type: Rural Municipality
Incorporated: Jan. 3, 1884 *Area:* 539.96 sq km
Population in 2006: 840
Provincial Electoral District(s): Russell
Federal Electoral District(s): Dauphin-Swan River-Marquette
Next Election: Oct. 2014 (4 year terms)
Ken Wozney, Reeve
Shelley Glenn, Chief Administrative Officer

Strathcona
P.O. Box 100
101 Albert St. East
Belmont, MB R0K 0C0
Tel: 204-537-2241; *Fax:* 204-537-2364
caostrathcona@inethome.ca
Municipal Type: Rural Municipality
Incorporated: Jan. 2, 1906 *Area:* 485.56 sq km
Population in 2006: 727
Provincial Electoral District(s): Turtle Mountain

Federal Electoral District(s): Brandon-Souris
Next Election: Oct. 2014 (4 year terms)
Dennis Schram, Reeve
Carolyn Davies, Chief Administrative Officer

Stuartburn
P.O. Box 59
108 Main St. North
Vita, MB R0A 2K0
Tel: 204-425-3218; *Fax:* 204-425-3513
612rm@mts.net
Municipal Type: Rural Municipality
Incorporated: Jan. 4, 1997 *Area:* 1,161.65 sq km
Population in 2006: 1,629
Provincial Electoral District(s): Emerson
Federal Electoral District(s): Provencher
Next Election: Oct. 2014 (4 year terms)
Jim Swidersky, Reeve
Jennifer Blatz, Chief Administrative Officer

Swan River
P.O. Box 610
216 Main St. West
Swan River, MB R0L 1Z0
Tel: 204-734-3344; *Fax:* 204-734-3701
ruralm@mts.net
www.rmofswanriver.com
Municipal Type: Rural Municipality
Incorporated: Jan. 3, 1901 *Area:* 1,719.58 sq km
Population in 2006: 2,784
Provincial Electoral District(s): Swan River
Federal Electoral District(s): Dauphin-Swan River-Marquette
Next Election: Oct. 2014 (4 year terms)
Lorne Henkelman, Reeve
Debbie Reich, Chief Administrative Officer

Taché
P.O. Box 100
1294 Dawson Rd.
Lorette, MB R0A 0Y0
Tel: 204-878-3321; *Fax:* 204-878-9977
info@rmtache.ca
Municipal Type: Rural Municipality
Incorporated: Jan. 5, 1880 *Area:* 581.52 sq km
Population in 2006: 9,083
Provincial Electoral District(s): La Verendrye
Federal Electoral District(s): Provencher
Next Election: Oct. 2014 (4 year terms)
William Danylchuk, Reeve
Dan Poersch, Chief Administrative Officer

Thompson
P.O. Box 190
531 Norton Ave.
Miami, MB R0G 1H0
Tel: 204-435-2114; *Fax:* 204-435-2067
rmthompson@cici.mb.ca
Municipal Type: Rural Municipality
Incorporated: Jan. 6, 1909 *Area:* 528.57 sq km
Population in 2006: 1,259
Provincial Electoral District(s): Carman
Federal Electoral District(s): Portage-Lisgar
Next Election: Oct. 2014 (4 year terms)
Jason Vanstone, Reeve
Diane Chatwin, Chief Administrative Officer

Victoria
P.O. Box 40
130 Broadway St.
Holland, MB R0G 0X0
Tel: 204-526-2423; *Fax:* 204-526-2028
office@rmofvictoria.com
rmofvictoria.com
Municipal Type: Rural Municipality
Incorporated: Jan. 4, 1902 *Area:* 697.63 sq km
Population in 2006: 1,149
Provincial Electoral District(s): Carman
Federal Electoral District(s): Portage-Lisgar
Next Election: Oct. 2014 (4 year terms)
Harold W. Purkess, Reeve
Ivan Bruneau, Chief Administrative Officer

Victoria Beach
#303, 960 Portage Ave.
Winnipeg, MB R3G 0R4
Tel: 204-774-4263; *Fax:* 204-774-9834
vicbeach@mts.net
Municipal Type: Rural Municipality
Incorporated: Jan. 4, 1902 *Area:* 20.28 sq km
Population in 2006: 388
Provincial Electoral District(s): Selkirk
Federal Electoral District(s): Selkirk-Interlake
Next Election: Oct. 2014 (4 year terms)
Tom Farrell, Reeve
Raymond Moreau, Chief Administrative Officer

Wallace
P.O. Box 2200
305 Nelson St. West
Virden, MB R0M 2C0
Tel: 204-748-1239; *Fax:* 204-748-3450
don.wallace@mts.net
Municipal Type: Rural Municipality
Incorporated: Jan. 6, 1909 *Area:* 1,148.75 sq km
Population in 2006: 1,501
Provincial Electoral District(s): Arthur-Virden
Federal Electoral District(s): Brandon-Souris
Next Election: Oct. 2014 (4 year terms)
Vacant, Reeve
Don Stephenson, Chief Administrative Officer

West St. Paul
3550 Main St.
West St Paul, MB R4A 5A3
Tel: 204-338-0306; *Fax:* 204-334-9362
info@weststpaul.com
www.weststpaul.com
Municipal Type: Rural Municipality
Incorporated: Jan. 7, 1916 *Area:* 87.66 sq km
Population in 2006: 4,357
Provincial Electoral District(s): Gimli
Federal Electoral District(s): Kildonan-St. Paul
Next Election: Oct. 2014 (4 year terms)
Bruce Henley, Reeve
Brent Olynyk, Chief Administrative Officer

Westbourne
P.O. Box 150
Hwy. 16 West
Gladstone, MB R0J 0T0
Tel: 204-385-2388; *Fax:* 204-385-2780
info@rmwestbourne.mb.ca
Municipal Type: Rural Municipality
Incorporated: Jan. 2, 1877 *Area:* 1,261.79 sq km
Population in 2006: 1,906
Provincial Electoral District(s): Ste. Rose
Federal Electoral District(s): Dauphin-Swan River-Marquette
Next Election: Oct. 2014 (4 year terms)
David Single, Reeve
Patricia McCaskill, Municipal Administrator

Whitehead
P.O. Box 107
517 - 2nd Ave.
Alexander, MB R0K 0A0
Tel: 204-752-2261; *Fax:* 204-752-2129
rmwhitehead@mts.net
Municipal Type: Rural Municipality
Incorporated: Jan. 2, 1883 *Area:* 562.82 sq km
Population in 2006: 1,402
Provincial Electoral District(s): Minnedosa
Federal Electoral District(s): Brandon-Souris
Next Election: Oct. 2014 (4 year terms)
Wayne D. Dobbie, Reeve
John B. MacLellan, Chief Administrative Officer

Whitemouth
P.O. Box 248
47 Railway Ave.
Whitemouth, MB R0E 2G0
Tel: 204-348-2221; *Fax:* 204-348-2576
rmwhite@mymts.net
www.rmwhitemouth.com
Municipal Type: Rural Municipality
Incorporated: Jan. 1, 1905 *Area:* 703.02 sq km
Population in 2006: 1,480
Provincial Electoral District(s): Lac du Bonnet
Federal Electoral District(s): Provencher
Next Election: Oct. 2014 (4 year terms)
Kevin Lavallee, Reeve
kevin@rmwhitemouth.com
Jenny Peterson, Chief Administrative Officer

Whitewater
P.O. Box 53
201 South Railway St.
Minto, MB R0K 1M0
Tel: 204-776-2172; *Fax:* 204-776-2252
cao@whitewaterrm.ca
whitewaterrm.ca
Municipal Type: Rural Municipality
Incorporated: Jan. 6, 1897 *Area:* 584.25 sq km
Population in 2006: 648
Provincial Electoral District(s): Minnedosa
Federal Electoral District(s): Brandon-Souris
Next Election: Oct. 2014 (4 year terms)
Blair Woods, Reeve
Lisa Scott, Chief Administrative Officer

Winchester
P.O. Box 387
129 Broadway St. North
Deloraine, MB R0M 0M0
Tel: 204-747-2572; *Fax:* 204-747-2883
pamela@winchester.ca
Municipal Type: Rural Municipality
Area: 725.58 sq km
Population in 2006: 594
Provincial Electoral District(s): Arthur-Virden
Federal Electoral District(s): Brandon-Souris
Next Election: Oct. 2014 (4 year terms)
Michael Dillabough, Reeve
Pamela Hainsworth, Chief Administrative Officer

Woodlands
P.O. Box 10
57 Railway Ave.
Woodlands, MB R0C 3H0
Tel: 204-383-5679; *Fax:* 204-383-5169
rmwdlds1@mts.net
www.rmwoodlands.info
Municipal Type: Rural Municipality
Incorporated: Jan. 5, 1880 *Area:* 1,160.45 sq km
Population in 2006: 3,562
Provincial Electoral District(s): Lakeside
Federal Electoral District(s): Selkirk-Interlake
Next Election: Oct. 2014 (4 year terms)
Donald Walsh, Reeve
Lynn Kauppila, Chief Administrative Officer

Woodworth
P.O. Box 148
220 Cornwall St.
Kenton, MB R0M 0Z0
Tel: 204-838-2317; *Fax:* 204-838-2000
rmwdwo@inetlink.ca
Municipal Type: Rural Municipality
Incorporated: Jan. 2, 1883 *Area:* 817.84 sq km
Population in 2006: 890
Provincial Electoral District(s): Arthur-Virden
Federal Electoral District(s): Brandon-Souris
Next Election: Oct. 2014 (4 year terms)
Denis Carter, Reeve
Carol-Ann Brethour, Chief Administrative Officer

NEW BRUNSWICK

The provincial government of New Brunswick provides all services of a municipal nature for the rural area of the province while municipalities provide these services to their residents. For the rural area, an advisory committee may be elected at public meetings biennially to assist and advise the Minister. Municipal councils are elected to look after the affairs of the municipalities.

Acts of the legislature governing municipalities are the Municipalities Act, the Municipal Assistance Act, the Community Planning Act, the Assessment Act, the Municipal Capital Borrowing Act, the Municipal Elections Act, and the Control of Municipalities Act.

Population requirements for incorporation of municipalities are 10,000 for cities and 1,500 for towns. There are no specified requirements for villages.

Municipal elections are held every four years on the second Monday in May (May 2008, May 2012, etc.).

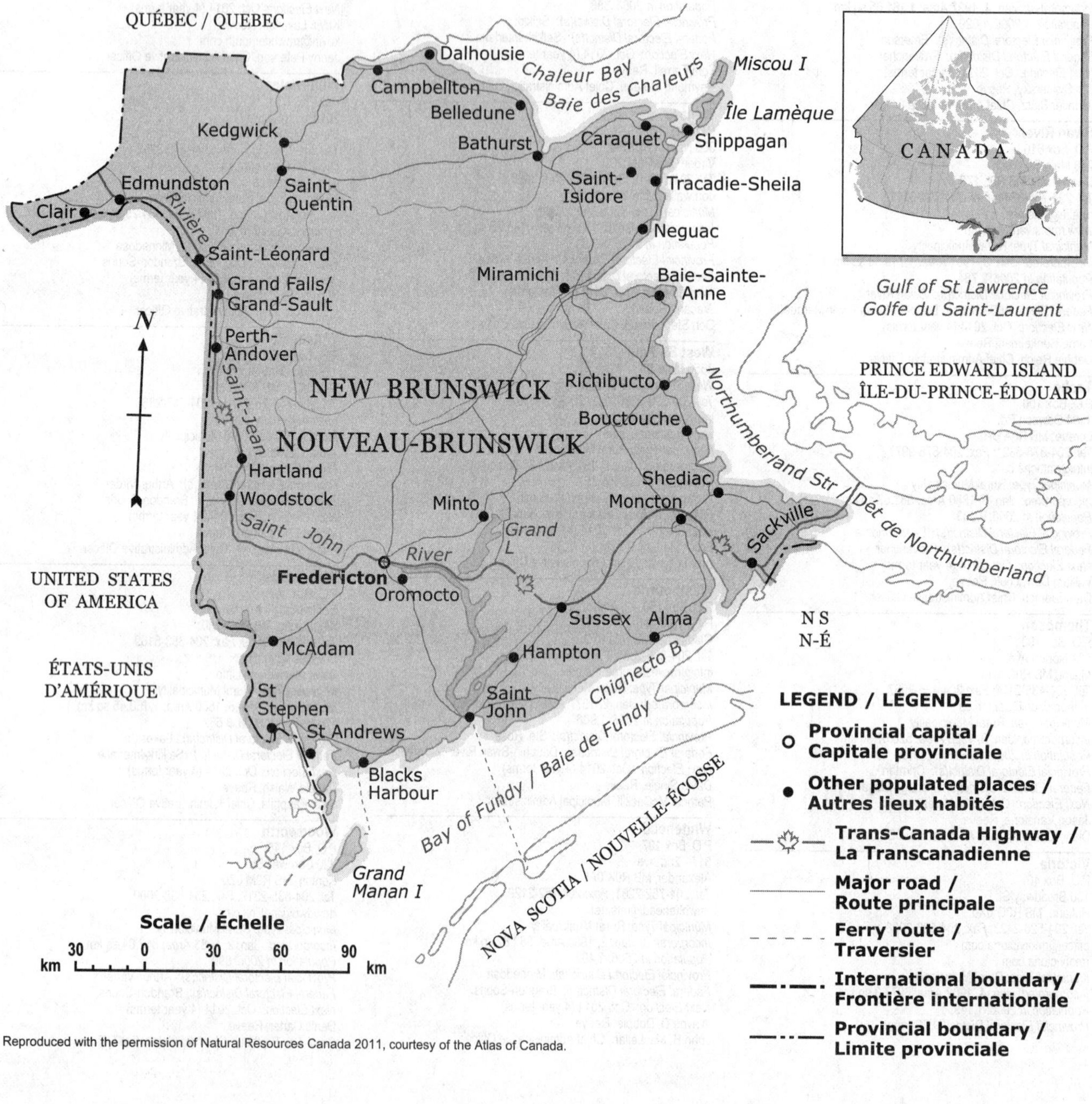

New Brunswick

Major Municipalities in New Brunswick

Bathurst
150 St. George St.
Bathurst, NB E2A 1B5
Tel: 506-548-0400; *Fax:* 506-548-0581
city@bathurst.ca
www.bathurst.ca
Municipal Type: City
Area: 91.55 sq km
County or District: Gloucester; *Population in 2006:* 12,714
Provincial Electoral District(s): Bathurst
Federal Electoral District(s): Acadie-Bathurst
Next Election: May 2012 (4 year terms)
Stephen J. Brunet, Mayor
506-548-2171
Lola Doucet, City Clerk
506-548-0417
Bob Anderson, Councillor
506-548-3536
bobelva@nb.sympatico.ca
André Doucet, City Manager
506-548-0733
Hugh L. Comeau, Councillor
506-548-2255
2868@nb.sympatico.ca
Gerald Pettigrew, Manager, Operations, Parks, Recreation & Tourism Department
506-548-0410
kcregionalcenter@bathurst.ca
Scott A. Ferguson, Councillor
506-547-8993
scott.ferguson@nbed.nb.ca
Vincent Wood, General Foreman, Utilities
506-548-0444
Vincent.Wood@bathurst.ca
Anne-Marie Gammon, Councillor
506-545-6821
amgammon@nbnet.nb.ca
Daniel (Danny) Roy, Councillor
506-546-1588
Paul Godin, General Engineer
Gordon Roy, Councillor
506-546-4590
roygo@rogers.com
Graham Wiseman, Councillor
506-548-3600
gwiseman3600@rogers.com
Hugh J. Young, Councillor
506-548-1815
HughJYoung@GMAIL.com
Danny White, Manager, Operation Planning
Barry Veniot, Supervisor, Purchasing
506-548-0700
Barry.Veniot@bathurst.ca
Lucien Cormier, Building Inspector
Lucien.Cormier@bathurst.ca
Donald McLaughlin, Technician, Planning
Dave Moran, General Foreman, Above Ground Operational Services

Dieppe
333, av Acadie
Dieppe, NB E1A 1G9
Tel: 506-877-7900; *Fax:* 506-877-7910
info@dieppe.ca, communications@dieppe.ca
www.dieppe.ca
Municipal Type: City
Incorporated: Jan. 1, 1952 *Area:* 51.17 sq km
County or District: Westmorland; *Population in 2006:* 18,565
Provincial Electoral District(s): Dieppe Centre-Lewisville
Federal Electoral District(s): Moncton-Riverview-Dieppe; Beauséjour
Next Election: May 2012 (4 year terms)
Jean G. LeBlanc, Mayor
jean.leblanc@dieppe.ca
Pierre LaForest, Assistant Chief Administrative Officer/City Clerk
Pierre.laForest@dieppe.ca
Yvon Comeau, Councillor at Large
506-388-3245
yvon.comeau@dieppe.ca
Nicole Rioux, Treasurer
Jody Dallaire, Councillor at Large
506-387-8738
jody.dallaire@dieppe.ca
Jacques LeBlanc, Director, Public Works
Jean J. Gaudet, Councillor at Large
506-854-8409
jean.gaudet@dieppe.ca
Isabelle LeBlanc, Director, Communications
communications@dieppe.ca
Dave A. Maltais, Councillor, Ward(s): 1
506-855-4299
dave.maltais@dieppe.ca
Luc St-Jules, Director, Municipal Buildings and Environment
luc.stjules@dieppe.ca
Paul J.L. LeBlanc, Councillor, Ward(s): 2
506-853-3974
paul.leblanc@dieppe.ca
Charles LeBlanc, Fire Chief, Fire Department
506-877-7970
charles.leblanc@dieppe.ca
Nicole Melanson, Coordinator, Planning and Development
506-877-7855
Paul N. Belliveau, Councillor, Ward(s): 3
506-855-2637
paul.belliveau@dieppe.ca
Hélène Boudreau, Councillor, Ward(s): 4
506-866-2739
helene.boudreau@dieppe.ca
Roger J. LeBlanc, Councillor, Ward(s): 5
506-850-1604
roger.leblanc@dieppe.ca

Edmundston
7, Canada Road
Edmundston, NB E3V 1T7
Tel: 506-739-4636; *Fax:* 506-737-6902
communication@edmundston.ca
www.ville.edmundston.nb.ca
Municipal Type: City
Area: 106.92 sq km
County or District: Madawaska; *Population in 2006:* 16,643
Provincial Electoral District(s): Edmundston-Saint-Basile
Federal Electoral District(s): Madawaska-Restigouche
Next Election: May 2012 (4 year terms)
Jacques P. Martin, Mayor
Marc Michaud, Acting Chief Administrative Officer
André Lang, Councillor, Ward(s): 1
Paul Dionne, Director, Public Works and Environment
506-739-2103
Aldéo D. Nadeau, Councillor, Ward(s): 1
Ben Beaulieu, Councillor, Ward(s): 2
Denis M. Pelletier, Councillor, Ward(s): 2
Martin (Tin) Albert, Councillor, Ward(s): 3
Gérald G. Morneault, Councillor, Ward(s): 3
Michel Dubé, Councillor, Ward(s): 4
Jean Guy Marquis, Councillor, Ward(s): 4

Fredericton
City Hall
P.O. Box 130
397 Queen St.
Fredericton, NB E3B 4Y7
Tel: 506-460-2020; *Fax:* 506-460-2042
www.fredericton.ca
Municipal Type: City
Incorporated: 1848 *Area:* 130.68 sq km
County or District: York; *Population in 2006:* 50,535
Provincial Electoral District(s): Fredericton-Lincoln; Fredericton-Silverwood; Fredericton-Fort Nashwaak; Fredericton-Nashwaaksis
Federal Electoral District(s): Fredericton
Next Election: May 2012 (4 year terms)
Brad S. Woodside, Mayor
506-460-2085, Fax: 506-460-2134
Pamela G. Hargrove, City Clerk
pam.hargrove@fredericton.ca
Daniel R. Keenan, Councillor, Ward(s): 1
506-472-6046
Marven Grant, City Treasurer & Director, Financial Services
marven.grant@fredericton.ca
Bruce N. Grandy, Deputy Mayor & Councillor, Ward(s): 2
506-459-5378
Bruce A. Noble, City Solicitor
bruce.noble@fredericton.ca
Michael G. O'Brien, Councillor, Ward(s): 3
506-472-4527
Paul R. Stapleton, City Administrator
cityadmin@fredericton.ca
Eric Megarity, Councillor, Ward(s): 4
506-472-6594
Barry MacKnight, Police Chief & Director, Emergency Measures Organization
506-460-2300
policechief@fredericton.ca
Steven Hicks, Councillor, Ward(s): 5
506-458-1973
Philip E. Toole, Fire Chief & Deputy Director, Emergency Measures Organization
506-460-2500
fire@fredericton.ca
Marilyn K. Kerton, Councillor, Ward(s): 6
506-453-9704
Jane Blakely, Director, Corporate Services
jane.blakely@fredericton.ca
Scott McConaghy, Councillor, Ward(s): 7
506-450-9183
W. Frank Flanagan, Director, Development Services
planning@fredericton.ca
Tony J. Whalen, Councillor, Ward(s): 8
506-450-5579
Murray Jamer, P.Eng., Director, Engineering & Public Works
publicworks@fredericton.ca
Stephen A. Chase, Councillor, Ward(s): 9
506-455-0711
Wayne Tallon, Director, Community Services
wayne.tallon@fredericton.ca
Stephen T. Kelly, Councillor, Ward(s): 10
506-455-1064
Ken Forrest, Manager, Policy & Planning
506-460-2110, Fax: 506-460-2894
Jordan S. Graham, Councillor, Ward(s): 11
506-454-5911
Sandy MacNeill, Manager, Transit
506-460-2200
transit@fredericton.ca
David A.J. Kelly, Councillor, Ward(s): 12
506-458-8518
Andy Holyoke, Superintendent, Water & Sewer
publicworks@fredericton.ca
Brian Cochrane, Superintendent, Parks & Trees Division
506-460-2230
recreation@fredericton.ca

Miramichi
141 Henry St.
Miramichi, NB E1V 2N5
Tel: 506-623-2200; *Fax:* 506-623-2201
jim.lamkey@miramichi.org
www.miramichi.org
Municipal Type: City
Incorporated: Jan. 1, 1995 *Area:* 179.84 sq km
County or District: Northumberland; *Population in 2006:* 18,129
Provincial Electoral District(s): Miramichi-Bay du Vin; Miramichi-Centre; Miramichi Bay-Neguac; Southwest Miramichi
Federal Electoral District(s): Miramichi
Next Election: May 2012 (4 year terms)
Gerry Cormier, Mayor
Rhonda Haining, Acting City Clerk
506-623-2208
Rupert Bernard, Councillor
David Dick, City Manager
506-623-2205
Derek Burchill, Councillor
Darlene O'shea, City Treasurer, Finance
506-623-2200, Fax: 506-623-2434
Joan M. Cripps, Councillor
Ian Gavet, Fire Chief
506-623-2225, Fax: 506-623-2226
Csaba Kazamer, Clerk, Engineering
506-623-2021, Fax: 506-623-2201
Suzanne Watters, Clerk, Community Wellness and Recreation
506-623-2300, Fax: 506-623-2306
Jason J. Harris, Councillor
Brian J. King, Councillor
Nancy Lordon, Councillor
Michael J. (Tanker) Malley, Councillor
Michael J. McCoombs, Councillor
Bill Treadwell, Councillor
Robert B. Trevors, Councillor

Moncton / Ville de Moncton
655 Main St.
Moncton, NB E1C 1E8
Tel: 506-853-3333; *Fax:* 506-389-5904
info@moncton.ca
www.moncton.ca
Municipal Type: City
Incorporated: 1890 *Area:* 141.17 sq km
County or District: Westmorland; *Population in 2006:* 64,128
Provincial Electoral District(s): Moncton East; Moncton North; Moncton West; Moncton Crescent
Federal Electoral District(s): Moncton-Riverview-Dieppe; Beauséjour
Next Election: May 2012 (4 year terms)

George H. LeBlanc, Mayor
506-856-4343, Fax: 506-853-3553
info.mayor@moncton.ca
Jacques Dubé, City Manager, Legislative Support
506-843-3498, Fax: 506-859-4225
Kathryn M. Barnes, Councillor at Large
John Martin, City Treasurer & CFO
506-853-3566
john.martin@moncton.ca
Pierre A. Boudreau, Councillor at Large
Steven Boyce, Councillor, Ward(s): 1
Stephen Trueman, City Solicitor
stephen.trueman@moncton.ca
Paulette Thériault, Councillor, Ward(s): 1
Eric Arsenault, Fire Chief
506-857-8800, Fax: 506-856-4353
info.fire@moncton.ca
Merrill A. Henderson, Councillor, Ward(s): 2
B. Butler, Constable, Codiac Regional RCMP
Nancy L. Hoar, Councillor, Ward(s): 2
Bill Budd, Director, District Planning
Daniel Bourgeois, Councillor, Ward(s): 3
C. Despres, Director, Corporate Planning & Policy Development
506-859-2608
info.support@moncton.ca
Brian A.Q. Hicks, Councillor, Ward(s): 3
D. Morehouse, Director, Engineering Operations
info.engineering@moncton.ca
René (Pepsi) Landry, Councillor, Ward(s): 4
A. Richard, Director, Design & Construction
Paul A. Pellerin, Councillor, Ward(s): 4
S. Sparks, Director, Building Inspection
info.inspection@moncton.ca
Paul Thomson, Director, Corporate Communications
info.communications@moncton.ca
Ian Fowler, General Manager, Economic Development, Tourism and Culture
506-853-3516
ian.fowler@moncton.ca
J. MacDonald, General Manager, Engineering & Public Works
info.publicworks@moncton.ca
T. Carter, Manager, Purchasing
506-853-3535
info.purchasing@moncton.ca
Catherine Dallaire, General Manager, Corporate Services
catherine.dallaire@moncton.ca
Donald MacLellan, General Manager, Community Safety Services
don.maclellan@moncton.ca
Rod Higgins, General Manager, Recreation, Parks, Tourism & Culture
rod.higgins@moncton.ca

Quispamsis

P.O. Box 21085
12 Landing Ct.
Quispamsis, NB E2E 4Z4
Tel: 506-849-5778; *Fax:* 506-849-5799
quispamsis@quispamsis.ca
www.quispamsis.ca
Municipal Type: City
Area: 57.06 sq km
County or District: Kings; *Population in 2006:* 15,239
Provincial Electoral District(s): Quispamsis
Federal Electoral District(s): Fundy Royal; Saint John
Next Election: May 2012 (4 year terms)
Chris Vriezen, Superintendent, Utility
506-849-5734
cvriezen@quispamsis.ca
Phil Shedd, Superintendent, Works
506-849-5742
pshedd@quispamsis.ca
Margie McGrath, Secretary, Planning Advisory Committee
506-849-5745
mmcgrath@quispamsis.ca
Paul Kirkpatrick, Fleet Foreman, Kennebecasis Valley Fire Dept.
506-849-5726
Gary Losier, Director, Engineering & Works
506-849-5749
glosier@quispamsis.ca
Murray Driscoll, Mayor
506-849-5992
mayor@quispamsis.ca
Catherine Snow, Clerk
506-849-5738
Jo-Anne McGraw, Town Treasurer
506-849-5738
Emil Olsen, Deputy Mayor
506-847-5197
Daryl Bishop, Councillor
506-849-3150
Gary Clark, Councillor
506-847-3700
Lisa Loughery, Councillor
506-847-6165
Libby O'Hara, Councillor
506-847-5078
Pierre Rioux, Councillor
506-847-4925
Beth Thompson, Councillor
506-849-2852

Riverview

30 Honour House Ct.
Riverview, NB E1C3Y9
Tel: 506-387-2020; *Fax:* 506-387-2033
www.town.riverview.nb.ca
Municipal Type: City
Area: 33.88 sq km
County or District: Albert; *Population in 2006:* 17,832
Provincial Electoral District(s): Riverview
Federal Electoral District(s): Moncton-Riverview-Dieppe; Fundy Royal
Next Election: May 2012 (4 year terms)
Clarence O. Sweetland, Mayor
506-386-1703
csweetland@town.riverview.nb.ca
David Muir, Chief Administrative Officer
506-387-2021
Claude Curwin, Councillor, Ward(s): 1
506-860-6873
ccurwin@town.riverview.nb.ca
Denyse Richard, Deputy Town Clerk
506-387-2043
Ian Macdonald, Councillor, Ward(s): 2
506-386-8756
imacdonald@town.riverview.nb.ca
Robert Higson, Director, Finance
506-387-2023
Bob Hyslop, Councillor, Ward(s): 3
506-866-2273
rhyslop@town.riverview.nb.ca
Tina Smith, Director, Human Resources
506-387-2163
Wayne Bennett, Councillor, Ward(s): 4
506-386-3295
Cole Gerry, Director, Parks, Recreation & Community Relations
506-387-2031
Don Lenehan, Councillor at Large
506-386-4483
lenehandon@yahoo.ca
Denis Pleau, Chief, Fire & Rescue
506-387-2201
rivefire@nbnet.nb.ca
Martha Shaw-Murphy, Councillor at Large
506-387-4248
mshawmurphy@town.riverview.nb.ca
Michel Ouellet, Director, Works & Engineering
506-387-2220
Ann Seamans, Councillor at Large
506-386-4558
aseamans@town.riverview.nb.ca

Rothesay

70 Hampton Rd.
Rothesay, NB E2E 5L5
Tel: 506-848-6600; *Fax:* 506-848-6677
info@rothesay.ca
www.rothesay.ca
Municipal Type: City
Incorporated: Jan. 1, 1998 *Area:* 34.73 sq km
County or District: Kings; *Population in 2006:* 11,637
Provincial Electoral District(s): Rothesay
Federal Electoral District(s): Saint John; Fundy Royal
Next Election: May 2012 (4 year terms)
William J. Bishop, Mayor
506-847-8607, Fax: 506-849-4121
BillBishop@rothesay.ca
Mary Jane Banks, Clerk
MaryJaneBanks@rothesay.ca
Scott Cochrane, Councillor
jassco@rogers.com
Susan Johnson, Treasurer, Operations
susanjohnson@rothesay.ca
Pat Gallagher Jette, Councillor
patgall@nbnet.nb.ca
Charles Jensen, Director, Recreation
charlesjensen@rothesay.ca
Terry Kilfoil, Councillor
kilfoilt@nbnet.nb.ca
Gay Drescher, Director, Development Services
gaydrescher@rothesay.ca
Norma Mullett, Councillor
normamullett@hotmail.com
Corinne Bexson, Senior GIS Technician, Engineering
corrinebexson@rothesay.ca
Don Shea, Councillor
sheadoj@nbnet.nb.ca
Tom Young, Councillor
tomyoung@rogers.com

Saint John

City Hall
P.O. Box 1971
15 Market Sq.
Saint John, NB E2L 4L1
Tel: 506-649-6000;
inquiries@saintjohn.ca
www.saintjohn.ca
Municipal Type: City
Incorporated: May 18, 1785 *Area:* 315.49 sq km
County or District: Saint John; *Population in 2006:* 68,043
Provincial Electoral District(s): Saint John East; Saint John Harbour; Saint John Portland; Saint John Lancaster; Saint John-Fundy
Federal Electoral District(s): Saint John
Next Election: May 2012 (4 year terms)
Ivan Court, Mayor
ivan.court@saintjohn.ca
J. Patrick Woods, City Manager
506-658-2913, Fax: 506-658-2802
citymanager@saintjohn.ca
Stephen Chase, Deputy Mayor & Councillor
stephen.chase@saintjohn.ca
Greg Yeomans, Treasurer & Commissioner, Finance & Corporate Services
506-658-2951, Fax: 506-649-7901
finance@saintjohn.ca
Christopher Titus, Councillor at Large
christopher.titus@saintjohn.ca
James R. Baird, Commissioner, Planning & Development
506-658-2835, Fax: 506-658-2837
planning@saintjohn.ca
Bill Farren, Councillor, Ward(s): 1
bill.farren@saintjohn.ca
William Edwards, Commissioner, Buildings & Inspection Services
506-658-2911, Fax: 506-632-6199
buildinginspection@saintjohn.ca
Peter McGuire, Councillor, Ward(s): 1
peter.mcguire@saintjohn.ca
Paul Groody, P.Eng., Commissioner, Municipal Operations
506-658-4455, Fax: 506-658-4740
municipaloperations@saintjohn.ca
Patricia (Patty) Higgins, Councillor, Ward(s): 2
patty.higgins@saintjohn.ca
Margaret Totten, Manager, Tourism Saint John
506-658-2990, Fax: 506-632-6118
visitsj@saintjohn.ca
H. Gary Sullivan, Councillor, Ward(s): 2
gary.sullivan@saintjohn.ca
John Nugent, City Solicitor
506-658-2860, Fax: 506-649-7939
legal@saintjohn.ca
Mel Norton, Councillor, Ward(s): 3
mel.norton@saintjohn.ca
Allen Bodechon, Police Chief
506-648-3200, Fax: 506-648-3304
police@saintjohn.ca
Donnie Snook, Councillor, Ward(s): 3
donnie.snook@saintjohn.ca
Rob Simonds, Fire Chief
506-658-2910, Fax: 506-658-2916
fire@saintjohn.ca
Bruce Court, Councillor, Ward(s): 4
bruce.court@saintjohn.ca
Shayne Galbraith, Director, Works
506-658-2852
works@saintjohn.ca
Joe Mott, Councillor, Ward(s): 4
joe.mott@saintjohn.ca
Peter J. Hanlon, P.Eng., Manager, Water & Sewerage Services
506-658-2811, Fax: 506-658-4740
waterandsewerage@cityofsaintjohn.com
David Logan, Purchasing Agent, Material & Fleet Management
506-658-2930, Fax: 506-658-4742
mat-man@saintjohn.ca

Other Municipalities in New Brunswick

Alma
8 School St.
Alma, NB E4H 1L2
Tel: 506-887-6123; *Fax:* 506-887-6124
almavill@nb.aibn.com
Municipal Type: Village
Area: 47.64 sq km
County or District: Albert; *Population in 2006:* 301
Provincial Electoral District(s): Albert
Federal Electoral District(s): Fundy Royal
Next Election: May 2012 (4 year terms)
Louise Butland, Clerk-Treasurer
Hilyard G. Rossiter, Mayor

Aroostook
383 Main St.
Aroostook, NB E7H 2Z4
Tel: 506-273-6443; *Fax:* 506-273-3025
varoostk@nb.aibn.com
Municipal Type: Village
Area: 2.24 sq km
County or District: Victoria; *Population in 2006:* 346
Provincial Electoral District(s): Victoria-Tobique
Federal Electoral District(s): Tobique-Mactaquac
Next Election: May 2012 (4 year terms)
Marven Demmings, Mayor

Atholville
247, rue Notre-Dame
Atholville, NB E3N 4T1
Tél: 506-789-2944; *Téléc:* 506-789-2925
lyssa@nb.aibn.com
www.atholville.net
Entité municipal: Village
Incorporation: 1966 *Area:* 10.25 sq km
Comté ou district: Restigouche; *Population au 2006:* 1,317
Circonscription(s) électorale(s) provinciale(s): Campbellton-Restigouche Centre
Circonscription(s) électorale(s) fédérale(s): Madawaska-Restigouche
Prochaines élections: May 2012 (4 year terms)
Lyssa Leclerc, Clerk-Administrator
J. Raymond Lagacé, Mayor

Baker Brook
3677, rue Principale, #A
Baker Brook, NB E7A 1V3
Tél: 506-258-3030; *Téléc:* 506-258-3017
villagebakerbrook@nb.aibn.com
Entité municipal: Village
Area: 12.4 sq km
Comté ou district: Madawaska; *Population au 2006:* 525
Circonscription(s) électorale(s) provinciale(s): Madawaska-les-Lacs
Circonscription(s) électorale(s) fédérale(s): Madawaska-Restigouche
Prochaines élections: May 2012 (4 year terms)
Francine Caron, Maire

Balmoral
CP 2531
1447, av des Pionniers
Balmoral, NB E8E 2W7
Tél: 506-826-6060; *Téléc:* 506-826-6037
vilbal@nbnet.nb.ca
www.balmoralnb.com
Entité municipal: Village
Incorporation: 1972 *Area:* 43.51 sq km
Comté ou district: Restigouche; *Population au 2006:* 1,706
Circonscription(s) électorale(s) provinciale(s): Dalhousie-Restigouche-East
Circonscription(s) électorale(s) fédérale(s): Madawaska-Restigouche
Prochaines élections: May 2012 (4 year terms)
Gilles LePage, Greffier-Administrateur
Hébert Donald Arsenault, Mayor

Bas-Caraquet
8185, rue St-Paul
Bas-Caraquet, NB E1W 6C4
Tél: 506-726-2776; *Téléc:* 506-726-2770
vilbasca@nbnet.nb.ca
www.bascaraquet.com
Entité municipal: Village
Area: 31 sq km
Comté ou district: Gloucester; *Population au 2006:* 1,471
Circonscription(s) électorale(s) provinciale(s): Caraquet
Circonscription(s) électorale(s) fédérale(s): Acadie-Bathurst
Prochaines élections: May 2012 (4 year terms)
Richard Frigault, Gérant
Agnes Doiron, Mairesse

Bath
161 School St.
Bath, NB E7J 1C3
Tel: 506-278-5293; *Fax:* 506-278-5932
bath@nbnet.nb.ca
Municipal Type: Village
Area: 2.03 sq km
County or District: Carleton; *Population in 2006:* 512
Provincial Electoral District(s): Carleton
Federal Electoral District(s): Tobique-Mactaquac
Next Election: May 2012 (4 year terms)
Troy F.J. Stone, Mayor
Christa Walton, Clerk

Belledune
P.O. Box 1006
2330 Main St.
Belledune, NB E8G 2X9
Tel: 506-522-3700; *Fax:* 506-522-3704
bell001@nbnet.nb.ca
www.belledune.com
Municipal Type: Village
Incorporated: Jan. 1, 1968 *Area:* 189.03 sq km
County or District: Gloucester; *Population in 2006:* 1,711
Provincial Electoral District(s): Nigadoo-Chaleur
Federal Electoral District(s): Miramichi
Next Election: May 2012 (4 year terms)
Nick Duivenvoorden, Mayor
Brenda Cormier, Clerk-Treas.

Beresford
#2, 855, rue Principale
Beresford, NB E8K 1T3
Tél: 506-542-2727; *Téléc:* 506-542-2702
beresfor@nbnet.nb.ca
www.acadie-bathurst.com
Entité municipal: Town
Area: 19.2 sq km
Comté ou district: Gloucester; *Population au 2006:* 4,264
Circonscription(s) électorale(s) provinciale(s): Nigadoo-Chaleur
Circonscription(s) électorale(s) fédérale(s): Acadie-Bathurst
Prochaines élections: May 2012 (4 year terms)
Raoul Charest, Mayor
Norval Godin, Administrateur

Bertrand
#1, 651, boul des Acadiens
Bertrand, NB E1W 1G5
Tél: 506-726-2442; *Téléc:* 506-726-2449
bertrand@nb.aibn.com
Entité municipal: Village
Area: 46.45 sq km
Comté ou district: Gloucester; *Population au 2006:* 1,179
Circonscription(s) électorale(s) provinciale(s): Caraquet
Circonscription(s) électorale(s) fédérale(s): Acadie-Bathurst
Prochaines élections: May 2012 (4 year terms)
Yvon Godin, Maire
Mélanie Arseneau, Chief Administrative Officer

Blacks Harbour
65 Wallace Cove Rd.
Blacks Harbour, NB E5H 1G9
Tél: 506-456-4870; *Téléc:* 506-456-4872
blkhvill@nbnet.nb.ca
www.villageofblacksharbour.com
Entité municipal: Village
Area: 8.9 sq km
Comté ou district: Charlotte; *Population au 2006:* 952
Circonscription(s) électorale(s) provinciale(s): Charlotte
Circonscription(s) électorale(s) fédérale(s): New Brunswick Southwest
Prochaines élections: May 2012 (4 year terms)
Terry James, Mayor
Deanna Hunter, Manager

Blackville
12 South Bartholomew Road
Blackville, NB E9B 1N2
Tel: 506-843-6337; *Fax:* 506-843-6043
blackvl@nb.sympatico.ca
www.villageofblackville.com
Municipal Type: Village
Area: 21.73 sq km
County or District: Northumberland; *Population in 2006:* 931
Provincial Electoral District(s): Southwest Miramichi
Federal Electoral District(s): Miramichi
Next Election: May 2012 (4 year terms)
Glen A. Hollowood, Mayor
Kurt Marks, Clerk-Administrator

Bouctouche
211, boul Irving
Bouctouche, NB E4S 3K6
Tél: 506-743-7260; *Téléc:* 506-743-7261
ville@bouctouche.ca
www.bouctouche.org
Entité municipal: Town
Area: 18.34 sq km
Comté ou district: Kent; *Population au 2006:* 2,383
Circonscription(s) électorale(s) provinciale(s): Kent
Circonscription(s) électorale(s) fédérale(s): Beauséjour
Prochaines élections: May 2012 (4 year terms)
Aldéo Saulnier, Maire
Marc Landry, Gérant-Greffier

Cambridge-Narrows
Municipal Bldg.
6 Municipal Lane
Cambridge-Narrows, NB E4C 4P4
Tel: 506-488-3155; *Fax:* 506-488-1018
office@nbnet.nb.ca
www.cambridge-narrows.ca
Municipal Type: Village
Area: 106.94 sq km
County or District: Queens; *Population in 2006:* 717
Provincial Electoral District(s): Grand Lake-Gagetown
Federal Electoral District(s): New Brunswick Southwest
Next Election: May 2012 (4 year terms)
Peter W. Knight, Mayor
Alexis Trebble, Clerk

Campbellton
Campbellton City Centre
P.O. Box 100
76 Water St.
Campbellton, NB E3N 3G1
Tel: 506-789-2700; *Fax:* 506-759-7403
manon.cloutier@campbellton.org
www.campbellton.org
Municipal Type: Town
Incorporated: 1889 *Area:* 18.66 sq km
County or District: Restigouche; *Population in 2006:* 7,384
Provincial Electoral District(s): Campbellton-Restigouche Centre
Federal Electoral District(s): Madawaska-Restigouche
Next Election: May 2012 (4 year terms)
Bruce N. MacIntosh, Mayor
mayor@campbellton.org
Monique Cormier, Clerk
monique.cormier@campbellton.org
Stephanie Marie Anglehart, Councillor
Diane M. Cyr, Councillor
Gilbert E. Cyr, Councillor
Sterling (Fuzzy) Loga, Councillor
Denis Turcotte, Councillor

Canterbury
199 Main St.
Canterbury, NB E6H 1M6
Tel: 506-279-6248; *Fax:* 506-279-9019
Municipal Type: Village
Area: 5.34 sq km
County or District: York; *Population in 2006:* 360
Provincial Electoral District(s): Woodstock
Federal Electoral District(s): Tobique-Mactaquac
Next Election: May 2012 (4 year terms)
Léo Joseph Cloutier, Mayor
Cara Hatton, Clerk

Cap-Pelé
33, ch St-André
Cap-Pelé, NB E4N 1Z4
Tél: 506-577-2030; *Téléc:* 506-577-2035
cappele@nb.aibn.com
www.cap-pele.com
Entité municipal: Village
Incorporation: E969 *Area:* 23.78 sq km
Comté ou district: Westmorland; *Population au 2006:* 2,279
Circonscription(s) électorale(s) provinciale(s): Shediac-Cap-Pelé
Circonscription(s) électorale(s) fédérale(s): Beauséjour
Prochaines élections: May 2012 (4 year terms)
Debbie Dodier, Mairesse
Stéphane Dallaire, Administrateur/Greffier
stephane.dallaire@cappele.com

Caraquet
CP 5695
10, rue du Colisée
Caraquet, NB E1W 1B7
Tél: 506-726-2727; *Téléc:* 506-726-2660
caraquet@nbnet.nb.ca
www.ville.caraquet.nb.ca

Entité municipal: Town
Incorporation: Nov. 15, 1961 *Area:* 68.26 sq km
Comté ou district: Gloucester; *Population au 2006:* 4,156
Circonscription(s) électorale(s) provinciale(s): Caraquet
Circonscription(s) électorale(s) fédérale(s): Acadie-Bathurst
Prochaines élections: May 2012 (4 year terms)
Antonio (Antoine) Landry, Maire
antoinel@nb.aibn.com
Lucien Sonier, Directeur général
luciensonier@nb.aibn.com

Centreville
836 Central St.
Centreville, NB E7K 2E7
Tel: 506-276-3671; *Fax:* 506-276-9891
clerk@nbnet.nb.ca
www.villageofcentreville.ca
Municipal Type: Village
Area: 2.69 sq km
County or District: Carleton; *Population in 2006:* 523
Provincial Electoral District(s): Carleton
Federal Electoral District(s): Tobique-Mactaquac; New Brunswick Southwest
Next Election: May 2012 (4 year terms)
Gary R. Thomas, Mayor
Teresa Burtt, Administrator

Charlo
614, rue Chaleur
Charlo, NB E8E 2G6
Tél: 506-684-7850; *Téléc:* 506-684-7855
vcharlo@nbnet.nb.ca
www.villagecharlo.com
Entité municipal: Village
Incorporation: 1966 *Area:* 30.75 sq km
Comté ou district: Restigouche; *Population au 2006:* 1,376
Circonscription(s) électorale(s) provinciale(s): Dalhousie-Restigouche East
Circonscription(s) électorale(s) fédérale(s): Madawaska-Restigouche
Prochaines élections: May 2012 (4 year terms)
André J.C. Carrier, Maire
Joanne McIntyre Levesque, Administrateur

Chipman
#1, 10 Civic Ct.
Chipman, NB E4A 2H9
Tel: 506-339-6601; *Fax:* 506-339-6197
mail@chipmannb.org
www.chipmannb.com
Municipal Type: Village
Area: 19.58 sq km
County or District: Queens; *Population in 2006:* 1,291
Provincial Electoral District(s): Grand Lake-Gagetown
Federal Electoral District(s): Fredericton
Next Election: May 2012 (4 year terms)
Edward L. Farris, Mayor
Susan Kennedy, Clerk

Clair
809E, rue Principale
Clair, NB E7A 2H7
Tél: 506-992-6030; *Téléc:* 506-992-6041
vgeclair@nbnet.nb.ca
www.villagedeclair.com
Entité municipal: Village
Area: 10.46 sq km
Comté ou district: Madawaska; *Population au 2006:* 848
Circonscription(s) électorale(s) provinciale(s): Madawaska-les-Lacs
Circonscription(s) électorale(s) fédérale(s): Madawaska-Restigouche
Prochaines élections: May 2012 (4 year terms)
Ludger Lang, Maire
Nicole Michaud, Greffière-Trés.

Dalhousie
#1, 111 Hall St.
Dalhousie, NB E8C 1X2
Tel: 506-684-7600; *Fax:* 506-684-7613
reception@dalhousienb.com
www.dalhousienb.com
Municipal Type: Town
Incorporated: 1905 *Area:* 14.51 sq km
County or District: Restigouche; *Population in 2006:* 3,676
Provincial Electoral District(s): Dalhousie-Restigouche East
Federal Electoral District(s): Madawaska-Restigouche
Next Election: May 2012 (4 year terms)
Clem Tremblay, Mayor
Roland Dumont, Deputy Mayor

Doaktown
8 Miramichi St.
Doaktown, NB E9C 1C8
Tel: 506-365-7970; *Fax:* 506-365-7111
doaktown@nbnet.nb.ca
www.doaktown.com
Municipal Type: Village
Area: 28.74 sq km
County or District: Northumberland; *Population in 2006:* 888
Provincial Electoral District(s): Southwest Miramichi
Federal Electoral District(s): Miramichi
Next Election: May 2012 (4 year terms)
Charles Eric Stewart, Mayor
Marilyn E. Price, Clerk-Administrator
marilyn.price@nb.aibn.com

Dorchester
4984 Main St.
Dorchester, NB E4K 2Z1
Tel: 506-379-3030; *Fax:* 506-379-3033
vilofdor@nb.sympatico.ca
www.dorchester.ca
Municipal Type: Village
Area: 5.74 sq km
County or District: Westmorland; *Population in 2006:* 1,119
Provincial Electoral District(s): Tantramar
Federal Electoral District(s): Beauséjour
Next Election: May 2012 (4 year terms)
Melvin J. Goodland, Mayor
Simonne Malenfant-Edgett, Clerk-Treas.

Drummond
1412, ch Tobique
Drummond, NB E3Y 1H7
Tél: 506-475-4000; *Téléc:* 506-475-4010
vildrum@nb.sympatico.ca
www.sn2000.nb.ca/comp/drummond
Entité municipal: Village
Area: 8.91 sq km
Comté ou district: Victoria; *Population au 2006:* 839
Circonscription(s) électorale(s) provinciale(s): Grand Falls-Drummond-Saint-André
Circonscription(s) électorale(s) fédérale(s): Tobique-Mactaquac
Prochaines élections: May 2012 (4 year terms)
Cyril Rioux, Maire
Annie Gagné, Administratrice

Eel River Crossing
CP 159
20, rue Savoie
Eel River Crossing, NB E8E 1T8
Tél: 506-826-6080; *Téléc:* 506-826-6088
voerc@nbnet.nb.ca
Entité municipal: Village
Area: 17.43 sq km
Population au 2006: 1,168
Circonscription(s) électorale(s) provinciale(s): Dalhousie-Restigouche East
Circonscription(s) électorale(s) fédérale(s): Madawaska-Restigouche
Prochaines élections: May 2012 (4 year terms)
Denis D. Savoie, Maire
Kim Bujold, Administrateure

Florenceville-Bristol
4724 Juniper Rd.
Bristol, NB E7L 2W9
Tel: 506-392-6013; *Fax:* 506-392-5211
vbristol@nb.sympatico.ca
www.florencevillebristol.ca
Municipal Type: Village
Incorporated: 2008
County or District: Carleton
Provincial Electoral District(s): Carleton
Federal Electoral District(s): Tobique-Mactaquac
Next Election: May 2012 (4 year terms)
Note: The villages of Florenceville & Bristol amalgamated to create the municipality of Florenceville-Bristol.
Darrell R. Giggie, Mayor
Nancy Shaw, Chief Administrative Officer

Fredericton Junction
102 Wilsey Rd.
Fredericton Junction, NB E5L 1W7
Tel: 506-368-2628; *Fax:* 506-368-1900
fredjct@nbnet.nb.ca
www.frederictonjunction.com
Municipal Type: Village
Area: 23.86 sq km
County or District: Sunbury; *Population in 2006:* 715
Provincial Electoral District(s): New Maryland-Sunbury West
Federal Electoral District(s): New Brunswick Southwest
Next Election: May 2012 (4 year terms)
Gary W. Mersereau, Mayor
Jocelyn Nason, Clerk

Gagetown
68 Babbit St.
Gagetown, NB E5M 1C8
Tel: 506-488-3567; *Fax:* 506-488-3543
gagetnvl@nbnet.nb.ca
www.villageofgagetown.ca
Municipal Type: Village
Incorporated: 1966 *Area:* 49.48 sq km
County or District: Queens; *Population in 2006:* 719
Provincial Electoral District(s): Grand Lake-Gagetown
Federal Electoral District(s): New Brunswick Southwest
Next Election: May 2012 (4 year terms)
Randy A. Smith, Mayor
Connie May, Clerk-Administrator

Grand Bay-Westfield
P.O. Box 3001
609 River Valley Dr.
Grand Bay-Westfield, NB E5K 4V3
Tel: 506-738-6400; *Fax:* 506-738-6424
sgautreau@town.grandbay-westfield.nb.ca
www.town.grandbay-westfield.nb.ca
Municipal Type: Town
Incorporated: 1998 *Area:* 59.73 sq km
County or District: Kings; *Population in 2006:* 4,981
Provincial Electoral District(s): Fundy-River Valley
Federal Electoral District(s): New Brunswick Southwest
Next Election: May 2012 (4 year terms)
Grace Losier, Mayor
losier@town.grandbay-westfield.nb.ca
Sandra M. Gautreau, Town Manager & Clerk
smgautreau2002@yahoo.ca

Grand Falls / Grand-Sault
#200, 131, rue Pleasant
Grand-Sault, NB E3Z 1G6
Tél: 506-475-7777; *Téléc:* 506-475-7779
tgf@nbnet.nb.ca
www.grandfalls.com
Entité municipal: Town
Area: 18.06 sq km
Comté ou district: Victoria; *Population au 2006:* 5,650
Circonscription(s) électorale(s) provinciale(s): Grand Falls-Drummond-Saint-André
Circonscription(s) électorale(s) fédérale(s): Tobique-Mactaquac
Prochaines élections: May 2012 (4 year terms)
Marcel Yvon Deschênes, Mayor
Peter Michaud, CAO-Clerk
petergf@nb.aibn.com

Grand Manan
#4, 1021 rte 776
Grand Manan, NB E5G 4E5
Tel: 506-662-7059; *Fax:* 506-662-7060
grandmanan@villageofgrandmanan.com
www.villageofgrandmanan.com
Municipal Type: Village
Incorporated: May 8, 1995 *Area:* 150.78 sq km
County or District: Charlotte; *Population in 2006:* 2,460
Provincial Electoral District(s): Charlotte-The Isles
Federal Electoral District(s): New Brunswick Southwest
Next Election: May 2012 (4 year terms)
Dennis Clifton Greene, Mayor
dennisgreene@villageofgrandmanan.com
Rob MacPherson, CAO
Melanie Frost, Clerk/Assistant Treasurer

Grande-Anse
393, rue Acadie
Grande-Anse, NB E8N 1E2
Tél: 506-732-3242; *Téléc:* 506-732-3217
grande-anse@i-web.net
www.grande-anse.net
Entité municipal: Village
Incorporation: 1968 *Area:* 24.42 sq km
Comté ou district: Gloucester; *Population au 2006:* 758
Circonscription(s) électorale(s) provinciale(s): Caraquet
Circonscription(s) électorale(s) fédérale(s): Acadie-Bathurst
Prochaines élections: May 2012 (4 year terms)
Roméo Thériault, Maire
Rhéal Paulin, Administrateur

Hampton
P.O. Box 1066
27 Centennial Rd.
Hampton, NB E5N 8H1
Tel: 506-832-6065; *Fax:* 506-832-6098
brenda.collings@nb.aibn.com
www.townofhampton.ca
Municipal Type: Town
Area: 21 sq km
County or District: Kings; *Population in 2006:* 4,004
Provincial Electoral District(s): Hampton-Kings
Federal Electoral District(s): Fundy Royal
Next Election: May 2012 (4 year terms)
Kenneth A. Chorley, Mayor
hampton@nbnet.nb.ca
Brenda Collings, CAO
Megan O'Brien Harrison, Clerk & Development Officer
megan.obrienharrison@nb.aibn.com

Hartland
#1, 31 Orser St.
Hartland, NB E7P 1R4
Tel: 506-375-4357; *Fax:* 506-375-8265
hartland@nbnet.nb.ca
www.town.hartland.nb.ca
Municipal Type: Town
Area: 9.63 sq km
County or District: Carleton; *Population in 2006:* 947
Provincial Electoral District(s): Carleton
Federal Electoral District(s): Tobique-Mactaquac
Next Election: May 2012 (4 year terms)
Judy Dee, Clerk
Wayne D. Britton, Mayor

Harvey Station
58 Hanselpacker Rd.
Harvey Station, NB E6K 1A3
Tel: 506-366-6240; *Fax:* 506-366-6242
harveyst@nbnet.nb.ca
www.village.harvey-station.nb.ca
Municipal Type: Village
Incorporated: Nov. 9, 1966 *Area:* 2.46 sq km
County or District: York; *Population in 2006:* 352
Provincial Electoral District(s): York
Federal Electoral District(s): New Brunswick Southwest
Next Election: May 2012 (4 year terms)
Richard Corey, Mayor
506-366-3039
Roy Bird, EMO
506-366-5733

Hillsborough
#1, 2849 Main St.
Hillsborough, NB E4H 2X7
Tel: 506-734-3733; *Fax:* 506-734-3711
hillsborough@rogers.com
www.villageofhillsborough.ca
Municipal Type: Village
Incorporated: 1966 *Area:* 12.98 sq km
County or District: Albert; *Population in 2006:* 1,292
Provincial Electoral District(s): Albert
Federal Electoral District(s): Fundy Royal
Next Election: May 2012 (4 year terms)
Donna M. Bennett, Mayor
Shari Collins, Administrator-Clerk

Kedgwick
114, rue Notre-Dame
Kedgwick, NB E8B 1H8
Tél: 506-284-2160; *Téléc:* 506-284-2859
villkedg@nbnet.nb.ca
www.village.kedgwick.nb.ca
Entité municipal: Village
Area: 4.28 sq km
Comté ou district: Restigouche; *Population au 2006:* 1,146
Circonscription(s) électorale(s) provinciale(s):
Restigouche-La-Vallée
Circonscription(s) électorale(s) fédérale(s):
Madawaska-Restigouche
Prochaines élections: May 2012 (4 year terms)
Jean Paul Savoie, Maire
Suzanne J. Cyr, Greffière

Lac-Baker
69, rue De La Pointe
Lac Baker, NB E7A 1J1
Tél: 506-992-6060; *Téléc:* 506-992-6061
lacbacac@nbnet.nb.ca
Entité municipal: Village
Area: 4.02 sq km
Comté ou district: Madawaska; *Population au 2006:* 169
Circonscription(s) électorale(s) provinciale(s):
Madawaska-les-Lacs
Circonscription(s) électorale(s) fédérale(s):
Madawaska-Restigouche
Prochaines élections: May 2012 (4 year terms)
Jean-Marc Nadeau, Mayor
Doris Blanchard, Supervisor

Lamèque
CP 2037
28, rue de l'Hôpital
Lamèque, NB E8T 3N4
Tél: 506-344-3222; *Téléc:* 506-344-3266
info@lameque.ca
www.lameque.ca
Entité municipal: Town
Area: 12.45 sq km
Comté ou district: Gloucester; *Population au 2006:* 1,422
Circonscription(s) électorale(s) provinciale(s):
Lamèque-Shippagan-Miscou
Circonscription(s) électorale(s) fédérale(s): Acadie-Bathurst
Prochaines élections: May 2012 (4 year terms)
Rénald Haché, Maire
Henri-Paul Guignard, Administrateur
hplameque@nb.aibn.com

Le Goulet
1295, rue Principale
Le Goulet, NB E8S 2E9
Tél: 506-336-3272; *Téléc:* 506-336-3281
villagelegoulet@nb.aibn.com
www.legoulet.peninsuleacadienne.ca
Entité municipal: Village
Incorporation: May 12, 1986 *Area:* 5.46 sq km
Comté ou district: Gloucester; *Population au 2006:* 908
Circonscription(s) électorale(s) provinciale(s):
Lamèque-Shippagan-Miscou
Circonscription(s) électorale(s) fédérale(s): Acadie-Bathurst
Prochaines élections: May 2012 (4 year terms)
Ulysse Haché, Maire
Line Roussel, Sec.-trés. adjointe

Maisonnette
1512, rue Châtillon
Maisonnette, NB E8N 1S4
Tél: 506-726-2717; *Téléc:* 506-726-2718
maisonet@nbnet.nb.ca
www.maisonnette.ca
Entité municipal: Village
Incorporation: May 12, 1986 *Area:* 12.88 sq km
Comté ou district: Gloucester; *Population au 2006:* 599
Circonscription(s) électorale(s) provinciale(s): Caraquet
Circonscription(s) électorale(s) fédérale(s): Acadie-Bathurst
Prochaines élections: May 2012 (4 year terms)
Lucio Cordisco, Maire
Lynne-Andrée Galarneau, Greffière

McAdam
146 Saunders Rd.
McAdam, NB E6J 1L2
Tel: 506-784-2293; *Fax:* 506-784-1402
villageofmcadam@nb.aibn.com
www.mcadamnb.com
Municipal Type: Village
Area: 14.47 sq km
County or District: York; *Population in 2006:* 1,404
Provincial Electoral District(s): York
Federal Electoral District(s): New Brunswick Southwest
Next Election: May 2012 (4 year terms)
Frank M. Carroll, Mayor
Ann Donahue, Clerk/ Treasurer

Meductic
320 Rte. 165
Meductic, NB E6H 1J5
Tel: 506-272-2098; *Fax:* 506-272-1883
villageofmeductic@nb.aibn.com
Municipal Type: Village
Area: 5.57 sq km
County or District: York; *Population in 2006:* 155
Provincial Electoral District(s): Woodstock
Federal Electoral District(s): Tobique-Mactaquac
Next Election: May 2012 (4 year terms)
Pamela E. Gavel, Mayor
Pamela Grant, Clerk-Treas.

Memramcook
540, rue Centrale
Memramcook, NB E4K 3S6
Tél: 506-758-4078; *Téléc:* 506-758-4079
village@memramcook.com
www.memramcook.com/English/index.html
Entité municipal: Village
Incorporation: 1995 *Area:* 185.71 sq km
Comté ou district: Westmorland; *Population au 2006:* 4,638
Circonscription(s) électorale(s) provinciale(s):
Memramcook-Lakeville-Dieppe
Circonscription(s) électorale(s) fédérale(s): Beauséjour
Prochaines élections: May 2012 (4 year terms)
Donald Oscar LeBlanc, Maire
Monique Bourque, Secrétaire Municipale
monique@memramcook.com

Millville
39 Howland Ridge Rd.
Millville, NB E6E 1Y3
Tel: 506-463-2719; *Fax:* 506-463-8262
villageofmillville@nb.aibn.com
Municipal Type: Village
Area: 12.16 sq km
County or District: York; *Population in 2006:* 303
Provincial Electoral District(s): York North
Federal Electoral District(s): Tobique-Mactaquac
Next Election: May 2012 (4 year terms)
Beverly Herbert Forbes, Mayor
Karen Cooney, Clerk-Treas.

Minto
420 Pleasant Dr.
Minto, NB E4B 2T3
Tel: 506-327-3383; *Fax:* 506-327-3041
minto@nb.aibn.com
www.village.minto.nb.ca
Municipal Type: Village
Area: 31.53 sq km
County or District: Sunbury-Queens; *Population in 2006:* 2,681
Provincial Electoral District(s): Grand Lake-Gagetown
Federal Electoral District(s): Fredericton
Next Election: May 2012 (4 year terms)
Eric G. Barnett, Mayor
Trila McKenelley, Clerk-Administrator

Nackawic
115 Otis Dr.
Nackawic, NB E6G 2P1
Tel: 506-575-2241; *Fax:* 506-575-2035
townhall@nackawic.com
www.nackawic.com
Municipal Type: Town
Area: 8.4 sq km
County or District: York; *Population in 2006:* 977
Provincial Electoral District(s): York North
Federal Electoral District(s): Tobique-Mactaquac
Next Election: May 2012 (4 year terms)
Rowena E. Simpson, Mayor
Kathryn Clark, Acting Chief Administrative Officer
townhall@nackawic.com

Néguac
#1, 1175, rue Principale
Néguac, NB E9G 1T1
Tél: 506-776-3950; *Téléc:* 506-776-3975
village@nbnet.nb.ca
www.neguac.com
Entité municipal: Village
Incorporation: Aug. 23, 1967 *Area:* 26.69 sq km
Comté ou district: Northumberland; *Population au 2006:* 1,623
Circonscription(s) électorale(s) provinciale(s): Miramichi
Bay-Neguac
Circonscription(s) électorale(s) fédérale(s): Miramichi
Prochaines élections: May 2012 (4 year terms)
Roger Ward, Maire
Albertine Savoie, Administrateur
village.denis@nb.aibn.com

New Maryland
584 New Maryland Hwy.
New Maryland, NB E3C 1K1
Tel: 506-451-8508; *Fax:* 506-450-1605
office@vonm.ca
www.vonm.ca
Municipal Type: Village
Incorporated: 1991 *Area:* 21.23 sq km
County or District: York; *Population in 2006:* 4,248
Provincial Electoral District(s): New Maryland-Sunbury West
Federal Electoral District(s): Fredericton; New Brunswick
Southwest
Next Election: May 2012 (4 year terms)
Frank C. Dunn, Mayor
mayor@vonm.ca
Cynthia Geldart, CAO-Clerk
cynthia.geldart@vonm.ca

Nigadoo
#1, 385, rue Principale
Nigadoo, NB E8K 3R6
Tél: 506-542-2626; *Téléc:* 506-542-2678
nigadoov@nbnet.nb.ca
www.acadie-bathurst.com
Entité municipal: Village
Incorporation: 1967 *Area:* 7.69 sq km
Comté ou district: Gloucester; *Population au 2006:* 927
Circonscription(s) électorale(s) provinciale(s): Nigadoo-Chaleur
Circonscription(s) électorale(s) fédérale(s): Acadie-Bathurst
Prochaines élections: May 2012 (4 year terms)
Gilberte Boudreau, Mairesse
Aline Morrison, Secrétaire

Norton
P.O. Box 335
Norton, NB E5T 1J7
Tel: 506-839-3011; *Fax:* 506-839-3015
vnorton@nbnet.nb.ca
Municipal Type: Village
Area: 75.35 sq km
County or District: Kings; *Population in 2006:* 1,314
Provincial Electoral District(s): Hampton-Kings; Kings East
Federal Electoral District(s): Fundy Royal; New Brunswick Southwest
Next Election: May 2012 (4 year terms)
Wendy L. Alcorn, Mayor
Anita Pollock, Clerk-Treas.

Oromocto
4 Doyle Dr.
Oromocto, NB E2V 2V3
Tel: 506-357-4400; *Fax:* 506-357-2266
gengov@oromocto.ca
www.oromocto.ca
Municipal Type: Town
Area: 22.37 sq km
County or District: Sunbury; *Population in 2006:* 8,402
Provincial Electoral District(s): Oromocto
Federal Electoral District(s): Fredericton
Next Election: May 2012 (4 year terms)
Fay L. Tidd, Mayor
Dick Isabelle, CAO-Clerk

Paquetville
1094, rue du Parc
Paquetville, NB E8R 1J4
Tél: 506-764-2500; *Téléc:* 506-764-2504
loulou.blanchard@nb.aibn.com
www.paquetville.com
Entité municipal: Village
Incorporation: 1966 *Area:* 9.4 sq km
Comté ou district: Gloucester; *Population au 2006:* 642
Circonscription(s) électorale(s) provinciale(s): Centre-Péninsule-Saint-Sauveur
Circonscription(s) électorale(s) fédérale(s): Acadie-Bathurst
Prochaines élections: May 2012 (4 year terms)
André Gozzo, Maire
elitec@nbnet.nb.ca
Marie-Louise (Loulou) Blanchard, Greffière & Secrétaire

Perth-Andover
1131 West Riverside Dr.
Perth-Andover, NB E7H 5G5
Tel: 506-273-4959; *Fax:* 506-273-4947
info@perth-andover.com
www.perth-andover.com
Municipal Type: Village
Incorporated: 1966 *Area:* 8.89 sq km
County or District: Victoria; *Population in 2006:* 1,797
Provincial Electoral District(s): Victoria-Tobique
Federal Electoral District(s): Tobique-Mactaquac
Next Election: May 2012 (4 year terms)
Rickey Allen Beaulieu, Mayor
Daniel Dionne, Chief Administrative Officer
dan.dionne@perth-andover.com

Petit-Rocher
582, rue Principale
Petit-Rocher, NB E8J 1S5
Tél: 506-542-2686; *Téléc:* 506-542-2708
petit-rocher@nb.aibn.com
www.acadie-bathurst.com
Entité municipal: Village
Area: 4.49 sq km
Comté ou district: Gloucester; *Population au 2006:* 1,949
Circonscription(s) électorale(s) provinciale(s): Nigadoo-Chaleur
Circonscription(s) électorale(s) fédérale(s): Acadie-Bathurst
Prochaines élections: May 2012 (4 year terms)
Pierre Godin, Maire
Guy Clavette, Gérant

Petitcodiac
P.O. Box 2507
63 Main St.
Petitcodiac, NB E4Z 6H4
Tel: 506-756-3140; *Fax:* 506-756-3142
vop@nbnet.nb.ca
www.petitcodiac.ca
Municipal Type: Village
Area: 17.22 sq km
County or District: Westmorland; *Population in 2006:* 1,368
Provincial Electoral District(s): Petitcodiac
Federal Electoral District(s): Fundy Royal
Next Election: May 2012 (4 year terms)
Peter J. Saunders, Mayor
Janice Conley, Clerk

Plaster Rock
159 Main St.
Plaster Rock, NB E7G 2H2
Tel: 506-356-6070; *Fax:* 506-356-6081
vilprock@nb.sympatico.ca
www.plasterrock.com
Municipal Type: Village
Area: 3.09 sq km
County or District: Victoria; *Population in 2006:* 1,150
Provincial Electoral District(s): Victoria-Tobique
Federal Electoral District(s): Tobique-Mactaquac
Next Election: May 2012 (4 year terms)
Judy A. St. Peter, Mayor
Barbara Wishart-Fawcett, Clerk
wishartbl@hotmail.com

Pointe-Verte
375, rue Principale
Pointe-Verte, NB E8J 2S8
Tél: 506-542-2606; *Téléc:* 506-542-2638
pverte@nbnet.nb.ca
www.acadie-bathurst.com
Entité municipal: Village
Area: 13.79 sq km
Comté ou district: Gloucester; *Population au 2006:* 971
Circonscription(s) électorale(s) provinciale(s): Nigadoo-Chaleur
Circonscription(s) électorale(s) fédérale(s): Acadie-Bathurst
Prochaines élections: May 2012 (4 year terms)
Paul Desjardins, Maire
Marie-Eve Cyr, Directrice generale

Port Elgin
41 East Main St.
Port Elgin, NB E4M 2X8
Tel: 506-538-2120; *Fax:* 506-538-2126
prtelgin@nbnet.nb.ca
www.villageofportelgin.com
Municipal Type: Village
Incorporated: 1922 *Area:* 2.61 sq km
County or District: Westmorland; *Population in 2006:* 451
Provincial Electoral District(s): Tantramar
Federal Electoral District(s): Beauséjour
Next Election: May 2012 (4 year terms)
Judy Scott, Mayor
Sonia M. Wells, Clerk-Treas.

Rexton
#1, 79 Main St.
Rexton, NB E4W 1Z9
Tel: 506-523-6921; *Fax:* 506-523-7383
villageofrexton@nb.aibn.com
www.villageofrexton.com
Municipal Type: Village
Incorporated: Nov. 9, 1966 *Area:* 6.14 sq km
County or District: Kent; *Population in 2006:* 862
Provincial Electoral District(s): Kent
Federal Electoral District(s): Beauséjour
Next Election: May 2012 (4 year terms)
David L. Hanson, Mayor
Barry Glencross, General Manager

Richibucto
9235, rue Main
Richibucto, NB E4W 4B4
Tél: 506-523-7870; *Téléc:* 506-523-7850
vtrcto@nbnet.nb.ca
www.richibucto.org
Entité municipal: Town
Incorporation: 1967 *Area:* 11.83 sq km
Comté ou district: Kent; *Population au 2006:* 1,290
Circonscription(s) électorale(s) provinciale(s): Rogersville-Kouchibouguac
Circonscription(s) électorale(s) fédérale(s): Beauséjour
Prochaines élections: May 2012 (4 year terms)
Meldric J. Mazerolle, Mayor
Gilles Belleau, Gérant

Riverside-Albert
5823 King St.
Riverside-Albert, NB E4H 4B4
Tel: 506-882-3022; *Fax:* 506-882-3016
villra@nbnet.nb.ca
www.bay-of-fundy.com/riverside-albert
Municipal Type: Village
Area: 3.41 sq km
County or District: Albert; *Population in 2006:* 320
Provincial Electoral District(s): Albert
Federal Electoral District(s): Fundy Royal
Next Election: May 2012 (4 year terms)
Deborah Murray, Clerk
C.Dale Elliot, Mayor

Rivière-Verte
78, rue Principale
Rivière-Verte, NB E7C 2T8
Tél: 506-263-1060; *Téléc:* 506-263-1065
evelyne@nbnet.nb.ca
Entité municipal: Village
Area: 7 sq km
Comté ou district: Madawaska; *Population au 2006:* 798
Circonscription(s) électorale(s) provinciale(s): Restigouche-La-Vallée
Circonscription(s) électorale(s) fédérale(s): Madawaska-Restigouche
Prochaines élections: May 2012 (4 year terms)
Michel Leblond, Maire
Evelyn Therrien, Greffière

Rogersville
#2, 28, rue de l'École
Rogersville, NB E4Y 1V7
Tél: 506-775-2080; *Téléc:* 506-775-2090
rogervil@nbnet.nb.ca
www.rogersville.info
Entité municipal: Village
Incorporation: Nov. 9, 1966 *Area:* 7.23 sq km
Comté ou district: Kent; *Population au 2006:* 1,165
Circonscription(s) électorale(s) provinciale(s): Rogersville-Kouchibouguac
Circonscription(s) électorale(s) fédérale(s): Miramichi
Prochaines élections: May 2012 (4 year terms)
Hélène LeBlanc, Greffière & Administratrice
Bertrand LeBlanc, Maire

Sackville
P.O. Box 6191
110 East Main St.
Sackville, NB E4L 1G6
Tel: 506-364-4930; *Fax:* 506-364-4976
b.carroll@sackville.com
www.sackville.com
Municipal Type: Town
Incorporated: Jan. 1903 *Area:* 74.32 sq km
County or District: Westmorland; *Population in 2006:* 5,411
Provincial Electoral District(s): Tantramar
Federal Electoral District(s): Beauséjour
Next Election: May 2012 (4 year terms)
Pat A. Estabrooks, Mayor
Eric Mourant, CAO
e.mourant@sackville.com
Rhonda Tower, Clerk
r.tower@sackville.com

Saint Léonard
108, rue du Pont
Saint Léonard, NB E7E 1Y1
Tél: 506-423-3111; *Téléc:* 506-423-3115
sleonard@nbnet.nb.ca
www.saint-leonard.ca
Entité municipal: Town
Incorporation: 1920 *Area:* 5.2 sq km
Comté ou district: Madawaska; *Population au 2006:* 1,352
Circonscription(s) électorale(s) provinciale(s): Restigouche-La-Vallée
Circonscription(s) électorale(s) fédérale(s): Madawaska-Restigouche
Prochaines élections: May 2012 (4 year terms)
Carmel St-Amand, Maire
Charles Boucher, Directeur général

Saint-André
438, rue Lévesque
Saint-André, NB E3Y 3C7
Tél: 506-473-7580; *Téléc:* 506-473-7585
vilstand@nbnet.nb.ca
www.sn2000.nb.ca/comp/saint-andre
Entité municipal: Village
Area: 3.72 sq km
Comté ou district: Madawaska; *Population au 2006:* 404

Circonscription(s) électorale(s) provinciale(s): Grand Falls-Drummond-Saint-André
Circonscription(s) électorale(s) fédérale(s): Tobique-Mactaquac
Prochaines élections: May 2012 (4 year terms)
Lionel Poitras, Maire
Gisèle Ouellette, Sec.-Tres.

Saint-Antoine
4599, rue Principale
Saint-Antoine, NB E4V 1P8
Tél: 506-525-4020; *Téléc:* 506-525-4027
village@village.stantoine.nb.ca
www.village.stantoine.nb.ca
Entité municipal: Village
Area: 6.43 sq km
Comté ou district: Kent; *Population au 2006:* 1,546
Circonscription(s) électorale(s) provinciale(s): Kent South
Circonscription(s) électorale(s) fédérale(s): Beauséjour
Prochaines élections: May 2012 (4 year terms)
Roseline M. Maillet, Mairesse
Bernadine Maillet-LeBlanc, Directrice générale
berniem@village.stantoine.nb.ca

Saint-François-de-Madawaska
2033, rue Commerciale
Saint-François-de-Madawaska, NB E7A 1B3
Tél: 506-992-6050; *Téléc:* 506-992-6049
munstf@nb.aibn.com
Entité municipal: Village
Area: 6.34 sq km
Comté ou district: Madawaska; *Population au 2006:* 585
Circonscription(s) électorale(s) provinciale(s): Madawaska-les-Lacs
Circonscription(s) électorale(s) fédérale(s): Madawaska-Restigouche
Prochaines élections: May 2012 (4 year terms)
Raoul Cyr, Maire
Colette Lévesque, Greffière

Saint-Hilaire
2190, rue Centrale
Saint-Hilaire, NB E3V 4W1
Tél: 506-258-3307; *Téléc:* 506-258-1802
Entité municipal: Village
Area: 5.67 sq km
Comté ou district: Madawaska; *Population au 2006:* 231
Circonscription(s) électorale(s) provinciale(s): Madawaska-les-Lacs
Circonscription(s) électorale(s) fédérale(s): Madawaska-Restigouche
Prochaines élections: May 2012 (4 year terms)
Benoit Dumont, Maire
Cécile Renaud, Mairesse
Dave Cowan, Directeur général
davecowan@t2way.com

Saint-Isidore
3906, boul des Fondateurs
Saint-Isidore, NB E8M 1C2
Tel: 506-358-6005; *Fax:* 506-358-6010
villasti@nbnet.nb.ca
www.saintisidore.ca
Municipal Type: Village
Incorporated: June 1, 1991 *Area:* 22.58 sq km
Population in 2006: 796
Provincial Electoral District(s): Centre-Péninsule-Saint-Sauveur
Federal Electoral District(s): Acadie-Bathurst
Next Election: May 2012 (4 year terms)

Saint-Léolin
117, rue des Prés
Saint-Léolin, NB E8N 2P9
Tél: 506-732-3266; *Téléc:* 506-732-3267
stleolin@nb.aira.com
www.villagesaintleolin.ca
Entité municipal: Village
Area: 19.78 sq km
Comté ou district: Gloucester; *Population au 2006:* 733
Circonscription(s) électorale(s) provinciale(s): Caraquet
Circonscription(s) électorale(s) fédérale(s): Acadie-Bathurst
Prochaines élections: May 2012 (4 year terms)
Joseph Lanteigne, Maire
Gérard Battah, Administrateur

Saint-Louis-de-Kent
83, rue Beauséjour, #A
Saint-Louis-de-Kent, NB E4X 1A6
Tél: 506-876-3420; *Téléc:* 506-876-3477
vstlouis@nbnet.nb.ca
www.st-louis-de-kent.ca
Entité municipal: Village
Area: 2 sq km
Comté ou district: Kent; *Population au 2006:* 960
Circonscription(s) électorale(s) provinciale(s): Rogersville-Kouchibouguac
Circonscription(s) électorale(s) fédérale(s): Beauséjour
Prochaines élections: May 2012 (4 year terms)
Louis J. Arsenault, Maire
Léo-Paul Frigault, Administrateur

Saint-Quentin
10, rue Deschênes
Saint-Quentin, NB E8A 1M1
Tél: 506-235-2425; *Téléc:* 506-235-1952
ville@saintquentin.nb.ca
www.saintquentin.nb.ca
Entité municipal: Town
Incorporation: 1947 *Area:* 4.3 sq km
Comté ou district: Restigouche; *Population au 2006:* 2,250
Circonscription(s) électorale(s) provinciale(s): Restigouche-La-Vallée
Circonscription(s) électorale(s) fédérale(s): Madawaska-Restigouche
Prochaines élections: May 2012 (4 year terms)
Note: Proclaimed as a town in 1992.
Robert Beaulieu, Maire
Suzanne Coulombe, Greffière

St. Andrews
212 Water St.
St Andrews, NB E5B 1B4
Tel: 506-529-5120; *Fax:* 506-529-5183
thenderson@townofstandrews.ca
www.townofstandrews.ca
Municipal Type: Town
Area: 8.35 sq km
County or District: Charlotte; *Population in 2006:* 1,798
Provincial Electoral District(s): Charlotte-Campobello
Federal Electoral District(s): New Brunswick Southwest
Next Election: May 2012 (4 year terms)
John D. Craig, Mayor
W. Timothy Henderson, CAO & Development Officer

Sainte-Anne-de-Madawaska
75, rue Principale
Sainte-Anne-de-Madawaska, NB E7E 1A8
Tél: 506-445-2449; *Téléc:* 506-445-2405
Entité municipal: Village
Area: 9.21 sq km
Comté ou district: Madawaska; *Population au 2006:* 1,073
Circonscription(s) électorale(s) provinciale(s): Restigouche-La-Vallée
Circonscription(s) électorale(s) fédérale(s): Madawaska-Restigouche
Prochaines élections: May 2012 (4 year terms)
Guy Bellefleur, Maire
Lise Deschênes, Clerk-Très.

Sainte-Marie-Saint-Raphaël
1541, boul de la Mer
Sainte-Marie-Saint-Raphaël, NB E8T 1P5
Tél: 506-344-3210; *Téléc:* 506-344-3213
smsr@nbnet.nb.ca
www.ste-marie-st-raphael.ca
Entité municipal: Village
Incorporation: May 12, 1986 *Area:* 15.61 sq km
Comté ou district: Gloucester; *Population au 2006:* 993
Circonscription(s) électorale(s) provinciale(s): Lamèque-Shippagan-Miscou
Circonscription(s) électorale(s) fédérale(s): Acadie-Bathurst
Prochaines élections: May 2012 (4 year terms)
Henri Pierre Duguay, Maire
Denis Ducharme, Directeur général

St. George
1 School St.
St George, NB E5C 3N2
Tel: 506-755-4320; *Fax:* 506-755-4329
stgeonb@nbnet.nb.ca
www.town.stgeorge.nb.ca
Municipal Type: Town
Incorporated: Oct. 17, 1904 *Area:* 16.13 sq km
County or District: Charlotte; *Population in 2006:* 1,309
Provincial Electoral District(s): Charlotte-The Isles
Federal Electoral District(s): New Brunswick Southwest
Next Election: May 2012 (4 year terms)
Sharon E. Tucker, Mayor
Ross A. Norman, Manager

St. Martins
#2, 73 Main St.
St Martins, NB E5R 1B4
Tel: 506-833-2010; *Fax:* 506-833-2008
vilstmar@nbnet.nb.ca
www.stmartinscanada.com
Municipal Type: Village
Incorporated: Nov. 9, 1967 *Area:* 2.29 sq km
County or District: Saint John; *Population in 2006:* 386
Provincial Electoral District(s): Saint John-Fundy
Federal Electoral District(s): Fundy-Royal
Next Election: May 2012 (4 year terms)
James Huttges, Mayor
Sandra Roy, Clerk

St. Stephen
73 Milltown Blvd.
St Stephen, NB E3L 1G5
Tel: 506-466-7700; *Fax:* 506-466-7701
jflewelling@town.ststephen.nb.ca
www.town.ststephen.nb.ca
Municipal Type: Town
County or District: Charlotte; *Population in 2006:* 4,780
Provincial Electoral District(s): Charlotte-Campobello
Federal Electoral District(s): New Brunswick Southwest
Next Election: May 2012 (4 year terms)
G.L. (Jed) Purcell, Mayor
Joan Flewelling, Clerk

Salisbury
56, rue Douglas
Salisbury, NB E4J 3E3
Tel: 506-372-3230; *Fax:* 506-372-3225
vilsalisbury@nb.aibn.com
www.salisburynb.ca
Municipal Type: Village
Incorporated: 1966 *Area:* 13.68 sq km
County or District: Westmorland; *Population in 2006:* 2,036
Provincial Electoral District(s): Petitcodiac
Federal Electoral District(s): Fundy Royal
Next Election: May 2012 (4 year terms)
Terry A. Keating, Mayor
Pamela Cochrane, Clerk-Administrator

Shediac
#300, 290, rue Main
Shediac, NB E4P 2E3
Tél: 506-532-7000; *Téléc:* 506-532-6156
info@shediac.org
www.shediac.org
Entité municipal: Town
Area: 11.97 sq km
Comté ou district: Westmorland; *Population au 2006:* 5,497
Circonscription(s) électorale(s) provinciale(s): Shediac-Cap-Pelé
Circonscription(s) électorale(s) fédérale(s): Beauséjour
Prochaines élections: May 2012 (4 year terms)
Raymond Cormier, Mayor
Jeannette Bourque, Greffière

Shippagan
200, av Hôtel de Ville
Shippagan, NB E8S 1M1
Tél: 506-336-3900; *Téléc:* 506-336-3901
shipadm@nbnet.nb.ca
www.ville.shippagan.com
Entité municipal: Town
Incorporation: 1947 *Area:* 9.94 sq km
Comté ou district: Gloucester; *Population au 2006:* 2,754
Circonscription(s) électorale(s) provinciale(s): Lamèque-Shippagan-Miscou
Circonscription(s) électorale(s) fédérale(s): Acadie-Bathurst
Prochaines élections: May 2012 (4 year terms)
Note: Proclaimed as a town in 1958.
Jonathan Roch Noël, Maire
Nathalie Robichaud, Clerk
nathalie.robichaud@shippagan.com

Stanley
20 Main St.
Stanley, NB E6B 1A2
Tel: 506-367-3245; *Fax:* 506-367-0006
vstanley@nbnet.nb.ca
www.villageofstanley.com
Municipal Type: Village
Area: 17.34 sq km
County or District: York; *Population in 2006:* 433
Provincial Electoral District(s): York North
Federal Electoral District(s): Tobique-Mactaquac
Next Election: May 2012 (4 year terms)
Richard A. Storey, Mayor
Lorna Pinnock, Clerk-Administrator

Sussex
524 Main St.
Sussex, NB E4E 3E4
Tel: 506-432-4540; *Fax:* 506-432-4566
townofsussex@sussex.ca
www.sussex.ca
Municipal Type: Town
Incorporated: 1904 *Area:* 9.03 sq km
County or District: Kings; *Population in 2006:* 4,241
Provincial Electoral District(s): Kings East
Federal Electoral District(s): Fundy Royal
Next Election: May 2012 (4 year terms)
Ralph A. Carr, Mayor
Paul Maguire, Clerk-Treas.
paul.maguire@sussex.ca

Sussex Corner
1067 Main St.
Sussex Corner, NB E4E 3A1
Tel: 506-433-5184; *Fax:* 506-433-3785
sussex.corner@nb.aibn.com
www.sussexcorner.com
Municipal Type: Village
Incorporated: 1966 *Area:* 9.43 sq km
County or District: Kings; *Population in 2006:* 1,413
Provincial Electoral District(s): Kings East
Federal Electoral District(s): Fundy Royal
Next Election: May 2012 (4 year terms)
Eric C. Cunningham, Mayor
Don Smith, Clerk-Treas.

Tide Head
6 Mountain St.
Tide Head, NB E3N 4J9
Tel: 506-789-6550; *Fax:* 506-789-6553
viltide@nb.sympatico.ca
www.tidehead.ca
Municipal Type: Village
Area: 19.57 sq km
County or District: Restigouche; *Population in 2006:* 1,075
Provincial Electoral District(s): Campbellton-Restigouche Centre
Federal Electoral District(s): Madawaska-Restigouche
Next Election: May 2012 (4 year terms)
Randy Hunter, Mayor
Christine Babcock, Clerk-Administrator

Tracadie-Sheila
CP 3600 Main
3620, rue Principale
Tracadie-Sheila, NB E1X 1G5
Tél: 506-394-4020; *Téléc:* 506-394-4025
info@tracadie-sheila.ca
www.tracadie-sheila.ca
Entité municipal: Town
Incorporation: Jan. 1, 1992 *Area:* 24.64 sq km
Comté ou district: Gloucester; *Population au 2006:* 4,474
Circonscription(s) électorale(s) provinciale(s): Tracadie-Sheila
Circonscription(s) électorale(s) fédérale(s): Acadie-Bathurst
Prochaines élections: May 2012 (4 year terms)
Aldéoda Losier, Maire
Denis Poirier, Executive Director

Tracy
4435 Heritage Dr.
Tracy, NB E5L 1C1
Tel: 506-368-2878; *Fax:* 506-368-1014
Municipal Type: Village
Area: 29.36 sq km
County or District: Sunbury; *Population in 2006:* 619
Provincial Electoral District(s): New Maryland-Sunbury West
Federal Electoral District(s): New Brunswick-Southwest
Next Election: May 2012 (4 year terms)
Dale W. Mowry, Mayor
Susan Phillips, Clerk

Woodstock
824 Main St.
Woodstock, NB E7M 2E8
Tel: 506-325-4600; *Fax:* 506-325-4308
townhall@town.woodstock.nb.ca
www.town.woodstock.nb.ca
Municipal Type: Town
Incorporated: 1856 *Area:* 13.41 sq km
County or District: Carleton; *Population in 2006:* 5,113
Provincial Electoral District(s): Woodstock
Federal Electoral District(s): Tobique-Mactaquac
Next Election: May 2012 (4 year terms)
Arthur L. Slipp, Mayor
Ken Harding, CAO
ken.harding@town.woodstock.nb.ca

NEWFOUNDLAND & LABRADOR

The provincial government of Newfoundland and Labrador exercises control over the activities of all municipalities in accordance with the Executive Council Act and the Municipal Affairs Act. Under the provisions of the Municipalities Act, the Department exercises a certain degree of financial and administrative control over all municipalities with the exception of the cities of St. John's, Corner Brook and Mount Pearl. The towns incorporated under the Municipalities Act do not require ministerial approval of their annual budgets, but the Department employs Municipal Analysts to oversee municipal activities. The province assumes responsibility for public health, welfare and law enforcement which are elsewhere generally considered to be municipal functions.

The cities and towns incorporated in Newfoundland are authorized to levy taxes and to provide a wide range of municipal services and to make appropriate bylaws or regulations for the implementation and administration of these services.

City and town councils in Newfoundland are elected on the last Tuesday in September every four years (2009, 2013, etc.).

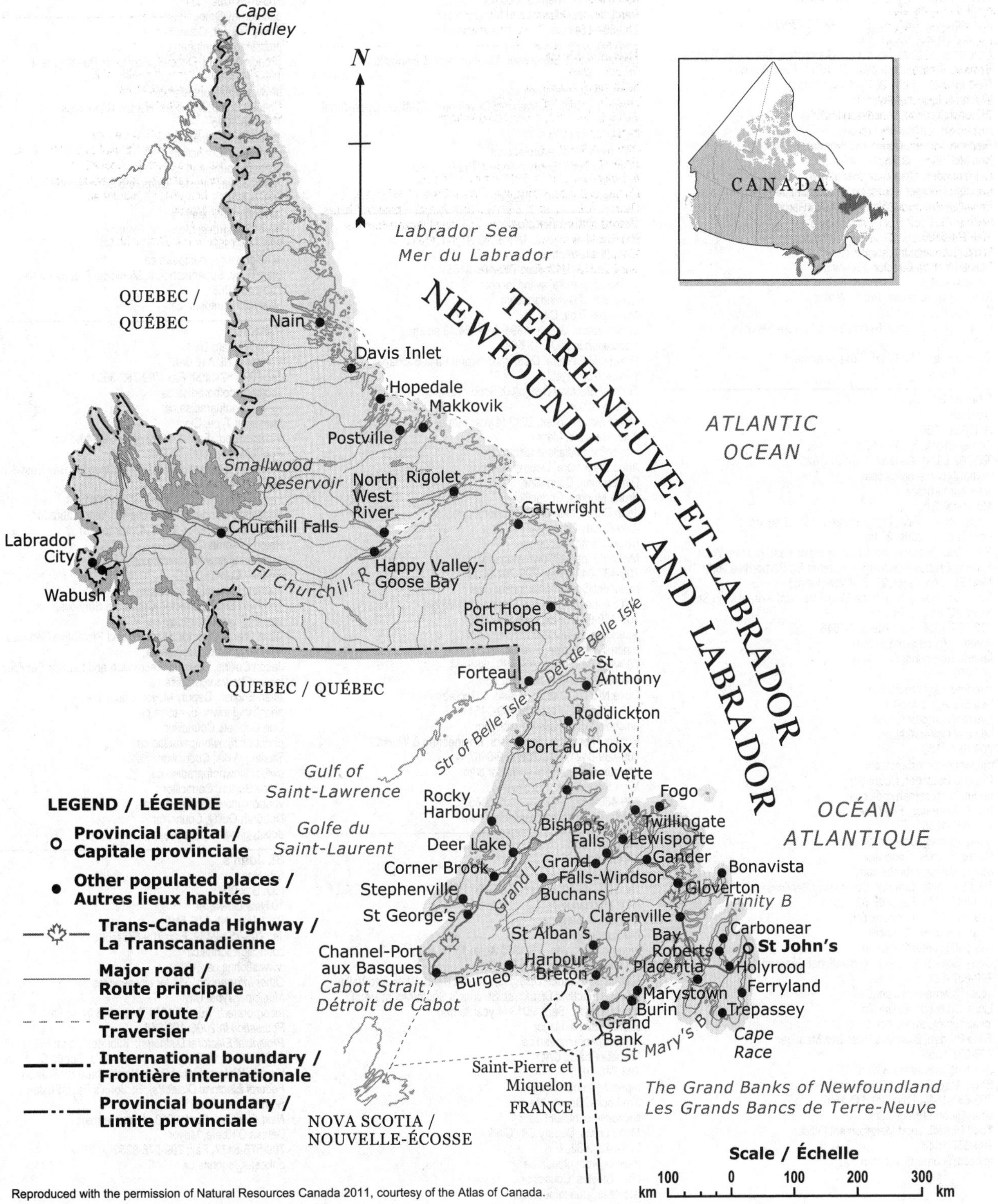

Reproduced with the permission of Natural Resources Canada 2011, courtesy of the Atlas of Canada.

Newfoundland & Labrador

Major Municipalities in Newfoundland & Labrador

Conception Bay South
106 Conception Bay Hwy.
Conception Bay South, NL A1W 3A5
Tel: 709-834-6500; *Fax:* 709-834-8337
jmiller@conceptionbaysouth.ca
www.conceptionbaysouth.ca
Municipal Type: City
Incorporated: Sept. 1, 1971 *Area:* 59.27 sq km
Population in 2006: 21,966
Provincial Electoral District(s): Conception Bay South; Topsail
Federal Electoral District(s): St. John's East; Avalon
Next Election: Sept. 2013 (4 year terms)
Woodrow French, Mayor
WFrench@conceptionbaysouth.ca
Rex Hillier, Councillor, Ward(s): 1
Stephen Tessier, Councillor, Ward(s): 2
Ken McDonald, Councillor, Ward(s): 3
Kirk Younden, Councillor, Ward(s): 4
Kenneth George, Councillor, Ward(s): at large
Beverly Rowe, Councillor, Ward(s): at large
Keith Arns, CAO
709-834-6506
karns@conceptionbaysouth.ca
Elaine Mitchell, Director, Planning
709-834-6553
Ron Franey, Director, Public Works
709-834-6523
Dave Tibbo, Director, Recreation & Leisure Services
709-834-6534
Todd Brophy, Fire Chief, Fire Department
709-834-6543

Corner Brook
City Hall
P.O. Box 1080
Corner Brook, NL A2H 6E1
Tel: 709-637-1500; *Fax:* 709-637-1625
cityhall@cornerbrook.com
www.cornerbrook.com
Municipal Type: City
Incorporated: April 27, 1955 *Area:* 148.27 sq km
Population in 2006: 20,083
Provincial Electoral District(s): Humber East; Humber West
Federal Electoral District(s): Humber-St. Barbe-Baie Verte
Next Election: Sept. 2013 (4 year terms)
Note: City Hall is located on Mount Bernard Ave. at Main St.
Neville Greeley, Mayor
709-637-1537, Fax: 709-637-1543
ngreeley@cornerbrook.com
Marina Redmond, City Clerk
709-637-1534
mredmond@cornerbrook.com
Leo Bruce, Councillor
lbruce@cornerbrook.com
Michael Dolter, CAO
709-637-1532
mdolter@cornerbrook.com
Priscilla Boutcher, Councillor
pboutcher@cornerbrook.com
Neville Wheaton, Fire Chief
709-637-1615
nmwheaton@cornerbrook.com
Donna Francis, Councillor
dfrancis@cornerbrook.com
Paul Barnable, Director, Community Services
709-637-1548, Fax: 709-637-1514
pbarnable@cornerbrook.com
Charlie Renouf, Councillor
crenouf@cornerbrook.com
Gerry Cole, Supervisor, Recreational Services
709-637-1232
gcole@cornerbrook.com
Linda Chaisson, Councillor
lchaisson@cornerbrook.com
Trina Burden, Business Resource Manager
709-637-1558
tburden@cornerbrook.com
Steve May, Director, Operational Services
709-637-1541, Fax: 709-637-1502
smay@cornerbrook.com
Todd Pickett, Land Management Officer
709-637-1544
tpickett@cornerbrook.com
Colleen Humphries, Supervisor, Planning
709-637-1553
chumphries@cornerbrook.com
James Warford, P.Eng., Coordinator, Engineering Services
709-637-1626
jwarford@cornerbrook.com
Keith Costello, Superintendent, Water & Sewer
709-637-1595
kcostello@cornerbrook.com
Barry Ellsworth, Manager, Public Works
709-637-1509
bellsworth@cornerbrook.com
Percy Joyce, Officer, Land Management
709-637-1544
pjoyce@cornerbrook.com
Deon Rumbolt, Supervisor, Development & Inspection
709-637-1552
drumbolt@cornerbrook.com
Rhea Hutchings, Sustainable Development Officer, Operational Services
709-637-1574
rhutchings@cornerbrook.com
Craig Kennedy, Superintendent, Public Works
709-637-1607
ckennedy@cornerbrook.com

Grand Falls-Windsor
P.O. Box 439
Grand Falls-Windsor, NL A2A 2J8
Tel: 709-489-0412; *Fax:* 709-489-0465
jrowsell@grandfallswindsor.com
www.grandfallswindsor.com
Municipal Type: City
Incorporated: Jan. 1, 1991 *Area:* 54.48 sq km
Population in 2006: 13,558
Provincial Electoral District(s): Grand Falls-Buchans; Windsor-Springdale
Federal Electoral District(s): Bonavista-Gander-Grand Falls-Windsor
Next Election: Sept. 2013 (4 year terms)
Allan Hawkins, Mayor
mayor@grandfallswindsor.com
Anne Blackmore, Deputy Mayor
Darren Finn, Councillor
Bruce Moores, Councillor
Jean Buffett-Mercer, Councillor
Amy Coady-Davis, Councillor
Roger Barnett, Councillor
Michael Pinsent, Town Manager
709-487-0407, Fax: 709-292-0018
mpinsent@grandfallswindsor.com
Jeff Saunders, Director, Engineering Works
709-489-0427, Fax: 709-489-0465
jsaunders@grandfallswindsor.com
Vince J. McKenzie, Fire Chief
709-489-0431, Fax: 709-489-0885
firechief@grandfallswindsor.com
Dave Nichols, Director, Parks & Recreation
709-489-0450, Fax: 709-489-0454
dnichols@grandfallswindsor.com
Robert Thompson, Supervisor, Engineering & Works
709-489-0421, Fax: 709-489-0467
rthompson@grandfallswindsor.com
Mark Kelly, Clerk, Purchasing
709-489-0422, Fax: 709-489-0465
purchasing@grandfallswindsor.com

Mount Pearl
3 Centennial St.
Mount Pearl, NL A1N 1G4
Tel: 709-748-1006; *Fax:* 709-748-1150
info@mtpearl.nf.ca
www.mountpearl.ca
Municipal Type: City
Incorporated: Jan. 11, 1955 *Area:* 15.75 sq km
Population in 2006: 24,671
Provincial Electoral District(s): Mount Pearl; Waterford Valley
Federal Electoral District(s): St. John's South-Mount Pearl
Next Election: Sept. 2013 (4 year terms)
Randy Simms, Mayor
rsimms@mountpearl.ca
Michele Peach, CAO
709-748-1025
mpeach@mountpearl.ca
Jim Locke, Deputy Mayor
jlocke@mountpearl.ca
Mona Lewis, Deputy City Clerk
709-748-1032
mlewis@mountpearl.ca
Lucy Stoyles, Councillor
lstoyless@mountpearl.ca
Stephen Jewcyzk, Director, Planning & Development
709-748-1029
sjewczyk@mountpearl.ca
John Walsh, Councillor
jwalsh@mountpearl.ca
Scott Lush, Director, Infrastructure & Public Works
709-748-1028
slush@mountpearl.ca
Paul Lane, Councillor
plane@mountpearl.ca
Brian Chmarney, Director, Community Services
709-748-1027
bchmarney@mountpearl.ca
Paula Tessier, Councillor
ptessier@mountpearl.ca
Bronda Aylward, Director, Economic Development
709-748-1096
baylward@mountpearl.ca
Colleen Butler, Manager, Human Resources
709-748-1095
cbutler@mountpearl.ca
Dave Aker, Councillor
daker@mountpearl.ca
Jason Silver, Director, Corporate Services
709-748-1026
jsilver@mountpearl.ca
Norm Snelgrove, Manager, Finance
709-748-1159
nsnelgrove@mountpearl.ca
Blair Tilley, Superintendent, Municipal Enforcement
709-748-1068
btilley@mountpearl.ca

Paradise
28 McNamara Dr.
Paradise, NL A1L 0A6
Tel: 709-782-1400; *Fax:* 709-782-3601
info@townofparadise.ca
www.townofparadise.ca
Municipal Type: City
Incorporated: Feb. 1, 1992 *Area:* 29.24 sq km
Population in 2006: 12,584
Provincial Electoral District(s): Conception Bay East & Bell Island; Topsail
Federal Electoral District(s): St. John's East; Bonavista-Gander-Grand Falls-Windsor; Labrador
Next Election: Sept. 2013 (4 year terms)
Ralph Wiseman, Mayor
rwiseman@townofparadise.ca
Rodney Cumby, CAO
rcumby@townofparadise.ca
Terrilynn Smith, Director, Corporate Services
tlsmith@townofparadise.ca
Alton Glenn, Director, Planning and Protective Services
aglenn@townofparadise.ca
Jason Collins, Director, Recreation and Leisure Services
jcolins@townofparadise.ca
Allan English, Deputy Mayor, Councillor
aenglish@townofparadise.ca
Dan Bobbett, Councillor
dbobbett@townofparadise.ca
Sterling Willis, Councillor
swillis@townofparadise.ca
Vince Burton, Councillor
vburton@townofparadise.ca
Deborah Quilty, Councillor
dquilty@townofparadise.ca

St. John's
City Hall
P.O. Box 908
10 New Gower St.
St. John's, NL A1C 5M2
Tel: 709-754-2489; *Fax:* 709-576-7688
council@stjohns.ca
www.stjohns.ca
Other Information: 311 for city services
Municipal Type: City
Incorporated: Aug. 7, 1921 *Area:* 446.04 sq km
Population in 2006: 100,646
Provincial Electoral District(s): Kilbride; Signal Hill-Quidi Vidi; St. J. Centre; St. J. East; St. J. North; St. J. South; St. J. West; Virginia Waters; Mount Pearl North; Cape St. Francis
Federal Electoral District(s): St. John's East; St. John's South-Mount Pearl
Next Election: Sept. 2013 (4 year terms)
Dennis O'Keefe, Mayor
709-576-8477, Fax: 709-576-8250
dokeefe@stjohns.ca

Neil Martin, City Clerk, Director & Associate Commissioner, Corporate Services
709-576-8446, Fax: 709-576-8474
Shannie Duff, Deputy Mayor & Councillor
709-576-8583, Fax: 709-576-8474
sduff@stjohns.ca
Robert Bishop, C.A., Treasurer & Director, Finance
709-576-8696, Fax: 709-576-8564
Gerry Colbert, Councillor at Large
709-576-7689, Fax: 709-576-8474
gcolbert@stjohns.ca
Ronald Penney, City Solicitor & City Manager
709-576-8557, Fax: 709-576-8561
legal@stjohns.ca
Sheilagh O'Leary, Councillor at Large
709-576-8567, Fax: 709-576-8474
soleary@stjohns.ca
Walt Mills, Director, Engineering
709-576-8658, Fax: 709-576-8625
Tom Hann, Councillor at Large
709-576-8219, Fax: 709-576-8474
thann@stjohns.ca
David Blackmore, Director, Building & Property Management
709-576-8701, Fax: 709-576-8160
Sandy Hickman, Councillor at Large
709-576-8045, Fax: 709-576-8474
shickman@stjohns.ca
Kevin Breen, Director, Human Resources
709-576-8213, Fax: 709-576-8575
Danny Breen, Councillor, Ward(s): 1
709-576-2332, Fax: 709-576-8474
dbreen@stjohns.ca
Jill Brewer, Director, Recreation
709-576-8405, Fax: 709-576-8469
Frank Galgay, Councillor, Ward(s): 2
709-576-8577, Fax: 709-576-8474
fgalgay@stjohns.ca
Cliff Johnston, Director, Planning
709-576-8383, Fax: 709-576-8625
Bruce Tilley, Councillor, Ward(s): 3
709-576-8643, Fax: 709-576-8474
btilley@stjohns.ca
Elizabeth Lawrence, Director, Economic Development, Tourism & Culture
709-576-8203, Fax: 709-576-8246
Debbie Hanlon, Councillor, Ward(s): 4
709-576-2383, Fax: 709-576-8474
dhanlon@stjohns.ca
Paul Mackey, Director, Public Works & Parks
709-576-8303, Fax: 709-576-8026
Wally Collins, Councillor, Ward(s): 5
709-576-8584, Fax: 709-576-8474
wcollins@stjohns.ca
Jim Clarke, Manager, Streets & Parks
709-576-8541, Fax: 709-576-8026
P.J. (Jim) Ford, Manager, Regulatory Services
709-576-8294, Fax: 709-576-8160
Gareth Griffiths, C.E.T., Manager, Real Estate Services
709-576-8440, Fax: 709-576-8561
Kevin Gushue, Manager, Tourism Development
709-567-8545, Fax: 709-576-8246
Geraldine King, Manager, Environmental Initiatives
709-576-8613, Fax: 709-576-8625
Joe Sampson, Manager, Development
Bob Wilson, Manager, Energy Efficiency
709-576-8238, Fax: 709-576-8160
Robin King, Transportation Engineer
709-576-8232, Fax: 709-576-8625

Other Municipalities in Newfoundland & Labrador

Admiral's Beach
P.O. Box 196
Admiral's Beach, NL A0B 3A0
Tel: 709-521-2671; *Fax:* 709-521-2671
Municipal Type: Town
Incorporated: Jan. 16, 1968 *Area:* 24.42 sq km
Population in 2006: 185
Provincial Electoral District(s): Placentia & St. Mary's
Federal Electoral District(s): Avalon
Next Election: Sept. 2013 (4 year terms)
Keith Guitar, Mayor
Mary Dobbin, Clerk

Anchor Point
P.O. Box 117
Anchor Point, NL A0K 1A0
Tel: 709-456-2011; *Fax:* 709-456-2364
anchorpoint@nf.aibn.com
Municipal Type: Town
Incorporated: Sept. 10, 1974 *Area:* 2.41 sq km
Population in 2006: 309
Provincial Electoral District(s): St. Barbe
Federal Electoral District(s): Humber-St. Barbe-Baie Verte
Next Election: Sept. 2013 (4 year terms)
Gerry Gros, Mayor
Sharon Gaulton, Clerk

Appleton
PO Box 31, Site 4
Appleton, NL A0G 2K0
Tel: 709-679-2289; *Fax:* 709-679-5552
townofappleton@personainternet.com
Municipal Type: Town
Incorporated: Feb. 27, 1962 *Area:* 6.39 sq km
Population in 2006: 582
Provincial Electoral District(s): Gander
Federal Electoral District(s): Bonavista-Gander-Grand Falls-Windsor
Next Election: Sept. 2013 (4 year terms)
Derm Flynn, Mayor
Pat Barnes, Clerk

Aquaforte
General Delivery
Aquaforte, NL A0A 1A0
Tel: 709-363-2618;
townofaqaquaforte@hotmail.com
Municipal Type: Town
Incorporated: April 25, 1972 *Area:* 6.82 sq km
Population in 2006: 103
Provincial Electoral District(s): Ferryland
Federal Electoral District(s): Avalon
Next Election: Sept. 2013 (4 year terms)
Carol Ann Case, Mayor
Kathleen Hayes, Clerk

Arnold's Cove
P.O. Box 70
Arnolds Cove, NL A0B 1A0
Tel: 709-463-2323; *Fax:* 709-463-2326
townofarnoldscove@nf.aibn.com
www.townofarnoldscove.com
Municipal Type: Town
Incorporated: June 3, 1967 *Area:* 4.93 sq km
Population in 2006: 1,003
Provincial Electoral District(s): Bellevue
Federal Electoral District(s): Avalon
Next Election: Sept. 2013 (4 year terms)
Thomas Osbourne, Mayor
Wayne Slade, Clerk

Avondale
P.O. Box 59
Avondale, NL A0A 1B0
Tel: 709-229-4201; *Fax:* 709-229-4446
townofavondale@persona.ca
Municipal Type: Town
Incorporated: Nov. 26, 1974 *Area:* 29.93 sq km
Population in 2006: 667
Provincial Electoral District(s): Harbour Main-Whitbourne
Federal Electoral District(s): Avalon
Next Election: Sept. 2013 (4 year terms)
Bern Hickey, Mayor
Jennifer Lewis, Clerk

Badger
P.O. Box 130
Badger, NL A0H 1A0
Tel: 709-539-2406; *Fax:* 709-539-5262
townofbadger@gmail.com
Municipal Type: Town
Incorporated: Sept. 24, 1963 *Area:* 1.96 sq km
Population in 2006: 813
Provincial Electoral District(s): Grand Falls-Buchans
Federal Electoral District(s): Bonavista-Gander-Grand Falls-Windsor
Next Election: Sept. 2013 (4 year terms)
Michael Patey, Mayor
Pansy Hurley, Clerk

Baie Verte
P.O. Box 218
Baie Verte, NL A0K 1B0
Tel: 709-532-8222; *Fax:* 709-532-4134
info@townofbaieverte.ca
www.townofbaieverte.ca
Municipal Type: Town
Incorporated: April 29, 1958 *Area:* 371.07 sq km
Population in 2006: 1,275
Provincial Electoral District(s): Baie Verte
Federal Electoral District(s): Humber-St. Barbe-Baie Verte
Next Election: Sept. 2013 (4 year terms)
Gerald Acreman, Mayor
Angela Furey, Clerk

Baine Harbour
General Delivery
Baine Harbour, NL A0E 1A0
Tel: 709-443-2980; *Fax:* 709-443-2355
Municipal Type: Town
Incorporated: Dec. 1, 1970 *Area:* 4.82 sq km
Population in 2006: 134
Provincial Electoral District(s): Burin-Placentia West
Federal Electoral District(s): Random-Burin-St. George's
Next Election: Sept. 2013 (4 year terms)
Harold Kenway, Mayor
Dinah Smith, Clerk

Bauline
2 Brook Path
Bauline, NL A1K 1E9
Tel: 709-335-2483; *Fax:* 709-335-2053
baulinetowncouncil@nf.aibn.com
Municipal Type: Town
Incorporated: July 1, 1988 *Area:* 15.95 sq km
Population in 2006: 379
Provincial Electoral District(s): Cape St. Francis
Federal Electoral District(s): St. John's East
Next Election: Sept. 2013 (4 year terms)
Christopher Dredge, Mayor
Raylene Manning, Clerk

Bay Bulls
P.O. Box 70
Bay Bulls, NL A0A 1C0
Tel: 709-334-3454; *Fax:* 709-334-3477
townofbaybulls@nf.aibn.com
www.baybulls.com
Municipal Type: Town
Incorporated: Jan. 1, 1986 *Area:* 30.74 sq km
Population in 2006: 1,078
Provincial Electoral District(s): Ferryland
Federal Electoral District(s): Avalon
Next Election: Sept. 2013 (4 year terms)
Harold Mullowney, Mayor
Janet O'Brien, Clerk

Bay de Verde
P.O. Box 10
Bay de Verde, NL A0A 1E0
Tel: 709-587-2260; *Fax:* 709-587-2049
towncouncilbdv@persona.ca
www.baydeverde.com
Municipal Type: Town
Incorporated: Aug. 22, 1950 *Area:* 13.28 sq km
Population in 2006: 470
Provincial Electoral District(s): Trinity-Bay de Verde
Federal Electoral District(s): Avalon
Next Election: Sept. 2013 (4 year terms)
Gerald Murphy, Mayor
Molly Walsh, Clerk

Bay L'Argent
P.O. Box 29
Bay L'Argent, NL A0E 1B0
Tel: 709-461-2606; *Fax:* 709-461-2608
townofbaylargent@nf.aibn.com
Municipal Type: Town
Incorporated: July 13, 1971 *Area:* 3.56 sq km
Population in 2006: 287
Provincial Electoral District(s): Bellevue
Federal Electoral District(s): Random-Burin-St. George's
Next Election: Sept. 2013 (4 year terms)
Rhonda Baker, Mayor
Viola Pardy, Clerk

Bay Roberts
P.O. Box 114
Bay Roberts, NL A0A 1G0
Tel: 709-786-2126; *Fax:* 709-786-2128
shawe@town.bayroberts.nf.ca
www.bayroberts.com
Municipal Type: Town
Incorporated: Feb. 17, 1951 *Area:* 23.92 sq km
Population in 2006: 5,414
Provincial Electoral District(s): Port de Grave
Federal Electoral District(s): Avalon
Next Election: Sept. 2013 (4 year terms)
Glenn Littlejohn, Mayor
glennlittlejohn@bayroberts.com
Shirley Hawe, Clerk

Baytona
P.O. Box 29
Baytona, NL A0G 2J0
Tel: 709-659-6101; *Fax:* 709-659-6101
thetownofbaytona@eastlink.ca
Municipal Type: Town
Incorporated: Aug. 1, 1975 *Area:* 15.38 sq km
Population in 2006: 276
Provincial Electoral District(s): Lewisporte
Federal Electoral District(s): Bonavista-Gander-Grand Falls-Windsor
Next Election: Sept. 2013 (4 year terms)
Rex Quinlan, Mayor
Patsy Lewis, Clerk

Beachside
112 Bayview Rd.
Beachside, NL A0J 1T0
Tel: 709-267-5251; *Fax:* 709-267-5251
Municipal Type: Town
Incorporated: July 7, 1961 *Area:* 2.61 sq km
Population in 2006: 183
Provincial Electoral District(s): Baie Verte
Federal Electoral District(s): Humber-St. Barbe-Baie Verte
Next Election: Sept. 2013 (4 year terms)
Ada Locke, Mayor
Robert Stone, Clerk

Bellburns
General Delivery
Bellburns, NL A0K 1H0
Tel: 709-898-2468; *Fax:* 709-898-2442
Municipal Type: Town
Incorporated: May 13, 1969 *Area:* 7.39 sq km
Population in 2006: 83
Provincial Electoral District(s): St. Barbe
Federal Electoral District(s): Humber-St. Barbe-Baie Verte
Next Election: Sept. 2013 (4 year terms)
Baxter House, Mayor
Pauline House, Clerk

Belleoram
P.O. Box 29
Belleoram, NL A0H 1B0
Tel: 709-881-6161; *Fax:* 709-881-6161
belloeam1946@yahoo.ca
Municipal Type: Town
Incorporated: March 19, 1946 *Area:* 2.1 sq km
Population in 2006: 421
Provincial Electoral District(s): Fortune Bay-Cape La Hune
Federal Electoral District(s): Random-Burin-St. George's
Next Election: Sept. 2013 (4 year terms)
Steward May, Mayor
Evelyn Savoury, Clerk

Birchy Bay
P.O. Box 40
Birchy Bay, NL A0G 1E0
Tel: 709-659-3221; *Fax:* 709-659-2121
office@birchybay.ca
Municipal Type: Town
Incorporated: Aug. 27, 1974 *Area:* 49.52 sq km
Population in 2006: 618
Provincial Electoral District(s): Lewisporte
Federal Electoral District(s): Bonavista-Gander-Grand Falls-Windsor
Next Election: Sept. 2013 (4 year terms)
Seymour Quinlan, Mayor
Cynthia Baker, Clerk

Bird Cove
67 Michael's Dr.
Bird Cove, NL A0K 1L0
Tel: 709-247-2256; *Fax:* 709-247-2254
tobc@nf.aibn.com
Municipal Type: Town
Incorporated: April 15, 1977 *Area:* 9.39 sq km
Population in 2006: 137
Provincial Electoral District(s): St. Barbe
Federal Electoral District(s): Humber-St. Barbe-Baie Verte
Next Election: Sept. 2013 (4 year terms)
Richard May, Mayor
Wanda Pittman, Clerk

Bishop's Cove
P.O. Box 36
Bishop's Cove, NL A0A 3X0
Tel: 709-589-2195
Municipal Type: Town
Incorporated: June 24, 1969 *Area:* 1.89 sq km
Population in 2006: 329
Provincial Electoral District(s): Port de Grave
Federal Electoral District(s): Avalon
Next Election: Sept. 2013 (4 year terms)
Lori Ann King, Mayor
Irene Menchions, Clerk

Bishop's Falls
P.O. Box 310
Bishops Falls, NL A0H 1C0
Tel: 709-258-6581; *Fax:* 709-258-6346
info@bishopsfalls.com
Municipal Type: Town
Incorporated: Nov. 1, 1961 *Area:* 28.12 sq km
Population in 2006: 3,399
Provincial Electoral District(s): Exploits
Federal Electoral District(s): Bonavista-Gander-Grand Falls-Windsor
Next Election: Sept. 2013 (4 year terms)
Robert Hobbs, Mayor
Randy Drover, Clerk

Bonavista
P.O. Box 279
Bonavista, NL A0C 1B0
Tel: 709-468-7816; *Fax:* 709-468-2495
town.bonavista@nf.sympatico.ca
Municipal Type: Town
Incorporated: Nov. 24, 1964 *Area:* 31.5 sq km
Population in 2006: 3,764
Provincial Electoral District(s): Bonavista South
Federal Electoral District(s): Bonavista-Gander-Grand Falls-Windsor
Next Election: Sept. 2013 (4 year terms)
Elizabeth Fitzgerald, Mayor
David Hiscock, Clerk

Botwood
P.O. Box 490
Botwood, NL A0H 1E0
Tel: 709-257-2839; *Fax:* 709-257-3330
botwoodtowncouncil@nf.aibn.com
www.town.botwood.nl.ca
Municipal Type: Town
Incorporated: June 21, 1960 *Area:* 15.05 sq km
Population in 2006: 3,052
Provincial Electoral District(s): Exploits
Federal Electoral District(s): Bonavista-Gander-Grand Falls-Windsor
Next Election: Sept. 2013(4 year terms)
Jerry Dean, Mayor
Audrey Rowsell, Clerk

Branch
P.O. Box 129
Branch, NL A0B 1E0
Tel: 709-338-2920; *Fax:* 709-338-2921
townofbranch@nf.aibn.com
Municipal Type: Town
Incorporated: May 17, 1966 *Area:* 16.15 sq km
Population in 2006: 309
Provincial Electoral District(s): Placentia & St. Mary's
Federal Electoral District(s): Avalon
Next Election: Sept. 2013 (4 year terms)
Priscilla Corcoran Mooney, Mayor
Augustine Power, Clerk

Brent's Cove
General Delivery
Brents Cove, NL A0K 1R0
Tel: 709-661-5301; *Fax:* 709-661-5216
Municipal Type: Town
Incorporated: April 12, 1966 *Area:* 1.02 sq km
Population in 2006: 204
Provincial Electoral District(s): Baie Verte
Federal Electoral District(s): Humber-St. Barbe-Baie Verte
Next Election: Sept. 2013 (4 year terms)
Ellen Butler, Clerk
Richard Andrews, Mayor

Brighton
General Delivery
Brighton, NL A0J 1B0
Tel: 709-263-7391; *Fax:* 709-263-7391
Other Information: townofbrighton@hotmail.com
Municipal Type: Town
Incorporated: Jan. 1, 1986 *Area:* 2.23 sq km
Population in 2006: 203
Provincial Electoral District(s): Windsor-Springdale
Federal Electoral District(s): Humber-St. Barbe-Baie Verte
Next Election: Sept. 2013 (4 year terms)
Lindy Fudge, Mayor
Jane Fudge, Clerk

Brigus
P.O. Box 220
Brigus, NL A0A 1K0
Tel: 709-528-4588; *Fax:* 709-528-4588
brigus@eastlink.ca
www.brigus.net
Municipal Type: Town
Incorporated: July 21, 1964 *Area:* 11.57 sq km
Population in 2006: 794
Provincial Electoral District(s): Harbour Main-Whitbourne
Federal Electoral District(s): Avalon
Next Election: Sept. 2013(4 year terms)
Byron Rodway, Mayor
709-528-3201
byronrodway@personainternet.com
Wayne Rose, Town Clerk & Manager

Bryant's Cove
PO Box 5, Site 3
Bryant's Cove, NL A0A 3P0
Tel: 709-596-2291; *Fax:* 709-596-0015
Other Information: bryantscove@eastlink.ca
Municipal Type: Town
Incorporated: July 29, 1977 *Area:* 4.87 sq km
Population in 2006: 417
Provincial Electoral District(s): Port de Grave
Federal Electoral District(s): Avalon
Next Election: Sept. 2013 (4 year terms)
Kim Sheppard, Mayor
Michelle Antle, Clerk

Buchans
P.O. Box 190
Buchans, NL A0H 1G0
Tel: 709-672-3972; *Fax:* 709-672-3702
townofbuchans@nf.aibn.com
Municipal Type: Town
Incorporated: April 24, 1963 *Area:* 4.88 sq km
Population in 2006: 761
Provincial Electoral District(s): Grand Falls-Buchans
Federal Electoral District(s): Bonavista-Gander-Grand Falls-Windsor
Next Election: Sept. 2013 (4 year terms)
Derm Corbett, Mayor
David Whalen, Clerk

Burgeo
P.O. Box 220
Burgeo, NL A0N 2H0
Tel: 709-886-2250; *Fax:* 709-886-2166
townofburgeo@bbsict.ca
Municipal Type: Town
Incorporated: June 17, 1950 *Area:* 31.34 sq km
Population in 2006: 1,607
Provincial Electoral District(s): Burgeo & La Poile
Federal Electoral District(s): Random-Burin-St. George's
Next Election: Sept. 2013 (4 year terms)
Gerald MacDonald, Mayor
Michael Ballard, Clerk

Burin
P.O. Box 370
Burin, NL A0E 1E0
Tel: 709-891-1760; *Fax:* 709-891-2069
townofburin@eastlink.ca
www.burincanada.com
Municipal Type: Town
Incorporated: July 18, 1950 *Area:* 34.05 sq km
Population in 2006: 2,483
Provincial Electoral District(s): Burin-Placentia West; Grand Bank
Federal Electoral District(s): Random-Burin-St. George's
Next Election: Sept. 2013(4 year terms)
Kevin Lundrigan, Mayor
Beth Hanrahan, Clerk
bhanrahan@persona.ca

Burlington
General Delivery
Burlington, NL A0K 1S0
Tel: 709-252-2607; *Fax:* 709-252-2161
mbartlett@townofburlington.ca
www.townofburlington.ca
Municipal Type: Town
Incorporated: Oct. 20, 1953 *Area:* 4.1 sq km
Population in 2006: 376
Provincial Electoral District(s): Baie Verte
Federal Electoral District(s): Humber-St. Barbe-Baie Verte
Next Election: Sept. 2013 (4 year terms)
George Kelly, Mayor
gkelly@townofburlington.ca
Mary Lou Bartlett, Clerk

Burnt Islands
P.O. Box 39
Burnt Islands, NL A0M 1B0
Tel: 709-698-3512; *Fax:* 709-698-3512
townofburntislands@hotmail.com
Municipal Type: Town
Incorporated: Oct. 31, 1975 *Area:* 9.52 sq km
Population in 2006: 703
Provincial Electoral District(s): Burgeo & La Poile
Federal Electoral District(s): Random-Burin-St. George's
Next Election: Sept. 2013 (4 year terms)
Alfred Taylor, Mayor
Linda Thorne, Clerk

Campbellton
P.O. Box 70
Campbellton, NL A0G 1L0
Tel: 709-261-2300; *Fax:* 709-261-2375
townofcampbellton@nf.aibn.com
Municipal Type: Town
Incorporated: Oct. 21, 1972 *Area:* 35.71 sq km
Population in 2006: 494
Provincial Electoral District(s): Lewisporte
Federal Electoral District(s): Bonavista-Gander-Grand Falls-Windsor
Next Election: Sept. 2013 (4 year terms)
Maisie Clarke, Mayor
Gail Osmond, Clerk

Cape Broyle
P.O. Box 69
Cape Broyle, NL A0A 1P0
Tel: 709-432-2288; *Fax:* 709-432-2794
townofcapebroyle@nf.aibn.com
Municipal Type: Town
Incorporated: Jan. 1, 1990 *Area:* 10.05 sq km
Population in 2006: 545
Provincial Electoral District(s): Ferryland
Federal Electoral District(s): Avalon
Next Election: Sept. 2013 (4 year terms)
Donald Graham, Mayor
Wendy Duggan, Clerk

Cape St. George
876 Oceanview Drive
Cape St George, NL A0N 1T1
Tel: 709-644-2290; *Fax:* 709-644-2291
townofcapestgeorge@eastlink.ca
Municipal Type: Town
Incorporated: June 24, 1969 *Area:* 33.46 sq km
Population in 2006: 893
Provincial Electoral District(s): Port au Port
Federal Electoral District(s): Random-Burin-St. George's
Next Election: Sept. 2013 (4 year terms)
Peter Fenwick, Mayor
Ina Renouf, Clerk

Carbonear
P.O. Box 999
Carbonear, NL A1Y 1C5
Tel: 709-596-3831; *Fax:* 709-596-5021
info@carbonear.ca
www.carbonear.ca
Municipal Type: Town
Incorporated: July 13, 1948 *Area:* 11.81 sq km
Population in 2006: 4,723
Provincial Electoral District(s): Carbonear-Harbour Grace
Federal Electoral District(s): Avalon
Next Election: Sept. 2013 (4 year terms)
Sam Slade, Mayor
Cathy Somers, Clerk
csomers@@nf.aibn.com

Carmanville
P.O. Box 239
Carmanville, NL A0G 1N0
Tel: 709-534-2814; *Fax:* 709-534-2425
townofcarmanville@nf.aibn.com
Municipal Type: Town
Incorporated: March 29, 1955 *Area:* 43.08 sq km
Population in 2006: 753
Provincial Electoral District(s): Bonavista North
Federal Electoral District(s): Bonavista-Gander-Grand Falls-Windsor
Next Election: Sept. 2013 (4 year terms)
Sam Winsor, Mayor
Dianne Goodyear, Clerk

Cartwright
P.O. Box 129
Cartwright, NL A0K 1V0
Tel: 709-938-7259; *Fax:* 709-938-7454
shopkins@nf.aibn.com
Municipal Type: Town
Incorporated: Oct. 10, 1956 *Area:* 3.27 sq km
Population in 2006: 552
Provincial Electoral District(s): Cartwright-L'Anse au Clair
Federal Electoral District(s): Labrador
Next Election: Sept. 2013 (4 year terms)
Rosetta Holwell, Mayor
Shirley Hopkins, Clerk

Centreville-Wareham-Trinity
P.O. Box 130
Centreville, NL A0G 4P0
Tel: 709-678-2840; *Fax:* 709-678-2536
townofcentreville@nf.aibn.com
Municipal Type: Town
Incorporated: Jan. 1, 1992 *Area:* 37.25 sq km
Population in 2006: 1,122
Provincial Electoral District(s): Bonavista North
Federal Electoral District(s): Bonavista-Gander-Grand Falls-Windsor
Next Election: Sept. 2013 (4 year terms)
Churence Rogers, Mayor
Gertrude Brown, Clerk

Chance Cove
P.O. Box 133
Chance Cove, NL A0B 1K0
Tel: 709-460-4151; *Fax:* 709-460-5580
townofchancecove@nf.aibn.com
Municipal Type: Town
Incorporated: Feb. 8, 1972 *Area:* 18.2 sq km
Population in 2006: 310
Provincial Electoral District(s): Bellevue
Federal Electoral District(s): Avalon
Next Election: Sept. 2013 (4 year terms)
Edgar Crann, Mayor
Glenis Rowe, Clerk

Change Islands
P.O. Box 67
Change Islands, NL A0G 1R0
Tel: 709-621-4181; *Fax:* 709-621-3202
townclerk@changeislands.ca
www.changeislands.ca
Municipal Type: Town
Incorporated: Oct. 16, 1951 *Area:* 5.31 sq km
Population in 2006: 300
Provincial Electoral District(s): Twillingate & Fogo
Federal Electoral District(s): Bonavista-Gander-Grand Falls-Windsor
Next Election: Sept. 2013 (4 year terms)
Stephen Brinson, Mayor
709-621-3401
Sherry Diamond, Clerk

Channel-Port aux Basques
P.O. Box 67
Port aux Basques, NL A0G 1R0
Tel: 709-621-4181; *Fax:* 709-621-3202
townclerk@changeislands.ca
www.portauxbasques.ca
Municipal Type: Town
Incorporated: Nov. 6, 1945 *Area:* 38.77 sq km
Population in 2006: 4,319
Provincial Electoral District(s): Burgeo & La Poile
Federal Electoral District(s): Random-Burin-St. George's
Next Election: Sept. 2013 (4 year terms)
Stephen Brinson, Mayor
Sherry Diamond, Clerk

Chapel Arm
68 Main Rd.
Chapel Arm, NL A0B 1L0
Tel: 709-592-2720; *Fax:* 709-592-2800
ppretty@eastlink.ca
Municipal Type: Town
Incorporated: Nov. 24, 1970 *Area:* 28.17 sq km
Population in 2006: 451
Provincial Electoral District(s): Bellevue
Federal Electoral District(s): Avalon
Next Election: Sept. 2013 (4 year terms)
Larry Reid, Mayor
Phyllis Pretty, Clerk

Charlottetown
P.O. Box 151
Charlottetown, NL A0K 5Y0
Tel: 709-949-0299; *Fax:* 709-949-0377
ctown@nf.aibn.com
Municipal Type: Town
Incorporated: March 4, 1988 *Area:* 30.53 sq km
Population in 2006: 366
Provincial Electoral District(s): Cartwright-L'Anse au Clair
Federal Electoral District(s): Bonavista-Gander-Grand Falls-Windsor; Labrador
Next Election: Sept. 2013 (4 year terms)
Charmaine Powell, Mayor
Zillah Kippenhuck, Clerk

Clarenville
99 Pleasant St.
Clarenville, NL A5A 1V9
Tel: 709-466-7937; *Fax:* 709-466-2276
info@clarenville.net
www.clarenville.net
Municipal Type: Town
Incorporated: June 12, 1951 *Area:* 140.79 sq km
Population in 2006: 5,274
Provincial Electoral District(s): Trinity North
Federal Electoral District(s): Random-Burin-St.George's
Next Election: Sept. 2013 (4 year terms)
Fred Best, Mayor
Marie Blackmore, Clerk

Clarke's Beach
P.O. Box 159
Clarkes Beach, NL A0A 1W0
Tel: 709-786-3993; *Fax:* 709-786-3994
joanwilcox@nf.aibn.com
Municipal Type: Town
Incorporated: Aug. 24, 1965 *Area:* 12.71 sq km
Population in 2006: 1,289
Provincial Electoral District(s): Harbour Main-Whitbourne
Federal Electoral District(s): Avalon
Next Election: Sept. 2009 (4 year terms)
Betty Moore, Mayor
Joan Wilcox, Clerk

Coachman's Cove
General Delivery
Coachmans Cove, NL A0K 1X0
Tel: 709-253-5161; *Fax:* 709-253-5161
Municipal Type: Town
Incorporated: Nov. 24, 1970 *Area:* 18.15 sq km
Population in 2006: 93
Provincial Electoral District(s): Baie Verte
Federal Electoral District(s): Humber-St. Barbe-Baie Verte
Next Election: Sept. 2013 (4 year terms)
Martin Breen, Mayor
Johanna Breen, Clerk

Colinet
P.O. Box 8
Colinet, NL A0B 1M0
Tel: 709-521-2300; *Fax:* 709-521-2482
Municipal Type: Town
Incorporated: Sept. 24, 1974 *Area:* 6.23 sq km
Population in 2006: 165
Provincial Electoral District(s): Placentia & St. Mary's
Federal Electoral District(s): Avalon
Next Election: Sept. 2013 (4 year terms)
Linda Hearn, Mayor
Marie Bonia, Clerk

Colliers
P.O. Box 84
Colliers, NL A0A 1Y0
Tel: 709-229-4333; *Fax:* 709-229-4033
townofcolliers@nl.aibn.com
Municipal Type: Town
Incorporated: Oct. 31, 1972 *Area:* 26.16 sq km
Population in 2006: 722
Provincial Electoral District(s): Harbour Main-Whitbourne
Federal Electoral District(s): Avalon
Next Election: Sept. 2009 (4 year terms)
Waneta Whelan, Clerk
Patrick L. Phillips, Mayor

Come By Chance
P.O. Box 89
Come By Chance, NL A0B 1N0
Tel: 709-542-3240; *Fax:* 709-542-3121
townofcbc@xplornet.com
Municipal Type: Town
Incorporated: July 22, 1969 *Area:* 41.16 sq km
Population in 2006: 260

Provincial Electoral District(s): Bellevue
Federal Electoral District(s): Avalon
Next Election: Sept. 2013 (4 year terms)
Joan Cleary, Mayor
Stephanie Eddy, Clerk

Comfort Cove-Newstead
P.O. Box 10
Comfort Cove, NL A0G 3K0
Tel: 709-244-4125; *Fax:* 709-244-4122
ccntown@eastlink.ca
Municipal Type: Town
Incorporated: Oct. 24, 1967 *Area:* 29.83 sq km
Population in 2006: 451
Provincial Electoral District(s): Lewisporte
Federal Electoral District(s): Bonavista-Gander-Grand Falls-Windsor
Next Election: Sept. 2013 (4 year terms)
Stanley Reid, Mayor
Mona Lane, Clerk

Conception Harbour
P.O. Box 128
Conception Harbour, NL A0A 1Z0
Tel: 709-229-4781; *Fax:* 709-229-0432
charbour@eastlink.ca
Municipal Type: Town
Incorporated: Oct. 31, 1972 *Area:* 21.62 sq km
Population in 2006: 743
Provincial Electoral District(s): Harbour Main-Whitbourne
Federal Electoral District(s): Avalon
Next Election: Sept. 2013 (4 year terms)
John Curran, Mayor
Lillian Connors, Clerk

Conche
P.O. Box 59
Conche, NL A0K 1Y0
Tel: 709-622-4531; *Fax:* 709-622-4491
townofconche@nf.aibn.com
Municipal Type: Town
Incorporated: Sept. 13, 1960 *Area:* 9.09 sq km
Population in 2006: 225
Provincial Electoral District(s): The Straits & White Bay North
Federal Electoral District(s): Humber-St. Barbe-Baie Verte
Next Election: Sept. 2013 (4 year terms)
Gary Carroll, Mayor
Alice Flynn, Clerk

Cook's Harbour
P.O. Box 69
Cooks Harbour, NL A0K 1Z0
Tel: 709-249-3111; *Fax:* 709-249-4105
r.short@nf.aibn.com
Municipal Type: Town
Incorporated: Oct. 10, 1956 *Area:* 1.95 sq km
Population in 2006: 190
Provincial Electoral District(s): The Straits & White Bay North
Federal Electoral District(s): Humber-St. Barbe-Baie Verte
Next Election: Sept. 2013 (4 year terms)
Barry Decker, Mayor
Regina Short, Clerk

Cormack
280 Veteran'S Dr.
Cormack, NL A8A 2R4
Tel: 709-635-7025; *Fax:* 709-635-7363
townofcormack@nf.aibn.com
Municipal Type: Town
Incorporated: April 14, 1964 *Area:* 135.23 sq km
Population in 2006: 657
Provincial Electoral District(s): Humber Valley
Federal Electoral District(s): Humber-St.Barbe-Baie Verte
Next Election: Sept. 2013 (4 year terms)
Melvin Rideout Sr., Mayor
Cynthia Fry, Clerk

Cottlesville
P.O. Box 10
Cottlesville, NL A0G 1S0
Tel: 709-629-3505; *Fax:* 709-629-7411
vecassell@yahoo.ca
www.cottlesville.com
Municipal Type: Town
Incorporated: Oct. 24, 1972 *Area:* 11.17 sq km
Population in 2006: 279
Provincial Electoral District(s): Twillingate & Fogo
Federal Electoral District(s): Bonavista-Gander-Grand Falls-Windsor
Next Election: Sept. 2013 (4 year terms)
Larry Peddle, Mayor
Shelly Abbott, Clerk

Cow Head
P.O. Box 40
Cow Head, NL A0K 2A0
Tel: 709-243-2446; *Fax:* 709-243-2590
townofcowhead@eastlink.ca
www.cowhead.ca
Municipal Type: Town
Incorporated: Feb. 1, 1964 *Area:* 17.84 sq km
Population in 2006: 493
Provincial Electoral District(s): St. Barbe
Federal Electoral District(s): Humber-St. Barbe-Baie Verte
Next Election: Sept. 2013 (4 year terms)
Garland Hutchings, Mayor
Ruth Payne, Clerk

Cox's Cove
P.O. Box 100
Coxs Cove, NL A0L 1C0
Tel: 709-688-2900; *Fax:* 709-688-2929
coxcove@eastlink.ca
Municipal Type: Town
Incorporated: Nov. 11, 1969 *Area:* 7.21 sq km
Population in 2006: 646
Provincial Electoral District(s): Bay of Islands
Federal Electoral District(s): Humber-St. Barbe-Baie Verte
Next Election: Sept. 2013 (4 year terms)
Tony Oxford, Mayor
Tonya Sheppard, Clerk

Crow Head
P.O. Box 250
Crow Head, NL A0G 4M0
Tel: 709-884-5651; *Fax:* 709-884-2344
Municipal Type: Town
Incorporated: Sept. 13, 1960 *Area:* 2.98 sq km
Population in 2006: 205
Provincial Electoral District(s): Twillingate & Fogo
Federal Electoral District(s): Bonavista-Gander-Grand Falls-Windsor
Next Election: Sept. 2013 (4 year terms)
Meta J. Hamlyn, Clerk
John Hamlyn, Mayor

Cupids
P.O. Box 99
Cupids, NL A0A 2B0
Tel: 709-528-4428; *Fax:* 709-528-4430
townofcupids@eastlink.ca
Municipal Type: Town
Incorporated: April 13, 1965 *Area:* 11.02 sq km
Population in 2006: 790
Provincial Electoral District(s): Harbour Main-Whitbourne
Federal Electoral District(s): Avalon
Next Election: Sept. 2013 (4 year terms)
Ivy King, Clerk
Ronald Laracy, Mayor

Daniel's Harbour
P.O. Box 68
Daniels Harbour, NL A0K 2C0
Tel: 709-898-2300; *Fax:* 709-898-2311
townofdanielshr@eastlink.ca
Municipal Type: Town
Incorporated: March 9, 1965 *Area:* 8.19 sq km
Population in 2006: 288
Provincial Electoral District(s): St. Barbe
Federal Electoral District(s): Humber-St. Barbe-Baie Verte
Next Election: Sept. 2013 (4 year terms)
Melda Hann, Clerk
Ross Humber, Mayor

Deer Lake
6 Crescent St.
Deer Lake, NL A8A 1E9
Tel: 709-635-2451; *Fax:* 709-635-5857
deerlake@nf.aibn.com
www.town.deerlake.nf.ca
Municipal Type: Town
Incorporated: May 27, 1950 *Area:* 73.23 sq km
Population in 2006: 4,827
Provincial Electoral District(s): Humber Valley
Federal Electoral District(s): Humber-St. Barbe-Baie Verte
Next Election: Sept. 2013 (4 year terms)
Kimberley Reid, Clerk
Dean Ball, Mayor

Dover
P.O. Box 10
Dover, NL A0G 1X0
Tel: 709-537-2139; *Fax:* 709-537-2190
townofdover@persona.ca
Municipal Type: Town
Incorporated: July 13, 1971 *Area:* 11.55 sq km
Population in 2006: 688
Provincial Electoral District(s): Terra Nova
Federal Electoral District(s): Bonavista-Gander-Grand Falls-Windsor
Next Election: Sept. 2013 (4 year terms)
Wendy Elms, Clerk
Tony R. Keats, Mayor

Duntara
P.O. Box 15
Duntara, NL A0C 1M0
Tel: 709-447-3106; *Fax:* 709-447-3107
Municipal Type: Town
Incorporated: Nov. 14, 1961 *Area:* 17.78 sq km
Population in 2006: 72
Provincial Electoral District(s): Bonavista South
Federal Electoral District(s): Bonavista-Gander-Grand Falls-Windsor
Next Election: Sept. 2013 (4 year terms)

Eastport
P.O. Box 119
Eastport, NL A0G 1Z0
Tel: 709-677-2161; *Fax:* 709-677-2144
cynthia@eastport.ca
www.eastport.ca
Municipal Type: Town
Incorporated: Oct. 20, 1959 *Area:* 18.64 sq km
Population in 2006: 499
Provincial Electoral District(s): Terra Nova
Federal Electoral District(s): Bonavista-Gander-Grand Falls-Windsor
Next Election: Sept. 2013 (4 year terms)
Genevieve Squire, Mayor
Cynthia Bull, Clerk

Elliston
P.O. Box 115
Elliston, NL A0C 1N0
Tel: 709-468-2649; *Fax:* 709-468-2867
town_elliston@yahoo.ca
www.rootcellars.com
Municipal Type: Town
Incorporated: June 15, 1965 *Area:* 10.05 sq km
Population in 2006: 306
Provincial Electoral District(s): Bonavista South
Federal Electoral District(s): Bonavista-Gander-Grand Falls-Windsor
Next Election: Sept. 2013 (4 year terms)
Gary Baker, Mayor
Wendy Baker, Clerk

Embree
P.O. Box 81
General Delivery
Embree, NL A0G 2A0
Tel: 709-535-8712; *Fax:* 709-535-8716
Municipal Type: Town
Incorporated: Sept. 28, 1971 *Area:* 18.16 sq km
Population in 2006: 703
Provincial Electoral District(s): Lewisporte
Federal Electoral District(s): Bonavista-Gander-Grand Falls-Windsor
Next Election: Sept. 2013 (4 year terms)
Donald Bennett, Mayor
Verma Bursey, Clerk

Englee
P.O. Box 160
Englee, NL A0K 2J0
Tel: 709-866-2711; *Fax:* 709-866-2357
dorisenglee@nf.aibn.com
Municipal Type: Town
Incorporated: Dec. 23, 1948 *Area:* 28.76 sq km
Population in 2006: 618
Provincial Electoral District(s): The Straits & White Bay North
Federal Electoral District(s): Humber-St. Barbe-Baie Verte
Next Election: Sept. 2013 (4 year terms)
Rudy Porter, Mayor
Doris Randell, Clerk

English Harbour East
P.O. Box 21
General Delivery
English Harbour East, NL A0E 1M0
Tel: 709-245-4346; *Fax:* 709-245-4556
Municipal Type: Town
Incorporated: Feb. 5, 1974 *Area:* 3.2 sq km
Population in 2006: 169
Provincial Electoral District(s): Bellevue

Federal Electoral District(s): Random-Burin-St. George's
Next Election: Sept. 2013 (4 year terms)
Janet Rideout, Mayor
Dorothy Evans, Clerk

Fermeuse
General Delivery
Fermeuse, NL A0A 2G0
Tel: 709-363-2400; *Fax:* 709-363-2308
townoffermeuse@gmail.com
Municipal Type: Town
Incorporated: Nov. 28, 1967 *Area:* 38.73 sq km
Population in 2006: 284
Provincial Electoral District(s): Ferryland
Federal Electoral District(s): Avalon
Next Election: Sept. 2013 (4 year terms)
Perry Oates, Mayor
Mary Kenny, Clerk

Ferryland
P.O. Box 75
Ferryland, NL A0A 2H0
Tel: 709-432-2127; *Fax:* 709-432-2209
town.ferryland@nf.aibn.com
Municipal Type: Town
Incorporated: Oct. 19, 1971 *Area:* 13.62 sq km
Population in 2006: 529
Provincial Electoral District(s): Ferryland
Federal Electoral District(s): Avalon
Next Election: Sept. 2013 (4 year terms)
Leo Moriarty, Mayor
Doris Kavanagh, Clerk

Flatrock
663 Wind Gap Rd.
Flatrock, NL A1K 1C7
Tel: 709-437-6312; *Fax:* 709-437-6311
townmanager@nf.aibn.ca
www.townofflatrock.com
Municipal Type: Town
Incorporated: Oct. 31, 1975 *Area:* 18.12 sq km
Population in 2006: 1,214
Provincial Electoral District(s): Cape St. Francis
Federal Electoral District(s): St. John's East
Next Election: Sept. 2013 (4 year terms)
Kevin Butt, Mayor
Rita Farrell, Clerk

Fleur de Lys
General Delivery
Fleur de Lys, NL A0K 2M0
Tel: 709-253-3131; *Fax:* 709-253-2146
fleurdelys@nf.aibn.com
Municipal Type: Town
Incorporated: April 18, 1967 *Area:* 39.77 sq km
Population in 2006: 320
Provincial Electoral District(s): Baie Verte
Federal Electoral District(s): Humber-St. Barbe-Baie Verte
Next Election: Sept. 2013 (4 year terms)
Millie Walsh, Mayor
Esther Lewis, Clerk

Flower's Cove
P.O. Box 149
Flowers Cove, NL A0K 2N0
Tel: 709-456-2124; *Fax:* 709-456-2086
townofflowerscove@nf.aibn.net
Municipal Type: Town
Incorporated: Dec. 12, 1961 *Area:* 7.64 sq km
Population in 2006: 270
Provincial Electoral District(s): The Straits & White Bay North
Federal Electoral District(s): Humber-St. Barbe-Baie Verte
Next Election: Sept. 2013 (4 year terms)
Keith Billard, Mayor
Bruce Way, Clerk

Fogo Island
P.O. Box 100
Seldom, NL A0G 3Z0
Tel: 709-266-1320; *Fax:* 709-266-1323
townclerk@townoffogoisland.ca
Municipal Type: Town
Incorporated: Dec.2010 *Area:* 29.4
Population in 2006: 2706
Provincial Electoral District(s): The Isles of Notre Dame
Federal Electoral District(s): Bonavista-Gander-Grand Falls-Windsor
Next Election: Feb. 2015 (4 year terms)
Note: Effective Dec.2010, the towns of Fogo, Joe Batt's Arm-Barr'd Islands-Shoal Bay, Seldom-Little Seldom, Tilting and Fogo Island Region amalgamated to form the new Town of Fogo Island.

Gerald Foley, Mayor
Blanche Bennett, Clerk

Forteau
P.O. Box 99
Forteau, NL A0K 2P0
Tel: 709-931-2241; *Fax:* 709-931-2037
gflynn2006@hotmail.com
Municipal Type: Town
Incorporated: Dec. 7, 1971 *Area:* 7.44 sq km
Population in 2006: 448
Provincial Electoral District(s): Cartwright-L'Anse au Clair
Federal Electoral District(s): Labrador
Next Election: Sept. 2013 (4 year terms)
Reginald Hancock, Mayor
Gail Flynn, Clerk

Fortune
P.O. Box 159
Fortune, NL A0E 1P0
Tel: 709-832-2810; *Fax:* 709-832-2210
fortune@nf.aibn.com
Municipal Type: Town
Incorporated: Sept. 3, 1946 *Area:* 54.85 sq km
Population in 2006: 1,458
Provincial Electoral District(s): Grand Bank
Federal Electoral District(s): Random-Burin-St. George's
Next Election: Sept. 2013 (4 year terms)
Charles Penwell, Mayor
Norma Stacey, Clerk

Fox Cove-Mortier
PO Box 17, Site 25, RR#1
Fox Cove-Mortier, NL A0E 1E0
Tel: 709-891-1500; *Fax:* 709-891-1999
Municipal Type: Town
Incorporated: June 2, 1970 *Area:* 25.6 sq km
Population in 2006: 351
Provincial Electoral District(s): Burin-Placentia West
Federal Electoral District(s): Random-Burin-St. George's
Next Election: Sept. 2013 (4 year terms)
Wanda Antle, Mayor
Gladys Kavanagh, Clerk

Fox Harbour
P.O. Box 64
Fox Harbour PB, NL A0B 1V0
Tel: 709-227-2271; *Fax:* 709-227-2271
Municipal Type: Town
Incorporated: Oct. 13, 1964 *Area:* 19.78 sq km
Population in 2006: 314
Provincial Electoral District(s): Placentia & St. Mary's
Federal Electoral District(s): Avalon
Next Election: Sept. 2013 (4 year terms)
John Maher, Mayor
Patricia Quilty, Clerk

Frenchman's Cove
P.O. Box 20
Frenchman's Cove, NL A0E 1R0
Tel: 709-826-2190; *Fax:* 709-826-2190
townoffrenchmanscove@persona.ca
Municipal Type: Town
Incorporated: May 28, 1974 *Area:* 68.55 sq km
Population in 2006: 166
Provincial Electoral District(s): Grand Bank; Bay of Islands
Federal Electoral District(s): Humber-St. Barbe-Baie Verte; Random-Burin-St. George's
Next Election: Sept. 2013 (4 year terms)
Leah Sperry, Mayor
Corina Thorne, Clerk

Gallants
General Delivery
Gallants, NL A0L 1G0
Tel: 709-646-2115; *Fax:* 709-646-2627
marion21@xplornet.ca
Municipal Type: Town
Incorporated: Aug. 16, 1966 *Area:* 6.34 sq km
Population in 2006: 54
Provincial Electoral District(s): Humber West
Federal Electoral District(s): Random-Burin-St. George's
Next Election: Sept. 2013 (4 year terms)
James Collier, Mayor
Marion Collier, Clerk

Gambo
P.O. Box 250
Gambo, NL A0G 1T0
Tel: 709-674-4476; *Fax:* 709-674-5399
lgtownofgambo@nf.aibn.com
www.townofgambo.com
Municipal Type: Town
Incorporated: July 10, 1962 *Area:* 92.07 sq km
Population in 2006: 2,072
Provincial Electoral District(s): Terra Nova
Federal Electoral District(s): Bonavista-Gander-Grand Falls-Windsor
Next Election: Sept. 2013 (4 year terms)
Peter Lush, Mayor
Jean Blackwood, Acting Town Clerk & Manager

Gander
100 Elizabeth Dr.
Gander, NL A1V 1G7
Tel: 709-651-2930; *Fax:* 709-256-5809
info@gandercanada.com
www.gandercanada.com
Municipal Type: Town
Incorporated: Dec. 28, 1954 *Area:* 104.25 sq km
Population in 2006: 9,951
Provincial Electoral District(s): Gander
Federal Electoral District(s): Bonavista-Gander-Grand Falls-Windsor
Next Election: Sept. 2013 (4 year terms)
Claude Elliott, Mayor
Garry Brown, Town Clerk & Director, Finance

Garnish
P.O. Box 70
Garnish, NL A0E 1T0
Tel: 709-826-2330; *Fax:* 709-826-2173
townclerk@eastlink.ca
Municipal Type: Town
Incorporated: Aug. 25, 1971 *Area:* 39.11 sq km
Population in 2006: 578
Provincial Electoral District(s): Grand Bank
Federal Electoral District(s): Random-Burin-St. George's
Next Election: Sept. 2013 (4 year terms)
Reuben Noseworthy, Mayor
Ruth Cluett, Clerk

Gaskiers-Point La Haye
P.O. Box 434
St Marys, NL A0B 3B0
Tel: 709-525-2430; *Fax:* 709-525-2431
townofgaskiers@nf.aibn.com
Municipal Type: Town
Incorporated: Aug. 25, 1970 *Area:* 23.81 sq km
Population in 2006: 302
Provincial Electoral District(s): Placentia & St. Mary's
Federal Electoral District(s): Avalon
Next Election: Sept. 2013 (4 year terms)
Pearl Kielly, Mayor
Jeanette Critch, Clerk

Gaultois
P.O. Box 101
Gaultois, NL A0H 1N0
Tel: 709-841-6546; *Fax:* 709-841-3521
Other Information: townofgaultois@hotmail.com
Municipal Type: Town
Incorporated: Jan. 1, 1962 *Area:* 4.33 sq km
Population in 2006: 265
Provincial Electoral District(s): Fortune Bay-Cape La Hune
Federal Electoral District(s): Random-Burin-St. George's
Next Election: Sept. 2013 (4 year terms)
Gordon Hunt, Mayor
Sylvin Rose, Clerk

Gillams
P.O. Box 3968
RR#2
Corner Brook, NL A2H 6B9
Tel: 709-783-2800; *Fax:* 709-783-2800
townofgillams@nf.aibn.com
Municipal Type: Town
Incorporated: Aug. 17, 1971 *Area:* 6.7 sq km
Population in 2006: 402
Provincial Electoral District(s): Bay of Islands
Federal Electoral District(s): Humber-St. Barbe-Baie Verte
Next Election: Sept. 2013 (4 year terms)
Newton Pritchett, Mayor
Shelly Penny, Clerk

Glenburnie-Birchy Head-Shoal Brook
General Delivery
Birchy Head, NL A0K 1K0
Tel: 709-453-7220; *Fax:* 709-453-7220
Municipal Type: Town
Incorporated: Sept. 1, 1978 *Area:* 6.57 sq km
Population in 2006: 275
Provincial Electoral District(s): Humber Valley

Federal Electoral District(s): Humber-St. Barbe-Baie Verte
Next Election: Sept. 2009 (4 year terms)
Marilyn Wight, Mayor
Myrna Hynes, Clerk

Glenwood
P.O. Box 130
Glenwood, NL A0G 2K0
Tel: 709-679-2159; *Fax:* 709-679-5470
Municipal Type: Town
Incorporated: June 12, 1962 *Area:* 6.92 sq km
Population in 2006: 762
Provincial Electoral District(s): Gander
Federal Electoral District(s): Bonavista-Gander-Grand Falls-Windsor
Next Election: Sept. 2009 (4 year terms)
Darren Bursey, Mayor
Susan Gillingham, Clerk

Glovertown
P.O. Box 224
Glovertown, NL A0G 2L0
Tel: 709-533-2351; *Fax:* 709-533-2225
jperry@personainternet.com
www.glovertown.net
Municipal Type: Town
Incorporated: Dec. 28, 1954 *Area:* 70.33 sq km
Population in 2006: 2,062
Provincial Electoral District(s): Terra Nova
Federal Electoral District(s): Bonavista-Gander-Grand Falls-Windsor
Next Election: Sept. 2009 (4 year terms)
David Saunders, Mayor
Joanne Perry, Clerk

Goose Cove East
P.O. Box 208
Goose Cove, NL A0K 4S0
Tel: 709-454-8393; *Fax:* 709-454-8393
Municipal Type: Town
Incorporated: Oct. 19, 1971 *Area:* 2.69 sq km
Population in 2006: 234
Provincial Electoral District(s): The Straits & White Bay North
Federal Electoral District(s): Humber-St. Barbe-Baie Verte
Next Election: Sept. 2013 (4 year terms)
Marie Reardon, Mayor
Patricia Reardon, Clerk

Grand Bank
P.O. Box 640
56 Main St.
Grand Bank, NL A0E 1W0
Tel: 709-832-1600; *Fax:* 709-832-1636
townofgrandbank@townofgrandbank.net
www.townofgrandbank.com
Municipal Type: Town
Incorporated: Dec. 28, 1943 *Area:* 16.97 sq km
Population in 2006: 2,580
Provincial Electoral District(s): Grand Bank
Federal Electoral District(s): Random-Burin-St. George's
Next Election: Sept. 2013 (4 year terms)
Darrell LeFosse, Mayor
Cathy Follett, Town Clerk & Treas.

Grand Le Pierre
P.O. Box 35
Grand Le Pierre, NL A0E 1Y0
Tel: 709-662-2702; *Fax:* 709-662-2076
Municipal Type: Town
Incorporated: June 17, 1969 *Area:* 153.59 sq km
Population in 2006: 264
Provincial Electoral District(s): Bellevue
Federal Electoral District(s): Random-Burin-St. George's
Next Election: Sept. 2013 (4 year terms)
Willoughby Bolt, Mayor
Rhonda Bolt, Clerk

Greenspond
P.O. Box 100
Greenspond, NL A0G 2N0
Tel: 709-269-3111; *Fax:* 709-269-3191
greenspond@eastlink.ca
Municipal Type: Town
Incorporated: Aug. 15, 1951 *Area:* 2.85 sq km
Population in 2006: 365
Provincial Electoral District(s): Bonavista North
Federal Electoral District(s): Bonavista-Gander-Grand Falls-Windsor
Next Election: Sept. 2013 (4 year terms)
Kevin Blackwood, Mayor
Derrick Bragg, Clerk

Hampden
P.O. Box 9
Hampden, NL A0K 2Y0
Tel: 709-455-4212; *Fax:* 709-455-2117
townofhampden@eastlink.ca
Municipal Type: Town
Incorporated: Dec. 8, 1959 *Area:* 32.97 sq km
Population in 2006: 489
Provincial Electoral District(s): Humber Valley
Federal Electoral District(s): Humber-St. Barbe-Baie Verte
Next Election: Sept. 2013 (4 year terms)
Jerry Martin, Mayor
Ruth Jenkins, Clerk

Hant's Harbour
P.O. Box 40
Hants Harbour, NL A0B 1Y0
Tel: 709-586-2741; *Fax:* 709-586-2680
Municipal Type: Town
Incorporated: Oct. 13, 1970 *Area:* 32.31 sq km
Population in 2006: 401
Provincial Electoral District(s): Trinity-Bay de Verde
Federal Electoral District(s): Avalon
Next Election: Sept. 2013 (4 year terms)
Donald G. Green, Mayor
Doris J. Short, Clerk

Happy Adventure
PO Box 1, Site 2
Happy Adventure, NL A0G 1Z0
Tel: 709-677-2593; *Fax:* 709-677-2594
happyadventure@aibn.com
Municipal Type: Town
Incorporated: May 10, 1960 *Area:* 9.62 sq km
Population in 2006: 227
Provincial Electoral District(s): Terra Nova
Federal Electoral District(s): Bonavista-Gander-Grand Falls-Windsor
Next Election: Sept. 2013 (4 year terms)
James Warren, Mayor
Kim Babstock, Clerk

Happy Valley-Goose Bay
P.O. Box 40 B
Happy Valley-Goose Bay, NL A0P 1E0
Tel: 709-896-3321; *Fax:* 709-896-9454
townclerk@happyvalley-goosebay.com
www.happyvalley-goosebay.com
Municipal Type: Town
Incorporated: March 15, 1955 *Area:* 305.85 sq km
Population in 2006: 7,572
Provincial Electoral District(s): Lake Melville
Federal Electoral District(s): Labrador
Next Election: Sept. 2013 (4 year terms)
Leo Abbass, Mayor
labbass@cdli.ca
Valerie Sheppard, Clerk
townclerk@happyvalley-goosebay.com

Harbour Breton
P.O. Box 130
Harbour Breton, NL A0H 1P0
Tel: 709-885-2354; *Fax:* 709-885-2095
bernice@harbourbreton.com
www.harbourbreton.com
Municipal Type: Town
Incorporated: Dec. 16, 1952 *Area:* 13.74 sq km
Population in 2006: 1,877
Provincial Electoral District(s): Fortune Bay-Cape La Hune
Federal Electoral District(s): Random-Burin-St. George's
Next Election: Sept. 2013 (4 year terms)
Eric Skinner, Mayor
Bernice Herritt, Clerk

Harbour Grace
P.O. Box 310
Harbour Grace, NL A0A 2M0
Tel: 709-596-3631; *Fax:* 709-596-1991
thg@nf.sympatico.ca
www.hrgrace.ca
Municipal Type: Town
Incorporated: July 10, 1945 *Area:* 33.71 sq km
Population in 2006: 3,074
Provincial Electoral District(s): Carbonear-Harbour Grace
Federal Electoral District(s): Avalon
Next Election: Sept. 2013 (4 year terms)
Don Coombs, Mayor
Lester Forward, Clerk

Harbour Main-Chapel Cove-Lakeview
P.O. Box 40
Harbour Main, NL A0A 2P0
Tel: 709-229-6822; *Fax:* 709-229-6234
hmcouncil@eastlink.ca
Municipal Type: Town
Incorporated: June 1, 1965 *Area:* 21.05 sq km
Population in 2006: 1,090
Provincial Electoral District(s): Harbour Main-Whitbourne
Federal Electoral District(s): Avalon
Next Election: Sept. 2013 (4 year terms)
Raymond Parsley, Mayor
Marian Hawco, Clerk

Hare Bay
P.O. Box 130
Hare Bay BB, NL A0G 2P0
Tel: 709-537-2187; *Fax:* 709-537-2987
Municipal Type: Town
Incorporated: Oct. 20, 1964 *Area:* 34.06 sq km
Population in 2006: 1,020
Provincial Electoral District(s): Terra Nova
Federal Electoral District(s): Bonavista-Gander-Grand Falls-Windsor
Next Election: Sept. 2013 (4 year terms)
James Payne, Mayor
George R. Collins, Clerk

Hawke's Bay
P.O. Box 33
Hawkes Bay, NL A0K 3B0
Tel: 709-248-5216; *Fax:* 709-248-5201
hbcouncil@nf.aibn.com
Municipal Type: Town
Incorporated: Aug. 21, 1956 *Area:* 46.55 sq km
Population in 2006: 391
Provincial Electoral District(s): St. Barbe
Federal Electoral District(s): Humber-St. Barbe-Baie Verte
Next Election: Sept. 2013 (4 year terms)
Lloyd Bennett, Mayor
Emily Smith, Clerk

Heart's Content
P.O. Box 31
Hearts Content, NL A0B 1Z0
Tel: 709-583-2491; *Fax:* 709-583-2226
townofheartscontent@persona.ca
Municipal Type: Town
Incorporated: Aug. 25, 1967 *Area:* 62.81 sq km
Population in 2006: 418
Provincial Electoral District(s): Trinity-Bay de Verde
Federal Electoral District(s): Avalon
Next Election: Sept. 2013 (4 year terms)
Donald Blundon, Mayor
Alice Cumby, Clerk

Heart's Delight-Islington
P.O. Box 129
Hearts Delight, NL A0B 2A0
Tel: 709-588-2708; *Fax:* 709-588-2235
heartsdelightislington@persona.ca
Municipal Type: Town
Incorporated: Oct. 24, 1972 *Area:* 27.27 sq km
Population in 2006: 663
Provincial Electoral District(s): Trinity-Bay de Verde
Federal Electoral District(s): Avalon
Next Election: Sept. 2013 (4 year terms)
Denzil Sheppard, Mayor
Emily Harnum, Clerk

Heart's Desire
P.O. Box 10
Hearts Desire, NL A0B 2B0
Tel: 709-588-2280; *Fax:* 709-588-2343
townofheartsdesire@persona.ca
Municipal Type: Town
Incorporated: Sept. 28, 1971 *Area:* 17.27 sq km
Population in 2006: 226
Provincial Electoral District(s): Trinity-Bay de Verde
Federal Electoral District(s): Avalon
Next Election: Sept. 2013 (4 year terms)
Patrick Coombs, Mayor
Eleanor Andrews, Clerk

Hermitage-Sandyville
P.O. Box 160
Hermitage, NL A0H 1S0
Tel: 709-883-2343; *Fax:* 709-883-2150
jsimms@nf.aibn.com
www.hermitage-sandyville.ca
Municipal Type: Town
Incorporated: Oct. 22, 1960 *Area:* 28.91 sq km

Population in 2006: 499
Provincial Electoral District(s): Fortune Bay-Cape La Hune
Federal Electoral District(s): Random-Burin-St. George's
Next Election: Sept. 2013 (4 year terms)
Douglas Rose, Mayor
Josephine (Josie) Rideout Simms, Town Manager

Holyrood
P.O. Box 100
Holyrood, NL A0A 2R0
Tel: 709-229-7252; *Fax:* 709-229-7269
cturnbull@townofholyrood.com
www.townofholyrood.com
Municipal Type: Town
Incorporated: March 23, 1969 *Area:* 125.57 sq km
Population in 2006: 2,005
Provincial Electoral District(s): Conception Bay South
Federal Electoral District(s): Avalon
Next Election: Sept. 2013 (4 year terms)
Gary Goobie, Mayor
Marie Searle, CAO-Clerk

Hopedale
P.O. Box 189
Hopedale, NL A0P 1G0
Tel: 709-933-3864; *Fax:* 709-933-3800
towncouncilhopedale@nf.aibn.com
Municipal Type: Town
Incorporated: Sept. 30, 1969 *Area:* 3.36 sq km
Population in 2006: 530
Provincial Electoral District(s): Torngat Mountains
Federal Electoral District(s): Labrador
Next Election: Sept. 2013 (4 year terms)
Judy Dicker, Mayor
Jullian Mistuk, Clerk

Howley
P.O. Box 40
Howley, NL A0K 3E0
Tel: 709-635-5555; *Fax:* 709-635-5850
Municipal Type: Town
Incorporated: Feb. 4, 1958 *Area:* 19.91 sq km
Population in 2006: 241
Provincial Electoral District(s): Humber Valley
Federal Electoral District(s): Humber-St. Barbe-Baie Verte
Next Election: Sept. 2013 (4 year terms)
Calvin Samms, Mayor
Blanche Gilley, Clerk

Hughes Brook
P.O. Box 2527
RR#2
Corner Brook, NL A2H 6B9
Tel: 709-783-2921; *Fax:* 709-783-2921
Municipal Type: Town
Incorporated: July 25, 1975 *Area:* 1.6 sq km
Population in 2006: 197
Provincial Electoral District(s): Bay of Islands
Federal Electoral District(s): Humber-St. Barbe-Baie Verte
Next Election: Sept. 2013 (4 year terms)
Maurice Osborne, Mayor
Gloria Loder, Clerk

Humber Arm South
General Delivery
Benoits Cove, NL A0L 1A0
Tel: 709-789-2981; *Fax:* 709-789-2918
humberarmsouth@nf.aibn.com
Municipal Type: Town
Incorporated: June 15, 1971 *Area:* 65.05 sq km
Population in 2006: 1,854
Provincial Electoral District(s): Bay of Islands
Federal Electoral District(s): Humber-St. Barbe-Baie Verte
Next Election: Sept. 2013 (4 year terms)
Arch Mitchell, Mayor
Marion Evoy, Clerk

Indian Bay
General Delivery
Indian Bay, NL A0G 2V0
Tel: 709-678-2727; *Fax:* 709-678-2727
Municipal Type: Town
Incorporated: Oct. 19, 1971 *Area:* 86.24 sq km
Population in 2006: 196
Provincial Electoral District(s): Bonavista North
Federal Electoral District(s): Bonavista-Gander-Grand Falls-Windsor
Next Election: Sept. 2013 (4 year terms)
Ronald Collins, Mayor
Thomas Easton, Clerk

Irishtown-Summerside
P.O. Box 2795
RR#2
Corner Brook, NL A2H 6B9
Tel: 709-783-2146; *Fax:* 709-783-2146
Municipal Type: Town
Incorporated: Jan. 1, 1991 *Area:* 11.89 sq km
Population in 2006: 1,290
Provincial Electoral District(s): Bay of Islands
Federal Electoral District(s): Humber-St. Barbe-Baie Verte
Next Election: Sept. 2013 (4 year terms)
Ralph Loder, Mayor
Rita Blanchard, Clerk

Isle aux Morts
P.O. Box 110
Isle-aux-Morts, NL A0M 1J0
Tel: 709-698-3441; *Fax:* 709-698-3449
townhalliam@nf.aibn.com
Municipal Type: Town
Incorporated: Nov. 5, 1956 *Area:* 7.66 sq km
Population in 2006: 718
Provincial Electoral District(s): Burgeo & La Poile
Federal Electoral District(s): Random-Burin-St. George's
Next Election: Sept. 2013 (4 year terms)
Raymond LeFrense, Mayor
Lydia Francis, Clerk

Jackson's Arm
P.O. Box 10
Jacksons Arm, NL A0K 3H0
Tel: 709-459-3122; *Fax:* 709-459-3173
info@townofjacksonsarm.com
Municipal Type: Town
Incorporated: June 19, 1982 *Area:* 7.02 sq km
Population in 2006: 374
Provincial Electoral District(s): Humber Valley
Federal Electoral District(s): Humber-St. Barbe-Baie Verte
Next Election: Sept. 2013 (4 year terms)
Claude Jones, Mayor
Carmel Wicks, Clerk

Keels
P.O. Box 20
Keels, NL A0C 1R0
Tel: 709-447-3127; *Fax:* 709-447-6186
Municipal Type: Town
Incorporated: June 14, 1966 *Area:* 6.54 sq km
Population in 2006: 73
Provincial Electoral District(s): Bonavista South
Federal Electoral District(s): Bonavista-Gander-Grand Falls-Windsor
Next Election: Sept. 2013 (4 year terms)
Annie Fitzgerald, Mayor
Crystal Taylor, Clerk

King's Cove
General Delivery
Kings Cove, NL A0C 1S0
Tel: 709-447-4361; *Fax:* 709-448-2004
Municipal Type: Town
Incorporated: June 14,1966 *Area:* 21.48 sq km
Population in 2006: 121
Provincial Electoral District(s): Bonavista South
Federal Electoral District(s): Bonavista-Gander-Grand Falls-Windsor; Humber-St. Barbe-Baie Verte; Labrador
Next Election: Sept. 2013 (4 year terms)
Tom Maddox, Mayor
Gerald Barron, Clerk

King's Point
P.O. Box 10
Kings Point, NL A0J 1H0
Tel: 709-268-3838; *Fax:* 709-268-3856
d.snow@eastlink.ca
Municipal Type: Town
Incorporated: Oct. 1, 1957 *Area:* 46.31 sq km
Population in 2006: 670
Provincial Electoral District(s): Baie Verte
Federal Electoral District(s): Humber-St. Barbe-Baie Verte
Next Election: Sept. 2013 (4 year terms)
Ed Wright, Mayor
Don Snow, Clerk

Kippens
2 Juniper Ave.
Kippens, NL A2N 3H8
Tel: 709-643-5281; *Fax:* 709-643-9773
kippens@nf.aibn.com
www.kippens.ca
Municipal Type: Town
Incorporated: Dec. 31, 1968 *Area:* 14.32 sq km
Population in 2006: 1,739
Provincial Electoral District(s): Port au Port
Federal Electoral District(s): Random-Burin-St. George's
Next Election: Sept. 2013 (4 year terms)
Cator Best, Mayor
Debbie Cormier, Acting Clerk

L'Anse au Clair
P.O. Box 83
L'Anse au Clair, NL A0K 3K0
Tel: 709-931-2481; *Fax:* 709-931-2488
townoflanseauclair@hotmail.com
Municipal Type: Town
Incorporated: June 2, 1970 *Area:* 61.92 sq km
Population in 2006: 226
Provincial Electoral District(s): Cartwright-L'Anse au Clair
Federal Electoral District(s): Labrador
Next Election: Sept. 2013 (4 year terms)
Nath Moores, Mayor
Loretta Griffin, Clerk

L'Anse au Loup
P.O. Box 101
L'Anse au Loup, NL A0K 3L0
Tel: 709-927-5573; *Fax:* 709-927-5263
lanseauloup@nf.aibn.com
www.lanseauloup.ca
Municipal Type: Town
Incorporated: April 11, 1975 *Area:* 3.48 sq km
Population in 2006: 593
Provincial Electoral District(s): Cartwright-L'Anse au Clair
Federal Electoral District(s): Labrador; Random-Burin-St. George's
Next Election: Sept. 2013 (4 year terms)
Headley Ryland, Mayor
Lawrence Normore, Town Clerk, Manager & Officer, Community Economic Development

La Scie
P.O. Box 130
La Scie, NL A0K 3M0
Tel: 709-675-2266; *Fax:* 709-675-2168
townoflascie@eastlink.ca
Municipal Type: Town
Incorporated: May 25, 1955 *Area:* 29.14 sq km
Population in 2006: 955
Provincial Electoral District(s): Baie Verte
Federal Electoral District(s): Humber-St. Barbe-Baie Verte
Next Election: Sept. 2013 (4 year terms)
Clyde Saunders, Mayor
Rowena Morey, Clerk

Labrador City
P.O. Box 280
Labrador City, NL A2V 2K5
Tel: 709-944-5537; *Fax:* 709-944-2810
www.labradorwest.com
Municipal Type: Town
Incorporated: June 27, 1961 *Area:* 38.83 sq km
Population in 2006: 7,240
Provincial Electoral District(s): Labrador West
Federal Electoral District(s): Labrador
Next Election: Sept. 2013 (4 year terms)
Janice Barnes, Mayor
Diane Gear, Town Clerk

Lamaline
P.O. Box 40
Lamaline, NL A0E 2C0
Tel: 709-857-2341; *Fax:* 709-857-2210
barbking70@hotmail.com
Municipal Type: Town
Incorporated: April 24, 1963 *Area:* 81.69 sq km
Population in 2006: 315
Provincial Electoral District(s): Grand Bank
Federal Electoral District(s): Random-Burin-St. George's
Next Election: Sept. 2013 (4 year terms)
Maureen Fleming, Mayor
Barbara King, Clerk

Lark Harbour
P.O. Box 40
Lark Harbour, NL A0L 1H0
Tel: 709-681-2270; *Fax:* 709-681-2900
Municipal Type: Town
Incorporated: Jan. 22, 1974 *Area:* 12.92 sq km
Population in 2006: 565
Provincial Electoral District(s): Bay of Islands
Federal Electoral District(s): Humber-St. Barbe-Baie Verte
Next Election: Sept. 2013 (4 year terms)
John Parsons, Mayor
Debra Park, Clerk

Louise Darrigan, Co-Clerk

Lawn
P.O. Box 29
Lawn, NL A0E 2E0
Tel: 709-873-2439; *Fax:* 709-873-3006
townoflawn@nf.aibn.com
Municipal Type: Town
Incorporated: Sept. 30, 1952 *Area:* 3.61 sq km
Population in 2006: 705
Provincial Electoral District(s): Grand Bank
Federal Electoral District(s): Random-Burin-St. George's
Next Election: Sept. 2013 (4 year terms)
William Lockyer, Mayor
Ruth M. Bennett, Clerk

Leading Tickles
P.O. Box 39
Leading Tickles West, NL A0H 1T0
Tel: 709-483-2180; *Fax:* 709-483-2185
leadingtickles@nf.aibn.com
www.leadingtickles.ca
Municipal Type: Town
Incorporated: July 11, 1961 *Area:* 26.73 sq km
Population in 2006: 407
Provincial Electoral District(s): Exploits
Federal Electoral District(s): Bonavista-Gander-Grand Falls-Windsor
Next Election: Sept. 2013 (4 year terms)
Harry Hallet, Mayor
Doreen Haggett, Clerk

Lewin's Cove
P.O. Box 40
Lewins Cove, NL A0E 2G0
Tel: 709-894-4777; *Fax:* 709-894-4952
townoflewinscove@bellaliant.com
Municipal Type: Town
Incorporated: May 1, 1973 *Area:* 6.52 sq km
Population in 2006: 566
Provincial Electoral District(s): Grand Bank
Federal Electoral District(s): Random-Burin-St. George's
Next Election: Sept. 2013 (4 year terms)
William Wakeley, Mayor
Barbara Mullett, Clerk

Lewisporte
P.O. Box 219
Lewisporte, NL A0G 3A0
Tel: 709-535-2737; *Fax:* 709-535-2695
elaine@lewisportecanada.com
www.lewisportecanada.com
Municipal Type: Town
Incorporated: July 2, 1946 *Area:* 36.91 sq km
Population in 2006: 3,308
Provincial Electoral District(s): Lewisporte
Federal Electoral District(s): Bonavista-Gander-Grand Falls-Windsor
Next Election: Sept. 2013 (4 year terms)
Brian Peckford, Mayor
Elaine Bursey, Clerk
elaine@lewisportecanada.com

Little Bay
P.O. Box 39
Little Bay, NL A0J 1J0
Tel: 709-267-3200; *Fax:* 709-267-3200
Municipal Type: Town
Incorporated: April 19, 1966 *Area:* 1.45 sq km
Population in 2006: 116
Provincial Electoral District(s): Baie Verte
Federal Electoral District(s): Humber-St. Barbe-Baie Verte; Random-Burin-St. George's
Next Election: Sept. 2013 (4 year terms)
Bronson Webber, Mayor
Jamie Winsor, Clerk

Little Bay East
P.O. Box 15
Little Bay East, NL A0E 2J0
Tel: 709-461-2724; *Fax:* 709-461-2724
Municipal Type: Town
Incorporated: April 27, 1979 *Area:* 1.48 sq km
Population in 2006: 140
Provincial Electoral District(s): Bellevue
Federal Electoral District(s): Random-Burin-St. George's
Next Election: Sept. 2013 (4 year terms)
Earl Thornhill, Mayor
Gail Clarke, Clerk

Little Bay Islands
P.O. Box 64
Little Bay Islands, NL A0J 1K0
Tel: 709-626-3511; *Fax:* 709-626-3512
lbtowncouncil@eastlink.ca
Municipal Type: Town
Incorporated: Oct. 25, 1955 *Area:* 7.16 sq km
Population in 2006: 152
Provincial Electoral District(s): Baie Verte
Federal Electoral District(s): Humber-St. Barbe-Baie Verte
Next Election: Sept. 2013 (4 year terms)
Kelly Roberts, Clerk
Perry Locke, Mayor

Little Burnt Bay
P.O. Box 40
Little Burnt Bay, NL A0G 3B0
Tel: 709-535-6415; *Fax:* 709-535-6490
lbbtowncouncil@bellaliant.com
Municipal Type: Town
Incorporated: Sept. 19, 1975 *Area:* 8.5 sq km
Population in 2006: 325
Provincial Electoral District(s): Lewisporte
Federal Electoral District(s): Bonavista-Gander-Grand Falls-Windsor
Next Election: Sept. 2013 (4 year terms)
Laverne Suppa, Mayor
Maisie Wells, Clerk

Little Catalina
P.O. Box 59
Little Catalina, NL A0C 1W0
Tel: 709-469-2795; *Fax:* 709-469-2795
thetownoflittlecatalina@hotmail.com
www.littlecatalina.com
Municipal Type: Town
Incorporated: May 18, 1965 *Area:* 11.15 sq km
Population in 2006: 458
Provincial Electoral District(s): Bonavista South
Federal Electoral District(s): Bonavista-Gander-Grand Falls-Windsor
Next Election: Sept. 2013 (4 year terms)
Annie G. Johnson, Mayor
Marilyn Reid, Clerk

Logy Bay-Middle Cove-Outer Cove
744 Logy Bay Rd.
Logy Bay, NL A1K 3B5
Tel: 709-726-7930; *Fax:* 709-726-2178
office@lbmcoc.ca
Municipal Type: Town
Incorporated: Sept. 1, 1986 *Area:* 16.98 sq km
Population in 2006: 1,978
Provincial Electoral District(s): Cape St. Francis
Federal Electoral District(s): St. John's East
Next Election: Sept. 2013 (4 year terms)
John Kennedy, Mayor
Richard Roache, Clerk

Long Harbour-Mount Arlington Heights
P.O. Box 40
Long Harbour, NL A0B 2J0
Tel: 709-228-2920; *Fax:* 709-228-2900
towncouncil@longharbour.net
Municipal Type: Town
Incorporated: Oct. 22, 1968 *Area:* 18.41 sq km
Population in 2006: 211
Provincial Electoral District(s): Bellevue
Federal Electoral District(s): Avalon
Next Election: Sept. 2013 (4 year terms)
Gary Keating, Mayor
Harriet Bruce, Clerk

Lord's Cove
General Delivery
Lord's Cove, NL A0E 2C0
Tel: 709-857-2316; *Fax:* 709-857-2031
Municipal Type: Town
Incorporated: May 17, 1966 *Area:* 30.91 sq km
Population in 2006: 207
Provincial Electoral District(s): Grand Bank
Federal Electoral District(s): Random-Burin-St. George's
Next Election: Sept. 2013 (4 year terms)
Eileen Harnett, Acting Clerk

Lourdes
P.O. Box 29
Lourdes, NL A0N 1R0
Tel: 709-642-5812; *Fax:* 709-642-5812
townoflourdes@yahoo.ca
Municipal Type: Town
Incorporated: July 17, 1969 *Area:* 8.1 sq km
Population in 2006: 550
Provincial Electoral District(s): Port au Port
Federal Electoral District(s): Random-Burin-St. George's
Next Election: Sept. 2013 (4 year terms)
Henry Gaudon, Mayor
Angela Young, Clerk

Lumsden
P.O. Box 100
Lumsden, NL A0G 3E0
Tel: 709-530-2309; *Fax:* 709-530-2144
townoflumsden@nf.aibn.com
www.lumsdennl.ca
Municipal Type: Town
Incorporated: April 16, 1968 *Area:* 20.43 sq km
Population in 2006: 533
Provincial Electoral District(s): Bonavista North
Federal Electoral District(s): Bonavista-Gander-Grand Falls-Windsor
Next Election: Sept. 2013 (4 year terms)
Danny Gibbons, Mayor
Jeanie Stokes, Clerk

Lushes Bight-Beaumont-Beaumont North
P.O. Box 40
Beaumont, NL A0J 1A0
Tel: 709-264-3271; *Fax:* 709-264-3191
townoflushesbightbeaumont@nf.aibn.com
Municipal Type: Town
Incorporated: Oct. 15, 1968 *Area:* 34.38 sq km
Population in 2006: 275
Provincial Electoral District(s): Windsor-Springdale
Federal Electoral District(s): Humber-St. Barbe-Baie Verte
Next Election: Sept. 2013 (4 year terms)
Clyde Croucher, Mayor
Joan Pittman, Clerk

Main Brook
P.O. Box 130
Main Brook, NL A0K 3N0
Tel: 709-865-6561; *Fax:* 709-865-3279
townofmainbrook@nf.aibn.com
Municipal Type: Town
Incorporated: June 1, 1948 *Area:* 28.51 sq km
Population in 2006: 293
Provincial Electoral District(s): The Straits & White Bay North
Federal Electoral District(s): Humber-St. Barbe-Baie Verte
Next Election: Sept. 2013 (4 year terms)
Leander Pilgrim, Mayor
Karen Pilgrim, Clerk

Makkovik
P.O. Box 132
Makkovik, NL A0P 1J0
Tel: 709-923-2221; *Fax:* 709-923-2126
townmanager@makkovik.ca
Municipal Type: Town
Incorporated: April 7, 1970 *Area:* 1.97 sq km
Population in 2006: 362
Provincial Electoral District(s): Torngat Mountains
Federal Electoral District(s): Labrador
Next Election: Sept. 2013 (4 year terms)
Herbert R. Jacque, Mayor
Doreen Winters, Clerk

Mary's Harbour
P.O. Box 134
Mary's Harbour, NL A0K 3P0
Tel: 709-921-6281; *Fax:* 709-921-6255
maryshbr@nf.aibn.com
Municipal Type: Town
Incorporated: April 11, 1975 *Area:* 38.16 sq km
Population in 2006: 417
Provincial Electoral District(s): Cartwright-L'Anse au Clair
Federal Electoral District(s): Labrador
Next Election: Sept. 2013 (4 year terms)
Larry Rumbolt, Mayor
Sheena Rumbolt, Clerk

Marystown
P.O. Box 1118
Marystown, NL A0E 2M0
Tel: 709-279-1661; *Fax:* 709-279-2862
info@townofmarystown.ca
www.townofmarystown.ca
Municipal Type: Town
Incorporated: Dec. 18, 1951 *Area:* 61.97 sq km
Population in 2006: 5,436
Provincial Electoral District(s): Burin-Placentia West
Federal Electoral District(s): Random-Burin-St. George's
Next Election: Sept. 2013 (4 year terms)

Sam Synard, Mayor
ssynard@townofmarystown.ca
Dennis P. Kelly, Clerk & Manager
dkelly@townofmarystown.ca

Massey Drive
85 Massey Dr.
Massey Drive, NL A2H 7A2
Tel: 709-634-2742; *Fax:* 709-634-2899
townmasseydr@nf.aibn.com
Municipal Type: Town
Incorporated: Sept. 28, 1971 *Area:* 2.48 sq km
Population in 2006: 1,170
Provincial Electoral District(s): Humber East
Federal Electoral District(s): Humber-St. Barbe-Baie Verte
Next Election: Sept. 2013 (4 year terms)
Gord Davis, Mayor
Rodger Hunt, Town Manager/Clerk

McIvers
P.O. Box 4375
RR#2
Corner Brook, NL A2H 6B9
Tel: 709-688-2603; *Fax:* 709-688-2680
mciverscouncil@eastlink.ca
Municipal Type: Town
Incorporated: June 15, 1971 *Area:* 12.06 sq km
Population in 2006: 571
Provincial Electoral District(s): Bay of Islands
Federal Electoral District(s): Humber-St. Barbe-Baie Verte
Next Election: Sept. 2013 (4 year terms)
Warren Blanchard, Mayor
Bernice E. Parsons, Clerk

Meadows
P.O. Box 3529
RR#2
Corner Brook, NL A2H 6B9
Tel: 709-783-2339; *Fax:* 709-783-2501
townofmeadows@nf.aibn.com
Municipal Type: Town
Incorporated: Jan. 13, 1970 *Area:* 3.79 sq km
Population in 2006: 637
Provincial Electoral District(s): Bay of Islands
Federal Electoral District(s): Humber-St. Barbe-Baie Verte
Next Election: Sept. 2013 (4 year terms)
Kenneth March, Mayor
Joy Taylor, Clerk

Middle Arm
P.O. Box 51
Middle Arm, NL A0K 3R0
Tel: 709-252-2521; *Fax:* 709-252-2521
townofmiddlearm@nf.aibn.com
Municipal Type: Town
Incorporated: Nov. 29, 1966 *Area:* 25.19 sq km
Population in 2006: 517
Provincial Electoral District(s): Baie Verte
Federal Electoral District(s): Avalon; Humber-St. Barbe-Baie Verte
Next Election: Sept. 2013 (4 year terms)
Nevil Robinson, Mayor
Loretta Budgell, Clerk

Miles Cove
General Delivery
Miles Cove, NL A0J 1L0
Tel: 709-652-3685; *Fax:* 709-652-3695
Municipal Type: Town
Incorporated: Sept. 22, 1970 *Area:* 4.03 sq km
Population in 2006: 140
Provincial Electoral District(s): Windsor-Springdale
Federal Electoral District(s): Humber-St. Barbe-Baie Verte
Next Election: Sept. 2013 (4 year terms)
Melvin Morey, Mayor
Gloria Reid, Clerk

Millertown
P.O. Box 56
Millertown, NL A0H 1V0
Tel: 709-852-6216; *Fax:* 709-852-5431
townofmillertown@nf.aibn.com
Municipal Type: Town
Incorporated: Dec. 15, 1959 *Area:* 3.24 sq km
Population in 2006: 100
Provincial Electoral District(s): Grand Falls-Buchans
Federal Electoral District(s): Bonavista-Gander-Grand Falls-Windsor
Next Election: Sept. 2013 (4 year terms)
Kevin Greene, Mayor
Eileen M. Scott, Clerk

Milltown-Head of Bay D'Espoir
P.O. Box 70
Milltown, NL A0H 1W0
Tel: 709-882-2232; *Fax:* 709-882-2636
townofmill@bellaliant.com
Municipal Type: Town
Incorporated: Dec. 16, 1952 *Area:* 25.02 sq km
Population in 2006: 865
Provincial Electoral District(s): Fortune Bay-Cape La Hune
Federal Electoral District(s): Random-Burin-St. George's
Next Election: Sept. 2013 (4 year terms)
Georgina Brushett, Mayor
Kimberly Kendell, Clerk

Ming's Bight
P.O. Box 59
Mings Bight, NL A0K 3S0
Tel: 709-254-6516; *Fax:* 709-254-6516
townmingsbight@xplornet.ca
Municipal Type: Town
Incorporated: June 6, 1970 *Area:* 3.78 sq km
Population in 2006: 347
Provincial Electoral District(s): Baie Verte
Federal Electoral District(s): Humber-St. Barbe-Baie Verte
Next Election: Sept. 2013 (4 year terms)
Danny Regular, Mayor
Glenda Regular, Clerk

Morrisville
P.O. Box 19
Morrisville, NL A0H 1W0
Tel: 709-882-2831; *Fax:* 709-882-2831
Municipal Type: Town
Incorporated: June 1, 1971 *Area:* 14.26 sq km
Population in 2006: 128
Provincial Electoral District(s): Fortune Bay-Cape La Hune
Federal Electoral District(s): Random-Burin-St. George's
Next Election: Sept. 2013 (4 year terms)
Helen Kendell, Mayor
Karl Kendell, Clerk

Mount Carmel-Mitchell's Brook-St. Catherines
General Delivery
Mount Carmel, NL A0B 2M0
Tel: 709-521-2040; *Fax:* 709-521-2258
Municipal Type: Town
Incorporated: Oct. 6, 1970 *Area:* 61.55 sq km
Population in 2006: 438
Provincial Electoral District(s): Placentia & St. Mary's
Federal Electoral District(s): Avalon
Next Election: Sept. 2013 (4 year terms)
Kim Mercer, Mayor
Geraldine Nolan, Clerk

Mount Moriah
P.O. Box 31
Mount Moriah, NL A0L 1J0
Tel: 709-785-5232; *Fax:* 709-785-5332
mtmoriahtowncouncil@nf.aibn.com
Municipal Type: Town
Incorporated: Oct. 12, 1971 *Area:* 15.71 sq km
Population in 2006: 752
Provincial Electoral District(s): Bay of Islands
Federal Electoral District(s): Humber-St. Barbe-Baie Verte
Next Election: Sept. 2013 (4 year terms)
James Gillam, Mayor
Carol Skeard, Clerk

Musgrave Harbour
P.O. Box 159
Musgrave Harbour, NL A0G 3J0
Tel: 709-655-2119; *Fax:* 709-655-2064
musgravetowncouncil@nf.aibn.com
www.musgraveharbour.com
Municipal Type: Town
Incorporated: Jan. 1, 1954 *Area:* 69.94 sq km
Population in 2006: 1,085
Provincial Electoral District(s): Bonavista North
Federal Electoral District(s): Bonavista-Gander-Grand Falls-Windsor
Next Election: Sept. 2013 (4 year terms)
Raymond Stokes, Mayor
Sharla Abbott, Clerk

Musgravetown
P.O. Box 129
Musgravetown, NL A0C 1Z0
Tel: 709-467-2726; *Fax:* 709-467-2109
townofmusg@nf.aibn.com
Municipal Type: Town
Incorporated: March 1, 1974 *Area:* 13.63 sq km
Population in 2006: 583
Provincial Electoral District(s): Terra Nova
Federal Electoral District(s): Bonavista-Gander-Grand Falls-Windsor
Next Election: Sept. 2013 (4 year terms)
Jim Brown, Mayor
Linda Fitzgerald, Clerk

Nain
P.O. Box 400
Nain, NL A0P 1L0
Tel: 709-922-2842; *Fax:* 709-922-2295
towncouncilnain@nf.aibn.com
Municipal Type: Town
Incorporated: Nov. 24, 1970 *Area:* 94.58 sq km
Population in 2006: 1,034
Provincial Electoral District(s): Torngat Mountains
Federal Electoral District(s): Labrador
Next Election: Sept. 2013 (4 year terms)
Sarah Erickson, Mayor
Karen Dicker, Clerk

New Perlican
P.O. Box 130
New Perlican, NL A0B 2S0
Tel: 709-583-2500; *Fax:* 709-583-2554
townofnewperlican@persona.ca
Municipal Type: Town
Incorporated: Sept. 28, 1971 *Area:* 24.47 sq km
Population in 2006: 188
Provincial Electoral District(s): Trinity-Bay de Verde
Federal Electoral District(s): Avalon
Next Election: Sept. 2013 (4 year terms)
Linda Moyles, Mayor
Courtney Clarke, Clerk

New-Wes-Valley
P.O. Box 64
Badgers Quay, NL A0G 1B0
Tel: 709-536-2010; *Fax:* 709-536-3481
new-wes-valley@nf.aibn.com
www.townofnewwesvalley.com
Municipal Type: Town
Incorporated: Jan. 1, 1992 *Area:* 133.59 sq km
Population in 2006: 2,485
Provincial Electoral District(s): Bonavista North
Federal Electoral District(s): Bonavista-Gander-Grand Falls-Windsor
Next Election: Sept. 2013 (4 year terms)
Grant Burry, Mayor
Harry Winter, Clerk & Manager

Nipper's Harbour
P.O. Box 10
Nippers Harbour, NL A0K 3T0
Tel: 709-255-3151; *Fax:* 709-255-3151
Municipal Type: Town
Incorporated: Nov. 10, 1964 *Area:* 1.93 sq km
Population in 2006: 151
Provincial Electoral District(s): Baie Verte
Federal Electoral District(s): Humber-St. Barbe-Baie Verte
Next Election: Sept. 2013 (4 year terms)
Ted Noble, Mayor
Beth Prole, Clerk

Norman's Cove-Long Cove
P.O. Box 70
Normans Cove, NL A0B 2T0
Tel: 709-592-2490; *Fax:* 709-592-2106
townofnclc@eastlink.ca
Municipal Type: Town
Incorporated: June 2, 1970 *Area:* 19.98 sq km
Population in 2006: 773
Provincial Electoral District(s): Bellevue
Federal Electoral District(s): Avalon
Next Election: Sept. 2013 (4 year terms)
Eva Bennett, Mayor
Dianne Hudson, Clerk

Norris Arm
P.O. Box 70
Norris Arm, NL A0G 3M0
Tel: 709-653-2519; *Fax:* 709-653-2163
norrisarm@gmail.com
www.norrisarm.com
Municipal Type: Town
Incorporated: April 20, 1971 *Area:* 41.49 sq km
Population in 2006: 911
Provincial Electoral District(s): Lewisporte
Federal Electoral District(s): Bonavista-Gander-Grand Falls-Windsor
Next Election: Sept. 2013 (4 year terms)
Chris Manuel, Mayor

Beverly Peyton, Clerk

Norris Point
P.O. Box 119
Norris Point, NL A0K 3V0
Tel: 709-458-2896; *Fax:* 709-458-2883
norrispointcouncil@nf.aibn.com
www.norrispoint.ca
Municipal Type: Town
Incorporated: Oct. 25, 1960 *Area:* 4.91 sq km
Population in 2006: 699
Provincial Electoral District(s): St. Barbe
Federal Electoral District(s): Humber-St. Barbe-Baie Verte
Next Election: Sept. 2013 (4 year terms)
Howard Neil, Mayor
mayor@norrispoint.ca
Regina Organ, Clerk

North River
P.O. Box 104
North River, NL A0A 3C0
Tel: 709-786-6216; *Fax:* 709-786-1955
Municipal Type: Town
Incorporated: Aug. 11, 1964 *Area:* 4.32 sq km
Population in 2006: 557
Provincial Electoral District(s): Harbour Main-Whitbourne
Federal Electoral District(s): Avalon; Labrador
Next Election: Sept. 2013 (4 year terms)
Sheila Power, Mayor
Sheila Hall, Clerk

North West River
P.O. Box 100
North West River, NL A0P 1M0
Tel: 709-497-8533; *Fax:* 709-497-8228
manager@townofnwr.ca
www.townofnwr.ca
Municipal Type: Town
Incorporated: March 11, 1958 *Area:* 3.2 sq km
Population in 2006: 492
Provincial Electoral District(s): Lake Melville
Federal Electoral District(s): Labrador
Next Election: Sept. 2013 (4 year terms)
Lowell Barkman, Mayor

Northern Arm
P.O. Box 2006
Northern Arm, NL A0H 1E0
Tel: 709-257-3482; *Fax:* 709-257-3482
ella@townofnorthernarm.ca
www.townofnorthernarm.ca
Municipal Type: Town
Incorporated: July 18, 1972 *Area:* 25.64 sq km
Population in 2006: 385
Provincial Electoral District(s): Exploits
Federal Electoral District(s): Bonavista-Gander-Grand Falls-Windsor
Next Election: Sept. 2013 (4 year terms)
Deanna Gail Hancock, Mayor
Ella Humphries, Clerk

Old Perlican
P.O. Box 39
Old Perlican, NL A0A 3G0
Tel: 709-587-2266; *Fax:* 709-587-2261
townofoldperlican@persona.ca
Municipal Type: Town
Incorporated: March 30, 1971 *Area:* 14.47 sq km
Population in 2006: 676
Provincial Electoral District(s): Trinity-Bay de Verde
Federal Electoral District(s): Avalon
Next Election: Sept. 2013 (4 year terms)
Harry Strong, Mayor
Judi Barter, Clerk

Pacquet
General Delivery
Pacquet, NL A0K 3X0
Tel: 709-251-5496; *Fax:* 709-251-5497
pacquet@eastlink.ca
Municipal Type: Town
Incorporated: June 12, 1962 *Area:* 14.48 sq km
Population in 2006: 210
Provincial Electoral District(s): Baie Verte
Federal Electoral District(s): Humber-St. Barbe-Baie Verte
Next Election: Sept. 2013 (4 year terms)
Morris Geenham, Mayor
Janet Sacrey, Clerk

Parker's Cove
General Delivery
Parker's Cove, NL A0E 1H0
Tel: 709-443-2216; *Fax:* 709-443-2216
council@eatlink.ca
Municipal Type: Town
Incorporated: Jan. 25, 1966 *Area:* 4.85 sq km
Population in 2006: 308
Provincial Electoral District(s): Burin-Placentia West
Federal Electoral District(s): Random-Burin-St. George's
Next Election: Sept. 2013 (4 year terms)
Cyril Synard, Mayor
Jeanette Murphy, Clerk

Parson's Pond
P.O. Box 39
Parsons Pond, NL A0K 3Z0
Tel: 709-243-2564; *Fax:* 709-243-2500
towncouncilpp@nf.aibn.com
Municipal Type: Town
Incorporated: March 29, 1966 *Area:* 12.63 sq km
Population in 2006: 387
Provincial Electoral District(s): St. Barbe
Federal Electoral District(s): Humber-St. Barbe-Baie Verte
Next Election: Sept. 2013 (4 year terms)
Brenda Biggin, Mayor
Joan Parsons, Clerk

Pasadena
18 Tenth Ave.
Pasadena, NL A0L 1K0
Tel: 709-686-2075; *Fax:* 709-686-2507
pasadena@nf.aibn.com
www.town.pasadena.nf.ca
Municipal Type: Town
Incorporated: Oct. 25, 1955 *Area:* 49.16 sq km
Population in 2006: 3,180
Provincial Electoral District(s): Humber East
Federal Electoral District(s): Humber-St. Barbe-Baie Verte
Next Election: Sept. 2013 (4 year terms)
Jim Merrigan, Mayor
bmercer@nf.aibn.com
Jim Merrigan, Clerk & Manager
jimmerrigan@nf.aibn.com

Peterview
P.O. Box 10
Peterview, NL A0H 1Y0
Tel: 709-257-2926; *Fax:* 709-257-2926
townofpeterview@nf.aibn.com
Municipal Type: Town
Incorporated: June 12, 1962 *Area:* 6.72 sq km
Population in 2006: 807
Provincial Electoral District(s): Exploits
Federal Electoral District(s): Bonavista-Gander-Grand Falls-Windsor
Next Election: Sept. 2013 (4 year terms)
James Samson, Mayor
Venus Samson, Clerk

Petty Harbour-Maddox Cove
P.O. Box 434
Petty Harbour, NL A0A 3H0
Tel: 709-368-3959; *Fax:* 709-368-3994
ncostello@phmc.nf.net
www.pettyharbourmaddoxcove.ca
Municipal Type: Town
Incorporated: March 25, 1969 *Area:* 4.51 sq km
Population in 2006: 915
Provincial Electoral District(s): Ferryland
Federal Electoral District(s): St. John's South-Mount Pearl
Next Election: Sept. 2013(4 year terms)
Nath Hutchings, Mayor
Noreen Costello, Clerk

Pilley's Island
P.O. Box 70
Pilleys Island, NL A0J 1M0
Tel: 709-652-3555; *Fax:* 709-652-3852
pilleysisland@nf.aibn.com
Municipal Type: Town
Incorporated: April 11, 1975 *Area:* 34.67 sq km
Population in 2006: 317
Provincial Electoral District(s): Windsor-Springdale
Federal Electoral District(s): Humber-St. Barbe-Baie Verte
Next Election: Sept. 2013 (4 year terms)
Fern Roberts, Mayor
Paulette Callahan, Clerk

Pinware
P.O. Box 37
Pinware, NL A0K 5S0
Tel: 709-927-5422; *Fax:* 709-927-5422
Municipal Type: Town
Incorporated: May 18, 1978 *Area:* 4.37 sq km
Population in 2006: 114
Provincial Electoral District(s): Cartwright-L'Anse au Clair
Federal Electoral District(s): Labrador
Next Election: Sept. 2013 (4 year terms)
Joanne Dorey, Mayor
Gina Winslow, Clerk

Placentia
P.O. Box 99
Placentia, NL A0B 2Y0
Tel: 709-227-2151; *Fax:* 709-227-2323
townofplacentia@placentia.ca
www.placentia.ca
Municipal Type: Town
Incorporated: Nov. 6, 1945 *Area:* 58.05 sq km
Population in 2006: 3,898
Provincial Electoral District(s): Placentia & St. Mary's
Federal Electoral District(s): Avalon
Next Election: Sept. 2013 (4 year terms)
William P. Hogan, Mayor
wph@placentia.ca
Ed O'Keefe, Clerk

Point au Gaul
P.O. Box 11
Point au Gaul, NL A0E 2C0
Tel: 709-857-2514
Municipal Type: Town
Incorporated: Jan. 4, 1966 *Area:* 3.84 sq km
Population in 2006: 85
Provincial Electoral District(s): Grand Bank
Federal Electoral District(s): Random-Burin-St. George's
Next Election: Sept. 2013 (4 year terms)
Elizabeth Hillier, Mayor
Theresa Dodge, Clerk

Point Lance
P.O. Box 15
Point Lance, NL A0B 1E0
Tel: 709-338-2186; *Fax:* 709-338-2186
j_power@xplornet.ca
Municipal Type: Town
Incorporated: Dec. 7, 1971 *Area:* 29.14 sq km
Population in 2006: 119
Provincial Electoral District(s): Placentia & St. Mary's
Federal Electoral District(s): Avalon
Next Election: Sept. 2013 (4 year terms)
Melvin Careen, Mayor
Jane Power, Clerk

Point Leamington
P.O. Box 39
Point Leamington, NL A0H 1Z0
Tel: 709-484-3421; *Fax:* 709-484-3556
ptleamington@nf.aibn.com
Municipal Type: Town
Incorporated: Aug. 25, 1970 *Area:* 28.81 sq km
Population in 2006: 649
Provincial Electoral District(s): Exploits
Federal Electoral District(s): Bonavista-Gander-Grand Falls-Windsor
Next Election: Sept. 2013 (4 year terms)
Roosevelt Thompson, Mayor
Patricia Lanning, Clerk

Point May
P.O. Box 19
Point May, NL A0E 2C0
Tel: 709-857-2640; *Fax:* 709-857-2640
janicehaley@hotmail.com
Municipal Type: Town
Incorporated: Dec. 4, 1962 *Area:* 64.89 sq km
Population in 2006: 260
Provincial Electoral District(s): Grand Bank
Federal Electoral District(s): Random-Burin-St. George's
Next Election: Sept. 2013 (4 year terms)
Janice Haley, Clerk

Point of Bay
P.O. Box 9
Point of Bay, NL A0H 2A0
Tel: 709-257-3171; *Fax:* 709-257-3192
Municipal Type: Town
Incorporated: April 18, 1967 *Area:* 21.94 sq km
Population in 2006: 163
Provincial Electoral District(s): Exploits

Federal Electoral District(s): Bonavista-Gander-Grand Falls-Windsor
Next Election: Sept. 2013 (4 year terms)
Clarence Sparkes, Mayor
Sybil Boone, Clerk

Pool's Cove
P.O. Box 10
Pools Cove, NL A0H 2B0
Tel: 709-665-3371; *Fax:* 709-665-3372
Municipal Type: Town
Incorporated: Nov. 25, 1969 *Area:* 2.64 sq km
Population in 2006: 189
Provincial Electoral District(s): Fortune Bay-Cape La Hune
Federal Electoral District(s): Random-Burin-St. George's
Next Election: Sept. 2013 (4 year terms)
Melvin Perham, Mayor
Sharon May, Clerk

Port Anson
General Delivery
Port Anson, NL A0J 1N0
Tel: 709-652-3683; *Fax:* 709-652-3680
townofportanson@hotmail.com
Municipal Type: Town
Incorporated: Dec. 12, 1961 *Area:* 7.69 sq km
Population in 2006: 155
Provincial Electoral District(s): Windsor-Springdale
Federal Electoral District(s): Humber-St. Barbe-Baie Verte
Next Election: Sept. 2013 (4 year terms)
Shawn Burton, Mayor
Grace Burton, Clerk

Port au Choix
P.O. Box 89
Port au Choix, NL A0K 4C0
Tel: 709-861-3409; *Fax:* 709-861-3061
portauchoix@nf.aibn.com
Municipal Type: Town
Incorporated: July 26, 1966 *Area:* 35.61 sq km
Population in 2006: 893
Provincial Electoral District(s): St. Barbe
Federal Electoral District(s): Humber-St. Barbe-Baie Verte
Next Election: Sept. 2013 (4 year terms)
Carolyn Lavers, Mayor
Annette Payne, Clerk

Port au Port East
P.O. Box 160
Port au Port East, NL A0N 1T0
Tel: 709-648-2731; *Fax:* 709-648-9481
townofp.a.p.e@cablerocket.com
Municipal Type: Town
Incorporated: Dec. 16, 1952 *Area:* 24.76 sq km
Population in 2006: 608
Provincial Electoral District(s): Port au Port
Federal Electoral District(s): Random-Burin-St. George's
Next Election: Sept. 2013 (4 year terms)
Eileen Hann, Mayor
Joanne Ryan, Clerk

Port au Port West-Aguathuna-Felix Cove
P.O. Box 89
Aguathuna, NL A0N 1T0
Tel: 709-648-2891; *Fax:* 709-648-9292
papwaf@nf.aibn.com
Municipal Type: Town
Incorporated: Oct. 6, 1970 *Area:* 16.72 sq km
Population in 2006: 386
Provincial Electoral District(s): Port au Port
Federal Electoral District(s): Random-Burin-St. George's
Next Election: Sept. 2013 (4 year terms)
Vanessa Glasgow, Clerk

Port Blandford
P.O. Box 70
Port Blandford, NL A0C 2G0
Tel: 709-543-2170; *Fax:* 709-543-2153
vgreening@nf.aibn.com
www.portblandford.com
Municipal Type: Town
Incorporated: Sept. 28, 1971 *Area:* 50.56 sq km
Population in 2006: 521
Provincial Electoral District(s): Terra Nova
Federal Electoral District(s): Bonavista-Gander-Grand Falls-Windsor
Next Election: Sept. 2013 (4 year terms)
Reginald Penney, Mayor
Vida Greening, Town Clerk & Manager

Port Hope Simpson
P.O. Box 130
Port Hope Simpson, NL A0K 4E0
Tel: 709-960-0236; *Fax:* 709-960-0387
porthopesimpson@nf.aibn.com
Municipal Type: Town
Incorporated: May 1, 1973 *Area:* 32.52 sq km
Population in 2006: 529
Provincial Electoral District(s): Cartwright-L'Anse au Clair
Federal Electoral District(s): Labrador
Next Election: Sept. 2013 (4 year terms)
Margaret Burden, Mayor
Michelle Clarke, Clerk

Port Kirwan
PO Box 40, Site 2
Port Kirwan, NL A0A 2G0
Tel: 709-363-2207
Municipal Type: Town
Incorporated: June 15, 1965 *Area:* 9.19 sq km
Population in 2006: 85
Provincial Electoral District(s): Ferryland
Federal Electoral District(s): Avalon
Next Election: Sept. 2013 (4 year terms)
Eugene Brothers, Mayor
Dana Boland, Clerk

Port Rexton
P.O. Box 55
Port Rexton, NL A0C 2H0
Tel: 709-464-2006; *Fax:* 709-464-2006
portrexton@bellaliant.com
Municipal Type: Town
Incorporated: April 22, 1969 *Area:* 11.78 sq km
Population in 2006: 351
Provincial Electoral District(s): Trinity North
Federal Electoral District(s): Bonavista-Gander-Grand Falls-Windsor
Next Election: Sept. 2013 (4 year terms)
Alvin Piercey, Mayor
Lois Long, Clerk

Port Saunders
P.O. Box 39
Port Saunders, NL A0K 4H0
Tel: 709-861-3105; *Fax:* 709-861-2137
townofportsaunders@nf.aibn.com
Municipal Type: Town
Incorporated: Aug. 21, 1956 *Area:* 38.81 sq km
Population in 2006: 747
Provincial Electoral District(s): St. Barbe
Federal Electoral District(s): Humber-St. Barbe-Baie Verte
Next Election: Sept. 2013 (4 year terms)
Tony Ryan, Mayor
Judy Quinlan, Clerk
Helen Hamlyn, Co-clerk

Portugal Cove South
PO Box 8, Site 11
Trepassey, NL A0A 4B0
Tel: 709-438-2092; *Fax:* 709-438-2092
townofpcs@live.ca
Municipal Type: Town
Incorporated: Aug. 6, 1963 *Area:* 1.14 sq km
Population in 2006: 222
Provincial Electoral District(s): Ferryland
Federal Electoral District(s): Avalon
Next Election: Sept. 2013 (4 year terms)
Clarence Molloy, Mayor
Ida Perry, Clerk

Portugal Cove-St Philip's
1119 Thorburn Rd.
Portugal Cove-St Philips, NL A1M 1T6
Tel: 709-895-8000; *Fax:* 709-895-3780
pcsp@pcsp.ca
www.pcsp.ca
Municipal Type: Town
Incorporated: Feb. 1, 1992 *Area:* 57.35 sq km
Population in 2006: 6,575
Provincial Electoral District(s): Conception Bay East & Bell Island
Federal Electoral District(s): St. John's East
Next Election: Sept. 2013 (4 year terms)
Bill Fagan, Mayor
Judy Squires, Town Clerk & Treas.

Postville
P.O. Box 74
Postville, NL A0P 1N0
Tel: 709-479-9830; *Fax:* 709-479-9888
communitycouncil@nf.aibn.com
Municipal Type: Town
Incorporated: Aug. 1, 1975 *Area:* 1.96 sq km
Population in 2006: 219
Provincial Electoral District(s): Torngat Mountains
Federal Electoral District(s): Labrador
Next Election: Sept. 2013 (4 year terms)
Diane Gear, Mayor
Melanie Gear, Clerk

Pouch Cove
P.O. Box 59
Pouch Cove, NL A0A 3L0
Tel: 709-335-2848; *Fax:* 709-335-2840
pouchcove@nf.aibn.com
www.pouchcove.ca
Municipal Type: Town
Incorporated: Dec. 22, 1970 *Area:* 58.34 sq km
Population in 2006: 1,756
Provincial Electoral District(s): Cape St. Francis
Federal Electoral District(s): St. John's East
Next Election: Sept. 2013 (4 year terms)
Sarah Patten, Mayor
709-335-2464
Kim Osmond, Clerk

Raleigh
P.O. Box 119
Raleigh, NL A0K 4J0
Tel: 709-452-4461; *Fax:* 709-452-2135
townofraleigh@nf.aibn.com
Municipal Type: Town
Incorporated: Oct. 2, 1973 *Area:* 11.12 sq km
Population in 2006: 248
Provincial Electoral District(s): The Straits & White Bay North
Federal Electoral District(s): Humber-St. Barbe-Baie Verte
Next Election: Sept. 2013 (4 year terms)
Millicent Taylor, Mayor
Angela Taylor, Clerk

Ramea
P.O. Box 69
Ramea, NL A0N 2J0
Tel: 709-625-2280; *Fax:* 709-625-2010
rameatowncouncil@nf.aibn.com
Municipal Type: Town
Incorporated: March 20, 1951 *Area:* 1.89 sq km
Population in 2006: 618
Provincial Electoral District(s): Fortune Bay-Cape La Hune
Federal Electoral District(s): Random-Burin-St. George's
Next Election: Sept. 2009 (4 year terms)
Minnie Organ, Clerk
Lloyd Rossiter, Mayor

Red Bay
P.O. Box 108
Red Bay, NL A0K 4K0
Tel: 709-920-2197; *Fax:* 709-920-2103
redbaytowncouncil@nf.aibn.com
Municipal Type: Town
Incorporated: May 22, 1973 *Area:* 1.58 sq km
Population in 2006: 227
Provincial Electoral District(s): Cartwright-L'Anse au Clair
Federal Electoral District(s): Labrador
Next Election: Sept. 2013 (4 year terms)
Wade Earle, Mayor
Liz Yetman, Clerk

Red Harbour
General Delivery
Red Harbour PB, NL A0E 2R0
Tel: 709-443-2599; *Fax:* 709-443-2599
townofredhr@yahoo.ca
Municipal Type: Town
Incorporated: Nov. 9, 1969 *Area:* 11.35 sq km
Population in 2006: 210
Provincial Electoral District(s): Burin-Placentia West
Federal Electoral District(s): Random-Burin-St. George's
Next Election: Sept. 2013 (4 year terms)
Kevin Paddle, Clerk

Reidville
2 Community Sq.
Reidville, NL A8A 2V7
Tel: 709-635-5232; *Fax:* 709-635-4498
townofreidville@nf.aibn.com
www.reidville-nl.ca
Municipal Type: Town
Incorporated: Oct. 3, 1975 *Area:* 58.41 sq km
Population in 2006: 511
Provincial Electoral District(s): Humber Valley
Federal Electoral District(s): Humber-St. Barbe-Baie Verte
Next Election: Sept. 2013 (4 year terms)

Helen Reid, Mayor
Connie Reid, Clerk

Rencontre East
P.O. Box 56
Rencontre East, NL A0H 2C0
Tel: 709-848-3171; *Fax:* 709-848-4194
Municipal Type: Town
Incorporated: Feb. 8, 1972 *Area:* 2.62 sq km
Population in 2006: 165
Provincial Electoral District(s): Fortune Bay-Cape La Hune
Federal Electoral District(s): Random-Burin-St. George's
Next Election: Sept. 2013 (4 year terms)
Tom Caines, Mayor
Barbara Caines, Clerk

Renews-Cappahayden
P.O. Box 40
Renews, NL A0A 3N0
Tel: 709-363-2500; *Fax:* 709-363-2143
townofrenewscappahayden@nf.aibn.com
Municipal Type: Town
Incorporated: Sept. 19, 1967 *Area:* 127.84 sq km
Population in 2006: 421
Provincial Electoral District(s): Ferryland
Federal Electoral District(s): Avalon
Next Election: Sept. 2013 (4 year terms)
Donna Dinn, Mayor
Susan Perry, Clerk

Rigolet
P.O. Box 69
Rigolet, NL A0P 1P0
Tel: 709-947-3382; *Fax:* 709-947-3360
sherri.wolfrey@rigolet.ca
www.thebigland.ca
Municipal Type: Town
Incorporated: Jan. 7, 1977 *Area:* 3.61 sq km
Population in 2006: 269
Provincial Electoral District(s): Torngat Mountains
Federal Electoral District(s): Labrador
Next Election: Sept. 2013 (4 year terms)
Max Pottle, Acting Mayor
Sherri Wolfrey, Town Clerk

River of Ponds
P.O. Box 10
River of Ponds, NL A0K 4M0
Tel: 709-225-3161; *Fax:* 709-225-3162
Municipal Type: Town
Incorporated: May 26, 1970 *Area:* 4.69 sq km
Population in 2006: 251
Provincial Electoral District(s): St. Barbe
Federal Electoral District(s): Humber-St. Barbe-Baie Verte
Next Election: Sept. 2013 (4 year terms)
Eric Patey, Mayor
Cynthia Wheaton, Clerk

Riverhead
P.O. Box 426
St Marys, NL A0B 3B0
Tel: 709-525-2600; *Fax:* 709-525-2106
Municipal Type: Town
Incorporated: Dec. 20, 1966 *Area:* 105.6 sq km
Population in 2006: 220
Provincial Electoral District(s): Placentia & St. Mary's
Federal Electoral District(s): Avalon
Next Election: Sept. 2013 (4 year terms)
Gloria White, Mayor
Anne Lee, Clerk

Robert's Arm
P.O. Box 10
Roberts Arm, NL A0J 1R0
Tel: 709-652-3331; *Fax:* 709-652-3079
townofrobertsarm@eastlink.ca
Municipal Type: Town
Incorporated: Sept. 7, 1954 *Area:* 35.79 sq km
Population in 2006: 841
Provincial Electoral District(s): Windsor-Springdale
Federal Electoral District(s): Humber-St. Barbe-Baie Verte
Next Election: Sept. 2013 (4 year terms)
Lloyd Coulbourne, Mayor
Stephanie Ryan, Clerk

Rocky Harbour
P.O. Box 24
Rocky Harbour, NL A0K 4N0
Tel: 709-458-2376; *Fax:* 709-458-2293
rockyharbour@msn.com
www.rockyharbour.ca
Municipal Type: Town
Incorporated: April 5, 1966 *Area:* 12.08 sq km
Population in 2006: 978
Provincial Electoral District(s): St. Barbe
Federal Electoral District(s): Humber-St. Barbe-Baie Verte
Next Election: Sept. 2013 (4 year terms)
Walter Nicolle, Mayor
Kay Reid, Clerk

Roddickton-Bide Arm
P.O. Box 10
Roddickton, NL A0K 4P0
Tel: 709-457-2413; *Fax:* 709-457-2663
roddickton@nf.aibn.com
Municipal Type: Town
Incorporated: April 7, 1953 *Area:* 47.71 sq km
Population in 2006: 1103
Provincial Electoral District(s): The Straits & White Bay North
Federal Electoral District(s): Humber-St. Barbe-Baie Verte
Next Election: Sept. 2013 (4 year terms)
Raymond Norman, Mayor
Denise Adams, Clerk

Rose Blanche-Harbour Le Cou
P.O. Box 159
Rose Blanche, NL A0M 1P0
Tel: 709-956-2540; *Fax:* 709-956-2541
townofroseblanche@nf.aibn.com
Municipal Type: Town
Incorporated: Aug. 25, 1971 *Area:* 4.44 sq km
Population in 2006: 547
Provincial Electoral District(s): Burgeo & La Poile
Federal Electoral District(s): Random-Burin-St. George's
Next Election: Sept. 2013 (4 year terms)
Christine Nussey, Mayor
Tammy Farrell, Clerk

Rushoon
General Delivery
Rushoon, NL A0E 2S0
Tel: 709-443-2572; *Fax:* 709-443-2572
townofrushoon@bellaliant.com
Municipal Type: Town
Incorporated: Jan. 18, 1966 *Area:* 6.15 sq km
Population in 2006: 319
Provincial Electoral District(s): Burin-Placentia West
Federal Electoral District(s): Random-Burin-St. George's
Next Election: Sept. 2013 (4 year terms)
Jill Mulrooney, Mayor
Jacqueline Gaulton, Clerk

St. Alban's
P.O. Box 10
St Albans, NL A0H 2E0
Tel: 709-538-3132; *Fax:* 709-538-3683
st.albans@nf.aibn.com
www.stalbans.ca
Municipal Type: Town
Incorporated: Sept. 1, 1953 *Area:* 20.85 sq km
Population in 2006: 1,278
Provincial Electoral District(s): Fortune Bay-Cape La Hune
Federal Electoral District(s): Random-Burin-St. George's
Next Election: Sept. 2013 (4 year terms)
Rodney Kendall, Mayor
Genevieve Tremblett, Clerk & Manager

St. Anthony
P.O. Box 430
St Anthony, NL A0K 4S0
Tel: 709-454-3454; *Fax:* 709-454-4154
stanthony@nf.aibn.com
www.town.stanthony.nf.ca
Municipal Type: Town
Incorporated: July 18, 1945 *Area:* 37.02 sq km
Population in 2006: 2,476
Provincial Electoral District(s): The Straits & White Bay North
Federal Electoral District(s): Humber-St. Barbe-Baie Verte
Next Election: Sept. 2013 (4 year terms)
Ernest Simms, Mayor
Wallace Green, Clerk

St. Bernard's-Jacques Fontaine
P.O. Box 70
St Bernards, NL A0E 2T0
Tel: 709-461-2257; *Fax:* 709-461-2179
townofsbjf@eastlink.ca
Municipal Type: Town
Incorporated: Nov. 21, 1967 *Area:* 16.44 sq km
Population in 2006: 525
Provincial Electoral District(s): Bellevue
Federal Electoral District(s): Random-Burin-St. George's
Next Election: Sept. 2013 (4 year terms)
Clifford Allen, Mayor
Pauline Smith, Clerk

St. Brendan's
P.O. Box 43
St Brendans, NL A0G 3V0
Tel: 709-669-4271; *Fax:* 709-669-4271
Municipal Type: Town
Incorporated: Sept. 1, 1953 *Area:* 10.14 sq km
Population in 2006: 203
Provincial Electoral District(s): Terra Nova
Federal Electoral District(s): Bonavista-Gander-Grand Falls-Windsor
Next Election: Sept. 2013 (4 year terms)
Rita White, Clerk

St. Bride's
General Delivery
St Brides, NL A0B 2Z0
Tel: 709-337-2160; *Fax:* 709-337-2160
Municipal Type: Town
Incorporated: May 2, 1972 *Area:* 5.84 sq km
Population in 2006: 386
Provincial Electoral District(s): Placentia & St. Mary's
Federal Electoral District(s): Avalon
Next Election: Sept. 2013 (4 year terms)
Eugene Manning, Mayor
Joan Morrissey, Clerk

St. George's
P.O. Box 250
St Georges, NL A0N 1Z0
Tel: 709-647-3283; *Fax:* 709-647-3180
townofstgeorges@nf.aibn.com
www.townofstgeorges.com
Municipal Type: Town
Incorporated: May 18, 1965 *Area:* 25.83 sq km
Population in 2006: 1,246
Provincial Electoral District(s): St. George's-Stephenville East
Federal Electoral District(s): Random-Burin-St. George's
Next Election: Sept. 2013 (4 year terms)
Fintan Alexander, Mayor
Ray Chant, Clerk

St. Jacques-Coomb's Cove
P.O. Box 102
English Harbour West, NL A0H 1M0
Tel: 709-888-6141; *Fax:* 709-888-6102
sjcctc@gmail.com
Municipal Type: Town
Incorporated: Nov. 15, 1971 *Area:* 83.76 sq km
Population in 2006: 669
Provincial Electoral District(s): Fortune Bay-Cape La Hune
Federal Electoral District(s): Random-Burin-St. George's
Next Election: Sept. 2013 (4 year terms)
Max Taylor, Mayor
Frances Courtney, Clerk

St. Joseph's
P.O. Box 9
St Josephs, NL A0B 3A0
Tel: 709-521-2440; *Fax:* 709-521-2440
Municipal Type: Town
Incorporated: Aug. 18, 1970 *Area:* 32.31 sq km
Population in 2006: 144
Provincial Electoral District(s): Placentia & St. Mary's
Federal Electoral District(s): Avalon
Next Election: Sept. 2013 (4 year terms)
Anthony Healey, Mayor
Maureen Healey, Clerk

St. Lawrence
P.O. Box 128
St Lawrence, NL A0E 2V0
Tel: 709-873-2222; *Fax:* 709-873-3352
townofstlawrence@nf.aibn.com
www.discoverstlawrence.com
Municipal Type: Town
Incorporated: Nov. 15, 1949 *Area:* 35.5 sq km
Population in 2006: 1,349
Provincial Electoral District(s): Grand Bank
Federal Electoral District(s): Random-Burin-St. George's
Next Election: Sept. 2013 (4 year terms)
Wayde Rowsell, Mayor
Gregory Quirke, Clerk

St. Lewis
P.O. Box 106
St. Lewis, NL A0K 4W0
Tel: 709-939-2282; *Fax:* 709-939-2210
Municipal Type: Town
Incorporated: July 17, 1981 *Area:* 9.25 sq km
Population in 2006: 252
Provincial Electoral District(s): Cartwright-L'Anse au Clair

Federal Electoral District(s): Labrador
Next Election: Sept. 2013 (4 year terms)
Annie Rumbolt, Mayor
Lorraine Poole, Clerk

St. Lunaire-Griquet
P.O. Box 9
St Lunaire-Griquet, NL A0K 2X0
Tel: 709-623-2323; *Fax:* 709-623-2170
stlunaire.griquet@nf.aibn.com
Municipal Type: Town
Incorporated: June 10, 1958 *Area:* 16.68 sq km
Population in 2006: 666
Provincial Electoral District(s): The Straits & White Bay North
Federal Electoral District(s): Humber-St. Barbe-Baie Verte
Next Election: Sept. 2013 (4 year terms)
Gerald Hillier, Mayor
Linda Hillier, Clerk

St. Mary's
P.O. Box 348
St Marys, NL A0B 3B0
Tel: 709-525-2586; *Fax:* 709-525-2587
theresap@nf.aibn.com
Municipal Type: Town
Incorporated: Dec. 13, 1966 *Area:* 37.05 sq km
Population in 2006: 482
Provincial Electoral District(s): Placentia & St. Mary's
Federal Electoral District(s): Avalon
Next Election: Sept. 2013 (4 year terms)
Joseph Dillon, Mayor
Theresa Power, Clerk

St. Pauls
P.O. Box 9
St Pauls, NL A0K 4Y0
Tel: 709-243-2279; *Fax:* 709-243-2299
Municipal Type: Town
Incorporated: July 30, 1968 *Area:* 5.35 sq km
Population in 2006: 309
Provincial Electoral District(s): St. Barbe
Federal Electoral District(s): Humber-St. Barbe-Baie Verte
Next Election: Sept. 2013 (4 year terms)
Jerry Bennett, Mayor
Monica Pittman, Clerk

St. Shott's
General Delivery
St Shotts, NL A0A 3R0
Tel: 709-438-2694; *Fax:* 709-438-2617
Municipal Type: Town
Incorporated: May 21, 1963 *Area:* 1.14 sq km
Population in 2006: 109
Provincial Electoral District(s): Placentia & St. Mary's
Federal Electoral District(s): Avalon
Next Election: Sept. 2013 (4 year terms)
Patrick Hewitt, Mayor
Elizabeth Hewitt, Clerk

St. Vincent's-St. Stephen's-Peter's River
P.O. Box 39
St Vincents, NL A0B 3C0
Tel: 709-525-2540; *Fax:* 709-525-2110
svstpr@nf.aibn.com
Municipal Type: Town
Incorporated: Aug. 1, 1971 *Area:* 87.5 sq km
Population in 2006: 363
Provincial Electoral District(s): Placentia & St. Mary's
Federal Electoral District(s): Avalon
Next Election: Sept. 2013 (4 year terms)
Gus Stamp, Mayor
Marilyn Gibbons, Clerk

Salmon Cove
P.O. Box 240
Salmon Cove, NL A0A 3S0
Tel: 709-596-2101; *Fax:* 709-596-1170
townofsalmoncove@nf.aibn.com
Municipal Type: Town
Incorporated: Aug. 27, 1974 *Area:* 4.21 sq km
Population in 2006: 707
Provincial Electoral District(s): Carbonear-Harbour Grace
Federal Electoral District(s): Avalon
Next Election: Sept. 2013 (4 year terms)
Roy Rose, Mayor
Juanita Korpan, Clerk

Salvage
General Delivery
Salvage, NL A0G 3X0
Tel: 709-677-3535; *Fax:* 709-677-3535
Municipal Type: Town
Incorporated: Oct. 24, 1972 *Area:* 15.86 sq km
Population in 2006: 174
Provincial Electoral District(s): Terra Nova
Federal Electoral District(s): Bonavista-Gander-Grand Falls-Windsor
Next Election: Sept. 2013 (4 year terms)
Dave Brown, Mayor
Beverly Hunter, Clerk

Sandringham
43-47Main St.
Sandringham, NL A0G 3Y0
Tel: 709-677-2317; *Fax:* 709-677-2317
townofsandringham@yahoo.ca
Municipal Type: Town
Incorporated: April 30, 1968 *Area:* 9.6 sq km
Population in 2006: 255
Provincial Electoral District(s): Terra Nova
Federal Electoral District(s): Bonavista-Gander-Grand Falls-Windsor
Next Election: Sept. 2013 (4 year terms)
Glenn Arnold, Mayor
Audrey Penney, Clerk

Sandy Cove
PO Box 37, Site 8
Eastport, NL A0G 1Z0
Tel: 709-677-2731; *Fax:* 709-677-2731
sandycove@nf.sympatico.ca
www3.nf.sympatico.ca/sandycove
Municipal Type: Town
Incorporated: Sept. 18, 1956 *Area:* 9.01 sq km
Population in 2006: 133
Provincial Electoral District(s): Terra Nova; The Straits & White Bay North
Federal Electoral District(s): Bonavista-Gander-Grand Falls-Windsor; Humber-St. Barbe-Baie Verte
Next Election: Sept. 2013 (4 year terms)
Tony Parsons, Mayor
Anne Benger, Clerk

Seal Cove Fortune Bay
P.O. Box 156
Seal Cove Fortune Bay, NL A0H 2G0
Tel: 709-851-4431; *Fax:* 709-851-6174
sealcovecc@nf.aibn.com
Municipal Type: Town
Incorporated: Jan. 25, 1972 *Area:* 2.42 sq km
Population in 2006: 315
Provincial Electoral District(s): Fortune Bay-Cape La Hune
Federal Electoral District(s): Random-Burin-St. George's
Next Election: Sept. 2013 (4 year terms)
Junior Abbott, Mayor
Emily Loveless, Clerk

Seal Cove White Bay
P.O. Box 119
Seal Cove White Bay, NL A0K 5E0
Tel: 709-531-2550; *Fax:* 709-531-2551
sealcovewb@nf.aibn.com
Municipal Type: Town
Incorporated: Dec. 16, 1958 *Area:* 10.79 sq km
Population in 2006: 331
Provincial Electoral District(s): Baie Verte
Federal Electoral District(s): Humber-St. Barbe-Baie Verte
Next Election: Sept. 2013 (4 year terms)
Winston May, Mayor
Vanessa Osbourne, Clerk

Small Point-Adam's Cove-Blackhead-Broad Cove
P.O. Box 160
Broad Cove, NL A0A 1L0
Tel: 709-598-2610; *Fax:* 709-598-2618
towncouncil@eastlink.ca
Municipal Type: Town
Incorporated: Oct. 24, 1972 *Area:* 22.22 sq km
Population in 2006: 438
Provincial Electoral District(s): Tinity-Bay de Verde
Federal Electoral District(s): Avalon
Next Election: Sept. 2013 (4 year terms)
Leslie Grover, Mayor
Dana Reid, Clerk

South Brook
P.O. Box 63
South Brook, NL A0J 1S0
Tel: 709-657-2206; *Fax:* 709-657-2202
townofsbrk@yahoo.ca
Municipal Type: Town
Incorporated: July 6, 1965 *Area:* 9.07 sq km
Population in 2006: 531
Provincial Electoral District(s): Windsor-Springdale
Federal Electoral District(s): Humber-St. Barbe-Baie Verte
Next Election: Sept. 2013 (4 year terms)
Paul Mills, Mayor
Michelle Morey, Clerk

South River
P.O. Box 40
South River, NL A0A 3W0
Tel: 709-786-6761; *Fax:* 709-786-6760
townofsouthriver@persona.com
Municipal Type: Town
Incorporated: June 7, 1966 *Area:* 6.06 sq km
Population in 2006: 649
Provincial Electoral District(s): Harbour Main-Whitbourne
Federal Electoral District(s): Avalon
Next Election: Sept. 2013 (4 year terms)
Arthur Petten, Mayor
Terrie Lynn Aisien, Town Clerk & Manager

Southern Harbour
P.O. Box 10
Southern Harbour PB, NL A0B 3H0
Tel: 709-463-2329; *Fax:* 709-463-2208
twnsouthernharbour@nf.aibn.com
Municipal Type: Town
Incorporated: Aug. 20, 1968 *Area:* 5.41 sq km
Population in 2006: 474
Provincial Electoral District(s): Bellevue
Federal Electoral District(s): Avalon
Next Election: Sept. 2013 (4 year terms)
Joan Hickey, Mayor
Bernadette Power, Clerk

Spaniard's Bay
P.O. Box 190
Spaniards Bay, NL A0A 3X0
Tel: 709-786-3568; *Fax:* 709-786-7273
spaniardsbay@persona.ca
www.townofspaniardsbay.ca
Municipal Type: Town
Incorporated: June 8, 1965 *Area:* 65.73 sq km
Population in 2006: 2,540
Provincial Electoral District(s): Port de Grave
Federal Electoral District(s): Avalon
Next Election: Sept. 2013 (4 year terms)
John W. Drover, Mayor
Tony Ryan, Clerk & Manager

Springdale
P.O. Box 57
Springdale, NL A0J 1T0
Tel: 709-673-3439; *Fax:* 709-673-4969
townoffice.springdale@nf.aibn.com
www.townofspringdale.ca
Municipal Type: Town
Incorporated: Oct. 23, 1961 *Area:* 17.6 sq km
Population in 2006: 2,764
Provincial Electoral District(s): Windsor-Springdale
Federal Electoral District(s): Humber-St. Barbe-Baie Verte
Next Election: Sept. 2013 (4 year terms)
Harvey Tizzard, Mayor
Daphne Earle, Clerk & Manager

Steady Brook
P.O. Box 117
Steady Brook, NL A2H 2N2
Tel: 709-634-7601; *Fax:* 709-634-7547
townoffice@steadybrook.com
www.steadybrook.com
Municipal Type: Town
Incorporated: April 7, 1953 *Area:* 1.22 sq km
Population in 2006: 435
Provincial Electoral District(s): Humber East
Federal Electoral District(s): Humber-St. Barbe-Baie Verte
Next Election: Sept. 2013 (4 year terms)
Donna Thistle, Mayor
Robert Gosse, Clerk & Manager
townclerk@steadybrook.com

Stephenville
P.O. Box 420
Stephenville, NL A2N 2Z5
Tel: 709-643-8360; *Fax:* 709-643-2770
manager@town.stephenville.nf.ca
www.town.stephenville.nf.ca
Municipal Type: Town
Incorporated: Oct. 1, 1952 *Area:* 35.69 sq km
Population in 2006: 6,588
Provincial Electoral District(s): St. George's-Stephenville East; Port au Port
Federal Electoral District(s): Random-Burin-St. George's
Next Election: Sept. 2013 (4 year terms)

Tom O'Brien, Mayor
mayor@town.stephenville.nf.ca
Carolyn Lindstone, Clerk

Stephenville Crossing
P.O. Box 68
Stephenville Crossing, NL A0N 2C0
Tel: 709-646-2600; *Fax:* 709-646-2065
yyounge@nf.aibn.com
Municipal Type: Town
Incorporated: Oct. 20, 1958 *Area:* 31.2 sq km
Population in 2006: 1,960
Provincial Electoral District(s): St. George's-Stephenville East
Federal Electoral District(s): Random-Burin-St. George's
Next Election: Sept. 2013 (4 year terms)
Leona Webb, Mayor
Yvonne Young, Clerk

Summerford
P.O. Box 59
Summerford, NL A0G 4E0
Tel: 709-629-3419; *Fax:* 709-629-7532
townofsummerford@nf.aibn.com
www.townofsummerford.com
Municipal Type: Town
Incorporated: Sept. 28, 1971 *Area:* 16.06 sq km
Population in 2006: 976
Provincial Electoral District(s): Twillingate & Fogo
Federal Electoral District(s): Bonavista-Gander-Grand Falls-Windsor
Next Election: Sept. 2013 (4 year terms)
Clayton LeDrew, Mayor
Vicky Anstey, Clerk

Sunnyside Trinity Bay
P.O. Box 89
Sunnyside, NL A0B 3J0
Tel: 709-472-4506; *Fax:* 709-472-4182
townofsunnyside@eastlink.ca
Municipal Type: Town
Incorporated: March 10, 1970 *Area:* 37.95 sq km
Population in 2006: 470
Provincial Electoral District(s): Bellevue
Federal Electoral District(s): Bonavista-Gander-Grand Falls-Windsor
Next Election: Sept. 2013 (4 year terms)
Robert Snook, Mayor
G. Philip Smith, Clerk

Terra Nova
1 River Road
Terra Nova, NL A0C 1L0
Tel: 709-265-6543; *Fax:* 709-265-6533
townofterranova@nf.aibn.com
Municipal Type: Town
Incorporated: Sept. 13, 1960 *Area:* 2.46 sq km
Population in 2006: 68
Provincial Electoral District(s): Terra Nova
Federal Electoral District(s): Bonavista-Gander-Grand Falls-Windsor
Next Election: Sept. 2013 (4 year terms)
Paul Noseworthy, Mayor
Tracie Crocker, Clerk

Terrenceville
P.O. Box 100
Terrenceville, NL A0E 2X0
Tel: 709-662-2204; *Fax:* 709-662-2071
terrancevilletownoffice@nf.aibn.com
Municipal Type: Town
Incorporated: Aug. 15, 1972 *Area:* 14.5 sq km
Population in 2006: 536
Provincial Electoral District(s): Bellevue
Federal Electoral District(s): Random-Burin-St. George's
Next Election: Sept. 2013 (4 year terms)
Sheila Cox, Mayor
Joan Rideout, Clerk

Tilt Cove
P.O. Box 22
Tilt Cove, NL A0K 3M0
Tel: 709-675-2641
Municipal Type: Town
Incorporated: March 4, 1969 *Area:* 3.1 sq km
Population in 2006: 5
Provincial Electoral District(s): Baie Verte
Federal Electoral District(s): Humber-St. Barbe-Baie Verte
Next Election: Sept. 2013 (4 year terms)
Donald Collins, Mayor
Margaret Collins, Clerk

Torbay
P.O. Box 1160
Torbay, NL A1K 1K4
Tel: 709-437-6532; *Fax:* 709-437-1309
dchaplin@torbay.ca
www.town.torbay.nf.ca
Municipal Type: Town
Incorporated: Oct. 24, 1972 *Area:* 34.88 sq km
Population in 2006: 6,281
Provincial Electoral District(s): Cape St. Francis
Federal Electoral District(s): St. John's East
Next Election: Sept. 2013 (4 year terms)
Robert Codner, Mayor
Dawn Chaplin, CAO-Clerk
dchaplin@town.torbay.nf.ca

Traytown
1 Poplar Lane
Traytown, NL A0G 4K0
Tel: 709-533-2156; *Fax:* 709-533-2155
traytown@thezone.net
Municipal Type: Town
Incorporated: June 15, 1971 *Area:* 13.31 sq km
Population in 2006: 302
Provincial Electoral District(s): Terra Nova
Federal Electoral District(s): Bonavista-Gander-Grand Falls-Windsor
Next Election: Sept. 2013 (4 year terms)
Leo Tulk, Mayor
Sarah Patten, Clerk

Trepassey
P.O. Box 129
Trepassey, NL A0A 4B0
Tel: 709-438-2641; *Fax:* 709-438-2749
jill@townoftrepassey.com
Municipal Type: Town
Incorporated: Aug. 1, 1967 *Area:* 55.81 sq km
Population in 2006: 763
Provincial Electoral District(s): Ferryland
Federal Electoral District(s): Avalon
Next Election: Sept. 2013 (4 year terms)
Dennis Pearce, Mayor
Jill McNeil, Clerk

Trinity
P.O. Box 42
Trinity, NL A0C 2S0
Tel: 709-464-3836; *Fax:* 709-464-3836
counciltrinity@netscape.net
Municipal Type: Town
Incorporated: May 13, 1969 *Area:* 12.92 sq km
Population in 2006: 191
Provincial Electoral District(s): Trinity North; Bonavista North
Federal Electoral District(s): Bonavista-Gander-Grand Falls-Windsor
Next Election: Sept. 2013 (4 year terms)
Jim Miller, Mayor
Linda Sweet, Clerk

Trinity Bay North
P.O. Box 91
Port Union, NL A0C 2J0
Tel: 709-469-2571; *Fax:* 709-469-3444
tbn@personainternet.com
www.trinitybaynorth.com
Municipal Type: Town
Incorporated: Jan. 1, 2005 *Area:* 14.28 sq km
Population in 2006: 1,539
Provincial Electoral District(s): Bonavista South
Federal Electoral District(s): Bonavista-Gander-Grand Falls-Windsor
Next Election: Sept. 2013 (4 year terms)
Note: Effective January 1, 2005, the towns of Catalina, Port Union & Melrose amalgamated to form the new town of Trinity Bay North.
Brendan Peters, Mayor
Valerie Rogers, Clerk
tbn@personainternet.com

Triton
P.O. Box 10
Triton, NL A0J 1V0
Tel: 709-263-2264; *Fax:* 709-263-2381
townoftriton@eastlink.ca
www.townoftriton.ca
Municipal Type: Town
Incorporated: March 11, 1958 *Area:* 7.55 sq km
Population in 2006: 1,029
Provincial Electoral District(s): Windsor-Springdale
Federal Electoral District(s): Humber-St. Barbe-Baie Verte
Next Election: Sept. 2013 (4 year terms)

Jason Roberts, Mayor
Sandy Windsor, Clerk

Trout River
P.O. Box 89
Trout River, NL A0K 5P0
Tel: 709-451-5376; *Fax:* 709-451-2127
townoftroutriver@nf.aibn.com
Municipal Type: Town
Incorporated: April 12, 1966 *Area:* 5.91 sq km
Population in 2006: 604
Provincial Electoral District(s): Humber Valley
Federal Electoral District(s): Humber-St. Barbe-Baie Verte
Next Election: Sept. 2013 (4 year terms)
Gertrude Hann, Mayor
Shelly Emily Butler, Clerk

Twillingate
P.O. Box 220
Twillingate, NL A0G 4M0
Tel: 709-884-2438; *Fax:* 709-884-5278
Municipal Type: Town
Incorporated: Jan. 1, 1992 *Area:* 25.74 sq km
Population in 2006: 2,448
Provincial Electoral District(s): Twillingate & Fogo
Federal Electoral District(s): Bonavista-Gander-Grand Falls-Windsor
Next Election: Sept. 2013 (4 year terms)
Gordon Noseworthy, Mayor
David Burton, Clerk

Upper Island Cove
P.O. Box 149
Upper Island Cove, NL A0A 4E0
Tel: 709-589-2503; *Fax:* 709-589-2522
townofuic@nf.aibn.com
Municipal Type: Town
Incorporated: Oct. 19, 1965 *Area:* 7.85 sq km
Population in 2006: 1,667
Provincial Electoral District(s): Port de Grave
Federal Electoral District(s): Avalon
Next Election: Sept. 2013 (4 year terms)
George Adams, Mayor
Neil Shute, Clerk

Victoria
P.O. Box 130
Victoria, NL A0A 4G0
Tel: 709-596-3783; *Fax:* 709-596-5020
townofvictoria@nf.aibn.com
Municipal Type: Town
Incorporated: July 1, 1971 *Area:* 17.64 sq km
Population in 2006: 1,769
Provincial Electoral District(s): Carbonear-Harbour Grace
Federal Electoral District(s): Avalon
Next Election: Sept. 2013 (4 year terms)
Arthur Burke, Mayor
Sharon Snooks, Clerk

Wabana
P.O. Box 1229
Wabana, NL A0A 4H0
Tel: 709-488-2990; *Fax:* 709-488-3181
council@bellisland.net
www.bellisland.net
Municipal Type: Town
Incorporated: Aug. 28, 1950 *Area:* 14.5 sq km
Population in 2006: 2,418
Provincial Electoral District(s): Conception Bay East & Bell Island
Federal Electoral District(s): St. John's East
Next Election: Sept. 2013 (4 year terms)
Gary Gosine, Mayor
Ben Noseworthy, Clerk
bennoseworthy@townofwabana.net

Wabush
P.O. Box 190
Wabush, NL A0R 1B0
Tel: 709-282-5696; *Fax:* 709-282-5142
info@wabush.ca
www.labradorwest.com
Municipal Type: Town
Incorporated: April 11, 1967 *Area:* 46.25 sq km
Population in 2006: 1,739
Provincial Electoral District(s): Labrador West
Federal Electoral District(s): Labrador
Next Election: Sept. 2013 (4 year terms)
Ronald Barron, Mayor
Brian Hudson, Clerk
townclerk@wabush.ca

West St. Modeste
P.O. Box 78
West St Modeste, NL A0K 5S0
Tel: 709-927-5583; *Fax:* 709-927-5898
sandraodell@hotmail.com
Municipal Type: Town
Incorporated: Aug. 1, 1975 *Area:* 7.78 sq km
Population in 2006: 140
Provincial Electoral District(s): Cartwright-L'Anse au Clair
Federal Electoral District(s): Labrador
Next Election: Sept. 2013 (4 year terms)
Agnes Pike, Mayor
Sandra O'Dell, Clerk

Westport
P.O. Box 29
Westport, NL A0K 5R0
Tel: 709-224-5501; *Fax:* 709-224-5501
Municipal Type: Town
Incorporated: July 18, 1967 *Area:* 5.13 sq km
Population in 2006: 246
Provincial Electoral District(s): Baie Verte
Federal Electoral District(s): Humber-St. Barbe-Baie Verte
Next Election: Sept. 2013 (4 year terms)
Maxwell Warren, Mayor
Peggy Randell, Clerk

Whitbourne
P.O. Box 119
Whitbourne, NL A0B 3K0
Tel: 709-759-2780; *Fax:* 709-759-2016
whit.towncouncil@eastlink.ca
Municipal Type: Town
Incorporated: April 16, 1968 *Area:* 21.41 sq km
Population in 2006: 855
Provincial Electoral District(s): Harbour Main-Whitbourne
Federal Electoral District(s): Avalon
Next Election: Sept. 2013 (4 year terms)
Lloyd Gosse, Mayor
Crystal Peddle, Clerk

Whiteway
Main St.
Whiteway, NL A0B 3L0
Tel: 709-588-2948; *Fax:* 709-588-2985
townofwhiteway@eastlink.ca
Municipal Type: Town
Incorporated: Oct. 3, 1975 *Area:* 22.64 sq km
Population in 2006: 220
Provincial Electoral District(s): Trinity-Bay de Verde
Federal Electoral District(s): Avalon
Next Election: Sept. 2013 (4 year terms)
Craig Whalen, Mayor
Melinda Legge, Clerk

Winterland
P.O. Box 10
Winterland, NL A0E 2Y0
Tel: 709-279-3701; *Fax:* 709-279-3702
townofwinterland@hotmail.com
Municipal Type: Town
Incorporated: Nov. 24, 1970 *Area:* 54.34 sq km
Population in 2006: 337
Provincial Electoral District(s): Grand Bank
Federal Electoral District(s): Random-Burin-St. George's
Next Election: Sept. 2013 (4 year terms)
Ches Kenway, Mayor
Marlyese Simms, Clerk

Winterton
P.O. Box 59
Winterton, NL A0B 3M0
Tel: 709-583-2010; *Fax:* 709-583-2099
wintertontowncouncil@persona.ca
Municipal Type: Town
Incorporated: April 15, 1964 *Area:* 10.52 sq km
Population in 2006: 518
Provincial Electoral District(s): Trinity-Bay de Verde
Federal Electoral District(s): Avalon
Next Election: Sept. 2013 (4 year terms)
Jim Harnum, Mayor
Adella Green, Clerk

Witless Bay
P.O. Box 130
Witless Bay, NL A0A 4K0
Tel: 709-334-3407; *Fax:* 709-334-2377
townofwitlessbay@nf.aibn.com
Municipal Type: Town
Incorporated: Jan. 1, 1986 *Area:* 17.49 sq km
Population in 2006: 1,070
Provincial Electoral District(s): Ferryland
Federal Electoral District(s): Avalon
Next Election: Sept. 2013 (4 year terms)
Patrick Curran, Mayor
Geraldine Caul, Clerk

Woodstock
19 Park St.
Woodstock, NL A0K 5X0
Tel: 709-251-3176; *Fax:* 709-251-3176
townofwoodstock@nf.aibn.com
Municipal Type: Town
Incorporated: Sept. 29, 1970 *Area:* 10.09 sq km
Population in 2006: 199
Provincial Electoral District(s): Baie Verte
Federal Electoral District(s): Humber-St. Barbe-Baie Verte
Next Election: Sept. 2013 (4 year terms)
Terry Decker, Mayor
Norma Mitchell, Clerk

Woody Point
P.O. Box 100
Woody Point, NL A0K 1P0
Tel: 709-453-2273; *Fax:* 709-453-2270
woodypoint@nf.aibn.com
www.townofwoodypoint.ca
Municipal Type: Town
Incorporated: March 27, 1956 *Area:* 2.91 sq km
Population in 2006: 355
Provincial Electoral District(s): Humber Valley
Federal Electoral District(s): Humber-St. Barbe-Baie Verte
Next Election: Sept. 2013 (4 year terms)
Ken Thomas, Mayor
Heather Coates, Clerk

York Harbour
136-138 Main St.
York Harbour, NL A0L 1L0
Tel: 709-681-2280; *Fax:* 709-681-2799
yorkharbourcouncil@nf.aibn.com
Municipal Type: Town
Incorporated: June 27, 1972 *Area:* 3.9 sq km
Population in 2006: 346
Provincial Electoral District(s): Bay of Islands
Federal Electoral District(s): Humber-St. Barbe-Baie Verte
Next Election: Sept. 2013 (4 year terms)
Marie Byrne, Mayor
Michelle Sheppard, Clerk

NORTHWEST TERRITORIES

LEGISLATION: Cities, Towns and Villages Act; Hamlets Act; Charter Communities Act; Effective August 4, 2005, establishment of Tlicho Community Governments as a result of implementation of the Tlicho Self-Government and Land Claim; Settlements Act; Property Assessment and Taxation Act; Local Authorities Elections Act; Fire Protection Act; Civil Emergencies Act; Commissioner's Lands Act; Planning Act; Religious Societies Lands Act; Senior Citizens and Disabled Persons Property Tax Relief Act.

Incorporation as a city, town or village is determined by the value of all assessable land. Incorporation values: Village, $10 million; Town, $50 million; City, $200 million. All tax-based. Hamlets and Charter Communities may request tax-based status.

Local Authorities Elections: three years for cities, towns and villages; two years/staggered terms for hamlets and settlements; two to three years for charter communities. The Minister may extend or shorten terms on applications. Except for settlement councils, heads of councils are elected by separate ballot. First nations conduct their own electoral process.

Heads of Councils: Mayor, K'wati, Ehk'Wahtide, Chief, Chairperson.

First Nations provide municipal services as the main governing authority in several communities.

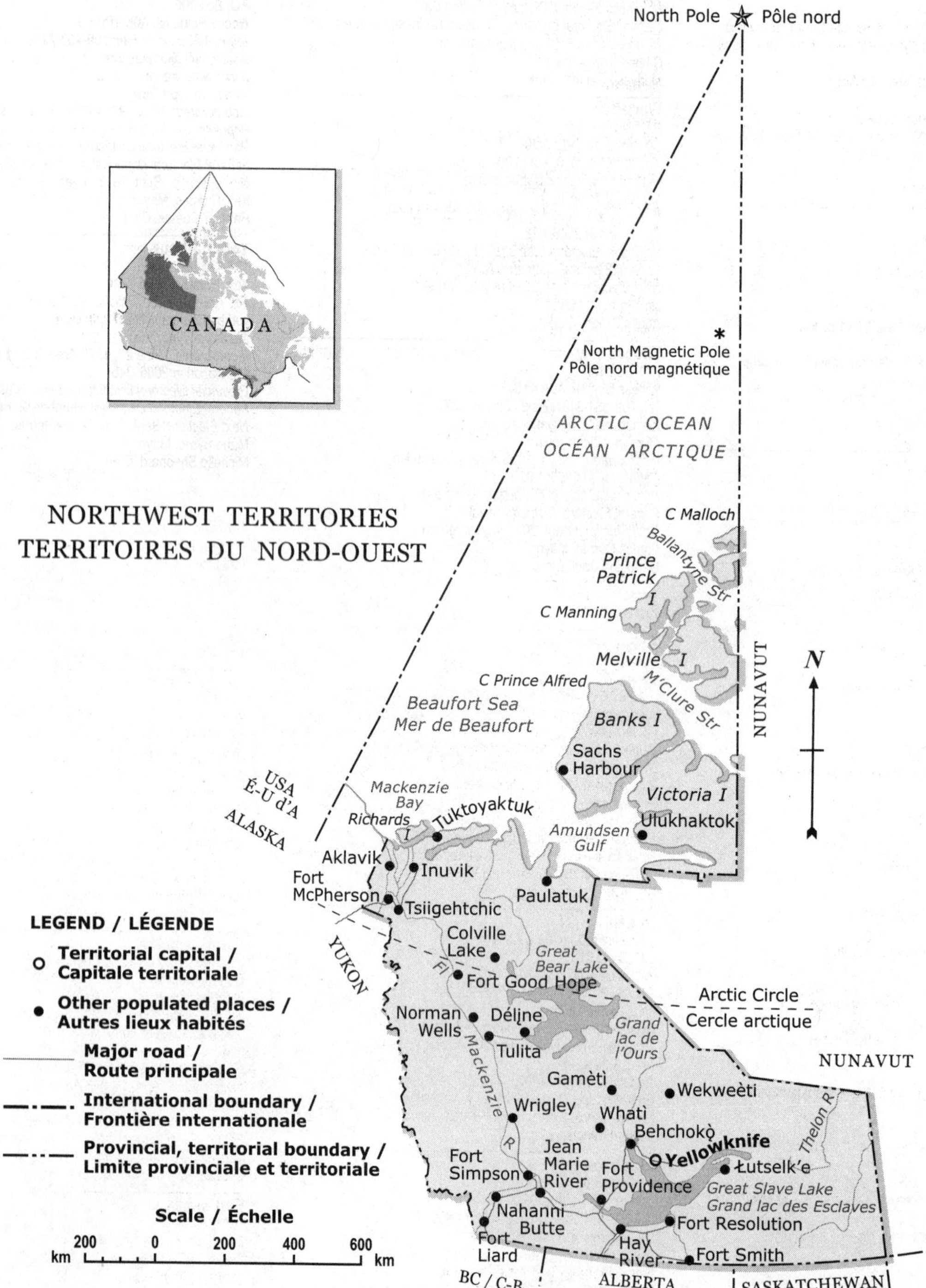

Reproduced with the permission of Natural Resources Canada 2011, courtesy of the Atlas of Canada.

www.atlas.gc.ca

Northwest Territories

Major Municipalities in Northwest Territories

Yellowknife
P.O. Box 580
4807 - 52 St.
Yellowknife, NT X1A 2N4
Tel: 867-920-5600; *Fax:* 867-920-5649
cityclerk@yellowknife.ca
www.yellowknife.ca
Municipal Type: City
Incorporated: Jan. 1, 1970 *Area:* 105.22 sq km
Population in 2009: 19,711
Provincial Electoral District(s): Yellowknife South; Yellowknife Centre; Frame Lake; Great Slave; Weledeh; Kam Lake, Range Lake
Federal Electoral District(s): Western Arctic
Next Election: Oct. 19, 2011
Gordon Van Tighem, Mayor
gvantighem@yellowknife.ca
Debbie Gillard, City Clerk
867-920-5646
debbie.gillard@yellowknife.ca
Lydia Bardak, City Councillor
lbardak@yellowknife.ca
Max Hall, City Administrator
867-920-5624
mhall@yellowknife.ca
Bob Brooks, City Councillor
bbrooks@yellowknife.ca
Darcy Hernblad, Fire Chief
867-766-5501
dhernblad@yellowknife.ca
Paul Falvo, City Councillor
pfalvo@yellowknife.ca
Carl Bird, Director, Corporate Services
867-920-5666
cbird@yellowknife.ca
Mark Heyck, City Councillor
mheyck@yellowknife.ca
Jeffrey Humble, Director, Planning & Lands
867-920-5633
jhumble@yellowknife.ca
Amanda Mallon, City Councillor
amallon@yellowknife.ca
Dennis Kefalas, Director, Public Works
867-920-5639
dkefalas@yellowknife.ca
Shelagh Montgomery, City Councillor
smontgomery@yellowknife.ca
Dennis Marchiori, Director, Public Safety
867-920-5661
dmarchiori@yellowknife.ca
Cory Vanthuyne, City Councillor
cvanthuyne@yellowknife.ca
Peter Neugebauer, Director, Economic Development
867-920-5660
pneugebauer@yellowknife.ca
David Wind, City Councillor
dwind@yellowknife.ca
Grant White, Director, Community Services
867-920-5636
gwhite@yellowknife.ca
Kerry Penney, Manager, Legal Services
kpenney@yellowknife.ca
Nalini Naidoo, Manager, Planning & Lands
867-920-5675
nnaidoo@yellowknife.ca
Marie Couturier, Manager, Human Resources
mcouturier@yellowknife.ca
Clem Hand, Manager, Procurement Services
867-920-5617
chand@yellowknife.ca
Bruce Underhay, Manager, Solid Waste Management Facility
867-669-3404
bunderhay@yellowknife.ca
Sharolynn Woodward, Manager, Information Technology
867-920-5651
swoodward@yellowknife.ca
Dennis Althouse, Superintendent, Operations & Maintenance
867-766-5512
dalthouse@yellowknife.ca

Other Municipalities in Northwest Territories

Aklavik
P.O. Box 88
Aklavik, NT X0E 0A0
Tel: 867-978-2351; *Fax:* 867-978-2434
saoaklavik@permafrost.com
www.aklavik.ca
Other Information: Additional Phone: 867-978-2361
Municipal Type: Hamlet
Incorporated: Jan. 1, 1974 *Area:* 8.16 sq km
Population in 2006: 594
Provincial Electoral District(s): Mackenzie Delta
Federal Electoral District(s): Western Arctic
Next Election: Dec. 13, 2010
William Storr, Mayor
Evelyn Storr, Sr. Admin. Officer

Behchoko
P.O. Box 68
Behchoko, NT X0E 0Y0
Tel: 867-392-6500; *Fax:* 867-392-6139
finance@behchoko.ca
www.tlicho.ca/communities/behchoko, www.behchoko.lgant.ca
Other Information: Additional Phone: 867-392-6561
Municipal Type: Tlicho Community Government
Area: 75.08 sq km
Population in 2006: 1,894
Provincial Electoral District(s): Monfwi
Federal Electoral District(s): Western Arctic
Next Election: June 2011
Craig Yeo, Sr. Admin. Officer
Clifford Daniels, Chief

Colville Lake
Behdzi Ahda First Nation
P.O. Box 53
Colville Lake, NT X0E 0L0
Tel: 867-709-2200; *Fax:* 867-709-2202
Joseph_Kochon@airware.ca
www.colvillelake.lgant.ca
Municipal Type: Settlement Corporation
Incorporated: Nov. 30, 1995 *Area:* 128.3 sq km
Population in 2006: 126
Provincial Electoral District(s): Sahtu
Federal Electoral District(s): Western Arctic
Next Election: Dec. 8, 2010
Joseph Kochon, Band Manager
Richard Kochon, Chief

Déline
General Delivery
Deline, NT X0E 0G0
Tel: 867-589-4800; *Fax:* 867-589-4106
erma_baton@gov.deline.ca
www.deline.ca
Other Information: Additional Phone: 867-589-3604
Municipal Type: Charter Community
Incorporated: April 1, 1993 *Area:* 79.33 sq km
Population in 2006: 525
Provincial Electoral District(s): Sahtu
Federal Electoral District(s): Western Arctic
Note: Déline sets its election date through its community charter.
Christina Gaudet, Sr. Admin. Officer
Raymond Tutcho, Mayor

Dettah
Yellowknife Dene First Nation
P.O. Box 2514
Yellowknife, NT X1A 2P8
Tel: 867-873-4307; *Fax:* 867-873-5969
ceo@ykdene.com
www.ykdene.com, www.dettahandndilo.lgant.ca
Municipal Type: First Nations/Governing Authority
Area: 1.34 sq km
Population in 2006: 247
Provincial Electoral District(s): Weledeh
Federal Electoral District(s): Western Arctic
Edward Sangris, Chief

Enterprise
526 Robin Rd.
Enterprise, NT X0E 0R1
Tel: 867-984-3491; *Fax:* 867-984-3400
sao_enterprise@northwestel.net
www.enterprise.lgant.ca
Municipal Type: Settlement Corporation
Incorporated: July 1, 1988 *Area:* 286.9 sq km
Population in 2006: 97
Provincial Electoral District(s): Deh Cho
Federal Electoral District(s): Western Arctic
Next Election: Dec. 8, 2010
Allan Flamand, Mayor
Peter Groenen, Sr. Admin Officer

Fort Good Hope
K'asho Got'ine Charter Community
P.O. Box 80
Fort Good Hope, NT X0E 0H0
Tel: 867-598-2231; *Fax:* 867-598-2024
greglaboucan@hotmail.com
www.fortgoodhope.lgant.ca
Other Information: Additional Phone: 867-598-2232
Municipal Type: Charter Community
Incorporated: April 1, 1995 *Area:* 52.82 sq km
Population in 2006: 557
Provincial Electoral District(s): Sahtu
Federal Electoral District(s): Western Arctic
Note: Fort Good Hope sets its election date through its community charter.
Arthur Tobac, Chief
Greg Labourcan, Sr. Admin. Officer

Fort Liard
General Delivery
Fort Liard, NT X0G 0A0
Tel: 867-770-4104; *Fax:* 867-770-4004
sao@fortliard.com
www.fortliard.com
Municipal Type: Hamlet
Incorporated: April 1, 1987 *Area:* 67.96 sq km
Population in 2006: 583
Provincial Electoral District(s): Nahendeh
Federal Electoral District(s): Western Arctic
Next Election: Dec. 13, 2010
Julie Capot-Blanc, Mayor
myr@fortliard.com
John McKee, Sr. Admin. Officer

Fort McPherson
P.O. Box 57
Fort McPherson, NT X0E 0J0
Tel: 867-952-2428; *Fax:* 867-952-2725
sao@fortmcpherson.ca
www.fortmcpherson.ca, www.fortmcpherson.lgant.ca
Municipal Type: Hamlet
Incorporated: Nov. 1, 1986 *Area:* 53.06 sq km
Population in 2006: 776
Provincial Electoral District(s): Mackenzie Delta
Federal Electoral District(s): Western Arctic
Next Election: Dec. 13, 2010
Hazel Nerysoo, Mayor
Troy Jenkins, Sr. Admin. Officer

Fort Providence
P.O. Box 290
Fort Providence, NT X0E 0L0
Tel: 867-699-3441; *Fax:* 867-699-3360
sao@fortprovidence.ca
www.fortprovidence.lgant.ca
Municipal Type: Hamlet
Incorporated: Jan. 1, 1987 *Area:* 256.33 sq km
Population in 2006: 727
Provincial Electoral District(s): Deh Cho
Federal Electoral District(s): Western Arctic
Next Election: Dec. 13, 2010
Raymond Bonnetrouge, Mayor
Susan Christie, Sr. Admin. Officer

Fort Resolution
c/o Deninoo Community Council
General Delivery
Fort Resolution, NT X0E 0M0
Tel: 867-394-4556; *Fax:* 867-394-5415
tausia.sao@gmail.com
fortresolution.lgant.ca
Municipal Type: Settlement Corporation
Incorporated: April 1, 1988 *Area:* 455.06 sq km
Population in 2006: 484
Provincial Electoral District(s): Tu Nedhe
Federal Electoral District(s): Western Arctic
Tausia Kaitu-Lal, Sr. Admin. Officer
Elizabeth Ann Mckay, Mayor

Fort Simpson
P.O. Box 438
Fort Simpson, NT X0E 0N0
Tel: 867-695-2253; *Fax:* 867-695-2005
saoftsim@northwestel.net
www.fortsimpson.com
Municipal Type: Village
Incorporated: Jan. 1, 1973 *Area:* 78.32 sq km

Population in 2006: 1,216
Provincial Electoral District(s): Nahendeh
Federal Electoral District(s): Western Arctic
Next Election: Oct. 19, 2011
John Ivey, Senior Administrative Officer
Sean Whelly, Mayor
mayor@fortsimpson.com

Fort Smith
P.O. Box 147
174 McDougal Rd.
Fort Smith, NT X0E 0P0
Tel: 867-872-8400; *Fax:* 867-872-8401
bblack@fortsmith.ca
www.fortsmith.ca
Municipal Type: Town
Incorporated: Oct. 1, 1966 *Area:* 92.79 sq km
Population in 2006: 2,364
Provincial Electoral District(s): Thebacha
Federal Electoral District(s): Western Arctic
Next Election: Oct. 19, 2011
Jane Hobart, Mayor
Brenda Black, Sr. Admin. Officer

Gamèti
Gameti First Nation
P.O. Box 1
Gameti, NT X0E 1R0
Tel: 867-997-3441; *Fax:* 867-997-3411
sao@gameti.org
www.tlicho.ca/communities/gameti, www.gameti.lgant.ca
Municipal Type: Tlicho Community Government
Incorporated: Aug. 4, 2005 *Area:* 9.18 sq km
Population in 2006: 283
Provincial Electoral District(s): Monfwi
Federal Electoral District(s): Western Arctic
Next Election: June 2011
Eddie Chocolate, Chief
Gregory Morash, Sr. Admin. Officer

Hay River
73 Woodland Dr.
Hay River, NT X0E 1G1
Tel: 867-874-6522; *Fax:* 867-874-3237
molenkamp@hayriver.com
www.hayriver.com
Municipal Type: Town
Incorporated: June 16, 1963 *Area:* 132.58 sq km
Population in 2006: 3,648
Provincial Electoral District(s): Hay River North; Hay River South
Federal Electoral District(s): Western Arctic
Next Election: Oct. 19, 2011
Kelly Schofield, Mayor
Terry Molenkemp, Sr. Admin Officer
molenkamp@hayriver.com

Hay River Reserve - K'atlodeeche First Nation
Katlodeechee First Nation
P.O. Box 3060
Hay River, NT X0E 1G0
Tel: 867-874-6701; *Fax:* 867-874-3229
kfnceo@katlodeeche.com
www.hayriverreserve.lgant.ca
Municipal Type: Reserve
Area: 134.21 sq km
Population in 2006: 309
Provincial Electoral District(s): Deh Cho
Federal Electoral District(s): Western Arctic
Roy Fabien, Chief
Scotty Edgerton, Band Manager

Inuvik
P.O. Box 1160
2 Firth St.
Inuvik, NT X0E 0T0
Tel: 867-777-8600; *Fax:* 867-777-8601
sao@town.inuvik.nt.ca
www.inuvik.ca
Municipal Type: Town
Incorporated: Jan. 1, 1979 *Area:* 49.76 sq km
Population in 2006: 3,484
Provincial Electoral District(s): Inuvik Twin Lakes; Inuvik Boot Lake
Federal Electoral District(s): Western Arctic
Next Election: Oct. 19, 2011
Denny Rodgers, Mayor
dlindsay@town.inuvik.nt.ca
Grant Hood, Sr. Admin. Officer

Jean Marie River
TthedzedK'edili First Nation
General Delivery
Fort Simpson, NT X0E 0N0
Tel: 867-809-2000; *Fax:* 867-809-2002
sao@jmrfn.ca
www.jmrfn.ca, www.jeanmarieriver.lgant.ca
Municipal Type: First Nations/Governing Authority
Area: 37.26 sq km
Population in 2006: 81
Provincial Electoral District(s): Nahendeh
Federal Electoral District(s): Western Arctic
Stanley Sanguez, Chief
Tammy Neal, Band Manager

Kakisa
Ka'a'gee Tu First Nation
P.O. Box 4428
Hay River, NT X0E 1G4
Tel: 867-825-2000; *Fax:* 867-825-2002
R_landry@airware.ca
www.kakisa.lgant.ca
Municipal Type: First Nations/Governing Authority
Area: 94.82 sq km
Population in 2006: 52
Provincial Electoral District(s): Deh Cho
Federal Electoral District(s): Western Arctic
Lloyd Chicot, Chief
Ruby Landry, Council Manager

Lutsel K'e
Lutsel K'e Dene Band
P.O. Box 28
Lutselk'e, NT X0E 1A0
Tel: 867-370-7000; *Fax:* 867-370-3010
cyberia@mts.net
www.lutselke.lgant.ca
Municipal Type: First Nations/Governing Authority
Area: 43.01 sq km
Population in 2006: 318
Provincial Electoral District(s): Tu Nedhe
Federal Electoral District(s): Western Arctic
Antoine Michel, Chief
Ray Griffith, Sr. Admin. Officer & Band Manager

Nahanni Butte
Nahanni Butte First Nation
General Delivery
Fort Simpson, NT X0E 0N0
Tel: 867-602-2900; *Fax:* 867-602-2910
manager@nahadeh.org
nahannibutte.lgant.ca
Municipal Type: First Nations/Governing Authority
Area: 78.96 sq km
Population in 2006: 115
Provincial Electoral District(s): Nahendeh
Federal Electoral District(s): Western Arctic
Fred Tesou, Chief

Norman Wells
P.O. Box 5
Norman Wells, NT X0E 0V0
Tel: 867-587-3700; *Fax:* 867-587-3701
townmgr@normanwells.com
www.normanwells.com
Municipal Type: Town
Incorporated: April 12, 1992 *Area:* 93.28 sq km
Population in 2006: 761
Provincial Electoral District(s): Sahtu
Federal Electoral District(s): Western Arctic
Next Election: Oct. 19, 2011
Dudley C. Johnson, Mayor
Ian Fremantle, Town Manager
townmgr@normanwells.com

Paulatuk
P.O. Box 98
Paulatuk, NT X0E 1N0
Tel: 867-580-3531; *Fax:* 867-580-3703
hopaulatuk@hotmail.com
www.paulatuk.lgant.ca
Municipal Type: Hamlet
Incorporated: April 1, 1987 *Area:* 66.76 sq km
Population in 2006: 294
Provincial Electoral District(s): Nunakput
Federal Electoral District(s): Western Arctic
Next Election: Dec. 13, 2010
Ray Ruben, Mayor
Debbie Gordon-Ruben, Sr. Admin. Officer

Sachs Harbour
General Delivery
P.O. Box 90
Sachs Harbour, NT X0E 0Z0
Tel: 867-690-4351; *Fax:* 867-690-4802
hamlet_sachs@airware.ca
sachsharbour.lgant.ca
Municipal Type: Hamlet
Incorporated: April 1, 1986 *Area:* 290.94 sq km
Population in 2006: 122
Provincial Electoral District(s): Nunakput
Federal Electoral District(s): Western Arctic
Next Election: Dec. 13, 2010
Priscilla Haogak, Mayor
Jackie Coultier, Sr. Admin. Officer

Trout Lake
Sambaa K'e Dene Band
P.O. Box 10
Trout Lake, NT X0E 1Z0
Tel: 867-206-2800; *Fax:* 867-206-2828
manager@sambaake.org
troutlake.lgant.ca
Municipal Type: First Nations/Governing Authority
Area: 119.42 sq km
Population in 2006: 86
Provincial Electoral District(s): Nahendeh
Federal Electoral District(s): Western Arctic
Dolphus Jumbo, Chief
Ruby Jumbo, Sr. Admin. Officer

Tsiigehtchic
General Delivery
Tsiigehtchic, NT X0E 0B0
Tel: 867-953-3201; *Fax:* 867-953-3302
sao@tsiigehtchic.ca
www.tsiigehtchic.lgant.ca
Municipal Type: Charter Community
Incorporated: June 21, 1993 *Area:* 48.98 sq km
Population in 2006: 175
Provincial Electoral District(s): Mackenzie Delta
Federal Electoral District(s): Western Arctic
Note: Tsiigehtchic sets its election date through its community charter.
Frederick Blake, Chief
Carolyn Lennie, Sr. Admin. Officer

Tuktoyaktuk
P.O. Box 120
Tuktoyaktuk, NT X0E 1C0
Tel: 867-977-2286; *Fax:* 867-977-2110
tuksao@netkaster.ca
www.tuktoyaktuk.lgant.ca
Municipal Type: Hamlet
Incorporated: April 1, 1970 *Area:* 11.07 sq km
Population in 2006: 870
Provincial Electoral District(s): Nunakput
Federal Electoral District(s): Western Arctic
Next Election: Dec. 13, 2010
Mervin Gruben, Mayor
Tom Matus, Sr. Admin. Officer

Tulita
General Delivery
P.O. Box 91
Tulita, NT X0E 0K0
Tel: 867-588-4471; *Fax:* 867-588-4908
sao@hamletoftulita.ca
www.tulita.lgant.ca
Other Information: Alt 867-588-4351
Municipal Type: Hamlet
Incorporated: April 1, 1984 *Area:* 51.74 sq km
Population in 2006: 505
Provincial Electoral District(s): Sahtu
Federal Electoral District(s): Western Arctic
Next Election: Dec. 13, 2010
Danny Yakeleya, Mayor
Brad Carlson, Sr. Admin. Officer

Ulukhaktok
P.O. Box 157
Ulukhaktok, NT X0E 0S0
Tel: 867-396-8000; *Fax:* 867-396-8001
ulukhaktok_sao@airware.ca
www.ulukhaktok.lgant.ca
Municipal Type: Hamlet
Incorporated: April 1, 1984 *Area:* 124.43 sq km
Population in 2006: 398
Provincial Electoral District(s): Nunakput
Federal Electoral District(s): Western Arctic
Next Election: Dec. 13, 2010
Note: Formerly known as Holman.

Janet Kanayok, Mayor
Lena Egotak, Sr. Admin. Officer

Wekweeti
Community Government of Wekweeti
P.O. Box 69
Wekweeti, NT X1A 1W0
Tel: 867-713-2010; *Fax:* 867-713-2030
saowekweti@netkaster.ca
www.tlicho.ca/communities/wekweeti, www.weweeti.lgant.ca
Municipal Type: Tlicho Community Government
Incorporated: Aug. 4, 2005 *Area:* 14.66 sq km
Population in 2006: 137
Provincial Electoral District(s): Monfwi
Federal Electoral District(s): Western Arctic
Next Election: June 2011
Charlie Football, Chief
Grace Angel, Sr. Admin. Officer

Whati
Community Government of Whati
P.O. Box 71
Whati, NT X0E 1P0
Tel: 867-573-3401; *Fax:* 867-573-3018
sao@whati.ca
www.tlicho.ca/communities/whati, www.whati.lgant.ca
Municipal Type: Tlicho Community Government
Incorporated: Aug. 4, 2005 *Area:* 15.18 sq km
Population in 2006: 460
Provincial Electoral District(s): Monfwi
Federal Electoral District(s): Western Arctic
Next Election: June 2011
Alfonz Nitsiza, Chief
Grant Scott, Sr. Admin. Officer

Wrigley
Pehdzeh Ki First Nation
General Delivery
Wrigley, NT X0E 1E0
Tel: 867-581-3321; *Fax:* 867-581-3329
bandmanager@pehdzehki.ca
www.whati.lgant.ca
Other Information: Additional Phone: 867-581-3581
Municipal Type: First Nations/Governing Authority
Area: 55.83 sq km
Population in 2006: 122
Provincial Electoral District(s): Nahendeh
Federal Electoral District(s): Western Arctic
Tim Lennie, Chief

NOVA SCOTIA

Nova Scotia is geographically divided into 18 counties. Twelve of these constitute separate municipalities (three are regional municipalities). The remaining six are each divided into two districts and each of these constitutes a separate municipality. Thus there are 21 rural municipalities. Within each of these areas are 31 autonomous incorporated towns and other local organizations with limited jurisdiction, including school boards, boards of school trustees, village commissions, local service commissions, rural fire districts and other special purpose forms.

Incorporation of a town is governed by the Municipal Government Act, Sections 383 to 393 (dissolution is governed by Sections 394 to 402).

The organization of municipalities and villages is governed by the Municipal Government Act. Additional regulation is provided by the Municipal Finance Corporation Act.

All general and special municipal elections, including elections for school board members, are governed by the Municipal Elections Act, 1979. The term of office for mayors, councillors, aldermen, and elective school board members is four years. Elections take place on the third Saturday in October in every fourth year (October 2008, October 2012, etc.).

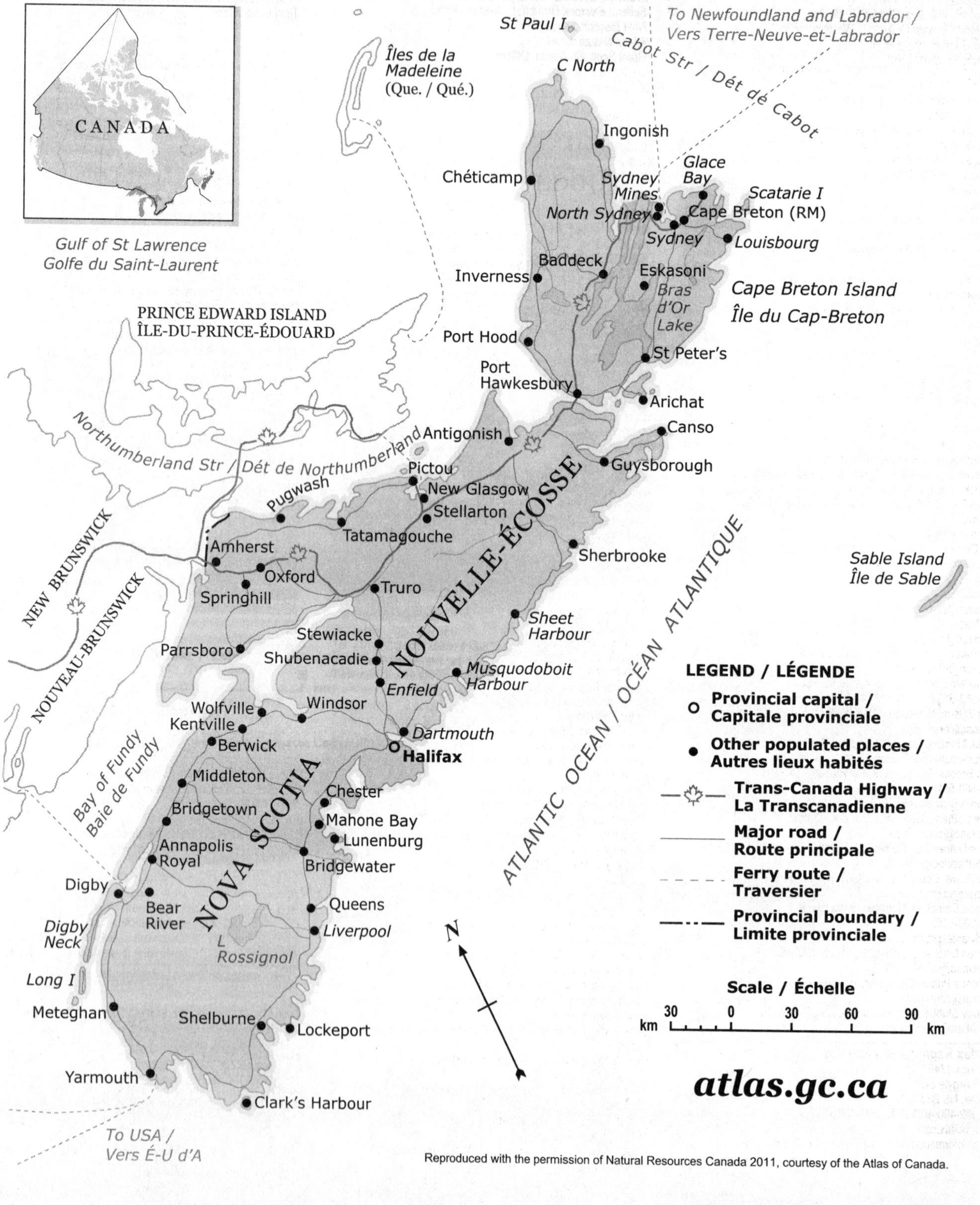

Reproduced with the permission of Natural Resources Canada 2011, courtesy of the Atlas of Canada.

Nova Scotia

Counties & Municipal Districts in Nova Scotia

Cape Breton
Civic Centre
320 Esplanade
Sydney, NS B1P 7B9
Tel: 902-563-5005; *Fax:* 902-564-0481
cbrm@cbrm.ns.ca
www.cbrm.ns.ca
Municipal Type: Regional Municipality
Incorporated: Aug. 1, 1995 *Area:* 2,433.33 sq km
County or District: Cape Breton; *Population in 2006:* 102,250
Provincial Electoral District(s): Cape Breton Centre; Cape Breton East; Cape Breton North; Cape Breton Nova; Cape Breton South; Cape Breton-The Lakes
Federal Electoral District(s): Cape Breton-Canso; Sydney-Victoria
Next Election: Oct. 2012 (4 year terms)
John W. Morgan, Mayor, Fax: 902-563-5585
jwmorgan@cbrm.ns.ca
Bernie White, Municipal Clerk
902-563-5010
bjwhite@cbrm.ns.ca
Brian Lahey, Councillor, Ward(s): District 1
blahey@cbrm.ns.ca
Marie Walsh, Director, Finance
902-563-5014
Kevin Saccary, Councillor, Ward(s): District 2
ksaccary@cbrm.ns.ca
Jerry Ryan, Chief Administrative Officer
Lee McNeil, Councillor, Ward(s): District 3
lmcneil@cbrm.ns.ca
Robin B. Campbell, Regional Solicitor
902-563-5045
rbcampbell@cbrm.ns.ca
George MacDonald, Councillor, Ward(s): District 4
gmmacdonald@cbrm.ns.ca
Edgar MacLeod, Police Chief
902-563-5095
eamacleod@cbrmps.cape-breton.ns.ca
Darren Bruckschwaiger, Councillor, Ward(s): District 5
drbruckschwaiger@cbrm.ns.ca
Angus Fleming, Director, Human Resources
902-563-5058
acfleming@cbrm.ns.ca
Kim Desveaux, Councillor, Ward(s): District 6
kadesveaux@cbrm.ns.ca
Doug Foster, Director, Planning
902-563-5070
dbfoster@cbrm.ns.ca
Jim MacLeod, Councillor, Ward(s): District 7
jmacleod@cbrm.ns.ca
Ray Paruch, Councillor, Ward(s): District 8
frparuch@cbrm.ns.ca
Bernie MacKinnon, Director, Fire Services
902-563-5132
Tom Wilson, Councillor, Ward(s): District 9
twilson@cbrm.ns.ca
Derek Mombourquette, Councillor, Ward(s): District 10
dcmombourquette@cbrm.ns.ca
Fred Brooks, Sr. Manager, Recreation
902-563-5510
ftbrooks@cbrm.ns.ca
Dave LeBlanc, Councillor, Ward(s): District 11
dfleblanc@cbrm.ns.ca
Claire Detheridge, Councillor, Ward(s): District 12
mcdetheridge@cbrm.ns.ca
Mae Rowe, Councillor, Ward(s): District 13
mjrowe@cbrm.ns.ca
Francis Campbell, Manager, Solid Waste
902-563-5182
solidwaste@cbrm.ns.ca
Gordon MacLeod, Councillor, Ward(s): District 14
gmacleod@cbrm.ns.ca
Clarence Prince, Councillor, Ward(s): District 15
cprince@cbrm.ns.ca
Wesley Stubbert, Councillor, Ward(s): District 16
wstubbert@cbrm.ns.ca

Halifax Regional Municipality
P.O. Box 1749
1841 Argyle St.
Halifax, NS B3J 3A5
Tel: 902-490-4000; *Fax:* 902-490-4208
www.halifax.ca
Other Information: Toll Free Phone: 1-800-835-6428
Municipal Type: Regional Municipality
Incorporated: April 1, 1996 *Area:* 5,490.18 sq km
Population in 2006: 372,679
Provincial Electoral District(s): Bedford-Birch Cove; Cole Harbour; Cole Harbour-Eastern Passage; Dartmouth E.; Dartmouth N.; Dartmouth S.-Portland Valley; Eastern Shore; Hlfx Atlantic; Hlfx Chebucto; Hlfx Citadel-Sable Island; Hlfx-Clayton Park; Hlfx Fairview; Hlfx Needham; Hammonds Plains-Upper Sackville; Preston; Sackville-Cobequid; Timberlea-Prospect; Waverly-Fall River-Beaver Bank
Federal Electoral District(s): Central Nova; Cumberland-Colchester-Musquodoboit Valley; Dartmouth-Cole Harbour; Halifax; Halifax West; Sackville-Eastern Shore; South Shore-St. Margaret's
Next Election: Oct. 2012 (4 year terms)
Peter J. Kelly, M.B.A., Mayor
902-490-4010
kellyp@halifax.ca
Cathy Mellett, Acting Municipal Clerk
902-490-4210
clerks@halifax.ca
Steve Streatch, Councillor, Ward(s): District 1
streats@halifax.ca
James Cooke, C.G.A., Director, Finance
Barry Dalrymple, Councillor, Ward(s): District 2
barry.dalrymple@halifax.ca
Richard Butts, Chief Administrative Officer
902-490-6430
David Hendsbee, Councillor, Ward(s): District 3
david.hendsbee@halifax.ca
Lorelei Nicoll, Councillor, Ward(s): District 4
lorelei.nicoll@halifax.ca
Gloria McCluskey, Councillor, Ward(s): District 5
mcclusg@halifax.ca
Frank Beazley, Chief, Halifax Regional Police
902-490-6500
Darren Fisher, Councillor, Ward(s): District 6
darren.fisher@halifax.ca
Bill Mosher, Chief Director, Fire & Emergency Services
Bill Karsten, Councillor, Ward(s): District 7
karsteb@halifax.ca
Phillip Townsend, Director, Infrastructure & Asset Management
Jackie Barkhouse, Councillor, Ward(s): District 8
barkhoj@halifax.ca
Brad Anguish, Director, Business Planning & Information Management & Harbour Solutions Project
Jim Smith, Councillor, Ward(s): District 9
smithj@halifax.ca
Mary Ellen Donovan, B.Sc., LL.B., Director, Legal Services
902-490-4226
Mary Wile, Councillor, Ward(s): District 10
wilema@halifax.ca
Vacant, Director, Community Development
Jerry Blumenthal, Councillor, Ward(s): District 11
blumenj@halifax.ca
Ken Reashor, Director, Transportation & Public Works
Dawn Marie Sloane, Councillor, Ward(s): District 12
sloaned@halifax.ca
Catherine Mullally, Director, Human Resources
Sue Uteck, Councillor, Ward(s): District 13
utecks@halifax.ca
Jennifer Watts, Councillor, Ward(s): District 14
jennifer.watts@halifax.ca
Gord Helm, Manager, Solid Waste Resources
902-490-6606
Carl Yates, Manager, Halifax Water
902-490-4827, Fax: 902-490-4808
general.manager@hrwc.ca
Russell Walker, Councillor, Ward(s): District 15
walkerr@halifax.ca
Alan Brady, Manager, Wastewater Treatment
302-835-9566
Debbie Hum, Councillor, Ward(s): District 16
humd@halifax.ca
Jim Donovan, Project Manager, Economic Strategy
902-490-1742
Linda Mosher, Councillor, Ward(s): District 17
mosherl@halifax.ca
Shaune MacKinlay, Manager, Public Affairs
Stephen Adams, Councillor, Ward(s): District 18
adamss@halifax.ca
Larry Munroe, Municipal Auditor General, Business Systems & Control
Brad Johns, Councillor, Ward(s): District 19
brad.johns@halifax.ca
John P. Sheppard, P.Eng., Manager, Environmental Engineering Services
902-490-6958, Fax: 902-490-4858
sheppaj@halifax.ca
Robert (Bob) P. Harvey, Councillor, Ward(s): District 20
harveyb@halifax.ca
Tim Outhit, Councillor, Ward(s): District 21
outhitt@halifax.ca
John Sibbald, Coordinator, Pollution Prevention
902-490-5527
sibbalj@halifax.ca
Reg Rankin, Councillor, Ward(s): District 22
rankinr@halifax.ca
Peter Lund, Councillor, Ward(s): District 23
peter.lund@halifax.ca

Queens
P.O. Box 1264
249 White Point Rd.
Liverpool, NS B0T 1K0
Tel: 902-354-3453; *Fax:* 902-354-7473
info@regionofqueens.com
www.regionofqueens.com
Municipal Type: Regional Municipality
Incorporated: April 1, 1996 *Area:* 2,386.58 sq km
County or District: Queens; *Population in 2006:* 11,177
Provincial Electoral District(s): Queens
Federal Electoral District(s): South Shore-St. Margaret's
Next Election: Oct. 2012 (4 year terms)
John G. Leefe, Mayor
jleefe@regionofqueens.com
Jennifer Keating-Hubley, Director, Finance
jkeating@regionofqueens.com
Brad Rowter, Director, Finance
902-354-3455
browter@regionofqueens.com
Darlene Norman, Councillor, Ward(s): District 1
ross.surf@ns.sympatico.ca
Sheldon Brannen, Councillor, Ward(s): District 2
sheldonbrannen@gmail.com
Owen Hamlin, Councillor, Ward(s): District 3
mrh@ns.sympatico.ca
Bruce Inglis, Councillor, Ward(s): District 4
bruceinglis@live.ca
Mervin Hartlen, Councillor, Ward(s): District 5
m.hartlen@eastlink.ca
Randi Dickie, Councillor, Ward(s): District 6
randidickie@eastlink.ca
John Croft, Councillor, Ward(s): District 7
jfcroft@ns.sympatico.ca
R. Douglas Adams, Councillor, Ward(s): District 8
radams@eastlink.ca
Peter Waterman, Councillor, Ward(s): District 9
pmwaterman@eastlink.ca

Major Municipalities in Nova Scotia

Truro
P.O. Box 427
695 Prince St.
Truro, NS B2N 5C5
Tel: 902-895-4484; *Fax:* 902-893-0501
town@truro.ca
www.truro.ca
Municipal Type: City
Incorporated: May 6, 1875 *Area:* 37.63 sq km
County or District: Colchester; *Population in 2006:* 11,765
Provincial Electoral District(s): Truro-Bible Hill
Federal Electoral District(s): Cumberland-Colchester-Musquodoboit Valley
Next Election: Oct. 2012 (4 year terms)
W.R. (Bill) Mills, Mayor
902-893-2438
Diane Bennett Cook, Councillor, Ward(s): 1
Raymond Tynes, Councillor, Ward(s): 1
Charles Cox, Councillor, Ward(s): 2
Brian Kinsman, Councillor, Ward(s): 2
Sharron Byers, Councillor, Ward(s): 3
Greg MacArthur, Councillor, Ward(s): 3
Jim Langille, Chief Administrative Officer
jlangille@truro.ca
Andrew McKinnon, Director, Public Works & Traffic Authority
902-895-4243, Fax: 902-893-6091
amackinnon@truro.ca
Chuck Roberts, Senior Engineer
Doug MacKenzie, Director, Parks & Recreation Committee
902-893-6078, Fax: 902-893-6099
dmackenzie@truro.ca
Tom Bremner, Chief, Fire
902-895-8645, Fax: 902-895-8063
Juanita Bigelow, Administrator, Planning
902-895-1148, Fax: 902-893-6091

Other Municipalities in Nova Scotia

Amherst
P.O. Box 516
5 Ratchford St.
Amherst, NS B4H 4A1
Tel: 902-667-3352; *Fax:* 902-667-3356
www.town.amherst.ns.ca
Municipal Type: Town
Incorporated: Dec. 18, 1889 *Area:* 12.02 sq km
County or District: Cumberland; *Population in 2006:* 9,505
Provincial Electoral District(s): Cumberland North
Federal Electoral District(s):
Cumberland-Colchester-Musquodoboit Valley
Next Election: Oct. 2012 (4 year terms)
Gregory D. Herrett, CA, Chief Administrative Officer
902-667-6513, Fax: 902-667-2090
gherrett@town.amherst.ns.ca
Rebecca Purdy, Mayor
902-667-6510
rpurdy@amherst.ca

Annapolis Royal
P.O. Box 310
285 St. George St.
Annapolis Royal, NS B0S 1A0
Tel: 902-532-2043; *Fax:* 902-532-7443
admin@annapolisroyal.com
www.annapolisroyal.com
Municipal Type: Town
Incorporated: Nov. 29, 1892 *Area:* 2.04 sq km
County or District: Annapolis; *Population in 2006:* 444
Provincial Electoral District(s): Annapolis
Federal Electoral District(s): West Nova
Next Election: Oct. 2012 (4 year terms)
Phil Roberts, Mayor
Amery Boyer, Chief Administrative Officer
cao@annapolisroyal.com

Antigonish
274 Main St.
Antigonish, NS B2G 2C4
Tel: 902-863-1312; *Fax:* 902-863-9201
www.townofantigonish.ca
Municipal Type: Town
Incorporated: Jan. 9, 1889 *Area:* 5.15 sq km
County or District: Antigonish; *Population in 2006:* 4,236
Provincial Electoral District(s): Antigonish
Federal Electoral District(s): Central Nova
Next Election: Oct. 2012 (4 year terms)
Carl Chisholm, Mayor
T. Wadden, Chief Administrative Officer

Aylesford
P.O. Box 91
Aylesford, NS B0P 1C0
Tel: 902-847-0827; *Fax:* 902-847-0827
aylesfordvillage@eastlink.ca
Municipal Type: Village
County or District: Kings
Provincial Electoral District(s): Kings West
Federal Electoral District(s): West Nova
Next Election: Oct. 2012 (4 year terms)
Rhonda Carey, Chair
Trudie Spinney, Clerk-Treasurer

Baddeck
P.O. Box 63
Baddeck, NS B0E 1B0
Tel: 902-295-3666; *Fax:* 902-295-1729
webmasters@vccaps.com
www.baddeck.com
Municipal Type: Village
County or District: Victoria; *Population in 2006:* 982
Provincial Electoral District(s): Victoria-The Lakes
Federal Electoral District(s): Sydney-Victoria
Next Election: Oct. 2012 (4 year terms)
Eddie Keeling, Chair
Erin Bradley, Clerk-Treasurer

Berwick
P.O. Box 130
236 Commercial St.
Berwick, NS B0P 1E0
Tel: 902-538-8068; *Fax:* 902-538-3724
general@town.berwick.ns.ca
www.town.berwick.ns.ca
Municipal Type: Town
Incorporated: May 25, 1923 *Area:* 6.8 sq km
County or District: Kings; *Population in 2006:* 2,454
Provincial Electoral District(s): Kings West
Federal Electoral District(s): West Nova
Next Election: Oct. 2012 (4 year terms)
John P. Prall, Mayor
902-583-4008
mayor@town.berwick.ns.ca
Bob Ashley, Chief Administrative Officer
902-583-4007
bashley.berwick@gmail.com

Bible Hill
67 Pictou Rd.
Bible Hill, NS B2N 2R9
Tel: 902-893-8083; *Fax:* 902-897-0430
office@biblehill.ca
www.biblehill.ca
Municipal Type: Village
County or District: Colchester; *Population in 2006:* 5,500
Provincial Electoral District(s): Truro-Bible Hill
Federal Electoral District(s):
Cumberland-Colchester-Musquodoboit Valley
Next Election: Oct. 2012 (4 year terms)
Robert Christianson, Clerk-Treas.
chris@biblehill.ca
Tom Burke, Chair

Bridgetown
P.O. Box 609
271 Granville St.
Bridgetown, NS B0S 1C0
Tel: 902-665-4637; *Fax:* 902-665-5011
bridgetown@ns.sympatico.ca
www.town.bridgetown.ns.ca
Municipal Type: Town
Incorporated: Sept. 15, 1897 *Area:* 3.54 sq km
County or District: Annapolis; *Population in 2006:* 972
Provincial Electoral District(s): Annapolis
Federal Electoral District(s): West Nova
Next Election: Oct. 2012 (4 year terms)
Darrell Hiltz, Chief Administrative Officer
Robert Fowler, Mayor

Bridgewater
60 Pleasant St.
Bridgewater, NS B4V 3X9
Tel: 902-543-4651; *Fax:* 902-543-6876
admin@town.bridgewater.ns.ca
www.town.bridgewater.ns.ca
Municipal Type: Town
Incorporated: Feb. 13, 1899 *Area:* 13.6 sq km
County or District: Lunenburg; *Population in 2006:* 7,944
Provincial Electoral District(s): Lunenburg West
Federal Electoral District(s): South Shore-St. Margaret's
Next Election: Oct. 2012 (4 year terms)
Carroll Publicover, Mayor
Ken Smith, Town Manager

Canning
P.O. Box 9
2229 North Ave.
Canning, NS B0P 1H0
Tel: 902-582-3768; *Fax:* 902-582-3068
village.canning@xcountry.tv
www.canningnovascotia.ca
Municipal Type: Village
County or District: Kings
Provincial Electoral District(s): Kings North
Federal Electoral District(s): Kings-Hants
Next Election: Oct. 2012 (4 year terms)
Kim MacQuarrie, Chair
kpphalen@hotmail.com
Gloria Porter, Clerk-Treasurer

Canso
P.O. Box 189
11 Telegraph St.
Canso, NS B0H 1H0
Tel: 902-366-2525; *Fax:* 902-366-3093
michelle@townofcanso.com
www.townofcanso.com
Municipal Type: Town
Incorporated: May 14, 1901 *Area:* 5.42 sq km
County or District: Guysborough; *Population in 2006:* 911
Provincial Electoral District(s): Guysborough-Sheet Harbour
Federal Electoral District(s): Cape Breton-Canso
Next Election: Oct. 2012 (4 year terms)
Frank Fraser, Mayor
mayor@townofcanso.com
Michelle Hart, Town Clerk-Treas.
mhart@townofcanso.com

Chester
P.O. Box 620
Chester, NS B0J 1J0
Tel: 902-275-4482; *Fax:* 902-275-2021
admin@chesterareans.ca
www.chesterns.com
Municipal Type: Village
County or District: Lunenburg
Provincial Electoral District(s): Chester-St.Margaret's
Federal Electoral District(s): South Shore-St. Margaret's
Next Election: Oct. 2012 (4 year terms)
Tony Howlett, Chair
Iris Tolliver, Clerk-Treas.

Clark's Harbour
P.O. Box 160
2648 Main St.
Clarks Harbour, NS B0W 1P0
Tel: 902-745-2390; *Fax:* 902-745-1772
www.clarksharbour.com
Municipal Type: Town
Incorporated: March 4, 1919 *Area:* 2.9 sq km
County or District: Shelburne; *Population in 2006:* 860
Provincial Electoral District(s): Shelburne
Federal Electoral District(s): South Shore-St. Margaret's
Next Election: Oct. 2012 (4 year terms)
Leigh B. Stoddart, Mayor
leighstoddart@eastlink.ca
Brian Crowell, Clerk-Treasurer
briancrowell@eastlink.ca

Cornwallis Square
P.O. Box 129
1415 Country Home Rd., Cambridge
Waterville, NS B0P 1V0
Tel: 902-538-0325; *Fax:* 902-538-1683
Municipal Type: Village
County or District: Kings
Provincial Electoral District(s): Kings North
Federal Electoral District(s): Kings-Hants
Next Election: Oct. 2012 (4 year terms)
George Foote, Chair
Bill Farrell, Clerk-Treas.

Digby
P.O. Box 579
147 First Ave.
Digby, NS B0V 1A0
Tel: 902-245-4769; *Fax:* 902-245-2121
www.digby.ca
Municipal Type: Town
Incorporated: Feb. 28, 1890 *Area:* 3.14 sq km
County or District: Digby; *Population in 2006:* 2,092
Provincial Electoral District(s): Digby-Annapolis
Federal Electoral District(s): West Nova
Next Election: Oct. 2012 (4 year terms)
Ben Cleveland, Mayor
Tom Ossinger, Chief Administrative Officer
eossinger@digby.ca

Freeport
P.O. Box 31
Freeport, NS B0V 1B0
Tel: 902-839-2144
Municipal Type: Village
County or District: Digby
Provincial Electoral District(s): Digby-Annapolis
Federal Electoral District(s): West Nova
Next Election: Oct. 2012 (4 year terms)
Peter Morehouse, Chair
Vacant, Clerk-Treasurer

Greenwood
P.O. Box 1068
904 Central Ave.
Greenwood, NS B0P 1N0
Tel: 902-765-8788; *Fax:* 902-765-4369
greenwoodns@eastlink.ca
www.greenwoodnovascotia.com
Municipal Type: Village
County or District: Kings; *Population in 2006:* 4,500
Provincial Electoral District(s): Kings West
Federal Electoral District(s): West Nova
Next Election: Oct. 2012 (4 year terms)
Don MacDonald, Chair
902-765-2894
Marian Elsworth, Clerk-Treasurer

Hantsport
P.O. Box 399
20 Main St.
Hantsport, NS B0P 1P0
Tel: 902-684-3211; *Fax:* 902-684-3227
www.hantsportnovascotia.com
Municipal Type: Town
Incorporated: April 1, 1895 *Area:* 2.13 sq km
County or District: Hants; *Population in 2006:* 1,191
Provincial Electoral District(s): Hants West
Federal Electoral District(s): Kings-Hants
Next Election: Oct. 2012 (4 year terms)
Jeffrey Lawrence, Chief Administrative Officer
H. Wayne Folker, Mayor
mayor@hantsportnovascotia.com

Havre Boucher
1318 Cape Jack Rd.
Havre Boucher, NS B0P 1P0
Tel: 902-234-3088;
www.havreboucher.com
Municipal Type: Village
County or District: Antigonish
Provincial Electoral District(s): Antigonish
Federal Electoral District(s): Central Nova
Next Election: Oct. 2012 (4 year terms)
Chuck Tibbo, Chair
Raymond Carpenter, Clerk

Hebbville
47 Catidian Pl., RR#4
Bridgewater, NS B4V 2W3
Tel: 902-543-5786; *Fax:* 902-543-7006
Municipal Type: Village
County or District: Lunenburg
Provincial Electoral District(s): Lunenburg West
Federal Electoral District(s): South Shore-St. Margaret's
Next Election: Oct. 2012 (4 year terms)
Glen Whitehouse, Chair
Vernon Cornish, Clerk-Treasurer

Kentville
354 Main St.
Kentville, NS B4N 1K6
Tel: 902-679-2500; *Fax:* 902-679-2375
info@town.kentville.ns.ca
www.town.kentville.ns.ca
Municipal Type: Town
Incorporated: May 1, 1886 *Area:* 17.35 sq km
County or District: Kings; *Population in 2006:* 5,815
Provincial Electoral District(s): Kings North
Federal Electoral District(s): Kings-Hants
Next Election: Oct. 2012 (4 year terms)
David Corkum, Mayor
dcorkum@kentville.ca
Keith Robichaud, Chief Administrative Officer
cao@kentville.ca

Kings County
P.O. Box 100
87 Cornwallis St.
Kentville, NS B4N 3W3
Tel: 902-678-6141; *Fax:* 902-678-9279
inquiry@county.kings.ns.ca
www.county.kings.ns.ca
Municipal Type: Municipality
Incorporated: April 17, 1879 *Area:* 2,122.18 sq km
County or District: Kings; *Population in 2006:* 60,035
Provincial Electoral District(s): Kings North; Kings South; Kings West
Federal Electoral District(s): Kings-Hants; West Nova
Next Election: Oct. 2012 (4 year terms)
Diana Brothers, Warden
902-690-6132
warden.brothers@county.kings.ns.ca
Vacant, Municipal Clerk
Jim Taylor, Councillor, Ward(s): District 1
councillor.taylor@county.kings.ns.ca
Bob Ashley, Chief Administrative Officer
902-690-6131, Fax: 902-678-9279
bashley@county.kings.ns.ca
Janet Newton, Councillor & Deputy Warden, Ward(s): District 2
councillor.newton@county.kings.ns.ca
Dick Killam, Councillor, Ward(s): District 3
councillor.killam@county.kings.ns.ca
Trish Javorek, Manager, Development & Building Services
902-690-6167
pjavorek@county.kings.ns.ca
Scott Quinn, Manager, Engineering & Public Works
902-690-6194
squinn@county.kings.ns.ca
Fred Whalen, Councillor, Ward(s): District 4
councillor.whalen@county.kings.ns.ca
Wayne Atwater, Councillor, Ward(s): District 5
councillor.atwater@county.kings.ns.ca
Kathleen Leslie, Manager, Information Technology
902-690-6155, Fax: 902-690-6165
kleslie@county.kings.ns.ca
Diana Brothers, Councillor, Ward(s): District 6
councillor.brothers@county.kings.ns.ca
Gary Smith, Manager, Protective Services
902-690-6117
gsmith@county.kings.ns.ca
Dale Lloyd, Councillor, Ward(s): District 8
councillor.lloyd@county.kings.ns.ca
Bob Suffron, Coordinator, Parks & Open Spaces
902-690-6153
bsuffron@county.kings.ns.ca
Basil Hall, Councillor, Ward(s): District 9
councillor.hall@county.kings.ns.ca
Ben Sivak, Manager, Planning
902-690-6102
bsivak@county.kings.ns.ca
Chris Parker, Councillor, Ward(s): District 10
councillor.parker@county.kings.ns.ca
Eric Smith, Councillor, Ward(s): District 11
councillor.smith@county.kings.ns.ca
Mike Ennis, Councillor, Ward(s): District 12
902-542-5217
councillor.ennis@county.kings.ns.ca

Kingston
P.O. Box 254
671 Main St.
Kingston, NS B0P 1R0
Tel: 902-765-2800; *Fax:* 902-765-0807
info@kingstonnovascotia.ca
www.kingstonnovascotia.ca
Municipal Type: Village
Incorporated: 1957
County or District: Kings; *Population in 2006:* 4,000
Provincial Electoral District(s): Kings West
Federal Electoral District(s): West Nova
Next Election: Oct. 2012 (4 year terms)
Jaki Fraser, Chair
902-584-3501
Kelly Rice, Clerk-Treasurer

Lawrencetown
P.O. Box 38
12 Prince St.
Lawrencetown, NS B0S 1M0
Tel: 902-584-3559; *Fax:* 902-584-3878
villagelawrencetown@ns.aliantzinc.ca
www.lawrencetownnovascotia.com
Municipal Type: Village
County or District: Annapolis; *Population in 2006:* 750
Provincial Electoral District(s): Annapolis
Federal Electoral District(s): West Nova
Next Election: Oct. 2012 (4 year terms)
Jaki Fraser, Chair
902-584-3501
jaki@ns.sympatico.ca
Kelly Rice, Clerk-Treasurer

Lockeport
P.O. Box 189
26 North St.
Lockeport, NS B0T 1L0
Tel: 902-656-2216; *Fax:* 902-656-2935
townoflockeport@ns.sympatico.ca
www.lockeport.ns.ca
Municipal Type: Town
Incorporated: Feb. 26, 1907 *Area:* 2.32 sq km
County or District: Shelburne; *Population in 2006:* 646
Provincial Electoral District(s): Shelburne
Federal Electoral District(s): South Shore-St. Margaret's
Next Election: Oct. 2012 (4 year terms)
Darian Huskilson, Mayor
902-875-7747
Joyce Y. Young, Clerk-Treas.

Lunenburg
P.O. Box 129
119 Cumberland St.
Lunenburg, NS B0J 2C0
Tel: 902-634-4410; *Fax:* 902-634-4416
explorelunenburg@ns.sympatico.ca
www.explorelunenburg.ca
Municipal Type: Town
Incorporated: Oct. 29, 1888 *Area:* 4.01 sq km
County or District: Lunenburg; *Population in 2006:* 2,317
Provincial Electoral District(s): Lunenburg
Federal Electoral District(s): South Shore-St. Margaret's
Next Election: Oct. 2012 (4 year terms)
Laurence Mawhinney, Mayor
lmawhinney@explorelunenburg.ca
Beatrice Renton, Town Manager & Clerk
brenton@explorelunenburg.ca

Mahone Bay
P.O. Box 530
493 Main St.
Mahone Bay, NS B0J 2E0
Tel: 902-624-8327; *Fax:* 902-624-8069
Municipal Type: Town
Incorporated: March 31, 1919 *Area:* 3.13 sq km
County or District: Lunenburg; *Population in 2006:* 904
Provincial Electoral District(s): Lunenburg
Federal Electoral District(s): South Shore-St. Margaret's
Next Election: Oct. 2012 (4 year terms)
Jim Wentzell, Chief Administrative Officer
C. Joseph Feeney, Mayor
cjfeeney@ns.sympatico.ca

Middleton
P.O. Box 340
131 Commercial St.
Middleton, NS B0S 1P0
Tel: 902-825-4841; *Fax:* 902-825-6460
www.town.middleton.ns.ca
Municipal Type: Town
Incorporated: May 31, 1909 *Area:* 5.44 sq km
County or District: Annapolis; *Population in 2006:* 1,829
Provincial Electoral District(s): Annapolis
Federal Electoral District(s): West Nova
Next Election: Oct. 2012 (4 year terms)
Clayton MacMurty, Chief Administrative Officer
cao@town.middleton.ns.ca
Calvin Eddy, Mayor
callyn@ns.sympatico.ca

Mulgrave
P.O. Box 129
457 MacLeod St.
Mulgrave, NS B0E 2G0
Tel: 902-747-2243; *Fax:* 902-747-2585
info@townofmulgrave.ca
www.townofmulgrave.ca
Municipal Type: Town
Incorporated: Dec. 1, 1923 *Area:* 17.81 sq km
County or District: Guysborough; *Population in 2006:* 879
Provincial Electoral District(s): Guysborough-Sheet Harbour
Federal Electoral District(s): Cape Breton-Canso
Next Election: Oct. 2012 (4 year terms)
Marney Simmons, Mayor
902-747-2662
J. Hugh Landry, Chief Administrative Officer
902-747-2243
hugh.landry@townofmulgrave.ca

New Glasgow
P.O. Box 7
111 Provost St.
New Glasgow, NS B2H 5E1
Tel: 902-755-7788; *Fax:* 902-755-6242
newglasgow@newglasgow.ca
www.newglasgow.ca
Municipal Type: Town
Incorporated: May 6, 1875 *Area:* 9.93 sq km
County or District: Pictou; *Population in 2006:* 9,455
Provincial Electoral District(s): Pictou Centre
Federal Electoral District(s): Central Nova
Next Election: Oct. 2012 (4 year terms)
Barrie MacMillan, Mayor
902-752-4550, Fax: 902-755-6242
barrie.macmillan@newglasgow.ca
Lisa M. MacDonald, Chief Administrative Officer
902-755-8333
lisa.macdonald@newglasgow.ca

New Minas
9209 Commercial St.
New Minas, NS B4N 3G1
Tel: 902-681-6972; *Fax:* 902-681-0779
newminas@ns.aliantzinc.ca
www.newminas.com
Municipal Type: Village
County or District: Kings; *Population in 2006:* 4,200
Provincial Electoral District(s): Kings South
Federal Electoral District(s): Kings-Hants
Next Election: Oct. 2012 (4 year terms)
Dave Chaulk, Chair
902-681-2387
dchaulk@av.eastlink.ca

Terry Silver, Clerk-Treasurer
902-681-0292
newminas@ns.sympatico.ca

Oxford
P.O. Box 338
105 Lower Main St.
Oxford, NS B0M 1P0
Tel: 902-447-2170; *Fax:* 902-447-2485
dwhite@town.oxford.ns.ca
www.town.oxford.ns.ca
Municipal Type: Town
Incorporated: April 19, 1904 *Area:* 10.76 sq km
County or District: Cumberland; *Population in 2006:* 1,178
Provincial Electoral District(s): Cumberland South
Federal Electoral District(s):
Cumberland-Colchester-Musquodoboit Valley
Next Election: Oct. 2012 (4 year terms)
Lloyd Jenkins, Mayor
ljenkins@townofoxford.ns.ca
Darrell White, Chief Administrative Officer
dwhite@town.oxford.ns.ca

Parrsboro
P.O. Box 400
4030 Eastern Ave.
Parrsboro, NS B0M 1S0
Tel: 902-254-2036; *Fax:* 902-254-2313
town@town.parrsboro.ns.ca
www.town.parrsboro.ns.ca
Municipal Type: Town
Incorporated: July 15, 1889 *Area:* 14.88 sq km
County or District: Cumberland; *Population in 2006:* 1,401
Provincial Electoral District(s): Cumberland South
Federal Electoral District(s):
Cumberland-Colchester-Musquodoboit Valley
Next Election: Oct. 2012 (4 year terms)
Dawn McCully, Mayor
J. Raymond Hickey, Chief Administrative Officer

Pictou
P.O. Box 640
40 Water St.
Pictou, NS B0K 1H0
Tel: 902-485-4372; *Fax:* 902-485-8110
town.pictou@north.nsis.com
www.townofpictou.com
Municipal Type: Town
Incorporated: May 4, 1874 *Area:* 7.94 sq km
County or District: Pictou; *Population in 2006:* 3,813
Provincial Electoral District(s): Pictou West
Federal Electoral District(s): Central Nova
Next Election: Oct. 2012 (4 year terms)
Joseph F. Hawes, Mayor
902-485-6025
joe.hawes@townofpictou.ca
Scott Conrad, Chief Administrative Officer
902-485-4372
scott.conrad@townofpictou.com

Port Hawkesbury
#1, 606 Reeves St.
Port Hawkesbury, NS B9A 2R7
Tel: 902-625-2746; *Fax:* 902-625-0040
www.townofporthawkesbury.ca
Municipal Type: Town
Incorporated: Jan. 22, 1889 *Area:* 8.11 sq km
County or District: Inverness; *Population in 2006:* 3,517
Provincial Electoral District(s): Inverness
Federal Electoral District(s): Cape Breton-Canso
Next Election: Oct. 2012 (4 year terms)
W.J. (Billy Joe) MacLean, Mayor
902-625-1800
billyjoe.maclean@townofporthawkesbury.ca
Maria Freimanis, Chief Administrative Officer
902-625-7890
maria.freimanis@townofhawkesbury.ca

Port Williams
P.O. Box 153
1045 Main St.
Port Williams, NS B0P 1T0
Tel: 902-542-4411; *Fax:* 902-542-4566
villageoffice@ns.aliantzinc.ca
www.portwilliams.com
Municipal Type: Village
County or District: Kings
Provincial Electoral District(s): Kings North
Federal Electoral District(s): Kings-Hants
Next Election: Oct. 2012 (4 year terms)
Kim Cogswell, Vice-Chair
kimcogswell@eastlink.ca

Vacant, Clerk

Pugwash
P.O. Box 220
124 Water St.
Pugwash, NS B0K 1L0
Tel: 902-243-2946; *Fax:* 902-243-2126
villagecommission@pugwashvillage.com
www.pugwashvillage.com
Municipal Type: Village
County or District: Cumberland; *Population in 2006:* 900
Provincial Electoral District(s): Cumberland North
Federal Electoral District(s):
Cumberland-Colchester-Musquodoboit Valley
Next Election: Oct. 2012 (4 year terms)
Rod Benjamin, Chair
Lisa Betts, Clerk-Treas.
lisabetts@pugwashvillage.com

River Hebert
2724 Taylor Rd.
River Hebert, NS B0L 1G0
Tel: 902-251-2250
Municipal Type: Village
County or District: Cumberland
Provincial Electoral District(s): Cumberland South
Federal Electoral District(s):
Cumberland-Colchester-Musquodoboit Valley
Next Election: Oct. 2012 (4 year terms)
Dale Porter, Chair
Judy Jollymore, Clerk-Treas.

St. Peter's
P.O. Box 452
60 Deny St.
St. Peters, NS B0E 3B0
Tel: 902-535-2155; *Fax:* 902-535-2330
info@visitstpeters.com
www.visitstpeters.com
Municipal Type: Village
County or District: Richmond; *Population in 2006:* 1200
Provincial Electoral District(s): Richmond
Federal Electoral District(s): Cape Breton-Canso
Next Election: Oct. 2012 (4 year terms)
Rena Burke, Clerk-Treasurer
Esther McDonnell, Chair

Shelburne
P.O. Box 670
168 Water St.
Shelburne, NS B0T 1W0
Tel: 902-875-2991; *Fax:* 902-875-3932
shelburnetown@ns.aliantzinc.ca
www.town.shelburne.ns.ca
Municipal Type: Town
Incorporated: April 4, 1907 *Area:* 9 sq km
County or District: Shelburne; *Population in 2006:* 1,879
Provincial Electoral District(s): Shelburne
Federal Electoral District(s): South Shore-St. Margaret's
Next Election: Oct. 2012 (4 year terms)
Al Delaney, Mayor
902-875-4747
mayordelaney@town.shelburne.ns.ca
Rhonda Henneberry, Chief Administrative Officer
rhenneberry@town.shelburne.ca

Springhill
P.O. Box 1000
43 Main St.
Springhill, NS B0M 1X0
Tel: 902-597-3751; *Fax:* 902-597-3637
www.town.springhill.ns.ca
Municipal Type: Town
Incorporated: March 30, 1889 *Area:* 11.15 sq km
County or District: Cumberland; *Population in 2006:* 3,941
Provincial Electoral District(s): Cumberland South
Federal Electoral District(s):
Cumberland-Colchester-Musquodoboit Valley
Next Election: Oct. 2012 (4 year terms)
Allen Dill, Mayor
Donald F. Tabor, Chief Administrative Officer
dtabor@townofspringhill.ns.ca

Stellarton
P.O. Box 2200
250 Foord St.
Stellarton, NS B0K 1S0
Tel: 902-752-2114; *Fax:* 902-755-4105
townoffice@town.stellarton.ns.ca
www.stellarton.ca
Municipal Type: Town
Incorporated: Oct. 22, 1889 *Area:* 8.99 sq km
County or District: Pictou; *Population in 2006:* 4,717
Provincial Electoral District(s): Pictou Centre
Federal Electoral District(s): Central Nova
Next Election: Oct. 2012 (4 year terms)
Joe Gennoe, Mayor
mayor@town.stellarton.ns.ca
Joyce Eaton, Clerk-Treas.
jeaton@town.stellarton.ns.ca

Stewiacke
P.O. Box 8
295 George St.
Stewiacke, NS B0N 2J0
Tel: 902-639-2231; *Fax:* 902-639-2221
sdorey@stewiacke.net
www.stewiacke.net
Municipal Type: Town
Incorporated: Aug. 30, 1906 *Area:* 17.67 sq km
County or District: Colchester; *Population in 2006:* 1,421
Provincial Electoral District(s): Colchester-Musqodoboit Valley
Federal Electoral District(s):
Cumberland-Colchester-Musquodoboit Valley
Next Election: Oct. 2012 (4 year terms)
Dereck Rhoddy, Mayor
drhoddy@stewiacke.net
Sheldon Dorey, Chief Administrative Officer
sdorey@stewiacke.net

Tatamagouche
P.O. Box 119
423 Main St.
Tatamagouche, NS B0K 1V0
Tel: 902-657-3696;
www.tatamagouchetoday.com
Municipal Type: Village
County or District: Colchester; *Population in 2006:* 2,069
Provincial Electoral District(s): Colchester North
Federal Electoral District(s):
Cumberland-Colchester-Musquodoboit Valley
Next Election: Oct. 2012 (4 year terms)
Marilyn Ebsary, Clerk-Treasurer
Dale Semple, Chair

Tiverton
P.O. Box 16
RR#1
Tiverton, NS B0V 1G0
Tel: 902-839-2369;
www.hometowncanada.com/ns/Tiverton.html
Municipal Type: Village
County or District: Digby
Provincial Electoral District(s): Digby-Annapolis
Federal Electoral District(s): West Nova
Next Election: Oct. 2012 (4 year terms)
Mary Cossaboom, Clerk-Treasurer
Woodrow Outhouse, Chair

Trenton
P.O. Box 328
120 Main St.
Trenton, NS B0K 1X0
Tel: 902-752-5311; *Fax:* 902-752-0090
trenton@town.trenton.ns.ca
www.town.trenton.ns.ca
Other Information: www.facebook.com/TrentonNS
Municipal Type: Town
Incorporated: March 18, 1911 *Area:* 6 sq km
County or District: Pictou; *Population in 2006:* 2,741
Provincial Electoral District(s): Pictou Centre
Federal Electoral District(s): Central Nova
Next Election: Oct. 2012 (4 year terms)
Glen MacKinnon, Mayor
glen.mackinnon@sobeys.com
Cathy MacGillivary, Chief Administrative Officer
cabugden@town.trenton.ns.ca

Westport
The Spouter Inn
P.O. Box 1192
263 Water St.
Westport, NS B0V 1H0
Tel: 902-839-2219; *Fax:* 902-839-2219
Municipal Type: Village
County or District: Digby
Provincial Electoral District(s): Digby-Annapolis
Federal Electoral District(s): West Nova
Next Election: Oct. 2012 (4 year terms)
Glenda Welch, Chair
Caroline Norwood, Clerk-Treasurer

Westville
P.O. Box 923
2042 Queen St.
Westville, NS B0K 2A0
Tel: 902-396-1500; *Fax:* 902-396-3986
www.westville.ca
Municipal Type: Town
Incorporated: Aug. 20, 1894 *Area:* 14.39 sq km
County or District: Pictou; *Population in 2006:* 3,805
Provincial Electoral District(s): Pictou East
Federal Electoral District(s): Central Nova
Next Election: Oct. 2012 (4 year terms)
Roger McKay, Mayor
rmackay@westville.ca
Scott Fraser, Chief Administrative Officer
sfraser@westville.ca

Weymouth
P.O. Box 121
5108 Hwy. 1
Weymouth, NS B0W 3T0
Tel: 902-837-4976;
village@weymouthnovascotia.com
www.weymouthnovascotia.com
Municipal Type: Village
County or District: Digby
Provincial Electoral District(s): Digby-Annapolis
Federal Electoral District(s): West Nova
Next Election: Oct. 2008 (4 year terms)
Murray Betts, Clerk-Treas.
Suzanne MacLean, Chair

Windsor
P.O. Box 158
100 King St.
Windsor, NS B0N 2T0
Tel: 902-798-2275; *Fax:* 902-798-5679
info@town.windsor.ns.ca
www.town.windsor.ns.ca
Municipal Type: Town
Incorporated: April 4, 1878 *Area:* 9.06 sq km
County or District: Hants; *Population in 2006:* 3,709
Provincial Electoral District(s): Hants West
Federal Electoral District(s): Kings-Hants
Next Election: Oct. 2012 (4 year terms)
Paul Beazley, Mayor
pbeazley@town.windsor.ns.ca
Louis Coutinho, Chief Administrative Officer
902-798-6675
lcoutinho@town.windsor.ns.ca

Wolfville
359 Main St.
Wolfville, NS B4P 1A1
Tel: 902-542-5767; *Fax:* 902-542-4789
www.town.wolfville.ns.ca
Municipal Type: Town
Incorporated: March 4, 1893 *Area:* 6.45 sq km
County or District: Kings; *Population in 2006:* 3,772
Provincial Electoral District(s): Kings South
Federal Electoral District(s): Kings-Hants
Next Election: Oct. 2012 (4 year terms)
Robert A. (Bob) Stead, Mayor
Rachel Turner, Interim Chief Administrative Officer
902-542-8842, Fax: 902-542-4789
rturner@wolfville.ca

Yarmouth
400 Main St.
Yarmouth, NS B5A 1G2
Tel: 902-742-8565; *Fax:* 902-742-6244
www.yarmouth-town.com
Municipal Type: Town
Incorporated: Aug. 6, 1890 *Area:* 10.56 sq km
County or District: Yarmouth; *Population in 2006:* 7,162
Provincial Electoral District(s): Yarmouth
Federal Electoral District(s): West Nova
Next Election: Oct. 2012 (4 year terms)
Charles Crosby, Mayor
mayor.mooney@townofyarmouth.ca
Jeffrey Gushue, Chief Administrative Officer
902-742-8565, Fax: 902-742-6244
cao@townofyarmouth.ca

Rural Municipality

Annapolis County
P.O. Box 100
752 George St.
Annapolis Royal, NS B0S 1A0
Tel: 902-532-2331; *Fax:* 902-532-2096
info@annapoliscounty.ns.ca
www.annapoliscounty.ns.ca
Municipal Type: Rural Municipality
Incorporated: April 17, 1879 *Area:* 3,184.97 sq km
County or District: Annapolis; *Population in 2006:* 21,438
Provincial Electoral District(s): Annapolis; Digby-Annapolis
Federal Electoral District(s): West Nova
Next Election: Oct. 2012 (4 year terms)
Reg Ritchie, Warden
902-532-3137
rritchie@annapoliscounty.ns.ca
Marilyn Wilkins, Councillor, Ward(s): 1
mwilkins@ns.sympatico.ca
Brian Connell, Councillor, Ward(s): 2
mwilkins@ns.sympatico.ca
R. Wayne Fowler, Councillor, Ward(s): 3
Brenda Orchard, Chief Administrative Officer
902-532-3130
admin@annapoliscounty.ns.ca
Carolyn Young, Clerk & Executive Assistant
cyoung@annapoliscounty.ns.ca
Stephen McInnis, Director
902-532-3141
smcinnis@annapoliscounty.ns.ca

Antigonish County
285 Beech Hill Rd.
Antigonish, NS B2G 0B4
Tel: 902-863-1117; *Fax:* 902-863-5751
clerk@antigonishcounty.ns.ca
www.antigonishcounty.ns.ca
Municipal Type: Rural Municipality
Incorporated: April 17, 1879 *Area:* 1,457.82 sq km
County or District: Antigonish; *Population in 2006:* 18,836
Provincial Electoral District(s): Antigonish
Federal Electoral District(s): Central Nova
Next Election: Oct. 2012 (4 year terms)
Herbert J. DeLorey, Warden & Councillor, Ward(s): 8. Tracadie/Monastery
warden@antigonishcounty.ns.ca
Mary MacLellan, Councillor, Ward(s): 1. Arisaig
Donnie MacDonald, Councillor, Ward(s): 2
Jerome Grant, Councillor, Ward(s): 3. St. Joseph's
Vaughan Chisholm, Councillor, Ward(s): 4. Fringe Area West
Rémi Deveau, Councillor, Ward(s): 5. Pomquet
Owen McCarron, Councillor, Ward(s): 6. St. Andrew's
Angus Bowie, Councillor, Ward(s): 7. Heatherton
Havre Boucher, Councillor, Ward(s): 9. Havre Boucher
Bill MacFarlane, Councillor, Ward(s): 10. Fringe Area South
Alan J. Bond, Clerk & Treasurer
clerk@antigonishcounty.ns.ca
John Bain, Director & Development Officer, Eastern District Planning Commission
902-625-5364
jdbain@edpc.ca
Michael O'Leary, Director, Public Works
902-863-5004
publicworks@antigonishcounty.ns.ca
Michael O'Leary, Director, Public Works
902-863-5004
solidwaste@antigonishcounty.ns.ca

Argyle District
P.O. Box 10
27 Courthouse St.
Tusket, NS B0W 3M0
Tel: 902-648-2311; *Fax:* 902-648-0367
admin@munargyle.com
www.munargyle.com
Municipal Type: Rural Municipality
Incorporated: April 17, 1879 *Area:* 1,527.1 sq km
County or District: Yarmouth; *Population in 2006:* 8,656
Provincial Electoral District(s): Argyle
Federal Electoral District(s): West Nova
Next Election: Oct. 2012 (4 year terms)
Aldric D'Entremont, Warden & Councillor, Ward(s): 8. West Pubnico
902-762-2195
Alain Muise, Chief Administrative Officer
902-648-3293
admuise@munargyle.com

Barrington District
P.O. Box 100
2447 Hwy. 3
Barrington, NS B0W 1E0
Tel: 902-637-2015; *Fax:* 902-637-2075
www.barringtonmunicipality.com
Municipal Type: Rural Municipality
Incorporated: April 17, 1879 *Area:* 631.94 sq km
County or District: Shelburne; *Population in 2012:* 7,331
Provincial Electoral District(s): Shelburne
Federal Electoral District(s): South Shore-St. Margaret's
Next Election: Oct. 2008 (4 year terms)
George El-Jakl, Warden
Brian Holland, Clerk
mobclerk@eastlink.ca

Chester District
P.O. Box 369
151 King St.
Chester, NS B0J 1J0
Tel: 902-275-3554; *Fax:* 902-275-4771
administration@district.chester.ns.ca
www.chester.ca
Municipal Type: Rural Municipality
Incorporated: April 17, 1879 *Area:* 1,120.75 sq km
County or District: Lunenburg; *Population in 2006:* 10,741
Provincial Electoral District(s): Chester-St. Margaret's
Federal Electoral District(s): South Shore-St. Margaret's
Next Election: Oct. 2012 (4 year terms)
Allen Webber, Warden
awebber@district.chester.ns.ca
Floyd Shatford, Deputy Warden
fshatford@district.chester.ns.ca
Marshal Hector, Councillor, Ward(s): 1
mhector@district.chester.ns.ca
Brad Armstrong, Councillor, Ward(s): 3
barmstrong@chester.ca
Allen Webber, Councillor, Ward(s): 4
awebber@chester.ca
Robert Myra, Councillor, Ward(s): 5
myra@chester.ca
Cheryl Scott, Councillor, Ward(s): 6
cscott@chester.ca
Sharon Church-Cornelius, Councillor, Ward(s): 6
scornelius@chester.ca
Erin Beaudin, Chief Administrative Officer
ebeaudin@chester.ca
Pam Myra, Municipal Clerk
pmyra@chester.ca
Matthew Davidson, Director, Public Works
902-275-1312
Bruce Forest, Director, Solid Waste
bforest@chester.ca
Cliff Gall, Director, Information Services
cgall@chester.ca
Steve Graham, Treasurer & Director, Finance
sgraham@chester.ca
Chad Haughn, Director, Recreation & Parks
chaughn@chester.ca
Geoff MacDonald, Planning Director
902-275-2599
gmacdonald@chester.ca
Karen Newton, Development Officer
knewton@chester.ca
Arden Weagle, Fire Inspector
aweagle@chester.ca
Earl Woodworth, Building Inspector
ewoodworth@chester.ca

Clare District
P.O. Box 458
1185 Hwy. 1
Little Brook, NS B0W 1Z0
Tel: 902-769-2031; *Fax:* 902-769-3773
council@municipality.clare.ns.ca
www.clarenovascotia.com
Municipal Type: Rural Municipality
Incorporated: April 17, 1879 *Area:* 852.82 sq km
County or District: Digby; *Population in 2006:* 8,813
Provincial Electoral District(s): Clare
Federal Electoral District(s): West Nova
Next Election: Oct. 2012 (4 year terms)
Jean Melanson, Warden & Councillor, Ward(s): 8
jeanmelanson@gmail.com
Connie Saulnier, Chief Administrative Officer

Colchester County
P.O. Box 697
1 Church St.
Truro, NS B2N 5E7
Tel: 902-897-3160; *Fax:* 902-895-9983
www.colchester.ca
Other Information: 866-728-5144 (toll-free)
Municipal Type: Rural Municipality
Incorporated: April 17, 1879 *Area:* 3,627.69 sq km
County or District: Colchester; *Population in 2006:* 50,023
Provincial Electoral District(s): Colchester-Musquodoboit Valley; Colchester North; Truro-Bible Hill
Federal Electoral District(s):
Cumberland-Colchester-Musquodoboit Valley
Next Election: Oct. 2012 (4 year terms)
Bob Taylor, Mayor
mayor@colchester.ca
Ron Cavanaugh, Deputy Mayor, Ward(s): 8
councillordistrict8@colchester.ca
Christine Blair, Councillor, Ward(s): 1
councillordistrict1@colchester.ca
Bill Masters, Councillor, Ward(s): 2
councillordistrict2@colchester.ca
Gerald Buott, Councillor, Ward(s): 3
councillordistrict3@colchester.ca
Mike Cooper, Councillor, Ward(s): 4
councillordistrict4@colchester.ca
Glen Edwards, Councillor, Ward(s): 5
councillordistrict5@colchester.ca
Karen MacKenzie, Councillor, Ward(s): 6
councillordistrict6@colchester.ca
Jimmie Le Fresne, Councillor, Ward(s): 7
councillordistrict7@colchester.ca
Dan McDougall, Chief Administrative Officer
dmcdougall@colchester.ca
Crawford Macpherson, Director, Community Development
902-897-3170
cmacpherson@colchester.ca
Bruce Purchase, Director, Corporate Services
bpurchase@colchester.ca
Ramesh Ummat, Director, Public Works
rummat@colchester.ca
Wayne Wamboldt, Director, Public Works
wwamboldt@colchester.ca

Cumberland County
E.D. Fullerton Municipal Bldg.
P.O. Box 428
1395 Blair Lake Rd., RR#6
Amherst, NS B4H 3Y4
Tel: 902-667-2313; *Fax:* 902-667-1352
info@cumberlandcounty.ns.ca
www.cumberlandcounty.ns.ca
Other Information: Toll Free Phone: 1-888-756-6262
Municipal Type: Rural Municipality
Incorporated: April 17, 1879 *Area:* 4,271.14 sq km
County or District: Cumberland; *Population in 2006:* 32,046
Provincial Electoral District(s): Cumberland North; Cumberland South
Federal Electoral District(s):
Cumberland-Colchester-Musquodoboit Valley
Next Election: Oct. 2012 (4 year terms)
Keith Hunter, Warden & Councillor, Ward(s): 3
khunter@cumberlandcounty.ns.ca
Gerald Read, Councillor, Ward(s): 2
gread@cumberlandcounty.ns.ca
Allison Gillis, Councillor, Ward(s): 3
agillis@cumberlandcounty.ns.ca
Ron MacNutt, Councillor, Ward(s): 5
rmacnutt@cumberlandcounty.ns.ca
Kathy Redmond, Councillor, Ward(s): 6
kredmond@cumberlandcounty.ns.ca
Phillip Donkin, Councillor, Ward(s): 7
pdonkin@cumberlandcounty.ns.ca
Ernest Gilbert, Councillor, Ward(s): 7
egilbert@cumberlandcounty.ns.ca
John Reid, Councillor, Ward(s): 7
jreid@cumberlandcounty.ns.ca
Ratchford Merriam, Councillor, Ward(s): 7
rmerriam@cumberlandcounty.ns.ca
Rennie Bugley, Chief Administrative Officer
rbugley@cumberlandcounty.ns.ca
Shelley Hoeg, Executive Assistant
shoeg@cumberlandcounty.ns.ca
Steve Ferguson, Director, Policy & Research
sferguson@cumberlandcounty.ns.ca
Penny Henneberry, Director, Planning & Development
phenneberry@cumberlandcounty.ns.ca
Andrew MacDonald, Director, Finance & Administration
amacdonald@cumberlandcounty.ns.ca
Robert Streatch, Director, Public Works
902-667-3029
rstreatch@cumberlandcounty.ns.ca

Digby District
P.O. Box 429
Digby, NS B0V 1A0
Tel: 902-245-4777; *Fax:* 902-245-5748
www.digbydistrict.ca
Municipal Type: Rural Municipality
Incorporated: April 17, 1879 *Area:* 1,655.93 sq km
County or District: Digby; *Population in 2006:* 7,986
Provincial Electoral District(s): Digby-Annapolis
Federal Electoral District(s): West Nova
Next Election: Oct. 2012 (4 year terms)
Linda Gregory, Warden
warden.mundigby@tartannet.ns.ca
Linda Fraser, Chief Administrative Officer
lfraser@municipality.digby.ns.ca

Guysborough District
Municipal Bldg.
P.O. Box 79
33 Pleasant St.
Guysborough, NS B0H 1N0
Tel: 902-533-3705; *Fax:* 902-533-2749
district@modg.ca
www.municipality.guysborough.ns.ca
Municipal Type: Rural Municipality
Incorporated: April 17, 1879 *Area:* 2,111.42 sq km
County or District: Guysborough; *Population in 2006:* 4,681
Provincial Electoral District(s): Guysborough-Sheet Harbour
Federal Electoral District(s): Cape Breton-Canso
Next Election: Oct. 2012 (4 year terms)
Lloyd P. Hines, Warden
lhines@modg.ca
Barry Carrollll, Chief Administrative Officer
902-533-3705
bcarroll@modg.ca

Hants East District
P.O. Box 190
2361 Hwy. 2, Milford
Shubenacadie, NS B0N 2H0
Tel: 902-758-2299; *Fax:* 902-758-3497
info@easthants.ca
www.easthants.ca
Municipal Type: Rural Municipality
Incorporated: April 17, 1879 *Area:* 1,787.64 sq km
County or District: Hants; *Population in 2006:* 21,387
Provincial Electoral District(s): Hants East
Federal Electoral District(s): Kings-Hants
Next Election: Oct. 2012 (4 year terms)
John Patterson, Warden & Councillor, Ward(s): 13
Fred Bannister, Councillor, Ward(s): 1. Enfield
fbannister@easthants.ca
Norval Mitchell, Councillor, Ward(s): 2. Elmsdale
nmitchell@easthants.ca
Willy Versteeg, Councillor, Ward(s): 3. Milford
wversteeg@easthants.ca
Pam MacInnis, Councillor, Ward(s): 4. Shubenacadie
pmacinnis@easthants.ca
Keith Ryno, Councillor, Ward(s): 5. Maitland
kryhno@easthants.ca
Wayne Greene, Councillor, Ward(s): 6. Noel
wgreene@easthants.ca
John A. MacDonald, Councillor, Ward(s): 6. Noel
jamacdonald@easthants.ca
Greg Grant, Councillor, Ward(s): 8. Gore
ggrant@easthants.ca
Eldon Hebb, Councillor, Ward(s): 9. Nine Mile River
ehebb@easthants.ca
Jim D. Smith, Councillor, Ward(s): 10. Enfield/Horne Settlement
jdsmith@easthants.ca
Eleanor Roulston, Councillor, Ward(s): 11. Rawdon
eroulston@easthants.ca
Rosanne Bland, Councillor, Ward(s): 11. Rawdon
rbland@easthants.ca
Connie Nolan, Chief Administrative Officer
902-883-7098
cnolan@easthants.ca
Janice VanTol, Executive Assitant & Deputy Clerk
902-883-7098
jvantol@easthants.ca
Lew Landers, P.Eng., Director, Engineering Services
llanders@easthants.ca
Terry Matheson, MA Sc.E., Officer, Environmental Compliance
tmatheson@easthants.ca
Andrea Trask, Coordinator & Educator, Waste Reduction
atrask@easthants.ca
John Woodford, Director, Planning & Development
902-758-2715
jwoodford@easthants.ca
Heidi Achenbach, Manager, Solid Waste
902-758-2299
hachenbach@easthants.ca
Jim Ashley, Manager, Public Works
jashley@easthants.ca
Mike Brown, Centre Foreman, Solid Waste Management
902-261-2178
Edward McQuillan, Operator, Water Distribution
emcquillan@easthants.ca

Hants West District
Windsor-West Hants Industrial Park
P.O. Box 3000
76 Morrison Dr.
Windsor, NS B0N 2T0
Tel: 902-798-8391; *Fax:* 902-798-8553
west.hants@westhants.ca
www.westhants.ca
Municipal Type: Rural Municipality
Incorporated: April 17, 1879 *Area:* 1,238.12 sq km
County or District: Hants; *Population in 2006:* 13,881
Provincial Electoral District(s): Hants West
Federal Electoral District(s): Kings-Hants
Next Election: Oct. 2012 (4 year terms)
Richard B. Dauphinee, Warden & Councillor, Ward(s): 6
902-798-4908
admin@westhants.ca
Reed W. Allen, Councillor, Ward(s): 1
rallen@ns.sympatico.ca
Shirley Pineo, Councillor, Ward(s): 2
councillorpineo@eastlink.ca
Randall Matheson, Councillor, Ward(s): 2
matheson007@eastlink.ca
Thomas Brown, Councillor, Ward(s): 2
councillorthomasb@gmail.com
Gary Cochrane, Councillor, Ward(s): 2
garycochrane@eastlink.ca
Gloria Shanks, Councillor, Ward(s): 7
gkshanks@ns.sympatico.ca
Rick Gaudet, Councillor, Ward(s): 8
rickgaudet@eastlink.ca
Pam Ainslie, Councillor, Ward(s): 8
painslie@eastlink.ca
Cheryl Chislett, Chief Administrative Officer
cao@westhants.ca
Lynn Davis, Director, Planning
902-798-6900
ldavis@windsorwesthantsplanning.ns.ca
Paul DeMont, Operator, Water Treatment
drc@westhants.ca
Christine McClare, Coordinator, Waste Reduction
waste@westhants.ca
Rick Sherrard, Director, Public Works
public.works@westhants.ca

Inverness County
Municipal Bldg.
P.O. Box 179
375 Main St.
Port Hood, NS B0E 2W0
Tel: 902-787-2274; *Fax:* 902-787-3110
www.invernesscounty.ca
Municipal Type: Rural Municipality
Incorporated: April 17, 1879 *Area:* 3,830.4 sq km
County or District: Inverness; *Population in 2006:* 19,036
Provincial Electoral District(s): Guysborough-Sheet Harbour; Inverness; Victoria-The Lakes
Federal Electoral District(s): Cape Breton-Canso; Sydney-Victoria
Next Election: Oct. 2012 (4 year terms)
Duart MacAulay, Warden & Councillor, Ward(s): 4
duartmaca@ns.sympatico.ca
Daniel Boudreau, Councillor, Ward(s): 1
Gloria Leblanc, Councillor, Ward(s): 2
James Mustard, Councillor, Ward(s): 3
Susan Mallette, Councillor, Ward(s): 5
Dwayne MacDonald, Councillor, Ward(s): 6
Joe O'Connor, Chief Administrative Officer
joe.oconnor@invernesscounty.ca
Joe O'Connor, Director, Public Works
902-787-3502, Fax: 902-787-2339
invworks@ns.sympatico.ca
William Gillis, Officer, Bylaw Enforcement

Lunenburg District
P.O. Box 200
210 Aberdeen Rd.
Bridgewater, NS B4V 2W8
Tel: 902-543-8181; *Fax:* 902-543-7123
admin@municipality.lunenburg.ca
www.lunenburgdistrict.com
Municipal Type: Rural Municipality
Incorporated: April 17, 1879 *Area:* 1,759.14 sq km
County or District: Lunenburg; *Population in 2006:* 25,164
Provincial Electoral District(s): Chester-St. Margaret's
Lunenburg; Lunenburg West
Federal Electoral District(s): South Shore-St. Margaret's
Next Election: Oct. 2012 (4 year terms)
Don Downe, Mayor
902-543-5357
Martin Bell, Deputy Mayor
902-543-5357
Martin Bell, Deputy Mayor
902-543-5357
Milton Countway, Councillor
Frank Fawson, Councillor
Erik Hustvedt, Councillor
Cathy Moore, Councillor
Lee Nauss, Councillor
Basil Oickle, Councillor
Sandra Statton, Councillor
John Veinot, Councillor
April Whynot-Lohnes, Municipal Clerk
902-541-1323
Tammy Wilson, Chief Administrative Officer
902-541-1320
twilson@modl.ca
Jim Annand, Manager, Solid Waste Operations
902-541-1325
jannand@modl.ca
Laura Barkhouse, Coordinator, Trails
902-541-1352
lbarkhouse@modl.ca
Jeff Merrill, Planner, Planning & Development
902-541-1340
jmerrill@modl.ca
Norma Schiefer, Officer, Development
902-541-1334
nschiefer@modl.ca
Roger Stein, Municipal Engineer & Director, Engineering
Kevin Wentzell, Supervisor, Compost Plant
902-543-0151
kwentzell@modl.ca

Pictou County
P.O. Box 910
46 Municipal Dr.
Pictou, NS B0K 1H0
Tel: 902-485-4311; *Fax:* 902-485-6475
cmacintosh@county.pictou.ns.ca
www.county.pictou.ns.ca
Municipal Type: Rural Municipality
Incorporated: April 17, 1879 *Area:* 2,845.26 sq km
County or District: Pictou; *Population in 2006:* 46,513
Provincial Electoral District(s): Pictou Centre; Pictou East;
Pictou West
Federal Electoral District(s): Central Nova
Next Election: Oct. 2012 (4 year terms)
Ronald Baillie, Warden & Councillor, Ward(s): 4
normabaillie@northnovacable.ca
Kelly McVicar, Councillor, Ward(s): 2
kmcvicar@county.pictou.ns.ca
Edward MacMaster, Councillor
edwardmacmaster@county.pictou.ns.ca
Robert Parker, Councillor, Ward(s): 5
rparker@county.pictou.ns.ca
Jim Turple, Councillor, Ward(s): 6
jturple@county.pictou.ns.ca
David Parker, Councillor, Ward(s): 7
dparker@county.pictou.ns.ca
Leonard Fraser, Councillor, Ward(s): 8
lfraser@county.pictou.ns.ca
Lori Kilburn, Councillor, Ward(s): 9
lkilburn@county.pictou.ns.ca
Allister MacDonald, Councillor, Ward(s): 10
amacdonald@county.pictou.ns.ca
Andy Thompson, Councillor, Ward(s): 11
athompson@county.pictou.ns.ca
Chester Dewar, Councillor, Ward(s): 12
cdewar@county.pictou.ns.ca
Randy Palmer, Councillor, Ward(s): 13
rpalmer@county.pictou.ns.ca
Fielding Smith, Councillor, Ward(s): 13
fsmith@county.pictou.ns.ca
Brian Cullen, Chief Administrative Officer
bcullen@county.pictou.ns.ca
Carol MacKenzie, Manager, Waste Reduction Program
902-396-1495
cmackenzie@pcwastemgmt.com

Richmond County
P.O. Box 120
2357 Hwy. 206
Arichat, NS B0E 1A0
Tel: 902-226-2400; *Fax:* 902-226-1510
ldigout@richmondcounty.ca
www.richmondcounty.ca
Municipal Type: Rural Municipality
Incorporated: April 17, 1879 *Area:* 1,244.24 sq km
County or District: Richmond; *Population in 2006:* 9,740
Provincial Electoral District(s): Richmond
Federal Electoral District(s): Cape Breton-Canso
Next Election: Oct. 2012 (4 year terms)
John Boudreau, Warden
902-226-3380, Fax: 902-226-1510
jboudreau@richmondcounty.ca
Warren Olsen, Chief Adminstrative Officer
902-226-3970, Fax: 902-226-2824
wolsen@richmondcounty.ca

St. Mary's District
P.O. Box 296
16 Main St.
Sherbrooke, NS B0J 3C0
Tel: 902-522-2049; *Fax:* 902-522-2309
council@saint-marys.ca
www.saint-marys.ca
Municipal Type: Rural Municipality
Incorporated: April 17, 1879 *Area:* 1,909.59 sq km
County or District: Guysborough; *Population in 2006:* 2,587
Provincial Electoral District(s): Guysborough-Sheet Harbour
Federal Electoral District(s): Central Nova
Next Election: Oct. 2012 (4 year terms)
David Clark, Warden
902-522-2049, Fax: 902-522-2309
dp.clark@nis.sympatico.ca
David Gillis, Clerk-Treasurer
902-522-2049, Fax: 902-522-2309
davidgillis@munet.ns.ca

Shelburne District
P.O. Box 280
136 Hammond Rd.
Shelburne, NS B0T 1W0
Tel: 902-875-3083; *Fax:* 902-875-1278
ademings@municipalityofshelburne.ca
Municipal Type: Rural Municipality
Incorporated: April 17, 1879 *Area:* 1,818.49 sq km
County or District: Shelburne; *Population in 2006:* 4,828
Provincial Electoral District(s): Shelburne
Federal Electoral District(s): South Shore-St. Margaret's
Next Election: Oct. 2012 (4 year terms)
Vacant, Warden
902-875-3544
Penny Smith, Clerk
902-875-3544

Victoria County
P.O. Box 370
495 Chebucto St.
Baddeck, NS B0E 1B0
Tel: 902-295-3231; *Fax:* 902-295-3331
heather.maclean@countyvictoria.ns.ca
www.countyvictoria.ns.ca
Municipal Type: Rural Municipality
Incorporated: April 17, 1879 *Area:* 2,870.85 sq km
County or District: Victoria; *Population in 2006:* 7,594
Provincial Electoral District(s): Victoria-The Lakes
Federal Electoral District(s): Sydney-Victoria
Next Election: Oct. 2012 (4 year terms)
Bruce Morrison, Warden
902-565-8229, Fax: 902-295-1311
bruce.morrison@countyvictoria.ns.ca
Alexander (Sandy) W. Hudson, Chief Administrative Officer
902-295-3660, Fax: 902-295-3331
sandy.hudson@countyvictorian.ns.ca

Yarmouth District
P.O. Box 21
932, Hwy 1
Hebron, NS B0W 1X0
Tel: 902-742-7159; *Fax:* 902-742-3164
admin@district.yarmouth.ns.ca
www.district.yarmouth.ns.ca
Municipal Type: Rural Municipality
Incorporated: April 17, 1879 *Area:* 585.27 sq km
County or District: Yarmouth; *Population in 2006:* 10,304
Provincial Electoral District(s): Yarmouth
Federal Electoral District(s): West Nova
Next Election: Oct. 2012 (4 year terms)
Leland Anthony, Warden & Councillor, Ward(s): 7
warden@district.yarmouth.ns.ca
Murray Goodwin, Deputy Warden & Councillor, Ward(s): 2
murray@district.yarmouth.ns.ca
John Cunningham, Councillor, Ward(s): 1
johnc@district.yarmouth.ns.ca
Ken Crosby, Councillor, Ward(s): 3
kenc@district.yarmouth.ns.ca
Trevor Cunningham, Councillor, Ward(s): 5
trevor@district.yarmouth.ns.ca
Heather MacDonald, Councillor, Ward(s): 4
heather@district.yarmouth.ns.ca
Ken Moses, Chief Administrative Officer
cao@district.yarmouth.ns.ca
Trudy LeBlanc, Deputy Chief Administrative Officer
trudy@district.yarmouth.ns.ca
Greg Shay, Director, Finance
greg@district.yarmouth.ns.ca

NUNAVUT

The Department of Community and Government Services has legislative responsibility for 27 Territorial Acts and Regulations. These Acts include: Area Development; Business Licenses; Cities, Town and Villages; Civil Emergency Measures; Commissioner's Land; Community Employees Benefits Program Transfer; Conflict of Interest; Consumer Protection; Curfew; Dog; Film Classification; Fire Prevention; Hamlet; Homeowners Property; Local Authorities Election; Lotteries; Pawnbrokers and Second-hand Dealers; Planning; Property Assessments and Taxation; Real Estate Agents Licensing; Religious Societies; Residential Tenancies; Technical Standards and Safety; Senior Citizens and Disabled Persons Property Tax Relief Act; Settlement; Western Canada Lottery.

Incorporation as a city, town or village is determined by the value of all assessable land. Incorporation values: Village, $10 million; Town, $50 million; City, $200 million, all tax-based. Hamlets may request tax-based status. There is one city and 24 hamlets in Nunavut.

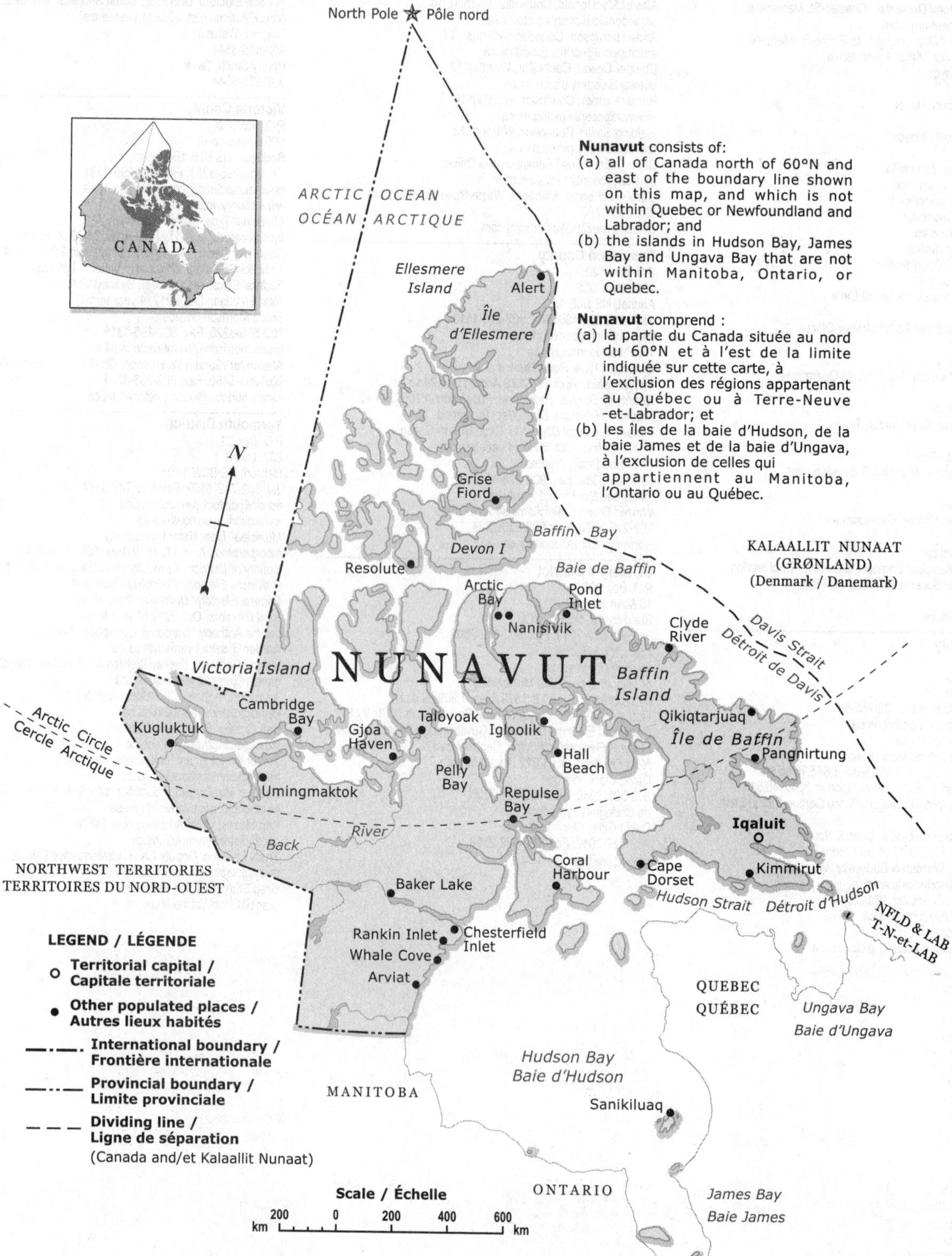

Reproduced with the permission of Natural Resources Canada 2011, courtesy of the Atlas of Canada.

www.atlas.gc.ca

Nunavut

Major Municipalities in Nunavut

Iqaluit
P.O. Box 460
Iqaluit, NU X0A 0H0
Tel: 867-979-5600; *Fax:* 867-979-5922
info@city.iqaluit.nu.ca
www.city.iqaluit.nu.ca
Municipal Type: City
Incorporated: 2001 *Area:* 52.34 sq km
Population in 2006: 6,184
Provincial Electoral District(s): Iqaluit East; Iqaluit West; Iqaluit Centre
Federal Electoral District(s): Nunavut
Next Election: 2012 (3 year terms)
Note: Formerly known as Frobisher Bay.
John Hussey, Chief Administration Officer
867-979-5666
j.hussey@city.iqaluit.nu.ca
Elisapee Sheutiapik, Mayor
mayor@city.iqaluit.nu.ca
Mary Akpalialuk, Councillor
John Mabberi-Mudonyi, Director, Corporate Services
867-979-5675
j.mabberi-mudonyi@city.iqaluit.nu.ca
Jimmy Kilabuk, Councillor
Doug Vincent, Chief Enforcement Officer
867-979-6363
d.vincent@city.iqaluit.nu.ca
Natsiq Kango, Councillor
Michèle Bertol, Director, Planning & Lands
867-979-6363
m.bertol@city.iqaluit.nu.ca
Mat Knicklebein, Councillor
Amy Elgersma, Director, Recreation
867-979-5616
a.elgersma@city.iqaluit.nu.ca
Simon Nattaq, Councillor
Vacant, Director, Engineering & Public Works
Mary Ekho Wilman, Councillor
Meagan Leach, Director, Engineering & Sustainability
867-979-6363
m.leach@city.iqaluit.nu.ca
David Ell, Councillor
Sean Tiessen, Coordinator, Materials
s.tiessen@city.iqaluit.nu.ca
Romeyn Stevenson, Councillor
Vacant, Superintendent, Operations
Geneva Chislett, Controller
867-979-5610
g.chislett@city.iqaluit.nu.ca
Walter Oliver, Fire Chief, Emergency Services
867-976-5657
w.oliver@city.iqaluit.nu.ca
Joamie Eegeesiak, Officer, Community Economic Development
867-979-6363
j.eegeesiak@city.iqaluit.nu.ca
Rob Hogan, Foreman, Utilidor Water Treatment Plant
867-975-8509

Other Municipalities in Nunavut

Arctic Bay
General Delivery
Arctic Bay, NU X0A 0A0
Tel: 867-439-8483; *Fax:* 867-439-8916
sao_ab@qiniq.com
Other Information: Additional Phone: 867-439-9918
Municipal Type: Hamlet
Area: 247.5 sq km
Population in 2006: 690
Provincial Electoral District(s): Quttiktuq
Federal Electoral District(s): Nunavut
Andrew Taqtu, Mayor
mayor_ab@qiniq.com
Joeli Qamanirq, Sr. Admin. Officer

Arviat
P.O. Box 150
Arviat, NU X0C 0E0
Tel: 867-857-2841; *Fax:* 867-857-2519
arviatsao@qiniq.com
www.arviat.ca
Municipal Type: Hamlet
Incorporated: 1977 *Area:* 132 sq km
Population in 2006: 2,060
Provincial Electoral District(s): Arviat
Federal Electoral District(s): Nunavut
Note: Formerly known as Eskimo Point.
Bob Leonard, Mayor
Ed Murphy, Sr. Admin. Officer

Baker Lake
P.O. Box 149
Baker Lake, NU X0C 0A0
Tel: 867-793-2874; *Fax:* 867-793-2509
bledo@netkaster.ca
www.bakerlake.org
Municipal Type: Hamlet
Incorporated: 1977 *Area:* 182.22 sq km
Population in 2006: 1,728
Provincial Electoral District(s): Baker Lake
Federal Electoral District(s): Nunavut
David Aksawnee, Mayor
blmayor@netkaster.ca
Dennis Zettler, Sr. Admin. Officer

Cambridge Bay
P.O. Box 16
Cambridge Bay, NU X0B 0C0
Tel: 867-983-4650; *Fax:* 867-983-2193
sking@cambridgebay.ca
www.cambridgebay.ca
Municipal Type: Hamlet
Incorporated: 1984 *Area:* 202.2 sq km
Population in 2006: 1,477
Provincial Electoral District(s): Cambridge Bay
Federal Electoral District(s): Nunavut
Michelle Gillis, Mayor
mayorycb@qiniq.com
Stephen King, Sr. Admin. Officer

Cape Dorset
P.O. Box 30
Cape Dorset, NU X0A 0C0
Tel: 867-897-8943; *Fax:* 867-897-8030
info@capedorset.ca
www.capedorset.ca
Other Information: Additional Phone: 867-897-8981
Municipal Type: Hamlet
Incorporated: 1982 *Area:* 9.74 sq km
Population in 2006: 1,236
Provincial Electoral District(s): South Baffin
Federal Electoral District(s): Nunavut
Cary Merritt, Mayor
Art Stewart, Sr. Admin. Officer

Chesterfield Inlet
P.O. Box 10
Chesterfield Inlet, NU X0C 0B0
Tel: 867-898-9206; *Fax:* 867-898-9108
edo_hamlet@qiniq.com
www.chesterfieldinlet.net
Municipal Type: Hamlet
Incorporated: 1980 *Area:* 141.08 sq km
Population in 2006: 332
Provincial Electoral District(s): Nanulik
Federal Electoral District(s): Nunavut
Harry Aqqark, Mayor
Richard Van Horne, Sr. Admin. Officer

Clyde River
P.O. Box 89
Clyde River, NU X0A 0E0
Tel: 867-924-6220; *Fax:* 867-924-6293
saoclyde2004@yahoo.ca
Other Information: Additional Phone: 867-924-6301
Municipal Type: Hamlet
Area: 106.48 sq km
Population in 2006: 820
Provincial Electoral District(s): Uqqummiut
Federal Electoral District(s): Nunavut
Apiusie Apak, Mayor
Terry Kalluk, Acting Sr. Admin. Officer

Coral Harbour
P.O. Box 30
Coral Harbour, NU X0C 0C0
Tel: 867-925-8867; *Fax:* 867-925-8233
munch@qiniq.com
Municipal Type: Hamlet
Area: 137.83 sq km
Population in 2006: 769
Provincial Electoral District(s): Nanulik
Federal Electoral District(s): Nunavut
Jerry Pianiyuk, Mayor
Ronald Ladd, Sr. Admin. Officer

Gjoa Haven
P.O. Box 200
Gjoa Haven, NU X0B 1J0
Tel: 867-360-7141; *Fax:* 867-360-6309
saogjoa@qiniq.com
Municipal Type: Hamlet
Incorporated: 1981 *Area:* 28.47 sq km
Population in 2006: 1,064
Provincial Electoral District(s): Nattilik
Federal Electoral District(s): Nunavut
Allen Aqlukkaq, Mayor
Enuk Pauloosie, Sr. Admin. Officer

Grise Fiord
P.O. Box 77
Grise Fiord, NU X0A 0J0
Tel: 867-980-9959; *Fax:* 867-980-9052
gfsao@nv.sympatico.ca
Other Information: Additional Phone: 867-980-9060
Municipal Type: Hamlet
Incorporated: 1987 *Area:* 332.7 sq km
Population in 2006: 141
Provincial Electoral District(s): Quttiktuq
Federal Electoral District(s): Nunavut
Meeka Kigutak, Mayor
Marty Kuluguaqtuq, Sr. Admin. Officer

Hall Beach
P.O. Box 3
Hall Beach, NU X0A 0K0
Tel: 867-928-8829; *Fax:* 867-928-8871
hbhamlet@sympatico.ca
Other Information: Additional Phone: 867-928-8945
Municipal Type: Hamlet
Area: 16.52 sq km
Population in 2006: 654
Provincial Electoral District(s): Amittuq
Federal Electoral District(s): Nunavut
Ammie Kipsigak, Mayor

Igloolik
P.O. Box 30
Igloolik, NU X0A 0L0
Tel: 867-934-8940; *Fax:* 867-934-8757
igloolik@magma.ca
Other Information: Additional Phone: 867-934-8830
Municipal Type: Hamlet
Incorporated: 1976 *Area:* 102.87 sq km
Population in 2006: 1,538
Provincial Electoral District(s): Amittuq
Federal Electoral District(s): Nunavut
Lucassie Ivalu, Mayor
Brian Fleming, Sr. Admin. Officer

Kimmirut
P.O. Box 120
Kimmirut, NU X0A 0N0
Tel: 867-939-2247; *Fax:* 867-939-2045
cedkimm@qiniq.com
www.kimmirut.ca
Other Information: Additional Phone: 867-939-2002
Municipal Type: Hamlet
Area: 2.27 sq km
Population in 2006: 411
Provincial Electoral District(s): South Baffin
Federal Electoral District(s): Nunavut
Jamesie Kootoo, Mayor
Akeego Ikkidluak, Sr. Admin. Officer

Kugaaruk
P.O. Box 205
General Delivery
Kugaaruk, NU X0B 1K0
Tel: 867-769-6281; *Fax:* 867-769-6069
pellybay@polarnet.ca
Municipal Type: Hamlet
Incorporated: 1972 *Area:* 4.97 sq km
Population in 2006: 688
Provincial Electoral District(s): Akulliq
Federal Electoral District(s): Nunavut
Note: Formerly known as Pelly Bay.
Makabe Nartok, Mayor
Andre Larabie, Sr. Admin. Officer

Kugluktuk
P.O. Box 271
Kugluktuk, NU X0B 0E0
Tel: 867-982-6500; *Fax:* 867-982-3060
saokug@qiniq.com
Other Information: Additional Phone: 867-982-6505
Municipal Type: Hamlet
Incorporated: 1981 *Area:* 549.61 sq km

Population in 2006: 1,302
Provincial Electoral District(s): Kugluktuk
Federal Electoral District(s): Nunavut
Note: Formerly known as Coppermine.
Ernie Bernhardt, Mayor
Derrick Power, Sr. Admin. Officer

Pangnirtung
P.O. Box 253
Pangnirtung, NU X0A 0R0
Tel: 867-473-8953; *Fax:* 867-473-8832
pang_sao@qiniq.com
Municipal Type: Hamlet
Incorporated: 1972 *Area:* 7.54 sq km
Population in 2006: 1,325
Provincial Electoral District(s): Pangnirtung
Federal Electoral District(s): Nunavut
Moses Qarpik, Mayor
Ron Mongeau, Sr. Admin. Officer

Pond Inlet
P.O. Box 180
Pond Inlet, NU X0A 0S0
Tel: 867-899-8934; *Fax:* 867-899-8940
hamletpond_sao@qiniq.com
www.pondinlet.ca
Other Information: Additional Phone: 867-899-8935
Municipal Type: Hamlet
Area: 173.36 sq km
Population in 2006: 1,315
Provincial Electoral District(s): Tunnuniq
Federal Electoral District(s): Nunavut
Jaykolasie Killiktee, Mayor
Mike Richards, Sr. Admin. Officer

Qikiqtarjuaq
P.O. Box 4
Qikiqtarjuaq, NU X0A 0B0
Tel: 867-927-8832; *Fax:* 867-927-8120
munQik@qiniq.com
Other Information: Additional Phone: 867-927-8178
Municipal Type: Hamlet
Area: 130.65 sq km
Population in 2006: 473
Provincial Electoral District(s): Uqqummiut
Federal Electoral District(s): Nunavut
Note: Formerly Broughton Island.
Hannah Audlakiak, Mayor
Qikmayor@qiniq.com
Rick Van Horne, Sr. Admin. Officer

Rankin Inlet
P.O. Box 310
Rankin Inlet, NU X0C 0G0
Tel: 867-645-2895; *Fax:* 867-645-2146
sao@rankininlet.ca
www.rankininlet.net
Municipal Type: Hamlet
Incorporated: 1975 *Area:* 20.24 sq km
Population in 2006: 2,358
Provincial Electoral District(s): Rankin Inlet North; Rankin Inlet South/Whale Cove
Federal Electoral District(s): Nunavut
Pujjutt Towtongie, Mayor
Hilda Price, Sr. Admin. Officer

Repulse Bay
P.O. Box 10
Repulse Bay, NU X0C 0H0
Tel: 867-462-4014; *Fax:* 867-462-4411
saorepulse@qiniq.com
Municipal Type: Hamlet
Incorporated: 1978 *Area:* 423.74 sq km
Population in 2006: 748
Provincial Electoral District(s): Akulliq
Federal Electoral District(s): Nunavut
Donaty Milortok, Mayor
Bob Aymont, Sr. Admin. Officer

Resolute Bay
P.O. Box 60
Resolute Bay, NU X0A 0V0
Tel: 867-252-3616; *Fax:* 867-252-3749
hamletsao@qiniq.com
Other Information: Additional Phone: 867-252-3689
Municipal Type: Hamlet
Incorporated: 1987 *Area:* 116.89 sq km
Population in 2006: 229
Provincial Electoral District(s): Quttiktuq
Federal Electoral District(s): Nunavut
Ludy Pudluk, Mayor
Josh Hunter, Sr. Admin. Officer

Sanikiluaq
General Delivery
Sanikiluaq, NU X0A 0W0
Tel: 867-266-7900; *Fax:* 867-266-8903
sanisao@qiniq.com
Other Information: Additional Phone: 867-266-7901
Municipal Type: Hamlet
Incorporated: 1976 *Area:* 114.98 sq km
Population in 2006: 744
Provincial Electoral District(s): Hudson Bay
Federal Electoral District(s): Nunavut
Joe Aragutina, Mayor
Thomas Kutluk, Sr. Admin. Officer

Taloyoak
P.O. Box 8
Taloyoak, NU X0B 1B0
Tel: 867-561-6341; *Fax:* 867-561-5057
hamoftal@qiniq.com
www.polarnet.ca/~taloyoak
Municipal Type: Hamlet
Incorporated: 1981 *Area:* 37.65 sq km
Population in 2006: 809
Provincial Electoral District(s): Nattilik
Federal Electoral District(s): Nunavut
Note: Formerly known as Spence Bay.
Tommy Aiyout, Mayor
Stephen King, Sr. Admin. Officer

Whale Cove
P.O. Box 120
Whale Cove, NU X0C 0J0
Tel: 867-896-9961; *Fax:* 867-896-9109
saowc@qiniq.com
Municipal Type: Hamlet
Incorporated: 1976 *Area:* 283.65 sq km
Population in 2006: 353
Provincial Electoral District(s): Rankin Inlet South/Whale Cove
Federal Electoral District(s): Nunavut
Percy Kabloona, Mayor

ONTARIO

There are two types of municipal government structure in Ontario: two-tier municipalities, which consist of upper-tier municipalities, known as either regions or counties, plus their constituent lower-tier municipalities; and single-tier municipalities.

One-half of Ontario's population lives in the single-tier cities of Toronto, Ottawa and Hamilton and in areas with a regional system of government. The regional system was created for the more densely populated areas of this province. Regions have more servicing responsibilities than a county, and while there are variations, services usually provided by regions include arterial roads, transit, policing, sewer and water systems, waste disposal, region-wide land use planning and development, health and social services. Lower-tier municipalities within regions are generally responsible for local roads, fire protection, tax collection, garbage collection, recreation and local land use planning. All municipalities in a region participate in the regional system.

Counties exist only in southern Ontario. Lower-tier municipalities (known as cities, towns, villages, townships) within counties provide the majority of municipal services to their residents. The services provided by county governments are usually limited to arterial roads, health and social services and county land use planning. Local municipalities raise taxes for their own purposes, as well as for upper-tier and school board purposes.

Generally, membership of the upper-tier council comprises representatives from the lower tiers, although heads of council can be directly elected.

Single-tier municipalities exist across Ontario and include separated municipalities that are located within a county but are not part of the county for municipal purposes (e.g. City of Windsor, Town of Smiths Falls, Township of Pelee). Single-tier municipalities also include all northern municipalities (e.g. City of Thunder Bay, Town of Blind River, Township of Cockburn Island). Single-tier municipalities also include those former counties or regional municipalities that have amalgamated into single-tier municipalities (e.g. Municipality of Chatham-Kent, County of Prince Edward, County of Brant, City of Kawartha Lakes, City of Toronto, City of Hamilton, City of Ottawa, City of Greater Sudbury, Haldimand County, Norfolk County). Single-tier municipalities have responsibilities for their residents.

The more populated areas are incorporated into municipalitites; only 40,000 people (not including aboriginal peoples on reserves) live in areas not incorporated as municipalities. Services in the northern regions have been structured to optimize efficiencies in service delivery. District Social Service Administration Boards deliver core services in social assistance, child care and social housing, and may also provide optional health services, land ambulances and public health. Some services in a limited number of unincorporated areas are provided by local service boards and local roads which are funded by the province.

Under the Municipal Elections Act, local government elections are held on the fourth Monday in October, for a four-year term (2010, 2014, etc.). The preliminary list of electors is compiled by the Municipal Property Assessment Corporation from assessment and other data. The Municipal Elections Act provides for alternative methods of voting, including touch screen, vote by mail, vote by telephone, and internet voting.

Reproduced with the permission of Natural Resources Canada 2011, courtesy of the Atlas of Canada.

Ontario

Counties & Municipal Districts in Ontario

Brant
P.O. Box 160
26 Park Ave.
Burford, ON N0E 1A0
Tel: 519-449-2451; *Fax:* 519-449-2454
brant@county.brant.on.ca
www.brant.ca
Other Information: Toll Free Phone: 1-888-250-2297
Municipal Type: County
Incorporated: Jan. 1, 1999 *Area:* 843.1 sq km
Population in 2006: 34,415
Provincial Electoral District(s): Brant
Federal Electoral District(s): Brant
Next Election: Oct. 2014 (4 year terms)
Ron Eddy, Mayor
Steve Schmitt, Councillor, Ward(s): 1
John Wheat, Councillor, Ward(s): 1
Roy Haggart, Councillor, Ward(s): 2
Shirley Simons, Councillor, Ward(s): 2
Cliff Atfield, Councillor, Ward(s): 3
Murray Powell, Councillor, Ward(s): 3
Robert Chambers, Councillor, Ward(s): 4
Kevin Hodge, Councillor, Ward(s): 4
Brian Coleman, Councillor, Ward(s): 5
Joan Gatward, Councillor, Ward(s): 5
Jayne Carman, Clerk & Coordinator, Council Committee
Don Glassford, Chief Administrative Officer
Heather Mifflin, Treasurer
Fran Bell, Director, Corporate Services
Cynthia Compeau, Director, Public Works
David Johnston, Director, Development Services
Paul Boissonneault, Fire Chief
Kathy Ballantyne, Manager, Parks & Facilities
Alex Davidson, Manager, Water Division
Lee Robinson, Manager, Infrastructure Services
Ed Sharp, Manager, Environmental Services
Mike Tout, Manager, Roads Operations

Bruce
P.O. Box 70
30 Park St.
Walkerton, ON N0G 2V0
Tel: 519-881-1291; *Fax:* 519-881-1619
www.brucecounty.on.ca
Municipal Type: County
Area: 4,079.17 sq km
Population in 2006: 65,349
Next Election: Oct. 2014 (4 year terms)
Mike Smith, Warden & Councillor, Ward(s): Saugeen Shores
J. Wayne Jamieson, Chief Administrative Officer
wjamieson@brucecounty.on.ca
Paul Eagleson, Councillor, Ward(s): Arran-Elderslie
Bettyanne Cobean, C.M.O., Clerk-Treasurer, Corporate Services
bcobean@brucecounty.on.ca
Bill Goetz, Councillor, Ward(s): South Bruce
Doug Harris, Director, Human Resources
Milt McIver, Councillor, Ward(s): Northern Bruce Peninsula
Chris LaForest, Director, Planning
Terry Sanderson, Director, Social Services & Social Housing
Larry Kraemer, Councillor, Ward(s): Kincardine
John Close, Councillor, Ward(s): South Bruce Peninsula
Doug Smith, Director, Emergency Services
Mitch Twolan, Councillor, Ward(s): Huron-Kinloss
Brian Knox, County Engineer
David Inglis, Councillor, Ward(s): Brockton

Dufferin
51 Zina St.
Orangeville, ON L9W 1E5
Tel: 519-941-2816; *Fax:* 519-941-4565
info@dufferincounty.on.ca; treasury@dufferincounty.on.ca
www.dufferincounty.on.ca
Other Information: Toll-Free Phone: 1-877-941-6991
Municipal Type: County
Incorporated: Jan. 24, 1881 *Area:* 1,485.58 sq km
Population in 2006: 54,436
Next Election: Oct. 2014 (4 year terms)
Warren Maycock, Warden & Councillor, Ward(s): Orangeville
warden@dufferincounty.on.ca
Pam Hillock, Clerk & Director, Corporate Services
clerk@dufferincounty.on.ca
Don MacIver, Councillor, Ward(s): Amaranth
Sonya Pritchard, Chief Administrative Officer
cao@dufferincounty.on.ca
Walter Kolodziechuk, Councillor, Ward(s): Amaranth
Alan Selby, Treasurer
treasurer@dufferincounty.on.ca
John Oosterhof, Councillor, Ward(s): East Luther Grand Valley
Trevor Lewis, Director, Public Works
directorofpublicworks@dufferincounty.on.ca
Bill Hill, Councillor, Ward(s): Melancthon
Michael A. Giles, Chief Building Official
cbo@dufferincounty.on.ca
Darren White, Councillor, Ward(s): Melancthon
Mark Bialkowski, Manager, Human Resources
hr@dufferincounty.on.ca
Ken McGhee, Councillor, Ward(s): Mono
Melissa Kovacs-Reid, Coordinator, Waste Management
wastemgmt@dufferincounty.on.ca
Laura Ryan, Councillor, Ward(s): Mono
Shara Bagnell, Officer, Health & Safety
health&safety@dufferincounty.on.ca
Rhonda Campbell Moon, Councillor, Ward(s): Mulmur
Paul Mills, Councillor, Ward(s): Mulmur
Rob Adams, Councillor, Ward(s): Orangeville
Ken Bennington, Councillor, Ward(s): Shelburne
Ed Crewson, Councillor, Ward(s): Shelburne

Durham
P.O. Box 623
605 Rossland Rd. East
Whitby, ON L1N 6A3
Tel: 905-668-7711; *Fax:* 905-668-9963
info@durham.ca; cishelp@durham.ca (Corporate Information)
www.durham.ca
Other Information: Toll-Free Phone: 1-800-372-1102
Municipal Type: Regional Municipality
Incorporated: Jan. 1, 1974 *Area:* 2,523.15 sq km
Population in 2006: 561,258
Next Election: Oct. 2014 (4 year terms)
Roger Anderson, Regional Chair & Chief Executive Officer, Councillor, Fax: 905-668-1567
chair@durham.ca
Patricia M. Madill, Regional Clerk, Fax: 905-668-9963
clerks@durham.ca
Garry H. Cubitt, M.S.W., Chief Administrative Officer
cao@durham.ca
Shaun Collier, Councillor, Ward(s): Ajax
R. Jim Clapp, Treasurer/Commissioner, Finance Department, Fax: 905-666-6256
Colleen Jordan, Councillor, Ward(s): Ajax
Cliff Curtis, Commissioner, Works Department, Fax: 905-668-2051
works@durham.ca
Debbie Bath, Councillor, Ward(s): Brock
Hugh A. Drouin, Commissioner, Social Services Department, Fax: 905-666-6219
socserv@durham.ca
Alex L. Georgieff, Commissioner, Planning Department, Fax: 905-666-6208
planning@durham.ca
Adrian Foster, Councillor, Ward(s): Clarington
Mary Novak, Councillor, Ward(s): Clarington
Garth S. Johns, Commissioner, Human Resources, Fax: 905-666-3327
Willie Woo, Councillor, Ward(s): Clarington
Robert J. Kyle, Commissioner, Health Department & Medical Officer of Health, Fax: 905-666-3327
health@durham.ca
John R. Aker, Councillor, Ward(s): Oshawa
Pat W. Olive, Commissioner, Economic Development & Tourism 800-413-0017, Fax: 905-666-6228
business@durham.ca; tourism@durham.ca
Bob Chapman, Councillor, Ward(s): Oshawa
Ivan Ciuciura, Director, Durham Emergency Management Office 905-430-2792, Fax: 905-430-8635
demo@durham.ca
Nancy Diamond, Councillor, Ward(s): Oshawa
Sherri Munns-Audet, Director, Corporate Communications, Fax: 905-668-1468
corporatecommunications@durham.ca
Amy England, Councillor, Ward(s): Oshawa
Ted Galinis, General Manager, Durham Region Transit, Fax: 905-666-6193
transit@durham.ca
Tito-Dante Marimpietri, Councillor, Ward(s): Oshawa
John Neal, Councillor, Ward(s): Oshawa
Nester Pidwerbecki, Councillor, Ward(s): Oshawa
Jennifer O'Connell, Councillor, Ward(s): Pickering 1
Bill McLean, Councillor, Ward(s): Pickering 2
Peter Rodrigues, Councillor, Ward(s): Pickering 3
Bobbie Drew, Councillor, Ward(s): Scugog
Jack Ballinger, Councillor, Ward(s): Uxbridge
Lorne Earle Coe, Councillor, Ward(s): Whitby
Joe Drumm, Councillor, Ward(s): Whitby
Don Mitchell, Councillor, Ward(s): Whitby

Elgin
450 Sunset Dr.
St Thomas, ON N5R 5V1
Tel: 519-631-1460; *Fax:* 519-633-7661
www.elgin-county.on.ca
Municipal Type: County
Incorporated: 1852 *Area:* 1,880.84 sq km
Population in 2006: 85,351
Next Election: Oct. 2014 (4 year terms)
Note: Restructuring of the county occurred in 1998.
Dave Mennill, Warden & Councillor, Ward(s): Malahide
Mark G. McDonald, Chief Administrative Officer
mmcdonald@elgin-county.on.ca
Jack Couckuyt, Councillor, Ward(s): Aylmer
Jim Bundschuh, Director, Financial Services
jbundschuh@elgin-county.on.ca
Paul Ens, Councillor, Ward(s): Bayham
Brian Masschaele, Director, Community & Cultural Services
bmasschaele@elgin-county.on.ca
David Marr, Councillor, Ward(s): Central Elgin
Rob Bryce, Director, Human Resources
Bill Walters, Councillor, Ward(s): Central Elgin
Clayton Watters, Director, Engineering Services
Cameron McWilliam, Councillor, Ward(s): Dutton/Dunwich
Jim Jenkins, Councillor, Ward(s): Malahide
James McIntyre, Councillor, Ward(s): Southwold
Bernie Wiehle, Councillor, Ward(s): West Elgin

Essex
360 Fairview Ave. West
Essex, ON N8M 1Y6
Tel: 519-776-6441; *Fax:* 519-776-4455
www.countyofessex.on.ca
Other Information: Planning Department, Fax: 519-776-1253
Municipal Type: County
Incorporated: 1999 *Area:* 1,851.34 sq km
Population in 2006: 393,402
Next Election: Oct. 2014 (4 year terms)
Tom Bain, Warden & Councillor, Ward(s): Lakeshore
tbain@lakeshore.ca
Mary S. Brennan, Clerk & Director, Council Services
Gary McNamara, Deputy Warden & Councillor, Ward(s): Tecumseh
gmcnamara@tecumseh.ca
Brian Gregg, Chief Administrative Officer
Wayne Hurst, Councillor, Ward(s): Amherstburg
519-736-7646
whurst@amherstburg.ca
Robert Maisonville, Director, Corporate Services & Treasurer
Ron Sutherland, Councillor, Ward(s): Amerstburg
519-736-8092
rsutherland@amherstburg.ca
Greg Schlosser, Director, Human Resources
Ron McDermott, Councillor, Ward(s): Essex
519-776-8150
rmcdermott@essex.ca
Bill King, Manager, Planning Services
Richard Meloche, Councillor, Ward(s): Essex
519-776-5726
rmeloche@essex.ca
Tom Bateman, County Engineer
Nelson Santos, Councillor, Ward(s): Kingsville
519-733-9936
nsantos@kingsville.ca
Phillip Berthiaume, Planner, Emergency Measures
Tamara Stomp, Councillor, Ward(s): Kingsville
519-733-5254
stomp@mnsi.net
Al Fazio, Councillor, Ward(s): Lakeshore
519-728-0490
afazio@lakeshore.ca
Ken Antaya, Councillor, Ward(s): LaSalle
mayor@town.lasalle.on.ca
Mark Carrick, Councillor, Ward(s): LaSalle
mcarrick@town.lasalle.on.ca
John Peterson, Councillor, Ward(s): Leamington
519-322-8470
jpaterson@leamington.ca
Charles Wright, Councillor, Ward(s): Leamington
519-324-5455
cwright@leamington.ca
Cheryl Hardcastle, Councillor, Ward(s): Tecumseh
519-817-4864
chardcastle@tecumseh.ca

Frontenac
2069 Battersea Rd., RR#1
Glenburnie, ON K0H 1S0
Tel: 613-548-9400; *Fax:* 613-546-8460
info@frontenaccounty.ca
www.frontenaccounty.ca

Municipal Type: County
Incorporated: Jan. 1, 1998 *Area:* 3,672.49 sq km
Population in 2006: 143,865
Next Election: Oct. 2014 (4 year terms)
Gary Davison, Warden & Councillor, Ward(s): South Frontenac
sfmayor@frontenaccounty.ca
Liz Savill, Chief Administrative Officer & Clerk
Janet Gutowski, Deputy Warden & Councillor, Ward(s): Central Frontenac
Marian Van Bruinessen, Treasurer
John Purden, Councillor, Ward(s): Central Frontenac
Paul Charbonneau, Director, Emergency & Transportation Services & Chief, Paramedics
Denis Doyle, Councillor, Ward(s): Frontenac Islands
David Jones, Councillor, Ward(s): Frontenac Islands
Bud Clayton, Councillor, Ward(s): North Frontenac
John Inglis, Councillor, Ward(s): North Frontenac
John McDougall, Councillor, Ward(s): South Frontenac
Joe Gallivan, Manager, Sustainability Planning
Anne Marie Young, Manager, Economic Development

Grey
County Administration Bldg.
595 Ninth Ave. East
Owen Sound, ON N4K 3E3
Tel: 519-376-2205;
www.greycounty.ca
Other Information: Toll-Free Phone: 1-800-567-4739
Municipal Type: County
Incorporated: Jan. 1, 1852 *Area:* 4,508.12 sq km
Population in 2006: 92,411
Next Election: Oct. 2014 (4 year terms)
Arlene Wright, Warden & Councillor
warden@grey.ca
Sharon Vokes, C.M.O., County Clerk & Director, Council Services
svokes@greycounty.ca
Bob Pringle, Mayor, Councillor, Ward(s): Chatsworth
bob.pringle@grey.ca
Lance Thurston, Chief Administrative Officer
lance.thurston@grey.ca
Terry McKay, Deputy Mayor & Councillor, Ward(s): Chatsworth
terry.mckay@grey.ca
Kevin Weppler, Director, Finance
kevin.weppler@grey.ca
Alan Barfoot, Mayor, Councillor, Ward(s): Georgian Bluffs
alan.barfoot@grey.ca
Barb Fedy, BA, Director, Social Services
barb.fedy@grey.ca
Dwight Burley, Deputy Mayor & Councillor, Ward(s): Georgian Bluffs
dwight.burley@grey.ca
Geoff Hogan, BSc, Director, Information Technology
geoff.hogan@grey.ca
Wayne Fitzgerald, Mayor, Councillor, Ward(s): Grey Highlands
wayne.fitzgerald@grey.ca
Randy Scherzer, BES, MCIP, RPP, Director, Planning & Development
randy.scherzer@grey.ca
Paul McQueen, Deputy Mayor & Councillor, Ward(s): Grey Highlands
paul.mcqueen@grey.ca
Grant McLevy, Director, Human Resources
grant.mclevy@grey.ca; employment@grey.ca
Kathi Maskell, Mayor, Councillor, Ward(s): Hanover
kathi.maskell@grey.ca
Bob White, Deputy Mayor & Councillor, Ward(s): Hanover
bob.white@grey.ca
Francis Richardson, Mayor, Councillor, Ward(s): Meaford
francis.richardson@grey.ca
Harley Greenfield, Deputy Mayor & Councillor, Ward(s): Meaford
harley.greenfield@grey.ca
Deborah Haswell, Mayor, Councillor, Ward(s): Owen Sound
deb.haswell@grey.ca
Arlene Wright, City / County Councillor, Councillor, Ward(s): Owen Sound
arlene.wright@grey.ca
Brian Milne, Mayor, Councillor, Ward(s): Southgate
brian.milne@grey.ca
Norman Jack, Deputy Mayor & Councillor, Ward(s): Southgate
norman.jack@grey.ca
Ellen Anderson, Mayor, Councillor, Ward(s): The Blue Mountains
ellen.anderson@grey.ca
Duncan McKinlay, Deputy Mayor & Councillor, Ward(s): The Blue Mountains
duncan.mckinlay@grey.ca
Kevin Eccles, Mayor, Councillor, Ward(s): West Grey
kevin.eccles@grey.ca
John Bell, Deputy Mayor & Councillor, Ward(s): West Grey
john.bell@grey.ca

Haldimand
Cayuga Administration Bldg.
45 Munsee St. North
Cayuga, ON N0A 1E0
Tel: 905-318-5932; *Fax:* 905-772-3542
www.haldimandcounty.on.ca
Municipal Type: County
Incorporated: Jan. 1, 2001 *Area:* 1,251.58 sq km
Population in 2006: 45,212
Provincial Electoral District(s): Haldimand-Norfolk
Federal Electoral District(s): Haldimand-Norfolk
Next Election: Oct. 2014 (4 year terms)
Ken Hewitt, Mayor
khewitt@haldimandcounty.on.ca
Leroy Bartlett, Councillor, Ward(s): 1
lbartlett@haldimandcounty.on.ca
Fred Morison, Councillor, Ward(s): 2
fmorison@haldimandcounty.on.ca
Craig Grice, Councillor, Ward(s): 3
cgrice@haldimandcounty.on.ca
Tony Dalimonte, Councillor, Ward(s): 4
tdalimonte@haldimandcounty.on.ca
Rob Shirton, Councillor, Ward(s): 5
rshirton@haldimandcounty.on.ca
Lorne Boyko, Councillor, Ward(s): 6
lpboyko@haldimandcounty.on.ca
Evelyn Eichenbaum, Clerk
eeichenbaum@haldimandcounty.on.ca
Donald Boyle, Chief Administrative Officer
dboyle@haldimandcounty.on.ca
Karen General, General Manager, Corporate Services
kgeneral@haldimandcounty.on.ca
Hugh Hanly, General Manager, Community Services
hhanly@haldimandcounty.on.ca
Craig Manley, General Manager, Planning & Economic Development
cmanley@haldimandcounty.on.ca
Paul Mungar, Director, Environemtnal Services & Fleet & Facility Asset Management
pmungar@haldimandcounty.on.ca

Haliburton
P.O. Box 399
11 Newcastle St.
Minden, ON K0M 2K0
Tel: 705-286-1333; *Fax:* 705-286-4829
aballe@county.haliburton.on.ca
www.haliburtoncounty.ca
Other Information: Toll-Free: 1-866-886-8815
Municipal Type: County
Incorporated: Jan. 1, 2001 *Area:* 4,025.27 sq km
Population in 2006: 16,147
Next Election: Oct. 2014 (4 year terms)
Murray Fearrey, Warden & Councillor, Ward(s): Dysart et al
mfearrey@dysartetal.ca
Jim Wilson, County Clerk & Chief Administrative Officer
jwilson@county.haliburton.on.ca
Carol Moffatt, Councillor, Ward(s): Algonquin Highlands
cmoffatt@algonquinhighlands.ca
Liz Danielsen, Councillor, Ward(s): Algonquin Highlands
ldanielsen@algonquinhighlands.ca
Laura Janke, Treasurer
ljanke@county.haliburton.on.ca
Pat Kennedy, Director, Emergency Services
pkennedy@county.haliburton.on.ca
Bill Davis, Councillor, Ward(s): Dysart et al
billdavis@dysartetal.ca
Doug Ray, Director, Public Works
dray@county.haliburton.on.ca
Dave Burton, Councillor, Ward(s): Highlands East
dburton@highlandseast.ca
Robert Smith, Director, Economic Development & Tourism
rsmith@county.haliburton.on.ca
Suzanne Partridge, Councillor, Ward(s): Highlands East
spartridge@highlandseast.ca
Barb Reid, Councillor, Ward(s): Minden Hills
breid@mindenhills.ca
Jane Tousaw, Director, Planning
jtousaw@county.haliburton.on.ca
Cheryl Murdoch, Councillor, Ward(s): Minden Hills
705-286-1701
Roy Haig, Manager, Engineering & 911 Services
rhaig@county.haliburton.on.ca
Jim Young, Manager, Operations
jyoung@county.haliburton.on.ca

Halton
1151 Bronte Rd.
Oakville, ON L6M 3L1
Tel: 905-825-6000; *Fax:* 905-825-9010
accesshalton@halton.ca
www.halton.ca
Other Information: Toll-Free Phone: 1-866-442-5866; TTY: 905-827-9833
Municipal Type: Regional Municipality
Incorporated: Jan. 1, 1974 *Area:* 967.17 sq km
Population in 2006: 439,256
Next Election: Oct. 2014 (4 year terms)
Gary Carr, Regional Chair, Councillor
905-825-6115, Fax: 905-825-8273
gary.carr@halton.ca
Susan Lathan, Regional Clerk & Director, Council Services
regionalclerk@halton.ca; susan.lathan@halton.ca
Rick Goldring, Councillor, Ward(s): Burlington Mayor
Pat Moyle, Chief Administrative Officer
Rick Craven, Councillor, Ward(s): Burlington 1
J.E. MacCaskill, Regional Treasurer & Commissioner, Corporate Services
Marianne Meed Ward, Councillor, Ward(s): Burlington 2
Mark Meneray, Commissioner, Legislative & Planning Services & Corporate Counsel
John Taylor, Councillor, Ward(s): Burlington 3
Robert Nosal, Commissioner & Medical Officer of Health
Jack Dennison, Councillor, Ward(s): Burlington 4
S. Wolfson, Commissioner, Social & Community Services
Paul Sharman, Councillor, Ward(s): Burlington 5
M. Zamojc, Commissioner, Public Works
Blair Lancaster, Councillor, Ward(s): Burlington 6
Rick Bonnette, Councillor, Ward(s): Halton Hills Mayor
Clark Somerville, Councillor, Ward(s): Halton Hills 1 & 2
Jane Fogal, Councillor, Ward(s): Halton Hills 3 & 4
Gordon Krantz, Councillor, Ward(s): Milton Mayor
Tony Lambert, Councillor, Ward(s): Milton 1, 6, 7, 8
Colin Best, Councillor, Ward(s): Milton 2, 3, 4, 5
Rob Burton, Councillor, Ward(s): Oakville Mayor
Alan Johnston, Councillor, Ward(s): Oakville 1
Cathy Duddeck, Councillor, Ward(s): Oakville 2
F. Keith Bird, Councillor, Ward(s): Oakville 3
Allan Elgar, Councillor, Ward(s): Oakville 4
Jeff Knoll, Councillor, Ward(s): Oakville 5
Tom Adams, Councillor, Ward(s): Oakville 6

Hastings
County Administration Bldg.
P.O. Box 4400
235 Pinnacle St.
Belleville, ON K8N 3A9
Tel: 613-966-1319; *Fax:* 613-966-2574
www.hastingscounty.com
Other Information: Toll-Free Phone: 1-800-510-3306
Municipal Type: County
Incorporated: 1850 *Area:* 5,977.64 sq km
Population in 2006: 130,474
Next Election: Oct. 2014 (4 year terms)
Jo-Anne Albert, Warden & Councillor, Ward(s): Tweed
albertj@hastingscounty.com
James Pine, Chief Administrative Officer & Clerk
pinej@hastingscounty.com
Bernice Jenkins, Councillor, Ward(s): Bancroft
Sue Horwood, Treasurer, Director, Finance, Asset Management & Services
Bonnie Adams, Councillor, Ward(s): Carlow/Mayo
Shaune Lightfoot, Director, Human Resources
Owen Ketcheson, Councillor, Ward(s): Centre Hastings
Brian McComb, Director, Planning
Norm Clark, Councillor, Ward(s): Deseronto
Carl Tinney, Councillor, Ward(s): Faraday
Ron Emond, Councillor, Ward(s): Hastings Highlands
Dave Golem, Councillor, Ward(s): Limerick
Bob Sager, Councillor, Ward(s): Madoc
Terry Clemens, Councillor, Ward(s): Marmora & Lake
Rodney Cooney, Councillor, Ward(s): Stirling-Rawdon
Wanda Donaldson, Councillor, Ward(s): Tudor & Cashel
Rick Phillips, Councillor, Ward(s): Tyendinaga
Dan McCaw, Councillor, Ward(s): Wollaston

Huron
1 Court House Sq.
Goderich, ON N7A 1M2
Tel: 519-524-8394; *Fax:* 519-524-2044
huronadmin@huroncounty.ca
www.huroncounty.ca
Other Information: Toll-Free Phone: 1-888-524-8394 (in 519 area)
Municipal Type: County
Area: 3,396.68 sq km

Population in 2006: 59,325
Next Election: Oct. 2014 (4 year terms)
Neil Vincent, Warden & Councillor, Ward(s): North Huron
Barbara Wilson, Clerk
Ben Van Diepenbeek, Councillor, Ward(s): Ashfield-Colborne-Wawanosh
Dave Laurie, Director, Public Works
Neil Rintoul, Councillor, Ward(s): Ashfield-Colborne-Wawanosh
Scott Tousaw, Director, Planning & Development
Paul Klopp, Councillor, Ward(s): Bluewater
Nancy Cameron, Medical Officer of Health
Tyler Hessel, Councillor, Ward(s): Bluewater
Jim Ginn, Councillor, Ward(s): Central Huron
David Jewitt, Councillor, Ward(s): Central Huron
Brian Barnim, Councillor, Ward(s): Central Huron
Deb Shewfelt, Councillor, Ward(s): Goderich
John Grace, Councillor, Ward(s): Goderich
Art Versteeg, Councillor, Ward(s): Howick
Bernie MacLellan, Councillor, Ward(s): Huron East
Joe Steffler, Councillor, Ward(s): Huron East
Bill Siemon, Councillor, Ward(s): Huron East
Paul Gowing, Councillor, Ward(s): Morris-Turnberry
Dave Riach, Councillor, Ward(s): North Huron
George Robertson, Councillor, Ward(s): South Huron
Jim Dietrich, Councillor, Ward(s): South Huron
David Frayne, Councillor, Ward(s): South Huron

Lambton

P.O. Box 3000
789 Broadway St.
Wyoming, ON N0N 1T0
Tel: 519-845-0801; *Fax:* 519-845-3160
www.lambtononline.com
Other Information: Toll-Free Phone: 1-866-324-6912
Municipal Type: County
Incorporated: 1853 *Area:* 3,001.7 sq km
Population in 2006: 128,204
Next Election: Oct. 2014 (4 year terms)
Steve Arnold, Warden & Councillor, Ward(s): St. Clair
sarnold1@rogers.blackberry.net
Ronald G. Van Horne, Chief Administrative Officer
ron.vanhorne@county-lambton.on.ca
Anne Marie Gillis, Councillor, Ward(s): Sarnia
sarcouncillor@gmail.com
Andrew Taylor, Acting General Manager, Public Health Services
Don McGugan, Councillor, Ward(s): Brooke-Alvinston
jdmcgugan@hotmail.com
Jim Kutyba, P.Eng., General Manager, Infrastructure & Development Services
jim.kutyba@county-lambton.on.ca
William (Bill) Bilton, Councillor, Ward(s): Dawn-Euphemia
mayor@dawneuphemia.on.ca
Jim Burns, Councillor, Ward(s): Enniskillen
jim.burns@county-lambton.on.ca
Robert Tremain, General Manager, Cultural Services
robert.tremain@county-lambton.on.ca
Bill Weber, Councillor, Ward(s): Lambton Shores
bweber@lambtonshores.ca
Elizabeth Davis-Dagg, Councillor, Ward(s): Lambton Shores
edavis-dagg@lambtonshores.ca
Jason Cole, P.Eng., Manager, Public Works
jason.cole@county-lambton.on.ca
Ian Veen, Councillor, Ward(s): Oil Springs
ianveen1@hotmail.com
John McCharles, Councillor, Ward(s): Petrolia
johnnyremax@bellnet.ca
Lonny Napper, Deputy Warden & Councillor, Ward(s): Plympton-Wyoming
lnapper@xcelco.on.ca
Dick Kirkland, Councillor, Ward(s): Point Edward
dkirkland@villageofpointedward.com
Mike Bradley, Councillor, Ward(s): Sarnia
mayor@sarnia.ca
David Boushy, Councillor, Ward(s): Sarnia
d.boushy@cogeco.ca
Jim Foubister, Councillor, Ward(s): Sarnia
jfoubister1@cogeco.ca
Bev MacDougall, Councillor, Ward(s): Sarnia
bevmacdougall@ebtech.net
Peter Gilliland, Councillor, Ward(s): St. Clair
pgillila@rivernet.net
Todd Case, Councillor, Ward(s): Warwick
cases@execulink.com

Lanark

County Administration Bldg.
P.O. Box 37
99 Christie Lake Rd.
Perth, ON K7H 3E2
Tel: 613-267-4200; *Fax:* 613-267-2964
info@county.lanark.on.ca
www.county.lanark.on.ca
Other Information: Toll-Free Phone: 1-888-952-6275
Municipal Type: County
Incorporated: Jan. 1st 1998 *Area:* 2,979.14 sq km
Population in 2006: 63,785
Next Election: Oct. 2014 (4 year terms)
Bill Dobson, Councillor, Ward(s): Montague
bdobson@ripnet.com
Sharon Mousseau, Warden & Councillor, Ward(s): Beckwith
Cathie Ritchie, Clerk
clerk@county.lanark.on.ca
Richard Kidd, Councillor, Ward(s): Beckwith Township
rkidd@ripnet.com
Peter Wagland, Chief Administrative Officer
cao@county.lanark.on.ca
Kurt Greaves, Treasurer & Director, Finance
Wendy Leblanc, Councillor, Ward(s): Carleton Place
wendyjleblanc@gmail.com
Ed Sonnenburg, Councillor, Ward(s): Carleton Place
e.sonnenburg@rogers.com
Aubrey Churchill, Councillor, Ward(s): Drummond/North Elmsley
achurchill@storm.ca
Lisa Crosbie-Larmon, Director, Human Resources
Gail Code, Councillor, Ward(s): Drummond/North Elmsley
gmcconnell@ripnet.com
Nancy Green, Director, Social Services
Peter McLaren, Councillor, Ward(s): Lanark Highlands
p.mclarenfarms@sympatico.ca
Sam Law, Director, Information Technology
Brian Stewart, Councillor, Ward(s): Lanark Highlands
brian_stewart@sympatico.ca
John Levi, Councillor, Ward(s): Mississippi Mills
johnlevi.mm@gmail.com
Val Wilkinson, Councillor, Ward(s): Mississippi Mills
vwilkinson@storm.ca
Pat Dolan, Councillor, Ward(s): Montague
pdolan.montague@bell.net
John Fenik, Councillor, Ward(s): Perth
jfenik@cogeco.ca
John Gemmell, Councillor, Ward(s): Perth
jgemmell2@cogeco.ca
Keith Kerr, Councillor, Ward(s): Tay Valley Township
kmkk@ripnet.com
Susan Freeman, Councillor, Ward(s): Tay Valley Township
susan@cysh.ca

Lennox & Addington

P.O. Box 1000
97 Thomas St. East
Napanee, ON K7R 3S9
Tel: 613-354-4883; *Fax:* 613-354-3112
www.lennox-addington.on.ca
Municipal Type: County
Area: 2,776.48 sq km
Population in 2006: 40,542
Next Election: Oct. 2014 (4 year terms)
Henry Hogg, Warden & Councillor, Ward(s): Addington Highlands
613-336-0227
warden@lennox-addington.on.ca
Larry Keech, Chief Administrative Officer & Clerk
lkeech@lennox-addington.on.ca
Bill Cox, Councillor, Ward(s): Addington Highlands
613-336-8491
Stephen Fox, Director, Financial & Physical Services
sfox@lennox-addington.on.ca
Bill Bishop, Director, Human Resources
bbishop@lennox-addington.on.ca
Brian Elo-Shepherd, Director, Social Services
Roger Cole, Councillor, Ward(s): Greater Napanee
613-354-7634
Gordon Schermerhorn, Councillor, Ward(s): Greater Napanee
613-354-0429
Mary Anne Evans, Director, Information Services
mevans@lennox-addington.on.ca
Bill Lowry, Councillor, Ward(s): Loyalist
613-583-2412
Mark Schjerning, Chief, Emergency Services
Ric Bresee, Councillor, Ward(s): Loyalist
613-634-5544
Stephen Paul, Manager, Economic Development
Doug Bearance, Councillor, Ward(s): Stone Mills
613-375-8874
Eric Smith, Councillor, Ward(s): Stone Mills
613-379-2366

Middlesex

399 Ridout St. North
London, ON N6A 2P1
Tel: 519-434-7321; *Fax:* 519-434-0638
www.middlesex.ca
Municipal Type: County
Area: 3,317.15 sq km
Population in 2006: 422,333
Next Election: Oct. 2014 (4 year terms)
Joanne Vanderheyden, Warden & Councillor, Ward(s): Thames Centre
519-434-7321
Kathy Bunting, Clerk
David Bolton, Councillor, Ward(s): Adelaide Metcalfe
Bill Rayburn, Chief Administrative Officer
Paul Hodgins, Councillor, Ward(s): Lucan Biddulph
Jim Gates, Treasurer
Al Edmondson, Councillor, Ward(s): Middlesex Centre
Sally Bennett, Director, Social Services
Clare Bloomfield, Councillor, Ward(s): Middlesex Centre
Steve Evans, Director, Planning & Economic Development
Don Whipway, Councillor, Ward(s): North Middlesex
Neal Roberts, Director, Emergency Services
Chuck Hall, Councillor, Ward(s): North Middlesex
Chris Traini, County Engineer
Doug Reycraft, Councillor, Ward(s): Southwest Middlesex
Doug Spettigue, Human Resource Officer
Vance Blackmore, Councillor, Ward(s): Southwest Middlesex
John Trott, Woodlands Conservation Officer & Weed Inspector
Brad Richards, Councillor, Ward(s): Strathroy Caradoc
Jim Maudsley, Councillor, Ward(s): Thames Centre
Marcel Meyer, Councillor, Ward(s): Thames Centre

Muskoka

70 Pine St.
Bracebridge, ON P1L 1N3
Tel: 705-645-2231; *Fax:* 705-645-5319
info@muskoka.on.ca
www.muskoka.on.ca
Other Information: Toll-Free Phone: 1-800-461-4210 (In 705 area code)
Municipal Type: Regional Municipality
Incorporated: Jan. 1, 1971 *Area:* 3,890.24 sq km
Population in 2006: 57,563
Next Election: Oct. 2014 (4 year terms)
John Klinck, District Chair & Councillor, Ward(s): Gravenhurst
jklinck@muskoka.on.ca
Debbie Crowder, District Clerk
Jim Green, Chief Administrative Officer
Steven Clement, Councillor, Ward(s): Bracebridge
Stephen Cairns, Commissioner, Finance & Corporate Services
Lori-Lynn Giaschi-Pacini, Councillor, Ward(s): Bracebridge
Tony White, Commissioner, Engineering & Public Works
705-645-6764
Graydon Smith, Councillor, Ward(s): Bracebridge
Marg French, Commissioner, Planning Economic Development
Rick Williams, Commissioner, Community Services
705-645-2100
Scott Young, Deputy Chair & Councillor, Ward(s): Bracebridge
Geoff Bache, Director, Environmental Services
Larry Braid, Councillor, Ward(s): Georgian Bay
Terri Burton, Director, Emergency Services
Mike Kennedy, Councillor, Ward(s): Georgian Bay
Paul Wiancko, Councillor, Ward(s): Georgian Bay
Anna Landry, Director, Human Resources
alandry@muskoka.on.ca
Paisley Donaldson, Councillor, Ward(s): Gravenhurst
Herman Clemens, Director, Water & Sewer Operations
Sandy Cairns, Councillor, Ward(s): Gravenhurst
Bob Colhoun, Councillor, Ward(s): Gravenhurst
Rosemary King, Councillor, Ward(s): Gravenhurst
Claude Doughty, Councillor, Ward(s): Huntsville
Scott Aitchison, Councillor, Ward(s): Huntsville
Fran Coleman, Councillor, Ward(s): Huntsville
Brian Thompson, Councillor, Ward(s): Huntsville
Bob Young, Councillor, Ward(s): Lake of Bays
Shane Baker, Councillor, Ward(s): Lake of Bays
Bob Lacroix, Councillor, Ward(s): Lake of Bays
Alice Murphy, Councillor, Ward(s): Muskoka Lakes
Allen Edwards, Councillor, Ward(s): Muskoka Lakes
Phil Harding, Councillor, Ward(s): Muskoka Lakes
Ruth-Ellen Nishikawa, Councillor, Ward(s): Muskoka Lakes

Niagara

P.O. Box 1042
2201 St. David's Rd.
Thorold, ON L2V 4T7
Tel: 905-685-1571; *Fax:* 905-687-4977
www.niagararegion.ca
Other Information: Toll-Free Phone: 1-800-263-7215; TTY: 905-984-3613
Municipal Type: Regional Municipality
Incorporated: Jan. 1, 1970 *Area:* 1,854.17 sq km
Population in 2006: 427,421
Next Election: Oct. 2014 (4 year terms)
Gary Burroughs, Regional Chair & Councillor, Ward(s): Niagara-on-the-Lake
Kevin Bain, Regional Clerk
905-685-4225
Douglas Martin, Councillor, Ward(s): Fort Erie
905-871-1600
Michael Trojan, Chief Administrative Officer
John Teal, Councillor, Ward(s): Fort Erie
905-871-5796
Gord Lockyer, Treasurer & Director, Financial Management & Reporting
Bob Bentley, Councillor, Ward(s): Grimsby
905-945-9634
Brian Hutchings, Commissioner, Corporate Services
Debbie M. Zimmerman, Councillor, Ward(s): Grimsby
905-945-9516
Cathy Cousins, Acting Commissioner, Community Services
Bill Hodgson, Councillor, Ward(s): Lincoln
905-562-4464
Patrick Robson, Commissioner, Integrated Community Planning
Mark Bylsma, Councillor, Ward(s): Lincoln
905-562-0064
Valerie Jaeger, Commissioner, Public Health & Medical Officer of Health
Jim Diodati, Councillor, Ward(s): Niagara Falls
905-356-7521
Ken Bothers, Commissioner, Public Works
Barbara Greenwood, Councillor, Ward(s): Niagara Falls
905-358-7226
Andrew Pollock, Director, Waste Management Services
Bart Meaves, Councillor, Ward(s): Niagara Falls
289-241-3785
Denise Papaiz, Senior Manager, Corporate Communications
905-685-4225
Selina Volpeti, Councillor, Ward(s): Niagara Falls
905-358-0333
Dave Eke, Councillor, Ward(s): Niagara-on-the-Lake
905-468-7320
Dave Lepp, Councillor, Ward(s): Niagara on the Lake
905-468-2980
Dave Augustyn, Councillor, Ward(s): Pelham
905-892-2607
Brian Baty, Councillor, Ward(s): Pelham
905-892-5317
Vance Badawey, Councillor, Ward(s): Port Colborne
905-835-2900
David Barrick, Councillor, Ward(s): Port Colborne
905-328-5126
Brian McMullan, Councillor, Ward(s): St Catharines
905-688-5600
Alan Caslin, Councillor, Ward(s): St Catharines
289-407-0137
Brian Heit, Councillor, Ward(s): St Catharines
905-935-8377
Ronna Katzman, Councillor, Ward(s): St Catharines
905-688-1993
Andrew Petrowski, Councillor, Ward(s): St Catharines
289-241-6098
Tim Rigby, Councillor, Ward(s): St Catharines
905-328-8508
D. Bruce Timms, Councillor, Ward(s): St Catharines
905-934-6816
Ted Luciani, Councillor, Ward(s): Thorold
905-227-8733
Henry D'Angela, Councillor, Ward(s): Thorold
905-227-8298
April Jeffs, Councillor, Ward(s): Wainfleet
905-834-9052
Barry Sharpe, Councillor, Ward(s): Welland
905-735-1700
Cindy Forster, Councillor, Ward(s): Welland
905-714-7999
George Marshall, Councillor, Ward(s): Welland
905-734-4851
Douglas Joyner, Councillor, Ward(s): West Lincoln
905-957-4926

Norfolk

50 Colborne St. South
Simcoe, ON N3Y 4N5
Tel: 519-426-5870; *Fax:* 519-426-8573
www.norfolkcounty.on.ca
Other Information: Delhi Customer Service Ctr., Phone: 519-582-2100
Municipal Type: County
Incorporated: Jan. 1, 2001 *Area:* 1,606.91 sq km
Population in 2006: 62,563
Provincial Electoral District(s): Haldimand-Norfolk
Federal Electoral District(s): Haldimand-Norfolk
Next Election: Oct. 2014 (4 year terms)
Dennis Travale, Mayor
dennis.travale@norfolkcounty.ca
Betty Chanyi, Councillor, Ward(s): 1
betty.chanyi@norfolkcounty.ca
Roger Geysens, Councillor, Ward(s): 2
roger.geysens@norfolkcounty.ca
Michael J. Columbus, Councillor, Ward(s): 3
michael.columbus@norfolkcounty.ca
Jim Oliver, Councillor, Ward(s): 4
jim.oliver@norfolkcounty.ca
Peter Black, Councillor, Ward(s): 5
peter.black@norfolkcounty.ca
Charlie Luke, Councillor, Ward(s): 5
charlie.luke@norfolkcounty.ca
John Wells, Councillor, Ward(s): 6
john.wells@norfolkcounty.ca
Harold Sonnenberg, Councillor, Ward(s): 7
harold.sonnenberg@norfolkcounty.ca
Beverley D. Wood, Clerk & Manager, Council Services
bev.wood@norfolkcounty.ca
Keith Robicheau, County Manager
keith.robicheau@norfolkcounty.ca
John Ford, Treasurer & Manager, Financial Services
john.ford@norfolkcounty.ca
Christopher D. Baird, CET, CMMIII, Ec.D., General Manager, Planning & Economic Development
chris.baird@norfolkcounty.ca
Eric R. D'Hondt, P.Eng., General Manager, Public Works & Environmental Services, Fax: 519-582-4571
eric.dhondt@norfolkcounty.ca
Frank Gelinas, General Manager, Corporate Services
frank.gelinas@norfolkcounty.ca
Kevin Lichach, General Manager, Community Services
Patti Moore, General Manager, Health & Social Services
patti.moore@haldimand-norfolk.org
Bob Fields, Manager, Environmental Services
bob.fields@norfolkcounty.ca
John Hamilton, Manager, Engineering
john.hamilton@norfolkcounty.ca
Marlene L. Ireland, Manager, Fleets & Facilities
marlene.ireland@norfolkcounty.ca
Terry Dicks, Fire Chief
519-426-4115, Fax: 519-426-4140
terry.dicks@norfolkcounty.ca

Northumberland

555 Courthouse Rd.
Cobourg, ON K9A 5J6
Tel: 905-372-3329; *Fax:* 905-372-1746
www.northumberlandcounty.ca
Other Information: Toll-Free Phone: 1-800-354-7050
Municipal Type: County
Area: 1,902.97 sq km
Population in 2006: 80,963
Next Election: Oct. 2014 (4 year terms)
Mark Lovshin, Warden & Councillor, Ward(s): Hamilton
lovshinm@northumberlandcounty.ca
Diane Cane, CMO, County Clerk
caned@northumberlandcounty.ca
Dalton McDonald, Councillor, Ward(s): Alnwick/Haldimand
mcdonaldd@northumberlandcounty.ca
Bill Pyatt, Chief Administrative Officer
pyattb@northumberlandcounty.ca
Mark Walas, Councillor, Ward(s): Brighton
walasm@northumberlandcounty.ca
Jennifer Moore, Treasurer & Director, Finance
moorej@northumberlandcounty.ca
Gil Brocanier, Councillor, Ward(s): Cobourg
BrocanierG@northumberlandcounty.ca
James Rogers, By-Law Officer, Forest Conservation
705-799-2470
Marc Coombs, Councillor, Ward(s): Cramahe
coombsm@northumberlandcounty.ca
Ken Stubbings, Coordinator, Emergency Management
stubbingsk@northumberlandcounty.ca
Linda Thompson, Councillor, Ward(s): Hamilton
mayor@porthope.ca
Hector Macmillan, Councillor, Ward(s): Trent Hills
macmillanh@northumberlandcounty.ca

Peel

70 Peel Centre Dr.
Brampton, ON L6T 4B9
Tel: 905-791-7800; *Fax:* 905-791-7871
info@peelregion.ca
www.peelregion.ca
Other Information: Toll-Free Phone: 1-888-919-7800
Municipal Type: Regional Municipality
Incorporated: Oct. 15, 1973 *Area:* 1,242.40 sq km
Population in 2006: 1,159,405
Next Election: Oct. 2014 (4 year terms)
Emil Kolb, Regional Chair & Councillor
905-791-7800, Fax: 905-791-2567
Carol Reid, Regional Clerk
David Szwarc, Chief Administrative Officer
Susan Fennell, Mayor & Councillor, Ward(s): Brampton
susan.fennell@brampton.ca
Norma Trim, Chief Financial Officer & Commissioner, Corporate Services
Elaine Moore, Councillor, Ward(s): Brampton 1 & 5
elaine.moore@brampton.ca
Kent Gillespie, Commissioner, Employee & Business Services
Paul Palleschi, Councillor, Ward(s): Brampton 2 & 6
paul.palleschi@brampton.ca
Dan Labrecque, Commissioner, Public Works
Janette Smith, Commissioner, Health Services
John Sanderson, Councillor, Ward(s): Brampton 3 & 4
john.sanderson@brampton.ca
Janet Menard, Commissioner, Human Services
Sandra Hames, Councillor, Ward(s): Brampton 7 & 8
sandra.hames@brampton.ca
Gael Miles, Councillor, Ward(s): Brampton 7 & 8
gael.miles@brampton.ca
David Mowat, Medical Officer of Health
John Sprovieri, Councillor, Ward(s): Brampton 9 & 10
john.sprovieri@brampton.ca
Marolyn Morrison, Mayor, Ward(s): Caledon
marolyn.morrison@caledon.ca
Arvin Prasad, Director, Planning Policy & Research
Richard Paterak, Councillor, Ward(s): Caledon 1
richard.paterak@caledon.ca
Norman Lee, Director, Waste Management
Allan Thompson, Councillor, Ward(s): Caledon 2
allan.thompson@caledon.ca
Richard Whitehead, Councillor, Ward(s): Caledon 3 & 4
r.whitehead@sympatico.ca
Patti Foley, Councillor, Ward(s): Caledon 5
patti.foley@caledon.ca
Hazel McCallion, Mayor & Councillor, Ward(s): Mississauga
mayor@mississauga.ca
Jim Tovey, Councillor, Ward(s): Mississauga 1
jim.tovey@mississauga.ca
Patricia Mullin, Councillor, Ward(s): Mississauga 2
pat.mullin@mississauga.ca
Chris Fonseca, Councillor, Ward(s): Mississauga 3
chris.fonseca@mississauga.ca
Frank Dale, Councillor, Ward(s): Mississauga 4
frank.dale@mississauga.ca
Ron Starr, Councillor, Ward(s): Mississauga 6
ron.starr@mississauga.ca
Nando Iannicca, Councillor, Ward(s): Mississauga 7
nando.iannicca@mississauga.ca
Katie Mahoney, Councillor, Ward(s): Mississauga 8
katie.mahoney@mississauga.ca
Pat Saito, Councillor, Ward(s): Mississauga 9
pat.saito@mississauga.ca
Sue McFadden, Councillor, Ward(s): Mississauga 10
sue.mcfadden@mississauga.ca
George Carlson, Councillor, Ward(s): Mississauga 11
george.carlson@mississauga.ca

Perth

Courthouse
1 Huron St.
Stratford, ON N5A 5S4
Tel: 519-271-0531; *Fax:* 519-271-6265
www.perthcounty.ca
Municipal Type: County
Incorporated: Jan. 1850 *Area:* 2,218.41 sq km
Population in 2006: 74,344
Next Election: Oct. 2014 (4 year terms)
Note: Restructuring occurred in Jan. 1998.
Julie Behrns, Warden & Councillor, Ward(s): North Perth
Kerri Ann O'Rourke, Clerk
Bill Arthur, Chief Administrative Officer
barthur@perthcounty.ca
Vince Judge, Councillor, Ward(s): North Perth
519-291-3877

Renato Pullia, Treasurer & Director, Corporate Services
rpullia@perthcounty.ca
Meredith Schneider, Councillor, Ward(s): North Perth
519-343-2849
Matt Ash, Director, Public Works
mash@perthcounty.ca
Ian Forrest, Councillor, Ward(s): Perth East
519-595-4031
Dave Hanly, Director, Planning & Development
dhanly@perthcounty.ca
Bob McMillan, Councillor, Ward(s): Perth East
519-656-2839
Linda Rockwood, Director, Emergency Medical Services
lrockwood@perthcounty.ca
Rhonda Ehgoetz, Councillor, Ward(s): Perth East
519-393-6888
Cliff Eggleton, Manager, EMS Operations
ceggleton@perthcounty.ca
Robert Wilhelm, Councillor, Ward(s): Perth South
519-225-2304
Ann McKnight Duralia, Manager, Human Resources
amcknight@perthcounty.ca
James Aitcheson, Councillor, Ward(s): Perth South
519-393-5298
Walter McKenzie, Councillor, Ward(s): West Perth
519-348-4236
Bill French, Councillor, Ward(s): West Perth
519-348-8749

Peterborough

County Court House
470 Water St.
Peterborough, ON K9H 3M3
Tel: 705-743-0380; *Fax:* 705-876-1730
www.county.peterborough.on.ca
Other Information: Toll-Free Phone: 1-800-710-9586
Municipal Type: County
Area: 3,805.71 sq km
Population in 2006: 133,080
Next Election: Oct. 2014 (4 year terms)
James Jones, Warden & Councillor, Ward(s): Douro-Dummer
dumnews@nexicom.net
Sally Saunders, Clerk
ssaunders@county.peterborough.on.ca
Douglas Pearcy, Councillor, Ward(s): Asphodel-Norwood
dpearcy@accel.net
Gary King, Chief Administrative Officer & Deputy Clerk
gking@county.peterborough.on.ca
Joseph Crowley, Councillor, Ward(s): Asphodel-Norwood
jwcrowley2010@gmail.com
John Butler, Treasurer
jbutler@county.peterborough.on.ca
John Fallis, Councillor, Ward(s): Cavan Monaghan
jbfallis@nexicom.net
Chris Bradley, Director, Public Works
cbradley@county.peterborough.on.ca
Scott McFadden, Councillor, Ward(s): Cavan Monaghan
smcfadden@cavanmonaghan.net
Patti Kraft, Director, Human Resources
pkraft@county.peterborough.on.ca
Bryan Weir, Director, Planning
bweir@county.peterborough.on.ca
Sheridan Graham, General Manager, Strategic Services & Corporate Projects
sgraham@county.peterborough.on.ca
Karl Moher, Councillor, Ward(s): Douro-Dummer
kmoher@nexicom.net
Laurie Westaway, Manager, Environmental Services
lwestaway@county.peterborough.on.ca
Janet Clarkson, Councillor, Ward(s): Galway-Cavendish & Harvey
gallery@baysideboutique.com
Bill Linnen, Manager, Operations
blinnen@county.peterborough.on.ca
Ron Windover, Councillor, Ward(s): Galway-Cavendish & Harvey
windover@bell.net
Bob English, Chief, Emergency Medical Services (EMS)
benglish@county.peterborough.on.ca
Ronald Gerow, Councillor, Ward(s): Havelock-Belmont-Methuen
ron.gerow@sympatico.ca
Andy Sharpe, Councillor, Ward(s): Havelock-Belmont-Methuen
2andysharpe@gmail.com
Mark Cross, Specialist, Waste Diversion Operations
mcross@county.peterborough.on.ca
Jim Whelan, Councillor, Ward(s): North Kawartha
reeve@northkawartha.on.ca
Barry Rand, Councillor, Ward(s): North Kawartha
dreeve@northkawartha.on.ca
David Nelson, Councillor, Ward(s): Otonabee-South Monaghan
dnelson@nexicom.net
Joe Taylor, Councillor, Ward(s): Otonabee-South Monaghan
jtaylor@osmtownship.ca
Mary Smith, Councillor, Ward(s): Smith-Ennismore-Lakefield
mjsmith@peterboro.net
Andy Mitchell, Councillor, Ward(s): Smith-Ennismore-Lakefield
mmitchell12@sympatico.ca

Prince Edward

332 Main St.
Picton, ON K0K 2T0
Tel: 613-476-2148; *Fax:* 613-476-8356
council@pecounty.on.ca
www.pecounty.on.ca
Municipal Type: County
Incorporated: Jan. 1, 1998 *Area:* 1,050.14 sq km
Population in 2006: 25,496
Provincial Electoral District(s): Prince Edward-Hastings
Federal Electoral District(s): Prince Edward-Hastings
Next Election: Oct. 2014 (4 year terms)
Peter Mertensn, Mayor
pmertens@pecounty.on.ca
Bev Campbell, Councillor, Ward(s): 1 - Picton
bcampbell@pecounty.on.ca
Brian Marisett, Councillor, Ward(s): 1 - Picton
bmarisett@pecounty.on.ca
Barry Turpin, Councillor, Ward(s): 2 - Bloomfield
bturpin@pecounty.on.ca
Jim Dunlop, Councillor, Ward(s): 3 - Wellington
jdunlop@pecounty.on.ca
Janice Maynard, Councillor, Ward(s): 4 - Ameliasburgh
jmaynard@pecounty.on.ca
Dianne O'Brien, Councillor, Ward(s): 4 - Ameliasburgh
dobrien@pecounty.on.ca
Nick Nowitski, Councillor, Ward(s): 4 - Ameliasburgh
nnowitski@pecounty.on.ca
Jamie Forrester, Councillor, Ward(s): 5 - Athol
jforrester@pecounty.on.ca
Heather Campbell, Councillor, Ward(s): 6 - Hallowell
hcampbell@pecounty.on.ca
Keith MacDonald, Councillor, Ward(s): 6 - Hallowell
kmacdonald@pecounty.on.ca
Alec Lunn, Councillor, Ward(s): 7 - Hillier
alunn@pecounty.on.ca
Robert Quaiff, Councillor, Ward(s): 8 - North Marysburgh
rquaiff@pecounty.on.ca
Barbara Proctor, Councillor, Ward(s): 9 - South Marysburgh
bproctor@pecounty.on.ca
Kevin Gale, Councillor, Ward(s): 10 - Sophiasburgh
kgale@pecounty.on.ca
Terry Shortt, Councillor, Ward(s): 10 - Sophiasburgh
tshortt@pecounty.on.ca
Victoria Leskie, Clerk
vleskie@pecounty.on.ca
Gerry Murphy, Acting Chief Administrative Officer & Commissioner, Planning Services
gmurphy@pecounty.on.ca
James Hepburn, Treasurer
jhepburn@pecounty.on.ca
Barry Braun, Commissioner, Recreation, Parks, & Culture Department
bbraun@pecounty.on.ca
Robert McAuley, Commissioner, Public Works Department
rmcauley@pecounty.on.ca
Susan Turnbull, Commissioner, Corporate Services & Finance
sturnbull@pecounty.on.ca
Kimberly Pierce, Manager, Human Resources, Corporate Services & Finance
kpierce@pecounty.on.ca
Scott Manlow, Fire Chief
smanlow@pecounty.on.ca

Renfrew

9 International Dr.
Pembroke, ON K8A 6W5
Tel: 613-735-7288; *Fax:* 613-735-2081
info@countyofrenfrew.on.ca
www.countyofrenfrew.on.ca
Other Information: Toll-Free Phone: 1-800-273-0183
Municipal Type: County
Incorporated: June 8, 1861 *Area:* 7,403.46 sq km
Population in 2006: 97,545
Next Election: Oct. 2014 (4 year terms)
Bob Sweet, Warden & Councillor, Ward(s): Petawawa
warden@countyofrenfrew.on.ca
Jim Hutton, Chief Administrative Officer & Clerk
Raye-Anne Briscoe, Councillor, Ward(s): Admaston/Bromley
613-432-2885
James D. Kutschke, CA, Treasurer & Deputy Clerk
jkutschke@countyofrenfrew.on.ca
Walter Stack, Councillor, Ward(s): Arnprior
613-623-4231
Bruce Beakley, Director, Human Resources
Jennifer Murphy, Councillor, Ward(s): Bonnechere Valley
613-628-3101
Dave Darch, Director, Public Works & Engineering
Norm Lentz, Councillor, Ward(s): Brudenell, Lyndoch, & Raglan
613-758-2061
Michael Nolan, Director, Emergency Services
Dave Thompson, Councillor, Ward(s): Deep River
613-584-2000
Jeff Muzzi, Manager, Forestry Services
613-735-3204
jmuzzi@countyofrenfrew.on.ca
Peter Emon, Councillor, Ward(s): Greater Madawaska
613-752-2222
Tammy Stewart, Councillor, Ward(s): Head, Clara & Maria
613-586-2526
Robert A. Johnston, Councillor, Ward(s): Horton
613-432-6271
Janice Visneskie, Councillor, Ward(s): Killaloe, Hagarty & Richards
613-757-2300
Dick Rabishaw, Councillor, Ward(s): Laurentian Hills
613-584-3114
Jack Wilson, Councillor, Ward(s): Laurentian Valley
613-735-6291
David Shulist, Councillor, Ward(s): Madawaska Valley
613-756-2747
Mary Campbell, Councillor, Ward(s): McNab/Braeside
613-623-5756
Harold Weckworth, Councillor, Ward(s): North Algona Wilberforce
613-628-2080
Audrey R. Green, Councillor, Ward(s): Renfrew
613-432-4848

Simcoe

County of Simcoe Administration Centre
1110 Hwy. 26
Midhurst, ON L0L 1X0
Tel: 705-735-6901; *Fax:* 705-719-4626
info@simcoe.ca
www.simcoe.ca
Other Information: Toll-Free Phone: 1-800-263-3199
Municipal Type: County
Incorporated: Jan. 1, 1850 *Area:* 4,840.56 sq km
Population in 2006: 422,204
Next Election: Oct. 2014 (4 year terms)
Cal Patterson, Warden & Councillor, Ward(s): Wasaga Beach
cal.patterson@simcoe.ca
Brenda Clark, Clerk
brenda.clark@simcoe.ca
Mary Small Brett, Councillor, Ward(s): Adjala-Tosorontio
mary.smallbrett@simcoe.ca
Mark Aitken, Chief Administrative Officer
Tom Walsh, Councillor, Ward(s): Adjala-Tosorontio
tom.walsh@simcoe.ca
Craig Elliott, General Manager, Finance & Administration
craig.elliott@simcoe.ca
Doug White, Councillor, Ward(s): Bradford West Gwillimbury
doug.white@simcoe.ca
Rick Newlove, General Manager, Engineering, Planning & Environment
rick.newlove@simcoe.ca
Rob Keffer, Councillor, Ward(s): Bradford West Gwillimbury
rob.keffer@simcoe.ca
Jane Sinclair, General Manager, Health & Emergency Services
jane.sinclair@simcoe.ca
Ken Ferguson, Councillor, Ward(s): Clearview
ken.ferguson@simcoe.ca
Terry Talon, General Manager, Social & Community Services
terry.talon@simcoe.ca
Alicia Savage, Councillor, Ward(s): Clearview
alicia.savage@simcoe.ca
Dawn Hipwell, Director, Procurement, Fleet & Property
dawn.hipwell@simcoe.ca
Sandra Cooper, Councillor, Ward(s): Collingwood
sandra.cooper@simcoe.ca
Jim Hunter, Director, Transportation Construction
jim.hunter@simcoe.ca
Rick Lloyd, Councillor, Ward(s): Collingwood
rick.lloyd@simcoe.ca
Bryan MacKell, Director, Planning, Development & Tourism
bryan.macKell@simcoe.ca
Terry Dowdall, Councillor, Ward(s): Essa
terry.dowdall@simcoe.ca
Sandie Macdonald, Councillor, Ward(s): Essa
sandie.macdonald@simcoe.ca
Michael Moffatt, Director, Human Resources
michael.moffatt@simcoe.ca
Barb Baguley, Councillor, Ward(s): Innisfil
barb.baguley@simcoe.ca

Dan Davidson, Councillor, Ward(s): Innisfil
dan.davidson@simcoe.ca
Gord McKay, Councillor, Ward(s): Midland
gord.mckay@simcoe.ca
Stephan Kramp, Councillor, Ward(s): Midland
stephan.kramp@simcoe.ca
Mike MacEachern, Councillor, Ward(s): New Tecumseth
mike.maceachern@simcoe.ca
Rick Milne, Councillor, Ward(s): New Tecumseth
rick.milne@simcoe.ca
Harry Huges, Councillor, Ward(s): Oro-Medonte
harry.hughes@simcoe.ca
Ralph Hough, Councillor, Ward(s): Oro-Medonte
ralph.hough@simcoe.ca
Gerry Marshall, Councillor, Ward(s): Penetanguishene
gerry.marshall@simcoe.ca
Patrick Marion, Councillor, Ward(s): Penetanguishene
patrick.marion@simcoe.ca
Bill Duffy, Councillor, Ward(s): Ramara
bill.duffy@simcoe.ca
Basil Clarke, Councillor, Ward(s): Ramara
basil.clarke@simcoe.ca
Mike Burkett, Councillor, Ward(s): Severn
mike.burkett@simcoe.ca
Judith Cox, Councillor, Ward(s): Severn
judith.cox@simcoe.ca
Linda Collins, Councillor, Ward(s): Springwater
linda.collins@simcoe.ca
Tony Hope, Councillor, Ward(s): Springwater
dan.mclean@simcoe.ca
Scott Warnock, Councillor, Ward(s): Tay
scott.warnock@simcoe.ca
Bill Rawson, Councillor, Ward(s): Tay
bill.rawson@simcoe.ca
Ray Millar, Councillor, Ward(s): Tiny
ray.millar@simcoe.ca
George Lawrence, Councillor, Ward(s): Tiny
george.lawrence@simcoe.ca
David Foster, Councillor, Ward(s): Wasaga Beach
david.foster@simcoe.ca

Waterloo

Regional Administration Bldg.
P.O. Box 9051 C
150 Frederick St.
Kitchener, ON N2G 4J3
Tel: 519-575-4400; *Fax:* 519-575-4481
regionalinquiries@region.waterloo.on.ca
www.region.waterloo.on.ca
Other Information: Phone, Regional Councillors: 519-575-4581
Municipal Type: Regional Municipality
Incorporated: Jan. 1, 1973 *Area:* 1,368.64 sq km
Population in 2006: 478,121
Next Election: Oct. 2014 (4 year terms)
Ken Seiling, Regional Chair & Councillor
519-575-4585, Fax: 519-575-4440
kseiling@regionofwaterloo.ca
Kris Fletcher, Regional Clerk & Director, Council & Administrative Services
Jane Brewer, Councillor, Ward(s): Cambridge
jbrewer@regionofwaterloo.ca
Mike Murray, Chief Administrative Officer
Doug Craig, Councillor, Ward(s): Cambridge
dcraig@regionofwaterloo.ca
Larry Ryan, Chief Financial Officer
Claudette Millar, Councillor, Ward(s): Cambridge
cmillar@regionofwaterloo.ca
Rob Horne, Commissioner, Planning, Housing & Community Services
Tom Galloway, Councillor, Ward(s): Kitchener
tgalloway@regionofwaterloo.ca
Thomas Schmidt, Commissioner, Transportation & Environmental Services
Jean Haalboom, Councillor, Ward(s): Kitchener
jhaalboom@regionofwaterloo.ca
Michael Schuster, Commissioner, Social Services
Geoff Lorentz, Councillor, Ward(s): Kitchener
glorentz@regionofwaterloo.ca
Penny Smiley, Commissioner, Human Resources
Jim Wideman, Councillor, Ward(s): Kitchener
jwideman@regionofwaterloo.ca
Gary Sosnoski, Commissioner, Corporate Resources
Carl Zehr, Councillor, Ward(s): Kitchener
czhr@regionofwaterloo.ca
Jon Arsenault, Director, Waste Management
Rob Deutschmann, Councillor, Ward(s): North Dumfries
rdeutschmann@regionofwaterloo.ca
Debra Arnold, Director, Legal Services & Regional Solicitor
Brenda Halloran, Councillor, Ward(s): Waterloo
bhalloran@regionofwaterloo.ca
Lucille Bish, Director, Community Services
Jane Mitchell, Councillor, Ward(s): Waterloo
jmitchell@regionofwaterloo.ca
Amanda Kutler, Director, Community Planning
Sean Strickland, Councillor, Ward(s): Waterloo
sstrickland@regionofwaterloo.ca
Eric Gillespie, Director, Transit Services
Ross Kelterborn, Councillor, Ward(s): Wellesley
rkelterborn@regionofwaterloo.ca
Nancy Kodousek, Director, Water Services
Les Armstrong, Councillor, Ward(s): Wilmot
lesarmstrong@regionofwaterloo.ca
Ellen McGaghey, Director, Facilities Management & Fleet Services
Todd Cowan, Councillor, Ward(s): Woolwich
tcowan@regionofwaterloo.ca
Graham Vincent, Director, Transportation Planning
Liana Nolan, Medical Officer of Health

Wellington

74 Woolwich St.
Guelph, ON N1H 3T9
Tel: 519-837-2600; *Fax:* 519-837-1909
finance@county.wellington.on.ca (Treasury)
www.wellington.ca
Other Information: Toll-Free Phone: 1-800-663-0750
Municipal Type: County
Incorporated: Jan. 1, 1852 *Area:* 2,656.66 sq km
Population in 2006: 200,425
Next Election: Oct. 2014 (4 year terms)
Note: The council of the County of Wellington is comprised of the mayors of its seven municipalities, plus nine elected county ward councillors.
Chris White, Warden & Councillor, Ward(s): Guelph/Eramosa
warden@wellington.ca
Donna Bryce, County Clerk
donnab@wellington.ca
Joanne Ross-Zuj, Councillor, Ward(s): Centre Wellington
Lou Maieron, Councillor, Ward(s): Erin
Scott Wilson, Chief Administrative Officer
scottw@wellington.ca
Craig Dyer, Treasurer
craigd@county.wellington.on.ca
Bruce Whale, Councillor, Ward(s): Mapleton
Andrea Lawson, Administrator, Human Resources, Fax: 519-837-8882
andreal@county.wellington.on.ca
George Bridge, Councillor, Ward(s): Minto
Heather Burke, Director, Housing
heatherb@wellington.ca; wghsinfo@wellington.ca
Dennis Lever, Councillor, Ward(s): Puslinch
Gary Cousins, Director, Planning, Fax: 519-823-1694
garyc@wellington.ca
Raymond Trout, Councillor, Ward(s): Wellington North
Luisa Della Croce, Director, Child Care Services
luisad@wellington.ca
Mark MacKenzie, Councillor, Ward(s): 1
John Green, Councillor, Ward(s): 2
Linda Dickson, Coordinator, Community Emergency Management
519-846-8058, Fax: 519-846-8482
lindad@wellington.ca
Gary Williamson, Ward(s): 3
Rob Johnson, Coordinator, Forestry
Linda White, Ward(s): 4
Jean Innes, Councillor, Ward(s): 5
Shawn Watters, Councillor, Ward(s): 6
Don McKay, Councillor, Ward(s): 7
Gordon Tosh, Councillor, Ward(s): 8
Ken Chapman, Councillor, Ward(s): 9

York

17250 Yonge St.
Newmarket, ON L3Y 6Z1
Tel: 905-895-1231; *Fax:* 905-895-1238
info@york.ca; twgeneral@york.ca (Transportation & Works)
www.york.ca
Other Information: Toll-Free Phone: 1-877-464-9675
Municipal Type: Regional Municipality
Incorporated: Jan. 1, 1971 *Area:* 1,761.84 sq km
Population in 2006: 892,712
Next Election: Oct. 2014 (4 year terms)
Bill Fisch, Regional Chair & Councillor
regional.chair@york.ca
Denis Kelly, Regional Clerk
regionalclerk@york.ca
Geoff Dawe, Councillor, Ward(s): Aurora
Bruce Macgregor, Chief Administrative Officer
Virginia Hackson, Councillor, Ward(s): East Gwillimbury
Bill Hughes, Regional Treasurer & Commissioner, Finance
Robert Grossi, Councillor, Ward(s): Georgina
Jim Davidson, Commissioner, Corporate Services
Danny Wheeler, Councillor, Ward(s): Georgina
Kathleen Llewellyn-Thomas, Commissioner, Transportation Services
Steve Pellegrini, Councillor, Ward(s): King
Erin Mahoney, Commissioner, Environmental Services
Frank Scarpitti, Councillor, Ward(s): Markham
Adelina Urbanski, Commissioner, Community & Health Services
Jack Heath, Councillor, Ward(s): Markham
John Walker, Acting Commissioner, Planning & Development Services
Jim Jones, Councillor, Ward(s): Markham
Patrick Casey, Director, Corporate Communications
patrick.casey@york.ca
Gordon Landon, Councillor, Ward(s): Markham
Karen Close, Director, Human Resources
Joe Li, Councillor, Ward(s): Markham
Karim Kurji, Medical Officer of Health & Director, Public Health Programs
A.J. (Tony) Van Bynen, Councillor, Ward(s): Newmarket
John Taylor, Councillor, Ward(s): Newmarket
David Barrow, Councillor, Ward(s): Richmond Hill
Brenda Hogg, Councillor, Ward(s): Richmond Hill
Vito Spatafora, Councillor, Ward(s): Richmond Hill
Maurizio Bevilacqua, Councillor, Ward(s): Vaughan
Michael Di Biase, Councillor, Ward(s): Vaughan
Deb Schulte, Councillor, Ward(s): Vaughan
Gino Rosati, Councillor, Ward(s): Vaughan
Wayne Emmerson, Councillor, Ward(s): Whitchurch-Stouffville

Major Municipalities in Ontario

Ajax

65 Harwood Ave. South
Ajax, ON L1S 2H9
Tel: 905-683-4550; *Fax:* 905-683-1061
contactus@townofajax.com; info@townofajax.com
www.townofajax.com
Other Information: Corporate Communications: 905-619-2529, ext. 3362
Municipal Type: City
Incorporated: 1955 *Area:* 67.09 sq km
County or District: Durham Regional Municipality; *Population in 2006:* 90,167
Provincial Electoral District(s): Ajax-Pickering
Federal Electoral District(s): Ajax-Pickering
Next Election: Oct. 2014 (4 year terms)
Steve Parish, Mayor
905-619-2529, Fax: 905-683-9450
steve.parish@townofajax.com
Brian J. Skinner, Chief Administrative Officer
brian.skinner@townofajax.com
Shaun Collier, Regional Councillor, Ward(s): 1 & 2
shaun.collier@townofajax.com
Rob Ford, Director, Finance & Treasurer
rob.ford@townofajax.com
Colleen Jordan, Regional Councillor, Ward(s): 3 & 4
colleen.jordan@townofajax.com
John Fleck, Director, Human Resource Services
905-619-2529
Marilyn Crawford, Councillor, Ward(s): 1
Dave Meredith, Director, Operations & Environmental Services
operations@townofajax.com
Renrick Ashby, Councillor, Ward(s): 2
renrick.ashby@townofajax.com
Joanne Dies, Councillor, Ward(s): 3
joanne.dies@townofajax.com
Pat Brown, Councillor, Ward(s): 4
pat.brown@townofajax.com

Amherstburg

271 Sandwich St. South
Amherstburg, ON N9V 2A5
Tel: 519-736-0012; *Fax:* 519-736-5403
www.amherstburg.ca
Other Information: TTY: 519-736-9860
Municipal Type: City
Incorporated: 1851 *Area:* 185.65 sq km
County or District: Essex; *Population in 2006:* 21,748
Provincial Electoral District(s): Essex
Federal Electoral District(s): Essex
Next Election: Oct. 2014 (4 year terms)
Note: Incorporated as a town in 1878.
Wayne Hurst, Mayor
519-736-7646
whurst@amherstburg.ca
Brenda Percy, Clerk/Manager of Council & Legislative Services
bpercy@amherstburg.ca
Pam Malott, Chief Administrative Officer
pmalott@amherstburg.ca

Carolyn Davies, Councillor
cdavies@amherstburg.ca
Lou Zarlenga, P.Eng, Manager, Public Works
John Sutton, Councillor
jsutton@amherstburg.ca
Antonietta Giofu, P.Eng, Engineer, Environmental Services
Bart DiPasquale, Councillor
bdipasquale@amherstburg.ca
Dwayne Grondin, Superintendent, Sewer & Watermain
Diane Pouget, Councillor
dpouget@amherstburg.ca
Todd Hewitt, Superintendent, Roads
Robert (Bob) Pillon, Councillor
rpillon@amherstburg.ca
Ron Sutherland, Councillor
rsutherland@amherstburg.ca

Aurora
P.O. Box 1000
100 John Way West
Aurora, ON L4G 6J1
Tel: 905-727-1375; *Fax:* 905-726-4738
info@aurora.ca
www.aurora.ca
Other Information: Alternative Phone: 905-727-3123; TTY: 905-726-4766
Municipal Type: City
Area: 49.62 sq km
County or District: York Regional Municipality; *Population in 2006:* 47,629
Provincial Electoral District(s): Newmarket-Aurora
Federal Electoral District(s): Newmarket-Aurora
Next Election: Oct. 2014 (4 year terms)
Geoff Dawe, Mayor
mayor@aurora.ca
John D. Leach, Town Clerk & Director, Customer & Legislative Services
905-727-3123
jleach@aurora.ca
John Abel, Councillor
jabel@aurora.ca
Neil Garbe, Chief Administrative Officer
ngarbe@aurora.ca
Chris Ballard, Councillor
chris@chrisballard.ca
Evelyn Buck, Councillor
ebuck@aurora.ca
Wendy Gaertner, Councillor
wgaertner@aurora.ca
John Gallo, Councillor
jgallo@aurora.ca
Sandra Humphries, Councillor
shumfryes@aurora.ca
Paul Pirri, Councillor
ppirri@aurora.ca
Michael Thompson, Councillor
mthompson@aurora.ca

Barrie
P.O. Box 400
70 Collier St.
Barrie, ON L4M 4T5
Tel: 705-726-4242; *Fax:* 705-739-4243
cityinfo@barrie.ca
www.barrie.ca; www.facebook.com/cityofbarrie
Other Information: TTY: 705-792-7910; Council Info: 705-739-4204
Municipal Type: City
Incorporated: 1853 *Area:* 76.99 sq km
County or District: Simcoe; *Population in 2006:* 128,430
Provincial Electoral District(s): Barrie
Federal Electoral District(s): Barrie
Next Election: Oct. 2014 (4 year terms)
Jeff Lehman, Mayor
705-792-7900
officeofthemayor@barrie.ca
Dawn McAlpine, City Clerk
705-739-4204
Bonnie J. Ainsworth, Councillor, Ward(s): 1
bainsworth@barrie.ca
Jon Babulic, Chief Administrative Officer
Lynn M. Strachan, Councillor, Ward(s): 2
lstrachan@barrie.ca
Ed Archer, CMA, General Manager, Corporate Services
Doug Shipley, Councillor, Ward(s): 3
dshipley@barrie.ca
Richard Forward, M.Sc., P.Eng., General Manager, Infrastructure, Development & Culture Division
Barry J. Ward, Councillor, Ward(s): 4
bward@barrie.ca
J.W. (Jim) Sales, General Manager, Community Operations
Peter Silveira, Councillor, Ward(s): 5
psilveira@barrie.ca
G. Allison, Director, Building Services & Chief Building Official
Michael Prowse, Councillor, Ward(s): 6
mprowse@barrie.ca
Sandy Coulter, B.Sc., Acting Director, Operations - Water, Wastewater & Environmental
John Brassard, Councillor, Ward(s): 7
jbrassard@barrie.ca
Dave Friary, Acting Director, Operations - Roads, Parks & Fleet Operations
Jennifer Robinson, Councillor, Ward(s): 8
psilveira@barrie.ca
Hany Kirolos, Director, Strategy & Economic Development
Brian H. Jackson, Councillor, Ward(s): 9
bjackson@barrie.ca
Wendell McArthur, Director, Engineering
Alexander Nuttall, Councillor, Ward(s): 10
anuttall@barrie.ca
Debbie McKinnon, Director, Finance
Barbara Roth, Director, Leisure, Transit & Facilities
J. Taylor, Director, Planning Services Department
John Lynn, Fire Chief
Bruce L. Griffin, Community Emergency Planner

Belleville
City Hall
169 Front St.
Belleville, ON K8N 2Y8
Tel: 613-968-6481; *Fax:* 613-967-3206
www.city.belleville.on.ca
Other Information: TTY: 613-967-3768
Municipal Type: City
Area: 246.76 sq km
County or District: Hastings; *Population in 2006:* 48,821
Provincial Electoral District(s): Prince Edward-Hastings
Federal Electoral District(s): Prince Edward-Hastings
Next Election: Oct. 2014 (4 year terms)
Neil R. Ellis, Mayor
613-967-3267, Fax: 613-967-3209
mayor.ellis@city.belleville.on.ca
Julie C. Oram, City Clerk & Director, Corporate Services
613-967-3271
joram@city.belleville.on.ca
Egerton Boyce, Councillor, Ward(s): 1
councillor.boyce@city.belleville.on.ca
Rick Kester, Chief Administrative Officer
rkester@city.belleville.on.ca
Pat Culhane, Councillor, Ward(s): 1
councillor.culhane@city.belleville.on.ca
Brian Cousins, Director, Finance & Treasurer
bcousins@city.belleville.on.ca
Jodie Jenkins, Councillor, Ward(s): 1
councillor.jenkins@city.belleville.on.ca
Mark Fluhrer, Director, Recreation Culture & Community Services
mfluhrer@city.belleville.on.ca
Tom Lafferty, Councillor, Ward(s): 1
councillor.lafferty@city.belleville.on.ca
Rod Bovay, Acting Director, Engineering & Development Services
rbovay@city.belleville.on.ca
Jack Miller, Councillor, Ward(s): 1
councillor.miller@city.belleville.on.ca
John Martin, Director, Human Resources
jmartin@city.belleville.on.ca
Garnet Thompson, Councillor, Ward(s): 1
councillor.thompson@city.belleville.on.ca
Brad Wilson, Director, Environmental & Operational Services
bwilson@city.belleville.on.ca
Taso Christopher, Councillor, Ward(s): 2
councillor.christopher@city.belleville.on.ca
Ted Marecak, Chief Building Official
tmarecak@city.belleville.on.ca
Jackie Denyes, Councillor, Ward(s): 2
councillor.denyes@city.belleville.on.ca
Rhéaume Chaput, Fire Chief
rchaput@city.belleville.on.ca
Peter Hodgson, Manager, Transit Operations
phodgson@city.belleville.on.ca
Art MacKay, Manager, Policy Planning
amackay@city.belleville.on.ca
Pat McNulty, Manager, Transportation
pmcnulty@city.belleville.on.ca
Richard Reinert, Manager, Environmental Services (Water Operations)
rreinert@city.belleville.on.ca

Bracebridge
1000 Taylor Ct.
Bracebridge, ON P1L 1R6
Tel: 705-645-5264; *Fax:* 705-645-1262
www.bracebridge.ca
Other Information: Fax, Public Works: 705-645-7525
Municipal Type: City
Area: 617.42 sq km
County or District: Muskoka Dist. Mun.; *Population in 2006:* 15,652
Provincial Electoral District(s): Parry Sound-Muskoka
Federal Electoral District(s): Parry Sound-Muskoka
Next Election: Oct. 2014 (4 year terms)
Graydon Smith, Mayor
gsmith@bracebridge.ca
Lori McDonald, Clerk
lmcdonald@bracebridge.ca
Steve Clement, District Councillor
sclement@bracebridge.ca
John R. Sisson, Chief Administrative Officer
jsisson@bracebridge.ca
Liam Cragg, Councillor
lcragg@bracebridge.ca
Carol Wakefield, Treasurer
cwakefield@bracebridge.ca
Lori-Lynn Giaschi-Pacini, District Councillor
lgiaschi-pacini@bracebridge.ca
Kim Horrigan, Director, Development Services
khorrigan@bracebridge.ca
Rick Maloney, Councillor
rmaloney@bracebridge.ca
Cheryl Kelley, Director, Economic Development
ckelley@bracebridge.ca
Barb McMurray, Councillor
bmcmurray@bracebridge.ca
Ron Walton, Municipal Engineer
rwalton@bracebridge.ca
Mark Quemby, Councillor
mquemby@bracebridge.ca
Murray Medley, Fire Chief
firechief@bracebridgefire.com
Gerry Tryon, Councillor
gtryon@bracebridge.ca
Scott Young, District Councillor
syoung@bracebridge.ca

Bradford West Gwillimbury
Administration Centre
P.O. Box 100
100 Dissette St.
Bradford, ON L3Z 2A7
Tel: 905-775-5366; *Fax:* 905-775-0153
www.town.bradfordwestgwillimbury.on.ca
Municipal Type: City
Incorporated: 1857 *Area:* 201.03 sq km
County or District: Simcoe; *Population in 2006:* 24,039
Provincial Electoral District(s): York-Simcoe
Federal Electoral District(s): York-Simcoe
Next Election: Oct. 2014 (4 year terms)
Note: Incorporated as a town in 1960.
Doug White, Mayor
dwhite@townofbwg.com
Rob Keffer, Deputy Mayor & Councillor
rkeffer@townofbwg.com
Jay Currier, Chief Administrative Officer
jcurrier@townofbwg.com
Raj Sandhu, Councillor, Ward(s): 1
rsandhu@townofbwg.com
Ian Goodfellow, Director, Finance & Treasurer
igoodfellow@townofbwg.com
Del Crake, Councillor, Ward(s): 2
dcrake@townofbwg.com
Debbie Korolnek, Director, Engineering Services
dkorolnek@townofbwg.com
Gary R. Lamb, Councillor, Ward(s): 3
glamb@townofbwg.com
Geoff McKnight, Director, Planning & Development
gmcknight@townofbwg.com
Carl Hordyk, Councillor, Ward(s): 4
chordyk@townofbwg.com
Paul Feehely, Superintendent, Public Works
pfeehely@townofbwg.com
Ron Simpson, Councillor, Ward(s): 5
rsimpson@townofbwg.com
Edward O'Donnell, Supervisor, Water
eodonnell@townofbwg.com
James Leduc, Councillor, Ward(s): 6
jleduc@townofbwg.com
Rick Way, Supervisor, Waste Water
rway@townofbwg.com

Peter Dykie, Jr., Councillor, Ward(s): 7
pdykie@townofbwg.com
Lorne Arscott, Fire Chief
kgallant@townofbwg.com

Brampton

2 Wellington St. West
Brampton, ON L6Y 4R2
Tel: 905-874-2000; *Fax:* 905-874-2119
cityhall@brampton.ca; tourism@brampton.ca (Tourism)
www.brampton.ca
Other Information: E-mail, Economic Development: edo@brampton.ca
Municipal Type: City
Incorporated: Jan. 1, 1974 *Area:* 266.71 sq km
County or District: Peel Reg. Mun.; *Population in 2006:* 433,806
Provincial Electoral District(s): Bramalea-Gore-Malton; Brampton Springdale; Brampton West; Brampton South-Mississauga
Federal Electoral District(s): Bramalea-Gore-Malton; Brampton Springdale; Brampton West; Mississauga-Brampton South
Next Election: Oct. 2014 (4 year terms)
Susan Fennell, Mayor
mayor@brampton.ca
Peter Fay, City Clerk
905-874-2100, Fax: 905-874-2119
cityclerksoffice@brampton.ca
Grant Gibson, City Councillor, Ward(s): 1 & 5
grant.gibson@brampton.ca
Deborah Dubenofsky, City Manager
John Hutton, City Councillor, Ward(s): 2 & 6
john.hutton@brampton.ca
Mo Lewis, Commissioner, Finance
Bob Callahan, City Councillor, Ward(s): 3 & 4
bob.callahan@brampton.ca
John Corbett, Commissioner, Planning, Design & Development
Sandra Hames, City Councillor, Ward(s): 7 & 8
sandra.hames@brampton.ca
Dennis Cutajar, Commissioner, Economic Development & Communications
Vicky Dhillon, City Councillor, Ward(s): 9 & 10
vicky.dhillon@brampton.ca
Jamie Lowery, Commissioner, Community Services
Elaine Moore, Regional Councillor, Ward(s): 1 & 5
elaine.moore@brampton.ca
Tom Mulligan, Commissioner, Works & Transportation
Paul Palleschi, Regional Councillor, Ward(s): 2 & 6
paul.palleschi@brampton.ca
Julian Patteson, Commissioner, Buildings & Property Management
John Sanderson, Regional Councillor, Ward(s): 3 & 4
john.sanderson@brampton.ca
Kathy Zammit, Commissioner, Corporate Services
Gael Miles, Regional Councillor, Ward(s): 7 & 8
gael.miles@brampton.ca
John Sprovieri, Regional Councillor, Ward(s): 9 & 10
john.sprovieri@brampton.ca

Brantford

City Hall
P.O. Box 818
100 Wellington Sq.
Brantford, ON N3T 2M3
Tel: 519-759-4150;
webmaster@brantford.ca
www.brantford.ca
Municipal Type: City
Incorporated: May 31, 1877 *Area:* 72.47 sq km
County or District: Brant; *Population in 2006:* 90,192
Provincial Electoral District(s): Brant
Federal Electoral District(s): Brant
Next Election: Oct. 2014 (4 year terms)
Chris Friel, Mayor
cfriel@brantford.ca
Charlene Touzel, Acting City Clerk
ctouzel@brantford.ca
Larry M. Kings, Councillor, Ward(s): 1
lkings@brantford.ca
Ted Salisbury, Chief Administrative Officer & General Manager, Community Development Services
Jan C. Vander Stelt, Councillor, Ward(s): 1
jvanderstelt@brantford.ca
Greg Dworak, Acting General Manager, Engineering & Operational Services
Vince Bucci, Councillor, Ward(s): 2
vbucci@brantford.ca
John K. Utley, Councillor, Ward(s): 2
jutley@brantford.ca
Dan Temprile, General Manager, Public Health, Safety, & Social Services
Debi Dignan-Rumble, Councillor, Ward(s): 3
ddignan-rumble@brantford.ca
Dan McCreary, Councillor, Ward(s): 3
dmccreary@brantford.ca
Richard Carpenter, Councillor, Ward(s): 4
rcarpenter@brantford.ca
Dave Wrobel, Councillor, Ward(s): 4
dwrobel@brantford.ca
Marguerite Ceschi-Smith, Councillor, Ward(s): 5
mceschi-smith@brantford.ca
David E. Neumann, Councillor, Ward(s): 5
dneumann@brantford.ca

Brighton

P.O. Box 189
35 Alice St.
Brighton, ON K0K 1H0
Tel: 613-475-0670; *Fax:* 613-475-3453
general@brighton.ca
www.brighton.ca
Other Information: Phone, Public Works & Planning: 613-475-1162
Municipal Type: City
Area: 222.52 sq km
County or District: Northumberland; *Population in 2006:* 10,253
Provincial Electoral District(s): Northumberland-Quinte West
Federal Electoral District(s): Northumberland-Quinte West
Next Election: Oct. 2014 (4 year terms)
Mark Walas, Mayor
mayor@brighton.ca
Gayle J. Frost, Chief Administrative Officer
gfrost@brighton.ca
Andrew Drzewiecki, Director, Public Works & Development
adrzewiecki@brighton.ca
Jim Millar, Director, Parks & Recreation
millar@brighton.ca
Linda Widdifield, Director, Finance & Administrative Services
linda@brighton.ca
Lloyd Hutchinson, Fire Chief
lhutchinson@brighton.ca
Craig Kerr, Councillor
ckerr@brighton.ca
John Martinello, Councillor
jmartinello@brighton.ca
Thomas Rittwage, Councillor
trittwage@brighton.ca
Emily Rowley, Councillor
erowley@brighton.ca
Mary Tadman, Councillor
mtadman@brighton.ca
Mike Vandertoorn, Councillor
mvandertoorn@brighton.ca

Brockville

Victoria Bldg.
P.O. Box 5000
1 King St. West
Brockville, ON K6V 7A5
Tel: 613-342-8772; *Fax:* 613-342-8780
info@brockville.com; tourism@brockvillechamber.com
www.brockville.com
Municipal Type: City
Area: 20.74 sq km
County or District: Leeds & Grenville; *Population in 2006:* 21,957
Provincial Electoral District(s): Leeds-Grenville
Federal Electoral District(s): Leeds-Grenville
Next Election: Oct. 2014 (4 year terms)
David L. Henderson, Mayor
themayor@brockville.com
Sandra M. Seale, City Clerk
sseale@brockville.com
Jason Baker, Councillor
jwbaker@rogers.blackberry.net
Bob Casselman, City Manager
bcasselman@brockville.com
David E. Beatty, Councillor
dbeatty@canarm.ca
Donna Cyr, Director, Finance
dcyr@brockville.com
Leigh Z. Bursey, Councillor
leighbursey@gmail.com
Jim Baker, Director, Human Resources
jbaker@brockville.com
Jeffery Earle, Councillor
jearle@brockville.com
Peter Raabe, Director, Environmental Services
praabe@brockville.com
Jane Fullerton, Councillor
jane@mentoringmatters.ca
David C. Paul, Director, Economic Development
dpaul@brockville.com
Larry F. Journal, Councillor
ljournal@cogeco.ca
Maureen Pascoe Merkley, Director, Planning
mpmerkley@brockville.com
Mike Kalivas, Councillor
mkalivas@ripnet.com
Harry Jones, Fire Chief
hjones@brockville.com
David D. LeSueur, Councillor
dlesueur@cogeco.ca
Mary Jane McFall, Councillor
mjm@tmlegal.ca

Burlington

City Hall
P.O. Box 5013
426 Brant St.
Burlington, ON L7R 3Z6
Tel: 905-335-7600; *Fax:* 905-335-7881
cob@burlington.ca
www.burlington.ca
Other Information: Toll-Free Phone: 1-877-213-3609
Municipal Type: City
Incorporated: 1914 *Area:* 185.74 sq km
County or District: Halton Regional Municipality; *Population in 2006:* 164,415
Provincial Electoral District(s): Ancaster-Dundas-Flamborough-Westdale; Burlington; Halton
Federal Electoral District(s): Burlington; Halton; Ancaster-Dundas-Flamborough-Westdale
Next Election: Oct. 2014 (4 year terms)
Note: Incorporated as a city in 1974.
Rick Goldring, Mayor
905-335-7607, Fax: 905-335-7708
mayor@burlington.ca
Kim Phillips, City Clerk
905-335-7698, Fax: 905-335-7881
cityclerks@burlington.ca; phillipsk@burlington.ca
Rick Craven, Councillor, Ward(s): 1
cravenr@burlington.ca
Scott Stewart, Acting City Manager
stewarts@burlington.ca
Marianne Meed Ward, Councillor, Ward(s): 2
meedwardm@burlington.ca
John Taylor, Councillor, Ward(s): 3
taylorj@burlington.ca
Jack Dennison, Councillor, Ward(s): 4
dennisonj@burlington.ca
Paul Sharman, Councillor, Ward(s): 5
sharmanp@burlington.ca
Blair Lancaster, Councillor, Ward(s): 6
lancasterb@burlington.ca

Caledon

Town Hall
6311 Old Church Rd.
Caledon, ON L7C 1J6
Tel: 905-584-2272; *Fax:* 905-584-4325
www.caledon.ca
Other Information: Toll-Free Phone: 1-888-225-3366
Municipal Type: City
Incorporated: Jan. 1, 1974 *Area:* 687.17 sq km
County or District: Peel Regional Municipality; *Population in 2006:* 57,050
Provincial Electoral District(s): Dufferin-Caledon
Federal Electoral District(s): Dufferin-Caledon
Next Election: Oct. 2014 (4 year terms)
Marolyn Morrison, Mayor
marolyn.morrison@caledon.ca
Karen Landry, Town Clerk & Director, Administration
Richard Paterak, Regional Councillor, Ward(s): 1
richard.paterak@caledon.ca
Douglas Barnes, Chief Administrative Officer
Allan Thompson, Regional Councillor, Ward(s): 2
allan.thompson@caledon.ca
Ron Kaufman, Chief Financial Officer, Deputy CAO, & Director, Corporate Services
Richard Whitehead, Regional Councillor, Ward(s): 3 & 4
richard.whitehead@caledon.ca
Craig Campbell, Director, Public Works
public.works@caledon.ca
Patti Foley, Regional Councillor, Ward(s): 5
patti.foley@caledon.ca
Doug Beffort, Area Councillor, Ward(s): 1
doug.beffort@caledon.ca
Glenn Middlebrook, Chief Building Official
glenn.middlebrook@caledon.ca
Gord McClure, Area Councillor, Ward(s): 2
gord.mcclure@caledon.ca

Sara Peckford, Officer, Envrionmental Progress
sara.peckford@caledon.ca
Jeremy Schembri, Coordinator, Energy & Environment
jeremy.schembri@caledon.ca
Nick deBoer, Area Councillor, Ward(s): 3 & 4
nick.deboer@caledon.ca
Rob Mezzapelli, Area Councillor, Ward(s): 5
rob.mezzapelli@caledon.ca

Cambridge
P.O. Box 669
50 Dickson St.
Cambridge, ON N1R 5W8
Tel: 519-623-1340; *Fax:* 519-740-3011
questions@cambridge.ca; csd@cambridge.ca (Community Svs.)
www.cambridge.ca
Other Information: E-mail, Corporate Services: corpserv@cambridge.ca
Municipal Type: City
Incorporated: Jan. 1973 *Area:* 112.86 sq km
County or District: Waterloo Regional Municipality; *Population in 2006:* 120,371
Provincial Electoral District(s): Cambridge
Federal Electoral District(s): Cambridge
Next Election: Oct. 2014 (4 year terms)
Doug Craig, Mayor
mayor@cambridge.ca; council@cambridge.ca
Alex Mitchell, City Clerk
519-740-4680
clerks@cambridge.ca
Donna Reid, City Councillor, Ward(s): 1
reidd@cambridge.ca
Jim King, Chief Administrative Officer
519-740-4683
cao@cambridge.ca
Rick Cowsill, City Councillor, Ward(s): 2
cowsillr@cambridge.ca
Bill Chesney, Fire Chief
Karl Kiefer, City Councillor, Ward(s): 3
kieferk@cambridge.ca
Janet Babcock, Commisssioner, Planning Services
Ben Tucci, City Councillor, Ward(s): 4
tuccib@cambridge.ca
Steven Fairweather, Commisssioner, Corporate Services
Pam Wolf, City Councillor, Ward(s): 5
wolfp@cambridge.ca
George Elliott, Commisssioner, Transportation & Public Works
Gary Price, City Councillor, Ward(s): 6
priceg@cambridge.ca
Kent McVittie, Commisssioner, Community Services
Frank Monteiro, City Councillor, Ward(s): 7
monteirof@cambridge.ca
Nicholas Ermeta, City Councillor, Ward(s): 8
ermetan@cambridge.ca
Jane Brewer, Regional Councillor
bjane@regionofwaterloo.ca
Claudette Millar, Regional Councillor
mclaudette@regionofwaterloo.ca

Clarence-Rockland
1560 Laurier St.
Rockland, ON K4K 1P7
Tel: 613-446-6022; *Fax:* 613-446-1497
www.clarence-rockland.com
Municipal Type: City
Incorporated: Jan. 1, 1998 *Area:* 296.53 sq km
County or District: Prescott & Russell; *Population in 2006:* 20,790
Provincial Electoral District(s): Glengarry-Prescott-Russell
Federal Electoral District(s): Glengarry-Prescott-Russell
Next Election: Oct. 2014 (4 year terms)
Note: Amalgamation of the Town of Rockland and the Township of Clarence.
Marcel Guibord, Mayor
613-446-0240
mguibord@xplornet.com
Monique Ouellet, Clerk
mouellet@clarence-rockland.com
Michel Thivierge, Councillor, Ward(s): 1
Chantal McLean-Leroux, Treasurer
cmcleanleroux@clarence-rockland.com
André Henrie, Councillor, Ward(s): 2
Thérèse Lefaivre, Director, Community Services
tlefaivre@clarence-rockland.com
Bernard Payer, Councillor, Ward(s): 3
Michael Michaud, Director, Planning
mmichaud@clarence-rockland.com
Raymond Serrurier, Councillor, Ward(s): 4
Yves Rivard, Director, By-law Enforcement
yrivard@clarence-rockland.com
Guy Félio, Councillor, Ward(s): 5
Yves Rousselle, Director, Physical Services
yrousselle@clarence-rockland.com
Guy Desjardins, Councillor, Ward(s): 6
Pierre Sabourin, Fire Chief
psabourin@clarence-rockland.com
René Campeau, Councillor, Ward(s): 7
Denis Longpré, Manager, Environment
dlongpre@clarence-rockland.com
Diane Choinière, Councillor, Ward(s): 8

Cobourg
55 King St. West
Cobourg, ON K9A 2M2
Tel: 905-372-4301; *Fax:* 905-372-7421
webmaster@cobourg.ca
www.cobourg.ca
Other Information: Toll-Free Phone: 1-888-262-6874
Municipal Type: City
Area: 22.37 sq km
County or District: Northumberland; *Population in 2006:* 18,210
Provincial Electoral District(s): Northumberland-Quinte West
Federal Electoral District(s): Northumberland-Quinte West
Next Election: Oct. 2014 (4 year terms)
Gil Brocanier, Mayor
gbrocanier@cobourg.ca
Lorraine Brace, Municipal Clerk
lbrace@cobourg.ca
Stephen E. Peacock, P.Eng., Chief Administrative Officer
speacock@cobourg.ca
Stan Frost, Deputy Mayor & Councillor
sfrost@cobourg.ca
Ian Davey, Director, Corporate Services
idavey@cobourg.ca
John Henderson, Councillor
jhenderson@cobourg.ca
Glenn J. McGlashon, Director, Planning & Development Services
gmcglashon@cobourg.ca
Miriam Mutton, Councillor
mmutton@cobourg.ca
Bill Watson, Director, Public Works
bwatson@cobourg.ca
Forrest Rowden, Councillor
frowden@cobourg.ca .
Larry E. Sherwin, Councillor
lsherwin@cobourg.ca
Donna Todd, Councillor
dtodd@cobourg.ca

Collingwood
P.O. Box 157
97 Hurontario St.
Collingwood, ON L9Y 3Z5
Tel: 705-445-1030; *Fax:* 705-445-2448
www.collingwood.ca
Municipal Type: City
Incorporated: 1858 *Area:* 33.46 sq km
County or District: Simcoe; *Population in 2006:* 17,290
Provincial Electoral District(s): Simcoe-Grey
Federal Electoral District(s): Simcoe-Grey
Next Election: Oct. 2014 (4 year terms)
Sandra Cooper, Mayor
705-445-8451
scooper@collingwood.ca
Sara J. Almas, Clerk
salmas@collingwood.ca
Rick Lloyd, Deputy Mayor & Councillor
rlloyd@collingwood.ca
Kim Wingrove, Chief Administrative Officer
kwingrove@collingwood.ca
Ian Chadwick, Councillor
ichadwick@collingwood.ca
Marjory Leonard, Treasurer
mleonard@collingwood.ca
Sandy Cunningham, Councillor
scunningham@collingwood.ca
Ed Houghton, Executive Director, Public Works
ehoughton@collingwood.ca
Mike Edwards, Councillor
medwards@collingwood.ca
Joe Gardhouse, Councillor
jgardhouse@collingwood.ca
Larry Irwin, Director, Information Technology
lirwin@collingwood.ca
Keith Hull, Councillor
khull@collingwood.ca
Bill Plewes, Chief Building Official & Director, Building Services
bplewes@collingwood.ca
Kevin Lloyd, Councillor
klloyd@collingwood.ca
Nancy Farrer, Director, Planning Services
nfarrer@collingwood.ca
Dale West, Councillor
dwest@collingwood.ca
Trent Elyea, Fire Chief
telyea@collingwood.ca
Donald Green, Manager, Environmental Services
dgreen@collingwood.ca
Wendy Martin, Manager, Parks
wmartin@collingwood.ca

Cornwall
P.O. Box 877
360 Pitt St.
Cornwall, ON K6H 5T9
Tel: 613-932-6252; *Fax:* 613-932-8145
www.cornwall.ca
Municipal Type: City
Incorporated: 1834 *Area:* 61.52 sq km
County or District: Stormont, Dundas & Glengarry; *Population in 2006:* 45,965
Provincial Electoral District(s): Stormont-Dundas-South Glengarry
Federal Electoral District(s): Stormont-Dundas-South Glengarry
Next Election: Oct. 2014 (4 year terms)
Note: Incorporated as a city in 1945.
Bob Kilger, Mayor
mayor@cornwall.ca
Denise Labelle-Gelinas, City Clerk
Denis Carr, Councillor
dcarr@cornwall.ca
Paul Fitzpatrick, Chief Administrative Officer
Bernadette Clément, Councillor
bclement@cornwall.ca
Maureen Adams, General Manager, Financial Services
Maurice Dupelle, Councillor
mdupelle@cornwall.ca
Stephen Alexander, General Manager, Planning, Parks & Recreation Services
Syd Gardiner, Councillor
sgardiner@cornwall.ca
Norm Levac, General Manager, Infrastructure & Municipal Works
Glen Grant, Councillor
gggrant@cornwall.ca
Jean Cousineau, Division Manager, Municipal Works
Elaine MacDonald, Councillor
emacdonald@cornwall.ca
Morris McCormick, Division Manager, Environment
David Murphy, Councillor
dmurphy@cornwall.ca
Len Tapp, Division Manager, Transit
Leslie O'Shaugnessy, Councillor
loshaughnessy@cornwall.ca
Mark Boileau, Manager, Economic Development
André Rivette, Councillor
arivette@cornwall.ca
Myles Cassidy, Fire Chief & Manager, Emergency Services
Denis Thibault, Councillor
dthibault@cornwall.ca
Patrick Carrière, Supervisor, Waste Water Treatment Facility
Owen O'Keefe, Supervisor, Water Purification Plant

East Gwillimbury
19000 Leslie St.
Sharon, ON L0G 1V0
Tel: 905-478-4282; *Fax:* 905-478-2808
town@eastgwillimbury.ca; engineering@eastgwillimbury.ca
www.eastgwillimbury.ca
Other Information: Alternate Fax: 905-478-8545
Municipal Type: City
Incorporated: 1850 *Area:* 245.06 sq km
County or District: York Regional Municipality; *Population in 2006:* 21,069
Provincial Electoral District(s): York-Simcoe
Federal Electoral District(s): York-Simcoe
Next Election: Oct. 2014 (4 year terms)
Virginia Hackson, Mayor
vhackson@eastgwillimbury.ca
Kathleen Foster, Municipal Clerk
kfoster@eastgwillimbury.ca
John Eaton, Councillor
jeaton@eastgwillimbury.ca
Thomas R. Webster, Chief Administrative Officer
twebster@eastgwillimbury.ca
Marlene Johnston, Councillor
mjohnston@eastgwillimbury.ca
Mark Valcic, General Manager, Corporate & Financial Services & Treasurer
mvalcic@eastgwillimbury.ca

Cathy Morton, Councillor
cmorton@eastgwillimbury.ca
Wayne Hunt, General Manager, Community Programs & Infrastructure
whunt@eastgwillimbury.ca
Tara Roy-Diclemente, Councillor
troydiclemente@eastgwillimbury.ca
Don Sinclair, General Manager, Legal & Council Support Services/Town Solicitor
dsinclair@eastgwillimbury.ca
Don Allan, Manager, Engineering Branch
dallan@eastgwillimbury.ca
Carolyn Kellington, Manager, Community Planning & Development Branch
ckellington@eastgwillimbury.ca
Steve Krystal, Manager, Capital Programs & Traffic Engineering Branch
skrystal@eastgwillimbury.ca
Gary Shropshire, Manager, Community Parks & Programs Branch
gshropshire@eastgwillimbury.ca
Tim Gibson, Chief Building Official & Director, Building Approvals & Inspections
tgibson@eastgwillimbury.ca
Christopher Kalimootoo, Director, Engineering & Environmental Services
ckalimootoo@eastgwillimbury.ca
Robin Prentice, Environmental Planner
rprentice@eastgwillimbury.ca

Elliot Lake
45 Hillside Dr. North
Elliot Lake, ON P5A 1X5
Tel: 705-848-2287;
www.cityofelliotlake.com
Municipal Type: City
Area: 698.12 sq km
County or District: Algoma District; *Population in 2006:* 11,549
Provincial Electoral District(s): Algoma-Manitoulin
Federal Electoral District(s): Algoma-Manitoulin-Kapuskasing
Next Election: Oct. 2014 (4 year terms)
Rick Hamilton, Mayor
Lesley Sprague, City Clerk
Al Collett, Councillor
Rob deBortoli, Chief Administrative Officer
Tom Farquhar, Councillor
Dawn Halcrow, Director, Finance
Sandy Finamore, Councillor
Norman Mann, Councillor
Chris Patrie, Councillor
Paul Officer, Fire Chief
Ken Rastin, Councillor

Erin
5684 Wellington Rd., RR#2
Hillsburgh, ON N0B 1Z0
Tel: 519-855-4407; *Fax:* 519-855-4821
council@erin.ca; cao@erin.ca (Town Manager)
www.erin.ca
Other Information: Toll-Free Phone: 1-877-818-2888
Municipal Type: City
Incorporated: 1997 *Area:* 296.98 sq km
County or District: Wellington; *Population in 2006:* 11,148
Provincial Electoral District(s): Wellington-Halton Hills
Federal Electoral District(s): Wellington-Halton Hills
Next Election: Oct. 2014 (4 year terms)
Lou Maieron, Mayor, Fax: 519-833-2492
lou.maieron@erin.ca
Kathryn Ironmonger, Clerk
John Brennan, Councillor
john.brennan@erin.ca
Lisa Hass, Town Manager
Deb Callaghan, Councillor
deb.callaghan@erin.ca
Sharon Marshall, Director, Finance
Barb Tocher, Councillor
barb.tocher@erin.ca
Josie Wintersinger, Councillor
josie.wintersinger@erin.ca
Louise Warn, Administrator, Water Compliance
Dan Callaghan, Fire Chief
Andrew Hartholt, Chief Building Official
Larry Van Wyck, Superintendent, Roads

Essex
33 Talbot St. South
Essex, ON N8M 1A8
Tel: 519-776-7336; *Fax:* 519-776-8811
www.essex.ca
Municipal Type: City
Incorporated: 1883 *Area:* 277.95 sq km
County or District: Essex; *Population in 2006:* 20,032
Provincial Electoral District(s): Essex
Federal Electoral District(s): Essex
Next Election: Oct. 2014 (4 year terms)
Note: Incorporated as a town in 1890. Restructuring occurred in 1999.
Ron McDermott, Mayor
519-776-8150
rmcdermott@essex.ca
Cheryl Bondy, Clerk & Deputy-Treasurer
cbondy@essex.ca
Morley Bowman, Councillor, Ward(s): 1
mbowman@essex.ca
Randy Voakes, Councillor, Ward(s): 1
rvoakes@essex.ca
Wayne Miller, Chief Administrative Officer
wmiller@essex.ca
Donna Hunter, Director, Finance & Administration & Treasurer
dhunter@essex.ca
Richard Meloche, Deputy Mayor & Councillor, Ward(s): 2
rmeloche@essex.ca
Richard Beausoleil, Director, Public Works
rbeausoleil@essex.ca
Bill Baker, Councillor, Ward(s): 3
bbaker@essex.ca
John Scott, Councillor, Ward(s): 3
jscott@essex.ca
Sherry Bondy, Councillor, Ward(s): 4
sbondy@essex.ca
Chris Nepszy, Director, Infastructure & Development
cnepszy@essex.ca
Ed Pillon, Fire Chief
519-776-6476, Fax: 519-776-7171
epillon@essex.ca
Heather Jablonski, Town Planner
hjablonski@essex.ca
Dan Boudreau, Superintendent, Drainage
dboudreau@essex.ca
Andy Graf, Superintendent, Water
agraf@essex.ca

Fort Erie
1 Municipal Centre Dr.
Fort Erie, ON L2A 2S6
Tel: 905-871-1600; *Fax:* 905-871-4022
www.forterie.on.ca
Other Information: Fax, Corporate Services: 905-871-9984
Municipal Type: City
Incorporated: 1857 *Area:* 166.35 sq km
County or District: Niagara Regional Municipality; *Population in 2006:* 29,925
Provincial Electoral District(s): Niagara Falls
Federal Electoral District(s): Niagara Falls
Next Election: Oct. 2014 (4 year terms)
Douglas G. Martin, Mayor
905-871-1600
Carolyn J. Kett, Town Clerk
Stephen Passero, Councillor, Ward(s): 1
H. Schlange, Chief Administrative Officer
Richard Shular, Councillor, Ward(s): 2
Helen Chamberlain, Director, Financial Services
Bob Steckley, Councillor, Ward(s): 3
Richard Brady, Director, Community & Development Services
John Hill, Councillor, Ward(s): 4
Heather Salter, B.E.S., LL.B., Director, Legal & Legislative Services & Town Solicitor
Don Lubberts, Councillor, Ward(s): 5
Ron Tripp, Director, Infrastructure Services
Paul Collard, Councillor, Ward(s): 6
John Teal, Regional Councillor
Larry Coplen, Fire Chief & Coordinator, Community Emergency Management
D. Heyworth, Manager, Land Use Policy

Georgina
Georgina Civic Centre
26557 Civic Centre Rd., RR#2
Keswick, ON L4P 3G1
Tel: 905-476-4301; *Fax:* 905-476-8100
info@georgina.ca; events@georgina.ca
www.georgina.ca
Other Information: Alternative Phones: 905-722-6516; 705-437-2210
Municipal Type: City
Area: 287.72 sq km
County or District: York Reg. Mun.; *Population in 2006:* 42,346
Provincial Electoral District(s): York-Simcoe
Federal Electoral District(s): York-Simcoe
Next Election: Oct. 2014 (4 year terms)
Note: Amalgamation of the Village of Keswick, the Township of Georgina & Village of Sutton.
Robert Grossi, Mayor, Fax: 905-476-1475
rgrossi@georgina.ca
Roland Chénier, A.M.C.T., Town Clerk
rchenier@georgina.ca
Danny Wheeler, Deputy Mayor & Regional Councillor
dwheeler@georgina.ca
Robert Magloughlen, Interim Chief Administrative Officer
rmagloughlen@georgina.ca
Naomi Davison, Councillor, Ward(s): 1
ndavison@georgina.ca
Rebecca Mathewson, C.G.A., Director, Administrative Services
rmathewson@georgina.ca
Phil Craig, Councillor, Ward(s): 2
pcraig@georgina.ca
Harold Lenters, M.Sc.Pl., MCIP, RPP, Director, Planning & Building
hlenters@georgina.ca
Dave Szollosy, Councillor, Ward(s): 3
dszollosy@georgina.ca
Robert Magloughlen, P.Eng., Director, Engineering & Public Works
rmagloughlen@georgina.ca
Ken Hackenbrook, Councillor, Ward(s): 4
khackenbrook@georgina.ca
Bill O'Neill, C.M.M. III, Director, Emergency Services & Fire Chief
boneill@georgina.ca
Brad Smockum, Councillor, Ward(s): 5
bsmockum@georgina.ca
Faye Richardson, Director, Parks & Culture
frichardson@georgina.ca
Claire Marsden, C.H.R.P., C.M.M. I, Manager, Human Resources
cmarsden@georgina.ca

Gravenhurst
3 - 5 Pineridge Gate
Gravenhurst, ON P1P 1Z3
Tel: 705-687-3412; *Fax:* 705-687-7016
reception@gravenhurst.ca
www.gravenhurst.ca
Municipal Type: City
Area: 517.99 sq km
County or District: Muskoka District Municipality; *Population in 2006:* 11,046
Provincial Electoral District(s): Parry Sound-Muskoka
Federal Electoral District(s): Parry Sound-Muskoka
Next Election: Oct. 2014 (4 year terms)
Paisley Donaldson, Mayor
705-689-5659
pdonaldson@gravenhurst.ca
Candace Thwaites, Clerk
D. Weldon, Interim Chief Administrative Officer
Sandy Cairns, District Councillor
sanmar@cogeco.ca
Kenneth Watson, Treasurer
kwatson@gravenhurst.ca
Bob Colhoun, District Councillor
colhoun@muskoka.com
D. Broderick, Manager, Recreation, Community Services, & Centennial Ctr. Ops.
Rosemary King, District Councillor
rosemary@rosemaryking.net
S. Lucas, Manager, Development Services
Heidi Lorenz, Councillor, Ward(s): 1
heidi.lorenz@cogeco.ca
Lola Bratty, Councillor, Ward(s): 2
lola@lolabratty.ca
G. Carelton, Manager, Public Works & Operations
Joe Donoghue, Councillor, Ward(s): 3
shamrocktrailerpark@gmail.com
Randy Jorgensen, Councillor, Ward(s): 4
randy@randyjorgensen.com
Jeff Watson, Deputy Mayor & Councillor, Ward(s): 5
jwatson17@cogeco.ca

Greater Napanee
P.O. Box 97
124 John St.
Napanee, ON K7R 3L4
Tel: 613-354-3351; *Fax:* 613-354-6545
info@greaternapanee.com; roads@greaternapanee.com
www.greaternapanee.com
Other Information: E-mail, Programs: recreation@greaternapanee.com
Municipal Type: City
Area: 459.71 sq km
County or District: Lennox-Addington; *Population in 2006:* 15,400
Provincial Electoral District(s): Lanark-Frontenac-Lennox & Addington

Federal Electoral District(s): Lanark-Frontenac-Lennox & Addington
Next Election: Oct. 2014 (4 year terms)
Gord Schermerhorn, Mayor
613-354-0429
Rebecca Murphy, Clerk & Director, Corporate & Legal Services
rmurphy@greaternapanee.com
Roger Cole, Deputy Mayor & Councillor
613-354-7634
Raymond Callery, Chief Administrative Officer
rcallery@greaternapanee.com
Mark Day, Director, Finance & Treasurer
mday@greaternapanee.com
Michael Schenk, Councillor, Ward(s): 1
Shane Grant, Councillor, Ward(s): 2
Vern Amey, Director, Public Works
vamey@greaternapanee.com
Marg Isbester, Councillor, Ward(s): 3
Bill Pierson, Councillor, Ward(s): 4
Terry Gervais, Fire Chief
tgervais@greaternapanee.com
Kevin Hill, Director, Parks, Recreation & Culture
khill@greaternapanee.com
Shaune Lucas, Councillor, Ward(s): 5
Charles McDonald, Director, Development Services
cmcdonald@greaternapanee.com
Ron Vankoughnet, Supervisor, Roads & Landfill

Greater Sudbury / Grand Sudbury

Tom Davies Square
P.O. Box 5000 A
200 Brady St.
Sudbury, ON P3A 5P3
Tel: 705-671-2489; *Fax:* 705-671-8118
www.greatersudbury.ca
Other Information: Phone, Local Calls: 3-1-1
Municipal Type: City
Incorporated: Jan. 1, 2001 *Area:* 3,200.56 sq km
Population in 2006: 157,857
Provincial Electoral District(s): Nickel Belt; Sudbury
Federal Electoral District(s): Nickel Belt; Sudbury
Next Election: Oct. 2014 (4 year terms)
Marianne Matichuk, Mayor
705-674-4455, Fax: 705-673-3096
mayor@greatersudbury.ca
Angie Hache, City Clerk
705-674-4455, Fax: 705-671-8118
angie.hache@greatersudbury.ca
Joe Cimino, Councillor, Ward(s): 1
joe.cimino@greatersudbury.ca
Doug Nadorozny, Chief Administrative Officer
doug.nadorozny@greatersudbury.ca
Jacques Barbeau, Councillor, Ward(s): 2
jacques.barbeau@greatersudbury.ca
Lorella M. Hayes, B.Comm., CA, Chief Financial Officer & Treasurer
lorella.hayes@greatersudbury.ca
Claude Berthiaume, Councillor, Ward(s): 3
claude.berthiaume@greatersudbury.ca
Greg Clausen, P. Eng, General Manager, Infrastructure Services
greg.clausen@greatersudbury.ca
Evelyn Dutrisac, Councillor, Ward(s): 4
claude.berthiaume@greatersudbury.ca
Bill Lautenbach, General Manager, Growth & Development
bill.lautenbach@greatersudbury.ca
Ron Dupuis, Councillor, Ward(s): 5
ron.dupuis@greatersudbury.ca
Catherine Matheson, General Manager, Community Development
catherine.matheson@greatersudbury.ca
André Rivest, Councillor, Ward(s): 6
andre.rivest@greatersudbury.ca
Bruno Mangiardi, Chief Information Officer
bruno.mangiardi@greatersudbury.ca
Dave Kilgour, Councillor, Ward(s): 7
dave.kilgour@greatersudbury.ca
Tim P. Beadman, Chief, Emergency Services
tim.beadman@greatersudbury.ca
Fabio Belli, Councillor, Ward(s): 8
fabio.belli@greatersudbury.ca
Marc Leduc, Fire Chief
marc.leduc@greatersudbury.ca
Doug Craig, Councillor, Ward(s): 9
doug.craig@greatersudbury.ca
Nick Benkovich, Director, Water & Wastewater
nick.benkovich@greatersudbury.ca
Frances Caldarelli, Councillor, Ward(s): 10
frances.caldarelli@greatersudbury.ca
Robert Falcioni, Director, Roads & Transportation
robert.falcioni@greatersudbury.ca
Terry Kett, Councillor, Ward(s): 11
terry.kett@greatersudbury.ca
Guido Mazza, Director, Building Services
guido.mazza@greatersudbury.caa
Joscelyne Landry-Altmann, Councillor, Ward(s): 12
joscelyne.landry-altmann@greatersudbury.ca
Roger Sauvé, Director, Greater Sudbury Transit
roger.sauve@greatersudbury.ca
Kevin Shaw, Director, Engineering Services
kevin.shaw@greatersudbury.ca

Grimsby

160 Livingston Ave.
Grimsby, ON L3M 4G3
Tel: 905-945-9634; *Fax:* 905-945-5010
www.town.grimsby.on.ca
Municipal Type: City
Area: 68.94 sq km
County or District: Niagara Reg. Mun.; *Population in 2006:* 23,937
Provincial Electoral District(s): Niagara West-Glanbrook
Federal Electoral District(s): Niagara West-Glanbrook
Next Election: Oct. 2014 (4 year terms)
Robert N. Bentley, Mayor
905-945-2710
bbentley@grimsby.ca
Hazel Soady-Easton, Town Clerk
905-309-2003
Steve Berry, Alderman, Ward(s): 1
905-945-2578
sberry@grimsby.ca
Keith Vogl, Town Manager
Dave Wilson, Alderman, Ward(s): 1
905-309-0905
dwilson@grimsby.ca
Stephen Gruninger, CGA, Town Treasurer & Director, Finance
Bruce Atkinson, CGA, Director, Recreation, Facilities, & Culture
Dave Kadwell, Alderman, Ward(s): 2
905-945-8259
dkadwell@grimsby.ca
Michelle Seaborn, Alderman, Ward(s): 2
905-945-7963
mseaborn@grimsby.ca
Robert LeRoux, P.Eng., Director, Public Works
David Finch, Alderman, Ward(s): 3
905-945-7074
dfinch@grimsby.ca
Joanne Johnston, Alderman, Ward(s): 3
905-945-9851
jjohnston@grimsby.ca
Michael Seaman, Director, Planning
Nick DiFlavio, Alderman, Ward(s): 4
905-309-4133
ndiflavio@grimsby.ca
M. Cain, Fire Chief
Carolyn Mullins, Alderman, Ward(s): 4
289-235-9460
cmullins@grimsby.ca
Brandon Wartman, Manager, EHS Compliance
905-309-2016

Guelph

City Hall
1 Carden St.
Guelph, ON N1H 3A1
Tel: 519-822-1260; *Fax:* 519-763-1269
info@guelph.ca; communications@guelph.ca
www.guelph.ca
Other Information: TTY: 519-826-9771
Municipal Type: City
Incorporated: 1879 *Area:* 86.72 sq km
County or District: Wellington; *Population in 2006:* 114,943
Provincial Electoral District(s): Guelph; Wellington-Halton Hills
Federal Electoral District(s): Guelph; Wellington-Halton Hills
Next Election: Oct. 2014 (4 year terms)
Karen Farbridge, Mayor
519-837-5643, Fax: 519-822-8277
mayor@guelph.ca
Lois Giles, City Clerk & Director, Information Services
clerks@guelph.ca
Bob Bell, Councillor, Ward(s): 1
bob.bell@guelph.ca
Ann Pappert, Chief Administrative Officer
administration@guelph.ca
Jim J. Furfaro, Councillor, Ward(s): 1
jim.furfaro@guelph.ca
Margaret Neubauer, Chief Financial Officer
finance@guelph.ca; margaret.neubauer@guelph.ca
Ian Findlay, Councillor, Ward(s): 2
ian.findlay@guelph.ca
Mark Amorosi, Executive Director, Human Resources & Legal Services
mark.amorosi@guelph.ca
Andy Van Hellemond, Councillor, Ward(s): 2
andy.vanhellemond@guelph.ca
Shawn Armstrong, General Manager, Emergency Services
June Hofland, Councillor, Ward(s): 3
june.hofland@guelph.ca
Janet Laird, Executive Director, Environmental Services
janet.laird@guelph.ca
Maggie Laidlaw, Councillor, Ward(s): 3
maggie.laidlaw@guelph.ca
Derek McCaughan, Executive Director, Operations
operations@guelph.ca
Cam Guthrie, Councillor, Ward(s): 4
cam.guthrie@guelph.ca
Gloria Kovach, Councillor, Ward(s): 4
gloria.kovach@guelph.ca
Lise Burcher, Councillor, Ward(s): 5
lise.burcher@guelph.ca
Leanne Piper, Councillor, Ward(s): 5
leanne.piper@guelph.ca
Todd Dennis, Councillor, Ward(s): 6
todd.dennis@guelph.ca
Karl Wettstein, Councillor, Ward(s): 6
karl.wettstein@guelph.ca

Halton Hills

1 Halton Hills Dr.
Georgetown, ON L7G 5G2
Tel: 905-873-2600; *Fax:* 905-873-2347
www.haltonhills.ca
Other Information: TTY: 905-873-0644
Municipal Type: City
Area: 276.26 sq km
County or District: Halton Reg. Mun.; *Population in 2006:* 55,289
Provincial Electoral District(s): Wellington-Halton Hills
Federal Electoral District(s): Wellington-Halton Hills
Next Election: Oct. 2014 (4 year terms)
Rick Bonnette, Mayor
mayor@haltonhills.ca
S. Jones, Town Clerk
Clark A. Somerville, Regional Councillor, Ward(s): 1 & 2
clarks@haltonhills.ca
D. Perlin, Chief Administrative Officer
Jane Fogal, Regional Councillor, Ward(s): 3 & 4
janefogal@haltonhills.ca
Ed DeSousa, Treasurer & Director, Corporate Services
Jon Hurst, Councillor, Ward(s): 1
jon@haltonhills.ca
Terry Alyman, Director, Recreation & Parks
Mike O'Leary, Councillor, Ward(s): 1
mikeo@haltonhills.ca
John Linhardt, Director, Planning, Development, & Sustainability
Joan Robson, Councillor, Ward(s): 2
joanr@haltonhills.ca
Chris Mills, Director, Infrastructure Services & Town Engineer
Bryan Lewis, Councillor, Ward(s): 2
bryanlewis@haltonhills.ca
D. Szybalski, Coordinator, Sustainability
Moya Johnson, Councillor, Ward(s): 3
moyajohnson@haltonhills.ca
David Kentner, Councillor, Ward(s): 3
davek@haltonhills.ca
Bob Inglis, Councillor, Ward(s): 4
b_inglis@sympatico.ca
Ann Lawlor, Councillor, Ward(s): 4
annl@haltonhills.ca

Hamilton

Hamilton City Centre
P.O. Box 2040 LCD1
#220, 77 James St. North
Hamilton, ON L8R 2K3
Tel: 905-546-2489; *Fax:* 905-546-2095
askCITY@hamilton.ca; communications@hamilton.ca
www.hamilton.ca
Other Information: E-mail, Dev.: economicdevelopment@hamilton.ca
Municipal Type: City
Incorporated: 1846 *Area:* 1,117.21 sq km
Population in 2006: 504,559
Provincial Electoral District(s): Ancaster-Dundas-Flamborough-Westdale; Hamilton Centre; Hamilton East-Stoney Creek; Hamilton Mountain; Niagara West-Glanbrook
Federal Electoral District(s): Hamilton Centre; Hamilton East-Stoney Creek; Hamilton Mountain; Niagara West-Glanbrook; Ancaster-Dundas-Flamborough-Westdale

Next Election: Oct. 2014 (4 year terms)
Note: Incorporated as a city on Jan. 1, 2001.
Bob Bratina, Mayor
mayor@hamilton.ca
Rose Caterini, City Clerk
clerk@hamilton.ca
Brian McHattie, Councillor, Ward(s): 1
brian.mchattie@hamilton.ca
Chris Murray, City Manager
905-540-5420
Jason Farr, Councillor, Ward(s): 2
jason.farr@hamilton.ca
Roberto Rossini, General Manager, Finance & Corporate Services
Bernie Morelli, Councillor, Ward(s): 3
bernie.morelli@hamilton.ca
Jim Kay, General Manager, Hamilton Emergency Services
Sam Merulla, Councillor, Ward(s): 4
sam.merulla@hamilton.ca
Tim McCabe, General Manager, Planning & Economic Development
Chad Collins, Councillor, Ward(s): 5
chad.collins@hamilton.ca
Joe-Anne Priel, General Manager, Community Services
Tom Jackson, Councillor, Ward(s): 6
tom.jackson@hamilton.ca
Scott Stewart, C.E.T., General Manager, Public Works
Scott Duvall, Councillor, Ward(s): 7
scott.duvall@hamilton.ca
Terry Whitehead, Councillor, Ward(s): 8
terry.whitehead@hamilton.ca
Brad Clark, Councillor, Ward(s): 9
brad.clark@hamilton.ca
Maria Pearson, Councillor, Ward(s): 10
maria.pearson@hamilton.ca
Brenda Johnson, Councillor, Ward(s): 11
brenda.johnson@hamilton.ca
Lloyd Ferguson, Councillor, Ward(s): 12
lloyd.ferguson@hamilton.ca
Russ Powers, Councillor, Ward(s): 13
russ.powers@hamilton.ca
Robert Pasuta, Councillor, Ward(s): 14
robert.pasuta@hamilton.ca
Judi Partridge, Councillor, Ward(s): 15
judi.partridge@hamilton.ca

Hawkesbury

600 Higginson St.
Hawkesbury, ON K6A 1H1
Tel: 613-632-0106;
www.hawkesbury.ca
Municipal Type: City
Area: 9.46 sq km
County or District: Prescott & Russell; *Population in 2006:* 10,869
Provincial Electoral District(s): Glengarry-Prescott-Russell
Federal Electoral District(s): Glengarry-Prescott-Russell
Next Election: Oct. 2014 (4 year terms)
Rene Berthiaume, Mayor
rberthiaume@hawkesbury.ca
Christine Groulx, Clerk
Michel A. Beaulne, Councillor
mbeaulne@hawkesbury.ca
Normand Beaulieu, Chief Administrative Officer & Treasurer
André Chamaillard, Councillor
achamaillard@hawkesbury.ca
Liette Valade, Director, Recreation & Culture
Alain Fraser, Councillor
afraser@hawkesbury.ca
Gérald Campbell, Superintendent, Public Works
Johanne Portelance, Councillor
jportelance@hawkesbury.ca
Richard Guertin, Superintendent, Water Treatment Plant
Michel Thibodeau, ouncillor
mthibodeau@hawkesbury.ca
Jean-Claude Miner, Chief Building Official
Marc Tourangeau, Councillor
mtourangeau@hawkesbury.ca
Ghislain Pigeon, Fire Chief
Danielle Fredette-Thériault, Officer, Human Resources
Manon Belle-Isle, Planner

Huntsville

37 Main St. East
Huntsville, ON P1H 1A1
Tel: 705-789-1751; *Fax:* 705-789-6689
administration@huntsville.ca
www.huntsville.ca
Other Information: TTY: 705-789-1768
Municipal Type: City
Area: 703.23 sq km
County or District: Muskoka Dist. Mun.; *Population in 2006:* 18,280
Provincial Electoral District(s): Parry Sound-Muskoka
Federal Electoral District(s): Parry Sound-Muskoka
Next Election: Oct. 2014 (4 year terms)
Claude Doughty, Mayor
mayor@huntsville.ca
Kathleen Gilchrist, Municipal Clerk
Fran Coleman, District & Town Councillor
Kelly Pender, Chief Administrative Officer
Brian Thompson, District & Town Councillor
Dianne Leeder, Treasurer
Scott Aitchison, District & Town Councillor/Deputy Mayor
Brian Crozier, Director, Community Services
Tim Withey, Councillor, Ward(s): Brunel
Mike Gooch, Director, Building & Chief Building Official
John Davis, Councillor, Ward(s): Chaffey
Steve Hernen, Director, Protective Services & Fire Chief
Karin Terziano, Councillor, Ward(s): Huntsville
Steve Keeley, Director, Public Works
Det Schumacher, Councillor, Ward(s): Stisted/Stephenson/Port Sydney
Colleen MacDonald, Manager, Parks & Cemeteries
Chris Zanetti, Councillor, Ward(s): Stisted/Stephenson/Port Sydney
Lisa Smith, Manager, Human Resources

Ingersoll

130 Oxford St., 2nd Fl.
Ingersoll, ON N5C 2V5
Tel: 519-485-0120; *Fax:* 519-485-3543
www.ingersoll.ca
Municipal Type: City
Area: 12.9 sq km
County or District: Oxford; *Population in 2006:* 11,760
Provincial Electoral District(s): Oxford
Federal Electoral District(s): Oxford
Next Election: Oct. 2014 (4 year terms)
Ted J. Comiskey, Mayor
mayor@ingersoll.ca
Marsha Paley, Clerk & Deputy Chief Administrative Officer
clerks@ingersoll.ca
Fred Freeman, Deputy Mayor & Councillor
ffreeman@ingersoll.ca
James Timlin, Chief Administrative Officer
jtimlin@ingersoll.ca
John F. Fortner, Councillor
jfortner@ingersoll.ca
Gary Seitz, Treasurer & Director, Finance
Gord Lesser, Councillor
glesser@ingersoll.ca
Gene McLaren, Director, Engineering Services
Dave McLeod, Councillor
dmcleod@ingersoll.ca
Cathy Mott, Councillor
cmott@ingersoll.ca
Bonnie Ward, Director, Parks & Recreation
Kristy Van Kooten-Bossence, Councillor
kvankootenbossence@ingersoll.ca
Darell Parker, Fire Chief & Deputy Chief Administrative Officer

Innisfil

2101 Innisfil Beach Rd.
Innisfil, ON L9S 1A1
Tel: 705-436-3710; *Fax:* 705-436-7120
www.innisfil.ca
Municipal Type: City
Incorporated: 1850 *Area:* 284.18 sq km
County or District: Simcoe; *Population in 2006:* 31,175
Provincial Electoral District(s): York Simcoe
Federal Electoral District(s): York-Simcoe; Barrie
Next Election: Oct. 2014 (4 year terms)
Barb Baguley, Mayor
bbaguley@innisfil.ca
Jason Reynar, Clerk & Director, Legal Services
Dan Davidson, Deputy Mayor & Councillor
ddavidson@innisfil.ca
John Skorobohacz, Chief Administrative Officer
Doug Lougheed, Councillor, Ward(s): 1
dlougheed@innisfil.ca
Lockie Davis, Chief Financial officer & Director, Finance & Customer Service
Richard Simpson, Councillor, Ward(s): 2
rsimpson@innisfil.ca
Kerry Columbus, Director, Community Services
Ken Simpson, Councillor, Ward(s): 3
ksimpson@innisfil.ca
Susan Downs, Director, Strategic Planning
Rod Boynton, Councillor, Ward(s): 4
rboynton@innisfil.ca
Jim Zimmerman, Director, Infrastructure & Engineering Services
Bill Loughead, Councillor, Ward(s): 5
bloughead@innisfil.ca
Michelle Collette, Director, Human Resources
Maria Baier, Councillor, Ward(s): 6
mbaierinnisfil.ca
Ross Cotton, Manager, Planning
Lynn Dollin, Councillor, Ward(s): 7
ldollin@innisfil.ca
R. Wayne Young, Manager, Operational Services
Randy Smith, Fire Chief

Kawartha Lakes

P.O. Box 9000
26 Francis St.
Lindsay, ON K9V 5R8
Tel: 705-324-9411; *Fax:* 705-324-8110
info@city.kawarthalakes.on.ca
www.city.kawarthalakes.on.ca
Other Information: Toll-Free Phone: 1-888-822-2225
Municipal Type: City
Incorporated: Jan. 1, 2001 *Area:* 3,059.47 sq km
Population in 2006: 74,561
Provincial Electoral District(s): Haliburton-Kawartha Lakes-Brock
Federal Electoral District(s): Haliburton-Kawartha Lakes-Brock
Next Election: Oct. 2014 (4 year terms)
Note: Formerly the County of Victoria.
Ric McGee, Mayor
rmcgee@city.kawarthalakes.on.ca
Judy Currins, City Clerk
John Macklem, Councillor, Ward(s): 1
jmacklem@city.kawarthalakes.on.ca
Albert Horsman, Chief Administrative Officer
Emmett Yeo, Councillor, Ward(s): 2
eyeo@city.kawarthalakes.on.ca
Rudy Huisman, Director, Financial Services
rhuisman@city.kawarthalakes.on.ca
David Hodgson, Councillor, Ward(s): 3
dhodgson@city.kawarthalakes.on.ca
Michelle Hendry, Director, Public Works
mhendry@city.kawarthalakes.on.ca
Glenn Campbell, Councillor, Ward(s): 4
gcampbell@city.kawarthalakes.on.ca
Ron Taylor, Director, Development Services
rtaylor@city.kawarthalakes.on.ca
Stephen Strangway, Councillor, Ward(s): 5
sstrangway@city.kawarthalakes.on.ca
Bob Knight, Director, Health & Social Services
bknight@city.kawarthalakes.on.ca
Doug Elmslie, Councillor, Ward(s): 6
delmslie@city.kawarthalakes.on.ca
Brian Junkin, Councillor, Ward(s): 7
bjunkin@city.kawarthalakes.on.ca
Kevin Williams, Director, Community Services
kwilliams@city.kawarthalakes.on.ca
Donna Villemaire, Councillor, Ward(s): 8
dvillemaire@city.kawarthalakes.on.ca
Mark Pankhurst, Fire Chief
mpankhurst@city.kawarthalakes.on.ca
Andy Luff, Councillor, Ward(s): 9
aluff@city.kawarthalakes.on.ca
Pat Dunn, Councillor, Ward(s): 10
pdunn@city.kawarthalakes.on.ca
Patrick O'Reilly, Councillor, Ward(s): 11
poreilly@city.kawarthalakes.on.ca
Gord James, Councillor, Ward(s): 12
gjames@city.kawarthalakes.on.ca
Pat Warren, Councillor, Ward(s): 13
pwarren@city.kawarthalakes.on.ca
Ron Ashmore, Councillor, Ward(s): 14
rashmore@city.kawarthalakes.on.ca
Gerald McGregor, Councillor, Ward(s): 15
gmcgregor@city.kawarthalakes.on.ca
Heather Stauble, Councillor, Ward(s): 16
hstauble@city.kawarthalakes.on.ca

Kenora

1 Main St. South
Kenora, ON P9N 3X2
Tel: 807-467-2000; *Fax:* 807-467-2009
service@kenora.ca
www.kenora.ca
Municipal Type: City
Area: 210.91 sq km
County or District: Kenora District; *Population in 2006:* 15,177
Provincial Electoral District(s): Kenora-Rainy River
Federal Electoral District(s): Kenora
Next Election: Oct. 2014 (4 year terms)
David S. Canfield, Mayor
dcanfield@kenora.ca

Joanne L. McMillin, Clerk
jmcmillin@kenora.ca
Charito V. Drinkwalter, Councillor
cdrinkwalter@kenora.ca
Karen Brown, Chief Administrative Officer
kbrown@kenora.ca
Ron Lunny, Councillor
rlunny@kenora.ca
Charlotte Edie, Treasurer
cedie@kenora.ca
Rod McKay, Councillor
rmckay@kenora.ca
Warren Brinkman, Manager, Emergency Services
wbrinkman@kenora.ca
Rory McMillan, Councillor
rmcmillan@kenora.ca
Sharen McDowall, Manager, Human Resources
smcdowall@kenora.ca
Louie Roussin, Councillor
lroussin@kenora.ca
Sharon L. Smith, Councillor
ssmith@kenora.ca
Colleen Neil, Manager, Recreation
cneil@kenora.ca
Rick Perchuk, Manager, Operations
rperchuk@kenora.ca
Mike Mostow, Supervisor, Fleet & Solid Waste
mmostow@kenora.ca
Warren Ortlieb, Supervisor, Sewer & Water
wortlieb@kenora.ca
Kevin Robertson, Chief Building Official
krobertson@kenora.ca
Marco Vogrig, Municipal Engineer
mvogrig@kenora.ca

Kingston
City Hall
216 Ontario St.
Kingston, ON K7L 2Z3
Tel: 613-546-0000; *Fax:* 613-546-5232
www.cityofkingston.ca
Other Information: TTY: 613-546-4889
Municipal Type: City
Incorporated: Jan. 1, 1998 *Area:* 450.39 sq km
County or District: Frontenac; *Population in 2006:* 117,207
Provincial Electoral District(s): Kingston & the Islands
Federal Electoral District(s): Kingston & the Islands
Next Election: Oct. 2014 (4 year terms)
Mark Gerretsen, Mayor
mgerretsen@cityofkingston.ca
John Bolognone, City Clerk
Rick Downes, Councillor, Ward(s): Cataraqui District
rdownes@cityofkingston.ca
Gerard Hunt, Chief Administrative Officer
Lisa Osanic, Councillor, Ward(s): Collins-Bayridge District
losanic@cityofkingston.ca
Desiree Kennedy, Treasurer & Director, Financial Services
Jeff Scott, Councillor, Ward(s): Countryside District
jscott@cityofkingston.ca
Cynthia Beach, Commissioner, Sustainability & Growth
Rob Hutchinson, Councillor, Ward(s): King's Town District
rhutchison@cityofkingston.ca
Denis Leger, Commissioner, Transportation, Properties & Emergency Services
Sandy Berg, Councillor, Ward(s): Kingscourt-Strathcona District
sberg@cityofkingston.ca
Dorothy Hector, Councillor, Ward(s): Lakeside District
dhector@cityofkingston.ca
Lanie Hurdle, Commissioner, Community Services & Director, Recreation & Leisure Services
Kevin George, Councillor, Ward(s): Loyalist-Cataraqui District
kgeorge@cityofkingston.ca
Paul MacLatchy, Director, Strategy, Environment, & Communications
Brian Reitzel, Councillor, Ward(s): Pittsburgh District
breitzel@cityofkingston.ca
Liz Schell, Councillor, Ward(s): Portsmouth District
lschell@cityofkingston.ca
Mark Van Buren, Director, Engineering
Bill Glover, Councillor, Ward(s): Sydenham District
bglover@cityofkingston.ca
George Wallace, Project Manager, Sustainability & Growth
Bryan Paterson, Councillor, Ward(s): Trillium District
bpaterson@cityofkingston.ca
Damon Wells, Director, Public Works
Jim Neill, Councillor, Ward(s): Williamsville District
jneill@cityofkingston.ca
Terry Willing, Director, Building & Licensing
Harold Tulk, Fire Chief
John Cross, Manager, Emergency Planning
John Giles, Manager, Solid Waste

Kingsville
2021 Division Rd. North
Kingsville, ON N9Y 2Y9
Tel: 519-733-2305; *Fax:* 519-733-8108
www.kingsville.ca
Municipal Type: City
Incorporated: 1874 *Area:* 246.84 sq km
County or District: Essex; *Population in 2006:* 20,908
Provincial Electoral District(s): Essex
Federal Electoral District(s): Essex
Next Election: Oct. 2014 (4 year terms)
Note: Incorporated as a town in 1901. Restructuring occurred in 1999.
Nelson Santos, Mayor
nsantos@kingsville.ca
Ruth Orton-Pert, Clerk & Director, Corporate Services
rorton-pert@kingsville.ca
Tamara Stomp, Deputy Mayor & Councillor
stomp@mnsi.net
Dan DiGiovanni, Chief Administrative Officer
ddigiovanni@kingsville.ca
Ron Colasanti, Councillor
ronaldcolasanti@gmail.com
Sandra Ingratta, Director, Financial Services
singratta@kingsville.ca
Gord Queen, Councillor
pgordonqueen@msn.com
Andrew Plancke, C.E.T., Director, Municipal Services
aplancke@kingsville.ca
Bob Peterson, Councillor
rpeterson9@cogeco.ca
Michael Arthur, Chief Building Official
marthur@kingsville.ca
Sandi McIntyre, Councillor
sandygmcintyre@hotmail.com
Bob Kissner, Fire Chief
bkissner@kingsville.ca
Gail Stiffler, Councillor
g.stiffler@sympatico.ca
Andy Coghill, Manager, Public Works
acoghill@kingsville.ca
Dan Wood, Manager, Parks & Recreation
dwood@kingsville.ca

Kitchener
City Hall
P.O. Box 1118
200 King St. West
Kitchener, ON N2G 4G7
Tel: 519-741-2345;
www.kitchener.ca
Other Information: TTY: 1-866-969-9994
Municipal Type: City
Incorporated: June 9, 1912 *Area:* 136.89 sq km
County or District: Waterloo Regional Municipality; *Population in 2006:* 204,668
Provincial Electoral District(s): Kitchener Centre; Kitchener-Waterloo; Waterloo-Wellington
Federal Electoral District(s): Kitchener Centre; Kitchener-Waterloo; Kitchener-Conestoga
Next Election: Oct. 2014 (4 year terms)
Carl Zehr, Mayor
519-741-2300
mayor@kitchener.ca
Carla Ladd, Chief Administrative Officer
carla.ladd@kitchener.ca
Scott Davey, Councillor, Ward(s): 1
scott.davey@kitchener.ca
Dan Chapman, City Treasurer & General Manager, Financial Services
Berry Vrbanovic, Councillor, Ward(s): 2
berryv@kitchener.ca
Pauline Houston, General Manager, Community Services
John Gazzola, Councillor, Ward(s): 3
john.gazzola@kitchener.ca
Troy Speck, General Manager, Corporate Services
Yvonne Fernandes, Councillor, Ward(s): 4
yvonne.fernandes@kitchener.ca
Jeff Willmer, General Manager, Development & Technical Services
Kelly Galloway, Councillor, Ward(s): 5
kelly.galloway@kitchener.ca
Grant Murphy, Director, Engineering Services
Paul Singh, Councillor, Ward(s): 6
paul.singh@kitchener.ca
Alain Pinard, Director, Planning
Bil Ioannidis, Councillor, Ward(s): 7
bil.ioannidis@kitchener.ca
Mike Seiling, Director, Building
Zyg Janecki, Councillor, Ward(s): 8
zyg.janecki@kitchener.ca
Tim Beckett, Fire Chief
519-741-2495
Frank Etherington, Councillor, Ward(s): 9
frank.etherington@kitchener.ca
Daniel Glenn-Graham, Councillor, Ward(s): 10
dan.glenn-graham@kitchener.ca

Environmental Committee, Dept. of Corporate Services
Colin Goodeve, Committee Administrator

Lakeshore
419 Notre Dame Rd.
Belle River, ON N0R 1A0
Tel: 519-728-2700; *Fax:* 519-728-9530
webmaster@lakeshore.ca
www.lakeshore.ca
Municipal Type: City
Incorporated: 1999 *Area:* 530.32 sq km
County or District: Essex; *Population in 2006:* 33,245
Provincial Electoral District(s): Essex
Federal Electoral District(s): Essex
Next Election: Oct. 2014 (4 year terms)
Note: Amalgamation of the former Town of Belle River & the former Townships of Maidstone, Rochester, Tilbury North & Tilbury West.
Tom Bain, Mayor
tbain@lakeshore.ca
Mary Masse, Town Clerk
mmasse@lakeshore.ca
Al Fazio, Deputy Mayor & Councillor
afazio@lakeshore.ca
Kirk Foran, Acting Chief Administrative Officer & Director, Corporate Services
kforan@lakeshore.ca
Len Janisse, Councillor, Ward(s): 1
ljanisse@lakeshore.ca
Sylvia Rammelaere, Director, Finance & Performance Service
srammelaere@lakeshore.ca
Dave Monk, Councillor, Ward(s): 2
dmonk@lakeshore.ca
Charles W. McLean, Councillor, Ward(s): 3
cmclean@lakeshore.ca
Lee Holling, Director, Community & Development Services
lholling@lakeshore.ca
Steven Bezaire, Councillor, Ward(s): 4
sbezaire@lakeshore.ca
Tom Touralias, Director, Engineering & Infrastructure Services
ttouralias@lakeshore.ca
Dan Diemer, Councillor, Ward(s): 5
ddiemer@lakeshore.ca
Chuck Chevalier, Manager, Public Works
cchevalier@lakeshore.ca
Linda McKinlay, Councillor, Ward(s): 6
lmckinlay@lakeshore.ca
Kim Darroch, Manager, Development Services
kdarroch@lakeshore.ca
Tony DiCiocco, Manager, Engineering Services
tdiciocco@lakeshore.ca
Tony Francisco, Manager, Environmental Services
tfrancisco@lakeshore.ca
Don Williamson, Fire Chief
dwilliamson@lakeshore.ca
Maureen Lesperance, Coordinator, Planning
mlesperance@lakeshore.ca

LaSalle
5950 Malden Rd.
Lasalle, ON N9H 1S4
Tel: 519-969-7770; *Fax:* 519-969-4469
webmaster@town.lasalle.on.ca
www.town.lasalle.on.ca
Municipal Type: City
Incorporated: 1924 *Area:* 65.25 sq km
County or District: Essex; *Population in 2006:* 27,652
Provincial Electoral District(s): Essex
Federal Electoral District(s): Essex
Next Election: Oct. 2014 (4 year terms)
Note: Dissolved into Township of Sandwich West in 1959. Status & name change to Town of LaSalle in 1991.
Ken Antaya, Mayor
mayor@town.lasalle.on.ca
Brenda Andreatta, Clerk
bandreat@town.lasalle.on.ca
Mark Carrick, Deputy Mayor & Councillor
mcarrick@town.lasalle.on.ca
Kevin Miller, Chief Administrative Officer
kmiller@town.lasalle.on.ca
Marc Bondy, Councillor
mbondy@town.lasalle.on.ca
Joe Milicia, Treasurer
jmilicia@town.lasalle.on.ca

Terry Burns, Councillor
tburns@town.lasalle.on.ca
Larry Silani, Director, Planning & Development Services
lsilani@town.lasalle.on.ca
Sue Desjarlais, Councillor
sdesjarl@town.lasalle.on.ca
Robert Hayes, P. Eng, Town Engineer
rhayes@town.lasalle.on.ca
Crystal B. Meloche, Councillor
cmeloche@town.lasalle.on.ca
Ray Renaud, Councillor
rrenaud@town.lasalle.on.ca

Lincoln
4800 South Service Rd.
Beamsville, ON L0R 1B1
Tel: 905-563-8205; *Fax:* 905-563-6566
info@lincoln.ca
www.lincoln.ca
Municipal Type: City
Incorporated: Jan. 1, 1970 *Area:* 162.86 sq km
County or District: Niagara Reg. Mun.; *Population in 2006:* 21,722
Provincial Electoral District(s): Niagara West-Glanbrook
Federal Electoral District(s): Niagara West-Glanbrook
Next Election: Oct. 2014 (4 year terms)
Note: Amalgamation of the Town of Beamsville, the Township of Clinton, & part of the Township of Louth.
Bill Hodgson, Mayor
bhodgson@lincoln.ca
William J. Kolasa, Clerk & Director, Corporate Services
wkolasa@lincoln.ca
Dianne Rintjema, Councillor, Ward(s): 1
drintjema@lincoln.ca
Anne Louise Heron, Chief Administrative Officer
aheron@lincoln.ca
Robert Foster, Councillor, Ward(s): 1
rfoster@lincoln.ca
Robert Spadoni, Director, Finance
bspadoni@lincoln.ca
John A. Kralt, Councillor, Ward(s): 2
jkralt@lincoln.ca
Kathleen Dale, Director, Planning & Development
kdale@lincoln.ca
John D. Pachereva, Councillor, Ward(s): 2
jdpachereva@lincoln.ca
Doug Kerr, Director, Public Works
dkerr@lincoln.ca
Robert Condotta, Councillor, Ward(s): 3
rcondotta@lincoln.ca
Judy Pease, Director, Community Services
jpease@lincoln.ca
Dave A. Thomson, Councillor, Ward(s): 3
Scott Blake, Fire Chief
sblake@lincoln.ca
Geoffrey Barlow, Councillor, Ward(s): 4
gbarlow@lincoln.ca
Andrew Greenaway, Chief Building Official
agreenaway@lincoln.ca
Wayne MacMillan, Councillor, Ward(s): 4
wmacmillan@lincoln.ca
Greg Lancaster, Manager, Facilities & Parks
glancaster@lincoln.ca

London
City Hall
P.O. Box 5035
300 Dufferin Ave.
London, ON N6A 4L9
Tel: 519-661-4500; *Fax:* 519-661-4892
webmaster@london.ca
www.london.ca
Municipal Type: City
Incorporated: 1855 *Area:* 420.57 sq km
County or District: Middlesex; *Population in 2006:* 352,395
Provincial Electoral District(s): London-Fanshawe; Elgin-Middlesex-London; London North Centre; London West
Federal Electoral District(s): London-Fanshawe; Elgin-Middlesex-London; London North Centre; London West
Next Election: Oct. 2014 (4 year terms)
Joe Fontana, Mayor
jfontana@london.ca
Bud Polhill, Councillor, Ward(s): 1
bpolhill@london.ca
Cathy Saunders, City Clerk
csaunder@london.ca
Bill Armstrong, Councillor, Ward(s): 2
barmstro@london.ca
Jeff Fielding, Chief Administrative Officer
jfielding@london.ca
Joe Swan, Councillor, Ward(s): 3
jswan@london.ca
Martin Hayward, City Treasurer & Chief Financial Officer
Stephen Orser, Councillor, Ward(s): 4
sorser@london.ca
Joni Baechler, Councillor, Ward(s): 5
jbaechle@london.ca
Ross Fair, Executive Director, Community Services
rfair@london.ca
Nancy Ann Branscombe, Councillor, Ward(s): 6
nbransco@london.ca
Patrick McNally, P.Eng., Executive Director, Planning, Environmental & Engineering Services
Matt Brown, Councillor, Ward(s): 7
mbrown@london.ca
Paul Hubert, Councillor, Ward(s): 8
phubert@london.ca
William Coxhead, Director, Parks & Recreation
bcoxhead@london.ca
Dale Henderson, Councillor, Ward(s): 9
dhenders@london.ca
Joseph Edward, Chief Technology Officer
jedward@london.ca
Paul Van Meerbergen, Councillor, Ward(s): 10
pvanmeer@london.ca
Denise Brown, Councillor, Ward(s): 11
dbrown@london.ca
Veronica McAlea Major, Chief Human Resources Officer
vmcaleamajor@london.ca
Harold Usher, Councillor, Ward(s): 12
husher@london.ca
Ronald Standish, Director, Wastewater & Treatment
rstandis@london.ca
Judy Bryant, Councillor, Ward(s): 13
jbryant@london.ca
Jay Stanford, Director, Environmental Programs & Solid Waste
jstanfor@london.ca
Sandy White, Councillor, Ward(s): 14
sawhite@london.ca

Markham
Markham Civic Centre
101 Town Centre Blvd.
Markham, ON L3R 9W3
Tel: 905-477-7000; *Fax:* 905-479-7771
customerservice@markham.ca; webmaster@markham.ca
www.markham.ca
Other Information: Customer Service: 905-477-5530
Municipal Type: City
Incorporated: Jan. 1, 1971 *Area:* 212.58 sq km
County or District: York Reg. Mun.; *Population in 2006:* 261,573
Provincial Electoral District(s): Markham-Unionville; Oak Ridges-Markham; Thornhill
Federal Electoral District(s): Markham-Unionville; Oak Ridges-Markham; Thornhill
Next Election: Oct. 2014 (4 year terms)
Frank Scarpitti, Mayor
905-475-4702
fscarpitti@markham.ca
Kimberly Kitteringham, Town Clerk
905-475-4729
kkitteringham@markham.ca
Jack Heath, Deputy Mayor & Regional Councillor
905-475-4872
jheath@markham.ca
John Livey, Chief Administrative Officer
905-479-7755
jlivey@markham.ca
Jim Jones, Regional Councillor
905-479-7757
jjones@markham.ca
Joel Lustig, Treasurer
905-475-4715
jlustig@markham.ca
Gordon Landon, Regional Councillor
905-415-7534
glandon@markham.ca
Jim Baird, Commissioner, Development Services
905-475-4875
jbaird@markham.ca
Joe Li, Regional Councillor
905-479-7749
joeli@markham.ca
Brenda Librecz, Commissioner, Community & Fire Services
905-479-7761
blibrecz@markham.ca
Valerie Burke, Councillor, Ward(s): 1
vburke@markham.ca
Andy Taylor, Commissioner, Corporate Services
905-475-4705
ataylor@markham.ca
Howard Shore, Councillor, Ward(s): 2
hshore@markham.ca
Nasir Kenea, Chief Information Officer
905-475-4733
nkenea@markham.ca
Don Hamilton, Councillor, Ward(s): 3
dhamilton@markham.ca
Bill Snowball, Fire Chief, Fire & Emergency Services
905-305-5982
bsnowball@markham.ca
Carolina Moretti, Councillor, Ward(s): 4
cmoretti@markham.ca
Alan Brown, Director, Engineering
905-415-7507
abrown@markham.ca
Colin Campbell, Councillor, Ward(s): 5
ccampbell@markham.ca
Sharon Laing, Director, Human Resources
905-475-4725
slaing@markham.ca
Alan Ho, Councillor, Ward(s): 6
alan.ho@markham.ca
Peter Loukes, Director, Operations
905-475-4894
ploukes@markham.ca
Logan Kanapathi, Councillor, Ward(s): 7
lkanapathi@markham.ca
Alex Chiu, Councillor, Ward(s): 8
achiu@markham.ca
Tim Moore, Director, Building Standards
905-475-4712
tmoore@markham.ca
Claudia Marsales, Senior Manager, Waste Management & Environment
cmarsales@markham.ca

Midland
575 Dominion Ave.
Midland, ON L4R 1R2
Tel: 705-526-4275; *Fax:* 705-526-9971
clerks@midland.ca
www.midland.ca
Other Information: TTY: 705-526-4276, ext. 2824
Municipal Type: City
Area: 29.09 sq km
County or District: Simcoe; *Population in 2006:* 16,300
Provincial Electoral District(s): Simcoe North
Federal Electoral District(s): Simcoe North
Next Election: Oct. 2014 (4 year terms)
Gordon A. McKay, Mayor
mayor@midland.ca; gmckay@midland.ca
Karen Desroches, Acting Deputy Clerk
Stephan M. Kramp, Deputy Mayor & Councillor
skramp@midland.ca
Ted Walker, Chief Administrative Officer
Jim Attwood, Councillor, Ward(s): 1
jattwood@midland.ca
Sue Gignac, Treasurer & Director, Finance
treasury@midland.ca
Patricia A. File, Councillor, Ward(s): 1
pfile@midland.ca
Wes Crown, Director, Planning & Development
wcrown@midland.ca; planning@midland.ca
Zena Pendlebury, Councillor, Ward(s): 1
zpendlebury@midland.ca
Shawn Berriault, Director, Public Works
engineering@midland.ca
Jack H. Charlebois, Councillor, Ward(s): 2
jcharlebois@midland.ca
Bob Jeffery, Councillor, Ward(s): 2
bjeffery@midland.ca
Mike Ross, Councillor, Ward(s): 2
mross@midland.ca
Glen M. Canning, Councillor, Ward(s): 3
gcanning@midland.ca

Milton
150 Mary St.
Milton, ON L9T 6Z5
Tel: 905-878-7252; *Fax:* 905-878-6995
info@milton.ca
www.milton.ca
Municipal Type: City
Incorporated: 1857 *Area:* 366.61 sq km
County or District: Halton Regional Municipality; *Population in 2006:* 53,939
Provincial Electoral District(s): Halton
Federal Electoral District(s): Halton
Next Election: Oct. 2014 (4 year terms)
Gordon A. Krantz, Mayor

Troy McHarg, Clerk
townclerk@milton.ca
Tony Lambert, Local & Regional Councillor, Ward(s): South
tonylambert2010@yahoo.com
William Mann, P.Eng., Director, Planning & Development
Colin Best, Local & Regional Councillor, Ward(s): North
Linda Leeds, Treasurer & Director, Corporate Services
Sharon Barkley, Councillor, Ward(s): 1
sharon@sharonbarkley.ca
Jennifer Reynolds, Director, Community Services
Brian Ellsworth, P.Eng., Fire Chief
Greg Nelson, Councillor, Ward(s): 2
Cindy Lunau, Councillor, Ward(s): 3
Rick Malboeuf, Councillor, Ward(s): 4
Arnold Huffman, Councillor, Ward(s): 5
Mike Cluett, Councillor, Ward(s): 6
Rick Di Lorenzo, Councillor, Ward(s): 7
rick@dilorenzo.com
Zeeshan Hamid, Councillor, Ward(s): 8
mail@zhamid.ca

Mississauga

Civic Centre
300 City Centre Dr.
Mississauga, ON L5B 3C1
Tel: 905-615-4311; *Fax:* 905-615-4081
public.info@mississauga.ca
www.mississauga.ca
Other Information: TTY: 905-896-5151
Municipal Type: City
Incorporated: Jan. 1, 1974 *Area:* 288.53 sq km
County or District: Peel Reg. Mun.; *Population in 2006:* 668,549
Provincial Electoral District(s): Bramalea-Gore-Malton; Mississauga-Brampton South; Mississauga-Erindale; Mississauga East-Cooksville; Mississauga South; Mississauga-Streetsville
Federal Electoral District(s): Bramalea-Gore-Malton; Mississauga-Brampton South; Mississauga-Erindale; Mississauga East-Cooksville; Mississauga South; Mississauga-Streetsville
Next Election: Oct. 2014 (4 year terms)
Hazel McCallion, Mayor
mayor@mississauga.ca
Crystal Greer, City Clerk & Director, Legislative Services
Jim Tovey, Councillor, Ward(s): 1
jim.tovey@mississauga.ca
Janice Baker, City Manager & Chief Administrative Officer
city.manager@mississauga.ca
Patricia Mullin, Councillor, Ward(s): 2
pat.mullin@mississauga.ca
Brenda Breault, Commissioner, Corporate Services, & Treasurer
Chris Fonseca, Councillor, Ward(s): 3
chris.fonseca@mississauga.ca
Paul Mitcham, Commissioner, Community Services
Frank Dale, Councillor, Ward(s): 4
frank.dale@mississauga.ca
Martin Powell, Commissioner, Transportation & Works
Ed Sajecki, Commissioner, Planning & Building
Ron Starr, Councillor, Ward(s): 6
ron.starr@mississauga.ca
John McDougall, Fire Chief
Nando Iannicca, Councillor, Ward(s): 7
nando.iannicca@mississauga.ca
Katie Mahoney, Councillor, Ward(s): 8
katie.mahoney@mississauga.ca
Pat Saito, Councillor, Ward(s): 9
pat.saito@mississauga.ca
Sue McFadden, Councillor, Ward(s): 10
sue.mcfadden@mississauga.ca
George Carlson, Councillor, Ward(s): 11
george.carlson@mississauga.ca

Mississippi Mills

P.O. Box 400
3131 Old Perth Rd., RR#2
Almonte, ON K0A 1A0
Tel: 613-256-2064; *Fax:* 613-256-4887
town@mississippimills.ca
www.mississippimills.ca
Other Information: Toll-Free Phone: 1-888-779-8666
Municipal Type: City
Incorporated: Jan. 1, 1998 *Area:* 509.05 sq km
County or District: Lanark; *Population in 2006:* 11,734
Provincial Electoral District(s): Carleton-Mississippi Mills
Federal Electoral District(s): Carleton-Mississippi Mills
Next Election: Oct. 2014 (4 year terms)
Note: Merger of the Town of Almonte with the townships of Ramsay & Pakenham.
John Levi, Mayor
Shawna Stone, Town Clerk
sstone@mississippimills.ca
Garry Dalgity, Councillor, Ward(s): Almonte
Diane Smithson, Chief Administrative Officer
dsmithson@mississippimills.ca
Rick Minnille, Councillor, Ward(s): Almonte
Rhonda Whitmarsh, Treasurer
rwhitmarsh@mississippimills.ca
Bernard Cameron, Councillor, Ward(s): Almonte
Troy Dunlop, Director, Roads & Public Works
tdunlop@mississippimills.ca
Alex Gillis, Councillor, Ward(s): Almonte
Rod Cameron, Manager, Operations
rcameron@mississippimills.ca
Duncan A. Abbott, Councillor, Ward(s): Pakenham
Art Brown, Fire Chief
abrown@mississippimills.ca
Denzil Ferguson, Councillor, Ward(s): Pakenham
Sherry Morrison, Chief Building Official
smorrison@mississippimills.ca
John H. Edwards, Councillor, Ward(s): Ramsay
Shaun J. McLaughlin, Councillor, Ward(s): Ramsay
Paul J. Watters, Councillor, Ward(s): Ramsay
Val Wilkinson, Councillor, Ward(s): Ramsay

New Tecumseth

Town Administration Centre
P.O. Box 910
10 Wellington St. East
Alliston, ON L9R 1A1
Tel: 705-435-6219; *Fax:* 705-435-2873
www.town.newtecumseth.on.ca
Other Information: Alternative Phone: 905-729-0057
Municipal Type: City
Incorporated: Jan. 1991 *Area:* 274.18 sq km
County or District: Simcoe; *Population in 2006:* 27,701
Provincial Electoral District(s): Simcoe-Grey
Federal Electoral District(s): Simcoe-Grey
Next Election: Oct. 2014 (4 year terms)
Mike MacEachern, Mayor
mayor@town.newtecumseth.on.ca
Cheryl McCarroll, Clerk & Manager, Administration
Rick Milne, Deputy Mayor & Councillor
deputymayor@town.newtecumseth.on.ca
Terri Caron, Chief Administrative Officer
Bob Marrs, Councillor, Ward(s): 1
ward.1@town.newtecumseth.on.ca
Mark Sirr, Treasurer & Manager, Finance
Jamie Smith, Councillor, Ward(s): 2
ward.2@town.newtecumseth.on.ca
Eric Chandler, Manager, Planning
J.J. Paul Whiteside, Councillor, Ward(s): 3
ward.3@town.newtecumseth.on.ca
Ray Osmond, Manager, Parks, Recreation & Culture
Fran Sainsbury, Councillor, Ward(s): 4
ward.4@town.newtecumseth.on.ca
Chad Horan, Manager, Public Works
Donna Jebb, Councillor, Ward(s): 5
ward.5@town.newtecumseth.on.ca
Hilary McCormack, Manager, Human Resources
Richard Norcross, Councillor, Ward(s): 6
ward.6@town.newtecumseth.on.ca
John Miller, Manager, Building Standards & Chief Building Official
Bruce Haire, Councillor, Ward(s): 7
ward.7@town.newtecumseth.on.ca
Rick Vatri, Manager, Engineering
Jim Stone, Councillor, Ward(s): 8
ward.8@town.newtecumseth.on.ca
Dan Heydon, Fire Chief

Newmarket

P.O. Box 328
395 Mulock Dr.
Newmarket, ON L3Y 4X7
Tel: 905-895-5193; *Fax:* 905-953-5100
info@newmarket.ca
www.newmarket.ca
Municipal Type: City
Incorporated: 1857 *Area:* 38.08 sq km
County or District: York Regional Municipality; *Population in 2006:* 74,295
Provincial Electoral District(s): Newmarket-Aurora
Federal Electoral District(s): Newmarket-Aurora
Next Election: Oct. 2014 (4 year terms)
Note: Incorporated as a town in 1880.
Tony Van Bynen, Mayor
905-898-2876, Fax: 905-953-5102
mayor@newmarket.ca
Anita Moore, Clerk & Director, Legislative Services
John Taylor, Regional Councillor
jtaylor@newmarket.ca
Robert N. Shelton, Chief Administrative Officer
Tom Vegh, Councillor, Ward(s): 1
tomvegh@gmail.com
Mike Mayes, Treasurer & Director, Financial Services
finance@newmarket.ca
Dave Kerwin, Councillor, Ward(s): 2
dkerwin@newmarket.ca
Robert Dixon, Commissioner, Corporate & Financial Services
Jane Twinney, Councillor, Ward(s): 3
jtwinney@newmarket.ca
Robert Prentice, Commissioner, Community Services
Tom Hempen, Councillor, Ward(s): 4
thempen@newmarket.ca
Brian Jones, Director, Public Works Services
Joe Sponga, Councillor, Ward(s): 5
jsponga@newmarket.ca
Jim Koutroubis, Director, Engineering Services
engineering@newmarket.ca
Maddie Di Muccio, Councillor, Ward(s): 6
mdimuccio@newmarket.ca
Ian McDougall, Director, Recreation & Culture Services
Chris Emanuel, Councillor, Ward(s): 7
cemanuel@newmarket.ca
Rick Nethery, BES, MCIP, RPP, Director, Planning
905-953-5321, Fax: 905-953-5140
planning@newmarket.ca
David Potter, Chief Building Official
buildings@newmarket.ca
Wanda Bennett, Director, Corporate Communications
communications@newmarket.ca
Lynn Georgeff, Director, Human Resources

Niagara Falls

City Hall
P.O. Box 1023
4310 Queen St.
Niagara Falls, ON L2E 6X5
Tel: 905-356-7521; *Fax:* 905-356-9083
www.niagarafalls.ca
Municipal Type: City
Incorporated: Jan. 1, 1904 *Area:* 209.58 sq km
County or District: Niagara Reg. Mun.; *Population in 2006:* 82,184
Provincial Electoral District(s): Niagara Falls
Federal Electoral District(s): Niagara Falls
Next Election: Oct. 2014 (4 year terms)
Jim Diodati, Mayor
jdiodati@niagarafalls.ca
Dean Iorfida, City Clerk & Director, Council Services
diorfida@niagarafalls.ca
Wayne Thomson, City Councillor
wthomson@niagarafalls.ca
Ken Todd, Chief Administrative Officer
ktodd@niagarafalls.ca
Victor Pietrangelo, City Councillor
vpietrangelo@niagarafalls.ca
Carolynn Ioannoni, City Councillor
ioannoni@niagarafalls.ca
Vince A. Kerrio, City Councillor
kerrio@overlookingthefalls.com s
Serge Felicetti, Director, Business Development
sfelicetti@niagarafalls.ca
Wayne Gates, City Councillor
wgates@niagarafalls.ca
Alex Herlovitch, Director, Planning & Development
planning@niagarafalls.ca
Joyce Morocco, City Councillor
joycemorocco@niagarafalls.ca
Geoffrey Holman, Director, Municipal Works
Janice Wing, City Councillor
jwing@niagarafalls.ca
Bart Maves, City Councillor
wmaves@cogeco.ca
Lee Smith, Fire Chief

Fire Dept.
Patrick Burke, Fire Chief

Niagara-on-the-Lake

P.O. Box 100
1593 Four Mile Creek Rd.
Virgil, ON L0S 1T0
Tel: 905-468-3266; *Fax:* 905-468-2959
webinquiry@notl.org
www.notl.org
Municipal Type: City
Area: 132.83 sq km
County or District: Niagara Reg. Mun.; *Population in 2006:* 14,587
Provincial Electoral District(s): Niagara Falls
Federal Electoral District(s): Niagara Falls
Next Election: Oct. 2014 (4 year terms)

David Eke, Mayor
deke@notl.org
Holly Dowd, Town Clerk
hdowd@notl.org
Dave Lepp, Regional Councillor
dave.lepp@niagararegion.ca
Mike Galloway, Chief Administrative Officer
mgalloway@notl.org
Dennis Dick, Councillor
ddick@notl.org
Sheldon Randall, CMA, Director, Corporate Services
srandall@notl.org
Terry Flynn, Councillor
tflynn@notl.org
Will Walker, Interim Director, Community & Development Services
wwalker@notl.org
Andrea Kaiser, Councillor
akaiser@notl.org
Clive Buist, Director, Parks & Recreation
cbuist@notl.org
Jamie R. King, Councillor
jking@notl.org
E. Kuczera, Director, Public Works
ekuczera@notl.org
Martin Mazza, Councillor
mmazza@notl.org
Greg Warner, Acting Fire Chief
Gary Zalepa, Jr., Councillor
gzalepajr@notl.org
Larry Higgins, Supervisor, Water & Wastewater
lhiggins@notl.org
Maria Bau-Coote, Deputy Mayor & Councillor
mbau-coote@notl.org
Jim Collard, Councillor
jcollard@notl.org
J. Darren MacKenzie, Superintendent, Irrigation & Drainage
dmackenzie@notl.org

North Bay

City Hall
P.O. Box 360
200 McIntyre St. East
North Bay, ON P1B 8H8
Tel: 705-474-0400; *Fax:* 705-495-4353
info@cityofnorthbay.ca
www.city.north-bay.on.ca
Other Information: Toll-Free Phone: 1-800-465-1882
Municipal Type: City
Incorporated: 1925 *Area:* 314.91 sq km
County or District: Nipissing District; *Population in 2006:* 53,966
Provincial Electoral District(s): Nipissing
Federal Electoral District(s): Nipissing-Timiskaming
Next Election: Oct. 2014 (4 year terms)
Al McDonald, Mayor
mayor@cityofnorthbay.ca
Cathy Conrad, City Clerk
cathy.conrad@cityofnorthbay.ca
Peter Chirico, Councillor
peter.chirico@cityofnorthbay.ca
Dave Linkie, Chief Administration Officer
dave.linkie@cityofnorthbay.ca
Mike Anthony, Councillor
mike.anthony@cityofnorthbay.ca
Margaret Karpenko, Chief Financial Officer & Treasurer
margaret.karpenko@cityofnorthbay.ca
Mac Bain, Councillor
mac.bain@cityofnorthbay.ca
Sean Lawlor, Councillor
sean.lawlor@cityofnorthbay.ca
Jerry Knox, Managing Director, Community Services
jerry.knox@cityofnorthbay.ca
George Maroosis, Councillor
george.maroosis@cityofnorthbay.ca
Alan Korell, Managing Director, Engineering, Environmental & Works
alan.korell@cityofnorthbay.ca
Judy Koziol, Councillor
judy.koziol@cityofnorthbay.ca
David Euler, Director, Sewer & Water
david.euler@cityofnorthbay.ca
Chris Mayne, Councillor
chris.mayne@cityofnorthbay.ca
Jamie Houston, Director, Parks, Recreation, & Leisure Services
jamie.houston@cityofnorthbay.ca
Dave Mendicino, Councillor
dave.mendicino@cityofnorthbay.ca
Lea Janisse, Director, Human Resources
lea.janisse@cityofnorthbay.ca
Daryl Vaillancourt, Councillor
daryl.vaillancourt@cityofnorthbay.ca
John Severino, Manager, Environmental Services
john.severino@cityofnorthbay.ca
Tanya Vrebosch Merry, Councillor
tanya.vrebosch-merry@cityofnorthbay.ca
Dorothea Carvell, Manager, Transit
dorothea.carvell@cityofnorthbay.ca
Joe Germano, Manager, Road & Traffic
joe.germano@cityofnorthbay.ca
Ian Kilgour, Manager, Planning Services
ian.kilgour@cityofnorthbay.ca
Shawn Killins, Chief Building Official
shawn.killins@cityofnorthbay.ca
Peter Leckie, City Solicitor
peter.leckie@cityofnorthbay.ca
Grant Love, Fire Chief
grant.love@cityofnorthbay.ca

North Perth

330 Wallace Ave. North
Listowel, ON N4W 1L3
Tel: 519-291-2950;
town@northperth.ca
www.northperth.ca
Other Information: Toll-Free Phone: 1-888-714-1993
Municipal Type: City
Incorporated: 1998 *Area:* 493.18 sq km
County or District: Perth; *Population in 2006:* 12,254
Provincial Electoral District(s): Perth-Wellington
Federal Electoral District(s): Perth-Wellington
Next Election: Oct. 2014 (4 year terms)
Note: Amalgamation of Elma Township, Town of Listowel & Wallace Township.
Julie Behrns, Mayor
juliebehrns@northperth.ca
Patricia Berfelz, Clerk
519-292-2062
pberfelz@northperth.ca
Vince Judge, Deputy Mayor & Councillor
vincejudge@northperth.ca
Frances Hale, Treasurer & Director, Finance
519-292-2045, Fax: 519-291-5611
fhale@northperth.ca
Doug Kellum, Councillor, Ward(s): Listowel
dougkellum@northperth.ca
Steve Hardie, Director, Parks & Recreation
519-292-2055
shardie@northperth.ca
Warren Howard, Councillor, Ward(s): Listowel
warrenhoward@northperth.ca
Mark Hackett, Manager, Environmental Services
519-292-2069
mhackett@northperth.ca
Matt Richardson, Councillor, Ward(s): Listowel
mattrichardson@northperth.ca
Ed Podniewicz, Chief Building Official & Administrator, Zoning
519-292-2058
epodniewicz@northperth.ca
Kenneth Buchanan, Councillor, Ward(s): Elma
kenbuchanan@northperth.ca
Ed Smith, Fire Chief
519-291-6825
esmith@northperth.ca
David Ludington, Councillor, Ward(s): Elma
davidludington@northperth.ca
Matt Duncan, Councillor, Ward(s): Elma
mattduncan@northperth.ca
Meredith Schneider, Councillor, Ward(s): Wallace
Paul Horn, Councillor, Ward(s): Wallace
paulhorn@northperth.ca

Oakville

1225 Trafalgar Rd.
Oakville, ON L6J 5A6
Tel: 905-845-6601; *Fax:* 905-815-2025
publicinquiry@oakville.ca; communications@oakville.ca
www.oakville.ca
Other Information: TTY: 905-338-4200
Municipal Type: City
Incorporated: May 27, 1857 *Area:* 138.56 sq km
County or District: Halton Regional Municipality; *Population in 2006:* 165,613
Provincial Electoral District(s): Halton; Oakville
Federal Electoral District(s): Halton; Oakville
Next Election: Oct. 2014 (4 year terms)
Rob Burton, Mayor, Fax: 905-815-2001
mayor@oakville.ca
Cathie Best, Town Clerk
clerks@oakville.ca; cbest@oakville.ca
Alan Johnston, Town & Regional Councillor, Ward(s): 1
ajohnston@oakville.ca
Ray Green, Chief Administrative Officer
rgreen@oakville.ca
Ralph Robinson, Town Councillor, Ward(s): 1
rrobinson@oakville.ca
Patricia Elliott-Spencer, M.B.A., CMA, Treasurer & Director, Finance
pelliott-spencer@oakville.ca; finance@oakville.ca
Cathy Duddeck, Town & Regional Councillor, Ward(s): 2
cduddeck@oakville.ca
David Bloomer, Commissioner, Infrastructure & Transportation Services
dbloomer@oakville.ca
Pam Damoff, Town Councillor, Ward(s): 2
pdamoff@oakville.ca
Jane Clohecy, Commissioner, Planning & Development Services
jclohecy@oakville.ca; planning@oakville.ca
F. Keith Bird, Town & Regional Councillor, Ward(s): 3
kbird@oakville.ca
Gord Lalonde, Commissioner, Corporate Services
glalonde@oakville.ca
Dave Gittings, Town Councillor, Ward(s): 3
dgittings@oakville.ca
Domenic Lunardo, Commissioner, Community Services
dlunardo@oakville.ca
Allan Elgar, Town & Regional Councillor, Ward(s): 4
aelgar@oakville.ca
Elizabeth Bourns, Director, Human Resources
ebourns@oakville.ca; humanresources@oakville.ca
Roger Lapworth, Town Councillor, Ward(s): 4
rlapworth@oakville.ca
Barry Cole, Director, Transit Services
bcole@oakville.ca; transit@oakville.ca
Jeff Knoll, Town & Regional Councillor, Ward(s): 5
jknoll@oakville.ca
Daniel Cozzi, P.Eng., Director, Roads & Works Operations
dcozzi@oakville.ca
Marc Grant, Town Councillor, Ward(s): 5
mgrant@oakville.ca
Darnell Lambert, C.E.T., Director, Engineering & Construction
dlambert@oakville.ca
Tom Adams, Town & Regional Councillor, Ward(s): 6
tadams@oakville.ca
Chris Mark, Director, Parks & Open Space
cmark@oakville.ca; parks@oakville.ca
Max Khan, Town Councillor, Ward(s): 6
mkhan@oakville.ca
Cindy Toth, Director, Environmental Policy
ctoth@oakville.ca; environment@oakville.ca
Sheldon Switzer, Director, Building Services & Chief Building Official
sswitzer@oakville.ca; building@oakville.ca
John McNeil, Manager, Forestry & Cemetery Services
jmcneil@oakville.ca; forestry@oakville.ca
Richard Boyes, Fire Chief
rboyes@oakville.ca; fire@oakville.ca

Orangeville

87 Broadway St.
Orangeville, ON L9W 1K1
Tel: 519-941-0440; *Fax:* 519-941-9033
info@orangeville.ca
www.orangeville.ca
Other Information: Toll-Free Phone: 1-866-941-0440; TTY: 519-943-0782
Municipal Type: City
Incorporated: Dec. 22, 1863 *Area:* 15.57 sq km
County or District: Dufferin; *Population in 2006:* 26,925
Provincial Electoral District(s): Dufferin-Caledon
Federal Electoral District(s): Dufferin-Caledon
Next Election: Oct. 2014 (4 year terms)
Note: Incorporated as a town on Dec. 15, 1873.
Rob Adams, Mayor
radams@orangeville.ca
Cheryl Johns, Clerk
cjohns@orangeville.ca
Warren Maycock, Deputy Mayor & Councillor
Rick Schwarzer, Chief Administrative Officer
rschwarzer@orangeville.ca
Sylvia Bradley, Councillor
Bill McKennan, Treasurer
bmckennan@orangeville.ca
Gail Campbell, Councillor
Vern Douglas, Director, Building & By-law Enforcement
vdouglas@orangeville.ca
Patrick D'Almada, Director, Parks & Recreation
pdalmada@orangeville.ca
Mary Rose, Councillor
Jeremy Williams, Councillor
James Stiver, Director, Planning
jstiver@orangeville.ca
Scott Wilson, Councillor

Jack Tupling, Director, Public Works
jtupling@orangeville.ca
Ed Gill, Managing Director, Operations & Transportation
egill@orangeville.ca
Doug Jones, Managing Director, Environmental & Development Services
djones@orangeville.ca
Jennifer Gohn, Manager, Human Resources
jgohn@orangeville.ca
Andy Macintosh, Fire Chief
amacintosh@orangeville.ca

Orillia

Administration Office
#300, 50 Andrew St. South
Orillia, ON L3V 7T5
Tel: 705-325-1311; *Fax:* 705-325-5178
corporate@city.orillia.on.ca
www.orillia.ca
Municipal Type: City
Incorporated: 1867 *Area:* 28.61 sq km
County or District: Simcoe; *Population in 2006:* 30,259
Provincial Electoral District(s): Simcoe North
Federal Electoral District(s): Simcoe North
Next Election: Oct. 2014 (4 year terms)
Note: Incorporated as a town in 1875 & as a city in 1969.
Angelo Orsi, Mayor
mayor@city.orillia.on.ca
Gayle Jackson, City Clerk
clerks@orillia.ca; gjackson@orillia.ca
Patrick F. Kehoe, Councillor, Ward(s): 1
Bob Ripley, Interim City Manager/Treasurer
treas@orillia.ca
Donald W. Jenkins, Councillor, Ward(s): 1
Linda Murray, Councillor, Ward(s): 2
Lori Bolton, Director, Human Resources
lbolton@orillia.ca
Pete Bowen, Councillor, Ward(s): 2
Peter Dance, Director, Public Works
publicworks@orillia.ca; pdance@orillia.ca
Michael Fogarty, Councillor, Ward(s): 3
Ray Merkley, Director, Parks & Recreation
parks@orillia.ca; rmerkley@orillia.ca
Paul Spears, Councillor, Ward(s): 3
Craig Metcalf, Director, Culture & Heritage
cmetcalf@orillia.ca
Tony Madden, Councillor, Ward(s): 4
Ian Sugden, Director, Planning & Development
planning@orillia.ca; isugden@orillia.ca
Andrew Hill, Councillor, Ward(s): 4
Ralph Dominell, Fire Chief
ofd@orillia.ca; rdominelli@orillia.ca
Kelly Smith, Chief Building Official
ksmith@orillia.ca
Jack Green, Manager, Transportation
jgreen@orillia.ca
Andrew Schell, Manager, Environmental Services
aschell@orillia.ca
Percival Thomas, Manager, Water & Wastewater Systems
pthomas@orillia.ca

Oshawa

City Hall
50 Centre St. South
Oshawa, ON L1H 3Z7
Tel: 905-436-3311; *Fax:* 905-436-5642
service@oshawa.ca
www.oshawa.ca
Other Information: Toll-Free Phone: 1-800-667-4292; TTY: 905-436-5627
Municipal Type: City
Incorporated: March 8, 1924 *Area:* 145.67 sq km
County or District: Durham Reg. Mun.; *Population in 2006:* 141,590
Provincial Electoral District(s): Whitby-Oshawa; Oshawa
Federal Electoral District(s): Whitby-Oshawa; Oshawa
Next Election: Oct. 2014 (4 year terms)
John Henry, Mayor
jhenry@oshawa.ca
Sandra Kranc, City Clerk, Fax: 905-436-5697
service@oshawa.ca
John Aker, Regional Councillor
jaker@oshawa.ca
Bob Duignan, City Manager
905-436-3311, Fax: 905-436-5623
Bob Chapman, Regional Councillor
bchapman@oshawa.ca
Chris Brown, Director, Finance Services, Fax: 905-436-5664
Nancy Diamond, Regional Councillor
ndiamond@oshawa.ca
Garth Johns, Interim Commissioner, Community Services Department
Amy England, Regional Councillor
aengland@oshawa.ca
Tom Hodgins, Commissioner, Development Services Department
Tito-Dante Marimpietri, Regional Councillor
tdmarimpietri@oshawa.ca
Rick Stockman, Commissioner, Corporate Services Department
John Neal, Regional Councillor
jneal@oshawa.ca
Ron Foster, Auditor General
905-436-5688, Fax: 905-436-5652
rfoster@oshawa.ca
Nester Pidwerbecki, Regional Councillor
npidwerbecki@oshawa.ca
Tracy Adams, Director, Corporate Communications & Marketing
Roger Bouma, City Councillor
rbouma@oshawa.ca
Jamie Bronsema, Director, Strategic & Business Services
Doug Sanders, City Councillor
dsanders@oshawa.ca
Jacqueline Long, Director, Human Resource Services
humanresources@oshawa.ca
Bruce Wood, City Councillor
bwood@oshawa.ca
Gary Carroll, Director, Engineering Services
Denyse Morrissey, Director, Recreation & Culture Services
recreation@oshawa.ca
Craig Kelly, Director, Works & Transportation Services
Paul Ralph, Director, Planning Services
Mike Leonard, Chief Building Official
buildings@oshawa.ca
Steve Meringer, Fire Chief

Ottawa

City Hall
110 Laurier Ave. West
Ottawa, ON K1P 1J1
Tel: 613-580-2400; *Fax:* 613-560-1380
info@ottawa.ca
www.ottawa.ca
Other Information: Toll Free Phone: 1-866-261-9799; or 311
Municipal Type: City
Incorporated: Jan. 1, 1855 *Area:* 2,778.13 sq km
Population in 2006: 812,129
Provincial Electoral District(s): Glengarry-Prescott-Russell; Nepean-Carleton; Ottawa Centre; Ottawa South; Ottawa-Vanier; Ottawa West-Nepean; Ottawa-Orléans; Carleton-Mississippi Mills
Federal Electoral District(s): Glengarry-Prescott-Russell; Nepean-Carleton; Ottawa Centre; Ottawa South; Ottawa-Vanier; Ottawa West-Nepean; Ottawa-Orléans; Carleton-Mississippi Mills
Next Election: Oct. 2014 (4 year terms)
Jim Watson, Mayor
613-580-2496
jim.watson@ottawa.ca
M. Rick O'Connor, City Clerk & Solicitor
Bob Monette, Councillor, Ward(s): 1 - Orléans
613-580-2471
bob.monette@ottawa.ca
Kent Kirkpatrick, City Manager
Rainer Bloess, Councillor, Ward(s): 2 - Innes
613-580-2472
rainer.bloess@ottawa.ca
Marian Simulik, City Treasurer
Jan Harder, Councillor, Ward(s): 3 - Barrhaven
613-580-2473
jan.harder@ottawa.ca
Steve Kanellakos, Deputy City Manager
Marianne Wilkinson, Councillor, Ward(s): 4 - Kanata North
613-580-2474
marianne.wilkinson@ottawa.ca
Nancy Schepers, Deputy City Manager
Eli El-Chantiry, Councillor, Ward(s): 5 - West Carleton-March
613-580-2475
eli.el-chantiry@ottawa.ca
Chris Day, Chief, Corporate Communications
Shad Qadri, Councillor, Ward(s): 6 - Stittsville-Kanata West
613-580-2476
shad.qadri@ottawa.ca
Catherine Frederick, Director, Human Resources
Mark Taylor, Councillor, Ward(s): 7 - Bay
613-580-2477
mark.taylor@ottawa.ca
Donna L. Gray, Director, Organizational Development & Performance
Rick Chiarelli, Councillor, Ward(s): 8 - College
613-580-2478
rick.chiarelli@ottawa.ca
Guy Michaud, Director, Information Technology & Chief Information Officer
Keith Egli, Councillor, Ward(s): 9 - Knoxdale-Merivale
613-580-2479
ward9@ottawa.ca
Johanne Levesque, Director, Community Sustainability
Diane Deans, Councillor, Ward(s): 10 - Gloucester-Southgate
613-580-2480
diane.deans@ottawa.ca
Wayne Newell, Director, Infrastructure Services
Tim Tierney, Councillor, Ward(s): 11 - Beacon Hill-Cyrville
613-580-2481
tim.tierney@ottawa.ca
Aaron Burry, General Manager, Community & Social Services
Mathieu Fleury, Councillor, Ward(s): 12 - Rideau-Vanier
613-580-2482
mathieu.fleury@ottawa.ca
Dan Chenier, General Manager, Parks, Recreation & Cultural Service
Peter Clark, Councillor, Ward(s): 13 - Rideau-Rockcliffe
613-580-2483
peter.clark@ottawa.ca
Susan Jones, General Manager, Emergency & Protective Services
Diane Holmes, Councillor, Ward(s): 14 - Somerset
613-580-2484
diane.holmes@ottawa.ca
John Manconi, General Manager, Public Works
Katherine Hobbs, Councillor, Ward(s): 15 - Kitchissippi
613-580-2485
katherine.hobbs@ottawa.ca
Alain Mercier, General Manager, Transit Services
Maria McRae, Councillor, Ward(s): 16 - River
613-580-2486
maria.mcrae@ottawa.ca
John Moser, General Manager, Planning & Growth Management
David Chernushenko, Councillor, Ward(s): 17 - Capital
613-580-2487
david.chernushenko@ottawa.ca
Dixon A. Weir, General Manager, Environmental Services
Peter Hume, Councillor, Ward(s): 18 - Alta Vista
613-580-2488
peter.hume@ottawa.ca
Isra Levy, Medical Officer of Health
Stephen Blais, Councillor, Ward(s): 19 - Cumberland
613-580-2489
stephen.blais@ottawa.ca
Michel Chevalier, Manager, Wastewater & Drainage Operations
Doug Thompson, Councillor, Ward(s): 20 - Osgoode
613-580-2490
doug.thompson@ottawa.ca
Felice Petti, Manager, Strategic & Environmental Services
Scott Moffatt, Councillor, Ward(s): 21 - Rideau-Goulbourn
613-580-2491
scott.moffatt@ottawa.ca
Tammy Rose, Manager, Drinking Water Services
Steve Desroches, Councillor, Ward(s): 22 - Gloucester-South
613-580-2751
steve.desroches@ottawa.ca
Allan Hubley, Councillor, Ward(s): 23 - Kanata South
613-580-2752
allan.hubley@ottawa.ca

Fire Department

Owen Sound

City Hall
808 - 2nd Ave. East
Owen Sound, ON N4K 2H4
Tel: 519-376-1440; *Fax:* 519-371-0511
cityadmin@e-owensound.com;
communityservices@e-owensound.com
www.owensound.ca
Municipal Type: City
Incorporated: Jan. 1, 2001 *Area:* 24.22 sq km
County or District: Grey; *Population in 2006:* 21,753
Provincial Electoral District(s): Bruce-Grey-Owen Sound
Federal Electoral District(s): Bruce-Grey-Owen Sound
Next Election: Oct. 2014 (4 year terms)
Deborah Haswell, Mayor
Marion Koepke, C.M.O., City Clerk
mkoepke@owensound.ca
David Adair, Councillor
Jim Harrold, City Manager
Ian C. Boddy, Councillor
Wayne Ritchie, CGA, Director, Financial Services
writchie@e-owensound.com
Jan Chamberlain, Councillor
Pam Coulter, Director, Community Services
pcoulter@e-owensound.com
Peter Lemon, Councillor

Glen Henry, C.M.O., Director, Corporate Services
ghenry@owensound.ca
Jim McManaman, Councillor
John D. Johnston, C.E.T., Director, Operations
jdjohnson@e-owensound.com
Colleen Purdon, Councillor
Steve Furness, Manager, Economic Development & Tourism
business@e-owensound.com
Bill Twaddle, Councillor
Chris Webb, P.Eng., Manager, Engineering Services
Arlene Wright, City & County Councillor
Ed Nowak, Fire Chief
enowak@e-owensound.com

Pelham
P.O. Box 400
20 Pelham Town Sq.
Fonthill, ON L0S 1E0
Tel: 905-892-2607;
www.pelham.ca
Municipal Type: City
Incorporated: 1970 *Area:* 126.42 sq km
County or District: Niagara Reg. Mun.; *Population in 2006:* 16,155
Provincial Electoral District(s): Niagara West-Glanbrook
Federal Electoral District(s): Niagara West-Glanbrook
Next Election: Oct. 2014 (4 year terms)
Dave Augustyn, Mayor
mayordave@pelham.ca
Nancy J. Bozzato, Clerk
njbozzato@pelham.ca
Larry Clark, Councillor, Ward(s): 1
lclark@pelham.ca
Martin Yamich, Chief Administrative Officer
myamich@pelham.ca
Richard Rybiak, Councillor, Ward(s): 1
rrybiak@pelham.ca
Cari Pupo, Treasurer
cpupo@pelham.ca
Gary Accursi, Councillor, Ward(s): 2
gaccursi@pelham.ca
Craig Larmour, Director, Planning & Development
clarmour@pelham.ca
Catherine King, Councillor, Ward(s): 2
cking@pelham.ca
John Durley, Councillor, Ward(s): 3
jjdurley@sympatico.ca
Keegan Gennings, Chief Building Official & Manager, By-law Enforcement
kgennings@pelham.ca
Peter Papp, Councillor, Ward(s): 3
ppapp@pelham.ca
Jim Phelps, Acting Fire Chief
jphelps@pelham.ca
Alan Mannell, Manager, Engineering
amannell@pelham.ca

Pembroke
1 Pembroke St. East
Pembroke, ON K8A 3J5
Tel: 613-735-6821; *Fax:* 613-735-3660
pembroke@pembroke.ca
www.pembroke.ca
Municipal Type: City
Incorporated: 1877 *Area:* 14.35 sq km
County or District: Renfrew; *Population in 2006:* 13,930
Provincial Electoral District(s): Renfrew-Nipissing-Pembroke
Federal Electoral District(s): Renfrew-Nipissing-Pembroke
Next Election: Oct. 2014 (4 year terms)
Note: Incorporated as a city in 1971.
Ed Jacyno, Mayor
Terry Lapierre, Chief Administrative Officer
tlapierre@pembroke.ca
Dan Callaghan, Councillor
LeeAnn McIntyre, Treasurer
lmcintyre@pembroke.ca
Ronald Gervais, Deputy Mayor & Councillor, Councillor
Susan Ellis, Manager, Economic Development, Recreation, & Tourism
sellis@pembroke.ca
Bob Hackett, Councillor
Patricia Lafreniere, Councillor
Colleen Sauriol, Coordinator, Emergency Management
csauriol@pembroke.ca
Terry O'Neill, Councillor
Douglas Sitland, Manager, Operations
dsitland@pembroke.ca
Les Scott, Councillor
Daniel Herback, Fire Chief
dherback@pembroke.ca
Gary Severin, Councillor
Robert Hughes, Chief Building Official
rhughes@pembroke.ca
Colonel Towriss, Councillor
Ron Conroy, Supervisor, Parks & Facilities
rconroy@pembroke.ca
Chris Mantha, Supervisor, Roads & Fleet
cmantha@pembroke.ca
Curtis Mick, Supervisor, Water & Sewer
cmick@pembroke.ca

Petawawa
1111 Victoria St.
Petawawa, ON K8H 2E6
Tel: 613-687-5536; *Fax:* 613-687-5973
www.petawawa.ca
Municipal Type: City
Incorporated: July 1, 1997 *Area:* 164.68 sq km
County or District: Renfrew; *Population in 2006:* 14,651
Provincial Electoral District(s): Renfrew-Nipissing-Pembroke
Federal Electoral District(s): Renfrew-Nipissing-Pembroke
Next Election: Oct. 2014 (4 year terms)
Note: Amalgamation of Petawawa Village & Petawawa Township.
Robert Sweet, Mayor
mayor@petawawa.ca
Mitchell Stillman, Chief Administrative Officer & Clerk
Tom Mohns, Deputy Mayor & Councillor
tmohns@petawawa.ca
Daniel Scissons, Treasurer & Deputy Clerk
James Carmody, Councillor
jcarmody@petawawa.ca
Randy Mohns, Chief Building Official
Frank Cirella, Councillor
fcirella@petawawa.ca
Steve Knott, Fire Chief
Treena Lemay, Councillor
tlemay@petawawa.ca
Tom Renaud, Supervisor, Public Works
Murray Rutz, Councillor
mrutz@petawawa.ca
Cyndy Phillips McCann, Coordinator, Economic Development
Theresa Sabourin, Councillor
tsabourin@petawawa.ca
Karen Cronier, Coordinator, Planning

Peterborough
500 George St. North
Peterborough, ON K9H 3R9
Tel: 705-742-7777; *Fax:* 705-742-4138
cityptbo@peterborough.ca; clerk@peterborough.ca
www.peterborough.ca
Other Information: E-mail, Human Resources: hr@peterborough.ca
Municipal Type: City
Incorporated: 1850 *Area:* 58.40 sq km
County or District: Peterborough; *Population in 2006:* 74,898
Provincial Electoral District(s): Peterborough
Federal Electoral District(s): Peterborough
Next Election: Oct. 2014 (4 year terms)
Daryl Bennett, Mayor
dbennett@peterborough.ca
Nancy Wright-Laking, City Clerk
nwright-laking@peterborough.ca
Dan McWilliams, Councillor, Ward(s): 1 - Otonabee
dmcwilliams@peterborough.ca
Brian Horton, Chief Administrative Officer
cao@peterborough.ca
Lesley Parnell, Councillor, Ward(s): 1 - Otonabee
lparnell@peterborough.ca
Sandra Clancy, Director, Corporate Services
sclancy@peterborough.ca
Henry Clarke, Councillor, Ward(s): 2 - Monaghan
hclarke@peterborough.ca
Ken Doherty, Director, Community Services
kdoherty@peterborough.ca
Jack Doris, Councillor, Ward(s): 2 - Monaghan
jdoris@peterborough.ca
Malcolm Hunt, Director, Planning & Development Services
mhunt@peterborough.ca
Bill J. Juby, Councillor, Ward(s): 3 - Town
bjuby@peterborough.ca
Wayne Jackson, Director, Utility Services & Deputy CAO
wjackson@peterborough.ca
Dean Pappas, Councillor, Ward(s): 3 - Town
dpappas@peterborough.ca
Trent Gervais, Fire Chief
Keith G. Riel, Councillor, Ward(s): 4 - Ashburnham
kriel@peterborough.ca
Len Vass, Councillor, Ward(s): 4 - Ashburnham
lvass@peterborough.ca
Andrew Beamer, Councillor, Ward(s): 5 - Northcrest
arbeamer@peterborough.ca
Bob Hall, Councillor, Ward(s): 5 - Northcrest
bhall@peterborough.ca

Pickering
1 The Esplanade
Pickering, ON L1V 6K7
Tel: 905-420-2222;
info@cityofpickering.com; customercare@cityofpickering.com
www.cityofpickering.com
Other Information: Toll-Free Phone: 1-866-683-2760; TTY: 905-420-1739
Municipal Type: City
Incorporated: 1849 *Area:* 231.59 sq km
County or District: Durham Reg. Mun.; *Population in 2006:* 87,838
Provincial Electoral District(s): Ajax-Pickering; Pickering-Scarborough East
Federal Electoral District(s): Ajax-Pickering; Pickering-Scarborough East
Next Election: Oct. 2014 (4 year terms)
Note: Incorporated as a town in 1974 & as a city in 2000.
Dave Ryan, Mayor
905-420-4600, Fax: 905-420-6064
mayor@cityofpickering.com
Debbie Shields, City Clerk
dshields@cityofpickering.com
Jennifer O'Connell, Regional Councillor, Ward(s): 1
jenniferoconnell@sympatico.ca
Tony Prevedel, Chief Administrative Officer
cao@cityofpickering.com
Kevin Ashe, City Councillor, Ward(s): 1
Gilles A. Paterson, Treasurer & Director, Corporate Services
905-420-4634
gpaterson@cityofpickering.com
Bill McLean, Regional Councillor, Ward(s): 2
bmclean@cityofpickering.com
Everett Buntsma, Director, Community Services
905-420-4624
ebuntsma@cityofpickering.com
Doug Dickerson, City Councillor, Ward(s): 2
ddickerson@cityofpickering.com
Neil Carroll, Director, Planning & Development
905-420-4617
ncarroll@cityofpickering.com
Peter Rodrigues, Regional Councillor, Ward(s): 3
prodrigues@cityofpickering.com
Thomas E. Melymuk, Director, Office of Sustainability
905-420-4636
tmelymuk@cityofpickering.com
David Pickles, City Councillor, Ward(s): 3
dpickles@cityofpickering.com
Richard W. Holborn, Division Head, Engineering Services Division
90-542-2049
rholborn@cityofpickering.com
Jennifer Parent, Division Head, Human Resources
905-420-2160
Stephen Reynolds, Division Head, Culture & Recreation
905-420-4620
sreynolds@cityofpickering.com
William T. Douglas, Fire Chief
905-839-9968, Fax: 905-839-6327
fire@cityofpickering.com
Kyle Bentley, Chief Building Official
905-420-2070
kbentley@cityofpickering.com
Paul Bigioni, City Solicitor
905-420-2048
pbigioni@cityofpickering.com

Port Colborne
66 Charlotte St.
Port Colborne, ON L3K 3C8
Tel: 905-835-2900; *Fax:* 905-834-5746
www.portcolborne.ca
Municipal Type: City
Incorporated: 1870 *Area:* 121.97 sq km
County or District: Niagara Reg. Mun.; *Population in 2006:* 18,599
Provincial Electoral District(s): Welland
Federal Electoral District(s): Welland
Next Election: Oct. 2014 (4 year terms)
Note: Incorporated as a town in 1918 & as a city in 1966.
Vance Badawey, Mayor, Fax: 905-835-2969
mayor@portcolborne.ca
Ashley Grigg, City Clerk
ashleygrigg@portcolborne.ca
David Barrick, Regional Councillor
david.barrick@niagararegion.ca

Carrie McIntosh, Chief Administrative Officer
carriemcintosh@portcolborne.ca
David B. Elliott, Councillor, Ward(s): 1
daveelliott@portcolborne.ca
Dan Aquilina, Director, Planning & Development
danaquilina@portcolborne.ca
Bill Steele, Councillor, Ward(s): 1
billsteele@portcolborne.ca
Ron Hanson, Director, Engineering & Operations
hanson@portcolborne.cane.ca
Yvon A. Doucet, Councillor, Ward(s): 2
yvondoucet@portcolborne.ca
Peter Senese, Director, Community & Corporate Services
petersenese@portcolborne.ca
Angie Desmarais, Councillor, Ward(s): 2
angiedesmarais@portcolborne.ca
Stephen Thompson, General Manager, Economic Development, Tourism & Marketing
stephenthompson@portcolborne.ca
Frank M. Danch, Councillor, Ward(s): 3
frankdanch@portcolborne.ca
Thomas Cartwright, Fire Chief
firechief@portcolborne.ca
Bea Kenny, Councillor, Ward(s): 3
beakenny@portcolborne.ca
Ernie Cronier, Chief Building Official
erniecronier@portcolborne.ca
Ron Bodner, Councillor, Ward(s): 4
ronbodner@portcolborne.ca
Rick Marshall, Coordinator, Human Resources
rickmarshall@portcolborne.ca
Barbara Butters, Councillor, Ward(s): 4
barbarabutters@portcolborne.ca
Darlene Suddard, Coordinator, Water & Waste Water Compliance
darlenesuddard@portcolborne.ca
Randy Chamberlain, Coordinator, Health & Safety
randychamberlain@portcolborne.ca

Quinte West

P.O. Box 490
7 Creswell Dr.
Trenton, ON K8V 5R6
Tel: 613-392-2841; *Fax:* 613-392-5608
www.city.quintewest.on.ca
Other Information: Toll-Free Phone: 1-866-485-2841
Municipal Type: City
Incorporated: Jan. 1, 1998 *Area:* 493.85 sq km
County or District: Hastings; *Population in 2006:* 42,697
Provincial Electoral District(s): Northumberland-Quinte West
Federal Electoral District(s): Northumberland-Quinte West
Next Election: Oct. 2014 (4 year terms)
Note: Amalgamation of the former municipalities of Trenton, Sidney, Murray & Frankford.
John R. Williams, Mayor
DonnaLee Craig, Clerk & Manager, Corporate Services
Gary Dyke, Chief Administrative Officer
Sally Freeman, Councillor, Ward(s): 1 - Trenton
613-965-6769
David Clazie, Treasurer & Director, Corporate & Financial Services
Fred Kuypers, Councillor, Ward(s): 1 - Trenton
613-392-8588
Chris Angelo, Director, Public Works & Environmental Services
Leslie Roseblade, Councillor, Ward(s): 1 - Trenton
613-394-3492
Charlie Murphy, Director, Planning & Development Services
Bob Wannamaker, Councillor, Ward(s): 1 - Trenton
613-392-8548
Tim Colasante, Manager, Engineering Services
Doug Whitney, Councillor, Ward(s): 1 - Trenton
613-392-4779
Matt Tracey, Manager, Water & Wastewater
Terry R.F. Cassidy, Councillor, Ward(s): 2 - Sidney
613-395-2031
Tim Osborne, Manager, Human Resources
Ron Hamilton, Councillor, Ward(s): 2 - Sidney
613-392-5369
Phillip Lappan, Chief Building Official
Don Kuntze, Councillor, Ward(s): 2 - Sidney
613-962-6122
John Whelan, Fire Chief
Paul Kyte, Councillor, Ward(s): 2 - Sidney
613-967-2134
Jim Alyea, Councillor, Ward(s): 3 - Murray
613-475-1519
Jim Harrison, Councillor, Ward(s): 3 - Murray
613-392-9437
Keith Reid, Councillor, Ward(s): 4 - Frankford
613-398-7991

Richmond Hill

225 East Beaver Creek Rd.
Richmond Hill, ON L4B 3P4
Tel: 905-771-8800; *Fax:* 905-771-2500
www.richmondhill.ca
Municipal Type: City
Incorporated: 1873 *Area:* 100.89 sq km
County or District: York Reg. Mun.; *Population in 2006:* 162,704
Provincial Electoral District(s): Richmond Hill; Oak Ridges-Markham
Federal Electoral District(s): Richmond Hill; Oak Ridges-Markham
Next Election: Oct. 2014 (4 year terms)
Dave Barrow, Mayor
officemayor@richmondhill.ca
D. McLarty, Town Clerk
clerks@richmondhill.ca
Brenda Hogg, Regional & Local Councillor
bhogg@richmondhill.ca
Joan Anderton, Chief Administrative Officer
cao@richmondhill.ca
Vito Spatafora, Regional & Local Councillor
vspatafora@richmondhill.ca
David Dexter, Treasurer & Director, Financial Services
revenue@richmondhill.ca; budget@richmondhill.ca
Greg Beros, Councillor, Ward(s): 1
gberos@richmondhill.ca
A. Bassios, Commissioner, Planning
planning@richmondhill.ca
Carmine Perrelli, Councillor, Ward(s): 2
cperrelli@richmondhill.ca
Italo Brutto, Commissioner, Environment & Infrastructure Services
905-771-8830
eis@richmondhill.ca
Catro Liu, Councillor, Ward(s): 3
cliu@richmondhill.ca
Dean Miller, Commissioner, Corporate & Financial Services
905-771-2497
dmiller@richmondhill.ca
Lynn Foster, Councillor, Ward(s): 4
lfoster@richmondhill.ca
J. DeVries, Director, Building Services, & Chief Building Official
Nick Papa, Councillor, Ward(s): 5
npapa@richmondhill.ca
D. Joslin, Director, Recreation & Culture
Godwin Chan, Councillor, Ward(s): 6
gchan@richmondhill.ca
P. Lee, Director, Planning Policy

St. Catharines

City Hall
P.O. Box 3012
50 Church St.
St Catharines, ON L2R 7C2
Tel: 905-688-5600; *Fax:* 905-682-3631
info@stcatharines.ca
www.stcatharines.ca
Other Information: TTY: 905-688-4889
Municipal Type: City
Incorporated: 1876 *Area:* 96.11 sq km
County or District: Niagara Reg. Mun.; *Population in 2006:* 131,989
Provincial Electoral District(s): St. Catharines; Welland
Federal Electoral District(s): St. Catharines; Welland
Next Election: Oct. 2014 (4 year terms)
Brian McMullan, Mayor
Bonnie Nistico-Dunk, City Clerk
Jeff Burch, Councillor, Ward(s): 1. Merritton
Colin Briggs, Chief Administrative Officer
Jennifer Stevens, Councillor, Ward(s): 1. Merritton
Shelley Chemnitz, Director, Financial Management Services
fms@stcatharines.ca
Matthew J. Harris, Councillor, Ward(s): 2. St. Andrew's
Paul Chapman, Director, Planning Services
Joseph Kushner, Councillor, Ward(s): 2. St. Andrew's
Richard Lane, Director, Recreation & Community Services
rcs@stcatharines.ca
Peter Secord, Councillor, Ward(s): 3. St. Georges
Mark Mehlenbacher, Director, Fire & Emergency Management Services
fs@stcatharines.ca
Greg Washuta, Councillor, Ward(s): 3. St. Georges
Paul Mustard, Director, Transportation & Environmental Services
tes@stcatharines.ca
Mark Elliott, Councillor, Ward(s): 4. St. Patricks
David Oakes, Director, Economic Development & Tourism Services
edt@stcatharines.ca
Mathew D. Siscoe, Councillor, Ward(s): 4. St. Patricks
Nicole Auty, City Solicitor

Dawn Dodge, Councillor, Ward(s): 5. Grantham
Bill Phillips, Councillor, Ward(s): 5. Grantham
Len Stack, Councillor, Ward(s): 6. Port Dalhousie
Bruce Williamson, Councillor, Ward(s): 6. Port Dalhousie

St. Thomas

City Hall
P.O. Box 520
545 Talbot St.
St Thomas, ON N5P 3V7
Tel: 519-631-1680;
www.city.st-thomas.on.ca
Municipal Type: City
Incorporated: March 4, 1881 *Area:* 35.48 sq km
County or District: Elgin; *Population in 2006:* 36,110
Provincial Electoral District(s): Elgin-Middlesex-London
Federal Electoral District(s): Elgin-Middlesex-London
Next Election: Oct. 2014 (4 year terms)
Heather Jackson-Chapman, Mayor
hchapman@city.st-thomas.on.ca
Wendell Graves, City Clerk
wgraves@city.st-thomas.on.ca
Lori Baldwin-Sands, Alderman
loribaldwinsands@live.com
Bill Day, City Treasurer
bday@city.st-thomas.on.ca
Gord Campbell, Alderman
jcampbell384@rogers.com
Graham Dart, Director, Human Resources
gdart@city.st-thomas.on.ca
Mark Cosens, Alderman
mark@markyourx.com
John Dewancker, Director, Environmental Services, & City Engineer
jdewancker@city.st-thomas.on.ca
Tom Johnston, Alderman
tomjohnston@execulink.com
Patrick Keenan, Director, Planning
pkeenan@city.st-thomas.on.ca
Jeff Kohler, Alderman
jkohler67@live.com
Brian Clement, Manager, Engineering
bclement@city.st-thomas.on.ca
David Warden, Alderman
warden_dave@hotmail.com
Edward Soldo, Manager, Operations & Compliance
esoldo@city.st-thomas.on.ca
Sam Yusuf, Alderman
sam@samyusuf.ca
Ross Tucker, Director, Parks & Recreation
rtucker@city.st-thomas.on.ca
Rob Broadbent, Fire Chief
rbroadbent@city.st-thomas.on.ca
Leon Bach, Chief Building Official
lbach@city.st-thomas.on.ca
Cyril McCready, Supervisor, Water & Wastewater
cmccready@city.st-thomas.on.ca
Dave White, Supervisor, Roads & Transportation
dwhite@city.st-thomas.on.ca

Sarnia

City Hall
P.O. Box 3018
255 North Christina St.
Sarnia, ON N7T 7N2
Tel: 519-332-0330;
clerks@sarnia.ca; bylaws@sarnia.ca; legal@sarnia.ca
www.sarnia.ca
Other Information: TTY: 519-332-2664
Municipal Type: City
Incorporated: May 7, 1914 *Area:* 164.63 sq km
County or District: Lambton; *Population in 2006:* 71,419
Provincial Electoral District(s): Sarnia-Lambton
Federal Electoral District(s): Sarnia-Lambton
Next Election: Oct. 2014 (4 year terms)
Mike Bradley, Mayor
mayor@sarnia.ca
Brian Knott, Clerk & Solicitor
brian.knott@sarnia.ca
Dave Boushy, City / County Councillor
dave.boushy@sarnia.ca
Lloyd Fennell, City Manager
lloyd.fennell@sarnia.ca
Jim Foubister, City / County Councillor
jim.foubister@sarnia.ca
Brian McKay, Director, Finance
finance@.sarnia.ca; brian.mckay@sarnia.ca
Anne Marie Gillis, City / County Councillor
sarcouncillor@gmail.com
Kim Bresee, Director, Planning & Building
planning@sarnia.ca; kim.bresee@sarnia.ca

Bev MacDougall, City / County Councillor
bevmacdougall@ebtech.net
Ian Smith, Director, Community Services
comserv@sarnia.ca; ian.smith@sarnia.ca
Andy Bruziewicz, City Councillor
andybruziewicz@hotmail.com
Jim Stevens, Director, Transit
transit@sarnia.ca; jim.stevens@sarnia.ca
Terry Burrell, City Councillor
terry@terryburrell.ca
Peter Hungerford, Manager, Economic Development & Corporate Planning
economic@sarnia.ca; peter.hungerford@sarnia.ca
Mike Kelch, City Councillor
mjkelch@mac.com
Chris Armstrong, Manager, Human Resources
hr@sarnia.ca; chris.armstrong@sarnia.ca
Jon McEachran, City Councillor
jonmceachran@hotmail.com
Andre Morin, City Engineer
engineer@sarnia.ca; andre.morin@sarnia.ca
Doug Robertson, Superintendent, Public Works Department
doug.robertson@sarnia.ca
Pat Cayen, Fire Chief, Fire Rescue Services
firerescue@sarnia.ca; pat.cayen@sarnia.ca

Saugeen Shores

P.O. Box 820
600 Tomlinson Dr.
Port Elgin, ON N0H 2C0
Tel: 519-832-2008; *Fax:* 519-832-2140
www.saugeenshores.ca
Municipal Type: City
Area: 170.58 sq km
County or District: Bruce; *Population in 2006:* 11,720
Provincial Electoral District(s): Huron-Bruce
Federal Electoral District(s): Huron-Bruce
Next Election: Oct. 2014 (4 year terms)
Mike Smith, Mayor
mayor@saugeenshores.ca
Linda White, Clerk
whitel@saugeenshores.ca
Luke Charbonneau, Deputy Mayor & Councillor
lcharbonneau@bmts.com
Lawrence Allison, Chief Administrative Officer
allisonl@saugeenshores.ca
Doug Gowanlock, Vice Deputy Mayor & Councillor
beaglerun@bmts.com
Lori Sweiger, Treasurer
sweigerl@saugeenshores.ca
Marcel Legault, Ward(s): Port Elgin
mlegaul@bmts.com
Dave Burnside, Director, Engineering Services
burnsided@saugeenshores.ca
Fred Schildroth, Councillor, Ward(s): Port Elgin
schildrf@bmts.com
Stuart Doyle, Director, Public Works
doyles@saugeenshores.ca
Gary R. Brown, Councillor, Ward(s): Saugeen
cargar@bmts.com
Mike Myatt, Director, Community Services
myattm@saugeenshores.ca
Taun Frosst, Councillor, Ward(s): Saugeen
sunset.taun@gmail.com
Lynn Worsley, Officer, Human Resources
worsleyl@saugeenshores.ca
Diane Huber, Councillor, Ward(s): Southampton
dianehuber@bmts.com
Jim Bell, Chief Building Official
bellj@saugeenshores.ca
Thead Seaman, Councillor, Ward(s): Southampton
t.j.seaman@bmts.com
Phil Eagleson, Fire Chief
shores.fire@bmts.com
Cassie Coulson, Coordinator, Water & Sewer
coulsonc@saugeenshores.ca

Sault Ste. Marie

Civic Centre
P.O. Box 580
99 Foster Dr.
Sault Ste Marie, ON P6A 5N1
Tel: 705-759-2500; *Fax:* 705-759-2310
webmaster@cityssm.on.
www.cityssm.on.ca
Municipal Type: City
Incorporated: 1912 *Area:* 221.71 sq km
County or District: Algoma District; *Population in 2006:* 74,948
Provincial Electoral District(s): Sault Ste. Marie
Federal Electoral District(s): Sault Ste. Marie
Next Election: Oct. 2014 (4 year terms)
Debbie Amaroso, Mayor
mayor.amaroso@cityssm.on.ca
Malcolm White, City Clerk
705-759-5388
cityclerk@cityssm.on.ca
Steve Butland, Councillor, Ward(s): 1
s.butland@cityssm.on.ca
Joseph M. (Joe) Fratesi, B.A., LL.B., Chief Administrative Officer
705-759-5347
j.fratesi@cityssm.on.ca
Paul Christian, Councillor, Ward(s): 1
p.christian@cityssm.on.ca
William Freiburger, Treasurer & Commissioner, Finance
705-759-5349
b.freiburger@cityssm.on.ca
Terry Sheehan, Councillor, Ward(s): 2
t.sheehan@cityssm.on.ca
Nicholas J. Apostle, Commissioner, Community Services
n.apostle@cityssm.on.ca
Susan Myers, Councillor, Ward(s): 2
s.myers@cityssm.on.ca
Jerry Dolcetti, Commissioner, Engineering & Planning
j.dolcetti@cityssm.on.ca
Pat Mick, Councillor, Ward(s): 3
p.mick@cityssm.on.ca
John R. Luszka, Commissioner, Human Resources
j.luszka@cityssm.on.ca
Brian Watkins, Councillor, Ward(s): 3
ab.watkins@cityssm.on.ca
Larry Girardi, Commissioner, Public Works & Transportation
l.girardi@cityssm.on.ca
Lou Turco, Councillor, Ward(s): 4
l.turco@cityssm.on.ca
Kim Streich-Poser, Commissioner, Social Services
k.streich-poser@cityssm.on.ca
Rick Niro, Councillor, Ward(s): 4
r.niro@cityssm.on.ca
Nuala Kenny, City Solicitor
n.kenny@cityssm.on.ca
Frank Fata, Councillor, Ward(s): 5
f.fata@cityssm.on.ca
Marcel Provenzano, Fire Chief
m.provenzano@cityssm.on.ca
Marchy Bruni, Councillor, Ward(s): 5
m.bruni@cityssm.on.ca
Frank Manzo, Councillor, Ward(s): 6
Joe Krmpotich, Councillor, Ward(s): 6
j.krmpotich@cityssm.on.ca

Stratford

City Hall
P.O. Box 818
1 Wellington St.
Stratford, ON N5A 6W1
Tel: 519-271-0250; *Fax:* 519-273-5041
general@city.stratford.on.ca
www.city.stratford.on.ca
Other Information: TTY: 519-271-5241
Municipal Type: City
Incorporated: 1854 *Area:* 25.28 sq km
County or District: Perth; *Population in 2006:* 30,461
Provincial Electoral District(s): Perth-Wellington
Federal Electoral District(s): Perth-Wellington
Next Election: Oct. 2014 (4 year terms)
Note: Incorporated as a city in 1886.
Daniel Mathieson, Mayor
519-271-2783
dmathieson@city.stratford.on.ca
Joan Thomson, Clerk
clerks@city.stratford.on.ca
Brad Beatty, Councillor
bbeatty@city.stratford.on.ca
Ronald R. Shaw, Chief Administrative Officer
cao@city.stratford.on.ca
George Brown, Councillor
gbrowny1@gmail.com
Larry Appel, Director, Economic Development
lappel@city.stratford.on.ca
Tom Clifford, Councillor
tclifford@brownclimatecare.com
George Bowa, Director, Engineering & Public Works
Keith Culliton, Councillor
CBL@cullitonbrothers.com
Bonnie Henderson, Councillor
bonnie48henderson@yahoo.ca
Barbara Dembek, Director, Building & Planning
Frank Mark, Councillor
frank.mark@schaeffler.com
David St. Louis, Director, Community Services
Kerry McManus, Councillor
kmcmanus@city.stratford.on.ca
Bill Tigert, Director, Social Services
Paul Nickel, Councillor
nickel@sympatico.ca
Rick Young, Fire Chief
Martin Ritsma, Councillor
martinritsma@gmail.com
Jeff Bannon, City Planner
Karen Smythe, Councillor
k.smythe@rogers.com
Randy Mattice, Economic Development Officer

Tecumseh

917 Lesperance Rd.
Tecumseh, ON N8N 1W9
Tel: 519-735-2184; *Fax:* 519-735-6712
info@tecumseh.ca
www.tecumseh.ca
Municipal Type: City
Incorporated: 1921 *Area:* 94.71 sq km
County or District: Essex; *Population in 2006:* 24,224
Provincial Electoral District(s): Windsor-Tecumseh
Federal Electoral District(s): Windsor-Tecumseh
Next Election: Oct. 2014 (4 year terms)
Note: Restructuring occurred in 1999.
Gary McNamara, Mayor
gmcnamara@tecumseh.ca
Laura Moy, Clerk & Director, Staff Services
Tony Haddad, Chief Administrative Officer
Cheryl M. Hardcastle, Deputy Mayor & Councillor
519-818-2047
Luc Gagnon, Treasurer & Director, Financial Services
Marcel (Pat) Blais, Councillor, Ward(s): 1
519-735-2686
Dan Piescic, Director, Public Works & Environmental Services
Rita Ossington, Councillor, Ward(s): 1
519-735-8251
Shaun Fuerth, Director, Information Systems
Guy Dorion, Councillor, Ward(s): 2
519-735-8580
Brian Hillman, Director, Planning & Building Services
Joe Bachetti, Councillor, Ward(s): 3
519-979-3339
Doug Pitre, Director, Fire Services
Tania C. Jobin, Councillor, Ward(s): 4
519-791-4213
Denis Berthiume, Manager, Water Services
Casey Colthurst, Manager, Parks & Horticulture
Rob Filipov, Manager, Engineering Services
Kerri Rice, Manager, Recreation Programs & Events

Temiskaming Shores

Temiskaming Shores Administration Office
P.O. Box 2050
325 Farr Ave.
Haileybury, ON P0J 1K0
Tel: 705-672-3363; *Fax:* 705-672-3200
www.temiskamingshores.ca
Municipal Type: City
Incorporated: Jan. 1, 2004 *Area:* 177 sq km
County or District: Timiskaming District; *Population in 2006:* 10,732
Provincial Electoral District(s): Timiskaming-Cochrane
Federal Electoral District(s): Nipissing-Timiskaming
Next Election: Oct. 2014 (4 year terms)
Note: Amalgamation of the Town of Haileybury, the Town of New Liskeard & the Township of Dymond.
Carman Kidd, Mayor
Sue Weiss, Clerk
Bob Hobbs, Councillor
Christopher W. Oslund, City Manager
Doug Jelly, Councillor
Laura Lee McLeod, Treasurer
Mike McArthur, Councillor
Dan Harvey, Acting Director, Public Works
Jamie Morrow, Councillor
Tammie Caldwell, Director, Leisure Services
Brian Thornton, Councillor
Danny Whalen, Councillor
James Sheppard, Manager, Public Works Operations
David Treen, Manager, Environmental & Engineering Services
Tim Uttley, Fire Chief

Thorold

Thorold City Hall
P.O. Box 1044
3540 Schmon Pkwy.
Thorold, ON L2V 4A7
Tel: 905-227-6613; *Fax:* 905-227-5590
secr@thorold.com (Administrative Assistant)
www.thorold.com
Other Information: E-mail, Deputy City Clerk: depclerk@thorold.com

Municipal Type: City
Incorporated: 1798 *Area:* 83 sq km
County or District: Niagara Reg. Mun.; *Population in 2006:* 18,224
Provincial Electoral District(s): Welland
Federal Electoral District(s): Welland
Next Election: Oct. 2014 (4 year terms)
Note: Incorporated as a village in 1850, as a town in 1875, as a new town (amalgamating the Township of Thorold & the Town of Thorold) in 1970, & as a city in 1975.
Ted Luciani, Mayor
mayor@thorold.com
Susan M. Daniels, AMCT, City Clerk
clerk@thorold.com
Henry D'Angela, Regional Councillor
Frank A. Fabiano, Chief Administrative Officer
adm@thorold.com
Arlene Arch, Councillor
councillorarch@cogeco.ca
Maria J. Mauro, Director, Finance
finance@thorold.com
Becky Day, Councillor
beckyday@hotmail.com
Adele Arbour, Director, Planning & Building Services
aarbour@thorold.com
Jennifer Ferry, Councillor
jenniferlynnferry@gmail.com
Mike Sauchuk, Director, Operations
905-227-3535
theoreng@thorold.com
Mike Murphy, Councillor
m__murphy7@sympatico.ca
Sergio Paone, Councillor
spaone@cogeco.ca
Jeff Menard, A.Sc.T., B.Tech, Chief Building Official
jmenard@thorold.com
Norbert Preiner, Councillor
norbert.preiner@ncdsb.com
Dave Akrigg, Manager, Parks, Cemetary & Arena Operations
905-227-1911
dave@thorold.com
Tim Whalen, Councillor
twhalen1@cogeco.ca
Shawn Wilson, Councillor
councillorshawnwilson@gmail.com

Thunder Bay

City Hall
P.O. Box 800
500 Donald St. East
Thunder Bay, ON P7C 5K4
Tel: 807-625-2230; *Fax:* 807-623-5468
cityinfo@thunderbay.ca
www.thunderbay.ca
Other Information: TTY: 807-625-2230
Municipal Type: City
Incorporated: Jan 1, 1970 *Area:* 328.48 sq km
County or District: Thunder Bay District; *Population in 2006:* 109,140
Provincial Electoral District(s): Thunder Bay-Superior North; Thunder Bay-Atikokan
Federal Electoral District(s): Thunder Bay-Rainy River; Thunder Bay-Superior North
Next Election: Oct. 2014 (4 year terms)
Keith Hobbs, Mayor
John S. Hannam, City Clerk
807-623-2238, Fax: 807-623-5468
jhannam@thunderbay.ca
Iain Angus, Councillor at Large
Tim Commisso, City Manager
807-625-2224, Fax: 807-623-1164
tcommisso@thunderbay.ca
Ken Boshcoff, Councillor at Large
Carol Busch, C.G.A., Treasurer & General Manager, Finance
807-625-2242
cbusch@thunderbay.ca
Larry Hebert, Councillor at Large
Greg Alexander, General Manager, Community Services
807-625-2315, Fax: 807-623-3292
galexander@thunderbay.ca
Rebecca Johnson, Councillor at Large
Rosalie Evans, General Manager, Corporate Services & City Solicitor
807-625-2405, Fax: 807-623-2256
revans@thunderbay.ca
Aldo. V. Ruberto, Councillor at Large
Alan Fydirchuk, General Manager, Facilities & Fleet
807-684-2774, Fax: 807-345-1909
afydirchuk@thunderbay.ca
Andrew Foulds, Ward Councillor, Ward(s): Current River
Darrell Matson, General Manager, Transportation & Works
dmatson@thunderbay.ca
Trevor Giertuga, Ward Councillor, Ward(s): McIntyre
Mark Smith, General Manager, Development Services
807-625-2544, Fax: 807-625-2206
msmith@thunderbay.ca
Paul Pugh, Ward Councillor, Ward(s): McKellar
Norm Gale, Chief, Emergency Medical Services
807-625-3259, Fax: 807-625-2698
ngale@thunderbay.ca
Linda Rydholm, Ward Councillor, Ward(s): Neebing
John Hay, Fire Chief
jhay@thunderbay.ca
Mark Bentz, Ward Councillor, Ward(s): Northwood
Brad Loroff, Manager, Transit
807-684-2187
bloroff@thunderbay.ca
Brian McKinnon, Ward Councillor, Ward(s): Red River
Alan Hjorth, Manager, Human Resources
807-625-2585, Fax: 807-625-3585
ahjorth@thunderbay.ca
Joe Virdiramo, Ward Councillor, Ward(s): Westfort
Karen Lewis, Manager, Corporate Communications & Strategic Initiatives
807-625-3859, Fax: 807-625-0181
klewis@thunderbay.ca
Kerri Marshall, Manager, Environment
807-625-2836, Fax: 807-625-3588
kmarshall@thunderbay.ca
Pat Mauro, Manager, Engineering
807-625-3022, Fax: 807-625-3588
pmauro@thunderbay.ca

Tillsonburg

200 Broadway St., 2nd Fl.
Tillsonburg, ON N4G 5A7
Tel: 519-842-9200; *Fax:* 519-688-0759
www.tillsonburg.ca
Municipal Type: City
Incorporated: 1872 *Area:* 22.34 sq km
County or District: Oxford; *Population in 2006:* 14,822
Provincial Electoral District(s): Oxford
Federal Electoral District(s): Oxford
Next Election: Oct. 2014 (4 year terms)
John Lessif, Mayor
jlessif@tillsonburg.ca
Donna Hemeryck, Clerk
dhemeryck@tillsonburg.ca
Kelley Coulter, Chief Administrative Officer
kcoulter@tillsonburg.ca
Darrell Eddington, Director, Finance
deddington@town.tillsonburg.on.ca
Mark Renaud, Deputy Mayor & Councillor
mrenaud@tillsonburg.ca
Steve Lund, Director, Operations
slund@town.tillsonburg.on.ca
Dave Beres, Councillor
dberes@tillsonburg.ca
Geno Vanhaelewyn, Chief Building Official
gvanhaelewyn@tillsonburg.ca
Mel Getty, Councillor
mgetty@tillsonburg.ca
Bryan Drinkwater, Manager, Operations Utility
bdrinkwater@town.tillsonburg.on.ca
Marty Klein, Councillor
mklein@tillsonburg.ca
Peter Fung, Manager, Engineering
pfung@town.tillsonburg.on.ca
Chris (Chrissy) Rosehart, Councillor
crosehart@tillsonburg.ca
Kelly Batt, Manager, Parks & Facilities
kbatt@town.tillsonburg.on.ca
Brian Stephenson, Councillor
bstephenson@tillsonburg.ca
Bob Parsons, Fire Chief
bparsons@town.tillsonburg.on.ca

Timmins

220 Algonquin Blvd. East
Timmins, ON P4N 1B3
Tel: 705-264-1331; *Fax:* 705-360-2674
www.timmins.ca
Municipal Type: City
Incorporated: 1973 *Area:* 2,961.58 sq km
County or District: Cochrane District; *Population in 2006:* 42,997
Provincial Electoral District(s): Timmins-James Bay
Federal Electoral District(s): Timmins-James Bay
Next Election: Oct. 2014 (4 year terms)
Thomas B. Laughren, Mayor
mayor@timmins.ca
R. Jack Watson, Clerk
Gary Scripnick, Councillor, Ward(s): 1
gary.scripnick@timmins.ca
Joe Torlone, Chief Administrative Officer
cao@timmins.ca
John P. Curley, Councillor, Ward(s): 2
john.curley@timmins.ca
Bernie Christian, City Treasurer
Noella C. Rinaldo, Councillor, Ward(s): 3
noella.rinaldo@timmins.ca
Luc Duval, Director, Public Works & Engineering
Pat Bamford, Councillor, Ward(s): 4
pat.bamford@timmins.ca
Steven L. Black, Councillor, Ward(s): 5
steven.black@timmins.ca
Michael J.J. Doody, Councillor, Ward(s): 5
michael.doody@timmins.ca
David Laneville, Director, Information Technology
Todd Lever, Councillor, Ward(s): 5
todd.lever@timmins.ca
Mike Pintar, Fire Chief
Andrew Marks, Councillor, Ward(s): 5
andrew.marks@timmins.ca

Toronto

City Hall
100 Queen St. West
Toronto, ON M5H 2N2
Tel: 416-392-2489; *Fax:* 416-338-0685
311@toronto.ca
www.toronto.ca
Other Information: In Toronto: 311; TTY: 416-338-0889
Municipal Type: City
Incorporated: March 6, 1834 *Area:* 630.18 sq km
Population in 2006: 2,503,281
Provincial Electoral District(s): Beaches-East York; To.-Danforth; Davenport; Don V. East; Don V. West; Eglinton-Lawrence; Etob. Centre; Etob.-Lakeshore; Etob. North; Parkdale-High Park; St. Paul's; Scarb.-Agincourt; Scarb. Centre; Scarb. Southwest; Scarb.-Guildwood; Scarb.-Rouge River; To. Centre; Trinity-Spadina; Willowdale; York Centre; York South-Weston; York West
Federal Electoral District(s): Beaches-East York; Davenport; Don V. East; Don V. West; Eglinton-Lawrence; Etob. Centre; Etob.-Lakeshore; Etob. North; Parkdale-High Park; St. Paul's; Scarb.-Agincourt; Scarb. Centre; Scarb. Southwest; Scarb.-Guildwood; Scarb.-Rouge River; To. Centre; To.-Danforth; Trinity-Spadina; Willowdale; York Centre; York South-Weston, York West
Next Election: Oct. 2014 (4 year terms)
Note: Incorporated as a city on Jan. 1, 1998, & comprising the 6 former municipalities of: Etobicoke; North York; York; East York; Scarborough; & Old Toronto
Rob Ford, Mayor
mayor_ford@toronto.ca
Ulli S. Watkiss, City Clerk
416-392-8010, Fax: 416-392-2980
Vincent Crisanti, Councillor, Ward(s): 1 - Etobicoke North
councillor_crisanti@toronto.ca
Joseph Pennachetti, City Manager
416-392-3551, Fax: 416-392-1827
Doug Ford, Councillor, Ward(s): 2 - Etobicoke North
councillor_dford@toronto.ca
Cam Weldon, Chief Financial Officer & Deputy City Manager
416-392-8773, Fax: 416-397-5236
Doug Holyday, Councillor, Ward(s): 3 - Etobicoke Centre
councillor_holyday@toronto.ca
Richard Butts, Deputy City Manager
416-338-7200, Fax: 416-392-4540
Gloria Lindsay Luby, Councillor, Ward(s): 4 - Etobicoke Centre
councillor_lindsay_luby@toronto.ca
Sue Corke, Deputy City Manager
416-338-7205, Fax: 416-395-0388
Peter Milczyn, Councillor, Ward(s): 5 - Etobicoke-Lakeshore
councillor_milczyn@toronto.ca
Bruce L. Anderson, Executive Director, Human Resources
416-397-4112, Fax: 416-392-1524
Mark Grimes, Councillor, Ward(s): 6 - Etobicoke-Lakeshore
councillor_grimes@toronto.ca
Ann Borooah, Executive Director, Toronto Building, & Chief Building Official
416-397-4446, Fax: 416-397-4383
Giorgio Mammoliti, Councillor, Ward(s): 7 - York West
councillor_mammoliti@toronto.ca
Jim Hart, Executive Director, Municipal Licensing & Standards
416-392-8445, Fax: 416-397-5463
Anthony Perruzza, Councillor, Ward(s): 8 - York West
councillor_perruzza@toronto.ca
Gary Wright, Executive Director, City Planning, & Chief Planner
416-392-8772, Fax: 416-392-8115
Maria Augimeri, Councillor, Ward(s): 9 - York Centre
councillor_augimeri@toronto.ca

Phil Brown, General Manager, Shelter, Support, & Housing Administration
416-392-7885, Fax: 416-392-0548
James Pasternak, Councillor, Ward(s): 10 - York Centre
councillor_pasternak@toronto.ca
Lou Di Gironimo, General Manager, Toronto Water
416-392-8200, Fax: 416-302-4540
Frances Nunziata, Councillor, Ward(s): 11 - York South-Weston
councillor_nunziata@toronto.ca
Bruce K. Farr, General Manager, Emergency Medical Services, & EMS Chief
416-397-9240, Fax: 416-392-2115
Frank Di Giorgio, Councillor, Ward(s): 12 - York South-Weston
councillor_digiorgio@toronto.ca
Heather MacVicar, General Manager, Employment & Social Services
416-392-8952, Fax: 416-392-4214
Sarah Doucette, Councillor, Ward(s): 13 - Parkdale-High Park
councillor_doucette@toronto.ca
Brenda Patterson, General Manager, Parks, Forestry, & Recreation
416-392-8182, Fax: 416-392-8565
parks@toronto.ca
Gord Perks, Councillor, Ward(s): 14 - Parkdale-High Park
councillor_perks@toronto.ca
Geoff Rathbone, General Manager, Solid Waste Management Services
416-392-4715, Fax: 416-392-4754
Josh Colle, Councillor, Ward(s): 15 - Eglinton-Lawrence
councillor_colle@toronto.ca
William (Bill) Stewart, General Manager, Fire Services & Fire Chief
416-338-9051, Fax: 416-338-9060
Karen Stintz, Councillor, Ward(s): 16 - Eglinton-Lawrence
councillor_stintz@toronto.ca
Gary Welsh, General Manager, Transportation Services
416-392-8431, Fax: 416-392-4455
Cesar Palacio, Councillor, Ward(s): 17 - Davenport
councillor_palacio@toronto.ca
Anna Kinastowski, City Solicitor
416-392-0080, Fax: 416-397-5624
Ana Bailao, Councillor, Ward(s): 18 - Davenport
councillor_bailao@toronto.ca
David McKeown, Medical Officer of Health
416-338-7820, Fax: 416-392-0713
Mike Layton, Councillor, Ward(s): 19 - Trinity-Spadina
councillor_layton@toronto.ca
Adam Vaughan, Councillor, Ward(s): 20 - Trinity-Spadina
councillor_vaughan@toronto.ca
Joe Mihevc, Councillor, Ward(s): 21 - St. Paul's
councillor_mihevc@toronto.ca
Josh Matlow, Councillor, Ward(s): 22 - St. Paul's
councillor_matlow@toronto.ca
John Filion, Councillor, Ward(s): 23 - Willowdale
councillor_filion@toronto.ca
David Shiner, Councillor, Ward(s): 24 - Willowdale
councillor_shiner@toronto.ca
Jaye Robinson, Councillor, Ward(s): 25 - Don Valley West
councillor_robinson@toronto.ca
John Parker, Councillor, Ward(s): 26 - Don Valley West
councillor_parker@toronto.ca
Kristyn Wong-Tam, Councillor, Ward(s): 27 - Toronto Centre-Rosedale
councillor_wongtam@toronto.ca
Pam McConnell, Councillor, Ward(s): 28 - Toronto Centre-Rosedale
councillor_mcconnell@toronto.ca
Mary Fragedakis, Councillor, Ward(s): 29 - Toronto-Danforth
councillor_fragedakis@toronto.ca
Paula Fletcher, Councillor, Ward(s): 30 - Toronto-Danforth
councillor_fletcher@toronto.ca
Janet Davis, Councillor, Ward(s): 31 - Beaches-East York
councillor_davis@toronto.ca
Mary-Margaret McMahon, Councillor, Ward(s): 32 - Beaches-East York
councillor_mcmahon@toronto.ca
Shelley Carroll, Councillor, Ward(s): 33 - Don Valley East
councillor_carroll@toronto.ca
Denzil Minnan-Wong, Councillor, Ward(s): 34 - Don Valley East
councillor_minnan-wong@toronto.ca
Michelle Berardinetti, Councillor, Ward(s): 35 - Scarborough Southwest
councillor_berardinetti@toronto.ca
Gary Crawford, Councillor, Ward(s): 36 - Scarborough Southwest
councillor_crawford@toronto.ca
Michael Thompson, Councillor, Ward(s): 37 - Scarborough Centre
councillor_thompson@toronto.ca
Glenn De Baeremaeker, Councillor, Ward(s): 38 - Scarborough Centre
councillor_debaeremaeker@toronto.ca
Mike Del Grande, Councillor, Ward(s): 39 - Scarborough-Agincourt
councillor_delgrande@toronto.ca
Norm Kelly, Councillor, Ward(s): 40 - Scarborough-Agincourt
councillor_kelly@toronto.ca
Chin Lee, Councillor, Ward(s): 41 - Scarborough-Rouge River
councillor_lee@toronto.ca
Raymond Cho, Councillor, Ward(s): 42 - Scarborough-Rouge River
councillor_cho@toronto.ca
Paul Ainslie, Councillor, Ward(s): 43 - Scarborough East
councillor_ainslie@toronto.ca
Ron Moeser, Councillor, Ward(s): 44 - Scarborough East
councillor_moeser@toronto.ca

Vaughan

2141 Major Mackenzie Dr.
Vaughan, ON L6A 1T1
Tel: 905-832-2281; *Fax:* 905-832-8535
clerks@vaughan.ca; humanresources@vaughan.ca
www.vaughan.ca
Other Information: Phone (Automated): 905-832-8585
Municipal Type: City
Incorporated: Jan. 1, 1971 *Area:* 273.58 sq km
County or District: York Regional Municipality; *Population in 2006:* 238,866
Provincial Electoral District(s): Vaughan; Thornhill
Federal Electoral District(s): Vaughan; Thornhill
Next Election: Oct. 2014 (4 year terms)
Maurizio Bevilacqua, Mayor
mayor@vaughan.ca
Jeffrey A. Abrams, City Clerk
jeffrey.abrams@vaughan.ca
Michael Di Biase, Regional Councillor
michael.dibiase@vaughan.ca
Clayton Harris, City Manager
clayton.harris@vaughan.ca
Gino Rosati, Regional Councillor
gino.rosati@vaughan.ca
Barbara Cribbett, Treasurer & Commissioner, Finance
Deb Schulte, Regional Councillor
deb.schulte@vaughan.ca
Janice Atwood-Petkovski, Commissioner, Legal & Administrative Services
Marilyn Iafrate, Councillor, Ward(s): 1
marilyn.iafrate@vaughan.ca
Marlon Kallideen, Commissioner, Community Services
marlon.kallideen@vaughan.ca
Tony Carella, Councillor, Ward(s): 2
tony.carella@vaughan.ca
Paul Jankowski, Commissioner, Engineering & Public Works
Rosanna Defrancesca, Councillor, Ward(s): 3
rosanna.defrancesca@vaughan.ca
John Zipay, Commissioner, Planning
john.mackenzie@vaughan.ca
Sandra Yeung Racco, Councillor, Ward(s): 4
sandra.racco@vaughan.ca
Marjie Fraser, Director, Parks & Forestry Operations
parks@vaughan.ca
Alan Shefman, Councillor, Ward(s): 5
alan.shefman@vaughan.ca
Jack Graziosi, Director, Engineering Services
jack.graziosi@vaughan.ca
Leo Grellette, Director, Building Standards
leo.grellette@vaughan.ca
Andrew D. Pearce, Director, Development & Transportation Engineering
andrew.pearce@vaughan.ca
Mary Reali, Director, Recreation & Culture
rec@vaughan.ca
Madeline Zito, Director, Corporate Communications
madeline.zito@vaughan.ca
Gregory R. Senay, Fire Chief
firerescue@vaughan.ca

Wasaga Beach

30 Lewis St.
Wasaga Beach, ON L9Z 1A1
Tel: 705-429-3844; *Fax:* 705-429-7603
www.wasagabeach.com
Municipal Type: City
Incorporated: 1947 *Area:* 58.43 sq km
County or District: Simcoe; *Population in 2006:* 15,029
Provincial Electoral District(s): Simcoe-Grey
Federal Electoral District(s): Simcoe-Grey
Next Election: Oct. 2014 (4 year terms)
Note: Incorporated as a village in 1951 & as a town in 1974.
Cal Patterson, Mayor
mayor@wasagabeach.com
Twyla Nicholson, Clerk
clerk@wasagabeach.com
George Vadeboncoeur, Chief Administrative Officer
Monica Quinlan, Treasurer
treasurer@wasagabeach.com
David Foster, Deputy Mayor & Councillor
deputymayor@wasagabeach.com
Kevin Lalonde, Director, Public Works
publicworksdirector@wasagabeach.com
Ron Anderson, Councillor
council2@wasagabeach.com
Gerry Reinders, Manager
parksandfac@wasagabeach.com
Morley Bercovitch, Councillor
council3@wasagabeach.com
Ray Kelso, Manager, Planning & Development
rkelso@wasagabeach.com
Barrie Vickers, Chief Building Officer
cbo@wasagabeach.com
Nina Bifolchi, Councillor
council4@wasagabeach.com
Jenny Legget, Economic Development Officer
edo@wasagabeach.com
George Watson, Councillor
Mike McWilliam, Fire & Emergency Management Chief
firechief@wasagabeach.com
Stan Wells, Councillor
council5@wasagabeach.com

Waterloo

City Hall
100 Regina St. South
Waterloo, ON N2J 4A8
Tel: 519-886-1550; *Fax:* 519-747-8500
www.city.waterloo.on.ca
Other Information: TTY Toll Free: 1-866-786-3941
Municipal Type: City
Incorporated: Jan. 15, 1857 *Area:* 64.1 sq km
County or District: Waterloo Regional Municipality; *Population in 2006:* 97,475
Provincial Electoral District(s): Kitchener-Waterloo
Federal Electoral District(s): Kitchener-Waterloo
Next Election: Oct. 2014 (4 year terms)
Note: Incorporated as a town in 1876 & as a city on Jan 1, 1948.
Brenda Halloran, Mayor
brenda.halloran@waterloo.ca
Susan Greatrix, City Clerk
519-747-8705, Fax: 519-747-8510
Scott Witmer, Councillor, Ward(s): 1
scott.witmer@waterloo.ca
Tim Anderson, Chief Administrative Officer
519-747-8702, Fax: 519-747-8500
Karen Scian, Councillor, Ward(s): 2
karen.scian@waterloo.ca
Bob Mavin, Chief Financial Officer
bob.mavin@waterloo.ca
Angela Veith, Councillor, Ward(s): 3
angela.vieth@waterloo.ca
David Calder, General Manager, Corporate Services
Diane Freeman, Councillor, Ward(s): 4
diane.freeman@waterloo.ca
Cameron Rapp, General Manager, Development Services
Mark Whaley, Councillor, Ward(s): 5
mark.whaley@waterloo.ca
David Smith, General Manager, Recreation & Leisure Services
Jeff Henry, Councillor, Ward(s): 6
jeff.henry@waterloo.ca
Mark Dykstra, Director, Environment & Parks Services
Melissa Durrell, ouncillor, Ward(s): 7
melissa.durrell@waterloo.ca
Bill Garibaldi, Director, Water Services
Phil Hewitson, Director, Transportation
Patti McKague, Director, Corporate Communications
Murray Kieswetter, Manager, Parks Operations
519-747-8607, Fax: 519-886-5788
Mary Thorpe, Manager, Human Resources
John DeHooge, Fire Chief

Welland

60 East Main St.
Welland, ON L3B 3X4
Tel: 905-735-1700; *Fax:* 905-732-1919
www.welland.ca
Municipal Type: City
Incorporated: July 24, 1858 *Area:* 81.09 sq km
County or District: Niagara Regional Municipality; *Population in 2006:* 50,331
Provincial Electoral District(s): Welland
Federal Electoral District(s): Welland

Next Election: Oct. 2014 (4 year terms)
Note: Incorporated as a town on Jan. 1, 1878 & as a city on July 1, 1917.
Barry Sharpe, Mayor
mayor@welland.ca
Christine Mintoff, City Clerk
clerk@welland.ca
Mark Carl, Councillor, Ward(s): 1
mark.carl@welland.ca
Craig A. Stirtzinger, City Manager
craig.stirtzinger@welland.ca
Mary Ann Grimaldi, Councillor, Ward(s): 1
maryann.grimaldi@welland.ca
Kristine Douglas, Treasurer & General Manager, Financial & Corporate Services
kristine.douglas@welland.ca
Frank Campion, Councillor, Ward(s): 2
frank.campion@welland.ca
Bill Fenwick, General Manager, Parks, Facilities & Leisure Services
bill.fenwick@welland.ca
David McLeod, Councillor, Ward(s): 2
david.mcleod@welland.ca
Sal Iannello, General Manager, Engineering, Public Works, & Transportation Svs.
sal.iannello@welland.ca
Dan Fortier, Councillor, Ward(s): 3
dan.fortier@welland.ca
Rosanne Mantesso, General Manager, Human Resources
rosanne.mantesso@welland.ca
Paul Grenier, Councillor, Ward(s): 3
paul.grenier@welland.ca
Donald Thorpe, General Manager, Planning & Development Services
don.thorpe@welland.ca
Pat Chiocchio, Councillor, Ward(s): 4
pat.chiocchio@welland.ca
Dan Degazio, Manager, Economic Development
Tony Dimarco, Councillor, Ward(s): 4
tony.dimarco@welland.ca
Mike Mantesso, Chief Building Official
mike.mantesso@welland.ca
Rocky G. Létourneau, Councillor, Ward(s): 5
rocky.letourneau@welland.ca
Denys Prevost, Fire Chief
denys.prevost@welland.ca
Michael Petrachenko, Councillor, Ward(s): 5
michael.petrachenko@welland.ca
Jim Larouche, Councillor, Ward(s): 6
jim.larouche@welland.ca
Bob Wright, Councillor, Ward(s): 6
bob.wright@welland.ca

Whitby

575 Rossland Rd. East
Whitby, ON L1N 2M8
Tel: 905-668-5803; *Fax:* 905-686-7005
www.whitby.ca
Other Information: TTY: 905-430-1942
Municipal Type: City
Incorporated: 1855 *Area:* 146.52 sq km
County or District: Durham Reg. Mun.; *Population in 2006:* 111,184
Provincial Electoral District(s): Whitby-Oshawa
Federal Electoral District(s): Whitby-Oshawa
Next Election: Oct. 2014 (4 year terms)
Pat Perkins, Mayor
council@whitby.ca
D. Wilcox, Town Clerk
clerks@whitby.ca
Tracy Hanson, Councillor, Ward(s): 1 - North
R. Petrie, Chief Administrative Officer
Elizabeth Roy, Councillor, Ward(s): 2 - West
Robert B. Short, Director, Planning
planning@whitby.ca
Michael G. Emm, Councillor, Ward(s): 3 - Centre
Peter LeBel, Director, Community & Marketing Services
lebelp@whitby.ca
Ken Montague, Councillor, Ward(s): 4 - East
Suzanne Beale, Director, Public Works
engineering@whitby.ca
Lorne Earl Coe, Regional Councillor
Sheila McGrory, Manager, Economic Development
905-430-4312
mcgrorys@whitby.ca
Joe Drumm, Regional Councillor
Don Mitchell, Regional Councillor
Steve Edwards, Manager, Parks, Marina, Long Range Planning, Special Events & Tourism
edwardss@whitby.ca
M. Gerrard, Fire Chief
fire@whitby.ca

Whitchurch-Stouffville

111 Sandiford Dr.
Stouffville, ON L4A 0Z8
Tel: 905-640-1900; *Fax:* 905-640-7957
www.townofws.com
Other Information: Toll-Free Phone: 1-855-642-8696
Municipal Type: City
Incorporated: 1877 *Area:* 206.74 sq km
County or District: York Reg. Mun.; *Population in 2006:* 24,390
Provincial Electoral District(s): Oak Ridges-Markham
Federal Electoral District(s): Oak Ridges-Markham
Next Election: Oct. 2014 (4 year terms)
Note: Incorporated as a town in 1971, with the amalgamation of Whitchurch Township & the Village of Stouffville.
Wayne Emmerson, Mayor
mayor.emmerson@townofws.ca
Michele Kennedy, Clerk
michele.kennedy@townofws.ca
David J. Cash, Cheif Administrative Officer
Ken Ferdinands, Councillor, Ward(s): 1
ken.ferdinands@townofws.ca
Marc J. Pourvahidi, Treasurer & Director, Finance
Mike Molinari, P.Eng., Director, Engineering & Capital Projects
Phil Bannon, Councillor, Ward(s): 2
phil.bannon@townofws.ca
Clyde Smith, Councillor, Ward(s): 3
clyde.smith@townofws.ca
Paul Whitehouse, Director
paul.whitehouse@townofws.com
Susanne Hilton, Councillor, Ward(s): 4
susanne.hilton@townofws.ca
Rob Raycroft, Manager
leisure.services@townofws.com
Richard Bartley, Councillor, Ward(s): 5
richard.bartley@townofws.ca
Rob Hargrave, Councillor, Ward(s): 6
rob.hargrave@townofws.ca
Andrew McNeely, Manager, Planning Services
andrew.mcneely@townofws.com
Rob McKenzie, Fire Chief

Windsor

City Hall
P.O. Box 1607
350 City Hall Sq. West
Windsor, ON N9A 6S1
Fax: 519-255-6868
311@city.windsor.on.ca; hrdiv@city.windsor.on.ca (HR Dept.)
www.citywindsor.ca
Other Information: Phone: 311; Toll Free Phone: 1-877-746-4311
Municipal Type: City
Incorporated: 1854 *Area:* 146.91 sq km
County or District: Essex; *Population in 2006:* 216,473
Provincial Electoral District(s): Windsor-Tecumseh; Windsor-West
Federal Electoral District(s): Windsor-Tecumseh; Windsor-West
Next Election: Oct. 2014 (4 year terms)
Note: Incorporated as a town in 1858 & as a city in 1892.
Eddie Francis, Mayor
mayoro@city.windsor.on.ca
Valerie Critchley, City Clerk
519-255-6868
clerks@city.windsor.on.ca
Drew Dilkens, Councillor, Ward(s): 1
ddilkens@city.windsor.on.ca
Helga Reidel, Chief Administrative Officer
519-255-6349
caodept@city.windsor.on.ca
Ronald Jones, Councillor, Ward(s): 2
rjones@city.windsor.on.ca
Michael Duben, General Manager, Community & Protective Services
Fulvio Valentinis, Councillor, Ward(s): 3
fvalentinis@city.windsor.on.ca
Dev Tyagi, General Manager, Public Works
pubwork@city.windsor.on.ca
Alan Halberstadt, Councillor, Ward(s): 4
ahalberstadt@city.windsor.on.ca
Ronna Warsh, General Manager, Social & Health Services
socserv@city.windsor.on.ca
Ed Sleiman, Councillor, Ward(s): 5
esleiman@city.windsor.on.ca
Thom Hunt, MCIP, RPP, City Planner
thunt@city.windsor.on.ca
Jo-Anne Gignac, Councillor, Ward(s): 6
joagignac@city.windsor.on.ca
Mario Sonego, P. Eng., City Engineer
engineeringdept@city.windsor.on.ca
Percy Hatfield, Councillor, Ward(s): 7
phatfield@city.windsor.on.ca
David T. Fields, Fire Chief, Windsor Fire & Rescue Service
519-253-6573, Fax: 519-255-6832
Bill (Biagio) Marra, Councillor, Ward(s): 8
bmarra@city.windsor.on.ca
Josette Eugeni, Manager, Transportation Planning
Hilary Payne, Councillor, Ward(s): 9
hpayne@city.windsor.on.ca
Bill Lacasse, Manager, Lou Romano Water Reclamation Plant
519-253-7217
Al Maghneih, Councillor, Ward(s): 10
amaghnieh@city.windsor.on.ca
Jack MacRae, Manager, Little River Pollution Control Plant
519-948-1751
Jim Yanchula, MCIP, RPP, Manager, Urban Design & Community Development
jyanchula@city.windsor.on.ca

Fire Dept.
David Fields, Fire Chief
Glenn Stannard, Chief of Police
Ronna Warsh, General Manager
Allen Heimann, Medical Officer of Health

Police Dept.

Social Services

Metro Windsor Essex County Health Unit

Building & Planning Dept.

Woodstock

City Hall
P.O. Box 1539
500 Dundas St.
Woodstock, ON N4S 7W5
Tel: 519-539-1291;
aash@city.woodstock.on.ca (Assistant to Mayor & CAO)
www.city.woodstock.on.ca
Municipal Type: City
Incorporated: Jan. 1, 1851 *Area:* 43.79 sq km
County or District: Oxford; *Population in 2006:* 35,480
Provincial Electoral District(s): Oxford
Federal Electoral District(s): Oxford
Next Election: Oct. 2014 (4 year terms)
Note: Incorporated as a city on July 1, 1901.
Pat Sobeski, Mayor
mayor@city.woodstock.on.ca
Louise Gartshore, City Clerk
lgartshore@city.woodstock.on.ca
Deb A. Tait, City / County Councillor
519-421-7449
dtait@city.woodstock.on.ca
David Creery, Chief Administrative Officer
dcreery@city.woodstock.on.ca
Sandra J. Talbot, City / County Councillor
519-788-0639
stalbot@city.woodstock.on.ca
Patrice Hilderley, Treasurer
philderley@city.woodstock.on.ca
Bill M. Bes, City Councillor
bbes@city.woodstock.on.ca
Len Magyar, Commissioner, Development
lmagyar@city.woodstock.on.ca
Ron Fraser, City Councillor
rfraser@city.woodstock.on.ca
Bob McFarland, Director, Community Services
bmcfarland@city.woodstock.on.ca
Jim Northcott, City Councillor
519-539-3698
jnorthcott@city.woodstock.on.ca
Harold deHaan, City Engineer
hdehaan@city.woodstock.on.ca
Paul D. Plant, City Councillor
pplant@city.woodstock.on.ca
Filippo D'Emilio, Engineer, Development
fdemilio@city.woodstock.on.ca
Scott Tegler, Fire Chief
stegler@city.woodstock.on.ca
Terry Harrington, Supervisor, Water Distribution
tharrington@city.woodstock.on.ca
Laird Crooks, Manager, Human Resources
lcrooks@city.woodstock.on.ca
Alex Piggott, Superintendent, Works
apiggott@city.woodstock.on.ca
Dan Major, Supervisor, Parks
dmajor@city.woodstock.on.ca

Other Municipalities in Ontario

Addington Highlands
P.O. Box 89
Flinton, ON K0H 1P0
Tel: 613-336-2286; *Fax:* 613-336-2847
www.addingtonhighlands.ca
Municipal Type: Township
Area: 1,288.47 sq km
County or District: Lennox & Addington; *Population in 2006:* 2,512
Provincial Electoral District(s): Lanark-Frontenac-Lennox & Addington
Federal Electoral District(s): Lanark-Frontenac-Lennox & Addington
Next Election: Oct. 2014 (4 year terms)
Henry Hogg, Reeve
henryh@sympatico.ca
Jack Pauhl, Clerk
clerk@addingtonhighlands.ca

Adelaide Metcalfe
2340 Egremont Dr., RR#5
Strathroy, ON N7G 3H6
Tel: 519-247-3687; *Fax:* 519-247-3411
info@adelaidemetcalfe.on.ca
www.adelaidemetcalfe.on.ca
Municipal Type: Township
Incorporated: Jan. 1, 2001 *Area:* 331.26 sq km
County or District: Middlesex; *Population in 2006:* 3,117
Provincial Electoral District(s): Lambton-Kent-Middlesex
Federal Electoral District(s): Lambton-Kent-Middlesex
Next Election: Oct. 2014 (4 year terms)
Note: Amalgamation of the former Township of Adelaide & the Township of Metcalfe.
David Bolton, Reeve
mayor@adelaidemetcalfe.on.ca
Fran Urbshott, Clerk, Administrator, & Treasurer
fran@adelaidemetcalfe.on.ca

Adjala-Tosorontio
7855 Sideroad 30, RR#1
Alliston, ON L9R 1V1
Tel: 705-434-5055; *Fax:* 705-434-5051
www.townshipadjtos.on.ca
Municipal Type: Township
Incorporated: Jan. 1, 1994 *Area:* 372.33 sq km
County or District: Simcoe; *Population in 2006:* 10,695
Provincial Electoral District(s): Simcoe-Grey
Federal Electoral District(s): Simcoe-Grey
Next Election: Oct. 2014 (4 year terms)
Note: Amalgamation of the former Township of Adjala & the former Township of Tosorontio.
Tom Walsh, Mayor
905-729-2132
twalsh@townshipadjtos.on.ca
Mary Small Brett, Deputy Mayor & Councillor
519-941-5828
marysmallbrett@sympatico.ca
Floyd Pinto, Councillor, Ward(s): 1
905-936-9616
marysmallbrett@sympatico.ca
Ambrose J. Keenan, Councillor, Ward(s): 2
905-729-3361
tundraathome@295.ca
Doug Little, Councillor, Ward(s): 3
705-435-9020
dlittle@townshipadjtos.on.ca
Tom Gauley, Councillor, Ward(s): 4
705-435-1437
tomlisegauley@rogers.com
Scott W. Anderson, Councillor, Ward(s): 5
705-424-0769
scott@andersonward5.ca
Barbara Kane, Clerk
bkane@townshipadjtos.on.ca
Eric Wargel, Chief Administrative Officer
ewargel@townshipadjtos.on.ca
Dorthy Bulman, Treasurer & Deputy Clerk
dbulman@townshipadjtos.on.ca
Jacquie Tschekalin, Director, Planning
jtschekalin@townshipadjtos.on.ca

Admaston/Bromley
477 Stone Rd., RR#2
Renfrew, ON K7V 3Z5
Tel: 613-432-2885; *Fax:* 613-432-4052
www.admastonbromley.com
Municipal Type: Township
Incorporated: Jan. 1, 2000 *Area:* 520.5 sq km
County or District: Renfrew; *Population in 2006:* 2,716
Provincial Electoral District(s): Renfrew-Nipissing-Pembroke
Federal Electoral District(s): Renfrew-Nipissing-Pembroke
Next Election: Oct. 2014 (4 year terms)
Note: Amalgamation of Admaston Township & Bromley Township.
Raye-Anne Briscoe, Mayor
613-432-5728
Beverly Briscoe, Clerk-Treasurer
bbriscoe@admastonbromley.com

Alberton
#B2, RR#1
Fort Frances, ON P9A 3M2
Tel: 807-274-6053; *Fax:* 807-274-8449
alberton@jam21.net
www.alberton.ca
Municipal Type: Township
Area: 115.3 sq km
County or District: Rainy River District; *Population in 2006:* 958
Provincial Electoral District(s): Kenora-Rainy River
Federal Electoral District(s): Thunder Bay-Rainy River; Ancaster-Dundas-Flamborough-Westdale
Next Election: Oct. 2014 (4 year terms)
Michael Hammond, Reeve
Dawn Hayes, CAO & Clerk-Treasurer

Alfred & Plantagenet
P.O. Box 350
205 Old Hwy. 17
Plantagenet, ON K0B 1L0
Tel: 613-673-4797; *Fax:* 613-673-4812
www.alfred-plantagenet.com
Municipal Type: Township
Incorporated: Jan. 1, 1997 *Area:* 391.68 sq km
County or District: Prescott & Russell; *Population in 2006:* 8,654
Provincial Electoral District(s): Glengarry-Prescott-Russell
Federal Electoral District(s): Glengarry-Prescott-Russell
Next Election: Oct. 2014 (4 year terms)
Note: Amalgamation of the Township of Alfred, the Village of Alfred, the Township of North Plantagenet & the Village of Plantagenet.
Jean-Yves Lalonde, Mayor
jean-yves.lalonde@sympatico.ca
Marc Daigneault, Chief Administrative Officer & Clerk

Algoma
c/o Algoma District Svs. Administration Bd.
1 Collver Rd., RR#1
Thessalon, ON P0R 1L0
Tel: 705-842-3370; *Fax:* 705-842-3747
www.adsab.on.ca
Municipal Type: District
Area: 48,734.66 sq km
Population in 2006: 117,461
Provincial Electoral District(s): Algoma-Manitoulin
Federal Electoral District(s): Algoma-Manitoulin-Kapuskasing
Keith Bell, Chief Administrative Officer
kbell@adsab.on.ca

Algonquin Highlands
1123 North Shore Rd., RR#2
Minden, ON K0M 1J1
Tel: 705-489-2379; *Fax:* 705-489-3491
info@algonquinhighlands.ca
www.algonquinhighlands.ca
Other Information: Phone, Dorset Satellite Office: 705-766-2211
Municipal Type: Township
Area: 1,002.12 sq km
County or District: Haliburton; *Population in 2006:* 1,976
Provincial Electoral District(s): Haliburton-Kawartha Lakes-Brock
Federal Electoral District(s): Haliburton-Kawartha Lakes-Brock
Next Election: Oct. 2014 (4 year terms)
Carol Moffat, Reeve
cmoffatt@algonquinhighlands.ca
Angela Bird, Clerk & Chief Administrative Officer
abird@algonquinhighlands.ca

Alnwick-Haldimand
P.O. Box 70
10836 County Rd. No. 2
Grafton, ON K0K 2G0
Tel: 905-349-2822; *Fax:* 905-349-3259
alnhald@alnwickhaldimand.ca
www.alnwickhaldimand.ca
Other Information: Phone, Roseneath Satellite Office: 905-352-3949
Municipal Type: Township
Area: 398.08 sq km
County or District: Northumberland; *Population in 2006:* 6,435
Provincial Electoral District(s): Northumberland-Quinte West
Federal Electoral District(s): Northumberland-Quinte West
Next Election: Oct. 2014 (4 year terms)
Dalton McDonald, Mayor
905-349-2747
mayor@alnwickhaldimand.ca
Robin van de Moosdyk, A.M.C.T., Clerk
rvandemoosdyk@alnwickhaldimand.ca

Amaranth
374028 - 6th Line, RR#7
Orangeville, ON L9W 2Z3
Tel: 519-941-1007; *Fax:* 519-941-1802
township@amaranth-eastgary.ca
www.amaranth-eastgary.ca
Municipal Type: Township
Incorporated: Jan. 2, 1854 *Area:* 264.35 sq km
County or District: Dufferin; *Population in 2006:* 3,845
Provincial Electoral District(s): Dufferin-Caledon
Federal Electoral District(s): Dufferin-Caledon
Next Election: Oct. 2014 (4 year terms)
Don MacIver, Mayor
519-925-3457
mayor.maciver@hotmail.com
Susan M. Stone, A.M.C.T., Chief Administrative Officer & Clerk-Treasurer
suestone@amaranth-eastgary.ca

Armour
Municipal Office
P.O. Box 533
56 Ontario St.
Burks Falls, ON P0A 1C0
Tel: 705-382-3332; *Fax:* 705-382-2068
info@armourtownship.ca
www.armourtownship.ca
Other Information: Alternative Phone: 705-382-2954
Municipal Type: Township
Area: 164.1 sq km
County or District: Parry Sound District; *Population in 2006:* 1,249
Provincial Electoral District(s): Parry Sound-Muskoka
Federal Electoral District(s): Parry Sound-Muskoka
Next Election: Oct. 2014 (4 year terms)
Bob MacPhail, Reeve
705-636-7678
aberdeen@surenet.net
Wendy Whitwell, Clerk-Administrator
clerk@armourtownship.ca

Armstrong
P.O. Box 546
35 Tenth St.
Earlton, ON P0J 1E0
Tel: 705-563-2375; *Fax:* 705-563-2093
www.armstrongtownship.com
Municipal Type: Township
Area: 90.33 sq km
County or District: Timiskaming District; *Population in 2006:* 1,155
Provincial Electoral District(s): Timiskaming-Cochrane
Federal Electoral District(s): Timmins-James Bay
Next Election: Oct. 2014 (4 year terms)
Jules Gravel, Reeve
Reynald Rivard, Clerk-Treasurer
reynaldrivard@nt.net

Arnprior
P.O. Box 130
105 Elgin St. West
Arnprior, ON K7S 0A8
Tel: 613-623-4231; *Fax:* 613-623-8091
arnprior@arnprior.ca
www.arnprior.ca
Municipal Type: Town
Area: 13.04 sq km
County or District: Renfrew; *Population in 2006:* 7,158
Provincial Electoral District(s): Renfrew-Nipissing-Pembroke
Federal Electoral District(s): Renfrew-Nipissing-Pembroke
Next Election: Oct. 2014 (4 year terms)
Terry Gibeau, Mayor
tgibeau@arnprior.ca
Jacquie Farrow-Lawrence, Town Clerk
jfarrow-lawrence@arnprior.ca

Arran-Elderslie
P.O. Box 70
1925 Bruce Rd. 10
Chesley, ON N0G 1L0
Tel: 519-363-3039; *Fax:* 519-363-2203
areld@bmts.com
www.arran-elderslie.com

Municipal Type: Municipality
Area: 460.13 sq km
County or District: Bruce; *Population in 2006:* 6,747
Provincial Electoral District(s): Bruce-Grey-Owen Sound
Federal Electoral District(s): Bruce-Grey-Owen Sound
Next Election: Oct. 2014 (4 year terms)
Paul Eagleson, Mayor
519-363-3559
Peggy Rouse, Clerk

Ashfield-Colborne-Wawanosh
82133 Council Line, RR#5
Goderich, ON N7A 3Y2
Tel: 519-524-4669; *Fax:* 519-524-1951
www.acwtownship.ca
Municipal Type: Township
Area: 587.07 sq km
County or District: Huron; *Population in 2006:* 5,409
Provincial Electoral District(s): Huron-Bruce
Federal Electoral District(s): Huron-Bruce
Next Election: Oct. 2014 (4 year terms)
Ben Van Diepenbeek, Reeve
519-529-7830
Mark Becker, Administrator & Clerk-Treasurer
clerk@acwtownship.ca

Asphodel-Norwood
P.O. Box 29
2357 County Rd. 45
Norwood, ON K0L 2V0
Tel: 705-639-5343; *Fax:* 705-639-1880
www.asphodelnorwood.com
Municipal Type: Township
Incorporated: 1998 *Area:* 160.85 sq km
County or District: Peterborough; *Population in 2006:* 4,247
Provincial Electoral District(s): Peterborough
Federal Electoral District(s): Peterborough
Next Election: Oct. 2014 (4 year terms)
Note: Amalgamation of the Village of Norwood & the Township of Asphodel.
Doug Pearcy, Reeve
705-639-5510, Fax: 705-639-5388
dpearcy@accel.net
Valerie Przybilla, Chief Administrative Officer, Clerk & Treasurer
valeriep@asphodelnorwood.com

Assiginack
P.O. Box 238
25B Spragge St.
Manitowaning, ON P0P 1N0
Tel: 705-859-3196; *Fax:* 705-859-3010
assiginackinfo@amtelecom.net
www.assiginack.ca
Other Information: Toll-Free Phone: 1-800-540-0179
Municipal Type: Township
Area: 227.44 sq km
County or District: Manitoulin District; *Population in 2006:* 914
Provincial Electoral District(s): Algoma-Manitoulin
Federal Electoral District(s): Algoma-Manitoulin-Kapuskasing
Next Election: Oct. 2014 (4 year terms)
Clyde Rohn, Reeve
Alton Hobbs, Clerk-Treasurer

Athens
P.O. Box 189
1 Main St. West
Athens, ON K0E 1B0
Tel: 613-924-2044; *Fax:* 613-924-2091
athens@ripnet.com
www.athenstownship.ca
Municipal Type: Township
Incorporated: 2001 *Area:* 126.46 sq km
County or District: Leeds & Grenville; *Population in 2006:* 3,086
Provincial Electoral District(s): Leeds-Grenville
Federal Electoral District(s): Leeds-Grenville
Next Election: Oct. 2014 (4 year terms)
Herb Scott, Mayor
613-924-2133
Darlene Noonan, Chief Administrative Officer & Clerk Treasurer

Atikokan
P.O. Box 1330
120 Marks St.
Atikokan, ON P0T 1C0
Tel: 807-597-1234; *Fax:* 807-597-6186
info@atikokan.ca
www.atikokan.ca
Municipal Type: Township
Area: 316.75 sq km
County or District: Rainy River District; *Population in 2006:* 3,293
Provincial Electoral District(s): Thunder Bay-Atikokan
Federal Electoral District(s): Thunder Bay-Rainy River
Next Election: Oct. 2014 (4 year terms)
Dennis Brown, Mayor
denbrown@tbaytel.net
Angela Sharbot, Clerk
angela.sharbot@atikokan.ca

Augusta
3560 County Rd. 26, RR#2
Prescott, ON K0E 1T0
Tel: 613-925-4231; *Fax:* 613-925-3499
www.augusta.ca
Municipal Type: Township
Area: 314.06 sq km
County or District: Leeds & Grenville; *Population in 2006:* 7,510
Provincial Electoral District(s): Leeds-Grenville
Federal Electoral District(s): Leeds-Grenville
Next Election: Oct. 2014 (4 year terms)
Mel Campbell, Reeve
613-342-6962
John Trudgen, Acting Chief Administrative Officer & Clerk

Aylmer
46 Talbot St. West
Aylmer, ON N5H 1J7
Tel: 519-773-3164; *Fax:* 519-765-1446
www.aylmer.ca
Municipal Type: Town
Area: 6.22 sq km
County or District: Elgin; *Population in 2006:* 7,069
Provincial Electoral District(s): Elgin-Middlesex-London
Federal Electoral District(s): Elgin-Middlesex-London
Next Election: Oct. 2014 (4 year terms)
Jack Couckuyt, Mayor
mayor@town.aylmer.on.ca
Nancie Irving, Clerk & Officer, Lottery Licensing
nirving@town.aylmer.on.ca

Baldwin
P.O. Box 7095
11 Spooner St.
McKerrow, ON P0P 1M0
Tel: 705-869-0225;
www.townshipofbaldwin.ca
Municipal Type: Township
Area: 81.82 sq km
County or District: Sudbury District; *Population in 2006:* 554
Provincial Electoral District(s): Algoma-Manitoulin
Federal Electoral District(s): Algoma-Manitoulin-Kapuskasing
Next Election: Oct. 2014 (4 year terms)
Archie Boivin, Reeve
Joan Seidel, Clerk & Treasurer
joanseidel@townshipofbaldwin.ca

Bancroft
P.O. Box 790
24 Flint Ave.
Bancroft, ON K0L 1C0
Tel: 613-332-3331; *Fax:* 613-332-0384
bancroft@town.bancroft.on.ca
www.town.bancroft.on.ca
Municipal Type: Town
Incorporated: 1904 *Area:* 227.84 sq km
County or District: Hastings; *Population in 2006:* 3,838
Provincial Electoral District(s): Prince Edward-Hastings
Federal Electoral District(s): Prince Edward-Hastings
Next Election: Oct. 2014 (4 year terms)
Bernice Jenkins, Mayor
613-332-1041
bjenkins@town.bancroft.on.ca
Barry Wannamaker, Chief Administrative Officer & Clerk
bwannamaker@town.bancroft.on.ca

Bayham
P.O. Box 160
9344 Plank Rd.
Straffordville, ON N0J 1Y0
Tel: 519-866-5521; *Fax:* 519-866-3884
bayham@bayham.on.ca
www.bayham.on.ca
Municipal Type: Municipality
Area: 244.99 sq km
County or District: Elgin; *Population in 2006:* 6,727
Provincial Electoral District(s): Elgin-Middlesex-London
Federal Electoral District(s): Elgin-Middlesex-London
Next Election: Oct. 2014 (4 year terms)
Paul Ens, Mayor
ens@porchlight.ca
Lynda Millard, Clerk
lmillard@bayham.on.ca

Beckwith
1702 - 9th Line, RR#2
Carleton Place, ON K7C 3P2
Tel: 613-257-1539; *Fax:* 613-257-8996
www.twp.beckwith.on.ca
Other Information: Toll-Free Phone: 1-800-535-4532 (in 613 area code)
Municipal Type: Township
Area: 240.12 sq km
County or District: Lanark; *Population in 2006:* 6,387
Provincial Electoral District(s): Lanark-Frontenac-Lennox & Addington
Federal Electoral District(s): Lanark-Frontenac-Lennox & Addington
Next Election: Oct. 2014 (4 year terms)
Richard Kidd, Reeve
613-257-5409
rkidd@ripnet.com
Cynthia Moyle, Chief Administrative Officer
cmoyle@twp.beckwith.on.ca

Billings
Municipal Office
P.O. Box 34
15 Old Mill Rd.
Kagawong, ON P0P 1J0
Tel: 705-282-2611; *Fax:* 705-282-3199
billingsadmin@xplornet.com
www.billingstwp.ca
Municipal Type: Township
Incorporated: 1884 *Area:* 209.15 sq km
County or District: Manitoulin District; *Population in 2006:* 539
Provincial Electoral District(s): Algoma-Manitoulin
Federal Electoral District(s): Algoma-Manitoulin-Kapuskasing
Next Election: Oct. 2014 (4 year terms)
Austin Hunt, Reeve
705-282-2684
Katherine McDonald, Clerk-Treasurer
clerktreasurer@billingstwp.ca

Black River-Matheson
P.O. Box 601
429 Park Lane
Matheson, ON P0K 1N0
Tel: 705-273-2313;
reception@blackriver-matheson.com
www.blackriver-matheson.com
Municipal Type: Township
Area: 1,161.67 sq km
County or District: Cochrane District; *Population in 2006:* 2,619
Provincial Electoral District(s): Timiskaming-Cochrane
Federal Electoral District(s): Timmins-James Bay
Next Election: Oct. 2014 (4 year terms)
Mike Milinkovich, Mayor
Heather Smith, Clerk & Treasurer
705-273-2313

Blandford-Blenheim
P.O. Box 100
47 Wilmot St. South
Drumbo, ON N0J 1G0
Tel: 519-463-5347; *Fax:* 519-463-5881
generalmail@twp.bla-ble.on.ca
www.blandfordblenheim.ca
Municipal Type: Township
Area: 382.34 sq km
County or District: Oxford; *Population in 2006:* 7,149
Provincial Electoral District(s): Oxford
Federal Electoral District(s): Oxford
Next Election: Oct. 2014 (4 year terms)
Marion Wearn, Mayor
mwearn@blandfordblenheim.ca
Fran Bell, Chief Administrative Officer & Clerk
fbell@blandfordblenheim.ca

Blind River
P.O. Box 640
11 Hudson St.
Blind River, ON P0R 1B0
Tel: 705-356-2251; *Fax:* 705-356-7343
www.blindriver.ca
Municipal Type: Town
Incorporated: 1906 *Area:* 520.59 sq km
County or District: Algoma District; *Population in 2006:* 3,780
Provincial Electoral District(s): Algoma-Manitoulin
Federal Electoral District(s): Algoma-Manitoulin-Kapuskasing
Next Election: Oct. 2014 (4 year terms)
Sue Jensen, Mayor
sue.jensen@blindriver.ca
Ken Corbiere, Clerk
kencorb@blindriver.ca

Bluewater, Municipality of
P.O. Box 250
14 Mill Ave.
Zurich, ON N0M 2T0
Tel: 519-236-4351; *Fax:* 519-236-4329
www.town.bluewater.on.ca
Other Information: Toll-Free: 1-877-236-4351
Municipal Type: Town
Area: 416.99 sq km
County or District: Huron; *Population in 2006:* 7,120
Provincial Electoral District(s): Huron-Bruce
Federal Electoral District(s): Huron-Bruce
Next Election: Oct. 2014 (4 year terms)
Bill Dowson, Mayor
wjdowson@tcc.on.ca
Lori Wolfe, Chief Administrative Officer & Clerk
l.wolfe@town.bluewater.on.ca

Bonfield
365 Hwy. 531
Bonfield, ON P0H 1E0
Tel: 705-776-2641; *Fax:* 705-776-1154
www.ebonfield.org
Municipal Type: Township
Incorporated: 1975 *Area:* 205.75 sq km
County or District: Nipissing District; *Population in 2006:* 2,009
Provincial Electoral District(s): Nipissing
Federal Electoral District(s): Nipissing-Timiskaming
Next Election: 2014 (4 year terms)
Randall McLaren, Mayor
rmclaren@ebonfield.org
Lise B. McMillan, A.M.C.T., Administrator, Clerk & Treasurer
lise@ebonfield.org

Bonnechere Valley
P.O. Box 100
49 Bonnechere St. East
Eganville, ON K0J 1T0
Tel: 613-628-3101; *Fax:* 613-628-1336
admin@eganville.com
www.bonnecherevalleytwp.com
Municipal Type: Township
Incorporated: Jan. 1, 2001 *Area:* 589.87 sq km
County or District: Renfrew; *Population in 2006:* 3,665
Provincial Electoral District(s): Renfrew-Nipissing-Pembroke
Federal Electoral District(s): Renfrew-Nipissing-Pembroke
Next Election: Oct. 2014 (4 year terms)
Note: Amalgamation of Eganville Village, Grattan Township, Sebastopol Township & Algona South Township.
Jennifer Murphy, Mayor
613-628-3295
jenniferm@eganville.com
Bryan Martin, Chief Administrative Officer
bryanm@eganville.com

Brethour
P.O. Box 537
51476 Brethour Rd.
Belle Vallee, ON P0J 1A0
Tel: 705-647-1712; *Fax:* 705-647-6851
brethourtwp@ntl.sympatico.ca
Municipal Type: Township
Area: 82.05 sq km
County or District: Timiskaming District; *Population in 2006:* 117
Provincial Electoral District(s): Timiskaming-Cochrane
Federal Electoral District(s): Timmins-James Bay
Next Election: Oct. 2014 (4 year terms)
Maurice Chabot, Reeve
Pam Bennewies, Clerk-Treasurer

Brock
P.O. Box 10
1 Cameron St. East
Cannington, ON L0E 1E0
Tel: 705-432-2355; *Fax:* 705-432-3487
brock@townshipofbrock.ca
www.townshipofbrock.ca
Other Information: Toll-Free Phone: 1-866-223-7668
Municipal Type: Township
Incorporated: 1973 *Area:* 423.31 sq km
County or District: Durham Reg. Mun.; *Population in 2006:* 11,979
Provincial Electoral District(s): Haliburton-Kawartha Lakes-Brock
Federal Electoral District(s): Haliburton-Kawartha Lakes-Brock
Next Election: Oct. 2014 (4 year terms)
W. Terry Clayton, Mayor
tclayton@townshipofbrock.ca
Debbie Bath, Regional Coucillor
dbath@townshipofbrock.ca
Mike Manchester, Councillor, Ward(s): 1
mmanchester@townshipofbrock.ca
Randy Skinner, Councillor, Ward(s): 2
rskinner@townshipofbrock.ca
Walter Schummer, Councillor, Ward(s): 3
wschummer@townshipofbrock.ca
Keith Shier, Councillor, Ward(s): 4
kshier@townshipofbrock.ca
W.E. Ted Smith, Councillor, Ward(s): 5
tsmith@townshipofbrock.ca
Thomas G. Gettinby, MA, MCIP, RPP, CMO, Chief Administrative Officer & Municipal Clerk
tgettinby@townshipofbrock.ca
Laura Barta, CMA, Treasurer
lbarta@townshipofbrock.ca
Nick Colucci, P.Eng., Director, Public Works
ncolucci@townshipofbrock.ca
Joseph J. Bonura, Chief Building Offical
jbonura@townshipofbrock.ca
Rick Harrison, Chief, Fire
rharrison@townshipofbrock.ca

Brockton
P.O. Box 68
100 Scott St.
Walkerton, ON N0G 2V0
Tel: 519-881-2223;
info@brockton.ca
www.brockton.ca
Other Information: Toll-Free Phone: 1-877-885-8084
Municipal Type: Municipality
Incorporated: Jan. 1, 1999 *Area:* 565.07 sq km
County or District: Bruce; *Population in 2006:* 9,641
Provincial Electoral District(s): Huron-Bruce
Federal Electoral District(s): Huron-Bruce
Next Election: Oct. 2014 (4 year terms)
Note: Amalgamation of the Town of Walkerton, Township of Brant, & the Township of Greenock.
David Inglis, Mayor
dinglis@brockton.ca
Debra Roth, Clerk
droth@brockton.ca

Brooke-Alvinston
P.O. Box 28
3236 River St.
Alvinston, ON N0N 1A0
Tel: 519-898-2173; *Fax:* 519-898-5653
info@brookealvinston.com
www.brookealvinston.com
Other Information: Toll-Free Phone, Enforcement Unit: 1-866-344-9119
Municipal Type: Township
Area: 311.3 sq km
County or District: Lambton; *Population in 2006:* 2,661
Provincial Electoral District(s): Lambton-Kent-Middlesex
Federal Electoral District(s): Lambton-Kent-Middlesex
Next Election: Oct. 2014 (4 year terms)
Don McGugan, Mayor
519-847-5606, Fax: 519-847-5607
jdmcgugan@hotmail.com
Cathy Case, Clerk
cathycase@amtelecom.net

Bruce Mines
P.O. Box 220
9180 Hwy. 17 East
Bruce Mines, ON P0R 1C0
Tel: 705-785-3493; *Fax:* 705-785-3170
brucemines@bellnet.ca
www.brucemines.ca
Municipal Type: Town
Incorporated: 1903 *Area:* 6.13 sq km
County or District: Algoma District; *Population in 2006:* 584
Provincial Electoral District(s): Algoma-Manitoulin
Federal Electoral District(s): Sault Ste Marie
Next Election: Oct. 2014 (4 year terms)
Gordon Post, Mayor
Donna Brunke, Town Clerk
dbrunke@bellnet.ca

Brudenell, Lyndoch & Raglan
P.O. Box 40
42 Burnt Bridge Rd.
Palmer Rapids, ON K0J 2E0
Tel: 613-758-2061; *Fax:* 613-758-2235
blrtownship@xplornet.com
www.countyofrenfrew.on.ca
Municipal Type: Township
Incorporated: Jan. 1, 1999 *Area:* 702.77 sq km
County or District: Renfrew; *Population in 2006:* 1,497
Provincial Electoral District(s): Renfrew-Nipissing-Pembroke
Federal Electoral District(s): Renfrew-Nipissing-Pembroke
Next Election: Oct. 2014 (4 year terms)
Norman Lentz, Reeve
Michelle Mantifel, Clerk-Treasurer

Burk's Falls
P.O. Box 160
172 Ontario St.
Burks Falls, ON P0A 1C0
Tel: 705-382-3138; *Fax:* 705-382-2273
villofbf@bellnet.ca
www.burksfalls.net
Municipal Type: Village
Incorporated: 1890 *Area:* 3.12 sq km
County or District: Parry Sound District; *Population in 2006:* 893
Provincial Electoral District(s): Parry Sound-Muskoka
Federal Electoral District(s): Parry Sound-Muskoka
Next Election: Oct. 2014 (4 year terms)
Cathy Still, Reeve
Kim Dunnett, Clerk

Burpee & Mills
RR#1
Evansville, ON P0P 1E0
Tel: 705-282-0624; *Fax:* 705-282-0624
burpeemills@xplornet.com
www.burpeemills.com
Municipal Type: Township
Area: 218.48 sq km
County or District: Manitoulin District; *Population in 2006:* 329
Provincial Electoral District(s): Algoma-Manitoulin
Federal Electoral District(s): Algoma-Manitoulin-Kapuskasing
Next Election: Oct. 2014 (4 year terms)
Ken Noland, Reeve
Bonnie J. Bailey, Clerk-Treasurer

Callander, Municipality of
P.O. Box 100
280 Main St. North
Callander, ON P0H 1H0
Tel: 705-752-1410; *Fax:* 705-752-3116
www.callander.ca
Municipal Type: Township
Area: 100.96 sq km
County or District: Parry Sound District; *Population in 2006:* 3,249
Provincial Electoral District(s): Nipissing
Federal Electoral District(s): Nipissing-Timiskaming
Next Election: Oct. 2014 (4 year terms)
Note: Formerly North Himsworth Township.
Hector Lavigne, Mayor
705-845-5010
Jeffrey Celentano, Chief Administration Officer & Clerk

Calvin
1355 Peddlers Dr., RR#2
Mattawa, ON P0H 1V0
Tel: 705-744-2700; *Fax:* 705-744-0309
administration@calvintownship.ca
www.calvintownship.ca
Municipal Type: Township
Area: 139.17 sq km
County or District: Nipissing District; *Population in 2006:* 608
Provincial Electoral District(s): Nipissing
Federal Electoral District(s): Nipissing-Timiskaming
Next Election: Oct. 2014 (4 year terms)
Wayne Brown, Mayor
mayor@calvintownship.ca
Lynda Kovacs, Clerk-Treasurer
clerk@calvintownship.ca

Carleton Place
175 Bridge St.
Carleton Place, ON K7C 2V8
Tel: 613-257-6200; *Fax:* 613-257-8170
info@carletonplace.ca; bylaw@carletonplace.ca (Bylaws)
www.carletonplace.ca
Other Information: E-mail, Public Works: dyoung@carletonplace.ca
Municipal Type: Town
Area: 8.83 sq km
County or District: Lanark; *Population in 2006:* 9,453
Provincial Electoral District(s): Lanark-Frontenac-Lennox & Addington
Federal Electoral District(s): Lanark-Frontenac-Lennox & Addington
Next Election: Oct. 2014 (4 year terms)
Wendy LeBlanc, Mayor
613-257-6206
wendyleblanc@sympatico.ca
Duncan H. Rogers, Clerk
613-257-6211
drogers@carletonplace.ca

Carling
2 West Carling Bay Rd., RR#1
Nobel, ON P0G 1G0
Tel: 705-342-5856; *Fax:* 705-342-9527
www.carlingtownship.ca
Municipal Type: Township
Area: 243.94 sq km
County or District: Parry Sound District; *Population in 2006:* 1,123
Provincial Electoral District(s): Parry Sound-Muskoka
Federal Electoral District(s): Parry Sound-Muskoka
Next Election: Oct. 2014 (4 year terms)
Gord Harrison, Mayor
705-342-5230
gordharrison@carlingtownship.ca
Stephen Kaegi, Chief Administrative Officer & Clerk
cao@carlingtownship.ca

Carlow/Mayo
General Delivery, 3987 Boulter Rd.
Boulter, ON K0L 1G0
Tel: 613-332-1760; *Fax:* 613-332-2175
carlowmayo@hughes.net
www.carlowmayo.ca
Municipal Type: Township
Incorporated: Jan. 1, 2001 *Area:* 388.36 sq km
County or District: Hastings; *Population in 2006:* 950
Provincial Electoral District(s): Prince Edward-Hastings
Federal Electoral District(s): Prince Edward-Hastings
Next Election: Oct. 2014 (4 year terms)
Note: Amalgamation of the former townships of Carlow & Mayo.
Bonnie Adams, Reeve
Arlene Cox, Clerk-Administrator

Casey
P.O. Box 460
Belle Vallee, ON P0J 1A0
Tel: 705-647-7257; *Fax:* 705-647-6373
harlytwp@parolink.net; lise_chhk@parolink.net
harley.ca/casey/index.html
Municipal Type: Township
Incorporated: 1909 *Area:* 80.75 sq km
County or District: Timiskaming District; *Population in 2006:* 385
Provincial Electoral District(s): Timiskaming-Cochrane
Federal Electoral District(s): Timmins-James Bay
Next Election: Oct. 2014 (4 year terms)
Guy Labonté, Reeve
Michel Lachapelle, Clerk-Treasurer

Casselman
P.O. Box 710
751 St. Jean St.
Casselman, ON K0A 1M0
Tel: 613-764-3139; *Fax:* 613-764-5709
info@casselman.ca
www.casselman.ca
Municipal Type: Village
Area: 5.15 sq km
County or District: Prescott & Russell; *Population in 2006:* 3,294
Provincial Electoral District(s): Glengarry-Prescott-Russell
Federal Electoral District(s): Glengarry-Prescott-Russell
Next Election: Oct. 2014 (4 year terms)
Claude Levac, Mayor
maire@casselman.ca
Gilles R. Lortie, Clerk
glortie@casselman.ca

Cavan Monaghan
988 County Rd. 10, RR#3
Millbrook, ON L0A 1G0
Tel: 705-932-2929; *Fax:* 705-932-3458
info@cavanmonaghan.net
www.cavanmonaghan.net
Other Information: Toll-Free Phone: 1-877-906-5556
Municipal Type: Township
Area: 306.13 sq km
County or District: Peterborough; *Population in 2006:* 8,828
Provincial Electoral District(s): Haliburton-Kawartha Lakes-Brock
Federal Electoral District(s): Haliburton-Kawartha Lakes-Brock
Next Election: Oct. 2014 (4 year terms)
Note: Formerly The Corporation of the Township of Cavan-Millbrook-North Monaghan.
John Fallis, Mayor
705-932-5568
jfallis@cavanmonaghan.net
Gail Empey, Clerk
705-932-9326
gempey@cavanmonaghan.net

Central Elgin
450 Sunset Dr.
St Thomas, ON N5R 5V1
Tel: 519-631-4860; *Fax:* 519-631-4036
www.centralelgin.org
Municipal Type: Municipality
Area: 280.22 sq km
County or District: Elgin; *Population in 2006:* 12,723
Provincial Electoral District(s): Elgin-Middlesex-London
Federal Electoral District(s): Elgin-Middlesex-London
Next Election: Oct. 2014 (4 year terms)
Bill Walters, Mayor
519-631-8110
billwalters@amtelecom.net
David Marr, Deputy Mayor & Councillor
grvalley@rogers.com
Dan McNeil, Councillor, Ward(s): 1
dkmcneil@rogers.com
Sally Martyn, Councillor, Ward(s): 2
tcg@execulink.com
Stephen Carr, Councillor, Ward(s): 3
secarr40@yahoo.ca
Russell Matthews, Councillor, Ward(s): 4
russellm@rogers.com
Robert McFarlan, Councillor, Ward(s): 5
rdmcfarlan@rogers.com
Donald N. Leitch, Chief Administrative Officer & Clerk
dleitch@centralelgin.org
Sharon Larmour, Treasurer & Director, Financial Services
slarmour@centralelgin.org
Donald Crocker, Director, Fire & Rescue Services
dcrocker@centralelgin.org
Lloyd Perrin, Director, Physical Services
lperrin@centralelgin.org

Central Frontenac
P.O. Box 89
1084 Elizabeth S.
Sharbot Lake, ON K0H 2P0
Tel: 613-279-2935; *Fax:* 613-279-2422
township@centralfrontenac.com
www.centralfrontenac.com
Municipal Type: Township
Incorporated: Jan. 1, 1998 *Area:* 970.07 sq km
County or District: Frontenac; *Population in 2006:* 4,665
Provincial Electoral District(s): Lanark-Frontenac-Lennox & Addington
Federal Electoral District(s): Lanark-Frontenac-Lennox & Addington
Next Election: Oct. 2014 (4 year terms)
Janet Gutowski, Mayor
613-374-1355
j.gutowski@sympatico.ca
John DuChene, Chief Administrative Officer & Clerk
jduchene@centralfrontenac.com

Central Huron, Municipality of
P.O. Box 400
23 Albert St.
Clinton, ON N0M 1L0
Tel: 519-482-3997; *Fax:* 519-482-9183
www.centralhuron.com
Municipal Type: Township
Incorporated: Jan. 1, 2001 *Area:* 447.6 sq km
County or District: Huron; *Population in 2006:* 7,641
Provincial Electoral District(s): Huron-Bruce
Federal Electoral District(s): Huron-Bruce
Next Election: Oct. 2014 (4 year terms)
Note: Amalgamation of the Town of Clinton, the Township of Hullett, & the Township of Goderich.
Jim Ginn, Reeve
519-524-2522, Fax: 519-524-2755
jginn@centralhuron.com
Brenda MacIsaac, Clerk
clerk@centralhuron.com

Central Manitoulin
P.O. Box 187
6020 Hwy. 542
Mindemoya, ON P0P 1S0
Tel: 705-377-5726; *Fax:* 705-377-5585
centralm@amtelecom.net; centralinspections@amtelecom.net
www.centralmanitoulin.ca
Other Information: E-mail, Economic Dev.: centralecdev@amtelecom.net
Municipal Type: Township
Area: 431.53 sq km
County or District: Manitoulin District; *Population in 2006:* 1,944
Provincial Electoral District(s): Algoma-Manitoulin
Federal Electoral District(s): Algoma-Manitoulin-Kapuskasing
Next Election: Oct. 2014 (4 year terms)
Gerry Strong, Reeve
cmreeve@eastlink.ca
Ruth Frawley, Chief Administrative Officer & Clerk

Centre Hastings
P.O. Box 900
7 Furnace St.
Madoc, ON K0K 2K0
Tel: 613-473-4030; *Fax:* 613-473-5444
www.centrehastings.com
Municipal Type: Municipality
Area: 222.09 sq km
County or District: Hastings; *Population in 2006:* 4,386
Provincial Electoral District(s): Prince Edward-Hastings
Federal Electoral District(s): Prince Edward-Hastings
Next Election: Oct. 2014 (4 year terms)
Owen Ketcheson, Reeve
613-477-2527
Matt MacDonald, Chief Administrative officer & Clerk
mmacdonald@centrehastings.com

Centre Wellington
P.O. Box 10
1 MacDonald Sq.
Elora, ON N0B 1S0
Tel: 519-846-9691; *Fax:* 519-846-2190
www.centrewellington.ca
Municipal Type: Township
Area: 407.33 sq km
County or District: Wellington; *Population in 2006:* 26,049
Provincial Electoral District(s): Wellington-Halton Hills
Federal Electoral District(s): Wellington-Halton Hills
Next Election: Oct. 2014 (4 year terms)
Joanne Ross-Zuj, Mayor
519-846-0213, Fax: 519-846-2825
Kelly Linton, Councillor, Ward(s): 1
Kirk McElwain, Councillor, Ward(s): 2
Mary Lloyd, Councillor, Ward(s): 3
Fred Morris, Councillor, Ward(s): 4
Walt Visser, Councillor, Ward(s): 5
Steven VanLeeuwen, Councillor, Ward(s): 6
Marion Morris, Clerk
Michael K. Wood, Chief Administrative Officer
Wes Snarr, Chief Financial Officer & Treasurer
Andrew Goldie, Director, Parks & Recreation
Brett Salmon, Director, Planning
Brad Patton, Fire Chief
Ken Elder, Contact, Public Works

Chamberlain
467501 Chamberlain Rd. 5
Englehart, ON P0J 1H0
Tel: 705-544-8088; *Fax:* 705-544-1118
twpchamb@ntl.sympatico.ca
www.twpofchamberlain.com
Municipal Type: Township
Incorporated: 1908 *Area:* 110.13 sq km
County or District: Timiskaming District; *Population in 2006:* 322
Provincial Electoral District(s): Timiskaming-Cochrane
Federal Electoral District(s): Timmins-James Bay
Next Election: Oct. 2014 (4 year terms)
William Dickinson, Reeve
Barbara Cook, Township Clerk-Treasurer

Champlain
948 Pleasant Corners Rd. East
Vankleek Hill, ON K0B 1R0
Tel: 613-678-3003; *Fax:* 613-678-3363
info@champlain.ca
www.champlain.ca
Municipal Type: Township
Incorporated: Jan. 1, 1998 *Area:* 207.15 sq km
County or District: Prescott & Russell; *Population in 2006:* 8,683
Provincial Electoral District(s): Glengarry-Prescott-Russell
Federal Electoral District(s): Glengarry-Prescott-Russell
Next Election: Oct. 2014 (4 year terms)
Note: Amalgamation of the Village of L'Orignal, the Township of West Hawkesbury, the Township of Longueuil & the Village of Vankleek Hill.
Gary J. Barton, Mayor
613-678-3101
gary.barton@champlain.ca
Jean Thériault, Chief Administrative Officer & Clerk-Treasurer
jean.theriault@champlain.ca

Chapleau
Civic Centre
P.O. Box 129
20 Pine St.
Chapleau, ON P0M 1K0
Tel: 705-864-1330; *Fax:* 705-864-1824
www.chapleau.ca

Municipal Type: Township
Area: 14.27 sq km
County or District: Sudbury District; *Population in 2006:* 2,354
Provincial Electoral District(s): Algoma-Manitoulin
Federal Electoral District(s): Algoma-Manitoulin-Kapuskasing
Next Election: Oct. 2014 (4 year terms)
Andre Byham, Mayor
mayorbyham@township.chapleau.on.ca
Allan D. Pellow, Chief Administrative Officer
apellow@township.chapleau.on.ca

Chapple
P.O. Box 4
Barwick, ON P0W 1A0
Tel: 807-487-2354; *Fax:* 807-487-2406
info@chapple.on.ca
www.chapple.on.ca
Municipal Type: Township
Area: 529.02 sq km
County or District: Rainy River District; *Population in 2006:* 856
Provincial Electoral District(s): Kenora-Rainy River
Federal Electoral District(s): Thunder Bay-Rainy River
Next Election: Oct. 2014 (4 year terms)
Peter Van Heyst, Reeve
Peggy Johnson, Chief Administrative Officer & Clerk-Treasurer

Charlton & Dack
RR#2
Englehart, ON P0J 1H0
Tel: 705-544-7525; *Fax:* 705-544-2369
dack@ntl.sympatico.ca
www.charltonanddack.com
Municipal Type: Municipality
Incorporated: Jan. 1, 2003 *Area:* 92.33 sq km
County or District: Timiskaming District; *Population in 2006:* 613
Provincial Electoral District(s): Timiskaming-Cochrane
Federal Electoral District(s): Timmins-James Bay
Next Election: Oct. 2014 (4 year terms)
Note: Amalgamation of the Town of Charlton & the Township of Dack.
Wayne Pawson, Reeve

Chatham-Kent
Civic Centre
P.O. Box 640
315 King St. West
Chatham, ON N7M 5K8
Tel: 519-360-1998; *Fax:* 519-436-3237
ckinfo@chatham-kent.ca
www.chatham-kent.ca
Other Information: Toll-Free Phone: 1-800-714-7497
Municipal Type: Municipality
Incorporated: Jan. 1, 1998 *Area:* 2,458.06 sq km
Population in 2006: 108,177
Provincial Electoral District(s): Chatham-Kent-Essex; Lambton-Kent-Middlesex
Federal Electoral District(s): Chatham-Kent-Essex; Lambton-Kent-Middlesex
Next Election: Oct. 2014 (4 year terms)
Note: Formerly the County of Kent.
Randy Hope, Mayor & Chief Executive Officer
519-436-3219, Fax: 519-436-3236
ckmayor@chatham-kent.ca
Bryon Fluker, Councillor, Ward(s): 1 - West Kent
bryon.fluker@chatham-kent.ca
Brian W. King, Councillor, Ward(s): 1 - West Kent
brian.king@chatham-kent.ca
Karen Herman, Councillor, Ward(s): 2 - South Kent
karen.herman@chatham-kent.ca
Art Sterling, Councillor, Ward(s): 2 - South Kent
art.stirling@chatham-kent.ca
Frank Vercouteren, Councillor, Ward(s): 2 - South Kent
frank.vercouteren@chatham-kent.ca
Jim Brown, Councillor, Ward(s): 3 - East Kent
jim.brown@chatham-kent.ca
Steve Pinsonneault, Councillor, Ward(s): 3 - East Kent
steve.pinsonneault@chatham-kent.ca
Joe Faas, Councillor, Ward(s): 4 - North Kent
joe.faas@chatham-kent.ca
Leon Leclair, Councillor, Ward(s): 4 - North Kent
leon.leclair@chatham-kent.ca
Sheldon Parsons, ouncillor, Ward(s): 5 - Wallaceburg
sheldon.parsons@chatham-kent.ca
Jeff Wesley, Councillor, Ward(s): 5 - Wallaceburg
jeff.wesley@chatham-kent.ca
Michael Bondy, Councillor, Ward(s): 6 - Chatham
michael.bondy@chatham-kent.ca
Marjorie Crew, Councillor, Ward(s): 6 - Chatham
marjorie.crew@chatham-kent.ca
Anne Gilbert, Councillor, Ward(s): 6 - Chatham
anne.gilbert@chatham-kent.ca
Bob Myers, Councillor, Ward(s): 6 - Chatham
bob.myers@chatham-kent.ca
Derek Robertson, Councillor, Ward(s): 6 - Chatham
derek.robertson@chatham-kent.ca
Douglas Sulman, Councillor, Ward(s): 6 - Chatham
doug.sulman@chatham-kent.ca
Elinor Mifflin, Clerk
Rob Browning, Chief Administrative Officer
Stuart Wood, CMA, Director, Financial Services & Treasurer
Lucy Brown, General Manager, Health & Family Services
Leo Denys, General Manager, Infrastruture & Engineering Systems
Don Shropshire, General Manager. Community Development & Planning Services

Chatsworth
#316837, Hwy. 6, RR#1
Chatsworth, ON N0H 1G0
Tel: 519-794-3232; *Fax:* 519-794-4499
office@chatsworth.ca
www.chatsworth.ca
Municipal Type: Township
Incorporated: Jan. 1, 2001 *Area:* 595.35 sq km
County or District: Grey; *Population in 2006:* 6,392
Provincial Electoral District(s): Bruce-Grey-Owen Sound
Federal Electoral District(s): Bruce-Grey-Owen Sound
Next Election: Oct. 2014 (4 year terms)
Note: Amalgamation of the Townships of Holland & Sullivan & the Village of Chatsworth.
Bob Pringle, Mayor
519-794-2579
bob.pringle@grey.ca
Will Moore, Chief Administrative Officer & Clerk
519-794-3232
wmoore@chatsworth.ca

Chisholm
2847 Chiswick Line, RR#4
Powassan, ON P0H 1Z0
Tel: 705-724-3526; *Fax:* 705-724-5099
info@chisholm.ca; twpchisholm@ontera.ca
www.chisholm.ca
Other Information: Phone, Public Works: 705-724-5530
Municipal Type: Township
Incorporated: 1912 *Area:* 205.26 sq km
County or District: Nipissing District; *Population in 2006:* 1,318
Provincial Electoral District(s): Nipissing
Federal Electoral District(s): Nipissing-Timiskaming
Next Election: Oct. 2014 (4 year terms)
Leo Jobin, Mayor
Linda M. Ringler, Clerk-Treasurer

Clarington
40 Temperance St.
Bowmanville, ON L1C 3A6
Tel: 905-623-3379; *Fax:* 905-623-6506
info@clarington.net; communications@clarington.net
www.clarington.net
Other Information: Toll-Free Phone: 1-800-563-1195
Municipal Type: Municipality
Area: 611.1 sq km
County or District: Durham Reg. Mun.; *Population in 2006:* 77,820
Provincial Electoral District(s): Durham
Federal Electoral District(s): Durham
Next Election: Oct. 2014 (4 year terms)
Adrian Foster, Mayor
mayor@clarington.net
Mary Novak, Regional Councillor, Ward(s): 1 & 2
mnovak@clarington.net
Willie Woo, Regional Councillor, Ward(s): 3 & 4
wwoo@clarington.net
Joe Neal, Local Councillor, Ward(s): 1
jneal@clarington.net
Ron Hooper, Local Councillor, Ward(s): 2
rhooper@clarington.net
Corinna Trail, Local Councillor, Ward(s): 3
ctraill@clarington.net
Wendy Partner, Local Councillor, Ward(s): 4
wpartner@clarington.net
Patti L. Barrie, Municipal Clerk
pbarrie@clarington.net; clerks@clarington.net
Franklin Wu, Chief Administrative Officer
cao@clarington.net
Nancy Taylor, Treasurer & Director, Finance
ntaylor@clarington.net; finance@clarington.net
Tony Cannella, Director, Engineering Services
tcannella@clarington.net
Joseph Caruana, Director, Community Services
jcaruana@clarington.net
David Crome, Director, Planning Services
dcrome@clarington.net; planning@clarington.net
Fred Horvath, Director, Operations
fhorvath@clarington.net; operations@clarington.net
Marie Marano, Director, Corporate Services
mmarano@clarington.net
Gord Weir, Director, Emergency & Fire Services
gweir@clarington.net

Clearview
P.O. Box 200
217 Gideon St.
Stayner, ON L0M 1S0
Tel: 705-428-6230; *Fax:* 705-428-0288
www.clearview.ca
Municipal Type: Township
Area: 557.32 sq km
County or District: Simcoe; *Population in 2006:* 14,088
Provincial Electoral District(s): Simcoe-Grey
Federal Electoral District(s): Simcoe-Grey
Next Election: Oct. 2014 (4 year terms)
Ken Ferguson, Mayor
kferguson@clearview.ca
Alicia Savage, Deputy Mayor & Councillor
asavage@clearview.ca
Doug Measures, Councillor, Ward(s): 1
dmeasures@clearview.ca
Orville Brown, Councillor, Ward(s): 2
obrown@clearview.ca
Brent Preston, Councillor, Ward(s): 3
mroyal@clearview.ca
Thom Paterson, Councillor, Ward(s): 4
tpaterson@clearview.ca
Robert Walker, Councillor, Ward(s): 5
rwalker@clearview.ca
Deborah Bronée, Councillor, Ward(s): 6
dbronee@clearview.ca
Shawn Davidson, Councillor, Ward(s): 7
sdavidson@clearview.ca
Bob Campbell, Clerk
bcampbell@clearview.ca
Susan McKenzie, Chief Administrative Officer
smckenzie@clearview.ca
Edward Henley, Treasurer
ehenley@clearview.ca
Richard Spraggs, Director, Public Works
rspraggs@clearview.ca
Michael Wynia, Director, Planning & Development
mwynia@clearview.ca
Bob McKean, Fire Chief
bmckean@clearview.ca

Cobalt
P.O. Box 70
18 Silver St.
Cobalt, ON P0J 1C0
Tel: 705-679-8877;
www.cobalt.ca
Municipal Type: Town
Area: 2.11 sq km
County or District: Timiskaming District; *Population in 2006:* 1,229
Provincial Electoral District(s): Timiskaming-Cochrane
Federal Electoral District(s): Nipissing-Timiskaming
Next Election: Oct. 2014 (4 year terms)
Tina Sartoretto, Mayor
Steph Palmateer, Chief Administrative Officer & Clerk-Treasurer

Cochrane
P.O. Box 490
171 Fourth Ave.
Cochrane, ON P0L 1C0
Tel: 705-272-4361; *Fax:* 705-272-6068
townhall@town.cochrane.on.ca
www.town.cochrane.on.ca
Municipal Type: Town
Incorporated: 1910 *Area:* 538.76 sq km
County or District: Cochrane District; *Population in 2006:* 5,487
Provincial Electoral District(s): Timiskaming-Cochrane
Federal Electoral District(s): Timmins-James Bay
Next Election: Oct. 2014 (4 year terms)
Peter Politis, Mayor
peter.politis@town.cochrane.on.ca
Jean-Pierre Ouellette, Chief Administrative Officer & Clerk

Cochrane
Cochrane, ON
www.cdssab.on.ca
Municipal Type: District
Area: 141,247.30 sq km
Population in 2006: 82,503
David Landers, CAO, Cochrane District Social Services Administration Board

705-268-7722, Fax: 705-268-8290
cao@cdssab.on.ca

Cockburn Island
General Delivery
Walford, ON P0P 2E0
Tel: 705-844-2289; *Fax:* 705-844-1101
Municipal Type: Township
Area: 167.6 sq km
County or District: Manitoulin District; *Population in 2006:* 10
Provincial Electoral District(s): Algoma-Manitoulin
Federal Electoral District(s): Algoma-Manitoulin-Kapuskasing
Next Election: Oct. 2014 (4 year terms)
David Haight, Reeve
Austin Clipperton, Clerk-Treasurer

Coleman
937907 Marsh Bay Rd.
Coleman, ON P0J 1C0
Tel: 705-679-8833; *Fax:* 705-679-8300
toc@ontera.net
www.colemantownship.ca
Municipal Type: Township
Incorporated: 1906 *Area:* 177.6 sq km
County or District: Timiskaming District; *Population in 2006:* 431
Provincial Electoral District(s): Timiskaming-Cochrane
Federal Electoral District(s): Nipissing-Timiskaming
Next Election: Oct. 2014 (4 year terms)
Dan Cleroux, Mayor
danc@ntl.sympatico.ca
Claire Bigelow, Clerk-Treasurer

Conmee
19 Holland Rd. West, RR#1
Kakabeka Falls, ON P0T 1W0
Tel: 807-475-5229; *Fax:* 807-475-4793
info@conmee.com
www.conmee.com
Municipal Type: Township
Area: 167.53 sq km
County or District: Thunder Bay District; *Population in 2006:* 740
Provincial Electoral District(s): Thunder Bay-Atikokan
Federal Electoral District(s): Thunder Bay-Rainy River
Next Election: Oct. 2014 (4 year terms)
Kevin Holland, Reeve
Patricia Maxwell, Clerk-Treasurer

Cramahe
P.O. Box 357
1 Toronto St.
Colborne, ON K0K 1S0
Tel: 905-355-2821; *Fax:* 905-355-3430
www.visitcramahe.ca
Other Information: Toll-Free Phone: 1-877-272-4263
Municipal Type: Township
Area: 201.56 sq km
County or District: Northumberland; *Population in 2006:* 5,950
Provincial Electoral District(s): Northumberland-Quinte West
Federal Electoral District(s): Northumberland-Quinte West
Next Election: Oct. 2014 (4 year terms)
Marc Coombs, Mayor
marc.coombs@airnet.ca
Christie Alexander, Chief Administrative Officer & Clerk
christie@cramahetownship.ca

Dawn-Euphemia
4591 Lambton Line, RR#4
Dresden, ON N0P 1M0
Tel: 519-692-5148; *Fax:* 519-692-5511
admin@dawneuphemia.on.ca
www.lambtononline.ca/county_councillors
Municipal Type: Township
Area: 445.05 sq km
County or District: Lambton; *Population in 2006:* 2,190
Provincial Electoral District(s): Lambton-Kent-Middlesex
Federal Electoral District(s): Lambton-Kent-Middlesex
Next Election: Oct. 2014 (4 year terms)
William E. Bilton, Mayor
mayor@dawneuphemia.on.ca
Michael Schnare, Administrator-Clerk

Dawson
P.O. Box 427
211 Fourth St.
Rainy River, ON P0W 1L0
Tel: 807-852-3529; *Fax:* 807-852-3529
Municipal Type: Township
Area: 338.35 sq km
County or District: Rainy River District; *Population in 2006:* 620
Provincial Electoral District(s): Kenora-Rainy River
Federal Electoral District(s): Thunder Bay-Rainy River
Next Election: Oct. 2014 (4 year terms)

Eltjo Wiersema, Reeve
Patrick W. Giles, Clerk-Treasurer

Deep River
P.O. Box 400
100 Deep River Rd.
Deep River, ON K0J 1P0
Tel: 613-584-2000; *Fax:* 613-584-3237
townmail@deepriver.ca
www.deepriver.ca
Municipal Type: Town
Area: 50.84 sq km
County or District: Renfrew; *Population in 2006:* 4,216
Provincial Electoral District(s): Renfrew-Nipissing-Pembroke
Federal Electoral District(s): Renfrew-Nipissing-Pembroke
Next Election: Oct. 2014 (4 year terms)
Dave Thompson, Mayor
Michelle Larose, Chief Administrative Officer & Clerk
mlarose@deepriver.ca

Deseronto
P.O. Box 310
331 Main St.
Deseronto, ON K0K 1X0
Tel: 613-396-2440; *Fax:* 613-396-3141
jcarter@deseronto.ca (Public Works)
www.deseronto.ca
Other Information: E-mail, Economic Dev.: mconger@deseronto.ca
Municipal Type: Town
Incorporated: 1889 *Area:* 2.52 sq km
County or District: Hastings; *Population in 2006:* 1,824
Provincial Electoral District(s): Prince Edward-Hastings
Federal Electoral District(s): Prince Edward-Hastings
Next Election: Oct. 2014 (4 year terms)
Norm Clark, Mayor
nnclark@sympatico.ca
Bryan Brooks, Clerk-Treasurer
bbrooks@deseronto.ca

Dorion
170 Dorion Loop Rd., RR#1
Dorion, ON P0T 1K0
Tel: 807-857-2289; *Fax:* 807-857-2203
office@doriontownship.ca
www.doriontownship.ca
Municipal Type: Township
Area: 212.07 sq km
County or District: Thunder Bay District; *Population in 2006:* 379
Provincial Electoral District(s): Thunder Bay-Superior North
Federal Electoral District(s): Thunder Bay-Superior North
Next Election: Oct. 2014 (4 year terms)
Dave Harris, Reeve
dharris@doriontownship.ca
Helena Tamminen, Clerk-Treasurer
helena@doriontownship.ca

Douro-Dummer
P.O. Box 92
894 South St.
Warsaw, ON K0L 3A0
Tel: 705-652-8392; *Fax:* 705-652-5044
info@dourodummer.on.ca
www.dourodummer.on.ca
Other Information: Toll-Free Phone: 1-800-899-8785
Municipal Type: Township
Area: 458.36 sq km
County or District: Peterborough; *Population in 2006:* 6,954
Provincial Electoral District(s): Peterborough
Federal Electoral District(s): Peterborough
Next Election: Oct. 2014 (4 year terms)
J. Murray Jones, Reeve
705-652-6325, Fax: 705-652-6325
jjones@dourodummer.on.ca
Linda G. Moher, Clerk & Coordinator, Planning
lindamo@dourodummer.on.ca

Drummond-North Elmsley
310 Port Elmsley Rd., RR#5
Perth, ON K7H 3L7
Tel: 613-267-6500; *Fax:* 613-267-2083
admin@drummondnorthelmsley.com
www.drummondnorthelmsley.com
Municipal Type: Township
Incorporated: 1998 *Area:* 364.78 sq km
County or District: Lanark; *Population in 2006:* 7,118
Provincial Electoral District(s): Lanark-Frontenac-Lennox & Addington
Federal Electoral District(s): Lanark-Frontenac-Lennox & Addington
Next Election: Oct. 2014 (4 year terms)
Note: Amalgamation of the Townships of Drummond and North Elmsley.
Aubrey Churchill, Reeve
613-264-8404
Cindy Halcrow, Clerk-Administrator
cindy@drummondnorthelmsley.com

Dryden
30 Van Horne Ave.
Dryden, ON P8N 2A7
Tel: 807-223-1147; *Fax:* 807-223-1126
generalinquiries@dryden.ca
www.dryden.ca
Other Information: Alternative Phone: 807-223-1126
Municipal Type: Town
Area: 65.2 sq km
County or District: Kenora; *Population in 2006:* 8,195
Provincial Electoral District(s): Kenora-Rainy River
Federal Electoral District(s): Kenora
Next Election: Oct. 2014 (4 year terms)
Craig Nuttall, Mayor
cnuttall@dryden.ca
Colleen Brosseau, City Clerk
807-223-1127
cbrosseau@dryden.ca

Dubreuilville
P.O. Box 367
23 Pine St.
Dubreuilville, ON P0S 1B0
Tel: 705-884-2340; *Fax:* 705-884-2626
www.dubreuilville.ca
Municipal Type: Township
Incorporated: 1978 *Area:* 89.57 sq km
County or District: Algoma District; *Population in 2006:* 773
Provincial Electoral District(s): Algoma-Manitoulin
Federal Electoral District(s): Algoma-Manitoulin-Kapuskasing
Next Election: Oct. 2014 (4 year terms)
Louise Perrier, Mayor
lperrier@dubreuilville.ca
Réjean Raymond, Chief Administrative Officer & Clerk
rraymond@dubreuilville.ca

Dutton-Dunwich
P.O. Box 329
199 Currie Rd.
Dutton, ON N0L 1J0
Tel: 519-762-2204; *Fax:* 519-762-2278
htuffin@duttondunwich.on.ca (Office assistant)
www.duttondunwich.on.ca
Municipal Type: Municipality
Area: 294.63 sq km
County or District: Elgin; *Population in 2006:* 3,821
Provincial Electoral District(s): Elgin-Middlesex-London
Federal Electoral District(s): Elgin-Middlesex-London
Next Election: Oct. 2014 (4 year terms)
Cameron McWilliam, Mayor
csmcwilliam@gmail.com
Ken Loveland, Administrator & Clerk-Treasurer
kloveland@duttondunwich.on.ca

Dysart et al
P.O. Box 389
135 Maple Ave.
Haliburton, ON K0M 1S0
Tel: 705-457-1740; *Fax:* 705-457-1964
www.dysartetal.ca
Municipal Type: Township
Incorporated: Jan. 7, 1867 *Area:* 1,474.07 sq km
County or District: Haliburton; *Population in 2006:* 5,526
Provincial Electoral District(s): Haliburton-Kawartha Lakes-Brock
Federal Electoral District(s): Haliburton-Kawartha Lakes-Brock
Next Election: Oct. 2014 (4 year terms)
Murray Fearrey, Reeve
Cheryl Coulson, Chief Administrative Officer & Clerk
ccoulson@dysartetal.ca

Ear Falls
P.O. Box 309
Ear Falls, ON P0V 1T0
Tel: 807-222-3624; *Fax:* 807-222-2384
eftownship@ear-falls.com
www.ear-falls.com
Other Information: E-mail, Public Services & Ops: pdyck@ear-falls.com
Municipal Type: Township
Area: 330.99 sq km
County or District: Kenora District; *Population in 2006:* 1,153
Provincial Electoral District(s): Kenora-Rainy River
Federal Electoral District(s): Kenora
Next Election: Oct. 2014 (4 year terms)

Kevin Kahoot, Mayor
kkahoot@ear-falls.com
Kimberly Ballance, Clerk-Treasurer & Administrator
kballance@ear-falls.com

East Ferris
390 Hwy. 94
Corbeil, ON P0H 1K0
Tel: 705-752-2740;
eastferris.ca
Municipal Type: Township
Area: 149.76 sq km
County or District: Nipissing District; *Population in 2006:* 4,200
Provincial Electoral District(s): Nipissing
Federal Electoral District(s): Nipissing-Timiskaming
Next Election: Oct. 2014 (4 year terms)
William Vrebosch, Mayor
John B. Fior, Clerk
john.fior@eastferris.ca

East Garafraxa
374028 6th Line, RR#3
Orton, ON L0N 1N0
Tel: 519-928-5298; *Fax:* 519-941-1802
township@amaranth-eastgary.ca
www.amaranth-eastgary.ca
Other Information: Alternative Phone: 519-941-1007
Municipal Type: Township
Incorporated: Jan. 1, 1869 *Area:* 165.72 sq km
County or District: Dufferin; *Population in 2006:* 2,389
Provincial Electoral District(s): Dufferin-Caledon
Federal Electoral District(s): Dufferin-Caledon
Next Election: Oct. 2014 (4 year terms)
Allen Taylor, Mayor
519-941-4047
Susan M. Stone, AMCT, Chief Administrative Officer & Clerk-Treasurer
suestone@amaranth-eastgary.ca

East Hawkesbury
P.O. Box 340
5151 County Rd. 14
St Eugene, ON K0B 1P0
Tel: 613-674-2170; *Fax:* 613-674-2989
www.easthawkesbury.ca
Municipal Type: Township
Incorporated: Jan. 1, 1850 *Area:* 235.09 sq km
County or District: Prescott & Russell; *Population in 2006:* 3,368
Provincial Electoral District(s): Glengarry-Prescott-Russell
Federal Electoral District(s): Glengarry-Prescott-Russell
Next Election: Oct. 2014 (4 year terms)
Robert Kirby, Mayor
613-632-4841, Fax: 613-632-4841
Linda Rozon, Chief Administrative Officer & Clerk-Treasurer
lrozon@easthawkesbury.ca

East Luther Grand Valley
P.O. Box 249
5 Main St. North
Grand Valley, ON L0N 1G0
Tel: 519-928-5652; *Fax:* 519-928-2275
mail@eastluthergrandvalley.ca
www.eastluthergrandvalley.ca
Municipal Type: Township
Incorporated: Dec. 27, 1880 *Area:* 158.2 sq km
County or District: Dufferin; *Population in 2006:* 2,844
Provincial Electoral District(s): Dufferin-Caledon
Federal Electoral District(s): Dufferin-Caledon
Next Election: Oct. 2014 (4 year terms)
Note: Amalgamation of the Township of East Luther & the Village of Grand Valley on Jan. 1, 1995.
John K. Oosterhof, Mayor
519-928-3117
joosterhof@eastluthergrandvalley.ca
Jane M. Wilson, Chief Administrative Officer & Clerk-Treasurer
jwilson@eastluthergrandvalley.ca

East Zorra-Tavistock
P.O. Box 100
90 Loveys St.
Hickson, ON N0J 1L0
Tel: 519-462-2697; *Fax:* 519-462-2961
ezt@twp.ezt.on.ca
www.twp.ezt.on.ca
Municipal Type: Township
Area: 247.42 sq km
County or District: Oxford; *Population in 2006:* 7,350
Provincial Electoral District(s): Oxford
Federal Electoral District(s): Oxford
Next Election: Oct. 2014 (4 year terms)
Don McKay, Mayor
519-532-2500
dmckay@twp.ezt.on.ca
Brenda Junker, Municipal Clerk & Tax Collector
bjunker@twp.ezt.on.ca

Edwardsburgh/Cardinal
P.O. Box 129
18 Centre St.
Spencerville, ON K0E 1X0
Tel: 613-658-3055; *Fax:* 613-658-3445
www.twpec.ca
Other Information: Toll-Free Phone: 1-866-848-9099
Municipal Type: Township
Area: 311.83 sq km
County or District: Leeds & Grenville; *Population in 2006:* 6,689
Provincial Electoral District(s): Leeds-Grenville
Federal Electoral District(s): Leeds-Grenville
Next Election: Oct. 2014 (4 year terms)
Bill Sloane, Mayor
613-802-0797
mayor@twpec.ca
Debra McKinstry, Clerk & Administrator, Planning
dmckinstry@twpec.ca

Elizabethtown-Kitley
6544 New Dublin Rd., RR#2
Addison, ON K0E 1A0
Tel: 613-345-7480; *Fax:* 613-345-7235
mail@elizabethtown-kitley.on.ca
www.elizabethtown-kitley.on.ca
Other Information: Toll-Free Phone: 1-800-492-3175
Municipal Type: Township
Area: 554.24 sq km
County or District: Leeds & Grenville; *Population in 2006:* 10,201
Provincial Electoral District(s): Leeds-Grenville
Federal Electoral District(s): Leeds-Grenville
Next Election: Oct. 2014 (4 year terms)
Jim Pickard, Mayor
613-342-5721
jimpickard@ripnet.com
Earl Brayton, Councillor
613-345-2650
Dan Downey, Councillor
613-275-1460
John Johnston, Councillor
613-342-8952
Susan Prettejohn, Councillor
613-498-2842
Elenor Renaud, Councillor
613-275-2091
Rob Smith, Councillor
613-498-0827
Yvonne L. Robert, Administrator-Clerk
Melanie Kirkby, Director, Finance & Treasurer
Barbara Kalivas, Director, Planning & Development
Dale Kulp, Director, Public Works
Jim Donovan, Fire Chief
613-498-2460
Ray Scissons, Chief Building Official
cbo@elizabethtown-kitley.on.ca

Emo
P.O. Box 520
39 Roy St.
Emo, ON P0W 1E0
Tel: 807-482-2378; *Fax:* 807-482-2741
township@emo.ca
www.emo.ca
Municipal Type: Township
Incorporated: 1899 *Area:* 203.54 sq km
County or District: Rainy River District; *Population in 2006:* 1,305
Provincial Electoral District(s): Kenora-Rainy River
Federal Electoral District(s): Thunder Bay-Rainy River
Next Election: Oct. 2014 (4 year terms)
Vince Sheppard, Mayor
Brenda J. Cooke, Chief Administrative Officer & Clerk-Treasurer

Englehart
P.O. Box 399
61 Fifth Ave.
Englehart, ON P0J 1H0
Tel: 705-544-2244;
englehrt@ntl.sympatico.ca
www.englehart.ca
Municipal Type: Town
Incorporated: 1908 *Area:* 3.04 sq km
County or District: Timiskaming District; *Population in 2006:* 1,494
Provincial Electoral District(s): Timiskaming-Cochrane
Federal Electoral District(s): Timmins-James Bay
Next Election: Oct. 2014 (4 year terms)
Nina Wallace, Mayor
Jana Van Oosten, Clerk

Enniskillen
4465 Rokeby Line, RR#1
Petrolia, ON N0N 1R0
Tel: 519-882-2490;
www.enniskillen.ca
Municipal Type: Township
Area: 338.18 sq km
County or District: Lambton; *Population in 2006:* 3,122
Provincial Electoral District(s): Sarnia-Lambton
Federal Electoral District(s): Sarnia-Lambton
Next Election: Oct. 2014 (4 year terms)
Jim Burns, Mayor
jim.tara.burns@cogeco.ca
Duncan McTavish, Administrator-Clerk
dmctavish@enniskillen.ca

Espanola
#2, 100 Tudhope St.
Espanola, ON P5E 1S6
Tel: 705-869-1540; *Fax:* 705-869-0083
town@town.espanola.on.ca
www.town.espanola.on.ca
Other Information: E-mail, Public Works: jyusko@town.espanola.on.ca
Municipal Type: Town
Incorporated: March 1, 1958 *Area:* 82.37 sq km
County or District: Sudbury District; *Population in 2006:* 5,314
Provincial Electoral District(s): Algoma-Manitoulin
Federal Electoral District(s): Algoma-Manitoulin-Kapuskasing
Next Election: Oct. 2014 (4 year terms)
Mike Lehoux, Mayor
Joel Mackenzie, Clerk-Treasurer & Administrator
jmackenzie@town.espanola.on.ca

Essa
5786 County Rd. 21
Utopia, ON L0M 1T0
Tel: 705-424-9770; *Fax:* 705-424-2367
info@essatownship.on.ca
www.essatownship.on.ca
Other Information: TTY: 705-424-5302
Municipal Type: Township
Incorporated: 1850 *Area:* 279.57 sq km
County or District: Simcoe; *Population in 2006:* 16,901
Provincial Electoral District(s): Simcoe-Grey
Federal Electoral District(s): Simcoe-Grey
Next Election: Oct. 2014 (4 year terms)
Terry Dowdall, Mayor
705-423-1154
tdowdall@essatownship.on.ca
Sandie Macdonald, Deputy Mayor & Councillor
705-424-6844
smacdonald@essatownship.on.ca
Keith White, Councillor, Ward(s): 1
705-424-2727
kwhite@essatownship.on.ca
Michael Smith, Councillor, Ward(s): 2
705-794-3230
msmith@essatownship.on.ca
Ron Henderson, Councillor, Ward(s): 3
705-424-9752
rhenderson@essatownship.on.ca
Bonnie Sander, Clerk
Greg Murphy, Chief Administrative Officer & Manager, Public Works
gmurphy@essatownship.on.ca
Julie Barrett, Treasurer & Deputy Chief Administrative Officer
jbarrett@essatownship.on.ca
Colleen Healey, Manager, Planning & Development
chealey@essatownship.on.ca
Paul Macdonald, Fire Chief
fire@essatownship.on.ca
Heather Rutherford, Chief Building Official
hrutherford@essatownship.on.ca

Evanturel
P.O. Box 209
245453 Hwy. 659
Englehart, ON P0J 1H0
Tel: 705-544-8200; *Fax:* 705-544-8206
www.evanturel.com
Other Information: E-mail, Building: cbo@ntl.sympatico.ca
Municipal Type: Township
Incorporated: Jan. 1, 1904 *Area:* 88.99 sq km
County or District: Timiskaming District; *Population in 2006:* 473
Provincial Electoral District(s): Timiskaming-Cochrane

Federal Electoral District(s): Timmins-James Bay
Next Election: Oct. 2014 (4 year terms)
Jack Briggs, Reeve
Amy Vickery-Menard, Clerk-Treasurer
evanturelclerk@parolink.net

Faraday
P.O. Box 929
29860 Hwy. 28 South
Bancroft, ON K0L 1C0
Tel: 613-332-3638; *Fax:* 613-332-3006
faraday@reztel.net
www.faraday.ca
Municipal Type: Township
Area: 215.23 sq km
County or District: Hastings; *Population in 2006:* 1,578
Provincial Electoral District(s): Prince Edward-Hastings
Federal Electoral District(s): Prince Edward-Hastings
Next Election: Oct. 2014 (4 year terms)
Carl A. Tinney, Reeve
613-332-2050
Brenda Vader, Clerk-Treasurer & Tax Collector

Fauquier-Strickland
P.O. Box 40
25 Grzela Rd.
Fauquier, ON P0L 1G0
Tel: 705-339-2521; *Fax:* 705-339-2421
info@fauquierstrickland.com
fauquierstrickland.com
Municipal Type: Township
Area: 1,013.54 sq km
County or District: Cochrane District; *Population in 2006:* 568
Provincial Electoral District(s): Timmins-James Bay
Federal Electoral District(s): Algoma-Manitoulin-Kapuskasing
Next Election: Oct. 2014 (4 year terms)
Madeleine Tremblay, Reeve
Robert Courchesne, Administrator & Clerk-Treasurer

Fort Frances
320 Portage Ave.
Fort Frances, ON P9A 3P9
Tel: 807-274-5323; *Fax:* 807-274-8479
town@fort-frances.com
www.fort-frances.com
Municipal Type: Town
Incorporated: 1903 *Area:* 26.85 sq km
County or District: Rainy River District; *Population in 2006:* 8,103
Provincial Electoral District(s): Kenora-Rainy River
Federal Electoral District(s): Thunder Bay-Rainy River
Next Election: Oct. 2014 (4 year terms)
Roy Avis, Mayor
ravis@fort-frances.com
Glenn Treftlin, Clerk
gtreftlin@fort-frances.com

French River, Municipality of / Municipalité de la Rivière des Français
P.O. Box 156
#1, 44 St. Christophe St.
Noëlville, ON P0M 2N0
Tel: 705-898-2294; *Fax:* 705-898-2181
www.frenchriver.ca
Municipal Type: Town
Incorporated: Jan. 1, 1999 *Area:* 734.26 sq km
County or District: Sudbury District; *Population in 2006:* 2,659
Provincial Electoral District(s): Timiskaming-Cochrane; Nickle Belt
Federal Electoral District(s): Nickel Belt
Next Election: Oct. 2014 (4 year terms)
Claude Bouffard, Mayor
cbouffard@frenchriver.ca
Michel V. Monette, CMA, Chief Administrative Officer & Clerk
mmonette@frenchriver.ca

Front of Yonge
P.O. Box 130
1514 County Rd. 2
Mallorytown, ON K0E 1R0
Tel: 613-923-2251; *Fax:* 613-923-2421
admin@frontofyonge.com
www.frontofyonge.com
Other Information: Phone, Public Works: 613-923-5074
Municipal Type: Township
Area: 127.85 sq km
County or District: Leeds & Grenville; *Population in 2006:* 2,803
Provincial Electoral District(s): Leeds-Grenville
Federal Electoral District(s): Leeds-Grenville
Next Election: Oct. 2014 (4 year terms)
Roger Haley, Reeve
rogerhaley@frontofyonge.com
Elaine A. Covey, Clerk
ecovey@frontofyonge.com

Frontenac Islands
P.O. Box 130
Rd. 96
Wolfe Island, ON K0H 2Y0
Tel: 613-385-2216; *Fax:* 613-385-1032
www.municipality.frontenacislands.on.ca
Municipal Type: Township
Incorporated: Jan. 1, 1998 *Area:* 174.99 sq km
County or District: Frontenac; *Population in 2006:* 1,862
Provincial Electoral District(s): Kingston & the Islands
Federal Electoral District(s): Kingston & the Islands
Next Election: Oct. 2014 (4 year terms)
Note: Amalgamation of Howe Island & Wolfe Island.
Dennis Doyle, Mayor
613-385-2763
denisdoyle@kos.net
Terry J. O'Shea, AMCT, Chief Administrative Officer & Clerk
tjoshea@kos.net

Galway-Cavendish-Harvey
P.O. Box 820
701 County Rd. 36, RR#3
Bobcaygeon, ON K0M 1A0
Tel: 705-738-3800; *Fax:* 705-738-3801
www.galwaycavendishharvey.ca
Other Information: Toll-Free Phone: 1-800-374-4009
Municipal Type: Township
Area: 848.26 sq km
County or District: Peterborough; *Population in 2006:* 5,284
Provincial Electoral District(s): Haliburton-Kawartha Lakes-Brock
Federal Electoral District(s): Haliburton-Kawartha Lakes-Brock
Next Election: Oct. 2014 (4 year terms)
Janet Clarkson, Reeve
705-657-9932
jclarkson@galwaycavendishharvey.ca
Lynn Holtz, Clerk
lholtz@galwaycavendishharvey.ca

Gananoque
Town Hall
P.O. Box 100
30 King St. East
Gananoque, ON K7G 2T6
Tel: 613-382-2149; *Fax:* 613-382-8587
www.townofgananoque.com
Municipal Type: Separated for Municipal Purposes Only
Area: 7.01 sq km
County or District: Leeds & Grenville; *Population in 2006:* 5,285
Provincial Electoral District(s): Leeds-Grenville
Federal Electoral District(s): Leeds-Grenville
Next Election: Oct. 2014 (4 year terms)
Erika Demchuk, Mayor
mayor@townofgananoque.ca
Robert W. Small, Chief Administrative Officer
rsmall@gananoque.ca

Gauthier
P.O. Box 65
92 McPherson St.
Dobie, ON P0K 1B0
Tel: 705-568-8951; *Fax:* 705-568-8951
Municipal Type: Township
Area: 88.36 sq km
County or District: Timiskaming District; *Population in 2006:* 133
Provincial Electoral District(s): Timiskaming-Cochrane
Federal Electoral District(s): Timmins-James Bay
Next Election: Oct. 2014 (4 year terms)
Dave Fraser, Reeve
Dianne Quinn, Clerk-Treasurer
quinner@ntl.sympatico.ca

Georgian Bay
99 Lone Pine Rd.
Port Severn, ON L0K 1S0
Tel: 705-538-2337; *Fax:* 705-538-1850
clerks@township.georgianbay.on.ca
www.township.georgianbay.on.ca
Other Information: Toll-Free Phone: 1-800-567-0187
Municipal Type: Township
Area: 535.48 sq km
County or District: Muskoka District Municipality; *Population in 2006:* 2,340
Provincial Electoral District(s): Parry Sound-Muskoka
Federal Electoral District(s): Parry Sound-Muskoka
Next Election: Oct. 2014 (4 year terms)
Larry Braid, Mayor
Susan Boonstra, Clerk
sboonstra@gbtownship.ca

Georgian Bluffs
177964 Grey Rd. 18, RR#3
Owen Sound, ON N4K 5N5
Tel: 519-376-2729; *Fax:* 519-372-1620
office@georgianbluffs.on.ca
www.georgianbluffs.on.ca
Municipal Type: Township
Incorporated: Jan. 1, 2001 *Area:* 603.58 sq km
County or District: Grey; *Population in 2006:* 10,506
Provincial Electoral District(s): Bruce-Grey-Owen Sound
Federal Electoral District(s): Bruce-Grey-Owen Sound
Next Election: Oct. 2014 (4 year terms)
Note: Amalgamation of the Townships of Derby, Keppel & Sarawak.
Alan Barfoot, Mayor
abarfoot@georgianbluffs.on.ca
Dwight Burley, Deputy Mayor & Councillor
dburley@georgianbluffs.on.ca
Carol Barfoot, Councillor
cbarfoot@georgianbluffs.on.ca
Judy Gay, Councillor
jgay@georgianbluffs.on.ca
Robert Lennox, Councillor
rlennox@georgianbluffs.on.ca
Ryan Thompson, Councillor
rthompson@georgianbluffs.on.ca
Tom Wiley, Councillor
twiley@georgianbluffs.on.ca
Bruce Hoffman, Clerk
bhoffman@georgianbluffs.on.ca
Bill White, Chief Administrative Officer
Holly Morrison, Treasurer
hmorrison@georgianbluffs.on.ca
Bill Klingenberg, Chief Building Official
Martin Timmerman, Supervisor, Operations

Gillies
1092 Hwy. 595, RR#1
South Gillies, ON P0T 1W0
Tel: 807-475-3185; *Fax:* 807-473-0767
gillies@tbaytel.net
www.gilliestownship.ca
Other Information: E-mail, Building: cmaki@xplornet.com
Municipal Type: Township
Area: 92.67 sq km
County or District: Thunder Bay District; *Population in 2006:* 544
Provincial Electoral District(s): Thunder Bay-Atikokan
Federal Electoral District(s): Thunder Bay-Rainy River
Next Election: Oct. 2014 (4 year terms)
Rick Kieri, Reeve
Karen Caren, Clerk-Treasurer
gillies@tbaytel.net

Goderich
Municipal Office, Town Hall
57 West St.
Goderich, ON N7A 2K5
Tel: 519-524-8344; *Fax:* 519-524-7209
townhall@goderich.ca
www.goderich.ca
Municipal Type: Town
Area: 7.91 sq km
County or District: Huron; *Population in 2006:* 7,563
Provincial Electoral District(s): Huron-Bruce
Federal Electoral District(s): Huron-Bruce
Next Election: Oct. 2014 (4 year terms)
Delbert (Deb) Shewfelt, Mayor
519-524-9581
Larry J. McCabe, Clerk-Administrator

Gordon / Barrie Island
P.O. Box 680
29 Noble Side Rd.
Gore Bay, ON P0P 1H0
Tel: 705-282-2702; *Fax:* 705-282-2722
adminoffice@gordonbarrieisland.ca
gordontownship.manitoulin-link.com
Municipal Type: Municipality
Incorporated: Jan. 1, 2009
County or District: Manitoulin District; *Population in 2006:* 459
Provincial Electoral District(s): Algoma-Manitoulin
Federal Electoral District(s): Algoma-Manitoulin-Kapuskasing
Next Election: Oct. 2014 (4 year terms)
Note: Amalgamation of the former Township of Gordon & Allan West & the Township of Barrie Island.
Art Madore, Reeve
Carrie Lewis, Clerk-Treasurer
clerk@gordonbarrieisland.ca

Gore Bay
P.O. Box 590
15 Water St.
Gore Bay, ON P0P 1H0
Tel: 705-282-2420; *Fax:* 705-282-3076
www.gorebay.ca
Other Information: E-mail, Treasury: pbond@gorebay.ca
Municipal Type: Town
Incorporated: 1890 *Area:* 5.27 sq km
County or District: Manitoulin District; *Population in 2006:* 924
Provincial Electoral District(s): Algoma-Manitoulin
Federal Electoral District(s): Algoma-Manitoulin-Kapuskasing
Next Election: Oct. 2014 (4 year terms)
Ron Lane, Mayor
mayor@gorebay.ca
Annette Clarke, Clerk
aclarke@gorebay.ca

Greater Madawaska
P.O. Box 180
1101 Francis St.
Calabogie, ON K0J 1H0
Tel: 613-752-2222; *Fax:* 613-752-2617
admin@greatermadawaska.com
www.townshipofgreatermadawaska.com
Municipal Type: Township
Incorporated: Jan. 1, 2001 *Area:* 1,011.67 sq km
County or District: Renfrew; *Population in 2006:* 2,751
Provincial Electoral District(s): Renfrew-Nipissing-Pembroke
Federal Electoral District(s): Renfrew-Nipissing-Pembroke
Next Election: Oct. 2014 (4 year terms)
Note: Amalgamation of Bagot, Blythfield & Brougham Township & Griffith & Matawatchan Township.
Peter Emon, Reeve
613-752-2922
peteremon@somuchmore.ca
Angela Yolkowskie, Chief Administrative Officer
ayolkowskie@greatermadawaska.com

Greenstone, Municipality of
P.O. Box 70
301 East St.
Geraldton, ON P0T 1M0
Tel: 807-854-1100; *Fax:* 807-854-1947
www.greenstone.ca
Municipal Type: Town
Area: 2,780.99 sq km
County or District: Thunder Bay; *Population in 2006:* 4,906
Provincial Electoral District(s): Thunder Bay-Superior North
Federal Electoral District(s): Thunder Bay-Superior North
Next Election: Oct. 2014 (4 year terms)
Renald Beaulieu, Mayor
Elizabeth (Lisa) Slomke, Clerk
lisa.slomke@greenstone.ca

Grey Highlands, Municipality of
P.O. Box 409
#1, 206 Toronto St. South
Markdale, ON N0C 1H0
Tel: 519-986-2811; *Fax:* 519-986-3643
info@greyhighlands.ca
www.greyhighlands.ca
Other Information: Toll-Free Phone: 1-888-342-4059
Municipal Type: Township
Incorporated: Jan. 1, 2001 *Area:* 880.6 sq km
County or District: Grey; *Population in 2006:* 9,480
Provincial Electoral District(s): Bruce-Grey-Owen Sound
Federal Electoral District(s): Bruce-Grey-Owen Sound
Next Election: Oct. 2014 (4 year terms)
Note: Amalgamation of Flesherton, Artemesia, Euphrasia, Markdale & Osprey.
Wayne Fitzgerald, Mayor
519-986-3898
Debbie Robertson, Clerk
519-986-1216
robertson@greyhighlands.ca

Guelph / Eramosa
P.O. Box 700
8348 Wellington Rd. 124
Rockwood, ON N0B 2K0
Tel: 519-856-9951; *Fax:* 519-856-2240
general@get.on.ca
www.get.on.ca
Other Information: Toll-Free Phone: 1-800-267-1465
Municipal Type: Township
Incorporated: Jan. 1, 1999 *Area:* 291.73 sq km
County or District: Wellington; *Population in 2006:* 12,066
Provincial Electoral District(s): Wellington-Halton Hills
Federal Electoral District(s): Wellington-Halton Hills
Next Election: Oct. 2014 (4 year terms)
Note: Amalgamation of the Townships of Guelph, Eramosa, Pilkington & Nichol.
Chris White, Mayor
whitecj@sympatico.ca
Meaghen Reid, Clerk
mreid@get.on.ca
Shawn Armstrong, Fire Chief
519-824-6590
Brad Roelfson, Manager, Property & Leisure Services
broelofson@get.on.ca
Ken Gagnon, Manager, Public Works
kgagnon@get.on.ca
Mark Thorpe, Officer, Bylaw Enforcement
mthorpe@get.on.ca
Mike Newark, Chief Building Official
mnewark@get.on.ca

Hamilton
P.O. Box 1060
8285 Majestic Hills Dr.
Cobourg, ON K9A 4W5
Tel: 905-342-2810; *Fax:* 905-342-2818
info@hamiltontownship.ca
www.hamiltontownship.ca
Municipal Type: Township
Area: 256.11 sq km
County or District: Northumberland; *Population in 2006:* 10,972
Provincial Electoral District(s): Northumberland-Quinte West
Federal Electoral District(s): Northumberland-Quinte West
Next Election: Oct. 2014 (4 year terms)
Mark Lovshin, Mayor
mlovshin@cogeco.ca
Isobel Hie, Deputy Mayor & Councillor
ihie@hamiltontownship.ca
Donna Cole, Councillor
dcole@hamiltontownship.ca
John Davison, Councillor
jdavison@hamiltontownship.ca
Gary Woods, Councillor
gwoods@hamiltontownship.ca
Kate Surerus, Clerk
ksurerus@hamiltontownship.ca
Bill Winegard, Interim Chief Administrative Officer
bwinegard@hamiltontownship.ca
Fran Aird, Acting Tax Collector & Treasurer
faird@hamiltontownship.ca
Doug Murray, Director, Public Works
dmurray@hamiltontownship.ca
Ken Clapperton, Fire Chief, Baltimore
baltimorefire@hamiltontownship.ca
Reg Jackson, Fire Chief, Bewdley
bewdleyfire@hamiltontownship.ca
Pete Staples, Fire Chief, Harwood
harwoodfire@hamiltontownship.ca
Scott Jibb, Chief Building Official
sjibb@hamiltontownship.ca
Sandra Stothart, Coordinator, Planning
sstothart@hamiltontownship.ca
Doug Thompson, Manager, Water Operations
dthompson@hamiltontownship.ca

Hanover
341 - 10th St.
Hanover, ON N4N 1P5
Tel: 519-364-2780; *Fax:* 519-364-6456
civic@hanover.ca
www.hanover.ca
Municipal Type: Town
Incorporated: Jan. 1, 2001 *Area:* 9.81 sq km
County or District: Grey; *Population in 2006:* 7,147
Provincial Electoral District(s): Bruce-Grey-Owen Sound
Federal Electoral District(s): Bruce-Grey-Owen Sound
Next Election: Oct. 2014 (4 year terms)
Kathi Maskell, Mayor
kmaskell@hanover.ca
Mike Dunlop, Chief Administrative Officer & Clerk
mdunlop@hanover.ca

Harley
903303 Hanbury Rd., RR#2
New Liskeard, ON P0J 1P0
Tel: 705-647-5439; *Fax:* 705-647-6373
harleytwp@parolink.net
www.harley.ca
Municipal Type: Township
Incorporated: 1904 *Area:* 91.73 sq km
County or District: Timiskaming District; *Population in 2006:* 551
Provincial Electoral District(s): Timiskaming-Cochrane
Federal Electoral District(s): Timmins-James Bay
Next Election: Oct. 2014 (4 year terms)
Pauline Archambault, Reeve
Michel Lachapelle, Clerk-Treasurer

Harris
Site 4-96, RR#3
New Liskeard, ON P0J 1P0
Tel: 705-647-5094; *Fax:* 705-647-0041
harris@ntl.sympatico.ca
Municipal Type: Township
Area: 50.17 sq km
County or District: Timiskaming District; *Population in 2006:* 512
Provincial Electoral District(s): Timiskaming-Cochrane
Federal Electoral District(s): Nipissing-Timiskaming
Next Election: Oct. 2014 (4 year terms)
Martin Auger, Reeve

Hastings Highlands
P.O. Box 130
33011 Hwy. 62 North
Maynooth, ON K0L 2S0
Tel: 613-338-2811; *Fax:* 613-338-3292
office@hastingshighlands.ca
www.hastingshighlands.ca
Other Information: Toll-Free Phone: 1-877-338-2818
Municipal Type: Municipality
Area: 967.34 sq km
County or District: Hastings; *Population in 2006:* 4,033
Provincial Electoral District(s): Prince Edward-Hastings
Federal Electoral District(s): Prince Edward-Hastings
Next Election: Oct. 2014 (4 year terms)
Ronald J. Emond, Mayor
remond@hastingshighlands.ca
Craig Davidson, Chief Administrative Officer & Clerk-Treasurer
cdavidson@hastingshighlands.ca

Havelock-Belmont-Methuen
P.O. Box 10
1 Ottawa St. East
Havelock, ON K0L 1Z0
Tel: 705-778-2308; *Fax:* 705-778-5248
havbelmet@hbmtwp.ca
www.havelockbelmontmethuen.on.ca
Other Information: Toll-Free Phone: 1-877-767-2795
Municipal Type: Township
Area: 526.02 sq km
County or District: Peterborough; *Population in 2006:* 4,637
Provincial Electoral District(s): Peterborough
Federal Electoral District(s): Peterborough
Next Election: Oct. 2014 (4 year terms)
Ronald Gerow, Reeve
705-778-2092
rgerow@hbmtwp.ca
Glenn Girven, Clerk
ggirven@hbmtwp.ca

Head, Clara & Maria
15 Township Hall Rd.
Stonecliffe, ON K0J 2K0
Tel: 613-586-2526; *Fax:* 613-586-2596
twpshcm@xplornet.com
www.townshipsofheadclaramaria.ca
Other Information: Phone, Building Inspection: 613-586-1950
Municipal Type: Township
Area: 727.96 sq km
County or District: Renfrew; *Population in 2006:* 228
Provincial Electoral District(s): Renfrew-Nipissing-Pembroke
Federal Electoral District(s): Renfrew-Nipissing-Pembroke
Next Election: Oct. 2014 (4 year terms)
Tammy Lea Stewart, Reeve
613-586-2750
Melinda Reith, Municipal Clerk

Hearst
Town Hall
P.O. Box 5000
925 Alexandra St.
Hearst, ON P0L 1N0
Tel: 705-362-4341; *Fax:* 705-362-5902
townofhearst@hearst.ca
www.hearst.ca
Municipal Type: Town
Incorporated: 1922 *Area:* 98.67 sq km
County or District: Cochrane District; *Population in 2006:* 5,620
Provincial Electoral District(s): Timmins-James Bay
Federal Electoral District(s): Algoma-Manitoulin-Kapuskasing
Next Election: Oct. 2014 (4 year terms)
Roger Sigouin, Mayor
Claude J. Laflamme, Chief Administrative Officer & Clerk
705-372-2817

Highlands East, Municipality of
P.O. Box 295
County Rd. 648
Wilberforce, ON K0L 3C0
Tel: 705-448-2981; *Fax:* 705-448-2532
www.highlandseast.ca
Municipal Type: Township
Incorporated: Jan. 1, 2001 *Area:* 701.32 sq km
County or District: Haliburton; *Population in 2006:* 3,089
Provincial Electoral District(s): Haliburton-Kawartha Lakes-Brock
Federal Electoral District(s): Haliburton-Kawartha Lakes-Brock
Next Election: Oct. 2014 (4 year terms)
Note: Amalgamation of the Townships of Bicroft, Cardiff, Glamorgan & Monmouth.
Dave Burton, Reeve
705-448-9355
dburton@highlandseast.ca
Irene Cook, CMO, Clerk, Fax: 705-448-3211
icook@highlandseast.ca

Hilliard
P.O. Box 12
RR#3
Thornloe, ON P0J 1S0
Tel: 705-563-2593; *Fax:* 705-563-2593
twphill@ntl.sympatico.ca
Municipal Type: Township
Area: 91.17 sq km
County or District: Timiskaming District; *Population in 2006:* 222
Provincial Electoral District(s): Timiskaming-Cochrane
Federal Electoral District(s): Timmins-James Bay
Next Election: Oct. 2014 (4 year terms)
Morgan Carson, Reeve
Janet Gore, Clerk-Treasurer

Hilton
P.O. Box 205
2983 Base Line
Hilton Beach, ON P0R 1G0
Tel: 705-246-2472; *Fax:* 705-246-0132
admin@hiltontownship.ca; hiltontownship@xplornet.com
www.hiltontownship.ca
Other Information: Phone, Roads: 705-246-1781
Municipal Type: Township
Incorporated: 1883 *Area:* 115.78 sq km
County or District: Algoma District; *Population in 2006:* 243
Provincial Electoral District(s): Algoma-Manitoulin
Federal Electoral District(s): Sault Ste Marie
Next Election: Oct. 2014 (4 year terms)
James See, Reeve
see@hiltontownship.ca
Valerie Obarymskyj, Clerk-Treasurer
clerk@hiltontownship.ca

Hilton Beach
P.O. Box 25
3100 Bowker St.
Hilton Beach, ON P0R 1G0
Tel: 705-246-2242; *Fax:* 705-246-2913
info@hiltonbeach.com
www.hiltonbeach.com
Municipal Type: Village
Area: 2.46 sq km
County or District: Algoma District; *Population in 2006:* 172
Provincial Electoral District(s): Algoma-Manitoulin
Federal Electoral District(s): Sault Ste Marie
Next Election: Oct. 2014 (4 year terms)
Wilfred Stevens, Mayor
Gloria Fischer, Clerk

Hornepayne
P.O. Box 370
68 Front St.
Hornepayne, ON P0M 1Z0
Tel: 807-868-2020; *Fax:* 807-868-2787
www.hornepayne.com/township
Municipal Type: Township
Area: 204.52 sq km
County or District: Algoma District; *Population in 2006:* 1,209
Provincial Electoral District(s): Algoma-Manitoulin
Federal Electoral District(s): Algoma-Manitoulin-Kapuskasing
Next Election: Oct. 2014 (4 year terms)
Gene Belanger, Mayor
Susan Smith, Township Clerk
smith.hpayne@xplornet.com

Horton
2253 Johnston Rd., RR#5
Renfrew, ON K7V 3Z8
Tel: 613-432-6271; *Fax:* 613-432-7298
mjmhorton@xplornet.com
www.hortontownship.ca
Municipal Type: Township
Area: 158.38 sq km
County or District: Renfrew; *Population in 2006:* 2,803
Provincial Electoral District(s): Renfrew-Nipissing-Pembroke
Federal Electoral District(s): Renfrew-Nipissing-Pembroke
Next Election: Oct. 2014 (4 year terms)
Don Eady, Mayor
Mackie J. McLaren, Chief Administrative Officer & Clerk

Howick
P.O. Box 89
Hwy 87
Gorrie, ON N0G 1X0
Tel: 519-335-3208; *Fax:* 519-335-6208
office@town.howick.on.ca
www.town.howick.on.ca
Municipal Type: Township
Area: 287.17 sq km
County or District: Huron; *Population in 2006:* 3,882
Provincial Electoral District(s): Huron-Bruce
Federal Electoral District(s): Huron-Bruce
Next Election: Oct. 2014 (4 year terms)
Art Versteeg, Reeve
versteeg@wightman.ca
Genevieve Scharback, Clerk
clerk@town.howick.on.ca

Hudson
903303 Hanbury Rd., RR#2
New Liskeard, ON P0J 1P0
Tel: 705-647-5439; *Fax:* 705-647-6373
harleytwp@parolink.net
www.hudson.ca
Municipal Type: Township
Area: 90.46 sq km
County or District: Timiskaming District; *Population in 2006:* 305
Provincial Electoral District(s): Timiskaming-Cochrane
Federal Electoral District(s): Nipissing-Timiskaming
Next Election: Oct. 2014 (4 year terms)
Larry Craig, Reeve
Michel Lachapelle, Clerk-Treasurer

Huron East, Municipality of
P.O. Box 610
72 Main St. South
Seaforth, ON N0K 1W0
Tel: 519-527-0160; *Fax:* 519-527-2561
webmaster@huroneast.com
www.huroneast.com
Other Information: Toll-Free Phone: 1-888-868-7513
Municipal Type: Town
Incorporated: Jan. 1, 2001 *Area:* 669.16 sq km
County or District: Huron; *Population in 2006:* 9,310
Provincial Electoral District(s): Huron-Bruce
Federal Electoral District(s): Huron-Bruce
Next Election: Oct. 2014 (4 year terms)
Note: Amalgamation of the Town of Seaforth, the Village of Brussels, & the Townships of Grey, McKillop and Tuckersmith.
Bernie MacLellan, Mayor
519-233-7489, Fax: 519-233-3405
mayor@huroneast.com
Brad Knight, Clerk-Administrator
bknight@huroneast.com

Huron Shores
P.O. Box 460
7 Bridge St.
Iron Bridge, ON P0R 1H0
Tel: 705-843-2033; *Fax:* 705-843-2035
email@huronshores.ca
www.huronshores.ca
Municipal Type: Municipality
Area: 455.33 sq km
County or District: Algoma District; *Population in 2006:* 1,696
Provincial Electoral District(s): Algoma-Manitoulin
Federal Electoral District(s): Algoma-Manitoulin-Kapuskasing
Next Election: Oct. 2014 (4 year terms)
Lionel Reeves, Mayor
Deborah Tonelli, AMCT, Administrator-Clerk

Huron-Kinloss
P.O. Box 130
21 Queen St.
Ripley, ON N0G 2R0
Tel: 519-395-3735; *Fax:* 519-395-4107
info@huronkinloss.com
www.huronkinloss.com
Municipal Type: Township
Incorporated: 1999 *Area:* 440.59 sq km
County or District: Bruce; *Population in 2006:* 6,515
Provincial Electoral District(s): Huron-Bruce
Federal Electoral District(s): Huron-Bruce
Next Election: Oct. 2014 (4 year terms)
Note: Amalgamation of the Village of Lucknow & the Townships of Ripley-Huron & Kinloss.
Mitch Twolan, Mayor
519-395-0717
mitch.twolan@remax-lx.ca
Sonya Watson, Clerk
clerk@huronkinloss.com

Ignace
P.O. Box 248
34 Hwy. 17 West
Ignace, ON P0T 1T0
Tel: 807-934-2202; *Fax:* 807-934-2864
ecdev@tbaytel.net
www.town.ignace.on.ca
Municipal Type: Township
Incorporated: 1908 *Area:* 72.66 sq km
County or District: Kenora District; *Population in 2006:* 1,431
Provincial Electoral District(s): Kenora-Rainy River
Federal Electoral District(s): Kenora
Next Election: Oct. 2014 (4 year terms)
Lee Kennard, Mayor
elkennard@yahoo.com
Wayne Hanchard, Administrator & Treasurer
admintreasurer@tbaytel.net

Iroquois Falls
P.O. Box 230
253 Main St.
Iroquois Falls, ON P0K 1G0
Tel: 705-232-5700; *Fax:* 705-232-4241
www.iroquoisfalls.com
Municipal Type: Town
Area: 599.43 sq km
County or District: Cochrane District; *Population in 2006:* 4,729
Provincial Electoral District(s): Timiskaming-Cochrane
Federal Electoral District(s): Timmins-James Bay
Next Election: Oct. 2014 (4 year terms)
Gilles Forget, Mayor
mayor@iroquoisfalls.com
Michel S. Morrissette, Administrator-Clerk
morrissm@iroquoisfalls.com

James
P.O. Box 10
372 Third St.
Elk Lake, ON P0J 1G0
Tel: 705-678-2237; *Fax:* 705-678-2495
elklake@ntl.sympatico.ca
www.elklake.ca
Municipal Type: Township
Incorporated: 1909 *Area:* 86.19 sq km
County or District: Timiskaming District; *Population in 2006:* 414
Provincial Electoral District(s): Timiskaming-Cochrane
Federal Electoral District(s): Timmins-James Bay
Next Election: Oct. 2014 (4 year terms)
Terry Fiset, Reeve
Myrna J. Hayes, Clerk-Treasurer

Jocelyn
RR#1
Richards Landing, ON P0R 1J0
Tel: 705-246-2025; *Fax:* 705-246-3282
jocelynt@soonet.ca
Municipal Type: Township
Area: 131.37 sq km
County or District: Algoma District; *Population in 2006:* 277
Provincial Electoral District(s): Algoma-Manitoulin
Federal Electoral District(s): Sault Ste Marie
Next Election: Oct. 2014 (4 year terms)
Mark Henderson, Reeve
Janet Boucher, Clerk

Johnson
P.O. Box 160
1 Johnson Dr.
Desbarats, ON P0R 1E0
Tel: 705-782-6601; *Fax:* 705-782-6780
johnsontwp@bellnet.ca
www.johnsontwp.ca
Municipal Type: Township
Area: 119.67 sq km
County or District: Algoma District; *Population in 2006:* 701
Provincial Electoral District(s): Algoma-Manitoulin
Federal Electoral District(s): Sault Ste Marie
Next Election: Oct. 2014 (4 year terms)
Ted Hicks, Mayor
705-782-6348
Ruth Kelso, Clerk & Chief Administrative Officer

Joly
P.O. Box 519
871 Forest Lake Rd.
Sundridge, ON P0A 1Z0
Tel: 705-384-5428; *Fax:* 705-384-0845
twpjoly@on.aibn.com
Municipal Type: Township
Area: 193.82 sq km
County or District: Parry Sound District; *Population in 2006:* 280
Provincial Electoral District(s): Parry Sound-Muskoka
Federal Electoral District(s): Parry Sound-Muskoka
Next Election: Oct. 2014 (4 year terms)
Mario Campese, Reeve
Gerry Whittington, Chief Administrative Officer & Clerk

Kapuskasing
Civic Centre
88 Riverside Dr.
Kapuskasing, ON P5N 1B3
Tel: 705-335-2341; *Fax:* 705-337-1741
townkap@ntl.sympatico.ca
www.kapuskasing.ca
Municipal Type: Town
Incorporated: 1921 *Area:* 83.98 sq km
County or District: Cochrane District; *Population in 2006:* 8,509
Provincial Electoral District(s): Timmins-James Bay
Federal Electoral District(s): Algoma-Manitoulin-Kapuskasing
Next Election: Oct. 2014 (4 year terms)
Alan Spacek, Mayor
Yvan Brousseau, Chief Administrative Officer

Kearney
P.O. Box 38
8 Main St.
Kearney, ON P0A 1M0
Tel: 705-636-7752; *Fax:* 705-636-0527
kearney1@vianet.ca
www.townofkearney.com
Municipal Type: Town
Incorporated: 1908 *Area:* 529.5 sq km
County or District: Parry Sound District; *Population in 2006:* 798
Provincial Electoral District(s): Parry Sound-Muskoka
Federal Electoral District(s): Parry Sound-Muskoka
Next Election: Oct. 2014 (4 year terms)
Paul Tomlinson, Mayor
kearneytomlinson@gmail.com
Yvonne Aubichon, Clerk Administrator
clerkadministrator@townofkearney.com

Kenora
Kenora District Services Board Admin Office
#1, 211 Princess St.
Dryden, ON P8N 3L5
Tel: 807-223-2100; *Fax:* 807-223-6500
kdsb@kdsb.on.ca
www.kdsb.on.ca
Municipal Type: District
Area: 407,192.66 sq km
Population in 2006: 64,419
Phil Vinet, Chair, Kenora District Services Board of Directors, & Councillor
Dan McNeill, Chief Administrative Officer, Kenora District Services Board
dmcneill@kdsb.on.ca

Kerns
903303 Hanbury Rd., RR#2
New Liskeard, ON P0J 1P0
Tel: 705-647-5439; *Fax:* 705-647-6373
harleytwp@parolink.net
www.kerns.ca
Municipal Type: Township
Incorporated: 1904 *Area:* 90.44 sq km
County or District: Timiskaming District; *Population in 2006:* 325
Provincial Electoral District(s): Timiskaming-Cochrane
Federal Electoral District(s): Timmins-James Bay
Next Election: Oct. 2014 (4 year terms)
Terry Phillips, Reeve
Michel Lachapelle, Clerk-Treasurer

Killaloe, Hagarty & Richards
P.O. Box 39
1 John St.
Killaloe, ON K0J 2A0
Tel: 613-757-2300; *Fax:* 613-757-3634
info@khrtownship.ca
www.killaloe-hagarty-richards.ca
Municipal Type: Township
Incorporated: July 1, 2000 *Area:* 395.91 sq km
County or District: Renfrew; *Population in 2006:* 2,550
Provincial Electoral District(s): Renfrew-Nipissing-Pembroke
Federal Electoral District(s): Renfrew-Nipissing-Pembroke
Next Election: Oct. 2014 (4 year terms)
Note: Amalgamation of the Township of Hagarty & Richards & the former Village of Killaloe.
Janice Visneskie, Mayor
moorevisneskie@hotmail.com
Lorna Hudder, Chief Administrative Officer & Clerk-Treasurer
lhudder@khrtownship.ca

Killarney, Municipality of
32 Commissioner St.
Killarney, ON P0M 2A0
Tel: 705-287-2424; *Fax:* 705-287-2660
townkill@vianet.on.ca
www.municipality.killarney.on.ca
Other Information: Toll-Free Phone: 1-888-597-2721
Municipal Type: Town
Incorporated: Jan. 1, 1999 *Area:* 1,513.58 sq km
County or District: Sudbury District; *Population in 2006:* 454
Provincial Electoral District(s): Algoma-Manitoulin
Federal Electoral District(s): Nickel Belt
Next Election: Oct. 2014 (4 year terms)
Morgan Pitfield, Mayor
Candy Beavais, Clerk-Treasurer

Kincardine
1475 Conc. 5, RR#5
Kincardine, ON N2Z 2X6
Tel: 519-396-3468; *Fax:* 519-396-8288
ssmith@kincardine.net
www.kincardine.net
Municipal Type: Municipality
Area: 537.65 sq km
County or District: Bruce; *Population in 2006:* 11,173
Provincial Electoral District(s): Huron-Bruce
Federal Electoral District(s): Huron-Bruce
Next Election: Oct. 2014 (4 year terms)
Larry Kraemer, Mayor
519-396-3130
mayor@kincardine.net
Anne Eadie, Deputy Mayor & Councillor
519-396-6927
aeadie@brucetelecom.com
Ron Coristine, Councillor at Large
519-396-5458
ronc@tnt21.com
Maureen Couture, Councillor at Large
519-395-3629
ronc@tnt21.com
Kenneth Craig, Councillor at Large
519-396-8767
kencraig@bmts.com
Jacqueline Faubert, Councillor, Ward(s): 1
519-396-7240
jfauberb@sfu.ca
Mike Leggett, Councillor, Ward(s): 1
519-396-4529
ff1221@tnt21.com
Candy Hewitt, Councillor, Ward(s): 2
519-395-2461
candyhewitt@hotmail.com
Randy Roppel, Councillor, Ward(s): 3
519-368-7792
Donna MacDougall, Clerk & Acting Chief Administrative Officer
clerk@kincardine.net; cao@kincardine.net
Brenda French, Treasurer
519-396-3468
treasurer@kincardine.net
Michele Barr, Manager, Building & Planning
cbo@kincardine.net
Jim O'Rourke, Manager, Public Works
pwmgr@kincardine.net
Jamie MacKinnon, Fire Chief
kinfirechief@bmts.com
Steve Murray, Coordinator, Community Services
smurray@kincardine.net
Roberta Trelford, Coordinator, Community Emergency Management, & Health & Safety
kinfirecemc@bmts.com
Donna Hardman, Compliance Officer, Public Works
519-396-4660
dhardman@bmts.com

King
2075 King Rd.
King City, ON L7B 1A1
Tel: 905-833-5321; *Fax:* 905-833-2300
online@king.ca
www.king.ca
Municipal Type: Township
Incorporated: 1850 *Area:* 333.04 sq km
County or District: York Reg. Mun.; *Population in 2006:* 19,487
Provincial Electoral District(s): Oak Ridges-Markham; York-Simcoe
Federal Electoral District(s): Oak Ridges-Markham; York-Simcoe
Next Election: Oct. 2014 (4 year terms)
Steve Pellegrini, Mayor
spellegrini@king.ca
Cleve Mortelliti, Councillor, Ward(s): 1
cmortelliti@king.ca
Peter Grandilli, Councillor, Ward(s): 2
pgrandilli@king.ca
Linda Pabst, Councillor, Ward(s): 3
lpabst@king.ca
Bill Cober, Councillor, Ward(s): 4
bcober@king.ca
Debbie Schaefer, Councillor, Ward(s): 5
dschaefer@king.ca
Avia Eek, Councillor, Ward(s): 6
aeek@king.ca
Kathryn Smyth, Clerk
ksmyth@king.ca
Susan Plamondon, Chief Administrative Officer
splamondon@king.ca
Jeff Schmidt, Director, Finance
jschmidt@king.ca
Judy Laplante, Director, Engineering & Development
jlaplante@king.ca
David Clark, Director, Parks, Recreation & Culture
dclark@king.ca
Marilyn Loan, Manager, Human Resources
mloan@king.ca
Gaspare Ritacca, Manager, Planning & Development
gritacca@king.ca
Bryan Burbidge, Fire Chief
bburbidge@king.ca
Jamie Smyth, Community Development Officer
jsmyth@king.ca

Kirkland Lake
P.O. Box 1757
3 Kirkland St. West
Kirkland Lake, ON P2N 3P4
Tel: 705-567-9361; *Fax:* 705-567-3535
edd@tkl.ca
www.discoverkl.ca
Municipal Type: Town
Incorporated: 1972 *Area:* 262.24 sq km
County or District: Timiskaming District; *Population in 2006:* 8,248
Provincial Electoral District(s): Timiskaming-Cochrane
Federal Electoral District(s): Timmins-James Bay
Next Election: Oct. 2014 (4 year terms)
Note: Formerly known as the Township of Teck.
William Enouy, Mayor
bill.enouy@tkl.ca
Jo Ann Ducharme, Clerk, Department of Corporate Services
joann.ducharme@tkl.ca

La Vallée
P.O. Box 99
56 Church Rd.
Devlin, ON P0W 1C0
Tel: 807-486-3452; *Fax:* 807-486-3863
lavalley@nwonet.net
www.lavallee.ca
Municipal Type: Township
Area: 237.26 sq km
County or District: Rainy River District; *Population in 2006:* 1,067
Provincial Electoral District(s): Kenora-Rainy River
Federal Electoral District(s): Thunder Bay-Rainy River
Next Election: Oct. 2014 (4 year terms)
Ross Donaldson, Reeve
Sylvia Smeeth, Municipal Clerk

Laird
3 Pumpkin Point Rd., RR#4
Echo Bay, ON P0S 1C0
Tel: 705-248-2395; *Fax:* 705-248-1138
lairdtwp@soonet.ca
www.lairdtownship.ca
Municipal Type: Township
Incorporated: 1891 *Area:* 101.77 sq km
County or District: Algoma District; *Population in 2006:* 1,078
Provincial Electoral District(s): Algoma-Manitoulin
Federal Electoral District(s): Sault Ste Marie
Next Election: Oct. 2014 (4 year terms)
Richard (Dick) Beitz, Mayor
Phyllis L. MacKay, Clerk-Treasurer, Tax Collector, & License Issuing Officer

Lake of Bays
1012 Dwight Beach Rd., RR#1
Dwight, ON P0A 1H0
Tel: 705-635-2272; *Fax:* 705-635-2132
contact@lakeofbays.on.ca
www.lakeofbays.on.ca
Other Information: Toll-Free Phone: 1-877-566-0005
Municipal Type: Township
Incorporated: 1971 *Area:* 671.46 sq km
County or District: Muskoka Dist. Mun.; *Population in 2006:* 3,570
Provincial Electoral District(s): Parry Sound-Muskoka
Federal Electoral District(s): Parry Sound-Muskoka
Next Election: Oct. 2014 (4 year terms)
Note: Amalgamation of the former Townships of Franklin, Ridout, McLean & Sinclair/Finlayson.
Bob Young, Mayor
705-635-1845
ryoung@lakeofbays.on.ca
Don Chevalier, Chief Administrative Officer & Treasurer

Lake of the Woods
P.O. Box 427
211 Fourth St.
Rainy River, ON P0W 1L0
Tel: 807-852-3529; *Fax:* 807-852-3529
www.lakeofthewoods.ca
Municipal Type: Township
Incorporated: Jan. 1, 1998 *Area:* 751.17 sq km
County or District: Rainy River District; *Population in 2006:* 323
Provincial Electoral District(s): Kenora-Rainy River
Federal Electoral District(s): Thunder Bay-Rainy River
Next Election: Oct. 2014 (4 year terms)
Note: Amalgamation of the Township of Morson & McCrosson-Tovell.
Valerie Pizey, Mayor
Patrick W. Giles, Clerk-Treasurer
gilesp@tbaytel.net

Lambton Shores
P.O. Box 610
7883 Amtelecom Pkwy.
Forest, ON N0N 1J0
Tel: 519-786-2335; *Fax:* 519-786-2135
administration@lambtonshores.ca
www.lambtonshores.ca
Other Information: Toll-Free Phone: 1-877-786-2335
Municipal Type: Municipality
Incorporated: 2001 *Area:* 331.08 sq km
County or District: Lambton; *Population in 2006:* 11,150
Provincial Electoral District(s): Lambton-Kent-Middlesex
Federal Electoral District(s): Lambton-Kent-Middlesex
Next Election: Oct. 2014 (4 year terms)
Note: Amalgamation of the Towns of Bosanquet & Forest, & the Villages of Thedford, Arkona & Grand Bend.
Bill Weber, Mayor
519-238-1313
bweber@lambtonshores.ca
Elizabeth Davis-Dagg, Deputy Mayor & Councillor
519-899-2535
edavis-dagg@lambtonshores.ca
Dave Maguire, Councillor, Ward(s): 1
dmaguire@lambtonshores.ca
Doug Bonesteel, Councillor, Ward(s): 2
dbonesteel@lambtonshores.ca
Lorie Scott, Councillor, Ward(s): 3
lscott@lambtonshores.ca
Ruth Illman, Councillor, Ward(s): 4
rillman@lambtonshores.ca
Martin Underwood, Councillor, Ward(s): 5
munderwood@lambtonshores.ca
Doug Cook, Councillor, Ward(s): 6
dcook@lambtonshores.ca
John Russell, Councillor, Ward(s): 7
jrussell@lambtonshores.ca
Carol McKenzie, Clerk
cpmckenzie@lambtonshores.ca
John Byrne, Chief Administrative Officer
jbyrne@lambtonshores.ca
Janet Ferguson, Treasurer
jferguson@lambtonshores.ca
Peggy Van Mierlo-West, Director, Community Services
pvmwest@lambtonshores.ca
Patti Richardson, Planner
prichardson@lambtonshores.ca
Allan Little, Superintendent, Drainage, & Construction Inspector
alittle@lambtonshores.ca

Lanark Highlands
P.O. Box 340
75 George St.
Lanark, ON K0G 1K0
Tel: 613-259-2398; *Fax:* 613-259-2291
mailbag@lanarkhighlands.ca
www.lanarkhighlands.ca
Other Information: Toll-Free Phone: 1-800-239-4695
Municipal Type: Township
Incorporated: July 1, 1997 *Area:* 1,033.3 sq km
County or District: Lanark; *Population in 2006:* 5,180
Provincial Electoral District(s): Lanark-Frontenac-Lennox & Addington
Federal Electoral District(s): Lanark-Frontenac-Lennox & Addington
Next Election: Oct. 2014 (4 year terms)
Note: Amalgamation of North West Lanark Township & Darling Township.
Peter McLaren, Mayor
Ross Trimble, Chief Administrative Officer & Clerk
rtrimble@lanarkhighlands.ca

Larder Lake
P.O. Box 40
13 Godfrey St.
Larder Lake, ON P0K 1L0
Tel: 705-643-2158; *Fax:* 705-643-2311
www.larderlake.net
Municipal Type: Township
Area: 228.73 sq km
County or District: Timiskaming District; *Population in 2006:* 735
Provincial Electoral District(s): Timiskaming-Cochrane
Federal Electoral District(s): Timmins-James Bay
Next Election: Oct. 2014 (4 year terms)
Patricia Bodick, Reeve
Jim Roman, Clerk-Treasurer
jroman@ntl.sympatico.ca

Latchford
P.O. Box 10
10 Main St.
Latchford, ON P0J 1N0
Tel: 705-676-2416; *Fax:* 705-676-2121
www.latchford.ca
Municipal Type: Town
Incorporated: 1907 *Area:* 153.27 sq km
County or District: Timiskaming District; *Population in 2006:* 446
Provincial Electoral District(s): Timiskaming-Cochrane
Federal Electoral District(s): Nipissing-Timiskaming
Next Election: Oct. 2014 (4 year terms)
George Lefebvre, Mayor
glefebvre@latchford.ca
Jaime Allen, Municipal Clerk
jallen@latchford.ca

Laurentian Hills
34465 Hwy. 17, RR#1
Deep River, ON K0J 1P0
Tel: 613-584-3114; *Fax:* 613-584-3285
info@laurentianhills.ca
www.laurentianhills.ca
Municipal Type: Town
Incorporated: Jan. 1, 2000 *Area:* 640.37 sq km
County or District: Renfrew; *Population in 2006:* 2,789
Provincial Electoral District(s): Renfrew-Nipissing-Pembroke
Federal Electoral District(s): Renfrew-Nipissing-Pembroke
Next Election: Oct. 2014 (4 year terms)
Note: Amalgamation of the United Townships of Rolph, Buchanan, Wylie & McKay & the Village of Chalk River.
Richard Rabishaw, Mayor
mayor@laurentianhills.ca
Wayne T. Kirby, Chief Administrative Officer & Clerk
cao@laurentianhills.ca

Laurentian Valley
460 Witt Rd., RR#4
Pembroke, ON K8A 6W5
Tel: 613-735-6291; *Fax:* 613-735-5820
laurentian@laurvall.on.ca
www.laurentianvalleytwsp.on.ca
Municipal Type: Township
Incorporated: Jan. 1, 2000 *Area:* 552.44 sq km
County or District: Renfrew; *Population in 2006:* 9,265
Provincial Electoral District(s): Renfrew-Nipissing-Pembroke
Federal Electoral District(s): Renfrew-Nipissing-Pembroke
Next Election: Oct. 2014 (4 year terms)
Note: Amalgamation of the former Townships of Stafford-Pembroke & Alice & Fraser.
Jack Wilson, Mayor
613-732-9281
John Baird, Chief Administrative Officer & Clerk

Leamington
111 Erie St. North
Leamington, ON N8H 2Z3
Tel: 519-326-5761; *Fax:* 519-326-2481
info@leamington.ca
www.leamington.ca
Other Information: E-mail, Public Works: publicworks@leamington.ca
Municipal Type: Municipality
Incorporated: 1874 *Area:* 261.92 sq km
County or District: Essex; *Population in 2006:* 28,833
Provincial Electoral District(s): Chatham-Kent-Essex
Federal Electoral District(s): Chatham-Kent-Essex
Next Election: Oct. 2014 (4 year terms)
Note: Incorporated as a town in 1890. Restructuring occurred in 1999.
John Paterson, Mayor
519-326-5761
councilmembers@leamington.ca
Charlie Wright, Deputy Mayor & Councillor
Rick Atkin, Councillor
Chris Chopchik, Councillor
John Jacobs, Councillor
Hilda MacDonald, Councillor
Larry Verbeke, Councillor
Brian R. Sweet, B.A., LL.B, Municipal Clerk, Corporate Counsel & Director, Corporate Services
clerk@leamington.ca
William J. Marck, B.A., LL.B, Chief Administrative Officer
bmarck@leamington.ca
Cheryl L. Horrobin, B.Comm, CA, AMCT, Director, Finance & Business Services
Tracey Pillon-Abbs, Director, Development Services
Robert Sharon, Director, Community Services
Chuck Parsons, Fire Chief
Bechara Daher, Manager, Building Services
Allan Botham, Manager, Engineering
Cameron McKay, Manager, Public Works
Kit Woods, Manager, Environmental Services
Gary Foisy, Superintendent, Water Services

Leeds & Grenville
#100, 25 Central Ave. West
Brockville, ON K6V 4N6
Tel: 613-342-3840; *Fax:* 613-342-2101
www.uclg.ca
Other Information: Toll-Free Phone: 1-800-770-2170
Municipal Type: United County
Area: 3,350.18 sq km
Population in 2006: 99,206
Next Election: Oct. 2014 (4 year terms)
Mel Campbell, Warden & Councillor, Ward(s): Augusta Township
Lesley Todd, Clerk
Herb Scott, Councillor, Ward(s): Athens Township
Steven Silver, Chief Administrative Officer
William Sloan, Councillor, Ward(s): Edwardsburgh/Cardinal Township
Nigel White, Treasurer & Director, Corporate Services
Jim Pickard, Councillor, Ward(s): Elizabethtown-Kitley Township
Leslie Shepherd, Director, Works, Planning Services & Asset Management
Roger Haley, Councillor, Ward(s): Front of Yonge Township
Alison Tutak, Director, Human Services
Bruce Bryan, Councillor, Ward(s): Leeds & the Thousand Islands
James Alexander (Sandy) Hay, County Planner
J. Douglas Struthers, Councillor, Ward(s): Merrickville-Wolford
Ann Weir, Manager, Economic Development
David Gordon, Councillor, Ward(s): North Grenville Municipality
Dan Chevrier, Manager, Emergency Medical Services (EMS) Division
Ronald E. Holman, Councillor, Ward(s): Rideau Lakes Township
Kristen Hobbs, Manager, Human Resources

William (Bill) L. Thake, Councillor, Ward(s): Westport
Geoff McVey, Manager, Forest

Leeds & The Thousand Islands

P.O. Box 129
1233 Prince St.
Lansdowne, ON K0E 1L0
Tel: 613-659-2415;
www.townshipleeds.on.ca
Other Information: Toll-Free Phone: 1-866-220-2327
Municipal Type: Township
Incorporated: Jan. 1, 2001 *Area:* 607.18 sq km
County or District: Leeds & Grenville; *Population in 2006:* 9,435
Provincial Electoral District(s): Leeds-Grenville
Federal Electoral District(s): Leeds-Grenville
Next Election: Oct. 2014 (4 year terms)
Note: Amalgamation of Front of Leeds & Lansdowne, Rear of Leeds & Lansdowne & Front of Escott.
Bruce Bryan, Mayor
bbryan@townshipleeds.on.ca
Vanessa Latimer, AMCT, Clerk
vanessa@townshipleeds.on.ca

Limerick

89 Limerick Lake Rd., RR#2
Gilmour, ON K0L 1W0
Tel: 613-474-2863; *Fax:* 613-474-0478
assistant@township.limerick.on.ca
www.township.limerick.on.ca
Municipal Type: Township
Incorporated: 1887 *Area:* 200.59 sq km
County or District: Hastings; *Population in 2006:* 364
Provincial Electoral District(s): Prince Edward-Hastings
Federal Electoral District(s): Prince Edward-Hastings
Next Election: Oct. 2014 (4 year terms)
David Golem, Reeve
613-474-0803
Jennifer Trumble, Clerk-Treasurer
613-474-2863
clerk@township.limerick.on.ca

Loyalist

P.O. Box 70
263 Main St.
Odessa, ON K0H 2H0
Tel: 613-386-7351; *Fax:* 613-386-3833
www.loyalisttownship.ca
Municipal Type: Township
Incorporated: 1998 *Area:* 340.02 sq km
County or District: Lennox & Addington; *Population in 2006:* 15,062
Provincial Electoral District(s): Lanark-Frontenac-Lennox & Addington
Federal Electoral District(s): Lanark-Frontenac-Lennox & Addington
Next Election: Oct. 2014 (4 year terms)
Note: Amalgamation of the Townships of Ernestown, Amherst Island & the Village of Bath.
Bill Lowry, Mayor
blowry@loyalist.ca
Ric Bresee, Deputy Mayor
rbresee@gmail.com
Duncan Ashley, Councillor, Ward(s): 1 Amherst Island
Ed Daniliunas, Councillor, Ward(s): 2 Bath
Jim Hegadorn, Councillor, Ward(s): 3 Ernestown
John Ibey, Councillor, Ward(s): 3 Ernestown
Penny Porter, Councillor, Ward(s): 3 Ernestown
Brenda Hamilton, Township Clerk
Diane Pearce, Chief Administrative Officer
Alida Moffatt, Director, Finance
Cindy Lawson, Director, Recreation
David Thompson, Director, Engineering Services
Murray Beckel, Chief Building Official & Planner
Wayne Calver, Fire Chief
Ed Adams, Manager, Transportaton & Solid Waste
Lorie McFarland, Manager, Utilities
Brenda Martineau, Coordinator, Employee Relations

Lucan Biddulph

P.O. Box 190
33351 Richmond St., RR#3
Lucan, ON N0M 2J0
Tel: 519-227-4491; *Fax:* 519-227-4998
info@lucanbiddulph.on.ca
www.lucanbiddulph.on.ca
Municipal Type: Township
Incorporated: Jan. 1, 1999 *Area:* 169.15 sq km
County or District: Middlesex; *Population in 2006:* 4,187
Provincial Electoral District(s): Lambton-Kent-Middlesex
Federal Electoral District(s): Lambton-Kent-Middlesex
Next Election: Oct. 2014 (4 year terms)
Note: Amalgamation of the Village of Lucan and the Township of Biddulph.
Paul Hodgins, Mayor
phodgins@lucanbiddulph.on.ca
Lisa deBoer, Clerk
ldeboer@lucanbiddulph.on.ca

MacDonald, Meredith & Aberdeen Additional

P.O. Box 10
208 Church St.
Echo Bay, ON P0S 1C0
Tel: 705-248-2441;
twpmacd@onlink.net
www.echobay.ca
Municipal Type: Township
Incorporated: 1899 *Area:* 161.73 sq km
County or District: Algoma District; *Population in 2006:* 1,550
Provincial Electoral District(s): Algoma-Manitoulin
Federal Electoral District(s): Sault Ste Marie
Next Election: Oct. 2014 (4 year terms)
Lynn Watson, Mayor
Lynne Duguay, Clerk

Machar

P.O. Box 70
73 Municipal Rd. North
South River, ON P0A 1X0
Tel: 705-386-7741; *Fax:* 705-386-0765
www.machartownship.net
Municipal Type: Township
Area: 184.38 sq km
County or District: Parry Sound District; *Population in 2006:* 866
Provincial Electoral District(s): Parry Sound-Muskoka
Federal Electoral District(s): Parry Sound-Muskoka
Next Election: Oct. 2014 (4 year terms)
Douglas Maeck, Mayor
Brenda Paul, AMCT, Clerk-Treasurer
bpaulmachar@vianet.ca

Machin

P.O. Box 249
75 Spruce St.
Vermilion Bay, ON P0V 2V0
Tel: 807-227-2633; *Fax:* 807-227-5443
deputyclerk@visitmachin.com
www.visitmachin.com
Municipal Type: Township
Area: 288.85 sq km
County or District: Kenora District; *Population in 2006:* 978
Provincial Electoral District(s): Kenora-Rainy River
Federal Electoral District(s): Kenora
Next Election: Oct. 2014 (4 year terms)
Joe Ruete, Acting Mayor
Tammy Rob, Clerk-Treasurer
clerktreasurer@visitmachin.com

Madawaska Valley

P.O. Box 1000
85 Bay St.
Barrys Bay, ON K0J 1B0
Tel: 613-756-2747; *Fax:* 613-756-0553
info@madawaskavalley.on.ca
www.madawaskavalley.on.ca
Other Information: Toll-Free Phone: 1-866-222-8699
Municipal Type: Township
Incorporated: Jan. 1, 2001 *Area:* 670.11 sq km
County or District: Renfrew; *Population in 2006:* 4,381
Provincial Electoral District(s): Renfrew-Nipissing-Pembroke
Federal Electoral District(s): Renfrew-Nipissing-Pembroke
Next Election: Oct. 2014 (4 year terms)
Note: Amalgamation of Barry's Bay Village, Radcliffe Township & Sherwood, Jones & Burns Township.
David M. Shulist, Mayor
613-756-5200
mayor@madawaskavalley.ca
Pat Pilgrim, C.M.O., Chief Administrative Officer & Clerk
ppilgrim@madawaskavalley.on.ca

Madoc

P.O. Box 503
15651 Hwy. 62, RR#2
Madoc, ON K0K 2K0
Tel: 613-473-2677; *Fax:* 613-473-5580
www.madoc.ca
Other Information: E-mail, Building: building@madoc.ca
Municipal Type: Township
Incorporated: 1850 *Area:* 269.98 sq km
County or District: Hastings; *Population in 2006:* 2,069
Provincial Electoral District(s): Prince Edward-Hastings
Federal Electoral District(s): Prince Edward-Hastings
Next Election: Oct. 2014 (4 year terms)
Robert Sager, Reeve
twpmad@sympatico.ca
W.G. (Bill) Lebow, B.A., AMCT, Clerk Administrator
clerk@madoc.ca

Magnetawan, Municipality of

P.O. Box 70
4304 Hwy. 520
Magnetawan, ON P0A 1P0
Tel: 705-387-3947; *Fax:* 705-387-4875
admin@magnetawan.com
www.magnetawan.com
Other Information: E-mail, Roads: roads@magnetawan.com
Municipal Type: Township
Incorporated: July 4, 1997 *Area:* 523.07 sq km
County or District: Parry Sound District; *Population in 2006:* 1,610
Provincial Electoral District(s): Parry Sound-Muskoka
Federal Electoral District(s): Parry Sound-Muskoka
Next Election: Oct. 2014 (4 year terms)
Sam Dunnett, Mayor
mayor@magnetawan.com
Roger Labelle, Clerk
clerk@magnetawan.com

Malahide

87 John St. South
Aylmer, ON N5H 2C3
Tel: 519-773-5344; *Fax:* 519-773-5334
www.malahide.ca
Municipal Type: Township
Incorporated: Jan. 1, 1998 *Area:* 395.07 sq km
County or District: Elgin; *Population in 2006:* 8,828
Provincial Electoral District(s): Elgin-Middlesex-London
Federal Electoral District(s): Elgin-Middlesex-London
Next Election: Oct. 2014 (4 year terms)
Note: Amalgamation of the Township of Malahide, Village of Springfield & Township of South Dorchester.
Dave Mennill, Mayor
519-773-8850
davemennill@eastlink.ca
Michelle M. Casavecchia, Chief Administrative Officer & Clerk
mcasavecchia@malahide.ca

Manitoulin

Gore Bay, ON
Municipal Type: District
Area: 4,759.74 sq km
Population in 2006: 13,090
Provincial Electoral District(s): Algoma-Manitoulin
Federal Electoral District(s): Algoma-Manitoulin-Kapuskasing
Note: The District incorporates the towns of Gore Bay, & Northeastern Manitoulin & the Islands; communities in the townships of Assiginack, Barrie Isl., Billing, Burpe & Mills, Central Manitoulin, Cockburn Isl., Gordon, & Tehkummah; & 1st Nations reserves

Manitouwadge

1 Mississauga Rd.
Manitouwadge, ON P0T 2C0
Tel: 807-826-3227; *Fax:* 807-826-4592
www.manitouwadge.ca
Municipal Type: Township
Area: 351.97 sq km
County or District: Thunder Bay District; *Population in 2006:* 2,300
Provincial Electoral District(s): Algoma-Manitoulin
Federal Electoral District(s): Algoma-Manitoulin-Kapuskasing
Next Election: Oct. 2014 (4 year terms)
John MacEachern, Mayor
mayor@manitouwadge.ca
Cecile Kerster, Municipal Manager Clerk & Acting Treasurer
ckerster@manitouwadge.ca

Mapleton

P.O. Box 160
7275 Sideroad 3
Drayton, ON N0G 1P0
Tel: 519-638-3313; *Fax:* 519-638-5113
www.mapleton.ca
Other Information: Toll-Free Phone: 1-800-385-7248
Municipal Type: Township
Incorporated: Jan. 1, 1999 *Area:* 534.71 sq km
County or District: Wellington; *Population in 2006:* 9,851
Provincial Electoral District(s): Perth-Wellington
Federal Electoral District(s): Perth-Wellington
Next Election: Oct. 2014 (4 year terms)
Note: Amalgamation of the Townships of Maryborough & Peel & the Village of Drayton.
Bruce Whale, Mayor
519-638-2230

Patty Sinnamon, Chief Administrative Officer & Clerk
psinnamon@town.mapleton.on.ca

Marathon
P.O. Box TM
4 Hemlo Dr.
Marathon, ON P0T 2E0
Tel: 807-229-1340; *Fax:* 807-229-1999
info@marathon.ca; clerk@marathon.ca
www.marathon.ca
Municipal Type: Town
Area: 170.48 sq km
County or District: Thunder Bay District; *Population in 2006:* 3,863
Provincial Electoral District(s): Thunder Bay-Superior North
Federal Electoral District(s): Thunder Bay-Superior North
Next Election: Oct. 2014 (4 year terms)
Rick Dumas, Mayor
mayor@marathon.ca
Brian Tocheri, Chief Administrative Officer & Clerk
cao@marathon.ca

Markstay-Warren, Municipality of
P.O. Box 79
21 Main St. South
Markstay, ON P0M 2G0
Tel: 705-853-4536; *Fax:* 705-853-4964
info@markstay-warren.ca
www.markstay-warren.ca
Other Information: Toll-Free Phone: 1-866-710-1065
Municipal Type: Town
Incorporated: Jan. 1, 1999 *Area:* 510.12 sq km
County or District: Sudbury District; *Population in 2006:* 2,475
Provincial Electoral District(s): Timiskaming-Cochrane
Federal Electoral District(s): Nickel Belt
Next Election: Oct. 2014 (4 year terms)
Note: Amalgamation of the Towns of Warren, Markstay & the Townships of Awrey, Street, Hawley, Loughrin & Henry.
Sonja Flynn, Mayor
sflynn@msdsb.net
Denis Turcot, Chief Administrative Officer & Clerk
dturcot@markstay-warren.ca

Marmora & Lake, Municipality of
P.O. Box 459
12 Bursthall St.
Marmora, ON K0K 2M0
Tel: 613-472-2629; *Fax:* 613-472-5330
www.marmoraandlake.ca
Other Information: Toll-Free Phone: 1-866-518-2282
Municipal Type: Township
Area: 533.75 sq km
County or District: Hastings; *Population in 2006:* 3,912
Provincial Electoral District(s): Prince Edward-Hastings
Federal Electoral District(s): Prince Edward-Hastings
Next Election: Oct. 2014 (4 year terms)
Terry Clemens, Reeve
t.clemens@marmoraandlake.ca
Judy Durbatch, Municipal Clerk
j.durbatch@marmoraandlake.ca

Matachewan
P.O. Box 177
Matachewan, ON P0K 1M0
Tel: 705-565-2274; *Fax:* 705-565-2564
township@ntl.sympatico.ca
www.matachewan.com
Municipal Type: Township
Area: 543.63 sq km
County or District: Timiskaming District; *Population in 2006:* 375
Provincial Electoral District(s): Timiskaming-Cochrane
Federal Electoral District(s): Timmins-James Bay
Next Election: Oct. 2014 (4 year terms)
Beverley Hine, Reeve
Andrew Van Oosten, Chief Administrative Officer & Clerk-Treasurer

Mattawa
P.O. Box 390
160 Water St.
Mattawa, ON P0H 1V0
Tel: 705-744-5611; *Fax:* 705-744-0104
info@mattawa.info
www.mattawa.info
Municipal Type: Town
Area: 3.66 sq km
County or District: Nipissing District; *Population in 2006:* 2,003
Provincial Electoral District(s): Nipissing
Federal Electoral District(s): Nipissing-Timiskaming
Next Election: Oct. 2014 (4 year terms)
Dean Backer, Mayor
Wayne P. Belter, Administrator, Clerk & Treasurer

Mattawan
P.O. Box 610
Mattawa, ON P0H 1V0
Tel: 705-744-5680; *Fax:* 705-744-4141
info@mattawan.info
www.mattawan.info
Municipal Type: Township
Area: 199.52 sq km
County or District: Nipissing District; *Population in 2006:* 147
Provincial Electoral District(s): Nipissing
Federal Electoral District(s): Nipissing-Timiskaming
Next Election: Oct. 2014 (4 year terms)
Peter Murphy, Mayor
Deborah Miller, Clerk

Mattice-Val Côté
P.O. Box 129
500 Hwy. 11
Mattice, ON P0L 1T0
Tel: 705-364-6511; *Fax:* 705-364-6431
mattice@ntl.sympatico.ca
www.nt.net/mattice
Municipal Type: Township
Area: 414.64 sq km
County or District: Cochrane District; *Population in 2006:* 772
Provincial Electoral District(s): Timmins-James Bay
Federal Electoral District(s): Algoma-Manitoulin-Kapuskasing
Next Election: Oct. 2014 (4 year terms)
Jean Louis Brunet, Reeve
Gilbert Brisson, Administrator-Clerk

McDougall
5 Barager Blvd., RR#3
Parry Sound, ON P2A 2W9
Tel: 705-342-5252; *Fax:* 705-342-5573
www.municipalityofmcdougall.com
Municipal Type: Township
Incorporated: May 1, 1872 *Area:* 262.69 sq km
County or District: Parry Sound District; *Population in 2006:* 2,704
Provincial Electoral District(s): Parry Sound-Muskoka
Federal Electoral District(s): Parry Sound-Muskoka
Next Election: Oct. 2014 (4 year terms)
Dale Robinson, Mayor
Tammy Hazzard, Clerk & Secretary

McGarry
P.O. Box 99
27 Webster St.
Virginiatown, ON P0K 1X0
Tel: 705-634-2145; *Fax:* 705-634-2700
admin@mcgarry.ca
www.mcgarry.ca
Municipal Type: Township
Area: 86.05 sq km
County or District: Timiskaming District; *Population in 2006:* 674
Provincial Electoral District(s): Timiskaming-Cochrane
Federal Electoral District(s): Timmins-James Bay
Next Election: Oct. 2014 (4 year terms)
Clermont Lapointe, Reeve
Gary Cunnington, Clerk-Treasurer

McKellar
P.O. Box 69
701 Hwy. 124
McKellar, ON P0G 1C0
Tel: 705-389-2842; *Fax:* 705-389-1244
www.township.mckellar.on.ca
Municipal Type: Township
Incorporated: 1873 *Area:* 177.48 sq km
County or District: Parry Sound District; *Population in 2006:* 1,080
Provincial Electoral District(s): Parry Sound-Muskoka
Federal Electoral District(s): Parry Sound-Muskoka
Next Election: Oct. 2014 (4 year terms)
Peter Hopkins, Reeve
705-389-2842
Shawn Boggs, AMCT, Clerk Administrator

McMurrich-Monteith
P.O. Box 70
31 William St.
Sprucedale, ON P0A 1Y0
Tel: 705-685-7901; *Fax:* 705-685-7393
mcmurric@surenet.net
www.mcmurrichmonteith.com
Municipal Type: Township
Area: 273.33 sq km
County or District: Parry Sound District; *Population in 2006:* 791
Provincial Electoral District(s): Parry Sound-Muskoka
Federal Electoral District(s): Parry Sound-Muskoka
Next Election: Oct. 2014 (4 year terms)
Glynn Robinson, Reeve
705-685-7779
Cheryl Marshall, Clerk

McNab-Braeside
2508 Russett Dr., RR#2
Arnprior, ON K7S 3G8
Tel: 613-623-5756; *Fax:* 613-623-9138
info@mcnabbraeside.com
www.mcnabbraeside.com
Other Information: Toll-Free Phone: 1-800-957-4621
Municipal Type: Township
Incorporated: Jan. 1, 1998 *Area:* 253.87 sq km
County or District: Renfrew; *Population in 2006:* 7,222
Provincial Electoral District(s): Renfrew-Nipissing-Pembroke
Federal Electoral District(s): Renfrew-Nipissing-Pembroke
Next Election: Oct. 2014 (4 year terms)
Note: Amalgamation of Braeside Village & McNab Township.
Mary M. Campbell, Mayor
mcampbell@mcnabbraeside.com
Noreen C. Mellema, CMO, Chief Administrative Officer & Clerk
nmellema@mcnabbraeside.com

Meaford
21 Trowbridge St. West
Meaford, ON N4L 1A1
Tel: 519-538-1060; *Fax:* 519-538-5240
www.meaford.ca
Other Information: Alternate Fax: 519-538-1556
Municipal Type: Municipality
Incorporated: Jan. 1, 2001 *Area:* 588.47 sq km
County or District: Grey; *Population in 2006:* 10,948
Provincial Electoral District(s): Bruce-Grey-Owen Sound
Federal Electoral District(s): Bruce-Grey-Owen Sound
Next Election: Oct. 2014 (4 year terms)
Note: Formerly the Town of Georgian Highlands. Amalgamation of Sydenham, St. Vincent & Meaford.
Francis Richardson, Mayor
519-538-1060
frichardson@meaford.ca
Harley Greenfield, Deputy Mayor & Councillor
519-538-2570
hgreenfield@meaford.ca
Barb Clumpus, Councillor
519-538-3345
bclumpus@meaford.ca
James McIntosh, Councillor
519-538-2306
jmcintosh@meaford.ca
Mike Poetker, Councillor
519-538-4075
mpoetker@meaford.ca
Lynda Stephens, Councillor
519-538-9239
lstephens@meaford.ca
Deborah Young, Councillor
519-379-9646
dyoung@meaford.ca
Pamela Fettes, Clerk
pfettes@meaford.ca
Frank Miele, Chief Administrative Officer
fmiele@meaford.ca
Robert Armstrong, Director, Planning & Building
rarmstrong@meaford.ca
Karen Davies, Director, Human Resources
kdavies@meaford.ca
Stephen Vokes, Director, Operations
svokes@meaford.ca
Rick Carefoot, Chief Building Official
rcarefoot@meaford.ca
Chris Collyer, Chief Operator, Environmental Services
jcollyer@meaford.ca
Steve Nickels, Fire Chief
mmolloy@meaford.ca

Melancthon
157101 Hwy. 10, RR#6
Shelburne, ON L0N 1S9
Tel: 519-925-5525; *Fax:* 519-925-1110
info@melancthontownship.ca
www.melancthontownship.ca
Municipal Type: Township
Incorporated: Jan. 1, 1853 *Area:* 310.88 sq km
County or District: Dufferin; *Population in 2006:* 2,895
Provincial Electoral District(s): Dufferin-Caledon
Federal Electoral District(s): Dufferin-Caledon
Next Election: Oct. 2014 (4 year terms)
Bill Hill, Mayor
519-925-1161
bhill@melancthontownship.ca

Denise B. Holmes, Chief Administrative Officer & Clerk-Treasurer
dholmes@melancthontownship.ca

Merrickville-Wolford
P.O. Box 340
317 Brock St. West
Merrickville, ON K0G 1N0
Tel: 613-269-4791; *Fax:* 613-269-3095
reception@merrickville-wolford.ca
www.merrickville-wolford.ca
Other Information: E-mail, Admin.: admin@merrickville-wolford.ca
Municipal Type: Village
Area: 213.77 sq km
County or District: Leeds-Grenville; *Population in 2006:* 2,867
Provincial Electoral District(s): Leeds-Grenville
Federal Electoral District(s): Leeds-Grenville
Next Election: Oct. 2014 (4 year terms)
J. Douglas Struthers, Mayor
mayor@merrickville-wolford.ca
Jill Eagle, Chief Administrative Officer & Clerk
cao@merrickville-wolford.ca

Middlesex Centre
10227 Ilderton Rd., RR#2
Ilderton, ON N0M 2A0
Tel: 519-666-0190; *Fax:* 519-666-0271
cormans@middlesexcentre.on.ca
www.middlesexcentre.on.ca
Other Information: Toll-Free Phone: 1-800-220-8968
Municipal Type: Township
Incorporated: Jan. 1, 1998 *Area:* 588.05 sq km
County or District: Middlesex; *Population in 2006:* 15,589
Provincial Electoral District(s): Lambton-Kent-Middlesex
Federal Electoral District(s): Lambton-Kent-Middlesex
Next Election: Oct. 2014 (4 year terms)
Note: Amalgamation of the former Townships of Delaware, Lobo, & London.
Al Edmondson, Mayor
edmondson@middlesexcentre.on.ca
Stephanie Troyer-Boyd, Clerk
boyds@middlesexcentre.on.ca
Michelle Smibert, Chief Administrative Officer
smibert@middlesexcentre.on.ca
Clare Bloomfield, Deputy Mayor
bloomfield@middlesexcentre.on.ca
Greg Watterton, Director, Finance & Community Services
watterton@middlesexcentre.on.ca
Stephen Harvey, Councillor, Ward(s): 1
harvey@middlesexcentre.on.ca
Maureen A. Looby, Director, Public Works & Engineering
loobym@middlesexcentre.on.ca
John Brennan, Councillor, Ward(s): 2
brennan@middlesexcentre.on.ca
Arnie Marsman, Director, Planning & Development Svs., & Chief Building Official
marsmana@middlesexcentre.on.ca
Sharon McMillan, Councillor, Ward(s): 3
mcmillan@middlesexcentre.on.ca
Wayne Shipley, Fire Chief
shipley@middlesexcentre.on.ca
Aina DeViet, Councillor, Ward(s): 4
deviet@middlesexcentre.on.ca
Jim Reeve, Superintendent, Drainage
reevej@middlesexcentre.on.ca
Frank Berze, Councillor, Ward(s): 5
berze@middlesexcentre.on.ca
Mauro Castrilli, Coordinator, Transportation
castrilli@middlesexcentre.on.ca
Laura Snobelen, Environmental Technologist
snobelen@middlesexcentre.on.ca

Minden Hills
P.O. Box 359
7 Milne St.
Minden, ON K0M 2K0
Tel: 705-286-1260; *Fax:* 705-286-4917
admin@mindenhills.ca
www.mindenhills.ca
Other Information: Treasury/Bldg./By-law/Planning, Fax: 705-286-6005
Municipal Type: Township
Area: 847.76 sq km
County or District: Haliburton; *Population in 2006:* 5,556
Provincial Electoral District(s): Haliburton-Kawartha Lakes-Brock
Federal Electoral District(s): Haliburton-Kawartha Lakes-Brock
Next Election: Oct. 2014 (4 year terms)
Barb Reid, Reeve
breid@mindenhills.ca
Laura Cunliffe, Clerk
lcunliffe@mindenhills.ca

Minto
5941 Hwy. 89
Harriston, ON N0G 1Z0
Tel: 519-338-2511; *Fax:* 519-338-2005
peg@town.minto.on.ca (Clerical Assistant)
www.town.minto.on.ca
Other Information: E-mail, Treasury: gordon@town.minto.on.ca
Municipal Type: Town
Area: 300.37 sq km
County or District: Wellington; *Population in 2006:* 8,504
Provincial Electoral District(s): Perth-Wellington
Federal Electoral District(s): Perth-Wellington
Next Election: Oct. 2014 (4 year terms)
George Bridge, Mayor
georgeabridge@gmail.com
Bill White, Chief Administrative Officer & Clerk

Mono
347209 MonoCenter Rd., RR#1
Orangeville, ON L9W 2Y8
Tel: 519-941-3599; *Fax:* 519-941-9490
info@townofmono.com
www.townofmono.com
Municipal Type: Town
Incorporated: June 1, 1999 *Area:* 277.67 sq km
County or District: Dufferin; *Population in 2006:* 7,071
Provincial Electoral District(s): Dufferin-Caledon
Federal Electoral District(s): Dufferin-Caledon
Next Election: Oct. 2014 (4 year terms)
Laura Ryan, Mayor
mayor@townofmono.com
Keith J. McNenly, Chief Administrative Officer & Clerk
keith@townofmono.com

Montague
P.O. Box 755
6547 Roger Stevens Dr.
Smiths Falls, ON K7A 4W6
Tel: 613-283-7478; *Fax:* 613-283-3112
info@township.montague.on.ca
www.township.montague.on.ca
Municipal Type: Township
Area: 277.03 sq km
County or District: Lanark; *Population in 2006:* 3,595
Provincial Electoral District(s): Lanark-Frontenac-Lennox & Addington
Federal Electoral District(s): Lanark-Frontenac-Lennox & Addington
Next Election: Oct. 2014 (4 year terms)
Bill Dobson, Reeve
bdobson@ripnet.com
Katie Valentin, Clerk
kvalentin@township.montague.on.ca

Moonbeam
P.O. Box 330
53 St. Aubin Ave.
Moonbeam, ON P0L 1V0
Tel: 705-367-2244; *Fax:* 705-367-2610
moonbeam@moonbeam.ca
www.moonbeam.ca
Municipal Type: Township
Area: 235.17 sq km
County or District: Cochrane District; *Population in 2006:* 1,298
Provincial Electoral District(s): Timmins-James Bay
Federal Electoral District(s): Algoma-Manitoulin-Kapuskasing
Next Election: Oct. 2014 (4 year terms)
Gilles Audet, Mayor
Carole Gendron, Clerk-Treasurer
cgendron@moonbeam.ca

Moosonee
P.O. Box 727
5 First St.
Moosonee, ON P0L 1Y0
Tel: 705-336-2993; *Fax:* 705-336-2426
www.moosonee.ca
Municipal Type: Town
Area: 555.35 sq km
County or District: Cochrane District; *Population in 2006:* 2,006
Provincial Electoral District(s): Timmins-James Bay
Federal Electoral District(s): Timmins-James Bay
Next Election: Oct. 2014 (4 year terms)
Victor Mitchell, Mayor
Shelley L. Petten, Clerk-Treasurer

Morley
P.O. Box 40
Stratton, ON P0W 1N0
Tel: 807-483-5455; *Fax:* 807-483-5882
morley@nwonet.net
www.townshipofmorley.ca
Municipal Type: Township
Incorporated: 1903 *Area:* 375.61 sq km
County or District: Rainy River District; *Population in 2006:* 492
Provincial Electoral District(s): Kenora-Rainy River
Federal Electoral District(s): Thunder Bay-Rainy River
Next Election: Oct. 2014 (4 year terms)
Gary Gamsby, Reeve
Anna H.M. Boily, CMO, Clerk-Treasurer

Morris-Turnberry
41342 Morris Rd., RR#4
Brussels, ON N0G 1H0
Tel: 519-887-6137; *Fax:* 519-887-6424
morris@scsinternet.com
www.morris-turnberry.on.ca
Municipal Type: Township
Incorporated: Jan. 1, 2001 *Area:* 376.45 sq km
County or District: Huron; *Population in 2006:* 3,403
Provincial Electoral District(s): Huron-Bruce
Federal Electoral District(s): Huron-Bruce
Next Election: Oct. 2014 (4 year terms)
Note: Amalgamation of the Township of Morris & the Township of Turnberry.
Paul Gowing, Mayor
pgowing@hurontel.on.ca
Nancy Michie, Administrator & Clerk-Treasurer
nmichie@morristurnberry.ca

Mulmur
758070 2nd Line East, RR#2
Lisle, ON L0M 1M0
Tel: 705-466-3341; *Fax:* 705-466-2922
info@mulmurtownship.ca
www.mulmurtownship.ca
Other Information: Toll-Free Phone: 1-866-472-0417 (In 519 area code)
Municipal Type: Township
Incorporated: 1851 *Area:* 286.73 sq km
County or District: Dufferin; *Population in 2006:* 3,318
Provincial Electoral District(s): Dufferin-Caledon
Federal Electoral District(s): Dufferin-Caledon
Next Election: Oct. 2014 (4 year terms)
Paul Mills, Mayor
pmills@mulmurtownship.ca
Terry M. Horner, AMCT, Chief Administrative Officer & Clerk
thorner@mulmurtownship.ca

Muskoka Lakes
P.O. Box 129
1 Bailey St.
Port Carling, ON P0B 1J0
Tel: 705-765-3156; *Fax:* 705-765-6755
www.muskokalakes.ca
Municipal Type: Township
Incorporated: Jan. 1971 *Area:* 781.55 sq km
County or District: Muskoka Dist. Mun.; *Population in 2006:* 6,467
Provincial Electoral District(s): Parry Sound-Muskoka
Federal Electoral District(s): Parry Sound-Muskoka
Next Election: Oct. 2014 (4 year terms)
Alice Murphy, Mayor
amurphy@muskokalakes.ca
Cheryl Mortimer, AMCT, Clerk
cmortimer@muskokalakes.ca

Nairn & Hyman
64 McIntyre St.
Nairn Centre, ON P0M 2L0
Tel: 705-869-4232;
information@nairncentre.ca
www.nairncentre.ca
Municipal Type: Township
Incorporated: 1896 *Area:* 159.03 sq km
County or District: Sudbury District; *Population in 2006:* 493
Provincial Electoral District(s): Algoma-Manitoulin
Federal Electoral District(s): Algoma-Manitoulin-Kapuskasing
Next Election: Oct. 2014 (4 year terms)
Laurier P. Falldien, Mayor
laurierfalldien@nairncentre.ca
Robert Deschene, Chief Administrative Officer & Clerk-Treasurer

Neebing, Municipality of
4766 Hwy. 61
Thunder Bay, ON P7L 0B5
Tel: 807-474-5331; *Fax:* 807-474-5332
neebing@neebing.org
www.neebing.org
Other Information: Information Phone Line: 807-474-5338
Municipal Type: Town
Area: 875.51 sq km
County or District: Thunder Bay District; *Population in 2006:* 2,184
Provincial Electoral District(s): Thunder Bay-Atikokan
Federal Electoral District(s): Thunder Bay-Rainy River
Next Election: Oct. 2014 (4 year terms)
Ziggy Polkowski, Mayor
Delma Stajkowski, AMCT, Clerk

Newbury
P.O. Box 130
22910 Hagerty Rd.
Newbury, ON N0L 1Z0
Tel: 519-693-4941; *Fax:* 519-693-4340
vnewbury@on.aibn.com
www.newbury.ca
Municipal Type: Village
Incorporated: 1873 *Area:* 1.85 sq km
County or District: Middlesex; *Population in 2006:* 439
Provincial Electoral District(s): Lambton-Kent-Middlesex
Federal Electoral District(s): Lambton-Kent-Middlesex
Next Election: Oct. 2014 (4 year terms)
Diane Brewer, Reeve
Betty D. Gordon, Clerk-Treasurer

Nipigon
P.O. Box 160
52 Front St.
Nipigon, ON P0T 2J0
Tel: 807-887-3135; *Fax:* 807-887-3564
info@nipigon.net
www.nipigon.net
Other Information: E-mail, Recreation Inquiries: nipigonrec@shaw.ca
Municipal Type: Township
Area: 109.14 sq km
County or District: Thunder Bay District; *Population in 2006:* 1,752
Provincial Electoral District(s): Thunder Bay-Superior North
Federal Electoral District(s): Thunder Bay-Superior North
Next Election: Oct. 2014 (4 year terms)
Richard Harvey, Mayor
richardharvey@nipigon.net
Lindsay Mannila, Chief Administrative Officer

Nipissing
45 Beatty St.
Nipissing, ON P0H 1W0
Tel: 705-724-2144; *Fax:* 705-724-5385
www.nipissingtownship.com
Municipal Type: Township
Area: 387.4 sq km
County or District: Parry Sound District; *Population in 2006:* 1,642
Provincial Electoral District(s): Nipissing; Timiskaming-Cochrane
Federal Electoral District(s): Nipissing-Timiskaming
Next Election: Oct. 2014 (4 year terms)
Pat Haufe, Mayor
705-729-5343
Charles H. Barton, Chief Administrative Officer & Clerk

Nipissing
District Social Services Administration Bd.
P.O. Box 750
200 McIntyre St. East
North Bay, ON P1B 8J8
Municipal Type: District
Area: 17,065.07 sq km
Population in 2006: 84,688
George Maroosis, Chair, District of Nipissing Social Services Administration Board
705-474-2151, Fax: 705-474-0136
Leo Deloyde, CAO, District of Nipissing Social Services Administration Board
705-474-2151, Fax: 705-474-7155
Leo.deloyde@dnssab.on.ca

North Algona Wilberforce
1091 Shaw Woods Rd., RR#1
Eganville, ON K0J 1T0
Tel: 613-628-2080; *Fax:* 613-628-3341
naw@nalgonawil.com
www.nalgonawil.com
Municipal Type: Township
Incorporated: Jan. 1, 1999 *Area:* 378.53 sq km
County or District: Renfrew; *Population in 2006:* 2,840
Provincial Electoral District(s): Renfrew-Nipissing-Pembroke
Federal Electoral District(s): Renfrew-Nipissing-Pembroke
Next Election: Oct. 2014 (4 year terms)
Note: Amalgamation of North Algona Township & Wilberforce Township.
Harold Weckworth, Mayor
Marilyn M. Schruder, Clerk-Treasurer

North Dumfries
1171 Greenfield Rd., RR#4
Cambridge, ON N1R 5S5
Tel: 519-621-0340; *Fax:* 519-623-7641
www.northdumfries.ca
Other Information: Toll-Free Phone: 1-800-563-5595
Municipal Type: Township
Area: 187.22 sq km
County or District: Waterloo Regional Municipality; *Population in 2006:* 9,063
Provincial Electoral District(s): Cambridge
Federal Electoral District(s): Cambridge
Next Election: Oct. 2014 (4 year terms)
Robert Deutschmann, Mayor
519-574-4001
Roger Mordue, Chief Administrative Officer & Clerk
519-621-0340

North Dundas
P.O. Box 489
636 St. Lawrence St.
Winchester, ON K0C 2K0
Tel: 613-774-2105; *Fax:* 613-774-5699
info@northdundas.com
www.northdundas.com
Other Information: Toll-Free Phone: 1-800-795-0437
Municipal Type: Township
Incorporated: Jan. 1, 1998 *Area:* 503.18 sq km
County or District: Stormont, Dundas & Glengarry; *Population in 2006:* 11,095
Provincial Electoral District(s): Stormont-Dundas-South Glengarry
Federal Electoral District(s): Stormont-Dundas-South Glengarry
Next Election: Oct. 2014 (4 year terms)
Note: Amalgamation of the former Townships of Winchester & Mountain & the villages of Chesterville & Winchester.
Eric Duncan, Mayor
613-774-1081
eduncan2@gmail.com
Jo-Anne McCaslin, Clerk
613-774-2105
jmccaslin@northdundas.com
Gerry Boyce, Deputy Mayor
613-989-2330
glboyce@hotmail.com
Howard F. Smith, Chief Administrative Officer
613-774-2105
hsmith@northdundas.com
Allan Armstrong, Councillor
613-774-0752
alarmstrong@bell.net
John J. Gareau, CA, AMCT, Treasurer
jgareau@northdundas.com
Greg Trizisky, Chief Building Official & Officer, Property Standards
613-774-2105
gtrizisky@northdundas.com
Tony Fraser, Councillor
613-774-2182
tonyfraser@personainternet.com
Arden Carruthers, Director, Public Works, & Fire Chief, Morewood
613-774-2105
acarruthers@northdundas.com
John Thompson, Councillor
613-448-2963
jthompsonelect@hotmail.com
Mark Guy, Director, Recreation & Culture
mguy@northdundas.com
Calvin Pol, BES, MCIP, RPP, Director, Planning, Building, & Enforcement
613-774-2105
cpol@northdundas.com
Rob Hunter, Officer, Economic Development & Communications
613-774-2105
rhunter@northdundas.com
Doug Froats, Coordinator, Waste Management
dfroats@northdundas.com
Dan Kelly, Fire Chief, Winchester
Mike Gruich, Fire Chief, Chesterville
Scott Patterson, Fire Chief, Mountain

North Frontenac
P.O. Box 97
6648 Rd. 506
Plevna, ON K0H 2M0
Tel: 613-479-2231; *Fax:* 613-479-2352
info@northfrontenac.ca
www.northfrontenac.com
Other Information: Toll-Free Phone: 1-800-234-3953
Municipal Type: Township
Incorporated: Jan. 1, 1998 *Area:* 1,135.75 sq km
County or District: Frontenac; *Population in 2006:* 1,904
Provincial Electoral District(s): Hastings-Frontenac-Lennox & Addington
Federal Electoral District(s): Lanark-Frontenac-Lennox & Addington
Next Election: Oct. 2014 (4 year terms)
Bud Clayton, Mayor
613-966-9222
dundiggin@xplornet.ca
Jenny Duhamel, Clerk & Manager, Planning
613-479-2231
clerkplanning@northfrontenac.ca

North Glengarry
P.O. Box 700
90 Main St. South
Alexandria, ON K0C 1A0
Tel: 613-525-1110; *Fax:* 613-525-1649
www.northglengarry.ca
Municipal Type: Township
Area: 642.4 sq km
County or District: Stormont, Dundas & Glengarry; *Population in 2006:* 10,635
Provincial Electoral District(s): Glengarry-Prescott-Russell
Federal Electoral District(s): Glengarry-Prescott-Russell
Next Election: Oct. 2014 (4 year terms)
Grant E. Crack, Mayor
613-525-1110, Fax: 613-525-1649
Daniel Gagnon, Chief Administrative Officer
613-525-1110
Chris McDonell, Deputy Mayor & Councillor
613-525-1110
Johanna (Annie) Levac, Treasurer
613-525-1110
Gary Shepherd, Councillor at Large
613-525-1110
André Bachand, Manager, Public Works
613-525-1110
Dean McDonald, Manager, Water Works
613-525-1110
Jamie MacDonald, Councillor, Ward(s): Alexandria
613-525-1110
Gerry Murphy, Manager, Planning & By-law Enforcement, & Chief Building Official
613-525-1110
Jim Picken, Councillor, Ward(s): Kenyon
613-525-1110
Stephane Ouimet, Director, Recreation
613-525-0614
Eric MacSweyn, Councillor, Ward(s): Lochiel
613-525-1110
Manson Barton, Superintendent, Drainage & Beaver Management
613-525-1110
Carma Williams, Councillor, Ward(s): Maxville
613-525-1110

North Grenville
P.O. Box 130
285 County Rd. 44
Kemptville, ON K0G 1J0
Tel: 613-258-9569; *Fax:* 613-258-9620
www.northgrenville.ca
Municipal Type: MN
Incorporated: July 14, 2003 *Area:* 350.14 sq km
County or District: Leeds-Grenville; *Population in 2006:* 14,198
Provincial Electoral District(s): Leeds-Grenville
Federal Electoral District(s): Leeds-Grenville
Next Election: Oct. 2014 (4 year terms)
David Gordon, Mayor
613-258-9569
dgordon@northgrenville.on.ca
Cahl Pominville, Clerk & Director, Corporate Services
cpominville@northgrenville.on.ca
Terry Butler, Councillor
613-258-9569, Fax: 613-258-9620
tbutler@northgrenville.on.ca
Andy Brown, Chief Administrative Officer
abrown@northgrenville.on.ca

Tim Sutton, Councillor
613-258-9569, Fax: 613-258-9620
tsutton@northgrenville.on.ca
Sheila Kehoe, Treasurer
skehoe@northgrenville.on.ca
Barb Tobin, Councillor
613-258-9569, Fax: 613-258-9620
btobin@northgrenville.on.ca
Karen Dunlop, Director, Public Works
kdunlop@northgrenville.on.ca
Ken Finnerty, Deputy Mayor
613-258-9569
kfinnerty@northgrenville.on.ca
Darren Patmore, Director, Parks, Recreation & Culture
dpatmore@northgrenville.on.ca
Forbes Symon, Director, Planning & Development
fsymon@northgrenville.on.ca
Paul Hutt, Fire Chief
phutt@northgrenville.on.ca
Randy Wilkinson, Chief Building Official
rwilkinson@northgrenville.on.ca
Gary Boal, Superintendent, Waste Site
613-258-9677
Doug Scott, Superintendent, Roads
dscott@northgrenville.on.ca
Mark Tenbult, Engineering Technologist
mtenbult@northgrenville.on.ca
Gary Simser, Technician, Regulatory Water / Wastewater Compliance
gsimser@magma.ca

North Huron
P.O. Box 90
274 Josephine St.
Wingham, ON N0G 2W0
Tel: 519-357-3550; *Fax:* 519-357-1110
www.northhuron.ca
Municipal Type: Township
Incorporated: Jan. 1, 2001 *Area:* 178.98 sq km
County or District: Huron; *Population in 2006:* 5,015
Provincial Electoral District(s): Huron-Bruce
Federal Electoral District(s): Huron-Bruce
Next Election: Oct. 2014 (4 year terms)
Note: Amalgamation of the Village of Blyth, the Township of East Wawanosh & the Town of Wingham.
Neil Vincent, Reeve
519-357-2336
nvincent@northhuron.ca
Gary Long, Clerk Administrator
519-357-3550

North Kawartha
P.O. Box 550
280 Burleigh St.
Apsley, ON K0L 1A0
Tel: 705-656-4445; *Fax:* 705-656-4446
d.page@northkawartha.on.ca (Reception)
www.northkawartha.on.ca
Other Information: Toll-Free Phone: 1-800-755-6931
Municipal Type: Township
Area: 765.02 sq km
County or District: Peterborough; *Population in 2006:* 2,342
Provincial Electoral District(s): Haliburton-Kawartha Lakes-Brock
Federal Electoral District(s): Haliburton-Kawartha Lakes-Brock
Next Election: Oct. 2014 (4 year terms)
Jim Whelan, Reeve
reeve@northkawartha.on.ca
Connie Parent, Clerk
c.parent@northkawartha.on.ca

North Middlesex
Administrative Centre
P.O. Box 9
229 Parkhill Main St.
Parkhill, ON N0M 2K0
Tel: 519-294-6244; *Fax:* 519-294-0573
clerk@northmiddlesex.on.ca
www.northmiddlesex.on.ca
Other Information: Toll-Free Phone: 1-888-793-9637
Municipal Type: Municipality
Incorporated: Jan. 1, 2001 *Area:* 597.86 sq km
County or District: Middlesex; *Population in 2006:* 6,740
Provincial Electoral District(s): Lambton-Kent-Middlesex
Federal Electoral District(s): Lambton-Kent-Middlesex
Next Election: Oct. 2014 (4 year terms)
Note: Amalgamation of the Townships of East Williams, West Williams & McGillivray, the Town of Parkhill & the Village of Ailsa Craig.
Don F. Shipway, Mayor
519-293-3219
donshipway@execulink.com
Linda Creaghe, Chief Administrative Officer
519-294-6244
lindacr@northmiddlesex.on.ca

North Stormont
P.O. Box 99
15 Union St.
Berwick, ON K0C 1G0
Tel: 613-984-2821; *Fax:* 613-984-2908
www.northstormont.ca
Other Information: Toll-Free Phone: 1-877-984-2821
Municipal Type: Township
Area: 515.55 sq km
County or District: Stormont, Dundas & Glengarry; *Population in 2006:* 6,769
Provincial Electoral District(s): Stormont-Dundas-South Glengarry
Federal Electoral District(s): Stormont-Dundas-South Glengarry
Next Election: Oct. 2014 (4 year terms)
Dennis Fife, Mayor
613-984-2821, Fax: 613-984-2908
Karen McPherson, Municipal Clerk
613-984-2821, Fax: 613-984-2908

Northeastern Manitoulin & the Islands
P.O. Box 2000
15 Manitowaning Rd.
Little Current, ON P0P 1K0
Tel: 705-368-3500; *Fax:* 705-368-2245
info@townofnemi.on.ca
www.townofnemi.on.ca
Municipal Type: Town
Area: 495.04 sq km
County or District: Manitoulin District; *Population in 2006:* 2,711
Provincial Electoral District(s): Algoma-Manitoulin
Federal Electoral District(s): Algoma-Manitoulin-Kapuskasing
Next Election: Oct. 2014 (4 year terms)
Joe Chapman, Mayor
705-968-0193
jchapman@townofnemi.on.ca
Janet Moore, Clerk
705-368-3500

Northern Bruce Peninsula
56 Lindsay Rd. 5, RR#2
Lion's Head, ON N0H 1W0
Tel: 519-793-3552; *Fax:* 519-793-3823
northernbrucepen@amtelecom.net
www.northbrucepeninsula.ca
Municipal Type: Municipality
Incorporated: Jan. 1999 *Area:* 781.51 sq km
County or District: Bruce; *Population in 2006:* 3,850
Provincial Electoral District(s): Bruce-Grey-Owen Sound
Federal Electoral District(s): Bruce-Grey-Owen Sound
Next Election: Oct. 2014 (4 year terms)
Note: Amalgamation of of the former Townships of St. Edmunds, Lindsay, Eastnor & the Village of Lion's Head.
Milton McIver, Mayor
519-592-3076
mayor.nbp@eastlink.ca
Mary Lynn Standen, Municipal Clerk
519-793-3522
marylynn.nbp@amtelecom.net

Norwich
P.O. Box 100
210 Main St. East
Otterville, ON N0J 1R0
Tel: 519-863-2709; *Fax:* 519-879-6385
www.twp.norwich.on.ca
Other Information: Alternative Phone: 519-879-6568
Municipal Type: Township
Area: 431.28 sq km
County or District: Oxford; *Population in 2006:* 10,481
Provincial Electoral District(s): Oxford
Federal Electoral District(s): Oxford
Next Election: Oct. 2014 (4 year terms)
Donald Doan, Mayor
519-468-5609
ddoan@twp.norwich.on.ca
Michael Graves, Chief Administrativve Officer & Clerk
519-879-6568
mgraves@twp.norwich.on.ca
Pat Lee, Councillor, Ward(s): 1
519-842-9635
plee@twp.norwich.on.ca
Mike Legge, Treasurer & Director, Finance
519-879-6568
mlegge@twp.norwich.on.ca
Lynne DePlancke, Councillor, Ward(s): 2
519-468-6728
ldeplancke@twp.norwich.on.ca
Brian Reid, Chief Building Official, Property Standards
519-879-6568
breid@twp.norwich.on.ca
Patrick Hovorka, Director, Community Development Services
519-863-3733
phovorka@twp.norwich.on.ca
Russell Jull, Councillor, Ward(s): 3
519-468-5648
rjull@twp.norwich.on.ca
Susan Hampson, Councillor, Ward(s): 4
519-424-9784
shampson@twp.norwich.on.ca
Ron Smith, Superintendent, Public Works
519-879-6568
ronsmith@twp.norwich.on.ca
Monica Bratley, Coordinator, Customer Service & Records Management
519-879-6568
mbratley@twp.norwich.on.ca
Jason Brander, Planner
519-539-9800
jbrander@county.oxford.on.ca

O'Connor
RR#1
Kakabeka Falls, ON P0T 1W0
Tel: 807-476-1451; *Fax:* 807-473-0891
twpoconn@tbaytel.net
www.oconnortownship.ca
Municipal Type: Township
Incorporated: January 1, 1907 *Area:* 108.58 sq km
County or District: Thunder Bay District; *Population in 2006:* 720
Provincial Electoral District(s): Thunder Bay-Atikokan
Federal Electoral District(s): Thunder Bay-Rainy River
Next Election: Oct. 2014 (4 year terms)
Ron Nelson, Mayor
807-475-9213
Lorna Buob, Clerk-Treasurer
twpoconn@tbaytel.net

Oil Springs
P.O. Box 22
4591 Oil Springs Line
Oil Springs, ON N0N 1P0
Tel: 519-834-2939; *Fax:* 519-834-2333
oilsprings@ciaccess.com
www.oilsprings.ca
Municipal Type: Village
Incorporated: 1865 *Area:* 8.18 sq km
County or District: Lambton; *Population in 2006:* 717
Provincial Electoral District(s): Sarnia-Lambton
Federal Electoral District(s): Sarnia-Lambton
Next Election: Oct. 2014 (4 year terms)
Ian Veen, Mayor
Christine Poland, Clerk-Treasurer

Oliver Paipoonge, Municipality of
P.O. Box 10
4569 Oliver Rd.
Murillo, ON P0T 2G0
Tel: 807-935-2613; *Fax:* 807-935-2161
sharron.martyn@oliverpaipoonage.on.ca
www.oliverpaipoonge.on.ca
Municipal Type: Township
Incorporated: Jan. 1, 1998 *Area:* 350.27 sq km
County or District: Thunder Bay District; *Population in 2006:* 5,757
Provincial Electoral District(s): Thunder Bay-Atikokan
Federal Electoral District(s): Thunder Bay-Rainy River
Next Election: Oct. 2014 (4 year terms)
Note: Amalgamation of the Township of Oliver & the Township of Paipoonge.
Lucy Kloosterhuis, Mayor
807-473-5658, Fax: 807-935-2161
lakbusiness@xplornet.com
Jamie Cressman, Chief Administrative Officer & Clerk
807-935-2613, Fax: 807-935-2123
jamie.cressman@oliverpaipoonge.on.ca

Opasatika
P.O. Box 100
50 Government Rd.
Opasatika, ON P0L 1Z0
Tel: 705-369-4531; *Fax:* 705-369-2002
twpopas@persona.ca
www.opasatika.net
Municipal Type: Township
Area: 329.98 sq km
County or District: Cochrane District; *Population in 2006:* 280
Provincial Electoral District(s): Timmins-James Bay
Federal Electoral District(s): Algoma-Manitoulin-Kapuskasing
Next Election: Oct. 2014 (4 year terms)

Françoise Lambert, Mayor
Denis Dorval, Clerk-Treasurer
705-369-4531, Fax: 705-369-2002

Oro-Medonte
148 Line 7 South
Oro, ON L0L 2X0
Tel: 705-487-2171; *Fax:* 705-487-0133
www.oro-medonte.ca
Municipal Type: Township
Area: 586.65 sq km
County or District: Simcoe; *Population in 2006:* 20,031
Provincial Electoral District(s): Simcoe North
Federal Electoral District(s): Simcoe North
Next Election: Oct. 2014 (4 year terms)
Harry Hughes, Mayor
705-487-2128
Doug Irwin, Clerk & Director, Corporate Services
Ralph Hough, Deputy Mayor
705-835-2770
Robin Dunn, Chief Administrative Officer
Mel Coutanche, Councillor, Ward(s): 1
705-835-5728
Paul Gravelle, Treasurer, Deputy CAO, & Director, Finance
Kelly Meyer, Councillor, Ward(s): 2
705-835-2656
Jerry Ball, Director, Transportation & Environmental Services
Marty Lancaster, Councillor, Ward(s): 3
705-220-5410
Shawn Binns, Director, Recreation & Community Services
Donna Hewitt, Director, Corporate & Strategic Initiatives
John Crawford, Councillor, Ward(s): 4
705-487-3373
Andria Leigh, Director, Development Services
Kim Allen, Chief Building Official
Dwight Evans, Councillor, Ward(s): 5
705-325-1653
Lisa McNiven, Manager, Engineering & Environmental Services
Tamara Obee, Manager, Health & Safety & Human Resources
Brian Roubos, Manager, Transportation Services
Glenn White, Manager, Planning Services
Hugh Murray, Deputy Fire Chief
705-835-5568, Fax: 705-487-0133

Otonabee-South Monaghan
Municipal Office
P.O. Box 70
20 Third St.
Keene, ON K0L 2G0
Tel: 705-295-6852; *Fax:* 705-295-6405
info@osmtownship.ca
www.osmtownship.ca
Other Information: Toll-Free Phone: 1-800-999-4861 (In 705 area code)
Municipal Type: Township
Area: 349.22 sq km
County or District: Peterborough; *Population in 2006:* 6,934
Provincial Electoral District(s): Peterborough
Federal Electoral District(s): Peterborough
Next Election: Oct. 2014 (4 year terms)
David Nelson, Reeve
705-295-4628
dnelson@osmtownship.ca
Heather Scott, Clerk
705-295-6852
hscott@osmtownship.ca

Oxford
P.O. Box 1614
21 Reeve St.
Woodstock, ON N4S 7Y3
Tel: 519-539-9800;
www.oxfordcounty.ca
Municipal Type: Restructured County
Area: 2,039.46 sq km
Population in 2006: 102,756
Next Election: Oct. 2014 (4 year terms)
Don McKay, Warden & Councillor, Ward(s): East Zorra-Tavistock
519-539-9800, Fax: 519-421-4712
Michael Bragg, Chief Administrative Officer & Clerk
519-539-9800
Marion Wearn, Councillor, Ward(s): Blandford-Blenheim
519-463-5347
Lynn Buchner, Director, Corporate Services
519-539-9800
Lynn Beath, Director, Public Health & Emergency Services
519-539-9800
Ted J. Comiskey, Councillor, Ward(s): Ingersoll
519-485-0120
Robert Walton, Director, Public Works
519-539-9800
Donald Doan, Councillor, Ward(s): Norwich
519-863-2709, Fax: 519-468-3229
Gordon K. Hough, Corporate Manager, Community & Strategic Planning
519-539-9800
David Mayberry, Councillor, Ward(s): South-West Oxford
519-485-0477
Janice Kubiak, Corporate Manager, Human Resources
519-539-9800
John Lessif, Councillor, Ward(s): Tillsonburg
519-688-3009
Pat Sobeski, Councillor, Ward(s): Woodstock
519-539-2382
Deb A. Tait, Councillor, Ward(s): Woodstock
519-421-7449
Sandra J. Talbot, Councillor, Ward(s): Woodstock
519-539-6685, Fax: 519-539-4526
Margaret E. Lupton, Councillor, Ward(s): Zorra
519-485-2490

Papineau-Cameron
P.O. Box 630
4861 Hwy. 17
Mattawa, ON P0H 1V0
Tel: 705-744-5610; *Fax:* 705-744-0434
www.papineaucameron.ca
Municipal Type: Township
Area: 561.37 sq km
County or District: Nipissing District; *Population in 2006:* 1,058
Provincial Electoral District(s): Nipissing
Federal Electoral District(s): Nipissing-Timiskaming
Next Election: Oct. 2014 (4 year terms)
Robert Corriveau, Mayor
Sandra J. Morin, Clerk-Treasurer

Parry Sound
52 Seguin St.
Parry Sound, ON P2A 1B4
Tel: 705-746-2101; *Fax:* 705-746-7461
middaugh@townofparrysound.com (Economic Dev. & Leisure Svs.)
www.townofparrysound.com
Municipal Type: Town
Area: 13.33 sq km
County or District: Parry Sound District; *Population in 2006:* 5,818
Provincial Electoral District(s): Parry Sound-Muskoka
Federal Electoral District(s): Parry Sound-Muskoka
Next Election: Oct. 2014 (4 year terms)
Jamie McGarvey, Mayor
jmcgarvey@townofparrysound.com
Rob Mens, Chief Administrative Officer
rmens@townofparrysound.com

Parry Sound
District Social Services Administration Bd.
1 Beechwood Dr., 2nd Fl.
Parry Sound, ON P2A 1J2
Tel: 705-746-7777; *Fax:* 705-746-7783
Municipal Type: District
Area: 9,222.04 sq km
Population in 2006: 40,918
Rick Zanussi, Chair, Parry Sound District Social Services Administration Board
Janet Patterson, Chief Administrative Officer, District Social Service Admin Board
705-746-7777

Pelee
1045 West Shore Rd.
Pelee Island, ON N0R 1M0
Tel: 519-724-2931; *Fax:* 519-724-2470
info@pelee.ca
www.pelee.org
Other Information: Toll-Free Phone: 1-866-889-5203
Municipal Type: Township
Incorporated: 1869 *Area:* 41.79 sq km
County or District: Essex; *Population in 2006:* 287
Provincial Electoral District(s): Essex
Federal Electoral District(s): Essex
Next Election: Oct. 2014 (4 year terms)
Rick Masse, Mayor
Ann Mitchell, Clerk-Treasurer

Penetanguishene
P.O. Box 5009
10 Robert St. West
Penetanguishene, ON L9M 2G2
Tel: 705-549-7453; *Fax:* 705-549-3743
www.penetanguishene.ca
Other Information: Public Works, Phone: 705-549-7992
Municipal Type: Town
Incorporated: Feb. 22, 1882 *Area:* 25.38 sq km
County or District: Simcoe; *Population in 2006:* 9,354
Provincial Electoral District(s): Simcoe North
Federal Electoral District(s): Simcoe North
Next Election: Oct. 2014 (4 year terms)
Gerry Marshall, Mayor
Holly Bryce, Town Clerk
hbryce@penetanguishene.ca

Perry
P.O. Box 70
1695 Emsdale Rd.
Emsdale, ON P0A 1J0
Tel: 705-636-5941; *Fax:* 705-636-5759
info@townshipofperry.ca; perrylib@ontera.net (library)
www.townshipofperry.ca
Other Information: Public Works Email: publicworks@townshipofperry.ca
Municipal Type: Township
Area: 186.63 sq km
County or District: Parry Sound District; *Population in 2006:* 2,010
Provincial Electoral District(s): Parry Sound-Muskoka
Federal Electoral District(s): Parry Sound-Muskoka
Next Election: Oct. 2014 (4 year terms)
John Dunn, Mayor
705-636-5727
john.dunn@townshipofperry.ca
Beth Morton, Clerk & Planning Administrator
705-636-5941
beth.morton@townshipofperry.ca

Perth
Town Hall
80 Gore St. East
Perth, ON K7H 1H9
Tel: 613-267-3311; *Fax:* 613-267-5635
www.perthcanada.com
Other Information: After hour water & sewer emergencies: 613-267-1072
Municipal Type: Town
Area: 10.36 sq km
County or District: Lanark; *Population in 2006:* 5,907
Provincial Electoral District(s): Lanark-Frontenac-Lennox & Addington
Federal Electoral District(s): Lanark-Frontenac-Lennox & Addington
Next Election: Oct. 2014 (4 year terms)
John Fenik, Mayor
613-267-3311
jfenik@perth.ca
Lauren Walton, Clerk
613-267-3311
lwalton@perth.ca

Perth East
P.O. Box 455
25 Mill St. East
Milverton, ON N0K 1M0
Tel: 519-595-2800; *Fax:* 519-595-2801
township@pertheast.on.ca
www.pertheast.on.ca
Municipal Type: Township
Area: 715.07 sq km
County or District: Perth; *Population in 2006:* 12,041
Provincial Electoral District(s): Perth-Wellinton
Federal Electoral District(s): Perth-Wellington
Next Election: Oct. 2014 (4 year terms)
Note: Amalgamation of North Easthope Township, South Easthope Township, Ellice Township, Village of Milverton & Mornington Township.
Ian Forrest, Mayor
iforrest@pertheast.on.ca
Theresa Campbell, Municipal Clerk
519-595-2800
tcampbell@pertheast.on.ca
Bob McMillan, Deputy Mayor
mcmillan@cyg.net
Glenn Schwendinger, Chief Administrative Officer
519-595-2800
Rhonda Ehgoetz, Councillor, Ward(s): Ellice
rhonda.ehgoetz@hotmail.com
Rhonda Fischer, Municipal Treasurer & Manager, Finance Department
519-595-2800
Jeremy Matheson, Councillor, Ward(s): Milverton
jmatheson@zehrinsurance.com
Wes Kuepfer, Manager, Public Works & Parks
519-595-2800
Don Brunk, Councillor, Ward(s): Mornington
morningtonward@hotmail.com

Donna Chaffe, Coordinator, Human Resources
519-595-2800
Hugh McDermid, Councillor, Ward(s): North Easthope
mcdermid2020hotmail.com
Andrew MacAlpine, Councillor, Ward(s): South Easthope
a.macalpine@sympatico.ca
Bill Hunter, Fire Chief
519-595-2800
519-595-2801
Grant Schwartzentruber, Chief Building Official
519-595-2800
Becky Boertien, Manager, Perth East Recreation Complex
519-595-2244, Fax: 519-595-4067
Martin Feeney, By-law Enforcement Officer & Building & Sewage Inspector
519-595-2800
Geoff VanderBaaren, Planner
519-271-0531

Perth South
3191 Rd. 122
St. Pauls, ON N0K 1V0
Tel: 519-271-0619; *Fax:* 519-271-0647
township@perthsouth.ca
www.perthsouth.ca
Other Information: Toll-Free Phone: 1-866-771-0619
Municipal Type: Township
Area: 393.01 sq km
County or District: Perth; *Population in 2006:* 4,132
Provincial Electoral District(s): Perth-Wellington
Federal Electoral District(s): Perth-Wellington
Next Election: Oct. 2014 (4 year terms)
Note: Amalgamation of Blanshard Township & Downie Township.
Robert Wilhelm, Mayor
519-225-2304
ulchtran@quadro.net
Lizet Scott, Clerk
519-271-0619
lscott@perthsouth.ca

Petrolia
P.O. Box 1270
411 Greenfield St.
Petrolia, ON N0N 1R0
Tel: 519-882-2350; *Fax:* 519-882-3373
petrolia@town.petrolia.on.ca
www.town.petrolia.on.ca
Other Information: After Hours Emergency, Phone: 519-882-2351
Municipal Type: Town
Area: 12.68 sq km
County or District: Lambton; *Population in 2006:* 5,222
Provincial Electoral District(s): Lambton-Kent-Middlesex
Federal Electoral District(s): Sarnia-Lambton
Next Election: Oct. 2014 (4 year terms)
John McCharles, Mayor
519-882-2455
johnnyremax@bellnet.ca
Dianne Caryn, Chief Administrative Officer & Clerk
dcaryn@town.petrolia.on.ca

Pickle Lake
P.O. Box 340
2 Anne St.
Pickle Lake, ON P0V 3A0
Tel: 807-928-2034; *Fax:* 807-928-2708
reception@picklelake.org
www.picklelake.ca
Other Information: Toll-Free Phone: 1-800-565-9189
Municipal Type: Township
Incorporated: Dec. 1980 *Area:* 255.08 sq km
County or District: Kenora District; *Population in 2006:* 479
Provincial Electoral District(s): Kenora-Rainy River
Federal Electoral District(s): Kenora
Next Election: Oct. 2014 (4 year terms)
Roy Hoffman, Mayor
mayor@picklelake.org
Paul Panciw, Clerk-Treasurer
clerktreasurer@picklelake.org

Plummer Additional
38 Railway Cres., RR#2
Bruce Mines, ON P0R 1C0
Tel: 705-785-3479; *Fax:* 705-785-3135
plumtwsp@onlink.net
www.plummertownship.ca
Municipal Type: Township
Area: 221.31 sq km
County or District: Algoma District; *Population in 2006:* 625
Provincial Electoral District(s): Algoma-Manitoulin
Federal Electoral District(s): Sault Ste Marie
Next Election: Oct. 2014 (4 year terms)
Beth West, Mayor
Vicky Goertzen-Cooke, Clerk-Treasurer

Plympton-Wyoming
P.O. Box 250
546 Niagara St.
Wyoming, ON N0N 1T0
Tel: 519-845-3939; *Fax:* 519-845-0597
feedback@plympton-wyoming.ca
www.plympton-wyoming.com
Other Information: Toll-Free Phone: 1-877-313-3939
Municipal Type: Town
Incorporated: Jan. 1, 2001 *Area:* 318.76 sq km
County or District: Lambton; *Population in 2006:* 7,506
Provincial Electoral District(s): Sarnia-Lambton
Federal Electoral District(s): Sarnia-Lambton
Next Election: Oct. 2014 (4 year terms)
Note: Amalgamation of the Village of Wyoming & the Township of Plympton.
Lonny Napper, Mayor
lnapper@xcelco.on.ca
Caroline DeSchutter, Clerk & Deputy Chief Administrative Officer
cdeschutter@plympton-wyoming.ca

Point Edward
Municipal Office
135 Kendall St.
Point Edward, ON N7V 4G6
Tel: 519-337-3021; *Fax:* 519-337-5963
info@villageofpointedward.com
www.villageofpointedward.com
Municipal Type: Village
Incorporated: 1878 *Area:* 3.27 sq km
County or District: Lambton; *Population in 2006:* 2,019
Provincial Electoral District(s): Sarnia-Lambton
Federal Electoral District(s): Sarnia-Lambton
Next Election: Oct. 2014 (4 year terms)
Dick Kirkland, Mayor
518-344-8755
dkirkland@villageofpointedward.com
Peggy Cramp, Chief Administrative Officer &
519-337-3021
pcramp@villageofpointedward.com

Port Hope
Town Hall
56 Queen St.
Port Hope, ON L1A 3Z9
Tel: 905-885-4544; *Fax:* 905-885-7698
admin@porthope.ca
www.porthope.ca
Municipal Type: Municipality
Incorporated: March 6, 1834 *Area:* 278.97 sq km
County or District: Northumberland; *Population in 2006:* 16,390
Provincial Electoral District(s): Northumberland-Quinte West
Federal Electoral District(s): Northumberland-Quinte West
Next Election: Oct. 2014 (4 year terms)
Linda M. Thompson, Mayor
905-885-4544
mayor@porthope.ca
Sue Dawe, Clerk & Director, Corporate Services
905-885-4544
sdawe@porthope.ca
Rick Austin, Councillor, Ward(s): 1
905-376-9050
raustin@porthope.ca
Mary Lou Ellis, Councillor, Ward(s): 1
905-885-0376
mellis@porthope.ca
R. Carl Cannon, Chief Administrative Officer
905-885-4544
ccannon@porthope.ca
David Turck, Councillor, Ward(s): 1
905-885-8927
dturck@porthope.ca
Liz Araujo, Treasurer & Director, Finance
905-885-4544
laraujo@porthope.ca
Jeff G. Lees, Councillor, Ward(s): 1
905-885-8977
jlees@porthope.ca; jefflees@sympatico.ca
Peter Angelo, P.Eng., Director, Public Works
905-885-2431
pangelo@porthope.ca
Greg W. Burns, Councillor, Ward(s): 2
905-797-9616
gburns@porthope.ca
Rob Collins, Director, Fire & Emergency Services
905-885-5323
rcollins@porthope.ca
Judy Selvig, Director, Economic Development & Tourism
905-885-2431
jselvig@porthope.ca
Jeffrey S. Gilmer, Deputy Mayor & Councillor, Ward(s): 2
905-753-2685
jgilmer@porthope.ca
Karen Sharpe, Director, Parks, Recreation, & Culture
905-753-2230, Fax: 905-753-2434
ksharpe@porthope.ca
Ron Warne, Director, Planning & Development Services
905-885-2431, Fax: 905-885-0507
rwarne@porthope.ca
Ken Andrus, Chief Building Official
905-885-2431
kandrus@porthope.ca
Gina Jackson, Manager, Human Resources
905-885-4544
gjackson@porthope.ca
Sandra Weeks, Coordinator, Communications
905-885-4544
sweeks@porthope.ca

Powassan, Municipality of
P.O. Box 250
466 Main St.
Powassan, ON P0H 1Z0
Tel: 705-724-2813; *Fax:* 705-724-5533
info@powassan.net
www.powassan.net
Municipal Type: Town
Incorporated: Nov. 30, 1904 *Area:* 222.75 sq km
County or District: Parry Sound District; *Population in 2006:* 3,309
Provincial Electoral District(s): Nipissing
Federal Electoral District(s): Nipissing-Timiskaming
Next Election: Oct. 2014 (4 year terms)
Peter McIsaac, Mayor
705-491-0374
pmcisaac@powassan.net
Maureen Lang, Clerk-Treasurer
795-724-2813, Fax: 705-724-5533
mlang@powassan.netet

Prescott
P.O. Box 160
360 Dibble St. West
Prescott, ON K0E 1T0
Tel: 613-925-2812; *Fax:* 613-925-4381
info@prescott.ca
www.prescott.ca
Municipal Type: Town
Area: 4.95 sq km
County or District: Leeds & Grenville; *Population in 2006:* 4,180
Provincial Electoral District(s): Leeds-Grenville
Federal Electoral District(s): Leeds-Grenville
Next Election: Oct. 2014 (4 year terms)
Brett Todd, Mayor
613-925-2812
btodd@prescott.ca
Randy Haller, Chief Administrative Officer & Clerk
613-925-2812, Fax: 613-925-4381
rhaller@prescott.ca

Prescott & Russell
P.O. Box 304
59 Court St.
L'Orignal, ON K0B 1K0
Tel: 613-675-4661; *Fax:* 613-675-2519
support@prescott-russell.on.ca
www.prescott-russell.on.ca
Other Information: Toll-Free Phone: 1-800-667-6307
Municipal Type: United County
Incorporated: 1820 *Area:* 2,001.18 sq km
Population in 2006: 80,184
Next Election: Oct. 2014 (4 year terms)
Jean-Yves Lalonde, Warden & Mayor, Township of Alfred & Plantagenet
613-673-4797, Fax: 613-673-4812
jean-yves.lalonde@sympatico.ca
Stéphane P. Parisien, Chief Administrative Officer & Clerk
613-675-4661
spparisien@prescott-russell.on.ca
Louise Lepage-Gareau, Treasurer
613-675-4661, Fax: 613-675-4547
llgareau@prescott-russell.on.ca
Claude Levac, Council Member & Mayor, Village of Casselman
613-764-3139, Fax: 613-764-5709
maire@casselman.ca
Michel Chrétien, Director, Emergency Services
613-673-5139, Fax: 613-673-1401
mchretien@prescott-russell.on.ca

Gary J. Barton, Council Member & Mayor, Township of Champlain
613-678-3003, Fax: 613-678-3363
gary.barton@champlain.ca
Marc Clermont, Director, Public Works
613-675-4661, Fax: 613-675-1007
mclermont@prescott-russell.on.ca
Jonathan B. Roy, Director, Human Resources
613-675-4661, Fax: 613-675-4547
jbroy@prescott-russell.on.ca
Anne Comtois Lalonde, Administrator, Social Services Management
613-675-4642, Fax: 613-675-2030
aclalonde@prescott-russell.on.ca
Marcel Guibord, Council Member & Mayor, City of Clarence-Rockland
613-446-6022, Fax: 613-446-1497
mguibord@clarence-rockland.com
Louis Prévost, Director, Planning & Forestry
613-675-4661, Fax: 613-675-1007
lprevost@prescott-russell.on.ca
Robert Kirby, Council Member & Mayor, Township of East Hawkesbury
613-674-2170, Fax: 613-632-4841
René Berthiaume, Council Member & Mayor, Town of Hawkesbury
613-632-0106, Fax: 613-636-2096
rberthiaume@hawkesbury.ca
François St. Amour, Council Member & Mayor, Nation Municipality
613-764-5444
fstamour@nationmun.ca
Jean-Paul Saint-Pierre, Council Member & Mayor, Township of Russell
613-443-3066, Fax: 613-443-1042
jpstpierre@russell.ca

Prince
3042 2nd Line West
Sault Ste Marie, ON P6A 6K4
Tel: 705-779-2992; *Fax:* 705-779-2725
www.princetwp.ca
Municipal Type: Township
Area: 84.28 sq km
County or District: Algoma District; *Population in 2006:* 971
Provincial Electoral District(s): Algoma Manitoulin
Federal Electoral District(s): Sault Ste Marie
Next Election: Oct. 2014 (4 year terms)
Ken Lamming, Reeve
705-779-2875
kenlamming@sympatico.ca
Peggy Greco, Chief Administrative Officer & Administrator

Puslinch
7404 Wellington Rd. 34, RR#3
Guelph, ON N1H 6H9
Tel: 519-763-1226; *Fax:* 519-763-5846
admin@twp.puslinch.on.ca
www.twp.puslinch.on.ca
Municipal Type: Township
Incorporated: Jan. 1, 1850 *Area:* 214.44 sq km
County or District: Wellington; *Population in 2006:* 6,689
Provincial Electoral District(s): Wellington-Halton Hills
Federal Electoral District(s): Wellington-Halton Hills; Guelph
Next Election: Oct. 2014 (4 year terms)
Dennis Lever, Mayor
226-971-2067
dennisl@wellington.ca
Brenda Law, Chief Administrative Officer & Clerk-Treasurer
519-763-1226
brendal@twp.puslinch.on.ca

Rainy River
P.O. Box 488
Rainy River, ON P0W 1L0
Tel: 807-852-3244; *Fax:* 807-852-3553
rainyriver@tbaytel.net
www.rainyriver.ca
Municipal Type: Town
Incorporated: 1904 *Area:* 2.99 sq km
County or District: Rainy River District; *Population in 2006:* 909
Provincial Electoral District(s): Kenora-Rainy River
Federal Electoral District(s): Thunder Bay-Rainy River
Next Election: Oct. 2014 (4 year terms)
Deborah Ewald, Mayor
Veldron Vogan, Chief Administrative Officer

Rainy River
District Social Services Administration Bd.
450 Scott St.
Fort Frances, ON P9A 1H2
Tel: 807-274-5349; *Fax:* 807-274-0678
Other Information: Toll-Free Phone: 1-800-265-5349
Municipal Type: District
Area: 15,472.94 sq km
Population in 2006: 21,564
Ross Donaldson, Chair, Rainy River District Social Services Administration Board
Donna Dittaro, CAO, Rainy River District Social Services Administration Board
donnad@rrdssab.on.ca

Ramara
Ramara Administration Building
P.O. Box 130
2297 Hwy. 12
Brechin, ON L0K 1B0
Tel: 705-484-5374; *Fax:* 705-484-0441
ramara@ramara.ca
www.ramara.ca
Other Information: Toll-Free Phone: 1-800-663-4054 (for 689 exchange)
Municipal Type: Township
Area: 417.25 sq km
County or District: Simcoe; *Population in 2006:* 9,427
Provincial Electoral District(s): Simcoe North
Federal Electoral District(s): Simcoe North
Next Election: Oct. 2014 (4 year terms)
Bill Duffy, Mayor
705-326-3915
council@ramara.ca
Janice McKinnon, Clerk
705-484-5374
jmckinnon@ramara.ca

Red Lake
P.O. Box 1000
2 Fifth St.
Balmertown, ON P0V 1C0
Tel: 807-735-2096; *Fax:* 807-735-2286
municipality@red-lake.com
www.red-lake.com
Municipal Type: Municipality
Incorporated: July 1, 1998 *Area:* 610.38 sq km
County or District: Kenora District; *Population in 2006:* 4,526
Provincial Electoral District(s): Kenora-Rainy River
Federal Electoral District(s): Kenora
Next Election: Oct. 2014 (4 year terms)
Note: Amalgamation of the former Unorganized Territory of Madsen, the Township of Red Lake, & the Township of Golden.
Phil T. Vinet, Mayor
807-735-2096, Fax: 807-735-2286
Shelly Kocis, Clerk
807-735-2096, Fax: 807-735-2286
shelly@red-lake.com

Red Rock
P.O. Box 447
Red Rock, ON P0T 2P0
Tel: 807-886-2245; *Fax:* 807-886-2793
info@redrocktownship.com
www.redrocktownship.com
Other Information: Phone, Public Works: 807-886-2524
Municipal Type: Township
Area: 62.93 sq km
County or District: Thunder Bay District; *Population in 2006:* 1,063
Provincial Electoral District(s): Thunder Bay-Superior North
Federal Electoral District(s): Thunder Bay-Superior North
Next Election: Oct. 2014 (4 year terms)
Gary Nelson, Mayor
807-886-2503
Kal Pristanski, CAO, Clerk-Treasurer, Tax Collector, & Commissioner of Oaths
cao@shawbiz.ca

Renfrew
127 Raglan St. South
Renfrew, ON K7V 1P8
Tel: 613-432-4848; *Fax:* 613-432-7245
info@town.renfrew.on.ca
www.town.renfrew.on.ca
Municipal Type: Town
Area: 12.77 sq km
County or District: Renfrew; *Population in 2006:* 7,846
Provincial Electoral District(s): Renfrew-Nipissing-Pembroke
Federal Electoral District(s): Renfrew-Nipissing-Pembroke
Next Election: Oct. 2014 (4 year terms)
Bill Ringrose, Mayor
613-432-4848
bringrose@town.renfrew.on.ca
Kim R. Bulmer, Town Clerk
613-432-4848
kbulmer@town.renfrew.on.ca

Rideau Lakes
1439 County Rd. 8
Delta, ON K0E 1G0
Tel: 613-928-2251; *Fax:* 613-928-3097
info@twprideaulakes.on.ca
www.twprideaulakes.on.ca
Other Information: Toll-Free Phone: 1-800-928-2250
Municipal Type: Township
Incorporated: Jan. 1, 1998 *Area:* 710.25 sq km
County or District: Leeds-Grenville; *Population in 2006:* 10,350
Provincial Electoral District(s): Leeds-Grenville
Federal Electoral District(s): Leeds-Grenville
Next Election: Oct. 2014 (4 year terms)
Note: Amalgamation of the former Townships of North Crosby, South Crosby, Bastard & South Burgess, South Elmsley & the Village of Newboro.
Ron Holman, Mayor
613-283-0724, Fax: 613-283-5517
mayor@twprideaulakes.on.ca
Dianna Bresee, Clerk
613-928-2251
dianna@twprideaulakes.on.ca
Anders Carson, Councillor, Ward(s): Bastard & South Burgess
613-272-3354
anderscarson77@gmail.com
Robert Maddocks, Chief Administrative Officer
613-928-2251
cao@twprideaulakes.on.ca
Rob Dunfield, Councillor, Ward(s): Bastard & South Burgess
613-272-2179
dunfield.robert@gmail.com
Joseph Whyte, Treasurer
613-928-2251
joe@twprideaulakes.on.ca
Cathy Monck, Councillor, Ward(s): Newboro
613-272-3453
monck.cathy@bell.net
Susan Dunfield, Manager, Community & Leisure Services
613-928-2251
susan@twprideaulakes.on.ca
Ron Pollard, Deputy Mayor & Councillor, Ward(s): North Crosby
613-273-5491
pollard.ron@kingston.net
Sheldon Laidman, Manager, Development Services
613-928-2251
slaidman@twprideaulakes.on.ca
Bob Lavoie, Councillor, Ward(s): North Crosby
613-273-8177
BobLavoie@kingston.net
Michael Touw, Manager, Public Works & Superintendent, Drainage
613-928-2251
mtouw@twprideaulakes.on.ca
Linda Carr, Councillor, Ward(s): South Crosby
613-272-2227
councillorlinda@gmail.com
Jay DeBernardi, Fire Chief
613-928-2251
fire.j@twprideaulakes.on.ca
Robert Taylor, Councillor, Ward(s): South Crosby
613-359-5118
robert.roy.taylor@hotmail.ca
Jeff Banks, Councillor, Ward(s): South Elmsley
613-800-2790
jeffbanks@xplornet.com
Paul A.L. Smith, Councillor, Ward(s): South Elmsley
613-283-6265
smith.paul@sympatico.ca

Russell
717 Notre Dame St.
Embrun, ON K0A 1W1
Tel: 613-443-3066; *Fax:* 613-443-1042
info@russell.ca; publicworks.voirie@russell.ca
www.russell.ca
Other Information: Bylaws, E-mail: bylaws.reglements@russell.ca
Municipal Type: Township
Area: 198.96 sq km
County or District: Prescott & Russell; *Population in 2006:* 13,883
Provincial Electoral District(s): Glengarry-Prescott-Russell
Federal Electoral District(s): Glengarry-Prescott-Russell
Next Election: Oct. 2014 (4 year terms)

JP St-Pierre, Mayor
jpstpierre@russell.ca
Eric Bazinet, Councillor
ericbazinet@russell.ca
Craig Cullen, Councillor
craigcullen@russell.ca
Jamie Laurin, Councillor
jlaurin@russell.ca
Pierre Leroux, Councillor
pierreleroux@russell.ca
Ginette Bertrand, Municipal Clerk
clerk.greffe@russell.ca
Jean Leduc, Chief Administrative Officer
Christiane B. Brault, Treasurer & Director, Finance
finances@russell.ca
Millie Bourdeau, Director, Public Safety & Enforcement
Graham Gorman, Director, Environmental Services & Public Utilities
Jacques Lortie, Director, Public Works, Parks, & Recreation
recreation@russell.ca
Dominique Tremblay, Director, Planning & Building
planning.amenagement@russell.ca
Bruce Armstrong, Fire Chief, Russell
Jean-Luc Bourgie, Fire Chief, Embrun

Ryerson

28 Midlothian Rd., RR#1
Burks Falls, ON P0A 1C0
Tel: 705-382-3232; *Fax:* 705-382-3286
admin@ryersontownship.ca
www.ryersontownship.ca
Municipal Type: Township
Area: 186.79 sq km
County or District: Parry Sound District; *Population in 2006:* 686
Provincial Electoral District(s): Parry Sound-Muskoka
Federal Electoral District(s): Parry Sound-Muskoka
Next Election: Oct. 2014 (4 year terms)
Glenn Miller, Reeve
705-382-2898
Judy Kosowan, Chief Administrative Officer & Clerk-Treasurer

Sables-Spanish Rivers

PO Box 5, Site 1, 11 Birch Lake Rd. RR#3
Massey, ON P0P 1P0
Tel: 705-865-2646; *Fax:* 705-865-2736
inquiries@sables-spanish.ca
www.sables-spanish.ca
Municipal Type: Township
Incorporated: July 1998 *Area:* 806.27 sq km
County or District: Sudbury District; *Population in 2006:* 3,237
Provincial Electoral District(s): Algoma-Manitoulin
Federal Electoral District(s): Algoma-Manitoulin-Kapuskasing
Next Election: Oct. 2014 (4 year terms)
Leslie Gamble, Mayor
705-865-2655
Kim Sloss, Clerk-Administrator
705-865-2646, Fax: 705-865-2736
kasloss@sables-spanish.ca

St. Clair

Civic Centre
1155 Emily St.
Mooretown, ON N0N 1M0
Tel: 519-867-2021; *Fax:* 519-867-5509
webmaster@twp.stclair.on.ca; publicworks@twp.stclair.on.ca
www.twp.stclair.on.ca
Other Information: Toll-Free Phone: 1-800-809-0301 (Sombra & Lambton)
Municipal Type: Township
Area: 619.3 sq km
County or District: Lambton; *Population in 2006:* 14,649
Provincial Electoral District(s): Sarnia-Lambton
Federal Electoral District(s): Sarnia-Lambton
Next Election: Oct. 2014 (4 year terms)
Steve Arnold, Mayor
519-381-7440
John DeMars, Clerk, Deputy CAO, & Director, Administration
519-867-2021
Peter Gilliland, Deputy Mayor
519-862-3534
John Rodey, MCIP, RPP, Chief Administrative Officer
519-867-2021, Fax: 519-867-5509
jrodey@twp.stclair.on.ca
Jeff Agar, Councillor, Ward(s): 1
519-862-5062
Charles Quenneville, B.Com., CMA, Treasurer
519-867-2024
cquenneville@twp.stclair.on.ca
Patricia Carswell-Alexander, Councillor, Ward(s): 1
519-864-4006
Jim DeGurse, Councillor, Ward(s): 1
519-862-3060
Roy Dewhirst, Fire Chief
rdewhirst@twp.stclair.on.ca
Steve Miller, Councillor, Ward(s): 2
519-677-5676
Gary Hackett, Director, Community Services
ghackett@twp.stclair.on.ca
J. Baranek, Coordinator, Planning
Rick McClemens, Coordinator, Facilities & Parks
rmcclemens@twp.stclair.on.ca
Darrell Randell, Councillor, Ward(s): 2
519-627-3764

St. Joseph

P.O. Box 187
1669 Arthur St.
Richards Landing, ON P0R 1J0
Tel: 705-246-2625; *Fax:* 705-246-3142
stjosephtownship@bellnet.ca
www.stjosephtownship.com
Municipal Type: Township
Area: 129.18 sq km
County or District: Algoma District; *Population in 2006:* 1,129
Provincial Electoral District(s): Algoma-Manitoulin
Federal Electoral District(s): Sault Ste Marie
Next Election: Oct. 2014 (4 year terms)
Jody Wildman, Mayor
705-246-0616
Carol O. Trainor, A.M.C.T., Clerk Administrator
stjoeadmin@bellnet.ca

St. Marys

P.O. Box 998
175 Queen St. East, 2nd Fl.
St. Marys, ON N4X 1B6
Tel: 519-284-2340; *Fax:* 519-284-3881
www.townofstmarys.com
Municipal Type: Town
Area: 12.48 sq km
County or District: Perth; *Population in 2006:* 6,617
Provincial Electoral District(s): Perth-Wellington
Federal Electoral District(s): Perth-Wellington
Next Election: Oct. 2014 (4 year terms)
Steve Grose, Mayor
519-284-2340
sgrose@town.stmarys.on.ca
Robert Brindley, Chief Administrative Officer
519-284-2340
rbrindley@town.stmarys.on.ca

Schreiber

P.O. Box 40
204 Alberta St.
Schreiber, ON P0T 2S0
Tel: 807-824-2711; *Fax:* 807-824-3231
executiveassistant@schreiber.ca
www.schreiber.ca
Municipal Type: Township
Area: 36.79 sq km
County or District: Thunder Bay District; *Population in 2006:* 901
Provincial Electoral District(s): Thunder Bay-Superior North
Federal Electoral District(s): Thunder Bay-Superior North
Next Election: Oct. 2014 (4 year terms)
Don McArthur, Mayor
807-824-2711
mayor@schreiber.ca
Jon Hall, Clerk & Deputy Treasurer
807-824-2711
clerk@schreiber.ca

Scugog

P.O. Box 780
181 Perry St.
Port Perry, ON L9L 1A7
Tel: 905-985-7346; *Fax:* 905-985-9914
www.scugog.ca
Municipal Type: Township
Area: 474.63 sq km
County or District: Durham Regional Municipality; *Population in 2006:* 21,439
Provincial Electoral District(s): Durham
Federal Electoral District(s): Durham
Next Election: Oct. 2014 (4 year terms)
Chuck Mercier, Mayor
905-985-7346
mayormercier@scugog.ca
Bobbie Drew, Regional Councillor
905-985-7183
bdrew@scugog.ca
Bev Hendry, Chief Administrative Officer
905-985-7346, Fax: 905-985-9914
T. DeBruijn, Treasurer & Director, Finance
Larry Corrigan, Councillor, Ward(s): 1
905-985-7215
lcorrigan@scugog.ca
D. Gordon, Director, Community Services
John Hancock, Councillor, Ward(s): 2
905-985-8083
jhancock@scugog.ca
Jim Howard, Councillor, Ward(s): 3
905-442-0448
jhoward@scugog.ca
I. Roger, Director, Public Works & Parks
Wilma Wotten, Councillor, Ward(s): 4
905-986-4975
wwotten@scugog.ca
Richard Miller, Fire Chief
905-985-2384
Howard Danson, Councillor, Ward(s): 5
905-982-2724
hdanson@scugog.ca

Seguin

5 Humphrey Dr., RR#2
Parry Sound, ON P2A 2W8
Tel: 705-732-4300; *Fax:* 705-732-6347
info@seguin.ca
www.seguin.ca
Other Information: Toll-Free Phone: 1-877-473-4846
Municipal Type: Township
Incorporated: May 8, 1997 *Area:* 586.17 sq km
County or District: Parry Sound District; *Population in 2006:* 4,276
Provincial Electoral District(s): Parry Sound-Muskoka
Federal Electoral District(s): Parry Sound-Muskoka
Next Election: Oct. 2014 (4 year terms)
David Conn, Mayor, Fax: 705-732-2730
connd@rogers.com
Craig Jeffery, Clerk & Officer, Lottery Licensing
cjeffery@seguin.ca

Severn

P.O. Box 159
1024 Hurlwood Lane
Orillia, ON L3V 6J3
Tel: 705-325-2315; *Fax:* 705-327-5818
severn@encode.com
www.townshipofsevern.com
Municipal Type: Township
Incorporated: Jan. 1, 1994 *Area:* 534.78 sq km
County or District: Simcoe; *Population in 2006:* 12,030
Provincial Electoral District(s): Simcoe North
Federal Electoral District(s): Simcoe North
Next Election: Oct. 2014 (4 year terms)
Mike Burkett, Mayor
MBurkett@townshipofsevern.com
Henry Sander, Clerk-Treasurer & Director, Corporate Services
705-325-2315
Judith Cox, Deputy Mayor
JCox@townshipofsevern.com
Mark Taylor, Councillor, Ward(s): 1
MTaylor@townshipofsevern.com
Clayton Cameron, Director, Public Works
Jane Dunlop, Councillor, Ward(s): 2
JDunlop@townshipofsevern.com
Eric Dowell, Director, Fire & Emergency Services
Ian Crichton, Councillor, Ward(s): 3
ICrichton@townshipofsevern.com
David Parks, Director, Planning & Development
705-325-2315
James Oakley, Chief Building Official
705-325-2315
Rob Martel, Officer, Municipal Law Enforcement
Ron Stevens, Councillor, Ward(s): 4
RStevens@townshipofsevern.com
Rob Ferguson, Councillor, Ward(s): 5
RFerguson@townshipofsevern.com

Shelburne

Town of Shelburne Municipal Office
203 Main St. East
Shelburne, ON L0N 1S0
Tel: 519-925-2600; *Fax:* 519-925-6134
www.townofshelburne.on.ca
Municipal Type: Town
Incorporated: March 22, 1879 *Area:* 6.44 sq km
County or District: Dufferin; *Population in 2006:* 5,149
Provincial Electoral District(s): Dufferin-Caledon
Federal Electoral District(s): Dufferin-Caledon
Next Election: Oct. 2014 (4 year terms)
Note: Incorporated as a town on Dec. 31, 1976.
Ed Crewson, Mayor
519-925-2600, Fax: 519-925-6134

John Telfer, AMCT, Chief Administrative Officer & Town Clerk
519-925-2600
jtelfer@townofshelburne.on.ca

Shuniah
420 Leslie Ave.
Thunder Bay, ON P7A 1X8
Tel: 807-683-4545;
shuniah@shuniah.org
www.shuniah.org
Municipal Type: Township
Incorporated: 1873 *Area:* 569.18 sq km
County or District: Thunder Bay District; *Population in 2006:* 2,913
Provincial Electoral District(s): Thunder Bay-Superior North
Federal Electoral District(s): Thunder Bay-Superior North
Next Election: Oct. 2014 (4 year terms)
Maria Harding, Reeve
807-983-2276
mharding@tbaytel.net
Wendy Hamlin, Clerk
whamlin@shuniah.org

Sioux Lookout, Municipality of
P.O. Box 158
25 Fifth Ave.
Sioux Lookout, ON P8T 1A4
Tel: 807-737-2700;
admin@siouxlookout.ca
www.siouxlookout.ca
Municipal Type: Town
Incorporated: 1912 *Area:* 378.61 sq km
County or District: Kenora District; *Population in 2006:* 5,183
Provincial Electoral District(s): Kenora-Rainy River
Federal Electoral District(s): Kenora
Next Election: Oct. 2014 (4 year terms)
Dennis Leney, Mayor
dleney@siouxlookout.ca
Mary L. MacKenzie, Municipal Clerk
clerk@siouxlookout.ca

Sioux Narrows-Nestor Falls
P.O. Box 417
Sioux Narrows, ON P0X 1N0
Tel: 807-226-5241; *Fax:* 807-226-5712
www.siouxnarrows-nestorfalls.ca
Municipal Type: Township
Area: 1,221.56 sq km
County or District: Kenora District; *Population in 2006:* 672
Provincial Electoral District(s): Kenora-Rainy River
Federal Electoral District(s): Kenora
Next Election: Oct. 2014 (4 year terms)
William (Bill) Thompson, Mayor
Wanda Kabel, Chief Administrative Officer

Smith-Ennismore-Lakefield
P.O. Box 270
1310 Centre Line, RR#4
Bridgenorth, ON K0L 1H0
Tel: 705-292-9507; *Fax:* 705-292-8964
www.smithennismorelakefield.on.ca
Other Information: Toll-Free Phone: 1-877-213-7419 (in 705 area code)
Municipal Type: Township
Area: 318.77 sq km
County or District: Peterborough; *Population in 2006:* 17,413
Provincial Electoral District(s): Peterborough
Federal Electoral District(s): Peterborough
Next Election: Oct. 2014 (4 year terms)
Mary Smith, Reeve
705-652-0784
Angela Chittick, Clerk
705-292-9507
Andy Mitchell, Deputy Reeve
705-931-4873
Janice Lavalley, Chief Administrative Officer
705-292-9507
Donna Ballantyne, Councillor, Ward(s): Ennismore
705-292-7174
R. Lane Vance, Treasurer & Manager, Financial Services
705-292-9507
Anita Locke, Councillor, Ward(s): Lakefield
705-652-1086
Ed Barber, Manager, Recreation, s
705-292-9507
Sherry Senis, Councillor, Ward(s): Smith
705-657-1166
Stephen Crough, Manager, Public Works
705-292-9507
Robert Lamarre, Manager, Building & Planning
705-292-9507
Gord Jopling, Fire Chief
705-292-7282
Kim Berry, Coordinator, Human Resources
705-292-9507

Smiths Falls
77 Beckwith St. North
Smiths Falls, ON K7A 4T6
Tel: 613-283-4124;
info@smithsfalls.ca
www.smithsfalls.ca
Municipal Type: Separated for Municipal Purposes Only
Incorporated: 1854 *Area:* 8.2 sq km
County or District: Lanark; *Population in 2006:* 8,777
Provincial Electoral District(s): Lanark-Frontenac-Lennox & Addington
Federal Electoral District(s): Lanark-Frontenac-Lennox & Addington
Next Election: Oct. 2014 (4 year terms)
Note: Incorporated as a town on Jan. 1, 1883. In Dec. 1902, the Town of Smiths Falls became the Separated Town of Smiths Falls.
Dennis Staples, Mayor
613-283-4124, Fax: 613-283-4764
mayor@smithsfalls.ca
Kerry Costello, Clerk
613-283-4124
kcostello@smithsfalls.ca

Smooth Rock Falls
P.O. Box 249
142 First St.
Smooth Rock Falls, ON P0L 2B0
Tel: 705-338-2717; *Fax:* 705-338-2584
comments@townsrf.ca
www.townofsmoothrockfalls.ca
Municipal Type: Town
Incorporated: 1929 *Area:* 199.79 sq km
County or District: Cochrane District; *Population in 2006:* 1,473
Provincial Electoral District(s): Timmins-James Bay
Federal Electoral District(s): Algoma-Manitoulin-Kapuskasing
Next Election: Oct. 2014 (4 year terms)
Michel Arseneault, Mayor
Luc Denault, Chief Administrative Officer
luc.denault@townsrf.ca

South Algonquin
P.O. Box 217
Hay Creek Rd.
Whitney, ON K0J 2M0
Tel: 613-637-2650; *Fax:* 613-637-5368
southalgonquin@xplornet.com
www.township.southalgonquin.on.ca
Other Information: Toll-Free Phone: 1-888-307-3187
Municipal Type: Township
Area: 871.31 sq km
County or District: Nipissing District; *Population in 2006:* 1,253
Provincial Electoral District(s): Renfrew-Nipissing-Pembroke
Federal Electoral District(s): Renfrew-Nipissing-Pembroke
Next Election: Oct. 2014 (4 year terms)
Jane A.E. Dumas, Mayor
613-637-5261
mayor.tsa@xplornet.ca
Harold Luckasavitch, Clerk-Treasurer
613-637-2650, Fax: 613-637-5368

South Bruce
P.O. Box 540
21 Gordon St. East
Teeswater, ON N0G 2S0
Tel: 519-392-6623; *Fax:* 519-392-6266
clerk@town.southbruce.on.ca
www.town.southbruce.on.ca
Municipal Type: Municipality
Incorporated: 1999 *Area:* 487.17 sq km
County or District: Bruce; *Population in 2006:* 5,939
Provincial Electoral District(s): Huron-Bruce
Federal Electoral District(s): Huron-Bruce
Next Election: Oct. 2014 (4 year terms)
Note: Amalgamation of the Village of Mildmay, the Township of Carrick, the Village of Teeswater, & the Township of Culross.
William Goetz, Mayor
519-367-5509
Sharon Chambers, Chief Administrative Officer & Clerk
519-392-6623

South Bruce Peninsula
P.O. Box 310
315 George St.
Wiarton, ON N0H 2T0
Tel: 519-534-1400; *Fax:* 519-534-4862
admin@southbrucepeninsula.com
www.southbrucepeninsula.com
Other Information: Toll-Free Phone: 1-877-534-1400
Municipal Type: Town
Area: 531.9 sq km
County or District: Bruce; *Population in 2006:* 8,415
Provincial Electoral District(s): Bruce-Grey-Owen Sound
Federal Electoral District(s): Bruce-Grey-Owen Sound
Next Election: Oct. 2014 (4 year terms)
John D. Close, B.SC.(Agri), Mayor
519-534-1589
John.Close@southbrucepeninsula.com
Angie Cathrae, Clerk
519-534-1400
sbpen@bmts.com

South Dundas
P.O. Box 160
4296 County Rd. 31
Williamsburg, ON K0C 2H0
Tel: 613-535-2673; *Fax:* 613-535-2099
mail@southdundas.com
www.southdundas.com
Other Information: Toll-Free Phone: 1-800-265-0619
Municipal Type: Township
Area: 519.98 sq km
County or District: Stormont, Dundas & Glengarry; *Population in 2006:* 10,535
Provincial Electoral District(s): Stormont-Dundas-South Glengarry
Federal Electoral District(s): Stormont-Dundas-South Glengarry
Next Election: Oct. 2014 (4 year terms)
Steven J. Byvelds, Mayor, Fax: 613-535-2746
mayor@southdundas.com
Brenda M. Brunt, Clerk
bbrunt@southdundas.com
Jim Locke, Deputy Mayor, Fax: 613-652-2233
jp.locke@hotmail.com
Stephen McDonald, Chief Administrative Officer
smcdonald@southdundas.com
Evonne Delegarde, Councillor
evonne_delegarde@hotmail.com
Shannon Geraghty, Treasurer
sgeraghty@southdundas.com
Archie L. Mellan, Councillor
amellan@ripnet.com
Hugh Garlough, Manager, Public Works
hgarlough@southdundas.com
Jim Graham, Councillor
jwg60@xplornet.com
Don J.W. Lewis, Manager, Planning & Enforcement
dlewis@southdundas.com
Don W. Lewis, Manager, Recreation
arena@southdundas.com
Chris McDonough, Fire Chief
cmcdonough@southdundas.com

South Frontenac
P.O. Box 100
4432 George St.
Sydenham, ON K0H 2T0
Tel: 613-376-3027; *Fax:* 613-376-6657
admin@township.southfrontenac.on.ca
www.township.southfrontenac.on.ca
Other Information: Toll-Free Phone: 1-800-559-5862
Municipal Type: Township
Incorporated: Jan. 1, 1998 *Area:* 941.28 sq km
County or District: Frontenac; *Population in 2006:* 18,227
Provincial Electoral District(s): Lanark-Frontenac-Lennox & Addington
Federal Electoral District(s): Lanark-Frontenac-Lennox & Addington
Next Election: Oct. 2014 (4 year terms)
Gary Davison, Mayor
613-376-3027, Fax: 613-376-6657
davison4544@yahoo.ca
Wayne Orr, Chief Administrative Officer
613-376-3027
worr@township.southfrontenac.on.ca
Del Stowe, Councillor, Ward(s): Bedford
delstowe@yahoo.com
Deborah Bracken, Treasurer
613-376-3027
dbracken@township.southfrontenac.on.ca
Mark Tinlin, Councillor, Ward(s): Bedford
marktinlin@rideau.net

Mark Segsworth, Manager, Public Works
613-376-3027
msegsworth@township.southfrontenac.on.ca
Allan G. McPhail, Councillor, Ward(s): Loughborough
mcphail@queensu.ca
Lindsay Mills, Coordinator, Planning
613-376-3027
lmills@township.southfrontenac.on.ca
Ron W. Vandewal, Councillor, Ward(s): Loughborough
lakevalley@kos.net
Rick Chesebrough, Fire Chief
613-376-3027
rchesebrough@township.southfrontenac.on.ca
John R. McDougall, Councillor, Ward(s): Portland
john.mcdougall@xplornet.ca
Alan Revill, Chief Building Inspector
613-376-3027
arevill@township.southfrontenac.on.ca
Bill W.L. Robinson, Councillor, Ward(s): Portland
wlrobinson@bell.net
Cam L. Naish, Councillor, Ward(s): Storrington
camnaish@kingston.net
Larry W. York, Councillor, Ward(s): Storrington
blue@reztel.net

South Glengarry
6 Oak St.
Lancaster, ON K0C 1N0
Tel: 613-347-1166;
info@southglengarry.com
www.southglengarry.com
Municipal Type: Township
Incorporated: Jan. 1, 1998 *Area:* 604.91 sq km
County or District: Stormont, Dundas & Glengarry; *Population in 2006:* 12,880
Provincial Electoral District(s): Stormont-Dundas-South Glengarry
Federal Electoral District(s): Stormont-Dundas-South Glengarry
Next Election: Oct. 2014 (4 year terms)
Jim McDonell, Mayor, Fax: 613-347-3411
jim.mcdonell@bell.net
Marilyn Lebrun, Clerk
613-347-1166, Fax: 613-347-3411
marilyn@southglengarry.com
Ian McLeod, Deputy Mayor
613-933-5602, Fax: 613-933-2620
ian.mcleod@genivar.com
Derik Brandt, Chief Administrative Officer
613-347-1166, Fax: 613-347-3411
derik@southglengarry.com
Trevor Bougie, Councillor
tx_bougie@laurentian.ca
Michel J. Samson, Treasurer & Deputy Clerk
613-347-1166, Fax: 613-347-3411
mike@southglengarry.com
Joyce Gravelle, Councillor
joyceg50@bell.net
Joanne Haley, General Manager, Community Services
613-347-1166, Fax: 613-347-3411
jhaley@southglengarry.com
Bill McKenzie, Councillor
613-347-3254, Fax: 613-347-3119
Ewen MacDonald, General Manager, Infrastructure Services
613-347-2040, Fax: 613-347-3411
ewen@southglengarry.com
Dwane Crawford, Director, Development
613-347-1166, Fax: 613-347-3411
dwane@southglengarry.com
Shawn Killoran, Director, Water & Wastewater
613-931-3036
shawnkilloran@on.aibn.com
Roger Lapierre, Director, Roads
613-930-3445, Fax: 613-347-3411
roger.southglengarry@bellnet.ca
Gary Poupart, Manager, Property Standards & Enforcement
613-347-1166, Fax: 613-347-3411
gary@southglengarry.com

South Huron
P.O. Box 759
322 Main St. South
Exeter, ON N0M 1S6
Tel: 519-235-0310; *Fax:* 519-235-3304
info@southhuron.ca
www.southhuron.ca
Other Information: Toll-Free: 1-877-204-0747
Municipal Type: Municipality
Incorporated: 2001 *Area:* 425.35 sq km
County or District: Huron; *Population in 2006:* 9,982
Provincial Electoral District(s): Huron-Bruce
Federal Electoral District(s): Huron-Bruce
Next Election: Oct. 2014 (4 year terms)
George Robertson, Mayor
519-235-2030
g.robertson@southhuron.ca
Michael Di Lullo, Clerk & Manager, Corporate Services
519-235-0310
m.dilullo@southhuron.ca

South River
P.O. Box 310
63 Marie St.
South River, ON P0A 1X0
Tel: 705-386-2573;
info@southriverontario.com
www.southriverontario.com
Other Information: Public Works, Phone: 705-386-0245
Municipal Type: Village
Incorporated: 1907 *Area:* 4.04 sq km
County or District: Parry Sound District; *Population in 2006:* 1,069
Provincial Electoral District(s): Parry Sound-Muskoka
Federal Electoral District(s): Parry Sound-Muskoka
Next Election: Oct. 2014 (4 year terms)
Jim Coleman, Mayor
Susan Arnold, Administrator & Clerk

South Stormont
P.O. Box 84
2 Mille Roches Rd.
Long Sault, ON K0C 1P0
Tel: 613-534-8889; *Fax:* 613-534-2280
info@southstormont.ca
www.southstormont.ca
Other Information: Toll-Free Phone: 1-800-265-3915
Municipal Type: Township
Area: 447.46 sq km
County or District: Stormont, Dundas & Glengarry; *Population in 2006:* 12,520
Provincial Electoral District(s): Stormont-Dundas-South Glengarry
Federal Electoral District(s): Stormont-Dundas-South Glengarry
Next Election: Oct. 2014 (4 year terms)
Bryan McGillis, Mayor
613-577-0753, Fax: 613-937-3116
mayor@southstormont.ca
Betty de Haan, Chief Administrative Officer & Clerk
613-534-8889
betty@southstormont.ca
Tammy Hart, Deputy Mayor
613-984-2543
tammy.farms@xplornet.com
Johanna Barkley, Treasurer
613-534-8889
johanna@southstormont.ca
Barry Brownlee, Councillor
613-537-9753
Dan Pilon, Manager, Public Works
613-534-8889
dan@southstormont.ca
Richard F. Waldroff, Councillor
613-537-8226, Fax: 613-362-7596
rwaldroff@bell.net
Hilton Cryderman, Manager, Building & Development
613-534-8889
hilton@southstormont.ca
Cindy Woods, Councillor
613-537-2977
cindy_woods@xplornet.com
Roger Desjardins, Fire Chief
613-534-8889
roger@southstormont.ca
Harry Hutchinson, Deputy Chief Building Official & Superintendent, Drainage
613-534-8889
buildinginspector@southstormont.ca
Gord Ramsay, Officer, Law Enforcement
613-534-8889
bylawofficer@southstormont.ca

South-West Oxford
312915 Dereham Line
Mount Elgin, ON N0J 1N0
Tel: 519-485-0477; *Fax:* 519-485-2932
dbarnes@swox.org (Office)
www.swox.org
Other Information: Phone, Works Department: 519-877-2702
Municipal Type: Township
Area: 370.63 sq km
County or District: Oxford; *Population in 2006:* 7,589
Provincial Electoral District(s): Oxford
Federal Electoral District(s): Oxford
Next Election: Oct. 2014 (4 year terms)
David Mayberry, Mayor
519-485-3642
mayor@swox.org
Mary Ellen Greb, Chief Administrative Officer
519-877-2702
cao@swox.org

Southgate
185667 Grey Rd. 9, RR#1
Dundalk, ON N0C 1B0
Tel: 519-923-2110; *Fax:* 519-923-9262
info@town.southgate.on.ca
www.town.southgate.on.ca
Other Information: Toll-Free Phone: 1-888-560-6607
Municipal Type: Township
Incorporated: Jan. 1, 2001 *Area:* 643.95 sq km
County or District: Grey; *Population in 2006:* 7,167
Provincial Electoral District(s): Bruce-Grey-Owen Sound
Federal Electoral District(s): Bruce-Grey-Owen Sound
Next Election: Oct. 2014 (4 year terms)
Note: Amalgamation of the Village of Dundalk, the Township of Proton & the Township of Egremont.
Brian A. Milne, Mayor
519-334-3712, Fax: 519-334-9836
brian.milne@grey.ca
Carol Watson, Clerk
519-923-9262
cwatson@town.southgate.on.ca

Southwest Middlesex, Municipality of
P.O. Box 218
153 McKellar St.
Glencoe, ON N0L 1M0
Tel: 519-287-2015; *Fax:* 519-287-2359
info@southwestmiddlesex.ca
www.southwestmiddlesex.ca
Municipal Type: Township
Incorporated: Jan. 1, 2001 *Area:* 427.92 sq km
County or District: Middlesex; *Population in 2006:* 5,890
Provincial Electoral District(s): Lambton-Kent-Middlesex
Federal Electoral District(s): Lambton-Kent-Middlesex
Next Election: Oct. 2014 (4 year terms)
Note: Amalgamation of the Villages of Glencoe & Wardsville & the Townships of Ekfrid & Mosa.
Doug Reycraft, Mayor
519-287-2015, Fax: 519-287-2359
dreycraft@southwestmiddlesex.ca
Janneke Newitt, Administrator & Clerk
519-287-2015
jnewitt@southwestmiddlesex.ca

Southwold
General Delivery
35663 Fingal Line
Fingal, ON N0L 1K0
Tel: 519-769-2010; *Fax:* 519-769-2837
southwold@twp.southwold.on.ca
www.twp.southwold.on.ca
Municipal Type: Township
Area: 301.71 sq km
County or District: Elgin; *Population in 2006:* 4,724
Provincial Electoral District(s): Elgin-Middlesex-London
Federal Electoral District(s): Elgin-Middlesex-London
Next Election: Oct. 2014 (4 year terms)
James McIntyre, Mayor
519-764-9764
Donna Ethier, Chief Administrative Officer, Clerk, & Deputy Treasurer
cao@twp.southwold.on.ca

Spanish
P.O. Box 70
8 Trunk Rd.
Spanish, ON P0P 2A0
Tel: 705-844-2300; *Fax:* 705-844-2622
info@town.spanish.on.ca
www.town.spanish.on.ca
Municipal Type: Town
Area: 106.02 sq km
County or District: Algoma District; *Population in 2006:* 728
Provincial Electoral District(s): Algoma-Manitoulin
Federal Electoral District(s): Algoma-Manitoulin-Kapuskasing
Next Election: Oct. 2014 (4 year terms)
Note: Formerly the Township of Shedden. Effective Oct. 1, 2004, the name was changed to the Town of Spanish.
Gary Bishop, Mayor
Brent St. Denis, Chief Administrative Officer & Clerk-Treasurer
brent.st.denis@ontera.net

Springwater
Township of Springwater Administrative Ctr.
2231 Nursery Rd.
Minesing, ON L0L 1Y2
Tel: 705-728-4784; *Fax:* 705-728-6957
info@springwater.ca; council@springwater.ca
www.springwater.ca
Municipal Type: Township
Incorporated: Jan. 1, 1994 *Area:* 536.3 sq km
County or District: Simcoe; *Population in 2006:* 17,456
Provincial Electoral District(s): Simcoe-Grey
Federal Electoral District(s): Simcoe-Grey
Next Election: Oct. 2014 (4 year terms)
Linda Collins, Mayor
705-728-4784, Fax: 705-728-6957
linda.collins@springwater.ca
John Daly, Clerk & Director, Corporate Services
705-728-4784, Fax: 705-728-6957
Dan McLean, Deputy Mayor
705-728-4784, Fax: 705-728-6957
dan.mclean@springwater.ca
Winanne Grant, Chief Administrative Officer
705-728-4784, Fax: 705-728-6957
Dan Clement, Councillor, Ward(s): 1
705-728-4784, Fax: 705-728-6957
dan.clement@springwater.ca
Laurie Kennard, CA, Treasurer & Director, Finance
705-728-4784
finance@springwater.ca
Perry Ritchie, Councillor, Ward(s): 2
705-728-4784, Fax: 705-728-6957
perry.ritchie@springwater.ca
Ron Belcourt, Director, Recreation Services
705-728-4784
recreation@springwater.ca
Rick Webster, Councillor, Ward(s): 3
705-728-4784, Fax: 705-728-6957
rick.webster@springwater.ca
Brad Sokach, Director, Public Works
705-728-4784
publicworks@springwater.ca
Sandy McConkey, Councillor, Ward(s): 4
705-728-4784, Fax: 705-737-4729
sandy.mcconkey@springwater.ca
Jack Hanna, Councillor, Ward(s): 5
705-728-4784, Fax: 705-728-6957
jack.hanna@springwater.ca
Tony Van Dam, Director, Fire & Emergency Services
705-728-4784, Fax: 705-726-7223
fire@springwater.ca
Nick Ippolito, Chief Building Official
705-728-4784, Fax: 705-728-2759
building@springwater.ca
Barb Fralick, Manager, Human Resources
705-728-4784, Fax: 705-728-6957
Jennett Mays, Coordinator, Communications
705-728-4784, Fax: 705-728-6957
jennett.mays@springwater.ca
Brent Spagnol, Planner
705-728-4784, Fax: 705-728-6957
planning@springwater.ca

St.-Charles, Municipality of
P.O. Box 70
2 King St. East
St Charles, ON P0M 2W0
Tel: 705-867-2032; *Fax:* 705-867-5789
cta@stcharlesontario.ca; tourism@stcharlesontario.ca
www.stcharlesontario.ca
Other Information: Toll-Free Phone: 1-877-867-2032
Municipal Type: Town
Area: 318.47 sq km
County or District: Sudbury District; *Population in 2006:* 1,159
Provincial Electoral District(s): Timiskaming-Cochrane
Federal Electoral District(s): Nickel Belt
Next Election: Oct. 2014 (4 year terms)
Paul Schoppman, Mayor
mayor@stcharlesontario.ca
Theresa Niemi, Clerk-Treasurer & Administrator

Stirling-Rawdon
P.O. Box 40
14 Demorest Rd.
Stirling, ON K0K 3E0
Tel: 613-395-3380; *Fax:* 613-395-0864
info@stirling-rawdon.com
www.stirling-rawdon.com
Municipal Type: Township
Area: 280.63 sq km
County or District: Hastings; *Population in 2006:* 4,906
Provincial Electoral District(s): Prince Edward-Hastings
Federal Electoral District(s): Prince Edward-Hastings
Next Election: Oct. 2014 (4 year terms)
Rodney Cooney, Mayor
613-395-3947
Kevin Heath, Clerk-Administrator
cao@stirling-rawdon.com

Stone Mills
4504 County Rd. 4
Centreville, ON K0K 1N0
Tel: 613-378-2475; *Fax:* 613-378-0033
caoclerk@stonemills.com
www.stonemills.com
Municipal Type: Township
Incorporated: Jan. 1, 1998 *Area:* 688.28 sq km
County or District: Lennox-Addington; *Population in 2006:* 7,568
Provincial Electoral District(s): Lanark-Frontenac-Lennox & Addington
Federal Electoral District(s): Lanark-Frontenac-Lennox & Addington
Next Election: Oct. 2014 (4 year terms)
Note: Amalgamation of the former Township of Camden East, Township of Sheffield & Village of Newburgh.
Douglas Bearance, Reeve
613-375-8874
bearance@frontenac.net
Darlene Plumley, Chief Administrative Officer & Municipal Clerk
613-378-2475
caoclerk@stonemills.com

Stormont, Dundas & Glengarry
26 Pitt St.
Cornwall, ON K6J 3P2
Tel: 613-932-1515; *Fax:* 613-936-2913
info@sdgcounties.ca
www.sdgcounties.ca
Other Information: Toll-Free Phone: 1-800-267-7158
Municipal Type: United County
Area: 3,306.86 sq km
Population in 2006: 110,399
Next Election: Oct. 2014 (4 year terms)
Eric Duncan, Mayor, Ward(s): North Dundas
eduncan2@gmail.com
Gerry Boyce, Deputy Mayor, Ward(s): North Dundas
glboyce@hotmail.com
Helen Thomson, Clerk
Grant Crack, Mayor, Ward(s): North Glengarry
613-525-1110
grantcrack@northglengarry.ca
Chris McDonell, Deputy Mayor, Ward(s): North Glengarry
cy.mcdonell@sympatico.ca
Tim J. Simpson, Chief Administrative Officer
Vanessa Bennett, Treasurer
Denis Fife, Mayor, Ward(s): North Stormont
613-984-2059
fifeag@plantpioneer.com
Bill McGimpsey, Deputy Mayor, Ward(s): North Stormont
mcgimpsey@ontarioeast.net
Benjamin deHaan, P.Emg., County Engineer
Steven Byvelds, Warden & Mayor, Ward(s): South Dundas
mayor@southdundas.com
James Locke, Deputy Mayor, Ward(s): South Dundas
jp.locke@hotmail.com
Michael Otis, County Planner
Jim McDonell, Mayor, Ward(s): South Glengarry
jim.mcdonell@bell.net
Ian McLeod, Deputy Mayor, Ward(s): South Glengarry
613-933-5602
ian.mcleod@genivar.com
Bryan McGillis, Mayor, Ward(s): South Stormont
mayor@southstormont.ca
Tammy Hart, Deputy Mayor, Ward(s): South Stormont
tammy.farms@xplornet.com

Strathroy-Caradoc
52 Frank St.
Strathroy, ON N7G 2R4
Tel: 519-245-1070; *Fax:* 519-245-6353
general@strathroy-caradoc.ca
www.strathroy-caradoc.ca
Municipal Type: Township
Incorporated: 2001 *Area:* 274.19 sq km
County or District: Middlesex; *Population in 2006:* 19,977
Provincial Electoral District(s): Lambton-Kent-Middlesex
Federal Electoral District(s): Lambton-Kent-Middlesex
Next Election: Oct. 2014 (4 year terms)
Note: Amalgamation of the Town of Strathroy & the Township of Caradoc.
Joanne Vanderheyden, Mayor
519-245-1105, Fax: 519-245-6353
jvanderheyden@strathroy-caradoc.ca
Angela Toth, Clerk & Director, Corporate Services
519-245-1105, Fax: 224- -
atoth@strathroy-caradoc.ca
Brad Richards, Deputy Mayor
519-245-1105, Fax: 519-245-6353
brichards@strathroy-caradoc.ca
Marie Baker, Councillor, Ward(s): 1 - Strathroy
519-245-8696, Fax: 519-245-0076
mbaker@strathroy-caradoc.caadoc.ca
Jane McPherson, Treasurer & Director, Financial Services
519-245-1105, Fax: 519-245-2177
jmcpherson@strathroy-caradoc.ca
John G. Brennan, Councillor, Ward(s): 1 - Strathroy
519-245-2680
jbrennan@strathroy-caradoc.ca
Steve Pelkman, Councillor, Ward(s): 1 - Strathroy
519-245-5277
spelkman@strathroy-caradoc.ca
Tim Hanna, Director, Recreation & Leisure Services
519-245-1105, Fax: 519-245-9534
thanna@strathroy-caradoc.ca
Dave Cameron, Councillor, Ward(s): 1 - Strathroy
dcameron@strathroy-caradoc.ca
Tom Gibson, Director, Fire Services & Fire Chief
519-245-1990
tgibson@strathroy-caradoc.ca
Mark Harris, Director, Environmental Services
519-245-2010
mharris@strathroy-caradoc.ca
Matthew Stephenson, Director, Building & Waste Services
519-245-1105
mstephenson@strathroy-caradoc.ca
Steve Dausett, Councillor, Ward(s): 2 - Caradoc
519-246-1900
sdausett@strathroy-caradoc.ca
Brad Dausett, Manager, Roads
519-245-1105, Fax: 519-245-6353
bdausett@strathroy-caradoc.ca
Andrew Meyer, Manager, Community Development
519-245-0492, Fax: 519-245-1073
agmeyer@strathroymuseum.ca
Larry Cowan, Councillor, Ward(s): 2 - Caradoc
lcowan@strathroy-caradoc.ca
Paul Hicks, Planner
519-245-1105, Fax: 519-245-6353
phicks@strathroy-caradoc.ca
Neil Flegel, Councillor, Ward(s): 2 - Caradoc
nflegel@strathroy-caradoc.ca
Leslie Pommer, Coordinator, Customer Services & Concession
519-245-7557
lpommer@strathroy-caradoc.ca

Strong
P.O. Box 1120
28 Municipal Lane
Sundridge, ON P0A 1Z0
Tel: 705-384-5819; *Fax:* 705-384-5892
www.strongtownship.com
Municipal Type: Township
Area: 158.73 sq km
County or District: Parry Sound District; *Population in 2006:* 1,327
Provincial Electoral District(s): Parry Sound-Muskoka
Federal Electoral District(s): Parry Sound-Muskoka
Next Election: Oct. 2014 (4 year terms)
Christine Ellis, Mayor
705-384-5243
Linda Maurer, Clerk & Treausurer
705-384-5819

Sudbury District
c/o Manitoulin-Sudbury District Services Bd
210 Mead Blvd.
Espanola, ON P5E 1R9
www.msdsb.net
Municipal Type: District
Area: 38,504.53 sq km
Population in 2006: 21,392
Provincial Electoral District(s): Algoma-Manitoulin; Nickel Belt
Federal Electoral District(s): Nickel Belt; Algoma-Manitoulin-Kapuskasing
Les Gamble, Board Chair, Manitoulin-Sudbury District Services Board
705-865-2646
lgamble@msdsb.nett
Fern Dominelli, Chief Administrative Officer, Manitoulin-Sudbury District Svs Bd
705-862-7850, Fax: 705-862-7866
fern.dominelli@msdsb.net; cao@msdsb.net

Sundridge
P.O. Box 129
110 Main St.
Sundridge, ON P0A 1Z0
Tel: 705-384-5316; *Fax:* 705-384-7874
villageoffice@sundridge.ca
www.sundridge.ca
Municipal Type: Village
Incorporated: 1889 *Area:* 2.23 sq km
County or District: Parry Sound District; *Population in 2006:* 942
Provincial Electoral District(s): Parry Sound-Muskoka
Federal Electoral District(s): Parry Sound-Muskoka
Next Election: Oct. 2014 (4 year terms)
Elgin Schneider, Mayor
705-384-5883
elgin28@sympatico.ca
Lillian S. Fowler, Chief Administrative Officer & Clerk
705-384-5316

Tarbutt & Tarbutt Additional
27 Barr Rd. South
Desbarats, ON P0R 1E0
Tel: 705-782-6776; *Fax:* 705-782-4274
tarbutttownship@bellnet.ca
www.tarbutttownship.com
Municipal Type: Township
Incorporated: 1889 *Area:* 52.82 sq km
County or District: Algoma District; *Population in 2006:* 388
Provincial Electoral District(s): Algoma-Manitoulin
Federal Electoral District(s): Sault Ste Marie
Next Election: Oct. 2014 (4 year terms)
Ken Richie, Mayor
705-782-4386
Glenn Martin, Clerk-Treasurer

Tay
P.O. Box 100
450 Park St.
Victoria Harbour, ON L0K 2A0
Tel: 705-534-7248; *Fax:* 705-534-4493
taytownship@tay.ca
www.tay.ca
Municipal Type: Township
Area: 138.93 sq km
County or District: Simcoe; *Population in 2006:* 9,748
Provincial Electoral District(s): Simcoe North
Federal Electoral District(s): Simcoe North
Next Election: Oct. 2014 (4 year terms)
Scott Warnock, Mayor
swarnock@tay.ca
Alison Thomas, Clerk
795-534-7248
athomas@tay.ca

Tay Valley
217 Harper Rd., RR#4
Perth, ON K7H 3C6
Tel: 613-267-5353; *Fax:* 613-264-8516
cao@tayvalleytwp.ca; treasurer@tayvalleytwp.ca
www.tayvalleytwp.ca
Other Information: Toll-Free Phone: 1-800-810-0161
Municipal Type: Township
Area: 527.46 sq km
County or District: Lanark; *Population in 2006:* 5,634
Provincial Electoral District(s): Lanark-Frontenac-Lennox & Addington
Federal Electoral District(s): Lanark-Frontenac-Lennox & Addington
Next Election: Oct. 2014 (4 year terms)
Note: Formerly the Township of Bathurst Burgess Sherbrooke.
Keith Kerr, Reeve
613-267-4025
Amanda Mabo, Clerk & Returning Officer
613-267-5353
clerk@tayvalleytwp.ca

Tehkummah
Municipal Building
456 Hwy. 542A
Tehkummah, ON P0P 2C0
Tel: 705-859-3293; *Fax:* 705-859-2605
www.manitoulin-island.com/tehkummah/
Municipal Type: Township
Incorporated: 1881 *Area:* 132.48 sq km
County or District: Manitoulin District; *Population in 2006:* 382
Provincial Electoral District(s): Algoma-Manitoulin
Federal Electoral District(s): Algoma-Manitoulin-Kapuskasing
Next Election: Oct. 2014 (4 year terms)
Gary Brown, Reeve

Temagami
P.O. Box 220
Temagami, ON P0H 2H0
Tel: 705-569-3421; *Fax:* 705-569-2834
visit@temagami.ca; finance@temagami.ca
www.temagami.ca
Other Information: E-mail, Public Works: publicworks@temagami.ca
Municipal Type: Municipality
Incorporated: Jan. 1, 1998 *Area:* 1,906.42 sq km
County or District: Nipissing District; *Population in 2006:* 934
Provincial Electoral District(s): Timiskaming-Cochrane
Federal Electoral District(s): Nipissing-Timiskaming
Next Election: Oct. 2014 (4 year terms)
John Hodgson, Mayor
mayor@temagami.ca
Elaine Gunnell, Municipal Clerk
705-569-3421
clerk@temagami.ca

Terrace Bay
P.O. Box 40
1 Selkirk Ave.
Terrace Bay, ON P0T 2W0
Tel: 807-825-3315; *Fax:* 807-825-9576
info@terracebay.ca
www.terracebay.ca
Municipal Type: Township
Incorporated: Sept. 1, 1947 *Area:* 151.04 sq km
County or District: Thunder Bay District; *Population in 2006:* 1,625
Provincial Electoral District(s): Thunder Bay-Superior North
Federal Electoral District(s): Thunder Bay-Superior North
Next Election: Oct. 2014 (4 year terms)
Note: Incorporated as a municipality on July 1, 1959.
Michael King, Mayor
807-825-3501
m.king@terracebay.ca
Carmelo Notarbartolo, Chief Administrative Officer
807-825-3315
cao@terracebay.ca

Thames Centre
4305 Hamilton Rd.
Dorchester, ON N0L 1G3
Tel: 519-268-7334; *Fax:* 519-268-3928
inquiries@thamescentre.on.ca
www.thamescentre.on.ca
Other Information: Toll-Free Phone: 1-866-425-7306
Municipal Type: Municipality
Incorporated: Jan. 1, 2001 *Area:* 433.8 sq km
County or District: Middlesex; *Population in 2006:* 13,085
Provincial Electoral District(s): Elgin-Middlesex-London
Federal Electoral District(s): Elgin-Middlesex-London
Next Election: Oct. 2014 (4 year terms)
Note: Amalgamation of the former Township of West Nissouri & the Township of North Dorchester.
Jim Maudsley, Mayor
jmaudsley@thamescentre.on.ca
Marcel Meyer, Deputy Mayor
mmeyer@thamescentre.on.ca
Mike Bontje, Councillor, Ward(s): 1
mbontje@thamescentre.on.ca
Chris Patterson, Councillor, Ward(s): 2
cpatterson@thamescentre.on.ca
Angelo Suffoletta, Councillor, Ward(s): 3
asuffoletta@thamescentre.on.ca
Margaret Lewis, Clerk & Manager, Cemetery
519-268-7334, Fax: 519-268-3928
mlewis@thamescentre.on.ca
Greg Borduas, Chief Administrative Officer
519-268-7334, Fax: 519-268-3928
gborduas@thamescentre.on.ca
John Cummings, Treasurer & Director, Financial Services
519-268-7334, Fax: 519-268-3928
jcummings@thamescentre.on.ca
Eric Boere, Director, Environmental Services
519-268-7334, Fax: 519-268-3928
eboere@thamescentre.on.ca
Stewart Findlater, Director, Community Services & Development
519-268-7334, Fax: 519-268-3928
sfindlater@thamescentre.on.ca
Randy Kalan, Fire Chief
519-268-7334
rkalan@thamescentre.on.ca
Dave Murray, Chief Building Official
519-268-7334, Fax: 519-268-3928
dmurray@thamescentre.on.ca
Dave Armstrong, Manager, Information Systems
519-268-7334, Fax: 519-268-3928
darmstrong@thamescentre.on.ca
Matt Jenner, Manager, Roads
519-268-7982
mjenner@thamescentre.on.ca
Liz Murray, Manager, Recreation & Facilities
519-268-7334, Fax: 519-268-3928
lizmurray@thamescentre.on.ca
Jarrod Craven, Superintendent, Environmental Services
519-268-7334, Fax: 519-268-3928
jcraven@thamescentre.on.ca
Dennis Shand, Superintendent, Drainage
519-268-7334, Fax: 519-268-3928
dshand@thamescentre.on.ca

The Archipelago
9 James St.
Parry Sound, ON P2A 1T4
Tel: 705-746-4243; *Fax:* 705-746-7301
www.thearchipelago.on.ca
Municipal Type: Township
Incorporated: April 1, 1980 *Area:* 602.3 sq km
County or District: Parry Sound District; *Population in 2006:* 576
Provincial Electoral District(s): Parry Sound-Muskoka
Federal Electoral District(s): Parry Sound-Muskoka
Next Election: Oct. 2014 (4 year terms)
Note: Amalgamation of the Township of Georgian Bay South Archipelago & the Township of Georgian Bay North Archipelago.
Peter Ketchum, Reeve
416-944-1116
peter.ketchum@sympatico.ca
Stephen Kaegi, Chief Administrative Officer & Clerk
705-746-4243
skaegi@thearchipelago.on.ca

The Blue Mountains
P.O. Box 310
32 Mill St.
Thornbury, ON N0H 2P0
Tel: 519-599-3131; *Fax:* 519-599-7723
info@town.thebluemountains.on.ca
www.thebluemountains.ca
Other Information: Toll-Free Phone: 1-888-258-6867
Municipal Type: Town
Incorporated: Jan. 1, 2001 *Area:* 286.78 sq km
County or District: Grey; *Population in 2006:* 6,825
Provincial Electoral District(s): Simcoe-Grey
Federal Electoral District(s): Simcoe-Grey
Next Election: Oct. 2014 (4 year terms)
Note: Amalgamation of Collingwood & Thornbury.
Ellen Anderson, Mayor
519-599-3131
mayor@thebluemountains.ca
Corrina Giles, Town Clerk
519-599-3131
cgiles@thebluemountains.ca

The Nation
958 Rte. 500 West
Casselman, ON K0A 1M0
Tel: 613-764-5444; *Fax:* 613-764-3310
mmccuaig@nationmun.ca
www.nationmun.ca
Other Information: Toll-Free Phone: 1-800-475-2855
Municipal Type: Municipality
Incorporated: Jan. 1, 1998 *Area:* 657.16 sq km
County or District: Prescott & Russell; *Population in 2006:* 10,643
Provincial Electoral District(s): Glengarry-Prescott-Russell
Federal Electoral District(s): Glengarry-Prescott-Russell
Next Election: Oct. 2014 (4 year terms)
Note: Amalgamation of the Townships of Cambridge, South Plantagenet, Caledonia & the Village of St. Isidore.
François St. Amour, Mayor
fstamour@nationmun.ca
Raymond Lalande, Councillor, Ward(s): 1
613-673-1013
raylalande@nationmun.ca
Marcel Legault, Councillor, Ward(s): 2
613-524-2873
mlegault@nationmun.ca
Danika Bourgeois-Desnoyers, Councillor, Ward(s): 3
dbourgeoisdesnoyers@nationmun.ca
Richard Legault, Councillor, Ward(s): 4
613-443-3000
rlegault@nationmun.ca
Mary J. McCuaig, Chief Administrative Officer & Clerk
613-764-5444, Fax: 613-764-3310
mmccuaig@nationmun.ca
Cécile Lortie, Treasurer
613-764-5444, Fax: 613-764-3310
clortie@nationmun.ca

Marc Legault, Director, Public Works
613-524-2932, Fax: 613-524-1140
marclegault@nationmun.ca
Carol Ann Scott, Director, Recreation
613-524-2529
cscott@nationmun.ca
Todd Bayly, Chief Building Official
613-764-5444, Fax: 613-764-3310
tbayly@nationmun.ca
Jocelyn Ferguson, Manager, LAN
613-764-5444, Fax: 613-764-3310
webmaster@nationmun.ca
Guylain Laflèche, Municipal Planner
613-764-5444, Fax: 613-764-3310
glafleche@nationmun.ca
Yves Roy, Senior Officer, Municipal Law Enforcement Officer
613-524-2932
yvesroy@nationmun.ca
Roger Parent, Coordinator, Landfill Sites
613-524-2932, Fax: 613-524-1140
Doug Renaud, Senior Technician, Water & Sewers
613-524-2740, Fax: 613-524-5379
drenaud@nationmun.ca

The North Shore

P.O. Box 108
1385 Hwy. 17 West
Algoma Mills, ON P0R 1A0
Tel: 705-849-2213; *Fax:* 705-849-2428
www.townshipofthenorthshore.ca
Municipal Type: Township
Incorporated: March 1, 1973 *Area:* 230.79 sq km
County or District: Algoma District; *Population in 2006:* 549
Provincial Electoral District(s): Algoma-Manitoulin
Federal Electoral District(s): Algoma-Manitoulin-Kapuskasing
Next Election: Oct. 2014 (4 year terms)
Note: Incorporated as a township on Dec. 1, 1978.
Randi Condie, Mayor
705-849-2489
mayor.northshore@ontera.net
Brenda Green, Clerk
bgreen@ontera.net

Thessalon

P.O. Box 220
169 Main St.
Thessalon, ON P0R 1L0
Tel: 705-842-2217; *Fax:* 705-842-2572
townthess@bellnet.ca
townthessalon.ca
Municipal Type: Town
Area: 4.37 sq km
County or District: Algoma District; *Population in 2006:* 1,312
Provincial Electoral District(s): Algoma-Manitoulin
Federal Electoral District(s): Algoma-Manitoulin-Kapuskasing
Next Election: Oct. 2014 (4 year terms)
Brent Rankin, Mayor
Robert P. MacLean, Clerk-Treasurer

Thornloe

P.O. Box 30
Main St.
Thornloe, ON P0J 1S0
Tel: 705-563-8303; *Fax:* 705-563-8303
thorn@ntl.sympatico.ca
Municipal Type: Village
Area: 6.49 sq km
County or District: Timiskaming District; *Population in 2006:* 105
Provincial Electoral District(s): Timiskaming-Cochrane
Federal Electoral District(s): Timmins-James Bay
Next Election: Oct. 2014 (4 year terms)
Ron Vottero, Reeve
Janet Gore, Clerk-Treasurer

Thunder Bay

District Social Services Administration Bd.
34 North Cumberland St., 4th Fl.
Thunder Bay, ON P7A 8B9
Municipal Type: District
Area: 103,706.27 sq km
Population in 2006: 149,063
Iain Angus, Chair, District of Thunder Bay Social Services Administration Bd.
807-474-0926, Fax: 807-474-0881
Melissa Harrison, CAO, District of Thunder Bay Social Services Administration Board
807-766-2103, Fax: 807-345-6146

Timiskaming

District Social Services Administrative Bd.
P.O. Box 310
29 Duncan Ave. North
Kirkland Lake, ON P2N 3H7
Tel: 705-567-9366;
Other Information: Toll-Free Phone: 1-888-544-5555
Municipal Type: District
Area: 13,279.88 sq km
Population in 2006: 33,283
Jim Whipple, Chair, District of Timiskaming Social Services Administration Bd.
Don Studholme, CAO, District of Timiskaming Social Services Administration Board
705-567-9366, Fax: 705-567-3908
studholmed@dtssab.com

Tiny

130 Balm Beach Rd. West, RR#1
Perkinsfield, ON L0L 2J0
Tel: 705-526-4204; *Fax:* 705-526-2372
www.tiny.ca
Other Information: Toll-Free Phone: 1-866-939-8469
Municipal Type: Township
Area: 343.19 sq km
County or District: Simcoe; *Population in 2006:* 10,784
Provincial Electoral District(s): Simcoe North
Federal Electoral District(s): Simcoe North
Next Election: Oct. 2014 (4 year terms)
Ray Millar, Mayor
George Lawrence, Deputy Mayor
André Claire, Councillor
Nigel Warren, Councillor
Gibb Wishart, Councillor
Doug Luker, Chief Administrative Officer-Clerk
Doug Taylor, Treasurer & Manager, Administrative Services
Henk Blom, Manager, Public Works
Roger E. Robitaille, Manager, Planning & Development
Randy Smith, Fire Chief
Steven Harvey, Chief Municipal Law Enforcement Officer
705-526-4136

Trent Hills

P.O. Box 1030
66 Front St. South
Campbellford, ON K0L 1L0
Tel: 705-653-1900; *Fax:* 705-653-5203
info@trenthills.ca
www.trenthills.ca
Other Information: Public Works Emergency, Phone: 705-653-2610
Municipal Type: Municipality
Area: 510.83 sq km
County or District: Northumberland; *Population in 2006:* 12,247
Provincial Electoral District(s): Northumberland-Quinte West
Federal Electoral District(s): Northumberland-Quinte West
Next Election: Oct. 2014 (4 year terms)
Hector MacMillan, Mayor
705-653-1900
hector.macmillan@trenthills.ca
Rosemary Kelleher-MacLennan, Deputy Mayor, Ward(s): 1 - Campbellford / Seymour
705-653-3456, Fax: 705-653-5300
rosemary.kelleher-maclennan@trenthills.ca
Eugene Brahaney, Councillor, Ward(s): 1 - Campbellford / Seymour, Fax: 705-653-1879
gene.brahaney@trenthills.ca
William J. Thompson, Councillor, Ward(s): 1 - Campbellford / Seymour
705-653-3540, Fax: 705-653-5360
bill.thompson@trenthills.ca
Meirion Jones, Councillor, Ward(s): 2 - Percy
meirion.jones@trenthills.ca
Kim MacNeil, Councillor, Ward(s): 2 - Percy
kim.macneil@trenthills.ca
Robert Crate, Councillor, Ward(s): 3 - Hastings
bob.crate@trenthills.ca
Marg Montgomery, Clerk
705-653-1900
marg.montgomery@trenthills.ca
Mike Rutter, Chief Administrative Officer
705-653-1900
mike.rutter@trenthills.ca
Shelley Eliopoulos, Treasurer & Director, Finance
705-653-1900
shelleyeli@trenthills.ca
Richard Bolduc, Director, Public Works
705-653-1900
richard.bolduc@trenthills.ca
Jim Peters, Director, Planning & Development
705-653-1900
jim.peters@trenthills.ca
David Rogers, Chief Building Official
705-653-1900
dave.rogers@trenthills.ca
Neil Allanson, Manager, Roads & Urban Services
Scott White, Manager, Water & Wastewater Operations
Joanne Chartrand, Officer, Bylaw Enforcement
705-653-1900
joanne.chartrand@trenthills.ca
Scott Rose, Officer, Community Services
705-653-1900
scott.rose@trenthills.ca
Shari Lang, Coordinator, Health & Safety
705-653-1900
shari.lang@trenthills.ca
Kari Petherick, Coordinator, Human Resources & Special Projects
705-653-1900
kari.petherick@trenthills.ca

Tudor & Cashel

P.O. Box 436
371 Weslemkoon Lake Rd., RR#2
Gilmour, ON K0L 1W0
Tel: 613-474-2583; *Fax:* 613-474-0664
clerk@tudorandcashel.com
www.tudorandcashel.com
Municipal Type: Township
Incorporated: 1869 *Area:* 433.49 sq km
County or District: Hastings; *Population in 2006:* 682
Provincial Electoral District(s): Prince Edward-Hastings
Federal Electoral District(s): Prince Edward-Hastings
Next Election: Oct. 2014 (4 year terms)
Wanda Donaldson, Reeve
613-473-4806
Bernice Crocker, Chief Administrative Officer
613-474-2583
clerk@tudorandcashel.com

Tweed

P.O. Box 729
255 Metcalf St.
Tweed, ON K0K 3J0
Tel: 613-478-2535; *Fax:* 613-478-6457
info@twp.tweed.on.ca
www.twp.tweed.on.ca
Municipal Type: Municipality
Incorporated: 1998 *Area:* 896.98 sq km
County or District: Hastings; *Population in 2006:* 5,614
Provincial Electoral District(s): Prince Edward-Hastings
Federal Electoral District(s): Prince Edward-Hastings
Next Election: Oct. 2014 (4 year terms)
Jo-Anne Albert, Reeve
reeve@twp.tweed.on.ca
Patricia Bergeron, Chief Administrative Officer & Clerk
plb@twp.tweed.on.ca

Tyendinaga

859 Melrose Rd., RR#1
Shannonville, ON K0K 3A0
Tel: 613-396-1944; *Fax:* 613-396-2080
info@tyendinagatownship.com
www.tyendinagatownship.com
Municipal Type: Township
Area: 311.94 sq km
County or District: Hastings; *Population in 2006:* 4,070
Provincial Electoral District(s): Prince Edward-Hastings
Federal Electoral District(s): Prince Edward-Hastings
Next Election: Oct. 2014 (4 year terms)
Rick Phillips, Reeve
613-477-3129
phillipsr@xplornet.ca
Steve Mercer, Clerk-Treasurer
clerk@tyendinagatownship.com

Uxbridge

P.O. Box 190
51 Toronto St. South
Uxbridge, ON L9P 1T1
Tel: 905-852-9181; *Fax:* 905-852-9674
info@town.uxbridge.on.ca
www.town.uxbridge.on.ca
Municipal Type: Township
Incorporated: 1872 *Area:* 420.65 sq km
County or District: Durham Reg. Mun.; *Population in 2006:* 19,169
Provincial Electoral District(s): Durham
Federal Electoral District(s): Durham
Next Election: Oct. 2014 (4 year terms)

Note: Incorporated as a town in 1885, & town became part of Uxbridge Township in 1973.
Gerri Lynn O'Connor, Mayor
905-852-9181
gloconnor@town.uxbridge.on.ca
Jack Ballinger, Regional Councillor
416-320-0585
johnhballinger@gmail.com
Beverly Northeast, Councillor, Ward(s): 1
905-640-3966
bnortheast@powergate.ca
Pat Molloy, Councillor, Ward(s): 2
905-852-9181
pmolloy@town.uxbridge.on.ca
Pat Mikuse, Councillor, Ward(s): 3
905-852-0206
prmikuse@sympatico.ca
Jacob Mantle, Councillor, Ward(s): 4
905-852-9181
jmantle@town.uxbridge.on.ca
Gordon Highet, Councillor, Ward(s): 5
905-852-9181
ghighet@town.uxbridge.on.ca
Debbie Leroux, Clerk
905-852-9181, Fax: 905-852-9674
Ingrid Svelnis, Chief Administrative Officer
905-852-9181, Fax: 905-852-9674
isvelnis@town.uxbridge.on.ca
Alan Shultz, Treasurer
ashultz@town.uxbridge.on.ca
Ben Kester, C.E.T., Director, Public Works
905-852-9181, Fax: 905-852-9674
bkester@town.uxbridge.on.ca
Amanda Ferraro, Manager, Recreation, Culture, & Tourism
905-852-0095
aferraro@town.uxbridge.on.ca
Richard Vandezand, Manager, Development Services
905-852-9181, Fax: 905-852-9674
rvandezande@town.uxbridge.on.ca
Brian Pigozzo, Chief Building Official
905-852-9181, Fax: 905-852-9674
bpigozzo@town.uxbridge.on.ca
Scott Richardson, Fire Chief
srichardson@town.uxbridge.on.ca
Andre Gratton, MLEO (C), C.P.S.O., Supervisor, Municipal Law Enforcement
905-852-9181, Fax: 905-852-9674
agratton@town.uxbridge.on.ca

Val Rita-Harty
P.O. Box 100
2 Eglise Ave.
Val Rita, ON P0L 2G0
Tel: 705-335-6146; *Fax:* 705-337-6292
www.valharty.ca
Municipal Type: Township
Area: 382.64 sq km
County or District: Cochrane District; *Population in 2006:* 939
Provincial Electoral District(s): Timmins-James Bay
Federal Electoral District(s): Algoma-Manitoulin-Kapuskasing
Next Election: Oct. 2014 (4 year terms)
Laurier Bourgeois, Mayor
Christiane Potvin, Clerk-Treasurer

Wainfleet
P.O. Box 40
31940 Hwy. 3
Wainfleet, ON L0S 1V0
Tel: 905-899-3463; *Fax:* 905-899-2340
sluey@township.wainfleet.on.ca
www.wainfleet.ca
Municipal Type: Township
Area: 217.29 sq km
County or District: Niagara Reg. Mun.; *Population in 2006:* 6,601
Provincial Electoral District(s): Welland
Federal Electoral District(s): Welland
Next Election: Oct. 2014 (4 year terms)
April Jeffs, Mayor
905-899-3463, Fax: 905-899-2340
ajeffs@wainfleet.ca
Tanya Lamb, Township Clerk
905-899-3463
tlamb@township.wainfleet.on.ca

Warwick
6332 Nauvoo Rd.
Watford, ON N0M 2S0
Tel: 519-849-3926; *Fax:* 519-849-6136
info@warwicktownship.ca
www.warwicktownship.ca
Municipal Type: Township
Incorporated: 1998 *Area:* 290.2 sq km
County or District: Lambton; *Population in 2006:* 3,945
Provincial Electoral District(s): Lambton-Kent-Middlesex
Federal Electoral District(s): Lambton-Kent-Middlesex
Next Election: Oct. 2014 (4 year terms)
Todd Case, Mayor
Don R. Bruder, Administrator-Treasurer
dbruder@warwicktownship.ca

Wawa
P.O. Box 500
40 Broadway Ave.
Wawa, ON P0S 1K0
Tel: 705-856-2244; *Fax:* 705-856-2120
info@wawa.cc
www.wawa.cc
Other Information: Toll-Free Phone: 1-800-367-9292
Municipal Type: Township
Area: 417.78 sq km
County or District: Algoma District; *Population in 2006:* 3,204
Provincial Electoral District(s): Algoma-Manitoulin
Federal Electoral District(s): Algoma-Manitoulin-Kapuskasing
Next Election: Oct. 2014 (4 year terms)
Linda Nowicki, Mayor
Chris Wray, Chief Administrative Officer & Clerk-Treasurer
705-856-2244
cwray@wawa.cc

Wellesley
Administration Office
4639 Lobsinger Line, RR#1
St Clements, ON N0B 2M0
Tel: 519-699-4611; *Fax:* 519-699-4540
www.township.wellesley.on.ca
Municipal Type: Township
Area: 277.84 sq km
County or District: Waterloo Regional Municipality; *Population in 2006:* 9,789
Provincial Electoral District(s): Kitchener-Conestoga
Federal Electoral District(s): Kitchener-Conestoga
Next Election: Oct. 2014 (4 year terms)
Ross Kelterborn, Mayor
519-656-2445
kross@region.waterloo.on.ca
Susan Duke, Clerk & Executive Director, Corporate Services
sduke@wellesley.ca

Wellington North
P.O. Box 125
7490 Sideroad 7 West
Kenilworth, ON N0G 2E0
Tel: 519-848-3620;
township@wellington-north.com
www.wellington-north.com
Other Information: Toll-Free Phone: 1-866-848-3620
Municipal Type: Township
Incorporated: Jan. 1, 1999 *Area:* 524.38 sq km
County or District: Wellington; *Population in 2006:* 11,175
Provincial Electoral District(s): Perth-Wellington
Federal Electoral District(s): Perth-Wellington
Next Election: Oct. 2014 (4 year terms)
Note: Amalgamation of the Township of Arthur, Arthur Village, the Township of West Luther & the Town of Mount Forest.
Raymond T. Tout, Mayor
519-323-9146
rtout@wellington-north.ca
Dan Yake, Councillor, Ward(s): 1
519-323-2334
dyake@wellington-north.ca
Sherry Burke, Councillor, Ward(s): 2
519-323-2604
sburke@wellington-north.ca
Mark Goetz, Councillor, Ward(s): 3
519-848-3380
mgoetz@wellington-north.ca
Andy Lennox, Councillor, Ward(s): 4
519-848-9948
alennox@wellington-north.ca
Lorraine (Lori) Heinbuch, Chief Administrative Officer & Clerk
519-848-3620
lheinbuch@wellington-north.com
John W. Jeffery, Treasurer
519-848-3620
jjeffery@wellington-north.com
Barry Trood, Director, Public Works
519-848-3620
btrood@wellington-north.com
Darren Jones, Chief Building Official
519-848-3620
djones@wellington-north.com
Dale Clark, Superintendent, Roads
519-848-3620
dclark@wellington-north.com
Mark Van Patter, Senior Planner
519-837-2600
markv@county.wellington.on.ca

West Elgin
P.O. Box 490
22413 Hoskins Line
Rodney, ON N0L 2C0
Tel: 519-785-0560; *Fax:* 519-785-0644
westelgin@westelgin.net
www.westelgin.net
Municipal Type: Municipality
Area: 322.52 sq km
County or District: Elgin; *Population in 2006:* 5,349
Provincial Electoral District(s): Elgin-Middlesex-London
Federal Electoral District(s): Elgin-Middlesex-London
Next Election: Oct. 2014 (4 year terms)
Bernhard Wiehle, Mayor
519-785-0560, Fax: 519-785-0644
bwiehle@sympatico.ca
Norma Bryant, AMCT, Clerk
519-785-0560
nbryant@westelgin.net

West Grey
402813 Grey Rd., RR#2
Durham, ON N0G 1R0
Tel: 519-369-2200; *Fax:* 519-369-5962
info@westgrey.com
www.westgrey.com
Other Information: Toll-Free Phone: 1-800-538-9647
Municipal Type: Municipality
Incorporated: Jan 1, 2001 *Area:* 875.37 sq km
County or District: Grey; *Population in 2006:* 12,193
Provincial Electoral District(s): Bruce-Grey-Owen Sound
Federal Electoral District(s): Bruce-Grey-Owen Sound
Next Election: Oct. 2014 (4 year terms)
Note: Amalgamation of Bentinck, Glenelg, Normanby, Neustadt & Durham.
Kevin Eccles, Mayor
519-799-5476
mayor@westgrey.com
John A. Bell, Deputy Mayor
519-369-6894
deputymayor@westgrey.com
Bev Cutting, Councillor
519-986-4635
bevcutting@westgrey.com
John Eccles, Councillor
519-369-3618
johneccles@westgrey.com
Carol Lawrence, Councillor
519-369-3816
Don Marshall, Councillor
519-369-7221
donmarshall@westgrey.com
David Mollison, Councillor
519-369-5337
davemollison@westgrey.com
Mark Rapke, Councillor
519-986-4498
markrapke@westgrey.com
Rob Thompson, Councillor
519-369-3052
robthompson@westgrey.com
Mark Turner, Clerk
519-369-2200
mturner@westgrey.com
Christine Robinson, Chief Administrative Officer
519-369-2200
robinsonc@westgrey.com
Kerri Mighton, Treasurer & Director, Finance
519-369-2200
kmighton@westgrey.com
Ken Gould, Director, Infrastructure & Public Works
519-369-2200
kgould@westgrey.com

West Lincoln
P.O. Box 400
318 Canborough St.
Smithville, ON L0R 2A0
Tel: 905-957-3346; *Fax:* 905-957-3219
reception@westlincoln.ca
www.westlincoln.ca
Other Information: Toll-Free Phone: 1-800-350-3876; TTY: 905-957-0680
Municipal Type: Township
Incorporated: Jan. 1, 1970 *Area:* 387.72 sq km

County or District: Niagara Reg. Mun.; Population in 2006: 13,167
Provincial Electoral District(s): Niagara West-Glanbrook
Federal Electoral District(s): Niagara West-Glanbrook
Next Election: Oct. 2014 (4 year terms)
Note: Amalgamation of the former Townships of South Grimsby, Caistor, & Gainsborough.
Douglas Joyner, Mayor
905-957-4926
djoyner@westlincoln.ca
Eric Leith, Alderman, Ward(s): 1
905-957-1626
eleith@westlincoln.ca
Sue-Ellen Merritt, Alderman, Ward(s): 1
905-869-0939
smerritt@westlincoln.ca
Joann Chechalk, Alderman, Ward(s): 2
905-386-6412
jchechalk@westlincoln.ca
Alexander Micallef, Alderman, Ward(s): 2
289-668-8654
amicallef@westlincoln.ca
Luciano (Lou) Di Leonardo, Alderman, Ward(s): 3
905-957-8435
ldileonardo@westlincoln.ca
John Glazier, Alderman, Ward(s): 3
905-957-1140
jglazier@westlincoln.ca
Carolyn Langley, Clerk
905-957-3346
carolynlangley@westlincoln.ca
Derrick Thomson, Chief Administrative Officer
905-957-3346
dthomson@westlincoln.ca
Stephanie Nagel, Treasurer & Director, Finance
905-957-3346
snagel@westlincoln.ca
Brian Treble, Director, Planning & Building
905-957-3346
btreble@westlincoln.ca
Dennis Fisher, Fire Chief
905-957-3346
dfisher@westlincoln.ca

West Nipissing

Municipal Office
#101, 225 Holditch St.
Sturgeon Falls, ON P2B 1T1
Tel: 705-753-2250; Fax: 705-753-3950
www.westnipissingouest.ca
Municipal Type: Municipality
Area: 1,989.57 sq km
County or District: Nipissing District; Population in 2006: 13,410
Provincial Electoral District(s): Timiskaming-Cochrane
Federal Electoral District(s): Nickel Belt
Next Election: Oct. 2014 (4 year terms)
Joanne Savage, Mayor
705-753-2250, Fax: 705-753-3950
jsavage@westnipissing.ca
Denise Brisson, Councillor, Ward(s): 1
705-753-3136
dbrisson@westnipissing.ca
Léo Malette, Councillor, Ward(s): 2
705-753-3568
lmalette@westnipissing.ca
Don Fortin, Councillor, Ward(s): 3
705-753-2844
dfortin@westnipissing.ca
Jamie Restoule, Councillor, Ward(s): 4
705-753-9396
jrestoule@westnipissing.ca
Guilles Tessier, Councillor, Ward(s): 5
705-753-3559
gtessier@westnipissing.ca
Paul Finley, Councillor, Ward(s): 6
705-594-2882
pfinley@westnipissing.ca
Normand Roberge, Councillor, Ward(s): 7
705-594-9486
nroberge@westnipissing.ca
Guy Fortier, Councillor, Ward(s): 8
705-594-2301
gfortier@westnipissing.ca
Mélanie Ducharme, Municipal Clerk & Planner
705-753-2250
mducharme@westnipissing.ca
Jean-Pierre (Jay) Barbeau, Chief Administrative Officer
705-753-2250
jbarbeau@westnipissing.ca
Serge Ducharme, Director, Museum
705-753-4716
admin@sturgeonriverhouse.com
Marc Gagnon, Director, Operations
705-753-2250
mgagnon@westnipissing.ca
Stephan Poulin, Director, Economic Development & Community Services
705-753-2250
spoulin@westnipissing.ca
Alain Bazinet, Chief Building Official & Officer, Property Maintenance
705-753-2250
abazinet@westnipissing.ca
Richard Savage, Fire Chief
705-753-1171
rsavage@wnfs.ca
Denis Lafreniere, Manager, Solid Waste
705-753-6913
dlafreniere@westnipissing.ca
Raymond Lortie, Manager, Power Generation
705-753-6364
westnipissingpower@bellnet.ca
Peter Ming, Manager, Water & Wastewater Operations
705-753-6454
pming@westnipissing.ca
Ginette Rochon, Manager, Ancillary Operations
705-753-6939
grochon@westnipissing.ca

West Perth, Municipality of

169 St. David St.
Mitchell, ON N0K 1N0
Tel: 519-348-8429;
info@westperth.com
www.westperth.com
Municipal Type: Township
Area: 579.4 sq km
County or District: Perth; Population in 2006: 8,839
Provincial Electoral District(s): Perth-Wellington
Federal Electoral District(s): Perth-Wellington
Next Election: Oct. 2014 (4 year terms)
Note: Amalgamation of Fullarton Township, Hibbert Township, Logan Township & the Town of Mitchell.
Walter McKenzie, Mayor
wmckenzie@westperth.com
Susan Cronin, Municipal Clerk
519-348-8429

Westport

P.O. Box 68
30 Bedford St.
Westport, ON K0G 1X0
Tel: 613-273-2191; Fax: 613-273-3460
westport@rideau.net
www.village.westport.on.ca
Municipal Type: Village
Incorporated: 1904 Area: 1.71 sq km
County or District: Leeds & Grenville; Population in 2006: 645
Provincial Electoral District(s): Leeds-Grenville
Federal Electoral District(s): Leeds-Grenville
Next Election: Oct. 2014 (4 year terms)
William (Bill) L. Thake, Mayor
Scott Bryce, Clerk-Treasurer

White River

P.O. Box 307
102 Durham St.
White River, ON P0M 3G0
Tel: 807-822-2450; Fax: 807-822-2719
info@whiteriver.ca
www.whiteriver.ca
Municipal Type: Township
Area: 96.94 sq km
County or District: Algoma District; Population in 2006: 841
Provincial Electoral District(s): Algoma-Manitoulin
Federal Electoral District(s): Algoma-Manitoulin-Kapuskasing
Next Election: Oct. 2014 (4 year terms)
Angelo Bazzoni, Mayor
Marilyn Parent Lethbridge, Clerk Administrator
807-822-2450, Fax: 807-822-2179

Whitestone, Municipality of

General Delivery
21 Church St.
Dunchurch, ON P0A 1G0
Tel: 705-389-2466; Fax: 705-389-1855
general@whitestone.ca; confidential@whitestone.ca
www.whitestone.ca
Municipal Type: Township
Incorporated: 2000 Area: 946.56 sq km
County or District: Parry Sound District; Population in 2006: 1,030
Provincial Electoral District(s): Parry Sound-Muskoka
Federal Electoral District(s): Parry Sound-Muskoka
Next Election: Oct. 2014 (4 year terms)
Chris Armstrong, Mayor
705-389-3721
mayor.armstrong@whitestone.ca
Liliane Nolan, Chief Administrative Officer & Clerk
705-389-2466
clerk.administrator@whitestone.ca

Whitewater Region

P.O. Box 40
44 Main St.
Cobden, ON K0J 1K0
Tel: 613-646-2282; Fax: 613-646-2283
info@whitewaterregion.ca
www.whitewaterregion.ca
Other Information: Toll-Free Phone: 1-877-646-2282
Municipal Type: Township
Incorporated: Jan. 1, 2001 Area: 537.96 sq km
County or District: Renfrew; Population in 2006: 6,631
Provincial Electoral District(s): Renfrew-Nipissing-Pembroke
Federal Electoral District(s): Renfrew-Nipissing-Pembroke
Next Election: Oct. 2014 (4 year terms)
Note: Amalgamation of Beachburg Village, Cobden Village, Westmeath Township & Ross Township.
Jim Labow, Mayor
613-582-3969, Fax: 613-582-3338
jlabow@whitewaterregion.ca
Donald Rathwell, Reeve
613-646-7924, Fax: 613-646-7417
djr@nrtco.net
Dean Sauriol, Chief Administrative Officer & Clerk
dsauriol@whitewaterregion.ca

Wilmot

60 Snyder's Rd. West
Baden, ON N3A 1A1
Tel: 519-634-8444; Fax: 519-634-5522
info@wilmot.ca
www.wilmot.ca
Other Information: Toll-Free Phone: 1-800-469-5576
Municipal Type: Township
Area: 263.73 sq km
County or District: Waterloo Regional Municipality; Population in 2006: 17,097
Provincial Electoral District(s): Kitchener-Conestoga
Federal Electoral District(s): Kitchener-Conestoga
Next Election: Oct. 2014 (4 year terms)
Les Armstrong, Mayor, Fax: 519-662-2764
les.armstrong@wilmot.ca
Al Junker, Councillor, Ward(s): 1
519-696-3922
al.junker@wilmot.ca
Peter Roe, Councillor, Ward(s): 2
519-886-6395, Fax: 519-886-6395
peter.roe@wilmot.ca
Barry Fisher, Councillor, Ward(s): 3
519-634-8916
barry.fisher@wilmot.ca
Jeff Gerber, Councillor, Ward(s): 4
519-662-6658
jeff.gerber@wilmot.ca
Mark Murray, Councillor, Ward(s): 4
519-662-2625, Fax: 519-662-2601
mark.murray@wilmot.ca
Barbara McLeod, Director, Clerk's Services
519-634-8444, Fax: 519-634-5522
barb.mcleod@wilmot.ca
Grant Whittington, Chief Administrative Officer
519-634-8444, Fax: 519-634-5522
grant.whittington@wilmot.ca
Rosita Tse, Treasurer & Director, Finance
519-634-8444, Fax: 519-634-5522
rosita.tse@wilmot.ca
Gary Charbonneau, Director, Public Works
519-634-8444, Fax: 519-634-5044
gary.charbonneau@wilmot.ca
Scott Nancekivell, Director, Facilities & Recreation
519-634-8444, Fax: 519-634-5044
scott.nancekivell@wilmot.ca
Harold O'Krafka, Director, Development Services
519-634-8444, Fax: 519-634-5044
harold.okrafka@wilmot.ca
John Ritz, Fire Chief
519-634-8444, Fax: 519-634-5660
john.ritz@wilmot.ca
Doug Robertson, Chief Building Official
519-634-8444, Fax: 519-634-5044
doug.robertson@wilmot.ca

Derek Wallace, Senior Officer, Municipal Law Enforcement
519-634-8444, Fax: 519-634-5522
derek.wallace@wilmot.ca
Andrew Martin, Planner & Officer, Economic Development
519-634-8444, Fax: 519-634-5044
andrew.martin@wilmot.ca

Wollaston
P.O. Box 99
90 Wollaston Lake Rd.
Coe Hill, ON K0L 1P0
Tel: 613-337-5731; *Fax:* 613-337-5789
wollaston@bellnet.ca
www.township.wollaston.on.ca
Municipal Type: Township
Incorporated: 1880 *Area:* 215.22 sq km
County or District: Hastings; *Population in 2006:* 730
Provincial Electoral District(s): Prince Edward-Hastings
Federal Electoral District(s): Prince Edward-Hastings
Next Election: Oct. 2014 (4 year terms)
Dan McCaw, Reeve
613-337-5705
danandedithm@yahoo.ca
Christine FitzSimons, Chief Administrative Officer & Clerk
wollaston@bellnet.ca

Woolwich
P.O. Box 158
24 Church St. West
Elmira, ON N3B 2Z6
Tel: 519-669-1647; *Fax:* 519-669-1820
woolwich.mail@woolwich.ca
www.woolwich.ca
Other Information: Phone from 648 exchange: 519-664-2613
Municipal Type: Township
Incorporated: Jan. 1, 1973 *Area:* 326 sq km
County or District: Waterloo Regional Municipality; *Population in 2006:* 19,658
Provincial Electoral District(s): Kitchener-Conestoga
Federal Electoral District(s): Kitchener-Conestoga
Next Election: Oct. 2014 (4 year terms)
Todd A. Cowan, Mayor
519-669-0591
Julie-Anne Herteis, Councillor, Ward(s): 1
519-669-4740
Allan Poffenroth, Councillor, Ward(s): 1
519-669-8074
Mark Bauman, Councillor, Ward(s): 2
519-664-3318
Bonnie Bryant, Councillor, Ward(s): 3
519-648-3608
Christine Broughton, Clerk & Director, Council & Information Services
519-669-1647
David Brenneman, Chief Administrative Officer
519-669-1647
Richard Petherick, Treasurer & Director, Finance
519-669-1647
Larry Devitt, Director, Recreation & Facilities Services
519-669-1647
Dan Kennaley, Director, Engineering & Planning Services
519-669-1647
Rick Pedersen, Township Fire Chief
519-664-2887
Peter vanderBeek, Chief Building Official
519-669-1647
Barry Baldasaro, Superintendent, Public Works
519-669-1647
Laurel Davies-Snyder, Officer, Economic Development & Tourism
519-669-1647

Zorra
Municipal Office
P.O. Box 306
274620 - 27th Line, RR#3
Ingersoll, ON N5C 3K5
Tel: 519-485-2490; *Fax:* 519-485-2520
admin@zorra.on.ca
www.zorra.on.ca
Other Information: Toll-Free Phone: 1-888-699-3868
Municipal Type: Township
Area: 528.78 sq km
County or District: Oxford; *Population in 2006:* 8,125
Provincial Electoral District(s): Oxford
Federal Electoral District(s): Oxford
Next Election: Oct. 2014 (4 year terms)
Margaret Lupton, Mayor
519-475-4443, Fax: 519-485-2520
mlupton@zorra.on.ca
Karen Graham, Clerk
519-485-2490, Fax: 519-485-2520
kgraham@zorra.on.ca

PRINCE EDWARD ISLAND

Enabling legislation in P.E.I. includes the Charlottetown Area Municipalities Act, the City of Summerside Act, and the Municipalities Act. The first provides governance for three municipalities, the second provides governance for one municipality, and the third provides the framework for 71 municipalities. There are no population considerations for incorporation of a municipality, but a petition must be made by at least 25 residents of an area indicating their desire to incorporate; stating the boundaries of the area, whether it is to be a town or a community, and the services which are to be provided.

Municipal Elections are held every three or four years in November.

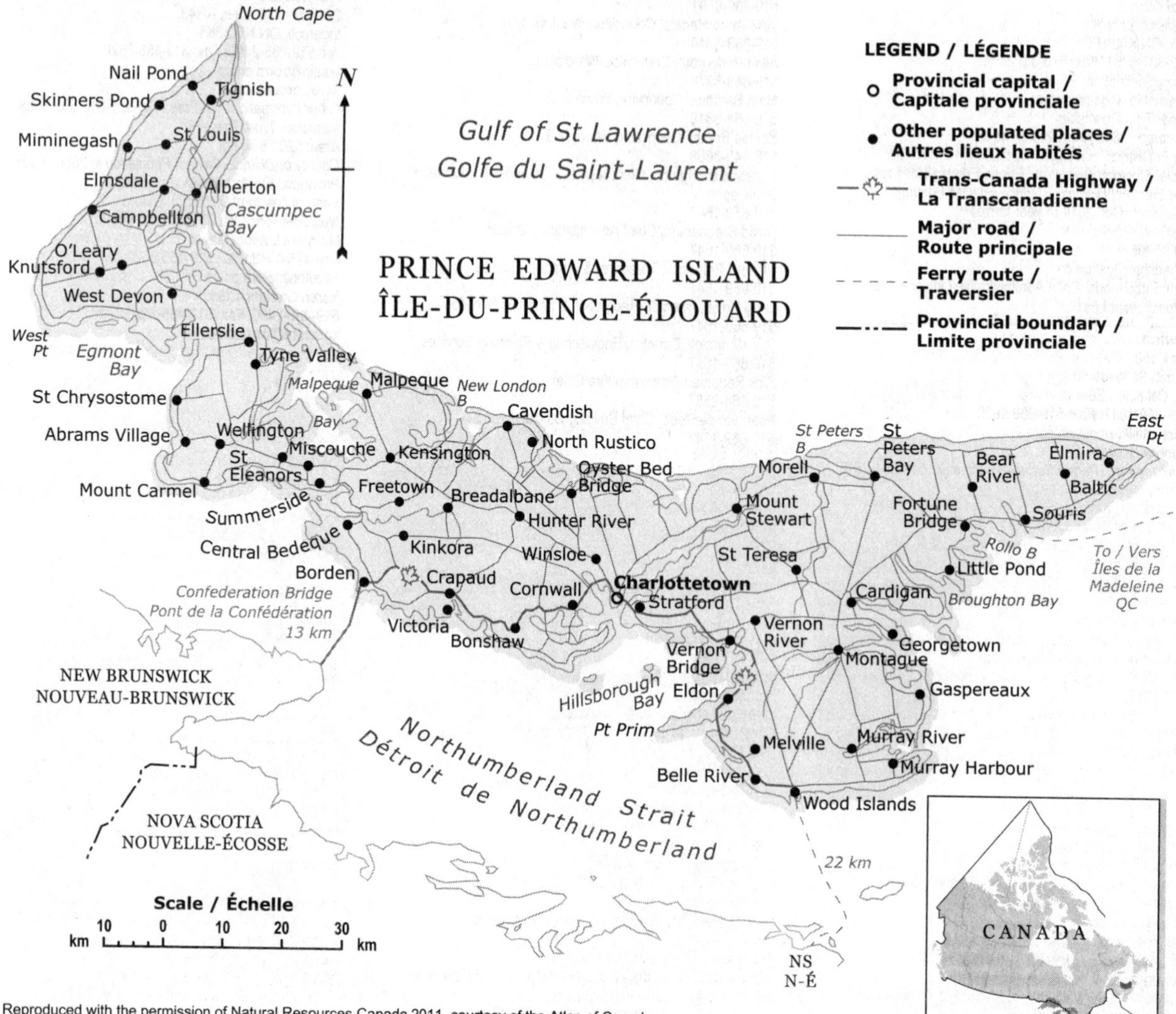

Reproduced with the permission of Natural Resources Canada 2011, courtesy of the Atlas of Canada.

Prince Edward Island

Major Municipalities in Prince Edward Island

Charlottetown
P.O. Box 98
199 Queen St.
Charlottetown, PE C1A 4B7
Tel: 902-566-5548; *Fax:* 902-566-4701
city@city.charlottetown.pe.ca
www.city.charlottetown.pe.ca
Municipal Type: City
Incorporated: 1855 *Area:* 44.33 sq km
County or District: Hillsborough; *Population in 2006:* 32,174
Provincial Electoral District(s): Charlottetown-Sherwood; Charlottetown-Parkdale; Charlottetown-Victoria Park; Charlottetown-Brighton; Charlottetown-Lewis Point
Federal Electoral District(s): Charlottetown
Next Election: Nov. 2010 (four year terms)
Clifford J. Lee, Mayor
mayor@city.charlottetown.pe.ca
Roy Main, Chief Administrative Officer
rmain@city.charlottetown.pe.ca
Kim Devine, B.A., Councillor, Ward(s): 1
kdevine@city.charlottetown.pe.ca
Joseph Coady, Director, Public Services
jcoady@city.charlottetown.pe.ca
Daniel (Danny) J. Redmond, B.A., Councillor, Ward(s): 2
dredmond@city.charlottetown.pe.ca
Donna Waddell, Director, Corporate Services
dwaddell@city.charlottetown.pe.ca
Rob Lantz, B.Sc., Councillor, Ward(s): 3
rlantz@city.charlottetown.pe.ca
Phil Handrahan, Director, Fiscal & Development Services
phandrahan@city.charlottetown.pe.ca
Mitchell G. Tweel, B.A., Councillor, Ward(s): 4
mitchell.tweel@pei.sympatico.ca
Craig Walker, Manager, Water & Sewer Utility
902-629-4014
cwalker@city.charlottetown.pe.ca
Sterling MacFadyen, Deputy Mayor & Councillor, Ward(s): 5
smacfadyen@city.charlottetown.pe.ca
Bill Clair, Works Superintendent, Water & Sewer Utility
902-629-4015
bclair@city.charlottetown.pe.ca
David MacDonald, Councillor, Ward(s): 6
dmacdonald@city.charlottetown.pe.ca
Herman Van Omme, Superintendent, Waste Water Treatment Plant
902-628-6647, Fax: 902-628-6684
hvanomme@city.charlottetown.pe.ca
Cecil F. Villard, Councillor, Ward(s): 7
cvillard@city.charlottetown.pe.ca
Ron Atkinson, Economic Development Officer, Economic Development, Tourism & Events
ratkinson@city.charlottetown.pe.ca
Dan Hughes, Manager, Human Resources
Peter F. McCloskey, Councillor, Ward(s): 8
pmccloskey@city.charlottetown.pe.ca
Don Poole, Manager of Planning, Planning & Development
dpoole@city.charlottetown.pe.ca
Melissa Hilton, B.A., Councillor, Ward(s): 9
mhilton@city.charlottetown.pe.ca
Vada Fernandez, Purchasing Officer, Finance
vfernandez@city.charlottetown.pe.ca
Terence H. Bernard, Councillor, Ward(s): 10
tbernard@city.charlottetown.pe.ca
Mel Cheverie, Chief Building Inspector, Planning & Development
mcheverie@city.charlottetown.pe.ca
Jim Molyneux, Field Works Coordinator, Public Works
jmolyneux@city.charlottetown.pe.ca
Blair Kinch, Sr. Superintendent, Public Works
bkinch@city.charlottetown.pe.ca
Lance Jones, Streets Maintenance Supervisor, Public Works
ljones@city.charlottetown.pe.ca
Nancy McMinn, Parks Superintendent, Parks & Recreation
nmcminn@city.charlottetown.pe.ca
Scott Ryan, M.B.A., CMA, FCMA, Manager, Finance
sryan@city.charlottetown.pe.ca
Randy MacDonald, Fire Chief, Fire Services
rmacdonald@city.charlottetown.pe.ca
Paul Johnston, Manager, Public Works
902-894-5208
pjohnston@city.charlottetown.pe.ca
Sue Hendricken, Manager, Parks & Recreation
902-368-1025
shendricken@city.charlottetown.pe.ca
Paul Smith, Chief of Police
psmith@city.charlottetown.pe.ca

Saint-Lambert
55, avenue Argyle
Saint-Laurent, QB J4P 2H3
Tél: 450-672-444; *Téléc:* 450-672-3732
direction.generale@ville.saint-lambert.qc.ca
www.ville.saint-lambert.qc.ca
Entité municipal: City
Incorporation: 1er janvier 2006 *Area:* 6,43 km2
Population au 2006: 21,599
Circonscription(s) électorale(s) provinciale(s): Laporte
Circonscription(s) électorale(s) fédérale(s): Saint-Lambert
Prochaines élections: 3e novembre 2013
Philippe Brunet, Maire
Myriam Pellerin, Greffière

Summerside
275 Fitzroy St.
Summerside, PE C1N 1H9
Tel: 902-432-1230; *Fax:* 902-436-9296
cityhall@city.summerside.pe.ca
www.city.summerside.pe.ca
Municipal Type: City
Incorporated: 1995 *Area:* 28.36 sq km
County or District: Egmont; *Population in 2006:* 14,500
Provincial Electoral District(s): Wilmot-Summerside; St. Eleanors-Summerside
Federal Electoral District(s): Egmont
Next Election: Nov. 2010 (four year terms)
Basil Stewart, Mayor
902-432-1244
mayor@city.summerside.pe.ca
Terry Murphy, Chief Administrative Officer
tmurphy@city.summerside.pe.ca
Bruce MacDougall, Deputy Mayor & Councillor, Ward(s): 1. St. Eleanors-Bayview
bmacdougall@city.summerside.pe.ca
Malcolm Millar, Director, Financial Services
902-432-1250
mmillar@city.summerside.pe.ca
Frank Costa, Councillor, Ward(s): 2. St. Eleanors-Slemon Park
frank.costa@city.summerside.pe.ca
Paul Gallant, Program & Scheduling Coordinator, Community Services, Recreation
902-432-1294
pgallant@city.summerside.pe.ca
Peter Holman, Councillor, Ward(s): 3. Summerside-North
peter.holman@city.summerside.pe.ca
James Peters, Director, Fire Services
902-432-1224
jpeters@city.summerside.pe.ca
Jim Steele, Councillor, Ward(s): 4. Clifton/Market
jim.steele@city.summerside.pe.ca
J. David Poirier, Director, Police Services
902-432-1330
dpoirier@city.summerside.pe.ca
Ron Dowling, Councillor, Ward(s): 5. Hillcrest-Platte River
rondowling@hotmail.com
Gordon MacFarlane, Director, Human Resources
902-432-1240
gmacfarlane@city.summerside.pe.ca
Jeff Sullivan, Councillor, Ward(s): 6. Centre East-Downtown
jeff.sullivan@city.summerside.pe.ca
Michael Thususka, Director, Economic Development
902-432-1255
miket@city.summerside.pe.ca
Tina Mundy, Councillor, Ward(s): 7. Greenhouse-Three Oaks
tina.mundy@city.summerside.pe.ca
Aaron MacDonald, Director, Technical Services
902-432-1258
aaronmac@city.summerside.pe.ca
Cory Thomas, Councillor, Ward(s): 8. Wilmot
cthomas@city.summerside.pe.ca

Other Municipalities in Prince Edward Island

Abrams Village
P.O. Box 104
Wellington, PE C0B 2E0
Tel: 902-854-4111; *Fax:* 902-854-2740
Municipal Type: Community
Incorporated: 1974 *Area:* 1.37 sq km
Population in 2006: 266
Provincial Electoral District(s): Evangeline-Miscouche
Federal Electoral District(s): Egmont
Next Election: Nov. 2010 (four year terms)
Roger Gallant, Chairperson
Karen Gallant, Chief Administrative Officer

Afton
P.O. Box 836
Cornwall, PE C0A 1H0
Tel: 902-675-3515;
afton.cic@gmail.com
Municipal Type: Community
Incorporated: 1974
Population in 2006: 826
Provincial Electoral District(s): Tracadie-Fort Augustus
Federal Electoral District(s): Malpeque
Next Election: Nov. 2010 (four year terms)
Gina Rankin, Chairperson
Joseph Clow, Chief Administrative Officer

Alberton
P.O. Box 153
Alberton, PE C0B 1B0
Tel: 902-853-2720; *Fax:* 902-853-2314
info@townofalberton.ca
www.townofalberton.ca
Municipal Type: Town
Incorporated: May 1913 *Area:* 4.50 sq km
County or District: Egmont; *Population in 2006:* 1,081
Provincial Electoral District(s): Alberton-Miminegash
Federal Electoral District(s): Egmont
Next Election: Nov. 2010 (four year terms)
Michael Murphy, Mayor
Susan Wallace-Flynn, Chief Administrative Officer

Alexandra
P.O. Box 2683
Charlottetown, PE C1A 8C3
Tel: 902-569-4760
Municipal Type: Community
Incorporated: 1972
County or District: Cardigan; *Population in 2006:* 259
Provincial Electoral District(s): Belfast-Pownal Bay
Federal Electoral District(s): Cardigan
Next Election: Nov. 2010 (four year terms)
John Brehaut, Chairperson
Sheila Whiteway-McNeill, Chief Administrative Officer

Annandale-Little Pond-Howe Bay
75 Ross Rd., RR#2
Vernon Bridge, PE C0A 2B0
Tel: 902-583-2865
Municipal Type: Community
Incorporated: 1975
County or District: Cardigan; *Population in 2006:* 370
Provincial Electoral District(s): Georgetown-Baldwin's Road
Federal Electoral District(s): Cardigan
Next Election: Nov. 2010 (four year terms)
Edwin McKie, Chairperson
Florence Sutherland, Chief Administrative Officer

Bedeque
P.O. Box 4109
Bedeque, PE C0B 1C0
Tel: 902-887-2909; *Fax:* 902-887-3226
jlkimmet@pei.sympatico.ca
Municipal Type: Community
Incorporated: 1978 *Area:* 0.68 sq km
County or District: Malpeque; *Population in 2006:* 139
Provincial Electoral District(s): Borden-Kinkora
Federal Electoral District(s): Malpeque
Next Election: Nov. 2010 (four year terms)
Karen McLenithan, Chairperson
Dianna Linder, Chief Administrative Officer

Belfast
RR#3
Belle River, PE C0A 1B0
Tel: 902-659-2989; *Fax:* 902-659-2813
add_belfast_here.cap@pei.sympatico.ca
www3.pei.sympatico.ca/belfast.cap/public_html/
Municipal Type: Community
Incorporated: 1972
County or District: Cardigan; *Population in 2006:* 1,839
Provincial Electoral District(s): Belfast-Pownal Bay
Federal Electoral District(s): Cardigan
Next Election: Nov. 2010 (four year terms)
Norman Gillis, Chairperson
Janice MacDonald, Chief Administrative Officer

Bonshaw
599 Riverdale Rd., RR#3
Bonshaw, PE C0A 1C0
Tel: 902-675-3670; *Fax:* 902-368-1239
dianne_dowling@hotmail.com
Municipal Type: Community
Incorporated: 1977
County or District: Malpeque; *Population in 2006:* 186

Provincial Electoral District(s): Crapaud-Hazel Grove
Federal Electoral District(s): Malpeque
Next Election: Nov. 2010 (four year terms)
John Jamieson, Chairperson
Dianne Dowling, Chief Administrative Officer

Borden-Carleton
P.O. Box 89
167 Industrial Dr.
Borden-Carleton, PE C0B 1X0
Tel: 902-437-2225; *Fax:* 902-437-2610
bcadmin@borden-carleton.ca
www.borden-carleton.ca
Municipal Type: Community
Incorporated: July 1, 1995 *Area:* 13.16 sq km
County or District: Malpeque; *Population in 2006:* 786
Provincial Electoral District(s): Borden-Kinkora
Federal Electoral District(s): Malpeque
Next Election: Nov. 2010 (four year terms)
Fred Leard, Chairperson
Charles McNally, Chief Administrative Officer

Brackley
576 Brackley Point Rd.
Brackley, PE C1E 1Z3
Tel: 902-368-8274
Municipal Type: Community
Incorporated: 1983 *Area:* 8.92 sq km
County or District: Malpeque; *Population in 2006:* 336
Provincial Electoral District(s): Stanhope-East Royalty
Federal Electoral District(s): Malpeque
Next Election: Nov. 2010 (four year terms)
Leonard MacCormack, Chairperson
Maureen Cudmore, Chief Administrative Officer

Breadalbane
20 Grafton St.
Breadalbane, PE C0A 1E0
Tel: 902-964-2730;
admin@peicaps.org
Municipal Type: Community
Incorporated: 1991 *Area:* 12.57 sq km
Population in 2006: 172
Provincial Electoral District(s): Crapaud-Hazel Grove
Federal Electoral District(s): Malpeque
Next Election: Nov. 2010 (four year terms)
Dawna MacLeod, Chairperson
Kim MacLeod, Chief Administrative Officer

Brudenell
415 Brudenell Point Rd., RR#5
Montague, PE C0A 1R0
Tel: 902-838-4160;
lindabarry.brudenell@gmail.com
Municipal Type: Community
Incorporated: 1973
County or District: Cardigan; *Population in 2006:* 358
Provincial Electoral District(s): Montague-Kilmuir
Federal Electoral District(s): Cardigan
Next Election: Nov. 2010 (four year terms)
Peggy Coffin, Chairperson
Linda Barry, Chief Administrative Officer

Cardigan
P.O. Box 40
Cardigan, PE C0A 1G0
Tel: 902-583-2198; *Fax:* 902-583-3198
villageofcardigan@gmail.com
Municipal Type: Community
Incorporated: 1954 *Area:* 5.28 sq km
County or District: Cardigan; *Population in 2006:* 374
Provincial Electoral District(s): Georgetown-Baldwin's Road
Federal Electoral District(s): Cardigan
Next Election: Nov. 2010 (four year terms)
Darlene Stewart, Chairperson
Jimmy Mooney, Chief Administrative Officer

Central Bedeque
246 Walker Ave.
Summerside, PE C1N 5P2
Tel: 902-436-8894;
doug.macmurdo@pei.sympatico.ca
Municipal Type: Community
Incorporated: 1966 *Area:* 1.89 sq km
County or District: Malpeque; *Population in 2006:* 149
Provincial Electoral District(s): Borden-Kinkora
Federal Electoral District(s): Malpeque
Next Election: Nov. 2010 (four year terms)
Earl Smith, Chairperson
Douglas MacMurdo, Chief Administrative Officer

Central Kings
Bridgetown, RR#5
Cardigan, PE C0A 1G0
Tel: 902-583-2248;
michdowne@hotmail.com
Municipal Type: Community
Incorporated: 1975
Population in 2006: 563
Provincial Electoral District(s): Morell-Fortune Bay
Federal Electoral District(s): Cardigan
Next Election: Nov. 2010 (four year terms)
Craig Jackson, Chairperson
Micheline Downe, Chief Administrative Officer

Clyde River
P.O. Box 644
Cornwall, PE C0A 1H0
Tel: 902-675-4747;
clyderiver.cic@pei.sympatico.ca
Municipal Type: Community
Incorporated: 1974 *Area:* 16.05 sq km
County or District: Malpeque; *Population in 2006:* 618
Provincial Electoral District(s): Crapaud-Hazel Grove
Federal Electoral District(s): Malpeque
Next Election: Nov. 2010 (four year terms)
Ferne Halman, Chairperson
Bruce Brine, Chief Administrative Officer

Cornwall
P.O. Box 430
Cornwall, PE C0A 1H0
Tel: 902-566-2354; *Fax:* 902-566-5228
town.cornwall@town.cornwall.pe.ca
www.town.cornwall.pe.ca
Municipal Type: Town
Incorporated: 1995 *Area:* 28.2 sq km
County or District: Malpeque; *Population in 2006:* 4,677
Provincial Electoral District(s): North River-Rice Point
Federal Electoral District(s): Malpeque
Next Election: Nov. 2010 (four year terms)
Glen (Barney) Fullerton, Mayor
902-566-2354
gfullerton@town.cornwall.pe.ca
Kevin McCarville, Chief Administrative Officer
902-566-2354
kmccarville@town.cornwall.pe.ca

Crapaud
P.O. Box 30
Crapaud, PE C0A 1J0
Tel: 902-658-2983;
crapaudadmin@pei.aibn.com
Municipal Type: Community
Incorporated: 1950 *Area:* 2.16 sq km
County or District: Malpeque; *Population in 2006:* 353
Provincial Electoral District(s): Crapaud-Hazel Grove
Federal Electoral District(s): Malpeque
Next Election: Nov. 2010 (four year terms)
Lyndon Mayhew, Chairperson
Kathy Nicholson, Chief Administrative Officer

Darlington
760 Darlington Rd., RR#4
North Wiltshire, PE C0A 1Y0
Tel: 902-964-2438
Municipal Type: Community
Incorporated: 1983
County or District: Malpeque; *Population in 2006:* 78
Provincial Electoral District(s): Crapaud-Hazel Grove
Federal Electoral District(s): Malpeque
Next Election: Nov. 2010 (four year terms)
Warren MacDonald, Chairperson
Bonnie MacDonald, Chief Administrative Officer

Eastern Kings
RR#1
Elmira, PE C0A 1K0
Tel: 902-357-2534; *Fax:* 902-357-2386
easternkingscommunitycouncil@pei.sympatico.ca
Municipal Type: Community
Incorporated: 1974
County or District: Cardigan; *Population in 2006:* 1,272
Provincial Electoral District(s): Souris-Elmira
Federal Electoral District(s): Cardigan
Next Election: Nov. 2010 (four year terms)
Sheila Eastman, Chairperson
Kay Sweeney, Chief Administrative Officer

Ellerslie-Bideford
P.O. Box 13
Ellerslie, PE C0B 1J0
Tel: 902-831-3268;
mandj@pei.sympatico.ca
Municipal Type: Community
Incorporated: 1977
County or District: Egmont; *Population in 2006:* 463
Provincial Electoral District(s): Cascumpec-Grand River
Federal Electoral District(s): Egmont
Next Election: Nov. 2010 (four year terms)
Nan Ferrier, Chairperson
Julie Ellisworth-Enman, Chief Administrative Officer

Georgetown
P.O. Box 89
36 Kent St.
Georgetown, PE C0A 1L0
Tel: 902-652-2924; *Fax:* 902-652-2701
georgetown@pei.sympatico.ca
www.georgetown.ca
Municipal Type: Town
Incorporated: 1912 *Area:* 1.65 sq km
County or District: Cardigan; *Population in 2006:* 634
Provincial Electoral District(s): Georgetown-Baldwin's Road
Federal Electoral District(s): Cardigan
Next Election: Nov. 2010 (four year terms)
Lewis Lavandier, Mayor
lewis.lavandier@georgetown.ca
Tonya Cameron, Chief Administrative Officer
tonya.cameron@georgetown.ca

Grand Tracadie
York, PE C0A 1P0
Tel: 902-672-3429
Municipal Type: Community
Incorporated: 1984
County or District: Cardigan; *Population in 2006:* 543
Provincial Electoral District(s): Tracadie-Fort Augustus
Federal Electoral District(s): Cardigan
Next Election: Nov. 2010 (four year terms)
Kim Meunier, Chairperson
Patsy MacKinnon, Chief Administrative Officer

Greenmount-Montrose
1981 Union Rd., RR#2
Alberton, PE C0B 1B0
Tel: 902-853-3949; *Fax:* 902-853-2583
Municipal Type: Community
Incorporated: 1977
County or District: Egmont; *Population in 2006:* 319
Provincial Electoral District(s): Tignish-DeBlois
Federal Electoral District(s): Egmont
Next Election: Nov. 2010 (four year terms)
David Pizio, Chairperson
Donna Gallant, Chief Administrative Officer

Hampshire
RR#2
North Wiltshire, PE C0A 1Y0
Tel: 902-368-1144
Municipal Type: Community
Incorporated: 1974
County or District: Malpeque; *Population in 2006:* 327
Provincial Electoral District(s): North River-Rice Point; Crapaud-Hazel Grove
Federal Electoral District(s): Malpeque
Next Election: Nov. 2010 (four year terms)
Florence Nicholson, Chairperson
Gail Stewart, Chief Administrative Officer

Hazelbrook
1011 Donagh Rd, RR#5
Charlottetown, PE C1A 7J8
Tel: 902-892-5918; *Fax:* 902-892-5760
rbrunell@telusplanet.net
Municipal Type: Community
Incorporated: 1974
County or District: Cardigan; *Population in 2006:* 216
Provincial Electoral District(s): Belfast-Pownal Bay; Tracadie-Fort Augustus
Federal Electoral District(s): Cardigan
Next Election: Nov. 2010 (four year terms)
Brian Gallant, Chairperson
Ruth Copeland, Chief Administrative Officer

Hunter River
P.O. Box 154
Hunter River, PE C0A 1N0
Tel: 902-621-2170;
admin.hunter.river@gmail.com
www.peicaps.org/~hunterriver

Municipal Type: Community
Incorporated: 1974 *Area:* 6.08 sq km
County or District: Malpeque; *Population in 2006:* 319
Provincial Electoral District(s): Crapaud-Hazel Grove; Park Corner-Oyster Bed
Federal Electoral District(s): Malpeque
Next Election: Nov. 2010 (four year terms)
Paul Ellis, Chairperson
Zoe Kunschner, Chief Administrative Officer

Kensington
P.O. Box 418
55 Victoria St.
Kensington, PE C0B 1M0
Tel: 902-836-3781; *Fax:* 902-836-3741
mail@townofkensington.com
www.townofkensington.com
Municipal Type: Town
Incorporated: 1914 *Area:* 2.26 sq km
County or District: Malpeque; *Population in 2006:* 1,485
Provincial Electoral District(s): Kensington-Malpeque
Federal Electoral District(s): Malpeque
Next Election: Nov. 2010 (four year terms)
Gordon Coffin, Mayor
mayor@townofkensington.com
Geoff Baker, Chief Administrative Officer
townmanager@townofkensington.com

Kingston
P.O. Box 648
Cornwall, PE C0A 1H0
Tel: 902-675-3670; *Fax:* 902-628-4024
Municipal Type: Community
Incorporated: 1974
County or District: Malpeque; *Population in 2006:* 685
Provincial Electoral District(s): North River-Rice Point; Crapaud-Hazel Grove
Federal Electoral District(s): Malpeque
Next Election: Nov. 2010 (four year terms)
Kimberlee Trainor, Chairperson
Dianne Dowling, Chief Administrative Officer

Kinkora
P.O. Box 38
Kinkora, PE C0B 1N0
Tel: 902-887-2868; *Fax:* 902-887-3514
communityofkinkora@bellaliant.com
www.kinkorapei.com
Municipal Type: Community
Incorporated: 1955 *Area:* 3.82 sq km
County or District: Malpeque; *Population in 2006:* 326
Provincial Electoral District(s): Borden-Kinkora
Federal Electoral District(s): Malpeque
Next Election: Nov. 2010 (four year terms)
Roger Savoie, Chairperson
Vacant, Chief Administrative Officer

Lady Slipper
RR#2
Tyne Valley, PE C0B 2C0
Tel: 902-831-3496
Municipal Type: Community
Incorporated: 1983
County or District: Egmont; *Population in 2006:* 1,076
Provincial Electoral District(s): Casumpec-Grand River
Federal Electoral District(s): Egmont
Next Election: Nov. 2010 (four year terms)
Julie Smith, Chairperson
Douglas MacLeod, Chief Administrative Officer

Linkletter
211 Glenn Dr.
Linkletter, PE C1N 5N2
Tel: 902-888-5465; *Fax:* 902-436-1520
Municipal Type: Community
Incorporated: 1972 *Area:* 9.05 sq km
County or District: Egmont; *Population in 2006:* 321
Provincial Electoral District(s): St. Eleanors-Summerside
Federal Electoral District(s): Egmont
Next Election: Nov. 2010 (four year terms)
David Linkletter, Chairperson
Gary Linkletter, Chief Administrative Officer

Lorne Valley
c/o Karen McLeod
RR#3
Cardigan, PE C0A 1G0
Tel: 902-838-4160
Municipal Type: Community
Incorporated: 1978
County or District: Cardigan; *Population in 2006:* 91
Provincial Electoral District(s): Georgetown-Baldwin's Road
Federal Electoral District(s): Cardigan
Next Election: Nov. 2010 (four year terms)
Karen MacLeod, Chairperson
Rhonda Fisher, Chief Administrative Officer

Lot 11 & Area
RR#2
Ellerslie, PE C0B 1J0
Tel: 902-831-2787;
www.lot11andarea.org
Municipal Type: Community
Incorporated: 1982
County or District: Egmont; *Population in 2006:* 780
Provincial Electoral District(s): Cascumpec-Grand River
Federal Electoral District(s): Egmont
Next Election: Nov. 2010 (four year terms)
Alfred Bridges, Chairperson
Mary Williams, Chief Administrative Officer

Lower Montague
P.O. Box 821
Montague, PE C0A 1R0
Tel: 902-838-5405; *Fax:* 902-838-3617
administrator@lowermontague.ca
Municipal Type: Community
Incorporated: 1974
County or District: Cardigan; *Population in 2006:* 450
Provincial Electoral District(s): Montague-Kilmuir
Federal Electoral District(s): Cardigan
Next Election: Nov. 2010 (four year terms)
Scott Annear, Chairperson
Elizabeth Nicholson, Chief Administrative Officer

Malpeque Bay
P.O. Box 405
Kensington, PE C0B 1M0
Tel: 902-836-5029;
cic@isnhighspeed.ca
www.malpequebay.ca
Municipal Type: Community
Incorporated: 1973
County or District: Malpeque; *Population in 2006:* 1,238
Provincial Electoral District(s): Kensington-Malpeque
Federal Electoral District(s): Malpeque
Next Election: Nov. 2010 (four year terms)
David Smith, Chairperson
Joanne McCarvill, Chief Administrative Officer

Meadowbank
P.O. Box 316
RR#2
Cornwall, PE C0A 1H0
Tel: 902-566-3215
Municipal Type: Community
Incorporated: 1974 *Area:* 9.25 sq km
County or District: Malpeque; *Population in 2006:* 364
Provincial Electoral District(s): North River-Rice Point
Federal Electoral District(s): Malpeque
Next Election: Nov. 2010 (four year terms)
Helen MacPhail, Chairperson
Alan MacCormac, Chief Administrative Officer

Miltonvale Park
P.O. Box 38
Winsloe, PE C1E 1Z2
Tel: 902-368-3090; *Fax:* 902-368-1152
admin@miltonvalepark.com
www.miltonvalepark.com
Municipal Type: Community
Incorporated: 1974 *Area:* 35.32 sq km
County or District: Malpeque; *Population in 2006:* 1,163
Provincial Electoral District(s): Winsloe-West Royalty
Federal Electoral District(s): Malpeque
Next Election: Nov. 2010 (four year terms)
Betty Pryor, Chairperson
Shari MacDonald, Chief Administrative Officer

Miminegash
General Delivery
Miminegash, PE C0B 1S0
Tel: 902-882-4298;
ydeagle@islandtelecom.com
Municipal Type: Community
Incorporated: 1968 *Area:* 1.85 sq km
County or District: Egmont; *Population in 2006:* 176
Provincial Electoral District(s): Alberton-Miminegash
Federal Electoral District(s): Egmont
Next Election: Nov. 2010 (four year terms)
Charlie Murphy, Chairperson
Yvonne Deagle, Chief Administrative Officer

Miscouche
P.O. Box 70
Miscouche, PE C0B 1T0
Tel: 902-436-4962; *Fax:* 902-436-4962
communityofmiscouche@pei.aibn.com
Municipal Type: Community
Incorporated: 1957 *Area:* 2.81 sq km
County or District: Egmont; *Population in 2006:* 769
Provincial Electoral District(s): Evangeline-Miscouche
Federal Electoral District(s): Egmont
Next Election: Nov. 2010 (four year terms)
Wayne Poirier, Chairperson
Judy Gallant, Chief Administrative Officer

Montague
24 Queens Rd.
Montague, PE C0A 1R0
Tel: 902-838-2528; *Fax:* 902-838-3392
cgill@montaguepei.ca
www.townofmontaguepei.com
Municipal Type: Town
Incorporated: 1917 *Area:* 3.04 sq km
County or District: Cardigan; *Population in 2006:* 1,802
Provincial Electoral District(s): Montague-Kilmuir
Federal Electoral District(s): Cardigan
Next Election: Nov. 2010 (four year terms)
Richard Collins, Mayor
racollins@montaguepei.ca
Andrew Daggett, Chief Administrative Officer
adaggett@montaguepei.ca

Morell
P.O. Box 173
Morell, PE C0A 1S0
Tel: 902-961-2900;
morellcommunity@eastlink.ca
members.tripod.com/~Mrcap
Municipal Type: Community
Incorporated: 1953 *Area:* 1.40 sq km
County or District: Cardigan; *Population in 2006:* 306
Provincial Electoral District(s): Morell-Fortune Bay
Federal Electoral District(s): Cardigan
Next Election: Nov. 2010 (four year terms)
Jean Eldershaw, Chairperson
Paula Sinnott, Chief Administrative Officer

Mount Stewart
P.O. Box 143
Mount Stewart, PE C0A 1T0
Tel: 902-676-2881; *Fax:* 902-731-3111
mountstewart@eastlink.ca
Municipal Type: Community
Incorporated: 1953 *Area:* 1.22 sq km
County or District: Cardigan; *Population in 2006:* 261
Provincial Electoral District(s): Tracadie-Fort Augustus
Federal Electoral District(s): Cardigan
Next Election: Nov. 2010 (four year terms)
Connie Doucette, Chairperson
Christine Watts, Chief Administrative Officer

Murray Harbour
P.O. Box 72
Murray Harbour, PE C0A 1V0
Tel: 902-962-3835; *Fax:* 902-962-3835
villoffice@eastlink.ca
www.murrayharbourpei.com
Municipal Type: Community
Incorporated: 1953 *Area:* 4.01 sq km
County or District: Cardigan; *Population in 2006:* 358
Provincial Electoral District(s): Murray River-Gaspereaux
Federal Electoral District(s): Cardigan
Next Election: Nov. 2010 (four year terms)
Faye Fraser, Chairperson
Joan Young, Chief Administrative Officer

Murray River
P.O. Box 266
Murray River, PE C0A 1W0
Tel: 902-962-2820; *Fax:* 902-962-3671
mrvillage@isnhighspeed.ca
www.murrayriverpei.com
Municipal Type: Community
Incorporated: 1955 *Area:* 1.43 sq km
County or District: Cardigan; *Population in 2006:* 430
Provincial Electoral District(s): Murray River-Gaspereaux
Federal Electoral District(s): Cardigan
Next Election: Nov. 2010 (four year terms)
Anne Petley, Chairperson
Dianne MacDonald, Chief Administrative Officer

New Haven-Riverdale
599 Riverdale Rd., RR#3
Bonshaw, PE C0A 1C0
Tel: 902-675-3670; *Fax:* 902-368-1239
dianne_dowling@hotmail.com
Municipal Type: Community
Incorporated: 1974
County or District: Malpeque; *Population in 2006:* 500
Provincial Electoral District(s): Crapaud-Hazel Grove
Federal Electoral District(s): Malpeque
Next Election: Nov. 2010 (four year terms)
Stephen Gould, Chairperson
Dianne Dowling, Chief Administrative Officer

North Rustico
P.O. Box 38
North Rustico, PE C0A 1X0
Tel: 902-963-3211; *Fax:* 902-963-3321
northrustico@pei.aibn.com
www.northrustico.net
Municipal Type: Community
Incorporated: 1954 *Area:* 2.45 sq km
County or District: Malpeque; *Population in 2006:* 599
Provincial Electoral District(s): Park Corner-Oyster Bed
Federal Electoral District(s): Malpeque
Next Election: Nov. 2010 (four year terms)
Giles Gallant, Chairperson
Patsy Gamauf, Chief Administrative Officer

North Shore
P.O. Box 134 Post Office
York, PE C0A 1P0
Tel: 902-672-2363; *Fax:* 902-672-1766
nscouncil@stanhopecovehead.pe.ca
www.stanhopecovehead.pe.ca
Municipal Type: Community
Incorporated: 1974
County or District: Malpeque; *Population in 2006:* 737
Provincial Electoral District(s): Stanhope-East Royalty
Federal Electoral District(s): Malpeque
Next Election: Nov. 2010 (four year terms)
Sandy Gallant, Chairperson
argallant@edu.pe.ca
Joanne Smith, Chief Administrative Officer
nscc@pei.aibn.com

North Wiltshire
North Wiltshire, PE C0A 1Y0
Tel: 902-621-1908
Municipal Type: Community
Incorporated: 1974
County or District: Egmont; *Population in 2006:* 208
Provincial Electoral District(s): Crapaud-Hazel Grove
Federal Electoral District(s): Malpeque
Next Election: Nov. 2010 (four year terms)
Robert Bertram, Chairperson
Charlene Waddell, Chief Administrative Officer

Northport
P.O. Box 466
Alberton, PE C0B 1B0
Tel: 902-853-2551
Municipal Type: Community
Incorporated: 1974
County or District: Egmont; *Population in 2006:* 210
Provincial Electoral District(s): Alberton-Miminegash
Federal Electoral District(s): Egmont
Next Election: Nov. 2010 (four year terms)
Wendy McNeil, Chairperson
Paula Foley, Chief Administrative Officer

O'Leary
P.O. Box 130
O'Leary, PE C0B 1V0
Tel: 902-859-3311; *Fax:* 902-859-2341
olearyadm@eastlink.ca
www.community.oleary.pe.ca
Municipal Type: Community
Incorporated: 1951 *Area:* 1.57 sq km
County or District: Egmont; *Population in 2006:* 861
Provincial Electoral District(s): West Point-Bloomfield
Federal Electoral District(s): Egmont
Next Election: Nov. 2010 (four year terms)
Nancy Wallace, Chairperson
Beverley Shaw, Chief Administrative Officer

Pleasant Grove
1118 Pleasant Grove, RR#2
York, PE C0A 1P0
Tel: 902-672-3472
Municipal Type: Community
Incorporated: 1980
County or District: Malpeque; *Population in 2006:* 194
Provincial Electoral District(s): Stanhope-East Royalty
Federal Electoral District(s): Malpeque
Next Election: Nov. 2010 (four year terms)
Doyle Eugene, Chairperson
Kim Doyle, Chief Administrative Officer

Resort Municipality
RR#2
Hunter River, PE C0A 1N0
Tel: 902-963-2698; *Fax:* 902-963-2932
resort@pei.aibn.com
Municipal Type: Community
Incorporated: 1990 *Area:* 37.74 sq km
Population in 2006: 272
Provincial Electoral District(s): Park Corner-Oyster Bed
Federal Electoral District(s): Malpeque
Next Election: Nov. 2010 (four year terms)
Mel Gass, Chairperson
Brenda MacDonald, Chief Administrative Officers

Richmond
P.O. Box 18
Richmond, PE C0B 1Y0
Tel: 902-854-2298; *Fax:* 902-854-3621
p_cbrown@airtechca.com
Municipal Type: Community
Incorporated: 1979
County or District: Egmont; *Population in 2006:* 248
Provincial Electoral District(s): Cascumpec-Grand River; Evangeline-Miscouche
Federal Electoral District(s): Egmont
Next Election: Nov. 2010 (four year terms)
Leonard Gallant, Chairperson
Carol Brown, Chief Administrative Officer

St. Felix
P.O. Box 22
Tignish, PE C0B 2B0
Tel: 902-882-4015
Municipal Type: Community
Incorporated: 1977
County or District: Egmont; *Population in 2006:* 359
Provincial Electoral District(s): Tignish-DeBlois
Federal Electoral District(s): Egmont
Next Election: Nov. 2010 (four year terms)
Claude Gaudette, Chairperson
Joanne Gaudette, Chief Administrative Officer

St. Louis
P.O. Box 40
St. Louis, PE C0B 1Z0
Tel: 902-882-2447
Municipal Type: Community
Incorporated: 1964 *Area:* 0.62 sq km
County or District: Egmont; *Population in 2006:* 80
Provincial Electoral District(s): Alberton-Miminegash; Tignish-DeBlois
Federal Electoral District(s): Egmont
Next Election: Nov. 2010 (four year terms)
Everett Wedge, Chairperson
Linda McCue, Chief Administrative Officer

St. Nicholas
3699 St. Nicholas
Miscouche, PE C0B 1T0
Tel: 902-854-2731
Municipal Type: Community
Incorporated: 1991
Population in 2006: 177
Provincial Electoral District(s): Evangeline-Miscouche
Federal Electoral District(s): Egmont
Next Election: Nov. 2010 (four year terms)
Pam Dawson, Chairperson
Corina Mundy, Chief Administrative Officer

St. Peter's Bay
P.O. Box 51
St. Peter's Bay, PE C0A 2A0
Tel: 902-961-2268; *Fax:* 902-961-3148
stpeters@eastlink.ca
Municipal Type: Community
Incorporated: 1953 *Area:* 4.24 sq km
County or District: Cardigan; *Population in 2006:* 248
Provincial Electoral District(s): Morell-Fortune Bay
Federal Electoral District(s): Cardigan
Next Election: Nov. 2010 (four year terms)
Ron MacInnis, Chairperson
Mary Burge, Chief Administrative Officer

Sherbrooke
P.O. Box 1344
Summerside, PE C1N 4K2
Tel: 902-436-7005; *Fax:* 902-436-7005
Municipal Type: Community
Incorporated: 1972 *Area:* 8.83 sq km
Population in 2006: 168
Provincial Electoral District(s): Wilmot-Summerside
Federal Electoral District(s): Egmont
Next Election: Nov. 2010 (four year terms)
Ron Chappell, Chair
Peggy Kilbride, Chief Administrative Officer

Souris
P.O. Box 628
75 Main St.
Souris, PE C0A 2B0
Tel: 902-687-2157; *Fax:* 902-687-4426
town@sourispei.com
www.sourispei.com
Municipal Type: Town
Incorporated: 1910 *Area:* 3.42 sq km
County or District: Cardigan; *Population in 2006:* 1,232
Provincial Electoral District(s): Souris-Elmira
Federal Electoral District(s): Cardigan
Next Election: Nov. 2010 (four year terms)
David McDonald, Mayor
902-969-3361
Shelley LaVie, Chief Administrative Officer
902-687-2157
smacinnis@sourispei.com

Souris West
P.O. Box 680
Souris, PE C0A 2B0
Tel: 902-215-0513
Municipal Type: Community
Incorporated: 1972
County or District: Cardigan; *Population in 2006:* 327
Provincial Electoral District(s): Souris-Elmira
Federal Electoral District(s): Cardigan
Next Election: Nov. 2010 (four year terms)
Mark Kickham, Chairperson
Susan Wrabiutza-Smith, Chief Administrative Officer

Stratford
234 Shakespeare Dr.
Stratford, PE C1B 2V8
Tel: 902-569-1995; *Fax:* 902-569-5000
info@town.stratford.pe.ca
www.town.stratford.pe.ca
Municipal Type: Town
Incorporated: April 1, 1995 *Area:* 22.48 sq km
Population in 2006: 7,083
Provincial Electoral District(s): Glen Stewart-Bellevue Cove
Federal Electoral District(s): Cardigan
Next Election: Nov. 2010 (four year terms)
David Dunphy, Mayor
902-569-2149
ddunphy@town.stratford.pe.ca
Robert Hughes, Chief Administrative Officer
902-569-6251
rhughes@town.stratford.pe.ca

Tignish
P.O. Box 57
209 Phillip St.
Tignish, PE C0B 2B0
Tel: 902-882-2600; *Fax:* 902-882-2414
karen@village.tignish.pe.ca
www.tignish.com
Municipal Type: Community
Incorporated: 1952 *Area:* 5.86 sq km
County or District: Egmont; *Population in 2006:* 758
Provincial Electoral District(s): Tignish-DeBlois
Federal Electoral District(s): Egmont
Next Election: Nov. 2010 (four year terms)
Gerard LeClair, Chairperson
Karen Gaudet-Gavin, Chief Administrative Officer

Tignish Shore
Kildare Cape
Tignish, PE C0B 2B0
Tel: 902-882-3811
Municipal Type: Community
Incorporated: 1975
Population in 2006: 72
Provincial Electoral District(s): Tignish-DeBlois
Federal Electoral District(s): Egmont
Next Election: Nov. 2010 (four year terms)
Ronnie McRae, Chairperson
Donna MacKay, Chief Administrative Officer

Tyne Valley
P.O. Box 39
Tyne Valley, PE C0B 2C0
Tel: 902-831-2938
Municipal Type: Community
Incorporated: 1966 *Area:* 1.74 sq km
County or District: Egmont; *Population in 2006:* 226
Provincial Electoral District(s): Cascumpec-Grand River
Federal Electoral District(s): Egmont
Next Election: Nov. 2010 (four year terms)
Kevin Kadey, Chairperson
Marie Barlow, Chief Administrative Officer

Union Road
P.O. Box 5908
2257 Horne Cross Rd., RR#3
Union Road, PE C1A 7J7
Tel: 902-566-4097
Municipal Type: Community
Incorporated: 1977 *Area:* 9.95 sq km
County or District: Malpeque; *Population in 2006:* 245
Provincial Electoral District(s): Georgetown-Baldwin's Road
Federal Electoral District(s): Malpeque
Next Election: Nov. 2010 (four year terms)
Fern Yeo, Chairperson
Vicki Cotton, Chief Administrative Officer

Valleyfield
RR#3
Montague, PE C0A 1R0
Tel: 902-838-4447
Municipal Type: Community
Incorporated: 1974
County or District: Cardigan; *Population in 2006:* 648
Provincial Electoral District(s): Georgetown-Baldwin's Road; Montague-Kilmuir; Belfast-Pownal Bay
Federal Electoral District(s): Cardigan
Next Election: Nov. 2010 (four year terms)
Graham Jones, Chairperson
Margaret Campion, Chief Administrative Officer

Victoria
P.O. Box 7
Victoria, PE C0A 2G0
Tel: 902-658-2541; *Fax:* 902-658-2541
victoriaadmin@eastlink.ca
Municipal Type: Community
Incorporated: 1951 *Area:* 1.40 sq km
County or District: Malpeque; *Population in 2006:* 77
Provincial Electoral District(s): Crapaud-Hazel Grove
Federal Electoral District(s): Malpeque
Next Election: Nov. 2010 (four year terms)
Ben Smith, Chairperson
Hilary Dunsmore, Chief Administrative Officer

Warren Grove
P.O. Box 963
Cornwall, PE C0A 1H0
Tel: 902-675-2788;
rodr@isnhighspeed.ca
Municipal Type: Community
Incorporated: 1985 *Area:* 10.32 sq km
County or District: Malpeque; *Population in 2006:* 341
Provincial Electoral District(s): North River-Rice Point
Federal Electoral District(s): Malpeque
Next Election: Nov. 2010 (four year terms)
Ambre Tawil, Chairperson
Rod Raper, Chief Administrative Officer

Wellington
P.O. Box 26
Wellington, PE C0B 2E0
Tel: 902-854-2920
Municipal Type: Community
Incorporated: 1959 *Area:* 1.80 sq km
County or District: Egmont; *Population in 2006:* 401
Provincial Electoral District(s): Cascumpec-Grand River; Evangeline-Miscouche
Federal Electoral District(s): Egmont
Next Election: Nov. 2010 (four year terms)
Gilles Painchaud, Chairperson
Claudette Gallant, Chief Administrative Officer

West River
#12, 10 Mutch Dr.
Stratford, PE C1B 1S5
Tel: 902-566-9179; *Fax:* 902-368-0327
Municipal Type: Community
Incorporated: 1974
County or District: Malpeque; *Population in 2006:* 296
Provincial Electoral District(s): North River-Rice Point
Federal Electoral District(s): Malpeque
Next Election: Nov. 2010 (four year terms)
Eric MacArthur, Chairperson
Bill Grant, Chief Administrative Officer

Winsloe South
RR#9
Winsloe, PE C1E 1Z3
Tel: 902-368-1444
Municipal Type: Community
Incorporated: 1986 *Area:* 9.63 sq km
County or District: Malpeque; *Population in 2006:* 198
Provincial Electoral District(s): Winsloe-West Royalty
Federal Electoral District(s): Malpeque
Next Election: Nov. 2010 (four year terms)
Brian Turner, Chairperson
Joanne Turner, Chief Administrative Officer

York
53 Andrews Ct.
Charlottetown, PE C1C 1B2
Tel: 902-566-5653;
cakellough@hotmail.com
Municipal Type: Community
Incorporated: 1986
Population in 2006: 296
Provincial Electoral District(s): Stanhope-East Royalty
Federal Electoral District(s): Malpeque
Next Election: Nov. 2010 (four year terms)
Robert Adams, Chairperson
Robert Jourdain, Chief Administrative Officer

QUÉBEC

Québec legislation recognizes two levels of municipal organization: the local and the regional.

Major municipal reform has reduced the number of local municipalities from nearly 1,400 in 1998 to 1,087 on April 1, 2005. Of this number, 201 towns fall under the jurisdiction of the Cities and Towns Act (RSQ, chap. C-19). Nine of them have over 100,000 inhabitants and account for 53% of the Québec population. The 886 other local municipalities, which go by a variety of designations (township, united township, parish, municipality, village) are governed by the Municipal Code of Québec (RSQ, chap. C-27.1). Québec also has 96 unorganized territories, 39 Indian reserves, 14 Northern villages, eight Cree villages and one Naskapi village.

The regional level of municipal territorial organization includes the Montréal and Québec City metropolitan communities, the 86 regional county municipalities (RCMs), and the Kativik Regional Government. The metropolitan communities and RCMs are made up of local municipalities. RCMs may also include unorganized territories. As for the area under the administration of the Kativik Regional Government, it includes the Northern villages, the Naskapi village and one unorganized territory.

The regional organizations were created to ensure that issues that go beyond local boundaries were handled at the regional or metropolitan level. Although their structures, operation and powers vary, they are based on identical principles. The Montréal and Québec City metropolitan communities are responsible at their level for land use planning, economic development, international economic promotion, artistic and cultural development, regional orientations in public transit, waste management planning, establishing a tax base sharing program, as well as for determining and financing regional facilities, infrastructures, activities, and services. RCMs also meet regional needs, including land use planning and the pooling of services. In addition, they exercise certain powers in the areas of economic development, public security and the environment. The Kativik Regional Government is in charge of local administration, police, transport, communications and labour force training and use, and may also set minimum standards by ordinance for things like house and building construction.

Eight local municipalities belong neither to a metropolitan community nor to one of the regional county municipalities. They do, however, wield some of the same powers as RCMs. This also holds true for six other cities, which although situated within one of the two metropolitan communities, nonetheless exercise certain of the powers of an RCM.

Ten cities are divided into boroughs. The boroughs have consultative and decision-making powers, are responsible for delivering certain neighbourhood services, and are represented by an elected borough council.

Source: Ministère des Affaires municipales, Régions et Occupation du territoire.

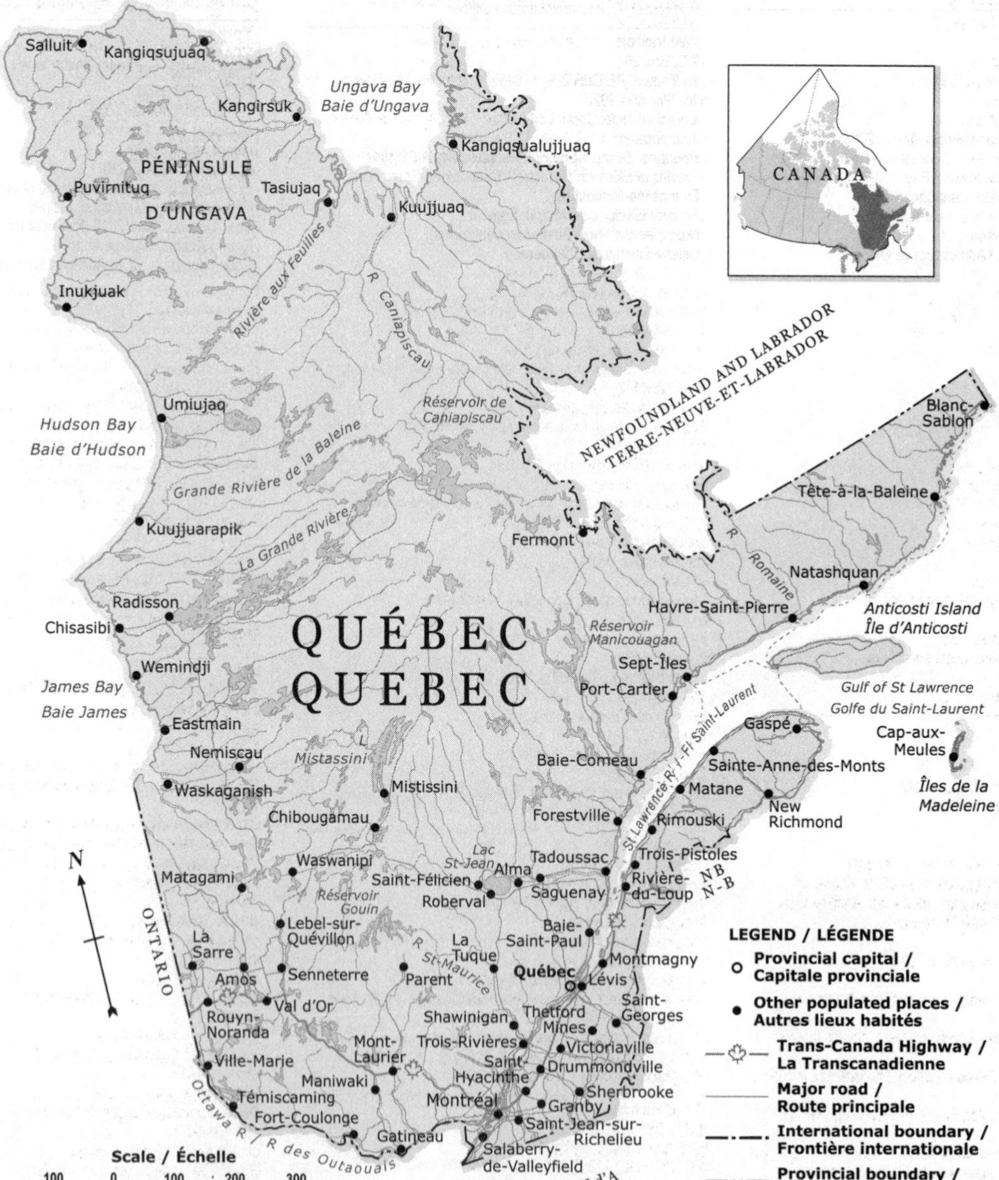

Reproduced with the permission of Natural Resources Canada 2011, courtesy of the Atlas of Canada.

Québec

Major Municipalities in Québec

Alma
140, rue St-Joseph
Alma, QC G8B 3R1
Tél: 418-669-5000; *Téléc:* 418-669-5019
info@ville.alma.qc.ca
www.ville.alma.qc.ca
Entité municipal: City
Incorporation: 21 février 2001 *Area:* 202,10 km2
Comté ou district: Lac-St-Jean-Est; *Population au 2006:* 29,998
Circonscription(s) électorale(s) provinciale(s): Lac-Saint-Jean
Circonscription(s) électorale(s) fédérale(s): Jonquière-Alma
Prochaines élections: 1er novembre 2013
Marc Asselin, Maire
418-669-5005, Fax: 418-668-8923
marc.asselin@ville.alma.qc.ca
Lucien Boily, Conseiller, Ward(s): 1
418-669-1070
lucien.boily@ville.alma.qc.ca
Jocelyn Fradette, Conseillère, Ward(s): 2
418-450-1359
jocelyn.fradette@ville.alma.qc.ca
Gilles Girard, Conseiller, Ward(s): 3
418-668-6815
gilles.girard@ville.alma.qc.ca
Frédéric Tremblay, Conseiller, Ward(s): 4
418-668-5014
frederic.tremblay@ville.alma.qc.ca
Gino Villeneuve, Conseiller, Ward(s): 5
418-321-3458
gino.villeneuve@ville.alma.qc.ca
Sylvie Beaumont, Conseillère, Ward(s): 6
418-668-0919
sylvie.beaumont@ville.alma.qc.ca
Pascal Pilote, Conseiller, Ward(s): 7
418-480-1417
pascal.pilote@ville.alma.qc.ca
Alain Fortin, Conseiller, Ward(s): 8
418-669-1083
alain.fortin@ville.alma.qc.ca
Jean Paradis, Greffier
418-669-5001
jean.paradis@ville.alma.qc.ca
Yves Thériault, Trésorier, Trésorerie
418-669-5001
yves.theriault@ville.alma.qc.ca
Jean-Yves Lessard, Directeur
418-669-5001, Fax: 418-669-5180
jeanyves.lessard@ville.alma.qc.ca
Guy Simard, Directeur général
418-669-5001
guy.simard@ville.alma.qc.ca
Bernard Dallaire, Directeur, Prévention des incendies
418-669-5059
bernard.dallaire@ville.alma.qc.ca
Jocelyn Tremblay, Directrice, Loisirs & culture
418-669-5111
jocelyn.tremblay@ville.alma.qc.ca

Amos
182, 1re Rue est
Amos, QC J9T 2G1
Tél: 819-732-3254; *Téléc:* 819-727-9792
master@ville.amos.qc.ca
www.ville.amos.qc.ca
Entité municipal: City
Incorporation: 17 janvier 1987 *Area:* 430,84 km2
Comté ou district: Abitibi; *Population au 2006:* 12,584
Circonscription(s) électorale(s) provinciale(s): Abitibi-Ouest
Circonscription(s) électorale(s) fédérale(s): Abitibi-Témiscamingue
Prochaines élections: 3e novembre 2013
Ulrick Chérubin, Maire
Sébastien D'Astous, Conseiller, Infrastructures & services aux citoyens, Ward(s): 1
Amélie Mercier, Conseillère, Environnement, culture & services à la population, Ward(s): 2
Éric Mathieu, Conseiller, Développement économique, industriel & commercial, Ward(s): 3
Denis Chandonnet, Conseiller, Administration & sports, Ward(s): 4
Benoit Deshaies, Conseiller, Qualité de vie & famille, Ward(s): 5
Julie Cazes, Conseillère, Administration, développement communautaire & social & service à la population, Ward(s): 6
Alain Plante, Greffier
819-732-3254, Fax: 819-727-9792
Gérald Lavoie, Trésorier
819-732-3254, Fax: 819-727-9792
Régis Fortin, Directeur, Service de l'environnement
819-732-3254, Fax: 819-732-9675

Baie-Comeau
19, av Marquette
Baie-Comeau, QC G4Z 1K5
Tél: 418-296-4931; *Téléc:* 418-296-3759
vbc@ville.baie-comeau.qc.ca
www.ville.baie-comeau.qc.ca
Entité municipal: City
Incorporation: 23 juin 1982 *Area:* 371,69 km2
Comté ou district: Manicouagan; *Population au 2006:* 22,554
Circonscription(s) électorale(s) provinciale(s): René-Lévesque
Circonscription(s) électorale(s) fédérale(s): Manicouagan
Prochaines élections: 3e novembre 2013
Christine Brisson, Mairesse
418-296-8109, Fax: 418-296-4194
mairie@ville.baie-comeau.qc.ca
Alain Larouche, Conseiller, Ward(s): Saint-Sacrement
418-589-2107
Richard Bélanger, Conseiller, Ward(s): Mgr-Bélanger
418-589-9979
Denise Arsenault, Conseillère, Ward(s): Trudel
418-589-6795
Carole Deschênes, Conseillère, Ward(s): N.-A.-Labrie
418-589-8734
André Veillette, Conseiller, Ward(s): La Chasse
418-296-6070
Léa Thibault, Conseillère, Ward(s): Saint-Nom-de-Marie
418-296-4654
Reina Savoie Jourdain, Conseillère, Ward(s): Sainte-Amélie
418-296-5231
Régis Deschênes, Conseiller, Ward(s): Saint-Georges
418-296-5989
Lorna Pineault, Greffière
418-296-8898, Fax: 418-296-8194
lpineault@ville.baie-comeau.qc.ca
Danielle Bernatchez, Trésorière
418-296-8128, Fax: 418-296-3759
dbernatchez@ville.baie-comeau.qc.ca
François Corriveau, Directeur général (par intérim)
418-296-8104, Fax: 418-296-8121
jviens@ville.baie-comeau.qc.ca
Jacques Comeau, Directeur, Service des communications
418-296-8142, Fax: 418-296-3759
jcomeau@ville.baie-comeau.qc.ca
François LeBlond, Directeur, Loisirs, sports & vie communautaire
418-296-8358, Fax: 418-296-8399
fleblond@ville.baie-comeau.qc.ca
Ghislain Gauthier, Directeur, Service des travaux publics
418-296-8180, Fax: 418-296-3095
ggauthier@ville.baie-comeau.qc.ca
David Pollock, Maire
514-428-4410
Michael Montagano, Conseiller, Ward(s): 1
514-697-9558
Karin Essen, Conseiller, Ward(s): 2
514-693-5024
Wade Staddon, Conseiller, Ward(s): 3
514-448-1349
Brian Ross, Conseiller, Ward(s): 4
514-865-3176
Roy Baird, Conseiller, Ward(s): 5
514-630-1576
Rhonda Massad, Conseiller, Ward(s): 6
514-830-6694

Beaconsfield
303, boul Beaconsfield
Beaconsfield, QC H9W 4A7
Tél: 514-428-4400; *Téléc:* 514-428-4424
info@beaconsfield.ca
www.beaconsfield.ca
Entité municipal: City
Incorporation: 1er janvier 2006 *Area:* 10,64 km2
Comté ou district: Communauté métropolitaine de Montréal; *Population au 2006:* 19,194
Circonscription(s) électorale(s) provinciale(s): Jacques-Cartier
Circonscription(s) électorale(s) fédérale(s): Lac-Saint-Louis
Prochaines élections: 3e novembre 2013

Beauharnois
#100, 660, rue Ellice
Beauharnois, QC J6N 1Y1
Tél: 450-429-3546; *Téléc:* 450-429-2478
direction.generale@ville.beauharnois.qc.ca
www.ville.beauharnois.qc.ca
Entité municipal: City
Incorporation: 1er janvier 2002 *Area:* 73,05 km2
Comté ou district: Beauharnois-Salaberry; *Population au 2006:* 11,918
Circonscription(s) électorale(s) provinciale(s): Beauharnois
Circonscription(s) électorale(s) fédérale(s): Beauharnois-Salaberry
Prochaines élections: 3e novembre 2013
Claude Haineault, Maire
450-429-3546
Gaëtan Dagenais, Conseiller, Ward(s): 1
Michel Quevillon, Conseiller, Ward(s): 2
Guillaume Lévesque-Sauvé, Conseiller, Ward(s): 3
Patrick Laniel, Conseiller, Ward(s): 4
Jocelyne Rajotte, Conseillère, Ward(s): 5
Bruno Tremblay, Conseiller, Ward(s): 6
Manon Fortier, Greffière
manon.fortier@ville.beauharnois.qc.ca
Alain Gravel, Directeur général
alain.gravel@ville.beauharnois.qc.ca
Guylaine Côte, Trésorière
guylaine.cote@ville.beauharnois.qc.ca
Yves Magnan, Directeur, Travaux publics
450-225-0650
yves.magnan@ville.beauharnois.qc.ca
Richard Plouffe, Directeur, Urbanisme
450-429-3546
richard.plouffe@ville.beauharnois.qc.ca
Jean-Maurice Marleau, Directeur, Service des incendies
450-225-2222
directeur.incendie@ville.beauharnois.qc.ca
Daniel Leblanc, Directeur, Environnement
450-429-3959
daniel.leblanc@ville.beauharnois.qc.ca

Bécancour
1295, av Nicolas-Perrot
Bécancour, QC G9H 1A1
Tél: 819-294-6500; *Téléc:* 819-294-6535
becancour@ville.becancour.qc.ca
www.becancour.net
Entité municipal: City
Incorporation: 17 octobre 1965 *Area:* 434,28 km2
Comté ou district: Bécancour; *Population au 2006:* 11,011
Circonscription(s) électorale(s) provinciale(s): Nicolet-Yamaska
Circonscription(s) électorale(s) fédérale(s): Bas-Richelieu-Nicolet-Bécancour
Prochaines élections: 3e novembre 2013
Maurice Richard, Maire
Fernand Croteau, Conseiller, Ward(s): Bécancour
Gaétane Désilets, Conseillère, Ward(s): Saint-Grégoire
Alain Lévesque, Conseiller, Ward(s): Sainte-Angèle
Guy Richard, Conseiller, Ward(s): Sainte-Gertrude
Mario Gagné, Conseiller, Ward(s): Précieux-Sang
Karl Grondin, Conseiller, Ward(s): Gentilly
France Leclerc, Greffière
Daniel Brunelle, Trésorier
819-294-6500, Fax: 819-294-6535
finances@ville.becancour.qc.ca
Gaston Bélanger, Directeur général

Beloeil
777, rue Laurier
Beloeil, QC J3G 4S9
Tél: 450-467-2835; *Téléc:* 450-464-5445
info@ville.beloeil.qc.ca
www.ville.beloeil.qc.ca
Entité municipal: City
Incorporation: 9e décembre 1903 *Area:* 24 km2
Comté ou district: La Vallée-du-Richelieu; *Population au 2006:* 18,927
Circonscription(s) électorale(s) provinciale(s): Borduas
Circonscription(s) électorale(s) fédérale(s): Chambly-Borduas
Prochaines élections: 3e novembre 2013
Diane Lavoie, Mairesse
450-464-3095
dlavoie@ville.beloeil.qc.ca
Louise Allie, Conseillère, Ward(s): 1
450-446-4201
zoize@hotmail.com
Renée Trudel, Conseillère, Ward(s): 2
514-823-3722
rtrudel@ville.beloeil.qc.ca
Lyse Girard, Conseillère, Ward(s): 3
450-446-8624
lgirard@ville.beloeil.qc.ca
Denis Corriveau, Conseiller, Ward(s): 4
450-464-2435
dcorriveau@ville.beloeil.qc.ca
Guy Bédard, Conseiller, Ward(s): 5
450-446-7837
gbedard@ville.beloeil.qc.ca

Pierre Verret, Conseiller, Ward(s): 6
450-467-0630
pierre-verret@hotmail.com
Lise Touchette, Conseillère, Ward(s): 7
450-467-4645
toulise@videotron.ca
Jean-Yves Labadie, Conseiller, Ward(s): 8
450-446-0347
jylabadie@ville.beloeil.qc.ca
Sylvie Piérard, Greffière
450-467-2835, Fax: 450-464-5445
Cathy Goyette, Directrice, Finances
450-467-2835, Fax: 450-464-5445
Martine Vallières, Directrice générale
450-467-2835, Fax: 450-464-5445
direction@ville.beloeil.qc.ca

Blainville
1000, ch du Plan-Bouchard
Blainville, QC J7C 3S9
Tél: 450-434-5200; *Téléc:* 450-434-8295
accueil@ville.blainville.qc.ca
www.ville.blainville.qc.ca
Entité municipal: City
Incorporation: 1er juillet 1968 *Area:* 54,62 km2
Comté ou district: Thérèse-De Blainville; *Population au 2006:* 46,493
Circonscription(s) électorale(s) provinciale(s): Blainville
Circonscription(s) électorale(s) fédérale(s): Terrebonne-Blainville
Prochaines élections: 3e novembre 2013
François Cantin, Maire
francois.cantin@ville.blainville.qc.ca
Liza Poulin, Conseillère, Ward(s): 1. Fontainebleu
liza.poulin@ville.blainville.qc.ca
Alain Portelance, Conseiller, Ward(s): 2. Côte-Saint-Louis
alain.portelance@ville.blainville.qc.ca
Serge Paquette, Conseiller, Ward(s): 3. Saint-Rédempteur
serge.paquette@ville.blainville.qc.ca
Guy Frigon, Conseiller, Ward(s): 4. Plan-Bouchard
guy.frigon@ville.blainville.qc.ca
Normand Dupont, Conseiller, Ward(s): 5. Notre-Dame-de-l'Assomption
normand.dupont@ville.blainville.qc.ca
Nicole Ruel, Conseillère, Ward(s): 6. Chante-Bois
nicole.ruel@ville.blainville.qc.ca
Louis Lamarre, Conseiller, Ward(s): 7. Hirondelles
louis.lamarre@ville.blainville.qc.ca
Richard Perreault, Conseiller, Ward(s): 8. Alençon
richard.perreault@ville.blainville.qc.ca
François Garand, Conseiller, Ward(s): 9. Renaissance
francois.garand@ville.blainville.qc.ca
Marie-Claude Collin, Conseillère, Ward(s): 10. Blainvillier
marie-claude.collin@ville.blainville.qc.ca
Claude Bertrand, Greffier
Lorraine Barry, Trésorière
Paul Allard, Directeur général

Boisbriand
940, boul de la Grande-Allée
Boisbriand, QC J7G 2J7
Tél: 450-435-1954; *Téléc:* 450-435-6398
www.ville.boisbriand.qc.ca
Entité municipal: City
Incorporation: 1er janvier 1946 *Area:* 26,43 km2
Comté ou district: Thérèse-De Blainville; Communauté métropolitaine de Montréal; *Population au 2009:* 26,674
Circonscription(s) électorale(s) provinciale(s): Groulx
Circonscription(s) électorale(s) fédérale(s): Rivière-des-Mille-Iles
Prochaines élections: 1er novembre 2013
Lucie Mongeau, Greffière
Sylvie St-Jean, Mairesse
sstjean@ville.boisbriand.qc.ca
Michel Lacasse, Directeur général
André Drainville, Directeur, Finances & Trésorerie
Lyne Levert, Conseillers et Districts, Ward(s): 1 Sanche
llevert@ville.boisbriand.qc.ca
Gilles Sauriol, Conseillers et Districts, Ward(s): 2 Du Gué
gsauriol@ville.broisbriand.qc.ca
Robert Frégeau, Conseillers et Districts, Ward(s): 3 Filion
rfregeau@ville.boisbriand.qc.ca
Patrick Thifault, Conseillers et Districts, Ward(s): 4 Dubois
pthifault@ville.boisbriand.qc.ca
Louise Gauthier, Conseillers et Districts, Ward(s): 5 Brosseau
lgauthier@ville.boisbriand.qc.ca
Louise Lemay, Conseillers et Districts, Ward(s): 6 Labelle
llemay@ville.boisbriand.qc.ca
Mario Lavallée, Conseillers et Districts, Ward(s): 7 Desjardins
mlavallee@ville.boisbriand.qc.ca
Marlene Cordato, Conseillers et Districts, Ward(s): 8 Dion
mcordato@ville.boisbriand.qc.ca

Boucherville
500, rue de la Rivière-aux-Pins
Boucherville, QC J4B 2Z7
Tél: 450-449-8100; *Téléc:* 450-655-0086
information@boucherville.ca
www.ville.boucherville.qc.ca
Entité municipal: City
Incorporation: 1er janvier 2006 *Area:* 69,33 km2
Comté ou district: Communauté métropolitaine de Montréal; *Population au 2006:* 39,062
Circonscription(s) électorale(s) provinciale(s): Marguerite-D'Youville
Circonscription(s) électorale(s) fédérale(s): Longueuil—Pierre-Boucher; Verchères—Les Patriotes
Prochaines élections: 3e novembre 2013
Jean Martel, Maire
450-449-8105
mairie@boucherville.ca
Yan Savaria-Laquerre, Conseiller, Ward(s): 1. Pierre-Viger
yan.savaria-laquerre@boucherville.ca
Francine Crevier Bélair, Conseillère, Ward(s): 2. Père-Le Jeune
francine.crevierbelair@boucherville.ca
Alexandra Capone, Conseillère, Ward(s): 3. Sainte Famille
alexandra.capone@boucherville.ca
Anne Barabé, Conseillère, Ward(s): 4. Découvreurs
anne.barabe@boucherville.ca
Dominic Lévesque, Conseiller, Ward(s): 5. Seigneurie
dominic.levesque@boucherville.ca
Magalie Queval, Conseillère, Ward(s): 6. Saint-Louis
magalie.queval@boucherville.ca
Jacqueline Boubane, Conseillère, Ward(s): 7. Mortagne
jacqueline.boubane@boucherville.ca
Lise Roy, Conseillère, Ward(s): 8. Normandie
lise.roy@boucherville.ca
Claude Caron, Greffier
450-449-8605, Fax: 450-655-0086
greffe@boucherville.ca

Brossard
2001, boul Rome
Brossard, QC J4W 3K5
Tél: 450-923-6300; *Téléc:* 450-923-7009
information@brossard.ca
www.ville.brossard.qc.ca
Entité municipal: City
Incorporation: 1er janvier 2006 *Area:* 44,77 km2
Comté ou district: Communauté métropolitaine de Montréal; *Population au 2006:* 71,154
Circonscription(s) électorale(s) provinciale(s): La Pinière
Circonscription(s) électorale(s) fédérale(s): Brossard—La Prairie
Prochaines élections: 3e novembre 2013
Paul Leduc, Maire
450-923-6325
mairie@brossard.ca
Doreen Assaad, Conseillère, Ward(s): 1
450-923-6304
doreen.assaad@brossard.ca
Pierre O'Donoughue, Conseiller, Ward(s): 2
450-923-6304
pierre.odonoughue@brossard.ca
Monique Gagné, Conseillère, Ward(s): 3
450-923-6304
monique.gagne@brossard.ca
Alexandre Plante, Conseiller, Ward(s): 4
450-923-6304
alexandre.plante@brossard.ca
Serge Séguin, Conseiller, Ward(s): 5
450-923-6304
serge.seguin@brossard.ca
Claudio Benedetti, Conseiller, Ward(s): 6
450-923-6304
claudio.benedetti@brossard.ca
Zaki Thomas, Conseiller, Ward(s): 7
450-923-6304
zaki.thomas@brossard.ca
Antoine Assaf, Conseiller, Ward(s): 8
450-923-6304
antoine.assaf@brossard.ca
Pascal Forget, Conseiller, Ward(s): 9
450-923-6304
pascal.forget@brossard.ca
Daniel Lucier, Conseiller, Ward(s): 10
450-923-6304
daniel.lucier@brossard.ca
Diane Lebrun, Greffière
450-923-6305, Fax: 450-923-7009

Candiac
100, boul Montcalm nord
Candiac, QC J5R 3L8
Tél: 450-444-6000; *Téléc:* 450-444-6009
info@ville.candiac.qc.ca
www.ville.candiac.qc.ca
Entité municipal: City
Incorporation: 31 janvier 1957 *Area:* 16,40 km2
Comté ou district: Roussillon; *Population au 2006:* 15,947
Circonscription(s) électorale(s) provinciale(s): La Prairie
Circonscription(s) électorale(s) fédérale(s): Brossard—La Prairie
Prochaines élections: 3e novembre 2013
André J. Côté, Maire
mairie@ville.candiac.qc.ca
Thérèse Gatien, Conseillère, Ward(s): La Promenade
tgatien@ville.candiac.qc.ca
Vincent Chatel, Conseiller, Ward(s): Saint-Laurent
vchatel@ville.candiac.qc.ca
Kevin Vocino, Conseiller, Ward(s): Champlain
kvocino@ville.candiac.qc.ca
Anne Scott, Conseillère, Ward(s): Taschereau
ascott@ville.candiac.qc.ca
Charles-André Fortier, Conseiller, Ward(s): Montcalm
cafortier@ville.candiac.qc.ca
Normand Dyotte, Conseiller, Ward(s): Jean-Leman
ndyotte@ville.candiac.qc.ca
Carole Lemaire, Greffière
450-444-6398, Fax: 450-444-0789
greffe@ville.candiac.qc.ca
David Johnstone, Directeur général
450-444-6006, Fax: 450-444-2480
directiongenerale@ville.candiac.qc.ca
Sylvie Landry, Trésorière
450-444-6018, Fax: 450-444-6009
finances@ville.candiac.qc.ca

Chambly
56, rue Martel
Chambly, QC J3L 1V3
Tél: 450-658-8788; *Téléc:* 450-447-4525
information@ville.chambly.qc.ca
www.ville.chambly.qc.ca
Entité municipal: City
Incorporation: 26 octobre 1848 *Area:* 25,01 km2
Comté ou district: La Vallée-du-Richelieu; *Population au 2006:* 22,608
Circonscription(s) électorale(s) provinciale(s): Chambly
Circonscription(s) électorale(s) fédérale(s): Chambly-Borduas
Prochaines élections: 3e novembre 2013
Denis Lavoie, Maire
450-658-8788
maire@ville.chambly.qc.ca
Denise Grégoire, Conseillère, Ward(s): Canton
450-447-2549
denise.gregoire@cstjean.qc.ca
Normand Perrault, Conseiller, Ward(s): Bassin
450-447-2336, Fax: 514-971-5439
normandperrault@videotron.ca
Lucette Robert, Conseillère, Ward(s): Charles-Michel-de Salaberry
514-799-3575
lucette.robert@usherbrooke.ca
Richard Tetreault, Conseiller, Ward(s): La Petite Rivière
450-658-4282, Fax: 514-891-4282
rtetreault@videotron.qc.ca
Serge Gélinas, Conseiller, Ward(s): Antoine-Louis-Fréchette
514-462-0151
sergelinas01@hotmail.com
Luc Ricard, Conseiller, Ward(s): Louis-Franquet
450-447-1829
lucricard@videotron.ca
Jean Roy, Conseiller, Ward(s): Ruisseau
450-447-6152
jeanrr@hotmail.com
Steeves Demers, Conseiller, Ward(s): Grandes-Terres
514-250-9960
steeves.demers@hotmail.com
Louise Bouvier, Greffière
450-658-8788, Fax: 450-658-4214
greffe@ville.chambly.qc.ca
Jean Lacroix, Directeur général
450-658-8788, Fax: 450-447-4525
jean.lacroix@ville.chambly.qc.ca
Annie Nepton, Directrice & trésorière, Service des finances
450-658-8788, Fax: 450-447-4525
finances@ville.chambly.qc.ca

Châteauguay
5, boul d'Youville
Châteauguay, QC J6J 2P8
Tél: 450-698-3000; *Téléc:* 450-698-3019
info@ville.chateauguay.qc.ca
www.ville.chateauguay.qc.ca
Entité municipal: City
Incorporation: 3e novembre 1975 *Area:* 35,37 km2
Comté ou district: Roussillon; *Population au 2006:* 42,786
Circonscription(s) électorale(s) provinciale(s): Châteauguay
Circonscription(s) électorale(s) fédérale(s):
Châteauguay—St-Constant
Prochaines élections: 3e novembre 2013
Nathalie Simon, Mairesse
450-698-3008
mairie@ville.chateauguay.qc.ca
Barry Doyle, Conseiller, Ward(s): 1
450-699-1984
barry.doyle@ville.chateauguay.qc.ca
Pierre Gloutnay, Conseiller, Ward(s): 2
514-706-1582
pierre.gloutnay@ville.chateauguay.qc.ca
Esther Salomon, Conseillère, Ward(s): 3
450-844-0507
esther.salomon@ville.chateauguay.qc.ca
Guillaume Dumas, Conseiller, Ward(s): 4
450-691-3177
guillaume.dumas@ville.chateauguay.qc.ca
Marcel Deschamps, Conseiller, Ward(s): 5
450-699-1120
marcel.deschamps@ville.chateauguay.qc.ca
Michel Gendron, Conseiller, Ward(s): 6
514-829-1986
mike.gendron@ville.chateauguay.qc.ca
Ginette Gendron, Conseillère, Ward(s): 7
450-692-3302
ginette.gendron@ville.chateauguay.qc.ca
Alain Côté, Conseiller, Ward(s): 8
450-692-8877
alain.cote@ville.chateauguay.qc.ca
Paul G. Brunet, Greffier & Directeur général
Manon Tourigny, Trésorière

Côte-Saint-Luc
5801, boul Cavendish
Côte-Saint-Luc, QC H4W 3C3
Tél: 514-485-6800; *Téléc:* 514-485-6963
info@cotesaintluc.org
www.cotesaintluc.org
Entité municipal: City
Incorporation: 1er janvier 2006 *Area:* 7,35 km2
Comté ou district: Communauté métropolitaine de Montréal;
Population au 2006: 31,395
Circonscription(s) électorale(s) provinciale(s): D'Arcy-McGee
Circonscription(s) électorale(s) fédérale(s): Mount Royal
Prochaines élections: 3e novembre 2013
Anthony Housefather, Maire
514-485-6936
ahousefather@cotesaintluc.org
Sam Goldbloom, Conseiller, Ward(s): 1
514-485-6945
sgoldbloom@cotesaintluc.org
Mike Cohen, Counseiller, Ward(s): 2
mcohen@cotesaintluc.org
Dida Berku, Conseillère, Ward(s): 3
dberku@cotesaintluc.org
Steven Erdelyi, Conseillère, Ward(s): 4
serdelyi@cotesaintluc.org
Allan J. Levine, Conseiller, Ward(s): 5
alevine@cotesaintluc.org
Glenn J. Nashen, Conseiller, Ward(s): 6
gjnashen@cotesaintluc.org
Mitchell Brownstein, Conseiller, Ward(s): 7
mbrownstein@cotesaintluc.org
Ruth Kovac, Conseillère, Ward(s): 8
rkovac@cotesaintluc.org
Jonathan Shecter, Greffier
514-485-6800
jshecter@cotesaintluc.org
Tanya Abramovitch, Directrice générale
tabramovitch@cotesaintluc.org
Raymond LeBlanc, Trésorier
514-485-6922

Cowansville
220, place Municipale
Cowansville, QC J2K 1T4
Tél: 450-263-0141; *Téléc:* 450-263-9357
hoteldeville@ville.cowansville.qc.ca
www.ville.cowansville.qc.ca
Entité municipal: City
Incorporation: 1er janvier 1876 *Area:* 48,79 km2
Comté ou district: Brome-Missisquoi; *Population au 2006:* 12,182
Circonscription(s) électorale(s) provinciale(s): Brome-Missisquoi
Circonscription(s) électorale(s) fédérale(s): Brome-Missisquoi
Prochaines élections: 3e novembre 2013
Arthur Fauteux, Maire
450-263-0141
afauteux@ville.cowansville.qc.ca
Guy Patenaude, Conseiller, Ward(s): Ruiter
450-263-7327
gpatenaude@ville.cowansville.qc.ca
Lucille Robert, Conseillère, Ward(s): Sweetsburg
450-263-3779
lrobert@ville.cowansville.qc.ca
Ghyslain Vallières, Conseiller, Ward(s): Vilas
450-260-5703
gvallières@ville.cowansville.qc.ca
Michel Charbonneau, Conseiller, Ward(s): Bruck
450-266-1146
mcharbonneau@ville.cowansville.qc.ca
Yvon Pepin, Conseiller, Ward(s): Davignon
450-263-1426
ypepin@ville.cowansville.qc.ca
Sylvie Beauregard, Conseillère, Ward(s): Fordyce
450-266-4312
sbeauregard@ville.cowansville.qc.ca
Sandra Ruel, Greffière
Pierre Belle, Trésorier
450-263-0141

Deux-Montagnes
803, ch d'Oka
Deux-Montagnes, QC J7R 1L8
Tél: 450-473-2796; *Téléc:* 450-473-2417
info@ville.deux-montagnes.qc.ca
www.ville.deux-montagnes.qc.ca
Entité municipal: City
Incorporation: 18 août 1921 *Area:* 5,82 km2
Comté ou district: Deux-Montagnes; *Population au 2006:* 17,402
Circonscription(s) électorale(s) provinciale(s): Deux-Montagnes
Circonscription(s) électorale(s) fédérale(s): Rivière-des-Mille-îles
Prochaines élections: 3e novembre 2013
Marc Lauzon, Maire
450-473-8898
mlauzon@ville.deux-montagnes.qc.ca
Suzette Bigras, Conseillère, Ward(s): Grand-Moulin
sbigras@ville.deux-montagnes.qc.ca
Mario Saint-Charles, Conseiller, Ward(s): Lac
mst-charles@ville.deux-montagnes.qc.ca
Tom Whitton, Conseiller, Ward(s): Olympia
twhitton@ville.deux-montagnes.qc.ca
Nathalie Chayer, Conseillère, Ward(s): Gare
nchayer@ville.deux-montagnes.qc.ca
Guillaume Bouvrette, Conseiller, Ward(s): Coteau
gbouvrette@ville.deux-montagnes.qc.ca
James McAllister, Conseiller, Ward(s): Golf
jmcallister@ville.deux-montagnes.qc.ca
Jacques Robichaud, Greffier
450-473-2796, Fax: 450-473-4434
Jean Langevin, Directeur général
450-473-2796, Fax: 450-473-2417
Marie-Josée Boissonneault, Directrice, Finances & Trésorerie,
Fax: 450-473-3412

Dolbeau-Mistassini
1100, boul Wallberg
Dolbeau-Mistassini, QC G8L 1G7
Tél: 418-276-0160; *Téléc:* 418-276-8312
hotelville@ville.dolbeau-mistassini.qc.ca
www.ville.dolbeau-mistassini.qc.ca
Entité municipal: City
Incorporation: 17 décembre 1997 *Area:* 296,57 km2
Comté ou district: Maria-Chapdelaine; *Population au 2006:* 14,546
Circonscription(s) électorale(s) provinciale(s): Roberval
Circonscription(s) électorale(s) fédérale(s):
Roberval—Lac-St-Jean
Prochaines élections: 3e novembre 2013
Georges Simard, Maire
maire@ville.dolbeau-mistassini.qc.ca
Richard Hébert, Conseiller, Ward(s): 1
r.hebert@bellnet.ca
Claude Ouellet, Conseiller, Ward(s): 2
mairie-greffe@ville.dolbeau-mistassini.qc.ca
Daniel Savard, Conseiller, Ward(s): 3
conseillers@ville.dolbeau-mistassini.qc.ca
Daniel Lambert, Conseiller, Ward(s): 4
conseillers@ville.dolbeau-mistassini.qc.ca
Claire Néron, Conseillère, Ward(s): 5
cneron@mrcmaria.qc.ca
Pierre Lavoie, Conseiller, Ward(s): 6
mairie-greffe@ville.dolbeau-mistassini.qc.ca
André Côté, Greffier
418-276-0160
acote@ville.dolbeau-mistassini.qc.ca
Frédéric Lemieux, Directeur général
418-276-0160
flemieux@ville.dolbeau-mistassini.qc.ca
Suzie Gagnon, Directrice, Finances & trésorier
418-276-0160
sgagnon@ville.dolbeau-mistassini.qc.ca

Dollard-Des-Ormeaux
12001, boul De Salaberry
Dollard-des-Ormeaux, QC H9B 2A7
Tél: 514-684-1010; *Téléc:* 514-684-6894
ville@ddo.qc.ca
www.ville.ddo.qc.ca
Entité municipal: City
Incorporation: 1er janvier 2006 *Area:* 15,20 km2
Comté ou district: Communauté métropolitaine de Montréal;
Population au 2006: 48,930
Circonscription(s) électorale(s) provinciale(s): Robert-Baldwin
Circonscription(s) électorale(s) fédérale(s): Pierrefonds—Dollard
Prochaines élections: 3e novembre 2013
Ed Janiszewski, Maire
Zoé Bayouk, Conseillère, Ward(s): 1
Errol Johnson, Conseiller, Ward(s): 2
Mickey Max Guttman, Conseiller, Ward(s): 3
Herbert Brownstein, Conseiller, Ward(s): 4
Morris Vesely, Conseiller, Ward(s): 5
Peter Prassas, Conseiller, Ward(s): 6
Alex Bottausci, Conseiller, Ward(s): 7
Colette Gauthier, Conseillère, Ward(s): 8
Chantale Bilodeau, Greffière
514-684-9244
cbilodeau@ddo.qc.ca
Jack Benzaquen, Directeur général
514-684-8060
jbenzaquen@ddo.qc.ca
Caroline Thall, Trésorière
514-684-9391
cthall@ddo.qc.ca

Dorval
60, av Martin
Dorval, QC H9S 3R4
Tél: 514-633-4040; *Téléc:* 514-633-4138
dorval@ville.dorval.qc.ca
www.ville.dorval.qc.ca
Entité municipal: City
Incorporation: 1er janvier 2006 *Area:* 20,64 km2
Comté ou district: Communauté métropolitaine de Montréal;
Population au 2006: 18,088
Circonscription(s) électorale(s) provinciale(s): Marquette
Circonscription(s) électorale(s) fédérale(s):
Notre-Dame-de-Grâce—Lachine
Prochaines élections: 3e novembre 2013
Edgar Rouleau, Maire
erouleau@ville.dorval.qc.ca
Claude Valiquet, Conseiller, Ward(s): 1
cvaliquet@ville.dorval.qc.ca
Michel Hébert, Conseiller, Ward(s): 2
mhebert@ville.dorval.qc.ca
Daniel da Chão, Conseiller, Ward(s): 3
ddachao@ville.dorval.qc.ca
Marc Doret, Conseiller, Ward(s): 4
mdoret@ville.dorval.qc.ca
Heather Allard, Conseillère, Ward(s): 5
hallard@ville.dorval.qc.ca
Margo Heron, Conseillère, Ward(s): 6
mheron@ville.dorval.qc.ca
Colette Gauthier, Greffière
514-633-4142
Robert Bourbeau, Directeur général
514-633-4044
André Girard, Trésorier
514-633-4040

Drummondville
CP 398
415, rue Lindsay
Drummondville, QC J2B 6W3
Tél: 819-478-6550;
communications@ville.drummondville.qc.ca
www.ville.drummondville.qc.ca
Entité municipal: City
Incorporation: 7e juillet 2004 *Area:* 249,80 km2
Comté ou district: Drummond; *Population au 2006:* 67,392
Circonscription(s) électorale(s) provinciale(s): Drummond

Circonscription(s) électorale(s) fédérale(s): Drummond
Prochaines élections: 3e novembre 2013
Note: Effective July 7, 2004, the municipalities of St-Charles-de-Drummond & St-Joachim-de-Courval & the cities of St-Nicéphore & Drummondville regrouped to form the new city of Drummondville
Francine Ruest Jutras, Mairesse
mairie@ville.drummondville.qc.ca
Mario Jacques, Conseiller, Ward(s): 1
mjacques@ville.drummondville.qc.ca
Roberto Léveillée, Conseiller, Ward(s): 2
rleveillee@ville.drummondville.qc.ca
Jocelyn Gagné, Conseiller, Ward(s): 3
jgagne@ville.drummondville.qc.ca
Isabelle Marquis, Conseillère, Ward(s): 4
imarquis@ville.drummondville.qc.ca
John Husk, Conseiller, Ward(s): 5
jhusk@ville.drummondville.qc.ca
Marie-Eve Le Gendre, Conseillère, Ward(s): 6
melegendre@ville.drummondville.qc.ca
Alain Martel, Conseiller, Ward(s): 7
amartel@ville.drummondville.qc.ca
Yves Grondin, Conseiller, Ward(s): 8
ygrondin@ville.drummondville.qc.ca
Annick Bellavance, Conseillère, Ward(s): 9
abellavance@ville.drummondville.qc.ca
Vincent Chouinard, Conseiller, Ward(s): 10
vchouinard@ville.drummondville.qc.ca
Philippe Mercure, Conseiller, Ward(s): 11
pmercure@ville.drummondville.qc.ca
Pierre Levasseur, Conseiller, Ward(s): 12
plevasseur@ville.drummondville.qc.ca
Thérèse Cajolet, Greffière
819-478-6554, Fax: 819-478-3363
greffe@ville.drummondville.qc.ca
Claude Proulx, Directeur général
819-478-6557, Fax: 819-478-3363
direction@ville.drummondville.qc.ca
Gilles Bélisle, Trésorier
819-478-6559, Fax: 819-478-3164
tresor@ville.drummondville.qc.ca

Gaspé

25, rue de l'Hôtel-de-Ville
Gaspé, QC G4X 2A5
Tél: 418-368-2104; *Téléc:* 418-368-8532
direction.generale@ville.gaspe.qc.ca
www.ville.gaspe.qc.ca
Entité municipal: City
Incorporation: 1er janvier 1971 *Area:* 1446,95 km2
Comté ou district: La Côte-de-Gaspé; *Population au 2006:* 14,819
Circonscription(s) électorale(s) provinciale(s): Gaspé
Circonscription(s) électorale(s) fédérale(s): Gaspésie—Îles-de-la-Madeleine
Prochaines élections: 3e novembre 2013
François Roussy, Maire
Luc Savage, Conseiller, Ward(s): 1
Charles Aspirault, Conseiller, Ward(s): 2
Nelson O'Connor, Conseiller, Ward(s): 3
Patrice Quenneville, Conseiller, Ward(s): 4
Aline Perry, Conseillère, Ward(s): 5
Ghislain Smith, Conseiller, Ward(s): 6
Doreen Savage, Adjointe de direction, Greffe et services juridiques
greffe@ville.gaspe.qc.ca
Daniel Côté, Coordonnateur municipal, Direction générale et mairie
daniel.cote@ville.gaspe.qc.ca
Yvanne Huet, Adjointe de direction, Finances
serv.administratif@ville.gaspe.qc.ca

Gatineau

CP 1970 Hull
25, rue Laurier
Gatineau, QC J8X 3Y9
Tél: 819-595-2002;
info@gatineau.ca
www.ville.gatineau.qc.ca
Entité municipal: City
Incorporation: 1er janvier 2002 *Area:* 344,16 km2
Population au 2006: 242,124
Circonscription(s) électorale(s) provinciale(s): Gatineau; Chapleau; Hull; Papineau; Pontiac
Circonscription(s) électorale(s) fédérale(s): Gatineau
Prochaines élections: 3e novembre 2013
Marc Bureau, Maire
819-595-7100
maire@gatineau.ca
Stefan Psenak, Conseiller, Ward(s): 1. Aylmer
psenak.stefan@gatineau.ca
André Laframboise, Conseiller, Ward(s): 2. Lucerne
laframboise.andre@gatineau.ca
Alain Riel, Conseiller, Ward(s): 3. Deschênes
riel.alain@gatineau.ca
Maxime Tremblay, Conseiller, Ward(s): 4. Plateau-Manoir-des-Trembles
tremblay.maxime@gatineau.ca
Patrice Martin, Conseiller, Ward(s): 5. Wright—Parc-de-la-Montagne
martin.patrice@gatineau.ca
Mireille Apollon, Conseillère, Ward(s): 6. Orée-du-Parc
apollon.mireille@gatineau.ca
Pierre Philion, Conseiller, Ward(s): 7. Saint-Raymond—Vanier
philion.pierre@gatineau.ca
Denise Laferrière, Conseillère, Ward(s): 8. Hull—Val-Tétreau
laferriere.denise@gatineau.ca
Nicole Champagne, Conseillère, Ward(s): 9. Limbour
champagne.nicole@gatineau.ca
Denis Tassé, Conseiller, Ward(s): 10. Touraine
tasse.denis@gatineau.ca
Luc Angers, Conseiller, Ward(s): 11. Pointe-Gatineau
angers.luc@gatineau.ca
Patsy Bouthillette, Conseillère, Ward(s): 12. Carrefour-de-l'Hôpital
bouthillette.patsy@gatineau.ca
Joseph De Sylva, Conseiller, Ward(s): 13. Versant
desylva.joseph@gatineau.ca
Sylvie Goneau, Conseillère, Ward(s): 14. Bellevue
goneau.sylvie@gatineau.ca
Stéphane Lauzon, Conseiller, Ward(s): 15. Lac-Beauchamp
lauzon.stephane@gatineau.ca
Yvon Boucher, Conseiller, Ward(s): 16. Rivière-Blanche
boucher.yvon@gatineau.ca
Luc Montreuil, Conseiller, Ward(s): 17. Masson-Angers
montreuil.luc@gatineau.ca
Maxime Pedneaud-Jobin, Conseiller, Ward(s): 18. Buckingham
pedneaud-jobin.maxime@gatineau.ca
Suzanne Ouellet, Greffière
819-595-7180, Fax: 819-595-7192
ouellet.suzanne@ville.gatineau.qc.ca
Robert F. Weemaes, Directeur général
Marco Lalonde, Directeur, Service des travaux publics
Louise Lavoie, Directrice, Service de l'environnement
Marc Pageau, Directeur, Service des ressources humaines
André Bonneau, Directeur, Service de sécurité incendie
Marie-Claude Martel, Directrice, Service de l'urbanisme et du développement durable
André Barbeau, Directeur, Service des finances
Nicole Dumoulin, Directrice, Service des communications
Mario Harel, Directeur, Service de police

Granby

87, rue Principale
Granby, QC J2G 2T8
Tél: 450-776-8282; *Téléc:* 450-776-8231
communication@ville.granby.qc.ca
www.ville.granby.qc.ca
Entité municipal: City
Incorporation: 1er janvier 2007 *Area:* 156,68 km2
Comté ou district: La Haute-Yamaska; *Population au 2006:* 47,637
Circonscription(s) électorale(s) provinciale(s): Shefford
Circonscription(s) électorale(s) fédérale(s): Shefford
Prochaines élections: 3e novembre 2013
Richard Goulet, Maire
450-776-8228, Fax: 450-378-0010
mairie@ville.granby.qc.ca
Louise B. Comeau, Conseillère, Ward(s): 1
450-378-2645
Éliette Jenneau, Conseillère, Ward(s): 2
450-531-8526
Pierre Breton, Conseiller, Ward(s): 3
450-777-7695
Patrick Girard, Conseiller, Ward(s): 4
450-578-4808
Denis Choinière, Conseiller, Ward(s): 5
Serges Ruel, Conseiller, Ward(s): 6
450-405-4446
Pascal Bonin, Conseiller, Ward(s): 7
450-776-1285
Guy Gaudor, Conseiller, Ward(s): 8
450-379-5949
Yves Pronovost, Conseiller, Ward(s): 9
450-577-2439
Michel Mailhot, Conseiller, Ward(s): 10
450-372-8317
Catherine Bouchard, Greffière
450-776-8275, Fax: 450-776-8278
greffe@ville.granby.qc.ca
Michel Pineault, Directeur général
450-776-8232, Fax: 450-776-8279
direction.generale@ville.granby.qc.ca
Jean-Pierre Renaud, Trésorier
450-776-8287, Fax: 450-776-8384
tresorerie@ville.granby.qc.ca
André Jean, Directeur, Travaux publics
450-776-8366, Fax: 450-776-8370
travaux.publics@ville.granby.qc.ca
Pierre Lacombe, Directeur, Incendies
450-776-8344, Fax: 450-839-0370
incendie@ville.granby.qc.ca
Patrice Faucher, Directeur, Loisir, arts, culture et vie communautaire
450-776-8224
pfaucher@ville.granby.qc.ca
Claude Ouimette, Coordonnateur, Station d'épuration des eaux usées
450-776-8371, Fax: 450-776-8373
epuration@ville.granby.qc.ca

Joliette

614, boul Manseau
Joliette, QC J6E 3E4
Tél: 450-753-8000; *Téléc:* 450-753-8199
www.ville.joliette.qc.ca
Entité municipal: City
Incorporation: 12 novembre 1966 *Area:* 22,36 km2
Comté ou district: Joliette; *Population au 2006:* 19,044
Circonscription(s) électorale(s) provinciale(s): Joliette
Circonscription(s) électorale(s) fédérale(s): Joliette
Prochaines élections: 3e novembre 2013
René Laurin, Maire
450-753-8020
mairie@ville.joliette.qc.ca
Alain Beaudry, Conseiller, Ward(s): 1
Normand-Guy Lépine, Conseiller, Ward(s): 2
Alain Lozeau, Conseiller, Ward(s): 3
Diane Nicoletti, Conseillère, Ward(s): 4
Jean-François Courteau, Conseiller, Ward(s): 5
Yves Liard, Conseiller, Ward(s): 6
Richard Leduc, Conseiller, Ward(s): 7
Pierrick Sylvestre, Greffier
450-753-8030
greffier@ville.joliette.qc.ca
Renald Gravel, Directeur général
450-753-8031
renald.gravel@ville.joliette.qc.ca
France Venne, Directrice, Opérations financières
450-753-8185
service.finances@ville.joliette.qc.ca
François Pépin, Directeur, Travaux publics et services techniques
450-753-8080
francois.pepin@ville.joliette.qc.ca
Terry Rousseau, Directeur, Incendies
450-753-8154
service.incendies@ville.joliette.qc.ca

L'Assomption

399, rue Dorval
L'Assomption, QC J5W 1A1
Tél: 450-589-5671; *Téléc:* 450-589-4512
information@ville.lassomption.qc.ca
www.ville.lassomption.qc.ca
Entité municipal: City
Incorporation: 1er juillet 2000 *Area:* 100,09 km2
Comté ou district: L'Assomption; *Population au 2006:* 16,738
Circonscription(s) électorale(s) provinciale(s): L'Assomption et Rousseau
Circonscription(s) électorale(s) fédérale(s): Repentigny
Prochaines élections: 3e novembre 2013
Louise T. Francoeur, Maire
450-589-5671
lfrancoeur@ville.lassomption.qc.ca
René Langlais, Conseiller, Ward(s): 1. Hector-Charland
rlanglais@ville.lassomption.qc.ca
Micheline Martel-Richard, Conseillère, Ward(s): 2. Wilfrid-Laurier
mmartel@ville.lassomption.qc.ca
Laurette Jobin-Morin, Conseillère, Ward(s): 3. J.-Edouard-Faribault
ljobin@ville.lassomption.qc.ca
Eugène Vincent, Conseiller, Ward(s): 4. L.-Michel-Viger
evincent@ville.lassomption.qc.ca
Nicole Martel, Conseillère, Ward(s): 5. Pierre-LeSueur
nmartel@ville.lassomption.qc.ca
Valérie Couturier, Conseillère, Ward(s): 6. Louis-Laberge
vcouturier@ville.lassomption.qc.ca
Charles Asselin, Conseiller, Ward(s): 7. Albert-Racette
casselin@ville.lassomption.qc.ca

Chantal Bédard, Greffière
greffe@ville.lassomption.qc.ca
Martin Levièvre, Directeur général
directiongenerale@ville.lassomption.qc.ca
Dominique Valiquette, Trésorier
tresorerie@ville.lassomption.qc.ca

L'île-Perrot

110, boul Perrot
L'Ile-Perrot, QC J7V 3G1
Tél: 514-453-1751; *Téléc:* 514-453-2432
ville@ile-perrot.qc.ca
www.ileperrot.qc.ca
Entité municipal: City
Incorporation: 1er juillet 1855 *Area:* 4,86 km2
Comté ou district: Vaudreuil-Soulanges; *Population au 2006:* 9,927
Circonscription(s) électorale(s) provinciale(s): Vaudreuil
Circonscription(s) électorale(s) fédérale(s): Vaudreuil-Soulanges
Prochaines élections: 3e novembre 2013
Marc Roy, Maire
514-453-6975
mroy@ile-perrot.qc.ca
André Legault, Conseiller, Ward(s): 1
514-453-6337
alegault@ile-perrot.qc.ca
Daniel Taillefer, Conseiller, Ward(s): 2
514-453-4774
dtaillefer@ile-perrot.qc.ca
Marcel Rainville, Conseiller, Ward(s): 3
514-902-1352
mrainville@ile-perrot.qc.ca
Michelle L. LeCavalier, Conseillère, Ward(s): 4
514-453-2599
mlecavalier@ile-perrot.qc.ca
René Pinsonneault, Conseiller, Ward(s): 5
514-453-7405
rpinsonneault@ile-perrot.qc.ca
Daniel Leblanc, Conseiller, Ward(s): 6
514-425-0403
dleblanc@ile-perrot.qc.ca
Lucie Coallier, Greffière
514-453-1751
lcoallier@ile-perrot.qc.ca
André Morin, Directeur général
514-453-1751
amorin@ile-perrot.qc.ca
Danielle Rioux, Trésorière
514-453-1751
drioux@ile-perrot.qc.ca

La Prairie

#400, 170, boul Taschereau
La Prairie, QC J5R 5H6
Tél: 450-444-6600; *Téléc:* 450-444-6636
info@ville.laprairie.qc.ca
www.ville.laprairie.qc.ca
Entité municipal: City
Incorporation: 30 mars 1846 *Area:* 43,53 km2
Comté ou district: Roussillon; *Population au 2006:* 21,763
Circonscription(s) électorale(s) provinciale(s): La Prairie
Circonscription(s) électorale(s) fédérale(s): Brossard-La Prairie
Prochaines élections: 3e novembre 2013
Lucie F. Roussel, Mairesse
Donat Serres, Conseiller, Ward(s): 1. Milice
Christian Caron, Conseiller, Ward(s): 2. Christ-Roi
Laurent Blais, Conseiller, Ward(s): 3. Vieux La Prairie
Jacques Bourbonnais, Conseiller, Ward(s): 4. Citière
Yvon Brière, Conseiller, Ward(s): 5. Clairière
Pierre Vocino, Conseiller, Ward(s): 6. Magdeleine
Yves Senécal, Conseiller, Ward(s): 7. Bataille
Suzanne Perron, Conseillère, Ward(s): 8. Briqueterie
Manon Thériault, Greffière
450-444-6625
greffe@ville.laprairie.qc.ca
Jean Bergeron, Directeur général
450-444-6619
dg@ville.laprairie.qc.ca
Nathalie Guérin, Trésorière
450-444-6603
finances@ville.laprairie.qc.ca
Guy Trahan, Directeur, Travaux publics
450-444-6684, Fax: 450-444-6692
tp@ville.laprairie.qc.ca

La Tuque

375, rue St-Joseph
La Tuque, QC G9X 1L5
Tél: 819-523-8200; *Téléc:* 819-523-5419
dg@ville.latuque.qc.ca
www.ville.latuque.qc.ca
Entité municipal: City
Incorporation: 26 mars 2003 *Area:* 28 421,48 km2
Population au 2006: 11,821
Circonscription(s) électorale(s) provinciale(s): Laviolette
Circonscription(s) électorale(s) fédérale(s): St-Maurice-Champlain
Prochaines élections: 3e novembre 2013
Note: Dès le 26 mars 2003, la nouvelle ville de La Tuque regroupe La Tuque, les municipalités de La Croche, La Bostonnais, & Lac-Édouard, le village de Parent, & 8 autres territoires.
Normand Beaudoin, Maire
819-523-8200
mairie@ville.latuque.qc.ca
Sylvie Lachapelle, Conseillère, Ward(s): 1. Parent
819-667-2323, Fax: 819-667-2542
parent@tlb.sympatico.ca
Line Pilote, Conseillère, Ward(s): 2. Croche/Couronee rurale
lpilote@ville.latuque.qc.ca
Luc Martel, Conseiller, Ward(s): 3. Jacques-Buteux
lmartel@ville.latuque.qc.ca
Jean-Marc Dumont, Conseiller, Ward(s): 4. Polyvalente
jdumont@ville.latuque.qc.ca
Jean Duchesneau, Conseiller, Ward(s): 5. Bel-Air—Centre-ville
jduchesneau@ville.latuque.qc.ca
Roch Lepage, Conseiller, Ward(s): 6. Aéroport
rlepage@ville.latuque.qc.ca
Jean-Sébastien Poirier, Greffier
greffe@ville.latuque.qc.ca
Marco Lethiecq, Directeur général
mlethiecq@ville.latuque.qc.ca
Pierre Bouchard, Trésorier
tresorerie@ville.latuque.qc.ca

Lachute

380, rue Principale
Lachute, QC J8H 1Y2
Tél: 450-562-3781; *Téléc:* 450-562-1431
lachute@ville.lachute.qc.ca
www.ville.lachute.qc.ca
Entité municipal: City
Incorporation: 30 avril 1966 *Area:* 111,20 km2
Comté ou district: Argenteuil; *Population au 2006:* 11,832
Circonscription(s) électorale(s) provinciale(s): Argenteuil
Circonscription(s) électorale(s) fédérale(s): Argenteuil-Papineau-Mirabel
Prochaines élections: 3e novembre 2013
Daniel Mayer, Maire
Marcelle L. Louis-Seize, Conseillère, Ward(s): 1
Mario Beaudin, Conseiller, Ward(s): 2
Guy Léger, Conseiller, Ward(s): 3
Stéphane Braney, Conseiller, Ward(s): 4
Guy Desforges, Conseiller, Ward(s): 5
Paul Cleary, Conseiller, Ward(s): 6
Louise Beaulieu, Greffière
450-562-3781
lbeaulieu@ville.lachute.qc.ca
Pierre Gionet, Directeur général
450-562-3781
pgionet@ville.lachute.qc.ca
Nathalie Piret, Trésorière
450-562-3781
npiret@ville.lachute.qc.ca

Laval

Hôtel de Ville
CP 422 St-Martin
1, Place du Souvenir
Laval, QC H7V 3Z4
Tél: 450-978-8000; *Téléc:* 450-978-5943
info@ville.laval.qc.ca
www.ville.laval.qc.ca
Entité municipal: City
Incorporation: 6e août 1965 *Area:* 245,40 km2
Population au 2009: 377,332
Circonscription(s) électorale(s) provinciale(s): Chomedey; Fabre; Laval-des-Rapides; Mille-Iles; Vimont
Circonscription(s) électorale(s) fédérale(s): Laval; Marc-Aurèle-Fortin; Alfred-Pellan; Laval-Les Iles
Prochaines élections: 3e novembre 2013
Gilles Vaillancourt, Maire
Jacques St-Jean, Conseiller, Ward(s): 1. Saint-François
450-666-2509
j.stjean@ville.laval.qc.ca
Sylvie Clermont, Conseillère, Ward(s): 2. Saint-Vincent-de-Paul
450-664-2776
s.clermont@ville.laval.qc.ca
Madeleine Sollazzo, Conseillère, Ward(s): 3. Val-des-Arbres
450-661-8248
info@madeleinesollazzo.com
Michèle des Trois Maisons, Conseillère, Ward(s): 4. Duvernay-Pont-Viau
450-975-2493
m.destroismaisons@ville.laval.qc.ca
Francine Légaré, Conseillère, Ward(s): 5. Marigot
450-661-9730
fr.legare@ville.laval.qc.ca
Claire Le Bel, Conseillère, Ward(s): 6. Concorde-Bois-de-Boulogne
450-663-8039
cl.lebel@ville.laval.qc.ca
Benoit Fradet, Conseiller, Ward(s): 7. Renaud
450-662-4140
b.fradet@ville.laval.qc.ca
Norman Girard, Conseiller, Ward(s): 8. Vimont
450-967-1633
n.girard@ville.laval.qc.ca
Yvon Martineau, Conseiller, Ward(s): 9. Saint-Bruno
450-629-8803
ymartineau@live.ca
Lucie Hill Larocque, Conseillère, Ward(s): 10. Auteuil
450-625-1821
l.hill@ville.laval.qc.ca
Ginette Grisé, Conseillère, Ward(s): 11. Laval-des-Rapides
450-967-7373
g.grise@ville.laval.qc.ca
Jocelyne Guertin, Conseillère, Ward(s): 12. Souvenir-Labelle
450-662-4140
j.guertin@ville.laval.qc.ca
Ginette Legault Bernier, Conseillère, Ward(s): 13. Abord-à-Plouffe
450-681-9468
glbernier@yahoo.com
Basile Angelopoulos, Conseiller, Ward(s): 14. Chomedey
450-662-4140
b.angelopoulos@ville.laval.qc.ca
Alexandre Duplessis, Conseiller, Ward(s): 15. Saint-Martin
514-944-2961
a.duplessis@ville.laval.qc.ca
Pierre Cléroux, Conseiller, Ward(s): 16. Sainte-Dorothée
450-689-7331
p.cleroux@ville.laval.qc.ca
Jean-Jacques Beldié, Conseiller, Ward(s): 17. Laval-les-îles
514-945-4700
j-j.beldie@ville.laval.qc.ca
France Dubreuil, Conseillère, Ward(s): 18. Orée-des-bois
514-239-1396
f.dubreuil@ville.laval.qc.ca
Yvon Bromley, Conseiller, Ward(s): 19. Marc-Aurèle-Fortin
450-628-4799
y.bromley@ville.laval.qc.ca
Martine Beaugrand, Conseillère, Ward(s): 20. Fabreville
450-736-3086
m.beaugrand@ville.laval.qc.ca
Denis Robillard, Conseiller, Ward(s): 21. Sainte-Rose
450-628-3055
d.robillard@ville.laval.qc.ca
Guy Collard, Greffier et secrétaire-trésorier
450-978-3950
Gaétan Turbide, Directeur général
450-978-3676
Robert Cadieux, Directeur, Contentieux
450-978-5866
Gilles Benoit, Directeur, Environnement
450-978-8000
Ernest Lépine, Directeur, Évaluation
450-978-8777
Suzanne Deshaies, Directrice, Finances
450-978-6888
Gérard Poirier, Directeur, Ingénierie
450-680-2999
Jean-Pierre Gariépy, Directeur, Protection des citoyens
450-662-4242
Martin Fiset, Directeur, Ressources humaines
450-978-6560
Lise Poirier, Directrice, Systèmes & technologies
450-662-4040
Michel Toutant, Directeur, Travaux publics
450-978-8000
Sylvain Dubois, Directeur, Urbanisme
450-680-5500
Marc Deblois, Directeur, Vie communautaire, culture et communications
450-978-2900
Martine Lachambre, Vérificateur général
450-978-8715

Lavaltrie
1370, rue Notre-Dame
Lavaltrie, QC J0K 1H0
Tél: 450-586-2921; *Téléc:* 450-586-3939
mairie@ville.lavaltrie.qc.ca
www.ville.lavaltrie.qc.ca
Entité municipal: City
Incorporation: 16 mai 2001 *Area:* 68,61 km2
Comté ou district: D'Autray; *Population au 2006:* 12,120
Circonscription(s) électorale(s) provinciale(s): Berthier
Circonscription(s) électorale(s) fédérale(s): Berthier-Maskinongé
Prochaines élections: 3e novembre 2013
Jean-Claude Gravel, Maire
Michele Dawe, Conseillère, Ward(s): 1. Terrasses
Robert Pellerin, Conseiller, Ward(s): 2. Rivière
Louise Martel, Conseillère, Ward(s): 3. Chemin du Roy
Lynda Pelletier, Conseillère, Ward(s): 4. Érablière
Georges Bonin, Conseiller, Ward(s): 5. Boisé
Sophie Hervieux, Conseillère, Ward(s): 6. Golf
Yves Deguire, Conseiller, Ward(s): 7. Chasse-galerie
Gaétan Bérard, Conseiller, Ward(s): 8. Saint-Antoine
Madeleine Barbeau, Greffière
450-586-2921, Fax: 450-586-3939
mbarbeau@ville.lavaltrie.qc.ca
Yvon Mousseau, Directeur général
450-586-2921, Fax: 450-586-3939
ymousseau@ville.lavaltrie.qc.ca
Réjean Nantais, Trésorier
450-586-2921, Fax: 450-586-4060
tresorerie@ville.lavaltrie.qc.ca
André Houle, Directeur, Travaux publics
450-586-2921, Fax: 450-586-3540
travauxpublics@ville.lavaltrie.qc.ca

Lévis
2175, ch du Fleuve
Lévis, QC G6W 7W9
Tél: 418-839-2002; *Téléc:* 418-839-5548
levis@ville.levis.qc.ca
www.ville.levis.qc.ca
Entité municipal: City
Incorporation: 1er janvier 2002 *Area:* 443,65 km2
Population au 2006: 130,006
Circonscription(s) électorale(s) provinciale(s):
Chutes-de-la-Chaudière; Lévis
Circonscription(s) électorale(s) fédérale(s): Lévis-Bellechasse; Lotbinière—Chutes-de-la-Chaudière
Prochaines élections: 3e novembre 2013
Danielle Roy Marinelli, Mairesse
dmarinelli@ville.levis.qc.ca
Mario Fortier, Conseiller, Ward(s): 1
mfortier@ville.levis.qc.ca
Dominique Maranda, Conseillère, Ward(s): 2
dmaranda@ville.levis.qc.ca
Anne Ladouceur, Conseillère, Ward(s): 3
aladouceur@ville.levis.qc.ca
Réjean Lamontagne, Conseiller, Ward(s): 4
rlamontagne@ville.levis.qc.ca
Michel Patry, Conseiller, Ward(s): 5
michel.patry@ville.levis.qc.ca
Michel Turner, Conseiller, Ward(s): 6
mturner@ville.levis.qc.ca
Guy Dumoulin, Conseiller, Ward(s): 7
gdumoulin@ville.levis.qc.ca
Jean-Pierre Bazinet, Conseiller, Ward(s): 8
jpbazinet@ville.levis.qc.ca
Jean-Luc Daigle, Conseiller, Ward(s): 9
jldaigle@ville.levis.qc.ca
Simon Théberge, Conseiller, Ward(s): 10
stheberge@ville.levis.qc.ca
Serge Côté, Conseiller, Ward(s): 11
scote@ville.levis.qc.ca
Janet Jones, Conseillère, Ward(s): 12
jjones@ville.levis.qc.ca
Robert Maranda, Conseiller, Ward(s): 13
rmaranda@ville.levis.qc.ca
Jean-Claude Bouchard, Conseiller, Ward(s): 14
jcbouchard@ville.levis.qc.ca
Ann Jeffrey, Conseillère, Ward(s): 15
ajeffrey@ville.levis.qc.ca
Danielle Bilodeau, Greffière
418-839-2002
levis@ville.levis.qc.ca
Jean Dubé, Directeur général
418-839-2002
jdube@ville.levis.qc.ca
Marcel Rodrigue, Trésorier
418-839-2002, Fax: 418-835-8522
Claude Pelletier, Chef de police
Christian Brière, Directeur, Communications
Claude Guérin, Directeur, Ressources humaines
René Tremblay, Directeur, Culture et des loisirs
Alain Francoeur, Directeur, Travaux publics
Pierre Boulay, Directeur, Environnement
André Matte, Vérificateur général
Robert Cooke, Directeur, Urbanisme
Philippe Meurant, Directrice, Planification et du développement
Yves Després, Directeur, Sécurité incendie

Longueuil
4250, ch de la Savane
Longueuil, QC J3Y 9G4
Tél: 450-463-7000; *Téléc:* 450-463-7403
www.longueuil.ca
Entité municipal: City
Incorporation: 1er janvier 2002 *Area:* 111,50 km2
Population au 2006: 230,949
Circonscription(s) électorale(s) provinciale(s): Marie-Victorin; Taillon; Laporte; Vachon
Circonscription(s) électorale(s) fédérale(s): Saint-Lambert; Longueuil-Pierre-Boucher; Saint-Bruno-Saint Hubert
Prochaines élections: 3e novembre 2013
Caroline St-Hilaire, Mairesse
Michel Desjardins, Conseiller, Ward(s): 1. Vieux-Longueuil
450-463-7081
Sylvie Parent, Conseillère, Ward(s): 2. Vieux-Longueuil
Benôit L'Ecuyer, Conseiller, Ward(s): 3. Vieux-Longueuil
450-468-6650
André Groleau, Conseiller, Ward(s): 4. Vieux-Longueuil
450-748-1015
Albert Beaudry, Conseiller, Ward(s): 5. Vieux-Longueuil
Michel Lanctôt, Conseiller, Ward(s): 6. Vieux-Longueuil
Marie-Lise Sauvé, Conseillère, Ward(s): 7. Vieux-Longueuil
450-448-7777
Manon D. Hénault, Conseillère, Ward(s): 8. Vieux-Longueuil
450-679-0931
Nicole Lafontaine, Conseillère, Ward(s): 9. Vieux-Longueuil
450-928-3616
Claude Jr. Gladu, Conseiller, Ward(s): 10. Vieux-Longueuil
450-651-7959
Johane Fontaine-Deshaies, Conseillère, Ward(s): 11. Vieux-Longueuil
450-677-2157
Monique Bastien, Conseillère, Ward(s): 12. Vieux-Longueuil
Monique Brisson, Conseillère, Ward(s): 13. Vieux-Longueuil
Robert Gladu, Conseiller, Ward(s): 14. Vieux-Longueuil
450-646-7671
Gilles Grégoire, Conseiller, Ward(s): 15. Vieux-Longueuil, Le Moyne
450-671-2149
Mireille Carrière, Conseillère, Ward(s): 16. Greenfield Park
Robert Myles, Conseiller, Ward(s): 17. Greenfield Park
450-465-6703
Michael O'Grady, Conseiller, Ward(s): 18. Greenfield Park
Jacques Lemire, Conseiller, Ward(s): 19. St-Hubert
450-445-2216
Roger Roy, Conseiller, Ward(s): 20. St-Hubert
450-676-8529
Jacques E. Poitras, Conseiller, Ward(s): 21. St-Hubert
Éric Beaulieau, Conseiller, Ward(s): 22. St-Hubert
450-463-7001
Suzanne Lachance, Conseillère, Ward(s): 23. St-Hubert
Nathalie Boisclair, Conseillère, Ward(s): 24. St-Hubert
Lorraine Guay-Boivin, Conseillère, Ward(s): 25. St-Hubert
450-463-7100
Michel Latendresse, Conseiller, Ward(s): 26. St-Hubert
Daniel Carrier, Directeur, Services juridiques
Guy Benedetti, Directeur général
Sylvie Toupin, Directrice, Finances
Pierre Archambault, Directeur, Ressources informationnelles & matérielles
Sylvie Cossette, Directrice, Développement durable et de la planification du territoire
Linda Rivard, Directrice, Communications et relations avec le citoyen
Denis Desroches, Directeur, Service de police
Claude Chevalier, Directeur, Service de sécurité incendie
Alain Cyr, Directeur, Travaux publics
Hélène Ladouceur, Directrice, Urbanisme
Michel Vallée, Directeur, Évaluation
André Lachapelle, Directeur général adjoint, Services administratifs
Alain Desgagné, Directeur, Ressources humaines
Francine Brunette, Vérificatrice générale

Magog
7, rue Principale est
Magog, QC J1X 1Y4
Tél: 819-843-6501; *Téléc:* 819-843-1091
info@ville.magog.qc.ca
www.ville.magog.qc.ca
Entité municipal: City
Incorporation: 9e octobre 2002 *Area:* 145,68 km2
Comté ou district: Memphrémagog; *Population au 2006:* 23,880
Circonscription(s) électorale(s) provinciale(s): Orford
Circonscription(s) électorale(s) fédérale(s): Brome-Missisquoi
Prochaines élections: 3e novembre 2013
Note: Depuis le 9 oct., le canton de Magog, le village d'Omerville & la ville de Magog sont regroupés pour former la nouvelle ville de Magog.
Vicki May Hamm, Mairesse
819-843-2880
vm.hamm@ville.magog.qc.ca
Michel Bombardier, Conseiller, Ward(s): 1. La Rivière
819-843-0370
mbom@cgocable.ca
Yvon Lamontagne, Conseiller, Ward(s): 2. Omerville
819-843-7250
info@ville.magog.qc.ca
Denise Poulin-Marcotte, Conseillère, Ward(s): 3. Des Sommets
819-843-1146
denisepmarcotte@hotmail.com
Olivier Tremblay, Conseiller, Ward(s): 4. Du Marais
819-847-4191
olitremblay@hotmail.com
Robert Ranger, Conseiller, Ward(s): 5. Canton Ouest
819-620-4134
rangerconseiller@live.ca
Jacques Laurendeau, Conseiller, Ward(s): 6. Des Pionniers
819-843-3244
info@ville.magog.qc.ca
Gilbert Kurt Boucher, Conseiller, Ward(s): 7. Centre
819-868-2006
bouc7@sympatico.ca
Nathalie Bélanger, Conseillère, Ward(s): 8. Monseigneur Vel
819-868-0256
nathbel30@hotmail.com
Nathalie Pelletier, Conseillère, Ward(s): 9. Des Marinas
819-868-5126
natp@cgocable.ca
Diane Pelletier, Conseillère, Ward(s): 10. Des Deux lacs
819-570-7597
diane.pelletier@cgocable.ca
Martine Savard, Greffière
819-843-6501
greffe@ville.magog.qc.ca
Armand Comeau, Directeur général
819-843-2880
dg@ville.magog.qc.ca
Anne Couturier, Trésorière
819-843-6501
finances@ville.magog.qc.ca

Mascouche
3034, ch Ste-Marie
Mascouche, QC J7K 1P1
Tél: 450-474-4133; *Téléc:* 450-474-6401
www.ville.mascouche.qc.ca
Entité municipal: City
Incorporation: 1er juillet 1855 *Area:* 107,95 km2
Comté ou district: Les Moulins; *Population au 2006:* 33,764
Circonscription(s) électorale(s) provinciale(s): Masson
Circonscription(s) électorale(s) fédérale(s): Montcalm
Prochaines élections: 3e novembre 2013
Richard Marcotte, Maire
450-474-4133
Normand Pagé, Conseiller, Ward(s): 1. Louis-Hébert
450-966-6326
Lise Gagnon, Conseillère, Ward(s): 2. Laurier
450-474-4501
Jacques Tremblay, Conseiller, Ward(s): 3. Le Gardeur
514-591-8710
Donald Mailly, Conseiller, Ward(s): 4. La Vérendrye
450-966-1413
Sylvain Picard, Conseiller, Ward(s): 5. Du Coteau
450-966-9233
Chantal Laurin, Conseillère, Ward(s): 6. Des Hauts-Bois
450-477-4953
Nathalie Filion, Conseillère, Ward(s): 7. Du Rucher
514-461-3065
Denise Paquette, Conseillère, Ward(s): 8. Du Manoir
450-966-6044
Yvan Laberge, Greffier
450-474-4133
Luc Tremblay, Directeur général
450-474-4133
Michel Gobeil, Trésorier, Finances
450-474-4133

Matane
230, av St-Jérôme
Matane, QC G4W 3A2
Tél: 418-562-2333; *Téléc:* 418-562-4869
mairie@ville.matane.qc.ca
www.ville.matane.qc.ca
Entité municipal: City
Incorporation: 26 septembre 2001 *Area:* 214,63 km2
Comté ou district: Matane; *Population au 2006:* 14,742
Circonscription(s) électorale(s) provinciale(s): Matane
Circonscription(s) électorale(s) fédérale(s): Haute-Gaspésie-La Mitis-Matane-Matapédia
Prochaines élections: 3e novembre 2013
Claude Canuel, Maire
mairie@ville.matane.qc.ca
Anick Fortin, Conseiller, Ward(s): 1
418-562-7334
Monique Fournier, Conseillère, Ward(s): 2
colombo@cgocable.ca
Claude Harrison, Conseiller, Ward(s): 3
charrison@globetrotter.net
Mario Hamilton, Conseiller, Ward(s): 4
mhjm@globetrotter.net
Martin Lefrançois, Conseiller, Ward(s): 5
martin@lefrancoisfrancoeur.ca
Steve Girard, Conseiller, Ward(s): 6
418-562-4975
sgirard.matane@globetrotter.net
Nicolas Leclerc, Greffier (par intérim)
n.leclerc@ville.matane.qc.ca
Michel Barriault, Directeur général
418-562-2333
m.barriault@ville.matane.qc.ca
Marie Pelletier, Trésorière
418-562-2333
m.pelletier@ville.matane.qc.ca

Mercier
869, boul St-Jean-Baptiste, 2e étage
Mercier, QC J6R 2L3
Tél: 450-691-6090; *Téléc:* 450-691-6529
info@ville.mercier.qc.ca
www.ville.mercier.qc.ca
Entité municipal: City
Incorporation: 1er juillet 1855 *Area:* 45,89 km2
Comté ou district: Roussillon; *Population au 2006:* 10,121
Circonscription(s) électorale(s) provinciale(s): Châteauguay
Circonscription(s) électorale(s) fédérale(s):
Châteauguay—St-Constant
Prochaines élections: 3e novembre 2013
Jacques Lambert, Maire
450-691-6090
jacques.lambert@ville.mercier.qc.ca
Stéphane Roy, Conseiller, Ward(s): 1
stephane.roy@ville.mercier.qc.ca
Jeannine Breault, Conseillère, Ward(s): 2
jeannine.breault@ville.mercier.qc.ca
Gilles Desponts, Conseiller, Ward(s): 3
gilles.desponts@ville.mercier.qc.ca
Daniel Pilon, Conseiller, Ward(s): 4
daniel.pilon@ville.mercier.qc.ca
Louis Cimon, Conseiller, Ward(s): 5
louis.cimon@ville.mercier.qc.ca
Pierre Hébert, Conseiller, Ward(s): 6
pierre.hebert@ville.mercier.qc.ca
Marc Rouleau, Greffier et directeur général
450-691-6090
marc.rouleau@ville.mercier.qc.ca
Nadia René, Trésorière
450-691-6090
nadia.rene@ville.mercier.qc.ca

Mirabel
14111, rue Saint-Jean
Mirabel, QC J7J 1Y3
Tél: 450-475-8653; *Téléc:* 450-475-7195
communications@ville.mirabel.qc.ca
ville.mirabel.qc.ca
Entité municipal: City
Incorporation: 1er janvier 1971 *Area:* 477,86 km2
Comté ou district: Mirabel; *Population au 2006:* 34,626
Circonscription(s) électorale(s) provinciale(s): Mirabel
Circonscription(s) électorale(s) fédérale(s):
Argenteuil-Papineau-Mirabel
Prochaines élections: 3e novembre 2013
Hubert Meilleur, Maire
Michel Lauzon, Conseiller, Ward(s): 1
Gérald Forget, Conseiller, Ward(s): 2
Jean Bouchard, Conseiller, Ward(s): 3
François Bélanger, Conseiller, Ward(s): 4
Daniel Gauthier, Conseiller, Ward(s): 5
Pierre-Paul Meloche, Conseiller, Ward(s): 6
Luc St-Jean, Conseiller, Ward(s): 7
Guy Laurin, Conseiller, Ward(s): 8
Suzanne Mireault, Greffière
450-475-2002
s.mireault@ville.mirabel.qc.ca
Louis Prud'homme, Directeur général
450-475-2000, Fax: 450-475-2013
l.prud'homme@ville.mirabel.qc.ca
Germain Paquette, Trésorier
450-475-2003
g.paquette@ville.mirabel.qc.ca
Bernard Poulin, Directeur, Communications
450-475-2001
b.poulin@ville.mirabel.qc.ca
Jean Gaudreault, Directeur, Loisirs, la culture et la vie
450-475-8656
j.gaudreault@ville.mirabel.qc.ca
Denis Maurice, Directeur adjoint, Sécurité incendie
450-475-2010
d.maurice@ville.mirabel.qc.ca

Mont-Laurier
485, rue Mercier
Mont-Laurier, QC J9L 3N8
Tél: 819-623-1221; *Téléc:* 819-623-4840
info@villemontlaurier.qc.ca
www.villemontlaurier.qc.ca
Entité municipal: City
Incorporation: 8e janvier 2003 *Area:* 590,64 km2
Comté ou district: Antoine-Labelle; *Population au 2006:* 13,405
Circonscription(s) électorale(s) provinciale(s): Labelle
Circonscription(s) électorale(s) fédérale(s): Laurentides-Labelle
Prochaines élections: 3e novembre 2013
Note: Dès le 8 janvier 2003, la ville de Mont-Laurier regroupe les municipalités de Des Ruisseaux & Saint-Aimé-du-Lac-des-Iles.
Michel Adrien, Maire
Denis Ethier, Conseiller, Ward(s): 1
Frank Crépeau, Conseiller, Ward(s): 2
Jocelyne Cloutier, Conseillère, Ward(s): 3
Benoit Pagé, Conseiller, Ward(s): 4
Louis-Pierre Blais, Conseiller, Ward(s): 5
Lise St-Louis, Conseillère, Ward(s): 6
Blandine Boulianne, Greffière
Jean-Yves Forget, Directeur général
Johanne Nantel, Trésorière

Mont-St-Hilaire
100, rue du Centre-Civique
Mont-Saint-Hilaire, QC J3H 3M8
Tél: 450-467-2854; *Téléc:* 450-467-6460
information@villemsh.ca
www.ville.mont-saint-hilaire.qc.ca
Entité municipal: City
Incorporation: 12 mars 1966 *Area:* 38,96 km2
Comté ou district: La Vallée-du-Richelieu; *Population au 2006:* 15,720
Circonscription(s) électorale(s) provinciale(s): Borduas
Circonscription(s) électorale(s) fédérale(s): Chambly-Borduas
Prochaines élections: 3e novembre 2013
Michel Gilbert, Maire
450-446-9511
michel.gilbert@villemsh.ca
Guy Boulé, Conseiller, Ward(s): 1. Déboulis
450-467-6631
guy.boule@villemsh.ca
Rémi H. Lair, Conseiller, Ward(s): 2. Patriotes
450-536-0960
remi.h.lair@villemsh.ca
André Ricard, Conseiller, Ward(s): 3. Piémont
450-446-5774
andre.ricard@villemsh.ca
Valéry Lapointe, Conseillère, Ward(s): 4. Rouville
450-714-1351
valery.lapointe@villemsh.ca
Jean-Luc Halde, Conseiller, Ward(s): 5. Montagne
450-467-6535
jean-luc.halde@villemsh.ca
Fernand Brillant, Conseiller, Ward(s): 6. Pommeraie
450-467-4699
fernand.brillant@villemsh.ca
Estelle Simard, Greffière
450-467-2854
greffe@villemsh.ca
Vacant, Directeur général
450-467-2854
direction.generale@villemsh.ca
Carmel Constant, Trésorier
450-467-2854
finances@villemsh.ca
Pierre Bergeron, Directeur, Loisir, culture et communication

Montmagny
143, rue St-Jean-Baptiste est
Montmagny, QC G5V 1K4
Tél: 418-248-3361; *Téléc:* 418-248-4870
info@ville.montmagny.qc.ca
www.ville.montmagny.qc.ca
Entité municipal: City
Incorporation: 2e avril 1966 *Area:* 125,76 km2
Comté ou district: Montmagny; *Population au 2006:* 11,353
Circonscription(s) électorale(s) provinciale(s): Montmagny-L'Islet
Circonscription(s) électorale(s) fédérale(s):
Montmagny-L'Islet-Kamouraska-Rivière-du-Loup
Prochaines élections: 3e novembre 2013
Jean-Guy Desrosiers, Maire
Jean-Paul Boivin, Conseiller, Ward(s): 1
Gaston Caron, Conseiller, Ward(s): 2
Michel Coulombe, Conseiller, Ward(s): 3
Michel Mercier, Conseiller, Ward(s): 4
Michel Paquet, Conseiller, Ward(s): 5
Rémy Langevin, Conseiller, Ward(s): 6
Félix Michaud, Greffier
418-248-3362
felix.michaud@ville.montmagny.qc.ca
Bernard Létourneau, Directeur général
418-248-3362
bernard.letourneau@ville.montmagny.qc.ca
André Lévesque, Directeur, Finances et approvisionnement
418-248-3361, Fax: 418-248-8468
finances@ville.montmagny.qc.ca
Yves Chayer, Directeur, Protection contre les incendies
418-248-5813, Fax: 418-248-2266
yves.chayer@ville.montmagny.qc.ca

Montréal
Hôtel de Ville
275, rue Notre-Dame est
Montréal, QC H2Y 1C6
Tél: 514-872-3142; *Téléc:* 514-872-5655
www.ville.montreal.qc.ca
Entité municipal: City
Incorporation: 1er janvier 2002 *Area:* 363,52 km2
Population au 2006: 1,620,693
Circonscription(s) électorale(s) provinciale(s):
Acadie;Anjou;Bourassa-Sauvé;Bourget;Crémazie;D'Arcy McGee;Gouin;Hochelaga-Maisonneuve;Jeanne-Mance-Viger;La Fontaine;Laurier-Dorion;Marguerite-Bourgeoys;Mercier;Marquette;Mont-Royal;Nelligan;Notre-Dame-de-Grâce;Outremont;Pointe-aux-Trembles;Robert-Baldwin;Rosemont;St-Henri-Ste-Anne;St-Laurent;Ste-Marie -St-Jacques;Westmount-St-Louis;Verdun;Viau
Circonscription(s) électorale(s) fédérale(s): Ahuntsic; Bourassa; Hochelaga; Honoré-Mercier; Jeanne-Le Ber; Lac-Saint-Louis; LaSalle-Émard; Laurier-Ste-Marie; Mount Royal; Notre-Dame-de-Grâce-Lachine; Outremont; Papineau; Rosemont-La Petite-Patrie; Westmount-Ville-Marie; St-Laurent-Cartierville; St-Léonard-St-Michel; La Pointe-de-l'Ile; Pierrefonds-Dollard
Prochaines élections: 3e novembre 2013
Gérald Tremblay, Maire
514-872-3101, Fax: 514-872-4059
Yves Saindon, Greffier
514-872-3007
yvessaindon@ville.montreal.qc.ca
Louis Roquet, Directeur général
Robert Lamontagne, Directeur, Finances
Pierre Villeneuve, Directeur (par intérim), Relations avec les citoyens
Jean Yves Hinse, Directeur, Service du capital humain
Jacques Bergeron, Vérificateur général

Conseiller de la ville
Élaine Ayotte, Conseillère de la ville, Marie-Victorin, Ward(s): Rosemont—La Petite—Patrie
514-868-3931, Fax: 514-868-3932
Frantz Benjamin, Conseillère de la ville, Saint-Michel, Ward(s): Villeray-St-Michel-Parc-Ext.
514-872-3103, Fax: 514-872-2196
Richard Bergeron, Conseiller de la ville, Jeanne-Mance, Ward(s): Le Plateau-Mont-Royal
514-872-8023, Fax: 514-868-4077
richardbbergeron@ville.montreal.qc.ca
Laurent Blanchard, Conseiller de la ville, Hochelaga, Ward(s): Mercier—Hochelaga-Maisonneuve
514-872-9899, Fax: 514-872-7125
laurentblanchard@ville.montreal.qc.ca
Caroline Bourgeois, Conseillère de la ville, La Pointe-aux-Prairies, Ward(s): Riv.-des-Prairies-Pte-aux-Trem
514-868-4356, Fax: 514-868-4353
Étienne Brunet, Conseiller de la ville, Sault-au-Récollet, Ward(s): Ahuntsic-Cartierville
514-872-0430, Fax: 514-868-3324

Daniel Bélanger, Conseiller de la ville, Saint-Paul—Émard, Ward(s): Le Sud-Ouest
514-872-6814, Fax: 514-872-3705
Maria Calderone, Conseillère de la ville, Rivière-des-Prairies, Ward(s): Riv.-des-Prairies-Pte-aux-Trem
514-868-4052, Fax: 514-872-3709
mariacalderone@ville.montreal.qc.ca
Jocelyn Ann Campbell, Conseillère de la ville, Saint-Sulpice, Ward(s): Ahuntsic-Cartierville
514-872-2246, Fax: 514-868-3324
jacampbell@ville.montreal.qc.ca
Harout Chitilian, Conseiller de la ville, Bordeaux-Cartierville, Ward(s): Ahuntsic-Cartierville
514-872-2246, Fax: 514-868-3324
Susan Clarke, Conseillère de la ville, Loyola, Ward(s): Côte-des-Neiges-N.-D.-de-Grâce
514-872-4863, Fax: 514-868-3327
Jane Cowell-Poitras, Conseillère de la ville, Ward(s): Lachine
514-634-3471, Fax: 514-634-8164
Mary Deros, Conseillère de la ville, Parc-Extension, Ward(s): Villeray-St-Michel-Parc-Extens
514-872-3103, Fax: 514-872-2196
mderos@ville.montreal.qc.ca
Richard Deschamps, Conseiller de la ville, Sault-St-Louis, Ward(s): LaSalle
514-872-4879, Fax: 514-367-6600
richarddeschamps@ville.montreal.qc.ca
Christian G. Dubois, Conseiller de la ville, Bois-de-Liesse, Ward(s): Pierrefonds-Roxboro
514-624-1488, Fax: 514-624-1415
christiangdubois@ville.montreal.qc.ca
Josée Duplessis, Conseillère de la ville, De Lorimier, Ward(s): Le Plateau-Mont-Royal
514-868-5196, Fax: 514-868-4118
joseeduplessis@ville.montreal.qc.ca
Suzanne Décarie, Conseillère de la ville, Pointe-aux-Trembles, Ward(s): Riv.-des-Prairies-Pte-aux-Trem
514-868-4350, Fax: 514-868-4353
suzannedecarie@ville.montreal.qc.ca
Alvaro Farinacci, Conseiller de la ville, Cecil-P.-Newman, Ward(s): LaSalle
514-367-6208, Fax: 514-367-6600
genesee@qc.aira.com
Sammy Forcillo, Conseiller de la ville, Peter-McGill, Ward(s): Ville-Marie
514-868-5858, Fax: 514-872-8347
sforcillo@ville.montreal.qc.ca
Helen Fotopulos, Conseillère de la ville, Côte-des-Neiges, Conseillers et Districts, Ward(s): Côte-de-Neiges-N.-D.-de-Grâce
hfotopulos@ville.montreal.qc.ca
Véronique Fournier, Conseillère de la ville, St-Henri-Petite-Bourgogne-Pte-St-Charles, Ward(s): Le Sud-Ouest
514-872-6814, Fax: 514-872-3705
Marc-André Gadoury, Conseiller de la ville, Étienne-Desmarteau, Ward(s): Rosemont—La Petite-Patrie
514-872-8390, Fax: 514-868-3932
Jean-Marc Gibeau, Conseiller de la ville, Ovide-Clermont, Ward(s): Montréal-Nord
514-328-4000, Fax: 514-325-4025
jgibeau@ville.montreal.qc.ca
Louise Harel, Conseillère de la ville, Maisonneuve—Longue-Pointe, Ward(s): Mercier-Hochelaga-Maisonneuve
514-872-7123, Fax: 514-872-7125
Andrée Hénault, Conseillère de la ville, Ward(s): Anjou
514-493-8051, Fax: 514-493-8013
ahenault@ville.montreal.qc.ca
Pierre Lampron, Conseiller de la ville, Vieux-Rosemont, Ward(s): Rosemont—La Petite-Patrie
514-868-3907, Fax: 514-868-3932
Elsie Lefebvre, Conseillère de la ville, Villeray, Ward(s): Villeray St-Michel-Parc-Extens
514-872-3103, Fax: 514-872-2196
François Limoges, Conseiller de la ville, Saint-Édouard, Ward(s): Rosemont—La Petite-Patrie
514-872-8234, Fax: 514-868-3932
Pierre Mainville, Conseiller de la ville, Ste-Marie, Ward(s): Ville-Marie
514-868-5169, Fax: 514-868-5963
pierremainville@ville.montreal.qc.ca
Ginette Marotte, Conseillère de la ville, Champlain-L'île-des-Soeurs, Ward(s): Verdun
514-765-7010, Fax: 514-765-7013
ginette.marotte@verdun.ca
Peter McQueen, Conseiller de la ville, Notre-Dame-de-Grâce, Ward(s): Côte-des-Neiges-N.-D.-de-Grâce
514-868-4281, Fax: 514-868-3327
Francesco Miele, Conseiller de la ville, Côte-de-Liesse, Ward(s): Saint-Laurent
514-855-6000, Fax: 514-855-6049
Alex Norris, Conseiller de la ville, Mile End, Ward(s): Le Plateau-Mont-Royal
514-872-8023, Fax: 514-868-4077
Lionel Perez, Conseiller de la ville, Darlington, Ward(s): Côte-des-Neiges-N.-D.-de-Grâce
514-872-4863, Fax: 514-868-3327
Dominic Perri, Conseiller de la ville, St-Léonard-Ouest, Ward(s): Saint-Léonard
514-328-8410, Fax: 514-328-8419
dperri@ville.montreal.qc.ca
Gaëtan Primeau, Conseiller de la ville, Tétreaultville, Ward(s): Mercier—Hochelaga-Maisonneuve
514-872-8241, Fax: 514-872-7125
gaetanprimeau@ville.montreal.qc.ca
François Robillard, Conseiller de la ville, St-Jacques, Ward(s): Ville-Marie
514-868-5178, Fax: 514-872-8347
Marvin Rotrand, Conseiller de la ville, Snowdon, Ward(s): Côte-des-Neiges-N.-D.-de-Grâce
514-872-4863, Fax: 514-868-3327
mrotrand@ville.montreal.qc.ca
Aref Salem, Conseiller de la ville, Norman-McLaren, Ward(s): Saint-Laurent
514-855-6000, Fax: 514-855-6049
Alain Tassé, Conseiller de la ville, Desmarchais-Crawford, Ward(s): Verdun
514-765-7010, Fax: 514-765-7013
alain.tasse@verdun.ca
Clementina Teti-Tomassi, Conseillère de la ville, Marie-Clarac, Ward(s): Montréal-Nord
514-328-4000, Fax: 514-325-4025
clementinatetitomassi@ville.montreal.qc.ca
Émilie Thuillier, Conseillère de la ville, Ward(s): Ahuntsic-Cartierville
514-872-2246, Fax: 514-868-3324
Lyn Thériault, Conseillère de la Ville, Ward(s): Mercier-Hochelaga-Maisonneuve
514-872-7123, Fax: 514-872-7125
lyn.theriault@ville.montreal.qc.ca
Frank Venneri, Conseiller de la ville, François-Perrault, Ward(s): Villeray St-Michel-Parc-Extens
514-872-3103, Fax: 514-872-2196
mfvenneri@ville.montreal.qc.ca
Bertrand A. Ward, Conseiller de la ville, Cap-Saint-Jacques, Ward(s): Pierrefonds-Roxboro
514-624-1053, Fax: 514-624-1415
bward@ville.montreal.qc.ca
Robert L. Zambito, Conseiller de la ville, St-Léonard-Est, Ward(s): Saint-Léonard
514-328-8410, Fax: 514-328-8419
rzambito@ville.montreal.qc.ca

Maire d'arrondissement/Conseiller de la ville

Michael Applebaum, Maire d'arrondissement/Conseiller de la ville, Ward(s): Côte-des-Neiges-N.-D.-de-Grâce
514-872-4863, Fax: 514-868-3327
mapplebaum@ville.montreal.qc.ca
Manon Barbe, Mairesse d'arrondissement/Conseillère de la ville, Ward(s): LaSalle
514-367-6206, Fax: 514-367-6600
mbarbe@ville.montreal.qc.ca
Michel Bissonnet, Maire d'arrondissement/Conseiller de la ville, Ward(s): Saint-Léonard
514-328-8410, Fax: 514-328-8419
Richard Bélanger, Maire d'arrondissement/Conseiller de la ville, Ward(s): L'île-Bizard—Ste-Geneviève
514-620-7592, Fax: 514-620-4543
richardbelanger@ville.montreal.qc.ca
Marie Cinq-Mars, Mairesse d'arrondissement/Conseillère de la ville, Ward(s): Outremont
514-495-6220, Fax: 514-495-6290
mariecinq-mars@ville.montreal.qc.ca
François W. Croteau, Maire d'arrondissement/Conseiller de la ville, Ward(s): Rosemont—La Petite-Patrie
514-868-3934, Fax: 514-868-3932
Claude Dauphin, Maire d'arrondissement/Conseiller de la ville, Ward(s): Lachine
514-634-3471, Fax: 514-634-8164
Alan DeSousa, Maire d'arrondissement/Conseiller de la ville, Ward(s): Saint-Laurent
514-855-6000, Fax: 514-855-6049
adesousa@ville.montreal.qc.ca
Gilles Deguire, Maire d'arrondissement/Conseiller de la ville, Ward(s): Montréal-Nord
514-328-4000, Fax: 514-328-5577
Benoit Dorais, Maire d'arrondissement/Conseiller de la ville, Ward(s): Le Sud-Ouest
514-872-6814, Fax: 514-872-3705
Luc Ferrandez, Maire d'arrondissement/Conseiller de la ville, Ward(s): Le Plateau-Mont-Royal
514-872-8023, Fax: 514-868-4118
Pierre Gagnier, Maire d'arrondissement/Conseiller de la ville, Ward(s): Ahuntsic-Cartierville
514-872-0430, Fax: 514-868-3324
Luis Miranda, Maire d'arrondissement/Conseiller de la ville, Ward(s): Anjou
514-493-8010, Fax: 514-493-8013
lmiranda@ville.montreal.qc.ca
Réal Ménard, Maire d'arrondissement/Conseiller de la ville, Ward(s): Mercier—Hochelaga-Maisonneuve
514-872-8759, Fax: 514-869-4451
Chantal Rouleau, Mairesse d'arrondissement/Conseillère de la ville, Ward(s): Riv.-des-Prairies-Pte-aux-Trem
514-868-4050, Fax: 514-868-4353
Anie Samson, Mairesse d'arrondissement/Conseillère de la ville, Ward(s): Villeray St-Michel-Parc-Extens
514-872-3103, Fax: 514-872-2196
asamson@ville.montreal.qc.ca
Claude Trudel, Maire d'arrondissement/Conseiller de la ville, Ward(s): Verdun
514-765-7010, Fax: 514-765-7013
claude.trudel@verdun.ca
Monique Worth, Mairesse d'arrondissement/Conseillère de la ville, Ward(s): Pierrefonds-Roxboro
514-624-1400, Fax: 514-624-1415
mworth@ville.montreal.qc.ca

Conseiller d'arrondissement

Gilles Beaudry, Conseiller d'arrondissement, Ouest, Ward(s): Anjou
514-493-8019, Fax: 514-493-8013
gillesbeaudry@ville.montreal.qc.ca
Paul Beaupré, Conseiller d'arrondissement, Champlain-L'île-des-Soeurs, Ward(s): Verdun
514-765-7010, Fax: 514-765-7013
Dimitrios Jim Beis, Conseiller d'arrondissement, Bois-de-Liesse, Ward(s): Pierrefonds-Roxboro
514-624-1175, Fax: 514-624-1415
Michèle D. Biron, Conseillère d'arrondissement, Norman-McLaren, Ward(s): Saint-Laurent
514-855-6000, Fax: 514-855-6049
Ross Blackhurst, Conseiller d'arrondissement, Sault-St-Louis, Ward(s): LaSalle
514-794-7677, Fax: 514-367-6600
Bernard Blanchet, Conseiller d'arrondissement, J.-Émery-Provost, Ward(s): Lachine
514-634-3471, Fax: 514-634-8164
Mario Blanchet, Conseiller d'arrondissement, La Pointe-aux-Prairies, Ward(s): Riv.-des-Prairies-Pte-aux-Trem
514-868-4350, Fax: 514-868-4353
Carl Boileau, Conseillère d'arrondissement, De Lorimier, Ward(s): Le Plateau-Mont-Royal
514-872-8023, Fax: 514-868-4077
Vincenzo Cesari, Conseiller d'arrondissement, Cecil-P.-Newman, Ward(s): LaSalle
514-367-6216, Fax: 514-367-6600
Andrée Champoux, Conseillère d'arrondissement, Champlain-L'île-des-Soeurs, Ward(s): Verdun
514-765-7010, Fax: 514-765-7013
Jean-François Cloutier, Conseiller d'arrondissement, Fort-Rolland, Ward(s): Lachine
514-634-3471, Fax: 514-634-8164
Catherine Clément-Talbot, Conseillère d'arrondissement, Cap-St-Jacques, Ward(s): Pierrefonds-Roxboro
514-624-1174, Fax: 514-624-1415
catherineclementtalbot@ville.montreal.qc.ca
Maurice Cohen, Conseiller d'arrondissement, Côte-de-Liesse, Ward(s): Saint-Laurent
514-855-6000, Fax: 514-855-6049
mcohen@ville.montreal.qc.ca
Michèle Di Genova Zammit, Conseillère d'arrondissement, Centre, Ward(s): Anjou
514-493-8085, Fax: 514-493-8013
mzammit@ville.montreal.qc.ca
Éric Dugas, Conseiller d'arrondissement, Ste-Geneviève, Ward(s): L'île-Bizard—Ste-Geneviève
514-620-6896, Fax: 514-620-4543
Gilles Déziel, Conseiller d'arrondissement, Pointe-aux-Trembles, Ward(s): Riv.-des-Prairies-Pte-aux-Trem
514-868-4350, Fax: 514-868-4353
Céline Forget, Conseillère d'arrondissement, Joseph-Beaubien, Ward(s): Outremont
514-495-7430, Fax: 514-872-5655
Diane Gibb, Conseillère d'arrondissement, Pierre-Foretier, Ward(s): L'île-Bizard—Ste-Geneviève
514-620-6896, Fax: 514-620-4543
dianegibb@ville.montreal.qc.ca

Ann Guy, Conseillère d'arrondissement, Desmarchais-Crawford, Ward(s): Verdun
514-765-7010, Fax: 514-765-7013
Piper Huggins, Conseillère d'arrondissement, Jeanne-Mance, Ward(s): Le Plateau-Mont-Royal
514-872-8023, Fax: 514-868-4077
Christopher Little, Conseiller d'arrondissement, Denis-Benjamin-Viger, Ward(s): L'île-Bizard—Ste-Geneviève
514-620-6896, Fax: 514-620-4543
littlechristopher@ville.montreal.qc.ca
Louis Moffatt, Conseiller d'arrondissement, Claude-Ryan, Ward(s): Outremont
514-495-6230, Fax: 514-495-6290
louismoffatt@ville.montreal.qc.ca
Ana Nunes, Conseillère d'arrondissement, Jeanne-Sauvé, Ward(s): Outremont
514-495-6228, Fax: 514-495-6290
anunes@ville.montreal.qc.ca
Laura-Ann Palestini, Conseillère d'arrondissement, Sault-St-Louis, Ward(s): LaSalle
514-367-6216, Fax: 514-367-6600
Paul-Yvon Perron, Conseiller d'arrondissement, Est, Ward(s): Anjou
514-493-8017, Fax: 514-493-8013
Marie Potvin, Conseillère d'arrondissement, Robert-Bourassa, Ward(s): Outremont
514-495-6248, Fax: 514-495-6290
marie.potvin@ville.montreal.qc.ca
Lise Poulin, Conseillère d'arrondissement, Canal, Ward(s): Lachine
514-634-3471, Fax: 514-634-8164
Giovanni Rapanà, Conseiller d'arrondissement, Rivière-des-Prairies, Ward(s): Riv.-des-Prairies-Pte-aux-Trem
514-868-5558, Fax: 514-872-3709
Monica Ricourt, Conseillère d'arrondissement, Ovide-Clermont, Ward(s): Montréal-Nord
514-328-4000, Fax: 514-325-4025
François Robert, Conseiller d'arrondissement, Jacques-Bizard, Ward(s): L'île-Bizard—Ste-Geneviève
514-620-6896, Fax: 514-620-4543
francoisrobert@ville.montreal.qc.ca
Chantal Rossi, Conseillère d'arrondissement, Marie-Clarac, Ward(s): Montréal-Nord
514-328-4000, Fax: 514-325-4025
Huguette Roy, Conseil. d'arrondissmnt., St-Henri-Pte-Bourgogne-Pte-St-Charles, Ward(s): Le Sud-Ouest
514-872-6814, Fax: 514-872-3705
Richard Ryan, Conseiller d'arrondissement, Mile End, Ward(s): Le Plateau-Mont-Royal
514-872-8023, Fax: 514-868-4077
André Savard, Conseiller d'arrondissement, Desmarchais-Crawford, Ward(s): Verdun
514-765-7010, Fax: 514-765-7013
Sophie Thiébaut, Conseil. d'arrondissmnt., St-Henri-Pte-Bourgogne-Pte-St-Charles, Ward(s): Le Sud-Ouest
514-872-6814, Fax: 514-872-3705
Lili-Anne Tremblay, Conseillère d'arrondissement, Saint-Léonard-Est, Ward(s): Saint-Léonard
514-328-8410, Fax: 514-328-8419
Josée Troilo, Conseillère d'arrondissement, Cecil-P.-Newman, Ward(s): LaSalle
514-367-6216, Fax: 514-367-6600

Bureau du vérificateur général
Jacques Bergeron, CA, MBA, M.Sc., Vérificateur général
Robert Duquette, CA, Vérificateur général adjoint, Optimisation des ressources et conformité réglementair
Serge Vaillancourt, Vérificateur général adjoint, Technologies de l'information, éthique et administration
Denis Tremblay, Vérificateur général adjoint, Certification des états financiers Ville et autres organismes municipaux
Denis Tremblay, Chef de division, Vérification -Autre organismes municipaux

Service de sécurité incendie de Montréal
Serge Tremblay, Directeur

Service du capital humain
Jean Yves Hinse, Directeur

Direction générale
Louis Roquet, Directeur général

Service de police de la Ville de Montréal
Marc Parent, Directeur

Pincourt

919, ch Duhamel
Pincourt, QC J7V 4G8
Tél: 514-453-8981; *Téléc:* 514-453-8401
pincourtinfo@videotron.ca
www.villepincourt.qc.ca
Entité municipal: City
Incorporation: 1er janvier 1950 *Area:* 8,36 km2
Comté ou district: Vaudreuil-Soulanges; *Population au 2006:* 11,197
Circonscription(s) électorale(s) provinciale(s): Vaudreuil
Circonscription(s) électorale(s) fédérale(s): Vaudreuil-Soulanges
Prochaines élections: 3e novembre 2013
Yvan Cardinal, Maire
Stéphane Boyer, Conseiller, Ward(s): 1
Marie-Andrée G. Laliberté, Conseillère, Ward(s): 2
John Kinnear, Conseiller, Ward(s): 3
Michel Pratte, Conseiller, Ward(s): 4
Jim Miron, Conseiller, Ward(s): 5
André D'Aragon, Conseiller, Ward(s): 6
Nicole Drouin, Greffière
514-453-8981
Michel Perrier, Directeur général
514-453-8981, Fax: 514-453-0934
Nathalie Boisvert, Trésorière
514-453-8981

Prévost

2870, boul du Curé-Labelle
Prévost, QC J0R 1T0
Tél: 450-224-8888; *Téléc:* 450-224-8323
info@ville.prevost.qc.ca
www.ville.prevost.qc.ca
Entité municipal: City
Incorporation: 20 janvier 1973 *Area:* 34,32 km2
Comté ou district: La Rivière-du-Nord; *Population au 2006:* 10,132
Circonscription(s) électorale(s) provinciale(s): Prévost
Circonscription(s) électorale(s) fédérale(s): Rivière-du-Nord
Prochaines élections: 3e novembre 2013
Germain Richer, Maire
450-224-8888
maire@ville.prevost.qc.ca
Gaétan Bordeleau, Conseiller, Ward(s): 1
450-224-8888
gbordeleau@ville.prevost.qc.ca
Jean-Pierre Joubert, Conseiller, Ward(s): 2
450-224-8888
jpjoubert@ville.prevost.qc.ca
Diane Berthiaume, Conseillère, Ward(s): 3
450-224-8888
diane.berthiaume@ville.prevost.qc.ca
Claude Leroux, Conseiller, Ward(s): 4
450-224-8888
claude.leroux@ville.prevost.qc.ca
Brigitte Paquette, Conseillère, Ward(s): 5
450-224-8888
brigitte.paquette@ville.prevost.qc.ca
Stéphane Parent, Conseiller, Ward(s): 6
450-224-8888
sparent@ville.prevost.qc.ca
Laurent Laberge, Greffier
450-224-8888
greffe@ville.prevost.qc.ca
Réal Martin, Directeur général
450-224-8888
dg@ville.prevost.qc.ca
Jean-Yves Crispin, Trésorier
450-224-8888
tresor@ville.prevost.qc.ca

Québec

Hôtel de Ville
CP 700 Haute-Ville
2, rue des Jardins
Québec, QC G1R 4S9
Tél: 418-641-6000; *Téléc:* 418-641-6463
renseignements@ville.quebec.qc.ca
www.ville.quebec.qc.ca
Entité municipal: City
Incorporation: 1er janvier 2002 *Area:* 451,79 km2
Population au 2006: 491,142
Circonscription(s) électorale(s) provinciale(s): Charlesbourg-Haute-Saint-Charles; Chauveau; Jean-Lesage; Jean-Talon; La Peltrie; Louis-Hébert; Montmorency; Taschereau; Vanier
Circonscription(s) électorale(s) fédérale(s): Québec; Louis-St-Laurent
Prochaines élections: 3e novembre 2013
Régis Labeaume, Maire
418-641-6434
Sylvain Ouellet, Greffier
418-641-6212
greffearchives@ville.quebec.qc.ca
Alain Marcoux, Directeur général
418-641-6373
directiongenerale@ville.quebec.qc.ca
Jacques Grantham, Directeur, Environnement
418-641-6189
environnement@ville.quebec.qc.ca
Chantale Giguère, Directrice, Rssources humaines
418-641-6234
ressourceshumaines@ville.quebec.qc.ca
Denis Deslauriers, Directeur, Technologies de l'information/télécomm.
418-641-6239
technologies@ville.quebec.qc.ca
Rhonda Rioux, Directrice, Culture
418-641-6181
culture@ville.quebec.qc.ca
Fernand Martin, Directeur, Aménagement du territoire
418-641-6160
amenageterrit@ville.quebec.qc.ca
Marcel Roy, Directeur, Travaux publics
418-641-6240
travauxpublics@ville.quebec.qc.ca
Pierre Huot, Directeur, Évaluation
418-641-6193
evaluation@ville.quebec.qc.ca
Guy Bélanger, Directeur, Loisirs, sports & vie communautaire
418-641-6224
loisirs@ville.quebec.qc.ca
Jean-Yves Tellier, Directeur, Développement économique
418-641-6183
deveconomique@ville.quebec.qc.ca
Daniel Lessard, Directeur, Ingénierie
418-641-6217
ingenierie@ville.quebec.qc.ca
Richard Poitras, Directeur, Protection contre l'incendie
418-641-6231
protectionincendie@ville.quebec.qc.ca
Serge Bélisle, Directeur, Police
418-641-6292
police@ville.quebec.qc.ca
Vacant, Directeur, Communications
418-641-6651
communications@ville.quebec.qc.ca
Daniel Maranda, Directeur, Service des approvisionnements
418-641-6164
approvisionnements@ville.quebec.qc.ca
Gabriel Savard, Directeur, Office du tourisme de Québec
418-522-3511
François Gagnon, Vérificateur général
Serge Giasson, Directeur, Affaires juridiques
418-641-6156
Gilles Noël, Directeur général adjoint, Services de soutien
Suzanne Canac Marquis, Directrice générale adjointe, Développement culturel, touristique, sportif & social
Alain Thériault, Directeur général adjoint (par intérim), Développement durable
Chantale Giguère, Directrice générale adjointe, Sécurité publique
Alain Thériault, Directeur général adjoint, Coordination des arrondissements
Yves Courchesne, Directeur, Services des finances
418-641-6203
finances@ville.quebec.qc.ca

Arrondissement de Beauport
Counseil
Lisette Lepage, Conseillère, Ward(s): Seigneurial
418-641-6501
Julie Lemieux, Conseillère, Ward(s): Chute-Montmorency
418-641-6501
Marc Simoneau, Conseiller, Ward(s): Robert-Giffard
418-641-6501
Marie France Trudel, Conseillère, Ward(s): Sainte-Thérèse-de-Lisieux
418-641-6501

Arrondissement de Charlesbourg
Administration
Jean-Marie Laliberté, Conseiller, Ward(s): Monts
418-641-6401
Michelle Morin-Doyle, Conseillère, Ward(s): Trait-Carré
418-641-6401
Odette Simoneau, Conseillère, Ward(s): Sentiers
418-641-6401
Denise Trudel, Conseillère, Ward(s): Saint-Rodrigue
418-641-6401

Arrondissement de La Cité-Limoilou
Yvon Bussières, Conseiller, Ward(s): Saint-Sacrement-Belvédère
418-641-6101
Chantal Gilbert, Conseillère, Ward(s): Faubourgs
418-641-6411
Anne Guérette, Conseillère, Ward(s): Vieux-Québec-Montcalm
418-641-6411

Geneviève Hamelin, Conseillère, Ward(s): Saint-Sauveur
418-641-6411
Ginette Picard-Lavoie, Conseillère, Ward(s): Maizerets-Lairet
418-641-6411
Suzanne Verrault, Conseillère, Ward(s): Sylvain-Lelièvre
418-641-6411

Arrondissement de La Haute-Saint-Charles
Simon Brouard, Conseiller, Ward(s): Châtels
418-641-6701
Raymond Dion, Conseiller, Ward(s): Loretteville
418-641-6701
Sylvain Légaré, Conseiller, Ward(s): Val-Bélair
418-641-6411
Steeve Verret, Conseiller, Ward(s): Lac-Saint-Charles—Saint-Émile
418-641-6701

Arrondissement de Sainte-Foy—Sillery—Cap-Rouge
Christiane Bois, Conseillère, Ward(s): Cité-Universitaire
418-641-6301
Jean Guilbault, Conseiller, Ward(s): Laurentien
418-641-6301
Francine Lortie, Conseillère, Ward(s): Saint-Louis-Sillery
418-641-6301
Marie-Josée Savard, Conseillère, Ward(s): Plateau
418-641-6411
Denise Tremblay Blanchette, Conseillère, Ward(s): Cap-Rouge
418-641-6301

Arrondissement des Rivières
Richard Côté, Conseiller, Ward(s): Vanier
418-641-6411
Patrick Pauqet, Conseiller, Ward(s): Neufchâtel
418-641-6201
François Picard, Conseiller, Ward(s): Lebourgneuf
418-641-6411
Gérald Poirier, Conseiller, Ward(s): Duberger—Les Saules
418-641-6201

Service de la planification stratégique & du développement organisationnel
Michel Beauchemin, Directeur

Repentigny
435, boul Iberville
Repentigny, QC J6A 2B6
Tél: 450-470-3000; *Téléc:* 450-470-3082
communication@ville.repentigny.qc.ca
www.ville.repentigny.qc.ca
Entité municipal: City
Incorporation: 1er juin 2002 *Area:* 68,42 km2
Comté ou district: L'Assomption; *Population au 2006:* 76,237
Circonscription(s) électorale(s) provinciale(s): L'Assomption; Masson
Circonscription(s) électorale(s) fédérale(s): Repentigny
Prochaines élections: 3e novembre 2013
Chantal Deschamps, Mairesse
450-470-3103
deschampsc@ville.repentigny.qc.ca
André Cyr, Conseiller, Ward(s): 1
450-585-3410
cyra@ville.repentigny.qc.ca
Georges Robinson, Conseiller, Ward(s): 2
450-654-9746
robinsong@ville.repentigny.qc.ca
Denyse Peltier, Conseillère, Ward(s): 3
450-581-5733
peltierd@ville.repentigny.qc.ca
Cécile Hénault, Conseillère, Ward(s): 4
450-654-3046
henaultc@ville.repentigny.qc.ca
Éric Laporte, Conseiller, Ward(s): 5
450-581-5026
laportee@ville.repentigny.qc.ca
Sylvain Benoit, Conseiller, Ward(s): 6
514-602-4793
benoits@ville.repentigny.qc.ca
Raymond Hénault, Conseiller, Ward(s): 7
450-581-0319
henaultr@ville.repentigny.qc.ca
Mario Morais, Conseiller, Ward(s): 8
450-654-4018
moraism@ville.repentigny.qc.ca
Serge Gauthier, Conseiller, Ward(s): 9
450-585-6616
gauthiers@ville.repentigny.qc.ca
Luc Gauthier, Conseiller, Ward(s): 10
514-713-8337
gauthierl@ville.repentigny.qc.ca
Francine Payer, Conseillère, Ward(s): 11
450-582-7711
payerf@ville.repentigny.qc.ca
Sylvie Langlois-Brouillette, Conseillère, Ward(s): 12
514-295-8376
langlois-brouillettes@ville.repentigny.qc.ca
Louis-André Garceau, Greffier
450-470-3130
greffe@ville.repentigny.qc.ca
Daniel L'Écuyer, Directeur général
450-470-3110
direction-generale@ville.repentigny.qc.ca
Diane Pelchat, Trésorière
450-470-3200
finance@ville.repentigny.qc.ca
Michel Mailhot, Directeur, Ressources humaines
450-470-3700
ressources-humaines@ville.repentigny.qc.ca
Helen Dion, Directrice, Police (Quartier général)
450-470-3600
securite-publique@ville.repentigny.qc.ca
David Legault, Directeur, Permis, inspections et urbanisme
450-470-3840
permis@ville.repentigny.qc.ca
Denis Larose, Directeur, Incendie
450-470-3620
incendie@ville.repentigny.qc.ca
Sylvie Bouchard, Directrice, Travaux publics
450-470-3800
travaux-publics@ville.repentigny.qc.ca
Vacant, Directeur, Communications
450-470-3140
communication@ville.repentigny.qc.ca
Sylviane DiFolco, Directrice, Loisirs, culture et vie communautaire
450-470-3400
loisirs@ville.repentigny.qc.ca
Ghislain Bélanger, Directeur, Développement économique et services techniques
450-470-3150
belangerg@ville.repentigny.qc.ca

Rimouski
CP 710
205, av de la Cathédrale
Rimouski, QC G5L 7C7
Tél: 418-724-3126; *Téléc:* 418-724-3183
communications@ville.rimouski.qc.ca
www.ville.rimouski.qc.ca
Entité municipal: City
Incorporation: 1er janvier 2002 *Area:* 254,16 km2
Comté ou district: Rimouski-Neigette; *Population au 2006:* 42,240
Circonscription(s) électorale(s) provinciale(s): Rimouski
Circonscription(s) électorale(s) fédérale(s): Rimouski-Neigette-Témiscouata-Les Basques
Prochaines élections: 3e novembre 2013
Éric Forest, Maire
418-724-3126
mairie@ville.rimouski.qc.ca
Marc St-Laurent, Conseiller, Ward(s): 1. Sacré-Coeur
418-722-0326
marc.st-laurent@ville.rimouski.qc.ca
Rodrigue Joncas, Conseiller, Ward(s): 2. Nazareth
418-725-4991
rodrigue.joncas@ville.rimouski.qc.ca
Jennifer Murray, Conseillère, Ward(s): 3. Saint-Germain
418-721-7752
jennifer.murray@ville.rimouski.qc.ca
Denise Banville, Conseillère, Ward(s): 4. Rimouski-Est
418-723-6477
denise.banville@ville.rimouski.qc.ca
Raymond-Marie Murray, Conseiller, Ward(s): 5. Pointe-au-Père
418-724-7250
raymond-marie.murray@ville.rimouski.qc.ca
Donald Bélanger, Conseiller, Ward(s): 6. Sainte-Odile
418-723-3467
donald.belanger@ville.rimouski.qc.ca
Christian Tremblay, Conseiller, Ward(s): 7. Saint-Robert
418-723-8299
christian.tremblay@ville.rimouski.qc.ca
Jean Yves Beaulieu, Conseiller, Ward(s): 8. Terrasse Arthur-Buies
418-722-9372
jeanyves.beaulieu@ville.rimouski.qc.ca
Karol Francis, Conseiller, Ward(s): 9. Saint-Pie-X
418-721-4262
karol.francis@ville.rimouski.qc.ca
Bernard Lepage, Conseiller, Ward(s): 10. Sainte-Blanche/Mont-Lebel
418-735-5611
bernard.lepage@ville.rimouski.qc.ca
Marc Doucet, Greffier
418-724-3125, Fax: 418-724-9795
greffe@ville.rimouski.qc.ca
Jean Matte, Directeur général
418-724-3171, Fax: 418-724-3183
direction.generale@ville.rimouski.qc.ca
Jean-Charles Fournier, Directeur, Service des finances
418-724-3111, Fax: 418-724-3180
finances@ville.rimouski.qc.ca

Rivière-du-Loup
CP 37
65, rue de l'Hôtel-de-Ville
Rivière-du-Loup, QC G5R 3Y7
Tél: 418-867-6700; *Téléc:* 418-862-2817
www.ville.riviere-du-loup.qc.ca
Entité municipal: City
Incorporation: 30 décembre 1998 *Area:* 83,39 km2
Comté ou district: Rivière-du-Loup; *Population au 2006:* 18,586
Circonscription(s) électorale(s) provinciale(s): Rivière-du-Loup
Circonscription(s) électorale(s) fédérale(s): Montmagny-L'Islet-Kamouraska-Rivière-du-Loup
Prochaines élections: 3e novembre 2013
Michel Morin, Maire
418-867-6625
maire@ville.riviere-du-loup.qc.ca
Amélie Dionne, Conseillère, Ward(s): Rivière
Jacques Minville, Conseiller, Ward(s): Fraserville
Sylvie Vignet, Conseillère, Ward(s): Plaine
Gaétan St-Pierre, Conseiller, Ward(s): Estuaire
Denis Tardif, Conseiller, Ward(s): Saint-Patrice
Georges Deschênes, Greffier
418-867-6715
georges.deschenes@ville.riviere-du-loup.qc.ca
Jacques Poulin, Directeur général
418-867-6707
jacques.poulin@ville.riviere-du-loup.qc.ca
Marie Lapointe, Directrice, Finances et Trésorerie
418-867-6711
marie.lapointe@ville.riviere-du-loup.qc.ca
Gérald Tremblay, Directeur, Travaux publics
418-862-2121, Fax: 418-867-6096
gerald.tremblay@ville.riviere-du-loup.qc.ca
Éric Côté, Directeur, Environnement et développement durable
418-867-6663
eric.cote@ville-riviere-du-loup.qc.ca
Benoît Ouellet, Directeur, Loisirs, culture et vie communautaire
418-862-0906
benoit.ouellet@ville.riviere-du-loup.qc.ca

Roberval
851, boul St-Joseph
Roberval, QC G8H 2L6
Tél: 418-275-0202; *Téléc:* 418-275-5031
vroberval@ville.roberval.qc.ca
www.ville.roberval.qc.ca
Entité municipal: City
Incorporation: 23 décembre 1976 *Area:* 168,27 km2
Comté ou district: Le Domaine-du-Roy; *Population au 2006:* 10,544
Circonscription(s) électorale(s) provinciale(s): Roberval
Circonscription(s) électorale(s) fédérale(s): Roberval-Lac-St-Jean
Prochaines élections: 3e novembre 2013
Michel Larouche, Maire
Jocelyn Bouchard, Conseiller, Ward(s): 1
Nancy Guillemette, Conseillère, Ward(s): 2
Gilles Otis, Conseiller, Ward(s): 3
Michèle Claveau, Conseillère, Ward(s): 4
Rémy Leclerc, Conseiller, Ward(s): 5
Jacques Dion, Conseiller, Ward(s): 6
Jean-Guy Tardif, Greffier
jgtardif@ville.roberval.qc.ca
Jeannot Gagnon, Directeur général
jeannotgagnon@ville.roberval.qc.ca
Nancy Boutin, Trésorière
nboutin@ville.roberval.qc.ca

Rosemère
100, rue Charbonneau
Rosemère, QC J7A 3W1
Tél: 450-621-3500; *Téléc:* 450-621-7601
info@ville.rosemere.qc.ca
ville.rosemere.qc.ca
Entité municipal: City
Incorporation: 1er janvier 1947 *Area:* 10,35 km2
Comté ou district: Thérèse-De Blainville; *Population au 2006:* 14,173
Circonscription(s) électorale(s) provinciale(s): Groulx
Circonscription(s) électorale(s) fédérale(s): Marc-Aurèle-Fortin
Prochaines élections: 3e novembre 2013
Hélène Daneault, Mairesse

Normand Bleau, Conseiller, Ward(s): 1
Pierre Roussel, Conseiller, Ward(s): 2
Madeleine Leduc, Conseillère, Ward(s): 3
Normand Corriveau, Conseiller, Ward(s): 4
Eric Westram, Conseiller, Ward(s): 5
Claude Roy, Conseiller, Ward(s): 6
Patrick St-Amour, Greffier
450-621-3500
pstamour@ville.rosemere.qc.ca
Michel Gagné, Directeur général
450-621-3500
mgagne@ville.rosemere.qc.ca
Luce Jacques, Trésorière
450-621-3500
ljacques@ville.rosemere.qc.ca

Rouyn-Noranda
CP 220
100, rue Taschereau est
Rouyn-Noranda, QC J9X 5C3
Tél: 819-797-7110; *Téléc:* 819-797-7108
www.ville.rouyn-noranda.qc.ca
Entité municipal: City
Incorporation: 1er janvier 2002 *Area:* 6435,64 km2
Population au 2006: 39,924
Circonscription(s) électorale(s) provinciale(s):
Rouyn-Noranda—Témiscamingue
Circonscription(s) électorale(s) fédérale(s):
Abitibi-Témiscamingue
Prochaines élections: 3e novembre 2013
Mario Provencher, Maire
info@rouyn-noranda.ca
Marc Bibeau, Conseiller, Ward(s): Noranda-Nord/Lac-Dufault
Sylvie Turgeon, Conseillère, Ward(s): Noranda-Ouest
André Philippon, Conseiller, Ward(s): Rouyn-Sud
Yves Gauthier, Conseiller, Ward(s): Centre-Ville
Robert B. Brière, Conseiller, Ward(s): Vieux-Noranda
robertbbriere@royallepage.ca
Bernard Duchesneau, Conseiller, Ward(s): Université
Luc Lacroix, Conseiller, Ward(s): Granada
Philippe Marquis, Conseiller, Ward(s): Marie-Victorin/Du Sourire
André Tessier, Conseiller, Ward(s): Évain
Marcel Maheux, Conseiller, Ward(s): Sud-Ouest
François Cotnoir, Conseiller, Ward(s): Dallaire
Marc Paquin, Conseiller, Ward(s): Nord
paquin2009@gmail.com
Jean Olivier, Conseiller, Ward(s): Bellecombe/McWatters
Yvon Hurtubise, Conseiller, Ward(s): Cadillac
yvon.hurtubise@cablevision.qc.ca
Daniel Samson, Greffier
819-797-7110, Fax: 819-797-7108
Denis Charron, Directeur général
819-797-7110, Fax: 819-797-7108
Hélène Piuze, Directrice, Finances
819-797-7110, Fax: 819-797-7120
Noël Lanouette, Directeur, Travaux publics et services techniques
819-797-7110, Fax: 819-797-7153

Saguenay
CP 129
201, rue Racine est
Chicoutimi, QC G7H 5B8
Tél: 418-698-3000; *Téléc:* 418-541-4524
info@ville.saguenay.qc.ca
www.ville.saguenay.qc.ca
Entité municipal: City
Incorporation: 18 février 2002 *Area:* 1,166 km2
Population au 2006: 143,692
Circonscription(s) électorale(s) provinciale(s): Dubuc; Chicoutimi; Jonquière
Circonscription(s) électorale(s) fédérale(s): Chicoutimi-Le Fjord
Prochaines élections: 3e novembre 2013
Jean Tremblay, Maire
418-698-3330, Fax: 418-541-4510
maire@ville.saguenay.qc.ca
Paul-Roger Cantin, Conseiller, Ward(s): 1
paul-roger.cantin@ville.saguenay.qc.ca
Réjean Laforest, Conseiller, Ward(s): 2
rejean.laforest@ville.saguenay.qc.ca
Sylvie Gaudreault, Conseillère, Ward(s): 3
sylvie.gaudreault@ville.saguenay.qc.ca
Georges Bouchard, Conseiller, Ward(s): 4
georges.bouchard@ville.saguenay.qc.ca
Bernard Noël, Conseiller, Ward(s): 5
bernard.noel@ville.saguenay.qc.ca
Carl Dufour, Conseiller, Ward(s): 6
carl.dufour@ville.saguenay.qc.ca
Claude Tremblay, Conseiller, Ward(s): 7
claude.tremblay@ville.saguenay.qc.ca
Fabien Hovington, Conseiller, Ward(s): 8
fabien.hovington@ville.saguenay.qc.ca
Jean-Yves Provencher, Conseiller, Ward(s): 9
jean-yves.provencher@ville.saguenay.qc.ca
Marc Pettersen, Conseiller, Ward(s): 10
marc.pettersen@ville.saguenay.qc.ca
Marina Larouche, Conseillère, Ward(s): 11
marina.larouche@ville.saguenay.qc.ca
Marcel Jean, Conseiller, Ward(s): 12
marcel.jean@ville.saguenay.qc.ca
Jacques Cleary, Conseiller, Ward(s): 13
jacques.cleary@ville.saguenay.qc.ca
Denis Dahl, Conseiller, Ward(s): 14
denis.dahl@ville.saguenay.qc.ca
Jacques Fortin, Conseiller, Ward(s): 15
jacques.fortin@ville.saguenay.qc.ca
Luc Blackburn, Conseiller, Ward(s): 16
luc.blackburn@ville.saguenay.qc.ca
Martine Gauthier, Conseillère, Ward(s): 17
martine.gauthier@ville.saguenay.qc.ca
Luc Boivin, Conseiller, Ward(s): 18
luc.boivin@ville.saguenay.qc.ca
Jean-Eudes Simard, Conseiller, Ward(s): 19
jean-eudes.simard@ville.saguenay.qc.ca
Caroline Dion, Greffière
418-698-3260, Fax: 418-541-5961
Jean-François Boivin, Directeur général
418-698-3320, Fax: 418-541-4524
Christine Tremblay, Trésorière
418-698-3030, Fax: 418-698-3049
Serges Chamberland, Directeur général adjoint, Opérations
Francine Maltais, Directrice, Arts, culture, communautaire et bibliothèque
418-698-3000, Fax: 418-698-3129
Daniel Larouche, Directeur, Arrondissement de Jonquière
418-698-3356, Fax: 418-546-2058
André Martin, Directeur, Arrondissement de Chicoutimi
418-698-3355, Fax: 418-698-3129
Gaétan Bergeron, Directeur, Arrondissement de La Baie
418-698-3357, Fax: 418-697-5059
Jeannot Allard, Directeur, Communications
418-698-3350, Fax: 418-541-4545
Sylvie Jean, Directrice, Approvisionnements
418-698-3055, Fax: 418-546-2114
Pierre A. Tremblay, Directeur, Ressources informationnelles
418-698-3335, Fax: 418-697-5187
Robert Pépin, Directeur, Affaires juridiques et du greffe
418-698-3260, Fax: 418-541-5961
Denis Coulombe, Directeur, Aménagement du territoire et urbanisme
418-698-3130, Fax: 418-698-1158
Claude Bouchard, Directeur, Hydro-Jonquière
418-698-3370, Fax: 418-546-2068
Jean Morneau, Directeur, Immeubles et équipements motorisés
418-698-3060, Fax: 418-698-3069
Pierre Racine, Directeur, Sports et du plein air
418-698-3000, Fax: 418-699-6095
Carol Girard, Directeur, Sécurité incendie
418-698-3380, Fax: 418-698-3389
Mario Giroux, Directeur, Sécurité publique
418-699-6000, Fax: 418-699-8206
Denis Simard, Directeur, Travaux publics
418-698-3180, Fax: 418-698-3189

Saint-Basile-le-Grand
204, rue Principale
Saint-Basile-le-Grand, QC J3N 1M1
Tél: 450-461-8000; *Téléc:* 450-461-8029
communciations@ville.saint-basile-le-grand.qc.ca
www.ville.saint-basile-le-grand.qc.ca
Entité municipal: City
Incorporation: 15 juin 1871 *Area:* 34,82 km2
Comté ou district: La Vallée-du-Richelieu; *Population au 2006:* 15,605
Circonscription(s) électorale(s) provinciale(s): Chambly
Circonscription(s) électorale(s) fédérale(s): Chambly-Borduas
Prochaines élections: 3e novembre 2013
Bernard Gagnon, Maire
450-461-8000
bernardgagnon@villesblg.ca
Marie Ginette Lafrance, Conseillère
marieginette.lafrance@villesblg.ca
Jacques Fafard, Conseiller
jacques.fafard@villesblg.ca
Norman Perreault, Conseiller
normanperreault@videotron.ca
Maurice Cantin, Conseiller
maurice.cantin@villesblg.ca
Guylaine Yelle, Conseillère
guylaine.yelle@villesblg.ca
Geneviève Desrosiers, Conseillère
genevieve.desrosiers@villesblg.ca
Sophie Deslauriers, Greffière
450-461-8000, Fax: 450-461-8029
greffe@ville.saint-basile-le-grand.qc.ca
Jean-Marie Beaupré, Directeur général
450-461-8000, Fax: 450-461-8039
direction.generale@ville.saint-basile-le-grand.qc.
Normand Lalande, Trésorier
450-461-8000, Fax: 450-653-4394
finances@ville.saint-basile-le-grand.qc.ca
Marc-André Lehoux, Directeur, Loisirs, culture et vie communautaire

Saint-Constant
147, rue St-Pierre
Saint-Constant, QC J5A 2G2
Tél: 450-638-2010; *Téléc:* 450-638-5919
communications@ville.saint-constant.qc.ca
www.ville.saint-constant.qc.ca
Entité municipal: City
Incorporation: 1er juillet 1855 *Area:* 57,04 km2
Comté ou district: Roussillon; *Population au 2006:* 23,957
Circonscription(s) électorale(s) provinciale(s): La Prairie
Circonscription(s) électorale(s) fédérale(s):
Châteauguay—St-Constant
Prochaines élections: 3e novembre 2013
Gilles Pepin, Maire
Jonathan Bédard, Conseiller, Ward(s): 1
Pierre Lalonde, Conseiller, Ward(s): 2
Gilles Lapierre, Conseiller, Ward(s): 3
France Hébert, Conseillère, Ward(s): 4
André Sauvé, Conseiller, Ward(s): 5
Ginette Bourget, Conseillère, Ward(s): 6
Pascal Bédard, Conseiller, Ward(s): 7
Mario Arsenault, Conseiller, Ward(s): 8
Sophie Laflammme, Greffière
450-638-2010, Fax: 450-638-5919
greffe@ville.saint-constant.qc.ca
Sylvain Boulianne, Directeur général
450-638-2010, Fax: 450-638-5919
direction_generale@ville.saint-constant.qc.ca
Frédéric Thifault, Trésorier
450-638-2010, Fax: 450-638-4764
finances@ville.saint-constant.qc.ca
Vacant, Responsable, Travaux publics
450-638-2010, Fax: 450-632-0072
travaux_publics@ville.saint-constant.qc.ca
Jean Gariépy, Directeur et chef, Brigade des pompiers
Sylvain Boulianne, Coordonnateur, Mesures d'urgence

Saint-Eustache
145, rue St-Louis
Saint-Eustache, QC J7R 1X9
Tél: 450-974-5000; *Téléc:* 450-974-5229
communications@ville.saint-eustache.qc.ca
www.ville.saint-eustache.qc.ca
Entité municipal: City
Incorporation: 15 janvier 1972 *Area:* 70,61 km2
Comté ou district: Deux-Montagnes; Communauté métropolitaine de Montréal; *Population au 2006:* 42,062
Circonscription(s) électorale(s) provinciale(s): Deux-Montagnes
Circonscription(s) électorale(s) fédérale(s): Rivière-des-Mille-Îles
Prochaines élections: 3e novembre 2013
Pierre Charron, Maire
450-974-5014, Fax: 450-974-5203
maire@ville.saint-eustache.qc.ca
Denis Paré, Conseiller, Ward(s): 1. Vieux-Saint-Eustache
450-472-2533
dpare@ville.saint-eustache.qc.ca
André Biard, Conseiller, Ward(s): 2. Carrefour
450-473-2214
abiard@ville.saint-eustache.qc.ca
Patrice Paquette, Conseiller, Ward(s): 3. Rivière-Nord
450-974-1120
ppaquette@ville.saint-eustache.qc.ca
Daniel Goyer, Conseiller, Ward(s): 4. Des Érables
450-974-9104
dgoyer@ville.saint-eustache.qc.ca
Marc Lamarre, Conseiller, Ward(s): 5. Clair Matin
450-473-4792
mlamarre@ville.saint-eustache.qc.ca
Germain Lalonde, Conseiller, Ward(s): 6. Seigneurie
450-472-5890
glalonde@ville.saint-eustache.qc.ca
Pauline Harrison, Conseillère, Ward(s): 7. Moissons
450-473-8141
pharrison@ville.saint-eustache.qc.ca
Raymond Tessier, Conseiller, Ward(s): 8. Îles
450-472-3951
rtessier@ville.saint-eustache.qc.ca

Nicole Carignan Lefebvre, Conseillère, Ward(s): 9. Plateau-des-Chênes
450-623-5730
ncarignan-lefebvre@ville.saint-eustache.qc.ca
Sylvie Cloutier, Conseillère, Ward(s): 10. Jardins
450-974-9379
scloutier@ville.saint-eustache.qc.ca
Marc Tourangeau, Greffier
Christian Bellemare, Directeur général
450-974-5280, Fax: 450-974-5229
Ginette Lacoix, Trésorière
450-974-5070, Fax: 450-974-5077
Yves Guillemette, Directeur général adjoint
Bastien Morin, Directeur, Services municipaux
450-974-5284, Fax: 450-974-5229
Stéphanie Bouchard, Directrice, Communications
450-974-5220, Fax: 450-974-5223
communications@ville.saint-eustache.qc.ca

Saint-Félicien

CP 7000
1209, boul Sacré-Coeur
Saint-Félicien, QC G8K 2R5
Tél: 418-679-0251; *Téléc:* 418-679-1449
dir.general@ville.stfelicien.qc.ca
www.ville.stfelicien.qc.ca
Entité municipal: City
Incorporation: 12 juin 1996 *Area:* 359,69 km2
Comté ou district: Le Domaine-du-Roy; *Population au 2006:* 10,477
Circonscription(s) électorale(s) provinciale(s): Roberval
Circonscription(s) électorale(s) fédérale(s): Roberval—Lac-St-Jean
Prochaines élections: 3e novembre 2013
Gilles Potvin, Maire
maire@ville.stfelicien.qc.ca
Luc Imbeault, Conseiller, Ward(s): 1
Bernard Boivin, Conseiller, Ward(s): 2
Camil Guy, Conseiller, Ward(s): 3
Luc Gibbons, Conseiller, Ward(s): 4
Sonia Boudreault, Conseiller, Ward(s): 5
Michel Gagnon, Conseiller, Ward(s): 6
Louise Ménard, Greffière
418-679-2100, Fax: 418-679-1449
louise.menard@ville.stfelicien.qc.ca
Mario Ménard, Directeur général (par intérim)
418-679-2100, Fax: 418-679-1449
mmenard@ville.stfelicien.qc.ca
Dany Coudé, Trésorier
418-679-2100, Fax: 418-679-2178
tresorerie@ville.stfelicien.qc.ca
Olivier de Launière, Directeur, Protection contre les incendies
418-679-0313, Fax: 418-679-8217
sincendie@ville.st-felicien.qc.ca
Jacynthe Duplain, Secrétaire administrative, Aménagement et entretien du territoire
418-679-2100, Fax: 418-679-4083
urbanisme@ville.stfelicien.qc.ca

Saint-Georges

11700, boul Lacroix
Saint-Georges, QC G5Y 1L3
Tél: 418-228-5555; *Téléc:* 418-228-3855
www.ville.saint-georges.qc.ca
Entité municipal: City
Incorporation: 26 septembre 2001 *Area:* 199,51 km2
Comté ou district: Beauce-Sartigan; *Population au 2006:* 29,616
Circonscription(s) électorale(s) provinciale(s): Beauce-Sud
Circonscription(s) électorale(s) fédérale(s): Beauce
Prochaines élections: 3e novembre 2013
François Fecteau, Maire
maire@ville.saint-georges.qc.ca
Serge Thomassin, Conseiller, Ward(s): 1
Manon Tousignant, Conseillère, Ward(s): 2
Jean Perron, Conseiller, Ward(s): 3
Irma Quirion, Conseillère, Ward(s): 4
Manon Bougie, Conseillère, Ward(s): 5
Marie-Ève Dutil, Conseillère, Ward(s): 6
Marcel Drouin, Conseiller, Ward(s): 7
Lionel Bisson, Conseiller, Ward(s): 8
Jean McCollough, Greffier
jean.mccollough@ville.saint-georges.qc.ca
Marcel Grondin, Directeur général
marcel.grondin@ville.saint-georges.qc.ca
Isabelle Déchêne, Trésorière

Saint-Hyacinthe

CP 10
700, av de l'Hôtel-de-Ville
Saint-Hyacinthe, QC J2S 5B2
Tél: 450-778-8300; *Téléc:* 450-778-8628
communications@ville.st-hyacinthe.qc.ca
www.ville.st-hyacinthe.qc.ca
Entité municipal: City
Incorporation: 27 décembre 2001 *Area:* 189,11 km2
Comté ou district: Les Maskoutains; *Population au 2006:* 51,616
Circonscription(s) électorale(s) provinciale(s): St-Hyacinthe
Circonscription(s) électorale(s) fédérale(s): St-Hyacinthe—Bagot
Prochaines élections: 3e novembre 2013
Claude Bernier, Maire
450-778-8302, Fax: 450-778-5800
claude.bernier@ville.st-hyacinthe.qc.ca
Donald Côté, Conseiller, Ward(s): 1. Sainte-Rosalie
donald.cote@ville.st-hyacinthe.qc.ca
Sylvain Savoie, Conseiller, Ward(s): 2. Laurier
sylvain.savoie@ville.st-hyacinthe.qc.ca
Louise Arpin, Conseillère, Ward(s): 3. Saint-Joseph
louise.arpin@ville.st-hyacinthe.qc.ca
Bernard Barré, Conseiller, Ward(s): 4. Providence
bernard.barre@ville.st-hyacinthe.qc.ca
André Beauregard, Conseiller, Ward(s): 5. Douville
andre.beauregard@ville.st-hyacinthe.qc.ca
Guylain Coulombe, Conseiller, Ward(s): 6. Saint-Thomas-d'Aquin
guylain.coulombe@ville.st-hyacinthe.qc.ca
Brigitte Sansoucy, Conseillère, Ward(s): 7. Saint-Sacrement
brigitte.sansoucy@ville.st-hyacinthe.qc.ca
Alain Leclerc, Conseiller, Ward(s): 8. Bois-Joli
alain.leclerc@ville.st-hyacinthe.qc.ca
David Bousquet, Conseiller, Ward(s): 9. Sacré-Coeur
david.bousquet@ville.st-hyacinthe.qc.ca
Sylvie Adam, Cascades, Ward(s): 10. Cascades
sylvie.adam@ville.st-hyacinthe.qc.ca
Nicole Dion-Audette, Conseillère, Ward(s): 11. Hertel-Notre-Dame
n.dion-audette@ville.st-hyacinthe.qc.ca
Hélène Beauchesne, Greffière
450-778-8317, Fax: 450-778-2514
Louis Bilodeau, Directeur général
louis.bilodeau@ville.st-hyacinthe.qc.ca
Michel Tradif, OMA, Trésorier
450-778-8306
finances@ville.st-hyacinthe.qc.ca
Chantal Frigon, Directrice générale adjointe
450-778-8304
chantal.frigon@ville.st-hyacinthe.qc.ca
Yvan Gatien, Directeur, Urbanisme
450-778-8321, Fax: 450-778-5820
urbanisme@ville.st-hyacinthe.qc.ca
Daniel Dubois, Directeur, Sécurité incendie
450-778-8550, Fax: 450-778-5853
daniel.dubois@ville.st.hyacinthe.qc.ca

Saint-Jean-sur-Richelieu

CP 1025
188, rue Jacques-Cartier nord
Saint-Jean-sur-Richelieu, QC J3B 7B2
Tél: 450-357-2100; *Téléc:* 450-357-2362
info@ville.saint-jean-sur-richelieu.qc.ca
www.ville.saint-jean-sur-richelieu.qc.ca
Entité municipal: City
Incorporation: 24 janvier 2001 *Area:* 225,61 km2
Comté ou district: Le Haut-Richelieu; *Population au 2006:* 87,492
Circonscription(s) électorale(s) provinciale(s): St-Jean; Iberville
Circonscription(s) électorale(s) fédérale(s): St-Jean
Prochaines élections: 3e novembre 2013
Gilles Dolbec, Maire
450-357-2095, Fax: 450-357-2079
mairie@ville.saint-jean-sur-richelieu.qc.ca
Philippe Lasnier, Conseiller, Ward(s): 1
450-347-1299
p.lasnier@ville.saint-jean-sur-richelieu.qc.ca
Justin Bessette, Conseiller, Ward(s): 2
514-718-5675
j.bessette@ville.saint-jean-sur-richelieu.qc.ca
Gaétan Gagnon, Conseiller, Ward(s): 3
450-347-3209
g.gagnon@ville.saint-jean-sur-richelieu.qc.ca
Jean Fontaine, Conseiller, Ward(s): 4
450-346-3063
j.fontaine@ville.saint-jean-sur-richelieu.qc.ca
Stéphane Legrand, Conseiller, Ward(s): 5
450-545-9515
s.legrand@ville.saint-jean-sur-richelieu.qc.ca
Germain Poissant, Conseiller, Ward(s): 6
450-347-8703
g.poissant@ville.saint-jean-sur-richelieu.qc.ca
Christiane Marcoux, Conseillère, Ward(s): 7
450-347-5277
c.marcoux@ville.saint-jean-sur-richelieu.qc.ca
Marco Savard, Conseiller, Ward(s): 8
450-349-0473
m.savard@ville.saint-jean-sur-richelieu.qc.ca
Yvan Berthelot, Conseiller, Ward(s): 9
450-349-0685
y.berthelot@ville.saint-jean-sur-richelieu.qc.ca
Alain Paradis, Conseiller, Ward(s): 10
450-348-8046
a.paradis@ville.saint-jean-sur-richelieu.qc.ca
Alain Laplante, Conseiller, Ward(s): 11
450-349-1312
a.laplante@ville.saint-jean-sur-richelieu.qc.ca
Robert Cantin, Conseiller, Ward(s): 12
450-349-6661
r.cantin@ville.saint-jean-sur-richelieu.qc.ca
François Lapointe, Greffier
450-357-2077, Fax: 450-357-2362
greffe@ville.saint-jean-sur-richelieu.qc.ca
Daniel Desroches, Directeur général
450-357-2383, Fax: 450-357-2385
Pierre Beauvais, Trésorier
finances@ville.saint-jean-sur-richelieu.qc.ca
Roch Arbour, Directeur, Travaux publics
450-357-2238, Fax: 450-357-2290
Michelle Hébert, Directrice générale adjointe
Serge Boulerice, Directeur, Police
450-359-2529
police@ville.saint-jean-sur-richelieu.qc.ca
Luc Castonguay, Directeur, Urbanisme
urbanisme@ville.saint-jean-sur-richelieu.qc.ca

Saint-Jérôme

#301, 10, rue St-Joseph
Saint-Jérôme, QC J7Z 7G7
Tél: 450-436-1511; *Téléc:* 450-436-6626
info@vsj.ca
www.ville.saint-jerome.qc.ca
Entité municipal: City
Incorporation: 1er janvier 2002 *Area:* 89,37 km2
Comté ou district: La Rivière-du-Nord; *Population au 2006:* 63,729
Circonscription(s) électorale(s) provinciale(s): Prévost
Circonscription(s) électorale(s) fédérale(s): Rivière-du-Nord
Prochaines élections: 3e novembre 2013
Marc Gascon, Maire
450-436-1511
Renée Arsenault, Conseillère, Ward(s): 1
450-592-3469
Guy Lalande, Conseiller, Ward(s): 2
450-438-2021
Bernard Bougie, Conseiller, Ward(s): 3
450-431-7227
Alain Langlois, Conseiller, Ward(s): 4
450-569-2242
Robert Carrière, Conseiller, Ward(s): 5
450-432-5629
Benoît Delage, Conseiller, Ward(s): 6
450-436-6134
Marcel Lachance, Conseiller, Ward(s): 7
450-432-4399
Michel Des Chênes, Conseiller, Ward(s): 8
450-565-0693
Martin Pigeon, Conseiller, Ward(s): 9
450-436-1787
François Boyer, Conseiller, Ward(s): 10
450-224-1148
Tommy Kulczyk, Conseiller, Ward(s): 11
450-432-3700
Manon Labrèche, Conseillère, Ward(s): 12
450-432-2733
Luc Savoie, Conseiller, Ward(s): 13
450-592-3921
Michèle Céclier, Conseillère, Ward(s): 14
450-438-1073
Marcel Bélanger, Greffier
Éric Lachapelle, Directeur général
Johanne Coursol, Trésorière
Fernand Boudreault, Directeur, Travaux publics
Louis Bruneault, Directeur, Police
Marc Lapointe, Directeur, Sécurité incendie
Marc Lapointe, Directeur, Mesures d'urgence
Érick Frigon, Directeur, Ingénierie
Yvan Patenaude, Directeur, Communications
Richard St-Jean, Directeur, Urbanisme

Saint-Lazare

1960, ch Ste-Angélique
Saint-Lazare, QC J7T 3A3
Tél: 450-424-8000; *Téléc:* 450-455-4712
info@ville.saint-lazare.qc.ca
www.ville.saint-lazare.qc.ca
Entité municipal: City
Incorporation: 29 décembre 1875 *Area:* 67,59 km2
Comté ou district: Vaudreuil-Soulanges; *Population au 2006:* 17,016
Circonscription(s) électorale(s) provinciale(s): Soulanges
Circonscription(s) électorale(s) fédérale(s): Vaudreuil-Soulanges
Prochaines élections: 3e novembre 2013
Pierre Kary, Maire
pkary@ville.saint-lazare.qc.ca
Jean-Pierre Giguère, Conseiller, Ward(s): 1
jpgiguere@ville.saint-lazare.qc.ca
Nathalie Richard, Conseillère, Ward(s): 2
nrichard@ville.saint-lazare.qc.ca
Brigitte Asselin, Conseillère, Ward(s): 3
basselin@ville.saint-lazare.qc.ca
Michel Lambert, Conseiller, Ward(s): 4
mlambert@ville.saint-lazare.qc.ca
Gilbert Arsenault, Conseiller, Ward(s): 5
garsenault@ville.saint-lazare.qc.ca
Jean-Claude Gauthier, Conseiller, Ward(s): 6
jcgauthier@ville.saint-lazare.qc.ca
Nathaly Rayneault, Greffière
François Vaillancourt, Directeur général
fvaillancourt@ville.saint-lazare.qc.ca
Claude La Rue, Directeur, Travaux publics

Saint-Lin-Laurentides

900, 12e av
Saint-Lin-Laurentides, QC J5M 2W2
Tél: 450-439-3130; *Téléc:* 450-439-1525
saint-lin-laurentides.com
Entité municipal: City
Incorporation: 1er mars 2000 *Area:* 117,52 km2
Comté ou district: Montcalm; *Population au 2006:* 14,159
Circonscription(s) électorale(s) provinciale(s): Rousseau
Circonscription(s) électorale(s) fédérale(s): Montcalm
Prochaines élections: 3e novembre 2013
André Auger, Maire
450-439-3130, Fax: 450-439-2876
Luc Cyr, Conseiller, Ward(s): 1
450-439-6588
Mathieu Maisonneuve, Conseiller, Ward(s): 2
450-772-1849
André Malouin, Conseiller, Ward(s): 3
450-439-2352
Patrick Massé, Conseiller, Ward(s): 4
450-891-1423
Jean-Luc Arène, Conseiller, Ward(s): 5
450-431-1465
Pierre Lortie, Conseiller, Ward(s): 6
450-439-8230
Richard Dufort, Greffier & Directeur général
Sylvain Martel, Trésorier
André Héroux, Directeur, Travaux publics
Jean-Pierre Desjardins, Directeur, Incendies

Sainte-Adèle

1381, boul de Sainte-Adèle
Sainte-Adèle, QC J8B 1A3
Tél: 450-229-2921; *Téléc:* 450-229-4179
dirgenerale@ville.sainte-adele.qc.ca
sainte-adele.net
Entité municipal: City
Incorporation: 27 août 1997 *Area:* 122,19 km2
Comté ou district: Les Pays-d'en-Haut; *Population au 2006:* 10,634
Circonscription(s) électorale(s) provinciale(s): Bertrand
Circonscription(s) électorale(s) fédérale(s): Laurentides-Labelle
Prochaines élections: 3e novembre 2013
Réjean Charbonneau, Maire
Nadine Brière, Conseillère, Ward(s): 1
Roch Bédard, Conseiller, Ward(s): 2
Lise Gendron, Conseillère, Ward(s): 3
John Butler, Conseiller, Ward(s): 4
Robert Lagacé, Conseiller, Ward(s): 5
Pierre Morabito, Conseiller, Ward(s): 6
Michel Rousseau, Greffier
Pierre Dionne, Directeur général

Sainte-Anne-des-Plaines

139, boul Ste-Anne
Sainte-Anne-des-Plaines, QC J0N 1H0
Tél: 450-478-0211; *Téléc:* 450-478-5660
info@ville.ste-anne-des-plaines.qc.ca
www.ville.ste-anne-des-plaines.qc.ca
Entité municipal: City
Incorporation: 1er juillet 1855 *Area:* 92,22 km2
Comté ou district: Thérèse-De Blainville; *Population au 2006:* 13,412
Circonscription(s) électorale(s) provinciale(s): Blainville
Circonscription(s) électorale(s) fédérale(s): Terrebonne-Blainville
Prochaines élections: 3e novembre 2013
Guy Charbonneau, Mairesse
Julie Bellerose, Conseillère, Ward(s): 1
France Majeau, Conseiller, Ward(s): 2
Alain Cassista, Conseiller, Ward(s): 3
Denys Gagnon, Conseiller, Ward(s): 4
Mario Gauthier, Conseiller, Ward(s): 5
Stéphane Chouinard, Conseiller, Ward(s): 6
Serge Lepage, Greffier et Directeur général
Christiane Joyal, Trésorière
Paul Fournier, Directeur, Travaux publics

Sainte-Catherine

5465, boul Marie-Victorin
Sainte-Catherine, QC J5C 1M1
Tél: 450-632-0590; *Téléc:* 450-632-3298
information@ville.sainte-catherine.qc.ca
www.ville.sainte-catherine.qc.ca
Entité municipal: City
Incorporation: 30 octobre 1937 *Area:* 9,06 km2
Comté ou district: Roussillon; *Population au 2006:* 16,211
Circonscription(s) électorale(s) provinciale(s): La Prairie
Circonscription(s) électorale(s) fédérale(s): Châteauguay—St-Constant
Prochaines élections: 3e novembre 2013
Jocelyne Bates, Mairesse
Daniel Lamanque, Conseiller, Ward(s): 1
Martin Gélinas, Conseiller, Ward(s): 2
Jocelyne Brossard, Conseillère, Ward(s): 3
Louise Cormier, Conseillère, Ward(s): 4
Michel Béland, Conseiller, Ward(s): 5
Daniel Gagnon, Conseiller, Ward(s): 6
Jacques Foucher, Greffier
Danielle Chevrette, Directrice générale
Serge Courchesne, Trésorier

Sainte-Julie

1580, ch du Fer-à-Cheval
Sainte-Julie, QC J3E 2M1
Tél: 450-922-7111; *Téléc:* 450-922-7108
communications@ville.sainte-julie.qc.ca
www.ville.sainte-julie.qc.ca
Entité municipal: City
Incorporation: 1er juillet 1855 *Area:* 47,78 km2
Comté ou district: Lajemmerais; *Population au 2006:* 29,561
Circonscription(s) électorale(s) provinciale(s): Verchères
Circonscription(s) électorale(s) fédérale(s): Verchères-Les Patriotes
Prochaines élections: 3e novembre 2013
Suzanne Roy, Mairesse
450-922-7053
mairesse@ville.sainte-julie.qc.ca
Isabelle Poulet, Conseillère, Ward(s): 1. Belle-Rivière/Ringuet
André Lemay, Conseiller, Ward(s): 2. Moulin
Donald Savaria, Conseiller, Ward(s): 3. Vallée
Nicole Marchand, Conseillère, Ward(s): 4. Rucher
Mario Lemay, Conseiller, Ward(s): 5. Vieux-Village
Normand Varin, Conseiller, Ward(s): 6. Grand-Coteau
Henri Corbin, Conseiller, Conseillers et Districts, Ward(s): 7. Arc-en-Ciel
Lucie Bisson, Conseillère, Ward(s): 8. Montagne
bissonlucie@videotron.ca
Jean-François Gauthier, Greffier
450-922-7050
greffe@ville.sainte-julie.qc.ca
Pierre Bernardin, Directeur général
450-922-7102
dirgen@ville.sainte-julie.qc.ca
Jean-Pierre Duplin, Trésorier
450-922-7062
finances@ville.sainte-julie.qc.ca
Denyse Journault, Directrice, Communications
450-922-7092
communications@ville.sainte-julie.qc.ca
Pierre-Luc Blanchard, Directeur, Urbanisme
450-922-7142
urbanisme@ville.sainte-julie.qc.ca
Daniel Chagnon, Directeur, Loisirs
450-922-7122
loisirs@ville.sainte-julie.qc.ca

Sainte-Marie

270, av Marguerite-Bourgeoys
Sainte-Marie, QC G6E 3Z3
Tél: 418-387-2301; *Téléc:* 418-387-2454
info@sainte-marie.ca
www.ville.sainte-marie.qc.ca
Entité municipal: City
Incorporation: 15 avril 1978 *Area:* 106,65 km2
Comté ou district: La Nouvelle-Beauce; *Population au 2006:* 11,584
Circonscription(s) électorale(s) provinciale(s): Beauce-Nord
Circonscription(s) électorale(s) fédérale(s): Beauce
Prochaines élections: 3e novembre 2013
Harold Guay, Maire
Christian Laroche, Conseiller, Ward(s): 1
Mélanie Boissonneault, Conseillère, Ward(s): 2
Rosaire Simoneau, Conseiller, Ward(s): 3
Patrice Cossette, Conseiller, Ward(s): 4
Paulin Nappert, Conseiller, Ward(s): 5
Yves Chassé, Conseiller, Ward(s): 6
Hélène Gagné, Greffière
418-387-2301
helene.gagne@ville.sainte-marie.qc.ca
Louis Normand, Directeur général
418-387-2301
Jacques Boutin, Trésorier
418-387-2301
Maurice Mercier, Directeur, Travaux publics
418-387-6111

Sainte-Marthe-sur-le-Lac

3000, ch d'Oka
Sainte-Marthe-sur-le-Lac, QC J0N 1P0
Tél: 450-472-7310; *Téléc:* 450-472-0109
info@ville.sainte-marthe-sur-le-lac.qc.ca
www.sainte-marthe-sur-le-lac.qc.ca
Entité municipal: City
Incorporation: 1er janvier 1960 *Area:* 9,01 km2
Comté ou district: Deux-Montagnes; Communauté métropolitaine de Montréal; *Population au 2009:* 12,089
Circonscription(s) électorale(s) provinciale(s): Mirabel
Circonscription(s) électorale(s) fédérale(s): Rivière-des-Mille-Iles
Prochaines élections: 1er novembre 2013
Sylvie Brunet, Greffière
Sonia Paulus, Mairesse
Valérie Vivier, Trésorière
Marisol Charland, Directrice générale

Sainte-Thérèse

CP 100
6, rue de l'Église
Sainte-Thérèse, QC J7E 4H7
Tél: 450-434-1440; *Téléc:* 450-434-1499
info@sainte-therese.ca
www.ville.sainte-therese.qc.ca
Entité municipal: City
Incorporation: 1er juin 1849 *Area:* 8,62 km2
Comté ou district: Thérèse-De Blainville; *Population au 2006:* 25,224
Circonscription(s) électorale(s) provinciale(s): Groulx
Circonscription(s) électorale(s) fédérale(s): Marc-Aurèle-Fortin
Prochaines élections: 3e novembre 2013
Sylvie Surprenant, Mairesse
mairie@sainte-therese.ca
Denise Perreault-Théberge, Conseillère, Ward(s): 1. Sève
d.perreault-theberge@sainte-therese.ca
Patrick Morin, Conseiller, Ward(s): 2. Verschelden
p.morin@sainte-therese.ca
Marie-Andrée Petelle, Conseillère, Ward(s): 3. Morris
ma.petelle@sainte-therese.ca
Normand Toupin, Conseiller, Ward(s): 4. Chapleau
n.toupin@sainte-therese.ca
Luc Vézina, Conseiller, Ward(s): 5. Lonergan
l.vezina@sainte-therese.ca
Michel Milette, Conseiller, Ward(s): 6. Ducharme
m.milette@sainte-therese.ca
Louis Lauzon, Conseiller, Ward(s): 7 Blanchard
l.lauzon@sainte-therese.ca
Vincent Arseneau, Conseiller, Ward(s): 8. Marie-Thérèse
v.arseneau@sainte-therese.ca
Jean-Luc Berthiaume, Greffier
jl.berthiaume@sainte-therese.ca
Chantal Gauvreau, Directrice générale
450-434-1440, Fax: 450-434-1499
c.gauvreau@sainte-therese.ca
Jean Pierre Gendron, Trésorier
450-434-1440, Fax: 450-434-1499
jp.gendron@sainte-therese.ca

Salaberry-de-Valleyfield
61, rue Ste-Cécile
Salaberry-de-Valleyfield, QC J6T 1L8
Tél: 450-370-4300;
communications@ville.valleyfield.qc.ca
www.ville.valleyfield.qc.ca
Entité municipal: City
Incorporation: 24 avril 2002 *Area:* 100,96 km2
Comté ou district: Beauharnois-Salaberry; *Population au 2006:* 39,672
Circonscription(s) électorale(s) provinciale(s): Beauharnois
Circonscription(s) électorale(s) fédérale(s): Beauharnois-Salaberry
Prochaines élections: 3e novembre 2013
Denis Lapointe, Maire
450-370-4801
denis.lapointe@ville.valleyfield.qc.ca
Denis Laître, Conseiller, Ward(s): 1. Grande-Île
450-373-0954
denis.laitre@ville.valleyfield.qc.ca
Jean-Marc Rochon, Conseiller, Ward(s): 2. Nitro
450-377-2774
jean-marc.rochon@ville.valleyfield.qc.ca
Louise Sauvé, Conseillère, Ward(s): 3. Georges-Leduc
450-377-8597
louise.sauvé@ville.valleyfield.qc.ca
Robert Savard, Conseiller, Ward(s): 4. Champlain
450-371-1173
robert.savard@ville.valleyfield.qc.ca
Jean-Jacques Leduc, Conseiller, Ward(s): 5. La Baie
450-371-5099
jean-jacques.leduc@ville.valleyfield.qc.ca
Jacques Smith, Conseiller, Ward(s): 6. Robert-Cauchon
450-371-4975
jacques.smith@ville.valleyfield.qc.ca
Pierre-Paul Messier, Conseiller, Ward(s): 7. Jules-Léger
450-373-5459
pierre-paul.messier@ville.valleyfield.qc.ca
Normand Amesse, Conseiller, Ward(s): 8. Saint-Timothée
450-371-6895
normand.amesse@ville.valleyfield.qc.ca
Alain Gagnon, Greffier
450-370-4304, Fax: 450-370-4388
alain.gagnon@ville.valleyfield.qc.ca
Pierre Chevrier, Directeur général
450-370-4800, Fax: 450-370-4343
pierre.chevrier@ville.valleyfield.qc.ca
Jacques Lemieux, CA, OMA, Trésorier
450-370-4320, Fax: 450-370-4316
jacques.lemieux@ville.valleyfield.qc.ca
Michel Ménard, Directeur, Sécurité incendie
450-370-4750, Fax: 450-370-4755
securiteincendie@ville.valleyfield.qc.ca
Denis Larochelle, Directeur, Eau et environnement/Travaux publics
450-370-4820, Fax: 450-370-4370
gestionduterritoire@ville.valleyfield.qc.ca
Danielle Prieur, Coordonnatrice
450-370-4875, Fax: 450-370-4343
communications@ville.valleyfield.qc.ca
René Monette, Directeur, Récréatif et communautaire
450-370-4390, Fax: 450-370-4888
src@ville.valleyfield.qc.ca

Sept-Îles
546, av De Quen
Sept-Îles, QC G4R 2R4
Tél: 418-962-2525; *Téléc:* 418-964-3213
info@ville.sept-iles.qc.ca
www.ville.sept-iles.qc.ca
Entité municipal: City
Incorporation: 12 février 2003 *Area:* 1 969,42 km2
Comté ou district: Sept-Rivières; *Population au 2006:* 25,514
Circonscription(s) électorale(s) provinciale(s): Duplessis
Circonscription(s) électorale(s) fédérale(s): Manicouagan
Prochaines élections: 3e novembre 2013
Note: En 1970, Clarke City est fusionnée à Sept-Iles; le 12 fév., 2003, Moisie & Gallix sont fusionnées à Sept-Iles.
Serge Lévesque, Maire
maire@ville.sept-iles.qc.ca
Gervais Gagné, Conseiller, Ward(s): 1. Ste-Marguerite
district1@ville.sept-iles.qc.ca
Maurice Gagné, Conseiller, Ward(s): 2. Ferland
district2@ville.sept-iles.qc.ca
Jean Masse, Conseiller, Ward(s): 3. L'Anse
district3@ville.sept-iles.qc.ca
Denis Miousse, Conseiller, Ward(s): 4. Marie-Immaculée
district4@ville.sept-iles.qc.ca
Gaby Gauthier, Conseiller, Ward(s): 5. Vieux-Quai
district5@ville.sept-iles.qc.ca
Lorraine Dubuc-Johnson, Conseillère, Ward(s): 6. Mgr-Blanche
district6@ville.sept-iles.qc.ca
Jean-François Martin, Conseiller, Ward(s): 7. Jacques-Cartier
district7@ville.sept-iles.qc.ca
Martial Lévesque, Conseiller, Ward(s): 8. Sainte-Famille
district8@ville.sept-iles.qc.ca
Claude Lessard, Conseiller, Ward(s): 9. Moisie-Plages
district9@ville.sept-iles.qc.ca
Valérie Haince, Greffière
418-964-3205
greffe@ville.sept-iles.qc.ca
Claude Bureau, Directeur général
418-964-3201
directiongenerale@ville.sept-iles.qc.ca
Serge Gagné, Directeur, Finances
418-964-3215
finances@ville.sept-iles.qc.ca

La Corporation de protection de l'environnement de Sept-Iles (CPESI)
Stéphanie Prévost, Directrice générale
sprevost@cpesi@cgocable.ca

Shawinigan
CP 400
550, av de l'Hôtel-de-Ville
Shawinigan, QC G9N 6V3
Tél: 819-536-7200; *Téléc:* 819-536-7255
information@shawinigan.ca
www.shawinigan.ca
Entité municipal: City
Incorporation: 1er janvier 2002 *Area:* 781,81 km2
Population au 2006: 51,904
Circonscription(s) électorale(s) provinciale(s): Saint-Maurice; Laviolette
Circonscription(s) électorale(s) fédérale(s): Saint-Mauricie—Champlain
Prochaines élections: 3e novembre 2013
Note: 8 nouveaux districts seront en vigueur lors des élections municipal de nov/09.
Michel Angers, Mairesse
819-536-7211
cabinetdumaire@shawinigan.ca
Josette Allard-Gignac, Conseillère, Ward(s): Almaville
819-537-4727
jallard-gignac@shawinigan.ca
Bernard Cayouette, Conseiller, Ward(s): Boisés
819-835-2874
bcayouette@shawinigan.ca
Alain Lord, Conseiller, Ward(s): Cité
819-539-8462
bcayouette@shawinigan.ca
Jean-Yves Tremblay, Conseiller, Conseillers et Districts, Ward(s): Hêtres
819-536-7211
jytremblay@shawinigan.ca
Serge Aubry, Conseiller, Ward(s): Montagnes
819-539-9474
saubry@shawinigan.ca
Jacques Grenier, Conseiller, Ward(s): Rivière
819-269-2161
jgrenier@shawinigan.ca
Lucie de Bons, Conseillère, Ward(s): Rocher
819-538-7348
ldebons@shawinigan.ca
Pierre Giguère, Conseiller, Ward(s): Val-Mauricie
819-537-6043
pgiguere@shawinigan.ca
Yves Vincent, Greffier
819-536-7211
greffe@shawinigan.ca
Gaétan Béchard, Directeur général
819-536-7211
directiongenerale@shawinigan.ca
Sylvie Lavoie, Directrice, Finances
servicesadministratifs@shawinigan.ca
Réal Beauchamp, Directeur général adjoint
819-536-7211
directiongenerale@shawinigan.ca
Vacant, Directeur, Aménagement et de l'environnement
819-536-7211
urbanisme@shawinigan.ca
François St-Onge, Directeur, Communications
819-536-7211
fstonge@shawinigan.ca
Pierre Godin, Directeur, Travaux publics
819-536-7211
travauxpublics@shawinigan.ca
Robert Y. Desjardins, Directeur, Loisirs, culture et vie communautaire
819-536-7211
loisirs@shawinigan.ca
François Garceau, Directeur, Ressources humaines
ressourceshumaines@shawinigan.ca
Claude Larocque, Directeur, Techniques
819-536-7211
servicestechniques@shawinigan.ca
François Lelièvre, Directeur, Sécurité incendie
819-538-2248
incendie@shawinigan.ca

Sherbrooke
CP 610
191, rue du Palais
Sherbrooke, QC J1H 5H9
Tél: 819-821-5500; *Téléc:* 819-822-6064
www.ville.sherbrooke.qc.ca
Entité municipal: City
Incorporation: 1er janvier 2002 *Area:* 366,00 km2
Population au 2006: 147,427
Circonscription(s) électorale(s) provinciale(s): St-François; Sherbrooke; Orford; Johnson
Circonscription(s) électorale(s) fédérale(s): Sherbrooke
Prochaines élections: 3e novembre 2013
Bernard Sévigny, Maire
819-821-5969, Fax: 819-822-6131
mairie@ville.sherbrooke.qc.ca
Isabelle Sauvé, Greffière
819-821-5500, Fax: 819-822-6064
Claude Marcoux, Directeur général
819-821-5618, Fax: 819-823-5121
Claude Périnet, Directeur général adjoint
François Poulette, Trésorier
819-821-5490, Fax: 819-822-6091
Colette Ouellet, Directrice, Communications
819-821-5572, Fax: 819-823-5153
communications@ville.sherbrooke.qc.ca
Jacques Leduc, Directeur, Ressources humaines
819-821-5677, Fax: 819-822-6086
ressources.humaines@ville.sherbrooke.qc.ca
Gaétan Labbé, Directeur, Protection des incendies
819-821-5514, Fax: 819-821-5516
protection.incendies@ville.sherbrooke.qc.ca

Arrondissement de Brompton Counseil
Nicole Bergeron, Conseillère, Ward(s): Brompton
819-846-2757
nicole.bergeron@ville.sherbrooke.qc.ca
Benoit Dionne, Conseiller, Ward(s): Beauvoir
819-846-4725
dionneb@csrs.qc.ca
Michel Lamontagne, Conseiller, Ward(s): Moulins
819-846-3257

Arrondissement de Fleurimont Administration
Louisda Brochu, Conseiller, Ward(s): Lavigerie
819-565-9954
louida.brochu@ville.sherbrooke.qc.ca
Jean-Guy Demers, Conseiller, Ward(s): Desranleau
819-432-2562
jgdemers01@hotmail.com
Rémi Demers, Conseiller, Ward(s): Marie-Rivier
819-565-1066
remi.demers@videotron.qc.ca
Mariette Fugère, Conseillère, Ward(s): Pin-Solitaire
819-562-7064
mariette.fugere@sympatico.ca
Roger Labrecque, Conseiller, Ward(s): Quatre-Saisons
819-823-2125
labrecqueniro@videotron.ca

Arrondissement de Lennoxville
David W. Price, Conseiller, Ward(s): Lennoxville
819-569-9388
david.price@ville.sherbrooke.qc.ca
Mark McLaughlin, Conseiller, Ward(s): Fairview
819-212-5851
mark.mclaughlin@videotron.ca
William Smith, Conseiller, Ward(s): Uplands
819-569-8175

Arrondissement du Mont-Bellevue
Serge Paquin, Conseiller, Ward(s): Centre-Sud
819-346-9312
paquin.serge@videotron.ca
Pierre Boisvert, Conseiller, Ward(s): Croix-Lumineuse
819-564-8924
pboisvert2005@sympatico.ca
Robert Y. Pouliot, Conseiller, Ward(s): Ascot
819-563-1848
r.pouliot@bobpouliotinc.ca

Jean-François Rouleau, Conseiller, Ward(s): Université
819-569-0208
jean-francois.rouleau@ville.sherbrooke.qc.ca

Arrondissement de Rock Forest-Saint-Élie-Deauville
Julien Lachance, Conseiller, Ward(s): Saint-Élie
819-566-7886
jlach@videotron.ca
Diane Délisle, Conseillère, Ward(s): Deauville
819-864-4656
ddelisle@abacom.com
Serge Foreste, Conseillère, Ward(s): Rock Forest
819-823-0062
serge.forest@videotron.ca
Bruno Vachon, Conseiller, Ward(s): Châteaux-d'Eau
819-212-5688
bruno.vachon@ville.sherbrooke.qc.ca

Arrondissement de Jacques-Cartier
Chantal L'Espérance, Conseillère, Ward(s): Domaine Howard
819-565-8089
chantal.lesperance@ville.sherbrooke.qc.ca
Marc Denault, Conseiller, Ward(s): Montcalm
819-565-5555
denaultm@abacom.com
Nathalie Goguen, Conseillère, Ward(s): Beckett
819-348-1929
nathalie.goguen@videotron.ca
Pierre Tardif, Conseiller, Ward(s): Carrefour
819-566-7926
pierrectardif@videotron.ca

Sorel-Tracy
CP 368
71, rue Charlotte
Sorel-Tracy, QC J3P 7K1
Tél: 450-780-5600; *Téléc:* 450-780-5625
info@ville.sorel-tracy.qc.ca
www.ville.sorel.qc.ca
Entité municipal: City
Incorporation: 15 mars 2000 *Area:* 56,58 km2
Comté ou district: Pierre-De Saurel; *Population au 2006:* 34,076
Circonscription(s) électorale(s) provinciale(s): Richelieu
Circonscription(s) électorale(s) fédérale(s): Bas-Richelieu—Nicolet—Bécancour
Prochaines élections: 3e novembre 2013
Réjean Dauplaise, Maire
Sophie Chevalier, Conseillère, Ward(s): 1. Bourgchemin
450-746-3858
sophie.chevalier@ville.sorel-tracy.qc.ca
André Potvin, Conseiller, Ward(s): 2. Saint-Laurent
450-746-2536
andre.potvin@ville.sorel-tracy.qc.ca
Yvon Bibeau, Conseiller, Ward(s): 3. Saint-Laurent
450-746-8987
yvon.bibeau@ville.sorel-tracy.qc.ca
Corina Bastiani, Conseillère, Ward(s): 4. Vieux-Sorel
450-780-2252
corina.bastiani@ville.sorel-tracy.qc.ca
Alain Maher, Conseiller, Ward(s): 5. Du Faubourg
450-743-8749
alain.maher@ville.sorel-tracy.qc.ca
Gilles Jr. Lemieux, Conseiller, Ward(s): 6. Gouverneurs
450-780-2225
gilles.lemieux@ville.sorel-tracy.qc.ca
Michèle Lacombe-Gauthier, Conseillère, Ward(s): 7. Patriotes
450-746-7710
michele.lacombe@ville.sorel-tracy.qc.ca
Dominique Ouellet, Conseillère, Ward(s): 8. Pierre-De Saurel
450-780-1248
dominique.ouellet@ville.sorel-tracy.qc.ca
René Chevalier, Greffier
450-780-5600
Mario Lazure, Directeur général
450-780-5600
Diane Robillard, Directrice, Finances & Trésorerie
450-780-5600
Alain Rouleau, Directeur, Sécurité incendie
450-780-5600

Terrebonne
775, rue St-Jean-Baptiste
Terrebonne, QC J6W 1B5
Tél: 450-961-2001; *Téléc:* 450-471-4482
information@ville.terrebonne.qc.ca
www.ville.terrebonne.qc.ca
Entité municipal: City
Incorporation: 27 juin 2001 *Area:* 155,44 km2
Comté ou district: Les Moulins; *Population au 2006:* 94,703
Circonscription(s) électorale(s) provinciale(s): Terrebonne; Masson
Circonscription(s) électorale(s) fédérale(s): Terrebonne-Blainville
Prochaines élections: 3e novembre 2013
Jean-Marc Robitaille, Maire
Nathalie Bellavance, Conseillère, Ward(s): 1
Daniel L'Espérance, Conseiller, Ward(s): 2
Marie-Claude Lamarche, Conseillère, Ward(s): 3
Réal Leclerc, Conseiller, Ward(s): 4
Denis Poitras, Conseiller, Ward(s): 5
Michel Morin, Conseiller, Ward(s): 6
Paul Asselin, Conseiller, Ward(s): 7
Marie-Josée Beaupré, Conseillère, Ward(s): 8
Marc Campagna, Conseiller, Ward(s): 9
Frédéric Asselin, Conseiller, Ward(s): 10
Clermont Lévesque, Conseiller, Ward(s): 11
Jean-Luc Labrecque, Conseiller, Ward(s): 12
Sylvain Tousignant, Conseiller, Ward(s): 13
Michel Lefebvre, Conseiller, Conseillers et Districts, Ward(s): 14
Stéphane Berthe, Conseiller, Ward(s): 15
Jean-Guy Sénécal, Conseiller, Ward(s): 16
Denis Bouffard, Greffier
Denis Lévesque, Directeur général
Francine Blain, Trésorière
Guy Dubois, Chef de police
Jacques Bérubé, Directeur, Incendie
Michel Sarrazin, Directeur, Travaux publics

Thetford Mines
CP 489
144, rue Notre-Dame sud
Thetford Mines, QC G6G 5T3
Tél: 418-335-2981; *Téléc:* 418-335-7089
infos@ville.thetfordmines.qc.ca
www.ville.thetfordmines.qc.ca
Entité municipal: City
Incorporation: 17 octobre 2001 *Area:* 224,37 km2
Comté ou district: Des Appalaches; *Population au 2006:* 25,704
Circonscription(s) électorale(s) provinciale(s): Frontenac
Circonscription(s) électorale(s) fédérale(s): Mégantic-L'Érable
Prochaines élections: 3e novembre 2013
Luc Berthold, Maire
Clément Boudreau, Conseiller, Ward(s): 1. Black Lake
418-423-2257
Renaud Legendre, Conseiller, Ward(s): 2. Black Lake-Mitchell/Lacs
418-423-2349
renaudlegendre@hotmail.com
Ghyslain Cliche, Conseiller, Ward(s): 3. Thetford Mines
418-335-9267
ghcliche@hotmail.com
Luc Champagne, Conseiller, Ward(s): 4. Thetford Mines
418-338-2812
Carmen Jalbert-Jacques, Conseillère, Ward(s): 5. Thetford Mines
418-338-1901
cjalbertjacques@sympatico.ca
Louis-Philippe Champagne, Conseiller, Ward(s): 6. Thetford Mines
418-335-7119
lphilchampagne@hotmail.com
Marco Tanguay, Conseiller, Ward(s): 7. Thetford Mines
418-338-8819
tanguaymarco@sympatico.ca
Marc Vachon, Conseiller, Ward(s): 8. Thetford Mines
418-334-0340
marcf.vachon@cgocable.ca
Paul-André Marchand, Conseiller, Ward(s): 9. Thetford-Sud
418-335-9871
paul.marchand@cgocable.ca
Gaétan Vachon, Conseiller, Ward(s): 10. Robertsonville/Pontbriand
418-335-9543
Réjean Martin, Greffier
greffe@ville.thetfordmines.qc.ca
René Soucy, Directeur général
dirgen@ville.thetfordmines.qc.ca
Sylvain Tremblay, Trésorier
s.tremblay@ville.thetfordmines.qc.ca
François Gagnon, Directeur, Sécurité publique
secpub@ville.thetfordmines.qc.ca

Trois-Rivières
CP 368
1325, place de l'Hôtel-de-Ville
Trois-Rivières, QC G9A 5H3
Tél: 819-374-2002; *Téléc:* 819-372-4631
info@v3r.net
www.v3r.net
Entité municipal: City
Incorporation: 1er janvier 2002 *Area:* 288,50 km2
Population au 2006: 129,100
Circonscription(s) électorale(s) provinciale(s): Trois-Rivières; Maskinongé; Champlain
Circonscription(s) électorale(s) fédérale(s): Trois-Rivières
Prochaines élections: 3e novembre 2013
Yves Lévesque, Maire
André Noël, Conseiller, Ward(s): Carmel
anoel@v3r.net
Monique Leclerc, Conseillère, Ward(s): Châteaudun
Marie-Claude Camirand, Conseillère, Ward(s): Chavigny
mccamirand@v3r.net
Fernand Lajoie, Conseiller, Ward(s): Estacades
flajoie@v3r.net
Guy Daigle, Conseiller, Ward(s): Laviolette
gdaigle@v3r.net
René Goyette, Conseiller, Ward(s): Madeleine
rgoyette@v3r.net
Sylvie Tardif, Conseillère, Ward(s): Marie de l'Incarnation
stardif@v3r.net
Marie-Josée Tardif, Conseillère, Ward(s): Plateaux
mjtardif@v3r.net
Michel Veillette, Conseiller, Ward(s): Pointe-du-lac
michel.veillette@v3r.net
Ginette Bellemare, Conseillère, Ward(s): Rigaud
gbellemare@v3r.net
Michel Bronsard, Conseiller, Ward(s): St-Louis-de-France
mbronsard@v3r.net
Catherine Dufresne, Conseillère, Ward(s): Ste-Marguerite
cdufresne@v3r.net
Micheline Courteau, Conseillère, Ward(s): Ste-Marthe
Alain Croteau, Conseiller, Ward(s): Sanctuaire
acroteau@v3r.net
Yves Landry, Conseiller, Ward(s): Terrasses
ylandry@v3r.net
Françoise H. Viens, Conseillère, Ward(s): Vieilles-Forges
fviens@v3r.net
Gilles Poulin, Directeur, Greffe/Services juridiques
819-372-4604, Fax: 819-372-4636
greffe@v3r.net
Michel Byette, Directeur général
819-372-4608, Fax: 819-372-4631
directiongenerale@v3r.net
Daniel Thibault, Directeur général adjoint
France Cinq-Mars, Directrice, Finances
819-374-2002, Fax: 819-372-4630
finances@v3r.net
Éric Chevalier, Directeur, Ressources humaines
819-372-4603, Fax: 819-374-9005
ressourceshumaines@v3r.net
Francis Gobeil, Directeur, Sécurité publique
819-370-6700, Fax: 819-374-3506
policeincendie@v3r.net
Michel Jutras, Directeur, Arts et culture
Pierre Desjardins, Directeur, Aménagement, gestion et développement durable du territoire
819-372-4626, Fax: 819-375-5865
urbanisme@v3r.net
Vincent Fortier, Directeur, Techniques
819-372-4627, Fax: 819-374-6646
Michel Lemieux, Directeur, Loisirs et communautaires
819-372-4621, Fax: 819-374-7133
François Roy, Directeur, Communications
819-372-4602, Fax: 819-374-0210
relationspubliques@v3r.net
Ghislain Lachance, Directeur, Travaux publics
819-379-3733

Val-d'Or
CP 400
855, 2e av
Val-d'Or, QC J9P 4P4
Tél: 819-824-9613; *Téléc:* 819-825-6650
info@ville.valdor.qc.ca
www.ville.valdor.qc.ca
Entité municipal: City
Incorporation: 1er janvier 2002 *Area:* 3 958,13 km2
Comté ou district: La Vallée-de-l'Or; *Population au 2006:* 31,123
Circonscription(s) électorale(s) provinciale(s): Abitibi-Est
Circonscription(s) électorale(s) fédérale(s): Abitibi-Baie-James-Nunavik-Eeyou
Prochaines élections: 3e novembre 2013
Fernand Trahan, Maire
Suzanne Couture Bordeleau, Conseillère, Ward(s): 1. Lac Blouin-Centre-ville
Michael Prince, Conseiller, Ward(s): 2. Paquinville-Fatima
Pierre Potvin, Conseiller, Ward(s): 3. Belvédère
Céline Brindamour, Conseillère, Ward(s): 4. Sullivan
Gilles Bérubé, Conseiller, Ward(s): 5. Val-Senneville-Vassan
Francis Murphy, Conseiller, Ward(s): 6. Bourlamaque-Louvicourt
Bernard Gauthier, Conseiller, Ward(s): 7. Lemoine-Baie-Carrière
Robert Quesnal, Conseiller, Ward(s): 8. Dubuisson
Sophie Gareau, Greffière
819-824-9613

Guy Faucher, Directeur général
819-824-9613
Chantale Gilbert, Trésorier
819-824-9613
Alain Cloutier, Directeur, Ressources humaines et Communications
819-824-9613
Danny Burbridge, Directeur, Infrastructures urbaines
819-824-9613
Robert Migué, Directeur, Culturel
819-824-9613

Varennes
CP 5000
175, rue Ste-Anne
Varennes, QC J3X 1T5
Tél: 450-652-9888; *Téléc:* 450-652-2655
general@ville.varennes.qc.ca
ville.varennes.qc.ca
Entité municipal: City
Incorporation: 26 août 1972 *Area:* 93,96 km2
Comté ou district: Marguerite-D'Youville; *Population au 2006:* 20,950
Circonscription(s) électorale(s) provinciale(s): Verchères
Circonscription(s) électorale(s) fédérale(s): Verchères-Les Patriotes
Prochaines élections: 3e novembre 2013
Martin Damphousse, Maire
martin.damphousse@ville.varennes.qc.ca
Joël Beauchemin, Conseiller, Ward(s): 1. Guillaudière
joel.beauchemin@ville.varennes.qc.ca
Lyne Beaulieu, Conseillère, Ward(s): 2. Sitière
lyne.beaulieu@ville.varennes.qc.ca
Francis Rinfret, Conseiller, Ward(s): 3. Langloiserie
francis.rinfret@ville.varennes.qc.ca
Denis Le Blanc, Conseiller, Ward(s): 4. Notre-Dame
denis.leblanc@ville.varennes.qc.ca
Bruno Desjarlais, Conseiller, Ward(s): 5. Petite Prairie
bruno.desjarlais@ville.varennes.qc.ca
Natalie Parent, Conseillère, Ward(s): 6. Seigneuries
natalie.parent@ville.varennes.qc.ca
Gaétan Marcil, Conseiller, Ward(s): 7. Saint-Charles
gaetan.marcil@ville.varennes.qc.ca
Brigitte Collin, Conseillère, Ward(s): 8. Martigny
brigitte.collin@ville.varennes.qc.ca
Marc Giard, Greffier
Sébastien Roy, Directeur général
Denise Beauchemin, Trésorière
Denis Guay, Directeur, Travaux publics
Denis Marchand, Directeur, Urbanisme

Vaudreuil-Dorion
#200, 2555, rue Dutrisac
Vaudreuil-Dorion, QC J7V 7E6
Tél: 450-455-3371; *Téléc:* 450-424-8540
courriel@ville.vaudreuil-dorion.qc.ca
www.ville.vaudreuil-dorion.qc.ca
Entité municipal: City
Incorporation: 16 mars 1994 *Area:* 73,18 km2
Comté ou district: Vaudreuil-Soulanges; *Population au 2006:* 25,789
Circonscription(s) électorale(s) provinciale(s): Vaudreuil
Circonscription(s) électorale(s) fédérale(s): Vaudreuil-Soulanges
Prochaines élections: 3e novembre 2013
Guy Pilon, Maire
Claude Beaudoin, Conseiller, Ward(s): 1. Quinchien
François Séguin, Conseiller, Ward(s): 2. Harwood
Robert A. Laurence, Conseiller, Ward(s): 3. Fief-Cavagnal
Denis Vincent, Conseiller, Ward(s): 4. Seigneurie
Rénald Gabriele, Conseiller, Ward(s): 5. Chenaux
Gabriel Parent, Conseiller, Ward(s): 6. Cité-des-Jeunes
Guylène Duplessis, Conseillère, Ward(s): 7. Carrefour
Paul Dumoulin, Conseiller, Ward(s): 8. Baie
Jean St-Antoine, Greffier
Manon Bernard, Directrice générale
Marco Pilo, Trésorier
Luc Duval, Directeur, Travaux publics

Victoriaville
CP 370
1, rue Notre-Dame ouest
Victoriaville, QC G6P 6T2
Tél: 819-758-1571; *Téléc:* 819-758-9292
info@ville.victoriaville.qc.ca
www.ville.victoriaville.qc.ca
Entité municipal: City
Incorporation: 23 juin 1993 *Area:* 81,96 km2
Comté ou district: Arthabaska; *Population au 2006:* 40,486
Circonscription(s) électorale(s) provinciale(s): Arthabaska
Circonscription(s) électorale(s) fédérale(s): Richmond-Arthabaska
Prochaines élections: 3e novembre 2013
Alain Rayes, Maire
819-758-1571
alain.rayes@ville.victoriaville.qc.ca
Caroline Pilon, Conseillère, Ward(s): 1. Parc-de-l'Amitié
819-604-1600
caroline.pilon@ville.victoriaville.qc.ca
Jacques Gagnon, Conseiller, Ward(s): 2. Parc-de-l'île
819-758-8511
jacques.gagnon@ville.victoriaville.qc.ca
Jacques Nadeau, Conseiller, Ward(s): 3. Charles-Édouard-Mailhot
819-758-8530
jacques.nadeau@ville.victoriaville.qc.ca
Alexandre Côté, Conseiller, Ward(s): 4. Sainte-Famille
819-357-3272
alexandre.cote@ville.victoriaville.qc.ca
France Auger, Conseillère, Ward(s): 5. Parc-Terre-des-Jeunes
819-758-7330
france.auger@ville.victoriaville.qc.ca
Marc Mortin, Conseiller, Ward(s): 6. Parc-Victoria
819-758-1864
marc.morin@ville.victoriaville.qc.ca
Michel Allard, Conseiller, Ward(s): 7. Sainte-Victoire
819-752-6362
michel.allard@ville.victoriaville.qc.ca
Denis Morin, Conseiller, Ward(s): 8. Arthabaska-Nord
819-357-7821
denis.morin@ville.victoriaville.qc.ca
Gilles Lafontaine, Conseiller, Ward(s): 9. Arthabaska-Ouest
819-357-8712
gilles.lafontaine@ville.victoriaville.qc.ca
Christian Lettre, Conseiller, Ward(s): 10. Arthabaska-Est
819-357-8573
christian.lettre@ville.victoriaville.qc.ca
Jean Poirier, Greffier
819-758-1571
jean.poirier@ville.victoriaville.qc.ca
Martin Lessard, Directeur général
martin.lessard@ville.victoriaville.qc.ca
Yves Fréchette, Trésorier
yves.frechette@ville.victoriaville.qc.ca
Jean Mercier, Directeur, Ressources humaines
819-758-1571
jean.mercier@ville.victoriaville.qc.ca
André Charest, Directeur, Travaux publics
819-758-0651
andre.charest@ville.victoriaville.qc.ca
Jean Demers, Directeur, Gestion du territoire
819-758-1571
jean.demers@ville.victoriaville.qc.ca

Other Municipalities in Québec

Abercorn
10, ch des Églises ouest
Abercorn, QC J0E 1B0
Tél: 450-538-2664; *Téléc:* 450-538-6295
mun.abercorn@vivomail.ca
Entité municipal: Village
Incorporation: 25 juin 1929 *Area:* 27,84 km2
Comté ou district: Brome-Missisquoi; *Population au 2006:* 366
Circonscription(s) électorale(s) provinciale(s): Brome-Missisquoi
Circonscription(s) électorale(s) fédérale(s): Brome-Missisquoi
Prochaines élections: 3e novembre 2013
Jean-Charles Bisonnette, Maire
Danielle Corriveau, Directrice générale

Abitibi
CP 214
571, 1re Rue est
Amos, QC J9T 2H3
Tél: 819-732-5356; *Téléc:* 819-732-9607
mrc@mrcabitibi.qc.ca
www.mrcabitibi.qc.ca
Entité municipal: Regional County Municipality
Population au 2006: 24,275
Note: 17 municipalités & 2 autres territoires.
Jacques Riopel, Préfet
Michel Roy, Directeur général
michel.roy@mrcabitibi.qc.ca

Abitibi-Ouest
#105, 6, 8e Av est
La Sarre, QC J9Z 1N6
Tél: 819-339-5671; *Téléc:* 819-339-5400
mrcao@mrcao.qc.ca
www.mrc.ao.ca
Entité municipal: Regional County Municipality
Population au 2006: 20,792
Note: 21 municipalités & 2 autres territoires.
Daniel Rancourt, Préfet
Nicole Breton, Directrice générale
nicole.breton@lino.com

Acton
CP 99
1037, rue Beaugrand
Acton Vale, QC J0H 1A0
Tél: 450-546-3256; *Téléc:* 450-546-0525
mrc@mrcacton.qc.ca
www.mrcacton.qc.ca
Entité municipal: Regional County Municipality
Population au 2006: 15,289
Huguette St-Pierre-Beaulac, Préfète
Yvan Talbot, Directeur général
yvan.talbot@mrcacton.qc.ca

Acton Vale
1025, rue Boulay
Acton Vale, QC J0H 1A0
Tél: 450-546-2703; *Téléc:* 450-546-4865
actonvale@ville.actonvale.qc.ca
www.ville.actonvale.qc.ca
Entité municipal: Town
Incorporation: 26 janvier 2000 *Area:* 90,88 km2
Comté ou district: Acton; *Population au 2006:* 7,797
Circonscription(s) électorale(s) provinciale(s): Johnson
Circonscription(s) électorale(s) fédérale(s): St-Hyacinthe-Bagot
Prochaines élections: 3e novembre 2013
Éric Charbonneau, Maire
Rita Parent, Greffière

Adstock
35, rue Principale ouest
Adstock, QC G0N 1S0
Tél: 418-422-2135; *Téléc:* 418-422-2134
info@municipaliteadstock.qc.ca
www.municipaliteadstock.qc.ca
Entité municipal: Municipality
Incorporation: 24 octobre 2001 *Area:* 289,220 km2
Comté ou district: Des Appalaches; *Population au 2006:* 2,678
Circonscription(s) électorale(s) provinciale(s): Frontenac
Circonscription(s) électorale(s) fédérale(s): Mégantic-L'Érable
Prochaines élections: 3e novembre 2013
René Gosselin, Maire
Jean-Rock Turgeon, Directeur général

Aguanish
CP 47
106, rte Jacques-Cartier
Aguanish, QC G0G 1A0
Tél: 418-533-2323; *Téléc:* 418-533-2012
munag@xplornet.com
Entité municipal: Municipality
Incorporation: 1er janvier 1957 *Area:* 594,40 km2
Comté ou district: Minganie; *Population au 2006:* 303
Circonscription(s) électorale(s) provinciale(s): Duplessis
Circonscription(s) électorale(s) fédérale(s): Manicouagan
Prochaines élections: 3e novembre 2013
Richard Noël, Maire
Bernard Déraps, Directeur général

Akulivik
CP 50
Akulivik, QC J0M 1V0
Tél: 819-496-2222; *Téléc:* 819-496-2200
www.nvakulivik.ca
Entité municipal: Northern Village
Incorporation: 29 décembre 1979 *Area:* 79,37 km2
Comté ou district: Administration régionale Kativik; *Population au 2006:* 507
Circonscription(s) électorale(s) provinciale(s): Ungava
Circonscription(s) électorale(s) fédérale(s): Abitibi-Baie-James-Nunavik-Eeyou
Prochaines élections: 3e novembre 2013
Lucasi Alayco, Maire
Lydia Nappatuk, Directrice

Albanel
160, rue Principale
Albanel, QC G8M 3J5
Tél: 418-279-5250; *Téléc:* 418-279-3147
info@albanel.ca
www.albanel.ca
Entité municipal: Municipality
Incorporation: 11 avril 1990 *Area:* 195,69 km2
Comté ou district: Maria-Chapdelaine; *Population au 2006:* 2,326
Circonscription(s) électorale(s) provinciale(s): Roberval
Circonscription(s) électorale(s) fédérale(s): Roberval—Lac-Saint-Jean
Prochaines élections: 3e novembre 2013

Évangéline Plourde, Mairesse
Réjean Hudon, Directeur général

Albertville
CP 9
1058, rue Principale
Albertville, QC G0J 1A0
Tél: 418-756-3554; *Téléc:* 418-756-3554
albertville@mrcmatapedia.qc.ca
Entité municipal: Municipality
Incorporation: 29 novembre 1930 *Area:* 104,55 km2
Comté ou district: La Matapédia; *Population au 2006:* 319
Circonscription(s) électorale(s) provinciale(s): Matapédia
Circonscription(s) électorale(s) fédérale(s): Haute-Gaspésie-La Mitis-Matane-Matapédia
Prochaines élections: 3e novembre 2013
Martin Landry, Maire
Claire Sénéchal, Directrice-générale

Alleyn-et-Cawood
10, ch Jondée
Alleyn-et-Cawood, QC J0X 1P0
Tél: 819-467-2941; *Téléc:* 819-467-3133
administration@municipalite.alleyn-et-cawood.qc.ca
Entité municipal: United Township (Cantons)
Incorporation: 1er janvier 1877 *Area:* 346,64 km2
Comté ou district: Pontiac; *Population au 2006:* 248
Circonscription(s) électorale(s) provinciale(s): Pontiac
Circonscription(s) électorale(s) fédérale(s): Pontiac
Prochaines élections: 3e novembre 2013
Charlene Scharf-Lafleur, Mairesse
Annie Beauregard, Directrice générale

Amherst
CP 30
124, rue St-Louis
Amherst, QC J0T 2L0
Tél: 819-687-3355; *Téléc:* 819-687-8430
bdavidson@municipalite.amherst.qc.ca
Entité municipal: Township
Incorporation: 9e mars 1887 *Area:* 260,82 km2
Comté ou district: Les Laurentides; *Population au 2006:* 1,421
Circonscription(s) électorale(s) provinciale(s): Labelle
Circonscription(s) électorale(s) fédérale(s): Laurentides-Labelle
Prochaines élections: 3e novembre 2013
Bernard Lapointe, Maire
Bernard Davidson, Directeur général

Amqui
20, promenade de l'Hôtel-de-Ville
Amqui, QC G5J 1A1
Tél: 418-629-4242; *Téléc:* 418-629-4090
administration@ville.amqui.qc.ca
www.matapedia.net/amqui
Entité municipal: Town
Incorporation: 16 janvier 1991 *Area:* 127,90 km2
Comté ou district: La Matapédia; *Population au 2006:* 6,261
Circonscription(s) électorale(s) provinciale(s): Matapédia
Circonscription(s) électorale(s) fédérale(s): Haute-Gaspésie-La Mitis-Matane-Matapédia
Prochaines élections: 3e novembre 2013
Gaëtan Ruest, Maire
Marie-Claude Gagnon, Greffière

Ange-Gardien
249, rue St-Joseph
Ange-Gardien, QC J0E 1E0
Tél: 450-293-7575; *Téléc:* 450-293-6635
municipalite.ange-gardien@videotron.ca
Entité municipal: Municipality
Incorporation: 31 décembre 1997 *Area:* 89,07 km2
Comté ou district: Rouville; *Population au 2006:* 1,987
Circonscription(s) électorale(s) provinciale(s): Iberville
Circonscription(s) électorale(s) fédérale(s): Shefford
Prochaines élections: 3e novembre 2013
Odette Ménard, Mairesse
Robert Taylor, Directeur général

Angliers
CP 9
14, rue de la Baie Miller
Angliers, QC J0Z 1A0
Tél: 819-949-4351; *Téléc:* 819-949-4351
angliers@lino.com
Entité municipal: Village
Incorporation: 24 mai 1945 *Area:* 378,20 km2
Comté ou district: Témiscamingue; *Population au 2006:* 308
Circonscription(s) électorale(s) provinciale(s): Rouyn-Noranda-Témiscamingue
Circonscription(s) électorale(s) fédérale(s): Abitibi-Témiscamingue
Prochaines élections: 3e novembre 2013

Lyne Pine, Mairesse
Micheline Champoux, Directrice générale

Antoine-Labelle
425, rue du Pont
Mont-Laurier, QC J9L 2R6
Tél: 819-623-3485; *Téléc:* 819-623-5052
administration@mrc-antoine-labelle.qc.ca
www.mrc-antoine-labelle.qc.ca
Entité municipal: Regional County Municipality
Population au 2006: 34,999
Note: 17 municipalités & 11 autres territoires.
Roger Lapointe, Préfet
Jackline Williams, Directrice générale

Argenteuil
430, rue Grace
Lachute, QC J8H 1M6
Tél: 450-562-2474; *Téléc:* 450-562-1911
mrc@argenteuil.qc.ca
www.argenteuil.qc.ca
Entité municipal: Regional County Municipality
Population au 2006: 29,992
Note: 9 municipalités.
Ronald Tittlit, Préfet
Marc Carrière, Directeur général
mcarriere@argenteuil.qc.ca

Armagh
CP 87
5, rue de la Salle
Armagh, QC G0R 1A0
Tél: 418-466-2916; *Téléc:* 418-466-2409
www.armagh.ca
Entité municipal: Municipality
Incorporation: 29 décembre 1993 *Area:* 168,15 km2
Comté ou district: Bellechasse; *Population au 2006:* 1,613
Circonscription(s) électorale(s) provinciale(s): Bellechasse
Circonscription(s) électorale(s) fédérale(s): Lévis-Bellechasse
Prochaines élections: 3e novembre 2013
Guylain Chamberland, Maire
Sylvie Vachon, Directrice générale

Arthabaska
40, rte de la Grande-Ligne
Victoriaville, QC G6T 0E6
Tél: 819-752-2444; *Téléc:* 819-752-3623
info@mrc-arthabaska.qc.ca
www.mrc-arthabaska.qc.ca
Entité municipal: Regional County Municipality
Population au 2006: 66,247
Note: 24 municipalités.
Lionel Fréchette, Préfet
Frédérick Michaud, Directeur général

Arundel
2, rue du Village
Arundel, QC J0T 1A0
Tél: 819-687-3991; *Téléc:* 819-687-8760
info@municipalite.arundel.qc.ca
Entité municipal: Township
Incorporation: 1er janvier 1878 *Area:* 64,43 km2
Comté ou district: Les Laurentides; *Population au 2006:* 601
Circonscription(s) électorale(s) provinciale(s): Argenteuil
Circonscription(s) électorale(s) fédérale(s): Laurentides-Labelle
Prochaines élections: 3e novembre 2013
Johanna Earle, Mairesse
Bernice Goulet, Directrice générale

Asbestos
185, rue du Roi
Asbestos, QC J1T 1S4
Tél: 819-879-7171; *Téléc:* 819-879-2343
adm.mun@ville.asbestos.qc.ca
www.ville.asbestos.qc.ca
Entité municipal: Town
Incorporation: 8e décembre 1999 *Area:* 29,55 km2
Comté ou district: Des Sources; *Population au 2006:* 6,819
Circonscription(s) électorale(s) provinciale(s): Richmond
Circonscription(s) électorale(s) fédérale(s): Richmond-Arthabaska
Prochaines élections: 3e novembre 2013
Hugues Grimard, Maire
adm.mun@ville.asbestos.qc.ca
Georges-André Gagné, Directeur général
gagagne@ville.asbestos.qc.ca

Ascot Corner
5655, rte 112
Ascot-Corner, QC J0B 1A0
Tél: 819-566-5436; *Téléc:* 819-566-8526
ascot.corner@hsfqc.ca
www.ascot-corner.qc.ca
Entité municipal: Municipality
Incorporation: 28 mars 1901 *Area:* 83,38 km2
Comté ou district: Le Haut-St-François; *Population au 2006:* 2,595
Circonscription(s) électorale(s) provinciale(s): Mégantic-Compton
Circonscription(s) électorale(s) fédérale(s): Compton-Stanstead
Prochaines élections: 3e novembre 2013
Fabien Morin, Maire
Daniel St-Onge, Directeur général
daniel.st-onge@hsfqc.ca

Aston-Jonction
1300, rue Principale
Aston-Jonction, QC G0Z 1A0
Tél: 819-226-3459; *Téléc:* 819-226-3459
mun.astonjonction@lino.com
www.municipalite.aston-jonction.qc.ca
Entité municipal: Municipality
Incorporation: 26 mars 1997 *Area:* 26,43 km2
Comté ou district: Nicolet-Yamaska; *Population au 2006:* 377
Circonscription(s) électorale(s) provinciale(s): Nicolet-Yamaska
Circonscription(s) électorale(s) fédérale(s): Bas-Richelieu-Nicolet-Bécancour
Prochaines élections: 3e novembre 2013
Pierre Gaudet, Maire
Jacqueline Leblanc, Directrice générale

Auclair
773A, rue du Clocher
Auclair, QC G0L 1A0
Tél: 418-899-2834; *Téléc:* 418-899-6958
info@municipaliteauclair.ca
Entité municipal: Municipality
Incorporation: 1er janvier 1954 *Area:* 106,66 km2
Comté ou district: Témiscouata; *Population au 2006:* 510
Circonscription(s) électorale(s) provinciale(s): Kamouraska-Témiscouata
Circonscription(s) électorale(s) fédérale(s): Rimouski-Neigette-Témiscouata-Les-Basques
Prochaines élections: 3e novembre 2013
Jean-Guy Robert, Maire
Ryna St-Pierre, Directrice générale

Audet
CP 27
266, rue Principale
Audet, QC G0Y 1A0
Tél: 819-583-1596; *Téléc:* 819-583-1596
munaudet@axion.ca
Entité municipal: Municipality
Incorporation: 26 novembre 1903 *Area:* 132,86 km2
Comté ou district: Le Granit; *Population au 2006:* 662
Circonscription(s) électorale(s) provinciale(s): Mégantic-Compton
Circonscription(s) électorale(s) fédérale(s): Mégantic-L'Érable
Prochaines élections: 3e novembre 2013
André Grenier, Maire
France Larochelle, Directrice générale

Aumond
679, rte Principale
Aumond, QC J0W 1W0
Tél: 819-449-4006; *Téléc:* 819-449-7448
mun.aumond@lino.com
Entité municipal: Township
Incorporation: 12 décembre 1877 *Area:* 215,12 km2
Comté ou district: La Vallée-de-la-Gatineau; *Population au 2006:* 775
Circonscription(s) électorale(s) provinciale(s): Gatineau
Circonscription(s) électorale(s) fédérale(s): Pontiac
Prochaines élections: 3e novembre 2013
Denis Charron, Maire
Rénald Mongrain, Directeur général

Aupaluk
CP 4
Aupaluk, QC J0M 1X0
Tél: 819-491-7070; *Téléc:* 819-491-7035
sectre@nvaupaluk.ca
www.nvaupaluk.ca
Entité municipal: Northern Village
Incorporation: 2e février 1980 *Area:* 32,93 km2
Comté ou district: Administration régionale Kativik; *Population au 2006:* 174
Circonscription(s) électorale(s) provinciale(s): Ungava
Circonscription(s) électorale(s) fédérale(s): Abitibi-Baie-James-Nunavik-Eeyou
Prochaines élections: 3e novembre 2013
David Lucassie, Maire
Jessica Kulula, Directrice générale

Austin
21, ch Millington
Austin, QC J0B 1B0
Tél: 819-843-2388; *Téléc:* 819-843-8211
dg_@municipalite.austin.qc.ca
Entité municipal: Municipality
Incorporation: 5 novembre 1938 *Area:* 72,62 km2
Comté ou district: Memphrémagog; *Population au 2006:* 1,404
Circonscription(s) électorale(s) provinciale(s): Brome-Missisquoi
Circonscription(s) électorale(s) fédérale(s): Brome-Missisquoi
Prochaines élections: 3e novembre 2013
Roger Nicolet, Maire
Anne-Marie Ménard, Directrice générale

Authier
605, av Principale
Authier, QC J0Z 1C0
Tél: 819-782-3093; *Téléc:* 819-782-3203
authier.ao.ca
Entité municipal: Municipality
Incorporation: 20 septembre 1918 *Area:* 139,72 km2
Comté ou district: Abitibi-Ouest; *Population au 2006:* 247
Circonscription(s) électorale(s) provinciale(s): Abitibi Ouest
Circonscription(s) électorale(s) fédérale(s):
Abitibi-Témiscamingue
Prochaines élections: 3e novembre 2013
Pierre Lambert, Maire
Louise Lambert, Directrice générale

Authier-Nord
452, rue Principale
Authier-Nord, QC J0Z 1E0
Tél: 819-782-3914; *Téléc:* 819-782-3914
authier-nord@mrcao.qc.ca
authier-nord.ao.ca
Entité municipal: Municipality
Incorporation: 1er janvier 1983 *Area:* 289,79 km2
Comté ou district: Abitibi-Ouest; *Population au 2006:* 317
Circonscription(s) électorale(s) provinciale(s): Abitibi-Ouest
Circonscription(s) électorale(s) fédérale(s):
Abitibi-Témiscamingue
Prochaines élections: 3e novembre 2013
Alain Gagnon, Maire
Élyse Gagnon, Directrice générale

Avignon
CP 128
470, rue Francoeur
Nouvelle, QC G0C 2E0
Tél: 418-794-2221; *Téléc:* 418-794-2076
info@mrcavignon.com
www.mrcavignon.com
Entité municipal: Regional County Municipality
Incorporation: 18 mars 1981
Population au 2006: 14,643
Note: 11 municipalités & 2 autres territoires.
Bertrand Berger, Préfet
Gaétan Bernatchez, Directeur général
gaetan.bernatchez@mrcavigon.com

Ayer's Cliff
958, rue Main
Ayer's Cliff, QC J0B 1C0
Tél: 819-838-5006; *Téléc:* 819-838-4411
ayerclif@abacom.com
Entité municipal: Village
Incorporation: 24 février 1909 *Area:* 11,15 km2
Comté ou district: Memphrémagog; *Population au 2006:* 1,096
Circonscription(s) électorale(s) provinciale(s): Orford
Circonscription(s) électorale(s) fédérale(s): Compton-Stanstead
Prochaines élections: 3e novembre 2013
Vincent Gérin, Maire
Ghislaine Poulin-Doherty, Directrice générale

Baie-D'Urfé
20410, ch Lakeshore
Baie-D'Urfé, QC H9X 1P7
Tél: 514-457-5324; *Téléc:* 514-457-5671
info@baie-durfe.qc.ca
www.baie-durfe.qc.ca
Entité municipal: Town
Incorporation: 1er janvier 2006 *Area:* 6,70 km2
Population au 2006: 3,902
Circonscription(s) électorale(s) provinciale(s): Jacques-Cartier
Circonscription(s) électorale(s) fédérale(s): Lac-Saint-Louis
Prochaines élections: 3e novembre 2013
Maria Tutino, Mairesse
mtutino@baie-durfe.qc.ca
Nathalie Hadida, Greffière

Baie-des-Sables
CP 39
20, rue du Couvent
Baie-des-Sables, QC G0J 1C0
Tél: 418-772-6218; *Téléc:* 418-772-6455
infobaiedessables@lac-megantic.qc.ca
www.baiedessables.com
Entité municipal: Municipality
Incorporation: 1er janvier 1859 *Area:* 64,54 km2
Comté ou district: Matane; *Population au 2006:* 614
Circonscription(s) électorale(s) provinciale(s): Matane
Circonscription(s) électorale(s) fédérale(s): Haute-Gaspésie-La Mitis-Matane-Matapédia
Prochaines élections: 3e novembre 2013
Denis Santerre, Maire
Adam Coulombe, Directeur général

Baie-du-Febvre
CP 10
298, rte Marie-Victorin
Baie-du-Febvre, QC J0G 1A0
Tél: 450-783-6422; *Téléc:* 450-783-6423
municipalite@baie-du-febvre.net
www.baie-du-febvre.net
Entité municipal: Municipality
Incorporation: 26 mars 1983 *Area:* 96,04 km2
Comté ou district: Nicolet-Yamaska; *Population au 2006:* 1,063
Circonscription(s) électorale(s) provinciale(s): Nicolet-Yamaska
Circonscription(s) électorale(s) fédérale(s):
Bas-Richelieu-Nicolet-Bécancour
Prochaines élections: 3e novembre 2013
Claude Biron, Maire
450-783-6735
Maryse Baril, Directeur général

Baie-James
CP 500
110, boul de Matagami
Matagami, QC J0Y 2A0
Tél: 819-739-2030; *Téléc:* 819-739-2713
municipalite@baie-james.net
municipalite.baie-james.qc.ca
Entité municipal: Municipality
Incorporation: 14 juillet 1971 *Area:* 333 255,55 km2
Population au 2006: 1,394
Circonscription(s) électorale(s) provinciale(s): Ungava
Circonscription(s) électorale(s) fédérale(s):
Abitibi-Baie-James-Nunavik-Eeyou
Prochaines élections: 3e novembre 2013
Gérald Lemoyne, Maire
Stéphane Simard, Greffier

Baie-Johan-Beetz
20, rue Johan-Beetz
Baie-Johan-Beetz, QC G0G 1B0
Tél: 418-539-0125; *Téléc:* 418-539-0205
munbjb@globetrotter.net
Entité municipal: Municipality
Incorporation: 1er janvier 1966 *Area:* 425,31 km2
Comté ou district: Minganie; *Population au 2006:* 95
Circonscription(s) électorale(s) provinciale(s): Duplessis
Circonscription(s) électorale(s) fédérale(s): Manicouagan
Prochaines élections: 3e novembre 2013
Martin Côté, Maire
Sylvain Roy, Directeur général

Baie-Saint-Paul
15, rue Forget
Baie-Saint-Paul, QC G3Z 3G1
Tél: 418-435-2205; *Téléc:* 418-435-2688
ville@baiesaintpaul.com
www.baiesaintpaul.com
Entité municipal: Town
Incorporation: 3e janvier 1996 *Area:* 546,73 km2
Comté ou district: Charlevoix; *Population au 2006:* 7,288
Circonscription(s) électorale(s) provinciale(s): Charlevoix
Circonscription(s) électorale(s) fédérale(s):
Montmorency-Charlevoix-Haute-Côte-Nord
Prochaines élections: 3e novembre 2013
Jean Fortin, Maire
Émilien Bouchard, Greffier

Baie-Ste-Catherine
CP 10
308, rue Leclerc
Baie-Sainte-Catherine, QC G0T 1A0
Tél: 418-237-4241; *Téléc:* 418-237-4223
municipalite@baiestecatherine.com
baiestecatherine.com
Entité municipal: Municipality
Incorporation: 4e novembre 1903 *Area:* 232,16 km2
Comté ou district: Charlevoix-Est; *Population au 2006:* 227
Circonscription(s) électorale(s) provinciale(s): Charlevoix
Circonscription(s) électorale(s) fédérale(s):
Montmorency-Charlevoix-Haute-Côte-Nord
Prochaines élections: 3e novembre 2013
Albert Boulianne, Maire
Brigitte Boulianne, Directrice générale

Baie-Trinité
CP 100
28, rte 138
Baie-Trinité, QC G0H 1A0
Tél: 418-939-2231; *Téléc:* 418-939-2616
municipalite.baie.trinite@globetrotter.net
Entité municipal: Village
Incorporation: 1er janvier 1955 *Area:* 536,33 km2
Comté ou district: Manicouagan; *Population au 2006:* 526
Circonscription(s) électorale(s) provinciale(s): René-Lévesque
Circonscription(s) électorale(s) fédérale(s): Manicouagan
Prochaines élections: 3e novembre 2013
Denis Lejeune, Maire
Manon Comeau, Greffière

Barkmere
CP 11
182, ch de Barkmere
Barkmere, QC J0T 1A0
Tél: 819-687-3373; *Téléc:* 819-687-3383
dg@barkmere.org
www.barkmere.org
Entité municipal: Village
Incorporation: 24 mars 1926 *Area:* 18,07 km2
Comté ou district: Les Laurentides; *Population au 2006:* 87
Circonscription(s) électorale(s) provinciale(s): Argenteuil
Circonscription(s) électorale(s) fédérale(s): Laurentides-Labelle
Prochaines élections: 3e novembre 2013
Luc Trépanier, Maire
Caroline Dion, Directrice générale

Barnston-Ouest
741, ch Hunter
Ayer's Cliff, QC J0B 1C0
Tél: 819-838-4334; *Téléc:* 819-838-1717
barnston.ouest@xittel.ca
barnston-ouest.ca
Entité municipal: Municipality
Incorporation: 1er janvier 1946 *Area:* 97,90 km2
Comté ou district: Coaticook; *Population au 2006:* 583
Circonscription(s) électorale(s) provinciale(s): Orford
Circonscription(s) électorale(s) fédérale(s): Compton-Stanstead
Prochaines élections: 3e novembre 2013
Ghislaine Leblond, Mairesse
Manon Bergeron, Directrice générale

Barraute
CP 299
481, 8e Av
Barraute, QC J0Y 1A0
Tél: 819-734-6574; *Téléc:* 819-734-5186
mun.barraute@cableamos.com
Entité municipal: Municipality
Incorporation: 5e janvier 1994 *Area:* 495,51 km2
Comté ou district: Abitibi; *Population au 2006:* 2,062
Circonscription(s) électorale(s) provinciale(s): Abitibi-Est
Circonscription(s) électorale(s) fédérale(s):
Abitibi-Témiscamingue
Prochaines élections: 3e novembre 2013
Lionel Pelchat, Maire
Richard Nantel, Directeur général

Batiscan
395, rue Principale
Batiscan, QC G0X 1A0
Tél: 418-362-2421; *Téléc:* 418-362-3174
municipalite@batiscan.ca
www.batiscan.ca
Entité municipal: Municipality
Incorporation: 1er juillet 1855 *Area:* 44,02 km2
Comté ou district: Les Chenaux; *Population au 2006:* 949
Circonscription(s) électorale(s) provinciale(s): Champlain
Circonscription(s) électorale(s) fédérale(s):
St-Maurice-Champlain
Prochaines élections: 3e novembre 2013
Christian Fortin, Maire
Johanne Faucher, Directrice générale

Béarn
CP 369
28, 2e rue nord
Béarn, QC J0Z 1G0
Tél: 819-726-4121; *Téléc:* 819-726-2121
dg.bearn@mrctemiscamingue.qc.ca
www.temiscamingue.net/bearn

Entité municipal: Municipality
Incorporation: 3e octobre 1912 *Area:* 566,48 km2
Comté ou district: Témiscamingue; *Population au 2006:* 883
Circonscription(s) électorale(s) provinciale(s):
Rouyn-Noranda-Témiscamingue
Circonscription(s) électorale(s) fédérale(s):
Abitibi-Témiscamingue
Prochaines élections: 3e novembre 2013
Luc Lalonde, Maire
Lynda Gaudet, Directrice générale

Beauce-Sartigan
2727, 6e Av
Saint-Georges, QC G5Y 3Y1
Tél: 418-228-8418; *Téléc:* 418-228-3709
mrcbsart@globetrotter.net
Entité municipal: Regional County Municipality
Population au 2006: 49,611
Note: 16 municipalités.
Luc Lemieux, Préfet
Éric Paquet, Directeur général

Beauceville
540, boul Renault
Beauceville, QC G5X 1N1
Tél: 418-774-9137; *Téléc:* 418-774-9141
beauceville@ville.beauceville.qc.ca
www.ville.beauceville.qc.ca
Entité municipal: Town
Incorporation: 25 février 1998 *Area:* 167,76 km2
Comté ou district: Robert-Cliche; *Population au 2006:* 6,226
Circonscription(s) électorale(s) provinciale(s): Beauce-Nord
Circonscription(s) électorale(s) fédérale(s): Beauce
Prochaines élections: 3e novembre 2013
Luc Provençal, Maire
Madeleine Poulin, Greffière

Beauharnois-Salaberry
#200, 660, rue Ellice
Beauharnois, QC J6N 1Y1
Tél: 450-225-0870; *Téléc:* 450-225-0872
info@mrc-beauharnois-salaberry.com
www.mrc-beauharnois-salaberry.com
Entité municipal: Regional County Municipality
Population au 2006: 60,802
Note: 7 municipalités.
Yves Daoust, Préfet
Linda Phaneuf, Directrice générale
l.phaneuf@mrc-beauharnois-salaberry.com

Beaulac-Garthby
96, rte 112
Beaulac-Garthby, QC G0Y 1B0
Tél: 418-458-2375; *Téléc:* 418-458-1127
municipalitedebeaulac@bellnet.ca
www.beaulac-garthby.com
Entité municipal: Municipality
Incorporation: 15 mars 2000 *Area:* 76,81 km2
Comté ou district: Des Appalaches; *Population au 2006:* 900
Circonscription(s) électorale(s) provinciale(s): Richmond
Circonscription(s) électorale(s) fédérale(s): Mégantic-L'Érable
Prochaines élections: 3e novembre 2013
Loic Lenoir, Maire
Cynthia Gagné, Directrice générale

Beaumont
48, ch du Domaine
Beaumont, QC G0R 1C0
Tél: 418-833-3369; *Téléc:* 418-833-4788
info.generale@municipalite.beaumont.qc.ca
www.municipalitedebeaumont.com
Entité municipal: Municipality
Incorporation: 1er juillet 1855 *Area:* 45,29 km2
Comté ou district: Bellechasse; *Population au 2006:* 2,180
Circonscription(s) électorale(s) provinciale(s): Bellechasse
Circonscription(s) électorale(s) fédérale(s): Lévis-Bellechasse
Prochaines élections: 3e novembre 2013
André Goulet, Maire
Patrice Bissonnette, Directeur général

Beaupré
216, rue Prévost
Beaupré, QC G0A 1E0
Tél: 418-827-4541; *Téléc:* 418-827-3818
mairie@ville.beaupre.qc.ca
www.ville.beaupre.qc.ca
Entité municipal: Town
Incorporation: 23 avril 1928 *Area:* 22,53 km2
Comté ou district: La Côte-de-Beaupré; *Population au 2006:* 3,006
Circonscription(s) électorale(s) provinciale(s): Charlevoix
Circonscription(s) électorale(s) fédérale(s):
Montmorency-Charlevoix-Haute-Côte-Nord
Prochaines élections: 3e novembre 2013
Michel Paré, Maire
Johanne Gagnon, Greffière

Bécancour
#1, 3689, boul Bécancour
Bécancour, QC G9H 3W7
Tél: 819-298-2070; *Téléc:* 819-298-2041
info@mrcbecancour.qc.ca
Entité municipal: Regional County Municipality
Incorporation: 1er janvier 1982
Population au 2006: 18,806
Note: 12 municipalités.
Maurice Richard, Préfet
Laval Dubois, Directeur général
l.dubois@mrcbecancour.qc.ca

Bedford
237, rte 202 est
Canton de Bedford, QC J0J 1A0
Tél: 450-248-7576; *Téléc:* 450-248-0135
canton.bedford@qc.aira.com
www.cantondebedford.ca
Entité municipal: Township
Incorporation: 4e mars 1919 *Area:* 31,06 km2
Comté ou district: Brome-Missisquoi; *Population au 2006:* 736
Circonscription(s) électorale(s) provinciale(s): Brome-Missisquoi
Circonscription(s) électorale(s) fédérale(s): Brome-Missisquoi
Prochaines élections: 3e novembre 2013
Gilles St-Jean, Maire
Linda Payment, Directrice générale

Bedford
1, rue Principale
Bedford, QC J0J 1A0
Tél: 450-248-0550; *Téléc:* 450-248-3220
corpobedford@bellnet.ca
www.bedfordplus.com
Entité municipal: Town
Incorporation: 21 novembre 1866 *Area:* 4,57 km2
Comté ou district: Brome-Missisquoi; *Population au 2006:* 2,612
Circonscription(s) électorale(s) provinciale(s): Brome-Missisquoi
Circonscription(s) électorale(s) fédérale(s): Brome-Missisquoi
Prochaines élections: 3e novembre 2013
Claude Dubois, Maire
Yvon Labonté, Directeur général

Bégin
126, rue Brassard
Bégin, QC G0V 1B0
Tél: 418-672-4270; *Téléc:* 418-672-6161
munbegin@hotmail.com
www.begin.ca
Entité municipal: Municipality
Incorporation: 8e février 1922 *Area:* 191,81 km2
Comté ou district: Le Fjord-du-Saguenay; *Population au 2006:* 862
Circonscription(s) électorale(s) provinciale(s): Dubuc
Circonscription(s) électorale(s) fédérale(s): Jonquière-Alma
Prochaines élections: 3e novembre 2013
Gérald Savard, Maire
Peggy Lemieux, Directrice générale

Belcourt
CP 22
219, rue Communautaire
Belcourt, QC J0Y 2M0
Tél: 819-737-8894; *Téléc:* 819-737-8894
g.m.a@munbelcourt.ca
Entité municipal: Municipality
Incorporation: 24 octobre 1918 *Area:* 411,23 km2
Comté ou district: La Vallée-de-l'Or; *Population au 2006:* 256
Circonscription(s) électorale(s) provinciale(s): Abitibi-Est
Circonscription(s) électorale(s) fédérale(s):
Abitibi-Baie-James-Nunavik-Eeyou
Prochaines élections: 3e novembre 2013
Carol Nolet, Maire
Nathalie Lizotte, Directrice

Bellechasse
100, rue Monseigneur-Bilodeau
Saint-Lazare-de-Bellechasse, QC G0R 3J0
Tél: 418-883-3347; *Téléc:* 418-883-2555
clement@mrcbellechasse.qc.ca
www.mrcbellechasse.qc.ca
Entité municipal: Regional County Municipality
Incorporation: 1er janvier 1982
Population au 2006: 33,330
Note: 20 municipalités.
Hervé Blais, Préfet
Clément Fillion, Directeur général
clement@mrcbellechasse.qc.ca

Belleterre
CP 130
265, 1re av
Belleterre, QC J0Z 1L0
Tél: 819-722-2122; *Téléc:* 819-722-2527
villebelleterre@hotmail.com
Entité municipal: Village
Incorporation: 13 mai 1942 *Area:* 606,33 km2
Comté ou district: Témiscamingue; *Population au 2006:* 350
Circonscription(s) électorale(s) provinciale(s):
Rouyn-Noranda-Témiscamingue
Circonscription(s) électorale(s) fédérale(s):
Abitibi-Témiscamingue
Prochaines élections: 3e novembre 2013
Bruno Boyer, Maire
Liliane Rochon, Directrice générale

Berry
274, rte 399
Berry, QC J0Y 2G0
Tél: 819-732-1815; *Téléc:* 819-732-3289
direction.berry@mrcabitibi.qc.ca
Entité municipal: Municipality
Incorporation: 1er janvier 1982 *Area:* 583,36 km2
Comté ou district: Abitibi; *Population au 2006:* 560
Circonscription(s) électorale(s) provinciale(s): Abitibi-Ouest
Circonscription(s) électorale(s) fédérale(s):
Abitibi-Témiscamingue
Prochaines élections: 3e novembre 2013
Jean-Pierre Naud, Maire
Sandra Boutin, Directrice générale

Berthier-sur-Mer
5, rue du Couvent
Berthier-sur-Mer, QC G0R 1E0
Tél: 418-259-7343; *Téléc:* 418-259-2038
berthier-sur-mer@montmagny.com
www.berthiersurmer.ca
Entité municipal: Municipality
Incorporation: 1er juillet 1855 *Area:* 26,05 km2
Comté ou district: Montmagny; *Population au 2006:* 1,239
Circonscription(s) électorale(s) provinciale(s): Montmagny-L'Islet
Circonscription(s) électorale(s) fédérale(s):
Montmagny-L'Islet-Kamouraska-Rivière-du-Loup
Prochaines élections: 3e novembre 2013
Rosario Bossé, Maire
Suzanne G. Blais, Directrice générale

Berthierville
CP 269
588, rue De Montcalm
Berthierville, QC J0K 1A0
Tél: 450-836-7035; *Téléc:* 450-836-1446
info@ville.berthierville.qc.ca
www.ville.berthierville.qc.ca
Entité municipal: Town
Incorporation: 14 avril 1852 *Area:* 7,20 km2
Comté ou district: D'Autray; *Population au 2006:* 4,007
Circonscription(s) électorale(s) provinciale(s): Berthier
Circonscription(s) électorale(s) fédérale(s): Berthier-Maskinongé
Prochaines élections: 3e novembre 2013
Bernard Grégoire, Maire
Lincoln Le Breton, Greffier

Béthanie
1321, ch de Béthanie
Béthanie, QC J0H 1E1
Tél: 450-548-2826; *Téléc:* 450-548-5693
bethanie@cooptel.qc.ca
municipalite.bethanie.qc.ca
Entité municipal: Municipality
Incorporation: 2e mars 1920 *Area:* 47,29 km2
Comté ou district: Acton; *Population au 2006:* 331
Circonscription(s) électorale(s) provinciale(s): Johnson
Circonscription(s) électorale(s) fédérale(s): St-Hyacinthe-Bagot
Prochaines élections: 3e novembre 2013
Chantal Beauregard Favreau, Mairesse
Heidi Bédard, Directrice générale

Biencourt
CP 70
2, rue St-Marc
Biencourt, QC G0K 1T0
Tél: 418-499-2423; *Téléc:* 418-499-2708
info@biencourt.ca
www.biencourt.ca
Entité municipal: Municipality
Incorporation: 1er janvier 1947 *Area:* 187,80 km2
Comté ou district: Témiscouata; *Population au 2006:* 596

Circonscription(s) électorale(s) provinciale(s): Rimouski
Circonscription(s) électorale(s) fédérale(s):
Rimouski-Neigette-Témiscouata-Les Basques
Prochaines élections: 3e novembre 2013
Daniel Boucher, Maire
Julie Vaillancourt, Directrice générale

Blanc-Sablon
CP 400
1149, boul Dr.-Camille-Marcoux
Lourdes-de-Blanc-Sablon, QC G0G 1W0
Tél: 418-461-2707; *Téléc:* 418-461-2529
mbsablon@globetrotter.net
Entité municipal: Municipality
Incorporation: 1er janvier 1990 *Area:* 254,49 km2
Population au 2006: 1,263
Circonscription(s) électorale(s) provinciale(s): Duplessis
Circonscription(s) électorale(s) fédérale(s): Manicouagan
Prochaines élections: 3e novembre 2013
Anthony Dumas, Maire
Réjean L. Dumas, Directeur général

Blue Sea
CP 99
7, rue Principale
Blue Sea, QC J0X 1C0
Tél: 819-463-2261; *Téléc:* 819-463-4345
info@bluesea.ca
www.bluesea.ca
Entité municipal: Municipality
Incorporation: 31 janvier 1921 *Area:* 76,89 km2
Comté ou district: La Vallée-de-la-Gatineau; *Population au 2006:* 608
Circonscription(s) électorale(s) provinciale(s): Gatineau
Circonscription(s) électorale(s) fédérale(s): Pontiac
Prochaines élections: 3e novembre 2013
Laurent Fortin, Maire
Josée Parsons, Directrice générale

Boileau
702, ch de Boileau
Boileau, QC J0V 1N0
Tél: 819-687-3436; *Téléc:* 819-687-3745
mun.boileau@mrcpapineau.com
www.municipaliteboileau.ca
Entité municipal: Municipality
Incorporation: 8e mars 1882 *Area:* 136,22 km2
Comté ou district: Papineau; *Population au 2006:* 499
Circonscription(s) électorale(s) provinciale(s): Papineau
Circonscription(s) électorale(s) fédérale(s):
Argenteuil-Papineau-Mirabel
Prochaines élections: 3e novembre 2013
Henri Gariépy, Maire
Ghyslaine Lauzon, Directrice générale

Bois-des-Filion
375, boul Adophe-Chapleau
Bois-des-Filion, QC J6Z 1H1
Tél: 450-621-1460; *Téléc:* 450-621-8483
ville@ville.bois-des-filion.qc.ca
ville.bois-des-filion.qc.ca
Entité municipal: Town
Incorporation: 1er janvier 1949 *Area:* 4,34 km2
Comté ou district: Thérèse-De Blainville; *Population au 2006:* 8,383
Circonscription(s) électorale(s) provinciale(s): Blainville
Circonscription(s) électorale(s) fédérale(s): Marc-Aurèle-Fortin
Prochaines élections: 3e novembre 2013
Paul Larocque, Maire
Robert L'Africain, Greffière

Bois-Franc
466, rte 105
Bois-Franc, QC J9E 3A9
Tél: 819-449-2252; *Téléc:* 819-449-4407
mun.bois-franc@ireseau.com
www.bois-franc.ca
Entité municipal: Municipality
Incorporation: 17 novembre 1920 *Area:* 73,24 km2
Comté ou district: La Vallée-de-la-Gatineau; *Population au 2006:* 449
Circonscription(s) électorale(s) provinciale(s): Gatineau
Circonscription(s) électorale(s) fédérale(s): Pontiac
Prochaines élections: 3e novembre 2013
Armand Hubert, Maire
Claudette Rochon, Directrice générale

Boischatel
45, rue Bédard
Boischatel, QC G0A 1H0
Tél: 418-822-4500; *Téléc:* 418-822-4512
info@municipalitedeboischatel.ca
www.municipalitedeboischatel.ca
Entité municipal: Municipality
Incorporation: 3e avril 1920 *Area:* 19,64
Comté ou district: La Côte de Beaupré; *Population au 2006:* 5,287
Circonscription(s) électorale(s) provinciale(s): Montmorency
Circonscription(s) électorale(s) fédérale(s):
Montmorency-Charlevoix-Haute-Côte-Nord
Prochaines élections: 3e novembre 2013
Yves Germain, Maire
Carl Michaud, Directeur général

Bolton-Est
858, rte Missisquoi
Bolton-Est, QC J0E 1G0
Tél: 450-292-3444; *Téléc:* 450-292-4224
info@boltonest.ca
www.boltonest.ca
Entité municipal: Municipality
Incorporation: 28 décembre 1876 *Area:* 80,78
Comté ou district: Memphrémagog; *Population au 2006:* 704
Circonscription(s) électorale(s) provinciale(s): Brome-Missisquoi
Circonscription(s) électorale(s) fédérale(s): Brome-Missisquoi
Prochaines élections: 3e novembre 2013
Royal Dupuis, Maire
Monique Pépin, Directrice générale (par intérim)

Bolton-Ouest
9, ch Town Hall
Bolton-Ouest, QC J0E 2T0
Tél: 450-242-2704; *Téléc:* 450-242-2705
info@municipalitedeboltonouest.com
www.municipalitedeboltonouest.com
Entité municipal: Municipality
Incorporation: 28 décembre 1876 *Area:* 103,59
Comté ou district: Brome-Missisquoi; *Population au 2006:* 723
Circonscription(s) électorale(s) provinciale(s): Brome-Missisquoi
Circonscription(s) électorale(s) fédérale(s): Brome-Missisquoi
Prochaines élections: 3e novembre 2013
Donald Badger, Maire
Carrol Kralik, Directrice générale

Bonaventure
127, av de Louisbourg
Bonaventure, QC G0C 1E0
Tél: 418-534-2313; *Téléc:* 418-534-4336
adm@bonaventuregaspesie.com
bonaventuregaspesie.com
Entité municipal: Town
Incorporation: 1er janvier 1884 *Area:* 109,20 km2
Comté ou district: Bonaventure; *Population au 2006:* 2,673
Circonscription(s) électorale(s) provinciale(s): Bonaventure
Circonscription(s) électorale(s) fédérale(s):
Gaspésie—Îles-de-la-Madeleine
Prochaines élections: 3e novembre 2013
Serge Arsenault, Maire
Rollande Roy, Greffière

Bonaventure
CP 310
51, rue Notre-Dame
New Carlisle, QC G0C 1Z0
Tél: 418-752-6601; *Téléc:* 418-752-6657
mrcbonav@globetrotter.net
www.mrcbonaventure.com
Entité municipal: Regional County Municipality
Incorporation: 8e avril 1981
Population au 2006: 17,948
Note: 13 municipalités & 1 autre territoire.
Jean-Guy Poirier, Préfet
Anne-Marie Flowers, Directrice générale
mrcbonavaflowers@globetrotter.net

Bonne-Espérance
CP 40
100, rue Whiteley
Rivière-Saint-Paul, QC G0G 2P0
Tél: 418-379-2911; *Téléc:* 418-379-2959
bonneesperance@xplornet.com
Entité municipal: Municipality
Incorporation: 1er janvier 1990 *Area:* 721,28 km2
Comté ou district: Le Golfe-du-Saint-Laurent; *Population au 2006:* 834
Circonscription(s) électorale(s) provinciale(s): Duplessis
Circonscription(s) électorale(s) fédérale(s): Manicouagan
Prochaines élections: 3e novembre 2013
Bryce Douglas Fequet, Maire
René Fequet, Directeur général

Bonsecours
691, rte 220
Bonsecours, QC J0E 1H0
Tél: 450-532-3139; *Téléc:* 450-532-3953
mbonsecours@cooptel.qc.ca
www.bonsecours.ca
Entité municipal: Municipality
Incorporation: 20 mars 1905 *Area:* 59,92 km2
Comté ou district: Le Val-St-François; *Population au 2006:* 547
Circonscription(s) électorale(s) provinciale(s): Brome-Missisquoi
Circonscription(s) électorale(s) fédérale(s): Shefford
Prochaines élections: 3e novembre 2013
Cécile Laliberté, Mairesse
Lyne Gaudreau, Directrice générale

Bouchette
CP 59
36, rue Principale
Bouchette, QC J0X 1E0
Tél: 819-465-2555; *Téléc:* 819-465-2318
mun.bouchette@ireseau.com
www.bouchette.ca
Entité municipal: Municipality
Incorporation: 22 mars 1980 *Area:* 131,97 km2
Comté ou district: La Vallée-de-la-Gatineau; *Population au 2006:* 718
Circonscription(s) électorale(s) provinciale(s): Gatineau
Circonscription(s) électorale(s) fédérale(s): Pontiac
Prochaines élections: 3e novembre 2013
Réjean Major, Maire
Claudia Lacroix, Directrice générale

Bowman
214, rte 307
Bowman, QC J0X 3C0
Tél: 819-454-2421; *Téléc:* 819-454-2133
bowman01@mrcpapineau.com
www.bowman.ca
Entité municipal: Municipality
Incorporation: 27 juin 1913 *Area:* 166,99 km2
Comté ou district: Papineau; *Population au 2006:* 676
Circonscription(s) électorale(s) provinciale(s): Papineau
Circonscription(s) électorale(s) fédérale(s):
Argenteuil-Papineau-Mirabel
Prochaines élections: 3e novembre 2013
Michel David, Maire
Mylène Groulx, Directrice générale

Brébeuf
217, rte 323
Brébeuf, QC J0T 1B0
Tél: 819-425-9833; *Téléc:* 819-425-6611
secretariat@brebeuf.ca
www.brebeuf.ca
Entité municipal: Parish (Paroisse)
Incorporation: 4e juin 1910 *Area:* 36,71 km2
Comté ou district: Les Laurentides; *Population au 2006:* 939
Circonscription(s) électorale(s) provinciale(s): Labelle
Circonscription(s) électorale(s) fédérale(s): Laurentides-Labelle
Prochaines élections: 3e novembre 2013
Ronald Provost, Maire
Pascal Caron, Directeur général

Brigham
118, av des Cèdres
Brigham, QC J2K 4K4
Tél: 450-263-5942; *Téléc:* 450-263-8380
info@brigham.ca
www.brigham.ca
Entité municipal: Municipality
Incorporation: 1er juillet 1855 *Area:* 84,80 km2
Comté ou district: Brome-Missisquoi; *Population au 2006:* 2,408
Circonscription(s) électorale(s) provinciale(s): Brome-Missisquoi
Circonscription(s) électorale(s) fédérale(s): Brome-Missisquoi
Prochaines élections: 3e novembre 2013
Steven Neil, Maire
Jean-François Grandmont, Directeur général

Bristol
32, ch d'Aylmer
Bristol, QC J0X 1G0
Tél: 819-647-5555; *Téléc:* 819-647-2424
info@bristolmunicipality.qc.ca
www.bristolmunicipality.qc.ca
Entité municipal: Municipality
Incorporation: 1er juillet 1855 *Area:* 224,08 km2
Comté ou district: Pontiac; *Population au 2006:* 1,210
Circonscription(s) électorale(s) provinciale(s): Pontiac
Circonscription(s) électorale(s) fédérale(s): Pontiac
Prochaines élections: 3e novembre 2013

Brent Orr, Maire
Christina Peck, Directrice générale

Brome
330, ch Stagecoach
Brome, QC J0E 1K0
Tél: 450-243-0489; *Téléc:* 450-243-1091
bromevillage@axion.ca
Entité municipal: Village
Incorporation: 20 juin 1923 *Area:* 11,75 km2
Comté ou district: Brome-Missisquoi; *Population au 2006:* 286
Circonscription(s) électorale(s) provinciale(s): Brome-Missisquoi
Circonscription(s) électorale(s) fédérale(s): Brome-Missisquoi
Prochaines élections: 3e novembre 2013
L. Thomas Selby, Maire
Paul McKeogh, Directeur général

Brome-Missisquoi
749, rue Principale
Cowansville, QC J2K 1J8
Tél: 450-266-4900; *Téléc:* 450-266-6141
administration@mrcbm.qc.ca
www.brome-missisquoi.ca
Entité municipal: Regional County Municipality
Population au 2006: 46,720
Note: 20 municipalités.
Arthur Fauteux, Préfet
prefet@mrcbm.qc.ca
Robert Desmarais, Directeur général
rdesmarais@mrcbm.qc.ca

Bromont
88, boul de Bromont
Bromont, QC J2L 1A1
Tél: 450-534-2021; *Téléc:* 450-534-1025
ville@bromont.com
www.bromont.com
Entité municipal: Town
Incorporation: 27 janvier 1973 *Area:* 108,36 km2
Comté ou district: Brome-Missisquoi; *Population au 2006:* 6,049
Circonscription(s) électorale(s) provinciale(s): Brome-Missisquoi
Circonscription(s) électorale(s) fédérale(s): Brome-Missisquoi
Prochaines élections: 3e novembre 2013
Pauline Quinlan, Mairesse
Joanne Skelling, Greffière

Brownsburg-Chatham
300, rue de l'Hôtel-de-Ville
Brownsburg-Chatham, QC J8G 3B4
Tél: 450-533-6687; *Téléc:* 450-533-5795
secretariat@brownsburgchatham.ca
www.brownsburgchatham.ca
Entité municipal: Town
Incorporation: 6e octobre 1999 *Area:* 249,31 km2
Comté ou district: Argenteuil; *Population au 2006:* 6,664
Circonscription(s) électorale(s) provinciale(s): Argenteuil
Circonscription(s) électorale(s) fédérale(s):
Argenteuil-Papineau-Mirabel
Prochaines élections: 3e novembre 2013
Georges Dinel, Maire
Marie-Josée Larocque, Greffière

Bryson
CP 190
833, rue Principale
Bryson, QC J0X 1H0
Tél: 819-648-5940; *Téléc:* 819-648-5297
bryson@mrcpontiac.qc.ca
Entité municipal: Municipality
Incorporation: 1er janvier 1873 *Area:* 3,10 km2
Comté ou district: Pontiac; *Population au 2006:* 618
Circonscription(s) électorale(s) provinciale(s): Pontiac
Circonscription(s) électorale(s) fédérale(s): Pontiac
Prochaines élections: 3e novembre 2013
John Griffin, Maire
Tracey Hérault, Directrice générale

Bury
563, rue Main
Bury, QC J0B 1J0
Tél: 819-560-8414; *Téléc:* 819-872-3675
information.bury@hsfqc.ca
www.municipalitedebury.qc.ca
Entité municipal: Municipality
Incorporation: 1er juillet 1855 *Area:* 232,52 km2
Comté ou district: Le Haut-St-François; *Population au 2006:* 1,249
Circonscription(s) électorale(s) provinciale(s):
Mégantic-Compton
Circonscription(s) électorale(s) fédérale(s): Compton-Stanstead
Prochaines élections: 3e novembre 2013
Walter Dougherty, Maire

Suzanne Ménard, Directrice générale

Cacouna
415, rue St-Georges
Cacouna, QC G0L 1G0
Tél: 418-867-1781; *Téléc:* 418-867-5677
municipalite@cacouna.ca
www.cacouna.ca
Entité municipal: Municipality
Incorporation: 22 mars 2006 *Area:* 62,49 km2
Comté ou district: Rivière-du-Loup; *Population au 2006:* 1,847
Circonscription(s) électorale(s) provinciale(s): Rivière-du-Loup
Circonscription(s) électorale(s) fédérale(s):
Montmagny—L'Islet—Kamouraska—Rivière-du-Loup
Prochaines élections: 3e novembre 2013
Ghislaine Daris, Maire
Madeleine Lévesque, Directrice générale

Calixa-Lavallée
771, ch de la Beauce
Calixa-Lavallée, QC J0L 1A0
Tél: 450-583-6470; *Téléc:* 450-583-5508
directeur@calixa-lavallee.ca
www.calixa-lavallee.ca
Entité municipal: Parish (Paroisse)
Incorporation: 24 juillet 1878 *Area:* 32,42 km2
Comté ou district: Marguerite-D'Youville; *Population au 2006:* 533
Circonscription(s) électorale(s) provinciale(s): Verchères
Circonscription(s) électorale(s) fédérale(s): Verchères-Les Patriotes
Prochaines élections: 3e novembre 2013
Claude Jutras, Maire
Alain Beauregard, Directeur général

Campbell's Bay
CP 157
59, rue Leslie
Campbell's Bay, QC J0X 1K0
Tél: 819-648-5811; *Téléc:* 819-648-2045
administration@municipalite.campbellsbay.qc.ca
Entité municipal: Municipality
Incorporation: 23 février 1904 *Area:* 3,08 km2
Comté ou district: Pontiac; *Population au 2006:* 745
Circonscription(s) électorale(s) provinciale(s): Pontiac
Circonscription(s) électorale(s) fédérale(s): Pontiac
Prochaines élections: 3e novembre 2013
William Stewart, Maire
Colleen Larivière, Directrice générale

Caniapiscau
CP 1420
100, place Daviault
Fermont, QC G0G 1J0
Tél: 418-287-5339; *Téléc:* 418-287-3420
mrc@caniapiscau.net
www.caniapiscau.net
Entité municipal: Regional County Municipality
Incorporation: 1er janvier 1982
Population au 2006: 3,948
Note: 2 municipalités & 4 autres territoires.
Lise Pelletier, Préfète
Jimmy Morneau, Directeur général

Cantley
8, ch River
Cantley, QC J8V 2Z9
Tél: 819-827-3434; *Téléc:* 819-827-4328
municipalite@cantley.ca
www.cantley.ca
Entité municipal: Municipality
Incorporation: 1er janvier 1989 *Area:* 134,00 km2
Comté ou district: Les Collines-de-l'Outaouais; *Population au 2006:* 7,926
Circonscription(s) électorale(s) provinciale(s): Gatineau
Circonscription(s) électorale(s) fédérale(s): Pontiac
Prochaines élections: 3e novembre 2013
Steve Harris, Maire
Sylvie Loublier, Greffière

Cap-Chat
CP 279
53, rue Notre-Dame
Cap-Chat, QC G0J 1E0
Tél: 418-786-5537; *Téléc:* 418-786-5540
ville.capchat@globetrotter.net
Entité municipal: Town
Incorporation: 15 mars 2000 *Area:* 183,13 km2
Comté ou district: La Haute-Gaspésie; *Population au 2006:* 2,777
Circonscription(s) électorale(s) provinciale(s): Matane
Circonscription(s) électorale(s) fédérale(s): Haute-Gaspésie-La
Mitis-Matane-Matapédia
Prochaines élections: 3e novembre 2013
Judes Landry, Maire
Jacques Fournier, Greffier

Cap-Santé
194, rte 138
Cap-Santé, QC G0A 1L0
Tél: 418-285-1207; *Téléc:* 418-285-0009
villecapsante@globetrotter.net
www.capsante.qc.ca
Entité municipal: Town
Incorporation: 1er juillet 1855 *Area:* 54,38 km2
Comté ou district: Portneuf; *Population au 2006:* 2,666
Circonscription(s) électorale(s) provinciale(s): Portneuf
Circonscription(s) électorale(s) fédérale(s):
Portneuf-Jacques-Cartier
Prochaines élections: 3e novembre 2013
Jean-Yves Nobert, Maire
Jacques Blais, Directeur général

Cap-St-Ignace
850, rte du Souvenir
Cap-Saint-Ignace, QC G0R 1H0
Tél: 418-246-5631; *Téléc:* 418-246-5663
dg@capsaintignace.ca
www.capsaintignace.ca
Entité municipal: Municipality
Incorporation: 1er juillet 1855 *Area:* 227,76 km2
Comté ou district: Montmagny; *Population au 2006:* 3,204
Circonscription(s) électorale(s) provinciale(s): Montmagny-L'Islet
Circonscription(s) électorale(s) fédérale(s):
Montmagny-L'Islet-Kamouraska-Rivière-du-Loup
Prochaines élections: 3e novembre 2013
André Clavet, Maire
Sophie Boucher, Directrice générale

Capitale-Nationale
3, ch de l'Église
Sainte-Pétronille, QC G0A 4C0
Tél: 418-828-2270; *Téléc:* 418-828-1364
ste-petronille@qc.aira.com
Entité municipal: Village
Incorporation: 1er juillet 1874 *Area:* 4,50
Comté ou district: L'Ile-d'Orléans; *Population au 2006:* 1,060
Circonscription(s) électorale(s) provinciale(s): Montmorency
Circonscription(s) électorale(s) fédérale(s):
Montmorency-Charlevoix-Haute-Côte-Nord
Prochaines élections: 3e novembre 2013
Harold Noël, Maire
Jean-François Labbé, Directeur général

Caplan
CP 360
17, boul Perron est
Caplan, QC G0C 1H0
Tél: 418-388-2075; *Téléc:* 418-388-2429
caplan@globetrotter.net
www.municipalitecaplan.com
Entité municipal: Municipality
Incorporation: 1er janvier 1875 *Area:* 85,05 km2
Comté ou district: Bonaventure; *Population au 2006:* 1,884
Circonscription(s) électorale(s) provinciale(s): Bonaventure
Circonscription(s) électorale(s) fédérale(s):
Gaspésie—Îles-de-la-Madeleine
Prochaines élections: 3e novembre 2013
Doris Boissonnault, Mairesse
Lise Castilloux, Directrice générale

Carignan
2555, ch Bellevue
Carignan, QC J3L 6G8
Tél: 450-658-1066; *Téléc:* 450-658-6079
info@villedecarignan.org
www.villedecarignan.org
Entité municipal: Town
Incorporation: 1er juillet 1855 *Area:* 62,39 km2
Comté ou district: La Vallée-du-Richelieu; *Population au 2006:* 7,426
Circonscription(s) électorale(s) provinciale(s): Chambly
Circonscription(s) électorale(s) fédérale(s): Chambly-Borduas
Prochaines élections: 3e novembre 2013
Louise Lavigne, Mairesse
Rémi Raymond, Greffier

Carleton-sur-Mer
629, boul Perron
Carleton, QC G0C 1J0
Tél: 418-364-7073; *Téléc:* 418-364-6011
direction@carletonsurmer.com
www.carletonsurmer.com

Entité municipal: Town
Incorporation: 4e octobre 2000 *Area:* 214,78 km2
Comté ou district: Avignon; *Population au 2006:* 4,077
Circonscription(s) électorale(s) provinciale(s): Bonaventure
Circonscription(s) électorale(s) fédérale(s):
Gaspésie—Îles-de-la-Madeleine
Prochaines élections: 3e novembre 2013
Denis Henry, Maire
Caroline Asselin, Greffière

Cascapédia-St-Jules
55, rte Gallagher
Cascapédia-Saint-Jules, QC G0C 1T0
Tél: 418-392-4042; *Téléc:* 418-392-6004
cascapediastjules.loisirs@globetrotter.net
Entité municipal: Municipality
Incorporation: 2e juin 1999 *Area:* 168,00 km2
Comté ou district: Bonaventure; *Population au 2006:* 714
Circonscription(s) électorale(s) provinciale(s): Bonaventure
Circonscription(s) électorale(s) fédérale(s):
Gaspésie—Îles-de-la-Madeleine
Prochaines élections: 3e novembre 2013
Pat Saint-Onge, Maire
Susan Legouffe, Directrice générale

Causapscal
1, rue St-Jacques nord
Causapscal, QC G0J 1J0
Tél: 418-756-3444; *Téléc:* 418-756-3344
causapscal@mrcmatapedia.qc.ca
www.causapscal.net
Entité municipal: Town
Incorporation: 31 décembre 1997 *Area:* 163,88 km2
Comté ou district: La Matapédia; *Population au 2006:* 2,458
Circonscription(s) électorale(s) provinciale(s): Matapédia
Circonscription(s) électorale(s) fédérale(s): Haute-Gaspésie-La Mitis-Matane-Matapédia
Prochaines élections: 3e novembre 2013
Mario Côté, Maire
Jean-Noël Barriault, Directeur général

Cayamant
6, ch Lachapelle
Lac-Cayamant, QC J0X 1Y0
Tél: 819-463-3587; *Téléc:* 819-463-4020
mun.caymant@ireseau.com
Entité municipal: Municipality
Incorporation: 10 octobre 1906 *Area:* 411,13 km2
Comté ou district: La Vallée-de-la-Gatineau; *Population au 2006:* 811
Circonscription(s) électorale(s) provinciale(s): Gatineau
Circonscription(s) électorale(s) fédérale(s): Pontiac
Prochaines élections: 3e novembre 2013
Pierre Pedro Chartrand, Maire
Suzanne Vallières, Directrice générale

Chambord
1526, rue Principale
Chambord, QC G0W 1G0
Tél: 418-342-6274; *Téléc:* 418-342-8438
info@chambord.ca
www.chambord.ca
Entité municipal: Municipality
Incorporation: 8e décembre 1973 *Area:* 157,03 km2
Comté ou district: Le Domaine-du-Roy; *Population au 2006:* 1,690
Circonscription(s) électorale(s) provinciale(s): Roberval
Circonscription(s) électorale(s) fédérale(s):
Roberval-Lac-Saint-Jean
Prochaines élections: 3e novembre 2013
Gérard Savard, Maire
Sylvie Desmeules, Directrice générale

Champlain
CP 250
819, rue Notre-Dame
Champlain, QC G0X 1C0
Tél: 819-295-3979; *Téléc:* 819-295-3032
municipalite.champlain@infoteck.qc.ca
www.municipalite.champlain.qc.ca
Entité municipal: Municipality
Incorporation: 11 décembre 1982 *Area:* 58,59 km2
Comté ou district: Les Chenaux; *Population au 2006:* 1,566
Circonscription(s) électorale(s) provinciale(s): Champlain
Circonscription(s) électorale(s) fédérale(s):
St-Maurice-Champlain
Prochaines élections: 3e novembre 2013
Jean-Robert Barnes, Maire
Jean Houde, Directeur général

Champneuf
12, 6e av nord
Champneuf, QC J0Y 1E0
Tél: 819-754-2053; *Téléc:* 819-754-5749
munichampneuf@cableamos.com
Entité municipal: Municipality
Incorporation: 1er janvier 1964 *Area:* 241,38 km2
Comté ou district: Abitibi; *Population au 2006:* 130
Circonscription(s) électorale(s) provinciale(s): Abitibi-Ouest
Circonscription(s) électorale(s) fédérale(s):
Abitibi-Témiscamingue
Prochaines élections: 3e novembre 2013
Rosaire Guénette, Maire
Josée Beauregard, Directrice générale

Chandler
CP 459
35, rue Commerciale ouest
Chandler, QC G0C 1K0
Tél: 418-689-2221; *Téléc:* 418-689-3073
hdvchan@globetrotter.net
www.villedechandler.com
Entité municipal: Town
Incorporation: 27 juin 2001 *Area:* 424,90 km2
Comté ou district: Le Rocher-Percé; *Population au 2006:* 7,914
Circonscription(s) électorale(s) provinciale(s): Gaspé
Circonscription(s) électorale(s) fédérale(s):
Gaspésie—Îles-de-la-Madeleine
Prochaines élections: 3e novembre 2013
Louisette Langlois, Mairesse
Roch Giroux, Greffier et Directeur général

Chapais
CP 380
145, boul Springer
Chapais, QC G0W 1H0
Tél: 418-745-2511; *Téléc:* 418-745-3871
villedechapais@lino.com
www.villedechapais.com
Entité municipal: Village
Incorporation: 16 novembre 1955 *Area:* 62,78 km2
Population au 2006: 1,630
Circonscription(s) électorale(s) provinciale(s): Ungava
Circonscription(s) électorale(s) fédérale(s):
Abitibi-Baie-James-Nunavik-Eeyou
Prochaines élections: 3e novembre 2013
Steve Gamache, Maire
Yves Blackburn, Greffier

Charette
390, rue St-Édouard
Charette, QC G0X 1E0
Tél: 819-221-2095; *Téléc:* 819-221-3493
municipalitecharette@sogetel.net
Entité municipal: Municipality
Incorporation: 9e février 1918 *Area:* 42,55 km2
Comté ou district: Maskinongé; *Population au 2006:* 924
Circonscription(s) électorale(s) provinciale(s): Maskinongé
Circonscription(s) électorale(s) fédérale(s): Berthier-Maskinongé
Prochaines élections: 3e novembre 2013
Guy Diamond, Maire
Danielle D. Villemure, Directeur général

Charlemagne
84, rue du Sacré-Coeur
Charlemagne, QC J5Z 1W8
Tél: 450-581-2541; *Téléc:* 450-581-0597
info@ville.charlemagne.qc.ca
www.ville.charlemagne.qc.ca
Entité municipal: Town
Incorporation: 13 novembre 1906 *Area:* 1,95 km2
Comté ou district: L'Assomption; *Population au 2006:* 5,594
Circonscription(s) électorale(s) provinciale(s): Masson
Circonscription(s) électorale(s) fédérale(s): Repentigny
Prochaines élections: 3e novembre 2013
Normand Grenier, Maire
Bernard Boudreau, Greffier et Directeur général

Charlevoix
#201, 4, place de l'Église
Baie-Saint-Paul, QC G3Z 1T2
Tél: 418-435-2639; *Téléc:* 418-435-2666
mrc@charlevoix.net
www.mrc-charlevoix.com
Entité municipal: Regional County Municipality
Incorporation: 1er janvier 1982
Population au 2006: 13,190
Note: 6 municipalités & 1 autre territoire.
Dominic Tremblay, Préfet
Karine Horvath, Directrice générale

Charlevoix-Est
172, boul Notre-Dame
Clermont, QC G4A 1G1
Tél: 418-439-3947; *Téléc:* 418-439-2502
direction@mrccharlevoixest.ca
www.mrccharlevoixest.ca
Entité municipal: Regional County Municipality
Incorporation: 1er janvier 1982
Population au 2006: 16,372
Note: 7 municipalités & 2 autres territoires.
Jean-Luc Simard, Préfet
Pierre Girard, Directeur général

Chartierville
27, rue St-Jean-Baptiste
Chartierville, QC J0B 1K0
Tél: 819-560-8522; *Téléc:* 819-560-8523
chartierville@hsfqc.ca
www.chartierville.ca
Entité municipal: Municipality
Incorporation: 1er janvier 1879 *Area:* 139,13 km2
Comté ou district: Le Haut-St-François; *Population au 2006:* 378
Circonscription(s) électorale(s) provinciale(s):
Mégantic-Compton
Circonscription(s) électorale(s) fédérale(s): Compton-Stanstead
Prochaines élections: 3e novembre 2013
Jean Belhumeur, Maire
Maryse Prud'homme, Directrice générale

Château-Richer
8006, av Royale
Château-Richer, QC G0A 1N0
Tél: 418-824-4294; *Téléc:* 418-824-3277
chateau.richer@videotron.ca
www.chateauricher.qc.ca
Entité municipal: Town
Incorporation: 1er juillet 1855 *Area:* 228,99 km2
Comté ou district: La Côte-de-Beaupré; *Population au 2006:* 3,563
Circonscription(s) électorale(s) provinciale(s): Montmorency
Circonscription(s) électorale(s) fédérale(s):
Montmorency-Charlevoix-Haute-Côte-Nord
Prochaines élections: 3e novembre 2013
Frédéric Dancause, Maire
Lucie Gagnon, Greffière

Chazel
752, 1er Avenue ouest
Chazel, QC J0Z 1N0
Tél: 819-333-4758; *Téléc:* 819-333-3818
chazel@mrcao.qc.ca
www.chazel.ao.ca
Entité municipal: Municipality
Incorporation: 19 février 1938 *Area:* 134,57 km2
Comté ou district: Abitibi-Ouest; *Population au 2006:* 321
Circonscription(s) électorale(s) provinciale(s): Abitibi-Ouest
Circonscription(s) électorale(s) fédérale(s):
Abitibi-Témiscamingue
Prochaines élections: 3e novembre 2013
Daniel Favreau, Maire
Sandra Baillargeon, Directrice générale

Chelsea
100, ch d'Old Chelsea
Chelsea, QC J9B 1C1
Tél: 819-827-1124; *Téléc:* 819-827-2672
info@chelsea.ca
www.chelsea.ca
Entité municipal: Municipality
Incorporation: 1er janvier 1875 *Area:* 111,2 km2
Comté ou district: Les Collines-de-l'Outaouais; *Population au 2006:* 6,703
Circonscription(s) électorale(s) provinciale(s): Gatineau
Circonscription(s) électorale(s) fédérale(s): Pontiac
Prochaines élections: 3e novembre 2013
Caryl Green, Maire
Paul St-Louis, Directeur général

Chénéville
63, rue de l'Hôtel-de-Ville
Chénéville, QC J0V 1E0
Tél: 819-428-3583; *Téléc:* 819-428-4838
adm.cheneville@mrcpapineau.com
www.ville.cheneville.qc.ca
Entité municipal: Municipality
Incorporation: 21 août 1996 *Area:* 65,22 km2
Comté ou district: Papineau; *Population au 2006:* 784
Circonscription(s) électorale(s) provinciale(s): Papineau
Circonscription(s) électorale(s) fédérale(s):
Argenteuil-Papineau-Mirabel
Prochaines élections: 3e novembre 2013
Gilles Tremblay, Maire

Suzanne Prévost, Directrice générale

Chertsey
333, av de l'Amitié
Chertsey, QC J0K 3K0
Tél: 450-882-2920; *Téléc:* 450-882-3333
general@municipalite.chertsey.qc.ca
www.municipalite.chertsey.qc.ca
Entité municipal: Municipality
Incorporation: 13 novembre 1991 *Area:* 313,22 km2
Comté ou district: Matawinie; *Population au 2006:* 5,006
Circonscription(s) électorale(s) provinciale(s): Bertrand
Circonscription(s) électorale(s) fédérale(s): Joliette
Prochaines élections: 3e novembre 2013
Jocelyn Gravel, Maire
Pierre Mercier, Directeur général

Chesterville
472, rue de l'Accueil
Chesterville, QC G0P 1J0
Tél: 819-382-2059; *Téléc:* 819-382-2073
info@municipalite.chesterville.qc.ca
Entité municipal: Municipality
Incorporation: 18 décembre 1982 *Area:* 114,89 km2
Comté ou district: Arthabaska; *Population au 2006:* 894
Circonscription(s) électorale(s) provinciale(s): Arthabaska
Circonscription(s) électorale(s) fédérale(s):
Richmond-Arthabaska
Prochaines élections: 3e novembre 2013
Louis Lafleur, Maire
Lise Setlakwe, Directrice générale

Chibougamau
650, 3e rue
Chibougamau, QC G8P 1P1
Tél: 418-748-2688; *Téléc:* 418-748-6562
directiongenerale@ville.chibougamau.qc.ca
www.ville.chibougamau.qc.ca
Entité municipal: Town
Incorporation: 8e novembre 1952 *Area:* 1,041,97 km2
Population au 2006: 7,563
Circonscription(s) électorale(s) provinciale(s): Ungava
Circonscription(s) électorale(s) fédérale(s):
Abitibi-Baie-James-Nunavik-Eeyou
Prochaines élections: 3e novembre 2013
Manon Cyr, Maire
Mario Asselin, Greffier

Chichester
CP 158
75, rue Notre-Dame
Chapeau, QC J0X 1M0
Tél: 819-689-2266; *Téléc:* 819-689-5619
chichester@mrcpontiac.qc.ca
Entité municipal: Township
Incorporation: 1er janvier 1857 *Area:* 225,71 km2
Comté ou district: Pontiac; *Population au 2006:* 388
Circonscription(s) électorale(s) provinciale(s): Pontiac
Circonscription(s) électorale(s) fédérale(s): Pontiac
Prochaines élections: 3e novembre 2013
Donald Gagnon, Maire
Richard Vaillancourt, Directeur général

Chisasibi
CP 150
1, rue Riverside
Chisasibi, QC J0M 1E0
Tél: 819-855-2878; *Téléc:* 819-855-2875
kanatewat4@hotmail.com
www.chisasibi.ca
Entité municipal: Villages Cris
Incorporation: 28 juin 1978 *Area:* 500,20 km2
Population au 2006: 3,972
Circonscription(s) électorale(s) provinciale(s): Ungava
Circonscription(s) électorale(s) fédérale(s):
Abitibi-Baie-James-Nunavik-Eeyou
Prochaines élections: 14 octobre 2010
Roderick Pachanos, Maire
Nellie Pashagumeskum, Secrétaire

Chute-aux-Outardes
2, rue de l'École
Chute-aux-Outardes, QC G0H 1C0
Tél: 418-567-2144; *Téléc:* 418-567-4478
directeur@municao.com
www.mrcmanicouagan.qc.ca
Entité municipal: Village
Incorporation: 7e mars 1951 *Area:* 8,31 km2
Comté ou district: Manicouagan; *Population au 2006:* 1,853
Circonscription(s) électorale(s) provinciale(s): René-Lévesque
Circonscription(s) électorale(s) fédérale(s): Manicouagan
Prochaines élections: 3e novembre 2013
Arlette Girard, Mairesse
Rick Tanguay, Directeur général

Chute-Saint-Philippe
592, ch du Progrès
Chute-Saint-Philippe, QC J0W 1A0
Tél: 819-585-3397; *Téléc:* 819-585-4949
dg@chute-saint-philippe.ca
www.chute-saint-philippe.ca
Entité municipal: Municipality
Incorporation: 26 octobre 1940 *Area:* 282,28 km2
Comté ou district: Antoine-Labelle; *Population au 2006:* 890
Circonscription(s) électorale(s) provinciale(s): Labelle
Circonscription(s) électorale(s) fédérale(s): Laurentides-Labelle
Prochaines élections: 3e novembre 2013
Normand St-Amour, Maire
Ginette Ippersiel, Directrice générale

Clarendon
CP 777
C427, rte 148
Shawville, QC J0X 2Y0
Tél: 819-647-3862; *Téléc:* 819-647-3822
clarendon@mrcpontiac.qc.ca
Entité municipal: Municipality
Incorporation: 1er juillet 1855 *Area:* 327,27 km2
Comté ou district: Pontiac; *Population au 2006:* 1,248
Circonscription(s) électorale(s) provinciale(s): Pontiac
Circonscription(s) électorale(s) fédérale(s): Pontiac
Prochaines élections: 3e novembre 2013
John A. Lang, Maire
Ruth Potter Strutt, Directrice générale

Clermont
722, ch des 4e-et-5e-Rangs est
Saint-Vital-de-Clermont, QC J0Z 3M0
Tél: 819-333-6129; *Téléc:* 819-333-3811
clermont@mrcao.qc.ca
www.clermont.ao.ca
Entité municipal: Township
Incorporation: 4e mars 1936 *Area:* 155,89 km2
Comté ou district: Abitibi-Ouest; *Population au 2006:* 534
Circonscription(s) électorale(s) provinciale(s): Abitibi-Ouest
Circonscription(s) électorale(s) fédérale(s):
Abitibi-Témiscamingue
Prochaines élections: 3e novembre 2013
Robert Paquette, Maire
Mélissa Caron, Directrice générale

Clermont
2, rue Maisonneuve
Clermont, QC G4A 1G6
Tél: 418-439-3931; *Téléc:* 418-439-4889
info@ville.clermont.qc.ca
www.ville.clermont.qc.ca
Entité municipal: Town
Incorporation: 16 février 1935 *Area:* 52,99 km2
Comté ou district: Charlevoix-Est; *Population au 2006:* 3,041
Circonscription(s) électorale(s) provinciale(s): Charlevoix
Circonscription(s) électorale(s) fédérale(s):
Montmorency-Charlevoix-Haute-Côte-Nord
Prochaines élections: 3e novembre 2013
Jean-Pierre Gagnon, Maire
Brigitte Harvey, Directrice générale

Clerval
579, 2e rang
Clerval, QC J0Z 1R0
Tél: 819-783-2640; *Téléc:* 819-783-4001
clerval@mrcao.qc.ca
www.clerval.ao.ca
Entité municipal: Municipality
Incorporation: 12 septembre 1927 *Area:* 101,60 km2
Comté ou district: Abitibi-Ouest; *Population au 2006:* 358
Circonscription(s) électorale(s) provinciale(s): Abitibi-Ouest
Circonscription(s) électorale(s) fédérale(s):
Abitibi-Témiscamingue
Prochaines élections: 3e novembre 2013
Suzanne Théberge, Maire
Marielle Gauthier, Directrice générale

Cleveland
292, ch de la Rivière
Cleveland, QC J0B 2H0
Tél: 819-826-3546; *Téléc:* 819-826-2827
cleveland.dir.gen@b2b2c.ca
Entité municipal: Township
Incorporation: 1er juillet 1855 *Area:* 120,82 km2
Comté ou district: Le Val-St-François; *Population au 2006:* 1,590
Circonscription(s) électorale(s) provinciale(s): Richmond
Circonscription(s) électorale(s) fédérale(s):
Richmond-Arthabaska
Prochaines élections: 3e novembre 2013
Pierre Grandmont, Maire
Claudette Lapointe, Directrice générale

Cloridorme
CP 253
472, rte 132
Cloridorme, QC G0E 1G0
Tél: 418-395-2808; *Téléc:* 418-395-2228
dgclori@globetrotter.net
canton-de-cloridorme.com
Entité municipal: Township
Incorporation: 1er janvier 1885 *Area:* 162,10 km2
Comté ou district: La Côte-de-Gaspé; *Population au 2006:* 764
Circonscription(s) électorale(s) provinciale(s): Gaspé
Circonscription(s) électorale(s) fédérale(s):
Gaspésie—Îles-de-la-Madeleine
Prochaines élections: 3e novembre 2013
Jocelyne Huet, Mairesse
Marie Dufresne, Directrice générale

Coaticook
294, rue St-Jacques nord
Coaticook, QC J1A 2R3
Tél: 819-849-9166; *Téléc:* 819-849-4320
secretariat@mrcdecoaticook.qc.ca
www.mrcdecoaticook.qc.ca
Entité municipal: Regional County Municipality
Incorporation: 1er janvier 1982
Population au 2006: 18,467
Note: 12 municipalités.
Réjean Masson, Préfet
secretariat@mrcdecoaticook.qc.ca
Sylvie Harvey, Directrice générale
direction@mrcdecoaticook.qc.ca

Coaticook
150, rue Child
Coaticook, QC J1A 2B3
Tél: 819-849-2721; *Téléc:* 819-849-9669
hoteldeville@ville.coaticook.qc.ca
www.ville.coaticook.qc.ca
Entité municipal: Town
Incorporation: 30 décembre 1998 *Area:* 218,89 km2
Comté ou district: Coaticook; *Population au 2006:* 9,204
Circonscription(s) électorale(s) provinciale(s): St-François
Circonscription(s) électorale(s) fédérale(s): Compton-Stanstead
Prochaines élections: 3e novembre 2013
Bertrand Lamoureux, Maire
administration@ville.coaticook.qc.ca
Luc Marcoux, Conseiller, Ward(s): 1
Sonia Montminy, Conseillère, Ward(s): 2
Sylvain Véronneau, Conseiller, Ward(s): 3
Raynald Drolet, Conseiller, Ward(s): 4
Simon Madore, Conseiller, Ward(s): 5
François Lévesque, Conseiller, Ward(s): 6
Geneviève Dupras, Greffière
819-849-2721, Fax: 819-849-9669
greffe@ville.coaticook.qc.ca
Vincent Tanguay, Directeur général
directeurgeneral@ville.coaticook.qc.ca
Roger Garceau, Trésorier
rogergarceau@ville.coaticook.qc.ca

Colombier
CP 69
568, rue Principale
Colombier, QC G0H 1P0
Tél: 418-565-3343; *Téléc:* 418-565-3289
info@municipalite.colombier.qc.ca
www.municipalite.colombier.qc.ca
Entité municipal: Municipality
Incorporation: 1er janvier 1946 *Area:* 313,20 km2
Comté ou district: La Haute-Côte-Nord; *Population au 2006:* 817
Circonscription(s) électorale(s) provinciale(s): René-Lévesque
Circonscription(s) électorale(s) fédérale(s):
Montmorency-Charlevoix-Haute-Côte-Nord
Prochaines élections: 3e novembre 2013
Jean-Claude Degrace, Maire
Claire Savard, Directrice générale

Compton
3, ch de Hatley
Compton, QC J0B 1L0
Tél: 819-835-5584; *Téléc:* 819-835-5750
muncompton@bellnet.ca
www.compton.ca
Entité municipal: Municipality
Incorporation: 8e décembre 1999 *Area:* 205,72 km2
Comté ou district: Coaticook; *Population au 2006:* 2,818

Circonscription(s) électorale(s) provinciale(s): St-François
Circonscription(s) électorale(s) fédérale(s): Compton-Stanstead
Prochaines élections: 3e novembre 2013
Fernand Veilleux, Maire
Jacques Leblond, Directeur général

Contrecoeur
5000, rte Marie-Victorin
Contrecoeur, QC J0L 1C0
Tél: 450-587-5901; *Téléc:* 450-587-5855
mairie@ville.contrecoeur.qc.ca
www.ville.contrecoeur.qc.ca
Entité municipal: Town
Incorporation: 1er janvier 1976 *Area:* 61,56 km2
Comté ou district: Lajemmerais; *Population au 2006:* 5,678
Circonscription(s) électorale(s) provinciale(s): Verchères
Circonscription(s) électorale(s) fédérale(s): Verchères-Les Patriotes
Prochaines élections: 3e novembre 2013
Suzanne Dansereau, Mairesse
Yves Beaulieu, Directeur général

Cookshire-Eaton
220, rue Principale est
Cookshire, QC J0B 1M0
Tél: 819-560-8585; *Téléc:* 819-875-5311
cookshire-eaton@hsfqc.ca
www.cookshire-eaton.qc.ca
Entité municipal: Town
Incorporation: 24 juillet 2002 *Area:* 297,60 km2
Comté ou district: Le Haut-St-François; *Population au 2006:* 5,004
Circonscription(s) électorale(s) provinciale(s): Mégantic-Compton
Circonscription(s) électorale(s) fédérale(s): Compton-Stanstead
Prochaines élections: 3e novembre 2013
Noël Landry, Maire
Martin Tremblay, Directeur général

Côte-Nord-du-Golfe-du-St-Laurent
Chevery, QC G0G 1G0
Tél: 418-787-2244; *Téléc:* 418-787-2241
mcngsl@xplornet.com
Entité municipal: Municipality
Incorporation: 22 juin 1963 *Area:* 2783,59 km2
Comté ou district: Le Golfe-du-Saint-Laurent; *Population au 2006:* 1,028
Circonscription(s) électorale(s) provinciale(s): Duplessis
Circonscription(s) électorale(s) fédérale(s): Manicouagan
Prochaines élections: 3e novembre 2013
Jacques Lareau, Administrateur (par intérim)

Coteau-du-Lac
342, ch du Fleuve
Coteau-du-Lac, QC J0P 1B0
Tél: 450-763-5822; *Téléc:* 450-763-0938
info@coteau-du-lac.com
www.coteau-du-lac.com
Entité municipal: Municipality
Incorporation: 6e février 1982 *Area:* 46,57 km2
Comté ou district: Vaudreuil-Soulanges; *Population au 2006:* 6,346
Circonscription(s) électorale(s) provinciale(s): Soulanges
Circonscription(s) électorale(s) fédérale(s): Vaudreuil-Soulanges
Prochaines élections: 3e novembre 2013
Robert Sauvé, Maire
Claire Blais, Greffière

Courcelles
CP 160
116, av du Domaine
Courcelles, QC G0M 1C0
Tél: 418-483-5540; *Téléc:* 418-483-3540
municipal@telcourcelles.net
www.muncourcelles.qc.ca
Entité municipal: Parish (Paroisse)
Incorporation: 6e avril 1904 *Area:* 92,25 km2
Comté ou district: Le Granit; *Population au 2006:* 928
Circonscription(s) électorale(s) provinciale(s): Beauce-Sud
Circonscription(s) électorale(s) fédérale(s): Mégantic-L'Érable
Prochaines élections: 3e novembre 2013
Mario Quirion, Maire
Renée Mathieu, Directrice générale

Crabtree
CP 660
111, 4e Av
Crabtree, QC J0K 1B0
Tél: 450-754-3434; *Téléc:* 450-754-2172
info@municipalitecrabtree.qc.ca
www.municipalitecrabtree.qc.ca
Entité municipal: Municipality
Incorporation: 23 octobre 1996 *Area:* 24,71 km2
Comté ou district: Joliette; *Population au 2006:* 3,441
Circonscription(s) électorale(s) provinciale(s): Joliette
Circonscription(s) électorale(s) fédérale(s): Joliette
Prochaines élections: 3er novembre 2013
Denis Laporte, Maire
Pierre Rondeau, Directeur général

D'Autray
CP 1500
550, rue De Montcalm
Berthierville, QC J0K 1A0
Tél: 450-836-7007; *Téléc:* 450-836-1576
mrcautray@mrcautray.com
www.mrcautray.com
Entité municipal: Regional County Municipality
Incorporation: 1er janvier
Population au 2006: 40,321
Note: 15 municipalités.
Gaétan Gravel, Préfet
Danielle Joyal, Directrice générale

Danville
CP 310
150, rue Water
Danville, QC J0A 1A0
Tél: 819-839-2771; *Téléc:* 819-839-2918
info@villededanville.com
www.villededanville.com
Entité municipal: Town
Incorporation: 17 mars 1999 *Area:* 149,51 km2
Comté ou district: Les Sources; *Population au 2006:* 4,041
Circonscription(s) électorale(s) provinciale(s): Richmond
Circonscription(s) électorale(s) fédérale(s): Richmond-Arthabaska
Prochaines élections: 3e novembre 2013
Jacques Hémond, Maire
Michel Lecours, Directeur général

Daveluyville
CP 187
337, rue Principale
Daveluyville, QC G0Z 1C0
Tél: 819-367-3395; *Téléc:* 819-367-3550
info@ville.daveluyville.qc.ca
www.ville.daveluyville.qc.ca
Entité municipal: Village
Incorporation: 13 novembre 1901 *Area:* 2,25 km2
Comté ou district: Arthabaska; *Population au 2006:* 1,005
Circonscription(s) électorale(s) provinciale(s): Nicolet-Yamaska
Circonscription(s) électorale(s) fédérale(s): Richmond-Arthabaska
Prochaines élections: 3e novembre 2013
Réal Savoie, Directeur général
Gilles Labarre, Maire

Dégelis
369, av Principale
Dégelis, QC G5T 2G3
Tél: 418-853-2332; *Téléc:* 418-853-3464
info@ville.degelis.qc.ca
www.ville.degelis.qc.ca
Entité municipal: Town
Incorporation: 13 décembre 1969 *Area:* 562,84 km2
Comté ou district: Témiscouata; *Population au 2006:* 3,209
Circonscription(s) électorale(s) provinciale(s): Kamouraska-Témiscouata
Circonscription(s) électorale(s) fédérale(s): Rimouski-Neigette-Témiscouata-Les Basques
Prochaines élections: 3e novembre 2013
Claude Lavoie, Maire
Bernard Caron, Directeur général

Déléage
175, rte 107, RR#1
Déléage, QC J9E 3A8
Tél: 819-449-1979; *Téléc:* 819-449-7441
reception@deleage.ca
www.deleage.ca
Entité municipal: Municipality
Incorporation: 1er janvier 1881 *Area:* 249,44 km2
Comté ou district: La Vallée-de-la-Gatineau; *Population au 2006:* 1,964
Circonscription(s) électorale(s) provinciale(s): Gatineau
Circonscription(s) électorale(s) fédérale(s): Pontiac
Prochaines élections: 3e novembre 2013
Jean-Paul Barbe, Maire
Emmanuelle Michaud, Directrice générale

Delson
50, rue Ste-Thérèse
Delson, QC J5B 2B2
Tél: 450-632-1050; *Téléc:* 450-632-1571
info@ville.delson.qc.ca
www.ville.delson.qc.ca
Entité municipal: Town
Incorporation: 4e janvier 1918 *Area:* 7,76 km2
Comté ou district: Roussillon; *Population au 2006:* 7,322
Circonscription(s) électorale(s) provinciale(s): La Prairie
Circonscription(s) électorale(s) fédérale(s): Châteauguay-St-Constant
Prochaines élections: 3e novembre 2013
Gilles Meloche, Maire
Nicole Lafontaine, Greffière

Denholm
419, ch du Poisson-Blanc
Denholm, QC J8N 9C8
Tél: 819-457-2992; *Téléc:* 819-457-9862
info@municipalite.denholm.qc.ca
www.mundenholm.com
Entité municipal: Municipality
Incorporation: 27 février 1924 *Area:* 191,65 km2
Comté ou district: La Vallée-de-la-Gatineau; *Population au 2006:* 604
Circonscription(s) électorale(s) provinciale(s): Gatineau
Circonscription(s) électorale(s) fédérale(s): Pontiac
Prochaines élections: 3e novembre 2013
Pierre Nelson Renaud, Maire
Sandra Bélisle, Directrice générale

Des Sources
309, rue Chassé
Asbestos, QC J1T 2B4
Tél: 819-879-6643; *Téléc:* 819-879-5188
mrcdessources@mrcdessources.com
www.mrcdessources.com
Entité municipal: Regional County Municipality
Incorporation: 1er janvier 1982
Population au 2006: 14,466
Note: 7 municipalités.
Jacques Hémond, Préfet
Yvan Provencher, Directeur général

Desbiens
CP 9
925, rue Hébert
Desbiens, QC G0W 1N0
Tél: 418-346-5571; *Téléc:* 418-346-5422
administration@ville.desbiens.qc.ca
www.ville.desbiens.qc.ca
Entité municipal: Village
Incorporation: 16 août 1926 *Area:* 10,35 km2
Comté ou district: Lac-St-Jean-Est; *Population au 2006:* 1,074
Circonscription(s) électorale(s) provinciale(s): Lac-St-Jean
Circonscription(s) électorale(s) fédérale(s): Roberval-Lac-St-Jean
Prochaines élections: 3e novembre 2013
Nicolas Martel, Maire
Michaël Gagnon, Directeur général

Deschaillons-sur-St-Laurent
1596, rte Marie-Victorin
Deschaillons-sur-Saint-Laurent, QC G0S 1G0
Tél: 819-292-2085; *Téléc:* 819-292-3194
mun.deschaillons@qc.aira.com
Entité municipal: Municipality
Incorporation: 23 mai 1990 *Area:* 37,70 km2
Comté ou district: Bécancour; *Population au 2006:* 1,009
Circonscription(s) électorale(s) provinciale(s): Lotbinière
Circonscription(s) électorale(s) fédérale(s): Bas-Richelieu-Nicolet-Bécancour
Prochaines élections: 3e novembre 2013
Christian Baril, Maire
France Grimard, Directrice générale

Deschambault-Grondines
CP 220
120, rue St-Joseph
Deschambault, QC G0A 1S0
Tél: 418-286-4511; *Téléc:* 418-286-6511
deschambault@csportneuf.qc.ca
www.municipalite.deschambault.qc.ca
Entité municipal: Municipality
Incorporation: 27 février 2002 *Area:* 123,60 km2
Comté ou district: Portneuf; *Population au 2006:* 2,032
Circonscription(s) électorale(s) provinciale(s): Portneuf
Circonscription(s) électorale(s) fédérale(s): Portneuf-Jacques-Cartier
Prochaines élections: 3e novembre 2013
Gaston Arcand, Maire

Claire St-Arnaud, Directrice générale

Deux-Montagnes
1, place de la Gare
Saint-Eustache, QC J7R 0B4
Tél: 450-491-1818; *Téléc:* 450-491-3040
info@mrc2m.qc.ca
Entité municipal: Regional County Municipality
Incorporation: 1er janvier 1983
Population au 2006: 87,249
Note: 7 municipalités.
Marc Lauzon, Préfet
Nicole Loiselle, Directrice générale

Disraéli
550, av Jacques-Cartier
Disraéli, QC G0N 1E0
Tél: 418-449-2771; *Téléc:* 418-449-4299
hoteldeville@villededisraeli.com
www.villededisraeli.com
Entité municipal: Town
Incorporation: 19 novembre 1904 *Area:* 6,470 km2
Comté ou district: Les Appalaches; *Population au 2006:* 2,564
Circonscription(s) électorale(s) provinciale(s): Frontenac
Circonscription(s) électorale(s) fédérale(s): Mégantic-L'Érable
Prochaines élections: 3e novembre 2013
André Rodrigue, Maire
Francyne Gagné, Directrice générale

Disraéli
8306, rte 112
Disraéli, QC G0N 1E0
Tél: 418-449-5329; *Téléc:* 418-449-5459
paroissedisraeli@tlb.sympatico.ca
www.paroissedisraeli.com
Entité municipal: Parish (Paroisse)
Incorporation: 1er janvier 1883 *Area:* 93,880 km2
Comté ou district: Les Appalaches; *Population au 2006:* 1,055
Circonscription(s) électorale(s) provinciale(s): Frontenac
Circonscription(s) électorale(s) fédérale(s): Mégantic-L'Érable
Prochaines élections: 3e novembre 2013
André Gosselin, Maire
Caroline Picard, Directrice générale

Dixville
251, rue Parker
Dixville, QC J0B 1P0
Tél: 819-849-3037; *Téléc:* 819-849-9520
bureaumunicipal@dixville.ca
www.dixville.ca
Entité municipal: Municipality
Incorporation: 27 septembre 1995 *Area:* 76,17 km2
Comté ou district: Coaticook; *Population au 2006:* 685
Circonscription(s) électorale(s) provinciale(s):
Mégantic-Compton
Circonscription(s) électorale(s) fédérale(s): Compton-Stanstead
Prochaines élections: 3e novembre 2013
Réal Ouimette, Maire
Mary Brus, Directrice générale

Donnacona
138, av Pleau
Donnacona, QC G3M 1A1
Tél: 418-285-0110; *Téléc:* 418-285-0020
naudb@villededonnaconna.com
www.villededonnacona.com
Entité municipal: Town
Incorporation: 21 janvier 1967 *Area:* 20,12 km2
Comté ou district: Portneuf; *Population au 2006:* 5,564
Circonscription(s) électorale(s) provinciale(s): Portneuf
Circonscription(s) électorale(s) fédérale(s):
Portneuf-Jacques-Cartier
Prochaines élections: 3e novembre 2013
Sylvain Germain, Maire
Pierre-Luc Gignac, Greffier

Dosquet
183, rte St-Joseph
Dosquet, QC G0S 1H0
Tél: 418-728-3653; *Téléc:* 418-728-3338
mundosquet@videotron.ca
www.municipalitededosquet.com
Entité municipal: Municipality
Incorporation: 9e février 1918 *Area:* 67,26 km2
Comté ou district: Lotbinière; *Population au 2006:* 907
Circonscription(s) électorale(s) provinciale(s): Lotbinière
Circonscription(s) électorale(s) fédérale(s):
Lotbinière-Chutes-de-la-Chaudière
Prochaines élections: 3e novembre 2013
Yvan Charest, Maire
Paul Fillion, Directeur général

Drummond
436, rue Lindsay
Drummondville, QC J2B 1G6
Tél: 819-477-2230; *Téléc:* 819-477-8442
courriel@mrcdrummond.qc.ca
www.mrcdrummond.qc.ca
Entité municipal: Regional County Municipality
Incorporation: 1er janvier 1982
Population au 2006: 92,982
Note: 18 municipalités.
Francine Ruest Jutras, Préfète
Michel Gagnon, Directeur général
mgagnon@mrcdrummond.qc.ca

Dudswell
76, rue Main
Bishopton, QC J0B 1G0
Tél: 819-560-8484; *Téléc:* 819-884-5777
helene.leroux@hsfqc.ca
Entité municipal: Municipality
Incorporation: 11 octobre 1995 *Area:* 214,76 km2
Comté ou district: Le Haut-St-François; *Population au 2006:* 1,712
Circonscription(s) électorale(s) provinciale(s):
Mégantic-Compton
Circonscription(s) électorale(s) fédérale(s): Compton-Stanstead
Prochaines élections: 3e novembre 2013
Claude Corriveau, Maire
Hélène Leroux, Directrice générale

Duhamel
1890, rue Principale
Duhamel, QC J0V 1G0
Tél: 819-428-7100; *Téléc:* 819-428-1941
dg.duhamel@mrcpapineau.com
www.municipalite.duhamel.qc.ca
Entité municipal: Municipality
Incorporation: 15 août 1936 *Area:* 449,45 km2
Comté ou district: Papineau; *Population au 2006:* 483
Circonscription(s) électorale(s) provinciale(s): Papineau
Circonscription(s) électorale(s) fédérale(s):
Argenteuil-Papineau-Mirabel
Prochaines élections: 3e novembre 2013
David Pharand, Maire
Claire Dinel, Directrice générale

Duhamel-Ouest
361, rte 101 sud
Duhamel-Ouest, QC J9V 1A2
Tél: 819-629-2522; *Téléc:* 819-629-2422
duhamel.ouest@mrctemiscamingue.qc.ca
Entité municipal: Municipality
Incorporation: 20 février 1911 *Area:* 127,61 km2
Comté ou district: Témiscamingue; *Population au 2006:* 870
Circonscription(s) électorale(s) provinciale(s):
Rouyn-Noranda-Témiscamingue
Circonscription(s) électorale(s) fédérale(s):
Abitibi-Témiscamingue
Prochaines élections: 3e novembre 2013
Alain Sarrazin, Maire
Lise Perron, Directrice générale

Dundee
3296, montée Smallman
Dundee, QC J0S 1L0
Tél: 450-264-4674; *Téléc:* 450-264-8044
mun.dundee@sftl.ca
Entité municipal: Township
Incorporation: 1er juillet 1855 *Area:* 94,20 km2
Comté ou district: Le Haut-St-Laurent; *Population au 2006:* 436
Circonscription(s) électorale(s) provinciale(s): Huntingdon
Circonscription(s) électorale(s) fédérale(s):
Beauharnois-Salaberry
Prochaines élections: 3e novembre 2013
Jean Armstrong, Maire
Stéphan Landry, Directeur général

Dunham
CP 70
3777, rue Principale
Dunham, QC J0E 1M0
Tél: 450-295-2418; *Téléc:* 450-295-2182
info@ville.dunham.qc.ca
www.ville.dunham.qc.ca
Entité municipal: Town
Incorporation: 25 septembre 1971 *Area:* 200,99 km2
Comté ou district: Brome-Missisquoi; *Population au 2006:* 3,396
Circonscription(s) électorale(s) provinciale(s): Brome-Missisquoi
Circonscription(s) électorale(s) fédérale(s): Brome-Missisquoi
Prochaines élections: 3e novembre 2013
Jean Guy Demers, Maire
Pierre Loiselle, Greffier

Duparquet
86, rue Principale
Duparquet, QC J0Z 1W0
Tél: 819-948-2266; *Téléc:* 819-948-2466
duparquet@mrcao.qc.ca
www.duparquet.ao.ca
Entité municipal: Village
Incorporation: 13 avril 1933 *Area:* 157,40 km2
Comté ou district: Abitibi-Ouest; *Population au 2006:* 639
Circonscription(s) électorale(s) provinciale(s): Abitibi-Ouest
Circonscription(s) électorale(s) fédérale(s):
Abitibi-Témiscamingue
Prochaines élections: 3e novembre 2013
Gilbert Rivard, Maire
Jacques Taillefer, Greffier

Dupuy
2, av du Chemin-de-Fer
Dupuy, QC J0Z 1X0
Tél: 819-783-2595; *Téléc:* 819-783-2192
dupuy@mrcao.qc.ca
www.dupuy.ao.ca
Entité municipal: Municipality
Incorporation: 20 septembre 1918 *Area:* 123,48 km2
Comté ou district: Abitibi-Ouest; *Population au 2006:* 955
Circonscription(s) électorale(s) provinciale(s): Abitibi-Ouest
Circonscription(s) électorale(s) fédérale(s):
Abitibi-Témiscamingue
Prochaines élections: 3e novembre 2013
Marc-André Côté, Maire
Pascale Lavigne, Greffière

Durham-Sud
CP 70
70, rue de l'Hôtel-de-Ville
Durham-Sud, QC J0H 2C0
Tél: 819-858-2044; *Téléc:* 819-858-2044
mun@durham-sud.com
www.durham-sud.com
Entité municipal: Municipality
Incorporation: 1er novembre 1975 *Area:* 92,02 km2
Comté ou district: Drummond; *Population au 2006:* 1,018
Circonscription(s) électorale(s) provinciale(s): Johnson
Circonscription(s) électorale(s) fédérale(s): Drummond
Prochaines élections: 3e novembre 2013
Michel Noël, Maire
Christiane Bastien, Directrice générale

East Broughton
600, 10e av sud
East Broughton, QC G0N 1H0
Tél: 418-427-2608; *Téléc:* 418-427-3414
municipaliteeastbroughton@bellnet.ca
Entité municipal: Municipality
Incorporation: 5e janvier 1994 *Area:* 9,310 km2
Comté ou district: Les Appalaches; *Population au 2006:* 2,351
Circonscription(s) électorale(s) provinciale(s): Frontenac
Circonscription(s) électorale(s) fédérale(s): Mégantic-L'Érable
Prochaines élections: 3e novembre 2013
Kaven Mathieu, Maire
Normand Laplante, Directeur général

East Farnham
228, rue Principale
East Farnham, QC J2K 4T5
Tél: 450-263-4252; *Téléc:* 450-263-6131
eastfarnham@videotron.ca
www.municipalite.eastfarnham.qc.ca
Entité municipal: Village
Incorporation: 27 août 1914 *Area:* 5,29 km2
Comté ou district: Brome-Missisquoi; *Population au 2006:* 484
Circonscription(s) électorale(s) provinciale(s): Brome-Missisquoi
Circonscription(s) électorale(s) fédérale(s): Brome-Missisquoi
Prochaines élections: 3e novembre 2013
Sylvie D.-Raymond, Mairesse
Madelyn Marcoux, Directrice générale

East Hereford
15, rue de l'Église
East Hereford, QC J0B 1S0
Tél: 819-844-2463; *Téléc:* 819-844-2463
dlrioux@municipalite.easthereford.qc.ca
www.municipalite.easthereford.qc.ca
Entité municipal: Municipality
Incorporation: 1er juillet 1855 *Area:* 71,56 km2
Comté ou district: Coaticook; *Population au 2006:* 401
Circonscription(s) électorale(s) provinciale(s):
Mégantic-Compton
Circonscription(s) électorale(s) fédérale(s): Compton-Stanstead
Prochaines élections: 3e novembre 2013
Richard Belleville, Maire
Diane Lauzon-Rioux, Directrice générale

East-Angus
49, rue Angus nord
East Angus, QC J0B 1R0
Tél: 819-560-8600; *Téléc:* 819-560-8611
info.eastangus@hsfqc.ca
www.ville.east-angus.qc.ca
Entité municipal: Town
Incorporation: 14 mars 1912 *Area:* 8,10 km2
Comté ou district: Le Haut-St-François; *Population au 2006:* 3,357
Circonscription(s) électorale(s) provinciale(s): Mégantic-Compton
Circonscription(s) électorale(s) fédérale(s): Compton-Stanstead
Prochaines élections: 3e novembre 2013
Robert G. Roy, Maire
Normand Graillon, Directeur général

Eastmain
147, Shabow Meskino
Eastmain, QC J0M 1W0
Tél: 819-977-0211; *Téléc:* 819-977-0281
Entité municipal: Villages Cris
Incorporation: 28 juin 1978 *Area:* 334,70 km2
Population au 2006: 650
Circonscription(s) électorale(s) provinciale(s): Ungava
Circonscription(s) électorale(s) fédérale(s): Abitibi-Baie-James-Nunavik-Eeyou
Prochaines élections: 3e novembre 2013
Rusty Cheezo, Maire
Vacant, Trésorier

Eastman
160, ch George-Bonnallie
Eastman, QC J0E 1P0
Tél: 450-297-3440; *Téléc:* 450-297-3448
municipaliteeastman@bellnet.ca
www.muneastman.ca
Entité municipal: Municipality
Incorporation: 30 mai 2001 *Area:* 68,87 km2
Comté ou district: Memphrémagog; *Population au 2006:* 1,585
Circonscription(s) électorale(s) provinciale(s): Brome-Missisquoi
Circonscription(s) électorale(s) fédérale(s): Brome-Missisquoi
Prochaines élections: 3e novembre 2013
Gérard Marinovich, Maire
Caroline Rioux, Directrice générale

Egan-Sud
95, rte 105
Egan-Sud, QC J9E 3A9
Tél: 819-449-1702; *Téléc:* 819-449-7423
mun.egansud@ireseau.com
Entité municipal: Municipality
Incorporation: 17 novembre 1920 *Area:* 50,67 km2
Comté ou district: La Vallée-de-la-Gatineau; *Population au 2006:* 508
Circonscription(s) électorale(s) provinciale(s): Gatineau
Circonscription(s) électorale(s) fédérale(s): Pontiac
Prochaines élections: 3e novembre 2013
Neil Gagnon, Maire
Mariette Rochon, Directrice générale

Elgin
933,ch de la 2e Concession
Elgin, QC J0S 2E0
Tél: 450-264-2320; *Téléc:* 450-264-6846
munelgindir.gen@targo.ca
Entité municipal: Township
Incorporation: 1er juillet 1855 *Area:* 69,38 km2
Comté ou district: Le Haut-St-Laurent; *Population au 2006:* 458
Circonscription(s) électorale(s) provinciale(s): Huntingdon
Circonscription(s) électorale(s) fédérale(s): Beauharnois—Salaberry
Prochaines élections: 3e novembre 2013
Deborah Stewart, Mairesse
Danielle Sauvé, Directrice générale

Entrelacs
2351, ch d'Entrelacs
Entrelacs, QC J0T 2E0
Tél: 450-228-2529; *Téléc:* 450-228-4866
info@entrelacs.com
www.entrelacs.com
Entité municipal: Municipality
Incorporation: 1er janvier 1860 *Area:* 51,78 km2
Comté ou district: Matawinie; *Population au 2006:* 952
Circonscription(s) électorale(s) provinciale(s): Bertrand
Circonscription(s) électorale(s) fédérale(s): Joliette
Prochaines élections: 3e novembre 2013
Sylvain Breton, Maire
Ginette Brisebois, Directrice (par intérim)

Escuminac
13, rue de l'Église
Pointe-à-la-Garde, QC G0C 2M0
Tél: 418-788-5644; *Téléc:* 418-788-2613
munescuminac@globetrotter.net
Entité municipal: Municipality
Incorporation: 10 octobre 1907 *Area:* 109,55 km2
Comté ou district: Avignon; *Population au 2006:* 645
Circonscription(s) électorale(s) provinciale(s): Bonaventure
Circonscription(s) électorale(s) fédérale(s): Gaspésie—Îles-de-la-Madeleine
Prochaines élections: 3e novembre 2013
Bertrand Berger, Maire
Sylvie Bossé, Directrice générale

Esprit-Saint
121, rue Principale
Esprit-Saint, QC G0K 1A0
Tél: 418-779-2716; *Téléc:* 418-779-2716
muni.esprit@globetrotter.net
www.municipalite.esprit-saint.qc.ca
Entité municipal: Municipality
Incorporation: 13 mai 1972 *Area:* 169,28 km2
Comté ou district: Rimouski-Neigette; *Population au 2006:* 397
Circonscription(s) électorale(s) provinciale(s): Rimouski
Circonscription(s) électorale(s) fédérale(s): Rimouski-Neigette-Témicouata-Les Basques
Prochaines élections: 3e novembre 2013
Marlène Dubé, Mairesse
Diane Ouellet, Directrice générale

Estérel
115, ch Dupuis
Estérel, QC J0T 1E0
Tél: 450-228-3232; *Téléc:* 450-228-3737
info@villedesterel.com
www.villedesterel.com
Entité municipal: Village
Incorporation: 1er janvier 2006 *Area:* 12,06 km2
Comté ou district: Les Pays-d'en-Haut; *Population au 2006:* 256
Circonscription(s) électorale(s) provinciale(s): Bertrand
Circonscription(s) électorale(s) fédérale(s): Laurentides—Labelle
Prochaines élections: 3e novembre 2013
Jean-Pierre Nepveu, Maire
Luc Lafontaine, Directeur général

Farnham
477, rue de l'Hôtel-de-Ville
Farnham, QC J2N 2H3
Tél: 450-293-3178; *Téléc:* 450-293-2989
administration@ville.farnham.qc.ca
www.ville.farnham.qc.ca
Entité municipal: Town
Incorporation: 8e mars 2000 *Area:* 92,53 km2
Comté ou district: Brome-Missisquoi; *Population au 2006:* 7,809
Circonscription(s) électorale(s) provinciale(s): Brome-Missisquoi
Circonscription(s) électorale(s) fédérale(s): Brome-Missisquoi
Prochaines élections: 3e novembre 2013
Josef Hüsler, Maire
Marielle Benoit, Greffière

Fassett
19, rue Gendron
Fassett, QC J0V 1H0
Tél: 819-423-6943; *Téléc:* 819-423-5388
munfassett@mrcpapineau.com
www.village-fassett.com
Entité municipal: Municipality
Incorporation: 1er juillet 1855 *Area:* 13,98 km2
Comté ou district: Papineau; *Population au 2006:* 468
Circonscription(s) électorale(s) provinciale(s): Papineau
Circonscription(s) électorale(s) fédérale(s): Argenteuil-Papineau-Mirabel
Prochaines élections: 3e novembre 2013
Michel Rioux, Maire
Diane Leduc, Directrice générale

Ferland-et-Boileau
CP 260
461, rte 381
Ferland-et-Boilleau, QC G0V 1H0
Tél: 418-676-2282; *Téléc:* 418-676-3092
municipalite@ferlandetboilleau.com
www.ferlandetboilleau.com
Entité municipal: Municipality
Incorporation: 1er janvier 1978 *Area:* 418,85 km2
Comté ou district: Le Fjord-du-Saguenay; *Population au 2006:* 626
Circonscription(s) électorale(s) provinciale(s): Dubuc
Circonscription(s) électorale(s) fédérale(s): Chicoutimi-Le Fjord
Prochaines élections: 3e novembre 2013
Carmen Simard, Mairesse
Sylvie Gagnon, Directrice générale

Ferme-Neuve
125, 12e rue
Ferme-Neuve, QC J0W 1C0
Tél: 819-587-3400; *Téléc:* 819-587-4733
bureau@municipalite.ferme-neuve.qc.ca
www.municipalite.ferme-neuve.qc.ca
Entité municipal: Municipality
Incorporation: 24 décembre 1997 *Area:* 1031,55 km2
Comté ou district: Antoine-Labelle; *Population au 2006:* 3,006
Circonscription(s) électorale(s) provinciale(s): Labelle
Circonscription(s) électorale(s) fédérale(s): Laurentides-Labelle
Prochaines élections: 3e novembre 2013
Gilbert Pilote, Maire
Normand Bélanger, Directeur général

Fermont
CP 2010
100, place Daviault
Fermont, QC G0G 1J0
Tél: 418-287-5411; *Téléc:* 418-287-5413
administration@villedefermont.qc.ca
www.caniapiscau.net
Entité municipal: Town
Incorporation: 15 octobre 1974 *Area:* 497,45 km2
Comté ou district: Caniapiscau; *Population au 2006:* 2,633
Circonscription(s) électorale(s) provinciale(s): Duplessis
Circonscription(s) électorale(s) fédérale(s): Manicouagan
Prochaines élections: 3er novembre 2013
Lise Pelletier, Mairesse
Carolle Bourque, Greffière

Forestville
1, 2e av
Forestville, QC G0T 1E0
Tél: 418-587-2285; *Téléc:* 418-587-6212
forestville@forestville.ca
www.forestville.ca
Entité municipal: Town
Incorporation: 5e janvier 1980 *Area:* 241,73 km2
Comté ou district: La Haute Côte-Nord; *Population au 2006:* 3,543
Circonscription(s) électorale(s) provinciale(s): René-Lévesque
Circonscription(s) électorale(s) fédérale(s): Montmorency-Charlevoix-Haute-Côte-Nord
Prochaines élections: 3e novembre 2013
Micheline Anctil, Mairesse
Jacques Beaulieu, Directeur général

Fort-Coulonge
CP 640
134, rue Principale
Fort-Coulonge, QC J0X 1V0
Tél: 819-683-2259; *Téléc:* 819-683-3627
administration@fortcoulonge.qc.ca
www.fortcoulonge.qc.ca
Entité municipal: Village
Incorporation: 15 décembre 1888 *Area:* 3,44 km2
Comté ou district: Pontiac; *Population au 2006:* 1,369
Circonscription(s) électorale(s) provinciale(s): Pontiac
Circonscription(s) électorale(s) fédérale(s): Pontiac
Prochaines élections: 3e novembre 2013
Raymond Durocher, Maire
Gilles Beaulieu, Directrice générale

Fortierville
198, rue de la Fabrique
Fortierville, QC G0S 1J0
Tél: 819-287-5922; *Téléc:* 819-287-0322
municipalite@fortierville.com
www.fortierville.com
Entité municipal: Municipality
Incorporation: 3e juin 1998 *Area:* 45,53 km2
Comté ou district: Bécancour; *Population au 2006:* 702
Circonscription(s) électorale(s) provinciale(s): Lotbinière
Circonscription(s) électorale(s) fédérale(s): Bas-Richelieu-Nicolet-Bécancour
Prochaines élections: 3e novembre 2013
Normand Gagnon, Maire
Annie Jacques, Directrice générale

Fossambault-sur-le-Lac
145, rue Gingras
Fossambault-sur-le-Lac, QC G0A 3M0
Tél: 418-875-3133; *Téléc:* 418-875-3544
fossam@coopcscf.com
www.fossambault-sur-le-lac.com
Entité municipal: Village
Incorporation: 10 mars 1949 *Area:* 10,96 km2
Comté ou district: La Jacques-Cartier; *Population au 2006:* 1,532

Circonscription(s) électorale(s) provinciale(s): Portneuf
Circonscription(s) électorale(s) fédérale(s):
Portneuf-Jacques-Cartier
Prochaines élections: 3e novembre 2013
Jean Laliberté, Maire
Jacques Arsenault, Greffier

Frampton
107, rue Ste-Anne
Frampton, QC G0R 1M0
Tél: 418-479-5363; *Téléc:* 418-479-5364
munframpton@globetrotter.net
www.nouvellebeauce.com/frampton
Entité municipal: Municipality
Incorporation: 1er juillet 1855 *Area:* 150,76 km2
Comté ou district: La Nouvelle-Beauce; *Population au 2006:* 1,314
Circonscription(s) électorale(s) provinciale(s): Beauce-Nord
Circonscription(s) électorale(s) fédérale(s): Beauce
Prochaines élections: 3e novembre 2013
Jacques Soucy, Maire
Josée Audet, Directrice générale

Franklin
1670, rte 202
Franklin, QC J0S 1E0
Tél: 450-827-2538; *Téléc:* 450-827-2640
franklin@qc.aira.com
Entité municipal: Municipality
Incorporation: 31 mars 1973 *Area:* 112,19 km2
Comté ou district: Le Haut-St-Laurent; *Population au 2006:* 1,651
Circonscription(s) électorale(s) provinciale(s): Huntingdon
Circonscription(s) électorale(s) fédérale(s):
Beauharnois-Salaberry
Prochaines élections: 3e novembre 2013
Suzanne Yelle Blair, Mairesse
Nancy Westerman, Directrice générale

Franquelin
CP 10
27, rue des Érables
Franquelin, QC G0H 1E0
Tél: 418-296-1406; *Téléc:* 418-296-6946
munic.franq@globetrotter.net
Entité municipal: Municipality
Incorporation: 1er janvier 1978 *Area:* 529,84 km2
Comté ou district: Manicouagan; *Population au 2006:* 346
Circonscription(s) électorale(s) provinciale(s): René-Lévesque
Circonscription(s) électorale(s) fédérale(s): Manicouagan
Prochaines élections: 3e novembre 2013
Michel Lévesque, Maire
Diane Cyr, Directrice générale

Frelighsburg
2, place de l'Hôtel-de-Ville
Frelighsburg, QC J0J 1C0
Tél: 450-298-5133; *Téléc:* 450-298-5557
municipalite@village.frelighsburg.qc.ca
Entité municipal: Municipality
Incorporation: 28 septembre 1985 *Area:* 123,27 km2
Comté ou district: Brome-Missisquoi; *Population au 2006:* 1,030
Circonscription(s) électorale(s) provinciale(s): Brome-Missisquoi
Circonscription(s) électorale(s) fédérale(s): Brome-Missisquoi
Prochaines élections: 3e novembre 2013
Roland Lemaire, Maire
Anne Pouleur, Directrice générale

Frontenac
2430, rue St-Jean
Frontenac, QC G6B 2S1
Tél: 819-583-3295; *Téléc:* 819-583-0855
adm@municipalitefrontenac.qc.ca
www.municipalitefrontenac.qc.ca
Entité municipal: Municipality
Incorporation: 1er janvier 1882 *Area:* 225,71 km2
Comté ou district: Le Granit; *Population au 2006:* 1,622
Circonscription(s) électorale(s) provinciale(s):
Mégantic-Compton
Circonscription(s) électorale(s) fédérale(s): Mégantic-L'Érable
Prochaines élections: 3e novembre 2013
Jean-Denis Cloutier, Maire
Bruno Turmel, Directeur général

Fugèreville
43, rue Principale
Fugèreville, QC J0Z 2A0
Tél: 819-748-3241; *Téléc:* 819-748-2422
dg.fugereville@mrctemiscamingue.qc.ca
Entité municipal: Municipality
Incorporation: 5e février 1904 *Area:* 163,79 km2
Comté ou district: Témiscamingue; *Population au 2006:* 301
Circonscription(s) électorale(s) provinciale(s):
Rouyn-Noranda-Témiscamingue
Circonscription(s) électorale(s) fédérale(s):
Abitibi-Témiscamingue
Prochaines élections: 3e novembre 2013
André Pâquet, Maire
Marguerite Lachance, Directrice générale

Gallichan
207, ch de la Rivière ouest
Gallichan, QC J0Z 2B0
Tél: 819-787-6092; *Téléc:* 819-787-6015
gallichan@mrca.qc.ca
www.gallichan.ao.ca
Entité municipal: Municipality
Incorporation: 1er janvier 1958 *Area:* 73,32 km2
Comté ou district: Abitibi-Ouest; *Population au 2006:* 458
Circonscription(s) électorale(s) provinciale(s): Abitibi-Ouest
Circonscription(s) électorale(s) fédérale(s): Abitibi-Témiscamigue
Prochaines élections: 3e novembre 2013
Émilien Larochelle, Maire
Johanne Shink, Directrice générale

Girardville
180, rue Principale
Girardville, QC G0W 1R0
Tél: 418-258-3293; *Téléc:* 418-258-3473
admin@ville.girardville.qc.ca
ville.girardville.qc.ca
Entité municipal: Municipality
Incorporation: 11 novembre 1921 *Area:* 125,80 km2
Comté ou district: Maria-Chapdelaine; *Population au 2006:* 1,186
Circonscription(s) électorale(s) provinciale(s): Roberval
Circonscription(s) électorale(s) fédérale(s):
Roberval-Lac-St-Jean
Prochaines élections: 3e novembre 2013
Jeanne Savard, Mairesse
Denis Desmeules, Directeur général

Godbout
CP 248
144, rue Pascal-Comeau
Godbout, QC G0H 1G0
Tél: 418-568-7581; *Téléc:* 418-568-7401
mgodbout144@hotmail.com
www.godbout.info
Entité municipal: Village
Incorporation: 1er janvier 1955 *Area:* 204,34 km2
Comté ou district: Manicouagan; *Population au 2006:* 361
Circonscription(s) électorale(s) provinciale(s): René-Lévesque
Circonscription(s) électorale(s) fédérale(s): Manicouagan
Prochaines élections: 3e novembre 2013
Alain Labrie, Maire
Carolle Vallée, Directrice générale

Godmanchester
2282, ch Ridge
Godmanchester, QC J0S 1H0
Tél: 450-264-4116; *Téléc:* 450-264-9749
godmanchester@intermobilex.com
Entité municipal: Township
Incorporation: 1er juillet 1855 *Area:* 138,77 km2
Comté ou district: Le Haut-St-Laurent; *Population au 2006:* 1,457
Circonscription(s) électorale(s) provinciale(s): Huntingdon
Circonscription(s) électorale(s) fédérale(s):
Beauharnois-Salaberry
Prochaines élections: 3e novembre 2013
Pierre Poirier, Maire
Élaine Duhème, Directrice générale

Gore
9, ch Cambria
Lakefield, QC J0V 1K0
Tél: 450-562-2025; *Téléc:* 450-562-5424
dchales@cantondegore.qc.ca
www.cantondegore.qc.ca
Entité municipal: Township
Incorporation: 1er juillet 1855 *Area:* 93,86 km2
Comté ou district: Argenteuil; *Population au 2006:* 1,540
Circonscription(s) électorale(s) provinciale(s): Argenteuil
Circonscription(s) électorale(s) fédérale(s):
Argenteuil-Papineau-Mirabel
Prochaines élections: 3e novembre 2013
Scott Pearce, Maire
Ron Kelley, Directeur général

Gracefield
CP 329
351, rte 105
Gracefield, QC J0X 1W0
Tél: 819-463-3458; *Téléc:* 819-463-4236
infos@gracefield.ca
www.gracefield.ca
Entité municipal: Town
Incorporation: 13 mars 2002 *Area:* 386,95 km2
Comté ou district: La Vallée-de-la-Gatineau; *Population au 2006:* 2,439
Circonscription(s) électorale(s) provinciale(s): Gatineau
Circonscription(s) électorale(s) fédérale(s): Pontiac
Prochaines élections: 3e novembre 2013
Note: Formerly known as Wright-Gracefield-Northfield.
Réal Rochon, Maire
Jean-Marie Gauthier, Greffier

Grand-Métis
70, ch Kempt
Grand-Métis, QC G0J 1Z0
Tél: 418-775-6485; *Téléc:* 418-775-3591
grandmetis@mitis.qc.ca
www.municipalite.grand-metis.qc.ca
Entité municipal: Municipality
Incorporation: 13 septembre 1855 *Area:* 25,85 km2
Comté ou district: La Mitis; *Population au 2006:* 268
Circonscription(s) électorale(s) provinciale(s): Matapédia
Circonscription(s) électorale(s) fédérale(s): Haute-Gaspésie-La Mitis-Matane-Matapédia
Prochaines élections: 3e novembre 2013
Richard Fournier, Maire
Chantal Tremblay, Directrice générale

Grand-Remous
1508, rte Transcanadienne
Grand-Remous, QC J0W 1E0
Tél: 819-438-2877; *Téléc:* 819-438-2364
info@grandremous.ca
www.grandremous.ca
Entité municipal: Municipality
Incorporation: 29 avril 1937 *Area:* 386,55 km2
Comté ou district: La Vallée-de-la-Gatineau; *Population au 2006:* 1,249
Circonscription(s) électorale(s) provinciale(s): Gatineau
Circonscription(s) électorale(s) fédérale(s): Pontiac
Prochaines élections: 3e novembre 2013
Betty McCarthy, Sec.-Trés.
Gérard Coulombe, Maire

Grand-St-Esprit
5410, rte Principale
Grand-Saint-Esprit, QC J0G 1B0
Tél: 819-289-2410; *Téléc:* 819-289-2029
municipalite@grandsaintesprit.qc.ca
www.grandsaintesprit.qc.ca
Entité municipal: Municipality
Incorporation: 14 mai 1938 *Area:* 28,41 km2
Comté ou district: Nicolet-Yamaska; *Population au 2006:* 466
Circonscription(s) électorale(s) provinciale(s): Nicolet-Yamaska
Circonscription(s) électorale(s) fédérale(s):
Bas-Richelieu-Nicolet-Bécancour
Prochaines élections: 3e novembre 2013
Julien Boudreault, Maire
Caludie Larochelle, Directrice générale

Grande-Rivière
CP 188
108, rue de l'Hôtel de Ville
Grande-Rivière, QC G0C 1V0
Tél: 418-385-2282; *Téléc:* 418-385-2290
villegr@globetrotter.net
www.ville.grande-riviere.qc.ca
Entité municipal: Town
Incorporation: 21 septembre 1974 *Area:* 87,15 km2
Comté ou district: Le Rocher Percé; *Population au 2006:* 3,409
Circonscription(s) électorale(s) provinciale(s): Gaspé
Circonscription(s) électorale(s) fédérale(s):
Gaspésie—Îles-de-la-Madeleine
Prochaines élections: 3e novembre 2013
Bernard Stevens, Maire
Éliane Hotton-Beaulieu, Greffière

Grande-Vallée
3, rue St-François-Xavier est
Grande-Vallée, QC G0E 1K0
Tél: 418-393-2161; *Téléc:* 418-393-2274
gvdiane@globetrotter.net
www.grande-vallee.ca
Entité municipal: Municipality
Incorporation: 15 septembre 1927 *Area:* 154,67 km2
Comté ou district: La Côte-de-Gaspé; *Population au 2006:*

1,230
Circonscription(s) électorale(s) provinciale(s): Gaspé
Circonscription(s) électorale(s) fédérale(s):
Gaspésie—Îles-de-la-Madeleine
Prochaines élections: 3e novembre 2013
Nathalie Côté, Mairesse
Ghislaine Bouthillette, Directrice générale

Grandes-Piles
630, 4e av
Grandes-Piles, QC G0X 1H0
Tél: 819-538-9708; *Téléc:* 819-538-6947
info@grandespiles.qc.ca
www.grandespiles.qc.ca
Entité municipal: Village
Incorporation: 10 août 1885 *Area:* 115,38 km2
Comté ou district: Mékinac; *Population au 2006:* 350
Circonscription(s) électorale(s) provinciale(s): Laviolette
Circonscription(s) électorale(s) fédérale(s):
St-Maurice-Champlain
Prochaines élections: 3e novembre 2013
Jean-Pierre Ratelle, Maire
Roger Lacaille, Directeur général

Grenville
21, rue Tri-Jean
Grenville, QC J0V 1J0
Tél: 819-242-2146; *Téléc:* 819-242-5891
info@grenville.ca
www.grenville.ca
Entité municipal: Village
Incorporation: 1er janvier 1876 *Area:* 3,05 km2
Comté ou district: Argenteuil; *Population au 2006:* 1,398
Circonscription(s) électorale(s) provinciale(s): Argenteuil
Circonscription(s) électorale(s) fédérale(s):
Argenteuil-Papineau-Mirabel
Prochaines élections: 3e novembre 2013
Ronald Tittlit, Maire
Alain Léveillé, Directeur général

Grenville-sur-la-Rouge
40, rue Maple
Grenville, QC J0V 1J0
Tél: 819-242-8762; *Téléc:* 819-242-9341
info@grenvillesurlarouge.ca
www.grenvillesurlarouge.ca
Entité municipal: Municipality
Incorporation: 24 avril 2002 *Area:* 321,81 km2
Comté ou district: Argenteuil; *Population au 2006:* 2,721
Circonscription(s) électorale(s) provinciale(s): Argenteuil
Circonscription(s) électorale(s) fédérale(s):
Argenteuil-Papineau-Mirabel
Prochaines élections: 3e novembre 2013
John Saywell, Maire
Pascal B. Surprenant, Directeur général

Gros-Mécatina
CP 9
30, rte Mecatina
La Tabatière, QC G0G 1T0
Tél: 418-773-2263; *Téléc:* 418-773-2696
mungrosmecatina@xplornet.com
Entité municipal: Municipality
Incorporation: 1er janvier 1994 *Area:* 961,46 km2
Comté ou district: Le Golfe-du-Saint-Laurent; *Population au 2006:* 566
Circonscription(s) électorale(s) provinciale(s): Duplessis
Circonscription(s) électorale(s) fédérale(s): Manicouagan
Prochaines élections: 3e novembre 2013
Randy Jones, Maire
Rita Collier, Directrice générale

Grosses-Roches
CP 69
122, rue de la Mer
Grosses-Roches, QC G0J 1K0
Tél: 418-733-4273; *Téléc:* 418-733-4273
grossesroches@mrcdematane.qc.ca
Entité municipal: Municipality
Incorporation: 19 août 1939 *Area:* 63,99 km2
Comté ou district: Matane; *Population au 2006:* 416
Circonscription(s) électorale(s) provinciale(s): Matane
Circonscription(s) électorale(s) fédérale(s): Haute-Gaspésie-La Mitis-Matane-Matapédia
Prochaines élections: 3e novembre 2013
Victoire Marin, Mairesse
Linda Imbeault, Directrice générale

Guérin
#101, 516, rue St-Gabriel ouest
Guérin, QC J0Z 2E0
Tél: 819-784-7011; *Téléc:* 819-784-7012
mun.guerin@mrctemiscamingue.qc.ca
Entité municipal: Township
Incorporation: 8e novembre 1911 *Area:* 203,10 km2
Comté ou district: Témiscamingue; *Population au 2006:* 295
Circonscription(s) électorale(s) provinciale(s):
Rouyn-Noranda-Témiscamingue
Circonscription(s) électorale(s) fédérale(s):
Abitibi-Témiscamingue
Prochaines élections: 3e novembre 2013
Maurice Laverdière, Maire
Doris Gauthier, Directrice générale

Ham-Nord
CP 1271
474, rue Principale
Ham-Nord, QC G0P 1A0
Tél: 819-344-2424; *Téléc:* 819-344-2806
info@ham-nord.ca
www.ham-nord.ca
Entité municipal: Township
Incorporation: 1er janvier 1864 *Area:* 101,60 km2
Comté ou district: Arthabaska; *Population au 2006:* 890
Circonscription(s) électorale(s) provinciale(s): Richmond
Circonscription(s) électorale(s) fédérale(s):
Richmond-Arthabaska
Prochaines élections: 3e novembre 2013
François Marcotte, Maire
Aline Lemieux, Directrice générale

Hampden
CP 1055
863, rte 257 nord
Hampden, QC J0B 1Y0
Tél: 819-560-8444; *Téléc:* 819-560-8445
muni.hampden@hsfqc.ca
www.cantonhampden.com
Entité municipal: Township
Incorporation: 1er janvier 1874 *Area:* 110,10 km2
Comté ou district: Le Haut-St-François; *Population au 2006:* 209
Circonscription(s) électorale(s) provinciale(s):
Mégantic-Compton
Circonscription(s) électorale(s) fédérale(s): Compton-Stanstead
Prochaines élections: 3e novembre 2013
Bertrand Prévost, Maire
Diane Carrier, Directrice générale

Harrington
2811, rte 327
Harrington, QC J8G 2T1
Tél: 819-687-2122; *Téléc:* 819-687-8610
r.lacroix@harrington.ca
www.harrington.ca
Entité municipal: Township
Incorporation: 1er juillet 1855 *Area:* 243,87 km2
Comté ou district: Argenteuil; *Population au 2006:* 777
Circonscription(s) électorale(s) provinciale(s): Argenteuil
Circonscription(s) électorale(s) fédérale(s):
Argenteuil-Papineau-Mirabel
Prochaines élections: 3e novembre 2013
Keith Robson, Maire
Robert Lacroix, Directeur général

Hatley
135, rue Main
North Hatley, QC J0B 2C0
Tél: 819-842-2977; *Téléc:* 819-842-2639
info@cantondehatley.ca
www.cantondehatley.ca
Entité municipal: Township
Incorporation: 1er juillet 1855 *Area:* 65,87 km2
Comté ou district: Memphrémagog; *Population au 2006:* 1,786
Circonscription(s) électorale(s) provinciale(s): Orford
Circonscription(s) électorale(s) fédérale(s): Compton-Stanstead
Prochaines élections: 3e novembre 2013
Pierre A. Levac, Maire
Liane Breton, Directrice générale

Hatley
2100, rte 143
Hatley, QC J0B 4B0
Tél: 819-838-5877; *Téléc:* 819-838-4646
hatley@xplornet.com
Entité municipal: Municipality
Incorporation: 27 juillet 1995 *Area:* 66,31 km2
Comté ou district: Memphrémagog; *Population au 2006:* 777
Circonscription(s) électorale(s) provinciale(s): Orford
Circonscription(s) électorale(s) fédérale(s): Compton-Stanstead
Prochaines élections: 3e novembre 2013

Roland Gascon, Directeur général
Jacques de Léséleuc, Maire

Havelock
481, rte 203
Havelock, QC J0S 2C0
Tél: 450-826-4741; *Téléc:* 450-826-4800
mun.havelock@xplornet.com
Entité municipal: Township
Incorporation: 1er avril 1863 *Area:* 87,98 km2
Comté ou district: Le Haut-St-Laurent; *Population au 2006:* 761
Circonscription(s) électorale(s) provinciale(s): Huntingdon
Circonscription(s) électorale(s) fédérale(s):
Beauharnois-Salaberry
Prochaines élections: 3e novembre 2013
Joanne Primeau, Administratrice
Daniel Pilon, Directeur général

Havre-Saint-Pierre
#01, 1235, rue de la Digue
Hâvre-Saint-Pierre, QC G0G 1P0
Tél: 418-538-2717; *Téléc:* 418-538-3439
info@havresaintpierre.com
www.havresaintpierre.com
Entité municipal: Municipality
Incorporation: 1er janvier 1873 *Area:* 3779,89 km2
Comté ou district: Minganie; *Population au 2006:* 3,150
Circonscription(s) électorale(s) provinciale(s): Duplessis
Circonscription(s) électorale(s) fédérale(s): Manicouagan
Prochaines élections: 3e novembre 2013
Berchmans Boudreau, Maire
Danys Jomphe, Directeur général

Hébertville
351, rue Turgeon
Hébertville, QC G8N 1S8
Tél: 418-344-1302; *Téléc:* 418-344-4618
guy@ville.hebertville.qc.ca
www.ville.hebertville.qc.ca
Entité municipal: Municipality
Incorporation: 16 décembre 1972 *Area:* 263,88 km2
Comté ou district: Lac-St-Jean-Est; *Population au 2006:* 2,421
Circonscription(s) électorale(s) provinciale(s): Lac-St-Jean
Circonscription(s) électorale(s) fédérale(s):
Roberval-Lac-St-Jean
Prochaines élections: 3e novembre 2013
Martin Bergeron, Maire
Christian Ouellet, Directeur général

Hébertville-Station
6, rue Tremblay
Hébertville-Station, QC G0W 1T0
Tél: 418-343-3961; *Téléc:* 418-343-2349
dg@hebertville-station.com
hebertville-station.com
Entité municipal: Village
Incorporation: 18 février 1903 *Area:* 33,28 km2
Comté ou district: Lac-St-Jean-Est; *Population au 2006:* 1,230
Circonscription(s) électorale(s) provinciale(s): Lac-St-Jean
Circonscription(s) électorale(s) fédérale(s):
Roberval-Lac-St-Jean
Prochaines élections: 3e novembre 2013
Réal Côté, Maire
Serge Martel, Directeur général

Hemmingford
#3, 505, rue Frontière
Hemmingford, QC J0L 1H0
Tél: 450-247-2050; *Téléc:* 450-247-3283
canton.township@hemmingford.ca
www.hemmingford.ca
Entité municipal: Township
Incorporation: 1er juillet 1855 *Area:* 155,78 km2
Comté ou district: Les Jardins-de-Napierville; *Population au 2006:* 1,763
Circonscription(s) électorale(s) provinciale(s): Huntingdon
Circonscription(s) électorale(s) fédérale(s):
Beauharnois-Salaberry
Prochaines élections: 3e novembre 2013
Paul Viau, Maire
Margaret Hess, Directrice générale

Hemmingford
#5, 505, rue Frontière
Hemmingford, QC J0L 1H0
Tél: 450-247-3310; *Téléc:* 450-247-2389
village@hemmingford.ca
www.hemmingford.ca
Entité municipal: Village
Incorporation: 1er janvier 1878 *Area:* 0,85 km2
Comté ou district: Les Jardins-de-Napierville; *Population au 2006:* 757

Circonscription(s) électorale(s) provinciale(s): Huntingdon
Circonscription(s) électorale(s) fédérale(s):
Beauharnois-Salaberry
Prochaines élections: 3e novembre 2013
Drew Somerville, Maire
Diane Lawrence, Directrice générale

Henryville
165, rue de l'Église
Henryville, QC J0J 1E0
Tél: 450-299-2655; *Téléc:* 450-299-2355
mcchoquette.munihenryville@netc.net
www.municipalite-henryville.com
Entité municipal: Municipality
Incorporation: 15 décembre 1999 *Area:* 64,87 km2
Comté ou district: Le Haut-Richelieu; *Population au 2006:* 1,529
Circonscription(s) électorale(s) provinciale(s): Iberville
Circonscription(s) électorale(s) fédérale(s): Brome-Missisquoi
Prochaines élections: 3e novembre 2013
Serges Lafrance, Maire
Marie-Claude Choquette, Directrice générale

Hérouxville
1060, rue St-Pierre sud
Hérouxville, QC G0X 1J0
Tél: 418-365-7135; *Téléc:* 418-365-7041
herouxville@regionmekinac.com
www.municipalite.herouxville.qc.ca
Entité municipal: Parish (Paroisse)
Incorporation: 13 avril 1904 *Area:* 54,51 km2
Comté ou district: Mékinac; *Population au 2006:* 1,235
Circonscription(s) électorale(s) provinciale(s): Laviolette
Circonscription(s) électorale(s) fédérale(s):
St-Maurice-Champlain
Prochaines élections: 3e novembre 2013
Bernard Thompson, Maire
Denise Cossette, Directrice générale

Hinchinbrooke
1056, ch Brook
Hinchinbrooke, QC J0S 1A0
Tél: 450-264-5353; *Téléc:* 450-264-3787
hinchinbrooke@targo.ca
Entité municipal: Township
Incorporation: 1er juillet 1855 *Area:* 148,95 km2
Comté ou district: Le Haut-St-Laurent; *Population au 2006:* 2,369
Circonscription(s) électorale(s) provinciale(s): Huntingdon
Circonscription(s) électorale(s) fédérale(s):
Beauharnois-Salaberry
Prochaines élections: 3e novembre 2013
Normand Crête, Maire
Kevin Neal, Directeur général

Honfleur
320, rue St-Jean
Honfleur, QC G0R 1N0
Tél: 418-885-9195; *Téléc:* 418-885-9195
livro@globetrotter.qc.ca
munhonfleur.net
Entité municipal: Municipality
Incorporation: 5e mars 1915 *Area:* 50,99 km2
Comté ou district: Bellechasse; *Population au 2006:* 794
Circonscription(s) électorale(s) provinciale(s): Bellechasse
Circonscription(s) électorale(s) fédérale(s): Lévis-Bellechasse
Prochaines élections: 3e novembre 2013
Marcel Blais, Maire
Jocelyne G. Paré, Directrice générale

Hope
330, rte 132
Hope, QC G0C 2K0
Tél: 418-752-3212; *Téléc:* 418-752-6986
mun.hope@globetrotter.net
Entité municipal: Township
Incorporation: 1er juillet 1855 *Area:* 71,45 km2
Comté ou district: Bonaventure; *Population au 2006:* 878
Circonscription(s) électorale(s) provinciale(s): Bonaventure
Circonscription(s) électorale(s) fédérale(s):
Gaspésie—îles-de-la-Madeleine
Prochaines élections: 3e novembre 2013
Hazen Whittom, Maire
Nancy Castilloux, Directrice générale

Hope Town
CP 146
209, rte 132 ouest
Hope Town, QC G0C 3C0
Tél: 418-752-2137; *Téléc:* 418-752-3789
hopetown@navigue.com
www.municipalitehopetown.com
Entité municipal: Municipality
Incorporation: 21 novembre 1936 *Area:* 49,80 km2
Comté ou district: Bonaventure; *Population au 2006:* 347
Circonscription(s) électorale(s) provinciale(s): Bonaventure
Circonscription(s) électorale(s) fédérale(s):
Gaspésie—îles-de-la-Madeleine
Prochaines élections: 3e novembre 2013
Lisa Marie MacWhirter, Maire
Gina Mei, Directrice générale

Howick
51, rue Colville
Howick, QC J0S 1G0
Tél: 450-825-2032; *Téléc:* 450-825-0026
municipalite@villagehowick.com
Entité municipal: Village
Incorporation: 29 octobre 1915 *Area:* 0,89 km2
Comté ou district: Le Haut-St-Laurent; *Population au 2006:* 606
Circonscription(s) électorale(s) provinciale(s): Huntingdon
Circonscription(s) électorale(s) fédérale(s):
Beauharnois-Salaberry
Prochaines élections: 3e novembre 2013
Denis Loiselle, Maire
Claudette Provost, Directrice générale

Huberdeau
101, rue du Pont
Huberdeau, QC J0T 1G0
Tél: 819-687-8321; *Téléc:* 819-687-8808
info@municipalite.huberdeau.qc.ca
www.municipalite.huberdeau.qc.ca
Entité municipal: Municipality
Incorporation: 8e juin 1926 *Area:* 57,18 km2
Comté ou district: Les Laurentides; *Population au 2006:* 924
Circonscription(s) électorale(s) provinciale(s): Labelle
Circonscription(s) électorale(s) fédérale(s): Laurentides-Labelle
Prochaines élections: 3e novembre 2013
Évelyne Charbonneau, Mairesse
Guylaine Maurice, Directrice générale

Hudson
481, rue Principale
Hudson, QC J0P 1H0
Tél: 450-458-5348; *Téléc:* 450-458-4922
louisev@ville.hudson.qc.ca
www.ville.hudson.qc.ca
Entité municipal: Town
Incorporation: 7e juin 1969 *Area:* 21,62 km2
Comté ou district: Vaudreuil-Soulanges; *Population au 2006:* 5,088
Circonscription(s) électorale(s) provinciale(s): Vaudreuil
Circonscription(s) électorale(s) fédérale(s): Vaudreuil-Soulanges
Prochaines élections: 3e novembre 2013
Michael Elliot, Maire
Louise L.-Villandré, Directrice générale

Huntingdon
23, rue King
Huntingdon, QC J0S 1H0
Tél: 450-264-5389; *Téléc:* 450-264-6826
dg@villehuntingdon.com
www.villehuntingdon.com
Entité municipal: Town
Incorporation: 9e octobre 1848 *Area:* 2,61 km2
Comté ou district: Le Haut-St-Laurent; *Population au 2006:* 2,587
Circonscription(s) électorale(s) provinciale(s): Huntingdon
Circonscription(s) électorale(s) fédérale(s):
Beauharnois-Salaberry
Prochaines élections: 3e novembre 2013
Stéphane Gendron, Maire
Denyse Jenneau, Greffière

Inukjuak
CP 234
Inukjuak, QC J0M 1M0
Tél: 819-254-8822; *Téléc:* 819-254-8779
jnaktialuk@nvinukjuak.ca
www.nvinukjuak.ca
Entité municipal: Northern Village
Incorporation: 7e juin 1980 *Area:* 64,45 km2
Comté ou district: Administration régionale Kativik; *Population au 2006:* 1,597
Circonscription(s) électorale(s) provinciale(s): Ungava
Circonscription(s) électorale(s) fédérale(s):
Abitibi-Baie-James-Nunavil-Eeyou
Prochaines élections: 7e novembre 2012
Sarollie Weetaluktuk, Mairesse
Caroline Naktialuk, Secrétaire-trésorière

Inverness
CP 129
1799, rte Dublin
Inverness, QC G0S 1K0
Tél: 418-453-2512; *Téléc:* 418-453-2554
info@municipaliteinverness.ca
www.municipaliteinverness.ca
Entité municipal: Municipality
Incorporation: 9e septembre 1998 *Area:* 176,35 km2
Comté ou district: L'Érable; *Population au 2006:* 838
Circonscription(s) électorale(s) provinciale(s): Lotbinière
Circonscription(s) électorale(s) fédérale(s): Mégantic-L'Érable
Prochaines élections: 3e novembre 2013
Gilles St-Pierre, Maire
Sonia Tardif, Directrice générale

Irlande
157, ch Gosford
Irlande, QC G6H 2N7
Tél: 418-428-9216; *Téléc:* 418-428-4262
mundirlande@bellnet.ca
Entité municipal: Municipality
Incorporation: 1er juillet 1855 *Area:* 110,200 km2
Comté ou district: Les Appalaches; *Population au 2006:* 942
Circonscription(s) électorale(s) provinciale(s): Frontenac
Circonscription(s) électorale(s) fédérale(s): Mégantic-L'Érable
Prochaines élections: 3e novembre 2013
Bruno Vézina, Maire
Christiane Laroche, Directrice générale

Ivujivik
CP 20
Ivujivik, QC J0M 1H0
Tél: 819-922-9940; *Téléc:* 819-922-3045
mayorivu@nvivujivik.ca
www.nvivujivik.ca
Entité municipal: Northern Village
Incorporation: 27 juin 1981 *Area:* 36,59 km2
Comté ou district: Kativik; *Population au 2006:* 349
Circonscription(s) électorale(s) provinciale(s): Ungava
Circonscription(s) électorale(s) fédérale(s):
Abitibi-Baie-James-Nunavik-Eeyou
Prochaines élections: 7e novembre 2012
Charlie Paningajak, Maire
Johnny Mark, Secrétaire-trésorier

Joliette
632, rue De Lanaudière
Joliette, QC J6E 3M7
Tél: 450-759-2237; *Téléc:* 450-759-2597
info@mrcjoliette.qc.ca
www.mrcjoliette.qc.ca
Entité municipal: Regional County Municipality
Incorporation: 1er janvier 1982
Population au 2006: 58,354
Note: 10 municipalités.
André Hénault, Préfet
prefet@mrcjoliette.qc.ca
Line Laporte, Directrice générale
llaporte@mrcjoliette.qc.ca

Kamouraska
67, av Morel
Kamouraska, QC G0L 1M0
Tél: 418-492-6523; *Téléc:* 418-492-9789
mychelle.levesque@kamouraska.ca
www.kamouraska.ca
Entité municipal: Municipality
Incorporation: 25 avril 1987 *Area:* 40,81 km2
Comté ou district: Kamouraska; *Population au 2006:* 705
Circonscription(s) électorale(s) provinciale(s):
Kamouraska-Témiscouata
Circonscription(s) électorale(s) fédérale(s):
Montmagny-L'Islet-Kamouraska-Rivière-du-Loup
Prochaines élections: 3e novembre 2013
Claude Langlais, Maire
Mychelle Lévesque, Directrice générale

Kamouraska
CP 1120
425, av Patry
Saint-Pascal, QC G0L 3Y0
Tél: 418-492-1660; *Téléc:* 418-492-2220
info@mrckamouraska.com
www.kamouraska.com
Entité municipal: Regional County Municipality
Incorporation: 1er janvier 1982
Population au 2006: 22,084
Note: 17 municipalités & 2 autres territoires.
Yvon Soucy, Préfet
Guy Lavoie, Directeur général
glavoie@mrckamouraska.com

Kangiqsualujjuaq
CP 120
Kangiqsualujjuaq, QC J0M 1N0
Tél: 819-337-5271; *Téléc:* 819-337-5200
tannanack@nvkangiqsualujjuaq.ca
www.nvkangiqsualujjuaq.ca
Entité municipal: Northern Village
Incorporation: 2e février 1980 *Area:* 36,23 km2
Comté ou district: Administration régionale Kativik; *Population au 2006:* 735
Circonscription(s) électorale(s) provinciale(s): Ungava
Circonscription(s) électorale(s) fédérale(s): Abitibi-Baie-James-Nunavik-Eeyou
Prochaines élections: 7e novembre 2012
Kitty Annanack, Mairesse
Tommy Annanack, Secrétaire-trésorier

Kangiqsujuaq
CP 60
901, ch Sinaitia
Kangiqsujuaq, QC J0M 1K0
Tél: 819-338-3342; *Téléc:* 819-338-3237
sectreasurer@nvkangiqsujuaq.ca
www.nvkangiqsujuaq.ca
Entité municipal: Northern Village
Incorporation: 20 septembre 1980 *Area:* 12,47 km2
Comté ou district: Administration régionale Kativik; *Population au 2006:* 605
Circonscription(s) électorale(s) provinciale(s): Ungava
Circonscription(s) électorale(s) fédérale(s): Abitibi-Baie-James-Nunavik-Eeyou
Prochaines élections: 7e novembre 2012
Mary A. Pilurtuut, Mairesse
Pasa Kiatainaq, Secrétaire-trésorière

Kangirsuk
CP 90
101, ch Kuuvviliariaq
Kangirsuk, QC J0M 1A0
Tél: 819-935-4388; *Téléc:* 819-935-4287
sectreasurer@nvkangirsuk.ca
www.nvkangirsuk.ca
Entité municipal: Northern Village
Incorporation: 17 janvier 1981 *Area:* 58,73 km2
Comté ou district: Administration régionale Kativik; *Population au 2006:* 466
Circonscription(s) électorale(s) provinciale(s): Ungava
Circonscription(s) électorale(s) fédérale(s): Abitibi-Baie-James-Nunavik-Eeyou
Prochaines élections: 7e novembre 2012
Tommy Nassak, Maire
Alec Kudluk, Secrétaire-trésorier

Kawawachikamach
CP 5111
Kawawachikamach, QC G0G 2Z0
Tél: 418-585-2686; *Téléc:* 418-585-3130
kawawa@naskapi.ca
www.naskapi.ca
Entité municipal: Villages Naskapi
Incorporation: 10 septembre 1981 *Area:* 284,7 km2
Comté ou district: Administration régionale Kativik
Circonscription(s) électorale(s) provinciale(s): Duplessis
Circonscription(s) électorale(s) fédérale(s): Manicouagan
Pillip Einish, Maire
John Mameamskum, Directeur général

Kazabazua
CP 10
30, ch Begley
Kazabazua, QC J0X 1X0
Tél: 819-467-2852; *Téléc:* 819-467-3872
munkaz@qc.aibn.com
www.kazabazua.ca
Entité municipal: Municipality
Incorporation: 1er janvier 1862 *Area:* 175,49 km2
Comté ou district: La Vallée-de-la-Gatineau; *Population au 2006:* 839
Circonscription(s) électorale(s) provinciale(s): Gatineau
Circonscription(s) électorale(s) fédérale(s): Pontiac
Prochaines élections: 3e novembre 2013
Ota Hora, Maire
Pierre Vaillancourt, Directeur général

Kiamika
3, ch Valiquette
Kiamika, QC J0W 1G0
Tél: 819-585-3225; *Téléc:* 819-585-3992
mun.kiamika@tlb.sympatico.ca
www.kiamika.ca
Entité municipal: Municipality
Incorporation: 3e janvier 1898 *Area:* 348,25 km2
Comté ou district: Antoine-Labelle; *Population au 2006:* 779
Circonscription(s) électorale(s) provinciale(s): Labelle
Circonscription(s) électorale(s) fédérale(s): Laurentides-Labelle
Prochaines élections: 3e novembre 2013
Michel Dion, Maire
Josée Lacasse, Directrice générale

Kingsbury
370, rue du Moulin
Kingsbury, QC J0B 1X0
Tél: 819-826-2527; *Téléc:* 819-826-2520
kingsbury@qc.aira.com
Entité municipal: Village
Incorporation: 7e juillet 1896 *Area:* 6,26 km2
Comté ou district: Le Val-St-François; *Population au 2006:* 99
Circonscription(s) électorale(s) provinciale(s): Richmond
Circonscription(s) électorale(s) fédérale(s): Richmond-Arthabaska
Prochaines élections: 3e novembre 2013
Jean Dandurand, Maire
Yves Barthe, Directeur général

Kingsey Falls
CP 270
15, rue Caron
Kingsey Falls, QC J0A 1B0
Tél: 819-363-3810; *Téléc:* 819-363-3819
villedekingseyfalls@kingseyfalls.ca
www.kingseyfalls.ca
Entité municipal: Town
Incorporation: 31 décembre 1997 *Area:* 70,14 km2
Comté ou district: Arthabaska; *Population au 2006:* 2,086
Circonscription(s) électorale(s) provinciale(s): Richmond
Circonscription(s) électorale(s) fédérale(s): Richmond-Arthabaska
Prochaines élections: 3e novembre 2013
Micheline Pinard-Lampron, Mairesse
Gino Dubé, Greffier

Kinnear's Mills
120, rue des Églises
Kinnear's Mills, QC G0N 1K0
Tél: 418-424-3377; *Téléc:* 418-424-3015
munikin@gabskycom.com
www.kinnearsmills.com
Entité municipal: Municipality
Incorporation: 1er juillet 1855 *Area:* 93,18 km2
Comté ou district: Les Appalaches; *Population au 2006:* 333
Circonscription(s) électorale(s) provinciale(s): Frontenac
Circonscription(s) électorale(s) fédérale(s): Mégantic-L'Érable
Prochaines élections: 3e novembre 2013
Paul Vachon, Maire
Claudette Perreault, Directrice générale

Kipawa
15, rue Principale
Kipawa, QC J0Z 2H0
Tél: 819-627-3500; *Téléc:* 819-627-1067
kipawa@mrctemiscamingue.qc.ca
www.kipawa.ca
Entité municipal: Municipality
Incorporation: 1er janvier 1985 *Area:* 47,20 km2
Comté ou district: Témiscamingue; *Population au 2006:* 565
Circonscription(s) électorale(s) provinciale(s): Rouyn-Noranda-Témiscamingue
Circonscription(s) électorale(s) fédérale(s): Abitibi-Témiscamingue
Prochaines élections: 3e novembre 2013
Norman Young, Maire
Danielle Gravelle, Directrice générale

Kuujjuaq
CP 210
528, ch de l'Airport
Kuujjuaq, QC J0M 1C0
Tél: 819-964-2943; *Téléc:* 819-964-2980
mayor@nvkuujjuaq.qc.ca
www.nvkuujjuaq.ca
Entité municipal: Northern Village
Incorporation: 29 décembre 1979 *Area:* 390,33 km2
Comté ou district: Administration régionale Kativik; *Population au 2006:* 2,132
Circonscription(s) électorale(s) provinciale(s): Ungava
Circonscription(s) électorale(s) fédérale(s): Abitibi-Baie-James-Nunavik-Eeyou
Prochaines élections: 7e novembre 2012
Paul Parsons, Maire
Ian D. Robertson, Secrétaire-trésorier

Kuujjuarapik
CP 360
412, av St-Edmund
Kuujjuarapik, QC J0M 1G0
Tél: 819-929-3360; *Téléc:* 819-929-3453
proussel@nkuujjaraapik.ca
Entité municipal: Northern Village
Incorporation: 7e juin 1980 *Area:* 7,46 km2
Comté ou district: Administration régionale Kativik; *Population au 2006:* 568
Circonscription(s) électorale(s) provinciale(s): Ungava
Circonscription(s) électorale(s) fédérale(s): Abitibi-Baie-James-Nunavik-Eeyou
Prochaines élections: 7e novembre 2012
Raymond Mickpegak, Maire
Pierre Roussel, Secrétaire-trésorier

L'Ange-Gardien
870, ch Donaldson
L'Ange-Gardien, QC J8L 0K8
Tél: 819-986-7470; *Téléc:* 819-986-8349
adm@ville.lange-gardien.qc.ca
www.ville.lange-gardien.qc.ca
Entité municipal: Municipality
Incorporation: 17 mai 1979 *Area:* 224,17 km2
Comté ou district: Les Collines-de-l'Outaouais; *Population au 2006:* 4,348
Circonscription(s) électorale(s) provinciale(s): Papineau
Circonscription(s) électorale(s) fédérale(s): Pontiac
Prochaines élections: 3e novembre 2013
Robert Goulet, Maire
Alain Descarreaux, Directeur général

L'Ange-Gardien
6405, av Royale
L'Ange-Gardien, QC G0A 2K0
Tél: 418-822-1555; *Téléc:* 418-822-2526
mun-langegardien@bellnet.ca
www.langegardien.qc.ca
Entité municipal: Parish (Paroisse)
Incorporation: 1er juillet 1855 *Area:* 50,67 km2
Comté ou district: La Côte-de-Beaupré; *Population au 2006:* 3,008
Circonscription(s) électorale(s) provinciale(s): Montmorency
Circonscription(s) électorale(s) fédérale(s): Montmorency-Charlevoix-Haute-Côte-Nord
Prochaines élections: 3e novembre 2013
Pierre Lefrançois, Maire
Lise Drouin, Directrice générale

L'Anse-St-Jean
3, rue du Couvent
L'Anse-Saint-Jean, QC G0V 1J0
Tél: 418-272-2633; *Téléc:* 418-544-3078
info@lanse-saint-jean.ca
www.lanse-saint-jean.ca
Entité municipal: Municipality
Incorporation: 1er janvier 1859 *Area:* 527,06 km2
Comté ou district: Le Fjord-du-Saguenay; *Population au 2006:* 1,088
Circonscription(s) électorale(s) provinciale(s): Dubuc
Circonscription(s) électorale(s) fédérale(s): Chicoutimi-Le Fjord
Prochaines élections: 3e novembre 2013
Claude Boucher, Maire
Marina Gagné, Directrice générale

L'Ascension
CP 30
59, rue de l'Hôtel-de-Ville
L'Ascension, QC J0T 1W0
Tél: 819-275-3027; *Téléc:* 819-275-3489
directiongenerale@municipalite-lascension.qc.ca
www.municipalite-lascension.qc.ca
Entité municipal: Municipality
Incorporation: 23 septembre 1905 *Area:* 342,83 km2
Comté ou district: Antoine-Labelle; *Population au 2006:* 861
Circonscription(s) électorale(s) provinciale(s): Labelle
Circonscription(s) électorale(s) fédérale(s): Laurentides-Labelle
Prochaines élections: 3e novembre 2013
Yves Meilleur, Maire
Hélène Beauchamp, Directrice générale

L'Ascension-de-Notre-Seigneur
CP 100
1000, 1re rue est
L'Ascension-de-Notre-Seigneur, QC G0W 1Y0
Tél: 418-347-3482; *Téléc:* 418-347-4253
normand.desgagne@ville.ascension.qc.ca
www.ville.ascension.qc.ca
Entité municipal: Parish (Paroisse)
Incorporation: 25 février 1919 *Area:* 131,83 km2
Comté ou district: Lac-St-Jean-Est; *Population au 2006:* 1,976

Circonscription(s) électorale(s) provinciale(s): Lac-St-Jean
Circonscription(s) électorale(s) fédérale(s):
Roberval-Lac-St-Jean
Prochaines élections: 3e novembre 2013
Louis Ouellet, Maire
Normand Desgagné, Directeur général

L'Ascension-de-Patapédia
CP 9
70, rue Principale
L'Ascension-de-Patapédia, QC G0J 1R0
Tél: 418-299-2024; *Téléc:* 418-299-2027
munlas-d-pat@globetrotter.net
www.matapedialesplateaux.com
Entité municipal: Municipality
Incorporation: 1er janvier 1968 *Area:* 95,38 km2
Comté ou district: Avignon; *Population au 2006:* 214
Circonscription(s) électorale(s) provinciale(s): Bonaventure
Circonscription(s) électorale(s) fédérale(s):
Gaspésie—îles-de-la-Madeleine
Prochaines élections: 3e novembre 2013
Rémi Gallant, Maire
Josiane Boucher, Directrice générale

L'Assomption
300A, rue Dorval
L'Assomption, QC J5W 3A1
Tél: 450-589-2288; *Téléc:* 450-589-9430
mrcinfo@mrclassomption.qc.ca
www.mrclassomption.qc.ca
Entité municipal: Regional County Municipality
Incorporation: 1er janvier 1983
Population au 2006: 109,6363
Note: 6 municipalités.
Chantal Deschamps, Préfète
Michel C. Gagnon, Directeur général

L'Avenir
545, rue Principale
L'Avenir, QC J0C 1B0
Tél: 819-394-2422; *Téléc:* 819-394-2222
info@municipalitelavenir.qc.ca
www.municipalitelavenir.qc.ca
Entité municipal: Municipality
Incorporation: 23 décembre 1976 *Area:* 96,47 km2
Comté ou district: Drummond; *Population au 2006:* 1,262
Circonscription(s) électorale(s) provinciale(s): Johnson
Circonscription(s) électorale(s) fédérale(s): Drummond
Prochaines élections: 3e novembre 2013
Jean Parenteau, Maire
Suzie Lemire, Directrice générale

L'Épiphanie
331, rang du Bas-de-l'Achigan
L'Épiphanie, QC J5X 1E1
Tél: 450-588-5547; *Téléc:* 450-588-6050
mun@paroisse-lepiphanie.com
www.paroisse-lepiphanie.com
Entité municipal: Parish (Paroisse)
Incorporation: 1er juillet 1855 *Area:* 55,32 km2
Comté ou district: L'Assomption; *Population au 2006:* 3,129
Circonscription(s) électorale(s) provinciale(s): Rousseau
Circonscription(s) électorale(s) fédérale(s): Repentigny
Prochaines élections: 3e novembre 2013
Denis Lévesque, Maire
Nicole Renaud, Directrice générale

L'Épiphanie
66, rue Notre-Dame
L'Épiphanie, QC J5X 1A1
Tél: 450-588-5515; *Téléc:* 450-588-6171
courrier@ville.lepiphanie.qc.ca
www.ville.lepiphanie.qc.ca
Entité municipal: Town
Incorporation: 30 juin 1967 *Area:* 2,46 km2
Comté ou district: L'Assomption; *Population au 2006:* 4,606
Circonscription(s) électorale(s) provinciale(s): Rousseau
Circonscription(s) électorale(s) fédérale(s): Repentigny
Prochaines élections: 3e novembre 2013
Benoît Verstraete, Maire
Claude Crépeau, Greffier

L'Érable
#300, 1783, av St-Édouard
Plessisville, QC G6L 3S7
Tél: 819-362-2333; *Téléc:* 819-362-9150
info@mrc-erable.qc.ca
www.mrc-erable.qc.ca
Entité municipal: Regional County Municipality
Incorporation: 1er janvier 1982
Population au 2006: 23,158
Note: 11 municipalités.
Donald Langlois, Préfet
Rick Lavergne, Directeur général
rlavergne@mrc-erable.qc.ca

L'île-Cadieux
50, ch de l'île
L'île-Cadieux, QC J7V 8P3
Tél: 450-424-4273; *Téléc:* 450-424-6327
secretaire.ilecadieux@videotron.ca
www.ilecadieux.ca
Entité municipal: Village
Incorporation: 21 mars 1922 *Area:* 0,62 km2
Comté ou district: Vaudreuil-Soulanges; *Population au 2006:* 128
Circonscription(s) électorale(s) provinciale(s): Vaudreuil
Circonscription(s) électorale(s) fédérale(s): Vaudreuil-Soulanges
Prochaines élections: 3e novembre 2013
Marc-André Léger, Maire
Gisèle Fournier, Directrice générale

L'île-d'Anticosti
CP 119
25B, ch des Forestiers
Port-Menier, QC G0G 2Y0
Tél: 418-535-0311; *Téléc:* 418-535-0381
munanticosti@xplornet.com
www.ile-anticosti.com
Entité municipal: Municipality
Incorporation: 1er janvier 1984 *Area:* 7923,16 km2
Comté ou district: Minganie; *Population au 2006:* 281
Circonscription(s) électorale(s) provinciale(s): Duplessis
Circonscription(s) électorale(s) fédérale(s): Manicouagan
Prochaines élections: 3e novembre 2013
Denis Duteau, Maire
Véronique Rodgers, Directrice générale

L'île-d'Orléans
3896, ch Royal
Sainte-Famille, QC G0A 3P0
Tél: 418-829-1011; *Téléc:* 418-829-2513
info@mrcio.qc.ca
mrcio.qc.ca
Entité municipal: Regional County Municipality
Incorporation: 1er janvier 1982
Population au 2006: 6,862
Note: 6 municipalités.
Jean-Pierre Turcotte, Préfet
Chantale Cormier, Directrice générale

L'île-du-Grand-Calument
CP 130
8, rue Brizard
L'île-du-Grand-Calumet, QC J0X 1J0
Tél: 819-648-5965; *Téléc:* 819-648-2659
ile-du-grand-calumet@mrcpontiac.qc.ca
Entité municipal: Municipality
Incorporation: 1er juillet 1855 *Area:* 130,61 km2
Comté ou district: Pontiac; *Population au 2006:* 785
Circonscription(s) électorale(s) provinciale(s): Pontiac
Circonscription(s) électorale(s) fédérale(s): Pontiac
Prochaines élections: 3e novembre 2013
Paul-Émile Maleau, Maire
Jacques Mantha, Directeur général

L'Isle-aux-Allumettes
CP 100
75, rue Notre-Dame
L'Isle-aux-Allumettes, QC J0X 1M0
Tél: 819-689-2266; *Téléc:* 819-689-5619
lisle-aux-allumettes@mrcpontiac.qc.ca
www.isle-aux-allumettes.com
Entité municipal: Municipality
Incorporation: 30 décembre 1998 *Area:* 190,19 km2
Comté ou district: Pontiac; *Population au 2006:* 1,443
Circonscription(s) électorale(s) provinciale(s): Pontiac
Circonscription(s) électorale(s) fédérale(s): Pontiac
Prochaines élections: 3e novembre 2013
Winston Sunstrum, Maire
Richard Vaillancourt, Directeur général

L'Isle-aux-Coudres
1026, ch des Coudriers
L'Isle-aux-Coudres, QC G0A 3J0
Tél: 418-760-1060; *Téléc:* 418-760-1061
contact@municipaliteiac.ca
Entité municipal: Municipality
Incorporation: 23 août 2000 *Area:* 29,54 km2
Comté ou district: Charlevoix; *Population au 2006:* 1,296
Circonscription(s) électorale(s) provinciale(s): Charlevoix
Circonscription(s) électorale(s) fédérale(s):
Montmorency-Charevoix-Haute-Côte-Nord
Prochaines élections: 3e novembre 2013
Dominic Tremblay, Maire
Johanne Fortin, Directrice générale

L'Isle-Verte
CP 159
141, rue St-Jean-Baptiste
L'Isle-Verte, QC G0L 1K0
Tél: 418-898-2812; *Téléc:* 418-898-2788
guyberube@lisle-verte.ca
www.municipalite.lisle-verte.qc.ca
Entité municipal: Municipality
Incorporation: 9 février 2000 *Area:* 112,33 km2
Comté ou district: Rivière-du-Loup; *Population au 2006:* 1,464
Circonscription(s) électorale(s) provinciale(s): Rivière-du-Loup
Circonscription(s) électorale(s) fédérale(s):
Montmagny-L'Islet-Kamouraska-Rivière-du-Loup
Prochaines élections: 1er novembre 2013
Serge Forest, Maire
Guy Bérubé, Directeur général

L'Islet
284, boul Nilus-Leclerc
L'Islet, QC G0R 2C0
Tél: 418-247-3060; *Téléc:* 418-247-5085
muni-islet@globetrotter.net
www.lislet.com
Entité municipal: Municipality
Incorporation: 1er janvier 2000 *Area:* 119,44 km2
Comté ou district: L'Islet; *Population au 2006:* 3,840
Circonscription(s) électorale(s) provinciale(s): Montmagny-L'Islet
Circonscription(s) électorale(s) fédérale(s):
Montmagny-L'Islet-Kamouraska-Rivière-du-Loup
Prochaines élections: 3e novembre 2013
André Caron, Maire
Colette Lord, Directrice générale

L'Islet
34-A, rue Fortin
Saint-Jean-Port-Joli, QC G0R 3G0
Tél: 418-598-3076; *Téléc:* 418-598-6880
administration@mrclislet.com
www.mrclislet.com
Entité municipal: Regional County Municipality
Incorporation: 1er janvier 1982
Population au 2006: 18,902
Note: 14 municipalités.
Réal Laverdière, Préfet
Michel Pelletier, Directeur général

La Conception
1371, rue du Centenaire
La Conception, QC J0T 1M0
Tél: 819-686-3016; *Téléc:* 819-686-5808
mbrisson@municipalite.laconception.qc.ca
www.municipalite.laconception.qc.ca
Entité municipal: Municipality
Incorporation: 1er janvier 1882 *Area:* 142,61 km2
Comté ou district: Les Laurentides; *Population au 2006:* 1,283
Circonscription(s) électorale(s) provinciale(s): Labelle
Circonscription(s) électorale(s) fédérale(s): Laurentides-Labelle
Prochaines élections: 3e novembre 2013
Maurice Plouffe, Maire
Marie-France Brisson, Directrice générale

La Corne
324, rte 111
La Corne, QC J0Y 1R0
Tél: 819-799-3571; *Téléc:* 819-799-3572
mun.lacorne@cableamos.com
www.lacorne.ca
Entité municipal: Municipality
Incorporation: 2e août 1975 *Area:* 331,54 km2
Comté ou district: Abitibi; *Population au 2006:* 682
Circonscription(s) électorale(s) provinciale(s): Abitibi-Ouest
Circonscription(s) électorale(s) fédérale(s):
Abitibi-Témiscamingue
Prochaines élections: 3e novembre 2013
Michel Lévesque, Maire
Diane St-Pierre, Directrice générale

La Côte-de-Beaupré
3, rue de la Seigneurie
Château-Richer, QC G0A 1N0
Tél: 418-824-3444; *Téléc:* 418-824-3917
info@mrccotedebeaupre.qc.ca
Entité municipal: Regional County Municipality
Incorporation: 1er janvier 1982
Population au 2006: 23,015
Note: 9 municipalités & 2 autres territoires.
Henri Cloutier, Préfet
Jacques Pichette, Directeur général

La Côte-de-Gaspé
#208, 19, rue Adams
Gaspé, QC G4X 1E5
Tél: 418-368-7000; *Téléc:* 418-368-8181
mrc@cotedegaspe.ca
mrc.cotedegaspe.ca
Entité municipal: Regional County Municipality
Incorporation: 1er janvier 1982
Population au 2006: 17,888
Note: 5 municipalités & 2 autres territoires.
François Roussy, Préfet
Pierre R. Charron, Directeur général

La Doré
5000, rue des Peupliers
La Doré, QC G8J 1E8
Tél: 418-256-3545; *Téléc:* 418-256-3496
info@municipalite.ladore.qc.ca
www.municipalite.ladore.qc.ca
Entité municipal: Parish (Paroisse)
Incorporation: 16 mars 1906 *Area:* 280,83 km2
Comté ou district: Le Domaine-du-Roy; *Population au 2006:* 1,454
Circonscription(s) électorale(s) provinciale(s): Roberval
Circonscription(s) électorale(s) fédérale(s): Roberval-Lac-St-Jean
Prochaines élections: 3e novembre 2013
Jacques Asselin, Maire
René Perron, Directeur général

La Durantaye
539, rue du Piedmont
La Durantaye, QC G0R 1W0
Tél: 418-884-3465; *Téléc:* 418-884-3048
par.ladurantaye@globetrotter.net
www.munladurantaye.qc.ca
Entité municipal: Parish (Paroisse)
Incorporation: 4e août 1910 *Area:* 33,78 km2
Comté ou district: Bellechasse; *Population au 2006:* 703
Circonscription(s) électorale(s) provinciale(s): Bellechasse
Circonscription(s) électorale(s) fédérale(s): Lévis-Bellechasse
Prochaines élections: 3e novembre 2013
Jean-Paul Lacroix, Maire
Cindy Breton, Directrice générale

La Guadeloupe
483, 9e rue est
La Guadeloupe, QC G0M 1G0
Tél: 418-459-3342; *Téléc:* 418-459-3507
dglagua@tlb.sympatico.ca
www.munlaguadeloupe.qc.ca
Entité municipal: Village
Incorporation: 6e août 1929 *Area:* 31,67 km2
Comté ou district: Beauce-Sartigan; *Population au 2006:* 1,758
Circonscription(s) électorale(s) provinciale(s): Beauce-Sud
Circonscription(s) électorale(s) fédérale(s): Beauce
Prochaines élections: 3e novembre 2013
Huguette Plante, Mairesse
Marc-André Doyle, Directeur général

La Haute-Côte-Nord
#101, 26, rue de la Rivière
Les Escoumins, QC G0T 1K0
Tél: 418-233-2102; *Téléc:* 418-233-3010
info@mrchcn.qc.ca
www.mrchcn.qc.ca
Entité municipal: Regional County Municipality
Incorporation: 1er janvier 1982
Population au 2006: 12,303
Note: 8 municipalités & 1 autre territoire.
Pierre Laurencele, Préfet
Alain Tremblay, Directeur général
atremblay@mrchcn.qc.ca

La Haute-Gaspésie
464, boul Ste-Anne ouest
Sainte-Anne-des-Monts, QC G4V 1T5
Tél: 418-763-7791; *Téléc:* 418-763-7737
mrchg.rdeschenes@globetrotter.net
www.hautegaspesie.com
Entité municipal: Regional County Municipality
Incorporation: 18 mars 1981
Population au 2006: 12,329
Note: 8 municipalités & 2 autres territoires.
Allen Cormier, Préfet
Renée Deschênes, Directrice générale

La Haute-Yamaska
#100, 142, rue Dufferin
Granby, QC J2G 4X1
Tél: 450-378-9975; *Téléc:* 450-378-2465
mrc@mrchauteyamaska.qc.ca
www.haute-yamaska.ca
Entité municipal: Regional County Municipality
Incorporation: 3e mars 1982
Population au 2006: 85,405
Note: 9 municipalités.
Pascal Russell, Préfet
Johanne Gaouette, Directrice générale
jgaouette@mrchauteyamaska.qc.ca

La Jacques-Cartier
60, rue St-Patrick
Shannon, QC G0A 4N0
Tél: 418-844-2160; *Téléc:* 418-844-2664
mrcjc@mrc.lajacquescartier.qc.ca
www.mrc.lajacquescartier.qc.ca
Entité municipal: Regional County Municipality
Incorporation: 1er avril 1981
Population au 2006: 29,738
Note: 9 municipalités & 1 autre territoire.
Jacques Marcotte, Préfet
Francine Breton, Directrice générale
fbreton@mrc.lajacquescartier.qc.ca

La Malbaie
280, rue John-Nairne
La Malbaie, QC G5A 1L9
Tél: 418-665-3747; *Téléc:* 418-665-4935
dg@ville.lamalbaie.qc.ca
www.ville.lamalbaie.qc.ca
Entité municipal: Town
Incorporation: 1er décembre 1999 *Area:* 470,57 km2
Comté ou district: Charlevoix-Est; *Population au 2006:* 8,959
Circonscription(s) électorale(s) provinciale(s): Charlevoix
Circonscription(s) électorale(s) fédérale(s): Montmorency-Charlevoix-Haute-Côte-Nord
Prochaines élections: 1er novembre 2013
Lise Lapointe, Mairesse
Caroline Tremblay, Greffière

La Martre
9, av du Phare
La Martre, QC G0E 2H0
Tél: 418-288-5605; *Téléc:* 418-288-5144
lamartre@globetrotter.net
Entité municipal: Municipality
Incorporation: 18 décembre 1923 *Area:* 185,69 km2
Comté ou district: La Haute-Gaspésie; *Population au 2006:* 253
Circonscription(s) électorale(s) provinciale(s): Matane
Circonscription(s) électorale(s) fédérale(s): Haute-Gaspésie-La Mitis-Matane-Matapédia
Prochaines élections: 3er novembre 2013
Claudette Robinson, Mairesse
Marie-Alexandrine Hudon, Directrice générale

La Matapédia
#501, 123, rue Desbiens
Amqui, QC G5J 3P9
Tél: 418-629-2053; *Téléc:* 418-629-3195
administration@mrcmatapedia.qc.ca
www.lamatapedia.com/mrc
Entité municipal: Regional County Municipality
Incorporation: 1er janvier 1982
Population au 2006: 19,199
Note: 18 municipalités & 7 autres territoires.
Chantale Lavoie, Préfète
Mario Lavoie, Directeur général

La Minerve
6, rue Mailloux
La Minerve, QC J0T 1S0
Tél: 819-274-2364; *Téléc:* 819-274-2031
bureau@municipalite.laminerve.qc.ca
www.municipalite.laminerve.qc.ca
Entité municipal: Municipality
Incorporation: 30 décembre 1892 *Area:* 297,78 km2
Comté ou district: Les Laurentides; *Population au 2006:* 1,295
Circonscription(s) électorale(s) provinciale(s): Labelle
Circonscription(s) électorale(s) fédérale(s): Laurentides-Labelle
Prochaines élections: 3e novembre 2013
Vacant, Maire
Pierre Gagnon, Directeur général (par intérim)

La Mitis
300, av du Sanatorium
Mont-Joli, QC G5H 1V7
Tél: 418-775-8445; *Téléc:* 418-775-9303
mrc.mitis@cgocable.ca
www.lamitis.ca
Entité municipal: Regional County Municipality
Incorporation: 1er janvier 1982
Population au 2006: 19,365
Note: 16 municipalités & 2 autres territoires.
Michel Côté, Préfet
Marcel Moreau, Directeur général
mmoreau@mitis.qc.ca

La Morandière
204, rte 397
La Morandière, QC J0Y 1S0
Tél: 819-734-6143; *Téléc:* 819-734-6143
lamo@cableamos.com
www.lamorandiere.ca
Entité municipal: Municipality
Incorporation: 1er janvier 1983 *Area:* 430 km2
Comté ou district: Abitibi; *Population au 2006:* 262
Circonscription(s) électorale(s) provinciale(s): Abitibi-Ouest
Circonscription(s) électorale(s) fédérale(s): Abitibi-Témiscamingue
Prochaines élections: 3e novembre 2013
Guy Lemire, Maire
Sandra Hardy, Directrice générale

La Motte
CP 644
349, ch St-Luc
La Motte, QC J0Y 1T0
Tél: 819-732-2878; *Téléc:* 819-727-4248
municipalite.lamotte@cableamos.com
www.municipalitedelamotte.ca
Entité municipal: Municipality
Incorporation: 30 mai 1921 *Area:* 224,03 km2
Comté ou district: Abitibi; *Population au 2006:* 395
Circonscription(s) électorale(s) provinciale(s): Abitibi-Ouest
Circonscription(s) électorale(s) fédérale(s): Abitibi-Témiscamingue
Prochaines élections: 3e novembre 2013
René Martineau, Maire
Rachel Cossette, Directrice générale

La Nouvelle-Beauce
#B, 700, rue Notre-Dame nord
Sainte-Marie, QC G6E 2K9
Tél: 418-387-3444; *Téléc:* 418-387-7060
mrc.lanouvellebeauce@nouvellebeauce.com
www.nouvellebeauce.com
Entité municipal: Regional County Municipality
Incorporation: 1er janvier 1982
Population au 2006: 31,415
Note: 11 municipalités.
Richard Lehoux, Préfet
Mario Caron, Directeur général
mariocaron@nouvellebeauce.com

La Patrie
18, rue Chartier
La Patrie, QC J0B 1Y0
Tél: 819-560-8535; *Téléc:* 819-888-2697
munilapatrie@hsfqc.ca
www.municipalite.lapatrie.qc.ca
Entité municipal: Municipality
Incorporation: 24 décembre 1997 *Area:* 206,95 km2
Comté ou district: Le Haut-St-François; *Population au 2006:* 805
Circonscription(s) électorale(s) provinciale(s): Mégantic-Compton
Circonscription(s) électorale(s) fédérale(s): Compton-Stanstead
Prochaines élections: 3e novembre 2013
Jacques Blais, Maire
Johanne Latendresse, Directrice générale

La Pêche
1, rue Principale ouest
La Pêche, QC J0X 2W0
Tél: 819-456-2161; *Téléc:* 819-456-4534
tchartrand@villelapeche.qc.ca
www.villelapeche.qc.ca
Entité municipal: Municipality
Incorporation: 1er janvier 1975 *Area:* 597,14 km2
Comté ou district: Les Collines-de-l'Outaouais; *Population au 2009:* 7,609
Circonscription(s) électorale(s) provinciale(s): Gatineau
Circonscription(s) électorale(s) fédérale(s): Pontiac
Prochaines élections: 3e novembre 2013
Robert Bussière, Maire
Charles Ricard, Directeur général

La Pocatière
412, 9e rue
La Pocatière, QC G0R 1Z0
Tél: 418-856-3394; *Téléc:* 418-856-5465
danielle.caron@lapocatiere.ca
www.lapocatiere.ca
Entité municipal: Town
Incorporation: 1er janvier 1960 *Area:* 22,71 km2
Comté ou district: Kamouraska; *Population au 2006:* 4,575
Circonscription(s) électorale(s) provinciale(s): Kamouraska-Témiscouata
Circonscription(s) électorale(s) fédérale(s): Montmagny-L'Islet-Kamouraska-Rivière-du-Loup
Prochaines élections: 3e novembre 2013
Sylvain Hudon, Maire
Danielle Caron, Greffière

La Présentation
772, rue Principale
La Présentation, QC J0H 1B0
Tél: 450-796-2317; *Téléc:* 450-796-1707
lapresentation@mrcmaskoutains.qc.ca
www.municipalitelapresentation.qc.ca
Entité municipal: Parish (Paroisse)
Incorporation: 1er juillet 1855 *Area:* 104,71 km2
Comté ou district: Les Maskoutains; *Population au 2006:* 2,115
Circonscription(s) électorale(s) provinciale(s): Verchères
Circonscription(s) électorale(s) fédérale(s): St-Hyacinthe-Bagot
Prochaines élections: 3e novembre 2013
Claude Roger, Maire
Lise Lapalme, Directrice générale

La Rédemption
CP 39
68, rue Soucy
La Rédemption, QC G0J 1P0
Tél: 418-776-5311; *Téléc:* 418-776-5711
redemption@mitis.qc.ca
www.municipalite.laredemption.qc.ca
Entité municipal: Parish (Paroisse)
Incorporation: 1er janvier 1956 *Area:* 116,29 km2
Comté ou district: La Mitis; *Population au 2006:* 515
Circonscription(s) électorale(s) provinciale(s): Matapédia
Circonscription(s) électorale(s) fédérale(s): Haute-Gaspésie-La Mitis-Matane-Matapédia
Prochaines élections: 3e novembre 2013
Isabelle Dupont, Mairesse
Nadine Roussy, Directrice générale

La Reine
1, 3e av ouest
La Reine, QC J0Z 2L0
Tél: 819-947-5271; *Téléc:* 819-947-5271
lareine@mrcao.qc.ca
www.lareine.ao.ca
Entité municipal: Municipality
Incorporation: 19 septembre 1981 *Area:* 100,01 km2
Comté ou district: Abitibi-Ouest; *Population au 2006:* 362
Circonscription(s) électorale(s) provinciale(s): Abitibi-Ouest
Circonscription(s) électorale(s) fédérale(s): Abitibi-Témiscamingue
Prochaines élections: 3e novembre 2013
Jean-Guy Boulet, Maire
Sylvie Germain, Directrice générale

La Rivière-du-Nord
#200, 161, rue de la Gare
Saint-Jérôme, QC J7Z 2B9
Tél: 450-436-9321; *Téléc:* 450-436-1977
info@mrcrivieredunord.qc.ca
www.mrcrivieredunord.qc.ca
Entité municipal: Regional County Municipality
Incorporation: 1er janvier 1983
Population au 2006: 101,571
Note: 5 municipalités.
Yvon Brière, Préfet
Pierre Godin, Directeur général
pgodindg@mrcrivieredunord.qc.ca

La Sarre
6, 4e av est
La Sarre, QC J9Z 1J9
Tél: 819-333-2282; *Téléc:* 819-333-3090
info@ville.lasarre.qc.ca
www.ville.lasarre.qc.ca
Entité municipal: Town
Incorporation: 19 avril 1980 *Area:* 148,21 km2
Comté ou district: Abitibi-Ouest; *Population au 2006:* 7,336
Circonscription(s) électorale(s) provinciale(s): Abitibi-Ouest
Circonscription(s) électorale(s) fédérale(s): Abitibi-Témiscamingue
Prochaines élections: 3e novembre 2013
Normand Houde, Maire
François Casaubon, Greffier

La Trinité-des-Monts
CP 9
12, rue Principale ouest
La Trinité-des-Monts, QC G0K 1B0
Tél: 418-779-2421; *Téléc:* 418-779-2454
muntrinite@globetrotter.net
trinite-des-monts.qc.ca
Entité municipal: Parish (Paroisse)
Incorporation: 1er janvier 1965 *Area:* 233,09 km2
Comté ou district: Rimouski-Neigette; *Population au 2006:* 278
Circonscription(s) électorale(s) provinciale(s): Rimouski
Circonscription(s) électorale(s) fédérale(s): Rimouski-Neigette-Témiscouata-Les Basques
Prochaines élections: 3e novembre 2013
Fernand Garon, Maire
Jacky Malenfant, Directrice générale

La Vallée-de-l'Or
42, place Hammond
Val-d'Or, QC J9P 3A9
Tél: 819-825-7733; *Téléc:* 819-825-4137
info@mrcvo.qc.ca
www.mrcvo.qc.ca
Entité municipal: Regional County Municipality
Incorporation: 8e avril 1981
Population au 2006: 41,896
Note: 6 municipalités & 5 autres territoires.
Fernand Trahan, Préfet
Louis Bourget, Directeur général
louisbourget@mrcvo.qc.ca

La Vallée-de-la-Gatineau
7, rue de la Polyvalente
Gracefield, QC J0X 1W0
Tél: 819-463-3241; *Téléc:* 819-463-3632
info@mrcvg.qc.ca
www.mrcvg.qc.ca
Entité municipal: Regional County Municipality
Incorporation: 1er janvieer 1983
Population au 2006: 20,518
Note: 17 municipalités & 5 autres territoires.
Pierre Rondeau, Préfet
André Beauchemin, Directeur général
abeauchemin@mrcvg.qc.ca

La Vallée-du-Richelieu
#100, 255, boul Laurier
McMasterville, QC J3G 0B7
Tél: 450-464-0339; *Téléc:* 450-464-3827
info@mrcvr.ca
www.vallee-du-richelieu.ca
Entité municipal: Regional County Municipality
Incorporation: 1er janvier 1982
Population au 2006: 106,762
Note: 13 municipalités.
Gilles Plante, Préfet
Bernard Roy, Directeur général

La Visitation-de-l'île-Dupas
113, rue de l'Église
La Visitation-de-l'île-Dupas, QC J0K 2P0
Tél: 450-836-6019; *Téléc:* 450-836-8266
admin@ile-dupas.ca
Entité municipal: Municipality
Incorporation: 1er juillet 1855 *Area:* 24,86 km2
Comté ou district: D'Autray; *Population au 2006:* 612
Circonscription(s) électorale(s) provinciale(s): Berthier
Circonscription(s) électorale(s) fédérale(s): Joliette
Prochaines élections: 3e novembre 2013
Maurice Désy, Maire
Sylive Toupin, Directrice générale

La Visitation-de-Yamaska
21, rue Principale
La Visitation, QC J0G 1C0
Tél: 450-564-2818; *Téléc:* 450-564-9923
info@lavisitationdeyamaska.net
www.lavisitationdeyamaska.net
Entité municipal: Municipality
Incorporation: 2 février 1899 *Area:* 41,86 km2
Comté ou district: Nicolet-Yamaska; *Population au 2006:* 348
Circonscription(s) électorale(s) provinciale(s): Nicolet-Yamaska
Circonscription(s) électorale(s) fédérale(s): Bas-Richelieu-Nicolet-Bécancour
Prochaines élections: 3e novembre 2013
Sylvain Laplante, Maire
Suzanne Bibeau, Directrice générale

Labelle
1, rue du Pont
Labelle, QC J0T 1H0
Tél: 819-681-3371; *Téléc:* 819-686-3820
info@municipalite.labelle.qc.ca
www.municipalite.labelle.qc.ca
Entité municipal: Municipality
Incorporation: 27 janvier 1973 *Area:* 217,11 km2
Comté ou district: Les Laurentides; *Population au 2006:* 2,258
Circonscription(s) électorale(s) provinciale(s): Labelle
Circonscription(s) électorale(s) fédérale(s): Laurentides-Labelle
Prochaines élections: 3e novembre 2013
Gilbert Brassard, Maire
Claire Coulombe, Directrice générale

Labrecque
3425, rue Ambroise
Labrecque, QC G0W 2S0
Tél: 418-481-2022; *Téléc:* 418-481-1210
municipalite@ville.labrecque.qc.ca
www.ville.labrecque.qc.ca
Entité municipal: Municipality
Incorporation: 6 octobre 1925 *Area:* 147,37 km2
Comté ou district: Lac-St-Jean-Est; *Population au 2006:* 1,295
Circonscription(s) électorale(s) provinciale(s): Lac-St-Jean
Circonscription(s) électorale(s) fédérale(s): Roberval-Lac-St-Jean
Prochaines élections: 3e novembre 2013
Daniel Perron, Maire
Suzanne Couture, Directrice générale

Lac-au-Saumon
CP 98
36, rue Bouillon
Lac-au-Saumon, QC G0J 1M0
Tél: 418-778-3378; *Téléc:* 418-778-3706
lacausaumon@mrcmatapedia.qc.ca
www.lacausaumon.com
Entité municipal: Municipality
Incorporation: 17 décembre 1997 *Area:* 79,74 km2
Comté ou district: La Matapédia; *Population au 2006:* 1,495
Circonscription(s) électorale(s) provinciale(s): Matapédia
Circonscription(s) électorale(s) fédérale(s): Haute-Gaspésie-La Mitis-Matane-Matapédia
Prochaines élections: 3e novembre 2013
Michel Chevarie, Maire
Chantale Gagné, Directrice générale

Lac-aux-Sables
820, rue St-Alphonse
Lac-aux-Sables, QC G0X 1M0
Tél: 418-336-2331; *Téléc:* 418-336-2500
lac-aux-sables@regionmekinac.com
www.lac-aux-sables.qc.ca
Entité municipal: Parish (Paroisse)
Incorporation: 24 avril 1899 *Area:* 285,45 km2
Comté ou district: Mékinac; *Population au 2006:* 1,312
Circonscription(s) électorale(s) provinciale(s): Portneuf
Circonscription(s) électorale(s) fédérale(s): St-Maurice-Champlain
Prochaines élections: 3e novembre 2013
Yvan Hamelin, Maire
Valérie Adm.A. Cloutier, Directrice générale

Lac-Beauport
65, ch du Tour-du-Lac
Lac-Beauport, QC G3B 0A1
Tél: 418-849-7141; *Téléc:* 418-849-0361
info@lacbeauport.net
www.lac-beauport.ca
Entité municipal: Municipality
Incorporation: 1er juillet 1855 *Area:* 62,72 km2
Comté ou district: La Jacques-Cartier; *Population au 2006:* 6,081
Circonscription(s) électorale(s) provinciale(s): Chauveau
Circonscription(s) électorale(s) fédérale(s): Portneuf—Jacques-Cartier
Prochaines élections: 3e novembre 2013
Michel Beaulieu, Maire
Richard Labrecque, Directeur général

Lac-Bouchette
249, rue Principale
Lac-Bouchette, QC G0W 1V0
Tél: 418-348-6306; *Téléc:* 418-348-9477
munilac@lac-bouchette.com
Entité municipal: Municipality
Incorporation: 25 septembre 1971 *Area:* 919,99 km2
Comté ou district: Le Domaine-du-Roy; *Population au 2006:* 1,311
Circonscription(s) électorale(s) provinciale(s): Roberval
Circonscription(s) électorale(s) fédérale(s):

Roberval-Lac-St-Jean
Prochaines élections: 3e novembre 2013
Benoît Gélinas, Maire
Jean-Pierre Tremblay, Directeur général

Lac-Brome
122, ch Lakeside
Lac-Brome, QC J0E 1V0
Tél: 450-243-6111; *Téléc:* 450-243-5300
reception@ville.lac-brome.qc.ca
ville.lac-brome.qc.ca
Entité municipal: Town
Incorporation: 2 janvier 1971 *Area:* 209,37 km2
Comté ou district: Brome-Missisquoi; *Population au 2006:* 5,629
Circonscription(s) électorale(s) provinciale(s): Brome-Missisquoi
Circonscription(s) électorale(s) fédérale(s): Brome-Missisquoi
Prochaines élections: 3e novembre 2013
Gilles Decelles, Maire
Alain Roy, Greffier

Lac-Delage
24, rue du Pied-des-Pentes
Lac-Delage, QC G3C 5A4
Tél: 418-848-2417; *Téléc:* 418-848-1948
villelacdelage@ccapcable.com
www.lacdelage.qc.ca
Entité municipal: Village
Incorporation: 11 février 1959 *Area:* 1,46 km2
Comté ou district: La Jacques-Cartier; *Population au 2006:* 530
Circonscription(s) électorale(s) provinciale(s): Chauveau
Circonscription(s) électorale(s) fédérale(s):
Portneuf-Jacques-Cartier
Prochaines élections: 3e novembre 2013
Marc Boiteau, Maire
Guylaine Thibault, Directrice générale

Lac-des-Aigles
CP 70
75, rue Principale
Lac-des-Aigles, QC G0K 1V0
Tél: 418-779-2300; *Téléc:* 418-779-3024
info@lacdesaigles.ca
Entité municipal: Municipality
Incorporation: 1er janvier 1948 *Area:* 85,10 km2
Comté ou district: Témiscouata; *Population au 2006:* 609
Circonscription(s) électorale(s) provinciale(s): Rimouski
Circonscription(s) électorale(s) fédérale(s):
Rimouski-Neigette-Témiscouata-Les Basques
Prochaines élections: 3e novembre 2013
Claude Breault, Maire
Francine Beaulieu, Directrice générale

Lac-des-Écorces
672, boul St-François
Lac-des-Écorces, QC J0W 1H0
Tél: 819-585-4600; *Téléc:* 819-585-4610
dg@lacdesecorces.ca
www.lacdesecorces.ca
Entité municipal: Municipality
Incorporation: 10 octobre 2002 *Area:* 143,59 km2
Comté ou district: Antoine-Labelle; *Population au 2006:* 2,884
Circonscription(s) électorale(s) provinciale(s): Labelle
Circonscription(s) électorale(s) fédérale(s): Laurentides-Labelle
Prochaines élections: 3e novembre 2013
Note: Effective October 10, 2002, the Municipality of Beaux-Rivages, the Village of Lac-des-Écorces & the Village of Val-Barrette amalgamated to create the new Municipality of Beaux-Rivages-Lac-des-Écorces-Val-Barrette. Effective June 21, 2003, name change
Pierre Flamand, Maire
Claude Meilleur, Directeur général

Lac-des-Plages
2053, ch Tour-du-Lac
Lac-des-Plages, QC J0T 1K0
Tél: 819-426-2391; *Téléc:* 819-426-2085
admin@lacdesplages.com
www.lacdesplages.com
Entité municipal: Municipality
Incorporation: 1er janvier 1950 *Area:* 121,78 km2
Comté ou district: Papineau; *Population au 2006:* 403
Circonscription(s) électorale(s) provinciale(s): Papineau
Circonscription(s) électorale(s) fédérale(s):
Argenteuil-Papineau-Mirabel
Prochaines élections: 3e novembre 2013
Josée Simon, Maire
Denis Dagenais, Directeur général

Lac-des-Seize-îles
47, rue de l'Église
Lac-des-Seize-îles, QC J0T 2M0
Tél: 450-226-3117; *Téléc:* 450-226-1461
munlac16iles@qc.aira.com
www.lac-des-seize-iles.ca
Entité municipal: Municipality
Incorporation: 19 février 1914 *Area:* 8,49 km2
Comté ou district: Les Pays-d'en-Haut; *Population au 2006:* 160
Circonscription(s) électorale(s) provinciale(s): Argenteuil
Circonscription(s) électorale(s) fédérale(s):
Argenteuil-Papineau-Mirabel
Prochaines élections: 3e novembre 2013
Luc Lamond, Maire
Luce Bergeron, Directrice générale

Lac-Drolet
685, rue Principale
Lac-Drolet, QC G0Y 1C0
Tél: 819-549-2332; *Téléc:* 819-549-2626
munlacdrolet@axion.ca
www.lacdrolet.ca
Entité municipal: Municipality
Incorporation: 1er janvier 1885 *Area:* 124,94 km2
Comté ou district: Le Granit; *Population au 2006:* 1,148
Circonscription(s) électorale(s) provinciale(s):
Mégantic-Compton
Circonscription(s) électorale(s) fédérale(s): Mégantic-L'Érable
Prochaines élections: 3e novembre 2013
Marielle Fecteau, Mairesse
Maryse Champagne, Directrice générale

Lac-du-Cerf
19, ch de l'Église
Lac-du-Cerf, QC J0W 1S0
Tél: 819-597-2424; *Téléc:* 819-597-4036
taxation@lac-du-cerf.ca
www.lac-du-cerf.info
Entité municipal: Municipality
Incorporation: 1er janvier 1955 *Area:* 78,45 km2
Comté ou district: Antoine-Labelle; *Population au 2006:* 424
Circonscription(s) électorale(s) provinciale(s): Labelle
Circonscription(s) électorale(s) fédérale(s): Laurentides-Labelle
Prochaines élections: 3e novembre 2013
Pauline Ouimet, Mairesse
Jacinthe Valiquette, Directrice générale

Lac-Etchemin
208, 2e Av
Lac-Etchemin, QC G0R 1S0
Tél: 418-625-4521; *Téléc:* 418-625-3175
munetchemin@sogetel.net
www.municipalite.lac-etchemin.qc.ca
Entité municipal: Municipality
Incorporation: 10 octobre 2001 *Area:* 160,57 km2
Comté ou district: Les Etchemins; *Population au 2006:* 4,045
Circonscription(s) électorale(s) provinciale(s): Bellechasse
Circonscription(s) électorale(s) fédérale(s): Lévis-Bellechasse
Prochaines élections: 3e novembre 2013
Harold Gagnon, Maire
Laurent Rheault, Directeur général

Lac-Frontière
22, rue de l'Église
Lac-Frontière, QC G0R 1T0
Tél: 418-245-3553; *Téléc:* 418-245-3552
municipalitelac-frontiere@globetrotter.net
www.lac-frontiere.ca
Entité municipal: Municipality
Incorporation: 7 février 1916 *Area:* 51,33 km2
Comté ou district: Montmagny; *Population au 2006:* 197
Circonscription(s) électorale(s) provinciale(s): Montmagny-L'Islet
Circonscription(s) électorale(s) fédérale(s):
Montmagny-L'Islet-Kamouraska-Rivière-du-Loup
Prochaines élections: 3e novembre 2013
Léon Laverdière, Maire
Dany Robert, Directrice générale

Lac-Mégantic
#200, 5527, rue Frontenac
Lac-Mégantic, QC G6B 1H6
Tél: 819-583-2441; *Téléc:* 819-583-5920
greffier@ville.lac-megantic.qc.ca
www.ville.lac-megantic.qc.ca
Entité municipal: Town
Incorporation: 14 mars 1907 *Area:* 20,33 km2
Comté ou district: Le Granit; *Population au 2006:* 5,967
Circonscription(s) électorale(s) provinciale(s):
Mégantic-Compton
Circonscription(s) électorale(s) fédérale(s): Mégantic-L'Érable
Prochaines élections: 3e novembre 2013
Colette Roy Laroche, Mairesse

Chantal Dion, Greffière

Lac-Poulin
CP 1019
Lac-Poulin, QC G0M 1P0
Tél: 418-228-7585; *Téléc:* 418-222-6931
munlacpoulin@globetrotter.net
Entité municipal: Village
Incorporation: 5 mars 1959 *Area:* 1,08 km2
Comté ou district: Beauce-Sartigan; *Population au 2006:* 135
Circonscription(s) électorale(s) provinciale(s): Beauce-Sud
Circonscription(s) électorale(s) fédérale(s): Beauce
Prochaines élections: 3e novembre 2013
Denis Drouin, Maire
Karina Bélanger, Directrice générale

Lac-Saguay
257A, rte 117
Lac-Saguay, QC J0W 1L0
Tél: 819-278-3972; *Téléc:* 819-278-0260
info@lacsaguay.qc.ca
www.lacsaguay.qc.ca
Entité municipal: Village
Incorporation: 1er juillet 1951 *Area:* 176,26 km2
Comté ou district: Antoine-Labelle; *Population au 2006:* 492
Circonscription(s) électorale(s) provinciale(s): Labelle
Circonscription(s) électorale(s) fédérale(s): Laurentides-Labelle
Prochaines élections: 3e novembre 2013
Francine Asselin-Bélisle, Mairesse
Richard Gagnon, Directeur général

Lac-Saint-Jean-Est
625, rue Bergeron ouest
Alma, QC G8B 1V3
Tél: 418-668-3023; *Téléc:* 418-668-5112
sabin.larouche@mrclac.qc.ca
www.mrclacsaintjeanest.qc.ca
Entité municipal: Regional County Municipality
Incorporation: 1er janvier 1982
Population au 2006: 51,170
Note: 14 municipalités & 4 autres territoires.
André Paradis, Préfet
Sabin Larouche, Directeur général
sabin.larouche@mrclac.qc.ca

Lac-Ste-Marie
CP 97
106, ch de Lac-Ste-Marie
Lac-Sainte-Marie, QC J0X 1Z0
Tél: 819-467-5437; *Téléc:* 819-467-3691
municipalite@lac-sainte-marie.com
www.lac-sainte-marie.com
Entité municipal: Municipality
Incorporation: 1er janvier 1872 *Area:* 211,13 km2
Comté ou district: La Vallée-de-la-Gatineau; *Population au 2006:* 647
Circonscription(s) électorale(s) provinciale(s): Gatineau
Circonscription(s) électorale(s) fédérale(s): Pontiac
Prochaines élections: 3e novembre 2013
Gary Lachapelle, Maire
Yvon Blanchard, Directeur général

Lac-Sergent
1149, ch Tour-du-Lac nord
Lac-Sergent, QC G0A 2J0
Tél: 418-875-4854; *Téléc:* 418-875-3805
lac-sergent@bellnet.ca
www.villelacsergent.com
Entité municipal: Village
Incorporation: 25 février 1921 *Area:* 3,52 km2
Comté ou district: Portneuf; *Population au 2006:* 423
Circonscription(s) électorale(s) provinciale(s): Portneuf
Circonscription(s) électorale(s) fédérale(s):
Portneuf-Jacques-Cartier
Prochaines élections: 3e novembre 2013
Denis Racine, Maire
Josée Brouillette, Directrice générale

Lac-Simon
CP 3550
849, ch du Tour-du-Lac
Chénéville, QC J0V 1E0
Tél: 819-428-3906; *Téléc:* 819-428-3455
mun.lacsimon@mrcpapineau.com
www.lac-simon.net
Entité municipal: Municipality
Incorporation: 1er janvier 1881 *Area:* 96,83 km2
Comté ou district: Papineau; *Population au 2006:* 869
Circonscription(s) électorale(s) provinciale(s): Papineau
Circonscription(s) électorale(s) fédérale(s):
Argenteuil-Papineau-Mirabel
Prochaines élections: 3e novembre 2013

Gaston A. Tremblay, Maire
Jacques Maillé, Directeur général

Lac-St-Joseph
1048, ch Thomas-Maher
Lac-St-Joseph, QC G3N 0B4
Tél: 418-875-3355; *Téléc:* 418-875-0444
villedelacstjoseph@coopcscf.com
www.villelacstjoseph.com
Entité municipal: Village
Incorporation: 10 juin 1936 *Area:* 32,81 km2
Comté ou district: La Jacques-Cartier; *Population au 2006:* 266
Circonscription(s) électorale(s) provinciale(s): Portneuf
Circonscription(s) électorale(s) fédérale(s):
Portneuf-Jacques-Cartier
Prochaines élections: 3e novembre 2013
O'Donnell Bédard, Maire
Vivian Viviers, Directrice générale

Lac-St-Paul
388, rue Principale
Lac-Saint-Paul, QC J0W 1K0
Tél: 819-587-4283; *Téléc:* 819-587-4892
dg@lac-saint-paul.ca
www.lac-saint-paul.ca
Entité municipal: Municipality
Incorporation: 11 septembre 1922 *Area:* 173,06 km2
Comté ou district: Antoine-Labelle; *Population au 2006:* 521
Circonscription(s) électorale(s) provinciale(s): Labelle
Circonscription(s) électorale(s) fédérale(s): Laurentides-Labelle
Prochaines élections: 3e novembre 2013
Claude Ménard, Maire
Suzanne Raymond, Directrice générale

Lac-Supérieur
1281, ch du Lac-Supérieur
Lac-Supérieur, QC J0T 1J0
Tél: 819-681-3370; *Téléc:* 819-688-3010
directiongenerale@muni.lacsuperieur.qc.ca
www.muni.lacsuperieur.qc.ca
Entité municipal: Municipality
Incorporation: 1er janvier 1881 *Area:* 380,36 km2
Comté ou district: Les Laurentides; *Population au 2006:* 1,745
Circonscription(s) électorale(s) provinciale(s): Labelle
Circonscription(s) électorale(s) fédérale(s): Laurentides-Labelle
Prochaines élections: 3e novembre 2013
Daniele Lagarde, Mairesse
Diane Taillon, Directrice générale

Lacolle
1, rue de l'Église sud
Lacolle, QC J0J 1J0
Tél: 450-246-3201; *Téléc:* 450-246-4412
admin@lacolle.com
www.lacolle.com
Entité municipal: Municipality
Incorporation: 13 septembre 2001 *Area:* 49,17 km2
Comté ou district: Le Haut-Richelieu; *Population au 2006:* 2,512
Circonscription(s) électorale(s) provinciale(s): Huntingdon
Circonscription(s) électorale(s) fédérale(s): St-Jean
Prochaines élections: 3e novembre 2013
Yves Duteau, Maire
Jacques Mireault, Directeur général

Laforce
CP 25
703, ch du Village
Laforce, QC J0Z 2J0
Tél: 819-722-2461; *Téléc:* 819-722-2462
dir.genlaforce@mrctemiscamingue.qc.ca
www.laforce.ca
Entité municipal: Municipality
Incorporation: 1er janvier 1979 *Area:* 612,65 km2
Comté ou district: Témiscamingue; *Population au 2006:* 174
Circonscription(s) électorale(s) provinciale(s):
Rouyn-Noranda-Témiscamingue
Circonscription(s) électorale(s) fédérale(s):
Abitibi-Témiscamingue
Prochaines élections: 3e novembre 2013
Gérald Charron, Maire
Daniel Lizotte, Directeur général

Lamarche
100, rue Principale
Lamarche, QC G0W 1X0
Tél: 418-481-2861; *Téléc:* 418-481-1412
mun.lamarche@ville.lamarche.qc.ca
www.ville.lamarche.qc.ca
Entité municipal: Municipality
Incorporation: 1er janvier 1967 *Area:* 94,79 km2
Comté ou district: Lac-St-Jean-Est; *Population au 2006:* 562
Circonscription(s) électorale(s) provinciale(s): Lac-St-Jean
Circonscription(s) électorale(s) fédérale(s):
Roberval-Lac-St-Jean
Prochaines élections: 3e novembre 2013
Claude Bourgault, Maire
Fabienne Girard, Directrice générale

Lambton
230, rue du Collège
Lambton, QC G0M 1H0
Tél: 418-486-7438; *Téléc:* 418-486-7440
dg@munilambton.qc.ca
www.lambton.ca
Entité municipal: Municipality
Incorporation: 23 décembre 1976 *Area:* 106,86 km2
Comté ou district: Le Granit; *Population au 2006:* 1,623
Circonscription(s) électorale(s) provinciale(s):
Mégantic-Compton
Circonscription(s) électorale(s) fédérale(s): Mégantic-L'Érable
Prochaines élections: 3e novembre 2013
Ghislain Bolduc, Maire
Sylvain Carrier, Directeur général

Landrienne
158, av Principale est
Landrienne, QC J0Y 1V0
Tél: 819-732-4357; *Téléc:* 819-732-3866
jperron@landrienne.com
www.landrienne.com
Entité municipal: Township
Incorporation: 15 juillet 1918 *Area:* 276,22 km2
Comté ou district: Abitibi; *Population au 2006:* 986
Circonscription(s) électorale(s) provinciale(s): Abitibi-Ouest
Circonscription(s) électorale(s) fédérale(s):
Abitibi-Témiscamingue
Prochaines élections: 3e novembre 2013
François Lemieux, Maire
Jacques Perron, Directeur général

Lanoraie
57, rue Laroche
Lanoraie, QC J0K 1E0
Tél: 450-887-1100; *Téléc:* 450-836-5221
info@lanoraie.ca
www.municipalite.lanoraie.qc.ca
Entité municipal: Municipality
Incorporation: 6 décembre 2000 *Area:* 102,04 km2
Comté ou district: D'Autray; *Population au 2006:* 4,067
Circonscription(s) électorale(s) provinciale(s): Berthier
Circonscription(s) électorale(s) fédérale(s): Berthier-Maskinongé
Prochaines élections: 3e novembre 2013
Jacinthe Brissette, Mairesse
Michel Dufort, Directeur général

Lantier
CP 39
118, croissant des Trois-Lacs
Lantier, QC J0T 1V0
Tél: 819-326-2674; *Téléc:* 819-326-5204
direction@municipalite.lantier.qc.ca
www.municipalite.lantier.qc.ca
Entité municipal: Municipality
Incorporation: 1er janvier 1948 *Area:* 43,57 km2
Comté ou district: Les Laurentides; *Population au 2006:* 825
Circonscription(s) électorale(s) provinciale(s): Bertrand
Circonscription(s) électorale(s) fédérale(s): Laurentides-Labelle
Prochaines élections: 3e novembre 2013
Richard Forget, Maire
Benoit Charbonneau, Directeur général

Larouche
709, rue Gauthier
Larouche, QC G0W 1Z0
Tél: 418-695-2201; *Téléc:* 418-693-2119
administration@villedelarouche.qc.ca
www.villedelarouche.qc.ca
Entité municipal: Municipality
Incorporation: 21 mars 1922 *Area:* 88 km2
Comté ou district: Le Fjord-du-Saguenay; *Population au 2006:* 1,200
Circonscription(s) électorale(s) provinciale(s): Lac-St-Jean
Circonscription(s) électorale(s) fédérale(s): Jonquière-Alma
Prochaines élections: 3e novembre 2013
Réjean Bédard, Maire
Martin Gagné, Directeur général

Latulipe-et-Gaboury
1B, rue Principale est
Latulipe-et-Gaboury, QC J0Z 2N0
Tél: 819-747-4281; *Téléc:* 819-747-2194
dir.gen_latulipe@mrctemiscamingue.qc.ca
www.latulipeetgaboury.net
Entité municipal: United Township (Cantons)
Incorporation: 18 novembre 1924 *Area:* 298,38 km2
Comté ou district: Témiscamingue; *Population au 2006:* 333
Circonscription(s) électorale(s) provinciale(s):
Rouyn-Noranda-Témiscamingue
Circonscription(s) électorale(s) fédérale(s):
Abitibi-Témiscamingue
Prochaines élections: 3e novembre 2013
Yvon Gingras, Maire
Julie Gilbert, Directrice générale

Launay
843, rue des Pionniers
Launay, QC J0Y 1W0
Tél: 819-796-2545; *Téléc:* 819-796-2546
canton.launay@cableamos.com
Entité municipal: Township
Incorporation: 18 mai 1921 *Area:* 252,44 km2
Comté ou district: Abitibi; *Population au 2006:* 226
Circonscription(s) électorale(s) provinciale(s): Abitibi-Ouest
Circonscription(s) électorale(s) fédérale(s):
Abitibi-Témiscamingue
Prochaines élections: 3e novembre 2013
Rémi Gilbert, Maire
Valérie Normand, Directrice générale

Laurier-Station
121, rue St-André
Laurier-Station, QC G0S 1N0
Tél: 418-728-3852; *Téléc:* 418-728-4801
info@ville.laurier-station.qc.ca
www.ville.laurier-station.qc.ca
Entité municipal: Village
Incorporation: 1er janvier 1951 *Area:* 12,43 km2
Comté ou district: Lotbinière; *Population au 2006:* 2,403
Circonscription(s) électorale(s) provinciale(s): Lotbinière
Circonscription(s) électorale(s) fédérale(s):
Lotbinière-Chutes-de-la-Chaudière
Prochaines élections: 3e novembre 2013
Pierrette Trépanier, Mairesse
Nancy Clavet, Directrice générale

Laurierville
140, rue Grenier
Laurierville, QC G0S 1P0
Tél: 819-365-4646; *Téléc:* 819-365-4200
rgingras@laurierville.ca
www.laurierville.net
Entité municipal: Municipality
Incorporation: 26 novembre 1997 *Area:* 110,62 km2
Comté ou district: L'Érable; *Population au 2006:* 1,404
Circonscription(s) électorale(s) provinciale(s): Lotbinière
Circonscription(s) électorale(s) fédérale(s): Mégantic-L'Érable
Prochaines élections: 3e novembre 2013
Marc Simoneau, Maire
Réjean Gingras, Directeur général

Laval
1, Place du Souvenir
Laval, QC H7V 3Z4
Tél: 450-978-3951; *Téléc:* 450-978-3966
info@ville.laval.qc.ca
www.ville.laval.qc.ca
Entité municipal: Regional County Municipality
Incorporation: 1er juin 1980
Population au 2006: 368,709
Gilles Vaillancourt, Préfet
Guy Collard, Directeur général

Laverlochère
CP 159
11, rue St-Isidore ouest
Laverlochère, QC J0Z 2P0
Tél: 819-765-5111; *Téléc:* 819-765-2564
dg.lave@mrctemiscamingue.qc.ca
www.temiscamingue.net/laverlochere
Entité municipal: Municipality
Incorporation: 3 octobre 1912 *Area:* 107,01 km2
Comté ou district: Témiscamingue; *Population au 2006:* 732
Circonscription(s) électorale(s) provinciale(s):
Rouyn-Noranda-Témiscamingue
Circonscription(s) électorale(s) fédérale(s):
Abitibi-Témiscamingue
Prochaines élections: 3e novembre 2013
Daniel Barrette, Maire
Monique Rivest, Directrice générale

Lawrenceville
2100, rue Dandenault
Lawrenceville, QC J0E 1W0
Tél: 450-535-6398; *Téléc:* 450-535-6537
munlaw@cooptel.qc.ca

Entité municipal: Village
Incorporation: 27 avril 1905 *Area:* 17,40 km2
Comté ou district: Le Val-St-François; *Population au 2006:* 642
Circonscription(s) électorale(s) provinciale(s): Brome-Missisquoi
Circonscription(s) électorale(s) fédérale(s): Shefford
Prochaines élections: 3e novembre 2013
Michel Carbonneau, Maire
Ginette Bergeron, Directrice générale

Le Domaine-du-Roy
901, boul St-Joseph
Roberval, QC G8H 2L8
Tél: 418-275-5044; *Téléc:* 418-275-4049
administration@mrcdomaineduroy.ca
www.domaineduroy.ca
Entité municipal: Regional County Municipality
Incorporation: 1er janvier 1983
Population au 2006: 31,956
Note: 9 municipalités & 1 autre territoire.
Bernard Généreux, Préfet
Denis Taillon, Directeur général
dtaillon@mrcdomaineduroy.ca

Le Fjord-du-Saguenay
3110, boul Martel
Saint-Honoré, QC G0V 1L0
Tél: 418-673-1705; *Téléc:* 418-673-7205
mrcdufjord@mrc-fjord.qc.ca
www.mrc-fjord.qc.ca
Entité municipal: Regional County Municipality
Population au 2006: 20,025
Note: 13 municipalités & 3 autres territoires.
Jean-Marie Claveau, Préfet
Christine Dufour, Directrice générale
christine.dufour@mrc-fjord.qc.ca

Le Granit
5090, rue Frontenac
Lac-Mégantic, QC G6B 1H3
Tél: 819-583-0181; *Téléc:* 819-583-5327
administration@mrcgranit.qc.ca
www.mrcgranit.qc.ca
Entité municipal: Regional County Municipality
Incorporation: 26 mai 1982
Population au 2011: 22,342
Note: 20 municipalités.
Maurice Bernier, Préfet
Serge Bilodeau, Directeur général

Le Haut-Richelieu
380, 4e av
Saint-Jean-sur-Richelieu, QC J2X 1W9
Tél: 450-346-3636; *Téléc:* 450-346-8464
info@mrchr.qc.ca
mrchr.qc.ca
Entité municipal: Regional County Municipality
Incorporation: 1er janvier 1982
Population au 2006: 108,892
Note: 14 municipalités.
Gilles Dolbec, Préfet
Joane Saulnier, Directrice générale

Le Haut-St-François
85, rue du Parc
Cookshire, QC J0B 1M0
Tél: 819-875-5451; *Téléc:* 819-875-3135
dominic.provost@hsfqc.ca
www.mrchsf.com
Entité municipal: Regional County Municipality
Incorporation: 1er janvier 1982
Population au 2006: 21,744
Note: 14 municipalités.
Nicole Robert, Préfète
nicole.robert@hsfqc.ca
Dominique Provost, Directeur général

Le Haut-St-Laurent
#400, 10, rue King
Huntingdon, QC J0S 1H0
Tél: 450-264-5411; *Téléc:* 450-264-6885
mrchsl@mrchsl.com
www.mrchsl.com
Entité municipal: Regional County Municipality
Incorporation: 1 janvier 1982
Population au 2006: 21,943
Note: 13 municipalités.
Alain Castagner, Préfet
François Landreville, Directeur général

Le Rocher-Percé
CP 128
129, boul René-Lévesque ouest
Chandler, QC G0C 1K0
Tél: 418-689-4313; *Téléc:* 418-689-5807
mrc@rocherperce.qc.ca
www.mrcrocherperce.qc.ca
Entité municipal: Regional County Municipality
Incorporation: 1 avril 1981
Population au 2006: 18,437
Note: 5 municipalités & 1 autre territoire.
Diane Lebouthillier, Préfet
Mario Grenier, Directeur général
418-689-4017

Le Val-St-François
CP 3160
810, montée du Parc
Richmond, QC J0B 2H0
Tél: 819-826-6505; *Téléc:* 819-826-3484
mrc@val-saint-francois.qc.ca
www.val-saint-francois.qc.ca
Entité municipal: Regional County Municipality
Incorporation: 26 mai 1982
Population au 2006: 29,023
Note: 18 municipalités.
Claude Boucher, Préfet
Manon Fortin, Directrice générale
manon.fortin@val-saint-francois.qc.ca

Lebel-sur-Quévillon
CP 430
500, place Quévillon
Lebel-sur-Quévillon, QC J0Y 1X0
Tél: 819-755-4826; *Téléc:* 819-755-8124
ville@lebel-sur-quevillon.com
www.lebel-sur-quevillon.com
Entité municipal: Town
Incorporation: 6 août 1965 *Area:* 44,74 km2
Population au 2006: 2,729
Circonscription(s) électorale(s) provinciale(s): Ungava
Circonscription(s) électorale(s) fédérale(s):
Abitibi-Baie-James-Nunavik-Eeyou
Prochaines élections: 3e novembre 2013
Gérald Lemoyne, Maire
Réal Lavigne, Greffier

Leclercville
1014, rue de l'Église
Leclercville, QC G0S 2K0
Tél: 819-292-2331; *Téléc:* 819-292-2639
mun.leclercville@videotron.ca
www.munleclercville.qc.ca
Entité municipal: Municipality
Incorporation: 26 janvier 2000 *Area:* 135,40 km2
Comté ou district: Lotbinière; *Population au 2006:* 524
Circonscription(s) électorale(s) provinciale(s): Lotbinière
Circonscription(s) électorale(s) fédérale(s):
Lotbinière-Chutes-de-la-Chaudière
Prochaines élections: 3e novembre 2013
Marcel Richard, Maire
Francine B. Demers, Directrice générale

Lefebvre
186, 10e rang
Lefebvre, QC J0H 2C0
Tél: 819-394-2782; *Téléc:* 819-394-2186
municipalite.lefebvre@xittel.ca
Entité municipal: Municipality
Incorporation: 10 octobre 1922 *Area:* 65,75 km2
Comté ou district: Drummond; *Population au 2006:* 806
Circonscription(s) électorale(s) provinciale(s): Johnson
Circonscription(s) électorale(s) fédérale(s): Drummond
Prochaines élections: 3e novembre 2013
Claude Bahl, Maire
Julie Yergeau, Directrice générale

Lejeune
CP 40
69, rue de la Grande-Coulée
Lejeune, QC G0L 1S0
Tél: 418-855-2428; *Téléc:* 418-855-2428
info@municipalitelejeune.ca
Entité municipal: Municipality
Incorporation: 1er janvier 1964 *Area:* 269,40 km2
Comté ou district: Témiscouata; *Population au 2006:* 357
Circonscription(s) électorale(s) provinciale(s):
Kamouraska-Témiscouata
Circonscription(s) électorale(s) fédérale(s):
Rimouski-Neigette-Témiscouata-Les Basques
Prochaines élections: 3e novembre 2013
Lucie Gilbert, Mairesse
Claudine Castonguay, Directrice générale

Lemieux
530, rue de l'Église
Lemieux, QC G0X 1S0
Tél: 819-283-2506; *Téléc:* 819-283-2029
info@municipalitelemieux.ca
Entité municipal: Municipality
Incorporation: 14 août 1922 *Area:* 74,79 km2
Comté ou district: Bécancour; *Population au 2006:* 323
Circonscription(s) électorale(s) provinciale(s): Lotbinière
Circonscription(s) électorale(s) fédérale(s):
Bas-Richelieu-Nicolet-Bécancour
Prochaines élections: 3e novembre 2013
Jean-Louis Bélisle, Maire
France Hénault, Directrice générale

Léry
1, rue de l'Hôtel-de-Ville
Léry, QC J6N 1E8
Tél: 450-692-6861; *Téléc:* 450-692-6881
villedelery@videotron.ca
Entité municipal: Town
Incorporation: 1er juin 1914 *Area:* 10,98 km2
Comté ou district: Roussillon; *Population au 2006:* 2,385
Circonscription(s) électorale(s) provinciale(s): Châteauguay
Circonscription(s) électorale(s) fédérale(s):
Châteauguay-St-Constant
Prochaines élections: 3e novembre 2013
Yvon Mailhot, Maire
Dale Stewart, Directeur général

Les Appalaches
3830, boul Frontenac ouest
Thetford Mines, QC G6H 2L8
Tél: 418-423-2757; *Téléc:* 418-423-5122
info@mrcdesappalaches.ca
www.mrcdesappalaches.ca
Entité municipal: Regional County Municipality
Incorporation: 1er janvier 1982
Population au 2006: 43,390
Note: 19 municipalités.
Ghislain Hamel, Préfet
Marie-Eve Mercier, Directrice générale
memercier@mrcdesappalaches.ca

Les Basques
#400, 2, rue Jean-Rioux
Trois-Pistoles, QC G0L 4K0
Tél: 418-851-3206; *Téléc:* 418-851-3171
mrc@mrcdesbasques.com
www.mrcdesbasques.com
Entité municipal: Regional County Municipality
Incorporation: 1er avril 1981
Population au 2006: 9,475
Note: 11 municipalités & 1 autre territoire.
Denis Bertin, Préfet
François Gosselin, Directeur général

Les Bergeronnes
CP 158
424, rue de la Mer
Les Bergeronnes, QC G0T 1G0
Tél: 418-232-6244; *Téléc:* 418-232-6602
info@bergeronnes.com
www.bergeronnes.net
Entité municipal: Municipality
Incorporation: 29 décembre 1999 *Area:* 291,89 km2
Comté ou district: La Haute Côte-Nord; *Population au 2006:* 655
Circonscription(s) électorale(s) provinciale(s): René-Lévesque
Circonscription(s) électorale(s) fédérale(s):
Montmorency-Charlevoix-Haute-Côte-Nord
Prochaines élections: 3e novembre 2013
Francis Bouchard, Maire
Lynda Tremblay, Directrice générale

Les Cèdres
1060, ch du Fleuve
Les Cèdres, QC J7T 1A1
Tél: 450-452-4651; *Téléc:* 450-452-4605
dgenerale@ville.lescedres.qc.ca
www.ville.lescedres.qc.ca
Entité municipal: Municipality
Incorporation: 9 mars 1985 *Area:* 78,31 km2
Comté ou district: Vaudreuil-Soulanges; *Population au 2006:* 5,732
Circonscription(s) électorale(s) provinciale(s): Soulanges
Circonscription(s) électorale(s) fédérale(s): Vaudreuil-Soulanges
Prochaines élections: 3e novembre 2013
Géraldine T. Quesnel, Mairesse
Jimmy Poulin, Directeur général

Les Chenaux
630, rue Principale
Saint-Luc-de-Vincennes, QC G0X 3K0
Tél: 819-840-0704; *Téléc:* 819-295-5117
info@mrcdeschenaux.ca
www.mrcdeschenaux.ca
Entité municipal: Regional County Municipality
Incorporation: 1er janvier 2002
Population au 2006: 16,944
Note: 10 municipalités.
Gérard Bruneau, Préfet
Pierre St-Onge, Directeur général
pierre.stonge@mrcdeschenaux.ca

Les Collines-de-l'Outaouais
216, ch Old Chelsea
Chelsea, QC J9B 1J4
Tél: 819-827-0516; *Téléc:* 819-827-4669
gpoulin@mrcdescollines.com
www.mrcdescollines.com
Entité municipal: Regional County Municipality
Incorporation: 4e décembre 1991
Population au 2006: 42,005
Note: 7 municipalités.
Robert Bussière, Préfet
Ghislain Poulin, Directeur général

Les Coteaux
65, rte 338
Les Coteaux, QC J7X 1A2
Tél: 450-267-3531; *Téléc:* 450-267-3532
municipalitedescoteaux@videotron.ca
www.les-coteaux.qc.ca
Entité municipal: Municipality
Incorporation: 18 mai 1994 *Area:* 12,11 km2
Comté ou district: Vaudreuil-Soulanges; *Population au 2006:* 3,764
Circonscription(s) électorale(s) provinciale(s): Soulanges
Circonscription(s) électorale(s) fédérale(s): Vaudreuil-Soulanges
Prochaines élections: 3e novembre 2013
Réal Boisvert, Maire
Claude Madore, Directeur général

Les Éboulements
248, rue du Village
Les Éboulements, QC G0A 2M0
Tél: 418-489-2988; *Téléc:* 418-489-2989
municipalite@leseboulements.com
www.leseboulements.com
Entité municipal: Municipality
Incorporation: 19 septembre 2001 *Area:* 153,99 km2
Comté ou district: Charlevoix; *Population au 2006:* 1,264
Circonscription(s) électorale(s) provinciale(s): Charlevoix
Circonscription(s) électorale(s) fédérale(s): Montmorency-Charlevoix-Haute-Côte-Nord
Prochaines élections: 3e novembre 2013
Bertrand Bouchard, Maire
Linda Gauthier, Directrice générale

Les Escoumins
2, rue Sirois
Les Escoumins, QC G0T 1K0
Tél: 418-233-2766; *Téléc:* 418-233-3273
administration.muni@escoumins.ca
www.escoumins.ca
Entité municipal: Municipality
Incorporation: 5 mai 1863 *Area:* 267,33 km2
Comté ou district: La Haute-Côte-Nord; *Population au 2006:* 2,073
Circonscription(s) électorale(s) provinciale(s): René-Lévesque
Circonscription(s) électorale(s) fédérale(s): Montmorency-Charlevoix-Haute-Côte-Nord
Prochaines élections: 3e novembre 2013
Pierre Laurencelle, Maire
Chantale Otis, Directrice générale

Les Etchemins
1137, rte 277
Lac-Etchemin, QC G0R 1S0
Tél: 418-625-9000; *Téléc:* 418-625-9005
mrcetchemins@sogetel.net
www.mrcetchemins.qc.ca
Entité municipal: Regional County Municipality
Incorporation: 1er janvier 1982
Population au 2006: 17,599
Note: 13 muncipalités.
Hector Provençal, Préfet
Fernand Heppell, Directeur général
fheppell@mrcetchemins.qc.ca

Les Hauteurs
50, rue de l'Église
Les Hauteurs, QC G0K 1C0
Tél: 418-798-8266; *Téléc:* 418-798-4707
leshauteurs@mitis.qc.ca
municipalite.leshauteurs.qc.ca
Entité municipal: Municipality
Incorporation: 7e novembre 1918 *Area:* 105,41 km2
Comté ou district: La Mitis; *Population au 2006:* 576
Circonscription(s) électorale(s) provinciale(s): Matapédia
Circonscription(s) électorale(s) fédérale(s): Haute-Gaspésie-La Mitis-Matane-Matapédia
Prochaines élections: 3e novembre 2013
Noël Lambert, Maire
Diane Bernier, Directrice générale

Les Îles-de-la-Madeleine
460, ch Principal
Cap-aux-Meules, QC G4T 1A1
Tel: 418-986-3100; *Fax:* 418-986-6962
jlebreux@muniles.ca
www.muniles.ca
Municipal Type: Municipality
Incorporated: 1er janvier 2002 *Area:* 166,39 km2
Population in 2006: 12,560
Provincial Electoral District(s): Îles-de-la-Madeleine
Federal Electoral District(s): Gaspésie—Îles-de-la-Madeleine
Next Election: 3e novembre 2013
Joël Arseneau, Maire
Jean-Yves Lebreux, Greffier

Les Jardins-de-Napierville
1767, rue Principale
Saint-Michel, QC J0L 2J0
Tél: 450-454-0559; *Téléc:* 450-454-0560
info@mrcjardinsdenapierville.ca
mrcjardinsdenapierville.ca
Entité municipal: Regional County Municipality
Incorporation: 1er janvier 1982
Population au 2006: 24,111
Circonscription(s) électorale(s) provinciale(s): Huntington
Circonscription(s) électorale(s) fédérale(s): Beauharnois-Salaberry
Note: 11 municipalités.
Michel Lavoie, Préfet
M. Michel Charbonneau, Directeur général
michel.c@cld-jardinsdenapierville.com

Les Laurentides
1255, ch des Lacs
Saint-Faustin-Lac-Carré, QC J0T 1J2
Tél: 819-425-5555; *Téléc:* 819-688-6590
adm@mrclaurentides.qc.ca
www.mrclaurentides.qc.ca
Entité municipal: Regional County Municipality
Incorporation: 1er janvier 1983
Population au 2006: 42,896
Note: 20 municipalités.
Ronald Provost, Préfet
Michel Bélanger, Directeur général
mbelanger@mrclaurentides.qc.ca

Les Maskoutains
805, av du Palais
Saint-Hyacinthe, QC J2S 5C6
Tél: 450-774-3141; *Téléc:* 450-774-7161
admin@mrcmaskoutains.qc.ca
www.mrcmaskoutains.qc.ca
Entité municipal: Regional County Municipality
Incorporation: 1er janvier 1982
Population au 2006: 80,694
Note: 17 municipalités.
Francine Morin, Préfète
Gabriel Michaud, Directeur général

Les Méchins
108, rte des Fonds
Les Méchins, QC G0J 1T0
Tél: 418-729-3952; *Téléc:* 418-729-3585
lesmechins@mrcdematane.qc.ca
www.lesmechins.com
Entité municipal: Municipality
Incorporation: 27 novembre 1982 *Area:* 452 km2
Comté ou district: Matane; *Population au 2006:* 1,148
Circonscription(s) électorale(s) provinciale(s): Matane
Circonscription(s) électorale(s) fédérale(s): Haute-Gaspésie-La Mitis-Matane-Matapédia
Prochaines élections: 3e novembre 2013
Jean-Sébastien Barriault, Maire
Lyne Fortin, Directrice générale

Les Moulins
148, rue St-André
Terrebonne, QC J6W 3C3
Tél: 450-471-9576; *Téléc:* 450-471-8193
info@mrclesmoulins.ca
www.mrclesmoulins.ca
Entité municipal: Regional County Municipality
Incorporation: 1er janvier 1982
Population au 2006: 128,467
Note: 2 municipalités.
Jean-Marc Robitaille, Préfet
Daniel Pilon, Directeur général
dpilon@mrclesmoulins.ca

Les Pays-d'en-Haut
1014, rue Valiquette
Sainte-Adèle, QC J8B 2M3
Tél: 450-229-6637; *Téléc:* 450-229-5203
info@mrcpdh.org
www.mrcpdh.com
Entité municipal: Regional County Municipality
Incorporation: 1er janvier 1983
Population au 2006: 36,573
Note: 10 municipalités.
Charles Garnier, Préfet
Yvan Genest, Directeur général

Lingwick
72, rte 108
Lingwick, QC J0B 2Z0
Tél: 819-560-8422; *Téléc:* 819-877-3315
canton.lingwick@hsfqc.ca
www.cantondelingwick.com
Entité municipal: Township
Incorporation: 1er juillet 1855 *Area:* 242,83 km2
Comté ou district: Le Haut-St-François; *Population au 2006:* 611
Circonscription(s) électorale(s) provinciale(s): Mégantic-Compton
Circonscription(s) électorale(s) fédérale(s): Compton-Stanstead
Prochaines élections: 3e novembre 2013
Céline Gagné, Mairesse
Monique Polard, Directrice générale

Litchfield
CP 340
1362, rte 148
Campbell's Bay, QC J0X 1K0
Tél: 819-648-5511; *Téléc:* 819-648-5575
litchfield@mrcpontiac.qc.ca
Entité municipal: Municipality
Incorporation: 1er juillet 1855 *Area:* 178,96 km2
Comté ou district: Pontiac; *Population au 2006:* 483
Circonscription(s) électorale(s) provinciale(s): Pontiac
Circonscription(s) électorale(s) fédérale(s): Pontiac
Prochaines élections: 3e novembre 2013
Michael McCrank, Maire
Jacqueline Brisebois, Directrice générale

Lochaber
164, rte 148 est
Lochaber, QC J0X 3B0
Tél: 819-985-3291; *Téléc:* 819-985-3291
munlochaber@qc.aira.com
Entité municipal: Township
Incorporation: 1er juillet 1855 *Area:* 62,17 km2
Comté ou district: Papineau; *Population au 2006:* 497
Circonscription(s) électorale(s) provinciale(s): Papineau
Circonscription(s) électorale(s) fédérale(s): Argenteuil-Papineau-Mirabel
Prochaines élections: 3e novembre 2013
Georges Leduc, Maire
Marthe Thibaudeau, Directrice générale

Lochaber-Partie-Ouest
#11, 161, rue Galipeau
Thurso, QC J0X 3B0
Tél: 819-985-1553; *Téléc:* 819-985-0790
mun.lochaberouest@mrcpapineau.com
Entité municipal: Township
Incorporation: 20 avril 1891 *Area:* 61,22 km2
Comté ou district: Papineau; *Population au 2006:* 514
Circonscription(s) électorale(s) provinciale(s): Papineau
Circonscription(s) électorale(s) fédérale(s): Argenteuil-Papineau-Mirabel
Prochaines élections: 3e novembre 2013
Michel Labreque, Maire
Alain Hotte, Directeur général

Longue-Pointe-de-Mingan
CP 68
878, ch du Roi
Longue-Pointe-de-Mingan, QC G0G 1V0
Tél: 418-949-2053; *Téléc:* 418-949-2166
munlpm@xplornet.com
Entité municipal: Municipality
Incorporation: 1er janvier 1966 *Area:* 417,60 km2
Comté ou district: Minganie; *Population au 2006:* 430
Circonscription(s) électorale(s) provinciale(s): Duplessis
Circonscription(s) électorale(s) fédérale(s): Manicouagan
Prochaines élections: 3e novembre 2013
Jean-Luc Burgess, Maire
Célyne B.-Loiselle, Directrice générale

Longue-Rive
3, rue de l'Église
Longue-Rive, QC G0T 1Z0
Tél: 418-231-2344; *Téléc:* 418-231-2577
munlonguerive@bellnet.ca
Entité municipal: Municipality
Incorporation: 28 mai 1997 *Area:* 295,35 km2
Comté ou district: La Haute-Côte-Nord; *Population au 2006:* 1,259
Circonscription(s) électorale(s) provinciale(s): René-Lévesque
Circonscription(s) électorale(s) fédérale(s): Montmorency-Charlevoix-Haute-Côte-Nord
Prochaines élections: 3e novembre 2013
Mario Tremblay, Maire
Hélène Boulianne, Sec.-Trés.

Lorraine
33, boul De Gaulle
Lorraine, QC J6Z 3W9
Tél: 450-621-8550; *Téléc:* 450-621-4763
communication@ville.lorraine.qc.ca
www.ville.lorraine.qc.ca
Entité municipal: Town
Incorporation: 4e février 1960 *Area:* 5,96 km2
Comté ou district: Thérèse-De Blainville; *Population au 2006:* 9,613
Circonscription(s) électorale(s) provinciale(s): Blainville
Circonscription(s) électorale(s) fédérale(s): Marc-Aurèle-Fortin
Prochaines élections: 3e novembre 2013
Ramez Ayoub, Maire
450-965-8717
mairie@ville.lorraine.qc.ca
Sylvie Trahan, Greffière
450-621-8550
greffe@ville.lorraine.qc.ca

Lorrainville
CP 218
2, rue St-Jean-Baptiste est
Lorrainville, QC J0Z 2R0
Tél: 819-625-2167; *Téléc:* 819-625-2380
lorrainville@mrctemiscamingue.qc.ca
www.lorrainville.ca
Entité municipal: Municipality
Incorporation: 16 février 1994 *Area:* 85,12 km2
Comté ou district: Témiscamingue; *Population au 2006:* 1,325
Circonscription(s) électorale(s) provinciale(s): Rouyn-Noranda-Témiscamingue
Circonscription(s) électorale(s) fédérale(s): Abitibi-Témiscamingue
Prochaines élections: 3e novembre 2013
Philippe Boutin, Maire
Francyne Bleau, Directrice générale

Lotbinière
7440, rue Marie-Victorin
Lotbinière, QC G0S 1S0
Tél: 418-796-2103; *Téléc:* 418-796-2198
info@municipalite.lotbiniere.qc.ca
www.municipalite.lotbiniere.qc.ca
Entité municipal: Municipality
Incorporation: 1er janvier 1979 *Area:* 78,47 km2
Comté ou district: Lotbinière; *Population au 2006:* 931
Circonscription(s) électorale(s) provinciale(s): Lotbinière
Circonscription(s) électorale(s) fédérale(s): Lotbinière-Chutes-de-la-Chaudière
Prochaines élections: 3e novembre 2013
Maurice Sénécal, Maire
Bernard Lepage, Directeur général

Lotbinière
6375, rue Garneau
Sainte-Croix, QC G0S 2H0
Tél: 418-926-3407; *Téléc:* 418-926-3409
info@mrclotbiniere.org
www.mrclotbiniere.org
Entité municipal: Regional County Municipality
Incorporation: 1 janvier 1982
Population au 2006: 27,425
Note: 18 municipalités.
Maurice Sénécal, Préfet
Daniel Patry, Directeur général
daniel.patry@mrclotbiniere.org

Louiseville
105, av St-Laurent
Louiseville, QC J5V 1J6
Tél: 819-228-9437; *Téléc:* 819-228-2263
directiongenerale@ville.louiseville.qc.ca
www.ville.louiseville.qc.ca
Entité municipal: Town
Incorporation: 31 décembre 1988 *Area:* 62,56 km2
Comté ou district: Maskinongé; *Population au 2006:* 7,433
Circonscription(s) électorale(s) provinciale(s): Maskinongé
Circonscription(s) électorale(s) fédérale(s): Berthier-Maskinongé
Prochaines élections: 3e novembre 2013
Guy Richard, Mairesse
Martine St-Yves, Greffière

Low
4A, ch d'Amour
Low, QC J0X 2C0
Tél: 819-422-3528; *Téléc:* 819-422-3796
info@lowquebec.ca
www.lowquebec.ca
Entité municipal: Township
Incorporation: 1er janvier 1858 *Area:* 259,95 km2
Comté ou district: La Vallée-de-la-Gatineau; *Population au 2006:* 956
Circonscription(s) électorale(s) provinciale(s): Gatineau
Circonscription(s) électorale(s) fédérale(s): Pontiac
Prochaines élections: 3e novembre 2013
Morris O'Connor, Maire
Liette Hickey, Directrice générale

Lyster
2375, rue Bécancour
Lyster, QC G0S 1V0
Tél: 819-389-5787; *Téléc:* 819-389-5981
info@municipalite.lyster.qc.ca
www.municipalite.lyster.qc.ca
Entité municipal: Municipality
Incorporation: 18 septembre 1976 *Area:* 162,35 km2
Comté ou district: L'Érable; *Population au 2006:* 1,644
Circonscription(s) électorale(s) provinciale(s): Lotbinière
Circonscription(s) électorale(s) fédérale(s): Mégantic-L'Érable
Prochaines élections: 3e novembre 2013
Sylvain Labrecque, Maire
Suzie Côté, Directrice générale

Macamic
70, rue Principale
Macamic, QC J0Z 2S0
Tél: 819-782-4604; *Téléc:* 819-782-4283
macamic@mrcao.qc.ca
www.villemacamic.qc.ca
Entité municipal: Town
Incorporation: 6 mars 2002 *Area:* 191,95 km2
Comté ou district: Abitibi-Ouest; *Population au 2006:* 2,726
Circonscription(s) électorale(s) provinciale(s): Abitibi-Ouest
Circonscription(s) électorale(s) fédérale(s): Abitibi-Témiscamingue
Prochaines élections: 3e novembre 2013
Daniel Rancourt, Maire
Denis Bédard, Directeur général

Maddington
86, rte 261 nord
Maddington, QC G0Z 1C0
Tél: 819-367-2577; *Téléc:* 819-367-3137
info@maddington.ca
Entité municipal: Township
Incorporation: 11 janvier 1902 *Area:* 23,38 km2
Comté ou district: Arthabaska; *Population au 2006:* 412
Circonscription(s) électorale(s) provinciale(s): Nicolet-Yamaska
Circonscription(s) électorale(s) fédérale(s): Richmond-Arthabaska
Prochaines élections: 3e novembre 2013
Normand Soucy, Maire
Martine Lebeau, Directrice générale

Malartic
CP 3090
901, rue Royale
Malartic, QC J0Y 1Z0
Tél: 819-757-3611; *Téléc:* 819-757-3084
cmaurice@ville.malartic.qc.ca
www.ville.malartic.qc.ca
Entité municipal: Town
Incorporation: 28 avril 1939 *Area:* 159,31 km2
Comté ou district: La Vallée-de-l'Or; *Population au 2006:* 3,640
Circonscription(s) électorale(s) provinciale(s): Abitibi-Est
Circonscription(s) électorale(s) fédérale(s): Abitibi-Baie-James-Nunavik-Eeyou
Prochaines élections: 3e novembre 2013
André Vezeau, Maire
Claudyne Maurice, Greffière

Mandeville
162, rue Desjardins
Mandeville, QC J0K 1L0
Tél: 450-835-2055; *Téléc:* 450-835-7795
mandeville@intermonde.net
www.mandeville.qc.ca
Entité municipal: Municipality
Incorporation: 20 avril 1904 *Area:* 330,85 km2
Comté ou district: D'Autray; *Population au 2006:* 2,221
Circonscription(s) électorale(s) provinciale(s): Berthier
Circonscription(s) électorale(s) fédérale(s): Joliette
Prochaines élections: 3e novembre 2013
Francine Bergeron, Mairesse
Hélène Plourde, Directrice générale

Manicouagan
768, rue Bossé
Baie-Comeau, QC G5C 1L6
Tél: 418-589-9594; *Téléc:* 418-589-6383
info@mrcmanicouagan.qc.ca
www.mrcmanicouagan.qc.ca
Entité municipal: Regional County Municipality
Incorporation: 1er avril 1981
Population au 2006: 33,052
Note: 8 municipalités & 1 autre territoire.
Christine Brisson, Préfète
Patricia Huet, Directrice générale
patricia.huet@globetrotter.net

Maniwaki
186, rue Principale sud
Maniwaki, QC J9E 1Z9
Tél: 819-449-2800; *Téléc:* 819-449-7078
maniwaki@ville.maniwaki.qc.ca
www.ville.maniwaki.qc.ca
Entité municipal: Town
Incorporation: 15 mars 1904 *Area:* 5,60 km2
Comté ou district: La Vallée-de-la-Gatineau; *Population au 2006:* 4,102
Circonscription(s) électorale(s) provinciale(s): Gatineau
Circonscription(s) électorale(s) fédérale(s): Pontiac
Prochaines élections: 3e novembre 2013
Robert Coulombe, Maire
Andrée Loyer, Greffière

Manseau
200, rue Roux
Manseau, QC G0X 1V0
Tél: 819-356-2450; *Téléc:* 819-356-2721
directiongenerale@manseau.ca
www.manseau.ca
Entité municipal: Municipality
Incorporation: 31 décembre 1997 *Area:* 102,5 km2
Comté ou district: Bécancour; *Population au 2006:* 934
Circonscription(s) électorale(s) provinciale(s): Lotbinière
Circonscription(s) électorale(s) fédérale(s): Bas-Richelieu-Nicolet-Bécancour
Prochaines élections: 3e novembre 2013
Guy St-Pierre, Maire
Nadine Watters, Directrice générale

Mansfield-et-Pontefract
300, rue Principale
Mansfield, QC J0X 1R0
Tél: 819-683-2944; *Téléc:* 819-683-3590
mansfield@personainternet.com
Entité municipal: Municipality
Incorporation: 1er janvier 1868 *Area:* 420,79 km2
Comté ou district: Pontiac; *Population au 2006:* 2,064
Circonscription(s) électorale(s) provinciale(s): Pontiac
Circonscription(s) électorale(s) fédérale(s): Pontiac
Prochaines élections: 3e novembre 2013
Leslie L. Bélair, Maire
Éric Rochon, Directeur général

Marguerite-D'Youville
609, rte Marie-Victorin
Verchères, QC J0L 2R0
Tél: 450-583-3301; *Téléc:* 450-583-3592
info@margueritedyouville.ca
www.margueritedyouville.ca

Entité municipal: Regional County Municipality
Incorporation: 1er janvier 1982
Population au 2009: 69,881
Note: 6 municipalités.
Suzanne Roy, Préfète
Sylvain Berthiaume, Directeur général

Maria

545, boul Perron
Maria, QC G0C 1Y0
Tél: 418-759-3883; *Téléc:* 418-759-3059
munmaria@globetrotter.net
www.mariaquebec.com
Entité municipal: Municipality
Incorporation: 1er juillet 1855 *Area:* 96,34 km2
Comté ou district: Avignon; *Population au 2006:* 2,401
Circonscription(s) électorale(s) provinciale(s): Bonaventure
Circonscription(s) électorale(s) fédérale(s): Gaspésie—îles-de-la-Madeleine
Prochaines élections: 3e novembre 2013
Normand Audet, Maire
Gilbert Leblanc, Directeur général

Maria-Chapdelaine

173, boul St-Michel
Dolbeau-Mistassini, QC G8L 4N9
Tél: 418-276-2131; *Téléc:* 418-276-7043
portail@mrcmaria.qc.ca
www.mrcdemaria-chapdelaine.ca
Entité municipal: Regional County Municipality
Incorporation: 1er janvier 1983
Population au 2006: 25,767
Note: 12 municipalités & 2 autres territoires.
Jean-Pierre Boivin, Préfet
Christian Bouchard, Directeur général
cbouchard@mrcmaria.qc.ca

Maricourt

1195, 3e rang nord
Maricourt, QC J0E 1Y0
Tél: 450-532-2243; *Téléc:* 450-532-2246
munmari@cooptel.qc.ca
Entité municipal: Municipality
Incorporation: 1er janvier 1864 *Area:* 62,03 km2
Comté ou district: Le Val-St-François; *Population au 2006:* 432
Circonscription(s) électorale(s) provinciale(s): Johnson
Circonscription(s) électorale(s) fédérale(s): Shefford
Prochaines élections: 3e novembre 2013
Réjean Paquette, Maire
Yves Barthe, Directeur général

Marieville

682, rue Saint-Charles
Marieville, QC J3M 1P9
Tél: 450-460-4444; *Téléc:* 450-460-2770
administration@ville.marieville.qc.ca
www.ville.marieville.qc.ca
Entité municipal: Town
Incorporation: 14 juin 2000 *Area:* 64,25 km2
Comté ou district: Rouville; *Population au 2006:* 7,904
Circonscription(s) électorale(s) provinciale(s): Iberville
Circonscription(s) électorale(s) fédérale(s): Chambly-Borduas
Prochaines élections: 3e novembre 2013
Alain Ménard, Maire
Nancy Forget, Greffière

Marsoui

CP 130
8, rte Principale est
Marsoui, QC G0E 1S0
Tél: 418-288-5552; *Téléc:* 418-288-5104
municipalite.marsoui@globetrotter.net
www.marsoui.com
Entité municipal: Village
Incorporation: 1er janvier 1950 *Area:* 182,95 km2
Comté ou district: La Haute-Gaspésie; *Population au 2006:* 341
Circonscription(s) électorale(s) provinciale(s): Matane
Circonscription(s) électorale(s) fédérale(s): Haute-Gaspésie-La Mitis-Matane-Matapédia
Prochaines élections: 3e novembre 2013
Jovette Gasse, Mairesse
Nancy Leclerc, Directrice générale

Marston

175, rte 263 sud
Marston, QC G0Y 1G0
Tél: 819-583-0435; *Téléc:* 819-583-6604
marston@axion.ca
www.munmarston.qc.ca
Entité municipal: Township
Incorporation: 1er janvier 1874 *Area:* 71,77 km2
Comté ou district: Le Granit; *Population au 2006:* 683
Circonscription(s) électorale(s) provinciale(s): Mégantic-Compton
Circonscription(s) électorale(s) fédérale(s): Mégantic-L'Érable
Prochaines élections: 3e novembre 2013
Jacques Lalonde, Maire
Francine Veilleux, Directrice générale

Martinville

233, rue Principale est
Martinville, QC J0B 2A0
Tél: 819-835-5390; *Téléc:* 819-835-0171
martinville@qc.aira.com
Entité municipal: Municipality
Incorporation: 21 décembre 1895 *Area:* 48,64 km2
Comté ou district: Coaticook; *Population au 2006:* 467
Circonscription(s) électorale(s) provinciale(s): Mégantic-Compton
Circonscription(s) électorale(s) fédérale(s): Compton-Stanstead
Prochaines élections: 3e novembre 2013
Réjean Masson, Maire
France Veilleux, Directrice générale

Maskinongé

154, boul Ouest, rte 138
Maskinongé, QC J0K 1N0
Tél: 819-227-2243; *Téléc:* 819-227-2097
fgervais@mun-maskinonge.ca
www.mun-maskinonge.ca
Entité municipal: Municipality
Incorporation: 25 avril 2001 *Area:* 75,98 km2
Comté ou district: Maskinongé; *Population au 2006:* 2,233
Circonscription(s) électorale(s) provinciale(s): Maskinongé
Circonscription(s) électorale(s) fédérale(s): Berthier-Maskinongé
Prochaines élections: 3e novembre 2013
Roger Michaud, Maire
France Gervais, Directrice générale

Maskinongé

651, boul St-Laurent est
Louiseville, QC J5V 1J1
Tél: 819-228-9461; *Téléc:* 819-228-2193
mrcinfo@mrc-maskinonge.qc.ca
www.mrc-maskinonge.qc.ca
Entité municipal: Regional County Municipality
Incorporation: 1er janvier 1982
Population au 2006: 35,637
Note: 17 municipalités.
Robert Lalonde, Préfet
Janyse L. Pichette, Directrice générale

Massueville

CP 90
881, rue Royale
Massueville, QC J0G 1K0
Tél: 450-788-2957; *Téléc:* 450-788-2050
massueville@bas-richelieu.net
www.massueville.net
Entité municipal: Village
Incorporation: 25 mars 1903 *Area:* 1,29 km2
Comté ou district: Pierre-De Saurel; *Population au 2006:* 520
Circonscription(s) électorale(s) provinciale(s): Richelieu
Circonscription(s) électorale(s) fédérale(s): Bas-Richelieu-Nicolet-Bécancour
Prochaines élections: 3e novembre 2013
Denis Marion, Maire
France Saint-Pierre, Directrice générale

Matagami

CP 160
195, boul Matagami
Matagami, QC J0Y 2A0
Tél: 819-739-2541; *Téléc:* 819-739-4278
matagami@matagami.com
www.matagami.com
Entité municipal: Village
Incorporation: 1er avril 1963 *Area:* 64,75 km2
Population au 2006: 1,555
Circonscription(s) électorale(s) provinciale(s): Ungava
Circonscription(s) électorale(s) fédérale(s): Abitibi-Baie-James-Nunavik-Eeyou
Prochaines élections: 3e novembre 2013
René Dubé, Maire
Pierre Deslauriers, Greffier

Matane

145, rue Soucy
Matane, QC G4W 2E1
Tél: 418-562-6734; *Téléc:* 418-562-7265
mrcmatane@mrcdematane.qc.ca
Entité municipal: Regional County Municipality
Incorporation: 1er janvier 1982
Population au 2006: 22,247
Note: 11 municipalités & 1 autre territoire.
Yvan Imbeault, Préfet
Line Ross, Directrice générale

Matapédia

CP 207
1, rue de l'Hôtel-de-Ville
Matapédia, QC G0J 1V0
Tél: 418-865-2917; *Téléc:* 418-865-2828
munmata@globetrotter.net
Entité municipal: Parish (Paroisse)
Incorporation: 4e novembre 1905 *Area:* 70,75 km2
Comté ou district: Avignon; *Population au 2006:* 696
Circonscription(s) électorale(s) provinciale(s): Bonaventure
Circonscription(s) électorale(s) fédérale(s): Gaspésie—îles-de-la-Madeleine
Prochaines élections: 3e novembre 2013
Louis Michaud, Maire
Carole Bélanger, Directrice générale

Matawinie

3184, 1re Av
Rawdon, QC J0K 1S0
Tél: 450-834-5441; *Téléc:* 450-834-6560
administration@matawinie.org
www.matawinie.org
Entité municipal: Regional County Municipality
Incorporation: 1er janvier 1982
Population au 2006: 49,717
Note: 15 municipalités & 12 autres territoires.
Gaétan Morin, Préfet
Lyne Arbour, Directrice générale

Mayo

CP 2936
20, ch McAlendin
Gatineau, QC J8L 4J7
Tél: 819-986-3199; *Téléc:* 819-986-8881
mun.mayo@mrcpapineau.com
Entité municipal: Municipality
Incorporation: 1er août 1864 *Area:* 72,67 km2
Comté ou district: Papineau; *Population au 2006:* 549
Circonscription(s) électorale(s) provinciale(s): Papineau
Circonscription(s) électorale(s) fédérale(s): Argenteuil-Papineau-Mirabel
Prochaines élections: 3e novembre 2013
Gaëtan Brunet, Maire
Yves Lafleur, Directeur général

McMasterville

255, boul Constable
McMasterville, QC J3G 6N9
Tél: 450-467-3580; *Téléc:* 450-467-2493
hoteldeville@municipalitemcmasterville.qc.ca
www.mcmasterville.ca
Entité municipal: Municipality
Incorporation: 31 juillet 1917 *Area:* 3,00 km2
Comté ou district: La Vallée-du-Richelieu; *Population au 2006:* 5,234
Circonscription(s) électorale(s) provinciale(s): Borduas
Circonscription(s) électorale(s) fédérale(s): Chambly-Borduas
Prochaines élections: 3e novembre 2013
Gilles Plante, Maire
Lyne Savaria, Directrice générale

Mékinac

560, rue Notre-Dame
Saint-Tite, QC G0X 3H0
Tél: 418-365-5151; *Téléc:* 418-365-7377
mrcmekinac@mrcmekinac.com
www.regionmekinac.com
Entité municipal: Regional County Municipality
Incorporation: 1 janvier 1982
Population au 2006: 12,672
Note: 10 municipalités & 4 autres territoires.
Lucien Mongrain, Préfet
Claude Beaulieu, Directeur général
claude.beaulieu@mrcmekinac.com

Melbourne

1257, rte 243
Melbourne, QC J0B 2B0
Tél: 819-826-3555; *Téléc:* 819-826-3981
melcan@qc.aibn.com
www.melbournecanton.ca
Entité municipal: Township
Incorporation: 1er juillet 1855 *Area:* 170,29 km2
Comté ou district: Le Val-St-François; *Population au 2006:* 1,095
Circonscription(s) électorale(s) provinciale(s): Richmond
Circonscription(s) électorale(s) fédérale(s):

Richmond-Arthabaska
Prochaines élections: 3e novembre 2013
James Johnston, Maire
Cindy Jones, Directrice générale

Memphrémagog
#200, 455, rue MacDonald
Magog, QC J1X 1M2
Tél: 819-843-9292; *Téléc:* 819-843-7295
info@mrcmemphremagog.com
www.mrcmemphremagog.com
Entité municipal: Regional County Municipality
Incorporation: 1er janvier 1982
Population au 2006: 45,310
Note: 17 municipalités.
Gérard Marinovich, Préfet
Guy Jauron, Directeur général
g.jauron@mrcmemphremagog.com

Messines
CP 69
70, rue Principale
Messines, QC J0X 2J0
Tél: 819-465-2323; *Téléc:* 819-465-2943
info@messines.ca
www.messines.ca
Entité municipal: Municipality
Incorporation: 19 août 1921 *Area:* 108,46 km2
Comté ou district: La Vallée-de-la-Gatineau; *Population au 2006:* 1,610
Circonscription(s) électorale(s) provinciale(s): Gatineau
Circonscription(s) électorale(s) fédérale(s): Pontiac
Prochaines élections: 3e novembre 2013
Ronald Cross, Maire
Jim Smith, Directeur général

Métabetchouan—Lac-à-la-Croix
87, rue St-André
Métabetchouan—Lac-à-la-Croix, QC G8G 1A1
Tél: 418-349-2060; *Téléc:* 418-349-2395
bouchard.mario@ville.metabetchouan.qc.ca
www.ville.metabetchouan.qc.ca
Entité municipal: Town
Incorporation: 6 janvier 1999 *Area:* 185,86 km2
Comté ou district: Lac-St-Jean-Est; *Population au 2006:* 4,084
Circonscription(s) électorale(s) provinciale(s): Lac-St-Jean
Circonscription(s) électorale(s) fédérale(s): Roberval-Lac-St-Jean
Prochaines élections: 3e novembre 2013
Lili Simard, Mairesse
Mario Bouchard, Greffier

Métis-sur-Mer
138, rue Principale
Métis-sur-Mer, QC G0J 1S0
Tél: 418-936-3255; *Téléc:* 418-936-3117
metissurmer@mitis.qc.ca
www.ville.metis-sur-mer.qc.ca
Entité municipal: Village
Incorporation: 4 juillet 2002 *Area:* 48,01 km2
Comté ou district: La Mitis; *Population au 2006:* 604
Circonscription(s) électorale(s) provinciale(s): Matapédia
Circonscription(s) électorale(s) fédérale(s): Haute-Gaspésie-La Mitis-Matane-Matapédia
Prochaines élections: 3e novembre 2013
Jean-Pierre Pelletier, Maire
Stéphane Marcheterre, Greffier

Milan
CP 54
403, rang Ste-Marie
Milan, QC G0Y 1E0
Tél: 819-657-4527; *Téléc:* 819-657-2987
munmilan@axion.ca
www.munmilan.qc.ca
Entité municipal: Municipality
Incorporation: 1er juin 1948 *Area:* 130,06 km2
Comté ou district: Le Granit; *Population au 2006:* 299
Circonscription(s) électorale(s) provinciale(s): Mégantic-Compton
Circonscription(s) électorale(s) fédérale(s): Mégantic-L'Érable
Prochaines élections: 3e novembre 2013
Claude Turcotte, Maire
Noëlla Bergeron, Directrice générale

Mille-Isles
1262, ch de Mille-Isles
Mille-Isles, QC J0R 1A0
Tél: 450-438-2958; *Téléc:* 450-438-6157
jringuette@mille-isles.ca
www.mille-isles.ca
Entité municipal: Municipality
Incorporation: 1er juillet 1855 *Area:* 59,98 km2
Comté ou district: Argenteuil; *Population au 2006:* 1,480
Circonscription(s) électorale(s) provinciale(s): Argenteuil
Circonscription(s) électorale(s) fédérale(s): Argenteuil-Papineau-Mirabel
Prochaines élections: 3e novembre 2013
Yvon Samson, Maire
Johanne Ringuette, Directrice générale

Minganie
1303, rue de la Digue
Hâvre-Saint-Pierre, QC G0G 1P0
Tél: 418-538-2732; *Téléc:* 418-538-3711
info@mrc.minganie.org
www.mrc.minganie.org
Entité municipal: Regional County Municipality
Incorporation: 1er janvier 1982
Population au 2006: 6,390
Note: 8 municipalités & 2 autres territoires.
Julien Boudreault, Prèfet
Nathalie de Grandpré, Directice générale

Mirabel
14111, rue Saint-Jean
Mirabel, QC J7J 1Y3
Tél: 450-475-8653; *Téléc:* 450-475-7195
communications@ville.mirabel.qc.ca
www.ville.mirabel.qc.ca
Entité municipal: Regional County Municipality
Incorporation: 1er janvier 1985
Population au 2006: 34,626
Note: 1 municipalité.
Hubert Meilleur, Préfet
Suzanne Mireault, Directrice générale
s.mireault@ville.mirabel.qc.ca

Mistissini
187, ch Main
Mistissini, QC G0W 1C0
Tél: 418-923-3461; *Téléc:* 418-923-3115
legislative@mistissini.ca
Entité municipal: Villages Cris
Incorporation: 28 juin 1978 *Area:* 526,13 km2
Circonscription(s) électorale(s) provinciale(s): Ungava
Circonscription(s) électorale(s) fédérale(s): Abitibi-Baie-James-Nunavik-Eeyou
Prochaines élections: 1er août 2010
Richard Shecapio, Maire
Thomas Neeposh, Directeur général

Moffet
CP 89
14D, rue Principale
Moffet, QC J0Z 2W0
Tél: 819-747-6116; *Téléc:* 819-747-6117
dg.moffet@mrctemiscamingue.qc.ca
www.moffet.ca
Entité municipal: Municipality
Incorporation: 1er janvier 1953 *Area:* 431,46 km2
Comté ou district: Témiscamingue; *Population au 2006:* 208
Circonscription(s) électorale(s) provinciale(s): Rouyn-Noranda-Témiscamingue
Circonscription(s) électorale(s) fédérale(s): Abitibi-Témiscamingue
Prochaines élections: 3e novembre 2013
Michel Paquette, Maire
Linda Roy, Directrice générale

Mont-Carmel
22, rue de la Fabrique
Mont-Carmel, QC G0L 1W0
Tél: 418-498-2050; *Téléc:* 418-489-2522
direction@mont-carmel.ca
www.mont-carmel.ca
Entité municipal: Municipality
Incorporation: 1er juillet 1855 *Area:* 435,29 km2
Comté ou district: Kamouraska; *Population au 2006:* 1,198
Circonscription(s) électorale(s) provinciale(s): Kamouraska-Témiscouata
Circonscription(s) électorale(s) fédérale(s): Montmagny-L'Islet-Kamouraska-Riviére-du-Loup
Prochaines élections: 3e novembre 2013
Denis Lévesque, Maire
Odile Soucy, Directrice générale

Mont-Joli
40, av de l'Hôtel-de-Ville
Mont-Joli, QC G5H 1W8
Tél: 418-775-7285; *Téléc:* 418-775-6320
mont-joli@ville.mont-joli.qc.ca
www.ville.mont-joli.qc.ca
Entité municipal: Town
Incorporation: 13 juin 2001 *Area:* 22,64 km2
Comté ou district: La Mitis; *Population au 2006:* 6,568
Circonscription(s) électorale(s) provinciale(s): Matapédia
Circonscription(s) électorale(s) fédérale(s): Huate-Gaspésie-La Mitis-Matane-Matapédia
Prochaines élections: 3e novembre 2013
Jean Bélanger, Maire
Yves Sénéchal, Greffier

Mont-St-Grégoire
225, rue St-Joseph
Mont-Saint-Grégoire, QC J0J 1K0
Tél: 450-347-5376; *Téléc:* 450-347-9200
taxes@mmsg.ca
www.mont-saint-gregoire.ca
Entité municipal: Municipality
Incorporation: 21 décembre 1994 *Area:* 79,92 km2
Comté ou district: Le Haut-Richelieu; *Population au 2006:* 2,922
Circonscription(s) électorale(s) provinciale(s): Iberville
Circonscription(s) électorale(s) fédérale(s): St-Jean
Prochaines élections: 3e novembre 2013
Suzanne Boulais, Mairesse
Christianne Pouliot, Directrice générale

Mont-St-Michel
94, rue de l'Église
Mont-Saint-Michel, QC J0W 1P0
Tél: 819-587-3093; *Téléc:* 819-587-3781
mun.mont-st-michel@tlb.sympatico.ca
Entité municipal: Municipality
Incorporation: 11 septembre 1928 *Area:* 137,65 km2
Comté ou district: Antoine-Labelle; *Population au 2006:* 625
Circonscription(s) électorale(s) provinciale(s): Labelle
Circonscription(s) électorale(s) fédérale(s): Laurentides-Labelle
Prochaines élections: 3e novembre 2013
Roger Lapointe, Maire
Lucie Gagnon, Directrice générale

Mont-St-Pierre
CP 9
102, rue Prudent-Cloutier
Mont-Saint-Pierre, QC G0E 1V0
Tél: 418-797-2898; *Téléc:* 418-797-2307
mont-st-pierre@globetrotter.net
www.mont-saint-pierre.ca
Entité municipal: Village
Incorporation: 1er janvier 1947 *Area:* 60,45 km2
Comté ou district: La Haute-Gaspésie; *Population au 2006:* 230
Circonscription(s) électorale(s) provinciale(s): Matane
Circonscription(s) électorale(s) fédérale(s): Haute-Gaspésie-La Mitis-Matane-Matapédia
Prochaines élections: 3e novembre 2013
Jean-Sébastien Cloutier, Maire
Jérôme Émond, Directeur général

Mont-Tremblant
1145, rue de St-Jovite
Mont-Tremblant, QC J8E 1V1
Tél: 819-425-8614; *Téléc:* 819-425-2528
info@villedemont-tremblant.qc.ca
www.villedemont-tremblant.qc.ca
Entité municipal: Town
Incorporation: 22 novembre 2000 *Area:* 235,97 km2
Comté ou district: Les Laurentides; *Population au 2006:* 8,892
Circonscription(s) électorale(s) provinciale(s): Labelle
Circonscription(s) électorale(s) fédérale(s): Laurentides-Labelle
Prochaines élections: 3e novembre 2013
Pierre Pilon, Maire
Isabelle Grenier, Greffière

Montcalm
10, rue de l'Hôtel-de-Ville
Montcalm, QC J0T 2V0
Tél: 819-687-2836;
direction@municipalite.montcalm.qc.ca
www.municipalite.montcalm.qc.ca
Entité municipal: Municipality
Incorporation: 6e mars 1907 *Area:* 119,65 km2
Comté ou district: Les Laurentides; *Population au 2006:* 652
Circonscription(s) électorale(s) provinciale(s): Argenteuil
Circonscription(s) électorale(s) fédérale(s): Laurentides-Labelle
Prochaines élections: 3e novembre 2013
Steven Larose, Maire
Lucie Côté, Directrice générale

Montcalm
1540, rue Albert
Sainte-Julienne, QC J0K 2T0
Tél: 450-831-2182; *Téléc:* 450-831-2647
info@mrcmontcalm.com
www.mrcmontcalm.com

Entité municipal: Regional County Municipality
Incorporation: 1er janvier 1982
Population au 2006: 42,558
Note: 11 municipalités.
Danielle Henri Allard, Préfet
Gaétan Hudon, Directeur général

Montcerf-Lytton
18, rue Principale nord
Montcerf-Lytton, QC J0W 1N0
Tél: 819-449-4578; *Téléc:* 819-449-7310
mun.montcerf@ireseau.com
www.montcerf-lytton.com
Entité municipal: Municipality
Incorporation: 19 septembre 2001 *Area:* 358,34 km2
Comté ou district: La Vallée-de-la-Gatineau; *Population au 2006:* 739
Circonscription(s) électorale(s) provinciale(s): Gatineau
Circonscription(s) électorale(s) fédérale(s): Pontiac
Prochaines élections: 3e novembre 2013
Alain Fortin, Maire
Liliane Crytes, Directrice générale

Montebello
550, rue Notre-Dame
Montebello, QC J0V 1L0
Tél: 819-423-5123; *Téléc:* 819-423-5703
mun.montebello@videotron.ca
www.ville.montebello.qc.ca
Entité municipal: Municipality
Incorporation: 29 août 1878 *Area:* 7,85 km2
Comté ou district: Papineau; *Population au 2006:* 987
Circonscription(s) électorale(s) provinciale(s): Papineau
Circonscription(s) électorale(s) fédérale(s):
Argenteuil-Papineau-Mirabel
Prochaines élections: 3e novembre 2013
Pierre Bertrand, Maire
Charles-Guy Beauchamp, Directeur général

Montmagny
159, rue Saint-Louis
Montmagny, QC G5V 1N5
Tél: 418-248-5985; *Téléc:* 418-248-4624
mrc@montmagny.com
www.montmagny.com
Entité municipal: Regional County Municipality
Incorporation: 1er janvier 1982
Population au 2006: 23,201
Note: 14 municipalités.
Jean-Guy Desrosiers, Préfet
Nancy Labrecque, Directrice générale

Montpellier
4, rue du Bosquet
Montpellier, QC J0V 1M0
Tél: 819-428-3663; *Téléc:* 819-428-1221
admin.montpellier@mrcpapineau.com
www.montpellier.ca
Entité municipal: Municipality
Incorporation: 11 octobre 1920 *Area:* 249,16 km2
Comté ou district: Papineau; *Population au 2006:* 966
Circonscription(s) électorale(s) provinciale(s): Papineau
Circonscription(s) électorale(s) fédérale(s):
Argenteuil-Papineau-Mirabel
Prochaines élections: 3e novembre 2013
Pierre Bernier, Maire
Manon Lanthier, Directrice générale (par intérim)

Morin-Heights
567, ch du Village
Morin-Heights, QC J0R 1H0
Tél: 450-226-3232; *Téléc:* 450-226-8786
municipalite@morinheights.com
www.morinheights.com
Entité municipal: Municipality
Incorporation: 1er juillet 1855 *Area:* 55,42 km2
Comté ou district: Les Pays-d'en-Haut; *Population au 2006:* 3,503
Circonscription(s) électorale(s) provinciale(s): Argenteuil
Circonscription(s) électorale(s) fédérale(s):
Argenteuil-Papineau-Mirabel
Prochaines élections: 3e novembre 2013
Timothy Watchorn, Maire
Yves Desmarais, Directeur général

Mulgrave-et-Derry
591, av de Buckingham
Gatineau, QC J8L 2H2
Tél: 819-986-9519; *Téléc:* 819-986-9954
mulgrave-derry@bellnet.ca
Entité municipal: Municipality
Incorporation: 1er janvier 1870 *Area:* 297,74 km2
Comté ou district: Papineau; *Population au 2006:* 389
Circonscription(s) électorale(s) provinciale(s): Papineau
Circonscription(s) électorale(s) fédérale(s):
Argenteuil-Papineau-Mirabel
Prochaines élections: 3e novembre 2013
Michael Kane, Maire
Isabelle Cusson, Directrice générale

Murdochville
CP 1120
635, 5e rue
Murdochville, QC G0E 1W0
Tél: 418-784-2536; *Téléc:* 418-784-2607
dgmurd@globetrotter.net
www.murdochville.com
Entité municipal: Village
Incorporation: 15 juillet 1953 *Area:* 64,68 km2
Comté ou district: La Côte-de-Gaspé; *Population au 2006:* 812
Circonscription(s) électorale(s) provinciale(s): Gaspé
Circonscription(s) électorale(s) fédérale(s):
Gaspésie—Îles-de-la-Madeleine
Prochaines élections: 3e novembre 2013
Délisca Ritchie Roussy, Mairesse
Jean-Pierre Cassivi, Greffier

Namur
996, rue du Centenaire
Namur, QC J0V 1N0
Tél: 819-426-2457; *Téléc:* 819-426-3074
dirgeneral.namur@mrcpapineau.com
Entité municipal: Municipality
Incorporation: 1er janvier 1964 *Area:* 57,07 km2
Comté ou district: Papineau; *Population au 2006:* 487
Circonscription(s) électorale(s) provinciale(s): Papineau
Circonscription(s) électorale(s) fédérale(s):
Argenteuil-Papineau-Mirabel
Prochaines élections: 3e novembre 2013
Gilbert Dardel, Maire
Diane Thibault, Directrice générale

Nantes
1244, rue Principale
Nantes, QC G0Y 1G0
Tél: 819-547-3655; *Téléc:* 819-547-3755
munantes@axion.ca
www.munantes.qc.ca
Entité municipal: Municipality
Incorporation: 1er janvier 1874 *Area:* 120,47 km2
Comté ou district: Le Granit; *Population au 2006:* 1,436
Circonscription(s) électorale(s) provinciale(s):
Mégantic-Compton
Circonscription(s) électorale(s) fédérale(s): Mégantic-L'Érable
Prochaines élections: 3e novembre 2013
Bernard Isabel, Maire
Lucie Lortitch, Directrice générale

Napierville
260, rue de l'Église
Napierville, QC J0J 1L0
Tél: 450-245-7210; *Téléc:* 450-245-7691
mun.napierville@qc.aira.com
www.napierville.ca
Entité municipal: Village
Incorporation: 1er janvier 1873 *Area:* 4,53 km2
Comté ou district: Les Jardins-de-Napierville; *Population au 2006:* 3,352
Circonscription(s) électorale(s) provinciale(s): Huntingdon
Circonscription(s) électorale(s) fédérale(s):
Beauharnois-Salaberry
Prochaines élections: 3e novembre 2013
Alain Fredette, Maire
Ginette Leblanc-Pruneau, Directrice générale

Natashquan
CP 99
29, ch d'en-Haut
Natashquan, QC G0G 2E0
Tél: 418-726-3362; *Téléc:* 418-726-3698
muninatashquan@globetrotter.net
www.natashquan.org
Entité municipal: Township
Incorporation: 16 septembre 1907 *Area:* 193,20 km2
Comté ou district: Minganie; *Population au 2006:* 264
Circonscription(s) électorale(s) provinciale(s): Duplessis
Circonscription(s) électorale(s) fédérale(s): Manicouagan
Prochaines élections: 3e novembre 2013
Léonard Landry, Sec.-Trés.
Jacques Landry, Maire

Nédélec
CP 70
33, rue Principale
Nédélec, QC J0Z 2Z0
Tél: 819-784-3311; *Téléc:* 819-784-2126
nedelec@mrctemiscamingue.qc.ca
municipalite.nedelec.qc.ca
Entité municipal: Township
Incorporation: 1er février 1909 *Area:* 369,90 km2
Comté ou district: Témiscamingue; *Population au 2006:* 416
Circonscription(s) électorale(s) provinciale(s):
Rouyn-Noranda-Témiscamingue
Circonscription(s) électorale(s) fédérale(s):
Abitibi-Témiscamingue
Prochaines élections: 3e novembre 2013
Carmen Rivard, Mairesse
Nancy Beaulé, Directrice générale

Némiscau
1, rue Lakeshore
Némiscau, QC J0Y 3B0
Tel: 819-673-2512; *Fax:* 819-673-2542
nation@nemaska.ca
www.nemaska.ca
Municipal Type: Villages Cris
Incorporated: 28 juin 1978 *Area:* 55,40 km2
Provincial Electoral District(s): Ungava
Federal Electoral District(s): Abitibi-Baie-James-Nunavik-Eeyou
Next Election: 3e novembre 2013
Josie Jimiken, Maire
Georges Wapachee, Directeur général

Neuville
230, rue du Père-Rhéaume
Neuville, QC G0A 2R0
Tél: 418-876-2280; *Téléc:* 418-876-3349
mun@ville.neuville.qc.ca
www.ville.neuville.qc.ca
Entité municipal: Town
Incorporation: 2 janvier 1997 *Area:* 72,04 km2
Comté ou district: Portneuf; *Population au 2006:* 3,638
Circonscription(s) électorale(s) provinciale(s): Portneuf
Circonscription(s) électorale(s) fédérale(s):
Portneuf-Jacques-Cartier
Prochaines élections: 3e novembre 2013
Bernard Gaudreau, Maire
Nicole Béland, Greffière

New Carlisle
CP 40
138, boul Gérard-D.-Levesque
New Carlisle, QC G0C 1Z0
Tél: 418-752-3141; *Téléc:* 418-752-3140
newcarlisle@globetrotter.net
www.new-carlisle.com
Entité municipal: Municipality
Incorporation: 1er février 1877 *Area:* 66,12 km2
Comté ou district: Bonaventure; *Population au 2006:* 1,370
Circonscription(s) électorale(s) provinciale(s): Bonaventure
Circonscription(s) électorale(s) fédérale(s):
Gaspésie—Îles-de-la-Madeleine
Prochaines élections: 3e novembre 2013
Cyrus Journeau, Maire
Denise Dallain, Directrice générale

New Richmond
99, place Suzanne-Guité
New Richmond, QC G0C 2B0
Tél: 418-392-7000; *Téléc:* 418-392-5331
scyr@villenewrichmond.com
www.villenewrichmond.com
Entité municipal: Town
Incorporation: 1er juillet 1855 *Area:* 168,63 km2
Comté ou district: Bonaventure; *Population au 2006:* 3,748
Circonscription(s) électorale(s) provinciale(s): Bonaventure
Circonscription(s) électorale(s) fédérale(s):
Gaspésie—Îles-de-la-Madeleine
Prochaines élections: 3e novembre 2013
Nicole Appleby, Mairesse
Stéphane Cyr, Greffier

Nicolet
180, rue Monseigneur-Panet
Nicolet, QC J3T 1S6
Tél: 819-293-6901; *Téléc:* 819-293-6767
p.genest@ville.nicolet.qc.ca
www.ville.nicolet.qc.ca
Entité municipal: Town
Incorporation: 27 décembre 2000 *Area:* 94,50 km2
Comté ou district: Nicolet-Yamaska; *Population au 2006:* 7,827
Circonscription(s) électorale(s) provinciale(s): Nicolet-Yamaska
Circonscription(s) électorale(s) fédérale(s):

Bas-Richelieu-Nicolet-Bécancour
Prochaines élections: 3e novembre 2013
Alain Drouin, Maire
Monique Corriveau, Greffière

Nicolet-Yamaska
#257, 1, rue de Mgr-Courchesne
Nicolet, QC J3T 2C1
Tél: 819-293-2997; *Téléc:* 819-293-5367
mrcny@mrcnicolet-yamaska.qc.ca
www.mrcnicolet-yamaska.qc.ca
Entité municipal: Regional County Municipality
Incorporation: 1 janvier 1982
Population au 2006: 23,007
Note: 16 municipalités.
Alain Drouin, Préfet
Donald Martel, Directeur général

Nominingue
2110, ch du Tour-du-Lac
Nominingue, QC J0W 1R0
Tél: 819-278-3384; *Téléc:* 819-278-4967
mun.nominingue@tlb.sympatico.ca
www.municipalitenominingue.qc.ca
Entité municipal: Municipality
Incorporation: 30 octobre 1971 *Area:* 308,34 km2
Comté ou district: Antoine-Labelle; *Population au 2006:* 2,317
Circonscription(s) électorale(s) provinciale(s): Labelle
Circonscription(s) électorale(s) fédérale(s): Laurentides-Labelle
Prochaines élections: 3e novembre 2013
Yves Généreux, Maire
Robert Généreux, Directeur général

Normandin
1048, rue St-Cyrille
Normandin, QC G8M 4R9
Tél: 418-274-2004; *Téléc:* 418-274-7171
admin@ville.normandin.qc.ca
www.ville.normandin.qc.ca
Entité municipal: Town
Incorporation: 10 mars 1979 *Area:* 211,96 km2
Comté ou district: Maria-Chapdelaine; *Population au 2006:* 3,220
Circonscription(s) électorale(s) provinciale(s): Roberval
Circonscription(s) électorale(s) fédérale(s): Roberval-Lac-St-Jean
Prochaines élections: 3e novembre 2013
Lucien Guillemette, Maire
Guy Mailloux, Greffier

Normétal
CP 308
59, 1re rue
Normétal, QC J0Z 3A0
Tél: 819-788-2550; *Téléc:* 819-788-2730
normetal@mrcao.qc.ca
www.normetal.ao.ca
Entité municipal: Municipality
Incorporation: 1er janvier 1945 *Area:* 55,89 km2
Comté ou district: Abitibi-Ouest; *Population au 2006:* 886
Circonscription(s) électorale(s) provinciale(s): Abitibi-Ouest
Circonscription(s) électorale(s) fédérale(s): Abitibi-Témiscamingue
Prochaines élections: 3e novembre 2013
Jocelyn Trottier, Maire
Lyne Blanchet, Directrice générale

North Hatley
3125, ch Capelton
North Hatley, QC J0B 2C0
Tél: 819-842-2754; *Téléc:* 819-842-4501
villagenorthhatley@qc.aira.com
www.northhatley.org
Entité municipal: Village
Incorporation: 25 octobre 1897 *Area:* 3,23 km2
Comté ou district: Memphrémagog; *Population au 2006:* 722
Circonscription(s) électorale(s) provinciale(s): Orford
Circonscription(s) électorale(s) fédérale(s): Compton-Stanstead
Prochaines élections: 3e novembre 2013
Michael Page, Maire
Léonard Castagner, Directeur général

Notre-Dame-Auxiliatrice-de-Buckland
4340, rue Principale
Buckland, QC G0R 1G0
Tél: 418-789-3119; *Téléc:* 418-789-3535
buckland@globetrotter.net
Entité municipal: Parish (Paroisse)
Incorporation: 1er janvier 1885 *Area:* 96,32 km2
Comté ou district: Bellechasse; *Population au 2006:* 815
Circonscription(s) électorale(s) provinciale(s): Bellechasse
Circonscription(s) électorale(s) fédérale(s): Lévis-Bellechasse
Prochaines élections: 3e novembre 2013
Juliette Laflamme, Mairesse
Jocelyne Nadeau, Directrice générale

Notre-Dame-de-Bonsecours
220A, rue Bonsecours
Montebello, QC J0V 1L0
Tél: 819-423-5575; *Téléc:* 819-423-5571
mun.ndbonsecours@mrcpapineau.com
www.ndbonsecours.com
Entité municipal: Municipality
Incorporation: 7 mars 1918 *Area:* 265,75 km2
Comté ou district: Papineau; *Population au 2006:* 275
Circonscription(s) électorale(s) provinciale(s): Papineau
Circonscription(s) électorale(s) fédérale(s): Argenteuil-Papineau-Mirabel
Prochaines élections: 3e novembre 2013
Denis Beauchamp, Maire
Suzie Latourelle, Directrice générale

Notre-Dame-de-Ham
25, rue de l'Église
Notre-Dame-de-Ham, QC G0P 1C0
Tél: 819-344-5806; *Téléc:* 819-344-5807
info@notre-dame-de-ham.ca
Entité municipal: Municipality
Incorporation: 7 octobre 1898 *Area:* 32,34 km2
Comté ou district: Arthabaska; *Population au 2006:* 424
Circonscription(s) électorale(s) provinciale(s): Richmond
Circonscription(s) électorale(s) fédérale(s): Richmond-Arthabaska
Prochaines élections: 3e novembre 2013
Diane Lefort, Mairesse
Christiane Leblanc, Directrice générale

Notre-Dame-de-l'Île-Perrot
21, rue de l'Église
Notre-Dame-de-l'Île-Perrot, QC J7V 8P4
Tél: 514-453-4128; *Téléc:* 514-453-8961
info@ndip.org
www.ndip.org
Entité municipal: Municipality
Incorporation: 14 avril 1984 *Area:* 28,14 km2
Comté ou district: Vaudreuil-Soulanges; *Population au 2006:* 9,885
Circonscription(s) électorale(s) provinciale(s): Vaudreuil
Circonscription(s) électorale(s) fédérale(s): Vaudreuil-Soulanges
Prochaines élections: 3e novembre 2013
Marie-Claude Beaulieu-Nichols, Maire
Katherine-Erika Vincent, Greffière

Notre-Dame-de-la-Merci
1900, montée de la Réserve
Notre-Dame-de-la-Merci, QC J0T 2A0
Tél: 819-424-2113; *Téléc:* 819-424-7347
municipaliteNDM@netaxis.ca
www.municipalitenotredamedelamerci.com
Entité municipal: Municipality
Incorporation: 1er janvier 1950 *Area:* 251,22 km2
Comté ou district: Matawinie; *Population au 2006:* 1,056
Circonscription(s) électorale(s) provinciale(s): Bertrand
Circonscription(s) électorale(s) fédérale(s): Joliette
Prochaines élections: 3e novembre 2013
Julien Alarie, Maire
Chantal Soucy, Directrice générale

Notre-Dame-de-la-Paix
267, rue Notre-Dame
Notre-Dame-de-la-Paix, QC J0V 1P0
Tél: 819-522-6610; *Téléc:* 819-522-6710
mun.ndlapaix@mrcpapineau.com
www.notredamedelapaix.qc.ca
Entité municipal: Municipality
Incorporation: 3 octobre 1902 *Area:* 105,90 km2
Comté ou district: Papineau; *Population au 2006:* 719
Circonscription(s) électorale(s) provinciale(s): Papineau
Circonscription(s) électorale(s) fédérale(s): Argenteuil-Papineau-Mirabel
Prochaines élections: 3e novembre 2013
Daniel Bock, Maire
Nadine Proulx, Directrice générale

Notre-Dame-de-la-Salette
CP 59
45, rue des Saules
Notre-Dame-de-la-Salette, QC J0X 2L0
Tél: 819-766-2533; *Téléc:* 819-766-2983
salette@muni-ndsalette.qc.ca
www.notredamedelasalette.ca
Entité municipal: Municipality
Incorporation: 17 mai 1979 *Area:* 117,54 km2
Comté ou district: Les Collines-de-l'Outaouais; *Population au 2006:* 774
Circonscription(s) électorale(s) provinciale(s): Papineau
Circonscription(s) électorale(s) fédérale(s): Pontiac
Prochaines élections: 3e novembre 2013
Daniel Malette, Maire
Sylvie Gratton, Directrice générale

Notre-Dame-de-Lorette
22, rue Principale
Notre-Dame-de-Lorette, QC G0W 1B0
Tél: 418-276-1934; *Téléc:* 418-276-1934
muni.lorette@hotmail.com
Entité municipal: Municipality
Incorporation: 1er janvier 1966 *Area:* 225,32 km2
Comté ou district: Maria-Chapdelaine; *Population au 2006:* 175
Circonscription(s) électorale(s) provinciale(s): Roberval
Circonscription(s) électorale(s) fédérale(s): Roberval-Lac-St-Jean
Prochaines élections: 3e novembre 2013
Daniel Tremblay, Maire
Michèle Tremblay, Directrice générale

Notre-Dame-de-Lourdes
830, rue Principale
Lourdes, QC G0S 1T0
Tél: 819-385-4315; *Téléc:* 819-385-4827
info@municipalitelourdes.com
www.municipalitelourdes.com
Entité municipal: Parish (Paroisse)
Incorporation: 7 octobre 1897 *Area:* 83,39 km2
Comté ou district: L'Érable; *Population au 2006:* 716
Circonscription(s) électorale(s) provinciale(s): Lotbinière
Circonscription(s) électorale(s) fédérale(s): Mégantic-L'Érable
Prochaines élections: 3e novembre 2013
Jocelyn Bédard, Maire
Danielle Bédard, Directrice générale

Notre-Dame-de-Lourdes
4050, rue Principale
Notre-Dame-de-Lourdes, QC J0K 1K0
Tél: 450-759-2277; *Téléc:* 450-759-2055
munindl@intermonde.net
www.notredamedelourdes.ca
Entité municipal: Municipality
Incorporation: 28 octobre 1925 *Area:* 35,48 km2
Comté ou district: Joliette; *Population au 2006:* 2,201
Circonscription(s) électorale(s) provinciale(s): Joliette
Circonscription(s) électorale(s) fédérale(s): Joliette
Prochaines élections: 3e novembre 2013
Céline Geoffroy, Maire
Micheline Miron, Directrice générale

Notre-Dame-de-Montauban
555, av des Loisirs
Notre-Dame-de-Montauban, QC G0X 1W0
Tél: 418-336-2640; *Téléc:* 418-336-2353
nd-montauban@regionmekinac.com
www.municipalite.notre-dame-de-montauban.qc.ca
Entité municipal: Municipality
Incorporation: 3 janvier 1976 *Area:* 163,53 km2
Comté ou district: Mékinac; *Population au 2006:* 846
Circonscription(s) électorale(s) provinciale(s): Portneuf
Circonscription(s) électorale(s) fédérale(s): St-Maurice-Champlain
Prochaines élections: 3e novembre 2013
Jean-Guy Lavoie, Maire
Manon Frenette, Directrice générale

Notre-Dame-de-Pontmain
5, rue de l'Église
Notre-Dame-de-Pontmain, QC J0W 1S0
Tél: 819-597-2382; *Téléc:* 819-597-2231
dg@munpontmain.qc.ca
www.munpontmain.qc.ca
Entité municipal: Municipality
Incorporation: 26 janvier 1894 *Area:* 267,92 km2
Comté ou district: Antoine-Labelle; *Population au 2006:* 712
Circonscription(s) électorale(s) provinciale(s): Labelle
Circonscription(s) électorale(s) fédérale(s): Laurentides-Labelle
Prochaines élections: 3e novembre 2013
Lyz Beaulieu, Mairesse
Daisy Constantineau, Directrice générale

Notre-Dame-de-Stanbridge
CP 209
900, rue Principale
Notre-Dame-de-Stanbridge, QC J0J 1M0
Tél: 450-296-4710; *Téléc:* 450-296-5001
notredamedestanbridge@videotron.ca
www.notredamedestanbridge.qc.ca

Entité municipal: Parish (Paroisse)
Incorporation: 21 mars 1889 *Area:* 44,57 km2
Comté ou district: Brome-Missisquoi; *Population au 2006:* 728
Circonscription(s) électorale(s) provinciale(s): Brome-Missisquoi
Circonscription(s) électorale(s) fédérale(s): Brome-Missisquoi
Prochaines élections: 3e novembre 2013
Ginette Simard Gendreault, Maire
Béatrice Travers, Directrice générale

Notre-Dame-des-Anges
260, boul Langelier
Québec, QC G1K 5N1
Tél: 418-529-0931; *Téléc:* 418-524-7162
mamj@mediom.com
Entité municipal: Parish (Paroisse)
Incorporation: 1er juillet 1855 *Area:* 0,06 km2
Population au 2006: 437
Circonscription(s) électorale(s) provinciale(s): Taschereau
Circonscription(s) électorale(s) fédérale(s): Québec
Prochaines élections: 3e novembre 2013
Aline Plante, Administratrice
Colette Huot, Directrice générale

Notre-Dame-des-Bois
35, rte de l'Église
Notre-Dame-des-Bois, QC J0B 2E0
Tél: 819-888-2724; *Téléc:* 819-888-2904
mun.notredamedesbois@axion.ca
www.notredamedesbois.qc.ca
Entité municipal: Municipality
Incorporation: 1er janvier 1877 *Area:* 190,90 km2
Comté ou district: Le Granit; *Population au 2006:* 964
Circonscription(s) électorale(s) provinciale(s):
Mégantic-Compton
Circonscription(s) électorale(s) fédérale(s): Mégantic-L'Érable
Prochaines élections: 3e novembre 2013
Jean-Louis Gobeil, Maire
Guylaine Blais, Directrice générale

Notre-Dame-des-Monts
15, rue Principale
Notre-Dame-des-Monts, QC G0T 1L0
Tél: 418-489-2011; *Téléc:* 418-489-2014
municipalitenddm@coopnddm.com
www.notredamedesmonts.com
Entité municipal: Municipality
Incorporation: 11 avril 1935 *Area:* 56,15 km2
Comté ou district: Charlevoix-Est; *Population au 2006:* 764
Circonscription(s) électorale(s) provinciale(s): Charlevoix
Circonscription(s) électorale(s) fédérale(s):
Montmorency-Charlevoix-Haute-Côte-Nord
Prochaines élections: 3e novembre 2013
Jean-Claude Simard, Maire
Marcelle Pedneault, Directrice générale

Notre-Dame-des-Neiges
4, 2e rang Centre
Trois-Pistoles, QC G0L 4K0
Tél: 418-851-3009; *Téléc:* 418-851-3169
admin@notredamedesneiges.qc.ca
www.notredamedesneiges.qc.ca
Entité municipal: Municipality
Incorporation: 1er juillet 1855 *Area:* 92,87 km2
Comté ou district: Les Basques; *Population au 2006:* 1,209
Circonscription(s) électorale(s) provinciale(s): Rivière-du-Loup
Circonscription(s) électorale(s) fédérale(s):
Rimouski-Neigette-Témiscouata-Les Basques
Prochaines élections: 3e novembre 2013
Jean Marie Lafrance, Maire
Danielle Ouellet, Directrice générale

Notre-Dame-des-Pins
CP 40
2790, 1re av
Notre-Dame-des-Pins, QC G0M 1K0
Tél: 418-774-9718; *Téléc:* 418-774-9728
notredamedespins@sogetel.net
www.notredamedespins.qc.ca
Entité municipal: Parish (Paroisse)
Incorporation: 29 juin 1926 *Area:* 24,60 km2
Comté ou district: Beauce-Sartigan; *Population au 2006:* 1,065
Circonscription(s) électorale(s) provinciale(s): Beauce-Sud
Circonscription(s) électorale(s) fédérale(s): Beauce
Prochaines élections: 3e novembre 2013
Pierre Bégin, Maire
Dominique Lamarre, Directrice générale

Notre-Dame-des-Prairies
225, boul Antonio-Barrette
Notre-Dame-des-Prairies, QC J6E 1E7
Tél: 450-759-7741; *Téléc:* 450-759-6255
prairies@notre-dame-des-prairies.org
www.notre-dame-des-prairies.org
Entité municipal: Town
Incorporation: 1er janvier 1957 *Area:* 17,74 km2
Comté ou district: Joliette; *Population au 2006:* 8,230
Circonscription(s) électorale(s) provinciale(s): Joliette
Circonscription(s) électorale(s) fédérale(s): Joliette
Prochaines élections: 3e novembre 2013
Alain Larue, Maire
Sylvie Malo, Greffière

Notre-Dame-des-Sept-Douleurs
6201, ch de l'île
Notre-Dame-des-Sept-Douleurs, QC G0L 1K0
Tél: 418-898-3451; *Téléc:* 418-898-3492
mun_ndsd-ileverte@ileverte.qc.ca
www.ileverte.qc.ca
Entité municipal: Parish (Paroisse)
Incorporation: 1er janvier 1874 *Area:* 11,18 km2
Comté ou district: Rivière-du-Loup; *Population au 2006:* 62
Circonscription(s) électorale(s) provinciale(s): Rivière-du-Loup
Circonscription(s) électorale(s) fédérale(s):
Montmagny-L'Islet-Kamouraska-Rivière-du-Loup
Prochaines élections: 3e novembre 2013
Gilbert Delage, Maire
Denis Cusson, Directeur général

Notre-Dame-du-Bon-Conseil
1428, rte 122
Notre-Dame-du-Bon-Conseil, QC J0C 1A0
Tél: 819-336-5374; *Téléc:* 819-336-2389
vaubin@cgocable.ca
Entité municipal: Parish (Paroisse)
Incorporation: 15 février 1898 *Area:* 86,42 km2
Comté ou district: Drummond; *Population au 2006:* 912
Circonscription(s) électorale(s) provinciale(s): Richmond
Circonscription(s) électorale(s) fédérale(s): Drummond
Prochaines élections: 3e novembre 2013
Michel Bourgeois, Maire
Valérie Aubin, Directrice générale

Notre-Dame-du-Bon-Conseil
541, rue Notre-Dame
Notre-Dame-du-Bon-Conseil, QC J0C 1A0
Tél: 819-336-2744; *Téléc:* 819-336-2030
nb.bonconseil@cgocable.ca
www.notre-dame-du-bon-conseil-village.qc.ca
Entité municipal: Village
Incorporation: 1er janvier 1957 *Area:* 4,22 km2
Comté ou district: Drummond; *Population au 2006:* 1,426
Circonscription(s) électorale(s) provinciale(s): Richmond
Circonscription(s) électorale(s) fédérale(s): Drummond
Prochaines élections: 3e novembre 2013
Yvon Lampron, Maire
Isabelle Dumont, Directrice générale

Notre-Dame-du-Laus
CP 10
66, rue Principale
Notre-Dame-du-Laus, QC J0X 2M0
Tél: 819-767-2247; *Téléc:* 819-767-3102
mun.notre-dame-du-laus@tlb.sympatico.ca
www.notre-dame-du-laus.ca
Entité municipal: Municipality
Incorporation: 1er janvier 1876 *Area:* 866,02 km2
Comté ou district: Antoine-Labelle; *Population au 2006:* 1,564
Circonscription(s) électorale(s) provinciale(s): Labelle
Circonscription(s) électorale(s) fédérale(s): Laurentides-Labelle
Prochaines élections: 3e novembre 2013
Ken Ménard, Maire
Yves Larocque, Directeur général

Notre-Dame-du-Mont-Carmel
3860, rue de l' Hôtel de Ville
Notre-Dame-du-Mont-Carmel, QC G0X 3J0
Tél: 819-375-9856; *Téléc:* 819-373-4045
municipalite@mont-carmel.org
www.mont-carmel.org
Entité municipal: Parish (Paroisse)
Incorporation: 30 décembre 1858 *Area:* 126,61 km2
Comté ou district: Les Chenaux; *Population au 2006:* 5,299
Circonscription(s) électorale(s) provinciale(s): St-Maurice
Circonscription(s) électorale(s) fédérale(s):
St-Maurice-Champlain
Prochaines élections: 3e novembre 2013
Pierre A. Bouchard, Maire
Jean Lachance, Directeur général

Notre-Dame-du-Nord
71, rue Principale nord
Notre-Dame-du-Nord, QC J0Z 3B0
Tél: 819-723-2294; *Téléc:* 819-723-2483
rejean.nddn@mrctemiscamingue.qc.ca
municipalite.notre-dame-du-nord.qc.ca
Entité municipal: Municipality
Incorporation: 23 septembre 1919 *Area:* 103,60 km2
Comté ou district: Témiscamingue; *Population au 2006:* 1,116
Circonscription(s) électorale(s) provinciale(s):
Rouyn-Noranda-Témiscamingue
Circonscription(s) électorale(s) fédérale(s):
Abitibi-Témiscamingue
Prochaines élections: 3e novembre 2013
Mychel Tremblay, Maire
Réjean Pelletier, Directeur général

Notre-Dame-du-Portage
560, rte de la Montagne
Notre-Dame-du-Portage, QC G0L 1Y0
Tél: 418-862-9163; *Téléc:* 418-862-5240
directiongenerale@notre-dame-du-portage.ca
www.municipalite.notre-dame-du-portage.qc.ca
Entité municipal: Municipality
Incorporation: 19 juillet 1856 *Area:* 39,55 km2
Comté ou district: Rivière-du-Loup; *Population au 2006:* 1,262
Circonscription(s) électorale(s) provinciale(s): Rivière-du-Loup
Circonscription(s) électorale(s) fédérale(s):
Montmagny-L'Islet-Kamouraska-Rivière-du-Loup
Prochaines élections: 3e novembre 2013
Louis Vadeboncoeur, Maire
Annie Lemieux, Directrice générale

Notre-Dame-du-Rosaire
144, rue Principale
Notre-Dame-du-Rosaire, QC G0R 2H0
Tél: 418-469-2802; *Téléc:* 418-469-2802
munndr@globetrotter.net
www.notredamedurosaire.com
Entité municipal: Municipality
Incorporation: 18 décembre 1894 *Area:* 158,53 km2
Comté ou district: Montmagny; *Population au 2006:* 394
Circonscription(s) électorale(s) provinciale(s): Montmagny-L'Islet
Circonscription(s) électorale(s) fédérale(s):
Montmagny-L'Islet-Kamouraska-Rivière-du-Loup
Prochaines élections: 3e novembre 2013
Gilles Giroux, Maire
Isabelle Lachance, Directrice générale

Notre-Dame-du-Sacré-Coeur-d'Issoudun
268, rue Principale
Issoudun, QC G0S 1L0
Tél: 418-728-2006; *Téléc:* 418-728-2303
munissoudun@videotron.ca
www.issoudun.qc.ca
Entité municipal: Parish (Paroisse)
Incorporation: 4 janvier 1909 *Area:* 60,81 km2
Comté ou district: Lotbinière; *Population au 2006:* 794
Circonscription(s) électorale(s) provinciale(s): Lotbinière
Circonscription(s) électorale(s) fédérale(s):
Lotbinière-Chutes-de-la-Chaudière
Prochaines élections: 3e novembre 2013
Annie Thériault, Mairesse
Suzanne Therrien-Croteau, Directrice générale

Nouvelle
CP 68
470, rue Francoeur
Nouvelle, QC G0C 2E0
Tél: 418-794-2253; *Téléc:* 418-794-2254
direction@nouvellegaspesie.com
nouvellegaspesie.com
Entité municipal: Municipality
Incorporation: 10 octobre 1907 *Area:* 230,63 km2
Comté ou district: Avignon; *Population au 2006:* 1,815
Circonscription(s) électorale(s) provinciale(s): Bonaventure
Circonscription(s) électorale(s) fédérale(s):
Gaspésie—Îles-de-la-Madeleine
Prochaines élections: 3e novembre 2013
Richard St-Laurent, Maire
Daniel Bujold, Directeur général

Noyan
1312, ch de la Petite-France
Noyan, QC J0J 1B0
Tél: 450-294-2689; *Téléc:* 450-294-2175
renseignements@ville.noyan.qc.ca
www.ville.noyan.qc.ca
Entité municipal: Municipality
Incorporation: 1er juillet 1855 *Area:* 43,79 km2
Comté ou district: Le Haut-Richelieu; *Population au 2006:* 1,354
Circonscription(s) électorale(s) provinciale(s): Iberville

Circonscription(s) électorale(s) fédérale(s): Brome-Missisquoi
Prochaines élections: 3e novembre 2013
Réal Ryan, Maire
Marie-France Saucier, Directrice générale

Ogden
70, ch Ogden
Ogden, QC J0B 3E3
Tél: 819-876-7117; *Téléc:* 819-876-2121
mun.ogden@gmail.com
Entité municipal: Municipality
Incorporation: 23 janvier 1932 *Area:* 75,49 km2
Comté ou district: Memphrémagog; *Population au 2006:* 762
Circonscription(s) électorale(s) provinciale(s): Orford
Circonscription(s) électorale(s) fédérale(s): Compton-Stanstead
Prochaines élections: 3e novembre 2013
Joe Stairs, Maire
Renée Donaldson, Directrice générale

Oka
183, rue des Anges
Oka, QC J0N 1E0
Tél: 450-479-8333; *Téléc:* 450-479-1886
info@municipalite.oka.qc.ca
www.municipalite.oka.qc.ca
Entité municipal: Municipality
Incorporation: 8 septembre 1999 *Area:* 67,21 km2
Comté ou district: Deux-Montagnes; *Population au 2006:* 3,300
Circonscription(s) électorale(s) provinciale(s): Mirabel
Circonscription(s) électorale(s) fédérale(s):
Argenteuil-Papineau-Mirabel
Prochaines élections: 3e novembre 2013
Richard Lalonde, Maire
Marie Daoust, Directrice générale

Orford
2530, ch du Parc
Orford, QC J1X 8R8
Tél: 819-843-3111; *Téléc:* 819-843-2707
info@canton.orford.qc.ca
www.canton.orford.qc.ca
Entité municipal: Township
Incorporation: 1er juillet 1855 *Area:* 135,25 km2
Comté ou district: Memphrémagog; *Population au 2006:* 2,979
Circonscription(s) électorale(s) provinciale(s): Orford
Circonscription(s) électorale(s) fédérale(s): Brome-Missisquoi
Prochaines élections: 3e novembre 2013
Pierre Bastien, Maire
Brigitte Boisvert, Greffière

Ormstown
81, rue Lambton
Ormstown, QC J0S 1K0
Tél: 450-829-2625; *Téléc:* 450-829-4162
ormstown@ormstown.ca
www.ormstown.ca
Entité municipal: Municipality
Incorporation: 26 janvier 2000 *Area:* 142,39 km2
Comté ou district: Le Haut-St-Laurent; *Population au 2006:* 3,651
Circonscription(s) électorale(s) provinciale(s): Huntingdon
Circonscription(s) électorale(s) fédérale(s):
Beauharnois-Salaberry
Prochaines élections: 3e novembre 2013
Jacques Lapierre, Maire
Daniel Théroux, Directeur général

Otter Lake
CP 70
15, av Palmer
Otter Lake, QC J0X 2P0
Tél: 819-453-7049; *Téléc:* 819-453-7311
otter-lake@mrcpontiac.qc.ca
www.otterlakequebec.ca
Entité municipal: Municipality
Incorporation: 1er janvier 1877 *Area:* 496,21 km2
Comté ou district: Pontiac; *Population au 2006:* 972
Circonscription(s) électorale(s) provinciale(s): Pontiac
Circonscription(s) électorale(s) fédérale(s): Pontiac
Prochaines élections: 3e novembre 2013
Graham Hawley, Maire
Andrea Lafleur, Directrice générale

Otterburn Park
601, ch Ozias-Leduc
Otterburn Park, QC J3H 2M6
Tél: 450-536-0303; *Téléc:* 450-467-8260
info@ville.otterburnpark.qc.ca
www.ville.otterburnpark.qc.ca
Entité municipal: Town
Incorporation: 1er juillet 1855 *Area:* 5,20 km2
Comté ou district: La Vallée-du-Richelieu; *Population au 2006:* 8,464
Circonscription(s) électorale(s) provinciale(s): Borduas
Circonscription(s) électorale(s) fédérale(s): Chambly-Borduas
Prochaines élections: 3e novembre 2013
Vacant, Maire
Julie Waite, Greffière

Oujé-Bougoumou
203, Opemiska Meskino
Oujé-Bougoumou, QC G0W 3C0
Tél: 888-745-3905; *Téléc:* 418-745-3544
tourism@ouje.ca
www.ouje.ca
Entité municipal: Villages Cris
Area: 2,54 km2
Population au 2006: 606
Circonscription(s) électorale(s) provinciale(s): Ungava
Circonscription(s) électorale(s) fédérale(s):
Roberval-Lac-St-Jean
Louise Wapachee, Chief

Packington
35A, rue Principale
Packington, QC G0L 1Z0
Tél: 418-853-2269; *Téléc:* 418-853-6427
info@packington.org
www.packington.org
Entité municipal: Parish (Paroisse)
Incorporation: 6 octobre 1925 *Area:* 117,89 km2
Comté ou district: Témiscouata; *Population au 2006:* 657
Circonscription(s) électorale(s) provinciale(s):
Kamouraska-Témiscouata
Circonscription(s) électorale(s) fédérale(s):
Rimouski-Neigette-Témiscouata-Les Basques
Prochaines élections: 3e novembre 2013
Emilien Beaulieu, Maire
Denis Moreau, Directeur général

Padoue
CP 15
215, rue Beaulieu
Padoue, QC G0J 1X0
Tél: 418-775-8188; *Téléc:* 418-775-8177
padoue@mitis.qc.ca
www.municipalite.padoue.qc.ca
Entité municipal: Municipality
Incorporation: 31 janvier 1911 *Area:* 67,57 km2
Comté ou district: La Mitis; *Population au 2006:* 283
Circonscription(s) électorale(s) provinciale(s): Matapédia
Circonscription(s) électorale(s) fédérale(s): Haute-Gaspésie-La Mitis-Matane-Matapédia
Prochaines élections: 3e novembre 2013
Gilles Laflamme, Maire
Line Fillion, Directrice générale

Palmarolle
CP 309
499, rte 393
Palmarolle, QC J0Z 3C0
Tél: 819-787-2303; *Téléc:* 819-787-2412
palmarolle@mrcao.qc.ca
www.palmarolle.ao.ca
Entité municipal: Municipality
Incorporation: 14 avril 1930 *Area:* 118,36 km2
Comté ou district: Abitibi-Ouest; *Population au 2006:* 1,453
Circonscription(s) électorale(s) provinciale(s): Abitibi-Ouest
Circonscription(s) électorale(s) fédérale(s):
Abitibi-Témiscamingue
Prochaines élections: 3e novembre 2013
Marcel Caron, Maire
Claude Marquis, Directeur général

Papineau
266, rue Viger
Papineauville, QC J0V 1R0
Tél: 819-427-6243; *Téléc:* 819-427-8318
info@mrcpapineau.com
www.mrcpapineau.com
Entité municipal: Regional County Municipality
Incorporation: 1er janvier 1983
Population au 2006: 21,863
Note: 24 municipalités.
Paulette Lalande, Préfète
Ghislain Ménard, Directeur général
menard@mrcpapineau.com

Papineauville
#100, 188, rue Jeanne-D'Arc
Papineauville, QC J0V 1R0
Tél: 819-427-5511; *Téléc:* 819-427-5590
papineauville@mrcpapineau.com
www.mun-papineauville.qc.ca
Entité municipal: Municipality
Incorporation: 29 novembre 2000 *Area:* 48,52 km2
Comté ou district: Papineau; *Population au 2006:* 2,167
Circonscription(s) électorale(s) provinciale(s): Papineau
Circonscription(s) électorale(s) fédérale(s):
Argenteuil-Papineau-Mirabel
Prochaines élections: 3e novembre 2013
Gilles Clément, Maire
Martine Joanisse, Greffier

Parisville
975, rte Principale ouest
Parisville, QC G0S 1X0
Tél: 819-292-2222; *Téléc:* 819-292-1514
dg@municipalite.parisville.qc.ca
www.municipalite.parisville.qc.ca
Entité municipal: Parish (Paroisse)
Incorporation: 18 mars 1901 *Area:* 36,85 km2
Comté ou district: Bécancour; *Population au 2006:* 487
Circonscription(s) électorale(s) provinciale(s): Lotbinière
Circonscription(s) électorale(s) fédérale(s):
Bas-Richelieu-Nicolet-Bécancour
Prochaines élections: 3e novembre 2013
Maurice Grimard, Maire
François Gaudreault, Directeur général

Paspébiac
CP 130
178, 9e rue
Paspébiac, QC G0C 2K0
Tél: 418-752-2277; *Téléc:* 418-752-6566
paspebia@globetrotter.net
www.ville.paspebiac.qc.ca
Entité municipal: Town
Incorporation: 20 août 1997 *Area:* 94,59 km2
Comté ou district: Bonaventure; *Population au 2006:* 3,159
Circonscription(s) électorale(s) provinciale(s): Bonaventure
Circonscription(s) électorale(s) fédérale(s):
Gaspésie—îles-de-la-Madeleine
Prochaines élections: 3e novembre 2013
Gino LeBrasseur, Maire
Paul Langlois, Directeur général

Percé
CP 99
137, rte 132 ouest
Percé, QC G0C 2L0
Tél: 418-782-2933; *Téléc:* 418-782-5487
renseignements@ville.perce.qc.ca
www.ville.perce.qc.ca
Entité municipal: Town
Incorporation: 1er janvier 1971 *Area:* 427,94 km2
Comté ou district: Le Rocher-Percé; *Population au 2006:* 3,419
Circonscription(s) électorale(s) provinciale(s): Gaspé
Circonscription(s) électorale(s) fédérale(s):
Gaspésie—îles-de-la-Madeleine
Prochaines élections: 3e novembre 2013
Bruno Cloutier, Maire
Gemma Vibert, Greffière

Péribonka
312, rue Édouard-Niquet
Péribonka, QC G0W 2G0
Tél: 418-374-2967; *Téléc:* 418-374-2355
sharvey@peribonka.ca
www.municipalite-peribonka.com
Entité municipal: Municipality
Incorporation: 19 septembre 1908 *Area:* 113,46 km2
Comté ou district: Maria-Chapdelaine; *Population au 2006:* 541
Circonscription(s) électorale(s) provinciale(s): Roberval
Circonscription(s) électorale(s) fédérale(s):
Roberval-Lac-St-Jean
Prochaines élections: 3e novembre 2013
Gilbert Goulet, Maire
Steve Harvey, Directeur général

Petit-Saguenay
35, ch du Quai
Petit-Saguenay, QC G0V 1N0
Tél: 418-272-2323; *Téléc:* 418-544-3077
munps@royaume.com
www.petit-saguenay.com
Entité municipal: Municipality
Incorporation: 12 août 1919 *Area:* 328,72 km2
Comté ou district: Le Fjord-du-Saguenay; *Population au 2006:* 780
Circonscription(s) électorale(s) provinciale(s): Dubuc
Circonscription(s) électorale(s) fédérale(s): Chicoutimi-Le Fjord
Prochaines élections: 3e novembre 2013
Thérèse Gaudreault, Maire
Alexis Lavoie, Directeur général

Petite-Rivière-St-François
CP 10
1067, rue Principale
Petite-Rivière-Saint-François, QC G0A 2L0
Tél: 418-760-1050; *Téléc:* 418-760-1051
francined@petiteriviere.com
www.petiteriviere.com
Entité municipal: Municipality
Incorporation: 1er juillet 1855 *Area:* 135,66 km2
Comté ou district: Charlevoix; *Population au 2006:* 703
Circonscription(s) électorale(s) provinciale(s): Charlevoix
Circonscription(s) électorale(s) fédérale(s):
Montmorency-Charlevoix-Haute-Côte-Nord
Prochaines élections: 3e novembre 2013
Gérald Maltais, Maire
Francine Dufour, Directrice générale

Petite-Vallée
CP 1067
45, rue Principale
Petite-Vallée, QC G0E 1Y0
Tél: 418-393-2949; *Téléc:* 418-393-2949
bibliopv@globetrotter.qc.ca
Entité municipal: Municipality
Incorporation: 1er janvier 1957 *Area:* 37,83 km2
Comté ou district: La Côte-de-Gaspé; *Population au 2006:* 248
Circonscription(s) électorale(s) provinciale(s): Gaspé
Circonscription(s) électorale(s) fédérale(s):
Gaspésie—îles-de-la-Madeleine
Prochaines élections: 3e novembre 2013
Rodrigue Brousseau, Maire
Simon Côté, Directeur général

Piedmont
670, rue Principale
Piedmont, QC J0R 1K0
Tél: 450-227-1888; *Téléc:* 450-227-6716
info@municipalite.piedmont.qc.ca
www.municipalite.piedmont.qc.ca
Entité municipal: Municipality
Incorporation: 22 septembre 1923 *Area:* 23,66 km2
Comté ou district: Les Pays-d'en-Haut; *Population au 2006:* 2,386
Circonscription(s) électorale(s) provinciale(s): Bertrand
Circonscription(s) électorale(s) fédérale(s): Laurentides-Labelle
Prochaines élections: 3e novembre 2013
Clément Cardin, Maire
Gilbert Aubin, Directeur général

Pierre-De Saurel
50, rue du Fort
Sorel-Tracy, QC J3P 7X7
Tél: 450-743-2703; *Téléc:* 450-743-7313
mrc@pierredesaurel.com
www.soreltracyregion.net
Entité municipal: Regional County Municipality
Incorporation: 1er janvier 1982
Population au 2006: 49,932
Note: 12 municipalités.
Raymond Arel, Préfet
Denis Boisvert, Directeur général

Pierreville
CP 300
26, rue Ally
Pierreville, QC J0G 1J0
Tél: 450-568-2139; *Téléc:* 450-568-0689
info@municipalitepierreville.qc.ca
www.pierreville.net
Entité municipal: Municipality
Incorporation: 13 juin 2001 *Area:* 79,54 km2
Comté ou district: Nicolet-Yamaska; *Population au 2006:* 2,337
Circonscription(s) électorale(s) provinciale(s): Nicolet-Yamaska
Circonscription(s) électorale(s) fédérale(s):
Bas-Richelieu-Nicolet-Bécancour
Prochaines élections: 3e novembre 2013
André Descôteaux, Maire
Micheline C. Laforce, Directrice générale

Piopolis
403, rue Principale
Piopolis, QC G0Y 1H0
Tél: 819-583-3953; *Téléc:* 819-583-1467
municipalite@piopolis.ca
www.piopolis.ca
Entité municipal: Municipality
Incorporation: 1er janvier 1880 *Area:* 104,14 km2
Comté ou district: Le Granit; *Population au 2006:* 376
Circonscription(s) électorale(s) provinciale(s):
Mégantic-Compton
Circonscription(s) électorale(s) fédérale(s): Mégantic-L'Érable
Prochaines élections: 3e novembre 2013
André St-Marseille, Maire
Julie Cloutier, Directrice générale

Plaisance
274, rue Desjardins
Plaisance, QC J0V 1S0
Tél: 819-427-5363; *Téléc:* 819-427-5015
ville.plaisance@videotron.ca
www.ville.plaisance.qc.ca
Entité municipal: Municipality
Incorporation: 31 octobre 1900 *Area:* 42,61 km2
Comté ou district: Papineau; *Population au 2006:* 1,024
Circonscription(s) électorale(s) provinciale(s): Papineau
Circonscription(s) électorale(s) fédérale(s):
Argenteuil-Papineau-Mirabel
Prochaines élections: 3e novembre 2013
Paulette Lalande, Mairesse
Benoit Hébert, Directeur général

Plessisville
CP 245
290, rte 165 sud
Plessisville, QC G6L 2Y7
Tél: 819-362-2712; *Téléc:* 819-362-9185
info@paroisseplessisville.com
www.paroisseplessisville.com
Entité municipal: Parish (Paroisse)
Incorporation: 1er juillet 1855 *Area:* 136,29 km2
Comté ou district: L'Érable; *Population au 2006:* 2,557
Circonscription(s) électorale(s) provinciale(s): Arthabaska
Circonscription(s) électorale(s) fédérale(s): Mégantic-L'Érable
Prochaines élections: 3e novembre 2013
Alain Dubois, Maire
Johanne Dubois, Directrice générale

Plessisville
1700, rue St-Calixte
Plessisville, QC G6L 1R3
Tél: 819-362-3284; *Téléc:* 819-362-6421
info@ville.plessisville.qc.ca
www.ville.plessisville.qc.ca
Entité municipal: Town
Incorporation: 27 avril 1855 *Area:* 4,44 km2
Comté ou district: L'Érable; *Population au 2006:* 6,677
Circonscription(s) électorale(s) provinciale(s): Arthabaska
Circonscription(s) électorale(s) fédérale(s): Mégantic-L'Érable
Prochaines élections: 3e novembre 2013
Réal Ouellet, Maire
Jean Marcoux, Dicecteur général

Pohénégamook
1309, rue Principale
Pohénégamook, QC G0L 1J0
Tél: 418-859-2222; *Téléc:* 418-859-3465
info.ville@pohenegamook.net
www.pohenegamook.net
Entité municipal: Town
Incorporation: 3 novembre 1973 *Area:* 351,97 km2
Comté ou district: Témiscouata; *Population au 2006:* 2,940
Circonscription(s) électorale(s) provinciale(s):
Kamouraska-Témiscouata
Circonscription(s) électorale(s) fédérale(s):
Rimouski-Neigette-Témiscouata-Les Basques
Prochaines élections: 3e novembre 2013
Louise Labonté, Mairesse
Denise Pelletier, Greffière

Pointe-à-la-Croix
CP 159
139, boul Inter-Provincial
Pointe-à-la-Croix, QC G0C 1L0
Tél: 418-788-2011; *Téléc:* 418-788-2916
pointe-a-la-croix@globetrotter.net
www.pointe-a-la-croix.com
Entité municipal: Municipality
Incorporation: 7 mai 1983 *Area:* 394,03 km2
Comté ou district: Avignon; *Population au 2006:* 1,587
Circonscription(s) électorale(s) provinciale(s): Bonaventure
Circonscription(s) électorale(s) fédérale(s):
Gaspésie—îles-de-la-Madeleine
Prochaines élections: 3e novembre 2013
Jean-Paul Audy, Maire
Claude Audet, Directeur général

Pointe-aux-Outardes
471, ch Principal
Pointe-aux-Outardes, QC G0H 1M0
Tél: 418-567-2203; *Téléc:* 418-567-4409
municipalite@pointe-aux-outardes.ca
www.pointe-aux-outardes.ca
Entité municipal: Village
Incorporation: 1er janvier 1964 *Area:* 71,56 km2
Comté ou district: Manicouagan; *Population au 2006:* 1,443
Circonscription(s) électorale(s) provinciale(s): René-Lévesque
Circonscription(s) électorale(s) fédérale(s): Manicouagan
Prochaines élections: 3e novembre 2013
André Lepage, Maire
Dania Hovington, Directrice générale

Pointe-Calumet
300, av Basile-Routhier
Pointe-Calumet, QC J0N 1G2
Tél: 450-473-5930; *Téléc:* 450-473-6571
info@municipalite.pointe-calumet.qc.ca
www.municipalite.pointe-calumet.qc.ca
Entité municipal: Municipality
Incorporation: 12 février 1953 *Area:* 4,89 km2
Comté ou district: Deux-Montagnes; *Population au 2006:* 6,574
Circonscription(s) électorale(s) provinciale(s): Mirabel
Circonscription(s) électorale(s) fédérale(s):
Argenteuil-Papineau-Mirabel
Prochaines élections: 3e novembre 2013
Jacques Séguin, Maire
Chantal Pilon, Directrice générale

Pointe-des-Cascades
105, ch du Fleuve
Pointe-des-Cascades, QC J0P 1M0
Tél: 450-455-3414; *Téléc:* 450-455-9671
pointe-des-cascades@videotron.ca
www.pointe-des-cascades.com
Entité municipal: Village
Incorporation: 1er mai 1961 *Area:* 2,66 km2
Comté ou district: Vaudreuil-Soulanges; *Population au 2006:* 1,046
Circonscription(s) électorale(s) provinciale(s): Soulanges
Circonscription(s) électorale(s) fédérale(s): Vaudreuil-Soulanges
Prochaines élections: 3e novembre 2013
Maryse M. Sauvé, Maire
Christiane Cyr, Directrice générale

Pointe-Fortune
694, rue du Tisseur
Pointe-Fortune, QC J0P 1N0
Tél: 450-451-5178; *Téléc:* 450-451-4649
mpf@qc.aira.com
pointefortune.ca
Entité municipal: Village
Incorporation: 28 août 1880 *Area:* 9,09 km2
Comté ou district: Vaudreuil-Soulanges; *Population au 2006:* 507
Circonscription(s) électorale(s) provinciale(s): Soulanges
Circonscription(s) électorale(s) fédérale(s): Vaudreuil-Soulanges
Prochaines élections: 3e novembre 2013
Jean-Pierre Daoust, Maire
Diane Héroux, Directrice générale

Pointe-Lebel
365, rue Granier
Pointe-Lebel, QC G0H 1N0
Tél: 418-589-8073; *Téléc:* 418-589-6154
nadiaptl@globetrotter.net
www.pointe-lebel.com
Entité municipal: Village
Incorporation: 1er janvier 1964 *Area:* 91,16 km2
Comté ou district: Manicouagan; *Population au 2006:* 1,958
Circonscription(s) électorale(s) provinciale(s): René-Lévesque
Circonscription(s) électorale(s) fédérale(s): Manicouagan
Prochaines élections: 3e novembre 2013
Ghislain Beaudin, Maire
Nadia Allard, Directrice générale

Pont-Rouge
212, rue Dupont
Pont-Rouge, QC G3H 1A1
Tél: 418-873-4481; *Téléc:* 418-873-3494
info@ville.pontrouge.qc.ca
www.ville.pontrouge.qc.ca
Entité municipal: Town
Incorporation: 3 janvier 1996 *Area:* 121,02 km2
Comté ou district: Portneuf; *Population au 2006:* 7,518
Circonscription(s) électorale(s) provinciale(s): Portneuf
Circonscription(s) électorale(s) fédérale(s):
Portneuf-Jacques-Cartier
Prochaines élections: 3e novembre 2013
Claude Bégin, Maire
Jocelyne Laliberté, Greffière

Pontiac
2024, rte 148
Pontiac, QC J0X 2G0
Tél: 819-455-2401; *Téléc:* 819-455-9756
dirgen@munpontiac.com
www.munpontiac.com

Entité municipal: Municipality
Incorporation: 1er janvier 1975 *Area:* 446,87 km2
Comté ou district: Les Collines-de-l'Outaouais; *Population au 2006:* 5,238
Circonscription(s) électorale(s) provinciale(s): Pontiac
Circonscription(s) électorale(s) fédérale(s): Pontiac
Prochaines élections: 3e novembre 2013
Edward McCann, Maire
Sylvain Bertrand, Directeur général

Pontiac
602, rte 301
Campbell's Bay, QC J0X 1K0
Tél: 819-648-5689; *Téléc:* 819-648-5810
mrc@mrcpontiac.qc.ca
www.mrcpontiac.qc.ca
Entité municipal: Regional County Municipality
Incorporation: 1er janvier 1983
Population au 2006: 14,586
Note: 18 municipalités & 1 autre territoire.
Michael McCrank, Préfet
Rémi Bertrand, Directeur général

Port-Cartier
40, av Parent
Port-Cartier, QC G5B 2G5
Tél: 418-766-2349; *Téléc:* 418-766-3390
directiongenerale@villeport-cartier.com
www.villeport-cartier.com
Entité municipal: Town
Incorporation: 19 février 2003 *Area:* 1073,70 km2
Comté ou district: Sept-Rivières; *Population au 2006:* 6,758
Circonscription(s) électorale(s) provinciale(s): Duplessis
Circonscription(s) électorale(s) fédérale(s): Manicouagan
Prochaines élections: 3e novembre 2013
Laurence Méthot, Mairesse
Andrée Bouffard, Greffière

Port-Daniel—Gascons
494, rte 132
Port-Daniel—Gascons, QC G0C 2N0
Tél: 418-396-5225; *Téléc:* 418-396-5588
municipalitedeport-daniel@globetrotter.net
www.port-daniel-gascons.ca
Entité municipal: Municipality
Incorporation: 17 janvier 2001 *Area:* 305,34 km2
Comté ou district: Le Rocher Percé; *Population au 2006:* 2,586
Circonscription(s) électorale(s) provinciale(s): Bonaventure
Circonscription(s) électorale(s) fédérale(s):
Gaspésie—îles-de-la-Madeleine
Prochaines élections: 3e novembre 2013
Maurice Anglehart, Maire
Thérèse Roussy, Directrice générale

Portage-du-Fort
CP 130
24, rue de l'Église
Portage-du-Fort, QC J0X 2T0
Tél: 819-647-2767; *Téléc:* 819-647-1910
therault@hotmail.com
Entité municipal: Village
Incorporation: 1er janvier 1863 *Area:* 4,24 km2
Comté ou district: Pontiac; *Population au 2006:* 280
Circonscription(s) électorale(s) provinciale(s): Pontiac
Circonscription(s) électorale(s) fédérale(s): Pontiac
Prochaines élections: 3e novembre 2013
Lynne Cameron, Mairesse
Tracey Hérault, Directrice générale

Portneuf
297, 1re Av
Portneuf, QC G0A 2Y0
Tél: 418-286-3844; *Téléc:* 418-286-4304
vilport@globetrotter.net
www.villedeportneuf.com
Entité municipal: Town
Incorporation: 4 juillet 2002 *Area:* 110,43 km2
Comté ou district: Portneuf; *Population au 2006:* 3,086
Circonscription(s) électorale(s) provinciale(s): Portneuf
Circonscription(s) électorale(s) fédérale(s):
Portneuf-Jacques-Cartier
Prochaines élections: 3e novembre 2013
Nelson Bédard, Maire
France Marcotte, Greffière
Yves Landry, Directeur général

Portneuf
185, rte 138
Cap-Santé, QC G0A 1L0
Tél: 418-285-3744; *Téléc:* 418-285-1703
portneuf@mrc-portneuf.qc.ca
www.portneuf.com
Entité municipal: Regional County Municipality
Incorporation: 1er janvier 1982
Population au 2006: 46,507
Note: 18 municipalités & 3 autres territoires.
Denis Langlois, Préfet
Josée Frenette, Directrice générale

Portneuf-sur-Mer
CP 98
170, rue Principale
Portneuf-sur-Mer, QC G0T 1P0
Tél: 418-238-2642; *Téléc:* 418-238-5319
muniport@bellnet.ca
www.portneuf-sur-mer.ca
Entité municipal: Municipality
Incorporation: 12 septembre 1902 *Area:* 241,23 km2
Comté ou district: La Haute-Côte-Nord; *Population au 2006:* 835
Circonscription(s) électorale(s) provinciale(s): René-Lévesque
Circonscription(s) électorale(s) fédérale(s):
Montmorency-Charlevoix-Haute-Côte-Nord
Prochaines élections: 3e novembre 2013
Jean-Marie Delaunay, Maire
Gontran Tremblay, Directeur général

Potton
CP 330
2, rue de Vale Perkins
Mansonville, QC J0E 1X0
Tél: 450-292-3313; *Téléc:* 450-292-5555
info@potton.ca
www.potton.ca
Entité municipal: Township
Incorporation: 1er juillet 1855 *Area:* 264,10 km2
Comté ou district: Memphrémagog; *Population au 2006:* 1,790
Circonscription(s) électorale(s) provinciale(s): Brome-Missisquoi
Circonscription(s) électorale(s) fédérale(s): Brome-Missisquoi
Prochaines élections: 3e novembre 2013
Jacques Marcoux, Maire
Thierry Gilbert, Directeur général

Poularies
CP 58
990, rue Principale
Poularies, QC J0Z 3E0
Tél: 819-782-5159; *Téléc:* 819-782-5063
poularies@mrcao.qc.ca
poularies.ao.ca
Entité municipal: Municipality
Incorporation: 7 mai 1924 *Area:* 164,95 km2
Comté ou district: Abitibi-Ouest; *Population au 2006:* 693
Circonscription(s) électorale(s) provinciale(s): Abitibi-Ouest
Circonscription(s) électorale(s) fédérale(s):
Abitibi-Témiscamingue
Prochaines élections: 3e novembre 2013
Claude Blais, Maire
Katy Rivard, Directrice générale

Preissac
6, rue des Rapides
Preissac, QC J0Y 2E0
Tél: 819-732-4938; *Téléc:* 819-732-4909
direction@preissac.com
www.preissac.com
Entité municipal: Municipality
Incorporation: 1er janvier 1979 *Area:* 489,50 km2
Comté ou district: Abitibi; *Population au 2006:* 726
Circonscription(s) électorale(s) provinciale(s): Abitibi-Ouest
Circonscription(s) électorale(s) fédérale(s):
Abitibi-Témiscamingue
Prochaines élections: 3e novembre 2013
Huguette Saucier, Mairesse
France Beaulieu, Directrice générale (par intérim)

Price
CP 340
18, rue Fournier
Price, QC G0J 1Z0
Tél: 418-775-2144; *Téléc:* 418-775-2459
price@mitis.qc.ca
www.municipaliteprice.com
Entité municipal: Village
Incorporation: 3 mars 1926 *Area:* 2,35 km2
Comté ou district: La Mitis; *Population au 2006:* 1,777
Circonscription(s) électorale(s) provinciale(s): Matapédia
Circonscription(s) électorale(s) fédérale(s):
Haute-Gaspésie-La-Mitis-Matane-Matapédia
Prochaines élections: 3e novembre 2013
Laurent Emond, Maire
Louise Furlong, Greffière

Princeville
50, rue St-Jacques ouest
Princeville, QC G6L 4Y5
Tél: 819-364-3333; *Téléc:* 819-364-5198
info@villedeprinceville.qc.ca
www.villedeprinceville.qc.ca
Entité municipal: Town
Incorporation: 23 février 2000 *Area:* 198,00 km2
Comté ou district: L'Érable; *Population au 2006:* 5,571
Circonscription(s) électorale(s) provinciale(s): Arthabaska
Circonscription(s) électorale(s) fédérale(s): Mégantic-L'Érable
Prochaines élections: 3e novembre 2013
Gilles Fortier, Maire
Mario Juaire, Greffier

Puvirnituq
CP 150
Puvirnituq, QC J0M 1P0
Tél: 819-988-2825; *Téléc:* 819-988-2751
sec.treasurer@nvpuvirnituq.ca
www.nvpuvirnituq.ca
Entité municipal: Northern Village
Incorporation: 2 septembre 1989 *Area:* 111,00 km2
Comté ou district: Kativik; *Population au 2006:* 1,457
Circonscription(s) électorale(s) provinciale(s): Ungava
Circonscription(s) électorale(s) fédérale(s):
Abitibi-Baie-James-Nunavik-Eeyou
Prochaines élections: 7e novembre 2012
Aisara Kenuajuak, Maire
Sarah Beaulne, Secrétaire-trésorière

Quaqtaq
CP 107
Quaqtaq, QC J0M 1J0
Tél: 819-492-9912; *Téléc:* 819-492-9935
stukkiapik@nvquaqtaq.ca
www.nvquaqtaq.ca
Entité municipal: Northern Village
Incorporation: 1er novembre 1980 *Area:* 26,49 km2
Comté ou district: Kativik; *Population au 2006:* 315
Circonscription(s) électorale(s) provinciale(s): Ungava
Circonscription(s) électorale(s) fédérale(s):
Abitibi-Baie-James-Nunavik-Eeyou
Prochaines élections: 7e novembre 2012
Bobby Putulik, Maire
Sammy Tukkiapik, Secrétaire-trésorier

Racine
348, rue de L'Église
Racine, QC J0E 1Y0
Tél: 450-532-2876; *Téléc:* 450-532-2865
reception@municipalite.racine.qc.ca
www.municipalite.racine.qc.ca
Entité municipal: Municipality
Incorporation: 15 février 1995 *Area:* 107,87 km2
Comté ou district: Le Val-St-François; *Population au 2006:* 1,265
Circonscription(s) électorale(s) provinciale(s): Johnson
Circonscription(s) électorale(s) fédérale(s): Jonquière-Alma
Prochaines élections: 3e novembre 2013
Rene Pelletier, Maire
André Courtemanche, Directeur général

Ragueneau
523, rte 138
Ragueneau, QC G0H 1S0
Tél: 418-567-2345; *Téléc:* 418-567-2344
ragueneau@satcomcolibri.com
www.municipalite.ragueneau.qc.ca
Entité municipal: Parish (Paroisse)
Incorporation: 7 mars 1951 *Area:* 215,92 km2
Comté ou district: Manicouagan; *Population au 2006:* 1,520
Circonscription(s) électorale(s) provinciale(s): René-Lévesque
Circonscription(s) électorale(s) fédérale(s): Manicouagan
Prochaines élections: 3e novembre 2013
Claude Lavoie, Maire
Audrey Morin, Directrice générale

Rapide-Danseur
535, rue du Village
Rapide-Danseur, QC J0Z 3G0
Tél: 819-948-2152; *Téléc:* 819-948-2265
rapide-danseur@mrcao.qc.ca
www.rapide-danseur.ao.ca
Entité municipal: Municipality
Incorporation: 1er janvier 1981 *Area:* 185,18 km2
Comté ou district: Abitibi-Ouest; *Population au 2006:* 273
Circonscription(s) électorale(s) provinciale(s): Abitibi-Ouest
Circonscription(s) électorale(s) fédérale(s):
Abitibi-Témiscamingue
Prochaines élections: 3e novembre 2013
Alain Gagnon, Maire

Mona Cyr, Directrice générale (par intérim)

Rapides-des-Joachims
CP 2-10
48, rue de l'Église
Rapides-des-Joachims, QC J0X 3M0
Tél: 613-586-2532; *Téléc:* 613-586-2720
rapides-des-joachims@mrcpontiac.qc.ca
www.rapidesdesjoachims.ca
Entité municipal: Municipality
Incorporation: 1er janvier 1955 *Area:* 248,92 km2
Comté ou district: Pontiac; *Population au 2006:* 172
Circonscription(s) électorale(s) provinciale(s): Pontiac
Circonscription(s) électorale(s) fédérale(s): Pontiac
Prochaines élections: 3e novembre 2013
James Gibson, Maire
Hélène Larente, Directrice générale

Rawdon
3647, rue Queen
Rawdon, QC J0K 1S0
Tél: 450-834-2596; *Téléc:* 450-834-3031
lmarsh@rawdon.ca
www.rawdon.ca
Entité municipal: Municipality
Incorporation: 28 mai 1998 *Area:* 179,73 km2
Comté ou district: Matawinie; *Population au 2006:* 10,058
Circonscription(s) électorale(s) provinciale(s): Rousseau
Circonscription(s) électorale(s) fédérale(s): Joliette
Prochaines élections: 3e novembre 2013
Jacques Beauregard, Maire
Georges Robitaille, Greffier adjoint

Rémigny
1304, ch de l'Église
Rémigny, QC J0Z 3H0
Tél: 819-761-2421; *Téléc:* 819-761-2421
mun.remigny@mrctemiscamingue.qc.ca
www.municipaliteremigny.qc.ca
Entité municipal: Municipality
Incorporation: 1er janvier 1978 *Area:* 985,03 km2
Comté ou district: Témiscamingue; *Population au 2006:* 318
Circonscription(s) électorale(s) provinciale(s): Rouyn-Noranda-Témiscamingue
Circonscription(s) électorale(s) fédérale(s): Abitibi-Témiscamingue
Prochaines élections: 3e novembre 2013
Jocelyn Aylwin, Maire
Josée Dubeau, Directrice générale

Richelieu
200, boul Richelieu
Richelieu, QC J3L 3R4
Tél: 450-658-1157; *Téléc:* 450-658-5096
n.poirier@villederichelieu.org
www.villederichelieu.org
Entité municipal: Town
Incorporation: 15 mars 2000 *Area:* 29,75 km2
Comté ou district: Rouville; *Population au 2006:* 5,208
Circonscription(s) électorale(s) provinciale(s): Chambly
Circonscription(s) électorale(s) fédérale(s): Chambly-Borduas
Prochaines élections: 3e novembre 2013
Jacques Ladouceur, Maire
Nancy Poirier, Greffière

Richmond
745, rue Gouin
Richmond, QC J0B 2H0
Tél: 819-826-3789; *Téléc:* 819-826-2813
admin@ville.richmond.qc.ca
www.ville.richmond.qc.ca
Entité municipal: Town
Incorporation: 29 décembre 1999 *Area:* 7,76 km2
Comté ou district: Le Val-St-François; *Population au 2006:* 3,336
Circonscription(s) électorale(s) provinciale(s): Richmond
Circonscription(s) électorale(s) fédérale(s): Richmond-Arthabaska
Prochaines élections: 3e novembre 2013
Marc-André Martel, Maire
Daniel Leduc, Directeur général

Rigaud
391, ch de la Mairie
Rigaud, QC J0P 1P0
Tél: 450-451-0869; *Téléc:* 450-451-4227
rigaud@ville.rigaud.qc.ca
www.ville.rigaud.qc.ca
Entité municipal: Municipality
Incorporation: 29 novembre 1995 *Area:* 97,15 km2
Comté ou district: Vaudreuil-Soulanges; *Population au 2006:* 6,780
Circonscription(s) électorale(s) provinciale(s): Soulanges
Circonscription(s) électorale(s) fédérale(s): Vaudreuil-Soulanges
Prochaines élections: 3e novembre 2013
Réal Brazeau, Maire
Hélène Therrien, Greffière

Rimouski-Neigette
#220, 23, rue de l'Évêché ouest
Rimouski, QC G5L 4H4
Tél: 418-724-5154; *Téléc:* 418-725-4567
administration@mrcrimouskineigette.qc.ca
Entité municipal: Regional County Municipality
Incorporation: 26 mai 1982
Population au 2006: 53,193
Note: 10 municipalités & 1 autre territoire.
Gilbert Pigeon, Préfet
Louise Audet, Directrice générale

Ripon
#101, 31, rue Coursol
Ripon, QC J0V 1V0
Tél: 819-983-2000; *Téléc:* 819-983-1327
information@ville.ripon.qc.ca
www.ville.ripon.qc.ca
Entité municipal: Municipality
Incorporation: 3 mai 2000 *Area:* 140,57 km2
Comté ou district: Papineau; *Population au 2006:* 1,497
Circonscription(s) électorale(s) provinciale(s): Papineau
Circonscription(s) électorale(s) fédérale(s): Argenteuil-Papineau-Mirabel
Prochaines élections: 3e novembre 2013
Luc Desjardins, Maire
Lorraine Sabourin, Directrice générale

Ristigouche-Partie-Sud-Est
35, ch Kempt, RR#2
Matapédia, QC G0J 1V0
Tél: 418-788-5769; *Téléc:* 418-788-2598
ristigouchesudest@globetrotter.net
www.ristigouchesudest.ca
Entité municipal: Township
Incorporation: 30 juin 1906 *Area:* 48,95 km2
Comté ou district: Avignon; *Population au 2006:* 173
Circonscription(s) électorale(s) provinciale(s): Bonaventure
Circonscription(s) électorale(s) fédérale(s): Gaspésie—îles-de-la-Madeleine
Prochaines élections: 3e novembre 2013
Annette Sénéchal, Mairesse
Suzanne Bourdages, Directrice générale

Rivière-à-Claude
520, rue Principale est
Rivière-à-Claude, QC G0E 1Z0
Tél: 418-797-2422; *Téléc:* 418-797-2455
munirac@globetrotter.net
Entité municipal: Municipality
Incorporation: 18 décembre 1923 *Area:* 155,39 km2
Comté ou district: La Haute-Gaspésie; *Population au 2006:* 171
Circonscription(s) électorale(s) provinciale(s): Matane
Circonscription(s) électorale(s) fédérale(s): Haute-Gaspésie-La Mitis-Matane-Matapédia
Prochaines élections: 3e novembre 2013
Réjean Normand, Maire
Claudine Auclair, Directrice générale

Rivière-à-Pierre
CP 648
830, rue Principale
Rivière-à-Pierre, QC G0A 3A0
Tél: 418-323-2112; *Téléc:* 418-323-2111
rivapier@globetrotter.net
www.riviereapierre.com
Entité municipal: Municipality
Incorporation: 11 octobre 1897 *Area:* 521,31 km2
Comté ou district: Portneuf; *Population au 2006:* 694
Circonscription(s) électorale(s) provinciale(s): Portneuf
Circonscription(s) électorale(s) fédérale(s): Portneuf-Jacques-Cartier
Prochaines élections: 3e novembre 2013
Ghislaine Noreau, Mairesse
Pascale Bonin, Directrice générale

Rivière-au-Tonnerre
CP 129
473, rue Jacques Cartier
Rivière-au-Tonnerre, QC G0G 2L0
Tél: 418-465-2255; *Téléc:* 418-465-2956
municipaliterivauton@globetrotter.net
Entité municipal: Municipality
Incorporation: 14 décembre 1925 *Area:* 1331,17 km2
Comté ou district: Minganie; *Population au 2006:* 390
Circonscription(s) électorale(s) provinciale(s): Duplessis
Circonscription(s) électorale(s) fédérale(s): Manicouagan
Prochaines élections: 3e novembre 2013
Jeannot Boudreau, Maire
Carmelle Anglehart, Directrice générale

Rivière-Beaudette
663, ch de la Frontière
Rivière-Beaudette, QC J0P 1R0
Tél: 450-269-2931; *Téléc:* 450-269-2815
munrivbeaudette@qc.aira.com
www.riviere-beaudette.com
Entité municipal: Municipality
Incorporation: 17 janvier 1990 *Area:* 19,62 km2
Comté ou district: Vaudreuil-Soulanges; *Population au 2006:* 1,720
Circonscription(s) électorale(s) provinciale(s): Soulanges
Circonscription(s) électorale(s) fédérale(s): Vaudreuil-Soulanges
Prochaines élections: 3e novembre 2013
Patrick Bousez, Maire
Céline Chayer, Directrice générale

Rivière-Bleue
32, rue des Pins est
Rivière-Bleue, QC G0L 2B0
Tél: 418-893-5559; *Téléc:* 418-893-5530
info@riviere-bleue.ca
www.riviere-bleue.ca
Entité municipal: Municipality
Incorporation: 14 juin 1975 *Area:* 179,93 km2
Comté ou district: Témiscouata; *Population au 2006:* 1,407
Circonscription(s) électorale(s) provinciale(s): Kamouraska-Témiscouata
Circonscription(s) électorale(s) fédérale(s): Rimouski-Neigette-Témiscouata-Les Basques
Prochaines élections: 3e novembre 2013
Claude H. Pelletier, Maire
Claudie Levasseur, Directrice générale

Rivière-du-Loup
310, rue St-Pierre
Rivière-du-Loup, QC G5R 3V3
Tél: 418-867-2485; *Téléc:* 418-867-3100
administration@mrc-riviere-du-loup.qc.ca
www.mrc-rdl.qc.ca
Entité municipal: Regional County Municipality
Incorporation: 1 janvier 1982
Population au 2006: 33,305
Note: 13 municipalités.
Michel Lagacé, Préfet
Raymond Duval, Directeur général

Rivière-Éternité
418, rte Principale
Rivière-Éternité, QC G0V 1P0
Tél: 418-272-2860; *Téléc:* 418-544-3085
municipalite@riviere-eternite.com
www.riviere-eternite.com
Entité municipal: Municipality
Incorporation: 20 juillet 1974 *Area:* 496,88 km2
Comté ou district: Le Fjord-du-Saguenay; *Population au 2006:* 557
Circonscription(s) électorale(s) provinciale(s): Dubuc
Circonscription(s) électorale(s) fédérale(s): Chicoutimi-Le Fjord
Prochaines élections: 3e novembre 2013
Rémi Gagné, Maire
Denis Houde, Directeur général

Rivière-Héva
CP 60
740, rte St-Paul nord
Rivière-Héva, QC J0Y 2H0
Tél: 819-735-3521; *Téléc:* 819-735-4251
nsavard@mun-r-h.com
Entité municipal: Municipality
Incorporation: 1er janvier 1982 *Area:* 166,09 km2
Comté ou district: La Vallée-de-l'Or; *Population au 2006:* 1,056
Circonscription(s) électorale(s) provinciale(s): Abitibi-Est
Circonscription(s) électorale(s) fédérale(s): Abitibi-Baie-James-Nunavik-Eeyou
Prochaines élections: 3e novembre 2013
Réjean Guay, Maire
Nathalie Savard, Directrice générale

Rivière-Ouelle
CP 99
106, rue de l'Église
Rivière-Ouelle, QC G0L 2C0
Tél: 418-856-3829; *Téléc:* 418-856-1790
dg@riviereouelle.ca
www.riviereouelle.ca
Entité municipal: Municipality
Incorporation: 1er juillet 1855 *Area:* 54,72 km2

Comté ou district: Kamouraska; *Population au 2006:* 1,165
Circonscription(s) électorale(s) provinciale(s):
Kamouraska-Témiscouata
Circonscription(s) électorale(s) fédérale(s):
Montmagny-L'Islet-Kamouraska-Rivière-du-Loup
Prochaines élections: 3e novembre 2013
Elizabeth Hudon, Mairesse
Adam Ménard, Directeur général

Rivière-Rouge
25, rue L'Annonciation sud
Rivière-Rouge, QC J0T 1T0
Tél: 819-275-2929; *Téléc:* 819-275-3676
greffe@riviere-rouge.ca
www.riviere-rouge.ca
Entité municipal: Town
Incorporation: 18 décembre 2002 *Area:* 463,18 km2
Comté ou district: Antoine-Labelle; *Population au 2006:* 4,152
Circonscription(s) électorale(s) provinciale(s): Labelle
Circonscription(s) électorale(s) fédérale(s): Laurentides-Labelle
Prochaines élections: 3e novembre 2013
Déborah Bélanger, Mairesse
Pierre St-Onge, Greffier

Rivière-St-Jean
116, rue du Quai
Rivière-Saint-Jean, QC G0G 2N0
Tél: 418-949-2464; *Téléc:* 418-949-2489
magpiest-jean@globetrotter.net
Entité municipal: Municipality
Incorporation: 1er janvier 1966 *Area:* 652,54 km2
Comté ou district: Minganie; *Population au 2006:* 260
Circonscription(s) électorale(s) provinciale(s): Duplessis
Circonscription(s) électorale(s) fédérale(s): Manicouagan
Prochaines élections: 3e novembre 2013
Michel Beaudin, Maire
Louise Rodgers, Directrice générale

Robert-Cliche
111A, 107e Rue
Beauceville, QC G5X 2P9
Tél: 418-774-9828; *Téléc:* 418-774-4057
mrc.robert.cliche@beaucerc.com
www.beaucerc.com
Entité municipal: Regional County Municipality
Incorporation: 1 janvier 1982
Population au 2006: 18,790
Note: 10 municipalités.
Jean-Rock Veilleux, Préfet
Gilbert Caron, Directeur général
gilbert.caron@beaucerc.com

Rochebaucourt
20, rue du Chanoine-Girard
Rochebaucourt, QC J0Y 2J0
Tél: 819-754-2083; *Téléc:* 819-754-5417
muniroche@cableamos.com
www.municipalite-rochebaucourt.org
Entité municipal: Municipality
Incorporation: 1er janvier 1983 *Area:* 185,00 km2
Comté ou district: Abitibi; *Population au 2006:* 177
Circonscription(s) électorale(s) provinciale(s): Abitibi-Ouest
Circonscription(s) électorale(s) fédérale(s):
Abitibi-Témiscamingue
Prochaines élections: 3e novembre 2013
Gaby Chiasson Yergeau, Maire
Nathalie Lyrette, Directrice générale

Roquemaure
15, rue Raymond est
Roquemaure, QC J0Z 3K0
Tél: 819-787-6311; *Téléc:* 819-787-6383
roquemaure@mrcao.qc.ca
www.roquemaure.ao.ca
Entité municipal: Municipality
Incorporation: 1er janvier 1952 *Area:* 121,67 km2
Comté ou district: Abitibi-Ouest; *Population au 2006:* 402
Circonscription(s) électorale(s) provinciale(s): Abitibi-Ouest
Circonscription(s) électorale(s) fédérale(s):
Abitibi-Témiscamingue
Prochaines élections: 3e novembre 2013
Léo Pinard, Maire
Annick Lavoie, Directrice générale

Rougemont
61, ch de Marieville
Rougemont, QC J0L 1M0
Tél: 450-469-3790; *Téléc:* 450-469-0309
reception@rougemont.ca
www.rougemont.ca
Entité municipal: Municipality
Incorporation: 26 janvier 2000 *Area:* 44,48 km2
Comté ou district: Rouville; *Population au 2006:* 2,622
Circonscription(s) électorale(s) provinciale(s): Iberville
Circonscription(s) électorale(s) fédérale(s): Shefford
Prochaines élections: 3e novembre 2013
Alain Brière, Maire
Kathia Joseph, Directrice générale

Roussillon
#200, 260, rue Saint-Pierre
Saint-Constant, QC J5A 2A5
Tél: 450-638-1221; *Téléc:* 450-638-4499
admin@mrcroussillon.qc.ca
www.mrcroussillon.qc.ca
Entité municipal: Regional County Municipality
Incorporation: 1er janvier 1982
Population au 2006: 149,996
Note: 11 municipalités.
Nathalie Simon, Préfète
Pierre Largy, Directeur général
p.largy@mrcroussillon.qc.ca

Rouville
#100, 500 rue Desjardins
Marieville, QC J3M 1E1
Tél: 450-460-2127; *Téléc:* 450-460-7169
mrcrouville@on.aira.com
www.mrcrouville.qc.ca
Entité municipal: Regional County Municipality
Incorporation: 1er janvier 1982
Population au 2006: 31,365
Note: 8 municipalités.
Michel Picotte, Préfet
Rosaire Marcil, Directeur général
r.marcil@mrcrouville.qc.ca

Roxton
216, rang Ste-Geneviève
Roxton Falls, QC J0H 1E0
Tél: 450-548-2500; *Téléc:* 450-548-2412
canrox@cooptel.qc.ca
www.cantonderoxton.qc.ca
Entité municipal: Township
Incorporation: 1er juillet 1855 *Area:* 149,07 km2
Comté ou district: Acton; *Population au 2006:* 1,016
Circonscription(s) électorale(s) provinciale(s): Johnson
Circonscription(s) électorale(s) fédérale(s): St-Hyacinthe-Bagot
Prochaines élections: 3e novembre 2013
Stéphane Beauregard, Maire
Deynse Viens, Directrice générale (par intérim)

Roxton Falls
26, rue du Marché
Roxton Falls, QC J0H 1E0
Tél: 450-548-5790; *Téléc:* 450-548-5881
roxton@roxtonfalls.ca
www.roxtonfalls.ca
Entité municipal: Village
Incorporation: 1er janvier 1863 *Area:* 5,25 km2
Comté ou district: Acton; *Population au 2006:* 1,305
Circonscription(s) électorale(s) provinciale(s): Johnson
Circonscription(s) électorale(s) fédérale(s): St-Hyacinthe-Bagot
Prochaines élections: 3e novembre 2013
Jean-Marie Laplante, Maire
Julie Gagné, Directrice générale

Roxton Pond
901, rue St-Jean
Roxton Pond, QC J0E 1Z0
Tél: 450-372-6875; *Téléc:* 450-372-1205
fgiasson@roxtonpond.ca
Entité municipal: Municipality
Incorporation: 17 décembre 1997 *Area:* 102,11 km2
Comté ou district: La Haute-Yamaska; *Population au 2006:* 3,599
Circonscription(s) électorale(s) provinciale(s): Johnson
Circonscription(s) électorale(s) fédérale(s): Shefford
Prochaines élections: 3e novembre 2013
Raymond Loignon, Maire
Francois Giasson, Directeur général

Sacré-Coeur
88, rue Principale nord
Sacré-Coeur, QC G0T 1Y0
Tél: 418-236-4621; *Téléc:* 418-236-9144
s-c@municipalite.sacre-coeur.qc.ca
www.municipalite.sacre-coeur.qc.ca
Entité municipal: Municipality
Incorporation: 30 juin 1976 *Area:* 341,74 km2
Comté ou district: La Haute-Côte-Nord; *Population au 2006:* 2,024
Circonscription(s) électorale(s) provinciale(s): René-Lévesque
Circonscription(s) électorale(s) fédérale(s):
Montmorency-Charlevoix-Haute-Côte-Nord
Prochaines élections: 3e novembre 2013
Gilles Pineault, Maire
Claudia Gauthier, Directrice générale

Sacré-Coeur-de-Jésus
4118, rte 112
East Broughton, QC G0N 1G0
Tél: 418-427-3447; *Téléc:* 418-427-4774
info@sacrecoeurdejesus.qc.ca
www.sacrecoeurdejesus.qc.ca
Entité municipal: Parish (Paroisse)
Incorporation: 11 décembre 1889 *Area:* 103,850 km2
Comté ou district: Les Appalaches; *Population au 2006:* 599
Circonscription(s) électorale(s) provinciale(s): Frontenac
Circonscription(s) électorale(s) fédérale(s): Mégantic-L'Érable
Prochaines élections: 3e novembre 2013
Guy Roy, Maire
Marie-France Létourneau, Directrice générale

Saint-Adalbert
55, rue Principale
Saint-Adalbert, QC G0R 2M0
Tél: 418-356-5271; *Téléc:* 418-356-5317
mstadalb@globetrotter.net
www.saintadalbert.qc.ca
Entité municipal: Municipality
Incorporation: 26 août 1911 *Area:* 213,95 km2
Comté ou district: L'Islet; *Population au 2006:* 596
Circonscription(s) électorale(s) provinciale(s): Montmagny-L'Islet
Circonscription(s) électorale(s) fédérale(s):
Montmagny-L'Islet-Kamouraska-Rivière-du-Loup
Prochaines élections: 3e novembre 2013
René Laverdière, Maire
Magguy Mathault, Directrice générale

Saint-Adelme
CP 39
138, rue Principale
Saint-Adelme, QC G0J 2B0
Tél: 418-733-4044; *Téléc:* 418-733-4111
st-adelme@mrcdematane.qc.ca
www.mrcdematane.qc.ca/stadelme.html
Entité municipal: Parish (Paroisse)
Incorporation: 9 septembre 1933 *Area:* 100,20 km2
Comté ou district: Matane; *Population au 2006:* 497
Circonscription(s) électorale(s) provinciale(s): Matane
Circonscription(s) électorale(s) fédérale(s): Haute-Gaspésie-La Mitis-Matane-Matapédia
Prochaines élections: 3e novembre 2013
Yvan Imbeault, Maire
Annick Hudon, Directrice générale

Saint-Adelphe
150, rue Baillargeon
Saint-Adelphe-de-Champlain, QC G0X 2G0
Tél: 418-322-5721; *Téléc:* 418-322-5434
st-adelphe@regionmekinac.com
www.st-adelphe.qc.ca/
Entité municipal: Parish (Paroisse)
Incorporation: 19 octobre 1891 *Area:* 135,35 km2
Comté ou district: Mékinac; *Population au 2006:* 1,013
Circonscription(s) électorale(s) provinciale(s): Laviolette
Circonscription(s) électorale(s) fédérale(s):
Saint-Maurice-Champlain
Prochaines élections: 3e novembre 2013
Paul Labranche, Maire
Daniel Bacon, Directeur général

Saint-Adolphe-d'Howard
1881, ch du Village
Saint-Adolphe-d'Howard, QC J0T 2B0
Tél: 819-327-2044; *Téléc:* 819-327-2282
info@stadolphedhoward.qc.ca
www.stadolphedhoward.qc.ca
Entité municipal: Municipality
Incorporation: 1er janvier 1883 *Area:* 144,41 km2
Comté ou district: Les Pays-d'en-Haut; *Population au 2006:* 3,563
Circonscription(s) électorale(s) provinciale(s): Argenteuil
Circonscription(s) électorale(s) fédérale(s):
Argenteuil-Papineau-Mirabel
Prochaines élections: 3e novembre 2013
Pierre Roy, Maire
maire@stadolphedhoward.qc.ca
Richard Daveluy, Directeur général
rdaveluy@stadolphedhoward.qc.ca

Saint-Adrien
1589, rue Principale
Saint-Adrien, QC J0A 1C0
Tél: 819-828-2872; *Téléc:* 819-828-0442
munstadrien@cgocable.ca
st-adrien.com
Entité municipal: Municipality
Incorporation: 1er janvier 1879 *Area:* 97,59 km2
Comté ou district: Les Sources; *Population au 2006:* 488
Circonscription(s) électorale(s) provinciale(s): Richmond
Circonscription(s) électorale(s) fédérale(s):
Richmond-Arthabaska
Prochaines élections: 3e novembre 2013
Pierre Therrien, Maire
Maryse Ducharme, Directrice générale

Saint-Adrien-d'Irlande
152, rue Municipale
Saint-Adrien-d'Irlande, QC G0N 1M0
Tél: 418-335-2585; *Téléc:* 418-335-4040
muadrien@hotmail.com
Entité municipal: Municipality
Incorporation: 1er janvier 1873 *Area:* 52,780 km2
Comté ou district: Les Appalaches; *Population au 2009:* 419
Circonscription(s) électorale(s) provinciale(s): Frontenac
Circonscription(s) électorale(s) fédérale(s): Mégantic-L'Érable
Prochaines élections: 3e novembre 2013
Jessika Lacombe, Mairesse
Ghislaine Leblanc, Directrice générale

Saint-Agapit
1186, rue Principale
Saint-Agapit, QC G0S 1Z0
Tél: 418-888-4620; *Téléc:* 418-888-4791
stagapit@globetrotter.net
st-agapit.qc.ca
Entité municipal: Municipality
Incorporation: 14 avril 1979 *Area:* 65,91 km2
Comté ou district: Lotbinière; *Population au 2006:* 2,965
Circonscription(s) électorale(s) provinciale(s): Lotbinière
Circonscription(s) électorale(s) fédérale(s):
Lotbinière-Chutes-de-la-Chaudière
Prochaines élections: 3e novembre 2013
Sylvie Fortin Graham, Mairesse
Isabelle Paré, Directrice générale
isabelle.pare@st-agapit.qc.ca

Saint-Aimé
CP 240
285, rue Bonsecours
Massueville, QC J0G 1K0
Tél: 450-788-2737; *Téléc:* 450-788-3337
staime@bas-richelieu.net
www.saintaime.qc.ca/
Entité municipal: Municipality
Incorporation: 1er juillet 1855 *Area:* 61,33 km2
Comté ou district: Pierre-De Saurel; *Population au 2006:* 523
Circonscription(s) électorale(s) provinciale(s): Richelieu
Circonscription(s) électorale(s) fédérale(s):
Bas-Richelieu-Nicolet-Bécancour
Prochaines élections: 3e novembre 2013
Maria Libert, Mairesse
Francine B. Lambert, Directrice générale

Saint-Aimé-des-Lacs
119, rue Principale
Saint-Aimé-des-Lacs, QC G0T 1S0
Tél: 418-439-2229; *Téléc:* 418-439-1475
info@saintaimedeslacs.ca
www.saintaimedeslacs.ca
Entité municipal: Municipality
Incorporation: 1er janvier 1950 *Area:* 101,57 km2
Comté ou district: Charlevoix-Est; *Population au 2006:* 1,076
Circonscription(s) électorale(s) provinciale(s): Charlevoix
Circonscription(s) électorale(s) fédérale(s):
Montmorency-Charlevoix-Haute-Côte-Nord
Prochaines élections: 3e novembre 2013
Bernard Maltais, Maire
maire@saintaimedeslacs.ca
Suzanne Gaudreault, Directrice générale

Saint-Aimé-du-Lac-des-Iles
871, chemin Diotte
Saint-Aimé-du-Lac-des-Iles, QC J0W 1J0
Tél: 819-597-2047; *Téléc:* 819-597-2554
munldi@tlb.sympatico.ca
www.saint-aime-du-lac-des-iles.ca
Entité municipal: Municipality
Incorporation: 1er janvier 2006 *Area:* 165,77 km2
Comté ou district: Antoine-Labelle; *Population au 2006:* 744
Circonscription(s) électorale(s) provinciale(s): Labelle
Circonscription(s) électorale(s) fédérale(s): Laurentides-Labelle
Prochaines élections: 3e novembre 2013
François Desjardins, Maire
mairieldi@tlb.sympatico.ca
Gisèle Lépine-Pilotte, Directrice générale
dgldi@tlb.sympatico.ca

Saint-Alban
204, rue Principale
Saint-Alban, QC G0A 3B0
Tél: 418-268-8026; *Téléc:* 418-268-5073
www.st-alban.qc.ca
Entité municipal: Municipality
Incorporation: 31 décembre 1991 *Area:* 150,55 km2
Comté ou district: Portneuf; *Population au 2006:* 1,138
Circonscription(s) électorale(s) provinciale(s): Portneuf
Circonscription(s) électorale(s) fédérale(s):
Portneuf-Jacques-Cartier
Prochaines élections: 3e novembre 2013
Lynn Audet, Mairesse
Andrée Gosselin, Directrice générale
a.gosselin@st-alban.qc.ca

Saint-Albert
CP 100
25, rue des Loisirs
Saint-Albert, QC J0A 1E0
Tél: 819-353-3300; *Téléc:* 819-353-3313
stalbert@munstalbert.ca
Entité municipal: Municipality
Incorporation: 1er janvier 1864 *Area:* 70,36 km2
Comté ou district: Arthabaska; *Population au 2006:* 1,501
Circonscription(s) électorale(s) provinciale(s): Richmond
Circonscription(s) électorale(s) fédérale(s):
Richmond-Arthabaska
Prochaines élections: 3e novembre 2013
Alain St-Pierre, Maire
Suzanne Corriveau-Crête, Directrice générale

Saint-Alexandre
453, rue St-Denis
Saint-Alexandre, QC J0J 1S0
Tél: 450-346-6641; *Téléc:* 450-346-0538
villedestalexandre@qc.aira.com
www.ville.saint-alexandre.qc.ca
Entité municipal: Municipality
Incorporation: 17 septembre 1988 *Area:* 76,55 km2
Comté ou district: Le Haut-Richelieu; *Population au 2006:* 2,340
Circonscription(s) électorale(s) provinciale(s): Iberville
Circonscription(s) électorale(s) fédérale(s): St-Jean
Prochaines élections: 3e novembre 2013
André Bergeron, Maire
Michèle Bertrand, Directrice générale

Saint-Alexandre-de-Kamouraska
CP 10
629, rte 289
Saint-Alexandre-de-Kamouraska, QC G0L 2G0
Tél: 418-495-2440; *Téléc:* 418-495-2659
stalex.kamouraska@bellnet.ca
www.stalex.kamouraska.qc.ca
Entité municipal: Municipality
Incorporation: 1er juillet 1855 *Area:* 115,95 km2
Comté ou district: Kamouraska; *Population au 2006:* 1,880
Circonscription(s) électorale(s) provinciale(s):
Kamouraska-Témiscouata
Circonscription(s) électorale(s) fédérale(s):
Montmagny-L'Islet-Kamouraska-Rivière-du-Loup
Prochaines élections: 3e novembre 2013
Luc Chouinard, Maire
Lyne Dumont, Directrice générale
ldumont@stalexkamouraska.com

Saint-Alexandre-des-Lacs
17, rue de l'Église
Saint-Alexandre-des-Lacs, QC G0J 2C0
Tél: 418-778-3532; *Téléc:* 418-778-1315
stalexandre@mrcmatapedia.qc.ca
Entité municipal: Parish (Paroisse)
Incorporation: 1er janvier 1965 *Area:* 92,98 km2
Comté ou district: La Matapédia; *Population au 2006:* 275
Circonscription(s) électorale(s) provinciale(s): Matapédia
Circonscription(s) électorale(s) fédérale(s): Haute-Gaspésie-La Mitis-Matane-Matapédia
Prochaines élections: 3e novembre 2013
Jean-Marc Roy, Maire
Caroline Savoie, Directrice générale

Saint-Alexis
232, rue Principale
Saint-Alexis, QC J0K 1T0
Tél: 450-839-7277; *Téléc:* 450-839-6241
info@st-alexis.com
Entité municipal: Parish (Paroisse)
Incorporation: 1er juillet 1855 *Area:* 36,59 km2
Comté ou district: Montcalm; *Population au 2006:* 722
Circonscription(s) électorale(s) provinciale(s): Rousseau
Circonscription(s) électorale(s) fédérale(s): Montcalm
Prochaines élections: 3e novembre 2013
Adélard Éthier, Maire
Rémy Lanoue, Directeur général

Saint-Alexis
232, rue Principale
Saint-Alexis, QC J0K 1T0
Tél: 450-839-7277; *Téléc:* 450-839-6241
info@st-alexis.com
Entité municipal: Village
Incorporation: 16 novembre 1920 *Area:* 6,60 km2
Comté ou district: Montcalm; *Population au 2006:* 556
Circonscription(s) électorale(s) provinciale(s): Rousseau
Circonscription(s) électorale(s) fédérale(s): Montcalm
Prochaines élections: 3e novembre 2013
Adélard Éthier, Maire
Rémy Lanoue, Directeur général

Saint-Alexis-de-Matapédia
CP 99
190, rue Principale
Saint-Alexis-de-Matapédia, QC G0J 2E0
Tél: 418-299-2030; *Téléc:* 418-299-3011
plateau1@globetrotter.qc.ca
www.matapedialesplateaux.com
Entité municipal: Municipality
Incorporation: 1er juillet 1855 *Area:* 83,37 km2
Comté ou district: Avignon; *Population au 2006:* 625
Circonscription(s) électorale(s) provinciale(s): Bonaventure
Circonscription(s) électorale(s) fédérale(s):
Gaspésie—Îles-de-la-Madeleine
Prochaines élections: 3e novembre 2013
Guy Gallant, Maire
Lise Pitre, Directrice générale

Saint-Alexis-des-Monts
101, rue de l'Hôtel-de-Ville
Saint-Alexis-des-Monts, QC J0K 1V0
Tél: 819-265-2046; *Téléc:* 819-265-2481
info@saint-alexis-des-monts.ca
www.saint-alexis-des-monts.ca
Entité municipal: Parish (Paroisse)
Incorporation: 21 avril 1984 *Area:* 1153,85 km2
Comté ou district: Maskinongé; *Population au 2006:* 3,118
Circonscription(s) électorale(s) provinciale(s): Maskinongé
Circonscription(s) électorale(s) fédérale(s): Berthier-Maskinongé
Prochaines élections: 3e novembre 2013
Madeleine L. Robert, Mairesse
Sylvie Clément, Directrice générale

Saint-Alfred
9, rte du Cap
Saint-Alfred, QC G0M 1L0
Tél: 418-774-2068; *Téléc:* 418-774-2068
municipalitestalfred@sogetel.net
www.st-alfred.qc.ca
Entité municipal: Municipality
Incorporation: 1er janvier 1950 *Area:* 42,42 km2
Comté ou district: Robert-Cliche; *Population au 2006:* 458
Circonscription(s) électorale(s) provinciale(s): Beauce-Nord
Circonscription(s) électorale(s) fédérale(s): Beauce
Prochaines élections: 3e novembre 2013
Jean-Roch Veilleux, Maire
Diane Jacques, Directrice générale

Saint-Alphonse
127, rue Principale est
Saint-Alphonse, QC G0C 2V0
Tél: 418-388-5214; *Téléc:* 418-388-2435
st-alphonsemuni@globetrotter.net
www.st-alphonsegaspesie.com
Entité municipal: Municipality
Incorporation: 9 mai 1902 *Area:* 113,13 km2
Comté ou district: Bonaventure; *Population au 2006:* 731
Circonscription(s) électorale(s) provinciale(s): Bonaventure
Circonscription(s) électorale(s) fédérale(s):
Gaspésie—Îles-de-la-Madeleine
Prochaines élections: 3e novembre 2013
Gérard Porlier, Maire
Reina Goulet, Directrice générale

Saint-Alphonse-de-Granby
360, rue Principale
Saint-Alphonse-de-Granby, QC J0E 2A0
Tél: 450-375-4570; *Téléc:* 450-375-4717
infos@st-alphonse.qc.ca
www.st-alphonse.qc.ca
Entité municipal: Parish (Paroisse)
Incorporation: 30 décembre 1890 *Area:* 50,52 km2
Comté ou district: La Haute-Yamaska; *Population au 2006:* 2,918
Circonscription(s) électorale(s) provinciale(s): Brome-Missisquoi
Circonscription(s) électorale(s) fédérale(s): Shefford
Prochaines élections: 3e novembre 2013
Clément Choinière, Maire
Réal Pitt, Directeur général

Saint-Alphonse-Rodriguez
101, rue de la Plage
Saint-Alphonse-Rodriguez, QC J0K 1W0
Tél: 450-883-2264; *Téléc:* 450-883-0833
info@munsar.ca
www.munsar.ca
Entité municipal: Municipality
Incorporation: 1er juillet 1855 *Area:* 101,37 km2
Comté ou district: Matawinie; *Population au 2006:* 3,152
Circonscription(s) électorale(s) provinciale(s): Berthier
Circonscription(s) électorale(s) fédérale(s): Joliette
Prochaines élections: 3e novembre 2013
Robert W. Desnoyers, Maire
François Dauphin, Directeur général

Saint-Amable
575, rue Principale
Saint-Amable, QC J0L 1N0
Tél: 450-649-3555; *Téléc:* 450-922-0728
ville@st-amable.qc.ca
www.st-amable.qc.ca
Entité municipal: Municipality
Incorporation: 13 juin 1921 *Area:* 38,04 km2
Comté ou district: Lajemmerais; *Population au 2006:* 8,398
Circonscription(s) électorale(s) provinciale(s): Verchères
Circonscription(s) électorale(s) fédérale(s): Verchères-Les-Patriotes
Prochaines élections: 3e novembre 2013
François Gamache, Maire
Carmen McDuff, Directrice générale

Saint-Ambroise
330, rue Gagnon
Saint-Ambroise, QC G7P 2P9
Tél: 418-672-4765; *Téléc:* 418-672-6126
info@st-ambroise.qc.ca
www.st-ambroise.qc.ca
Entité municipal: Municipality
Incorporation: 25 septembre 1971 *Area:* 148,61 km2
Comté ou district: Le Fjord-du-Saguenay; *Population au 2006:* 3,484
Circonscription(s) électorale(s) provinciale(s): Dubuc
Circonscription(s) électorale(s) fédérale(s): Jonquière-Alma
Prochaines élections: 3e novembre 2013
Marcel Claveau, Maire
Michel Perreault, Directeur général

Saint-Ambroise-de-Kildare
CP 57
850, rue Principale
Kildare, QC J0K 1C0
Tél: 450-755-4782; *Téléc:* 450-755-4784
info@saintambroise.ca
www.saintambroisedekildare.qc.ca
Entité municipal: Parish (Paroisse)
Incorporation: 1er juillet 1855 *Area:* 66,89 km2
Comté ou district: Joliette; *Population au 2006:* 3,491
Circonscription(s) électorale(s) provinciale(s): Joliette
Circonscription(s) électorale(s) fédérale(s): Joliette
Prochaines élections: 3e novembre 2013
René Laurin, Maire
Renald Gravel, Directeur général

Saint-Anaclet-de-Lessard
318, rue Principale ouest
Saint-Anaclet, QC G0K 1H0
Tél: 418-723-2816; *Téléc:* 418-723-0436
municipalite@stanaclet.qc.ca
stanaclet.qc.ca
Entité municipal: Parish (Paroisse)
Incorporation: 9 mai 1859 *Area:* 126,26 km2
Comté ou district: Rimouski-Neigette; *Population au 2006:* 2,644
Circonscription(s) électorale(s) provinciale(s): Rimouski
Circonscription(s) électorale(s) fédérale(s): Rimouski-Neigette-Témiscouata-Les Basques
Prochaines élections: 3e novembre 2013
Francis St-Pierre, Maire
Alain Lapierre, Directeur général

Saint-André
122A, rue Principale
Saint-André-de-Kamouraska, QC G0L 2H0
Tél: 418-493-2085; *Téléc:* 418-493-2373
munand@bellnet.ca
www.standredekamouraska.ca
Entité municipal: Municipality
Incorporation: 14 février 1987 *Area:* 68,94 km2
Comté ou district: Kamouraska; *Population au 2006:* 618
Circonscription(s) électorale(s) provinciale(s): Kamouraska-Témiscouata
Circonscription(s) électorale(s) fédérale(s): Montmagny-L'Islet-Kamouraska-Rivière-du-Loup
Prochaines élections: 3e novembre 2013
Gervais Darisse, Maire
Claudine Lévesque, Directrice générale

Saint-André-Avellin
119, rue Principale
Saint-André-Avellin, QC J0V 1W0
Tél: 819-983-2318; *Téléc:* 819-983-2344
info@ville.st-andre-avellin.qc.ca
www.ville.st-andre-avellin.qc.ca
Entité municipal: Municipality
Incorporation: 17 décembre 1997 *Area:* 131,05 km2
Comté ou district: Papineau; *Population au 2006:* 3,435
Circonscription(s) électorale(s) provinciale(s): Papineau
Circonscription(s) électorale(s) fédérale(s): Argenteuil-Papineau-Mirabel
Prochaines élections: 3e novembre 2013
Thérèse Whissell, Mairesse
Claire Tremblay, Directrice générale

Saint-André-d'Argenteuil
10, rue de la Mairie
Saint-André-d'Argenteuil, QC J0V 1X0
Tél: 450-537-3527; *Téléc:* 450-537-3070
info@saintandredargenteuil.ca
www.saintandredargenteuil.ca
Entité municipal: Municipality
Incorporation: 29 décembre 1999 *Area:* 98,45 km2
Comté ou district: Argenteuil; *Population au 2006:* 3,097
Circonscription(s) électorale(s) provinciale(s): Argenteuil
Circonscription(s) électorale(s) fédérale(s): Argenteuil-Papineau-Mirabel
Prochaines élections: 3e novembre 2013
André Jetté, Maire
Ronald Baidr, Directeur général

Saint-André-de-Restigouche
CP 4
163, rue Principale
Saint-André-de-Restigouche, QC G0J 2G0
Tél: 418-865-2234; *Téléc:* 418-865-1393
m.st.and.restigouche@globetrotter.net
www.matapedialesplateaux.com
Entité municipal: Municipality
Incorporation: 1er juillet 1855 *Area:* 146,07 km2
Comté ou district: Avignon; *Population au 2006:* 192
Circonscription(s) électorale(s) provinciale(s): Bonaventure
Circonscription(s) électorale(s) fédérale(s): Gaspésie—Îles-de-la-Madeleine
Prochaines élections: 3e novembre 2013
Doris Deschênes, Mairesse
Blandine Parent, Directrice générale

Saint-André-du-Lac-St-Jean
11, rue du Collège
Saint-André-du-Lac-Saint-Jean, QC G0W 2K0
Tél: 418-349-8167; *Téléc:* 418-349-1019
municipalite@standredulac.qc.ca
Entité municipal: Village
Incorporation: 29 novembre 1969 *Area:* 157,75 km2
Comté ou district: Le Domaine-du-Roy; *Population au 2006:* 484
Circonscription(s) électorale(s) provinciale(s): Lac-St-Jean
Circonscription(s) électorale(s) fédérale(s): Roberval-Lac-St-Jean
Prochaines élections: 3e novembre 2013
Gabriel Martel, Maire
Maude Tremblay, Directrice générale

Saint-Anicet
335, av Jules-Léger
Saint-Anicet, QC J0S 1M0
Tél: 450-264-2555; *Téléc:* 450-264-2395
saint.anicet@municipalite-saint-anicet.qc.ca
www.municipalite-saint-anicet.qc.ca
Entité municipal: Parish (Paroisse)
Incorporation: 1er juillet 1855 *Area:* 136,25 km2
Comté ou district: Le Haut-St-Laurent; *Population au 2006:* 2,717
Circonscription(s) électorale(s) provinciale(s): Huntingdon
Circonscription(s) électorale(s) fédérale(s): Beauharnois-Salaberry
Prochaines élections: 3e novembre 2013
Alain Castagner, Maire
Lyne Viau, Directrice générale

Saint-Anselme
134, rue Principale
Saint-Anselme, QC G0R 2N0
Tél: 418-885-4977; *Téléc:* 418-885-9834
municipalite@st-anselme.ca
www.st-anselme.ca
Entité municipal: Municipality
Incorporation: 7 janvier 1998 *Area:* 74,45 km2
Comté ou district: Bellechasse; *Population au 2006:* 3,220
Circonscription(s) électorale(s) provinciale(s): Bellechasse
Circonscription(s) électorale(s) fédérale(s): Lévis-Bellechasse
Prochaines élections: 3e novembre 2013
Michel Bonneau, Maire
Louis Felteau, Directeur général

Saint-Antoine de l'Isle-aux-Grues
107, ch de la Volière
L'Isle-aux-Grues, QC G0R 1P0
Tél: 418-248-8060; *Téléc:* 418-248-7955
municipaliteiag@globetrotter.net
www.isle-aux-grues.com
Entité municipal: Parish (Paroisse)
Incorporation: 1er janvier 1860 *Area:* 26,40 km2
Comté ou district: Montmagny; *Population au 2006:* 163
Circonscription(s) électorale(s) provinciale(s): Montmagny-L'Islet
Circonscription(s) électorale(s) fédérale(s): Montmagny-L'Islet-Kamouraska-Rivière-du-Loup
Prochaines élections: 3e novembre 2013
Frédéric Poulin, Maire
Hélène Painchaud, Directrice générale

Saint-Antoine-de-Tilly
CP 10
3870, ch de Tilly
Saint-Antoine-de-Tilly, QC G0S 2C0
Tél: 418-886-2441; *Téléc:* 418-886-2075
info@saintantoinedetilly.com
www.saintantoinedetilly.com
Entité municipal: Municipality
Incorporation: 1er juillet 1855 *Area:* 60,29 km2
Comté ou district: Lotbinière; *Population au 2006:* 1,449
Circonscription(s) électorale(s) provinciale(s): Lotbinière
Circonscription(s) électorale(s) fédérale(s): Lotbinière-Chutes-de-la-Chaudière
Prochaines élections: 3e novembre 2013
Ghislain Daigle, Maire
Diane Laroche, Directrice générale

Saint-Antoine-sur-Richelieu
1060, rue des Ormes
Saint-Antoine-sur-Richelieu, QC J0L 1R0
Tél: 450-787-3497; *Téléc:* 450-787-2852
municipalite@sasr.ca
www.saint-antoine-sur-richelieu.qc.ca
Entité municipal: Municipality
Incorporation: 6 novembre 1982 *Area:* 65,26 km2
Comté ou district: La Vallée-du-Richelieu; *Population au 2006:* 1,594
Circonscription(s) électorale(s) provinciale(s): Verchères
Circonscription(s) électorale(s) fédérale(s): Verchères-Les Patriotes
Prochaines élections: 3e novembre 2013
Martin Lévesque, Maire
Élise Guertin, Directrice générale

Saint-Antonin
CP 340
261, rue Principale
Saint-Antonin, QC G0L 2J0
Tél: 418-862-1056; *Téléc:* 418-862-3268
saintantonin@municipalitedesaintantonin.qc.ca
www.municipalite.saint-antonin.qc.ca
Entité municipal: Parish (Paroisse)
Incorporation: 30 août 1856 *Area:* 182,66 km2
Comté ou district: Rivière-du-Loup; *Population au 2006:* 3,780
Circonscription(s) électorale(s) provinciale(s): Rivière-du-Loup
Circonscription(s) électorale(s) fédérale(s): Montmagny-L'Islet-Kamouraska-Rivière-du-Loup
Prochaines élections: 3e novembre 2013
Réal Thibault, Maire
Louisiane Dubé, Directrice générale

Saint-Apollinaire
11, rue Industrielle
Saint-Apollinaire, QC G0S 2E0
Tél: 418-881-3996; *Téléc:* 418-881-4152
www.st-apollinaire.com
Entité municipal: Municipality
Incorporation: 6 avril 1974 *Area:* 96,63 km2
Comté ou district: Lotbinière; *Population au 2006:* 4,425
Circonscription(s) électorale(s) provinciale(s): Lotbinière
Circonscription(s) électorale(s) fédérale(s):
Lotbinière-Chutes-de-la-Chaudière
Prochaines élections: 3e novembre 2013
Ginette Moreau, Mairesse
Martine Couture, Directrice générale
martine.couture@st-apollinaire.com

Saint-Armand
444, ch Bradley
Saint-Armand, QC J0J 1T0
Tél: 450-248-2344; *Téléc:* 450-248-3820
starmand@bellnet.ca
www.municipalite.saint-armand.qc.ca
Entité municipal: Municipality
Incorporation: 3 février 1999 *Area:* 84,26 km2
Comté ou district: Brome-Missisquoi; *Population au 2006:* 1,166
Circonscription(s) électorale(s) provinciale(s): Brome-Missisquoi
Circonscription(s) électorale(s) fédérale(s): Brome-Missisquoi
Prochaines élections: 3e novembre 2013
Réal Pelletier, Maire
Jacqueline Chisholm, Directrice générale

Saint-Arsène
#101, 49, rue de l'Église
Saint-Arsène, QC G0L 2K0
Tél: 418-867-2205; *Téléc:* 418-867-2025
directiongenerale@saint-arsene.ca
www.municipalite.saint-arsene.qc.ca
Entité municipal: Parish (Paroisse)
Incorporation: 1er juillet 1855 *Area:* 71,01 km2
Comté ou district: Rivière-du-Loup; *Population au 2006:* 1,151
Circonscription(s) électorale(s) provinciale(s): Rivière-du-Loup
Circonscription(s) électorale(s) fédérale(s):
Montmagny-L'Islet-Kamouraska-Rivière-du-Loup
Prochaines élections: 3e novembre 2013
André Roy, Maire
François Michaud, Directeur général

Saint-Athanase
CP 108
6081, ch de l'Église
Saint-Athanase, QC G0L 2L0
Tél: 418-859-2575; *Téléc:* 418-859-3415
info@saint-athanase.com
www.saint-athanase.com
Entité municipal: Municipality
Incorporation: 1er janvier 1955 *Area:* 289,08 km2
Comté ou district: Témiscouata; *Population au 2006:* 321
Circonscription(s) électorale(s) provinciale(s):
Kamouraska-Témiscouata
Circonscription(s) électorale(s) fédérale(s):
Rimouski-Neigette-Témiscouata-Les Basques
Prochaines élections: 3e novembre 2013
Mario Patry, Maire
Francine Morin, Directrice générale

Saint-Aubert
14, rue des Loisirs
Saint-Aubert, QC G0R 2R0
Tél: 418-598-3368; *Téléc:* 418-598-3369
administration@saint-aubert.net
saint-aubert.net
Entité municipal: Municipality
Incorporation: 1er juillet 1857 *Area:* 97,15 km2
Comté ou district: L'Islet; *Population au 2006:* 1,468
Circonscription(s) électorale(s) provinciale(s): Montmagny-L'Islet
Circonscription(s) électorale(s) fédérale(s):
Montmagny-L'Islet-Kamouraska-Rivière-du-Loup
Prochaines élections: 3e novembre 2013
Germain Robichaud, Maire
Serge Roussel, Directeur général

Saint-Augustin
CP 279
Saint-Augustin, QC G0G 2R0
Tél: 418-947-2404; *Téléc:* 418-947-2533
generaldirector.msa@gmail.com
Entité municipal: Municipality
Incorporation: 1er janvier 1993 *Area:* 1435,82 km2
Population au 2006: 599
Circonscription(s) électorale(s) provinciale(s): Duplessis
Circonscription(s) électorale(s) fédérale(s):
Roberval-Lac-St-Jean
Prochaines élections: 3e novembre 2013
Randy Maurice, Maire
Jackie Gallibois, Directrice générale

Saint-Augustin
686, rue Principale
Saint-Augustin, QC G0W 1K0
Tél: 418-374-2147; *Téléc:* 418-374-2984
mun.sta@derytele.com
www.saint-augustin.net
Entité municipal: Parish (Paroisse)
Incorporation: 14 mai 1925 *Area:* 103,96 km2
Comté ou district: Maria-Chapdelaine; *Population au 2006:* 393
Circonscription(s) électorale(s) provinciale(s): Roberval
Circonscription(s) électorale(s) fédérale(s):
Roberval-Lac-St-Jean
Prochaines élections: 3e novembre 2013
Nicole Fortin, Mairesse
Maud Larouche, Directrice générale

Saint-Augustin-de-Woburn
590, rue St-Augustin
Woburn, QC G0Y 1R0
Tél: 819-544-4211; *Téléc:* 819-544-9236
mun.woburn@axion.ca
Entité municipal: Parish (Paroisse)
Incorporation: 13 janvier 1900 *Area:* 280,80 km2
Comté ou district: Le Granit; *Population au 2006:* 701
Circonscription(s) électorale(s) provinciale(s):
Mégantic-Compton
Circonscription(s) électorale(s) fédérale(s): Mégantic-L'Érable
Prochaines élections: 3e novembre 2013
Steve Charrier, Maire
Gaétane Allard, Directrice générale

Saint-Barnabé
CP 250
70, rue Duguay
Saint-Barnabé, QC G0X 2K0
Tél: 819-264-2085; *Téléc:* 819-264-2079
municipalitest-barnabe@telmilot.net
Entité municipal: Parish (Paroisse)
Incorporation: 1er juillet 1855 *Area:* 58,81 km2
Comté ou district: Maskinongé; *Population au 2006:* 1,207
Circonscription(s) électorale(s) provinciale(s): Maskinongé
Circonscription(s) électorale(s) fédérale(s): Berthier-Maskinongé
Prochaines élections: 3e novembre 2013
René Bourassa, Maire
Denis Gélinas, Directeur général

Saint-Barnabé-Sud
251, rang de Michaudville
Saint-Barnabé-Sud, QC J0H 1G0
Tél: 450-792-3030; *Téléc:* 450-792-3759
munstbarnabesud@mrcmaskoutains.qc.ca
Entité municipal: Municipality
Incorporation: 1er juillet 1855 *Area:* 57,08 km2
Comté ou district: Les Maskoutains; *Population au 2006:* 864
Circonscription(s) électorale(s) provinciale(s): St-Hyacinthe
Circonscription(s) électorale(s) fédérale(s): St-Hyacinthe-Bagot
Prochaines élections: 3e novembre 2013
Richard Leblanc, Maire
Nathalie Audette, Directrice générale

Saint-Barthélemy
1980, rue Bonin
Saint-Barthélémy, QC J0K 1X0
Tél: 450-885-3511; *Téléc:* 450-836-5220
municipalite@saint-barthelemy.ca
www.saint-barthelemy.ca
Entité municipal: Parish (Paroisse)
Incorporation: 1er juillet 1855 *Area:* 98,80 km2
Comté ou district: D'Autray; *Population au 2006:* 2,037
Circonscription(s) électorale(s) provinciale(s): Berthier
Circonscription(s) électorale(s) fédérale(s): Berthier-Maskinongé
Prochaines élections: 3e novembre 2013
Pierre Roy, Maire
Francine Rivest, Directrice générale

Saint-Basile
20, rue St-Georges
Saint-Basile, QC G0A 3G0
Tél: 418-329-2204; *Téléc:* 418-329-2788
greffe@saintbasile.qc.ca
www.saintbasile.qc.ca
Entité municipal: Town
Incorporation: 1er mars 2000 *Area:* 97,69 km2
Comté ou district: Portneuf; *Population au 2006:* 2,560
Circonscription(s) électorale(s) provinciale(s): Portneuf
Circonscription(s) électorale(s) fédérale(s):
Portneuf-Jacques-Cartier
Prochaines élections: 3e novembre 2013
Jean Poirier, Maire
Paulin Leclerc, Directeur général

Saint-Benjamin
CP 100
440, av du Collège
Saint-Benjamin, QC G0M 1N0
Tél: 418-594-8156; *Téléc:* 418-594-6068
munstbenjamin@aclcable.ca
www.st-benjamin.qc.ca
Entité municipal: Municipality
Incorporation: 9 janvier 1897 *Area:* 110,53 km2
Comté ou district: Les Etchemins; *Population au 2006:* 865
Circonscription(s) électorale(s) provinciale(s): Beauce-Sud
Circonscription(s) électorale(s) fédérale(s): Beauce
Prochaines élections: 3e novembre 2013
Martine Boulet, Maire
France Veilleux, Directrice générale

Saint-Benoît-du-Lac
1, rue Principale
Saint-Benoît-du-Lac, QC J0B 2M0
Tél: 819-843-4080; *Téléc:* 819-868-1861
muni.sbl@axion.ca
www.st-benoit-du-lac.com
Entité municipal: Municipality
Incorporation: 16 mars 1939 *Area:* 2,27 km2
Comté ou district: Memphrémagog; *Population au 2006:* 48
Circonscription(s) électorale(s) provinciale(s): Brome-Missisquoi
Circonscription(s) électorale(s) fédérale(s): Brome-Missisquoi
Prochaines élections: 3e novembre 2013
Jacques Duguay, Administrateur

Saint-Benoît-Labre
216, rte 271
Saint-Benoît-Labre, QC G0M 1P0
Tél: 418-228-9250; *Téléc:* 418-228-0518
munstben@globetrotter.net
www.saintbenoitlabre.qc.ca
Entité municipal: Municipality
Incorporation: 4 janvier 1894 *Area:* 83,92 km2
Comté ou district: Beauce-Sartigan; *Population au 2006:* 1,613
Circonscription(s) électorale(s) provinciale(s): Beauce-Sud
Circonscription(s) électorale(s) fédérale(s): Beauce
Prochaines élections: 3e novembre 2013
Marco Marois, Maire
Gaétane Vallée, Directrice générale

Saint-Bernard
CP 70
1512, rue St-Georges
Saint-Bernard, QC G0S 2G0
Tél: 418-475-6060; *Téléc:* 418-475-6069
stbernard@globetrotter.net
Entité municipal: Municipality
Incorporation: 9 mai 1987 *Area:* 87,56 km2
Comté ou district: La Nouvelle-Beauce; *Population au 2006:*
1,920
Circonscription(s) électorale(s) provinciale(s): Beauce-Nord
Circonscription(s) électorale(s) fédérale(s): Beauce
Prochaines élections: 3e novembre 2013
Liboire Lefebrve, Maire
Marie-Eve Parent, Directrice générale

Saint-Bernard-de-Lacolle
116, rang St-Claude
Saint-Bernard-de-Lacolle, QC J0J 1V0
Tél: 450-246-3348; *Téléc:* 450-246-4380
mun.st-bernard-de-lacolle@bellnet.ca
Entité municipal: Parish (Paroisse)
Incorporation: 1er juillet 1855 *Area:* 112,63 km2
Comté ou district: Les Jardins-de-Napierville; *Population au 2006:* 1,537
Circonscription(s) électorale(s) provinciale(s): Huntingdon
Circonscription(s) électorale(s) fédérale(s):
Beauharnois-Salaberry
Prochaines élections: 3e novembre 2013
Robert Duteau, Maire
Daniel Striletsky, Directeur général

Saint-Bernard-de-Michaudville
390, rue Principale
Saint-Bernard-de-Michaudville, QC J0H 1C0
Tél: 450-792-3190; *Téléc:* 450-792-3591
munstbernard@mrcmaskoutains.qc.ca
Entité municipal: Municipality
Incorporation: 31 août 1908 *Area:* 64,80 km2
Comté ou district: Les Maskoutains; *Population au 2006:* 486
Circonscription(s) électorale(s) provinciale(s): Richelieu

Circonscription(s) électorale(s) fédérale(s): St-Hyacinthe-Bagot
Prochaines élections: 3e novembre 2013
Francine Morin, Mairesse
Sylvie Chaput, Directrice générale

Saint-Blaise-sur-Richelieu
795, rue des Loisirs
Saint-Blaise-sur-Richelieu, QC J0J 1W0
Tél: 450-291-5944; *Téléc:* 450-291-3832
info@municipalite.saint-blaise-sur-richelieu.qc.ca
Entité municipal: Municipality
Incorporation: 20 juin 1892 *Area:* 68,42 km2
Comté ou district: Le Haut-Richelieu; *Population au 2006:* 2,050
Circonscription(s) électorale(s) provinciale(s): St-Jean
Circonscription(s) électorale(s) fédérale(s): St-Jean
Prochaines élections: 3e novembre 2013
Jacques Desmarais, Mairesse
Francine Milot, Directrice générale

Saint-Bonaventure
720, rue Plante
Saint-Bonaventure, QC J0C 1C0
Tél: 819-396-2335; *Téléc:* 819-396-2335
st-bonaventure@mrcdrummond.qc.ca
Entité municipal: Municipality
Incorporation: 1er janvier 1867 *Area:* 78,83 km2
Comté ou district: Drummond; *Population au 2006:* 983
Circonscription(s) électorale(s) provinciale(s): Nicolet-Yamaska
Circonscription(s) électorale(s) fédérale(s): Drummond
Prochaines élections: 3e novembre 2013
Félicien Cardin, Maire
Claire Côté, Directrice générale

Saint-Boniface
140, rue Guimont
Saint-Boniface, QC G0X 2L0
Tél: 819-535-3811; *Téléc:* 819-535-1242
lgauthier@ville.saint-boniface.ca
Entité municipal: Municipality
Incorporation: 1er janvier 1962 *Area:* 112,12 km2
Comté ou district: Maskinongé; *Population au 2006:* 4,180
Circonscription(s) électorale(s) provinciale(s): St-Maurice
Circonscription(s) électorale(s) fédérale(s): Berthier-Maskinongé
Prochaines élections: 3e novembre 2013
Claude Caron, Maire
Jacques Caron, Directeur général

Saint-Bruno
563, av St-Alphonse
Saint-Bruno, QC G0W 2L0
Tél: 418-343-2303; *Téléc:* 418-343-2662
info@ville.saint-bruno.qc.ca
www.ville.saint-bruno.qc.ca
Entité municipal: Municipality
Incorporation: 12 juillet 1975 *Area:* 77,88 km2
Comté ou district: Lac-St-Jean-Est; *Population au 2006:* 2,353
Circonscription(s) électorale(s) provinciale(s): Lac-St-Jean
Circonscription(s) électorale(s) fédérale(s):
Roberval-Lac-St-Jean
Prochaines élections: 3e novembre 2013
Réjean Bouchard, Maire
Gilles Boudreault, Directeur général

Saint-Bruno-de-Guigues
CP 130
21, rue Principale nord
Saint-Bruno-de-Guigues, QC J0Z 2G0
Tél: 819-728-2186; *Téléc:* 819-728-2404
dg.guigues@mrctemiscamingue.qc.ca
www.temiscamingue.net/guigues
Entité municipal: Municipality
Incorporation: 3 octobre 1912 *Area:* 188,99 km2
Comté ou district: Témiscamingue; *Population au 2006:* 1,076
Circonscription(s) électorale(s) provinciale(s):
Rouyn-Noranda-Témiscamingue
Circonscription(s) électorale(s) fédérale(s):
Abitibi-Témiscamingue
Prochaines élections: 3e novembre 2013
Joanne Larochelle, Maire
Serge Côté, Directeur général

Saint-Bruno-de-Kamouraska
CP 10
4, rue du Couvent
Saint-Bruno-de-Kamouraska, QC G0L 2M0
Tél: 418-492-2612; *Téléc:* 418-492-9076
mun.stbrunokam@globetrotter.net
www.stbrunokam.qc.ca
Entité municipal: Municipality
Incorporation: 1er janvier 1887 *Area:* 186,79 km2
Comté ou district: Kamouraska; *Population au 2006:* 534
Circonscription(s) électorale(s) provinciale(s):
Kamouraska-Témiscouata
Circonscription(s) électorale(s) fédérale(s):
Montmagny-L'Islet-Kamouraska-Rivière-du-Loup
Prochaines élections: 3e novembre 2013
Roger Lavoie, Maire
Constance Gagné, Directrice générale

Saint-Calixte
6230, rue de l'Hôtel-de-Ville
Saint-Calixte, QC J0K 1Z0
Tél: 450-222-2782; *Téléc:* 450-222-2789
lemay@mscalixte.qc.ca
www.municipalite.saint-calixte.qc.ca
Entité municipal: Municipality
Incorporation: 1er juillet 1855 *Area:* 147,68 km2
Comté ou district: Montcalm; *Population au 2006:* 5,687
Circonscription(s) électorale(s) provinciale(s): Rousseau
Circonscription(s) électorale(s) fédérale(s): Montcalm
Prochaines élections: 3e novembre 2013
Louis-Charles Thouin, Maire
Denis Lemay, Directeur général

Saint-Camille
87, rue Desrivières
Saint-Camille, QC J0A 1G0
Tél: 819-828-3222; *Téléc:* 819-828-3723
munstcamille@cgocable.ca
www.saint-camille.ca
Entité municipal: Township
Incorporation: 1er janvier 1860 *Area:* 81,27 km2
Comté ou district: Asbestos; *Population au 2006:* 448
Circonscription(s) électorale(s) provinciale(s): Richmond
Circonscription(s) électorale(s) fédérale(s):
Richmond-Arthabaska
Prochaines élections: 3e novembre 2013
Benoit Bourassa, Maire
Mélisa Camiré, Directrice générale

Saint-Camille-de-Lellis
CP 70
217, rue Principale
Saint-Camille-de-Lellis, QC G0R 2S0
Tél: 418-595-2233; *Téléc:* 418-595-2238
mustcam@sogetel.net
www.saint-camille.net
Entité municipal: Parish (Paroisse)
Incorporation: 11 janvier 1904 *Area:* 252,08 km2
Comté ou district: Les Etchemins; *Population au 2006:* 904
Circonscription(s) électorale(s) provinciale(s): Bellechasse
Circonscription(s) électorale(s) fédérale(s): Lévis-Bellechasse
Prochaines élections: 3e novembre 2013
Adélard Couture, Maire
Nicole Mathieu, Directrice générale

Saint-Casimir
CP 220
220, boul de la Montagne
Saint-Casimir, QC G0A 3L0
Tél: 418-339-2543; *Téléc:* 418-339-3105
st-casimir@infoteck.qc.ca
www.saint-casimir.com
Entité municipal: Municipality
Incorporation: 21 juin 2000 *Area:* 65,93 km2
Comté ou district: Portneuf; *Population au 2006:* 1,528
Circonscription(s) électorale(s) provinciale(s): Portneuf
Circonscription(s) électorale(s) fédérale(s): Portneuf-Jacques Cartier
Prochaines élections: 3e novembre 2013
Dominic Tessier Perry, Maire
René Savard, Directeur général

Saint-Célestin
990, rang du Pays-Brûlé
Saint-Célestin, QC J0C 1G0
Tél: 819-229-3745; *Téléc:* 819-229-1386
info@saint-celestin.net
www.saint-celestin.net
Entité municipal: Municipality
Incorporation: 1er juillet 1864 *Area:* 78,72 km2
Comté ou district: Nicolet-Yamaska; *Population au 2006:* 624
Circonscription(s) électorale(s) provinciale(s): Nicolet-Yamaska
Circonscription(s) électorale(s) fédérale(s):
Bas-Richelieu-Nicolet-Bécancour
Prochaines élections: 3e novembre 2013
Maurice Morin, Maire
Gisèle Plourde, Directrice générale

Saint-Célestin
510, rue Marquis
Saint-Célestin, QC J0C 1G0
Tél: 819-229-3642; *Téléc:* 819-229-1149
info@village-st-celestin.net
www.village-st-celestin.net
Entité municipal: Village
Incorporation: 25 novembre 1896 *Area:* 1,61 km22
Comté ou district: Nicolet-Yamaska; *Population au 2006:* 762
Circonscription(s) électorale(s) provinciale(s): Nicolet-Yamaska
Circonscription(s) électorale(s) fédérale(s):
Bas-Richelieu-Nicolet-Bécancour
Prochaines élections: 3e novembre 2013
Raymond Noël, Maire
Pascale Lamoureux, Directrice générale

Saint-Césaire
1111, av St-Paul
Saint-Césaire, QC J0L 1T0
Tél: 450-469-3108; *Téléc:* 450-469-5275
ville-st-cesaire@bellnet.ca
www.ville.saint-cesaire.qc.ca
Entité municipal: Town
Incorporation: 26 janvier 2000 *Area:* 84,14 km2
Comté ou district: Rouville; *Population au 2006:* 5,151
Circonscription(s) électorale(s) provinciale(s): Iberville
Circonscription(s) électorale(s) fédérale(s): Shefford
Prochaines élections: 3e novembre 2013
Serge Gendron, Maire
Louise Benoît, Greffière

Saint-Charles-Borromée
370, rue de la Visitation
Saint-Charles-Borromée, QC J6E 4P3
Tél: 450-759-4415; *Téléc:* 450-759-3393
info@st-charles-borromee.org
www.st-charles-borromee.org
Entité municipal: Municipality
Incorporation: 1er juillet 1855 *Area:* 18,60 km2
Comté ou district: Joliette; *Population au 2009:* 12,345
Circonscription(s) électorale(s) provinciale(s): Joliette
Circonscription(s) électorale(s) fédérale(s): Joliette
Prochaines élections: 3e novembre 2013
André Hénault, Maire
Denis Girard, Coordonnateur, Génie/Urbanisme
Jacques Fortin, Directeur, Services d'incendie/Protection civile
François Thériault, Directeur général

Saint-Charles-de-Bellechasse
2815, av Royale
Saint-Charles-de-Bellechasse, QC G0R 2T0
Tél: 418-887-6600; *Téléc:* 418-887-6779
munstcha@globetrotter.net
www.saint-charles.ca
Entité municipal: Municipality
Incorporation: 22 décembre 1993 *Area:* 94,73 km2
Comté ou district: Bellechasse; *Population au 2006:* 2,159
Circonscription(s) électorale(s) provinciale(s): Bellechasse
Circonscription(s) électorale(s) fédérale(s): Lévis-Bellechasse
Prochaines élections: 3e novembre 2013
Martin Lapierre, Maire
Denis Labbé, Directeur général

Saint-Charles-de-Bourget
357, 2e rang
Saint-Charles-de-Bourget, QC G0V 1G0
Tél: 418-672-2676; *Téléc:* 418-673-2118
info@stcharlesdebourget.ca
Entité municipal: Municipality
Incorporation: 29 septembre 1885 *Area:* 62,31 km2
Comté ou district: Le Fjord-du-Saguenay; *Population au 2006:* 659
Circonscription(s) électorale(s) provinciale(s): Dubuc
Circonscription(s) électorale(s) fédérale(s): Jonquière-Alma
Prochaines élections: 3e novembre 2013
Michel Ringuette, Maire
Audrey Thibeault, Directrice générale

Saint-Charles-Garnier
CP 39
38, rue Principale
Saint-Charles-Garnier, QC G0K 1K0
Tél: 418-798-4305; *Téléc:* 418-798-4499
stcharles@mitis.qc.ca
www.municipalite.saint-charles-garnier.qc.ca
Entité municipal: Parish (Paroisse)
Incorporation: 1er janvier 1966 *Area:* 83,73 km2
Comté ou district: La Mitis; *Population au 2006:* 298
Circonscription(s) électorale(s) provinciale(s): Matapédia
Circonscription(s) électorale(s) fédérale(s): Haute-Gaspésie-La Mitis-Matane-Matapédia
Prochaines élections: 3e novembre 2013

Jean-Pierre Bélanger, Maire
Josette Bouillon, Directrice générale

Saint-Charles-sur-Richelieu
#101, 405, ch des Patriotes
Saint-Charles-sur-Richelieu, QC J0H 2G0
Tél: 450-584-3484; *Téléc:* 450-584-2965
direction@saint-charles-sur-richelieu.ca
www.saint-charles-sur-richelieu.ca
Entité municipal: Municipality
Incorporation: 22 mars 1995 *Area:* 63,59 km2
Comté ou district: La Vallée-du-Richelieu; *Population au 2006:* 1,742
Circonscription(s) électorale(s) provinciale(s): Verchères
Circonscription(s) électorale(s) fédérale(s): Verchères-Les-Patriotes
Prochaines élections: 3e novembre 2013
Denis Miller, Maire
Nancy Fortier, Directrice générale

Saint-Christophe-d'Arthabaska
418, av Pie-X
Saint-Christophe-d'Arthabaska, QC G6R 0M9
Tél: 819-357-9031; *Téléc:* 819-357-9087
directiongenerale@saint-christophe-darthabaska.ca
www.saint-christophe-darthabaska.ca
Entité municipal: Parish (Paroisse)
Incorporation: 1er juillet 1855 *Area:* 74,87 km2
Comté ou district: Arthabaska; *Population au 2006:* 2,709
Circonscription(s) électorale(s) provinciale(s): Arthabaska
Circonscription(s) électorale(s) fédérale(s): Richmond-Arthabaska
Prochaines élections: 3e novembre 2013
Clémence LeMay Verville, Maire
Francine Moreau, Directrice générale

Saint-Chrysostome
624, rue Notre-Dame, 2e étage
Saint-Chrysostome, QC J0S 1R0
Tél: 450-826-3911; *Téléc:* 450-826-0568
dg@mun-sc.ca
www.mun-sc.ca
Entité municipal: Municipality
Incorporation: 29 septembre 1999 *Area:* 99,54 km2
Comté ou district: Le Haut-St-Laurent; *Population au 2006:* 2,584
Circonscription(s) électorale(s) provinciale(s): Huntingdon
Circonscription(s) électorale(s) fédérale(s): Beauharnois-Salaberry
Prochaines élections: 3e novembre 2013
Jocelyne Lefort, Maire
Céline Ouimet, Directrice générale

Saint-Claude
295, rte de l'Église
Saint-Claude, QC J0B 2N0
Tél: 819-845-7795; *Téléc:* 819-845-2479
directrice@st-claude.ca
www.municipalite.st-claude.ca
Entité municipal: Municipality
Incorporation: 15 novembre 1912 *Area:* 120,38 km2
Comté ou district: Le Val-St-François; *Population au 2006:* 1,104
Circonscription(s) électorale(s) provinciale(s): Richmond
Circonscription(s) électorale(s) fédérale(s): Richmond-Arthabaska
Prochaines élections: 3e novembre 2013
Hervé Provencher, Maire
France Lavertu, Directrice générale

Saint-Clément
CP 40
25A, rue St-Pierre
Saint-Clément, QC G0L 2N0
Tél: 418-963-2258; *Téléc:* 418-963-2619
admin@stclement.qc.ca
www.st-clement.ca
Entité municipal: Parish (Paroisse)
Incorporation: 1er janvier 1885 *Area:* 80,44 km2
Comté ou district: Les Basques; *Population au 2006:* 521
Circonscription(s) électorale(s) provinciale(s): Rivière-du-Loup
Circonscription(s) électorale(s) fédérale(s): Rimouski-Neigette-Témiscouata-Les Basques
Prochaines élections: 3e novembre 2013
Richard April, Maire
Line Caron, Directrice générale

Saint-Cléophas
350, rue Principale
Saint-Cléophas, QC G0J 3N0
Tél: 418-536-3023; *Téléc:* 418-536-1349
stcleophas@mrcmatapedia.qc.ca
Entité municipal: Parish (Paroisse)
Incorporation: 19 mai 1921 *Area:* 97,46 km2
Comté ou district: La Matapédia; *Population au 2006:* 367
Circonscription(s) électorale(s) provinciale(s): Matapédia
Circonscription(s) électorale(s) fédérale(s): Haute-Gaspésie-La Mitis-Matane-Matapédia
Prochaines élections: 3e novembre 2013
Jean-Paul Bélanger, Maire
Katie St-Pierre, Directrice générale

Saint-Cléophas-de-Brandon
750, rue Principale
Saint-Cléophas-de-Brandon, QC J0K 2A0
Tél: 450-889-5683; *Téléc:* 450-835-6076
dg@st-cleophas.qc.ca
www.st-cleophas.qc.ca
Entité municipal: Municipality
Incorporation: 7 octobre 1897 *Area:* 14,76 km2
Comté ou district: D'Autray; *Population au 2006:* 284
Circonscription(s) électorale(s) provinciale(s): Berthier
Circonscription(s) électorale(s) fédérale(s): Berthier-Maskinongé
Prochaines élections: 3e novembre 2013
Denis Gamelin, Maire
Chantal Piette, Directrice générale

Saint-Clet
4, rue du Moulin
Saint-Clet, QC J0P 1S0
Tél: 450-456-3363; *Téléc:* 450-456-3879
st-clet@videotron.ca
www.municipalite-st-clet.qc.ca
Entité municipal: Municipality
Incorporation: 31 août 1974 *Area:* 38,61 km2
Comté ou district: Vaudreuil-Soulanges; *Population au 2006:* 1,725
Circonscription(s) électorale(s) provinciale(s): Soulanges
Circonscription(s) électorale(s) fédérale(s): Vaudreuil-Soulanges
Prochaines élections: 3e novembre 2013
Gilles Farand, Maire
Nathalie Pharand, Directrice générale

Saint-Colomban
330, montée de l'Église
Saint-Colomban, QC J5K 1A1
Tél: 450-436-1453; *Téléc:* 450-436-5955
info@st-colomban.qc.ca
www.st-colomban.qc.ca
Entité municipal: Municipality
Incorporation: 1er juillet 1855 *Area:* 94,24 km2
Comté ou district: La Rivière-du-Nord; *Population au 2006:* 10,973
Circonscription(s) électorale(s) provinciale(s): Argenteuil
Circonscription(s) électorale(s) fédérale(s): Rivière-du-Nord
Prochaines élections: 3e novembre 2013
Jacques Labrosse, Maire
Claude Panneton, Directeur général

Saint-Côme
1673, 55e rue
Saint-Côme, QC J0K 2B0
Tél: 450-883-2726; *Téléc:* 450-883-6431
dg@stcomelanaudiere.ca
www.stcomelanaudiere.ca
Entité municipal: Parish (Paroisse)
Incorporation: 1er janvier 1873 *Area:* 167,26 km2
Comté ou district: Matawinie; *Population au 2006:* 2,161
Circonscription(s) électorale(s) provinciale(s): Berthier
Circonscription(s) électorale(s) fédérale(s): Joliette
Prochaines élections: 3e novembre 2013
Jocelyn Breault, Maire
Alice Riopel, Directrice générale

Saint-Côme-Linière
1375, 18e rue
Saint-Côme-Linière, QC G0M 1J0
Tél: 418-685-3825; *Téléc:* 418-685-2566
st-come@globetrotter.net
www.stcomeliniere.com
Entité municipal: Municipality
Incorporation: 13 avril 1994 *Area:* 151,24 km2
Comté ou district: Beauce-Sartigan; *Population au 2006:* 3,260
Circonscription(s) électorale(s) provinciale(s): Beauce-Sud
Circonscription(s) électorale(s) fédérale(s): Beauce
Prochaines élections: 3e novembre 2013
Gabriel Giguère, Maire
Yvan Bélanger, Directeur général

Saint-Cuthbert
CP 100
1891, rue Principale
Saint-Cuthbert, QC J0K 2C0
Tél: 450-836-4852; *Téléc:* 450-836-4833
mairie@st-cuthbert.qc.ca
www.st-cuthbert.qc.ca
Entité municipal: Municipality
Incorporation: 7 janvier 1998 *Area:* 133,71 km2
Comté ou district: D'Autray; *Population au 2006:* 1,938
Circonscription(s) électorale(s) provinciale(s): Berthier
Circonscription(s) électorale(s) fédérale(s): Berthier-Maskinongé
Prochaines élections: 3e novembre 2013
Bruno Vadnais, Maire
Richard Lauzon, Directeur général

Saint-Cyprien
CP 9
101B, rue Collin
Saint-Cyprien, QC G0L 2P0
Tél: 418-963-2730; *Téléc:* 418-963-3490
www.municipalite.saint-cyprien.qc.ca
Entité municipal: Municipality
Incorporation: 1er janvier 1883 *Area:* 136,14 km2
Comté ou district: Rivière-du-Loup; *Population au 2006:* 1,262
Circonscription(s) électorale(s) provinciale(s): Rivière-du-Loup
Circonscription(s) électorale(s) fédérale(s): Montmagny-L'Islet-Kamouraska-Rivière-du-Loup
Prochaines élections: 3e novembre 2013
Michel Lagacé, Maire
Sanny Beaulieu, Greffière
sanny@saintcyprien.ca

Saint-Cyprien
CP 100
399, rue Principale
Saint-Cyprien-des-Etchemins, QC G0R 1B0
Tél: 418-383-5274; *Téléc:* 418-383-5269
corpmun@sogetel.net
www.st-cyprien.qc.ca
Entité municipal: Parish (Paroisse)
Incorporation: 22 février 1918 *Area:* 92,82 km2
Comté ou district: Les Etchemins; *Population au 2006:* 630
Circonscription(s) électorale(s) provinciale(s): Bellechasse
Circonscription(s) électorale(s) fédérale(s): Lévis-Bellechasse
Prochaines élections: 3e novembre 2013
Poste vacant, Maire
Pauline Fortier, Directrice générale

Saint-Cyprien-de-Napierville
121, rang Cyr
Saint-Cyprien-de-Napierville, QC J0J 1L0
Tél: 450-245-3658; *Téléc:* 450-245-7824
www.st-cypriendenapierville.ca
Entité municipal: Parish (Paroisse)
Incorporation: 1er juillet 1855 *Area:* 97,62 km2
Comté ou district: Les Jardins-de-Napierville; *Population au 2006:* 1,570
Circonscription(s) électorale(s) provinciale(s): Huntingdon
Circonscription(s) électorale(s) fédérale(s): Beauharnois-Salaberry
Prochaines élections: 3e novembre 2013
André Tremblay, Maire
Nancy Trottier, Directrice générale
ntrottier@st-cypriendenapierville.ca

Saint-Cyrille-de-Lessard
282, rue Principale
Saint-Cyrille-de-Lessard, QC G0R 2W0
Tél: 418-247-5186; *Téléc:* 418-247-7086
munstcyrille@globetrotter.net
www.st-cyrille-de-lessard.ca
Entité municipal: Parish (Paroisse)
Incorporation: 1er juillet 1855 *Area:* 228,95 km2
Comté ou district: L'Islet; *Population au 2006:* 778
Circonscription(s) électorale(s) provinciale(s): Montmagny-L'Islet
Circonscription(s) électorale(s) fédérale(s): Montmagny-L'Islet-Kamouraska-Rivière-du-Loup
Prochaines élections: 3e novembre 2013
Luc Caron, Maire
Josée Godbout, Directrice générale

Saint-Cyrille-de-Wendover
4055, rue Principale
Saint-Cyrille-de-Wendover, QC J1Z 1C8
Tél: 819-397-4226; *Téléc:* 819-397-5505
municipalite@stcyrille.qc.ca
www.stcyrille.qc.ca
Entité municipal: Municipality
Incorporation: 6 septembre 1905 *Area:* 112,24 km2
Comté ou district: Drummond; *Population au 2006:* 4,079
Circonscription(s) électorale(s) provinciale(s): Richmond

Circonscription(s) électorale(s) fédérale(s): Drummond
Prochaines élections: 3e novembre 2013
Daniel Lafond, Maire
Mario Picotin, Directeur général

Saint-Damase
115, rue St-Étienne
Saint-Damase, QC J0H 1J0
Tél: 450-797-3341; *Téléc:* 450-797-3543
svfrechette@st-damase.qc.ca
www.st-damase.qc.ca
Entité municipal: Municipality
Incorporation: 5 octobre 2001 *Area:* 79,06 km2
Comté ou district: Les Maskoutains; *Population au 2006:* 2,486
Circonscription(s) électorale(s) provinciale(s): St-Hyacinthe
Circonscription(s) électorale(s) fédérale(s): St-Hyacinthe-Bagot
Prochaines élections: 3e novembre 2013
Note: Effective October 10, 2001, the Village & Parish of St-Damase amalgamated to create the Municipality of St-Damase.
Germain Chabot, Maire
Sylvie V. Fréchette, Directrice générale

Saint-Damase-de-L'Islet
CP 10
26, rue du Village est
Saint-Damase-de-L'Islet, QC G0R 2X0
Tél: 418-598-9370; *Téléc:* 418-598-9396
stdamase3@hotmail.com
Entité municipal: Municipality
Incorporation: 9 novembre 1898 *Area:* 259,72 km2
Comté ou district: L'Islet; *Population au 2006:* 593
Circonscription(s) électorale(s) provinciale(s): Montmagny-L'Islet
Circonscription(s) électorale(s) fédérale(s): Montmagny-L'Islet-Kamouraska-Rivière-du-Loup
Prochaines élections: 3e novembre 2013
Paulette Lord, Maire
Dany Marois, Directrice générale

Saint-Damien
6850, ch Montauban
Saint-Damien, QC J0K 2E0
Tél: 888-835-3419; *Téléc:* 450-835-5538
stdamien@intermonde.net
www.st-damien.com
Entité municipal: Parish (Paroisse)
Incorporation: 6 septembre 1870 *Area:* 260,38 km2
Comté ou district: Matawinie; *Population au 2006:* 2,178
Circonscription(s) électorale(s) provinciale(s): Berthier
Circonscription(s) électorale(s) fédérale(s): Joliette
Prochaines élections: 3e novembre 2013
Yves Giard, Mairesse
Josée Tellier, Directrice générale

Saint-Damien-de-Buckland
75, rte St-Gérard
Saint-Damien-de-Buckland, QC G0R 2Y0
Tél: 418-789-2526; *Téléc:* 418-789-2125
info@saint-damien.com
www.saint-damien.com
Entité municipal: Parish (Paroisse)
Incorporation: 20 décembre 1890 *Area:* 85,17 km2
Comté ou district: Bellechasse; *Population au 2006:* 1,946
Circonscription(s) électorale(s) provinciale(s): Bellechasse
Circonscription(s) électorale(s) fédérale(s): Lévis-Bellechasse
Prochaines élections: 3e novembre 2013
Hervé Blais, Maire
Jacques Thibault, Directeur général

Saint-David
16, rue Saint-Charles
Saint-David, QC J0G 1L0
Tél: 450-789-2288; *Téléc:* 450-789-3023
stdavid@bas-richelieu.net
www.stdavid.qc.ca
Entité municipal: Municipality
Incorporation: 1er juillet 1855 *Area:* 91,08 km2
Comté ou district: Pierre-De Saurel; *Population au 2009:* 812
Circonscription(s) électorale(s) provinciale(s): Nicolet-Yamaska
Circonscription(s) électorale(s) fédérale(s): Bas-Richelieu-Nicolet-Bécancour
Prochaines élections: 3e novembre 2013
Raymond Arel, Maire
Sylvie Letendre, Directrice générale

Saint-David-de-Falardeau
CP 130
140, boul St-David
Saint-David-de-Falardeau, QC G0V 1C0
Tél: 418-673-4647; *Téléc:* 418-673-3266
info@villefalardeau.ca
www.villefalardeau.ca
Entité municipal: Municipality
Incorporation: 1er janvier 1948 *Area:* 379,23 km2
Comté ou district: Le Fjord-du-Saguenay; *Population au 2006:* 2,555
Circonscription(s) électorale(s) provinciale(s): Dubuc
Circonscription(s) électorale(s) fédérale(s): Jonquière-Alma
Prochaines élections: 3e novembre 2013
Jean-Yves Dufour, Maire
Daniel Hudon, Directeur général

Saint-Denis
5, rte 287
Saint-Denis, QC G0L 2R0
Tél: 418-498-2968; *Téléc:* 418-498-2948
www.munstdenis.com
Entité municipal: Parish (Paroisse)
Incorporation: 1er juillet 1855 *Area:* 33,84 km2
Comté ou district: Kamouraska; *Population au 2006:* 523
Circonscription(s) électorale(s) provinciale(s): Kamouraska-Témiscouata
Circonscription(s) électorale(s) fédérale(s): Montmagny-L'Islet-Kamouraska-Rivière-du-Loup
Prochaines élections: 3e novembre 2013
Jean Dallaire, Mairesse
Anne Desjardins, Directrice générale
adesjardins@munstdenis.com

Saint-Denis-de-Brompton
CP 120
2050, rue Ernest-Camiré
Saint-Denis-de-Brompton, QC J0B 2P0
Tél: 819-846-2744; *Téléc:* 819-846-0915
mstdenis@videotron.ca
www.saintdenisdebrompton.com
Entité municipal: Parish (Paroisse)
Incorporation: 6 mars 1935 *Area:* 70,25 km2
Comté ou district: Le Val-St-François; *Population au 2006:* 3,090
Circonscription(s) électorale(s) provinciale(s): Johnson
Circonscription(s) électorale(s) fédérale(s): Brome-Missisquoi; Richmond-Arthabaska
Prochaines élections: 3e novembre 2013
Marc Laflamme, Sec.-Trés.
Mike Doyle, Maire

Saint-Denis-sur-Richelieu
599, ch des Patriotes
Saint-Denis-sur-Richelieu, QC J0H 1K0
Tél: 450-787-2244; *Téléc:* 450-787-2635
municipalitedestdenis@bellnet.ca
www.stdenissurrichelieu.ca
Entité municipal: Municipality
Incorporation: 24 décembre 1997 *Area:* 82,20 km2
Comté ou district: La Vallée-du-Richelieu; *Population au 2006:* 2,243
Circonscription(s) électorale(s) provinciale(s): Verchères
Circonscription(s) électorale(s) fédérale(s): Verchères-Les Patriotes
Prochaines élections: 3e novembre 2013
Jacques Villemaire, Maire
Pierre Pétrin, Directeur général

Saint-Didace
380, rue Principale
Saint-Didace, QC J0K 2G0
Tél: 450-835-4184; *Téléc:* 450-835-0602
info@saint-didace.com
www.saint-didace.com
Entité municipal: Parish (Paroisse)
Incorporation: 27 août 1863 *Area:* 99,66 km2
Comté ou district: D'Autray; *Population au 2006:* 668
Circonscription(s) électorale(s) provinciale(s): Berthier
Circonscription(s) électorale(s) fédérale(s): Berthier-Maskinongé
Prochaines élections: 3e novembre 2013
Guy Desjarlais, Maire
André Allard, Directeur général

Saint-Dominique
467, rue Deslandes
Saint-Dominique, QC J0H 1L0
Tél: 450-774-9939; *Téléc:* 450-774-1595
admin@municipalite.saint-dominique.qc.ca
www.municipalite.saint-dominique.qc.ca
Entité municipal: Municipality
Incorporation: 1er juillet 1855 *Area:* 70,16 km2
Comté ou district: Les Maskoutains; *Population au 2006:* 2,132
Circonscription(s) électorale(s) provinciale(s): St-Hyacinthe
Circonscription(s) électorale(s) fédérale(s): St-Hyacinthe-Bagot
Prochaines élections: 3e novembre 2013
Robert Houle, Maire
Diane G. Bélanger, Directrice générale

Saint-Dominique-du-Rosaire
235, rue Principale
Saint-Dominique-du-Rosaire, QC J0Y 2K0
Tél: 819-727-9544; *Téléc:* 819-727-4344
mun.stdomrosaire@cableamos.com
Entité municipal: Municipality
Incorporation: 1er janvier 1978 *Area:* 512,24 km2
Comté ou district: Abitibi; *Population au 2006:* 447
Circonscription(s) électorale(s) provinciale(s): Abitibi-Ouest
Circonscription(s) électorale(s) fédérale(s): Abitibi-Témiscamingue
Prochaines élections: 3e novembre 2013
Maurice Godbout, Maire
Nathalie Boire, Directrice générale

Saint-Donat
CP 70
194, av du Mont-Comi
Saint-Donat-de-Rimouski, QC G0K 1L0
Tél: 418-739-4634; *Téléc:* 418-739-5003
municipalite@saintdonat.ca
www.saintdonat.ca
Entité municipal: Parish (Paroisse)
Incorporation: 10 mars 1869 *Area:* 93,23 km2
Comté ou district: La Mitis; *Population au 2006:* 892
Circonscription(s) électorale(s) provinciale(s): Matapédia
Circonscription(s) électorale(s) fédérale(s): Haute-Gaspésie-La Mitis-Matane-Matapédia
Prochaines élections: 3e novembre 2013
Michel Côté, Maire
Gil Bérubé, Directeur général

Saint-Donat
490, rue Principale
Saint-Donat, QC J0T 2C0
Tél: 819-424-2383; *Téléc:* 819-424-5020
dg@saint-donat.ca
www.saint-donat.ca
Entité municipal: Municipality
Incorporation: 19 février 1904 *Area:* 361,42 km2
Comté ou district: Matawinie; *Population au 2006:* 4,297
Circonscription(s) électorale(s) provinciale(s): Bertrand
Circonscription(s) électorale(s) fédérale(s): Joliette
Prochaines élections: 3e novembre 2013
Richard Bénard, Maire
Michel Séguin, Directeur général

Saint-Edmond-de-Grantham
1393, rue Notre-Dame-de-Lourdes
Saint-Edmond-de-Grantham, QC J0C 1K0
Tél: 819-395-2562; *Téléc:* 819-395-2666
muned@tellabaie.net
www.st-edmond-de-grantham.qc.ca
Entité municipal: Parish (Paroisse)
Incorporation: 9 février 1918 *Area:* 48,79 km2
Comté ou district: Drummond; *Population au 2006:* 621
Circonscription(s) électorale(s) provinciale(s): Drummond
Circonscription(s) électorale(s) fédérale(s): Drummond
Prochaines élections: 3e novembre 2013
Marie-Andrée Auger, Mairesse
Julie Galarneau, Directrice générale

Saint-Edmond-les-Plaines
561, ch Principale
Saint-Edmond-les-Plaines, QC G0W 2M0
Tél: 418-274-3069; *Téléc:* 418-274-5629
stedmond@destination.ca
www.stedmond.ca
Entité municipal: Municipality
Incorporation: 3 septembre 1938 *Area:* 87,15 km2
Comté ou district: Maria-Chapdelaine; *Population au 2006:* 432
Circonscription(s) électorale(s) provinciale(s): Roberval
Circonscription(s) électorale(s) fédérale(s): Roberval-Lac-St-Jean
Prochaines élections: 3e novembre 2013
Rodrigue Cantin, Maire
Danielle Bernard, Directrice générale

Saint-Édouard
CP 120
405C, montée Lussier
Saint-Édouard, QC J0L 1Y0
Tél: 450-454-6333; *Téléc:* 450-454-4921
lucieriendeau@intermobilex.com
Entité municipal: Parish (Paroisse)
Incorporation: 1er juillet 1855 *Area:* 52,91 km2
Comté ou district: Les Jardins-de-Napierville; *Population au 2006:* 1,212
Circonscription(s) électorale(s) provinciale(s): Huntingdon
Circonscription(s) électorale(s) fédérale(s): Beauharnois-Salaberry
Prochaines élections: 3e novembre 2013

Poste vacant, Maire
Poste vacant, Directeur général

Saint-Édouard-de-Fabre
CP 70
620, rue de l'Église
Saint-Édouard-de-Fabre, QC J0Z 1Z0
Tél: 819-634-4441; *Téléc:* 819-634-2646
municipalitefabre@mrctemiscamingue.qc.ca
Entité municipal: Parish (Paroisse)
Incorporation: 3 octobre 1912 *Area:* 216,18 km2
Comté ou district: Témiscamingue; *Population au 2006:* 701
Circonscription(s) électorale(s) provinciale(s): Rouyn-Noranda-Témiscamingue
Circonscription(s) électorale(s) fédérale(s): Abitibi-Témiscamingue
Prochaines élections: 3e novembre 2013
Réjean Drouin, Maire
Gérard Pétrin, Directeur général

Saint-Édouard-de-Lotbinière
105, rte Soucy
Saint-Edouard-de-Lotbinière, QC G0S 1Y0
Tél: 418-796-2971; *Téléc:* 418-796-2228
st-edouar@municipalite.st-edouard.qc.ca
www.municipalite.st-edouard.qc.ca
Entité municipal: Parish (Paroisse)
Incorporation: 1er décembre 1862 *Area:* 98,57 km2
Comté ou district: Lotbinière; *Population au 2006:* 1,261
Circonscription(s) électorale(s) provinciale(s): Lotbinière
Circonscription(s) électorale(s) fédérale(s): Lotbinière-Chutes-de-la-Chaudière
Prochaines élections: 3e novembre 2013
Alain Soucy, Maire
Anna Blondin, Directrice générale

Saint-Édouard-de-Maskinongé
3851, rue Notre-Dame
Saint-Édouard-de-Maskinongé, QC J0K 2H0
Tél: 819-268-2833; *Téléc:* 819-268-2883
municipalitestedouard@telmilot.net
Entité municipal: Municipality
Incorporation: 1er janvier 1950 *Area:* 55,06 km2
Comté ou district: Maskinongé; *Population au 2006:* 800
Circonscription(s) électorale(s) provinciale(s): Maskinongé
Circonscription(s) électorale(s) fédérale(s): Berthier-Maskinongé
Prochaines élections: 3e novembre 2013
Denis Morin, Maire
Sylvie Vallières, Directrice générale

Saint-Élie-de-Caxton
52, ch des Loisirs
Saint-Élie, QC G0X 2N0
Tél: 819-221-2839; *Téléc:* 819-221-4039
saintelie@sogetel.com
www.saint-elie-de-caxton.com
Entité municipal: Municipality
Incorporation: 12 avril 1865 *Area:* 118,75 km2
Comté ou district: Maskinongé; *Population au 2006:* 1,676
Circonscription(s) électorale(s) provinciale(s): Maskinongé
Circonscription(s) électorale(s) fédérale(s): Berthier-Maskinongé
Prochaines élections: 3e novembre 2013
André Garant, Maire
Micheline Allard, Directrice générale

Saint-Éloi
CP 9
183, rue Principale
Saint-Éloi, QC G0L 2V0
Tél: 418-898-2734; *Téléc:* 418-898-2305
st-eloi@st-eloi.qc.ca
www.st-eloi.qc.ca
Entité municipal: Parish (Paroisse)
Incorporation: 1er juillet 1855 *Area:* 67,69 km2
Comté ou district: Les Basques; *Population au 2006:* 338
Circonscription(s) électorale(s) provinciale(s): Rivière-du-Loup
Circonscription(s) électorale(s) fédérale(s): Rimouski-Neigette-Témiscouata-Les Basques
Prochaines élections: 3e novembre 2013
Mario St-Louis, Maire
Annie Roussel, Directrice générale

Saint-Elphege
245, rang St-Antoine
Saint-Elphege, QC J0G 1J0
Tél: 450-568-0288; *Téléc:* 450-568-0288
mun.stelphege@sogetel.net
Entité municipal: Parish (Paroisse)
Incorporation: 12 mars 1886 *Area:* 40,32 km2
Comté ou district: Nicolet-Yamaska; *Population au 2006:* 271
Circonscription(s) électorale(s) provinciale(s): Nicolet-Yamaska
Circonscription(s) électorale(s) fédérale(s): Bas-Richelieu-Nicolet-Bécancour
Prochaines élections: 3e novembre 2013
France Dionne, Sec.-Trés.
Gérard Côté, Maire

Saint-Elzéar
CP 40
148, ch Principal
Saint-Elzéar-de-Bonaventure, QC G0C 2W0
Tél: 418-534-2611; *Téléc:* 866-499-8558
muni@saint-elzear.net
www.saint-elzear.org
Entité municipal: Municipality
Incorporation: 1er janvier 1965 *Area:* 198,75 km2
Comté ou district: Bonaventure; *Population au 2006:* 508
Circonscription(s) électorale(s) provinciale(s): Bonaventure
Circonscription(s) électorale(s) fédérale(s): Gaspésie—Îles-de-la-Madeleine
Prochaines élections: 3e novembre 2013
Damien Arsenault, Maire
Marjolaine St-Pierre, Directrice générale

Saint-Elzéar
672, av Principale
Saint-Elzéar, QC G0S 2J0
Tél: 418-387-2534; *Téléc:* 418-387-4378
munst-elzear@nouvellebeauce.com
Entité municipal: Municipality
Incorporation: 30 novembre 1994 *Area:* 85,12 km2
Comté ou district: La Nouvelle-Beauce; *Population au 2006:* 1,864
Circonscription(s) électorale(s) provinciale(s): Beauce-Nord
Circonscription(s) électorale(s) fédérale(s): Beauce
Prochaines élections: 3e novembre 2013
Richard Lehoux, Maire
Solange Marcoux, Directrice générale

Saint-Elzér-de-Témiscouata
209, rue de l'Église
Saint-Elzér-de-Témiscouata, QC G0L 2W0
Tél: 418-854-7690; *Téléc:* 418-854-3279
admin@saintelzear.ca
Entité municipal: Municipality
Incorporation: 19 novembre 1938 *Area:* 151,54 km2
Comté ou district: Témiscouata; *Population au 2006:* 334
Circonscription(s) électorale(s) provinciale(s): Kamouraska-Témiscouata
Circonscription(s) électorale(s) fédérale(s): Rimouski-Neigette-Témiscouata-Les Basques
Prochaines élections: 3e novembre 2013
Réjean Deschênes, Maire
Denise Dubé, Directrice générale

Saint-Émile-de-Suffolk
299, rte des Cantons
Saint-Émile-de-Suffolk, QC J0V 1Y0
Tél: 819-426-2987; *Téléc:* 819-426-3447
admstemile@mrcpapineau.com
www.st-emile-de-suffolk.com
Entité municipal: Municipality
Incorporation: 1er janvier 1881 *Area:* 54,07 km2
Comté ou district: Papineau; *Population au 2006:* 537
Circonscription(s) électorale(s) provinciale(s): Papineau
Circonscription(s) électorale(s) fédérale(s): Argenteuil-Papineau-Mirabel
Prochaines élections: 3e novembre 2013
Michel Samson, Maire
Gisèle Éthier, Directrice générale

Saint-Éphrem-de-Beauce
#3, 2, rue de la Clinique
Saint-Éphrem-de-Beauce, QC G0M 1R0
Tél: 418-484-5716; *Téléc:* 418-484-2305
munise@telstep.net
Entité municipal: Municipality
Incorporation: 24 décembre 1997 *Area:* 115,35 km2
Comté ou district: Beauce-Sartigan; *Population au 2006:* 2,627
Circonscription(s) électorale(s) provinciale(s): Beauce-Sud
Circonscription(s) électorale(s) fédérale(s): Beauce
Prochaines élections: 3e novembre 2013
Luc Lemieux, Maire
François Fontaine, Directeur général

Saint-Épiphane
280, rue Bernier
Saint-Épiphane, QC G0L 2X0
Tél: 418-862-0052; *Téléc:* 418-862-7753
direction@saint-epiphane.ca
www.saint-epiphane.ca
Entité municipal: Municipality
Incorporation: 1er juillet 1855 *Area:* 82,36 km2
Comté ou district: Rivière-du-Loup; *Population au 2006:* 874
Circonscription(s) électorale(s) provinciale(s): Rivière-du-Loup
Circonscription(s) électorale(s) fédérale(s): Montmagny-L'Islet-Kamouraska-Rivière-du-Loup
Prochaines élections: 3e novembre 2013
Jean-Pierre Gratton, Maire
Nicolas Dionne, Directrice générale

Saint-Esprit
21, rue Principale
Saint-Esprit, QC J0K 2L0
Tél: 450-831-2114; *Téléc:* 450-839-6070
dg@municipalite-saint-esprit.com
www.municipalite-saint-esprit.com
Entité municipal: Municipality
Incorporation: 1er juillet 1855 *Area:* 54,36 km2
Comté ou district: Montcalm; *Population au 2006:* 1,868
Circonscription(s) électorale(s) provinciale(s): Rousseau
Circonscription(s) électorale(s) fédérale(s): Montcalm
Prochaines élections: 3e novembre 2013
Michel Brisson, Mairesse
Diane Précourt, Directrice générale

Saint-Étienne-de-Beauharnois
489, ch St-Louis
Saint-Étienne-de-Beauharnois, QC J0S 1S0
Tél: 450-225-1000; *Téléc:* 450-225-1011
stetienne@videotron.ca
www.st-etiennedebeauharnois.qc.ca
Entité municipal: Municipality
Incorporation: 1er janvier 1867 *Area:* 41,62 km2
Comté ou district: Beauharnois-Salaberry; *Population au 2006:* 774
Circonscription(s) électorale(s) provinciale(s): Beauharnois
Circonscription(s) électorale(s) fédérale(s): Beauharnois-Salaberry
Prochaines élections: 3e novembre 2013
Louis Pouliot, Maire
Ginette Prud'Homme, Directrice générale

Saint-Étienne-de-Bolton
9, rang de la Montagne
Saint-Étienne-de-Bolton, QC J0E 2E0
Tél: 450-297-3353; *Téléc:* 450-297-0412
stetiennedebolton@axion.ca
www.sedb.qc.ca
Entité municipal: Municipality
Incorporation: 27 mai 1939 *Area:* 47,99 km2
Comté ou district: Memphrémagog; *Population au 2006:* 496
Circonscription(s) électorale(s) provinciale(s): Brome-Missisquoi
Circonscription(s) électorale(s) fédérale(s): Brome-Missisquoi
Prochaines élections: 3e novembre 2013
Pierre Patry, Maire
Pauline Desautels, Directrice générale

Saint-Étienne-des-Grès
1230, rue Principale
Saint-Étienne-des-Grès, QC G0X 2P0
Tél: 819-535-3113; *Téléc:* 819-535-1246
saint-etienne-des-gres@mun-stedg.qc.ca
www.mun-stedg.qc.ca
Entité municipal: Parish (Paroisse)
Incorporation: 14 avril 1859 *Area:* 103,52 km2
Comté ou district: Maskinongé; *Population au 2006:* 3,881
Circonscription(s) électorale(s) provinciale(s): Maskinongé
Circonscription(s) électorale(s) fédérale(s): Berthier-Maskinongé
Prochaines élections: 3e novembre 2013
Robert Landry, Maire
Nathalie Vallée, Directrice générale

Saint-Eugène
CP 120
1065, rang de l'Église
Saint-Eugène, QC J0C 1J0
Tél: 819-396-3000; *Téléc:* 819-396-3576
municipalite.steugene@xittel.ca
Entité municipal: Municipality
Incorporation: 31 octobre 1879 *Area:* 76,37 km2
Comté ou district: Drummond; *Population au 2006:* 1,133
Circonscription(s) électorale(s) provinciale(s): Drummond
Circonscription(s) électorale(s) fédérale(s): Drummond
Prochaines élections: 3e novembre 2013
Gilles Watier, Maire
Maryse Desbiens, Directrice générale

Saint-Eugène-d'Argentenay
CP 70
439, rue Principale
Saint-Eugène-d'Argentenay, QC G0W 1B0
Tél: 418-276-1787; *Téléc:* 418-276-9356
argentenay@derytele.com
Entité municipal: Municipality
Incorporation: 14 novembre 2009 *Area:* 83,37 km2

Comté ou district: Maria-Chapdelaine; *Population au 2006:* 572
Circonscription(s) électorale(s) provinciale(s): Roberval
Circonscription(s) électorale(s) fédérale(s):
Roberval-Lac-St-Jean
Prochaines élections: 1er novembre 2013
Françoise Boudreault, Mairesse
Karine Ouellet, Directrice générale

Saint-Eugène-de-Guigues
CP 1070
4, rue Notre-Dame ouest
Saint-Eugène-de-Guigues, QC J0Z 3L0
Tél: 819-785-2301; *Téléc:* 819-785-2302
munst-eugene@mrctemiscamingue.qc.ca
Entité municipal: Municipality
Incorporation: 20 novembre 1912 *Area:* 113,02 km2
Comté ou district: Témiscamingue; *Population au 2006:* 474
Circonscription(s) électorale(s) provinciale(s):
Rouyn-Noranda-Témiscamingue
Circonscription(s) électorale(s) fédérale(s):
Abitibi-Témiscamingue
Prochaines élections: 3e novembre 2013
Jacinthe Marcoux, Mairesse
Hugo Bellehumeur, Directeur général

Saint-Eugène-de-Ladrière
155, rue Principale
Saint-Eugène-de-Ladrière, QC G0L 1P0
Tél: 418-869-2582; *Téléc:* 418-869-2582
ladriere@globetrotter.net
www.ladriere.qc.ca
Entité municipal: Parish (Paroisse)
Incorporation: 1er janvier 1962 *Area:* 355,09 km2
Comté ou district: Rimouski-Neigette; *Population au 2006:* 441
Circonscription(s) électorale(s) provinciale(s): Rimouski
Circonscription(s) électorale(s) fédérale(s):
Rimouski-Neigette-Témiscouata-Les Basques
Prochaines élections: 3e novembre 2013
Gilbert Pigeon, Maire
Christiane Berger, Directrice générale

Saint-Euphémie-sur-Rivière-du-Sud
220, rue Principal est
Ste-Euphémie-sur-Rivière-du-Su, QC G0R 2Z0
Tél: 418-469-3427; *Téléc:* 418-469-3427
municipalitesteeuphemie@globetrotter.net
Entité municipal: Municipality
Incorporation: 20 juillet 1907 *Area:* 93,21 km2
Comté ou district: Montmagny; *Population au 2006:* 358
Circonscription(s) électorale(s) provinciale(s): Montmagny-L'Islet
Circonscription(s) électorale(s) fédérale(s):
Montmagny-L'Islet-Kamouraska-Rivière-du-Loup
Prochaines élections: 3e novembre 2013
Laurence Hallé, Maire
Chantal Lachance, Directrice générale

Saint-Eusèbe
222, rue Principale
Saint-Eusèbe, QC G0L 2Y0
Tél: 418-899-2762; *Téléc:* 418-899-0194
admin@sainteusebe.ca
sainteusebe.ca
Entité municipal: Parish (Paroisse)
Incorporation: 5 janvier 1911 *Area:* 120,12 km2
Comté ou district: Témiscouata; *Population au 2006:* 620
Circonscription(s) électorale(s) provinciale(s):
Kamouraska-Témiscouata
Circonscription(s) électorale(s) fédérale(s):
Rimouski-Neigette-Témiscouata-Les Basques
Prochaines élections: 3e novembre 2013
Gaston Chouinard, Maire
Chantal Bouchard, Directrice générale

Saint-Évariste-de-Forsyth
495, rue Principale
Saint-Évariste-de-Forsyth, QC G0M 1S0
Tél: 418-459-6488; *Téléc:* 418-459-6268
munstevar@tlb.sympatico.ca
www.st-evariste.qc.ca
Entité municipal: Municipality
Incorporation: 1er mars 1870 *Area:* 111,36 km2
Comté ou district: Beauce-Sartigan; *Population au 2006:* 647
Circonscription(s) électorale(s) provinciale(s): Beauce-Sud
Circonscription(s) électorale(s) fédérale(s): Beauce
Prochaines élections: 3e novembre 2013
Gaétan Bégin, Maire
Nathalie Poulin, Directrice générale

Saint-Fabien
CP 9
10, 7e av
Saint-Fabien, QC G0L 2Z0
Tél: 418-869-2950; *Téléc:* 418-869-3265
informations@saintfabien.net
www.saintfabien.net
Entité municipal: Parish (Paroisse)
Incorporation: 1er juillet 1855 *Area:* 128,07 km2
Comté ou district: Rimouski-Neigette; *Population au 2006:* 1,952
Circonscription(s) électorale(s) provinciale(s): Rimouski
Circonscription(s) électorale(s) fédérale(s):
Rimouski-Neigette-Témiscouata-Les Basques
Prochaines élections: 3e novembre 2013
Marnie Perreault, Mairesse
Yves Galbrand, Directeur général

Saint-Fabien-de-Panet
195, rue Bilodeau
Saint-Fabien-de-Panet, QC G0R 2J0
Tél: 418-249-4471; *Téléc:* 418-249-4470
munpanet@globetrotter.net
www.stfabiendepanet.com
Entité municipal: Parish (Paroisse)
Incorporation: 26 mars 1907 *Area:* 185,31 km2
Comté ou district: Montmagny; *Population au 2006:* 1,057
Circonscription(s) électorale(s) provinciale(s): Montmagny-L'Islet
Circonscription(s) électorale(s) fédérale(s):
Montmagny-L'Islet-Kamouraska-Rivière-du-Loup
Prochaines élections: 3e novembre 2013
Pierre Thibaudeau, Maire
Julie Lapointe, Directrice générale

Saint-Faustin-Lac-Carré
100, Place de la Mairie
Saint-Faustin-Lac-Carré, QC J0T 1J2
Tél: 819-688-2161; *Téléc:* 819-688-6791
dirgen@munipalite.stfaustin.qc.ca
www.municipalite.stfaustin.qc.ca
Entité municipal: Municipality
Incorporation: 3 janvier 1996 *Area:* 119,86 km2
Comté ou district: Les Laurentides; *Population au 2006:* 2,985
Circonscription(s) électorale(s) provinciale(s): Labelle
Circonscription(s) électorale(s) fédérale(s): Laurentides-Labelle
Prochaines élections: 3e novembre 2013
Pierre Poirier, Maire
Jacques Brisebois, Directeur général

Saint-Félix-d'Otis
455, rue Principale
Saint-Félix-d'Otis, QC G0V 1M0
Tél: 418-544-5543; *Téléc:* 418-544-9122
municipalite@st-felix-dotis.qc.ca
www.st-felix-dotis.qc.ca
Entité municipal: Municipality
Incorporation: 3 octobre 1923 *Area:* 235,94 km2
Comté ou district: Le Fjord-du-Saguenay; *Population au 2006:* 1,007
Circonscription(s) électorale(s) provinciale(s): Dubuc
Circonscription(s) électorale(s) fédérale(s): Chicoutimi-Le Fjord
Prochaines élections: 3e novembre 2013
Jean-Marie Claveau, Maire
Hélène Gagnon, Directrice générale

Saint-Félix-de-Dalquier
CP 219
41, rue de L'Aqueduc
Saint-Felix-de-Dalquier, QC J0Y 1G0
Tél: 819-727-1732; *Téléc:* 819-727-9685
mun.stfelixdedalquier@cableamos.com
Entité municipal: Municipality
Incorporation: 29 octobre 1932 *Area:* 112,12 km2
Comté ou district: Abitibi; *Population au 2006:* 936
Circonscription(s) électorale(s) provinciale(s): Abitibi-Ouest
Circonscription(s) électorale(s) fédérale(s):
Abitibi-Témiscamingue
Prochaines élections: 3e novembre 2013
Luc Pomerleau, Maire
Richard Michaud, Directeur général

Saint-Félix-de-Kingsey
CP 30
1205, rue de l'Église
Saint-Félix-de-Kingsey, QC J0B 2T0
Tél: 819-848-2321; *Téléc:* 819-848-2202
direction.generale@saintfelixdekingsey.ca
Entité municipal: Municipality
Incorporation: 1er juillet 1855 *Area:* 125,38
Comté ou district: Drummond; *Population au 2006:* 1,430
Circonscription(s) électorale(s) provinciale(s): Richmond
Circonscription(s) électorale(s) fédérale(s): Drummond
Prochaines élections: 3e novembre 2013
Joëlle Cardonne, Mairesse
Nancy Lussier, Directrice générale

Saint-Félix-de-Valois
600, ch de Joliette
Saint-Félix-de-Valois, QC J0K 2M0
Tél: 450-889-5589; *Téléc:* 450-889-5259
municipalite@st-felix-de-valois.com
www.st-felix-de-valois.com
Entité municipal: Municipality
Incorporation: 24 décembre 1997 *Area:* 85,79 km2
Comté ou district: Matawinie; *Population au 2006:* 5,755
Circonscription(s) électorale(s) provinciale(s): Berthier
Circonscription(s) électorale(s) fédérale(s): Joliette
Prochaines élections: 3e novembre 2013
Gyslain Loyer, Maire
René Charbonneau, Directeur général

Saint-Ferdinand
821, rue Principale
Saint-Ferdinand, QC G0N 1N0
Tél: 418-428-3480; *Téléc:* 418-428-9724
info@municipalite.saint-ferdinand.qc.ca
www.municipalite.saint-ferdinand.qc.ca
Entité municipal: Municipality
Incorporation: 29 novembre 2000 *Area:* 137,07 km2
Comté ou district: L'Érable; *Population au 2006:* 2,195
Circonscription(s) électorale(s) provinciale(s): Lotbinière
Circonscription(s) électorale(s) fédérale(s): Mégantic-L'Érable
Prochaines élections: 3e novembre 2013
Donald Langlois, Maire
Sylvie Tardif, Directrice générale

Saint-Ferréol-les-Neiges
33, rue de l'Église
Saint-Ferréol-les-Neiges, QC G0A 3R0
Tél: 418-826-2253; *Téléc:* 418-826-0489
info@saintferreollesneiges.qc.ca
www.saintferreollesneiges.qc.ca
Entité municipal: Municipality
Incorporation: 1er juillet 1855 *Area:* 82,28 km2
Comté ou district: La Côte-de-Beaupré; *Population au 2006:* 2,546
Circonscription(s) électorale(s) provinciale(s): Charlevoix
Circonscription(s) électorale(s) fédérale(s):
Montmorency-Charlevoix-Haute-Côte-Nord
Prochaines élections: 3e novembre 2013
Germain Tremblay, Maire
François Drouin, Directeur général

Saint-Flavien
177, rue Prinipale
Saint-Flavien, QC G0S 2M0
Tél: 418-728-4190; *Téléc:* 418-728-3775
municipalite@st-flavien.com
www.st-flavien.com
Entité municipal: Municipality
Incorporation: 29 décembre 1999 *Area:* 67,56 km2
Comté ou district: Lotbinière; *Population au 2006:* 1,585
Circonscription(s) électorale(s) provinciale(s): Lotbinière
Circonscription(s) électorale(s) fédérale(s):
Lotbinière-Chutes-de-la-Chaudière
Prochaines élections: 3e novembre 2013
Roland Gagnon, Maire
Mario Roy, Directeur général

Saint-Fortunat
156, rue Principale
Saint-Fortunat, QC G0P 1G0
Tél: 819-344-5399; *Téléc:* 819-344-5399
dg.stfortunat@gmail.com
www.st-fortunat.com
Entité municipal: Municipality
Incorporation: 1er janvier 1873 *Area:* 75,520 km2
Comté ou district: Les Appalaches; *Population au 2009:* 324
Circonscription(s) électorale(s) provinciale(s): Richmond
Circonscription(s) électorale(s) fédérale(s): Mégantic-L'Érable
Prochaines élections: 3e novembre 2013
Denis Fortier, Maire
Lise Henri, Directrice générale

Saint-François-d'Assise
457, ch Central
Saint-François-d'Assise, QC G0J 2N0
Tél: 418-299-2066; *Téléc:* 418-299-3037
munstfrs@globetrotter.net
Entité municipal: Municipality
Incorporation: 3 septembre 1926 *Area:* 171,97 km2
Comté ou district: Avignon; *Population au 2006:* 743
Circonscription(s) électorale(s) provinciale(s): Bonaventure

Circonscription(s) électorale(s) fédérale(s):
Gaspésie—Îles-de-la-Madeleine
Prochaines élections: 1er novembre 2013
Pauline Gallant, Sec.-Trés.
Michaud Ghislain, Maire

Saint-François-de-l'Ile-d'Orléans
337, ch Royal
Saint-François, QC G0A 3S0
Tél: 418-829-3100; *Téléc:* 418-829-1004
info@msfio.ca
www.msfio.ca
Entité municipal: Municipality
Incorporation: 1er juillet 1855 *Area:* 30,76 km2
Comté ou district: L'Ile-d'Orléans; *Population au 2006:* 573
Circonscription(s) électorale(s) provinciale(s): Montmorency
Circonscription(s) électorale(s) fédérale(s):
Montmorency-Charlevoix-Haute-Côte-Nord
Prochaines élections: 3e novembre 2013
Lina Labbé, Maire
Marco Langlois, Directeur général

Saint-François-de-la-Rivière-du-Sud
534, ch St-François ouest
St-François-de-la-Riv.-du-Sud, QC G0R 3A0
Tél: 418-259-7228; *Téléc:* 418-259-2056
munist-frs@globetrotter.net
stfrancoisdelarivieredusud.com
Entité municipal: Municipality
Incorporation: 1er juillet 1855 *Area:* 95,49 km2
Comté ou district: Montmagny; *Population au 2006:* 1,574
Circonscription(s) électorale(s) provinciale(s): Montmagny-L'Islet
Circonscription(s) électorale(s) fédérale(s):
Montmagny-L'Islet-Kamouraska-Rivière-du-Loup
Prochaines élections: 3e novembre 2013
Yves Laflamme, Maire
Yves Laflamme, Directeur général

Saint-François-de-Sales
541, rue Principale
Saint-François-de-Sales, QC G0W 1M0
Tél: 418-348-6736; *Téléc:* 418-348-9439
municipalite@stfrancoisdesales.qc.ca
Entité municipal: Municipality
Incorporation: 14 mai 1888 *Area:* 200,56 km2
Comté ou district: Le Domaine-du-Roy; *Population au 2006:* 731
Circonscription(s) électorale(s) provinciale(s): Roberval
Circonscription(s) électorale(s) fédérale(s):
Roberval-Lac-St-Jean
Prochaines élections: 3e novembre 2013
Louis-Joseph Gagnon, Maire
Renaud Blanchette, Directeur général

Saint-François-du-Lac
CP 60
400, rue Notre-Dame
Saint-François-du-Lac, QC J0G 1M0
Tél: 450-568-2124; *Téléc:* 450-568-7465
municipalite@saint-francois-du-lac.ca
www.saint-francois-du-lac.ca
Entité municipal: Municipality
Incorporation: 31 décembre 1997 *Area:* 63,11 km2
Comté ou district: Nicolet-Yamaska; *Population au 2006:* 2,002
Circonscription(s) électorale(s) provinciale(s): Nicolet-Yamaska
Circonscription(s) électorale(s) fédérale(s):
Bas-Richelieu-Nicolet-Bécancour
Prochaines élections: 3e novembre 2013
Georgette Critchley, Mairesse
Peggy Péloquin, Directrice générale

Saint-François-Xavier-de-Brompton
CP 10
94, rue Principale
St-François-Xavier-de-Brompton, QC J0B 2V0
Tél: 819-845-3954; *Téléc:* 819-845-7711
info@sfxb.qc.ca
www.municipalite.sfxb.qc.ca
Entité municipal: Parish (Paroisse)
Incorporation: 28 décembre 1887 *Area:* 96,11 km2
Comté ou district: Le Val-St-François; *Population au 2006:* 2,018
Circonscription(s) électorale(s) provinciale(s): Johnson
Circonscription(s) électorale(s) fédérale(s):
Richmond-Arthabaska
Prochaines élections: 3e novembre 2013
Claude Sylvian, Maire
Sylvie Champagne, Directrice générale

Saint-François-Xavier-de-Viger
123, rue Principale
Saint-François-Xavier-de-Viger, QC G0L 3C0
Tél: 418-497-2302; *Téléc:* 418-497-2302
munstfrancois@munstfrancoisxv.qc.ca
Entité municipal: Municipality
Incorporation: 1er janvier 1950 *Area:* 110,19 km2
Comté ou district: Rivière-du-Loup; *Population au 2006:* 277
Circonscription(s) électorale(s) provinciale(s): Rivière-du-Loup
Circonscription(s) électorale(s) fédérale(s):
Montmagny-L'Islet-Kamourask-Rivière-du-Loup
Prochaines élections: 3e novembre 2013
Yvon Caron, Maire
Yvette Beaulieu, Directrice générale

Saint-Frédéric
850, rue de l'Hôtel-de-Ville
Saint-Frédéric, QC G0N 1P0
Tél: 418-426-3357; *Téléc:* 418-426-1259
municipal@saint-frederic.com
www.saint-frederic.com
Entité municipal: Parish (Paroisse)
Incorporation: 1er juillet 1855 *Area:* 71,58 km2
Comté ou district: Robert-Cliche; *Population au 2006:* 1,049
Circonscription(s) électorale(s) provinciale(s): Beauce-Nord
Circonscription(s) électorale(s) fédérale(s): Beauce
Prochaines élections: 3e novembre 2013
Henri Gagné, Maire
Cathy Poulin, Directrice générale

Saint-Fulgence
253, rue du Saguenay
Saint-Fulgence, QC G0V 1S0
Tél: 418-674-2588; *Téléc:* 418-673-2116
admin@ville.st-fulgence.qc.ca
www.ville.st-fulgence.qc.ca
Entité municipal: Municipality
Incorporation: 1er mai 1973 *Area:* 354,68 km2
Comté ou district: Le Fjord-du-Saguenay; *Population au 2006:* 2,024
Circonscription(s) électorale(s) provinciale(s): Dubuc
Circonscription(s) électorale(s) fédérale(s): Chicoutimi-Le Fjord
Prochaines élections: 3e novembre 2013
Gilbert Simard, Maire
Daniel Gaudreault, Directeur général

Saint-Gabriel
45, rue Beausoleil
Saint-Gabriel, QC J0K 2N0
Tél: 450-835-2212; *Téléc:* 450-835-9852
mairie@ville.stgabriel.qc.ca
Entité municipal: Town
Incorporation: 17 décembre 1892 *Area:* 2,9 km2
Comté ou district: D'Autray; *Population au 2006:* 2,828
Circonscription(s) électorale(s) provinciale(s): Berthier
Circonscription(s) électorale(s) fédérale(s): Berthier-Maskinongé
Prochaines élections: 3e novembre 2013
Gaétan Gravel, Maire
Michel St-Laurent, Greffier & Directeur général

Saint-Gabriel-de-Brandon
5111, ch du Lac
Saint-Gabriel-de-Brandon, QC J0K 2N0
Tél: 450-835-3494; *Téléc:* 450-835-3495
info@munstgab.com
Entité municipal: Parish (Paroisse)
Incorporation: 30 juin 1864 *Area:* 95,87 km2
Comté ou district: D'Autray; *Population au 2006:* 2,800
Circonscription(s) électorale(s) provinciale(s): Berthier
Circonscription(s) électorale(s) fédérale(s): Berthier-Maskinongé
Prochaines élections: 3e novembre 2013
Roch Desrosiers, Maire
Jeanne Pelland, Directrice générale

Saint-Gabriel-de-Rimouski
248, rue Principale
Saint-Gabriel-de-Rimouski, QC G0K 1M0
Tél: 418-798-4938; *Téléc:* 418-798-4108
stgabriel@mitis.qc.ca
www.municipalite.saint-gabriel-de-rimouski.qc.ca
Entité municipal: Municipality
Incorporation: 7 janvier 1989 *Area:* 132,10 km2
Comté ou district: La Mitis; *Population au 2006:* 1,228
Circonscription(s) électorale(s) provinciale(s): Matapédia
Circonscription(s) électorale(s) fédérale(s): Haute-Gaspésie-La Mitis-Matane-Matapédia
Prochaines élections: 3e novembre 2013
Georges Deschenes, Maire
Martin Norman, Directeur générale

Saint-Gabriel-de-Valcartier
1743, boul Valcartier
Saint-Gabriel-de-Valcartier, QC G0A 4S0
Tél: 418-844-1218; *Téléc:* 418-844-3030
admin@munsgdv.ca
www.saint-gabriel-de-valcartier.ca
Entité municipal: Municipality
Incorporation: 5 octobre 1985 *Area:* 441,17 km2
Comté ou district: La Jacques-Cartier; *Population au 2006:* 2,827
Circonscription(s) électorale(s) provinciale(s): Chauveau
Circonscription(s) électorale(s) fédérale(s):
Portneuf-Jacques-Cartier
Prochaines élections: 3e novembre 2013
Brent Montgomery, Maire
Joan Sheehan, Directrice générale

Saint-Gabriel-Lalemant
12, ave des Érables
Saint-Gabriel-Lalemant, QC G0L 3E0
Tél: 418-852-2801; *Téléc:* 418-852-3390
munstgab@videotron.ca
www.saintgabriellalemant.qc.ca
Entité municipal: Municipality
Incorporation: 27 mai 1939 *Area:* 80,49 km2
Comté ou district: Kamouraska; *Population au 2006:* 788
Circonscription(s) électorale(s) provinciale(s):
Kamouraska-Témiscouata
Circonscription(s) électorale(s) fédérale(s):
Montmagny-L'Islet-Kamouraska-Rivière-du-Loup
Prochaines élections: 3e novembre 2013
Raymond Chouinard, Maire
Kathy Lévesque, Directrice générale

Saint-Gédéon
208, rue De Quen
Saint-Gédéon, QC G0W 2P0
Tél: 418-345-8001; *Téléc:* 418-345-2306
mairie@ville.st-gedeon.qc.ca
www.ville.st-gedeon.qc.ca
Entité municipal: Municipality
Incorporation: 6 décembre 1975 *Area:* 64,17 km2
Comté ou district: Lac-St-Jean-Est; *Population au 2006:* 1,931
Circonscription(s) électorale(s) provinciale(s): Lac-St-Jean
Circonscription(s) électorale(s) fédérale(s):
Roberval-Lac-St-Jean
Prochaines élections: 3e novembre 2013
Jean-Paul Boucher, Maire
Dany Dallaire, Directeur général

Saint-Gédéon-de-Beauce
102 - 1re av sud
Saint-Gédéon-de-Beauce, QC G0M 1T0
Tél: 418-582-3341; *Téléc:* 418-582-6016
stgedeon@globetrotter.net
www.st-gedeon-de-beauce.qc.ca
Entité municipal: Municipality
Incorporation: 12 février 1003 *Area:* 193,45 km2
Comté ou district: Beauce-Sartigan; *Population au 2006:* 2,351
Circonscription(s) électorale(s) provinciale(s): Beauce-Sud
Circonscription(s) électorale(s) fédérale(s): Beauce
Prochaines élections: 3e novembre 2013
Note: Effective October 12, 2003, the Municipality of St-Gédéon-de-Beauce & the Parish of St-Gédéon amalgamated to create the new Municipality of St-Gédéon-de-Beauce.
Eric Lachance, Maire
Pierre-Alain Pelchat, Directeur général

Saint-Georges-de-Clarenceville
1350, ch Middle
Saint-Georges-de-Clarenceville, QC J0J 1B0
Tél: 450-294-2464; *Téléc:* 450-294-2016
st-georges@qc.aira.com
Entité municipal: Municipality
Incorporation: 27 décembre 1989 *Area:* 63,76 km2
Comté ou district: Le Haut-Richelieu; *Population au 2006:* 1,106
Circonscription(s) électorale(s) provinciale(s): Iberville
Circonscription(s) électorale(s) fédérale(s): Brome-Missisquoi
Prochaines élections: 3e novembre 2013
Louis Hak, Maire
Thérèse Lacombe, Directrice générale

Saint-Georges-de-Windsor
485, rue Principale
Saint-Georges-de-Windsor, QC J0A 1J0
Tél: 819-828-2716; *Téléc:* 819-828-0213
mungeorges@cgocable.ca
Entité municipal: Municipality
Incorporation: 30 novembre 2009 *Area:* 126,57 km2
Comté ou district: Les Sources; *Population au 2006:* 911
Circonscription(s) électorale(s) provinciale(s): Richmond
Circonscription(s) électorale(s) fédérale(s):

Richmond-Arthabaska
Prochaines élections: 3e novembre 2013
René Perreault, Maire
Armande Perreault, Directrice générale

Saint-Gérard-Majella

435, rang St-Antoine
Saint-Gérard-Majella, QC J0G 1X0
Tél: 450-789-5777; *Téléc:* 450-789-1188
info@munistgerardmajella.com
Entité municipal: Parish (Paroisse)
Incorporation: 18 février 1907 *Area:* 37,81 km2
Comté ou district: Pierre-De Saurel; *Population au 2009:* 230
Circonscription(s) électorale(s) provinciale(s): Nicolet-Yamaska
Circonscription(s) électorale(s) fédérale(s):
Bas-Richelieu-Nicolet-Bécancour
Prochaines élections: 3e novembre 2013
Charles Lachapelle, Maire
Anny Boisjoli, Directeur général

Saint-Germain

146, rang des Côtes
Saint-Germain, QC G0L 3G0
Tél: 418-492-9771; *Téléc:* 418-492-9772
Entité municipal: Parish (Paroisse)
Incorporation: 29 juin 1893 *Area:* 26,70 km2
Comté ou district: Kamouraska; *Population au 2006:* 301
Circonscription(s) électorale(s) provinciale(s):
Kamouraska-Témiscouata
Circonscription(s) électorale(s) fédérale(s):
Montmagny-L'Islet-Kamouraska-Rivière-du-Loup
Prochaines élections: 3e novembre 2013
Daniel Laplante, Maire
Hélène B.-Bernier, Directrice générale
berubehelene@videotron.ca

Saint-Germain-de-Grantham

233, ch Yamaska
Saint-Germain-de-Grantham, QC J0C 1K0
Tél: 819-395-5496; *Téléc:* 819-395-5200
municipalitestgermain@cgocable.ca
www.st-germain.info
Entité municipal: Municipality
Incorporation: 22 février 1995 *Area:* 86,29 km2
Comté ou district: Drummond; *Population au 2006:* 3,993
Circonscription(s) électorale(s) provinciale(s): Drummond
Circonscription(s) électorale(s) fédérale(s): Drummond
Prochaines élections: 3e novembre 2013
Yvon Nault, Maire
Danielle Smith Gauthier, Directrice générale

Saint-Gervais

CP 9
150, rue Principale
Saint-Gervais, QC G0R 3C0
Tél: 418-887-6116; *Téléc:* 418-887-6312
mungerv@globetrotter.net
www.saint-gervais.ca
Entité municipal: Municipality
Incorporation: 1er juillet 1855 *Area:* 87,23 km2
Comté ou district: Bellechasse; *Population au 2006:* 1,926
Circonscription(s) électorale(s) provinciale(s): Bellechasse
Circonscription(s) électorale(s) fédérale(s): Lévis-Bellechasse
Prochaines élections: 3e novembre 2013
Gilles Nadeau, Maire
Patrick Côté, Directeur général

Saint-Gilbert

110, rue Principale
Saint-Gilbert, QC G0A 3T0
Tél: 418-268-8194; *Téléc:* 418-268-6466
saint-gilbert@globetrotter.net
www.municipalite.saint-gilbert.qc.ca
Entité municipal: Parish (Paroisse)
Incorporation: 27 avril 1893 *Area:* 36,95 km2
Comté ou district: Portneuf; *Population au 2006:* 292
Circonscription(s) électorale(s) provinciale(s): Portneuf
Circonscription(s) électorale(s) fédérale(s):
Portneuf-Jacques-Cartier
Prochaines élections: 3e novembre 2013
Luc Gignac, Maire
Réjeanne Plamondon, Directrice générale

Saint-Gilles

1540, rue Principale
Saint-Gilles, QC G0S 2P0
Tél: 418-888-3198; *Téléc:* 418-888-5145
info@stgilles.net
www.st-gilles.qc.ca
Entité municipal: Parish (Paroisse)
Incorporation: 1er juillet 1855 *Area:* 174,74 km2
Comté ou district: Lotbinière; *Population au 2006:* 1,813
Circonscription(s) électorale(s) provinciale(s): Lotbinière
Circonscription(s) électorale(s) fédérale(s):
Lotbinière-Chutes-de-la-Chaudière
Prochaines élections: 3e novembre 2013
Robert Samson, Maire
Lucie-Marie De Blois, Directrice générale

Saint-Godefroi

CP 157
109C, rte 132
Saint-Godefroi, QC G0C 3C0
Tél: 418-752-6316; *Téléc:* 418-752-6396
stgodefroi@navigue.com
Entité municipal: Township
Incorporation: 16 décembre 1913 *Area:* 60,32 km2
Comté ou district: Bonaventure; *Population au 2006:* 370
Circonscription(s) électorale(s) provinciale(s): Bonaventure
Circonscription(s) électorale(s) fédérale(s):
Gaspésie—Îles-de-la-Madeleine
Prochaines élections: 3e novembre 2013
Gérard-Raymond Blais, Maire
Céline Roussy, Directrice générale

Saint-Guillaume

106, rue St-Jean-Baptiste
Saint-Guillaume, QC J0C 1L0
Tél: 819-396-2403; *Téléc:* 819-396-0184
municipalite.st-guillaume@tellabaie.net
www.municipalite-st-guillaume.qc.ca
Entité municipal: Municipality
Incorporation: 8 novembre 1995 *Area:* 86,83 km2
Comté ou district: Drummond; *Population au 2006:* 1,578
Circonscription(s) électorale(s) provinciale(s): Nicolet-Yamaska
Circonscription(s) électorale(s) fédérale(s): Drummond
Prochaines élections: 3e novembre 2013
Jean-Pierre Vallée, Maire
Gaétan Bellerose, Directeur général

Saint-Guy

52, rue Principal
Saint-Guy, QC G0K 1W0
Tél: 418-963-2601; *Téléc:* 418-963-2601
admin@st-guy.qc.ca
Entité municipal: Municipality
Incorporation: 1er janvier 1958 *Area:* 140,09 km2
Comté ou district: Les Basques; *Population au 2006:* 89
Circonscription(s) électorale(s) provinciale(s): Rivière-du-Loup
Circonscription(s) électorale(s) fédérale(s):
Rimouski-Neigette-Témiscouata-Les Basques
Prochaines élections: 3e novembre 2013
Roger Rioux, Maire
Marie-Eve Chouinard, Directrice générale

Saint-Henri

219, rue Commerciale
Saint-Henri, QC G0R 3E0
Tél: 418-882-2401; *Téléc:* 418-882-0302
munhenri@globetrotter.net
www.municipalite.saint-henri.qc.ca
Entité municipal: Municipality
Incorporation: 9 octobre 1976 *Area:* 121,78 km2
Comté ou district: Bellechasse; *Population au 2006:* 4,094
Circonscription(s) électorale(s) provinciale(s): Bellechasse
Circonscription(s) électorale(s) fédérale(s): Lévis-Bellechasse
Prochaines élections: 3e novembre 2013
Yvon Bruneau, Maire
Jacques Risler, Directeur général

Saint-Henri-de-Taillon

401, rue de l'Hôtel-de-Ville
Saint-Henri-de-Taillon, QC G0W 2X0
Tél: 418-347-3243; *Téléc:* 418-347-1138
municipalite@ville.st-henri-de-taillon.qc.ca
www.ville.st-henri-de-taillon.qc.ca
Entité municipal: Municipality
Incorporation: 12 août 1903 *Area:* 62,95 km2
Comté ou district: Lac-St-Jean-Est; *Population au 2006:* 739
Circonscription(s) électorale(s) provinciale(s): Lac-St-Jean
Circonscription(s) électorale(s) fédérale(s):
Roberval-Lac-St-Jean
Prochaines élections: 3e novembre 2013
André Paradis, Maire
Rachel Bourget, Directrice générale

Saint-Herménégilde

776, rue Principale
Saint-Herménégilde, QC J0B 2W0
Tél: 819-849-4443; *Téléc:* 819-849-6924
municipalite@st-hermenegilde.qc.ca
www.st-hermenegilde.qc.ca
Entité municipal: Municipality
Incorporation: 12 octobre 1985 *Area:* 169,90 km2
Comté ou district: Coaticook; *Population au 2006:* 718
Circonscription(s) électorale(s) provinciale(s):
Mégantic-Compton
Circonscription(s) électorale(s) fédérale(s): Compton-Stanstead
Prochaines élections: 3e novembre 2013
Lucie Tremblay, Mairesse
Nathalie Isabelle, Directrice générale

Saint-Hilaire-de-Dorset

847, rue Principale
Saint-Hilaire-de-Dorset, QC G0M 1G0
Tél: 418-459-6872; *Téléc:* 418-459-6882
munsthilaire@hotmail.com
Entité municipal: Parish (Paroisse)
Incorporation: 12 avril 1916 *Area:* 252,52 km2
Comté ou district: Beauce-Sartigan; *Population au 2006:* 104
Circonscription(s) électorale(s) provinciale(s): Beauce-Sud
Circonscription(s) électorale(s) fédérale(s): Beauce
Prochaines élections: 3e novembre 2013
Jérôme Lacroix, Maire
Johanne Jacques, Directrice générale

Saint-Hilarion

306, ch Cartier Nord
Saint-Hilarion, QC G0A 3V0
Tél: 418-457-3463; *Téléc:* 418-457-3805
municipalite@sainthilarion.ca
Entité municipal: Parish (Paroisse)
Incorporation: 1er juillet 1855 *Area:* 97,77 km2
Comté ou district: Charlevoix; *Population au 2006:* 1,191
Circonscription(s) électorale(s) provinciale(s): Charlevoix
Circonscription(s) électorale(s) fédérale(s):
Montmorency-Charlevoix-Haute-Côte-du-Loup
Prochaines élections: 3e novembre 2013
Rosaire Lavoie, Maire
Madeleine Tremblay, Directrice générale

Saint-Hippolyte

2253, ch des Hauteurs
Saint-Hippolyte, QC J8A 1A1
Tél: 450-563-2505; *Téléc:* 450-563-2362
municipalite@saint-hippolyte.ca
www.saint-hippolyte.ca
Entité municipal: Parish (Paroisse)
Incorporation: 1er juillet 1855 *Area:* 121,19 km2
Comté ou district: La Rivière-du-Nord; *Population au 2006:* 7,219
Circonscription(s) électorale(s) provinciale(s): Bertrand
Circonscription(s) électorale(s) fédérale(s): Rivière-du-Nord
Prochaines élections: 3e novembre 2013
Bruno Laroche, Maire
Christiane Côté, Directrice générale

Saint-Honoré

3611, boul Martel
Saint-Honoré, QC G0V 1L0
Tél: 418-673-3405; *Téléc:* 418-673-3871
admin@ville.sthonore.qc.ca
www.ville.sthonore.qc.ca
Entité municipal: Municipality
Incorporation: 16 décembre 1972 *Area:* 189,82 km2
Comté ou district: Le Fjord-du-Saguenay; *Population au 2006:* 4,727
Circonscription(s) électorale(s) provinciale(s): Dubuc
Circonscription(s) électorale(s) fédérale(s): Chicoutimi-Le Fjord
Prochaines élections: 3e novembre 2013
Marie-Luce Demers-Martin, Mairesse
Stéphane Leclerc, Directeur général

Saint-Honoré-de-Shenley

CP 128
499, rue Principale
Saint-Honoré-de-Shenley, QC G0M 1V0
Tél: 418-485-6738; *Téléc:* 418-485-6171
st.honore@tlb.sympatico.ca
www.sthonoredeshenley.com
Entité municipal: Municipality
Incorporation: 19 avril 2000 *Area:* 136,46 km2
Comté ou district: Beauce-Sartigan; *Population au 2006:* 1,664
Circonscription(s) électorale(s) provinciale(s): Beauce-Sud
Circonscription(s) électorale(s) fédérale(s): Beauce
Prochaines élections: 3e novembre 2013
Herman Bolduc, Maire
Edith Quirion, Directrice générale

Saint-Honoré-de-Témiscouata

99, rue Principale
Saint-Honoré-de-Témiscouata, QC G0L 3K0
Tél: 418-497-2588; *Téléc:* 418-497-1656
admin@sainthonoredetemiscouata.ca
www.sainthonoredetemiscouata.ca

Entité municipal: Municipality
Incorporation: 1er janvier 1881 *Area:* 251,58 km2
Comté ou district: Témiscouata; *Population au 2006:* 807
Circonscription(s) électorale(s) provinciale(s): Kamouraska-Témiscouata
Circonscription(s) électorale(s) fédérale(s): Rimouski-Neigette-Témiscouata-Les Basques
Prochaines élections: 3e novembre 2013
Marin Lebel, Maire
Lucie April, Directrice générale

Saint-Hubert-Rivière-du-Loup
CP 218
10, rue Saint-Rosaire
Saint-Hubert-Rivière-du-Loup, QC G0L 3L0
Tél: 418-497-3394; *Téléc:* 418-497-1187
mun.st-hubert@sthubertrdl.qc.ca
www.municipalite.saint-hubert-de-riviere-du-loup.qc.ca
Entité municipal: Municipality
Incorporation: 4 janvier 1894 *Area:* 183,99 km2
Comté ou district: Rivière-du-Loup; *Population au 2006:* 1,422
Circonscription(s) électorale(s) provinciale(s): Rivière-du-Loup
Circonscription(s) électorale(s) fédérale(s): Montmagney-L'Islet-Kamouraska-Rivière-du-Loup
Prochaines élections: 3e novembre 2013
Napoléon Lévesque, Maire
Sylvie Samson, Directrice générale

Saint-Hugues
508, rue Notre-Dame
Saint-Hugues, QC J0H 1N0
Tél: 450-794-2030; *Téléc:* 450-794-2474
munst-huguesdirection@mrcmaskoutains.qc.ca
www.saint-hugues.com
Entité municipal: Municipality
Incorporation: 6 novembre 1982 *Area:* 89,39 km2
Comté ou district: Les Maskoutains; *Population au 2006:* 1,310
Circonscription(s) électorale(s) provinciale(s): St-Hyacinthe
Circonscription(s) électorale(s) fédérale(s): St-Hyacinthe-Bagot
Prochaines élections: 3e novembre 2013
Serge Picard, Maire
Yolande Simoneau, Directrice générale

Saint-Ignace-de-Loyola
25, rue Laforest
Saint-Ignace-de-Loyola, QC J0K 2P0
Tél: 450-836-3376; *Téléc:* 450-836-1400
st.ignace.loyola@intermonde.net
www.stignacedeloyola.qc.ca
Entité municipal: Parish (Paroisse)
Incorporation: 11 février 1897 *Area:* 30,76 km2
Comté ou district: D'Autray; *Population au 2006:* 1,925
Circonscription(s) électorale(s) provinciale(s): Berthier
Circonscription(s) électorale(s) fédérale(s): Berthier-Maskinongé
Prochaines élections: 3e novembre 2013
Jean-Luc Barthe, Maire
Fabrice St-Martin, Directeur général

Saint-Ignace-de-Stanbridge
678, rang de l'Église nord
Saint-Ignace-de-Stanbridge, QC J0J 1Y0
Tél: 450-296-4467; *Téléc:* 450-296-4461
stignace@citenet.net
www.saint-ignace-de-stanbridge.com
Entité municipal: Parish (Paroisse)
Incorporation: 21 mars 1889 *Area:* 69,33 km2
Comté ou district: Brome-Missisquoi; *Population au 2006:* 631
Circonscription(s) électorale(s) provinciale(s): Brome-Missisquoi
Circonscription(s) électorale(s) fédérale(s): Brome-Missisquoi
Prochaines élections: 3e novembre 2013
Albert Santerre, Maire
Mélanie Thibault, Directrice générale

Saint-Irénée
475, rue Principale
Saint-Irénée, QC G0T 1V0
Tél: 418-620-5015; *Téléc:* 418-620-5017
dg@saintirenee.ca
www.saintirenee.ca
Entité municipal: Parish (Paroisse)
Incorporation: 1er juillet 1855 *Area:* 60,29 km2
Comté ou district: Charlevoix-Est; *Population au 2006:* 727
Circonscription(s) électorale(s) provinciale(s): Charlevoix
Circonscription(s) électorale(s) fédérale(s): Montmorency-Charlevoix-Haute-Côte-Nord
Prochaines élections: 3e novembre 2013
Pierre Boudreault, Maire
Marie-Claude Lavoie, Directrice générale

Saint-Isidore
671, rue St-Régis
Saint-Isidore, QC J0L 2A0
Tél: 450-454-3919; *Téléc:* 450-454-7485
www.municipalite.saint-isidore.qc.ca
Entité municipal: Parish (Paroisse)
Incorporation: 1er juillet 1855 *Area:* 52,00 km2
Comté ou district: Roussillon; *Population au 2006:* 2,489
Circonscription(s) électorale(s) provinciale(s): Châteauguay
Circonscription(s) électorale(s) fédérale(s): Châteauguay-St Constant
Prochaines élections: 3e novembre 2013
Gilles Yelle, Maire
Daniel Vinet, Directeur général
daniel.vinet@municipalite.saint-isidore.qc.ca

Saint-Isidore
128, route Coulombe
Saint-Isidore, QC G0S 2S0
Tél: 418-882-5670; *Téléc:* 418-882-5902
info@saint-isidore.net
www.saint-isidore.net
Entité municipal: Municipality
Incorporation: 22 septembre 1993 *Area:* 101,18 km2
Comté ou district: La Nouvelle-Beauce; *Population au 2006:* 2,503
Circonscription(s) électorale(s) provinciale(s): Beauce-Nord
Circonscription(s) électorale(s) fédérale(s): Beauce
Prochaines élections: 3e novembre 2013
Réal Turgeon, Maire
Louise Trachy, Directrice générale

Saint-Isidore-de-Clifton
66, ch Auckland
Saint-Isidore-de-Clifton, QC J0B 2X0
Tél: 819-658-3637; *Téléc:* 819-658-9070
Bureau.StIsidoredeclifton@hsfqc.ca
www.st-isidore-clifton.qc.ca
Entité municipal: Municipality
Incorporation: 24 décembre 1997 *Area:* 178,43 km2
Comté ou district: Le Haut-St-François; *Population au 2006:* 781
Circonscription(s) électorale(s) provinciale(s): Mégantic-Compton
Circonscription(s) électorale(s) fédérale(s): Compton-Stanstead
Prochaines élections: 3e novembre 2013
André Perron, Maire
Gaétan Perron, Directeur général

Saint-Jacques
16, rue Maréchal
Saint-Jacques, QC J0K 2R0
Tél: 450-839-3671; *Téléc:* 450-839-2387
info@st-jacques.org
www.st-jacques.org
Entité municipal: Municipality
Incorporation: 20 mai 1998 *Area:* 64,69 km2
Comté ou district: Montcalm; *Population au 2006:* 3,706
Circonscription(s) électorale(s) provinciale(s): Joliette
Circonscription(s) électorale(s) fédérale(s): Montcalm
Prochaines élections: 3e novembre 2013
Pierre Beaulieu, Maire
Josée Favreau, Directrice générale

Saint-Jacques-de-Leeds
355, rue Principale
Saint-Jacques-de-Leeds, QC G0N 1J0
Tél: 418-424-3321; *Téléc:* 418-424-0126
mun.leeds@cableeds.com
www.stjacquesdeleeds.com
Entité municipal: Municipality
Incorporation: 23 septembre 1929 *Area:* 81,830 km2
Comté ou district: Les Appalaches; *Population au 2009:* 795
Circonscription(s) électorale(s) provinciale(s): Frontenac
Circonscription(s) électorale(s) fédérale(s): Mégantic-L'Érable
Prochaines élections: 3e novembre 2013
Philippe Chabot, Maire
Nathalie Laflamme, Directrice générale

Saint-Jacques-le-Majeur-de-Wolfstown
877, rte 263
Saint-Jacques-le-Majeur, QC G0N 1E0
Tél: 418-449-1531; *Téléc:* 418-449-1876
stjacqueslemajeur@hotmail.com
Entité municipal: Parish (Paroisse)
Incorporation: 30 septembre 1909 *Area:* 59,330 km2
Comté ou district: Les Appalaches; *Population au 2009:* 182
Circonscription(s) électorale(s) provinciale(s): Frontenac
Circonscription(s) électorale(s) fédérale(s): Mégantic-L'Érable
Prochaines élections: 3e novembre 2013
Steven Laprise, Maire
France Moisan, Directrice générale

Saint-Jacques-le-Mineur
91, rue Principale
Saint-Jacques-le-Mineur, QC J0J 1Z0
Tél: 450-347-5446; *Téléc:* 450-347-5754
info@sjlm.ca
Entité municipal: Parish (Paroisse)
Incorporation: 1er juillet 1855 *Area:* 65,19 km2
Comté ou district: Les Jardins-de-Napierville; *Population au 2006:* 1,628
Circonscription(s) électorale(s) provinciale(s): Huntingdon
Circonscription(s) électorale(s) fédérale(s): Beauharnois-Salaberry
Prochaines élections: 3e novembre 2013
Lise Trotter, Mairesse
Jean-Pierre Cayer, Directeur général

Saint-Janvier-de-Joly
729, rue des Loisirs
Saint-Janvier-de-Joly, QC G0S 1M0
Tél: 418-728-2984; *Téléc:* 418-728-2997
joly33065@globetrotter.net
www.municipalitedejoly.com
Entité municipal: Municipality
Incorporation: 1er janvier 1944 *Area:* 109,86 km2
Comté ou district: Lotbinière; *Population au 2006:* 890
Circonscription(s) électorale(s) provinciale(s): Lotbinière
Circonscription(s) électorale(s) fédérale(s): Lotbinière-Chutes-de-la-Chaudière
Prochaines élections: 3e novembre 2013
Bernard Fortier, Maire
Céline Biron, Directrice générale

Saint-Jean-Baptiste
3041, rue Principale
Saint-Jean-Baptiste, QC J0L 2B0
Tél: 450-467-3456; *Téléc:* 450-467-8813
info@msjb.qc.ca
www.msjb.qc.ca
Entité municipal: Municipality
Incorporation: 1er juillet 1855 *Area:* 75,98 km2
Comté ou district: La Vallée-du-Richelieu; *Population au 2006:* 3,035
Circonscription(s) électorale(s) provinciale(s): 2006uas
Circonscription(s) électorale(s) fédérale(s): Chambly-Borduas
Prochaines élections: 3e novembre 2013
Jacques Durand, Maire
Denis Meunier, Directeur général

Saint-Jean-de-Brébeuf
844, rue de l'Église
Saint-Jean-de-Brébeuf, QC G6G 0A1
Tél: 418-453-7774; *Téléc:* 418-453-2339
stjeandebrebeuf@bellnet.ca
Entité municipal: Municipality
Incorporation: 1er janvier 1946 *Area:* 79,680 km2
Comté ou district: Les Appalaches; *Population au 2009:* 378
Circonscription(s) électorale(s) provinciale(s): Frontenac
Circonscription(s) électorale(s) fédérale(s): Mégantic-L'Érable
Prochaines élections: 3e novembre 2013
Ghyslain Hamel, Maire
Paule Bizier, Directrice générale

Saint-Jean-de-Cherbourg
10, 8e rang
Saint-Jean-de-Cherbourg, QC G0J 2R0
Tél: 418-733-8177; *Téléc:* 418-733-8177
st-jeandecherbourg@mrcdematane.qc.ca
Entité municipal: Parish (Paroisse)
Incorporation: 1er mai 1954 *Area:* 113,23 km2
Comté ou district: Matane; *Population au 2006:* 218
Circonscription(s) électorale(s) provinciale(s): Matane
Circonscription(s) électorale(s) fédérale(s): Haute-Gaspésie-La Mitis-Matane-Matapédia
Prochaines élections: 3e novembre 2013
Jocelyn Bergeron, Maire
Jacinthe Imbeault, Directrice générale

Saint-Jean-de-Dieu
32, rue Principale sud
Saint-Jean-de-Dieu, QC G0L 3M0
Tél: 418-963-3529; *Téléc:* 418-963-2903
stjeandd@intermobilex.com
Entité municipal: Municipality
Incorporation: 1er janvier 1865 *Area:* 151,32 km2
Comté ou district: Les Basques; *Population au 2006:* 1,671
Circonscription(s) électorale(s) provinciale(s): Rivière-du-Loup
Circonscription(s) électorale(s) fédérale(s): Rimouski-Neigette-Témisouata-Les Basques
Prochaines élections: 3e novembre 2013
Jean-Marie Côté, Maire
Normand Morency, Directeur général

Saint-Jean-de-l'Ile-d'Orléans
8, ch des Côtes
Saint-Jean-de-l'Ile-d'Orléans, QC G0A 3W0
Tél: 418-829-2206; *Téléc:* 418-829-0997
stjeanio@bellnet.ca
Entité municipal: Municipality
Incorporation: 1er juillet 1855 *Area:* 43,64 km2
Comté ou district: L'Ile-d'Orléans; *Population au 2006:* 968
Circonscription(s) électorale(s) provinciale(s): Montmorency
Circonscription(s) électorale(s) fédérale(s):
Montmorency-Charlevoix-Haute-Côte-Nord
Prochaines élections: 3e novembre 2013
Jean-Claude Pouliot, Maire
Lucie Lambert, Directrice générale

Saint-Jean-de-la-Lande
810, rue Principale
Saint-Jean-de-la-Lande, QC G0L 3N0
Tél: 418-853-3703; *Téléc:* 418-853-3475
info@saintjeandelalande.ca
Entité municipal: Municipality
Incorporation: 1er janvier 1965 *Area:* 108,80 km2
Comté ou district: Témiscouata; *Population au 2006:* 293
Circonscription(s) électorale(s) provinciale(s):
Kamouraska—Témiscouata
Circonscription(s) électorale(s) fédérale(s):
Rimouski-Neigette-Témiscouata-Les Basques
Prochaines élections: 3e novembre 2013
Serge Boulet, Maire
Danielle Rousseau, Directrice générale

Saint-Jean-de-Matha
170, rue Ste-Louise
Saint-Jean-de-Matha, QC J0K 2S0
Tél: 450-886-3867; *Téléc:* 450-886-3398
matha@qc.aira.com
www.municipalitestjeandematha.com
Entité municipal: Municipality
Incorporation: 1er juillet 1855 *Area:* 117,01 km2
Comté ou district: Matawinie; *Population au 2006:* 4,152
Circonscription(s) électorale(s) provinciale(s): Berthier
Circonscription(s) électorale(s) fédérale(s): Joliette
Prochaines élections: 3e novembre 2013
Normand Champagne, Maire
Nicole D. Archambault, Directrice générale

Saint-Jean-Port-Joli
7, place de l'Église
Saint-Jean-Port-Joli, QC G0R 3G0
Tél: 418-598-3084; *Téléc:* 418-598-3085
munisjpj@globetrotter.net
www.saintjeanportjoli.com
Entité municipal: Municipality
Incorporation: 1er juillet 1855 *Area:* 68,55 km2
Comté ou district: L'Islet; *Population au 2006:* 3,363
Circonscription(s) électorale(s) provinciale(s): Montmagny-L'Islet
Circonscription(s) électorale(s) fédérale(s):
Montmagny-L'Islet-Kamouraska-Rivière-du-Loup
Prochaines élections: 3e novembre 2013
Jean-Pierre Dubé, Maire
Stéphen Lord, Directeur général

Saint-Joachim
172, rue de l'Église
Saint-Joachim, QC G0A 3X0
Tél: 418-827-3755; *Téléc:* 418-827-8574
dg@saintjoachim.qc.ca
www.saintjoachim.qc.ca
Entité municipal: Parish (Paroisse)
Incorporation: 1er juillet 1855 *Area:* 40,68 km2
Comté ou district: La Côte-de-Beaupré; *Population au 2006:* 1,362
Circonscription(s) électorale(s) provinciale(s): Charlevoix
Circonscription(s) électorale(s) fédérale(s):
Montmorency-Charlevoix-Haute-Côte-Nord
Prochaines élections: 3e novembre 2013
Marc Dubeau, Maire
Roger Carrier, Directeur général

Saint-Joachim-de-Shefford
567, 1er rang ouest
Saint-Joachim-de-Shefford, QC J0E 2G0
Tél: 450-539-3201; *Téléc:* 450-539-3145
mairie@st-joachim.ca
www.st-joachim.ca
Entité municipal: Parish (Paroisse)
Incorporation: 10 juin 1884 *Area:* 126,98 km2
Comté ou district: La Haute-Yamaska; *Population au 2006:* 1,089
Circonscription(s) électorale(s) provinciale(s): Johnson
Circonscription(s) électorale(s) fédérale(s): Shefford
Prochaines élections: 3e novembre 2013
René Beauregard, Maire
France Lagrandneur, Directrice générale

Saint-Joseph-de-Beauce
843, av du Palais
Saint-Joseph-de-Beauce, QC G0S 2V0
Tél: 418-397-4358; *Téléc:* 418-397-5715
info@vsjb.ca
www.ville.stjosephdebeauce.qc.ca
Entité municipal: Town
Incorporation: 27 janvier 1999 *Area:* 108,54 km2
Comté ou district: Robert-Cliche; *Population au 2006:* 4,454
Circonscription(s) électorale(s) provinciale(s): Beauce-Nord
Circonscription(s) électorale(s) fédérale(s): Beauce
Prochaines élections: 3e novembre 2013
Michel Cliche, Maire
Danielle Maheu, Greffière

Saint-Joseph-de-Coleraine
88, av St-Patrick
Saint-Joseph-de-Coleraine, QC G0N 1B0
Tél: 418-423-4000; *Téléc:* 418-423-4150
coleraine@bellnet.ca
www.coleraine.qc.ca
Entité municipal: Municipality
Incorporation: 11 novembre 1891 *Area:* 125,11 km2
Comté ou district: Les Appalaches; *Population au 2009:* 2,030
Circonscription(s) électorale(s) provinciale(s): Frontenac
Circonscription(s) électorale(s) fédérale(s): Mégantic-L'Érable
Prochaines élections: 3e novembre 2013
Gilles Gosselin, Maire
Martin Cadorette, Directeur général

Saint-Joseph-de-Ham-Sud
9, ch Gosford sud
Saint-Joseph-de-Ham-Sud, QC J0B 3J0
Tél: 819-877-3258; *Téléc:* 819-877-5121
hamsud@cgocable.ca
www.saint-joseph-de-ham-sud.ca
Entité municipal: Parish (Paroisse)
Incorporation: 1er janvier 1879 *Area:* 150,45 km2
Comté ou district: Les Sources; *Population au 2006:* 219
Circonscription(s) électorale(s) provinciale(s): Richmond
Circonscription(s) électorale(s) fédérale(s):
Richmond-Arthabaska
Prochaines élections: 3e novembre 2013
Langevin Gagnon, Maire
Caroline Poirier, Directrice générale

Saint-Joseph-de-Kamouraska
300, rue Principale ouest
Saint-Joseph-de-Kamouraska, QC G0L 3P0
Tél: 418-493-2214; *Téléc:* 418-493-1126
stjosephkam@bellnet.ca
www.stjosephkam.ca
Entité municipal: Parish (Paroisse)
Incorporation: 14 janvier 1924 *Area:* 84,61 km2
Comté ou district: Kamouraska; *Population au 2006:* 402
Circonscription(s) électorale(s) provinciale(s):
Kamouraska-Témiscouata
Circonscription(s) électorale(s) fédérale(s):
Montmagny-L'Islet-Kamouraska-Rivière-du-Loup
Prochaines élections: 3e novembre 2013
Sylvain Roy, Maire
Charles Montamat, Directeur général

Saint-Joseph-de-Lepage
70, rue de la Rivière
Saint-Joseph-de-Lepage, QC G5H 3N8
Tél: 418-775-4171; *Téléc:* 418-775-3004
stjoseph@mitis.qc.ca
www.municipalite.saint-joseph-de-lepage.qc.ca
Entité municipal: Parish (Paroisse)
Incorporation: 29 septembre 1873 *Area:* 30,27 km2
Comté ou district: La Mitis; *Population au 2006:* 545
Circonscription(s) électorale(s) provinciale(s): Matapédia
Circonscription(s) électorale(s) fédérale(s): Haute-Gaspésie-La Mitis-Matane-Matapédia
Prochaines élections: 3e novembre 2013
Réginald Morissette, Maire
Renée Roy, Directrice générale

Saint-Joseph-de-Sorel
700, rue Montcalm
Saint-Joseph-de-Sorel, QC J3R 1C9
Tél: 450-742-3744; *Téléc:* 450-742-1315
ville@vsjs.ca
www.vsjs.ca
Entité municipal: Village
Incorporation: 1er mai 1907 *Area:* 1,4 km2
Comté ou district: Pierre-De Saurel; *Population au 2009:* 1,669
Circonscription(s) électorale(s) provinciale(s): Richelieu
Circonscription(s) électorale(s) fédérale(s):
Bas-Richelieu-Nicolet-Bécancour
Prochaines élections: 3e novembre 2013
Olivar Gravel, Maire
Martin Valois, Directeur général

Saint-Joseph-des-Érables
370A, rang des Érables
Saint-Joseph-des-Érables, QC G0S 2V0
Tél: 418-397-4772; *Téléc:* 418-397-1555
municipalite@stjosephdeserables.com
www.stjosephdeserables.com
Entité municipal: Municipality
Incorporation: 26 novembre 2009 *Area:* 50,01 km2
Comté ou district: Robert-Cliche; *Population au 2006:* 417
Circonscription(s) électorale(s) provinciale(s): Beauce-Nord
Circonscription(s) électorale(s) fédérale(s): Beauce
Prochaines élections: 1er novembre 2013
Louis Jacques, Maire
Mélanie Jacques, Directrice générale

Saint-Joseph-du-Lac
1110, ch Principal
Saint-Joseph-du-Lac, QC J0N 1M0
Tél: 450-623-1072; *Téléc:* 450-623-2889
info@sjdl.qc.ca
www.sjdl.qc.ca
Entité municipal: Municipality
Incorporation: 1er juillet 1855 *Area:* 40,81 km2
Comté ou district: Deux-Montagne; *Population au 2006:* 4,958
Circonscription(s) électorale(s) provinciale(s): Mirabel
Circonscription(s) électorale(s) fédérale(s):
Argenteuil-Papineau-Mirabel
Prochaines élections: 3e novembre 2013
Alain Guindon, Maire
Guylaine Comtois, Directrice générale

Saint-Jude
940, rue du Centre
Saint-Jude, QC J0H 1P0
Tél: 450-792-3855; *Téléc:* 450-792-3828
munstjude@mrcmaskoutains.qc.ca
www.saint-jude.ca
Entité municipal: Municipality
Incorporation: 1er juillet 1855 *Area:* 77,36 km2
Comté ou district: Les Maskoutains; *Population au 2006:* 1,130
Circonscription(s) électorale(s) provinciale(s): Richelieu
Circonscription(s) électorale(s) fédérale(s): St-Hyacinthe-Bagot
Prochaines élections: 3e novembre 2013
Yves de Bellefeuille, Maire
Sylvie Beauregard, Directrice générale

Saint-Jules
390, rte Principale
Saint-Jules, QC G0N 1R0
Tél: 418-397-5444; *Téléc:* 418-397-5007
mun.st-jules@axion.ca
www.st-jules.qc.ca
Entité municipal: Parish (Paroisse)
Incorporation: 28 mai 1919 *Area:* 57,08 km2
Comté ou district: Robert-Cliche; *Population au 2006:* 534
Circonscription(s) électorale(s) provinciale(s): Beauce-Nord
Circonscription(s) électorale(s) fédérale(s): Beauce
Prochaines élections: 3e novembre 2013
Ghislaine Doyon, Mairesse
Claire Roy, Directrice générale

Saint-Julien
787, ch St-Julien
Saint-Julien, QC G0N 1B0
Tél: 418-423-4295; *Téléc:* 418-423-2384
municipalite@st-julien.ca
www.st-julien.ca
Entité municipal: Municipality
Incorporation: 1er juillet 1855 *Area:* 82,300 km2
Comté ou district: Les Appalaches; *Population au 2009:* 409
Circonscription(s) électorale(s) provinciale(s): Frontenac
Circonscription(s) électorale(s) fédérale(s): Mégantic-L'Érable
Prochaines élections: 3e novembre 2013
Jacques Laprise, Maire
Réjean Gouin, Directeur général

Saint-Juste-du-Lac
CP 38
28, ch Principal
Saint-Juste-du-Lac, QC G0L 3R0
Tél: 418-899-2855; *Téléc:* 418-899-2938
info@saintjustedulac.com
www.saintjustedulac.com
Entité municipal: Municipality
Incorporation: 23 mai 1923 *Area:* 170,11 km2
Comté ou district: Témiscouata; *Population au 2006:* 653

Circonscription(s) électorale(s) provinciale(s): Kamouraska-Témiscouata
Circonscription(s) électorale(s) fédérale(s): Montmagny-L'Islet-Kamouraska-Rivière-du-Loup
Prochaines élections: 3e novembre 2013
Jean-Jacques Bonenfant, Maire
Nicole Dubé-Chouinard, Directrice générale

Saint-Just-de-Bretenières
CP 668
250, rue Principale
Saint-Just-de-Bretenières, QC G0R 3H0
Tél: 418-244-3637; *Téléc:* 418-244-3637
st-just-de-bretenieres@globetrotter.net
www.saintjustdebretenieres.com
Entité municipal: Municipality
Incorporation: 27 mai 1918 *Area:* 132,35 km2
Comté ou district: Montmagny; *Population au 2006:* 794
Circonscription(s) électorale(s) provinciale(s): Montmagny-L'Islet
Circonscription(s) électorale(s) fédérale(s): Lévis-Bellechasse
Prochaines élections: 3e novembre 2013
Réal Bolduc, Maire
Isabelle Simard, Directrice générale

Saint-Justin
1281, rue Gérin
Saint-Justin, QC J0K 2V0
Tél: 819-227-2838; *Téléc:* 819-227-4876
dg@saint-justin.ca
www.saint-justin.ca
Entité municipal: Parish (Paroisse)
Incorporation: 1er juillet 1855 *Area:* 82,46 km2
Comté ou district: Maskinongé; *Population au 2006:* 1,051
Circonscription(s) électorale(s) provinciale(s): Maskinongé
Circonscription(s) électorale(s) fédérale(s): Berthier-Maskinongé
Prochaines élections: 3e novembre 2013
Denis McKinnon, Mairesse
Michel C. Cousineau, Directeur général

Saint-Lambert
CP 86
509, rte 5e-au-8e Rang
Des Méloizes, QC J0Z 1V0
Tél: 819-788-2491; *Téléc:* 819-788-2491
st-lambert@mrcao.qc.ca
www.st-lambert.ao.ca
Entité municipal: Parish (Paroisse)
Incorporation: 14 mai 1938 *Area:* 101,76 km2
Comté ou district: Abitibi-Ouest; *Population au 2006:* 222
Circonscription(s) électorale(s) provinciale(s): Abitibi-Ouest
Circonscription(s) électorale(s) fédérale(s): Abitibi-Témiscamingue
Prochaines élections: 3e novembre 2013
Emilien Rivard, Maire
Nataly Morin, Directrice générale

Saint-Lambert-de-Lauzon
1200, rue du Pont
Saint-Lambert-de-Lauzon, QC G0S 2W0
Tél: 418-889-9715; *Téléc:* 418-889-0660
info@municipalite.saint-lambert-de-lauzon.qc.ca
www.municipalite.saint-lambert-de-lauzon.qc.ca
Entité municipal: Parish (Paroisse)
Incorporation: 1er juillet 1855 *Area:* 107,32 km2
Comté ou district: La Nouvelle-Beauce; *Population au 2006:* 5,401
Circonscription(s) électorale(s) provinciale(s): Beauce-Nord
Circonscription(s) électorale(s) fédérale(s): Lotbinière-Chutes-de-la-Chaudière
Prochaines élections: 3e novembre 2013
François Barret, Maire
Magdalen Blanchet, Directrice générale

Saint-Laurent-de-l'Ile-d'Orléans
1430, ch Royal
St-Laurent-de-l'Ile-d'Orléans, QC G0A 3Z0
Tél: 418-828-2322; *Téléc:* 418-828-2170
stlaurentorleans@videotron.ca
st-laurent.iledorleans.com
Entité municipal: Municipality
Incorporation: 1er juillet 1855 *Area:* 35,32 km2
Comté ou district: L'Ile-d'Orléans; *Population au 2006:* 1,601
Circonscription(s) électorale(s) provinciale(s): Montmorency
Circonscription(s) électorale(s) fédérale(s): Montmorency-Charlevoix-Haute-Côte-Nord
Prochaines élections: 3e novembre 2013
Yves Coulombe, Maire
Claudette Pouliot, Directrice générale

Saint-Lazare-de-Bellechasse
116, rue de la Fabrique
Saint-Lazare-de-Bellechasse, QC G0R 3J0
Tél: 418-883-3841; *Téléc:* 418-883-2551
munstlaz@globetrotter.net
Entité municipal: Municipality
Incorporation: 1er juillet 1855 *Area:* 85,53 km2
Comté ou district: Bellechasse; *Population au 2006:* 1,155
Circonscription(s) électorale(s) provinciale(s): Bellechasse
Circonscription(s) électorale(s) fédérale(s): Lévis-Bellechasse
Prochaines élections: 3e novembre 2013
Martin J. Côté, Maire
Richard Côté, Directeur général

Saint-Léandre
2005, rue de l'Église
Saint-Léandre, QC G0J 2V0
Tél: 418-737-4973; *Téléc:* 418-737-4972
st-leandre@mrcdematane.qc.ca
Entité municipal: Parish (Paroisse)
Incorporation: 20 mars 1912 *Area:* 102,62 km2
Comté ou district: Matane; *Population au 2006:* 401
Circonscription(s) électorale(s) provinciale(s): Matane
Circonscription(s) électorale(s) fédérale(s): Haute-Gaspésie-La Mitis-Matane-Matapédia
Prochaines élections: 3e novembre 2013
Yvon Tremblay, Maire
Guylaine Ouellet, Directrice générale

Saint-Léon-de-Standon
CP 130
100A, rue St-Pierre
Saint-Léon-de-Standon, QC G0R 4L0
Tél: 418-642-5034; *Téléc:* 418-642-2570
mun.st-leon@globetrotter.net
www.stleondestandon.qc.ca
Entité municipal: Parish (Paroisse)
Incorporation: 1er janvier 1874 *Area:* 136,90 km2
Comté ou district: Bellechasse; *Population au 2006:* 1,237
Circonscription(s) électorale(s) provinciale(s): Bellechasse
Circonscription(s) électorale(s) fédérale(s): Lévis-Bellechasse
Prochaines élections: 3e novembre 2013
Bernard Morin, Maire
Michel Lacasse, Directeur général

Saint-Léon-le-Grand
CP 188
277, rue Plourde
Saint-Léon-le-Grand, QC G0J 2W0
Tél: 418-743-2914; *Téléc:* 418-743-2914
stleonlegrand@mrcmatapedia.qc.ca
www.saintleonlegrand.com
Entité municipal: Parish (Paroisse)
Incorporation: 12 août 1903 *Area:* 127,73 km2
Comté ou district: La Matapédia; *Population au 2006:* 1,073
Circonscription(s) électorale(s) provinciale(s): Matapédia
Circonscription(s) électorale(s) fédérale(s): Haute-Gaspésie-La Mitis-Matane-Matapédia
Prochaines élections: 3e novembre 2013
Steve Lamontagne, Maire
Suzanne Poirier, Directrice générale

Saint-Léon-le-Grand
49, rue de la Fabrique
Saint-Léon-le-Grand, QC J0K 2W0
Tél: 819-228-3236; *Téléc:* 819-228-8088
glessard@st-leon.com
Entité municipal: Parish (Paroisse)
Incorporation: 1er juillet 1855 *Area:* 72,57 km2
Comté ou district: Maskinongé; *Population au 2006:* 965
Circonscription(s) électorale(s) provinciale(s): Maskinongé
Circonscription(s) électorale(s) fédérale(s): Berthier-Maskinongé
Prochaines élections: 3e novembre 2013
Robert Lalonde, Maire
Gabrielle Lessard, Directrice générale

Saint-Léonard-d'Aston
370, rue Principale
Saint-Léonard-d'Aston, QC J0C 1M0
Tél: 819-399-2596; *Téléc:* 819-399-2333
municipalite@saint-leonard-daston.net
www.saint-leonard-daston.net
Entité municipal: Municipality
Incorporation: 13 avril 1994 *Area:* 81,83 km2
Comté ou district: Nicolet-Yamaska; *Population au 2006:* 2,146
Circonscription(s) électorale(s) provinciale(s): Nicolet-Yamaska
Circonscription(s) électorale(s) fédérale(s): Bas-Richelieu-Nicolet-Bécancour
Prochaines élections: 3e novembre 2013
Luc P. Balleux, Maire
Carmelle L. Dupuis, Directrice générale

Saint-Léonard-de-Portneuf
260, rue Pettigrew
Saint-Léonard-de-Portneuf, QC G0A 4A0
Tél: 418-337-6741; *Téléc:* 418-337-6742
saintleonard@derytele.com
www.municipalite.st-leonard.qc.ca
Entité municipal: Municipality
Incorporation: 22 juillet 1899 *Area:* 138,71 km2
Comté ou district: Portneuf; *Population au 2006:* 1,046
Circonscription(s) électorale(s) provinciale(s): Portneuf
Circonscription(s) électorale(s) fédérale(s): Portneuf-Jacques-Cartier
Prochaines élections: 3e novembre 2013
Denis Langlois, Maire
Eddy Alain, Directeur-général

Saint-Liboire
CP 120
21, place Mauriac
Saint-Liboire, QC J0H 1R0
Tél: 450-793-2811; *Téléc:* 450-793-4428
admin@municipalite.st-liboire.qc.ca
www.municipalite.st-liboire.qc.ca
Entité municipal: Municipality
Incorporation: 17 août 1994 *Area:* 72,90 km2
Comté ou district: Les Maskoutains; *Population au 2006:* 2,895
Circonscription(s) électorale(s) provinciale(s): St-Hyacinthe
Circonscription(s) électorale(s) fédérale(s): St-Hyacinthe-Bagot
Prochaines élections: 3e novembre 2013
Denis Chabot, Maire
Lucie Chevrier, Directrice générale

Saint-Liguori
750, rue Principale
Saint-Liguori, QC J0K 2X0
Tél: 450-753-3570; *Téléc:* 450-753-4638
info@saint-liguori.com
Entité municipal: Parish (Paroisse)
Incorporation: 1er juillet 1855 *Area:* 50,91 km2
Comté ou district: Montcalm; *Population au 2006:* 1,887
Circonscription(s) électorale(s) provinciale(s): Joliette
Circonscription(s) électorale(s) fédérale(s): Montcalm
Prochaines élections: 3e novembre 2013
Serge Rivest, Maire
Edith Gagné, Directrice générale

Saint-Louis
765B, rue St-Joseph
Saint-Louis, QC J0G 1K0
Tél: 450-788-2631; *Téléc:* 450-788-2231
mstlouis@mrcmaskoutains.qc.ca
mun-st-louis.qc.ca
Entité municipal: Parish (Paroisse)
Incorporation: 29 août 1881 *Area:* 45,92 km2
Comté ou district: Les Maskoutains; *Population au 2006:* 726
Circonscription(s) électorale(s) provinciale(s): Richelieu
Circonscription(s) électorale(s) fédérale(s): St-Hyacinthe-Bagot
Prochaines élections: 3e novembre 2013
Doris Gosselin, Mairesse
Pascale Dalcourt, Directrice générale

Saint-Louis-de-Blandford
CP 140
80-1, rue Principale
Saint-Louis-de-Blandford, QC G0Z 1B0
Tél: 819-364-7007; *Téléc:* 819-364-2781
info@saint-louis-de-blandford.ca
www.saint-louis-de-blandford.ca
Entité municipal: Parish (Paroisse)
Incorporation: 1er juillet 1855 *Area:* 106,70 km2
Comté ou district: Arthabaska; *Population au 2006:* 985
Circonscription(s) électorale(s) provinciale(s): Lotbinière
Circonscription(s) électorale(s) fédérale(s): Richmond-Arthabaska
Prochaines élections: 3e novembre 2013
Gilles Marchand, Maire
Mélisa Morissette, Directrice générale

Saint-Louis-de-Gonzague
108, rue de l'Église
Ravignan, QC G0R 2L0
Tél: 418-267-5931; *Téléc:* 418-267-5930
munstlouis@sogetel.net
www.st-louisdegonzague.qc.ca
Entité municipal: Municipality
Incorporation: 17 mars 1923 *Area:* 116,36 km2
Comté ou district: Les Etchemins; *Population au 2006:* 442
Circonscription(s) électorale(s) provinciale(s): Bellechasse
Circonscription(s) électorale(s) fédérale(s): Lévis-Bellechasse; Beauharnois-Salaberry
Prochaines élections: 3e novembre 2013
Suzanne Campeau Guenette, Mairesse

Odette Poulin, Directrice générale

Saint-Louis-de-Gonzague
CP 382
140, rue Principale
Saint-Louis-de-Gonzague, QC J0S 1T0
Tél: 450-371-0523; *Téléc:* 450-371-6229
munstlouisdegonzague@intermobilex.com
saint-louis-de-gonzague.com
Entité municipal: Parish (Paroisse)
Incorporation: 1er juillet 1855 *Area:* 78,52 km2
Comté ou district: Beauharnois-Salaberry; *Population au 2006:* 1,404
Circonscription(s) électorale(s) provinciale(s): Beauharnois
Circonscription(s) électorale(s) fédérale(s): Beauharnois-Salaberry
Prochaines élections: 3e novembre 2013
Yves Daoust, Maire
Micheline J.-Carrière, Directrice générale

Saint-Louis-de-Gonzague-du-Cap-Tourmente
CP 460 Haute-Ville
1, rue des Remparts
Québec, QC G1R 4R7
Tél: 418-692-3981; *Téléc:* 418-692-4345
jroberge@globetrotter.net
Entité municipal: Parish (Paroisse)
Incorporation: 1er janvier 1917
Comté ou district: La Côte-de-Beaupré; *Population au 2006:* 2
Circonscription(s) électorale(s) provinciale(s): Charlevoix
Circonscription(s) électorale(s) fédérale(s): Charlevoix-Montmorency-Haute-Côte-Nord
Prochaines élections: 3e novembre 2013
Jacques Roberge, Administrateur

Saint-Louis-du-Ha!-Ha!
95, rue St-Charles
Saint-Louis-du-Ha!-Ha!, QC G0L 3S0
Tél: 418-854-2260; *Téléc:* 418-854-0717
municipalite@saintlouisduhaha.com
www.saintlouisduhaha.com
Entité municipal: Parish (Paroisse)
Incorporation: 14 juillet 1874 *Area:* 114,45 km2
Comté ou district: Témiscouata; *Population au 2006:* 1,348
Circonscription(s) électorale(s) provinciale(s): Kamouraska-Témiscouata
Circonscription(s) électorale(s) fédérale(s): Rimouski-Neigette-Témiscouata-Les Basques
Prochaines élections: 3e novembre 2013
Louiselle Ouellet, Mairesse
Gratien Ouellet, Directeur général

Saint-Luc-de-Bellechasse
115, rue de la Fabrique
Saint-Luc-de-Bellechasse, QC G0R 1L0
Tél: 418-636-2176; *Téléc:* 418-636-2176
munstluc@sogetel.net
www.st-luc-bellechasse.qc.ca
Entité municipal: Municipality
Incorporation: 12 août 1921 *Area:* 160,03 km2
Comté ou district: Les Etchemins; *Population au 2006:* 490
Circonscription(s) électorale(s) provinciale(s): Bellechasse
Circonscription(s) électorale(s) fédérale(s): Lévis-Bellechasse
Prochaines élections: 3e novembre 2013
René Leclerc, Maire
Amélie Gagnon, Directrice générale

Saint-Luc-de-Vincennes
CP 450
660, rue Principale
Saint-Luc-de-Vincennes, QC G0X 3K0
Tél: 819-295-3782; *Téléc:* 819-295-3782
municipalite@stlucdevincennes.com
www.stlucdevincennes.com
Entité municipal: Municipality
Incorporation: 19 janvier 1865 *Area:* 52,73 km2
Comté ou district: Les Chenaux; *Population au 2006:* 553
Circonscription(s) électorale(s) provinciale(s): Champlain
Circonscription(s) électorale(s) fédérale(s): St-Maurice-Champlain
Prochaines élections: 3e novembre 2013
Jean-Claude Milot, Maire
Manon Shallow, Directrice générale

Saint-Lucien
5350, 7e rang
Saint-Lucien, QC J0C 1N0
Tél: 819-397-4679; *Téléc:* 819-397-2732
lynda.lalancette@municipalite.saint-lucien.qc.ca
Entité municipal: Parish (Paroisse)
Incorporation: 11 novembre 1907 *Area:* 113,61 km2
Comté ou district: Drummond; *Population au 2006:* 1,508
Circonscription(s) électorale(s) provinciale(s): Richmond
Circonscription(s) électorale(s) fédérale(s): Drummond
Prochaines élections: 3e novembre 2013
Suzanne Pinard Lebeau, Mairesse
Lynda Lalancette, Directrice générale

Saint-Ludger
212, rue La Salle
Saint-Ludger, QC G0M 1W0
Tél: 819-548-5408; *Téléc:* 819-548-5743
munstludger@sogetel.net
www.st-ludger.qc.ca
Entité municipal: Municipality
Incorporation: 25 février 1998 *Area:* 124,46 km2
Comté ou district: Le Granit; *Population au 2006:* 1,197
Circonscription(s) électorale(s) provinciale(s): Beauce-Sud
Circonscription(s) électorale(s) fédérale(s): Beauce
Prochaines élections: 3e novembre 2013
Diane Roy, Maire
Julie Létourneau, Directrice générale

Saint-Ludger-de-Milot
739, rue Gaudreault
Saint-Ludger-de-Milot, QC G0W 2B0
Tél: 418-373-2266; *Téléc:* 418-373-2554
administration@ville.st-ludger-de-milot.qc.ca
www.ville.st-ludger-de-milot.qc.ca
Entité municipal: Municipality
Incorporation: 1er janvier 1948 *Area:* 106,81 km2
Comté ou district: Lac-St-Jean-Est; *Population au 2006:* 727
Circonscription(s) électorale(s) provinciale(s): Lac-St-Jean
Circonscription(s) électorale(s) fédérale(s): Roberval-Lac-St-Jean
Prochaines élections: 3e novembre 2013
Marc Laliberté, Maire
Rita Ouellet, Directrice générale

Saint-Magloire
130, rue Principale
Saint-Magloire, QC G0R 3M0
Tél: 418-257-4421; *Téléc:* 418-257-4422
stmagloire@sogetel.net
www.saint-magloire.com
Entité municipal: Municipality
Incorporation: 1er janvier 1875 *Area:* 208,64 km2
Comté ou district: Les Etchemins; *Population au 2006:* 745
Circonscription(s) électorale(s) provinciale(s): Bellechasse
Circonscription(s) électorale(s) fédérale(s): Lévis-Bellechasse
Prochaines élections: 3e novembre 2013
Marcel Asselin, Maire
Huguette Lavigne, Directrice générale

Saint-Majorique-de-Grantham
1966, boul St-Joseph ouest
Saint-Majorique-de-Grantham, QC J2B 8A8
Tél: 819-478-7058; *Téléc:* 819-478-8479
municipalite.st-majorique@reseaualliance.com
Entité municipal: Parish (Paroisse)
Incorporation: 13 juillet 1901 *Area:* 57,26 km2
Comté ou district: Drummond; *Population au 2006:* 1,136
Circonscription(s) électorale(s) provinciale(s): Drummond
Circonscription(s) électorale(s) fédérale(s): Drummond
Prochaines élections: 3e novembre 2013
Réjean Rodier, Maire
Hélène Ruel, Directrice générale

Saint-Malachie
610, 7e rue
Saint-Malachie, QC G0R 3N0
Tél: 418-642-2102; *Téléc:* 418-642-2231
munimala@globetrotter.net
www.st-malachie.qc.ca
Entité municipal: Parish (Paroisse)
Incorporation: 1er juin 1874 *Area:* 100,59 km2
Comté ou district: Bellechasse; *Population au 2006:* 1,413
Circonscription(s) électorale(s) provinciale(s): Bellechasse
Circonscription(s) électorale(s) fédérale(s): Lévis-Bellechasse
Prochaines élections: 1er novembre 2013
Hélène Bissonnette, Sec.-Trés. & Directrice générale
Vital Labonté, Maire

Saint-Malo
228, rte 253 sud
Saint-Malo, QC J0B 2Y0
Tél: 819-658-2174; *Téléc:* 819-658-1169
saint-malo@axion.ca
Entité municipal: Municipality
Incorporation: 1er janvier 1870 *Area:* 129,30 km2
Comté ou district: Coaticook; *Population au 2006:* 516
Circonscription(s) électorale(s) provinciale(s): Mégantic-Compton
Circonscription(s) électorale(s) fédérale(s): Compton-Stanstead
Prochaines élections: 3e novembre 2013
Jacques Madore, Maire
Micheline Robert, Directrice générale

Saint-Marc-de-Figuery
CP 12
10, av Michaud
Saint-Marc-de-Figuery, QC J0Y 1J0
Tél: 819-732-8501; *Téléc:* 819-732-4324
mun.stmard@cableamos.com
Entité municipal: Parish (Paroisse)
Incorporation: 10 novembre 1926 *Area:* 91,10 km2
Comté ou district: Abitibi; *Population au 2006:* 692
Circonscription(s) électorale(s) provinciale(s): Abitibi-Ouest
Circonscription(s) électorale(s) fédérale(s): Abitibi-Témiscamingue
Prochaines élections: 3e novembre 2013
Jacques Riopel, Maire
Aline Guénette, Directrice générale

Saint-Marc-des-Carrières
965, av Bona-Dussault
Saint-Marc-des-Carrières, QC G0A 4B0
Tél: 418-268-3862; *Téléc:* 418-268-8776
info@villestmarc.com
www.st-marc-des-carrieres.qc.ca
Entité municipal: Town
Incorporation: 24 octobre 1918 *Area:* 16,73 km2
Comté ou district: Portneuf; *Population au 2006:* 2,774
Circonscription(s) électorale(s) provinciale(s): Portneuf
Circonscription(s) électorale(s) fédérale(s): Portneuf-Jacques-Cartier
Prochaines élections: 3e novembre 2013
Guy Denis, Maire
Maryon Leclerc, Directeur général

Saint-Marc-du-Lac-Long
12, rue de l'Église
Saint-Marc-du-Lac-Long, QC G0L 1T0
Tel: 418-893-2643; *Fax:* 418-893-7228
admin@saintmarcdulaclong.ca
Municipal Type: Parish (Paroisse)
Incorporated: 11 juin 1938 *Area:* 147,16 km2
County or District: Témiscouata; *Population in 2006:* 479
Provincial Electoral District(s): Kamouraska-Témiscouata
Federal Electoral District(s): Rimouski-Neigette-Témiscouata-Les Basques
Next Election: 3e novembre 2013
Adrien Kennedy, Maire
Karine Plourde, Directrice générale

Saint-Marc-sur-Richelieu
102, rue de la Fabrique
Saint-Marc-sur-Richelieu, QC J0L 2E0
Tél: 450-584-2258; *Téléc:* 450-584-2795
sburelle@ville.saint-marc-sur-richelieu.qc.ca
www.ville.saint.marc-sur-richelieu.qc.ca
Entité municipal: Municipality
Incorporation: 1er juillet 1855 *Area:* 59,51 km2
Comté ou district: Le Vallée-du-Richelieu; *Population au 2006:* 1,876
Circonscription(s) électorale(s) provinciale(s): Verchères
Circonscription(s) électorale(s) fédérale(s): Verchères-Les Patriotes
Prochaines élections: 3e novembre 2013
Jean Murray, Maire
Sylvie Burelle, Directrice générale

Saint-Marcel
48, ch Taché est
Saint-Marcel, QC G0R 3R0
Tél: 418-356-2691; *Téléc:* 418-356-2820
mun.sm@globetrotter.net
www.saintmarcel.qc.ca
Entité municipal: Municipality
Incorporation: 30 juillet 1904 *Area:* 178,86 km2
Comté ou district: L'Islet; *Population au 2006:* 527
Circonscription(s) électorale(s) provinciale(s): Montmagny-L'Islet
Circonscription(s) électorale(s) fédérale(s): Montmagny-L'Islet-Kamouraska-Rivière-du-Loup
Prochaines élections: 3e novembre 2013
Clément Bernier, Maire
Carole St-Hilaire, Directrice générale

Saint-Marcel-de-Richelieu
117, rue Saint-Louis
Saint-Marcel-de-Richelieu, QC J0H 1T0
Tél: 450-794-2832; *Téléc:* 450-794-1140
munst-marcel@mrcmaskoutains.qc.ca
Entité municipal: Municipality
Incorporation: 1er juillet 1855 *Area:* 50,21 km2

Comté ou district: Les Maskoutains; *Population au 2006:* 580
Circonscription(s) électorale(s) provinciale(s): Nicolet-Yamaska
Circonscription(s) électorale(s) fédérale(s): St-Hyacinthe-Bagot
Prochaines élections: 3e novembre 2013
Yvon Pesant, Maire
Christiane Janelle, Directrice générale

Saint-Marcellin
336, rte 234
Saint-Marcellin, QC G0K 1R0
Tél: 418-798-4382; *Téléc:* 418-798-4383
munstmar@globetrotter.net
www.st-marcellin.qc.ca
Entité municipal: Parish (Paroisse)
Incorporation: 19 novembre 1924 *Area:* 117,01 km2
Comté ou district: Rimouski-Neigette; *Population au 2006:* 357
Circonscription(s) électorale(s) provinciale(s): Rimouski
Circonscription(s) électorale(s) fédérale(s):
Rimouski-Neigette-Témiscouata-Les Basques
Prochaines élections: 3e novembre 2013
Sarto Roy, Maire
Brigitte Rouleau, Directrice générale

Saint-Martin
131, 1e av est
Saint-Martin, QC G0M 1B0
Tél: 418-382-5035; *Téléc:* 418-382-5561
municipalite@st-martin.qc.ca
www.st-martin.qc.ca
Entité municipal: Parish (Paroisse)
Incorporation: 12 octobre 1911 *Area:* 119,34 km2
Comté ou district: Beauce-Sartigan; *Population au 2006:* 2,543
Circonscription(s) électorale(s) provinciale(s): Beauce-Sud
Circonscription(s) électorale(s) fédérale(s): Beauce
Prochaines élections: 3e novembre 2013
Jean-Marc Paquet, Maire
Brigitte Quirion, Directrice générale

Saint-Mathias-sur-Richelieu
300, ch des Patriotes
Saint-Mathias-sur-Richelieu, QC J3L 6Z5
Tél: 450-658-2841; *Téléc:* 450-447-1416
information@st-mathias.org
Entité municipal: Municipality
Incorporation: 1er juillet 1855 *Area:* 48,22 km2
Comté ou district: Rouville; *Population au 2006:* 4,506
Circonscription(s) électorale(s) provinciale(s): Chambly
Circonscription(s) électorale(s) fédérale(s): Chambly-Borduas
Prochaines élections: 3e novembre 2013
Yanik Maheu, Maire
Catherine Chartrand, Directrice général

Saint-Mathieu
299, ch St-Édouard
Saint-Mathieu, QC J0L 2H0
Tél: 450-632-9528; *Téléc:* 450-632-9544
dg@municipalite.saint-mathieu.qc.ca
Entité municipal: Municipality
Incorporation: 1er août 1917 *Area:* 32,27 km2
Comté ou district: Roussillon; *Population au 2006:* 1,894
Circonscription(s) électorale(s) provinciale(s): La Prairie
Circonscription(s) électorale(s) fédérale(s):
Châteauguay-St-Constant
Prochaines élections: 3e novembre 2013
Lise Poissant-Charron, Mairesse
Louise Hébert, Directrice générale

Saint-Mathieu-d'Harricana
203, ch Lanoix
Saint-Mathieu-d'Harricana, QC J0Y 1M0
Tél: 819-727-9557; *Téléc:* 819-727-2052
mun.st-mathieu@cableamos.com
Entité municipal: Municipality
Incorporation: 1er janvier 1943 *Area:* 104,09 km2
Comté ou district: Abitibi; *Population au 2006:* 716
Circonscription(s) électorale(s) provinciale(s): Abitibi-Ouest
Circonscription(s) électorale(s) fédérale(s):
Abitibi-Témiscamingue
Prochaines élections: 3e novembre 2013
Martin Roch, Maire
Kathleen Guévin, Directrice générale

Saint-Mathieu-de-Beloeil
5000, rue des Loisirs
Saint-Mathieu-de-Beloeil, QC J3G 2C9
Tél: 450-467-7490; *Téléc:* 450-467-2999
reception@munstmathbel.ca
www.saint-mathieu-de-beloeil.com
Entité municipal: Municipality
Incorporation: 1er juillet 1855 *Area:* 39,26 km2
Comté ou district: La Vallée-du-Richelieu; *Population au 2006:* 2,288
Circonscription(s) électorale(s) provinciale(s): Borduas
Circonscription(s) électorale(s) fédérale(s): Chambly-Borduas
Prochaines élections: 3e novembre 2013
Michel Aubin, Maire
Doris Parent, Directrice générale

Saint-Mathieu-de-Rioux
41, rue de l'Église
Saint-Mathieu-de-Rioux, QC G0L 3T0
Tél: 418-738-2953; *Téléc:* 418-738-2454
admin@stmathieuderioux.qc.ca
www.st-mathieu-de-rioux.ca
Entité municipal: Parish (Paroisse)
Incorporation: 18 août 1865 *Area:* 102,35 km2
Comté ou district: Les Basques; *Population au 2006:* 672
Circonscription(s) électorale(s) provinciale(s): Rivière-du-Loup
Circonscription(s) électorale(s) fédérale(s):
Rimouski-Neigette-Témiscouata-Les Basques
Prochaines élections: 3e novembre 2013
Réal Côté, Maire
Michelle Lafontaine, Directrice générale

Saint-Mathieu-du-Parc
561, ch Déziel
Saint-Mathieu-du-Parc, QC G0X 1N0
Tél: 819-532-2205; *Téléc:* 819-532-2415
stmathieu@stmathieuduparc.org
www.stmathieuduparc.org
Entité municipal: Municipality
Incorporation: 30 juin 1886 *Area:* 196,45 km2
Comté ou district: Maskinongé; *Population au 2006:* 1,376
Circonscription(s) électorale(s) provinciale(s): St-Maurice
Circonscription(s) électorale(s) fédérale(s): Berthier-Maskinongé
Prochaines élections: 3e novembre 2013
Claude Mayrand, Maire
Sylvian Tousignant, Directeur général

Saint-Maurice
CP 9
2510, rang St-Jean
Saint-Maurice, QC G0X 2X0
Tél: 819-374-4525; *Téléc:* 819-374-9132
municipalite@st-maurice.ca
www.st-maurice.ca
Entité municipal: Parish (Paroisse)
Incorporation: 1er juillet 1855 *Area:* 90,33 km2
Comté ou district: Les Chenaux; *Population au 2006:* 2,338
Circonscription(s) électorale(s) provinciale(s): Champlain
Circonscription(s) électorale(s) fédérale(s):
St-Maurice-Champlain
Prochaines élections: 3e novembre 2013
Gérard Bruneau, Maire
Andrée Neault, Directrice générale

Saint-Maxime-du-Mont-Louis
CP 130
1, 1re av ouest
Saint-Maxime-du-Mont-Louis, QC G0E 1T0
Tél: 418-797-2310; *Téléc:* 418-797-2928
munst-maxime@globetrotter.net
www.municipalitest-maxime.qc.ca
Entité municipal: Municipality
Incorporation: 10 juin 1884 *Area:* 220,38 km2
Comté ou district: La Haute-Gaspésie; *Population au 2006:* 1,194
Circonscription(s) électorale(s) provinciale(s): Matane
Circonscription(s) électorale(s) fédérale(s): Haute-Gaspésie-La Mitis-Matane-Matapédia
Prochaines élections: 3e novembre 2013
Paul-Hébert Bernatchez, Maire
Hilaire Lemieux, Directeur général

Saint-Médard
1B, rue Principale est
Saint-Médard, QC G0L 3V0
Tél: 418-963-6276; *Téléc:* 418-963-6468
admin@st-medard.qc.ca
www.info-basques.com
Entité municipal: Municipality
Incorporation: 1er janvier 1949 *Area:* 67,59 km2
Comté ou district: Les Basques; *Population au 2006:* 252
Circonscription(s) électorale(s) provinciale(s): Rivière-du-Loup
Circonscription(s) électorale(s) fédérale(s):
Rimouski-Neigette-Témiscouata-Les Basques
Prochaines élections: 3e novembre 2013
Diane Marquis, Maire
Andrée O. Beaulieu, Directrice générale

Saint-Michel
1700, rue Principale
Saint-Michel, QC J0L 2J0
Tél: 450-454-4502; *Téléc:* 450-454-7508
stmichel@cstsm.net
Entité municipal: Parish (Paroisse)
Incorporation: 1er juillet 1855 *Area:* 57,36 km2
Comté ou district: Les Jardins-de-Napierville; *Population au 2006:* 2,637
Circonscription(s) électorale(s) provinciale(s): Huntingdon
Circonscription(s) électorale(s) fédérale(s): St-Léonard-St-Michel
Prochaines élections: 3e novembre 2013
Pierre Raymond Cloutier, Maire
Micheline Lemay, Directrice générale

Saint-Michel-de-Bellechasse
129, rte 132 est
Saint-Michel-de-Bellechasse, QC G0R 3S0
Tél: 418-884-2865; *Téléc:* 418-884-2866
munstmic@globetrotter.net
www.saintmicheldebellechasse.com
Entité municipal: Municipality
Incorporation: 1er juillet 1855 *Area:* 53,43 km2
Comté ou district: Bellechasse; *Population au 2006:* 1,669
Circonscription(s) électorale(s) provinciale(s): Bellechasse
Circonscription(s) électorale(s) fédérale(s): Lévis-Bellechasse
Prochaines élections: 3e novembre 2013
Suzanne Côté, Mairesse
Ronald Gonthier, Directeur général

Saint-Michel-des-Saints
441, rue Brassard
Saint-Michel-des-Saints, QC J0K 3B0
Tél: 450-886-4502; *Téléc:* 450-833-6081
info@saintmicheldessaints.com
www.saintmicheldesaints.com
Entité municipal: Municipality
Incorporation: 3 mars 1979 *Area:* 563,72 km2
Comté ou district: Matawinie; *Population au 2006:* 2,713
Circonscription(s) électorale(s) provinciale(s): Berthier
Circonscription(s) électorale(s) fédérale(s): Joliette
Prochaines élections: 3e novembre 2013
Jean-Pierre Bellerose, Maire
Alain Bellerose, Directeur général

Saint-Michel-du-Squatec
CP 280
150, rue St-Joseph
Saint-Michel-du-Squatec, QC G0L 4H0
Tél: 418-855-2185; *Téléc:* 418-855-2935
info@squatec.qc.ca
www.squatec.qc.ca
Entité municipal: Parish (Paroisse)
Incorporation: 16 avril 1928 *Area:* 363,10 km2
Comté ou district: Témiscouata; *Population au 2006:* 1,263
Circonscription(s) électorale(s) provinciale(s):
Kamouraska-Témiscouata
Circonscription(s) électorale(s) fédérale(s):
Rimouski-Neigette-Témiscouata-Les Basques
Prochaines élections: 3e novembre 2013
André Chouinard, Maire
Danielle Albert, Directrice générale

Saint-Modeste
312, rue Principale
Saint-Modeste, QC G0L 3W0
Tél: 418-867-2352; *Téléc:* 418-867-5359
municipalite@saint-modeste.ca
www.municipalite.saint-modeste.qc.ca
Entité municipal: Parish (Paroisse)
Incorporation: 1er juillet 1855 *Area:* 107,91 km2
Comté ou district: Rivière-du-Loup; *Population au 2006:* 942
Circonscription(s) électorale(s) provinciale(s): Rivière-du-Loup
Circonscription(s) électorale(s) fédérale(s):
Montmagny-L'Islet-Kamouraska-Rivière-du-Loup
Prochaines élections: 3e novembre 2013
Louis-Marie Bastille, Maire
Alain Vila, Directeur général

Saint-Moïse
CP 8
117-B, rue Principale
Saint-Moïse, QC G0J 2Z0
Tél: 418-776-2833; *Téléc:* 418-776-2835
Other Information: muni.moise@globetrotter.net
Entité municipal: Parish (Paroisse)
Incorporation: 1er janvier 1878 *Area:* 106,83 km2
Comté ou district: La Matapédia; *Population au 2006:* 625
Circonscription(s) électorale(s) provinciale(s): Matapédia
Circonscription(s) électorale(s) fédérale(s): Haute-Gaspésie-La Mitis-Matane-Matapédia
Prochaines élections: 3e novembre 2013

Paul Lepage, Maire
Monique Bouchard, Directrice générale

Saint-Narcisse
353, rue Notre-Dame
Saint-Narcisse, QC G0X 2Y0
Tél: 418-328-8645; *Téléc:* 418-328-4348
municipalite@saint-narcisse.com
Entité municipal: Parish (Paroisse)
Incorporation: 1er juillet 1855 *Area:* 103,49 km2
Comté ou district: Les Chenaux; *Population au 2006:* 1,806
Circonscription(s) électorale(s) provinciale(s): Champlain
Circonscription(s) électorale(s) fédérale(s):
St-Maurice-Champlain
Prochaines élections: 3e novembre 2013
Guy Veillette, Maire
André Carignan, Directeur général

Saint-Narcisse-de-Beaurivage
#1, 508, rue de l'École
Saint-Narcisse-de-Beaurivage, QC G0S 1W0
Tél: 418-475-6842; *Téléc:* 418-475-6880
saintnarcisse@globetrotter.net
www.saintnarcissedebeaurivage.ca
Entité municipal: Parish (Paroisse)
Incorporation: 1er mai 1874 *Area:* 60,83 km2
Comté ou district: Lotbinière; *Population au 2006:* 975
Circonscription(s) électorale(s) provinciale(s): Lotbinière
Circonscription(s) électorale(s) fédérale(s):
Lotbinière-Chutes-de-la-Chaudière
Prochaines élections: 3e novembre 2013
Denis Dion, Maire
Dany Lehoux, Directrice générale

Saint-Narcisse-de-Rimouski
7, rue du Pavillon
Saint-Narcisse-de-Rimouski, QC G0K 1S0
Tél: 418-735-2638; *Téléc:* 418-735-6021
informations@saintnarcisse.net
www.saintnarcisse.net
Entité municipal: Parish (Paroisse)
Incorporation: 13 février 1922 *Area:* 166,83 km2
Comté ou district: Rimouski-Neigette; *Population au 2006:* 1,088
Circonscription(s) électorale(s) provinciale(s): Rimouski
Circonscription(s) électorale(s) fédérale(s):
Rimouski-Neigette-Témiscouata-Les Basques
Prochaines élections: 3e novembre 2013
Laurent Proulx, Maire
Gilles Lepage, Directeur général

Saint-Nazaire
199, rue Principale
Saint-Nazaire, QC G0W 2V0
Tél: 418-662-4154; *Téléc:* 418-662-5467
ktremblay@ville.saint-nazaire.qc.ca
www.ville.saint-nazaire.qc.ca
Entité municipal: Municipality
Incorporation: 23 septembre 1905 *Area:* 147,78 km2
Comté ou district: Lac-St-Jean-Est; *Population au 2006:* 1,866
Circonscription(s) électorale(s) provinciale(s): Lac-St-Jean
Circonscription(s) électorale(s) fédérale(s):
Roberval-Lac-St-Jean
Prochaines élections: 3e novembre 2013
Martin Sauvé, Maire
Kathy Tremblay, Directrice générale

Saint-Nazaire-d'Acton
750, rue des Loisirs
Saint-Nazaire-d'Acton, QC J0H 1V0
Tél: 819-392-2347; *Téléc:* 819-392-2039
Entité municipal: Parish (Paroisse)
Incorporation: 8 janvier 1894 *Area:* 57,49 km2
Comté ou district: Acton; *Population au 2006:* 832
Circonscription(s) électorale(s) provinciale(s): Johnson
Circonscription(s) électorale(s) fédérale(s): St-Hyacinthe-Bagot
Prochaines élections: 3e novembre 2013
André Fafard, Maire
Guylaine Bourgoin, Directrice générale
gbourgoin@mun-nazaire.qc.ca

Saint-Nazaire-de-Dorchester
61A, rue Principale
Saint-Nazaire, QC G0R 3T0
Tél: 418-642-1305; *Téléc:* 418-642-2945
mun_st_nazaire@globetrotter.net
www.saint-nazaire-de-dorchester.org
Entité municipal: Parish (Paroisse)
Incorporation: 9 mars 1906 *Area:* 51,43 km2
Comté ou district: Bellechasse; *Population au 2006:* 385
Circonscription(s) électorale(s) provinciale(s): Bellechasse
Circonscription(s) électorale(s) fédérale(s): Lévis-Bellechasse
Prochaines élections: 3e novembre 2013
Claude Lachance, Maire
Francine Brochu, Directrice générale

Saint-Nérée
1990, rte Principale
Saint-Nérée, QC G0R 3V0
Tél: 418-243-2735; *Téléc:* 418-243-2136
muneree@globetrotter.net
www.st-neree.qc.ca
Entité municipal: Parish (Paroisse)
Incorporation: 29 mars 1887 *Area:* 75,73 km2
Comté ou district: Bellechasse; *Population au 2006:* 789
Circonscription(s) électorale(s) provinciale(s): Bellechasse
Circonscription(s) électorale(s) fédérale(s): Lévis-Bellechasse
Prochaines élections: 3e novembre 2013
Clément Vallières, Maire
Michael Couture, Directeur général

Saint-Noël
CP 99
51, rue de l'Église
Saint-Noël, QC G0J 3A0
Tél: 418-776-2936; *Téléc:* 418-776-5521
stnoel@mrcmatapedia.qc.ca
Entité municipal: Village
Incorporation: 2 octobre 1906 *Area:* 45,68 km2
Comté ou district: La Matapédia; *Population au 2006:* 459
Circonscription(s) électorale(s) provinciale(s): Matapédia
Circonscription(s) électorale(s) fédérale(s): Haute-Gaspésie-La Mitis-Matane-Matapédia
Prochaines élections: 3e novembre 2013
Gilbert Sénéchal, Maire
Manon Caron, Directrice générale

Saint-Norbert
2150, rue Principale
Saint-Norbert, QC J0K 3C0
Tél: 450-836-4700; *Téléc:* 450-836-4004
municipalite@saint-norbert.net
www.saint-norbert.net
Entité municipal: Parish (Paroisse)
Incorporation: 1er juillet 1855 *Area:* 77,31 km2
Comté ou district: D'Autray; *Population au 2006:* 1,067
Circonscription(s) électorale(s) provinciale(s): Berthier
Circonscription(s) électorale(s) fédérale(s): Berthier-Maskinongé
Prochaines élections: 3e novembre 2013
André Dauphin, Maire
Martine Laberge, Directrice générale

Saint-Norbert-d'Arthabaska
44, rue Landry
Saint-Norbert-d'Arthabaska, QC G0P 1B0
Tél: 819-369-9318; *Téléc:* 819-369-8686
Entité municipal: Municipality
Incorporation: 30 novembre 1994 *Area:* 113,66 km2
Comté ou district: Arthabaska; *Population au 2006:* 857
Circonscription(s) électorale(s) provinciale(s): Arthabaska
Circonscription(s) électorale(s) fédérale(s):
Richmond-Arthabaska
Prochaines élections: 3e novembre 2013
Ghislain Caouette, Maire
Linda Trottier, Directrice générale
ltrottier@saint-norbert-darthabaska.ca

Saint-Octave-de-Métis
201A, rue de l'Église
Saint-Octave-de-Métis, QC G0J 3B0
Tél: 418-775-2996; *Téléc:* 418-775-0099
stoctave@mitis.qc.ca
Entité municipal: Parish (Paroisse)
Incorporation: 25 avril 1908 *Area:* 74,63 km2
Comté ou district: La Mitis; *Population au 2006:* 488
Circonscription(s) électorale(s) provinciale(s): Matapédia
Circonscription(s) électorale(s) fédérale(s): Haute-Gaspésie-La Mitis-Matane-Matapédia
Prochaines élections: 3e novembre 2013
Mylène-Julie Lavoie, Maire
Maxime Richard-Dubé, Directeur général

Saint-Odilon-de-Cranbourne
CP 100
111, rue de l'Hôtel-de-Ville
Saint-Odilon, QC G0S 3A0
Tél: 418-464-4801; *Téléc:* 418-464-4800
info@saint-odilon.qc.ca
www.saint-odilon.qc.ca
Entité municipal: Parish (Paroisse)
Incorporation: 1er juillet 1855 *Area:* 128,77 km2
Comté ou district: Robert-Cliche; *Population au 2006:* 1,440
Circonscription(s) électorale(s) provinciale(s): Beauce-Nord
Circonscription(s) électorale(s) fédérale(s): Beauce
Prochaines élections: 3e novembre 2013
Marc-André Labbé, Maire
Suzie Turcotte, Directrice générale

Saint-Omer
243, rang des Pelletier
Saint-Omer, QC G0R 4R0
Tél: 418-356-5634; *Téléc:* 418-356-5634
municipalitest-omer@globetrotter.net
Entité municipal: Municipality
Incorporation: 1er janvier 1954 *Area:* 125,35 km2
Comté ou district: L'Islet; *Population au 2006:* 343
Circonscription(s) électorale(s) provinciale(s): Montmagny-L'Islet
Circonscription(s) électorale(s) fédérale(s):
Montmagny-L'Islet-Kamouraska-Rivière-du-Loup
Prochaines élections: 3e novembre 2013
Réjeanne Godbout, Mairesse
Lise Bastien, Directrice générale

Saint-Onésime-d'Ixworth
12, rue de l'Église
Saint-Onésime-d'Ixworth, QC G0R 3W0
Tél: 418-856-3018; *Téléc:* 418-856-6626
municipalite@stonesime.com
Entité municipal: Parish (Paroisse)
Incorporation: 13 mai 1895 *Area:* 103,59 km2
Comté ou district: Kamouraska; *Population au 2006:* 577
Circonscription(s) électorale(s) provinciale(s):
Kamouraska-Témiscouata
Circonscription(s) électorale(s) fédérale(s):
Montmagny-L'Islet-Kamouraska-Rivière-du-Loup
Prochaines élections: 3e novembre 2013
Jacques Dionne, Maire
Hélène Lessard, Directrice générale

Saint-Ours
CP 129
2540, rue de l'Immaculée-Conception
Saint-Ours, QC J0G 1P0
Tél: 450-785-2203; *Téléc:* 450-785-2254
Entité municipal: Village
Incorporation: 17 avril 1991 *Area:* 58,50 km2
Comté ou district: Pierre-De Saurel; *Population au 2009:* 1,704
Circonscription(s) électorale(s) provinciale(s): Richelieu
Circonscription(s) électorale(s) fédérale(s):
Bas-Richelieu-Nicolet-Bécancour
Prochaines élections: 3e novembre 2013
Robert Tremblay, Maire
Pierre Dion, Directeur général
pdion@pierredesaurel.com

Saint-Pacôme
CP 370
27, rue St-Louis
Saint-Pacôme, QC G0L 3X0
Tél: 418-852-2356; *Téléc:* 418-852-2977
stpacome@bellnet.ca
www.st-pacome.ca
Entité municipal: Municipality
Incorporation: 5 janvier 1980 *Area:* 29,31 km2
Comté ou district: Kamouraska; *Population au 2006:* 1,685
Circonscription(s) électorale(s) provinciale(s):
Kamouraska-Témiscouata
Circonscription(s) électorale(s) fédérale(s):
Montmagny-L'Islet-Kamouraska-Rivière-du-Loup
Prochaines élections: 3e novembre 2013
Gervais Lévesque, Maire
Fréderic Lee, Directeur général

Saint-Pamphile
3, rte Elgin sud
Saint-Pamphile, QC G0R 3X0
Tél: 418-356-5501; *Téléc:* 418-356-5502
pamphile@globetrotter.qc.ca
www.saintpamphile.ca
Entité municipal: Town
Incorporation: 21 janvier 1888 *Area:* 136,80 km2
Comté ou district: L'Islet; *Population au 2006:* 2,704
Circonscription(s) électorale(s) provinciale(s): Montmagny-L'Islet
Circonscription(s) électorale(s) fédérale(s):
Montmagny-L'Islet-Kamouraska-Rivière-du-Loup
Prochaines élections: 3e novembre 2013
Réal Laverdière, Maire
Richard Pelletier, Directeur général

Saint-Pascal
CP 250
405, rue Taché
Saint-Pascal, QC G0L 3Y0
Tél: 418-492-2312; *Téléc:* 418-492-9862
hoteldeville@villestpascal.com
www.villesaintpascal.qc.ca
Entité municipal: Town
Incorporation: 1er mars 2000 *Area:* 57,75 km2
Comté ou district: Kamouraska; *Population au 2006:* 3,504
Circonscription(s) électorale(s) provinciale(s): Kamouraska-Témiscouata
Circonscription(s) électorale(s) fédérale(s): Montmagny-L'Islet-Kamouraska-Rivière-du-Loup
Prochaines élections: 3e novembre 2013
Renald Bernier, Maire
Louise Saint-Pierre, Greffière

Saint-Patrice-de-Beaurivage
530, rue Principale
Saint-Patrice-de-Beaurivage, QC G0S 1B0
Tél: 418-596-2362; *Téléc:* 418-596-2430
st.patrice@globetrotter.net
www.ville.saint-patrice-de-beaurivage.qc.ca
Entité municipal: Municipality
Incorporation: 29 septembre 1984 *Area:* 86,18 km2
Comté ou district: Lotbinière; *Population au 2006:* 1,037
Circonscription(s) électorale(s) provinciale(s): Lotbinière
Circonscription(s) électorale(s) fédérale(s): Lotbinière-Chutes-de-la-Chaudière
Prochaines élections: 3e novembre 2013
Lewis Camden, Maire
Frédéric Desjardins, Directrice générale

Saint-Patrice-de-Sherrington
300, rue St-Patrice
Saint-Patrice-de-Sherrington, QC J0L 2N0
Tél: 450-454-4959; *Téléc:* 450-454-5677
municipalitesherrington@intermobilex.com
Entité municipal: Parish (Paroisse)
Incorporation: 1er juillet 1855 *Area:* 91,47 km2
Comté ou district: Les Jardins-de-Napierville; *Population au 2006:* 1,911
Circonscription(s) électorale(s) provinciale(s): Huntingdon
Circonscription(s) électorale(s) fédérale(s): Beauharnois-Salaberry
Prochaines élections: 3e novembre 2013
André Giroux, Maire
Francine Fleurent, Directrice générale

Saint-Paul
18, boul Brassard
Saint-Paul, QC J0K 3E0
Tél: 450-759-4040; *Téléc:* 450-759-6396
mairie@municipalitestpaul.qc.ca
www.municipalitestpaul.qc.ca
Entité municipal: Municipality
Incorporation: 1er juillet 1855 *Area:* 48,17 km2
Comté ou district: Joliette; *Population au 2006:* 3,987
Circonscription(s) électorale(s) provinciale(s): Joliette
Circonscription(s) électorale(s) fédérale(s): Joliette
Prochaines élections: 3e novembre 2013
Alain Bellemarre, Maire
Richard-B. Morasse, Directeur général

Saint-Paul-d'Abbotsford
926, rue Principale est
Saint-Paul-d'Abbotsford, QC J0E 1A0
Tél: 450-379-5408; *Téléc:* 450-379-9905
dg@stpauldabbotsford.qc.ca
www.saintpauldabbotsford.qc.ca
Entité municipal: Parish (Paroisse)
Incorporation: 1er juillet 1855 *Area:* 79,59 km2
Comté ou district: Rouville; *Population au 2006:* 2,824
Circonscription(s) électorale(s) provinciale(s): Iberville
Circonscription(s) électorale(s) fédérale(s): Shefford
Prochaines élections: 3e novembre 2013
Dean Thomson, Maire
Daniel-Eric St-Onge, Directeur général

Saint-Paul-de-l'Ile-aux-Noix
959, rue Principale
Saint-Paul-de-l'Ile-aux-Noix, QC J0J 1G0
Tél: 450-291-3166; *Téléc:* 450-291-5930
mairie_stpaul@netc.net
www.ile-aux-noix.qc.ca
Entité municipal: Parish (Paroisse)
Incorporation: 18 novembre 1898 *Area:* 29,47 km2
Comté ou district: Le Haut-Richelieu; *Population au 2006:* 1,996
Circonscription(s) électorale(s) provinciale(s): Huntingdon
Circonscription(s) électorale(s) fédérale(s): St-Jean
Prochaines élections: 1er novembre 2013
Marie-Lili Lenoir, Directrice générale & Sec.-Trés.
Gérard Dutil, Maire

Saint-Paul-de-la-Croix
CP 70
1A, rue du Parc
Saint-Paul-de-la-Croix, QC G0L 3Z0
Tél: 418-898-2031; *Téléc:* 418-898-2322
munstpaul@st-paul-de-la-croix.qc.ca
www.municipalite.saint-paul-de-la-croix.qc.ca
Entité municipal: Parish (Paroisse)
Incorporation: 1er janvier 1873 *Area:* 84,25 km2
Comté ou district: Rivière-du-Loup; *Population au 2006:* 370
Circonscription(s) électorale(s) provinciale(s): Rivière-du-Loup
Circonscription(s) électorale(s) fédérale(s): Montmagny-L'Islet-Kamouraska-Rivière-du-Loup
Prochaines élections: 3e novembre 2013
Phillipe Dionne, Maire
Hélène Malenfant, Directrice générale

Saint-Paul-de-Montminy
CP 160
309, 4e av
Saint-Paul-de-Montminy, QC G0R 3Y0
Tél: 418-469-3120; *Téléc:* 418-469-3358
municipalitest-paul@globetrotter.net
www.stpauldemontminy.com
Entité municipal: Municipality
Incorporation: 1er janvier 1862 *Area:* 162,80 km2
Comté ou district: Montmagny; *Population au 2006:* 840
Circonscription(s) électorale(s) provinciale(s): Montmagny-L'Islet
Circonscription(s) électorale(s) fédérale(s): Montmagny-L'Islet-Kamouraska-Rivière-du-Loup
Prochaines élections: 3e novembre 2013
Émile Tanguay, Maire
Claudette Aubé, Directrice générale

Saint-Paulin
CP 120
3051, rue Bergeron
Saint-Paulin, QC J0K 3G0
Tél: 819-268-2026; *Téléc:* 819-268-2890
munistpaulindg@telmilot.net
www.st-paulin.qc.ca
Entité municipal: Municipality
Incorporation: 27 février 1988 *Area:* 96,40 km2
Comté ou district: Maskinongé; *Population au 2006:* 1,622
Circonscription(s) électorale(s) provinciale(s): Maskinongé
Circonscription(s) électorale(s) fédérale(s): Berthier-Maskinongé
Prochaines élections: 3e novembre 2013
Brigitte Gagnon, Mairesse
Ghislain Lemay, Directeur général

Saint-Philémon
1531, rue Principale
Saint-Philémon, QC G0R 4A0
Tél: 418-469-2890; *Téléc:* 418-469-2726
munphile@globetrotter.net
www.saint-philemon.com
Entité municipal: Parish (Paroisse)
Incorporation: 1er janvier 1867 *Area:* 146,51 km2
Comté ou district: Bellechasse; *Population au 2006:* 790
Circonscription(s) électorale(s) provinciale(s): Bellechasse
Circonscription(s) électorale(s) fédérale(s): Lévis-Bellechasse
Prochaines élections: 3e novembre 2013
Daniel Pouliot, Maire
Diane Labrecque, Directrice générale

Saint-Philibert
403, rue Principale
Saint-Philibert, QC G0M 1X0
Tél: 418-228-8759; *Téléc:* 418-228-0432
www.st-philibert.qc.ca
Entité municipal: Municipality
Incorporation: 25 février 1921 *Area:* 57,26 km2
Comté ou district: Beauce-Sartigan; *Population au 2006:* 387
Circonscription(s) électorale(s) provinciale(s): Beauce-Sud
Circonscription(s) électorale(s) fédérale(s): Beauce
Prochaines élections: 3e novembre 2013
Marc Nasdeau, Maire
Chantale Gareau, Directrice générale
gareau.chantale@st-philibert.qc.ca3

Saint-Philippe
2225, rte Édouard-VII
Saint-Philippe, QC J0L 2K0
Tél: 450-659-7701; *Téléc:* 450-659-7702
administration@municipalite.saint-philippe.qc.ca
www.municipalite.saint-philippe.qc.ca
Entité municipal: Municipality
Incorporation: 1er juillet 1855 *Area:* 61,66 km2
Comté ou district: Roussillon; *Population au 2006:* 5,121
Circonscription(s) électorale(s) provinciale(s): La Prairie
Circonscription(s) électorale(s) fédérale(s): Brossard-La Prairie
Prochaines élections: 1er novembre 2013
Claudine Cormier, Greffière
Gaétan Brosseau, Maire

Saint-Philippe-de-Néri
CP 130
12, côte de l'Église
Saint-Philippe-de-Néri, QC G0L 4A0
Tél: 418-498-2744; *Téléc:* 418-498-2193
munic.s.phil.neri@qc.aira.com
Entité municipal: Parish (Paroisse)
Incorporation: 29 décembre 1875 *Area:* 33,08 km2
Comté ou district: Kamouraska; *Population au 2006:* 889
Circonscription(s) électorale(s) provinciale(s): Kamouraska-Témiscouata
Circonscription(s) électorale(s) fédérale(s): Montmagny-L'Islet-Kamouraska-Rivière-du-Loup
Prochaines élections: 3e novembre 2013
Gilles Lévesque, Maire
Pierre Leclerc, Directeur général

Saint-Pie
77, rue St-Pierre
Saint-Pie, QC J0H 1W0
Tél: 450-772-2488; *Téléc:* 450-772-2233
st-pie@villest-pie.ca
www.villest-pie.ca
Entité municipal: Town
Incorporation: 28 février 2003 *Area:* 106,47 km2
Comté ou district: Les Maskoutains; *Population au 2006:* 5,109
Circonscription(s) électorale(s) provinciale(s): Iberville
Circonscription(s) électorale(s) fédérale(s): St-Hyacinthe-Bagot
Prochaines élections: 3e novembre 2013
Note: Effective February 28, 2003, the Parish & the Village of St-Pie amalgamated to create the new City of St-Pie.
Pierre St-Onge, Maire
Denise Breton, Greffière

Saint-Pie-de-Guire
435, rue Principale
Saint-Pie-de-Guire, QC J0G 1R0
Tél: 450-784-2278; *Téléc:* 450-784-0133
stpiedeguire@bellnet.ca
www.stpiedeguire.ca
Entité municipal: Parish (Paroisse)
Incorporation: 14 juin 1866 *Area:* 52,34 km2
Comté ou district: Drummond; *Population au 2006:* 453
Circonscription(s) électorale(s) provinciale(s): Nicolet-Yamaska
Circonscription(s) électorale(s) fédérale(s): Drummond
Prochaines élections: 3e novembre 2013
Benoît Bourque, Maire
Claire Roy, Directrice générale

Saint-Pierre
485, ch du Village-de-St-Pierre nord
Joliette, QC J6E 3Z1
Tél: 450-756-2592; *Téléc:* 450-756-2735
villagestpierre@qc.aira.com
Entité municipal: Village
Incorporation: 24 avril 1922 *Area:* 10,60 km2
Comté ou district: Joliette; *Population au 2006:* 304
Circonscription(s) électorale(s) provinciale(s): Joliette
Circonscription(s) électorale(s) fédérale(s): Joliette
Prochaines élections: 3e novembre 2013
Roland Charest, Maire
Édith Gagné, Directrice générale

Saint-Pierre-Baptiste
532B, rte de l'Église
Saint-Pierre-Baptiste, QC G0P 1K0
Tél: 418-453-2286; *Téléc:* 418-453-2286
info@saintpierrebaptiste.qc.ca
www.saintpierrebaptiste.qc.ca
Entité municipal: Parish (Paroisse)
Incorporation: 1er janvier 1874 *Area:* 80,72 km2
Comté ou district: L'Érable; *Population au 2006:* 422
Circonscription(s) électorale(s) provinciale(s): Lotbinière
Circonscription(s) électorale(s) fédérale(s): Mégantic-L'Érable
Prochaines élections: 3e novembre 2013
Yvon Gingras, Maire
Annie Poirier, Directrice générale

Saint-Pierre-de-Broughton
CP 90
29, rue de la Fabrique
Saint-Pierre-de-Broughton, QC G0N 1T0
Tél: 418-424-3572; *Téléc:* 418-424-0389
muni.stpierre@ville.st-pierre-de-broughton.qc.ca
www.ville.st-pierre-de-broughton.qc.ca

Entité municipal: Municipality
Incorporation: 12 octobre 1974 *Area:* 147,460 km2
Comté ou district: Les Appalaches; *Population au 2009:* 838
Circonscription(s) électorale(s) provinciale(s): Frontenac
Circonscription(s) électorale(s) fédérale(s): Mégantic-L'Érable
Prochaines élections: 3e novembre 2013
Nicole Bourque, Mairesse
Sylvie Mercier, Directrice générale

Saint-Pierre-de-la-Rivière-du-Sud
645 - 2e av
St-Pierre-de-la-Rivière-du-Sud, QC G0R 4B0
Tél: 418-248-8277; *Téléc:* 418-248-7068
st-pierre.rivsud@globetrotter.net
www.stpierrerivieresud.net
Entité municipal: Parish (Paroisse)
Incorporation: 1er juillet 1855 *Area:* 92,28 km2
Comté ou district: Montmagny; *Population au 2006:* 1,014
Circonscription(s) électorale(s) provinciale(s): Montmagny-L'Islet
Circonscription(s) électorale(s) fédérale(s):
Montmagny-L'Islet-Kamouraska-Rivière-du-Loup
Prochaines élections: 3e novembre 2013
Marie Eve Proulx, Mairesse
Georges Baillargeon, Directeur général

Saint-Pierre-de-Lamy
115, rte de l'Église
Saint-Pierre-de-Lamy, QC G0L 4B0
Tél: 418-497-2447; *Téléc:* 418-497-2447
admin@saintpierredelamy.ca
Entité municipal: Municipality
Incorporation: 4 juin 1977 *Area:* 115,46 km2
Comté ou district: Témiscouata; *Population au 2006:* 123
Circonscription(s) électorale(s) provinciale(s):
Kamouraska-Témiscouata
Circonscription(s) électorale(s) fédérale(s):
Rimouski-Neigette-Témiscouata-Les Basques
Prochaines élections: 3e novembre 2013
Gaston Caron, Maire
Mireille Plourde, Directrice générale

Saint-Pierre-de-Véronne-à-Pike-River
CP 93
548, rte 202
St-Pierre-de-Véronne, QC J0J 1P0
Tél: 450-248-2120; *Téléc:* 450-248-4772
pikeriver@axion.ca
www.pikeriver.ca
Entité municipal: Municipality
Incorporation: 3 avril 1912 *Area:* 43,58 km2
Comté ou district: Brome-Missisquoi; *Population au 2006:* 542
Circonscription(s) électorale(s) provinciale(s): Brome-Missisquoi
Circonscription(s) électorale(s) fédérale(s): Brome-Missisquoi
Prochaines élections: 3e novembre 2013
Martin Bellefroid, Maire
Sonia Côté, Directrice générale

Saint-Pierre-Ile-d'Orléans
515, rte des Prêtres
Saint-Pierre-Ile-d'Orléans, QC G0A 4E0
Tél: 418-828-2855; *Téléc:* 418-828-0724
Entité municipal: Municipality
Incorporation: 1er juillet 1855 *Area:* 31,13 km2
Comté ou district: L'Ile-d'Orléans; *Population au 2006:* 1,816
Circonscription(s) électorale(s) provinciale(s): Montmorency
Circonscription(s) électorale(s) fédérale(s):
Montmorency-Charlevoix-Haute-Côte-Nord
Prochaines élections: 3e novembre 2013
Jacques Trudel, Maire
Gérard Cossette, Directeur général
gcossette@stpierreio.ca

Saint-Pierre-les-Becquets
110, rue des Loisirs
Saint-Pierre-les-Becquets, QC G0X 2Z0
Tél: 819-263-2622; *Téléc:* 819-263-0798
municipalite@st-pierre-les-becquets.qc.ca
www.st-pierre-les-becquets.qc.ca
Entité municipal: Municipality
Incorporation: 22 février 1986 *Area:* 43,00 km2
Comté ou district: Bécancour; *Population au 2006:* 1,183
Circonscription(s) électorale(s) provinciale(s): Lotbinière
Circonscription(s) électorale(s) fédérale(s):
Bas-Richelieu-Nicolet-Bécancour
Prochaines élections: 3e novembre 2013
Raymond Dion, Maire
Michèle Laquerre, Directrice générale

Saint-Placide
281, montée St-Vincent
Saint-Placide, QC J0V 2B0
Tél: 450-258-2305; *Téléc:* 450-258-3059
infosp@municipalite.st-placide.qc.ca
www.municipalite.saint-placide.qc.ca
Entité municipal: Municipality
Incorporation: 3 août 1994 *Area:* 41,95 km2
Comté ou district: Deux-Montagnes; *Population au 2006:* 1,642
Circonscription(s) électorale(s) provinciale(s): Mirabel
Circonscription(s) électorale(s) fédérale(s):
Argenteuil-Papineau-Mirabel
Prochaines élections: 3e novembre 2013
Denis Lavigne, Maire
Lise Lavigne, Directrice générale

Saint-Polycarpe
CP 380
1263, ch Élie-Auclair
Saint-Polycarpe, QC J0P 1X0
Tél: 450-265-3777; *Téléc:* 450-265-3010
mdery@munstpolycarpe.qc.ca
www.munstpolycarpe.qc.ca
Entité municipal: Municipality
Incorporation: 31 décembre 1988 *Area:* 70,80 km2
Comté ou district: Vaudreuil-Soulanges; *Population au 2006:* 1,708
Circonscription(s) électorale(s) provinciale(s): Soulanges
Circonscription(s) électorale(s) fédérale(s): Vaudreuil-Soulanges
Prochaines élections: 3e novembre 2013
Normand Ménard, Maire
Micheline Déry, Directrice générale

Saint-Prime
599, rue Principale
Saint-Prime, QC G8J 1T2
Tél: 418-251-2116; *Téléc:* 418-251-2823
rgirard@saint-prime.ca
www.saint-prime.ca
Entité municipal: Municipality
Incorporation: 29 juin 1968 *Area:* 147,43 km2
Comté ou district: Le Domaine-du-Roy; *Population au 2006:* 2,661
Circonscription(s) électorale(s) provinciale(s): Roberval
Circonscription(s) électorale(s) fédérale(s):
Roberval-Lac-St-Jean
Prochaines élections: 1er novembre 2013
Régis Girard, Sec.-Trés. & Directeur général
Bernard Généreux, Maire

Saint-Prosper
2025, 29e rue
Saint-Prosper, QC G0M 1Y0
Tél: 418-594-8135; *Téléc:* 418-594-8865
stpros@globetrotter.qc.ca
www.saint-prosper.com
Entité municipal: Municipality
Incorporation: 26 septembre 1887 *Area:* 136, 95 km2
Comté ou district: Les Etchemins; *Population au 2006:* 3,612
Circonscription(s) électorale(s) provinciale(s): Beauce-Sud
Circonscription(s) électorale(s) fédérale(s): Beauce
Prochaines élections: 3e novembre 2013
Richard Couët, Maire
Johanne Nadeau, Directrice générale

Saint-Prosper-de-Champlain
CP 68
375, rue St-Joseph
Saint-Prosper, QC G0X 3A0
Tél: 418-840-0461; *Téléc:* 418-328-4267
municipalite@st-prosper.ca
www.st-prosper.ca
Entité municipal: Parish (Paroisse)
Incorporation: 1er juillet 1855 *Area:* 92,03 km2
Comté ou district: Les Chenaux; *Population au 2006:* 541
Circonscription(s) électorale(s) provinciale(s): Champlain
Circonscription(s) électorale(s) fédérale(s):
St-Maurice-Champlain
Prochaines élections: 3e novembre 2013
Michel Grosleau, Maire
Francine Masse, Directrice générale

Saint-Raphaël
CP 1091
19, av Chanoine-Audet
Saint-Raphaël, QC G0R 4C0
Tél: 418-243-2853; *Téléc:* 418-243-2605
muraph@globetrotter.net
www.municipalite.saint-raphael.qc.ca
Entité municipal: Municipality
Incorporation: 8 décembre 1993 *Area:* 120,06 km2
Comté ou district: Bellechasse; *Population au 2006:* 2,301
Circonscription(s) électorale(s) provinciale(s): Bellechasse
Circonscription(s) électorale(s) fédérale(s): Lévis-Bellechasse
Prochaines élections: 3e novembre 2013
Gilles Breton, Maire
Paul Beaudoin, Directeur général

Saint-Raymond
375, rue St-Joseph
Saint-Raymond, QC G3L 1A1
Tél: 418-337-2202; *Téléc:* 418-337-2203
info@villesaintraymond.com
www.villesaintraymond.coma
Entité municipal: Town
Incorporation: 29 mars 1995 *Area:* 684,65 km2
Comté ou district: Portneuf; *Population au 2006:* 9,273
Circonscription(s) électorale(s) provinciale(s): Portneuf
Circonscription(s) électorale(s) fédérale(s):
Portneuf-Jacques-Cartier
Prochaines élections: 3e novembre 2013
Vacant, Maire
Chantal Plamandon, Greffière

Saint-Rémi
105, rue de la Mairie
Saint-Rémi, QC J0L 2L0
Tél: 450-454-3993; *Téléc:* 450-454-7978
administration@ville.saint-remi.qc.ca
www.ville.saint-remi.qc.ca
Entité municipal: Town
Incorporation: 20 septembre 1975 *Area:* 79,66 km2
Comté ou district: Les Jardins-de-Napierville; *Population au 2006:* 6,136
Circonscription(s) électorale(s) provinciale(s): Huntingdon
Circonscription(s) électorale(s) fédérale(s):
Beauharnois-Salaberry
Prochaines élections: 3e novembre 2013
Michel Lavoie, Maire
Diane Soucy, Greffier

Saint-Rémi-de-Tingwick
156A, rue Principale
Saint-Rémi-de-Tingwick, QC J0A 1K0
Tél: 819-359-2731; *Téléc:* 819-359-3532
info@st-remi-de-tingwick.qc.ca
Entité municipal: Parish (Paroisse)
Incorporation: 1er janvier 1882 *Area:* 72,18 km2
Comté ou district: Arthabaska; *Population au 2006:* 468
Circonscription(s) électorale(s) provinciale(s): Richmond
Circonscription(s) électorale(s) fédérale(s):
Richmond-Arthabaska
Prochaines élections: 3e novembre 2013
Estelle Luneau, Mairesse
Éva Fréchette, Directrice générale

Saint-René
778, rte Principale
Saint-René, QC G0M 1Z0
Tél: 418-382-5226; *Téléc:* 418-382-3655
muni.st.rene@globetrotter.net
Entité municipal: Parish (Paroisse)
Incorporation: 1er janvier 1945 *Area:* 61,53 km3
Comté ou district: Beauce-Sartigan; *Population au 2006:* 612
Circonscription(s) électorale(s) provinciale(s): Beauce-Sud
Circonscription(s) électorale(s) fédérale(s): Beauce
Prochaines élections: 3e novembre 2013
Jean-Guy Deblois, Maire
Michel Gilbert, Directeur général

Saint-René-de-Matane
CP 58
178, av St-René
Saint-René-de-Matane, QC G0J 3E0
Tél: 418-224-3306; *Téléc:* 418-224-3259
st-renedematane@mrcdematane.qc.ca
www.municipalite.st-rene-matane.qc.ca
Entité municipal: Municipality
Incorporation: 18 décembre 1982 *Area:* 255,58 km2
Comté ou district: Matane; *Population au 2006:* 1,070
Circonscription(s) électorale(s) provinciale(s): Matane
Circonscription(s) électorale(s) fédérale(s): Haute-Gaspésie-La Mitis-Matane-Matapédia
Prochaines élections: 3e novembre 2013
Roger Vaillancourt, Maire
Yvette Boulay, Directrice générale

Saint-Robert
CP 150
650, ch de St-Robert
Saint-Robert, QC J0G 1S0
Tél: 450-782-2844; *Téléc:* 450-782-2733
strobert@bas-richelieu.net
www.saintrobert.qc.ca

Entité municipal: Municipality
Incorporation: 17 octobre 1857 *Area:* 64,93 km2
Comté ou district: Pierre-De Saurel; *Population au 2009:* 1,757
Circonscription(s) électorale(s) provinciale(s): Richelieu
Circonscription(s) électorale(s) fédérale(s):
Bas-Richelieu-Nicolet-Bécanour
Prochaines élections: 3e novembre 2013
Gilles Salvas, Maire
Nathalie Lussier, Directrice générale

Saint-Robert-Bellarmin
10, rue Nadeau
Saint-Robert-Bellarmin, QC G0M 2E0
Tél: 418-582-3420; *Téléc:* 418-582-0052
mun-st-robert@bellarmin.ca
www.st-robertbellarmin.qc.ca
Entité municipal: Municipality
Incorporation: 1er janvier 1949 *Area:* 234,82 km2
Comté ou district: Le Granit; *Population au 2006:* 645
Circonscription(s) électorale(s) provinciale(s): Beauce-Sud
Circonscription(s) électorale(s) fédérale(s): Beauce
Prochaines élections: 3e novembre 2013
Jeannot Lachance, Maire
Suzanne Lescomb, Directrice générale

Saint-Roch-de-l'Achigan
CP 480
30, rue du Dr.-Wilfrid-Locat nord
Saint-Roch-de-l'Achigan, QC J0K 3H0
Tél: 450-588-2326; *Téléc:* 450-588-4478
mairie@saint-roch-de-lachigan.ca
www.strochlachigan.com
Entité municipal: Parish (Paroisse)
Incorporation: 1er juillet 1855 *Area:* 78,83 km2
Comté ou district: Montcalm; *Population au 2006:* 4,449
Circonscription(s) électorale(s) provinciale(s): Rousseau
Circonscription(s) électorale(s) fédérale(s): Montcalm
Prochaines élections: 3e novembre 2013
Georges Locas, Maire
Philippe Riopelle, Directeur général

Saint-Roch-de-Mékinac
1212, rue Principale
Saint-Roch-de-Mékinac, QC G0X 2E0
Tél: 819-646-5635; *Téléc:* 819-646-5635
st-roch@regionmekinac.com
www.strochdemekinac.com
Entité municipal: Parish (Paroisse)
Incorporation: 2 novembre 2009 *Area:* 155,39 km2
Comté ou district: Mékinac; *Population au 2006:* 324
Circonscription(s) électorale(s) provinciale(s): Laviolette
Circonscription(s) électorale(s) fédérale(s):
St-Maurice-Champlain
Prochaines élections: 3e novembre 2013
Guy Dessureault, Maire
Robert Jourdain, Directeur général

Saint-Roch-de-Richelieu
1111, rue du Parc
Saint-Roch-de-Richelieu, QC J0L 2M0
Tél: 450-785-2755; *Téléc:* 450-785-3098
stroch@pierredesaurel.com
www.saintrochderichelieu.qc.ca
Entité municipal: Municipality
Incorporation: 4 juin 1859 *Area:* 34,86 km2
Comté ou district: Pierre-De Saurel; *Population au 2006:* 1,870
Circonscription(s) électorale(s) provinciale(s): Verchères
Circonscription(s) électorale(s) fédérale(s):
Bas-Richelieu-Nicolet-Bécancour
Prochaines élections: 3e novembre 2013
Claude Pothier, Maire
Claude Gratton, Directeur général

Saint-Roch-des-Aulnaies
379, rte de l'Église
Saint-Roch-des-Aulnaies, QC G0R 4E0
Tél: 418-354-2892; *Téléc:* 418-354-2059
munirock@globetrotter.net
www.saintrochdesaulnaies.ca
Entité municipal: Parish (Paroisse)
Incorporation: 1er juillet 1855 *Area:* 48,28 km2
Comté ou district: L'Islet; *Population au 2006:* 939
Circonscription(s) électorale(s) provinciale(s):
Kamouraska-Témiscouata
Circonscription(s) électorale(s) fédérale(s):
Montmorency-Charlevoix-Haute-Côte-Nord
Prochaines élections: 3e novembre 2013
Cécile Morin, Directrice générale
Michel Castonguay, Maire

Saint-Roch-Ouest
806, rang de la Rivière sud, RR#2
Saint-Roch-Ouest, QC J0K 3H0
Tél: 450-588-6060; *Téléc:* 450-588-0975
stroch_ouest@hotmail.com
Entité municipal: Municipality
Incorporation: 4 juin 1921 *Area:* 20,90 km2
Comté ou district: Montcalm; *Population au 2006:* 285
Circonscription(s) électorale(s) provinciale(s): Rousseau
Circonscription(s) électorale(s) fédérale(s): Montcalm
Prochaines élections: 3e novembre 2013
Claude Mercier, Maire
Sherron Kollar, Directrice générale

Saint-Romain
355, rue Principale
Saint-Romain, QC G0Y 1L0
Tél: 418-486-7374; *Téléc:* 418-486-7875
municipalite-st-romain@tellambton.net
Entité municipal: Municipality
Incorporation: 1er janvier 1858 *Area:* 112,92 km2
Comté ou district: Le Granit; *Population au 2006:* 628
Circonscription(s) électorale(s) provinciale(s):
Mégantic-Compton
Circonscription(s) électorale(s) fédérale(s): Mégantic-L'Érable
Prochaines élections: 3e novembre 2013
Jean-Luc Filion, Maire
Nicole P. Roy, Directrice générale

Saint-Rosaire
208, 6e rang
Saint-Rosaire, QC G0Z 1K0
Tél: 819-752-6178; *Téléc:* 819-752-3959
info@municipalitestrosaire.qc.ca
www.municipalitestrosaire.qc.ca
Entité municipal: Parish (Paroisse)
Incorporation: 23 mai 1896 *Area:* 109,84 km2
Comté ou district: Arthabaska; *Population au 2007:* 776
Circonscription(s) électorale(s) provinciale(s): Arthabaska
Circonscription(s) électorale(s) fédérale(s):
Richmond-Arthabaska
Prochaines élections: 3e novembre 2013
Harold Poisson, Maire
Jacques Boucher, Directeur général

Saint-Samuel
140, rue de l'Église
Saint-Samuel, QC G0Z 1G0
Tél: 819-353-1242; *Téléc:* 819-353-1499
info@saint-samuel.ca
www.saint-samuel.ca
Entité municipal: Parish (Paroisse)
Incorporation: 9 mars 1878 *Area:* 42,89 km2
Comté ou district: Arthabaska; *Population au 2006:* 673
Circonscription(s) électorale(s) provinciale(s): Richmond
Circonscription(s) électorale(s) fédérale(s):
Richmond-Arthabaska
Prochaines élections: 3e novembre 2013
René Mongrain, Maire
Suzie Constant, Directrice générale

Saint-Sauveur
1, place de la Mairie
Saint-Sauveur, QC J0R 1R6
Tél: 450-227-4633; *Téléc:* 450-227-3834
directiongenerale@ville.saint-sauveur.qc.ca
www.ville.saint-sauveur.qc.ca
Entité municipal: Town
Incorporation: 11 septembre 2002 *Area:* 47,99 km2
Comté ou district: Les Pays-d'en-Haut; *Population au 2006:* 9,191
Circonscription(s) électorale(s) provinciale(s): Bertrand
Circonscription(s) électorale(s) fédérale(s): Laurentides-Labelle
Prochaines élections: 3e novembre 2013
Note: Effective September 9, 2002, the Parish of St-Sauveur & the Village of St-Sauveur-des-Monts amalgamated to create the City of St-Sauveur.
Michel Lagacé, Maire
Normand Patrice, Greffier

Saint-Sébastien
582, rue Principale
Saint-Sébastien, QC G0Y 1M0
Tél: 819-652-2727; *Téléc:* 819-652-2584
st-sebastien@bellnet.ca
www.st-sebastien.com
Entité municipal: Municipality
Incorporation: 15 mars 1975 *Area:* 91,19 km2
Comté ou district: Le Granit; *Population au 2006:* 752
Circonscription(s) électorale(s) provinciale(s):
Mégantic-Compton
Circonscription(s) électorale(s) fédérale(s): Mégantic-L'Érable
Prochaines élections: 3e novembre 2013
Marie Douce Morin, Mairesse
Martine Rouleau, Directrice générale

Saint-Sébastien
CP 126
176, rue Dussault
Saint-Sébastien, QC J0J 2C0
Tél: 450-244-5237; *Téléc:* 450-244-6264
muniseba@netc.net
www.paroisse-saint-sebastien.ca
Entité municipal: Parish (Paroisse)
Incorporation: 17 février 1865 *Area:* 62,56 km2
Comté ou district: Le Haut-Richelieu; *Population au 2006:* 682
Circonscription(s) électorale(s) provinciale(s): Iberville
Circonscription(s) électorale(s) fédérale(s): Brome-Missisquoi
Prochaines élections: 3e novembre 2013
Michel Surprenant, Maire
Manon Donais, Directrice générale

Saint-Sévère
47, rue Principale
Saint-Sévère, QC G0X 3B0
Tél: 819-264-5656; *Téléc:* 819-264-5656
paroissestsevere@hotmail.com
Entité municipal: Parish (Paroisse)
Incorporation: 1er juillet 1855 *Area:* 31,83 km2
Comté ou district: Maskinongé; *Population au 2006:* 329
Circonscription(s) électorale(s) provinciale(s): Maskinongé
Circonscription(s) électorale(s) fédérale(s): Berthier-Maskinongé
Prochaines élections: 1er novembre 2013
Anne-Marie Sauvageau, Sec.-Trés. & Directrice générale
Yves Gélinas, Maire

Saint-Séverin
900, rue des Lacs
Saint-Séverin, QC G0N 1V0
Tél: 418-426-2423; *Téléc:* 418-426-1274
munseverin@oricom.ca
www.st-severin.qc.ca
Entité municipal: Parish (Paroisse)
Incorporation: 24 décembre 1875 *Area:* 56,22 km2
Comté ou district: Robert-Cliche; *Population au 2006:* 279
Circonscription(s) électorale(s) provinciale(s): Beauce-Nord
Circonscription(s) électorale(s) fédérale(s): Beauce
Prochaines élections: 3e novembre 2013
Daniel Perron, Maire
Paul Baker, Directeur général

Saint-Séverin
CP 120
1986, place du Centre
Saint-Séverin, QC G0X 2B0
Tél: 418-365-5844; *Téléc:* 418-365-7544
st-severin@regionmekinac.com
Entité municipal: Parish (Paroisse)
Incorporation: 11 avril 1890 *Area:* 61,97 km2
Comté ou district: Mékinac; *Population au 2006:* 859
Circonscription(s) électorale(s) provinciale(s): Laviolette
Circonscription(s) électorale(s) fédérale(s):
St-Maurice-Champlain
Prochaines élections: 3e novembre 2013
Michel Champagne, Maire
Jocelyn St-Amant, Directeur général

Saint-Siméon
CP 98
502, rue St-Laurent
Saint-Siméon, QC G0T 1X0
Tél: 418-638-2691; *Téléc:* 418-638-5145
info@saintsimeon.ca
www.saintsimeon.ca
Entité municipal: Municipality
Incorporation: 25 avril 2001 *Area:* 289,73 km2
Comté ou district: Charlevoix-Est; *Population au 2006:* 1,360
Circonscription(s) électorale(s) provinciale(s): Charlevoix
Circonscription(s) électorale(s) fédérale(s):
Montmorency-Charlevoix-Haute-Côte-Nord
Prochaines élections: 3e novembre 2013
Sylvain Tremblay, Maire
Sylvie Foster, Directrice générale

Saint-Siméon
CP 39
111, av de l'Église
Saint-Siméon, QC G0C 3A0
Tél: 418-534-2155; *Téléc:* 418-534-3830
munsseon@globetrotter.net
Entité municipal: Parish (Paroisse)
Incorporation: 29 octobre 1914 *Area:* 56,12 km2
Comté ou district: Bonaventure; *Population au 2006:* 1,174

Circonscription(s) électorale(s) provinciale(s): Bonaventure
Circonscription(s) électorale(s) fédérale(s):
Gaspésie—Îles-de-la-Madeleine
Prochaines élections: 3e novembre 2013
Jean-Guy Poirier, Maire
Jean-Pierre Gauthier, Directeur général

Saint-Simon
CP 40
30, rue de l'Église
Saint-Simon, QC G0L 4C0
Tél: 418-738-2896; *Téléc:* 418-738-2934
admin@st-simon.qc.ca
www.st-simon.qc.ca
Entité municipal: Parish (Paroisse)
Incorporation: 1er juillet 1855 *Area:* 75,62 km2
Comté ou district: Les Basques; *Population au 2006:* 437
Circonscription(s) électorale(s) provinciale(s): Rivière-du-Loup
Circonscription(s) électorale(s) fédérale(s):
Rimouski-Neigette-Témiscouata-Les Basques
Prochaines élections: 3e novembre 2013
Jérôme Rouleau, Maire
Yolande Théberge, Directrice générale

Saint-Simon
49, rue du Couvent
Saint-Simon-de-Bagot, QC J0H 1Y0
Tél: 450-798-2276; *Téléc:* 450-798-2498
st-simon@mrcmaskoutains.qc.ca
www.saint-simon.ca
Entité municipal: Parish (Paroisse)
Incorporation: 1er juillet 1855 *Area:* 68,66 km2
Comté ou district: Les Maskoutains; *Population au 2006:* 1,228
Circonscription(s) électorale(s) provinciale(s): St-Hyacinthe
Circonscription(s) électorale(s) fédérale(s): St-Hyacinthe-Bagot
Prochaines élections: 3e novembre 2013
Normand Corbeil, Maire
France Desjardins, Directrice générale

Saint-Simon-les-Mines
3338, rue Principale
Saint-Simon-les-Mines, QC G0M 1K0
Tél: 418-774-3317; *Téléc:* 418-774-3362
municipalitestsimonlesmines@sogetel.net
Entité municipal: Municipality
Incorporation: 1er juin 1950 *Area:* 44,80 km2
Comté ou district: Beauce-Sartigan; *Population au 2006:* 473
Circonscription(s) électorale(s) provinciale(s): Beauce-Sud
Circonscription(s) électorale(s) fédérale(s): Beauce
Prochaines élections: 3e novembre 2013
Martin Busque, Maire
Francine Poulin, Directrice générale

Saint-Sixte
5, rue Emery
Saint-Sixte, QC J0X 3B0
Tél: 819-983-3155; *Téléc:* 819-983-3409
Entité municipal: Municipality
Incorporation: 7 février 1893 *Area:* 83,44 km2
Comté ou district: Papineau; *Population au 2006:* 466
Circonscription(s) électorale(s) provinciale(s): Papineau
Circonscription(s) électorale(s) fédérale(s):
Argenteuil-Papineau-Mirabel
Prochaines élections: 3e novembre 2013
André Bélisle, Maire
Alain Hotte, Directeur général
alain.saintsixte@mrcpapineau.com

Saint-Stanislas
33, rue du Pont
Saint-Stanislas, QC G0X 3E0
Tél: 819-840-0703; *Téléc:* 418-328-4121
municipalite@saint-stanislas.ca
www.saint-stanislas.ca
Entité municipal: Municipality
Incorporation: 17 avril 1976 *Area:* 86,37 km2
Comté ou district: Les Chenaux; *Population au 2006:* 1,033
Circonscription(s) électorale(s) provinciale(s): Champlain
Circonscription(s) électorale(s) fédérale(s):
St-Maurice-Champlain
Prochaines élections: 3e novembre 2013
Alain Guillemette, Maire
Marc-Claude Jean, Directrice générale

Saint-Stanislas
953, rue Principale
Saint-Stanislas, QC G8L 7B4
Tél: 418-276-4476; *Téléc:* 418-276-9947
admin@st-stanislas.qc.ca
Entité municipal: Municipality
Incorporation: 24 octobre 1931 *Area:* 159,45 km2
Comté ou district: Maria-Chapdelaine; *Population au 2006:* 345
Circonscription(s) électorale(s) provinciale(s): Roberval
Circonscription(s) électorale(s) fédérale(s):
Roberval-Lac-St-Jean
Prochaines élections: 3e novembre 2013
Mario Biron, Maire
Caroline Gagnon, Directrice générale

Saint-Stanislas-de-Kostka
CP 120
221, rue Centrale
Saint-Stanislas-de-Kostka, QC J0S 1W0
Tél: 450-373-8944; *Téléc:* 450-373-8949
info@st-stanislas-de-kostka.ca
www.st-stanislas-de-kostka.ca
Entité municipal: Parish (Paroisse)
Incorporation: 1er juillet 1855 *Area:* 62,16 km2
Comté ou district: Beauharnois-Salaberry; *Population au 2006:* 1,668
Circonscription(s) électorale(s) provinciale(s): Beauharnois
Circonscription(s) électorale(s) fédérale(s):
Beauharnois-Salaberry
Prochaines élections: 3e novembre 2013
Jean-Pierre Gaboury, Maire
Louise Maheu Denis, Directrice générale

Saint-Sulpice
1089, rue Notre-Dame
Saint-Sulpice, QC J5W 1G1
Tél: 450-589-4450; *Téléc:* 450-589-9647
mun.paroissestsulpice@videotron.ca
www.municipalitesaintsulpice.com
Entité municipal: Parish (Paroisse)
Incorporation: 1er juillet 1855 *Area:* 37 km2
Comté ou district: L'Assomption; *Population au 2006:* 3,332
Circonscription(s) électorale(s) provinciale(s): L'Assomption
Circonscription(s) électorale(s) fédérale(s): Repentigny
Prochaines élections: 3e novembre 2013
Jean Gendron, Maire
Marie-Josée Masson, Directrice générale

Saint-Sylvère
837, 8e rang
Saint-Sylvère, QC G0Z 1H0
Tél: 819-285-2075; *Téléc:* 819-285-2040
mun.st.sylvere@infoteck.qc.ca
www.saint-sylvere.ca
Entité municipal: Municipality
Incorporation: 18 septembre 1976 *Area:* 85,02 km2
Comté ou district: Bécancour; *Population au 2006:* 686
Circonscription(s) électorale(s) provinciale(s): Nicolet-Yamaska
Circonscription(s) électorale(s) fédérale(s):
Bas-Richelieu-Nicolet-Bécancour
Prochaines élections: 3e novembre 2013
Claude Beaudoin, Maire
Ginette Richard, Directrice générale

Saint-Sylvestre
CP 70
423B, rue Principale
Saint-Sylvestre, QC G0S 3C0
Tél: 418-596-2384; *Téléc:* 418-596-2375
munisylvestre@altanet.ca
www.ville.saint-sylvestre.qc.ca
Entité municipal: Municipality
Incorporation: 4 décembre 1996 *Area:* 143,34 km2
Comté ou district: Lotbinière; *Population au 2006:* 973
Circonscription(s) électorale(s) provinciale(s): Lotbinière
Circonscription(s) électorale(s) fédérale(s):
Lotbinière-Chutes-de-la-Chaudière
Prochaines élections: 3e novembre 2013
Mario Grenier, Maire
Ginette Roger, Directrice générale

Saint-Télesphore
1425, rte 340
Saint-Télesphore, QC J0P 1Y0
Tél: 450-269-2999; *Téléc:* 450-269-2257
st-telesphore@xittel.ca
Entité municipal: Parish (Paroisse)
Incorporation: 10 avril 1877 *Area:* 59,62 km2
Comté ou district: Vaudreuil-Soulanges; *Population au 2006:* 769
Circonscription(s) électorale(s) provinciale(s): Soulanges
Circonscription(s) électorale(s) fédérale(s): Vaudreuil-Soulanges
Prochaines élections: 3e
Yvon Bériault, Maire
Nicole St-Pierre, Directrice générale

Saint-Tharcisius
CP 10
55, rue Principale
Saint-Tharcisius, QC G0J 3G0
Tél: 418-629-4727; *Téléc:* 418-629-4727
sttharcisius@mrcmatapedia.qc.ca
Entité municipal: Parish (Paroisse)
Incorporation: 4 décembre 2009 *Area:* 79,61 km2
Comté ou district: La Matapédia; *Population au 2006:* 480
Circonscription(s) électorale(s) provinciale(s): Matapédia
Circonscription(s) électorale(s) fédérale(s): Haute-Gaspésie-La Mitis-Matane-Matapédia
Prochaines élections: 3e novembre 2013
Sophie Champagne, Mairesse
Joyce Kathie Collin, Directrice générale

Saint-Théodore-d-Acton
1661, rue Principale
Saint-Théodore-d-Acton, QC J0H 1Z0
Tél: 450-546-2634; *Téléc:* 450-546-2526
mun.st-theo@mrcacton.qc.ca
www.st-theodore.com
Entité municipal: Parish (Paroisse)
Incorporation: 1er janvier 1864 *Area:* 83,60 km2
Comté ou district: Acton; *Population au 2006:* 1,494
Circonscription(s) électorale(s) provinciale(s): Johnson
Circonscription(s) électorale(s) fédérale(s): St-Hyacinthe-Bagot
Prochaines élections: 3e novembre 2013
Dany Larivière, Maire
Marc Lévesque, Directeur générale

Saint-Théophile
CP 10
644, rue du Collège
Saint-Théophile, QC G0M 2A0
Tél: 418-597-3998; *Téléc:* 418-597-3015
muntheo@globetrotter.net
www.sainttheophile.qc.ca
Entité municipal: Municipality
Incorporation: 28 juin 1975 *Area:* 429,58 km2
Comté ou district: Beauce-Sartigan; *Population au 2006:* 776
Circonscription(s) électorale(s) provinciale(s): Beauce-Sud
Circonscription(s) électorale(s) fédérale(s): Beauce
Prochaines élections: 3e novembre 2013
Roland Boucher, Maire
Paula Lacoursière, Directrice générale

Saint-Thomas
1240, rte 158
Saint-Thomas, QC J0K 3L0
Tél: 450-759-3405; *Téléc:* 450-759-0059
municipalite@saintthomas.qc.ca
www.saintthomas.qc.ca
Entité municipal: Municipality
Incorporation: 1er juillet 1855 *Area:* 97,26 km2
Comté ou district: Joliette; *Population au 2006:* 2,861
Circonscription(s) électorale(s) provinciale(s): Joliette
Circonscription(s) électorale(s) fédérale(s): Joliette
Prochaines élections: 3e novembre 2013
Renè Vincent, Maire
Danielle Lambert, Directrice générale

Saint-Thomas-Didyme
9, av du Moulin
Saint-Thomas-Didyme, QC G0W 1P0
Tél: 418-274-3638; *Téléc:* 418-274-4176
www.stthomasdidyme.qc.ca
Entité municipal: Municipality
Incorporation: 11 mai 1923 *Area:* 325,36 km2
Comté ou district: Maria-Chapdelaine; *Population au 2006:* 708
Circonscription(s) électorale(s) provinciale(s): Roberval
Circonscription(s) électorale(s) fédérale(s):
Roberval-Lac-St-Jean
Prochaines élections: 3e novembre 2013
Denis Tremblay, Maire
Jean-Marc Paradis, Directeur général
jmparadis@stthomasdidyme.qc.ca

Saint-Thuribe
CP 69
385, rue Principale
Saint-Thuribe, QC G0A 4H0
Tél: 418-339-2171; *Téléc:* 418-339-3435
municipalitestthuribe@globetrotter.net
www.st-thuribe.net
Entité municipal: Parish (Paroisse)
Incorporation: 14 février 1898 *Area:* 50,81 km2
Comté ou district: Portneuf; *Population au 2006:* 303
Circonscription(s) électorale(s) provinciale(s): Portneuf
Circonscription(s) électorale(s) fédérale(s):
Portneuf-Jacques-Cartier
Prochaines élections: 3e novembre 2013

Richard Genest, Maire
Sylvie Groleau, Directrice générale

Saint-Tite
540, rue Notre-Dame
Saint-Tite, QC G0X 3H0
Tél: 418-365-5143; *Téléc:* 418-365-4020
www.villest-tite.com
Entité municipal: Town
Incorporation: 23 décembre 1998 *Area:* 91,01 km2
Comté ou district: Mékinac; *Population au 2006:* 3,826
Circonscription(s) électorale(s) provinciale(s): Laviolette
Circonscription(s) électorale(s) fédérale(s): St-Maurice-Champlain
Prochaines élections: 3e novembre 2013
André Léveillé, Maire
Pierre Massicotte, Directeur général
pmassicotte@villest-tite.com

Saint-Tite-des-Caps
1, rue Leclerc
Saint-Tite-des-Caps, QC G0A 4J0
Tél: 418-823-2239; *Téléc:* 418-823-2527
sainttitedescaps@videotron.ca
www.sainttitedescaps.com
Entité municipal: Municipality
Incorporation: 24 décembre 1872 *Area:* 130,01 km2
Comté ou district: La Côte-de-Beaupré; *Population au 2006:* 1,440
Circonscription(s) électorale(s) provinciale(s): Charlevoix
Circonscription(s) électorale(s) fédérale(s): Montmorency-Charlevoix-Haute-Côte-Nord
Prochaines élections: 3e novembre 2013
Pierre Dion, Maire
Marc Lachance, Directeur général

Saint-Ubalde
427B, boul Chabot
Saint-Ubalde, QC G0A 4L0
Tél: 418-277-2124; *Téléc:* 418-277-2055
info@saintubalde.com
www.st-ubalde.qc.ca
Entité municipal: Municipality
Incorporation: 3 mars 1973 *Area:* 141,28 km2
Comté ou district: Portneuf; *Population au 2006:* 1,458
Circonscription(s) électorale(s) provinciale(s): Portneuf
Circonscription(s) électorale(s) fédérale(s): Portneuf-Jacques-Cartier
Prochaines élections: 3e novembre 2013
Pierre Saint-Germain, Maire
Serge Deraspe, Directeur général

Saint-Ulric
128, av Ulric-Tessier
Saint-Ulric, QC G0J 3H0
Tél: 418-737-4341; *Téléc:* 418-737-9242
st-ulric@mrcdematane.qc.ca
www.st-ulric.ca
Entité municipal: Municipality
Incorporation: 12 janvier 2000 *Area:* 118,68 km2
Comté ou district: Matane; *Population au 2006:* 1,696
Circonscription(s) électorale(s) provinciale(s): Matane
Circonscription(s) électorale(s) fédérale(s): Haute-Gaspésie-La Mitis-Matane-Matapédia
Prochaines élections: 3e novembre 2013
Pierre Thibodeau, Maire
Louise Coll, Directrice générale

Saint-Urbain
CP 100
917, rue St-Édouard
Saint-Urbain, QC G0A 4K0
Tél: 418-639-2467; *Téléc:* 418-639-1056
munsturb@sainturbain.qc.ca
www.sainturbain.qc.ca
Entité municipal: Parish (Paroisse)
Incorporation: 1er juilllet 1855 *Area:* 327,68 km2
Comté ou district: Charlevoix; *Population au 2006:* 1,448
Circonscription(s) électorale(s) provinciale(s): Charlevoix
Circonscription(s) électorale(s) fédérale(s): Montmorency-Charlevoix-Haute-Côte-Nord
Prochaines élections: 3e novembre 2013
Claudette Siomard, Mairesse
Josée Desmeules, Directrice générale

Saint-Urbain-Premier
204, rue Principale
Saint-Urbain-Premier, QC J0S 1Y0
Tél: 450-427-3987; *Téléc:* 450-427-2056
dg.sainturbainpremier@videotron.ca
www.saint-urbain-premier.com
Entité municipal: Municipality
Incorporation: 1er juillet 1855 *Area:* 52,24
Comté ou district: Beauharnois-Salaberry; *Population au 2006:* 1,129
Circonscription(s) électorale(s) provinciale(s): Huntingdon
Circonscription(s) électorale(s) fédérale(s): Beauharnois-Salaberry
Prochaines élections: 3e novembre 2013
Réjean Beaulieu, Maire
Michael Morneau, Directeur général

Saint-Valentin
790, ch de la Quatrième-Ligne
Saint-Valentin, QC J0J 2E0
Tél: 450-291-5422; *Téléc:* 450-291-5327
administration@municipalite.saint-valentin.qc.ca
Entité municipal: Parish (Paroisse)
Incorporation: 1er juillet 1855 *Area:* 40,09 km2
Comté ou district: Le Haut-Richelieu; *Population au 2006:* 478
Circonscription(s) électorale(s) provinciale(s): Huntingdon
Circonscription(s) électorale(s) fédérale(s): St-Jean
Prochaines élections: 3e novembre 2013
Pierre Chamberland, Maire
Serge Gibeau, Directeur général

Saint-Valère
2, rue du Parc
Saint-Valère, QC G0P 1M0
Tél: 819-353-3450; *Téléc:* 819-353-3459
stvalere@msvalere.qc.ca
www.msvalere.qc.ca
Entité municipal: Municipality
Incorporation: 1er janvier 1862 *Area:* 108,13 km2
Comté ou district: Arthabaska; *Population au 2006:* 1,299
Circonscription(s) électorale(s) provinciale(s): Arthabaska
Circonscription(s) électorale(s) fédérale(s): Richmond-Arthabaska
Prochaines élections: 3e novembre 2013
Louis Hébert, Maire
Jocelyn Jutras, Directeur général

Saint-Valérien
CP 9
181, rte Centrale
Saint-Valérien-de-Rimouski, QC G0L 4E0
Tél: 418-736-5047; *Téléc:* 418-736-5922
valerien@globetrotter.net
www.municipalite.saint-valerien.qc.ca
Entité municipal: Parish (Paroisse)
Incorporation: 19 juin 1885 *Area:* 149,69 km2
Comté ou district: Rimouski-Neigette; *Population au 2006:* 835
Circonscription(s) électorale(s) provinciale(s): Rimouski
Circonscription(s) électorale(s) fédérale(s): Rimouski-Neigette-Témiscouata-Les Basques
Prochaines élections: 3e novembre 2013
Robert Savoie, Maire
Marie-Paule Cimon, Directrice générale

Saint-Valérien-de-Milton
960, ch de Milton
Saint-Valérien-de-Milton, QC J0H 2B0
Tél: 450-549-2463; *Téléc:* 450-549-2993
administration.st-valerien@mrcmaskoutains.qc.ca
www.st-valerien-de-milton.qc.ca
Entité municipal: Township
Incorporation: 1er janvier 1864 *Area:* 106,44 km2
Comté ou district: Les Maskoutains; *Population au 2006:* 1,718
Circonscription(s) électorale(s) provinciale(s): Johnson
Circonscription(s) électorale(s) fédérale(s): St-Hyacinthe-Bagot
Prochaines élections: 3e novembre 2013
Raymonde Plamondon, Mairesse
Robert Leclerc, Directeur général

Saint-Vallier
375, montée de la Station
Saint-Vallier, QC G0R 4J0
Tél: 418-884-2559; *Téléc:* 418-884-2454
svallier@globetrotter.net
www.stvallierbellechasse.qc.ca
Entité municipal: Municipality
Incorporation: 10 mars 1993 *Area:* 42,24 km2
Comté ou district: Bellechasse; *Population au 2006:* 1,044
Circonscription(s) électorale(s) provinciale(s): Bellechasse
Circonscription(s) électorale(s) fédérale(s): Lévis-Bellechasse
Prochaines élections: 3e novembre 2013
Gilbert Vallières, Maire
Claire St-Laurent, Directrice générale

Saint-Venant-de-Paquette
5, ch du Village
Saint-Venant-de-Paquette, QC J0B 1S0
Tél: 819-658-3660; *Téléc:* 819-658-0985
stvenant@axion.ca
www.regioncoaticook.qc.ca/stvenant
Entité municipal: Municipality
Incorporation: 11 juin 1917 *Area:* 58,17 km2
Comté ou district: Coaticook; *Population au 2006:* 81
Circonscription(s) électorale(s) provinciale(s): Mégantic-Compton
Circonscription(s) électorale(s) fédérale(s): Compton-Stanstead
Prochaines élections: 3e novembre 2013
Henri Pariseau, Maire
Manon Jacques, Directeur général

Saint-Vianney
CP 39
170, av Centrale
Saint-Vianney, QC G0J 3J0
Tél: 418-629-4082; *Téléc:* 418-629-4821
stvianney@mrcmatapedia.qc.ca
Entité municipal: Municipality
Incorporation: 27 août 1926 *Area:* 145,24 km2
Comté ou district: La Matapédia; *Population au 2006:* 489
Circonscription(s) électorale(s) provinciale(s): Matapédia
Circonscription(s) électorale(s) fédérale(s): Haute-Gaspésie-La Mitis-Matane-Matapédia
Prochaines élections: 3e novembre 2013
Georges Guénard, Maire
Roselle Caron, Directrice générale

Saint-Victor
CP 40
287, rue Marchand
Saint-Victor, QC G0M 2B0
Tél: 418-588-6854; *Téléc:* 418-588-6855
saint-vic@telvic.net
Entité municipal: Municipality
Incorporation: 31 décembre 1996 *Area:* 120,94 km2
Comté ou district: Robert-Cliche; *Population au 2006:* 2,553
Circonscription(s) électorale(s) provinciale(s): Beauce-Nord
Circonscription(s) électorale(s) fédérale(s): Beauce
Prochaines élections: 3e novembre 2013
Roland Giguère, Maire
Marc Bélanger, Directeur général

Saint-Wenceslas
1065, rue Richard
Saint-Wenceslas, QC G0Z 1J0
Tél: 819-224-7784; *Téléc:* 819-224-4036
mun.stwen@sogetel.net
www.municipalitestwenceslas.com
Entité municipal: Municipality
Incorporation: 11 octobre 1995 *Area:* 78,42 km2
Comté ou district: Nicolet-Yamaska; *Population au 2006:* 1,101
Circonscription(s) électorale(s) provinciale(s): Nicolet-Yamaska
Circonscription(s) électorale(s) fédérale(s): Bas-Richelieu-Nicolet-Bécancour
Prochaines élections: 3e novembre 2013
Raymond Bilodeau, Maire
Carole Hélie, Directrice générale

Saint-Zacharie
735, 15e rue
Saint-Zacharie, QC G0M 2C0
Tél: 418-593-3185; *Téléc:* 418-593-3085
munzac@cablezach.com
www.st-zacharie.qc.ca
Entité municipal: Municipality
Incorporation: 18 avril 1990 *Area:* 189,70 km2
Comté ou district: Les Etchemins; *Population au 2006:* 1,918
Circonscription(s) électorale(s) provinciale(s): Beauce-Sud
Circonscription(s) électorale(s) fédérale(s): Beauce
Prochaines élections: 3e novembre 2013
Jean Paradis, Maire
Brigitte Larivière, Dirctrice générale

Saint-Zénon
6101, rue Principale
Saint-Zénon, QC J0K 3N0
Tél: 450-884-5987; *Téléc:* 450-884-5285
municipalite@st-zenon.net
www.st-zenon.org
Entité municipal: Municipality
Incorporation: 7 octobre 1895 *Area:* 488,69 km2
Comté ou district: Matawinie; *Population au 2006:* 1,379
Circonscription(s) électorale(s) provinciale(s): Berthier
Circonscription(s) électorale(s) fédérale(s): Joliette
Prochaines élections: 3e novembre 2013
Murielle Richard, Mairesse
Alain St-Vincent-Rioux, Directeur général

Saint-Zénon-du-Lac-Humqui
CP 39
156, rte 195
Lac-Humqui, QC G0J 1N0
Tél: 418-743-2177; *Téléc:* 418-743-2177
lachumqui@mrcmatapedia.qc.ca
Entité municipal: Parish (Paroisse)
Incorporation: 28 avril 1920 *Area:* 112,97 km2
Comté ou district: La Matapédia; *Population au 2006:* 426
Circonscription(s) électorale(s) provinciale(s): Matapédia
Circonscription(s) électorale(s) fédérale(s): Haute-Gaspésie-La Mitis-Matane-Matapédia
Prochaines élections: 1er novembre 2013
Maryline Pronovost, Sec.-Trés. & Directrice générale
Réginald Duguay, Maire

Saint-Zéphirin-de-Courval
CP 40
1471, rue St-Pierre
Saint-Zéphirin-de-Courval, QC J0G 1V0
Tél: 450-564-2188; *Téléc:* 450-564-2339
municipalite@saint-zephirin.ca
www.saint-zephirin.ca
Entité municipal: Parish (Paroisse)
Incorporation: 1er juillet 1855 *Area:* 71,01 km2
Comté ou district: Nicolet-Yamaska; *Population au 2006:* 825
Circonscription(s) électorale(s) provinciale(s): Nicolet-Yamaska
Circonscription(s) électorale(s) fédérale(s): Bas-Richelieu-Nicolet-Bécancour
Prochaines élections: 3e novembre 2013
Raymond Lemaire, Maire
Hélène Chassé, Directrice générale

Saint-Zotique
1250, rue Principale
Saint-Zotique, QC J0P 1Z0
Tél: 450-267-9335; *Téléc:* 450-267-0907
dg@st-zotique.com
www.st-zotique.com
Entité municipal: Village
Incorporation: 27 mai 1967 *Area:* 24,24 km2
Comté ou district: Vaudreuil-Soulanges; *Population au 2006:* 5,251
Circonscription(s) électorale(s) provinciale(s): Soulanges
Circonscription(s) électorale(s) fédérale(s): Vaudreuil-Soulanges
Prochaines élections: 3e novembre 2013
Gaëtane Legault, Mairesse
Jean-François Messier, Directeur général

Sainte-Agathe-de-Lotbinière
CP 159
254, rue St-Pierre
Sainte-Agathe-de-Lotbinière, QC G0S 2A0
Tél: 418-599-2605; *Téléc:* 418-599-2905
administration@coopsteagathe.com
www.ste-agathelotb.qc.ca
Entité municipal: Municipality
Incorporation: 3 février 1999 *Area:* 169,50 km2
Comté ou district: Lotbinière; *Population au 2006:* 1,202
Circonscription(s) électorale(s) provinciale(s): Lotbinière
Circonscription(s) électorale(s) fédérale(s): Lotbinière-Chutes-de-la-Chaudière
Prochaines élections: 3e novembre 2013
Michel Champagne, Maire
André Castonguay, Directeur général

Sainte-Agathe-des-Monts
50, rue St-Joseph
Sainte-Agathe-des-Monts, QC J8C 1M9
Tél: 819-326-4595; *Téléc:* 819-326-5784
info@ville.sainte-agathe-des-monts.qc.ca
www.ville.sainte-agathe-des-monts.qc.ca
Entité municipal: Town
Incorporation: 27 février 2002 *Area:* 129,03 km2
Comté ou district: Les Laurentides; *Population au 2006:* 9,679
Circonscription(s) électorale(s) provinciale(s): Bertrand
Circonscription(s) électorale(s) fédérale(s): Laurentides-Labelle
Prochaines élections: 3e novembre 2013
Denis Chalifoux, Maire
Benoît Fugère, Greffier

Sainte-Angèle-de-Mérici
CP 129
23, rue de la Fabrique
Sainte-Angèle-de-Mérici, QC G0J 2H0
Tél: 418-775-7733; *Téléc:* 418-775-5722
steangele@mitis.qc.ca
www.municipalite.sainte-angele-de-merici.qc.ca
Entité municipal: Municipality
Incorporation: 26 avril 1989 *Area:* 108,41 km2
Comté ou district: La Mitis; *Population au 2006:* 1,068
Circonscription(s) électorale(s) provinciale(s): Matapédia
Circonscription(s) électorale(s) fédérale(s): Haute-Gaspésie-La Mitis-Matane-Matapédia
Prochaines élections: 3e novembre 2013
Alain Carrier, Maire
Marielle Dionne, Directrice générale

Sainte-Angèle-de-Monnoir
5, ch du Vide
Sainte-Angèle-de-Monnoir, QC J0L 1P0
Tél: 450-460-7838; *Téléc:* 450-460-3853
info@sainte-angele-de-monnoir.ca
www.municipalite.sainte-angele-de-monnoir.qc.ca
Entité municipal: Parish (Paroisse)
Incorporation: 15 mars 1865 *Area:* 45,49 km2
Comté ou district: Rouville; *Population au 2006:* 1,163
Circonscription(s) électorale(s) provinciale(s): Iberville
Circonscription(s) électorale(s) fédérale(s): Shefford
Prochaines élections: 1er novembre 2013
Jacqueline Houle, Directrice générale
Michel Picotte, Maire

Sainte-Angèle-de-Prémont
2451, rue Camirand
Sainte-Angèle-de-Prémont, QC J0K 1R0
Tél: 819-268-5526; *Téléc:* 819-268-5536
adminmuni@municpremont.ca
www.municpremont.ca
Entité municipal: Municipality
Incorporation: 28 août 1917 *Area:* 38,51 km2
Comté ou district: Maskinongé; *Population au 2006:* 663
Circonscription(s) électorale(s) provinciale(s): Maskinongé
Circonscription(s) électorale(s) fédérale(s): Berthier-Maskinongé
Prochaines élections: 3e novembre 2013
Barbara Paillé, Mairesse
Jean Charland, Directeur général

Sainte-Anne-de-Beaupré
9336, av Royale
Sainte-Anne-de-Beaupré, QC G0A 3C0
Tél: 418-827-3191; *Téléc:* 418-827-8275
info@sainteannedebeaupre.com
www.sainteannedebeaupre.com
Entité municipal: Town
Incorporation: 27 janvier 1973 *Area:* 64,38 km2
Comté ou district: La Côte-de-Beaupré; *Population au 2006:* 2,803
Circonscription(s) électorale(s) provinciale(s): Charlevoix
Circonscription(s) électorale(s) fédérale(s): Montmorency-Charlevoix-Haute-Côte-Nord
Prochaines élections: 3e novembre 2013
Jean-Luc Fortin, Maire
Frédéric Drolet-Gervais, Directeur général

Sainte-Anne-de-la-Pérade
200, rue Principale
Sainte-Anne-de-la-Pérade, QC G0X 2J0
Tél: 418-325-2841; *Téléc:* 418-325-3070
municipalite@sainteannedelaperade.net
www.sainteannedelaperade.net
Entité municipal: Municipality
Incorporation: 10 mai 1989 *Area:* 107,94 km2
Comté ou district: Les Chenaux; *Population au 2006:* 1,991
Circonscription(s) électorale(s) provinciale(s): Champlain
Circonscription(s) électorale(s) fédérale(s): St-Maurice-Champlain
Prochaines élections: 3e novembre 2013
Yvon Lafond, Maire
René Roy, Directeur général

Sainte-Anne-de-la-Pocatière
395, ch des Sables est
Sainte-Anne-de-la-Pocatière, QC G0R 1Z0
Tél: 418-856-3192; *Téléc:* 418-856-9936
paroisse@ste-anne-de-la-pocatiere.com
Entité municipal: Parish (Paroisse)
Incorporation: 1er juillet 1855 *Area:* 53,68 km2
Comté ou district: Kamouraska; *Population au 2006:* 1,843
Circonscription(s) électorale(s) provinciale(s): Kamouraska-Témiscouata
Circonscription(s) électorale(s) fédérale(s): Montmagny-L'Islet-Kamouraska-Rivière-du-Loup
Prochaines élections: 3e novembre 2013
François Lagacé, Maire
Sylvie Dionne, Directrice générale

Sainte-Anne-de-la-Rochelle
145, rue l'Église
Sainte-Anne-de-la-Rochelle, QC J0E 2B0
Tél: 450-539-1654; *Téléc:* 450-539-2317
mun.steannedelarochelle@axion.ca
Entité municipal: Municipality
Incorporation: 1er juillet 1855 *Area:* 60,96 km2
Comté ou district: Le Val-St-François; *Population au 2006:* 642
Circonscription(s) électorale(s) provinciale(s): Brome-Missisquoi
Circonscription(s) électorale(s) fédérale(s): Shefford
Prochaines élections: 3e novembre 2013
J. André Bourassa Gosselin, Maire
Majella René, Directrice générale

Sainte-Anne-de-Sabrevois
CP 60
1218, rte 133
Sabrevois, QC J0J 2G0
Tél: 450-347-0066; *Téléc:* 450-347-4040
info.sabrevois@videotron.ca
Entité municipal: Parish (Paroisse)
Incorporation: 1er mars 1888 *Area:* 45,24 km2
Comté ou district: Le Haut-Richelieu; *Population au 2006:* 1,889
Circonscription(s) électorale(s) provinciale(s): Iberville
Circonscription(s) électorale(s) fédérale(s): St-Jean
Prochaines élections: 3e novembre 2013
Clément Couture, Maire
Fredy Serreyn, Directeur général

Sainte-Anne-de-Sorel
1685, ch du Chenal-du-Moine
Sainte-Anne-de-Sorel, QC J3P 5N3
Tél: 450-742-1616; *Téléc:* 450-742-1118
info@sainteannedesorel.ca
www.sainteannedesorel.ca
Entité municipal: Municipality
Incorporation: 14 mai 1877 *Area:* 36,51 km2
Comté ou district: Pierre-De Saurel; *Population au 2009:* 2,803
Circonscription(s) électorale(s) provinciale(s): Richelieu
Circonscription(s) électorale(s) fédérale(s): Bas-Richelieu-Nicolet-Bécancour
Prochaines élections: 3e novembre 2013
Pierre Lacombe, Maire
Maxime Dauplaise, Directeur général

Sainte-Anne-des-Lacs
773, ch de Ste-Anne-des-Lacs
Sainte-Anne-des-Lacs, QC J0R 1B0
Tél: 450-224-2675; *Téléc:* 450-224-8672
info@sadl.qc.ca
www.sadl.qc.ca
Entité municipal: Parish (Paroisse)
Incorporation: 28 mars 1946 *Area:* 23,45 km2
Comté ou district: Les Pays-d'en-Haut; *Population au 2006:* 3,029
Circonscription(s) électorale(s) provinciale(s): Bertrand
Circonscription(s) électorale(s) fédérale(s): Laurentides-Labelle
Prochaines élections: 3e novembre 2013
Claude Boyer, Maire
Jean-François René, Directeur général

Sainte-Anne-des-Monts
6, 1re av ouest
Sainte-Anne-des-Monts, QC G4V 1A1
Tél: 418-763-5511; *Téléc:* 418-763-3473
sadmonts@globetrotter.net
www.villesainte-anne-des-monts.qc.ca
Entité municipal: Town
Incorporation: février 2000 *Area:* 263,62 km2
Comté ou district: La Haute-Gaspésie; *Population au 2006:* 6,772
Circonscription(s) électorale(s) provinciale(s): Matane
Circonscription(s) électorale(s) fédérale(s): Haute-Gaspésie-La Mitis-Matane-Matapédia
Prochaines élections: 3e novembre 2013
Micheline Pelletier, Mairesse
Sylvie Lepage, Greffière

Sainte-Anne-du-Lac
1, rue St-François-Xavier
Sainte-Anne-du-Lac, QC J0W 1V0
Tél: 819-586-2110; *Téléc:* 819-586-2203
sainte.anne.du.lac.municipalite@tlb.sympatico.ca
www.municipalite.sainte-anne-du-lac.qc.ca
Entité municipal: Municipality
Incorporation: 30 décembre 1976 *Area:* 345,28 km2
Comté ou district: Antoine-Labelle; *Population au 2006:* 613
Circonscription(s) électorale(s) provinciale(s): Labelle
Circonscription(s) électorale(s) fédérale(s): Laurentides-Labelle
Prochaines élections: 3e novembre 2013
Aimé Lachapelle, Maire
Denise Bélec, Directrice générale

Sainte-Anne-du-Sault
539, rte Principale
Sainte-Anne-du-Sault, QC G0Z 1C0
Tél: 819-367-2210; *Téléc:* 819-367-4011
munstann@tlb.sympatico.ca

Entité municipal: Municipality
Incorporation: 21 mars 1889 *Area:* 56,09 km2
Comté ou district: Arthabaska; *Population au 2006:* 1,315
Circonscription(s) électorale(s) provinciale(s): Nicolet-Yamaska
Circonscription(s) électorale(s) fédérale(s): Richmond-Arthabaska
Prochaines élections: 3e novembre 2013
Jean-Claude Bourassa, Maire
Lyne Bertrand, Directrice générale

Sainte-Apolline-de-Patton
105, rte de l'Église
Sainte-Apolline-de-Patton, QC G0R 2P0
Tél: 418-469-3031; *Téléc:* 418-469-3051
munapoli@globetrotter.net
www.sainteapollinedepatton.ca
Entité municipal: Parish (Paroisse)
Incorporation: 14 décembre 1909 *Area:* 255,70 km2
Comté ou district: Montmagny; *Population au 2006:* 678
Circonscription(s) électorale(s) provinciale(s): Montmagny-L'Islet
Circonscription(s) électorale(s) fédérale(s): Montamagny-L'Islet-Kamouraska-Rivière-du-Loup
Prochaines élections: 3e novembre 2013
Thérèse Mercier, Mairesse
Doris Godbout, Sec.-Trés.

Sainte-Aurélie
151A, ch des Bois Francs
Sainte-Aurélie, QC G0M 1M0
Tél: 418-593-3021; *Téléc:* 418-593-3961
munsteau@sogetel.net
www.ste-aurelie.qc.ca
Entité municipal: Municipality
Incorporation: 3 avril 1909 *Area:* 78,52 km2
Comté ou district: Les Etchemins; *Population au 2006:* 965
Circonscription(s) électorale(s) provinciale(s): Beauce-Sud
Circonscription(s) électorale(s) fédérale(s): Beauce
Prochaines élections: 3e novembre 2013
Mario Pouliot, Maire
Sophie Fortin, Directrice générale

Sainte-Barbe
470, ch de l'Église
Sainte-Barbe, QC J0S 1P0
Tél: 450-371-2504; *Téléc:* 450-371-2575
info@ste-barbe.com
www.ste-barbe.com
Entité municipal: Parish (Paroisse)
Incorporation: 12 juin 1882 *Area:* 39,78 km2
Comté ou district: Le Haut-St-Laurent; *Population au 2006:* 1,453
Circonscription(s) électorale(s) provinciale(s): Huntingdon
Circonscription(s) électorale(s) fédérale(s): Beauharnois-Salaberry
Prochaines élections: 3e novembre 2013
Jean-Claude Chantigny, Maire
Chantal Girouard, Sec.-Trés.

Sainte-Béatrix
861, rue de l'Église
Sainte-Béatrix, QC J0K 1Y0
Tél: 450-883-2245; *Téléc:* 450-883-1772
administration@stebeatrix.com
www.sainte-beatrix.com
Entité municipal: Municipality
Incorporation: 11 mai 1864 *Area:* 83,52 km2
Comté ou district: Matawinie; *Population au 2006:* 1,788
Circonscription(s) électorale(s) provinciale(s): Berthier
Circonscription(s) électorale(s) fédérale(s): Joliette
Prochaines élections: 3e novembre 2013
Normand Montagne, Maire
Patricia Labby, Directrice générale

Sainte-Brigide-d'Iberville
555, rue Principale
Sainte-Brigide-d'Iberville, QC J0J 1X0
Tél: 450-293-7511; *Téléc:* 450-293-1077
ste_brigide@bellnet.ca
www.sainte-brigide.qc.ca
Entité municipal: Municipality
Incorporation: 1er juillet 1855 *Area:* 68,89 km2
Comté ou district: Le Haut-Richelieu; *Population au 2006:* 1,223
Circonscription(s) électorale(s) provinciale(s): Iberville
Circonscription(s) électorale(s) fédérale(s): St-Jean
Prochaines élections: 3e novembre 2013
Patrick Bonvouloir, Maire
Murielle Papineau, Directrice générale

Sainte-Brigitte-de-Laval
414, av Ste-Brigitte
Sainte-Brigitte-de-Laval, QC G0A 3K0
Tél: 418-825-2515; *Téléc:* 418-825-3114
mairie@sbdl.net
www.sbdl.net
Entité municipal: Municipality
Incorporation: 11 février 1875 *Area:* 111,49 km2
Comté ou district: La Jacques-Cartier; *Population au 2006:* 3,790
Circonscription(s) électorale(s) provinciale(s): Montmorency
Circonscription(s) électorale(s) fédérale(s): Portneuf-Jacques Cartier
Prochaines élections: 3e novembre 2013
Gilbert Thomassin, Maire
Gaétan Bussières, Directeur général

Sainte-Brigitte-des-Saults
CP 1051
400, rue Principale
Sainte-Brigitte-des-Saults, QC J0C 1E0
Tél: 819-336-4460; *Téléc:* 819-336-4410
muni.ste-brigitte@mrcdrummond.qc.ca
www.saintebrigittedessaults.ca
Entité municipal: Parish (Paroisse)
Incorporation: 9 mars 1878 *Area:* 69,23
Comté ou district: Drummond; *Population au 2006:* 739
Circonscription(s) électorale(s) provinciale(s): Nicolet-Yamaska
Circonscription(s) électorale(s) fédérale(s): Drummond
Prochaines élections: 3e novembre 2013
Jean-Guy Hébert, Maire
Manon Lemaire, Directrice générale

Sainte-Catherine-de-Hatley
CP 30
35, ch de North Hatley
Sainte-Catherine-de-Hatley, QC J0B 1W0
Tél: 819-843-1935; *Téléc:* 819-843-8527
munstecatherinehatley@qc.aira.com
www.sainte-catherine-de-hatley.ca
Entité municipal: Municipality
Incorporation: 28 mars 1901 *Area:* 81,43 km2
Comté ou district: Memphrémagog; *Population au 2006:* 2,318
Circonscription(s) électorale(s) provinciale(s): Orford
Circonscription(s) électorale(s) fédérale(s): Compton-Stanstead
Prochaines élections: 3e novembre 2013
Jacques Demers, Maire
Serge Caron, Directeur général

Sainte-Catherine-de-la-Jacques-Cartier
CP 250
1, rue Rouleau
Ste-Catherine-de-la-J-Cartier, QC G0A 3M0
Tél: 418-875-2758; *Téléc:* 418-875-2170
sainte-catherine-de-la-jacques-cartier@coopcscf.com
www.villescjc.com
Entité municipal: Town
Incorporation: 1er juillet 1855 *Area:* 120,61 km2
Comté ou district: La Jacques-Cartier; *Population au 2006:* 5,021
Circonscription(s) électorale(s) provinciale(s): Portneuf
Circonscription(s) électorale(s) fédérale(s): Portneuf-Jacques-Cartier
Prochaines élections: 3e novembre 2013
Jacques Marcotte, Maire
Marcel Grenier, Directeur général

Sainte-Cécile-de-Lévrard
235, rue Principale
Sainte-Cécile-de-Lévrard, QC G0X 2M0
Tél: 819-263-2104; *Téléc:* 819-263-1043
info@munstececilevrd.ca
Entité municipal: Parish (Paroisse)
Incorporation: 11 septembre 1908 *Area:* 33,35 km2
Comté ou district: Bécancour; *Population au 2006:* 417
Circonscription(s) électorale(s) provinciale(s): Lotbinière
Circonscription(s) électorale(s) fédérale(s): Bas-Richelieu-Nicolet-Bécancour
Prochaines élections: 3me novembre 2013
Simon Brunelle, Maire
Réjean Poisson, Directeur général

Sainte-Cécile-de-Milton
CP 195
136, rue Principale
Sainte-Cécile-de-Milton, QC J0E 2C0
Tél: 450-378-1942; *Téléc:* 450-378-4621
mun@stececiledemilton.qc.ca
Entité municipal: Township
Incorporation: 1er janvier 1864 *Area:* 74,04 km2
Comté ou district: La Haute-Yamaska; *Population au 2006:* 2,024
Circonscription(s) électorale(s) provinciale(s): Johnson
Circonscription(s) électorale(s) fédérale(s): Shefford
Prochaines élections: 3e novembre 2013
Sylvain Beaudoin, Maire
Monique Fortin, Directrice générale

Sainte-Cécile-de-Whitton
4557, rue Principale
Sainte-Cécile-de-Whitton, QC G0Y 1J0
Tél: 819-583-0770; *Téléc:* 819-583-4149
muncecilewhitton@axion.ca
www.stececiledewhitton.qc.ca
Entité municipal: Municipality
Incorporation: 19 septembre 1889 *Area:* 146,59 km2
Comté ou district: Le Granit; *Population au 2006:* 899
Circonscription(s) électorale(s) provinciale(s): Mégantic-Compton
Circonscription(s) électorale(s) fédérale(s): Mégantic-L'Érable
Prochaines élections: 3e novembre 2013
Diane Turgeon, Maire
Françoise Audet, Directrice générale

Sainte-Christine
629, rue des Loisirs
Sainte-Christine, QC J0H 1H0
Tél: 819-858-2828; *Téléc:* 819-858-9911
stechristine@cooptel.qc.ca
Entité municipal: Parish (Paroisse)
Incorporation: 8 janvier 1894 *Area:* 89,40 km2
Comté ou district: Acton; *Population au 2006:* 560
Circonscription(s) électorale(s) provinciale(s): Johnson
Circonscription(s) électorale(s) fédérale(s): St-Hyacinthe-Bagot
Prochaines élections: 3e novembre 2013
Huguette St-Pierre-Beaulac, Mairesse
Caroline Lamothe, Directrice-générale

Sainte-Christine-d'Auvergne
80, rue Principale
Sainte-Christine-d'Auvergne, QC G0A 1A0
Tél: 418-329-3304; *Téléc:* 418-329-3356
ste-christine@globetrotter.net
www.ste-christine.qc.ca
Entité municipal: Municipality
Incorporation: 10 avril 1896 *Area:* 145,58 km2
Comté ou district: Portneuf; *Population au 2006:* 462
Circonscription(s) électorale(s) provinciale(s): Portneuf
Circonscription(s) électorale(s) fédérale(s): Portneuf-Jacques Cartier
Prochaines élections: 3e novembre 2013
Pierre Tourigny, Maire
Louise Quintin, Directrice générale (interim)

Sainte-Claire
135, rue Principale
Sainte-Claire, QC G0R 2V0
Tél: 418-883-3314; *Téléc:* 418-883-3845
msclaire@globetrotter.qc.ca
www.municipalite.sainte-claire.qc.ca
Entité municipal: Municipality
Incorporation: 1er octobre 1977 *Area:* 88,63 km2
Comté ou district: Bellechasse; *Population au 2006:* 3,097
Circonscription(s) électorale(s) provinciale(s): Bellechasse
Circonscription(s) électorale(s) fédérale(s): Lévis-Bellechasse
Prochaines élections: 3e novembre 2013
Fernand Fortier, Maire
Serge Gagnon, Directeur général

Sainte-Clotilde-de-Beauce
307B, rue du Couvent
Sainte-Clotilde-de-Beauce, QC G0N 1C0
Tél: 418-427-2637; *Téléc:* 418-427-4303
steclotilde@hotmail.com
www.ste-clotilde.com
Entité municipal: Municipality
Incorporation: 19 novembre 1938 *Area:* 58,680 km2
Comté ou district: Les Appalaches; *Population au 2006:* 601
Circonscription(s) électorale(s) provinciale(s): Beauce-Sud
Circonscription(s) électorale(s) fédérale(s): Mégantic-L'Érable
Prochaines élections: 3e novembre 2013
Gérald Grenier, Maire
Sandy Grenier, Directrice générale

Sainte-Clotilde-de-Châteauguay
2452, ch de l'Église
Sainte-Clotilde-de-Châteauguay, QC J0L 1W0
Tél: 450-826-3129; *Téléc:* 450-826-3217
mun.steclotilde@rocler.qc.ca
Entité municipal: Parish (Paroisse)
Incorporation: 2 avril 1885 *Area:* 78,96 km2
Comté ou district: Les Jardins-de-Napierville; *Population au 2006:* 1,608
Circonscription(s) électorale(s) provinciale(s): Huntingdon

Circonscription(s) électorale(s) fédérale(s):
Beauharnois-Salaberry
Prochaines élections: 3e novembre 2013
Clément Lemieux, Maire
Nicole Marcil, Directrice générale

Sainte-Clotilde-de-Horton
CP 29
17, rte 122
Sainte-Clotilde-de-Horton, QC J0A 1H0
Tél: 819-336-5344; *Téléc:* 819-336-5440
info@steclotildehorton.ca
www.steclotildehorton.ca
Entité municipal: Municipality
Incorporation: 26 mars 1997 *Area:* 118,44 km2
Comté ou district: Arthabaska; *Population au 2006:* 1,560
Circonscription(s) électorale(s) provinciale(s): Richmond
Circonscription(s) électorale(s) fédérale(s):
Richmond-Arthabaska
Prochaines élections: 3e novembre 2013
Marie Désilets, Mairesse
Marlène Langlois, Directrice générale

Sainte-Croix
6310, rue Principale
Sainte-Croix, QC G0S 2H0
Tél: 418-926-3494; *Téléc:* 418-926-2570
www.ville.sainte-croix.qc.ca
Entité municipal: Municipality
Incorporation: 5 octobre 2001 *Area:* 69,64 km2
Comté ou district: Lotbinière; *Population au 2006:* 2,390
Circonscription(s) électorale(s) provinciale(s): Lotbinière
Circonscription(s) électorale(s) fédérale(s):
Lotbinière-Chutes-de-la-Chaudière
Prochaines élections: 3e novembre 2013
Jacques Gauthier, Maire
Bertrand Fréchette, Directeur général
bertrand.frechette@ville.sainte-croix.qc.ca

Sainte-Edwidge-de-Clifton
1439, chemin Favreau
Sainte-Edwidge-de-Clifton, QC J0B 2R0
Tél: 819-849-7740; *Téléc:* 819-849-4212
info@ste-edwidge.ca
www.ste-edwidge.ca
Entité municipal: Township
Incorporation: 21 décembre 1895 *Area:* 99,35 km2
Comté ou district: Coaticook; *Population au 2006:* 440
Circonscription(s) électorale(s) provinciale(s):
Mégantic-Compton
Circonscription(s) électorale(s) fédérale(s): Compton-Stanstead
Prochaines élections: 3e novembre 2013
Linda Ouellet, Mairesse
Réjean Fauteux, Directeur général

Sainte-Élisabeth
2270, rue Principale
Sainte-Élisabeth, QC J0K 2J0
Tél: 450-759-2875; *Téléc:* 450-756-4312
steelisabeth@qc.aira.com
www.ste-elisabeth.qc.ca
Entité municipal: Parish (Paroisse)
Incorporation: 1er juillet 1855 *Area:* 81,66 km2
Comté ou district: D'Autray; *Population au 2006:* 1,440
Circonscription(s) électorale(s) provinciale(s): Berthier
Circonscription(s) électorale(s) fédérale(s): Joliette
Prochaines élections: 3e novembre 2013
Mario Houle, Maire
Lorraine C. Garnelin, Directrice générale

Sainte-Élizabeth-de-Warwick
243, rue Principale
Sainte-Élizabeth-de-Warwick, QC J0A 1M0
Tél: 819-358-5162; *Téléc:* 819-358-9192
info@sainte-elizabeth-de-warwick.ca
Entité municipal: Parish (Paroisse)
Incorporation: 18 mai 1887 *Area:* 50,51 km2
Comté ou district: Arthabaska; *Population au 2006:* 368
Circonscription(s) électorale(s) provinciale(s): Richmond
Circonscription(s) électorale(s) fédérale(s):
Richmond-Arthabaska
Prochaines élections: 3e novembre 2013
Luc Le Blanc, Maire
Josée Leblond, Directrice générale

Sainte-Émélie-de-l'Énergie
241, rue Coutu
Sainte-Émélie-de-l'Énergie, QC J0K 2K0
Tél: 450-886-3823; *Téléc:* 450-886-9175
stemelie@intermonde.net
www.ste-emelie-de-lenergie.qc.ca
Entité municipal: Municipality
Incorporation: 10 juin 1884 *Area:* 170,68 km2
Comté ou district: Matawinie; *Population au 2006:* 1,681
Circonscription(s) électorale(s) provinciale(s): Berthier
Circonscription(s) électorale(s) fédérale(s): Joliette
Prochaines élections: 3e novembre 2013
Atchez Arbour, Maire
Brigitte Belleville, Directrice générale

Sainte-Eulalie
757, rue des Bouleaux
Sainte-Eulalie, QC G0Z 1E0
Tél: 819-225-4345; *Téléc:* 819-225-4078
info@municipalite.sainte-eulalie.qc.ca
www.municipalite.sainte-eulalie.qc.ca
Entité municipal: Municipality
Incorporation: 1er juillet 1864 *Area:* 90,79 km2
Comté ou district: Nicolet-Yamaska; *Population au 2006:* 894
Circonscription(s) électorale(s) provinciale(s): Nicolet-Yamaska
Circonscription(s) électorale(s) fédérale(s):
Bas-Richelieu-Nicolet-Bécancour
Prochaines élections: 3e novembre 2013
André Demers, Maire
Yvon Douville, Directeur général

Sainte-Famille
3894, ch Royal
Sainte-Famille, QC G0A 3P0
Tél: 418-829-3572; *Téléc:* 418-829-2513
info@munstefamille.org
Entité municipal: Parish (Paroisse)
Incorporation: 1er juillet 1855 *Area:* 46,43 km2
Comté ou district: L'Ile-d'Orléans; *Population au 2006:* 844
Circonscription(s) électorale(s) provinciale(s): Montmorency
Circonscription(s) électorale(s) fédérale(s):
Montmorency-Charlevoix-Haute-Côte-Nord
Prochaines élections: 3e novembre 2013
Jean-Pierre Turcotte, Maire
Sylvie Beaulieu, Directrice générale

Sainte-Félicité
5, rte de l'Église nord
Sainte-Félicité, QC G0R 4P0
Tél: 418-359-2321; *Téléc:* 418-359-2321
mun.ste-felicite@globetrotter.net
Entité municipal: Municipality
Incorporation: 1er janvier 1950 *Area:* 95,82 km2
Comté ou district: L'Islet; *Population au 2006:* 422
Circonscription(s) électorale(s) provinciale(s): Montmagny-L'Islet
Circonscription(s) électorale(s) fédérale(s):
Montmagny-l'Islet-Kamouraska-Rivière-du-Loup
Prochaines élections: 3e novembre 2013
Georges Gagnon, Maire
Julie Bélanger, Directrice générale

Sainte-Félicité
CP 9
192, rue St-Joseph
Sainte-Félicité, QC G0J 2K0
Tél: 418-733-4628; *Téléc:* 418-733-8377
ste-felicite@mrcdematane.qc.ca
Entité municipal: Municipality
Incorporation: 10 janvier 1996 *Area:* 89,76 km2
Comté ou district: Matane; *Population au 2006:* 1,201
Circonscription(s) électorale(s) provinciale(s): Matane
Circonscription(s) électorale(s) fédérale(s): Haute-Gaspésie-La Mitis-Matane-Matapédia
Prochaines élections: 3e novembre 2013
Réginald Desrosiers, Maire
Yves Chassé, Directeur général

Sainte-Flavie
775, rte Flavie-Drapeau
Sainte-Flavie, QC G0J 2L0
Tél: 418-775-7050; *Téléc:* 418-775-5672
info@sainte-flavie.net
www.sainte-flavie.net
Entité municipal: Parish (Paroisse)
Incorporation: 1er juillet 1855 *Area:* 37,62 km2
Comté ou district: La Mitis; *Population au 2006:* 943
Circonscription(s) électorale(s) provinciale(s): Matapédia
Circonscription(s) électorale(s) fédérale(s): Haute-Gaspésie-La Mitis-Matane-Matapédia
Prochaines élections: 3e novembre 2013
Damien Ruest, Maire
Francine Roy, Directrice générale

Sainte-Florence
CP 9
29, rue des Loisirs
Sainte-Florence, QC G0J 2M0
Tél: 418-756-3491; *Téléc:* 418-756-5079
steflorence@mrcmatapedia.qc.ca
www.sainte-florence.com
Entité municipal: Municipality
Incorporation: 12 avril 1911 *Area:* 103,00 km2
Comté ou district: La Matapédia; *Population au 2006:* 458
Circonscription(s) électorale(s) provinciale(s): Matapédia
Circonscription(s) électorale(s) fédérale(s): Haute-Gaspésie-La Mitis-Matane-Matapédia
Prochaines élections: 3e novembre 2013
Réjeanne Doiron, Mairesse
Huguette Gagné, Directrice générale

Sainte-Françoise
563, 10e-et-11e rang est
Sainte-Françoise-de-Lotbinière, QC G0S 2N0
Tél: 819-287-5755; *Téléc:* 819-287-5838
municipalite@ste-francoise.com
www.visitedefermeeducative.com
Entité municipal: Municipality
Incorporation: 1er janvier 1947 *Area:* 89,12 km2
Comté ou district: Bécancour; *Population au 2006:* 471
Circonscription(s) électorale(s) provinciale(s): Lotbinière
Circonscription(s) électorale(s) fédérale(s):
Bas-Richelieu-Nicolet-Bécancour
Prochaines élections: 3e novembre 2013
Mario Lyonnais, Maire
Isabelle Dubois, Directrice générale

Sainte-Françoise
156, rue Jérémie-Beaulieu
Sainte-Françoise, QC G0L 3B0
Tél: 418-851-1502; *Téléc:* 418-851-0926
municipal@ste-francoise.qc.ca
Entité municipal: Parish (Paroisse)
Incorporation: 6 décembre 1873 *Area:* 88,54 km2
Comté ou district: Les Basques; *Population au 2006:* 431
Circonscription(s) électorale(s) provinciale(s): Rivière-du-Loup
Circonscription(s) électorale(s) fédérale(s):
Rimouski-Neigette-Témiscouata-Les Basques
Prochaines élections: 3e novembre 2013
Bernard D'Amours, Maire
Véronique Pelletier, Directrice générale

Sainte-Geneviève-de-Batiscan
30, rue St-Charles
Sainte-Geneviève-de-Batiscan, QC G0X 2R0
Tél: 418-362-2078; *Téléc:* 418-362-2111
municipalite@stegenevieve.ca
www.stegenevieve.ca
Entité municipal: Parish (Paroisse)
Incorporation: 1er juillet 1855 *Area:* 97,09 km2
Comté ou district: Les Chenaux; *Population au 2006:* 1,036
Circonscription(s) électorale(s) provinciale(s): Champlain
Circonscription(s) électorale(s) fédérale(s):
St-Maurice-Champlain
Prochaines élections: 3e novembre 2013
Christian Gendron, Maire
Line Blais, Directrice générale

Sainte-Geneviève-de-Berthier
400, rang de la Rivière-Bayonne sud
Sainte-Geneviève-de-Berthier, QC J0K 1A0
Tél: 450-836-4333; *Téléc:* 450-836-7260
munisgb@autray.net
Entité municipal: Parish (Paroisse)
Incorporation: 1er juillet 1855 *Area:* 74,67
Comté ou district: D'Autray; *Population au 2006:* 2,307
Circonscription(s) électorale(s) provinciale(s): Berthier
Circonscription(s) électorale(s) fédérale(s): Berthier-Maskinongé
Prochaines élections: 3e novembre 2013
Richard Giroux, Maire
Réjean Marsolais, Directeur général

Sainte-Germaine-Boulé
CP 5 Boulé
199, rue Roy
Sainte-Germaine-Boulé, QC J0Z 1M0
Tél: 819-787-6221; *Téléc:* 819-787-2560
stegermaine@ste-germaine.ao.ca
www.ste-germaine.ao.ca
Entité municipal: Municipality
Incorporation: 1er janvier 1954 *Area:* 108,46 km2
Comté ou district: Abitibi-Ouest; *Population au 2006:* 942
Circonscription(s) électorale(s) provinciale(s): Abitibi-Ouest
Circonscription(s) électorale(s) fédérale(s):
Abitibi-Témiscamingue
Prochaines élections: 3e novembre 2013

Jaclin Bégin, Maire
Gisèle Bisson-Lapointe, Directrice générale

Sainte-Gertrude-Manneville
391, rte 395
Sainte-Gertrude-Manneville, QC J0Y 2L0
Tél: 819-727-2244; *Téléc:* 819-727-3293
stegertman@cableamos.com
Entité municipal: Municipality
Incorporation: 1er janvier 1980 *Area:* 329,84 km2
Comté ou district: Abitibi; *Population au 2006:* 811
Circonscription(s) électorale(s) provinciale(s): Abitibi-Ouest
Circonscription(s) électorale(s) fédérale(s): Abitibi-Témiscamingue
Prochaines élections: 3e novembre 2013
Pascal Rheault, Maire
Laurence Demers, Directrice générale

Sainte-Hedwidge
1090, rue Principale
Sainte-Hedwidge, QC G0W 2R0
Tél: 418-275-3020; *Téléc:* 418-275-4163
Entité municipal: Municipality
Incorporation: 10 mars 1909 *Area:* 469,07 km2
Comté ou district: Le Domaine-du-Roy; *Population au 2006:* 820
Circonscription(s) électorale(s) provinciale(s): Roberval
Circonscription(s) électorale(s) fédérale(s): Roberval-Lac-St-Jean
Prochaines élections: 3e novembre 2013
Gilles Toulouse, Maire
Sylvain Privé, Directeur général
sylvain.prive@ste-hedwidge.qc.ca

Sainte-Hélène
CP 216
531, rue de l'Église sud
Sainte-Hélène, QC G0L 3J0
Tél: 418-492-6830; *Téléc:* 418-492-1854
munhel@bellnet.ca
www.sainte-helene.net
Entité municipal: Parish (Paroisse)
Incorporation: 1er juillet 1855 *Area:* 60,34 km2
Comté ou district: Kamouraska; *Population au 2006:* 897
Circonscription(s) électorale(s) provinciale(s): Kamouraska-Témiscouata
Circonscription(s) électorale(s) fédérale(s): Montmagny-L'Islet-Kamourask-Rivière-du-Loup
Prochaines élections: 3e novembre 2013
Marcel Guay, Maire
Maryse Oullet, Directrice générale

Sainte-Hélène-de-Bagot
379, 7e av
Sainte-Hélène-de-Bagot, QC J0H 1M0
Tél: 450-791-2455; *Téléc:* 450-791-2550
line.lupien@mrcmaskoutains.qc.ca
Entité municipal: Municipality
Incorporation: 9 juillet 1977 *Area:* 73,53 km2
Comté ou district: Les Maskoutains; *Population au 2006:* 1,446
Circonscription(s) électorale(s) provinciale(s): Johnson
Circonscription(s) électorale(s) fédérale(s): St-Hyacinthe-Bagot
Prochaines élections: 3e novembre 2013
Yves Petit, Maire
Line Lupien, Directrice générale

Sainte-Hélène-de-Mancebourg
451, rang 2e-et-3e
Mancebourg, QC J0Z 2T0
Tél: 819-333-5766; *Téléc:* 819-333-9514
mancebourg@mrcao.qc.ca
www.ste-helene.ao.ca
Entité municipal: Parish (Paroisse)
Incorporation: 10 mai 1941 *Area:* 68,29 km2
Comté ou district: Abitibi-Ouest; *Population au 2006:* 375
Circonscription(s) électorale(s) provinciale(s): Abitibi-Ouest
Circonscription(s) électorale(s) fédérale(s): Abitibi-Témiscamingue
Prochaines élections: 3e novembre 2013
Florent Bédard, Maire
Sylvie Boutin-Bergeron, Directrice générale

Sainte-Hénédine
CP 6
111, rue Principale
Sainte-Hénédine, QC G0S 2R0
Tél: 418-935-7125; *Téléc:* 418-935-3113
munisthe@globetrotter.net
Entité municipal: Parish (Paroisse)
Incorporation: 1er juillet 1855 *Area:* 53,06
Comté ou district: La Nouvelle-Beauce; *Population au 2006:* 1,073
Circonscription(s) électorale(s) provinciale(s): Beauce-Nord
Circonscription(s) électorale(s) fédérale(s): Beauce
Prochaines élections: 3e novembre 2013
Yvon Asselin, Maire
Yvon Marcoux, Sec.-Trés.

Sainte-Irène
362, rue de la Fabrique
Sainte-Irène, QC G0J 2P0
Tél: 418-629-5705; *Téléc:* 418-629-3220
steirene@mrcmatapedia.qc.ca
Entité municipal: Parish (Paroisse)
Incorporation: 1er janvier 1953 *Area:* 134,03
Comté ou district: La Matapédia; *Population au 2006:* 350
Circonscription(s) électorale(s) provinciale(s): Matapédia
Circonscription(s) électorale(s) fédérale(s): Haute-Gaspésie-La Mitis-Matane-Matapédia
Prochaines élections: 3e novembre 2013
Alain Duchemin, Maire
Lucie Desjardins, Directrice générale

Sainte-Jeanne-d'Arc
CP 40
205, rue Principale
Sainte-Jeanne-d'Arc, QC G0J 2T0
Tél: 418-776-5660; *Téléc:* 418-776-5660
stejeanne@mitis.qc.ca
www.municipalite.sainte-jeanne-darc.qc.ca
Entité municipal: Parish (Paroisse)
Incorporation: 30 janvier 1922 *Area:* 110,82 km2
Comté ou district: La Mitis; *Population au 2006:* 322
Circonscription(s) électorale(s) provinciale(s): Matapédia
Circonscription(s) électorale(s) fédérale(s): Haute-Gaspésie-La Mitis-Matane-Matapédia
Prochaines élections: 3e novembre 2013
Maurice Chrétien, Maire
Louise Boivin, Directrice générale

Sainte-Jeanne-d'Arc
378, rue François-Bilodeau
Sainte-Jeanne-d'Arc, QC G0W 1E0
Tél: 418-276-3166; *Téléc:* 418-276-7648
jeannerm@destination.ca
Entité municipal: Village
Incorporation: 24 janvier 1970 *Area:* 270,88 km2
Comté ou district: Maria-Chapdelaine; *Population au 2006:* 1,139
Circonscription(s) électorale(s) provinciale(s): Roberval
Circonscription(s) électorale(s) fédérale(s): Roberval-Lac-St-Jean
Prochaines élections: 1er novembre 2013
Gaston Morin, Maire
Régis Martin, Directeur général

Sainte-Julienne
1400, rte 125
Sainte-Julienne, QC J0K 2T0
Tél: 450-831-2688; *Téléc:* 450-831-4433
municipalite@sainte-julienne.com
www.sainte-julienne.com
Entité municipal: Municipality
Incorporation: 1er juillet 1855 *Area:* 102,10 km2
Comté ou district: Montcalm; *Population au 2006:* 7,983
Circonscription(s) électorale(s) provinciale(s): Rousseau
Circonscription(s) électorale(s) fédérale(s): Montcalm
Prochaines élections: 3e novembre 2013
Marcel Jetté, Maire
Diane Desjardins, Directrice générale

Sainte-Justine
167, rte 204
Sainte-Justine, QC G0R 1Y0
Tél: 418-383-5397; *Téléc:* 418-383-5398
sjustine@sogetel.net
www.stejustine.net
Entité municipal: Municipality
Incorporation: 1er janvier 1870 *Area:* 124,55 km2
Comté ou district: Les Etchemins; *Population au 2006:* 1,825
Circonscription(s) électorale(s) provinciale(s): Bellechasse
Circonscription(s) électorale(s) fédérale(s): Lévis-Bellechasse
Prochaines élections: 3e novembre 2013
Denis Beaulieu, Maire
Gilles Vézina, Directeur général

Sainte-Justine-de-Newton
CP 270
2627, rue Principale
Sainte-Justine-de-Newton, QC J0P 1T0
Tél: 450-764-3573; *Téléc:* 450-764-3180
ste-justine@rocler.qc.ca
Entité municipal: Parish (Paroisse)
Incorporation: 1er juillet 1855 *Area:* 84,14 km2
Comté ou district: Vaudreuil-Soulanges; *Population au 2006:* 929
Circonscription(s) électorale(s) provinciale(s): Soulanges
Circonscription(s) électorale(s) fédérale(s): Vaudreuil-Soulanges
Prochaines élections: 3e novembre 2013
Patricia Domingos, Mairesse
Denis Perrier, Directeur général

Sainte-Louise
CP 2130
80, rte de la Station
Sainte-Louise, QC G0R 3K0
Tél: 418-354-2509; *Téléc:* 418-354-7730
ste-louise@globetrotter.net
www.saintelouise.qc.ca
Entité municipal: Parish (Paroisse)
Incorporation: 11 décembre 1860 *Area:* 73,03 km2
Comté ou district: L'Islet; *Population au 2006:* 704
Circonscription(s) électorale(s) provinciale(s): Kamouraska-Témiscouata
Circonscription(s) électorale(s) fédérale(s): Montmagny-L'Islet-Kamouraska-Rivière-du-Loup
Prochaines élections: 3e novembre 2013
Denis Gagnon, Maire
Marie-Hélène Viau, Directeur générale

Sainte-Luce
1, rue Langlois
Sainte-Luce, QC G0K 1P0
Tél: 418-739-4317; *Téléc:* 418-739-4823
sainte-luce@sainteluce.ca
www.sainteluce.ca
Entité municipal: Municipality
Incorporation: 29 octobre 2001 *Area:* 74,88 km2
Comté ou district: La Mitis; *Population au 2006:* 2,934
Circonscription(s) électorale(s) provinciale(s): Matapédia
Circonscription(s) électorale(s) fédérale(s): Haute-Gaspédie-La Mitis-Matane-Matapédia
Prochaines élections: 3e novembre 2013
Gaston Gaudreault, Maire
Jean Robidoux, Directeur général

Sainte-Lucie-de-Beauregard
21, rte des Chutes
Sainte-Lucie-de-Beauregard, QC G0R 3L0
Tél: 418-223-3122; *Téléc:* 418-223-3121
ste-lucie@globetrotter.net
www.saintelluciedebeauregard.net
Entité municipal: Municipality
Incorporation: 18 novembre 1924 *Area:* 80,18 km2
Comté ou district: Montmagny; *Population au 2006:* 336
Circonscription(s) électorale(s) provinciale(s): Montagny-L'Islet
Circonscription(s) électorale(s) fédérale(s): Montmagny-L'Islet-Kamouraska-Rivière-du-Loup
Prochaines élections: 3e novembre 2013
Louis Lachance, Maire
Bianca Deschênes, Directrice générale

Sainte-Lucie-des-Laurentides
2121, ch des Hauteurs
Sainte-Lucie-des-Laurentides, QC J0T 2J0
Tél: 819-326-3198; *Téléc:* 819-326-0592
dg@municipalite.sainte-lucie-des-laurentides.qc.ca
Entité municipal: Municipality
Incorporation: 1er janvier 1874 *Area:* 115,15 km2
Comté ou district: Les Laurentides; *Population au 2006:* 1,138
Circonscription(s) électorale(s) provinciale(s): Bertrand
Circonscription(s) électorale(s) fédérale(s): Laurentides-Labelle
Prochaines élections: 3e novembre 2013
Ghislain Schoeb, Maire
Denis Malouin, Directeur général

Sainte-Madeleine
850, rue St-Simon
Sainte-Madeleine, QC J0H 1S0
Tél: 450-795-3822; *Téléc:* 450-795-3736
administration@villestemadeleine.qc.ca
www.villestemadeleine.qc.ca
Entité municipal: Village
Incorporation: 30 décembre 1919 *Area:* 5,39 km2
Comté ou district: Les Maskoutains; *Population au 2006:* 2,175
Circonscription(s) électorale(s) provinciale(s): Verchères
Circonscription(s) électorale(s) fédérale(s): St-Hyacinthe-Bagot
Prochaines élections: 3e novembre 2013
Alain Paradis, Maire
Carole Dulude, Directrice générale

Sainte-Madeleine-de-la-Rivière-Madeleine
104, rte Principale
Madeleine-Centre, QC G0E 1P0
Tél: 418-393-2428; *Téléc:* 418-393-2869
munste-madeleine@globetrotter.net

Entité municipal: Municipality
Incorporation: 27 février 1915 *Area:* 269,35 km2
Comté ou district: La Haute-Gaspésie; *Population au 2006:* 373
Circonscription(s) électorale(s) provinciale(s): Matane
Circonscription(s) électorale(s) fédérale(s): Haute-Gaspésie-La Mitis-Matane-Matapédia
Prochaines élections: 3e novembre 2013
Joel Côté, Maire
Suzanne Roy, Directrice générale

Sainte-Marcelline-de-Kildare
500, rue Principale
Sainte-Marcelline-de-Kildare, QC J0K 2Y0
Tél: 450-883-2241; *Téléc:* 450-883-2242
info@ste-marcelline.com
www.ste-marcelline.com
Entité municipal: Municipality
Incorporation: 1er janvier 1956 *Area:* 33,66 km2
Comté ou district: Matawinie; *Population au 2006:* 1,423
Circonscription(s) électorale(s) provinciale(s): Joliette
Circonscription(s) électorale(s) fédérale(s): Joliette
Prochaines élections: 3e novembre 2013
Gaétan Morin, Maire
Catherine Haulard, Directrice générale

Sainte-Marguerite
15, rte de La Vérendrye
Sainte-Marguerite-Marie, QC G0J 2Y0
Tél: 418-756-3364; *Téléc:* 418-756-3364
stemarguerite@mrcmatapedia.qc.ca
Entité municipal: Municipality
Incorporation: 1er janvier 1957 *Area:* 83,94 km2
Comté ou district: La Matapédia; *Population au 2006:* 222
Circonscription(s) électorale(s) provinciale(s): Matapédia
Circonscription(s) électorale(s) fédérale(s): Haute-Gaspésie-La Mitis-Matane-Matapédia
Prochaines élections: 1er novembre 2013
Marlène Landry, Mairesse
Odette Corbin, Directrice générale

Sainte-Marguerite
235, rue St-Jacques
Sainte-Marguerite, QC G0S 2X0
Tél: 418-935-7103; *Téléc:* 418-935-3709
munste-marguerite@nouvellebeauce.com
Entité municipal: Parish (Paroisse)
Incorporation: 1er juillet 1855 *Area:* 82,56 km2
Comté ou district: La Nouvelle-Beauce; *Population au 2006:* 1,060
Circonscription(s) électorale(s) provinciale(s): Beauce-Nord
Circonscription(s) électorale(s) fédérale(s): Beauce
Prochaines élections: 3e novembre 2013
Adrienne Gagné, Mairesse
Nicole Chabot, Directrice générale

Sainte-Marguerite-du-Lac-Masson
414, rue de Baron-Louis-Empain
Ste-Marguerite-du-Lac-Masson, QC J0T 1L0
Tél: 450-228-2543; *Téléc:* 450-228-4008
adm@lacmasson.com
www.ste-marguerite.qc.ca
Entité municipal: Town
Incorporation: 17 octobre 2001 *Area:* 98,65 km2
Comté ou district: Les Pays-d'en-Haut; *Population au 2006:* 2,498
Circonscription(s) électorale(s) provinciale(s): Bertrand
Circonscription(s) électorale(s) fédérale(s): Laurentides-Labelle
Prochaines élections: 3e novembre 2013
Linda Fortier, Mairesse
Francine Labelle, Directrice générale

Sainte-Marie-de-Blandford
492, rte des Bosquets
Sainte-Marie-de-Blandford, QC G0X 2W0
Tél: 819-283-2127; *Téléc:* 819-283-2169
mun@saintemariedeblandford.qc.ca
Entité municipal: Municipality
Incorporation: 23 décembre 1976 *Area:* 68,29 km2
Comté ou district: Bécancour; *Population au 2006:* 517
Circonscription(s) électorale(s) provinciale(s): Lotbinière
Circonscription(s) électorale(s) fédérale(s): Bas-Richelieu-Nicolet-Bécancour
Prochaines élections: 3e novembre 2013
Vacant, Mairesse
Galina Papantcheva, Directrice générale

Sainte-Marie-Madeleine
3541, boul Laurier
Sainte-Marie-Madeleine, QC J0H 1S0
Tél: 450-795-6272; *Téléc:* 450-795-3180
info@stemariemadeleine.qc.ca
Entité municipal: Parish (Paroisse)
Incorporation: 13 août 1879 *Area:* 49,53 km2
Comté ou district: Les Maskoutains; *Population au 2006:* 2,678
Circonscription(s) électorale(s) provinciale(s): Verchères
Circonscription(s) électorale(s) fédérale(s): St-Hyacinthe-Bagot
Prochaines élections: 3e novembre 2013
Simon Lacombe, Maire
Carole Simpson, Directrice générale

Sainte-Marie-Salomé
690, ch St-Jean
Sainte-Marie-Salomé, QC J0K 2Z0
Tél: 450-839-6212; *Téléc:* 450-839-6106
smsalome@pandore.qc.ca
Entité municipal: Parish (Paroisse)
Incorporation: 27 décembre 1888 *Area:* 34,44 km2
Comté ou district: Montcalm; *Population au 2006:* 1,256
Circonscription(s) électorale(s) provinciale(s): Joliette
Circonscription(s) électorale(s) fédérale(s): Montcalm
Prochaines élections: 3e novembre 2013
Maurice Richard, Maire
Denise Desmarais, Directrice générale

Sainte-Marthe
776, rue des Loisirs
Sainte-Marthe, QC J0P 1W0
Tél: 450-459-4284; *Téléc:* 450-459-4627
municipalite-stemarthe@sympatico.ca
www.sainte-marthe.ca
Entité municipal: Municipality
Incorporation: 27 décembre 1980 *Area:* 80,23 km2
Comté ou district: Vaudreuil-Soulanges; *Population au 2006:* 1,080
Circonscription(s) électorale(s) provinciale(s): Soulanges
Circonscription(s) électorale(s) fédérale(s): Vaudreuil-Soulanges
Prochaines élections: 3e novembre 2013
Aline Guillotte, Mairesse
Bernard Charlebois, Directeur général

Sainte-Martine
3, rue des Copains
Sainte-Martine, QC J0S 1V0
Tél: 450-427-3050; *Téléc:* 450-427-7331
saintemartine@videotron.ca
www.municipalite.sainte-martine.qc.ca
Entité municipal: Municipality
Incorporation: 8 septembre 1999 *Area:* 59,79 km2
Comté ou district: Beauharnois-Salaberry; *Population au 2006:* 4,237
Circonscription(s) électorale(s) provinciale(s): Huntingdon
Circonscription(s) électorale(s) fédérale(s): Beauharnois-Salaberry
Prochaines élections: 3e novembre 2013
François Candau, Maire
Luc Laberge, Directeur général

Sainte-Mélanie
10, rue Louis-Charles-Panet
Sainte-Mélanie, QC J0K 3A0
Tél: 450-889-5871; *Téléc:* 450-889-4527
info@sainte-melanie.ca
www.sainte-melanie.ca
Entité municipal: Municipality
Incorporation: 1er juillet 1855 *Area:* 77,05 km2
Comté ou district: Joliette; *Population au 2006:* 2,765
Circonscription(s) électorale(s) provinciale(s): Berthier
Circonscription(s) électorale(s) fédérale(s): Joliette
Prochaines élections: 3e novembre 2013
Yves Beaulieu, Maire
Claude Gagné, Directrice générale

Sainte-Monique
101, rue Honfleur
Sainte-Monique-de-Honfleur, QC G0W 2T0
Tél: 418-347-3592; *Téléc:* 418-347-3335
ste-monique@qc.aira.com
Entité municipal: Municipality
Incorporation: 30 octobre 1930 *Area:* 155,15 km2
Comté ou district: Lac-St-Jean-Est; *Population au 2006:* 914
Circonscription(s) électorale(s) provinciale(s): Lac-St-Jean
Circonscription(s) électorale(s) fédérale(s): Roberval-Lac-St-Jean
Prochaines élections: 3e novembre 2013
Georges Bouchard, Maire
Jean-Claude Duchesne, Directeur général

Sainte-Monique
247, rue Principale
Sainte-Monique, QC J0G 1N0
Tél: 819-289-2051; *Téléc:* 819-289-2344
municipalite@municipalitesaintemonique.com
Entité municipal: Municipality
Incorporation: 3 janvier 1996 *Area:* 58,79 km2
Comté ou district: Nicolet-Yamaska; *Population au 2006:* 536
Circonscription(s) électorale(s) provinciale(s): Nicolet-Yamaska
Circonscription(s) électorale(s) fédérale(s): Bas-Richelieu-Nicolet-Bécancour
Prochaines élections: 3e novembre 2013
Denis Jutras, Maire
Line Camiré, Directrice générale

Sainte-Paule
191, rue de l'Église
Sainte-Paule, QC G0J 3C0
Tél: 418-737-4296; *Téléc:* 418-737-9460
ste-paule@mrcdematane.qc.ca
www.municipalite.sainte-paule.qc.ca
Entité municipal: Municipality
Incorporation: 1er janvier 1968 *Area:* 86,64 km2
Comté ou district: Matane; *Population au 2006:* 229
Circonscription(s) électorale(s) provinciale(s): Matane
Circonscription(s) électorale(s) fédérale(s): Haute-Gaspésie-La Mitis-Matane-Matapédia
Prochaines élections: 3e novembre 2013
Yvan Côté, Maire
Gilles Desjardins, Directeur général

Sainte-Perpétue
#201, 366, rue Principale sud
Sainte-Perpétue, QC G0R 3Z0
Tél: 418-359-2966; *Téléc:* 418-359-2707
munistep@globetrotter.net
www.sainteperpetue.com
Entité municipal: Municipality
Incorporation: 21 janvier 1888 *Area:* 284,51 km2
Comté ou district: L'Islet; *Population au 2006:* 1,895
Circonscription(s) électorale(s) provinciale(s): Montmagny-L'Islet
Circonscription(s) électorale(s) fédérale(s): Montmagny-L'Islet-Kamouraska-Rivière-du-Loup; Bas-Richelieu-Nicolet-Bécancour
Prochaines élections: 3e novembre 2013
Céline Avoine Cloutier, Mairesse
Marie-Claude Chouinard, Directrice générale

Sainte-Perpétue
2197, rang St-Joseph
Sainte-Perpétue, QC J0C 1R0
Tél: 819-336-6740; *Téléc:* 819-336-6770
municipalite@ste-perpetue.qc.ca
Entité municipal: Parish (Paroisse)
Incorporation: 9 mars 1878 *Area:* 71,14 km2
Comté ou district: Nicolet-Yamaska; *Population au 2006:* 959
Circonscription(s) électorale(s) provinciale(s): Nicolet-Yamaska
Circonscription(s) électorale(s) fédérale(s): Bas-Richelieu-Nicolet-Bécancour
Prochaines élections: 3e novembre 2013
Line Théroux, Mairesse
Silvie Leclerc, Directrice générale

Sainte-Praxède
4795, rte 263
Sainte-Praxède, QC G0N 1E0
Tél: 418-449-2250; *Téléc:* 418-449-2251
mun.stepraxede@globetrotter.net
Entité municipal: Municipality
Incorporation: 1er janvier 1944 *Area:* 135,680 km2
Comté ou district: Les Appalaches; *Population au 2006:* 425
Circonscription(s) électorale(s) provinciale(s): Frontenac
Circonscription(s) électorale(s) fédérale(s): Mégantic-L'Érable
Prochaines élections: 3e novembre 2013
Daniel Talbot, Maire
Josée Vachon, Directrice générale

Sainte-Rita
CP 39
5, rue de l'Église ouest
Sainte-Rita, QC G0L 4G0
Tél: 418-963-2967; *Téléc:* 418-963-6539
info@municipalite.sainte-rita.qc.ca
www.municipalite.sainte-rita.qc.ca
Entité municipal: Municipality
Incorporation: 1er janvier 1948 *Area:* 142,88 km2
Comté ou district: Les Basques; *Population au 2006:* 355
Circonscription(s) électorale(s) provinciale(s): Rivière-du-Loup
Circonscription(s) électorale(s) fédérale(s): Rimouski-Neigette-Témiscouata-Les Basques
Prochaines élections: 3e novembre 2013
Francine Ouellet, Mairesse
Marguerite D. Michaud, Directrice générale

Sainte-Rose-de-Watford
CP 39
695, rue Carrier
Sainte-Rose-de-Watford, QC G0R 4G0
Tél: 418-267-5811; *Téléc:* 418-267-5812
municipaliteste-rose@sogetel.net
www.sainterosedewatford.qc.ca
Entité municipal: Municipality
Incorporation: 17 novembre 1897 *Area:* 112,74 km2
Comté ou district: Les Etchemins; *Population au 2006:* 750
Circonscription(s) électorale(s) provinciale(s): Bellechasse
Circonscription(s) électorale(s) fédérale(s): Lévis-Bellechasse
Prochaines élections: 3e novembre 2013
Hector Provençal, Maire
Lyse Audet, Directrice générale

Sainte-Rose-du-Nord
126, rue de la Descente-des-Femmes
Sainte-Rose-du-Nord, QC G0V 1T0
Tél: 418-675-2250; *Téléc:* 418-673-2115
admin@ste-rosedunord.qc.ca
www.ste-rosedunord.qc.ca
Entité municipal: Parish (Paroisse)
Incorporation: 1er janvier 1942 *Area:* 119,03 km2
Comté ou district: Le Fjord-du-Saguenay; *Population au 2006:* 441
Circonscription(s) électorale(s) provinciale(s): Dubuc
Circonscription(s) électorale(s) fédérale(s): Chicoutimi-Le Fjord
Prochaines élections: 3e novembre 2013
Laurent Thibeault, Maire
Maryse Girard, Directrice générale

Sainte-Sabine
4, rue St-Charles
Sainte-Sabine, QC G0R 4H0
Tél: 418-383-5488; *Téléc:* 418-383-5484
munisabine@sogetel.net
Entité municipal: Parish (Paroisse)
Incorporation: 26 août 1908 *Area:* 67,28 km2
Comté ou district: Les Etchemins; *Population au 2006:* 408
Circonscription(s) électorale(s) provinciale(s): Bellechasse
Circonscription(s) électorale(s) fédérale(s): Lévis-Bellechasse
Prochaines élections: 3e novembre 2013
Denis Boutin, Maire
Réjeanne Ruel, Directrice générale

Sainte-Sabine
185, rue Principale
Sainte-Sabine, QC J0J 2B0
Tél: 450-293-7686; *Téléc:* 450-293-7604
administration@saintesabine.ca
www.saintesabine.ca
Entité municipal: Municipality
Incorporation: 19 mars 1921 *Area:* 55,42 km2
Comté ou district: Brome-Missisquoi; *Population au 2006:* 1,053
Circonscription(s) électorale(s) provinciale(s): Brome-Missisquoi
Circonscription(s) électorale(s) fédérale(s): Brome-Missisquoi
Prochaines élections: 3e novembre 2013
Laurent Phoenix, Maire
Johanne Duval, Directrice générale

Sainte-Séraphine
2660, rue du Centre-Communautaire
Sainte-Séraphine, QC J0A 1E0
Tél: 819-336-3200; *Téléc:* 819-336-3800
info@munsainteseraphine.ca
www.munsainteseraphine.ca
Entité municipal: Parish (Paroisse)
Incorporation: 7 mars 1931 *Area:* 75,73 km2
Comté ou district: Arthabaska; *Population au 2006:* 401
Circonscription(s) électorale(s) provinciale(s): Richmond
Circonscription(s) électorale(s) fédérale(s): Richmond-Arthabaska
Prochaines élections: 3e novembre 2013
Claude Lampron, Maire
Julie Paris, Directrice générale

Sainte-Sophie
2212, rue de l'Hôtel-de-Ville
Sainte-Sophie, QC J5J 1A1
Tél: 450-438-7784; *Téléc:* 450-438-1080
courrier@ste-sophie.qc.ca
www.stesophie.ca
Entité municipal: Municipality
Incorporation: 3 mai 2000 *Area:* 108,98 km2
Comté ou district: La Rivière-du-Nord; *Population au 2006:* 10,355
Circonscription(s) électorale(s) provinciale(s): Rousseau
Circonscription(s) électorale(s) fédérale(s): Rivière-du-Nord
Prochaines élections: 3e novembre 2013
Yvon Brière, Maire
Matthieu Ledoux, Directeur général

Sainte-Sophie-d'Halifax
10, rue de l'Église
Sainte-Sophie-d'Halifax, QC G0P 1L0
Tél: 819-362-2225; *Téléc:* 819-362-2225
Entité municipal: Municipality
Incorporation: 17 décembre 1997 *Area:* 91,11 km2
Comté ou district: L'Érable; *Population au 2006:* 638
Circonscription(s) électorale(s) provinciale(s): Lotbinière
Circonscription(s) électorale(s) fédérale(s): Mégantic-L'Érable
Prochaines élections: 3e novembre 2013
Marc Nadeau, Maire
Suzanne Savage, Directrice générale

Sainte-Sophie-de-Lévrard
174A, rang St-Antoine
Sainte-Sophie-de-Lévrard, QC G0X 3C0
Tél: 819-288-5804; *Téléc:* 819-288-5804
municipalite@ste-sophie-de-levrard.com
Entité municipal: Parish (Paroisse)
Incorporation: 23 avril 1875 *Area:* 82,38 km2
Comté ou district: Bécancour; *Population au 2006:* 775
Circonscription(s) électorale(s) provinciale(s): Lotbinière
Circonscription(s) électorale(s) fédérale(s): Bas-Richelieu-Nicolet-Bécancour
Prochaines élections: 3e novembre 2013
Jean-Guy Beaudet, Maire
Micheline St-Onge, Directrice générale

Sainte-Thècle
301, rue St-Jacques
Sainte-Thècle, QC G0X 3G0
Tél: 418-289-2070; *Téléc:* 418-289-3014
ste-thecle@regionmekinac.com
www.ste-thecle.qc.ca
Entité municipal: Municipality
Incorporation: 7 juin 1989 *Area:* 216,64 km2
Comté ou district: Mékinac; *Population au 2006:* 2,486
Circonscription(s) électorale(s) provinciale(s): Laviolette
Circonscription(s) électorale(s) fédérale(s): St-Maurice-Champlain
Prochaines élections: 3e novembre 2013
Alain Valliée, Maire
Louise T.-Rompré, Sec.-Trés.

Sainte-Thérèse-de-Gaspé
CP 160
374, rte 132
Sainte-Thérèse-de-Gaspé, QC G0C 3B0
Tél: 418-385-3313; *Téléc:* 418-385-3799
muniste@globetrotter.net
Entité municipal: Municipality
Incorporation: 6 septembre 1930 *Area:* 34,36 km2
Comté ou district: Le Rocher-Percé; *Population au 2006:* 1,109
Circonscription(s) électorale(s) provinciale(s): Gaspé
Circonscription(s) électorale(s) fédérale(s): Gaspésie—Îles-de-la-Madeleine
Prochaines élections: 3e novembre 2013
Leo Lelièvre, Maire
Luc Lambert, Directeur général

Sainte-Thérèse-de-la-Gatineau
CP 155
27, ch Principal
Sainte-Thérèse-de-la-Gatineau, QC J0X 2X0
Tél: 819-449-4134; *Téléc:* 819-449-2194
info@ste-theresehg.ca
www.ste-theresehg.ca
Entité municipal: Municipality
Incorporation: 1er janvier 1946 *Area:* 67,85 km2
Comté ou district: La Vallée-de-la-Gatineau; *Population au 2006:* 335
Circonscription(s) électorale(s) provinciale(s): Gatineau
Circonscription(s) électorale(s) fédérale(s): Pontiac
Prochaines élections: 3e novembre 2013
Roch Carpentier, Maire
Mélanie Lyrette, Directrice générale

Sainte-Ursule
CP 60
215, rue Lessard
Sainte-Ursule, QC J0K 3M0
Tél: 819-228-4345; *Téléc:* 819-228-8326
dg@ste-ursule.ca
www.ste-ursule.ca
Entité municipal: Parish (Paroisse)
Incorporation: 1er juillet 1855 *Area:* 65,37 km2
Comté ou district: Maskinongé; *Population au 2006:* 1,419
Circonscription(s) électorale(s) provinciale(s): Maskinongé
Circonscription(s) électorale(s) fédérale(s): Berthier-Maskinongé
Prochaines élections: 3e novembre 2013
Réjean Carle, Maire
Diane Faucher, Directrice générale

Sainte-Victoire-de-Sorel
517, ch Ste-Victoire
Sainte-Victoire-de-Sorel, QC J0G 1T0
Tél: 450-782-3111; *Téléc:* 450-782-2687
info@saintevictoiredesorel.qc.ca
www.saintevictoiredesorel.qc.ca
Entité municipal: Parish (Paroisse)
Incorporation: 1er juillet 1855 *Area:* 74,90 km2
Comté ou district: Pierre-De Saurel; *Population au 2006:* 2,410
Circonscription(s) électorale(s) provinciale(s): Richelieu
Circonscription(s) électorale(s) fédérale(s): Bas-Richelieu-Nicolet-Bécancour
Prochaines élections: 3e novembre 2013
Solange Cournoyer, Mairesse
Michel Saint-Martin, Directeur général

Saints-Anges
CP 157
317, rue des Érables
Saints-Anges, QC G0S 3E0
Tél: 418-253-5230; *Téléc:* 418-253-5613
munsts-anges@nouvellebeauce.com
www.nouvellebeauce.com
Entité municipal: Parish (Paroisse)
Incorporation: 29 décembre 1880 *Area:* 68,61 km2
Comté ou district: La Nouvelle-Beauce; *Population au 2006:* 1,032
Circonscription(s) électorale(s) provinciale(s): Beauce-Nord
Circonscription(s) électorale(s) fédérale(s): Beauce
Prochaines élections: 3e novembre 2013
Jean-Marie Pouliot, Maire
Louise Turmel, Directrice générale

Saints-Martyrs-Canadiens
13, ch du Village
Saints-Martyrs-Canadiens, QC G0Y 1A1
Tél: 819-344-5171; *Téléc:* 819-344-2298
info@saints-martyrs-canadiens.ca
Entité municipal: Parish (Paroisse)
Incorporation: 1er janvier 1943 *Area:* 109,37 km2
Comté ou district: Arthabaska; *Population au 2006:* 253
Circonscription(s) électorale(s) provinciale(s): Richmond
Circonscription(s) électorale(s) fédérale(s): Richmond-Arthabaska
Prochaines élections: 3e novembre 2013
André Henri, Maire
Thérèse Lemay, Directrice générale

Salluit
CP 240
64, rue Aqqutituqaq
Salluit, QC J0M 1S0
Tél: 819-255-8953; *Téléc:* 819-255-8802
nvstreasurer@nvsalluit.ca
www.nvsalluit.ca
Entité municipal: Northern Village
Incorporation: 29 décembre 1979 *Area:* 14,33 km2
Comté ou district: Kativik; *Population au 2006:* 1,241
Circonscription(s) électorale(s) provinciale(s): Ungava
Circonscription(s) électorale(s) fédérale(s): Abitibi-Baie-James-Nunavik-Eeyou
Prochaines élections: 7 novembre 2012
Qalingo Angotigirk, Maire
Adamie Papigatuk, Conseiller régional

Sayabec
3, rue Keable
Sayabec, QC G0J 3K0
Tél: 418-536-5440; *Téléc:* 418-536-5572
www.municipalitesayabec.com
Entité municipal: Municipality
Incorporation: 24 décembre 1982 *Area:* 130,29 km2
Comté ou district: La Matapédia; *Population au 2006:* 1,953
Circonscription(s) électorale(s) provinciale(s): Matapédia
Circonscription(s) électorale(s) fédérale(s): Haute-Gaspésie-La Mitis-Matane-Matapédia
Prochaines élections: 3e novembre 2013
Danielle Marcoux, Mairesse
Francis Ouellet, Directeur général
francis.o@globetrotter.net

Schefferville
CP 1600
505, rue Fleming
Schefferville, QC G0G 2T0
Tél: 418-585-2471; *Téléc:* 418-585-2256
municipalite_schefferville@xplornet.ca
Entité municipal: Village
Incorporation: 1er août 1955 *Area:* 39,02 km2
Comté ou district: Caniapiscau; *Population au 2006:* 202
Circonscription(s) électorale(s) provinciale(s): Duplessis

Circonscription(s) électorale(s) fédérale(s): Manicouagan
Prochaines élections: 3e novembre 2013
Marcella Beaudoin, Maire
Marcella Beaudoin, Administratrice

Scotstown
101, ch Victoria ouest
Scotstown, QC J0B 3B0
Tél: 819-560-8433; *Téléc:* 819-560-8434
ville.scotstown@hsfgc.ca
www.scotstown-hsf.com
Entité municipal: Village
Incorporation: 24 juin 1892 *Area:* 12,40 km2
Comté ou district: Le Haut-St-François; *Population au 2006:* 588
Circonscription(s) électorale(s) provinciale(s):
Mégantic-Compton
Circonscription(s) électorale(s) fédérale(s): Compton-Stanstead
Prochaines élections: 3e novembre 2013
Vacant, Maire
Nicolle Gaudreau, Directrice générale

Scott
1070, rte Kennedy
Scott, QC G0S 3G0
Tél: 418-387-2037; *Téléc:* 418-387-1837
nthibodeau@municipalitescott.com
www.municipalitescott.com
Entité municipal: Municipality
Incorporation: 29 mars 1995 *Area:* 32,91 km2
Comté ou district: La Nouvelle-Beauce; *Population au 2006:* 1,796
Circonscription(s) électorale(s) provinciale(s): Beauce-Nord
Circonscription(s) électorale(s) fédérale(s): Beauce
Prochaines élections: 3e novembre 2013
Clément Marcoux, Maire
Nicole Thibodeau, Directrice générale

Senneterre
CP 700
100, rue le Portage
Senneterre, QC J0Y 2M0
Tél: 819-737-2842; *Téléc:* 819-737-4668
info@paroissesenneterre.qc.ca
www.paroissesenneterre.qc.ca
Entité municipal: Parish (Paroisse)
Incorporation: 23 mars 1923 *Area:* 432,98 km2
Comté ou district: Vallée-de-l'Or; *Population au 2006:* 1,186
Circonscription(s) électorale(s) provinciale(s): Abitibi-Est
Circonscription(s) électorale(s) fédérale(s):
Abitibi-Baie-James-Nunavik-Eeyou
Prochaines élections: 3e novembre 2013
Jacline Rouleau, Mairesse
Louise Leroux, Directrice générale

Senneterre
CP 789
551, 10e av
Senneterre, QC J0Y 2M0
Tél: 819-737-2296; *Téléc:* 819-737-4215
info@ville.senneterre.qc.ca
www.ville.senneterre.qc.ca
Entité municipal: Town
Incorporation: 13 juin 1919 *Area:* 16 524,89 km2
Comté ou district: Vallée-de-l'Or; *Population au 2006:* 2,993
Circonscription(s) électorale(s) provinciale(s): Abitibi-Est
Circonscription(s) électorale(s) fédérale(s):
Abitibi-Baie-James-Nunavik-Eeyou
Prochaines élections: 1er novembre 2013
Hélène Veillette, Greffière
Jean-Maurice Matte, Maire

Sept-Rivières
#400, 106, rue Napoléon
Sept-×les, QC G4R 3L7
Tél: 418-962-1900; *Téléc:* 418-962-3365
dg.mrc7riv@globetrotter.net
Entité municipal: Regional County Municipality
Incorporation: 18 mars 1981 *Area:* 32 153,95 km2
Population au 2006: 38,661
Note: 2 municipalités & 2 autres territoires.
Laurence Méthot-Losier, Préfet
Alain Lapierre, Directeur général

Shannon
50, rue St-Patrick
Shannon, QC G0A 4N0
Tél: 418-844-3778; *Téléc:* 418-844-2111
municipalite@shannon.ca
www.shannon.ca
Entité municipal: Municipality
Incorporation: 1er janvier 1947 *Area:* 61,79 km2
Comté ou district: La Jacques-Cartier; *Population au 2006:* 3,825
Circonscription(s) électorale(s) provinciale(s): Chauveau
Circonscription(s) électorale(s) fédérale(s):
Portneuf-Jacques-Cartier
Prochaines élections: 3e novembre 2013
Clive Kiley, Maire
Me Hugo Lépine, Directeur général

Shawville
CP 339
350, rue Main
Shawville, QC J0X 2Y0
Tél: 819-647-2979; *Téléc:* 819-647-6895
info@town.shawville.qc.ca
www.town.shawville.qc.ca
Entité municipal: Municipality
Incorporation: 1er janvier 1874 *Area:* 5,25 km2
Comté ou district: Pontiac; *Population au 2006:* 1,587
Circonscription(s) électorale(s) provinciale(s): Pontiac
Circonscription(s) électorale(s) fédérale(s): Pontiac
Prochaines élections: 3e novembre 2013
Albert Armstrong, Maire
Crystal Webb, Directrice générale

Sheenboro
59, ch de Sheenboro
Sheenboro, QC J0X 2Z0
Tél: 819-683-3862; *Téléc:* 819-683-3816
municsheenboro@hotmail.com
Entité municipal: Municipality
Incorporation: 1er janvier 1860 *Area:* 571,01 km2
Comté ou district: Pontiac; *Population au 2006:* 167
Circonscription(s) électorale(s) provinciale(s): Pontiac
Circonscription(s) électorale(s) fédérale(s): Pontiac
Prochaines élections: 3e novembre 2013
Dick Edwards, Maire
Donald Marion, Directeur général

Shefford
245, ch Picard
Shefford, QC J2M 1J2
Tél: 450-539-2258; *Téléc:* 450-539-4951
info@cantonshefford.qc.ca
www.cantonshefford.qc.ca
Entité municipal: Township
Incorporation: 1er juillet 1855 *Area:* 116,62 km2
Comté ou district: La Haute-Yamaska; *Population au 2006:* 5,941
Circonscription(s) électorale(s) provinciale(s): Shefford
Circonscription(s) électorale(s) fédérale(s): Shefford
Prochaines élections: 3e novembre 2013
Jean-Marc Desrochers, Maire
Sylvie Gougeon, Directrice générale

Shigawake
180, rte 132
Shigawake, QC G0C 3E0
Tél: 418-752-2474; *Téléc:* 418-752-7474
shigawake@navigue.com
Entité municipal: Municipality
Incorporation: 15 décembre 1924 *Area:* 77,36 km2
Comté ou district: Bonaventure; *Population au 2006:* 357
Circonscription(s) électorale(s) provinciale(s): Bonaventure
Circonscription(s) électorale(s) fédérale(s):
Gaspésie—Îles-de-la-Madeleine
Prochaines élections: 3e novembre 2013
Kenneth Duguay, Maire
Joann Ross, Directrice général

Stanbridge East
12, rue Maple
Stanbridge East, QC J0J 2H0
Tél: 450-248-3188; *Téléc:* 450-248-7744
stanbridge@axion.ca
www.stanbridgeeast.ca
Entité municipal: Municipality
Incorporation: 1er juillet 1855 *Area:* 49,05 km2
Comté ou district: Brome-Missisquoi; *Population au 2006:* 833
Circonscription(s) électorale(s) provinciale(s): Brome-Missisquoi
Circonscription(s) électorale(s) fédérale(s): Brome-Missisquoi
Prochaines élections: 3e novembre 2013
Greg Vaughan, Maire
Vera Gendreau, Directrice générale

Stanbridge Station
229, ch Principal
Stanbridge Station, QC J0J 2J0
Tél: 450-248-2125; *Téléc:* 450-248-1132
sergetherrien@bellnet.ca
Entité municipal: Municipality
Incorporation: 21 mars 1889 *Area:* 18,11 km2
Comté ou district: Brome-Missisquoi; *Population au 2006:* 309
Circonscription(s) électorale(s) provinciale(s): Brome-Missisquoi
Circonscription(s) électorale(s) fédérale(s): Brome-Missisquoi
Prochaines élections: 3e novembre 2013
Gilles Rioux, Maire
Serge Therrien, Directeur général

Stanstead
425, rue Dufferin
Stanstead, QC J0B 3E2
Tél: 819-876-7181; *Téléc:* 819-876-5560
info@stanstead.ca
www.stanstead.ca
Entité municipal: Town
Incorporation: 15 février 1995 *Area:* 21,93 km2
Comté ou district: Memphrémagog; *Population au 2006:* 2,957
Circonscription(s) électorale(s) provinciale(s): Orford
Circonscription(s) électorale(s) fédérale(s): Compton-Stanstead
Prochaines élections: 3e novembre 2013
Philippe Dutil, Maire
Edwin Johan Sullivan, Greffier

Stanstead
778, ch Sheldon
Fitch Bay, QC J1X 3W4
Tél: 819-876-2948; *Téléc:* 819-876-7007
cantonstanstead@axion.ca
Entité municipal: Township
Incorporation: 1er juillet 1855 *Area:* 113,93 km2
Comté ou district: Memphrémagog; *Population au 2006:* 1,065
Circonscription(s) électorale(s) provinciale(s): Orford
Circonscription(s) électorale(s) fédérale(s): Compton-Stanstead
Prochaines élections: 3e novembre 2013
Lionel Larochelle, Maire
Suzanne Ménard, Directrice générale

Stanstead-Est
7015, route 143
Stanstead-Est, QC J0B 3E0
Tél: 819-876-7292; *Téléc:* 819-876-7170
stansteadest@xittel.ca
Entité municipal: Municipality
Incorporation: 16 juillet 1932 *Area:* 111,70 km2
Comté ou district: Coaticook; *Population au 2006:* 628
Circonscription(s) électorale(s) provinciale(s): Orford
Circonscription(s) électorale(s) fédérale(s): Compton-Stanstead
Prochaines élections: 3e novembre 2013
Guy Lefebvre, Maire
Suzanne Boislard Côté, Directrice générale

Stoke
403, rue Principale
Stoke, QC J0B 3G0
Tél: 819-878-3790; *Téléc:* 819-878-3804
mun.stoke@videotron.ca
www.stoke.ca/Municipalite_de_Stoke/Bienvenue.html
Entité municipal: Municipality
Incorporation: 1er janvier 1864 *Area:* 239,89 km2
Comté ou district: Le Val-St-François; *Population au 2006:* 2,708
Circonscription(s) électorale(s) provinciale(s): Johnson
Circonscription(s) électorale(s) fédérale(s): Compton-Stanstead
Prochaines élections: 3e novembre 2013
Luc Cayer, Maire
Benoit Rousseau, Directrice générale

Stoneham-et-Tewkesbury
325, ch du Hibou
Stoneham-et-Tewkesbury, QC G3C 1R8
Tél: 418-848-2381; *Téléc:* 418-848-1748
mairie@villestoneham.com
www.villestoneham.com
Entité municipal: United Township (Cantons)
Incorporation: 1er juillet 1855 *Area:* 684,75 km2
Comté ou district: La Jacques-Cartier; *Population au 2006:* 5,866
Circonscription(s) électorale(s) provinciale(s): Chauveau
Circonscription(s) électorale(s) fédérale(s):
Portneuf-Jacques-Cartier
Prochaines élections: 3e novembre 2013
Robert Miller, Maire
Michel Chatigny, Directeur général

Stornoway
CP 98
507, rte 108 ouest
Stornoway, QC G0Y 1N0
Tél: 819-652-2800; *Téléc:* 819-652-2105
administration@munstornoway.gc.ca
www.munstornoway.qc.ca
Entité municipal: Municipality
Incorporation: 1er janvier 1858 *Area:* 178,32 km2
Comté ou district: Le Granit; *Population au 2006:* 584

Circonscription(s) électorale(s) provinciale(s): Mégantic-Compton
Circonscription(s) électorale(s) fédérale(s): Mégantic-L'Érable
Prochaines élections: 3e novembre 2013
Pierre-André Gagné, Maire
Sylvie Gauthier, Directrice générale

Stratford
165, av Centrale nord
Stratford, QC G0Y 1P0
Tél: 418-443-2307; *Téléc:* 418-443-2603
mun.stratford@qc.aira.com
www.munstratford.qc.ca
Entité municipal: Township
Incorporation: 1er janvier 1874 *Area:* 125,61 km2
Comté ou district: Le Granit; *Population au 2006:* 1,086
Circonscription(s) électorale(s) provinciale(s): Mégantic-Compton
Circonscription(s) électorale(s) fédérale(s): Mégantic-L'Érable
Prochaines élections: 3e novembre 2013
Jacques Fontaine, Maire
Manon Goulet, Directrice générale

Stukely-Sud
101, place de la Mairie
Stukely-Sud, QC J0E 2J0
Tél: 450-297-3407; *Téléc:* 450-297-3759
info@stukely-sud.com
www.stukely-sud.com
Entité municipal: Village
Incorporation: 19 septembre 1934 *Area:* 66,31 km2
Comté ou district: Memphrémagog; *Population au 2006:* 941
Circonscription(s) électorale(s) provinciale(s): Brome-Missisquoi
Circonscription(s) électorale(s) fédérale(s): Brome-Missisquoi
Prochaines élections: 3e novembre 2013
Gérald Allaire, Maire
Louisette Tremblay, Directrice générale

Sutton
11, rue Principale sud
Sutton, QC J0E 2K0
Tél: 450-538-2290; *Téléc:* 450-538-0930
p.menard@sutton.caa
www.sutton.ca
Entité municipal: Town
Incorporation: 4 juillet 2002 *Area:* 243,51 km2
Comté ou district: Brome-Missisquoi; *Population au 2006:* 3,805
Circonscription(s) électorale(s) provinciale(s): Brome-Missisquoi
Circonscription(s) électorale(s) fédérale(s): Brome-Missisquoi
Prochaines élections: 3e novembre 2013
Pierre Pelland, Maire
Jean-François D'Amour, Directrice générale

Tadoussac
162, rue des Jésuites
Tadoussac, QC G0T 2A0
Tél: 418-235-4446; *Téléc:* 418-235-4433
ville@tadoussac.com
www.tadoussac.com
Entité municipal: Village
Incorporation: 10 octobre 1899 *Area:* 74,59 km2
Comté ou district: La Haute-Côte-Nord; *Population au 2006:* 850
Circonscription(s) électorale(s) provinciale(s): René-Lévesque
Circonscription(s) électorale(s) fédérale(s): Montmorency-Charlevoix-Haute-Côte-Nord
Prochaines élections: 3e novembre 2013
Hugues Tremblay, Maire
Marie-Claude Guérin, Directeur général

Taschereau
CP 150
52, rue Morin
Taschereau, QC J0Z 3N0
Tél: 819-796-2219; *Téléc:* 819-796-2220
taschereau@mrcao.qc.ca
www.taschereau.ao.ca
Entité municipal: Municipality
Incorporation: 27 décembre 2001 *Area:* 265,62 km2
Comté ou district: Abitibi-Ouest; *Population au 2006:* 996
Circonscription(s) électorale(s) provinciale(s): Abitibi-Ouest
Circonscription(s) électorale(s) fédérale(s): Abitibi-Témiscamingue
Prochaines élections: 3e novembre 2013
Jean-Marie Poulin, Maire
Yves Aubut, Directeur général

Tasiujaq
CP 54
Tasiujaq, QC J0M 1T0
Tél: 819-633-9924; *Téléc:* 819-633-5026
www.nvtasiujaq.ca
Entité municipal: Northern Village
Incorporation: 2 février 1980 *Area:* 68,08 km2
Comté ou district: Kativik; *Population au 2006:* 248
Circonscription(s) électorale(s) provinciale(s): Ungava
Circonscription(s) électorale(s) fédérale(s): Abitibi-Baie-James-Nunavik-Eeyou
Prochaines élections: 7 novembre 2012
Willie Cain, Maire
Mary Berthe, Sec.-Trés.

Témiscaming
CP 730
20, rue Humphrey
Témiscaming, QC J0Z 3R0
Tél: 819-627-3273; *Téléc:* 819-627-3019
ville.temiscaming@temiscaming.net
www.temiscaming.net
Entité municipal: Town
Incorporation: 26 mars 1988 *Area:* 861,77 km2
Comté ou district: Témiscamingue; *Population au 2006:* 2,697
Circonscription(s) électorale(s) provinciale(s): Rouyn-Noranda-Témiscamingue
Circonscription(s) électorale(s) fédérale(s): Abitibi-Témiscamingue
Prochaines élections: 3e novembre 2013
Philippe Barette, Maire
Maurice Paquin, Directeur général

Témiscamingue
#209, 21, rue Notre-Dame-de-Lourdes
Ville-Marie, QC J9V 1X8
Tél: 819-629-2829; *Téléc:* 819-629-3472
mrc@mrctemiscamingue.qc.ca
www.temiscamingue.net
Entité municipal: Regional County Municipality
Incorporation: 15 avril 1981 *Area:* 19 243,88 km2
Population au 2006: 16,985
Note: 20 municipalités & 2 autres territoires.
Jean-Pierre Charron, Préfet
mrc@mrctemiscamingue.qc.ca
Denis Clermont, Directeur général
denis.clermont@mrctemiscamingue.qc.ca

Témiscouata
5, rue de l'Hôtel de Ville, 2e étage
Notre-Dame-du-Lac, QC G0L 1X0
Tél: 418-899-6725; *Téléc:* 418-899-2000
admin@mrctemis.ca
www.mrctemiscouata.qc.ca
Entité municipal: Regional County Municipality
Incorporation: 1 janvier 1982 *Area:* 3 920,90 km2
Population au 2006: 21,785
Note: 20 municipalités.
Jean-Pierre Laplante, Directeur général
Serge Fortin, Préfet

Témiscouata-sur-le-Lac
79, rue Commerciale
Témiscouata-sur-le-Lac, QC G0L 1E0
Tél: 418-854-2116; *Téléc:* 418-854-0118
info@ville.cabano.qc.ca
www.ville.cabano.qc.ca
Entité municipal: Town
Incorporation: 5e mai 2010 *Area:* 227,91 km2
Comté ou district: Témiscouata; *Population au 2006:* 5,259
Circonscription(s) électorale(s) provinciale(s): Kamouraska-Témiscouata
Note: Le 5e mai 2010, les villes de Cabano et Notre-Dame-du-Lac ont été amalgamé sous le nom de Témiscouata-sur-le-Lac.
Gilles Garon, Maire
Gilles Desrosiers, Directeur général

Terrasse-Vaudreuil
74, 7e av
Terrasse-Vaudreuil, QC J7V 3M9
Tél: 514-453-8120; *Téléc:* 514-453-1180
info@terrasse-vaudreuil.ca
www.terrasse-vaudreuil.ca
Entité municipal: Municipality
Incorporation: 1er janvier 1952 *Area:* 1,08 km2
Comté ou district: Vaudreuil-Soulanges; *Population au 2006:* 1,985
Circonscription(s) électorale(s) provinciale(s): Vaudreuil
Circonscription(s) électorale(s) fédérale(s): Vaudreuil-Soulanges
Prochaines élections: 3e novembre 2013
Manon Trudel, Mairesse
Ginette Roy, Directrice générale

Thérèse-de-Blainville
479, boul Adolphe-Chapleau
Bois-des-Filion, QC J6Z 1J9
Tél: 450-621-5546; *Téléc:* 450-621-2628
reception@mrc-tdb.org
www.mrctheresedeblainville.qc.ca
Entité municipal: Regional County Municipality
Population au 2006: 147,370
Note: 7 municipalités.
Paul Larocque, Préfet
Perrine Lapierre, Directrice générale

Thorne
775, rte 366
Ladysmith, QC J0X 2A0
Tél: 819-647-3206; *Téléc:* 819-647-2086
administration@municipalite.thorne.qc.ca
www.thornequebec.ca
Entité municipal: Municipality
Incorporation: 1er janvier 1860 *Area:* 177,33 km2
Comté ou district: Pontiac; *Population au 2006:* 427
Circonscription(s) électorale(s) provinciale(s): Pontiac
Circonscription(s) électorale(s) fédérale(s): Pontiac
Prochaines élections: 3e novembre 2013
Ross Vowles, Maire
Ginger Finan, Directrice générale

Thurso
161, rue Galipeau
Thurso, QC J0X 3B0
Tél: 819-985-2701; *Téléc:* 819-985-0134
ville.thurso@mrcpapineau.com
www.ville.thurso.qc.ca
Entité municipal: Town
Incorporation: 16 janvier 1886 *Area:* 6,77 km2
Comté ou district: Papineau; *Population au 2006:* 2,299
Circonscription(s) électorale(s) provinciale(s): Papineau
Circonscription(s) électorale(s) fédérale(s): Argenteuil-Papineau-Mirabel
Prochaines élections: 3e novembre 2013
Maurice Boivin, Maire
Mario Boyer, Directeur général & Greffier

Tingwick
CP 150
12, rue de l'Hôtel-de-Ville
Tingwick, QC J0A 1L0
Tél: 819-359-2454; *Téléc:* 819-359-2233
c.ramsay@tingwick.ca
www.tingwick.ca
Entité municipal: Municipality
Incorporation: 12 décembre 1981 *Area:* 168,93 km2
Comté ou district: Arthabaska; *Population au 2006:* 1,458
Circonscription(s) électorale(s) provinciale(s): Richmond
Circonscription(s) électorale(s) fédérale(s): Richmond-Arthabaska
Prochaines élections: 3e novembre 2013
Paul-Émile Simoneau, Maire
Chantale Ramsay, Directrice générale

Tourville
962, rue des Trembles
Tourville, QC G0R 4M0
Tél: 418-359-2106; *Téléc:* 418-359-3671
municipal.tourville@globetrotter.net
www.muntourville.qc.ca
Entité municipal: Municipality
Incorporation: 14 novembre 1918 *Area:* 161,51 km2
Comté ou district: L'Islet; *Population au 2006:* 730
Circonscription(s) électorale(s) provinciale(s): Montmagny-L'Islet
Circonscription(s) électorale(s) fédérale(s): Montmagny-L'Islet-Kamouraska-Rivière-du-Loup
Prochaines élections: 3e novembre 2013
Michel Guy Anctil, Maire
Normand Blier, Directeur général

Trécesson
314, rue Sauvé
Trécesson, QC J0Y 2S0
Tél: 819-732-8524; *Téléc:* 819-732-8322
mun.trecesson@cableamos.com
www.mrcabitibi.qc.ca
Entité municipal: Township
Incorporation: 15 juillet 1918 *Area:* 198,38 km2
Comté ou district: Abitibi; *Population au 2006:* 1,195
Circonscription(s) électorale(s) provinciale(s): Abitibi-Ouest
Circonscription(s) électorale(s) fédérale(s): Abitibi-Témiscamingue
Prochaines élections: 3e novembre 2013
Ghislain Nadeau, Maire
Joanie Lambert, Directrice générale

Très-St-Rédempteur
769, rte Principale
Très-St-Rédempteur, QC J0P 1P0
Tél: 450-451-5203; *Téléc:* 450-451-8894
dir@tressaintredemteur.ca
www.tressaintredempteur.ca
Entité municipal: Parish (Paroisse)
Incorporation: 30 décembre 1880 *Area:* 25,40 km2
Comté ou district: Vaudreuil-Soulanges; *Population au 2006:* 733
Circonscription(s) électorale(s) provinciale(s): Soulanges
Circonscription(s) électorale(s) fédérale(s): Vaudreuil-Soulanges
Prochaines élections: 3e novembre 2013
Jean Lalonde, Maire
Vacant, Directeur général

Très-St-Sacrement
CP 160
1180, rte 203
Howick, QC J0S 1G0
Tél: 450-825-0192; *Téléc:* 450-825-0193
mun-trst@videotron.ca
Entité municipal: Parish (Paroisse)
Incorporation: 2 avril 1885 *Area:* 97,30 km2
Comté ou district: Le Haut-Saint-Laurent; *Population au 2006:* 1,213
Circonscription(s) électorale(s) provinciale(s): Huntingdon
Circonscription(s) électorale(s) fédérale(s): Beauharnois-Salaberry
Prochaines élections: 3e novembre 2013
Albert Billette, Maire
Suzanne Côté, Directrice générale

Tring-Jonction
100, av Commerciale
Tring-Jonction, QC G0N 1X0
Tél: 418-426-2497; *Téléc:* 418-426-2498
tring@bellnet.ca
www.tringjonction.qc.ca
Entité municipal: Village
Incorporation: 21 novembre 1918 *Area:* 25,71 km2
Comté ou district: Robert-Cliche; *Population au 2006:* 1,380
Circonscription(s) électorale(s) provinciale(s): Beauce-Nord
Circonscription(s) électorale(s) fédérale(s): Beauce
Prochaines élections: 3e novembre 2013
Mario Groleau, Maire
Marcel Poulin, Directeur général

Trois-Pistoles
5, rue Notre-Dame est
Trois-Pistoles, QC G0L 4K0
Tél: 418-851-1995; *Téléc:* 418-851-3567
administration@ville-trois-pistoles.ca
www.ville-trois-pistoles.ca
Entité municipal: Town
Incorporation: 9 mars 1916 *Area:* 7,74 km2
Comté ou district: Les Basques; *Population au 2006:* 3,500
Circonscription(s) électorale(s) provinciale(s): Rivière-du-Loup
Circonscription(s) électorale(s) fédérale(s): Rimouski-Neigette-Témiscouata-Les Basques
Prochaines élections: 3e novembre 2013
Jean-Pierre Rioux, Maire
Cindy Lafrenière, Greffière

Trois-Rives
258, ch St-Joseph
Trois-Rives, QC G0X 2C0
Tél: 819-646-5686; *Téléc:* 819-646-5688
trois-rives@regionmekinac.com
www.trois-rives.com
Entité municipal: Municipality
Incorporation: 2 septembre 1972 *Area:* 675,09 km2
Comté ou district: Mékinac; *Population au 2006:* 411
Circonscription(s) électorale(s) provinciale(s): Laviolette
Circonscription(s) électorale(s) fédérale(s): St-Maurice-Champlain
Prochaines élections: 3e novembre 2013
Lucien Mongrain, Maire
Nicole Léveillé, Directrice générale

Ulverton
151, rte 143
Ulverton, QC J0B 2B0
Tél: 819-826-5049; *Téléc:* 819-826-5181
municipalite.ulverton@bellnet.ca
Entité municipal: Municipality
Incorporation: 1er juillet 1855 *Area:* 51,28 km2
Comté ou district: Le Val-St-François; *Population au 2006:* 363
Circonscription(s) électorale(s) provinciale(s): Johnson
Circonscription(s) électorale(s) fédérale(s): Richmond-Arthabaska
Prochaines élections: 3e novembre 2013
Vacant, Maire
Chantal Dubé, Directrice générale

Umiujaq
CP 108
Umiujaq, QC J0M 1Y0
Tél: 819-331-7000; *Téléc:* 819-331-7057
sec.treasurer@nvumiujaq.ca
www.nvumiujaq.ca
Entité municipal: Northern Village
Incorporation: 20 décembre 1986 *Area:* 25,50 km2
Comté ou district: Kativik; *Population au 2006:* 390
Circonscription(s) électorale(s) provinciale(s): Ungava
Circonscription(s) électorale(s) fédérale(s): Abitibi-Baie-James-Nunavik-Eeyou
Prochaines élections: 7 novembre 2012
Abelie Napartuk, Maire
Sam Nuktie, Sec.-Trés.

Upton
863, rue Lanoie
Upton, QC J0H 2E0
Tél: 450-549-5611; *Téléc:* 450-549-5045
dg@upton.ca
www.upton.ca
Entité municipal: Municipality
Incorporation: 25 février 1998 *Area:* 51,02 km2
Comté ou district: Acton; *Population au 2006:* 1,954
Circonscription(s) électorale(s) provinciale(s): Johnson
Circonscription(s) électorale(s) fédérale(s): St-Hyacinthe-Bagot
Prochaines élections: 3e novembre 2013
Yves Croteau, Maire
Cynthia Bossé, Directrice générale

Val-Alain
CP 10
1245, 2e rang
Val-Alain, QC G0S 3H0
Tél: 819-744-3222; *Téléc:* 819-744-1330
municipalitevalalain@globetrotter.net
www.val-alain.com
Entité municipal: Municipality
Incorporation: 1er janvier 1950 *Area:* 103,80 km2
Comté ou district: Lotbinière; *Population au 2006:* 901
Circonscription(s) électorale(s) provinciale(s): Lotbinière
Circonscription(s) électorale(s) fédérale(s): Lotbinière-Chutes-de-la-Chaudière
Prochaines élections: 3e novembre 2013
Rénald Grondin, Maire
France Bisson, Directrice générale

Val-Brillant
CP 220
11, rue St-Pierre ouest
Val-Brillant, QC G0J 3L0
Tél: 418-742-3212; *Téléc:* 418-742-3624
valbrillant@globetrotter.net
www.valbrillant.ca
Entité municipal: Municipality
Incorporation: 20 décembre 1986 *Area:* 80,00 km2
Comté ou district: La Matapédia; *Population au 2006:* 1,003
Circonscription(s) électorale(s) provinciale(s): Matapédia
Circonscription(s) électorale(s) fédérale(s): Haute-Gaspésie-La Mitis-Matane-Matapédia
Prochaines élections: 3e novembre 2013
Donald Malenfant, Maire
Lise Tremblay, Directrice générale

Val-David
2579, rue de l'Église
Val-David, QC J0T 2N0
Tél: 819-324-5678; *Téléc:* 819-322-6327
info@valdavid.com
www.valdavid.com
Entité municipal: Village
Incorporation: 10 mai 1921 *Area:* 43,17 km2
Comté ou district: Les Laurentides; *Population au 2006:* 4,216
Circonscription(s) électorale(s) provinciale(s): Bertrand
Circonscription(s) électorale(s) fédérale(s): Laurentides-Labelle
Prochaines élections: 3e novembre 2013
Nicole Davidson, Mairesse
Serge Pourreaux, Directeur général

Val-des-Bois
CP 69
595, rte 309
Val-des-Bois, QC J0X 3C0
Tél: 819-454-2280; *Téléc:* 819-454-2211
mun.valdesbois@mrcpapineau.com
www.val-des-bois.ca
Entité municipal: Municipality
Incorporation: 1er janvier 1885 *Area:* 224,34 km2
Comté ou district: Papineau; *Population au 2006:* 873
Circonscription(s) électorale(s) provinciale(s): Papineau
Circonscription(s) électorale(s) fédérale(s): Argenteuil-Papineau-Mirabel
Prochaines élections: 3e novembre 2013
Marcel Proulx, Maire
Line Sarrazin, Directrice générale

Val-des-Lacs
349, ch de Val-des-Lacs
Val-des-Lacs, QC J0T 2P0
Tél: 819-326-5624; *Téléc:* 819-326-7065
info@municipalite.val-des-lacs.qc.ca
municipalite.val-des-lacs.qc.ca
Entité municipal: Municipality
Incorporation: 6 février 1932 *Area:* 121,82 km2
Comté ou district: Les Laurentides; *Population au 2006:* 778
Circonscription(s) électorale(s) provinciale(s): Bertrand
Circonscription(s) électorale(s) fédérale(s): Laurentides-Labelle
Prochaines élections: 1er novembre 2013
Sylvain Michaudville, Sec.-Trés. & Directeur général
Berthe Béleanger, Maire

Val-des-Monts
1, rte du Carrefour
Val-des-Monts, QC J8N 4E9
Tél: 819-457-9400; *Téléc:* 819-457-4141
administration@val-des-monts.net
www.val-des-monts.net
Entité municipal: Municipality
Incorporation: 1er janvier 1975 *Area:* 457,31 km2
Comté ou district: Les Collines-de-l'Outaouais; *Population au 2006:* 9,539
Circonscription(s) électorale(s) provinciale(s): Papineau
Circonscription(s) électorale(s) fédérale(s): Pontiac
Prochaines élections: 3e novembre 2013
Jean Lafrenière, Maire
Patricia Fillet, Directrice générale

Val-Joli
500, rte 249
Val-Joli, QC J1S 2L5
Tél: 819-845-7663; *Téléc:* 819-845-4399
val-jolidg@axion.ca
Entité municipal: Municipality
Incorporation: 1er juillet 1855 *Area:* 90,61 km2
Comté ou district: Le Val-Saint-François; *Population au 2006:* 1,479
Circonscription(s) électorale(s) provinciale(s): Johnson
Circonscription(s) électorale(s) fédérale(s): Richmond-Arthabaska
Prochaines élections: 1er novembre 2013
Lucie Camiré, Sec.-Trés. & Directrice générale
Gilles Perron, Maire

Val-Morin
6120, rue Morin
Val-Morin, QC J0T 2R0
Tél: 819-322-5670; *Téléc:* 819-322-3923
municipalite@val-morin.ca
www.val-morin.ca
Entité municipal: Municipality
Incorporation: 27 juin 1922 *Area:* 39,00 km2
Comté ou district: Les Laurentides; *Population au 2006:* 2,756
Circonscription(s) électorale(s) provinciale(s): Bertrand
Circonscription(s) électorale(s) fédérale(s): Laurentides-Labelle
Prochaines élections: 3e novembre 2013
Jacques Brien, Maire
Pierre Delage, Directeur général

Val-Racine
CP 1
2991, ch St-Léon
Val-Racine, QC G0Y 1E0
Tél: 819-657-4790; *Téléc:* 819-657-4790
vracine@xplornet.com
www.municipalite.val-racine.qc.ca
Entité municipal: Parish (Paroisse)
Incorporation: 26 avril 1907 *Area:* 116,80 km2
Comté ou district: Le Granit; *Population au 2006:* 142
Circonscription(s) électorale(s) provinciale(s): Mégantic-Compton
Circonscription(s) électorale(s) fédérale(s): Mégantic-L'Érable
Prochaines élections: 3e novembre 2013
Chantal Grégoire, Directrice générale
Sonia Cloutier, Mairesse

Val-St-Gilles
801, rue Principale
Val-Saint-Gilles, QC J0Z 3T0
Tél: 819-333-2158; *Téléc:* 819-333-3116
valstgilles@mrcao.qc.ca
www.valst-gilles.ao.ca
Entité municipal: Municipality
Incorporation: 1er avril 1939 *Area:* 110,54 km2
Comté ou district: Abitibi-Ouest; *Population au 2006:* 171
Circonscription(s) électorale(s) provinciale(s): Abitibi-Ouest
Circonscription(s) électorale(s) fédérale(s): Abitibi-Témiscamingue
Prochaines élections: 3e novembre 2013
Réjean Lambert, Maire
Sylvie Lambert, Directrice générale

Valcourt
9040B, rue de la Montagne
Valcourt, QC J0E 2L0
Tél: 450-532-2688; *Téléc:* 450-532-5570
info@cantonvalcourt.qc.ca
Entité municipal: Township
Incorporation: 1er juillet 1855 *Area:* 79,64 km2
Comté ou district: Le Val-St-François; *Population au 2006:* 1,025
Circonscription(s) électorale(s) provinciale(s): Johnson
Circonscription(s) électorale(s) fédérale(s): Shefford
Prochaines élections: 1er novembre 2013
Patrice Desmarais, Maire
desmpat@cooptel.qc.ca
Sylvie Courtemanche, Directrice générale
directrice@catonvalcourt.qc.ca

Valcourt
1155, rue St-Joseph
Valcourt, QC J0E 2L0
Tél: 450-532-3313; *Téléc:* 450-532-3424
ville.valcourt@valcourt.ca
www.valcourt.ca
Entité municipal: Town
Incorporation: 19 octobre 1929 *Area:* 5,17 km2
Comté ou district: Le Val-St-François; *Population au 2006:* 2,349
Circonscription(s) électorale(s) provinciale(s): Johnson
Circonscription(s) électorale(s) fédérale(s): Shefford
Prochaines élections: 3e novembre 2013
Laurian Gagné, Maire
Manon Beauchemin, Greffière

Vallée-Jonction
259, blvd. Jean-Marie Rousseau
Vallée-Jonction, QC G0S 3J0
Tél: 418-253-5515; *Téléc:* 418-253-6731
munivj@globetrotter.net
www.valleejonction.qc.ca
Entité municipal: Municipality
Incorporation: 22 mars 1989 *Area:* 24,41 km2
Comté ou district: La Nouvelle-Beauce; *Population au 2006:* 1,868
Circonscription(s) électorale(s) provinciale(s): Beauce-Nord
Circonscription(s) électorale(s) fédérale(s): Beauce
Prochaines élections: 3e novembre 2013
Réal Bisson, Mairesse
Gervais Boily, Directeur général

Vaudreuil-Soulanges
420, av Saint-Charles
Vaudreuil-Dorion, QC J7V 2N1
Tél: 450-455-5753; *Téléc:* 450-455-0145
info@mrcvs.ca
www.mrcvs.ca
Entité municipal: Regional County Municipality
Population au 2009: 125,404
Note: 23 municipalités.
Guy-Lin Beaudoin, Directeur général
Gilles Farand, Préfet

Vaudreuil-sur-le-Lac
44, rue de l'Église
Vaudreuil-sur-le-Lac, QC J7V 8P3
Tél: 450-455-1133; *Téléc:* 450-455-8614
vsll@videotron.ca
www.vsll.ca
Entité municipal: Village
Incorporation: 29 mai 1920 *Area:* 1,73 km2
Comté ou district: Vaudreuil-Soulanges; *Population au 2006:* 1,290
Circonscription(s) électorale(s) provinciale(s): Vaudreuil
Circonscription(s) électorale(s) fédérale(s): Vaudreuil-Soulanges
Prochaines élections: 3e novembre 2013
Claude Pilon, Maire
Claudia Chebin, Directrice générale

Venise-en-Québec
CP 270
237, 16e av ouest
Venise-en-Québec, QC J0J 2K0
Tél: 450-244-5838; *Téléc:* 450-244-5550
begind@venise-en-quebec.ca
www.municipalite.venise-en-quebec.qc.ca
Entité municipal: Municipality
Incorporation: 1er janvier 1950 *Area:* 13,57 km2
Comté ou district: Le Haut-Richelieu; *Population au 2006:* 1,319
Circonscription(s) électorale(s) provinciale(s): Iberville
Circonscription(s) électorale(s) fédérale(s): Brome-Missisquoi
Prochaines élections: 3e novembre 2013
Jacques Landry, Maire
Diane Bégin, Directrice générale

Verchères
581, rte Marie-Victorin
Verchères, QC J0L 2R0
Tél: 450-583-3307; *Téléc:* 450-583-3637
mairie@ville.vercheres.qc.ca
www.ville.vercheres.qc.ca
Entité municipal: Municipality
Incorporation: 18 septembre 1971 *Area:* 7,277 km2
Comté ou district: Marguerite-D'Youville; *Population au 2006:* 5,243
Circonscription(s) électorale(s) provinciale(s): Verchères
Circonscription(s) électorale(s) fédérale(s): Verchères-Les Patriotes
Prochaines élections: 3e novembre 2013
Alexandre Bélisle, Maire
Luc Forcier, Directeur général

Ville-Marie
Édifice Gérard-Caron
21, rue St-Gabriel sud
Ville-Marie, QC J9V 1A1
Tél: 819-629-2881; *Téléc:* 819-629-3215
vvm.dgst@mrctemiscamingue.qc.ca
www.ville-marie.ca
Entité municipal: Town
Incorporation: 13 octobre 1897 *Area:* 11,94 km2
Comté ou district: Témiscamingue; *Population au 2006:* 2,696
Circonscription(s) électorale(s) provinciale(s): Rouyn-Noranda-Témiscamingue
Circonscription(s) électorale(s) fédérale(s): Abitibi-Témiscamingue
Prochaines élections: 3e novembre 2013
Bernard Flébus, Maire
Daniel Dufour, Directeur général

Villeroy
378, rue Principale
Villeroy, QC G0S 3K0
Tél: 819-385-4605; *Téléc:* 819-385-4754
info@municipalite-villeroy.ca
www.municipalite-villeroy.ca
Entité municipal: Municipality
Incorporation: 22 septembre 1924 *Area:* 100,41 km2
Comté ou district: L'Érable; *Population au 2006:* 496
Circonscription(s) électorale(s) provinciale(s): Lotbinière
Circonscription(s) électorale(s) fédérale(s): Mégantic-L'Érable
Prochaines élections: 3e novembre 2013
Michel Poisson, Maire
Angèle Germain, Directrice générale

Waltham
CP 160
69, rue de l'Hôtel-de-Ville
Waltham, QC J0X 3H0
Tél: 819-683-3027; *Téléc:* 819-683-1815
froytenuedelivres@yahoo.ca
Entité municipal: Municipality
Incorporation: 1er janvier 1859 *Area:* 451,43 km2
Comté ou district: Pontiac; *Population au 2006:* 360
Circonscription(s) électorale(s) provinciale(s): Pontiac
Circonscription(s) électorale(s) fédérale(s): Pontiac
Prochaines élections: 3e novembre 2013
Garry Marchand, Maire
Fernand Roy, Directeur-général

Warden
172, rue Principale
Warden, QC J0E 2M0
Tél: 450-539-1349; *Téléc:* 450-539-0096
info@village.warden.gc.ca
Entité municipal: Village
Incorporation: 31 mars 1916 *Area:* 5,28 km2
Comté ou district: La Haute-Yamaska; *Population au 2006:* 346
Circonscription(s) électorale(s) provinciale(s): Shefford
Circonscription(s) électorale(s) fédérale(s): Shefford
Prochaines élections: 3e novembre 2013
Philip Tétrault, Maire
Jacqueline Giroux, Directrice générale

Warwick
8, rue de l'Hôtel-de-Ville
Warwick, QC J0A 1M0
Tél: 819-358-4300; *Téléc:* 819-358-4319
ville@ville.warwick.qc.ca
www.ville.warwick.qc.ca
Entité municipal: Town
Incorporation: 15 mars 2000 *Area:* 114,01 km2
Comté ou district: Arthabaska; *Population au 2006:* 4,804
Circonscription(s) électorale(s) provinciale(s): Richmond
Circonscription(s) électorale(s) fédérale(s): Richmond-Arthabaska
Prochaines élections: 3e novembre 2013
Claude Desrochers, Maire
Lise Lemieux, Directrice générale

Waskaganish
CP 60
70, rue Waskaganish
Waskaganish, QC J0M 1R0
Tél: 819-895-8650; *Téléc:* 819-895-8901
Entité municipal: Villages Cris
Population au 2006: 1,864
Circonscription(s) électorale(s) provinciale(s): Ungava
Circonscription(s) électorale(s) fédérale(s): Abitibi-Baie-James-Nunavik-Eeyou
Steve Diamond, Maire
Susan Esau, Secrétaire-Trésorière

Waswanipi
Edifice Diom-Blacksmith
CP 8
Waswanipi, QC J0Y 3C0
Tél: 819-753-2587; *Téléc:* 819-753-2555
council@waswanipi.com
www.waswanipi.com
Entité municipal: Villages Cris
Population au 2006: 1,473
Circonscription(s) électorale(s) provinciale(s): Ungava
Circonscription(s) électorale(s) fédérale(s): Abitibi-Baie-James-Nunavik-Eeyou
Paul Gull, Maire
Samuel Gull, Directeur général

Waterloo
CP 50
417, rue de la Cour
Waterloo, QC J0E 2N0
Tél: 450-539-2282; *Téléc:* 450-539-3257
administration@ville.waterloo.gc.ca
www.ville.waterloo.qc.ca
Entité municipal: Town
Incorporation: 1er janvier 1867 *Area:* 11,52 km2
Comté ou district: La Haute-Yamaska; *Population au 2006:* 4,054
Circonscription(s) électorale(s) provinciale(s): Shefford
Circonscription(s) électorale(s) fédérale(s): Shefford
Prochaines élections: 3e novembre 2013
Pascal Russell, Maire
Luc Lafleur, Greffier

Waterville
170, rue Principale sud
Waterville, QC J0B 3H0
Tél: 819-837-2456; *Téléc:* 819-837-0786
kesmith@sympatico.ca
Entité municipal: Village
Incorporation: 1er janvier 1876 *Area:* 44,53 km2
Comté ou district: Coaticook; *Population au 2006:* 1,926
Circonscription(s) électorale(s) provinciale(s): St-François
Circonscription(s) électorale(s) fédérale(s): Compton-Stanstead
Prochaines élections: 3e novembre 2013
Gladys Bruun, Mairesse
François Fréchette, Directeur général

Weedon
525, 2e av
Weedon, QC J0B 3J0
Tél: 819-560-8550; *Téléc:* 819-560-8551
adm.weedon@hsfgc.ca
www.weedon.info
Entité municipal: Municipality
Incorporation: 9 février 2000 *Area:* 215,02 km2
Comté ou district: Le Haut-St-François; *Population au 2006:* 2,739
Circonscription(s) électorale(s) provinciale(s): Mégantic-Compton
Circonscription(s) électorale(s) fédérale(s): Compton-Stanstead
Prochaines élections: 3e novembre 2013

Jean-Claude Dumas, Maire
Émile Royer, Directeur général

Wemindji
CP 60
16, rue Beaver
Wemindji, QC J0M 1L0
Tél: 819-978-0264; *Téléc:* 819-978-0258
info@wemindji-nation.qc.ca
www.wemindji-nation.qc.ca
Entité municipal: Villages Cris
Incorporation: 28 juin 1978 *Area:* 186,22 km2
Population au 2006: 1,215
Circonscription(s) électorale(s) provinciale(s): Ungava
Circonscription(s) électorale(s) fédérale(s):
Abitibi-Baie-James-Nunavik-Eeyou
Prochaines élections: 1er septembre 2012
Rodney Mark, Maire
Karen Mistacheesick, Sec.-Trés.

Wentworth
114, ch Louisa
Wentworth, QC J8H 0C7
Tél: 450-562-0701; *Téléc:* 450-562-0703
info@wentworth.ca
Entité municipal: Township
Incorporation: 1er juillet 1855 *Area:* 88,99 km2
Comté ou district: Argenteuil; *Population au 2006:* 483
Circonscription(s) électorale(s) provinciale(s): Argenteuil
Circonscription(s) électorale(s) fédérale(s):
Argenteuil-Papineau-Mirabel
Prochaines élections: 1er novembre 2013
Paula Knudsen, Directrice générale
Normand Champoux, Maire

Wentworth-Nord
3488, rte Principale
Wentworth-Nord, QC J0T 1Y0
Tél: 450-226-2416; *Téléc:* 450-226-2109
info@wenworth-nord.ca
www.went-nord.ca
Entité municipal: Municipality
Incorporation: 1er janvier 1958 *Area:* 155,71 km2
Comté ou district: Les Pays-d'en-Haut; *Population au 2006:* 1,353
Circonscription(s) électorale(s) provinciale(s): Argenteuil
Circonscription(s) électorale(s) fédérale(s):
Argenteuil-Papineau-Mirabel
Prochaines élections: 3e novembre 2013
André Genest, Maire
Sophie Bélanger, Directrice générale

Westbury
168, rte 112
Westbury, QC J0B 1R0
Tél: 819-560-8450; *Téléc:* 819-560-8451
westbury@abacom.com
Entité municipal: Township
Incorporation: 16 août 1858 *Area:* 65,78 km2
Comté ou district: Le Haut-St-François; *Population au 2006:* 932
Circonscription(s) électorale(s) provinciale(s):
Mégantic-Compton
Circonscription(s) électorale(s) fédérale(s): Compton-Stanstead
Prochaines élections: 3e novembre 2013
Kenneth Coates, Maire
Adèle Madore, Directrice générale

Whapmagoostui
CP 390
Whapmagoostui, QC J0M 1G0
Tél: 819-929-3384; *Téléc:* 819-929-3203
chief@whapmagoostuifn.ca
www.whapmagoostuifn.ca
Entité municipal: Villages Cris
Incorporation: 28 juillet 1978 *Area:* 113,70 km2
Population au 2006: 812
Circonscription(s) électorale(s) provinciale(s): Ungava
Circonscription(s) électorale(s) fédérale(s):
Abitibi-Baie-James-Nunavik-Eeyou
Losty Mamianskum, Maire
Patricia-George Kawapit, Secrétaire

Wickham
893, rue Moreau
Wickham, QC J0C 1S0
Tél: 819-398-6878; *Téléc:* 819-398-7166
wickham@bellnet.ca
www.wickham.ca
Entité municipal: Municipality
Incorporation: 23 décembre 1972 *Area:* 97,72 km2
Comté ou district: Drummond; *Population au 2006:* 2,503
Circonscription(s) électorale(s) provinciale(s): Johnson
Circonscription(s) électorale(s) fédérale(s): Drummond
Prochaines élections: 3e novembre 2013
Carole Côté, Mairesse
Réal Dulmaine, Directeur général

Windsor
CP 90
22, rue St-Georges
Windsor, QC J1S 2L7
Tél: 819-845-7888; *Téléc:* 819-845-7606
info@villedewindsor.qc.ca
www.villedewindsor.qc.ca
Entité municipal: Town
Incorporation: 29 décembre 1999 *Area:* 13,78 km2
Comté ou district: Le Val-St-François; *Population au 2006:* 5,239
Circonscription(s) électorale(s) provinciale(s): Johnson
Circonscription(s) électorale(s) fédérale(s):
Richmond-Arthabaska
Prochaines élections: 3e novembre 2013
Sylvie Bureau, Mairesse
Sylvain Saint-Cyr, Directrice générale & Greffière

Wotton
CP 60
396, rue Monseigneur-L'Heureux
Wotton, QC J0A 1N0
Tél: 819-828-2112; *Téléc:* 819-828-3594
municipalite.wotton@cgocable.ca
www.wotton.ca
Entité municipal: Municipality
Incorporation: 10 mars 1993 *Area:* 142,41 km2
Comté ou district: Les Sources; *Population au 2006:* 1,540
Circonscription(s) électorale(s) provinciale(s): Richmond
Circonscription(s) électorale(s) fédérale(s):
Richmond-Arthabaska
Prochaines élections: 3e novembre 2013
Ghislain Drouin, Maire
Carole Vaillancourt, Directrice générale

Yamachiche
366, rue Ste-Anne
Yamachiche, QC G0X 3L0
Tél: 819-296-3795; *Téléc:* 819-296-3542
hoteldeville@yamachiche.ca
www.municipalite.yamachiche.qc.ca
Entité municipal: Municipality
Incorporation: 26 décembre 1987 *Area:* 106,30 km2
Comté ou district: Maskinongé; *Population au 2006:* 2,760
Circonscription(s) électorale(s) provinciale(s): Maskinongé
Circonscription(s) électorale(s) fédérale(s): Berthier-Maskinongé
Prochaines élections: 3e novembre 2013
Michel Isabelle, Maire
Linda Lafrenière, Directeur générale

Yamaska
CP 120
100, rue Guilbault
Yamaska, QC J0G 1X0
Tél: 450-789-2489; *Téléc:* 450-789-2970
yamaska@bas-richelieu.net
www.yamaska.ca
Entité municipal: Municipality
Incorporation: 19 décembre 2001 *Area:* 74,44 km2
Comté ou district: Pierre-De Saurel; *Population au 2006:* 1,643
Circonscription(s) électorale(s) provinciale(s): Richelieu;
Nicolet-Yamaska
Circonscription(s) électorale(s) fédérale(s):
Bas-Richelieu-Nicolet-Bécancour
Prochaines élections: 3e novembre 2013
Louis R. Joyal, Maire
450-789-2912
Brigitte Vachon, Directrice générale
bvachon@bas-richelieu.net

SASKATCHEWAN

Acts governing the municipal system in Saskatchewan are The Urban Municipality Act, 1984; The Rural Municipality Act, 1989; and The Northern Municipalities Act. In the province there are the following types of incorporated municipalities: Rural Municipalities, Villages, Resort Villages, Towns, and Cities, as well as Northern Towns, Northern Villages, Northern Hamlets, Northern Settlements, Resort Hamlets and Organized Hamlets. The incorporation of these municipalities is voluntary. Thus a Village that qualifies to be named a Town, can remain a Village if the population so wishes.

Rural Municipalities are divided into divisions. A Reeve is elected at large every two years. Councillors are also elected every two years but in "staggered" sequence. Rural municipal nominations are received until the third Monday in October and elections are held on the third Wednesday after the nomination period.

Villages are defined as communities with not less than 100 permanent residents and not less than 50 dwellings and/or business premises. The Village is represented by a Mayor and at least two Councillors.

Towns are defined as communities with not less that 500 permanent residents. They are represented by a Mayor and at least two Councillors.

Cities are defined as communities with not less than 5,000 residents. They are represented by a Mayor and Councillors (the number varies).

Elections for all members of council in urban municipalities occur every three years. Nominations are held in cities, towns, and villages on the second Wednesday in October and elections on the fourth Wednesday in October. In resort villages, nomination day will be the last Saturday in June and the election will be held on the fourth Saturday in July.

Northern Hamlets: have a population of 50 or more and must contain 25 or more separate dwelling units or business premises. They are governed by a Mayor and two Aldermen, although they may pass a bylaw to increase the number of Aldermen to four.

Northern Villages: contain a minimum population of 100 and at least 50 dwelling units or business premises. Their council consists of a Mayor and four Councillors; although they may pass bylaws to either decrease the number of Councillors to two, or increase the number of Councillors by any even number.

Northern Towns: will have a minimum population of 500 and are governed by a Mayor and six Councillors. The council may pass a bylaw increasing or decreasing the size of council by any even number, provided the number of Councillors does not fall below two.

Election for all members of council in northern municipalities occur every three years. Council will determine the date of the election, which shall be held the second last Wednesday in September, the last Wednesday in September, or the first Wednesday in October. Nomination day is five weeks prior to the date on which the election is to be held.

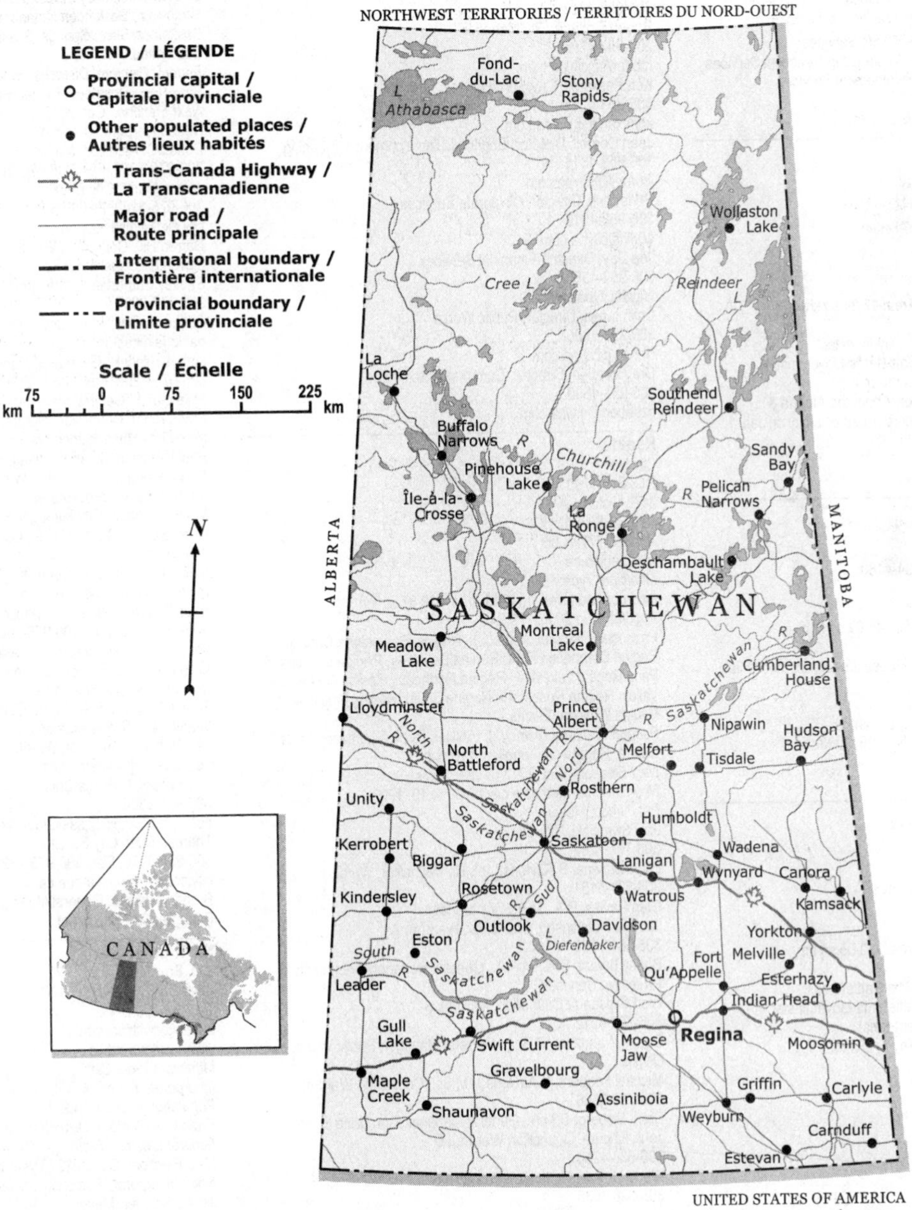

Reproduced with the permission of Natural Resources Canada 2011, courtesy of the Atlas of Canada.

Saskatchewan

Major Municipalities in Saskatchewan

Estevan
1102 - 4 St.
Estevan, SK S4A 0W7
Tel: 306-634-1800; *Fax:* 306-634-9790
citymanager@estevan.ca
www.estevan.ca
Municipal Type: City
Incorporated: Nov. 2, 1899 *Area:* 17.56 sq km
Population in 2006: 10,084
Provincial Electoral District(s): Estevan
Federal Electoral District(s): Souris-Moose Mountain
Next Election: Oct. 2012 (3 year terms)
Note: Incorporated as city on March 1, 1957.
Gary St. Onge, Mayor
mayor@estevan.ca
Lyndon Stachoski, Clerk
administration@estevan.ca
Zeshan Halder, Engineer, Engineering Services
Ron Tocker, Fire Chief
Del Block, Police Chief
Jim Puffalt, City Manager
306-634-1803
Tim Leson, Treasurer
Owen Green, Manager, Public Works Services
Kevin Sutter, Manager, Water/Wastewater Treatment Services
Rob Denys, Manager, Land Development Services
rdenys@estevan.ca
Helen Fornwald, Manager, Leisure Services

Lloydminster
City Hall
4420 - 50 Ave.
Lloydminster, SK T9V 0W2
Tel: 306-875-6184; *Fax:* 306-871-8346
tomlysyk@telusplanet.net
www.lloydminster.ca
Municipal Type: City
Incorporated: Nov. 25, 1903 *Area:* 17.34 sq km
Population in 2006: 24,028
Provincial Electoral District(s): Lloydminster
Federal Electoral District(s): Battlefords-Lloydminster
Next Election: Oct. 2012 (3 year terms)
Note: Population figure represents both the Alberta & Saskatchewan populations. Incorporated as a city on Jan. 1, 1958.
Ken Baker, Mayor
Tom Lysyk, City Clerk

Moose Jaw
228 Main St. North
Moose Jaw, SK S6H 3J8
Tel: 306-694-4400; *Fax:* 306-694-4480
www.moosejaw.ca
Municipal Type: City
Incorporated: Jan. 19, 1884 *Area:* 46.82 sq km
Population in 2006: 32,132
Provincial Electoral District(s): Moose Jaw North; Moose Jaw Wakamow
Federal Electoral District(s): Palliser
Next Election: Oct. 2012 (3 year terms)
Note: Incorporated as a city on Nov. 20, 1903.
Glen Hagel, Mayor
Garry McKay, City Manager

North Battleford
P.O. Box 460
1291 - 101st St.
North Battleford, SK S9A 2Y6
Tel: 306-445-1700; *Fax:* 306-445-0411
www.cityofnb.ca
Municipal Type: City
Incorporated: March 21, 1906 *Area:* 33.55 sq km
Population in 2006: 13,190
Provincial Electoral District(s): The Battlefords
Federal Electoral District(s): Battlefords-Lloydminster
Next Election: Oct. 2012 (3 year terms)
Note: Proclaimed as a city on May 1, 1913.
Ian Hamilton, Mayor
ihamilton@cityofnb.ca
Debbie Wohlberg, City Clerk
dwohlberg@cityofnb.ca
Jim Toye, City Manager
jtoye@cityofnb.ca
Tim LaFreniere, City Planner
tlafreniere@citynb.ca
Stewart Schafer, Director, Public Works
Keith Anderson, Director, Parks & Recreation
kanderson@cityofnb.ca
Pat MacIsaac, Fire Chief
pmacisaac@cityofnb.ca

Prince Albert
City Hall
1084 Central Ave.
Prince Albert, SK S6V 7P3
Tel: 306-953-4884;
www.citypa.ca
Municipal Type: City
Incorporated: Oct. 8, 1885 *Area:* 65.68 sq km
Population in 2006: 34,138
Provincial Electoral District(s): Prince Albert Carlton; Prince Albert Northcote
Federal Electoral District(s): Prince Albert
Next Election: Oct. 2012 (3 year terms)
Note: Incorporated as a city on Oct. 8, 1904.
Jim Scarrow, Mayor
mayor@citypa.com
Cliff Skauge, Clerk
cskauge@citypa.com
Les Karpluk, Fire Chief
306-953-4200
lkarpluk@citypa.com
Dale McFee, Police Chief
306-953-4222
Robert Cotterill, City Manager
306-953-4395
rcotterill@citypa.com
Ken Paskaruk, City Solicitor
306-953-4315
kpaskaruk@citypa.com
Jean Corneil, Director, Economic Development & Planning
306-953-4315
jcorneil@citypa.com
Chris Cvik, Director, Corporate Services
306-953-4310
ccvik@citypa.com
Joe Day, Director, Financial Services
306-953-4350
jday@citypa.com
Colin Innes, Director, Public Works
306-953-4900
cinnes@citypa.com
Greg Zeeben, Director, Community Services
306-953-4800
gzeeben@citypa.com

Regina
City Hall
P.O. Box 1790
2476 Victoria Ave.
Regina, SK S4P 3C8
Tel: 306-777-7000;
www.regina.ca
Municipal Type: City
Incorporated: Dec. 1, 1883 *Area:* 118.87 sq km
Population in 2006: 179,246
Provincial Electoral District(s): Regina Elphinstone-Centre; Regina Coronation Park; Regina Dewdney; Regina Douglas Park; Regina Lakeview; Regina Northeast; Regina Qu'Appelle Valley; Regina Rosemont; Regina South; Regina Walsh Acres; Regina Wascana Plains
Federal Electoral District(s): Palliser; Regina-Lumsden-Lake Centre; Regina-Qu'Appelle; Wascana
Next Election: Oct. 2012 (3 year terms)
Note: Incorporated as a city on June 19, 1903.
Pat Fiacco, Mayor
Joni Swidnicki, City Clerk
306-777-7262
Louis Browne, B.A.(Hons.), LL.B., Councillor, Ward(s): 1
306-531-5151
Glen Davies, B.A., M.A., City Manager
Jocelyn Hutchinson, Councillor, Ward(s): 2
306-584-1739
Bonny Bryant, B.A., M.P.A., General Manager, Community & Protective Services
Fred Clipsham, Councillor, Ward(s): 3
306-757-8212
Dorian Wandzura, P.Eng., General Manager, Public Works Division
Michael Fougere, B.A.(Hons.), M.Sc., Councillor, Ward(s): 4
306-789-5586
Brent Sjoberg, C.M.A., General Manager, Corporate Services
John Findura, Councillor, Ward(s): 5
306-536-4250
Wade Murray, Councillor, Ward(s): 6
306-596-1035
Jason Carlston, B.A., M.A., General Manager, Planning & Development
Sharron Bryce, R.N., Councillor, Ward(s): 7
306-949-5025
Troy Hagen, Chief, Regina Police Service
306-777-6500, Fax: 306-757-5461
rps@police.regina.sk.ca
Mike O'Donnell, Councillor, Ward(s): 8
306-545-7300
Jim Nicol, Chief of Staff, City Manager's Office
Terry Hincks, Councillor, Ward(s): 9
306-949-9690
Chris Szarka, Councillor, Ward(s): 10
306-551-2766

Saskatoon
City Hall
222 - 3rd Ave. North
Saskatoon, SK S7K 0J5
Tel: 306-975-3200;
www.saskatoon.ca
Municipal Type: City
Incorporated: Nov. 16, 1901 *Area:* 170.83 sq km
Population in 2006: 202,340
Provincial Electoral District(s): Saskatoon Centre; Saskatoon Eastview; Saskatoon Fairview; Saskatoon Greystone; Saskatoon Massey Place; Saskatoon Meewasin; Saskatoon Northwest; Saskatoon Nutana; Saskatoon Riversdale; Saskatoon Silver Springs; Saskatoon Southeast; Saskatoon Sutherland
Federal Electoral District(s): Blackstrap; Saskatoon-Humboldt; Saskatoon-Rosetown-Biggar; Saskatoon-Wanuskewin
Next Election: Oct. 2012 (3 year terms)
Note: Incorporated as a city on May 26, 1906.
Donald J. Atchison, Mayor
306-975-3202, Fax: 306-975-3144
Janice Mann, City Clerk
306-975-3240, Fax: 306-975-2784
city.clerks@saskatoon.ca
Darren Hill, Councillor, Ward(s): 1
darren.hill@saskatoon.ca
Shelley Sutherland, Treasurer
306-975-3692
Pat Lorje, B.A., M.A., Councillor, Ward(s): 2
pat.lorje@saskatoon.ca
Marlys Bilanski, General Manager, Corporate Services
306-975-3206, Fax: 306-975-7975
Mike Gutek, General Manager, Infrastructure Services
Myles Heidt, Councillor, Ward(s): 4
myles.heidt@saskatoon.ca
Paul Gauthier, General Manager, Community Services
Randy Donauer, Councillor, Ward(s): 5
randy.donauer@saskatoon.ca
Murray Totland, City Manager
Charlie Clark, B.Ed., M.E.S., Councillor, Ward(s): 6
charlie.clark@saskatcoon.ca
Mairin Loewen, B.A., Councillor, Ward(s): 7
mairin.loewen@saskatoon.ca
Brian Bentley, General Manager, Fire & Protective Services
306-975-2575, Fax: 306-975-2689
fire.protective.services@city.saskatoon.sk.ca
Glen Penner, B.Ed., M.Ed., Councillor, Ward(s): 8
glen.penner@saskatoon.ca
Tiffany Paulsen, B.A., LL.B., Councillor, Ward(s): 9
tiffany.paulsen@saskatoon.ca
Bev Dubois, Councillor, Ward(s): 10
bev.dubois@saskatoon.ca
Clive Weighill, Police Chief
306-975-8300
police.service@city.saskatoon.sk.ca
Theresa Dust, City Solicitor
306-975-3270, Fax: 306-975-7828
city.solicitor@saskatoon.ca
Brenda Wallace, General Manager, Utility Services
Brian Bentley, Fire Chief

Swift Current
P.O. Box 340
Swift Current, SK S9H 3W1
Tel: 306-778-2777;
admin@swiftcurrent.ca
www.swiftcurrent.ca
Municipal Type: City
Incorporated: Feb. 4, 1904 *Area:* 24.04 sq km
Population in 2006: 14,946
Provincial Electoral District(s): Swift Current
Federal Electoral District(s): Cypress Hills-Grasslands
Next Election: Oct. 2012 (3 year terms)
Note: Incorporated as a city on Jan. 15, 1914.
Jerrod Schafer, Mayor

Susan Motkaluk, Chief Administrative Officer
306-778-2723
Mac Forster, Director, Engineering
306-778-2740
eng@swiftcurrent.ca
Denis Pilon, Fire Chief
306-778-2760
Andy Toth, Manager, Parks
306-778-2787
Trevor Feicht, Manager, Engineering Services
306-778-2740
Dean Robson, Director, Recreation & Parks
306-778-2787

Weyburn
P.O. Box 370
157 - 3rd St. NE
Weyburn, SK S4H 2K6
questions@weyburn.ca
www.weyburn.ca
Municipal Type: City
Incorporated: Oct. 22, 1900 *Area:* 15.78 sq km
Population in 2006: 9,433
Provincial Electoral District(s): Weyburn-Big Muddy
Federal Electoral District(s): Souris-Moose Mountain
Next Election: Oct. 2012 (3 year terms)
Note: Incorporated as a city on Sept. 1, 1913.
Debra Button, Mayor
mayor@weyburn.ca
Donette Ritcher, City Clerk
drichter@weyburn.ca
Robert Smith, City Manager
rsmith@weyburn.ca
Jon Michaud, City Assessor/Director, Finance
jmichaud@weyburn.ca
Rene Richard, Director, Engineering
rrichard@weyburn.ca
Mathew Warren, Director, Engineering
mwarren@weyburn.ca
Doug Mulhall, Manager, Community Development
dmulhall@weyburn.ca
Katelyn Struthers, Manager, Parks Services
kstruthers@weyburn.ca
Claude Morin, Superintendent, Public Works & Parks
cmorin@weyburn.ca
Kim Wilkes, Foreman, Public Works
kwilkes@weyburn.ca
Steve Debienne, Fire Chief
sdebienne@weyburn.ca
Howard Georgeson, Police Chief
hgeorgeson@weyburn.ca

Yorkton
37 - 3rd Ave. North
Yorkton, SK S3N 2W3
Tel: 306-786-1700; *Fax:* 306-786-6880
www.yorkton.ca
Municipal Type: City
Incorporated: July 11, 1894 *Area:* 24.57 sq km
Population in 2006: 15,038
Provincial Electoral District(s): Yorkton
Federal Electoral District(s): Yorkton-Melville
Next Election: Oct. 2012 (3 year terms)
Note: Incorporated as a city on Feb. 1, 1928.
James Wilson, Mayor
mayor@yorkton.ca
Bonnie Schenher, City Clerk
bschenher@yorkton.ca
Lonnie Kaal, Director, Finance
306-786-1721
lkaal@yorkton.ca
Gord Shaw, Director, Planning & Engineering
306-786-1730
gshaw@yorkton.ca
Dean Clark, Fire Chief, Fire Protective Services
306-786-1795
dclark@yorkton.ca
Faisal Anwar, Officer, Economic Development
306-786-1747
fanwar@yorkton.ca
Trent Mandzuk, Director, Public Works
306-786-1762
tmanzuk@yorkton.ca
Michael Buchholzer, Director, Water Works
306-828-2470
mbuchholzer@yorkton.ca
Brant Hryhorczuk, Manager, Building Services
306-786-1710
bhryhorczuk@yorkton.ca

David Putz, City Manager
306-786-1703
dputz@yorkton.ca
Darcy McLeod, Director, Community Development, Parks & Recreation
306-786-1750
dmcleod@yorkton.ca

Other Municipalities in Saskatchewan

Abbey
P.O. Box 210
Abbey, SK S0N 0A0
Tel: 306-689-2412; *Fax:* 306-689-2901
rm229@sasktel.net
Municipal Type: Village
Incorporated: Sept. 2, 1913 *Area:* 0.77 sq km
Population in 2006: 130
Provincial Electoral District(s): Cypress Hills
Federal Electoral District(s): Cypress Hills-Grasslands
Next Election: Oct. 2012 (3 year terms)
Bruce Walker, Mayor
Jan Stern, Administrator

Aberdeen
P.O. Box 130
207 Main St.
Aberdeen, SK S0K 0A0
Tel: 306-253-4311; *Fax:* 306-253-4201
townaberdeen@sasktel.net
www.aberdeen.ca
Municipal Type: Town
Incorporated: March 13, 1907 *Area:* 1.95 sq km
Population in 2006: 527
Provincial Electoral District(s): Humboldt
Federal Electoral District(s): Saskatoon-Humboldt
Next Election: Oct. 2012 (3 year terms)
Note: Proclaimed as town on Nov. 1, 1988.
Glen Ogilvy, Mayor
Susan Thompson, Town Manager

Abernethy
P.O. Box 189
Abernethy, SK S0A 0A0
Tel: 306-333-2271; *Fax:* 306-333-2276
village@abernethy.ca
www.abernethy.ca
Municipal Type: Village
Incorporated: July 26, 1904 *Area:* 1.03 sq km
Population in 2006: 197
Provincial Electoral District(s): Last Mountain-Touchwood
Federal Electoral District(s): Regina-Qu'Appelle
Next Election: Oct. 2012 (3 year terms)
Janet Englot, Mayor
themayor@sasktel.net
Sheree Emmerson, Administrator

Air Ronge
P.O. Box 100
Air Ronge, SK S0J 3G0
Tel: 306-425-2107; *Fax:* 306-425-3108
www.villageofairronge.com
Municipal Type: Northern Village
Incorporated: Oct. 1, 1983 *Area:* 6.00 sq km
Population in 2006: 1,032
Provincial Electoral District(s): Cumberland
Federal Electoral District(s): Desnethé-Missinippi-Churchill River
Next Election: Oct. 2012 (3 year terms)
Gordon Stomp, Mayor
Rachel Kunz, Administrator

Alameda
P.O. Box 36
Alameda, SK S0C 0A0
Tel: 306-489-2077; *Fax:* 306-489-4602
townofalameda@sasktel.net
www.townofalameda.ca
Municipal Type: Town
Incorporated: Dec. 29, 1898 *Area:* 2.55 sq km
Population in 2006: 308
Provincial Electoral District(s): Cannington
Federal Electoral District(s): Souris-Moose Mountain
Next Election: Oct. 2012 (3 year terms)
Note: Proclaimed as town on April 15, 1907.
Allan Faber, Mayor
306-489-2047
Lynne Hewitt, Administrator

Albertville
General Delivery
Albertville, SK S0J 0A0
Tel: 306-929-2110; *Fax:* 306-929-4744
albertville@inet2000.com
Municipal Type: Village
Incorporated: Jan. 1, 1986 *Area:* 1.11 sq km
Population in 2006: 110
Provincial Electoral District(s): Saskatchewan Rivers
Federal Electoral District(s): Prince Albert
Next Election: Oct. 2012 (3 year terms)
Louis Hradecki, Mayor
Valerie Fidler, Clerk

Alida
P.O. Box 6
Alida, SK S0C 0B0
Tel: 306-443-2228; *Fax:* 306-443-2568
villageofalida@sasktel.net
Municipal Type: Village
Incorporated: Feb. 19, 1926 *Area:* 0.35 sq km
Population in 2006: 106
Provincial Electoral District(s): Cannington
Federal Electoral District(s): Souris-Moose Mountain
Next Election: Oct. 2012 (3 year terms)
James Boettcher, Mayor
Kathy Anthony, Administrator

Allan
P.O. Box 159
224 Main St.
Allan, SK S0K 0C0
Tel: 306-257-3272; *Fax:* 306-257-3337
www.allan.ca
Municipal Type: Town
Incorporated: June 9, 1910 *Area:* 1.78 sq km
Population in 2006: 631
Provincial Electoral District(s): Humboldt
Federal Electoral District(s): Blackstrap
Next Election: Oct. 2012 (3 year terms)
Note: Proclaimed as town on Dec. 1, 1965.
Larry Sommerfeld, Mayor
Christine Dyck, Administrator

Alsask
P.O. Box 219
Alsask, SK S0L 0A0
Tel: 306-968-2394; *Fax:* 306-968-2300
alsask.village@sasktel.net
Municipal Type: Village
Incorporated: Nov. 22, 1910 *Area:* 1.66 sq km
Population in 2006: 129
Provincial Electoral District(s): Kindersley
Federal Electoral District(s): Battlefords-Lloydminster
Next Election: Oct. 2012 (3 year terms)
Gordon Chiliak, Mayor
Sandy Nielsen, Acting Clerk

Alvena
P.O. Box 8
Alvena, SK S0K 0E0
Tel: 306-943-2101; *Fax:* 306-943-2155
villageofalvena@yahoo.ca
Municipal Type: Village
Incorporated: July 1, 1936 *Area:* 0.43 sq km
Population in 2006: 55
Provincial Electoral District(s): Batoche
Federal Electoral District(s): Saskatoon-Humboldt
Next Election: Oct. 2012 (3 year terms)
Ernie Sawitsky, Mayor
Lucille Cousin, Clerk

Aneroid
P.O. Box 226
Aneroid, SK S0N 0C0
Municipal Type: Village
Incorporated: Aug. 7, 1913 *Area:* 1.05 sq km
Population in 2006: 45
Provincial Electoral District(s): Wood River
Federal Electoral District(s): Cypress Hills-Grasslands
Next Election: Oct. 2012 (3 year terms)
Elton Meikle, Mayor

Annaheim
P.O. Box 130
Annaheim, SK S0K 0G0
Tel: 306-598-2006; *Fax:* 306-598-2008
villageofannaheim@sasktel.net
Municipal Type: Village
Incorporated: April 1, 1977 *Area:* 0.78 sq km
Population in 2006: 218
Provincial Electoral District(s): Melfort

Federal Electoral District(s): Saskatoon-Humboldt
Next Election: Oct. 2012 (3 year terms)
Donald Willenborg, Mayor
Debra Parry, Administrator

Antler
P.O. Box 83
Antler, SK S0C 0E0
Tel: 306-452-3533; *Fax:* 306-452-6114
ruttenranch@sasktel.net
Municipal Type: Village
Incorporated: March 15, 1905 *Area:* 0.72 sq km
Population in 2006: 40
Provincial Electoral District(s): Cannington
Federal Electoral District(s): Souris-Moose Mountain
Next Election: Oct. 2012 (3 year terms)
James Duncan, Mayor
Bonnie Rutten, Clerk

Arborfield
P.O. Box 280
201 Main St.
Arborfield, SK S0E 0A0
Tel: 306-769-8533; *Fax:* 306-769-8301
arborfieldrm456@sasktel.net
www.arborfieldsk.ca
Municipal Type: Town
Incorporated: June 16, 1933 *Area:* 0.88 sq km
Population in 2006: 329
Provincial Electoral District(s): Carrot River Valley
Federal Electoral District(s): Prince Albert
Next Election: Oct. 2012 (3 year terms)
Note: Proclaimed as town on June 1, 1950.
Alvin Alyea, Mayor
Allan Frisky, Administrator

Archerwill
P.O. Box 130
Archerwill, SK S0E 0B0
Tel: 306-323-2161; *Fax:* 306-323-2101
villageofarcherwill@sasktel.net
www.newsaskcfdc.ca/archerwill.htm
Municipal Type: Village
Incorporated: Jan. 1, 1947 *Area:* 0.83 sq km
Population in 2006: 185
Provincial Electoral District(s): Kelvington-Wadena
Federal Electoral District(s): Yorkton-Melville
Next Election: Oct. 2012 (3 year terms)
Robert Wilson, Mayor
Sheila Ottmann, Administrator

Arcola
P.O. Box 359
127 Main St.
Arcola, SK S0C 0G0
Tel: 306-455-2212; *Fax:* 306-455-2445
arcadmin@sasktel.net
Municipal Type: Town
Incorporated: April 11, 1901 *Area:* 2.59 sq km
Population in 2006: 504
Provincial Electoral District(s): Cannington
Federal Electoral District(s): Souris-Moose Mountain
Next Election: Oct. 2012 (3 year terms)
Note: Proclaimed as town on Nov. 20, 1903.
Adam Manastryski, Mayor
Glenda Johnson, Administrator

Arran
P.O. Box 40
Arran, SK S0A 0B0
Tel: 306-595-4521; *Fax:* 306-595-4531
rm331@sasktel.net
Municipal Type: Village
Incorporated: Sept. 21, 1916 *Area:* 0.69 sq km
Population in 2006: 40
Provincial Electoral District(s): Canora-Pelly
Federal Electoral District(s): Yorkton-Melville
Next Election: Oct. 2012 (3 year terms)
Rick Nahnybida, Mayor
Yvonne Bilsky, Administrator

Asquith
P.O. Box 160
Asquith, SK S0K 0J0
Tel: 306-329-4341; *Fax:* 306-329-4969
town.asquith@sasktel.net
townofasquith.com
Municipal Type: Town
Incorporated: Dec. 10, 1907 *Area:* 1.23 sq km
Population in 2006: 576
Provincial Electoral District(s): Biggar
Federal Electoral District(s): Saskatoon-Rosetown-Biggar
Next Election: Oct. 2012 (3 year terms)
Note: Proclaimed as a town on Aug. 15, 1908.
James Madden, Mayor
Holly Cross, Administrator

Assiniboia
P.O. Box 1470
Assiniboia, SK S0H 0B0
Tel: 306-642-5553; *Fax:* 306-642-3529
townofassiniboia@sasktel.net
www.assiniboia.net
Municipal Type: Town
Incorporated: Dec. 19, 1912 *Area:* 3.78 sq km
Population in 2006: 2,305
Provincial Electoral District(s): Wood River
Federal Electoral District(s): Cypress Hills-Grasslands
Next Election: Oct. 2012 (3 year terms)
Note: Proclaimed as a town on Oct. 1, 1913.
Paul Topola, Mayor
David Connauton, Chief Administrative Officer

Atwater
P.O. Box 45
Atwater, SK S0A 0C0
Tel: 306-793-2193;
villageofatwater@gmail.com
Municipal Type: Village
Incorporated: Aug. 12, 1910 *Area:* 1.79 sq km
Population in 2006: 25
Provincial Electoral District(s): Melville-Saltcoats
Federal Electoral District(s): Yorkton-Melville
Next Election: Oct. 2012 (3 year terms)
James Ferguson, Mayor
Sheila Shivak, Clerk

Avonlea
P.O. Box 209
Avonlea, SK S0H 0C0
Tel: 306-868-2221; *Fax:* 306-868-2221
avonlea@sasktel.net
www.avonlea.biz
Municipal Type: Village
Incorporated: Feb. 10, 1912 *Area:* 0.96 sq km
Population in 2006: 381
Provincial Electoral District(s): Indian Head-Milestone
Federal Electoral District(s): Palliser
Next Election: Oct. 2012 (3 year terms)
Alex Getzlaf, Mayor
Tim Forer, Administrator

Aylesbury
201 King St.
Aylesbury, SK S0G 0B0
Tel: 306-734-5125;
susy632@sasktel.net
www.craik.ca/aylesbury.html
Municipal Type: Village
Incorporated: March 31, 1910 *Area:* 1.28 sq km
Population in 2006: 45
Provincial Electoral District(s): Thunder Creek
Federal Electoral District(s): Regina-Lumsden-Lake Centre
Next Election: Oct. 2012 (3 year terms)
Douglas Watt, Mayor
Jeff Murry, Village Clerk

Aylsham
P.O. Box 64
Aylsham, SK S0E 0C0
Tel: 306-862-9415;
villageofaylsham@sasktel.net
Municipal Type: Village
Incorporated: Aug. 4, 1947 *Area:* 0.48 sq km
Population in 2006: 92
Provincial Electoral District(s): Carrot River Valley
Federal Electoral District(s): Prince Albert
Next Election: Oct. 2012 (3 year terms)
Elizabeth F. Archer, Mayor
Dorothy E. Blue, Clerk

Balcarres
P.O. Box 130
209 Main St.
Balcarres, SK S0G 0C0
Tel: 306-334-2566; *Fax:* 306-334-2907
balcarrestown@sasktel.net
www.townofbalcarres.ca
Municipal Type: Town
Incorporated: Nov. 21, 1904 *Area:* 1.57 sq km
Population in 2006: 598
Provincial Electoral District(s): Last Mountain-Touchwood
Federal Electoral District(s): Regina-Qu'Appelle
Next Election: Oct. 2012 (3 year terms)
Note: Proclaimed as a town on Jan. 1, 1951.
Dwight Dixon, Mayor
Bev Gelech, Administrator

Balgonie
P.O. Box 310
129 South Railway St. East
Balgonie, SK S0G 0E0
Tel: 306-771-2284; *Fax:* 306-771-2899
townofbalgonie@sasktel.net
www.townofbalgonie.ca
Municipal Type: Town
Incorporated: April 20, 1903 *Area:* 3.15 sq km
Population in 2006: 1,384
Provincial Electoral District(s): Indian Head-Milestone
Federal Electoral District(s): Regina-Qu'Appelle
Next Election: Oct. 2012 (3 year terms)
Note: Proclaimed as a town on Jan. 1, 1951.
Tim Sterzer, Mayor
Val Hubbard, Administrator

Bangor
P.O. Box 35
Bangor, SK S0A 0E0
Tel: 306-728-4084
Municipal Type: Village
Incorporated: June 8, 1911 *Area:* 1.65 sq km
Population in 2006: 50
Provincial Electoral District(s): Melville-Saltcoats
Federal Electoral District(s): Yorkton-Melville
Next Election: Oct. 2012 (3 year terms)
Jerome Bomberak, Mayor
Joan C. Bomberak, Clerk

Battleford
P.O. Box 40
Battleford, SK S0M 0E0
Tel: 306-937-6200; *Fax:* 306-937-2450
admin@battleford.ca
www.battleford.ca
Municipal Type: Town
Incorporated: Jan. 6, 1899 *Area:* 23.33 sq km
Population in 2006: 3,685
Provincial Electoral District(s): The Battlefords
Federal Electoral District(s): Battlefords-Lloydminster
Next Election: Oct. 2012 (3 year terms)
Note: Proclaimed as a town on June 15, 1904.
Chris Odishaw, Mayor
Sheryl Ballendine, Administrator

Beatty
P.O. Box 51
Beatty, SK S0J 0C0
Tel: 306-752-3980;
fhrainville@sasktel.net
www.newsaskcfdc.ca/beatty.htm
Municipal Type: Village
Incorporated: March 31, 1921 *Area:* 0.82 sq km
Population in 2006: 61
Provincial Electoral District(s): Melfort
Federal Electoral District(s): Prince Albert
Next Election: Oct. 2012 (3 year terms)
Harvey Rainville, Mayor
Linda Logan, Clerk

Beauval
P.O. Box 19
Lavoie St.
Beauval, SK S0M 0G0
Tel: 306-288-2110; *Fax:* 306-288-2348
admin.beauval@sasktel.net
Municipal Type: Northern Village
Incorporated: Oct. 1, 1983 *Area:* 6.71 sq km
Population in 2006: 806
Provincial Electoral District(s): Athabasca
Federal Electoral District(s): Desnethé-Missinippi-Churchill River
Next Election: Oct. 2012 (3 year terms)
Fred Roy, Mayor
Marie LaVallee, Administrator

Beechy
P.O. Box 153
Beechy, SK S0L 0C0
Tel: 306-859-2205; *Fax:* 306-859-2290
info@beechysask.ca; beechy@sasktel.net
www.beechysask.ca
Municipal Type: Village
Incorporated: May 11, 1925 *Area:* 1.06 sq km
Population in 2006: 243
Provincial Electoral District(s): Rosetown-Elrose

Federal Electoral District(s): Cypress Hills-Grasslands
Next Election: Oct. 2012 (3 year terms)
Francis Fleuter, Mayor
Mel Hanke, Administrator

Belle Plaine
P.O. Box 63
Belle Plaine, SK S0G 0G0
Tel: 306-693-0378
Municipal Type: Village
Incorporated: Aug. 12, 1910 *Area:* 1.34 sq km
Population in 2006: 64
Provincial Electoral District(s): Thunder Creek
Federal Electoral District(s): Palliser
Next Election: Oct. 2012 (3 year terms)
Donald Firomski, Mayor
Deborah Day, Clerk

Bengough
P.O. Box 188
181 Main St.
Bengough, SK S0C 0K0
Tel: 306-268-2927; *Fax:* 306-268-2988
town.bengough@sasktel.net
www.bengough.com
Municipal Type: Town
Incorporated: March 15, 1912 *Area:* 1.07 sq km
Population in 2006: 337
Provincial Electoral District(s): Weyburn-Big Muddy
Federal Electoral District(s): Souris-Moose Mountain
Next Election: Oct. 2012 (3 year terms)
Note: Proclaimed as a town on April 1, 1958.
Dennis Mazenc, Mayor
Penny Nergard, Administrator

Bethune
P.O. Box 209
Bethune, SK S0G 0H0
Tel: 306-638-3188; *Fax:* 306-638-3102
villageofbethune@sasktel.net
www.villageofbethune.com
Municipal Type: Village
Incorporated: Aug. 2, 1912 *Area:* 1.04 sq km
Population in 2006: 369
Provincial Electoral District(s): Thunder Creek
Federal Electoral District(s): Regina-Lumsden-Lake Centre
Next Election: Oct. 2012 (3 year terms)
Ron Gemmell, Mayor
Rodney Audette, Administrator

Bienfait
P.O. Box 220
Bienfait, SK S0C 0M0
Tel: 306-388-2969; *Fax:* 306-388-2449
bienfait@sasktel.net
Municipal Type: Town
Incorporated: April 16, 1912 *Area:* 3.09 sq km
Population in 2006: 748
Provincial Electoral District(s): Estevan
Federal Electoral District(s): Souris-Moose Mountain
Next Election: Oct. 2012 (3 year terms)
Note: Proclaimed as a town on March 1, 1957.
Jamie Bonokoski, Mayor
Laurel Gilroy, Administrator

Big River
P.O. Box 220
Big River, SK S0J 0E0
Tel: 306-469-2112; *Fax:* 306-469-4856
bigriver@sasktel.net
www.bigriver.ca
Municipal Type: Town
Incorporated: Aug. 18, 1923 *Area:* 2.11 sq km
Population in 2006: 728
Provincial Electoral District(s): Saskatchewan Rivers
Federal Electoral District(s): Desnethé-Missinippi-Churchill River
Next Election: Oct. 2012 (3 year terms)
Note: Proclaimed as a town on Oct. 1, 1966.
Brian Brownfield, Mayor
Gail Gear, Administrator

Biggar
P.O. Box 489
202 - 3rd Ave. West
Biggar, SK S0K 0M0
Tel: 306-948-3317; *Fax:* 306-948-5134
townoffice@townofbiggar.com
www.townofbiggar.com
Municipal Type: Town
Incorporated: May 18, 1909 *Area:* 15.75
Population in 2006: 2,033
Provincial Electoral District(s): Biggar
Federal Electoral District(s): Saskatoon-Rosetown-Biggar
Next Election: Oct. 2012 (3 year terms)
Note: Proclaimed as a town on Nov. 1, 1911.
Raymond Sadler, Mayor
Barb Barteski, Administrator

Birch Hills
P.O. Box 206
Birch Hills, SK S0J 0G0
Tel: 306-749-2232; *Fax:* 306-749-2545
birchhills.town@sasktel.net
www.birchhills.ca
Municipal Type: Town
Incorporated: July 19, 1907 *Area:* 1.82 sq km
Population in 2006: 935
Provincial Electoral District(s): Batoche
Federal Electoral District(s): Prince Albert
Next Election: Oct. 2012 (3 year terms)
Note: Proclaimed as a town on Aug. 1, 1960.
Alan Bzdel, Mayor
Darlene Cochrane, Administrator

Bjorkdale
P.O. Box 27
Bjorkdale, SK S0E 0E0
Tel: 306-886-2167; *Fax:* 306-886-2181
villageofbjorkdale@live.com
www.newsaskcfdc.ca/bjorkdale.htm
Municipal Type: Village
Incorporated: April 1, 1968 *Area:* 1.39 sq km
Population in 2006: 201
Provincial Electoral District(s): Kelvington-Wadena
Federal Electoral District(s): Yorkton-Melville
Next Election: Oct. 2012 (3 year terms)
Brian Wilkie, Mayor
Katherine Clarke, Administrator

Bladworth
P.O. Box 90
Bladworth, SK S0G 0J0
Tel: 306-567-5564; *Fax:* 306-567-4364
donna.haug@sasktel.net
Municipal Type: Village
Incorporated: July 27, 1906 *Area:* 0.84 sq km
Population in 2006: 70
Provincial Electoral District(s): Arm River-Watrous
Federal Electoral District(s): Blackstrap
Next Election: Oct. 2012 (3 year terms)
Ron Bessey, Mayor
Donna Bessey, Clerk

Blaine Lake
P.O. Box 10
Blaine Lake, SK S0J 0J0
Tel: 306-497-2531; *Fax:* 306-497-2511
blainelake@sasktel.net
www.blainelake.ca
Municipal Type: Town
Incorporated: March 15, 1912 *Area:* 1.75 sq km
Population in 2006: 472
Provincial Electoral District(s): Rosthern-Shellbrook
Federal Electoral District(s): Saskatoon-Wanuskewin
Next Election: Oct. 2012 (3 year terms)
Note: Proclaimed as a town on March 1, 1954.
Ernie Crowder, Mayor
Anna Brad, Administrator

Borden
P.O. Box 210
200 Shepard St.
Borden, SK S0K 0N0
Tel: 306-997-2134; *Fax:* 306-997-2201
borden@sasktel.net
www.bordensask.ca
Municipal Type: Village
Incorporated: July 19, 1907 *Area:* 0.76 sq km
Population in 2006: 223
Provincial Electoral District(s): Biggar
Federal Electoral District(s): Saskatoon-Wanuskewin
Next Election: Oct. 2012 (3 year terms)
Dave Buckingham, Mayor
Sandra Long, Administrator

Bracken
P.O. Box 41
Bracken, SK S0N 0G0
Tel: 306-293-2124; *Fax:* 306-293-2702
Municipal Type: Village
Incorporated: Jan. 4, 1926 *Area:* 0.60 sq km
Population in 2006: 25
Provincial Electoral District(s): Wood River
Federal Electoral District(s): Cypress Hills-Grasslands
Next Election: Oct. 2012 (3 year terms)
Steve Dueck, Mayor
Ron Johnson, Administrator

Bradwell
P.O. Box 100
Bradwell, SK S0K 0P0
Tel: 306-257-4141; *Fax:* 306-257-3303
rm343@sasktel.net
Municipal Type: Village
Incorporated: July 13, 1910 *Area:* 0.42 sq km
Population in 2006: 182
Provincial Electoral District(s): Humboldt
Federal Electoral District(s): Blackstrap
Next Election: Oct. 2012 (3 year terms)
Ken Hartz, Mayor
R. Doran Scott, Administrator

Bredenbury
P.O. Box 87
Bredenbury, SK S0A 0H0
Tel: 306-898-2055; *Fax:* 306-898-2103
bredenbury@sasktel.net
www.townofbredenbury.ca
Municipal Type: Town
Incorporated: May 3, 1911 *Area:* 4.80 sq km
Population in 2006: 329
Provincial Electoral District(s): Melville-Saltcoats
Federal Electoral District(s): Yorkton-Melville
Next Election: Oct. 2012 (3 year terms)
Note: Proclaimed as a town on May 1, 1913.
Fred Nicholson, Mayor
Kim Varga, Administrator

Briercrest
P.O. Box 25
Briercrest, SK S0H 0K0
Tel: 306-799-2066; *Fax:* 306-799-2067
villageofbriercrest@sasktel.net
villageofbriercrest.ca
Municipal Type: Village
Incorporated: April 17, 1912 *Area:* 0.62 sq km
Population in 2006: 117
Provincial Electoral District(s): Indian Head-Milestone
Federal Electoral District(s): Palliser
Next Election: Oct. 2012 (3 year terms)
Bill Duncan, Mayor
Lloyd Muma, Administrator

Broadview
P.O. Box 430
524 Main St.
Broadview, SK S0G 0K0
Tel: 306-696-2533; *Fax:* 306-696-3573
town.of.broadview@sasktel.net
www.broadview.ca
Municipal Type: Town
Incorporated: Dec. 29, 1898 *Area:* 2.45 sq km
Population in 2006: 611
Provincial Electoral District(s): Moosomin
Federal Electoral District(s): Souris-Moose Mountain
Next Election: Oct. 2012 (3 year terms)
Note: Proclaimed as a town on May 15, 1907.
Sidney Criddle, Mayor
Mervin J. Schmidt, Administrator

Brock
P.O. Box 70
Brock, SK S0L 0H0
Tel: 306-379-2116;
brockadmin@sasktel.net
Municipal Type: Village
Incorporated: July 7, 1910 *Area:* 0.74 sq km
Population in 2006: 115
Provincial Electoral District(s): Rosetown-Elrose
Federal Electoral District(s): Battlefords-Lloydminster
Next Election: Oct. 2012 (3 year terms)
David Wicks, Mayor
Shannon Beheil, Administrator

Broderick
P.O. Box 29
Broderick, SK S0H 0L0
Tel: 306-867-8578;
villageofbroderick@yourlink.ca
Municipal Type: Village
Incorporated: Sept. 13, 1909 *Area:* 0.91 sq km
Population in 2006: 77
Provincial Electoral District(s): Rosetown-Elrose
Federal Electoral District(s): Blackstrap
Next Election: Oct. 2012 (3 year terms)

Jacob Vanderschaaf, Mayor
Sylvia Klotz, Clerk

Brownlee
P.O. Box 89
Brownlee, SK S0H 0M0
Tel: 306-759-2302
Municipal Type: Village
Incorporated: Dec. 29, 1908 *Area:* 2.42 sq km
Population in 2006: 50
Provincial Electoral District(s): Thunder Creek
Federal Electoral District(s): Regina-Lumsden-Lake Centre
Next Election: Oct. 2012 (3 year terms)
Lyle Swanson, Mayor
Jackie Leggott, Clerk

Bruno
P.O. Box 370
Bruno, SK S0K 0S0
Tel: 306-369-2514; *Fax:* 306-369-2878
bruno@sasktel.net
sites.google.com/site/brunosaskatchewan
Municipal Type: Town
Incorporated: March 9, 1909 *Area:* 0.95 sq km
Population in 2006: 495
Provincial Electoral District(s): Humboldt
Federal Electoral District(s): Saskatoon-Humboldt
Next Election: Oct. 2012 (3 year terms)
Note: Proclaimed as a town on Jan. 1, 1962.
Audrey Ludwig, Mayor
Kim Sopotyk, Administrator

Buchanan
P.O. Box 479
300 Central Ave.
Buchanan, SK S0A 0J0
Tel: 306-592-2144; *Fax:* 306-592-4471
buchananvillage@sasktel.net
www.buchananvillage.sasktelwebsite.net
Municipal Type: Village
Incorporated: June 11, 1907 *Area:* 1.29 sq km
Population in 2006: 225
Provincial Electoral District(s): Canora-Pelly
Federal Electoral District(s): Yorkton-Melville
Next Election: Oct. 2012 (3 year terms)
Kent Zuravloff, Mayor
Nicole Monchamp, Administrator

Buena Vista
1050 Grand Ave.
Buena Vista, SK S2V 1A2
Tel: 306-729-4385; *Fax:* 306-729-4518
buenavista@sasktel.net
www.lumsden.ca/buenavista
Municipal Type: Village
Incorporated: Nov. 18, 1983 *Area:* 3.61 sq km
Population in 2006: 490
Provincial Electoral District(s): Thunder Creek
Federal Electoral District(s): Regina-Lumsden-Lake Centre
Next Election: Oct. 2012 (3 year terms)
Roni Goulet, Mayor
Cindy Baumgartner, Administrator

Buffalo Narrows
P.O. Box 98
Waite St.
Buffalo Narrows, SK S0M 0J0
Tel: 306-235-4225; *Fax:* 306-235-4699
chartier.t@sasktel.net
Municipal Type: Northern Village
Incorporated: Oct. 1, 1983 *Area:* 34.10 sq km
Population in 2006: 1,081
Provincial Electoral District(s): Athabasca
Federal Electoral District(s): Churchill River/Rivière Churchill
Next Election: Oct. 2012 (3 year terms)
Bobby Woods, Mayor
Therese Chartier, Administrator

Bulyea
P.O. Box 37
Bulyea, SK S0G 0L0
Tel: 306-725-4936;
info@bulyea.com
www.bulyea.com
Municipal Type: Village
Incorporated: March 9, 1909 *Area:* 1.28 sq km
Population in 2006: 104
Provincial Electoral District(s): Last Mountain-Touchwood
Federal Electoral District(s): Regina-Lumsden-Lake Centre
Next Election: Oct. 2012 (3 year terms)
Darren Cameron, Mayor
Jenna Johnson, Clerk

Burstall
P.O. Box 250
428 Martin St.
Burstall, SK S0N 0H0
Tel: 306-679-2000; *Fax:* 306-679-2275
burstall@sasktel.net
www.burstall.ca
Municipal Type: Town
Incorporated: May 31, 1921 *Area:* 1.11 sq km
Population in 2006: 315
Provincial Electoral District(s): Cypress Hills
Federal Electoral District(s): Cypress Hills-Grasslands
Next Election: Oct. 2012 (3 year terms)
Note: Proclaimed as a town on Nov. 1, 1976.
Ken Hook, Mayor
Lucein Stuebing, Administrator

Cabri
P.O. Box 200
Cabri, SK S0N 0J0
Tel: 306-587-2500; *Fax:* 306-587-2392
townofcabri@sasktel.net
Municipal Type: Town
Incorporated: May 13, 1912 *Area:* 1.33 sq km
Population in 2006: 439
Provincial Electoral District(s): Cypress Hills
Federal Electoral District(s): Cypress Hills-Grasslands
Next Election: Oct. 2012 (3 year terms)
Note: Proclaimed as a town on April 16, 1917.
David Gossard, Mayor
Kristi Jamieson, Administrator

Cadillac
P.O. Box 189
Cadillac, SK S0N 0K0
Tel: 306-785-2100; *Fax:* 306-785-2101
v.cadillac@sasktel.net
Municipal Type: Village
Incorporated: July 2, 1914 *Area:* 1.05 sq km
Population in 2006: 80
Provincial Electoral District(s): Wood River
Federal Electoral District(s): Cypress Hills-Grasslands
Next Election: Oct. 2012 (3 year terms)
Holly Franklin, Mayor
Betty Moller, Clerk

Calder
P.O. Box 47
Calder, SK S0A 0K0
Tel: 306-742-2158; *Fax:* 306-742-2158
caldervillage@sasktel.net
Municipal Type: Village
Incorporated: Jan. 18, 1911 *Area:* 0.75 sq km
Population in 2006: 80
Provincial Electoral District(s): Melville-Saltcoats
Federal Electoral District(s): Yorkton-Melville
Next Election: Oct. 2012 (3 year terms)
Walter Balabuk, Mayor
Kendra Busch, Administrator

Canora
P.O. Box 717
418 Main St.
Canora, SK S0A 0L0
Tel: 306-563-5773; *Fax:* 306-563-4336
admin.canora@sasktel.net
www.canora.com
Municipal Type: Town
Incorporated: April 8, 1905 *Area:* 7.31 sq km
Population in 2006: 2,013
Provincial Electoral District(s): Canora-Pelly
Federal Electoral District(s): Yorkton-Melville
Next Election: Oct. 2012 (3 year terms)
Note: Proclaimed as a town on Nov. 1, 1910.
Terry Dennis, Mayor
306-563-6485
Michael Mykytyshyn, Administrator
306-563-6466

Canwood
P.O. Box 172
Canwood, SK S0J 0K0
Tel: 306-468-2016; *Fax:* 306-468-2666
canwood.town@sasktel.net
Municipal Type: Village
Incorporated: July 18, 1916 *Area:* 2.56 sq km
Population in 2006: 337
Provincial Electoral District(s): Rosthern-Shellbrook
Federal Electoral District(s): Desnethé-Missinippi-Churchill River
Next Election: Oct. 2012 (3 year terms)
Gary Thall, Mayor
Lisa Quessy, Administrator

Carievale
P.O. Box 88
128 Broadway St.
Carievale, SK S0C 0P0
Tel: 306-928-2033; *Fax:* 306-928-2021
village.carievale@sasktel.net
Municipal Type: Village
Incorporated: March 14, 1903 *Area:* 0.88 sq km
Population in 2006: 241
Provincial Electoral District(s): Cannington
Federal Electoral District(s): Souris-Moose Mountain
Next Election: Oct. 2012 (3 year terms)
Katie Steenbruggen, Administrator
Eric Hoefer, Mayor

Carlyle
P.O. Box 10
Carlyle, SK S0C 0R0
Tel: 306-453-2363; *Fax:* 306-453-6380
towncarlyle@sasktel.net
www.townofcarlyle.com
Municipal Type: Town
Incorporated: March 13, 1902 *Area:* 3.03 sq km
Population in 2006: 1,257
Provincial Electoral District(s): Cannington
Federal Electoral District(s): Souris-Moose Mountain
Next Election: Oct. 2012 (3 year terms)
Note: Proclaimed as a town on Jan. 1, 1906.
Don Shirley, Mayor
Huguette Lutz, Chief Administrative Officer

Carmichael
P.O. Box 420
Gull Lake, SK S0N 1A0
Tel: 306-672-3501; *Fax:* 306-672-3879
rm109@sasktel.net
Municipal Type: Village
Incorporated: May 25, 1917 *Area:* 0.67 sq km
Population in 2006: 10
Provincial Electoral District(s): Cypress Hills
Federal Electoral District(s): Cypress Hills-Grasslands
Next Election: Oct. 2012 (3 year terms)
Miles C. Wells, Mayor
Collette Jones, Clerk

Carnduff
P.O. Box 100
Carnduff, SK S0C 0S0
Tel: 306-482-3300; *Fax:* 306-482-3422
town.carnduff@sasktel.net
www.carnduff.ca
Municipal Type: Town
Incorporated: March 29, 1899 *Area:* 2.05 sq km
Population in 2006: 1,012
Provincial Electoral District(s): Cannington
Federal Electoral District(s): Souris-Moose Mountain
Next Election: Oct. 2012 (3 year terms)
Note: Proclaimed as a town on Aug. 12, 1905.
Ross Apperley, Mayor
Annette Brown, Administrator

Caronport
P.O. Box 550
Caronport, SK S0H 0S0
Tel: 306-756-2225; *Fax:* 306-756-5007
vcoffice@sasktel.net
Municipal Type: Village
Incorporated: Jan. 1, 1988 *Area:* 1.90 sq km
Population in 2006: 919
Provincial Electoral District(s): Thunder Creek
Federal Electoral District(s): Palliser
Next Election: Oct. 2012 (3 year terms)
Paul Blankestijn, Mayor
Brenda Thiessen, Administrator

Carrot River
P.O. Box 147
5 Main St.
Carrot River, SK S0E 0L0
Tel: 306-768-2515; *Fax:* 306-768-2930
t.carrotriver@sasktel.net
www.town.carrotriver.sk.ca
Municipal Type: Town
Incorporated: Nov. 6, 1941 *Area:* 1.46 sq km
Population in 2006: 941
Provincial Electoral District(s): Carrot River Valley
Federal Electoral District(s): Prince Albert
Next Election: Oct. 2012 (3 year terms)
Note: Proclaimed as a town on April 1, 1948.
Robert Gagne, Mayor
Duril Touet, Administrator

Central Butte
P.O. Box 10
Central Butte, SK S0H 0T0
Tel: 306-796-2288; *Fax:* 306-796-4627
townofcentralbutte@sasktel.net
www.centralbutte.ca
Municipal Type: Town
Incorporated: April 9, 1915 *Area:* 2.24 sq km
Population in 2006: 372
Provincial Electoral District(s): Thunder Creek
Federal Electoral District(s): Cypress Hills-Grasslands
Next Election: Oct. 2012 (3 year terms)
Note: Proclaimed as a town on July 1, 1967.
Alvin Klassen, Mayor
Joyce Aitken, Administrator

Ceylon
P.O. Box 188
Ceylon, SK S0C 0T0
Tel: 306-454-2202; *Fax:* 306-454-2627
rmgap39@sasktel.net
Municipal Type: Village
Incorporated: Sept. 26, 1911 *Area:* 0.75 sq km
Population in 2006: 90
Provincial Electoral District(s): Weyburn-Big Muddy
Federal Electoral District(s): Souris-Moose Mountain
Next Election: Oct. 2012 (3 year terms)
Larry Harkes, Mayor
Yvonne Johnston, Administrator

Chamberlain
P.O. Box 8
Chamberlain, SK S0G 0R0
Tel: 306-638-4680; *Fax:* 306-638-3108
chamberlain@canwan.com
Municipal Type: Village
Incorporated: Jan. 31, 1911 *Area:* 0.70 sq km
Population in 2006: 108
Provincial Electoral District(s): Thunder Creek
Federal Electoral District(s): Regina-Lumsden-Lake Centre
Next Election: Oct. 2012 (3 year terms)
Rita Folk, Mayor
Donna Flavel, Clerk

Chaplin
P.O. Box 210
Chaplin, SK S0H 0V0
Tel: 306-395-2221; *Fax:* 306-395-2555
village.chaplin@sasktel.net
www.chaplin.ca
Municipal Type: Village
Incorporated: Oct. 8, 1912 *Area:* 1.26 sq km
Population in 2006: 235
Provincial Electoral District(s): Thunder Creek
Federal Electoral District(s): Cypress Hills-Grasslands
Next Election: Oct. 2012 (3 year terms)
Jack Doell, Mayor
Gina Hallborg, Administrator

Choiceland
P.O. Box 279
100 Railway Ave. East
Choiceland, SK S0J 0M0
Tel: 306-428-2070; *Fax:* 306-428-2071
choiceland.town@sasktel.net
choiceland.ca
Municipal Type: Town
Incorporated: Sept. 8, 1944 *Area:* 1.12 sq km
Population in 2006: 346
Provincial Electoral District(s): Saskatchewan Rivers
Federal Electoral District(s): Desnethé-Missinippi-Churchill River
Next Election: Oct. 2012 (3 year terms)
Note: Proclaimed as a town on Jan. 1, 1979.
Edna Dickson, Mayor
Elaine L. McLean, Administrator

Christopher Lake
P.O. Box 163
Christopher Lake, SK S0J 0N0
Tel: 306-982-4242; *Fax:* 306-982-4242
vilchr@sasktel.net
Municipal Type: Village
Incorporated: March 1, 1985 *Area:* 3.47 sq km
Population in 2006: 215
Provincial Electoral District(s): Saskatchewan Rivers
Federal Electoral District(s): Desnethé-Missinippi-Churchill River
Next Election: Oct. 2012 (3 year terms)
Denis Daughton, Mayor
Audrey Veer, Administrator

Churchbridge
P.O. Box 256
116 Vincent Ave.
Churchbridge, SK S0A 0M0
Tel: 306-896-2240; *Fax:* 306-896-2910
churchbridge@sasktel.net
www.churchbridge.com
Municipal Type: Town
Incorporated: Sept. 17, 1903 *Area:* 2.76 sq km
Population in 2006: 704
Provincial Electoral District(s): Melville-Saltcoats
Federal Electoral District(s): Yorkton-Melville
Next Election: Oct. 2012 (3 year terms)
Note: Proclaimed as a town on March 1, 1964.
Jim Gallant, Mayor
Carla Kaeding, Administrator

Clavet
P.O. Box 68
Clavet, SK S0K 0Y0
Tel: 306-933-2425; *Fax:* 306-933-1995
clavetvillage@sasktel.net
Municipal Type: Village
Incorporated: Dec. 21, 1908 *Area:* 0.61 sq km
Population in 2006: 345
Provincial Electoral District(s): Humboldt
Federal Electoral District(s): Blackstrap
Next Election: Oct. 2012 (3 year terms)
Blair Bentley, Mayor
Janet Patry, Administrator

Climax
P.O. Box 30
Climax, SK S0N 0N0
Tel: 306-293-2124; *Fax:* 306-293-2702
villageofclimax@sasktel.net
Municipal Type: Village
Incorporated: Dec. 11, 1923 *Area:* 1.00 sq km
Population in 2006: 182
Provincial Electoral District(s): Cypress Hills
Federal Electoral District(s): Cypress Hills-Grasslands
Next Election: Oct. 2012 (3 year terms)
Nancy Kirk, Mayor
Shawna-Lee Bertram, Administrator

Coderre
P.O. Box 9
Coderre, SK S0H 0X0
Tel: 306-394-2070;
vil.of.coderre@sasktel.net
Municipal Type: Village
Incorporated: Aug. 26, 1925 *Area:* 0.85 sq km
Population in 2006: 40
Provincial Electoral District(s): Wood River
Federal Electoral District(s): Cypress Hills-Grasslands
Next Election: Oct. 2012 (3 year terms)
David Duckworth, Mayor
Barbara Arnold, Clerk

Codette
P.O. Box 100
Codette, SK S0E 0P0
Tel: 306-862-9551; *Fax:* 306-862-2432
rm487@sasktel.net
Municipal Type: Village
Incorporated: March 9, 1929 *Area:* 0.37 sq km
Population in 2006: 221
Provincial Electoral District(s): Carrot River Valley
Federal Electoral District(s): Prince Albert
Next Election: Oct. 2012 (3 year terms)
Brad Reed, Mayor
Eunice Rudy, Clerk

Cole Bay
P.O. Box 80
Canoe Rd.
Cole Bay, SK S0M 0M0
Tel: 306-829-4232; *Fax:* 306-829-4312
Municipal Type: Northern Village
Incorporated: Jan. 1, 1990 *Area:* 4.95 sq km
Population in 2006: 156
Provincial Electoral District(s): Athabasca
Federal Electoral District(s): Desnethé-Missinippi-Churchill River
Next Election: Oct. 2012 (3 year terms)
Harold Aubichon, Mayor
Delphine Bouvier, Clerk

Coleville
P.O. Box 249
Coleville, SK S0L 0K0
Tel: 306-965-2281; *Fax:* 306-965-2466
rm320@sasktel.net; rmoakassist@sasktel.net
www.colevillesk.ca
Municipal Type: Village
Incorporated: July 1, 1953 *Area:* 1.27 sq km
Population in 2006: 248
Provincial Electoral District(s): Kindersley
Federal Electoral District(s): Battlefords-Lloydminster
Next Election: Oct. 2012 (3 year terms)
Mike Smith, Mayor
Gillian Lund, Administrator

Colonsay
P.O. Box 190
100 Jura St.
Colonsay, SK S0K 0Z0
Tel: 306-255-2313;
town.colonsay@sasktel.net
www.townofcolonsay.com
Municipal Type: Town
Incorporated: Oct. 6, 1910 *Area:* 2.46 sq km
Population in 2006: 425
Provincial Electoral District(s): Humboldt
Federal Electoral District(s): Blackstrap
Next Election: Oct. 2012 (3 year terms)
Note: Proclaimed as a town on Jan. 1, 1977.
James Gray, Mayor
Deborah Prosper, Administrator

Conquest
P.O. Box 250
202 Coulthard St.
Conquest, SK S0L 0L0
Tel: 306-856-2114; *Fax:* 306-856-2114
conquest@sasktel.net
www.conquest.ca
Municipal Type: Village
Incorporated: Oct. 24, 1911 *Area:* 1 sq km
Population in 2006: 167
Provincial Electoral District(s): Rosetown-Elrose
Federal Electoral District(s): Cypress Hills-Grasslands
Next Election: Oct. 2012 (3 year terms)
Doug Lemon, Mayor
Colleen Reilly, Clerk

Consul
P.O. Box 185
Consul, SK S0N 0P0
Tel: 306-299-2030; *Fax:* 306-299-2031
consul@sasktel.net
Municipal Type: Village
Incorporated: June 12, 1917 *Area:* 0.65 sq km
Population in 2006: 93
Provincial Electoral District(s): Cypress Hills
Federal Electoral District(s): Cypress Hills-Grasslands
Next Election: Oct. 2012 (3 year terms)
Linda Brown, Mayor
Carrie Funk, Administrator

Coronach
P.O. Box 90
Coronach, SK S0H 0Z0
Tel: 306-267-2150; *Fax:* 306-267-2296
townoffice@coronach.ca
www.coronach.ca
Municipal Type: Town
Incorporated: Feb. 3, 1928 *Area:* 2.33 sq km
Population in 2006: 770
Provincial Electoral District(s): Weyburn-Big Muddy
Federal Electoral District(s): Souris-Moose Mountain
Next Election: Oct. 2012 (3 year terms)
Note: Proclaimed as a town on Jan. 1, 1977.
Alexander McBain, Mayor
Murray Setrum, Administrator

Craik
P.O. Box 60
Craik, SK S0G 0V0
Tel: 306-734-2250; *Fax:* 306-734-2688
town.craik@sasktel.net
www.craik.ca
Municipal Type: Town
Incorporated: Oct. 22, 1903 *Area:* 5.41 sq km
Population in 2006: 408
Provincial Electoral District(s): Thunder Creek
Federal Electoral District(s): Regina-Lumsden-Lake Centre
Next Election: Oct. 2012 (3 year terms)
Note: Proclaimed as a town on Aug. 1, 1907.
Rick Rodgers, Mayor

Jeff Murray, Administrator

Craven
P.O. Box 30
Craven, SK S0G 0W0
Tel: 306-731-3452; *Fax:* 306-731-3162
villageofcraven@canwan.com
Municipal Type: Village
Incorporated: April 11, 1905 *Area:* 1.16 sq km
Population in 2006: 274
Provincial Electoral District(s): Last Mountain-Touchwood
Federal Electoral District(s): Regina-Lumsden-Lake Centre
Next Election: Oct. 2012 (3 year terms)
Adri Vandeven, Mayor
Wendy Dunn, Administrator

Creelman
P.O. Box 177
Creelman, SK S0G 0X0
Tel: 306-433-2011; *Fax:* 306-433-2011
creelmanvillage@sasktel.net
Municipal Type: Village
Incorporated: April 6, 1906 *Area:* 1.14 sq km
Population in 2006: 81
Provincial Electoral District(s): Cannington
Federal Electoral District(s): Souris-Moose Mountain
Next Election: Oct. 2012 (3 year terms)
Don Anslow, Mayor
Vernna Wiggins, Administrator

Creighton
123 Main St.
Creighton, SK S0P 0A0
Tel: 306-688-8253; *Fax:* 306-688-4764
townofcreighton@sasktel.net
www.townofcreighton.ca
Municipal Type: Northern Town
Incorporated: Oct. 1, 1983 *Area:* 14.39 sq km
Population in 2006: 1,502
Provincial Electoral District(s): Cumberland
Federal Electoral District(s): Desnethé-Missinippi-Churchill River
Next Election: Oct. 2012 (3 year terms)
Bruce Fidler, Mayor
Paula Muench, Administrator

Cudworth
P.O. Box 69
223 Main St.
Cudworth, SK S0K 1B0
Tel: 306-256-3492; *Fax:* 306-256-3515
town.cudworth@sasktel.net
www.townofcudworth.com
Municipal Type: Town
Incorporated: Oct. 23, 1911 *Area:* 2.21 sq km
Population in 2006: 738
Provincial Electoral District(s): Batoche
Federal Electoral District(s): Saskatoon-Humboldt
Next Election: Oct. 2012 (3 year terms)
Note: Proclaimed as a town on Oct. 1, 1961.
Harold Mueller, Mayor
Yvonne Gobolos, Administrator

Cumberland House
P.O. Box 190
Cumberland St.
Cumberland House, SK S0E 0S0
Tel: 306-888-2066; *Fax:* 306-888-2103
northernvillageofchouse@sasktel.net
Municipal Type: Northern Village
Incorporated: Oct. 1, 1983 *Area:* 15.69 sq km
Population in 2006: 810
Provincial Electoral District(s): Cumberland
Federal Electoral District(s): Desnethé-Missinippi-Churchill River
Next Election: Oct. 2012 (3 year terms)
Andy McKay, Mayor
Emily Nabess, Clerk

Cupar
P.O. Box 397
Cupar, SK S0G 0Y0
Tel: 306-723-4324; *Fax:* 306-723-4644
townofcupar1@sasktel.net
www.townofcupar.com
Municipal Type: Town
Incorporated: March 21, 1906 *Area:* 0.80 sq km
Population in 2006: 566
Provincial Electoral District(s): Last Mountain-Touchwood
Federal Electoral District(s): Regina-Qu'Appelle
Next Election: Oct. 2012 (3 year terms)
Note: Proclaimed as a town on Jan. 1, 1961.
Don Jeworski, Mayor
Linda Nameth, Administrator

Cut Knife
P.O. Box 70
Cut Knife, SK S0M 0N0
Tel: 306-398-2363; *Fax:* 306-398-2839
rm439@sasktel.net
Municipal Type: Town
Incorporated: May 17, 1912 *Area:* 1.99 sq km
Population in 2006: 532
Provincial Electoral District(s): Cut Knife-Turtleford
Federal Electoral District(s): Battlefords-Lloydminster
Next Election: Oct. 2012 (3 year terms)
Note: Proclaimed as a town on Aug. 1, 1968.
Germaine Vany, Mayor
Don McCallum, Administrator

Dafoe
P.O. Box 142
Dafoe, SK S0K 1C0
Tel: 306-554-3250
Municipal Type: Village
Incorporated: May 28, 1920 *Area:* 0.80 sq km
Population in 2006: 10
Provincial Electoral District(s): Rosetown-Elrose
Federal Electoral District(s): Regina-Qu'Appelle
Next Election: Oct. 2012 (3 year terms)
Bob Pilkey, Mayor
Lana M. Bolt, Clerk

Dalmeny
P.O. Box 400
301 Railway Ave.
Dalmeny, SK S0K 1E0
Tel: 306-254-2133; *Fax:* 306-254-2142
dalmenytownoffice@sasktel.net
www.dalmeny.ca
Municipal Type: Town
Incorporated: June 17, 1912 *Area:* 2.27 sq km
Population in 2006: 1,560
Provincial Electoral District(s): Weyburn-Big Muddy
Federal Electoral District(s): Saskatoon-Wanuskewin
Next Election: Oct. 2012 (3 year terms)
Note: Proclaimed as a town on April 1, 1983.
Allan Earle, Mayor
Shelley Funk, Administrator

Davidson
P.O. Box 340
Davidson, SK S0G 1A0
Tel: 306-567-2040; *Fax:* 306-567-4730
townofdavidson@sasktel.net
www.townofdavidson.com
Municipal Type: Town
Incorporated: March 7, 1904 *Area:* 4.49 sq km
Population in 2006: 958
Provincial Electoral District(s): Arm River-Watrous
Federal Electoral District(s): Regina-Lumsden-Lake Centre
Next Election: Oct. 2012 (3 year terms)
Note: Proclaimed as a town on Nov. 15, 1906.
Mary Jane Morrison, Mayor
Gary Edom, Administrator

Debden
P.O. Box 400
Debden, SK S0J 0S0
Tel: 306-724-2040; *Fax:* 306-724-2220
vdebden@sasktel.net
www.debden.net
Municipal Type: Village
Incorporated: June 7, 1922 *Area:* 1.39 sq km
Population in 2006: 348
Provincial Electoral District(s): Saskatchewan Rivers
Federal Electoral District(s): Desnethé-Missinippi-Churchill River
Next Election: Oct. 2012 (3 year terms)
Aline Hannon, Mayor
Carmen Jean, Administrator

Delisle
P.O. Box 40
201 - 1st St. West
Delisle, SK S0L 0P0
Tel: 306-493-2242; *Fax:* 306-493-2263
delisle@sasktel.net
www.townofdelisle.com
Municipal Type: Town
Incorporated: Dec. 29, 1908 *Area:* 2.35 sq km
Population in 2006: 898
Provincial Electoral District(s): Biggar
Federal Electoral District(s): Saskatoon-Rosetown-Biggar
Next Election: Oct. 2012 (3 year terms)
Note: Proclaimed as a town on Nov. 1, 1913.
Rita Pfoh, Mayor
306-493-2652

Mark Dubkowski, Administrator

Denare Beach
P.O. Box 70
512 - 7th Ave.
Denare Beach, SK S0P 0B0
Tel: 306-362-2054; *Fax:* 306-362-2257
denarebeach@aski.ca
www.denarebeach.net
Municipal Type: Northern Village
Incorporated: April 1, 1984 *Area:* 5.84 sq km
Population in 2006: 785
Provincial Electoral District(s): Cumberland
Federal Electoral District(s): Desnethé-Missinippi-Churchill River
Next Election: Oct. 2012 (3 year terms)
Carl Lentowicz, Mayor
Bev Wheeler, Administrator

Denholm
P.O. Box 71
Denholm, SK S0M 0R0
Tel: 306-446-0478
Municipal Type: Village
Incorporated: June 25, 1912 *Area:* 0.33 sq km
Population in 2006: 61
Provincial Electoral District(s): Biggar
Federal Electoral District(s): Battlefords-Lloydminster
Next Election: Oct. 2012 (3 year terms)
Terry Welch, Mayor
Lila Yuhasz, Clerk

Denzil
P.O. Box 100
Denzil, SK S0L 0S0
Tel: 306-358-2118; *Fax:* 306-358-4828
villageofdenzil@sasktel.net
www.villageofdenzil.com
Municipal Type: Village
Incorporated: May 3, 1911 *Area:* 0.55 sq km
Population in 2006: 142
Provincial Electoral District(s): Kindersley
Federal Electoral District(s): Battlefords-Lloydminster
Next Election: Oct. 2012 (3 year terms)
Murray Sieben, Mayor
Kathy Reschny, Administrator

Dilke
P.O. Box 100
Dilke, SK S0G 1C0
Tel: 306-488-4866; *Fax:* 306-488-4866
dilke@canwan.com
Municipal Type: Village
Incorporated: Dec. 30, 1912 *Area:* 1.28 sq km
Population in 2006: 80
Provincial Electoral District(s): Thunder Creek
Federal Electoral District(s): Regina-Lumsden-Lake Centre
Next Election: Oct. 2012 (3 year terms)
Arnold Ball, Mayor
Colleen R. Duesing, Clerk

Dinsmore
P.O. Box 278
100 Main St.
Dinsmore, SK S0L 0T0
Tel: 306-846-2220; *Fax:* 306-846-2999
dinsmore@sasktel.net
www.dinsmore.ca
Municipal Type: Village
Incorporated: Nov. 3, 1913 *Area:* 2.59 sq km
Population in 2006: 269
Provincial Electoral District(s): Rosetown-Elrose
Federal Electoral District(s): Cypress Hills-Grasslands
Next Election: Oct. 2012 (3 year terms)
Janice Thomson, Mayor
j.thomson.cma@sasktel.net
Jim Main, Administrator

Disley
R.R.#1
Lumsden, SK S0G 3C0
Tel: 306-731-3355;
villageofdisley@gmail.com
Municipal Type: Village
Incorporated: June 24, 1907 *Area:* 0.65 sq km
Population in 2006: 62
Provincial Electoral District(s): Thunder Creek
Federal Electoral District(s): Regina-Lumsden-Lake Centre
Next Election: Oct. 2012 (3 year terms)
Gord Wilson, Mayor
Rhonda Woelk, Clerk

Dodsland
P.O. Box 400
Dodsland, SK S0L 0V0
Tel: 306-356-2106; *Fax:* 306-356-2085
rm319@sasktel.net
Municipal Type: Village
Incorporated: Aug. 23, 1913 *Area:* 2.93 sq km
Population in 2006: 207
Provincial Electoral District(s): Rosetown-Elrose
Federal Electoral District(s): Battlefords-Lloydminster
Next Election: Oct. 2012 (3 year terms)
Kevin McCarthy, Mayor
Regan MacDonald, Administrator

Dore Lake
P.O. Box 608
Dore Ave.
Big River, SK S0J 0E0
Tel: 306-832-4528; *Fax:* 306-832-4525
northern.dore@sasktel.net
Municipal Type: Northern Hamlet
Incorporated: Jan. 11, 1985 *Area:* 8.03 sq km
Population in 2006: 30
Provincial Electoral District(s): Athabasca
Federal Electoral District(s): Desnethé-Missinippi-Churchill River
Next Election: Oct. 2012 (3 year terms)
Hilda McKay, Mayor
Eugenie Lafleur, Administrator

Dorintosh
P.O. Box 40
301 1st St. East
Dorintosh, SK S0M 0T0
Tel: 306-236-5166;
vill.dor@sasktel.net
www.villageofdorintosh.sasktelwebsite.net
Municipal Type: Village
Incorporated: Jan. 1, 1989 *Area:* 0.88 sq km
Population in 2006: 127
Provincial Electoral District(s): Meadow Lake
Federal Electoral District(s): Desnethé-Missinippi-Churchill River
Next Election: Oct. 2012 (3 year terms)
John Osborne, Mayor
Pam Dallyn, Administrator

Drake
P.O. Box 18
125 Francis St.
Drake, SK S0K 1H0
Tel: 306-363-2109; *Fax:* 306-363-2102
villageofdrake@sasktel.net
www.drake.ca
Municipal Type: Village
Incorporated: Sept. 19, 1910 *Area:* 0.72 sq km
Population in 2006: 232
Provincial Electoral District(s): Arm River-Watrous
Federal Electoral District(s): Blackstrap
Next Election: Oct. 2012 (3 year terms)
Peter Nicholson, Mayor
Stuart Jantz, Administrator

Drinkwater
P.O. Box 66
Drinkwater, SK S0H 1G0
Tel: 306-693-5093; *Fax:* 306-693-4410
villageofdrinkwater@sasktel.net
Municipal Type: Village
Incorporated: June 7, 1904 *Area:* 2.64 sq km
Population in 2006: 65
Provincial Electoral District(s): Indian Head-Milestone
Federal Electoral District(s): Palliser
Next Election: Oct. 2012 (3 year terms)
Ryan Briggs, Mayor
Lloyd Muma, Clerk

Dubuc
P.O. Box 126
Dubuc, SK S0A 0R0
Tel: 306-877-2172;
villageofdubuc@sasktel.net
www.spreda.sk.ca/community_Dubuc.htm
Municipal Type: Village
Incorporated: May 29, 1905 *Area:* 0.63 sq km
Population in 2006: 55
Provincial Electoral District(s): Melville-Saltcoats
Federal Electoral District(s): Yorkton-Melville
Next Election: Oct. 2012 (3 year terms)
Melba McAlpine, Mayor
Joan Kerr, Clerk

Duck Lake
P.O. Box 430
Duck Lake, SK S0K 1J0
Tel: 306-467-2277; *Fax:* 306-467-4434
www.ducklake.ca
Municipal Type: Town
Incorporated: Dec. 29, 1898 *Area:* 2.86 sq km
Population in 2006: 610
Provincial Electoral District(s): Batoche
Federal Electoral District(s): Saskatoon-Wanuskewin
Next Election: Oct. 2012 (3 year terms)
Note: Proclaimed as a town on Nov. 1, 1911.
Denis Poirier, Mayor
Betty Fiolleau, Administrator

Duff
P.O. Box 57
Duff, SK S0A 0S0
Tel: 306-728-3570;
www.spreda.sk.ca/community_Duff.htm
Municipal Type: Village
Incorporated: May 28, 1920 *Area:* 0.22 sq km
Population in 2006: 30
Provincial Electoral District(s): Last Mountain-Touchwood
Federal Electoral District(s): Yorkton-Melville
Next Election: Oct. 2012 (3 year terms)
David Hollinger, Mayor
Tracey Schuman, Clerk

Dundurn
P.O. Box 185
300 Third Ave.
Dundurn, SK S0K 1K0
Tel: 306-492-2202; *Fax:* 306-492-2360
town.dundurn@sasktel.net
www.townofdundurn.ca
Municipal Type: Town
Incorporated: July 7, 1905 *Area:* 0.88 sq km
Population in 2006: 647
Provincial Electoral District(s): Arm River-Watrous
Federal Electoral District(s): Blackstrap
Next Election: Oct. 2012 (3 year terms)
Note: Proclaimed as a town on Nov. 1, 1980.
Per Vinding, Mayor
Michelle Roepe, Administrator

Duval
P.O. Box 70
Duval, SK S0G 1G0
Tel: 306-725-3767; *Fax:* 306-725-4339
jeff.jones@sasktel.net
Municipal Type: Village
Incorporated: Dec. 21, 1910 *Area:* 0.75 sq km
Population in 2006: 94
Provincial Electoral District(s): Arm River-Watrous
Federal Electoral District(s): Regina-Lumsden-Lake Centre
Next Election: Oct. 2012 (3 year terms)
Dale Campbell, Mayor
Jeff Jones, Clerk

Dysart
P.O. Box 70
Dysart, SK S0G 1H0
Tel: 306-432-2100; *Fax:* 306-432-2265
dysartsk@sasktel.net
www.dysartsk.com
Municipal Type: Village
Incorporated: April 6, 1909 *Area:* 1.19 sq km
Population in 2006: 198
Provincial Electoral District(s): Last Mountain-Touchwood
Federal Electoral District(s): Regina-Qu'Appelle
Next Election: Oct. 2012 (3 year terms)
Brenda Macknak, Mayor
Gerry Burym, Administrator

Earl Grey
P.O. Box 100
Earl Grey, SK S0G 1J0
Tel: 306-939-2062; *Fax:* 306-939-2036
earlgreyvillage@sasktel.net
earl.sasktelwebhosting.com
Municipal Type: Village
Incorporated: July 27, 1906 *Area:* 1.31 sq km
Population in 2006: 264
Provincial Electoral District(s): Last Mountain-Touchwood
Federal Electoral District(s): Regina-Lumsden-Lake Centre
Next Election: Oct. 2012 (3 year terms)
Allan H. Johnson, Mayor
Murray Cook, Administrator

Eastend
P.O. Box 520
Eastend, SK S0N 0T0
Tel: 306-295-3322; *Fax:* 306-295-3571
eastend@sasktel.net
www.dinocountry.com
Municipal Type: Town
Incorporated: Feb. 26, 1914 *Area:* 2.71 sq km
Population in 2006: 471
Provincial Electoral District(s): Cypress Hills
Federal Electoral District(s): Cypress Hills-Grasslands
Next Election: Oct. 2012 (3 year terms)
Note: Proclaimed as a town on March 15, 1920.
Scott Morvik, Mayor
Deb Lewis, Administrator

Eatonia
P.O. Box 237
Eatonia, SK S0L 0Y0
Tel: 306-967-2251; *Fax:* 306-967-2267
eatonia@yourlink.ca
www.townofeatonia.com
Municipal Type: Town
Incorporated: Jan. 28, 1920 *Area:* 1.68 sq km
Population in 2006: 449
Provincial Electoral District(s): Kindersley
Federal Electoral District(s): Cypress Hills-Grasslands
Next Election: Oct. 2012 (3 year terms)
Note: Proclaimed as a town on Jan. 1, 1954.
R.W. (Bob) Peters, Mayor
Cheryl Bailey, Administrator

Ebenezer
P.O. Box 97
Ebenezer, SK S0A 0T0
Tel: 306-783-1217; *Fax:* 306-793-1218
village.ebenezer@sasktel.net
Municipal Type: Village
Incorporated: July 1, 1948 *Area:* 0.62 sq km
Population in 2006: 139
Provincial Electoral District(s): Canora-Pelly
Federal Electoral District(s): Yorkton-Melville
Next Election: Oct. 2012 (3 year terms)
Kelly Pfeifer, Mayor
Angela Filipchuk, Administrator

Edam
P.O. Box 203
Edam, SK S0M 0V0
Tel: 306-397-2223; *Fax:* 306-397-2626
edamvill@sasktel.net
villageofedam.ca
Municipal Type: Village
Incorporated: Oct. 12, 1911 *Area:* 1.13 sq km
Population in 2006: 399
Provincial Electoral District(s): Cut Knife-Turtleford
Federal Electoral District(s): Battlefords-Lloydminster
Next Election: Oct. 2012 (3 year terms)
Larry McDaid, Mayor
Trudy McMurphy, Administrator

Edenwold
P.O. Box 130
Edenwold, SK S0G 1K0
Tel: 306-771-4121; *Fax:* 306-771-2518
office@villageofedenwold.ca
www.villageofedenwold.ca
Municipal Type: Village
Incorporated: Oct. 3, 1912 *Area:* 0.68 sq km
Population in 2006: 242
Provincial Electoral District(s): Indian Head-Milestone
Federal Electoral District(s): Regina-Qu'Appelle
Next Election: Oct. 2012 (3 year terms)
Dean Josephson, Mayor
mayor@villageofedenwold.ca
Christine Galbraith, Administrator

Elbow
P.O. Box 8
Elbow, SK S0H 1J0
Tel: 306-854-2277; *Fax:* 306-854-2229
info@elbowsask.com
www.elbowsask.com
Municipal Type: Village
Incorporated: April 6, 1909 *Area:* 3.92 sq km
Population in 2006: 294
Provincial Electoral District(s): Thunder Creek
Federal Electoral District(s): Blackstrap
Next Election: Oct. 2012 (3 year terms)
David Cross, Mayor
Yvonne Jess, Administrator

Elfros
P.O. Box 40
Elfros, SK S0A 0V0
Tel: 306-328-2011; *Fax:* 306-328-4490
rm307@sasktel.net
Municipal Type: Village
Incorporated: Dec. 1, 1909 *Area:* 2.52 sq km
Population in 2006: 110
Provincial Electoral District(s): Kelvington-Wadena
Federal Electoral District(s): Regina-Qu'Appelle
Next Election: Oct. 2012 (3 year terms)
Karilee Zemlak, Mayor
Glenn Thompson, Administrator

Elrose
P.O. Box 458
101 Main St.
Elrose, SK S0L 0Z0
Tel: 306-378-2202; *Fax:* 306-378-2966
townofelrose@sasktel.net
www.elrose.ca
Municipal Type: Town
Incorporated: Oct. 24, 1913 *Area:* 2.76 sq km
Population in 2006: 453
Provincial Electoral District(s): Rosetown-Elrose
Federal Electoral District(s): Cypress Hills-Grasslands
Next Election: Oct. 2012 (3 year terms)
Note: Proclaimed as a town on Feb. 1, 1951.
June Hintze, Mayor
Chris Hopkins, Administrator

Elstow
P.O. Box 29
Elstow, SK S0K 1M0
Tel: 306-257-3889; *Fax:* 306-257-3709
villageofelstow@gmail.com
Municipal Type: Village
Incorporated: Dec. 17, 1908 *Area:* 0.58 sq km
Population in 2006: 91
Provincial Electoral District(s): Humboldt
Federal Electoral District(s): Blackstrap
Next Election: Oct. 2012 (3 year terms)
Jed Bruce, Mayor
J. Linda Barnes, Administrator

Endeavour
P.O. Box 307
Endeavour, SK S0A 0W0
Tel: 306-547-3484; *Fax:* 306-547-3484
endeavour@sasktel.net
Municipal Type: Village
Incorporated: April 29, 1953 *Area:* 0.99 sq km
Population in 2006: 118
Provincial Electoral District(s): Canora-Pelly
Federal Electoral District(s): Yorkton-Melville
Next Election: Oct. 2012 (3 year terms)
Roy Sheets, Mayor
Kathleen Ambrose, Administrator

Englefeld
P.O. Box 44
135 Main St.
Englefeld, SK S0K 1N0
Tel: 306-287-3151; *Fax:* 306-287-9902
vengle@sasktel.net
www.englefeld.ca
Municipal Type: Village
Incorporated: June 13, 1916 *Area:* 0.65 sq km
Population in 2006: 227
Provincial Electoral District(s): Melfort
Federal Electoral District(s): Saskatoon-Humboldt
Next Election: Oct. 2012 (3 year terms)
Darrell Athmer, Mayor
Lani Best, Administrator

Ernfold
P.O. Box 340
Morse, SK S0H 3C0
Tel: 306-629-3282; *Fax:* 306-629-3212
rm165@sasktel.net
Municipal Type: Village
Incorporated: Dec. 4, 1912 *Area:* 1.19 sq km
Population in 2006: 35
Provincial Electoral District(s): Thunder Creek
Federal Electoral District(s): Cypress Hills-Grasslands
Next Election: Oct. 2012 (3 year terms)
Christine Bauck, Mayor
Mark Wilson, Administrator

Esterhazy
P.O. Box 490
600 Sumner St.
Esterhazy, SK S0A 0X0
Tel: 306-745-3942; *Fax:* 306-745-6797
town.esterhazy@sasktel.net
www.town.esterhazy.sk.ca
Municipal Type: Town
Incorporated: Dec. 3, 1903 *Area:* 4.75 sq km
Population in 2006: 2,336
Provincial Electoral District(s): Melville-Saltcoats
Federal Electoral District(s): Yorkton-Melville
Next Election: Oct. 2012 (3 year terms)
Note: Proclaimed as a town on March 1, 1957.
Herb Hozjan, Mayor
Lois Kubik, Administrator
lois.esterhazy@sasktel.net

Eston
P.O. Box 757
Eston, SK S0L 1A0
Tel: 306-962-4444; *Fax:* 306-962-4224
townofeston@sasktel.net
www.eston.ca
Municipal Type: Town
Incorporated: March 28, 1916 *Area:* 2.72 sq km
Population in 2006: 971
Provincial Electoral District(s): Rosetown-Elrose
Federal Electoral District(s): Cypress Hills-Grasslands
Next Election: Oct. 2012 (3 year terms)
Note: Proclaimed as a town on Dec. 1, 1928.
Allan Heron, Mayor
bigbird70@sasktel.net
Gary Johnson, Administrator
gjohnson.towneston@sasktel.net

Eyebrow
P.O. Box 159
Eyebrow, SK S0H 1L0
Tel: 306-759-2167; *Fax:* 306-759-2388
eyebrowvillage@sasktel.net
villageofeyebrow.com
Municipal Type: Village
Incorporated: Jan. 8, 1909 *Area:* 2.70 sq km
Population in 2006: 135
Provincial Electoral District(s): Thunder Creek
Federal Electoral District(s): Regina-Lumsden-Lake Centre
Next Election: Oct. 2012 (3 year terms)
Don Linton, Mayor
Deanne Hartell, Clerk

Fairlight
P.O. Box 55
Fairlight, SK S0G 1M0
Tel: 306-646-2006; *Fax:* 306-646-2006
admin@villageoffairlight.ca
www.villageoffairlight.ca
Municipal Type: Village
Incorporated: Oct. 5, 1909 *Area:* 2.71 sq km
Population in 2006: 40
Provincial Electoral District(s): Cannington
Federal Electoral District(s): Souris-Moose Mountain
Next Election: Oct. 2012 (3 year terms)
Bary Metz, Mayor
Nadia Metz, Administrator

Fenwood
P.O. Box 66
Fenwood, SK S0A 0Y0
Tel: 306-728-2185;
www.spreda.sk.ca/community_Fenwood.htm
Municipal Type: Village
Incorporated: June 30, 1909 *Area:* 1.74 sq km
Population in 2006: 35
Provincial Electoral District(s): Last Mountain-Touchwood
Federal Electoral District(s): Yorkton-Melville
Next Election: Oct. 2012 (3 year terms)
Byron Dohms, Mayor
Doreen Dohms, Clerk

Fillmore
P.O. Box 185
Fillmore, SK S0G 1N0
Tel: 306-722-3330; *Fax:* 306-722-3340
v.fillmore@sasktel.net
Municipal Type: Village
Incorporated: June 10, 1905 *Area:* 1.33 sq km
Population in 2006: 193
Provincial Electoral District(s): Cannington
Federal Electoral District(s): Souris-Moose Mountain
Next Election: Oct. 2012 (3 year terms)
Marvin J. Chambers, Mayor
Kimberley A. Palmer, Administrator

Findlater
P.O. Box 10
Findlater, SK S0G 1P0
Tel: 306-638-4630; *Fax:* 306-638-4630
villageoffindlater@live.ca
Municipal Type: Village
Incorporated: Sept. 27, 1911 *Area:* 1.20 sq km
Population in 2006: 49
Provincial Electoral District(s): Thunder Creek
Federal Electoral District(s): Regina-Lumsden-Lake Centre
Next Election: Oct. 2012 (3 year terms)
Bob Lesperance, Mayor
Joanne Yates, Clerk

Flaxcombe
P.O. Box 136
Flaxcombe, SK S0L 1E0
Tel: 306-463-2004; *Fax:* 306-463-2004
flaxcombe@sasktel.net
Municipal Type: Village
Incorporated: June 4, 1913 *Area:* 1.49 sq km
Population in 2006: 111
Provincial Electoral District(s): Kindersley
Federal Electoral District(s): Battlefords-Lloydminster
Next Election: Oct. 2012 (3 year terms)
Dolores Doolittle, Mayor
Charlotte Helfrich, Clerk

Fleming
P.O. Box 129
Fleming, SK S0G 1R0
Tel: 306-435-4244; *Fax:* 306-435-3508
thetownoffleming@sasktel.net
Municipal Type: Town
Incorporated: July 2, 1896 *Area:* 2.17 sq km
Population in 2006: 75
Provincial Electoral District(s): Moosomin
Federal Electoral District(s): Souris-Moose Mountain
Next Election: Oct. 2012 (3 year terms)
Note: Proclaimed as a town on June 15, 1907.
Philip Hamm, Mayor
Helen Gurski, Administrator

Foam Lake
P.O. Box 57
Foam Lake, SK S0A 1A0
Tel: 306-272-3359; *Fax:* 306-272-3738
foamlaketown@sasktel.net
www.foamlake.com
Municipal Type: Town
Incorporated: Oct. 12, 1908 *Area:* 6.06 sq km
Population in 2006: 1,123
Provincial Electoral District(s): Kelvington-Wadena
Federal Electoral District(s): Yorkton-Melville
Next Election: Oct. 2012 (3 year terms)
Note: Proclaimed as a town on March 1, 1924.
Bob Johnson, Mayor
Gloria Leader, Administrator

Forget
P.O. Box 522
Stoughton, SK S0G 4T0
Tel: 306-457-2277; *Fax:* 306-457-3149
rmtec@sasktel.net
Municipal Type: Village
Incorporated: Nov. 21, 1904 *Area:* 1.39 sq km
Population in 2006: 40
Provincial Electoral District(s): Cannington
Federal Electoral District(s): Souris-Moose Mountain
Next Election: Oct. 2012 (3 year terms)
Leon Gilbertson, Mayor
Zandra Slater, Administrator

Fort Qu'Appelle
P.O. Box 309
Fort Qu'appelle, SK S0G 1S0
Tel: 306-332-5266; *Fax:* 306-332-5087
forttownoffice@sasktel.net
www.fortquappelle.com
Municipal Type: Town
Incorporated: June 25, 1898 *Area:* 5.28 sq km
Population in 2006: 1,919
Provincial Electoral District(s): Indian Head-Milestone
Federal Electoral District(s): Regina-Qu'Appelle
Next Election: Oct. 2012 (3 year terms)
Note: Proclaimed as a town on Jan. 1, 1951.
Ron Osika, Mayor
Ed Sigmeth, Administrator

Fosston
P.O. Box 160
Fosston, SK S0E 0V0
Tel: 306-322-4521; *Fax:* 306-322-4442
vilfos@sasktel.net
www.newsaskcfdc.ca/fosston.htm
Municipal Type: Village
Incorporated: Jan. 1, 1965 *Area:* 0.59 sq km
Population in 2006: 55
Provincial Electoral District(s): Kelvington-Wadena
Federal Electoral District(s): Yorkton-Melville
Next Election: Oct. 2012 (3 year terms)
Ron Einarson, Mayor
Valerie Bjerland, Administrator

Fox Valley
P.O. Box 207
Fox Valley, SK S0N 0V0
Tel: 306-666-3020; *Fax:* 306-666-3020
villoffoxvalley@sasktel.net
foxvalleysask.com
Municipal Type: Village
Incorporated: Aug. 30, 1928 *Area:* 0.60 sq km
Population in 2006: 295
Provincial Electoral District(s): Cypress Hills
Federal Electoral District(s): Cypress Hills-Grasslands
Next Election: Oct. 2012 (3 year terms)
Mark Hudec, Mayor
Michelle Sehn, Administrator

Francis
P.O. Box 128
Francis, SK S0G 1V0
Tel: 306-245-3624; *Fax:* 306-245-3326
town.francis@sasktel.net
Municipal Type: Town
Incorporated: Oct. 24, 1904 *Area:* 0.59 sq km
Population in 2006: 148
Provincial Electoral District(s): Indian Head-Milestone
Federal Electoral District(s): Wascana
Next Election: Oct. 2012 (3 year terms)
Note: Proclaimed as a town on Sept. 24, 1906.
Richard Senger, Mayor
Ila Connery, Administrator

Frobisher
P.O. Box 235
Frobisher, SK S0C 0Y0
Tel: 306-486-2140; *Fax:* 306-486-4504
vilfrob@sdcwireless.com
Municipal Type: Village
Incorporated: July 4, 1904 *Area:* 1.35 sq km
Population in 2006: 145
Provincial Electoral District(s): Cannington
Federal Electoral District(s): Souris-Moose Mountain
Next Election: Oct. 2012 (3 year terms)
Jerry Nashiem, Mayor
Bill Ringguth, Clerk

Frontier
P.O. Box 270
108 1st Ave. West
Frontier, SK S0N 0W0
Tel: 306-296-2250; *Fax:* 306-296-4586
village.frontier@sasktel.net
www.villageoffrontier.com
Municipal Type: Village
Incorporated: July 10, 1930 *Area:* 0.93 sq km
Population in 2006: 283
Provincial Electoral District(s): Cypress Hills
Federal Electoral District(s): Cypress Hills-Grasslands
Next Election: Oct. 2012 (3 year terms)
Connie Korsberg, Mayor
Barb Webber, Administrator

Gainsborough
P.O. Box 120
Gainsborough, SK S0C 0Z0
Tel: 306-685-2010; *Fax:* 306-685-2161
rm.1@sasktel.net
Municipal Type: Village
Incorporated: May 25, 1894 *Area:* 0.87 sq km
Population in 2006: 250
Provincial Electoral District(s): Cannington
Federal Electoral District(s): Souris-Moose Mountain
Next Election: Oct. 2012 (3 year terms)
Victor Huish, Mayor
Robert Trott, Administrator

Gerald
P.O. Box 155
Gerald, SK S0A 1B0
Tel: 306-745-6786; *Fax:* 306-745-6590
vofger@sasktel.net
Municipal Type: Village
Incorporated: March 25, 1953 *Area:* 0.80 sq km
Population in 2006: 124
Provincial Electoral District(s): Melville-Saltcoats
Federal Electoral District(s): Yorkton-Melville
Next Election: Oct. 2012 (3 year terms)
Rudy Lonoway, Mayor
Lila R.A. Sippola, Administrator

Gladmar
P.O. Box 54
Gladmar, SK S0C 1A0
Tel: 306-969-4952;
rhoimyr@gmail.com
Municipal Type: Village
Incorporated: Feb. 15, 1968 *Area:* 0.55 sq km
Population in 2006: 53
Provincial Electoral District(s): Weyburn-Big Muddy
Federal Electoral District(s): Souris-Moose Mountain
Next Election: Oct. 2012 (3 year terms)
Dale Ehrhardt, Mayor
Randy Hoimyr, Clerk

Glaslyn
P.O. Box 279
172 Main St.
Glaslyn, SK S0M 0Y0
Tel: 306-342-2144; *Fax:* 306-342-2135
villageofglaslyn@sasktel.net
glaslyn.ca
Municipal Type: Village
Incorporated: April 16, 1929 *Area:* 1.97 sq km
Population in 2006: 369
Provincial Electoral District(s): Cut Knife-Turtleford
Federal Electoral District(s): Battlefords-Lloydminster
Next Election: Oct. 2012 (3 year terms)
Ken Morrison, Mayor
Jamey Kuhmayer, Clerk

Glen Ewen
P.O. Box 99
Glen Ewen, SK S0C 1C0
Tel: 306-925-2211; *Fax:* 306-925-2210
rm3@sasktel.net
www3.telus.net/public/ketchs
Municipal Type: Village
Incorporated: March 24, 1904 *Area:* 2.77 sq km
Population in 2006: 120
Provincial Electoral District(s): Cannington
Federal Electoral District(s): Souris-Moose Mountain
Next Election: Oct. 2012 (3 year terms)
Glen Lewis, Mayor
Myrna-Jean Babbings, Administrator

Glenavon
104 Main St.
Glenavon, SK S0G 1Y0
Tel: 306-429-2110;
rmchester125@sasktel.net
www.glenavonsk.ca
Municipal Type: Village
Incorporated: April 13, 1910 *Area:* 1.32 sq km
Population in 2006: 183
Provincial Electoral District(s): Moosomin
Federal Electoral District(s): Souris-Moose Mountain
Next Election: Oct. 2012 (3 year terms)
Herb Schmidt, Mayor
James Hoff, Administrator

Glenside
P.O. Box 99
Glenside, SK S0H 1T0
Tel: 306-867-8932;
villageofglenside@xplornet.com
Municipal Type: Village
Incorporated: March 30, 1911 *Area:* 0.77 sq km
Population in 2006: 86
Provincial Electoral District(s): Rosetown-Elrose
Federal Electoral District(s): Blackstrap
Next Election: Oct. 2012 (3 year terms)
Rod Simonson, Mayor
Evelyn Swan, Administrator

Golden Prairie
P.O. Box 9
Golden Prairie, SK S0N 0Y0
Tel: 306-662-2883; *Fax:* 306-662-3954
rm141@sasktel.net
Municipal Type: Village
Incorporated: April 15, 1942 *Area:* 0.41 sq km
Population in 2006: 35
Provincial Electoral District(s): Cypress Hills
Federal Electoral District(s): Cypress Hills-Grasslands
Next Election: Oct. 2012 (3 year terms)
Daryl Martin, Mayor
Quinton Jacksteit, Administrator

Goodeve
P.O. Box 160
Goodeve, SK S0A 1C0
Tel: 306-795-2272; *Fax:* 306-795-3330
www.spreda.sk.ca/community_Goodeve.htm
Municipal Type: Village
Incorporated: Aug. 18, 1910 *Area:* 2.62 sq km
Population in 2006: 50
Provincial Electoral District(s): Last Mountain-Touchwood
Federal Electoral District(s): Yorkton-Melville
Next Election: Oct. 2012 (3 year terms)
Craig Sawchuk, Mayor
Diana Lee, Clerk

Goodsoil
P.O. Box 176
Goodsoil, SK S0M 1A0
Tel: 306-238-2094; *Fax:* 306-238-2098
villageofgoodsoil@sasktel.net
www.goodsoil.sasktelwebsite.net
Municipal Type: Village
Incorporated: Jan. 1, 1960 *Area:* 1.76 sq km
Population in 2006: 253
Provincial Electoral District(s): Meadow Lake
Federal Electoral District(s): Desnethé-Missinippi-Churchill River
Next Election: Oct. 2012 (3 year terms)
John Purves, Mayor
Linda Brophy, Administrator

Goodwater
P.O. Box 280
Weyburn, SK S4H 2K1
Tel: 306-456-2566; *Fax:* 306-456-2440
rm37@sasktel.net
Municipal Type: Village
Incorporated: May 8, 1911 *Area:* 0.59 sq km
Population in 2006: 25
Provincial Electoral District(s): Estevan
Federal Electoral District(s): Souris-Moose Mountain
Next Election: Oct. 2012 (3 year terms)
Greg Collins, Mayor
Kevin Melle, Administrator

Govan
P.O. Box 160
Govan, SK S0G 1Z0
Tel: 306-484-2011;
govan@parkland.lib.sk.ca
www.govansk.com
Municipal Type: Town
Incorporated: Aug. 21, 1907 *Area:* 1.35 sq km
Population in 2006: 232
Provincial Electoral District(s): Arm River-Watrous
Federal Electoral District(s): Regina-Lumsden-Lake Centre
Next Election: Oct. 2012 (3 year terms)
Note: Proclaimed as a town on Nov. 1, 1911.
Wesley Pearce, Mayor
Kelly Holbrook, Administrator

Grand Coulee
P.O. Box 72
GBS 200, RR#2
Regina, SK S4P 2Z2
Tel: 306-352-8694; *Fax:* 306-352-6659
grandcoulee.cap@sasktel.net
www.grandcoulee.ca
Municipal Type: Village
Incorporated: April 10, 1908 *Area:* 0.30 sq km
Population in 2006: 435
Provincial Electoral District(s): Regina Qu'Appelle Valley
Federal Electoral District(s): Regina-Lumsden-Lake Centre
Next Election: Oct. 2012 (3 year terms)
Irvin Brunas, Mayor
Tobi Duck, Administrator

Gravelbourg
P.O. Box 359
Gravelbourg, SK S0H 1X0
Tel: 306-648-3301; *Fax:* 306-648-3400
gravelbourg.adm@sasktel.net; info@gravelbourg.ca
www.gravelbourg.ca
Municipal Type: Town
Incorporated: Dec. 30, 1912 *Area:* 3.23 sq km
Population in 2006: 1,089
Provincial Electoral District(s): Wood River
Federal Electoral District(s): Cypress Hills-Grasslands
Next Election: Oct. 2012 (3 year terms)
Note: Proclaimed as a town on Nov. 1, 1916.
Réal Forest, Mayor
Gord Murray, Administrator

Grayson
P.O. Box 9
Railway Ave.
Grayson, SK S0A 1E0
Tel: 306-794-2011; *Fax:* 306-794-2261
villageofgrayson@sasktel.net
www.spreda.sk.ca/community_Grayson.htm
Municipal Type: Village
Incorporated: April 19, 1906 *Area:* 1.47 sq km
Population in 2006: 179
Provincial Electoral District(s): Melville-Saltcoats
Federal Electoral District(s): Yorkton-Melville
Next Election: Oct. 2012 (3 year terms)
Neil Ottenbreit, Mayor
Lawrence J. Kreiser, Administrator

Green Lake
P.O. Box 128
110 North St.
Green Lake, SK S0M 1B0
Tel: 306-832-2131; *Fax:* 306-832-2124
green.lake@sasktel.net
www.nvgreenlake.ca
Municipal Type: Northern Village
Incorporated: Oct. 1, 1983 *Area:* 121.92 sq km
Population in 2006: 361
Provincial Electoral District(s): Athabasca
Federal Electoral District(s): Desnethé-Missinippi-Churchill River
Next Election: Oct. 2012 (3 year terms)
Fred McCallum, Mayor
Tina Rasmussen, Administrator

Grenfell
P.O. Box 1120
Grenfell, SK S0G 2B0
Tel: 306-697-2815; *Fax:* 306-697-2484
townofgrenfell@sasktel.net
www.grenfell.ca
Municipal Type: Town
Incorporated: April 12, 1894 *Area:* 3.17 sq km
Population in 2006: 947
Provincial Electoral District(s): Moosomin
Federal Electoral District(s): Souris-Moose Mountain
Next Election: Oct. 2012 (3 year terms)
Note: Proclaimed as a town on Nov. 1, 1911.
Marc Saleski, Mayor
Suzanne Hawkshaw, Administrator

Gull Lake
P.O. Box 150
Gull Lake, SK S0N 1A0
Tel: 306-672-3361; *Fax:* 306-672-3777
gulllaketown@sasktel.net
www.gulllakesk.ca
Municipal Type: Town
Incorporated: Jan. 12, 1909 *Area:* 2.5 sq km
Population in 2006: 965
Provincial Electoral District(s): Cypress Hills
Federal Electoral District(s): Cypress Hills-Grasslands
Next Election: Oct. 2012 (3 year terms)
Note: Proclaimed as a town on Nov. 1, 1911.
Blake Campbell, Mayor
Dawnette Peterson, Administrator

Hafford
P.O. Box 220
Hafford, SK S0J 1A0
Tel: 306-549-2331; *Fax:* 306-549-2338
town.administrator@hafford.ca; hafto@littleloon.ca
www.hafford.ca
Municipal Type: Town
Incorporated: Dec. 16, 1913 *Area:* 0.80 sq km
Population in 2006: 360
Provincial Electoral District(s): Rosthern-Shellbrook
Federal Electoral District(s): Saskatoon-Wanuskewin
Next Election: Oct. 2012 (3 year terms)
Note: Proclaimed as a town on Jan. 1, 1981.
Peter Kingsmill, Mayor
Valerie Fendelet, Administrator

Hague
P.O. Box 180
Hague, SK S0K 1X0
Tel: 306-225-2155; *Fax:* 306-225-4410
town.hague@sasktel.net
www.townofhague.com
Municipal Type: Town
Incorporated: Aug. 25, 1903 *Area:* 1.03 sq km
Population in 2006: 707
Provincial Electoral District(s): Martensville
Federal Electoral District(s): Saskatoon-Wanuskewin
Next Election: Oct. 2012 (3 year terms)
Note: Proclaimed as a town on Nov. 1, 1991.
Patricia Wagner, Mayor
Deanna Braun, Administrator

Halbrite
P.O. Box 10
Halbrite, SK S0C 1H0
Tel: 306-458-2252; *Fax:* 306-458-2657
Municipal Type: Village
Incorporated: Feb. 26, 1904 *Area:* 1.20 sq km
Population in 2006: 98
Provincial Electoral District(s): Estevan
Federal Electoral District(s): Souris-Moose Mountain
Next Election: Oct. 2012 (3 year terms)
Dwayne Carlson, Mayor
Joy M. Guider, Clerk

Hanley
P.O. Box 270
Hanley, SK S0G 2E0
Tel: 306-544-2223; *Fax:* 306-544-2261
townoffice@townofhanley.ca
www.townofhanley.ca
Municipal Type: Town
Incorporated: April 27, 1905 *Area:* 2.65 sq km
Population in 2006: 464
Provincial Electoral District(s): Arm River-Watrous
Federal Electoral District(s): Blackstrap
Next Election: Oct. 2012 (3 year terms)
Note: Proclaimed as a town on Dec. 1, 1906.
Marvin Gerbrandt, Mayor
Darice Carlson, Administrator

Harris
P.O. Box 124
Harris, SK S0L 1K0
Tel: 306-656-2122; *Fax:* 306-656-2123
villageofharris@sasktel.net
Municipal Type: Village
Incorporated: Aug. 10, 1909 *Area:* 0.72 sq km
Population in 2006: 187
Provincial Electoral District(s): Rosetown-Elrose
Federal Electoral District(s): Saskatoon-Rosetown-Biggar
Next Election: Oct. 2012 (3 year terms)
Ron Genest, Mayor
Rhonda Leonard, Clerk

Hawarden
P.O. Box 7
Hawarden, SK S0H 1Y0
Tel: 306-855-2020; *Fax:* 306-855-2020
villageofhawarden@yourlink.ca
Municipal Type: Village
Incorporated: July 16, 1909 *Area:* 1.24 sq km
Population in 2006: 75
Provincial Electoral District(s): Arm River-Watrous
Federal Electoral District(s): Blackstrap
Next Election: Oct. 2012 (3 year terms)
Keith Carlson, Mayor
Judy Phillips, Clerk

Hazenmore
P.O. Box 36
Hazenmore, SK S0N 1C0
Tel: 306-264-3218; *Fax:* 306-264-3218
villageofkincaid@hotmail.com
Municipal Type: Village
Incorporated: Aug. 20, 1913 *Area:* 0.80 sq km
Population in 2006: 57
Provincial Electoral District(s): Wood River
Federal Electoral District(s): Cypress Hills-Grasslands
Next Election: Oct. 2012 (3 year terms)
Gary Loverin, Mayor
Barbara Hunter, Administrator

Hazlet
P.O. Box 150
Hazlet, SK S0N 1E0
Tel: 306-678-2131; *Fax:* 306-678-2132
hazlet@sasktel.net
hazletsk.com
Municipal Type: Village
Incorporated: Jan. 1, 1963 *Area:* 0.55 sq km
Population in 2006: 85
Provincial Electoral District(s): Cypress Hills
Federal Electoral District(s): Cypress Hills-Grasslands
Next Election: Oct. 2012 (3 year terms)
Terry Bailey, Mayor
Terry Erdelyan, Administrator

Hepburn
P.O. Box 217
311 Main St.
Hepburn, SK S0K 1Z0
Tel: 306-947-2170; *Fax:* 306-947-4202
hepburnvillage@sasktel.net
Municipal Type: Village
Incorporated: July 5, 1919 *Area:* 1.02 sq km
Population in 2006: 530
Provincial Electoral District(s): Martensville
Federal Electoral District(s): Saskatoon-Wanuskewin
Next Election: Oct. 2012 (3 year terms)
Barbara Adams-Eichendorf, Mayor
Andrew Spriggs, Administrator

Herbert
P.O. Box 370
218 Dennis St.
Herbert, SK S0H 2A0
Tel: 306-784-2400; *Fax:* 306-784-2402
t.o.herbert@sasktel.net
Municipal Type: Town
Incorporated: June 11, 1907 *Area:* 3.78 sq km
Population in 2006: 742
Provincial Electoral District(s): Thunder Creek
Federal Electoral District(s): Cypress Hills-Grasslands
Next Election: Oct. 2012 (3 year terms)
Note: Proclaimed as a town on Nov. 1, 1912.
Doreen Schroeder, Mayor
Reagan Funk, Administrator

Heward
P.O. Box 10
Heward, SK S0G 2G0
Tel: 306-457-2707; *Fax:* 306-457-3149
rmtec@sasktel.net
Municipal Type: Village
Incorporated: Nov. 21, 1904 *Area:* 0.99 sq km
Population in 2006: 20
Provincial Electoral District(s): Cannington
Federal Electoral District(s): Souris-Moose Mountain
Next Election: Oct. 2012 (3 year terms)
Murray Sabados, Mayor
Zandra Slater, Clerk

Hodgeville
P.O. Box 307
Hodgeville, SK S0H 2B0
Tel: 306-677-2223; *Fax:* 306-677-2466
Municipal Type: Village
Incorporated: June 22, 1921 *Area:* 1.35 sq km
Population in 2006: 142
Provincial Electoral District(s): Wood River
Federal Electoral District(s): Cypress Hills-Grasslands
Next Election: Oct. 2012 (3 year terms)
Clifford Culbert, Mayor
Michelle Mackow, Clerk

Holdfast
P.O. Box 160
Roberts St.
Holdfast, SK S0G 2H0
Tel: 306-488-2000; *Fax:* 306-488-4609
rm.sarnia@sasktel.net
Municipal Type: Village
Incorporated: Oct. 5, 1911 *Area:* 1.29 sq km
Population in 2006: 173
Provincial Electoral District(s): Thunder Creek
Federal Electoral District(s): Regina-Lumsden-Lake Centre
Next Election: Oct. 2012 (3 year terms)
Todd Thauberger, Mayor
Patti Vance, Administrator

Hubbard
P.O. Box 190
Ituna, SK S0A 1N0
Tel: 306-795-2202; *Fax:* 306-795-2202
rmofituna@sasktel.net
Municipal Type: Village
Incorporated: June 11, 1910 *Area:* 1.25 sq km
Population in 2006: 43
Provincial Electoral District(s): Last Mountain-Touchwood
Federal Electoral District(s): Regina-Qu'Appelle
Next Election: Oct. 2012 (3 year terms)
Ron Rokosh, Mayor
Diane M. Olech, Administrator

Hudson Bay
P.O. Box 730
304 Main St.
Hudson Bay, SK S0E 0Y0
Tel: 306-865-2261; *Fax:* 306-865-2800
hudson.bay@sasktel.net
www.townofhudsonbay.com
Municipal Type: Town
Incorporated: Sept. 25, 1907 *Area:* 17.35 sq km
Population in 2006: 1,646
Provincial Electoral District(s): Carrot River Valley
Federal Electoral District(s): Yorkton-Melville
Next Election: Oct. 2012 (3 year terms)
Note: Proclaimed as a town on Nov. 30, 1946.
Elvina Rumak, Mayor
hbmayor@sasktel.net
Richard Dolezsar, Administrator
rdolezsar@sasktel.net

Humboldt
P.O. Box 640
715 Main St.
Humboldt, SK S0K 2A0
Tel: 306-682-2525; *Fax:* 306-682-3144
www.cityofhumboldt.ca
Municipal Type: Town
Incorporated: June 30, 1905 *Area:* 11.72 sq km
Population in 2006: 4,998
Provincial Electoral District(s): Humboldt
Federal Electoral District(s): Saskatoon-Humboldt
Next Election: Oct. 2012 (3 year terms)
Note: Incorporated as a city on Nov. 7, 2000.
Malcolm Eaton, Mayor
mayor.cityofhumboldt@sasktel.net
Sandra Pauli, Director
spauli.cityofhumboldt@sasktel.net

Hyas
P.O. Box 40
Hyas, SK S0A 1K0
Tel: 306-594-2817; *Fax:* 306-594-2830
hyas@sasktel.net
Municipal Type: Village
Incorporated: May 23, 1919 *Area:* 1.17 sq km
Population in 2006: 111
Provincial Electoral District(s): Canora-Pelly
Federal Electoral District(s): Yorkton-Melville
Next Election: Oct. 2012 (3 year terms)
Lawrence Ostafichuk, Mayor
Denise Sorrell, Administrator

Ile à la Crosse
P.O. Box 280
Lajeunesse Ave.
Ile-a-la-Crosse, SK S0M 1C0
Tel: 306-833-2122; *Fax:* 306-833-2132
village.of.ilealacrosse@sasktel.net
www.sakitawak.ca
Municipal Type: Northern Village
Incorporated: Oct. 1, 1983 *Area:* 23.84 sq km
Population in 2006: 1,341
Provincial Electoral District(s): Athabasca
Federal Electoral District(s): Desnethé-Missinippi-Churchill River
Next Election: Oct. 2012 (3 year terms)
Duane Favel, Mayor
Dianne McCallum, Administrator

Imperial
P.O. Box 90
Imperial, SK S0G 2J0
Tel: 306-963-2220; *Fax:* 306-963-2445
town.imperial@sasktel.net
www.imperial.ca
Municipal Type: Town
Incorporated: July 4, 1911 *Area:* 1.23 sq km
Population in 2006: 321
Provincial Electoral District(s): Arm River-Watrous
Federal Electoral District(s): Regina-Lumsden-Lake Centre
Next Election: Oct. 2012 (3 year terms)
Note: Proclaimed as a town on April 1, 1962.
Harvey McLane, Mayor
Sheila Newlove, Administrator

Indian Head
P.O. Box 460
Indian Head, SK S0G 2K0
Tel: 306-695-3344;
office@townofindianhead.com
www.townofindianhead.com
Municipal Type: Town
Incorporated: April 19, 1902 *Area:* 3.17 sq km
Population in 2006: 1,634
Provincial Electoral District(s): Indian Head-Milestone
Federal Electoral District(s): Regina-Qu'Appelle
Next Election: Oct. 2012 (3 year terms)
Allan Hubbs, Mayor
mayor@townofindianhead.com
Cam Thauberger, Administrator

Invermay
P.O. Box 234
Invermay, SK S0A 1M0
Tel: 306-593-2242; *Fax:* 306-593-2242
villageofinvermay@sasktel.net
Municipal Type: Village
Incorporated: Sept. 1, 1908 *Area:* 1.22 sq km
Population in 2006: 262
Provincial Electoral District(s): Kelvington-Wadena
Federal Electoral District(s): Yorkton-Melville
Next Election: Oct. 2012 (3 year terms)
Kim C. Rioch, Mayor
Veronica L. Wolski, Clerk

Ituna
P.O. Box 580
Ituna, SK S0A 1N0
Tel: 306-795-2272; *Fax:* 306-795-3330
townofituna@sasktel.net
www.ituna.ca
Municipal Type: Town
Incorporated: May 30, 1910 *Area:* 1.56 sq km
Population in 2006: 622
Provincial Electoral District(s): Last Mountain-Touchwood
Federal Electoral District(s): Regina-Qu'Appelle
Next Election: Oct. 2012 (3 year terms)
Note: Proclaimed as a town on Oct. 1, 1961.
Glenn Leontowich, Mayor
Angela Romanson, Administrator

Jans Bay
Maurice Ave., General Delivery
Canoe Narrows, SK S0M 0K0
Tel: 306-829-4320; *Fax:* 306-829-4424
jansbay@sasktel.net
Municipal Type: Northern Village
Incorporated: Oct. 1, 1983 *Area:* 5.94 sq km
Population in 2006: 181
Provincial Electoral District(s): Athabasca
Federal Electoral District(s): Desnethé-Missinippi-Churchill River
Next Election: Oct. 2012 (3 year terms)
Tony Maurice, Mayor
Anne Marie Couillonneur, Clerk

Jansen
P.O. Box 116
Jansen, SK S0K 2B0
Tel: 306-364-2013; *Fax:* 306-364-2088
jansen@jansen.ca
www.jansen.ca
Municipal Type: Village
Incorporated: Oct. 19, 1908 *Area:* 0.85 sq km
Population in 2006: 140
Provincial Electoral District(s): Arm River-Watrous
Federal Electoral District(s): Blackstrap
Next Election: Oct. 2012 (3 year terms)
Albert Cardinal, Mayor
Dennis McBurney, Administrator

Kamsack
P.O. Box 729
161 Queen Elizabeth Blvd. West
Kamsack, SK S0A 1S0
Tel: 306-542-2155; *Fax:* 306-542-2975
www.kamsack.ca
Municipal Type: Town
Incorporated: March 14, 1905 *Area:* 5.85 sq km
Population in 2006: 1,713
Provincial Electoral District(s): Canora-Pelly
Federal Electoral District(s): Yorkton-Melville
Next Election: Oct. 2012 (3 year terms)
Note: Proclaimed as a town on Nov. 1, 1911.
Betty Dix, Mayor
Joanne Binsfeld, Acting Administrator

Keeler
P.O. Box 33
Keeler, SK S0H 2E0
Tel: 306-759-2302
Municipal Type: Village
Incorporated: July 5, 1910 *Area:* 1.02 sq km
Population in 2006: 5
Provincial Electoral District(s): Thunder Creek
Federal Electoral District(s): Regina-Lumsden-Lake Centre
Next Election: Oct. 2012 (3 year terms)
Duncan Keeler, Mayor
Jackie Leggott, Clerk

Kelliher
P.O. Box 190
406 - 2nd Ave.
Kelliher, SK S0A 1V0
Tel: 306-675-2226; *Fax:* 306-675-2240
villageofkelliher@sasktel.net
www.kelliher.ca
Municipal Type: Village
Incorporated: April 27, 1909 *Area:* 2.81 sq km
Population in 2006: 257
Provincial Electoral District(s): Last Mountain-Touchwood
Federal Electoral District(s): Regina-Qu'Appelle
Next Election: Oct. 2012 (3 year terms)
Darcy King, Mayor
Gerry Burym, Administrator

Kelvington
P.O. Box 10
201 Main St.
Kelvington, SK S0A 1W0
Tel: 306-327-4482; *Fax:* 306-327-4946
tkelv@sasktel.net
www.townofkelvington.com
Municipal Type: Town
Incorporated: Nov. 18, 1921 *Area:* 3.89 sq km
Population in 2006: 866
Provincial Electoral District(s): Kelvington-Wadena
Federal Electoral District(s): Yorkton-Melville
Next Election: Oct. 2012 (3 year terms)
Note: Proclaimed as a town on May 1, 1944.
Ed Tetelowski, Mayor
Loretta Nagy, Administrator

Kenaston
P.O. Box 129
Kenaston, SK S0G 2N0
Tel: 306-252-2211; *Fax:* 306-252-2248
kenaston@sasktel.net
www.kenaston.ca
Municipal Type: Village
Incorporated: July 18, 1910 *Area:* 1.17 sq km
Population in 2006: 259
Provincial Electoral District(s): Arm River-Watrous
Federal Electoral District(s): Blackstrap
Next Election: Oct. 2012 (3 year terms)
Dan O'Handley, Mayor
Carmen Fowler, Administrator

Kendal
P.O. Box 97
115 Main St.
Kendal, SK S0G 2P0
Tel: 306-424-2722; *Fax:* 306-424-2722
villageofkendal@sasktel.net
kendalsk.com
Municipal Type: Village
Incorporated: Feb. 17, 1919 *Area:* 0.65 sq km
Population in 2006: 59
Provincial Electoral District(s): Indian Head-Milestone
Federal Electoral District(s): Wascana
Next Election: Oct. 2012 (3 year terms)
Pammylyn Knickle, Mayor
Colleen Hoffman, Administrator

Kennedy
P.O. Box 93
Kennedy, SK S0G 2R0
Tel: 306-538-2194; *Fax:* 306-538-4522
village.kennedy@sasktel.net
www.angelfire.com/ca/kennedysk
Municipal Type: Village
Incorporated: Nov. 5, 1907 *Area:* 1.60 sq km
Population in 2006: 187
Provincial Electoral District(s): Moosomin

Federal Electoral District(s): Souris-Moose Mountain
Next Election: Oct. 2012 (3 year terms)
Clarence Bender, Mayor
Jane Johnson, Administrator

Kenosee Lake
P.O. Box 30
Kenosee Lake, SK S0C 2S0
Tel: 306-577-2139; *Fax:* 306-577-2261
village.kenosee@sasktel.net
Municipal Type: Village
Incorporated: Oct. 1, 1987 *Area:* 0.35 sq km
Population in 2006: 194
Provincial Electoral District(s): Cannington
Federal Electoral District(s): Souris-Moose Mountain
Next Election: Oct. 2012 (3 year terms)
Lyle Basken, Mayor
Peggy Fleck, Administrator

Kerrobert
P.O. Box 558
433 Manitoba Ave.
Kerrobert, SK S0L 1R0
Tel: 306-834-2361; *Fax:* 306-834-2633
kerrobert@sasktel.net
www.kerrobertsk.com
Municipal Type: Town
Incorporated: Nov. 9, 1910 *Area:* 7.49 sq km
Population in 2006: 1,001
Provincial Electoral District(s): Kindersley
Federal Electoral District(s): Battlefords-Lloydminster
Next Election: Oct. 2012 (3 year terms)
Note: Proclaimed as a town on Nov. 1, 1911.
Erhard Poggemiller, Mayor
Michele Schmidt, Administrator
kerrobert.admin@sasktel.net

Killaly
P.O. Box 69
Railway Ave.
Killaly, SK S0A 1X0
Tel: 306-748-2540;
rm185@sasktel.net
www.spreda.sk.ca/community_Killaly.htm
Municipal Type: Village
Incorporated: April 28, 1909 *Area:* 2.59 sq km
Population in 2006: 77
Provincial Electoral District(s): Melville-Saltcoats
Federal Electoral District(s): Yorkton-Melville
Next Election: Oct. 2012 (3 year terms)
Angie Rogalski, Mayor
Linda Hanowski, Administrator

Kincaid
P.O. Box 177
Kincaid, SK S0H 2J0
Tel: 306-264-3910; *Fax:* 306-264-3903
villageofkincaid@hotmail.com
www.villageofkincaid.ca
Municipal Type: Village
Incorporated: July 19, 1913 *Area:* 0.82 sq km
Population in 2006: 135
Provincial Electoral District(s): Wood River
Federal Electoral District(s): Cypress Hills-Grasslands
Next Election: Oct. 2012 (3 year terms)
Cynthia Gross, Mayor
Barbara Hunter, Administrator

Kindersley
P.O. Box 1269
106 - 5th Ave. East
Kindersley, SK S0L 1S0
Tel: 306-463-2675; *Fax:* 306-463-4577
office@kindersley.ca
www.kindersley.ca
Municipal Type: Town
Incorporated: Jan. 10, 1910 *Area:* 12.55 sq km
Population in 2006: 4,412
Provincial Electoral District(s): Kindersley
Federal Electoral District(s): Battlefords-Lloydminster
Next Election: Oct. 2012 (3 year terms)
Note: Proclaimed as a town on Nov. 1, 1910.
Wayne Foster, Mayor
waynefoster@kindersley.ca
Monica Shields, Chief Administrative Officer/Council Secretary
306-463-2675

Kinistino
P.O. Box 10
Kinistino, SK S0J 1H0
Tel: 306-864-2461; *Fax:* 306-864-2880
townofkinistino@sasktel.net
www.townofkinistino.ca
Municipal Type: Town
Incorporated: July 30, 1905 *Area:* 0.89 sq km
Population in 2006: 643
Provincial Electoral District(s): Batoche
Federal Electoral District(s): Prince Albert
Next Election: Oct. 2012 (3 year terms)
Note: Proclaimed as a town on Feb. 7, 1952.
Leonard Margolis, Mayor
Rhonda Bacon, Administrator

Kinley
P.O. Box 51
Kinley, SK S0K 2E0
Tel: 306-237-4601; *Fax:* 306-237-4605
villageofkinley@sasktel.net
Municipal Type: Village
Incorporated: Jan. 7, 1909 *Area:* 1.18 sq km
Population in 2006: 35
Provincial Electoral District(s): Biggar
Federal Electoral District(s): Saskatoon-Rosetown-Biggar
Next Election: Oct. 2012 (3 year terms)
Cindy Latta, Mayor
Lynne Tolley, Administrator

Kipling
P.O. Box 299
301 - 6th Ave.
Kipling, SK S0G 2S0
Tel: 306-736-2515; *Fax:* 306-736-8448
kiptown@sasktel.net; kiplingadmin@sasktel.net
www.townofkipling.ca
Municipal Type: Town
Incorporated: Sept. 13, 1909 *Area:* 2.15 sq km
Population in 2006: 973
Provincial Electoral District(s): Moosomin
Federal Electoral District(s): Souris-Moose Mountain
Next Election: Oct. 2012 (3 year terms)
Note: Proclaimed as a town on Jan. 1, 1954.
Kelly Fish, Mayor
glokel@sasktel.net
Gail Dakue, Administrator

Kisbey
P.O. Box 249
Kisbey, SK S0C 1L0
Tel: 306-462-2212; *Fax:* 306-462-2279
vill.kisbey@sasktel.net
Municipal Type: Village
Incorporated: May 8, 1907 *Area:* 2.77 sq km
Population in 2006: 185
Provincial Electoral District(s): Cannington
Federal Electoral District(s): Souris-Moose Mountain
Next Election: Oct. 2012 (3 year terms)
John Houston, Mayor
Judy Graham, Administrator

Krydor
P.O. Box 160
Hafford, SK S0J 1A0
Tel: 306-549-2333; *Fax:* 306-549-2435
rm435@littleloon.ca
Municipal Type: Village
Incorporated: Aug. 25, 1914 *Area:* 0.82 sq km
Population in 2006: 25
Provincial Electoral District(s): Rosthern-Shellbrook
Federal Electoral District(s): Saskatoon-Wanuskewin
Next Election: Oct. 2012 (3 year terms)
Arnold Bahniuk, Mayor
Alan J. Tanchak, Clerk

Kyle
P.O. Box 520
Kyle, SK S0L 1T0
Tel: 306-375-2525; *Fax:* 306-375-2534
townofkyle@sasktel.net
www.kylesaskatchewan.ca
Municipal Type: Town
Incorporated: April 13, 1926 *Area:* 1.01 sq km
Population in 2006: 423
Provincial Electoral District(s): Rosetown-Elrose
Federal Electoral District(s): Cypress Hills-Grasslands
Next Election: Oct. 2012 (3 year terms)
Note: Proclaimed as a town on Jan. 1, 1959.
Ansgar Tynning, Mayor
Audrey Blohm, Administrator

La Loche
P.O. Box 310
La Loche Ave.
La Loche, SK S0M 1G0
Tel: 306-822-2032; *Fax:* 306-822-2078
nor.vill.laloche@sasktel.net
Municipal Type: Northern Village
Incorporated: Oct. 1, 1983 *Area:* 15.59 sq km
Population in 2006: 2,348
Provincial Electoral District(s): Athabasca
Federal Electoral District(s): Desnethé-Missinippi-Churchill River
Next Election: Oct. 2012 (3 year terms)
Georgina Jolibois, Mayor
Doug Gailey, Clerk

La Ronge
P.O. Box 5680
1212 Hildebrandt Dr.
La Ronge, SK S0J 1L0
Tel: 306-425-2066; *Fax:* 306-425-3883
www.townoflaronge.ca; www.laronge.ca
Municipal Type: Northern Town
Incorporated: May 3, 1905 *Area:* 11.86 sq km
Population in 2006: 2,725
Provincial Electoral District(s): Cumberland
Federal Electoral District(s): Desnethé-Missinippi-Churchill River
Next Election: Oct. 2012 (3 year terms)
Note: Proclaimed as a northern town on Oct. 1, 1983.
Thomas Sierzycki, Mayor
laronge.mayor@sasktel.net
Davidie Zarazun, Administrator
laronge.administrator@sasktel.net

Lafleche
P.O. Box 250
35 - 2nd Ave. East
Lafleche, SK S0H 2K0
Tel: 306-472-5292; *Fax:* 306-472-3706
town.of.lafleche@sasktel.net
www.town.lafleche.sk.ca
Municipal Type: Town
Incorporated: Sept. 3, 1913 *Area:* 1.51 sq km
Population in 2006: 370
Provincial Electoral District(s): Wood River
Federal Electoral District(s): Cypress Hills-Grasslands
Next Election: Oct. 2012 (3 year terms)
Note: Proclaimed as a town on June 1, 1953.
Raymond Clermont, Mayor
Lorraine McIvor, Administrator

Laird
P.O. Box 189
220A Main St.
Laird, SK S0K 2H0
Tel: 306-223-4343; *Fax:* 306-223-4349
lairdvillage@sasktel.net
www.lairdvillage.ca
Municipal Type: Village
Incorporated: May 4, 1911 *Area:* 1.29 sq km
Population in 2006: 207
Provincial Electoral District(s): Rosthern-Shellbrook
Federal Electoral District(s): Saskatoon-Wanuskewin
Next Election: Oct. 2012 (3 year terms)
Doug Crowe, Mayor
Michelle Zurakowski, Administrator

Lake Alma
P.O. Box 163
Lake Alma, SK S0C 1M0
Tel: 306-447-2002
Municipal Type: Village
Incorporated: Jan. 1, 1949 *Area:* 0.47 sq km
Population in 2006: 30
Provincial Electoral District(s): Estevan
Federal Electoral District(s): Souris-Moose Mountain
Next Election: Oct. 2012 (3 year terms)
Wilfred Jacobson, Mayor
Kyla Robinson, Clerk

Lake Lenore
P.O. Box 148
Lake Lenore, SK S0K 2J0
Tel: 306-368-2344; *Fax:* 306-368-2226
lakelenorevil@sasktel.net
www.newsaskcfdc.ca/lakelenore.htm
Municipal Type: Village
Incorporated: April 28, 1921 *Area:* 0.97 sq km
Population in 2006: 306
Provincial Electoral District(s): Batoche
Federal Electoral District(s): Saskatoon-Humboldt
Next Election: Oct. 2012 (3 year terms)
Kerry Haeusler, Mayor

Barb Politeski, Clerk

Lampman
P.O. Box 70
215 Main St.
Lampman, SK S0C 1N0
Tel: 306-487-2462; *Fax:* 306-487-2285
browning.lampman@sasktel.net
www.lampman.sasktelwebsite.net
Municipal Type: Town
Incorporated: Aug. 16, 1910 *Area:* 2.23 sq km
Population in 2006: 634
Provincial Electoral District(s): Cannington
Federal Electoral District(s): Souris-Moose Mountain
Next Election: Oct. 2012 (3 year terms)
Note: Proclaimed as a town on June 1, 1963.
Scott Greening, Mayor
Greg Wallin, Administrator

Lancer
P.O. Box 3
Lancer, SK S0N 1G0
Tel: 306-689-2925; *Fax:* 306-689-2890
Municipal Type: Village
Incorporated: Sept. 11, 1913 *Area:* 1.33 sq km
Population in 2006: 65
Provincial Electoral District(s): Cypress Hills
Federal Electoral District(s): Cypress Hills-Grasslands
Next Election: Oct. 2012 (3 year terms)
Ernest Wagner, Mayor
Karen Hartman, Clerk

Landis
P.O. Box 153
Landis, SK S0K 2K0
Tel: 306-658-2155; *Fax:* 306-658-2156
villageoflandis@sasktel.net
www.landissask.ca
Municipal Type: Village
Incorporated: May 17, 1909 *Area:* 0.80 sq km
Population in 2006: 119
Provincial Electoral District(s): Biggar
Federal Electoral District(s): Battlefords-Lloydminster
Next Election: Oct. 2012 (3 year terms)
Joe Sarrasin, Mayor
Sandra Beckett, Administrator

Lang
P.O. Box 97
223 Main St.
Lang, SK S0G 2W0
Tel: 306-464-2024; *Fax:* 306-464-2024
voflang@sasktel.net
www.langsk.com
Municipal Type: Village
Incorporated: July 27, 1906 *Area:* 0.64 sq km
Population in 2006: 172
Provincial Electoral District(s): Indian Head-Milestone
Federal Electoral District(s): Souris-Moose Mountain
Next Election: Oct. 2012 (3 year terms)
Al Broderick, Mayor
Ernest Audette, Administrator

Langenburg
P.O. Box 400
Langenburg, SK S0A 2A0
Tel: 306-743-2432; *Fax:* 306-743-2723
langenburgt@sasktel.net
www.town.langenburg.sk.ca
Municipal Type: Town
Incorporated: March 30, 1903 *Area:* 3.46 sq km
Population in 2006: 1,048
Provincial Electoral District(s): Melville-Saltcoats
Federal Electoral District(s): Yorkton-Melville
Next Election: Oct. 2012 (3 year terms)
Note: Proclaimed as a town on Sept. 15, 1959.
Dave Schappert, Mayor
Howard McCullough, Administrator

Langham
P.O. Box 289
230 Main St. East
Langham, SK S0K 2L0
Tel: 306-283-4842; *Fax:* 306-283-4772
admin@langham.ca
www.langham.ca
Municipal Type: Town
Incorporated: June 8, 1906 *Area:* 3.98 sq km
Population in 2006: 1,120
Provincial Electoral District(s): Biggar
Federal Electoral District(s): Saskatoon-Rosetown-Biggar; Saskatoon-Wanuskewin
Next Election: Oct. 2012 (3 year terms)
Note: Proclaimed as a town on Aug. 1, 1907.
Glen Thiessen, Mayor
Randy J. Sherstobitoff, Administrator

Lanigan
P.O. Box 280
Lanigan, SK S0K 2M0
Tel: 306-365-2809; *Fax:* 306-365-2960
town.lanigan@sasktel.net
www.town.lanigan.sk.ca
Municipal Type: Town
Incorporated: Aug. 21, 1907 *Area:* 8.34 sq km
Population in 2006: 1,233
Provincial Electoral District(s): Humboldt
Federal Electoral District(s): Blackstrap
Next Election: Oct. 2012 (3 year terms)
Note: Proclaimed as a town on April 15, 1908.
Bernie Bishop, Mayor
Jack R. Dvernichuk, Administrator

Lashburn
P.O. Box 328
Lashburn, SK S0M 1H0
Tel: 306-285-3533; *Fax:* 306-285-3358
townoflashburn@sasktel.net
www.lashburn.ca
Municipal Type: Town
Incorporated: Dec. 8, 1906 *Area:* 3.11 sq km
Population in 2006: 914
Provincial Electoral District(s): Cut Knife-Turtleford
Federal Electoral District(s): Battlefords-Lloydminster
Next Election: Oct. 2012 (3 year terms)
Note: Proclaimed as a town on March 1, 1979.
Steven Turnbull, Mayor
Vicki Seabrook, Administrator

Leader
P.O. Box 39
151 - 1st St. West
Leader, SK S0N 1H0
Tel: 306-628-3868; *Fax:* 306-628-4337
town.leader@sasktel.net
www.leader.ca
Other Information: Toll Free Phone: 1-800-424-8335
Municipal Type: Town
Incorporated: Sept. 13, 1913 *Area:* 1.70 sq km
Population in 2006: 881
Provincial Electoral District(s): Cypress Hills
Federal Electoral District(s): Cypress Hills-Grasslands
Next Election: Oct. 2012 (3 year terms)
Note: Proclaimed as a town on May 1, 1947.
Craig Tondevold, Mayor
Rochelle Francis, Administrator

Leask
P.O. Box 40
15 Main St.
Leask, SK S0J 1M0
Tel: 306-466-2229; *Fax:* 306-466-2239
village.leask@sasktel.net
www.leask.ca
Municipal Type: Village
Incorporated: Sept. 3, 1912 *Area:* 0.75 sq km
Population in 2006: 418
Provincial Electoral District(s): Rosthern-Shellbrook
Federal Electoral District(s): Saskatoon-Wanuskewin
Next Election: Oct. 2012 (3 year terms)
Maurice Stieb, Mayor
Brenda Lockhart, Administrator
admin.464@sasktel.net

Lebret
P.O. Box 40
Lebret, SK S0G 2Y0
Tel: 306-332-6545; *Fax:* 306-332-5338
villageoflebret@sasktel.net
Municipal Type: Village
Incorporated: Oct. 14, 1912 *Area:* 1.32 sq km
Population in 2006: 203
Provincial Electoral District(s): Last Mountain-Touchwood
Federal Electoral District(s): Regina-Qu'Appelle
Next Election: Oct. 2012 (3 year terms)
Carl Olson, Mayor
Gwen Lowe, Administrator

Lemberg
P.O. Box 399
Lemberg, SK S0A 2B0
Tel: 306-335-2244; *Fax:* 306-335-2911
townoffice.lemberg@sasktel.net
www.spreda.sk.ca/community_Lemberg.htm
Municipal Type: Town
Incorporated: July 12, 1904 *Area:* 2.67 sq km
Population in 2006: 255
Provincial Electoral District(s): Last Mountain-Touchwood
Federal Electoral District(s): Yorkton-Melville
Next Election: Oct. 2012 (3 year terms)
Note: Proclaimed as a town on Sept. 1, 1907.
Herbert MacDonald, Mayor
Joyce Hauck, Clerk

Leoville
P.O. Box 280
Leoville, SK S0J 1N0
Tel: 306-984-2140; *Fax:* 306-984-2337
leoville@sasktel.net
Municipal Type: Village
Incorporated: June 26, 1944 *Area:* 1.11 sq km
Population in 2006: 341
Provincial Electoral District(s): Meadow Lake
Federal Electoral District(s): Desnethé-Missinippi-Churchill River
Next Election: Oct. 2012 (3 year terms)
Ron Craswell, Mayor
Mona Chalifour, Clerk

Leross
P.O. Box 68
Leross, SK S0A 2C0
Tel: 306-675-4429; *Fax:* 306-675-2097
villageofleross@sasktel.net
Municipal Type: Village
Incorporated: Dec. 1, 1909 *Area:* 1.21 sq km
Population in 2006: 42
Provincial Electoral District(s): Last Mountain-Touchwood
Federal Electoral District(s): Regina-Qu'Appelle
Next Election: Oct. 2012 (3 year terms)
Francis Klyne, Mayor
Elaine Klyne, Clerk

Leroy
P.O. Box 40
Leroy, SK S0K 2P0
Tel: 306-286-3288; *Fax:* 306-286-3400
leroy@bogend.ca
www.leroy.ca
Municipal Type: Town
Incorporated: Dec. 5, 1922 *Area:* 1.06 sq km
Population in 2006: 412
Provincial Electoral District(s): Melfort
Federal Electoral District(s): Saskatoon-Humboldt
Next Election: Oct. 2012 (3 year terms)
Note: Proclaimed as a town on March 1, 1963.
Morris Hartman, Mayor
Ann-Marie Block, Administrator

Lestock
P.O. Box 209
320 Touchwood Hills Ave.
Lestock, SK S0A 2G0
Tel: 306-274-2277; *Fax:* 306-274-2277
lestockv@sasktel.net
Municipal Type: Village
Incorporated: April 17, 1912 *Area:* 0.87 sq km
Population in 2006: 138
Provincial Electoral District(s): Last Mountain-Touchwood
Federal Electoral District(s): Regina-Qu'Appelle
Next Election: Oct. 2012 (3 year terms)
Kelly Komodowski, Mayor
Frank Kasa, Administrator

Liberty
P.O. Box 59
Liberty, SK S0G 3A0
Tel: 306-963-2402; *Fax:* 306-963-2405
rm251@sasktel.net
Municipal Type: Village
Incorporated: Jan. 23, 1912 *Area:* 1.37 sq km
Population in 2006: 73
Provincial Electoral District(s): Arm River-Watrous
Federal Electoral District(s): Regina-Lumsden-Lake Centre
Next Election: Oct. 2012 (3 year terms)
Terry Tannahill, Mayor
Yvonne (Bonny) Goodsman, Administrator

Limerick
P.O. Box 129
Limerick, SK S0H 2P0
Tel: 306-263-2020; *Fax:* 306-263-2013
rm73@sasktel.net
Municipal Type: Village
Incorporated: July 10, 1913 *Area:* 0.79 sq km
Population in 2006: 130
Provincial Electoral District(s): Wood River

Federal Electoral District(s): Cypress Hills-Grasslands
Next Election: Oct. 2012 (3 year terms)
Robert Smith, Mayor
Tammy Franks, Administrator

Lintlaw
P.O. Box 10
Lintlaw, SK S0A 2H0
Tel: 306-325-2006; *Fax:* 306-325-2006
villageoflintlaw@sasktel.net
Municipal Type: Village
Incorporated: Dec. 14, 1921 *Area:* 1.23 sq km
Population in 2006: 145
Provincial Electoral District(s): Kelvington-Wadena
Federal Electoral District(s): Yorkton-Melville
Next Election: Oct. 2012 (3 year terms)
Leonard Johnson, Mayor
Kathleen Ambrose, Administrator

Lipton
P.O. Box 219
Lipton, SK S0G 3B0
Tel: 306-336-2505; *Fax:* 306-336-2505
lipton@sasktel.net
www.villageoflipton.com
Municipal Type: Village
Incorporated: May 15, 1905 *Area:* 0.75 sq km
Population in 2006: 342
Provincial Electoral District(s): Last Mountain-Touchwood
Federal Electoral District(s): Regina-Qu'Appelle
Next Election: Oct. 2012 (3 year terms)
Marvis Seel, Mayor
Marlene L. Bausmer, Administrator

Loon Lake
P.O. Box 220
Loon Lake, SK S0M 1L0
Tel: 306-837-2090; *Fax:* 306-837-4735
loonlake@sasktel.net
Municipal Type: Village
Incorporated: Jan. 1, 1950 *Area:* 0.66 sq km
Population in 2006: 306
Provincial Electoral District(s): Meadow Lake
Federal Electoral District(s): Churchill River/Rivière Churchill
Next Election: Oct. 2012 (3 year terms)
Larry Heon, Mayor
Meredith Chuiko, Administrator

Loreburn
P.O. Box 177
Loreburn, SK S0H 2S0
Tel: 306-644-2097; *Fax:* 306-644-4847
villageofloreburn@yourlink.ca
Municipal Type: Village
Incorporated: May 20, 1909 *Area:* 0.62 sq km
Population in 2006: 113
Provincial Electoral District(s): Arm River-Watrous
Federal Electoral District(s): Blackstrap
Next Election: Oct. 2012 (3 year terms)
Bruce Hagen, Mayor
Muriel Stronski, Clerk

Love
P.O. Box 94
Love, SK S0J 1P0
Tel: 306-276-2525;
villageoflove@sasktel.net
www.villageoflove.ca
Municipal Type: Village
Incorporated: June 2, 1945 *Area:* 0.46 sq km
Population in 2006: 55
Provincial Electoral District(s): Saskatchewan Rivers
Federal Electoral District(s): Desnethé-Missinippi-Churchill River
Next Election: Oct. 2012 (3 year terms)
Jackie Hazelwood, Mayor
Yvonne Moore, Administrator

Lucky Lake
P.O. Box 99
Lucky Lake, SK S0L 1Z0
Tel: 306-858-2234; *Fax:* 306-858-2234
rm225.vll@sasktel.net
Municipal Type: Village
Incorporated: Nov. 23, 1920 *Area:* 0.66 sq km
Population in 2006: 295
Provincial Electoral District(s): Rosetown-Elrose
Federal Electoral District(s): Cypress Hills-Grasslands
Next Election: Oct. 2012 (3 year terms)
Kristopher Netzel, Mayor
D.B. (Blair) Cleaveley, Administrator

Lumsden
P.O. Box 160
300 James Street North
Lumsden, SK S0G 3C0
Tel: 306-731-2404; *Fax:* 306-731-3572
town.lumsden@sasktel.net
www.lumsden.ca
Municipal Type: Town
Incorporated: Dec. 29, 1898 *Area:* 3.82 sq km
Population in 2006: 1,523
Provincial Electoral District(s): Thunder Creek
Federal Electoral District(s): Regina-Lumsden-Lake Centre
Next Election: Oct. 2012 (3 year terms)
Note: Proclaimed as a town on March 15, 1905.
Bryan Matheson, Mayor
Darcie Cooper, Administrator

Luseland
P.O. Box 130
Luseland, SK S0L 2A0
Tel: 306-372-4218; *Fax:* 306-347-4700
luseland@sasktel.net
www.townofluseland.com
Municipal Type: Town
Incorporated: Dec. 10, 1910 *Area:* 1.53 sq km
Population in 2006: 571
Provincial Electoral District(s): Kindersley
Federal Electoral District(s): Battlefords-Lloydminster
Next Election: Oct. 2012 (3 year terms)
Note: Proclaimed as a town on Jan. 1, 1954.
Len Schlosser, Mayor
Karyl Richardson, Administrator

Macklin
P.O. Box 69
Macklin, SK S0L 2C0
Tel: 306-753-2256; *Fax:* 306-753-3234
town.macklin@sasktel.net
www.macklin.ca
Municipal Type: Town
Incorporated: Nov. 8, 1909 *Area:* 2.85 sq km
Population in 2006: 1,290
Provincial Electoral District(s): Kindersley
Federal Electoral District(s): Battlefords-Lloydminster
Next Election: Oct. 2012 (3 year terms)
Note: Proclaimed as a town on Nov. 1, 1912.
Patrick Doetzel, Mayor
Kim G. Gartner, Administrator

MacNutt
P.O. Box 10
MacNutt, SK S0A 2K0
Tel: 306-742-4391; *Fax:* 306-742-4391
macnutt2013@hotmail.com; macnuttvillage@iewireless.ca
www.macnuttsaskatchewan.com
Municipal Type: Village
Incorporated: Feb. 22, 1913 *Area:* 0.81 sq km
Population in 2006: 80
Provincial Electoral District(s): Melville-Saltcoats
Federal Electoral District(s): Yorkton-Melville
Next Election: Oct. 2012 (3 year terms)
Glen Cartwright, Mayor
Kendra Busch, Clerk

Macoun
P.O. Box 58
Macoun, SK S0C 1P0
Tel: 306-634-9352; *Fax:* 306-634-9377
macoun.sask@gmail.com
Municipal Type: Village
Incorporated: Oct. 16, 1903 *Area:* 1.68 sq km
Population in 2006: 168
Provincial Electoral District(s): Estevan
Federal Electoral District(s): Souris-Moose Mountain
Next Election: Oct. 2012 (3 year terms)
Stuart Sovdi, Mayor
Carmen Dodd, Administrator

Macrorie
P.O. Box 37
Main St.
Macrorie, SK S0L 2E0
Tel: 306-243-2010; *Fax:* 306-243-2010
villageofmacrorie@sasktel.net
www.macrorie.com
Municipal Type: Village
Incorporated: Feb. 8, 1912 *Area:* 0.77 sq km
Population in 2006: 78
Provincial Electoral District(s): Rosetown-Elrose
Federal Electoral District(s): Cypress Hills-Grasslands
Next Election: Oct. 2012 (3 year terms)
Lorne Arthur, Mayor
Treena Lammers, Clerk

Maidstone
P.O. Box 208
112 - 1st Ave. West
Maidstone, SK S0M 1M0
Tel: 306-893-2373; *Fax:* 306-893-4378
townofmaidstone@sasktel.net
www.townofmaidstone.com
Municipal Type: Town
Incorporated: July 19, 1907 *Area:* 4.56 sq km
Population in 2006: 1,037
Provincial Electoral District(s): Cut Knife-Turtleford
Federal Electoral District(s): Battlefords-Lloydminster
Next Election: Oct. 2012 (3 year terms)
Note: Proclaimed as a town on March 1, 1955.
Connie McCulloch, Mayor
Bernie Swanson, Administrator

Major
P.O. Box 179
Major, SK S0L 2H0
Tel: 306-834-5493;
www.major.ca
Municipal Type: Village
Incorporated: Sept. 29, 1914 *Area:* 2.78 sq km
Population in 2006: 67
Provincial Electoral District(s): Kindersley
Federal Electoral District(s): Battlefords-Lloydminster
Next Election: Oct. 2012 (3 year terms)
Veryl Richelhoff, Mayor
Margaret Ostrowski, Clerk
ostrowski@yourlink.ca

Makwa
P.O. Box 159
Makwa, SK S0M 1N0
Tel: 306-236-3919; *Fax:* 306-236-3913
villageofmakwa@sasktel.net
Municipal Type: Village
Incorporated: June 1, 1965 *Area:* 0.66 sq km
Population in 2006: 96
Provincial Electoral District(s): Meadow Lake
Federal Electoral District(s): Desnethé-Missinippi-Churchill River
Next Election: Oct. 2012 (3 year terms)
Maurice Jeannotte, Mayor
Raylene Barthel, Clerk

Mankota
P.O. Box 336
Mankota, SK S0H 2W0
Tel: 306-478-2331; *Fax:* 306-478-2525
village.mankota@sasktel.net
Municipal Type: Village
Incorporated: Feb. 3, 1941 *Area:* 1.55 sq km
Population in 2006: 238
Provincial Electoral District(s): Wood River
Federal Electoral District(s): Cypress Hills-Grasslands
Next Election: Oct. 2012 (3 year terms)
Judy Smith, Mayor
Maggie Brown, Administrator

Manor
P.O. Box 295
45 Main St.
Manor, SK S0C 1R0
Tel: 306-448-2273; *Fax:* 306-448-2274
admin.manor@sasktel.net
Municipal Type: Village
Incorporated: April 15, 1902 *Area:* 2.79 sq km
Population in 2006: 312
Provincial Electoral District(s): Cannington
Federal Electoral District(s): Souris-Moose Mountain
Next Election: Oct. 2012 (3 year terms)
Vickie Akins, Mayor
Joan Mills, Administrator

Maple Creek
P.O. Box 428
205 Jasper St.
Maple Creek, SK S0N 1N0
Tel: 306-662-2244; *Fax:* 306-662-4131
townofmaplecreek@sasktel.net
www.maplecreek.ca
Municipal Type: Town
Incorporated: April 28, 1896 *Area:* 4.42 sq km
Population in 2006: 2,198
Provincial Electoral District(s): Cypress Hills
Federal Electoral District(s): Cypress Hills-Grasslands
Next Election: Oct. 2012 (3 year terms)
Note: Proclaimed as a town on April 30, 1903.

Barry Rudd, Mayor
mayor@maplecreek.ca
Mark D. Caswell, Administrator

Marcelin
P.O. Box 39
100 - 1st Ave. North
Marcelin, SK S0J 1R0
Tel: 306-226-2168; *Fax:* 306-226-2171
vmarcelin@sasktel.net
Municipal Type: Village
Incorporated: Sept. 25, 1911 *Area:* 1.32 sq km
Population in 2006: 169
Provincial Electoral District(s): Rosthern-Shellbrook
Federal Electoral District(s): Saskatoon-Wanuskewin
Next Election: Oct. 2012 (3 year terms)
E.W. Dale Butler, Mayor
Nicole Pool, Administrator

Marengo
P.O. Box 70
Marengo, SK S0L 2K0
Tel: 306-968-2922; *Fax:* 306-968-2278
rm292.rm322@sasktel.net
Municipal Type: Village
Incorporated: Nov. 5, 1910 *Area:* 0.87 sq km
Population in 2006: 51
Provincial Electoral District(s): Kindersley
Federal Electoral District(s): Battlefords-Lloydminster
Next Election: Oct. 2012 (3 year terms)
Robert Lee, Mayor
Shelley Mohr, Administrator

Margo
P.O. Box 28
Margo, SK S0A 2M0
Tel: 306-324-2134; *Fax:* 306-324-4563
villagemargo@sasktel.net
Municipal Type: Village
Incorporated: April 24, 1911 *Area:* 0.80 sq km
Population in 2006: 90
Provincial Electoral District(s): Kelvington-Wadena
Federal Electoral District(s): Yorkton-Melville
Next Election: Oct. 2012 (3 year terms)
George Dawe, Mayor
Gail Selch, Administrator

Markinch
P.O. Box 29
Markinch, SK S0G 3J0
Tel: 306-726-4355; *Fax:* 306-726-4355
vofmarkinch@canwan.com
Municipal Type: Village
Incorporated: Feb. 16, 1911 *Area:* 0.68 sq km
Population in 2006: 59
Provincial Electoral District(s): Last Mountain-Touchwood
Federal Electoral District(s): Regina-Qu'Appelle
Next Election: Oct. 2012 (3 year terms)
Wendell Langford, Mayor
Rita T. Orb, Clerk

Marquis
P.O. Box 40
Marquis, SK S0H 2X0
Tel: 306-788-2022; *Fax:* 306-788-2168
rm191@sasktel.net
Municipal Type: Village
Incorporated: March 21, 1910 *Area:* 0.63 sq km
Population in 2006: 71
Provincial Electoral District(s): Thunder Creek
Federal Electoral District(s): Regina-Lumsden-Lake Centre
Next Election: Oct. 2012 (3 year terms)
Ken Marcyniuk, Mayor
Ronald J. Gasper, Administrator

Marsden
P.O. Box 69
Marsden, SK S0M 1P0
Tel: 306-826-5215; *Fax:* 306-826-5512
rm442@sasktel.net
Municipal Type: Village
Incorporated: April 24, 1931 *Area:* 0.94 sq km
Population in 2006: 234
Provincial Electoral District(s): Cut Knife-Turtleford
Federal Electoral District(s): Battlefords-Lloydminster
Next Election: Oct. 2012 (3 year terms)
Tracy Kurtz, Mayor
Joanne Loy, Administrator

Marshall
P.O. Box 125
Marshall, SK S0M 1R0
Tel: 306-387-6340; *Fax:* 306-387-6161
village.marshall@sasktel.net
Municipal Type: Town
Incorporated: Jan. 21, 1914 *Area:* 1.01 sq km
Population in 2006: 608
Provincial Electoral District(s): Lloydminster
Federal Electoral District(s): Battlefords-Lloydminster
Next Election: Oct. 2012 (3 year terms)
Note: Proclaimed as a town on Oct. 26, 2006.
Brad Douglas, Mayor
Lorne Kachur, Administrator

Martensville
P.O. Box 970
515 Centennial Dr. South
Martensville, SK S0K 2T0
Tel: 306-931-2166; *Fax:* 306-933-2468
manager@martensville.ca
www.martensville.ca
Municipal Type: Town
Incorporated: Sept. 1, 1966 *Area:* 4.78 sq km
Population in 2006: 4,968
Provincial Electoral District(s): Martensville
Federal Electoral District(s): Saskatoon-Wanuskewin
Next Election: Oct. 2012 (3 year terms)
Note: Proclaimed as a town on Jan. 1, 1969.
Gordon Rutten, Mayor
rutten@martensville.caca
Scott Blevins, City Manager

Maryfield
P.O. Box 58
Maryfield, SK S0G 3K0
Tel: 306-646-2143; *Fax:* 306-646-2193
vom.ward@sasktel.net
www.maryfieldsaskatchewan.com
Municipal Type: Village
Incorporated: Aug. 21, 1907 *Area:* 2.69 sq km
Population in 2006: 347
Provincial Electoral District(s): Cannington
Federal Electoral District(s): Souris-Moose Mountain
Next Election: Oct. 2012 (3 year terms)
David Hill, Mayor
Ward Frazer, Administrator

Maymont
P.O. Box 160
Maymont, SK S0M 1T0
Tel: 306-389-2077; *Fax:* 306-389-2078
villageofmaymont@sasktel.net
Municipal Type: Village
Incorporated: June 24, 1907 *Area:* 0.66 sq km
Population in 2006: 130
Provincial Electoral District(s): Biggar
Federal Electoral District(s): Saskatoon-Wanuskewin
Next Election: Oct. 2012 (3 year terms)
Denise Bernier, Mayor
Wendy Davis, Administrator

McLean
P.O. Box 56
McLean, SK S0G 3E0
Tel: 306-699-7279; *Fax:* 306-699-2347
villageofmclean@sasktel.net
www.mcleansask.com
Municipal Type: Village
Incorporated: Jan. 24, 1913 *Area:* 1.33 sq km
Population in 2006: 275
Provincial Electoral District(s): Indian Head-Milestone
Federal Electoral District(s): Regina-Qu'Appelle
Next Election: Oct. 2012 (3 year terms)
Cliff Ebenal, Mayor
Nadine Jensen, Administrator

McTaggart
P.O. Box 134
McTaggart, SK S0G 3G0
Tel: 306-793-2023
Municipal Type: Village
Incorporated: Oct. 5, 1909 *Area:* 0.69 sq km
Population in 2006: 114
Provincial Electoral District(s): Weyburn-Big Muddy
Federal Electoral District(s): Souris-Moose Mountain
Next Election: Oct. 2012 (3 year terms)
John Dyck, Mayor
Darlene Paquin, Administrator

Meacham
P.O. Box 9
Meacham, SK S0K 2V0
Tel: 306-376-2003; *Fax:* 306-376-2006
villageofmeacham@baudoux.ca
Municipal Type: Village
Incorporated: June 19, 1912 *Area:* 1.27 sq km
Population in 2006: 70
Provincial Electoral District(s): Humboldt
Federal Electoral District(s): Blackstrap
Next Election: Oct. 2012 (3 year terms)
Perry Thiessen, Mayor
Juaneta Bendig, Clerk

Meadow Lake
120 - 1st St. East
Meadow Lake, SK S9X 1P8
Tel: 306-236-3622; *Fax:* 306-236-4299
cityhall@meadowlake.ca
www.meadowlake.ca
Municipal Type: Town
Incorporated: Aug. 24, 1931 *Area:* 7.95 sq km
Population in 2006: 4,771
Provincial Electoral District(s): Meadow Lake
Federal Electoral District(s): Desnethé-Missinippi-Churchill River
Next Election: Oct. 2012 (3 year terms)
Note: Proclaimed as a town on Feb. 1, 1936.
Don Bradley, Mayor
Paul Listrom, City Clerk

Meath Park
P.O. Box 255
Meath Park, SK S0J 1T0
Tel: 306-929-2112; *Fax:* 306-929-2281
villpark@sasktel.net
Municipal Type: Village
Incorporated: May 23, 1938 *Area:* 0.77 sq km
Population in 2006: 179
Provincial Electoral District(s): Saskatchewan Rivers
Federal Electoral District(s): Prince Albert
Next Election: Oct. 2012 (3 year terms)
Warren Morley, Mayor
Elaine Esopenko, Administrator

Medstead
P.O. Box 148
Medstead, SK S0M 1W0
Tel: 306-342-4898; *Fax:* 306-342-2067
villageofmedstead@sasktel.net
Municipal Type: Village
Incorporated: April 23, 1931 *Area:* 0.67 sq km
Population in 2006: 148
Provincial Electoral District(s): Rosthern-Shellbrook
Federal Electoral District(s): Battlefords-Lloydminster
Next Election: Oct. 2012 (3 year terms)
Trevor Short, Mayor
Christie Stafford, Administrator

Melfort
City Hall
P.O. Box 2230
202 Burrows Ave. West
Melfort, SK S0E 1A0
Tel: 306-752-5911; *Fax:* 306-752-5556
city@cityofmelfort.ca
www.cityofmelfort.ca
Municipal Type: Town
Incorporated: Nov. 4, 1903 *Area:* 14.78 sq km
Population in 2006: 5,192
Provincial Electoral District(s): Melfort
Federal Electoral District(s): Prince Albert
Next Election: Oct. 2012 (3 year terms)
Note: Incorporated as a city on Sept. 2, 1980.
Kevin Phillips, Mayor
Heather Audette, Clerk
h.audette@cityofmelfort.ca

Melville
P.O. Box 1240
430 Main St.
Melville, SK S0A 2P0
Tel: 306-728-6840; *Fax:* 306-728-5911
cityhall@melville.ca
www.city.melville.sk.ca
Municipal Type: Town
Incorporated: Dec. 21, 1908 *Area:* 14.82 sq km
Population in 2006: 4,149
Provincial Electoral District(s): Melville-Saltcoats
Federal Electoral District(s): Yorkton-Melville
Next Election: Oct. 2012 (3 year terms)
Note: Incorporated as a city on Aug. 1, 1960.
Walter Streelasky, Mayor

Michael Hotsko, City Manager
mhotsko@melville.ca

Mendham
P.O. Box 69
Mendham, SK S0N 1P0
Tel: 306-679-2000; *Fax:* 306-679-2275
Municipal Type: Village
Incorporated: April 1, 1930 *Area:* 0.5 sq km
Population in 2006: 35
Provincial Electoral District(s): Cypress Hills
Federal Electoral District(s): Cypress Hills-Grasslands
Next Election: Oct. 2012 (3 year terms)
Kevin Angerman, Mayor
Lucein Stuebing, Clerk

Meota
P.O. Box 123
Meota, SK S0M 1X0
Tel: 306-892-2277; *Fax:* 306-892-2275
vmeota@sasktel.net
Municipal Type: Village
Incorporated: July 6, 1911 *Area:* 1.55 sq km
Population in 2006: 297
Provincial Electoral District(s): Cut Knife-Turtleford
Federal Electoral District(s): Battlefords-Lloydminster
Next Election: Oct. 2012 (3 year terms)
John MacDonald, Mayor
Jacquie Code, Clerk

Mervin
P.O. Box 35
Mervin, SK S0M 1Y0
Tel: 306-845-2784; *Fax:* 306-845-3563
villageofmervin@littleloon.ca
Municipal Type: Village
Incorporated: March 17, 1920 *Area:* 0.73 sq km
Population in 2006: 228
Provincial Electoral District(s): Cut Knife-Turtleford
Federal Electoral District(s): Battlefords-Lloydminster
Next Election: Oct. 2012 (3 year terms)
Kenneth Knowlton, Mayor
Lora Hundt, Administrator

Michel Village
Sylvestre Place
P.O. Box 250
Dillon, SK S0M 0S0
Tel: 306-282-4401; *Fax:* 306-282-2155
Municipal Type: Northern Hamlet
Incorporated: Nov. 1, 1983 *Area:* 3.73 sq km
Population in 2006: 79
Provincial Electoral District(s): Athabasca
Federal Electoral District(s): Desnethé-Missinippi-Churchill River
Next Election: Oct. 2012 (3 year terms)
Cliff Coombs, Mayor
Allison Janvier, Clerk

Midale
P.O. Box 128
233 Main St.
Midale, SK S0C 1S0
Tel: 306-458-2400; *Fax:* 306-458-2209
lindugan@sasktel.net
www.townofmidale.com
Municipal Type: Town
Incorporated: Aug. 10, 1907 *Area:* 1.53 sq km
Population in 2006: 462
Provincial Electoral District(s): Estevan
Federal Electoral District(s): Souris-Moose Mountain
Next Election: Oct. 2012 (3 year terms)
Note: Proclaimed as a town on March 1, 1962.
Allan Hauglum, Mayor
Linda M. Dugan, Administrator

Middle Lake
P.O. Box 119
Middle Lake, SK S0K 2X0
Tel: 306-367-2149; *Fax:* 306-367-4963
middlelake@sasktel.net
Municipal Type: Village
Incorporated: Jan. 1, 1963 *Area:* 1.26 sq km
Population in 2006: 277
Provincial Electoral District(s): Batoche
Federal Electoral District(s): Saskatoon-Humboldt
Next Election: Oct. 2012 (3 year terms)
Ken Herman, Mayor
Colette Hauser, Clerk

Milden
P.O. Box 70
202 Centre St.
Milden, SK S0L 2L0
Tel: 306-935-2131; *Fax:* 306-935-2020
vmilden@sasktel.net
www.villageofmilden.com
Municipal Type: Village
Incorporated: July 20, 1911 *Area:* 1.18 sq km
Population in 2006: 172
Provincial Electoral District(s): Rosetown-Elrose
Federal Electoral District(s): Cypress Hills-Grasslands
Next Election: Oct. 2012 (3 year terms)
Lester Wall, Mayor
Heather Maxemniuk, Clerk

Milestone
P.O. Box 74
105 Main St.
Milestone, SK S0G 3L0
Tel: 306-436-2130; *Fax:* 306-436-2051
milcal@sasktel.net
www.milestonesk.ca
Municipal Type: Town
Incorporated: March 14, 1903 *Area:* 2.17 sq km
Population in 2006: 562
Provincial Electoral District(s): Indian Head-Milestone
Federal Electoral District(s): Souris-Moose Mountain
Next Election: Oct. 2012 (3 year terms)
Note: Proclaimed as a town on Aug. 15, 1906.
Jeff Brown, Mayor
Stephen Schury, Administrator

Minton
P.O. Box 52
Minton, SK S0C 1T0
Tel: 306-969-2144; *Fax:* 306-969-2127
rmnine@sasktel.net
Municipal Type: Village
Incorporated: Jan. 1, 1951 *Area:* 0.3 sq km
Population in 2006: 60
Provincial Electoral District(s): Weyburn-Big Muddy
Federal Electoral District(s): Souris-Moose Mountain
Next Election: Oct. 2012 (3 year terms)
Dennis Simpart, Mayor
Joyce Axtenm, Clerk

Missinipe
c/o Ministry of Municipal Affairs
P.O. Box 5000
La Ronge, SK S0J 1L0
Tel: 306-425-4323; *Fax:* 306-425-2401
Municipal Type: Northern Hamlet
Incorporated: Feb. 1, 1984 *Area:* 1.87 sq km
Population in 2006: 5
Provincial Electoral District(s): Cumberland
Federal Electoral District(s): Desnethé-Missinippe-Churchill River
Next Election: Oct. 2012 (3 year terms)
Zack Adams, Chairman
Valerie Antoniuk, Advisor
valerie.antoniuk@gov.sk.ca

Mistatim
P.O. Box 145
Mistatim, SK S0E 1B0
Tel: 306-889-2008; *Fax:* 306-889-4439
villageofmistatim@yourlink.ca
www.newsaskcfdc.ca/mistatim.htm
Municipal Type: Village
Incorporated: July 1, 1952 *Area:* 0.47 sq km
Population in 2006: 89
Provincial Electoral District(s): Carrot River Valley
Federal Electoral District(s): Yorkton-Melville
Next Election: Oct. 2012 (3 year terms)
Gene Legare, Mayor
Ingrid Conway, Administrator

Montmartre
P.O. Box 146
Montmartre, SK S0G 3M0
Tel: 306-424-2040; *Fax:* 306-424-2065
rm126@sasktel.net
www.montmartre-sk.com
Municipal Type: Village
Incorporated: Oct. 19, 1908 *Area:* 1.63 sq km
Population in 2006: 413
Provincial Electoral District(s): Moosomin
Federal Electoral District(s): Wascana
Next Election: Oct. 2012 (3 year terms)
Robert Chittenden, Mayor
Dale Brenner, Administrator

Moosomin
P.O. Box 730
701 Main St.
Moosomin, SK S0G 3N0
Tel: 306-435-2988; *Fax:* 306-435-3343
twn.moosomin@sasktel.net
www.moosomin.com
Municipal Type: Town
Incorporated: March 20, 1889 *Area:* 5.97 sq km
Population in 2006: 2,257
Provincial Electoral District(s): Moosomin
Federal Electoral District(s): Souris-Moose Mountain
Next Election: Oct. 2012 (3 year terms)

Morse
P.O. Box 270
Morse, SK S0H 3C0
Tel: 306-629-3300; *Fax:* 306-629-3235
morse@sasktel.net
morsesask.com
Municipal Type: Town
Incorporated: March 11, 1910 *Area:* 1.45 sq km
Population in 2006: 236
Provincial Electoral District(s): Thunder Creek
Federal Electoral District(s): Cypress Hills-Grasslands
Next Election: Oct. 2012 (3 year terms)
Note: Proclaimed as a town on Nov. 1, 1912.
Louis Fafard, Mayor
Gloria Weppler, Administrator

Mortlach
P.O. Box 10
Mortlach, SK S0H 3E0
Tel: 306-355-2554; *Fax:* 306-355-2557
village.mortlach@sasktel.net
www.mortlach.ca
Municipal Type: Village
Incorporated: April 19, 1906 *Area:* 2.76 sq km
Population in 2006: 254
Provincial Electoral District(s): Thunder Creek
Federal Electoral District(s): Cypress Hills-Grasslands
Next Election: Oct. 2012 (3 year terms)
Gerald Forbes, Mayor
Tracey Gardner, Administrator

Mossbank
P.O. Box 370
Mossbank, SK S0H 3G0
Tel: 306-354-2294; *Fax:* 306-354-7725
townofmossbank@sasktel.net
www.mossbank.ca
Municipal Type: Town
Incorporated: Dec. 14, 1915 *Area:* 1.75 sq km
Population in 2006: 330
Provincial Electoral District(s): Wood River
Federal Electoral District(s): Palliser
Next Election: Oct. 2012 (3 year terms)
Note: Proclaimed as a town on May 15, 1959.
Carl Weiss, Mayor
Cindy Kimball, Administrator

Muenster
P.O. Box 98
Muenster, SK S0K 2Y0
Tel: 306-682-2794; *Fax:* 306-682-4179
muenster@sasktel.net
Municipal Type: Village
Incorporated: Aug. 18, 1908 *Area:* 1.24 sq km
Population in 2006: 342
Provincial Electoral District(s): Humboldt
Federal Electoral District(s): Saskatoon-Humboldt
Next Election: Oct. 2012 (3 year terms)
Benno Korte, Mayor
Rose M. Haeusler, Administrator

Naicam
P.O. Box 238
Naicam, SK S0K 2Z0
Tel: 306-874-2280; *Fax:* 306-874-5444
naicam.ced@sasktel.net
www.townofnaicam.ca
Municipal Type: Town
Incorporated: April 28, 1921 *Area:* 1.69 sq km
Population in 2006: 690
Provincial Electoral District(s): Melfort
Federal Electoral District(s): Saskatoon-Humboldt
Next Election: Oct. 2012 (3 year terms)
Note: Proclaimed as a town on Sept. 1, 1954.
Rodger Hayward, Mayor
Lowell Prefontaine, Administrator

Neilburg
P.O. Box 280
39 Centre St.
Neilburg, SK S0M 2C0
Tel: 306-823-4321; *Fax:* 306-823-4477
neilburg@sasktel.net
Municipal Type: Village
Incorporated: Jan. 1, 1947 *Area:* 1.16 sq km
Population in 2006: 394
Provincial Electoral District(s): Cut Knife-Turtleford
Federal Electoral District(s): Battlefords-Lloydminster
Next Election: Oct. 2012 (3 year terms)
Ernest Ducherer, Mayor
Janet L. Black, Administrator

Netherhill
P.O. Box 4
Netherhill, SK S0L 2M0
Tel: 306-379-2116;
brockadmin@sasktel.net
Municipal Type: Village
Incorporated: April 28, 1910 *Area:* 0.73 sq km
Population in 2006: 30
Provincial Electoral District(s): Rosetown-Elrose
Federal Electoral District(s): Battlefords-Lloydminster
Next Election: Oct. 2012 (3 year terms)
Winston Jones, Mayor
Shannon Beheil, Clerk

Neudorf
P.O. Box 187
Neudorf, SK S0A 2T0
Tel: 306-748-2551; *Fax:* 306-748-2647
vneudorf@sasktel.net
www.village.neudorf.sk.ca
Municipal Type: Village
Incorporated: April 25, 1905 *Area:* 2.05 sq km
Population in 2006: 281
Provincial Electoral District(s): Last Mountain-Touchwood
Federal Electoral District(s): Yorkton-Melville
Next Election: Oct. 2012 (3 year terms)
Murray J. Hanowski, Mayor
Crystal Campbell, Administrator

Neville
P.O. Box 88
Neville, SK S0N 1T0
Tel: 306-627-3255; *Fax:* 306-627-3546
village.neville@sasktel.net
Municipal Type: Village
Incorporated: July 5, 1912 *Area:* 1.10 sq km
Population in 2006: 65
Provincial Electoral District(s): Wood River
Federal Electoral District(s): Cypress Hills-Grasslands
Next Election: Oct. 2012 (3 year terms)
Harvey Linnen, Mayor
Linda Hornung, Clerk

Nipawin
P.O. Box 2134
210 Second Ave. East
Nipawin, SK S0E 1E0
Tel: 306-862-9866; *Fax:* 306-862-3076
townoffice@nipawin.com; info@nipawin.com
www.nipawin.com
Other Information: Toll Free Phone: 306-877-647-2946
Municipal Type: Town
Incorporated: May 7, 1925 *Area:* 8.03 sq km
Population in 2006: 4,061
Provincial Electoral District(s): Carrot River Valley
Federal Electoral District(s): Prince Albert
Next Election: Oct. 2012 (3 year terms)
Note: Proclaimed as a town on May 1, 1937.
Lawrence Rospad, Mayor
Steven Piermantier, Administrator
s.piermantier@nipawin.com

Nokomis
P.O. Box 189
101 - 3rd Ave. West
Nokomis, SK S0G 3R0
Tel: 306-528-2010;
townofnokomis@sasktel.net
nokomisweb.com
Municipal Type: Town
Incorporated: March 5, 1908 *Area:* 2.61 sq km
Population in 2006: 404
Provincial Electoral District(s): Arm River-Watrous
Federal Electoral District(s): Regina-Lumsden-Lake Centre
Next Election: Oct. 2012 (3 year terms)
Note: Proclaimed as a town on Aug. 15, 1908.
Fredard Wright, Mayor
Joanne Hamilton, Administrator

Norquay
P.O. Box 327
25 Main St.
Norquay, SK S0A 2V0
Tel: 306-594-2101; *Fax:* 306-594-2347
norquay@sasktel.net
www.townofnorquay.ca
Municipal Type: Town
Incorporated: June 4, 1913 *Area:* 1.69 sq km
Population in 2006: 412
Provincial Electoral District(s): Canora-Pelly
Federal Electoral District(s): Yorkton-Melville
Next Election: Oct. 2012 (3 year terms)
Note: Proclaimed as a town on March 1, 1963.
Don Tower, Mayor
Rona Seidle, Administrator

North Portal
P.O. Box 119
North Portal, SK S0C 1W0
Tel: 306-927-5050; *Fax:* 306-927-2033
villagen@sasktel.net
Municipal Type: Village
Incorporated: Nov. 16, 1903 *Area:* 2.49 sq km
Population in 2006: 123
Provincial Electoral District(s): Estevan
Federal Electoral District(s): Souris-Moose Mountain
Next Election: Oct. 2012 (3 year terms)
Murray Arnold, Mayor
Lindsay Davis, Clerk

Odessa
P.O. Box 91
Odessa, SK S0G 3S0
Tel: 306-957-2020; *Fax:* 306-957-4502
villageofodessa@sasktel.net
www.odessask.com
Municipal Type: Village
Incorporated: March 14, 1911 *Area:* 1.18 sq km
Population in 2006: 201
Provincial Electoral District(s): Indian Head-Milestone
Federal Electoral District(s): Wascana
Next Election: Oct. 2012 (3 year terms)
Larry Lockert, Mayor
Sheila Leurer, Clerk

Ogema
P.O. Box 159
Ogema, SK S0C 1Y0
Tel: 306-459-2262; *Fax:* 306-459-2762
townofogema@sasktel.net
www.ogema.ca
Municipal Type: Town
Incorporated: Jan. 18, 1911 *Area:* 1.43 sq km
Population in 2006: 304
Provincial Electoral District(s): Weyburn-Big Muddy
Federal Electoral District(s): Souris-Moose Mountain
Next Election: Oct. 2012 (3 year terms)
Note: Proclaimed as a town on Jan. 7, 1913.
Wayne Myren, Mayor
Peggy Tuchscherer, Administrator

Osage
P.O. Box 96
Osage, SK S0G 3T0
Tel: 306-722-3747;
garry.lindakreutzer@sasktel.net
Municipal Type: Village
Incorporated: May 8, 1906 *Area:* 0.59 sq km
Population in 2006: 20
Provincial Electoral District(s): Indian Head-Milestone
Federal Electoral District(s): Souris-Moose Mountain
Next Election: Oct. 2012 (3 year terms)
Garry Kreutzer, Mayor
Linda R. Kreutzer, Clerk

Osler
P.O. Box 190
228 Willow Dr.
Osler, SK S0K 3A0
Tel: 306-239-2155; *Fax:* 306-239-2194
info@townofosler.com
www.osler-sk.ca
Municipal Type: Town
Incorporated: April 9, 1904 *Area:* 0.98 sq km
Population in 2006: 926
Provincial Electoral District(s): Martensville
Federal Electoral District(s): Saskatoon-Wanuskewin
Next Election: Oct. 2012 (3 year terms)
Note: Proclaimed as a town on Nov. 1, 1985.
Ben Buhler, Mayor
Sandra MacArthur, Chief Administrative Officer

Outlook
P.O. Box 518
Outlook, SK S0L 2N0
Tel: 306-867-8663; *Fax:* 306-867-9898
town@town.outlook.sk.ca
www.town.outlook.sk.ca
Municipal Type: Town
Incorporated: Dec. 19, 1908 *Area:* 7.83 sq km
Population in 2006: 1,938
Provincial Electoral District(s): Rosetown-Elrose
Federal Electoral District(s): Blackstrap; Cypress Hills-Grasslands
Next Election: Oct. 2012 (3 year terms)
Note: Proclaimed as a town on Nov. 1, 1909.
Bob Stephenson, Mayor
Trent Michelman, Municipal Manager
michelman@town.outlook.sk.ca

Oxbow
P.O. Box 149
307 Main St.
Oxbow, SK S0C 2B0
Tel: 306-483-2300; *Fax:* 306-483-5277
oxbowtown@sasktel.net
www.oxbow.ca
Municipal Type: Town
Incorporated: March 7, 1899 *Area:* 3.1 sq km
Population in 2006: 1,139
Provincial Electoral District(s): Cannington
Federal Electoral District(s): Souris-Moose Mountain
Next Election: Oct. 2012 (3 year terms)
Note: Proclaimed as a town on May 30, 1904.
Doug Pierce, Mayor
Brad Vanbeselaere, Administrator

Paddockwood
P.O. Box 188
Paddockwood, SK S0J 1Z0
Tel: 306-989-2033; *Fax:* 306-989-2033
vpaddockwood@inet2000.com
Municipal Type: Village
Incorporated: Jan. 1, 1949 *Area:* 0.65 sq km
Population in 2006: 125
Provincial Electoral District(s): Saskatchewan Rivers
Federal Electoral District(s): Prince Albert
Next Election: Oct. 2012 (3 year terms)
Reg Hintz, Mayor
Diana Siurko, Clerk

Pangman
P.O. Box 189
Pangman, SK S0C 2C0
Tel: 306-442-2131; *Fax:* 306-442-2144
rm.69@sasktel.net
www.pangman.ca
Municipal Type: Village
Incorporated: May 17, 1911 *Area:* 0.73 sq km
Population in 2006: 200
Provincial Electoral District(s): Weyburn-Big Muddy
Federal Electoral District(s): Souris-Moose Mountain
Next Election: Oct. 2012 (3 year terms)
Cory Henheffer, Mayor
Wayne W. Lozinsky, Administrator

Paradise Hill
P.O. Box 270
Paradise Hill, SK S0M 2G0
Tel: 306-344-2206; *Fax:* 306-344-4941
paradisehill@sasktel.net
www.paradisehill.ca
Municipal Type: Village
Incorporated: Jan. 1, 1947 *Area:* 1.99 sq km
Population in 2006: 483
Provincial Electoral District(s): Lloydminster
Federal Electoral District(s): Battlefords-Lloydminster
Next Election: Oct. 2012 (3 year terms)
Larry Harland, Mayor
Marion Hougham, Clerk

Parkside
P.O. Box 48
Parkside, SK S0J 2A0
Tel: 306-747-2235; *Fax:* 306-747-3395
villageofparkside@yourlink.ca
Municipal Type: Village
Incorporated: Feb. 21, 1913 *Area:* 0.92 sq km
Population in 2006: 129
Provincial Electoral District(s): Rosthern-Shellbrook

Federal Electoral District(s): Saskatoon-Wanuskewin
Next Election: Oct. 2012 (3 year terms)
David K. Moe, Mayor
Gwen Olson, Clerk

Patuanak
P.O. Box 180
Shagwenaw Dr.
Patuanak, SK S0M 2H0
Tel: 306-396-2020; *Fax:* 306-396-2092
hamofpat@sasktel.net
Municipal Type: Northern Hamlet
Incorporated: Dec. 1, 1983 *Area:* 1.34 sq km
Population in 2006: 84
Provincial Electoral District(s): Athabasca
Federal Electoral District(s): Desnethé-Missinippi-Churchill River
Next Election: Oct. 2012 (3 year terms)
Hazel Maurice, Mayor
Miranda Wolverine, Clerk

Paynton
P.O. Box 100
Paynton, SK S0M 2J0
Tel: 306-895-2023; *Fax:* 306-895-2053
village470@sasktel.net
Municipal Type: Village
Incorporated: May 2, 1907 *Area:* 0.85 sq km
Population in 2006: 151
Provincial Electoral District(s): Cut Knife-Turtleford
Federal Electoral District(s): Battlefords-Lloydminster
Next Election: Oct. 2012 (3 year terms)
David Florizone, Mayor
Joan Caldwell, Administrator

Pelican Narrows
P.O. Box 10
Bear St.
Pelican Narrows, SK S0P 0E0
Tel: 306-632-2225; *Fax:* 306-632-2006
Municipal Type: Northern Village
Incorporated: Jan. 1, 1989 *Area:* 3.70 sq km
Population in 2006: 599
Provincial Electoral District(s): Cumberland
Federal Electoral District(s): Desnethé-Missinippi-Churchill River
Next Election: Oct. 2012 (3 year terms)
Horace Morin, Mayor
Doreen Linklater, Clerk

Pelly
P.O. Box 220
Pelly, SK S0A 2Z0
Tel: 306-595-2124; *Fax:* 306-595-2050
town.pelly@sasktel.net
www.pelly.ca
Municipal Type: Village
Incorporated: May 4, 1911 *Area:* 0.96 sq km
Population in 2006: 287
Provincial Electoral District(s): Canora-Pelly
Federal Electoral District(s): Yorkton-Melville
Next Election: Oct. 2012 (3 year terms)
Sharon Nelson, Mayor
Victoria Makohoniuk, Administrator

Pennant
P.O. Box 57
Pennant, SK S0N 1X0
Tel: 306-626-3255; *Fax:* 306-626-3661
villageofpennant@sasktel.net; rm168@sasktel.net
www.villageofpennant.com
Municipal Type: Village
Incorporated: July 29, 1912 *Area:* 0.65 sq km
Population in 2006: 119
Provincial Electoral District(s): Swift Current
Federal Electoral District(s): Cypress Hills-Grasslands
Next Election: Oct. 2012 (3 year terms)
Leslie Bayliss, Mayor
Brandi Trembath, Administrator

Pense
P.O. Box 125
243 Brunswick St.
Pense, SK S0G 3W0
Tel: 306-345-2332; *Fax:* 306-345-2340
pensevillage@sasktel.net
www.pense.ca
Municipal Type: Village
Incorporated: March 7, 1904 *Area:* 1.32 sq km
Population in 2006: 507
Provincial Electoral District(s): Thunder Creek
Federal Electoral District(s): Palliser
Next Election: Oct. 2012 (3 year terms)
Michele LeBlanc, Mayor
mayor@pense.ca
Jennifer Lendvay, Administrator
jlendvay@pense.ca

Penzance
P.O. Box 68
Penzance, SK S0G 3X0
Tel: 306-488-4669
Municipal Type: Village
Incorporated: July 13, 1912 *Area:* 0.62 sq km
Population in 2006: 30
Provincial Electoral District(s): Thunder Creek
Federal Electoral District(s): Regina-Lumsden-Lake Centre
Next Election: Oct. 2012 (3 year terms)
John Thorson, Mayor
Ellen Frohlick, Clerk

Perdue
P.O. Box 190
Perdue, SK S0K 3C0
Tel: 306-237-4337; *Fax:* 306-237-4874
www.villageofperdue.com
Municipal Type: Village
Incorporated: July 15, 1909 *Area:* 1.10 sq km
Population in 2006: 364
Provincial Electoral District(s): Biggar
Federal Electoral District(s): Saskatoon-Rosetown-Biggar
Next Election: Oct. 2012 (3 year terms)
Dave Miller, Mayor
Nancy Duns, Administrator

Pierceland
P.O. Box 39
177 Main St.
Pierceland, SK S0M 2K0
Tel: 306-839-2015; *Fax:* 306-839-2057
plandvillage@sasktel.net
Municipal Type: Village
Incorporated: Jan. 1, 1973 *Area:* 2.69 sq km
Population in 2006: 498
Provincial Electoral District(s): Lloydminster
Federal Electoral District(s): Desnethé-Missinippi-Churchill River
Next Election: Oct. 2012 (3 year terms)
Jim Krushelnitzky, Mayor
Jane Eistetter, Clerk

Pilger
P.O. Box 24
Pilger, SK S0K 3G0
Tel: 306-367-4631; *Fax:* 306-367-4621
Municipal Type: Village
Incorporated: Jan. 1, 1969 *Area:* 0.52 sq km
Population in 2006: 74
Provincial Electoral District(s): Batoche
Federal Electoral District(s): Saskatoon-Humboldt
Next Election: Oct. 2012 (3 year terms)
Joyce Bauer, Mayor
Gloria Struck, Clerk

Pilot Butte
P.O. Box 253
Pilot Butte, SK S0G 3Z0
Tel: 306-781-4547;
townofpilotbutte@sasktel.net
www.pilotbutte.ca
Municipal Type: Town
Incorporated: Nov. 8, 1913 *Area:* 4.69 sq km
Population in 2006: 1,867
Provincial Electoral District(s): Regina Wascana Plains
Federal Electoral District(s): Regina-Qu'Appelle
Next Election: Oct. 2012 (3 year terms)
Note: Proclaimed as a town on Nov. 1, 1980.
Sid Bowles, Mayor
Laurie Rudolph, Administrator

Pinehouse
P.O. Box 298
Pinehouse Ave.
Pinehouse, SK S0J 2B0
Tel: 306-884-2030; *Fax:* 306-884-2021
nvp@sasktel.net
career.kcdc.ca/comm/Pinehouse.php
Municipal Type: Northern Village
Incorporated: Oct. 1, 1983 *Area:* 6.84 sq km
Population in 2006: 1,076
Provincial Electoral District(s): Athabasca
Federal Electoral District(s): Desnethé-Missinippi-Churchill River
Next Election: Oct. 2012 (3 year terms)
Mike Natomagan, Mayor
Marie Smith, Clerk

Pleasantdale
P.O. Box 147
Pleasantdale, SK S0K 3H0
Tel: 306-874-5743; *Fax:* 306-874-5743
villageofpleasantdale@gmail.com
www.newsaskcfdc.ca/pleasantdale.htm
Municipal Type: Village
Incorporated: Jan. 1, 1987 *Area:* 0.56 sq km
Population in 2006: 85
Provincial Electoral District(s): Melfort
Federal Electoral District(s): Saskatoon-Humboldt
Next Election: Oct. 2012 (3 year terms)
Kenneth Myhre, Mayor
Rosmarie Zenner, Clerk

Plenty
P.O. Box 177
Plenty, SK S0L 2R0
Tel: 306-932-2045; *Fax:* 306-932-2044
vop@sasktel.net
Municipal Type: Village
Incorporated: March 25, 1911 *Area:* 0.65 sq km
Population in 2006: 126
Provincial Electoral District(s): Rosetown-Elrose
Federal Electoral District(s): Battlefords-Lloydminster
Next Election: Oct. 2012 (3 year terms)
Corey Kingwell, Mayor
Lorraine McDonald, Administrator

Plunkett
P.O. Box 149
Plunkett, SK S0K 3J0
Tel: 306-944-4514; *Fax:* 306-944-4512
Municipal Type: Village
Incorporated: Dec. 28, 1921 *Area:* 0.64 sq km
Population in 2006: 75
Provincial Electoral District(s): Humboldt
Federal Electoral District(s): Blackstrap
Next Election: Oct. 2012 (3 year terms)
Richard Hayes, Mayor
Helen Miller, Clerk
dhmiller@sasktel.net

Ponteix
P.O. Box 330
213 Centre St.
Ponteix, SK S0N 1Z0
Tel: 306-625-3222; *Fax:* 306-625-3204
town.ponteix@sasktel.net
www.townofponteix.com
Municipal Type: Town
Incorporated: June 24, 1914 *Area:* 1.09 sq km
Population in 2006: 531
Provincial Electoral District(s): Wood River
Federal Electoral District(s): Cypress Hills-Grasslands
Next Election: Oct. 2012 (3 year terms)
Note: Proclaimed as a town on April 1, 1957.
Etiennette Binette, Mayor
Lynne Lemieux, Administrator
admin@townofponteix.com

Porcupine Plain
P.O. Box 310
151 McAllister Ave.
Porcupine Plain, SK S0E 1H0
Tel: 306-278-2262; *Fax:* 306-278-3378
porcupineplain@sasktel.net
www.porcupineplain.com
Municipal Type: Town
Incorporated: April 9, 1942 *Area:* 2.27 sq km
Population in 2006: 783
Provincial Electoral District(s): Kelvington-Wadena
Federal Electoral District(s): Yorkton-Melville
Next Election: Oct. 2012 (3 year terms)
Note: Proclaimed as a town on Jan. 1, 1968.
Terry Zip, Mayor
Lousie Baht, Administrator

Preeceville
P.O. Box 560
239 Highway Ave. East
Preeceville, SK S0A 3B0
Tel: 306-547-2810; *Fax:* 306-547-3116
preeceville@sasktel.net
www.townofpreeceville.ca
Other Information: Toll Free Phone: 1-877-706-3196
Municipal Type: Town
Incorporated: Feb. 6, 1912 *Area:* 2.79 sq km
Population in 2006: 1,050
Provincial Electoral District(s): Canora-Pelly
Federal Electoral District(s): Yorkton-Melville

Next Election: Oct. 2012 (3 year terms)
Note: Incorporated as a town on Nov. 30, 1946.
Garth Harris, Mayor
Lorelei Karcha, Administrator

Prelate
P.O. Box 40
Prelate, SK S0N 2B0
Tel: 306-673-2340; *Fax:* 306-673-2340
prelate@chinook.lib.sk.ca
Municipal Type: Village
Incorporated: Oct. 25, 1913 *Area:* 0.87 sq km
Population in 2006: 126
Provincial Electoral District(s): Cypress Hills
Federal Electoral District(s): Cypress Hills-Grasslands
Next Election: Oct. 2012 (3 year terms)
Darrah Duchscherer, Mayor
Darlene Wagner, Clerk

Primate
P.O. Box 6
Primate, SK S0L 2S0
Tel: 306-753-3232; *Fax:* 306-753-2971
tjcl@lincsat.com
Municipal Type: Village
Incorporated: April 5, 1922 *Area:* 0.94 sq km
Population in 2006: 50
Provincial Electoral District(s): Kindersley
Federal Electoral District(s): Battlefords-Lloydminster
Next Election: Oct. 2012 (3 year terms)
Daniel Allen, Mayor
Dianne Latendresse, Clerk

Prud'homme
P.O. Box 38
Prud'Homme, SK S0K 3K0
Tel: 306-654-2001; *Fax:* 306-654-2001
voprud@sasktel.net
www.prudhommevillage.com
Municipal Type: Village
Incorporated: Nov. 15, 1922 *Area:* 0.84 sq km
Population in 2006: 167
Provincial Electoral District(s): Humboldt
Federal Electoral District(s): Saskatoon-Humboldt
Next Election: Oct. 2012 (3 year terms)
Preston Tkatch, Mayor
Holly Maas, Administrator

Punnichy
P.O. Box 250
Punnichy, SK S0A 3C0
Tel: 306-835-2135; *Fax:* 306-835-2401
punnichy@aski.ca
Municipal Type: Village
Incorporated: Oct. 22, 1909 *Area:* 0.68 sq km
Population in 2006: 277
Provincial Electoral District(s): Last Mountain-Touchwood
Federal Electoral District(s): Regina-Qu'Appelle
Next Election: Oct. 2012 (3 year terms)
Dean Schlosser, Mayor
Donna Colley, Administrator

Qu'Appelle
P.O. Box 60
Qu'Appelle, SK S0G 4A0
Tel: 306-699-2279; *Fax:* 306-699-2306
townquappelle@sasktel.net
www.townofquappelle.ca
Municipal Type: Town
Incorporated: Feb. 20, 1904 *Area:* 4.22 sq km
Population in 2006: 624
Provincial Electoral District(s): Indian Head-Milestone
Federal Electoral District(s): Regina-Qu'Appelle
Next Election: Oct. 2012 (3 year terms)
Tom Williams, Mayor
Carol Wickenheiser, Administrator

Quill Lake
P.O. Box 9
60 Main St.
Quill Lake, SK S0A 3E0
Tel: 306-383-2592; *Fax:* 306-383-2255
quilllake@sasktel.net
www.quill-lakes.com/quilllake/village
Municipal Type: Village
Incorporated: Dec. 8, 1906 *Area:* 1.30 sq km
Population in 2006: 413
Provincial Electoral District(s): Melfort
Federal Electoral District(s): Saskatoon-Humboldt
Next Election: Oct. 2012 (3 year terms)
Robert Walker, Mayor
Judy L. Kanak, Administrator

Quinton
P.O. Box 128
Quinton, SK S0A 3G0
Tel: 306-835-2515; *Fax:* 306-835-2515
quintonvillage@aski.ca
Municipal Type: Village
Incorporated: March 1, 1910 *Area:* 0.96 sq km
Population in 2006: 108
Provincial Electoral District(s): Arm River-Watrous
Federal Electoral District(s): Regina-Qu'Appelle
Next Election: Oct. 2012 (3 year terms)
Ralph Brockman, Mayor
Lorelei Paulsen, Administrator

Rabbit Lake
P.O. Box 9
Rabbit Lake, SK S0M 2L0
Tel: 306-824-2125; *Fax:* 306-824-2150
rabbitlake@yourlink.ca
Municipal Type: Village
Incorporated: April 13, 1928 *Area:* 0.92 sq km
Population in 2006: 113
Provincial Electoral District(s): Rosthern-Shellbrook
Federal Electoral District(s): Battlefords-Lloydminster
Next Election: Oct. 2012 (3 year terms)
Don Peters, Mayor
Brenda Aumack, Administrator

Radisson
P.O. Box 69
Radisson, SK S0K 3L0
Tel: 306-827-2218; *Fax:* 306-827-2218
tradisson@sasktel.net
radisson.sasktelwebhosting.com
Municipal Type: Town
Incorporated: Feb. 3, 1906 *Area:* 2.07 sq km
Population in 2006: 421
Provincial Electoral District(s): Biggar
Federal Electoral District(s): Saskatoon-Wanuskewin
Next Election: Oct. 2012 (3 year terms)
Note: Proclaimed as a town on July 1, 1913.
Walter Kyliuk, Mayor
Darrin Beaudoin, Administrator

Radville
P.O. Box 339
Radville, SK S0C 2G0
Tel: 306-869-2477; *Fax:* 306-869-3100
town.radville@sasktel.net
www.radville.ca
Municipal Type: Town
Incorporated: Jan. 3, 1911 *Area:* 1.86 sq km
Population in 2006: 755
Provincial Electoral District(s): Estevan
Federal Electoral District(s): Souris-Moose Mountain
Next Election: Oct. 2012 (3 year terms)
Note: Proclaimed as a town on May 1, 1913.
Shirley Cancade, Mayor
Shauna Bourassa, Administrator

Rama
P.O. Box 205
Rama, SK S0A 3H0
Tel: 306-593-6065; *Fax:* 306-593-2273
villagerama@yourlink.ca
Municipal Type: Village
Incorporated: Dec. 18, 1919 *Area:* 0.67 sq km
Population in 2006: 75
Provincial Electoral District(s): Kelvington-Wadena
Federal Electoral District(s): Yorkton-Melville
Next Election: Oct. 2012 (3 year terms)
Darrell Dutchak, Mayor
Nicole Monchamp, Administrator

Raymore
P.O. Box 10
107 Main St.
Raymore, SK S0A 3J0
Tel: 306-746-2100; *Fax:* 306-746-4314
raymoretown@aski.ca
www.raymore.ca
Municipal Type: Town
Incorporated: Aug. 11, 1909 *Area:* 2.75 sq km
Population in 2006: 581
Provincial Electoral District(s): Arm River-Watrous
Federal Electoral District(s): Regina-Qu'Appelle
Next Election: Oct. 2012 (3 year terms)
Note: Proclaimed as a town on Aug. 1, 1963.
Keith Bentz, Mayor
Gail R. Braman, Administrator

Redvers
P.O. Box 249
25 Railway Ave.
Redvers, SK S0C 2H0
Tel: 306-452-3533; *Fax:* 306-452-3701
town.of.redvers@sasktel.net
www.townofredvers.org
Municipal Type: Town
Incorporated: July 9, 1904 *Area:* 2.83 sq km
Population in 2006: 878
Provincial Electoral District(s): Cannington
Federal Electoral District(s): Souris-Moose Mountain
Next Election: Oct. 2012 (3 year terms)
Note: Proclaimed as a town on July 6, 1960.
Omer Carriere, Mayor
Janice Burnett, Administrator

Regina Beach
P.O. Box 10
218 Centre St.
Regina Beach, SK S0G 4C0
Tel: 306-729-2202; *Fax:* 306-729-3411
townofreginabeach@sasktel.net
www.reginabeach.ca
Municipal Type: Town
Incorporated: Sept. 30, 1920 *Area:* 2.58 sq km
Population in 2006: 1,195
Provincial Electoral District(s): Thunder Creek
Federal Electoral District(s): Regina-Lumsden-Lake Centre
Next Election: Oct. 2012 (3 year terms)
Note: Proclaimed as a town on Nov. 1, 1980.
George Solomon Schofield, Mayor
Christina Stanford, Administrator

Rhein
P.O. Box 40
Rhein, SK S0A 3K0
Tel: 306-273-2155; *Fax:* 306-273-2155
villageofrhein@yourlink.ca
Municipal Type: Village
Incorporated: March 10, 1913 *Area:* 1.09 sq km
Population in 2006: 161
Provincial Electoral District(s): Canora-Pelly
Federal Electoral District(s): Yorkton-Melville
Next Election: Oct. 2012 (3 year terms)
Ian Bugera, Mayor
Valerie Stricker, Administrator

Richard
P.O. Box 6
Richard, SK S0M 2P0
Tel: 306-549-2331;
vrichard@sasktel.net
Municipal Type: Village
Incorporated: Oct. 11, 1916 *Area:* 0.73 sq km
Population in 2006: 25
Provincial Electoral District(s): Rosthern-Shellbrook
Federal Electoral District(s): Saskatoon-Wanuskewin
Next Election: Oct. 2012 (3 year terms)
Merilyn Wawryk, Mayor
Valerie Fendelet, Administrator

Richmound
P.O. Box 29
Richmound, SK S0N 2E0
Tel: 306-669-4415; *Fax:* 306-669-2044
richmound.village@sasktel.net
www.richmound.ca
Municipal Type: Village
Incorporated: May 5, 1947 *Area:* 0.47 sq km
Population in 2006: 159
Provincial Electoral District(s): Cypress Hills
Federal Electoral District(s): Cypress Hills-Grasslands
Next Election: Oct. 2012 (3 year terms)
Barry Manz, Mayor
Al Korol, Alderman
Glen Nickell, Alderman
Laurie Baron, Administrator

Ridgedale
P.O. Box 27
Ridgedale, SK S0E 1L0
Tel: 306-277-2002; *Fax:* 306-277-2002
ridgedalevillage@sasktel.net
www.newsaskcfdc.ca/ridgedale.htm
Municipal Type: Village
Incorporated: Dec. 15, 1921 *Area:* 0.72 sq km
Population in 2006: 66
Provincial Electoral District(s): Carrot River Valley
Federal Electoral District(s): Prince Albert
Next Election: Oct. 2012 (3 year terms)
Beverley Sochaski, Mayor

Barbara Messenger, Clerk

Riverhurst
P.O. Box 116
324 Teck St.
Riverhurst, SK S0H 3P0
Tel: 306-353-2220; *Fax:* 306-353-2220
villageofriverhurst@sasktel.net
www.riverhurst.ca
Municipal Type: Village
Incorporated: June 22, 1916 *Area:* 0.91 sq km
Population in 2006: 121
Provincial Electoral District(s): Thunder Creek
Federal Electoral District(s): Cypress Hills-Grasslands
Next Election: Oct. 2012 (3 year terms)
Sylvia Matwe, Mayor
306-796-2006
Garry Gross, Administrator

Rocanville
P.O. Box 265
Rocanville, SK S0A 3L0
Tel: 306-645-2022; *Fax:* 306-645-4492
rocanville.town@sasktel.net
www.rocanville.ca
Municipal Type: Town
Incorporated: March 24, 1904 *Area:* 2.43 sq km
Population in 2006: 869
Provincial Electoral District(s): Moosomin
Federal Electoral District(s): Souris-Moose Mountain
Next Election: Oct. 2012 (3 year terms)
Note: Incorporated as a town on Aug. 1, 1967.
Daryl Fingas, Mayor
Monica M. Merkosky, Administrator

Roche Percée
P.O. Box 237
Bienfait, SK S0C 0M0
Tel: 306-634-4661
Municipal Type: Village
Incorporated: Jan. 12, 1909 *Area:* 2.59 sq km
Population in 2006: 149
Provincial Electoral District(s): Estevan
Federal Electoral District(s): Souris-Moose Mountain
Next Election: Oct. 2012 (3 year terms)
Reg Jahn, Mayor
Charlotte Wrigley, Administrator

Rockglen
P.O. Box 267
Rockglen, SK S0H 3R0
Tel: 306-476-2144; *Fax:* 306-476-2339
rockglen1@sasktel.net
www.rockglentourism.com
Municipal Type: Town
Incorporated: July 12, 1927 *Area:* 2.85 sq km
Population in 2006: 366
Provincial Electoral District(s): Wood River
Federal Electoral District(s): Cypress Hills-Grasslands
Next Election: Oct. 2012 (3 year terms)
Note: Proclaimed as a town on Sept. 1, 1957.
Richard Prefontaine, Mayor
Sherri Spagrud, Administrator

Rockhaven
P.O. Box 9
Rockhaven, SK S0M 2R0
Tel: 306-398-3775; *Fax:* 306-398-2083
Municipal Type: Village
Incorporated: March 19, 1913 *Area:* 1.58 sq km
Population in 2006: 20
Provincial Electoral District(s): Cut Knife-Turtleford
Federal Electoral District(s): Battlefords-Lloydminster
Next Election: Oct. 2012 (3 year terms)
Tom Hollman, Mayor
Karri Risling, Clerk

Rose Valley
P.O. Box 460
Rose Valley, SK S0E 1M0
Tel: 306-322-2232; *Fax:* 306-322-4461
rosevalley@sasktel.net
www.townofrosevalley.com
Municipal Type: Town
Incorporated: Sept. 24, 1940 *Area:* 1.12 sq km
Population in 2006: 338
Provincial Electoral District(s): Kelvington-Wadena
Federal Electoral District(s): Yorkton-Melville
Next Election: Oct. 2012 (3 year terms)
Note: Proclaimed as a town on Jan. 1, 1962.
Daniel Veilleux, Mayor
Marjorie A. Zarowny, Clerk

Rosetown
P.O. Box 398
417 Main St.
Rosetown, SK S0L 2V0
Tel: 306-882-2214; *Fax:* 306-882-3166
townofrosetown@sasktel.net
www.rosetown.ca
Municipal Type: Town
Incorporated: Aug. 24, 1909 *Area:* 10.59 sq km
Population in 2006: 2,277
Provincial Electoral District(s): Rosetown-Elrose
Federal Electoral District(s): Saskatoon-Rosetown-Biggar
Next Election: Oct. 2012 (3 year terms)
Note: Proclaimed as a town on Nov. 1, 1911.
Brian Gerow, Mayor
Darcy Olson, Administrator

Rosthern
P.O. Box 416
Rosthern, SK S0K 3R0
Tel: 306-232-4826; *Fax:* 306-232-5638
townofrosthern@sasktel.net
www.rosthern.com
Municipal Type: Town
Incorporated: Dec. 29, 1898 *Area:* 4.01 sq km
Population in 2006: 1,382
Provincial Electoral District(s): Rosthern-Shellbrook
Federal Electoral District(s): Saskatoon-Wanuskewin
Next Election: Oct. 2012 (3 year terms)
Note: Proclaimed as a town on Nov. 20, 1903.
Doug Knoll, Mayor
Nicole J. Lerat, Administrator

Rouleau
P.O. Box 250
Rouleau, SK S0G 4H0
Tel: 306-776-2270; *Fax:* 306-776-2482
info@townofrouleau.com
www.townofrouleau.com
Municipal Type: Town
Incorporated: July 23, 1903 *Area:* 1.65 sq km
Population in 2006: 400
Provincial Electoral District(s): Indian Head-Milestone
Federal Electoral District(s): Palliser
Next Election: Oct. 2012 (3 year terms)
Note: Proclaimed as a town on March 1, 1907.
Leroy (Pete) Westgard, Mayor
Guy Lagrandeur, Administrator

Ruddell
P.O. Box 7
Ruddell, SK S0M 2S0
Tel: 306-445-4601; *Fax:* 306-445-4611
Municipal Type: Village
Incorporated: March 18, 1914 *Area:* 0.47 sq km
Population in 2006: 20
Provincial Electoral District(s): Biggar
Federal Electoral District(s): Saskatoon-Wanuskewin
Next Election: Oct. 2012 (3 year terms)
Linda Mushka, Mayor
Les Klippentein, Administrator
Klipp1951@gmail.com

Rush Lake
P.O. Box 126
Rush Lake, SK S0H 3S0
Tel: 306-784-3504; *Fax:* 306-773-0331
Municipal Type: Village
Incorporated: Oct. 16, 1911 *Area:* 0.74 sq km
Population in 2006: 50
Provincial Electoral District(s): Thunder Creek
Federal Electoral District(s): Cypress Hills-Grasslands
Next Election: Oct. 2012 (3 year terms)
Stacey Beisel, Mayor
Adeline Steinley, Clerk
a.steinley@sasktel.net

Ruthilda
P.O. Box 90
Ruthilda, SK S0K 3S0
Tel: 306-932-4408
Municipal Type: Village
Incorporated: Feb. 3, 1921 *Area:* 0.67 sq km
Population in 2006: 5
Provincial Electoral District(s): Biggar
Federal Electoral District(s): Battlefords-Lloydminster
Next Election: Oct. 2012 (3 year terms)
Jerry Gilles, Mayor
Anita Gilles, Clerk
anita@sasktel.net

St. Benedict
P.O. Box 99
St Benedict, SK S0K 3T0
Tel: 306-289-2072; *Fax:* 306-289-2077
benedictvillage@gmail.com
Municipal Type: Village
Incorporated: Jan. 1, 1964 *Area:* 0.54 sq km
Population in 2006: 78
Provincial Electoral District(s): Batoche
Federal Electoral District(s): Saskatoon-Humboldt
Next Election: Oct. 2012 (3 year terms)
Edward Martin, Mayor
Helen Martinka, Clerk

St. Brieux
P.O. Box 249
300 Main St.
St Brieux, SK S0K 3V0
Tel: 306-275-2257; *Fax:* 306-275-4949
brieux@sasktel.net
Municipal Type: Town
Incorporated: Nov. 11, 1913 *Area:* 2.02 sq km
Population in 2006: 492
Provincial Electoral District(s): Batoche
Federal Electoral District(s): Saskatoon-Humboldt
Next Election: Oct. 2012 (3 year terms)
Note: Proclaimed as a town on Nov. 8, 2006.
Pauline Boyer, Mayor
Jennifer Thompson, Administrator

St. George's Hill
P.O. Box 160
Desjarlais St.
Dillon, SK S0M 0S0
Tel: 306-282-4408; *Fax:* 306-282-2002
sgh123@sasktel.net
Municipal Type: Northern Hamlet
Incorporated: Dec. 1, 1983 *Area:* 1.46 sq km
Population in 2006: 19
Provincial Electoral District(s): Athabasca
Federal Electoral District(s): Desnethé-Missinippi-Churchill River
Next Election: Oct. 2012 (3 year terms)
Doris Janvier, Mayor
Shirley Desjardin, Clerk

St. Gregor
P.O. Box 19
St Gregor, SK S0K 3X0
Tel: 306-366-2129; *Fax:* 306-366-2128
stgregorsk@sasktel.net
Municipal Type: Village
Incorporated: March 26, 1920 *Area:* 0.91 sq km
Population in 2006: 102
Provincial Electoral District(s): Melfort
Federal Electoral District(s): Saskatoon-Humboldt
Next Election: Oct. 2012 (3 year terms)
Doug Hogemann, Mayor
Darlene Kuz, Administrator

St. Louis
P.O. Box 40
172 Riverside Dr.
St Louis, SK S0J 2C0
Tel: 306-422-8471; *Fax:* 306-422-8450
villageofstlouis@sasktel.net
www.villageofstlouis.com
Municipal Type: Village
Incorporated: May 19, 1959 *Area:* 1.08 sq km
Population in 2006: 431
Provincial Electoral District(s): Batoche
Federal Electoral District(s): Saskatoon-Humboldt
Next Election: Oct. 2012 (3 year terms)
Les Rancourt, Mayor
Robin Boyer, Clerk

St. Walburg
P.O. Box 368
St Walburg, SK S0M 2T0
Tel: 306-248-3232; *Fax:* 306-248-3484
townofstwalburg@sasktel.net
www.stwalburg.com
Municipal Type: Town
Incorporated: Jan. 18, 1922 *Area:* 2.12 sq km
Population in 2006: 672
Provincial Electoral District(s): Meadow Lake
Federal Electoral District(s): Battlefords-Lloydminster
Next Election: Oct. 2012 (3 year terms)
Note: Proclaimed as a town on Feb. 1, 1953.
A. V. "Tony" Leeson, Mayor
Leah Mullis, Acting Administrator

Saltcoats
P.O. Box 120
Saltcoats, SK S0A 3R0
Tel: 306-744-2212; *Fax:* 306-744-2239
saltcoats.town@sasktel.net
townofsaltcoats.ca
Municipal Type: Town
Incorporated: April 4, 1894 *Area:* 1.35 sq km
Population in 2006: 467
Provincial Electoral District(s): Melville-Saltcoats
Federal Electoral District(s): Yorkton-Melville
Next Election: Oct. 2012 (3 year terms)
Note: Proclaimed as a town on Nov. 1, 1910.
Walter Farquharson, Mayor
Diane Jamieson, Administrator

Sandy Bay
P.O. Box 130
Hill St. & Sandy Bay Ave.
Sandy Bay, SK S0P 0G0
Tel: 306-754-2165; *Fax:* 306-754-2157
nvsb@sasktel.net
Municipal Type: Northern Village
Incorporated: Oct. 1, 1983 *Area:* 14.85 sq km
Population in 2006: 1,175
Provincial Electoral District(s): Cumberland
Federal Electoral District(s): Desnethé-Missinippi-Churchill River
Next Election: Oct. 2012 (3 year terms)
Daniel Bear, Mayor
Ramona Nateweyes, Administrator

Sceptre
P.O. Box 128
Sceptre, SK S0N 2H0
Tel: 306-623-4244; *Fax:* 306-623-4244
sceptrevillage@xplornet.com
Municipal Type: Village
Incorporated: April 30, 1913 *Area:* 1.23 sq km
Population in 2006: 99
Provincial Electoral District(s): Cypress Hills
Federal Electoral District(s): Cypress Hills-Grasslands
Next Election: Oct. 2012 (3 year terms)
Charlene King, Mayor
Sherry Egeland, Clerk

Scott
P.O. Box 96
104 Main St.
Scott, SK S0K 4A0
Tel: 306-247-2033; *Fax:* 306-247-2055
townofscott@xplornet.com
Municipal Type: Town
Incorporated: Nov. 17, 1908 *Area:* 4.39 sq km
Population in 2006: 91
Provincial Electoral District(s): Kindersley
Federal Electoral District(s): Battlefords-Lloydminster
Next Election: Oct. 2012 (3 year terms)
Note: Proclaimed as a town on Nov. 1, 1910.
Eric Schell, Mayor
Stacy Hawkins, Administrator

Sedley
P.O. Box 130
Sedley, SK S0G 4K0
Tel: 306-885-2133; *Fax:* 306-885-2132
villageofsedley@sasktel.net
Municipal Type: Village
Incorporated: Aug. 3, 1907 *Area:* 1.31 sq km
Population in 2006: 319
Provincial Electoral District(s): Indian Head-Milestone
Federal Electoral District(s): Wascana
Next Election: Oct. 2012 (3 year terms)
Bryan Leier, Mayor
Samantha Gillies, Clerk

Semans
P.O. Box 113
Semans, SK S0A 3S0
Tel: 306-524-2144; *Fax:* 306-524-2145
semans@aski.ca
www.semans-sask.com
Municipal Type: Village
Incorporated: Dec. 14, 1908 *Area:* 1.18 sq km
Population in 2006: 195
Provincial Electoral District(s): Arm River-Watrous
Federal Electoral District(s): Regina-Lumsden-Lake Centre
Next Election: Oct. 2012 (3 year terms)
Ray Lamontagne, Mayor
Charmayne Szatkowski, Administrator

Senlac
P.O. Box 93
Senlac, SK S0L 2Y0
Tel: 306-228-4330;
rm411@sasktel.net
Municipal Type: Village
Incorporated: Oct. 11, 1916 *Area:* 0.60 sq km
Population in 2006: 45
Provincial Electoral District(s): Cut Knife-Turtleford
Federal Electoral District(s): Battlefords-Lloydminster
Next Election: Oct. 2012 (3 year terms)
Joe Murrell, Mayor
Maureen Forbes, Clerk

Shackleton
P.O. Box 7
Shackleton, SK S0N 2L0
Tel: 306-587-2910; *Fax:* 306-587-2311
Municipal Type: Village
Incorporated: May 29, 1919 *Area:* 0.66 sq km
Population in 2006: 10
Provincial Electoral District(s): Cypress Hills
Federal Electoral District(s): Cypress Hills-Grasslands
Next Election: Oct. 2012 (3 year terms)
Ronald J. Heron, Mayor
Marjorie A. Cator, Clerk
marjorie.cator@gmail.com

Shamrock
P.O. Box 119
Shamrock, SK S0H 3W0
Tel: 306-648-2736; *Fax:* 306-648-2798
Municipal Type: Village
Incorporated: April 30, 1924 *Area:* 0.79 sq km
Population in 2006: 20
Provincial Electoral District(s): Wood River
Federal Electoral District(s): Cypress Hills-Grasslands
Next Election: Oct. 2012 (3 year terms)
Rene Fortin, Mayor
Cathy Marchessault, Clerk
rmarchessault@sasktel.net

Shaunavon
P.O. Box 820
Shaunavon, SK S0N 2M0
Tel: 306-297-2605; *Fax:* 306-297-2608
shaunavon@sasktel.net
www.shaunavon.com
Municipal Type: Town
Incorporated: Nov. 27, 1913 *Area:* 5.10 sq km
Population in 2006: 1,691
Provincial Electoral District(s): Cypress Hills
Federal Electoral District(s): Cypress Hills-Grasslands
Next Election: Oct. 2012 (3 year terms)
Note: Proclaimed as a town on Nov. 1, 1914.
Sharon J. Dickie, Mayor
Charmaine Bernath, Administrator
bernath.shaunavon@sasktel.net

Sheho
P.O. Box 130
Sheho, SK S0A 3T0
Tel: 306-849-2044;
shehovillage@sasktel.net
Municipal Type: Village
Incorporated: June 30, 1905 *Area:* 1.95 sq km
Population in 2006: 121
Provincial Electoral District(s): Kelvington-Wadena
Federal Electoral District(s): Yorkton-Melville
Next Election: Oct. 2012 (3 year terms)
Dennis Zoski, Mayor
Ron Sebulsky, Clerk

Shell Lake
P.O. Box 280
Shell Lake, SK S0J 2G0
Tel: 306-427-2272; *Fax:* 306-427-4800
village.sl@sasktel.net
www.rkc.ca/shell_lake/
Municipal Type: Village
Incorporated: Oct. 18, 1940 *Area:* 1.09 sq km
Population in 2006: 152
Provincial Electoral District(s): Rosthern-Shellbrook
Federal Electoral District(s): Desnethé-Missinippi-Churchill River
Next Election: Oct. 2012 (3 year terms)
Anita Weiers, Mayor
Tara Bueckert, Administrator

Shellbrook
P.O. Box 40
71 Main St.
Shellbrook, SK S0J 2E0
Tel: 306-747-4900; *Fax:* 306-747-3111
shellbrook@sasktel.net
www.shellbrook.net
Municipal Type: Town
Incorporated: Nov. 18, 1909 *Area:* 2.13 sq km
Population in 2006: 1,215
Provincial Electoral District(s): Rosthern-Shellbrook
Federal Electoral District(s): Prince Albert
Next Election: Oct. 2012 (3 year terms)
Note: Proclaimed as a town on April 1, 1948.
George Tomporowski, Mayor
Tara Kerber, Administrator

Silton
P.O. Box 1
Silton, SK S0G 4L0
Tel: 306-731-3222;
villageofsilton@xplornet.ca
Municipal Type: Village
Incorporated: July 2, 1914 *Area:* 1.07 sq km
Population in 2006: 91
Provincial Electoral District(s): Last Mountain-Touchwood
Federal Electoral District(s): Regina-Lumsden-Lake Centre
Next Election: Oct. 2012 (3 year terms)
Warren Wild, Mayor
Brenda Small, Clerk

Simpson
P.O. Box 10
303 George St.
Simpson, SK S0G 4M0
Tel: 306-836-2020; *Fax:* 306-836-4460
rm281@sasktel.net
www.simpsonsask.ca
Municipal Type: Village
Incorporated: July 11, 1911 *Area:* 1.41 sq km
Population in 2006: 118
Provincial Electoral District(s): Arm River-Watrous
Federal Electoral District(s): Regina-Lumsden-Lake Centre
Next Election: Oct. 2012 (3 year terms)
Donald Janzen, Mayor
Darlene Mann, Administrator

Sintaluta
P.O. Box 150
Sintaluta, SK S0G 4N0
Tel: 306-727-2100; *Fax:* 306-727-2100
sintaluta@yourlink.ca
Municipal Type: Town
Incorporated: Oct. 27, 1898 *Area:* 2.70 sq km
Population in 2006: 98
Provincial Electoral District(s): Indian Head-Milestone
Federal Electoral District(s): Regina-Qu'Appelle
Next Election: Oct. 2012 (3 year terms)
Note: Proclaimed as a town on June 1, 1907.
Keith Rathgerber, Mayor
Donna Pitre, Administrator

Smeaton
P.O. Box 70
Smeaton, SK S0J 2J0
Tel: 306-426-2044; *Fax:* 306-426-2291
smeaton@sasktel.net
www.newsaskcfdc.ca/smeaton.htm
Municipal Type: Village
Incorporated: March 7, 1944 *Area:* 1.38 sq km
Population in 2006: 183
Provincial Electoral District(s): Saskatchewan Rivers
Federal Electoral District(s): Desnethé-Missinippi-Churchill River
Next Election: Oct. 2012 (3 year terms)
Joe Bernhard, Mayor
Diana M. Jensen, Administrator

Smiley
P.O. Box 90
Smiley, SK S0L 2Z0
Tel: 306-838-2020; *Fax:* 306-838-4343
rm321@sasktel.net
Municipal Type: Village
Incorporated: Nov. 26, 1913 *Area:* 0.64 sq km
Population in 2006: 50
Provincial Electoral District(s): Kindersley
Federal Electoral District(s): Battlefords-Lloydminster
Next Election: Oct. 2012 (3 year terms)
William Wasylenchuk, Mayor
Charlotte Helfrich, Administrator

Southey
P.O. Box 248
Southey, SK S0G 4P0
Tel: 306-726-2202; *Fax:* 306-726-2916
townofsouthey@sasktel.net
www.southey.ca
Municipal Type: Town
Incorporated: Nov. 9, 1907 *Area:* 1 sq km
Population in 2006: 711
Provincial Electoral District(s): Last Mountain-Touchwood
Federal Electoral District(s): Regina-Qu'Appelle
Next Election: Oct. 2012 (3 year terms)
Note: Proclaimed as a town on Nov. 1, 1980.
Martin Lingelbach, Mayor
Karen Herman, Administrator

Spalding
P.O. Box 280
Spalding, SK S0K 4C0
Tel: 306-872-2276; *Fax:* 306-872-2275
spalding.village@sasktel.net
www.newsaskcfdc.ca/spalding.htm
Municipal Type: Village
Incorporated: March 11, 1924 *Area:* 1.18 sq km
Population in 2006: 237
Provincial Electoral District(s): Melfort
Federal Electoral District(s): Saskatoon-Humboldt
Next Election: Oct. 2012 (3 year terms)
Norman Foushe, Mayor
Cathy Holt, Administrator

Speers
P.O. Box 974
Speers, SK S0M 2V0
Tel: 306-246-2114; *Fax:* 306-246-2173
rm436@littleloon.ca
Municipal Type: Village
Incorporated: Dec. 24, 1915 *Area:* 0.69 sq km
Population in 2006: 74
Provincial Electoral District(s): Rosthern-Shellbrook
Federal Electoral District(s): Saskatoon-Wanuskewin
Next Election: Oct. 2012 (3 year terms)
Thomas E. Nicholson, Mayor
Dean Nicholson, Clerk

Spiritwood
P.O. Box 460
Spiritwood, SK S0J 2M0
Tel: 306-883-2161; *Fax:* 306-883-3212
www.townofspiritwood.ca
Municipal Type: Town
Incorporated: Oct. 1, 1935 *Area:* 2.95 sq km
Population in 2006: 911
Provincial Electoral District(s): Rosthern-Shellbrook
Federal Electoral District(s): Desnethé-Missinippi-Churchill River
Next Election: Oct. 2012 (3 year terms)
Note: Proclaimed as a town on Sept. 1, 1965.
Gary von Holwede, Mayor
Teri Scaife, Administrator

Springside
P.O. Box 414
Springside, SK S0A 3V0
Tel: 306-792-2022; *Fax:* 306-792-2210
springside.town@sasktel.net
www.townofspringside.com
Municipal Type: Town
Incorporated: Nov. 11, 1909 *Area:* 0.64 sq km
Population in 2006: 494
Provincial Electoral District(s): Canora-Pelly
Federal Electoral District(s): Yorkton-Melville
Next Election: Oct. 2012 (3 year terms)
Note: Proclaimed as a town on Nov. 1, 1985.
Jack Prychak, Mayor
Joan M. Popoff, Administrator

Spy Hill
P.O. Box 69
Spy Hill, SK S0A 3W0
Tel: 306-534-2255; *Fax:* 306-534-4520
spyhillvillage@sasktel.net
vila.sasktelwebsite.net
Municipal Type: Village
Incorporated: April 22, 1910 *Area:* 1.19 sq km
Population in 2006: 201
Provincial Electoral District(s): Melville-Saltcoats
Federal Electoral District(s): Yorkton-Melville
Next Election: Oct. 2012 (3 year terms)
Allan Perrin, Mayor
Tawnya Moore, Administrator

Star City
P.O. Box 250
145 - 4th St.
Star City, SK S0E 1P0
Tel: 306-863-2282; *Fax:* 306-863-2277
town.starcity@sasktel.net
www.townofstarcity.com
Municipal Type: Town
Incorporated: April 6, 1906 *Area:* 0.7 sq km
Population in 2006: 428
Provincial Electoral District(s): Melfort
Federal Electoral District(s): Prince Albert
Next Election: Oct. 2012 (3 year terms)
Note: Proclaimed as a town on Nov. 1, 1921.
Barry Petrie, Mayor
Ann Welton, Administrator

Stenen
P.O. Box 160
Stenen, SK S0A 3X0
Tel: 306-548-4334; *Fax:* 306-548-4334
villageofstenen@sasktel.net
Municipal Type: Village
Incorporated: Aug. 14, 1912 *Area:* 0.58 sq km
Population in 2006: 91
Provincial Electoral District(s): Canora-Pelly
Federal Electoral District(s): Yorkton-Melville
Next Election: Oct. 2012 (3 year terms)
Garry Giesbrecht, Mayor
Sharon Thompson, Administrator

Stewart Valley
P.O. Box 10
210 Charles St.
Stewart Valley, SK S0N 2P0
Tel: 306-778-3611; *Fax:* 306-778-3688
vlg.stvalley@sasktel.net
www.stewartvalley.ca
Municipal Type: Village
Incorporated: Jan. 1, 1958 *Area:* 0.86 sq km
Population in 2006: 100
Provincial Electoral District(s): Swift Current
Federal Electoral District(s): Cypress Hills-Grasslands
Next Election: Oct. 2012 (3 year terms)
Mike Moen, Mayor
Corie Lanceleve, Clerk

Stockholm
P.O. Box 265
Stockholm, SK S0A 3Y0
Tel: 306-793-2151; *Fax:* 306-793-4597
stockholm@sasktel.net
Municipal Type: Village
Incorporated: June 30, 1905 *Area:* 1.64 sq km
Population in 2006: 323
Provincial Electoral District(s): Melville-Saltcoats
Federal Electoral District(s): Yorkton-Melville
Next Election: Oct. 2012 (3 year terms)
Fran Herperger, Mayor
Joanne Barber, Administrator

Stony Rapids
P.O. Box 120
Johnson St.
Stony Rapids, SK S0J 2R0
Tel: 306-439-2173; *Fax:* 306-439-2098
nhstonyrap@sasktel.net
Municipal Type: Northern Hamlet
Incorporated: April 1, 1992 *Area:* 3.96 sq km
Population in 2006: 255
Provincial Electoral District(s): Athabasca
Federal Electoral District(s): Desnethé-Missinippi-Churchill River
Next Election: Oct. 2012 (3 year terms)
Sandra Hanson, Mayor
Shauna Sayazie, Clerk

Storthoaks
P.O. Box 40
Storthoaks, SK S0C 2K0
Tel: 306-449-2262; *Fax:* 306-449-2210
rm31@sasktel.net
Municipal Type: Village
Incorporated: June 5, 1940 *Area:* 0.49 sq km
Population in 2006: 82
Provincial Electoral District(s): Cannington
Federal Electoral District(s): Souris-Moose Mountain
Next Election: Oct. 2012 (3 year terms)
Sydney Chicoine, Mayor
Gisele Bouchard, Administrator

Stoughton
P.O. Box 397
232 Main St.
Stoughton, SK S0G 4T0
Tel: 306-457-2413; *Fax:* 306-457-3162
stoughtontown@sasktel.net
stoughtn.sasktelwebhosting.com
Municipal Type: Town
Incorporated: Feb. 26, 1904 *Area:* 2.13 sq km
Population in 2006: 653
Provincial Electoral District(s): Cannington
Federal Electoral District(s): Souris-Moose Mountain
Next Election: Oct. 2012 (3 year terms)
Note: Proclaimed as a town on June 1, 1960.
Heather Balon-Barmann, Mayor
Chris Miskolczi, Administrator

Strasbourg
P.O. Box 369
Strasbourg, SK S0G 4V0
Tel: 306-725-3707; *Fax:* 306-725-3613
strasbourg@sasktel.net
www.townofstrasbourg.ca
Municipal Type: Town
Incorporated: April 19, 1906 *Area:* 5.70 sq km
Population in 2006: 732
Provincial Electoral District(s): Last Mountain-Touchwood
Federal Electoral District(s): Regina-Lumsden-Lake Centre
Next Election: Oct. 2012 (3 year terms)
Note: Proclaimed as a town on July 1, 1907.
Carol Schultz, Mayor
Barbara Griffin, Administrator

Strongfield
P.O. Box 87
Strongfield, SK S0H 3Z0
Tel: 306-857-2200;
villageofstrongfield@yourlink.ca
Municipal Type: Village
Incorporated: May 3, 1912 *Area:* 0.8 sq km
Population in 2006: 47
Provincial Electoral District(s): Arm River-Watrous
Federal Electoral District(s): Blackstrap
Next Election: Oct. 2012 (3 year terms)
George Bristow, Mayor
Lora-Lee McKay, Administrator

Sturgis
P.O. Box 520
209 - 1st Ave. SE
Sturgis, SK S0A 4A0
Tel: 306-548-2108; *Fax:* 306-548-2948
townofsturgis@sasktel.net
www.townofsturgis.com
Municipal Type: Town
Incorporated: Sept. 3, 1912 *Area:* 3.39 sq km
Population in 2006: 575
Provincial Electoral District(s): Canora-Pelly
Federal Electoral District(s): Yorkton-Melville
Next Election: Oct. 2012 (3 year terms)
Note: Proclaimed as a town on March 1, 1951.
Don Olson, Mayor
Olivia (Bim) Bartch, Administrator

Success
P.O. Box 40
Success, SK S0N 2R0
Tel: 306-773-7934;
success1@yourlink.ca
Municipal Type: Village
Incorporated: Oct. 25, 1912 *Area:* 1.38 sq km
Population in 2006: 40
Provincial Electoral District(s): Swift Current
Federal Electoral District(s): Cypress Hills-Grasslands
Next Election: Oct. 2012 (3 year terms)
John Kroeker, Mayor
Donna Butler, Clerk

Tantallon
P.O. Box 70
Tantallon, SK S0A 4B0
Tel: 306-643-2112; *Fax:* 306-643-2113
tantallon@sasktel.net
Municipal Type: Village
Incorporated: June 17, 1904 *Area:* 0.84 sq km
Population in 2006: 105
Provincial Electoral District(s): Melville-Saltcoats
Federal Electoral District(s): Yorkton-Melville
Next Election: Oct. 2012 (3 year terms)
Michael Swanton, Mayor
Richelle Haanstra, Administrator

Tessier
P.O. Box 34
Tessier, SK S0L 3G0
Tel: 306-656-4580
Municipal Type: Village
Incorporated: Aug. 24, 1909 *Area:* 1 sq km
Population in 2006: 20
Provincial Electoral District(s): Rosetown-Elrose
Federal Electoral District(s): Saskatoon-Rosetown-Biggar
Next Election: Oct. 2012 (3 year terms)
L.B. Johnson, Mayor
Barbara Shaw, Clerk

Theodore
P.O. Box 417
102 Main St.
Theodore, SK S0A 4C0
Tel: 306-647-2315; *Fax:* 306-647-2476
theodore.village@sasktel.net
www.villageoftheodore.com
Municipal Type: Village
Incorporated: July 5, 1907 *Area:* 1.73 sq km
Population in 2006: 339
Provincial Electoral District(s): Kelvington-Wadena
Federal Electoral District(s): Yorkton-Melville
Next Election: Oct. 2012 (3 year terms)
Dennis Biblow, Mayor
Crystal Workman, Acting Administrator

Timber Bay
General Delivery
Timber Bay, SK S0J 2T0
Tel: 306-663-5885; *Fax:* 306-663-5052
northerntimberbay@sasktel.net
Municipal Type: Northern Hamlet
Incorporated: Oct. 1, 1983 *Area:* 4.44 sq km
Population in 2006: 139
Provincial Electoral District(s): Cumberland
Federal Electoral District(s): Desnethé-Missinippi-Churchill River
Next Election: Oct. 2012 (3 year terms)
Peggy Hennie, Mayor
Sylvia LaVallee, Clerk

Tisdale
P.O. Box 1090
901 - 100 St.
Tisdale, SK S0E 1T0
Tel: 306-873-2681; *Fax:* 306-873-5700
thetownoffice@townoftisdale.com
www.townoftisdale.com
Municipal Type: Town
Incorporated: May 15, 1905 *Area:* 4.62 sq km
Population in 2006: 2,981
Provincial Electoral District(s): Carrot River Valley
Federal Electoral District(s): Prince Albert
Next Election: Oct. 2012 (3 year terms)
Note: Proclaimed as a town on Nov. 1, 1920.
Roland (Rolly) Zimmer, Mayor
Brad Hvidston, Administrator

Togo
P.O. Box 100
Togo, SK S0A 4E0
Tel: 306-597-2114; *Fax:* 306-597-2114
villageoftogo@sasktel.net
Municipal Type: Village
Incorporated: Sept. 4, 1906 *Area:* 1.5 sq km
Population in 2006: 100
Provincial Electoral District(s): Canora-Pelly
Federal Electoral District(s): Yorkton-Melville
Next Election: Oct. 2012 (3 year terms)
Amanda Burback, Mayor
Carlotta Schwartz, Administrator

Tompkins
P.O. Box 247
5 - 2nd St.
Tompkins, SK S0N 2S0
Tel: 306-622-2020; *Fax:* 306-622-2025
villageoftompkins@sasktel.net
www.villageoftompkins.ca
Municipal Type: Village
Incorporated: June 2, 1910 *Area:* 2.65 sq km
Population in 2006: 173
Provincial Electoral District(s): Cypress Hills
Federal Electoral District(s): Cypress Hills-Grasslands
Next Election: Oct. 2012 (3 year terms)
John Woodward, Mayor
Tammy Todd, Administrator

Torquay
P.O. Box 6
Torquay, SK S0C 2L0
Tel: 306-923-2172; *Fax:* 306-923-2172
villageoftorquay@sasktel.net
Municipal Type: Village
Incorporated: Dec. 11, 1923 *Area:* 1.35 sq km
Population in 2006: 184
Provincial Electoral District(s): Estevan
Federal Electoral District(s): Souris-Moose Mountain
Next Election: Oct. 2012 (3 year terms)
Michael Strachan, Mayor
Thera-Lee Deschner, Administrator

Tramping Lake
P.O. Box 157
Tramping Lake, SK S0K 4H0
Tel: 306-755-2002; *Fax:* 306-755-2022
Municipal Type: Village
Incorporated: April 10, 1917 *Area:* 1.39 sq km
Population in 2006: 60
Provincial Electoral District(s): Kindersley
Federal Electoral District(s): Battlefords-Lloydminster
Next Election: Oct. 2012 (3 year terms)
Joe Fruhstuk, Mayor
Rose Simon, Clerk

Tribune
P.O. Box 61
Tribune, SK S0C 2M0
Tel: 306-456-2213; *Fax:* 306-456-2213
Municipal Type: Village
Incorporated: Feb. 18, 1914 *Area:* 1.61 sq km
Population in 2006: 35
Provincial Electoral District(s): Estevan
Federal Electoral District(s): Souris-Moose Mountain
Next Election: Oct. 2012 (3 year terms)
Glenn Walkeden, Mayor
Dallas Locken, Clerk

Tugaske
P.O. Box 159
Tugaske, SK S0H 4B0
Tel: 306-759-2211; *Fax:* 306-759-2249
info@tugaske.com
www.tugaske.com
Municipal Type: Village
Incorporated: May 7, 1909 *Area:* 0.76 sq km
Population in 2006: 105
Provincial Electoral District(s): Thunder Creek
Federal Electoral District(s): Regina-Lumsden-Lake Centre
Next Election: Oct. 2012 (3 year terms)
Kevin Wilson, Mayor
Daryl Dean, Administrator

Turnor Lake
P.O. Box 130
Turnor Lake, SK S0M 3E0
Tel: 306-894-2080; *Fax:* 306-894-2138
Municipal Type: Northern Hamlet
Incorporated: Oct. 1, 1984 *Area:* 4.62 sq km
Population in 2006: 115
Provincial Electoral District(s): Athabasca
Federal Electoral District(s): Desnethé-Missinippi-Churchill River
Next Election: Oct. 2012 (3 year terms)
Marius Montgrand, Mayor
Doreen Morin, Clerk
doreen9401morin@hotmail.com

Turtleford
P.O. Box 38
Turtleford, SK S0M 2Y0
Tel: 306-845-2156; *Fax:* 306-845-3320
townofturtleford@sasktel.net
Municipal Type: Town
Incorporated: Oct. 9, 1914 *Area:* 1.64 sq km
Population in 2006: 461
Provincial Electoral District(s): Cut Knife-Turtleford
Federal Electoral District(s): Battlefords-Lloydminster
Next Election: Oct. 2012 (3 year terms)
Note: Proclaimed as a town on July 1, 1983.
Roland Olson, Mayor
Deanna M. Kahl Lundberg, Administrator

Tuxford
P.O. Box 28
Tuxford, SK S0H 4C0
Tel: 306-691-0785; *Fax:* 306-395-2767
vtuxford@yahoo.ca
Municipal Type: Village
Incorporated: July 19, 1907 *Area:* 0.62 sq km
Population in 2006: 88
Provincial Electoral District(s): Thunder Creek
Federal Electoral District(s): Regina-Lumsden-Lake Centre
Next Election: Oct. 2012 (3 year terms)
Reg E. McKee, Clerk
Allison Koch, Mayor

Unity
P.O. Box 1030
#2, 100 First Ave. West
Unity, SK S0K 4L0
Tel: 306-228-2621; *Fax:* 306-228-4221
townofunity@sasktel.net
www.townofunity.com
Municipal Type: Town
Incorporated: May 18, 1909 *Area:* 9.77 sq km
Population in 2006: 2,147
Provincial Electoral District(s): Kindersley
Federal Electoral District(s): Battlefords-Lloydminster
Next Election: Oct. 2012 (3 year terms)
Note: Proclaimed as a town on Nov. 1, 1919.
Sylvia Maljan, Mayor
Aileen Garrett, Administrator

Val Marie
P.O. Box 178
Val Marie, SK S0N 2T0
Tel: 306-298-2022; *Fax:* 306-298-2224
villageofvalmarie@sasktel.net
Municipal Type: Village
Incorporated: Sept. 13, 1926 *Area:* 0.42 sq km
Population in 2006: 137
Provincial Electoral District(s): Wood River
Federal Electoral District(s): Cypress Hills-Grasslands
Next Election: Oct. 2012 (3 year terms)
Roland Facette, Mayor
Ken Hollinger, Administrator

Valparaiso
P.O. Box 473
Star City, SK S0E 1P0
Tel: 306-863-2522; *Fax:* 306-863-2255
r.m.starcity@sasktel.net
www.newsaskcfdc.ca/valparaiso.htm
Municipal Type: Village
Incorporated: July 18, 1924 *Area:* 0.69 sq km
Population in 2006: 20
Provincial Electoral District(s): Melfort
Federal Electoral District(s): Prince Albert
Next Election: Oct. 2012 (3 year terms)
Margaret Emro, Mayor
Ann Campbell, Clerk

Vanguard
P.O. Box 187
Vanguard, SK S0N 2V0
Tel: 306-582-2295; *Fax:* 306-582-2296
vill.vanguard@sasktel.net
Municipal Type: Village
Incorporated: July 8, 1912 *Area:* 1.86 sq km
Population in 2006: 152
Provincial Electoral District(s): Wood River
Federal Electoral District(s): Cypress Hills-Grasslands
Next Election: Oct. 2012 (3 year terms)
John Bickner, Mayor
Sandra Englot, Administrator

Vanscoy
P.O. Box 480
109 Main St.
Vanscoy, SK S0L 3J0
Tel: 306-668-2008; *Fax:* 306-978-0237
vanscoy@sasktel.net
Municipal Type: Village
Incorporated: June 17, 1919 *Area:* 1.49 sq km
Population in 2006: 339
Provincial Electoral District(s): Biggar
Federal Electoral District(s): Saskatoon-Rosetown-Biggar
Next Election: Oct. 2012 (3 year terms)
Jerome Robert, Mayor
Dawn Steeves, Administrator

Vibank
P.O. Box 204
101 - 2nd Ave.
Vibank, SK S0G 4Y0
Tel: 306-762-2130; *Fax:* 306-762-4722
village.of.vibank@sasktel.net
www.vibank.ca
Municipal Type: Village
Incorporated: June 23, 1911 *Area:* 0.73 sq km
Population in 2006: 361
Provincial Electoral District(s): Indian Head-Milestone

Federal Electoral District(s): Wascana
Next Election: Oct. 2012 (3 year terms)
Shane Henderson, Mayor
shane.henderson@vibank.ca
Jeanette Schaeffer, Administrator

Viscount
P.O. Box 99
319 Bangor Ave.
Viscount, SK S0K 4M0
Tel: 306-944-2199; *Fax:* 306-944-2198
viscount.office@sasktel.net
www.viscount.ca
Municipal Type: Village
Incorporated: Dec. 17, 1908 *Area:* 1.18 sq km
Population in 2006: 251
Provincial Electoral District(s): Humboldt
Federal Electoral District(s): Blackstrap
Next Election: Oct. 2012 (3 year terms)
Moe Kirzinger, Mayor
Valerie Schlosser, Clerk

Vonda
P.O. Box 308
204 Main St.
Vonda, SK S0K 4N0
Tel: 306-258-2035; *Fax:* 306-258-4420
vonda.to@baudoux.ca
www.townofvonda.ca
Municipal Type: Town
Incorporated: Aug. 29, 1905 *Area:* 2.86 sq km
Population in 2006: 322
Provincial Electoral District(s): Humboldt
Federal Electoral District(s): Saskatoon-Humboldt
Next Election: Oct. 2012 (3 year terms)
Note: Proclaimed as a town on May 6, 1907.
Daniel Sembalerus, Mayor
Linda Denis, Clerk

Wadena
P.O. Box 730
102 Main St. North
Wadena, SK S0A 4J0
Tel: 306-338-2145; *Fax:* 306-338-3804
wadadmin@sasktel.net
www.wadena.ca
Municipal Type: Town
Incorporated: Oct. 6, 1906 *Area:* 2.91 sq km
Population in 2006: 1,315
Provincial Electoral District(s): Kelvington-Wadena
Federal Electoral District(s): Yorkton-Melville
Next Election: Oct. 2012 (3 year terms)
Note: Proclaimed as a town on April 1, 1912.
Greg Linnen, Mayor
Diana Lee, Administrator

Wakaw
P.O. Box 669
121 Main St.
Wakaw, SK S0K 4P0
Tel: 306-233-4223; *Fax:* 306-233-5234
town.wakaw@sasktel.net
www.townofwakaw.com
Municipal Type: Town
Incorporated: Dec. 26, 1911 *Area:* 3.12 sq km
Population in 2006: 864
Provincial Electoral District(s): Batoche
Federal Electoral District(s): Saskatoon-Humboldt
Next Election: Oct. 2012 (3 year terms)
Note: Proclaimed as a town on Aug. 1, 1953.
Ed Kidd, Mayor
Rick Kindrachuk, Administrator

Waldeck
P.O. Box 97
Waldeck, SK S0H 4J0
Tel: 306-773-6275; *Fax:* 306-773-6275
villageofwaldeck@sasktel.net
Municipal Type: Village
Incorporated: Dec. 23, 1913 *Area:* 2 sq km
Population in 2006: 294
Provincial Electoral District(s): Thunder Creek
Federal Electoral District(s): Cypress Hills-Grasslands
Next Election: Oct. 2012 (3 year terms)
Bill Martens, Mayor
Barb Cornelson, Administrator

Waldheim
P.O. Box 460
Waldheim, SK S0K 4R0
Tel: 306-945-2161; *Fax:* 306-945-2360
town.waldheim@sasktel.net
www.waldheim.ca
Municipal Type: Town
Incorporated: June 10, 1912 *Area:* 1.97 sq km
Population in 2006: 868
Provincial Electoral District(s): Martensville
Federal Electoral District(s): Saskatoon-Wanuskewin
Next Election: Oct. 2012 (3 year terms)
Note: Proclaimed as a town on March 1, 1967.
Barbara Schultz, Mayor
D. Chris Adams, Chief Administrative Officer

Waldron
P.O. Box 87
Waldron, SK S0A 4K0
Tel: 306-728-2371;
www.spreda.sk.ca/community_Waldron.htm
Municipal Type: Village
Incorporated: July 17, 1909 *Area:* 1.45 sq km
Population in 2006: 20
Provincial Electoral District(s): Melville-Saltcoats
Federal Electoral District(s): Yorkton-Melville
Next Election: Oct. 2012 (3 year terms)
Raymond Kitch, Mayor
Arlene Maguire, Clerk

Wapella
P.O. Box 189
Wapella, SK S0G 4Z0
Tel: 306-532-4343; *Fax:* 306-532-4342
townofwapella@sasktel.net
www.townofwapella.com
Municipal Type: Town
Incorporated: Dec. 29, 1898 *Area:* 2.56 sq km
Population in 2006: 311
Provincial Electoral District(s): Moosomin
Federal Electoral District(s): Souris-Moose Mountain
Next Election: Oct. 2012 (3 year terms)
Note: Proclaimed as a town on Nov. 20, 1903.
Sandy Hintz, Mayor
Lila R.A. Sippola, Administrator
townoffice@townofwapella.com

Warman
P.O. Box 340
107 Central St. West
Warman, SK S0K 4S0
Tel: 306-933-2133; *Fax:* 306-933-1987
town.warman@sasktel.net
www.townofwarman.ca
Municipal Type: Town
Incorporated: Aug. 3, 1906 *Area:* 5.34 sq km
Population in 2006: 4,764
Provincial Electoral District(s): Martensville
Federal Electoral District(s): Saskatoon-Wanuskewin
Next Election: Oct. 2012 (3 year terms)
Note: Proclaimed as a town on July 1, 1966.
Sheryl Spence, Mayor
Ivan Gabrysh, Chief Administrative officer
ivang@warman.ca

Waseca
Douglas Place
P.O. Box 88
Waseca, SK S0M 3A0
Tel: 306-893-2211; *Fax:* 306-893-4193
villageofwaseca@sasktel.net
Municipal Type: Village
Incorporated: March 15, 1911 *Area:* 0.68 sq km
Population in 2006: 144
Provincial Electoral District(s): Cut Knife-Turtleford
Federal Electoral District(s): Battlefords-Lloydminster
Next Election: Oct. 2012 (3 year terms)
Curtis Sutherland, Mayor
Sandra Sutherland, Administrator

Watrous
P.O. Box 730
Watrous, SK S0K 4T0
Tel: 306-946-3369; *Fax:* 306-946-2974
townofwatrous@sasktel.net
www.townofwatrous.com; www.watrousmanitou.com
Municipal Type: Town
Incorporated: Oct. 15, 1908 *Area:* 11.17 sq km
Population in 2006: 1,743
Provincial Electoral District(s): Arm River-Watrous
Federal Electoral District(s): Blackstrap
Next Election: Oct. 2012 (3 year terms)
Note: Proclaimed as a town on Dec. 30, 1909.
Ed Collins, Mayor
Orrin Redden, Administrator

Watson
P.O. Box 276
Watson, SK S0K 4V0
Tel: 306-287-3224; *Fax:* 306-287-3442
contact@townofwatson.com
www.townofwatson.ca; www.quill-lakes.com/watson/town
Municipal Type: Town
Incorporated: Oct. 6, 1906 *Area:* 2.83 sq km
Population in 2006: 719
Provincial Electoral District(s): Melfort
Federal Electoral District(s): Saskatoon-Humboldt
Next Election: Oct. 2012 (3 year terms)
Note: Proclaimed as a town on Aug. 1, 1908.
Ted Reifferscheid, Mayor
Cathy Coleman, Administrator

Wawota
P.O. Box 58
308 Railway Ave.
Wawota, SK S0G 5A0
Tel: 306-739-2216; *Fax:* 306-739-2216
wawota.town@sasktel.net
www.wawota.com
Municipal Type: Town
Incorporated: Dec. 10, 1907 *Area:* 1.24 sq km
Population in 2006: 522
Provincial Electoral District(s): Cannington
Federal Electoral District(s): Souris-Moose Mountain
Next Election: Oct. 2012 (3 year terms)
Note: Proclaimed as a town on Feb. 1, 1975.
Norman Oliver, Mayor
Diane Smith, Administrator

Webb
P.O. Box 100
Webb, SK S0N 2X0
Tel: 306-674-2230; *Fax:* 306-674-2324
rm138@xplornet.com
Municipal Type: Village
Incorporated: June 18, 1910 *Area:* 1.41 sq km
Population in 2006: 44
Provincial Electoral District(s): Cypress Hills
Federal Electoral District(s): Cypress Hills-Grasslands
Next Election: Oct. 2012 (3 year terms)
John Martens, Mayor
Linda Boser, Administrator

Weekes
P.O. Box 159
Weekes, SK S0E 1V0
Tel: 306-278-2800; *Fax:* 306-278-2395
weekes123@xplornet.ca
www.newsaskcfdc.ca/weekes.htm
Municipal Type: Village
Incorporated: Jan. 13, 1947 *Area:* 0.59 sq km
Population in 2006: 55
Provincial Electoral District(s): Kelvington-Wadena
Federal Electoral District(s): Yorkton-Melville
Next Election: Oct. 2012 (3 year terms)
Kenneth Harris, Mayor
Betty Gagnon, Clerk

Weirdale
General Delivery
Albertville, SK S0J 0A0
Tel: 306-929-2625; *Fax:* 306-929-2197
weirdale@hotmail.com
Municipal Type: Village
Incorporated: April 1, 1948 *Area:* 1.36 sq km
Population in 2006: 83
Provincial Electoral District(s): Saskatchewan Rivers
Federal Electoral District(s): Prince Albert
Next Election: Oct. 2012 (3 year terms)
Rolena Krawec, Mayor
Betty Glatley, Clerk

Weldon
P.O. Box 190
Weldon, SK S0J 3A0
Tel: 306-887-2070; *Fax:* 306-752-3882
weldon@sk.sympatico.ca
www.newsaskcfdc.ca/weldon.htm
Municipal Type: Village
Incorporated: Jan. 24, 1914 *Area:* 1.1 sq km
Population in 2006: 205
Provincial Electoral District(s): Batoche

Federal Electoral District(s): Prince Albert
Next Election: Oct. 2012 (3 year terms)
Brenda Hadland, Mayor
Fanuela Lima, Administrator

Welwyn
P.O. Box 118
Welwyn, SK S0A 4L0
Tel: 306-733-2077; *Fax:* 306-733-2078
welwynvillage@hotmail.com
Municipal Type: Village
Incorporated: June 11, 1907 *Area:* 0.64 sq km
Population in 2006: 142
Provincial Electoral District(s): Moosomin
Federal Electoral District(s): Souris-Moose Mountain
Next Election: Oct. 2012 (3 year terms)
Joe Santer, Mayor
Monica Pethick, Administrator

Weyakwin
P.O. Box 295
Weyakwin Rd.
Weyakwin, SK S0J 1W0
Tel: 306-663-5820; *Fax:* 306-663-5112
weyakwin@sasktel.net
Municipal Type: Northern Hamlet
Incorporated: Dec. 1, 1983 *Area:* 8.2 sq km
Population in 2006: 99
Provincial Electoral District(s): Cumberland
Federal Electoral District(s): Desnethé-Missinippi-Churchill River
Next Election: Oct. 2012 (3 year terms)
Stella Brown, Mayor
Flora Kraus, Clerk

Weyburn No. 67
23 - 6 St. NE
Weyburn, SK S4H 1A7
Tel: 306-842-2314; *Fax:* 306-842-1002
rm.67@sasktel.net
Municipal Type: Municipality
Incorporated: Dec. 13, 1909 *Area:* 811.70 sq km
Population in 2006: 888
Next Election: Oct 2012; staggered 2 yr term
Note: URL:
www.saskbiz.ca/communityprofiles/CommunityProfile.Asp?CommunityID=1024
Carmen Sterling, Reeve
Kim McIvor, Administrator

White City
P.O. Box 220 Main
14 Ramm Ave. East
White City, SK S4L 5B1
Tel: 306-781-2355; *Fax:* 306-781-2194
townoffice@whitecity.ca
www.whitecity.ca
Municipal Type: Town
Incorporated: March 1, 1967 *Area:* 4.64 sq km
Population in 2006: 1,113
Provincial Electoral District(s): Regina Wascana Plains
Federal Electoral District(s): Regina-Qu'Appelle
Next Election: Oct. 2012 (3 year terms)
Note: Proclaimed as a town on Nov. 1, 2000.
Bruce Evans, Mayor
bevans@whitecity.ca
Shauna Bzdel, Office Manager
sbzdel@whitecity.ca

White Fox
P.O. Box 38
116 Main St.
White Fox, SK S0J 3B0
Tel: 306-276-2106; *Fax:* 306-276-2131
villageofwhitefox@sasktel.net
www.whitefox.ca
Municipal Type: Village
Incorporated: July 21, 1941 *Area:* 0.85 sq km
Population in 2006: 348
Provincial Electoral District(s): Saskatchewan Rivers
Federal Electoral District(s): Desnethé-Missinippi-Churchill River
Next Election: Oct. 2012 (3 year terms)
Gary Vidnes, Mayor
Kimberley Issacson, Administrator

Whitewood
P.O. Box 129
731 Lalonde St.
Whitewood, SK S0G 5C0
Tel: 306-735-2210; *Fax:* 306-735-2262
general@townofwhitewood.ca
www.townofwhitewood.ca

Municipal Type: Town
Incorporated: Dec. 31, 1892 *Area:* 3.04 sq km
Population in 2006: 869
Provincial Electoral District(s): Moosomin
Federal Electoral District(s): Souris-Moose Mountain
Next Election: Oct. 2012 (3 year terms)
Malcolm Green, Mayor
Sharon Rodgers, Administrator

Wilcox
P.O. Box 130
Wilcox, SK S0G 5E0
Tel: 306-732-2030; *Fax:* 306-732-4495
rm129@sasktel.net
www.wilcox.ca
Municipal Type: Village
Incorporated: April 20, 1907 *Area:* 1.48 sq km
Population in 2006: 222
Provincial Electoral District(s): Indian Head-Milestone
Federal Electoral District(s): Palliser
Next Election: Oct. 2012 (3 year terms)
Pat Vigneron, Mayor
Kevin Ritchie, Village Clerk

Wilkie
P.O. Box 580
206 - 2nd Ave. West
Wilkie, SK S0K 4W0
Tel: 306-843-2692; *Fax:* 306-843-3151
contact@townofwilkie.com
www.townofwilkie.com
Municipal Type: Town
Incorporated: July 18, 1908 *Area:* 9.48 sq km
Population in 2006: 1,222
Provincial Electoral District(s): Biggar
Federal Electoral District(s): Battlefords-Lloydminster
Next Election: Oct. 2012 (3 year terms)
Note: Proclaimed as a town on Nov. 1, 1910.
Sharon Armstrong, Mayor
Jason Chorneyko, Administrator

Willow Bunch
P.O. Box 189
16 - 5th Edouard Beaupre St. East
Willow Bunch, SK S0H 4K0
Tel: 306-473-2450; *Fax:* 306-473-2773
www.willowbunch.ca
Municipal Type: Town
Incorporated: Nov. 15, 1929 *Area:* 0.84 sq km
Population in 2006: 297
Provincial Electoral District(s): Weyburn-Big Muddy
Federal Electoral District(s): Cypress Hills-Grasslands
Next Election: Oct. 2012 (3 year terms)
Note: Proclaimed as a town on Oct. 1, 1960.
Renaud Bissonnette, Mayor
Margaret L. Brown, Administrator

Willowbrook
P.O. Box 98
Willowbrook, SK S0A 4P0
Municipal Type: Village
Incorporated: March 12, 1919 *Area:* 0.48 sq km
Population in 2006: 46
Provincial Electoral District(s): Yorkton
Federal Electoral District(s): Yorkton-Melville
Next Election: Oct. 2012 (3 year terms)
William Kish, Mayor
Shirley Biro, Clerk

Windthorst
P.O. Box 98
202 Angus St.
Windthorst, SK S0G 5G0
Tel: 306-224-2033; *Fax:* 306-224-4610
village.windthorst@sasktel.net
www.windthorstvillage.ca
Municipal Type: Village
Incorporated: Aug. 21, 1907 *Area:* 1.43 sq km
Population in 2006: 194
Provincial Electoral District(s): Moosomin
Federal Electoral District(s): Souris-Moose Mountain
Next Election: Oct. 2012 (3 year terms)
Norm Jones, Mayor
Denise Swallow, Administrator

Wiseton
P.O. Box 160
Wiseton, SK S0L 3M0
Tel: 306-357-2022; *Fax:* 306-357-2027
villageofwiseton@sasktel.net
Municipal Type: Village
Incorporated: Sept. 23, 1913 *Area:* 0.77 sq km

Population in 2006: 96
Provincial Electoral District(s): Rosetown-Elrose
Federal Electoral District(s): Cypress Hills-Grasslands
Next Election: Oct. 2012 (3 year terms)
Les Meyers, Mayor
Cheryl Joel, Administrator

Wolseley
P.O. Box 310
Wolseley, SK S0G 5H0
Tel: 306-698-2477; *Fax:* 306-698-2953
townofwolseley@sasktel.net; administrator@wolseley.ca
www.wolseley.ca
Municipal Type: Town
Incorporated: Oct. 20, 1898 *Area:* 5.93 sq km
Population in 2006: 782
Provincial Electoral District(s): Moosomin
Federal Electoral District(s): Regina-Qu'Appelle
Next Election: Oct. 2012 (3 year terms)
Denton Keating, Mayor
mayor@wolseley.ca
Ed Attridge, Administrator
edatt@sasktel.net

Wood Mountain
P.O. Box 89
Wood Mountain, SK S0H 4L0
Tel: 306-266-4810; *Fax:* 306-266-2020
wmtvillage@sasktel.net
www.woodmountain.ca
Municipal Type: Village
Incorporated: March 4, 1930 *Area:* 0.61 sq km
Population in 2006: 20
Provincial Electoral District(s): Wood River
Federal Electoral District(s): Cypress Hills-Grasslands
Next Election: Oct. 2012 (3 year terms)
Michael Klein, Mayor
Sherry Mielke, Clerk

Wynyard
P.O. Box 220
435 Bosworth St.
Wynyard, SK S0A 4T0
Tel: 306-554-2123; *Fax:* 306-554-3224
town.office.wynyard@sasktel.net
www.townofwynyard.com
Municipal Type: Town
Incorporated: Oct. 9, 1908 *Area:* 5.29 sq km
Population in 2006: 1,744
Provincial Electoral District(s): Arm River-Watrous
Federal Electoral District(s): Regina-Qu'Appelle
Next Election: Oct. 2012 (3 year terms)
Note: Proclaimed as a town on Nov. 1, 1911.

Yarbo
P.O. Box 96
Yarbo, SK S0A 4V0
Tel: 306-745-3532;
villageofyarbo@sasktel.net
Municipal Type: Village
Incorporated: July 1, 1964 *Area:* 0.83 sq km
Population in 2006: 72
Provincial Electoral District(s): Melville-Saltcoats
Federal Electoral District(s): Yorkton-Melville
Next Election: Oct. 2012 (3 year terms)
Nancy Prazma, Mayor
Leanne Rue, Clerk

Yellow Creek
P.O. Box 219
Yellow Creek, SK S0K 4X0
Tel: 306-279-2191
Municipal Type: Village
Incorporated: May 13, 1943 *Area:* 0.64 sq km
Population in 2006: 45
Provincial Electoral District(s): Batoche
Federal Electoral District(s): Saskatoon-Humboldt
Next Election: Oct. 2012 (3 year terms)
Ken Pacholko, Mayor
Betty Ann Fossen, Clerk

Yellow Grass
P.O. Box 270
102 Coteau Ave. West
Yellow Grass, SK S0G 5J0
Tel: 306-465-2400; *Fax:* 306-465-2802
yellowgrass@signaldirect.ca
www.yellowgrass.ca
Municipal Type: Town
Incorporated: July 22, 1903 *Area:* 2.68 sq km
Population in 2006: 371
Provincial Electoral District(s): Weyburn-Big Muddy

Federal Electoral District(s): Souris-Moose Mountain
Next Election: Oct. 2012 (3 year terms)
Note: Proclaimed as a town on Feb. 15, 1906.
William Wilke, Mayor
Wendy Carver, Administrator

Young
P.O. Box 359
Young, SK S0K 4Y0
Tel: 306-259-2242; *Fax:* 306-259-2247
villageoffice@young.ca
www.young.ca
Municipal Type: Village
Incorporated: June 7, 1910 *Area:* 2.51 sq km
Population in 2006: 263
Provincial Electoral District(s): Arm River-Watrous
Federal Electoral District(s): Blackstrap
Next Election: Oct. 2012 (3 year terms)
Garth Sebelius, Mayor
Belinda Rowan, Administrator

Zealandia
P.O. Box 52
Zealandia, SK S0L 3N0
Tel: 306-882-4177; *Fax:* 306-882-4178
townofzealandia@yahoo.com
Municipal Type: Town
Incorporated: May 22, 1909 *Area:* 1.38 sq km
Population in 2006: 90
Provincial Electoral District(s): Rosetown-Elrose
Federal Electoral District(s): Saskatoon-Rosetown-Biggar
Next Election: Oct. 2012 (3 year terms)
Note: Proclaimed as a town on Nov. 1, 1911.
Darren Haugen, Mayor
Lynn Farquharson, Clerk

Zelma
Zelma GMB #14
Allan, SK S0K 0C0
Tel: 306-257-3927; *Fax:* 306-257-4125
Municipal Type: Village
Incorporated: Aug. 10, 1910 *Area:* 0.72 sq km
Population in 2006: 30
Provincial Electoral District(s): Humboldt
Federal Electoral District(s): Blackstrap
Next Election: Oct. 2012 (3 year terms)
R. Glen Crockett, Mayor
Maxine A. Fischer, Clerk

Zenon Park
P.O. Box 278
Zenon Park, SK S0E 1W0
Tel: 306-767-2233; *Fax:* 306-767-2226
vofzenon@sasktel.net
www.newsaskcfdc.ca/zenonpark.htm
Municipal Type: Village
Incorporated: July 28, 1941 *Area:* 0.56 sq km
Population in 2006: 192
Provincial Electoral District(s): Carrot River Valley
Federal Electoral District(s): Prince Albert
Next Election: Oct. 2012 (3 year terms)
Cory Clapson, Mayor
Lisa e LeBlanc, Administrator

Rural Municipality

Aberdeen No. 373
P.O. Box 40
Aberdeen, SK S0K 0A0
Tel: 306-253-4312; *Fax:* 306-253-4445
rm373@sasktel.net
www.rmofaberdeen.ca
Municipal Type: Rural Municipality
Incorporated: Dec. 13, 1909 *Area:* 673.43 sq km
Population in 2006: 765
Next Election: Oct 2012; staggered 2 yr term
Real Hamoline, Reeve
Gary Dziadyk, Administrator

Abernethy No. 186
P.O. Box 249
Abernethy, SK S0A 0A0
Tel: 306-333-2044; *Fax:* 306-333-2285
rm186@sasktel.net
www.townofbalcarres.ca
Municipal Type: Rural Municipality
Incorporated: Dec. 11, 1911 *Area:* 779.42 sq km
Population in 2006: 375
Next Election: Oct 2012; staggered 2 yr term
George Noble, Reeve
Karissa Lingelbach, Administrator

Antelope Park No. 322
P.O. Box 70
Marengo, SK S0L 2K0
Tel: 306-968-2922; *Fax:* 306-968-2278
rm292.rm322@sasktel.net
Municipal Type: Rural Municipality
Incorporated: Dec. 11, 1911 *Area:* 612.66 sq km
Population in 2006: 151
Next Election: Oct 2012; staggered 2 yr term
Gordon Dommett, Reeve
Shelley Mohr, Administrator

Antler No. 61
P.O. Box 70
Redvers, SK S0C 2H0
Tel: 306-452-3263; *Fax:* 306-452-3518
rm61@sasktel.net
Municipal Type: Rural Municipality
Incorporated: Dec. 13, 1909 *Area:* 832.23 sq km
Population in 2006: 506
Next Election: Oct 2012; staggered 2 yr term
Ron Henderson, Reeve
Mike Wirges, Administrator

Arborfield No. 456
P.O. Box 280
Arborfield, SK S0E 0A0
Tel: 306-769-8533; *Fax:* 306-769-8301
arborfieldrm456@sasktel.net
www.arborfieldsk.ca/council.htm
Municipal Type: Rural Municipality
Incorporated: Jan. 1, 1913 *Area:* 1,416.01 sq km
Population in 2006: 429
Next Election: Oct 2012; staggered 2 yr term
Alec J. Black, Reeve
Allan Frisky, Administrator

Argyle No. 1
P.O. Box 120
Gainsborough, SK S0C 0Z0
Tel: 306-685-2010; *Fax:* 306-685-2161
rm.1@sasktel.net
saskbiz.ca/communityprofiles/communityprofile.asp?CommunityID=753
Municipal Type: Rural Municipality
Incorporated: Dec. 19, 1912 *Area:* 579.99 sq km
Population in 2006: 267
Next Election: Oct 2012; staggered 2 yr term
Robert Meredith, Reeve
Robert L. Trott, Administrator

Arlington No. 79
P.O. Box 1115
264 Centre St.
Shaunavon, SK S0N 2M0
Tel: 306-297-2108; *Fax:* 306-297-2144
rm79@sasktel.net
saskbiz.ca/communityprofiles/CommunityProfile.Asp?CommunityID=754
Municipal Type: Rural Municipality
Incorporated: Jan. 1, 1913 *Area:* 846.79 sq km
Population in 2006: 413
Next Election: Oct 2012; staggered 2 yr term
Donald L. Lundberg, Reeve
Richard E. Goulet, Administrator

Arm River No. 252
P.O. Box 250
Davidson, SK S0G 1A0
Tel: 306-567-3103; *Fax:* 306-567-3266
rm253@sasktel.net
Municipal Type: Rural Municipality
Incorporated: Dec. 13, 1909 *Area:* 725.26 sq km
Population in 2006: 240
Next Election: Oct 2012; staggered 2 yr term
Lorne Willner, Reeve
Yvonne (Bonny) Goodsman, Administrator

Auvergne No. 76
P.O. Box 60
Ponteix, SK S0N 1Z0
Tel: 306-625-3210; *Fax:* 306-625-3681
rm76@sasktel.net
Municipal Type: Rural Municipality
Incorporated: Jan. 1, 1913 *Area:* 853.40 sq km
Population in 2006: 329
Next Election: Oct 2012; staggered 2 yr term
Allan R. Oliver, Reeve
Roxanne Empey, Administrator

Baildon No. 131
P.O. Box 1902
Moose Jaw, SK S6H 7N6
Tel: 306-693-2166; *Fax:* 306-693-2166
rm131@sasktel.net
saskbiz.ca/communityprofiles/CommunityProfile.Asp?CommunityID=757
Municipal Type: Rural Municipality
Incorporated: Dec. 9, 1912 *Area:* 846.21 sq km
Population in 2006: 548
Next Election: Oct 2012; staggered 2 yr term
Sheldon Okerstrom, Reeve
Cal Shaw, Administrator

Barrier Valley No. 397
P.O. Box 246
Archerwill, SK S0E 0B0
Tel: 306-323-2101; *Fax:* 306-323-2106
rm397@sasktel.net
saskbiz.ca/communityprofiles/CommunityProfile.Asp?CommunityID=758
Municipal Type: Rural Municipality
Incorporated: Oct. 29, 1917 *Area:* 819.99 sq km
Population in 2006: 576
Next Election: Oct 2012; staggered 2 yr term
Quentin Ralph Hanson, Reeve
Glenda Smith, Administrator

Battle River No. 438
P.O. Box 159
Battleford, SK S0M 0E0
Tel: 306-937-2235; *Fax:* 306-937-2235
rm438@sasktel.net
saskbiz.ca/communityprofiles/CommunityProfile.Asp?CommunityID=759
Municipal Type: Rural Municipality
Incorporated: Dec. 12, 1910 *Area:* 1,061.40 sq km
Population in 2006: 1,053
Next Election: Oct 2012; staggered 2 yr term
Joseph Beckman, Reeve
Betty Johnson, Administrator

Bayne No. 371
P.O. Box 130
Bruno, SK S0K 0S0
Tel: 306-369-2511; *Fax:* 306-369-2528
rm371@sasktel.net
saskbiz.ca/communityprofiles/communityprofile.asp?CommunityID=760
Municipal Type: Rural Municipality
Incorporated: Dec. 12, 1910 *Area:* 802.93 sq km
Population in 2006: 505
Next Election: Oct 2012; staggered 2 yr term
Gerald Picouye, Reeve
Lonnie Sowa, Administrator

Beaver River No. 622
P.O. Box 129
159 Main St.
Pierceland, SK S0M 2K0
Tel: 306-839-2060; *Fax:* 306-839-2178
rm622@sasktel.net
www.rmofbeaverriver622.ca
Municipal Type: Rural Municipality
Incorporated: Jan. 1, 1978 *Area:* 2,370.25 sq km
Population in 2006: 1,108
Next Election: Oct 2012; staggered 2 yr term
Murray Rausch, Reeve
Rita Rogers, Administrator

Bengough No. 40
P.O. Box 429
Bengough, SK S0C 0K0
Tel: 306-268-2055; *Fax:* 306-268-2054
rm40@sasktel.net
www.rm40.com
Municipal Type: Rural Municipality
Incorporated: Jan. 1, 1913 *Area:* 1,036.91 sq km
Population in 2006: 337
Next Election: Oct 2012; staggered 2 yr term
Terry Gravelle, Reeve
Lara Scott, Administrator

Benson No. 35
P.O. Box 69
Benson, SK S0C 0L0
Tel: 306-634-9410; *Fax:* 306-634-8804
rm35@sasktel.net
saskbiz.ca/communityprofiles/CommunityProfile.Asp?CommunityID=762
Municipal Type: Rural Municipality
Incorporated: Dec. 13, 1909 *Area:* 836.39 sq km

Population in 2006: 434
Next Election: Oct 2012; staggered 2 yr term
David Hoffort, Reeve
Laureen Keating, Administrator

Big Arm No. 251
P.O. Box 10
Stalwart, SK S0G 4R0
Tel: 306-963-2402; *Fax:* 306-963-2405
rm251@sasktel.net
saskbiz.ca/communityprofiles/communityprofile.asp?CommunityID=763
Municipal Type: Rural Municipality
Incorporated: Dec. 11, 1911 *Area:* 699.47 sq km
Population in 2006: 237
Next Election: Oct 2012; staggered 2 yr term
Paul Remlinger, Reeve
Yvonne (Bonny) Goodsman, Administrator

Big Quill No. 308
P.O. Box 898
Wynyard, SK S0A 4T0
Tel: 306-554-2533; *Fax:* 306-554-3935
rm308@sasktel.net
Municipal Type: Rural Municipality
Incorporated: Dec. 13, 1909 *Area:* 739.86 sq km
Population in 2006: 635
Next Election: Oct 2012; staggered 2 yr term
Eugene McSymytz, Reeve
Gail Wolfe, Administrator

Big River No. 555
P.O. Box 219
Big River, SK S0J 0E0
Tel: 306-469-2323; *Fax:* 306-469-2428
rm555@sasktel.net
www.bigriver.ca/rm.html
Municipal Type: Rural Municipality
Incorporated: Oct. 1, 1977 *Area:* 2,488.22 sq km
Population in 2006: 851
Next Election: Oct 2012; staggered 2 yr term
Doug Panter, Reeve
Donna Tymiak, Administrator

Big Stick No. 141
P.O. Box 9
Golden Prairie, SK S0N 0Y0
Tel: 306-662-2883; *Fax:* 306-662-3954
rm141@sasktel.net
Municipal Type: Rural Municipality
Incorporated: Dec. 11, 1911 *Area:* 821.40 sq km
Population in 2006: 182
Next Election: Oct 2012; staggered 2 yr term
Edward Feil, Reeve
Quinton Jacksteit, Administrator

Biggar No. 347
P.O. Box 280
Biggar, SK S0K 0M0
Tel: 306-948-2422; *Fax:* 306-948-2250
rm347@sasktel.net
Municipal Type: Rural Municipality
Incorporated: Dec. 11, 1911 *Area:* 1,597.87 sq km
Population in 2006: 867
Next Election: Oct 2012; staggered 2 yr term
Louise Singer, Reeve
Adrienne Urban, Administrator

Birch Hills No. 460
P.O. Box 369
Birch Hills, SK S0J 0G0
Tel: 306-749-2233; *Fax:* 306-749-2220
rm460@sasktel.net
Municipal Type: Rural Municipality
Incorporated: Dec. 11, 1911 *Area:* 554.52 sq km
Population in 2006: 701
Next Election: Oct 2012; staggered 2 yr term
Earl Mickelson, Reeve
Sandra Barber, Administrator

Bjorkdale No. 426
P.O. Box 10
Crooked River, SK S0E 0R0
Tel: 306-873-2470; *Fax:* 306-873-2470
rm.426.bjork@xplornet.com
saskbiz.ca/communityprofiles/CommunityProfile.Asp?CommunityID=769
Municipal Type: Rural Municipality
Incorporated: Jan. 1, 1913 *Area:* 1,458.79 sq km
Population in 2006: 997
Next Election: Oct 2012; staggered 2 yr term
Wayne Dmytriw, Reeve
Lisa Hamelin, Administrator

Blaine Lake No. 434
P.O. Box 38
Blaine Lake, SK S0J 0J0
Tel: 306-497-2282; *Fax:* 306-497-2511
rm434@sasktel.net
saskbiz.ca/communityprofiles/CommunityProfile.Asp?CommunityID=770
Municipal Type: Rural Municipality
Incorporated: Dec. 9, 1912 *Area:* 799.89 sq km
Population in 2006: 302
Next Election: Oct 2012; staggered 2 yr term
Eugene Chudskov, Reeve
Tony Obrigewitch, Administrator

Blucher No. 343
P.O. Box 100
Bradwell, SK S0K 0P0
Tel: 306-257-3344; *Fax:* 306-257-3303
rm343@sasktel.net
www.rm343.com
Municipal Type: Rural Municipality
Incorporated: Dec. 13, 1909 *Area:* 789.28 sq km
Population in 2006: 1,593
Next Election: Oct 2012; staggered 2 yr term
Daniel Greschuk, Reeve
R. Doran Scott, Administrator

Bone Creek No. 108
P.O. Box 459
Shaunavon, SK S0N 2M0
Tel: 306-297-2570; *Fax:* 306-297-6270
rmbc@sasktel.net
Municipal Type: Rural Municipality
Incorporated: Dec. 11, 1911 *Area:* 847.16 sq km
Population in 2006: 321
Next Election: Oct 2012; staggered 2 yr term
Ben Lewans, Reeve
Rhonda Bellefeuille, Administrator

Bratt's Lake No. 129
P.O. Box 130
Wilcox, SK S0G 5E0
Tel: 306-732-2030; *Fax:* 306-732-4495
rm129@sasktel.net
Municipal Type: Rural Municipality
Incorporated: Jan. 1, 1913 *Area:* 844.94 sq km
Population in 2006: 362
Next Election: Oct 2012; staggered 2 yr term
J. Barry Hamdorf, Reeve
Kevin S. Ritchie, Administrator

Britannia No. 502
P.O. Box 661
4824 - 47th St.
Lloydminster, SK S9V 0Y7
Tel: 306-825-2610; *Fax:* 306-825-8894
rm502@sasktel.net
www.rmbritannia.com
Municipal Type: Rural Municipality
Incorporated: Dec. 13, 1909 *Area:* 950.87 sq km
Population in 2006: 1,501
Next Election: Oct 2012; staggered 2 yr term
Neil Johnson, Reeve
Patti Volk, Clerk
patti.rm502@sasktel.net

Brock No. 64
P.O. Box 247
Kisbey, SK S0C 1L0
Tel: 306-462-2010; *Fax:* 306-462-2016
rm64@signaldirect.ca
saskbiz.ca/communityprofiles/communityprofile.asp?CommunityID=775
Municipal Type: Rural Municipality
Incorporated: Dec. 12, 1910 *Area:* 827.53 sq km
Population in 2006: 279
Next Election: Oct 2012; staggered 2 yr term
Paul Cameron, Reeve
Michael Rattray, Administrator

Brokenshell No. 68
23 - 6th St. NE
Weyburn, SK S4H 1A7
Tel: 306-842-2314; *Fax:* 306-842-1002
rm.67@sasktel.net
saskbiz.ca/communityprofiles/CommunityProfile.Asp?CommunityID=776
Municipal Type: Rural Municipality
Incorporated: Dec. 13, 1909 *Area:* 850.01 sq km
Population in 2006: 324
Next Election: Oct 2012; staggered 2 yr term
Don Watson, Reeve
Kim McIvor, Administrator

Browning No. 34
P.O. Box 40
Lampman, SK S0C 1N0
Tel: 306-487-2444; *Fax:* 306-487-2496
browning.lampman@sasktel.net
saskbiz.ca/communityprofiles/communityprofile.asp?CommunityID=777
Municipal Type: Rural Municipality
Incorporated: Dec. 11, 1911 *Area:* 823.39 sq km
Population in 2006: 426
Next Election: Oct 2012; staggered 2 yr term
Randy Fleck, Reeve
Greg Wallin, Administrator

Buchanan No. 304
P.O. Box 10
Buchanan, SK S0A 0J0
Tel: 306-592-2055; *Fax:* 306-592-4436
rm304@sasktel.net
Municipal Type: Rural Municipality
Incorporated: Jan. 1, 1913 *Area:* 738.80 sq km
Population in 2006: 435
Next Election: Oct 2012; staggered 2 yr term
Gerald Wolkowski, Reeve
Twila Hadubiak, Administrator

Buckland No. 491
99 River St. East
Prince Albert, SK S6V 0A1
Tel: 306-763-2585; *Fax:* 306-763-6369
rm491@sasktel.net
www.rmbuckland.ca
Municipal Type: Rural Municipality
Incorporated: Dec. 11, 1911 *Area:* 791.55 sq km
Population in 2006: 3,429
Next Election: Oct 2012; staggered 2 yr term
Wes Stubbs, Reeve
reeve@rmbuckland.ca
Wendy Gowda, Administrator

Buffalo No. 409
P.O. Box 100
Wilkie, SK S0K 4W0
Tel: 306-843-2342; *Fax:* 306-843-2455
rm409@sasktel.net
saskbiz.ca/communityprofiles/communityprofile.asp?CommunityID=780
Municipal Type: Rural Municipality
Incorporated: Dec. 13, 1909 *Area:* 1,222.08 sq km
Population in 2006: 525
Next Election: Oct 2012; staggered 2 yr term
Leslie Krochinski, Reeve
Sherry Huber, Administrator

Calder No. 241
P.O. Box 10
Wroxton, SK S0A 4S0
Tel: 306-742-4233; *Fax:* 306-742-4559
calderrm@sasktel.net
Municipal Type: Rural Municipality
Incorporated: Jan. 1, 1913 *Area:* 807.15 sq km
Population in 2006: 423
Next Election: Oct 2012; staggered 2 yr term
Dennis Elaschuk, Reeve
Linda Napady, Administrator

Caledonia No. 99
P.O. Box 328
Milestone, SK S0G 3L0
Tel: 306-436-2050; *Fax:* 306-436-2051
milcal@sasktel.net
saskbiz.ca/communityprofiles/communityprofile.asp?CommunityID=782
Municipal Type: Rural Municipality
Incorporated: Dec. 13, 1909 *Area:* 845.68 sq km
Population in 2006: 286
Next Election: Oct 2012; staggered 2 yr term
Richard Linton, Reeve
Stephen Schury, Administrator

Cambria No. 6
P.O. Box 210
Torquay, SK S0C 2L0
Tel: 306-923-2000; *Fax:* 306-923-2099
rm.cambria@sasktel.net
saskbiz.ca/communityprofiles/CommunityProfile.Asp?CommunityID=783
Municipal Type: Rural Municipality
Incorporated: Dec. 13, 1909 *Area:* 814.14 sq km
Population in 2006: 268
Next Election: Oct 2012; staggered 2 yr term

James Phillips, Reeve
Graham Bell, Administrator

Cana No. 214
P.O. Box 550
Melville, SK S0A 2P0
Tel: 306-728-5645; *Fax:* 306-728-3807
rmcana@sasktel.net
www.spreda.sk.ca/community_RM_of_Cana.htm
Municipal Type: Rural Municipality
Incorporated: Dec. 13, 1909 *Area:* 820.81 sq km
Population in 2006: 850
Next Election: Oct 2012; staggered 2 yr term
Gordon Steffan, Reeve
Audrey Law, Administrator

Canaan No. 225
P.O. Box 99
Lucky Lake, SK S0L 1Z0
Tel: 306-858-2234; *Fax:* 306-858-2234
rm225.vll@sasktel.net
Municipal Type: Rural Municipality
Incorporated: Jan. 1, 1913 *Area:* 549.09 sq km
Population in 2006: 165
Next Election: Oct 2012; staggered 2 yr term
William Sheppard, Reeve
D.B. (Blair) Cleaveley, Administrator

Canwood No. 494
P.O. Box 10
Canwood, SK S0J 0K0
Tel: 306-468-2014; *Fax:* 306-468-2666
rm494@sasktel.net
Municipal Type: Rural Municipality
Incorporated: Jan. 1, 1913 *Area:* 1,945.20 sq km
Population in 2006: 1,535
Next Election: Oct 2012; staggered 2 yr term
Jason Bischler, Reeve
Lorna Benson, Administrator

Carmichael No. 109
P.O. Box 420
Gull Lake, SK S0N 1A0
Tel: 306-672-3501; *Fax:* 306-672-3295
rm109@sasktel.net
saskbiz.ca/communityprofiles/CommunityProfile.Asp?CommunityID=787
Municipal Type: Rural Municipality
Incorporated: Dec. 9, 1912 *Area:* 846.40 sq km
Population in 2006: 450
Next Election: Oct 2012; staggered 2 yr term
Howard Wedrick, Reeve
Collette Jones, Administrator

Caron No. 162
P.O. Box 85
Caron, SK S0H 0R0
Tel: 306-756-2353; *Fax:* 306-756-2250
rm162@sasktel.net
saskbiz.ca/communityprofiles/CommunityProfile.Asp?CommunityID=788
Municipal Type: Rural Municipality
Incorporated: Dec. 9, 1912 *Area:* 569.87 sq km
Population in 2006: 500
Next Election: Oct 2012; staggered 2 yr term
Gregory McKeown, Reeve
Sandra Thatcher, Administrator

Chaplin No. 164
P.O. Box 60
Chaplin, SK S0H 0V0
Tel: 306-395-2244; *Fax:* 306-395-2767
rm164@sasktel.net
saskbiz.ca/communityprofiles/CommunityProfile.Asp?CommunityID=789
Municipal Type: Rural Municipality
Incorporated: Jan. 1, 1913 *Area:* 802.74 sq km
Population in 2006: 138
Next Election: Oct 2012; staggered 2 yr term
Duane Doell, Reeve
Tammy Knight, Administrator

Chester No. 125
P.O. Box 180
Glenavon, SK S0G 1Y0
Tel: 306-429-2110; *Fax:* 306-429-2260
rmchester125@sasktel.net
saskbiz.ca/communityprofiles/communityprofile.asp?CommunityID=791
Municipal Type: Rural Municipality
Incorporated: Dec. 13, 1909 *Area:* 837.08 sq km
Population in 2006: 386
Next Election: Oct 2012; staggered 2 yr term
Stan Muchowski, Reeve
James R. Hoff, Administrator

Chesterfield No. 261
P.O. Box 70
Eatonia, SK S0L 0Y0
Tel: 306-967-2222; *Fax:* 306-967-2424
rm261@sasktel.net
saskbiz.ca/communityprofiles/CommunityProfile.Asp?CommunityID=790
Municipal Type: Rural Municipality
Incorporated: Dec. 9, 1912 *Area:* 1,942.72 sq km
Population in 2006: 475
Next Election: Oct 2012; staggered 2 yr term
Dennis Hyland, Reeve
Beverly Dahl, Administrator

Churchbridge No. 211
P.O. Box 211
Churchbridge, SK S0A 0M0
Tel: 306-896-2522; *Fax:* 306-896-2743
rmchurchbridge@sasktel.net
Municipal Type: Rural Municipality
Incorporated: Jan. 1, 1913 *Area:* 958.98 sq km
Population in 2006: 679
Next Election: Oct 2012; staggered 2 yr term
Neil Mehrer, Reeve
Brenda A. Goulden, Administrator

Clayton No. 333
P.O. Box 220
Hyas, SK S0A 1K0
Tel: 306-594-2832; *Fax:* 306-594-2944
rm333@sasktel.net
Municipal Type: Rural Municipality
Incorporated: Jan. 1, 1913 *Area:* 1,401.69 sq km
Population in 2006: 753
Next Election: Oct 2012; staggered 2 yr term
Wayne Lazaruk, Reeve
Kelly Kim Smith, Administrator

Clinworth No. 230
P.O. Box 120
Sceptre, SK S0N 2H0
Tel: 306-623-4229; *Fax:* 306-623-4229
rm230@xplornet.com
Municipal Type: Rural Municipality
Incorporated: Dec. 9, 1912 *Area:* 1,432.75 sq km
Population in 2006: 228
Next Election: Oct 2012; staggered 2 yr term
Ken Dietz, Reeve
Sherry Egeland, Administrator

Coalfields No. 4
P.O. Box 190
Bienfait, SK S0C 0M0
Tel: 306-388-2723; *Fax:* 306-388-2330
rm.04@sasktel.net
saskbiz.ca/communityprofiles/communityprofile.asp?CommunityID=795
Municipal Type: Rural Municipality
Incorporated: Jan. 1, 1913 *Area:* 819.76 sq km
Population in 2006: 396
Next Election: Oct 2012; staggered 2 yr term
Stanley Lainton, Reeve
Valerie Pelton, Administrator

Colonsay No. 342
P.O. Box 130
100 Jura St.
Colonsay, SK S0K 0Z0
Tel: 306-255-2233; *Fax:* 306-255-2291
rm342@sasktel.net
www.townofcolonsay.ca/rural-municipality
Municipal Type: Rural Municipality
Incorporated: Dec. 13, 1909 *Area:* 549.99 sq km
Population in 2006: 275
Next Election: Oct 2012; staggered 2 yr term
Jerry Spoatyk, Reeve
Deborah Prosper, Administrator

Connaught No. 457
P.O. Box 25
Tisdale, SK S0E 1T0
Tel: 306-873-2657; *Fax:* 306-873-4442
rm457@sasktel.net
saskbiz.ca/communityprofiles/CommunityProfile.Asp?CommunityID=797
Municipal Type: Rural Municipality
Incorporated: Dec. 11, 1911 *Area:* 853.11 sq km
Population in 2006: 656
Next Election: Oct 2012; staggered 2 yr term
Francis Chabot, Reeve
Tamie Jack, Administrator

Corman Park No. 344
111 Pinehouse Dr.
Saskatoon, SK S7K 5W1
Tel: 306-242-9303; *Fax:* 306-242-6965
rm344@rmcormanpark.ca
www.rmcormanpark.ca
Municipal Type: Rural Municipality
Incorporated: Jan. 1, 1970 *Area:* 1,978.14 sq km
Population in 2006: 8,349
Next Election: Oct 2012; staggered 2 yr term
Mel Henry, Reeve

Cote No. 271
P.O. Box 669
Kamsack, SK S0A 1S0
Tel: 306-542-2121; *Fax:* 306-542-2428
rm271@sasktel.net
Municipal Type: Rural Municipality
Incorporated: Dec. 12, 1910 *Area:* 880.23 sq km
Population in 2006: 551
Next Election: Oct 2012; staggered 2 yr term
Jim Tomochko, Reeve
Wendy Becenko, Administrator

Coteau No. 255
P.O. Box 30
Birsay, SK S0L 0G0
Tel: 306-573-2047; *Fax:* 306-573-2111
rm255@sasktel.net
Municipal Type: Rural Municipality
Incorporated: Dec. 12, 1910 *Area:* 899.27 sq km
Population in 2006: 468
Next Election: Oct 2012; staggered 2 yr term
Clayton Ylioja, Reeve
Linda Van Den Bosch, Administrator

Coulee No. 136
1680 Chaplin St. East
Swift Current, SK S9H 1K8
Tel: 306-773-5420; *Fax:* 306-773-1859
rm136@sasktel.net
Municipal Type: Rural Municipality
Incorporated: Dec. 12, 1910 *Area:* 842.95 sq km
Population in 2006: 509
Next Election: Oct 2012; staggered 2 yr term
Greg Targerson, Reeve
Laurel Dyck, Administrator

Craik No. 222
P.O. Box 420
Craik, SK S0G 0V0
Tel: 306-734-2242; *Fax:* 306-734-2257
rm222@sasktel.net
www.craik.ca/rm222.html
Municipal Type: Rural Municipality
Incorporated: Dec. 9, 1912 *Area:* 883.02 sq km
Population in 2006: 288
Next Election: Oct 2012; staggered 2 yr term
Hilton Spencer, Reeve
JoAnne Yates, Administrator

Cupar No. 218
P.O. Box 400
Cupar, SK S0G 0Y0
Tel: 306-723-4726; *Fax:* 306-723-4726
rm218@sasktel.net
saskbiz.ca/communityprofiles/communityprofile.asp?CommunityID=803
Municipal Type: Rural Municipality
Incorporated: Dec. 13, 1909 *Area:* 919.01 sq km
Population in 2006: 502
Next Election: Oct 2012; staggered 2 yr term
Raymond Orb, Reeve
Loretta Young, Administrator

Cut Knife No. 439
P.O. Box 70
Cut Knife, SK S0M 0N0
Tel: 306-398-2353; *Fax:* 306-398-2839
rm439@sasktel.net
saskbiz.ca/communityprofiles/communityprofile.asp?CommunityID=804
Municipal Type: Rural Municipality
Incorporated: Dec. 13, 1909 *Area:* 651.43 sq km
Population in 2006: 390
Next Election: Oct 2012; staggered 2 yr term
Milton Bingham, Reeve
Donald McCallum, Administrator

Cymri No. 36
P.O. Box 238
Midale, SK S0C 1S0
Tel: 306-458-2244; *Fax:* 306-458-2699
rmcymri@sasktel.net
saskbiz.ca/communityprofiles/CommunityProfile.Asp?CommunityID=805
Municipal Type: Rural Municipality
Incorporated: Dec. 13, 1909 *Area:* 832.36 sq km
Population in 2006: 455
Next Election: Oct 2012; staggered 2 yr term
Joe Vilcu, Reeve
Pamela Scott, Administrator

Deer Forks No. 232
P.O. Box 250
Burstall, SK S0N 0H0
Tel: 306-679-2000; *Fax:* 306-679-2275
rm232@sasktel.net
Municipal Type: Rural Municipality
Incorporated: Jan. 1, 1913 *Area:* 735.49 sq km
Population in 2006: 213
Next Election: Oct 2012; staggered 2 yr term
Doug Smith, Reeve
Tim C. Lozinsky, Administrator

Douglas No. 436
P.O. Box 964
Speers, SK S0M 2V0
Tel: 306-246-2171; *Fax:* 306-246-2173
rm436@littleloon.ca
saskbiz.ca/communityprofiles/CommunityProfile.Asp?CommunityID=807
Municipal Type: Rural Municipality
Incorporated: Dec. 13, 1909 *Area:* 820.37 sq km
Population in 2006: 383
Next Election: Oct 2012; staggered 2 yr term
Nick W. Partyka, Reeve
Charles W. Linnell, Administrator

Duck Lake No. 463
P.O. Box 250
Duck Lake, SK S0K 1J0
Tel: 306-467-2011; *Fax:* 306-476-4423
rm463@sasktel.net
ducklake.ca
Municipal Type: Rural Municipality
Incorporated: Jan. 1, 1913 *Area:* 1,046.57 sq km
Population in 2006: 776
Next Election: Oct 2012; staggered 2 yr term
Cathy Appelgren, Reeve
Amanda Harris, Administrator

Dufferin No. 190
P.O. Box 67
Bethune, SK S0G 0H0
Tel: 306-638-3112; *Fax:* 306-638-3102
190@sasktel.net
www.villageofbethune.com/pages/dufferin.php
Municipal Type: Rural Municipality
Incorporated: Dec. 9, 1912 *Area:* 961.44 sq km
Population in 2006: 540
Next Election: Oct 2012; staggered 2 yr term
Donald McDonald, Reeve
Rodney Audette, Administrator

Dundurn No. 314
P.O. Box 159
314 - 2nd St.
Dundurn, SK S0K 1K0
Tel: 306-492-2132; *Fax:* 306-492-4758
rm314@sasktel.net
www.rmdundurn.ca
Municipal Type: Rural Municipality
Incorporated: Dec. 13, 1909 *Area:* 800.91 sq km
Population in 2006: 632
Next Election: Oct 2012; staggered 2 yr term
R. Fred Wilson, Reeve
Violet P. Barna, Administrator

Eagle Creek No. 376
P.O. Box 278
Asquith, SK S0K 0J0
Tel: 306-237-4424; *Fax:* 306-237-4294
rm376eaglecreek@xplornet.ca
Municipal Type: Rural Municipality
Incorporated: Dec. 13, 1909 *Area:* 833.08 sq km
Population in 2006: 552
Next Election: Oct 2012; staggered 2 yr term
M.J. Northcote, Reeve
Lloyd Cross, Administrator

Edenwold No. 158
P.O. Box 10
Balgonie, SK S0G 0E0
Tel: 306-771-2522; *Fax:* 306-771-2631
rm158@sasktel.net
www.rmedenwold.ca
Municipal Type: Rural Municipality
Incorporated: Dec. 9, 1912 *Area:* 882.67 sq km
Population in 2006: 3,611
Next Election: Oct 2012; staggered 2 yr term
Mitchell Huber, Reeve
Gail Sloan, Administrator

Elcapo No. 154
P.O. Box 668
Broadview, SK S0G 0K0
Tel: 306-696-2474; *Fax:* 306-696-3573
rm154@sasktel.net
Municipal Type: Rural Municipality
Incorporated: Dec. 12, 1910 *Area:* 846.54 sq km
Population in 2006: 489
Next Election: Oct 2012; staggered 2 yr term
Larry Parrott, Reeve
Mervin J. Schmidt, Administrator

Eldon No. 471
P.O. Box 130
212 Main St.
Maidstone, SK S0M 1M0
Tel: 306-893-2391; *Fax:* 306-893-4644
rm471@sasktel.net
www.rmeldon.ca
Municipal Type: Rural Municipality
Incorporated: Dec. 13, 1909 *Area:* 1,007.59 sq km
Population in 2006: 750
Next Election: Oct 2012; staggered 2 yr term
Garry Taylor, Reeve
Ken E. Reiter, Administrator

Elfros No. 307
P.O. Box 40
Elfros, SK S0A 0V0
Tel: 306-328-2011; *Fax:* 306-328-4490
rm307@sasktel.net
Municipal Type: Rural Municipality
Incorporated: Dec. 13, 1909 *Area:* 696.71 sq km
Population in 2006: 481
Next Election: Oct 2012; staggered 2 yr term
Henry Bzdel, Reeve
Glenn Thompson, Administrator

Elmsthorpe No. 100
P.O. Box 240
Avonlea, SK S0H 0C0
Tel: 306-868-2221; *Fax:* 306-868-2040
rm.100@sasktel.net
saskbiz.ca/communityprofiles/communityprofile.asp?CommunityID=816
Municipal Type: Rural Municipality
Incorporated: Dec. 12, 1910 *Area:* 843.12 sq km
Population in 2006: 258
Next Election: Oct 2012; staggered 2 yr term
Tim Forer, Administrator
Ken Miller, Reeve

Emerald No. 277
P.O. Box 160
Wishart, SK S0A 4R0
Tel: 306-576-2002; *Fax:* 306-576-2132
rm277@sasktel.net
www.rm277emerald.ca
Municipal Type: Rural Municipality
Incorporated: Dec. 12, 1910 *Area:* 854.44 sq km
Population in 2006: 549
Next Election: Oct 2012; staggered 2 yr term
Morris Karakochuk, Reeve
Sharolyn Prisiak, Administrator

Enfield No. 194
P.O. Box 70
Central Butte, SK S0H 0T0
Tel: 306-796-2025; *Fax:* 306-796-2025
rm194@sasktel.net
Municipal Type: Rural Municipality
Incorporated: Dec. 13, 1909 *Area:* 1,014.10 sq km
Population in 2006: 301
Next Election: Oct 2012; staggered 2 yr term
Ron Kurz, Reeve
Joe Van Leuken, Administrator

Enniskillen No. 3
P.O. Box 179
307 Main St.
Oxbow, SK S0C 2B0
Tel: 306-483-2277; *Fax:* 306-483-2598
rm3@sasktel.net
www.oxbow.ca/rm-of-enniskillen
Municipal Type: Rural Municipality
Incorporated: Dec. 13, 1909 *Area:* 834.78 sq km
Population in 2006: 430
Next Election: Oct 2012; staggered 2 yr term
Brian Northeast, Reeve
Myrna-Jean Babbings, Administrator

Enterprise No. 142
P.O. Box 150
Richmound, SK S0N 2E0
Tel: 306-669-2000; *Fax:* 306-669-2052
rm142@sasktel.net
Municipal Type: Rural Municipality
Incorporated: April 18, 1913 *Area:* 988.80 sq km
Population in 2006: 160
Next Election: Oct 2012; staggered 2 yr term
Wayne Freitag, Reeve
Rolande Davis, Administrator

Estevan No. 5
#1, 322 - 4th St.
Estevan, SK S4A 2B7
Tel: 306-634-2222; *Fax:* 306-634-2223
rm5@sasktel.net
saskbiz.ca/communityprofiles/communityprofile.asp?CommunityID=821
Municipal Type: Rural Municipality
Incorporated: Dec. 12, 1910 *Area:* 774.67 sq km
Population in 2006: 1,051
Next Election: Oct 2012; staggered 2 yr term
Kelly Lafrentz, Reeve
Greg Hoffort, Administrator

Excel No. 71
P.O. Box 100
Viceroy, SK S0H 4H0
Tel: 306-268-4555; *Fax:* 306-268-4547
rm71@sasktel.net
saskbiz.ca/communityprofiles/communityprofile.asp?CommunityID=745
Municipal Type: Rural Municipality
Incorporated: Jan. 1, 1913 *Area:* 1,122.02 sq km
Population in 2006: 466
Next Election: Oct 2012; staggered 2 yr term
Glenn Roszell, Reeve
Mervin A. Guillemin, Administrator

Excelsior No. 166
P.O. Box 180
Rush Lake, SK S0H 3S0
Tel: 306-784-3121; *Fax:* 306-784-3479
rm166@sasktel.net
Municipal Type: Rural Municipality
Incorporated: Dec. 13, 1909 *Area:* 1,198.35 sq km
Population in 2006: 825
Next Election: Oct 2012; staggered 2 yr term
Harold Martens, Reeve
Christina Patoine, Administrator

Eye Hill No. 382
P.O. Box 69
Macklin, SK S0L 2C0
Tel: 306-753-2075; *Fax:* 306-753-2304
rm382@sasktel.net
saskbiz.ca/communityprofiles/CommunityProfile.Asp?CommunityID=823
Municipal Type: Rural Municipality
Incorporated: Dec. 12, 1910 *Area:* 797.96 sq km
Population in 2006: 650
Next Election: Oct 2012; staggered 2 yr term
Robert Brost, Reeve
Jason Pilat, Administrator

Eyebrow No. 193
P.O. Box 99
Eyebrow, SK S0H 1L0
Tel: 306-759-2101; *Fax:* 306-759-2026
rm193@sasktel.net
saskbiz.ca/communityprofiles/CommunityProfile.Asp?CommunityID=746
Municipal Type: Rural Municipality
Incorporated: Dec. 13, 1909 *Area:* 835.04 sq km
Population in 2006: 245
Next Election: Oct 2012; staggered 2 yr term
Raymond L. Carrick, Reeve

Chris Bueckert, Administrator

Fertile Belt No. 183
P.O. Box 190
100 Ohlen St.
Stockholm, SK S0A 3Y0
Tel: 306-793-2061; *Fax:* 306-793-2063
rm183@sasktel.net
www.yellowheadreda.com/rmfertilebelt.htm
Municipal Type: Rural Municipality
Incorporated: January 1, 1913 *Area:* 1,006.68 sq km
Population in 2006: 771
Next Election: Oct 2012; staggered 2 yr term
Robert Richards, Reeve
Lorie Jackson, Acting Administrator

Fertile Valley No. 285
P.O. Box 70
Conquest, SK S0L 0L0
Tel: 306-856-2037; *Fax:* 306-856-2211
rmfv285@yourlink.ca
Municipal Type: Rural Municipality
Incorporated: Dec. 13, 1909 *Area:* 1,016.37 sq km
Population in 2006: 609
Next Election: Oct 2012; staggered 2 yr term
Alvin Barrington, Reeve
L. Jean Jones, Administrator

Fillmore No. 96
P.O. Box 130
Fillmore, SK S0G 1N0
Tel: 306-722-3251; *Fax:* 306-722-3775
rm96@sasktel.net
saskbiz.ca/communityprofiles/CommunityProfile.Asp?CommunityID=826
Municipal Type: Rural Municipality
Incorporated: Dec. 13, 1909 *Area:* 828.33 sq km
Population in 2006: 256
Next Election: Oct 2012; staggered 2 yr term
Robert Clay, Reeve
Vernna Wiggins, Administrator

Fish Creek No. 402
P.O. Box 160
Wakaw, SK S0K 4P0
Tel: 306-233-4412; *Fax:* 306-233-5234
rm402@sasktel.net
Municipal Type: Rural Municipality
Incorporated: Jan. 1, 1913 *Area:* 597.90 sq km
Population in 2006: 307
Next Election: Oct 2012; staggered 2 yr term
Dennis Sawitsky, Reeve
Richard Kindrachuk, Administrator

Flett's Springs No. 429
P.O. Box 160
Melfort, SK S0E 1A0
Tel: 306-752-3606; *Fax:* 306-752-3882
rm429@sasktel.net
saskbiz.ca/communityprofiles/communityprofile.asp?CommunityID=828
Municipal Type: Rural Municipality
Incorporated: Dec. 13, 1909 *Area:* 844.61 sq km
Population in 2006: 736
Next Election: Oct 2012; staggered 2 yr term
Blaine Forsyth, Reeve
Shelley L. Holmes, Administrator

Foam Lake No. 276
P.O. Box 490
Foam Lake, SK S0A 1A0
Tel: 306-272-3334; *Fax:* 306-272-4722
rm276@sasktel.net
Municipal Type: Rural Municipality
Incorporated: Dec. 12, 1910 *Area:* 1,345.91 sq km
Population in 2006: 598
Next Election: Oct 2012; staggered 2 yr term
Chris Gislason, Reeve
Tina Douglas, Administrator

Fox Valley No. 171
P.O. Box 190
100 Centre St.
Fox Valley, SK S0N 0V0
Tel: 306-666-2055; *Fax:* 306-666-2074
rm171@sasktel.net
foxvalleysask.com/12.html
Municipal Type: Rural Municipality
Incorporated: Oct. 29, 1913 *Area:* 1,253.79 sq km
Population in 2006: 368
Next Election: Oct 2012; staggered 2 yr term
Anthony Hoffart, Reeve
Daniel Steven Buye, Administrator

Francis No. 127
P.O. Box 36
Francis, SK S0G 1V0
Tel: 306-245-3256; *Fax:* 306-245-3203
rm127@sasktel.net
saskbiz.ca/communityprofiles/communityprofile.asp?CommunityID=831
Municipal Type: Rural Municipality
Incorporated: Dec. 13, 1909 *Area:* 1,106.80 sq km
Population in 2006: 672
Next Election: Oct 2012; staggered 2 yr term
George R. Leier, Reeve
Megan Macomber, Administrator

Frenchman Butte No. 501
P.O. Box 180
Paradise Hill, SK S0M 2G0
Tel: 306-344-2034; *Fax:* 306-344-4434
rm501@sasktel.net
www.rmfrenchmanbutte.ca
Municipal Type: Rural Municipality
Incorporated: Jan. 1, 1954 *Area:* 1,928.32 sq km
Population in 2006: 1,223
Next Election: Oct 2012; staggered 2 yr term
B. Bonnie Mills Midgley, Reeve
Cindy Schreiber, Administrator

Frontier No. 19
P.O. Box 30
Frontier, SK S0N 0W0
Tel: 306-296-2030; *Fax:* 306-296-2175
rm19@sasktel.net
saskbiz.ca/communityprofiles/Select_a_Community.asp?Region_ID=5
Municipal Type: Rural Municipality
Incorporated: Jan. 1, 1913 *Area:* 1,675.02 sq km
Population in 2006: 323
Next Election: Oct 2012; staggered 2 yr term
Troy Heggestad, Reeve
Barb Webber, Administrator

Garden River No. 490
P.O. Box 70
Meath Park, SK S0J 1T0
Tel: 306-929-2020; *Fax:* 306-929-2281
rm490@sasktel.net
Municipal Type: Rural Municipality
Incorporated: Jan. 1, 1913 *Area:* 662.90 sq km
Population in 2006: 633
Next Election: Oct 2012; staggered 2 yr term
Bernard Zurkowski, Reeve
Elaine Esopenko, Administrator

Garry No. 245
P.O. Box 10
Jedburgh, SK S0A 1R0
Tel: 306-647-2450; *Fax:* 306-647-2450
rm245@yourlink.ca
Municipal Type: Rural Municipality
Incorporated: Jan. 1, 1913 *Area:* 853.59 sq km
Population in 2006: 426
Next Election: Oct 2012; staggered 2 yr term
Garry Dubiel, Reeve
Tanis Ferguson, Administrator

Glen Bain No. 105
P.O. Box 39
Glen Bain, SK S0N 0X0
Tel: 306-264-3607; *Fax:* 306-264-3956
rm105@xplornet.com
Municipal Type: Rural Municipality
Incorporated: Dec. 11, 1911 *Area:* 843.40 sq km
Population in 2006: 232
Next Election: Oct 2012; staggered 2 yr term
Ivan Braun, Reeve
Marilyn Scheller, Administrator

Glen McPherson No. 46
P.O. Box 277
Mankota, SK S0H 2W0
Tel: 306-478-2323; *Fax:* 306-478-2606
rm45.46@sasktel.net
Municipal Type: Rural Municipality
Incorporated: Jan. 1, 1913 *Area:* 848.29 sq km
Population in 2006: 112
Next Election: Oct 2012; staggered 2 yr term
Gordon Kruger, Reeve
Michael E. Sherven, Administrator

Glenside No. 377
P.O. Box 1084
Biggar, SK S0K 0M0
Tel: 306-948-3681; *Fax:* 306-948-3684
rm377@sasktel.net
saskbiz.ca/communityprofiles/CommunityProfile.Asp?CommunityID=838
Municipal Type: Rural Municipality
Incorporated: Dec. 13, 1909 *Area:* 905.74 sq km
Population in 2006: 367
Next Election: Oct 2012; staggered 2 yr term
Wade Parkinson, Reeve
Cheryl Forbes, Administrator

Golden West No. 95
P.O. Box 70
Corning, SK S0G 0T0
Tel: 306-224-4456; *Fax:* 306-224-2196
goldwest@sasktel.net
saskbiz.ca/communityprofiles/communityprofile.asp?CommunityID=839
Municipal Type: Rural Municipality
Incorporated: Dec. 13, 1909 *Area:* 790.13 sq km
Population in 2006: 322
Next Election: Oct 2012; staggered 2 yr term
J. Garth Allan, Reeve
Edward A. Mish, Administrator

Good Lake No. 274
P.O. Box 896
401 Main St.
Canora, SK S0A 0L0
Tel: 306-563-5244; *Fax:* 306-563-5005
rm274@sasktel.net
www.goodlakerm.com
Municipal Type: Rural Municipality
Incorporated: Jan. 1, 1913 *Area:* 800.06 sq km
Population in 2006: 748
Next Election: Oct 2012; staggered 2 yr term
David Popowich, Reeve
Grant Doupe, Administrator

Grandview No. 349
P.O. Box 39
Kelfield, SK S0K 2C0
Tel: 306-932-4911; *Fax:* 306-932-4923
rm349@xplornet.com
Municipal Type: Rural Municipality
Incorporated: Dec. 11, 1911 *Area:* 712.05 sq km
Population in 2006: 355
Next Election: Oct 2012; staggered 2 yr term
Sally Germsheid, Reeve
Patti J. Turk, Administrator

Grant No. 372
P.O. Box 190
Vonda, SK S0K 4N0
Tel: 306-258-2022; *Fax:* 306-258-2011
rm372@sasktel.net
Municipal Type: Rural Municipality
Incorporated: Dec. 13, 1909 *Area:* 666.16 sq km
Population in 2006: 406
Next Election: Oct 2012; staggered 2 yr term
Julien Denis, Reeve
Brenda Skakun, Administrator

Grass Lake No. 381
P.O. Box 40
Reward, SK S0K 3N0
Tel: 306-228-2988; *Fax:* 306-228-4188
rm381@sasktel.net
Municipal Type: Rural Municipality
Incorporated: Dec. 13, 1909 *Area:* 801.29 sq km
Population in 2006: 433
Next Election: Oct 2012; staggered 2 yr term
Scott Vetter, Reeve
Brenda M. Kasas, Administrator

Grassy Creek No. 78
P.O. Box 400
Shaunavon, SK S0N 2M0
Tel: 306-297-2520; *Fax:* 306-297-3162
rm77.78@sasktel.net
Municipal Type: Rural Municipality
Incorporated: Jan. 1, 1913 *Area:* 837.40 sq km
Population in 2006: 305
Next Election: Oct 2012; staggered 2 yr term
Kerry Kronberg, Reeve
Grace Potter, Administrator

Gravelbourg No. 104
P.O. Box 510
Gravelbourg, SK S0H 1X0
Tel: 306-648-2412; *Fax:* 306-648-2603
rm104@sasktel.net
saskbiz.ca/communityprofiles/CommunityProfile.Asp?CommunityID=744
Municipal Type: Rural Municipality
Incorporated: Dec. 9, 1912 *Area:* 842.08 sq km
Population in 2006: 329
Next Election: Oct 2012; staggered 2 yr term
Roland Levac, Reeve
Nicole C. Smith, Administrator

Grayson No. 184
P.O. Box 69
Boswell St.
Grayson, SK S0A 1E0
Tel: 306-794-2044; *Fax:* 306-794-4655
grayson184@sasktel.net
Municipal Type: Rural Municipality
Incorporated: Jan. 1, 1913 *Area:* 875.22 sq km
Population in 2006: 542
Next Election: Oct 2012; staggered 2 yr term
Wilfred Schultz, Reeve
Darlene Paquin, Administrator

Great Bend No. 405
P.O. Box 150
200 Shepard St.
Borden, SK S0K 0N0
Tel: 306-997-2101; *Fax:* 306-997-2201
rm405@sasktel.net
saskbiz.ca/communityprofiles/CommunityProfile.Asp?CommunityID=846
Municipal Type: Rural Municipality
Incorporated: Dec. 12, 1910 *Area:* 830.57 sq km
Population in 2006: 458
Next Election: Oct 2012; staggered 2 yr term
Ron Saunders, Reeve
Barry Hvidston, Administrator

Griffin No. 66
P.O. Box 70
Griffin, SK S0C 1G0
Tel: 306-842-6298; *Fax:* 306-842-6400
rm66@sasktel.net
saskbiz.ca/communityprofiles/communityprofile.asp?CommunityID=848
Municipal Type: Rural Municipality
Incorporated: Dec. 13, 1909 *Area:* 816.59 sq km
Population in 2006: 334
Next Election: Oct 2012; staggered 2 yr term
Stacey Lund, Reeve
Audrey L. Trombley, Administrator

Gull Lake No. 139
P.O. Box 180
Gull Lake, SK S0N 1A0
Tel: 306-672-4430; *Fax:* 306-672-3879
rm139@sasktel.net
saskbiz.ca/communityprofiles/CommunityProfile.Asp?CommunityID=849
Municipal Type: Rural Municipality
Incorporated: Jan. 1, 1913 *Area:* 836.41 sq km
Population in 2006: 221
Next Election: Oct 2012; staggered 2 yr term
Doug Steele, Reeve
Jeanette Kerr, Administrator

Happy Valley No. 10
P.O. Box 39
Big Beaver, SK S0H 0G0
Tel: 306-267-4540; *Fax:* 306-267-4540
rm10@sasktel.net
Municipal Type: Rural Municipality
Incorporated: Jan. 1, 1913 *Area:* 812.74 sq km
Population in 2006: 174
Next Election: Oct 2012; staggered 2 yr term
David Schwab, Reeve
Vernon R. Palmer, Administrator

Happyland No. 231
P.O. Box 339
Leader, SK S0N 1H0
Tel: 306-628-3800; *Fax:* 306-628-4228
rm231@sasktel.net
Municipal Type: Rural Municipality
Incorporated: Jan. 1, 1913 *Area:* 1,259 sq km
Population in 2006: 297
Next Election: Oct 2012; staggered 2 yr term
Timothy Geiger, Reeve
Tim C. Lozinsky, Administrator

Harris No. 316
P.O. Box 146
Harris, SK S0L 1K0
Tel: 306-656-2072; *Fax:* 306-656-2151
rm316@sasktel.net
Municipal Type: Rural Municipality
Incorporated: Dec. 12, 1910 *Area:* 805.42 sq km
Population in 2006: 195
Next Election: Oct 2012; staggered 2 yr term
Ted Gross, Reeve
Jim Angus, Administrator

Hart Butte No. 11
P.O. Box 210
Coronach, SK S0H 0Z0
Tel: 306-267-2005; *Fax:* 306-267-2391
rm11@accesscomm.ca
saskbiz.ca/communityprofiles/communityprofile.asp?CommunityID=742
Municipal Type: Rural Municipality
Incorporated: Jan. 1, 1913 *Area:* 841.98 sq km
Population in 2006: 272
Next Election: Oct 2012; staggered 2 yr term
Donald Kirby, Reeve
Vernon R. Palmer, Administrator

Hazel Dell No. 335
P.O. Box 87
Okla, SK S0A 2X0
Tel: 306-325-4315; *Fax:* 306-352-4314
rm335@sasktel.net
Municipal Type: Rural Municipality
Incorporated: Jan. 1, 1913 *Area:* 1,394.02 sq km
Population in 2006: 611
Next Election: Oct 2012; staggered 2 yr term
Richard Radawetz, Reeve
Miranda Serhan, Administrator

Hazelwood No. 94
P.O. Box 270
Kipling, SK S0G 2S0
Tel: 306-736-8121; *Fax:* 306-736-2496
rm94@sasktel.net
saskbiz.ca/communityprofiles/communityprofile.asp?CommunityID=854
Municipal Type: Rural Municipality
Incorporated: Jan. 1, 1913 *Area:* 780.68 sq km
Population in 2006: 272
Next Election: Oct 2012; staggered 2 yr term
Allan LaRose, Reeve
Gary Vargo, Administrator

Heart's Hill No. 352
P.O. Box 458
200 Strathcona St.
Luseland, SK S0L 2A0
Tel: 306-372-4224; *Fax:* 306-372-4770
rm352@sasktel.net
www.heartshill.ca
Municipal Type: Rural Municipality
Incorporated: Nov. 15, 1910 *Area:* 838.20 sq km
Population in 2006: 285
Next Election: Oct 2012; staggered 2 yr term
Gordon Stang, Reeve
Janet Fisher, Administrator

Hillsborough No. 132
403 Coteau St. West
Moose Jaw, SK S6H 5E1
Tel: 306-693-1329; *Fax:* 306-693-2810
rm.132@sasktel.net
Municipal Type: Rural Municipality
Incorporated: Jan. 1, 1913 *Area:* 445.25 sq km
Population in 2006: 122
Next Election: Oct 2012; staggered 2 yr term
Ernest Doyle, Reeve
Charlene Loos, Administrator

Hillsdale No. 440
P.O. Box 280
Neilburg, SK S0M 2C0
Tel: 306-823-4321; *Fax:* 306-823-4477
rm440@sasktel.net
saskbiz.ca/communityprofiles/CommunityProfile.Asp?CommunityID=857
Municipal Type: Rural Municipality
Incorporated: Jan. 1, 1913 *Area:* 1,028.75 sq km
Population in 2006: 530
Next Election: Oct 2012; staggered 2 yr term
Glenn Goodfellow, Reeve
Janet L. Black, Administrator

Hoodoo No. 401
P.O. Box 250
Cudworth, SK S0K 1B0
Tel: 306-256-3281; *Fax:* 306-256-7147
rm401@yourlink.ca
Municipal Type: Rural Municipality
Incorporated: Jan. 1, 1913 *Area:* 810.61 sq km
Population in 2006: 804
Next Election: Oct 2012; staggered 2 yr term
Linus Hackl, Reeve
David Yorke, Administrator

Hudson Bay No. 394
P.O. Box 520
Hudson Bay, SK S0E 0Y0
Tel: 306-865-2691; *Fax:* 306-865-2857
rm394@sasktel.net
saskbiz.ca/communityprofiles/CommunityProfile.Asp?CommunityID=859
Municipal Type: Rural Municipality
Incorporated: May 1, 1977 *Area:* 12,460.90 sq km
Population in 2006: 1,359
Next Election: Oct 2012; staggered 2 yr term
Neal Hardy, Reeve
Tracy Smith, Administrator

Humboldt No. 370
P.O. Box 420
Humboldt, SK S0K 2A0
Tel: 306-682-2242; *Fax:* 306-682-3239
r.m.humboldt@sasktel.net
Municipal Type: Rural Municipality
Incorporated: Jan. 1, 1913 *Area:* 798.51 sq km
Population in 2006: 842
Next Election: Oct 2012; staggered 2 yr term
Jordan Bergermann, Reeve
Corinne Richardson, Administrator

Huron No. 223
P.O. Box 159
Tugaske, SK S0H 4B0
Tel: 306-759-2211; *Fax:* 306-759-2249
rm223@sasktel.net
www.tugaske.com/contact.shtml
Municipal Type: Rural Municipality
Incorporated: Dec. 12, 1910 *Area:* 842.11 sq km
Population in 2006: 233
Next Election: Oct 2012; staggered 2 yr term
Corey Doerksen, Reeve
Daryl Dean, Administrator

Indian Head No. 156
P.O. Box 39
Indian Head, SK S0G 2K0
Tel: 306-695-3464; *Fax:* 306-695-3462
rm156@sasktel.net
Municipal Type: Rural Municipality
Incorporated: Aug. 6, 1884 *Area:* 759.98 sq km
Population in 2006: 356
Next Election: Oct 2012; staggered 2 yr term
Lorne Scott, Reeve
Lorelei Theaker, Administrator

Insinger No. 275
P.O. Box 179
Insinger, SK S0A 1L0
Tel: 306-647-2422; *Fax:* 306-647-2740
rm275@sasktel.net
Municipal Type: Rural Municipality
Incorporated: Jan. 1, 1913 *Area:* 849.38 sq km
Population in 2006: 373
Next Election: Oct 2012; staggered 2 yr term
Terry Eritz, Reeve
Sonya Butuk, Administrator

Invergordon No. 430
P.O. Box 40
Crystal Springs, SK S0K 1A0
Tel: 306-749-2852; *Fax:* 306-749-2499
rm430@sasktel.net
Municipal Type: Rural Municipality
Incorporated: Dec. 11, 1911 *Area:* 853.55 sq km
Population in 2006: 570
Next Election: Oct 2012; staggered 2 yr term
Dennis Shulhan, Reeve
Sally Wojcichowsky, Administrator

Invermay No. 305
P.O. Box 130
Invermay, SK S0A 1M0
Tel: 306-593-2152; *Fax:* 306-593-2152
rm.inv.305@sasktel.net

Municipal Type: Rural Municipality
Incorporated: Dec. 11, 1911 *Area:* 728.23 sq km
Population in 2006: 379
Next Election: Oct 2012; staggered 2 yr term
Jack Prychak, Reeve
Sandra Leitch, Administrator

Ituna Bon Accord No. 246
P.O. Box 190
Ituna, SK S0A 1N0
Tel: 306-795-2202; *Fax:* 306-795-2202
rmofituna@sasktel.net
Municipal Type: Rural Municipality
Incorporated: Jan. 1, 1913 *Area:* 837.23 sq km
Population in 2006: 453
Next Election: Oct 2012; staggered 2 yr term
Terry Berezny, Reeve
Wilma Hrenyk, Administrator

Kellross No. 247
P.O. Box 10
Leross, SK S0A 2C0
Tel: 306-675-4423; *Fax:* 306-675-2097
rm247@sasktel.net
saskbiz.ca/communityprofiles/CommunityProfile.Asp?CommunityID=867
Municipal Type: Rural Municipality
Incorporated: Dec. 13, 1909 *Area:* 834.09 sq km
Population in 2006: 390
Next Election: Oct 2012; staggered 2 yr term
John Olinik, Reeve
Edith Goddard, Administrator

Kelvington No. 366
P.O. Box 519
Kelvington, SK S0A 1W0
Tel: 306-327-4222; *Fax:* 306-327-4222
rm366@sasktel.net
saskbiz.ca/communityprofiles/CommunityProfile.Asp?CommunityID=868
Municipal Type: Rural Municipality
Incorporated: Jan. 1, 1913 *Area:* 907.37 sq km
Population in 2006: 514
Next Election: Oct 2012; staggered 2 yr term
Stanley Elmy, Reeve
Tim G. Leurer, Administrator

Key West No. 70
P.O. Box 159
Ogema, SK S0C 1Y0
Tel: 306-459-2262; *Fax:* 306-459-2762
rm.70@sasktel.net
Municipal Type: Rural Municipality
Incorporated: Dec. 12, 1910 *Area:* 825.26 sq km
Population in 2006: 309
Next Election: Oct 2012; staggered 2 yr term
Rick Dunn, Reeve
Peggy Tuchscherer, Administrator

Keys No. 303
P.O. Box 899
Canora, SK S0A 0L0
Tel: 306-563-5331; *Fax:* 306-563-6759
rm303@sasktel.net
Municipal Type: Rural Municipality
Incorporated: Jan. 1, 1913 *Area:* 661.61 sq km
Population in 2006: 397
Next Election: Oct 2012; staggered 2 yr term
James Hallick, Reeve
Sharon Ciesielski, Administrator

Kindersley No. 290
P.O. Box 1210
Kindersley, SK S0L 1S0
Tel: 306-463-2524; *Fax:* 306-463-4197
rm290@sasktel.net
Municipal Type: Rural Municipality
Incorporated: Dec. 12, 1910 *Area:* 2,113.36 sq km
Population in 2006: 1,042
Next Election: Oct 2012; staggered 2 yr term
Glen Harrison, Reeve
Glenda M. Giles, Administrator

King George No. 256
P.O. Box 100
Dinsmore, SK S0L 0T0
Tel: 306-846-2022; *Fax:* 306-846-2032
rm256@sasktel.net
Municipal Type: Rural Municipality
Incorporated: Dec. 11, 1911 *Area:* 831.97 sq km
Population in 2006: 234
Next Election: Oct 2012; staggered 2 yr term
James Thorpe, Reeve
Cheryl Joel, Administrator

Kingsley No. 124
P.O. Box 239
Kipling, SK S0G 2S0
Tel: 306-736-2272; *Fax:* 306-736-2798
rm124@sasktel.net
saskbiz.ca/communityprofiles/CommunityProfile.Asp?CommunityID=873
Municipal Type: Rural Municipality
Incorporated: Dec. 12, 1910 *Area:* 844.61 sq km
Population in 2006: 439
Next Election: Oct 2012; staggered 2 yr term
Lorne Rygh, Reeve
Holly Kemp, Administrator

Kinistino No. 459
P.O. Box 310
Kinistino, SK S0J 1H0
Tel: 306-864-2474; *Fax:* 306-864-2880
rm459@sasktel.net
Municipal Type: Rural Municipality
Incorporated: Dec. 11, 1911 *Area:* 949.13 sq km
Population in 2006: 713
Next Election: Oct 2012; staggered 2 yr term
Vance Shmyr, Reeve
Tina M. Douglas, Administrator

Lac Pelletier No. 107
P.O. Box 70
Neville, SK S0N 1T0
Tel: 306-627-3226; *Fax:* 306-627-3641
rm107@sasktel.net
Municipal Type: Rural Municipality
Incorporated: Jan. 1, 1913 *Area:* 849.27 sq km
Population in 2006: 524
Next Election: Oct 2012; staggered 2 yr term
Cornie Martens, Reeve
Rose Lawrence, Administrator

Lacadena No. 228
P.O. Box 39
Lacadena, SK S0L 1V0
Tel: 306-574-2008; *Fax:* 306-574-4753
rm228@xplornet.com
saskbiz.ca/communityprofiles/communityprofile.asp?CommunityID=876
Municipal Type: Rural Municipality
Incorporated: Dec. 12, 1910 *Area:* 1,890.08 sq km
Population in 2006: 613
Next Election: Oct 2012; staggered 2 yr term
Bradley Sander, Reeve
Wilma Moen, Administrator

Laird No. 404
P.O. Box 160
Waldheim, SK S0K 4R0
Tel: 306-945-2133; *Fax:* 306-945-4824
rmlaird@sasktel.net; info@rmoflaird.com
www.rmoflaird.com
Municipal Type: Rural Municipality
Incorporated: Dec. 12, 1910 *Area:* 729.98 sq km
Population in 2006: 1,136
Next Election: Oct 2012; staggered 2 yr term
Kenneth Petkau, Reeve
rmlaird@sasktel.net
Sandra Galambos, Administrator

Lajord No. 128
P.O. Box 36
Lajord, SK S0G 2V0
Tel: 306-781-2744; *Fax:* 306-781-1023
rm128@yourlink.ca
Municipal Type: Rural Municipality
Incorporated: Dec. 13, 1909 *Area:* 943.87 sq km
Population in 2006: 977
Next Election: Oct 2012; staggered 2 yr term
Erwin Beitel, Reeve
Rod J. Heise, Administrator

Lake Alma No. 8
P.O. Box 100
Lake Alma, SK S0C 1M0
Tel: 306-447-2022; *Fax:* 306-447-2023
rmalma@sasktel.net
saskbiz.ca/communityprofiles/communityprofile.asp?CommunityID=880
Municipal Type: Rural Municipality
Incorporated: May 5, 1913 *Area:* 822.47 sq km
Population in 2006: 240
Next Election: Oct 2012; staggered 2 yr term
Lyle Hoimyr, Reeve
Myrna Lohse, Administrator

Lake Johnston No. 102
P.O. Box 160
Mossbank, SK S0H 3G0
Tel: 306-354-2414; *Fax:* 306-354-7725
rm102.103@sasktel.net
Municipal Type: Rural Municipality
Incorporated: Dec. 9, 1912 *Area:* 567.24 sq km
Population in 2006: 161
Next Election: Oct 2012; staggered 2 yr term
Kevin Stark, Reeve
Sherry D. Green, Administrator

Lake Lenore No. 399
P.O. Box 280
St Brieux, SK S0K 3V0
Tel: 306-275-2066; *Fax:* 306-275-4667
rmll@sasktel.net
saskbiz.ca/communityprofiles/communityprofile.asp?CommunityID=883
Municipal Type: Rural Municipality
Incorporated: Jan. 1, 1913 *Area:* 724.06 sq km
Population in 2006: 513
Next Election: Oct 2012; staggered 2 yr term
Jean Kernaleguen, Reeve
Jennifer Thompson, Administrator

Lake of the Rivers No. 72
P.O. Box 610
Assiniboia, SK S0H 0B0
Tel: 306-642-3533; *Fax:* 306-642-4382
rm72@sasktel.net
saskbiz.ca/communityprofiles/CommunityProfile.Asp?CommunityID=747
Municipal Type: Rural Municipality
Incorporated: Dec. 11, 1911 *Area:* 677.51 sq km
Population in 2006: 326
Next Election: Oct 2012; staggered 2 yr term
William Welk, Reeve
Mervin A. Guillemin, Administrator

Lakeland No. 521
P.O. Box 27
Christopher Lake, SK S0J 0N0
Tel: 306-982-2010; *Fax:* 306-982-2589
office@rmlakeland521.ca
www.rmlakeland521.ca
Municipal Type: Rural Municipality
Incorporated: Aug. 1, 1977 *Area:* 494.06 sq km
Population in 2006: 1,043
Next Election: Oct 2012; staggered 2 yr term
Al Christensen, Reeve
al.christensen@yahoo.ca
Dave Dmytruk, Administrator

Lakeside No. 338
P.O. Box 9
Quill Lake, SK S0A 3E0
Tel: 306-383-2261; *Fax:* 306-383-2255
rm338@sasktel.net
saskbiz.ca/communityprofiles/communityprofile.asp?CommunityID=884
Municipal Type: Rural Municipality
Incorporated: Dec. 12, 1910 *Area:* 636.80 sq km
Population in 2006: 444
Next Election: Oct 2012; staggered 2 yr term
Arnold Boyko, Reeve
Judy Kanak, Administrator

Lakeview No. 337
P.O. Box 220
Wadena, SK S0A 4J0
Tel: 306-338-2341; *Fax:* 306-338-2595
rm337@sasktel.net
saskbiz.ca/communityprofiles/CommunityProfile.Asp?CommunityID=885
Municipal Type: Rural Municipality
Incorporated: Dec. 13, 1909 *Area:* 724.89 sq km
Population in 2006: 393
Next Election: Oct 2012; staggered 2 yr term
Mervin Kryzanowski, Reeve
Betty Ann Bjarnason, Administrator

Langenburg No. 181
P.O. Box 489
Langenburg, SK S0A 2A0
Tel: 306-743-2341; *Fax:* 306-743-5282
rm181@sasktel.net
saskbiz.ca/communityprofiles/CommunityProfile.Asp?CommunityID=886
Municipal Type: Rural Municipality
Incorporated: Jan. 1, 1913 *Area:* 675.66 sq km

Population in 2006: 558
Next Election: Oct 2012; staggered 2 yr term
Ken Apland, Reeve
Darwyn MacKenzie, Administrator

Last Mountain Valley No. 250
P.O. Box 160
Govan, SK S0G 1Z0
Tel: 306-484-2011; *Fax:* 306-484-2113
rm250@sasktel.net
Municipal Type: Rural Municipality
Incorporated: Dec. 13, 1909 *Area:* 871.17 sq km
Population in 2006: 362
Next Election: Oct 2012; staggered 2 yr term
Allan Magel, Reeve
Kelly Holbrook, Administrator

Laurier No. 38
P.O. Box 219
Radville, SK S0C 2G0
Tel: 306-869-2255; *Fax:* 306-869-2524
rm.38@sasktel.net
saskbiz.ca/communityprofiles/communityprofile.asp?CommunityID=888
Municipal Type: Rural Municipality
Incorporated: Dec. 13, 1909 *Area:* 840.86 sq km
Population in 2006: 350
Next Election: Oct 2012; staggered 2 yr term
Gene Gilmore, Reeve
Ursula Herman, Administrator

Lawtonia No. 135
P.O. Box 10
Hodgeville, SK S0H 2B0
Tel: 306-677-2266; *Fax:* 306-677-2446
rm135@sasktel.net
saskbiz.ca/communityprofiles/CommunityProfile.Asp?CommunityID=889
Municipal Type: Rural Municipality
Incorporated: Dec. 12, 1910 *Area:* 845.28 sq km
Population in 2006: 356
Next Election: Oct 2012; staggered 2 yr term
Barry Leisle, Reeve
Art Thompson, Administrator

Leask No. 464
P.O. Box 190
Leask, SK S0J 1M0
Tel: 306-466-2000; *Fax:* 306-466-2091
admin.464@sasktel.net
www.leask.ca/rmoffice.html
Municipal Type: Rural Municipality
Incorporated: Dec. 9, 1912 *Area:* 1,257.36 sq km
Population in 2006: 846
Next Election: Oct 2012; staggered 2 yr term
Len Cantin, Reeve
Sheri McHanson-Budd, Administrator

Leroy No. 339
P.O. Box 100
Leroy, SK S0K 2P0
Tel: 306-286-3261; *Fax:* 306-286-3400
rm339@sasktel.net
saskbiz.ca/communityprofiles/communityprofile.asp?CommunityID=891
Municipal Type: Rural Municipality
Incorporated: Jan. 1, 1913 *Area:* 840.40 sq km
Population in 2006: 544
Next Election: Oct 2012; staggered 2 yr term
Jerry McGrath, Reeve
Joan Fedak, Administrator

Lipton No. 217
P.O. Box 40
Lipton, SK S0G 3B0
Tel: 306-336-2244; *Fax:* 306-336-2322
rm.217@sasktel.net
Municipal Type: Rural Municipality
Incorporated: Dec. 11, 1911 *Area:* 813.69 sq km
Population in 2006: 427
Next Election: Oct 2012; staggered 2 yr term
Corey Senft, Reeve
Nikki Czemeres, Administrator

Livingston No. 331
P.O. Box 40
Arran, SK S0A 0B0
Tel: 306-595-4521; *Fax:* 306-595-4531
rm331@sasktel.net
Municipal Type: Rural Municipality
Incorporated: Jan. 1, 1913 *Area:* 1,338.64 sq km
Population in 2006: 355
Next Election: Oct 2012; staggered 2 yr term
Paul Abrahamson, Reeve
Yvonne Bilsky, Administrator

Lomond No. 37
P.O. Box 280
Weyburn, SK S4H 2K1
Tel: 306-456-2566; *Fax:* 306-456-2440
rm37@sasktel.net
saskbiz.ca/communityprofiles/CommunityProfile.Asp?CommunityID=894
Municipal Type: Rural Municipality
Incorporated: Dec. 11, 1911 *Area:* 833.95 sq km
Population in 2006: 301
Next Election: Oct 2012; staggered 2 yr term
John McKenzie, Reeve
Kevin Melle, Administrator

Lone Tree No. 18
P.O. Box 30
Climax, SK S0N 0N0
Tel: 306-293-2124; *Fax:* 306-293-2702
villageofclimax@sasktel.net
Municipal Type: Rural Municipality
Incorporated: Dec. 8, 1913 *Area:* 838 sq km
Population in 2006: 150
Next Election: Oct 2012; staggered 2 yr term
Larry Jarman, Reeve
Ronald J. Johnson, Administrator

Longlaketon No. 219
P.O. Box 100
Earl Grey, SK S0G 1J0
Tel: 306-939-2144; *Fax:* 306-939-2036
rm219@sasktel.net
Municipal Type: Rural Municipality
Incorporated: Dec. 12, 1910 *Area:* 1,024.61 sq km
Population in 2006: 899
Next Election: Oct 2012; staggered 2 yr term
Marilyn Gibson, Reeve
Murray Cook, Administrator

Loon Lake No. 561
P.O. Box 40
Loon Lake, SK S0M 1L0
Tel: 306-837-2076; *Fax:* 306-837-2282
rm561@sasktel.net
Municipal Type: Rural Municipality
Incorporated: Jan. 1, 1978 *Area:* 2,802.51 sq km
Population in 2006: 815
Next Election: Oct 2012; staggered 2 yr term
Harvey Dimond, Reeve
Laurie Lehoux, Administrator

Loreburn No. 254
P.O. Box 40
Loreburn, SK S0H 2S0
Tel: 306-644-2022; *Fax:* 306-644-2064
rm254@sasktel.net
www.rmloreburn.ca
Municipal Type: Rural Municipality
Incorporated: Dec. 12, 1910 *Area:* 966.78 sq km
Population in 2006: 350
Next Election: Oct 2012; staggered 2 yr term
Kevin Vollmer, Reeve
mbarv@sasktel.net
Nona Stronski, Administrator

Lost River No. 313
P.O. Box 159
Allan, SK S0K 0C0
Tel: 306-257-3272; *Fax:* 306-257-3337
rm313@sasktel.net
saskbiz.ca/communityprofiles/CommunityProfile.Asp?CommunityID=899
Municipal Type: Rural Municipality
Incorporated: Dec. 11, 1911 *Area:* 549.90 sq km
Population in 2006: 188
Next Election: Oct 2012; staggered 2 yr term
Charles E. Smith, Reeve
Christine Dyck, Administrator

Lumsden No. 189
P.O. Box 160
300 James Street North
Lumsden, SK S0G 3C0
Tel: 306-731-2404; *Fax:* 306-731-3572
rm189@sasktel.net
www.lumsden.ca
Municipal Type: Rural Municipality
Incorporated: Dec. 9, 1912 *Area:* 818.66 sq km
Population in 2006: 1,627
Next Election: Oct 2012; staggered 2 yr term
Jim Hipkin, Reeve
Darcy Cooper, Administrator

Manitou Lake No. 442
P.O. Box 69
Marsden, SK S0M 1P0
Tel: 306-826-5215; *Fax:* 306-826-5512
rm442@sasktel.net
saskbiz.ca/communityprofiles/CommunityProfile.Asp?CommunityID=901
Municipal Type: Rural Municipality
Incorporated: Dec. 12, 1910 *Area:* 850.32 sq km
Population in 2006: 590
Next Election: Oct 2012; staggered 2 yr term
Ian Lamb, Reeve
Joanne Loy, Administrator

Mankota No. 45
P.O. Box 148
Mankota, SK S0H 2W0
Tel: 306-478-2323; *Fax:* 306-478-2606
rm45.46@sasktel.net
Municipal Type: Rural Municipality
Incorporated: Jan. 1, 1913 *Area:* 1,696.22 sq km
Population in 2006: 382
Next Election: Oct 2012; staggered 2 yr term
Doug Williamson, Reeve
Michael E. Sherven, Administrator

Maple Bush No. 224
P.O. Box 160
Riverhurst, SK S0H 3P0
Tel: 306-353-2292; *Fax:* 306-353-2292
rm224@xplornet.com
Municipal Type: Rural Municipality
Incorporated: Dec. 13, 1909 *Area:* 811.95 sq km
Population in 2006: 186
Next Election: Oct 2012; staggered 2 yr term
Dennis R. O'Brien, Reeve
Garry L. Gross, Administrator

Maple Creek No. 111
P.O. Box 188
Maple Creek, SK S0N 1N0
Tel: 306-662-2300; *Fax:* 306-662-3566
rm111@sasktel.net
Municipal Type: Rural Municipality
Incorporated: Dec. 10, 1917 *Area:* 3,242.96 sq km
Population in 2006: 1,167
Next Election: Oct 2012; staggered 2 yr term
Greg Link, Reeve
Barbi-Rose Weisgerber, Administrator

Mariposa No. 350
P.O. Box 228
603 Atlantic Ave.
Kerrobert, SK S0L 1R0
Tel: 306-834-5037; *Fax:* 306-834-5047
rm350@sasktel.net
saskbiz.ca/communityprofiles/communityprofile.asp?CommunityID=905
Municipal Type: Rural Municipality
Incorporated: Dec. 12, 1910 *Area:* 636.73 sq km
Population in 2006: 225
Next Election: Oct 2012; staggered 2 yr term
Peter Volk, Reeve
Terry Bohn, Administrator

Marquis No. 191
P.O. Box 40
Marquis, SK S0H 2X0
Tel: 306-788-2022; *Fax:* 306-788-2168
rm191@sasktel.net
saskbiz.ca/communityprofiles/CommunityProfile.Asp?CommunityID=906
Municipal Type: Rural Municipality
Incorporated: Dec. 11, 1911 *Area:* 805.48 sq km
Population in 2006: 404
Next Election: Oct 2012; staggered 2 yr term
Kenneth Waldenberger, Reeve
Ronald J. Gasper, Administrator

Marriott No. 317
P.O. Box 366
Rosetown, SK S0L 2V0
Tel: 306-882-4030; *Fax:* 306-882-4401
rm317@sasktel.net
Municipal Type: Rural Municipality
Incorporated: Dec. 12, 1910 *Area:* 843.29 sq km
Population in 2006: 410
Next Election: Oct 2012; staggered 2 yr term
Colin Ahrens, Reeve
Michelle McQueen, Administrator

Martin No. 122
P.O. Box 1109
Moosomin, SK S0G 3N0
Tel: 306-532-3113; *Fax:* 306-435-4313
rm121@sasktel.net
saskbiz.ca/communityprofiles/CommunityProfile.Asp?CommunityID=908
Municipal Type: Rural Municipality
Incorporated: Jan. 1, 1913 *Area:* 556.50 sq km
Population in 2006: 339
Next Election: Oct 2012; staggered 2 yr term
David Garvey, Reeve
Elaine M. Olsen, Administrator

Maryfield No. 91
P.O. Box 70
Maryfield, SK S0G 3K0
Tel: 306-646-2033; *Fax:* 306-646-2033
rm91@sasktel.net
www.maryfieldsaskatchewan.com/map.html
Municipal Type: Rural Municipality
Incorporated: Dec. 9, 1912 *Area:* 759.63 sq km
Population in 2006: 341
Next Election: Oct 2012; staggered 2 yr term
Bruce Lemon, Reeve
Anna Macksymchuk, Administrator

Mayfield No. 406
P.O. Box 100
Maymont, SK S0M 1T0
Tel: 306-389-2112; *Fax:* 306-389-2162
rm406@sasktel.net
saskbiz.ca/communityprofiles/communityprofile.asp?CommunityID=910
Municipal Type: Rural Municipality
Incorporated: Dec. 13, 1909 *Area:* 782.50 sq km
Population in 2006: 394
Next Election: Oct 2012; staggered 2 yr term
Ernest Voegeli, Reeve
Laurie DuBois, Administrator

McCraney No. 282
P.O. Box 129
Kenaston, SK S0G 2N0
Tel: 306-252-2240; *Fax:* 306-252-2248
rm282@sasktel.net
Municipal Type: Rural Municipality
Incorporated: Dec. 13, 1909 *Area:* 948.36 sq km
Population in 2006: 346
Next Election: Oct 2012; staggered 2 yr term
Murray Kadlec, Reeve
Mark Zdunich, Administrator

McKillop No. 220
P.O. Box 369
Strasbourg, SK S0G 4V0
Tel: 306-725-3230; *Fax:* 306-725-3613
rm220@sasktel.net
saskbiz.ca/communityprofiles/CommunityProfile.Asp?CommunityID=912
Municipal Type: Rural Municipality
Incorporated: Dec. 13, 1909 *Area:* 668.45 sq km
Population in 2006: 566
Next Election: Oct 2012; staggered 2 yr term
Murray MacPheat, Reeve
Barbara Griffin, Administrator

McLeod No. 185
P.O. Box 130
Neudorf, SK S0A 2T0
Tel: 306-748-2233; *Fax:* 306-748-2647
www.village.neudorf.sk.ca/RM%20OF%20MCLEOD.htm
Municipal Type: Rural Municipality
Incorporated: Jan. 1, 1913 *Area:* 886.6 sq km
Population in 2006: 508
Next Election: Oct 2012; staggered 2 yr term
Wilfred G. Goebel, Reeve
Murray J. Hanowski, Administrator

Meadow Lake No. 588
P.O. Box 668
#1, 225 Centre St.
Meadow Lake, SK S9X 1L5
Tel: 306-236-5651; *Fax:* 306-236-3115
rm.588@sasktel.net
rmmeadowlake.com
Municipal Type: Rural Municipality
Incorporated: Feb. 1, 1976 *Area:* 6,303.31 sq km
Population in 2006: 2,627
Next Election: Oct 2012; staggered 2 yr term
John Lawson, Reeve
Gina Bernier, Administrator

Medstead No. 497
P.O. Box 148
Medstead, SK S0M 1W0
Tel: 306-342-4609; *Fax:* 306-342-2067
rm497@sasktel.net
saskbiz.ca/communityprofiles/communityprofile.asp?CommunityID=915
Municipal Type: Rural Municipality
Incorporated: Jan. 1, 1913 *Area:* 1,203.22 sq km
Population in 2006: 524
Next Election: Oct 2012; staggered 2 yr term
Albert Schmirler, Reeve
Christin Baynes, Administrator

Meeting Lake No. 466
P.O. Box 26
Mayfair, SK S0M 1S0
Tel: 306-246-4228; *Fax:* 306-246-4974
rm466@sasktel.net
saskbiz.ca/communityprofiles/communityprofile.asp?CommunityID=916
Municipal Type: Rural Municipality
Incorporated: Jan. 1, 1913 *Area:* 1,066.74 sq km
Population in 2006: 429
Next Election: Oct 2012; staggered 2 yr term
Lyle Prescesky, Reeve
Janelle Lavallee, Administrator

Meota No. 468
P.O. Box 80
Meota, SK S0M 1X0
Tel: 306-892-2061; *Fax:* 306-892-2449
rm.468@sasktel.net
saskbiz.ca/communityprofiles/CommunityProfile.Asp?CommunityID=917
Municipal Type: Rural Municipality
Incorporated: Dec. 13, 1909 *Area:* 651.09 sq km
Population in 2006: 984
Next Election: Oct 2012; staggered 2 yr term
Wilbert Fennig, Reeve
Maryann Germann, Administrator

Mervin No. 499
P.O. Box 130
Turtleford, SK S0M 2Y0
Tel: 306-845-2045; *Fax:* 306-845-2950
rm499@sasktel.net
saskbiz.ca/communityprofiles/CommunityProfile.Asp?CommunityID=918
Municipal Type: Rural Municipality
Incorporated: Jan. 1, 1913 *Area:* 1,594.64 sq km
Population in 2006: 1,331
Next Election: Oct 2012; staggered 2 yr term
Harold Kivimaa, Reeve
L. Ryan Domotor, Administrator

Milden No. 286
P.O. Box 160
113 Centre St.
Milden, SK S0L 2L0
Tel: 306-935-2181; *Fax:* 306-935-2046
rm286@sasktel.net
saskbiz.ca/communityprofiles/communityprofile.asp?CommunityID=919
Municipal Type: Rural Municipality
Incorporated: Dec. 12, 1910 *Area:* 735.31 sq km
Population in 2006: 215
Next Election: Oct 2012; staggered 2 yr term
Arnold Somerville, Reeve
Melody Nieman, Administrator

Milton No. 292
P.O. Box 70
Marengo, SK S0L 2K0
Tel: 306-968-2922; *Fax:* 306-968-2278
rm292.rm322@sasktel.net
saskbiz.ca/communityprofiles/communityprofile.asp?CommunityID=920
Municipal Type: Rural Municipality
Incorporated: Dec. 11, 1911 *Area:* 655.76 sq km
Population in 2006: 181
Next Election: Oct 2012; staggered 2 yr term
Shelley Mohr, Administrator
Kenneth Weisbrod, Reeve

Miry Creek No. 229
P.O. Box 210
Abbey, SK S0N 0A0
Tel: 306-689-2281; *Fax:* 306-689-2901
rm229@sasktel.net
saskbiz.ca/communityprofiles/CommunityProfile.Asp?CommunityID=921
Municipal Type: Rural Municipality
Incorporated: Jan. 1, 1913 *Area:* 1,220.38 sq km
Population in 2006: 458
Next Election: Oct 2012; staggered 2 yr term
Morgan Powell, Reeve
Jan Stern, Administrator

Monet No. 257
P.O. Box 370
Elrose, SK S0L 0Z0
Tel: 306-378-2212; *Fax:* 306-378-2212
rm257@sasktel.net
Municipal Type: Rural Municipality
Incorporated: Dec. 13, 1909 *Area:* 1,591.75 sq km
Population in 2006: 479
Next Election: Oct 2012; staggered 2 yr term
George Myers, Reeve
Lori A. McDonald, Administrator

Montmartre No. 126
P.O. Box 120
136 Central Ave.
Montmartre, SK S0G 3M0
Tel: 306-424-2040; *Fax:* 306-424-2065
rm126@sasktel.net
www.montmartre-sk.com
Municipal Type: Rural Municipality
Incorporated: Dec. 13, 1909 *Area:* 853.91 sq km
Population in 2006: 503
Next Election: Oct 2012; staggered 2 yr term
Rodney Baumgartner, Reeve
Dale Brenner, Administrator

Montrose No. 315
P.O. Box 755
Delisle, SK S0L 0P0
Tel: 306-493-2694; *Fax:* 306-493-2694
rm315@sasktel.net
Municipal Type: Rural Municipality
Incorporated: Dec. 13, 1909 *Area:* 898.38 sq km
Population in 2006: 648
Next Election: Oct 2012; staggered 2 yr term
Gordon Ross, Reeve
Tracey Macknak, Administrator

Moose Creek No. 33
P.O. Box 10
Alameda, SK S0C 0A0
Tel: 306-489-2044; *Fax:* 306-489-2112
rm33@sasktel.net
saskbiz.ca/communityprofiles/communityprofile.asp?CommunityID=925
Municipal Type: Rural Municipality
Incorporated: Dec. 12, 1910 *Area:* 842.03 sq km
Population in 2006: 365
Next Election: Oct 2012; staggered 2 yr term
Murray Rossow, Reeve
Sentura Freitag, Administrator

Moose Jaw No. 161
170 Fairford St. West
Moose Jaw, SK S6H 1V3
Tel: 306-692-3446; *Fax:* 306-691-0015
rm161@sasktel.net
www.moosejawrm161.ca
Municipal Type: Rural Municipality
Incorporated: Dec. 11, 1911 *Area:* 797.60 sq km
Population in 2006: 1,228
Next Election: Oct 2012; staggered 2 yr term
Jeff Crichton, Reeve
John Eberl, Administrator

Moose Mountain No. 63
P.O. Box 445
Carlyle, SK S0C 0R0
Tel: 306-453-6175; *Fax:* 306-453-2430
rm63@sasktel.net
saskbiz.ca/communityprofiles/communityprofile.asp?CommunityID=927
Municipal Type: Rural Municipality
Incorporated: Dec. 11, 1911 *Area:* 740.91 sq km
Population in 2006: 482
Next Election: Oct 2012; staggered 2 yr term
Note: URL: www.creda.sk.ca/moosemountain/moose_mountain_community_profile.htm
Lyle Brown, Reeve
Ron Matsalla, Administrator

Moose Range No. 486
P.O. Box 699
Carrot River, SK S0E 0L0
Tel: 306-768-2212; *Fax:* 306-768-2211
rm486@sasktel.net
www.rmmooserange.sasktelwebsite.net
Municipal Type: Rural Municipality
Incorporated: Dec. 11, 1916 *Area:* 2,419.06 sq km
Population in 2006: 1,086
Next Election: Oct 2012; staggered 2 yr term
Herman Enns, Reeve
Richard C. Colborn, Administrator

Moosomin No. 121
P.O. Box 1109
Moosomin, SK S0G 3N0
Tel: 306-435-3113; *Fax:* 306-435-4313
rm121@sasktel.net
saskbiz.ca/communityprofiles/CommunityProfile.Asp?CommunityID=929
Municipal Type: Rural Municipality
Incorporated: Jan. 1, 1913 *Area:* 566.39 sq km
Population in 2006: 518
Next Election: Oct 2012; staggered 2 yr term
Christopher Bell, Reeve
Kendra L. Lawrence, Administrator

Morris No. 312
P.O. Box 130
121 Main St.
Young, SK S0K 4Y0
Tel: 306-259-2211; *Fax:* 306-259-2225
rm312@sasktel.net
www.young.ca/rm-morris.htm
Municipal Type: Rural Municipality
Incorporated: Dec. 13, 1909 *Area:* 847.16 sq km
Population in 2006: 347
Next Election: Oct 2012; staggered 2 yr term
Gordon Dengler, Reeve
Pamela Garner, Administrator

Morse No. 165
P.O. Box 340
Morse, SK S0H 3C0
Tel: 306-629-3282; *Fax:* 306-629-3212
rm165@sasktel.net
Municipal Type: Rural Municipality
Incorporated: Dec. 11, 1911 *Area:* 1,244.38 sq km
Population in 2006: 435
Next Election: Oct 2012; staggered 2 yr term
Glen Solberg, Reeve
Mark Wilson, Administrator

Mount Hope No. 279
P.O. Box 190
Semans, SK S0A 3S0
Tel: 306-524-2055; *Fax:* 306-524-4526
rm279@sasktel.net
Municipal Type: Rural Municipality
Incorporated: Dec. 11, 1911 *Area:* 1,669.29 sq km
Population in 2006: 633
Next Election: Oct 2012; staggered 2 yr term
Ernie Oblander, Reeve
Jim Down, Administrator

Mount Pleasant No. 2
P.O. Box 278
820 Railway Ave.
Carnduff, SK S0C 0S0
Tel: 306-482-3313; *Fax:* 306-482-5278
rm.2@sasktel.net
Municipal Type: Rural Municipality
Incorporated: Dec. 11, 1911 *Area:* 781.48 sq km
Population in 2006: 418
Next Election: Oct 2012; staggered 2 yr term
Slade Boyes, Reeve
Valerie A. Olney, Administrator

Mountain View No. 318
P.O. Box 130
Herschel, SK S0L 1L0
Tel: 306-377-2144; *Fax:* 306-377-2023
rm318@sasktel.net
Municipal Type: Rural Municipality
Incorporated: Dec. 13, 1909 *Area:* 838.67 sq km
Population in 2006: 333
Next Election: Oct 2012; staggered 2 yr term
Rodney G. Wiens, Reeve
Karen F. Martin, Administrator

Newcombe No. 260
P.O. Box 40
Glidden, SK S0L 1H0
Tel: 306-463-3338; *Fax:* 306-463-4748
rm260@yourlink.ca
saskbiz.ca/communityprofiles/communityprofile.asp?CommunityID=935
Municipal Type: Rural Municipality
Incorporated: Dec. 11, 1911 *Area:* 1,075.6 sq km
Population in 2006: 361
Next Election: Oct 2012; staggered 2 yr term
Ken McBride, Reeve
Monica Buddecke, Administrator

Nipawin No. 487
P.O. Box 250
Codette, SK S0E 0P0
Tel: 306-862-9551; *Fax:* 306-862-2432
rm487@sasktel.net
Municipal Type: Rural Municipality
Incorporated: Dec. 9, 1912 *Area:* 886.73 sq km
Population in 2006: 1,166
Next Election: Oct 2012; staggered 2 yr term
Lyle L. Larsen, Reeve
Eunice Rudy, Administrator

North Battleford No. 437
#4, 1462 - 100th St.
North Battleford, SK S9A 0W2
Tel: 306-445-3604; *Fax:* 306-445-3694
rm437@sasktel.net
saskbiz.ca/communityprofiles/CommunityProfile.Asp?CommunityID=937
Municipal Type: Rural Municipality
Incorporated: Dec. 12, 1910 *Area:* 797.20 sq km
Population in 2006: 737
Next Election: Oct 2012; staggered 2 yr term
Jim Rogers, Reeve
Debbie Arsenault, Administrator

North Qu'Appelle No. 187
P.O. Box 99
Fort Qu'appelle, SK S0G 1S0
Tel: 306-332-5202; *Fax:* 306-332-6028
rm187@sasktel.net
www.fortquappelle.com/rm187
Municipal Type: Rural Municipality
Incorporated: Dec. 12, 1910 *Area:* 494.98 sq km
Population in 2006: 852
Next Election: Oct 2012; staggered 2 yr term
Lance Fehr, Reeve
Naomi Hrischuk, Administrator

Norton No. 69
P.O. Box 189
Pangman, SK S0C 2C0
Tel: 306-442-2131; *Fax:* 306-442-2144
rm.69@sasktel.net
www.pangman.ca/rural-municipality-of-norton-no-69-2
Municipal Type: Rural Municipality
Incorporated: Dec. 13, 1909 *Area:* 844.8 sq km
Population in 2006: 248
Next Election: Oct 2012; staggered 2 yr term
Chuck Jacques, Reeve
Wayne Lozinsky, Administrator

Oakdale No. 320
P.O. Box 249
Coleville, SK S0L 0K0
Tel: 306-965-2281; *Fax:* 306-965-2466
rm320@sasktel.net
www.colevillesk.ca
Municipal Type: Rural Municipality
Incorporated: Dec. 13, 1909 *Area:* 806.52 sq km
Population in 2006: 290
Next Election: Oct 2012; staggered 2 yr term
Darwin Whitfield, Reeve
Gillian Lund, Administrator

Old Post No. 43
P.O. Box 70
Wood Mountain, SK S0H 4L0
Tel: 306-266-2002; *Fax:* 306-266-2020
rm43@sasktel.net
Municipal Type: Rural Municipality
Incorporated: Jan. 1, 1967 *Area:* 1,757 sq km
Population in 2006: 394
Next Election: Oct 2012; staggered 2 yr term
Warren Spagrud, Reeve
Vickie Greffard, Clerk

Orkney No. 244
26 - 5 Ave. North
Yorkton, SK S3N 0Y8
Tel: 306-782-2333; *Fax:* 306-782-5177
orkney@sasktel.net
Municipal Type: Rural Municipality
Incorporated: Jan. 1, 1913 *Area:* 815.87 sq km
Population in 2006: 1,721
Next Election: Oct 2012; staggered 2 yr term
Barclay Westerhaug, Reeve
Donna Westerhaug, Administrator

Paddockwood No. 520
P.O. Box 187
Paddockwood, SK S0J 1Z0
Tel: 306-989-2124; *Fax:* 306-989-4625
rm520@sasktel.net
www.rmofpaddockwood.com
Municipal Type: Rural Municipality
Incorporated: Jan. 1, 1978 *Area:* 2,456.51 sq km
Population in 2006: 976
Next Election: Oct 2012; staggered 2 yr term

Parkdale No. 498
P.O. Box 310
Glaslyn, SK S0M 0Y0
Tel: 306-342-2015; *Fax:* 306-342-4442
rm498@sasktel.ca
saskbiz.ca/communityprofiles/CommunityProfile.Asp?CommunityID=944
Municipal Type: Rural Municipality
Incorporated: Jan. 1, 1913 *Area:* 1,388.91 sq km
Population in 2006: 711
Next Election: Oct 2012; staggered 2 yr term
Bob Gourlay, Reeve
Linda Sandwick, Administrator

Paynton No. 470
P.O. Box 10
Paynton, SK S0M 2J0
Tel: 306-895-2020; *Fax:* 306-895-4800
rm470@sasktel.net
saskbiz.ca/communityprofiles/communityprofile.asp?CommunityID=945
Municipal Type: Rural Municipality
Incorporated: Jan. 1, 1913 *Area:* 593.95 sq km
Population in 2006: 254
Next Election: Oct 2012; staggered 2 yr term
Don Ferguson, Reeve
Elaine Knowlson, Administrator

Pense No. 160
P.O. Box 190
324 Elder St.
Pense, SK S0G 3W0
Tel: 306-345-2303; *Fax:* 306-345-2583
rm160@sasktel.net
www.pense160.ca
Municipal Type: Rural Municipality
Incorporated: Jan. 1, 1913 *Area:* 841.48 sq km
Population in 2006: 490
Next Election: Oct 2012; staggered 2 yr term
Tom Lemon, Reeve
Carolynn Meadows, Administrator

Perdue No. 346
P.O. Box 208
Perdue, SK S0K 3C0
Tel: 306-237-4202; *Fax:* 306-237-4202
rm346@sasktel.net
Municipal Type: Rural Municipality
Incorporated: Dec. 13, 1909 *Area:* 826.14 sq km
Population in 2006: 432
Next Election: Oct 2012; staggered 2 yr term
Bill Peters, Reeve
Allan Kirzinger, Administrator

Piapot No. 110
P.O. Box 100
Piapot, SK S0N 1Y0
Tel: 306-558-2011; *Fax:* 306-558-2125
rm110@sasktel.net
www.rmofpiapot.ca
Municipal Type: Rural Municipality
Incorporated: Dec. 8, 1913 *Area:* 1,912.81 sq km
Population in 2006: 392
Next Election: Oct 2012; staggered 2 yr term
John Wagner, Reeve
Lana Bavle, Administrator

Pinto Creek No. 75
P.O. Box 239
Kincaid, SK S0H 2J0
Tel: 306-264-3277; *Fax:* 306-264-3254
rm75@sasktel.net
Municipal Type: Rural Municipality
Incorporated: Jan. 1, 1913 *Area:* 845.01 sq km
Population in 2006: 204
Next Election: Oct 2012; staggered 2 yr term
Darryl Smith, Reeve
Roxanne Empey, Administrator

Pittville No. 169
P.O. Box 150
Hazlet, SK S0N 1E0
Tel: 306-678-2131; *Fax:* 306-678-2132
rm169@sasktel.net
hazletsk.com/contact.htm
Municipal Type: Rural Municipality
Incorporated: Jan. 1, 1913 *Area:* 1,258.06 sq km
Population in 2006: 216
Next Election: Oct 2012; staggered 2 yr term
Larry Sletten, Reeve
Terry Erdelyan, Administrator

Pleasant Valley No. 288
P.O. Box 2080
Rosetown, SK S0L 2V0
Tel: 306-882-4030; *Fax:* 306-882-4401
rm317@sasktel.net
Municipal Type: Rural Municipality
Incorporated: Dec. 11, 1911 *Area:* 830.53 sq km
Population in 2006: 346
Next Election: Oct 2012; staggered 2 yr term
Blake Jeffries, Reeve
Michelle McQueen, Administrator

Pleasantdale No. 398
P.O. Box 70
Naicam, SK S0K 2Z0
Tel: 306-874-5732; *Fax:* 306-874-2225
rm398@sasktel.net
saskbiz.ca/communityprofiles/CommunityProfile.Asp?CommunityID=951
Municipal Type: Rural Municipality
Incorporated: Dec. 11, 1911 *Area:* 757.91 sq km
Population in 2006: 607
Next Election: Oct 2012; staggered 2 yr term
Forrest Pederson, Reeve
Lowell Prefontaine, Administrator

Ponass Lake No. 367
P.O. Box 98
Rose Valley, SK S0E 1M0
Tel: 306-322-2162; *Fax:* 306-322-2168
rm367@sasktel.net
saskbiz.ca/communityprofiles/CommunityProfile.Asp?CommunityID=953
Municipal Type: Rural Municipality
Incorporated: Jan. 1, 1913 *Area:* 770.21 sq km
Population in 2006: 618
Next Election: Oct 2012; staggered 2 yr term
Allan Nelson, Reeve
Loretta Prevost, Administrator

Poplar Valley No. 12
P.O. Box 190
Rockglen, SK S0H 3R0
Tel: 306-476-2062; *Fax:* 306-476-2175
rm12@sasktel.net
Municipal Type: Rural Municipality
Incorporated: Jan. 1, 1913 *Area:* 769.37 sq km
Population in 2006: 245
Next Election: Oct 2012; staggered 2 yr term
Nairn Nielsen, Reeve
Carol Allingham, Administrator

Porcupine No. 395
P.O. Box 190
Porcupine Plain, SK S0E 1H0
Tel: 306-278-2368; *Fax:* 306-278-3473
rm395@sasktel.net
saskbiz.ca/communityprofiles/CommunityProfile.Asp?CommunityID=955
Municipal Type: Rural Municipality
Incorporated: Feb. 28, 1944 *Area:* 2,339.96 sq km
Population in 2006: 949
Next Election: Oct 2012; staggered 2 yr term
Wes Black, Reeve
Roxanne Serhan, Administrator

Prairie Rose No. 309
P.O. Box 89
Main St.
Jansen, SK S0K 2B0
Tel: 306-364-2013; *Fax:* 306-364-2088
rm309@sasktel.net
www.jansen.ca/map.htm
Municipal Type: Rural Municipality
Incorporated: Dec. 12, 1910 *Area:* 839.08 sq km
Population in 2006: 292
Next Election: Oct 2012; staggered 2 yr term
Bruce Elke, Reeve
306-364-2077
Joni Mack, Administrator

Prairiedale No. 321
P.O. Box 90
Smiley, SK S0L 2Z0
Tel: 306-838-2020; *Fax:* 306-838-4343
rm321@sasktel.net
saskbiz.ca/communityprofiles/CommunityProfile.Asp?CommunityID=956
Municipal Type: Rural Municipality
Incorporated: Dec. 13, 1909 *Area:* 546.74 sq km
Population in 2006: 271
Next Election: Oct 2012; staggered 2 yr term
Tim Richelhoff, Reeve
Charlotte Helfrich, Administrator

Preeceville No. 334
P.O. Box 439
Preeceville, SK S0A 3B0
Tel: 306-547-2029; *Fax:* 306-547-2081
rm334@sasktel.net
saskbiz.ca/communityprofiles/CommunityProfile.Asp?CommunityID=958
Municipal Type: Rural Municipality
Incorporated: Jan. 1, 1913 *Area:* 1,394.80 sq km
Population in 2006: 960
Next Election: Oct 2012; staggered 2 yr term
Richard Pristie, Reeve
Lisa Peterson, Administrator

Prince Albert No. 461
99 River St. East
Prince Albert, SK S6V 0A1
Tel: 306-763-2469; *Fax:* 306-763-6369
rm461@sasktel.net
rmprincealbert.ca
Municipal Type: Rural Municipality
Incorporated: Dec. 9, 1912 *Area:* 1,019.01 sq km
Population in 2006: 2,918
Next Election: Oct 2012; staggered 2 yr term
Norma Sheldon, Reeve
Terry-Lynn Zahara, Administrator

Progress No. 351
P.O. Box 460
Luseland, SK S0L 2A0
Tel: 306-372-4322; *Fax:* 306-372-4146
rm351@sasktel.net
saskbiz.ca/communityprofiles/communityprofile.asp?CommunityID=960
Municipal Type: Rural Municipality
Incorporated: Dec. 12, 1910 *Area:* 803.09 sq km
Population in 2006: 289
Next Election: Oct 2012; staggered 2 yr term
Dennis Gintaut, Reeve
Janet Bosch, Administrator

Reciprocity No. 32
P.O. Box 70
Alida, SK S0C 0B0
Tel: 306-443-2212; *Fax:* 306-443-2287
rm.of.reciprocity@sasktel.net
Municipal Type: Rural Municipality
Incorporated: Dec. 11, 1911 *Area:* 733.06 sq km
Population in 2006: 352
Next Election: Oct 2012; staggered 2 yr term
Alan Arthur, Reeve
Marilyn J. Larsen, Administrator

Redberry No. 435
P.O. Box 160
Hafford, SK S0J 1A0
Tel: 306-549-2333; *Fax:* 306-549-2435
rm435@sasktel.net
saskbiz.ca/communityprofiles/CommunityProfile.Asp?CommunityID=962
Municipal Type: Rural Municipality
Incorporated: Jan. 1, 1913 *Area:* 1,015.53 sq km
Population in 2006: 451
Next Election: Oct 2012; staggered 2 yr term
Victor Hupaelo, Reeve
Alan Tanchak, Administrator

Redburn No. 130
P.O. Box 250
Rouleau, SK S0G 4H0
Tel: 306-776-2270; *Fax:* 306-776-2482
redrou@sasktel.net
Municipal Type: Rural Municipality
Incorporated: Jan. 1, 1913 *Area:* 847.91 sq km
Population in 2006: 245
Next Election: Oct 2012; staggered 2 yr term
Ronald Hughes, Reeve
Guy Lagrandeur, Administrator

Reford No. 379
P.O. Box 100
Wilkie, SK S0K 4W0
Tel: 306-843-2342; *Fax:* 306-843-2455
rm409@sasktel.net
saskbiz.ca/communityprofiles/communityprofile.asp?CommunityID=964
Municipal Type: Rural Municipality
Incorporated: Dec. 12, 1910 *Area:* 707.06 sq km
Population in 2006: 296
Next Election: Oct 2012; staggered 2 yr term
Charles Robert Clay, Reeve
Sherry Huber, Administrator

Reno No. 51
P.O. Box 90
Consul, SK S0N 0P0
Tel: 306-299-2133; *Fax:* 306-299-4433
rm51@sasktel.net
Municipal Type: Rural Municipality
Incorporated: Dec. 11, 1911 *Area:* 3,460.66 sq km
Population in 2006: 462
Next Election: Oct 2012; staggered 2 yr term
Brian McMillan, Reeve
Kim Lacelle, Administrator

Riverside No. 168
P.O. Box 129
Pennant, SK S0N 1X0
Tel: 306-626-3255; *Fax:* 306-626-3661
rm168@sasktel.net
saskbiz.ca/communityprofiles/CommunityProfile.Asp?CommunityID=966
Municipal Type: Rural Municipality
Incorporated: Jan. 1, 1913 *Area:* 1,295.21 sq km
Population in 2006: 511
Next Election: Oct 2012; staggered 2 yr term
Richard Bye, Reeve
Brandi Prentice, Administrator

Rocanville No. 151
P.O. Box 298
Rocanville, SK S0A 3L0
Tel: 306-645-2055; *Fax:* 306-645-2697
rm151@sasktel.net
www.rocanville.ca/service.htm
Municipal Type: Rural Municipality
Incorporated: Dec. 9, 1912 *Area:* 758.64 sq km
Population in 2006: 554
Next Election: Oct 2012; staggered 2 yr term
Murray D. Reid, Reeve
Sylvia Anderson, Administrator

Rodgers No. 133
P.O. Box 70
Courval, SK S0H 1A0
Tel: 306-394-4305; *Fax:* 306-394-4981
rm133@sasktel.net
saskbiz.ca/communityprofiles/CommunityProfile.Asp?CommunityID=968
Municipal Type: Rural Municipality
Incorporated: Dec. 9, 1912 *Area:* 719.80 sq km
Population in 2006: 115
Next Election: Oct 2012; staggered 2 yr term
Lawrence Johnstone, Reeve
Linda K. Coates, Administrator

Rosedale No. 283
P.O. Box 150
107 Lincoln St.
Hanley, SK S0G 2E0
Tel: 306-544-2202; *Fax:* 306-544-2252
rm283@sasktel.net
Municipal Type: Rural Municipality
Incorporated: Dec. 13, 1909 *Area:* 921.50 sq km

Population in 2006: 455
Next Election: Oct 2012; staggered 2 yr term
Nick Patkau, Reeve
Paulette Wolkowski, Administrator

Rosemount No. 378
P.O. Box 184
Landis, SK S0K 2K0
Tel: 306-658-2034; *Fax:* 306-658-2028
rm378@sasktel.net
saskbiz.ca/communityprofiles/communityprofile.asp?CommunityID=970
Municipal Type: Rural Municipality
Incorporated: Dec. 12, 1910 *Area:* 571.35 sq km
Population in 2006: 230
Next Election: Oct 2012; staggered 2 yr term
A. Ed Egert, Reeve
Kara Kirilenko, Administrator

Rosthern No. 403
P.O. Box 126
2022 - 6th St.
Rosthern, SK S0K 3R0
Tel: 306-232-4393; *Fax:* 306-232-5321
rm403@sasktel.net
www.rmofrosthern.ca
Municipal Type: Rural Municipality
Incorporated: Dec. 9, 1912 *Area:* 954.66 sq km
Population in 2006: 1,840
Next Election: Oct 2012; staggered 2 yr term
Bruce K. Fehr, Reeve
Wendy Penner, Administrator

Round Hill No. 467
P.O. Box 9
Rabbit Lake, SK S0M 2L0
Tel: 306-824-2044; *Fax:* 306-824-2044
rm467@yourlink.ca
Municipal Type: Rural Municipality
Incorporated: Dec. 11, 1911 *Area:* 815.21 sq km
Population in 2006: 374
Next Election: Oct 2012; staggered 2 yr term
William Geates, Reeve
Cindy Miller, Administrator

Round Valley No. 410
P.O. Box 538
Unity, SK S0K 4L0
Tel: 306-228-2248; *Fax:* 306-228-3483
rm410@sasktel.net
saskbiz.ca/communityprofiles/CommunityProfile.Asp?CommunityID=973
Municipal Type: Rural Municipality
Incorporated: Dec. 13, 1909 *Area:* 810.57 sq km
Population in 2006: 355
Next Election: Oct 2012; staggered 2 yr term
Francis Boskill, Reeve
Mervin Bosch, Administrator

Rudy No. 284
P.O. Box 1010
400 Saskatchewan Ave. West
Outlook, SK S0L 2N0
Tel: 306-867-9349; *Fax:* 306-867-9898
rmrudy@sasktel.net
www.rmrudy.ca
Municipal Type: Rural Municipality
Incorporated: Dec. 13, 1909 *Area:* 813.86 sq km
Population in 2006: 434
Next Election: Oct 2012; staggered 2 yr term
D. Wayne Vaxvick, Reeve
Trent Michelman, Administrator

St. Andrews No. 287
P.O. Box 488
Rosetown, SK S0L 2V0
Tel: 306-882-2314; *Fax:* 306-882-3287
rm.287@sasktel.net
Municipal Type: Rural Municipality
Incorporated: Dec. 12, 1910 *Area:* 805.30 sq km
Population in 2006: 582
Next Election: Oct 2012; staggered 2 yr term
Garry Nisbet, Reeve
Joan Babecy, Administrator

St. Louis No. 431
P.O. Box 28
Hoey, SK S0J 1E0
Tel: 306-422-6170; *Fax:* 306-422-8520
rm431@sasktel.net
Municipal Type: Rural Municipality
Incorporated: Jan. 1, 1913 *Area:* 790.18 sq km
Population in 2006: 1,006
Next Election: Oct 2012; staggered 2 yr term
Henry Gareau, Reeve
Louise Hodgson, Administrator

St. Peter No. 369
P.O. Box 70
Annaheim, SK S0K 0G0
Tel: 306-598-2122; *Fax:* 306-598-4526
rm369@sasktel.net
Municipal Type: Rural Municipality
Incorporated: Dec. 11, 1911 *Area:* 823.22 sq km
Population in 2006: 901
Next Election: Oct 2012; staggered 2 yr term
Danny Breker, Reeve
Brenda Nagy, Administrator

St. Philips No. 301
P.O. Box 220
Pelly, SK S0A 2Z0
Tel: 306-595-2050; *Fax:* 306-595-2050
rm301@sasktel.net
Municipal Type: Rural Municipality
Incorporated: Jan. 1, 1913 *Area:* 655.79 sq km
Population in 2006: 258
Next Election: Oct 2012; staggered 2 yr term
Ron Sorrell, Reeve
Victoria Makohoniuk, Administrator

Saltcoats No. 213
P.O. Box 150
Saltcoats, SK S0A 3R0
Tel: 306-744-2202; *Fax:* 306-744-2455
rm.saltcoats@sasktel.net
saskbiz.ca/communityprofiles/communityprofile.asp?CommunityID=979
Municipal Type: Rural Municipality
Incorporated: Dec. 9, 1912 *Area:* 830.58 sq km
Population in 2006: 746
Next Election: Oct 2012; staggered 2 yr term
Don Taylor, Reeve
Ronald R. Risling, Administrator

Sarnia No. 221
P.O. Box 160
Roberts St.
Holdfast, SK S0G 2H0
Tel: 306-488-2033; *Fax:* 306-488-4609
rm.sarnia@sasktel.net
Municipal Type: Rural Municipality
Incorporated: Dec. 13, 1909 *Area:* 870.11 sq km
Population in 2006: 254
Next Election: Oct 2012; staggered 2 yr term
Brian Gottselig, Reeve
Patti Vance, Administrator

Saskatchewan Landing No. 167
P.O. Box 40
Stewart Valley, SK S0N 2P0
Tel: 306-778-2105; *Fax:* 306-778-2152
rm167@sasktel.net
Municipal Type: Rural Municipality
Incorporated: Jan. 1, 1913 *Area:* 797.52 sq km
Population in 2006: 480
Next Election: Oct 2012; staggered 2 yr term
Darwin Johnsgaard, Reeve
Corrie Lanceleve, Administrator

Sasman No. 336
P.O. Box 130
Kuroki, SK S0A 1Y0
Tel: 306-338-2263; *Fax:* 306-338-2048
rm336@yourlink.ca
saskbiz.ca/communityprofiles/CommunityProfile.Asp?CommunityID=982
Municipal Type: Rural Municipality
Incorporated: Jan. 1, 1913 *Area:* 1,006.49 sq km
Population in 2006: 960
Next Election: Oct 2012; staggered 2 yr term
Borden Woloshyn, Reeve
Sandy Wegwitz, Administrator

Scott No. 98
P.O. Box 210
Yellow Grass, SK S0G 5J0
Tel: 306-465-2512; *Fax:* 306-465-2802
rm98@signaldirect.ca
Municipal Type: Rural Municipality
Incorporated: Dec. 13, 1909 *Area:* 850.08 sq km
Population in 2006: 176
Next Election: Oct 2012; staggered 2 yr term
Douglas Watson, Reeve
Paul P. Thiele, Administrator

Senlac No. 411
P.O. Box 130
Senlac, SK S0L 2Y0
Tel: 306-228-3339; *Fax:* 306-228-2264
rm411@sasktel.net
saskbiz.ca/communityprofiles/communityprofile.asp?CommunityID=984
Municipal Type: Rural Municipality
Incorporated: Jan. 1, 1913 *Area:* 1,026.25 sq km
Population in 2006: 225
Next Election: Oct 2012; staggered 2 yr term
Della Purser, Reeve
Pauline Herle, Administrator

Shamrock No. 134
P.O. Box 40
Shamrock, SK S0H 3W0
Tel: 306-648-3594; *Fax:* 306-648-3687
rm134@sasktel.net
www.shamrockpark.ca/html/rm134.html
Municipal Type: Rural Municipality
Incorporated: Dec. 9, 1912 *Area:* 757.52 sq km
Population in 2006: 226
Next Election: Oct 2012; staggered 2 yr term
Dwayne James, Reeve
Jody Kennedy, Administrator

Shellbrook No. 493
P.O. Box 250
Shellbrook, SK S0J 2E0
Tel: 306-747-2178; *Fax:* 306-747-4315
rm493@sasktel.net
www.shellbrook.net
Municipal Type: Rural Municipality
Incorporated: Jan. 1, 1913 *Area:* 1,237.29 sq km
Population in 2006: 1,636
Next Election: Oct 2012; staggered 2 yr term
Robert Ernst, Reeve
Karen Beauchesne, Administrator

Sherwood No. 159
1840 Cornwall St.
Regina, SK S4P 2K2
Tel: 306-525-5237; *Fax:* 306-352-1760
admin@rmsherwood.ca
www.rmofsherwood.ca
Municipal Type: Rural Municipality
Incorporated: Dec. 11, 1911 *Area:* 719.32 sq km
Population in 2006: 1,075
Next Election: Oct 2012; staggered 2 yr term
Kevin Eberle, Reeve
Ron Hilton, Administrator

Silverwood No. 123
P.O. Box 700
Whitewood, SK S0G 5C0
Tel: 306-735-2500; *Fax:* 306-735-2524
rm123@sasktel.net
Municipal Type: Rural Municipality
Incorporated: Oct. 31, 1911 *Area:* 844.61 sq km
Population in 2006: 449
Next Election: Oct 2012; staggered 2 yr term
William MacPherson, Reeve
Jennalee Beutler, Administrator

Sliding Hills No. 273
P.O. Box 70
Mikado, SK S0A 2R0
Tel: 306-563-5285; *Fax:* 306-563-4447
slidinghills_rm273@sasktel.net
Municipal Type: Rural Municipality
Incorporated: Jan. 1, 1913 *Area:* 853.76 sq km
Population in 2006: 462
Next Election: Oct 2012; staggered 2 yr term
Harvey Malanowich, Reeve
Todd Steele, Administrator

Snipe Lake No. 259
P.O. Box 786
Eston, SK S0L 1A0
Tel: 306-962-3214; *Fax:* 306-962-4330
rm259admin@sasktel.net
saskbiz.ca/communityprofiles/communityprofile.asp?CommunityID=990
Municipal Type: Rural Municipality
Incorporated: Dec. 11, 1911 *Area:* 1,573.80 sq km
Population in 2006: 427
Next Election: Oct 2012; staggered 2 yr term
T. A. (Ted) Koester, Reeve
Debbie Shaw, Administrator

Souris Valley No. 7
P.O. Box 40
Oungre, SK S0C 1Z0
Tel: 306-456-2676; *Fax:* 306-456-2480
rm07@eclipsewireless.ca
Municipal Type: Rural Municipality
Incorporated: Dec. 13, 1909 *Area:* 817.52 sq km
Population in 2006: 230
Next Election: Oct 2012; staggered 2 yr term
Dallas Pederson, Reeve
Jo Ann Larsen, Administrator

South Qu'Appelle No. 157
P.O. Box 66
Qu'Appelle, SK S0G 4A0
Tel: 306-699-2257; *Fax:* 306-699-2856
rm157@sasktel.net
www.rm157.ca
Municipal Type: Rural Municipality
Incorporated: Aug. 6, 1884 *Area:* 889.73 sq km
Population in 2006: 1,066
Next Election: Oct 2012; staggered 2 yr term
Ken MacPherson, Reeve
Darlene Tyson, Administrator

Spalding No. 368
P.O. Box 10
Spalding, SK S0K 4C0
Tel: 306-872-2166; *Fax:* 306-872-2275
bob368@sasktel.net
saskbiz.ca/communityprofiles/CommunityProfile.Asp?CommunityID=993
Municipal Type: Rural Municipality
Incorporated: Dec. 11, 1911 *Area:* 811.47 sq km
Population in 2006: 425
Next Election: Oct 2012; staggered 2 yr term
Eugene Eggerman, Reeve
Cathy Holt, Administrator

Spiritwood No. 496
P.O. Box 340
Spiritwood, SK S0J 2M0
Tel: 306-883-2034; *Fax:* 306-883-2557
rm496@sasktel.net
saskbiz.ca/communityprofiles/communityprofile.asp?CommunityID=994
Municipal Type: Rural Municipality
Incorporated: Dec. 9, 1929 *Area:* 2,410.62 sq km
Population in 2006: 1,277
Next Election: Oct 2012; staggered 2 yr term
Grant Cadieu, Reeve
Gloria Teer, Administrator

Spy Hill No. 152
P.O. Box 129
Spy Hill, SK S0A 3W0
Tel: 306-534-2022; *Fax:* 306-534-2230
rm152@sasktel.net
Municipal Type: Rural Municipality
Incorporated: Dec. 11, 1911 *Area:* 679.28 sq km
Population in 2006: 365
Next Election: Oct 2012; staggered 2 yr term
Bernard Mikolas, Reeve
Carey Nicholauson, Administrator

Stanley No. 215
P.O. Box 70
238 - 3rd Ave. West
Melville, SK S0A 2P0
Tel: 306-728-2818; *Fax:* 306-728-2818
rm.ofstanley@sasktel.net
Municipal Type: Rural Municipality
Incorporated: Jan. 1, 1913 *Area:* 855.40 sq km
Population in 2006: 509
Next Election: Oct 2012; staggered 2 yr term
Kenneth Petlock, Reeve
Marie Steiner, Administrator

Star City No. 428
P.O. Box 370
Star City, SK S0E 1P0
Tel: 306-863-2522; *Fax:* 306-863-2255
r.m.starcity@sasktel.ca
saskbiz.ca/communityprofiles/CommunityProfile.Asp?CommunityID=997
Municipal Type: Rural Municipality
Incorporated: Jan. 1, 1913 *Area:* 824.85 sq km
Population in 2006: 936
Next Election: Oct 2012; staggered 2 yr term
Kenneth Naber, Reeve
Ann T. Campbell, Administrator

Stonehenge No. 73
P.O. Box 129
Limerick, SK S0H 2P0
Tel: 306-263-2020; *Fax:* 306-263-2013
rm73@sasktel.net
www.rmstonehenge.ca
Municipal Type: Rural Municipality
Incorporated: Dec. 11, 1911 *Area:* 985.74 sq km
Population in 2006: 442
Next Election: Oct 2012; staggered 2 yr term
Larry Lethbridge, Reeve
Tammy A. Franks, Administrator

Storthoaks No. 31
P.O. Box 40
Storthoaks, SK S0C 2K0
Tel: 306-449-2262; *Fax:* 306-449-2210
rm31@sasktel.net
Municipal Type: Rural Municipality
Incorporated: Dec. 11, 1911 *Area:* 582.57 sq km
Population in 2006: 312
Next Election: Oct 2012; staggered 2 yr term
James E. Lorette, Reeve
Elissa Henrion, Administrator

Surprise Valley No. 9
P.O. Box 52
Minton, SK S0C 1T0
Tel: 306-969-2144; *Fax:* 306-969-2127
rmnine@sasktel.net
Municipal Type: Rural Municipality
Incorporated: Jan. 1, 1913 *Area:* 813.38 sq km
Population in 2006: 199
Next Election: Oct 2012; staggered 2 yr term
Note: URL:
www.saskbiz.ca/communityprofiles/CommunityProfile.Asp?CommunityID=1000
Herb Axten, Reeve
Joyce Axten, Administrator

Sutton No. 103
P.O. Box 100
Mossbank, SK S0H 3G0
Tel: 306-354-2414; *Fax:* 306-354-7725
rm102.103@sasktel.net
Municipal Type: Rural Municipality
Incorporated: Dec. 11, 1911 *Area:* 822.40 sq km
Population in 2006: 294
Next Election: Oct 2012; staggered 2 yr term
Richard Nagel, Reeve
Sherry D. Green, Administrator

Swift Current No. 137
2024 South Service Rd. West
Swift Current, SK S9H 5J5
Tel: 306-773-7314; *Fax:* 306-773-9538
rmsc137@sasktel.net
Municipal Type: Rural Municipality
Incorporated: Dec. 12, 1910 *Area:* 1,107.7 sq km
Population in 2006: 1,587
Next Election: Oct 2012; staggered 2 yr term
Robert Neufeld, Reeve
Linda Boser, Administrator

Tecumseh No. 65
P.O. Box 300
Stoughton, SK S0G 4T0
Tel: 306-457-2277; *Fax:* 306-457-3149
rmtec@sasktel.net
Municipal Type: Rural Municipality
Incorporated: Dec. 13, 1909 *Area:* 826.11 sq km
Population in 2006: 270
Next Election: Oct 2012; staggered 2 yr term
Zandra Slater, Reeve
Kathy Rasmussen, Administrator

Terrell No. 101
P.O. Box 60
Spring Valley, SK S0H 3X0
Tel: 306-475-2803; *Fax:* 306-475-2805
street101@sasktel.net
Municipal Type: Rural Municipality
Incorporated: Jan. 1, 1913 *Area:* 864.06 sq km
Population in 2006: 257
Next Election: Oct 2012; staggered 2 yr term
M. Owen Labuik, Reeve
Kimberly Sippola, Administrator

The Gap No. 39
P.O. Box 188
Ceylon, SK S0C 0T0
Tel: 306-454-2202; *Fax:* 306-454-2627
rmgap39@sasktel.net
Municipal Type: Rural Municipality
Incorporated: Dec. 12, 1903 *Area:* 830.92 sq km
Population in 2006: 245
Next Election: Oct 2012; staggered 2 yr term
Yvonne Johnston, Administrator
Keith Kaufmann, Reeve

Three Lakes No. 400
P.O. Box 100
Middle Lake, SK S0K 2X0
Tel: 306-367-2172; *Fax:* 306-367-2011
rm400@sasktel.net
Municipal Type: Rural Municipality
Incorporated: Jan. 1, 1913 *Area:* 772.49 sq km
Population in 2006: 659
Next Election: Oct 2012; staggered 2 yr term
Allen Baumann, Reeve
Tim Schmidt, Administrator

Tisdale No. 427
P.O. Box 128
Tisdale, SK S0E 1T0
Tel: 306-873-2334; *Fax:* 306-873-4442
rm427@sasktel.net
Municipal Type: Rural Municipality
Incorporated: Dec. 9, 1912 *Area:* 849.24 sq km
Population in 2006: 938
Next Election: Oct 2012; staggered 2 yr term
Robert C. Jackson, Reeve
Fern Lucas, Administrator

Torch River No. 488
P.O. Box 40
White Fox, SK S0J 3B0
Tel: 306-276-2066; *Fax:* 306-276-2099
rm488@sasktel.net
Municipal Type: Rural Municipality
Incorporated: Jan. 1, 1950 *Area:* 5,179 sq km
Population in 2006: 1,559
Next Election: Oct 2012; staggered 2 yr term
Note: URL:
www.saskbiz.ca/communityprofiles/CommunityProfile.Asp?CommunityID=1008
Dennis Scott, Reeve
Barry Katschke, Administrator

Touchwood No. 248
P.O. Box 160
Punnichy, SK S0A 3C0
Tel: 306-835-2110; *Fax:* 306-835-2100
rm248@aski.ca
Municipal Type: Rural Municipality
Incorporated: Dec. 12, 1910 *Area:* 706.72 sq km
Population in 2006: 287
Next Election: Oct 2012; staggered 2 yr term
Ernest Matai, Reeve
Lorelei Paulsen, Administrator

Tramping Lake No. 380
P.O. Box 129
104 Main St.
Scott, SK S0K 4A0
Tel: 306-247-2033; *Fax:* 306-247-2055
rmtrampinglake@xplornet.com
Municipal Type: Rural Municipality
Incorporated: Dec. 12, 1910 *Area:* 615.56 sq km
Population in 2006: 403
Next Election: Oct 2012; staggered 2 yr term
Peter Volk, Reeve
Stacy Hawkins, Administrator

Tullymet No. 216
P.O. Box 190
Balcarres, SK S0G 0C0
Tel: 306-334-2366; *Fax:* 306-334-2930
rm216@sasktel.net
www.townofbalcarres.ca
Municipal Type: Rural Municipality
Incorporated: Jan. 1, 1913 *Area:* 562.99 sq km
Population in 2006: 245
Next Election: Oct 2012; staggered 2 yr term
Larry Jankoski, Reeve
Darwin Catterson, Administrator

Turtle River No. 469
P.O. Box 128
Edam, SK S0M 0V0
Tel: 306-397-2311; *Fax:* 306-397-2346
rm469@sasktel.net
Municipal Type: Rural Municipality
Incorporated: Dec. 9, 1912 *Area:* 664.49 sq km
Population in 2006: 336
Next Election: Oct 2012; staggered 2 yr term

Louis McCaffrey, Reeve
Nicole Walker, Administrator

Usborne No. 310
P.O. Box 310
Lanigan, SK S0K 2M0
Tel: 306-365-2924; *Fax:* 306-365-2129
rm310@sasktel.net
Municipal Type: Rural Municipality
Incorporated: Dec. 13, 1909 *Area:* 810.38 sq km
Population in 2006: 566
Next Election: Oct 2012; staggered 2 yr term
Don Bowman, Reeve
Keith Schulze, Administrator

Val Marie No. 17
P.O. Box 59
Val Marie, SK S0N 2T0
Tel: 306-298-2009; *Fax:* 306-298-2224
rm17@sasktel.net
Municipal Type: Rural Municipality
Incorporated: Jan. 1, 1969 *Area:* 3,105.26 sq km
Population in 2006: 479
Next Election: Oct 2012; staggered 2 yr term
Mike Waldner, Reeve
Cathy Legault, Administrator

Vanscoy No. 345
P.O. Box 187
Vanscoy, SK S0L 3J0
Tel: 306-668-2060; *Fax:* 306-668-1338
rm345@sasktel.net
rmvanscoy.ca
Municipal Type: Rural Municipality
Incorporated: Dec. 13, 1909 *Area:* 866.68 sq km
Population in 2006: 2,629
Next Election: Oct 2012; staggered 2 yr term
Floyd Chapple, Reeve
Shawn Antosh, Administrator

Victory No. 226
P.O. Box 100
Beechy, SK S0L 0C0
Tel: 306-859-2270; *Fax:* 306-859-2271
rm.226@yourlink.ca
Municipal Type: Rural Municipality
Incorporated: Dec. 8, 1919 *Area:* 1,375.44 sq km
Population in 2006: 428
Next Election: Oct 2012; staggered 2 yr term
Wes Jansen, Reeve
Diane Watt, Administrator

Viscount No. 341
P.O. Box 100
215 Bangor Ave.
Viscount, SK S0K 4M0
Tel: 306-944-2044; *Fax:* 306-944-2016
patrm341@sasktel.net
Municipal Type: Rural Municipality
Incorporated: Dec. 13, 1909 *Area:* 831.23 sq km
Population in 2006: 386
Next Election: Oct 2012; staggered 2 yr term
Russell Deneiko, Reeve
Patrick T. Clavelle, Administrator

Wallace No. 243
26 - 5 Ave. North
Yorkton, SK S3N 0Y8
Tel: 306-782-2455; *Fax:* 306-782-5177
wallace@sasktel.net
Municipal Type: Rural Municipality
Incorporated: Dec. 11, 1911 *Area:* 832.01 sq km
Population in 2006: 901
Next Election: Oct 2012; staggered 2 yr term
Garry Liebrecht, Reeve
Kim Waddell, Administrator

Walpole No. 92
P.O. Box 117
Wawota, SK S0G 5A0
Tel: 306-739-2545; *Fax:* 306-739-2777
rm92@sasktel.net
Municipal Type: Rural Municipality
Incorporated: Dec. 12, 1910 *Area:* 844.66 sq km
Population in 2006: 348
Next Election: Oct 2012; staggered 2 yr term
Hugh Smyth, Reeve
Rhonda M. Hall, Administrator

Waverley No. 44
P.O. Box 70
Glentworth, SK S0H 1V0
Tel: 306-266-4920; *Fax:* 306-266-2077
rm44@yourlink.ca
Municipal Type: Rural Municipality
Incorporated: Feb. 1, 1913 *Area:* 1,429.30 sq km
Population in 2006: 422
Next Election: Oct 2012; staggered 2 yr term
Lloyd Anderson, Reeve
Deidre Nelson, Administrator

Wawken No. 93
P.O. Box 90
Wawota, SK S0G 5A0
Tel: 306-739-2332; *Fax:* 306-739-2222
rm93@sasktel.net
Municipal Type: Rural Municipality
Incorporated: Jan. 1, 1913 *Area:* 766.53 sq km
Population in 2006: 613
Next Election: Oct 2012; staggered 2 yr term
Lester Brickley, Reeve
Debbie Saville, Administrator

Webb No. 138
P.O. Box 100
Webb, SK S0N 2X0
Tel: 306-674-2230; *Fax:* 306-674-2324
rm138@xplornet.com
Municipal Type: Rural Municipality
Incorporated: Dec. 13, 1909 *Area:* 1,098.78 sq km
Population in 2006: 556
Next Election: Oct 2012; staggered 2 yr term
Dennis Fiddler, Reeve
Raylene Packet, Administrator

Wellington No. 97
P.O. Box 1390
Weyburn, SK S4H 3J9
Tel: 306-842-5606; *Fax:* 306-842-5601
rm97@sasktel.net
Municipal Type: Rural Municipality
Incorporated: Dec. 13, 1909 *Area:* 838.68 sq km
Population in 2006: 357
Next Election: Oct 2012; staggered 2 yr term
Bernie Kot, Reeve
Tammie Kwochka, Administrator

Wheatlands No. 163
P.O. Box 129
Mortlach, SK S0H 3E0
Tel: 306-355-2233; *Fax:* 306-355-2351
rm163@sasktel.net
Municipal Type: Rural Municipality
Incorporated: Dec. 13, 1909 *Area:* 827.4 sq km
Population in 2006: 164
Next Election: Oct 2012; staggered 2 yr term
Gary Stirling, Reeve
Julie Gerbrandt, Administrator

Whiska Creek No. 106
P.O. Box 10
Vanguard, SK S0N 2V0
Tel: 306-582-2133; *Fax:* 306-582-4950
rm106@sasktel.net
Municipal Type: Rural Municipality
Incorporated: Jan. 1, 1913 *Area:* 851.89 sq km
Population in 2006: 520
Next Election: Oct 2012; staggered 2 yr term
Keith Carleton, Reeve
Teresa Richards, Administrator

White Valley No. 49
P.O. Box 520
Eastend, SK S0N 0T0
Tel: 306-295-3553; *Fax:* 306-295-3571
rm49@sasktel.net
Municipal Type: Rural Municipality
Incorporated: Jan. 1, 1913 *Area:* 2,026.88 sq km
Population in 2006: 518
Next Election: Oct 2012; staggered 2 yr term
Note: URL:
www.saskbiz.ca/communityprofiles/CommunityProfile.Asp?CommunityID=1027
James Leroy, Reeve
Edna Laturnus, Administrator

Willner No. 253
P.O. Box 250
Davidson, SK S0G 1A0
Tel: 306-567-3103; *Fax:* 306-567-3266
rm253@sasktel.net

Municipal Type: Rural Municipality
Incorporated: Jan. 1, 1913 *Area:* 834.97 sq km
Population in 2006: 254
Next Election: Oct 2012; staggered 2 yr term
Len Palmer, Reeve
Yvonne (Bonny) Goodsman, Administrator

Willow Bunch No. 42
P.O. Box 220
16 Edouard Beaupré St.
Willow Bunch, SK S0H 4K0
Tel: 306-473-2302; *Fax:* 306-473-2312
www.willowbunch.ca/wb/rm
Municipal Type: Rural Municipality
Incorporated: Nov. 21, 1912 *Area:* 1,047.8 sq km
Population in 2006: 407
Next Election: Oct 2012; staggered 2 yr term
David Kirby, Reeve
Margaret L. Brown, Administrator

Willow Creek No. 458
P.O. Box 5
Brooksby, SK S0E 0H0
Tel: 306-863-4143; *Fax:* 306-863-2366
rm458@staffcomm.com
Municipal Type: Rural Municipality
Incorporated: Dec. 9, 1912 *Area:* 845.18 sq km
Population in 2006: 719
Next Election: Oct 2012; staggered 2 yr term
Note: URL:
www.saskbiz.ca/communityprofiles/CommunityProfile.Asp?CommunityID=1030
John Deck, Reeve
Vicki Baptist, Administrator

Willowdale No. 153
P.O. Box 58
Whitewood, SK S0G 5C0
Tel: 306-735-2344; *Fax:* 306-735-4495
rm153@sasktel.net
Municipal Type: Rural Municipality
Incorporated: Jan. 1, 1913 *Area:* 605.06 sq km
Population in 2006: 333
Next Election: Oct 2012; staggered 2 yr term
Kenneth Aldous, Reeve
Robert Laing, Administrator

Wilton No. 472
P.O. Box 40
Marshall, SK S0M 1R0
Tel: 306-387-6244; *Fax:* 306-387-6598
rm472@sasktel.net
Municipal Type: Rural Municipality
Incorporated: Dec. 13, 1909 *Area:* 1,042.72 sq km
Population in 2006: 1,473
Next Election: Oct 2012; staggered 2 yr term
Glen Dow, Reeve
Darren Elder, Administrator

Winslow No. 319
P.O. Box 310
Dodsland, SK S0L 0V0
Tel: 306-356-2106; *Fax:* 306-356-2085
rm319@sasktel.net
Municipal Type: Rural Municipality
Incorporated: Dec. 13, 1909 *Area:* 798.07 sq km
Population in 2006: 296
Next Election: Oct 2012; staggered 2 yr term
Martin McGrath, Reeve
Regan MacDonald, Administrator

Wise Creek No. 77
P.O. Box 400
Shaunavon, SK S0N 2M0
Tel: 306-297-2520; *Fax:* 306-297-3162
rm77.78@sasktel.net
Municipal Type: Rural Municipality
Incorporated: Jan. 1, 1913 *Area:* 843.85 sq km
Population in 2006: 222
Next Election: Oct 2012; staggered 2 yr term
Frank Dunham, Reeve
Grace Potter, Administrator

Wolseley No. 155
P.O. Box 370
Wolseley, SK S0G 5H0
Tel: 306-698-2522; *Fax:* 306-698-2664
rm155@sasktel.net
Municipal Type: Rural Municipality
Incorporated: Dec. 13, 1909 *Area:* 774.26 sq km
Population in 2006: 438
Next Election: Oct 2012; staggered 2 yr term
Edward Dureault, Reeve

Rose Zimmer, Administrator

Wolverine No. 340
P.O. Box 28
Burr, SK S0K 0T0
Tel: 306-682-3640; *Fax:* 306-682-3640
rm340@sasktel.net
Municipal Type: Rural Municipality
Incorporated: Dec. 13, 1909 *Area:* 834.78 sq km
Population in 2006: 480
Next Election: Oct 2012; staggered 2 yr term
Bryan Gibney, Reeve
Sandi Dunne, Administrator

Wood Creek No. 281
P.O. Box 10
303 George St.
Simpson, SK S0G 4M0
Tel: 306-836-2020; *Fax:* 306-836-4460
rm281@sasktel.net
Municipal Type: Rural Municipality
Incorporated: Dec. 13, 1909 *Area:* 832.34 sq km
Population in 2006: 274
Next Election: Oct 2012; staggered 2 yr term
John McArthur, Reeve
Darlene Mann, Administrator

Wood River No. 74
P.O. Box 250
35 - 2nd Ave. East
Lafleche, SK S0H 2K0
Tel: 306-472-5235; *Fax:* 306-472-3706
rm74@sasktel.net
Municipal Type: Rural Municipality
Incorporated: Dec. 9, 1912 *Area:* 838.45 sq km
Population in 2006: 387
Next Election: Oct 2012; staggered 2 yr term
Duane Filson, Reeve
Brekke Massé, Administrator

Wreford No. 280
P.O. Box 99
Nokomis, SK S0G 3R0
Tel: 306-528-2202; *Fax:* 306-528-4411
rm280@sasktel.net
Municipal Type: Rural Municipality
Incorporated: Dec. 12, 1910 *Area:* 798.55 sq km
Population in 2006: 175
Next Election: Oct 2012; staggered 2 yr term
Dean Hobman, Reeve
Melanie Rich, Administrator

YUKON TERRITORY

LEGISLATION: Municipal Act, Municipal Finance and Community Grants Act, Assessment and Taxation Act.

Requirements for municipal incorporation in the Yukon are based on population: town 300–2,500, city over 2,500. Any community may become a Local Advisory Area, an advisory body to the minister, as a first step in local governance. A community may also incorporate as a Rural Government with limited powers, as a developmental step in becoming a full municipality. The Yukon Municipal Act does not include provisions for unorganized settlements or First Nation communities.

Municipal elections are held every three years and polling day is the third Thursday of October in each election year. Mayors and councillors are elected for a three-year period (2009, 2012, etc.).

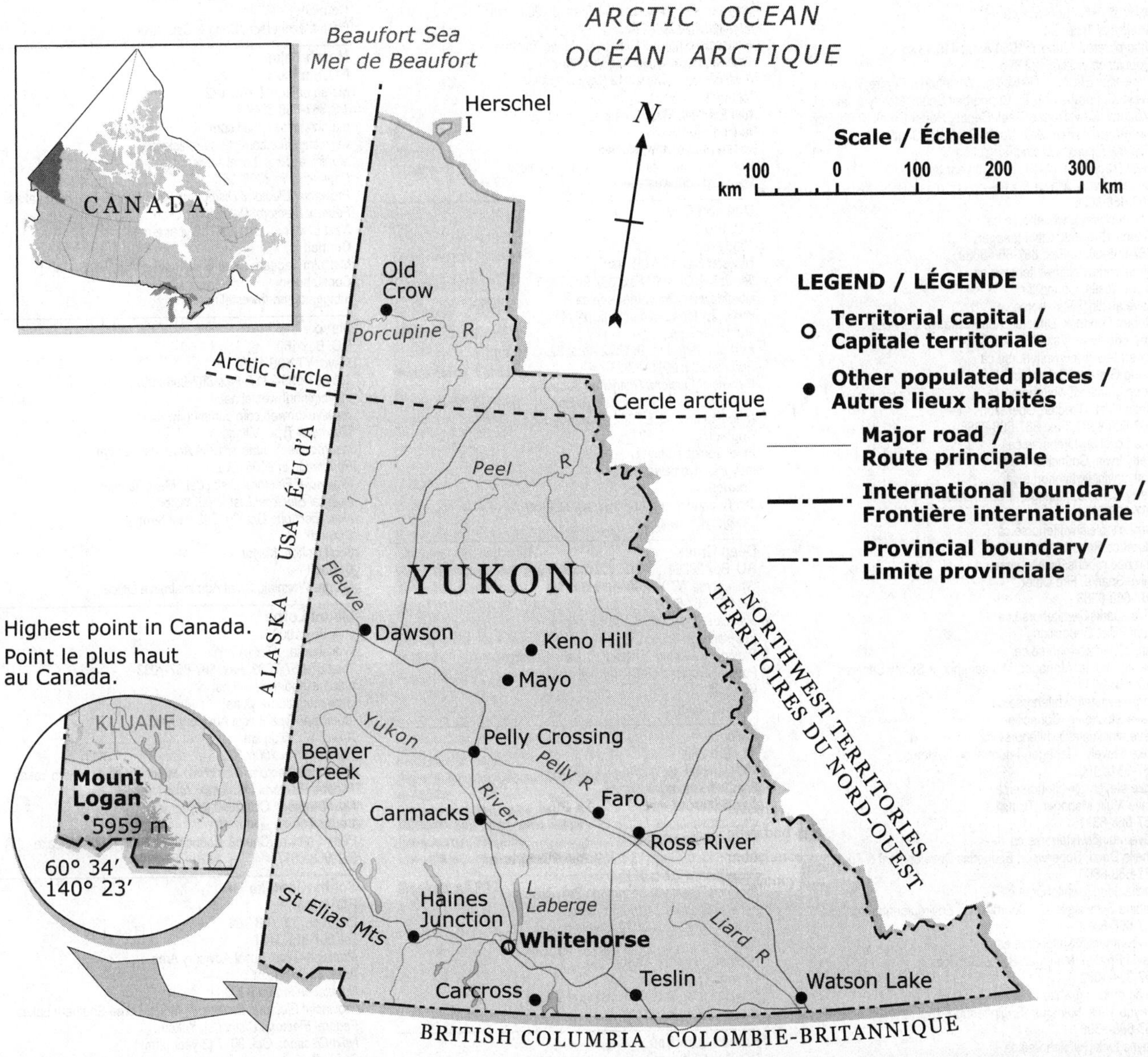

Reproduced with the permission of Natural Resources Canada 2011, courtesy of the Atlas of Canada.

www.atlas.gc.ca

Yukon Territory

Major Municipalities in Yukon Territory

Whitehorse
2121 Second Ave.
Whitehorse, YT Y1A 1C2
Tel: 867-667-6401; *Fax:* 867-668-8384
council.services@whitehorse.ca
www.city.whitehorse.yk.ca
Municipal Type: City
Incorporated: June 1, 1950 *Area:* 416.43 sq km
Population in 2006: 22,898
Provincial Electoral District(s): Whitehorse Centre; Whitehorse West; Copperbelt North; Copperbelt South; McIntyre-Takhini; Mountainview; Porter Creek Centre; Porter Creek North; Porter Creek South; Riverdale North; Riverdale South
Federal Electoral District(s): Yukon
Next Election: Oct. 18, 2012 (3 year terms)
Bev Buckway, Mayor
867-668-8626
bev.buckway@whitehorse.ca
Dennis Shewfelt, City Manager
867-668-8650, Fax: 867-668-8639
dennis.shewfelt@whitehorse.ca
Dave Austin, Councillor
dave.austin@whitehorse.ca
Robert Fendrick, Director, Administrative Services
867-668-8612, Fax: 867-668-8384
robert.fendrick@whitehorse.ca
Doug Graham, Councillor
doug.graham@whitehorse.ca
Brian Crist, Director, Operations
867-668-8301, Fax: 867-668-8386
brian.crist@whitehorse.ca
Betty Irwin, Councillor
betty.irwin@whitehorse.ca
Terry O'Toole, Manager, Public Works
867-668-8351
terry.o'toole@whitehorse.ca
Florence Roberts, Councillor
florence.roberts@whitehorse.ca
Clive Sparks, Fire Chief
867-668-8383
clive.sparks@whitehorse.ca
Ranj Pillai, Councillor
ranj.pillai@whitehorse.ca
George White, Manager, Maintenance & Safety Services
867-668-8345
george.white@whitehorse.ca
Dave Stockdale, Councillor
dave.stockdale@whitehorse.ca
Mike Stevely, Manager, Information Systems
867-334-2100
mike.stevely@whitehorse.ca
Dave Muir, Manager, Transit
867-668-8391
dave.muir@whitehorse.ca
Sheila Dodd, Supervisor, Economic Development & Tourism
867-668-8660
sheila.dodd@whitehorse.ca
Sabine Schweiger, Co-Coordinator, Environmental Services
867-668-8312
environment@whitehorse.ca
David Pruden, Manager, Bylaw Services
867-334-1082
david.pruden@whitehorse.ca
Wayne Tuck, Manager, Engineering & Environmental Services
867-668-8306
wayne.tuck@whitehorse.ca
Linda Rapp, Manager, Parks & Recreation
867-668-8325, Fax: 867-668-8675
parks.recreation@whitehorse.ca
Mike Gau, Manager, Planning & Development Services
867-668-8333, Fax: 867-668-8395
planning.services@whitehorse.ca
Pippa McNeil, Co-Coordinator, Environmental Services
867-668-8312
environment@whitehorse.ca
Ray Osborne, Supervisor, Utility Stations
867-668-8669
ray.osborne@whitehorse.ca

Other Municipalities in Yukon Territory

Carmacks
P.O. Box 113
Carmacks, YT Y0B 1C0
Tel: 867-863-6271; *Fax:* 867-863-6606
carmacks@northwestel.net
www.carmacks.ca
Municipal Type: Village
Incorporated: Nov. 1, 1984 *Area:* 36.90 sq km
Population in 2006: 425
Provincial Electoral District(s): Mayo-Tatchun
Federal Electoral District(s): Yukon
Next Election: Oct. 2012 (3 year terms)
Council
Elaine Wyatt, Mayor
867-863-6211
vocmayor@northwestel.net
Cory Bellmore, Chief Administrative Officer
voccao@northwestel.net

Dawson City
P.O. Box 308
1336 Front St.
Dawson City, YT Y0B 1G0
Tel: 867-993-7400; *Fax:* 867-993-7434
cityofdawson@cityofdawson.ca
www.cityofdawson.ca/municipalinfo
Municipal Type: Town
Incorporated: Jan. 9, 1902 *Area:* 32.45 sq km
Population in 2006: 1,327
Provincial Electoral District(s): Klondike
Federal Electoral District(s): Yukon
Next Election: Oct. 2012 (3 year terms)
Council
Peter Jenkins, Mayor
mayor@cityofdawson.ca
Council
Jeff Renaud, Chief Administrative Officer
cao@cityofdawson.ca

Deep Creek
P.O. Box 20264
Whitehorse, YT Y1A 7V2
Tel: 867-667-6966
Municipal Type: Local Advisory Area
Population in 2006: 150
Provincial Electoral District(s): Lake LaBerge
Federal Electoral District(s): Yukon
Council
Vacant, Chair

Faro
P.O. Box 580
200 Campbell St.
Faro, YT Y0B 1K0
Tel: 867-994-2728; *Fax:* 867-994-3154
www.faroyukon.ca
Municipal Type: Town
Incorporated: June 13, 1969 *Area:* 203.57 sq km
Population in 2006: 341
Provincial Electoral District(s): Pelly-Nisutlin
Federal Electoral District(s): Yukon
Next Election: Oct. 2012 (3 year terms)
Council
Heather Campbell, Mayor
Council
Ken Hodgins, Chief Administrative Officer
cao-faro@faroyukon.ca

Haines Junction
P.O. Box 5339
Haines Junction, YT Y0B 1L0
Tel: 867-634-7100; *Fax:* 867-634-2008
www.hainesjunctionyukon.com
Municipal Type: Village
Incorporated: Oct. 1, 1984 *Area:* 34.08 sq km
Population in 2006: 589
Provincial Electoral District(s): Kluane
Federal Electoral District(s): Yukon
Next Election: Oct. 2012 (3 year terms)
Council
George Nassiopoulos, Mayor
mayor06-vhj@yknet.ca
Council
Michael Riseborough, Chief Administrative Officer
vhj@yknet.yk.ca

Ibex Valley
P.O. Box 20624
Whitehorse, YT Y1A 7A2
Tel: 867-667-7844; *Fax:* 867-393-1966
Municipal Type: Local Advisory Area
Area: 209.06 sq km
Population in 2006: 376
Provincial Electoral District(s): Kluane-Lake LaBerge
Federal Electoral District(s): Yukon
Next Election: Oct. 2012 (3 year terms)
Council
Trish Macpherson, Chair & Councillor

Marsh Lake
P.O. Box 1325
Marsh Lake, YT Y0B 1Y2
Tel: 867-660-5347;
marshlakelac@mail.com
www.angelfire.com/yt2/marshlakelac
Municipal Type: Local Advisory Area
Population in 2006: 367
Provincial Electoral District(s): Mount Lorne-Southern Lakes
Federal Electoral District(s): Yukon
Next Election: Oct. 2012 (3 year terms)
Council
Malcolm Taggart, Chair & Councillor, Ward(s): 3. Old Constabulary
mtaggart@northwestel.net

Mayo
P.O. Box 160
Mayo, YT Y0B 1M0
Tel: 867-996-2317; *Fax:* 867-996-2907
mayo@northwestel.net
www.yukonweb.com/community/mayo
Municipal Type: Village
Incorporated: June 1, 1984 *Area:* 0.87 sq km
Population in 2006: 248
Provincial Electoral District(s): Mayo/Tatchun
Federal Electoral District(s): Yukon
Next Election: Oct. 2012 (3 year terms)
Council
Scott Bolton, Mayor
Council
Margrit Wozniak, Chief Administrative Officer

Mount Lorne
P.O. Box 10009
Whitehorse, YT Y1A 7A1
Tel: 867-667-7083; *Fax:* 867-667-7083
mtlorne@northwestel.net
www.mountlorne.yk.net
Municipal Type: Local Advisory Area
Area: 160.15 sq km
Population in 2006: 370
Provincial Electoral District(s): Mount Lorne-Southern Lakes
Federal Electoral District(s): Yukon
Next Election: Oct. 2012 (3 year terms)
Council
Peter Percival, Chair & Councillor, Ward(s): Cowley Lake
867-668-6817

South Klondike
P.O. Box 4
Carcross, YT Y0B 1B0
Tel: 867-821-3431
Municipal Type: Local Advisory Area
Area: 15.96 sq km
Population in 2006: 331
Provincial Electoral District(s): Mount Lorne-Southern Lakes
Federal Electoral District(s): Yukon
Next Election: Oct. 2012 (3 year terms)
Council
Linda Pringle, Chair & Councillor, Ward(s): 3
blpringle@northwestel.net

Tagish
P.O. Box 92
Tagish, YT Y0B 1T0
Tel: 867-399-4002; *Fax:* 867-399-3006
tagishclub@northwestel.net
Other Information: tac@northwestel.net
Municipal Type: Local Advisory Area
Incorporated: 2005 *Area:* 43.38 sq km
Population in 2006: 222
Provincial Electoral District(s): Mount Lorne-Southern Lakes
Federal Electoral District(s): Yukon
Next Election: Oct. 2012 (3 year terms)
Council
Paul Dabbs, Chair

Teslin
P.O. Box 32
Teslin, YT Y0A 1B0
Tel: 867-390-2530; *Fax:* 867-390-2104
vteslin@northwestel.net
www.teslin.ca
Municipal Type: Village
Incorporated: Aug. 1, 1984 *Area:* 2.22 sq km
Population in 2006: 141
Provincial Electoral District(s): Pelly-Nisutlin
Federal Electoral District(s): Yukon
Next Election: Oct. 2012 (3 year terms)
Council
Clara Jules, Mayor
Council
Frank Thomas, Chief Administrative Officer
frank.thomas@northwestel.net

Watson Lake
P.O. Box 590
Watson Lake, YT Y0A 1C0
Tel: 867-536-8000; *Fax:* 867-536-7522
twl@northwestel.net
www.watsonlake.ca
Municipal Type: Town
Incorporated: April 1, 1984 *Area:* 5.16 sq km
Population in 2006: 846
Provincial Electoral District(s): Watson Lake
Federal Electoral District(s): Yukon
Next Election: Oct. 2012 (3 year terms)
Council
Richard Durocher, Mayor
Council
Stephen Conway, Chief Administrative Officer

SECTION 9
GOVERNMENT/JUDICIAL

Following the federal listings, this section is arranged by province. Within each province, listings are by type of court, then by city.

Federal

Supreme Court of Canada
301 Wellington St., Ottawa, ON K1A 0J1
Tel: 613-995-4330; *Fax:* 613-996-3063
Toll-Free: 888-551-1185
reception@scc-csc.gc.ca; media@scc-csc.gc.ca
www.scc-csc.gc.ca
Other information: TTY: 613-944-7895; Registry, E-mail: registry-greffe@scc-csc.gc.ca; Court Library, E-mail: library-bibliotheque@scc-csc.gc.ca; Tours, E-mail: tour-visite@scc-csc.gc.ca

In 1875, the Supreme Court of Canada was created by an Act of Parliament. The Court is a general court of appeal, which consists of nine judges. The Governor in Council appoints the judges, who remain in the position until the age of seventy-five. There is a Chief Justice of Canada, plus eight puisne judges. A Registrar is also appointed by the Governor in Council. The Registrar is responsible for all the administrative work in the Court, & answers directly to the Chief Justice. There are approximately 200 employees of the Supreme Court. The Supreme Court sits in Ottawa where, each year, three sessions are held. Approximately eighty appeals are heard by the Court every year. The hearings are open to the public. Cases for review come from the provincial & territorial appellate courts & the Federal Court of Appeal, in criminal, civil, constitutional, & administrative law matters. Decisions of the Supreme Court of Canada may be unanimous, or a majority may decide.

Chief Justice of Canada: The Rt. Hon. Madam Chief Justice Beverley McLachlin, 613-992-6940, Fax: 613-952-3092
Puisne Judges (The Honourable Mr. / Madam Justice)
Louis LeBel
Marie Deschamps
Morris J. Fish
Rosalie Silberman Abella
Marshall Rothstein
Thomas Albert Cromwell
Michael J. Moldaver (pending)
Andromache Karakatsanis (pending)
Administration:
Registrar: Roger Bilodeau, 613-996-9277, Fax: 613-996-9138
Deputy Registrar: Louise Meagher, 613-996-7521, Fax: 613-941-5817
Director General: Corporate Services Sector, Lynn Potter, 613-996-0429, Fax: 613-947-2860
Director: Library Branch, Rosalie Fox, 613-996-9971, Fax: 613-991-0258
Director: Finance & Administrative Branch, Cathy Gaudet, 613-992-1765, Fax: 613-947-2860
Director: Information Management & Technology, Catherine Laforce, 613-947-0682, Fax: 613-991-0258
Director: Human Resources, Anne-Marie Larivière, 613-995-4224, Fax: 613-996-7266
Director: Security Services Branch, Louis Lahaie, 613-947-3700

Federal Court of Appeal
Cour d'appel fédérale
Courts Administration Service, Ottawa, ON K1A 0H9
Tel: 613-996-6795; *Fax:* 613-952-7226
Media Enquiries: media-fca@fca-caf.gc.ca
www.fca-caf.gc.ca
Other information: TTY: 613-995-4640

The Federal Court of Appeal was established by Parliament in accordance with provision of section 101 of the Constitution Act, 1867. The Court is a bilingual tribunal, which sits & hears cases anywhere in Canada. Both common law & civil law are administered by the Federal Court of Appeal. Decisions of the Federal Court of Appeal impact all Canadians. Responsibilities of the Court include enforcing rights & obligations between Canadians & the federal government, & interpreting & implementing Canada's international obligations.

Chief Justice of the Federal Court of Appeal: The Hon. Pierre Blais, 613-995-5106
Judges (The Hon. Mr. / Madam Justice):
Gilles Létourneau(Supernumerary)
Marc Noël
Marc Nadon
J. Edgar Sexton(Supernumerary)
John Maxwell Evans
Karen Sharlow
J.D. Denis Pelletier
Eleanor R. Dawson
Carolyn Layden-Stevenson
Johanne Trudel
David W. Stratas
Robert M. Mainville
Administration:
Judicial Administrator: Suzelle Bazinet, 613-995-5117, Fax: 613-952-6439

Court Martial Appeal Court of Canada
Cour d'Appel de la Cour Mart
Thomas D'Arcy McGee Building, 90 Sparks St., Ottawa, ON K1A 0H9
Tel: 613-996-6795; *Fax:* 613-952-7226
Media enquiries: media-fca@fca-caf.gc.ca
www.cmac-cacm.ca
Other information: TTY: 613-947-0407

The Court Martial Appeal Court of Canada was established by the Parliament of Canada, pursuant to its authority under section 101 of the Constitution Act,1867. The Court administers the National Defence Act & the Criminal Code. The Court Martial Appeal Court of Canada hears appeals from military courts. Military courts, known as courts martial, try members of the Canadian Forces, as well as civilians accompanying military personnel abroad, for crimes & offences against the Code of Service Discipline. The Code of Service Discipline is found in Part III & Part VII of the National Defence Act. Military personnel are subjected to military law, except when the offence has little to do with their military role. Offences, such as murder & manslaughter, are tried in civilian courts. There is a right of appeal to the Supreme Court of Canada from the Court Martial Appeal Court of Canada on questions of law.

Chief Justice: The Hon. Mr. Justice Edmond P. Blanchard, 613-995-7886
Designated Judges (The Hon. Mr. / Madam Justice):
Edward C. Malone
Yvon Pinard
Elizabeth McFadyen
Joanne B. Veit(Supernumerary Judge)
Gilles Létourneau
Marc Noël
Sandra J. Simpson
Marc Nadon
Danièle Tremblay-Lamer
Karen M. Weiler
Eugene Glen Ewaschuk
Douglas R. Campbell
Allan Lutfy
J. Edgar Sexton
Pierre Blais
John Maxwell Evans
François Lemieux
Karen Sharlow
Carol Mahood Huddart
Ross Goodwin
Elizabeth A. Bennett
John A. O'Keefe
J.D. Denis Pelletier
Eleanor R. Dawson
Dolores M. Hansen
Elizabeth Heneghan
Michael A. Kelen
Michel Beaudry
Luc Martineau
Luc Martineau
Carloyn Layden-Stevenson
Simon Noël
Judith A. Snider
Johanne Gauthier
James O'Reilly
James Russell
J. David Watt
A. Donald K. MacKenzie
Joseph T. Robertson
Deborah J. McCawley
Sean J. Harrington
Richard G. Mosley
Michel M.J. Shore
Michael L. Phelan
Anne L. Mactavish
Yves de Montigny
Roger T. Hughes
Robert L. Barnes
Johanne Trudel
Leonard S. Mandamin
Russel W. Zinn
Alexandre Deschênes
J. Douglas Cunningham
Guy Cournoyer
Douglas N. Abra
Richard Boivin
David Near
Robert Mainvile
Jamie W.S. Saunders
Administration:
Administrator of the Court: Raymond P. Guenette, 613-996-4778
Assistant Administrator: Suzanne Labbé, 613-947-5506
Judicial Administratorr: Dorothée Paquin, 613-995-7886
Contact: Media, Chantelle Bowers, 613-995-5063, Fax: 613-941-9454
media-fca@fca-caf.gc.ca

Tax Court of Canada
200 Kent St., Ottawa, ON K1A 0H9
Tel: 613-992-0901; *Fax:* 613-957-9034
Toll-Free: 800-927-5499
www.tcc-cci.gc.ca
Other information: TTY: 613-943-0946; After Hours, Phone: 613-850-5021

In 1983, the Tax Court of Canada was established, pursuant to the Tax Court of Canada Act. The Court operates independently of the Canada Revenue Agency & other departments of the Government of Canada. Many of the appeals to the Tax Court of Canada are related to income tax, the goods & services tax, & employment insurance. References are also heard from the Canada Revenue Agency to provide interpretations of the legislation within its jurisdiction.

Chief Justice: The Honourable Mr. Justice Gerald J. Rip, 613-992-1994
Associate Chief Justice: The Honourable Mr. Justice Eugene P. Rossiter, 613-992-2159
Judges in order of seniority (The Honourable Mr./Madam Justice):
Theodore E. Margeson(Supernumerary Judge)
Pierre Archambault
Cameron Hugh McArthur(Supernumerary Judge)
Lucie Lamarre
Alain Tardif
Eric A. Bowie(Supernumerary Judge)
Joe E. Hershfield
Diane Campbell
Campbell J. Miller
François M. Angers
Leslie M. Little
Brent Paris
Judith Woods
Georgette Anne Sheridan
Paul Bédard
Réal Favreau
Wyman W. Webb
Gaston Jorré
Patrick J. Boyle
Valerie Miller
Robert James Hogan
Steven K. D'Arcy
Frank J. Pizzitelli
Administration:
Registrar of the Court: Roula Eatrides, 613-944-7758
roula.eatrides@cas-satj.gc.ca
Judicial Administrator: Louise Rochon, 613-992-0942
Legal Information Officer: Danielle Lebeau, 613-947-3691

Federal Court
Cour fédérale
Courts Administration Service, 90 Sparks St., Ottawa, ON K1A 0H9
Tel: 613-992-4238; *Fax:* 613-952-3653
Media Enquiries: media-fct@fct-cf.gc.ca
www.fct-cf.gc.ca
Other information: TTY: 613-995-4640

The Federal Court is a trial court. The jurisdiction of the Federal Court is conferred by the Federal Courts Act, as well as close to one hundred other applicable federal statutes. Its broad federal jurisdiction includes the following: Crown litigation, access to information, admiralty & maritime disputes, citizenship, communications, customs, immigration & refugee matters, intellectual property rights, labour relations, national security, parole & penitentiary proceedings, tax, transportation & aeronautics, war veterans, & limited criminal jurisdiction. The Court conducts hearings & renders decisions in disputes anywhere in Canada.

Chief Justice of the Federal Court: The Hon. Mr. Justice Allan Lufty, 613-996-5901
Yvon Pinard(Supernumerary)
Sandra J. Simpson
Danièle Tremblay-Lamer(Supernumerary)
Douglas R. Campbell
François Lemieux(Supernumerary)
John A. O'Keefe
Elizabeth Heneghan
Dolores Hansen
Edmond P. Blanchard
Michael A. Kelen
Michel Beaudry
Luc Martineau
Simon Noël
Judith A. Snider
James Russell
Johanne Gauthier
James W. O'Reilly

Sean J. Harrington
Richard Mosley
Michel M.J. Shore
Michael L. Phelan
Anne L. Mactavish
Yves de Montigny
Roger T. Hughes
Robert L. Barnes
Leonard S. Mandamin
Russel W. Zinn
David G. Near
Richard Boivin
Paul S. Crampton
Marie-Josée Bédard
James K. Hugessen
Max M. Teitelbaum
Frederick E. Gibson
Maurice E. Lagacé
Orville Frenette
Louis S. Tannenbaum
Prothonotaries:
Richard Morneau, 514-496-7840
Roza Aronovitch, 613-947-3356
Roger Lafrenière, 604-666-7435
Mireille Tabib, 613-947-2453
Martha Milczynski, 416-954-9006
Kevin R. Aalto, 416-954-9009
Registrar of the Federal Court: Manon Pitre
Judicial Administrator: Giovanna Calamo, 613-995-1285

Courts Administration Service
Service administratif des tr
434 Queen St., Ottawa, ON K1A 0H9
Tel: 613-996-4778; *Fax:* 613-941-6197
Media Enquiries: reception@cas-satj.gc.ca
www.cas-satj.gc.ca
Other information: Internal Audit Division, Tel: 613-996-4778; TTY: (613) 995-4640

In 2003, the Courts Administration Service was established by the Courts Administration Service Act, S.C. 2002, c. 8. The Courts Administration Service provides administrative services to the following courts of law: the Federal Court, the Federal Court of Appeal, the Tax Court of Canada, & the Court Martial Appeal Court of Canada. Examples of the duties of the Courts Administration Service are as follows: providing support services, such as library services, to judges, prothonotaries, & staff; maintaining courts records; providing facilities & security for judges, prothonotaries, & staff; & informing litigants on rules of practice & procedures.

Administration:
Chief Administrator: Raymond P. Guenette, 613-996-4778
Deputy Chief Administrator, Registry Services: Murielle Brazeau, 613-943-3458
Deputy Chief Administrator, Corporate Services: Francine Côté, 613-996-1611
Deputy Chief Administrator, Judicial Services: Suzanne Labbé, 613-992-4439
Registrar, Registry of the Tax Court of Canada: Roula Eatrides, 613-944-7758
roula.eatrides@tcc-cci.gc.ca
Registrar: Federal Court of Appeal & Court Martial Appeal Court, Alain Le Gal, 613-992-8867
alain.le_gal@cas-satj.gc.ca
Registrar, Registry of the Federal Court: Manon Pitre, 613-992-4238
manon.pitre@cas-satj.gc.ca
Executive Director, Project Management: Gerry R. Montpetit, 613-992-9104
Director General: Information Management & Information Technology, Eric Cloutier, 613-992-9393
Director General: Administrative, Facilities, & Security Services, Eric R. Delage, 613-944-6614, Fax: 613-943-7948
Director General, Human Resources: Nathalie Dunn, 613-995-4453
Director General, Finance & Contracting Services: Paul Waksberg, 613-992-1745, Fax: 613-941-4915
Director, Corporate Secretariat: Alan Ritchie, 613-943-4782
Director, Library Services: Jean Weerasinghe, 613-995-1382
Manager, Communications: Isabelle Rodier, 613-943-4355
isabelle.rodier@cas-satj.gc.ca

Registry of the Courts Administration Service
Principal Office, Ottawa, ON K1A 0H9
Other information: Federal Court of Appeal: 613-996-6795; Federal Court: 613-992-4238; Court Martial Appeal Court of Canada: 613-996-6795; Tax Court of Canada: 613-992-0901; Duty Officers (after hours): 613-769-3079

Local Offices:
Calgary
Canadian Occidental Tower, 635 - Eighth Ave. SW, Calgary, AB T2P 3M3
Tel: 403-292-5329; *Toll-Free:* 800-665-3329
Other information: TTY: 403-292-5992; Duty Officers (for matters of an urgent nature which arise after regular business hours), Phone: 403-292-5920
Director: Cheryl Braden, 403-292-5328
Senior Registry Officer: Nancy Gagné, 403-292-5417

Charlottetown
Sir Henry Louis Davies Law Courts, 42 Water St., P.O. Box 2000, Charlottetown, PE C1A 8B9
Tel: 902-368-0179; *Fax:* 902-368-0266
Toll-Free: 800-565-0541
Registry Officer: Marjorie M. MacDonald, 902-368-0179
Registry Officer: Gloria Panting, 902-368-0179

Edmonton
Tower 1, Scotia Place, #530, 10060 Jasper Ave., P.O. Box 51, Edmonton, AB T5J 3R8
Fax: 780-495-4681
Toll-Free: 800-665-3329
Other information: TTY: 780-495-2428; Duty Officers (for matters of an urgent nature which arise after regular business hours), Phone: 780-495-4651
Director: Kathy Dobransky, 780-495-2216

Fredericton
Westmorland Place, #100, 82 Westmorland St., Fredericton, NB E3B 3L3
Fax: 506-452-3584
Toll-Free: 800-565-0541
Other information: TTY: 506-452-3036; Duty Officers (for matters of an urgent nature which arise after regular business hours), Phone: 506-452-3016
Director: Willa Doyle, 506-452-3016
Registry Officer: Michel Morneault, 506-452-3016

Halifax
#1720, 1801 Hollis St., 17th Fl., Halifax, NS B3J 3N4
Fax: 902-426-5514
Toll-Free: 800-565-0541
Other information: TTY: 902-426-9776; Duty Officers (for matters of an urgent nature which arise after regular business hours), Phone: 902-229-3719
Director: Elizabeth Caverly, 902-426-3282
Registry Officer: Michael Kowalchuk, 902-426-3282

Montréal
Registry of the Federal Courts, 30, rue McGill, Montréal, QC H2Y 3Z7
Toll-Free: 800-927-5499
Other information: Duty Officers (for matters of an urgent nature which arise after regular business hours), Phone: 514-346-7884

Québec
Palais de Justice, #500A, 300, boul Jean Lesage, Québec, QC G1K 8K6
Fax: 418-648-4051
Other information: TTY: 418-648-4644; Duty Officers (for matters of an urgent nature which arise after regular business hours), Phone: 418-648-4920
Director: Claire Drolet, 418-648-7778
Registry Officer: Donald Ringuette, 418-648-5127
Registry Officer: Isabelle Sanfacon, 418-648-8469

Regina
Court House, 2425 Victoria Ave., Regina, SK S4P 3V7
Tel: 306-780-5268; *Fax:* 306-787-7217
Toll-Free: 800-663-2096
Director: Gordon C. Dauncey, 306-787-5380
Registry Officer: Gregory Jenkins, 306-787-5403
Registry Officer: Margaret Pelletier, 306-787-5421

Toronto
Registry of the Federal Courts, #200, 180 Queen St. West, Toronto, ON M5V 3L6
Tel: 416-973-3356; *Toll-Free:* 800-927-5499
Other information: Duty Officers (for matters of an urgent nature which arise after regular business hours), Phone: 416-677-1054
Regional Director General: Ontario, Gerry Montpetit

Saint John
Provincial Building, #413, 110 Charlotte St., 4th Fl., Saint John, NB E2L 2J4
Tel: 506-636-4990; *Fax:* 506-658-3070
Toll-Free: 800-565-0541
Registry Officer: Edward Joas, 506-636-4990
Registry Officer: Kathy Tobin, 506-636-4990

St. John's
The Court House, Duckworth St., P.O. Box 937, St. John's, NL A1C 5M3
Tel: 709-772-2884; *Fax:* 709-772-6351
Toll-Free: 800-565-0541
Deputy District Administrator: Darlene Wells, 709-772-2811
Registry Officer: Daphne Lewis, 709-772-2884

Saskatoon
The Court House, 520 Spadina Cres. East, Saskatoon, SK S7K 2H6
Tel: 306-975-4509; *Fax:* 306-975-4818
Toll-Free: 800-663-2096
Director: Dennis Berezowsky, 306-933-5139
Registry Officer: Diane Papuzynski, 306-933-6642

Vancouver
The Pacific Centre, 701 West Georgia St., P.O. Box 10065, Vancouver, BC V7Y 1B6
Tel: 604-666-3232
Other information: Duty Officers (for matters of an urgent nature which arise after regular business hours), Phone: 604-512-4471
Regional Director General: Western, Gail MacIver

Whitehorse
Andrew A. Phillipsen Law Centre, 2134 Second Ave., P.O. Box 2703, Whitehorse, YT Y1A 2C6
Tel: 867-667-5441; *Fax:* 867-393-6212
Toll-Free: 800-665-3329
District Administrator: Shauna Curtin, 867-667-5441
Registry Officer: Sue Bergren, 867-667-5441

Winnipeg
363 Broadway St., 4th Fl., Winnipeg, MB R3C 3N9
Fax: 204-983-7636
Other information: TTY: 204-984-4440; Duty Officers (for matters of an urgent nature which arise after regular business hours), Phone: 204-983-2509
Director: Jennifer MacGillivray, 204-983-7610
Registry Officer: Robert M'vondo, 204-983-2509
Registry Officer: Renée Taillefer, 204-983-2509

Yellowknife
Court House, 4905 - 49th St., P.O. Box 1320, Yellowknife, NT X1A 2L9
Tel: 867-873-2044; *Fax:* 867-873-0291
Toll-Free: 800-665-3329
District Administrator: Robin Anne Mould, 867-873-2044
Registry Officer: Bernice Dillman, 867-873-2044

Alberta

Alberta Court of Appeal
Law Courts, 1A Sir Winston Churchill Sq., Edmonton, AB T5J 0R2
Tel: 780-422-2416; *Fax:* 780-422-4127
www.albertacourts.ab.ca/ca

The Alberta Court of Appeal hears appeals from the following courts: the Provincial Court; the Court of Queen's Bench; & administrative tribunals. The Court of Appeal also provides opinions on questions referred from the Lieutenant Governor under the Judicature Act. Court of Appeal justices are appointed by the federal government. Sittings are held in Edmonton & Calgary.

Chief Justice of Alberta: The Honourable Catherine A. Fraser
Justices of the Court of Appeal (The Hon. Mr. / Madam Justice):
Jean E. Côté
Ellen I. Picard
Ronald L. Berger
Peter T. Costigan
Keith G. Ritter
Jack Watson
Frans F. Slatter
Myra B. Bielby
Administration:
Registrar: Sue Stushnoff, 780-422-7710, Fax: 780-427-5507
sue.stushnoff@gov.ab.ca
Deputy Registrar: Danielle Umrysh, 780-422-7714, Fax: 780-422-4127
danielle.umrysh@gov.ab.ca
Office Manager: Julie Ulmer, 780-422-4223, Fax: 780-422-4127
julie.ulmer@gov.ab.ca

Courts:
Calgary: Court of Appeal
TransCanada Pipelines Tower, #2600, 450 - 1st St. SW, Calgary, AB T2P 5H1
Tel: 403-297-2206; *Fax:* 403-297-5294
www.albertacourts.ab.ca/ca
Justices of the Court of Appeal (The Hon. Mr. / Madam Justice):
Carole M. Conrad
Elizabeth A. McFadyen
Constance D. Hunt
Marina S. Paperny
Constance D. O'Brien
Peter W.L. Martin

Justices of the Court of Appeal (The Hon. Mr. / Madam Justice):
Patricia A. Rowbotham
J.D. Bruce McDonald
Administration:
Deputy Registrar: Ileen Moore, 403-297-3949, Fax: 403-297-5294
ileen.moore@gov.ab.ca
Administration:
Director, Operations: Bev Thomson, 403-297-6077, Fax: 403-297-7528
bev.thomson@gov.ab.ca

Alberta Court of Queen's Bench

Calgary Courts Centre, #705N, 601 - 5th St. SW, Calgary, AB T2P 5P7
Tel: 403-297-7538; *Fax:* 403-297-8617
www.albertacourts.ab.ca

In Alberta, the Court of Queen's Bench is the Superior Trial Court. The Court hears trials in both civil & criminal matters, as well as appeals from decisions of the Provincial Court. The Chief Justice & other Justices are also judges of Surrogate Matters. Sittings of the Court of Queen's Bench are held in various areas throughout Alberta.

Chief Justice: The Honourable Neil C. Wittmann
Associate Chief Justice: The Honourable J.D. Rooke
Justices (The Honourable Mr. / Madam Justice):
Allen B. Sulatycky
Arthur M. Lutz
Bonnie L. Rawlins
T.F. McMahon
Suzanne M. Bensler
Lloyd David Wilkins(Supernumerary Judge)
C. Adele Kent
Peter J. McIntyre
Carolyn S. Phillips
Peter Macdonnell Clark
Sal Joseph LoVecchio
William P. Sullivan
Colleen Lynn Kenny
Gerard C. Hawco
C. Scott Brooker
Barbara E.C. Romaine
Rosemary E. Nation
Aexander G. Park
Bryan E. Mahoney
Elizabeth A. Hughes
Marshsa C. Erb
Karen M. Horner
Sheilah L. Martin
Alan D. Macleod
K.M. Eidsvik
E.C. Wilson
J. Strekaf
R.G. Stevens
P.R. Jeffrey
S.L. Hunt McDonald
J.T. McCarthy
R.J. Hall
G.H. Poelman
Administration:
Kathleen McAusland(Senior Manager)
Bonita Dueck(Director, Judicial Administration)
Shoana Holt(Criminal Supervisor)
Audrey Jeske(Exhibits Supervisor)
Lise Spilloway(Administrator, Procedure Control)
Christine Urquhart(Supervisor, Judicial Assistants)

Courts:

Drumheller: Court of Queen's Bench
Court House, 511 - 3 Ave. West, P.O. Box 759, Drumheller, AB T0J 0Y0
Tel: 403-820-7300; *Fax:* 403-823-6073
www.albertacourts.ab.ca
Manager: Janice McGuckin, 403-820-7300, Fax: 403-823-6073
janice.mcguckin@gov.ab.ca

Edmonton: Court of Queen's Bench
Law Courts, 1A Sir Winston Churchill Sq., Edmonton, AB T5J 0R2
Tel: 780-422-2492; *Fax:* 780-422-9742
www.albertacourts.ab.ca
Justices (The Honourable Mr. / Madam Justice):
Joanne B. Veit
Edward P. MacCallum(Supernumerary Judge)
Ernest A. Marshall(Supernumerary Judge)
Myra B. Bielby
Lawrie J. Smith
Donald Lee
Mary T. Moreau
Richard P. Marceau
R. Paul Belzil
Mel A. Binder
Sterling M. Sanderman
Doreen A. Sulyma
Brian R. Burrows
Gerald A. Verville
L. Darlene Acton
Terrance D. Clackson
Andrea B. Moen
S.J. Greckol
Eric F. Macklin
Vital O. Ouellette
Donna C. Read
Stephen D. Hillier
Juliana E. Topolniski
Adam W. Germain
June M. Ross
John J. Gill
Dennis R.G. Thomas
R.A. Graesser
D.L. Shelley
K.G. Nielsen
M.G. Crighton
D.J. Manderscheid
K.D. Yamauchi
Beverley A. Browne
J.H. Goss
Senior Manager: Maria Lavorato, 780-422-2492, Fax: 780-427-0629
maria.lavorato@gov.ab.ca
Manager: Diane Royan, 780-422-2492, Fax: 780-427-0629
diane.royan@gov.ab.ca
Manager: Susan Logan, 780-422-9475, Fax: 780-427-0629
susan.logan@gov.ab.ca
Administrator: Leanne Malcolm, 780-415-2672, Fax: 780-422-9742
leanne.malcolm@gov.ab.ca

Fort McMurray: Court of Queen's Bench
Court House, 9700 Franklin Ave., Fort McMurray, AB T9H 4W3
Tel: 780-743-7136; *Fax:* 780-743-7135
www.albertacourts.ab.ca
Manager: M. Campbell

Grande Prairie: Court of Queen's Bench
Court House, 10260 - 99 St., Grande Prairie, AB T8V 2H4
Tel: 780-538-5340; *Fax:* 780-538-5493
www.albertacourts.ab.ca
Manager: Rogena Hunt, 780-538-5340, Fax: 780-538-5493
rogena.hunt@gov.ab.ca
Senior Judicial Clerk: Jaime Bressler, 780-538-5340, Fax: 780-538-5493
jaime.bressler@gov.ab.ca
Senior Judicial Clerk: Chervaughn Shirto, 780-538-5340, Fax: 780-538-5493
chervaughn.shirto@gov.ab.ca
Senior Judicial Clerk: Michelle Wilmott, 780-538-5340, Fax: 780-538-5493
michelle.wilmott@gov.ab.ca

High Level: Court of Queen's Bench
Court House, 10106 - 100 Ave., P.O. Box 1560, High Level, AB T0H 1Z0
Tel: 780-926-3715; *Fax:* 780-926-4068
www.albertacourts.ab.ca
Criminal sittings are held as required.
Manager: S. Rendle

Hinton: Court of Queen's Bench
Court House, 237 Jasper St. West, P.O. Box 6450, Hinton, AB T7V 1X7
Tel: 780-865-8280; *Fax:* 780-865-8253
www.albertacourts.ab.ca
Administration
Manager: K. Hanington

Lethbridge: Court of Queen's Bench
Court House, 320 - 4 St. South, Lethbridge, AB T1J 1Z8
Tel: 403-381-5196; *Fax:* 403-381-5128
www.albertacourts.ab.ca
W. Vaughan Hembroff
Justices (The Honourable Mr. / Madam Justice):
J.H. Langston
D.K. Miller
Administration:
Gwen Chadsey(Manager)
Evina Frankish(Senior Judicial Clerk)

Medicine Hat: Court of Queen's Bench
Law Courts, 460 First St. SE, Medicine Hat, AB T1A 0A8
Tel: 403-529-8710; *Fax:* 403-529-8607
www.albertacourts.ab.ca
Manager: Shauna Jobagyu, 403-529-8710, Fax: 403-529-8607
shauna.jobagy@gov.ab.ca

Peace River: Court of Queen's Bench
Court House, 9905 - 97 Ave., P.O. Box 900-34, Peace River, AB T8S 1T4
Tel: 780-624-6256; *Fax:* 780-624-7101
www.albertacourts.ab.ca
Manager: Pam Testawich, 780-624-6256, Fax: 780-624-7101
pam.testawich@gov.ab.ca

Red Deer: Court of Queen's Bench
Court House, 4909 - 48 Ave., Red Deer, AB T4N 3T5
Tel: 403-340-5220; *Fax:* 403-340-7984
www.albertacourts.ab.ca
Justices (The Honourable Mr. / Madam Justice):
James L. Foster
K.L. Sisson
Monica R. Bast
Administration:
Sandra Mitchell(Senior Manager)
W. Darda(Manager)

St. Paul: Court of Queen's Bench
Court House, 4704 - 50 St., P.O. Box 1900, St Paul, AB T0A 3A0
Tel: 780-645-6324; *Fax:* 780-645-6273
www.albertacourts.ab.ca
Manager: Wanda Whelan, 780-645-6324, Fax: 780-645-6273
wanda.whelan@gov.ab.ca

Wetaskiwin: Court of Queen's Bench
Law Courts, 4605 - 51 St., Wetaskiwin, AB T9A 1K7
Tel: 780-361-1258; *Fax:* 780-361-1319
www.albertacourts.ab.ca
Manager: Edwina Segboer, 780-361-1204, Fax: 780-361-1338
edwina.segboer@gov.ab.ca

Alberta Provincial Court

Law Courts, 1A Sir Winston Churchill Sq., Edmonton, AB T5J 0R2
Tel: 780-427-8713; *Fax:* 780-422-9736
www.albertacourts.ab.ca

The Provincial Court of Alberta serves as the point of entry to the justice system in the following areas of law: civil matters (Small Claims Court), related to damages & debt & pretrial conferences; criminal law; family law, such as Parenting & Contact Orders; traffic offences, under federal statutes, provincial statutes, & municipal bylaws; & Criminal Code offences committed by youth from ages twelve to seventeen. Circuit point courts are situated throughout the province.

A.G. Vickery(Chief Judge)
A.H. Lefever(Deputy Chief Judge)
J.M. Fililce(Assistant Chief Judge (Family & Youth))
N.R. Hess(Assistant Chief Judge (Civil))

Courts:

Calgary - Civil, Criminal, Family, Regional, Traffic, & Youth
Calgary Courts Centre, #402S, 601 - 5th St. SW, Calgary, AB T2P 5P7
Tel: 403-297-3122; *Fax:* 403-297-2932
www.albertacourts.ab.ca
A.G Vickery(Chief Judge)
N.R. Hess(Assistant Chief Judge (Civil))
V.T. Tousignant(Assistant Chief Judge (Family & Youth))
Administration:
Senior Manager: Basem Hage, 403-297-3681, Fax: 403-592-4896
basem.hage@gov.ab.ca

Calgary - Civil
Calgary Courts Centre, #606S, 601 - 5th St. SW, Calgary, AB T2P 5P7
Tel: 403-297-7217; *Fax:* 403-297-7374
www.albertacourts.ab.ca
N.R. Hess(Assistant Chief Judge)
L.L. Burt
M.A. McCorquodale
B.K. O'Ferrall
Administrator: Marilyn Clisdell, 403-297-7217, Fax: 403-297-7374
marilyn.clisdell@gov.ab.ca

Calgary - Criminal
Calgary Courts Centre, #402S, 601 5th St. SW, Calgary, AB T2P 5P7
Tel: 403-297-3122; *Fax:* 403-297-3179
www.albertacourts.ab.ca
A.G. Vickery(Chief Judge)
R.J. Wilkins(Assistant Chief Judge (Calgary & Calgary Region))
Administration:
Manager: Barb McCullough, 403-297-3122, Fax: 403-297-3106
barb.mccullough@gov.ab.ca
Administrator, Criminal Hearing Office & Document Control: Julia Hiebert, 403-297-3127, Fax: 403-297-6405
Administrator: Criminal Justice Clerks, Jo-Ann Larson, 403-297-3128, Fax: 403-297-3179

Calgary - Family
Calgary Courts Centre, #704N, 601 - 5th St. SW, Calgary, AB T2P 5P7
Tel: 403-297-3471; *Fax:* 403-297-3461
www.albertacourts.ab.ca
Judges:
V.T. Tousignant(Assistant Chief Judge)
G.J. Burrell
E.R.R. Carruthers
L.T.L. Cook-Stanhope
K.J. Jordan
T. LaRochelle
S.E. Lipton
L.K. McLellan
R.J. O'Gorman
S. Prowse O'Ferrall
J.R. Shaw
Administration:
Manager: Lisa Lindquist, 403-297-3926, Fax: 403-297-3461
lisa.lindquist@gov.ab.ca
Administrator: Nadia Gates, 403-297-3925, Fax: 403-297-4892
nadia.gates@gov.ab.ca

Calgary - Regional
Calgary Courts Centre, #607S, 601 - 5th St. SW, Calgary, AB T2P 5P7
Tel: 403-297-3010; *Fax:* 403-297-3237
www.albertacourts.ab.ca
Circuit point courts are located in the following places: Airdrie (#113, 104 - 1 Ave.), Banff (#350, 208 Wolf St.), Canmore (#101, 800 Railway Ave.), Cochrane (213 - 1 St., West), Didsbury (1611 - 15 Ave.), Okotoks (98 McRae St.), & Tsuu T'ina Nation (9911 Chula Blvd., Sarcee).
Judges:
R.J. Wilkins(Assistant Chief Judge, Calgary & Calgary Regional)
P.B. Barley
E.J. Creighton
L.R. Grieve
P.M. McIlhargey
J. Shriar
Administration:
Manager, Victims Services: Carol Lemieux, 780-422-3566, Fax: 780-422-4213
carol.lemieux@gov.ab.ca

Calgary - Traffic
Calgary Courts Centre, #203S, 601 - 5th St. SW, Calgary, AB T2P 5P7
Tel: 403-297-2283; *Fax:* 403-297-2220
www.albertacourts.ab.ca
Traffic Commissioner: M.A. Brown
Traffic Commissioner: J.K. Conley
Traffic Commissioner: D.C. Elliott
Traffic Commissioner: J.G. Szekeres
Administrator: Lynn Quinton, 403-297-4771, Fax: 403-591-4820
lynn.quinton@gov.ab.ca

Calgary - Youth
Calgary Courts Centre, #201N, 601 - 5th St. SW, Calgary, AB T2P 5P7
Tel: 403-297-3473; *Fax:* 403-297-4892
www.albertacourts.ab.ca
V.T. Tousignant(Assistant Chief Judge)
G.J. Burrell
E.R.R. Carruthers
L.T.L. Cook-Stanhope
K.J. Jordan
T. LaRochelle
S.E. Lipton
L.K. McLellan
R.J. O'Gorman
S. Prowse O'Ferrall
J.R. Shaw
Manager: Lisa Lindquist, 403-297-3926, Fax: 403-297-3461
lisa.lindquist@gov.ab.ca
Administrator: Nadia Gates, 403-297-3925, Fax: 403-297-4892
nadia.gates@gov.ab.ca

Camrose
Court House, 5210 - 49 Ave., Camrose, AB T4V 3Y2
Tel: 780-679-1240; *Fax:* 780-679-1253
www.albertacourts.ab.ca
A circuit point court is located in Killam (4903 - 50 St.).
Judges:
H.D. Gaede
Judges:
W.A. Andreassen
Judges:
K.L. Rostad
Administration:
Manager: Debbie Tkachuk, 780-644-8411, Fax: 780-644-8424
debbie.tkachuk@gov.ab.ca

Drumheller
Court House, 511 - 3 Ave. West, P.O. Box 759, Drumheller, AB T0J 0Y0
Tel: 403-820-7300; *Fax:* 403-823-6073
www.albertacourts.ab.ca
Circuit point courts are situated in the following places: Hanna (401 Centre St.), Siksika Nation (Junction of Highways 901 & 547), & Strathmore (226 - 2 Ave.).
Administration:
Manager: Janice McGuckin, 403-820-7300, Fax: 403-823-6073
janice.mcguckin@gov.ab.ca

Edmonton - Civil, Criminal, Family & Youth, & Traffic
Law Courts, 1A Sir Winston Churchill Sq., Edmonton, AB T5J 0R2
Tel: 780-427-8713; *Fax:* 780-422-9736
www.albertacourts.ab.ca
A.G. Vickery(Chief Judge)
A.H. Lefever(Deputy Chief Judge)
J.M. Filice(Assistant Chief Judge (Family & Youth))
N.R. Hess(Assistant Chief Judge (Civil))
D.R. Pahl(Assistant Chief Judge (Edmonton Region))
Senior Manager: Brenda Haynes, 780-427-7869, Fax: 780-422-9736
brenda.haynes@gov.ab.ca

Edmonton - Civil
Law Courts, 1A Sir Winston Churchill Sq., Edmonton, AB T5J 0R2
Tel: 780-422-2508; *Fax:* 780-427-4348
www.albertacourts.ab.ca
N.R. Hess(Assistant Chief Judge)
M.M. Donnelly
K. Haymour
K.D. Hope
J.L. Skitsko
L.D. Young
Administration:
Administrator: Clarice Cameron, 780-422-2508, Fax: 780-427-4348
clarice.cameron@gov.ab.ca

Edmonton - Criminal
Law Courts, 1A Sir Winston Churchill Sq., Edmonton, AB T5J 0R2
Tel: 780-427-7868; *Fax:* 780-422-9736
www.albertacourts.ab.ca
A.G. Vickery(Chief Judge)
A.H. Lefever(Deputy Chief Judge)
J.K. Wheatley(Assistant Chief Judge)
D.R. Pahl(Assistant Chief Judge (Edmonton Region))
Administration:
Manager: Kerri McPhee, 780-427-7869, Fax: 780-422-9736
kerri.mcphee@gov.ab.ca

Edmonton - Family & Youth
Law Courts, 1A Sir Winston Churchill Sq., Edmonton, AB T5J 0R2
Tel: 780-427-2743; *Fax:* 780-427-5797
www.albertacourts.ab.ca
J.M. Filice(Assistant Chief Judge)
D.J. Buchanan
M.J. Burch
D. Dalton
J.G. Easton
J.D. Franklin
G.B.N. Ho
J.C. Koshman
P.E. Kvill
S.C. Miller
L.S. Witten
Manager: Barbara Petryk, 780-427-2743, Fax: 780-427-5797
barb.petryk@gov.ab.ca
Administrator: Donna Blauel, 780-427-8337, Fax: 780-427-5797
donna.blauel@gov.ab.ca

Edmonton - Traffic & Civil
Law Courts, 1A Sir Winston Churchill Sq., Edmonton, AB T5J 0R2
Tel: 780-427-5913; *Fax:* 780-427-5791
www.albertacourts.ab.ca
Traffic Commissioner: D.R. Ackroyd
Traffic Commissioner: W.S. Andrew
Traffic Commissioner: I. Yaverbaum
Linda Hawryluk, 780-427-5913, Fax: 780-427-5791
linda.hawryluk@gov.ab.ca

Fort McMurray
Court House, 9700 Franklin Ave., Fort McMurray, AB T9H 4W3
Tel: 780-743-7195; *Fax:* 780-743-7395
www.albertacourts.ab.ca
A circuit point court is located in Fort Chipewyan (Multi-Plex, Flett St.).
S.A. Cleary
J.R. Jacques
Manager: Michelle Campbell, 780-743-7136, Fax: 780-743-7395
michelle.l.campbell@gov.ab.ca

Fort Saskatchewan
Court House, 10504 - 100 Ave., Fort Saskatchewan, AB T8L 3S9
Tel: 780-998-1200; *Fax:* 780-998-7222
www.albertacourts.ab.ca
A circuit point court is located in Boyle (5006 - 3 St.).
D.G. Rae
Manager: Bonnie Matvichuk, 780-998-1200, Fax: 780-998-7222
bonnie.matvichuk@gov.ab.ca

Grande Prairie
Court House, 10260 - 99 St., Grande Prairie, AB T8V 6J4
Tel: 780-538-5360; *Fax:* 780-538-5454
www.albertacourts.ab.ca
Circuit point courts are located in the following places: Fox Creek (100 - 4 Ave.) & Valleyview (5102 - 50 Ave.).
M.B. Golden
B.R. Hougestol
J.A. Watson
Manager: Rogena Hunt, 780-538-5360, Fax: 780-538-5454
rogena.hunt@gov.ab.ca

High Level
Court House, 10106 - 100 Ave., P.O. Box 1560, High Level, AB T0H 1Z0
Tel: 780-926-3715; *Fax:* 780-926-4068
www.albertacourts.ab.ca
Circuit point courts are located in the following places: Assumption (Court House, Chateh) & Fort Vermilion (4607 River Rd.).
Administrator: Shelly Rendle, 780-926-3715, Fax: 780-926-4068
shelly.rendle@gov.ab.ca

High Prairie
Court House, 4911 - 53 Ave., P.O. Box 1470, High Prairie, AB T0G 1E0
Tel: 780-523-6600; *Fax:* 780-523-6643
www.albertacourts.ab.ca
Circuit point courts are located in the following places: Red Earth Creek (122 Forestry Rd.), Slave Lake (101 - 3 St., SW), & Wabasca-Desmarais (867 Stony Point Rd.).
T.R. Goodson
Manager: Mae Fjeld, 780-523-6600, Fax: 780-523-6643
mae.fjeld@gov.ab.ca

Hinton
Court House, 237 Jasper St. West, P.O. Box 6450, Hinton, AB T7V 1X7
Tel: 780-865-8280; *Fax:* 780-865-8253
www.albertacourts.ab.ca
Circuit point courts are located in the following places: Edson (111 - 54 St.), Grande Cache (Provincial Building, Hoppe Ave.), & Jasper (629 Patricia St.).
D.C. Norheim
Administrator: Karen Hanington, 780-865-8280, Fax: 780-865-8253
karen.hanington@gov.ab.ca

Leduc
Court House, 4612 - 50 St., Leduc, AB T9E 6L1
Tel: 780-986-6911; *Fax:* 780-986-0345
www.albertacourts.ab.ca
Circuit point courts are located in the following places: Breton (4911 - 50 Ave.) & Drayton Valley (5136 - 51 Ave.).
M.M. White
Manager: Marilea McMullen, 780-986-6911, Fax: 780-986-0345
marilea.mcmullen@gov.ab.ca

Lethbridge
Court House, 320 - 4th St. South, Lethbridge, AB T1J 1Z8
Tel: 403-381-5223; *Fax:* 403-381-5763
www.albertacourts.ab.ca
Circuit point courts are located in the following places: Cardston (576 Main St.), Fort Macleod (244 Chief Red Crow Blvd.), Pincher Creek (782 Main St.), & Taber (5126 - 49 Ave.).
E.W. Peterson(Assistant Chief Judge, Southern Region)
F.W. Coward
G.R. DeBow
T.G. Hironaka
L.B. Hogan
R.A. Jacobson
J.N. LeGrandeur
S.L. Oishi
D.G. Redman
Administrator: M, McCulloch, 403-381-5525, Fax: 403-381-5763
maria.mcculloch@gov.ab.ca

Medicine Hat
Law Courts, 460 - First St. SE, Medicine Hat, AB T1A 0A8
Tel: 403-529-8644; *Fax:* 403-529-8606
www.albertacourts.ab.ca
A circuit point court is located in Brooks (220 - 4 Ave., West).

Dietrich Brand
F.C. Fisher
D.J. Greaves
G.K. Krinke
Administrator: Miles Weatherall, 403-529-8647, Fax: 403-529-8606
miles.weatherall@gov.ab.ca

Peace River
Court House, 9905 - 97 Ave., P.O. Box 900-34, Peace River, AB T8S 1T4
Tel: 780-624-6256; *Fax:* 780-624-6175
www.albertacourts.ab.ca
Circuit point courts are located in the following places: Fairview (10209 - 109 St.) & Falher (028 Main St., SE).
E.J. Simpson(Assistant Chief Judge, Northern Region)
J.R. McIntosh
G.W. Paul
Administrator: Pam Testawich, 780-624-6256, Fax: 780-624-6175
pam.testawich@gov.ab.ca

Red Deer
Court House, 4909 - 48 Ave., Red Deer, AB T4N 3T5
Tel: 403-340-5250; *Fax:* 403-340-7985
www.albertacourts.ab.ca
Circuit point courts are located in the following places: Coronation (4909 Royal St.), Rimbey (5025 - 55 St.), Rocky Mountain House (4919 - 51 St.), & Stettler (4705 - 49 Ave.).
W.A. Skinner(Assistant Chief Judge, Central Region)
N.P. Lawrence
T.G. Schollie
G.E. Deck
J.D. Holmes
J.A. Hunter
J.B. Mitchell
D.J. Plosz
E.D. Riemer
Manager: Sandra Mitchell, 403-340-5250, Fax: 403-340-7985
sandra.mitchell@gov.ab.ca

St Albert
Court House, 3 St. Anne St., St Albert, AB T8N 2E8
Tel: 780-458-7305; *Fax:* 780-460-2963
www.albertacourts.ab.ca
Circuit point courts are located in the following places: Athabasca (4903 - 50 St.), Barrhead (6203 - 49 St.), Morinville (10008 - 107 St.), & Westlock (10003 - 100 St.).
B.H. Fraser
N.A.F. Mackie
Manager: Joanne McNeilly, 780-458-7300, Fax: 780-460-2963
joanne.mcneilly@gov.ab.ca

St Paul
Court House, 4704 - 50 St., P.O. Box 1900, St Paul, AB T0A 3A0
Tel: 780-645-6324; *Fax:* 780-645-6273
www.albertacourts.ab.ca
Circuit point courts are located in the following places: Bonnyville (4902 - 50 Ave.), Cold Lake (5323 - 48 Ave.), & Lac La Biche (9503 Beaver Hill Rd.).
D.E. Demetrick
K.D. Williams
Manager: Wanda Whelan, 780-645-6324, Fax: 780-645-6273
wanda.whelan@gov.ab.ca

Sherwood Park
Court House, 190 Chippewa Rd., Sherwood Park, AB T8A 4H5
Tel: 780-464-0114; *Fax:* 780-449-1490
www.albertacourts.ab.ca
J. Maher
S.G. Peck
Administrator: Bonnie Matvichuk, 780-464-0114, Fax: 780-449-1490
bonnie.matvichuk@gov.ab.ca

Stony Plain
Court House, 4711 - 44 Ave., Stony Plain, AB T7Z 1N5
Tel: 780-963-6205; *Fax:* 780-963-6402
www.albertacourts.ab.ca
Circuit point courts are located in the following places: Evansburg (4921 - 50 St.), Glenevis (Administration Office, Alexis Reserve), Mayerthorpe (5013 - 50 St.), & Whitecourt (5020 - 52 Ave.).
P. Ayotte
H.W.A. Fuller
V.H. Myers
K.E. Tjosvold
Manager: Brenda Majeau, 780-968-6401, Fax: 780-963-6402
brenda.majeau@gov.ab.ca

Vermilion
Provincial Building, 4701 - 52nd St., P.O. Box 30, Vermilion, AB T9X 1J9
Tel: 780-853-8130; *Fax:* 780-853-8200
www.albertacourts.ab.ca
Circuit point courts are located in the following places: Lloydminster (5124 - 50 St.), Vegreville (4809 - 50 St.), & Wainwright (738 - 2 Ave.).
R.L. Tibbitt
P.T. Johnston
Administrator: Ruth Westman, 780-853-8130, Fax: 780-853-8200
ruth.westman@gov.ab.ca

Wetaskiwin
Law Courts, 4605 - 51 St., Wetaskiwin, AB T9A 1K7
Tel: 780-361-1204; *Fax:* 780-361-1338
www.albertacourts.ab.ca
A circuit point court is located in Ponoka (5110 - 49 Ave.).
B.D. Rosborough
Manager: Edwina Segboer, 780-361-1204, Fax: 780-361-1338
edwina.segboer@gov.ab.ca

British Columbia

British Columbia Court of Appeal
The Law Courts, #400, 800 Hornby St., Vancouver, BC V6Z 2C5
Tel: 604-660-2468; *Fax:* 604-660-1951
www.courts.gov.bc.ca/Court_of_Appeal
The Court of Appeal is the highest court in the province. It hears appeals from the Supreme Court, & from the Provincial Court on some criminal matters. It also hears reviews and appeals from some administrative boards and tribunals.
Chief Justice: The Hon. Lance S.G. Finch
Justices of Appeal (The Hon. Mr./Madam Justice):
E.A. Bennett
E.C. Chiasson
I.T. Donald
S.D. Frankel
N.J. Garson
H.M. Groberman
J.E. Hall
C.E. Hinkson
C.M. Huddart
P.A. Kirkpatrick
R.E. Levine
R.T.A. Low
P.D. Lowry
K.C. Mackenzie
K.E. Neilson
M.V. Newbury
J.E. Prowse
M. Rowles
C.A. Ryan
M. Saunders
D.M. Smith
K.J. Smith
D.F. Tysoe
Administration:
Registrar: Jennifer Jordan, 604-660-2729

British Columbia Supreme Court
The Law Courts, 800 Smithe St., Vancouver, BC V6Z 2E1
Tel: 604-660-2800; *Fax:* 604-660-1723
www.courts.gov.bc.ca/supreme_court
The Supreme Court is a trial court of original jurisdiction for all civil & criminal matters arising in B.C., save & except matters expressly excluded by statute. It hears most appeals from the Provincial Court.
Chief Justice: The Hon. Robert J. Bauman
Assoc. Chief Justice: The Hon. Anne W. MacKenzie
Judges (The Hon. Mr./Madam Justice):
E.J. Adair
M.J. Allan
W.G. Baker
S.K. Ballance
G.T.W. Bowden
M. Boyd
B. Brown
C.J. Bruce
G.D. Burnyeat
B. Butler
B.I. Cohen
F.W. Cole
A.F. Cullen
V.R. Curtis
D.J. Dardi
B.M. Davies
G. Dickson
J.R. Dillon
W. Ehrcke
L.A. Fenlon
B. Fisher
S.C. Fitzpatrick
L.B. Gerow
R.B.T. Goepel
J.C. Grauer
V. Gray
B.M. Greyell
S.A. Griffin
J.M. Gropper
J.R. Groves
D.D. Harris
H.J. Holmes
M.A. Humphries
S.F. Kelleher
D. Kloegman
P.D. Leask
L.A. Loo
M.A. Mainsonville
D.M. Masuhara
N. Morrison
E.M. Myers
P.J. Pearlman
E. Rice
S.R. Romilly
C.J. Ross
L.D. Russell
J.E.D. Savage
R.J. Sewell
J.S. Sigurdson
A.H. Silverman
H.A. Slade
W.B. Smart
C.L. Smith
N.H. Smith
A.M. Stewart
S.S. Stromberg-Stein
P.G. Voith
Paul W. Walker
C.A. Wedge
P.M. Willcock
R.S.K. Wong

Courts:
Campbell River
500 - 13 Ave., Campbell River, BC V9W 6P1
Tel: 250-286-7510; *Fax:* 250-286-7512
Registry (County): Vancouver Island
District Manager: Michael Hammell
michael.hammell@gov.bc.ca

Chilliwack
Court House, 46085 Yale Rd., Chilliwack, BC V2P 2L8
Tel: 604-795-8350; *Fax:* 604-795-8393
Registry (County): Westminster
W. Grist
B. Joyce
District Manager: Marian Moore, 604-795-8300, Fax: 604-795-8345

Courtenay
Court House, #100, 420 Cumberland Rd., Courtenay, BC V9N 2C4
Tel: 250-334-1115; *Fax:* 250-334-1191
Registry (County): Vancouver Island
District Manager: R. Krayenhoff
rolph.krayenhoff@gov.bc.ca

Cranbrook
Court House, 102 - 11 Ave. South, Cranbrook, BC V1C 2P3
Tel: 250-426-1234; *Fax:* 250-426-1352
Registry (County): Kootenay
T. Melnick
Deputy District Registrar: Debbie Schroeter
debbie.schroeter@gov.bc.ca

Duncan
Court House, 238 Government St., Duncan, BC V9L 1A5
Tel: 250-746-1227; *Fax:* 250-746-1244
Registry (County): Vancouver Island
District Manager: Joanne Power
joanne.power@gov.bc.ca

Fort Nelson
4604 Sunset Dr., P.O. Box 1000, Fort Nelson, BC V0C 1R0
Tel: 250-774-5999; *Fax:* 250-774-6904
Registry (County): Cariboo
Court Administrator: Linda Brekelmans
linda.brekelmans@gov.bc.ca

Fort St. John
Court House, 10600 - 100 St., Fort St John, BC V1J 4L6
Tel: 250-787-3231; *Fax:* 250-787-3518
Registry (County): Cariboo

Deputy Registrar: Gloria Carew
gloria.carew@gov.bc.ca

Golden
837 Park Dr., P.O. Box 1500, Golden, BC V0A 1H0
Tel: 250-344-7581; *Fax:* 250-344-7715
Registry (County): Kootenay
Court Administrator: Lori-Ann Roseberry
loriann.roseberry@gov.bc.ca

Kamloops
Court House, #223 - 455 Columbia St., Kamloops, BC V2C 6K4
Tel: 250-828-4344; *Fax:* 250-828-4332
Registry (County): Yale
R. Blair
S.D. Dley
H. Hyslop
I.C. Meiklem
R. Powers
Manager, Scheduling: David McCoy, 250-828-4021, Fax: 250-828-4080
sc.scheduling_ka@courts.gov.bc.ca

Kelowna
Court House, 1355 Water St., Kelowna, BC V1Y 9R3
Tel: 250-470-6900; *Fax:* 250-470-6939
Registry (County): Yale
G. Barrow
A. Beames
T. Brooke
P. Rogers
Manager, Scheduling: Barb Turik
sc.scheduling_ok@courts.gov.bc.ca

Nanaimo
Court House, 35 Front St., Nanaimo, BC V9R 5J1
Tel: 250-741-3805; *Fax:* 250-741-3809
Registry (County): Vancouver Island
D.A. Halfyard
B.D. MacKenzie
J. Power
S. Shabbits
Senior Manager: Tanya Hingley, 250-741-3812, Fax: 250-741-3809
tanya.hingley@gov.bc.ca

Nelson
Court House, 320 Ward St., Nelson, BC V1L 1S6
Tel: 250-354-6165; *Fax:* 250-354-6133
Registry (County): Kootenay
T. McEwan
District Manager: Wendy Schwab, 250-354-6165, Fax: 250-354-6539
wendy.schwab@gov.bc.ca

New Westminster
Court House, Begbie Sq., 651 Carnarvon St., New Westminster, BC V3M 1C9
Tel: 604-660-8551; *Fax:* 604-660-2072
Registry (County): Vancouver
E. Arnold-Bailey
L. Bernard
N. Brown
R. Crawford
J.S. Harvey
I.B. Josephson
K.M. Ker
R. McKinnon
A. Saunders
T. Schultes
J. Truscott
F. Verhoeven
J. Williams
L.P. Williamson
Administrator: Laura Mayes, 604-660-8557, Fax: 604-660-2047
laura.mayes@gov.bc.ca

Penticton
Court House, #116, 100 Main St., Penticton, BC V2A 5A5
Tel: 250-492-1231; *Fax:* 250-492-1378
Toll-Free: 888-526-8555
Registry (County): Yale
District Manager: Sylvia Judge
sylvia.judge@gov.bc.ca

Port Alberni
2999 - 4 Ave., Port Alberni, BC V9Y 8A5
Tel: 250-720-2424; *Fax:* 250-720-2426
Toll-Free: 877-741-3820
Registry (County): Vancouver Island
District Manager: Lowell Boran
lowell.boran@gov.bc.ca

Powell River
#103, 6953 Alberni St., Powell River, BC V8A 2B8
Tel: 604-485-3630; *Fax:* 604-485-3637
Toll-Free: 877-741-3820
Registry (County): Vancouver Island
District Manager: Bryna Ary
bryna.ary@gov.bc.ca

Prince George
Court House
J.O. Wilson Sq., 250 George St., Prince George, BC V2L 5S2
Tel: 250-614-2700; *Fax:* 250-614-2737
Registry (County): Cariboo
W. Parrett
Senior District Manager: Patty Walker, 250-614-2700, Fax: 250-614-2737
patricia.walker@gov.bc.ca

Prince Rupert
Court House, 100 Market Pl., Prince Rupert, BC V8J 1B8
Tel: 250-624-7525; *Fax:* 250-624-7538
Registry (County): Prince Rupert
R.D. Punnett
Manager, Scheduling: Crystal Foerster, 250-624-7474, Fax: 250-624-7538
sc.scheduling_pr@courts.gov.bc.ca

Quesnel
Court House, #305, 350 Barlow Ave., Quesnel, BC V2J 2C1
Tel: 250-992-4256; *Fax:* 250-992-4171
Registry (County): Cariboo
District Manager: Einar Gunnarson
einar.gunnarson@gov.bc.ca

Rossland
Court House, 2288 Columbia Ave., P.O. Box 639, Rossland, BC V0G 1Y0
Tel: 250-362-7368; *Fax:* 250-362-9632
Registry (County): Kootenay
District Manager: Trudy Williams
trudy.williams@gov.bc.ca

Salmon Arm
Court House, #550, 2nd Ave. NE, Salmon Arm, BC V1E 4S4
Tel: 250-832-1610; *Fax:* 250-832-1749
Registry (County): Yale
Manager, Scheduling: David McCoy
sc.scheduling_ka@courts.gov.bc.ca

Smithers
3793 Alfred St., P.O. Box 5000, Smithers, BC V0J 2N0
Tel: 250-847-7376; *Fax:* 250-847-7710
Registry (County): Prince Rupert
District Manager: J. Caird
janet.caird@gov.bc.ca

Terrace
Court House, 3408 Kalum St., Terrace, BC V8G 2N6
Tel: 250-638-2111; *Fax:* 250-638-2123
Registry (County): Prince Rupert
District Manager: Laura Pistell
laura.pistell@gov.bc.ca

Vernon
Court House, 3001 - 27th St., Vernon, BC V1T 4W5
Tel: 250-549-5422; *Fax:* 205-549-5621
Registry (County): Yale
District Manager: Sheree Marshall, 250-549-5420
sheree.marshall@gov.bc.ca

Victoria
Court House, #2, 850 Burdett Ave., Victoria, BC V8W 1B4
Tel: 250-356-1478; *Fax:* 250-356-6279
Registry (County): Vancouver Island
K. Bracken
J. Dorgan
R. Johnston
M.D. Macaulay
R.W. Metzger
D. Wilson
R. Wilson
Senior District Manager: Charlene Kornaga, 250-356-1461
charlene.kornaga@gov.bc.ca

Williams Lake
Court House, 540 Borland St., Williams Lake, BC V2G 1R8
Tel: 250-398-4301; *Fax:* 250-398-4459
Registry (County): Cariboo
Deputy Registrar: Rhonda Hykawy, 250-398-4308, Fax: 250-398-4459

British Columbia Provincial Court

Pacific Centre, #602, 700 West Georgia St., P.O. Box 10287, Vancouver, BC V7Y 1E8
Tel: 604-660-2864; *Fax:* 604-660-1108
www.provincialcourt.bc.ca

The Provincial Court is a statutory, trial court. It hears cases in criminal, family, youth, small claims & traffic matters.
Acting Chief Judge: The Hon. Jim Threlfall
Assoc. Chief Judge: The Hon. Gurmail Gill
Assoc. Chief Judge: The Hon. Nancy Phillips
Judges (The Hon.):
T. Crabtree
T. Shupe
K. Walker
Ad Hoc Judicial Justices of the Peace:
Cheryl Harvey
David Maihara
Linda Mayner
Candice Rogers
Jane Wakefield
Administration:
Executive Director: Judicial Administration, Jan Rossley
Administrator: Justice of the Peace Program, Kevin Purdy

Courts:

Abbotsford
32203 South Fraser Way, Abbotsford, BC V2T 1W6
Tel: 604-855-3200; *Fax:* 604-855-3232
R.B. Caryer
D. Gardner
B.G. Hoy
C.G. Maltby
R.R. Romano
J. Rounthwaite
K.D. Skilnick
Judicial Case Manager: Healther Holt

Campbell River
500 - 13 Ave., Campbell River, BC V9W 6P1
Tel: 250-286-7650; *Fax:* 250-286-7512
B. Saunderson
Judicial Case Manager: Christine M. Ballman

Chilliwack
46085 Yale Rd., Chilliwack, BC V2P 2L8
Tel: 604-795-8350; *Fax:* 604-795-8345
T.J. Crabtree
R. MacKay
W.A. Young
Judicial Case Manager: Andrea Schulz

Courtenay
#100, 420 Cumberland Rd., Courtenay, BC V9N 2C4
Tel: 250-334-1115; *Fax:* 250-334-1191
P. Doherty
Judicial Case Manager: Christine M. Ballman

Cranbrook
#147, 102 - 11 Ave. South, Cranbrook, BC V1C 2P3
Tel: 250-426-1234; *Fax:* 250-426-1352
W.G. Sheard
R.J. Webb
Judicial Case Manager: Megan Jensen

Dawson Creek
#205, 1201 - 103 Ave., Dawson Creek, BC V1G 4J2
Tel: 250-784-2278; *Fax:* 250-784-2339
R.R. Blaskovits
Judicial Case manager: Faye Campbell

Duncan
238 Government St., Duncan, BC V9L 1A5
Tel: 250-746-1219; *Fax:* 250-746-1244
J. Wood
Judicial Case Manager: Shannon L. Cole

Fort St. John
10600 - 100 St., Fort St John, BC V1J 4L6
Tel: 250-787-3231; *Fax:* 250-787-3518
R.S. Bowry
B.A. Daley
Judicial Case Manager: Faye Campbell

Golden
837 Park Dr., P.O. Box 1500, Golden, BC V0A 1H0
Tel: 250-344-7581; *Fax:* 250-344-7715

Kamloops
#223, 455 Columbia St., Kamloops, BC V2C 6K4
Tel: 250-828-4344; *Fax:* 250-828-4332
C.D. Cleaveley
D. Dley
S. Frame(Admin. Judge)
S.R. Harrison
H. Rohrmoser
J.E. Hughes
Judicial Case Manager: Sheila D. Paul

Kelowna
#1, 1355 Water St., Kelowna, BC V1Y 9R3
Tel: 250-470-6900; *Fax:* 250-470-6939
E.M. Burdett

J.P. Cartwright
B.J. Chapman
P.V. Hogan
W.W. Klinger
R.R. Smith
J.J. Threlfall(Acting Chief Judge)
A. Wallace
Judicial Case Manager: Kathy Bullach

Mackenzie
64 Centennial Dr., P.O. Box 2050, Mackenzie, BC V0J 2C0
Tel: 250-997-3377; *Fax:* 250-997-5617

Masset
1666 Orr St., P.O. Box 230, Masset, BC V0T 1M0
Tel: 250-626-5512; *Fax:* 250-626-5491

Nakusp
415 Broadway St., P.O. Box 328, Nakusp, BC V0G 1R0
Tel: 250-265-4253; *Fax:* 250-265-4413

Nanaimo
Court House, 35 Front St., Nanaimo, BC V9R 5J1
Tel: 250-741-3805; *Fax:* 250-741-3809

J.D. Cowling
T.A. Dohm(Admin. Judge)
R.A. Gould
E.L. Iverson
J.I.D. Joe
B.R. Klaver
John Dodd
Judicial Case Manager: Veronica Mitchell

Nelson
320 Ward St., Nelson, BC V1L 1S6
Tel: 250-354-6165; *Fax:* 250-354-6539

L.J. Mrozinski
Judicial Case Manager: Sandra Hadikin

New Westminster
Law Courts, Begbie Sq., New Westminster, BC V3M 1C9
Tel: 604-660-8522; *Fax:* 604-660-8977

T. Alexander
G.P. Angelomatis
D.M.B. Steinberg
C.M. Proctor
Judicial Case Manager: Lila MacDonald

North Vancouver
200 East 23 St., North Vancouver, BC V7L 4R4
Tel: 604-981-0200; *Fax:* 604-981-0234

J. Auxier
C.C. Baird Ellan
J. Challenger
J. Gedye
D.E. Moss
W.J. Rodgers(Admin. Judge)
Phillip Lim
Judicial Case Manager: Suzanne McLarty

Penticton
100 Main St., Penticton, BC V2A 5A5
Tel: 250-492-1231; *Fax:* 250-492-1378

G.G. Sinclair
Judicial Case Manager: Mar Warwick

Port Alberni
2999 - 4 Ave., Port Alberni, BC V9Y 8A5
Tel: 250-720-2424; *Fax:* 250-720-2426

J.E. Saunders

Port Coquitlam
2620 Mary Hill Rd., #A, Port Coquitlam, BC V3C 3B2
Tel: 604-927-2100; *Fax:* 604-927-2222

M.R. Buller-Bennett
P.L.J. de Couto
S. Dossa
A. Dyer
D.D. Pothecary
D.A. St. Pierre
A.J. Spence
D. Stone
Judicial Case Manager: Marylynn deKeruzec

Port Hardy
9300 Trustee Rd., P.O. Box 279, Port Hardy, BC V0N 2P0
Tel: 604-949-6122; *Fax:* 604-949-9283

Powell River
#103, 6953 Alberni St., Powell River, BC V8A 2B8
Tel: 604-485-3630; *Fax:* 604-485-3637

Prince George
J.O. Wilson Square, 250 George St., Prince George, BC V2L 5S2
Tel: 250-614-2700; *Fax:* 250-614-2717

M.J. Brecknell
B.L. Dollis
M.A. Gray
D. O'Byrne(Admin. Judge)
R.S. Tindale
R.E. Walker
D.H. Weatherly
C.D. Jolly
Judicial Case Manager: Debra Pillipow

Prince Rupert
#200, 100 Market Pl., Prince Rupert, BC V8J 1B8
Tel: 250-624-7525; *Fax:* 250-627-7538

A.K. Krantz
H.J. Seidemann III(Admin. Judge)
Judicial Case Manager: Crystal M. Foerster

Quesnel
#115, 350 Barlow Ave., Quesnel, BC V2J 2C2
Tel: 250-992-4256; *Fax:* 250-992-4171

R.D. Morgan
Judicial Case Manager: Sherry Jasper

Richmond
7577 Elmridge Way, Richmond, BC V6X 4J2
Tel: 604-660-6900; *Fax:* 604-660-1797

R.D. Fratkin
J.E. McKinnon
P.R. Meyers
M. Rae
E.D. Schmidt
P.L. Dodwell
Judicial Case Manager: Candace Goodrich

Rossland
Court House, 2288 Columbia Ave., P.O. Box 639, Rossland, BC V0G 1Y0
Tel: 250-362-7368; *Fax:* 250-362-9632

D.L. Sperry

Salmon Arm
#550, 2nd Ave. NE, P.O. Box 100 Main, Salmon Arm, BC V1E 4S4
Tel: 250-832-1610; *Fax:* 250-832-1749

E.F. de Walle

Sechelt
5480 Shorncliffe Ave., Sechelt, BC V0N 3A0
Tel: 604-740-8929; *Fax:* 604-740-8924

A. Rounthwaite

Smithers
3793 Alfred St., P.O. Box 5000, Smithers, BC V0J 2N0
Tel: 250-847-7376; *Fax:* 250-847-7710

C. Birnie
J.R. Milne
Judicial Case Manager: Sharon Portsch

Surrey
14340 - 57 Ave., Surrey, BC V3X 1B2
Tel: 604-572-2200; *Fax:* 604-572-2280

K.W. Ball
M.C. Borowicz
J.G. Cohen
P.M. Dohm
H. Field
G. Gill(Assoc. Chief Judge)
E. Gordon
P. Gulbransen(Admin. Judge)
R.P. Harris
M.B. Hicks
P.A. Hyde
J.F. Lenaghan
J.R. Lytwyn
W.G. MacDonald
S.K. MacGregor
R.D. Miller
R. Raven
A. Rounthwaite
W.F. Stewart
K. Walker
J.O. Wingham
Judicial Case Manager: Doreen J. Hodge
Judicial Case Manager: Judith Jenvey
Judicial Case Manager: Sandra Thorne
Judicial Case Manager: Bianca L. West

Terrace
3408 Kalum St., Terrace, BC V8G 2N6
Tel: 250-638-2111; *Fax:* 250-638-2123

Judicial Case Manager: Lyne Leonardes

Valemount
38 Dogwood St., Valemount, BC V0E 2Z0
Tel: 250-566-4652; *Fax:* 250-566-9732

Vancouver
Robson Sq., 800 Hornby St., P.O. Box 21, Vancouver, BC V6Z 2C5
Tel: 604-660-8989; *Fax:* 604-660-8950

B.K. Davis
H.K. Dhillon
A. Ehrcke
E.A. Ferbey
R.M. Gallagher
D.R. Pendleton
N.N. Phillips(Assoc. Chief Judge)
V. Romilly
A.R. Tweedale
J.F. Werier
W.F.W. Yee
J. Arntsen
M. Kobiljski
Z. Makhdoom
Judicial Case Manager: Barbara Brown
Judicial Case Manager: Clare Mayhew
Judicial Case Manager: Judith Norton

Vancouver - Criminal Division
222 Main St., Vancouver, BC V6A 2S8
Tel: 604-660-4200; *Fax:* 604-775-1134

C.L. Bagnall
B.E. Bastin
G.T.W. Bowden
E. Burgess
R.P. Chen
J. Galati
M.F. Giardini
J.E. Godfrey
T.J. Gove
F.E. Howard
W.J. Kitchen
R.R. Low(Admin. Judge)
M.O. MacLean
T.D. McGee
M. McMillan
J.F. Palmer
G.M. Rideout
D. Senniw
D.I. Smyth
C.E. Warren
J.E. Watchuk
H. Weitzel
Judicial Case Manager: Kelly Butler
Judicial Case Manager: Laura Caporale
Judicial Case Manager: Johnny Ceraldi
Judicial Case Manager: Teresa L. Hill
Judicial Case Manager: Catherine J. Johnstone
Judicial Case Manager: Jovanka Mihic
Judicial Case Manager: Lori Stokes

Vernon
3001 - 27 St., Vernon, BC V1T 4W5
Tel: 250-549-5422; *Fax:* 250-549-5621

D.A. Betton(Admin. Judge)
M.G. Takahashi
Judicial Case Manager: D.C. Krenz

Victoria
#2, 850 Burdett Ave., Victoria, BC V8W 1B4
Tel: 250-356-1478; *Fax:* 250-356-6279

E.C. Blake
A.F. Brooks
L.F.E. Chaperon
L.J.M. Harvey
R.A. Higinbotham
J.M. Hubbard
J.N. Kay
B.D. MacKenzie
B.M. Neal
E.J. Quantz(Admin. Judge)
L.W. Smith
S.E. Wishart
G.E. Madrick
Judicial Case Manager: A. Bruce
Judicial Case Manager: Deborah Henry
Judicial Case Manager: Yvonne Locke

Victoria - Western Communities
1756 Island Hwy., Victoria, BC V9B 1H8
Tel: 250-391-2888; *Fax:* 250-391-2877

A.J. Palmer
Judicial Case Manager: Shannon Cole

Williams Lake
540 Borland St., Williams Lake, BC V2G 1R8
Tel: 250-398-4310; *Fax:* 250-398-4459

E.L. Bayliff
R. Walters
Judicial Case Manager: Sherry Jasper

Manitoba

Manitoba Court of Appeal

Law Courts Bldg., #100E, 408 York Ave., Winnipeg, MB R3C 0P9

Tel: 204-945-2647; *Fax:* 204-948-2072
www.manitobacourts.mb.ca

The Court is the senior & final court in the province & has appellate jurisdiction in all civil & criminal cases adjudicated by the Court of Queen's Bench & indictable offences adjudicated by the Provincial Court. The Court hears, in limited circumstances & as mandated by statute, appeals from professional bodies & some government boards & tribunals.

Chief Justice: The Hon. Mr. Richard J. Scott
Justices of Appeal (The Hon. Mr./Madam Justice):
Martin H. Freedman
Barbara M. Hamilton
Richard J.F. Chartier
Alan D. MacInnes
Michael A. Monnin
Freda M. Steel
Holly C. Beard

Manitoba Court of Queen's Bench

Law Courts Bldg., 408 York Ave., Winnipeg, MB R3C 0P9

Tel: 204-945-0344; *Fax:* 204-948-2369
www.manitobacourts.mb.ca

The highest trial court for the province, The Court of Queen's Bench is a court of original jurisdiction & hears all civil & criminal cases arising in Manitoba, except matters expressly excluded by statute. The Court is comprised of the General Division, and the Family Division; it also has appellate jurisdiction & hears appeals from decisions of the Provincial Court in less serious criminal & quasi-criminal matters, decisions of the Hearing Officers in small claims matters, & decisions made by Masters of the court.

Chief Justice: The Hon. Mr. Marc M. Monnin
Assoc. Chief Justice: General Division, The Hon. Mr. Glenn D. Joyal
Assoc. Chief Justice: Family Division, The Hon. Madam A. Lori Douglas
Robert Carr(Supernumerary)
A.R. Clearwater(Supernumerary)
Léa A. Duval
Shawn D. Greenberg
Kenneth R. Hanssen(Supernumerary)
Morris Kaufman
Brenda L. Keyser
Deborah J. McCawley
Rodney H. Mykle
Perry Schulman(Supernumerary)
Karen I. Simonsen
C. Murray Sinclair
Lori T. Spivak
Colleen Suche
Laurie P. Allen
Frank Aquila
Douglas N. Abra
Robert A. Dewar
Robyn M. Diamond
Robert B. Doyle
A. Catherine Everett
Marilyn E. Goldberg
Sylvia Guertin-Riley(Supernumerary)
William Johnston
Donald M. Little
Joan G. McKelvey
Joan A. MacPhail
Chris W. Martin
John A. Menzies
Gerald W. Mercier
Brian Midwinter
Jeffrey J. Oliphant(Supernumerary)
Marianne Rivoalen
Richard A. Saull
Kris Stefanson(Supernumerary)
Michael A. Thomson
Douglas D. Yard
Donald P. Bryk
William J. Burnett
Robert G. Cummings

Courts:

Brandon
Court of Queen's Bench, 1104 Princess Ave., P.O. Box 68, Brandon, MB R7A 0P9
Tel: 204-726-6240; *Fax:* 204-726-6547
R. Mykle
J.A. Menzies
Master/Registrar in Bankruptcy: Errick G. Harrison

Dauphin
Court of Queen's Bench, 114 River Ave. West, Dauphin, MB R7N 0J7
Tel: 204-622-2087; *Fax:* 204-622-2099
D. Bryk

Portage la Prairie
Court of Queen's Bench, 20 3rd St. SE, Portage la Prairie, MB R1N 1M9
Tel: 204-239-3383; *Fax:* 204-239-3402

The Pas
Court of Queen's Bench, 300 - 3rd St. East, P.O. Box 1259, The Pas, MB R9A 1L2
Tel: 204-627-8420; *Fax:* 204-623-6528

Thompson
Court of Queen's Bench, 59 Elizabeth Dr., P.O. Box 34, Thompson, MB R8N 1X4
Tel: 204-677-6757; *Fax:* 204-677-6686

Manitoba Provincial Court

Law Courts Bldg., 408 York Ave., Main Fl., Winnipeg, MB R3C 0P9

Tel: 204-945-3454; *Fax:* 204-945-7130

The Provincial Court has jurisdiction in youth & select family & criminal matters, including summary conviction offences.

Chief Judge: The Hon. Kenneth Champagne
Assoc. Chief Judge: The Hon. Murray Thompson
Assoc. Chief Judge: The Hon. Janice leMaistre
Assoc. Chief Judge: Michel L.J. Chartier
Judges (His/Her Hon.):
Herbert Lawrence Allen
Catherine Carlson
Sandra L. Chapman
Brian G. Colli
John Combs
Brian M. Corrin
Kathlyn Mary A. Curtis
Judith A. Elliott
Robin A. Finlayson
Marvin F. Garfinkel
Wanda M. Garreck
John P. Guy
Christine Harapiak
Mary Kate Harvie
Robert M. Heinrichs
Shauna Hewitt-Michta
Sidney B. Lerner
Theodore J. Lismer
Tracey M. Lord
Lee Ann M. Martin
Jean McBride
Malcolm W. McDonald
Kelly Moar
Timothy Preston
Heather R. Pullan
Doreen Redhead
Fred H. Sandhu
Dale C. Schille
Donald R. Slough
Marva J. Smith
Lynn A. Stannard
Brent D. Stewart
Krystyna D. Tarwid
Patti-Anne L. Umpherville
Raymond E. Wyant

Courts:

Brandon
Provincial Court, 1104 Princess Ave., Brandon, MB R7A 0P9
J. Combs
B.D. Giesbrecht
K. Tarwid
Sheriff: M. Drosdoski, 204-726-6552

Dauphin
Provincial Court, 114 River Ave. West, Dauphin, MB R7N 0J7
R.W. Thompson
C. Harapiak
Sheriff: D. Werbiski, 204-622-2088

Portage la Prairie
Provincial Court, 25 Tupper St., Portage la Prairie, MB R1N 3K1
R.G. Cummings
Sheriff: R. Sim, 204-239-3379

The Pas
300 - 3 St. East, The Pas, MB R9A 1L2
Roger Grégoire
B.D. Stewart
Sheriff: R.A. Gray, 204-627-8431

Thompson
Provincial Court, 59 Elizabeth Dr., Thompson, MB R8N 1X4
B.G. Colli
M. Thompson
Sheriff: Dale Manning, 204-677-6764

New Brunswick

New Brunswick Court of Appeal

Justice Bldg., #202, 427 Queen St., P.O. Box 6000, Fredericton, NB E3B 5H1

Tel: 506-453-2452; *Fax:* 506-453-7921
www.gnb.ca/cour

The Court of Appeal has appellate jurisdiction in civil & criminal matters.

Chief Justice: The Hon. Mr. J. Ernest Drapeau
Justices of Appeal (The Hon. Mr./Madam Justice):
Alexandre Deschênes(Supernumerary)
Joseph Z. Daigle
Margaret E.L. Larlee(Supernumerary)
J.C. Marc Richard
Joseph T. Robertson
Wallace S. Turnbull(Supernumerary)
B. Richard Bell
Kathleen A. Quigg
Bradley V. Green

New Brunswick Court of Queen's Bench

Justice Bldg., 427 Queen St., P.O. Box 6000, Fredericton, NB E3B 5H1

www.gnb.ca/cour

The Court of Queen's Bench is a court of original jurisdiction, having jurisdiction in all civil & criminal matters arising in New Brunswick, except those expressly excluded by statute. The Court is comprised of two divisions: Trial & Family.

Moncton: **Chief Justice:** The Hon. David D. Smith, 506-856-2300, Fax: 506-856-2751
Administration:
Registrar: Bankruptcy/Divorce & Matrimonial Causes, Michael J. Bray, 506-453-2452
Deputy Registrar: Bankruptcy, Elizabeth Nicholas, 506-453-2452

Courts:

Bathurst
Court House, 254 St. Patrick St., P.O. Box 5001, Bathurst, NB E2A 3Z9
Tel: 506-547-2151; *Fax:* 506-547-2966
G.W. Boisvert
Réginald Léger
J.R. McIntyre
Regional Manager: R.G. Boudreau
Clerk (Trial Division) & Administrator (Family Division): Donald Arseneau
Sheriff/Coroner: Edgar Aubé

Campbellton
Court House, 157 Water St., P.O. Box 5001, Campbellton, NB E3N 3H5
Tel: 506-789-2368; *Fax:* 506-789-2062
Raymond J. Guerette
Gladys J. Young
Clerk (Trial Division) & Administrator (Family Division): Johanne Martin
Sheriff/Coroner: Walter Thompson

Edmundston
121 Church St., P.O. Box 5001, Edmundston, NB E3V 3L3
Tel: 506-753-2025; *Fax:* 506-737-4419
Thomas E. Cyr
Lucie Lavigne
Clerk, Administrator (Family Division) & Regional Manager: Jean-François Cyr
Clerk, Administrator (Family Division) & Regional Manager: Sylvie Dumont
Sheriff/Coroner: Paul Ringuette

Fredericton
Court House, 427 Queen St., P.O. Box 6000, Fredericton, NB E3B 5H1
Tel: 506-453-2015
Other information: Fax: 506/453-7921 (Family); 506/444-4392 (Trial)
Myrna Athey
Paulette Garnett
D.H. Russell
Regional Manager: Dominique Laundry
Sheriff/Coroner: Keith Ball
Clerk (Trial Division) & Administrator (Family Division): Jean-Marie Goguen
Clerk (Trial Division) & Administrator (Family Division): Joy Toole

Moncton
770 Main St., P.O. Box 5001, Moncton, NB E1C 8R3
Tel: 506-856-2305; *Fax:* 506-856-2951

Colette M. d'Entremont
B.M. Robichaud
P.S. Creaghan
J. Alfred Landry
Guy A. Richard
George S. Rideout
Roger Savoie
Jacques A. Sirois
C.J. David D. Smith
Regional Director, Court Services: David Léger
Clerk (Trial Division) & Administrator (Family Division): Anne Richard
Sheriff/Coroner: Rhéal LeBlanc

Miramichi
Court House, 599 King George Hwy., Miramichi, NB E1V 1N6
Tel: 506-627-4021; *Fax:* 506-627-4134
Thomas Riordon
Stephen J. McNally
Administrator: Cynthia Goulette
Clerk: Matthew Cripps
Sheriff/Coroner:Vacant

Saint John
110 Charlotte St., P.O. Box 5001, Saint John, NB E2L 4Y9
Tel: 506-658-2400; *Fax:* 506-658-3070
Anne D. Wooder
Robert L. Tuck
P.S. Glennie
William T. Grant
Robert J. Higgins
H.H. McLellan
J.W. Turnbull
Regional Manager: Tom Bishop
Clerk (Trial Division) & Administrator (Family Division): Sharon LeBlanc
Clerk (Trial Division) & Administrator (Family Division): George S. Thériault
Sheriff/Coroner: Joan Collins

Woodstock
Court House, 689 Main St., P.O. Box 5001, Woodstock, NB E7M 5C6
Tel: 506-325-4414; *Fax:* 506-325-4447
Judy L. Clendening
Deputy Clerk (Trial Division) & Deputy Administrator (Fam: Andrea Hull
Sheriff/Coroner: Tim Wiebe

New Brunswick Provincial Court

Justice Bldg., #105, 427 Queen St., P.O. Box 6000, Fredericton, NB E3B 5H1
Tel: 506-453-2935
www.gnb.ca/cour
The Provincial Court has jurisdiction in select criminal matters as well as youth matters.
Chief Judge: His Hon. R. Leslie Jackson
Assoc. Chief Judge: The Hon. Pierre W. Arseneault

Courts:
Carleton County
689 Main St., P.O. Box 5001, Woodstock, NB E7M 5C6
Tel: 506-325-4415; *Fax:* 506-325-3906
R. Leslie Jackson(Chief Judge)

Charlotte County
41 King St., P.O. Box 5001, St Stephen, NB E3L 2C1
Tel: 506-466-7507; *Fax:* 506-466-7508
David C. Walker

Gloucester County (Bathurst)
#223, 254 St. Patrick St., P.O. Box 5001, Bathurst, NB E2A 3Z9
Tel: 506-547-2155; *Fax:* 506-547-7448
Frederic Arsenault(Supernumerary)

Gloucester County (Tracadie-Sheila)
Place Tracadie, 3514 Main St., 1st Fl., Tracadie, NB E1X 1C9
Tel: 506-394-3700; *Fax:* 506-394-3696
Donald J. LeBlanc

Kent County
#1, 9358 Main St., P.O. Box 5001, Richibucto, NB E4W 5R5
Tel: 506-523-7611; *Fax:* 506-526-7155
Joseph C. Michaud(Supernumerary)

Kings County
#2, 648 Main St., Hampton, NB E5N 6C8
Tel: 506-832-6015; *Fax:* 506-832-6079
Henrik G. Tonning

Madawaska County
Carrefour Assomption, #235, 121 rue de l'Église, P.O. Box 5001, Edmundston, NB E3V 3L3
Tél: 506-735-2026; *Téléc:* 506-735-2396
George S. Pérusse(Surnuméraire)

Northumberland County
673 King George Hwy., Miramichi, NB E1V 1N6
Tel: 506-627-4018
Denis T. Lordon
John C. Friel

Restigouche County
#202, 157 Water St., P.O. Box 5001, Campbellton, NB E3N 3H5
Tel: 506-789-2337; *Fax:* 506-789-2186
Pierre F. Dubé
Steven M. Hutchinson

Saint John County
15 Market Square, 3rd Fl., P.O. Box 5001, Saint John, NB E2L 1E8
Tel: 506-658-2568
Alfred H. Brien
Anne M. Jeffries
William J. McCarroll
James G. McNamee(Supernumerary)
W. Andrew LeMesurier

Sunbury-Queens Counties
P.O. Box 94, Oromocto, NB E2V 2G4
Tel: 506-347-4020; *Fax:* 506-357-4032
The courthouse is located at 23 Route 102 Highway, River Road, in Burton, NB.
Patricia L. Cumming

Victoria County
426 Broadway, P.O. Box 5001, Grand Falls, NB E3Z 1G1
Tel: 506-473-7700; *Fax:* 506-473-7379
Jacques Desjardins(Supernumerary)

Westmorland County
Assumption Place, 770 Main St., P.O. Box 5001, Moncton, NB E1C 8R3
Tel: 506-856-2301; *Fax:* 506-856-3226
Pierre W. Arseneault(Assoc. Chief Judge)
Jolène Richard
Anne Dugas-Horsman
Irwin E. Lampert
Michael McKee(Supernumerary)
J. Camille Vautour

York County
Justice Bldg., #105, 427 Queen St., P.O. Box 6000, Fredericton, NB E3B 5H1
Tel: 506-453-2120
Mary Jane Richards
Julian Dickson

New Brunswick Probate Court

Justice Bldg., 423 Queen St., P.O. Box 6000, Fredericton, NB E3B 5H1
Tel: 506-453-2015
www.gnb.ca/cour
The Probate Court has jurisdiction in estate matters. Clerks of the Court of Queen's Bench are, ex officio, Clerks of Probate Court. Court locations throughout New Brunswick; contact: Clerk of Probate, Court Services Office (Queen's Bench).

Newfoundland & Labrador

Supreme Court of Newfoundland & Labrador: Judicial Centres

Courthouse, 309 Duckworth St., P.O. Box 937, St. John's, NL A1C 5M3
Tel: 709-729-1137; *Fax:* 709-729-6623
The Supreme Court also has jurisdiction in Bankruptcy.
Administration:
Registrar: Christopher P. Curran
Senior Deputy Registrar: Bankruptcy, Darlene Wells darlenewells@gov.nl.ca
Director: Supreme Court Services, William F. Barron
Estate Administrator: W.H. John Baird

Courts:
Corner Brook
Courthouse, 82 Mt. Bernard Ave., P.O. Box 2006, Corner Brook, NL A2H 6J8
Tel: 709-637-2485; *Fax:* 709-637-2569
W.H.N. Goodridge
D. Peddle
Deputy Registrar: Sandra Oxford, 709-637-2224, Fax: 709-637-2569

Gander
Law Court Bldg., 98 Airport Blvd., P.O. Box 2222, Gander, NL A1V 2N9
Tel: 709-256-1115; *Fax:* 709-256-1120
R.P. Whalen
Asst. Deputy Registrar: Lynetta Payne, 709-256-1115, Fax: 709-256-1120

Grand Bank
T. Alex Hickman Courthouse, P.O. Box 910, Grand Bank, NL A0E 1W0
Tel: 709-832-1720; *Fax:* 709-832-2755
G.A. Handrigan
Asst. Deputy Registrar: Wilson Crowley, 709-832-1720, Fax: 709-832-2755

Grand Falls - Windsor
The Law Courts, 55 Cromer Ave., Grand Falls, NL A2A 1W9
Tel: 709-292-4260; *Fax:* 709-292-4224
A. Schwartz(Supernumerary)
K.J. Goulding
Asst. Deputy Registrar: Edward Lannon, 709-292-4260, Fax: 709-292-4224

Happy Valley - Goose Bay
Courthouse, 214 Hamilton River Rd., P.O. Box 1139 B, Happy Valley-Goose Bay, NL A0P 1E0
Tel: 709-896-7892; *Fax:* 709-896-9212
R.P. Stack
Asst. Deputy Registrar: Paula Parsons, 709-896-7891, Fax: 709-896-9212

Supreme Court of Newfoundland & Labrador: Court of Appeal

287 Duckworth St., P.O. Box 937, St. John's, NL A1C 5M3
Tel: 709-729-0066; *Fax:* 709-729-7909
The Court of Appeal has appellate jurisdiction in criminal & civil matters from decisions of the lower courts & designated administrative boards & tribunals.
Chief Justice: The Hon. J.D. Green
Justices of Appeal (The Hon. Mr./Madam Justice):
L. Barry
M.F. Harrington
L.R. Hoegg
K.J. Mercer
M. Rowe
C.K. Wells
G. Welsh
C.W. White

Supreme Court of Newfoundland & Labrador: Trial Division

Court House, 309 Duckworth St., P.O. Box 937, St. John's, NL A1C 5M3
Tel: 709-729-1137; *Fax:* 709-729-6623
www.court.nl.ca/supreme/trial
The Trial Division is a court of original jurisdiction having jurisdiction in all civil & criminal matters arising in Newfoundland, except those excluded by statute. With the exception of the judicial area of St. John's, the Trial Division's original jurisdiction extends to particular family matters. The Registrar,and staff in the Estates Division of the Supreme Court, carrys out public guardian, guardian ad litem and public trustree functions.
Chief Justice: The Hon. David B. Orsborn
Judges (The Hon.):
J.S. Adams
G.D. Butler
W.G. Dymond
A.E. Faour
R.A. Fowler
D.E. Fry
R.M. Hall
R.J. Halley
L.R. Hoegg(Supernumerary)
R.D. LeBlanc
D.L. Russell
C.R. Thompson

Supreme Court of Newfoundland & Labrador: United Family Court

21 King's Bridge Rd., St. John's, NL A1C 3K4
Tel: 709-729-2258; *Fax:* 709-729-0784
Judicial matters regarding families are shared/divided between the Supreme & Provincial Courts along geographical boundaries. The United Family Court, a division of the Supreme Court, has exclusive jurisdiction for all family matters on the Avalon Peninsula (including Bell Is.). In the "expanded service area" of the United Family Court (from Holyrood to Port Blandford & Bonavista Peninsula), however, there is concurrent jurisdiction.
Judges (The Hon.):
J.D. Cook
M. Dunn
S.B. O'Regan

Provincial Court of Newfoundland & Labrador

Atlantic Place, 215 Water St., P.O. Box 68, St. John's, NL A1C 6C9
Tel: 709-729-1004; *Fax:* 709-729-2161
inquiries@provincial.court.nl.ca
www.court.nl.ca/provincial

The Provincial Court has jurisdiction in select criminal & family (outside the judicial area of St. John's) matters as well as small claims & youth matters.
Chief Judge: The Hon. D. Mark Pike
Assoc. Chief Judge: The Hon. Robert B. Hyslop
Judges (The Hon.):
G.O. Brown
C.J. Flynn
G. Harding
D. Orr
D. Power
L. Skanes
R. Smith
L. Spracklin
J. Woodrow
Administration:
Director: Court Services, Pamela Ryder-Lahey
plahey@provincial.court.nl

Courts:
Clarenville
47 Marine Dr., Clarenville, NL A5A 1M5
Tel: 709-466-2635; *Fax:* 709-466-3147
P.J. Kennedy

Corner Brook
84 Mt. Bernard Ave., P.O. Box 2006, Corner Brook, NL A2H 6J8
Tel: 709-637-2323; *Fax:* 709-637-2656
C. Allen-Westby
W. Gorman
K. Howe

Gander
98 Airport Rd., P.O. Box 2222, Gander, NL A1V 2N9
Tel: 709-256-1100; *Fax:* 709-256-1097
M. Madden
B. Short

Happy Valley-Goose Bay
P.O. Box 3014 B, Happy Valley-Goose Bay, NL A0P 1E0
Tel: 709-896-7870; *Fax:* 709-896-8767
W. English
J. Joy

Grand Bank
Grand Bank-Fortune Hwy., P.O. Box 339, Grand Bank, NL A0E 1W0
Tel: 709-832-1450; *Fax:* 709-832-1758
H. Porter

Grand Falls
Law Courts Bldg., Grand Falls, NL A2A 1W9
Tel: 709-292-4212; *Fax:* 709-292-4388
T. Chalker
R.J. Whiffen

Harbour Grace
Harvey St., P.O. Box 519, Harbour Grace, NL A0A 2M0
Tel: 709-596-6141; *Fax:* 709-596-4304
www.hrgrace.ca/court.html
J. Brazil

Stephenville
35 Alabama Dr., Stephenville, NL A2N 3K9
Tel: 709-643-2966; *Fax:* 709-643-4022
J. Jenkins

Wabush
Whiteway Dr., P.O. Box 1060, Wabush, NL A0R 1B0
Tel: 709-282-6617; *Fax:* 709-282-6905
W.A. Trahey

Northwest Territories

Northwest Territories Court of Appeal
Court House, P.O. Box 550, Yellowknife, NT X1A 2N4
Tel: 867-873-7643; *Fax:* 867-873-0291
The Court of Appeal has appellate jurisdiction in criminal & civil matters from the Supreme Court & Territorial Court.
Chief Justice: The Hon. C.A. Fraser
Justices of Appeal (The Hon. Mr./Madam Justice):
Ronald L. Berger
Beverley A. Browne
J.E. Côté
C.M. Conrad
Peter T. Costigan
Adelle Fruman
L.F. Gower
C. Hunt
E.D. Johnson
Robert G. Kilpatrick
P. Martin
J.W. McClung
E.A. McFadyen
C.D. O'Brien
W. O'Leary
M.S. Paperny
E. Picard
J.E. Richard
K.G. Ritter
A.H. Russell
Virginia A. Schuler
Ronald S. Veale
J.Z. Vertes
Neil C. Wittmann
Administration:
Registrar: Anne Mould

Northwest Territories Supreme Court
P.O. Box 550, Yellowknife, NT X1A 2N4
Tel: 867-873-7643; *Fax:* 867-873-0291
The Supreme Court is a court of original jurisdiction & has jurisdiction in all civil & criminal matters arising in the Northwest Territories, except those expressly excluded by statute.
Senior Judge: The Hon. J.E. Richard
Judges (The Hon. Mr./Madam Justice):
V.A. Schuler
J.Z. Vertes
Deputy Judges (The Hon. Mr./Madam Justice):
Lucien Beaulieu
Jean-Guy Boilard
C. Scott Brooker
Paul Chrumka
Carole M. Conrad
Alan T. Cooke
Wallace M. Darichuk
R.P. Foisy
Tellex W. Gallant
J.K. Hugessen
Howard L. Irving
Cecilia I. Johnstone
Daniel P. Kennedy
Colleen L. Kenny
Douglas H. Lissaman
Arthur M. Lutz
E.P. MacCallum
Elizabeth McFadyen
Ernest A. Marshall
Mary Moreau
Mary E. Noonan
Terrance P. O'Connor
Vital Ouellette
R.F. Paul
Ellen I. Picard
M.L. Rothman
P. Lawrie J. Smith
William J. Vancise
Joanne B. Veit
A.H. Wachowich
Randall S.K. Wong
Ex-Officio Judges (The Hon. Mr./Madam Justice):
B.A. Browne
E.D. Johnson
Leigh F. Gower
R.G. Kilpatrick
Ronald S. Veale
Administration:
Court Administrator: Anne Mould

Northwest Territorial Court
P.O. Box 550, Yellowknife, NT X1A 2N4
Tel: 867-873-7643; *Fax:* 867-873-0291
The Territorial Court has jurisdiction in small claims, youth, family & select criminal matters.
Chief Judge: The Hon. B.A. Bruser
Judges (His/Her Hon.):
R.D. Gorin
B.A. Schmaltz
Administration:
Court Administrator: Anne Mould

Northwest Territories: Justice of the Peace Court
P.O. Box 550, Yellowknife, NT X1A 2N4
Tel: 867-920-8020; *Fax:* 867-873-0203
The Justices of the Peace have jurisdiction in summary conviction matters arising out of territorial statute, municipal by-law & select criminal matters.
Administration:
JP Program Administrator: The Hon. Judge Vacant
JP Coordinator: Ramona Sorenson

Nova Scotia

Nova Scotia Court of Appeal
The Law Courts Bldg., 1815 Upper Water St., Halifax, NS B3J 1S7
Tel: 902-424-4900; *Fax:* 902-424-0524
www.courts.ns.ca/Appeals/index_ca.htm
The Nova Scotia Court of Appeal is the province's highest court and has appellate jurisdiction in civil & criminal matters. It sits only in Halifax and hears appeals from both the Supreme and Provincial Courts.
Chief Justice: The Hon. Michael MacDonald
Justices of Appeal (The Hon. Justice):
Duncan R. Beveridge
Peter M.S. Bryson
David P.S. Farrar
Joel E. Fichaud
M. Jill Hamilton
Linda L. Oland
Jamie W.S. Saunders
Administration:
Registrar: Court of Appeal, Annette M. Boucher, 902-424-6187
boucheam@gov.ns.ca

Nova Scotia Supreme Court
The Law Courts Bldg., 1815 Upper Water St., Halifax, NS B3J 1S7
Tel: 902-424-4900; *Fax:* 902-424-0524
www.courts.ns.ca/supreme/index_sc.htm
The Supreme Court is the highest trial court in the province with jurisdiction in all civil & criminal matters, except those expressly excluded by statute. It hears appeals on Provincial Court, Small Claims Court and Residential Tenancies Board matters.
Chief Justice: The Hon. Joseph P. Kennedy, 902-424-6939, Fax: 902-424-0536
Assoc. Chief Justice: The Hon. Deborah K. Smith
Assoc. Chief Justice: Family Division, The Hon. Robert Ferguson
Judges (The Hon. Mr./Madam Justice):
A.P. Boudreau(Supernumerary)
F.A. Cacchione(Supernumerary)
K. Coady
C.R. Coughlan
P.J. Duncan(Supernumerary)
S.M. Hood
A.J. LeBlanc
A.D. MacAdam(Supernumerary)
G.G. McDougall
G. Moir
J.D. Murphy
A.W.D. Pickup
M.H. Robertson
P. Rosinski
Robert Wright
Judges, Family Division (The Hon. Mr./Madam Justice):
D.C. Campbell
L.J. Dellapinna
D. Gass
E. Jollimore
M.C. Legere-Sers
M. Lynch
B.A. MacDonald
L.I. O'Neil
R.J. Williams
Administration:
Registrar in Bankruptcy: Richard W. Cregan, 902-424-6908

Courts:
Amherst
16 Church St., 3 Fl., Amherst, NS B4H 3A6
Tel: 902-667-2256; *Fax:* 902-667-5498
J.E. Scanlon

Annapolis Royal
Justice Centre, 377 St. George St., Annapolis Royal, NS B0S 1A0
Tel: 902-532-5462; *Fax:* 902-532-7225
C.E. Haliburton(Supernumerary)

Antigonish
Justice Centre, 11 James St., Antigonish, NS B2G 1R6
Tel: 902-863-7394; *Fax:* 902-863-7479
D.L. MacLellan(Supernumerary)
N.M. Scaravelli

Bridgewater
Court House, 141 High St., Bridgewater, NS B4V 1W2
Tel: 902-543-4679; *Fax:* 902-543-0678
M. Stewart

Digby
Justice Centre, 119 Queen St., Digby, NS B0V 1A0
Tel: 902-245-7134; *Fax:* 902-245-6722
C.E. Haliburton(Supernumerary)

P.L. Muise

Kentville
Justice Centre, 87 Cornwallis St., Kentville, NS B4N 2E5
Tel: 902-679-6070; *Fax:* 902-679-6178

G.M. Warner

Pictou/New Glasgow
Court House, 69 Water St., P.O. Box 1750, Pictou, NS B0K 1H0
Tel: 902-485-6373; *Fax:* 902-485-6737

D.L. MacLellan(Supernumerary)
N.M. Scaravelli

Port Hawkesbury
#201, 15 Kennedy St., Port Hawkesbury, NS B9A 2Y1
Tel: 902-625-4218; *Fax:* 902-625-4084

Sydney
Justice Centre, #6, 136 Charlotte St., Sydney, NS B1P 1C3
Tel: 902-563-3550; *Fax:* 902-563-2224

C.A. Bourgeois
F.C. Edwards(Supernumerary)
S.J. MacDonald
P.J. Murray
T.M. Forgeron
K. Haley
M.C. MacLellan
D.W. Wilson

Truro
Justice Centre, 1 church St., Truro, NS B2N 3Z5
Tel: 902-893-3953; *Fax:* 902-893-6114

J.E. Scanlan

Yarmouth
Justice Centre, 164 Main St., Yarmouth, NS B5A 1C2
Tel: 902-742-0500; *Fax:* 902-742-0678

P.L. Muise

Nova Scotia: Probate Court

Law Courts Bldg, 1815 Upper Water St., Halifax, NS B3J 1S7
Tel: 902-424-7422; *Fax:* 902-424-0524

The Probate Court has jurisdiction in respect of estate matters.

Courts:

Amherst
Justice Centre, 16 Church St., 3rd Fl., Amherst, NS B4H 3A6
Tel: 902-667-2256; *Fax:* 902-667-1108

Registrar: Anne Marie LeBlanc

Annapolis Royal
Justice Centre, 377 St. George St., P.O. Box 129, Annapolis Royal, NS B0S 1A0
Tel: 902-532-5462; *Fax:* 902-532-7225

Registrar: Sandra Gennette

Antigonish
Justice Centre, 11 James St., Antigonish, NS B2G 1R6
Tel: 902-863-7396; *Fax:* 902-863-7479

Registrar: Lorna Chisholm

Bridgewater
Justice Centre, 141 High St., Bridgewater, NS B4V 1W2
Tel: 902-543-0816; *Fax:* 902-543-0678

Registrar: Claire Feener

Digby
Court House, Queen St., P.O. Box 1089, Digby, NS B0V 1A0
Tel: 902-245-7134; *Fax:* 902-245-6722

Registrar: Sandra Gennette

Halifax
Law Courts Bldg., 1815 Upper Water St., Halifax, NS B3J 1S7
Tel: 902-424-7422; *Fax:* 902-424-0524

Registrar: Sharron Atton

Kentville
Justice Centre, 87 Cornwallis St., Kentville, NS B4N 2E5
Tel: 902-679-5540; *Fax:* 902-679-6178

Registrar: Susan Campbell-Baltzer

Pictou/New Glasgow
69 Water St., P.O. Box 1750, Pictou, NS B0K 1H0
Tel: 902-485-4351; *Fax:* 902-485-6737

Registrar: Laura Lannon

Port Hawkesbury
Justice Centre, #201, 15 Kennedy St., Port Hawkesbury, NS B9A 2Y1
Tel: 902-625-4269; *Fax:* 902-625-4084

Registrar: Karen Gillies

Sydney
Justice Centre, #6, 136 Charlotte St., Sydney, NS B1P 1C3
Tel: 902-563-3545; *Fax:* 902-563-5701

Registrar: Shauna Wilson

Truro
Justice Centre, 1 Church St., Truro, NS B2N 3Z5
Tel: 902-893-5870; *Fax:* 902-893-6114

Registrar: Anne Marie LeBlanc

Yarmouth
Justice Centre, 164 Main St., Yarmouth, NS B5A 1C2
Tel: 902-742-5469; *Fax:* 902-742-0678

Registrar: Ruth Hulbert

Nova Scotia Provincial Court

5250 Spring Garden Rd., Halifax, NS B3J 1E7
Tel: 902-424-8718; *Fax:* 902-424-0551
www.courts.ns.ca/provincial/index_pc.htm

The Provincial Court has jurisdiction over almost all indictable charges under provincial & federal statutes and regulations. When judges are not available, presiding Justices of the Peace deal with release or detention of those arrested.

Chief Judge: The Hon. Patrick H. Curran
Judges (The Hon.):
B.J. Beach
J.S. Campbell
M.C. Chisholm
A.S. Derrick
W.B. Digby
T. Gabriel
G.H. Randall
M.B. Sherar
C.H.F. Williams

Courts:

Amherst
16 church St., 3rd Fl., Amherst, NS B4H 3A6
Tel: 902-667-2256; *Fax:* 902-667-1108

C.A. Beaton

Annapolis Royal
Justice Centre, 377 St. George St., Annapolis Royal, NS B0S 1A0
Tel: 902-245-4567

Antigonish
11 James St., Antigonish, NS B2G 1R6
Tel: 902-863-3676; *Fax:* 902-863-7479

J.D. Embree

Bridgewater
Justice Centre, 141 High St., Bridgewater, NS B4V 1W2
Tel: 902-543-4679; *Fax:* 902-543-0678

J.H. Burrill
A. Crawford

Dartmouth
#200, 277 Pleasant St., Dartmouth, NS B2Y 3S2
Tel: 902-424-2390; *Fax:* 902-424-0677

F.I. Buchan
R.B. Gibson
F.P. Hoskins
W. MacDonald
A. Murphy
T.K. Tax
P.S. Williams

Digby
119 Queen St., P.O. Box 1089, Digby, NS B0V 1A0
Tel: 902-245-4567; *Fax:* 902-245-6722

J. Batiot

Kentville
Justice Centre, 87 Cornwallis St., Kentville, NS B4N 2E5
Tel: 902-679-6070; *Fax:* 902-679-6190

C. MacDonald
M.L. Melvin
A.T. Tufts

New Glasgow
Justice Centre, 115 MacLean St., New Glasgow, NS B2H 4M5
Tel: 902-755-5106; *Fax:* 902-755-7181

Port Hawkesbury
Justice Centre, #201, 15 Kennedy St., Port Hawkesbury, NS B9A 2Y1
Tel: 902-625-2605; *Fax:* 902-625-4084

L. Halfpenny-MacQuarrie

Sydney
Harbour Place, #6, 136 Charlotte St., Sydney, NS B1P 1C3
Tel: 902-563-3510; *Fax:* 902-563-3421

A.P. Ross
D.J. Ryan
J.M. Whalen
B.D. Williston

Truro
Justice Centre, 540 Prince St., Truro, NS B2N 1G1
Tel: 902-893-5840; *Fax:* 902-893-6261

J.G. MacDougall
R.J. MacKinnon

Yarmouth
Justice Centre, 164 Main St., Yarmouth, NS B5A 1C2
Tel: 902-742-0500; *Fax:* 902-742-0678

R.M.J. Prince

Nova Scotia: Family Court

1815 Upper Water St., Halifax, NS B3J 1S7

The Family Court has jurisdiction in family matters & also functions as a Youth Court for cases involving youths aged 12 to 15 years.

Chief Judge: His Hon. Patrick H. Curran
Administration:
Director: Court Services, Judith McPhee, 902-424-4632, Fax: 902-424-7596
mcpheeja@gov.ns.ca

Courts:

Amherst
Justice Centre, 16 Church St., 3rd Fl., Amherst, NS B4H 3A6
Tel: 902-667-2256; *Fax:* 902-667-1108

C.A. Beaton
J.M. Dewolfe
Senior Officer: Patrick Dornan

Antigonish
Justice Centre, 11 James St., Antigonish, NS B2G 1R6
Tel: 902-863-7312; *Fax:* 902-863-7479

James C. Wilson

Bridgewater
Justice Centre, 141 High St., Bridgewater, NS B4V 1W2
Tel: 902-543-4679; *Fax:* 902-543-0678

J.H. Burrill
W. Dyer

Kentville
136 Exhibition St., Kentville, NS B4N 4E5
Tel: 902-679-6075; *Fax:* 902-679-6081

R. Levy
M.L. Melvin

Truro
542 Prince St., Truro, NS B2N 1G1
Tel: 902-893-5840; *Fax:* 902-893-6261

D.R. Hubley
J.G. MacDonald
R.J. MacKinnon
Officer: Keith Mumford

Yarmouth
Justice Centre, 164 Main St., Yarmouth, NS B5A 1C2
Tel: 902-742-0550; *Fax:* 902-742-0678

J.D. Comeau
Officer: Bob LeBlanc

Nova Scotia Justice Centres
NS

Amherst
16 Church St., 3rd Fl., Amherst, NS B4H 3A6
Tel: 902-667-2256; *Fax:* 902-667-1108

Court Administrator: Lynn Sorensen

Antigonish
11 James St., Antigonish, NS B2G 1R6
Tel: 902-863-3676; *Fax:* 902-863-7479

Court Administrator: Janice Gillis-MacLean

Bridgewater
141 High St., Bridgewater, NS B4V 1W2
Tel: 902-543-4679; *Fax:* 902-543-0678

Court Administrator: Paul Fay

Digby/Annapolis
119 Queen St., P.O. Box 1089, Digby, NS B0V 1A0
Tel: 902-245-4567; *Fax:* 902-245-6722

Court Administrator: Alan Hamilton

Halifax
1815 Upper Water St., Halifax, NS B3J 1S7
Tel: 902-424-6900; *Fax:* 902-424-0524

Prothonotary: Annette Boucher
Court Administrator: Court of Appeal/Supreme Court, Wayne Stewart
Court Administrator: Supreme Court, Family Div., John Campbell
Court Administrator: Provincial Court, Peter James

Kentville
87 Cornwallis St., Kentville, NS B4N 2E5
Tel: 902-679-6070; *Fax:* 902-679-6178

Court Administrator: Laurie Wanamaker

Pictou/New Glasgow
115 MacLean St., 1st Fl., New Glasgow, NS B2H 4M5
Tel: 902-755-7364; *Fax:* 902-755-7783

Court Administrator: Jim Hahnen

Port Hawkesbury
#201, 15 Kennedy St., Port Hawkesbury, NS B9A 2Y1
Tel: 902-625-4793; *Fax:* 902-625-4084
Acting Court Administrator: Janice Gillis-MacLean

Sydney
Harbour Place, #6, 136 Charlotte St., Sydney, NS B1P 1C3
Tel: 902-563-3510; *Fax:* 902-563-3421
Court Administrator: Pam Kachafanas

Truro
540 Prince St., Truro, NS B2N 1G1
Tel: 902-893-5840; *Fax:* 902-893-6261
Court Administrator: Lynn Sorensen

Yarmouth
Court House, 164 Main St., Yarmouth, NS B5A 1C2
Tel: 902-742-0500; *Fax:* 902-742-0678
Court Administrator: Alan Hamilton

Nunavut

Nunavut Court of Appeal
#224, Arnakallak Bldg., P.O. Box 297, Iqaluit, NU X0A 0H0
Tel: 867-975-6100; *Fax:* 867-975-6168
www.nunavutcourtofjustice.ca

Chief Justice: The Hon. Catherine Anne Fraser
Justices of Appeal (The Hon. Mr./Madam Justice):
Carole Conrad
Adelle Fruman
Constance D. Hunt
Peter Martin
Clifton O'Brien
Neil C. Wittmann
Ronald L. Berger
Peter T. Costigan
Jean E. Côté
Keith Ritter
Anne Helen Russell
Beverley Browne
Earl Johnson
Robert Kilpatrick
Ronald Veale
John Edward Richard
Virginia A. Schuler
John Z. Vertes

Nunavut Court of Justice
#224, Arnakallak Bldg., P.O. Box 297, Iqaluit, NU X0A 0H0
Tel: 867-975-6120; *Fax:* 867-975-6169
www.nunavutcourtofjustice.ca

Deputy Judges appointed as required.
Resident Judges (The Hon. Mr./Madam Justice):
Beverley A. Browne(Sr. Judge)
Earl D. Johnson
Robert G. Kilpatrick

Ontario

Court of Appeal for Ontario
Osgoode Hall, 130 Queen St. West, Toronto, ON M5H 2N5
Tel: 416-327-5020; *Fax:* 416-327-5032
www.ontariocourts.on.ca/coa/en/index.htm

The Court of Appeal is the final court of appeal for Ontario. Appeals from the Court of Appeal may be pursued in the Supreme Court of Canada.

Chief Justice: The Hon. Mr. Warren K. Winkler
Assoc. Chief Justice: The Hon. Mr. Dennis R. O'Connor
Justices (The Hon. Mr./Madam Justice):
Robert P. Armstrong
Robert A. Blair
Eleanore A. Cronk
David H. Doherty
Gloria J. Epstein
Kathryn N. Feldman
Eileen E. Gillese
Stephen T. Goudge
Russell G. Juriansz
Harry S. LaForme
Susan E. Lang
John I. Laskin
Jean L. MacFarland
James MacPherson
Marc Rosenberg
Paul S. Rouleau
Robert J. Sharpe
Janet M. Simmons
David Watt
Karen M. Weiler
Administration:
Senior Legal Officer: John Kromkamp, 416-327-5276
Registrar & Manager: Court Operations, Huguette Thomson
Deputy Registrar & Supervisor of Court Operations: Sandra Theroulde
Deputy Registrar & Acting Supervisor of Judicial Support: Carole Ibsen

Ontario Superior Court of Justice
Osgoode Hall, 130 Queen St. West, Toronto, ON M5H 2N5
Fax: 416-327-6209
www.ontariocourts.on.ca/scj/en/index.htm

In addition to its regular trial court functions, the Superior Court of Justice has two branches: the Divisional Court which generally hears appeals from a final order of a Judge of the Superior Court involving disputes of up to $25,000, & the Small Claims Court which generally hears cases involving claims up to $10,000. The Governor General appoints the Judges to all but the Ontario Court of Justice.

Chief Justice: The Hon. Heather F. Smith, 416-327-5000
Assoc. Chief Justice: The Hon. J. Douglas Cunningham, 416-327-5000

Central East Region
50 Eagle St. West, 4th Fl., Newmarket, ON L3Y 6B1
Tel: 905-853-4801
Regional Senior Justice: Michael Brown
R.C. Boswell
J.C. Corkery
G.P. DiTomaso
M.P. Eberhard
M.L. Edwards
J.E. Ferguson
M.K. Fuerst
C.A. Gilmore
B. Glass
F. Graham
D.S. Gunsolus
M.J. Hatton
S.E. Healey
P.H. Howden
A.P. Ingram
R.P. Kaufman
M.L. Lack
P. Lauwers
B.G. MacDougall
J.R. MacKinnon
P.Z. Magda
T.J. McEwen
H.A. McGee
J.R. McIsaac
E.B. Minden
G.M. Mulligan
A. Mullins
C.S. Nelson
H.K. O'Connell
L. Olah
E. Quinlan
S. Rogers
A.R. Rowsell
D. Salmers
M.A.C. Scott
J.B. Shaughnessy
A. Sosna
A.J. Stong
D.R. Timms
R.A. Wildman
T.M. Wood

Central South Region
45 Main St. East, Hamilton, ON L8N 2B7
Tel: 905-645-5252
Regional Senior Justice: C. Stephen Glithero
H.S. Arrell
C.E. Brown
K.A. Carpenter-Gunn
J.J. Cavarzan
David S. Crane
W.J. Festeryga
P.J. Flynn
D.J. Gordon
P.B. Hambly
C.R. Harris
J.R. Henderson
J.C. Kent
C. Lafrenière
T.R. Lofchik
W.L. MacPherson
T. Maddalena
B.H. Matheson
Randolph Mazza
M.J. McLaren
J.A. Milanetti
D. Parayeski
A. Pazaratz
J.W. Quinn
J.A. Ramsay
R.D. Reilly
J.W. Scott
D.M. Steinberg
D.J. Taliano
C.A. Tucker
J.R.H. Turnbull
L.M. Walters
A.C.R. Whitten

Central West Region
#100, 7755 Hurontario St., Brampton, ON L6W 4T1
Tel: 905-456-4700
Regional Senior Justice: Francine E. Van Melle
D.F. Baltman
J.R. Bellegham
T.A. Bielby
J.H. Clarke
K.D. Coats
D.L. Corbett
P.A. Daley
F. Dawson
T.M. Dunn
S.B. Durno
J.M. Fragomeni
D.K. Gray
C.N. Herold
S.C. Hill
C.W. Hourigan
E. Kruzick
K.A. Langdon
G.D. Lemon
A.D.K. MacKenzie
G.M. Miller
N.M. Mossip
C. Murray
T.P. O'Connor
D. Price
M.G. Quigley
L. Ricchetti
S.S. Seppi
L.L. Snowie
J.R. Sproat
R.G. Thomas
R.M. Thompson
M.H. Tulloch
K.M. van Rensburg
B.J. Wein

East Region
161 Elgin St., Ottawa, ON K2P 2K1
Tel: 613-239-1560
Regional Senior Justice: Charles T. Hackland
C.D. Aitken
P.B. Annis
R.N. Beaudoin
D.M. Belch
J.A. Blishen
W.J.L. Brennan
R.G. Byers
M.Z. Charbonneau
R.C. Desmarais
J.A. Forget
M.S. James
P.B. Kane
R. Kealey
S.J. Kershman
J. Lafrance-Cardinal
P.F. Lalonde
R. Leroy
H.S. Levenson Polowin
M.T. Linhares de Sousa
V.J. MacKinnon
H.K. MacLeod-Beliveau
B.J. Manton
R.L. Maranger
C. McKinnon
H.R. McLean
J.A. McMunagle
J. McNamara
M. Métivier
J.A. Parfett
K.D. Pedlar
R. Pelletier
D. Power
M. Quigley
L.D. Ratushny
T.D. Ray
C. Robertson
G.T. Roccamo
A.J. Roy
D.J.A. Rutherford
R.F. Scott

A.D. Sheffield
R.J. Smith
A.C. Trousdale

Metropolitan Toronto
361 University Ave., Toronto, ON M5G 1T3
Tel: 416-327-5990; *Fax:* 416-327-6056
Regional Senior Justice: The Hon. Edward F. Then
B.A. Allen
T.L. Archibald
D. Aston
N.L. Backhouse
D. Bellamy
E.P. Belobaba
M. Benotto
D.M. Brown
C.L. Campbell
S. Chapnik
R.A. Clark
M. Code
B.A. Conway
K.B. Corrick
B.L. Croll
P.A. Cumming
G. Czutrin
M.R. Dambrot
T. Ducharme
T. Dunnet
R.S. Echlin
E.G. Ewaschuk
L.K. Ferrier
M.D. Forestell
E.E. Frank
A.M. Gans
N.E. Garton
S.R. Goodman
A.D. Grace
S.E. Greer
P.A. Grossi
J.F. Hamilton
A.L. Harvison Young
T.P. Herman
S. Himel
C. Horkins
A. Hoy
P.G. Jarvis
J.R.R. Jennings
J.E. Kelly
F.P. Kiteley
G.R. Klowak
J. Lax
T.R. Lederer
S.N. Lederman
W. Low
E.M. Macdonald
J.A.B. Macdonald
I.A. MacDonnell
F.N. Marrocco
P.T. Matlow
J.D. McCombs
J.B. McMahon
F.E. McWatt
R.E. Mesbur
A.M. Molloy
J.P. Moore
G.B. Morawetz
F.J.C. Newbould
I.V.B. Nordheimer
A.J. O'Marra
V. Paisley
G.I. Pardu
L.A. Pattillo
M.A. Penny
S.E. Pepall
P.M. Perell
C. Perkins
R.W.M. Pitt
A. Pollack
L.B. Roberts
H.E. Sachs
M.A. Sanderson
H.J.W. Siegel
G.F. Speigel
C.M. Speyer
N.J. Spies
N.J. Spence
E.M. Stewart
D.G. Stinson
G.R. Strathy
K. Swinton
J.A. Thornburn
W.B. Trafford
G.T. Trotter
J.C. Wilkins
D.A. Wilson
J. Wilson

Northeast Region
155 Elm St. West, Sudbury, ON P3C 1T9
Tel: 705-564-7600
Regional Senior Justice: Louise L. Gauthier
R.P. Boissonneault
F.R Caputo
R.R.D. Cornell
R.G. Del Frate
E.E. Gareau
R.D. Gordon
I.M. Gordon
P.C. Hennessy
N.M.J. Karam
E.J. Koke
C.A.M. Macdonald
I.S. McMillan
D.J. Nadeau
J.S. O'Neill
J.S. Poupore
R.A. Riopelle
P.U. Rivard
G.W. Tranmer
G.T. Valin
W.L. Whalen
J.A.S. Wilcox

Northwest Region
277 Camelot St., Thunder Bay, ON P7A 4B3
Tel: 807-343-2710
Regional Senior Justice: Helen M. Pierce
J. dePencier Wright
J.S. Fregeau
J.F. McCartney
T.A. Platana
D.C. Shaw
G.P. Smith
E.W. Stach
B. Warkentin

Southwest Region
80 Dundas St. East, London, ON N6A 6A3
Tel: 519-660-3000; *Fax:* 519-660-3087
Regional Senior Justice: Edward Ducharme
A.W. Bryant
G.A. Campbell
S.K. Campbell
A.E. Cusinato
John Desotti
J.M.W. Donohue
R.C. Gates
K.A. Gorman
B.T. Granger
J. Harper
R.J. Haines
T.A. Heeney
Peter B. Hockin
W.A. Jenkins
J.C. Kennedy
L. Leitch
T.D. Little
M. Marshman
D.R. McDermid
J.F. McGarry
J.N. Morissette
M.J. Nolan
T.L.J. Patterson
R.M. Pomerance
J.G. Quinn
H.A. Rady
S. Rogin
W. Tausendfreund
L.C. Templeton
B.G. Thomas
G.I. Thomson
H. Vogelsang

Ontario Court of Justice
#2300, 1 Queen St. East, P.O. Box 91, Toronto, ON M5C 2W5
Tel: 416-327-5660
www.ontariocourts.on.ca/ocj/en/index.htm
The Ontario Court of Justice generally performs functions assigned to it by Acts such as the *Criminal Code* the *Provincial Offences Act* the *Family Law Act* the *Children's Law Reform Act* & the *Child & Family Services Act* & is a youth court. The Lieutenant Governor in Council, on the recommendation of the Attorney General, appoints the justices.
Chief Justice: The Hon. Annemarie E. Bonkalo
Assoc. Chief Justice: The Hon. Peter D. Griffiths
Assoc. Chief Justice: The Hon. John A. Payne

Central East Region
440 Kent St. West, Lindsay, ON K9V 6G8
Tel: 705-324-1400
Regional Senior Justice: Gregory Regis
S.C. Armstrong
G.W. Beatty
R.W. Beninger
P.L. Bellefontaine
M. Block
R. Blouin
P.N. Bourque
L.E. Chester
H.I. Chisvin
J.C. Crawford
N.A. Dawson
J.A. De Filippis
P. De Freitas
M.T.E. Devlin
J.A. Douglas
J.D. Evans
L. Favret
W.A. Gorewich
R. Graydon
D.J. Halikowski
M. Harpur
C.R. Harris
A. Hourigan
J.F. Kenkel
G.D. Krelove
S.C. MacLean
R.P. Main
R. McCreary
R.A. Minard
J.R. Morgan
K. Mulligan
R.J. Richards
E. Rosenberg
D.M. Stone
Peter Tetley
G. Wakefield
P.C. West
T.C. Whetung
J.B. Wilson
P.J. Wright

Central West Region
#762, 45 Main St. East, Hamilton, ON L8N 2B7
Tel: 905-645-5252
Regional Senior Justice: The Hon. Kathryn L. Hawke
P.H.M. Agro
J.E. Allen
I.W. André
H.K. Atwood
J.C. Baldock
L.M. Baldwin
J.C. Blacklock
L. Botham
S.D. Brown
F.M. Campling
S.R. Clark
T. Colvin
D.S. Cooper
S. Coroza
I. Cowan
T.A. Culver
P.R. Currie
B. Duncan
P.W. Dunn
G.B. Edward
F.L. Forsyth
G.S. Gage
D. Harris
R. Jennis
N.S. Kastner
J.J. Keaney
R. Kelly
J. Kerrigan Brownridge
M.F. Khoorshed
R.J. LeDressay
K.G. Lenz
J. Maresca
E. Martin
D.B. Maund
K.L. McLeod
J. Nadel
C.A. Nelson
M. Pawagi
B.E. Pugsley
E. Ready
R.H.K. Schwarzl
B.R. Shilton

M. Speyer
J.D. Takach
L.P. Thibideau
D.T. Vyse
A. Watson
P.H. Wilkie
B.E. Zabel
R. Zisman
M. Ziolak

East Region
161 Elgin St., 6th Fl., Ottawa, ON K2P 2L1
Tel: 613-239-1560
Regional Senior Justice: The Hon. Judith C. Beaman
P.R. Adams
A. Alder
C.D. Anderson
E. Deluzio
D.W. Dempsey
C.S. Dorval
R.N. Fournier
H.L. Fraser
G. Griffin
S.J. Hunter
C.A. Kehoe
R. Lajoie
B.W. Lennox
W. Malcolm
B.E. MacPhee
L. Maisonneuve
S.A.J. March
R.G. Masse
P.H. Megginson
J.D. Nadelle
D.M. Nicholas
H.E. Perkins-Walters
S.G. Radley-Walters
G. Renaud
R.G. Selkirk
J.D. Wake
J.D.G. Waugh
J.N. Wilson
J.P. Wright

Northeast Region
#303, 159 Cedar St., Sudbury, ON P3E 6A5
Tel: 705-564-7600
Regional Senior Justice: The Hon. Annemarie E. Bonkalo
E.K. Bignell
R.D.J. Boivin
P.J. Boucher
A. Buttazzoni
R.E.W. Carr
L. Duchesneau-McLachlan
W.F. Fitzgerald
G.N. Glaude
N. Gregson
A.L. Guay
J.D. Keast
L. Klein
J. Kukurin
R.W. Lalande
M.P. Lambert
J. Lebel
M. McLeod
Y. Renaud
M. Rocheleau
G.P. Rodgers
L. Serré
R.P. Villeneuve

Northwest Region
1805 East Arthur St., 1st Fl., Thunder Bay, ON P7E 5N7
Tel: 807-625-1620
Regional Senior Justice: The Hon. Marc L.G.H. Bode
D.P. Baig
P.T. Bishop
J. Elder
D. Di Giuseppe
D.G. Fraser
J.R. Hoshizaki
J. Little
A.T. McKay
J.L. Pelletier
F. Valente

Toronto
Old City Hall, 60 Queen St. West, Toronto, ON M5H 2M4
Tel: 416-327-6064
Regional Senior Justice: The Hon. Robert G. Bigelow
K.N. Barnes
W.P. Bassel
P. Bentley
F. Bhabha
M. Bloomenfeld
H. Borenstein
J.W. Bovard
C. Brewer
B.A. Brown
Harvey P. Brownstone
L.M. Budzinski
K.J. Caldwell
B. Cavion
A.P. Chapin
T.P. Cleary
S.F. Clements
M.L. Cohen
D.P. Cole
C. Curtis
A. Di Zio
S.G. Dobney
D. Fairgrieve
L.T. Feldman
F.M. Finnestad
R.J. Flaherty
S.E. Foster
P. French
M. Green
M.B. Greene
J.M. Grossman
D.G. Hackett
P.A.J. Harris
M.L. Hogan
W.B. Horkins
P. Hryn
P. Jones
H.L. Katarynych
R. Khawly
B. Knazan
N.L. Kozloff
A.T. Lacavera
G.S. Lapkin(Senior Judge)
E.N. Libman
S.B. Linden
T.R. Lipson
S.E. Marin
S. Merenda
C. Mocha
J.C. Moore
E.B. Murray
S.S. Nakatsuru
P.E. Newton
F.C. O'Donnell
D.I. Oleskiw
M. Omatsu
E.F. Ormston
R.J. Otter
D.A.W. Paulseth
L.C. Pringle
S. Ray
P.H. Reinhardt
J.M. Ritchie
P. Robertson
R. Rutherford
R. Schneider
B.M. Scully
S.R. Shamai
S.B. Sherr
G. Sparrow
R.J. Spence
J. Sutherland
P.M. Taylor
A. Tuck-Jackson
C.H. Vaillancourt
G. Waldman
B. Weagant
F.M. Weinper
W.R. Wolski
M. Wong
K.. Wright
B.J. Young
M.A. Zuker

West Region
80 Dundas St. East, 15th Fl., #G, London, ON N6A 6A3
Tel: 519-660-3013; *Fax:* 519-660-3087
Regional Senior Justice: The Hon. Kathleen E. McGowan
D.J. Austin
S.S. Bondy
G.J. Brophy
G.A. Campbell
D.G. Carr
J. Caspers
L.C. Dean
G.F. DeMarco
N. Douglas
M. Epstein
B. Frazer
S.J. Fuerth
J.L. Getliffe
L. Glenn
P.A. Hardman
G.F. Hearn
G.M. Hornblower
M. Hoffman
R.G.E. Hunter
P.R.W. Isaacs
P.J.S. Kowalyshyn
D.K. Livingstone
J.T. Lynch
R.S. MacKenzie
A.E.E. McFadyen
E.J. McGrath
K.L. McKerlie
M.A. McSorley
J. Morneau
S.M. Nicklas
M. O'Dea
D.W. Phillips
G.A. Pockele
W.G. Rabley
M. Rawlins
M.L.D. Roberts
L.J. Rogers
R.W. Rogerson
E.M. Schnall
J.S. Skowronski
B. Tobin
C.R. Westman
M.F. Woolcott

Court Services Division
McMurtry-Scott Bldg., #204, 720 Bay St., Toronto, ON M7A 2S9
Tel: 416-326-4263; *Fax:* 416-326-2652
www.attorneygeneral.jus.gov.on.ca/english/courts

Court Services Division manages the court offices in communities across Ontario: scheduling court cases, maintaining records & files, collecting fines & fees, enforcing civil orders, and providing information to the public. It also provides administration support to judicial offices in the Superior Court of Justice & the Ontario Court of Justice: providing clerks, court reporters, registrars and interpreters for court proceedings.

Regional Court: Central East
#210, 1091 Gorham St., Newmarket, ON L3Y 8X7
Tel: 905-836-5621; *Fax:* 905-836-5620
Areas served include: Barrie, Bracebridge, Huntsville, Lindsay, Kawartha Lakes, Muskoka, Newmarket, Orillia, Peterborough, Whitby, York Region. Total court locations: 24.
Acting Director: Court Operations, Sarina Kashak

Regional Court: Central West
John Sopinka Courthouse, #518B, 45 Main St. East, Hamilton, ON L8N 2B7
Tel: 905-645-5333; *Fax:* 905-645-5375
Areas served include: Brampton, Brantford, Burlington, Hamilton, Niagara Region, Oakville, Orangeville, St. Catharines, Welland. Total court locations: 15.
Director: Court Operations, Joanne Spriet

Regional Court: East
#100, Preston St., Ottawa, ON K1S 1N4
Tel: 613-239-1551; *Fax:* 613-239-1273
Areas served include: Bancroft, Belleville, Brockville, Cornwall, Kingston, Ottawa, Pembroke, Perth. Total court locations: 29.
Director: Court Operations, Thomas Fagan

Regional Court: North East
#501, 159 Cedar St., Sudbury, ON P3E 6A5
Tel: 705-564-7675; *Fax:* 705-564-7664
Areas served include: Kapuskasing, Kirkland Lake, Moosonee, North Bay, Parry Sound, Sault Ste. Marie, Sturgeon Falls, Sudbury, Timmins. Court services are regularly provided in French, Ojibway & Cree. Total court locations: 35.
Director: Court Operations, Paul Langlois

Regional Court: North West
277 Camelot St., Thunder Bay, ON P7A 4B3
Tel: 807-343-2747; *Fax:* 807-345-6383
Areas served include: Dryden, Fort Severn, Kenora, Nipigon, Rainy River, Thunder. There are significant Aboriginal populations in this region and court services are regularly provided in Ojibway and Oji-Cree. Many locations are fly-in. Total court locations: 42.
Director: Court Operations, Robert Gordon

Regional Court: Toronto
#1601, 720 Bay St., Toronto, ON M5G 1Z6
Tel: 416-326-4249; *Fax:* 416-326-2073
Areas served: Greater Toronto Area. Total court locations: 11.

Acting Director: Court Operations, Lou Bartucci

Regional Court: West
80 Dundas St., #D, London, ON N6A 6A4
Tel: 519-660-3090; *Fax:* 519-660-3098
Areas served include: Cambridge, Chatham, Fergus, Guelph, Kitchener, London, Owen Sound, Sarnia, Waterloo, Windsor.
Total court locations: 24.
Director: Court Operations, Len Griffiths

Prince Edward Island

Prince Edward Island Supreme Court: Trial Division
Sir Louis Davies Law Courts Bldg., 42 Water St., P.O. Box 2000, Charlottetown, PE C1A 7N8
The Supreme Court is a Court of original jurisdiction & has jurisdiction in all civil (including family, estate & small claims) & criminal matters arising in Prince Edward Island.
Chief Justice: The Hon. Madam Jacqueline Matheson
Justices (The Hon. Mr./Madam Justice):
Gordon Campbell
Wayne Cheverie
David Jenkins
Benjamin Taylor
Administration:
Registrar: Charles Thompson, 902-368-6669
Deputy Registrar: Estates Section, Gloria Panting
Deputy Registrar: General Section, Marjorie MacDonald
Deputy Registrar: Small Claims Section, Roxanne Smith
Deputy Registrar: Family Section, Sandra Mitchell
Deputy Registrar: Trial Division, Mary MacLeod
Court Services Manager: Tanya Tynski, 902-368-6005

Prince Edward Island Supreme Court
Sir Louis Henry Davies Law Courts, 42 Water St., P.O. Box 2000, Charlottetown, PE C1A 7N8
Tel: 902-368-6000; *Fax:* 902-368-0266
Chief Justice: The Hon. Gerard E. Mitchell

Prince Edward Island Supreme Court: Court of Appeal
Sir Louis Henry Davies Law Courts, 42 Water St., P.O. Box 2000, Charlottetown, PE C1A 7N8
The Court of Appeal has appellate jurisdiction in criminal & civil matters.
Chief Justice: The Hon. Mr. Gerard E. Mitchell
John McQuaid
Linda Webber
Deputy Registrar: Appeal Division, Gloria Panting

Prince Edward Island Provincial Court
Kelly Bldg., 3 Harbourside Access Rd., Charlottetown, PE C1A 8R4
Tel: 902-368-6000
The Provincial Court has jurisdiction in select criminal matters as well as youth matters.
Chief Judge: The Hon. John R. Douglas, 902-368-6011

Courts:
Queens & Kings Counties: Provincial Court
Law Courts Bldg., P.O. Box 2290, Charlottetown, PE C1A 8C1
Jeffrey Lantz
Nancy K. Orr

Prince County: Provincial Court
Law Courts Bldg., P.O. Box 2020, Summerside, PE C1N 4M1

Prince Edward Island: Judicial Officers
PE

Courts:
Kings County
Court House, Kent St., P.O. Box 89, Georgetown, PE C0A 1L0
Tel: 902-652-2924; *Fax:* 902-652-2701
georgetown@pei.sympatico.ca
www.georgetown.ca/courthouse.html
Deputy Registrar: Shirley Clory, 902-652-8990

Queens County
Law Courts, P.O. Box 2000, Charlottetown, PE C1A 7N8
Chief Sheriff: Frank Driscoll, 902-368-6055
Prothonotary: Charles P. Thompson
Court Services Manager: Tanya Tynski, 902-368-6005

Prince County
Court House, P.O. Box 2020, Summerside, PE C1N 4M1
Sheriff: Ron Dowling, 902-888-8191

Québec

Cour Supérieure du Québec
Québec Superior Court
300, boul Jean-Lesage, Québec, QC G1K 8K6
Tél: 418-649-3400; *Téléc:* 418-528-0932
www.tribunaux.qc.ca/c-superieure
Affaires civiles et commerciales dont l'enjeu est de 70 000$ ou plus; litiges en matières administratives et familiale, faillite, procès devant jury en matière pénale, et appels en matière de poursuites sommaires
Juge en chef: L'hon. François Rolland
Juge en chef associé: L'hon. Robert Pidgeon
Juge en chef adjoint: L'hon. André Wery

Abitibi—Rouyn-Noranda—Témiscamingue
QC
Robert Dufresne
Jocelyn Geoffroy
Laurent Guertin
Ivan St-Julien(Juge surnuméraire)
Jacques Viens(Juge surnuméraire)

Alma
QC
Gratien Duchesne

Arthabaska
QC
Jules Allard(Juge surnuméraire)

Baie-Comeau—Mingan
QC
Paul Corriveau

Bonaventure
QC
Jean-Roch Landry

Chicoutimi
QC
Jacques Babin
Roger Banford(Juge surnuméraire)
Martin Dallaire
Carl Lachance
Jean-Claude Larouche(Juge surnuméraire)

Granby
Paul-Marcel Bellavance
Suzanne Mireault

Hull—Pontiac—Labelle
QC
Martin Bédard
Pierre Dallaire
Dominique Goulet
Pierre Isabelle
Louis-Philippe Landry(Juge surnuméraire)
Jean-Pierre Plouffe(Juge surnuméraire)
Suzanne Tessier

Laval
QC
Michel Déziel
Jacques R. Fournier
Pierre Journet(Juges surnuméraire)

Longueuil
QC
Jean-Jude Chabot
Carole Julien
Gilles Mercure
Réjean F. Paul(Juge surnuméraire)

Montréal
QC
Christiane Alary
Louisa Arcand
Claude Auclair
Roger E. Baker(Juge surnuméraire)
Guylène Beaugé
Pierre Béliveau
Nicole Bénard(Juge surnuméraire)
Marc-André Blanchard
Jean-Guy Boilard(Juge surnuméraire)
Sylviane W. Borenstein(Juge surnuméraire)
Sophie Bourque
James L. Brunton
Jean-François Buffoni
Pepita G. Capriolo
Michel A. Caron
Kirkland Casgrain
Robert Castiglio
Martin Castonguay
Claude Champagne
Paul G. Chaput(Juge surnuméraire)
France Charbonneau
Jean-Pierre Chrétien
Carol Cohen
Chantal Corriveau
Guy Cournoyer
Suzanne Courteau
Marie-France Courville
Louis Crête(Juge surnuméraire)
Louis-Paul Cullen
Claude Dallaire
Marc David
Wilbrod Claude Décarie
Jean-François de Grandpré
Michel Delorme
André Denis(Juge surnuméraire)
Sylvie Devito
Marc De Wever
Kevin Downs(Juge surnuméraire)
Gérard Dugré
Benoît Emery
Lucie Fournier
William Fraiberg
Pierre-C. Gagnon
Clément Gascon
Marie Gaudreau
Jacques Gauthier
Nicole M. Gibeau
Danielle Grenier(Juge surnuméraire)
Jean Guibault(Juge surnuméraire)
Carole Hallée
Gilles Hébert(Juge surnuméraire)
Pierre Jasmin(Juge surnuméraire)
Marie-Christine Laberge
Louis Lacoursière
Jean-Yves Lalonde
Julien Lanctôt
Hélène Langlois
Claude Larouche(Juge surnuméraire)
Hélène Le Bel(Juge surnuméraire)
Luc Lefebvre
Louise Lemelin
Johanne Mainville(Juge surnuméraire)
Catherine Mandeville
Diane Marcelin(Juge surnuméraire)
Geneviève Marcotte
J. Fraser Martin(Juge surnuméraire)
Israel Mass(Juge surnuméraire)
Chantal Masse
Lise Matteau
Paul Mayer
Danièle Mayrand
Michèle Monast
Richard Mongeau
Robert Mongeon
Richard Nadeau
Francine Nantel
Pierre Nollet
Daniel W. Payette
Mark G. Peacock
Micheline Perrault
Eva Petras
Claudette Picard
Sophie Picard
Ginette Piché(Juge surnuméraire)
Yves Poirier
Hélène Poulin
André Prévost
Steve J. Reimnitz
Danielle Richer
Brian J. Riordan
Jeannine M. Rousseau(Juge surnuméraire)
André Roy
Claudine Roy
Manon Savard
Jean-Pierre Sénécal
Joel Avery Silcoff
Marie St-Pierre
Pierre Tessier(Juge surnuméraire)
Daniel H. Tingley(Juge surnuméraire)
Anne-Marie Trahan
Clément Trudel(Juge surnuméraire)
Danielle Turcotte
Martin Vauclair
Jocelyn Verrier
André Vincent
Richard Wagner
Dionysia Zerbisias(Juge surnuméraire)
Jerry Zigman(Juge surnuméraire)

Rimouski
QC
Gilles Blanchet
Claude-Henri Gendreau

Sherbrooke
QC
Pierre Boily(Juge surnuméraire)
Martin Bureau
Léo Daigle
Gaétan Dumas
Line Samoisette
Yves Tardif
François Tôth

St-Maurice
QC
Raymond W. Pronovost

Trois-Rivières
850, rue Hart, Trois-Rivières, QC G9A 1T9
Tél: 819-372-4153
www.justice.gouv.qc.ca; www.tribunaux.qc.ca/c-superieure
Alain Bolduc
Ivan Godin
Guy Lebrun(Juge surnuméraire)
Robert Legris(Juge surnuméraire)
Michel Richard
Marc St-Pierre

Cour du Québec
Court of Québec
300, boul Jean-Lesage, Québec, QC G1K 8K6
Tél: 418-649-3400; *Téléc:* 418-528-0932
www.tribunaux.qc.ca/c-quebec/
Composée d'au plus 270 juges dont la juge en chef, le juge en chef associé, 4 juges en chef adjoints, et 18 juges coordonnateurs et coordonnateurs adjoints; matières civile, criminelle et pénale; matière de jeunesse; matière administrative ou en appel dans les cas prévus par la loi; cour d'archives.
Juge en chef: L'honorable Élizabeth Corte
Juge en chef associé: L'honorable Mario Tremblay
Juge en chef adjoint: Chambre civile, L'honorable Michel Simard
Juge en chef adjoint: Chambre criminelle et pénale, L'honorable Maurice Galarneau
Juge en chef adjoint: Chambre jeunesse, L'honorable Claude C. Boulanger
Juge en chef adjoint: Cours municipales, L'honorable André Perreault
Maurice Abud(Juge coordonnateur)
Paul Chevalier(Juge coordonnateur)
Jean-Paul Decoste(Juge coordonnateur)
Pierre Labbé(Juge coordonnateur)
Micheline Laliberté(Juge coordonnatrice)
Daniel Bédard(Juge coordonnateur)
Lynne Landry(Juge coordonnatrice)
Patrick Théroux(Juge coordonnateur)
Ruth Veillet(Juge coordonnatrice)
Suzanne Villeneuve(Juge coordonnatrice)
Normand Amyot(Juge coordonnateur adjoint)
Pierre E. Audet(Juge coordonnateur adjoint)
Marc Bisson(Juge coordonnateur adjoint)
Claude Parent(Juge coordonnateur adjoint)
Charles-G. Grenier(Juge coordonnateur adjoint)
Chantale Pelletier(Juge coordonnatrice adjointe)
Jean Lebel(Juge coordonnateur adjoint)
Denis Saulnier(Juge coordonnateur adjoint)
Anne Bélanger(Directrice déléguée à l'administration)
Juges (Les honorables):
Michel Auger
Andrée Bergeron
Lina Bond
Rémi Bouchard
Hélène Bouillon
Christian Boulet
Peter Bradley
André-J. Brochet
Gilles Charest
André Cloutier
Pierre Coderre
René de la Sablonnière
Jean-François Dionne
Colette Duford
Jean-Pierre Dumais
Paule Gaumond
Marie-Claude Gilbert
François Godbout
Line Gosselin
Charles G. Grenier(Juge coordonnateur adjoint)
Anne Laberge
Judith Landry
Daniel Lavoie
Jean Lebel(Juge coordonnateur adjoint)
Jean-Louis Lemay
Bernard Lemieux
Alain Morand
Chantale Pelletier(Juge coordonnatrice adjointe)
André Plante
Lucie Rondeau
Pierre-L. Rousseau
Carol St-Cyr
Claude Tremblay
Jacques Tremblay
Alain Turgeon
Suzanne Villeneuve(Juge coordonnatrice)
Réna Émond(Juge de paix magistrat)
Sylvie Marcotte(Juge de paix magistrat)
Nicole Martin(Juge de paix magistrat)

Abitibi-Témiscamingue - Amos
Claude P. Bigué
Lucille Chabot
Jean-Pierre Gervais

Abitibi-Témiscamingue - Rouyn-Noranda
Marc E. Grimard
Richard Laflamme
Nancy McKenna
Marie-Claude Bélanger(Juge de paix magistrat)

Abitibi-Témiscamingue - Val d'Or
Daniel Bédard(Juge coordonnateur)
Denyse Leduc
Renée Lemoine

Est du Québec - Baie-Comeau
François Boisjoli
Michel Dionne

Est du Québec - Matane
VACANTE

Est du Québec - New-Carlisle
Jean Bécu
Robert Lévesque
Luc Marchildon(Juge de paix magistrat)

Est du Québec - Percé
Embert Whittom

Est du Québec - Rimouski
Richard Côté
Jean-Paul Decoste(Juge coordonnateur)
James Rondeau
Lucie Morissette(Juge de paix magistrat)

Est du Québec - Rivière-du-Loup
Martin Gagnon
Luce Kennedy
Guy Ringuet
Julie Dionne(Juge de paix magistrat)

Est du Québec - Sept-Iles
Nathalie Aubry
Gabriel de Pokomandy(Coordonnateur)
Michel Parent
Louise Gallant(Juge de paix magistrat)

Estrie - Drummondville
Gilles Lafrenière
Marie-Josée Ménard

Estrie - Granby
Pierre Bachand
Serge Champoux
Johanne Denis
François Marchand
Monique Perron(Juge de paix magistrat)

Estrie - Sherbrooke
Michel Beauchemin
Conrad Chapdelaine
Danielle Côté
Alain Désy
Michel DuBois
Paul Dunnigan
Michel Durand
Hélène Fabi
Lise Gagnon
Patrick Théroux(Juge coordonnateur)
Sylvie Desmeules(Juge de paix magistrat)

Laval—Lanaudière—Laurentides - Joliette
Normand Bonin
François Landry
Richard Landry
Denis Le Reste
Maurice Parent
Jean Roy
Marc Vanasse
Danielle Michaud(Juge de paix magistrat)

Laval—Lanaudière—Laurentides - Laval
Jean-Pierre Archambault
Lise Gaboury
Françoise Garneau-Fournier
Dominique Larochelle
Marie-Suzanne Lauzon
Julie Messier
Micheline Sasseville
Gaby Dumas(Juge de paix magistrat)

Laval—Lanaudière—Laurentides - Saint-Jérôme
Pierre E. Audet(Juge coordonnateur adjoint)
François Beaudoin
Jean R. Beaulieu
Valmont Beaulieu
Omer Boudreau
Paul Chevalier(Juge coordonnateur)
Antoine Cloutier
Monique Fradette
Jean-Claude Gagnon
Diane Girard
Normand Lafond
Marie Lapointe
Jean La Rue
Ginette Maillet
Georges Massol
Claude Melançon
Carol Richer
Jean Sirois
Michèle Toupin
Nathalie DuPerron Roy(Juge de paix magistrat)
Jean-Georges Laliberté(Juge de paix magistrat)

Mauricie—Bois-Francs - Shawinigan
Richard Poudrier

Mauricie—Bois-Francs - Trois-Rivières
Yvan Cousineau
Jacques Lacoursière
Guy Lambert
Nicole Mallette
Daniel Perreault
Jacques Rioux
Dominique Slater
Guylaine Tremblay
Alain Trudel
Jacques Trudel
Pierre Verrette(Juge de paix magistrat)

Mauricie—Bois-Francs - Victoriaville
Pierre Labbé(Juge coordonnateur)
Gaétan Ratté(Juge de paix magistrat)

Montérégie - Longueuil
Mireille Allaire
Pierre Bélisle
Marc Bisson(Juge coordonnateur adjoint)
Virgile Buffoni
Mario Gervais
Jean Gravel
Anne-Marie Jacques
Micheline Laliberté(Juge coordonnatrice)
Claude Laporte
Louise Leduc
Richard Marleau
Nancy Moreau
Denys Noël
Ellen Paré
Robert Proulx
Claude Provost
Jean-Pierre Saintonge
Chantal Sirois
Marie-Josée Hénault(Juge de paix magistrat)
Marc Renaud(Juge de paix magistrat)

Montérégie - Saint-Hyacinthe
Guy Fortier
Yves Morier
Viviane Primeau
Robert Lanctôt(Juge de paix magistrat)

Montérégie - Saint-Jean-sur-Richelieu
Michel Bédard
Éric Simard

Montérégie - Salaberry-de-Valleyfield
Linda Despots
Marie-Chantal Doucet
Gilbert Lanthier
Michel Mercier
Claude Montpetit
Odette Perron
Marie-Andrée Villeneuve
Patricia Compagnone(Juge de paix magistrat)

Montérégie - Sorel-Tracy
VACANTE

Montréal
Juges (Les honorables):
Normand Amyot(Juge coordonnateur adjoint)

Denis Asselin
Armando Aznar
Normand Bastien
Lucille Beauchemin
Michel Bellehumeur
Serge Boisvert
Louise Bourdeau
François Bousquet
Jean-Pierre Boyer
Jean-Paul Braun
Alain Breault
Carole Brosseau
Gilles Cadieux
David L. Cameron
Brigitte Charron
Louise Comeau
Suzanne Coupal
Sylvain Coutlée
Antonio De Michele
Taya Di Pietro
Daniel Dortélus
Sylvie Durand
Jean-B. Falardeau
Gilles Garneau
Lucie Godin
Brigitte Gouin
Louis Grégoire
Yves Hamel
Suzanne Handman
Patrick Healy
Martin Hébert
Patrice Hurtubise
Michel Jasmin
Ann-Marie Jones
Jean-F. Keable
Pierre E. Labelle
Céline Lacerte-Lamontagne
Gilson Lachance
Sylvie Lachapelle
Claude Lamoureux
Gilles Lareau
Denis Lavergne
Daniel Lavery
Marie Michelle Lavigne
Claude Leblond
Guy Lecompte
Michèle Lefebvre
Louis A. Legault
Gérald Locas
Robert Marchi
Eliana Marengo
Salvatore Mascia
Rolande Matte
Claude Millette
Hélène V. Morin
Jacques A. Nadeau
Gilles L. Ouellet
Manon Ouimet
Jacques Paquet
Claude Parent(Juge coordonnateur adjoint (criminelle/pénale))
Michèle Pauzé(Présidente)
Michel A. Pinsonnault(Président)
Louise Provost(Présidente)
Diane Quenneville
André Renaud
Isabelle Rheault
Henri Richard
Robert Sansfaçon
Denis Saulnier(Juge coordonnateur adjoint (jeunesse))
Mark Shamie
Christian M. Tremblay
Suzanne Vadboncoeur
Ruth Veillet(Juge coordonnatrice)
Julie Veilleux
Louise Villemure
Lori Renée Weitzman
Juanita Westmoreland-Traoré
Dominique Wilhelmy
Gaétan Zonato

Outaouais - Gatineau
Gatien Fournier
Nicole Gibeault
Jean-François Gosselin
Lynne Landry(Juge coordonnatrice)
Réal R. Lapointe
Serge Laurin
Rosemarie Millar
Michel Séguin
Louise Turpin
Christine Auger(Juge de paix magistrat)
Georges Benoît(Juge de paix magistrat)

Québec—Chaudière-Appalaches - Montmagny
Jogues Lavoie

Québec—Chaudière-Appalaches - Saint-Joseph-de-Beauce
Hubert Couture
Yannick Couture(Juge de paix magistrat)

Saguenay—Lac-Saint-Jean - Alma
Maurice Abud(Juge coordonnateur)

Saguenay—Lac-Saint-Jean - Saguenay (Chicoutimi)
Jean-Paul Aubin
Paul Casgrain
Richard P. Daoust
Pierre Lortie
Micheline Paradis
Johanne Roy
Pierre Simard
Doris Thibault
Réjean Bédard(Juge de paix magistrat)

Saguenay—Lac-Saint-Jean - Roberval
Rosaire Larouche
Michel Boissonneault(Juge de paix magistrat)

Québec: Les Palais de justice et Points de service de justice
Courts & Judicial Service Ce

QC Alma
725, rue Harvey ouest, Alma, QC G8B 1P5
Tél: 418-668-3334; *Téléc:* 418-662-3697

Amos
891, rue 3e ouest, Amos, QC J9T 2T4
Tél: 819-444-5063; *Téléc:* 819-444-5204

Baie Comeau
71, av Mance, Baie-Comeau, QC G4Z 1N2
Tél: 418-296-5534; *Téléc:* 418-294-8717
Ligne sans frais: 866-854-4075

Campbell's Bay
30, rue John, Campbell's Bay, QC J0X 1K0
Tél: 819-648-5222; *Téléc:* 819-648-5931

Chicoutimi
227, rue Racine est, 1er étage, Chicoutimi, QC G7H 7B4
Tél: 418-696-9926; *Téléc:* 418-698-3558

Cowansville
920, rue Principale, Cowansville, QC J2K 0E3
Tél: 450-263-3520; *Téléc:* 450-266-1415

Drummondville
1680, boul St-Joseph, Drummondville, QC J2C 2G3
Tél: 819-478-2513; *Téléc:* 819-475-8459

Granby
Édifice Roger-Paré, #1.32, 77, rue Principale, Granby, QC J2G 9B3
Tél: 450-776-7110; *Téléc:* 450-776-4080

Hâvre-Aubert
#102, 405, ch d'En-Haut, Hâvre-Aubert, QC G4T 9A7
Tél: 418-937-2201; *Téléc:* 418-937-9038

Hull
17, rue Laurier, Gatineau, QC J8X 4C1
Tél: 819-776-8100; *Téléc:* 819-772-3347

Joliette
200, rue Saint-Marc, Joliette, QC J6E 8C2
Tél: 450-753-4807; *Téléc:* 450-752-1733

Lac-Mégantic
#316, 5527, rue Frontenac, Lac-Mégantic, QC G6B 1H6
Tél: 819-583-1268; *Téléc:* 819-583-0703

La Malbaie
30, ch de la Vallée, La Malbaie, QC G5A 1A3
Tél: 418-665-3991; *Téléc:* 418-665-1125

La Tuque
290, rue Saint-Joseph, P.O. Box 6, La Tuque, QC G9X 3Z8
Tél: 819-523-9533; *Téléc:* 819-523-3603

Laval
2800, boul Saint-Martin ouest, Laval, QC H7T 2S9
Tél: 450-686-5015; *Téléc:* 450-686-5005

Longueuil
1111, boul Jacques-Cartier est, Longueuil, QC J4M 2J6
Tél: 450-646-4010; *Téléc:* 450-928-7982

Maniwaki
266, rue Notre-Dame, 1er étage, Maniwaki, QC J9E 2J8
Tél: 819-449-3222; *Téléc:* 819-449-6085

Mont-Laurier
645, rue de la Madone, Mont-Laurier, QC J9L 1T1
Tél: 819-623-9666; *Téléc:* 819-623-6859

Montmagny
25, rue du Palais de Justice, Montmagny, QC G5V 1P6
Tél: 418-248-0909; *Téléc:* 418-248-2437

Montréal
1, rue Notre-Dame est, Montréal, QC H2Y 1B6
Tél: 514-393-2721; *Téléc:* 514-873-4760

New Carlisle
87, rue Gérard-D.-Lévesque, New Carlisle, QC G0C 1Z0
Tél: 418-752-3376; *Téléc:* 418-752-6979

Percé
124, rte 132, P.O. Box 188, Percé, QC G0C 2L0
Tél: 418-782-2055; *Téléc:* 418-782-2906

Québec
300, boul Jean-Lesage, Québec, QC G1K 8K6
Tél: 418-649-3400; *Téléc:* 418-528-0932

Rimouski
183, av de la Cathédrale, Rimouski, QC G5L 5J1
Tél: 418-727-3852; *Téléc:* 418-727-3635

Rivière-du-Loup
33, rue de la Cour, Rivière-du-Loup, QC G5R 1J1
Tél: 418-862-3579; *Téléc:* 418-867-8794
Ligne sans frais: 800-463-8009

Roberval
750, boul St-Joseph, Roberval, QC G8H 2L5
Tél: 418-275-3666; *Téléc:* 418-275-6169

Rouyn-Noranda
2, av du Palais, Rouyn-Noranda, QC J9X 2N9
Tél: 819-763-3058; *Téléc:* 819-763-3389

Saint-Hyacinthe
1550, rue Dessaulles, Saint-Hyacinthe, QC J2S 2S8
Tél: 450-778-6559; *Téléc:* 450-778-6557

Saint-Jean-sur-Richelieu
109, rue Saint-Charles, Saint-Jean-sur-Richelieu, QC J3B 2C2
Tél: 450-347-1392; *Téléc:* 450-346-8437

Saint-Jérôme
25, rue de Martigny ouest, Saint-Jérôme, QC J7Y 4Z1
Tél: 514-431-4406; *Téléc:* 514-569-3143

Saint-Joseph-de-Beauce
795, av du Palais, Saint-Joseph-de-Beauce, QC G0S 2V0
Tél: 418-397-7187; *Téléc:* 418-397-7968

Salaberry-de-Valleyfield
180, rue Salaberry ouest, Salaberry-de-Valleyfield, QC J6T 2J2
Tél: 450-370-4006; *Téléc:* 450-370-3022

Sept-Iles
425, boul Laure, Sept-Iles, QC G4R 1X6
Tél: 418-962-3044; *Téléc:* 418-964-8714
Ligne sans frais: 866-405-7951

Shawinigan
212, 6e rue, Shawinigan, QC G9N 8B6
Tél: 819-536-2571; *Téléc:* 819-536-2992

Sherbrooke
375, rue King ouest, Sherbrooke, QC J1H 6B9
Tél: 819-822-6910; *Téléc:* 819-820-3134

Sorel-Tracy
46, rue Charlotte, Sorel-Tracy, QC J3P 6N5
Tél: 450-742-2786; *Téléc:* 450-746-7394

Thetford Mines
#1.23, 693, rue St-Alphonse ouest, Thetford Mines, QC G6G 3X3
Tél: 418-338-2118; *Téléc:* 418-335-7756

Trois-Rivières
850, rue Hart, Trois-Rivières, QC G9A 1T9
Other information: Fax civile: 819/371-6096; Fax criminel: 819/371-6111

Victoriaville
800, boul Bois-Francs sud, Victoriaville, QC G6P 5W5
Tél: 819-357-2054; *Téléc:* 819-357-5517

Ville-Marie
8, rue Saint-Gabriel nord, Ville-Marie, QC J9V 1Z9
Tél: 819-629-6473; *Téléc:* 819-622-6367

Points de service:

Amqui
29, boul Saint-Benoît ouest, Amqui, QC G5J 2E4
Tél: 418-629-4488; *Téléc:* 418-629-6450

Carleton
17, rue Lacroix, Carleton, QC G0C 1J0
Tél: 418-364-3442; *Téléc:* 418-364-7036

Dolbeau-Mistassini
1420, boul Walberg, 1er étage, Dolbeau-Mistassini, QC G8L 1H4
Tel: 418-276-0683; *Fax:* 418-276-6110

Forestville
Édifice Renato, 24, rte 138 ouest, P.O. Box 400, Forestville, QC G0T 1E0
Tél: 418-587-4471; *Téléc:* 418-587-6639
Ligne sans frais: 866-854-4075

Gaspé
11, rue de la Cathédrale, Gaspé, QC G4X 2V9
Tél: 418-368-5756; *Téléc:* 416-360-8030

Jonquière
Édifice Marguerite-Belley, 3950, boul Harvey, RC, Jonquière, QC G7X 8L6
Tel: 418-695-7991; *Fax:* 418-698-3558

Lachute
#216, 505, rue Béthany, Lachute, QC J8H 4A6
Tél: 450-562-3711; *Téléc:* 450-569-7645

Magog
Hôtel de Ville, #127, 7, rue Principale est, Magog, QC J1X 1Y4
Tél: 819-843-7323; *Téléc:* 819-843-4533

Matane
382, av Saint-Jérôme, Matane, QC G4W 3B3
Tél: 418-562-2497; *Téléc:* 418-560-8746

Mont-Joli
40, rue de l'Hôtel-de-Ville, Mont-Joli, QC G5H 1W8
Tél: 418-775-8811; *Téléc:* 418-775-7517

Sainte-Agathe-des-Monts
85, rue Saint-Vincent, Sainte-Agathe-des-Monts, QC J8C 2A8
Tél: 819-326-6462; *Téléc:* 819-569-7645

Sainte-Anne-des-Monts
10-B, boul Sainte-Anne ouest, Sainte-Anne-des-Monts, QC G4V 1P3
Tél: 418-763-2791; *Téléc:* 418-763-3107

Cour d'Appel du Québec
Québec Court of Appeal
Édifice Ernest-Cormier, 100, rue Notre-Dame Est, Montréal, QC H2Y 4B6
Tél: 514-393-2022
courdappelqc@justice.gouv.qc.ca
www.tribunaux.qc.ca/c-appel

Le plus haut tribunal du Québec; la cour est la gardienne de l'intégrité du droit civil de la province; en matière civile, la cour entend les appels des jugements finals de la Cour supérieure et de la Cour du Québec lorsque la valeur de l'objet du litige en appel est to 50 000$ ou plus; outrage, adoption, évaluation psychiatrique, garde en établissement, faillite, et divorce.

Juge en chef: L'hon. J.J. Michel Robert
Juges (Les honorables):
Marc Beauregard(Juge surnuméraire)
Marie-France Bich
Jean Bouchard
André Brossard(Juge surnuméraire)
Jacques Chamberland
Lise Côté
Pierre J. Dalphond
François Doyon
Jacques Dufresne
Julie Dutil
Nicole Duval Hesler
André Forget(Juge surnuméraire)
Guy Gagnon
Paul-Arthur Gendreau(Juge surnuméraire)
Lorne Giroux
Allan Ross Hilton
Nicholas Kasirer
Jacques A. Léger
Benoît Morin(Juge surnuméraire)
Yves-Marie Morissette
François Pelletier
Louis Rochette
André Rochon
France Thibault
Paul Vézina(Juge surnuméraire)

Montréal
Édifice Ernest-Cormier, #2.22, 100, rue Notre-Dame est, Montréal, QC H2Y 4B6
Tél: 514-393-2022; *Téléc:* 514-864-7270
Coordonnatrice juridique: Lysanne P. Legault

Québec
Palais de justice de Québec, #4.27, 300, boul Jean-Lesage, Québec, QC G1K 8K6
Tél: 418-649-3401; *Téléc:* 418-646-6961
Coordonnatrice juridique: Claire Roberge

Cours municipales du Québec
Québec Municipal Courts
Ministère de la Justice du Québec, 1200, route de l'Église, 6e étage, Québec, QC G1K 8K6
Tél: 418-643-5140; *Ligne sans frais:* 866-536-5140
informations@justice.gouv.qc.ca
www.justice.gouv.qc.ca

Les cours municipales ont une compétence limitée en matière civile, notamment dans le domaine des réclamations de taxes; en matière pénale en ce qui concerne les infractions aux règlements municipaux et les infractions aux lois québécoises; et pour entendre et juger les infractions visées par la partie XXVII du Code criminel.. infractions punissables sur déclaration de culpabilité par procédure sommaire.
Juge responsable: André Perreault

Courts:

Lévis
5333, rue de la Symphonie, Charny, QC G6X 3B6
Tél: 418-832-4695
www.ville.levis.qc.ca
Jacques Ouellet

Bedford
1, rue Principale, Bedford, QC J0J 1A0
Tél: 450-248-7742; *Téléc:* 450-248-3220
www.paquette.qc.ca
Alain Boisvert

Bellechasse MRC
100, Monseigneur Bilodeau, P.O. Box 130, St-Lazare-de-Bellechasse, QC G0R 3J0
Tél: 418-883-3347
www.paquette.qc.ca
Claude Fortin

Beloeil
777, rue Laurier, Beloeil, QC J3G 4S9
Tél: 450-467-2835; *Téléc:* 450-464-5445
cour-mun@ville.beloeil.qc.ca
www.paquette.qc.ca
Luc Alarie

Mascouche
3034, Ste-Marie, Mascouche, QC J7K 1P1
Tél: 450-474-4133
www.paquette.qc.ca
Claude Lemire

Blainville
Hôtel de ville, 1000, ch du Plan-Bouchard, Blainville, QC J7C 3S9
Tél: 450-434-5224; *Téléc:* 450-434-8285
www.ville.blainville.qc.ca, www.paquette.qc.ca
Guy Saulnier

Longueuil
100, Place Charles-Lemoyne, Longueuil, QC J4K 2T4
Tél: 450-463-7006; *Téléc:* 450-646-8897
www.longueuil.qc.ca
Richard Alary
Guy Houle
Bruno Themens

Ste-Marie
270, av Marguerite Bourgeos, P.O. Box 1750, Sainte-Marie, QC G6E 3C7
Tél: 418-387-2301; *Téléc:* 418-387-2454
www.paquette.qc.ca
Paul Routhier

Boisbriand
940, boul de la Grande-Allée, Boisbriand, QC J7G 2J7
Tél: 450-435-1954; *Téléc:* 450-435-6398
service.cour.municipale@ville.boisbriand.qc.ca
www.paquette.qc.ca
André Hotte

L'Islet MRC
364, rue Verreault, Saint-Jean-Port-Joli, QC G0R 3G0
Tél: 418-598-3076; *Téléc:* 418-598-6880
www.paquette.qc.ca
Jacques Ouellet

Loretteville
305, rue Racine, Loretteville, QC G2B 1E7
Tél: 418-842-1921
www.paquette.qc.ca
Louis-M. Vachon
Claude Fournier
Jean-Pierre Gignac
Paulin Cloutier

Louiseville
105, av St-Laurent ouest, Louiseville, QC J5V 1J6
Tél: 819-228-9437
Jocelyn Crête

Magog
7, rue Principale E., Magog, QC J1X 1Y4
Tél: 819-843-6501; *Téléc:* 819-843-3599
www.paquette.qc.ca
Pierre Geoffroy

St-Rédempteur
85, rue 19e, St-Rédempteur, QC G6K 1C3
Tél: 418-836-4400
www.paquette.qc.ca; www.barreau.qc.ca
Commune St-Nicholas, St-Rédempteur, Bernières et St-Étienne de Lauzon.
Jacques Ouellet
Louis-Marie Vachon

Marieville
682, rue St-Charles, Marieville, QC J3M 1P9
Tél: 450-460-4444
www.paquette.qc.ca
Louis-B. Grignon

Mirabel
14 026, boul du Curé-Labelle, Mirabel, QC J7J 1A1
Tél: 450-435-6408
www.paquette.qc.ca
Michel Paquin

Mistassini
173, St-Michel, P.O. Box 219, Mistissini, QC G0W 2C0
Michel J. Lapointe
Jacquelin Légaré

St-Pierre
69, av 5e, Saint-Pierre, QC H8R 1P1
Tél: 514-364-5153
www.paquette.qc.ca
Pierre G. Bouchard

Montmagny
134, rue St-Jean-Baptiste est, Montmagny, QC G5V 1K6
Tél: 418-248-3361
www.paquette.qc.ca
Louis-Marie Vachon

Candiac
100, boul Montcalm N., Candiac, QC J5R 3L8
Tél: 450-444-6060; *Téléc:* 450-444-0789
www.paquette.qc.ca
Jean-Pierre Dépelteau

St-Raymond
375, rue St-Joseph, Saint-Raymond, QC G3L 1A1
Tél: 418-337-2202; *Téléc:* 418-337-2203
Jean-R. Côté

Chambly
1, Place de la Mairie, Chambly, QC J3L 4X1
Tél: 450-658-8788; *Téléc:* 450-658-4214
www.paquette.qc.ca
Gilles R. Pelletier

St-Rémi
105, Perras, Saint-Rémi, QC J0L 2L0
Tél: 450-454-3994; *Téléc:* 450-454-6898
www.paquette.qc.ca
Pascal Pillarella

Charlesbourg
160, rue 76e est, Charlesbourg, QC G1H 7H5
Tél: 418-641-6179; *Téléc:* 418-641-6594
Jean-Pierre Gignac

Charny
5333, rue de la Symphonie, Charny, QC G6X 3B6
Raymond Lavoie

Ste-Thérèse
6, rue de l'Église, P.O. Box 100, Sainte-Thérèse, QC J7E 4H7
Tél: 450-434-1440; *Téléc:* 450-434-1499
www.paquette.qc.ca
Guy Saulnier

Châteauguay
#101, 265, boul d'Anjou, Châteauguay, QC J6J 5J9
Tél: 450-698-3245; *Téléc:* 450-698-3259
courmun@ville.chateauguay.qc.ca
www.ville.chateauguay.qc.ca
La cour a le mandat de veiller à l'application des lois et des règlements municipaux, provinciaux et fédéraux pour Châteauguay, Mercier, Léry et Beauharnois.
Paul Lemieux

Chibougamau
650, 3e rue, Chibougamau, QC G8P 1P1
Tél: 418-748-3132; *Téléc:* 418-748-6562
www.paquette.qc.ca
Frédérique Lalancette

St-Tite
540, rue Notre-Dame, Saint-Tite, QC G0X 3H0
Tél: 418-365-5143
Claude Trudel

Saguenay
201, rue Racine est, P.O. Box 129, Chicoutimi, QC G7H 5B8
Tél: 418-698-3161
www.paquette.qc.ca

Salaberry-de-Valleyfield
61, Sainte-Cécile, Salaberry-de-Valleyfield, QC J6T 1L8
Tél: 450-370-4305; *Téléc:* 450-370-4868
www.paquette.qc.ca
Paul Lemieux

Montréal-Est
11 370, rue Notre-Dame est, Montréal, QC H1B 2W6
Tél: 514-645-7431
www.paquette.qc.ca
Florent Bisson
Jean Hébert

Montréal-Nord
11 211 av. Hébert, Montréal-Nord, QC H1H 3X5
Tél: 514-328-4079
www.paquette.qc.ca
Jacques Lamontagne
Robert Diamond

Montréal-Ouest
50, av Westminster S., Montréal, QC H4X 1Y7
Tél: 514-481-8125
Frank Schlesinger

Mont-Royal
20, av Roosevelt, Mount-Royal, QC H3R 1Z4
Tél: 514-734-2907
Pierre-G. Bouchard
Jacques Laurier

Mont-Saint-Hilaire
Hôtel de Ville, 100, rue du Centre-Civique, Mont-Saint-Hilaire, QC J3H 3M8
Tél: 450-467-2854
courmunicipale@villemsh.ca
www.ville.mont-saint-hilaire.qc.ca

Nicolet
180, Mgr. Panet, Nicolet, QC J3T 1S6
Tél: 819-293-6901; *Téléc:* 819-293-6767
www.paquette.qc.ca
Jacques Desaulniers

Outremont
1433. ave. Van Horne, Outremont, QC H2V 1K9
Tél: 514-495-6250
www.paquette.qc.ca
Pierre-J. Raîche
Georges-E. Laurin

Pierrefonds
13 665, boul Pierrefonds, Pierrefonds, QC H9H 2Z4
Tél: 514-624-1124
www.paquette.qc.ca
Philippe Clément
Pierre Mondor

Pincourt
919, ch Duhamel, Pincourt, QC J7V 4G8
Robert La Haye

Plessisville
1700, rue St-Calixte, Plessisville, QC G6L 1R3
Tél: 819-362-3284
www.paquette.qc.ca
Jules Bellavance

Pointe-Claire
401, boul. Saint-Jean, Pointe-Claire, QC H9R 3J2
Tél: 514-630-1205
www.paquette.qc.ca
Pierre Mondor
Philippe Clément

Princeville
50, St-Jacques ouest, Princeville, QC G6L 4Y5
Tél: 819-364-5179; *Téléc:* 819-364-5198
www.paquette.qc.ca
Claude Caron

Repentigny
435, boul d'Iberville, Repentigny, QC J6A 2B6
Tél: 450-654-2358
www.paquette.qc.ca
Gilles Thouin

Rimouski
205, av de la Cathédrale, P.O. Box 710, Rimouski, QC G5L 7C7
Tél: 418-724-3181; *Téléc:* 418-724-9795
greffe@ville.rimouski.qc.ca
www.paquette.qc.ca
Jean Blouin

Roberval
851, boul Saint-Joseph, Roberval, QC G8H 2L6
Tél: 418-275-0202; *Téléc:* 418-275-5031
www.paquette.qc.ca
Jacquelin Légaré

Rosemère
100, rue Charbonneau, Rosemère, QC J7A 3W1
Tél: 450-621-3500; *Téléc:* 450-472-3607
www.paquette.qc.ca
Robert Diamond

Roxboro
13 Centre Commercial, Roxboro, QC H8Y 2N9
Tél: 514-684-0555
www.paquette.qc.ca
Ronald J. Montcalm
Philippe Clément

Ste-Adèle
1381, boul Sainte-Adele, Sainte-Adèle, QC J8B 1A3
Tél: 450-229-2921; *Téléc:* 450-229-4179
www.paquette.qc.ca
Jacques Laverdure

Ste-Agathe-des-Monts
50, rue St-Joseph, Sainte-Agathe-des-Monts, QC J8C 1M9
Tél: 819-326-4595; *Téléc:* 819-326-6331
www.paquette.qc.ca
J.H. Denis Gagnon

Ste-Anne-de-Bellevue
109, Ste-Anne, P.O. Box 40, Sainte-Anne-de-Bellevue, QC H9X 1M2
Tél: 514-457-5500
www.paquette.qc.ca
Pascal Pillarella
Jacques Ghanimé

St-Bruno-de-Montarville
1585, boul Montarville, St-Bruno-de-Montarville, QC J3V 3T8
Tél: 450-441-8303
www.paquette.qc.ca
Guy Houle
Marc Gravel

St-Césaire
1111, St-Paul, Saint-Césaire, QC J0L 1T0
Tél: 450-469-3108; *Téléc:* 450-469-5275
www.paquette.qc.ca
Michel Brun

St-Constant
147, rue St-Pierre, P.O. Box 130, Saint-Constant, QC J5A 2G2
Tél: 450-638-2010; *Téléc:* 450-632-0788
www.paquette.qc.ca
Jacques Laurier

St-Eustache
168, Dorion, Saint-Eustache, QC J7R 2G2
Tél: 450-472-4440
Guy Saulnier

St-Félicien
1058, boul. Sacré-Coeur, P.O. Box 7000, Saint-Félicien, QC G8K 2R5
Tél: 418-679-0251; *Téléc:* 418-679-1449
www.paquette.qc.ca
Frédérique Lalancette

Sainte-Foy
1130, rte de l'Église, Sainte-Foy, QC G1V 4X6
Tél: 418-641-6179; *Téléc:* 418-641-6539
www.ville.quebec.qc.ca

St-Georges
11 700, boul. LaCroix, St-Georges, QC G5Y 1L3
Tél: 418-228-5555; *Téléc:* 418-226-2282
www.paquette.qc.ca
Gabriel Garneau

St-Hubert
4800, Leckie, Saint-Hubert, QC J3Z 1H4
Tél: 450-445-7862
www.paquette.qc.ca
Jean Herbert
Claude Céré

Saint-Hyacinthe
700, de l'Hôtel-de-Ville, Saint-Hyacinthe, QC J2S 5B2
Tél: 450-778-8319; *Téléc:* 450-778-8628
cour-municipale@ville.st-hyacinthe.qc.ca
www.paquette.qc.ca
Gilles Charpentier

St-Jean-Chrysostome
959, rue de l'Hotel de Ville, St-Jean-Chrysostome-de-Lév, QC G6Z 2N8
Tél: 418-839-9417
www.paquette.qc.ca
Claude Fortin
Jean-Pierre Gignac

Saint-Jean-sur-Richelieu
188, Jacques-Cartier N., P.O. Box 1025, Saint-Jean-sur-Richelieu, QC J3B 7B2
Tél: 450-357-2087; *Téléc:* 450-357-2750
cour.municipale@ville.saint-jean-sur-richelieu.qc.ca
www.paquette.qc.ca
Pierre-Armand Tremblay

St-Jérôme MRC
280, Labelle, Saint-Jérome, QC J7Z 5L1
Tél: 450-436-1511; *Téléc:* 450-436-4506
Jacques Laverdure

St-Lambert
55, Argyle, Saint-Lambert, QC J4P 2H3
Tél: 450-923-6555
www.paquette.qc.ca
Marc Gravel
Guy Houle

Saint-Laurent
1405, de l'Église, Saint-Laurent, QC H4L 2H4
Tél: 514-855-6060
www.paquette.qc.ca
Pierre G. Bouchard
Lison Asseraf

St-Léonard-de-Port-Maurice
8400, boul Lacordaire, St-Léonard, QC H1R 3B1
Tél: 514-328-8447
www.paquette.qc.ca
Robert LaHaye
Richard Chassé

St-Luc
347, boul St-Luc, Saint-Luc, QC J2W 2A2
Tél: 450-359-2444
www.paquette.qc.ca
Denis Boudrias
Pascal Pillarella

Acton Vale
1025, rue Boulay, P.O. Box 640, Acton Vale, QC J0H 1A0
Tél: 450-546-2704
www.paquette.qc.ca
Louis-B. Grignon

Alma
140, rue St-Joseph S., Alma, QC G8B 3R1
Tél: 418-669-5020; *Téléc:* 418-669-5019
www.paquette.qc.ca
Jean-M. Morency

Asbestos
#201, 185, rue du Roi, Asbestos, QC J1T 1S4
Tél: 819-879-6971; *Téléc:* 819-879-4102
www.paquette.qc.ca
Pierre G. Geoffroy

Barkmère
RR#1, P.O. Box 11, Argenteuil, QC J0T 1A0

Coaticook
14, rue Adams, #14, Coaticook, QC J1A 1K3
Tél: 819-849-2721; *Téléc:* 819-849-4883
www.paquette.qc.ca
Pierre A. Cloutier

Cowansville
220, Place Municipale, Cowansville, QC J2K 1T4
Tél: 450-263-5434; *Téléc:* 450-263-4332
www.paquette.qc.ca
Pierre Raiche

Delson
50, Ste-Thérèse, Delson, QC J0L 1G0
Jacques Laurier

Deux-Montagnes
#101, 400, boul Deux-Montagnes, Deux-Montagnes, QC J7R 5C2
Tél: 450-473-8688; *Téléc:* 450-473-0094
www.paquette.qc.ca
Jacques Lamontagne

Dolbeau-Mistassini
1100, boul Walberg, Dolbeau-Mistassini, QC J7R 5C2
Tél: 450-473-8688
www.paquette.qc.ca
Jacquelin Légaré

Donnacona
138, av Pleau, P.O. Box 609, Donnacona, QC G01 1T0
Tél: 418-285-3163; *Téléc:* 418-285-0020
www.paquette.qc.ca
Claude Fournier

Dorion
190, St-Charles, P.O. Box 70, Dorion, QC J7V 5V8
Manon Bourbonnais

Dorval
530, boul Bouchard, Dorval, QC H9S 1B2
Tél: 514-633-4146
www.paquette.qc.ca
Georges É. Laurin
Jean-Pierre Dépelteau

Drummondville
415, rue Lindsay, P.O. Box 398, Drummondville, QC J2B 6W3
Tél: 819-478-6556; *Téléc:* 819-478-0920
courmunicipale@ville.drummondville.qc.ca
www.paquette.qc.ca
Michel Houle

Haut-St-François MRC
146, Angus Nord, East Angus, QC J0B 1R0
Tél: 819-832-2868; *Téléc:* 819-832-2868
Pierre-A. Cloutier

Farnham
477, de l'Hôtel-de-Ville, Farnham, QC J2N 2H3
Tél: 450-293-3178; *Téléc:* 450-260-1376
www.paquette.qc.ca
Claude Hamann

Gatineau
La Mairie- 280, boul. Maloney E., Gatineau, QC J8P 1C6
Tél: 819-243-2345; *Téléc:* 819-595-4289
www.paquette.qc.ca
François Gravel
Yves Daoust

Granby
125, Simonds S., Granby, QC J2J 1P7
Tél: 450-776-8340; *Téléc:* 450-776-8342
www.paquette.qc.ca
Pierre G. Geoffroy

Grand'Mère
333, av 5e, P.O. Box 350, Grand-Mère, QC G9T 5L1
Tél: 819-538-1614
www.paquette.qc.ca
Jean-Marc Champagne
Jocelyn Crête

Greenfield Park
156, boul Churchill, Greenfield Park, QC J4V 2M3
Tél: 450-446-8108
www.paquette.qc.ca
Jean-Guy Clément
Denis Boudrias

Hampstead
5569, ch. De la Reine-Marie, Hampstead, QC H3X 1W5
Tél: 514-369-8200
www.paquette.qc.ca
Lison Asseraf
Pierre Mondor

Hudson
rue Principale, Hudson, QC J0P 1H0
Robert La Haye

Iberville
855, 1ère, Iberville, QC J2X 3C7
Tél: 450-357-2744
www.paquette.qc.ca
Pierre-Armand Tremblay
Denis Boudrias

Ile-Perrot
110, boul Perrot, Ile-Perrot, QC J7V 3G1
Jacques Laverdure

Joliette
245, Papineau, Joliette, QC J6E 2K8
Tél: 450-753-8123
www.paquette.qc.ca
Other information: Email: cour.municipale@ville.joliette.qc.ca
Louis Laporte

Jonquière
2201, rue de Montfort, P.O. Box 278, Jonquière, QC G7X 4P6
Tél: 418-546-2238
www.paquette.qc.ca
Jean-Jacques Turcotte
Alain Côté

La-Baie
422, rue Victoria, La Baie, QC G7B 3M4
Tél: 418-697-5000
www.paquette.qc.ca
Alain Côté
Jean-Jacques Turcotte

Lachine
1800, boul St-Joseph, Lachine, QC H8S 2N4
Tél: 514-634-3471
www.paquette.qc.ca
Sophie Beauchemin
Manon Bourbonnais

Lachute
380, rue Principale, Lachute, QC J8H 1Y2
Tél: 450-562-3781; *Téléc:* 450-562-1431
www.paquette.qc.ca
Guy Saulnier

Lac Mégantic
#201, 5527, rue Frontenac, Lac-Mégantic, QC G6B 1H6
Tél: 819-583-2815; *Téléc:* 819-583-2841
cour.municipale@ville.lac-megantic.qc.ca
www.ville.lac-megantic.qc.ca; www.paquette.qc.ca
Gabriel Garneau

La Pocatière
412, 9e rue, P.O. Box 668, La Pocatière, QC G0R 1Z0
Tél: 418-856-3394; *Téléc:* 418-856-5465
www.paquette.qc.ca
Jacques Ouellet

La Prairie
170, boul. Taschereau, #400, La Prairie, QC J5R 5H6
Tél: 450-444-0540
www.paquette.qc.ca
Claude Céré

Lasalle
55, av Dupras, Lasalle, QC H8R 4A8
Tél: 514-367-6270
www.paquette.qc.ca
Denis Laberge

L'Assomption
399, rue Dorval, L'Assomption, QC J5W 1A1
Tél: 450-589-5671; *Téléc:* 450-589-4512
courmunicipale@ville.lassomption.qc.ca
www.ville.lassomption.qc.ca; www.paquette.qc.ca
Gilles Thouin

La Tuque
558, rue Commerciale, La Tuque, QC G9X 3A9
Tél: 819-523-2052; *Téléc:* 819-523-4536
www.paquette.qc.ca
Claude Trudel

Senneville
35, ch. Senneville, Senneville, QC H9X 1B8
Tél: 514-457-6020
www.paquette.qc.ca
Pierre Mondor
Philippe Clément

Sept-Iles
546, av Dequen, Sept-Iles, QC G4R 2R4
Tél: 418-964-3249; *Téléc:* 418-964-3259
www.paquette.qc.ca
Guy Pettigrew

Shawinigan MRC
550, de l'Hôtel de Ville, P.O. Box 400, Shawinigan, QC G9N 6V3
Tél: 819-536-7216; *Téléc:* 819-536-2797
Claude Trudel

Shawinigan
1550, rue 118e, P.O. Box 400, Shawinigan, QC G9P 3V3
Tél: 819-536-7216
www.paquette.qc.ca
Claude Trudel
Jocelyn Crête

Sherbrooke
191, rue Palais, P.O. Box 1614, Sherbrooke, QC J1H 5M4
Tél: 819-821-5600; *Téléc:* 819-821-5599
www.paquette.qc.ca
Roland Lamoureux

Sillery
1445, av Maguire, Sillery, QC G1T 2W9
Tél: 418-684-2134
www.paquette.qc.ca
René Paquet
Jean-Pierre Gignac

Sorel-Tracy
3025, boul de Tracy, Sorel-Tracy, QC J3R 1C2
Tél: 450-742-7775; *Téléc:* 450-742-2420
www.agcmq.qc.ca
Jacques Guertin

Terrebonne
Édifice Louis Lepage, 754, rue Saint-Pierre, Terrebonne, QC J6W 1E4
Tél: 450-471-4192
www.paquette.qc.ca
Michel Paquin

Thetford-Mines
144, rue Notre-Dame ouest, P.O. Box 489, Thetford Mines, QC G6G 5T3
Tél: 418-335-2981; *Téléc:* 418-335-7089
www.paquette.qc.ca
Gilles Ouellet

Trois-Rivières
1401, Royale, 2 étage, P.O. Box 969, Trois-Rivières, QC G9A 5K2
Tél: 819-372-4628; *Téléc:* 819-379-7551
www.paquette.qc.ca
Jocelyn Crête

Trois-Rivières-Ouest
500, Côte du Richelieu, Trois-Rivières, QC G9A 2Z1
Tél: 819-375-7731
www.paquette.qc.ca
Jocelyn Crête
Claude Trudel

Val-Bélair
1105, av de l'Église N., Val-Bélair, QC G3K 1X5
Tél: 418-842-7184
www.paquette.qc.ca
Jean-Pierre Gignac
Claude Fortin

Val-d'Or
855, 2e Ave., P.O. Box 400, Val-d'Or, QC J9P 4P4
Tél: 819-824-9613; *Téléc:* 819-825-6650
courmunicipale@ville.valdor.
www.paquette.qc.ca
Jacques Barbès

Verdun
#104, 4555, av Verdun, Verdun, QC H4G 1M4
Tél: 514-765-7060
www.paquette.qc.ca
Jacques Ghanimé
Pascal Pillarella

Victoriaville
1, Notre-Dame O., P.O. Box 370, Victoriaville, QC G6P 6T2
Tél: 819-758-4338; *Téléc:* 819-758-9292
www.paquette.qc.ca
Michel Houle

Waterloo
417, rue de la Cour, #210, P.O. Box 430, Waterloo, QC J0E 2N0
Tél: 450-539-2422; *Téléc:* 450-539-3257
www.paquette.qc.ca
Michel Brun

Westmount
21, rue Stanton, Westmount, QC H3Y 3B1
Tél: 514-989-5260
www.paquette.qc.ca
Keith A. Ham
Ronald Montcalm

Matawinie MRC
3184, 1e av, P.O. Box 1239, Rawdon, QC J0K 1S0
Tél: 450-834-5441
cour@mrcmatawinie.qc.ca
www.paquette.qc.ca
Michel Lalande

Montcalm
1530, rue Albert, P.O. Box 308, Sainte-Julienne, QC J0K 2T0
Tél: 450-831-2182
www.paquette.qc.ca
Marguerite M. Brochu

Baie-Comeau
1000, rue de Mingan, Baie-Comeau, QC G5C 3C3
Tel: 418-589-1518; *Fax:* 418-589-1556
www.paquette.qc.ca
Micheline Fournier

D'Autray MRC
118, Notre-Dame, Le Gardeur, QC J5Z 3C3
Téléc: 450-585-7035
Marguerite M. Brochu

Haut-Saint Laurent MRC
23, Laurier, 6e étage, Hull, QC J8X 4C8
Tél: 819-595-7272
www.paquette.qc.ca
Vacant

Val-St-François MRC
#101, 3, Greenlay S., Sainte-Grégoire-de-Greenlay, QC J1S 2J1
Tel: 819-845-2016; *Fax:* 819-845-3209
www.paquette.qc.ca
Pierre G. Geoffroy

Vaudreuil-Soulanges MRC
190, Saint-Charles, Vaudreuil-Dorion, QC J7V 2L3
Tel: 450-455-9480; *Fax:* 450-373-7967
www.paquette.qc.ca
Manon Bourbonnais

Colline-de-L'Outaouais
216, ch Haute-Chelsea, Chelsea, QC J9B 1J4
Tel: 819-827-0516; *Fax:* 819-827-5712
lst-pierre@mrcdescollines.co
www.paquette.qc.ca
Slobodan Delev

Lotbinière MRC
#4, 372, rue St-Joseph, P.O. Box 40, Laurier-Station, QC G0S 1N0
Tél: 418-728-2787; *Téléc:* 418-728-2501
www.paquette.qc.ca
Paulin Cloutier

Côte-de-Beaupré MRC
3, rue de la Seigneurie, Château-Richer, QC G0A 1N0
Tél: 418-824-3444; *Téléc:* 418-824-3917
M. Jacques Ouellet

Montréal
#101, 775, rue Gosford, Montréal, QC H2Y 3B9
Tél: 514-872-2534; *Téléc:* 514-872-8271
cour-municipale@ville.montreal.qc.ca
www.ville.montreal.qc.ca; www.paquette.qc.ca
Morton S. Minc(Juge-président)
Nathalie Haccoun
Richard Starck

Québec
285, rue de la Maréchausée, Québec, QC G1K 8W5
Tél: 418-691-6340; *Téléc:* 418-641-6512
greffecourmunicipale@ville.quebec.qc.ca
www.ville.quebec.qc.ca
Paulin Cloutier(Juge-président)

Laval
55, boul des Laurentides, Laval, QC H7G 2T1
Tél: 450-662-4466; *Téléc:* 450-662-8501
www.paquette.qc.ca
Bernard Caron
Jean H. Charbonneau
Yves Fournier

Saskatchewan

Saskatchewan: Court of Appeal
Court House, 2425 Victoria Ave., Regina, SK S4P 3V7
Tel: 306-787-5382; *Fax:* 306-787-5817
www.sasklawcourts.ca
The Court of Appeal has appellate jurisdiction with respect to any judgement, order or decree made by the Court of Queen's Bench & any matter granted to it by statute.
Chief Justice of Saskatchewan: The Hon. John Klebuc
Justices of Appeal (The Hon. Mr./Madam Justice):
S.J. Cameron
W.J. Vancise
M.A. Gerwing
R.G. Richards
N.W. Sherstobitoff
G.A. Smith
J.G. Lane
G.R. Jackson
Administration:
Registrar: Maurice Herauf

Saskatchewan Court of Queen's Bench
2425 Victoria Ave., Regina, SK S4P 3V7
Tel: 306-787-5377; *Fax:* 306-787-7217
www.sasklawcourts.ca/default.asp?pg=queens_ben
The Court of Queen's Bench is a court of original jurisdiction having jurisdiction in civil & criminal matters arising in Saskatchewan, except those matters expressly excluded by statute.
Chief Justice: The Hon. R.D. Laing
Justices (The Hon. Mr./Madam Justice):
D.P. Ball
R.L. Barclay(Supernumerary)
C.L. Dawson
W.F. Gerein(Supernumerary)
E.J. Gunn
D.C. Hunter
G.M. Kraus
L.A. Kyle
F.J. Kovach
E.C. Malone(Supernumerary)
D.E.W. McIntyre
I.D. McLellan(Supernumerary)
J.E. McMurtry
N.S. Sandomirsky
E.A. Scheibel(Supernumerary)
D.L. Wilson
C.R. Wimmer(Supernumerary)
T.C. Zarzeczny
Administration:
Registrar, the Court of Queen's Bench & Provincial Court: Sharon Pratchler
Local Registrar: Gordon Dauncey
Sheriff: J. Rhinelander

Courts:

Battleford
Court House, 291 - 23 St. West, P.O. Box 340, Battleford, SK S0M 0E0
Tel: 306-446-7670; *Fax:* 306-446-7737
Sheriff, Local Registrar: Linda Popp

Estevan
Court House, 1016 - 4 St., Estevan, SK S4A 0W5
Tel: 306-637-4530; *Fax:* 306-637-4536
G.A. Chicoine
Deputy Sheriff & Local Registrar: Peggy Boxrud
Sheriff & Local Registrar: Patricia Buttner

Humboldt
Court House, 805 - 8 Ave., P.O. Box 490, Humboldt, SK S0K 2A0
Tel: 306-682-6730; *Fax:* 306-682-3536
Sheriff & Local Registrar: Eleanor Neigel
Deputy Sheriff & Deputy Local Registrar: Elaine Lange

Melfort
Court House, 409 Main St., P.O. Box 850, Melfort, SK S0E 1A0
Tel: 306-752-6265; *Fax:* 306-752-6264
Deputy Sheriff & Deputy Local Registrar: D. Willenborg

Moose Jaw
Court House, 64 Ominica St. West, Moose Jaw, SK S6H 1W9
Tel: 306-694-3602; *Fax:* 306-694-3056
L.B. MacDonald

Prince Albert
Court House, Prince Albert, SK S6V 4W7
Tel: 306-953-3200; *Fax:* 306-953-3210
R.D. Maher
A.R. Rothery
Sheriff & Local Registrar: Maria Lynn Freeland

Saskatoon
520 Spadina Cres. East, Saskatoon, SK S7K 2H6
Tel: 306-933-5137; *Fax:* 306-975-4818
G.N. Allbright
G.W. Baynton(Supernumerary)
G.M. Currie
M.L. Dovell
P. Foley
N.G. Gabrielson
I. Goldenberg(Supernumerary)
P. Hrabinsky(Supernumerary)
J. Klebuc
J.D. Koch
R.C. Mills
G.A. Smith
D.H. Wright(Supernumerary)
Local Registrar: D. Berezowsky
Sheriff: G. Laing

Swift Current
Court House, 121 Lorne St. West, Swift Current, SK S9H 0J4
Tel: 306-778-8400; *Fax:* 306-778-8581
D.B. Konkin
Sheriff & Local Registrar: R. Peterson

Weyburn
Court House, 301 Prairie Ave., Weyburn, SK S4H 0L4
Tel: 306-848-2359; *Fax:* 306-848-2540
Sheriff & Local Registrar: Patricia Buttner

Wynyard
Court House, 410 Ave. C East, P.O. Box 369, Wynyard, SK S0A 4T0
Tel: 306-554-2561; *Fax:* 306-554-3405
Deputy Sheriff/Local Registrar & Court Clerk: Stan Urbanoski

Yorkton
Court House, 29 Darlington St. East, Yorkton, SK S3N 0C2
Tel: 306-786-1515; *Fax:* 306-786-1521
J.L.G. Pritchard
Sheriff, Court Clerk & Local Registrar: S. Urbanoski

Saskatoon Family Law Division
224 - 4 Ave. South, 9th Fl., Saskatoon, SK S7K 5M5
Tel: 306-933-5174; *Fax:* 306-933-5703
J.A. Ryan-Froslie
R.S. Smith
Y.G.K. Wilkinson
M.R. Wright
Local Registrar: Dennis Berezowsky
Deputy Local Registrar: Kathy Brower

Saskatchewan Provincial Court
1815 Smith St., Regina, SK S4P 3V7
Tel: 306-787-5500; *Fax:* 306-787-3933
www.sasklawcourts.ca/default.asp?pg=provincial
The Provincial Court has jurisdiction in both civil (including small claims & family) & select criminal (including young offender) matters.
Chief Judge: The Hon. G.T.G. Seniuk

Courts:

Estevan
Court House, 1016 - 4th St., Estevan, SK S4A 0W5
Tel: 306-637-4528; *Fax:* 306-637-4536
J. Benison

La Ronge
1320 La Ronge Ave., P.O. Box 5000, La Ronge, SK S0J 1L0
Tel: 306-425-4505; *Fax:* 306-425-4269
Sid Robinson
W.K. Tucker

Lloydminster
4815 - 50 St., Lloydminster, SK S9V 0M8
Tel: 306-825-6420; *Fax:* 306-825-6497
K.J. Young

Meadow Lake
#3, 212 - 1 St. East, Meadow Lake, SK S9X 1T7
Tel: 306-236-7575; *Fax:* 306-236-7598
J. Nightingale
E. Kalenith

Melfort
107 Crawford Ave. East, P.O. Box 6500, Melfort, SK S0E 1A0
Tel: 306-752-6230; *Fax:* 306-752-6126
L. Dyck
B. Morgan

Moose Jaw
#211, 110 Ominica St. West, Moose Jaw, SK S6H 6V2
Tel: 306-694-3612; *Fax:* 306-694-3043
D. Kovatch
D. Orr

North Battleford
3 Railway Ave. East, North Battleford, SK S9A 2P9
Tel: 306-446-7400; *Fax:* 306-446-7432
D. Kaiser
V.H. Meekma
D. O'Hanlon

Prince Albert
188 -11th St. West, P.O. Box 3003, Prince Albert, SK S6V 6G1
Tel: 306-953-2640; *Fax:* 306-953-2819
T.B. Bekolay
Stephen Carter
T.W. Ferris
H.W. Goliath
G.M. Morin
H.R.E. Weisgerber

Regina
1815 Smith St., Regina, SK S4P 3V7
Tel: 306-787-5250; *Fax:* 306-787-7037
K.E. Bellerose
D. Bogdasavich
A. Crugnole-Reid
D.E. Fenwick
L. Halliday
B.D. Henning
D. Morris
L.J. Smith
L.C.A. Snell
C. Toth

Saskatoon
220 - 19 St. East, Saskatoon, SK S7K 2H6
Tel: 306-933-5250; *Fax:* 306-933-7043
R.G. Bell
B.P. Carey
B.L. Huculak
R.D. Jackson
M.D. Irwin
P. Kolenick
D.A. Lavoie
G.T. Seniuk
B. Singer

M.E. Turpel-Lafond
S.P. Whelan
T.W. White

Swift Current
Court House, 121 Lorne St. West, Swift Current, SK S9H 0J4
Tel: 306-778-8390; *Fax:* 306-778-8581

L.A. Matsulla

Wynyard
Court House, 410 Ave. C East, P.O. Box 1449, Wynyard, SK S0A 4T0
Tel: 306-554-2155; *Fax:* 306-554-3405

D. Ebert

Yorkton
Court House, 120 Smith St. East, Yorkton, SK S3N 3V3
Tel: 306-786-1400; *Fax:* 306-786-1422

K.A. Andrychuck
R. Green
P.R. Koskie

Yukon Territory

Yukon Territory: Court of Appeal

Court Registry, 2134 Second Ave. (Ground Fl.), Whitehorse, YT Y1A 5H6
Tel: 867-667-3429; *Fax:* 867-393-6212
Toll-Free: 800-661-0408
courtservices@gov.yk.ca
www.yukoncourts.ca/courts/appeal

The Court of Appeal has appellate jurisdiction in all civil & criminal matters from decisions by the Territorial Court & Supreme Court.

Justices of Appeal (The Hon. Mr./Madam Justice):
Beverley A. Browne
Earl Johnson
Robert G. Kilpatrick
T. Braidwood
I.T. Donald
William A. Esson
L.S.G. Finch
J. Hall
H.A. Hollinrake
C. Huddart
J.D. Lambert
R.E. Levine
R.T.A. Low
P.D. Lowry
K. Mackenzie
M. Newbury
W.T. Oppal
J. Prowse
M.A. Rowles
C.A. Ryan
M.E. Saunders
K.J. Smith
M.F. Southin
A.D. Thackray
L.F. Gower
R.S. Veale
John Edward Richard
V.A. Schuler
John Z. Vertes

Administration:
Acting Registrar: Sharon Kerr

Yukon Territory: Supreme Court

Court Services J-3, 2134 Second Ave., P.O. Box 2703, Whitehorse, YT Y1A 2C6
Tel: 867-667-3524; *Fax:* 867-667-3079
Toll-Free: 800-661-0408
courtserivces@gov.yk.ca
www.justice.gov.yk.ca/prog/cs/supr/supremecrt.html

The Supreme Court is a superior court of record having original jurisdiction in all civil & criminal matters arising in the Yukon, unless excluded by statute.

Judges (The Hon. Mr./Madam Justice):
Leigh F. Gower
Ronald S. Veale

Ex-Officio Judges (The Hon. Mr./Madam Justice):
Beverley A. Browne
Earl Johnson
Robert G. Kilpatrick
John Edward Richard
Virginia A. Schuler
John Z. Vertes

Deputy Judges (The Hon. Mr./Madam Justice):
C. Scott Brooker
Paul S. Chrumka
Carole M. Conrad
Mary M. Hetherington
Colleen L. Kenny
Arthur M. Lutz
Peter McIntyre
René P. Foisy
William J. Girgulis
Cecilia I. Johnstone
Edward P. MacCallum
Richard P. Marceau
Ernest A. Marshall
Mary Moreau
Allan H. Wachowich
R.J. Haines
James D. Taylor
Ross Goodwin
Edward D. Bayda
Lucien A. Beaulieu
Stephen Borins
Dennis O'Connor
John D. Watt
Marion Jean Allan
George Peter Fraser
D.J. Martinson
Kathryn E. Neilson
Wallace T. Oppal
Randall S.K. Wong
John C. Bouck
David Vickers
Wallace M. Darichuk
Guy J. Kroft

Administration:
Acting Registrar: Bankruptcy, Sue Christianson
Acting Sheriff: Linda Balcaen

Yukon Territory: Territorial Court

Court Services J-3, 2134 Second Ave., P.O. Box 2703, Whitehorse, YT Y1A 2C6
Tel: 867-667-5441; *Fax:* 867-393-6212
Toll-Free: 800-661-0408
courtservices@gov.yk.ca
www.justice.gov.yk.ca/prog/cs/terr/index.html

The Territorial Court has jurisdiction in family, youth & select criminal matters.

Chief Judge: The Hon. John E. Faulkner
Judges (The Hon. Mr./Madam Justice):
Heino Lilles
K. Ruddy

Administration:
Senior Court Clerk: Sharon Kerr
Territorial Court Clerk: Tara Boland
Territorial Court Clerk: Dawson City, Susan Coulson
Territorial Court Clerk: Lucretia Flemming
Territorial Court Clerk: Watson Lake, Stella Hearty
Territorial Court Clerk: Dorothy Irwin
Territorial Court Clerk: Karin Keeley-Eriksson
Territorial Court Clerk: Sharon Kerr
Territorial Court Clerk: Arlene Ogden

SECTION 10
HOSPITALS & HEALTH CARE FACILITIES

Listings in this section are arranged by province, and then by city. Each provincial section includes the following six categories.

Government Department

Regional Health Authorities

Hospitals

Community Health Centres

Long Term/Retirement Care

Mental Health Facilities

Alberta

Government Departments in Charge

ALBERTA: Alberta Health & Wellness
Telus Plaza North Tower, PO Box 1360 Main, 10025 Jasper Ave., 22nd Fl., Edmonton, AB T5J 2N3
Tel: 780-427-7164; *Fax:* 780-427-1171
TTY: 780-427-9999
health.ahinform.gov.ab.ca
www.health.gov.ab.ca

Hon. Ronald Liepert, Minister of Health

Regional Health Authorities

***Edmonton:* Alberta Health Services (AHS)**
AHS Corporate Office, Manulife Place, #700, 10180 - 101 St., Edmonton, AB T5J 3S4
Tel: 780-342-2000; *Fax:* 780-342-2060
www.albertahealthservices.ca

Year Founded: 2009
Note: Specialty: Provincial governance board, overseeing hospitals, other health facilities, & ground ambulance service in Alberta. Number of Employees: 90,000 (7,200 physicians). Note: Alberta Health Services brings together the following former Alberta health entities: Chinook Health, Palliser Health Region, Calgary Health Region, David Thompson Health Region, East Central Health, Capital Health, Aspen Regional Health, Peace Country Health, Northern Lights Health Region, Alberta Mental Health Board, Alberta Alcohol & Drug Abuse Commission, & the Alberta Cancer Board.
J.M. Turc, President; CEO

Hospitals

Hospitals - General

***Athabasca:* Athabasca Healthcare Centre**
Affiliated with: Alberta Health Services
3100 - 48 Ave., Athabasca, AB T9S 1M9
Tel: 780-675-6000; *Fax:* 780-675-7050
www9.albertahealthservices.ca

Number of Beds: 26 acute care beds; 1 palliative care bed; 23 continuing care beds
Note: Hospital Specialties: Emergency services; Diagnostic imaging; Laboratory services; Acute care; Obstetrics; Pediatrics; Continuing care; Rehabilitation; Recreation services; Palliative care
Mary Proskie, Manager, Healthcare Centre
Dr. Brian Oldale, Chief, Medical Staff

***Banff:* Banff Mineral Springs Hospital**
Covenant Health
PO Box 1050, 305 Lynx St., Banff, AB T1L 1H7
Tel: 403-762-2222; *Fax:* 403-762-4193
info@banffmineralspringshospital.ca
www.banffmineralspringshospital.ca

Year Founded: 1930
Note: Hospital Specialties: Emergency services; Surgery; Acute care; Maternal & child care; Physiotherapy; Occupational therapy; Recreation therapy; Music therapy; Mental health services; P.A.R.T.Y. program, to Prevent Alcohol & Risk-Related Trauma in Youth; Continuing care; Outpatient clinics; Palliative care
Cindy Mulherin, Executive Director

***Barrhead:* Barrhead Healthcare Centre**
Affiliated with: Alberta Health Services
4815 - 51 Ave., Barrhead, AB T7N 1M1
Tel: 780-674-2221; *Fax:* 780-674-3541
www.albertahealthservices.ca

Number of Beds: 34 beds
Note: Hospital specialties: Emergency services; Diagnostic imaging; Laboratory Services; Obstetrics; Community cancer centre; Rehabilitation services; Social work; Diet counselling; Education programs; Outpatient clinics; Palliative care
Heather Thompson, Manager, Healthcare Centre
Dr. Elizabeth Thompson, Chief, Medical Staff

***Bassano:* Bassano Health Centre**
Affiliated with: Alberta Health Services
608 - 5 Ave., Bassano, AB T0J 0B0
Tel: 403-641-6100; *Fax:* 403-641-2157
www.albertahealthservices.ca

Year Founded: 1914
Number of Beds: 3 acute care beds; 7 continuting care beds; 1 palliative care bed
Note: Hospital specialties: Emergency services; Diagnostic imaging; Acute care; Physiotherapy; Occupational therapy; Physiotherapy; Mental health services; Nutrition services; Social work; Continuing care; Respite care; Palliative care

***Beaverlodge:* Beaverlodge Municipal Hospital**
Affiliated with: Alberta Health Services
PO Box 480, 422 - 10A St., Beaverlodge, AB T0H 0C0
Tel: 780-354-2136; *Fax:* 780-354-8355
www.albertahealthservices.ca

Number of Beds: 18 acute care beds
Note: Hospital Specialties: Emergency services; Radiology; Medical laboratory; Acute care; Obstetrics; Physiotherapy; Occupational therapy; Palliative care

***Black Diamond:* Oilfields General Hospital**
Affiliated with: Alberta Health Services
717 Government Rd., Black Diamond, AB T0L 0H0
Tel: 403-933-2222
www.albertahealthservices.ca

Note: Specialties: Acute care; Long-term care; Public health; Mental health services; Adult day support program; Physical therapy; Occupational therapy; Tuberculosis testing & immunization; Palliative care
Tom Sawyer, Maintenance

***Black Diamond:* Oilfields General Hospital**
PO Box 1, 717 Government Rd., Black Diamond, AB T0L 0H0
Tel: 403-933-2222; *Fax:* 403-933-2031

Murray Kobe, Administrator

***Blairmore:* Crowsnest Pass Health Centre**
Affiliated with: Alberta Health Services
2001 - 107th St., Blairmore, AB T0K 0E0
Tel: 403-562-5011; *Fax:* 403-562-8992
www.albertahealthservices.ca

Note: Specialties: Emergency services (403-562-2831); Diagnostic imaging services; Laboratory services; Surgery; Obstetrics; Neonatal intensive care nursery; Pediatrics; Critical care services; Acute care; Rehabilitation services, including occupational therapy & therapeutic recreation; Southern Alberta Renal Program (403-564-4661); Continuing care; Palliative care

***Bonnyville:* Bonnyville Healthcare Centre**
Affiliated with: Alberta Health Services
5001 Lakeshore Dr., Bonnyville, AB T9N 2J7
Tel: 780-826-3311; *Fax:* 780-826-6526
www.albertahealthservices.ca

Year Founded: 1986
Number of Beds: 24 acute care beds; 30 continuing care beds; 9 day care beds
Note: Hospital Specialties: Emergency services; Regional laboratory services (780-826-3311 ext. 265); Diagnostic imaging; Pathology; Surgery; Acute care; Community Cancer Centre (780-826-3311, ext. 227); Cardiac stress testing(780-826-3311, ext. 255); Obstetrics; Rehabilitation; Medical accupunture; Occupational therapy (780-826-8266); Respiratory therapy (780-826-3311, ext. 304); Continuing care (780-826-3311, Ext 272); Palliative care (780-826-3311, ext. 286); Number of Employees: 281

***Bow Island:* Bow Island Health Centre**
Affiliated with: Alberta Health Services
938 Centre St., Bow Island, AB T0K 0G0
Tel: 403-545-3200; *Fax:* 403-545-2281
www.albertahealthservices.ca

Number of Beds: 10 acute care beds; 20 continuing care beds
Note: Hospital Specialties: Emergency services; Diagnostic imaging & laboratory services (403-545-3209); Acute care; Maternal child services; Physiotherapy (403-545-3207); Occupational therapy (403-529-8851); Continuing care; Respite Services (403-545-3208)

***Boyle:* Boyle Healthcare Centre**
Affiliated with: Alberta Health Services
PO Box 330, 5004 Lakeview Rd., Boyle, AB T0A 0M0
Tel: 780-689-3731; *Fax:* 780-689-3951
www.albertahealthservices.ca

Year Founded: 1966
Number of Beds: 19 acute care beds; 1 palliative care bed
Note: Hospital specialties: Emergency services; Diagnostic imaging; Laboratory services; Acute care services; Nutrition services (780-675-2231); Community health; Social work; Palliative care
Carol Ulliac, Manager, Healthcare Centre
Dr. Marthinius Doman, Chief, Medical Staff

***Brooks:* Brooks Health Centre**
Affiliated with: Alberta Health Services
440 - 3rd St. East, Brooks, AB T1R 1B3
Tel: 403-501-3232; *Fax:* 403-362-6039

Number of Beds: 40 acute care beds; 75 long term care beds
Note: Hospital Specialties: Emergency services; Ambulatory care; Acute care; Obstetrics; Pediatrics (403-501-3211); Physiotherapy; Occupational therapy; Recreational therapy; Living Healthy Program / Cardiac rehabilitation (403-793-6659); Diabetes education; Community health; Social work (403-501-3266); Continuing care (403-501-3227); Palliative care

***Calgary:* Alberta Children's Hospital**
Affiliated with: Alberta Health Services
Former Name: Alberta Crippled Children's Hospital; Junior Red C
West Campus, University of Calgary, 2888 Shaganappi Trail NW, Calgary, AB T3B 6A8
Tel: 403-955-7211
TTY: 1-866-408-54
943.Link@calgaryhealthregion.ca
www.calgaryhealthregion.ca/ACH

Year Founded: 1922
Note: Hospital Specialties: Pediatrics (birth to age 18); Emergency services (403-955-7070); Sugery; Complex Pain Service (403-955-7430); Diagnostic imaging (403-955-7656); Burn treatment (403-955-7853); Eating disorder program - day treatment (403-943-1500); Therapeutic arts; Child health information (Family & Community Resource Centre)

***Calgary:* Foothills Medical Centre**
Affiliated with: Alberta Health Services
1403 - 29 St. NW, Calgary, AB T2N 2T9
Tel: 403-944-1110
www.albertahealthservices.ca

Note: Hospital Specialties: Emergency services (403-944-1405); Trauma services (403-944-4339); Diagnostic imaging; Acute care; Gynecology (403-944-1301); Newborn care (403-944-1352); Cardiology (403-944-1381); Gastrointestinal services (403-944-4711); Hematology (403-944-1157); Adult neuropsychology service (403-944-1340); Neurology (403-944-1312); Psychiatry (403-944-1321); Renal services (403-944-1137); Movement Disorders Program (403-944-4364); Occupational therapy (403-944-1432); Respiratory services (403-944-1319); Social work (403-944-1560); Addiction services (403-943-1500)

***Calgary:* Peter Lougheed Centre**
Affiliated with: Alberta Health Services
3500 - 26 Ave. NE, Calgary, AB T1Y 6J4
Tel: 403-943-4555; *Fax:* 403-943-4878
Number of Beds: 513 beds

***Calgary:* Rockyview General Hospital**
Affiliated with: Alberta Health Services
7007 - 14 St. SW, Calgary, AB T2V 1P9
Tel: 403-943-3000; *Fax:* 403-943-3434
www.albertahealthservices.ca/facilities.asp?pid=facility&rid=3
Number of Beds: 566 beds
Note: Services include: emergency, acute care, addiction network, CT imaging, cardiac intensive care/coronary care units, colorectal surgery, cystoscopy, diagnostic imaging, electroencephalography, endoscopy, geriatric assessment and rehabilitation, obstetrics/gynecology outpatient.
Dr. Stephen Duckett, President/CEO, AHS
Nancy Guebert, Vice-President
Teresa Davidson, Site Director

***Camrose:* St. Mary's Hospital**
Affiliated with: Alberta Health Services
4607 - 53 St., Camrose, AB T4V 1Y5
Tel: 780-679-6100; *Fax:* 780-679-6196
www.stmaryscamrose.com

Year Founded: 1924
Number of Beds: 76 beds
Note: An acute care facility with services including emergency, cardiology, diabetic education, diagnostic imaging (CT scans, fluoroscopy, radiology, mammography, ultrasound), community cancer clinic, women's health, pediatrics, palliative care, respiratory therapy, occupational therapy, mental health, urology. The facility operates under the governance of Covenant Health, a Catholic provider of healthcare.
Mr. R. Patrick Dumelie, President/CEO, Covenant Health
Ms. Rosa Rudelich, Vice-President/CFO, Covenant Health
Ms. Fran Ross, Vice-President, Communications, Covenant Health

***Canmore:* Canmore General Hospital**
Affiliated with: Alberta Health Services
1100 Hospital Pl., Canmore, AB T1W 1N2
Tel: 403-678-5536; *Fax:* 403-678-9874
www.albertahealthservices.ca

Note: Hospital Specialties: Emergency services; Diagnostic imaging (403-678-7216); Laboratory services; Surgical services; Obstetrics; Newborn care; Acute care; Cardiology; Audiology; Chemotherapy treatments; Wound centre; Occupational therapy; Physical therapy; Recreation therapy; Speech language pathology; Mental health; Aboriginal hospital Liaison; Diabetes prevention; Adult day support program (403-678-7200); Respite care; Long term care; Palliative care

***Castor:* Our Lady of the Rosary Hospital**
Affiliated with: Alberta Health Services
PO Box 329, 5402 - 47 St., Castor, AB T0C 0X0
Tel: 403-882-3434; *Fax:* 403-882-2751
Number of Beds: 5 acute care, 20 continuing care beds, 2 respite
Marilyn Weber, Executive Director
Barry Straub, Maintenance

***Claresholm:* Claresholm General Hospital**
Affiliated with: Alberta Health Services
221 - 43 Ave., Claresholm, AB T0L 0T0
Tel: 403-682-3750
www.albertahealthservices.ca
Note: Hospital Specialties: Emergency services (403-682-3700); Diagnostic imaging (403-682-3725); Cardiology electrocardiogram services; Acute care; Occupational therapy (403-625-8640); Physiotherapy (403-625-8617); Recreation therapy (403-625-8613); Mental health services; Respite care; Palliative care

***Cold Lake:* Cold Lake Healthcare Centre**
Affiliated with: Alberta Health Services
314 - 25 St., Cold Lake, AB T9M 1G6
Tel: 780-639-3322; *Fax:* 780-639-2255
www.albertahealthservices.ca
Number of Beds: 31 continuing care beds; 24 acute care beds; 2 palliative care beds
Note: Hospital Specialties: Emergency services; Diagnostic imaging services; Laboratory services; Surgical services; Acute care; Ambulatory care; Obstetrics; Pediatrics; Eating disorder services (780-998-5225); Rehabilitation services, including physiotherapy, occupational therapy, recreation therapy, & respiratory therapy; Continuing care (780-639-6515); Dementia care; Respite services; Palliative care
James Murray, Manager, Cold Lake Healthcare Centre
Dr. Siegfried Heydenrych, Chief, Medical Staff

***Consort:* Consort Hospital & Care Centre**
Affiliated with: Alberta Health Services
5402 - 52 Ave., Consort, AB T0C 1B0
Tel: 403-577-3555; *Fax:* 403-577-3950
www.albertahealthservices.ca
Note: Hospital Specialties: Emergency services; Diagnostic imaging; Laboratory services; Acute care; Occupational therapy; Physiotherapy; Recreation therapy; Continuing care; Palliative care

***Coronation:* Coronation Hospital & Care Centre**
Affiliated with: Alberta Health Services
5000 Municipal Rd., Coronation, AB T0C 1C0
Tel: 403-577-3803; *Fax:* 403-578-3474
www.albertahealthservices.ca
Note: Hospital Specialties: Emergency services (403-578-3200); Diagnostic imaging (403-578-3804); Laboratory services (403-578-3804, ext. 308); Acute care; Nutrition services (403-309-6199); Diabetes education (403-314-5780); Occupational therapy; Physical therapy; Recreation therapy; Speech language pathology (403-343-4822); Continuing care (403-343-4822); Supportive living; Seniors Mental Health Program; Palliative care (403-578-3680)

***Daysland:* Daysland Health Centre**
Affiliated with: Alberta Health Services
5920 - 51st Ave., Daysland, AB T0B 1A0
Tel: 780-374-3746; *Fax:* 780-374-2111
www.albertahealthservices.ca
Number of Beds: 16 acute care beds; 10 rehabilitation beds
Note: Hospital Specialties: Emergency services; Laboratory services; Surgery; Acute care; Obstetrics; Rehabilitation services, including occupational therapy, physiotherapy, & respiratory therapy; Pediatric speech language services; Social work; Respite care; Palliative care
Mariann Wolbeck, Health Centre Coordinator
mariann.wolbeck@albertahealthservice

***Devon:* Devon General Hospital**
Affiliated with: Alberta Health Services
101 Erie St. South, Devon, AB T9G 1A6
Tel: 780-342-7000
www.albertahealthservices.ca
Number of Beds: 9 acute care beds; 10 continuing care beds; 2 respite beds
Note: Hospital Specialties: Emergency services; Laboratory services; Radiology services (780-342-7075); Acute care; Rehabilitation services; Mental health therapy (780-963-6151); Public health (780-342-7069); Tuberculosis testing & immunization (780-342-7069); Diabetes education; Nutrition information; Social work (780-987-8200); Adult day program; Home care (780-342-7020); Continuing care

***Devon:* Devon Health Unit**
Affiliated with: Alberta Health Services
101 Erie St. South, Devon, AB T9G 1A6
Tel: 780-987-8224; *Fax:* 780-987-8232
www.capitalhealth.ca

***Didsbury:* Didsbury District Health Services**
Affiliated with: Alberta Health Services
1210 - 20th Ave., Didsbury, AB T0M 0W0
Tel: 403-335-9393; *Fax:* 403-335-4816
www.albertahealthservices.ca
Note: Hospital Specialties: Emergency services; Laboratory services (403-335-7224;); Diagnostic imaging; Acute care; Rehabilitation, including occupational therapy & physiotherapy; Speech language pathology (403-335-7623); Clinical nutrition services (403-335-9437); Public health services; Respite care; Long term care; Palliative care

***Drayton Valley:* Drayton Valley Hospital & Care Centre**
Affiliated with: Alberta Health Services
4550 Madsen Ave., Drayton Valley, AB T7A 1N8
Tel: 780-542-5321; *Fax:* 780-621-4966
www.albertahealthservices.ca
Number of Beds: 34 acute care beds; 50 long term care beds
Note: Hospital Specialties: Emergency services; Diagnostic imaging (780-621-4945); Laboratory services (780-542-5321); Acute care; Obstetrics (780-542-5321); Northern Alberta Renal Program (780-542-2010); Occupational therapy, physiotherapy, & recreation therapy (780-542-4415); Asthma education (780-621-4866); Diabetes education(403-314-5780); Nutrition services (403-309-6199); Long-term care; Palliative care (780-621-4917)

***Drumheller:* Drumheller Health Centre**
Affiliated with: Alberta Health Services
351 - 9 St. NW, Drumheller, AB T0J 0Y1
Tel: 403-823-6500; *Fax:* 403-823-5076
www.albertahealthservices.ca
Note: Hospital services: Emergency services; Diagnostic imaging; Acute care; Obstetrics; Cardiac Rehabilitation Program (403-820-7201); Chemotherapy treatments (403-820-7985); Occupational therapy, physical therapy, & recreation therapy; Mental health services (403-820-7863); Nutrition Services (403-309-6199); Public health (403-820-6004); Diabetes education (403-314-5780); Asthma education (403-820-7264); Continuing care (403-820-7245); Respite care (403-820-6020); Home care (403-820-6004); Palliative care (403-820-7241)

***Edmonton:* Grey Nuns Community Hospital**
Affiliated with: Alberta Health Services
Former Name: Grey Nuns Community Hospital & Health Centre
1100 Youville Dr. West, Edmonton, AB T6L 5X8
Tel: 780-735-7000
www.capitalhealth.ca
Number of Beds: 267 beds

***Edmonton:* Misericordia Community Hospital**
Affiliated with: Alberta Health Services
Former Name: Misericordia Community Hospital & Health Centre
16940 - 87 Ave., Edmonton, AB T5R 4H5
Tel: 780-735-2611; *Fax:* 780-930-5774
www.capitalhealth.ca
Number of Beds: 259 beds

***Edmonton:* Royal Alexandra Hospital**
Affiliated with: Alberta Health Services
10240 Kingsway Ave., Edmonton, AB T5H 3V9
Tel: 780-735-4111
www.albertahealthservices.ca/facilities.asp?pid=facility&rid=6598
Number of Beds: 678 beds
Note: Emergency, acute care of the elderly, adolescent pregnancy clinic, otolaryngology, angiography, child & adolescent psychiatry, colonoscopy, diabetic foot clinic, diagnostic imaging, electroencephalography, gastroscopy, radiology, intensive care unit, liver clinic, mental health clinic, ophthalmology, prenatal nutrition counselling, plastics surgery, recto/colo Clinic, rehabilitation services, rheumatology, sexual assault response team, ultrasound, urology. Located in this hospital is the Lois Hole Hospital for Women.
Dr. Stephen Duckett, President/CEO, AHS
Joanna Pawlyshyn, Vice-President
Lois Stefaniuk, Site Director

***Edmonton:* University of Alberta Hospital & Stollery Children's Hospital**
Affiliated with: Alberta Health Services
8440 - 112 St. NW, Edmonton, AB T6G 2B7
Tel: 780-735-7000
www.albertahealthservices.ca/facilities.asp?pid=facility&rid=6600
Number of Beds: 687 beds
Note: A clinical, research and teaching facility, its specialized services include cardiac sciences, neurosciences, surgery, medicine, renal, critical and trauma care, burn unit. Other areas of focus include amyotrophic lateral sclerosis, anaesthesiology, angiography, audiology, bronchoscopy, cardiology, cardiovascular intensive care unit, CT scans, continence, dental clinic, E. Garner King Critical Care Unit, ECG/Holter monitoring, ENT, ears nose & throat surgery, eating disorders, echocardiography, endoscopy, fluoroscopy, gastroenterology and hepatology, general surgery, geriatric assessment, hemodialysis, hepatitis, laboratory, MRI, medical microbiology, multiple sclerosis, neurosurgery, nuclear medicine, nutrition counselling, occupational therapy, orthopaedic surgery, palliative care, pediatric chronic pain, physical therapy, plastic surgery, psychiatry, pulmonary medicine, radiology, respiratory therapy, rheumatology, sexual assault response, social work, speech language pathology, spine assessment, spiritual care, stress, stroke, surgery, pediatric sleep disturbance, teleStroke, transplantation, tuberculosis, ultrasound, urology. Also located within the facility are the Mazankowski Alberta Heart Institute and the Stollery Children's Hospital, specializing in pediatric cardiac surgery and organ transplantation.
Dr. Stephen Duckett, President/CEO, AHS
Dr. David Megren, CMO/Executive Vice-President, AHS
Ms. Glenda Coleman-Miller, Site Vice-President
Ms. Amelda Foster, Site Director

***Edson:* Edson Healthcare Centre**
Affiliated with: Alberta Health Services
4716 - 5th Ave., Edson, AB T7E 1S8
Tel: 780-723-3331; *Fax:* 780-723-7787
www.albertahealthservices.ca
Note: Hospital Specialties: Emergency services; Diagnostic imaging; Laboratory services (780-712-6840); Surgical services & recovery; Acute care; Ambulatory care; Obstetrics; Pediatrics; Rehabilitation services; Social work (780-712-6862, ext. 324); Respite care; Continuing care (780-723-2229); Palliative care

***Elk Point:* Elk Point Healthcare Centre**
Affiliated with: Alberta Health Services
5310 - 50th Ave., Elk Point, AB T0A 1A0
Tel: 780-724-3847; *Fax:* 780-724-3085
www.albertahealthservices.ca
Number of Beds: 30 continuing care beds; 11 acute care beds; 1 palliative care bed
Note: Hospital Specialties: Diagnostic imaging; Laboratory services; Acute care; Ambulatory care; Obstetrics; Rehabilitation services, including physical therapy & recreation therapy; Community health services; Social work (780-645-3396); Continuing care; Respite care; Palliative care
Paulette Levasseur, Manager, Healthcare Centre
Dr. D. Ramful, Medical Director

***Fairview:* Fairview Health Centre**
Affiliated with: Alberta Health Services
PO Box 2201, 10628 - 110 St., Fairview, AB T0H 1L0
Tel: 780-835-4951; *Fax:* 780-835-5789
Cal Kindon, Director, Health Services

***Fairview:* Fairview Health Complex**
Affiliated with: Alberta Health Services
10628 - 110 St., Fairview, AB T0H 1L0
Tel: 780-835-6100
www.albertahealthservices.ca
Number of Beds: 25 beds
Note: Hospital Specialties: Emergency services; Intensive care unit; Acute care; Obstetrics; Pediatrics; Rehabilitation services, including occupational therapy, physiotherapy, & therapeutic recreation; Mental health services (780-835-6149); Cardiac education (780-835-6117); Prenatal education & counselling (780-835-4951); Healthy Families Program (780-835-6139); Diabetes Prevention & Wellness Program (780-835-6117); Environmental Public Health Program (780-835-4951); Social work (780-835-6112); Nutrition services; Continuing care (780-835-6180); Palliative care (780-835-4951)

***Fairview:* Fairview Mental Health Clinic**
Affiliated with: Alberta Health Services
Bag 2201, Fairview, AB T0H 1L0
Tel: 780-835-6149; *Fax:* 780-835-3879

***Fort McMurray:* Northern Lights Regional Health Centre**
Affiliated with: Alberta Health Services
7 Hospital St., Fort McMurray, AB T9H 1P2
Tel: 780-791-6161; *Fax:* 780-791-6029
Number of Beds: 94 beds
Patricia L. Eelton, CEO

***Fort Saskatchewan:* Fort Saskatchewan Health Centre**
Affiliated with: Alberta Health Services
9430 - 95 St., Fort Saskatchewan, AB T8L 1R8
Tel: 780-998-2256
www.albertahealthservices.ca
Number of Beds: 32 beds
Note: Specialties: Emergency services; Surgical services; Acute care; Obstetrics; Respiratory therapy; COPD Rehabilitation Program (780 992-5801); Neurological physical therapy services (780-992-5824); Occupational therapy; Nutritional counselling (780-992-5812); Social work

***Fort Vermilion:* St. Theresa General Hospital**
Affiliated with: Alberta Health Services
4506 - 46 Ave., Fort Vermilion, AB T0H 1N0
Tel: 780-927-3761; *Fax:* 780-927-4271
www.albertahealthservices.ca/facilities.asp?pid=facility&rid=1000199
Number of Beds: 10 long-term care, 21 acute care beds
Note: Services include emergency, blood collection, clinical nutrition, continuing care, diagnostic imaging, interpretive services, lab, maternity, mental health, occupational therapy, palliative care, pediatrics, physical therapy, school dental services, spiritual care.
Dr. Stephen Duckett, President/CEO, AHS
Dr. David Megren, Executive Vice-President/CMO, AHS
Kerry Williamson, Senior Media Relations Advisor, AHS 780-407-2602

***Fox Creek:* Fox Creek Health Care Centre**
Affiliated with: Alberta Health Services
600 - 3rd St., Fox Creek, AB T0H 1P0
Tel: 780-622-3545
www.albertahealthservices.ca
Number of Beds: 4 acute care beds
Note: Specialties: Emergency services; Laboratory services; Acute care; Prenatal classes & Healthy Beginnings Program (780-622-3730); Pediatrics; Cardiac & diabetes education (780-524-7027); Home care & palliative care (780-622-3730)

***Grande Cache:* Grande Cache Community Health Complex**
Affiliated with: Alberta Health Services
PO Box 629, 10200 Shand Ave., Grande Cache, AB T0E 0Y0
Tel: 780-827-3701; *Fax:* 780-827-2859
tracy.peddy@pchr.ca
Number of Beds: 12 acute care, 4 continuing care beds
Tracy Peddy, Director, Health Services

***Grande Prairie:* Queen Elizabeth II Hospital**
Affiliated with: Alberta Health Services
10409 - 98 St., Grande Prairie, AB T8V 2E8
Tel: 780-538-7100; *Fax:* 780-538-1500
Number of Beds: 48 med, 10 NICU, 22 Obs/Gen, 14 Ped, 26 psy, 8 rehab, 40 sur
Diane Calvert, Chief Operating Officer

***Grimshaw:* Grimshaw/Berwyn & District Community Health Centre**
Affiliated with: Alberta Health Services
PO Box 648, 5612 Wilcox Rd., Grimshaw, AB T0H 1W0
Tel: 780-332-6500; *Fax:* 780-618-4522
Number of Beds: 4 beds, 10 continuing care beds
Carmen Johnson, Chairperson

***Hanna:* Hanna Health Centre**
Affiliated with: Alberta Health Services
PO Box 730, 904 Centre St. North, Hanna, AB T0J 1P0
Tel: 403-854-3331; *Fax:* 403-854-3253
Number of Beds: 18 acute care, 49 continuing care beds, 12 assisted living beds
Ken Hansenen, Site Leader

***Hardisty:* Hardisty Health Centre**
Affiliated with: Alberta Health Services
PO Box 269, 4531 - 47 Ave., Hardisty, AB T0B 1V0
Tel: 780-888-3742; *Fax:* 780-888-2427
evelyn.scott@eastcentralhealth.com
www.ech.ab.ca
Number of Beds: 5 acute care, 15 continuing care beds
Evelyn Scott, Health Centre Coordinator

***High Level:* Ranchlands Village Mall**
Affiliated with: Alberta Health Services
Former Name: High Level General Hospital; Northwest Health Cent
1829 Ranchlands Blvd. NW, High Level, AB T0H 1Z0
Tel: 403-943-9700; *Fax:* 403-943-9735
Number of Beds: 30 beds
Patricia Pelton, CEO

***High Prairie:* High Prairie Health Complex**
Affiliated with: Alberta Health Services
4620 - 53 Ave, High Prairie, AB T0G 1E0
Tel: 780-523-6440; *Fax:* 780-523-6642
Number of Beds: 25 acute care, 35 long-term care, continuing care 35
Kate Butler, Director, Health Services

***High River:* High River General Hospital**
Affiliated with: Alberta Health Services
560 - 9 Ave. SW, High River, AB T1V 1B3
Tel: 403-652-2200; *Fax:* 403-652-0199
www.calgaryhealthregion.ca
Number of Beds: 103 beds
Rosemary Burness, Community Health Services Leader
Gesina Allan, Purchasing Manager
Geraldine Polanchek, Director, Finance & Support Services

***Hinton:* Hinton Healthcare Centre**
Affiliated with: Alberta Health Services
1280 Switzer Dr., Hinton, AB T7V 1V2
Tel: 780-865-3333; *Fax:* 780-865-1099
lisa.mcconnell@aspenrha.com
aspenrha.com
Number of Beds: 21 beds
Lisa McConnell, Health Centre Manager
Doug Johnson, Supervisor, Environmental Services

***Innisfail:* Innisfail Health Centre**
Affiliated with: Alberta Health Services
5023 - 42 St., Innisfail, AB T4G 1A9
Tel: 403-227-7800; *Fax:* 403-227-7801
Number of Beds: 102 beds
Cindy Mulherin, Site Leader

***Jasper:* Seton Jasper Healthcare Centre**
Affiliated with: Alberta Health Services
PO Box 310, 518 Robson St., Jasper, AB T0E 1E0
Tel: 780-852-3344; *Fax:* 780-852-3413
www9.albertahealthservices.ca/Default.aspx?cid=156&lang=1
Number of Beds: 11 beds; 10 for acute care and 1 for palliative care
Note: Emergency, acute care services, diagnostic imaging, eating disorder services, mental health services, occupational therapy, palliative care, physiotherapy, social work
Dr. Stephen Duckett, President; CEO, AHS
Lorna Chisholm, Site Manager
Dr. Mark Addison, Chief, Medical Staff

***Killam:* Killam Healthcare Centre**
Affiliated with: Alberta Health Services
PO Box 40, 5203 - 49 Ave., Killam, AB T0B 2L0
Tel: 780-385-3741; *Fax:* 780-385-3904
www.ech.ab.ca
Number of Beds: 5 acute care, 45 continuing care beds, 4 other
Geri Clark, Chief Executive Director

***Lac La Biche:* William J. Cadzow Health Centre**
Affiliated with: Alberta Health Services
PO Box 507, 9200 - 95 St., Lac La Biche, AB T0A 2C0
Tel: 780-623-4404; *Fax:* 780-623-5904
Number of Beds: 23 acute care, 41 long-term care beds

***Lac La Biche:* William J. Cadzow Lac La Biche Healthcare Centre**
Affiliated with: Alberta Health Services
Former Name: Lac La Biche Health Care Centre
PO Box 507, 9110 - 93 St., Lac La Biche, AB T0A 2C0
Tel: 780-623-4404; *Fax:* 780-623-5904
Number of Beds: 65 beds
Gislind Moehrle, Healthcare Centre Manager

***Lamont:* Lamont Health Care Centre**
Affiliated with: Alberta Health Services
5216 - 53 St., Lamont, AB T0B 2R0
Tel: 780-895-2211; *Fax:* 780-895-7305
www.ech.ab.ca
Number of Beds: 14 acute, 105 continuing care beds
Harold James, Executive Director

***Leduc:* Leduc Community Hospital**
Affiliated with: Alberta Health Services
Former Name: Leduc Community Hospital & Health Centre
4210 - 48 St., Leduc, AB T9E 5Z3
Tel: 780-986-7711
www.capitalhealth.ca
Number of Beds: 54 beds

***Lethbridge:* Lethbridge Regional Hospital**
Affiliated with: Alberta Health Services
960 - 19 St. South, Lethbridge, AB T1J 1W5
Tel: 403-382-6111; *Fax:* 403-388-6011
Number of Beds: 236 acute care, 41 mental health
Cheryl Dick, CEO

***Magrath:* Magrath Hospital**
Affiliated with: Alberta Health Services
PO Box 550, 37E - 2 Ave. North, Magrath, AB T0K 1J0
Tel: 403-758-3331; *Fax:* 403-758-3332
Number of Beds: 3 acute care beds, 21 auxiliary beds
Pam Whitnack, CEO
Grace Navratil, Housekeeping Supervisor

***Manning:* Manning Community Health Centre**
Affiliated with: Alberta Health Services
Bag 1260, 600 - 2 St. NE, Manning, AB T0H 2M0
Tel: 780-836-3391; *Fax:* 780-836-7352
Number of Beds: 11 acute care, 16 long-term care beds
Jo Kelemen, Director of Health Services

***Mayerthorpe:* Mayerthorpe Healthcare Centre**
Affiliated with: Alberta Health Services
PO Box 30, 4417 - 45 St., Mayerthorpe, AB T0E 1N0
Tel: 780-786-2261; *Fax:* 780-786-2023
Number of Beds: 25 acute care, 30 long-term care beds
Karen Kyle, Facility Supervisor
Gwen Hunt, Purchasing Agent

***McLennan:* McLennan Sacred Heart Community Health Centre**
Affiliated with: Alberta Health Services
Bag 2000, McLennan, AB T0H 2L0
Tel: 780-324-3730; *Fax:* 780-324-4206
barbara.mader@pchr.ca
www.pchr.ca
Number of Beds: 20 acute care, 45 long-term care beds
Note: community health centre; nursing home
Barbara Mader, Director, Health Services

***Medicine Hat:* Medicine Hat Regional Hospital**
Affiliated with: Alberta Health Services
666 - 5 St. SW, Medicine Hat, AB T1A 4H6
Tel: 403-529-8000; *Fax:* 403-529-8998
www.palliserhealth.ca
Number of Beds: 177 beds
L. Iwasiw, Senior Vice-President
G. Lukasiewich, Director, Physical Plant/Maintenance

***Milk River:* Milk River Health Centre**
Affiliated with: Alberta Health Services
Former Name: Milk River Hospital
PO Box 90, 517 Centre Ave. East, Milk River, AB T0K 1M0
Tel: 403-647-3500
Number of Beds: 21 auxiliary beds, 3 community support beds, 1 respite
Brad Moser, Head, Housekeeping

***Mundare:* Mary Immaculate Hospital**
Affiliated with: Alberta Health Services
PO Box 349, Mundare, AB T0B 3H0
Tel: 780-764-3730; *Fax:* 780-764-3039
www.ech.ab.ca
Number of Beds: 30 continuing care
Note: auxiliary/clinic (out patient)
Rhonda McCarty, Executive Director

***New Westminster:* Royal Columbian Hospital**
Affiliated with: Fraser Health Authority
330 East Columbia St., New Westminster, AB V3L 3W7
Tel: 604-520-4253; *Fax:* 604-520-4827
feedback@fraserhealth.ca
www.fraserhealth.ca/find_us/locations/our_locations?site_id=1789
Year Founded: 1862
Number of Beds: 352 acute care beds
Note: Emergency, acute care services, care for the elderly, angiography, antepartum care services, bone densitometry, cardiac services, diabetes education, bronchoscopy services, ultrasound, fluoroscopy, respiratory unit, radiography, surgery unit, hand clinic, haemodialysis, psychiatry, intensive care unit, intrapartum care, magnetic resonance imaging, mammography, oncology, neonatal intensive care, neurological services,

orthopaedic surgery, paediatrics, pantomography, family counselling, physiotherapy, plastic surgery, respiratory therapy, social work services, ultrasound, vascular and thoracic surgery
Dr. Nigel Murray, President/CEO, FHA
Dr. Andrew Webb, Vice-President, FHA, Medicine
Brian Woods, CFO, FHA
Gillian Harwood, Executive Director, FHA
Miriam Stewart, Director, Health Services

Olds: Olds Hospital & Care Centre
Affiliated with: Alberta Health Services
3901 - 57 Ave., Olds, AB T4H 1T4
Tel: 403-556-3381; *Fax:* 403-556-2199
Number of Beds: 81 beds
Colleen Simon, Site Leader

Oyen: Big Country Hospital
Affiliated with: Alberta Health Services
312 - 3 Ave. East, Oyen, AB T0J 2J0
Tel: 403-664-3651; *Fax:* 403-502-8649
Number of Beds: 10 acute care, 30 continuing care beds
Lynne Baisley, Director, Health Services Northern Area
Wayne Trembley, Supervisor, Physical Plant

Peace River: Peace River Community Health Centre
Affiliated with: Alberta Health Services
Bag 400, 10101 - 68 St., Peace River, AB T8S 1T6
Tel: 780-624-7500; *Fax:* 780-618-3472
hrabb@telusplanet.net
www.pchr.ca
Number of Beds: 30 acute care, 40 long-term care beds
Note: long-term care facility, nursing home, outpatient services, treatment centre, community health centre, home care office
Sandra Herritt, Director, Health Services

Picture Butte: Piyami Place
Affiliated with: Alberta Health Services
Former Name: Picture Butte Hospital
301 Cowan Ave., Picture Butte, AB T0K 1V0
Tel: 403-732-4811; *Fax:* 403-388-6011
Number of Beds: 15 suites
Pam Whitnack, CEO

Pincher Creek: Pincher Creek Health Centre
Affiliated with: Alberta Health Services
Former Name: Pincher Creek Hospital
1222 Bev McLachlin Dr., Pincher Creek, AB T0K 1W0
Tel: 403-627-1234; *Fax:* 403-627-5275
www.chr.ab.ca
Number of Beds: 16 acute care beds, 3 auxiliary beds
Pam Whitnack, CEO
Brian Meaney, Acting Maintenance Supervisor

Ponoka: Ponoka Hospital & Healthcare Centre
Affiliated with: Alberta Health Services
5800 - 57 Ave., Ponoka, AB T4J 1P1
Tel: 403-783-3341; *Fax:* 403-783-6907
Number of Beds: 75 beds
Sue MacKenzie, Site Leader
Hardy Kohlman, Director, Physical Plant

Provost: Provost Health Centre
Affiliated with: Alberta Health Services
PO Box 270, 5002 - 54 Ave., Provost, AB T0B 3S0
Tel: 780-753-2291; *Fax:* 780-608-8850
www.ech.ab.ca
Number of Beds: 15 acute care, 37 continuing care beds, 10 alternative housing
Lana Clark, Health Services Coordinator

Raymond: Raymond Hospital
Affiliated with: Alberta Health Services
PO Box 599, 150 North 4th St. E, Raymond, AB T0K 2S0
Tel: 403-752-4561; *Fax:* 403-627-5275
www.albertahealthservices.ca/facilities.asp?pid=facility&rid=3306
Number of Beds: 12 acute care, 35 auxiliary beds
Note: Emergency, obstetrics, and palliative care, diagnostic imaging, rehabilitation
Dr. Stephen Duckett, President; CEO, AHS
Dr. David Megran, Executive Vice-President, CMO, AHS

Red Deer: Red Deer Regional Hospital Centre
Affiliated with: Alberta Health Services
3942 - 50A Ave., Red Deer, AB T4N 4E7
Tel: 403-343-4422; *Fax:* 403-341-8632
www.albertahealthservices.ca/facilities.asp?pid=facility&rid=1000342
Number of Beds: 365 beds
Note: Emergency, dialysis clinic, cancer clinic and a pediatric and special care nursery
Dr. Stephen Duckett, President/ CEO, AHS
Dr. David Megran, Executive Vice-President, CMO, AHS

Redwater: Redwater Health Centre
Affiliated with: Alberta Health Services
4812 - 58 St., Redwater, AB T0A 2W0
Tel: 780-942-3932; *Fax:* 780-942-2373
www.albertahealthservices.ca/facilities.asp?pid=facility&rid=8928
Number of Beds: 13 beds
Note: 24-hour emergency services, palliative care, lab services, respiratory services, radiology, nutritional counselling, and a visiting optometrist office
David S. Diamond, Chief Operating Officer, AHS

Slave Lake: Slave Lake Healthcare Centre
Affiliated with: Alberta Health Services
309 - 6 St. NE, Slave Lake, AB T0G 2A2
Tel: 780-805-3500; *Fax:* 780-805-3574
www.albertahealthservices.ca/facilities.asp?pid=facility&rid=1024257
Number of Beds: 43 beds (24 acute care beds including 2 labor and delivery beds, 1 palliative care bed, 2 special care beds, plus 20 continuing care beds)
Note: Emergency, acute care, continuing care, pharmacy, renal dialysis, rehabilitation, obstetrics, occupational therapy, pediatrics, respiratory therapy, social work, ultrasound and X-Ray
Dr. Stephen Duckett, President/CEO, AHS
Mr. Steve Marcotte, Healthcare Centre Manager
Dr. Paul Caffaro, Chief, Medical Staff

Smoky Lake: Smoky Lake - George McDougall Memorial Healthcare Centre
Affiliated with: Alberta Health Services
PO Box 340, 4212 - 55 Ave., Smoky Lake, AB T0A 3C0
Tel: 780-656-3034; *Fax:* 780-656-5010
www.albertahealthservices.ca
Number of Beds: 12 acute care beds, including 1 palliative care bed; 23 continuing care beds
Note: Hospital Specialties: Emergency services; Diagnostic imaging; Laboratory services; Ambulatory services; Acute care; Rehabilitation; Occupational therapy; Physical therapy services; Respiratory therapy; Therapeutic recreation; Community health services; Nutrition services; Social work; Continuing care; Palliative care
David Ponich, Manager, Healthcare Centre
Dr. Anton Raubenheimer, Chief, Medical Staff

Spirit River: Central Peace Health Complex
Affiliated with: Alberta Health Services
5010 - 45th Ave., Spirit River, AB T0H 3G0
Tel: 780-864-3993
www.albertahealthservices.ca
Number of Beds: 10 acute care beds; 16 continuing care beds
Note: Hospital Specialties: Emergency care; Laboratory services; Acute care; Newborn hearing screening program; Pediatrics; Rehabilitation; Physical therapy; Nutrition counselling (780-864-3063); Continuing care; Palliative care

St Albert: Sturgeon Community Hospital
Affiliated with: Alberta Health Services
Former Name: Sturgeon Community Hospital & Health Centre
201 Boudreau Rd., St Albert, AB T8N 6C4
Tel: 780-418-8200; *Fax:* 780-460-6262
www.albertahealthservices.ca/facilities.asp?pid=facility&rid=1000932
Number of Beds: 167 beds
Note: A comprehensive health facility with services including emergency, cardiac rehabilitation, diagnostic imaging (CT scans, radiology, fluoroscopy), geriatric evaluation, intensive care unit, mental health emergency, nutrition counselling, obstetrical outpatient clinic, physical therapy/occupational therapy, prenatal program, sexual assault response team, spiritual care, surgery.
Dr. Stephen Duckett, President/CEO, AHS
Ms. Linda Cargill, Executive Director, Community & Rural Hospitals, AHS

St. Paul: St. Therese/St. Paul Healthcare Centre
Affiliated with: Alberta Health Services
4713 - 48 Ave., St. Paul, AB T0A 3A3
Tel: 780-645-3331; *Fax:* 780-645-1702
www9.albertahealthservices.ca/Default.aspx?cid=162&lang=1
Number of Beds: 80 beds (30 acute care beds, including 3 special care beds, 2 palliative care beds; there is also a 30-bed continuing care facility and a 20-bed psych
Note: Services include emergency, diagnostic imaging (ultrasound, x-ray), eating disorder services, obstetrics, pharmacy, rehabilitation, renal dialysis, and laboratory.
Dr. Stephen Duckett, President/CEO, AHS
Ms. Bev Belland, Site Manager
Dr. Albert Harmse, Chief of Medical Staff

Stettler: Stettler Hospital & Care Centre
Affiliated with: Alberta Health Services
5912 - 47 Ave., Stettler, AB T0C 2L0
Tel: 403-742-7400; *Fax:* 403-742-1244
www.albertahealthservices.ca/services.asp?pid=facility&rid=1000353
Number of Beds: 150 beds (with 50 acute care, 40 long-term care, 2 respite beds)
Note: Services include emergency, continuing care, diabetes education, diagnostic imaging, enterostomal therapy, homecare, mental health, obstetrics, occupational therapy (for acute & continuing care), palliative care, pharmacy, physical therapy, respiratory therapy, sleep program, speech language pathology
Dr. Stephen Duckett, President/CEO, AHS
Ms. Donna Stelmachovich, Vice-President, Seniors Health, AHS
Ms. Diane Ecklund, Site Program Supervisor

Stony Plain: Westview Health Centre
Affiliated with: Alberta Health Services
4405 South Park Dr., Stony Plain, AB T7Z 0A1
Tel: 780-968-3600; *Fax:* 780-963-7612
www.capitalhealth.ca
Number of Beds: 68 beds
Joy Myskiw, Area Team Leader

Strathmore: Strathmore District Health Services
Affiliated with: Alberta Health Services
200 Brent Blvd., Strathmore, AB T1P 1J9
Tel: 403-934-4204; *Fax:* 403-934-3948
www.albertahealthservices.ca/facilities.asp?pid=facility&rid=1000943
Number of Beds: 25 acute care, 23 long-term care beds
Note: An acute care hospital with services including cardiology, nutrition services, continuing care, diabetes education, diagnostic imaging, fluoroscopy, Holter monitoring, home care, laboratory, medical genetics, occupational therapy, palliative care, pharmacy, physical therapy, psychiatric assessment, respiratory services, respite care, speech language pathology
Dr. Stephen Duckett, President/CEO, AHS
Ms. Donna Stelmachovich, Vice-President, Seniors Health, AHS
Dr. Jim Silvius, Senior Medical Director, AHS

Sundre: Sundre Hospital & Care Centre
Affiliated with: Alberta Health Services
709 - 1 St. NE, Sundre, AB T0M 1X0
Tel: 403-638-3033; *Fax:* 403-638-4971
www.albertahealthservices.ca/facilities.asp?pid=facility&rid=1000359
Number of Beds: 13 acute care, 15 continuing care beds
Note: A facility offering long-term and acute care with services including emergency, clinical nutrition, continuing care counseling, diabetes education, diagnostic imaging, enterostomal therapy, laboratory, obstetrics, occupational therapy, palliative care, pharmacy, physical therapy, speech language pathology.
Dr. Stephen Duckett, President/CEO, AHS
Ms. Linda Cargill, Executive Director, Community & Rural Hospitals, AHS
Ms. Bonny Jones, Site Coordinator

Swan Hills: Swan Hills Healthcare Centre
Affiliated with: Alberta Health Services
PO Box 266, 29 Freeman Dr., Swan Hills, AB T0G 2C0
Tel: 780-333-7000; *Fax:* 780-333-7009
www9.albertahealthservices.ca/Default.aspx?cid=163&lang=1
Year Founded: 1985
Number of Beds: 4 acute care beds
Note: A community centre with services including emergency, general medicine, laboratory, nutrition services pharmacy, radiology.
Dr. Stephen Duckett, President/CEO, AHS
Ms. Patricia Baker, Site Manager
Dr. J. Hankinson, Site Medical Director

Taber: Taber Health Centre
Affiliated with: Alberta Health Services
Former Name: Taber Hospital
4326 - 50 Ave., Taber, AB T0K 2G0
Tel: 403-223-7211; *Fax:* 403-388-6011
www.albertahealthservices.ca/facilities.asp?pid=facility&rid=3307
Number of Beds: 19 acute care, 15 auxiliary, 55 nursing home beds
Note: This acute and continuing care facility has services including emergency, diagnostic imaging, home care, laboratory, neonatal intensive care, occupational therapy, pediatrics, therapeutic recreation.
Dr. Stephen Duckett, CEO, AHS
Mr. Bruce Conway, Senior Media Relations Advisor, South, AHS
403-943-1212

Tofield: Tofield Health Centre
Affiliated with: Alberta Health Services
PO Box 1200, 5543 - 44 St., Tofield, AB T0B 4J0
Tel: 780-662-3263; *Fax:* 780-662-3835
www.albertahealthservices.ca/facilities.asp?pid=facility&rid=1000176
Number of Beds: 16 acute care, 50 continuing care beds
Note: Services include emergency, acute care, communicable disease control, continuing care, home care, laboratory, occupational therapy, palliative care, physiotherapy, prenatal education, radiology, respiratory therapy, respite care, speech language services, surgery
Dr. Stephen Duckett, President/CEO, AHS
Dr. Dave Megren, Executive Vice-President/CMO, AHS
Mr. Roman Cooney, Senior Vice-President, Communications, AHS
Ms. Betty Kolewaski, Site Administrator

Two Hills: Two Hills Health Centre
Affiliated with: Alberta Health Services
PO Box 458, 4401 - 53 Ave., Two Hills, AB T0B 4K0
Tel: 780-657-3344; *Fax:* 780-657-2508
www.albertahealthservices.ca/facilities.asp?pid=facility&rid=1001613
Year Founded: 1986
Number of Beds: 75 beds (6 acute care, 60 continuing care, 9 stroke rehabilitation beds)
Note: A multi-level care complex with services including emergency, acute care, communicable disease control, genetics, mental health clinics, nutrition, continuing care, diabetes education, home care, laboratory, occupational therapy, adult community rehab program, oral health, palliative care, pharmacy, prenatal education, radiology, respiratory therapy, respite care, social work, stroke & geriatric empowerment unit
Dr. Stephen Duckett, President/CEO, AHS
Ms. Cheryl Knight, Executive Director, Continuing Care, Integrated Services Rural, AHS
Ms. Kathy Miskew, Interm Site Coordinator

Valleyview: Valleyview Health Complex
Affiliated with: Alberta Health Services
4802 Highway St., Valleyview, AB T0H 3N0
Tel: 780-524-3356; *Fax:* 780-524-4462
Number of Beds: 15 acute care, 17 long-term care beds
Tracy Brown, Site Manager
Debbie Stewart, Chairman

Vegreville: St. Joseph's General Hospital
Affiliated with: Alberta Health Services
5241 - 43 St., Vegreville, AB T9C 1R5
Tel: 780-632-2811; *Fax:* 780-603-4401
www.albertahealthservices.ca/facilities.asp?pid=facility&rid=1000160
Number of Beds: 35 beds; 6 station dialysis unit
Note: An acute care facility offering services in emergency, medicine, laboratory, diagnostic imaging (x-ray, ultrasound), dialysis, diabetic education, occupational therapy, respiratory therapy, surgery and day support
Dr. Stephen Duckett, President/CEO, AHS
Dr. David Megren, Executive Vice-President/CMO, AHS
Mr. Kerry Williamson, Senior Media Relations Advisor, North Region, AHS
780-407-2602

Vermilion: Vermilion Health Centre
Affiliated with: Alberta Health Services
5720 - 50 Ave., Vermilion, AB T9X 1K7
Tel: 780-853-5305; *Fax:* 780-853-4786
www.ech.ab.ca
Number of Beds: 25 acute care, 48 continuing care beds
Debora Okrainetz, Health Centre Coordinator

Viking: Viking Health Centre
Affiliated with: Alberta Health Services
PO Box 60, 5110 - 57 Ave., Viking, AB T0B 4N0
Tel: 780-336-4786; *Fax:* 780-336-4983
www.ech.ab.ca
Number of Beds: 16 acute care beds
Note: Community health care services; acute & continuing care facilities
Kathryn Miskew, Health Centre Coordinator

Vulcan: Vulcan Community Health Centre
610 Elizabeth St. South, Vulcan, AB T0L 2B0
Tel: 403-485-3333; *Fax:* 403-485-2336
Number of Beds: 8 acute care, 15 long-term care beds
Patty Greene, Executive Leader

Wabasca: Wabasca/Desmarais Healthcare Centre
Affiliated with: Alberta Health Services
Former Name: Wabasca/Desmarais General Hospital
PO Box 450, Wabasca, AB T0G 2K0
Tel: 780-891-3007; *Fax:* 780-891-3784
trisslin@aspenrha.ab.ca
www.aspenrha.ab.ca
Number of Beds: 10 beds
Kirk Richardson

Wainwright: Wainwright Health Centre
Affiliated with: Alberta Health Services
530 - 6 Ave., Wainwright, AB T9W 1R6
Tel: 780-842-3324; *Fax:* 780-842-4290
www.ech.ab.ca
Number of Beds: 25 acute care, 69 continuing care beds
Cheryl Huxley, Health Centre Coordinator

Westlock: Westlock Healthcare Centre
Affiliated with: Alberta Health Services
#103, 10030 - 106 St., Westlock, AB T7P 2G4
Tel: 780-349-3301; *Fax:* 780-349-6973
Number of Beds: 45 beds
Joyce Nadeau, Site Supervisor
Richard Baker, Director of Plant Operations; Maintenance

Wetaskiwin: Wetaskiwin Hospital & Health Centre
Affiliated with: Alberta Health Services
Former Name: Crossroads Hospital & Health Centre - Wetaskiwin
6910 - 47 St., Wetaskiwin, AB T9A 3N3
Tel: 780-361-7100; *Fax:* 780-361-4107
www.dthr.ab.ca
Number of Beds: 76 acute care, 79 long-term care beds
Bruce Finkel, Site Leader

Whitecourt: Whitecourt Healthcare Centre
Affiliated with: Alberta Health Services
20 Sunset Blvd., Whitecourt, AB T7S 1M8
Tel: 780-778-2285; *Fax:* 780-778-5161
Number of Beds: 24 beds
Marj Stockwell, Facility Supervisor

Auxiliary Hospitals

Breton: Breton Health Centre
Affiliated with: Alberta Health Services
4919 - 49th Ave., Breton, AB T0C 0P0
Tel: 780-696-4701; *Fax:* 780-696-4747
www.albertahealthservices.ca
Year Founded: 1994
Number of Beds: 23 long term care beds
Note: Hospital Specialties: Laboratory services (780-696-3731); Occupational therapy; Physical therapy; Recreational therapy; Speech language pathology; Clinical nutrition services (403-309-6199); Continuing care (780-696-3731); Home care; Palliative care (780-696-4713)

Cardston: Cardston Health Centre
Affiliated with: Alberta Health Services
PO Box 1440, 144 - 2nd St. West, Cardston, AB T0K 0K0
Tel: 403-653-5234
www.albertahealthservices.ca
Note: Hospital Specialties: Emergency services; Diagnostic imaging (403-653-4399); Surgery; Obstetrics: Acute care; Rehabilitation; Therapeutic Recreation (403-653-5253); Speech language pathology; Continuing care (403-653-5262); Palliative care
Cindy Baker, Manager, Cardston Acute Care
403-653-4411, CBaker@chr.ab.ca

Carmangay: Little Bow Continuing Care Centre
316 Armstrong St., Carmangay, AB T0L 0N0
Tel: 403-643-3511; *Fax:* 403-643-4222
Number of Beds: 20 beds
Pete Sherstabetoff, Supervisor, Plant Maintenance

Claresholm: Willow Creek Continuing Care Centre
Affiliated with: Alberta Health Services
4221 - 8 St., Claresholm, AB T0L 0T0
Tel: 403-625-3361; *Fax:* 403-625-3822
Number of Beds: 100 beds
Pat Manderville, Health Services Leader
Pat Manderville, Community Care Leader

Lacombe: Lacombe Community Health Centre
Affiliated with: Alberta Health Services
5010 - 51 St., Lacombe, AB T4L 1W2
Tel: 403-782-3218; *Fax:* 403-782-2866
Kerry Bales, Community Care Home Care Manager

Lethbridge: St. Michael's Health Centre
Affiliated with: Alberta Health Services
1400 - 9 Ave. South, Lethbridge, AB T1J 4V5
Tel: 403-382-6400; *Fax:* 403-382-6433
Year Founded: 1929
Number of Beds: 202 beds (148 continuing care, 36 rehabilitation, 18 palliative)
Note: A long-term care (continuing care) facility focusing on assisted living, palliative care, post-acute rehabilitative program, Bridges program (care for the elderly in their own home). It operates under the governance of Covenant Health, a Catholic healthcare provider.
Mr. R. Patrick Dumelie, President/CEO, Covenant Health
Mr. Al Pierog, Vice-President, Seniors Health, Covenant Health
Ms. Fran Ross, Vice-President, Communications, Covenant Health

Trochu: St. Mary's Health Care Centre
Affiliated with: Alberta Health Services
PO Box 100, 451 de Chauney Ave., Trochu, AB T0M 2C0
Tel: 403-442-3955; *Fax:* 403-341-8632
Number of Beds: 28 beds
Kathryn Kane-Upton, CEO

Westlock: Westlock Long Term Care Centre
Affiliated with: Alberta Health Services
9732 - 100 Ave., Westlock, AB T7P 2G3
Tel: 780-349-3306; *Fax:* 780-349-5647
Number of Beds: 103 beds
Susan Gokiert, Coninuing Care Centre Manager
Brian Hyndman, Supervisor, Plant Maintenance

Community Health Centres

Community Health Care Centres

Airdrie: Airdrie Regional Health Centre
Affiliated with: Alberta Health Services
604 Main St. South, Airdrie, AB T4B 1C9
Tel: 403-912-8400; *Fax:* 403-948-6284
www.calgaryhealthregion.ca

Athabasca: Athabasca Community Health Services
Affiliated with: Alberta Health Services
3401 - 48 Ave., Athabasca, AB T9S 1M7
Tel: 780-675-2231; *Fax:* 780-675-3111
Rosalie Stobee, Supervisor

Banff: Banff Public Health & Community Care
PO Box 1266, 301 Lynx St., Banff, AB T1L 1B3
Tel: 403-762-2990; *Fax:* 403-762-5570
Dr. Judith MacDonald, Designated Physician

Barrhead: Barrhead Community Health Services
Affiliated with: Alberta Health Services
6203 - 49 Ave., Barrhead, AB T7N 1A1
Tel: 780-674-3408; *Fax:* 780-674-3941
Lorraine Lindberg, CHS Supervisor

Bashaw: Bashaw
Affiliated with: Alberta Health Services
4909 - 50 St., Bashaw, AB T0B 0H0
Tel: 780-372-3731; *Fax:* 780-372-4050
www.ech.ab.ca
Lee Fredeen-Kohlert, Contact

Bashaw: Hospital Bashaw
Affiliated with: Alberta Health Services
PO Box 449, 4909 - 50 St., Bashaw, AB T0B 0H0
Tel: 780-372-3731; *Fax:* 780-372-4050
www.ech.ab.ca
Number of Beds: 25 beds, 4 program beds
Evelyn Kraft, Interim Health Centre Coordinator

Beaumont: Beaumont Public Health Authority
Affiliated with: Alberta Health Services
4918 - 50 Ave., Beaumont, AB T4X 1J9
Tel: 780-929-4822; *Fax:* 780-929-4828
www.capitalhealth.ca

Beaverlodge: Beaverlodge Public Health Centre
Affiliated with: Alberta Health Services
PO Box 120, 412 - 10A St., Beaverlodge, AB T0H 0C0
Tel: 780-354-2647; *Fax:* 780-354-1550
Janet Wallace, Director, Health Services

***Black Diamond:* Black Diamond Health Unit**
Affiliated with: Alberta Health Services
PO Box 1, 717 Government Rd. S, Black Diamond, AB T0L 0H0
Tel: 403-933-8505; *Fax:* 403-933-2031

***Blairmore:* Community Health - Crowsnest Pass**
Affiliated with: Alberta Health Services
12501 - 26 St., Blairmore, AB T0K 0E0
Tel: 403-388-6009; *Fax:* 403-388-6011

Pam Whitnack, CEO

***Bonnyville:* Bonnyville Community Health Services**
Affiliated with: Alberta Health Services
4904 - 50 Ave., Bonnyville, AB T9N 2G4
Tel: 780-826-3381; *Fax:* 780-826-6470

Joan Panteluk, Community Health Services Supervisor

***Bow Island:* Bow Island Public Health/Home Care**
Affiliated with: Alberta Health Services
PO Box 949, Bow Island, AB T0K 0G0
Tel: 403-525-2296; *Fax:* 403-525-6357
www.palliserhealth.org

***Boyle:* Boyle Community Health Services**
Affiliated with: Alberta Health Services
5004 Lakeview Rd., Boyle, AB T0A 0M0
Tel: 780-689-2677; *Fax:* 780-689-2835
Note: home care office

***Brooks:* Brooks Home Care**
Affiliated with: Alberta Health Services
#11 - 311 Ninth St. SE, Brooks, AB T1A 8E3
Tel: 403-362-7766; *Fax:* 403-362-7778

***Calgary:* 8th & 8th Health Centre**
Affiliated with: Alberta Health Services
912 - 8 Ave. SW, Calgary, AB T2P 1H9
Tel: 403-781-1200; *Fax:* 403-205-4979

***Calgary:* Bowness Community Health Centre**
Affiliated with: Alberta Health Services
6328 - 35 Ave. NW, Calgary, AB T3B 1S4
Tel: 403-288-7744; *Fax:* 403-288-3223

***Calgary:* East Community Health Centre**
Affiliated with: Alberta Health Services
112 - 28 St. SE, Calgary, AB T2A 5J9
Tel: 403-248-8868; *Fax:* 403-273-3219

***Calgary:* Forest Lawn District Office**
Affiliated with: Alberta Health Services
3810 - 17 Ave. SE, Calgary, AB T1X 1E1
Tel: 403-944-7300; *Fax:* 403-248-0429

Lisa Oake, Secretary

***Calgary:* Millican-Odgen Community Health Centre**
Affiliated with: Alberta Health Services
2880 Glenmore Trail SE, Calgary, AB T2C 2E6
Tel: 403-944-7225

Lorraine Dunn, Manager

***Calgary:* North Hill Community Health Centre**
Affiliated with: Alberta Health Services
1920 - 14 Ave. NW, Calgary, AB T2N 1M5
Tel: 403-282-1612; *Fax:* 403-282-0039

***Calgary:* Northwest Health Centre**
Affiliated with: Alberta Health Services
#109, 1829 Ranchlands Blvd. NW, Calgary, AB T3G 2A7
Tel: 403-943-9700; *Fax:* 403-943-9735

***Calgary:* Shaganappi District Office**
Affiliated with: Alberta Health Services
3415 - 8th Ave. SW, Calgary, AB T3C 0E8
Tel: 403-944-7373; *Fax:* 403-246-0326

***Calgary:* South Calgary Health District**
Affiliated with: Alberta Health Services
31 Sunpark Plaza SE, Calgary, AB T2X 3W5
Tel: 403-943-9501; *Fax:* 403-944-2224

***Calgary:* Thornhill District Office**
Affiliated with: Alberta Health Services
6617 Centre St. NW, Calgary, AB T2K 4Y5
Tel: 403-274-4515; *Fax:* 403-944-2224

***Calgary:* Village Square Community Health Centre**
Affiliated with: Alberta Health Services
2623 - 56 St. NE, Calgary, AB T1Y 6E7
Tel: 403-944-7000; *Fax:* 403-285-6304

***Calling Lake:* Calling Lake Community Health Services**
Affiliated with: Alberta Health Services
Highway 813, Calling Lake, AB T0G 0G0
Tel: 780-331-3760; *Fax:* 780-331-2200

***Camrose:* Camrose Public Health, Home Care, Rehab**
Affiliated with: Alberta Health Services
4615 - 56 St., Camrose, AB T4V 4M5
Tel: 780-679-2900; *Fax:* 780-679-2929
www.ech.ab.ca

Monica O'Gorman

***Canmore:* Canmore Public Health Office**
Provincial Building, #104, 800 Railway Ave., Canmore, AB T1W 1P1
Tel: 403-678-5656; *Fax:* 403-678-5068
Note: public health programs

***Cardston:* Cardston Community & Wellness Site**
Affiliated with: Alberta Health Services
Provincial Bldg., PO Box 1590, 576 Main St., Cardston, AB T0K 0K0
Tel: 403-388-6099; *Fax:* 403-388-6011
Note: community health centre & home care office
Pam Whitnack, CEO

***Claresholm:* Claresholm Public Health & Community Care**
Affiliated with: Alberta Health Services
PO Box 1391, 5221 - 2nd St. West, Claresholm, AB T0L 0T0
Tel: 403-625-4061; *Fax:* 403-625-4062

Pat Manderville, Facility Coordinator

***Coaldale:* Coaldale Community Health**
Affiliated with: Alberta Health Services
PO Box 1000, 2012 - 18 St., Coaldale, AB T1M 1M8
Tel: 403-345-6507; *Fax:* 403-345-2043
Number of Beds: 40 continuing care, 4 community care beds
Bob Parker, Environmental Services

***Coaldale:* Community Health - Coaldale**
Affiliated with: Alberta Health Services
PO Box 1000, 2012 - 18 St., Coaldale, AB T1M 1M8
Tel: 403-345-3000; *Fax:* 403-345-2043
Toll-Free: 866-345-8800

***Cochrane:* Cochrane Community Health Centre**
Affiliated with: Alberta Health Services
Provincial Bldg., 213 - 1 St. West, Cochrane, AB T4C 1A6
Tel: 403-932-8700; *Fax:* 403-932-7219
Note: home care public health programs

***Cold Lake:* Cold Lake Community Health Services**
Affiliated with: Alberta Health Services
4720 - 55 St., Cold Lake, AB T9M 1V9
Tel: 780-594-4404; *Fax:* 780-594-2404

Anne Tucker, Supervisor

***Cold Lake:* Elizabeth Settlement Community Health Services**
Affiliated with: Alberta Health Services
4720 - 55 St., Cold Lake, AB T9M 1V8
Tel: 780-594-3383

Anne Tucker, Supervisor

***Consort:* Consort Community Health Centre**
Affiliated with: Alberta Health Services
5410 - 52 Ave., Consort, AB T0C 1B0
Tel: 403-577-3770; *Fax:* 403-577-2235
www.albertahealthservices.ca
Note: Specialties: Public health promotion & services, including nutrition services & postnatal follow-up; Education programs, including diabetes & car seat education; Immunization clinics; Alberta Aids to Daily Living Program; Home care; Respite care; Continuing care counselling & placement coordination

***Coronation:* Coronation Community Health Centre**
Affiliated with: Alberta Health Services
PO Box 338, 4909 Royal St., Coronation, AB T0C 1C0
Tel: 403-578-3803; *Fax:* 403-578-2702

Carolee Tkach

***Drayton Valley:* Drayton Valley Community Health Centre**
Affiliated with: Alberta Health Services
4110 - 50 Ave., Drayton Valley, AB T7A 0B3
Tel: 780-542-4415; *Fax:* 780-621-4998
www.dthr.ab.ca

***Drumheller:* Drumheller Health Unit**
Affiliated with: Big Country Health Unit
601 - 7 St. East, Drumheller, AB T0J 0Y5
Tel: 403-823-3341; *Fax:* 403-823-6657

***Eckville:* Eckville Community Health Centre**
Affiliated with: Alberta Health Services
PO Box 150, 5120 - 51 Ave., Eckville, AB T0M 0X0
Tel: 403-746-2201; *Fax:* 403-341-8632
Number of Beds: 20 beds
Kevin McEntee, Administrator
Ken Kissick, Maintenance

***Edmonton:* Bonnie Doon Public Health Centre**
Affiliated with: Alberta Health Services
8314 - 88 Ave. NW, Edmonton, AB T6C 1L1
Tel: 780-413-5670; *Fax:* 780-466-3110
www.capitalhealth.ca

***Edmonton:* Capital Health Home Care**
Affiliated with: Alberta Health Services
10216 - 124th St., Edmonton, AB T5N 4A3
Tel: 780-408-5465; *Fax:* 780-488-3401
www.capitalhealth.ca

Linda Killick, Director

***Edmonton:* Castle Downs Public Health Centre**
Affiliated with: Alberta Health Services
214-10807 Castle Downs Rd. NW, Edmonton, AB T5X 3N7
Tel: 780-413-5787; *Fax:* 780-413-9746
www.capitalhealth.ca

***Edmonton:* Eastwood Public Health Centre**
Affiliated with: Alberta Health Services
7919 - 118 Ave. NW, Edmonton, AB T5B 0R5
Tel: 780-413-5645; *Fax:* 780-474-5760
www.capitalhealth.ca

***Edmonton:* Mill Woods Public Health Centre**
Affiliated with: Alberta Health Services
7525 - 38 Ave. NW, Edmonton, AB T6K 3X9
Tel: 780-413-5685; *Fax:* 780-461-2504
www.capitalhealth.ca

Marianne Stewart, Sr. Operating Officer

***Edmonton:* North Central Public Health Centre**
Affiliated with: Alberta Health Services
25-9204 - 144th Ave. NW, Edmonton, AB T5E 6A3
Tel: 780-413-5600; *Fax:* 780-457-5638
www.capitalhealth.ca

***Edmonton:* Northeast Community Health Centre**
Affiliated with: Alberta Health Services
14007 - 50 St., Edmonton, AB T5A 5E4
Tel: 780-472-5000; *Fax:* 780-472-5188
Toll-Free: 866-408-5465
www.capitalhealth.ca

***Edmonton:* Twin Brooks Public Health Centre**
Affiliated with: Alberta Health Services
201-1110 - 113 St. NW, Edmonton, AB T6J 7J4
Tel: 780-413-5630; *Fax:* 780-437-6270
www.capitalhealth.ca

***Edmonton:* West Jasper Place Public Health Centre**
Affiliated with: Alberta Health Services
9720 - 182 St. NW, Edmonton, AB T5T 3T9
Tel: 780-413-5700; *Fax:* 780-484-9516
www.capitalhealth.ca

***Edmonton:* Woodcroft Public Health Centre**
Affiliated with: Alberta Health Services
13221 - 115 Ave. NW, Edmonton, AB T5M 4B7
Tel: 780-413-5720; *Fax:* 780-451-5886
www.capitalhealth.ca

***Edson:* Edson Community Health Services**
Affiliated with: Alberta Health Services
5028 - 3 Ave., Edson, AB T7E 1X4
Tel: 780-723-4421; *Fax:* 780-852-3413

Margaret Fern, CHS Supervisor

***Elk Point:* Elk Point Community Health Services**
Affiliated with: Alberta Health Services
5310 - 50 Ave., Elk Point, AB T0A 1A0
Tel: 780-724-3532; *Fax:* 780-943-2575

Joan Panteluk, Community Health Services Supervisor

***Elnora:* Elnora Community Health Centre**
Affiliated with: Alberta Health Services
PO Box 659, 425 - 8 Ave., Elnora, AB T0M 0Y0
Tel: 403-773-3636; *Fax:* 403-341-8632

***Evansburg:* Evansburg Health Centre**
Affiliated with: Alberta Health Services
5225 - 50 St., Evansburg, AB T0E 0T0
Tel: 780-727-2288; *Fax:* 780-727-2809
www.capitalhealth.ca

***Fishing Lake:* Fishing Lake Community Health Services**
Affiliated with: Alberta Health Services
General Delivery, Fishing Lake, AB T0A 3G0
Tel: 780-943-2202; *Fax:* 780-943-2575
community.dev@gishinglake.ca

Joan Panteluk, Community Health Services Supervisor

***Fort MacLeod:* Fort Macleod Community Health**
Affiliated with: Alberta Health Services
Fort Macleod Health Centre, PO Box 820, 744 - 26 St. South, Fort MacLeod, AB T0L 0Z0
Tel: 403-553-5351; *Fax:* 403-553-4567
www.albertahealthservices.ca

Note: Specialties: Community mental health services (403-553-5340); Home care services (403-553-5300); Prenatal education & immunization program (403-553-5351)

***Fort MacLeod:* Fort Macleod Health Centre**
Affiliated with: Alberta Health Services
744 - 26 St. South, Fort MacLeod, AB T0L 0Z0
Tel: 403-553-5311
www.albertahealthservices.ca

Note: Specialties: Emergency services (403-553-4487); Diagnostic imaging services (403-553-4487); Laboratory services (403-553-4487); Occupational therapy; Services to persons with developmental disabilities; Southern Alberta Renal Program (403-553-3690)

***Fort Saskatchewan:* Fort Saskatchewan Health Unit**
Affiliated with: Alberta Health Services
10420 - 98th Ave., Fort Saskatchewan, AB T8L 2N6
Tel: 780-998-3366
www.albertahealthservices.ca

Note: Specialties: Audiology service (780-992-5801); Mental health services (780-342-2388); Health for Two Program (780-342-2366); Immunization services (780-342-2366)

***Fort Vermilion:* Fort Vermilion Mental Health Clinic**
PO Box 68, Fort Vermilion, AB T0H 1N0
Tel: 780-927-3391; *Fax:* 780-927-4440

***Fox Creek:* Aspen Health Services**
PO Box 430, Fox Creek, AB T0H 1P0
Tel: 780-622-3730; *Fax:* 780-622-4169

***Gibbons:* Gibbons Health Unit**
Affiliated with: Alberta Health Services
4720 50 Ave., Gibbons, AB T0A 1N0
Tel: 780-923-3700; *Fax:* 780-923-2373
www.capitalhealth.ca

***Gift Lake:* Public Health Centre**
Affiliated with: Alberta Health Services
PO Box 60, Gift Lake, AB T0G 1B0
Tel: 780-767-2101; *Fax:* 780-767-2095

Kate Butler, Director, Health Services

***Glendon:* Glendon Community Health Clinic**
Affiliated with: Alberta Health Services
PO Box 570, Glendon, AB T0A 1P0
Tel: 780-635-3861; *Fax:* 780-635-4213

Joan Panteluk, Home Care Services Manager

***Grande Cache:* Public Health Centre/Mistahia Health Unit**
Affiliated with: Alberta Health Services
1001 Hoppe Ave., Grande Cache, AB T0E 0Y0
Tel: 780-827-3504; *Fax:* 780-827-2728

Tracy Peddy, Director, Health Services

***Grande Prairie:* College & Community Health Centre**
Affiliated with: Alberta Health Services
10620 - 104 Ave., Grande Prairie, AB T8V 8J8
Tel: 780-518-7500; *Fax:* 780-538-4400

Dr. Peter Lindsay

***Grande Prairie:* Public Health Centre**
Affiliated with: Alberta Health Services
10320 - 99 St., Grande Prairie, AB T8V 6J4
Tel: 780-513-7500; *Fax:* 780-532-1550

***Grande Prairie:* Public Health Centre**
Affiliated with: Alberta Health Services
10121 - 97 Ave., Grande Prairie, AB T8V 0N5
Tel: 780-532-4447; *Fax:* 780-864-4187

***Hanna:* Hanna Health Unit**
Affiliated with: Alberta Health Services
Former Name: Hanna Health Unit
PO Box 730, 904 Centre St. North, Hanna, AB T0J 1P0
Tel: 403-854-3331; *Fax:* 403-854-3233

***High Level:* Health Care Centre**
PO Box 2000, 10207 - 103 St., High Level, AB T0H 1Z0
Tel: 780-926-7000; *Fax:* 780-926-7001

***High Level:* Paddle Prairie Health Centre**
Affiliated with: Alberta Health Services
PO Box 46, High Level, AB T0H 2W0
Tel: 780-981-2188; *Fax:* 780-981-2190
www.capitalhealth.ca

***High Prairie:* Community Health Services**
PO Bag 1, High Prairie, AB T0G 1E0
Tel: 780-523-6450; *Fax:* 780-523-6458

***High River:* High River Public Health**
PO Box 5638, 310 Macleod Trail, High River, AB T1V 1M7
Tel: 403-652-5450; *Fax:* 403-652-5455

Lori Anderson
403/652-0142

***Hobbema:* Hobbema Community Health Clinic**
Affiliated with: Carewest Health Authority
PO Box 189, Hobbema, AB T0C 1N0
Tel: 780-585-2020; *Fax:* 780-585-3965

Helen Littlechild, Nurse in Charge

***Hughenden:* Hughenden Public Health: Home Care**
Affiliated with: Alberta Health Services
PO Box 25, 33 Mackenzie Ave., Hughenden, AB T0B 2E0
Tel: 780-753-6180; *Fax:* 780-753-2064
www.ech.ab.ca

Lana Clark

***Jasper:* Jasper Community Health Services**
Affiliated with: Alberta Health Services
529 Turret St., Jasper, AB T0E 1E0
Tel: 780-852-4759; *Fax:* 780-852-3413

Joan Connors, Supervisor

***Kinuso:* Kinuso Public Health Centre**
Affiliated with: Alberta Health Services
PO Box 208, Kinuso, AB T0G 1K0
Tel: 780-775-3501; *Fax:* 780-775-3944

Kate Butler, Director, Health Services

***Kitscoty:* Kitscoty Public Health**
Affiliated with: Alberta Health Services
PO Box 508, 4922 - 59 Ave., Kitscoty, AB T0B 2P0
Tel: 780-846-2824; *Fax:* 780-846-2731
www.ech.ab.ca

Note: community health & home care office
Randey Ferster

***La Crete:* La Crete Health Centre**
Affiliated with: Alberta Health Services
PO Box 295, 10601 - 100th Ave., La Crete, AB T0H 1H0
Tel: 780-928-3242; *Fax:* 780-928-3080

***Lac La Biche:* Buffalo Lake Settlement Health Unit**
Affiliated with: Alberta Health Services
c/o Lac La Biche Health Unit, PO Box 869, 9503 Beaverhill Rd., Lac La Biche, AB T0A 2C0
Tel: 780-689-4471; *Fax:* 780-689-2615

Tracy Smith, Supervisor

***Lac La Biche:* Community Health Services**
Affiliated with: Alberta Health Services
PO Box 297, 9503 Beaver Hill Rd., Lac La Biche, AB T0A 2C0
Tel: 780-623-4471; *Fax:* 780-623-4212

Tracy Smith, Supervisor

***Lac La Biche:* Kikino Settlement Community Health Services**
Affiliated with: Alberta Health Services
c/o Lac La Biche Health Unit, PO Box 869, 9503 Beaverhill Rd., Lac La Biche, AB T0A 2C0
Tel: 780-623-7797; *Fax:* 780-623-4212

Tracy Smith, Supervisor

***Lacombe:* Lacombe Hospital & Care Centre**
Affiliated with: Alberta Health Services
5430 - 47 Ave., Lacombe, AB T4L 1G8
Tel: 403-782-3336; *Fax:* 403-782-2818

Number of Beds: 101 beds
M. Stotz, Site Leader
Rob Grodaes, Plant Maintenance Director

***Lamont:* Lamont Public Health, Home Care**
Affiliated with: Alberta Health Services
Bag 10, 5216 - 53 St., Lamont, AB T0B 2R0
Tel: 780-895-2211; *Fax:* 780-895-2200
www.ech.ab.ca

Janet Kiist, Contact

***Leduc:* Leduc Public Health Centre**
Affiliated with: Alberta Health Services
4219 - 50 St., Leduc, AB T9E 8C9
Tel: 780-980-4644; *Fax:* 780-980-4666
www.capitalhealth.ca

***Lethbridge:* Community Health**
Affiliated with: Alberta Health Services
960 19 St. South, Lethbridge, AB T1J 0C6
Tel: 403-388-6009; *Fax:* 403-388-6011

Pam Whitnack, CEO

***Lethbridge:* Lethbridge Community Health - Lethbridge Centre Tower**
Affiliated with: Alberta Health Services
400 - 4th Ave. South, Lethbridge, AB T1J 4E1
Tel: 403-388-6009; *Fax:* 403-388-6011

Pam Whitnack, CEO

Lethbridge: **Lethbridge Community Health Site/Health Unit**
Affiliated with: Alberta Health Services
806 - 2 Ave. South, Lethbridge, AB T1J 4L5
Tel: 403-388-6666; *Fax:* 403-627-5275

Pam Whitnack, CEO
Brian Dalshary, Coordinator, Environmental Services

Magrath: **Magrath Community & Wellness Site**
Affiliated with: Alberta Health Services
PO Box 126, 135 West Civic Ave., Magrath, AB T0K 1J0
Tel: 403-388-6009; *Fax:* 403-388-6011

Pam Whitnack, CEO

Manning: **Peace Country Health Unit**
Affiliated with: Alberta Health Services
PO Box 1260, 118 - 2 Ave., Manning, AB T0H 2M0
Tel: 780-836-3391; *Fax:* 780-836-2860

Mannville: **Mannville Home Care, Public Health/Rehab**
Affiliated with: Alberta Health Services
PO Box 1000, 5007 - 46 St., Mannville, AB T0B 2W0
Tel: 780-763-3989; *Fax:* 780-736-3678
www.ech.ab.ca

Gladys Burrows
780/632-3331

Mayerthorpe: **Mayerthorpe Community Health Services**
Affiliated with: Alberta Health Services
4417 - 45 St., Mayerthorpe, AB T0E 1N0
Tel: 780-786-4198; *Fax:* 780-786-2023

Doug Kemp, Supervisor

McLennan: **Peace Country Health Unit - McLennan**
Affiliated with: Alberta Health Services
c/o Sacred Heart Community Health Centre, 350 - 3 Ave., McLennan, AB T0H 2L0
Tel: 780-324-3750; *Fax:* 780-324-4256

Medicine Hat: **Medicine Hat Community Health Services**
Affiliated with: Alberta Health Services
2948 Dunmore Rd. SE, Medicine Hat, AB T1A 8E3
Tel: 403-502-8200; *Fax:* 403-528-2250

Milk River: **Milk River/Warner Community & Wellness Site**
Affiliated with: Alberta Health Services
PO Box 90, 517 Centre Ave., Milk River, AB T0K 1M0
Tel: 403-647-3500; *Fax:* 403-627-5275

Morinville: **Morinville Public Health Centre**
Affiliated with: Alberta Health Services
Former Name: Morinville Health Services
10008 - 107 St., Morinville, AB T8R 1L3
Tel: 780-939-3388; *Fax:* 780-939-7126
www.capitalhealth.ca

Myrnam: **Myrnam Home Care**
Affiliated with: Alberta Health Services
PO Box 220, 4802 - 49 Ave., Myrnam, AB T0B 3K0
Tel: 780-366-3891; *Fax:* 780-366-3919
www.ech.ab.ca

Judy Flessau, Contact
780/632-3331

Okotoks: **Okotoks Health & Wellness Centre**
Affiliated with: Alberta Health Services
11 Cimarron Common, Okotoks, AB T1S 2E9
Tel: 403-995-2600

Peer Mikelsen, Public Health Inspector

Olds: **Olds Community Health Centre**
Affiliated with: Alberta Health Services
#103, 5030 - 50th St., Olds, AB T4H 1S1
Tel: 403-556-8441; *Fax:* 403-556-6842

Denise McBain, Vice-President, Community Health Services

Onoway: **Onoway Community Health Servics**
Affiliated with: Alberta Health Services
PO Box 1047, 4919 Lac Ste Anne Trail, Onoway, AB T0E 1V0
Tel: 780-967-4440; *Fax:* 780-967-2547

Doug Kemp, Supervisor

Oyen: **Oyen Community Health Services**
Affiliated with: Alberta Health Services
c/o Big Country Hospital, PO Box 296, 315 - 3 St. East, Oyen, AB T0J 2J0
Tel: 403-664-3651; *Fax:* 403-664-2934

Peerless Lake: **Peerless Lake Community Health Services**
Affiliated with: Alberta Health Services
PO Box 90, Peerless Lake, AB T0G 2W0
Tel: 780-869-3930; *Fax:* 780-869-2053

Cindy Harmata, Supervisor

Picture Butte: **Community Health**
Affiliated with: Alberta Health Services
301 Cowan Ave., Picture Butte, AB T0K 1V0
Tel: 403-732-4762; *Fax:* 403-627-5275

Pincher Creek: **Community Health**
Affiliated with: Alberta Health Services
1222 Bev McLachlin Dr., Pincher Creek, AB T0K 1W0
Tel: 403-388-6009; *Fax:* 403-388-6011

Pam Whitnack, CEO

Ponoka: **Ponoka Community Health Centre**
Affiliated with: Alberta Health Services
5900 Hwy. 2A, Ponoka, AB T4J 1P6
Tel: 403-783-4491; *Fax:* 403-341-8632

Denise McBain, Vice-President, Community Health Services

Provost: **Provost Public Health, Home Care**
Affiliated with: Alberta Health Services
5419 - 44 St., Provost, AB T0B 3S0
Tel: 780-753-6180; *Fax:* 780-753-2064
www.ech.ab.ca

Lana Clark

Rainbow Lake: **Rainbow Lake Health Centre**
Affiliated with: Alberta Health Services
PO Box 177, Rainbow Lake, AB T0H 2Y0
Tel: 780-956-3646; *Fax:* 780-926-3338
www.nlhr.ca

Raymond: **Community Health**
Affiliated with: Alberta Health Services
PO Box 251, 200N - 2nd St. West, Raymond, AB T0K 2S0
Tel: 403-752-3303; *Fax:* 403-752-4655

Pam Whitnack, CEO

Red Deer: **Red Deer 49th Street Community Health Centre**
Affiliated with: Alberta Health Services
4755 - 49th St., Red Deer, AB T4N 1T6
Tel: 403-314-5225
www.albertahealthservices.ca

Note: Specialties: Public health; Diabetes education (403-314-5780); Audiology (403-314-5225); Pediatric rehabilitation (403-314 5240); Speech language pathology (403-314-5250); Hanen parent program (403-314-5250)

Red Deer: **Red Deer Community Health Centre**
Affiliated with: Alberta Health Services
2845 Bremner Ave., Red Deer, AB T4R 1S2
Tel: 403-341-2100; *Fax:* 403-341-8632

John Vogelzans, President/CEO

Red Earth Creek: **Red Earth Creek Community Health Services**
Affiliated with: Alberta Health Services
PO Box 109, Red Earth Creek, AB T0G 1X0
Tel: 780-649-2242; *Fax:* 780-649-2029

Cindy Harmata

Redwater: **Redwater Health Care Centre**
Affiliated with: Alberta Health Services
4812 - 58 St., Redwater, AB T0A 2W0
Tel: 780-942-3801; *Fax:* 780-942-2024
www.capitalhealth.ca

Rimbey: **Rimbey Community Health Centre**
Affiliated with: Alberta Health Services
4709 - 51 Ave., Rimbey, AB T0C 2J0
Tel: 403-843-2288; *Fax:* 403-843-3050

Denise McBain, Administrator

Rocky Mountain House: **Rocky Mountain House Community Health Centre**
Affiliated with: Alberta Health Services
5016 - 52 Ave., Rocky Mountain House, AB T0M 1T0
Tel: 403-845-3030; *Fax:* 403-845-4975
Number of Beds: 30 continuing care beds

Sedgewick: **Sedgewick Public Health, Home Care, Rehab**
Affiliated with: Alberta Health Services
PO Box 12, 4822 - 50 St., Sedgewick, AB T0B 4C0
Tel: 780-384-3652; *Fax:* 780-608-8850
www.ech.ab.ca

Marlene Adam

Sherwood Park: **Health First Strathcona Primary Care Centre**
Affiliated with: Alberta Health Services
140 - 80 Chippewa Rd., Sherwood Park, AB T0B 4C0
Tel: 780-449-5380; *Fax:* 780-942-2373
www.capitalhealth.ca

Sherwood Park: **Strathcona County Health Centre**
Affiliated with: Alberta Health Services
2 Brower Dr., Sherwood Park, AB T8H 1V4
Tel: 780-467-5571; *Fax:* 780-449-1338

Slave Lake: **Slave Lake Community Health Services**
Affiliated with: Alberta Health Services
309 - 6 St. NE, Slave Lake, AB T0G 2A4
Tel: 780-849-3947; *Fax:* 780-805-3550

Cindy Harmata, Community Health Services Supervisor

Smoky Lake: **Smoky Lake Community Health Services**
Affiliated with: Alberta Health Services
4212 - 55 Ave., Smoky Lake, AB T0A 3C0
Tel: 780-656-3595; *Fax:* 780-943-2575

Gloria Strachan, Supervisor

Spirit River: **Public Health Centre**
Affiliated with: Alberta Health Services
Former Name: Mistahia Health Unit - Spirit River
PO Box 187, Spirit River, AB T0H 3G0
Tel: 780-864-3063; *Fax:* 780-864-4187

Karen Osborne, Director, Health Services

St Albert: **St. Albert Public Health Centre**
Affiliated with: Alberta Health Services
23 Sir Winston Churchill Ave., St Albert, AB T8N 2S7
Tel: 780-459-6671; *Fax:* 780-460-7062
www.capitalhealth.ca

St Paul: **St Paul Community Health Services**
Affiliated with: Alberta Health Services
5610 - 50 Ave., St Paul, AB T0A 3A1
Tel: 780-645-3396; *Fax:* 780-943-2575

Leanne Betts, Community Health Services Supervisor

Stettler: **Stettler Community Health Center**
Affiliated with: Alberta Health Services
5911 - 50 Ave. SS 2, Stettler, AB T0C 2L0
Tel: 403-742-3326; *Fax:* 403-641-8632
www.dthr.ab.ca

Jenn Currie, Director of Public Health

Sundre: **Sundre Community Health Centre**
Affiliated with: Alberta Health Services
212 - 6 Ave. NE, Sundre, AB T0M 1X0
Tel: 403-638-4063; *Fax:* 403-341-8632

Note: health unit
Dr. Rudy Zimmer

Swan Hills: Swan Hills Community Health Services
Affiliated with: Alberta Health Services
29 Freeman Dr., Swan Hills, AB T0G 2C0
Tel: 780-333-7077; *Fax:* 780-891-3784

Lorraine Lindberg, Supervisor

Sylvan Lake: Sylvan Lake Community Health Centre
Affiliated with: Alberta Health Services
4602 - 49 Ave, Sylvan Lake, AB T4S 1M7
Tel: 403-887-2241
www.albertahealthservices.ca
Note: Specialties: Public health services; Health promotion; Car seat education program; Child & adolescent services; Speech language pathology; Mental health services; Continuing care counselling; Environmental public health program; Breast health program; Prenatal education program; Communicable disease control; Home care; Physiotherapy; Immunization clinics; Tobacco reduction program; Respite care
Lori Sparrow, Coordinator

Taber: Community Health
Affiliated with: Alberta Health Services
5009 - 56th St., Taber, AB T1G 1M8
Tel: 403-223-4403; *Fax:* 403-627-5275

Pam Whitnack, CEO

Thorhild: Thorhild Community Health Services
Affiliated with: Alberta Health Services
302 - 2 Ave., Thorhild, AB T0A 3J0
Tel: 780-398-3879; *Fax:* 780-398-2671

Gloria Strachan, Supervisor

Thorsby: Thorsby Public Health Centre
Affiliated with: Alberta Health Services
4825 Hankin St., Thorsby, AB T0C 2P0
Tel: 780-789-4800; *Fax:* 780-789-4811
www.capitalhealth.ca

Two Hills: Two Hills Public Health, Home Care, Rehab
Affiliated with: Alberta Health Services
c/o Two Hills Health Centre, PO Box 458, 4401 - 53 Ave., Two Hills, AB T0B 4K0
Tel: 780-657-3361; *Fax:* 780-608-8850
www.ech.ab.ca

Judy Flessau, Contact
780/632-3331,

Valleyview: Valleyview Public Health Centre
Affiliated with: Alberta Health Services
Former Name: Mistahia Health Unit, Valleyview; Valleyview Distr
5112 - 50 Ave., Valleyview, AB T0H 3N0
Tel: 780-524-3338; *Fax:* 780-524-3153

Tracy Brown, Director, Health Services

Vauxhall: Vauxhall Community Care
Affiliated with: Alberta Health Services
408 - 1 Ave., Vauxhall, AB T0K 2K0
Tel: 403-388-6009; *Fax:* 403-388-6011
Note: home care office, public health office
Pam Whitnack, CEO

Vegreville: Vegreville Public Health, Home Care, Rehab
Affiliated with: Alberta Health Services
5318 - 50 St., Vegreville, AB T9C 1R1
Tel: 780-632-3331; *Fax:* 780-632-4334
www.ech.ab.ca

Bonnie Litwin, Contact

Vermilion: Vermilion Public Health, Home Care, Rehab
Affiliated with: Alberta Health Services
4701 - 52nd St., Vermilion, AB T9X 1J9
Tel: 780-853-5270; *Fax:* 780-853-7362
www.ech.ab.ca

Note: community health & home care office
Gladys Burrows

Viking: Viking Home Care/Public Health/Rehab Office
Affiliated with: Alberta Health Services
5110 - 57 Ave., Viking, AB T0B 4N0
Tel: 780-336-4782; *Fax:* 780-608-8850
www.ech.ab.ca

Hilda Tucker

Vilna: Vilna Community Health Services
Former Name: Our Lady's Health Centre
5103 Dr. Frobb Ave., Vilna, AB T0A 3L0
Tel: 780-636-3533; *Fax:* 780-943-2575

Vulcan: Vulcan Health Unit
Affiliated with: Alberta Health Services
Vulcan Community Health Centre, PO Box 214, Vulcan, AB T0L 2B0
Tel: 403-485-2285; *Fax:* 403-485-2639

Wendy Shearer, Health Services Access Coordinator

Wabasca: Wabasca/Desmarais Community Health Services
Affiliated with: Alberta Health Services
PO Box 9, Wabasca, AB T0G 2K0
Tel: 780-891-3931; *Fax:* 780-891-3011

Brenda Jenkins, Supervisor

Wainwright: Wainwright Public Health, Home Care
Affiliated with: Alberta Health Services
Public Health #22, 810 - 14 Ave., Wainwright, AB T9W 1R2
Tel: 780-842-4077; *Fax:* 780-842-3151
www.ech.ab.ca

Randey Ferster

Westlock: Westlock Community Health Services
Affiliated with: Alberta Health Services
10024 - 107 St., Westlock, AB T7P 1H7
Tel: 780-349-3316; *Fax:* 780-349-5725

Rick Saint, Community Health Services Supervisor

Wetaskiwin: Wetaskiwin Community Health Centre
Affiliated with: Alberta Health Services
5610 - 40 Ave., Wetaskiwin, AB T9A 3E4
Tel: 780-361-4333; *Fax:* 780-361-8554

Malcolm Maxwell, CEO
Lucy Beck, Coordinator, Environmental Services

Whitecourt: Whitecourt Community Health Services
Affiliated with: Alberta Health Services
20 Sunset Blvd., Whitecourt, AB T7S 1M8
Tel: 780-778-5555; *Fax:* 780-778-3852

Willingdon: Willingdon Home Care
Affiliated with: Alberta Health Services
Former Name: Mary Immaculate Hospital
5303 - 49 St., Willingdon, AB T0B 4R0
Tel: 780-367-2928; *Fax:* 780-367-2379
www.ech.ab.ca

Judy Flessau, Manager, Health Services

Winfield: Winfield Community Health Centre
Affiliated with: Alberta Health Services
Former Name: Crossroads Health Unit - Winfield
PO Box 114, Winfield, AB T0C 2X0
Tel: 780-682-4757; *Fax:* 780-682-4750

Nursing Stations

Chateh: Assumption Nursing Station
PO Box 90, Chateh, AB T0H 0S0
Tel: 780-321-3971; *Fax:* 780-321-3820
Number of Beds: 1 bed
Joanne Smith, Nurse in Charge

Fort Chipewyan: Fort Chipewyan Nursing Station
PO Box 350, Fort Chipewyan, AB T0P 1B0
Tel: 780-697-3650; *Fax:* 780-697-3565
ftchipmedical@hotmail.com

Rocky Mountain House: Rocky Mountain House
Big Horn Health Station, PO Box 1617, Rocky Mountain House, AB T4T 1A1
Tel: 403-845-3660; *Fax:* 403-845-3011

Trout Lake: Trout Lake Health Station
Affiliated with: Alberta Health Services
General Delivery, Trout Lake, AB T0G 2N0
Tel: 780-869-3922; *Fax:* 780-869-2054
www.albertahealthservices.ca
Note: Specialties: Public health services; Community care nursing; Health education; Environmental health services; Healthy Beginnings, a support program for families with new infants; Immunization; Nutrition services; Social work; Rehabilitation services

Worsley: Worsley Health Centre
Affiliated with: Alberta Health Services
General Delivery, Worsley, AB T0H 3W0
Tel: 780-685-3752; *Fax:* 780-685-2007
rmacdonald@mhr.ab.ca

Rose Mary McDonald, Nurse

Special Treatment Centres

Calgary: Carewest Dr. Vernon Fanning Extended Care Centre
Affiliated with: Alberta Health Services
722 - 16 Ave. NE, Calgary, AB T2E 6V7
Tel: 403-230-6900; *Fax:* 403-230-6902
www.carewest.org

Number of Beds: 294 beds
Mark Ewan, Director

Calgary: Tom Baker Cancer Centre (TBCC)
Affiliated with: Alberta Health Services
1331 - 29 St. NW, Calgary, AB T2N 4N2
Tel: 403-521-3723; *Fax:* 403-521-3245
Toll-Free: 866-238-3735
support@albertabreast.com (Alberta Breast Cancer Program)
www.albertahealthservices.ca
Note: Specialties: Medical oncology; Surgery (E-mail, Alberta Radiosurgery Centre: arcinfo@cancerboard.ab.ca); Radiation oncology; Radiology; Chemotherapy treatments; Psychosocial resources; Pathology; Genetics; Research
Dr. George Browman, Director

Calgary: Women's Health Centre
Affiliated with: Alberta Health Services
Former Name: Grace Women's Health Centre
1441 - 29 St. NW, Calgary, AB T2N 4JB
Tel: 403-944-2200; *Fax:* 403-944-2190
www.crha-health.ab.ca/clin/women

Patricia DeWitt, Manager

Camrose: Rosehaven Care Center (The Bethany Group)
Affiliated with: Alberta Health Services
4612 - 53 St., Camrose, AB T4V 1Y5
Tel: 780-679-2000; *Fax:* 780-679-2001
www.thebethanygroup.ca

Number of Beds: 100 beds
Note: Faith-based organization that operates a wide range of homes and services for older, disabled and vulnerable people in the Central Alberta area, serving over 1000 residents through over 600 staff members.
Marilyn Wood, Administrator

Edmonton: Cross Cancer Institute
Affiliated with: Alberta Health Services
11560 University Ave. NW, Edmonton, AB T6G 1Z2
Tel: 780-432-8771; *Fax:* 780-432-8411
www.cancerboard.ab.ca

Number of Beds: 46 beds
Note: cancer treatment
Dr. Carol Cass

Edmonton: Glenrose Rehabilitation Hospital
Affiliated with: Alberta Health Services
10230 - 111 Ave., Edmonton, AB T5G 0B7
Tel: 780-735-7999; *Fax:* 780-735-7976
ihender@cha.ab.ca
www.cha.ab.ca/glenrose

Number of Beds: 240 beds
Note: rehabilitation centre

Edmonton: McConnell Place North
9113 - 144 Ave., Edmonton, AB T5E 6K2
Tel: 780-496-2575; *Fax:* 780-472-6699

Year Founded: 1995
Number of Beds: 36 beds
Note: Specialty: Residential care for persons with Alzheimer disease; Reminiscence therapy
Nat Mitchell, Manager

***Edmonton:* Woman's Health Options**
Former Name: Morgentaler Clinic of Edmonton
12409 - 109A Ave., Edmonton, AB T5M 4A7
Tel: 780-484-1124; *Fax:* 780-489-3379
info@whol.ca
www.womanshealthoptions.com
Note: abortion clinic
Kim Cholewa, Manager

***Grande Prairie:* Grande Prairie Cancer Centre**
Affiliated with: Alberta Health Services
10409 - 98 St., Grande Prairie, AB T8V 2E8
Tel: 780-538-7588; *Fax:* 780-532-9120
Note: cancer treatment; outpatient facility
Dr. Marie Moreau, Medical Director

***Lethbridge:* Children's Centre**
Affiliated with: Alberta Health Services
#A252, 200 - 5 Ave. South, 2nd Fl., Lethbridge, AB T1J 4C7
Tel: 403-388-6009; *Fax:* 403-388-6011
Note: children's assessment, rehabilitation & education centre
Pam Whitnack, CEO

***Lethbridge:* Lethbridge Cancer Centre**
Affiliated with: Alberta Health Services
#2H209, 960 - 19th St. South, Lethbridge, AB T1J 1W5
Tel: 403-329-0633; *Fax:* 403-320-0508
Note: cancer treatment
Dr. David R. Holland, Medical Director

***Medicine Hat:* Medicine Hat Cancer Clinic**
Affiliated with: Alberta Health Services
Medicine Hat Regional Hospital, 666 - 5th St. SW, Medicine Hat, AB T1A 4H6
Tel: 403-529-8817
Year Founded: 1989
Number of Beds: 4 treatment beds + 10 treatment chairs
Note: Specialties: Colposcopy screening; Diagnostic imaging; Chemotherapy; Pain management; Counselling; Palliative treatment
Dr. Josh Foley, Director

***Peace River:* Peace River Community Cancer Centre**
PO Box Bag 400, 10101, 68 St., Peace River, AB T8S 1T6
Tel: 780-624-7500; *Fax:* 780-624-7593
jillwood@cancerboard.ab.ca
Number of Beds: 3 treatment chairs
Note: cancer treatment

***Red Deer:* Central Alberta Cancer Centre**
Affiliated with: Alberta Health Services
3942 - 50A Ave., Red Deer, AB T4N 4E7
Tel: 403-343-4526; *Fax:* 403-346-1160
Note: cancer treatment outpatient facility
Dr. Neil Graham, Director

Nursing Homes

***Athabasca:* Athabasca Extendicare**
Affiliated with: Alberta Health Services
PO Box 119, 4517 - 53 St., Athabasca, AB T9S 1K4
Tel: 780-675-2291; *Fax:* 780-675-3833
Number of Beds: 50 beds
Note: Private; affiliated with Regional Health Authority
Joan Cody, Administrator

***Barrhead:* Barrhead Continuing Care Centre**
Affiliated with: Alberta Health Services
Former Name: Keir Care Centre
5336 - 59 Ave., Barrhead, AB T7N 1L2
Tel: 780-674-4506; *Fax:* 780-674-3003
Number of Beds: 115 beds
Note: auxiliary
Susan Oleskiw, Site Supervisor

***Blairmore:* York Creek Lodge**
Affiliated with: Alberta Health Services
1810 - 112 St., Blairmore, AB T0K 0J0
Tel: 403-562-2102; *Fax:* 403-562-2106
Number of Beds: 20 beds

***Bonnyville:* Extendicare - Bonnyville**
Affiliated with: Alberta Health Services
4602 - 47 Ave., Bonnyville, AB T9N 2E8
Tel: 780-826-3341; *Fax:* 780-826-4890
www.extendicare.com
Number of Beds: 50 beds
Steve Krim, Administrator

***Calgary:* Beverly Centre - Glenmore**
Affiliated with: Alberta Health Services
1729 - 90 Ave. SW, Calgary, AB T2V 4S1
Tel: 403-253-8806; *Fax:* 403-212-3532
Number of Beds: 200 beds

***Calgary:* Bow View Manor**
Affiliated with: Alberta Health Services
4628 Montgomery Blvd. NW, Calgary, AB T3B 0K7
Tel: 403-288-4446; *Fax:* 403-288-8522
Number of Beds: 193 beds
Norma J. Jackson, Administrator

***Calgary:* Bow-Crest Health Centre**
Affiliated with: Alberta Health Services
5927 Bowness Rd. NW, Calgary, AB T3B 0C7
Tel: 403-288-2373; *Fax:* 403-288-2403
bowcrestcare@shaw.ca
Number of Beds: 150 beds
Michael Harris, Administrator

***Calgary:* Carewest George Boyack**
Affiliated with: Alberta Health Services
1203 Centre Ave. NE, Calgary, AB T2E 0A5
Tel: 403-267-2750; *Fax:* 403-267-2757
www.carewest.org
Number of Beds: 221 beds
Marg Marlin, Administrator

***Calgary:* Extendicare - Cedars Villa**
Affiliated with: Alberta Health Services
3330 - 8 Ave. SW, Calgary, AB T3C 0E7
Tel: 403-249-8915; *Fax:* 403-246-7561
Number of Beds: 248 beds
Lori Young, Administrator

***Calgary:* Extendicare - Hillcrest**
Affiliated with: Alberta Health Services
1512 - 8 Ave. NW, Calgary, AB T2N 1C1
Tel: 403-289-0236; *Fax:* 403-289-2350
Number of Beds: 112 beds
Pierre Poirier, Administrator

***Calgary:* Father Lacombe Nursing Home**
Affiliated with: Alberta Health Services
332 - 146 Ave. SE, Calgary, AB T2X 2A3
Tel: 403-256-4641; *Fax:* 403-254-6297
Number of Beds: 110 beds
Note: adult day support program offered M-F, 15 clients/day
Bill Ruckdashel, Site Pastoral Care Coordinator

***Calgary:* Forest Grove Care Centre, Ltd.**
Affiliated with: Alberta Health Services
4726 - 8 Ave. SE, Calgary, AB T2A 0A8
Tel: 403-272-9831; *Fax:* 403-248-5788
fgcc@fgcc.ab.ca
www.fgcc.ab.ca
Number of Beds: 246 beds
Jack A. King, Administrator

***Calgary:* Glamorgan Care Centre**
Affiliated with: Alberta Health Services
105 Galbraith Dr. S, Calgary, AB T3E 4Z5
Tel: 403-242-5911; *Fax:* 403-242-7613
glamorgan@shaw.ca
Number of Beds: 52 beds
Joel Bond, Administrator

***Calgary:* Intercare/Brentwood Care Centre**
Affiliated with: Alberta Health Services
2727 - 16 Ave. NW, Calgary, AB T2N 3Y6
Tel: 403-289-2576; *Fax:* 403-282-7027
Number of Beds: 120 beds
Michela Smith, Director, Care

***Calgary:* Intercare/Chinook Care Centre**
Affiliated with: Alberta Health Services
1261 Glenmore Trail SW, Calgary, AB T2V 4Y8
Tel: 403-252-0141; *Fax:* 403-253-0292
Number of Beds: 149 beds
Lorraine Nygard, Director, Care

***Calgary:* Intercare/Southwood Care Centre**
Affiliated with: Alberta Health Services
211 Heritage Dr. SE, Calgary, AB T2H 1M9
Tel: 403-252-1194; *Fax:* 403-253-0393
Number of Beds: 177 beds
Oriel Morrison, Regional Director

***Calgary:* Mayfair Nursing Home**
Affiliated with: Alberta Health Services
211 Heritage Dr. SW, Calgary, AB T2H 1M9
Tel: 403-252-1194; *Fax:* 403-253-0393
Number of Beds: 142 beds
Joel Bond, Administrator

***Calgary:* Mount Royal Care Centre**
Affiliated with: Alberta Health Services
1813 - 9 St. SW, Calgary, AB T2T 3C2
Tel: 403-244-8994; *Fax:* 403-244-5939
Number of Beds: 107 beds
Colin McMillan, Administrator

***Camrose:* Bethany Long Term Care Centre**
Affiliated with: Alberta Health Services
4501 - 47 St., Camrose, AB T4V 1H9
Tel: 780-679-1000; *Fax:* 780-679-1020
www.ech.ab.ca
Number of Beds: 130 beds; 78 supportive housing
B. Olsen, Manager, Health Support Services

***Cardston:* Chinook Lodge**
Affiliated with: Alberta Health Services
451 - 3rd St. West, Cardston, AB T0K 0K0
Tel: 403-653-4324; *Fax:* 403-653-1506
Number of Beds: 20 beds

***Cardston:* Grandview Nursing Home**
Affiliated with: Alberta Health Services
PO Box 1440, 990 Main St., Cardston, AB T0K 0K0
Tel: 403-653-4054; *Fax:* 403-627-5275
Number of Beds: 40 nursing home beds
Pam Whitnack, CEO
Ron Schow, Director, Physical Plant

***Coaldale:* Sunny South Lodge**
Affiliated with: Alberta Health Services
Green Acres Foundation Housing for Seniors, 1122 - 20 Ave., Coaldale, AB T1M 1L4
Tel: 403-345-5955
Number of Beds: 20 beds

***Edmonton:* Good Samaritan Millwoods Centre**
Mill Woods Centre, 101 Youville Dr. East NW, Edmonton, AB T6L 7A4
Tel: 780-413-3501; *Fax:* 780-963-9808
Number of Beds: 60 beds

***Fort MacLeod:* Extendicare - Fort Macleod**
Affiliated with: Alberta Health Services
654 - 29 St., Fort MacLeod, AB T0L 0Z0
Tel: 403-553-3955; *Fax:* 403-553-2812
www.extendicare.com
Number of Beds: 50 beds
Greg Guyn, Administrator

***Grande Prairie:* Grande Prairie Care Centre**
Affiliated with: Alberta Health Services
10039 - 98 St., Grande Prairie, AB T8V 2E7
Tel: 780-532-3525; *Fax:* 780-532-6504
Number of Beds: 60 beds
Dorothy Brown, Administrator; Director, Nursing

***High Prairie:* J.B. Wood Extended Care Unit**
Affiliated with: Alberta Health Services
Bag 1, High Prairie, AB T0G 1E0
Tel: 780-523-6470; *Fax:* 780-523-6642
Number of Beds: 35 beds
Ron Benson, CEO

***Lethbridge:* Columbia House - Enhanced**
Affiliated with: Alberta Health Services
785 Columbia Blvd. West, Lethbridge, AB T1K 4T8
Number of Beds: 50 beds

***Lethbridge:* Edith Cavell Care Centre**
Affiliated with: Alberta Health Services
1255 - 5 Ave. South, Lethbridge, AB T1J 0V6
Tel: 403-328-6631; *Fax:* 403-627-5275
Number of Beds: 120 beds
Marian Teierle, Administrator

***Lethbridge:* Extendicare - Lethbridge**
Affiliated with: Alberta Health Services
1821 - 13 St. North, Lethbridge, AB T1H 2V4
Tel: 403-328-6664; *Fax:* 403-328-9294
Number of Beds: 120 beds
Joyce Adachi, Administrator

***Lethbridge:* Golden Acres Lodge**
Affiliated with: Alberta Health Services
1615 - 13 St. North, Lethbridge, AB T1H 2V2
Tel: 403-328-5111; *Fax:* 403-327-8909
Number of Beds: 45 beds

***Lethbridge:* Good Sam's - Park Meadow**
Affiliated with: Alberta Health Services
1511 - 15th Ave. North, Lethbridge, AB T1H 1W2
Tel: 403-328-9404; *Fax:* 403-328-8208

Number of Beds: 40 nursing home, 44 DAL, 1 community support beds

***Lethbridge:* Good Sam's - West Highlands**
Affiliated with: Alberta Health Services
2867 Gary Dr. West, Lethbridge, AB T1J 5A3
Tel: 403-380-6275; *Fax:* 403-380-6732
Number of Beds: 10 nursing home, 60 DAL, 30 enhanced beds

***Linden:* Linden Nursing Home**
Affiliated with: Alberta Health Services
PO Box 220, Linden, AB T0M 1J0
Tel: 403-546-3966; *Fax:* 403-546-4061
http://www.dthr.ab.ca/
Number of Beds: 37 beds
Roland Toews, Administrator
Leonard Toeurs, Director, Physical Plant

***Mayerthorpe:* Mayerthorpe Extendicare**
Affiliated with: Alberta Health Services
4706 - 54 St., Mayerthorpe, AB T0E 1N0
Tel: 780-786-2211; *Fax:* 780-786-4710
Number of Beds: 50 beds
Note: private, affiliated with Regional Health Authority
Michael Belanger, Administrator

***Picture Butte:* Piyami Lodge**
Affiliated with: Green Acres Foundation
301 Rogers Ave., Picture Butte, AB T0K 1V0
Tel: 403-732-4811
info@greenacres.ab.ca
www.greenacres.ab.ca
Number of Beds: 32 rooms
Note: Independent living & enhanced care options
Linda McFalls, Manager

***Pincher Creek:* Good Sam's - Vista Villa**
Affiliated with: Alberta Health Services
1240 Ken Thornton Blvd., Pincher Creek, AB T0K 1W0
Tel: 403-627-1900; *Fax:* 403-627-3939
Number of Beds: 10 nursing home, 40 DAL, 5 community support beds

***Ponoka:* Northcott Care Centre**
Affiliated with: Alberta Health Services
4209 - 48 Ave., Ponoka, AB T4J 1P4
Tel: 403-783-4764; *Fax:* 403-341-8632
Number of Beds: 72 beds
Arthur Ulveland, Managing Director

***Red Deer:* Red Deer Nursing Home**
Affiliated with: Alberta Health Services
Bag 5030, 4736 - 30 St., Red Deer, AB T4N 5H8
Tel: 403-343-4458; *Fax:* 403-341-4988
Number of Beds: 117 beds
Chris Hume, Clinical Manager

***Spruce Grove:* Good Samaritan Spruce Grove Care Centre**
5600 - 50 St., Spruce Grove, AB T7X 3Y8
Tel: 780-962-3415; *Fax:* 780-962-3416
www.gss.org
Number of Beds: 30 beds
Alice Sears, Director, Operations

***St Paul:* Extendicare - St. Paul**
Affiliated with: Alberta Health Services
4614 - 47 Ave., St Paul, AB T0A 3A0
Tel: 780-645-3375; *Fax:* 780-645-4290
Number of Beds: 75 beds
Steve Krim, Administrator

***Stony Plain:* Good Samaitan George Henning Place**
4808 - 57 Ave., Stony Plain, AB T7Z 2J9
Tel: 780-963-3403; *Fax:* 780-963-9808
www.gss.org
Number of Beds: 30 beds
Alice Sears, Director, Operations

***Taber:* Clearview Lodge - Enhanced**
Affiliated with: Alberta Health Services
4730 - 50th Ave., Taber, AB T1G 1N6
Tel: 780-963-3403; *Fax:* 780-963-9808
Number of Beds: 20 beds

***Viking:* Extendicare - Vicking**
Affiliated with: Alberta Health Services
PO Box 430, 5020 - 57 Ave., Viking, AB T0B 4N0
Tel: 780-336-4790; *Fax:* 780-336-4004
www.ech.ab.ca
Number of Beds: 60 beds
Brant Poirier, Administrator

Long Term/Retirement Care

Long Term Care Facilities

***Airdrie:* Bethany Airdrie**
Affiliated with: Alberta Health Services
1736 - 1st Ave. NW, Airdrie, AB T4B 2C4
Tel: 403-948-6022; *Fax:* 403-912-0958
info@bethanycare.com
www.bethanycare.com
Number of Beds: 124 beds
Heath Miller, Administrator

***Bentley:* Bentley Care Centre**
Affiliated with: Alberta Health Services
4834 - 52 Ave., Bentley, AB T0C 0J0
Tel: 403-748-4115; *Fax:* 403-748-2727
www.albertahealthservices.ca
Note: Specialties: Continuing Care services; Physiotherapy; Occupational therapy; Recreational therapy; Palliative care

***Blackie:* Nanton Mountain View Estates**
PO Box 50, Blackie, AB T0L 0J0
Tel: 403-684-3805
Note: private support home

***Bon Accord:* Oak Hills Boys Ranch**
PO Box 97, Bon Accord, AB T0A 0K0
Tel: 403-921-2121; *Fax:* 403-921-2379
www.oakhillboysranch.ca
Number of Beds: 30 beds
Note: group home
Anton Smith, Executive Director

***Calgary:* Bethany Calgary**
Affiliated with: Alberta Health Services
916 - 18A St. NW, Calgary, AB T2N 1C6
Tel: 403-284-6000; *Fax:* 403-284-6085
info@bethanycare.com
www.bethanycare.com
Number of Beds: 476 beds
Note: respite care
Ian West, Administrator

***Calgary:* Bethany Harvest Hills**
Affiliated with: Alberta Health Services
19 Harvest Gold Manor NE, Calgary, AB T3K 4Y1
Tel: 403-226-8200; *Fax:* 403-226-7265
info@bethanycare.com
Number of Beds: 60 long-term care beds
Note: provides a familiar home environment for residents in middle to late stages of Alzheimer disease & related dementias
Shelagh Slater, Administrator

***Calgary:* Bow Park Court**
Affiliated with: Alberta Health Services
200 - 200 Scenic Bow Pl. NW, Calgary, AB T3L 1S5
Tel: 403-297-6539; *Fax:* 403-287-4651
Number of Beds: 24 beds
D. Grant, Manager

***Calgary:* Carewest - Cross Bow**
Affiliated with: Alberta Health Services
1011 Centre Ave. NE, Calgary, AB T2E 0A3
Tel: 403-267-2950; *Fax:* 403-267-2995
Number of Beds: 98 beds
Note: continuing care

***Calgary:* Carewest - Glenmore Park**
Affiliated with: Alberta Health Services
6909 - 14 St. SW, Calgary, AB T2V 1P8
Tel: 403-258-7650; *Fax:* 403-258-7676
Number of Beds: 147 beds
Note: continuing care

***Calgary:* Carewest - Royal Park**
Affiliated with: Alberta Health Services
4222 Sarcee Rd. SW, Calgary, AB T3E 7J8
Tel: 403-240-7475; *Fax:* 403-240-7476
Number of Beds: 50 beds

***Calgary:* Margaret House Residential Treatment Centre**
Affiliated with: Alberta Health Services
404 - 94 Ave. SE, Calgary, AB T2J 0E8
Tel: 403-253-2291; *Fax:* 403-253-6974
astc@autism.ca
www.autism.ca
Number of Beds: 20 beds
Note: group home
Dave Mikkelsen, Executive Director

***Calgary:* Salvation Army Agape Hospice**
Affiliated with: Alberta Health Services
1302 - 8 Ave. NW, Calgary, AB T2N 1B8
Tel: 403-282-6588; *Fax:* 403-284-1778
ab.salvationarmy.ca/calgary/health.html
Number of Beds: 18 beds
Note: hospice for terminally ill
David Luginbuhl, Executive Director

***Camrose:* Bethany Group**
Affiliated with: Alberta Health Services
4612 - 53 St., Camrose, AB T4V 1Y6
Tel: 780-679-2000; *Fax:* 780-679-2001
www.thebethanygrp.ca
Number of Beds: 288 beds
Marilyn Wood, Director Health Services

***Cochrane:* Bethany Cochrane**
Affiliated with: Alberta Health Services
302 Quigley Dr., Cochrane, AB T4C 1X9
Tel: 403-932-6422; *Fax:* 403-932-4617
info@bethanycare.com
www.bethanycare.com
Number of Beds: 78 long-term care, 50 residential care beds
Note: adult day support program; residential care
Barb Fredrich, Administrator

***Edmonton:* Allen Gray Continuing Care Centre**
Affiliated with: Alberta Health Services
5005 - 28 Ave. NW, Edmonton, AB T6L 7G1
Tel: 780-469-2371; *Fax:* 780-465-2073
www.capitalhealth.ca

***Edmonton:* L'Arche Association of Edmonton**
Affiliated with: Alberta Health Services
7708 - 83 St., Edmonton, AB T6C 2Y8
Tel: 780-465-0618; *Fax:* 780-465-8091
edmoffice@larcheedmonton.org
www.larcheedmonton.org
Number of Beds: 24 beds
Note: group home
Grant Kaminski, Executive Director

***Edmonton:* CapitalCare Dickinsfield**
Affiliated with: Alberta Health Services
14225 - 94 St. NW, Edmonton, AB T5E 6C6
Tel: 780-496-3300; *Fax:* 780-476-4585
www.albertahealthservices.ca; www.capitalcare.net
Year Founded: 1979
Number of Beds: 275
Note: Specialties: Continuing care; Secure units for residents with dementia; Supportive & comfort units fo residents in middle to later stages of dementia; Care for young adults who are disabled; Young adult day support program
Betty Thompson, Administrator

***Edmonton:* CapitalCare Grandview**
Affiliated with: Alberta Health Services
6215 - 124 St. NW, Edmonton, AB T6H 3V1
Tel: 780-496-7100; *Fax:* 780-496-7150
www.albertahealthservices.ca; www.capitalcare.net
Year Founded: 1973
Number of Beds: 149 beds
Note: Specialties: Continuing care for persons with dementia & who are chronically disabled; Secure unit for residents wtih dementia who are at risk of leaving the building; Supportive & comfort units for residents in middle to later stages of dementia; Orthopedic sub-acute program

***Edmonton:* CapitalCare Lynnwood**
Affiliated with: Alberta Health Services
8740 - 165 St., Edmonton, AB T5R 2R8
Tel: 780-496-2500; *Fax:* 780-484-8089
www.albertahealthservices.ca; www.capitalcare.net
Year Founded: 1966
Number of Beds: 296 beds
Note: Specialties: Continuing care; Behavioural assessment & stabilization uit; Secure unit for residents with dementia; Supportive & comfore care units for rsidents in middle to later stages of dementia; Mental health services
Iris Neumann, Administrator
Ralph Anderson, Manager, Maintenance

***Edmonton:* CapitalCare Norwood**
Affiliated with: Alberta Health Services
10410 - 111 Ave., Edmonton, AB T5G 3A2
Tel: 780-496-3200; *Fax:* 780-474-9806
www.albertahealthservices.ca; www.capitalcare.net
Year Founded: 1963
Number of Beds: 235 beds
Note: Specialties: Continuing care; Brian injury unit; Chronic

ventilator unit; Medical sub-acute program; Transition program; Palliative care

Edmonton: Devonshire Care Centre
Affiliated with: Alberta Health Services
1808 - 142 St., Edmonton, AB T6R 3H2
Tel: 780-665-8050; Fax: 780-665-8051
www.capitalhealth.ca

Edmonton: Edmonton Chinatown Care Centre
Affiliated with: Alberta Health Services
9539 - 102A Ave. NW, Edmonton, AB T5H 0G2
Tel: 780-429-0888
www.capitalhealth.ca

Edmonton: Edmonton General Continuing Care Centre
Affiliated with: Alberta Health Services
11111 Jasper Ave., Edmonton, AB T5K 0L4
Tel: 780-482-8111
www.caritas.ab.ca

Edmonton: Eric Cormack Centre
9835 - 112 St., Edmonton, AB T5K 2E7
Tel: 403-427-2764; Fax: 403-422-2815
paulette.killam@gov.ab.ca
Number of Beds: 80 beds
Note: institution
Paulette Killam, Executive Director

Edmonton: Extendicare - Holyrood
Affiliated with: Alberta Health Services
8008 - 95 Ave., Edmonton, AB T6C 2T1
Tel: 780-469-1307; Fax: 780-469-5196
www.capitalhealth.ca
Note: continuing care centre

Edmonton: Extendicare - Somerset
Affiliated with: Alberta Health Services
13210 - 114 St., Edmonton, AB T5E 5E2
Tel: 780-454-8616; Fax: 780-447-5906
www.capitalhealth.ca

Edmonton: Good Samaritan Dr. Gerald Zetter Centre
Affiliated with: Alberta Health Services
9649 - 71 Ave., Edmonton, AB T6E 5J2
Tel: 780-431-3621; Fax: 780-431-3699
qchoo@gss.org
www.gss.org

Edmonton: Good Samaritan Mount Pleasant Care Centre
Affiliated with: Alberta Health Services
10530 - 56 Ave. NW, Edmonton, AB T6H 0X7
Tel: 780-431-3600; Fax: 780-431-3949
goodsaminfo@gss.org
www.gss.org

Edmonton: Good Samaritan Southgate Care Centre
Affiliated with: Alberta Health Services
4225 - 107 St. NW, Edmonton, AB T6J 2P1
Tel: 780-431-3600; Fax: 780-431-3898
goodsaminfo@gss.org
www.gss.org

Edmonton: Hardisty Nursing Home
Affiliated with: Alberta Health Services
6420 - 101 Ave. NW, Edmonton, AB T6A 0H5
Tel: 780-466-9267; Fax: 780-450-9457
www.capitalhealth.ca

Edmonton: Kensington Village
Affiliated with: Alberta Health Services
12603 - 135 Ave., Edmonton, AB T5L 5B1
Tel: 780-447-3840; Fax: 780-482-6532
www.capitalhealth.ca

Edmonton: Kipnes Centre for Veterans
Affiliated with: Alberta Health Services
4470 McCrae Ave., Edmonton, AB T5E 6M8
Tel: 780-442-5700; Fax: 780-442-5711
www.capitalhealth.ca

Edmonton: McConnell Place West
Affiliated with: Alberta Health Services
8720 - 165 St., Edmonton, AB T5R 5Y8
Tel: 780-413-4770; Fax: 780-413-4773
www.capitalhealth.ca
Number of Beds: 36 beds
Gwenne Tweddle, Manager

Edmonton: Miller Crossing Continuing Care Services
Affiliated with: Alberta Health Services
145251 - 50 St., Edmonton, AB T5E 6M8
Tel: 780-478-9212; Fax: 780-478-2894
www.capitalhealth.ca

Edmonton: Millwoods Shepherd's Care Centre
Affiliated with: Alberta Health Services
6620 - 28th Ave. NW, Edmonton, AB T6K 2R1
Tel: 780-463-9810; Fax: 780-462-1643
www.capitalhealth.ca

Edmonton: Rosecrest Home
Affiliated with: Alberta Health Services
10205 - 134 Ave., Edmonton, AB T5E 1J2
Tel: 403-427-0927; Fax: 403-427-4408
www.capitalhealth.ca
Number of Beds: 22 beds
Note: institution
MaryAnn Sinclair, Executive Director

Edmonton: St. Joseph's Auxiliary Hospital
Affiliated with: Alberta Health Services
10707 - 29 Ave. NW, Edmonton, AB T6J 6W1
Tel: 780-430-9110; Fax: 780-430-9777
www.stjosephs.ab.ca

Edmonton: St. Michael's Long Term Care Centre
Affiliated with: Alberta Health Services
7404 - 139 Ave. NW, Edmonton, AB T5C 3H7
Tel: 780-473-5621; Fax: 780-472-4506
smeccs@smhg.ca
www.smhg.ca
Number of Beds: 153 beds
Stan C. Fisher, President; CEO

Edmonton: Salvation Army Sunset Lodge
Affiliated with: Alberta Health Services
11034 - 124 St., Edmonton, AB T5X 6C4
Tel: 780-454-5484; Fax: 780-455-7196
www.capitalhealth.ca
Number of Beds: 108 beds
Note: intermediate care
Maj. Blake Mooney, Executive Director

Edmonton: South Terrace Continuing Care Centre
Affiliated with: Alberta Health Services
5905 - 112 St. NW, Edmonton, AB T6H 3J4
Tel: 780-434-1451; Fax: 780-436-4300
www.capitalhealth.ca
Number of Beds: 134 beds
C.W. Dillane, President/CEO

Edmonton: South Terrace Continuing Care Centre
5905 - 112 St. NW, Edmonton, AB T6H 3J4
Tel: 780-434-1451; Fax: 780-436-4300
southterrace@reveraliving.com
www.reveraliving.com

Edmonton: Venta Nursing Home
Affiliated with: Alberta Health Services
Former Name: Venta Nursing Home
13525 - 102 St. NW, Edmonton, AB T5E 4K3
Tel: 780-476-6633; Fax: 780-476-6943
www.capitalhealth.ca

Edmonton: Victoria: Salvation Army Sunset Lodge
Affiliated with: Vancouver Island Health Authority
952 Arm Street, Edmonton, AB V9A 4G7
Tel: 250-385-3422; Fax: 250-385-3183
Number of Beds: 41 beds
Note: seniors' lodge with residential mental health program
Blake Mooney, Executive Director

Evansburg: Good Samaritan Pembina Village
Affiliated with: Alberta Health Services
5225 - 50 St., Evansburg, AB T0E 0T0
Tel: 780-727-4441; Fax: 780-727-2410
www.capitalhealth.ca

Fort Saskatchewan: Rivercrest Care Centre
Affiliated with: Alberta Health Services
Former Name: Rivercrest Lodge Nursing Home
10104 - 101 Ave., Fort Saskatchewan, AB T8L 2A5
Tel: 780-998-2425; Fax: 780-992-9432
www.capitalhealth.ca
Eleanor Low, Administrator

Grande Prairie: Mackenzie Place Continuing Care
Affiliated with: Alberta Health Services
10409 - 98 St., Grande Prairie, AB T8V 2E8
Tel: 780-538-7100; Fax: 780-538-1500
www.capitalhealth.ca
Number of Beds: 128 beds
Shana Hammy-Bugarin, Director, Continuing Care

Hythe: Hythe Continuing Care Centre
Affiliated with: Alberta Health Services
PO Box 100, Hythe, AB T0H 2C0
Tel: 780-356-3818; Fax: 780-356-3633
Number of Beds: 29 long-term care beds
Note: continuing care centre
Donna Turner, Director, Health Services

Islay: Islay Care Centre
Affiliated with: Alberta Health Services
PO Box 55, Islay, AB T0B 2J0
Tel: 780-744-3795; Fax: 780-608-8850
www.ech.ab.ca
Number of Beds: 12 continuing care beds, 8 assisted living
Audrey Cusack, Health Centre Coordinator

Leduc: Extendicare - Leduc
Affiliated with: Alberta Health Services
PO Box 280, 4309 - 50 St., Leduc, AB T9E 6K6
Tel: 780-986-2245; Fax: 780-986-0669
www.capitalhealth.ca

Leduc: Salem Manor Nursing Home
Affiliated with: Alberta Health Services
4419 - 46 St., Leduc, AB T9E 6L2
Tel: 780-986-8654; Fax: 780-986-4130
www.capitalhealth.ca
Bernie Pankonin, Administrator

Lethbridge: Sifton Family & Youth Services
528 Stafford Dr. North, Lethbridge, AB T1H 2B2
Tel: 403-381-5411; Fax: 403-382-4565
Number of Beds: 12 beds
Note: group home
Ross Wakelen, Director

Mannville: Mannville Care Centre
Affiliated with: Alberta Health Services
5007 - 46 St., Mannville, AB T0B 2W0
Tel: 780-763-3621; Fax: 780-608-8850
www.ech.ab.ca
Number of Beds: 23 beds
Debora Okrainetz, Nursing Manager

Medicine Hat: Dr. Dan McCharles Extended Care Centre
Affiliated with: Alberta Health Services
666 - 5 St. SW, Medicine Hat, AB T1A 4H6
Tel: 403-529-7000; Fax: 403-529-8950
Number of Beds: 42 beds
Barb Cameron, Manager, Extended/Home Care

Medicine Hat: Riverview
603 Prospect Dr. SW, Medicine Hat, AB T1A 4C2
Tel: 403-527-5531; Fax: 403-527-5175
riverview@reveraliving.com
www.reveraliving.com
Goldie Boyd, Administrator
Audrey Powers, Care Coordinator

Morinville: Aspen House
9706 - 100 Ave., Morinville, AB T8R 1T2
Tel: 780-939-7482; Fax: 780-939-6144
Number of Beds: 40 beds; 4 respite beds
Note: assisted living
Grace Regnier, Site Manager

Radway: Radway Continuing Care Centre
Affiliated with: Alberta Health Services
PO Box 70, 5002 - 52 St., Radway, AB T0A 2V0
Tel: 780-736-3740; Fax: 780-736-2353
Number of Beds: 20 permanent, 4 waiting beds

Gloria Strachan

Red Deer: Valley Park Manor
Affiliated with: Alberta Health Services
5505 - 60 Ave., Red Deer, AB T4N 4W2
Tel: 403-343-4722; *Fax:* 403-341-5938
Number of Beds: 100 beds
Note: elderly, medically frail
Candace Spurell, Vice-President

Red Deer: West Park Lodge
Affiliated with: Alberta Health Services
5715 - 41 St. Crescent, Red Deer, AB T4N 1B3
Tel: 403-343-7471; *Fax:* 403-343-3424
westparklodge@telusplanet.net
www.westparklodge.com
Number of Beds: 37 beds
Note: senior's lodge; assisted living
Evelyne Gaudet, Administrator

Sherwood Park: CapitalCare Strathcona
Affiliated with: Alberta Health Services
12 Brower Dr., Sherwood Park, AB T8H 1V3
Tel: 780-467-3366; *Fax:* 780-467-4095
www.albertahealthservices.ca; www.capitalcare.net
Year Founded: 1994
Number of Beds: 75 beds
Note: Specialties: Continuing care; Secure dementia unit; Eden Alternative philosophy of care; Recreational programs; Occupational therapy; Respite program; Adult community day support program

Sherwood Park: Sherwood Park Care Center
Affiliated with: Alberta Health Services
2020 Brentwood Blvd., Sherwood Park, AB T8A 0X1
Tel: 780-467-2281; *Fax:* 780-449-1529
admin@advhealth.org

Smoky Lake: Smoky Lake Continuing Care Centre
Affiliated with: Alberta Health Services
47607 - 52 Ave., Smoky Lake, AB T0A 3C0
Tel: 780-656-3818; *Fax:* 780-656-3010
Number of Beds: 32 beds
David Ponich, Continuing Care Centre Supervisor

St Albert: Youville Home
Affiliated with: Alberta Health Services
9 St Vital Ave., St Albert, AB T8N 1K1
Tel: 780-460-6900; *Fax:* 780-459-4139
youville@telusplanet.net
www.capitalhealth.ca

Standoff: Kainai Continuing Care Centre
PO Box 380, Standoff, AB T0L 1Y0
Tel: 403-737-3652; *Fax:* 403-737-3487
ceciliabthealth@telusplanet.net
Number of Beds: 50 beds
Note: Blood Tribe Dept. of Health
Cecilia Black Water, Director, Health Services

Stony Plain: Good Samaritan Care Centre
Affiliated with: Alberta Health Services
5600 - 50 St., Stony Plain, AB T7Z 1P8
Tel: 780-963-2261; *Fax:* 780-963-5156
goodsaminfo@gss.org
www.gss.org
Bob Taillefer, Coordinator, Environmental Services

Vegreville: Heritage Home
Affiliated with: Alberta Health Services
4570 Maple St., Vegreville, AB T9C 1X2
Tel: 780-603-0853; *Fax:* 780-603-0867
www.ech.ab.ca
Wanda White, Site Manager

Vegreville: Vegreville Care Centre
Affiliated with: Alberta Health Services
5225 - 43 St., Vegreville, AB T9C 1S1
Tel: 780-632-2871; *Fax:* 780-632-6680
www.ech.ab.ca
Number of Beds: 87 beds
Peggy Standen, Coordinator, Health Care

Youngstown: Youngstown House
PO Box 9, Youngstown, AB T0J 3P0
Tel: 403-779-3920; *Fax:* 403-779-3946
Number of Beds: 50 beds
Note: group home
Dianne Bradley, Manager

Nursing Homes

Calgary: Carewest Sarcee
Affiliated with: Alberta Health Services
3504 - 29th St. SW, Calgary, AB T3E 2L3
Tel: 403-686-8100; *Fax:* 403-686-8104
www.carewest.ca; www.albertahealthservices.ca
Note: Specialties: Comprehensive community care for seniors; Short stay rehabilitation; Long term care; Alzheimer's & dementia services; Palliative care at Sarcee Hospice, which has 15 hospice rooms

Galahad: Galahad Care Centre
Affiliated with: Alberta Health Services
PO Box 88, 1 Main St., Galahad, AB T0B 1R0
Tel: 780-583-3788; *Fax:* 780-583-2105
Note: Specialties: Continuing care; Respite care; Palliative care

Retirement Residences

Calgary: Carewest Colonel Belcher Veterans' Care Centre & Seniors' Care Residence
Affiliated with: Alberta Health Services
1939 Veterans Way NW, Calgary, AB T3B 5Y8
Tel: 403-944-7800
www.carewest.ca; www.albertahealthservices.ca
Year Founded: 2003
Number of Beds: 175 residents in seniors' residence, most of whom are veterans
Note: Specialties: Continuing care services; Care centre offering areas for persons with Alzheimer's disease & other dementias; Day support program for seniors (403-944-7852)

Mental Health Facilities

Mental Health Hospitals/Facilities

Airdrie: Airdrie Mental Health Clinic
Affiliated with: Alberta Health Services
112 - 1 Ave. NW, Airdrie, AB T4B 2B3
Tel: 403-948-3878; *Fax:* 403-948-7926
maureen.gilberg@calgaryhealthregion.ca

Athabasca: Athabasca Mental Health Clinic
Affiliated with: Alberta Health Services
3401 - 48 Ave., Athabasca, AB T9S 1M7
Tel: 780-675-5404; *Fax:* 780-675-3994

Banff: Banff Mental Health Clinic
301 Lynx St., Banff, AB T1L 1A1
Tel: 403-762-4451; *Fax:* 403-762-5570
Note: outpatient clinic

Barrhead: Barrhead Mental Health Clinic
Affiliated with: Alberta Health Services
PO Box 4054, 6203 - 49 St., Barrhead, AB T7N 1A1
Tel: 780-674-8243; *Fax:* 780-674-8352
Lorraine Lindberg

Black Diamond: Black Diamond Mental Health Clinic
Oilfields General Hospital, PO Box 1, 717 Government Road, Black Diamond, AB T0L 0H0
Tel: 403-933-3800; *Fax:* 403-933-4353
Toll-Free: 1-877-652-4700

Blairmore: Community Health
Affiliated with: Alberta Health Services
PO Box 67, 12501 - 20 Ave., Blairmore, AB T0K 0E0
Tel: 403-562-7378; *Fax:* 403-562-7379

Bonnyville: Bonnyville Mental Health Clinic
Affiliated with: Alberta Health Services
PO Box 6917, 5201 - 44 St., Bonnyville, AB T9N 2H4
Tel: 780-826-2404; *Fax:* 780-826-6114
Joan Panteluk

Bow Island: Bow Island Mental Health Clinic
Affiliated with: Alberta Health Services
802 - 6 St., Bow Island, AB T0K 0G0
Tel: 403-545-5120; *Fax:* 403-545-6357

Brooks: Brooks Community Mental Health Services
Affiliated with: Alberta Health Services
Bag 300, Brooks, AB T1R 1C5
Tel: 403-793-6655; *Fax:* 403-795-6656

Calgary: Central Calgary Mental Health Clinic
Affiliated with: Alberta Health Services
1000 - 8 Ave. SW, Calgary, AB T2P 3M7
Tel: 403-297-7311; *Fax:* 403-297-5354

Calgary: Northwest Calgary Mental Health Clinic
Affiliated with: Alberta Health Services
#280, 1620 - 29th St. NW, Calgary, AB T2N 4L7
Tel: 403-297-7345; *Fax:* 403-297-4543

Calgary: Wood's Homes (Alberta) Mental Health & Child Welfare Services
Affiliated with: Alberta Health Services
9400 - 48 Ave. NW, Calgary, AB T3B 2B2
Tel: 403-247-6751; *Fax:* 403-268-0878
jane.matheson@woodshomes.ca
www.woodshomes.ca
Number of Beds: 110 beds
Dr. Jane Matheson, CEO

Calgary: Wood's Homes Child & Adolescent Mental Health Services
Affiliated with: Alberta Health Services
805 - 37 St. NW, Calgary, AB T2N 4N8
Tel: 403-270-4102; *Fax:* 403-286-0878
kathryn.osterberg@woodshomes.ca
www.woodshomes.ca
Number of Beds: 150 beds
Note: day treatment, educational, outreach services; longterm care: permanent care (child welfare services) residential; treatment centre for adolescents & families; services for street youth, educational/day treatment services, caregiver services
Dr. Jane Matheson, CEO

Camrose: Mental Health Centre
Affiliated with: Alberta Health Services
4911 - 49 St., Camrose, AB T4V 1J9
Tel: 780-679-1764; *Fax:* 780-608-8850
www.ech.ab.ca
Brenda Nelson
780/679-1765

Canmore: Mental Health Clinic
Affiliated with: Alberta Health Services
Provincial Building, 3rd Floor, 302 - 800 Railway Ave., Canmore, AB T1W 1P1
Tel: 403-678-4696; *Fax:* 403-678-1951
www.ech.ab.ca

Cardston: Cardston Mental Health Clinic
Affiliated with: Alberta Health Services
Provincial Building, PO Box 1590, 576 Main St., Cardston, AB T0K 0K0
Tel: 403-653-5115; *Fax:* 403-653-2926

Chestermere: Chestermere Lake Mental Health Clinic
Affiliated with: Alberta Health Services
#250, 124 East Chestermere Dr., Chestermere, AB T1X 1M1
Tel: 403-207-8770; *Fax:* 403-944-2224

Claresholm: Claresholm Care Centre
Affiliated with: Alberta Health Services
PO Box 490, 139 - 43 Ave. West, Claresholm, AB T0L 0T0
Tel: 403-625-8500; *Fax:* 403-625-4318
Darrell Contes, Administrator

Claresholm: Claresholm Mental Health Clinic
PO Box 2198, 4901 - 2 St. West, Claresholm, AB T0L 0T0
Tel: 403-625-4068; *Fax:* 403-625-4177

Cochrane: Cochrane Mental Health Clinic
Affiliated with: Alberta Health Services
PO Box 807, Cochrane, AB T4C 1A9
Tel: 403-932-3455; *Fax:* 403-932-2971

Cold Lake: Cold Lake Mental Health Clinic
Affiliated with: Alberta Health Services
#208, 314 - 25th St., Cold Lake, AB T9M 1G6
Tel: 780-639-4922; *Fax:* 780-639-4990
Anne Tucker

Consort: **Consort Mental Health Clinic**
Affiliated with: Alberta Health Services
5410 - 52 Ave., Consort, AB T0C 1B0
Tel: 403-577-3770; *Fax:* 403-577-2235

Didsbury: **Didsbury Mental Health Clinic**
Affiliated with: Alberta Health Services
1210 - 20 Ave., Didsbury, AB T0M 0W0
Tel: 403-335-7285; *Fax:* 403-335-7227

Drayton Valley: **Drayton Valley Mental Health Clinic**
Affiliated with: Alberta Health Services
PO Box 7276, 5136 - 51 Ave., Drayton Valley, AB T7A 1S5
Tel: 780-542-3140; *Fax:* 780-542-4461
www.dthr.ab.ca

Edmonton: **Alberta Hospital Edmonton**
Affiliated with: Alberta Health Services
PO Box 307, 17480 Fort Rd., Edmonton, AB T5J 2J7
Tel: 780-472-5555; *Fax:* 780-472-5508
www.capitalhealth.ca
Year Founded: 1923
Number of Beds: 410 beds
Note: Provides assessment, diagnosis, treatment, education & consultation. Conducts research. Programs include: Adult Psychiatry, Geriatric Psychiatry, & the Northern Alberta Forensic Psychiatry Program.

Edmonton: **Edmonton Mental Health Clinic**
Affiliated with: Alberta Health Services
9942 - 108th St., Edmonton, AB T5K 2J5
Tel: 780-427-4444; *Fax:* 780-427-0424
www.capitalhealth.ca

Edson: **Edson Mental Health Centre**
Affiliated with: Alberta Health Services
Provincial Bldg., #100, 111 - 54 St., Edson, AB T7E 1T2
Tel: 780-723-8294; *Fax:* 780-723-8297

Margaret Fern

Fort McMurray: **Fort McMurray Mental Health Services**
Affiliated with: Alberta Health Services
7 Hospital St., Fort McMurray, AB T9H 1P2
Tel: 780-791-6194; *Fax:* 780-791-6219

Gibbons: **Gibbons Mental Health Clinic**
5018 - 50 St., Gibbons, AB T0A 1N0
Tel: 780-923-3700; *Fax:* 780-923-3939

Grande Cache: **Grande Cache Mental Health Clinic**
702 Pine Plaza, Grande Cache, AB T0E 0Y0
Tel: 780-827-4998; *Fax:* 780-827-4787
Note: community clinic

Grande Prairie: **Grande Prairie Mental Health Clinic**
#600, 10014 - 99th St., Grande Prairie, AB T8V 3N4
Tel: 780-538-5160; *Fax:* 780-538-6279

Hanna: **Hanna Mental Health Clinic**
Affiliated with: Alberta Health Services
904 Centre St. North, Hanna, AB T0J 1P0
Tel: 403-854-5276; *Fax:* 403-854-5280

Hardisty: **Hardisty Mental Health Clinic**
Affiliated with: Alberta Health Services
PO Box 269, 4531 - 47 St., Hardisty, AB T0B 1V0
Tel: 780-888-8306; *Fax:* 780-888-2427
carol.roberts@ech.ab.ca
www.ech.ab.ca

Brenda Nelson
780/679-1765

High Level: **High Level Mental Health Clinic**
Affiliated with: Alberta Health Services
PO Box 400, High Level, AB T0H 1Z0
Tel: 780-926-3791; *Fax:* 780-926-2944
www.capitalhealth.ca

High Prairie: **High Prairie Mental Health Clinic**
Affiliated with: Alberta Health Services
High Prairie Health Complex, PO Box 1, 4444 - 53 Ave., High Prairie, AB T0G 1E0
Tel: 780-926-3791; *Fax:* 780-767-6491
www.capitalhealth.ca

High River: **High River Mental Health Clinic**
PO Box 5309, 310 Macleod Trail, 2nd Floor, High River, AB T1V 1M5
Tel: 403-652-8340; *Fax:* 403-652-1456

Hinton: **Hinton Mental Health Clinic**
Affiliated with: Alberta Health Services
Former Name: Hinton Mental Health Centre
1280A Switzer Dr., Hinton, AB T7V 1T5
Tel: 780-865-8247; *Fax:* 780-865-8327

Louise Maurik

Innisfail: **Innisfail Mental Health Clinic**
Affiliated with: Alberta Health Services
5023 - 42 St., Innisfail, AB T4G 1A9
Tel: 403-227-4601; *Fax:* 403-227-5683

Jasper: **Jasper Mental Health Clinc**
Affiliated with: Alberta Health Services
PO Box 310, 518 Robson St., Jasper, AB T0E 1E0
Tel: 780-852-6616; *Fax:* 780-852-3413

Joan Connors

Killam: **Killam Mental Health Club**
Affiliated with: Alberta Health Services
4811 - 49 Ave., Killam, AB T0B 2L0
Tel: 780-385-7160; *Fax:* 780-608-8850
www.ech.ab.ca

Brenda Nelson
780-679-1765,

La Crete: **La Crete Mental Health Club**
Affiliated with: Alberta Health Services
Unit 2, 10001 - 100 Av., La Crete, AB T0H 2H0
Tel: 780-928-4215; *Fax:* 780-928-4237
www.nlhr.ca

Lac La Biche: **Lac La Biche Mental Health Clinic**
Affiliated with: Alberta Health Services
9503 Beaver Hill Rd., Lac La Biche, AB T0A 2C0
Tel: 780-623-5230; *Fax:* 780-623-5232

Tracy Smith

Leduc: **Leduc Mental Health Clinic**
Affiliated with: Alberta Health Services
4210 - 48 St., Leduc, AB T9E 5Z3
Tel: 780-986-2660; *Fax:* 780-986-9292
www.capitalhealth.ca

Lethbridge: **Lethbridge Mental Health Clinic**
200 - 5 Ave. South, Lethbridge, AB T1K 4L1
Tel: 403-381-5260; *Fax:* 403-382-4518
mhc-leth@amhb.ab.ca

Diane Conley, Administrator

Mayerthorpe: **Mayerthorpe Mental Health Clinic**
Affiliated with: Alberta Health Services
PO Box 30, 4417 - 45 St., Mayerthorpe, AB T0E 1N0
Tel: 780-786-2279; *Fax:* 780-786-2023

Doug Kemp

Medicine Hat: **Medicine Hat Mental Health Clinic**
#4, 181 Carry Dr. SE, Medicine Hat, AB T1B 3T2
Tel: 403-529-3500; *Fax:* 403-529-3562

Morinville: **Morinville Mental Health Clinic**
Affiliated with: Alberta Health Services
10008 - 107 St., Morinville, AB T8R 1L3
Tel: 780-939-3388; *Fax:* 780-939-1216
www.capitalhealth.ca

Olds: **Olds Mental Health Centre**
Affiliated with: Alberta Health Services
Olds Provincial Bldg., 5025 - 50th St., Olds, AB T4H 1R9
Tel: 403-556-4204
www.albertahealthservices.ca
Note: Specialties: Mental health services; Crisis response; Counselling; Telemental health psychiatric consultation service

Onoway: **Onoway Mental Health Clinic**
Affiliated with: Alberta Health Services
PO Box 1047, 5115 Lac Ste Anne Trail, Onoway, AB T0E 1V0
Tel: 780-967-9117; *Fax:* 780-967-2547

Doug Kemp

Oyen: **Oyen Mental Health Clinic**
Affiliated with: Alberta Health Services
312 - 3 Ave. E, Oyen, AB T0J 2J0
Tel: 403-664-3651; *Fax:* 403-664-2934

Peace River: **Peace River Mental Health Clinic**
Affiliated with: Alberta Health Services
10015 - 98 St., 3rd Floor, Peace River, AB T8S 1T4
Tel: 780-624-6151; *Fax:* 780-624-6565

Brenda Nelson

Pincher Creek: **Pincher Creek Mental Health Clinic**
PO Box 1052, 696 Kerrle Street, Pincher Creek, AB T0K 1W0
Tel: 403-627-1121; *Fax:* 403-627-1145
mhc-pinchercreek@amhb.ab.ca

Ponoka: **Ponoka Mental Health Clinic**
Affiliated with: Alberta Health Services
#223, 5110 - 49th Ave., Ponoka, AB T4J 1R6
Tel: 403-783-7903; *Fax:* 403-783-7926
dorothy.ranta@amhb.ab.ca

Provost: **Provost Mental Health Centre**
Affiliated with: Alberta Health Services
5419 - 44 St., Provost, AB T0B 3S0
Tel: 780-753-2575; *Fax:* 780-753-8096
www.ech.ab.ca

Brenda Nelson
780/679-1765,

Raymond: **Raymond Care Centre**
Affiliated with: Alberta Health Services
PO Box 260, Raymond, AB T0K 2S0
Tel: 403-752-3316; *Fax:* 403-752-4147
Number of Beds: 30 beds
Note: geriatric psychiatric facility (longterm & rehab)

Raymond: **Raymond Mental Health Clinic**
Affiliated with: Alberta Health Services
150N - 4 St. East, Raymond, AB T0K 2S0
Tel: 403-752-7960; *Fax:* 403-627-5275

Red Deer: **Red Deer Mental Health Centre**
Affiliated with: Alberta Health Services
4755 - 49 St., Red Deer, AB T4N 1T6
Tel: 403-340-5466; *Fax:* 403-340-4874

Di Uosburgh, Executive Director

Rimbey: **Rimbey Mental Health Centre**
Affiliated with: Alberta Health Services
PO Box 471, 5025 - 55 St., Rimbey, AB T0C 2J0
Tel: 403-843-2406; *Fax:* 403-843-2337

Sherwood Park: **Sherwood Park Mental Health Clinic**
Capital Health Region
2 Brower Dr., Sherwood Park, AB T8A 3Y1
Tel: 780-449-5380; *Fax:* 780-464-3705
mhcsherwoodpark@cha.ab.ca
www.capitalhealth.ca

Anita Murphy, Manager

Slave Lake: **Slave Lake Mental Health Clinic**
Affiliated with: Alberta Health Services
309 - 6 St., Slave Lake, AB T0G 2A2
Tel: 780-805-3502; *Fax:* 780-805-3550

Cindy Harmata

Smoky Lake: **Smoky Lake Mental Health Clinic**
Affiliated with: Alberta Health Services
4212 - 55 Ave., Smoky Lake, AB T0A 3C0
Tel: 780-656-3034; *Fax:* 780-656-5010

Gloria Strachan

St Albert: **St. Albert Mental Health Clinic**
Affiliated with: Alberta Health Services
Sir Winston Churchill Ave., St Albert, AB T8N 3A4
Tel: 780-459-2820; *Fax:* 780-460-7152
www.capitalhealth.ca

St Paul: **St. Paul Mental Health Clinic**
Affiliated with: Alberta Health Services
4713 - 48 Ave., St Paul, AB T0A 3A4
Tel: 780-645-1850; *Fax:* 780-645-2788

Leanne Betts

Stettler: **Stettler Mental Health Clinic**
Affiliated with: Alberta Health Services
PO Box 600, 4835 - 50 Ave. SS, Stettler, AB T0C 2L0
Tel: 403-742-7591; *Fax:* 403-742-7916

Stony Plain: **Stony Plain Mental Health Clinic**
Westview Health Centre, 4405 South Park Dr., Stony Plain, AB T7Z 1A1
Tel: 780-968-3600; *Fax:* 780-963-7186

Strathmore: **Strathmore Mental Health Clinic**
Former Name: Strathmore Mental Health Centre
Hilton Plaza, PO Box 2002, 209 - 3 St., Strathmore, AB T1P 1K2
Tel: 403-934-5174; *Fax:* 403-934-2685

Swan Hills: **Swan Hills Mental Health Clinic**
Affiliated with: Alberta Health Services
PO Box 261, 29 Freeman Dr., Swan Hills, AB T0G 2C0
Tel: 780-333-4241; *Fax:* 780-333-7009

Lorraine Lindberg

Sylvan Lake: **Sylvan Lake Mental Health Centre**
Affiliated with: Alberta Health Services
4602 - 49 Ave., Sylvan Lake, AB T4S 1M7
Tel: 403-887-2241; *Fax:* 403-887-2641

Taber: **Taber Mental Health Clinic**
5011 - 49 Ave., Taber, AB T1G 1V9
Tel: 403-223-7932; *Fax:* 403-223-7902

Three Hills: **Three Hills Mental Health Centre**
Affiliated with: Alberta Health Services
PO Box 1717, 160 - 3 Ave. South, Three Hills, AB T0M 2A0
Tel: 403-443-8532; *Fax:* 403-443-8541

Tofield: **Tofield Mental Health Clinic & Children's Resource Centre**
Affiliated with: Alberta Health Services
5024 - 51 Ave., Tofield, AB T0B 4J0
Tel: 780-662-7061; *Fax:* 780-662-3854
www.albertahealthservices.ca

Brenda Nelson

Valleyview: **Valleyview Mental Health Clinic**
Affiliated with: Alberta Health Services
PO Box 358, 4802 Highway St., Valleyview, AB T0H 3N0
Tel: 780-524-7050

Vegreville: **Vegreville Mental Health Clinic**
Affiliated with: Alberta Health Services
5318 - 50 Ave., Vegreville, AB T9C 1R1
Tel: 780-632-2714; *Fax:* 780-632-4954

Brenda Nelson
780/679-1765

Vegreville: **Vegreville Mental Health Clinic**
Affiliated with: Alberta Health Services
PO Box 90, 5318 - 50 St., Vegreville, AB T9C 1R1
Tel: 780-632-2714; *Fax:* 780-632-4954
www.ech.ab.ca

Note: 24-hour crisis line: 780-632-7070
Brenda Nelson

Vermilion: **Vermilion Mental Health Clinic**
Affiliated with: Alberta Health Services
Provincial Building, PO Box 14, 4701 - 52 St., Vermilion, AB T9X 1J9
Tel: 780-853-8168; *Fax:* 780-853-8279
www.ech.ab.ca

Brenda Nelson
780/679-1765

Wainwright: **Wainwright Mental Health Clinic**
Affiliated with: Alberta Health Services
PO Box 20, 810 - 14 Ave., Wainwright, AB T9W 1R2
Tel: 780-842-7522; *Fax:* 780-842-7520
www.ech.ab.ca

Brenda Nelson

Wetaskiwin: **Wetaskiwin Mental Health Clinic**
Affiliated with: Alberta Health Services
5201 - 50 Ave., Wetaskiwin, AB T9A 0S7
Tel: 780-361-1245; *Fax:* 780-361-1387
mhc-wetaskiwin@amhb.ab.ca

Special Care Homes

Lloydminster: **Dr. Cooke Extended Care Centre**
Affiliated with: Prairie North Health Region
3915 - 56 Ave., Lloydminster, AB T9V 0Z7
Tel: 780-871-7900; *Fax:* 780-875-3505
Number of Beds: 105 beds
Joan Zimmer, Director, Continuing Care

British Columbia

Government Departments in Charge

BRITISH COLUMBIA: Ministry of Health Services Performance Management & Improvement Division
1515 Blanshard St., 6th Fl., Victoria, BC V8W 3C8
Tel: 250-952-1297; *Fax:* 250-952-1052
www.gov.bc.ca/health

Regional Health Authorities

Kelowna: **Interior Health Authority**
Corporate Office, 220-1815 Kirschner Rd., Kelowna, BC V1Y 4N7
Tel: 250-862-4200; *Fax:* 250-862-4201
feedback@interiorhealth.ca; patient.concerns@interiorhealth.ca
www.interiorhealth.ca
Note: Facilities: 20 community health centres; 16 community hospitals; 4 service area hospitals; 2 tertiary referral hospitals. Area Served: Thompson Cariboo Shuswap Health Service Area; Okanagan Health Service Area; Kootenay Boundary Health Service Area; East Kootenay Health Service Area
Dr. Robert Halpenny, President; Chief Executive Officer
Norman Embree, Board Chair
Dr. Keith Hutchison, Chair, Health Authority Medical Advisory Committee
Donna Lommer, Chief Financial Officer & Vice-President, Residential Services
Dr. Jeremy Etherington, Vice-President, Medicine / Quality
Joanne Konnert, Vice-President, Tertiary Services
Martin McMahon, Vice-President, Planning / Strategic Services
Andrew Neuner, Vice-President, Community Integration
Brenda Rebman, Vice-President, People / Clinical Services
Cathy Renkas, Vice-President, Communications / Public Affairs
Allan Sinclair, Vice-President, Acute Services

Prince George: **Northern Health Authority**
299 Victoria St., Prince George, BC V2L 5B8
Tel: 250-565-2649; *Fax:* 250-565-2640
Toll-Free: 866-565-2999
communications@northernhealth.ca
www.northernhealth.ca
Note: Formerly Northern Interior Health Board; services administered through 3 service delivery areas: Northwest, Northeast, Northern Interior
Malcolm Maxwell, CEO

Surrey: **Fraser Health Authority**
Corporate Office, #300, 10233 - 152A St., Surrey, BC V3R 7P8
Tel: 604-587-4600; *Fax:* 604-587-4666
Toll-Free: 1-877-935-5669
feedback@fraserhealth.ca
www.fraserhealth.ca
Note: Number of Employees: 23,000 employees, 2,300 physicians, & approximately 5,000 volunteers. Population Served: 1,600,000+. Area Served: Burnaby to White Rock to Hope in British Columbia
Dr. Nigel Murray, President; Chief Executive Officer
Gordon Barefoot, Board Chair
Brian Woods, Chief Financial Officer; Vice-President, Corporate Services Integration
Philip Barker, Vice-President, Information Management
Geoffrey Crampton, Vice-President, People & Organization Development
Peter Goldthorpe, Vice-President, Capital Projects, Real Estate, & Facilities, Lo
Barbara Korabek, Vice-President, Clinical Operations
Marc Pelletier, Vice-President, Clinical Operations & Clinical Support
Dr. Andrew Webb, Vice-President, Medicine
Kathleen Butler, Director, Corporate Communications
David Plug, Director, Public Affairs

Vancouver: **Provincial Health Services Authority (PHSA)**
700 - 1380 Burrard St., Vancouver, BC V6Z 2H3
Tel: 604-675-7400; *Fax:* 604-708-2000
www.phsa.ca
Note: Manages BC Cancer Agency, BC Centre for Disease Control, BC Drug & Poison Information Centre, BC Mental Health Society (Riverview Hospital), BC Provincial Renal Agency, BC Transplant Society, BC Cardiac Program; Children's & Women's Health Centre of British Columbia, Forensic Psychiatric Services Commission
Lynda Cranston, President/CEO

Vancouver: **Vancouver Coastal Health**
Vancouver Coastal Health Corporate Office, 601 West Broadway, 11th Fl., Vancouver, BC V5Z 4C2
Tel: 604-736-2033; *Fax:* 604-736-7601
Toll-Free: 1-866-884-0888
feedback@vch.ca; pcqo@vch.ca (Patient Care Quality Office)
www.vch.ca
Note: Number of Employees: 22,000 staff; 2,500 physicians; 5,000 volunteers. Population Served: 1,000,000+. Area Served: Vancouver; Richmond; the North Shore; Coast Garibaldi; Sea-to-Sky; Sunshine Coast; Powell River; Bella Bella; Bella Coola
Kip Woodward, Board Chair
Dr. David N. Ostrow, President; Chief Executive Officer
Mary Ackenhusen, Chief Operating Officer
Duncan Campbell, Chief Financial Officer; Vice-President, Systems Development; Performance
Dr. Patricia Daly, Chief Medical Health Officer; Vice-President, Public Health
Susan Wannamaker, Chief Nursing Officer; Executive Lead, Professional Practice
Clay Adams, Vice-President, Communications & Public Affairs
Dr. Jeff Coleman, Vice-President, Regional Programs & Service Integration
Dr. Patrick O'Connor, Vice-President, Medicine, Quality, & Safety
Maureen Whyte, Vice-President, Strategic Community Initiatives
Gavin Wilson, Director, Public Affairs
604-708-5312, gavin.wilson@vch.ca

Victoria: **Vancouver Island Health Authority**
1952 Bay St., Victoria, BC V8R 1J8
Tel: 250-370-8000; *Fax:* 250-370-8750
Toll-Free: 877-370-8699
info@viha.ca
www.viha.ca
Number of Beds: 1307 acute care; 4593 residential, VIHA & contracted beds
Note: Formerly Capital Health Region
Howard Waldner, President; CEO

Hospitals

Hospitals - General

Alert Bay: **Cormorant Island Health Centre**
Affiliated with: Vancouver Island Health Authority
PO Box 223, 49 School Rd., Alert Bay, BC V0N 1A0
Tel: 250-974-5585; *Fax:* 250-974-5422
info@viha.ca
www.viha.ca
Number of Beds: 10 multi-purpose beds
Note: Hospital Specialties: Emergency services; Acute care; Medical imaging; General laboratory services (250-974-5585, ext. 3); Adult mental health & addiction services; Care to adults with developmental or physical disabilities; Public health services; Rural health services (250-755-6281)
Dr. Richard Stanwick, Chief Medical Health Officer, Vancouver Island Health Authority

***Ashcroft:* Ashcroft & District General Hospital**
Affiliated with: Interior Health Authority
700 Ash-Cache Creek Hwy., Ashcroft, BC V0K 1A0
Tel: 250-453-2211; *Fax:* 250-453-9685
www.interiorhealth.ca
Year Founded: 1970
Number of Beds: Number of beds: 24

***Bella Bella:* R.W. Large Memorial Hospital**
Affiliated with: Vancouver Coastal Health Authority
88 Waglisla St., Bella Bella, BC V0T 1Z0
Tel: 250-957-2314; *Fax:* 250-957-2612
feedback@vch.ca
www.vch.ca/EN/find_locations/find_locations/?&site_id=2136
Number of Beds: 16 beds
Note: Provincial hospital offering ltc/acute care, pharmacy, diagnostic imaging services, telehealth services
Dr. David N. Ostrow, President; CEO, VCH

***Bella Coola:* Bella Coola General Hospital (BCGH)**
PO Box 434, 1025 Elcho St., Bella Coola, BC V0T 1C0
Tel: 250-799-5311; *Fax:* 250-799-5635
feedback@vch.ca
www.vch.ca
Number of Beds: 10 acute care beds; 5 extended care beds
Note: Hospital Specialties: Emergency services; Walk-in clinic; Laboratory services; Acute care; Long term care; Mental health services; Public health; Physiotherapy; Home support
Michel Bazille, Administrator, Health Services
250-799-5308, ext. 2
Lorinda Andersen, Director, Patient Care
250-799-5311, ext. 2, lorinda.andersen@vch.ca

***Burnaby:* Burnaby Hospital**
Affiliated with: Fraser Health Authority
3935 Kincaid St., Burnaby, BC V5G 2X6
Tel: 604-412-6131; *Fax:* 604-412-6190
www.fraserhealth.ca
Number of Beds: 309 acute care beds
Note: Hospital Specialties: Emergency services; Diagnostic testing; General surgery; Perinatal services; Neonatal intensive care; Oncology; Mental health services; Critical care; Palliative care
Arden Krystal, Executive Director

***Campbell River:* Campbell River & District Regional Hospital**
Affiliated with: Vancouver Island Health Authority
Also Known As: Campbell River General Hospital
375 - 2nd Ave., Campbell River, BC V9W 3V1
Tel: 250-850-2141; *Fax:* 250-286-9675
www.viha.ca
Note: Hospital Specialties: Emergency care; Surgical services: Intensive care; Cardiac care; Laboratory services; Acute care; Rehabilitation services (250-286-7045); Aboriginal health; Diabetes education (250-850-2607); Nutrition services (250-286-7013)
Dr. Richard Crow, Executive Vice-President; Chief Medical Officer, Vancouver Island Health Authority
Sandy Murphy, Nurse, Aboriginal Health
250-850-2602, sandy.murphy@viha.ca

***Chetwynd:* Chetwynd Hospital & Health Centre**
Affiliated with: Northern Health Authority
PO Box 507, 5500 Hospital Rd., Chetwynd, BC V0C 1J0
Tel: 250-788-2236; *Fax:* 250-788-7247
hello@northernhealth.ca
www2.northernhealth.ca
Note: Hospital Specialty: Acute care
Betty McCracken Morris, Chief Operating Officer, Northeast Health Service Delivery Area

***Chilliwack:* Chilliwack General Hospital**
Affiliated with: Fraser Health Authority
45600 Menholm Rd., Chilliwack, BC V2P 1P7
Tel: 604-795-4141; *Fax:* 604-795-4110
feedback@fraserhealth.ca
www.fraserhealth.ca
Note: Hospital Specialties: Emergency services; Laboratory services; Ambulatory care; Rehabilitation services
Dr. Andrew Webb, Vice-President, Medicine, Fraser Health

***Clearwater:* Dr. Helmcken Memorial Hospital (DHM)**
Affiliated with: Interior Health Authority
640 Park Dr., RR#1, Clearwater, BC V0E 1N0
Tel: 250-674-2244; *Fax:* 250-674-2477
www.interiorhealth.ca
Number of Beds: 6 beds
Note: Hospital Specialties: Community hospital level 1 services; Emergency services; Acute care; Physiotherapy; Recreation therapy; Dietician services; Public health; Environmental health protection services; Home care nursing
Nicole Lacroix, Coordinator, Recreation Therapy
Nicole.Lacroix@interiorhealth.ca

***Comox:* St. Joseph's General Hospital**
Affiliated with: Vancouver Island Health Authority
2137 Comox Ave., Comox, BC V9M 1P2
Tel: 250-339-2242; *Fax:* 250-339-1432
www.sjghcomox.ca
Year Founded: 1913
Number of Beds: 235 beds (110 in acute care and 125 in complex care)
Note: A comprehensive health facility with services in emergency, colposcopy, dermatology, diabetes, diagnostic imaging (mammography, radiology, ultrasound), extended care, general surgery, gastroenterology, internal medicine, maternity, obstetrics/gynaecology, oncology, ophthalmology, orthopaedics, paediatrics, palliative care, pathology, psychiatry and urology
Michael Pontus, President /CEO
250-339-1409
Dr. Stefan Schovanek, President, Medical Staff

***Cranbrook:* East Kootenay Regional Hospital (EKRH)**
Affiliated with: Interior Health Authority
13 - 24th Ave. North, Cranbrook, BC V1C 3H9
Tel: 250-426-5281; *Fax:* 250-426-5285
Toll-Free: 866-288-8082
www.interiorhealth.ca
Note: Hospital Specialties: Emergency services; Laboratory services; Diagnostic imaging; General surgery; Intensive care unit; Obstetrics; Pediatrics; Oncology (250-417-6228); Ophthalmology; Orthopedics; Urology; Otolaryncology; Rehabilitation services; Psychiatry
Dr. Jeremy Etherington, Vice-President, Medicine / Quality, Interior Health
Allan Sinclair, Vice-President, Acute Services, Interior Health
Kate Fox, Coordinator, Volunteers, East Kootenay Regional Hospital
250-417-2746, katefox@shaw.ca

***Creston:* Creston Valley Hospital (CVH)**
Affiliated with: Interior Health Authority
PO Box 3000, 312 - 15th Ave. North, Creston, BC V0B 1G0
Tel: 250-428-2286; *Fax:* 250-428-4860
www.interiorhealth.ca
Number of Beds: 16 beds
Note: Hospital Specialties: Emergency services; Trauma care; Diagnostic imaging; Laboratory services; Acute care; Ambulatory care; Obstetrics; Pediatrics; Rehabilitation services, including occupational therapy & physiotherapy; Mental health services; Diabetes education; Dietitian services; Outpatient renal dialysis unit; Chronic disease management; Adult day care; Number of Employees: 150
Cindy Kozak-Campbell, Interior Health Authority Health Services Administrator, Creston
Dr. Atma Persad, Chief of Staff
Deryn Collier, Coordinator, Recruitment

***Dawson Creek:* Dawson Creek & District Hospital**
Affiliated with: Northern Health Authority
11100 - 13th St., Dawson Creek, BC V1G 3W8
Tel: 250-782-8501; *Fax:* 250-783-7301
hello@northernhealth.ca
www2.northernhealth.ca
Number of Beds: 62 acute care beds
Note: Hospital Specialties: Emergency services (250-784-7393); Diagnostic imaging; Laboratory services; General surgery; Intensive care unit; Acute care; Maternity services; Rehabilitation services, including physiotherapy, occupational, & respiratory therapy; Adult psychiatry inpatient unit (250-784-7369); Diabetes education
Cathy Ulrich, Chief Executive Officer, Northern Health
Betty McCracken Morris, Chief Operating Officer, Northern Health Northeast Health Service Delivery A

***Delta:* Delta Hospital**
Affiliated with: Fraser Health Authority
5800 Mountain View Blvd., Delta, BC V4K 3V6
Tel: 604-946-1121; *Fax:* 604-538-3320
feedback@fraserhealth.ca
www.fraserhealth.ca
Note: Hospital Specialties: Emergency services; General surgery; Ambulatory care; Cardiac services; Occupational therapy; Physiotherapy; Respiratory therapy; Speech language pathology services; Diabetes education; Asthma education; Nutrition counselling; Social work; Palliative care
Arden Krystal, Vice-President, Clinical Operations, Fraser Health
Dr. Andrew Webb, Vice-President, Medicine, Fraser Health
Andrew.Webb@fraserhealth.ca

***Duncan:* Cowichan District Hospital (CDH)**
Affiliated with: Vancouver Island Health Authority
3045 Gibbins Rd., Duncan, BC V9L 1E5
Tel: 250-737-2030; *Fax:* 250-715-1212
www.viha.ca
Number of Beds: 95 beds
Note: Hospital Specialties: Emergency services; Laboratory services; Medical imaging: Intensive care unit; Acute care; Maternity; Rehabilitation services; Adult mental health & addiction services; Breast Health Hereditary Cancer Program; Hemodialysis; Occupational therapy & physiotherapy (250-709-3000); Nutrition services (250-370-8111); Respiratory ambulatory service; Palliative care
Dr. Richard Crow, Chief Medical Officer; Executive Vice-President, Vancouver Island Health Authority
Catherine Mackay, Chief Operating Officer; Executive Vice President, Vancouver Island Health Authority
Gerry Giles, Chair, Cowichan Valley Regional Hospital District
Jim Potts, Manager, CDH Pharmacy

***Fernie:* Elk Valley Hospital**
Affiliated with: Interior Health Authority
PO Box 670, 1501 - 5th Ave., Fernie, BC V0B 1M0
Tel: 250-423-4453; *Fax:* 250-423-3732
www.interiorhealth.ca
Number of Beds: 20 beds
Note: Hospital Specialties: Emergency services; Diagnostic imaging; Laboratory services; Ambulatory care; Acute care; Obstetrics; Pediatrics; Occupational therapy; Physiotherapy; Mental health services; Dietitian services; Pain management education; Public health; Home support services. Number of Employees: 100

***Fort Nelson:* Fort Nelson Hospital**
Affiliated with: Northern Health Authority
PO Box 60, 5315 Liard Street, Fort Nelson, BC V0C 1R0
Tel: 250-774-8100; *Fax:* 250-774-8110
hello@northernhealth.ca
www2.northernhealth.ca
Note: Hospital Specialties: Emergency care; Intensive care; Medical imaging; Addictions counselling services (250-565-2649); Adult day centre (250-565-7451); Diabetes education (250-774-6916)
Betty McCracken Morris, Chief Operating Officer, Northern Health, Northeast Health Service Delivery

***Fort St James:* Stuart Lake Hospital**
Affiliated with: Northern Health Authority
PO Box 1060, 600 Stuart Dr. East, Fort St James, BC V0J 1P0
Tel: 250-996-8201; *Fax:* 250-996-8777
hello@northernhealth.ca
www2.northernhealth.ca/Contact_Us/Northern_Interior/FraserLakeandVanderhoofcontacts.asp
Number of Beds: 12 beds (6 acute care, 6 long-term care beds)
Note: Services include emergency, laboratory and x-ray facilities.
Ms. Cathy Ulrich, CEO, NHA
250-565-2649
Mr. Michael McMillan, COO, Northern Interior, NHA
Ms. Bruna Schnepf., Director, Patient Care
250-567-2211

***Fort St John:* Fort St. John Hospital & Health Centre**
Affiliated with: Northern Health Authority
9636 - 100th Ave., Fort St John, BC V1J 1Y3
Tel: 250-262-5200; *Fax:* 250-262-5294
www2.northernhealth.ca
Number of Beds: 44 beds
Note: Hospital Specialties: Diagnostics; Surgery; Intensive care; Acute care; Maternity services; Rehabilitation; Hemo dialysis; Palliative care
Betty McCracken Morris, Chief Operating Officer, Northern Health, Northeast Health Service Delivery

***Golden:* Golden & District General Hospital**
Affiliated with: Interior Health Authority
835 - 9th St. North RR 2, Golden, BC V0A 1H2
Tel: 250-344-5271; *Fax:* 250-344-2511
Number of Beds: 8 beds
Tish Smith

***Grand Forks:* Boundary Hospital**
Affiliated with: Interior Health Authority
7649 - 22nd St., Grand Forks, BC V0H 1H2
Tel: 250-443-2100; *Fax:* 250-442-8331
www.interiorhealth.ca
Number of Beds: 12 acute care beds
Note: Hospital specialties: Emergency services; Laboratory services; Radiology; Acute care; Chemotherapy; Renal dialysis; Ambulatory care

Louise Fitzgerald, Social Worker
250-443-2162, Louise.Fitzgerald@interiorhealth.ca

Hazelton: Wrinch Memorial Hospital
Affiliated with: Northern Health Authority
#999, 2510 Highway 62, Hazelton, BC V0J 1Y0
Tel: 250-842-5339; *Fax:* 250-842-5685

Hope: Fraser Canyon Hospital
Affiliated with: Fraser Health Authority
1275 - 7th Ave., Hope, BC V0X 1L4
Tel: 604-869-5656; *Fax:* 604-860-7732
feedback@fraserhealth.ca
www.fraserhealth.ca
Note: Hospital Specialties: Emergency services; Diagnostic laboratory services (604-860-7702); Acute care; Social work; Nutrition counselling; Palliative care (604-860-7713)

Invermere: Invermere & District Hospital
Affiliated with: Interior Health Authority
850 - 10th Ave., Invermere, BC V0A 1K0
Tel: 250-342-9201; *Fax:* 250-342-6303
Number of Beds: 8 acute care, 35 residential beds
Colleen Wagner, Contact
250-342-9201 ext. 24

Kamloops: Royal Inland Hospital
Affiliated with: Interior Health Authority
311 Columbia St., Kamloops, BC V2C 2T1
Tel: 250-374-5111; *Fax:* 250-314-2333
Toll-Free: 877-288-5688
patient.concerns@interiorhealth.ca
www.interiorhealth.ca/health-services.aspx?id=284
Number of Beds: 226 beds
Note: Tertiary acute care hospital; angiography/interventional radiology, bone density, CT scan, mammography, MRI, nuclear medicine, ultrasound, X-Ray
Dr. Robert Halpenny, President/CEO, IHA
Donna Lommer, CFO, IHA, Medical Services

Kelowna: Kelowna General Hospital
Affiliated with: Interior Health Authority
2268 Pandosy St., Kelowna, BC V1Y 1T2
Tel: 250-862-4000; *Fax:* 250-862-4201
www.interiorhealth.ca
Number of Beds: 329 beds
Rick Riley, COO
Dave Macintosh, Director, Purchasing Services

Kitimat: Kitimat General Hospital & Health Centre
Affiliated with: Northern Health Authority
920 Lahakas Blvd. South, Kitimat, BC V8C 2S3
Tel: 250-632-2121; *Fax:* 250-632-8726
Number of Beds: 54 beds

Ladysmith: Ladysmith & District General Hospital
Affiliated with: Vancouver Island Health Authority
1111 - 4 Ave., Ladysmith, BC V0R 2E0
Tel: 250-739-5777; *Fax:* 250-245-3238
Number of Beds: 42 beds
Chuck Rowe, CEO

Langley: Langley Memorial Hospital
Affiliated with: Fraser Health Authority
Former Name: Langley Health Services
22051 Fraser Hwy., Langley, BC V3A 4H4
Tel: 604-534-4121; *Fax:* 604-534-8283
Number of Beds: 166 acute care beds, 230 residential care beds
Leanne Heppill, Executive Director
Harry Berglund, Director of Purchasing

Lillooet: Lillooet District Hospital & Community Health Programs
Affiliated with: Interior Health Authority
951 Murray St., Lillooet, BC V0K 1V0
Tel: 250-256-4233; *Fax:* 250-256-1336
Number of Beds: 6 beds
Jennifer Thur

MacKenzie: MacKenzie & District Hospital
Affiliated with: Northern Health Authority
45 Centennial Dr., MacKenzie, BC V0J 2C0
Tel: 250-997-3263; *Fax:* 250-997-3940
Number of Beds: 5 beds
Raelene Shea, Exec. Dir.

Maple Ridge: Ridge Meadows Hospital
Affiliated with: Fraser Health Authority
Former Name: Ridge Meadows Hospice Society
PO Box 5000, 11666 Laity St., Maple Ridge, BC V2X 7G5
Tel: 604-463-4111; *Fax:* 604-463-1888
feedback@fraserhealth.ca
www.fraserhealth.ca/find_us/locations/our_locations?site_id=178 7
Number of Beds: 104 acute care, 150 residential care beds, 20-bed psychiatric care unit
Dr. Nigel Murray, President/CEO, FHA
Dr. Greg Kotylak, Head, Surgery
Valerie Spurrell, Director, Acute Care

McBride: McBride & District Hospital
Affiliated with: Northern Health Authority
1126, 5th Ave., McBride, BC V0J 2E0
Tel: 250-569-2251; *Fax:* 250-569-3369
Number of Beds: 16 beds
Vic Chicoine, Administrator

Merritt: Nicola Valley General Hospital
Affiliated with: Interior Health Authority
3451 Voght St., Merritt, BC V1K 1C6
Tel: 250-378-3271; *Fax:* 250-378-3287
Number of Beds: 8 beds
Doug Sage

Mission: Mission Memorial Hospital
Affiliated with: Fraser Health Authority
7324 Hurd St., Mission, BC V2V 3H5
Tel: 604-826-6261; *Fax:* 604-826-9513
Number of Beds: 20 acute care, 75 residential care beds
Vivian Giglio, Executive Director, Health Services

Nakusp: Arrow Lakes Hospital
Affiliated with: Interior Health Authority
97 East 1st Ave., Nakusp, BC V0G 1R0
Tel: 250-265-3622; *Fax:* 250-265-4435
www.interiorhealth.ca
Number of Beds: 6 acute inpatient beds; 14 residential beds (Minto House residential unit)
Note: Hospital Specialties: Emergency services; Acute care; Public health; Physiotherapy; Occupational therapy; Home care; Mental health services; Palliative care Number of Employees: 50

Nanaimo: Nanaimo Regional General Hospital
Affiliated with: Vancouver Island Health Authority
1200 Dufferin Cres., Nanaimo, BC V9S 2B7
Tel: 250-754-2141; *Fax:* 250-755-7633
Number of Beds: 329 beds
Allison Cutler, Executive Director, Medicine, Chronic Disease Management/Primary Health

Nelson: Kootenay Lake Hospital
Affiliated with: Interior Health Authority
3 View St., Nelson, BC V1L 2V1
Tel: 250-352-3111; *Fax:* 250-354-2320
Toll-Free: 866-352-3111
www.interiorhealth.ca
Number of Beds: 30 beds
Dorothy Wayling, Site Director

New Denver: Slocan Community Health Centre
Affiliated with: Interior Health Authority
401 Galena Ave., New Denver, BC V0G 1S0
Tel: 250-358-7911; *Fax:* 250-358-7117
www.interiorhealth.ca/health-services.aspx?id=350&terms=sloca n
Number of Beds: 30 beds
Note: Primary, long-term care faciltiy with services including emergency, mental health services, occupational therapy, physiotherapy, podiatry, respiratory therapy, X-ray & ECG
Dr. Robert Halpenny, CEO, IHA
Ms. Ann Weir, Health Centre Manager
Fax: 250-358-7801, ann.weir@interiorhealth.ca

North Vancouver: Lions Gate Hospital
Affiliated with: Vancouver Coastal Health Authority
231 - 15 St. East, North Vancouver, BC V7L 2L7
Tel: 604-988-3131; *Fax:* 604-984-5838
www.vch.ca
Number of Beds: 268 beds
Ellen Pekeles, COO

Oliver: South Okanagan General Hospital
Affiliated with: Interior Health Authority
7139 - 362nd Ave., Oliver, BC V0H 1T0
Tel: 250-498-5000; *Fax:* 250-498-5004
www.interiorhealth.ca/health-services.aspx?id=11846
Number of Beds: 18 beds
Note: A level 1, community hospital with services including emergency, radiology, acute care, outpatient ambulatory care
Dr. Robert Halpenny, President/CEO, IHA
Mr. Allan Sinclair, Vice-President, Acute Services, IHA
Ms. Mary Doughtery, Patient Care Quality Officer, South Okanagan
250-862-4300, mary.dougherty@interiorhealth.ca

Penticton: Penticton Regional Hospital
Affiliated with: Interior Health Authority
550B Carmi Ave., Penticton, BC V2A 3G6
Tel: 250-492-4000; *Fax:* 250-492-9068
Number of Beds: 148 beds
Lorraine Ferguson

Port Alberni: West Coast General Hospital
Affiliated with: Vancouver Island Health Authority
3949 Port Alberni Hwy., Port Alberni, BC V9Y 7L1
Tel: 250-723-2135; *Fax:* 250-723-8805
Number of Beds: 43 acute care, 32 extended care beds
Jim Latham, Director, Physical Plant

Port Alice: Port Alice Hospital
Affiliated with: Vancouver Island Health Authority
1090 Marine Dr., Port Alice, BC V0N 2N0
Tel: 250-284-3555; *Fax:* 250-284-6163
pahospital@capescott.net
Number of Beds: 3 beds
Jean Wheeler, Manager

Port Hardy: Port Hardy Hospital
Affiliated with: Vancouver Island Health Authority
9120 Granville, Port Hardy, BC V0N 2P0
Tel: 250-949-6161; *Fax:* 250-949-7000
phhospital@capescott.net
Number of Beds: 17 beds
Ron Benson, CEO

Port McNeill: Port McNeill & District Hospital
Affiliated with: Vancouver Island Health Authority
2750 Kingcome Place, Port McNeill, BC V0N 2R0
Tel: 250-956-4461; *Fax:* 250-956-4823
pmhosp@island.net
Number of Beds: 10 beds

Port Moody: Eagle Ridge Hospital (ERH)
Affiliated with: Fraser Health Authority
475 Guildford Way, Port Moody, BC V3H 3W9
Tel: 604-461-2022; *Fax:* 604-461-9972
feedback@fraserhealth.ca
www.fraserhealth.ca
Year Founded: 1984
Note: Hospital Specialties: Emergency services; General surgery unit; Acute care; Ambulatory care; Cardiac care; Medical oncology unit; Rehabilitation services, including physiotherapy & occupational therapy; Respiratory therapy; Diabetes education; Asthma education; Nutrition counselling; Palliative care
Arden Krystal, Vice-President, Clinical Operations
Dr. Andrew Webb, Vice-President, Medicine, Fraser Health

Powell River: Powell River General Hospital
Affiliated with: Vancouver Coastal Health Authority
5000 Joyce Ave., Powell River, BC V8A 5R3
Tel: 604-485-3211; *Fax:* 604-485-3245
Number of Beds: 33 beds
Jerry Causier, Manager, Acute Services

Prince George: Prince George Regional Hospital
Affiliated with: Northern Health Authority
1475 Edmonton St., Prince George, BC V2M 1S2
Tel: 250-565-2000; *Fax:* 250-565-2343
Number of Beds: 338 beds
Ginger Brown, Executive Director
Adrian Van Peenen, Director, Physical Plant

Prince Rupert: Prince Rupert Regional Hospital
Affiliated with: Northern Health Authority
1305 Summit Ave., Prince Rupert, BC V8J 2A6
Tel: 250-624-2171; *Fax:* 250-624-2195
Number of Beds: 71 beds

Princeton: Princeton General Hospital
Affiliated with: Interior Health Authority
98 Ridgewood Ave., Princeton, BC V0X 1W0
Tel: 250-295-3233; *Fax:* 250-295-3344
mharkness@oshr.org
Number of Beds: 6 acute care beds
Marilyn Harkness, Administrator
Alex Smith, Head, Plant Maintenance

***Queen Charlotte:* Queen Charlotte Islands General Hospital**
Queen Charlotte City Site
Affiliated with: Northern Health Authority
PO Box 9, 3203 3rd Ave., Queen Charlotte, BC V0T 1S0
Tel: 250-559-4300; *Fax:* 250-559-4312
chcexec@qcislands.net
Number of Beds: 21 beds
George Cheyne, CEO

***Quesnel:* GR Baker Memorial Hospital**
Affiliated with: Northern Health Authority
543 Front St., Quesnel, BC V2J 2K7
Tel: 250-985-5600; *Fax:* 250-992-5652
www2.northernhealth.ca
Year Founded: 1955
Number of Beds: 38 beds
Note: Hospital Specialties: Emergency services; Intensive care; Crisis stabilization; Acute care; Maternity services; Occupational therapy; Physiotherapy
Michael McMillan, Chief Operating Officer, Northern Health, Northern Interior Health Service D

***Revelstoke:* Queen Victoria Hospital & Health Centre**
Affiliated with: Interior Health Authority
1200 Newlands Rd., Revelstoke, BC V0E 2S0
Tel: 250-837-2131; *Fax:* 250-837-4788
www.interiorhealth.ca
Number of Beds: 38 beds
Dorothy Schiller
Andrew Neuner
Ron Hawkins, Maintenance Supervisor

***Richmond:* Richmond Hospital**
Affiliated with: Vancouver Coastal Health Authority
Former Name: The Richmond Hospital
7000 Westminster Hwy., Richmond, BC V6X 1A2
Tel: 604-278-9711; *Fax:* 604-244-5191
feedback@vch.ca
www.vch.ca/find_locations/find_locations/?&site_id=135
Number of Beds: 175 beds
Note: Emergency, ambulatory care, diagnostics, intensive care and coronary care, maternity, psychiatry and surgery
Dr. David N. Ostrow, President/CEO, VCH
Duncan Adams, Vice-President, Communications & Public Affairs, VCH

***Saanichton:* Saanich Peninsula Hospital**
Affiliated with: Vancouver Island Health Authority
2166 Mount Newton Cross Rd., Saanichton, BC V8M 2B2
Tel: 250-544-7676; *Fax:* 250-652-7521
www.viha.ca/finding_care/facilities/saanich_peninsula_hospital.htm
Number of Beds: 48 acute beds, 144 extended care beds
Note: Emergency, breast surgical oncology, imaging - bone mineral densitometry, CT scan; 10-bed palliative care unit; acute & extended care
Howard Waldner, President; CEO, VIHA
William Boomer, Vice-President; CFO, VIHA
Catherine Mackay, Executive Vice-President; COO, VIHA

***Salmon Arm:* Shuswap Lake General Hospital**
Affiliated with: Interior Health Authority
601 - 10th St. NE, Salmon Arm, BC V1E 4N6
Tel: 250-833-3600; *Fax:* 250-833-3611
Toll-Free: 877-299-1599
lab.interiorhealth.ca/site_gi.aspx?id=32
Number of Beds: 40 beds
Note: Emergency, acute care beds, diagnostic imaging, radiology, obstetrical care
Dr. Robert Halpenny, CEO, IHA
Dr. Warren Bell, President, Medical Staff

***Salt Spring Island:* The Lady Minto Gulf Islands Hospital**
Affiliated with: Vancouver Island Health Authority
Former Name: Lady Minto Hospital
135 Crofton Rd., Salt Spring Island, BC V8K 1T1
Tel: 250-538-4800; *Fax:* 250-538-4870
www.viha.ca/finding_care/facilities/lady_minto_gulf_islands_hospital.htm
Number of Beds: 50 beds (19 acute care, 31 extended care beds)
Note: Services include emergency, laboratory, diagnostic imaging (fluoroscope, ultrasound, x-rays), breast oncology, surgery
Mr. Howard Waldner, President/CEO, VIHA
250-370-8692
Mr. Bill Boomer, Vice-President/CFO, VIHA
250-370-8602
Ms. Shannon Marshall, Communications Officer, VIHA
250-370-8270, shannon.marshall@viha.ca
Mr. Bill Relph, Site Manager

***Sechelt:* St. Mary's Hospital**
Affiliated with: Vancouver Coastal Health Authority
5544 Sunshine Coast Highway, Sechelt, BC V0N 3A0
Tel: 604-885-2224; *Fax:* 604-885-8628
feedback@vch.ca
www.vch.ca/EN/find_locations/find_locations/?&site_id=152
Number of Beds: 31 beds
Note: Services include emergency, tomography, fluoroscopy, mammography, renal program (dialysis units), ultrasound, laboratory, radiology, youth clinic.
Dr. David N. Ostrow, President/CEO, VCHA
Mr. Duncan Campbell, CFO/Vice-President, Systems Devlopment, VCHA
Ms. Trudi Beutel, Public Affairs Officer, VCHA
604 -08-5282, trudi.beutel@vch.ca

***Smithers:* Bulkley Valley District Hospital**
Affiliated with: Northern Health Authority
PO Box 370, 3950 - 8th Ave., Smithers, BC V0J 2N0
Tel: 250-847-2611; *Fax:* 250-847-2446
www.northernhealth.ca
Number of Beds: 25 beds
Note: Hospital Specialties: Emergency services; Medical imaging; Acute care; Maternity services; Long term care; Palliative care

***Sparwood:* Sparwood General Hospital & Health Care Centre**
Affiliated with: Interior Health Authority
PO Box 9, 570 Pine Ave., Sparwood, BC V0B 2G0
Tel: 250-425-6212; *Fax:* 250-425-2313
www.interiorhealth.ca/health-services.aspx?id=352
Note: A primary health care centre with services including emergency, medical clinic, on-site lab & x-ray, dialysis, wellness centre focusing on diabetic, cardiac and respiratory education, as well as nutrition counselling and pain management counselling
Dr. Robert Halpenny, President/CEO, IHA
Dr. Jeremy Etherington, Vice-President, Medicine/Quality, IHA
Ms. Donna Lommer, CFO/Vice-President, Residential Services, IHA

***Squamish:* Squamish General Hospital**
Affiliated with: Vancouver Coastal Health Authority
38140 Behrner Dr., Squamish, BC V0N 3G0
Tel: 604-892-5211; *Fax:* 604-892-9417
feedback@vch.ca
www.vch.ca/EN/find_locations/find_locations/?&site_id=150
Number of Beds: 21 beds
Note: Services include emergency, general medicine and surgery, obstetrics, palliative care, physiotherapy, pharmacy, diagnostic imaging, laboratory, ambulatory care, chemotherapy, fluoroscopy, diabetic day clinic, residential care
Dr. David N. Ostrow, President/CEO, VCHA
Mr. Duncan Campbell, CFO/Vice-President, Systems Development, VCHA
Ms. Tina Hua, Manager, Acute Services, VCHA

***Stewart:* Stewart Health Centre**
Affiliated with: Northern Health Authority
PO Box 8, 904 Brightwell St., Stewart, BC V0T 1W0
Tel: 250-636-2221; *Fax:* 250-636-2715
www2.northernhealth.ca/Contact_Us/Northwest/Stewartcontacts.asp
Number of Beds: 3 beds
Note: Services include acute care, home support, physicians, counseling services, pharmacy, visiting specialists, mammography, ambulance services.
Ms. Cathy Ulrich, CEO, NHA
Mr. Shawn Terlson, CFO, NHA
Ms. Marina Ellinson, COO, Northwest, NHA
Dr. Ronald Chapman, Chief Medical Health Officer, NHA
Dr. Suzanne Johnston, Chief Nursing Officer, NHA

***Summerland:* Summerland Memorial Health Centre**
Affiliated with: Interior Health Authority
Former Name: Summerland General Hospital
Also Known As: Summerland Health Centre
PO Box 869, 12815 Atkinson Rd., Summerland, BC V0H 1Z0
Tel: 250-404-8000; *Fax:* 250-404-8005
www.interiorhealth.ca/health-services.aspx?id=268
Year Founded: 1967
Number of Beds: 50 beds
Note: A community health and residential care facility with services including surgery (cataract, ear, nose & throat, and dental), occupational therapy, physical therapy, laboratory services, x-ray, home support, social work, diabetes education, long-term case management.
Dr. Robert Halpenny, President/CEO, IHA
Ms. Cathy Renkas, Vice-President, Communications/Public Affairs, IHA
Mr. Bob Heise, Community Health Services Administrator

***Surrey:* Matsqui-Sumas-Abbotsford General Hospital**
Affiliated with: Fraser Health Authority
10334, 152A Street, Surrey, BC V3R 7P8
Tel: 604-587-4600; *Fax:* 604-587-4666
Number of Beds: 202 beds
Vivian Giglio, Executive Director
Ed Towndow, Supervisor, Building Services/Environmental Dept.
Jeri Lynch, Purchasing Agent

***Surrey:* Surrey Memorial Hospital**
Affiliated with: Fraser Health Authority
13750 - 96 Ave., Surrey, BC V3V 1Z2
Tel: 604-581-2211; *Fax:* 604-588-3320
feedback@fraserhealth.ca
www.fraserhealth.ca/find_us/locations/our_locations?site_id=1792
Number of Beds: 450 acute care, 186 residential care beds
Note: A comprehensive health centre with services including emergency, adolescent psychiatry, angiography, antepartum care, asthma education, diagnostic imaging (CT scans, bone densitometry, fluoroscopy, mammography, MRI, radiology, ultrasound), cardiology, outpatient speech language pathology, dental surgery, drug and alcohol resource team, hospice palliative care, intensive care, neonatal intensive care, ophthalmology, otolaryngology, paediatric oncology, pharmacy, plastic surgery, postpartum care, psychiatry, respiratory therapy, STI/HIV clinic, sexual assault, sleep lab, social work, speech language pathology, spiritual care, urological surgery, vascular and thoracic surgery, youth wellness centre.
Dr. Nigel Murray, President/CEO, FHA
Dr. Andrew Webb, Vice-President, Medicine, FHA
Ms. Loretta Solomon, Site Executive Director
Loretta.Solomon@fraserhealth.ca
Dr. Urbain Ip, Site Medical Director

***Terrace:* Mills Memorial Hospital**
Affiliated with: Northern Health Authority
4720 Haugland Ave., Terrace, BC V8G 2W7
Tel: 250-635-2211; *Fax:* 250-635-7639
cholly.boland@northernhealth.ca
Number of Beds: 52 beds
Cholly Boland, Health Services Administrator

***Tofino:* Tofino General Hospital**
Affiliated with: Vancouver Island Health Authority
PO Box 190, 261 Neill St., Tofino, BC V0R 2Z0
Tel: 250-725-3212; *Fax:* 250-725-3150
info@viha.ca
www.viha.ca/finding_care/facilities/tofino_general_hospital.htm
Year Founded: 1954
Number of Beds: 10 beds
Note: Services include emergency, echocardiography, laboratory, mental health, physiotherapy, radiology
Mr. Howard Waldner, President/CEO, VIHA
250-370-8692
Mr. Brian Jackson, Director, Rural Health Services, VIHA
Ms. Kathryn Kilpatrick, Site Manager
Ms. Monica E. MacDonald, Site Administrative Assistant
250-725.3204, monica.macdonald@viha.ca

***Trail:* Kootenay Boundary Regional Hospital**
Affiliated with: Interior Health Authority
Former Name: Trail Regional Hospital
1200 Hospital Bench, Trail, BC V1R 4M1
Tel: 250-368-3311; *Fax:* 250-364-3422
Toll-Free: 866-368-2314
info@kbrh.ca
www.kbrh.ca
Number of Beds: 75 beds
Lynn Johnstone

***Vancouver:* Children's & Women's Health Centre of British Columbia**
BC Children's Hospital
Affiliated with: Provincial Health Services Authority
4500 Oak St., Vancouver, BC V6H 3N1
Tel: 604-875-2345; *Fax:* 604-875-5381
www.bcwomens.ca
Sharon Toohey, President

***Vancouver:* Children's & Women's Heatlh Centre of British Columbia**
BC Children's Hospital
Affiliated with: Provincial Health Services Authority
4480 Oak St., Vancouver, BC V6H 3V4
Tel: 604-875-2345; *Fax:* 604-875-5381
www.bcchildrens.ca
Sharon Toohey, President

***Vancouver:* Providence Health Care**
Holy Family Hospital
Affiliated with: Vancouver Coastal Health Authority
7801 Argyle St., Vancouver, BC V5P 3L6
Tel: 604-321-2661; *Fax:* 604-321-6886
www.providencehealthcare.org
Number of Beds: 218 beds
Note: Rehabilitation
Dianne Doyle, President; CEO

***Vancouver:* Providence Health Care**
Mount Saint Joseph Hospital
Affiliated with: Vancouver Coastal Health Authority
3080 Prince Edward St., Vancouver, BC V5T 3N4
Tel: 604-874-1141; *Fax:* 604-877-8125
www.providencehealthcare.org
Number of Beds: 208 beds
Dianne Doyle, President; CEO

***Vancouver:* Providence Health Care**
St. Paul's Hospital
Affiliated with: Vancouver Coastal Health Authority
1081 Burrard St., Vancouver, BC V6Z 1Y6
Tel: 604-682-2344; *Fax:* 604-684-6532
Number of Beds: 520 acute care beds
Dianne Doyle, President; CEO

***Vancouver:* UBC Hospital**
Affiliated with: Vancouver Coastal Health Authority
Also Known As: UBC Health Sciences Centre Hospital
2211 Westbrook Mall, Vancouver, BC V6T 2B5
Tel: 604-822-7121; *Fax:* 604-822-7268
feedback@vch.ca
www.vch.ca/EN/find_locations/find_locations/?&site_id=164
Year Founded: 1968
Number of Beds: 191 beds
Note: Divided into 3 buildings, the Detwiller Pavilion is known for its psychiatric unit, the Purdy Pavilion offers operational stress injury clinic, MRI, movement disorder clinic, residential care, while the Koerner Pavilion offers acute neurology, Alzheimer clinic, angiography, bladder care, brain research, breast reconstruction, CT scans, fluoroscopy, Huntington disease clinic, laboratory, multiple sclerosis clinic, nuclear medicine, nutrition counselling, radiology, sleep disorders program, speech language pathology, spirometry, surgical clinic, ultrasound, urgent care centre.
Dr. David N. Ostrow, President/CEO, VCHA
Ms. Anne Sutherland Boal, COO, Vancouver Acute, VCHA
Dr. Susan Stromberg, Medical Director, Urgent Care Centre, UBC
Ms. Tiffany Akins, Regional Communications Leader, VCHA
604-319-7530

***Vancouver:* Vancouver General Hospital**
Affiliated with: Vancouver Coastal Health Authority
855 West 12th Avenue, Vancouver, BC V5Z 1M9
Tel: 604-875-4111; *Fax:* 604-875-4035
http://www.vanhosp.bc.ca/
Number of Beds: 583 beds
Susan Wannamaker, Senior Operating Officer
C. Roach, Manager, Physical Plant
Maggie Sinclair, Waste Management, Physical Plant

***Vanderhoof:* St. John Hospital**
Affiliated with: Northern Health Authority
3255 Hospital Rd., Vanderhoof, BC V0J 3A0
Tel: 250-567-2211; *Fax:* 250-567-9713
hello@northernhealth.ca
www.northernhealth.ca
Year Founded: 1941
Number of Beds: 24 acute care
Note: Services include emergency, labor & delivery, diagnostic imaging (X-ray, ultrasound), orthopedic surgery, general surgeries, physiotherapy, visiting specialists
Ms. Cathy Ulrich, CEO, NHA
Mr. Michael McMillan, COO, Northern Interior Region, NHA

***Vernon:* Vernon Jubilee Hospital**
Affiliated with: Interior Health Authority
2101 - 32 St. South, Vernon, BC V1T 5L2
Tel: 250-558-1200; *Fax:* 250-545-0369
Number of Beds: 123 beds
Peter Dutoit
R. Lediet, Manager, Physical Plant

***Victoria:* Glengarry Extended Care Hospital**
Affiliated with: Vancouver Island Health Authority
1780 Fairfield Rd., Victoria, BC V8S 1G7
Tel: 250-595-4321; *Fax:* 250-370-5727
Number of Beds: 212 beds
Carrie Peter, Coordinator, Volunteer Resources

***Victoria:* Mount Tolmie Extended Care Hospital**
Affiliated with: Vancouver Island Health Authority
3690 Richmond Rd., Victoria, BC V8P 4R6
Tel: 250-370-5626; *Fax:* 250-370-5755
Number of Beds: 75 beds
Note: extended care hospital

***Victoria:* Priory Hospital**
Affiliated with: Vancouver Island Health Authority
567 Goldstream Ave., Victoria, BC V9B 2W4
Tel: 250-370-5626; *Fax:* 250-370-5779
Number of Beds: 75 beds
Note: extended care hospital

***Victoria:* Queen Alexandra Centre for Children's Health**
Affiliated with: Vancouver Island Health Authority
2400 Arbutus Rd., Victoria, BC V8N 1V7
Tel: 250-519-5390; *Fax:* 250-721-6837
Number of Beds: 20 beds
Note: acute & extended care

***Victoria:* Royal Jubilee Hospital**
Affiliated with: Vancouver Island Health Authority
1952 Bay St., Victoria, BC V8R 1J8
Tel: 250-370-8000; *Fax:* 250-370-8804
info@viha.ca
www.viha.ca/finding_care/facilities/royal_jubilee_hospital.htm
Number of Beds: 425 beds
Note: Acute care, cystic fibrosis clinic, rehabilitation services, breast physiotherapy, breast surgical oncology. Located in Memorial Pavilion.
Howard Waldner, President/CEO, VIHA
Catherine Mackay, Executive Vice-President/COO, VIHA
Shannon Marshall, Media Contact, Communications, VIHA
250-370-8270

***Victoria:* Victoria General Hospital**
Affiliated with: Vancouver Island Health Authority
1 Hospital Way, Victoria, BC V8Z 6R5
Tel: 250-727-4212; *Fax:* 250-727-4106
Number of Beds: 349 including 50 paeds
Note: acute care

***White Rock:* Peace Arch Hospital**
Affiliated with: Fraser Health Authority
15521 Russell Ave., White Rock, BC V4B 2R4
Tel: 604-531-5512; *Fax:* 604-531-0726
www.peacearchhospital.com
Number of Beds: 475 acute care, 300 residential care beds
Jackie Smith, Executive Director

***Williams Lake:* Cariboo Memorial Hospital**
Affiliated with: Interior Health Authority
517 North 6th Ave., Williams Lake, BC V2G 2G8
Tel: 250-392-4411; *Fax:* 250-392-2157
www.interiorhealth.ca
Note: Hospital Specialties: Emergency services: Diagnostic imaging; Laboratory services (250-392-8215); Ambulatory care; Acute care; Obstetrics
Deb Runge, Site Manager
Deborah.Runge@interiorhealth.ca

Federal Hospitals

***Abbotsford:* Pacific Institution / Regional Treatment Centre**
Correctional Services Canada, Dept. of the Solicitor General
Former Name: Regional Health Centre (Pacific)
Also Known As: Pacific Institution
PO Box 3000, 33344 King Rd., Abbotsford, BC V2S 4P4
Tel: 604-870-7700; *Fax:* 604-870-7746
www.csc-scc.gc.ca/text/facilit/institutprofiles/pacific-eng.shtml
Year Founded: 1972
Number of Beds: 122 beds
Note: Psychiatric care unit, health centre, rehabilitation unit, regional reception/assessment centre and intensive program unit; a mens' facility
Dr. Zender Katz, Executive Director

Private Hospitals

***Abbotsford:* Menno Hospital**
Affiliated with: Fraser Health Authority
32945 Marshall Rd., Abbotsford, BC V2S 1K1
Tel: 604-859-7631; *Fax:* 604-859-6931
www.mennoplace.ca
Number of Beds: 150 beds
Robert V. Turnbull, Chief Operating Officer
Chris Dean, Director, Environmental Services

***Burnaby:* Willingdon Park Hospital**
Affiliated with: Fraser Health Authority
Former Name: Willingdon Private Hospital
4435 Grange St., Burnaby, BC V5H 1P4
Tel: 604-433-2455; *Fax:* 604-433-5804
Number of Beds: 95 beds
Arnold Bennewith, Administrator
Joy Lee, Superintendent

***Coquitlam:* Como Lake Private Hospital & Nursing Home**
657 Gatensbury St., Coquitlam, BC V3J 5G9
Tel: 604-939-9277; *Fax:* 604-939-6518
Number of Beds: 95 beds
Note: Specialties: Complex health care & personal assistance in a residential setting; Adult day program

***Coquitlam:* Lakeshore Care Centre**
Affiliated with: Fraser Health Authority
657 Gatensbury St., Coquitlam, BC V3J 5G9
Tel: 604-939-9277; *Fax:* 604-939-6518
Number of Beds: 95 beds
Lynn Aarvold, Administrator

***Kelowna:* Still Waters Private Hospital**
1450 Sutherland Ave., Kelowna, BC V1Y 5Y5
Tel: 250-860-2216; *Fax:* 250-860-3655
Number of Beds: 79 beds
Note: A long-term care home for seniors and the disabled. Rooms are rented and geared to income. Licensed care included. Other services include 24-hr. emergency response, laundry, housekeeping. There is a fulltime resident manager.
David Kornell, Executive Director

***Langley:* Simpson Manor**
Affiliated with: Fraser Health Authority
Former Name: Simpsons Private Hospital
PO Box 40, 8838 Glover Rd., Langley, BC V1M 2R4
Tel: 604-888-0711; *Fax:* 604-888-1218
inquiries@simpsonmanor.ca
www.simpsonmanor.ca
Note: Long-term care for seniors, permanent and semi-premament residency; adult day program, 9-5 pm weekdays; a 2-storey facility with 42 resident rooms per floor, mostly single occupancy, and 18 double rooms
Ms. Debbie Eglsaer, Director, Resident Care
Director@SimpsonManor.ca
Mr. Ingo Riesen, Administrator
604-888-4699, Administrator@SimpsonManor.ca

***Maple Ridge:* Holyrood Manor**
Affiliated with: Fraser Health Authority
22710 Holyrood Ave., Maple Ridge, BC V2X 3E6
Tel: 604-467-8831; *Fax:* 604-467-8262
holyrood@reveraliving.com
Number of Beds: 123 beds
Ann MacMillan, Administrator

***North Vancouver:* North Shore Private Hospital & Lynn Valley Care Centre**
1070 Lynn Valley Rd., North Vancouver, BC V7J 1Z8
Tel: 604-988-4181; *Fax:* 604-988-0814
gailwilson@nsph.ca
www.lynnvalleycare.com
Number of Beds: 142 beds
Dr. Mehdi Sherkat, Administrator

***Vancouver:* Amherst Private Hospital & Nursing Home**
375 West 59th Ave., Vancouver, BC V5X 1X3
Tel: 604-321-6777; *Fax:* 604-322-0123
Year Founded: 1964
Number of Beds: 74 beds
Note: Hospital Specialties: Complex care

***Vancouver:* Point Grey Private Hospital**
2423 Cornwall Ave., Vancouver, BC V6K 1B9
Tel: 604-733-7133; *Fax:* 604-733-8298
pghosp@telus.net
Number of Beds: 52 beds
Maureen McIntosh, Administrator

***Victoria:* Wayside House**
Christian Science Care Facility
Affiliated with: Vancouver Island Health Authority
550 Foul Bay Rd., Victoria, BC V8S 4H1
Tel: 250-598-4521; *Fax:* 250-598-4547
inquiries@waysidehousevictoria.org
Number of Beds: 9 beds
Susan Waterman, Administrator

Auxiliary Hospitals

***100 Mile House:* 100 Mile District General Hospital**
Affiliated with: Interior Health Authority
South Cariboo Health Centre, PO Box 399, 555 Cedar Ave. South, 100 Mile House, BC V0K 2E0
Tel: 250-395-7600; *Fax:* 250-395-7578
www.interiorhealth.ca
Note: Hospital Specialties: Maternity; Diagnostic imaging; Physiotherapy; MMental health; Public health; Diabetic education; Adult day service; Home support
Gayle Dunsmuir, Contact, Hospice
gayle.hospice@shawbiz.ca
Wendy Reilly, Contact, Residential Care
Wendy.Reilly@interiorhealth.ca

***Vancouver:* BC Children's Hospital**
Affiliated with: Provincial Health Services Authority
Former Name: Crippled Children's Hospital; Children's Hospital
4480 Oak St., Vancouver, BC V6H 3N1
Tel: 604-875-2000; *Toll-Free:* 888-300-3088
comm@cw.bc.ca
www.bcchildrens.ca
Year Founded: 1928
Note: Hospital Specialties: Emergency services; Ambulatory care; Pediatric surgery; Specialized pediatric health services; Intensive & trauma care; Specialized programs for children with congenital or acquired heart disease; Oncology; Kidney transplants; Bone marrow transplants; Cochlear implant service; Medical genetics program; Mental health services for children & youth; Assessment & diagnosis for children with complex developmental behavioural conditions; Healthy Buddies, a child-centred health promotion program; Centre for Healthy Weights; Safe Start, an injury prevention program; Research; Child health information (Family Resource Library)
Larry Gold, President

***Vancouver:* BC Women's Hospital & Health Centre**
Affiliated with: Provincial Health Services Authority
4500 Oak St., Vancouver, BC V6H 3N1
Tel: 604-875-2424; *Toll-Free:* 1-888-300-3088
comm@cw.bc.ca (Communications)
www.bcwomens.ca
Note: Hospital Specialties: Health care for women, newborn, & families; Gynecological & reproductive health services; Sexual assault service; HIV care of women & children; Birth control & abortion support & counselling; Substance dependency; Psychology; Social work; Aboriginal Health Program; Osteoporois
Dr. Jan Christilaw, President

***Victoria:* Aberdeen Hospital**
Affiliated with: Vancouver Island Health Authority
1450 Hillside Ave., Victoria, BC V8T 2B7
Tel: 250-370-5626; *Fax:* 250-370-5612
www.viha.ca
Note: Hospital Specialty: Extended care for the elderly & young adults with neurological challenges
Helene Driscoll, Coordinator, Therapy / Seniors Health

Community Health Centres

Community Health Care Centres

***Alexis Creek:* Alexis Creek Health Centre**
Affiliated with: Interior Health Authority
2591 Morton St., Alexis Creek, BC V0L 1A0
Tel: 250-394-4313; *Fax:* 250-964-5179

***Armstrong:* Pleasant Valley Health Centre**
Affiliated with: Interior Health Authority
3800 Patten Dr., Armstrong, BC V0E 1B2
Tel: 250-546-4720; *Fax:* 250-546-9821
Number of Beds: 40 beds
Peter DuToit

***Barriere:* Barriere & District Health Centre**
Affiliated with: Interior Health Authority
PO Box 659, 537 Barriere Town Rd., Barriere, BC V0E 1M0
Tel: 250-672-9731; *Fax:* 250-672-5144
Linda Basran

***Castlegar:* Castlegar & District Community Health Centre**
Affiliated with: Interior Health Authority
709 - 10th St., Castlegar, BC V1N 2H7
Tel: 250-365-7711; *Fax:* 250-365-1236
www.interiorhealth.ca
Note: Specialties: Ambulatory care; Family medicine; Laboratory services

***Chase:* Chase Health Centre**
Affiliated with: Interior Health Authority
825 Thompson Ave., Chase, BC V0E 1M0
Tel: 250-679-3312; *Fax:* 250-679-5329
Bonnie Lee

***Chemainus:* Chemainus Health Centre**
Affiliated with: Vancouver Island Health Authority
PO Box 499, 9909 Esplanade St., Chemainus, BC V0R 1K0
Tel: 250-246-3291; *Fax:* 250-246-3844
Number of Beds: 75 beds
Note: diagnostic & treatment centre, multilevel care facility
Joan Roberts, Director

***Cumberland:* Cumberland Health Care Centre**
Affiliated with: Vancouver Island Health Authority
PO Box 400, 2696 Windermere Ave., Cumberland, BC V0R 1S0
Tel: 250-336-8531; *Fax:* 250-336-2100
Number of Beds: 75 beds
Don Brown, CEO

***Elkford:* Elkford Health Centre**
Affiliated with: Interior Health Authority
PO Box 640, 212 Alpine Way, Elkford, BC V0B 1H0
Tel: 250-865-2247; *Fax:* 250-865-2797
Number of Beds: 4 beds
Wendy Timmerman, Site Manager

***Fort Smith:* Fort Smith Public Health Unit**
Affiliated with: Fort Smith Health & Social Services Authority
PO Box 1080, Fort Smith, BC Z0E 0P0
Tel: 867-872-6203; *Fax:* 867-872-6260

***Fraser Lake:* Fraser Lake Community Health Centre**
Affiliated with: Northern Health Authority
130 Chowsunket St., Fraser Lake, BC V0J 1S0
Tel: 250-699-7742; *Fax:* 250-699-6987
Kay Scott, CEO

***Gold River:* Gold River Health Clinic**
Affiliated with: Vancouver Island Health Authority
601 Trumpeter Dr., Gold River, BC V0P 1G0
Tel: 250-283-2626; *Fax:* 250-283-7561
Enid O'Hara, Area Director of Rural Services, Campbell River/Nootka/Comac Valley

***Hudson's Hope:* Hudson's Hope Gething Diagnostic & Treatment Centre**
Affiliated with: Northern Health Authority
PO Box 599, 10309 Kyllo St., Hudson's Hope, BC V0C 1V0
Tel: 250-783-9991; *Fax:* 250-783-9125
Number of Beds: 2 emergency beds
Andrew Neuner, CEO
Susan Mochoruk, Nurse Manager

***Kaslo:* Victorian Community Health Centre of Kaslo**
Affiliated with: Interior Health Authority
Former Name: Victoria Hospital of Kaslo
673 A Ave., Kaslo, BC V0G 1M0
Tel: 250-353-2291; *Fax:* 250-353-2738
Number of Beds: 20 beds
Christie Heuston, Site Director

***Logan Lake:* Logan Lake Primary Health Care Organization**
Affiliated with: Interior Health Authority
Former Name: Logan Lake Health Centre
5 Beryl Ave., Logan Lake, BC V0K 1W0
Tel: 250-523-9414; *Fax:* 250-523-6869
Number of Beds: 4 beds
Marsha Wilson, Care Coordinator

***Lytton:* St. Bartholomew's Health & Healing Centre**
Affiliated with: Interior Health Authority
PO Box 1089, Lytton, BC V0K 1Z0
Tel: 250-455-2221; *Fax:* 250-455-6621
Jennifer Thur, Manager, Health Services

***Pemberton:* Pemberton Health Centre**
Affiliated with: Vancouver Coastal Health Authority
Former Name: Pemberton Diagnostic & Treatment Centre
PO Box 8, 1403 Portage Rd., Pemberton, BC V0N 2L0
Tel: 604-894-6939; *Fax:* 604-894-6918
Number of Beds: 5 beds
Dr. Rebecca Lindley, President, Med Staff

***Sparwood:* Sparwood General Healthcare Centre**
Affiliated with: Interior Health Authority
PO Box 9, 570 Pine Ave., Sparwood, BC V0B 2G0
Tel: 250-425-6212; *Fax:* 250-425-2313
wendy.timmerman@interiorhealth.ca
Number of Beds: 12 beds
Wendy Timmerman, Site Manager

***Tahsis:* Tahsis Health Centre**
Affiliated with: Vancouver Island Health Authority
PO Box 399, 1085 Maquinna Dr., Tahsis, BC V0P 1X0
Tel: 250-934-6322; *Fax:* 250-934-6404
Enid O'Hara, Area Director of Rural Health Services, Campbell River/Nootka/Comoc Valley

***Tatla Lake:* West Chilcotin Health Centre**
Affiliated with: Interior Health Authority
Tatla Lake Nursing Station, 16452 Chilcotin Highway 20, Tatla Lake, BC V0L 1V0
Tel: 250-476-1114; *Fax:* 250-476-1266

***Tumbler Ridge:* Tumbler Ridge Health Care Centre**
Affiliated with: Northern Health Authority
PO Box 80, 220 Front St., Tumbler Ridge, BC V0C 2W0
Tel: 250-242-5271; *Fax:* 250-242-3889
Number of Beds: 2 holding beds
Note: diagnostic & treatment centre
Beth Kidd, COO

***Valemount:* Valemount Health Centre**
Affiliated with: Northern Health Authority
PO Box 697, 1445 - 5 Ave., Valemount, BC V0E 2Z0
Tel: 250-566-9138; *Fax:* 250-566-4319
health@valemount.com
www.nirhb.bc.ca
Note: outpatient health centre
Marilyn Harknes, Administrator
Vic Chicoine, Executive Director

Nursing Stations

***Alexis Creek:* Red Cross Outpost Nursing Station**
PO Box 39, 2591 Morton Rd., Alexis Creek, BC V0L 1A0
Tel: 250-394-4313; *Fax:* 250-394-5179
Number of Beds: 1 beds
Note: Red Cross Outpost Nursing Stations correspondence should be sent to Manager of Outpost Hospital Program, Canadian Red Cross Society, 4750 Oak St., 3rd Fl., Vancouver BC V6H 2N9
Pat Kermeen, Manager

***Anahim Lake:* Anahim Lake Nursing Station**
Affiliated with: Interior Health Authority
Hudson Rd., Anahim Lake, BC V0L 1C0
Tel: 250-742-3305; *Fax:* 250-742-3336
anahim_lake_nursing_station@hc-sc.gc.ca

***Atlin:* Atlin Health Centre**
Former Name: Red Cross Outpost Hospital
PO Box 330, 3rd St., Atlin, BC V0W 1A0
Tel: 250-651-7677; *Fax:* 250-651-7687
atlinoph@atlin.net
Number of Beds: 1 bed

***Bamfield:* Red Cross Outpost Nursing Station**
Affiliated with: Vancouver Island Health Authority
353 Bamfield Rd., Bamfield, BC V0R 1B0
Tel: 250-728-3312; *Fax:* 250-728-3054
Number of Beds: 3 beds
Pat Kermeen, Manager, Outpost Hospital Program

***Blue River:* Red Cross Outpost Hospital**
PO Box 18, 858 Main St., Blue River, BC V0E 1J0
Tel: 250-673-8311; *Fax:* 250-673-2380
Pat Kermeen, Manager, Outpost Hospital Program

Edgewood: **Red Cross Outpost Nursing Station**
322 Monashee Ave., Edgewood, BC V0G 1J0
Tel: 250-269-7313; *Fax:* 250-269-7520

Pat Kermeen, Manager, Outpost Hospital Program

Hartley Bay: **Hartley Bay Nursing Station**
General Delivery, Hartley Bay, BC V0V 1A0
Tel: 250-841-2556; *Fax:* 250-841-2554
angelacliftonrhealth@yahoo.ca

Number of Beds: 1 bed
Angela Clifton, Health Director

Iskut: **Iskut Nursing Station**
Affiliated with: Northern Health Authority
PO Box 9, Iskut, BC V0J 1K0
Tel: 250-234-3511; *Fax:* 250-234-3512
Toll-Free: 866-660-6607
feddie.louie@ivhs.ca
www.ivhs.ca

Freddie Carlick, Health Director

Kincolith: **Kincolith Nursing Station**
General Delivery, Kincolith, BC V0V 1B0
Tel: 250-326-4258

Kitkatla: **Kitkatla Nursing Station**
General Delivery, Kitkatla, BC V0V 1C0
Tel: 250-848-2254; *Fax:* 250-848-2263
kitkatla_nursing_station@hc-sc.gc.ca

Klemtu: **Klemtu Nursing Station**
General Delivery, Klemtu, BC V0T 1L0
Tel: 250-839-1221; *Fax:* 250-839-1184
alma_wert@hc-sc.gc.ca

Kyuquot: **Red Cross Outpost Nursing Station**
100 Okime Island, Kyuquot, BC V0P 1J0
Tel: 250-332-5289; *Fax:* 250-332-5215

Pat Kermeen, Manager, Outpost Hospital Program

Takla Landing: **Takla Landing Nursing Station**
General Delivery, Takla Landing, BC V0J 2T0
Tel: 250-564-9334; *Fax:* 250-564-9334

Telegraph Creek: **Telegraph Creek Nursing Station**
PO Box 112, Telegraph Creek, BC V0J 2W0
Tel: 250-235-3211; *Fax:* 250-235-3213

Special Treatment Centres

Burnaby: **Burnaby Family Court Centre - Outpatient Clinic**
3405 Willingdon Ave., Burnaby, BC V5G 3H4
Tel: 604-660-5870; *Fax:* 604-660-1109
Number of Beds: 9 beds
Fred Bannon, Director

Houston: **Houston Health Centre**
Affiliated with: Northern Health Authority
3150 - 14 St., Houston, BC V0J 1Z0
Tel: 250-845-2294; *Fax:* 250-845-2005
Number of Beds: 2 holding beds
Hanna White, Administrator

Kamloops: **Phoenix Centre**
922 - 3 Ave., Kamloops, BC V2C 6W5
Tel: 250-374-4634; *Fax:* 250-374-4621
ksad@phoenixcentre.org
www.phoenixcentre.org
Number of Beds: 20 beds
Note: detox centre

Vancouver: **Arthritis Society**
Affiliated with: Vancouver Coastal Health Authority
895 - 10 Ave. West, Vancouver, BC V5Z 1L7
Tel: 604-879-7511; *Fax:* 604-871-4500

Melanie Crombie, Executive Director

Vancouver: **British Columbia Cancer Agency**
Affiliated with: Provincial Health Services Authority
600 - 10 Ave. West, Vancouver, BC V5Z 4E6
Tel: 604-877-6000; *Fax:* 604-872-4596
www.bccancer.bc.ca
Note: cancer treatment
Simon B. Sutcliffe, President
Mohan Bains, Supervisor, Biomedical Waste
Tom Bennett, Supervisor, Waste Management

Vancouver: **Elizabeth Bagshaw Women's Clinic**
Affiliated with: Vancouver Coastal Health Authority
200 - 1177 West Broadway, Vancouver, BC V6H 1G3
Tel: 604-736-7878; *Fax:* 604-736-8081
Toll-Free: 877-736-7171
www.elizabethbagshawclinic.ca
Note: abortion clinic
Cheryl Davies, Administrator

Vancouver: **Everywoman's Health Centre Abortion Control Clinic**
Affiliated with: Vancouver Coastal Health Authority
210 - 2525 Commercial Dr., Vancouver, BC V5A 4C1
Tel: 604-322-6692; *Fax:* 604-322-6632
ehc@axion.net
www.everywomanshealthcentre.ca
Number of Beds: 6 recovery room, 2 procedure room beds
Note: abortion clinic
J. Foley, Executive Director

Vancouver: **G.F. Strong Centre**
Affiliated with: Vancouver Coastal Health Authority
4255 Laurel St., Vancouver, BC V5Z 2G9
Tel: 604-734-1313; *Fax:* 604-737-6359
www.gfstrong.com
Number of Beds: 92 beds
Note: rehabilitation treatment centre
Patti Flaherty, Senior Operation Officer

Vancouver: **Sunny Hill Health Centre for Children**
Affiliated with: Provincial Health Services Authority
3644 Slocan St., Vancouver, BC V5M 3E8
Tel: 604-453-8300; *Fax:* 604-453-8301
Number of Beds: 18 beds
Note: Provincial rehabilitation & assessment centre for children with disabilities

Victoria: **British Columbia Cancer Agency**
Affiliated with: Vancouver Coastal Health Authority
2410 Lee Ave., Victoria, BC V8R 6V5
Tel: 250-519-5500; *Fax:* 250-519-2012
Toll-Free: 800-670-3322
www.bccancer.bc.ca
Note: comprehensive cancer centre
B. Weinerman, Vice-President

Whistler: **Diagnostic & Treatment Centre**
Affiliated with: Vancouver Coastal Health Authority
Former Name: Whistler Diagnostic & Treatment Centre
4380 Lorimer Rd., Whistler, BC V0N 1B4
Tel: 604-932-4911; *Fax:* 604-932-4992
Number of Beds: 13 beds
Tina Hua, Manager, Acute Services

Nursing Homes

Abbotsford: **Menno Home**
Affiliated with: Fraser Health Authority
32910 Brundige Ave., Abbotsford, BC V2S 1N2
Tel: 604-853-2411; *Fax:* 604-859-0751
Number of Beds: 196 beds
Arthur J. Enns, Administrator

Abbotsford: **Sunrise Special Care Facility**
2411 Railway St., Abbotsford, BC V2S 2E3
Tel: 604-853-3078
Number of Beds: 8 beds
Mona McMillan, Head Nursing

Burnaby: **St. Michael's Centre**
Affiliated with: Fraser Health Authority
7451 Sussex Ave., Burnaby, BC V5J 5C2
Tel: 604-434-1323; *Fax:* 604-434-6469
reception@stmichaels.bc.ca
www.saintmichaelscentre.org
Number of Beds: 128 extended care, 16 hospice beds
Helene Elias, Acting Executive Director
Severino Tolfo, Director, Environmental Services

Chilliwack: **Eden Care Centre**
Affiliated with: Fraser Health Authority
Former Name: Eden Rest Home
9100 Charles St., Chilliwack, BC V2P 5K6
Tel: 604-792-8166; *Fax:* 604-792-1111
edencare@telus.net
Number of Beds: 89 beds
Elaine Price, Administrator

Coquitlam: **Burquitlam Lions Care Centre**
Affiliated with: Fraser Health Authority
560 Sydney Ave., Coquitlam, BC V3K 6A4
Tel: 604-939-6485; *Fax:* 604-939-4728
ceo@burquitlamlionscare.com
www.burquitlamlionscare.com
Number of Beds: 76 beds
Renee Danylczuk, Administrator

Duncan: **Cowichan Lodge**
Affiliated with: Vancouver Island Health Authority
3045 Gibbins Rd., Duncan, BC V9L 1E5
Tel: 250-748-3331; *Fax:* 250-748-3032
www.viha.ca
Number of Beds: 85 beds
, Laurie, Chisholm

Gibsons: **Kiwanis Village Care Home**
841 Kiwanis Way, Gibsons, BC V0N 1V9
Tel: 604-886-8132; *Fax:* 604-886-8483
kiwanis@uniserve.com
Number of Beds: 37 beds
Dennis Regnier, Site Manager

Kamloops: **Extendicare - Pine Grove Lodge**
Affiliated with: Interior Health Authority
313 McGowan Ave., Kamloops, BC V2B 2N8
Tel: 250-376-5701; *Fax:* 250-376-5770
cnh-pinegrove@extendicare.com
www.motimahal.ca
Number of Beds: 75 beds
Robert S. Moffitt, Administrator

Kamloops: **Kamloops Personal Care Home Ltd. - Garden Manor**
63 Nicola St. West, Kamloops, BC V2C 1J5
Tel: 250-374-7612; *Fax:* 250-374-7605
Number of Beds: 24 beds
John H. Stewart, Administrator

Kamloops: **Overlander Extended Care Hospital**
Affiliated with: Interior Health Authority
953 Southill St., Kamloops, BC V2B 7Z9
Tel: 250-554-2323; *Fax:* 250-554-5557
Number of Beds: 189 beds

Kelowna: **Gordon House**
3091 Walnut Rd., Kelowna, BC V1W 3V2
Tel: 250-763-5290; *Fax:* 250-763-5207
Number of Beds: 8 beds
Valerie Bosch, Administrator

Langley: **Murrayville Manor Ltd.**
21616 - 46 Ave., Langley, BC V3A 3J4
Tel: 604-530-9033; *Fax:* 604-530-9023
Number of Beds: 39 beds
Wayne Mills, Administrator

Nanaimo: **Columbian Centre Society**
2356 Rosstown Rd., Nanaimo, BC V9T 3R7
Tel: 250-758-8711; *Fax:* 250-751-1128
Number of Beds: 10 beds
Tom Grauman, Administrator

Nelson: **Mount St. Francis Hospital**
Affiliated with: Interior Health Authority
1300 Gordon Rd., Nelson, BC V1L 3M5
Tel: 250-352-3531; *Fax:* 250-352-6942
Number of Beds: 79 beds
Cydney Higgins

Parksville: **Trillium Lodge**
Affiliated with: Vancouver Island Health Authority
PO Box 940, 401 Moilliet St., Parksville, BC V9P 2G9
Tel: 250-248-8353; *Fax:* 250-248-8388
Number of Beds: 106 beds
Gillian Forsyth, Director, Care

Pouce Coupe: **Pouce Coupe Care Home**
Affiliated with: Northern Helath Authority
PO Box 98, 5216 - 50 Ave., Pouce Coupe, BC V0C 2C0
Tel: 250-786-6116; *Fax:* 250-786-0197
Number of Beds: 55 beds
Dave Price, Resident Care Manager

Salmon Arm: **Bastion Place**
700 - 11 St. NE, Salmon Arm, BC V1E2S5
Tel: 250-833-3616; *Fax:* 250-833-3605
Number of Beds: 101 beds
Brenda Veerman

Sidney: **Rest Haven Lodge**
2281 Mills Rd., Sidney, BC V8L 2C3
Tel: 250-656-0717; *Fax:* 250-656-4745

Number of Beds: 75 beds
Bernard Skoretz, Administrator

Surrey: Argyll Lodge
14590 - 106A Ave., Surrey, BC V3R 1T4
Tel: 604-581-4174; *Fax:* 604-582-6348
Number of Beds: 25 beds
Baljit Kandola, Administrator

Surrey: Cherington Place
Affiliated with: Fraser Health Authority
13453 - 111A Ave., Surrey, BC V3R 2C5
Tel: 604-581-2885; *Fax:* 604-582-9028
cherington@telus.net
seniorshome.com
Number of Beds: 75 beds
Annamae Clarke, Administrator

Surrey: K & C Care Ltd.
1504 - 160 St., Surrey, BC V4A 4N9
Tel: 604-531-7900; *Fax:* 604-531-2338
Number of Beds: 10 beds
Kwan-Ying Jen, President

Terrace: Terraceview Lodge
Affiliated with: Northern Health Authority
4103 North Sparks South, Terrace, BC V8G 5G9
Tel: 250-638-0223; *Fax:* 250-635-9775
Number of Beds: 75 beds
Doris Mitchell, Administrator

Vancouver: Ananda
1249 - 8 Ave. East, Vancouver, BC V5T 1V3
Tel: 604-872-7134; *Fax:* 604-872-8420
Number of Beds: 20 beds
Darrell Burnham, Executive Director

Vancouver: Britannia Lodge
1090 Victoria Dr., Vancouver, BC V5L 4G2
Tel: 604-255-3711; *Fax:* 604-255-3712
britannia.lodge@shaw.ca
Number of Beds: 45 beds
A. Filsoof, Administrator

Vancouver: Louis Brier Home & Hospital
Affiliated with: Vancouver Coastal Health Authority
1055 West 41st Ave., Vancouver, BC V6M 1W9
Tel: 604-261-9376; *Fax:* 604-266-8712
Number of Beds: 93 beds
Peter Kafka, CEO
Patrick Chan, Director, Administration

Vancouver: St. Jude's Anglican Home
Affiliated with: Vancouver Coastal Health Authority
810 - 27 Ave. East, Vancouver, BC V5Z 2G7
Tel: 604-874-3200; *Fax:* 604-874-3459
info@stjudes.ca
www.stjudes.ca
Number of Beds: 55 beds
Chris Norman, Administrator

Vernon: Sunshine Lodge
9604 Shamanski Dr., Vernon, BC V1B 2L7
Tel: 250-542-9350
Number of Beds: 18 beds
C. Baziw, Administrator

Vernon: Twin Cedars Rest Home
3201 - 37 Ave., Vernon, BC V1T 2Y4
Tel: 250-542-4983; *Fax:* 250-542-4924
Number of Beds: 29 beds
Charlene Fair, Administrator

Victoria: Glenwarren Lodge
1230 Balmoral Rd., Victoria, BC V8T 1B3
Tel: 250-383-2323; *Fax:* 250-383-6359
glenwarren@cplodges.com
www.cplcanada.com
Number of Beds: 131 beds
Note: intermediate & extended care
Norman Carelius, Administrator

West Vancouver: Capilano Care Centre
Affiliated with: Vancouver Coastal Health Authority
525 Clyde Ave., West Vancouver, BC V7T 1C4
Tel: 604-926-6856; *Fax:* 604-926-9169
Number of Beds: 215 beds
Ann MacMillan, Administrator

West Vancouver: West Vancouver Care Centre
Affiliated with: Vancouver Coastal Health Authority
1675 - 27 St., West Vancouver, BC V7V 4K9
Tel: 604-925-1247; *Fax:* 604-925-3507
Number of Beds: 75 beds

Courtenay Woodworth, Administrator

White Rock: Buena Vista Rest Home
15109 Buena Vista Ave., White Rock, BC V4B 1Y2
Tel: 604-536-6752
Number of Beds: 12 beds
Elaine Lasoto, Administrator

Long Term/Retirement Care

Long Term Care Facilities

100 Mile House: Mill Site Lodge
76 Horse Lake Road, 100 Mile House, BC V0K 2E0
Tel: 250-395-3366; *Fax:* 250-395-7692
Number of Beds: 26 beds
Allison Ruault, Director, Health Services

Abbotsford: Bevan Lodge
Affiliated with: Fraser Health Authority
33386 Bevan Ave., Abbotsford, BC V2S 5G6
Tel: 604-850-5416; *Fax:* 604-850-5418
Number of Beds: 15 beds
Hendrik Van Ryk, Administrator

Abbotsford: M.S.A. Manor Society
Affiliated with: Fraser Health Authority
2510 Gladwin Rd., Abbotsford, BC V2T 3N9
Tel: 604-853-5831; *Fax:* 604-853-1647
Number of Beds: 34 beds
Dennis Magnusson, Administrator

Abbotsford: Maplewood House
Affiliated with: Fraser Health Authority
1919 Jackson St., Abbotsford, BC V2S 2Z8
Tel: 604-853-5585; *Fax:* 604-853-4224
Number of Beds: 76 beds
Dennis Magnusson, Director

Abbotsford: Sherwood Crescent Manor Ltd.
Affiliated with: Fraser Health Authority
32073 Sherwood Cres., Abbotsford, BC V2T 1C1
Tel: 604-853-7854; *Fax:* 604-853-9910
sherwoodcrescentmanor@telus.net
Number of Beds: 41 permanent, 10 transitional care, 3 respite beds
Note: intermediate/residential care
Marilyn Smart, Director, Care

Abbotsford: Tabor Home
Affiliated with: Fraser Health Authority
31944 Sunrise Cres., Abbotsford, BC V2T 1N5
Tel: 604-859-8715; *Fax:* 604-859-6695
Number of Beds: 121 beds
Jack Pauls, Administrator

Abbotsford: Valhaven Rest Home
Affiliated with: Fraser Health Authority
4212 Balmoral St., Abbotsford, BC V4X 1Y5
Tel: 604-856-2812; *Fax:* 604-856-3243
Number of Beds: 22 beds
Barb Schmidt

Agassiz: Glenwood Home
PO Box 15, 1458 Glenwood Dr., RR#2, Agassiz, BC V0M 1A2
Tel: 604-796-9202
Number of Beds: 19 beds
Anne Marie Leyen, Administrator

Agassiz: Glenwood Home
Affiliated with: Fraser Health Authority
PO Box 15, Agassiz, BC V0M 1A0
Tel: 604-796-9202; *Fax:* 604-796-9186
Number of Beds: 37 beds complete care; 32 units assisted living
Anne Marie Leyen, Administrator

Aldergrove: Jackman Manor
Affiliated with: Fraser Health Authority
27447 - 28 Ave., Aldergrove, BC V4W 3L9
Tel: 604-856-4161; *Fax:* 604-856-2562
Number of Beds: 87 beds
Sheila Bridger, Administrator

Aldergrove: La Rosa de Matsqui
28711 Huntington Rd., Aldergrove, BC V0X 1A0
Tel: 604-856-1555; *Fax:* 604-856-3252
Number of Beds: 15 beds
Carlos Arthur, Manager

Armstrong: Pioneer Square
Affiliated with: Willowdale Guest Home
2865 Willowdale Dr., Armstrong, BC V0E 1B1
Tel: 250-546-3396; *Fax:* 250-546-9033
Number of Beds: 20 beds

Kevin Svoboda, Administrator

Burnaby: L'Arche Greater Vancouver
7401 Sussex Ave., Burnaby, BC V5J 3V6
Tel: 604-435-9544; *Fax:* 604-434-1933
larchez@larchevancouver.org
www.larchevancouver.org
Number of Beds: 27 beds
Note: services for developmentally disabled adults
Landys Klyne, Executive Director

Burnaby: Canada Way Care Centre & Lodge
Affiliated with: Fraser Health Authority
7195 Canada Way, Burnaby, BC V5E 3R7
Tel: 604-525-9444; *Fax:* 604-526-4746
hmannis@agecare.ca
www.agecare.ca
Number of Beds: 80 beds
Note: intermediate care facility
Heidi Mannis, Administrator

Burnaby: Carlton Gardens
Affiliated with: Fraser Health Authority
4125 Canada Way, Burnaby, BC V5G 1G9
Tel: 604-438-8224; *Fax:* 604-438-6571
Number of Beds: 152 beds
Gwen Gordon, General Manager

Burnaby: Dania Home Society
Affiliated with: Fraser Health Authority
4279 Norland Ave., Burnaby, BC V5G 3Z6
Tel: 604-299-2414; *Fax:* 604-299-7775
margaretd@dania.bc.ca
Number of Beds: 67 beds
Margaret Douglas-Matthews, Administrator

Burnaby: Fair Haven United Church Homes
Affiliated with: Fraser Health Authority
7557 Sussex Ave., Burnaby, BC V5J 3V6
Tel: 604-435-0525; *Fax:* 604-435-7031
mharrison@fairhaven.bc.ca
Number of Beds: 100 beds
Maureen Harrison, Administrator

Burnaby: Fellburn Care Centre
Affiliated with: Fraser Health Authority
6050 Hastings St. East, Burnaby, BC V5B 1R6
Tel: 604-412-6510; *Fax:* 604-299-1015
Number of Beds: 110 beds
Note: extended care facility
Carol Wheeler, Administrator

Burnaby: Finnish Manor
Affiliated with: Fraser Health Authority
3460 Kalyk Ave., Burnaby, BC V5G 3B2
Tel: 604-434-2666; *Fax:* 604-439-7448
Number of Beds: 60 beds
Sinikka Seppanen, Administrator

Burnaby: George Derby Centre
Affiliated with: Fraser Health Authority
7550 Cumberland St., Burnaby, BC V3N 3X5
Tel: 604-521-2676; *Fax:* 604-521-0220
www.georgederbycentre.ca
Number of Beds: 300 beds
Janice Mitchell, Executive Director

Burnaby: New Vista Care Home
Affiliated with: Fraser Health Authority
7550 Rosewood St., Burnaby, BC V5E 3Z3
Tel: 604-521-7764; *Fax:* 604-527-6001
patk@newvista.bc.ca
www.newvista.bc.ca
Number of Beds: 236 beds
Pat Kasprow, CEO

Burnaby: Normanna Rest Home
Affiliated with: Fraser Health Authority
7725 - 4 St., Burnaby, BC V3N 5B6
Tel: 604-522-5812; *Fax:* 604-522-5803
Number of Beds: 100 beds
Note: multi level care
Margaret Douglas-Matthews, Administrator

Burns Lake: Pines Care Home
Affiliated with: Northern Health Authority
PO Box 479, 800 Center St., Burns Lake, BC V0J 1E0
Tel: 250-692-7752; *Fax:* 250-692-7462
Number of Beds: 30 beds
Note: multi-level care

***Campbell River:* Yucalta Lodge**
Affiliated with: Vancouver Island Health Authority
555 - 2 Ave., Campbell River, BC V9W 3V1
Tel: 250-286-1051; *Fax:* 250-850-0328
linda.harley@crncare.org
Number of Beds: 100 beds
Note: multi-level care
Linda Harley, Manager, Residential services

***Castlegar:* Castleview Care Centre**
Affiliated with: Interior Health Authority
2300 - 14 Ave., Castlegar, BC V1N 4A6
Tel: 250-365-7277; *Fax:* 250-365-3291
Number of Beds: 61 beds
Kimberly Hunter, Administrator

***Castlegar:* Talarico Place**
Affiliated with: Interior Health Authority
709 - 10 St., Castlegar, BC V1N 1A1
Tel: 250-365-7221; *Fax:* 250-304-1238
Number of Beds: 60 beds
Meg Milner

***Chilliwack:* McIntosh Lodge**
Affiliated with: Fraser Health Authority
44586 McIntosh Dr., Chilliwack, BC V2P 7W8
Tel: 604-795-2500; *Fax:* 604-795-5693
Number of Beds: 25 beds
Lynda Marlett, Administrator

***Chilliwack:* Valleyhaven Guest Home**
Affiliated with: Fraser Health Authority
45450 Menholm Rd., Chilliwack, BC V2P 1M2
Tel: 604-792-0037; *Fax:* 604-792-6766
Number of Beds: 52 beds
Gillian McCunnie, Director of Care

***Chilliwack:* Waverly of Chilliwack**
Affiliated with: Fraser Health Authority
8445 Young Rd. South, Chilliwack, BC V2P 4P2
Tel: 604-792-6340; *Fax:* 604-792-5611
Number of Beds: 15 beds
Debbie Davidson, Administrator

***Coquitlam:* Cartier House**
Affiliated with: Fraser Health Authority
1419 Cartier Ave., Coquitlam, BC V3K 2C6
Tel: 604-939-4654; *Fax:* 604-939-6442
Number of Beds: 78 beds
Linda Clary, Administrator

***Coquitlam:* Foyer Maillard**
Affiliated with: Fraser Health Authority
1010 Alderson Ave., Coquitlam, BC V3K 1W1
Tel: 604-937-5578; *Fax:* 604-937-7133
services@foyermaillard.com
Number of Beds: 45 beds
Doris Brisebois, Administrator

***Courtenay:* Glacier View Lodge**
2450 Back Rd., Courtenay, BC V9N 9G8
Tel: 250-338-1451; *Fax:* 250-338-1115
swolden@sjgh.hnet.bc.ca
Number of Beds: 100 beds
Michael Pontus, President/CEO

***Courtenay:* Laurel Lodge**
280 - 2nd St., Courtenay, BC V9N 1B7
Tel: 250-334-3083; *Fax:* 250-338-2253
Number of Beds: 27 beds
Note: seniors' support home
David Reghr, Administrator

***Cranbrook:* F.W. Green Memorial Home**
1700 - 4th St. South, Cranbrook, BC V1C 6E1
Tel: 250-426-3710; *Fax:* 250-426-3622
Number of Beds: 86 beds
Allan Sinclair

***Cranbrook:* Rocky Mountain Lodge**
20 - 23rd Ave. South, Cranbrook, BC V1C 5V1
Tel: 250-489-3361; *Fax:* 250-489-3545
Number of Beds: 63 beds
Allan Sinclair

***Creston:* Pioneer Villa**
Affiliated with: Interior Health Authority
1909 Ash St., RR#5, Creston, BC V0B 1G5
Tel: 250-428-7188; *Fax:* 250-428-5192
Number of Beds: 31 beds
Cheryl Comin, Manager

***Creston:* Swan Valley Lodge**
Affiliated with: Interior Health Authority
818 Vancouver St., Creston, BC V0B 1G0
Tel: 250-428-2283; *Fax:* 250-428-9318
Number of Beds: 105 beds
Note: residential care
Cindy Kozak-Campbell

***Dawson Creek:* Rotary Manor**
Affiliated with: Northern Health Authority
1121 - 90 Ave., Dawson Creek, BC V1G 5A3
Tel: 250-719-3480; *Fax:* 250-719-3781
rmanor@pris.ca
Number of Beds: 44 beds
Elaine Washington, Residential Program Manager

***Delta:* Delta Lodge**
4501 Arthur Dr., Delta, BC V4K 2X3
Tel: 604-946-6221; *Fax:* 604-946-6542
Number of Beds: 21 beds
Jesus Supnet, Administrator

***Delta:* Delta View Habilitation Centre**
9341 Burns Dr., Delta, BC V4K 3N3
Tel: 604-596-8842; *Fax:* 604-596-8858
jdevji@deltaview.ca
www.deltaview.ca
Number of Beds: 80 beds
Note: cares for peoples with Alzheimer's disease; specializing in caring for people with difficult behaviour
Jane Devji, Manager

***Delta:* Heritage Home**
Affiliated with: Fraser Health Authority
5681 Ladner Trunk Rd., Delta, BC V4K 1X3
Tel: 604-946-4013; *Fax:* 604-946-4034
heritagehome@dccnet.com
Number of Beds: 29 beds
Jasmine Barredo, Director of Care

***Delta:* Kinsmen Retirement Centre**
Affiliated with: Fraser Health Authority
5410 - 10 Ave., Delta, BC V4M 3X8
Tel: 604-943-0155; *Fax:* 604-943-0947
kinsmen@istar.ca
Number of Beds: 101 beds
Gerald Arksey, Chairman

***Delta:* Northcrest Care Centre**
Affiliated with: Fraser Health Authority
6771 - 120th St., Delta, BC V4E 2A7
Tel: 604-597-7878; *Fax:* 604-597-7805
general@northcrestcare.ca
Number of Beds: 106 beds
Sue Emmons, Executive Director

***Delta:* West Shore Laylum**
Affiliated with: Fraser Health Authority
4900 Central Ave., Delta, BC V4K 2G7
Tel: 604-946-2822; *Fax:* 604-946-2217
Number of Beds: 55 beds
Kris Coonfer, Administrator

***Duncan:* Cairnsmore Place**
Affiliated with: Vancouver Island Health Authority
250 Cairnsmore St., Duncan, BC V9L 4H2
Tel: 250-709-3080; *Fax:* 250-746-0351
Number of Beds: 100 beds

***Enderby:* Parkview Place**
Affiliated with: Interior Health Authority
PO Box 129, Granville St., Enderby, BC V0E 1V0
Tel: 250-546-6131; *Fax:* 250-546-9943
Number of Beds: 31 beds
Peter DuToit

***Fort Langley:* Simpson Private Hospital**
Affiliated with: Fraser Health Authority
PO Box 40, 8838 Glover Rd., Fort Langley, BC V1M 2R4
Tel: 604-888-0711; *Fax:* 604-888-1218
Number of Beds: 55 beds
Note: intermediate & extended care
Ingo Riesen, Controller

***Fort St John:* North Peace Care Centre**
Affiliated with: Northern Health Authority
9907 - 110 Ave., Fort St John, BC V1J 2S9
Tel: 250-785-8941; *Fax:* 250-785-2296
www.northernhealth.ca
Number of Beds: 95 beds
Note: complex care special care unit
Larry Tokarchuk, COO
Bob Smalley, Director, Plant Services

***Golden:* Durand Manor**
8th Ave. & 9th St., Golden, BC V0A 1H0
Tel: 250-344-5271; *Fax:* 250-344-2511
Number of Beds: 27 beds
Note: group home for the elderly mainly who are no longer able to live in the community

***Grand Forks:* Boundary Lodge Assisted Living**
7130 - 9th St., Grand Forks, BC V0H 1H4
Tel: 250-443-0006; *Fax:* 250-443-0015
Number of Beds: 18 assisted living units

***Grand Forks:* Hardy View Lodge**
Affiliated with: Interior Health Authority
2320 - 78 Ave., Grand Forks, BC V0H 1H0
Tel: 250-443-2080; *Fax:* 250-442-3663
Number of Beds: 35 beds
Trish Hallstrom, Director of Care

***Invermere:* Columbia House**
850 - 10th St., Invermere, BC V0A 1K0
Tel: 250-342-2329; *Fax:* 250-342-2319
Number of Beds: 20 beds
Rose Bard

***Kamloops:* Liberty Manor**
470 Hilltop Ave., Kamloops, BC V2B 2S3
Tel: 250-376-3788
Note: group home
Claire Ann Brodie, Executive Director, Continuing Care Services

***Kamloops:* Panderosa Lodge**
425 Columbia St., Kamloops, BC V2C 2T4
Tel: 250-374-5671; *Fax:* 250-374-8873
Number of Beds: 157 beds
Claire Ann Brodie, Director

***Kelowna:* Avonlea Care Centre Limited**
Avonlea House
Affiliated with: Interior Health Authority
1658 Blondeaux Cres., Kelowna, BC V1Y 4J7
Tel: 250-762-4378; *Fax:* 250-762-0167
avonleahouse@avonleacare.com
www.avonleacare.com
Number of Beds: 14 beds
Note: specialized care home for severely brain-injured
Dr. Abbas Moledina, Managing Director/Administrator
Lunda Asselstine, Director of Care/Manager

***Kelowna:* David Lloyd Jones Home**
934 Bernard Ave., Kelowna, BC V1Y 6P8
Tel: 250-762-2706; *Fax:* 250-762-5961
Number of Beds: 64 beds
Rick Riley

***Kelowna:* May Bennett Home**
Affiliated with: Interior Health Authority
965 West Highway 33, Kelowna, BC V1X 1Y8
Tel: 250-763-6277; *Fax:* 250-763-6262
Number of Beds: 24 beds
Nancy Kilpatrick, Director

***Kelowna:* Parkside Residence Ltd.**
Affiliated with: Interior Health Authority
265 Gray Rd., Kelowna, BC V1X 1W8
Tel: 250-765-8482; *Fax:* 250-765-8213
Number of Beds: 23 beds
Alena Merhaut, Administrator

***Kelowna:* Sutherland Hills Rest Home**
Affiliated with: Interior Health Authority
3081 Hall Rd., Kelowna, BC V1W 2R5
Tel: 250-860-2330; *Fax:* 250-860-2399
shrhbob@silk.net
Number of Beds: 100 beds
Wendy Calhoun, Facility Director

***Kelowna:* Three Links Manor**
Affiliated with: Interior Health Authority
1449 Kelglen Cres., Kelowna, BC V1Y 8P4
Tel: 250-763-2585; *Fax:* 250-763-6773
Number of Beds: 81 beds
Rick Riley

***Kelowna:* Windsor Manor Care Centre**
Affiliated with: Interior Health Authority
355 Terai Ct., Kelowna, BC V1X 5X6
Tel: 250-979-6000; *Fax:* 250-979-6002
Number of Beds: 149 beds
Bev Powell, Administrator

Kimberley: **Kimberley Special Care Home**
Affiliated with: Interior Health Authority
386 - 2nd Ave., Kimberley, BC V1A 2Z8
Tel: 250-427-4807; *Fax:* 250-427-5377
Number of Beds: 51 beds, 15 mental health
Allan Sinclair, Site Manager

Ladysmith: **Four All Seasons Retirement Lodge**
Affiliated with: Vancouver Island Health Authority
3464 Yellowpoint Rd., Ladysmith, BC V0R 1E6
Tel: 250-245-4237; *Fax:* 250-245-7757
4allseasons@telus.net
Number of Beds: 22 beds
Gerard B. Huard, Administrator

Langley: **Highland Lodge**
Affiliated with: Fraser Health Authority
20619 Eastleigh Cres., Langley, BC V3A 4C3
Tel: 604-534-7186; *Fax:* 604-534-7139
hlodge@idirect.ca
Number of Beds: 60 beds
Dave Stott, Director, Care

Langley: **Langley Gardens**
Affiliated with: Fraser Health Authority
8888 - 202nd St., Langley, BC V1M 4A7
Tel: 604-881-8122; *Fax:* 604-881-8199
www.cpac-care.com
Number of Beds: 73 beds
Lisa Kachur, General Manager

Langley: **Langley Lodge**
Affiliated with: Fraser Health Authority
5451 - 204th St., Langley, BC V3A 5M9
Tel: 604-530-2305; *Fax:* 604-532-4205
wpauls@langleylodge.org
www.langleylodge.org
Number of Beds: 153 beds
Note: seniors
Werner Pauls, Administrator

Lillooet: **Mountain View Lodge**
Affiliated with: Interior Health Authority
844 Main Street, Lillooet, BC V0K 1V0
Tel: 250-455-2221; *Fax:* 250-455-6621
Number of Beds: 22 beds
Jennifer Thur

Maple Ridge: **Golden Ears Retirement Centre**
Affiliated with: Fraser Health Authority
12155 Edge St., Maple Ridge, BC V2X 6G7
Tel: 604-467-5511; *Fax:* 604-467-0510
Number of Beds: 52 beds
Doreen Fleming, Administrator

Merritt: **Coquihalla/Gillis House**
Affiliated with: Interior Health Authority
3451 Voght St., Merritt, BC V1K 1C6
Tel: 250-378-3271; *Fax:* 250-378-3252
Number of Beds: 92 beds
Doug Sage, Administrator

Mission: **Grand Street Lodge**
Affiliated with: Fraser Health Authority
7755 Grand St., Mission, BC V2V 3T6
Tel: 604-826-6646; *Fax:* 604-820-8550
Number of Beds: 23 beds
Annamae Clark, Administrator

Mission: **Pleasant View Care Home**
Affiliated with: Fraser Health Authority
7530 Hurd St., Mission, BC V2V 3H9
Tel: 604-826-2154; *Fax:* 604-826-8672
j.ray@pvhs.ca
www.pvhs.ca
Number of Beds: 76 beds
Judith E. Ray, Administrator

Nakusp: **Halcyon Community Home**
PO Box 910, 83 - 8th Ave., Nakusp, BC V0G 1R0
Tel: 250-265-3692; *Fax:* 250-265-4141
Number of Beds: 14 beds
Note: Intermediate care
Deborah Austin

Nanaimo: **Kiwanis Village Lodge**
Affiliated with: Vancouver Island Health Authority
1221 Kiwanis Crescent, Nanaimo, BC V9S 5Y1
Tel: 250-753-6471; *Fax:* 250-740-2816
Number of Beds: 102 beds
Virginia Ostrand, Administrator

Nanaimo: **Malaspina Gardens Inc.**
Affiliated with: Vancouver Island Health Authority
388 Machleary St., Nanaimo, BC V9R 2G9
Tel: 250-754-7711; *Fax:* 250-754-2175
Number of Beds: 133 beds
Diane DeRepentigny, General Manager

Nanaimo: **Travellers Lodge**
Affiliated with: Vancouver Island Health Authority
1298 Nelson St., Nanaimo, BC V9S 2K5
Tel: 250-758-4676; *Fax:* 250-758-4698
ot@nantralodge.bc.ca
Number of Beds: 93 beds
Sandra Rummy, Administrator/Director

Nelson: **Nelson Jubilee Manor**
Affiliated with: Interior Health Authority
500 Beasley St., Nelson, BC V1L 6G9
Tel: 250-352-7011; *Fax:* 250-352-7044
Number of Beds: 39 beds
Kim Irving

New Westminster: **Blue Spruce Cottage**
Affiliated with: Fraser Health Authority
509 St. George St., New Westminster, BC V3L 1L1
Tel: 604-521-4316; *Fax:* 604-521-6600
Number of Beds: 15 beds
Betty Dewitte, Manager

New Westminster: **Buchanan Lodge**
Affiliated with: Fraser Health Authority
409 Blair Ave., New Westminster, BC V3L 4A4
Tel: 604-522-7033; *Fax:* 604-522-3689
Number of Beds: 112 beds
Penny Lang, Administrator

New Westminster: **Kiwanis Intermediate Care Centre**
Affiliated with: Fraser Health Authority
35 Clute St., New Westminster, BC V3L 1Z5
Tel: 604-525-6471; *Fax:* 604-525-8522
sbrowne@kiwaniscarecentre.com
Number of Beds: 74 beds, 2 respite beds
Note: intermediate care
Shirley Brown, Administrator

New Westminster: **Queen's Park Care Centre**
Affiliated with: Fraser Health Authority
260 Sherbrooke St., New Westminster, BC V3L 5E8
Tel: 604-520-0911; *Fax:* 604-517-8651
cspeers@sfhr.hnet.bc.ca
Number of Beds: 219 beds
Note: extended care facility
Carol Wheeler, Director

New Westminster: **Royal City Manor**
77 Jamieson Ct., New Westminster, BC V3L 5P8
Tel: 604-522-6699; *Fax:* 604-522-1022
royalcitymanor@reveraliving.com
www.reveraliving.com
Kevin Perry, Administrator

New Westminster: **Salvation Army Buchanan Lodge**
Affiliated with: Fraser Health Authority
409 Blair Ave., New Westminster, BC V3L 4A4
Tel: 604-522-7033; *Fax:* 604-522-3689
Number of Beds: 112 beds
Capt. Penny Lang

North Vancouver: **Cedarview Lodge**
Affiliated with: Vancouver Coastal Health Authority
1200 Cedar Village Close, North Vancouver, BC V7J 3P3
Tel: 604-904-6400; *Fax:* 604-904-6411
Number of Beds: 90 beds, 30 assisted living units
Note: intermediate care
Lynne Pentland, Manager

North Vancouver: **Evergreen House**
Affiliated with: Vancouver Coastal Health Authority
231 - 15 St. East, North Vancouver, BC V7L 2L7
Tel: 604-988-3131; *Fax:* 604-984-5838
Number of Beds: 293 beds
Rizwan Damji, Director of Seniors

North Vancouver: **H & H Total Care Services**
Affiliated with: Vancouver Coastal Health Authority
4530 Meadowbank Close, North Vancouver, BC V7K 2L2
Tel: 604-987-7569; *Fax:* 604-597-8032
Note: specializing in Huntington & brain injury care
Hank Van Ryk, Manager

North Vancouver: **N.S. Kiwanis Care Centre**
Affiliated with: Vancouver Coastal Health Authority
2444 Burr Pl., North Vancouver, BC V7H 3A5
Tel: 604-924-8300; *Fax:* 604-924-8325
Number of Beds: 192 beds
Carol Mothersill, Admin.
Cathy Baxter, Clinical Manager

North Vancouver: **United Lodge**
Affiliated with: Vancouver Coastal Health Authority
116 West 23rd St., North Vancouver, BC V7M 2A9
Tel: 604-987-5010; *Fax:* 604-987-9378
Number of Beds: 22 beds
Abraham Calaguian, Administrator

Oliver: **Sunnybank Retirement Centre**
36657 - 79th St., Oliver, BC V0H 1T0
Tel: 250-498-4951; *Fax:* 250-498-2287
Number of Beds: 51 beds
Janice Little, Care Coordinator

Osoyoos: **Country Squire Retirement Villa**
9707 - 87th St., RR#2, Osoyoos, BC V0H 1V0
Tel: 250-495-6568; *Fax:* 250-495-7466
Number of Beds: 31 beds
G. Munro, Administrator

Osoyoos: **Sagebrush Lodge**
Affiliated with: Vancouver Island Health Authority
4816 - 89 St., Osoyoos, BC V0H 1V1
Tel: 250-495-2666; *Fax:* 250-495-2605
Number of Beds: 52 beds
Lorraine Ferguson

Parksville: **Arrowsmith Lodge**
Affiliated with: Vancouver Island Health Authority
266 Moilliet St., Parksville, BC V9P 1M9
Tel: 250-248-4331; *Fax:* 250-248-4813
Number of Beds: 58 beds
Pam Swanson, Administrator

Parksville: **Halliday House of BC**
Affiliated with: Vancouver Island Health Authority
188 McCarter St., Parksville, BC V9P 1A1
Tel: 250-248-2835; *Fax:* 250-248-2403
Number of Beds: 20 beds
Louise Hughes, Manager

Penticton: **Haven Hill Retirement Centre**
Affiliated with: Interior Health Authority
415 Haven Hill Rd., Penticton, BC V2A 4E9
Tel: 250-492-2600; *Fax:* 250-492-2498
bwyatt@shawcable.com
Number of Beds: 83 beds
Brian Wyatt, Administrator

Penticton: **Penticton & District Retirement Centre**
Affiliated with: Interior Health Authority
439 Winnipeg St., Penticton, BC V2A 6P5
Tel: 250-770-7400; *Fax:* 250-492-1091
Number of Beds: 101 beds
Betty Ashton, Care Unit Coordinator

Port Alberni: **Echo Village**
Affiliated with: Vancouver Island Health Authority
4200 - 10th Ave., Port Alberni, BC V9Y 4X3
Tel: 250-724-1090; *Fax:* 250-724-2115
Number of Beds: 65 beds
Barbara A. Stevenson, Administrator

Port Alberni: **Fir Park Village**
Affiliated with: Vancouver Island Health Authority
4411 Wallace St., Port Alberni, BC V9Y 7Y5
Tel: 250-724-6541; *Fax:* 250-724-6543
bstevenson@acccs.ca
Number of Beds: 62 beds
Barb Stevenson, Executive Director

Port Alberni: **Tsawaayuus-Rainbow Gardens**
Affiliated with: Vancouver Island Health Authority
6151 Russell Pl., Port Alberni, BC V9Y 7W3
Tel: 250-724-5655; *Fax:* 250-724-5666
Number of Beds: 30 beds
Lillian Thomas, Administrator

Port Coquitlam: **Hawthorne Care Centre**
Affiliated with: Fraser Health Authority
2111 Hawthorne Ave., Port Coquitlam, BC V3C 1W3
Tel: 604-941-4051; *Fax:* 604-941-5829
Number of Beds: 125 beds
Lenore Pickering, Administrator

***Port Coquitlam:* Melissa Park Lodge**
Affiliated with: Fraser Health Authority
2175 Mary Hill Rd., Port Coquitlam, BC V3C 3A2
Tel: 604-942-4325; *Fax:* 604-526-2984
Number of Beds: 20 beds
Ronald Wong, Manager

***Pouce Coupe:* Peace River Haven**
Affiliated with: Northern Health Authority
PO Box 188, 5213 - 50th Ave., Pouce Coupe, BC V0C 2C0
Tel: 250-786-6100; *Fax:* 250-786-6107
Number of Beds: 60 beds
Note: intermediate level
Elaine Washington, Resident Care Manager

***Prince George:* AiMHi - Prince George Association for Community Living**
500 Victoria St., 3rd Fl., Prince George, BC V2L 2J9
Tel: 250-564-6408; *Fax:* 250-564-6801
aimhi@aimhi.ca
www.aimhi.ca
Number of Beds: 47 beds
Note: non-profit, supports individuals with developmental disabilities & children with special needs
Carol Burbee, Contact

***Prince George:* Simon Fraser Lodge**
2410 Laurier Cres., Prince George, BC V2M 2B3
Tel: 250-563-3413; *Fax:* 250-563-7209
Number of Beds: 131 beds
Kathy Giene, Administrator

***Prince Rupert:* Acropolis Manor**
Affiliated with: Northern Health Authority
1325 Summit Ave., Prince Rupert, BC V8J 4C1
Tel: 250-627-8497; *Fax:* 250-627-1490
Number of Beds: 50 beds
Karen Inkpen, Clinical Coordinator

***Princeton:* Ridgewood Lodge**
98 Ridgewood Dr., Princeton, BC V0X 1W0
Tel: 250-295-5551; *Fax:* 250-295-4081
Number of Beds: 37 beds
Marilyn Harkness, Administrator

***Qualicum Beach:* Arranglen Lodge**
Affiliated with: vancouver Island Health Authority
2300 Fowler Rd., Qualicum Beach, BC V9K 2A5
Tel: 250-752-9277; *Fax:* 250-752-5525
dderepentigny@cpac-care.com
Number of Beds: 85 beds
Diane Derepentigny, Administrator

***Qualicum Beach:* Eagle Park Health Care Facility**
Affiliated with: Vancouver Island Health Authority
777 Jones St., Qualicum Beach, BC V9K 2L1
Tel: 250-752-7075; *Fax:* 250-752-8316
Number of Beds: 10 beds
Jill Forsythe, Director, Residential Care

***Quesnel:* Dunrovin Park Lodge**
Affiliated with: Northern Health Authority
351 Murphy St., Quesnel, BC V2J 3S3
Tel: 250-992-5263; *Fax:* 250-992-5277
Number of Beds: 75 beds
Val Waymark, Program Manager, Home & Community Care

***Revelstoke:* Shuswap Lake General Hospital**
Affiliated with: Interior Health Authority
601 - 10th St. NE, Revelstoke, BC V1E 4N6
Tel: 250-833-3600; *Fax:* 250-833-3611
Number of Beds: 21 beds
Dorothy Schiller

***Richmond:* Courtyard Gardens**
Affiliated with: Vancouver Coastal Health Authority
7051 Moffatt Rd., Richmond, BC V6Y 3W2
Tel: 604-273-1225; *Fax:* 604-273-9253
courtyardgardens_info@diversicare.ca
www.diversicare.ca
Number of Beds: 31 intermediate care beds, 107 assisted living apts, 1 respi
Note: 107 suites of assisted living
Maggie Keatley, General Manager

***Richmond:* Fraserview Intermediate Care Lodge Co. Ltd.**
Affiliated with: Vancouver Coastal Health Authority
9580 Williams Rd., Richmond, BC V7A 1H2
Tel: 604-274-3510; *Fax:* 604-275-0996
Number of Beds: 105 beds
A.M. Baron, Administrator

***Richmond:* Pinegrove Place**
Affiliated with: Vancouver Coastal Health Authority
11331 Mellis Dr., Richmond, BC V6X 1L8
Tel: 604-278-1296; *Fax:* 604-273-0050
Number of Beds: 75 beds
Gordon Milner, Administrator

***Richmond:* Richmond Lions Manor**
Affiliated with: Vancouver Coastal Health Authority
11771 Fentiman Pl., Richmond, BC V7E 3M4
Tel: 604-274-6311; *Fax:* 604-274-2543
Number of Beds: 132 beds
S. Garrison, Medical Coordinator

***Richmond:* Rosewood Manor**
Affiliated with: Vancouver Coastal Health Authority
6260 Blundell Rd., Richmond, BC V7C 5C4
Tel: 604-271-3590; *Fax:* 604-271-3551
Number of Beds: 120 beds
Note: intermediate & complex care
Deborah Goegan, Administrator

***Salt Spring Island:* Greenwoods**
Affiliated with: Vancouver Island Health Authority
133 Blain Rd., Salt Spring Island, BC V8K 1Z9
Tel: 250-537-5561; *Fax:* 250-537-1124
catherinb53@yahoo.ca
Number of Beds: 50 beds
Andrew Brown, Administrator

***Sechelt:* Shorncliffe**
5847 Medusa St., Sechelt, BC V0N 3A0
Tel: 604-885-5126; *Fax:* 604-885-5140
dennis.regnier@cgh.bc.ca
Number of Beds: 60 beds
Dennis Regnier, Coordinator

***Shawnigan Lake:* Acacia Ty Mawr Lodge**
2655 Shawnigan Lake Rd. East, Shawnigan Lake, BC V0R 2W0
Tel: 250-743-2124; *Fax:* 250-743-2130
administration@acaciatymawr.com
Number of Beds: 35 beds
J. Neil Stuart, Administrator

***Sidney:* Sidney Intermediate Care Home Ltd.**
9888 - 5th St., Sidney, BC V8L 2X3
Tel: 250-656-0121; *Fax:* 250-656-0189
Number of Beds: 52 beds
Susan Irvine, Administrator

***Smithers:* Buckley Lodge**
Affiliated with: Northern Health Authority
3668 - 11th Ave., Smithers, BC V0J 2N0
Tel: 250-847-4443; *Fax:* 250-847-3895
Number of Beds: 73 beds
Heather Hodson, Administrator

***South Surrey:* Peace Portal Lodge**
Affiliated with: Fraser Health Authority
15441 - 16th Ave., South Surrey, BC V4A 8T8
Tel: 604-535-2273; *Fax:* 604-535-3051
swilson@retirementconcepts.com
www.retirementconcepts.com
Number of Beds: 27 beds
Susan Wilson, Administrator

***Squamish:* Hilltop House**
Affiliated with: Vancouver Coastal Health Authority
38146 Behrner Dr., Squamish, BC V8B 0J3
Tel: 604-892-9337; *Fax:* 604-892-6091
Number of Beds: 10 beds for dementia care, 31 intermediate care, 20 extended
Note: long term care
Marian Biln

***Summerland:* Kelly Care Centre**
12801 Kelly Ave., Summerland, BC V0H 1Z0
Tel: 250-494-7911; *Fax:* 250-494-4027
Number of Beds: 79 beds
Lorraine Ferguson

***Surrey:* Bear Creek Lodge**
Affiliated with: Fraser Health Authority
13646 - 94A Ave., Surrey, BC V3V 1N1
Tel: 604-581-4028; *Fax:* 604-581-8523
info@bearcreek-lodge.com
www.bearcreek-lodge.com
Number of Beds: 115 beds
Hendrik Van Ryk, COO

***Surrey:* Centennial Park Lodge**
Affiliated with: Fraser Health Authority
11861 - 99 Ave., Surrey, BC V3V 2M3
Tel: 604-584-6811; *Fax:* 604-581-4768
kahmon@telus.net
Number of Beds: 26 beds
Kevin Ahmon, Administrator

***Surrey:* Crescent Gardens**
Affiliated with: Fraser Health Authority
1222 King George Hwy., Surrey, BC V4A 9W6
Tel: 604-541-8861; *Fax:* 604-541-8871
bcosta@cpac-care.com
www.chartwellreit.ca
Number of Beds: 53 beds
Ann Varona, Director of Care

***Surrey:* Evergreen Cottages**
Affiliated with: Fraser Health Authority
15660 - 84th Ave., Surrey, BC V3A 2N5
Tel: 604-597-7906; *Fax:* 604-597-9025
www.evergreen-cottages.com
Number of Beds: 33 beds
Marion Butte, Administrator

***Surrey:* Fleetwood Place**
Affiliated with: Fraser Health Authority
16011 - 83rd Ave., Surrey, BC V3S 8M2
Tel: 604-590-6860; *Fax:* 604-590-6861
messages@fleetwoodplace.ca
Number of Beds: 75 beds
Kevin Ahmon, Administrator

***Surrey:* Guildford Seniors Village**
Affiliated with: Fraser Health Authority
14584 - 104A Ave., Surrey, BC V3R 1R3
Tel: 604-582-0808; *Fax:* 604-582-7011
Number of Beds: 60 beds
Leslie Karmazinuk, Administrator

***Surrey:* Hilton Villa Care Centre**
Affiliated with: Fraser Health Authority
13525 Hilton Rd., Surrey, BC V3R 5J3
Tel: 604-588-3424; *Fax:* 604-588-3433
Number of Beds: 124 beds
Al Jina, Administrator

***Surrey:* Kinsmen Place Lodge**
Affiliated with: Fraser Health Authority
13333 Old Yale Rd., Surrey, BC V3T 5A2
Tel: 604-588-0445; *Fax:* 604-588-7211
www.kinsmenplace.org
Number of Beds: 143 beds
Note: intermediate care
Karen Holt, Director, Resident Care

***Surrey:* Morgan Place**
Affiliated with: Fraser Health Authority
3288 - 156A St., Surrey, BC V3S 9T1
Tel: 604-535-7328; *Fax:* 604-535-7386
www.morganplace.ca
Number of Beds: 122 beds
Betty Ahmon, Administrator

***Surrey:* Newton Regency**
Affiliated with: Fraser Health Authority
13855 - 68 Ave., Surrey, BC V3W 2G9
Tel: 604-597-9333; *Fax:* 604-597-8032
reception@newtonregency.ca
www.newtonregency.ca
Number of Beds: 136 beds
Note: adults, resdential care
Rudy Young, Director of Care
Rudi Young, Manager of Facility

***Surrey:* Zion Park Manor**
Affiliated with: Fraser Health Authority
5939 - 180th St., Surrey, BC V3S 4L2
Tel: 604-576-2891; *Fax:* 604-576-8046
Number of Beds: 142 beds
Thomas Crump, Administrator

***Trail:* Columbia View Lodge**
Affiliated with: Interior Health Authority
2920 Laburnum Dr., Trail, BC V1R 4N2
Tel: 250-364-1271; *Fax:* 250-364-0911
Number of Beds: 77 beds
Note: complex care facility
Norma Mildenberger, Director, Residential Care

***Trail:* Kiro Manor**
Affiliated with: Interior Health Authority
1500 Columbia Ave., Trail, BC V1R 1J9
Tel: 250-364-1214; *Fax:* 250-364-1261
Number of Beds: 9 beds
Norman Mildenberger

***Trail:* Poplar Ridge Pavillion**
Affiliated with: Interior Health Authority
1200 Hospital Bench, Trail, BC V1R 4M1
Tel: 250-368-3311; *Fax:* 250-364-3422
Number of Beds: 50 beds
Frank Marino, Health Service Administrator

***Vancouver:* Adanac Park Lodge**
Affiliated with: Vancouver Coastal Health Authority
851 Boundary Rd., Vancouver, BC V5K 4T2
Tel: 604-299-7567; *Fax:* 604-299-7424
Number of Beds: 72 beds
Dan Levitt, Executive Director

***Vancouver:* Amica at Arbutus Manor**
Affiliated with: Vancouver Coastal Health Authority
2125 Eddington Dr., Vancouver, BC V6L 3A9
Tel: 604-736-8936; *Fax:* 604-731-8933
Number of Beds: 125 beds
Holly Goldsmith, Facilities Manager

***Vancouver:* Arbutus Care Centre**
Affiliated with: Vancouver Coastal Health Authority
4505 Valley Dr., Vancouver, BC V6L 2L1
Tel: 604-261-4292; *Fax:* 604-261-7849
arbutus@reveraliving.com
www.reveraliving.com
Number of Beds: 161 beds
Note: Specialty: Complex residential care; Nursing care; Foot care; Social work; Recreational therapy; Music therapy

***Vancouver:* Balfour House**
Affiliated with: Vancouver Coastal Health Authority
1490 Balfour St., Vancouver, BC V6H 1Y1
Tel: 604-733-0222; *Fax:* 604-714-1386
Number of Beds: 18 beds
D. Morton, Administrator

***Vancouver:* Blenheim Lodge**
Affiliated with: Vancouver Coastal Health Authority
3263 Blenheim St., Vancouver, BC V6L 2X7
Tel: 604-732-8717; *Fax:* 604-732-7316
Number of Beds: 109 beds
Derek Morton, Administrator

***Vancouver:* Braddan Private Hospital**
Affiliated with: Vancouver Coastal Health Authority
2450 - 2nd Ave., Vancouver, BC V6K 1J6
Tel: 604-731-2127; *Fax:* 604-731-0283
mcintosh@axion.net
Number of Beds: 51 beds
Maureen McIntosh, Administrator

***Vancouver:* Broadway Pentecostal Lodge**
Affiliated with: Vancouver Coastal Health Authority
1377 Lamey's Mill Rd., Vancouver, BC V6H 3S9
Tel: 604-733-1441; *Fax:* 604-731-1484
Number of Beds: 114 beds
Jeanette Thompson, Administrator

***Vancouver:* Chalmers Lodge Personal Care Home**
Affiliated with: Vancouver Coastal Health Authority
1450 - 12th Ave. West, Vancouver, BC V6H 1M9
Tel: 604-731-3178; *Fax:* 604-731-3140
info@chalmerslodge.ca
www.chalmerslodge.ca
Number of Beds: 130 beds
Note: personal care home
K.P.S. Aujlay, CEO

***Vancouver:* City Centre Care Society - Central City Lodge**
Affiliated with: Vancouver Coastal Health Authority
415 West Pender St., Vancouver, BC V6B 1V2
Tel: 604-681-9111; *Fax:* 604-681-5546
Number of Beds: 122 beds
Note: multilevel care; supportive housing - addictions recovery
Catherine Adair, Executive Director

***Vancouver:* City Centre Care Society - Cooper Place**
Affiliated with: Vancouver Coastal Health Authority
306 Cordova St. East, Vancouver, BC V6A 1L5
Tel: 604-684-2545; *Fax:* 604-684-2575
Number of Beds: 72 beds
Antonia Reynolds, Manager, Assisted Living

***Vancouver:* Columbus Residence**
Affiliated with: Vancouver Coastal Health Authority
704 West 69th Ave., Vancouver, BC V6P 2W3
Tel: 604-321-4405; *Fax:* 604-321-4543
Number of Beds: 76 beds
Peter Horsfield, Executive Director

***Vancouver:* Crofton Manor**
Affiliated with: Vancouver Coastal Health Authority
2803 - 41 Ave. West, Vancouver, BC V6N 4B4
Tel: 604-263-0921; *Fax:* 604-263-7719
cm.mkg@lra.ca
www.lrc.ca/crofton.asp
Number of Beds: 194 suites
Carol Omstead, General Manager

***Vancouver:* Dogwood Lodge**
Affiliated with: Vancouver Coastal Health Authority
500 West 57th Ave., Vancouver, BC V6P 6E8
Tel: 604-324-6882; *Fax:* 604-324-7226
Number of Beds: 113 beds
Susan Fong, Administrator

***Vancouver:* Fair Haven United Church Home**
Affiliated with: Vancouver Coastal Health Authority
2720 East 48th St., Vancouver, BC V5S 1G7
Tel: 604-433-2939; *Fax:* 604-433-4547
mharrison@fairhaven.bc.ca
Number of Beds: 69 beds
Maureen Harrison, COO

***Vancouver:* False Creek Residence**
Affiliated with: Vancouver Coastal Health Authority
1167 Forge Walk, Vancouver, BC V6H 3R1
Tel: 604-731-0401; *Fax:* 604-731-9546
info@rils.ca
www.rils.ca
Number of Beds: 24 beds
Kathleen Mason, Executive Director

***Vancouver:* George Pearson Centre**
Affiliated with: Vancouver Coastal Health Authority
700 West 57th Ave., Vancouver, BC V6P 1S1
Tel: 604-321-3231; *Fax:* 604-321-7833
Number of Beds: 120 beds
Maureen White, COO

***Vancouver:* German-Canadian Care Home**
Affiliated with: Vancouver Coastal Health Authority
2010 Harrison Dr., Vancouver, BC V5P 2P6
Tel: 604-713-6500; *Fax:* 604-713-6548
Number of Beds: 144 beds
Donna Dougan, CEO

***Vancouver:* Haro Park Centre**
Affiliated with: Vancouver Coastal Health Authority
1233 Haro St., Vancouver, BC V6E 3Y5
Tel: 604-687-5584; *Fax:* 604-687-0645
info@haropark.org
www.haropark.org
Number of Beds: 190 suites
Shayne Ramsay, Chief Executive Officer

***Vancouver:* Icelandic Care Home**
Affiliated with: Vancouver Coastal Health Authority
2020 Harrison Dr., Vancouver, BC V5P 2P6
Tel: 604-321-3812; *Fax:* 604-321-3863
Number of Beds: 64 beds
Marlene Wynes, Administrator

***Vancouver:* Kopernik Lodge**
Kopernik Nicolaus Foundation
Affiliated with: Vancouver Coastal Health Authority
3150 Rosemont Dr., Vancouver, BC V5S 2C9
Tel: 604-438-2474; *Fax:* 604-438-5344
admin@kopernik-lodge.bc.ca
www.kopernik-foundation.org
Number of Beds: 87 beds
Note: intermediate care facility
Diana Ollmann, Administrator/CEO

***Vancouver:* L & T Rehabilitation Services Ltd.**
Affiliated with: Vancouver Coastal Health Authority
3103 Kings Way, Vancouver, BC V5R 5J9
Tel: 604-439-7545; *Fax:* 604-439-1326
Number of Beds: 19 beds
Joan Grimsrud, Administrator

***Vancouver:* Lakeview Care Centre**
3490 Porter St., Vancouver, BC V5N 4H2
Tel: 604-874-2803; *Fax:* 604-874-7744
Number of Beds: 165 beds
Pat May, Administrator

***Vancouver:* Little Mountain Place**
Affiliated with: Vancouver Coastal Health Authority
330 East 36th Ave., Vancouver, BC V5W 3Z4
Tel: 604-325-2298; *Fax:* 604-325-3655
www.littlemountaincare.ca
Number of Beds: 117 beds
Dan Levitt, Executive Director

***Vancouver:* Providence Health Care**
St. Vincent's Hospital Langara
Affiliated with: Vancouver Coastal Health Authority
255 - 62nd Ave. West, Vancouver, BC V5X 4V4
Tel: 604-325-4116; *Fax:* 604-877-3081
www.providencehealthcare.org
Number of Beds: 221 beds
Note: long-term care facility
Carl Roy, President; CEO

***Vancouver:* Providence Health Care**
St. Vincent's Hospital
Affiliated with: Vancouver Coastal Health Authority
4650 Oak St., Vancouver, BC V6H 4J4
Tel: 604-877-3220; *Fax:* 604-877-3215
Number of Beds: 150 beds
Note: extended care facility
Carl Roy, President; CEO

***Vancouver:* Providence Health Care**
Youville Residence
Affiliated with: Vancouver Coastal Health Authority
4950 Heather, Vancouver, BC V5Z 3L9
Tel: 604-261-9371; *Fax:* 604-261-9047
www.providencehealthcare.org
Number of Beds: 84 beds
Note: intermediate care facility with Alzheimer ward
Carl Roy, President; CEO

***Vancouver:* Renfrew Care Centre**
Affiliated with: Vancouver Coastal Health Authority
1880 Renfrew St., Vancouver, BC V5M 3H9
Tel: 604-255-7723; *Fax:* 604-255-2045
Number of Beds: 88 beds
Loraine Coffin, Administrator

***Vancouver:* Royal Arch Masonic Home**
Affiliated with: Vancouver Coastal Health Authority
7850 Champlain Cres., Vancouver, BC V5S 4C7
Tel: 604-437-7343; *Fax:* 604-437-7373
Number of Beds: 151 beds
Gregory Runzer, Administrator

***Vancouver:* Royal Ascot Care Centre**
Affiliated with: Vancouver Coastal Health Authority
2455 Broadway East, Vancouver, BC V5M 1Y7
Tel: 604-254-5559; *Fax:* 604-254-5523
Number of Beds: 82 beds
Cheryl Scarlett, Administrator

***Vancouver:* St. Bernard House**
Affiliated with: Vancouver Coastal Health Authority
547 - 12th Ave. East, Vancouver, BC V5T 2H6
Tel: 604-874-8657; *Fax:* 604-984-7933
Number of Beds: 12 beds
David A. Russell, Administrator

***Vancouver:* Salvation Army Southview Terrace**
Affiliated with: Vancouver Coastal Health Authority
3131 East 58th Ave., Vancouver, BC V5S 4V2
Tel: 604-438-3367; *Fax:* 604-438-0262
Note: personal care facility

***Vancouver:* South Granville Park Lodge**
Affiliated with: Vancouver Coastal Health Authority
1645 West 14th Ave., Vancouver, BC V6J 2J4
Tel: 604-732-8633; *Fax:* 604-732-9833
jack@smartt.com
www.sgplodge.com
Number of Beds: 120 beds
Zdenka Votrubova, Director, Nursing

***Vancouver:* Three Links Care Centre**
Affiliated with: Vancouver Coastal Health Authority
2934 East 22nd Ave., Vancouver, BC V5M 2Y4
Tel: 604-434-7211; *Fax:* 604-438-7563
info@threelinks.com
www.threelinks.com
Number of Beds: 90 beds
Note: complex care facility
Tom Novak, CEO

Vancouver: **Villa Cathay Care Home**
Affiliated with: Vancouver Coastal Health Authority
970 Union St., Vancouver, BC V6A 3V1
Tel: 604-254-5621; *Fax:* 604-254-5230
www.villacathay.ca
Number of Beds: 188 beds
Hudson Chong, COO

Vancouver: **Windermere Care Centre**
Affiliated with: Vancouver Coastal Health Authority
900 West 12th Ave., Vancouver, BC V5Z 1N3
Tel: 604-736-8676; *Fax:* 604-736-8682
sugimoto@portal.ca
Number of Beds: 196 beds
Note: complex care
Ross Sugimoto, Administrator

Vancouver: **Yaletown House Society**
Affiliated with: Vancouver Coastal Health Authority
1099 Cambie St., Vancouver, BC V6B 5A8
Tel: 604-689-0022; *Fax:* 604-662-7954
Number of Beds: 130 beds
Carol Crichton, Executive Director

Vanderhoof: **Omineca Lodge**
Affiliated with: Northern Health Authority
Bag 5000, 242 Louvain St., Vanderhoof, BC V0J 3A0
Tel: 250-567-2216; *Fax:* 250-567-2677
Number of Beds: 36 beds
Note: intermediate care
Ray Scott, Administrator, Health Services

Vernon: **Bethany House**
Affiliated with: Interior Health Authority
3904 - 27 St., Vernon, BC V1T 4X7
Tel: 250-545-2060; *Fax:* 250-545-4060
Number of Beds: 37 beds
Kevin Svoboda, Facilities Manager

Vernon: **Birch Lodge**
Affiliated with: Interior Health Authority
7446 Hwy. 6, Vernon, BC V1B 3H4
Tel: 250-545-6849
Number of Beds: 29 beds
T. Huber, Facilities Manager

Vernon: **Gateby Intermediate Care Facility**
Affiliated with: Interior Health Authority
3000 Gateby Pl., Vernon, BC V1T 8V8
Tel: 250-545-4456; *Fax:* 250-545-4439
Number of Beds: 75 beds
Peter DuToit

Vernon: **Noric House Extended Care**
Affiliated with: Interior Health Authority
1400 Mission Rd., Vernon, BC V1T 9C3
Tel: 250-545-9167; *Fax:* 250-545-4980
mary.napier@interiorhealth.ca
Number of Beds: 85 beds
Peter DuToit

Victoria: **Beacon Hill Villa**
635 Superior St., Victoria, BC V8V 1V1
Tel: 250-383-5447; *Fax:* 250-361-4395
Number of Beds: 80 beds
May Sauder, Administrator

Victoria: **Beckley Farm Lodge**
Affiliated with: Vancouver Island Health Authority
530 Simcoe St., Victoria, BC V8V 1V1
Tel: 250-381-4421; *Fax:* 250-381-0112
jrobertson@beckleyfarmlodge.com
Number of Beds: 70 beds
Note: complex care & adult day centre
Jan Robertson, Administrator

Victoria: **Central Care Home**
Affiliated with: Vancouver Island Health Authority
844 Johnston St., Victoria, BC V8W 1N3
Tel: 250-384-1313; *Fax:* 250-384-9760
torr@baptisthousing.org
Number of Beds: 147 beds
Note: intermediate care
Tim Orr, Administrator

Victoria: **Chinatown Care Centre**
555 Herald St., Victoria, BC V8W 1S5
Tel: 250-381-4322; *Fax:* 250-920-0318
Number of Beds: 31 beds
May Sauder, Executive Director

Victoria: **Craigdarroch Care Home**
Affiliated with: Vancouver Island Health Authority
1048 Craigdarroch Rd., Victoria, BC V8W 1N3
Tel: 250-595-3813; *Fax:* 250-595-3836
Number of Beds: 18 beds
J.O. Scott, Administrator

Victoria: **Hart Home Seniors Residence**
Affiliated with: Vancouver Island Health Authority
1961 Fairfield Rd., Victoria, BC V8S 1H5
Tel: 250-598-3542; *Fax:* 250-598-2594
harthouse@shaw.ca
Number of Beds: 20 beds
Note: intermediate care home
Melanie Sundquist, Manager

Victoria: **James Bay Lodge**
Affiliated with: Vancouver Island Health Authority
336 Simcoe St., Victoria, BC V8V 1L2
Tel: 250-388-6457; *Fax:* 250-381-2969
Number of Beds: 208 beds
Note: intermediate care
Stan Dubas, Administrator

Victoria: **The Kensington**
3965 Shelbourne St., Victoria, BC V8N 6J4
Tel: 250-477-1232; *Fax:* 250-472-1271
kv.mkg@lrc.ca
www.lrc.ca
Number of Beds: 116 suites
Alaine Reimer, General Manager

Victoria: **Kiwanis Pavilion**
Affiliated with: Vancouver Island Health Authority
Former Name: Oak Bay Kiwanis Pavilion
3034 Cedar Hill Rd., Victoria, BC V8T 3J3
Tel: 250-598-2022; *Fax:* 250-598-0023
www.obkp.org
Number of Beds: 117 beds
Note: multi level care facility
William B. Cuthill, Administrator

Victoria: **Lodge at Broadmead**
Affiliated with: Vancouver Island Health Authority
4579 Chatterton Way, Victoria, BC V8X 4Y7
Tel: 250-658-0311; *Fax:* 250-658-0948
www.tvcs.ca
Number of Beds: 229 beds
Evelyn Stewart, Executive Director

Victoria: **Luther Court**
Affiliated with: Vancouver Island Health Authority
1525 Cedar Hill Cross Rd., Victoria, BC V8P 5M1
Tel: 250-477-7241; *Fax:* 250-477-5740
jsolomon@luthercourtsociety.org
Number of Beds: 66 beds
Joanne Solomonson, CEO

Victoria: **Mount Edwards Court Care Home**
Affiliated with: Vancouver Island Health Authority
1002 Vancouver St., Victoria, BC V8V 3V8
Tel: 250-385-2241; *Fax:* 250-385-4842
torr@baptisthousing.org
Number of Beds: 83 beds
Tim Orr, Administrator

Victoria: **Mount St. Mary Hospital**
Affiliated with: Vancouver Island Health Authority
861 Fairfield Rd., Victoria, BC V8V 5A9
Tel: 250-480-3100; *Fax:* 250-480-3110
www.mtstmary.victoria.bc.ca
Number of Beds: 200 beds
Note: extended care
Colleen Black, CEO
Doug Moffatt, Physical Plant

Victoria: **Oak Bay Lodge**
Affiliated with: Vancouver Island Health Authority
2251 Cadboro Bay Rd., Victoria, BC V8R 5H3
Tel: 250-370-6600; *Fax:* 250-370-6601
Number of Beds: 245 beds
Heather Cook
Heather.cook@gov.bc.ca

Victoria: **Rose Manor**
Affiliated with: Vancouver Island Health Authority
857 Rupert Terrace, Victoria, BC V8V 3E5
Tel: 250-383-0414; *Fax:* 250-360-2039
www.rosemanor.ca
Number of Beds: 128 beds
James Baird, Administrator

Victoria: **Sandringham Hospital**
Affiliated with: Vancouver Island Health Authority
1650 Fort St., Victoria, BC V8R 1H9
Tel: 250-595-2313; *Fax:* 250-595-4137
Number of Beds: 85 beds
Stan Dubas, Administrator

West Vancouver: **Capilano Care Centre**
Affiliated with: Vancouver Island Health Authority
525 Clyde Ave., West Vancouver, BC V7T 1C4
Tel: 604-926-6856; *Fax:* 604-926-0245
Number of Beds: 217 beds
Donna Moroz, Administrator

West Vancouver: **Hollyburn House**
Affiliated with: Vancouver Coastal Health Authority
2095 Marine Dr., West Vancouver, BC V7V 4V5
Tel: 604-922-7616; *Fax:* 604-922-9163
Number of Beds: 102 suites
June Messmer, General Manager

West Vancouver: **Inglewood Care Centre**
Affiliated with: Vancouver Coastal Health Authority
725 Inglewood Ave., West Vancouver, BC V7T 1X5
Tel: 604-922-9394; *Fax:* 604-922-2709
Number of Beds: 231 beds
Note: multi-level care
Nick Whittle, Administrator

Westbank: **Brookhaven Extended Care Centre**
Affiliated with: Interior Health Authority
1775 Shannon Lake Rd., Westbank, BC V4T 2N7
Tel: 250-862-4040; *Fax:* 250-862-4048
dolorese.rudnicki@interiorhealth.ca
www.interiorhealth.ca
Number of Beds: 168 beds
Dolorese Rudnicki, Primary Contact

Westbank: **Pine Acres Home**
Affiliated with: Interior Health Authority
1902 Pheasant Lane, Westbank, BC V4T 2H4
Tel: 250-768-7676; *Fax:* 250-768-3234
Number of Beds: 40 community beds, 23 private care beds
Note: complex care
JoAnn Derrickson, Administrator

Westbank: **Westside Care Centre**
Affiliated with: Interior Health Authority
3324 Old Okanagan Hwy., Westbank, BC V4T 1N3
Tel: 250-768-0488; *Fax:* 250-768-4777
Number of Beds: 98 beds
Elizabeth Harris, Managing Director

White Rock: **Bel Air Rest Home**
Affiliated with: Fraser Health Authority
14824 North Bluff Rd., White Rock, BC V4B 3E2
Tel: 604-536-1224; *Fax:* 604-536-1267
Number of Beds: 31 beds
Karen Armitage, Director

White Rock: **Evergreen Baptist Home**
Affiliated with: Fraser Health Authority
1550 Oxford St., White Rock, BC V4B 3R5
Tel: 604-536-3344; *Fax:* 604-541-3803
www.evergreen-home.com
Number of Beds: 157 beds
Linda Ingham, Administrator

White Rock: **Ocean View Care Home**
Affiliated with: Fraser Health Authority
15628 Buena Vista Ave., White Rock, BC V4B 1Z4
Tel: 604-531-2273; *Fax:* 604-531-8782
Number of Beds: 71 beds
Note: Specialty: Residential care for seniors; Secure unit for persons with dementia
Pat Mulcahy, Administrator

Williams Lake: **Jubilee Care Home**
Affiliated with: Interior Health Authority
196 - 2nd Ave. North, Williams Lake, BC V2G 1Z6
Tel: 250-398-7736; *Fax:* 250-398-7736
Number of Beds: 7 beds
Note: mental health group home
Doris Foote, Administrator

Winfield: **Lake Country Lodge**
10163 Konschuh Rd., Winfield, BC V4V 2M2
Tel: 250-766-3007; *Fax:* 250-766-3178
admin@lakecountrylodge.ca
www.lakecountrylodge.ca
Number of Beds: 34 beds
Cathy Redden, Facilities Manager

Nursing Homes

Coquitlam: Belvedere Care Centre
Affiliated with: Fraser Health Authority
Also Known As: Belvedere Care Centre & Residences at Belvedere
739 Alderson Ave., Coquitlam, BC V3K 7B3
Tel: 604-939-5991; *Fax:* 604-939-5910
belvederecare@telus.net
www.belvederecare.com
Number of Beds: 148 complex care beds at care centre; 114 units for seniors at assisted living centre, including a secure unit for 11 residents
Note: Specialties: Complex care for seniors; Assisted living for residents with mild cognitive impairment; Wellness programs; Diabetes management; Therapy; Rehabilitation; Dementia care; Chronic care; Palliative care
Berton B. Evertt, Chair; Chief Executive Officer
Annamae Clarke, Vice-President
Andrew Butler, Manager, Strategic Planning
Jennifer Cuvelier, Manager, Administration Services
Aileen Mellors-Luyt, Manager, Support Services
Karen Slutsken, Manager, Resident Relations
Fay Woodward, Manager, Resident Services
Dr. Azim Ladhani, Medical Coordinator
Linda Tod, Coordinator, Quality Improvement
Greg Graham, Controller
Gayle Vanags, Registered Dietitian

Coquitlam: Dufferin Care Centre
Retirement Concepts
1131 Dufferin St., Coquitlam, BC V3B 7X5
Tel: 604-552-1166; *Fax:* 604-552-3116
www.retirementconcepts.com
Number of Beds: 153 beds
Note: Specialties: Continuing care; Nursing care; Physiotherapy; Recreation therapy; Music therapy
Pat Kittler, General Manager
pkittler@retirementconcepts.com
Shannon Johnson, Director, Care
Elaine Drysdale, Coordinator, Administration
edrysdale@retirementconcepts.com
Doris Robinson, Coordinator, Marketing
604-375-9193, drobinson@retirementconcepts.com

Vancouver: George Pearson Centre (GPC)
Affiliated with: Vancouver Coastal Health Authority
700 West 57th Ave., Vancouver, BC V6P 1S1
Tel: 604-321-3231; *Fax:* 604-321-7833
feedback@vch.ca
www.vch.ca
Year Founded: 1952
Number of Beds: 120 beds; 1 respite bed
Note: Specialties: Residential & complex medical care for adults with severe disabilities, such as cerebral palsy, multiple sclerosis, & spinal cord & traumatic brain injury; Special care units for ventilator dependent residents & persons with tracheostomies; Occupational therapy, physical therapy, pool therapy, music therapy, & respiratory therapy; Speech language pathology; Social work

Retirement Residences

Burnaby: CPAC (Carlton Gardens) Inc.
4125 Canada Way, Burnaby, BC V5G 1G9
Tel: 604-438-8224; *Fax:* 604-438-6571
Note: Specialty: Care for the elderly

Coquitlam: Parkwood Manor
1142 Dufferin St., Coquitlam, BC V3B 6V4
Tel: 604-941-7651; *Fax:* 604-941-4223
parkwoodmanor@lrc.ca
www.reveraliving.com
Number of Beds: 139 suites
Note: Independent living, convalescent & respite options
Wilma Mitchell, General Manager

Surrey: Whitecliff
15501 - 16th Ave., Surrey, BC V4A 9M5
Tel: 604-538-7227; *Fax:* 604-538-4919
whiteclif@lrc.ca
www.reveraliving.com
Number of Beds: 133 suites; 18 beds
Note: Independent living, convalescent & respite options
Sherry Fossum, General Manager

Victoria: Parkwood Court
3000 Shelbourne St., Victoria, BC V8R 4M8
Tel: 250-598-1575; *Fax:* 250-598-7372
parkwoodcourt@lrc.ca
www.reveraliving.com
Number of Beds: 83 suites
Note: Assisted living, respite & convalescent options
Jan Bard, General Manager

Victoria: Parkwood Place
3051 Shelbourne St., Victoria, BC V8R 6T2
Tel: 250-598-1565; *Fax:* 250-598-8222
parkwoodplace@lrc.ca
www.reveraliving.com
Linda Bartel, Director, Marketing

Mental Health Facilities

Mental Health Hospitals/Facilities

Burnaby: Craigend Rest Home
5480 Patterson Ave., Burnaby, BC V5H 2M5
Tel: 604-433-8600
Number of Beds: 10 beds
Sayo Gardenia, Manager

Kamloops: Forensic Psychiatric Services Commission (B.C.)
Kamloops Clinic
#5, 1315 Summit Dr., Kamloops, BC V2C 5R9
Tel: 250-377-2660; *Fax:* 250-371-3894
www.bcmhas.ca/ForensicService/ForensicRegionalServices.htm
Rose Dumont, Coordinator

Kamloops: Kamloops Youth Forensic Psychiatric Services
#8, 1315 Summit Dr., Kamloops, BC V2C 5R9
Tel: 250-828-4940; *Fax:* 250-828-4946
Note: for young offenders directed by court/probation to assessment/treatment
Judie Hogg, Regional Office Manager
250/861-7601,

Kelowna: White Heather Manor
3728 Casorso Rd., Kelowna, BC V1W 4M8
Tel: 250-763-6554; *Fax:* 250-763-6754
Number of Beds: 24 beds
Peter White, Manager

Maple Ridge: Trejan Lodge Ltd.
25402 Johnson Ave., Maple Ridge, BC V4R 1G3
Tel: 604-467-3377; *Fax:* 604-467-0705
Note: Specialty: Long-term care
Mary Blume, Care Manager

Mission: Waddell's Haven Guest Home
12459 Dewdney Trunk Rd., Mission, BC V2V 5X4
Tel: 604-826-7420
Number of Beds: 30 beds
Betty Baird, Manager

Nanaimo: Forensic Psychiatric Services Commission (B.C.)
Nanaimo Clinic
Former Name: Nanaimo Adult Forensic Psychiatric Community Servi
#101, 190 Wallace St., Nanaimo, BC V9R 5B1
Tel: 250-739-5000; *Fax:* 250-739-5001
www.bcmhas.ca/ForensicService/ForensicRegionalServices.htm
Angus Monaghan, Regional Manager

Nanaimo: Nanaimo Youth Forensic Psychiatric Services
#101, 190 Wallace St., Nanaimo, BC V9R 5B1
Tel: 250-741-5733; *Fax:* 250-741-5740
Note: youth forensic psychiatric outpatient clinic
André Picard, Coordinator

Port Coquitlam: Forensic Psychiatric Services Commission (B.C.)
Forensic Psychiatric Hospital
70 Colony Farm Rd., Port Coquitlam, BC V3C 5X9
Tel: 604-524-7700; *Fax:* 604-524-7905
www.bcmhas.ca/ForensicService/ForensicHospital/default.htm
Number of Beds: 190 beds
Note: State-of-the-art facility which provides specialized clinical services & comprehensive rehabilitative & vocational programs.
Leslie Arnold, President, Mental Health

Port Coquitlam: Riverview Hospital
500 Lougheed Hwy., Port Coquitlam, BC V3C 4J2
Tel: 604-524-7000; *Fax:* 604-524-7016
www.bcmhs.bc.ca
Number of Beds: 256 beds
Note: psychiatric teaching hospital
Leslie Arnold, President, Mental Health

Prince George: Forensic Psychiatric Services Commission (B.C.)
Prince George Clinic
1594 - 7 Ave., 2nd Fl., Prince George, BC V2L 3P4
Tel: 250-561-8060; *Fax:* 250-561-8075
www.bcmhas.ca/ForensicService/ForensicRegionalServices.htm
Julia Thompson, Acting Regional Director

Richmond: Westminster House
Affiliated with: Vancouver Coastal Health Authority
11675 Bird Rd., Richmond, BC V6X 1N7
Tel: 604-270-9510; *Fax:* 604-270-3539
Number of Beds: 10 beds
André Chevrier, Director

Victoria: Pacific Operational Trauma & Stress Support Centre (OTSSC)
Canadian Forces Health Services
Also Known As: Canadian Forces Health Services, Operational Be
PO Box 17000 Forces, Victoria, BC V9A 7N2
Tel: 250-363-4411
Year Founded: 1999
Note: Specialties: Assistance to serving members of the Canadian Forces & their families, who are dealing with psychological, emotional, spiritual, & social problems stemming from military operations, especially deployments abroad; Psychiatry; Psychology; Social work; Community health nursing; Educational programs; Chaplain services

Victoria: Victoria Youth Forensic Psychiatric Services
1515 Quadra St., Victoria, BC V8V 3P3
Tel: 250-387-1465; *Fax:* 250-387-3217
www.mcf.gov.bc.ca/yfps/index.htm
Gregg Badger, Regional Manager

Manitoba

Government Departments in Charge

MANITOBA: Manitoba Health
Regional Affairs Division
300 Carlton St., Winnipeg, MB R3B 3M9
Tel: 204-786-7301; *Fax:* 204-775-3412
www.gov.mb.ca/health/index.html
Donna Forbes, Asst. Deputy Minister, Regional Affairs

Regional Health Authorities

Brandon: Brandon Regional Health Authority
150A - 7th St., Brandon, MB R7A 7M2
Tel: 204-571-8400; *Fax:* 204-726-8505
turnbullp@brandonrha.mb.ca
www.brandonrha.mb.ca
Number of Beds: 186 acute care, 430 PCH, 99 EPH beds
Note: Services include: public health, home care, long term care, mental health services, comprehensive health services (cancer care, cardiac, birthing & neonatal, rehabilitation, surgery).
Carmel Olson, CEO

Churchill: Churchill Regional Health Authority Inc. (Churchil)
Corporate Office, PO Box 2500, 162 Laverendrye St., Churchill, MB R0B 0E0
Tel: 204-675-8881; *Fax:* 204-675-2243 (
humanresources@churchillrha.mb.ca
www.churchillrha.com
Note: Area Served: Churchill; the communities of the Keewatin Region of the Territory of Nunavut
Verna Flett, Board Chair
Derry Martens, Chief Executive Officer
204-675-8325, dmartens@churchillrha.mb.ca
Bobbi Sigurdson, Chief Financial Officer
204-675-8305, bsigurds@churchillrha.mb.ca
Patti MacEwan, Director, Clinical Services
204-675-8312, pmacewan@churchillrha.mb.ca
Michel Petit, Director, Community Services & Planning
204-675-8387, mpetit@churchillrha.mb.ca
Ron Sweeney, Director, Human Resources
204-675-8307, rsweeney@churchillrha.mb.ca
Amy Goulet, Manager, EMS
204-675-8356, agoulet@churchillrha.mb.ca
Debbie Leggett, Manager, Community Wellness
204-675-8383, dleggett@churchillrha.mb.ca
Ken Slobodesky, Manager, Support Services
204-675-8333, kslobodesky@churchillrha.mb.ca

David Merry, Supervisor, Material Management
204-675-8332, dmerry@churchillrha.mb.ca
Jukeepa Nowdlak, Supervisor, Health Information Systems
204-675-8309, jnowdlak@churchillrha.mb.ca

***Dauphin:* Parkland Regional Health Authority Inc.**
#112, 27 - 2nd Ave. SW, Dauphin, MB R7N 3E5
Tel: 204-622-6222; *Fax:* 204-622-6232
Toll-Free: 800-259-7541
prha@prha.mb.ca
www.prha.mb.ca
Number of Beds: 214 acute care, 545 long-term care beds
Andre Remillard, CEO

***Flin Flon:* Nor-Man Regional Health Authority Inc.**
PO Box 130, 84 Church St., Flin Flon, MB R8A 1M7
Tel: 204-687-1300; *Fax:* 204-687-6405
nrha@normanrha.mb.ca
www.norman-rha.mb.ca
Number of Beds: 264 beds
Note: Serves a population of 26,000 across 72,000 square kilometers
Drew Lockhart, CEO

***La Broquerie:* South Eastman Health/Santé Sud-Est Inc.**
PO Box 470, La Broquerie, MB R0A 0W0
Tel: 204-424-5880; *Fax:* 204-424-5888
Toll-Free: 866-716-5633
corp@sehealth.mb.ca
www.sehealth.mb.ca
Monique Vielfaure MacKenz, CEO

***Pinawa:* North Eastman Health Association Inc.**
PO Box 339, 24 Aberdeen Ave., Pinawa, MB R0E 1L0
Tel: 204-753-2012; *Fax:* 204-753-2015
Toll-Free: 877-753-2012
neha@neha.mb.ca
www.neha.mb.ca
Note: Provides services to over 38,000 people
Jim Hayes, CEO

***Souris:* Assiniboine Regional Health Authority**
Office régional de la santé Assiniboine
Corporate Office, PO Box 579, 192 - 1st Ave. West, Souris, MB R0K 2C0
Tel: 204-483-5000; *Fax:* 204-483-5005
Toll-Free: 1-888-682-2253
assiniboinerha@arha.ca
www.assiniboine-rha.ca
Note: Facilities: 20 acute care facilities; 28 long term care facilities; 7 housing units for elderly persons; 1 transitional care unit. Number of Employees: 3,000+, including 64 physicians. Population served: 69,371
Penny Gilson, Chief Executive Officer
Michelle Clark, Executive Director, Primary Care & Medical Services
Garlen Maxwell, Executive Director, Facility Services
Glenda Short, Executive Director, Allied Health Services
Lara Bossert, Chief Officer, Human Resources & Communications
Deb Clevett, Vice-President, Community Health Services
Pat Cockburn, Vice-President, Programs & Standards
Kerry Takvam, Vice-President, Corporate Services

***Stonewall:* Interlake Regional Health Authority**
589 - 3rd Ave. South, Stonewall, MB R0C 2Z0
Tel: 204-467-4742; *Fax:* 204-467-4750
Toll-Free: 1-888-488-2299
info@irha.mb.ca
www.irha.mb.ca
Note: Population Served: 77,500. Area Served: 26,000 square kilometers, covering the R.M. of Rosser to the 53rd parallel, & Lake Manitoba on the west to Lake Winnipeg on the east (14 rural municipalities, 9 First Nation communities, 5 towns, 2 villages, 1 city, plus unorganized territories)
Kevin Beresford, Chief Executive Officer
204-467-4742, kberesford@irha.mb.ca
Jim Rodger, Chair, Board of Directors
Dr. Tim Hilderman, Medical Officer of Health
204-467-4400, Tim.Hilderman@gov.mb.ca
Dr. Cary Chapnick, Vice-President, Medical Services
204-642-4524, cchapnick@irha.mb.ca
Lorne Charbonneau, Vice-President, Health Services
204-467-4749, lcharbonneau@irha.mb.ca
Doreen Fey, Vice-President, Planning
204-467-4748, dfey@irha.mb.ca
Sherry Lees, Vice-President, Corporate Services
204-785-7431, slees@irha.mb.ca
Angela Charison, Director, Finance
204-785-7432, acharison@irha.mb.ca
Gary Dandeneau, Director, Physical Facilities
204-372-7318, gdandeneau@irha.mb.ca
Dela Irwin, Director, Human Resources
204-785-7436, dirwin@irha.mb.ca
Kim Olver, Director, Home Based Programs & Services to Seniors
204-785-5504, kolver@irha.mb.ca
Kevin O'Donovan, Manager, Public Relations
204-467-4747, kodonovan@irha.mb.ca

***Thompson:* Burntwood Regional Health Authority (BRHA)**
867 Thompson Dr. South, Thompson, MB R8N 1Z4
Tel: 204-677-5350; *Fax:* 204-778-1424
Toll-Free: 1-888-442-9264
brha@brha.mb.ca
www.brha.mb.ca
Info Line: 1-888-277-2763
Note: Population Served: 45,798
Gloria King, Chief Executive Officer
204-677-5399, gking@brha.mb.ca
Marion Ellis, Chief Nursing Officer; Vice-President, Acute Care
204-677-5351, mellis@brha.mb.ca
Paul Therrien, Chief Officer, Human Resources
204-778-1519, ptherrien@brha.mb.ca
Rajinder Thethy, Chief Officer, Finance & Operations
204-677-5346, rthethy@brha.mb.ca
Dr. Lisa Richards, Medical Officer of Health
204-778-1494, lrichards@brha.mb.ca
Dr. Hussam Azzam, Vice-President, Medical Services
204-677-5376, hazzam@brha.mb.ca
Rusty Beardy, Vice-President, Aboriginal Services
204-778-1435, rbeardy@brha.mb.ca

***Winnipeg:* Winnipeg Regional Health Authority**
#1800, 155 Carlton St., Winnipeg, MB R3C 4Y1
Tel: 204-926-7000; *Fax:* 204-926-7007
info@wrha.mb.ca
www.wrha.mb.ca
Dr. Brian Postl, President; CEO
Milton Sussman, Chief Operating Officer, Vice-President, Community Health Services

Hospitals

Hospitals - General

***Altona:* Altona Community Memorial Health Centre/Eastview Place**
Affiliated with: Regional Health Authority - Central Manitoba Inc.
PO Box 660, 240 - 5 Ave. NE, Altona, MB R0G 0B0
Tel: 204-324-6411; *Fax:* 204-324-8482
Number of Beds: 22 acute care, 65 long-term care beds
Edith Calder, Facility Contact
e.calder@ahc.rha-central.mb.ca

***Arborg:* Arborg & District Health Centre**
Affiliated with: Interlake Regional Health Authority Inc.
PO Box 10, Arborg, MB R0C 0A0
Tel: 204-376-5247; *Fax:* 204-376-5669
www.irha.mb.ca
Number of Beds: 16 beds + 40 long term care beds in an attached personal care home
Note: Specialties: Diagnostic services

***Ashern:* Lakeshore General Hospital**
Affiliated with: Interlake Regional Health Authority Inc.
PO Box 110, Ashern, MB R0C 0E0
Tel: 204-768-2461; *Fax:* 204-768-2337
Number of Beds: 15 beds
Jan O'Flanagan, District Director

***Beausejour:* Beausejour District Hospital**
Affiliated with: North Eastman Health Association Inc.
PO Box 1178, Beausejour, MB R0E 0C0
Tel: 204-268-1076; *Fax:* 204-268-1207
www.neha.mb.ca
Number of Beds: 30 acute care beds
Note: Hospital Specialties: Imaging; Physiotherapy; Occupational therapy; Number of Employees: 86
Glennda Gould, Manager, Care Team

***Boissevain:* Boissevain Health Centre**
Affiliated with: Assiniboine Regional Health Authority
PO Box 899, 305 Mill Rd., Boissevain, MB R0K 0E0
Tel: 204-534-2451; *Fax:* 204-534-6487
dgraham@arha.ca (Area Manager)
www.assiniboine-rha.ca
Number of Beds: 20 beds
Note: Specialties: Emergency services; Diagnostic services; Acute care; Mental health services; Public health services; Home care; Respite care

***Brandon:* Brandon Regional Health Centre**
Affiliated with: Brandon Regional Health Authority
150 McTavish Ave. East, Brandon, MB R7A 2B3
Tel: 204-578-4219; *Fax:* 204-578-4969
www.brandonrha.mb.ca
Number of Beds: 336 beds
Note: A regional referral acute care hospital & teaching facility. Services include in- & out-patient care, rehabilitation, diagnositics, & clinics.
Kathy McPhail, Vice-President, Acute Care & Diagnostic Services
K. Martinook, Director, Physical Plant

***Carman:* Carman Memorial Hospital**
Affiliated with: Regional Health Authority - Central Manitoba Inc.
PO Box 610, 350 - 4 St., SW, Carman, MB R0G 0J0
Tel: 204-745-2021; *Fax:* 204-745-2756
www.rha-central.mb.ca
Number of Beds: 25 beds
Note: Hospital Specialties: Surgerey; Acute care; Obstetrics Physiotherapy; Diabetes education; Dietitian service; Palliative care; Number of Employees: 190 at Carman Hospital & the nearby Boyne Lodge personal care home
Mary Heard, Director, Health Services - Carman
m.heard@rha-central.mb.ca

***Crystal City:* Rock Lake Hospital/Rock Lake Health District**
Affiliated with: Regional Health Authority - Central Manitoba Inc.
PO Box 130, 135 Machray Ave., Crystal City, MB R0K 0N0
Tel: 204-873-2132; *Fax:* 204-873-2185
pking@rlh.rha-central.mb.ca
Number of Beds: 16 acute care beds
Pam King, Facility Contact

***Dauphin:* Dauphin Regional Health Centre (DRHC)**
Affiliated with: Parkland Regional Health Authority Inc.
625 - 3rd St. SW, Dauphin, MB R7N 1R7
Tel: 204-638-3010; *Toll-Free:* 1-800-259-7541
www.prha.mb.ca
Note: Hospital Specialties: Emergency medical services; Computed Tomography (CT) services; Ultrasound service; Surgical services; Acute care; Obstetrics; Chemotherapy; Hemodialysis; 10 bed acute care psychiatric unit; Manitoba Telehealth site
Kevin McKnight, Chief Executive Officer, Parkland Regional Health Authority
Blaine Kraushaar, Coordinator, Community Relations
204-622-6237, Fax: 204-622-6232, bkraushaar@prha.mb.ca

***Deloraine:* Deloraine Health Centre**
Affiliated with: Assiniboine Regional Health Authority
PO Box 447, Deloraine, MB R0M 0M0
Tel: 204-747-2745; *Fax:* 204-747-2160
www.assiniboine-rha.ca
Note: Hospital Specialties: Emergency medical services; Diagnostic services (204-747-2431); Deloraine Community Cancer Program (204-747-1836); Acute care; Mental health services; Public health services; Home care
D. Graham, Area Manager
dgraham@arha.ca

***Eriksdale:* E.M. Crowe Memorial Hospital**
PO Box 130, 1st St. NE, Eriksdale, MB R0C 0W0
Tel: 204-739-2611; *Fax:* 204-739-2065
Note: Hospital Specialties: Emergency services; X-ray services; Doppler ultrasound carotid artery scans
Jan O'Flanagan, Director, North West District, Interlake Regional Health Auth
Kevin O'Donovan, Manager, Public Relations, Interlake Regional Health Authori

Eriksdale: **Elizabeth M. Crowe Memorial Hospital**
Affiliated with: Interlake Regional Health Authority Inc.
PO Box 130, Eriksdale, MB R0C 0W0
Tel: 204-739-2611; *Fax:* 204-739-2065
Jan O'Flanagan, District Director

Flin Flon: **Flin Flon General Hospital Inc.**
Affiliated with: Nor-Man Regional Health Authority Inc.
PO Box 340, Flin Flon, MB R8A 1N2
Tel: 204-687-7591; *Fax:* 204-687-8494
www.norman-rha.mb.ca
Number of Beds: 44 acute care beds
Note: Hospital Specialty: Acute care
Lois Moberly, Executive Director, Clinical Services
204-687-9610

Gillam: **Gillam Hospital Incorporated**
Affiliated with: Burntwood Regional Health Authority Inc.
PO Box 2000, 15 Gillam Dr., Gillam, MB R0B 0L0
Tel: 204-652-2600; *Fax:* 204-652-2536
Number of Beds: 10 beds, including 3 long term beds
Note: Hospital Specialties: Emergency services; Laboratory services; Acute care; Public health; Long term care

Gimli: **Gimli Community Health Centre (GCHC)**
Affiliated with: Interlake Regional Health Authority Inc.
Johnson Memorial Hospital, PO Box 250, 120 - 6th Ave., Gimli, MB R0C 1B0
Tel: 204-642-5116; *Fax:* 204-642-5860
info@irha.mb.ca
www.irha.mb.ca
Year Founded: 2004
Number of Beds: 14 acute beds; 4 special care beds; 2 palliative care beds
Note: Specialties: Diagnostic services (204-642-4519); Laboratory services; Acute care; Chemotherapy program (204-642-4520); Physiotherapy; Occupational therapy; Community health (204-642-6051); Adult day program; Palliative care
Dr. Cary Chapnick, Vice-President, Medical Services, Interlake Regional Health Authori
204-642-4524, cchapnick@irha.mb.ca
Lorne Charbonneau, Vice-President, Health Services, Interlake Regional Health Authorit
204-467-4749, lcharbonneau@irha.mb.ca

Gladstone: **Seven Regions Health Centre**
Affiliated with: Regional Health Authority - Central Manitoba Inc.
PO Box 1000, 24 Mill St., Gladstone, MB R0J 0T0
Tel: 204-385-2968; *Fax:* 204-385-3053
Number of Beds: 14 acute care beds
Dorothy Doell, Facility Contact
d.doell@srhc.rha-central.mb.ca

Grandview: **Grandview District Hospital**
Affiliated with: Parkland Regional Health Authority Inc.
PO Box 339, 644 Mill St., Grandview, MB R0L 0Y0
Tel: 204-546-2425; *Fax:* 204-546-3269
Number of Beds: 18 beds
John Kelly, COO

Hodgson: **Percy E. Moore Hospital**
Affiliated with: Interlake Regional Health Authority Inc.
PO Box 190, Hodgson, MB R0C 1N0
Tel: 204-372-8444; *Fax:* 204-372-6991
Number of Beds: 16 beds
Note: Specialties: Dialysis services
Carol Hartog, Acting Administrator
Joe Malenchak, Head of Maintenance
L. McCorrister, Purchasing Agent

Killarney: **Tri-Lake Health Centre**
Affiliated with: Assiniboine Regional Health Authority
PO Box 5000, Killarney, MB R0K 1G0
Tel: 204-523-3210; *Fax:* 204-523-8948
www.assiniboine-rha.ca
Number of Beds: 22 beds
Note: Specialties: Acute care; Diagnostic services; Mental health services; Public health services; Home care
Bev Towler, Area Manager

Lynn Lake: **Lynn Lake District Hospital**
Affiliated with: Burntwood Regional Health Authority Inc.
PO Box 2030, 640 Camp St., Lynn Lake, MB R0B 0W0
Tel: 204-356-2474; *Fax:* 204-356-8023
dtitterson@brha.mb.ca
www.thompson.ca/dbs/brha
Number of Beds: 11 general beds + 6 long term care beds + 2 chronic beds
Note: Specialties: Public health services; Mental health services; Medical clinic; Long-term care. Number of employees: 22

McCreary: **McCreary/Alonsa Health Centre**
Affiliated with: Parkland Regional Health Authority Inc.
PO Box 250, 613 Government Rd., McCreary, MB R0J 1B0
Tel: 204-835-2482; *Fax:* 204-835-2713
Number of Beds: 13 beds
Note: Specialties: Acute care; Diagnostic services
Charlie Sitwell, Administrator

Melita: **Melita Health Centre**
Affiliated with: Assiniboine Regional Health Authority
PO Box 459, Melita, MB R0M 1L0
Tel: 204-522-8197; *Fax:* 204-522-3161
Number of Beds: 11 beds
Note: Specialties: Diagnostic services; Acute care; Outreach services; Mental health services; Physiotherapy; Occupational therapy
Georgina Henuset, Area Manager

Morris: **Morris General Hospital**
Affiliated with: Regional Health Authority - Central Manitoba Inc.
PO Box 519, 215 Railroad Ave. East, Morris, MB R0G 1K0
Tel: 204-746-2301; *Fax:* 204-746-2197
www.rha-central.mb.ca
Number of Beds: 23 acute care beds
Brad Street, Facility Contact
b.street@mgh.rha-central.mb.ca

Norway House: **Norway House Hospital**
General Delivery, Norway House, MB R0B 1B0
Tel: 204-359-6731; *Fax:* 204-359-6599
www.nhhsinc.ca
Year Founded: 1925
Leonard York, Administrator

Pinawa: **Pinawa Hospital**
Affiliated with: North Eastman Health Association Inc.
PO Box 220, 30 Vanier Dr., Pinawa, MB R0E 1L0
Tel: 204-753-2334
Year Founded: 1964
Number of Beds: 17 beds
Note: Specialties: Acute care; Community cancer care program; Physiotherapy; Occupational therapy; Palliative care
May Fast, Care Team Manager

Pine Falls: **Pine Falls Health Complex**
Affiliated with: North Eastman Health Association Inc.
PO Box 2000, 37 Maple St., Pine Falls, MB R0E 1M0
Tel: 204-367-4441
www.neha.mb.ca
Number of Beds: 23 inpatient beds + 20 personal care home beds
Note: Specialties: Health & social services; Primary medical care combined with traditional aboriginal approaches to health care; Hemodialysis; Physiotherapy; Occupational therapy; Mental health services; Palliative care
Brenda Neufeld, Director of Acute Care

Portage la Prairie: **Portage District General Hospital**
Affiliated with: Regional Health Authority - Central Manitoba Inc.
524 - 5 St. SE, Portage la Prairie, MB R1N 3A8
Tel: 204 239-2211; *Fax:* 204-239-1941
Number of Beds: 89 acute care beds
Note: 660 staff
Pat Nodrick, Director, Health Services
p.nodrick@pdgh.rha-central.mb.ca

Roblin: **Roblin District Health Centre**
Affiliated with: Parkland Regional Health Authority Inc.
PO Box 940, 15 Hospital St., Roblin, MB R0L 1P0
Tel: 204-937-2142; *Fax:* 204-937-8892
rdhc@prha.mb.ca
www.prha.mb.ca
Number of Beds: 25 bed hospital, 60 bed personal care home
Note: Emergency & diagnostic services, X-ray and EKG testing, ultrasound & mammography, podiatry, speech therapy, occupational therapy, physiotherapy
Cheryl Jerome, COO

Russell: **Russell District Health Centre**
Affiliated with: Assiniboine Regional Health Authority
Bag Service 2, Russell, MB R0J 1W0
Tel: 204-773-2125; *Fax:* 204-773-2142
Number of Beds: 32 acute care beds; 40 PCH
Barb Kostesky, Community Health Director

Selkirk: **Selkirk & District General Hospital**
Affiliated with: Interlake Regional Health Authority Inc.
PO Box 5000, 100 Easton Dr., Selkirk, MB R1A 2M2
Tel: 204-482-5800; *Fax:* 204-785-9113
www.irha.mb.ca/programs.htm
Year Founded: 1907
Number of Beds: 49 beds
Note: Emergency & outpatient services, acute care, surgery, obstetrics, physiotherapy, diagnostic imaging, chemotherapy, dialysis, palliative care, mental health services
Kevin Beresford, CEO, IRHA
204-467-4742, kberesford@irha.mb.ca
Dianne Mestdagh, Director, South East District, IRHA
204-785-7430, dmestdagh@irha.mb.ca
Edie Telenko, Executive Assistant, Selkirk
204-785-7424, etelenko@irha.mb.ca

Shoal Lake: **Shoal Lake - Strathclair Health Centre**
PO Box 490, Shoal Lake, MB R0J 1Z0
Tel: 204-759-2336; *Fax:* 204-759-2230
assiniboinerha@arha.ca
www.assiniboine-rha.ca/index.php/health_sites/view?id=36
Number of Beds: 40 personal care home beds
Note: Emergency, acute care, diagnostic services, mental Health Services, home care services, regional palliative care program, regional occupational & physiotherapy services
Roseanne Yaremchuk, Area Manager
ryaremchuk@arha.ca

St Claude: **St. Claude Health District**
Affiliated with: Regional Health Authority - Central Manitoba Inc.
PO Box 400, 33 Roy St., St Claude, MB R0G 1Z0
Tel: 204-379-2585; *Fax:* 204-379-2655
Number of Beds: 10 beds; 18 long-term care beds
Mona Spencer, Facility Contact

Ste Anne: **Hôpital Ste Anne Hospital**
Affiliated with: South Eastman Health/Santé Sud-Est Inc.
52 St Gerard St., Ste Anne, MB R5H 1C4
Tel: 204-422-8837; *Fax:* 204-422-9929
clavack@schealth.mb.ca
Number of Beds: 21 beds
Carole Lavack, Facility Manager

Ste Rose du Lac: **Ste Rose General Hospital**
Hôpital général de Ste-Rose
PO Box 60, 480 - 3rd Ave. East, Ste Rose du Lac, MB R0L 1S0
Tel: 204-447-2131
Note: Specialty: Diagnostic services
Glen Kozak, Executive Director

Steinbach: **Bethesda Hospital / Bethesda Place Complex**
Affiliated with: South Eastman Health/Santé Sud-Est Inc.
316 Henry St., Steinbach, MB R5G 0P9
Tel: 204-326-6411
www.sehealth.mb.ca
Number of Beds: 64 acute care beds; 20 rehabilitation beds
Note: Specialties: Emergency services; Diagnostic services; Laboratory services; Acute care; Cardiac care; Cancer care; Obstetrics; Physiotherapy; Occupational therapy; Speech-language pathology services; Social work; Personal care at Bethesda Place; Palliative care; Number of Employees: 471
Patti Fries, Manager, Facility
204-346-5168
Don Fast, Clinical Manager, Medicine, ER, & CancerCare
Debbie Harms, Clinical Manager, Surgery, Obstetrics, Rehabilitation, & Therapy
Ginette Morgan, Clinical Manager, Long Term Care (Bethesda Place)
Wally Driedger, Manager, Physical Plant
Marie Lacey, Manager, Nutrition & Food Services

Pam Beaudoin, Coordinator, Recreation
Ruth Campbell, Coordinator, Human Resources

Swan Lake: Lorne Memorial Hospital
Affiliated with: Regional Health Authority - Central Manitoba Inc.
9 - 2nd St. North, Swan Lake, MB R0G 2S0
Tel: 204-836-2132; *Fax:* 204-836-2044
Number of Beds: 18 acute care beds
Note: Hospital Specialties: Imaging health unit; Advanced palliative care program. Number of Employees: 60
Kristal McKitrick-Bazin, Facility Contact
k.mckitrick-bazin@lmh.rha-central.mb

Swan River: Swan Valley Health Centre
Affiliated with: Parkland Regional Health Authority Inc.
PO Box 1450, 1011 Main St., Swan River, MB R0L 1Z0
Tel: 204-734-3441; *Fax:* 204-734-9081
www.prha.mb.ca/Hospitals.aspx
Year Founded: 2005
Number of Beds: 52 acute-care beds
Note: Services include acute care, ambulatory care, audiology, chemotherapy, diabetes education, diagnostics, dialysis, emergency service, mental health, physiotherapy, occupational therapy, speech language pathology, surgery.
Mr. Allan Bradley, CEO, PRHA
Mr. Blaine Kraushaar, Coordinator, Community Relations, PRHA
204-622-6237, Fax: 204-622-6232, bkraushaar@prha.mb.ca
Ms. Neoma Stiegler, Clinical Services Manager
204-734-6664, nstiegler@prha.mb.ca

Teulon: Teulon Hunter Memorial Hospital
Affiliated with: Interlake Regional Health Authority Inc.
PO Box 89, 3rd Ave. SE, Teulon, MB R0C 3B0
Tel: 204-886-2433; *Fax:* 204-886-2653
info@irha.mb.ca
www.irha.mb.ca
Number of Beds: 20 beds
Note: Services include emergency, ambulatory care, acute care, diagnostic imaging, laboratory, pharmacy, surgery, physiotherapy, dietary services, occupational therapy, opthamology.
Mr. Kevin Beresford, CEO, IRHA
204-467-4742, kberesford@irha.mb.ca
Ms. Shannon Montgomery, South West District Director, IRHA
smontgomery@irha.mb.ca
Mr. Kevin O'Donovan, Public Relations Manager, IRHA
204-467-4747, kodonovan@irha.mb.ca
Dr. Abdalla Rizk, Site Chief of Staff

The Pas: The Pas Health Complex Inc.
Affiliated with: Nor-Man Regional Health Authority Inc.
Former Name: St. Anthony's General Hospital
PO Box 240, 67 - 1st St. West, The Pas, MB R9A 1K4
Tel: 204-623-6431; *Fax:* 204-623-9263
Year Founded: 1969
Number of Beds: 118 beds
Note: Specialties: Acute care; Ambulatory clinic program; Dialysis; Physiotherapy; Occupational therapy; Social services; Chronic care; Long-term care
Drew Lockhart, CEO

Thompson: Thompson General Hospital
Affiliated with: Burntwood Regional Health Authority Inc.
871 Thompson Dr. South, Thompson, MB R8N 0C8
Tel: 204-677-2381; *Fax:* 204-778-1413
brha@brha.mb.ca
www.brha.mb.ca
Number of Beds: 74 beds
Note: A community facility with services including emergency, aboriginal interpretive services, cancer care, diagnostics, dialysis, obstetrics, palliative care, psychiatric acute care unit, rehabilitation, respiratory therapy, spiritual care, surgery
Ms. Gloria King, CEO, BRHA
204-677-5399, gking@brha.mb.ca
Dr. Hussam Azzam, Vice-President, Medical Services, BRHA
204-677-5376, hazzam@brha.mb.ca
Dr. Hisham Tassi, Site Head, Medical Services
204-677-5314, htassi@brha.mb.ca

Winkler: Boundary Trails Health Centre
Affiliated with: Regional Health Authority - Central Manitoba Inc.
PO Box 2000 Main, Winkler, MB R6W 1H8
Tel: 204-331-8800; *Fax:* 204-331-8801
www.rha-central.mb.ca
Number of Beds: 40 medical beds; 25 rehabilitation beds; 18 surgical services beds; 7 obstetrics / birthing beds; 4 intensive care unit beds
Note: Hospital specialties: Emergency services; Diagnostics, Laboratory services; Surgery; Intensive care; Acute care; Chemotherapy; Dialysis; Physiotherapy; Occupational therapy; Audiology; Mental health services; Public health; Home care
Number of Employees: 450
Linda Buhr, Director, Health Services
l.buhr@rha-central.mb.ca
Kristy Radke, Director, Support Services
k.radke@rha-central.mb.ca

Winnipeg: Concordia Hospital
Affiliated with: Winnipeg Regional Health Authority
1095 Concordia Ave., Winnipeg, MB R2K 3S8
Tel: 204-667-1560; *Fax:* 204-667-1049
www.concordiahospital.mb.ca
Note: Hospital Specialties: Emergency services; Diagnostic imaging; Laboratory services (204-661-7174); Surgery (a major centre for hip and knee replacements); Intensive care; A.M.I. (Acute Myocardial Infarct) Program; Occupational therapy (204-661-7216); Physiotherapy (204-661-7354); Respiratory therapy (204-661-7346); Oncology haematology service; Social work (204-661-7185); Cardiac Teaching Program (nurse home visit); Lifeline personal response & support services
Henry Tessman, President; Chief Operating Officer

Winnipeg: Health Sciences Centre
Affiliated with: Winnipeg Regional Health Authority
820 Sherbrook St., Winnipeg, MB R3A 1R9
Tel: 204-774-6511; *Fax:* 204-787-3912
www.hsc.mb.ca
Number of Beds: 850 beds
Note: teaching hospital
Adam Topp, COO
Dana Erickson, Vice-President; CAO
Dr. Perry Gray, Vice-President; Chief Medical Officer

Winnipeg: Riverview Health Centre
Affiliated with: Winnipeg Regional Health Authority
1 Morley Ave. East, Winnipeg, MB R3L 2P4
Tel: 204-478-6203; *Fax:* 204-478-6212
enquiries@rhc.mb.ca
www.rhc.mb.ca
Number of Beds: 388 beds
Note: Long-term care, catering to the needs of the elderly and rehabilitation patients
Norman R. Kasian, President/CEO
Sheldon Mindell, Development Officer
smindell@rhc.mb.ca

Winnipeg: St. Boniface General Hospital
L'Hôpital général Saint-Boniface
Affiliated with: Winnipeg Regional Health Authority
409 Taché Ave., Winnipeg, MB R2H 2A6
Tel: 204-233-8563; *Fax:* 204-231-0640
sbghweb@sbgh.mb.ca
www.sbgh.mb.ca
Year Founded: 1871
Number of Beds: 524 beds
Note: Catholic tertiary care facility & teaching hospital affiliated with the University of Manitoba & dedicated to the values of care of the Sisters of Charity of Montreal (Grey Nuns). Emergency services, family medicine, mental health, geriatrics & rehabilitation, surgery, women's health, paediatrics. Number of staff, including support & healthcare staff: 4,000+
Dr. Michel Tétreault, President/CEO

Winnipeg: The Salvation Army Grace General Hospital
Affiliated with: Winnipeg Regional Health Authority
300 Booth Dr., Winnipeg, MB R3J 3M7
Tel: 204-837-0111
hrs@ggh.mb.ca (Human Resources); pr@ggh.mb.ca (Public relations)
www.gracehospital.ca
Year Founded: 1904
Number of Beds: 270 beds
Note: Specialties: Emergency & critical care programs; Surgery program; Mental health services; Hospice care
Maj. John McFarlane, President; CEO
204/837-0143
Scott Wichenko, Director, Materials Management
Art Isaak, Director, Housekeeping

Winnipeg: Seven Oaks General Hospital
Affiliated with: Winnipeg Regional Health Authority
2300 McPhillips St., Winnipeg, MB R2V 3M3
Tel: 204-632-7133; *Fax:* 204-697-2106
www.sogh.winnipeg.mb.ca
Year Founded: 1981
Number of Beds: 275 beds
Note: Comprehensive health services, including emergency, surgery, rehabilitation/geriatric/mental health services, intensive care, dialysis, pulmonary rehabilitation program, hearing centre, dental services
Ms. Carrie Solmundson, President; COO
Dr. Ricardo Lobato de Faria, Chief Medical Officer
Ms. Monique Constant, Chief Administrative Officer

Winnipeg: Victoria General Hospital
Affiliated with: Winnipeg Regional Health Authority
2340 Pembina Hwy., Winnipeg, MB R3T 2E8
Tel: 204-269-3570; *Fax:* 204-261-0223
info@vgh.mb.ca
www.vgh.mb.ca
Number of Beds: 231 beds
Note: Comprehensive health care. Number of staff: 1,200
Ray J. Racette, President; CEO

Winnipegosis: Winnipegosis General Hospital
Affiliated with: Parkland Regional Health Authority Inc.
PO Box 280, 230 Bridge St., Winnipegosis, MB R0L 2G0
Tel: 204-656-4881; *Fax:* 204-656-4402
Number of Beds: 14 acute care, 20 long-term care beds
Glen Kozak, COO

Community Health Centres

Community Health Care Centres

Baldur: Baldur Health Centre/Baldur Health District
Affiliated with: Assiniboine Regional Health Authority
PO Box 128, Baldur, MB R0K 0B0
Tel: 204-535-2373; *Fax:* 204-535-2116
Number of Beds: 14 beds
Bev Towler

Benito: Benito Primary Health Centre
Affiliated with: Parkland Regional Health Authority Inc.
PO Box 490, 200 - 1st St. East, Benito, MB R0L 0C0
Tel: 204-539-2815; *Fax:* 204-539-2482
www.prha.mb.ca
Note: Specialties: Community health; Mental health services

Birtle: Birtle Health Centre
Affiliated with: Assiniboine Regional Health Authority
PO Box 10, Birtle, MB R0M 0C0
Tel: 204-842-3317; *Fax:* 204-842-3375
Number of Beds: 14 acute care, 20 long-term care beds
Roseanne Yaremchuk, Area Manager

Brandon: 7th Street Health Access Centre
Affiliated with: Brandon Regional Health Authority
20 - 7th St., Brandon, MB R7A 6M8
Tel: 204-578-4800; *Fax:* 204-578-4950
www.brandonrha.mb.ca
Note: Community Health Nurse; Adult Community Mental Health Worker; Community Social Worker; Addictions Services; Housing Resource Worker; Cultural Facilitators; Supports to Services in Group Living; Supports to Seniors living at Home; Mental Health Peer Support Educator; Community Volunteer Income Tax Program; YWCA Family Violence Outreach Program.
Vicky Legassie, Program Manager

Carberry: Carberry Plains District Health Centre
Affiliated with: Assiniboine Regional Health Authority
Bag Service #1, 1st Ave., Carberry, MB R0K 0H0
Tel: 204-834-2144; *Fax:* 204-834-3333
Number of Beds: 10 acute care, 36 PCH beds
Deb Obach, Director

Cartwright: Davidson Memorial Health Centre
Affiliated with: Assiniboine Regional Health Authority
Former Name: Cartwright & District Hospital
PO Box 118, Cartwright, MB R0K 0L0
Tel: 204-529-2483; *Fax:* 204-529-2562
Number of Beds: 10 beds
Bev Towler

Churchill: Churchill Health Centre
Affiliated with: Churchill Regional Health Authority Inc.
General Delivery, Churchill, MB R0B 0E0
Tel: 204-675-8318; *Fax:* 204-675-2243
www.churchillrha.com
Note: Specialties: Primary care; Public health services

Derry Martens, Chief Executive Officer, Churchill Regional Health Authority Inc.

***Deloraine:* Deloraine Health Centre**
PO Box 447, 109 Kellett St., Deloraine, MB R0M 0M0
Tel: 204-747-2745; *Fax:* 204-747-2160

John Rekai, Manager

***Emerson:* Emerson Hospital/Personal Care Home**
Affiliated with: Regional Health Authority - Central Manitoba Inc.
PO Box 428, 26 Main St., Emerson, MB R0A 0L0
Tel: 204-373-2109; *Fax:* 204-373-2748
Number of Beds: 4 acute care, 20 long-term care beds
Paulette Goossen, Facility Contact

***Erickson:* Erickson District Health Centre**
Affiliated with: Assiniboine Regional Health Authority
PO Box 25, Erickson, MB R0J 0P0
Tel: 204-636-7777; *Fax:* 204-636-2471
Number of Beds: 9 acute care, 16 PCH beds
Judith McDowell, Community Health Director

***Glenboro:* Glenboro Health District Hospital**
Affiliated with: Assiniboine Regional Health Authority
PO Box 310, Glenboro, MB R0K 0X0
Tel: 204-827-2438; *Fax:* 204-827-2199
Number of Beds: 11 beds
Note: acute care, personal home care
Marilyn McGregor, Manager

***Hamiota:* Hamiota District Health Centre**
Affiliated with: Assiniboine Regional Health Authority
177 Birch Ave., Hamiota, MB R0M 0T0
Tel: 204-764-2412; *Fax:* 204-764-2049
Number of Beds: 20 acute care, 30 PCH beds
Greg Paddock, Area Manager

***Hamiota:* Hamiota District Health Centre**
Affiliated with: Assiniboine Regional Health Authority
177 Birch Ave., Hamiota, MB R0M 0T0
Tel: 204-764-2412; *Fax:* 204-764-2049
mandrew@mrha.mb.ca

***Hartney:* Hartney Medical Nursing Unit**
PO Box 28, Hartney, MB R0M 0X0
Tel: 204-858-2054; *Fax:* 204-858-2303
Number of Beds: 9 beds
Shirley Kloon, Manager

***Lac du Bonnet:* Lac du Bonnet District Health Centre**
Affiliated with: North Eastman Health Association Inc.
PO Box 1030, Lac du Bonnet, MB R0E 1A0
Tel: 204-345-1219; *Fax:* 204-268-8609

Mary Power, Home Care Manager

***Leaf Rapids:* Leaf Rapids Health Centre**
Affiliated with: Burntwood Regional Health Authority Inc.
PO Box 370, Leaf Rapids, MB R0B 1W0
Tel: 204-473-2441; *Fax:* 204-473-8273
lrhcadm@cancom.net
Number of Beds: 8 beds
Bernette Alexander, Manager, Leaf Rapids Health Program

***MacGregor:* MacGregor Health Centre**
Affiliated with: Regional Health Authority - Central Manitoba Inc.
PO Box 250, 87 Grafton St. South, MacGregor, MB R0H 0R0
Tel: 204-685-2850; *Fax:* 204-685-2529
Number of Beds: 6 beds
Note: Specialties: Respite care; convalescent care; Palliative services; Number of Employees: 52
Sharon Stewart, Facility Contact

***Manitou:* Pembina-Manitou Health Centre**
Affiliated with: Regional Health Authority - Central Manitoba Inc.
PO Box 129, 232 Carrie St., Manitou, MB R0G 1G0
Tel: 204-242-2744; *Fax:* 204-242-3062
Number of Beds: 8 acute care, 18 long-term care beds
Linda Pearce, Facility Contact

***Minnedosa:* Minnedosa Health Centre**
Affiliated with: Assiniboine Regional Health Authority
PO Box 960, Minnedosa, MB R0J 1E0
Tel: 204-867-2701; *Fax:* 204-867-2239
Number of Beds: 27 acute care
Judith McDowell

***Neepawa:* Neepawa District Memorial Hospital**
Affiliated with: Assiniboine Regional Health Authority
PO Box 1240, Neepawa, MB R0J 1H0
Tel: 204-476-2394; *Fax:* 204-476-5007
Number of Beds: 38 beds
K.D. Braden, Community Health Director

***Notre Dame de Lourdes:* Notre Dame Medical Nursing Inc.**
Affiliated with: Regional Health Authority - Central Manitoba Inc.
PO Box 190, Notre Dame de Lourdes, MB R0G 1M0
Tel: 204-248-2112; *Fax:* 204-248-2499
Note: Specialty: Acute care
Cheryl Harrison, Facility Contact
c.harrison@fnd.rha-central.mb.ca

***Rivers:* Riverdale Health Centre/Riverdale Health Services District**
Affiliated with: Assiniboine Regional Health Authority
PO Box 428, 512 Quebec St., Rivers, MB R0K 1X0
Tel: 204-328-5321; *Fax:* 204-328-7130
Number of Beds: 14 acute care, 20 PCH beds, 12 Elderly Persons Housing units
Greg Paddock, Community Health Director

***Roblin:* Roblin District Health Centre**
Affiliated with: Parkland Regional Health Authority Inc.
PO Box 940, 15 Hospital St., Roblin, MB R0L 1P0
Tel: 204-937-2142; *Fax:* 204-937-8892
rdhc@prha.mb.ca
www.prha.mb.ca
Number of Beds: 25 bed hospital, 60 bed personal care home
Note: Emergency & diagnostic services, podiatry, speech therapy, physiotherapy, dietician. Number of employees: 125
Cheryl Jerome, COO

***Roblin:* Roblin District Health District**
Affiliated with: Parkland Regional Health Authority Inc.
PO Box 940, Roblin, MB R0L 1P0
Tel: 204-937-2142; *Fax:* 204-937-8892
Note: The Roblin District Health Centre is comprised of a 25 bed hospitaland a 60 bed personal care home, with 125 staff and 3.5 full time physicians
Cheryl Jerome, COO

***Rossburn:* Rossburn District Health Centre**
Affiliated with: Assiniboine Regional Health Authority
PO Box 40, Rossburn, MB R0J 1V0
Tel: 204-859-2413; *Fax:* 204-859-2526
Number of Beds: 10 acute care, 20 long-term care beds
Barb Kostesky, Area Manager

***Shoal Lake:* Shoal Lake-Strathclair Health Centre**
Affiliated with: Assiniboine Regional Health Authority
PO Box 490, Shoal Lake, MB R0J 1Z0
Tel: 204-759-2336; *Fax:* 204-759-2480
Number of Beds: 12 acute care, 40 long-term care beds
Roseanne Yaremchuk, Community Health Director

***Snow Lake:* Snow Lake Health Centre**
Affiliated with: Nor-Man Regional Health Authority Inc.
PO Box 453, Snow Lake, MB R0B 1M0
Tel: 204-358-2597; *Fax:* 204-358-7310
Number of Beds: 6 beds
Mae de Graff, Site Administrator

***Souris:* Souris Health District**
Affiliated with: Deloraine Health Centre
PO Box 10, Souris, MB R0K 2C0
Tel: 204-483-2121; *Fax:* 204-483-2310
Number of Beds: 30 beds
Shirley Kloon, Manager

***St Pierre Jolys:* Centre Medico-Social De Salaberry District Health Centre**
Affiliated with: South Eastman Health/Santé Sud-Est Inc.
PO Box 320, St Pierre Jolys, MB R0A 1V0
Tel: 204-433-7611; *Fax:* 204-433-7455
Number of Beds: 14 beds
Note: acute care & emergency with personal care home
Elaine McPherson, Facility Manager

***Stonewall:* Stonewall & District Health Centre**
Affiliated with: Interlake Regional Health Authority Inc.
589 - 3rd Ave. South, Stonewall, MB R0C 2Z0
Tel: 204-467-5514
Number of Beds: 15 beds
Note: Specialties: Clinic services; Community health services; Emergency outpatient services
Keith Bytheway, District Services

***Thompson:* Burntwood Community Health Resource Centre**
Affiliated with: Burntwood Regional Health Authority Inc.
50 Selkirk Avenue, Thompson, MB R8N 0M7
Tel: 204-677-1777; *Fax:* 204-677-1755
smacdonald@brha.mb.ca

Shane MacDonald, Manager
204/677-1796, smacdonald@brha.mb.ca

***Treherne:* Tiger Hills Health District**
Affiliated with: Assiniboine Regional Health Authority
PO Box 130, Treherne, MB R0G 2V0
Tel: 204-723-2133; *Fax:* 204-723-2869
Number of Beds: 13 acute beds; 20 pch
Deb Obach, Area Manager

***Virden:* Virdin Health Centre**
Affiliated with: Assiniboine Regional Health Authority
PO Box 400, Virden, MB R0M 2C0
Tel: 204-748-1230; *Fax:* 204-748-2053
mcarson@arha.ca
Number of Beds: 25 acute; 100 long-term care
Meegan Carson, Manager

***Vita:* Vita & District Health Centre Inc.**
Affiliated with: South Eastman Health/Santé Sud-Est Inc.
217 First Ave. West, Vita, MB R0A 2K0
Tel: 204-425-7763; *Fax:* 204-425-3545
Number of Beds: 10 acute care, 44 long-term care beds
Note: with personal care home
Shawny Elyk Prevost, Facility Manager

***Wawanesa:* Wawanesa & District Memorial Health Centre**
Affiliated with: Assiniboine Regional Health Authority
PO Box 309, Wawanesa, MB R0K 2G0
Tel: 204-824-2335; *Fax:* 204-824-2148
Number of Beds: 6 acute beds; 20 pch
Deb Obach, Manager

***Whitemouth:* Whitemouth District Health Centre**
Affiliated with: North Eastman Health Association Inc.
PO Box 160, Whitemouth, MB R0E 2G0
Tel: 204-348-7191; *Fax:* 204-348-7911
Number of Beds: 24 beds, 1 palliative, 1 respite
Heather Frederick, Care Team Manager

***Winnipeg:* Aboriginal Health & Wellness Centre**
Affiliated with: Winnipeg Regional Health Authority
#214-215, 181 Higgins Ave., Winnipeg, MB R3B 3G1
Tel: 204-925-3700; *Fax:* 204-925-3709
www.abcentre.org

Darlene Hall, Executive Director

***Winnipeg:* Centre de santé Saint-Boniface**
#D-1048, 409, av Taché, Winnipeg, MB R2H 2A6
Tel: 204-235-3910; *Fax:* 204-237-9057
access@centredesante.mb.ca
www.centredesante.mb.ca
Note: community health care office
Micheline St-Hilaire, Acting Executive Director

***Winnipeg:* Health Action Centre - Health Sciences Centre**
Affiliated with: Winnipeg Regional Health Authority
425 Elgin Ave., Winnipeg, MB R3A 1P2
Tel: 204-940-1626; *Fax:* 204-942-7828
healthac@mb.sympatico.ca
Note: community health care centre
Joan Dawkins, Community Area Director
Roy Becket, Manager of Administration
Dr. Kathryn Kisil, Medical Coordinator

***Winnipeg:* Hope Centre Health Care Inc.**
Affiliated with: Winnipeg Regional Health Authority
1644 Dublin Ave., Winnipeg, MB R3H 0X5
Tel: 204-982-4673; *Fax:* 204-953-3510
admin@hopecentreinc.org
www.hopecentreinc.org
Jeannette DeLong, Executive Director
jdelong@hopecentreinc.org

***Winnipeg:* Klinic Community Health Centre**
Affiliated with: Winnipeg Regional Health Authority
870 Portage Ave., Winnipeg, MB R3G 0P1
Tel: 204-784-4090; *Fax:* 204-772-7998
klinic@klinic.mb.ca
www.klinic.mb.ca
Note: community health centre & mental health facility
Lori Johnson, Executive Director

***Winnipeg:* MFL Occupational Health Centre, Inc.**
Affiliated with: Winnipeg Regional Health Authority
#102, 275 Broadway, Winnipeg, MB R3C 4M6
Tel: 204-949-0811; *Fax:* 204-956-0848
Toll-Free: 888-843-1229 (i
mflohc@mflohc.mb.ca
www.mflohc.mb.ca
Year Founded: 1983
Note: Specialties: Occupational health (health issues related to work experiences); Improvement of workplace health & safety conditions & elimination of hazards
Carol Loveridge, Executive Director

***Winnipeg:* Misericordia Health Centre**
Affiliated with: Winnipeg Regional Health Authority
99 Cornish Ave., Winnipeg, MB R3C 1A2
Tel: 204-774-6581; *Fax:* 204-783-6052
info@miseri.winnipeg.mb.ca
www.misericordia.mb.ca
Number of Beds: 250
Note: nursing home, outpatient services
Rosie Jacuzzi, President; CEO

***Winnipeg:* Mount Carmel Clinic**
Affiliated with: Winnipeg Regional Health Authority
886 Main St., Winnipeg, MB R2W 5L4
Tel: 204-582-2311; *Fax:* 204-582-1341
www.mountcarmel.ca
Brenda Slobozian, Executive Director

***Winnipeg:* Nine Circles Community Health Centre**
Affiliated with: Winnipeg Regional Health Authority
705 Broadway, Winnipeg, MB R3G 0X2
Tel: 204-940-6000; *Fax:* 204-940-6027
Toll-Free: 888-305-8647
ninecircles@ninecircles.ca
www.ninecircles.ca
Note: Non-profit centre specializing in STI/HIV prevention and care services
John C. Stinson, Executive Director

***Winnipeg:* Nor'west Cooperative Health & Social Service Centre Inc.**
Affiliated with: Winnipeg Regional Health Authority
#103, 61 Tyndall Ave., Winnipeg, MB R2X 2T4
Tel: 204-633-5955; *Fax:* 204-633-4666
Nancy Henrichs, Executive Director

***Winnipeg:* Women's Health Clinic Inc.**
Affiliated with: Winnipeg Regional Health Authority
419 Graham Ave., Unit A, Winnipeg, MB R3C 0M3
Tel: 204-947-1517; *Fax:* 204-943-3844
www.womenshealthclinic.org
Jennifer Howard, Executive Director
Carolyn Clarke, Nurse Practioner

***Winnipeg:* Youville Centre - Community Health Resource Centre**
33 Marion St., Winnipeg, MB R2H 0S8
Tel: 204-233-0262; *Fax:* 204-233-1520
www.youville.ca
Sylvia Oosterveen, Executive Director

Nursing Stations

***Bloodvein:* Bloodvein Nursing Station**
General Delivery, Bloodvein, MB R0C 0J0
Tel: 204-395-2161; *Fax:* 204-395-2087

***Brochet:* Brochet Nursing Station**
General Delivery, Brochet, MB R0B 0B0
Tel: 204-323-2120; *Fax:* 204-323-2650

***Cross Lake:* Cross Lake Nursing Station**
General Delivery, Cross Lake, MB R0B 0J0
Tel: 204-676-2011; *Fax:* 204-676-3179

***Easterville:* Easterville Nursing Station**
PO Box 122, Easterville, MB R0C 0V0
Tel: 204-329-2212; *Fax:* 204-329-2337
Ethel McKay, Community Health Representative

***Fisher Branch:* Fisher Medical Facilities Inc.**
PO Box 370, Fisher Branch, MB R0C 0Z0
Tel: 204-372-6228; *Fax:* 204-372-6207
Bev Fisher, Sec.-Treas.

***God's Narrows:* God's Lake Narrows Nursing Station**
General Delivery, God's Narrows, MB R0B 0M0
Tel: 204-335-2557

***Gods River:* God's River Health Station**
General Delivery, Gods River, MB R0B 0N0
Tel: 204-366-2355; *Fax:* 204-366-2474

***Grand Rapids:* Grand Rapids Nursing Station**
PO Box 53, Grand Rapids, MB R0C 1E0
Tel: 204-639-2215; *Fax:* 204-639-2448

***Ilford:* Ilford Nursing Station**
General Delivery, Ilford, MB R0B 0S0
Tel: 204-288-4348; *Fax:* 204-288-4360

***Island Lake:* Garden Hill Nursing Station**
General Delivery, Island Lake, MB R0B 0T0
Tel: 204-456-2454; *Fax:* 204-456-2866

***Lac Brochet:* Lac Brochet Nursing Station**
General Delivery, Lac Brochet, MB R0B 2E0
Tel: 204-337-2161; *Fax:* 204-337-2143

***Little Grand Rapids:* Little Grand Rapids Nursing Station**
General Delivery, Little Grand Rapids, MB R0B 0V0
Tel: 204-397-2115; *Fax:* 204-397-2016
Note: Number of Employees: 1 community health worker

***Little Grand Rapids:* Pauingassi Nursing Station**
PO Box 32, Little Grand Rapids, MB R0B 2G0
Tel: 204-397-2395; *Fax:* 204-397-2104

***Moose Lake:* Moose Lake Nursing Station**
General Delivery, Moose Lake, MB R0B 0Y0
Tel: 204-678-2252; *Fax:* 204-678-2343

***Negginan:* Poplar River Nursing Station**
General Delivery, Negginan, MB R0B 0Z0
Tel: 204-244-2102; *Fax:* 204-244-2001

***Oxford House:* Oxford House Nursing Station**
Affiliated with: Burntwood Regional Health Authority
General Delivery, Oxford House, MB R0B 1C0
Tel: 204-538-2347; *Fax:* 204-538-2445
Note: Specialties: Acute care; Public health programs. Number of Employees: 5 nurses + an administrative clerk + a maintenance person
Helen Weenusk, Secretary

***Pikwitonei:* Pikwitonei Health Centre**
Affiliated with: Burntwood Regional Health Authority Inc.
General Delivery, Pikwitonei, MB R0B 1E0
Tel: 204-288-4348; *Fax:* 204-458-2468
www.thompson.ca/dbs/brha
Marion Ellis, Director

***Pukatawagan:* Pukatawagan Nursing Station**
Also Known As: Nikawiy Nursing Station
General Delivery, Pukatawagan, MB R0B 1G0
Tel: 204-553-2271; *Fax:* 204-553-2402
Note: Serving the Mathias Colomb Cree Nation

***Red Sucker Lake:* Red Sucker Lake Nursing Station**
General Delivery, Red Sucker Lake, MB R0B 1H0
Tel: 204-469-5351; *Fax:* 204-469-5769
Note: Number of staff: 2 nurses, visiting physician, dentist, optometrist, pediatrician, & psychologist

***Shamattawa:* Shamattawa Nursing Station**
General Delivery, Shamattawa, MB R0B 1K0
Tel: 204-565-2370; *Fax:* 204-565-2519

***South Indian Lake:* South Indian Lake Nursing Station**
General Delivery, South Indian Lake, MB R0B 1N0
Tel: 204-374-2013; *Fax:* 204-374-2039

***Split Lake:* Split Lake Nursing Station**
General Delivery, Split Lake, MB R0B 1P0
Tel: 204-342-2033; *Fax:* 204-342-2319

***St Theresa Point:* St Theresa Point Nursing Station**
General Delivery, St Theresa Point, MB R0B 1J0
Tel: 204-462-2473; *Fax:* 204-462-2642
Richard Hopper, Clerk

***Thicket Portage:* Thicket Portage Health Centre**
PO Box 39, Thicket Portage, MB R0B 0L0
Tel: 204-286-3254; *Fax:* 204-286-3216
www.thompson.ca/dbs/brha
Marion Ellis, Director

***Wabowden:* Wabowden Health Centre**
PO Box 160, General Delivery, Wabowden, MB R0B 1S0
Tel: 204-689-2600; *Fax:* 204-689-2180
Marion Ellis, Director

***Wasagamack Bay:* Wasagamack Nursing Station**
General Delivery, Wasagamack Bay, MB R0B 1Z0
Tel: 204-457-2024; *Fax:* 204-457-2348

***York Landing:* York Landing Nursing Station**
General Delivery, York Landing, MB R0B 2B0
Tel: 204-341-2325; *Fax:* 204-341-2179

Special Treatment Centres

***Brandon:* Westman Crisis Centre**
Affiliated with: Brandon Regional Health Authority
Town Centre, B13 - 800 Rosser Avenue, Brandon, MB R7A 6N5
Toll-Free: 888-379-7699
Number of Beds: 8 beds
Allison Done, Program Manager

***Reston:* Reston District Health Centre**
Affiliated with: Assiniboine Regional Health Authority
PO Box 250, Reston, MB R0M 1X0
Tel: 204-877-3925; *Fax:* 204-877-3998
Number of Beds: 13 beds
Meegan Carson

***Winnipeg:* CancerCare Manitoba**
675 McDermot Ave., Winnipeg, MB R3E 0V9
Tel: 204-787-2241; *Fax:* 204-787-1184
www.cancercare.mb.ca
Note: cancer treatment, ambulatory care only

Dr. Dhali Dhaliwal, President; CEO
204/787-2241
Vivian Painter, Director of Nursing
204/787-4155

***Winnipeg:* Jane's Clinic**
883 Corydon Ave., Winnipeg, MB R3M 0W7
Tel: 204-477-1887; *Fax:* 204-447-1888
Note: abortion clinic

***Winnipeg:* Manitoba Cardiac Institute (Reh-Fit Centre)**
1390 Taylor Ave., Winnipeg, MB R3M 3V8
Tel: 204-488-8023; *Fax:* 204-488-4819
rehfit@reh-fit.com
www.reh-fit.com
Note: rehabilitation centre
Donald Fletcher, Executive Director
M. Grace, Director of Nursing
Al Coot, Maintenance Supervisor

***Winnipeg:* New Directions for Children, Youth, Adults & Families**
Former Name: Children's Home of Winnipeg
#400, 491 Portage Ave., Winnipeg, MB R3B 2E4
Tel: 204-786-7051; *Fax:* 204-774-6468
TTY: 204-774-8541
www.newdirections.mb.ca
Note: 19 programs: residential, day & family support services
Dr. Elizabeth Adkins, Executive Director

Long Term/Retirement Care

Long Term Care Facilities

***Arborg:* Riverdale Place Homes Inc.**
PO Box 968, Arborg, MB R0C 0A0
Tel: 204-376-2940; *Fax:* 204-376-5051
riverdale@mts.net
Number of Beds: 19 beds
Note: Provides residential services to adults with intellectual disabilities.
K. Finnson, Executive Director

***Saint Malo:* Chalet Malouin Inc.**
14 Hilaire St., Saint Malo, MB R0A 1T0
Tel: 204-347-5753; *Fax:* 204-347-5107
Number of Beds: 38 beds assisted living
Note: EPH & assisted living facility
Aline Sveinson, Administrator

***Swan River:* Association for Community Living - Swan River**
PO Box 1282, Swan River, MB R0L 1Z0
Tel: 204-734-9114; *Fax:* 204-734-3704
Number of Beds: 17 beds
G. Mitchell, Services Coordinator

***Winnipeg:* L'Arche Winnipeg Inc.**
118 Regent Ave. East., Winnipeg, MB R2C 0C1
Tel: 204-237-0300; *Fax:* 204-237-0316
office@larchewinnipeg.org
www.larchewinnipeg.org
Number of Beds: 28 beds
Note: group homes for persons with a developmental disability
Dennis Butcher, Executive Director

***Winnipeg:* Deer Lodge Centre**
Affiliated with: Winnipeg Regional Health Authority
2109 Portage Ave., Winnipeg, MB R3J 0L3
Tel: 204-837-1301
info@deerlodge.mb.ca
(www.deerlodge.mb.ca
Number of Beds: 487 beds, including 155 personal care beds for veterans
Note: Specialties: Rehabilitation services, including physiotherapy, occupational therapy, respiratory therapy, & therapeutic recreation services; Speech-language pathology; Services for ALS patients; Peritoneal dialysis; Operational Stress Injuries Clinic; Movement Disorders Clinic; Audiological services; Assistive technology products & services; Outreach programs in geriatric mental health; Social work; Day hospital & adult day care for cognitively impaired clients; Long term care; Geriatric research
Réal Cloutier, Chief Operating Officer; Winnipeg Regional Health, Long Term Care
204-831-2110, rcloutier@deerlodge.mb.ca
Ed Courcelles, Chief Financial Officer,
ecourcelles@deerlodge.mb.ca
204-831-2116
Jo-Ann LaPointe-McKenzie, Chief Nursing Officer
204-831-2529, JlapointeMcKenzie@deerlodge.mb.ca
Dr. David Strang, Chief Medical Officer
204-831-2920, dstrang@deerlodge.mb.ca
Janet Clark, Director, Allied Health Services
204-831-2570, jeclark@deerlodge.mb.ca
Cheryl LeBlue, Director, Human Resources
204-831-2103, cleblue@deerlodge.mb.ca
Sylvia Ptashnik, Director, Resident Services
204-831-2108, sptashnik@deerlodge.mb.ca

***Winnipeg:* Parkview Place**
440 Edmonton St., Winnipeg, MB R3B 2M4
Tel: 204-942-5291; *Fax:* 204-947-1969
parkviewplace@reveraliving.com
www.reveraliving.com
Number of Beds: 277 beds
Donald M. Solar, Administrator
Noel Gray, Director of Nursing

***Winnipeg:* Poseidon Care Centre**
70 Poseidon Bay, Winnipeg, MB R3M 3E5
Tel: 204-452-6204; *Fax:* 204-474-2173
poseidon@reveraliving.com
www.reveraliving.com
Number of Beds: 218 beds
Marg Fisher, Administrator

***Winnipeg:* St. Amant Inc.**
Affiliated with: Winnipeg Regional Health Authority
440 River Rd., Winnipeg, MB R2M 3Z9
Tel: 204-256-4301; *Fax:* 204-257-4349
inquiries@stamant.mb.ca
www.stamant.mb.ca
Number of Beds: 216 beds
Note: Developmental disability resource centre
Dr. Carl Stephens, President; CEO

***Winnipeg:* The Wellington**
3161 Grant Ave., Winnipeg, MB R3R 3R1
Tel: 204-831-0788; *Fax:* 204-896-0576
thewellington@lrc.ca
www.reveraliving.com
Number of Beds: 117 suites
Note: Independent living
Warren Stephenson, Executive Director

Retirement Residences

***Winnipeg:* Metropolitan Kiwanis Courts**
2300 Ness Ave., Winnipeg, MB R3J 1A2
Tel: 204-885-7700; *Fax:* 204-831-1022
shunter@kiwaniscourts.ca
Year Founded: 2000
Note: Specialties: Assisted living
Heather Ritchie, Exec. Dir.

Personal Care Homes

***Arborg:* Arborg Pioneer Health**
Affiliated with: Interlake Regional Health Authority
Former Name: Pioneer Health Services Inc
PO Box 10, Arborg, MB R0C 0A0
Tel: 204-376-5226; *Fax:* 204-376-5669
Number of Beds: 40 beds
Ruby Tretiak, District Director
C. Cherepak, Head Nurse

***Ashern:* Ashern Personal Care Home**
Affiliated with: Interlake Regional Health Authority
PO Box 110, Ashern, MB R0C 0E0
Tel: 204-768-2461; *Fax:* 204-768-2337
Number of Beds: 20 beds
Jan O'Flanagan, District Director

***Baldur:* Baldur Manor Inc.**
Affiliated with: Assiniboine Regional Health Authority
PO Box 128, Baldur, MB R0K 0B0
Tel: 204-535-2456; *Fax:* 204-535-2116
Number of Beds: 20 beds
Bev Towler

***Beausejour:* East-Gate Lodge**
Affiliated with: North Eastman Health Association Inc.
PO Box 1690, 646 James Ave., Beausejour, MB R0E 0C0
Tel: 204-268-1029; *Fax:* 204-268-3525
Number of Beds: 80 beds
Mary Ann Austman, Care Team Manager

***Benito:* Benito Health Centre Personal Care Home**
Affiliated with: Parkland Regional Health Authority
PO Box 490, Benito, MB R0L 0C0
Tel: 204-539-2815; *Fax:* 204-539-2482
Number of Beds: 20 beds

***Birtle:* Birtle Personal Care Home**
PO Box 10, Birtle, MB R0M 0C0
Tel: 204-842-3323; *Fax:* 204-842-3375
Number of Beds: 20 beds
Gerry Berry, Director

***Boissevain:* Evergreen Place**
Affiliated with: Assiniboine Regional Health Authority
PO Box 899, Boissevain, MB R0K 0E0
Tel: 204-534-2451; *Fax:* 204-534-6487
Number of Beds: 20 beds
Marilyn McGregor, Area Manager

***Boissevain:* Westview Lodge**
Affiliated with: Assiniboine Regional Health Authority
200 Student Street, Boissevain, MB R0K 0E0
Tel: 204-534-2455; *Fax:* 204-534-6633
Number of Beds: 42 beds

***Brandon:* Dinsdale Personal Care Home**
Affiliated with: Brandon Regional Health Authority
510 - 6th St., Brandon, MB R7A 3N9
Tel: 204-727-3636; *Fax:* 204-727-2103
Number of Beds: 60 beds
Maj. Wilson Perrin, Administrator

***Brandon:* Fairview Home**
Affiliated with: Brandon Regional Health Authority
1351 - 13th St., Brandon, MB R7A 4S5
Tel: 204-728-6696; *Fax:* 204-727-7616
Number of Beds: 248 beds
Trudy Curtis, Coordinator, Resident Services

***Brandon:* Hillcrest Place**
Affiliated with: Brandon Regional Health Authority
930 - 26th St., Brandon, MB R7B 2B8
Tel: 204-728-6690; *Fax:* 204-726-0089
Number of Beds: 100 beds
Kathy Traill, Administrator

***Brandon:* Rideau Park Personal Care Home**
Affiliated with: Brandon Regional Health Authority
525 Victoria Ave. East, Brandon, MB R7A 6S9
Tel: 204-727-1734; *Fax:* 204-726-6690
www.brandonrha.mb.ca
Number of Beds: 98 beds
Cheryl Bourdeau d'Hui, Coordinator, Resident Services

***Carberry:* Carberry Personal Care Home**
Bag Service #1, Carberry, MB R0K 0H0
Tel: 204-834-2144; *Fax:* 204-834-3333
Number of Beds: 36 beds

***Carman:* Boyne Lodge Personal Care Home**
Affiliated with: Central Regional Health Authority
120 - 4th Ave. SW, Carman, MB R0G 0J0
Tel: 204-745-6715; *Fax:* 204-745-6152
Number of Beds: 70 long-term care beds
Janet Wigley, Facility Contact
j.wigley@bvl.rha-central.mb.ca

***Dauphin:* Dauphin Personal Care Home Inc.**
Affiliated with: Parkland Regional Health Authority
625 Third St. SW, Dauphin, MB R7N 1R7
Tel: 204-638-3010; *Fax:* 204-638-2199
Number of Beds: 90 beds
Melodie Powell, Site Manager

***Dauphin:* St. Paul's Home**
Affiliated with: Parkland Regional Health Authority
703 Jackson St., Dauphin, MB R7N 2N2
Tel: 204-638-3129; *Fax:* 204-638-9294
Number of Beds: 70 beds
G. Karpinka, Administrator

***Deloraine:* Bren-Del-Win Lodge**
Affiliated with: Assiniboine Regional Health Authority
103 Kellet St. South, Deloraine, MB R0M 0M0
Tel: 204-747-2119; *Fax:* 204-747-2160
Number of Beds: 30 beds
Miriam Nichol, Community Health Manager

***Elkhorn:* Elkwood Manor Personal Care Home**
Affiliated with: Assiniboine Regional Health Authority
PO Box 70, Elkhorn, MB R0M 0N0
Tel: 204-845-2575; *Fax:* 204-845-2371
Number of Beds: 24 beds
Meegan Carson, Manager

Emerson: **Emerson Personal Care Home**
PO Box 428, 26 Main St., Emerson, MB R0A 0L0
Tel: 204-373-2109; *Fax:* 204-373-2748
Number of Beds: 20 beds
Paulette Goossen, Nurse Manager

Erickson: **Erickson Personal Care Home**
60 Queen E Rd., Erickson, MB R0J 0P0
Tel: 204-636-7777
Number of Beds: 16 beds

Eriksdale: **Eriksdale Personal Care Home**
Affiliated with: Interlake Regional Health Authority Inc.
PO Box 130, 40 Railway Ave., Eriksdale, MB R0C 0W0
Tel: 204-739-2611; *Fax:* 204-739-2065
Number of Beds: 20 beds
Patty Johnson, District Director
Helen Melville, Director of Nursing

Fisher Branch: **Fisher Personal Care Home**
Affiliated with: Interlake Regional Health Authority Inc.
PO Box 119, Fisher Branch, MB R0C 0Z0
Tel: 204-372-8703; *Fax:* 204-372-8710
Number of Beds: 30 beds
Ruby Tretiak, District Director

Flin Flon: **Flin Flon Personal Care Corporation**
Affiliated with: Nor-Man Regional Health Authority Inc.
PO Box 340, Flin Flon, MB R8A 1N2
Tel: 204-687-9630; *Fax:* 204-687-8494
Number of Beds: 30 beds

Flin Flon: **Northern Lights Manor**
Affiliated with: Nor-Man Regional Health Authority Inc.
PO Box 14, 274 Bracken St., Flin Flon, MB R8A 1P4
Tel: 204-687-7325; *Fax:* 204-687-8494
Number of Beds: 36 beds
Note: Personal care home
Shauna Cupples, Unit Manager

Gilbert Plains: **Gilbert Plains Health Centre**
Affiliated with: Parkland Regional Health Authority Inc.
PO Box 368, Gilbert Plains, MB R0L 0X0
Tel: 204-548-2161; *Fax:* 204-548-2516
gphc@mb.sympatico.ca
Number of Beds: 30 beds
Joan Gryba, Site Manager

Gimli: **Betel Home Foundation**
Affiliated with: Interlake Regional Health Authority Inc.
PO Box 10, Gimli, MB R0C 1B0
Tel: 204-642-5004; *Fax:* 204-642-7243
www.betelhomefoundation.ca
Number of Beds: 80 beds
Brenna Raemer, Executive Director

Gladstone: **Third Crossing Manor**
Affiliated with: Regional Health Authority - Central Manitoba Inc.
PO Box 1000, 24 Mill St., Gladstone, MB R0J 0T0
Tel: 204-385-2474; *Fax:* 204-385-2163
www.rha-central.mb.ca
Year Founded: 1974
Number of Beds: 50 residential capacity
Shirley Guenther, Facility Contact
s.guenther@tcm.rha-central.mb.ca

Glenboro: **Glenboro Personal Care Home Inc.**
Affiliated with: Assiniboine Regional Health Authority
PO Box 310, Glenboro, MB R0K 0X0
Tel: 204-827-2268; *Fax:* 204-827-2199
Number of Beds: 20 beds
Marilyn McGregor

Grandview: **Grandview Personal Care Home Inc.**
Affiliated with: Parkland Regional Health Authority Inc.
PO Box 130, 308 Jackson St., Grandview, MB R0L 0Y0
Tel: 204-546-2769; *Fax:* 204-546-2207
Number of Beds: 39 beds
John Kelly, COO

Grunthal: **Menno Home for the Aged**
Affiliated with: South Eastman Health / Santé Sud-Est Inc.
235 Park St., Grunthal, MB R0A 0R0
Tel: 204-434-6496
www.sehealth.mb.ca
Year Founded: 1960
Number of Beds: 40 beds
Ken Knaggs, Administrator

Hamiota: **Hamiota Personal Care Home**
177 Birch Ave., Hamiota, MB R0M 0T0
Tel: 204-764-2011; *Fax:* 204-764-2049
mandrew@mrha.mb.ca
Number of Beds: 30 beds
Marlene Andrew, Area Manager

Killarney: **Bayside Personal Care Home Inc.**
Affiliated with: Assiniboine Regional Health Authority
PO Box 400, Killarney, MB R0K 1G0
Tel: 204-523-4661; *Fax:* 204-523-8948
Number of Beds: 60 beds
L. Blixhavn, Head Nurse

Lac du Bonnet: **Lac du Bonnet Personal Care Home**
Affiliated with: North Eastman Health Association Inc.
PO Box 1030, Lac du Bonnet, MB R0E 1A0
Tel: 204-345-8675; *Fax:* 204-345-9245
Number of Beds: 30 beds
Merle Fischer, Care Team Manager

Lundar: **Lundar Personal Care Home**
Affiliated with: Interlake Regional Health Authority Inc.
97 - 1st St. South, Lundar, MB R0C 1Y0
Tel: 204-762-5663
Number of Beds: 20 beds
Patty Johnson, District Director
Patty Johnson, Director of Nursing

MacGregor: **MacGregor Personal Care Home**
Affiliated with: Regional Health Authority - Central Manitoba Inc.
PO Box 250, 87 Grafton St. South, MacGregor, MB R0H 0R0
Tel: 204-685-2850; *Fax:* 204-685-2529
Number of Beds: 20 beds
Garry Mattin, Executive Director

McCreary: **McCreary/Alonsa Personal Care Home Inc.**
Affiliated with: Parkland Regional Health Authority Inc.
PO Box 250, McCreary, MB R0J 1B0
Tel: 204-835-2482; *Fax:* 204-835-2713
Number of Beds: 20 beds
Charlie Sitwell, Administrator

Melita: **Melita & Area Personal Care Home**
Affiliated with: Assiniboine Regional Health Authority
147 Summit St., Melita, MB R0M 1L0
Tel: 204-522-3403
Number of Beds: 20 beds
Note: Specialties: Long-term care; Respite care
Georgina Henuset

Morden: **Tabor Home Inc.**
Affiliated with: Regional Health Authority - Central Manitoba Inc.
230 - 9th St. South, Morden, MB R6M 1Y3
Tel: 204-822-4848; *Fax:* 204-822-5289
info@taborhome.ca
www.taborhome.ca
Year Founded: 1951
Number of Beds: 60 residential capacity
Note: Specialties: Nursing services for persons who require long-term care; Activity program; Social work; Alternative needs area, for residents who experience difficulties in the areas of thought, memory, & perception; Adult day program
Sherry Hildebrand, Facility Director
s.hildebrand@taborhome.ca

Morris: **Red River Valley Lodge Inc.**
Affiliated with: Regional Health Authority - Central Manitoba Inc.
PO Box 507, 136 Ottawa St. West, Morris, MB R0G 1K0
Tel: 204-746-2394; *Fax:* 204-746-2123
Number of Beds: 40 long-term care beds
Clara Wiebe, Facility Contact
c.wiebe@rrvl.rha-central.mb.ca

Neepawa: **East View Lodge**
Affiliated with: Assiniboine Regional Health Authority
PO Box 1240, Neepawa, MB R0J 1H0
Tel: 204-476-2383; *Fax:* 204-476-3645
Number of Beds: 124 beds
Judy Gabler, Area Manager

Nelson House: **Nisichawaysihk Personal Care Home**
PO Box 460, Nelson House, MB R0B 1A0
Tel: 204-484-2350; *Fax:* 204-484-2011
Number of Beds: 24 beds

Norway House: **Pinaow Wachi Inc. Personal Care Home**
PO Box 98, Norway House, MB R0B 1B0
Tel: 204-359-6606; *Fax:* 204-359-6949
Number of Beds: 26 beds
B. Rowden, Administrator

Notre Dame de Lourdes: **Foyer Notre Dame Inc.**
Affiliated with: Regional Health Authority - Central Manitoba Inc.
PO Box 190, 40 Rodgers St., Notre Dame de Lourdes, MB R0G 1M0
Tel: 204-248-2092; *Fax:* 204-248-2499
Number of Beds: 60 long-term care beds
Marcie Dupasquier, Facility Contact
m.dupasquier@fnd.rha-central.mb.ca

Oakbank: **Kin Place**
Affiliated with: North Eastman Health Association Inc.
PO Box 28, Oakbank, MB R0E 1J0
Tel: 204-444-6128; *Fax:* 204-444-7868
Number of Beds: 40 beds
Liz Hogue, Care Team Manager

Pilot Mound: **Prairie View Lodge**
Affiliated with: Regional Health Authority - Central Manitoba Inc.
#26, 424 Broadway Ave. West, Pilot Mound, MB R0G 1P0
Tel: 204-825-2717; *Fax:* 204-825-2267
Number of Beds: 30 long-term care beds (24 EPH units)
Pam King, Health Services Leader
p.king@rlh.rha-central.mb.ca

Pilot Mound: **Rock Lake Personal Care Home Inc.**
Affiliated with: Regional Health Authority - Central Manitoba Inc.
#27, 115 Brown St. South, Pilot Mound, MB R0G 1P0
Tel: 204-825-2246; *Fax:* 204-825-2267
rlhd@mts.net
Number of Beds: 24 long-term care beds
Pam King, Health Services Leader
p.king@rlh.rha-central.mb.ca

Pine Falls: **Sunnywood Personal Care Home**
Affiliated with: North Eastman Health Association Inc.
PO Box 2000, Spruce St., Pine Falls, MB R0E 1M0
Tel: 204-367-8201
www.neha.mb.ca
Number of Beds: 20 beds
Note: Specialties: Nursing care; Recreation services; Occupational therapy; Physiotherapy; Podiatry; Mental health services; Respite care
Lorraine Dent-Prychun, Director of Long Term Care

Portage la Prairie: **Douglas Campbell Lodge**
Affiliated with: Regional Health Authority - Central Manitoba Inc.
150 - 9 St. SE, Portage la Prairie, MB R1N 3T6
Tel: 204-239-6006; *Fax:* 204-239-0055
Number of Beds: 60 long-term care beds
Colleen Fletcher, Facility Contact
c.fletcher@dcl.rha-central.mb.ca

Portage la Prairie: **Lions Prairie Manor**
Affiliated with: Regional Health Authority - Central Manitoba Inc.
24 - 9th St. SE, Portage la Prairie, MB R1N 3V4
Tel: 204-857-7864; *Fax:* 204-857-8207
Number of Beds: 150 beds
Cathy Asham, Facility Contact

Reston: **Willowview Home**
Affiliated with: Assiniboine Regional Health Authority
PO Box 250, Reston, MB R0M 1X0
Tel: 204-877-3921; *Fax:* 204-877-3998
Number of Beds: 20 beds
Meegan Carson

***Roblin:* Crocus Court Personal Care Home**
PO Box 940, 15 Hospital St., Roblin, MB R0L 1P0
Tel: 204-937-2142; *Fax:* 204-937-8892
Number of Beds: 60 beds
C. Jerome, Site Manager

***Rossburn:* Rossburn Personal Care Home Inc.**
PO Box 40, Rossburn, MB R0J 1V0
Tel: 204-859-2413; *Fax:* 204-859-2526
Number of Beds: 20 beds

***Russell:* Russell & District Personal Care Home Inc.**
Affiliated with: Assiniboine Regional Health Authority
PO Box 400, Russell, MB R0J 1W0
Tel: 204-773-3117; *Fax:* 204-773-2232
Number of Beds: 40 beds
Barb Kostesky, Area Manager

***Sandy Lake:* Sandy Lake Medical Nursing Home Inc.**
Affiliated with: Assiniboine Regional Health Authority
PO Box 7, Sandy Lake, MB R0J 1X0
Tel: 204-585-2107; *Fax:* 204-585-5352
gkowaluk@arha.ca
Number of Beds: 36 beds
Barb Kostesky, Area Manager

***Selkirk:* Betel Personal Care Home, Selkirk**
Affiliated with: Interlake Regional Health Authority Inc.
212 Manchester Ave., Selkirk, MB R1A 0B6
Tel: 204-482-4471; *Fax:* 204-482-4651
www.betelhomefoundation.ca/selkirk.html
Number of Beds: 92 beds
Brenna Raemer, Administrator
B. Armstrong, Plant Manager

***Selkirk:* Red River Place**
Affiliated with: Interlake Regional Health Authority Inc.
133 Manchester Ave., Selkirk, MB R1A 0B5
Tel: 204-482-3036; *Fax:* 204-482-9499
mgd_redriverplace@extendicare.com
www.ltcam.mb.ca
Number of Beds: 104 beds
Note: Personal care facility, member of the Long Term Care Association of Manitoba
M.S. Fages, Executive Director
J. Chennell, Director of Nursing

***Selkirk:* Tudor House Personal Care Home**
Affiliated with: Interlake Regional Health Authority Inc.
800 Manitoba Ave., Selkirk, MB R3C 2C9
Tel: 204-482-6601; *Fax:* 204-482-4369
tudor@geriatricare.ca
www.geriatricare.ca/tudorhouse
Year Founded: 1971
Number of Beds: 76 beds
Note: Specialties: Care for seniors, physically & mentally handicapped adults, & persons with dementia; Hospice-type care for the dying
Ashley Martyniw, CEO/Administrator

***Souris:* Souris District Personal Care Home**
Affiliated with: Assiniboine Regional Health Authority
PO Box 10, Souris, MB R0L 2C0
Tel: 204-483-2730; *Fax:* 204-483-2310
Number of Beds: 43 beds
Marilyn McGregor

***St Adolphe:* St. Adolphe Personal Care Home**
Affiliated with: South Eastman Health/Santé Sud-Est Inc.
PO Box 40, St Adolphe, MB R5A 1A1
Tel: 204-883-2181; *Fax:* 204-883-2394
stadolphepch@mts.net
Number of Beds: 42 beds
Robert Brosseau, Administrator

***St Pierre Jolys:* Repos Jolys**
Affiliated with: South Eastman Health/Santé Sud-Est Inc.
PO Box 320, St Pierre Jolys, MB R0A 1V0
Tel: 204-433-7611; *Fax:* 204-433-7455
Year Founded: 1995
Number of Beds: 22 beds
Note: this personal care home is justaposed to Centre Medico-Spcial De Salaberry District Health Centre
Elaine McPherson, Facility Manager

***Ste Anne:* Villa Youville Inc.**
Affiliated with: South Eastman Health/Santé Sud-Est Inc.
208 Central Ave., Ste Anne, MB R0A 1R0
Tel: 204-422-5624; *Fax:* 204-422-5842
Number of Beds: 66 beds
Claude Lachance, Executive Director
Noel Deslauriers, Coordinator, Environmental Services

***Ste Rose du Lac:* Dr. Gendreau Memorial Personal Care Home Inc.**
Affiliated with: Parkland Regional Health Authority Inc.
PO Box 420, Ste Rose du Lac, MB R0L 1S0
Tel: 204-447-2019; *Fax:* 204-447-2267
Number of Beds: 65 beds
Glen Kozak, Administrator

***Steinbach:* Rest Haven Care Services**
Affiliated with: South Eastman Health/Santé Sud-Est Inc.
185 Woodhaven Ave., Steinbach, MB R5G 1K7
Tel: 204-326-2206; *Fax:* 204-326-3521
Number of Beds: 60 long-term care beds
Note: Owned and operated by seven area Evangelical Mennonite Conference churches
Marlin J. Roth, CEO

***Stonewall:* Rosewood Lodge**
Affiliated with: Interlake Regional Health Authority Inc.
436 - 1 Ave. North, Stonewall, MB R0C 2Z0
Tel: 204-467-5257; *Fax:* 204-467-4763
knattrass@irha.mb.ca
www.irha.mb.ca
Number of Beds: 50 beds
Note: Personal care home
Keith Bytheway, South West District Director

***Swan River:* Swan River Valley Lodge (1991) Inc.**
Affiliated with: Parkland Regional Health Authority Inc.
1013 Main St., Swan River, MB R0L 1Z0
Tel: 204-734-3441; *Fax:* 204-734-9081
www.svhf.mb.ca
Number of Beds: 70 beds
Note: Number of staff: 7 Registered Nurses, 41 other staff
Mary Ellen Parsons, Clinical Services Manager
204-734-3441, mparsons@prha.mb.ca

***Swan River:* Swan River Valley Personal Care Home Inc.**
Affiliated with: Parkland Regional Health Authority Inc.
334 - 8 Ave. South, Swan River, MB R0L 1Z0
Tel: 204-734-4521; *Fax:* 204-734-9965
www.svhf.mb.ca
Number of Beds: 60 beds
Note: Personal care home. Number of staff: 8 Registered Nurses, 31 Nurses' Aides, 5 other staff
Michelle Vandepoele, Nurse Manager
mvandepoele@prha.mb.ca

***Teulon:* Goodwin Lodge**
Affiliated with: Interlake Regional Health Authority Inc.
PO Box 89, 3rd Ave. SE, Teulon, MB R0C 3B0
Tel: 204-886-2433; *Fax:* 204-886-2653
Number of Beds: 20 beds
Keith Bytheway, District Director

***The Pas:* St. Paul's Personal Care Home**
Former Name: St. Paul's Residence
PO Box 240, The Pas, MB R9A 1K4
Tel: 204-623-9226
Number of Beds: 60 beds
Shauna Cupples, Regional Manager

***Thompson:* Cambridge Residence**
PO Box 81, 65 McGill, Thompson, MB R8N 1M9
Tel: 204-778-7582
Number of Beds: 8 beds
Johanna Fudge, Manager

***Treherne:* Tiger Hills Manor Inc.**
Affiliated with: Assiniboine Regional Health Authority
PO Box 130, Treherne, MB R0G 2V0
Tel: 204-723-2023
www.assiniboine-rha.ca
Number of Beds: 22 beds
Note: Specialties: Long-term care
Deb Obach

***Virden:* Sherwood Nursing Home**
Affiliated with: Assiniboine Regional Health Authority
223 Hargrave St. East, Virden, MB R0M 2C0
Tel: 204-748-1546
www.assiniboine-rha.ca
Number of Beds: 50 beds
Note: Specialties: Long-term personal care; Respite care
Meegan Carson, Area Manager

***Virden:* West Man Nursing Home Inc.**
Affiliated with: Assiniboine Regional Health Authority
PO Box 1630, 427 Frame St. E, Virden, MB R0M 2C0
Tel: 204-748-1230; *Fax:* 204-748-3432
mcarson@arha.ca
Number of Beds: 50 beds
Meegan Carson

***Wawanesa:* Wawanesa Personal Care Home Inc.**
Affiliated with: Assiniboine Regional Health Authority
PO Box 309, Wawanesa, MB R0K 2G0
Tel: 204-824-2335; *Fax:* 204-824-2148
Number of Beds: 20 beds
Deb Obach, Area Manager

***Whitemouth:* Whitemouth District Health Centre Personal Care Home**
Affiliated with: North Eastman Health Association Inc.
PO Box 160, Whitemouth, MB R0E 2G0
Tel: 204-348-7191; *Fax:* 204-348-7911
Number of Beds: 24 PCH beds
Heather Frederick, Care Team Manager

***Winkler:* Salem Home Inc.**
Affiliated with: Regional Health Authority - Central Manitoba Inc.
165 - 15 St., Winkler, MB R6W 1T8
Tel: 204-325-4316; *Fax:* 204-325-5442
salem@salemhome.net
www.salemhome.net
Number of Beds: 145 long-term care beds
Note: Personal care home owned and operated by 14 Mennonite churches
Sherry Janzen, Facility Contact
s.janzen@salemhome.net

***Winnipeg:* Beacon Hill Lodge**
Affiliated with: Winnipeg Regional Health Authority
190 Fort St., Winnipeg, MB R3C 1C9
Tel: 204-942-7541; *Fax:* 204-944-0136
Number of Beds: 175 beds
Shelley Gurvey, Administrator

***Winnipeg:* Bethania Mennonite Personal Care Home Inc.**
Affiliated with: Winnipeg Regional Health Authority
1045 Concordia Ave., Winnipeg, MB R2K 3S7
Tel: 204-667-0795; *Fax:* 204-667-7078
Number of Beds: 148 beds
Anita Kampen, Executive Director

***Winnipeg:* Calvary Place Personal Care Home**
Affiliated with: Winnipeg Regional Health Authority
1325 Erin St., Winnipeg, MB R3E 3R6
Tel: 204-943-4424; *Fax:* 204-783-7524
Number of Beds: 100 beds
Dale Berry

***Winnipeg:* Charleswood Care Centre**
Affiliated with: Winnipeg Regional Health Authority
5501 Roblin Blvd., Winnipeg, MB R3R 0G8
Tel: 204-888-3363; *Fax:* 204-896-4763
Number of Beds: 155 beds

***Winnipeg:* Concordia Place Personal Care Home**
1000 Molson St., Winnipeg, MB R2K 4L5
Tel: 204-661-7372; *Fax:* 204-661-7297
Number of Beds: 140 beds
Les Janzen, COO

***Winnipeg:* Convalescent Home of Winnipeg**
Affiliated with: Winnipeg Regional Health Authority
276 Hugo St. North, Winnipeg, MB R3M 2N6
Tel: 204-453-4663; *Fax:* 204-453-7149
www.wrha.mb.ca
Number of Beds: 84 residents
Note: Specialty: Long-term care
A.L. (Tony) Fraser, Executive Director

Rhonda Crane, Director of Nursing

Winnipeg: Deaf Centre Manitoba
#101, 285 Pembina Hwy., Winnipeg, MB R3L 2E1
Tel: 204-284-0802; Fax: 204-284-9373
Number of Beds: 57 beds
Doug Momotiuk, Exec. Dir.

Winnipeg: Donwood Manor Personal Care Home
Affiliated with: Winnipeg Regional Health Authority
171 Donwood Dr., Winnipeg, MB R2G 0V9
Tel: 204-668-4410; Fax: 204-663-5429
jheinrichs@donwoodmanor.org
www.donwoodmanor.org
Number of Beds: 121 beds
James Heinrichs, Executive Director

Winnipeg: Extendicare - Oakview Place
Affiliated with: Winnipeg Regional Health Authority
2395 Ness Ave., Winnipeg, MB R3J 1A5
Tel: 204-888-3005; Fax: 204-831-8101
cnh_oakviewplace@extendicare.com
www.extendicarecanada.com
Number of Beds: 245 beds
Note: Specialties: Nursing & supportive care; Rehabilitation & rehabilitative services; Optometry services; Dental services; Social & therapeutic programs; Adult day program; Care for persons with Alzheimer's disease and related dementias; Palliative care
Terry Vanbocquestal, Administrator
Carol Rowley, Director of Care

Winnipeg: Extendicare - Tuxedo Villa
Affiliated with: Winnipeg Regional Health Authority
2060 Corydon Ave., Winnipeg, MB R3P 0N3
Tel: 204-889-2650; Fax: 204-896-0258
cnh_tuxedovilla@extendicare.com
www.extendicarecanada.com
Number of Beds: 213 beds
Note: Specialties: Professional nursing & supportive care; Rehabilitation services; Care for persons with Alzheimer's disease & related dementias; Optometry services; Social & therapeutic programs
Ronald Parent, Administrator

Winnipeg: Fort Garry Care Centre Ltd.
Affiliated with: Winnipeg Regional Health Authority
1776 Pembina Hwy., Winnipeg, MB R3T 2G2
Tel: 204-269-6939; Fax: 204-275-2192
Number of Beds: 64 beds
Gerald Kalef, Executive Director
Germain Sicotte, Maintenance Manager

Winnipeg: Foyer Valade Inc.
Affiliated with: Winnipeg Regional Health Authority
450 River Rd., Winnipeg, MB R2M 5M4
Tel: 204-254-3332; Fax: 204-254-0329
Number of Beds: 115 beds
Francis LaBossière, Executive Director
C. Dupuis, Environmental Services

Winnipeg: Fred Douglas Society Inc.
Affiliated with: Winnipeg Regional Health Authority
Former Name: Fred Douglas Lodge
1275 Burrows Ave., Winnipeg, MB R2X 0B8
Tel: 204-586-8541; Fax: 204-589-0110
www.freddouglassociety.com
Number of Beds: 136 beds
Theresa Jachnycky, Chief Executive Officer
Marilyn Allan, Director of Resident Care

Winnipeg: Golden Door Geriatric Centre
Affiliated with: Winnipeg Regional Health Authority
1679 Pembina Hwy., Winnipeg, MB R3T 2G6
Tel: 204-269-6308; Fax: 204-275-3185
Number of Beds: 78 beds
Lorrie LeBlanc, Administrator
Mary P. Entwistle, Director, Nursing

Winnipeg: Golden Links Lodge
Affiliated with: Winnipeg Regional Health Authority
PO Box 248, 2280 St. Mary's Rd., Winnipeg, MB R2M 4A5
Tel: 204-257-9947; Fax: 204-257-2405
Number of Beds: 88 beds
Dorene Rosmus, Administrator

Winnipeg: Golden West Centennial Lodge
Affiliated with: Winnipeg Regional Health Authority
811 School Rd., Winnipeg, MB R2Y 0S8
Tel: 204-888-3311; Fax: 204-831-0544
Number of Beds: 116 beds
Maj. Don Maye, Executive Director

Winnipeg: Heritage Lodge Personal Care Home
Former Name: Heritage Lodge Personal Care Home Inc
3555 Portage Ave., Winnipeg, MB R3K 0X2
Tel: 204-888-7940; Fax: 204-832-6544
heritagelodge@reveraliving.com
www.retirementresidencesreit.com/homes/82/
Number of Beds: 86 beds
Kim Hykawy, Administrator
Mary Baranski, Assistant Director of Nursing
Len Falco, Maintenance Supervisor

Winnipeg: Holy Family Nursing Home
165 Aberdeen Ave., Winnipeg, MB R2W 1T9
Tel: 204-589-7381; Fax: 204-589-8605
Number of Beds: 276 beds
Jean Piche, Executive Director
Mike Ostryniuk, Plant Supt.

Winnipeg: Kildonan Personal Care Centre Inc.
1970 Henderson Hwy., Winnipeg, MB R2G 1P2
Tel: 204-334-4633; Fax: 204-334-4632
kildonan@reveraliving.com
Number of Beds: 120 beds
Edward Bird, Administrator

Winnipeg: Lions Personal Care Centre
Affiliated with: Winnipeg Regional Health Authority
320 Sherbrook St., Winnipeg, MB R3B 2W6
Tel: 204-784-1240; Fax: 204-784-2723
Number of Beds: 116 rooms
Helmut Epp, CEO

Winnipeg: Luther Home
Affiliated with: Winnipeg Regional Health Authority
1081 Andrews St., Winnipeg, MB R2V 2G9
Tel: 204-338-4641; Fax: 204-338-4643
info@lutherhome.mb.ca
www.lutherhome.com
Year Founded: 1969
Number of Beds: 80 personal care home beds, including a respite bed
Note: Specialties: Physio, occupational, massage, & music therapy; Foot care
Ray Koop, Director of Care

Winnipeg: Maples Personal Care Home
Affiliated with: Winnipeg Regional Health Authority
500 Mandalay Dr., Winnipeg, MB R2P 1V4
Tel: 204-632-8570; Fax: 204-697-0249
Number of Beds: 200 beds
Linda Norton, Administrator
Nancy Coey, Director, Nursing

Winnipeg: Meadowood Manor
Affiliated with: Winnipeg Regional Health Authority
577 St. Anne's Rd., Winnipeg, MB R2M 5B2
Tel: 204-257-2394
info@meadowood.ca
www.meadowood.ca
Number of Beds: 88 beds
Note: Specialties: Long-term care; Rehabilitation services; Foot care services; Social work; Recreation programs; Respite care; Palliative care
Charles Kunze, Administrator
E. Verplaetse, Director of Resident Services

Winnipeg: Middlechurch Home of Winnipeg Inc.
Affiliated with: Winnipeg Regional Health Authority
280 Balderstone Ave., Winnipeg, MB R4A 4A6
Tel: 204-339-1947; Fax: 204-338-3498
www.middlechurchhome.mb.ca
Year Founded: 1884
Number of Beds: 197 beds
Note: Specialties: Care of older people; Activity centre; Physiotherapy; Occupational therapy; Pet therapy; Adult day program; Respite care. Number of employees: 320
Heather Temple, Executive Director

Winnipeg: Park Manor Personal Care Home Inc.
Affiliated with: Winnipeg Regional Health Authority
301 Redonda St., Winnipeg, MB R2C 1L7
Tel: 204-222-3251; Fax: 204-222-3237
www.parkmanor.ca
Number of Beds: 44 private rooms + 20 semi-private rooms + 4 four-bed rooms
Note: Specialties: Therapeutic recreation; Education sessions for residents & families; Adult day program; Palliative care
Charles L. Toop, Executive Director
Robert Ivany, Director, Nursing
B. Gmiterek, Maintenance Director

Winnipeg: Pembina Place Mennonite Personal Care Home
Affiliated with: Winnipeg Regional Health Authority
285 Pembina Hwy., Winnipeg, MB R3L 2E1
Tel: 204-284-0802; Fax: 204-474-0073
Number of Beds: 57 beds

Winnipeg: River East Personal Care Home Ltd.
Affiliated with: Winnipeg Regional Health Authority
1375 Molson St., Winnipeg, MB R2K 4K8
Tel: 204-668-7460; Fax: 204-668-7459
Number of Beds: 120 beds
Virginia Zazula, Administrator

Winnipeg: St. Joseph's Residence Inc.
Affiliated with: Winnipeg Regional Health Authority
1149 Leila Ave., Winnipeg, MB R2P 1S6
Tel: 204-697-8031; Fax: 204-697-8075
stjosephs@primus.ca
Number of Beds: 100 beds
Note: Personal care home
Marianna Muzyka, Executive Director
Luba Sirdar, Director, Nursing Services
Ben Korving, Director, Direct Services

Winnipeg: St. Norbert Personal Care Home
Affiliated with: Winnipeg Regional Health Authority
50 St Pierre St., Winnipeg, MB R3V 1J6
Tel: 204-269-4538; Fax: 204-269-6374
Number of Beds: 91 beds
Robert Brousseau, Administrator
Shirley Beaulieu, Director, Nursing

Winnipeg: The Sharon Home Inc.
The Saul and Claribel Simkin Centre
Affiliated with: Winnipeg Regional Health Authority
Also Known As: The Simkin Centre
1 Falconridge Dr., Winnipeg, MB R3Y 1V9
Tel: 204-586-9781; Fax: 204-589-9760
Year Founded: 2002
Number of Beds: 200 beds
Note: Specialties: Care for elders of Jewish community; Therapeutic recreation; Walking track for residents recovering from hip surgery or a stroke; Tracking program for resident safety; Adult day program

Winnipeg: Vista Park Lodge
Affiliated with: Winnipeg Regional Health Authority
144 Novavista Dr., Winnipeg, MB R2N 1P8
Tel: 204-257-6688; Fax: 204-257-0446
Year Founded: 1981
Number of Beds: 100 beds
Betty Jane Jones, Administrator; Director, Nursing

Winnipeg: West Park Manor
Affiliated with: Winnipeg Regional Health Authority
3199 Grant Ave., Winnipeg, MB R3R 1X2
Tel: 204-889-3330; Fax: 204-832-9555
krcimchewpm@mts.net
Number of Beds: 150 beds
K.D. Reimche, Administrator
M. Gutierrez, A/Director of Nursing

Winnipegosis: Winnipegosis-Mossey River Personal Care Home
Affiliated with: Parkland Regional Health Authority Inc.
PO Box 280, 230 Bridge St., Winnipegosis, MB R0L 2G0
Tel: 204-656-4481; Fax: 204-656-4402
Number of Beds: 20 beds
Glen Kozak, COO

Mental Health Facilities

Mental Health Hospitals/Facilities

Altona: Altona & District Association for the Mentally Handicapped Inc.
PO Box 330, 122 - 10th Ave. NW, Altona, MB R0G 0B0
Tel: 204-324-5401
otc@mts.net
Number of Beds: 5 beds
Anne Klassen, General Manager

Brandon: Centre for Adult Psychiatry
Affiliated with: Brandon Regional Health Authority
AP1, 150 McTavish Ave. East, Brandon, MB R7A 2B3
Tel: 204-726-2923; Fax: 204-728-9633
Number of Beds: 25 beds
Lynda Stiles, Program Manager

Brandon: **Centre for Geriatric Psychiatry**
Affiliated with: Brandon Regional Health Authority
Assiniboine Centre, 150 McTavish Ave. East, Brandon, MB R7A 2B3
Tel: 204-726-2900; *Fax:* 204-725-0911
Number of Beds: 22
Wendy Dryburgh, Program Manager

Brandon: **Child & Adolescent Treatment Centre**
Affiliated with: Brandon Regional Health Authority
1240 - 10 St., Brandon, MB R7A 7L6
Tel: 204-727-3445; *Fax:* 204-727-3451
Number of Beds: 10 beds
Doug Crookshanks, Program Manager

Brandon: **Community Mental Health Services**
The Town Centre, #B13, 800 Rosser Ave., Brandon, MB R7A 6N5
Tel: 204-571-8300; *Fax:* 204-726-8684
Albert Hajes, Coordinator

Portage la Prairie: **Manitoba Developmental Centre**
PO Box 1190, 3rd St. NE, Portage la Prairie, MB R1N 3C6
Tel: 204-856-4200; *Fax:* 204-856-4258
Toll-Free: 800/473-4603
dbjore@gov.mb.ca
Number of Beds: 375 beds
Note: developmental centre for residents with intellectual disabilities
Donna Bjore, CEO

Selkirk: **Selkirk Mental Health Centre**
PO Box 9600, 825 Manitoba Ave., Selkirk, MB R1A 2B5
Tel: 204-482-3810; *Fax:* 204-785-8936
Toll-Free: 800-881-3073
smhc@gov.mb.ca
www.gov.mb.ca/health/smhc/
Number of Beds: 269 beds
Note: Long term mental health inpatient care & rehabilitation
K. Nattrass, CEO

Winkler: **Eden Health Care Services**
Affiliated with: Regional Health Authority - Central Manitoba Inc.
PO Box 129, 204 Main St., Winkler, MB R6W 4A4
Tel: 204-325-5355; *Fax:* 204-325-8742
edencare@valleycable.com
edenhealth.mb.ca
Number of Beds: 40 beds
Eckhard Goerz, Facility Contact

Winkler: **Eden Mental Health Centre**
Affiliated with: Regional Health Authority - Central Manitoba Inc.
1500 Pembina Ave., Winkler, MB R6W 1T4
Tel: 204-325-4325; *Fax:* 204-325-8429
edenment@edenhealth.mb.ca
edenhealth.mb.ca
Number of Beds: 30 beds
Les Zacharias, Administrator
les.zacharias@edenhealth.mb.ca

Winnipeg: **Manitoba Adolescent Treatment Centre Inc.**
Affiliated with: Winnipeg Regional Health Authority
120 Tecumseh St., Winnipeg, MB R3E 2A9
Tel: 204-477-6391; *Fax:* 204-783-8948
info@matc.ca
www.matc.ca
Number of Beds: 25 beds
Note: Mental health services for children, youth, and families
Dr. Keith Hildahl, CEO

New Brunswick

Government Departments in Charge

NEW BRUNSWICK: Dept. of Health Communications
Former Name: Dept. of Health & Community Services
PO Box 5100, Fredericton, NB E3B 5G8
Tel: 506-453-2536; *Fax:* 506-444-4697
HealthInfo@gnb.ca; InfoSante@gnb.ca
Carole Payne, Director, Communications

Regional Health Authorities

Bathurst: **Vitalité Health Network**
Réseau de santé Vitalité
Former Name: Restigouche Health Authority/Régie de la santé du
#600, 275 Main St., Bathurst, NB E2A 1A9
Tel: 506-544-2133; *Fax:* 506-544-2145
Toll-Free: 1-888-472-2220
info@rrsa.ca
www.santevitalitehealth.ca
Year Founded: 2008
Number of Beds: 1,124
Note: The Vitalité Health Network amalgamates Regional Health Authority 4, the Restigouche Health Authority, the Acadie-Bathurst Health Authority, and the Beauséjour Health Authority; 7,600 employees; 470 physicians; 1,200 volunteers. The network is comprised of 11 hospitals, 6 community health centres, and a centre for psychiatric care.
Andrée Robichaud, President/CEO
Aldéa Landry, President of the Board of Directors

Miramichi: **Horizon Health Network**
Réseau de santé Horizon
Former Name: Regional Health Authority B
155 Pleasant St., Miramichi, NB E1V 1Y3
Tel: 506-623-5500; *Fax:* 506-623-5533
www.rhab-rrsb.ca
Year Founded: 2008
Number of Beds: 1,675 beds
Note: Along with the Vitalité Health Network, the Horizon Health Network amalgamates the 8 former regional health authorities in New Brunswick. Horizon Health Network servies the Moncton, Saint John, Fredericton and Miramichi areas, as well as communities in Nova Scotia and Prince Edward Island; 924 physicians; 5,000 nurses; 25 nurse practitioners; 2,175 health care professionals; 4,800 support staff; 3,500 volunteers.
Donald J. Peters, President/CEO

Hospitals

Hospitals - General

Bath: **Northern Carleton Hospital**
82 Hospital St., Bath, NB E7J 1B9
Tel: 506-278-2400; *Fax:* 506-278-2449
Number of Beds: 17 beds
Denise Gray, Facilities Manager
Peter Byron, Manager, Housekeeping

Bathurst: **Hôpital régional Chaleur**
Affiliée à: Regional Health Authority A
Ancien nom: Centre hospitalier régional
1745, promenade Vallée Lourdes, Bathurst, NB E2A 4L7
Tél: 506-544-3000; *Téléc:* 506-544-2440
Nombre de lits: 215 beds
Stéphane Legacy, Administrateur d'établissement

Blacks Harbour: **Fundy Health Centre**
Affiliated with: Horizon Health Network
34 Hospital St., Blacks Harbour, NB E5H 1K2
Tel: 506-456-4200; *Fax:* 506-456-4222
Note: Specialties: Primary care; Rehabilitation services

Campbellton: **Campbellton Regional Hospital**
Hôpital régional de Campbellton
Affiliated with: Regional Health Authority A
PO Box 880, 189 Lily Lake Rd., Campbellton, NB E3N 3H3
Tel: 506-789-5000; *Fax:* 506-789-5025
www.santerestigouchehealth.com; www.santevitalitehealth.ca
Year Founded: 1991
Number of Beds: 166 beds/lits
Note: The hospital is part of the Vitalité Health Network, one of 2 regional health authorities formed in 2008 to amalgamate the provincial health authority structure in New Brunswick; 900 employees; 17 family physicians; 200 nurses; 27 specialists; 35 health care professionals; emergency and ambulatory care; obstetrics and gynecology; pediatrics; psychiatry; geriatric medicine; rehabilitation; orthopedics; palliative care.
Ruth Lyons, Facility Director

Edmundston: **Hôpital régional d'Edmundston**
Edmundston Regional Hospital
Affiliée à: Regional Health Authority A
275, boul Hébert, Edmundston, NB E3V 4E4
Tél: 506-739-2200; *Téléc:* 506-739-2231
Nombre de lits: 169 lits
Dr. Édouard Hendriks, Administrateur d'établissement

Fredericton: **Dr. Everett Chalmers Regional Hospital**
PO Box 9000, 700 Priestman St., Fredericton, NB E3B 5N5
Tel: 506-452-5400; *Fax:* 506-452-5670
www.rhab-rrsb.ca
Year Founded: 1976
Number of Beds: 314 beds
Note: Hospital Specialties: Emergency services; Diagnostic services; Surgery; Intensive care; Primary care; Obstetrics; Neonatology; Pediatrics; Reconstructive & restorative medicine; Cardiac care; Rheumatology; Oncology; Dermatology; Gastroenterology; Neurology; Dialysis; Psychiatry; Geriatric care. Number of Employees: 2,000+ nurses, health care professionals, & support staff; 58 family physicians; 88 specialists
Dr. Ward Murdock, Chief of Staff, Fredericton, Horizon Health Network
Dr. Peter Feero, Chief of Surgery, Fredericton, Horizon Health Network
Dr. David Addleman, Chief of Psychiatry, Fredericton, Horizon Health Network

Grand Manan: **Grand Manan Hospital Ltd.**
Affiliated with: Regional Health Authority B
196 Rte. 776, Grand Manan, NB E5G 1A3
Tel: 506-662-4060; *Fax:* 506-662-4050
Number of Beds: 8 beds
Karen Thomas, Facility Manager

Grand-Sault: **Hôpital général de Grand-Sault inc.**
Grand Falls General Hospital Inc.
Affiliée à: Regional Health Authority A
CP 7061, 625, boul Evérard H. Daigle, Grand-Sault, NB E3Z 2R9
Tél: 506-473-7555; *Téléc:* 506-473-7530
Nombre de lits: 20 lits
Solange Bossé, Directrice d'établissement

Harvey Station: **Harvey Community Hospital Ltd.**
Affiliated with: Regional Health Authority B
2019 Rte. 3, Harvey Station, NB E6K 3E9
Tel: 506-366-6400; *Fax:* 506-366-6403
Shirley Moffatt, Nurse Manager

Lamèque: **Hôpital de Lamèque/Centre de santé communautaire de Lamèque**
Affiliée à: Regional Health Authority A
29, rue de l'Hôpital, Lamèque, NB E8T 1C5
Tél: 506-344-2261; *Téléc:* 506-344-3403
Nombre de lits: 12 lits
Dina Chiasson, Directrice d'établissement

Miramichi: **Miramichi Regional Hospital**
Affiliée à: Regional Health Authority B
500 Water St., Miramichi, NB E1V 3G5
Tél: 506-623-3000; *Téléc:* 506-623-3465
Nombre de lits: 161 beds
Gary Foley, Acting President/CEP

Moncton: **Hôpital régional Dr.-Georges-L.-Dumont**
Affiliée à: Regional Health Authority A
330, av Université, Moncton, NB E1C 2Z3
Tél: 506-862-4000; *Téléc:* 506-862-4256
www.beausejour-nb.ca
Nombre de lits: 362 lits
Dr. Louis-Marie Simard, Président et Directeur général par intérim
Blondine Arseneau, Conseillère en environnement

Moncton: **The Moncton Hospital**
L'Hôpital de Moncton
Affiliated with: Regional Health Authority B
135 MacBeath Ave., Moncton, NB E1C 6Z8
Tel: 506-857-5520; *Fax:* 506-857-5545
generalinquiries@serha.ca
www.serha.ca
Number of Beds: 381 beds
Note: Comprehensive health care, including trauma care, intensive care units for cardiac care, neonatal care, medical/surgical care; child & adolescent psychiatric unit; burn unit; ambulance service
Donald J. Peters, President/CEO

Oromocto: **Oromocto Public Hospital**
Affiliated with: Regional Health Authority B
103 Winnebago St., Oromocto, NB E2V 1C6
Tel: 506-357-4700; *Fax:* 506-357-4735
www.rivervalleyhealth.nb.ca
Number of Beds: 45 beds
Note: Specialties: Day surgery; Breast cancer screening centre; Close observation unit; William R. Duffie Unit, a healthy aging & restorative program. Number of employees: 15 family physicians

+ 1 radiologist + visiting surgeons + nurses, & professional & support staff
Darlene Cogswell, Facility Coordinator
John Swanwick, Lab Manager

Perth-Andover: Hôtel-Dieu of Saint-Joseph
Affiliated with: Regional Health Authority B
Former Name: Hôtel-Dieu Saint-Joseph de Perth-Andover
10 Woodland Hill, Perth-Andover, NB E7H 5H5
Tel: 506-273-7100; *Fax:* 506-273-7200
Number of Beds: 27 beds
Joy Van Tassel, Facility Manager

Plaster Rock: Tobique Valley Hospital Inc.
Affiliated with: Regional Health Authority B
120 Main St., Plaster Rock, NB E7G 2E5
Tel: 506-356-6600
www.rivervalleyhealth.nb.ca
Year Founded: 1957
Note: Specialties: Nursing care service; Physiotherapy
Susan Kukurski, Facility Coordinator
Ron Lewis, Plant Manager

Sackville: Sackville Memorial Hospital
L'Hôpital mémorial de Sackville
Affiliated with: Regional Health Authority B
8 Main St., Sackville, NB E4L 4A3
Tel: 506-364-4100; *Fax:* 506-536-1983
generalinquiries@serha.ca
www.serha.ca/sackville_hospital
Number of Beds: 21 beds
France Gauthier, Acting Manager

Saint John: Saint John Regional Hospital
Affiliated with: Regional Health Authority B
PO Box 2100, Tucker Park Rd., Saint John, NB E2L 4L2
Tel: 506-648-6000; *Fax:* 506-648-6364
Number of Beds: 524 beds
Note: Teaching hospital affiliated with Dalhousie University, New Brunswick Community College, University of New Brunswick and Memorial University in St. John's Newfoundland
Dora Nicinski, President/CEO

Saint John: Saint John Regional Hospital - Ridgewood Veterans Wing
Affiliated with: Regional Health Authority B
PO Box 2100, 422 Bay St., Saint John, NB E2L 4L2
Tel: 506-635-2420; *Fax:* 506-635-2425
www.ahsc.health.nb.ca/AboutUs/OurFacilities/facvets.shtml
Year Founded: 1976
Number of Beds: 80 beds
Note: A facility for veterans who require long-term care; maintains a close relationship with Veteran Affairs Canada and the Royal Canadian Legion.
Maxine Walsh, Regional Manager, Veterans Care, AHSC
506-635-2150, walma@reg2.health.nb.ca
Michael Park, Regional Manager, Long Term Mental Health Services, AHSC
parmi@reg2.health.nb.ca

Saint John: St. Joseph's Hospital
Affiliated with: Regional Health Authority B
130 Bayard Dr., Saint John, NB E2L 3L6
Tel: 506-632-5555; *Fax:* 506-632-5551
Number of Beds: 62 beds
Daryl Steeves, Facility Manager

Saint-Quentin: Hôtel-Dieu de St-Quentin
Affiliée à: Regional Health Authority A
21, rue Canada, Saint-Quentin, NB E8A 2P6
Tél: 506-235-2300; *Téléc:* 506-235-7201
nicole-d.labrie@rrs4.ca
Nombre de lits: 6 lits
Nicole Labrie, Directrice d'établissement
Monette Dupéré, Chef de service à l'entretien ménager

St Stephen: Charlotte County Hospital
Affiliated with: Regional Health Authority B
4 Garden St., St Stephen, NB E3L 2L9
Tel: 506-465-4444
Number of Beds: 44 beds
Note: Specialties: Ambulatory care; Diagnostic services; Rehabilitative services; Restorative health; Physiotherapy; Speech-language pathology; Respiratory therapy; Occupational therapy; Adult & youth addiction counselling; Diabetic education; Oncology outreach services; Sexual health clinic; Cardiac risk clinic; Healthy lung clinic; Palliative care
Yvonne Bartlette, Facility Manager

Ste-Anne-de-Kent: Hôpital Stella Maris de Kent
7714, rte 134, Ste-Anne-de-Kent, NB E4S 1H5
Tél: 506-743-7800; *Téléc:* 506-743-7813
www.beausejour-nb.ca
Nombre de lits: 20 lits
Lise Guerrette-Daigle, Directeur d'établissement
Gloria Melanson, Chef, Entretien mén.

Sussex: Sussex Health Centre
Affiliated with: Regional Health Authority B
75 Leonard Dr., Sussex, NB E4E 2P7
Tel: 506-432-3100
www.ahsc.health.nb.ca
Number of Beds: 25 beds
Note: Specialties: Acute care; Family medicine; Dialysis; IV therapy day hospital; Rehabilitative services; Palliative care
Elspeth Stanley, Facility Adminstrator

Tracadie-Sheila: Hôpital de Tracadie-Sheila
Affiliée à: Regional Health Authority A
400, rue des Hospitalières, Tracadie-Sheila, NB E1X 1G5
Tél: 506-394-3000; *Téléc:* 506-394-3034
Nombre de lits: 59 lits
Odette Robichaud, Directrice d'établissement
A. Saulnier, Directeur, Installations matériels

Community Health Centres

Community Health Care Centres

Baie-Sainte-Anne: Baie-Ste-Anne Health Centre
Centre de santé Baie-Ste-Anne
Affiliated with: Regional Health Authority B
13, rue de l'Église, Baie-Sainte-Anne, NB E9A 1A9
Tel: 506-228-2004; *Fax:* 506-228-2008
www.rha7.ca
Note: Patients may access the services of a physician who works 3 days per week, & a full time nurse on site; monthly public health & diabetic clinics; weekly lab.
Monica Lloyd, Contact

Bathurst: NB Extra Mural Program
Bathurst Unit
Affiliated with: Regional Health Authority A
1750 Sunset Dr., Bathurst, NB E2Z 4L7
Tel: 506-455-3030
Norma McGraw, Manager

Belledune: Centre de santé de Jacquet River Health Centre
Affiliated with: Regional Health Authority A
41 Mack St., Belledune, NB E8G 2R3
Tel: 506-237-3222; *Fax:* 506-237-3224
Lynn DeGroot, Administratrice d'établissement

Blackville: Blackville Health Centre
Affiliated with: Regional Health Authority B
2 Shaffer Lane, Blackville, NB E9B 1P4
Tel: 506-843-2910; *Fax:* 506-843-2911
Ann Dickison, Contact

Boiestown: Upper Miramichi Health Services Centre - Boiestown
Affiliated with: Regional Health Authority B
#2, 6154, rte 8, Boiestown, NB E6A 1M4
Tel: 506-369-2700; *Fax:* 506-369-2702
Lori Amos, Nurse Manager

Campobello: NB Extra Mural Program
St Stephen Unit - Campobello Office
Affiliated with: Regional Health Authority B
640, rte 774, Welshpool, Campobello, NB E5E 1A5
Tel: 506-752-4110; *Fax:* 506-752-4106
Sue Ness, Manager

Caraquet: Centre de santé communautaire de l'Enfant-Jésus
Affiliée à: Regional Health Authority A
Ancien nom: Hôpital de l'Enfant-Jésus-RHSJT
1, boul St-Pierre, Caraquet, NB E1W 1B7
Tél: 506-726-2100; *Téléc:* 506-726-2188
Dina Chiasson, Directrice d'établissement
Guy Gallien, Chef de service, Installations matériels

Caraquet: Programme extra mural du NB
Unite de la Penisule Acadienne - Bureau de Caraquet
Acadian Peninsula Unit
Affiliated with: Regional Health Authority A
442, blvd. Saint-Pierre ouest, Caraquet, NB E1W 1A3
Tel: 506-726-2800; *Fax:* 506-726-2808
Norma McGraw, Manager

Chipman: Chipman Health Centre
Affiliated with: Regional Health Authority B
9 Civic Ct., Chipman, NB E4A 2H8
Tel: 506-339-7650; *Fax:* 506-339-7652
Roddy Barton, Nurse Manager

Dalhousie: Centre de santé communautaire St. Joseph
St. Joseph Community Health Centre
Affiliated with: Regional Health Authority A
#1, 280, rue Victoria, Dalhousie, NB E8C 2R6
Tel: 506-684-7000; *Fax:* 506-684-4751
www.santerestigouchehealth.com; www.santevitalitehealth.ca
Note: Le Réseau de santé Vitalité regroupe les huit anciennes régies régionales dans la province. Le Centre a pour mission d'améliorer l'accès aux soins de santé primaires, et l'état de santé des collectivités; promotion de la santé, prévention des maladies et blessures, et traitement des maladies chroniques; services diagnostiques; soins ambulatoires.
Lynn Kelly deGroot, Directrice d'établissement

Dalhousie: NB Extra Mural Program
Restigouche Unit
Affiliated with: Regional Health Authority A
#2, 280 Victoria St., Dalhousie, NB E8C 2R6
Tel: 506-684-7060; *Fax:* 506-684-7334
Claire Dennie, Manager

Deer Island: Deer Island Health Centre
Affiliated with: Regional Health Authority B
999 Rte. 772, Deer Island, NB E5V 1P2
Tel: 506-747-4150; *Fax:* 506-747-4151
Susan Ness, Facility Manager

Dieppe: Programme extra mural du NB
Blanche Bourgeois Unit
Affiliated with: Regional Health Authority A
30, rue Englehart, Unité B, Dieppe, NB E1A 8H3
Tel: 506-862-4400; *Fax:* 506-862-4415
Rino Lang, Manager

Doaktown: Central Miramichi Community Health Centre
Affiliated with: Regional Health Authority B
Former Name: Upper Miramichi Health Services Centre - Doaktown
PO Box 1039, 8 Miramichi St., Doaktown, NB E9C 1C8
Tel: 506-365-6100; *Fax:* 506-365-6104
Lorri Amos, Nurse Manager

Edmundston: Programme extra mural du NB
Unite d'Edmundston
Affiliated with: Regional Health Authority A
275, boul Hebert, 4e étage, Edmundston, NB E3V 4N4
Tel: 506-739-2160; *Fax:* 506-739-2163
Carlene Pelletier, Manager

Fredericton: NB Extra Mural Program
Fredericton Unit
Affiliated with: Regional Health Authority B
PO Box 9000, 700 Priestman St., Fredericton, NB E3B 5N5
Tel: 506-452-5800; *Fax:* 506-452-5858
Christine DeJong, Manager

Fredericton: NB Extra Mural Program
Sussex Unit
Affiliated with: Regional Health Authority B
Health Services Complex, #4, 20 Kennedy Dr., Fredericton, NB E4E 2P1
Tel: 506-432-3280; *Fax:* 506-432-3250
Sue Ness, Manager

Fredericton: **NB Extra Mural Program**
Fredericton Unit - Boiestown Office
Affiliated with: Regional Health Authority B
c/o Fredericton Unit, PO Box 9000, 700 Priestman St., Fredericton, NB E3B 5N5
Tel: 506-369-2711; *Fax:* 506-369-2722
Christine DeJong, Manager

Fredericton Junction: **Fredericton Junction Health Centre**
Affiliated with: Regional Health Authority B
233 Sunbury Dr., Fredericton Junction, NB E3L 1S1
Tel: 506-368-6501; *Fax:* 506-368-6502
Ruth Richardson, Nurse Manager

Grand Manan: **NB Extra Mural Program**
Eastern Charlotte Unit - Grand Manan
Affiliated with: Regional Health Authority B
Grand Manan Hospital, 196 Rte. 776, Grand Manan, NB E5G 1A3
Tel: 506-662-4055; *Fax:* 506-662-4054
Sue Ness, Manager

Grand-Sault: **Programme extra mural du NB**
Unite de Grand-Sault
Affiliée à: Regional Health Authority A
CP 7812, 532, ch Madawaska, Grand-Sault, NB E3Z 3E8
Tél: 506-473-7492; *Téléc:* 506-473-7476
Carlene Pelletier, Manager

Kedgwick: **Programme extra mural du NB**
Unite de Grand-Sault - Kedgwick Office
CP 1002, Kedgwick, NB E8B 1Z7
Tél: 506-284-3444; *Téléc:* 506-284-3446
Carlene Pelletier, Manager

Lamèque: **Programme extra mural du NB**
Unte de la Peninsule Acadienne - Bureau de Lameque
Affiliated with: Regional Health Authority A
29, rue l'hopital Lemeque, Lamèque, NB E8T 1C5
Tel: 506-344-3000; *Fax:* 506-344-3001
Norma McGraw, Manager

McAdam: **MacLean Memorial Hospital**
PO Box 311, 15 Saunders Rd., McAdam, NB E6J 1K9
Tel: 506-784-6300; *Fax:* 506-784-6306
Shirley Moffat, Nurse Manager

Minto: **Queens North Community Health Centre**
Affiliated with: Regional Health Authority B
PO Box 1004, 1100 Pleasant Dr., Minto, NB E4B 3Y6
Tel: 506-327-7800; *Fax:* 506-327-7850
Sandra Parker, Nurse Manager
Kivon Snihur, Supervisor, Housekeeping

Miramichi: **NB Extra Mural Program**
Miramichi Unit
Affiliated with: Regional Health Authority B
500 Water St., Miramichi, NB E1V 3G5
Tel: 506-623-6350; *Fax:* 506-623-6370
Joanne Sonier, Manager

Miramichi: **NB Extra Mural Program**
Miramichi Unit - Blackville Office
Affiliated with: Regional Health Authority B
500 Water St., Miramichi, NB E1V 3G5
Tel: 506-623-6312; *Fax:* 506-623-6370
Joanne Sonier, Manager

Miramichi: **NB Extra Mural Program**
Miramichi Unit - Neguac Office
Affiliated with: Regional Health Authority B
500 Water St., Miramichi, NB E1V 3G5
Tel: 506-623-6311; *Fax:* 506-623-6370
Joanne Sonier, Manager

Miscou: **Centre de santé de Miscou Health Centre**
Affiliated with: Regional Health Authority A
10482, rte 113, Miscou, NB E8T 1Y8
Tel: 506-344-3434

Moncton: **NB Extra Mural Program**
Driscoll Unit
Programme extra-mural - unité Driscoll
Affiliated with: Regional Health Authority B
#107, 1600 Main St., Moncton, NB E1E 1G5
Tel: 506-867-6500; *Fax:* 506-867-6509
generalinquiries@serha.ca
www.serha.ca/extra_mural
Note: Home healthcare program for eligible residents
Fonda Kazi, Vice President, Community Health

Nackawic: **Nackawic Community Health Centre**
Affiliated with: Regional Health Authority B
Nackawic Shopping Centre, Upper Floor, #201, 135 Otis Dr., Nackawic, NB E6G 1H1
Tel: 506-575-6600; *Fax:* 506-575-6603
Shirley Moffatt, Nurse Manager

Néguac: **Neguac Health Centre**
38 Otho St., Néguac, NB E9C 4H3
Tel: 506-776-3876; *Fax:* 506-776-3877
Anna Stymiest, Contact

Oromocto: **NB Extra Mural Program**
Oromocto Unit
Affiliated with: Regional Health Authority B
275A Restigouche Rd., Oromocto, NB E2V 2H1
Tel: 506-357-4900; *Fax:* 506-357-4904
Christine DeJong, Manager

Oromocto: **NB Extra Mural Program**
Oromocto Unit - Minto Office
Affiliated with: Regional Health Authority B
c/o NB Extra Mural Program, 275A Restigouche Rd., Oromocto, NB E2V 2H1
Tel: 506-327-4900; *Fax:* 506-327-4904
Christine DeJong, Manager

Paquetville: **Centre de santé de Paquetville**
Affiliée à: Regional Health Authority A
1096, du Parc, Paquetville, NB E8R 1J4
Tél: 506-764-2424; *Téléc:* 506-764-2425

Perth-Andover: **NB Extra Mural Program**
Woodstock Unit - Perth-Andover Sub Unit
Affiliated with: Regional Health Authority B
#2, 500 East Riverside Dr., Perth-Andover, NB E7H 1Z1
Tel: 506-273-7222; *Fax:* 506-273-7220
Christine DeJong, Manager

Petitcodiac: **Petitcodiac Health Centre**
Centre de santé de Petitcodiac
Affiliated with: Regional Health Authority B
25 Railway Ave., Petitcodiac, NB E4Z 6H4
Tel: 506-756-3400; *Fax:* 506-756-3406
generalinquiries@serha.ca
www.serha.ca/petitcodiac
Note: Number of staff: 3 physicians, 1 dentist. Foot care & diabetes clinics by appointment, drop-in services, visiting dietician
Heather Steeves, Nurse Manager

Pointe-Verte: **Centre de santé de Chaleur Health Centre**
Affiliée à: Regional Health Authority A
Ancien nom: Centre de santé Pointe Verte
382, rue Principale, Pointe-Verte, NB E8J 2X6
Tél: 506-542-2434; *Téléc:* 506-783-8623

Quispamsis: **NB Extra Mural Program**
Kennebecasis Valley Unit
Affiliated with: Regional Health Authority B
PO Box 21025, 175 Old Hampton Hwy., Quispamsis, NB E2E 4Z4
Tel: 506-848-4600; *Fax:* 506-848-4620
Sue Ness, Manager

Rexton: **Health Services Centre Rexton**
Le Centre de santé de Rexton
Affiliated with: Regional Health Authority B
82 Main St., Rexton, NB E4W 5N4
Tel: 506-523-7940; *Fax:* 506-523-7949
generalinquiries@serha.ca
www.serha.ca
Year Founded: 1974
Note: Drop-in services, clinics, immunization, nutrition & diabetes education
Lucille Cormier, Nurse Manager

Riverside-Albert: **Albert County Health & Wellness Centre**
Le Centre de santé & de mieux-être du comté d'Albert
Affiliated with: Regional Health Authority B
8 Forestdale Rd., Riverside-Albert, NB E4H 3Y7
Tel: 506-882-3100; *Fax:* 506-882-3101
generalinquiries@serha.ca
www.serha.ca/albert_county
Year Founded: 1961
Note: Multidisciplinary, primary health care services
Marlene Hueston, Nurse Manager

Rogersville: **Rogersville Health Centre**
Affiliated with: Regional Health Authority B
9, rue des Ormes, Rogersville, NB E4Y 1S6
Tel: 506-775-2030; *Fax:* 506-775-2025
Glorine Caissie, Contact

Sackville: **NB Extra Mural Program**
Tantramar Unit
Programme extra-mural - unité Tantramar
Affiliated with: Regional Health Authority B
8 Main St., Sackville, NB E4L 4A3
Tel: 506-364-4400; *Fax:* 506-364-4405
generalinquiries@serha.ca
www.serha.ca/extra_mural
Year Founded: 1979
Note: Home healthcare program for eligible residents
Fonda Kazi, Vice President, Community Health

Saint John: **Hospice Greater Saint John**
Former Name: Hospice Saint John & Sussex
385 Dufferin Row, Saint John, NB E2M 2J9
Tel: 506-632-5593; *Fax:* 506-632-5592
info@hospicesj.ca
www.hospicesj.ca
Note: Number of employees: 4
Sandy Johnson, Executive Director

Saint John: **NB Extra Mural Program**
Saint John Unit
Affiliated with: Regional Health Authority B
West End Office Park, 1490 Manawagonish Rd., Saint John, NB E2M 3Y4
Tel: 506-649-2626; *Fax:* 506-649-2540
Note: in-home support
Sue Ness, Manager

Saint John: **St. Joseph's Community Health Centre**
Affiliated with: Regional Health Authority B
116 Coburg St., Saint John, NB E2L 3K1
Tel: 506-632-5537
www.ahsc.health.nb.ca/CHC
Dawn Marie Buck, Contact

Saint John: **Senior Watch Inc.**
33 Hanover St., Saint John, NB E2L 3G1
Tel: 506-634-8906; *Fax:* 506-633-2992
senior@seniorwatch.com
www.seniorwatch.com
Note: New Brunswick-based firm specializing in developing and managing new programs for Seniors
Jean E. Porter Mowatt, President/CEO

Sainte-Anne-de-Madawaska: **Centre de santé Ste-Anne**
Affiliated with: Regional Health Authority A
1, rue de la Clinique, Sainte-Anne-de-Madawaska, NB E7E 1B9
Tel: 506-445-6200; *Fax:* 506-445-6201
Dr. Édouard Hendriks, Administrateur d'établissement (par intérim)

Shediac: **Centre médical régional de Shédiac**
Affiliated with: Regional Health Authority A
419, rue Main, Shediac, NB E4P 2B8
Tel: 506-533-2700; *Fax:* 506-533-2710
Lise Guerrette-Daigle, Administrateur d'établissement

Shediac: **Programme extra mural du NB Shediac Unit**
Affiliated with: Regional Health Authority A
423 Main St., Shediac, NB E4P 2B6
Tel: 506-533-2800

Rino Lang, Manager

St George: **NB Extra Mural Program Eastern Charlotte Unit**
Affiliated with: Regional Health Authority B
#401, 124 Main St., St George, NB E5C 3S3
Tel: 506-755-4660; *Fax:* 506-755-4665

Sue Ness, Manager

St Stephen: **NB Extra Mural Program St Stephen Unit**
Affiliated with: Regional Health Authority B
#100, 73 Milltown Blvd., St Stephen, NB E3L 1G5
Tel: 506-465-4520; *Fax:* 506-465-4523

Sue Ness, Manager

Stanley: **Stanley Health Services Centre**
Affiliated with: Regional Health Authority B
PO Box 340, Stanley, NB E6B 2K5
Tel: 506-367-7730; *Fax:* 506-367-7738

Charlene Merrill, Nurse Manager
Penny Higgs, Director, Nursing
Ronald Hay, Maintenance Supervisor

Ste-Anne de Kent: **Programme extra mural du NB Kent Unit**
Affiliée à: Regional Health Authority A
7717, route 134, Livraison Générale, Ste-Anne de Kent, NB E4S 1H5
Tel: 506-743-2000

Rino Lang, Manager

Tracadie Sheila: **Progrmme extra mural du NB Unite de la Peninsule Acadienne - Bureau de Tracadie**
Affiliated with: Regional Health Authority A
Centre hospitalier de Tracadie, PO Box 3180 Bureau-Chef, 3512-2, rue Principale, Tracadie Sheila, NB E1X 1G5
Tel: 506-394-4100; *Fax:* 506-394-4117

Norma McGraw, Manager

Welshpool: **Campobello Health Centre**
Affiliated with: Regional Health Authority B
640, rte 774, Welshpool, NB E5E 1A5
Tel: 506-752-4100; *Fax:* 506-752-2654

Susan Ness, Facility Manager

Woodstock: **NB Extra Mural Program Woodstock Unit**
Affiliated with: Regional Health Authority B
Nurses' Residence, #310, 787 Main St., Woodstock, NB E7M 2E9
Tel: 506-325-6838; *Fax:* 506-325-6862

Christine DeJong, Manager

Special Treatment Centres

Edmundston: **Services de toxicomanie**
Affiliée à: Regional Health Authority A
62, rue Queen, Edmundston, NB E3V 1A1
Tél: 506-735-2092; *Téléc:* 506-835-2700
www.rrs4-rha4.nb.ca

Nombre de lits: 10 lits
Note: Service de désintoxification interne
Carmen Bouchard
Carmen.Bouchard@chr4.health.nb.ca

Fredericton: **Addiction Services**
c/o Victoria Health Centre, 65 Brunswick St., Fredericton, NB E3B 1G5
Tel: 506-452-5558; *Fax:* 506-452-5533

Gordon Skead, Regional Director

Fredericton: **The Morgentaler Clinic Fredericton Site**
554 Brunswick St., Fredericton, NB E3B 1H5
Tel: 506-451-9060; *Fax:* 506-451-9062
nbclinic@nb.aibn.com
www.morgentalernb.ca

Note: Specialties: Abortion care services; Abortion aftercare

Fredericton: **Stan Cassidy Centre for Rehabilitation**
Affiliated with: Regional Health Authority B
180 Woodbridge St., Fredericton, NB E3B 4R3
Tel: 506-452-5225; *Fax:* 506-452-5190

Number of Beds: 20 beds
Dr. Ron Harris, Administrative Director
Calvin Gesner, Maintenance Director

Moncton: **Addiction Services**
Services de traitement des dépendances
125 Mapleton Rd., Moncton, NB E1C 9G8
Tel: 506-856-2333; *Fax:* 506-856-6057
generalinquiries@serha.ca
www.serha.ca/addiction_services

Number of Beds: 20 beds
Note: Detoxification unit, methadone maintenance treatment program, addiction prevention & education, counseling, assessments
Michelina Mancuso, Regional Manager

Petit-Rocher: **Services Résidentiels Nepisiguit Inc.**
#312, 702, rue Principale, Petit-Rocher, NB E8J 1V1
Tél: 506-542-2404; *Téléc:* 506-542-2406
srninc@nb.aibn.com
www.gnb.ca

Nombre de lits: 22 lits
Note: Service résidentiel à toutes les personnes ayant des handicaps de la région Nepisiguit
Luc DeRoche, Directeur général

Saint John: **Workers' Rehabilitation Centre**
PO Box 160, 1 Portland St., Saint John, NB E2L 3X9
Tel: 506-738-8411; *Fax:* 506-738-3470
www.whscc.nb.ca

Note: occupational rehabilitation
Dr. R. Brian Connell, Vice-President, Compensation & Rehabilitation

Saint John West: **Ridgewood Addiction Services**
PO Box 3566 B, 416 Bay St., Saint John West, NB E2M 4Y1
Tel: 506-674-4300; *Fax:* 506-658-3774
www.ahsc.health.nb.ca

Number of Beds: 90 beds
Note: Comprehensive addiction treatment programs, detoxification, outpatient & short term residential services, addiction prevention & education, community reintegration
Bonnie Lambert, Executive Director
lambo@reg2.health.nb.ca

Nursing Homes

Albert: **Forest Dale Home Inc.**
5836 King St., Albert, NB E4H 4B9
Tel: 506-882-3015; *Fax:* 506-882-3014

Number of Beds: 40 beds
Debbie Smith, Administrator
506/882-3018
Ethel Duffy, Director, Nursing

Baker Brook: **Foyer Ste. Elizabeth Inc.**
25, rue des Ormes, Baker Brook, NB E7A 2J6
Tél: 506-258-3020; *Téléc:* 506-258-3010

Nombre de lits: 50 lits
Paul Couturier, Directeur général

Bath: **River View Manor Inc.**
96 Hospital St., Bath, NB E7J 1B9
Tel: 506-278-6030; *Fax:* 506-278-5962
www.riverviewmanor.ca

Year Founded: 1981
Number of Beds: 40 beds
Note: Nursing home
Kay Simonds, Administrator
Randy Giberson, Supervisor, Plant Maintenance

Bathurst: **Le Foyer Notre-Dame de Lourdes Inc.**
2055, Vallée-Lourdes, Bathurst, NB E2A 4P8
Tél: 506-549-5085; *Téléc:* 506-548-5052
dg.fndl@health.nb.ca

Nombre de lits: 100 lits
Claire Savoie, Directeur général
506/549-5071

Bathurst: **Robert L. Knowles Veterans Unit, Villa Chaleur**
795, rue Champlain, Bathurst, NB E2A 4M8
Tel: 506-549-5582; *Fax:* 506-545-6424

Number of Beds: 13 beds
Lucie Fournier, Administrator

Blacks Harbour: **Fundy Nursing Home**
34 Hospital St., Blacks Harbour, NB E5H 1C2
Tel: 506-456-4218; *Fax:* 506-456-4259

Number of Beds: 26 beds
Debbie Harris, Administrator
506/456-4213

Boiestown: **Central New Brunswick Nursing Home Inc.**
3458 Rte. 625, Boiestown, NB E6A 1C8
Tel: 506-369-7262; *Fax:* 506-369-2331

Number of Beds: 30 beds
Manley Black, Administrator

Bouctouche: **Manoir Saint-Jean Baptiste**
5, av Richard, Bouctouche, NB E4S 3T2
Tél: 506-743-7344; *Téléc:* 506-743-7343

Nombre de lits: 50 lits
Robert Allain, Administrateur
506/743-7346
Edmond Babineau, Chef, Installations matériels

Campbellton: **Campbellton Nursing Home Inc.**
PO Box 850, 101 Dover St., Campbellton, NB E3N 3K6
Tel: 506-789-7350; *Fax:* 506-789-7360

Number of Beds: 100 beds
Ken Murray, Executive Director
506/789-7351
Randy Johnson, Supervisor, Plant Maintenance

Caraquet: **Villa Beauséjour Inc.**
CP 5608, 253, boul St-Pierre ouest, Caraquet, NB E1W 1B7
Tél: 506-726-2744; *Téléc:* 506-726-2745

Nombre de lits: 62 lits
Roger Landry, Directeur général
506/726-2741
Annette Chiasson, Director, Nursing
Dennis Power, Maintenance Supervisor

Dalhousie: **Dalhousie Nursing Home Inc.**
#1, 296 Victoria St., Dalhousie, NB E8C 2R8
Tel: 506-684-7800; *Fax:* 506-684-7832

Number of Beds: 105 beds
Diane Léger, Administrator
506/684-7805
Maurice Savoie, Director, Physical Plant

Edmundston: **Villa des Jardins Inc.**
50, rue Queen, Edmundston, NB E3V 3N4
Tél: 506-735-2112; *Téléc:* 506-735-2462

Nombre de lits: 30 lits
Carole Ouellette, Administrateur
506/735-2115

Fredericton: **Pine Grove**
521 Woodstock Rd., Fredericton, NB E3B 2J2
Tel: 506-444-3400; *Fax:* 506-444-3407

Pam Bowen, Administrator

Fredericton: **York Manor Inc.**
100 Sunset Dr., Fredericton, NB E3A 1A3
Tel: 506-444-3880; *Fax:* 506-444-3544
info@yorkmanor.nb.ca
www.yorkmanor.nb.ca

Number of Beds: 198 beds
Ken McGeorge, Administrator

Fredericton Junction: **White Rapids Manor Inc.**
233 Sunbury Dr., Fredericton Junction, NB E5L 1S1
Tel: 613-368-6508; *Fax:* 613-368-6512

Number of Beds: 36 beds
Kathy Jenkins, Administrator

Gagetown: **Gagetown Nursing Home Ltd.**
2230 Rte 102, Gagetown, NB E5M 1A1
Tel: 506-488-3544; *Fax:* 506-488-3551
khamilto@health.nb.ca

Number of Beds: 40 beds
Kathy Hamilton, Administrator
506/488-3586
S. Douthwright, Maintenance Supervisor

Grand Falls: **Grand Falls Manor Inc.**
55, rue Gagnon, Grand Falls, NB E3Z 3E5
Tél: 506-473-7726; *Téléc:* 506-473-7849
manoirgs@health.nb.ca

Nombre de lits: 69 lits
Maurice Richard, Administrateur
506/473-7726
Gaetan Theriult, Director, Physical Plant

Grand Manan: Grand Manan Nursing Home Inc.
266, Rte. 776, Grand Manan, NB E5G 1A5
Tel: 506-662-7111; *Fax:* 506-662-7117
urquharts@nb.aibn.com

Number of Beds: 30 beds
Sharon Urquhart, Administrator
Larry Clowater, Maintenance Supervisor

Hampton: Dr. V.A. Snow Centre Inc.
54 Demille Ct., Hampton, NB E5N 5S7
Tel: 506-832-6210; *Fax:* 506-832-7674
adminvasnow@nb.aibn.com

Number of Beds: 50 beds
Terry MacNeill, Administrator
506/832-6214
Bill Bettle, Maintenance Supervisor

Hartland: Central Carleton Nursing Home Inc.
139 Rockland Rd., Hartland, NB E7P 1E9
Tel: 506-375-3033; *Fax:* 506-375-3035
cullinsg@health.nb.ca

Number of Beds: 30 beds
Gwen Cullins-Jones, Administrator

Inkerman: Résidences Inkerman Inc.
1171, ch Pallot, Inkerman, NB E8P 1C2
Tél: 506-336-3909; *Téléc:* 506-336-3912

Nombre de lits: 30 lits
Michel Haché, Directeur général
Paul Doucet, Coordinateur, Services environnementaux

Lamèque: Les Résidences Lucien Saindon Inc.
26, rue de l-Hôpital, Lamèque, NB E8T 1C3
Tél: 506-344-3232; *Téléc:* 506-344-3240
dir.gen.rlsaindon@health.nb.ca

Nombre de lits: 54 lits
Gaëtan Haché, Directeur général
506/344-3245

Memramcook: Foyer St. Thomas de la Vallée de Memramcook Inc.
100, rue Notre-Dame, Memramcook, NB E3K 3W3
Tél: 506-758-2110; *Téléc:* 506-758-9489

Nombre de lits: 30 lits
Pierre Landry, Directeur général
Alexandre Gaudet, Directrice, Installations matériels

Mill Cove: Mill Cove Nursing Home Inc.
5647 Rte 105, Mill Cove, NB E4C 3A5
Tel: 506-488-3033; *Fax:* 506-488-3037
mcceo@millcovenh.com
www.millcovenh.com

Note: Specialties: Nursing care for persons with special needs; Podiatry; Psychology; Rehabilitation; Snoezelen rooms
G. Paul Mills, Administrator
506/488-3033, ext. 2

Minto: W.G. Bishop Nursing Home
1100 Pleasant Dr., Minto, NB E4B 3Y6
Tel: 506-327-7853; *Fax:* 506-327-7812
llbetts@health.nb.ca
www.wgbishopnursinghome.org

Number of Beds: 30 beds
Kathy Donaldson, Acting CEO
506/327-7809

Miramichi: Miramichi Senior Citizens Home Inc.
1400 Water St., Miramichi, NB E1N 1A4
Tel: 506-778-6810; *Fax:* 506-778-6860
msch@nb.aibn.com
www.miramichiseniorshome.com

Number of Beds: 81 beds
Margaret Manderson, Administrator
Macrena Jardine, Director, Plant Maintenance

Miramichi: Mount Saint Joseph Nursing Home
PO Box 1002, 51 Lobban Ave., Miramichi, NB E1N 3W4
Tel: 506-778-6550; *Fax:* 506-778-0193

Number of Beds: 133 beds
Robert B. Stewart, Executive Director
506/778-6555
Jan Flieger, Director, Support Services

Moncton: Kenneth E. Spencer Memorial Home Inc.
35 Atlantic Baptist Ave., Moncton, NB E1E 4N3
Tel: 506-858-7870; *Fax:* 506-858-9674
info@abschi.com

Number of Beds: 200 beds
Barbara Cook, Administrator
Byron Cole, Director of Support Services

Moncton: Villa du Repos Inc.
474, promenade Elmwood, Moncton, NB E1A 2X3
Tél: 506-857-3560; *Téléc:* 506-859-1619

Nombre de lits: 126 lits
Paul Williams, Directeur général
Louis Audet, Directeur, Installations matériels

Paquetville: Manoir Édith B. Pinet Inc.
1189, rue des Fondateurs, Paquetville, NB E8R 1A9
Tél: 506-764-2444; *Téléc:* 506-764-2451
sec.mebp@health.nb.ca

Nombre de lits: 30 lits
Léonard Légère, Administrateur
506/764-2445
Guy Thériault, Directeur, Installations phys.

Perth-Andover: Victoria Glen Manor Inc.
30 Beech Glen Rd., Perth-Andover, NB E7H 1J9
Tel: 506-273-4885; *Fax:* 506-273-4975
office@vgm.ca
www.vgm.ca

Number of Beds: 65 beds
Note: Long-term care home
Eric Haddad, Administrator
506/273-4824,

Port Elgin: Westford Nursing Home
57 West Main St., Port Elgin, NB E4M 1L7
Tel: 506-538-2307; *Fax:* 506-538-7293
admwnh@nb.aibn.com
www.westfordnursinghome.com

Year Founded: 1986
Number of Beds: 30 beds
Note: Home for seniors and physically and mentally challenged adults
Judith White, Executive Director
Ian Hurley, Manager, Environmental Support Services

Rexton: Rexton Lions Nursing Home Inc.
84 Main St., Rexton, NB E4W 2B3
Tel: 506-523-7720; *Fax:* 506-523-7703
rex_general@nb.aibn.com

Number of Beds: 30 beds
Dianne Robichaud, Administrator
506/523-7778

Riverview: The Salvation Army Lakeview Manor
50 Suffolk St., Riverview, NB E1B 4K6
Tel: 506-387-2012; *Fax:* 506-387-7200
www.maritime.salvationarmy.ca

Number of Beds: 50 beds
Note: Specialties: Geriatric care; Care for persons with dementia
Maj. Shirley King, Executive Director

Rivière-Verte: Foyer de l'Age d'Or
55, rue Principale, Rivière-Verte, NB E7C 2T7
Tél: 506-263-8851

Rogersville: Foyer Assomption
CP 296, 62, rue Assomption, Rogersville, NB E4Y 1S5
Tél: 506-775-2040; *Téléc:* 506-775-2053

Nombre de lits: 50 lits
Anne Cormier, Directrice générale
506/775-2043
Ronald Poirier, Chef, Installations matériels

Saint John: Carleton-Kirk Lodge
3 Carleton Kirk Pl., Saint John, NB E2M 5B8
Tel: 506-635-7040; *Fax:* 506-635-7038

Number of Beds: 70 beds
Tim Stevens, Executive Director

Saint John: Church of St. John & St. Stephen Home Inc.
130 University Ave., Saint John, NB E2K 4K3
Tel: 506-634-6001; *Fax:* 506-634-6126

Note: Specialty: Long-term care
Darlene Cannell, Administrator

Saint John: Kennebec Manor Inc.
475 Woodward Ave., Saint John, NB E2K 4N1
Tel: 506-632-9628; *Fax:* 506-658-9376
kennebecman@health.nb.ca

Number of Beds: 70 beds
Judith Ann Lane, Administrator
506/658-0591

Saint John: Loch Lomond Villa, Inc.
185 Loch Lomond Rd., Saint John, NB E2J 3S3
Tel: 506-643-7175; *Fax:* 506-643-7198
bwilkins@lochlomondvilla.nb.ca (Executive Assistant)
www.lochlomondvilla.com

Year Founded: 1973
Number of Beds: 196 beds
Note: Specialties: Specialized units for Alzheimers & Psychogeriatric needs
Cindy Donovan, Administrator
506/643-7130
Valerie O'Leary, Director, Nursing
Paul Mills, Director, Operations

Saint John: Rocmaura Inc.
10 Park St., Saint John, NB E2K 4P1
Tel: 506-643-7050; *Fax:* 506-643-7053
reception@rocmaura.com
www.rocmaura.com

Year Founded: 1972
Number of Beds: 150 beds
Note: Christian nursing home; affiliated with the Sisters of Charity of the Immaculate Conception (SCIC)
Sr. Susan Quinn, Administrator
506/643-7060
Harry Seele, Maintenance Supervisor

Saint John: Turnbull Nursing Home Inc.
Former Name: Turnbull Home
231 Britain St., Saint John, NB E2L 0A4
Tel: 506-643-7200; *Fax:* 506-648-9786
turnbulloffice@nb.aibn.com

Number of Beds: 50 beds
Note: Specialty: Long-term care
Elizabeth Crouchman, Administrator
506/643-7211
Brian Worden, Director, Physical Plant

Saint-Antoine: Foyer Saint-Antoine
7, av de l'Église, Saint-Antoine, NB E4V 1L6
Tél: 506-525-4040; *Téléc:* 506-525-4090
dg_fsa@health.nb.ca
www3.nbnet.nb.ca/fsa

Nombre de lits: 30 lits
Gilles C. Ouellette, Administrateur
Gérard-Eugene Richard, Chef, Installations matériels

Saint-Basile: Foyer Saint-Joseph de Saint-Basile Inc.
475, rue Principale, Saint-Basile, NB E7C 1J2
Tél: 506-263-3462; *Téléc:* 506-263-3467

Nombre de lits: 126 lits
Louisette Landry-Bouchard, Directrice générale
506/263-3465
Roger Lévesque, Directeur, Installations matériels

Saint-Léonard: Foyer Notre-Dame de Saint-Léonard Inc.
604, rue Principale, Saint-Léonard, NB E7E 2H5
Tél: 506-423-3151; *Téléc:* 506-423-3152

Nombre de lits: 45 lits
Denis J. Michaud, Administrateur
506/423-3150

Saint-Louis-de-Kent: Villa Maria Inc.
19, rue du College, Saint-Louis-de-Kent, NB E4X 1C2
Tél: 506-876-3488; *Téléc:* 506-876-3466

Nombre de lits: 73 lits
Jean Paul Mazerolle, Administrateur
Sylvio Gigou, Directeur, Installations matériels

Saint-Quentin: Résidence Mgr. Melanson Inc.
11, rue Levesque, Saint-Quentin, NB E8A 1T1
Tél: 506-235-6030; *Téléc:* 506-235-6075

Nombre de lits: 42 lits
Susie Roy, Directrice générale
Rejeanne Chouinere, Superviseur
Claude Paquet, Chef, Installations

Shediac: Villa Providence Shédiac Inc.
403, rue Main, Shediac, NB E4P 2B9
Tél: 506-532-4484; *Téléc:* 506-532-5909
roger.hebert@vp-vr.ca

Nombre de lits: 190 lits
Roger T. Hébert, Directeur général
Regin LeBlanc, Chef, Entretien ménager

Shippagan: Les Résidences Mgr. Chiasson Inc.
128, rue Mgr Chiasson, Shippagan, NB E8S 1X7
Tél: 506-336-3266; *Téléc:* 506-336-3099

Nombre de lits: 100 lits
Octave Haché, Directeur général

St Andrews: Passamaquoddy Lodge Inc.
230 Sophia St., St Andrews, NB E5B 2C2
Tel: 506-529-5240; *Fax:* 506-529-5258
lezlie.leblanc@nb.aibn.com
www.passamaquoddylodge.ca

Number of Beds: 60 beds
Note: Nursing home

Catherine Smith, Administrator
506/529-5242
F. Meredith, Supervisor, Plant Maintenance

St Stephen: Lincourt Manor Inc.
PO Box 116, 1 Chipman St., St Stephen, NB E3L 2W9
Tel: 506-466-7855; Fax: 506-466-7853
Note: Specialty: Long term care
Jane Lyons, Administrator
Ron Hall, Maintenance Supervisor

St Stephen: Maria F. Ganong Seniors Residence
Former Name: Maria F. Ganong Old Folks Home
Also Known As: Lonicera Hall
28 Union St., St Stephen, NB E3L 1T1
Tel: 506-466-1471
lonicerahall@nb.aibn.com
www.lonicerahall.com
Number of Beds: 19 rooms
Pat Steves, Administrator

Stanley: Nashwaak Villa Inc.
PO Box 340, 32 Lime Kiln Rd., Stanley, NB E6B 2K5
Tel: 506-367-7731; Fax: 506-367-7745
Number of Beds: 30 beds
Bonnie MacNeil, Administrator
506/367-7734,

Sussex: Kiwanis Nursing Home Inc.
11 Bryant Dr., Sussex, NB E4E 2P3
Tel: 506-432-3118; Fax: 506-432-3104
knhi@nb.aibn.com
Number of Beds: 70 beds
Arthur Hetherington, Administrator
Ralph Mayfield, Director, Plant Maintenance

Tabusintac: Tabusintac Nursing Home
10 Old Manse Rd., Tabusintac, NB E9H 1G4
Tel: 506-779-4100; Fax: 506-779-8149
Betty Blake, Administrator

Tracadie-Sheila: Villa Saint-Joseph Inc.
3400, rue Albert, Tracadie-Sheila, NB E1X 1C8
Tél: 506-394-4800; Téléc: 506-394-4826
Nombre de lits: 64 lits
Paul Arseneau, Directeur général
506/394-4820

Welshpool: Campobello Lodge
640 Rte. 774, #2, Welshpool, NB ESE 1A5
Tel: 506-752-7101; Fax: 506-752-7105
Number of Beds: 30 beds
Sherry Johnston, Administrator
506/752-7030
Raye Brown, Maintenance Supervisor

Woodstock: Carleton Manor Inc.
106 Elizabeth St., Woodstock, NB E7M 1R1
Tel: 506-325-4373; Fax: 506-325-4618
macneilp@health.nb.ca
Number of Beds: 89 beds
Kay Simonds, Administrator
506/325-4376

Long Term/Retirement Care

Long Term Care Facilities

Acadieville: Villa Acadie Ltée
4057, rte. 480, Acadieville, NB E4Y 1Z3
Tél: 506-775-6088
Nombre de lits: 13 lits
Bernice Doiron, Proprietor

Baker Brook: Résidence Notre Dame
CP 38, 3741, rue Principale, Baker Brook, NB E7A 2A5
Tél: 506-258-3322
Nombre de lits: 18 lits
Roland Bouchard, Directeur général

Chatham: Howard Henderson House Inc.
225 Wellington St., Chatham, NB E1N 1N1
Tel: 506-773-6522
Number of Beds: 9 beds
Cathy McDonald, Executive Director

Kedgwick: Maison Notre-Dame
38, rue St. Paul, Kedgwick, NB E8B 2A7
Tél: 506-284-2318
Nombre de lits: 23 lits
Solange Borris, Administratrice

Moncton: Alternative Residences Inc.
257 Lutz St., Moncton, NB E1C 5G4
Tel: 506-854-7229; Fax: 506-853-6051
Number of Beds: 83 beds
Joanne LeBreton, Executive Director

Moncton: Birchmount Lodge
144 Birchmount Dr., Moncton, NB E1C 8E7
Tel: 506-384-7573; Fax: 506-384-8143
Number of Beds: 29 beds
Donald Vossburgh, Administrator

Moncton: Moncton Community Residences
357 Collishaw St., Moncton, NB E1C 9R2
Tel: 506-858-0550; Fax: 506-858-0271
mcri3@nb.aibn.com
Number of Beds: 30 beds
Jerry Kirkpatrick, General Manager

Moncton: Moncton Community Residences Inc.
Former Name: Reade House
357 Collishaw St., Moncton, NB E1C 9R2
Tel: 506-858-0550; Fax: 506-858-0271
mcri3@nb.aibn.com
Number of Beds: 5 beds
Note: Provides residential services to people with developmental challenges, ranging from group homes to assistance with independent living
Jerry Kirkpatrick, Administrator

Moncton: Moncton Community Residences Inc.
Former Name: West Lane House
357 Collishaw St., Moncton, NB E1C 9R2
Tel: 506-858-0550; Fax: 506-858-0271
mcri3@nb.aibn.com
Number of Beds: 8 beds
Note: Provides residential services to developmentally challenged adults
Jerry Kirkpatrick, Administrator

Moncton: Moncton Community Residences, Inc.
Former Name: Norwood House
357 Collishaw St., Moncton, NB E1C 9R2
Tel: 506-858-0550; Fax: 506-858-0271
mcri3@nb.aibn.com
Number of Beds: 6 beds
Note: Provides residential services to people with developmental challenges
Jerry Kirkpatrick, Administrator

Paquetville: Foyer Simonne Butler
1137, rue des Fondateurs, Paquetville, NB E8R 1B3
Tél: 506-764-2105
Nombre de lits: 5
Simonne Butler, Administratrice

Pennfield: Collingwood Home
RR#2, Pennfield, NB E0G 2R0
Tel: 506-456-3533
Number of Beds: 20 beds
Dan Drost, Administrator

Riverview: Grass Home
Former Name: N-Joy Homes Ltd.
774 Coverdale Rd., Riverview, NB E1B 3L5
Tel: 506-386-1740; Fax: 506-386-7040
Number of Beds: 24 beds
John Grass, Proprietor/Administrator

Robertville: La Villa Sormany Inc.
1730, ch. Ste Thérèse, Rte. 322, Robertville, NB E8K 2V8
Tél: 506-542-2731; Téléc: 506-542-2733
dg.vsormany@health.nb.ca
Nombre de lits: 40 lits
Lucie Marteau, Directrice générale

Sackville: Drew Nursing Home
165 Main St., Sackville, NB E4L 4S2
Tel: 506-364-4900; Fax: 506-364-4921
office@drewnursinghome.ca
www.drewnursinghome.ca
Number of Beds: 130 beds
Note: senior apartments
Linda Leroux, Administrator
506/364-4822
Ray Letcher, Director, Environmental Services

Saint John: New Direction Inc.
PO Box 549, Saint John, NB E2L 3Z8
Tel: 506-643-6207; Fax: 506-643-6209
newdir@nb.aibn.com
Number of Beds: 43 beds
Note: Provides housing and support services to persons suffering from mental illness

Gayle Capson, Executive Director

Saint John: Westport Residential Facility
427 Prince St., Saint John, NB E2M 1R2
Tel: 506-674-2069; Fax: 506-832-0808
beverlyr@nb.sympatico.ca
Number of Beds: 18 beds
Beverly Rideout, Administrator

Saint-Jacques: Foyer Georgette St-Onge
CP 484, 11, rue Babineau, Saint-Jacques, NB E0L 1K0
Tél: 506-735-8511
Nombre de lits: 6 lits
Georgette St-Onge, Propriétaire

Sainte-Anne-de-Madawaska: Foyer Mont St-Joseph
8, rue St-Joseph, Sainte-Anne-de-Madawaska, NB E7E 1L1
Tél: 506-445-2755
Nombre de lits: 16 lits
Florida Lavoie, Directrice générale

Tabusintac: Foyer Prime Breau
14 Covedell Rd., Tabusintac, NB E9H 1E6
Tél: 506-779-4445
Nombre de lits: 4 lits
Roséanna Breau, Propriétrice

Woodstock: Women's Institute Home
129 Chapel St., Woodstock, NB E7M 1G7
Tel: 506-328-2148
Number of Beds: 21 beds
Marion Briand, Supervisor

Mental Health Facilities

Mental Health Hospitals/Facilities

Campbellton: Centre Hospitalier Restigouche
Restigouche Hospital Centre
Affiliée à: Regional Health Authority A
CP 10, 63, ch Gallant, Campbellton, NB E3N 3G2
Tél: 506-789-7000; Téléc: 506-789-7065
www.santerestigouchehealth.com
Nombre de lits: 150 lits
Bertrand Collin, Directeur d'établissement
Jean Bouloy, Vice-President, Administration Services

Saint John: Centracare Saint John Inc.
Affiliated with: Regional Health Authority B
PO Box 3220 B, 414 Bay St., Saint John, NB E2M 4H7
Tel: 506-649-2550; Fax: 506-649-2570
Number of Beds: 50 beds
Joanne Lewis, Acting Regional Manager

Shippagan: Pavillon St-Jérôme Inc.
150, 17e rue, Shippagan, NB E8S 1G4
Tél: 506-336-8609; Téléc: 506-336-8652
Nombre de lits: 12 lits
Note: résidence pour adultes handicapés intellectuels
Louise Pichette, Directrice

Special Care Homes

Campbellton: Duguay's Special Care Home
20 Dover St., Campbellton, NB E3N 1P3
Tel: 506-789-1208
Number of Beds: 9 beds
Susan Duguay, Administrator

Harvey Station: Swanhaven Adult Residential Facility
1915, Rte. 3, Harvey Station, NB E6K 3K1
Tel: 506-366-2950; Fax: 506-366-1010
Number of Beds: 25 units
Note: Specialty: Long-term care
Frances P. Ward, Owner

Moncton: Castle Manor
271 Mountain Rd., Moncton, NB E1C 2L7
Tel: 506-382-5713; Fax: 506-383-4330
Number of Beds: 48 beds
Myrtle Rogers, Administrator

Moncton: Ritchie V Manor II
2031 Mountain Rd., Moncton, NB E1G 1B1
Tel: 506-384-7658
Number of Beds: 20 beds
Debbie Teakles, Proprietor

Moncton: Smith Special Care Home Ltd.
56 Dorchester St., Moncton, NB E1E 3A7
Tel: 506-383-2826; Fax: 506-383-2826
Number of Beds: 10 beds
Eric Smith

Ratter Corner: **Wilson's Special Care Home**
510 Drurys Cove Rd., Ratter Corner, NB E4E 3L4
Tel: 506-433-5532
Number of Beds: 3 beds
Sharon Wilson, Proprietor

Saint John: **Champlain House**
18 Hayes Ave., Saint John, NB E2M 5K3
Tel: 506-672-4651
Number of Beds: 8 beds
Barbara McMullin, Administrator

Saint John: **Forest Hills Special Care Home**
30 Mountain Rd., Saint John, NB E2J 2W8
Tel: 506-633-0743
Number of Beds: 10 beds
Janet Hebert, Proprietor

Saint John: **Seale Special Care Home**
295 Millidge Ave., Saint John, NB E2K 2M9
Tel: 506-693-3719
Number of Beds: 5 beds
Verna Seale, Proprietor

Titusville: **Yvonne's Special Care Home**
1773 Hwy. 860, Titusville, NB E0G 1Z0
Tel: 506-832-7186
Number of Beds: 14 beds
Yvonne Clark, Proprietor

Newfoundland & Labrador

Government Departments in Charge

NEWFOUNDLAND & LABRADOR: Newfoundland & Labrador Department of Health & Community Services
1st Floor West Block, Confederation Bldg., PO Box 8700, St. John's, NL A1B 4J6
Tel: 709-729-4984; *Fax:* 709-729-5824
healthinfo@gov.nl.ca
www.gov.nl.ca/health

Loretta Chard, Asst., Board Services

Regional Health Authorities

Corner Brook: **Western Health**
Former Name: Western Regional Integrated Health Authority
PO Box 2005, 1 Brookfield Ave., Western Memorial Hosp, Corner Brook, NL A2H 6C7
Tel: 709-637-5245; *Fax:* 709-637-5159
info@hcsw.nf.ca
www.westernhealth.nl.ca
Number of Beds: 226 acute care, 441 long-term care
Note: Provides health and community services to over 79,000 people
Susan Gillam, CEO

Grand Falls-Windsor: **Central Health**
Regional Office, 21 Carmelite Rd., Grand Falls-Windsor, NL A2A 1Y4
Tel: 709-292-1289
www.centralhealth.nl.ca
Number of Beds: 519 long term care beds; 269 acute care beds; 32 residential units; 28 bassinets
Note: Number of Employees: 3,179 (140 physicians). Population Served: 94,000
Karen McGrath, Chief Executive Officer
Dr. Ann Roberts, Medical Officer of Health
Sherry Freake, Chief Operating Officer, Gander
Sean Tulk, Chief Operating Officer, Grand Falls-Windsor
Trudy Stuckless, Chief Nursing Officer; Vice-President, Professional Standards
Rosemarie Goodyear, Senior Vice-President, Quality, Planning, & Priorities
Heather Brown, Vice-President, Rural Health
Terry Ings, Vice-President, Human Resources
John Kattenbusch, Vice-President, Finance & Corporate Services
Dr. Michael Zuckerman, Vice-President, Medical Services
Stephanie Power, Director, Communications

Happy Valley-Goose Bay: **Labrador-Grenfell Health**
PO Box 7000 C, Labrador Health Centre, Happy Valley-Goose Bay, NL A0P 1C0
Tel: 709-897-2349; *Fax:* 709-896-4032
www.hlc.nl.ca

Dr. Michael Jong, Vice-President, Medical Affairs
Boyd Rowe, CEO

St. John's: **Eastern Health Integrated Health Authority**
Also Known As: Eastern Health
Health Sciences Centre, Prince Philip Dr., St. John's, NL A1B 3V6
Tel: 709-777-1399; *Toll-Free:* 1-877-444-1399
employment@easternhealth.ca;
client.relations@easternhealth.ca
www.easternhealth.ca
Number of Beds: 1,696 long term care beds; 987 acute care beds; 9 observation beds
Note: Facilities: 80+ hospitals, health care centres, long-term care facilities, & community care sites. Number of Employees: 12,000+ health care & support services professionals. Population served: 293,790. Area Covered: Region of Newfoundland & Labrador east of Port Blandford, including Port Blandford, the Avalon, Burin, & Bonavista Peninsulas, & Bell Island (111 incorporated municipalities, 69 local service districts, & 66 unincorporated municipal units)
Vickie Kaminski, President; Chief Executive Officer
709-777-1301, ceo@easternhealth.ca
Michael J. O'Keefe, Chair
Norma Baker, Chief Operating Officer, Adult Acute Care (St. John's)
Beverley Clarke, Chief Operating Officer, Community, Children & Women, & Mental Healt
Pat Coish-Snow, Chief Operating Officer, Peninsulas
Alice Kennedy, Chief Operating Officer, Long Term Care (St. John's), Community Living &amp
Fay Matthews, Chief Operating Officer, Rural Avalon Child Youth & Family Services
George Butt, Vice-President, Corporate Services
Stephen Dodge, Vice-President, People & Information Services
Dr. Oscar Howell, Vice-President, Medical Services & Diagnostics
Wayne Miller, Vice-President, Planning, Quality, & Research

Hospitals

Hospitals - General

Burin: **Burin Peninsula Health Care Centre**
Affiliated with: Eastern Regional Integrated Health Authority
PO Box 340, Burin, NL A0E 1E0
Tel: 709-891-1040; *Fax:* 709-891-3375
www.easternhealth.ca
Number of Beds: 42 beds
Note: Hospital Specialties: Diagnostic imaging; Laboratory services; General surgery; Acute care; Gynecology; Obstetrics; Pediatrics; Psychiatry; Speech pathology, Physiotherapy, Occupational therapy; Respiratory therapy; Palliative care
Kim Green, Manager, Acute Care
709-891-3490, Fax: 709-891-3375, kim.green@easternhealth.ca

Clarenville: **Dr. G.B. Cross Memorial Hospital**
Affiliated with: Eastern Regional Integrated Health Authority
67 Manitoba Dr., Clarenville, NL A5A 1K3
Tel: 709-466-3411
www.easternhealth.ca
Note: Hospital Specialties: Surgery; Intensive care; Obstetrics; Respiratory therapy; Physiotherapy; Dietitian services; Palliative care
Dr. Oscar Howell, Vice-President, Medical Services & Diagnostics, Eastern Health

Corner Brook: **Western Memorial Regional Hospital**
Affiliated with: Western Health
PO Box 2005, Corner Brook, NL A2H 6J7
Tel: 709-637-5000; *Fax:* 709-637-5410
Number of Beds: 192 acute care beds
M. Wasmeier

Fogo: **Fogo Island Health Centre**
Affiliated with: Central Regional Integrated Health Authority
PO Box 9, Fogo, NL A0G 2B0
Tel: 709-266-2221
www.centralhealth.nl.ca
Year Founded: 1953
Note: Hospital Specialties: Primary care; Public health
Karen McGrath, Chief Executive Officer, Central Regional Health Authority

Gander: **James Paton Memorial Hospital**
Affiliated with: Central Regional Integrated Health Authority
125 TransCanada Hwy., Gander, NL A1V 1P7
Tel: 709-256-2500; *Fax:* 709-256-7800
Number of Beds: 92 acute care beds
J. Horwood

Grand Falls-Windsor: **Central Newfoundland Regional Health Centre**
Affiliated with: Central Regional Integrated Health Authority
50 Union St., Grand Falls-Windsor, NL A2A 2E1
Tel: 709-292-2500; *Fax:* 709-292-2249
www.centralhealth.nl.ca
Note: Hospital Specialties: Emergency services; Radiology; Surgical care; Ambulatory care services; Maternal / newborn unit; Cardiology; Neurology; Otolaryngology; Rehabilitation services; Physiotherapy; Occupational therapy; Pharmacy services
Janelle Hillier, Regional Director, Medical Services
709-292-2450, Fax: 709-292-2249, janelle.hillier@centralhealth.nl.ca

Happy Valley-Goose Bay: **Labrador Health Centre**
Affiliated with: Labrador-Grenfell Regional Integrated Health Authority
Former Name: Melville Hospital
PO Box 7000 C, Happy Valley-Goose Bay, NL A0P 1C0
Tel: 709-897-2000; *Fax:* 709-896-4032
Number of Beds: 25 beds
Note: Full diagnostic services; Rehabilitation
E. Harding
Ed Sharpe, Supervisor, Plant Maintenance

Labrador City: **Captain William Jackman Memorial Hospital (CWJ)**
Affiliated with: Labrador-Grenfell Regional Integrated Health Authority
410 Booth Ave., Labrador City, NL A2V 2K1
Tel: 709-944-2632
www.lghealth.ca
Year Founded: 1965
Number of Beds: 14 acute care beds; 6 long term care beds
Note: Hospital Specialties: Emergency services; Diagnostic imaging; Intensive care; Acute care; Obstetrics; Physiotherapy; Occupational therapy; Speech therapy; Respiratory therapy; Health education; Respite care; Long term care; Palliative care

St. Anthony: **Charles S. Curtis Memorial Hospital**
Affiliated with: Labrador-Grenfell Regional Integrated Health Authority
Also Known As: Curtis Hospital
178-200 West St., St. Anthony, NL A0K 4S0
Tel: 709-454-3333
www.lghealth.ca
Number of Beds: 50 hospital beds; 48 long term care beds at the John M. Gray Centre, which is adjoined to Charles S. Curtis Memorial Hospital
Note: Hospital Specialties: General surgery; Radiology; Pathology; Obstetrics; Gynecology; Genetics research; Pediatrics; Ophthalmology; Chemotherapy services; Orthopedics; Urology; Psychiatry; Rehabilitation services, including occupational therapy & physiotherapy; Acute care; Diabetes education; Social work
Michael Jong, Vice-President, Medical Services, Labrador-Grenfell Health

St. John's: **Dr. Leonard A. Miller Centre**
Former Name: Quidi Vidi Hospital
Also Known As: The Miller Centre
100 Forest Rd., St. John's, NL A1A 1E5
Tel: 709-777-6555
Year Founded: 1851
Note: Specialty: Continuing care; Rehabilitation; Residential care for veterans of Newfoundland & Labrador; Centre for Nursing Studies

St. John's: **The General Hospital/Health Sciences Centre**
Affiliated with: Eastern Regional Integrated Health Authority
300 Prince Phillip Dr., St. John's, NL A1B 3V6
Tel: 709-777-6300; *Fax:* 709-777-6770
www.easternhealth.ca/OurServices.aspx?d=2&id=118&p=75
Number of Beds: 344 acute care beds
Note: A tertiary acute care facility & teaching hospital affiliated with Memorial University Schools of Medicine, Nursing, & Pharmacy.
Ms. Vickie Kaminski, President/CEO, ERIHA
709-777-1301, ceo@easternhealth.ca
Ms. Deborah Collins, Manager, Media Relations, ERIHA
709-777-1339, deborah.collins@easternhealth.ca

St. John's: **Janeway Children's Health and Rehabilitation Centre**
Affiliated with: Eastern Regional Integrated Health Authority
300 Prince Philip Dr., St. John's, NL A1B 3V6
Tel: 709-777-6300; *Fax:* 709-777-4446
carol.chafe@easternhealth.ca
www.easternhealth.ca

Number of Beds: 83 beds
Note: teaching hospital
Carol Chafe, Program Director
Keith Collins, Environmental Services Manager
709/778-4222

St. John's: **St. Clare's Mercy Hospital**
Affiliated with: Eastern Regional Integrated Health Authority
154 LeMarchant Rd., St. John's, NL A1C 5B8
Tel: 709-777-1317; *Fax:* 709-777-5470
hcc.jonlo@hccsj.nf.ca

Year Founded: 1922
Number of Beds: 216 acute care beds
Note: tertiary hospital
Ernie Power, Director, Plant Maintenance
L. Jones, CEO

Stephenville: **Sir Thomas Roddick Hospital**
Affiliated with: Western Health
142 Minnesota Dr., Stephenville, NL A2N 1H0
Tel: 709-643-5111; *Fax:* 709-643-2700
westernhealth.nl.ca/index.php/locations/hospitals/sir-thomas-roddick-hospital

Year Founded: 2003
Number of Beds: 44 acute care beds
Note: A comprehensive care facility, with services including emergency, surgery, obstetrics, gynecaelogy, renal care
Ms. Karen Alexander, Site Manager
Dr. Alan McComiskey, Chief of Staff

Community Health Centres

Community Health Care Centres

Badgers Quay: **Brookfield/Bonnews Health Care Centre**
Affiliated with: Central Regional Integrated Health Authority
PO Box 209, Badgers Quay, NL A0G 1B0
Tel: 709-536-2405; *Fax:* 709-536-3334
www.cehcib.nf.ca

Year Founded: 1944
Number of Beds: 12 beds
Kevin Green, Facility Manager
Winston Perry, Director, Maintenance Services

Baie Verte: **Baie Verte Peninsula Health Centre**
Affiliated with: Central Regional Integrated Health Authority
Baie Verte, NL A0K 1B0
Tel: 709-532-4281; *Fax:* 709-532-4939

Number of Beds: 7 acute care, 18 long-term care beds, 1 respite bed
Joyce Barker, Facility Director

Bell Island: **Dr. Walter Templeman Community Health Centre**
Affiliated with: Eastern Regional Integrated Health Authority
PO Box 580, Wabana, Bell Island, NL A0A 4H0
Tel: 709-488-2821; *Fax:* 709-488-2600

Number of Beds: 20 Beds
T. O'Brien
Jerry Butler, Director, Plant Maintenance

Bonavista: **Bonavista Peninsula Health Centre**
Affiliated with: Eastern Regional Integrated Health Authority
Former Name: Bonavista Community Health Centre
PO Box 1, Bonavista, NL A0C 1B0
Tel: 709-468-7881; *Fax:* 709-468-7223

Pauline Pardy, Director, Patient/Resident Care

Burgeo: **Calder Health Care Centre**
Affiliated with: Western Health
PO Box 190, Burgeo, NL A0M 1A0
Tel: 709-886-3350; *Fax:* 709-886-3382

Number of Beds: 3 acute care, 18 continuing care beds
Laurie Porter, Director of Nursing/Site Coordinator

Churchill Falls: **Churchill Falls Community Health Centre**
Affiliated with: Labrador-Grenfell Regional Integrated Health Authority
General Delivery, Churchill Falls, NL A0R 1A0
Tel: 709-925-3381; *Fax:* 709-925-3246

Joan Paul Kent, Nurse in Charge

Flowers Cove: **Strait of Belle Isle Health Centre**
Affiliated with: Labrador-Grenfell Regional Integrated Health Authority
General Delivery, Flowers Cove, NL A0K 2N0
Tel: 709-456-2401
www.lghealth.ca

Number of Beds: 3 beds
Note: Specialties: Ambulatory care; Family medicine; Public health services; Pre-natal classes; Post-natal visiting; Preschool & baby assessments; Dental services; Rehabilitation services; Home care
Judy Applin Poole

Grand Bank: **Grand Bank Community Health Centre**
Affiliated with: Eastern Regional Integrated Health Authority
PO Box 310, Grand Bank, NL A0E 1W0
Tel: 709-832-2500; *Fax:* 709-832-1164

Joan Penney, Director, Patient/Resident Care
Cyril Parsons, Utility Supervisor

Harbour Breton: **Connaigre Peninsula Health Centre**
Affiliated with: Central Regional Integrated Health Authority
Former Name: Harbour Breton Health Centre
PO Box 70, Harbour Breton, NL A0H 1P0
Tel: 709-885-2359; *Fax:* 709-885-2358
www.cwhc.nl.ca/cp.htm
Number of Beds: 20 beds: 6 acute, 12 continuing, 1 palliative, 1 respite
Sharon Skinner, Facility Director

Norris Point: **Bonne Bay Health Centre**
Affiliated with: Western Health
Norris Point, NL A0K 3V0
Tel: 709-458-2201; *Fax:* 709-458-2074

Number of Beds: 8 acute care, 14 continuing care beds

Northwest River: **NorthWest River Clinic**
Affiliated with: Labrador-Grenfell Regional Integrated Health Authority
General Delivery, Northwest River, NL A0P 1M0
Tel: 709-497-8351; *Fax:* 709-497-8521

Old Perlican: **Dr. A.A. Wilkinson Memorial Health Centre**
Affiliated with: Eastern Regional Integrated Health Authority
PO Box 70, Old Perlican, NL A0A 3G0
Tel: 709-587-2200; *Fax:* 709-587-2275

Number of Beds: 4 beds
M. Oliver

Port Saunders: **Rufus Guinchard Health Care Centre**
Affiliated with: Western Health
PO Box 40, Port Saunders, NL A0K 4H0
Tel: 709-861-3533; *Fax:* 709-861-3772

Number of Beds: 1 palliative care, 6 acute care, 22 continuing care beds
Paulette Lavers, Director of Nursing/Site Coordinator

Port aux Basques: **Dr. Charles L. LeGrow Health Centre**
Affiliated with: Western Health
PO Box 250, Port aux Basques, NL A0M 1C0
Tel: 709-695-2175; *Fax:* 709-695-3118

Number of Beds: 14 acute care, 30 continuing care beds
S. Savoury, Director of Nursing/Site Coordinator

Springdale: **Green Bay Community Health Centre**
Affiliated with: Central Regional Integrated Health Authority
PO Box 280, Springdale, NL A0J 1T0
Tel: 709-673-3911; *Fax:* 709-673-3186

Number of Beds: 8 beds; 1 special care, 2 convalescent, 1 palliative
Rose Saunders, Facility Director

Twillingate: **Notre Dame Bay Memorial Health Centre**
Affiliated with: Central Regional Integrated Health Authority
General Delivery, Twillingate, NL A0G 4M0
Tel: 709-884-2131; *Fax:* 709-884-2586

Number of Beds: 31 long-term care beds + 18 acute care beds
Note: Specialties: Outpatient services; Social work; Physiotherapy; Recreation therapy; Dietetics; Diabetes education; Health promotion & protection; Respite care, for children with special needs
Katherine Walters, Director, Health Services
B. Hamlyn, Supervisor, Plant Maintenance

Whitbourne: **Dr. W. H. Newhook Community Health Centre**
Affiliated with: Eastern Regional Integrated Health Authority
General Delivery, Whitbourne, NL A0B 3K0
Tel: 709-759-2300; *Fax:* 709-759-2387

L. English

Nursing Stations

Black Tickle: **Black Tickle Nursing Station**
Affiliated with: Labrador-Grenfell Regional Integrated Health Authority
General Delivery, Black Tickle, NL A0K 1N0
Tel: 709-471-8872; *Fax:* 709-471-8893

Cartwright: **Cartwright Nursing Station**
Affiliated with: Labrador-Grenfell Regional Integrated Health Authority
General Delivery, Cartwright, NL A0K 1V0
Tel: 709-938-7285; *Fax:* 709-938-7286

Charlottetown: **Charlottetown Nursing Station**
Affiliated with: Labrador-Grenfell Regional Integrated Health Authority
Former Name: Charlottetown Nursing Station
Charlottetown, NL A0K 5Y0
Tel: 709-949-0259; *Fax:* 709-949-0259

Number of Beds: 3 beds

Forteau: **Labrador South Health Centre**
Affiliated with: Labrador-Grenfell Regional Integrated Health Authority
Forteau, NL A0K 2P0
Tel: 709-931-2450; *Fax:* 709-931-2000

Number of Beds: 15 long-term care beds; 5 in-patient beds
Cornelia Linstead

Hopedale: **Hopedale Nursing Station**
Affiliated with: Labrador-Grenfell Regional Integrated Health Authority
General Delivery, Hopedale, NL A0P 1G0
Tel: 709-933-3857; *Fax:* 709-933-3744

Number of Beds: 3 beds

Makkovik: **Makkovik Nursing Station & Community Service**
Affiliated with: Labrador-Grenfell Regional Integrated Health Authority
General Delivery, Makkovik, NL A0P 1J0
Tel: 709-923-2229; *Fax:* 709-923-2428

Note: Specialties: Pharmaceutical services; Social work.
Number of Employees: 2 nurses + 1 part time physician

Mary's Harbour: **Mary's Harbour Community Clinic**
Affiliated with: Labrador-Grenfell Regional Integrated Health Authority
Mary's Harbour, NL A0K 3P0
Tel: 709-921-6228; *Fax:* 709-921-6975
jbudgell@grhs.nf.ca
www.lghealth.ca

Number of Beds: 1 holding bed + 1 crib
Note: Number of Employees: 3 nurses + 1 social worker + 1 personal care attendant + 1 maintenance person

Nain: **Nain Nursing Station**
Affiliated with: Labrador-Grenfell Regional Integrated Health Authority
General Delivery, Nain, NL A0P 1L0
Tel: 709-922-2912; *Fax:* 709-922-2103

Natuashish: **Natuashish Nursing Station**
Affiliated with: Labrador-Grenfell Regional Integrated Health Authority
Former Name: Davis Inlet Nursing Station
General Delivery, Natuashish, NL A0P 1A0
Tel: 709-478-8842; *Fax:* 709-478-8817

Port Hope Simpson: **Port Hope Simpson Community Clinic**
Affiliated with: Labrador-Grenfell Health
General Delivery, Port Hope Simpson, NL A0K 4E0
Tel: 709-960-0271; *Fax:* 709-960-0392
www.lghealth.ca
Year Founded: 1975
Note: Specialties: Emergency room, basic trauma, cardiac monitoring & resuscitation, dental suite. Number of staff: 9

Postville: **Postville Community Clinic**
Affiliated with: Labrador-Grenfell Health
General Delivery, Postville, NL A0P 1N0
Tel: 709-479-9851; *Fax:* 709-479-9715
www.lghealth.ca
Number of Beds: 1 bed, 1 crib
Note: Number of staff: 3

Rigolet: **Rigolet Nursing Station**
Affiliated with: Labrador-Grenfell Regional Integrated Health Authority
General Delivery, Rigolet, NL A0P 1P0
Tel: 709-947-3386; *Fax:* 709-947-3401
Note: Number of staff: 2 Registered Nurses; visiting physician, dentist & specialists

Roddickton: **White Bay Central Health Centre**
Affiliated with: Labrador-Grenfell Regional Integrated Health Authority
Roddickton, NL A0K 4P0
Tel: 709-457-2215; *Fax:* 709-457-2076
Number of Beds: 5 beds

St Lewis: **St. Lewis Nursing Station**
Affiliated with: Labrador-Grenfell Regional Integrated Health Authority
General Delivery, St Lewis, NL A0K 4W0
Tel: 709-939-2230; *Fax:* 709-939-2342

Special Treatment Centres

St. John's: **Dr. H. Bliss Murphy Cancer Centre**
Newfoundland Cancer Treatment & Research Foundatio, 300 Prince Philip Dr., St. John's, NL A1B 3V6
Tel: 709-777-6480; *Fax:* 709-753-0927
www.nctrf.nf.ca
Bertha Paulse, CEO

St. John's: **The Morgentaler Clinic St. John's Site**
#408, 59 Hamlyn Rd. Plaza, St. John's, NL A1E 5X7
Tel: 709-754-3572; *Fax:* 709-754-6626
Toll-Free: 800-755-2044
sjmc@nf.aibn.com
Year Founded: 1990
Note: Specialties: Abortion services; Counselling

Nursing Homes

Botwood: **Dr. Hugh Twomey Health Care Centre**
Affiliated with: Central Regional Integrated Health Authority
PO Box 250, Botwood, NL A0H 1E0
Tel: 709-257-2874; *Fax:* 709-257-4613
Number of Beds: 77 long-term care, 2 respite, 1 palliative care beds
Brenda Kelly, Facility Director

Buchans: **A.M. Guy Memorial Health Centre**
Affiliated with: Central Regional Integrated Health Authority
PO Box 10, Buchans, NL A0H 1G0
Tel: 709-672-3326; *Fax:* 709-672-3390
Number of Beds: 22 beds: 18 long-term, 2 acute care, 1 holding, 1 palliative
Roslyn Lane, Facility Director

Carbonear: **Harbour Lodge Nursing Home**
Affiliated with: Eastern Regional Integrated Health Authority
86 Highroad South, Carbonear, NL A1Y 1A4
Tel: 709-945-5400
www.easternhealth.ca/OurServices.aspx?d=2&id=142&p=76
Number of Beds: 127 beds
Debbie Farrell, Facility Manager
Harry Meados, Director, Environmental Services

Carbonear: **Inter Faith Citizens Home**
Affiliated with: Eastern Regional Integrated Health Authority
41 Water St., Carbonear, NL A1Y 1B1
Tel: 709-945-5300; *Fax:* 709-945-5323
Number of Beds: 53 beds
Deborah Farrell, Facility Manager

Clarke's Beach: **Pentecostal Senior Citizen's Home**
Affiliated with: Eastern Regional Integrated Health Authority
PO Box 130, Clarke's Beach, NL A0A 1W0
Tel: 709-786-2993
www.easternhealth.ca
Number of Beds: 75 beds
Note: Specialties: Nursing care for persons who require Level I, II, & III type care; Social work; Physiotherapy; Occupational therapy; Podiatry; Hearing & vision care
Beverley Bellefleur, Facility Manager

Corner Brook: **Inter Faith Home for Senior Citizens**
Affiliated with: Western Health
Churchill St., Corner Brook, NL A2H 5L8
Tel: 709-639-9247; *Fax:* 709-639-1126
Number of Beds: 103 long-term care beds
P. Griffin, Director of Nursing/Site Coordinator

Corner Brook: **J.I. O'Connell Centre**
Affiliated with: Western Health
PO Box 2005, Corner Brook, NL A2H 6J7
Tel: 709-637-5606; *Fax:* 709-634-3047
Number of Beds: 104 beds
P. Griffin, Director of Nursing/Site Coordinator

Gander: **Lakeside Homes**
Affiliated with: Central Regional Integrated Health Authority
95 Airport Blvd., Gander, NL A1V 2L7
Tel: 709-256-8850; *Fax:* 709-256-4259
www.cehcib.nf.ca/web/lakeside.htm
Number of Beds: 102 beds; 1 respite
Marlyce Greene, Facility Manager
Sam Butt, Maintenance Supervisor

Gander Bay South: **Riverview Retirement Home Ltd.**
Also Known As: Gander Bay Retirement Home
Gander Bay South, NL A0G 2H0
Tel: 709-676-2773
Number of Beds: 40 beds
Shaun Lane

Goulds: **Hefferman Boarding Home**
PO Box 56, Goulds, NL A1S 1G3
Tel: 709-745-5398
Number of Beds: 15 beds
Theresa Hefferman, Administrator

Grand Bank: **Blue Crest Inter Faith Home**
Affiliated with: Eastern Regional Integrated Health Authority
PO Box 160, Grand Bank, NL A0E 1W0
Tel: 709-832-1660; *Fax:* 709-832-2103
Number of Beds: 70 long-term care beds
Joan Penney, Director, Patient/Resident Care
Cyril Parsons, Maintenance Manager

Grand Falls-Windsor: **Carmelite House**
Affiliated with: Central Regional Integrated Health Authority
50 Union St., Grand Falls-Windsor, NL A2A 2E4
Tel: 709-292-2528; *Fax:* 709-489-5778
Number of Beds: 60 longterm care beds
Cynthia Burt, Facility Director

Happy Valley-Goose Bay: **Harry L. Paddon Memorial Home**
Affiliated with: Labrador-Grenfell Regional Integrated Health Authority
PO Box 766 B, Happy Valley-Goose Bay, NL A0P 1E0
Tel: 709-896-3615; *Fax:* 709-896-5241
searle@hlc.nf.ca
Number of Beds: 48 beds
K. White
Ronald Lyall, Supervisor, Maintenance

Lewisporte: **North Haven Manor Senior Citizens' Home**
Affiliated with: Central Regional Integrated Health Authority
PO Box 880, 21 Centennial Dr., Lewisporte, NL A0G 3A0
Tel: 709-535-6767; *Fax:* 709-535-8383
Number of Beds: 62 long-term care, 1 palliative, 2 respite beds
Debbie Colbourne, Facility Director

Mount Pearl: **Masonic Park Nursing Home**
Affiliated with: Eastern Regional Integrated Health Authority
Former Name: Masonic Park Senior Citizen's Home
#4000, Bldg. 15, Masonic Park, Mount Carson Ave., Mount Pearl, NL A1N 3K6
Tel: 709-368-6081
www.masonicpark.ca; www.easternhealth.ca
Year Founded: 1982
Number of Beds: 40 long term beds + 200 self-contained cottage & apt. units
Note: Specialties: Long-term care for seniors
Rolanda Ryan, Resident Care Manager

Springdale: **Valley Vista Senior Citizens' Home**
Affiliated with: Central Regional Integrated Health Authority
PO Box 130, Springdale, NL A0J 1T0
Tel: 709-673-3936; *Fax:* 709-673-2832
Number of Beds: 75 long-term care beds, 3 respite
Rose Saunders, Facility Director

St Anthony: **John M. Gray Centre**
Affiliated with: Labrador-Grenfell Regional Integrated Health Authority
Former Name: St. Anthony Interfaith Home
PO Box 69, St Anthony, NL A0K 4S0
Tel: 709-454-0371; *Fax:* 709-454-4134
Year Founded: 1998
Number of Beds: 48 long-term care beds
Dr. Michael Jong, Vice President Medical Affairs
Boyd Rowe, Chief Executive Officer

St. John's: **Agnes Pratt Home**
Affiliated with: Eastern Regional Integrated Health Authority
239 Topsail Rd., St. John's, NL A1E 2B4
Tel: 709-579-0185; *Fax:* 709-739-5457
www.easternhealth.ca/AboutEH.aspx?d=2&id=150&p=76
Number of Beds: 128 long-term care beds
Linda Colllingwood, Administrator

St. John's: **Glenbrook Lodge**
Affiliated with: Eastern Regional Integrated Health Authority
105 Torbay Rd., St. John's, NL A1A 2G9
Tel: 709-726-1575; *Fax:* 709-726-0610
smatchem@sjnhb.nf.ca
www.sjnhb.nf.ca/glenbrooklodge.asp
Number of Beds: 114 beds
Maj. Charles Granter, Executive Director

St. John's: **Hoyles-Escasoni Complex**
Affiliated with: Eastern Regional Integrated Health Authority
10 Escasoni Pl., St. John's, NL A1A 3R6
Tel: 709-753-7590; *Fax:* 709-753-9620
Number of Beds: 377 beds
Annette Clarke, Manager, Resident Care

St. John's: **Saint Luke's Home**
Affiliated with: Eastern Regional Integrated Health Authority
24 Road Deluxe, St. John's, NL A1E 5Z3
Tel: 709-579-0052; *Fax:* 709-579-7317
Number of Beds: 126 beds
Note: Nursing homel also owns and operates 54 independent living cottages and the 76-unit Bishop John Meaden Manor Complex
Barbara Ivany, Administrator

St. John's: **St. Patrick's Mercy Home**
Affiliated with: Eastern Regional Integrated Health Authority
146 Elizabeth Ave., St. John's, NL A1B 1S5
Tel: 709-726-2687; *Fax:* 709-726-0722
Number of Beds: 214 beds
Note: Long-term care facility affiliated with the Roman Catholic Diocese of St. John's
Sr. Phyllis Corbett, Administrator

***Stephenville Crossing:* Bay St. George Long Term Care Centre**
Affiliated with: Western Health
Former Name: Bay St. George Senior Citizens Home
PO Box 250, Stephenville Crossing, NL A0N 2C0
Tel: 709-646-5800; *Fax:* 709-646-2375
Number of Beds: 114 beds
Anne Doyle, Nursing

Long Term/Retirement Care

Long Term Care Facilities

***Bonavista:* Golden Heights Manor**
Affiliated with: Eastern Regional Integrated Health Authority
Postal Service #1, Bonavista, NL A0C 1B0
Tel: 709-468-2043; *Fax:* 709-468-1549
Number of Beds: 62 beds
Pauline Pardy

***Placentia:* Placentia Health Centre**
Affiliated with: Eastern Regional Integrated Health Authority
PO Box 480, Placentia, NL A0B 2Y0
Tel: 709-227-2061; *Fax:* 709-227-5476
www.easternhealth.ca
Number of Beds: 10 acute care, 75 long term care beds
Note: Acute care, long term care (Lions Manor Nursing Home), on an in-patient & out-patient basis
Diane Reid, Facility Manager
W. Whittle, Director, Environmental Services

***St Brides:* Bay View Manor**
General Delivery, St Brides, NL A0B 2Z0
Tel: 709-337-2569
Number of Beds: 10 beds
Note: personal care home
Jerome Quinlan
Beverly Russell

***St Lawrence:* U.S. Memorial Community Health Centre**
Affiliated with: Eastern Regional Integrated Health Authority
PO Box 398, St Lawrence, NL A0E 2V0
Tel: 709-873-2220; *Fax:* 709-873-2390
www.easternhealth.ca
Number of Beds: 40 beds
Note: Long term & protective care units, ambulatory care clinic, nutritional services, pharmacy, visiting specialty clinics
Jocelyn Dunphy, Co-ordinator, Patient/Resident Care
Elizabeth Degruchy-Lace, Manager, Environmental Services

Personal Care Homes

***Arnolds Cove:* Hilltop Manor**
PO Box 280, Arnolds Cove, NL A0B 1A0
Tel: 709-463-5000; *Fax:* 709-463-1005
hollismetcalge@hotmail.com
Number of Beds: 32 beds
Trey Metcalfe

***Baie Verte:* Baie Verte Manor Ltd.**
PO Box 561, 20 High St., Baie Verte, NL A0K 1B0
Tel: 709-532-4615; *Fax:* 709-532-4643
Number of Beds: 30 beds
Donna Rideout, Owner/Administrator

***Baie Verte:* H. Pardy Manor**
PO Box 1, Baie Verte, NL A0K 1B0
Tel: 709-532-4603; *Fax:* 709-329-3281
Number of Beds: 22 beds
Kim Sacrey, Manager

***Bay Bulls:* Glynn's Rest Home**
Former Name: White's Rest Home
PO Box 6, Bay Bulls, NL A0A 1C0
Tel: 709-334-2241
Number of Beds: 13 beds
Kathy White, Contact

***Bay Bulls:* Walsh's Personal Care Home**
PO Box 42, Rte. 10, Bay Bulls, NL A0A 1C0
Tel: 709-334-2619
Number of Beds: 10 beds
Delores Walsh, Proprietor

***Bell Island:* Island Manor**
PO Box 728, Bell Island, NL A0A 4H0
Tel: 709-488-2966
Number of Beds: 10 beds
Jocelyn Russell

***Bishop's Cove:* Smith's Personal Care Home**
PO Box 86, RR#1, Bishop's Cove, NL A0A 3X0
Tel: 709-589-2189
Number of Beds: 4 beds
Mildred Naomi Smith

***Bishops Falls:* Exploits Manor**
PO Box 850, Bishops Falls, NL A0H 1C0
Tel: 709-258-6446
Number of Beds: 30 beds
Alex Faulkner

***Cape Anguille:* Hilliard's Personal Care Home**
PO Box 18, Cape Anguille, NL A0N 1H0
Tel: 709-955-2339
Number of Beds: 14 beds
Minnie Hilliard, Owner/Administrator

***Carmanville:* Carmanville Manor**
PO Box 42, Carmanville, NL A0G 1N0
Tel: 709-534-2244; *Fax:* 709-534-2337
carmanvillemanor@nf.sympatico.ca
Number of Beds: 21 beds
Jeanne Clarke

***Catalina:* Seaside Lodge**
PO Box 182, Catalina, NL A0C 1J0
Tel: 709-469-3160; *Fax:* 709-469-3161
Number of Beds: 50 beds
Note: Personal care home
Shirley Barney

***Catalina:* Shirley's Haven**
PO Box 182, Catalina, NL A0C 1J0
Tel: 709-469-3160; *Fax:* 709-469-3161
Number of Beds: 50 beds
Shirley Barney

***Clarenville:* Clarenville Rest Home**
PO Box 951, Clarenville, NL A0E 1J0
Tel: 709-466-2447
Number of Beds: 30 beds
Michelle Holloway, Proprietor/Administrator

***Clarkes Beach:* Brigus Personal Care Home**
PO Box 515, Clarkes Beach, NL A0A 1W0
Tel: 709-786-9693; *Fax:* 709-786-4757
Number of Beds: 9 beds
Denise Smith, Co-owner
Keith Smith, Co-owner

***Clarkes Beach:* Calling Wood Downs**
PO Box 160, Clarkes Beach, NL A0A 1W0
Tel: 709-786-1850
Number of Beds: 87 beds
Jerome Russell

***Clarkes Beach:* Smith's Country Villa Inc.**
PO Box 515, Clarkes Beach, NL A0A 1W0
Tel: 709-786-7861
Number of Beds: 17 beds
Denise Smith

***Conception Bay South:* Greenslade's Personal Care Home**
Former Name: Greenslade Special Care Home
12 Wettlaufer Rd., Conception Bay South, NL A1X 7P6
Tel: 709-834-3047; *Fax:* 709-834-3087
Number of Beds: 14 beds
Wayne Greenslade
Marilyn Greenslade

***Conception Bay South:* Halliday's Personal Care Home**
91 Cherry Lane, Conception Bay South, NL A1W 3B5
Tel: 709-834-2349
Number of Beds: 20 beds
Donna Meeker, Manager

***Corner Brook:* Brake's Personal Care Home**
292 Curling St., Corner Brook, NL A2H 3J7
Tel: 709-785-5092
Number of Beds: 6 beds
Vera Brake
Vivian Brake

***Corner Brook:* Mountain View Estates**
161 Premier Dr., Corner Brook, NL A2H 7M6
Tel: 709-637-7960; *Fax:* 709-634-0235
www.mountainviewestates.ca
Number of Beds: 84 beds
Note: Nursing home
Byron Brake

***Corner Brook:* Mountain View House**
PO Box 3850, RR#2, Corner Brook, NL A2H 6B9
Tel: 709-783-2019
Number of Beds: 30 beds
Note: Nursing home
Byron Brake

***Corner Brook:* Xavier House Inc.**
19 Mount Bernard Ave., Corner Brook, NL A2H 6K7
Tel: 709-634-2787
Number of Beds: 20 beds
Sr. Rosalie Carey, Administrator

***Cow Head:* Cowhead Personal Care Home**
PO Box 145, Cow Head, NL A0K 2A0
Tel: 709-243-2016
Number of Beds: 9 beds
Violet Nicolle

***Deer Lake:* Deer Lake Manor**
#119, 123 Nicholsville Rd., Deer Lake, NL A8A 1W6
Tel: 709-635-2868
Number of Beds: 31 Beds
Dwight Ball, Contact

***Dunville:* Gateway Residence**
PO Box 280, Dunville, NL A0B 1S0
Tel: 709-227-3814; *Fax:* 709-227-2346
polar@roadrunner.nf.net
Number of Beds: 22 beds
Maxine Dawe, Administrator

***Embree:* Parson's Retirement Home**
PO Box 82, Embree, NL A0G 2A0
Tel: 709-535-6094
Number of Beds: 16 beds
Robert Parsons

***Fermeuse:* Fahey's Personal Care Home**
Former Name: Fahey Boarding Home
General Delivery, Fermeuse, NL A0A 2G0
Tel: 709-363-2250; *Fax:* 709-363-2231
Number of Beds: 22 beds
Gerald Fahey

***Flowers Cove:* Ivey Durley Place**
Former Name: Straits-St Barbe Chronic Care
PO Box 157, Flowers Cove, NL A0K 2N0
Tel: 709-456-9104
Number of Beds: 20 beds
Judy Way, Contact
709-456-2022
Dennis Coates, Contact
704/456-2022

***Fogo:* Riverhead Manor**
PO Box 375, Fogo, NL A0G 2B0
Tel: 709-266-2336
Number of Beds: 17 beds
Luther Piercey

***Gander:* Nightingale Manor**
11 Hadfield St., Gander, NL A1V 2V6
Tel: 709-256-3711
Number of Beds: 60 beds
Lawrence Guy

***Glovertown:* Baywatch Manor**
PO Box 120, Glovertown, NL A0G 2M0
Tel: 709-533-2600
baywatchmanor@nf.aibn.com
www.baywatchmanor.ca
Number of Beds: 38 beds
Denise Button

***Glovertown:* Oram's Birchview Manor**
PO Box 10, Glovertown, NL A0G 2L0
Tel: 709-266-2336
Number of Beds: 50 beds
Note: Specialty: Personal care
Paul Oram

***Goulds:* Kelly's Personal Care Home**
Former Name: Kelly Boarding Home
478 Main Road, Goulds, NL A1S 1G3
Tel: 709-745-5343
Number of Beds: 19 beds
Linda Spurrell, Proprietor
709/745-5343

***Goulds:* Lawlor's Personal Care Home**
PO Box 419, Goulds, NL A1S 1G5
Tel: 709-745-1956
Number of Beds: 14 beds

Albert Lawlor

***Goulds:* Maloney's Personal Care Home**
PO Box 568, Barton's Rd., Goulds, NL A1S 1G3
Tel: 709-745-4986
Number of Beds: 10 beds
Note: Nursing Home
Mary Maloney, Contact

***Grand Falls-Windsor:* Golden Years Estate**
348 Grenfell Heights, Grand Falls-Windsor, NL A2H 2R8
Tel: 709-489-7263; *Fax:* 709-489-7306
zettalane@tgyestate.com
www.thegoldenyearsestate.com
Number of Beds: 67 beds
Zetta Lane, Owner

***Grand Falls-Windsor:* Islandside Manor**
PO Box 814, Grand Falls-Windsor, NL A2A 2P7
Tel: 709-483-2121
Number of Beds: 24 beds
Max Arnold

***Grand Falls-Windsor:* Twin Town Manor**
15 King St., Grand Falls-Windsor, NL A1B 1J6
Tel: 709-489-0988; *Fax:* 709-489-1880
Number of Beds: 96 beds
Guy Bailey, Contact

***Happy Valley-Goose Bay:* Pine Lodge Personal Care Home**
PO Box 264 C, 3 Spruce Ave., Happy Valley-Goose Bay, NL A0P 1C0
Tel: 709-896-5512; *Fax:* 709-896-5465
Note: Specialties: Personal care for seniors & person with an intellectual disability
Diane Oliver-Scales

***Harbour Breton:* Hillside Manor**
PO Box 687, Harbour Breton, NL A0H 1P0
Tel: 709-885-2693
Number of Beds: 16 beds
Luther Piercey

***Hickmans Harbour:* Blundons' Personal Care Home**
PO Box 90, Hickmans Harbour, NL A0C 1P0
Tel: 709-466-2189
Number of Beds: 20 beds
Effie Blundon, Proprietor

***Holyrood:* Kennedy's Riverside Boarding Home Ltd.**
Former Name: Kennedy's Riverside Manor Limited
PO Box 114, Holyrood, NL A0A 2R0
Tel: 709-229-6886
Number of Beds: 33 beds
Geneviève Kennedy

***Holyrood:* Tobin's Guest Home Inc.**
PO Box 95, Holyrood, NL A0A 2R0
Tel: 709-229-7464
Number of Beds: 30 beds
Betty Tobin
Walter Tobin

***Holyrood:* Woodford's Golden Care**
PO Box 158, Holyrood, NL A0A 2R0
Tel: 709-229-3343
Number of Beds: 10 beds
Josephine Woodford

***Holyrood:* Woodford's Golden Care Home**
PO Box 158, Holyrood, NL A0A 2R0
Tel: 709-229-3343
Number of Beds: 10 beds
Josephine Woodford, Contact

***Kelligrews:* Gully Pond Manor**
39 Gully Pond Rd., Kelligrews, NL A1X 6Z2
Tel: 709-834-8083
Number of Beds: 20 beds
Ruby Hennessey

***Kilbride:* Hennessey's Personal Care Home**
222 Old Bay Bulls Rd., Kilbride, NL A1G 1E1
Tel: 709-368-5558; *Fax:* 709-368-4910
Number of Beds: 16 beds
Catherine Hennessey, Proprietor

***Lark Harbour:* Guardian Angel Seniors Home**
PO Box 91, Lark Harbour, NL A0L 1L0
Tel: 709-681-2288
Number of Beds: 20 beds
Brian Park

***Lewisporte:* Pleasantville Manor**
PO Box 207, Lewisporte, NL A0G 3A0
Tel: 709-535-0941
Number of Beds: 60 beds
Ron Sheppard

***Long Pond:* Allison's Manor**
PO Box 14099, 332 Ancorage Rd., Long Pond, NL A0A 2Y0
Tel: 709-834-8541; *Fax:* 709-834-6336
Number of Beds: 42 beds
Sharon Stone, Administrator

***Mary's Harbour:* Harbourview Manor**
PO Box 153, Mary's Harbour, NL A0K 3P0
Tel: 709-921-6440
Number of Beds: 20 beds
Elaine Rumbolt

***Mount Carmel:* Silverdale Manor**
PO Box 86, Mount Carmel, NL A0B 2M0
Tel: 709-521-2377
Number of Beds: 25 beds
Angela DeCaria

***Mount Pearl:* Cradea Manor**
1234 Topsail Rd., Mount Pearl, NL A1N 2C1
Tel: 709-364-5265
Number of Beds: 20 beds
Madeline Sturge

***Mount Pearl:* Pearl House**
163 Park Ave., Mount Pearl, NL A1N 1K6
Tel: 709-368-3850
Number of Beds: 44 beds
Lawrence Guy

***Musgrave Harbour:* Hillcrest Manor**
PO Box 100, Musgrave Harbour, NL A0G 3J0
Tel: 709-655-2777
Number of Beds: 30 beds
Lawrence Guy

***Musgravetown:* Greenwood Rest Home Ltd.**
PO Box 9, Bunyan's Cove Rd., Musgravetown, NL A0C 1Z0
Tel: 709-467-5243; *Fax:* 709-467-5578
Number of Beds: 20 beds
Wilfred Greening

***New Harbour:* Honeysuckle Estates Inc.**
PO Box 46, New Harbour, NL A0B 2P0
Tel: 709-582-3604
Number of Beds: 14 beds
Joan Hillier

***New Harbour:* Jackson's Country Manor**
New Harbour Barrens, New Harbour, NL A0B 2P0
Tel: 709-588-2382
Number of Beds: 39 Beds
Wallace Jackson, Contact
709/582-2888,

***Norris Point:* Crockers Retirement Home**
PO Box 1, Norris Point, NL A0K 3V0
Tel: 709-458-2429
Number of Beds: 20 beds
Gerald Crocker

***Paradise:* Shady Rest Lodge**
PO Box 3034, Paradise, NL A1L 3W2
Tel: 709-895-6786
Number of Beds: 21 beds
Cavell Murphy, Contact

***Pollards Point:* Main River Manor Ltd.**
Former Name: Golden Crest Haven
General Delivery, Pollards Point, NL A0K 4B0
Tel: 709-482-2334
Number of Beds: 20 beds
Dale Gillingham, Contact

***Port aux Basques:* Mountain Hope Manor**
PO Box 957, Port aux Basques, NL A0M 1C0
Tel: 709-695-3458; *Fax:* 709-695-3751
Number of Beds: 32 beds
Ida Lawrence

***Porterville:* Bayside Manor**
PO Box 134, RR#1, Porterville, NL A0G 3A0
Tel: 709-654-3171; *Fax:* 709-654-2176
Number of Beds: 50 beds
Ron Sheppard, Proprietor

***Roddickton:* Roddickton House**
Former Name: Claudelle Manor
PO Box 40, Roddickton, NL A0K 4P0
Tel: 709-457-2166; *Fax:* 709-457-2079
Number of Beds: 22 beds
Note: Nursing home
Chris Decker

***Sheartown:* Maple Lodge**
PO Box 10, Sheartown, NL A0A 3V0
Tel: 709-786-7051
Number of Beds: 16 beds
Note: Nursing home
William Tetford, Proprietor

***St Albans:* K.M. Homes Limited**
8 Meadow Pl, St Albans, NL A0H 2E0
Tel: 709-538-3162
Number of Beds: 30 beds
Shirley Ingram

***St Anthony:* Shirley's Haven #2**
St Anthony, NL A0K 4S0
Tel: 709-454-1070
Number of Beds: 60 beds
Shirley Barney

***St Lawrence:* Mount Margaret Manor**
PO Box 278, St Lawrence, NL A0E 2V0
Tel: 709-873-3199
Number of Beds: 31 beds
Mildred Marsden

***St Marys:* Lewis' Personal Care Home, Inc.**
PO Box 219, St Marys, NL A0B 3B0
Tel: 709-525-2244
Number of Beds: 20 beds
Carolann Lewis, Proprietor

***St Marys:* Neville's Special Care Home**
General Delivery, St Marys, NL A0B 3B0
Tel: 709-525-2098
Number of Beds: 21 beds
Paul Neville

***St. John's:* Katherine House**
90 Lemarchant Rd., St. John's, NL A1E 1P1
Tel: 709-754-3864
Number of Beds: 10 beds
Barry Oliver
709/754-3864
Linda Ebsary, Proprietor
709/754-3864

***St. John's:* Margaret's Manor**
57 Bonaventure Ave., St. John's, NL A1C 3Z3
Tel: 709-722-4040
Number of Beds: 40 beds
Note: Nursing home
William Clarke

***St. John's:* North Pond Home**
34 Virginia Place, St. John's, NL A1A 3G6
Tel: 709-437-1415; *Fax:* 709-726-8187
Number of Beds: 35 beds
Maxine Isaacs
Barry Isaacs

***Stephenville:* Silverwood Manor**
42 Kippens Rd., Stephenville, NL A2N 1A7
Tel: 709-643-6550
Number of Beds: 30 beds
Judy Gallant

***Trepassey:* Ocean View Rest Home**
PO Box 5, Trepassey, NL A0A 4B0
Tel: 709-438-2227
Number of Beds: 19 beds
Anne Pennell, Contact
Jerome Devereaux, Contact

***Twillingate:* Sunset Manor**
PO Box 638, Twillingate, NL A0G 4M0
Tel: 709-884-5301
Number of Beds: 23 beds
Note: Rest home
Margaret Woods

***Wesleyville:* Otterbury Manor**
PO Box 42, 428 Main St., Wesleyville, NL A0G 4R0
Tel: 709-536-3383
Number of Beds: 30 beds
Elsie Carter

***White Bay:* Hamlyn Manor Inc.**
PO Box 59, Seal Cove, White Bay, NL A0K 5E0
Tel: 709-531-2085

Number of Beds: 17 beds
Calvin Hamlyn

***Witless Bay:* Alderwood Estates**
Former Name: Dunn's Personal Care Home
PO Box 10, Witless Bay, NL A0A 4K0
Tel: 709-334-2183; *Fax:* 709-334-2058
www.alderwoodestates.ca

Number of Beds: 52 beds
Debbie Dunne

Mental Health Facilities

Mental Health Hospitals/Facilities

***St. John's:* Waterford Hospital**
Affiliated with: Eastern Regional Integrated Health Authority
Waterford Bridge Rd., St. John's, NL A1E 4J8
Tel: 709-777-3300; *Fax:* 709-777-3993
www.easternhealth.ca

Number of Beds: 80 acute care, 104 continuing care beds
Note: Mental Health Program, acute & outpatient care; dialysis services, blood collection, x-ray clinics
Beverley Clarke, COO, Community & Children, Mental Health & Addic
Louise Jones, Interim President/CEO, Eastern Health

Northwest Territories

Government Departments in Charge

NORTHWEST TERRITORIES: Dept. of Health & Social Services
PO Box 1320, Centre Square Tower, Yellowknife, NT X1A 2L9
Tel: 867-920-6173; *Fax:* 867-873-0266
sandra_pearce@gov.nt.ca
www.hlthss.gov.nt.ca

Norman M. Hatlevik, Director, Population Health & Board Development

Regional Health Authorities

***Fort Simpson:* Dehcho Health & Social Services Authority (DHSSA)**
Former Name: Deh Cho Health & Social Services Board
PO Box 246, Fort Simpson, NT X0E 0N0
Tel: 867-695-3815; *Fax:* 867-695-2920
health_beat@gov.nt.ca
www.dhssa.ca

Year Founded: 1997
Note: Population Served: 3,409. Area Served: Fort Liard; Fort Providence; Fort Simpson; Hay River Reserve; Jean Marie River; Kakisa; Nahanni Butte; Trout Lake; Wrigley, Dehcho Region, NWT.
Allan J. Landry, Chair
Kathy Tsetso, Chief Executive Officer
KATHY_TSETSO@gov.nt.ca
David Humphrey, Director, Finance & Administration
Fax: 867-695-2054
Minnie Letcher, Director, Community Programs
MINNIE_LETCHER@gov.nt.ca
Claude Gingras, Manager, Social Services
Cindy MacDonald, Manager, Health Services
CINDY_MACDONALD@gov.nt.ca
Tracy Humphrey, Coordinator, Risk Management & Planning
TRACY_HUMPHREY@gov.nt.ca
Rene Lamothe, Coordinator, Traditional Healing
RENE_LAMOTHE@gov.nt.ca

***Hay River:* Hay River Health & Social Services Authority (HRHSSA)**
3 Gaetz Dr., Hay River, NT X0E 0R8
Tel: 867-874-7115; *Fax:* 867-874-7118
www.hrhssa.org
Note: Facilities: Hay River Emergency Group Home; Hay River Public Health Unit; Hay River Social Services Office; H.H. Williams Memorial Hospital (29 acute / extended care beds); Hay River Medical Clinic; Woodland Manor (15 long term care beds); Hay River Reserve Health Station; Hay River Reserve Social Services; Enterprise Social Services. Population Served: 3,832. Area Served: Southern shore of Great Slave Lake, Northwest Territories, including the communities of Enterprise & Hay River
Sue Cullen, Chief Executive Officer
867-874-7110, SUE_CULLEN@gov.nt.ca
George Blandford, Director, Finance & Administration
867-874-7119, GEORGE_BLANDFORD@gov.nt.ca
Joletta Larocque, Director, Employment & Community Service
867-874-7117, JOLETTA_LAROCQUE@gov.nt.ca
Jennifer Croucher, Physician Administrator
867-874-7160, JENNIFER_CROUCHER@gov.nt.ca
Sheryl Courtoreille, Coordinator, Quality Improvment
867-874-7168, SHERYL_COURTOREILLE@gov.nt.ca

***Inuvik:* Beaufort-Delta Health & Social Services Authority**
Former Name: Inuvik Regional Health & Social Services Authority
Bag 2, Inuvik, NT X0E 0T0
Tel: 867-777-8000; *Fax:* 867-777-8062
bdhssa.nt.ca
Note: Serves the communities of Aklavik, Fort McPherson, Inuvik, Paulatuk, Sachs Harbour, Tsiigehtchic, Tuktoyaktuk, & Ulukhaktok. Services provided through the Inuvik Regional Hospital & community clinics, & include continuing care, health promotion, counselling, social programs, nutrition, telehealth, rehabilitation & diabetes education.
Deborah Tynes, CEO
deborah_tynes@gov.nt.ca

***Norman Wells:* Sahtu Health & Social Services Authority**
PO Box 340, Norman Wells, NT X0E 0V0
Tel: 867-587-3438; *Fax:* 867-587-3436
www.shssa.org
Note: provides numerous health and social services to 2,700 people on the Mackenzie Valley
Chad Fehr, CEO
chad_fehr@gov.nt.ca

***Yellowknife:* Stanton Territorial Health Authority**
Former Name: Stanton Regional Health Board
PO Box 10, Yellowknife, NT X1A 2N1
Tel: 867-669-4224; *Fax:* 867-669-4128
www.srhb.org

Sylvia Haener, CEO
sylvia_haener@gov.nt.ca

***Yellowknife:* Yellowknife Health & Social Services Authority**
Former Name: Yellowknife Health & Social Services Board
PO Box 608, Yellowknife, NT X1A 2N5
Tel: 867-873-7276; *Fax:* 867-873-0289
greg_cummings@gov.nt.ca
Note: community health & social services board
Greg Cummings, CEO

Hospitals

Hospitals - General

***Hay River:* H.H. Williams Memorial Hospital**
Affiliated with: Hay River Health & Social Service Authority
3 Gaetz Dr., Hay River, NT X0E 0R8
Tel: 867-874-7100; *Fax:* 867-874-7118
Number of Beds: 23 acute, 8 extended care beds
Note: long-term care facility
Paul Vieira, CEO

***Inuvik:* Inuvik Regional Hospital**
Affiliated with: Beaufort-Delta Health & Social Services Authority
Bag 2, Inuvik, NT X0E 0T0
Tel: 867-777-8000; *Fax:* 867-777-8054
bdhssa.nt.ca

Number of Beds: 51 beds
Note: Location: 285 Mackenzie Rd., Inuvik. Provides emergency services, surgery, obstetrics, acute care, long term care, pharmacy, diagnostic imaging & lab, physician clinics, visiting specialists, & referral.

Community Health Centres

Community Health Care Centres

***Aklavik:* Susie Husky Health & Social Services Centre**
Affiliated with: Beaufort-Delta Health & Social Services Authority
Former Name: Susie Husky Health Centre
PO Box 114, Aklavik, NT X0E 0A0
Tel: 867-978-2516; *Fax:* 867-978-2160
www.bdhssa.nt.ca
Note: Specialties: Clinics, such as chronic disease & well child, woman, & man clinics; School health program; Health promotion; Dental therapy; Home care; Immunization programs; Rehabilitative services; Child protection; Child & family services; Palliative care. Number of Employees: 1 nurse in charge + 3 community health nurses + 2 community social service workers; 1 dental therapist + 1 community health representative + 1 home support worker + 1 clerk + 1 caretaker

***Behchoko:* Behchoko Health Centre**
Affiliated with: Dogrib Community Services Authority
Former Name: Rae Health Centre
General Delivery, Behchoko, NT X0E 0Y0
Tel: 867-392-6351; *Fax:* 867-392-6612

***Deline:* Deline Health Centre**
Affiliated with: Sahtu Health & Social Services Authority
PO Box 119, General Delivery, Deline, NT X0E 0G0
Tel: 867-589-3111; *Fax:* 867-589-3406

***Fort Good Hope:* Fort Good Hope Health Centre**
Affiliated with: Sahtu Health & Social Services Authority
PO Box 9, Fort Good Hope, NT X0E 0H0
Tel: 867-598-2211; *Fax:* 867-598-2605

***Fort Liard:* Fort Liard Health Centre**
Affiliated with: Deh Cho Health & Social Services Authority
General Delivery, Fort Liard, NT X0G 0A0
Tel: 867-770-4301; *Fax:* 867-770-3235

***Fort McPherson:* William Firth Health Centre**
Affiliated with: Beaufort-Delta Health & Social Services Authority
PO Box 56, Fort McPherson, NT X0E 0J0
Tel: 867-952-2586; *Fax:* 867-952-2620

***Fort Providence:* Fort Providence Health Centre**
Affiliated with: Deh Cho Health & Social Services Authority
PO Box 260, Fort Providence, NT X0E 0L0
Tel: 867-699-4311; *Fax:* 867-699-3811

***Fort Simpson:* Fort Simpson Health Centre**
Affiliated with: Deh Cho Health & Social Services Authority
PO Box 246, Fort Simpson, NT X0E 0N0
Tel: 867-695-7000; *Fax:* 867-695-7017

***Fort Smith:* Fort Smith Health Centre**
Affiliated with: Fort Smith Health & Social Services Authority
c/o Fort Smith Health & Social Services, PO Box 1080, Fort Smith, NT X0E 0P0
Tel: 867-872-6203; *Fax:* 867-872-6260
Number of Beds: 25 beds

***Gameti:* Gameti Health Centre**
Affiliated with: Dogrib Community Services Authority
Former Name: Gameti/Rae Lakes Outpatient Centre
General Delivery, Gameti, NT X0E 1R0
Tel: 867-997-3141; *Fax:* 867-997-3045

***Hay River:* Hay River Public Health Unit**
Affiliated with: Hay River Health & Social Service Authority
3 Gaetz Dr., Hay River, NT X0E 0R8
Tel: 867-874-7201; *Fax:* 867-874-7211

***Inuvik:* Inuvik Public Health Unit**
Affiliated with: Beaufort-Delta Health & Social Services Authority
PO Bag 2, Inuvik, NT X0E 0T0
Tel: 867-777-7246; *Fax:* 867-777-3255

***Inuvik:* Inuvik Public Health Unit**
Bag 2, Inuvik, NT X0E 0T0
Tel: 867-777-7246; *Fax:* 867-777-3255
Barb Lennie, Nurse-in-Charge

***Jean Marie River:* Jean Marie River Health Cabin**
General Delivery, Jean Marie River, NT X0E 0N0
Tel: 867-809-2900; *Fax:* 867-809-2902

***Lutselk'e:* Lutselk'e Health Centre**
Affiliated with: Yellowknife Health & Social Services Authority
PO Box 56, Lutselk'e, NT X0E 1A0
Tel: 867-370-3111; *Fax:* 867-370-3022
Note: Specialties: Public health programs; Counselling & crisis intervention & referrals

***Nahanni Butte:* Nahanni Butte Medical Health Clinic**
Affiliated with: Deh Cho Health & Social Services Authority
General Delivery, Nahanni Butte, NT X0E 0N0
Tel: 867-602-2203; *Fax:* 867-602-2021

***Norman Wells:* Norman Wells Health Centre**
Affiliated with: Sahtu Health & Social Services Authority
PO Box 8, Norman Wells, NT X0E 0V0
Tel: 867-587-2250; *Fax:* 867-587-2934

***Paulatuk:* Paulatuk Health Centre**
Affiliated with: Beaufort-Delta Health & Social Services Authority
PO Box 114, General Delivery, Paulatuk, NT X0E 1N0
Tel: 867-580-3231; *Fax:* 867-580-3300
Number of Beds: 1 bed

***Sachs Harbour:* Sachs Harbour Health Centre**
Affiliated with: Beaufort-Delta Health & Social Services Authority
PO Box 14, Sachs Harbour, NT X0E 0Z0
Tel: 867-690-4181; *Fax:* 867-690-3802

***Tuktoyaktuk:* Rosie Ovayouk Health Centre**
Affiliated with: Beaufort-Delta Health & Social Services Authority
Bag 1000, Tuktoyaktuk, NT X0E 1C0
Tel: 867-977-2321; *Fax:* 867-977-2535

***Tulita:* Tulita Health Centre**
Affiliated with: Sahtu Health & Social Services Authority
PO Box 145, Tulita, NT X0E 0K0
Tel: 867-588-4251; *Fax:* 867-588-3000
www.shssa.org
Note: Specialties: Primary care; Health promotion & prevention. Number of Employees: 3 nurses + 2 prevention & health promotion workers + 1 community social service worker + 1 mental health & addictions worker + 1 home support worker + support staff

***Ulukhaktok:* Emegak Health Centre**
Affiliated with: Beaufort-Delta Health & Social Services Authority
PO Box 160, Ulukhaktok, NT X0E 0S0
Tel: 867-396-3111; *Fax:* 867-396-3221

***Ulukhaktok:* Ulukhaktok Community Wellness Centre**
Affiliated with: Beaufort-Delta Health & Social Services Authority
c/o Emegak Health & Social Services Centre, PO Box 160, Ulukhaktok, NT X0E 0S0
Tel: 867-396-4688; *Fax:* 867-396-2934
Note: Specialties: Assessments; Crisis intervention; Therapeutic counselling; Education & awareness. Number of Employees: 1 mental health & addictions counsellor + 1 community wellness worker

***Wekweti:* Wekweti Health Centre**
General Delivery, Wekweti, NT X0E 1W0
Tel: 867-713-2904; *Fax:* 867-713-2904

***Wha Ti:* Wha Ti Health Centre**
Affiliated with: Dogrib Community Services Authority
Former Name: Wha Ti Outpatient Health Centre
General Delivery, Wha Ti, NT X0E 1P0
Tel: 867-573-3261; *Fax:* 867-573-3701

***Wrigley:* Wrigley Health Centre**
Affiliated with: Deh Cho Health & Social Services Authority
PO Box 58, General Delivery, Wrigley, NT X0E 1E0
Tel: 867-581-3441; *Fax:* 867-581-3200

***Yellowknife:* Yellowknife Public Health Centre**
Affiliated with: Yellowknife Health & Social Services Authority
PO Box 608, Yellowknife, NT X1A 2N5
Tel: 867-920-6570; *Fax:* 867-873-0158

Nursing Stations

***Colville Lake:* Colville Lake Health Station**
PO Box 50, General Delivery, Colville Lake, NT X0E 0L0
Tel: 867-709-2409; *Fax:* 867-709-2504

***Fort Resolution:* Fort Resolution Health Centre**
General Delivery, Fort Resolution, NT X0E 0M0
Tel: 867-394-4511; *Fax:* 867-394-3117

***Trout Lake:* Trout Lake Health Station**
Affiliated with: Deh Cho Health & Social Services Authority
Trout Lake Health Cabin, PO Box 39, Trout Lake, NT X0E 1Z0
Tel: 867-206-2838; *Fax:* 867-206-2024
Versa Vendron

***Tsiigehtchic:* Tsiigehtchic Health & Social Services Centre**
Affiliated with: Beaufort-Delta Health & Social Services Authority
General Delivery, Tsiigehtchic, NT X0E 0B0
Tel: 867-953-3361; *Fax:* 867-777-8049

Special Treatment Centres

***Fort Liard:* Fort Liard Mental Health & Addictions Program**
General Delivery, Fort Liard, NT X0G 0A0
Tel: 867-770-4770; *Fax:* 867-770-4813

***Fort Simpson:* Fort Simpson Mental Health & Addictions Program**
PO Box 246, Fort Simpson, NT X0E 0N0
Tel: 867-695-7085; *Fax:* 867-695-7071
Elsie Gresl, Coordinator

***Hay River:* Hay River Reserve Wellness Centre**
PO Box 3092, Hay River, NT X0E 1G4
Tel: 867-874-2838; *Fax:* 867-874-6305
Anne Firth-Jones, Community Wellness Worker

***Inuvik:* Inuvik Homeless Shelter**
PO Box 2570, Inuvik, NT X0E 0T0
Tel: 867-777-2726; *Fax:* 867-777-4597
Joanna Christie, Executive Director

Nursing Homes

***Fort Smith:* Northern Lights Special Care Home**
Affiliated with: Fort Smith Health & Social Services Authority
PO Box 1319, Fort Smith, NT X0E 0P0
Tel: 867-872-5403; *Fax:* 867-872-5404
Number of Beds: 21 beds
Suzanne Sihikal, Administrator

***Yellowknife:* Aven Manor**
Affiliated with: Yellowknife Health & Social Services Authority
#1, 5710 - 50th Ave., Yellowknife, NT X1A 1E9
Tel: 867-920-2443; *Fax:* 867-873-9915
yaccs@theedge.ca
Number of Beds: 29 beds
Greg Debogorski, Executive Director

Long Term/Retirement Care

Long Term Care Facilities

***Aklavik:* Joe Greenland Centre**
Affiliated with: Beaufort-Delta Health & Social Services Authority
PO Box 162, Aklavik, NT X0E 0A0
Tel: 867-978-2381; *Fax:* 867-978-2943
Number of Beds: 8 beds
Judy Semple, Facility Manager

***Fort Simpson:* Fort Simpson Long Term Care Home**
Affiliated with: Deh Cho Health & Social Services Authority
PO Box 246, Fort Simpson, NT X0E 0N0
Tel: 867-695-7080; *Fax:* 867-695-7083

***Fort Simpson:* Stanley Isaiah Support of Living Home**
Affiliated with: Deh Cho Health & Social Services Authority
PO Box 240, Fort Simpson, NT X0E 0N0
Tel: 867-695-2365; *Fax:* 867-695-2364
Note: independent living adult

***Hay River:* Judith Fabian Group Home**
Affiliated with: Deh Cho Health & Social Services Authority
PO Box 3052, Hay River, NT X0E 0R0
Tel: 867-874-3844; *Fax:* 867-847-3814

***Hay River:* Woodland Manor**
Affiliated with: Hay River Health & Social Service Authority
52 Woodland Dr., Hay River, NT X0E 0R8
Tel: 867-874-7226; *Fax:* 867-874-7234
ruth_budgel@gov.nt.ca
Number of Beds: 15 beds
Janet Leask, Coordinator, Residential Care

***Inuvik:* Billy Moore Home**
Affiliated with: Beaufort-Delta Health & Social Services Authority
PO Box 1078, Inuvik, NT X0E 0T0
Tel: 867-777-2472; *Fax:* 867-777-2472

***Inuvik:* Charlotte Vehus Home**
Affiliated with: Beaufort-Delta Health & Social Services Authority
PO Box 1800, Inuvik, NT X0E 0T0
Tel: 867-777-4780; *Fax:* 867-777-4687

Mental Health Facilities

Mental Health Hospitals/Facilities

***Yellowknife:* Yellowknife Mental Health Clinic**
PO Box 10, Yellowknife, NT X1A 2N5
Tel: 867-873-7042; *Fax:* 867-873-0487
Corliss McCloskey, Manager, Psychiatric Services

Nova Scotia

Government Departments in Charge

NOVA SCOTIA: Nova Scotia Department of Health
Joseph Howe Bldg., PO Box 488, 1690 Hollis St., Halifax, NS B3J 2R8
Tel: 902-424-5818; *Fax:* 902-424-0730
Toll-Free: 800-387-6665
dohweb@gov.ns.ca
www.gov.ns.ca/health
Nancy Maguire

Regional Health Authorities

Amherst: Cumberland Health Authority
PO Box CHA, 34 Prince Arthur St., Amherst, NS B4H 3B3
Tel: 902-661-1090; *Fax:* 902-667-1125
www.cha.nshealth.ca

Year Founded: 2001
Note: Area Served: Cumberland County, NS
Bruce Saunders, Chair
H. Bruce Quigley, Chief Executive Officer, bruce.quigley@cha.nshealth.ca
Darla MacPherson, Vice-President, Community Health
Darla.MacPherson@cha.nshealth.ca
Rakesh Minocha, Vice-President, Operations
rakesh.minocha@cha.nshealth.ca
Cheryl Northcott, Vice-President, Patient Care Services
cheryl.northcott@cha.nshealth.ca
Ann Keddy, Director, Public Relations
902-661-1090, ann.keddy@cha.nshealth.ca

Antigonish: Guysborough Antigonish Strait Health Authority #7 (GASHA)
25 Bay St., Antigonish, NS B2G 2G5
Tel: 902-867-4500; *Fax:* 902-863-1176
Toll-Free: 1-800-565-2511
Donalda.Macgillivary@gasha.nshealth.ca
www.gasha.nshealth.ca

Year Founded: 2001
Number of Beds: 89 beds at St. Martha's Regional Hospital; 31 beds at Strait Richmond Hospital; 10 beds at Guysborough Memorial Hospital; 6 beds at St. Mary's Memoria
Note: Facilities: St. Martha's Regional Hospital; Strait Richmond Hospital, Evanston, Richmond County; Guysborough Memorial Hospital; St. Mary's Memorial Hospital; Eastern Memorial Hospital, Canso. Number of Employees: 1,000+. Population Served: 44,515. Area Served: Town of Antigonish; Town of Canso; Town of Mulgrave; Town of Port Hawkesbury; Municipality of the County of Antigonish; Municipality of the District of Guysborough; Municipality of the County of Richmond; Municipality of the District of St. Mary's; Municipality of the County of Inverness, Nova Scotia
Kevin MacDonald, Chief Executive Officer
902-867-4500, ext. 4, Kevin.Macdonald@gasha.nshealth.ca
David Samson, Chair
Dr. Jeremy Hillyard, District Medical Chief of Staff
902-867-4500, ext. 4, Jeremy.Hillyard@gasha.nshealth.ca
Madonna MacDonald, Vice-President, Community Health
902-867-4500, ext.., Madonna.Macdonald@gasha.nshealth.ca
Heather MacKay, Director, Public Relations
902-867-4500, ext. 4, Fax: 902-867-1059, Heather.MacKay@gasha.nshealth.ca
David MacKenzie, Vice-President, Operations
902-867-4500, ext. 4, David.mackenzie@gasha.nshealth.ca
Liz Millett, Vice-President, Patient Care
902-867-4500, ext.., Liz.Millett@gasha.nshealth.ca
Helen Muir, Coordinator, Human Resources
902-867-4500, ext. 4, Fax: 902-863-6455, humanresources@gasha.nshealth.ca

Bridgewater: South Shore District Health Authority #1
90 Glen Allan Dr., Bridgewater, NS B4V 3S6
Tel: 902-527-2266; *Fax:* 902-527-5269
thawkesworth@ssdha.nshealth.ca
www.ssdha.nshealth.ca

Note: South Shore Regional Hospital (Bridgewater), Fishermen's Memorial Hospital (Lunenburg), & Queens General Hospital (Liverpool). Community-based programs for addiction services, palliative care, public health, mental health
Kevin McNamara, CEO

Halifax: Capital Health District
#2142, 1796 Summer St., Halifax, NS B3H 3A7
EXJW@cdha.nshealth.ca
www.cdha.nshealth.ca

Note: Number of Employees: 11,000. Population Served: 400,000
Chris Power, President; Chief Executive Officer
902-473-2240
Gaynor Watson-Creed, Medical Officer of Health
902-481-5800
Catherine Gaulton, General Counsel; Vice-President, Performance Excellence
902-473-2626
Paula Bond, Vice-President, People Centred Care
902-473-7084
Lea Bryden, Citizen Engagement; Accountability
902-473-2194
Brendan Carr, Vice-President, Medicine
902-473-7066
Ray LeBlanc, Vice-President, Innovation & Learning
902-473-7310
Kathy MacNeil, Vice-President, People
902-473-7995
Amanda Whitewood, Vice-President, Sustainability
902-473-3317
John McCarthy, Officer, Board Development
902-473-1143, Fax: 902-473-3368, John.McCarthy@cdha.nshealth.ca
Anne Bereziuk, Patient Representative
902-473-2133, anne.bereziuk@cdha.nshealth.ca

Kentville: Annapolis Valley Health (AVH)
15 Chipman Dr., Kentville, NS B4N 3V7
Tel: 902-678-7381; *Toll-Free:* 1-800-886-9757
www.avdha.nshealth.ca

Note: Number of Medical Staff: 170 physicians; Population Served: 84,000
Janet Knox, President; Chief Executive Officer
902-538-3431, Fax: 902-538-7609, ceo@avdha.nshealth.ca
David Logie, Board Chair
902-538-3431, Fax: 902-538-7609, lbobbitt@avdha.nshealth.ca (Linda Bo
Dr. Lynne Harrigan, Vice-President, Medicine
902-538-3424, Fax: 902-538-3432
Tamara Gilley, Director, Public Relations
902-538-3468, Fax: 902-678-9553, tgilley@avdha.nshealth.ca

New Glasgow: Pictou County District Health Authority #6
c/o Aberdeen Hospital, 835 East River Rd., New Glasgow, NS B2H 3S6
Tel: 902-752-7600
www.pcha.nshealth.ca

Patrick Flinn, CEO

Sydney: Cape Breton District Health Authority
1482 George St, Sydney, NS B1P 1P3
Tel: 902-567-8000; *Fax:* 902-563-2717
www.cbdha.nshealth.ca

Number of Beds: 466 acute care beds; 207 veteran & continuing care beds
Note: Number of Employees: 3,300 health care providers working with 270 hospital & community based physicians
John Malcom, Chief Executive Officer
902-567-7802
Yvon LeBlanc, Chair
Dr. M.A. Naqvi, Chief of Staff; Medical Director
902-567-7806
Evelyn Schaller, Chief Nursing Officer; Vice-President, Patient Services
902-567-7814
Jim Merkley, Vice-President, Diagnostic & Support Services
902-842-2842
Mary Lou O'Neil, Vice-President, Clinical Services
902-563-2711
Lindsay Peach, Vice-President, Population Health & Continuing Care
902-794-5449
Greg Boone, Director, Public Affairs
902-567-7791

Truro: Colchester East Hants Health Authority (CEHHA)
207 Willow St., Truro, NS B2N 5A1
Tel: 902-893-5554; *Fax:* 902-893-0040
Toll-Free: 1-800-460-2110
humanresources-cehha@cehha.nshealth.ca
www.cehha.nshealth.ca

Year Founded: 2001
Note: Facilities: Colchester Regional Hospital, Truro, NS; Lillian Fraser Memorial Hospital, Tatamagouche, NS; East Hants Resource Centre, Elmsdale, NS. Population Served: 73,000. Area Served: Colchester County; Municipality of East Hants
John K. MacDonald, Chair
Peter MacKinnon, Chief Executive Officer
Dr. Martin Dzierzanowski, Head, Surgery
Krista Wood, Director, Public Relations
902-893-5554, ext.., krista.wood@cehha.nshealth.ca
Wendy Mosher, Manager, Volunteer Resources
902-893-5554, ext. 2, Wendy.Mosher@cehha.nshealth.ca

Yarmouth: Southwest Health
Former Name: Western Regional Health Board
c/o Yarmouth Regional Hospital, 60 Vancouver St., Yarmouth, NS B4A 2P5
Tel: 902-742-3541; *Fax:* 902-742-0369
www.swndha.nshealth.ca

Number of Beds: 536 beds
Blaise MacNeil, CEO

Hospitals

Hospitals - General

Amherst: Cumberland Regional Health Care Centre (CRHCC)
Affiliated with: Cumberland Health Authority #5
19428 Hwy. #2, RR#6, Amherst, NS B4H 1N6
Tel: 902-667-3361; *Fax:* 902-667-6306
www.cha.nshealth.ca

Year Founded: 2002
Note: Hospital Specialties: Level 2 emergency services; Diagnostic imaging; Laboratory services; Surgery; Intensive care unit; Maternal / child unit (902-667-5400, ext. 6144); Acute care; Ambulatory care; Physiotherapy; Occupational therapy; Respiratory therapy; Diabetes education; Social work (902-667-5400, ext. 6219); Palliative care (902-667-5400, ext. 6373)
Dr. David Gass, Chief of Staff, Cumberland Health Authority
david.gass@cha.nshealth.ca
Cheryl Northcott, Vice-President, Patient Care Services, Cumberland Health Authority
cheryl.northcott@cha.nshealth.ca
Ann Keddy, Director, Public Relations, Cumberland Health Authority
902-661-1090, ann.keddy@cha.nshealth.ca

Antigonish: St. Martha's Regional Hospital
Affiliated with: Guysborough Antigonish Strait Health Authority #7
25 Bay St., Antigonish, NS B2G 2G5
Tel: 902-863-2830; *Fax:* 902-867-1059
www.erhb.ns.ca/Facilities/St_Marthas/default.htm

Number of Beds: 80 beds
Note: regional hospital
Liz Millett, Vice President, Patient Care
David MacKenzie, Vice President, Operations

Baddeck: Victoria County Memorial Hospital
Affiliated with: Cape Breton District Health Authority #8
PO Box 220, 30 Old Margaree Rd., Baddeck, NS B0E 1B0
Tel: 902-295-2112; *Fax:* 902-295-3432
www.cbdha.nshealth.ca

Number of Beds: 12 beds
Diane Grant, Administrator

Bridgewater: South Shore Regional Hospital
Affiliated with: South Shore District Health Authority #1
Former Name: Health Services Association of the South Shore
90 Glen Allan Dr., Bridgewater, NS B4V 3S6
Tel: 902-543-4603; *Fax:* 902-543-4719
www.ssdha.nshealth.ca/ssrh.htm

Number of Beds: 80 beds
Note: A primary and secondary care hospital and designated district trauma centre, services include emergency & ambulatory care, diagnostic imaging (radiography/fluoroscopy, ultrasound, mammography, CT scanning, nuclear medicine), intensive care, surgery, EKG, gastroenterology, mental health services, obstetrics, opthalmology, pediatrics, cardiac care, respiratory therapy, rheumatology, rehabilitation, palliative, pharmacy, walk-in clinic
Ms. Alice Leverman, CEO, SSDHA
aleverman@ssdha.nshealth.ca
Dr. Peter Vaughan, Medical Director, SSDHA
Ms. Theresa Hawkesworth, Communications Officer, SSDHA
902-527-2266, thawkesworth@ssdha.nshealth.ca

Canso: Eastern Memorial Hospital
Affiliated with: Guysborough Antigonish Strait Health Authority #7
PO Box 10, 1746 Union St., Canso, NS B0H 1H0
Tel: 902-366-2794; *Fax:* 902-366-2740
www.gasha.nshealth.ca

Year Founded: 1948
Number of Beds: 6 beds
Note: Hospital Specialties: Emergency services; Diagnostic imaging; Physiotherapy; Psychology services; Social services; Nutritional counselling; Diabetes education; Outreach nursing; Palliative care
Rose Richardson, Manager, Eastern Memorial Hospital Facility
Rose.Richardson@gasha.nshealth.ca

Cheticamp: Sacred Heart Community Health Centre
Affiliated with: Cape Breton District Health Authority #8
Former Name: Sacred Heart Hospital
PO Box 129, 15102 Cabot Trail, Cheticamp, NS B0E 1H0
Tel: 902-224-1500; *Fax:* 902-224-2903
www.cbdha.nshealth.ca

Number of Beds: 10 beds
Note: Emergency & outpatient services, lab, physiotherapy, nutrition counseling, foot & eye clinics, diagnostic imaging, palliative care
John Malcom, CEO, CBDHA
Mary Lou O'Neil, Vice-President, Clinical Services, CBDHA
Dr. M. A. Naqvi, Medical Director; Chief of Staff, CBDHA

Cleveland: Strait Richmond Hospital
Affiliated with: Guysborough Antigonish Strait Health Authority #7
138 Hospital Rd., RR#1, Cleveland, NS B0E 1J0
Tel: 902-625-3100; *Fax:* 902-625-3804
www.gasha.nshealth.ca
Year Founded: 1980
Number of Beds: 20 beds
Note: Specialties: Inpatient unit for addiction services; Mental health services; Social work services; Physiotherapy; Occupational therapy; Physicians clinics, such as pediatrics & orthopedics; Ambulatory care clinics, such as a living with stroke program, a well men's clinic, & a well women's clinic
Andrea Boyd-White, Facility Manager
Andy Parland, Director, Maintenance & Chief Engineer

Dartmouth: Dartmouth General Hospital (DGH)
Affiliated with: Capital District Health Authority #9
325 Pleasant St., Dartmouth, NS B2Y 4G8
Tel: 902-465-8300
www.cdha.nshealth.ca
Note: Hospital Specialties: Emergency services (902-465-8333); Diagnostic services; Laboratory services; Surgery; Critical care; Gynaecology; Urology; Orthopedics; Ophthalmology; Ear, nose, & throat; Renal dialysis; Nutrition counselling; Osteoporosis Multidisciplinary Education Program
Gaynor Watson-Creed, Medical Officer of Health, Capital Health
902-481-5800
Laura Brine, Patient Representative
902-460-4544, Fax: 902-465-2729,
laura.brine@cdha.nshealth.ca
Natalie Morris, Contact, Dartmouth Osteoporosis Multidisciplinary Education
902-860-3719, morrisn@cdha.nshealth.ca
Marlene Regan, Contact, DGH Nutrition Counselling Department
902-465-8514

Digby: Digby General Hospital
Affiliated with: Southwest Health
75 Warwick St., Digby, NS B0V 1A0
Tel: 902-245-2501; *Fax:* 902-245-5517
www.swndha.nshealth.ca
Note: Hospital Specialties: Emergency services (902-245-1303); Diagnostic imaging (1-877-742-2571); Laboratory services (902-245-2502, ext. 3213); Primary care; Ambulatory care; Cardiac & respiratory services (902-245-2502, ext. 3264); Restorative care (902-245-2502, ext. 3337); Physiotherapy & occupational therapy (902-245-2502, ext. 3257); Recreation therapy (902-245-2502, ext. 3280); Mental health services (902-245-4709); Diabetes education (902-245-2502, ext. 3274); Nutrition counselling (902-245-2502, ext. 3341); Public health (902-245-2557); Hearing & Speech Centre (902-245-2502, ext. 3265); Palliative care (902-245-2502, ext. 3335)
Hubert d'Entremont, Manager, Digby General Hospital Site
902)-245-2502, ext., Fax: 902-245-2803,
hubertdentremont@swndha.nshealth.ca

Guysborough: Guysborough Memorial Hospital
Affiliated with: Guysborough Antigonish Strait Health Authority #7
PO Box 170, Guysborough, NS B0H 1N0
Tel: 902-533-3702; *Fax:* 902-533-4066
Number of Beds: 10 beds
Elaine MacMaster, Facility Manager
emacmaster@gasha.nshealth.ca
Tom DeLorey, Supervisor, Plant Maintenance

Halifax: IWK Health Centre
PO Box 9700, 5980 University Ave., Halifax, NS B3K 6R8
Tel: 902-470-8888
feedback@iwk.nshealth.ca
www.iwk.nshealth.ca
Number of Beds: 324 beds
Anne McGuire, President/CEO
Anne Cogdon, Director, Primary Health
902/420-6770

Halifax: Queen Elizabeth II Health Sciences Centre
Affiliated with: Capital District Health Authority #9
1796 Summer St., Halifax, NS B3H 2A7
Tel: 902-473-2700; *Fax:* 902-473-4183
capitalnews@cdha.nshealth.ca
www.cdha.nshealth.ca
Number of Beds: 983 beds
Note: The largest teaching hospital in Atlantic Canada, the QEII provides general & specialized medical care, including mental health programs, cancer care, long-term care, geriatric assessment & restorative care
Karen MacRury-Sweet, Health Services Director, Nursing, Cardiac, Thoracic & Emergency Care

Inverness: Inverness Consolidated Memorial Hospital
Affiliated with: Cape Breton District Health Authority #8
Former Name: Inverness Consolidated Hospital
PO Box 610, 39 James St., Inverness, NS B0E 1N0
Tel: 902-258-2100; *Fax:* 902-258-3025
Number of Beds: 48 beds
Note: Acute & continuing care
Claire MacQuarrie, Facilities Manager
Sandy Gillis, Head, Plant Services

Kentville: Valley Regional Hospital
Affiliated with: Annapolis Valley District Health Authority #3
150 Exhibition St., Kentville, NS B4N 5E3
Tel: 902-678-7381; *Fax:* 902-679-1904
Year Founded: 1992
Note: Medicine, surgery, obstetrics, pediatrics, intensive care, emergency services, psychiatry, addictions. Number of staff: 700 staff, 100 physicians
Janet Knox, President/CEO, Annapolis Valley Health

Liverpool: Queens General Hospital
Affiliated with: South Shore District Health Authority #1
PO Box 370, 175 School St., Liverpool, NS B0T 1K0
Tel: 902-354-3436; *Fax:* 902-354-4614
Number of Beds: 22 beds
Anne Kelley, Site Manager

Lunenburg: Fishermen's Memorial Hospital
Affiliated with: South Shore District Health Authority #1
PO Box 1180, 14 High St., Lunenburg, NS B0J 2C0
Tel: 902-634-8801
www.ssdha.nshealth.ca
Number of Beds: 23 beds for veterans' care; 10 addiction services beds; 12 restorative care beds; 12 alternate level of care beds; 6 acute care beds; 2 observation be
Note: Hospital Specialties: Laboratory services; Diagnostic imaging; Acute care; Ambulatory care; Addiction services; Rehabilitation services; Restorative care; Respiratory therapy; Asthma Care Centre; Palliative care
Dr. Peter Vaughan, Medical Director, South Shore Health
902-527-5271, Fax: 902-527-5269
Phil Langford, Vice-President, Operations, South Shore Health
902-634-7308, Fax: 902-634-3668,
plangford@ssdha.nshealth.ca

Middle Musquodoboit: Musquodoboit Valley Memorial Hospital
Affiliated with: Capital District Health Authority #9
492 Archibald Brook Rd., Middle Musquodoboit, NS B0N 1X0
Tel: 902-384-2220; *Fax:* 902-384-3310
Number of Beds: 8 beds
Sheila Martin, Director, Health Services

Middleton: Soldiers Memorial Hospital
Affiliated with: Annapolis Valley District Health Authority #3
PO Box 730, Middleton, NS B0S 1P0
Tel: 902-825-3411; *Fax:* 902-825-0599
www.avdha.nshealth.ca/smh
Number of Beds: 62 beds (25 medical/surgical beds, 25 long term care beds, 12 beds for transitional patients)
Note: Services include emergency, acute care, addictions care, enterostomal therapy, surgery, diagnostic imaging, occupational & physiotherapy, nutrition services, diabetes education, speech language pathology services
Janet Knox, President/CEO, AVH
902-538-3431, ceo@avdha.nshealth.ca
Tamara Gilley, Public Relations Director, AVH
902-538-3468, Fax: 902-678-9553, tgilley@avdha.nshealth.ca
Joanne Wentzell, Site Manager

Musquodoboit Harbour: Twin Oaks Memorial Hospital
Affiliated with: Capital District Health Authority #9
7702 - 7 Hwy., Musquodoboit Harbour, NS B0J 2L0
Tel: 902-889-4110; *Fax:* 902-889-4144
www.cdha.nshealth.ca/default.aspx?page=SubPage&centerContent.Id.0=9233&category.Categories.1=22
Year Founded: 1976
Number of Beds: 14 beds
Note: Services include emergency, acute care, addiction services, diabetic and foot clinics, diagnostic imaging, hearing and speech clinic, Home Care Nova Scotia, laboratory, nutrition counseling, occupational therapy, outpatient services, palliative & respite care, physiotherapy, social services; Twin Oaks/Birches Continuting Care Centre. A helipad is located at the back of the hospital.
Mr. Chris Power, President/CEO, CDHA
Ms. Sheila Martin, Director, Health Services
902-889-2200, sheila.martin@cdha.nshealth.ca
Ms. Marilyn Cipak, Manager, Health Services
902-889-4106, Fax: 902-889-4140,
marilyn.cipak@cdha.nshealth.ca

Neils Harbour: Buchanan Memorial Community Health Centre
Affiliated with: Cape Breton District Health Authority #8
32610 Cabot Trail, Neils Harbour, NS B0C 1N0
Tel: 902-336-2200; *Fax:* 902-336-2399
www.cbdha.nshealth.ca
Note: Specialty: Acute care

North Sydney: Northside General Hospital
Affiliated with: Cape Breton District Health Authority #8
PO Box 399, 520 Purves St., North Sydney, NS B2A 3M4
Tel: 506-794-8521; *Fax:* 506-794-3355
Number of Beds: 21 beds
Note: Emergency & ambulatory care, diagnostic imaging, lab, day surgery, diabetic education, respiratory therapy, mental health clinic; Taigh Solas, a 21-bed continuing care facility, comprises the 3rd floor of the hospital
Sharon Sheppard, Director, Continuing Care

Pictou: Sutherland Harris Memorial Hospital
Affiliated with: Pictou County District Health Authority #6
PO Box 1059, 222 Haliburton Rd., Pictou, NS B0K 1H0
Tel: 902-485-4324; *Fax:* 902-485-8835
www.pcha.nshealth.ca/sutherlandharris/aboutus/default.htm
Year Founded: 1928
Number of Beds: 20 long-term beds for veterans, 12 restorative care beds
Note: A community facility with services incuding the Northumberland Veterans Unit, Restorative Care Unit, geriatric consultation, occupational therapy, palliative care, physiotherapy, social work, speech language therapy, special clinics (for dermatology, diabetes education, podiatry, vascularity, women's health).
Mr. Patrick Lee, CEO, PCHA
pat.lee@pcha.nshealth.ca
Dr. Nicole Boutilier, Interim Vice-President, Medical Affairs, PCHA
nicole.boutilier@pcha.nshealth.ca
Ms. Eileen MacIsaac, Public Relations Officer, PCHA
902-752-7600, eileen.macisaac@pcha.nshealth.ca

Sheet Harbour: Eastern Shore Memorial Hospital
Affiliated with: Capital District Health Authority #9
22737 Hwy. #7, Sheet Harbour, NS B0J 3B0
Tel: 902-885-2554; *Fax:* 902-885-3200
www.cdha.nshealth.ca
Year Founded: 1976
Number of Beds: 16 beds
Note: Hospital Specialties: Emergency services; Diagnostic imaging; Laboratory services; Ambulatory care; Acute care; Physiotherapy; Occupational therapy; Social services; Diabetes education (902-885-3606); Respite care; Palliative care
Harold Taylor, Manager, Health Services
902-885-3616, harold.taylor@cdha.nshealth.ca
Natasha Sharpe, Facility Secretary
902-885-3678, Fax: 902-885-3200,
natasha.sharpe@cdha.nshealth.ca

Shelburne: Roseway Hospital
Affiliated with: Southwest Nova District Health Authority #2
PO Box 610, 1606 Sandy Point Rd., Shelburne, NS B0T 1W0
Tel: 902-875-3011; *Fax:* 902-875-1580
www.swndha.nshealth.ca/pages/roseway.htm
Number of Beds: 19 beds
Note: Emergency, diagnostic services, physiotherapy, nutrition counseling, mental health & addiction services, speech therapy, continuing care, VON, visiting specialists
Jodi Ybarra, Site Manager
jybarra@swndha.nshealth.ca

***Sherbrooke:* St. Mary's Memorial Hospital**
Affiliated with: Guysborough Antigonish Strait Health Authority #7
PO Box 299, 91 Hospital Rd., Sherbrooke, NS B0J 3C0
Tel: 902-522-2882; *Fax:* 902-522-2556
Number of Beds: 6 beds
Teresa MacInnis, Facility Manager

***Sydney:* Cape Breton Regional Hospital**
Affiliated with: Cape Breton District Health Authority #8
1482 George St., Sydney, NS B1P 1P3
Tel: 902-567-8000
www.cbdha.nshealth.ca
Year Founded: 1995
Note: Hospital Specialties: Emergency services; Diagnostic imaging; Laboratory services; Ambulatory care; Surgery; Intensive care; Acute care; Obstetrics; Oncology; Renal dialysis; Physical therapy; Occupational therapy; Speech therapy; Respiratory therapy; Diabetes education; Social work; Mental health; Mi'kmaq liaison; Geriatrics; Palliative care

***Tatamagouche:* Lillian Fraser Memorial Hospital**
Affiliated with: Colchester East Hants Health Authority #4
PO Box 40, 110 Blair Ave., Tatamagouche, NS B0K 1V0
Tel: 902-657-2382; *Fax:* 902-657-3745
www.cehha.nshealth.ca/Lillian Fraser/index.cfm
Number of Beds: 10 beds
Bain Brown, Maintenance Supervisor

***Truro:* Colchester Regional Hospital**
Affiliated with: Colchester East Hants Health Authority #4
207 Willow St., Truro, NS B2N 5A1
Tel: 902-893-4321; *Fax:* 902-893-5559
Toll-Free: 1-800-460-2110
humanresources-cehha@cehha.nshealth.ca (Human Resources, Colchester
www.cehha.nshealth.ca
Number of Beds: 126 beds
Note: Hospital Specialties: Emergency services; Diagnostic imaging; Laboratory services; Acute care; Maternal / child services; Coronary care; Hearing & speech centre; Ophthalmology Occupational therapy; Physiotherapy; Wound management; Asthma care centre; Diabetes centre; Social work; Veterans' unit; Palliative care
Krista Wood, Director, Public Relations
902-893-5554, ext. 2, krista.wood@cehha.nshealth.ca

***Windsor:* Hants Community Hospital**
Affiliated with: Capital District Health Authority #9
89 Payzant Dr., Windsor, NS B0N 2T0
Tel: 902-792-2000; *Fax:* 902-798-6002
www.cdha.nshealth.ca
Number of Beds: 34 acute care beds
Sherri Parker, Director, Health Services
sherri.parker@cdha.nshealth.ca

***Yarmouth:* Yarmouth Regional Hospital**
Affiliated with: Southwest Nova District Health Authority #2
60 Vancouver St., Yarmouth, NS B5A 2P5
Tel: 902-742-3541; *Fax:* 902-742-0369
Number of Beds: 139 beds
Blaise MacNeil, President; CEO
John Sullivan, Director, Physical Plant
Chris Newell, Director, Environmental Services

Community Health Centres

Community Health Care Centres

***Annapolis Royal:* Annapolis Community Health Centre**
Affiliated with: Annapolis Valley District Health Authority #3
PO Box 426, 821 St. George St., Annapolis Royal, NS B0S 1A0
Tel: 902-532-2381; *Fax:* 902-532-2113
duggan.achc@avdha.nshealth.ca
www.avdha.nshealth.ca/achc/

***Berwick:* Western Kings Memorial Health Centre**
Affiliated with: Annapolis Valley District Health Authority #3
PO Box 490, 121 Orchard St., Berwick, NS B0P 1E0
Tel: 902-538-3111; *Fax:* 902-538-9590
www.avdha.nshealth.ca
Note: Outpatient department, lab, diagnostic imaging, physiotherapy, nutritional counseling, dialysis, mental health clinic, VON Adult Day Care
Cheryl Grosvold, Site Manager

***Dartmouth:* Regional Residential Services Society (RRSS)**
#LKD1, 202 Brownlow Ave., Dartmouth, NS B3B 1T5
Tel: 902-465-4022; *Fax:* 902-465-3124
beverley.wicks@rrss.ns.ca
www.rrss.ns.ca
Number of Beds: 185 beds
Note: Developmental residences & group homes, supported apartments, short & long term respite services, personal support planning, counseling, assessment. Number of staff: 400+
Carol Ann Brennan, Executive Director
carolann.brennan@rrss.ns.ca

***Lower Sackville:* Cobequid Community Health Centre**
Affiliated with: Capital District Health Authority #9
70 Memory Lane, Lower Sackville, NS B4C 2J3
Tel: 902-869-6100; *Fax:* 902-865-4816
Margaret Merlin, Health Facility Manager

***Parrsboro:* South Cumberland Community Care Centre**
Affiliated with: Cumberland Health Authority #5
PO Box 489, 50 Jenks Ave., Parrsboro, NS B0M 1S0
Tel: 902-254-2540; *Fax:* 902-254-2504
Number of Beds: 14 beds
Connie Ellis, Site Manager

***Pugwash:* North Cumberland Memorial Hospital**
Affiliated with: Cumberland Health Authority #5
PO Box 242, 260 Church St., Pugwash, NS B0K 1L0
Tel: 902-243-2521; *Fax:* 902-243-2941
Number of Beds: 4 beds
Beryl MacLean, Site Manager

***Springhill:* All Saints Springhill Hospital**
Affiliated with: Cumberland Health Authority #5
Former Name: All Saint's Hospital
PO Box 700, 10 Princess St., Springhill, NS B0M 1X0
Tel: 902-597-3773; *Fax:* 902-597-3440
Number of Beds: 20 beds
Note: Beds are provided for restorative care, transitional care, & palliative care. There is also a 10-bed inpatient addictions treatment program.
Beryl MacLean, Site Manager

***Sydney:* Public Health Services**
Affiliated with: Guysborough Antigonish Strait Health Authority #7
235 Townsend St., Sydney, NS B1P 5E7
Tel: 902-563-2400; *Fax:* 902-563-0508
Eileen Woodford

***Wolfville:* Eastern Kings Memorial Community Health Centre**
Affiliated with: Annapolis Valley District Health Authority #3
Former Name: Eastern Kings Community Health Centre
PO Box 1180, Wolfville, NS B0P 1X0
Tel: 902-542-2266; *Fax:* 902-542-4619
www.go.ednet.ns.ca/~healthque/
Marg Blakeney, Site Manager

Special Treatment Centres

***Halifax:* IWK Mental Health Program**
Former Name: Atlantic Child Guidance Center
#1001, 6080 Young St., Halifax, NS B3K 5L2
Tel: 902-464-4110; *Fax:* 902-464-3008
www.iwk.nshealth.ca
Wayne Hollett, Interim Executive Director

***Halifax:* Nova Scotia Hearing & Speech Centres**
Provincial Centre, Park Lane Terraces, PO Box 120, #401, 5657 Spring Garden Rd., Halifax, NS B3J 3R4
Tel: 902-492-8289; *Fax:* 902-423-0532
info@nshsc.ns.ca
www.nshsc.ns.ca
Note: Specialties: Speech-language pathology services; Audiology services Augmentative communication program; Cochlear implant program; Industrial & community audiology; Newborn hearing screening program
Anne Mason-Browne, Vice-President, Speech

***Waterville:* Kings Regional Rehabilitation Centre**
PO Box 128, 1349 County Home Rd., Waterville, NS B0P 1V0
Tel: 902-538-3103; *Fax:* 902-538-7022
Number of Beds: 199 beds
Note: residential rehab
Betty E. Mattson, Administrator

***Yarmouth:* Addiction Services**
District Health Authorities 1, 2, & 3
Former Name: Western Drug Dependency Program
c/o Yarmouth Regional Hospital, 60 Vancouver St., Yarmouth, NS B5A 2P5
Tel: 902-742-2406; *Fax:* 902-742-0684
addictions-yrh@swndha.nshealth.ca
Hubert Devine, Regional Program Manager

Nursing Homes

***Annapolis Royal:* Annapolis Royal Nursing Home**
9745, St. George St., RR#2, Annapolis Royal, NS B0S 1A0
Tel: 902-532-2240; *Fax:* 902-532-7151
arnh@tartannet.ns.ca
annapolisroyalnursinghome.ca
Number of Beds: 51 beds + 2 respite
Linda R. Bailey, Administrator

***Annapolis Royal:* Northhills Nursing Home Ltd.**
PO Box 220, 5038 Granville Rd., Annapolis Royal, NS B0S 1A0
Tel: 902-532-5555; *Fax:* 902-532-7449
nhnhltd@ns.sympatico.ca
Number of Beds: 50 beds
Note: adult residential centre
Leonard S. Tedds, Administrator

***Arichat:* St. Anne Community & Nursing Care Centre**
Affiliated with: Guysborough Antigonish Strait Health Authority #7
2313 Main St., PO Box Drawer 30, Arichat, NS B0E 1A0
Tel: 902-226-2826; *Fax:* 902-226-1529
eric.burke@sacentre.nshealth.ca
Number of Beds: 24 beds
Eric Burke, Administrator

***Beaverbank:* Scotia Nursing Homes Ltd.**
Affiliated with: Capital District Health Authority #9
Former Name: Scotia Nursing Homes Ltd.
125 Knowles Cres., Beaverbank, NS B4G 1E7
Tel: 902-865-6364; *Fax:* 902-865-3582
julie.frail@rosecrest.ca
www.scotianursinghomes.ca
Number of Beds: 49 beds + 1 respite
Patricia Bland, Administrator

***Berwick:* Grand View Manor**
110A Commercial St., Berwick, NS B0P 1E0
Tel: 902-538-3118; *Fax:* 902-538-3998
admin@grandviewmanor.org
www.grandviewmanor.org
Number of Beds: 142 beds
Graham E. Hardy, Administrator

***Bridgetown:* Mountain Lea Lodge**
170 Church St., RR#1, Bridgetown, NS B0S 1C0
Tel: 902-665-4489; *Fax:* 902-665-2900
larrymarsters@ns.sympatico.ca
Number of Beds: 106 beds + 1 respite
Larry Marsters, Administrator

***Bridgewater:* Hillside Pines**
77 Exhibition Dr., Bridgewater, NS B4V 3K6
Tel: 902-543-1525; *Fax:* 902-543-8083
Number of Beds: 50 beds
Sheila MacKinnon, Administrator

***Caledonia:* North Queens Nursing Home**
9565 Highway #8, Caledonia, NS B0T 1B0
Tel: 902-682-2553; *Fax:* 902-682-2602
www.nqnh.ca
Number of Beds: 42 beds + 2 respite
Note: adult residential centre
Norma Lenco, Administrator

***Canso:* Canso Seaside Manor**
PO Box 70, 1748 Union St., Canso, NS B0H 1H0
Tel: 902-366-3030; *Fax:* 902-366-2154
dbennett@gosha.nshealth.ca
Number of Beds: 15 beds
Darren Bennett, Administrator

***Chester:* Shoreham Village**
3777 North St., RR#1, Chester, NS B0J 1J0
Tel: 902-275-5631; *Fax:* 902-275-2586
www.shorehamvillage.com
Number of Beds: 83 beds
Brian M. Selig, Administrator
Joan Regimbal, Director, Environmental Services

***Dartmouth:* Oakwood Terrace**
Affiliated with: Capital District Health Authority #9
10 Mount Hope Ave., Dartmouth, NS B2Y 4K1
Tel: 902-469-3702; *Fax:* 902-469-3824
www.oakwoodterrace.ns.ca
Year Founded: 1982
Number of Beds: 111 beds
Note: Specialties: Physiotherapy; Adult Day Program; Medical services; Palliative care
Leonard Tedds, Administrator
Pat Nightingale, Nurse Manager
Gary Comeau, Coordinator, Recreation Therapy & Volunteer Services

***Dartmouth:* Woodside Manor**
351 Pleasant St., Dartmouth, NS B2Y 3S4
Tel: 902-463-5845
Number of Beds: 29 beds
Cathy Prothro, Site Manager

***Digby:* Tideview Terrace**
Affiliated with: Southwest Nova District Health Authority #2
PO Box 1120, 51 West St., Digby, NS B0V 1A0
Tel: 902-245-4718; *Fax:* 902-245-6674
Number of Beds: 89 beds
Note: Specialties: Long-term care (level II); Dementia care; Adult day programs; Respite care; Palliative care
Lynda Casey, Administrator

***Eastern Passage:* Ocean View Manor**
Affiliated with: Capital District Health Authority #9
PO Box 130, 1909 Caldwell Rd., Eastern Passage, NS B3G 1M4
Tel: 902-465-6020; *Fax:* 902-465-4929
admin@ovm.ca
www.ovm.ca
Year Founded: 1967
Number of Beds: 176 residents
Note: Specialties: Physiotherapy; Occupational therapy; Recreation therapy; Social work; Respite care; Palliative care
Dion Mouland, Administrator

***Glace Bay:* Victoria Haven Nursing Home**
PO Box 219, 5 Third St., Glace Bay, NS B1A 5V2
Tel: 902-849-4127; *Fax:* 902-849-8826
www.victoriahaven.ca
Number of Beds: 50 beds, 4 respite
Marie McPhee, Administrator

***Glenwood:* Nakile Home for Special Care**
Affiliated with: Southwest Nova District Health Authority #2
Former Name: Nakile Home for the Aged
35 Nakile Dr., RR#1, Glenwood, NS B0W 1W0
Tel: 902-643-2707; *Fax:* 902-643-2862
bertha@nakile.ns.ca
www.nakilehome.ca
Number of Beds: 35 beds + 1 respite
Bertha Brannen, Administrator

***Halifax:* Arborstone Enhanced Care**
Affiliated with: Capital District Health Authority #9
Former Name: Arbourstone Enhanced Care
126 Purcell's Cove Rd., Halifax, NS B3P 1B5
Tel: 902-477-8051; *Fax:* 902-477-5726
www.shannex.com
Number of Beds: 190 beds
Chris Labréche, Administrator
Sean Skinner, Director, Environmental Services

***Halifax:* Glades Lodge**
Affiliated with: Capital District Health Authority #9
25 Alton Dr., Halifax, NS B3N 1M1
Tel: 902-477-1777; *Fax:* 902-477-8174
glades.lodge@gemhealth.com
Number of Beds: 123 beds + 1 respite
Bonnie Kay-Griffin, Administrator

***Halifax:* Maplestone Enhanced Care**
Affiliated with: Capital District Health Authority #9
245 Main Ave., Halifax, NS B3M 1B7
Tel: 902-443-1971; *Fax:* 902-443-9037
Number of Beds: 87 beds
Note: Nursing home
Renee Donovan-Grey, Administrator
Debbie Thompson, Environmental Services

***Halifax:* Maplestone Enhanced Care**
Affiliated with: Capital District Health Authority #9
245 Main Ave., Halifax, NS B3M 1B7
Tel: 902-443-1971; *Fax:* 902-443-9037
Number of Beds: 87 beds
Renee Donovan-Gray, Administrator

***Halifax:* Melville Lodge Long Term Care Center**
50 Shoreham Lane, Halifax, NS B3P 2R3
Tel: 902-479-1030; *Fax:* 902-477-1663
www.gemhealth.com
Year Founded: 1984
Number of Beds: 122 beds
Bernice Clake-Dibblee, Administrator

***Halifax:* Northwoodcare Inc.**
Affiliated with: Capital District Health Authority #9
2615 Northwood Terrace, Halifax, NS B3K 3S5
Tel: 902-454-8311; *Fax:* 902-455-6408
information@nwood.ns.ca
www.nwood.ns.ca
Number of Beds: 406 beds
Note: Adult residential centre
Lloyd O. Brown, Administrator

***Halifax:* Parkstone Enhanced Care**
Affiliated with: Capital District Health Authority #9
156 Parkland Dr., Halifax, NS B3S 1N9
Tel: 902-446-7275; *Fax:* 902-446-4044
dryan@shannex.com
Number of Beds: 185 beds, 5 respite beds
Note: Nursing home
Carol Ann Gallant, Administrator

***Halifax:* Saint Vincent's Nursing Home**
Affiliated with: Capital District Health Authority #9
Former Name: Saint Vincent Guest Home
2080 Windsor St., Halifax, NS B3K 5B2
Tel: 902-429-0550; *Fax:* 902-492-3703
info@svnh.ca
www.svnh.ca
Number of Beds: 149 beds
Note: Nursing home affiliated with the Roman Catholic Archdiocese of Halifax
Kristin Schmitz, Administrator

***Inverness:* Inverary Manor**
Affiliated with: Cape Breton District Health Authority #8
PO Box 460, 72 Maple St., Inverness, NS B0E 1N0
Tel: 902-258-2842; *Fax:* 902-258-3865
inverary.manor@ns.sympatico.ca
Number of Beds: 60 beds
Joan MacLellan, Administrator

***Kentville:* Evergreen Home for Special Care**
655 Park St., Kentville, NS B4N 3V7
Tel: 902-678-7355; *Fax:* 902-678-5292
evergreen@evergreenhome.ns.ca
evergreenhome.ns.ca
Number of Beds: 97 beds plus 20 children's beds & 2 respite beds
Note: adult residential centre
Fred Houghton, Administrator

***Liverpool:* Queens Manor**
PO Box 1283, 20 Hollands Dr., Liverpool, NS B0T 1K0
Tel: 902-354-3451; *Fax:* 902-354-5383
www.queensmanor.ca
Number of Beds: 60 beds + 1 respite
Norma Lenco, Administrator

***Lockeport:* Surf Lodge Nursing Home**
Affiliated with: Southwest Nova District Health Authority #2
PO Box 160, 73 Howe St., Lockeport, NS B0T 1L0
Tel: 902-656-2014
www.surflodge.ca
Note: Specialties: Long-term care; Massage therapy; Activity program; Physiotherapy
Margaret Coates, Administrator

***Lunenburg:* Harbour View Haven**
PO Box 1480, 25 Blockhouse Hill Rd., Lunenburg, NS B0J 2C0
Tel: 902-634-8836; *Fax:* 902-634-8792
www.hvh.ca
Number of Beds: 129 beds + 1 respite
Barry Granter, Administrator

***Mahone Bay:* Mahone Nursing Home**
PO Box 320, 640 Main St., Mahone Bay, NS B0J 2E0
Tel: 902-624-8341; *Fax:* 902-624-6338
www.mahonenursinghome.com
Year Founded: 1965
Note: Specialties: Long-term care Physiotherapy & occupational therapy; Palliative care
Anne Kennedy, Administrator

***Meteghan:* Villa Acadienne**
Affiliée à: Southwest Nova District Health Authority #2
CP 248, 8403 Hwy. 1, Meteghan, NS B0W 2J0
Tél: 902-645-2065; *Téléc:* 902-645-3899
www.villaacadienne.com
Nombre de lits: 84 beds + 2 respite
Lucille Maillet, Administrator

***Middle Musquodoboit:* Musquodoboit Valley Home for Special Care (Braeside)**
Affiliated with: Capital District Health Authority #9
126 Higginsville Rd., Middle Musquodoboit, NS B0N 1X0
Tel: 902-384-3007; *Fax:* 902-384-3310
Number of Beds: 28 beds + 1 respite
Diana Graham-Lentz, Site Manager

***Musquodoboit Harbour:* The Birches Nursing Home**
Affiliated with: Capital District Health Authority #9
#7702, 7 Hwy. RR#2, Musquodoboit Harbour, NS B0J 2L0
Tel: 902-889-3474
Number of Beds: 42 residents
Note: Specialties: Long-term care for older adults; Community outreach adult day programs
Sheila Martin, Manager, Health Care Facility

***New Germany:* Rosedale Home for Special Care**
Former Name: Rosedale Home
Trunk 10, #4927, RR#2, New Germany, NS B0R 1E0
Tel: 902-644-2008; *Fax:* 902-644-3260
Year Founded: 1984
Number of Beds: 29 beds
Maureen Wade, Administrator

***New Glasgow:* Glen Haven Manor**
Affiliated with: Pictou County District Health Authority #6
739 East River Rd., New Glasgow, NS B2H 5E9
Tel: 902-752-2588; *Fax:* 902-752-0053
Number of Beds: 202 beds
Note: adult residential centre
James Ferguson, Administrator

***New Waterford:* Maple Hill Manor**
Affiliated with: Cape Breton District Health Authority #8
700 King St., New Waterford, NS B1H 3Z5
Tel: 902-862-6495; *Fax:* 902-862-9294
maplehillmanor1@ns.sympatico.ca
www.maplehillmanor.ca
Number of Beds: 50 beds
Note: Long term & secured care
Cathy MacPhee, Administrator

***North Sydney:* Northside Community Guest Home**
Affiliated with: Cape Breton District Health Authority #8
11 Queen St., North Sydney, NS B2A 1A2
Tel: 902-794-4733; *Fax:* 902-794-9021
www.northsideguesthome.com
Number of Beds: 105 beds
Joanne MacNeil, Administrator

***Pictou:* Maritime Odd Fellows Home**
Affiliated with: Pictou County District Health Authority #6
PO Box 850, 143 Haliburton Rd., Pictou, NS B0K 1H0
Tel: 902-485-5492; *Fax:* 902-485-6868
Number of Beds: 47 beds
Note: Specialty: Long-term care; Therapeutic recreation
Janet Johnston, Administrator

***Sheet Harbour:* Duncan MacMillan Nursing Home**
Affiliated with: Capital District Health Authority #9
Former Name: Duncan MacMillan Home for the Aged
PO Box 68, 22639 7 Hwy., Sheet Harbour, NS B0J 3B0
Tel: 902-885-2545; *Fax:* 902-885-3289
Number of Beds: 25 beds + 1 respite
Sheila Martin, Health Care Facility Manager

***Shelburne:* Roseway Manor Inc.**
Affiliated with: Southwest Nova District Health Authority #2
PO Box 518, 1604 Lake Rd., Sandy Point, Shelburne, NS B0T 1W0
Tel: 902-875-4707; *Fax:* 902-875-4105
admin@rosewaymanor.ca
Number of Beds: 65 beds + 1 respite
Jerry Fraser, Administrator

***Sherbrooke:* High-Crest Sherbrooke Home for Special Care**
Affiliated with: Guysborough Antigonish Strait Health Authority #7
PO Box 284, 53 Court St., Sherbrooke, NS B0J 3C0
Tel: 902-522-2147; *Fax:* 902-522-2628
high-crestsherbrooke@high-crest.com
www.high-crest.com/highcrester.html
Number of Beds: 39 beds
Marion Carroll, Administrator

***Stellarton:* Valley View Villa**
Affiliated with: Pictou County District Health Authority #6
6125 Trafalgar Rd., RR#1, Stellarton, NS B0K 1S0
Tel: 902-755-5780; *Fax:* 902-755-3104
jmacsonald@vvvilla.ca
www.valleyviewvilla.com
Year Founded: 1978
Number of Beds: 109 beds + 4 respite
Note: Home for special care
Norman Ferguson, Administrator

***Sydney:* Breton Bay Nursing Home**
70 St. Anthony Dr., Sydney, NS B1S 2R5
Tel: 902-539-4560; *Fax:* 902-567-6234
Number of Beds: 264 beds
Ellen Stoddard, Administrator

***Sydney:* Cove Guest Home**
Affiliated with: Cape Breton District Health Authority #8
320 Alexander St., Sydney, NS B1S 2G1
Tel: 902-539-5267; *Fax:* 902-539-7565
www.coveguesthome.com
Year Founded: 1944
Archie MacKeigan, CEO

***Sydney:* Harbourstone Enhanced Care**
Affiliated with: Cape Breton District Health Authority #8
84 Kenwood Dr., Sydney, NS B1S 3V7
Tel: 902-539-4560; *Fax:* 902-567-6234
www.shannex.com/enhanced_care/harbourstone.html
Year Founded: 2002
Number of Beds: 268 beds + 4 respite
Ellen Stoddard, Administrator

***Sydney:* New Dawn Guest Home**
50 Military Rd., Sydney, NS B1N 3K6
Tel: 902-539-2221; *Fax:* 902-564-8309
Number of Beds: 30 beds + 1 respite
Note: Residential care facility
Janet Gillis-Hussey, Administrator

***Sydney:* R.C. MacGillivray Guest Home Society**
Affiliated with: Cape Breton District Health Authority #8
25 Xavier Dr., Sydney, NS B1S 2R9
Tel: 902-539-6110; *Fax:* 902-567-0437
Number of Beds: 78 beds, 2 respite, 1 adult protection
John W. Coffey, Administrator

***Sydney Mines:* Miner's Memorial Manor**
Affiliated with: Cape Breton District Health Authority #8
15 Lorne St., Sydney Mines, NS B1V 3B9
Tel: 902-736-1992; *Fax:* 902-736-0667
Number of Beds: 35 beds + 2 respite
Harry Blinkhorn, Administrator

***Tatamagouche:* Willow Lodge**
Affiliated with: Colchester East Hants Health Authority #4
PO Box 249, 100 Blair Ave., Tatamagouche, NS B0X 1V0
Tel: 902-657-3101; *Fax:* 902-657-3859
douglas.cunningham@willowlodge.ca
Number of Beds: 51 beds
Douglas Cunningham, Administrator

***Truro:* Cedarstone Enhanced Care**
Affiliated with: Colchester East Hants Health Authority #4
378 Young St., Truro, NS B2N 7H2
Tel: 902-895-2891; *Fax:* 902-893-2361
powerk@shannex.acl.ca
Number of Beds: 122 beds + 2 respite
Kim Power, Administrator

***Truro:* The Mira Long Term Care Center**
426 Young St., Truro, NS B2N 7B1
Tel: 902-895-8715; *Fax:* 902-897-1903
mira@gemhealth.com
www.gemhealth.com
Year Founded: 1999
Number of Beds: 90 beds
Note: Specialty: Long-term care for seniors; Medication administration; Peritoneal dialysis unit; Seniors' dental clinic; Palliative care
Lynn Smith, Administrator

***Windsor:* Dykeland Lodge/Hants County Residence for Senior Citizens**
Affiliated with: Capital District Health Authority #9
Former Name: Dykeland Lodge
124 Cottage St., Windsor, NS B0N 2T0
Tel: 902-798-8346; *Fax:* 902-798-8312
dykelandlodge@ns.sympatico.ca
Number of Beds: 110 beds
M. Emily Samson, Administrator

***Windsor:* Haliburton Place**
Affiliated with: Capital District Health Authority #9
89 Payzant Dr., Windsor, NS B0N 2T0
Tel: 902-792-2026; *Fax:* 902-798-6002
Number of Beds: 30 beds + 2 respite
Theresa Fillatre, Healthcare Facility Manager

***Windsor:* Windsor Elms United Church Senior Citizens' Home**
Affiliated with: Capital District Health Authority #9
590 King St., Windsor, NS B0N 2T0
Tel: 902-798-2251; *Fax:* 902-798-0914
Number of Beds: 107 beds + 1 respite
Sherry Keen, Administrator

***Windsor:* Windsor House**
PO Box 938, 16 Wentworth St., Windsor, NS B0N 2T0
Tel: 902-798-2115
Number of Beds: 16 beds
Gordon Armsworthy, Proprietor

***Wolfville:* Wolfville Nursing Home**
601 Main St., Comp. C5, Site 11, RR#2, Wolfville, NS B0P 1X0
Tel: 902-542-2429; *Fax:* 902-542-4048
wnh.home@ns.sympatico.ca
Number of Beds: 66 beds + 1 respite bed
Paul MacDonald, Administrator

***Yarmouth:* Harbourside Lodge**
60 Vancouver St., Yarmouth, NS B5A 2P5
Tel: 902-742-3328; *Fax:* 902-742-1427
Number of Beds: 32 beds
Sandra M. Boudreau, Executive Director

***Yarmouth:* Villa Saint Joseph-du-Lac**
Affiliated with: Southwest Nova District Health Authority #2
PO Box 810, Yarmouth, NS B5A 4A5
Tel: 902-742-7128; *Fax:* 902-742-4230
rickatkinson@villasaintjoseph.com
www.villasaintjoseph.com
Number of Beds: 79 beds
Barry Granter, Administrator

***Yarmouth:* Villa St-Joseph-du-Lac**
Affiliée à: Southwest Nova District Health Authority #2
CP 810, RR#1, Yarmouth, NS B5A 4A5
Tél: 902-742-7128; *Téléc:* 902-742-4230
rickatkinson@villasaintjoseph.com
www.villasaintjoseph.com
Nombre de lits: 79 lits
Barry Granter, Administrator

Long Term/Retirement Care

Long Term Care Facilities

***Advocate Harbor:* Bayview Memorial Health Centre**
Affiliated with: Cumberland Health Authority #5
Advocate Harbor, NS B0M 1A0
Tel: 902-392-2859; *Fax:* 902-392-2625
Number of Beds: 12 beds
Note: also community health services
Connie Ells, Site Manager

***Advocate Harbour:* Chignecto Manor Co-op Ltd.**
Residential Care Facility, Box 63, Advocate Harbour, NS B0M 1A0
Tel: 902-392-2028; *Fax:* 902-392-2434
Number of Beds: 14 beds
Note: residential care facility
Shirley Morris, Administrator

***Antigonish:* L'Arche Antigonish**
4 West St., Antigonish, NS B2G 1R8
Tel: 902-863-5000; *Fax:* 902-863-8224
Number of Beds: 13 beds
Note: residential care facility
Gus Leuschner, Executive Director

***Antigonish:* Highland Crest Home**
Affiliated with: Guysborough Antigonish Strait Health Authority #7
44 Hillcrest St., Antigonish, NS B2G 1Z3
Tel: 902-863-3855; *Fax:* 902-863-1833
highlandcres@high-crest.com
www.high-crest.com/highlandcresthome.html
Number of Beds: 40 beds
Note: residential care facility
Mary Beaver, Administrator

***Barrington:* Bayside Home Adult Residential Centre**
PO Box 238, Barrington, NS B0W 1E0
Tel: 902-637-2098; *Fax:* 902-637-3151
Number of Beds: 20 beds
Note: adult residential centre
Joanne Rose, Administrator

***Bridgetown:* Annapolis County Adult Residential Centre**
PO Box 548, Bridgetown, NS B0S 1C0
Tel: 902-665-4566; *Fax:* 902-665-5265
Number of Beds: 34 beds
Note: adult residential centre
Patricia A. MacDougall, Administrator

***Bridgetown:* Grace Haven Enterprises Ltd.**
RR#4, Bridgetown, NS B0S 1C0
Tel: 902-665-4224; *Fax:* 902-825-1400
Number of Beds: 20 beds
Note: residential care facility
Donna Hatt, Administrator

***Bridgetown:* Saunders Rest Home**
PO Box 114, 9 Freeman St., Bridgetown, NS B0S 1C0
Tel: 902-665-4331; *Fax:* 902-665-4768
patricia_saunders@lycos.com
Number of Beds: 8 beds
Shaun Saunders, Administrator

***Bridgewater:* La Have Manor Corp. Adult Residential Centre**
PO Box 270, Bridgewater, NS B4V 2W9
Tel: 902-543-7851; *Fax:* 902-543-8332
Number of Beds: 97 beds
Note: adult residential centre
Thomas Wright, Executive Director

***Bridgewater:* LaHave Manor Corp. Group Home**
58 Alexandra Ave., Bridgewater, NS B4V 1H1
Tel: 902-543-7712; *Fax:* 902-543-1816
sclo@ns.sympatico.ca
Number of Beds: 9 beds
Note: group home for mentally challenged adults
Lorelei Mason, House Coordinator

***Bridgewater:* Pleasant Rest Home**
Affiliated with: Southwest Nova District Health Authority #2
45 Pleasant St., Bridgewater, NS B4V 1M9
Tel: 902-543-2675; *Fax:* 902-543-3779
djbreid@eastlink.ca
Number of Beds: 22 beds
Note: residential care facility
Deborah Reid, Administrator

***Chester:* Bonny Lea Farm**
PO Box 560, 5 Collicutt Rd., Chester, NS B0J 1J0
Tel: 902-275-5622; *Fax:* 902-275-2567
sscsa@tallships.ca
www.ChesterBound.com/bonnylea
Number of Beds: 35 beds
Note: adult residential centre; small option units & apartments
Jim MacFarlane, Director

***Dartmouth:* Harbour Glen Manor Ltd.**
229 Pleasant St., Dartmouth, NS B2Y 3R5
Tel: 902-465-5770
Number of Beds: 18 beds
Note: residential care facility
Deborah Morgan-Downey, Administrator

***Dartmouth:* Hilltop Villa**
Affiliated with: Capital District Health Authority #9
200 Main St., Dartmouth, NS B2X 1S3
Tel: 902-435-6186; *Fax:* 902-435-9354
hilltopvilla@hotmail.com
Number of Beds: 24 beds
Jin Young Jung, Administrator
Yoo Kyung Jung, Administrator

***Glace Bay:* Charlotte's Guest Home**
Affiliated with: Cape Breton District Health Authority #8
25 Dominion St., Glace Bay, NS B1A 3P6
Tel: 902-842-9797; *Fax:* 902-849-3774
charlottesguesthome@aliantzinc.com
Number of Beds: 10 beds + 1 respite
Martha Matheson, Administrator

***Glace Bay:* Terrace Manor**
208 South St., Glace Bay, NS B1A 1W1
Tel: 902-849-2849; *Fax:* 902-842-0359
John MacAulay, Administrator

***Greenfield:* Hillsview Acres**
PO Box 4, 14 Middlefield Rd., RR#1, Greenfield, NS B0T 1E0
Tel: 902-685-2966; *Fax:* 902-685-2446
Number of Beds: 28 beds + 1 respite
Mrs. Raymond Fiske, Administrator

***Halifax:* Basinview Drive Developmental Residence**
3838 Basinview Dr., Halifax, NS B3K 5A2
Tel: 902-455-7421
Number of Beds: 8 beds
Ruth McIver, Supervisor

***Halifax:* Haven Manor**
6411 Cobourg Rd., Halifax, NS B3H 2A6
Tel: 902-421-1167; *Fax:* 902-421-1168
Number of Beds: 17 beds
Hilda Stevens, Administrator

***Halifax:* Homes for Independent Living**
2505 Oxford St., Halifax, NS B3L 2T5
Tel: 902-422-9591; *Fax:* 902-425-3151
hil@hfx.eastlink.ca
www.nsnet.org/hil/
Year Founded: 1980
Number of Beds: 6 group home beds, with 1 respite bed
Note: Specialty: Programs & accommodation for young adults with physical disabilities; Community outreach programs
JoAnne Abraham, Supervisor

***Halifax:* Joseph Howe Drive Group Home**
Tower 1, #215, 7001 Mumford Rd., Halifax, NS B3L 4N9
Tel: 902-454-0630
Number of Beds: 9 beds
Note: group home
Cathy Krause, Executive Director

***Halifax:* Lynden Rest Home**
1019 Lucknow St., Halifax, NS B3H 2T2
Tel: 902-420-0697; *Fax:* 902-492-3936

***Halifax:* Melville Gardens Residential & Level 2 Nursing Care Facility**
11 Ramsgate Lane, Halifax, NS B3P 2S9
Tel: 902-477-3135; *Fax:* 902-477-2718
www.gemhealth.com
Year Founded: 1991
Paul Hussain, Administrator
Syed Hussain, GEM Management Group, Owner

***Halifax:* Point Pleasant Lodge**
1121 South Park St., Halifax, NS B3H 2W6
Tel: 902-421-1599; *Fax:* 902-429-9722
guestservices@pointpleasantlodge.com
www.pointpleasantlodge.com
Number of Beds: 104 guest rooms
Note: A specialty hotel, with guest rooms for people directly or indirectly associated with medical attention in the Halifax area
Robert S. Manuel, CEO

***Halifax:* Robert Allen Drive Development Residence**
31 Robert Allen Dr., Halifax, NS B3M 3G9
Tel: 902-443-6804
Number of Beds: 7 beds
Note: developmental residence
Angela Fraser, Supervisor

***Halifax:* Vernon St. Group Home**
1648 Vernon St., Halifax, NS B3H 3N1
Tel: 902-422-6742
Number of Beds: 7 beds
Note: group home

***Howie Center:* My Cape Breton Home for Seniors**
Affiliated with: Cape Breton District Health Authority #8
PO Box 856, 171 Curry St., Howie Center, NS B1P 6J1
Tel: 902-564-4461; *Fax:* 902-564-4247
Number of Beds: 7 beds
Sherry MacNeil, Owner/Operator

***Kentville:* Wedgewood House**
19 Leverett Ave., Kentville, NS B4N 2K5
Tel: 902-678-1242; *Fax:* 902-679-2808
Number of Beds: 15 beds
Note: Residential care facility
Ingrid Althouse, Administrator

***Lantz:* Corridor Community Options Society**
Former Name: Lantz Residential Programs
21 Convent Rd., Lantz, NS B2S 1T4
Tel: 902-883-9404; *Fax:* 902-883-1251
ccosdirector@gmail.com
Number of Beds: 14 beds
Note: group home/small options home
Robin C. Strickland, Executive Director

***Lower West Pubnico:* Pont du Marais Home Ltd.**
Affiliated with: Southwest Nova District Health Authority #2
PO Box 236, Lower West Pubnico, NS B0W 2C0
Tel: 902-762-3099; *Fax:* 902-762-2072
pdm@auracom.com
Number of Beds: 23 beds + 2 respite
Note: Residential care facility
Charlene LeBlanc, Administrator

***Margaree Valley:* Brookside Residential Care Facility**
PO Box 83, Margaree Valley, NS B0E 2C0
Tel: 902-248-2181; *Fax:* 902-248-2056
brook@ns.sympatico.ca
Number of Beds: 11 beds, 2 respite beds
Note: residential care facility
Lorraine Robertson, Administrator

***Meteghan:* Au Logis Meteghan Ltd.**
Affiliated with: Southwest Nova District Health Authority #2
PO Box 128, 8405 Hwy. 1, Meteghan, NS B0W 2J0
Tel: 902-645-3594; *Fax:* 902-645-3594
Number of Beds: 20 beds, 2 respite
Note: residential care
Joanne Deveau, Administrator

***Meteghan:* Cottage Celeste**
Affiliated with: Southwest Nova District Health Authority #2
PO Box 314, 8064 Hwy. 31, Meteghan, NS B0W 2J0
Tel: 902-645-2248
Number of Beds: 19 beds
Kathy MacDonald, Administrator

***Middle Musquodoboit:* Musquodoboit Valley Home for Special Care - Braeside**
126 Higginsville Rd., Middle Musquodoboit, NS B0N 1X0
Tel: 902-384-3007; *Fax:* 902-384-3310
Number of Beds: 28 beds
Diana Graham-Lentz, Site Manager

***New Glasgow:* High-Crest Home New Glasgow**
Affiliated with: Pictou County District Health Authority #6
Former Name: Sunset Haven Home
253 Forbes St., New Glasgow, NS B2G 4P5
Tel: 902-752-3461; *Fax:* 902-752-2672
high_crest@hotmail.com
www.high-crest.com
Number of Beds: 36 beds
Note: Specialties: Medication monitoring; Recreational program
Rosalie Parsons, Administrator

***New Glasgow:* Highland Community Residential Services**
483 East River Rd., New Glasgow, NS B2H 3R3
Tel: 902-752-1755; *Fax:* 902-752-4256
Number of Beds: 68 beds
Note: residential care facility
Hilary Amit, Executive Director

***Oxford:* Four Seasons Manor**
General Delivery, Oxford, NS B0M 1P0
Tel: 902-447-2819
Number of Beds: 24 beds
Note: residential care facility
Herbert Hochhold, Administrator

***Oxford:* Shady Rest Ltd.**
237 Water St., Oxford, NS B0M 1P0
Tel: 902-447-2786
Note: residential care facility

***Pugwash:* Residential & Rehabilitation Services Inc.**
PO Box 130, Pugwash, NS B0K 1L0
Tel: 902-243-2571; *Fax:* 902-243-3222
Note: Specialties: Residential care & support services for persons who are mentally challenged & disabled; Day programs; Life & vocational skills programs; Social development programs; Advocacy services
Ronald Langille, CEO

***Saulnierville:* La Maison au Coucher du Soleil Ltd.**
RR#1, Saulnierville, NS B0W 2Z0
Tél: 902-769-2270; *Téléc:* 902-769-3850
Nombre de lits: 32 lits
Note: residential care facility
Nicole Amirault, Administrator

***Shelburne:* Mary's Abide-A-While Home Ltd.**
Affiliated with: Southwest Nova District Health Authority #2
PO Box 609, 188 Water St., Shelburne, NS B0T 1W0
Tel: 902-875-4384; *Fax:* 902-875-4384
Number of Beds: 16 beds
Mary Davis, Administrator

***South Berwick:* New Visions Home for Seniors**
PO Box 566, 4507 Hwy. 1, South Berwick, NS B0P 1E0
Tel: 902-538-9579; *Fax:* 902-538-0390
newvision2@ns.sympatico.ca
www.newvision2.ca
Year Founded: 1993
Number of Beds: 25 beds + 1 respite
Helen B. Walsh, Administrator

***Stellarton:* Riverview Home Corp.**
6105 Trafalgar Rd., RR#1, Stellarton, NS B0K 1S0
Tel: 902-755-4884; *Fax:* 902-755-3207
riverview@eastlink.ca
Number of Beds: 106 beds + 3 community homes & supervised depts.
Note: Residential care facility for mentally and/or physically challenged adults, group homes, & developmental residence. Number of staff: 150
Nancy Clarke, CEO

***Stewiacke:* Elmwood Manor Limited**
PO Box 189, 98 Riverside Ave., Stewiacke, NS B0N 2J0
Tel: 902-639-9003
Number of Beds: 14 beds
Note: residential care facility
Germaine M. Roberts, Administrator

***Sydney:* Cape Breton Community Housing Association**
PO Box 1292, Sydney, NS B1P 6K3
Tel: 902-539-0025; *Fax:* 902-562-5476
communityhousing@auracom.com
Number of Beds: 50 beds
Note: residential care facility
Jane Crawley, Executive Director

***Sydney:* Mayfair Guest Home**
37 George St., Sydney, NS B1P 1H4
Tel: 902-539-5611
Rosemary Ingraham-MacEache, Proprietor/Administrator

***Sydney:* Resi-Care (Cape Breton) Association**
146 Vulcan Ave., Sydney, NS B1P 5W5
Tel: 902-539-0935; *Fax:* 902-562-0717
Number of Beds: 60 beds
Note: group home
Michael Walsh, Executive Director

***Sydney River:* Braemore Home**
PO Box 515, Sydney River, NS B1P 6H4
Tel: 902-539-7640; *Fax:* 902-539-5340
admin@braemorehome.ns.ca
www.braemorehome.ns.ca
Number of Beds: 124 beds
Note: adult residential & rehabilitation
Debra MacPherson, Administrator

***Tatamagouche:* Maplewood Manor**
Affiliated with: Colchester East Hants Health Authority #4
PO Box 208, 150 Blair Ave., Tatamagouche, NS B0K 1V0
Tel: 902-657-2876; *Fax:* 902-657-1022
maplewood.manor@ns.aliantzinc.ca
Number of Beds: 7 beds
Helen E. Williams, Administrator

***Truro:* Karlaine Place Ltd.**
Affiliated with: Colchester East Hants Health Authority #4
PO Box 691, 104 Pictou Rd., Truro, NS B2N 5E5
Tel: 902-895-5111; *Fax:* 902-893-1513
Number of Beds: 8 beds
Note: residential care facility
Robert Barnhill, Administrator

***Truro:* Townsview Estates**
Affiliated with: Colchester East Hants Health Authority #4
PO Box 1825, 310 Abenaki Rd., Truro, NS B2N 5Z5
Tel: 902-895-9559; *Fax:* 902-893-8094
sheila_peck@hotmail.com
Number of Beds: 85 beds
Note: Residential care facility
Sheila Peck, Administrator

***Truro:* Westside Villa**
Affiliated with: Colchester East Hants Health Authority #4
421 Prince St., Truro, NS B2N 1E6
Tel: 902-893-8463; *Fax:* 902-893-8107
Number of Beds: 26 beds
E. Louise Boyle, Administrator

***Windsor:* Kendall Lane Housing Society**
PO Box 556, Windsor, NS B0N 2T0
Tel: 902-798-4375; *Fax:* 902-798-4378
vpghinc@gmail.com
www.vpgh.ca/klhs.html
Year Founded: 1993
Number of Beds: 6 beds
Note: small option home
Dorothy Blakely, Manager

***Windsor:* Kings Meadows Residence**
RR#1, Windsor, NS B0N 2T0
Tel: 902-798-4657
kingsmeadow@ns.sympatico.ca
Number of Beds: 10 beds
Barbara Campbell, Administrator

***Windsor:* Victoria Park Guest House**
Affiliated with: Capital District Health Authority #9
PO Box 556, 350 King St., Windsor, NS B0N 2T0
Tel: 902-798-4375; *Fax:* 902-798-4378
vpghinc@@gmail.com
www.vpgh.ca
Year Founded: 1989
Number of Beds: 15 beds
Note: Adult residential care facility
Dorothy Blakely, Administrator
Tom Blakely, Administrator

***Wolfville:* Wolfville Elms Residential Care Facility**
705 Main St., Wolfville, NS B4P 2N4
Tel: 902-542-2420; *Fax:* 902-542-1048
wnh.home@ns.sympatico.ca
Number of Beds: 26 beds + 2 respite
Paul MacDonald, Administrator

***Yarmouth:* Glo Estates**
Affiliated with: Southwest Nova District Health Authority #2
36 Grove Rd., 143, Rte. 304, Yarmouth, NS B5A 4J7
Tel: 902-742-7583; *Fax:* 902-742-2463
holson@ns.sympatico.ca
Number of Beds: 12 beds
Evelyn Spurr, Assistant
Hazel Olson, Administrator

***Yarmouth:* Sunset Terrace**
8 James St., Yarmouth, NS B5A 2V1
Tel: 902-742-3322
Janet Doucette, Administration

Nursing Homes

***Antigonish:* R.K. MacDonald Nursing Home**
Affiliated with: Guysborough Antigonish Strait Health Authority #7
64 Pleasant St., Antigonish, NS B2G 1W7
Tel: 902-863-2578; *Fax:* 902-863-4437
lcrocker@rkmacdonald.ca
www.gov.ns.ca/health/
Number of Beds: 108 beds + 1 respite
Lorna Crocker, Administrator

***Cheticamp:* Foyer Père Fiset**
Affiliée à: Cape Breton District Health Authority #8
CP 219, 15092 Cabot Trail, Cheticamp, NS B0E 1H0
Tél: 902-224-2087; *Téléc:* 902-224-1188
www.cbdha.nshealth.ca
Nombre de lits: 60 lits
Betty Ann Aucoin, Administrator

***Glace Bay:* Seaview Manor**
Affiliated with: Cape Breton District Health Authority #8
275 South St., Glace Bay, NS B1A 1W6
Tel: 902-849-7300; *Fax:* 902-849-7401
seaviews@ns.sympatico.ca
www.seaviewmanor.ca
Number of Beds: 101 beds, 2 respite
Catherine Power, Administrator

***Glace Bay:* Taigh Na Mara**
Affiliated with: Cape Breton District Health Authority #8
974 Main St., Glace Bay, NS B1A 4L8
Tel: 902-842-3900; *Fax:* 902-842-3926
Number of Beds: 67 beds
Note: Continuing care for residents & veterans
Sharon Sheppard, Administrator

***Inverness:* Aite Curam**
Affiliated with: Cape Breton District Health Authority #8
PO Box 610, 39 James St., Inverness, NS B0E 1N0
Tel: 902-258-1914; *Fax:* 902-258-3025
www.cbdha.nshealth.ca/HL_AiteCuram.htm
Number of Beds: 11 beds
Note: Part of Inverness Consolidated Memorial Hospital
Clare MacQuarrie, Facility Manager

***New Waterford:* Waterford Heights**
Affiliated with: Cape Breton District Health Authority #8
c/o New Waterford Consolidated Hospital, 716 King St., New Waterford, NS B1H 3Z5
Tel: 902-862-6411; *Fax:* 902-862-8277
Number of Beds: 24 beds
Sharon Sheppard, Administrator

***Pictou:* Shiretown Nursing Home**
Affiliated with: Pictou County District Health Authority #6
PO Box 250, 270 Haliburton Rd., Pictou, NS B0K 1H0
Tel: 902-485-4341; *Fax:* 902-485-9203
bonniel@shiretown.ca
www.shiretown.ca
Number of Beds: 89 beds
Note: Nursing & residential care
Bonnie Linkletter, Administrator
Tammy MacKenzie, Director of Care

***Port Hawkesbury:* Port Hawkesbury Nursing Home**
Affiliated with: Guysborough Antigonish Strait Health Authority #7
2 MacQuarrie Dr. Extension, Port Hawkesbury, NS B9A 3A2
Tel: 902-625-1460; *Fax:* 902-625-3232
www.porthawkesburynursinghome.ca
Number of Beds: 50 beds + 4 respite
Note: Adult residential centre
Leona Wilneff, Administrator

***St Peters:* Richmond Villa**
Affiliated with: Guysborough Antigonish Strait Health Authority #7
PO Box 250, 9361 Pepperell St., St Peters, NS B0E 3B0
Tel: 902-535-3030; *Fax:* 902-535-2256
richmondvilla@ns.sympatico.ca
www.richmondvilla.ca
Number of Beds: 59 nursing home beds, 8 resident care beds
Note: Nursing & residential care centre
Margaret Morrison, Administrator
Heather MacQueen, Director of Care

Mental Health Facilities

Mental Health Hospitals/Facilities

***Dartmouth:* East Coast Forensic Psychiatric Hospital**
Affiliated with: Capital District Health Authority #9
88 Gloria McClusky Ave., Dartmouth, NS B3B 2B8
Tel: 902-460-7300; *Fax:* 902-460-7337
louise.bradley@cdha.nshealth.ca
Number of Beds: 92 beds
Louise Bradley, Director, Forensic Services

***Dartmouth:* Nova Scotia Hospital**
Affiliated with: Capital District Health Authority #9
PO Box 1004, 300 Pleasant St., Dartmouth, NS B2Y 3Z9
Tel: 902-464-3111; *Fax:* 902-464-6032
shelley.peterson@cdha.nshealth.ca (Volunteer services)
www.cdha.nshealth.ca
Note: Specialties: Mental health programs
Linda Judge, Director, Capital District Mental Health Programs

***Halifax:* Metro Community Housing Association**
Tower 1, #215, 7001 Mumford Rd., Halifax, NS B3L 4N9
Tel: 902-453-6444; *Fax:* 902-453-1188
info@mcha.ns.ca
www.mcha.ns.ca
Number of Beds: 165 residential capacity
Note: Specialties: Support & residential services to persons who have experienced mental health difficulties
Cathy Crouse, Executive Director

Special Care Homes

***Glace Bay:* Jones Manor**
Affiliated with: Cape Breton District Health Authority #8
1 Minto St., Glace Bay, NS B1Z 5B2
Tel: 902-849-1605
Number of Beds: 7 beds
Calvin Jones, Administrator

***Kingston:* Tibbetts Home Wilmot**
PO Box 519, 15074 Hwy. #1, Kingston, NS B0P 1R0
Tel: 902-765-6614; *Fax:* 902-765-3807
tibbco2001@yahoo.com
Number of Beds: 25 beds
Wanda Tibbetts, Administrator

Nunavut

Government Departments in Charge

NUNAVUT: Dept. of Health & Social Services
PO Box 1000 1000, 1107 Sivummut Bldg., 3rd Fl., Iqaluit, NU X0A 0H0
Tel: 867-975-5700; *Fax:* 867-975-5705
health@gov.nu.ca
www.gov.nu.ca/health

Regional Health Authorities

***Behchokö:* Tłįchǫ Community Services Agency**
Former Name: Dogrib Community Services Board; Dogrib Divisional
PO Box 5, Behchokö, NW X0E 0Y0
Tel: 867-392-3000; *Fax:* 867-392-3001
tcsa@tlicho.net
www.tlicho.ca/tlichocommunityservices
Year Founded: 2005
Note: Facilities: Rae Lakes Health Centre, Gamètì; Jimmy Erasmus Seniors Home, Rae; Mary Adele Bishop Health Centre, Rae; Tłįchǫ Healing Path Wellness Centre, Rae; Tłįchǫ Healing Path Wellness Centre, Whatì; Lac La Martre Health Centre,

Whatì; Dechi Laoti Health Centre, Wekweètì; Area Covered: Behchokǫ̀; Gamètì; Wekweètì; Whatì, Tłı̨chǫ Region, NWT
Alfonz Nitsiza, Chair
Jim Martin, Chief Executive Officer
jmartin@tlicho.net
Kevin Armstrong, Manager, Finance
karmstrong@tlicho.net
Dave Harnum, Manager, Ambulance
867-392-6075, Fax: 867-392-6612, dharnum@tlicho.net
Ryan Hewlett, Manager, Health Services
Nora Wedzin, Manager, Continuing Care & Independent Living
nwedzin@tlicho.net
Nancy Gibson, Coordinator, Community Health
ngibson@tlicho.net

***Fort Smith:* Fort Smith Health & Social Services Authority (Fort Smi)**
PO Box 1080, Fort Smith, NW X0E 0P0
Tel: 867-872-6200; *Fax:* 867-872-6275
www.hlthss.gov.nt.ca/english/our_system/authorities
Note: Facilities: Fort Smith Health & Social Services Centre; Northern Lights Special Care Home; Polar Crescent Group Home; Sutherland House; Tapwe House; Trailcross Treatment Centre; Fort Smith Wellness Centre. Population Served: 2,466. Area Covered: Southern Northwest Territories, including the Town of Fort Smith, Salt River First Nations, & Métis Nation Local 50
Robert Tordiff, Chief Executive Officer
867-872-6201, Fax: 867-872-6291,
ROBERT_TORDIFF@gov.nt.ca
Natalie Campbell, Director, Quality Assurance & Risk Management
867-872-6237, NATALIE_CAMPBELL@gov.nt.ca
Julie Lys, Director, Patient Services
867-872-6217, JULIE_LYS@gov.nt.ca
Phyllis Mawdsley, Director, Community Services
867-872-6300, PHYLLIS_MAWDSLEY@gov.nt.ca
Suzanne Sihikal, Director, Northern Lights Special Care Home
867-872-6296, SUZANNE_SIHIKAL@gov.nt.ca
Katerina Tsaknaki, Director, Finance
867-872-6235, KATERINA_TSAKNAKI@gov.nt.ca
Linda McDevitt, Officer, Human Resources
867-872-6507, LINDA_MCDEVITT@gov.nt.ca

Hospitals

Hospitals - General

***Dryden:* Dryden Regional Health Centre (DRHC)**
PO Box 3003, 58 Goodall St., Dryden, NU P8N 2Z6
Tel: 807-223-8200; *Fax:* 807-223-2370
TTY: 807-223-8295
www.dh.dryden.on.ca
Number of Beds: 31 acute care beds; 10 chronic / rehabilitation care beds
Note: Hospital Specialties: Emergency services; Diagnostic imaging (807-223-8253); Acute care; Obstetrics; Critical care; Mental health & addiction services (807-223-6678); Occupational therapy (807-223-8214); Physiotherapy (807-223-8259); Sexual assault & domestic violence services (807-223-7427); Diabetes education (807-223-8208); Counselling; Chronic care
Dr. Karen Mazurski, Chief of Staff
Dr. Mark Dahmer, Chief, Emergency
Dr. Steven Viherjoki, Chief, Inpatient Services
Siobain Moore, Administrative Director, Workplace Culture & Organizational Health
807-223-8829, smoore@dh.dryden.on.ca

***Iqaluit:* Baffin Regional Hospital**
PO Box 200, Iqaluit, NU X0A 0H0
Tel: 867-979-7300; *Fax:* 867-979-7347
Number of Beds: 25 inpatient beds; 19 acute care adult beds; 6 pediatric beds; 8 newborn bassinets
Note: Hospital Specialties: Emergency & outpatient department; X-ray department; Laboratory; Acute care; Pediatrics

***Iqaluit:* Qikiqtani General Hospital**
PO Box 1000 1040, Iqaluit, NU X0A 0H0
Tel: 867-975-8600
Number of Beds: 35 beds
Note: Birthing rooms, surgery, diagnostic imaging & lab, state-of-the-art community health care
Katherine Walters, Director

Community Health Centres

Community Health Care Centres

***Arctic Bay:* Arctic Bay Health Centre**
PO Box 60, Arctic Bay, NU X0A 0A0
Tel: 867-439-8816; *Fax:* 867-439-8315
Gail Redpath, Nurse Manager

***Arviat:* Arviat Health Centre**
General Delivery, Arviat, NU X0C 0E0
Tel: 867-857-2816; *Fax:* 867-857-2980
Sandy Ranahan, Nurse Manager

***Baker Lake:* Baker Lake Health Centre**
PO Box 120, Baker Lake, NU X0C 0A0
Tel: 867-793-2816; *Fax:* 867-793-2812
Donna Brown, Nurse Manager

***Cambridge Bay:* Cambridge Bay Health Centre**
PO Box 83, Cambridge Bay, NU X0E 0C0
Tel: 867-983-2531; *Fax:* 867-983-2262
Number of Beds: 2 beds

***Cape Dorset:* Cape Dorset Health Centre**
PO Box 40, Cape Dorset, NU X0A 0C0
Tel: 867-897-8820; *Fax:* 867-897-8914

***Chesterfield Inlet:* Chesterfield Inlet Health Centre**
PO Box 9, Chesterfield Inlet, NU X0C 0B0
Tel: 867-898-9968; *Fax:* 867-898-9122

***Clyde River:* Clyde River Health Centre**
PO Box 180, Clyde River, NU X0A 0E0
Tel: 867-924-6377; *Fax:* 867-924-6244

***Coral Harbour:* Coral Harbour Health Centre**
PO Box 120, Coral Harbour, NU X0C 0C0
Tel: 867-925-9916; *Fax:* 867-925-8380

***Gjoa Haven:* Gjoa Haven Haputtit Health Centre**
General Delivery, Gjoa Haven, NU X0E 1J0
Tel: 867-360-7441; *Fax:* 867-360-6110

***Grise Fjord:* Grise Fjord Health Centre**
PO Box 81, Grise Fjord, NU X0A 0J0
Tel: 867-980-9923; *Fax:* 867-980-9067

***Hall Beach:* Hall Beach Health Centre**
General Delivery, Hall Beach, NU X0A 0K0
Tel: 867-928-8827; *Fax:* 867-928-8847

***Igloolik:* Igloolik Health Centre**
PO Box 240, Igloolik, NU X0A 0L0
Tel: 867-934-8837; *Fax:* 867-934-8901

***Iqaluit:* Iqaluit Public Health Clinic**
PO Box 200, Iqaluit, NU X0A 0H0
Tel: 867-979-5306; *Fax:* 867-979-4830

***Kimmirut:* Kimmirut Health Centre**
PO Box 30, Kimmirut, NU X0A 0N0
Tel: 867-939-2217; *Fax:* 867-939-2068

***Kugaaruk:* St. Theresa Kugaaruk Health Centre**
General Delivery, Kugaaruk, NU X0E 1K0
Tel: 867-769-6441; *Fax:* 867-769-6059

***Kugluktuk:* Kugluktuk Health Centre**
General Delivery, Kugluktuk, NU X0E 0E0
Tel: 867-982-4531; *Fax:* 867-982-3115

***Pangnirtung:* Pangnirtung Health Centre**
PO Box 454, Pangnirtung, NU X0A 0R0
Tel: 867-473-8977; *Fax:* 867-473-8519
Note: Specialty: General health care by registered nurses; Individual counseling & referral; Massage therapy; Workshops for stress relief

***Pond Inlet:* Pond Inlet Health Centre**
PO Box 216, Pond Inlet, NU X0A 0S0
Tel: 867-899-8840; *Fax:* 867-899-8997
Year Founded: 2004
Note: Comprehensive health care. Number of employees: 20
Di Schulze, Supervisor, Health & Community Programs

***Qikiqtarjuaq:* Qikiqtarjuaq Health Centre**
PO Box 911, Qikiqtarjuaq, NU X0A 0B0
Tel: 867-927-8916; *Fax:* 867-927-8217

***Rankin Inlet:* Rankin Inlet Health Centre**
Bag 008, Rankin Inlet, NU X0C 0G0
Tel: 867-645-2816; *Fax:* 867-645-2688
gbecker@auroranet.nt.ca

***Repulse Bay:* Repulse Bay Health Centre**
General Delivery, Repulse Bay, NU X0C 0H0
Tel: 867-462-9916; *Fax:* 867-462-4212
Number of Beds: 2 beds

***Resolute:* Resolute Health Centre**
PO Box 180, Resolute, NU X0A 0V0
Tel: 867-252-3844; *Fax:* 867-252-3601

***Sanikiluaq:* Sanikiluaq Health Centre**
PO Box 145, Sanikiluaq, NU X0A 0W0
Tel: 867-266-8965; *Fax:* 867-266-8802
http://webmail.gov.nu.ca
Note: Provides general health care, counseling & referral. Services in Inuktitut & English
Joanne Watson, Nurse in Charge

***Taloyoak:* Taloyoak Judy Hill Memorial Health Centre**
General Delivery, Taloyoak, NU X0E 1B0
Tel: 867-561-5111

***Whale Cove:* Whale Cove Health Centre**
PO Box 3, Whale Cove, NU X0C 0J0
Tel: 867-896-9916; *Fax:* 867-896-9115

Nursing Stations

***Broughton Island:* Qikiqtarjuaq Health Centre**
PO Box 911, Broughton Island, NU X0A 0B0
Tel: 867-927-8916; *Fax:* 867-927-8217
Christine Kellett, Nursing Supervisor

Long Term/Retirement Care

Long Term Care Facilities

***Arviat:* Andy Aulatjut Elders' Centre**
PO Box 147, Arviat, NU X0C 0E0
Tel: 867-857-2667; *Fax:* 867-857-2668

***Chesterfield Inlet:* St. Therese Home**
PO Box 1, Chesterfield Inlet, NU X0C 0B0
Tel: 867-898-9917; *Fax:* 867-898-9080
Note: Homecare facility

***Iqaluit:* Iqaluit Elders' Facility**
Pairijait Tigumivik Society, PO Box 640, Iqaluit, NU X0A 0H0
Tel: 867-979-7408; *Fax:* 867-979-8864

Mental Health Facilities

Mental Health Hospitals/Facilities

***Iqaluit:* Akausisarvik Mental Health Facilty**
Baffin Hospital, PO Box 1000 1048, Iqaluit, NU X0A 0H0
Tel: 867-979-7379
Number of Beds: 13 beds
Katherine Walters, Director, Hospital Services

Ontario

Government Departments in Charge

ONTARIO: Ministry of Health & Long-Term Care
Hepburn Block, Queen's Park, 80 Grosvenor St., 10th Fl., Toronto, ON M7A 1S2
Tel: 416-327-4327; *Fax:* 416-314-8721
Toll-Free: 800-268-1153
www.health.gov.on.ca

Regional Health Authorities

Ajax: Central East Local Health Integration Network (Central)
Harwood Plaza, #204A, 314 Harwood Ave. South, Ajax, ON L1S 2J1
Tel: 905-427-5497; Fax: 905-427-9659
Toll-Free: 1-866-804-5446
centraleast@lhins.on.ca
www.centraleastlhin.on.ca
Note: Population Served: 1,400,000
Deborah Hammons, Chief Executive Officer
Foster Loucks, Chair
Paul Barker, Senior Director, Performance, Contracts, & Allocation
James Meloche, Senior Director, Planning, Integration & Community Engagement

Belleville: South East Local Health Integration Network
#2, 48 Dundas St. West, Belleville, ON K8P 1A3
Tel: 613-967-0196; Toll-Free: 866-831-5446
Paul Huras, CEO
Georgina Thompson, Chair

Brampton: Central West Local Health Integration Network (Central)
RLISS du Centre-Ouest
#300, 8 Nelson St. West, Brampton, ON L6X 4J2
Tel: 905-455-1281
centralwest@lhins.on.ca
www.centralwestlhin.on.ca
Note: Facilities: 23 long term care homes; 13 community support services; 8 mental health & addiction agencies; 2 hospitals (4 sites); 2 community health centres; 1 community care access centre. Population Served: 800,144
Mimi Lowi-Young, Chief Executive Officer
905-455-1281, ext. 2, Mimi.lowi-young@lhins.on.ca
Joe McReynolds, Chair
David Colgan, Senior Director, Planning, Integration, & Community Development
Pat Stoddart, Senior Director, Performance Contract & Allocation
Chuck Ferguson, Director, Communications & Community Engagement
905-455-1281, ext. 2, chuck.ferguson@lhins.on.ca

Chatham: Erie St. Clair Local Health Integration Network (Erie St.)
RLISS d'Érié St. Clair
180 Riverview Dr., Chatham, ON N7M 5Z8
Tel: 519-351-5677; Fax: 519-351-9672
Toll-Free: 1-866-231-5446
eriestclairlhin@lhins.on.ca
www.eriestclairlhin.on.ca
Note: Population Served: 649,000+. Area Served: Regions of Chatham-Kent, Sarnia / Lambton, & Windsor / Essex
Gary Switzer, Chief Executive Officer
1-866-231-5446, ext., gary.switzer@lhins.on.ca
Mina Grossman-Ianni, Chair
mailto:mina.grossman-ianni@lhins.on.
Ralph Ganter, Senior Director, Planning & Integration
1-866-231-5446, ext., ralph.ganter@lhins.on.ca
Brad Keeler, Senior Director, Performance, Contracts, & Allocation
1-866-231-5446, ext., brad.keeler@lhins.on.ca
Shannon Sasseville, Director, Communications & Community Engagement
1-866-231-5446, ext., shannon.sasseville@lhins.on.ca
Dr. Eli Malus, Lead, Critical Care
519-973-4411, ext. 3, eli.malus@hdgh.org
David Ng, Lead, Emergency Department
519-973-4411, ext. 3, dng14@cogeco.ca
Ruth Augi, Corporate Coordinator
1-866-231-5446, ext., ruth.augi@lhins.on.ca
Matthew Little, Corporate Controller; Manager, Business Support
1-866-231-5446, ext., matthew.little@lhins.on.ca

Grimsby: Hamilton Niagara Haldimand Brant Local Health Integration Network (HNHB LHI)
RLISS de Hamilton Niagara Haldimand Brant
264 Main St. East, Grimsby, ON L3M 1P8
Tel: 905-945-4930; Fax: 905-945-1992
Toll-Free: 1-866-363-5446
hamiltonniagarahaldimandbrant@lhins.on.ca
www.hnhblhin.on.ca
Note: Facilities: 88 long term care homes; 10 hospitals (23 hospital sites); 8 community health centres (10 sites); 1 community care access centre. Programs: 81 community support services; 50 community mental health & addictions programs. Area Served: Brant, Burlington, Haldimand, Hamilton, Niagara, Norfolk
Pat Mandy, Chief Executive Officer
905-945-4930, ext. 4, pat.mandy@lhins.on.ca
Juanita Gledhill, Chair
Marion Emo, Senior Director, Planning, Integration, & Community Engagement
905-945-4930, ext. 4, marion.emo@lhins.on.ca
Alan Iskiw, Senior Director, Performance, Contract, & Allocation
905-945-4930, ext. 4, alan.iskiw@lhins.on.ca
Patricia Ciccarelli, Team Lead, Funding & Allocation
905.945.4930, ext. 4, patricia.ciccarelli@lhins.on.ca
Jennifer Everson, Physician Lead, Planning & Integration
905.945.4930, ext. 4, jennifer.everson@lhins.on.ca
Trish Nelson, Team Lead, Communications
905-945-4930, ext. 4, trish.nelson@lhins.on.ca
Rosalind Tarrant, Team Lead, Performance & Integration
905-945-4930, ext. 4, rosalind.tarrant@lhins.on.ca

Guelph: Waterloo Wellington Local Health Integration Network
#212, 55 Wyndham St. North, Guelph, ON N1H 7T8
Tel: 519-822-6208; Fax: 519-822-5807
Toll-Free: 866-306-5446
waterloowellington@lhins.on.ca
www.waterloowellingtonlhin.on.ca
Note: Not-for-profit organization that works to plan, integrate, and fund local health services
Sandra Hanmer, CEO
Kathryn Durst, Chair

London: South West Local Health Integration Network
#700, 201 Queens Ave., London, ON N6A 1J1
Tel: 519-672-0445; Toll-Free: 866-294-5446
Tony Woolgar, CEO
Norm Gamble, Chair

Markham: Central Local Health Integration Network (Central)
#210, 140 Allstate Pkwy., Markham, ON L3R 5Y8
Tel: 905-948-1872; Fax: 905-948-8011
Toll-Free: 1-866-392-5446
Central@lhins.on.ca
www.centrallhin.on.ca
Note: Population Served: 1,600,000
Kim Baker, Chief Executive Officer
Kenneth A. Morrison, Chair
Shaukat Moloo, Senior Director, Performance, Contracts, & Allocations
Victoria van Hemert, Senior Director, Planning, Integration, &Community Engagement
Naj Hassam, Director, Performance & Funding, Hospital Programs
Frances Murphy, Director, Clinical Services Development & Organization
Frances.Murphy@lhins.on.ca
Thomas O'Shaughnessy, Director, System Integration & Engagement
Kate Blackwell, Coordinator, Communications
kate.blackwell@lhins.on.ca
Peter Sit, Controller
peter.sit@lhins.on.ca

North Bay: North East Local Health Integration Network
555 Oak St. East, 3rd Fl., North Bay, ON P1B 8E3
Tel: 705-840-2872; Toll-Free: 866-906-5446
www.nelhin.on.ca
Note: Provides services to over 560,000 people across 400,000 square kilometers
Dave Murray, CEO
Mathilde Gravelle, Chair

Oakville: Mississauga Halton Local Health Integration Network (MH LHIN)
#500, 700 Dorval Dr., Oakville, ON L6K 3V3
Tel: 905-337-7131; Fax: 905-337-8330
Toll-Free: 866-371-5446
mississaugahalton@lhins.on.ca
www.mississaugahaltonlhin.on.ca
Michael Fenn, CEO
John Magill, Chair

Orillia: North Simcoe Muskoka Local Health Integration Network
#127-130, 210 Memorial Ave., Orillia, ON L3V 7V1
Tel: 705-326-7750; Fax: 705-326-1392
Toll-Free: 866-903-5446
northsimcoemuskoka@lhins.on.ca
www.nsmlhin.on.ca
Note: Plans and funds health services for over 400,000 people in the District of Muskoka, County of Simcoe, and Grey County
Jean Trimnell, CEO
Ruben Rosen, Chair

Ottawa: Champlain Local Health Integration Network (Champlai)
RLISS de Champlain
#204, 1900 City Park Dr., Ottawa, ON K1J 1A3
Tel: 613-747-6784; Fax: 613-747-6519
Toll-Free: 1-866-902-5446
champlain@lhins.on.ca
www.champlainlhin.on.ca; www.rlisschamplain.on.ca
Year Founded: 2005
Note: Facilities: 100+ community support services, including mental health & addictions agencies; 61 long-term care homes; 21 hospitals; 7 community health centres plus satellites, 1 community care access centre. Population Served: 1,147,000. Area Served: Renfrew County; City of Ottawa; Prescott & Russell; Stormont; Dundas & Glengarry; North Grenville; four parts of North Lanark
Dr. Robert Cushman, Chief Executive Officer
613-747-6784
Michael LeMay, Board Chair
613-747-3201, Michael.LeMay@lhins.on.ca
Glenn Alexander, Chief Information Officer
613-747-3244, Glenn.Alexander@lhins.on.ca
Suzanne Dionne, Senior Director, Performance, Contract, & Allocation
Chantale LeClerc, Senior Director, Planning, Integration, & Community Engagement
Amir Afkham, Senior Manager, Projects
613-747-3235, Amir.Afkham@lhins.on.ca

Thunder Bay: North West Local Health Integration Network
#201, 975 Alloy Dr., Thunder Bay, ON P7B 5Z8
Tel: 807-684-9425; Fax: 807-684-9533
Toll-Free: 866-907-5446
northwest@lhins.on.ca.
www.northwestlhin.on.ca
Note: Works with healthcare providers, communities and the public to set prioritiesand plan health services in Northwestern Ontario
Gwen DuBois-Wing, CEO
John Whitfield, Chair

Toronto: Toronto Central Local Health Integration Network (LHIN)
#201, 425 Bloor St. East, Toronto, ON M4W 3R4
Tel: 416-921-7453; Fax: 416-921-0117
Toll-Free: 866-383-5446
torontocentral@lhins.on.ca
www.torontocentrallhin.on.ca
Note: Specialties: Planning, integrating, & funding local health services
Barry Monaghan, CEO
Penny Thomsen, Chair

Hospitals - General

Chapleau: Chapleau Health Services (SSCHS)
Services de sante de Chapleau
6 Broomhead Rd., Chapleau, ON P0M 1K0
Tel: 705-864-1520; Fax: 705-864-0449
chapleauhr@sschs.ca
Number of Beds: 14 acute care beds at Chapleau General Hospital; 19 long term care beds, 4 chronic care beds, & 2 respite beds at the Bignucolo Residence; 23 apartmen
Note: Specialties: Emergency services; Acute care; Occupational therapy; Rehabilitation services; Adult mental health services; Counselling; Services for the for the developmentally disabled; Diabetes education; Community services, such as Meals on Wheels, home support services, & Lifeline; Operation of a nursing station in Foleyet; Long term care; Chronic care; Respite care
Gail Bignucolo, Chief Executive Officer
705-864-3050
Robin Greer, Manager, Diabetes Education
rgreer@sschs.ca

Hospitals

Hospitals - General

Ajax: Rouge Valley Ajax & Pickering
Affiliated with: Rouge Valley Health System
580 Harwood Ave. South, Ajax, ON L1S 2J4
Tel: 905-683-2320; Fax: 905-683-2618
www.rougevalley.ca
Number of Beds: 130 beds
Note: Emergency, cancer care, cardiac care, continuing care & rehabilitation, diagnostic imaging, maternal, paediatrics, surgery

Rik Ganderton, President/CEO, RVHS
boardofdirectors@rougevalley.ca
David Brazeau, Director, RVHS, Public Affairs & Community Relations
647-294-8885, dbrazeau@rougevalley.ca

Alexandria: Glengarry Memorial Hospital
20260 County Road 43, Alexandria, ON K0C 1A0
Tel: 613-525-2222; *Fax:* 613-525-4515
www.hgmh.on.ca
Number of Beds: 37 beds
Linda Morrow, CEO

Alliston: Stevenson Memorial Hospital (SMH)
PO Box 4000, 200 Fletcher Cres., Alliston, ON L9R 1W7
Tel: 705-435-6281; *Fax:* 705-434-5138
information@smhosp.on.ca
www.smhosp.on.ca
Number of Beds: 36 beds
Note: Specialties: Acute care; Day surgery; Diagnostic imaging; Ambulatory care clinics; Obstetrics / Gynaecology
Edward Takacs, President/CEO

Almonte: Almonte General Hospital (AGH)
75 Spring St., Almonte, ON K0A 1A0
Tel: 613-256-2500; *Fax:* 613-256-8549
tmclelland@agh-fvm.com
www.almontegeneral.com
Note: Hospital Specialties: Emergency services; Diagnostic services; Acute care; Physiotherapy
Ray K. Timmons, Executive Director
613-256-2514, rtimmons@agh-fvm.com
Donna Leafloor, Assistant Executive Director, Patient & Resident Services
dleafloor@agh-fvm.com
Randy Shaw, Assistant Executive Director, Support Services
rshaw@agh-fvm.com
Jamie Welsford, Assistant Executive Director, Finance & Information Technology
jwelsford@agh-fvm.com
Rena L. Bowen, Director, Special Services
rbowen@agh-fvm.com
Michael Doyle, Director, Human Resources
mdoyle@agh-fvm.com
Beth Lepack, Director, Medical Records
blepack@agh-fvm.com
Nina Mukerjee, Director, Physiotherapy
nmukerjee@agh-fvm.com
Pam Murphy, Director, Long-Term Care
pmurphy@agh-fvm.com

Arnprior: Arnprior & District Memorial Hospital
350 John St. North, Arnprior, ON K7S 2P6
Tel: 613-623-3166; *Fax:* 613-623-4844
lab@arnpriorhospital.com
www.arnpriorhospital.com
Note: Hospital Specialties: Emergency services; Diagnostic imaging; Acute care; Ontario Breast Screening Program; Diabetes clinic; Physiotherapy; Speech therapy; Urotherapy; Palliative care
Eric Hanna, Chief Executive Officer
eric.hanna@arnpriorhospital.com
Leah Levesque, Director, Patient & Resident Services
Michelle Lewis, Director, Human Resources
michelle.lewis@arnpriorhospital.com
Tim Sonnenburg, Director, Finance & Support Services
tim.sonnenburg@arnpriorhospital.com
Wendy Knechtel, Manager, Public Relations & Fundraising
wknechtel@arnpriorhospital.com
Cindy O'Greysik, Manager, Health Records
cindy.ogreysik@arnpriorhospital.com
Karen Graham, Supervisor, Food Services
karen.graham@arnpriorhospital.com

Atikokan: Atikokan General Hospital
120 Dorothy St., Atikokan, ON P0T 1C0
Tel: 807-597-4215; *Fax:* 807-597-4305 (
www.aghospital.on.ca
Number of Beds: 41 beds
Note: Hospital services: Emergency services; Diagnostic services; Acute care; Cardiac care; Rehabilitation services; Counselling & addictions program; Diabetic counselling; Complex continuing care; Long-term care; Number of Employees: 100
Robert G. Wilson, Chief Executive Officer
robert.wilson@aghospital.on.ca
Kim Cross, Assistant Executive Director, Finance
kim.cross@aghospital.on.ca
Wayne Smith, Assistant Executive Director, Patient Care Services
wayne.smith@aghospital.on.ca
Marie Cornell, Manager, Lab
marie.cornell@aghospital.on.ca
Bridget Davidson, Manager, Health Records & Privacy
bridget.davidson@aghospital.on.ca
Donna Mallard, Nurse, Diabetic Health
donna.mallard@aghospital.on.ca

Attawapiskat: James Bay General Hospital
General Delivery, Attawapiskat, ON P0L 1A0
Tel: 705-997-2150; *Fax:* 705-997-2121
hr@jbgh.org
www.jbgh.org
Number of Beds: 16 beds
Cecile Rose, Wing Director

Bancroft: Quinte Health Care North Hastings
Quinte Health Care
Former Name: North Hastings District Hospital
PO Box 157, 1-H Manor Lane, Bancroft, ON K0L 1C0
Tel: 613-332-2825; *Fax:* 613-332-3847
www.qhc.on.ca/Default.aspx?cid=275&lang=1
Number of Beds: 6 beds
Note: Primary healthcare facility; acute care/emergency; dialysis unit
Pat Tresierra, Interim Site Administrator

Barrie: Royal Victoria Hospital
201 Georgian Dr., Barrie, ON L4M 6M2
Tel: 705-728-9802; *Fax:* 705-726-0822
TTY: 705-739-5618
webmaster@rvh.on.ca
www.rvh.on.ca
Number of Beds: 299 beds
Note: Comprehensive services, including emergency, cardiology, intensive care unit, renal services, chronic disease management, imaging (CT scans, MRIs, mammograms, BMDs, ultrasound, angiography); specializing in cancer care, surgical services, critical care, mental health rehabilitation services, as well as women and children's programs; 280 physicians, staff of 2,300.
Janice Skot, President; CEO
Laura Freeman, Senior Vice-President; CFO
Sandy McFarlane, Vice-President; Chief Nursing Executive, Patient Programs

Barry's Bay: St. Francis Memorial Hospital
PO Box 129, 7 St. Francis Memorial Dr., Barry's Bay, ON K0J 1B0
Tel: 613-756-3044; *Fax:* 613-756-0106
www.sfmhosp.com
Year Founded: 1960
Number of Beds: 27 beds (13 continuing care beds, 14 active care beds)
Note: A comprehensive care facility with services including emergency, complex continuing care, physiotherapy, dialysis, diagnostic imaging (ultrasound, mammography, bone densitometry), holter monitor, respirology, diabetic clinic, foot care clinic, general surgery, ear, nose & throat, mental health, orthotist. Private, semi-private and ward rooms are available.
Mr. Randy Penney, CEO
Mr. Jeremy Stevenson, COO
Ms. Joanne Pecarskie, Executive Assistant
pecarskiej@sfmhosp.com
Ms. Darlene Sernoskie, Director, Operations
Ms. Joan Kuiack, Director, Patient Care Services

Belleville: Quinte Health Care Belleville General
Quinte Health Care
265 Dundas St. East, Belleville, ON K8N 5A9
Tel: 613-969-7400; *Fax:* 613-968-8234
www.qhc.on.ca/Default.aspx?cid=273&lang=1
Year Founded: 1886
Number of Beds: 192 beds
Note: Emergency, cardiology, children's treatment centre, intensive care, obstetrics, oncology, outpatient clinics, orthopaedics, psychiatry/mental health services, rehabilitation, radiology, surgical services, District Stroke Centre
Ms. Mary Clare Egberts, President; CEO, Quinte Health Care
Dr. Mohamed Gaber, Chief of Staff

Blind River: Blind River District Health Centre (BRDHC)
Pavillion Santé du District de Blind River
Former Name: Robb Hospital; St. Joseph's General Hospital
525 Causley St., Blind River, ON P0R 1B0
Tel: 705-356-2265; *Fax:* 705-356-1220
webinfo@brdhc.on.ca
www.brdhc.on.ca
Year Founded: 1928
Number of Beds: 16 acute care beds
Note: Hospital Specialties: Emergency services; Acute care; Diagnostic imaging; Medical laboratory services; Long term care; Health promotion; Physiotherapy; Diabetes education; Dietician services; Social work; Palliative care
Gaston Lavigne, Chief Executive Officer
705-356-2265, ext. 2, glavigne@brdhc.on.ca
Dr. Chris Barnes, Chief of Staff
705-356-1666, cstjules@brdhc.on.ca
Mary Ellen Luukkonen, Chief Nursing Officer; Director, Clinical Services
705-356-2265, ext. 2, mluukkonen@brdhc.on.ca
Jennifer Stanton Smith, Chief Financial Officer
705-356-2265, ext. 2, jsmith@brdhc.on.ca
Dan Lewis, Director, Environmental Services
705-356-2265, ext., dlewis@brdhc.on.ca

Bowmanville: Lakeridge Health Corporation Bowmanville Site
47 Liberty St. South, Bowmanville, ON L1C 2N4
Tel: 905-623-3331; *Fax:* 905-623-0681
www.lakeridgehealth.on.ca
Number of Beds: 686 beds
C. Kooy, COO

Bracebridge: Muskoka Algonquin Healthcare - South Muskoka Memorial Hospital Site
Affiliated with: Muskoka Algonquin Healthcare
Also Known As: South Muskoka Memorial Hospital
75 Ann St., Bracebridge, ON P1L 2E4
Tel: 705-645-4400; *Fax:* 705-645-4594
info@mahc.ca
www.mahc.ca/Content.cfm?C=6169&SC=1&SCM=0&MI=4181&L1M=4150
Number of Beds: 75 beds
Note: Services include emergency, intensive care unit, surgery, endoscopy/gastroenterology, urology, ophthamology, oncology, obstetrics, antenatal, paediatrics, diabetes centre, social work, occupational therapy, speech/language therapy, pathology, complex continuing care, laboratory services, diagnostic imaging (radiography, tomography, ultrasound, bone densitometry, mammography), cardio-respiratory services, pharmacy
Mr. Barry Monaghan, CEO, MAHC
barry.monaghan@mahc.ca
Dr. David Mathies, Chief of Staff, MAHC
liz.parrott@mahc.ca
Ms. Bev McFarlane, Chief Nursing Officer, MAHC
bev.mcfarlane@mahc.ca

Brampton: William Osler Health Centre - Brampton Civic Hospital Campus
2100 Bovaird Dr. East, Brampton, ON L6R 3J7
Tel: 905-494-2120
www.williamoslerhc.on.ca
Year Founded: 2007
Number of Beds: 479
Note: Comprehensive health care. The William Osler Health Centre is comprised of the Brampton Civic Hospital, Etobicoke General, & the Peel Memorial Hospital (currently in re-development)
Ken White, Supervisor

Brantford: Brantford General Hospital Site
Brant Community Healthcare System
200 Terrace Hill St., Brantford, ON N3R 1G9
Tel: 519-752-7871
www.bchsys.org
Year Founded: 1885
Number of Beds: 300+ beds
Note: Hospital Specialties: Emergency medicine; Acute care; Critical care; Surgery; Ambulatory care; Obstetrics; Paediatrics; Brant Community Cancer Clinic; S.C. Johnson Dialysis Clinic; Mental health; Gynaecology; Number of Employees: 1,282 (175 physicians & 26 members of the Department of Dentistry)
James Hornell, President; Chief Executive Officer, Brant Community Healthcare System
519-751-5500
Lina Rinaldi, Vice-President, Patient Services
519-751-5544. ext. 2
Charmaine Roye, Chief, Medical Staff
519-751-5544, ext. 2
David Cameron, Director, Medical Affairs
519-751-5544, ext. 2
Patricia Debrusk, Director, Surgical & Ambulatory Services
519-751-5544, ext. 2
Diane Draper, Director, Critical Care, Maternal / Child Care, Dialysis, Med
519-751-5544, ext. 4
Don Manning, Director, Diagnostic Services
519-751-5544, ext. 2
Heather Riddell, Director, Emergency Services & Urgent Care
519-751-5544, ext. 2
Terry Dalimonte, Manager, Dialysis, Diabetic Education, Paediatrics, & Ma
519-751-5544, ext. 4
Robert Davidson, Manager, Human Resources
519-751-5544, ext. 2

Jill Randall, Manager, Critical Care
519-751-5544, ext. 2

Brockville: Brockville General Hospital (BGH)
75 Charles St., Brockville, ON K6V 1S8
Tel: 613-345-5649; *Fax:* 613-345-8336
www.bgh-on.ca

Year Founded: 1889
Number of Beds: 141 beds
Note: Hospital Specialties: Emergency services; Diagnostic services; Laboratory services; Acute care; Child development program; Rehabilitation services, including physiotherapy, occupational therapy, & speech therapy; Respiratory therapy; Stroke prevention clinic; Ontario breast screening clinic; Pain clinic; Complex continuing care; Palliative care
Hugh Bates, Chair
chair.of.the.board@bgh-on.ca
Ray Marshall, President; Chief Executive Officer
marra@bgh-on.ca
Dr. Robert Beveridge, Chief, Medical Staff
bevro@bgh-on.ca
Heather Crawford, Chief Nursing Executive; Vice-President, Clinical Services
Maggie Wheeler, Officer, Communications
613-345-5649, ext. 1

Burk's Falls: Burk's Falls & District Health Centre
Affiliated with: Muskoka Algonquin Healthcare
Former Name: Almaguin Health Centre
PO Box 520, 150 Huston St., Burk's Falls, ON P0A 1C0
Tel: 705-382-2900; *Fax:* 705-382-2257
Toll-Free: 1-800-661-2900
info@mahc.ca
www.mahc.ca

Number of Beds: 7 sub-acute care beds
Note: Specialties: Physiotherapy; Nutritional counselling; Palliative care
Barry Monaghan, Chief Executive Officer, Muskoka Algonquin Healthcare
705-789-0022, ext. 2, barry.monaghan@mahc.ca

Burlington: Joseph Brant Memorial Hospital
1230 North Shore Blvd., Burlington, ON L7R 4C4
Tel: 905-632-3730; *Fax:* 905-336-6480
corporatecommunications@jbmh.com
www.jbmh.com

Number of Beds: 285 beds
Don Scott, President/CEO

Cambridge: Cambridge Memorial Hospital
Former Name: South Waterloo Memorial Hospital
700 Coronation Blvd., Cambridge, ON N1R 3G2
Tel: 519-621-2330; *Fax:* 519-740-4938
TTY: 519-621-9180
information@cmh.org; patientrelations@cmh.org (Patient relations)
www.cmh.org

Year Founded: 1953
Note: Hospital Specialties: Emergency services; Surgical services; Women's & Children's Services; Cardio Respiratory Unit; Oncology; Rehabilitation; Palliative care; Number of Employees: 1,200 (283 medical staff)
Patrick Gaskin, Chief Executive Officer
519-621-2330, ext. 2
Dr. Michael Lawrie, Chief, Staff
519-621-2330, ext. 2
Katrina Power, Chief Finance Officer
519-621-2330, ext. 2
Susan Gregoroff, Chief Nursing Executive; Vice-President, Clinical Programs
519-621-2330, ext. 2
Ann Bartlett, Director, Patient Services
519-621-2330, ext. 3
Karen Anderson Keith, Program Manager, Mental Health
519-621-2330, ext. 3
Charles Bauman, Program Manager, Palliative Care, Rehabilitation & Oncology
519-621-2330, ext. 5, Fax: 519-740-4950
Alan Clay, Program Manager, Public Affairs & Communications
519-621-2330, ext. 2
Susan Harris-Howe, Program Manager, Emergency
519-621-2330, ext. 2
Scott Hutchings, Program Manager, ICU & Medicine
519-621-2330, ext. 5
Ruth McKinley, Program Manager, Diagnostic Imaging
519-621-2330, ext. 2
Deb Snider, Program Manager, Women's & Children's Health

Campbellford: Campbellford Memorial Hospital (CMH)
146 Oliver Rd., Campbellford, ON K0L 1L0
Tel: 705-653-1140; *Fax:* 705-653-4371 (ltinney@cmh.ca (The Office of the Board of Directors)
www.cmh.ca

Number of Beds: 34 beds
Note: Hospital Specialties: Emergency services; Radiology (705-653-1140, ext. 2125); Laboratory services; Ambulatory care (705-653-1140, ext. 2100); Acute care; Occupational therapy (705-653-1140, ext. 2111); Ontario Breast Screening Program (705-653-3104); Nutrition clinic (705-653-1140, ext. 2132)
Derek Nice, Chair
Kelly Isfan, President; Chief Executive Officer
Dr. Paul Williams, Chief, Staff
Dr. Norm Bartlett, Chief, Emergency Services
Dr. Glenn Gibson, President, Medical Staff

Carleton Place: Carleton Place & District Memorial Hospital
211 Lake Ave. East, Carleton Place, ON K7C 1J4
Tel: 613-257-2200; *Fax:* 613-257-3026
info@carletonplacehosp.com
www.carletonplacehospital.ca

Note: Hospital Specialties: Diagnostic imaging (613-253-3804); Laboratory services (613-257-2200, ext. 152); Physiotherapy (613-253-3822); Speech & language (613-253-3823)
Dr. Dewar Burnett, Chair
Dr. Martin White, Chief, Staff
Dr. Roger Drake, President, Medical Staff
Toni Surko, Secretary to the Board
613-253-3825, tsurko@carletonplacehosp.com

Chatham: Chatham-Kent Health Alliance
Former Name: Public General Hospital Society of Chatham
PO Box 2030, 80 Grand Ave. W., Chatham, ON N7M 5L9
Tel: 519-352-6400; *Fax:* 519-436-2543
www.ckha.on.ca

Number of Beds: 300 beds
Colin Patey, President/CEO

Chatham: Chatham-Kent Health Alliance (CKHA)
PO Box 2030, 80 Grand Ave. West, Chatham, ON N7M 5L9
Tel: 519-352-6400
howarewedoing@ckha.on.ca
www.ckha.on.ca

Year Founded: 1998
Number of Beds: 300 beds
Note: Hospital Specialties: Emergency services; District Stroke Centre; Sexual Assault Treatment Centre; Diagnostic imaging; Ontario Breast Screening Program; Surgery; Orthopedics; Women & children's health care services; Asthma Care Centre; Rehabilitation services, including physiotherapy & occupational therapy; Mental health services, including an Early Psychosis Intervention Program for youth; Dialysis; Post coronary classes; Diabetes education; Nutritional counselling; Complex continuing care; Number of Employees: 1,300
Colin Patey, President; Chief Executive Officer,
cpatey@ckha.on.ca
Anthony DiCaita, Chief Financial Officer& Vice-President
adicaita@ckha.on.ca
Shona Elliott, Chief Human Resource Officer& Vice-President
selliott@ckha.on.ca
Crystal Houze, Chief Nursing Executive; Chief Health Professions
chouze@ckha.on.ca
Dr. Gary Tithecott, Chief of Staff
chiefofstaff@ckha.on.ca
Kim Bossy, Director, Communications & Public Affairs
kbossy@ckha.on.ca

Chesley: Chesley Centre
PO Box 40, 39 Second St. SE, Chesley, ON N0G 1L0
Tel: 519-363-2340; *Fax:* 519-363-2340

Number of Beds: 20 beds
M. Jackson, CEO

Chesley: South Bruce Grey Health Centre - Chesley Site
Affiliated with: Chesley & District Memorial Hospital
39 - 2nd St. SE, Chesley, ON N0G 1L0
Tel: 519-363-2340; *Fax:* 519-363-9871
www.sbghc.on.ca

Year Founded: 1944
Number of Beds: 15 beds
Note: A rural health centre with services including emergency, internal medicine, nutrition services, diagnostic imaging (ultrasound, ECG, radiography), lab, physiotherapy, spirometry, healthy heart program, prenatal and postnatal care
Paul L. Davies, President/CEO, SBGHC
pdavies@sbghc.on.ca
Rhonda Ridgeway, Site Manager/Director, Patient Care
rridgeway@sbghc.on.ca

Clinton: Clinton Public Hospital
Affiliated with: Huron Perth Healthcare Alliance
98 Shipley St., Clinton, ON N0M 1L0
Tel: 519-482-3440; *Fax:* 519-482-5960
administration@hpha.ca; humanresources@hpha.ca
www.hpha.ca

Number of Beds: 17 acute care beds
Note: Hospital Specialties: Emergency services; Ambulatory care; Acute care; Physiotherapy; Diabetes education
Dr. Maarten Bokhout, Chief, Clinton Public Hospital Site
Bonnie Royal, Administrator, Clinton Public Hospital Site
bonnie.royal@hpha.ca
Greg Stewart, Chair, Local Advisory Committee

Cobourg: Northumberland Hills Hospital
Former Name: Northumberland Health Care Corp.
1000 DePalma Dr., Cobourg, ON K9A 5W6
Tel: 905-372-6811; *Fax:* 905-372-4243
info@nhh.ca
www.nhh.ca

Number of Beds: 80 acute care, 39 complex care, 18 rehabilitation beds
Note: community hospital
Joan Ross, CEO

Cochrane: The Lady Minto Hospital
PO Box 4000, 241 - 8 St., Cochrane, ON P0L 1C0
Tel: 705-272-7200; *Fax:* 705-272-5486
www.micsgroup.com/Site_Published/Micsgroup/minto_about.asp x

Year Founded: 1915
Number of Beds: 66 beds (20 acute, 8 complex continuing care, 2 OBS, 2 paediatrics, 1 special care and 33 long-term care beds)
Note: An acute general facility with services including emergency, complex continuing care, out-patient, ambulatory care, obstetrics, paediatrics, surgery, and long-term care services. The Villa Minto chronic care wing houses a long-term care unit.
Mr. Dan O'Mara, CEO, MICs Group of Health Services
dan.omara@micsgroup.com
Dr. Rita Affleck, Chief of Staff
Dr. Lawrence McPherrin, President, Medical Staff

Cornwall: Cornwall Community Hospital - McConnell Avenue Site
Hôpital communautaire de Cornwall
840 McConnell Ave., Cornwall, ON K6H 5S5
Tel: 613-938-4240; *Fax:* 613-930-4502
communications@cornwallhospital.ca
www.cornwallhospital.ca

Note: Hospital Specialties: Emergency services; Diagnostic imaging; Surgery; Cardio-respiratory therapy; Critical care; Maternal Child Program; Rehabilitation services, including occupational therapy, physiotherapy, social work, & speech-language pathology; Neurology; Orthopaedics; Ambulatory care; Geriatric services; Palliative care
Fernand Hamelin, Chair
Jeanette Despatie, Chief Executive Officer
Dr. Ashley Cook, Chief of Staff
Julie Lampron, Director, Diagnostic Imaging Department
julie.lampron@cornwallhospital.ca

Cornwall: Cornwall Community Hospital - Second Street Site
Hôpital communautaire de Cornwall
510 Second St. East, Cornwall, ON K6H 1Z6
Tel: 613-932-3300
www.cornwallhospital.ca

Note: Hospital Specialties: Assault & Sexual Abuse Program (Phone: 613-932-3300, ext. 4202; Toll-Free Phone: 1-866-263-1560; TTY: 613-936-4643; E-mail: asap@cornwallhospital.ca); Psychiatric care (613-932-3300, ext. 4204); Outpatient Mental Health Program (613-932-3300, ext. 4278); Withdrawal management services (613-938-8506)
Fernand Hamelin, Chair
Jeanette Despatie, Chief Executive Officer

Deep River: Deep River & District Hospital (DRDH)
117 Banting Dr., Deep River, ON K0J 1P0
Tel: 613-584-3333; *Fax:* 613-584-4920
Toll-Free: 1-866-571-8168
www.drdh.org

Year Founded: 1974
Note: Hospital Specialties: Emergency department (613-584-1266 ext. 166); Laboratory services (613-584-1266, ext 120); Diagnostic imaging (613-584-1266, ext 160); Cardiac care services; Physiotherapy; Nutritional counselling; Long term care
Paul Fehrenbach, Chair
Larry Schruder, Chief Executive Officer

Stacey Mortson, Chief Financial Officer
Dr. Elizabeth Noulty, Chief of Staff
Lianne Wheeler, Chief Nursing Officer
Allison Felix, Director, Rehabilitation Services
Terry Corbett, Manager, Laboratory / DI
Garry Hartlin, Manager, IT
Cara McGuire, Manager, Medical Records, Reception, & Admitting
Sean Patterson, Manager, Support Services
Ralph Roloff, Certified Orthotist
613-582-7219
Ericia Van Drunen, Contact, Clinical Nutrition
613-584-1266, ext. 1,

Dunnville: Haldimand War Memorial Hospital
206 John St., Dunnville, ON N1A 2P7
Tel: 905-774-7431; *Fax:* 905-774-6776
kanger@hwmh.ca
www.hwmh.ca
Number of Beds: 34 beds
David Montgomery, CEO

Durham: South Bruce Grey Health Centre - Durham Site
Affiliated with: Durham Memorial Hospital
PO Box 638, 320 College St., Durham, ON N0G 1R0
Tel: 519-369-2340; *Fax:* 519-369-6180
www.sbghc.on.ca
Year Founded: 1946
Number of Beds: 19 beds
Note: A rural health centre with services incuding emergency, audiology, cardiorespiratory care, bone densitometry, dermatology, ear/nose/throat, hearing aid testing, urology, nutrition services, diagnostic imaging (ultrasound, ECG, radiography), lab, physiotherapy, healthy heart program, prenatal and postnatal care
Paul L. Davies, President/CEO, SBGHC
pdavies@sbghc.on.ca
Maureen Rydall, Site Manager/Director, Patient Care
mrydall@sbghc.on.ca

Elliot Lake: St. Joseph's General Hospital
70 Spine Rd., Elliot Lake, ON P5A 1X2
Tel: 705-848-7181; *Fax:* 705-848-4414
www.sjgh.ca
Year Founded: 1958
Number of Beds: 57 beds, plus 12 day-surgery beds
Note: Services include emergency, bone density, cardiology, chemotherapy, chiropody, clinical nutrition, diabetes education, ears, nose, & throat, electrocardiogram, endoscopy, gastroenterology, gerontology, intensive care, mental health, nephrology, obstetrics, ophthamology, orthopedics, paediatrics, palliative care, pastoral care, physiotherapy, radiology, renal dialysis (as a satellite of Sudbury Regional Hospital), speech therapy, social work, surgery, urology, ultrasound. The hospital corporation also manages St. Joseph's Manor long term care facility, & the Oaks Substance Abuse Treatment Centre.
Mr. Michael Hukezalie, CEO
mhukezalie@sjgh.ca

Englehart: Englehart & District Hospital Inc.
PO Box 69, 61 Fifth St., Englehart, ON P0J 1H0
Tel: 705-544-2301; *Fax:* 705-544-5222
dmitchell@edhospital.on.ca
www.edhospital.on.ca
Note: Hospital Specialties: Emergency services; Diagnostic imaging; Laboratory services; Physiotherapy; Occupational therapy; Respiratory therapy; Chronic care (14 chronic care beds)
Mary Lynn Kirkey, Chair
Lois Kozak, Chief Executive Officer
Dr. A. Vera, Chief of Staff

Espanola: Espanola General Hospital (EGH)
Hôpital Général d' Espanola
825 McKinnon Dr., Espanola, ON P5E 1R4
Tel: 705-869-1420; *Fax:* 705-869-2608
info@esphosp.on.ca
www.esphosp.on.ca
Year Founded: 1949
Note: Hospital Specialties: Primary care; Therapeutic care; Preventive services; Diabetes education; Social work services; Assisted living; Long term care
Gisele Guenard, Chief Executive Officer
Catherine Gray, Director, Care

Exeter: South Huron Hospital Association
24 Huron St. West, Exeter, ON N0M 1S2
Tel: 519-235-2700; *Fax:* 519-235-3405
shha.administration@shha.on.ca
www.shha.on.ca
Year Founded: 1953
Number of Beds: 19 beds (11 acute, 4 rehab, 4 chronic care)
Note: Serving the municipalities of South Huron and Bluewater, services include emergency care, acute, in-patient services, diagnostic imaging (x-ray, ultrasound, bone mineral density, ECG, Holter monitors, pulmonary testing), physiotherapy, speech/language therapy, complex continuing care, and a range of out-patient clinics.
Debra Hunt, CEO/Chief Nursing Executive

Fergus: Groves Memorial Community Hospital
235 Union St. East, Fergus, ON N1M 1W3
Tel: 519-843-2010; *Fax:* 519-843-5331
info@gmch.fergus.net
www.gmch.ca
Number of Beds: 42 beds
Jerome Quenneville, President; CEO

Fort Albany: James Bay General Hospital
Fort Albany Wing
General Delivery, Fort Albany, ON P0L 1H0
Tel: 705-278-3330; *Fax:* 705-278-1121
hr@jbgh.org
www.jbgh.org
Number of Beds: 17 beds
Andrew Poonae, Wing Dir.
Alexandra Sutherland, Administrator

Fort Erie: Niagara Health System - Douglas Memorial Hospital Site in Fort Erie (NHS)
Niagara Health System / Système de santé de Niagara
230 Bertie St., Fort Erie, ON L2A 1Z2
Tel: 905-378-4647; *Fax:* 905-871-7765 (
www.niagarahealth.on.ca
Year Founded: 1931
Number of Beds: 46 beds
Note: Hospital Specialties: Urgent Care Centre; Acute care; Outpatient programs, including a methadone clinic & a satellite Ontario Breast Screening Program; Complex continuing care
Debbie Sevenpifer, President; Chief Executive Officer, Niagara Health System
Frank Demizio, Vice-President, Patient Services, Douglas Memorial Hospital
Christine Clark, Chief Communications Officer, Niagara Health System
Bala Kathiresan, Chief Operating Officer, Niagara Health System
Angela Zangari, Chief Financial Officer, Niagara Health System

Fort Frances: Riverside Health Care Facilities Inc.
110 Victoria Ave., Fort Frances, ON P9A 2B7
Tel: 807-274-3266; *Fax:* 807-274-2898
www.riversidehealthcare.ca
Year Founded: 1989
Number of Beds: 55 beds (Fort Frances), 15 beds (Emo), 24 beds (Rainy River)
Note: Operates the La Verendrye General Hospital (Fort Frances- acute care, continuing care, obstetrics & surgery); the Emo Health Centre (Emo- acute care, urgent care, long tern care, diagnostic imaging, physiotherapy, dental clinic); & Rainy River Health Centre (Rainy River- acute care, long term care, diagnostic imaging, dental clinic)
Wayne Woods, President/CEO

Georgetown: Halton Healthcare Services Corp. - Georgetown Hospital
Former Name: Georgetown & District Memorial Hospital
1 Princess Anne Dr., Georgetown, ON L7G 2B8
Tel: 905-873-0111; *Fax:* 905-873-9653
www.haltonhealthcare.com
Year Founded: 1961
Number of Beds: 33 acute care beds, 20 continuing care beds
Note: Number of staff: 346, 20 family physicians, 14 specialists
Cindy McDonell, COO

Geraldton: Geraldton District Hospital
500 Hogarth Ave., Geraldton, ON P0T 1M0
Tel: 807-854-1862; *Fax:* 807-854-1568
www.tbrhsc.net
Year Founded: 1963
Number of Beds: 23 acute care beds; 26 long term care beds
Note: Hospital Specialties: Emergency services; Diagnostic imaging; Laboratory services; Acute care; Physiotherapy; Occupational therapy; Social work; Diabetes education; Long term care
Kurt Pristanski, Chief Executive Officer
kpristanski@geraldtondh.com
Dr. R. Laine, Chief of Staff

Goderich: Alexandra Marine & General Hospital (AMGH)
120 Napier St., Goderich, ON N7A 1W5
Tel: 519-524-8689; *Fax:* 519-524-5579
stephanie.page@amgh.on.ca
www.amgh.on.ca
Number of Beds: 54 acute, long-term, & psychiatric care beds
Note: Hospital Specialties: Emergency services; Ambulatory care; Psychiatry; Diagnostic imaging; Physiotherapy; Occupational therapy; Speech & language pathology; Diabetes education; Social work; Number of employees: 250
William R. Thibert, President; Chief Executive Officer
william.thibert@amgh.on.ca
Dr. Patrick Conlon, Chief of Staff
Dr. Mike Dawson, President, Medical Staff

Grimsby: West Lincoln Memorial Hospital
169 Main St. East, Grimsby, ON L3M 1P3
Tel: 905-945-2253; *Fax:* 905-945-0504
comments@wlmh.on.ca
www.wlmh.on.ca
Number of Beds: 60 beds
Note: Number of staff: 385, 15 medical staff
David Bird, CEO

Guelph: Guelph General Hospital
115 Delhi St., Guelph, ON N1E 4J4
Tel: 519-822-5350; *Fax:* 519-822-2170
info@gghorg.ca
www.gghorg.ca
Number of Beds: 165 beds; 11 critical care, 55 surgery, 22 obstetrics
Note: Total employees: 1200, 224 physicians
Richard Ernst, President; CEO

Guelph: St. Joseph's Health Centre
100 Westmount Rd., Guelph, ON N1H 5H8
Tel: 519-824-6000; *Fax:* 519-763-0264
info@sjhcg.ca
www.sjhh.guelph.on.ca
Year Founded: 1861
Number of Beds: 235 beds (144 long-term care beds and 91 specialty beds)
Note: Residential long-term & respite care, complex continuing care, rehabilitation, community outreach, nutrition & food services, outpatient clinics, palliative care, recreation therapy, speech/language pathology services, social worker
Ms. Marianne Walker, President/CEO
president@sjhcg.ca

Hagersville: West Haldimand General Hospital
75 Parkview Rd., Hagersville, ON N0A 1H0
Tel: 905-768-3311; *Fax:* 905-768-1820
webmaster@whgh.ca
www.whgh.ca
Year Founded: 1964
Number of Beds: 33 beds
Note: Acute & complex continuing care, surgery, diagnostic imaging, senior support services
Paul Mailloux, CEO

Haliburton: Haliburton Highlands Health Service (HHHS)
Haliburton Site
PO Box 115, 7199 Gellert Rd., Haliburton, ON K0M 1S0
Tel: 705-457-1392; *Fax:* 705-457-2398
info@hhhs.on.ca; physio@hhhs.on.ca (Physiotherapy)
www.hhhs.on.ca
Year Founded: 2000
Number of Beds: 13 acute care beds + 1 maternity bed
Note: Specialties: Acute care; Physiotherapy
Keith Sansford, Pres./CEO

Hamilton: Hamilton Health Sciences
Chedoke Hospital
PO Box 2000 A, Sanitorium Road, MPO, Hamilton, ON L8N 3Z5
Tel: 905-521-2100; *Fax:* 905-521-7959
www.hamiltonhealthsciences.ca
Number of Beds: 129 beds
Murray T. Martin, President/CEO

Hamilton: Hamilton Health Sciences Corp.
Hamilton General Hospital
Former Name: Hamilton Health Sciences Corp, Hamilton General Di
237 Barton St. East, Hamilton, ON L8L 2X2
Tel: 905-521-2100; *Fax:* 905-527-1941
Year Founded: 1848
Number of Beds: 304 beds
Note: Hospital Specialty: Cardiac & Vascular; Neurosciences & Trauma; Population Health Institute.

***Hamilton:* Hamilton Health Sciences Corp. Juravinski Hospital**
711 Concession St., Hamilton, ON L8V 1C3
Tel: 905-527-4322; *Fax:* 905-575-2662
Year Founded: 1917
Number of Beds: 228
Note: Hospital Specialty: Oncology; Orthopedics; Rehabilitation; Palliative Care; Nuclear medecine; Infectious diseases; Diagnostic imaging; General surgery

***Hamilton:* St. Joseph's Healthcare**
50 Charlton Ave. East, Hamilton, ON L8N 4A6
Tel: 905-522-1155; *Fax:* 905-521-6066
www.stjosham.on.ca
Number of Beds: 600 acute care
Dr. Kevin Smith, President/CEO

***Hamilton:* St. Peter's Hospital**
88 Maplewood Ave., Hamilton, ON L8M 1W9
Tel: 905-777-3837; *Fax:* 905-549-7003
info@stpetes.ca
www.hhsc.ca/body.cfm?id=1575
Year Founded: 1890
Number of Beds: 250 beds
Note: A complex, continuing care hospital, with speciality programs in behavioural health, palliative care, rehabilitation, and community services. The facility operates under the umbrella of Hamilton Health Sciences.
Mr. Murray T. Martin, President/CEO, HHS
Mr. Murray Glendining, Executive Vice-President, Corporate Affairs, HHS
Ms. Donna Cripps, President, St. Peter's Hospital
Dr. Richard Seeley, Chief of Staff, St. Peter's Hospital

***Hanover:* Hanover & District Hospital**
90 - 7 Ave., Hanover, ON N4N 1N1
Tel: 519-364-2340; *Fax:* 519-364-6602
www.hanoverhospital.on.ca
Number of Beds: 80 beds; 36 acute care, 2 obstetrics, 2 palliative
Katrina Wilson, President; CEO

***Hawkesbury:* Hôpital Général de Hawkesbury & District General Hospital**
1111 Ghislain St., Hawkesbury, ON K6A 3J7
Tel: 613-632-1111; *Fax:* 613-636-6183
www.hawkesburyhospital.com
Year Founded: 1984
Number of Beds: 69 beds
Luc Séguin, Vice-President, Administration

***Hearst:* Hôpital Nôtre-Dame Hospital**
1405 Edward St., Bag 8000, Hearst, ON P0L 1N0
Tél: 705-362-4291; *Téléc:* 705-372-2923
www.ndh.on.ca
Nombre de lits: 44 lits
France Dallaire, CEO

***Hornepayne:* Hornepayne Community Hospital**
PO Box 190, 278 Front St., Hornepayne, ON P0M 1Z0
Tel: 807-868-2442; *Fax:* 807-868-2697
www.hornepayne.com/Hospital/hospital.htm
Number of Beds: 20 beds; 12 Long-term care, 8 Acute care
Lisa Verrino, CEO
Lisa.Verrino@hornepaynehospital.ca

***Huntsville:* Huntsville District Memorial Hospital Affiliated with: Muskoka Algonquin Healthcare**
100 Frank Miller Dr., Huntsville, ON P1H 1H7
Tel: 705-789-2311; *Fax:* 705-789-0557
info@mahc.ca
www.mahc.ca
Number of Beds: 76 beds, 6 special care beds
Barry Monaghan, CEO

***Ingersoll:* Alexandra Hospital**
29 Noxon St., Ingersoll, ON N5C 3V6
Tel: 519-485-1700; *Fax:* 519-485-9606
feedback@ah.tvh.ca; Robin.Schultz@ah.tvh.ca
www.alexandrahospital.on.ca
Year Founded: 1909
Number of Beds: 35 acute care beds
Note: Hospital Specialties: Emergency services; Diagnostic & laboratory services; Outpatient rehabilitation; Number of Employees: 168
Tom McHugh, Chief Executive Officer
519-485-1732, tom.mchugh@ah.tvh.ca
Jill Matsuo, President, Medical Staff
Martha Bancroft, Contact, Human Resources
519-485-9603, Martha.Bancroft@ah.tvh.ca

***Iroquois Falls:* Anson General Hospital**
58 Anson Dr., Iroquois Falls, ON P0K 1E0
Tel: 705-258-3911; *Fax:* 705-258-3221
Number of Beds: 21 active care beds; 15 chronic care beds; 4 palliative or long-term rehabilitation care beds
Note: Hospital Specialties: Emergency services; Chronic care; Diabetes education; Palliative care; Snoezelen room

***Kapuskasing:* Sensenbrenner Hospital**
101 Progress Cres., Kapuskasing, ON P5N 3H5
Tel: 705-337-6111; *Fax:* 705-337-4021
info@sensenbrennerhospital.on.ca
www.senhosp.ca
Number of Beds: 30 active care
Allan Yarush, CEO

***Kemptville:* Kemptville District Hospital**
PO Box 2007, 2675 Concession Rd., Kemptville, ON K0G 1J0
Tel: 613-258-6133
www.kdh.on.ca
Number of Beds: 23 acute care beds
Colin Goodfellow, Chief Executive Officer
613/258-6133 ext.132, Fax: 613/258-7853,

***Kenora:* Lake of the Woods District Hospital**
21 Sylvan St. West, Kenora, ON P9N 3W7
Tel: 807-468-9861; *Fax:* 807-468-3939
admin@lwdh.on.ca
www.lwdh.on.ca
Number of Beds: 104 beds
Mark Balcaen, CEO

***Kincardine:* South Bruce Grey Health Centre - Kincardine Site Kincardine & District General Hospital**
43 Queen St., Kincardine, ON N2Z 1G6
Tel: 519-396-3331; *Fax:* 519-396-3699
www.sbghc.on.ca
Year Founded: 1908
Number of Beds: 36 beds
Note: A rural health centre with services including emergency, cardiorespiratory care, dental services, bone densitometry, gynecology, internal medicine, pediatrics, respirology, rheumatology, surgery, urology, nutrition services, diagnostic imaging (ultrasound, ECG, radiography), lab, physiotherapy, pharmacy, healthy heart program, prenatal and postnatal care
Paul L. Davies, President/CEO, SBGHC
pdavies@sbgh.on.ca
Kate Kincaid, Site Manager/Director, Patient Care
kkincaid@sbghc.on.ca

***Kingston:* Kingston General Hospital**
76 Stuart St., Kingston, ON K7L 2V7
Tel: 613-548-3232; *Fax:* 613-548-6042
web@kgh.kari.net
www.kgh.kari.net
Year Founded: 1838
Number of Beds: 456 beds
Note: Teaching hospital; Research hospital; Total employees: 3,737; Medical Staff: 546
Janet Davidson, President/CEO
Dr. Paul Belliveau, President, Medical Staff

***Kingston:* The Religious Hospitaliers of Saint-Joseph of the Hotel Dieu of Kingston**
166 Brock St., Kingston, ON K7L 5G2
Tel: 613-544-3310; *Fax:* 613-544-9897
holdenc@hdh.kari.net
www.hoteldieu.com
Year Founded: 1845
Note: An ambulatory care teaching facility with services including emergency, audiology, breast assessment, detoxification centre, diabetes education, ophthalmology, pastoral care, pediatrics, psychiatry, sexual assault/domestic violence program, day surgery, urgent care and mental health programs. It is affiliated with Queen's University and is partnered with Kingston's university hospitals.
Dr. David Pichora, CEO
Mr. Steve Miller, CFO
Ms. Sandi Cox, Chief, Patient Care
Ms. Elizabeth Bardon, Chief, Pubilc Relations & Community Engagement

***Kirkland Lake:* Kirkland & District Hospital**
145 Government Rd. East, Kirkland Lake, ON P2N 3P4
Tel: 705-567-5251; *Fax:* 705-568-2115
www.kdhospital.com
Number of Beds: 62 beds
Hal Fjeldsted, CEO
hfjelsted@kdhospital.com
Dr. Mark Spiller, Chief of Staff
aallison@kdhospital.com
Louis Gravel, Manager, Information Systems
lgravel@kdhospital.com

***Kitchener:* Grand River Hospital Corp. Kitchener-Waterloo Health Centre**
PO Box 9056, 835 King St. West, Kitchener, ON N2G 1G3
Tel: 519-749-4300; *Fax:* 519-749-4208
info@grhosp.on.ca
www.grandriverhospital.on.ca
Number of Beds: 495 beds (including Freeport Health Centre site)
Note: Hospital Specialty: acute, complex continuing & cancer care
Malcolm Maxwell, President/CEO
malcolm.maxwell@grhosp.on.ca

***Kitchener:* Grand River Hospital Corp. Freeport Health Centre**
PO Box 9056, 3570 King St. East, Kitchener, ON N2A 2W1
Tel: 519-749-4300; *Fax:* 519-894-8349
www.grandriverhospital.on.ca
Number of Beds: 139 continuing care, 32 short-term rehab beds
Note: Complex continuing care, chronic care, rehabilitation & restoration
Malcolm Maxwell, President/CEO
malcolm.maxwell@grhosp.on.ca

***Kitchener:* St. Mary's General Hospital**
911 Queen's Blvd., Kitchener, ON N2M 1B2
Tel: 519-744-3311; *Fax:* 519-749-6426
info@smgh.ca
www.smgh.ca
Number of Beds: 191 acute care beds
Note: Catholic hospital, home to the Regional Cardiac Care Centre
Bruce M. Antonello, President/CEO

***Leamington:* Leamington District Memorial Hospital**
194 Talbot St. West, Leamington, ON N8H 1N9
Tel: 519-322-2501; *Fax:* 519-322-1677
www.leamingtonhospital.com
Number of Beds: 81 beds
Note: complex continuing care & rehab
J. Stenger, CEO

***Lindsay:* Ross Memorial Hospital**
10 Angeline St. North, Lindsay, ON K9V 4M8
Tel: 705-324-6111; *Fax:* 705-328-2817
Toll-Free: 800-510-7365
www.rmh.org
Year Founded: 1902
Number of Beds: 175 beds: 36 continuing care; 16 rehabilitation; 10 palliative; 8 intensive care; 40 adult beds; 36 adult surgical beds
Note: Emergency, mental health services, complex continuing care, rehabilitation, palliative care, surgery, women's health, pediatrics, physiotherapy, diagnostic imaging, cardiac & diabetes care, outpatient pain clinic
Brian Payne, President/CEO
Varouj Eskedjian, Vice-President, Diagnostics & Support

***Lions Head:* Grey Bruce Health Services Lion's Head Hospital**
22 Moore St., Lions Head, ON N0H 1W0
Tel: 519-793-3424
www.gbhs.on.ca/lionshead.php
Number of Beds: 6 inpatient beds
Note: Specialties: Acute care; Preschool speech therapy; Diabetes education; Physiotherapy Palliative care. Number of employees: 25
Sue McCutcheon, Site Director

***Listowel:* Listowel Memorial Hospital Affiliated with: Listowel & Wingham Hospitals Alliance**
255 Elizabeth St. East, Listowel, ON N4W 2P5
Tel: 519-291-3120; *Fax:* 519-291-5440
www.lwha.ca
Year Founded: 1919
Number of Beds: 51 beds
Note: Acute & complex continuing care. Number of staff: 10 physicians
Liz Phelan, CEO (Interim)
liz.phelan@lwha.ca

***Little Current:* Manitoulin Health Centre**
PO Box 640, 11-13 Meredith St. West, Little Current, ON P0P 1K0
Tel: 705-368-2300; *Fax:* 705-368-3566
www.mhc.on.ca
Number of Beds: 16 beds
James D. Van Camp, CEO

***London:* London Health Sciences Centre University Hospital Site**
339 Windermere Rd., London, ON N6A 5A5
Tel: 519-685-8500
motslhsc@lhsc.on.ca (general transplant inquiries)
www.lhsc.on.ca
Info Line: 519-685-8380
Note: Hospital Specialties: Emergency services; Medical-surgical intensive care; Cardiac surgery; Regional Stroke Centre for the Southwestern Ontario Region; London Health Sciences Centre cochlear implant program; Orthopaedics program; London Multiple Sclerosis Clinic; Multi-organ transplant program
Tony Dagnone, President/CEO

***London:* London Health Sciences Centre Victoria Hospital Site**
PO Box 5010, 800 Commissioners Rd. East, London, ON N6A 5W9
Tel: 519-685-8500
leanne.siebenmorgen@lhsc.on.ca (Trauma program)
www.lhsc.on.ca
Info Line: 519-685-8380
Year Founded: 1995
Note: Hospital Specialties: Emergency services; Critical Care Trauma Center; Bleeding disorders program; Maternal newborn care; Prostate cancer centre; Trauma progam
Dr. Tony Dagnone, President/CEO

***London:* London Health Sciences Centre South Street Hospital Site**
375 South St., London, ON N6A 4G5
Tel: 519-685-8500
www.lhsc.on.ca
Info Line: 519-685-8380
Note: Hospital Specialties: Adult mental health care program
Cliff Nordal, President; CEO

***London:* London Health Sciences Centre Children's Hospital Site**
Former Name: Children's Hospital of Western Ontario
800 Commissioners Rd. East, London, ON N6A 5W9
Tel: 519-685-8484
www.lhsc.on.ca
Info Line: 519-685-8380
Note: Hospital Specialties: Specialized paediatric inpatient & outpatient services; Paediatric critical care unit; Child & adolescent mental health care program; Acute paediatric rehabilitation services; Gastroenterology, transplant, hepatology, & nutrition; Medical genetics; Respiratory therapy; Asthma clinic; Cystic fibrosis; Hematology & oncology

***London:* Parkwood Hospital**
Affiliated with: St. Joseph's Health Care, London
801 Commissioners Rd. East, London, ON N6C 5J1
Tel: 519-685-4000; *Fax:* 519-685-4052
Communications.Department@sjhc.london.on.ca
www.sjhc.london.on.ca
Number of Beds: 530 beds

***London:* St. Joseph's Health Care, London**
268 Grosvenor St., London, ON N6A 4V2
Tel: 519-646-6000; *Fax:* 519-646-6006
www.sjhc.london.on.ca
Number of Beds: 1,660 beds
Note: Includes St. Joseph's Hospital; Mount Hope Centre for Long Term Care; Parkwood Hospital (chronic, longterm & veterans facility); Lawson Health Research Institute; Regional Mental Health Care, London & Regional Mental Health Care, St Thomas
Cliff Nordal, President/CEO

***London:* St. Joseph's Hospital**
Affiliated with: St. Joseph's Health Care, London
PO Box 5777, 268 Grosvenor St., London, ON N6A 4V2
Tel: 519-646-6000
Number of Beds: 177 beds

***Manitouwadge:* Manitouwadge General Hospital**
1 Health Care Lane, Manitouwadge, ON P0T 2C0
Tel: 807-826-3251; *Fax:* 807-826-4216
infoserv@mh.on.ca
www.mh.on.ca
Number of Beds: 18 beds
Judith C. Harris, CEO

***Marathon:* Wilson Memorial General Hospital**
26 Peninsula Rd., PO Bag W, Marathon, ON P0T 2E0
Tel: 807-229-1740; *Fax:* 807-229-1721
wilson@wmgh.net
www.wmgh.net
Year Founded: 1971
Number of Beds: 25 beds
Note: Number of staff: 7 physicians
Paul Paradis, CEO

***Markdale:* Grey Bruce Health Services Markdale Hospital**
Also Known As: Centre Grey Hospital
PO Box 406, 55 Isla St., Markdale, ON N0C 1H0
Tel: 519-986-3040
www.gbhs.on.ca/markdale.php
Number of Beds: 18 inpatient beds
Note: Specialties: Day surgery service; Acute care; Physiotherapy services; Diabetes education; Palliative care
Pat Campbell, President; CEO

***Markham:* Markham-Stouffville Hospital (MSH)**
PO Box 1800, 381 Church St., Markham, ON L3P 7P3
Tel: 905-472-7000
TTY: 905-472-7585
myhospital@msh.on.ca
www.msh.on.ca
Info Line: 905-472-7100
Year Founded: 1990
Note: Specialties: Emergency medicine; Surgical care; Child, adolescent, & adult mental health services; Genetics counselling; Obstetrical assessment; The Childbirth Centre; Paediatrics; Occupational therapy & Physiotherapy; Geriatrics; Sleep disorders; Speech language pathology; Palliative care. Number of Employees: 275 physicians + 1,700 staff
Janet M. Beed, President/CEO

***Matheson:* Bingham Memorial Hospital**
PO Box 70, 507 - 8th Ave., Matheson, ON P0K 1N0
Tel: 705-273-2424; *Fax:* 705-273-1617
Year Founded: 1955
Number of Beds: 11 acute care beds; 6 chronic care beds
Note: Hospital Specialties: Emergency services; Laboratory services; Radiology services; Acute care; Chemotherapy; Physiotherapy; Respiratory therapy; Dietician services; Diabetes education; Chronic care; Palliative care; Number of Employees: 72 (Bingham Memorial Hospital & adjoined Rosedale Centre)
Daniel O'Mara, Chief Executive Officer
705-273-2424, ext. 2, micsceo@puc.net
Sharon Hill, Coordinator, Human Resources
705-273-2424, ext. 3
Beverley Magee, Coordinator, Diabetes Program
Beverley.magee@micsgroup.com

***Mattawa:* Mattawa Hospital**
Hôpital de Mattawa
PO Box 70, 217 Turcotte Park Rd., Mattawa, ON P0H 1V0
Tel: 705-744-5511; *Fax:* 705-744-6020
admin@mattawahospital.ca
www.mhsmattawa.on.ca
Year Founded: 1878
Number of Beds: 19 beds
Note: Specialties: Primary care; Acute care; Ambulatory programs; Diabetic resource centre; Adult & children's mental health services; Paediatric, urology, psychiatry, & women's clinic; Physiotherapy services; Palliative care
Edward Darby, CEO

***Meaford:* Grey Bruce Health Services Meaford Hospital**
229 Nelson St. West, Meaford, ON N4L 1A3
Tel: 519-538-1311
www.gbhs.on.ca/meaford.php
Number of Beds: 20 inpatient beds
Note: Specialties: Diagnostic support; Laboratory services; Inpatient primary care; Ambulatory care services; Diabetes education; Physiotherapy; Palliative care. Number of Employees: 116
Carol Gouett, Site Director

***Midland:* Huronia District Hospital**
PO Box 760, 1112 St. Andrews Dr., Midland, ON L4R 4P4
Tel: 705-526-1300; *Fax:* 705-526-2007
www.nsha.on.ca
Number of Beds: 72 acute care beds, 8 ICU beds
Carol Lambie, Interim CEO

***Milton:* Halton Healthcare Services Corp. - Milton District Hospital**
30 Derry Rd. East, Milton, ON L9T 2X5
Tel: 905-878-2383; *Fax:* 905-878-7047
Number of Beds: 43 acute care beds, 25 complex continuing care beds
Note: Number of staff: 385, 29 physicians, 30 specialists
Allan Halls, COO

***Mindemoya:* Manitoulin Health Centre Mindemoya Medical Clinic**
PO Box 156, Mindemoya, ON P0P 1S0
Tel: 705-377-5371; *Fax:* 705-377-5372
Number of Beds: 14 beds
Dan Charette, Pat. Care Coord.

***Minden:* Haliburton Highlands Health Service (HHHS) Minden Site**
PO Box PO Box 30, 6 McPherson St, Minden, ON K0M 2K0
Tel: 705-286-2140; *Fax:* 705-286-6384
info@hhhs.on.ca; physio@hhhs.on.ca (Physiotherapy)
www.hhhs.on.ca
Note: Specialties: Physiotherapy; Diabetes education
Keith Sansford, Executive Director

***Mississauga:* The Credit Valley Hospital**
2200 Eglinton Ave. West, Mississauga, ON L5M 2N1
Tel: 905-813-2200; *Fax:* 905-813-4444
Toll-Free: 1-877-292-4284
cvhpr@cvh.on.ca
www.cvh.on.ca
Year Founded: 1985
Number of Beds: 471 beds
Note: A comprehensive health care facility with services including emergency, Addictions and Concurrent Disorders Centre, ambulatory care, asthma education, cancer care, cardiopulmonary, complex continuing care, critical care, diabetes care centre, diagnostic imaging, eating disorders program, endoscopy, genetics, geriatric assessment, laboratory, maternal child services, mental health, music therapy, occupational therapy, paediatrics, physiotherapy, psychology, renal program, social work, spiritual care, surgery.
Ms. Michelle DiEmanuele, President/CEO
905-813-1100, mdiemanuele@cvh.on.ca
Dr. Matt Gysler, Chief, Medical Staff
mgysler@cvh.on.ca
Ms. Wendy Johnson, Chief, Communications & Public Affairs
905-813-2617, wjohnson@cvh.on.ca

***Mississauga:* Trillium Health Centre - Mississauga Site**
Former Name: Queensway General Hospital
100 Queensway West, Mississauga, ON L5B 1B8
Tel: 905-848-7100; *Fax:* 905-848-7140
publicrelations@thc.on.ca
www.trilliumhealthcentre.org
Number of Beds: 748 beds (for acute, rehabilitation and chronic care)
Note: Inpatient services include emergency care centre, birthing centre, critical care, intensive care, neurosurgery, stroke & cardiac care, sexual assault & domestic violence services, women's & children's health (Colonel Harland Sanders Family Care Centre)
Ms. Janet M. Davidson, President /CEO
Ms. May Chang, CFO/Vice-President, Corporate Services
Dr. Gopal Bhatnagar, Chief of Staff
Mr. Larry Roberts, Media Relations Consultant
905-848-7580, lroberts@thc.on.ca

***Moose Factory:* Weeneebayko General Hospital**
PO Box 34, Moose Factory, ON P0L 1W0
Tel: 705-658-4544; *Fax:* 705-658-4917
pat.chilton@wha.on.ca
www.wha.on.ca
Number of Beds: 58 beds
Pat Chilton, CEO

***Moosonee:* James Bay General Hospital**
PO Box 370, Moosonee, ON P0L 1Y0
Tel: 705-336-2947; *Fax:* 705-336-2637
administrator@jbgh.org
www.jbgh.org
Year Founded: 1969
Number of Beds: 33 beds
Note: sites in Moosonee, Fort Albany, Attawapiska
Wes Drodge, Executive Director

***Mount Forest:* North Wellington Health Care Louise Marshall Hospital Site**
630 Dublin St., Mount Forest, ON N0G 2L3
Tel: 519-323-2210; *Fax:* 519-323-3741
www.nwhealthcare.ca
Number of Beds: 19 beds
Pierre Noel, CEO

***Napanee:* Lennox & Addington County General Hospital**
PO Box 300, 8 Richmond Park Dr., Napanee, ON K7R 2Z4
Tel: 613-354-3301; *Fax:* 613-354-7157
web.lacgh.napanee.on.ca

Number of Beds: 33 beds; 25 active care; 8 chronic care
Note: Number of employees: 200
Wayne Coveyduck, Executive Director
Dr. Tom Touzel, Chief of Staff

New Liskeard: Temiskaming Hospital
421 Shepherdson Rd., New Liskeard, ON P0J 1P0
Tel: 705-647-8121; *Fax:* 705-647-5800
www.temiskaming-hospital.com

Year Founded: 1980
Number of Beds: 59 beds (40 acute, 11 chronic, 5 obstetric & 3 special care unit beds)
Note: This community facility offers services including emergency, cardiac rehabilitation, diagnostic imaging (CT scans), laboratory, nutrition services, occupational therapy, pastoral care, pharmacy, physiotherapy, respiratory therapy, speech language pathology and Telestroke Program. Visiting specialists conduct services in neurology, nephrology, obstetrics and gynecology, orthotics, rehab/physical medicine, psychiatry, ophthalmology and pediatrics.
Mr. Bruce Cunningham, CEO
Mr. Lenord Alfred, Director, Support Services
Ms. Sylvie Lavictoire, Director, Clinical Services
Dr. Raymond Rahn, President, Medical Staff
Dr. Céline Léger-Nolet, Hospital Stroke Leader
705-647-1088

Newbury: Four Counties Health Services Site (FCHS)
Middlesex Hospital Alliance
1824 Concession Dr., RR#3, Newbury, ON N0L 1Z0
Tel: 519-693-7111
www.mhalliance.on.ca

Note: Specialties: Emergency care; Diagnostic services; Physiotherapy (519-693-7111, ext. 2441); Diabetes Education Centre (519-693-7111, ext. 2489); Adult Day Centre
Michael A. Mazza, Chief Executive Officer, Middlesex Hospital Alliance
Dr. Jon Dreyer, Chief of Staff, Four Counties Health Services Site

Newmarket: Southlake Regional Health Centre
Former Name: York County Hospital
596 Davis Dr., Newmarket, ON L3Y 2P9
Tel: 905-895-4521; *Fax:* 905-830-5972
communications@southlakeregional.org
www.southlakeregional.org

Year Founded: 1922
Number of Beds: 375 beds
Note: Comprehensive health care services including emergency, cancer care, cardiac care centre, arthritis care, birthing unit, diabetes education, diagnostic imaging (bone densitometry, CT scan, MRI, mammography, nuclear medicine, ultrasound, x-ray), eating disorders, mental health programs, neonatal intensive care unit, obstetrics, pediatrics & perinatal care, palliative care, respiratory therapy, thoracic surgery
Mr. Daniel P. Carriere, President/CEO
Mr. Terry Kuula, CFO/Vice-President, Finance
Mr. Paul Clarry, Vice-President, Facilities & Paramedical Services
Dr. Nancy Merrow, Chief of Staff

Niagara Falls: Niagara Health System - Greater Niagara General Site in Niagara Falls (NHS)
Niagara Health System / Système de santé de Niagara
5546 Portage Rd., Niagara Falls, ON L2E 6X2
Tel: 905-378-4647; *Fax:* 905-358-8435 (
www.niagarahealth.on.ca

Year Founded: 1907
Number of Beds: 180+ beds
Note: Hospital Specialties: Emergency services; Intensive care; Ambulatory care; Acute care; Maternal / child care services; Women's Health Centre, including the Ontario Breast Screening Program; Mental health services; Geriatric assessment; Regional Stroke Program; Complex continuing care
Debbie Sevenpifer, President; Chief Executive Officer, Niagara Health System
Frank Demizio, Vice-President, Patient Services, Greater Niagara General Site
Su Bolibruck, Director, Clinical Programs (Chronic Kidney Disease, Cardiolo
905-378-4647, ext. 3
Heather Scott, Director, Clinical Programs (Mental Health)
905-378-4647, ext. 5,

Niagara on the Lake: Niagara Health System - Niagara-on-the-Lake Site (NHS)
Niagara Health System / Système de santé de Niagara
176 Wellington St., Niagara on the Lake, ON L0S 1J0
Tel: 905-378-4647; *Fax:* 905-468-7690
www.niagarahealth.on.ca

Year Founded: 1921
Number of Beds: 22 beds
Note: Hospital Specialties: Acute care; Walk-in clinic; Complex continuing care
Debbie Sevenpifer, President; Chief Executive Officer, Niagara Health System
Linda Boich, Vice-President, Patient Services, Niagara-on-the-Lake Hospital Site
Dr. Joanna Hope, Chief of Staff, Niagara Health System

Nipigon: Nipigon District Memorial Hospital
PO Box 37, 125 Hogan Rd., Nipigon, ON P0T 2J0
Tel: 807-887-3026; *Fax:* 807-887-2800
lenders@ndmh.ca
www.ndmh.ca

Number of Beds: 37 beds
Lori Marshall, Site Administrator

North Bay: North Bay General Hospital
PO Box 2500, 750 Scollard St., North Bay, ON P1B 5A4
Tel: 705-474-8600; *Fax:* 705-495-7956
mhurst@nbgh.on.ca
www.nbgh.on.ca

Number of Beds: 204 beds
Mark Hurst, Pres./CEO

North Bay: North Bay General Hospital McLaren Site
PO Box 2500, 720 McLaren St., North Bay, ON P1B 3L9
Tel: 705-474-8600; *Toll-Free:* 888-602-2222
www.nbgh.on.ca

Denis Labelle, Executive Director

Oakville: Halton Healthcare Services Corp. - Oakville-Trafalgar Memorial Hospital
327 Reynolds St., Oakville, ON L6J 3L7
Tel: 905-845-2571; *Fax:* 905-338-4636
Number of Beds: 262 acute care beds, 39 rehab beds, 21 continuing care beds
Note: Full service acute care hospital. Number of staff: 2,056, 96 physicians, 101 specialists
Dale Clement, COO

Orangeville: Headwaters Orangeville
100 Rolling Hills Dr., Orangeville, ON L9W 4X9
Tel: 519-941-2410; *Fax:* 519-942-0483
www.headwatershealth.ca

Number of Beds: 108 beds
Cholly Boland, President; CEO

Orillia: Orillia Soldiers' Memorial Hospital (OSMH)
170 Colborne St. West, Orillia, ON L3V 2Z3
Tel: 705-325-2201
administration@osmh.on.ca; tadyni@osmh.on.ca (Community relations)
www.osmh.on.ca

Number of Beds: 230 inpatient beds
Note: Specialties: Paediatric & neonatal services; Regional diagnostic imaging centre of excellence; Surgical services; Critical care; Dialysis; Oncology; Chronic disease management; Complex continuing care; Diabetes education; Sexual & domestic violence services; Mental health services; Outpatient clinics. Number of Employees: 300 physicians + 1,200 staff + 400+ volunteers
Glen H. Penwarden, Executive Director

Oshawa: Lakeridge Health Corporation Oshawa Site
1 Hospital Ct., Oshawa, ON L1G 2B9
Tel: 905-576-8711; *Fax:* 905-721-4735
www.lakeridgehealth.on.ca

Number of Beds: 437 beds
J. Dusek, COO

Ottawa: Children's Hospital of Eastern Ontario (CHEO)
401 Smyth Rd., Ottawa, ON K1H 8L1
Tel: 613-737-7600
kouri@cheo.on.ca (Patient Representative Office)
www.cheo.on.ca

Year Founded: 1974
Number of Beds: 112 pediatric, oncology, adolescent medicine, & surgery beds; 25 psychiatry beds; 20 neonatal intensive care unit beds; 10 intensive care unit beds
Note: Hospital Specialties: Pediatric health for children & youth aged 0 to 18 years; Emergency services; Surgery; Ontario Newborn Screening Program; Neonatal intensive care; Genetics; Oncology; Dialysis; Cardiology; Neurology; Provincial Centre of Excellence for Child & Youth Mental Health; Number of Employees: 1,500 administrative, service, & allied health staff; 630 nursing staff; 183 physicians
Michel Bilodeau, President; Chief Executive Officer
Dr. Carrol Pitters, Chief of Staff
Jerry Bisson, Chief Financial Officer; Senior Vice-President
Pat Elliott-Miller, Chief Nursing Executive; Vice-President, Patient Services
Tyson Roffey, Chief Information Officer
Ginette Champagne, Vice-President, Human Resources
Dr. Martin H. Osmond, Vice-President, Research
Susan Richardson, Vice-President, Professional Services
Ann Fuller, Director, Public Relations

Ottawa: Hôpital Montfort
713, ch Montréal, Ottawa, ON K1K 0T2
Tél: 613-746-4621; *Téléc:* 613-748-4947
Ligne sans frais: 800-276-0161
montfort@montfort.on.ca
www.hopitalmontfort.com

Nombre de lits: 208 lits
Gérald Savoie, Président/Directeur général

Ottawa: The Ottawa Hospital Civic Campus
L'Hôpital d'Ottawa
1053 Carling Ave., Ottawa, ON K1Y 4E9
Tel: 613-722-7000
webmaster@ottawahospital.on.ca
www.ottawahospital.on.ca

Number of Beds: 1,066 beds across the system
Note: Comprehensive, patient-focussed care; University of Ottawa Heart Institute. Number of staff total TOH: 11,566 staff, 1,150 physicians
Dr. Jack Kitts, President/CEO
Dr. Jeffrey Turnbull, Chief of Staff

Ottawa: The Ottawa Hospital General Campus
L'Hôpital d'Ottawa
501 Smyth Rd., Ottawa, ON K1H 8L6
Tel: 613-722-7000; *Fax:* 613-737-8470
www.ottawahospital.on.ca

Number of Beds: 1,066 beds across the system
Note: Comprehensive, patient-focussed care, including the University of Ottawa Eye Institute. Number of staff total TOH: 11,566 staff, 1,150 physicians
Dr. Jack Kitts, President/CEO
Dr. Jeffrey Turnbull, Chief of Staff

Ottawa: The Ottawa Hospital Riverside Campus
L'Hôpital d'Ottawa
1967 Riverside Dr., Ottawa, ON K1H 7W9
Tel: 613-722-7000; *Fax:* 613-738-8526
Number of Beds: 1,066 beds across the system
Note: Comprehensive, patient-focussed care, including Eye Care Centre, & the Shirley E. Greenberg Women's Health Centre. Number of staff total TOH: 11,566 staff, 1,150 physicians
Dr. Jack Kitts, President/CEO
Dr. Jeffrey Turnbull, Chief of Staff

Ottawa: Queensway Carleton Hospital
3045 Baseline Rd., Ottawa, ON K2H 8P4
Tel: 613-721-2000; *Fax:* 613-721-4770
communications@qch.on.ca
www.qch.on.ca

Number of Beds: 264 beds
Note: Diagnostic imaging, emergency services, family medicine, geriatrics, lab, rehabilitation, obstetrics & gynaecology, paediatrics, psychiatry, surgery. Number of staff: 1,798, 234 physicians, 3 midwives.
Tom Schonberg, President/CEO
Dr. Andrew Falconer, Chief of Staff

Owen Sound: Grey Bruce Health Services
1800 - 8 St. East, Owen Sound, ON N4K 6M9
Tel: 519-376-2121
web@gbhs.on.ca
www.gbhs.on.ca

Pat Campbell, President; CEO

Owen Sound: Grey Bruce Health Services Owen Sound Hospital
PO Box 1800, 1800 - 8th St. East, Owen Sound, ON N4K 6M9
Tel: 519-376-2121
library@gbhs.on.ca
www.gbhs.on.ca/owensound.php

Note: Specialties: Community addiction treatment services; Community mental health services; Community outreach; Critical care services; Grey Bruce District Stroke Centre; Grey Bruce Huron paramedic base hospital program; Ontario breast screening program; Preschool speech & language service; Sleep lab; Sexual assault & partner abuse care; Surgical services; Nuclear medicine; Psychogeriatric unit; Palliative care. Number of Employees: 60 specialists + 21 family physicians + 1,129 nurses, therapists, technologists, & support staff

Palmerston: North Wellington Health Care Corporation
Palmerston & District Hospital Site
500 Whites Rd., Palmerston, ON N0G 2P0
Tel: 519-343-2030; *Fax:* 519-343-3821
www.nwhealthcare.ca

Number of Beds: 19 beds
Pierre Noel, Administrator/CEO

Paris: Willett Hospital Site
Brant Community Healthcare System (BCHS)
Also Known As: The Willett
238 Grand River St. North, Paris, ON N3L 2N7
Tel: 519-442-2251
www.bchsys.org

Year Founded: 1922
Number of Beds: A total of 350 beds are part of The Brant Community Healthcare System, which consists of The Willett Hospital in Paris, Ontario & the Brantford Genera
Note: Hospital Specialties: Urgent care; Diagnostic imaging; Recreational therapy; Physiotherapy; Occupational therapy; Counselling services; Community health, including health & wellness education
James Hornell, President; Chief Executive Officer, Brant Community Healthcare System
519-751-5500
Andrew McRobert, Director, Health & Addiction Services & Pastoral Care
519-751-5544, ext. 2
Heather Riddell, Director, Emergency Services / Urgent Care
519-751-5544, ext. 2
Jill Berridge, Manager, Rehabilitation Services
519-751-5544, ext. 2
Karen Kuzmich, Manager, Wellness & Healthcare Integration
519-442-4000, ext. 6
Nancy Wheeler, Manager, Imaging
519-751-5547

Pembroke: Pembroke General Hospital
705 MacKay St., Pembroke, ON K8A 1G8
Tel: 613-732-2811; *Fax:* 613-732-9986
pr@pemgenhos.org
www.pemgenhos.org

Number of Beds: 165 beds
Lloyd Koch, President/CEO

Penetanguishene: Penetanguishene General Hospital
25 Jeffery St., Penetanguishene, ON L9M 1K6
Tel: 705-549-7431; *Fax:* 705-549-4031
www.nsha.on.ca

Number of Beds: 51 beds
Note: hospital, regional rehab. & complex continuing care, dialysis
Doris Shirriff, Executive Director
Robert Robitaille, Director, Environmental Services

Perth: Perth & Smiths Falls District Hospital Perth Site
Also Known As: Great War Memorial Site
33 Drummond St. West, Perth, ON K7H 2K1
Tel: 613-267-1500; *Fax:* 613-264-0365
webinquiry@psfdh.on.ca
www.psfdh.on.ca

Note: Specialties: Acute care; Health promotion programs; Ambulatory care; Rehabilitation services; Chronic care; Palliative care

Peterborough: Peterborough Regional Health Centre (PRHC)
1 Hospital Dr., Peterborough, ON K9J 7C6
Tel: 705-743-2121; *Fax:* 705-876-5120
TTY: 705-876-5141
info@prhc.on.ca
www.prhc.on.ca

Number of Beds: 494 beds
Note: Specialties: Acute care; Emergency services; Diagnostic imaging; Surgical services; Regional renal program; Mental health services; Maternal child services. Number of Employees: 2,000 staff; 350 physicians with privileges; 600 volunteers
Wendy Fucile, Interim President/CEO

Petrolia: Charlotte Eleanor Englehart Hospital of Bluewater Health (CEEH of)
Bluewater Health
Former Name: Charlotte Eleanor Englehart Hospital
450 Blanche St., Petrolia, ON N0N 1R0
Tel: 519-882-4325; *Fax:* 519-882-3711
www.bluewaterhealth.ca

Year Founded: 1911
Number of Beds: 23 acute care beds; 18 continuing care beds
Note: Hospital Specialties: Emergency services; Acute care; Ambulatory care; Continuing care services
Sue Denomy, President; Chief Executive Officer, Bluewater Health
519-464-4400, ext. 4, Fax: 519-336-8780,
sdenomy@bluewaterhealth.ca

Picton: Quinte Health Care Prince Edward County Memorial
Quinte Health Care
403 Main St. East, Picton, ON K0K 2T0
Tel: 613-476-1008; *Fax:* 613-476-8600
www.qhc.on.ca/Default.aspx?cid=276&lang=1

Year Founded: 1959
Number of Beds: 24 beds
Note: Emergency services, obstetrics, physiotherapy, outpatient clinics, radiology, pharmacy
Mary Clare Egberts, President; CEO, Quinte Health Care

Port Colborne: Niagara Health System - Port Colborne Site (NHS)
Niagara Health System / Système de santé de Niagara
260 Sugarloaf St., Port Colborne, ON L3K 2N7
Tel: 905-378-4647; *Fax:* 905-834-0404 (
www.niagarahealth.on.ca

Year Founded: 1951
Number of Beds: 46 beds inpatient beds for complex continuing care; 35 beds at the New Port Centre for addiction recovery
Note: Hospital Specialties: Urgent Care Centre; Ontario Breast Screening Program; Eating Disorders Clinic; Addiction recovery, including a methadone clinic; Complex continuing care
Debbie Sevenpifer, President; Chief Executive Officer, Niagara Health System
Bala Kathiresan, Chief Operating Officer, Niagara Health System
Sue Matthews, Chief Nursing Executive; Vice-President, Patient Services, Port Colborne Site
Norma Medulun, Director, Clinical Program (Addiction Recovery)
905-378-4647, ext. 6

Port Perry: Lakeridge Health Corporation Port Perry Site
451 Paxton St., Port Perry, ON L9L 1A8
Tel: 905-985-7321; *Fax:* 905-985-5829
www.lakeridgehealth.on.ca

Number of Beds: 24 beds
Carol Anderson, Site Leader

Rainy River: Rainy River Health Centre
Affiliated with: Riverside Health Care Facilities Inc.
114 - 4th St., Rainy River, ON P0W 1L0
Tel: 807-852-3232; *Fax:* 807-852-3565
riverside@rhcf.on.ca
www.riversidehealthcare.ca

Number of Beds: 24 beds
Note: Emergency, diagnostic imaging, acute and long term care facility
Tammie McNally, Nurse Manager

Red Lake: Red Lake Margaret Cochenour Memorial Hospital
Also Known As: Red Lake Hospital
PO Box 5005, 51 Hwy. 105, Red Lake, ON P0V 2M0
Tel: 807-727-2066; *Fax:* 807-727-2923
info@redlakehospital.ca
www.redlakehospital.ca

Year Founded: 1973
Number of Beds: 14 acute care beds, 4 long term care beds
Note: Emergency services, lab, radiology & ultrasound, rehabilitation, sugery, endoscopy, nutritional services, chemotherapy, telehealth.
Ms. Janice Mullin, Chief Executive Officer

Renfrew: Renfrew Victoria Hospital
499 Raglan St. North, Renfrew, ON K7V 1P6
Tel: 613-432-4851; *Fax:* 613-432-8649
www.renfrewhosp.com

Year Founded: 1897
Number of Beds: 101 beds
Note: Birthing room & obstetrical care, pediatrics, chronic care, geriatric care, surgery, physiotherapy, palliative care, nephrology, urology, cardiac care, dialysis services, satellite oncology service, diagnostic imaging & ultrasound, dermatology, ophthalmology
Randy Penney, President/CEO
Julia Boudreau, Vice-President, Corporate Services

Richmond Hill: York Central Hospital
10 Trench St., Richmond Hill, ON L4C 4Z3
Tel: 905-883-1212; *Fax:* 905-883-2455
www.yorkcentral.on.ca

Number of Beds: 427 beds, 116 long-term care beds
Note: Total staff: 1732 Employees
William M. Leacy, President/CEO

Sarnia: Bluewater Health
Former Name: Charlotte Eleanor Englehart Hospital; Sarnia Gener
Norman Site, 89 Norman St., Sarnia, ON N7T 6S3
Tel: 519-464-4400; *Fax:* 519-336-8780
www.bluewaterhealth.ca

Year Founded: 2002
Number of Beds: 211 acute care beds; 88 complex continuing care beds
Note: Hospital Specialties: Emergency medicine; Laboratory services; Surgery; Acute care; Obstetrics; Pediatrics; Rehabilitation; Mental health services; Dialysis; Diabetes education; Nutrition services; Sexual & Domestic Assault Treatment Centre; Complex continuing care; Palliative care; Number of Employees: 2,070
Sue Denomy, President; Chief Executive Officer
519-464-4470, ext. 4, Fax: 519-336-8780,
sdenomy@bluewaterhealth.ca
Stephen Anema, Chief Financial Officer
519-464-4400, ext. 4, Fax: 519-346-4600,
sanema@bluewaterhealth.ca
Kim Bossy, Chief, Communications & Public Affairs
519-464-4400, ext. 4, Fax: 519-346-4600,
kbossy@bluewaterhealth.ca
Michael Lapaine, Chief Operating Officer; Vice-President, Operations
519-464-4400, ext. 4, Fax: 519-336-8780,
mlapaine@bluewaterhealth.ca
Dr. Martin Lees, Chief, Professional Staff & Quality / Risk Management
519-464-4400, ext. 4, Fax: 519-464-4501,
mlees@bluewaterhealth.ca
Barb O'Neil, Chief, Nursing, Interprofessional Practice & Organizat
519-464-4400, ext. 4, Fax: 519-346-4600,
boneil@bluewaterhealth.ca

Sault Ste Marie: Sault Area Hospital
969 Queen St. East, Sault Ste Marie, ON P6A 2C4
Tel: 705-759-3434; *Fax:* 705-759-3640
publicaffairs@sah.on.ca
www.sah.on.ca

Number of Beds: 289 beds
Note: Acute care hospital with over 1900 employees, 400 volunteers, and 125 physicians on staff.
Ron Gagnon, Interim President; CEO

Seaforth: Huron-Perth Healthcare Alliance
Seaforth Community Hospital
PO Box 99, 24 Centennial Dr., Seaforth, ON N0K 1W0
Tel: 519-527-1650; *Fax:* 519-527-8414
www.hpha.ca

Number of Beds: 34 beds
Andrew Williams, CEO
andrew.williams@hpha.ca

Seaforth: Seaforth Community Hospital
Affiliated with: Huron Perth Healthcare Alliance
PO Box 99, 24 Centennial Dr., Seaforth, ON N0K 1W0
Tel: 519-527-1650; *Fax:* 519-527-8414
administration@hpha.ca
www.hpha.ca/default.aspx?cid=48&lang=1

Year Founded: 1965
Number of Beds: 18 beds
Note: Emergency & ambulatory care, cardiorespiratory, diagnostic imaging, lab, physiotherapy, occupational therapy, chemotherapy, nutrition, diabetes education, dialysis, women's care & pediatrics, general surgery, intensive care & telemetry units, mental health services, dentistry. Heliport & Seaforth Medical Clinic
Andrew Williams, CEO, HPHA
519-272-8202, andrew.williams@hpha.ca
Ken Haworth, Vice-President; CFO, Operations, HPHA
519-272-8210, ken.haworth@hpha.ca
Bonnie Royal, Site Administrator; Program Director, Seaforth
519-527-3000, bonnie.royal@hpha.ca

Simcoe: Norfolk General Hospital
365 West St., Simcoe, ON N3Y 1T7
Tel: 519-426-0130; *Fax:* 519-429-6998
wlewis@ngh.on.ca
www.ngh.on.ca

Number of Beds: 121 beds
J. William C. Lewis, Executive Director

Sioux Lookout: Sioux Lookout Meno Ya Win Health Centre - 5th Avenue Site
PO Box 909, 5th Ave. South, Sioux Lookout, ON P8T 1B4
Tel: 807-737-3030; *Fax:* 807-737-3454
www.slmhc.on.ca

Year Founded: 2002
Number of Beds: 36 acute care beds, 5 chronic care beds, 20 extended care beds
Note: Emergency & ambulatory care, primary care services, specialized community-based programs, such as suicide prevention, addiction & mental health, long term care (William Bill George Extended Care facility), & integrated modern & traditional medicine. Services in English, Ojibway, Oji-Cree & Cree.
Mr. Douglas Semple, CEO (interim)
Mr. Doug Moynihan, Vice-President, Corporate Services
dmoynihan@slmhc.on.ca
Dr. Terry O'Driscoll, Chief of Staff
Ms. Renee Southwind, Manager, Communications and Community Development
807-737-5133, rsouthwind@slmhc.on.ca

Sioux Lookout: Sioux Lookout Meno Ya Win Health Centre - 7th Avenue Site
PO Box 909, 60 - 7th Ave., Sioux Lookout, ON P8T 1B4
Tel: 807-737-3030; *Fax:* 807-737-5127
www.slmhc.on.ca

Number of Beds: 35 beds
Note: Cancer care, cardiac care, lab, diagnostic imaging, pharmacy, telemedicine, library & education centre
Mr. Douglas Semple, CEO (interim)
Mr. Doug Moynihan, Vice-President, Corporate Services
Dr. Terry O'Driscoll, Chief of Staff
Ms. Renee Southwind, Manager, Communications & Community Development
807-737-5133, rsouthwind@slmhc.on.ca

Smiths Falls: Perth & Smiths Falls District Hospital Smiths Falls Site
60 Cornelia St. West, Smiths Falls, ON K7A 2H9
Tel: 613-283-2330; *Fax:* 613-283-8990
webinquiry@psfdh.on.ca
www.psfdh.on.ca
Note: Specialties: Acute care; Ambulatory care; Dialysis unit; Cataract surgery; Diabetes counselling; Children's mental health services; Sexual assault & domestic violence program; Vascular protection clinic; Chronic care; Palliative care. Number of Employees: 560
Todd Stepanuik, President/CEO

Smooth Rock Falls: Hôpital de Smooth Rock Falls Hospital
PO Box 219, 107 Kelly Road, Smooth Rock Falls, ON P0L 2B0
Tel: 705-338-2781; *Fax:* 705-338-4410
info@srfhosp.ca
www.srfhosp.ca
Number of Beds: 14 acute care beds, 23 long term care beds
Note: Primary care, including the North Cochrane Detoxification Centre. Number of staff: 85 staff, 1 FT & 3 PT physicians
Fabien L. Hébert, CEO

Southampton: Grey Bruce Health Services Southampton Hospital
340 High St., Southampton, ON N0H 2L0
Tel: 519-797-3230
www.gbhs.on.ca/southampton.php
Number of Beds: 16 inpatient beds
Note: Specialties: Day surgery services; Outpatient services, such as a women's health clinic; Home & community support services, such as the Day Away Program; Diabetes education; Physiotherapy; Palliative care. Number of employees: 105
Carolyn Zacharuk, Site Director

St Catharines: Niagara Health System - Ontario Street Site in St. Catharines
Niagara Health System / Système de santé de Niagara
Former Name: Hotel Dieu Hospital
155 Ontario St., St Catharines, ON L2R 5K3
Tel: 905-378-4647; *Fax:* 905-682-5533 (
www.niagarahealth.on.ca
Year Founded: 1948
Number of Beds: 43 beds for addiction management
Note: Hospital Specialties: Urgent Care Centre; Dialysis Program, including peritoneal dialysis, hemodialysis, & a pre-renal clinic; Addiction management services, including counselling, detoxification, & post-addiction services
Debbie Sevenpifer, President; Chief Executive Officer, Niagara Health System
Anne Atkinson, Vice-President, Patient Services, Ontario Street Site
Norma Medulun, Director, Clinical Program (Addiction Recovery)
905-378-4647, ext. 6

St Catharines: Niagara Health System - St. Catharines General Site (NHS)
Niagara Health System / Système de santé de Niagara
142 Queenston St., St Catharines, ON L2R 2Z7
Tel: 905-378-4647; *Fax:* 905-684-1468 (
www.niagarahealth.on.ca

Year Founded: 1865
Number of Beds: 200+ beds
Note: Hospital Specialties: Emergency services; Surgery; Acute care; Ambulatory care; Maternal & child services; Oncology; Ontario Breast Screening Program; Sexual Assault / Domestic Violence Treatment Centre; Mental health services; Critical care; Palliative care
Debbie Sevenpifer, President; Chief Executive Officer, Niagara Health System
Anne Atkinson, Vice-President, Patient Services, St. Catharines General Site
Terry McMahon, Vice-President, Human Resources, Niagara Health System
Dr. Joanna Hope, Chief of Staff, Niagara Health System
Bala Kathiresan, Chief Operating Officer, Niagara Health System
Donna Rothwell, Chief Nursing; Professional Practice Officer, Maternal; Child Care
Angela Zangari, Chief Financial Officer, Niagara Health System
Patricia Morka, Director, Clinical Program (Emergency & Critical Care)
905-378-4647, ext. 3
Heather Scott, Director, Clinical Program (Mental Health)
905-378-4647, ext. 5
Patty Welychka, Director, Clinical Program (Surgical Services)
905-378-4647, ext. 3

St Marys: St. Marys Memorial Hospital
Affiliated with: Huron Perth Healthcare Alliance
PO Box 940, 267 Queen St. West, St Marys, ON N4X 1B6
Tel: 519-284-1332; *Fax:* 519-284-8324
smmh.administration@hphp.org
www.hpha.ca

Year Founded: 1950
Number of Beds: 21 beds
Note: Primary care services include emergency, cardiac care, gynecology & pediatrics, rehabilitation, diagnostic imaging, orthopedic care
Mr. Andrew Williams, CEO, HPHA
519-272-8202, andrew.williams@hpha.ca.
Dr. Laurel Moore, Chief Of Staff, HPHA
519-272-8210, dr.laurel.moore@hpha.ca
Ms. Shirley Veenendaal, Site Administrator
shirley.veenendaal@hpha.ca

St Thomas: St. Thomas Elgin General Hospital
189 Elm St., St Thomas, ON N5R 5C4
Tel: 519-631-2020; *Fax:* 519-631-1825
publicrelations@stegh.on.ca
www.stegh.on.ca

Year Founded: 1954
Number of Beds: 166 beds
Note: A comprehensive health care facility with services including emergency, rehabiltation, complex Care, social work, diagnostic imaging, laboratory, pharmacy, surgery, diabetes education, cardiac intensive care, maternal care unit
Mr. Paul Collins, President /CEO
pcollins@stegh.on.ca
Mr. Malcolm Hopkins, Vice-President, Corporate Services
mhopkins@stegh.on.ca
Dr. Nancy Whitmore, Vice-President, Medical Affairs & Chief of Staff
nwhitmor@stegh.on.ca
Ms. Brenda Lambert, Vice-President, Patient Services
blambert@stegh.on.ca

Stratford: Stratford General Hospital
Affiliated with: Huron Perth Healthcare Alliance
46 General Hospital Dr., Stratford, ON N5A 2Y6
Tel: 519-271-2120; *Fax:* 519-271-7137
administration@hpha.ca
www.hpha.ca/default.aspx?cid=49&lang=1
Year Founded: 1896
Number of Beds: 153 beds (110 acute care beds, 25 chronic care beds, 15 rehab beds, 3 neonatal intensive care beds)
Note: A comprehensive care facility with services including emergency & ambulatory care, diagnostic imaging (CT scans, x-ray, ultrasound, mammography), obstetrics, gynecology, pediatrics, psychiatry, ophthalmology, complex continuing care, palliative care, rehabilitation, maternity, satellite dialysis unit, speech language pathology, surgery.
Mr. Andrew Williams, CEO, HPHA
519-272-8202, andrew.williams@hpha.ca
Dr. Laurel Moore, Chief of Staff, HPHA
519-272-8210, dr.laurel.moore@hpha.ca

Strathroy: Strathroy Middlesex General Hospital
Affiliated with: Middlesex Hospital Alliance
395 Carrie St., Strathroy, ON N7G 3J4
Tel: 519-245-5295; *Fax:* 519-245-0366
www.mhalliance.on.ca

Year Founded: 1914
Number of Beds: 77 beds (of which 60 are acute care beds)
Note: A full-service, community hospital with comprehensive outpatient services, primary & secondary care. Services include emergency & trauma care, cataract surgery, diagnostic imaging (bone mineral density, CT scans, x-rays, mammography, ultrasound), intensive care/coronary care unit, obstetrics, urology, orthopedics, gynecology, otolaryngology, ophthalmology and some operative dental.
Mr. Michael A. Mazza, CEO, MHA
Dr. Marc Raymond, President, Medical Staff
Dr. Paul Ferner, Chief of Staff

Sturgeon Falls: The West Nipissing General Hospital
L'Hôpital général de Nipissing Ouest
725 Coursol Rd., Sturgeon Falls, ON P2B 2Y6
Tel: 705-753-3110; *Fax:* 705-753-0210
marthe.levac@wngh.ca
www.wngh.ca

Year Founded: 1977
Number of Beds: 56 beds
Note: Number of staff: 9 physicians, 1 nurse practitioner
Yves Campeau, Executive Director

Sudbury: Sudbury Regional Hospital - Laurentian Site
Hôpital régional de Sudbury - Emplacement Laurentien
41 Ramsey Lake Rd., Sudbury, ON P3E 5J1
Tel: 705-523-7100; *Fax:* 705-523-7112
Toll-Free: 1-866-469-0822
communications@hrsrh.on.ca
www.hrsrh.on.ca
Number of Beds: 530 acute care beds
Note: Complex continuing care, assistive communication clinic, chiropody clinic, eating disorders clinic, HIV/AIDS clinic, intensive rehabilitation, physiotherapy, occupational therapy
Vickie Kaminski, President/CEO

Sudbury: Sudbury Regional Hospital - Memorial Site
Hôpital régional de Sudbury - Emplacement Mémorial
865 Regent St. South, Sudbury, ON P3E 3Y9
Tel: 705-523-7100; *Toll-Free:* 1-866-469-0822
communications@hrsrh.on.ca
www.hrsrh.on.ca
Number of Beds: 189 beds
Vickie Kaminski, CEO
Chris McKibbon, Chief of Staff

Sudbury: Sudbury Regional Hospital - St. Joseph's Health Centre
Hôpital régional de Sudbury - Centre de santé de St-Joseph
700 Paris St., Sudbury, ON P3B 3B5
Tel: 705-523-7100; *Fax:* 0
communications@hrsrh.on.ca
www.hrsrh.on.ca

Jo-Anne Palkovits, CEO

Terrace Bay: The McCausland Hospital
20B Cartier Rd., Terrace Bay, ON P0T 2W0
Tel: 807-825-3273; *Fax:* 807-825-9623
admin@mccauslandhospital.com
www.mccauslandhospital.com
Year Founded: 1980
Number of Beds: 45 beds (23 community beds, 22 long-term beds)
Note: Services include emergency, cancer care, diabetes program, diagnostic imaging (ECG, Holter monitors, radiology, ultrasound), laboratory, obstetrics & gynecology, physiotherapy, seniors drop-in program, surgery.
Mr. Paul Paradis, CEO
ceo@mccauslandhospital.com
Dr. David Hurst, Chief of Staff

***Thunder Bay:* Hogarth-Westmount Hospital**
300 Lillie St., Thunder Bay, ON P7C 4Y7
Tel: 807-625-1110; *Fax:* 807-623-4520
Number of Beds: 228 beds
Barry Brown, Executive Director
Richard Roberts, Director, Physical Plant

***Thunder Bay:* St. Joseph's Care Group**
Former Name: St. Joseph's Care Group
PO Box 3251, 35 North Algoma St., Thunder Bay, ON P7B 5G7
Tel: 807-343-2431; *Fax:* 807-345-4994
www.sjcg.net
Number of Beds: 224 beds
Carl White, President
Jack Tallon, Director, Materials Management

***Thunder Bay:* Thunder Bay Regional Health Sciences Centre**
980 Oliver Rd., Thunder Bay, ON P7B 6V4
Tel: 807-684-6000
tbrhsc@tbh.net
www.tbrhsc.com
Year Founded: 2004
Number of Beds: 375 acute care beds (28 beds for anesthetic recovery, 40 beds for day surgery recovery)
Note: A comprehensive, multi-disciplinary, acute care facility with services incuding emergency, ambulatory care, asthma education, cardiology, critical care unit, dentistry, diagnostic imaging (breast MRI, CT scans, radiology), dietitians, forensics, Holter monitoring, Hospice Northwest, ICU, laboratory, maternity, oncology (brachytherapy), paediatrics, renal program, respiratory therapy, surgery, trauma rooms. The TBRHSC amalgamates the former Port Arthur & McKellar sites of the Thunder Bay Regional Hospital.
Ms. Andrée Robichaud, President/CEO
Ms. Lori Marshall, Vice-President, Medicine, Cardiology, Mental Health and Maternal/Ch
Dr. Blair Schoales, Chief of Staff
Mr. Don Edwards, Director, Communications
807-684-6010

***Tillsonburg:* Tillsonburg District Memorial Hospital**
PO Box 3100, 167 Rolph St., Tillsonburg, ON N4G 3Y9
Tel: 519-842-3611; *Fax:* 519-688-1031
mail@tillsonburghospital.on.ca
www.tillsonburghospital.on.ca
Number of Beds: 79 beds
Note: Services include emergency, ambulatory care, Community Care Access Centre, complex continuing care, diagnostic imaging (ultrasound, nuclear medicine, mammography, x-ray, fluoroscopy), diabetes education, dialysis, dietitian, geriatric rehab therapy program, intensive coronary care, interpreter services, mental health, palliative care, pastoral care, pharmacy, physiotherapy, surgery.
Mr. Tom McHugh, President/CEO
Dr. Gerry Rowland, President, Medical Staff
Mr. Frank Deutsch, Senior Executive Leader/CFO
Ms. Julie Ellery, Senior Executive Leader, Patient Services

***Timmins:* Timmins & District Hospital**
L'Hôpital de Timmins et du district
700 Ross Ave. East, Timmins, ON P4N 8P2
Tel: 705-267-2131; *Fax:* 705-267-6311
evainio@tadh.com
www.tadh.com
Number of Beds: 159 beds
Note: Level C referral hospital, providing services in English & French; mental health services; medical, surgical, obstetrics & pediatrics, intensive care; complex continuing care & interim long term care
Esko Vainio, President/CEO

***Toronto:* The Hospital for Sick Children**
Also Known As: SickKids
555 University Ave., Toronto, ON M5G 1X8
Tel: 416-813-1500
inquiry.patientrep@sickkids.ca; hr.recruiter@sickkids.ca
www.sickkids.ca
Info Line: 416-813-6621
Note: Specialties: Paediatric academic health sciences; Paediatric emergency medicine; Trauma; Developmental paediatrics; Fetal cardiac program, cardiac transplants, cardiovascular surgery, & cardiac critical care; Neonatology; Clinical & metabolic genetics; Cleft lip & palate; Neurology & neurosurgery; Cochlear implants; Haematology / Oncology; Communication disorders; Infectious diseases; Immunology & allergy; Gastroenterology, hepatology, & nutrition; Orthotics & medical devices; Rehabilitation; Child & youth counselling; Program for international patients (cindy.fiore@sickkids.ca)
Mary Jo Haddad, Pres./CEO
Scott Menzies, Director, Environmental & Central Services
Valerie O'Grady, Waste Management Coordinator

***Toronto:* Humber River Regional Hospital Church St. Site**
200 Church St., Toronto, ON M9N 1N8
Tel: 416-249-8111; *Fax:* 416-243-4547
www.hrrh.on.ca
Reuben Devlin, President; CEO
Dr. Jack Barkin, Chief of Staff

***Toronto:* Humber River Regional Hospital Keele St. Site**
2175 Keele St., Toronto, ON M6M 3Z4
Tel: 416-249-8111
www.hrrh.on.ca

***Toronto:* Humber River Regional Hospital Finch Ave. Site**
2111 Finch Ave. West, Toronto, ON M3N 1N1
Tel: 416-744-2500; *Fax:* 416-747-3882
administration@hrrh.on.ca
www.hrrh.on.ca
Number of Beds: 610 beds
Reuben Devlin, President/CEO
Barbara Collins, COO; Vice-President, Planning; Support Services
Scott Jarrett, Vice-President, Patient Programs
Richard Kelly, Vice-President, Human Resources & Support Services
Peter Wegener, Vice-President, Finance & Information Systems

***Toronto:* Humber River Regional Hospital - Keele St. Site**
2175 Keele St., Toronto, ON M6M 3Z4
Tel: 416-651-6111; *Fax:* 416-658-2192
www.hrrh.on.ca

***Toronto:* Mount Sinai Hospital**
#334, 600 University Ave., Toronto, ON M5G 1X5
Tel: 416-596-4200; *Fax:* 416-586-8555
patientrelationsunit@mtsinai.on.ca
www.mountsinai.on.ca
Number of Beds: 472 beds
Note: Teaching and research Hospital; Home to five Centres of Excellence
Joseph Mapa, Pres./CEO

***Toronto:* North York General Hospital - Branson Site**
555 Finch Ave. West, Toronto, ON M2R 1N5
Tel: 416-633-9420; *Fax:* 416-635-2537
www.nygh.on.ca
Number of Beds: 205 beds
Note: Urgent & ambulatory care, Ontario Breast Screening Program site, pediatric speech & language services, diagnostic imaging, geriatric medicine & psychiatry, Gale & Graham Wright Prostrate Centre
Bonnie Adamson, President/CEO

***Toronto:* North York General Hospital - General Site**
4001 Leslie St., Toronto, ON M2K 1E1
Tel: 416-756-6000; *Fax:* 416-756-6384
www.nygh.on.ca
Number of Beds: 400 beds
Note: Community teaching hospital affiliated with the University of Toronto. Comprehensive health care services including full service emergency unit
Bonnie Adamson, President/CEO

***Toronto:* Rouge Valley Centenary**
Affiliated with: Rouge Valley Health System
2867 Ellesmere Rd., Toronto, ON M1E 4B9
Tel: 416-284-8131; *Fax:* 416-281-7323
www.rougevalley.ca
Year Founded: 1967
Number of Beds: 285 beds
Note: Emergency, cardiac care, mental health, paediatrics.
Rik Ganderton, President/CEO, RVHS
boardofdirectors@rougevalley.ca
David Brazeau, Director, RVHS, Public Affairs & Community Relations
647-294-8885, dbrazeau@rougevalley.ca

***Toronto:* St. Joseph's Health Centre**
30 The Queensway, Toronto, ON M6R 1B5
Tel: 416-530-6000; *Fax:* 416-530-6346
www.stjoe.on.ca
Year Founded: 1921
Number of Beds: 376 beds
Note: Services include emergency & critical care, women/children/family health, seniors' care, surgery, oncology, diagnostic imaging, rehabilitation. This teaching hospital was founded by the Sisters of St. Joseph.
Ms. Carolyn Baker, President/CEO
Mr. Dale McGregor, Executive Vice-President/CFO
Dr. Tom Harmantas, Chief of Staff

***Toronto:* St. Michael's Hospital**
1 Queen Wing, 30 Bond St., Toronto, ON M5B 1W8
Tel: 416-360-4000; *Fax:* 416-360-7304
www.stmichaelshospital.com
Number of Beds: 527 inpatient
Note: Catholic hospital with a focus on teaching and research affiliated with the University of Toronto
Jeffrey Lozon, President; CEO
William Rosenitsch, Director, Material Management

***Toronto:* The Salvation Army Toronto Grace Health Centre**
Also Known As: Toronto Grace Hospital
650 Church St., Toronto, ON M4Y 2G5
Tel: 416-925-2251; *Fax:* 416-925-3211
info@torontograce.org
www.torontograce.org
Year Founded: 1905
Number of Beds: 119 beds
Note: A patient-centred, palliative and complex continuing care facility focusing on holistic and respite care for patients, families and friends through inpatient and community outreach programs.
Ms. Marilyn Rook, President/CEO
Ms. Monica Codjoe, Vice-President, Patient Services
Dr. David Van Der Hout, Medical Director
Ms. Alexis Dishaw, Director, Communications, Community Engagement and Strategic
Ms. Beth D'Angelo, Manager, Patient Care
edangelo@torontograce.org
Mr. John P. Murray, Spokesperson, Public Relations and Development
416-998-0117, John_Murray@can.salvationarmy.org

***Toronto:* The Scarborough Hospital - Birchmount Campus**
Former Name: The Scarborough Hospital - Grace Campus
3030 Birchmount Rd., Toronto, ON M1W 3W3
Tel: 416-495-2400; *Fax:* 416-431-8204
info@tsh.to
www.tsh.to
Number of Beds: 650 beds total
Note: A health facility with emphasis on emergency outpatient psychiatric concerns, notably its Regional Crisis Program, an emergency response team to acute psychiatric crises. Total staff: 3,700
Dr. John Wright, President/CEO
Dr. Steven Jackson, Chief of Medical Staff
Ms. Ester Lipnicki, Executive Director, Patient Services & Quality Care
Mr. Dave Bourne, Manager, Corporate Communications
dbourne@tsh.to
Ms. Sara Kirkup, Manager, Regional Crisis Program
416-495-2891, Fax: 416-495-2880, skirkup@tsh.to

***Toronto:* The Scarborough Hospital - General Campus**
3050 Lawrence Ave. East, Toronto, ON M1P 2V5
Tel: 416-438-2911; *Fax:* 416-431-8204
www.tsh.to
Number of Beds: 556 beds (medical 266, surgical 134, paediatric 14, ICU/CCU 32, obstetric 44, mental health 50, rehab 16 beds)
Note: A comprehensive community facility with services including emergency, cardio-respiratory & critical care, specialized geriatrics, family medicine & community services, maternal/newborn & child care, mental health, nephrology & dialysis, oncology, surgery, sexual assault care & domestic violence program, orthopedics & rehabilitation. Total staff: 3,700
Dr. John Wright, President/CEO
Mr. Ralph Anstey, Vice-President/CFO
Ms. Lindsey Crawford, Vice-President, Patient Services
Ms. Cara Fleming, Vice-President/CIO, Performance
Dr. Steven Jackson, Chief of Medical Staff
Mr. Dave Bourne, Manager, Corporate Communications
dbourne@tsh.to

***Toronto:* Sunnybrook Health Sciences Centre**
2075 Bayview Ave., Toronto, ON M4N 3M5
Tel: 416-480-6100
questions@sunnybrook.ca
www.sunnybrook.ca
Year Founded: 1948
Number of Beds: 1,212 beds
Note: A comprehensive health facility with a focus on cancer care (Odette Cancer Centre), cardiac care (Schulich Heart Centre), musculoskeletal care (Holland Musculoskeletal

Program), brain science program (stroke, dementias, mood disorders), women's health, infertility, perinatal care, pediatrics, emergency services, trauma & critical care, veterans' care & residence, research & education. Number of staff: 10,000
Dr. Barry A. McLellan, President/CEO
Dr. Michael Julius, Vice-President, Research
Dr. Wendy Levinson, Physician-in-Chief
Dr. Gordon Rubenfeld, Chief, Trauma, Emergency and Critical Care

Toronto: Sunnybrook Health Sciences Centre - Perinatal & Gynaecology Unit
New Women's College Hospital, 76 Grenville St., Toronto, ON M5S 1B2
Tel: 416-323-6400; *Fax:* 416-323-7314
www.sunnybrook.ca
Note: The facility focuses on perinatal care (labour, delivery, newborn care), gynaecological conditions, mature women's health, infertility, cancers with an aim to high quality, individualized care. On site are a pregnancy & birth unit, high risk unit, NICU, HPV Vaccine Clinic.
Dr. Barry A. McLellan, President/CEO

Toronto: Toronto East General Hospital
825 Coxwell Ave., Toronto, ON M4C 3E7
Tel: 416-461-8272; *Fax:* 416-469-6106
ptrep@tegh.on.ca (Patients); community@tegh.on.ca (Community)
www.tegh.on.ca
Year Founded: 1929
Note: Specialties: Ambulatory & community services; Emergency; Diagnostic imaging; Laboratory medicine; Surgery; Maternal & newborn care; Diabetes education community network; Mental health services; Complex continuing care & rehabilitation; Progressive weaning centre
Robert Devitt, President; CEO
Joanne Holgate, Director, Environmental Services
416/469-6471,

Toronto: Trillium Health Centre - West Toronto Site
150 Sherway Dr., Toronto, ON M9C 1A5
Tel: 416-259-6671; *Fax:* 416-253-2500
publicrelations@thc.on.ca
www.trilliumhealthcentre.org
Note: An ambulatory care facility with services including urgent care centre (8:00 a.m.-10:00 p.m. only, daily), day surgery, diabetes management centre, cardiac wellness & rehabilitation, Kingsway Financial Spine Centre, The Betty Wallace Women's Health Centre (focusing on osteoporosis and breast disease). There is no emergency centre here; it is located at branch in Mississauga.
Ms. Janet M. Davidson, President /CEO
Ms. Ruby Brown, Executive Vice-President/COO
Dr. Gopal Bhatnagar, Chief of Staff
Mr. Larry Roberts, Media Relations Consultant
905-848-7580, lroberts@thc.on.ca

Toronto: University Health Network
Former Name: The Toronto Hospital
190 Elizabeth St., Toronto, ON M5G 2C4
Tel: 416-340-3388; *Fax:* 416-340-4896
uhn.info@uhn.on.ca
www.uhn.ca
Number of Beds: 1,093 beds (total, all sites)
Note: Comprised of Princess Margaret Hospital, Toronto General Hospital, & Toronto Western Hospital, UHN is a comprehensive health care, research & teaching facility with fields of focus including cancer care, cardiac care, musculoskeletal health & arthritis, neuroscience, ophthalmology, surgical & critical care, transplantation. The network is affiliated with the University of Toronto, Faculty of Medicine.
Dr. Robert S. Bell, President /CEO
416-340-3300
Mr. Kevin Empey, Executive Vice President, Clinical Support & Corporate Services
Dr. Mary Ferguson Paré, Chief Nurse Executive/Vice-President, Professional Affairs
Ms. Gillian Howard, Vice-President, Public Affairs & Communications
416-340-4838, gillian.howard@uhn.on.ca

Toronto: University Health Network - Toronto General Hospital
200 Elizabeth St., Toronto, ON M5G 2C4
Tel: 416-340-4800; *Fax:* 416-340-5054
uhn.info@uhn.on.ca
www.uhn.ca/applications/TGH/iNews/default.aspx
Year Founded: 1829
Number of Beds: 471 beds
Note: A comprehensive, health care and teaching facility, its specialties include cardiac care (Peter Munk Cardiac Centre), transplantation, kidney diseases & care, tropical disease, eating disorders, nephrology, psychiatry, HIV/AIDS care, telemedicine. It is home to the MaRS Discovery District, a not-for-profit research corporation with funding from both private and public sectors.
Dr. Robert Bell, President/CEO, UHN
416-340-3300
Dr. Charlie Chan, Vice-President, Medical Affairs, UHN
Ms. Marnie Escaf, Site Lead/Vice-President, UHN
Ms. Gillian Howard, Vice-President, Public Affairs & Communications, UHN
416-340-4838, gillian.howard@uhn.on.ca

Toronto: University Health Network - Toronto Western Hospital
399 Bathurst St., Toronto, ON M5T 2S8
Tel: 416-603-5800
uhn.info@uhn.on.ca
www.uhn.ca/applications/TWH/iNews/default.aspx
Year Founded: 1905
Number of Beds: 256 beds
Note: The facility focuses on neural/sensory science research & treatment, musculoskeletal health. Other fields of specialty include acupuncture for addictions, Asian Initiative in Mental Health program, asthma care, cardiac/pulmonary wellness centre, chronic pain, dermatology, diabetes education, epilepsy, geriatrics, memory, neuro-ophthalmology, neuro-otology, neurosurgery, occupational lung disease, outpatient physiotherapy, peritoneal dialysis, plastic surgery, Portuguese mental health & addictions, psychiatry, renal clinic, sleep, spinal cord, Tourette's syndrome, tuberculosis, urology.
Dr. Robert Bell, President/CEO, UHN
416-340-3300
Dr. Charlie Chan, Vice-President, Medical Affairs, UHN
Ms. Kathy Sabo, Site Lead/Vice-President
kathy.sabo@uhn.on.ca
Ms. Gillian Howard, Vice-President, Public Affairs & Communications, UHN
416-340-4838, gillian.howard@uhn.on.ca

Toronto: William Osler Health Centre - Etobicoke General Hospital Campus
101 Humber College Blvd., Toronto, ON M9V 1R8
Tel: 416-747-2120; *Fax:* 0
Number of Beds: 250 beds
Note: Comprehensive health care services. The William Osler Health Centre is comprised of the Etobicoke General Hospital, Brampton Civic Hospital, & the Peel Memorial Hospital (in re-development)
Dawne Barbiei, Site Executive; Chief Nursing Officer

Trenton: Quinte Health Care Trenton Memorial Quinte Health Care
242 King St., Trenton, ON K8V 5S6
Tel: 613-392-2540; *Fax:* 613-392-3749
www.qhc.on.ca/Default.aspx?cid=274&lang=1
Year Founded: 1951
Number of Beds: 33 beds
Note: Emergency services, intensive care, outpatient clinics, lab, pharmacy, radiology, surgical service, psychiatry
Wendy Parker, Site Administrator
Ext. 5376

Uxbridge: Markham-Stouffville Hospital Uxbridge Site
Former Name: Uxbridge Cottage Hospital
PO Box 5003, 4 Campbell Dr., Uxbridge, ON L9P 1S4
Tel: 905-852-9771
myhospital@msh.on.ca
www.msh.on.ca
Info Line: 905-852-9771
Year Founded: 1959
Number of Beds: 20 beds
Note: Specialties: Diagnostic services; Rhabilitation services, such as physiotherapy & diabetes education
Lorne Zen, Actg. COO

Walkerton: South Bruce Grey Health Centre - Walkerton Site
Walkerton Hospital
PO Box 1300, 21 McGivern St. W., Walkerton, ON N0G 2V0
Tel: 519-881-1220; *Fax:* 519-881-0452
www.sbghc.on.ca
Year Founded: 1900
Number of Beds: 38 beds
Note: A rural health centre with services including emergency, cardio-respiratory care, dental care, ear/nose/throat, family birthing centre, internal medicine, pediatrics, surgery, urology, nutrition services, diagnostic imaging, lab, physiotherapy, healthy heart program
Paul L. Davies, President/CEO, SBGHC
pdavies@sbghc.on.ca
Jill Machan, Site Manager/Director, Patient Care
jmachan@sbghc.on.ca

Wawa: Lady Dunn Health Centre
PO Box 179, 17 Government Rd., Wawa, ON P0S 1K0
Tel: 705-856-2335; *Fax:* 705-856-7533
Toll-Free: 866-832-3321
www.ldhc.com
Number of Beds: 26 beds
Sally Garland, CEO
Gary Trudeau, Chair, Environmental Committee
Holly Morrison-Smith, Manager, Environmental Services

Welland: Niagara Health System Welland Hospital Site
65 Third St., Welland, ON L3B 4W6
Tel: 905-378-4647; *Fax:* 905-732-3268
www.niagarahealth.on.ca
Number of Beds: 119 acure care; 56 continuing care; 16 mental health
K. Scott, Director, Environmental Services

Whitby: Lakeridge Health Corporation Whitby Site
300 Gordon St., Whitby, ON L1N 5T2
Tel: 905-668-6831; *Fax:* 905-665-2406
www.lakeridgehealth.on.ca
Number of Beds: 74 beds
Carol Anderson, Site Lead

Wiarton: Grey Bruce Health Services Wiarton Hospital
369 Mary St., Wiarton, ON N0H 2T0
Tel: 519-534-1260; *Fax:* 519-534-4450
www.gbhs.on.ca/wiarton.php
Number of Beds: 18 inpatient beds
Note: Specialties: Acute care; Dental surgery; Diabetes education; Physiotherapy; Mental health & addictions programs; Palliative care. Number of employees: 107
Pat Campbell, Pres./CEO

Winchester: Winchester District Memorial Hospital
566 Louise St., Winchester, ON K0C 2K0
Tel: 613-774-2422; *Fax:* 613-774-0453
www.wdmh.on.ca
Number of Beds: 70 beds
Note: Teaching hospital with emergency care, general surgery, cardiac & respiratory care, diabetes care, obstetrics & pediatrics, rehabilitation, palliative care, chemotherapy, diagnostic imaging
Trudy Reid, President/CEO
treid@wdmh.on.ca

Windsor: Hôtel Dieu Grace Hospital
1030 Ouellette Ave., Windsor, ON N9A 1E1
Tel: 519-973-4444; *Fax:* 519-973-0803
www.hdgh.org
Number of Beds: 305 beds
John Coughlin, Pres./CEO
Patricia Somers, Vice President of Operations

Windsor: The Windsor Regional Hospital - Metropolitan Campus
1995 Lens Ave., Windsor, ON N8W 1L9
Tel: 519-254-5577; *Fax:* 519-254-2317
www.wrh.on.ca
Year Founded: 1928
Number of Beds: 669 beds (total of all WRH sites)
Note: An acute care facility with services including emergency, ambulatory care, intensive care, Breast Health Centre, cardiac & critical care, diagnostic imaging (nuclear medicine/MRI), endoscopy, family birthing centre, Oncology Inpatient Program, paediatrics, regional cancer services, surgery
Mr. David Musyj, President/CEO
Dr. Gary Ing, Medical Chief of Staff
Ms. Karen McCullough, Vice-President/Chief Nursing Executive, Acute Care Services
Mr. Ron Foster, Vice-President, Public Affairs, Communication and Philanthropy
fosterr@wrh.on.ca

Windsor: The Windsor Regional Hospital - Western Campus
1453 Prince Rd., Windsor, ON N9C 3Z4
Tel: 519-254-5577; *Fax:* 519-254-2317
www.wrh.on.ca
Year Founded: 1910
Number of Beds: 669 beds (total of all WRH sites)
Note: Services include inter-disciplinary rehabilitation, complex continuing care, long term care, specialized mental health services, audiology, speech language pathology, acquired brain injury treatment, geriatric assessment & consultation program, physiotherapy, occupational therapy and chiropody. The Malden Park Continuing Care Centre is also located at this campus.
Mr. David Musyj, President/CEO
Dr. Gary Ing, Medical Chief of Staff

Ms. Sharon Pillon, Vice-President, Complex Continuing Care/Rehabilitation
Mr. Ron Foster, Vice-President, Public Affairs, Communications and Philanthropy
fosterr@wrh.on.ca

Wingham: Wingham & District Hospital
Affiliated with: Listowel & Wingham Hospitals Alliance
270 Carling Terrace, Wingham, ON N0G 2W0
Tel: 519-357-3210; *Fax:* 519-357-3522
www.lwha.ca
Number of Beds: 50 beds
Note: Acute care facility, emergency services, surgery, obstetrics & pediatrics, rehabilitation, specialist clinics; affiliated with the London Regional Cancer Centre; air ambulance service; medical clinic. Number of staff: 6 physicians, resident surgeon, 2 anesthetists
Margret Comack, CEO
margret.comack@lwha.ca

Woodstock: Woodstock General Hospital
270 Riddell St., Woodstock, ON N4S 6N4
Tel: 519-421-4211; *Fax:* 519-537-5142
www.wgh.on.ca
Number of Beds: 120 beds
Natasa Veljovic, President/CEO

Federal Hospitals

Ottawa: Canadian Forces Health Care Centre Ottawa (CF H Svc)
713 Montreal Rd., Ottawa, ON K1K 0T2
Tel: 945-1140; 61; *Fax:* 613-991-1543
www.forces.gc.ca/health-sante
Note: Hospital Specialties: Primary health care services to the military community in the National Capital Region (613-945-1502); Laboratory services; Surgery; Cardio Pulmonary Unit; Operational Trauma & Stress Support Centre (613-945-1060); Mental health (613-945-1060); Addiction counselling (613-945-1060); Ophthalmology (613-945-1550); Physiotherapy (613-945-1585); Preventive medicine (613-945-1604); Public health
LCol Gisele Fontaine, Commanding Officer
LCol Michel P. Deilgat, NCR Surgeon
CPO2 Mario Richard, Clinic Sergeant-Major
Cdr. Nathalie Tremblay, Officer, Patient Relations
Fax: 613-945-1836

Private Hospitals

Penetanguishene: Hôpital Privé Beechwood Private Hospital
58 Church St., Penetanguishene, ON L9M 1B3
Tel: 705-549-7473; *Fax:* 705-549-7194
bph@bellnet.ca
Number of Beds: 20 beds
L. Bellisle, CEO

Thornhill: Shouldice Hospital Ltd.
PO Box 370, 7750 Bayview Ave., Thornhill, ON L3T 4A3
Tel: 905-889-1125; *Fax:* 905-889-4216
Toll-Free: 800-291-7750
postoffice@shouldice.com
www.shouldice.com
Year Founded: 1945
Number of Beds: 89 beds
Note: Specializes in hernia repair; walk-in clinic
Dr. Cassim Degani, Chief Surgeon

Toronto: Don Mills Surgical Unit Inc. (DMSU)
Centric Health Group
#208, 20 Wynford Dr., Toronto, ON M3C 1J4
Tel: 416-441-2111; *Fax:* 416-441-2114
Toll-Free: 1-888-857-6069
info@dmsu.com
www.dmsu.com
Number of Beds: 20 in-patient beds
Note: Hospital Specialties: Opthamology; Orthopedic surgery; Plastic & reconstructive surgery; Number of Employees: 16 surgeons; 10 anesthesiologists
Dr. Robert G. Gordon, Superintendent

Toronto: St. Joseph's Infirmary
Former Name: St. Joseph's Morrow Park Infirmary & Private Hospi
3377 Bayview Ave., Toronto, ON M2M 2S4
Tel: 416-222-1101; *Fax:* 416-222-0186
Number of Beds: 57 beds
Catherine McDonough, Administrator
Diane Hibrant, Nursing Administrator

Woodbridge: Cosmetic Surgery Hospital (CSH)
The Manor, 4650 Hwy. 7, Woodbridge, ON L4L 1S7
Tel: 905-851-7701; *Fax:* 905-856-4406
info@cosmeticsurgeryhospital.com
www.cosmeticsurgeryhospital.com
Year Founded: 1970
Note: Hospital Specialties: Plastic & cosmetic surgery; Clinical obesity
Dr. Lloyd N. Carlsen, Director
Dr. Paul Braude, Medical Director, Ageless

Woodstock: Woodstock Private Hospital
369 Huron St., Woodstock, ON N4S 7A5
Tel: 519-537-8162; *Fax:* 519-537-7204
wph@gtn.net
Number of Beds: 16 beds
Note: Chronic care hospital
Irma C. Vander Zwaag, Administrator
Marg Atkinson, Head, Housekeeping

Auxiliary Hospitals

Toronto: Baycrest Hospital
Baycrest Geriatric Health Care System
3560 Bathurst St., Toronto, ON M6A 2E1
Tel: 416-785-2500; *Fax:* 416-785-2378
webmaster@baycrest.org
www.baycrest.org
Year Founded: 1986
Number of Beds: 300 hospital beds
Note: Hospital Specialties: Acute geriatric care; Rehabilitation; Psychiatry; Behavioural neurology; Complex continuing care for the elderly; Palliative care
William Reichman, President; Chief Executive Officer
David Conn, Vice-President, Education
Laurie Harrison, Chief Financial Officer & Vice-President, Corporate Services
Paul Katz, Chief of Staff & Vice-President, Medical Services
Joni Kent, Vice-President, Human Resources & Organizationa Effectiveness
Karima Velji, Chief Nursing Executive; Vice-President, Clinical; Residential Programs
Nancy Webb, Vice-President, Public Affairs &Stakeholders Relations

Welland: Niagara Health System - Welland Hospital Site (NHS)
Niagara Health System / Système de santé de Niagara
Third St., Welland, ON L3B 4W6
Tel: 905-378-4647; *Fax:* 905-732-3268 (
www.niagarahealth.on.ca
Year Founded: 1908
Number of Beds: 160 beds
Note: Hospital Specialties: Emergency service; Intensive care; Acute care; Ambulatory care; Maternal & child care services; Ontario Breast Screening Program; Dialysis; Nephrology; Mental health services; Complex continuing care
Debbie Sevenpifer, President; Chief Executive Officer, Niagara Health System
Christine Clark, Chief Communications Officer, Niagara Health System
Sue Matthews, Chief Nursing Executive; Vice-President, Patient Services, Welland Hospital Site
Su Bolibruck, Director, Clinical Programs (Chronic Kidney Disease, Cardiolo
905-378-4647, ext. 3
Patricia Morka, Director, Clinical Programs (Emergency & Critical Care)
905-378-4647, ext. 3
Debbie Smith, Director, Clinical Programs (Primary Care Services & Inpa
905-378-4647, ext. 5,

Community Health Centres

Community Health Care Centres

Ajax: Barbara Black Centre for Youth Resources
Also Known As: The Youth Centre
#5, 360 Bayly St. West, Ajax, ON L1S 1P1
Tel: 905-428-1212; *Fax:* 905-428-9151
Susan Bland, Executive Director

Barrie: Barrie Community Health Centre
56 Bayfield St., Barrie, ON L4M 3A5
Tel: 705-734-9690; *Fax:* 705-734-0239
bchc@csolve.net
www.bchc.ca
Note: Community-focused health promotion, illness prevention, & primary care services. Services provided by physicians, registered nurses, social workers, physiotherapists, & dietitians. North Innisfil office located at: 902 Lockhart Rd., 705-431-9245.
Carla Palmer, Executive Director

Barrie: CCAC North Simcoe Muskoka
#100, 15 Sperling Dr., Barrie, ON L4M 6K9
Tel: 705-721-8010; *Fax:* 705-792-6294
Toll-Free: 888-721-2222
www.ccac-ont.ca
Note: With offices in Barrie & Huntsville, provides health & personal support services for individuals living independently at home or making the transition to alternative care settings; information & referral, advocacy
Al Scarth, Board Chair

Belleville: CCAC South East - Belleville Branch Office
Bayview Mall, 470 Dundas St. East, Belleville, ON K8N 1G1
Tel: 613-966-3530; *Fax:* 613-966-0996
Toll-Free: 1-800-668-0901
www.ccac-ont.ca
John Hill, Board Chair

Brampton: CCAC Central West
199 County Court Blvd., 3rd Fl., Brampton, ON L6W 4P3
Tel: 905-796-0040; *Fax:* 905-796-5620
Toll-Free: 1-800-733-1177
www.ccac-ont.ca
David Lehtovaara, Board Chair

Brantford: CCAC Hamilton Niagara Haldimand Brant - Brant Branch Office
274 Colborne St., Brantford, ON N3T 2H5
Tel: 519-759-7752; *Fax:* 519-759-7130
Toll-Free: 1-866-759-7752
www.ccac-ont.ca
Note: Head office for the region
Melody Miles, Executive Director

Burlington: CCAC Hamilton Niagara Haldimand Brant - Burlington Branch Office
440 Elizabeth St., 4th Fl., Burlington, ON L7R 2M1
Tel: 905-639-5228; *Fax:* 905-639-5320
Toll-Free: 1-800-810-0000
www.ccac-ont.ca
Melody Miles, Executive Director

Cambridge: Langs Farm Village Association
#1, 887 Langs Dr., Cambridge, ON N3H 5K4
Tel: 519-653-1470; *Fax:* 519-653-1285
billd@langs.org
William Davidson, Executive Director

Chatham: CCAC Erie St. Clair
PO Box 306, 712 Richmond St., Chatham, ON N7M 5K4
Tel: 519-436-2222; *Toll-Free:* 888-447-4468
www.ccac-ont.ca
Note: Head Office located at the Chatham-Kent branch, with other branch offices located in Sarnia & Windsor. Provides access to in-home health & personal support services to help individuals live independently at home, & assists with the transition to long term care when living at home is no longer possible
Rose Scott, Board Chair

Cornwall: CCAC for Eastern Counties
709 Cotton Mill St., Cornwall, ON K6H 7K7
Tel: 613-936-1171; *Toll-Free:* 800-267-0852
www.ec.ccac-ont.ca
David Marshall, Executive Director

Cornwall: Centre de santé communautaire de l'Estrie
#6, 841, rue Sydney, Cornwall, ON K6H 3J7
Tél: 613-937-2683; *Téléc:* 613-937-2698
info@cscestrie.on.ca
www.cscestrie.on.ca
Marc Bisson

Emo: Emo Health Centre
Affiliated with: Riverside Health Care Facilities Inc.
PO Box 390, 260 Front St., Emo, ON P0W 1E0
Tel: 807-482-2881; *Fax:* 807-482-2493
www.riversidehealthcare.ca
Number of Beds: 12 long-term, 3 acute care beds
Wayne Woods

Forest: North Lambton Community Health Centre
Affiliated with: Erie St. Clair Local Health Integration Network
PO Box 1120, 59 King St. West, Forest, ON N0N 1J0
Tel: 519-786-4545; *Fax:* 519-786-6318
ninfo@nlchc.com
www.nlchc.com

Mac Redmond, Executive Director

Grand Bend: Grand Bend Area Community Health Centre
PO Box 1269, 29 Gill Rd., Grand Bend, ON N0M 1T0
Tel: 519-238-2362; *Fax:* 519-238-6478
www.gbachc.ca

Dan Steinwald, Executive Director

Guelph: CCAC Waterloo Wellington - Guelph Branch Office
#201, 450 Speedvale Ave. West, Guelph, ON N1H 7G7
Tel: 519-823-2550; *Fax:* 519-823-8682
Toll-Free: 1-800-265-8338
information@ww.ccac-ont.ca
www.ccac-ont.ca
Note: Long-term care placement services; information & referral to other community services; in-home health services; school health support services; access to long-term care facilities; access to adult day programs; mental health & palliative care services
Helene Ireton, Executive Assistant

Hamilton: CCAC Hamilton Niagara Haldimand Brant - Hamilton Branch Office
310 Limeridge Rd. West, Hamilton, ON L9C 2V2
Tel: 905-523-8600; *Fax:* 905-528-1883
Toll-Free: 1-800-450-8002
www.ccac-ont.ca

Melody Miles, Executive Director

Hamilton: Centre de santé communautaire Hamilton/Niagara
460, rue Main est, 2e étage, Hamilton, ON L8N 1K4
Tél: 905-528-0163; *Téléc:* 905-528-9196
cschwn@iaw.on.ca
www.centredesantecommunautaire.com

Robert Bisson, Directeur général

Hamilton: Hamilton Urban Core Community Health Centre
71 Rebecca St., Hamilton, ON L8R 1B6
Tel: 905-522-3233; *Fax:* 905-522-3433
dbrooks@hucchc.com
www.hucchc.com

Denise Brooks, Executive Director
dbrooks@hucchc.com

Hamilton: North Hamilton Community Health Centre
554 John St. North, Hamilton, ON L8L 4S1
Tel: 905-523-6611; *Fax:* 905-523-5173
www.northhamiltonchc.org
Year Founded: 1987
Note: Offers a variety of services and programs, including programs for men and women living with HIV/AIDS and programs for new immigrants/refugees
Beth Beader, Executive Director

Huntsville: Muskoka-East Parry Sound CCAC
100 Frank Miller Dr., Huntsville, ON P1H 1H7
Tel: 705-789-6451; *Fax:* 705-789-1982
ccac@muskoka.ccac-ont.ca
www.mahc.ca

Vaughn Adamson, Executive Director

Ignace: Mary Berglund Community Health Centre (MBCHC)
PO Box 450, Ignace, ON P0T 1T0
Tel: 807-934-6719; *Fax:* 807-934-6552
mbchced@bellnet.ca
www.maryberglundchc.com
Note: Specialties: Primary care; Public health nursing; Physiotherapy; Chronic disease follow-up; Health promotion; Men's & women's wellness clinics; Blood sugar & blood pressure screening programs; Chiropractic services; Massage therapy
Lillian Napierala, Executive Director

Kenora: CCAC North West - Kenora Branch Office
21 Wolsley St., 2nd Fl., Kenora, ON P9N 3W7
Tel: 807-467-4757; *Fax:* 807-468-1437
Toll-Free: 1-877-661-6621
www.ccac-ont.ca

Tuija Puiras, Executive Director
tuija.puiras@nw.ccac-ont.ca

Kingston: CCAC South East - Kingston Head Office
#300, 1471 John Counter Blvd., Kingston, ON K7M 8S8
Tel: 613-544-8200; *Fax:* 613-544-3888
www.ccac-ont.ca

John Hill, Board Chair

Kingston: North Kingston Community Health Centre
400 Elliot Ave., Kingston, ON K7K 6M9
Tel: 613-542-2949; *Fax:* 613-542-3872
info@nkchc.kchc.ca
www.kchc.ca/nkchc

Hersh Sehdev, Executive Director

Kirkland Lake: CCAC Timiskaming
PO Box 520, Kirkland Lake, ON P2N 3J5
Tel: 705-567-2222; *Fax:* 705-567-9407
www.timisk.ccac-ont.ca

Denis Labelle, Executive Director
denis.labelle@timisk.ccac-ont.ca

Kitchener: CCAC Waterloo Wellington
800 King St. West, Kitchener, ON N2G 1E8
Tel: 519-748-2222; *Fax:* 519-883-5555
Toll-Free: 1-888-883-3313
information@ww.ccac-ont.ca
www.ccac-ont.ca
Note: Head office for the region
Helene Ireton, Executive Assistant

Kitchener: Kitchener Downtown Community Health Centre
59 Frederick St., Kitchener, ON N2H 2L3
Tel: 519-745-4404; *Fax:* 519-745-3709
mail@kdchc.org
www.kdchc.org

Sheila Braidek, Executive Director

Lanark: North Lanark County Community Health Centre
207 Robertson Dr., Lanark, ON K0G 1K0
Tel: 613-259-2182; *Fax:* 613-259-5235
Toll-Free: 866-762-0496
info@northlanarkchc.on.ca
northlanarkchc.on.ca

Wanda MacDonald

Lindsay: CCAC Central East - Lindsay Branch Office
370 Kent St. W, Lindsay, ON K9V 6G8
Tel: 705-324-9165; *Fax:* 705-324-0884
Toll-Free: 1-800-347-0285
www.cacc-ont.ca

William N. Botshka, Board Chair

London: CCAC London & Eastern Middlesex
356 Oxford St. West, London, ON N6H 1T3
Tel: 519-473-2222; *Fax:* 519-472-4045
Toll-Free: 1-800-811-5146
info-london@sw.ccac-ont.ca
www.ccac-ont.ca
Note: Head office for the South West CCAC & regional office for London & E. Middlesex
Sandra Coleman, Executive Director, South West CCAC

London: London InterCommunity Health Centre
659 Dundas St. East, London, ON N5W 2Z1
Tel: 519-660-0874; *Fax:* 519-642-1532
mail@lihc.on.ca (General); orders@lihc.on.ca (Resources)
www.lihc.on.ca
Year Founded: 1989
Note: Specialties: Inclusive & equitable health & social services to persons who experience barriers to care; Mental health care; Diabetes program; Options clinic HIV anonymous testing; Health & youth outreach services. Number of employees: 70
Michelle Hurtubise

Longlac: NorWest Community Health Centre - Longlac Site
PO Box 910, 99 Skinner Ave., Longlac, ON P0T 1T0
Tel: 807-876-2271; *Fax:* 807-876-2473
www.norwestchc.org/longlac.htm

Merrickville: Merrickville District Community Health Centre
PO Box 550, 354 Read St., Merrickville, ON K0G 1N0
Tel: 613-269-3400; *Fax:* 613-269-4958
info@mdchc.on.ca
www.mdchc.on.ca
Note: Specialties: Social work; Dietitian services; Health education; Individual & family counselling; Case management, such as asthma; Foot care services; Flu clinics; Immunizations
Peter McKenna, Executive Director

New Liskeard: Centre de santé communautaire du Témiskaming
CP 38, 83, av Whitewood, New Liskeard, ON P0J 1P0
Tél: 705-647-5775; *Téléc:* 705-647-6011
jocelydg@csctim.on.ca

Jocelyne Maxwell, Directrice générale

Newmarket: CCAC Central - Newmarket Head Office
Former Name: Etobicoke & York CCAC
#1, 1100 Gorham St., Newmarket, ON L3Y 8Y8
Tel: 905-895-1240
info@central.ccac-ont.ca
www.ccac-ont.ca

Vikram Gulati, Board Chair

North Bay: Near North CCAC
1164 Devonshire Ave., North Bay, ON P1B 6X5
Tel: 705-476-2222; *Fax:* 705-476-6719
Toll-Free: 888-533-2222
nnccac@nnccac.on.ca
www.nearnorth.ccac-ont.ca

Lloy Schindeler, Executive Director

Oshawa: Oshawa Community Health Centre
Dr. Bryce A. Brown Wellness Centre, 115 Grassmere Ave., Oshawa, ON L1H 3X7
Tel: 905-723-0036; *Fax:* 905-432-3902
info@ochc.ca; help@ochc.ca (Volunteering & support
www.ochc.ca
Note: Specialties: Child development; Youth recreation; Women's wellness; Health promotion; Fmaily community outreach; Education services, such as the diabetes education program; Counselling; Parenting groups; Regular check-ups; Rehabilitation
Lee Kierstead, Executive Director

Ottawa: Bruyère Continuing Care
Soins continus Bruyère
Former Name: Sisters of Charity of Ottawa Health Service, Élisa
43 Bruyère St., Ottawa, ON K1N 5C8
Tel: 613-562-0050; *Fax:* 613-562-6367
communications@bruyere.org
www.bruyere.org
Year Founded: 1993
Number of Beds: 757 beds
Note: hospital with complex continuing care, rehabilitation, palliative care & long term care services; includes Elisabeth-Bruyere Health Centre, Saint-Vincent Hospital, Résidence Saint-Louis & Villa Marguerite
Jean Bartkowiak, President; CEO

Ottawa: Carlington Community & Health Services
900 Merivale Rd., Ottawa, ON K1Z 5Z8
Tel: 613-722-4000; *Fax:* 613-761-1805
mbirming@carlington.ochc.org
www.carlington.ochc.org

Michael Birmingham, Executive Director

Ottawa: CCAC Champlain
#100, 4200 Labelle St., Ottawa, ON K1J 1J8
Tel: 613-745-5525; *Fax:* 613-745-6984
Toll-Free: 1-800-538-0520
information@champlain.ccac-on.ca
www.ccac-ont.ca
Note: Health & personal support services for individuals living independently at home or recuperating from a hospital stay; advocacy for seniors; support for caregivers & families; assistance with transition to new care settings; information & referral. Serving communities of Renfrew County, Ottawa, & the Eastern Counties

Lynn Graham, Board Chair

Ottawa: Centretown Community Health Centre
420 Cooper St., Ottawa, ON K2P 2N6
Tel: 613-233-4443; *Fax:* 613-233-3987
info@centretownchc.org
www.centretownchc.org

Marguarite Keeley, Executive Director

Ottawa: Ottawa Community Care Access Centre (CCAC)
Centre d'accès aux soins communautaires
#100, 4200 Labelle St., Ottawa, ON K1J 1J8
Tel: 613-745-5525; *Fax:* 613-745-6984
Toll-Free: 800-538-0520
TTY: 613-745-0049
information@champlain.ccac-ont.ca
www.ottawa.ccac-ont.ca
Note: Specialties: Home care; Coordination of community care; Information about long-term care options
Sandra Golding, Executive Director

Ottawa: Pinecrest-Queensway Health & Community Services
1365 Richmond Rd., 2nd Fl., Ottawa, ON K2B 6R7
Tel: 613-820-4922; *Fax:* 613-820-2006
general@pqhcs.com
www.pqhcs.com

Wanda MacDonald, Executive Director

Ottawa: Sandy Hill Community Health Centre
211 Nelson St., Ottawa, ON K1N 1C7
Tel: 613-789-1500; *Fax:* 613-789-7962
info@sandyhillchc.on.ca
www.sandyhillchc.on.ca
Note: Provides a variety of Health and Social Services in the Eastern Ottawa region
Karen Patzer, Executive Director

Ottawa: Somerset West Community Health Centre
55 Eccles St., Ottawa, ON K1R 6S3
Tel: 613-238-8210; *Fax:* 613-238-7595
jmccarth@swchc.on.ca
www.swchc.on.ca

Jack McCarthy, Executive Director

Ottawa: South-East Ottawa Centre for a Healthy Community
#600, 1355 Bank St., Ottawa, ON K1H 8K7
Tel: 613-737-5115; *Fax:* 613-739-8199
office@seochc.on.ca

Owen Sound: CCAC North Bruce & Grey Counties
255 - 18th St. West, Owen Sound, ON N4K 6Y1
Tel: 519-371-2112; *Fax:* 519-371-5612
Toll-Free: 1-888-371-2112
info-owensound@sw.ccac-ont.ca
www.ccac-ont.ca

Sandra Coleman, Executive Director, South West CCAC

Parry Sound: West Parry Sound Health Centre
6 Albert St., Parry Sound, ON P2A 3A4
Tél: 705-746-9321
www.wpshc.com
Year Founded: 1897
Nombre de lits: 49 beds
Note: Acute & complex continuing care, rehabilitation, on-site Lakeland Long Term Care Facility (90 beds), Community Care Access Centre, emergency services, surgery, diagnostic imaging, chemotherapy, sleep disorder clinic, lab, telehealth, Base Hospital Program & nursing stations in Britt, Pointe au Baril, Rosseau, Whitestone, Argyle & Moosedeer, specialist clinics
Norm Maciver, CEO

Peterborough: CCAC Central East - Peterborough Branch Office
#202, 700 Clonsilla Ave., Peterborough, ON K9J 5Y3
Tel: 705-743-2212; *Fax:* 705-743-9559
Toll-Free: 1-888-235-7222
www.ccac-ont.ca

William N. Botshka, Board Chair

Portland: Country Roads Community Health Centre
PO Box 58, 4319 Cove Rd., Portland, ON K0G 1V0
Tel: 613-272-3443; *Fax:* 613-272-3463
schant@crchc.on.ca

Sandra Chant, Executive Director

Richmond Hill: CCAC Central - Richmond Hill Site
Former Name: York Region CCAC
#400, 9050 Yonge St., Richmond Hill, ON L4C 9S6
Tel: 905-763-9928
info@central.ccac-ont.ca
www.ccac-ont.ca

Vikram Gulati, Board Chair

Sault Ste Marie: Algoma Community Care Access Centre
390 Bay St. 2nd Fl., Sault Ste Marie, ON P6A 1X2
Tel: 705-949-1650; *Fax:* 705-949-1663
Toll-Free: 800-668-7705
marjo.keranen@algoma.ccac-ont.ca
www.ccac-ont.ca

Jim Dalgliesh, Executive Director

Sault Ste Marie: Group Health Centre Sault Ste. Marie
240 McNabb St., Sault Ste Marie, ON P6B 1Y5
Tel: 705-759-1234; *Fax:* 705-759-7469
Toll-Free: 800-461-2407
inquiries@ghc.on.ca
www.ghc.on.ca
Note: GHC is a progressive, multidisciplinary, consumer-sponsored health care facility, built by private funds donated by local union members. A partnership of the Sault Ste. Marie & District Group Health Association & the Algoma District Medical Group. Number of staff: 300+
Tom Bonell, Chairman, Group Health Association

Seaforth: CCAC Huron County
PO Box 580, 32 Centennial Dr., Seaforth, ON N0K 1W0
Tel: 519-527-0000; *Fax:* 519-527-1255
Toll-Free: 1-800-267-0535
info-seaforth@sw.ccac-ont.ca
www.ccac-ont.ca

Sandra Coleman, Executive Director, South West CCAC

Simcoe: CCAC Hamilton Niagara Haldimand Brant - Haldimand-Norfolk Branch Office
76 Victoria St., Simcoe, ON N3Y 1L5
Tel: 519-426-7400; *Fax:* 519-426-4384
Toll-Free: 1-800-265-8068
www.ccac-ont.ca

Melody Miles, Executive Director

Smiths Falls: CCAC South East - Smith Falls Branch Office
#1, 52 Abbott St. North, Smiths Falls, ON K7A 1W3
Tel: 613-283-8012; *Fax:* 613-283-0308
Toll-Free: 1-800-267-6041
www.ccac-ont.ca

John Hill, Board Chair

St Catharines: CCAC Hamilton Niagara Haldimand Brant - Niagara Branch Office
149 Hartzel Rd., St Catharines, ON L2P 1N6
Tel: 905-684-9441; *Fax:* 905-684-8463
Toll-Free: 1-800-263-5480
www.ccac-ont.ca

Melody Miles, Executive Director

St Jacobs: Woolwich Community Health Centre
10 Parkside Dr., St Jacobs, ON N0B 2N0
Tel: 519-664-3794; *Fax:* 519-664-2182
genmail@wchc.on.ca
www.wchc.on.ca

Denise Squire, Executive Director

St Thomas: CCAC Elgin County
294 Talbot St., St Thomas, ON N5P 4E3
Tel: 519-631-9907; *Fax:* 519-631-2236
Toll-Free: 1-800-563-3098
info-stthomas@sw.ccac-ont.ca
www.ccac-ont.ca

Sandra Coleman, Executive Director, South West CCAC

Stratford: CCAC Perth County
Former Name: Perth County Community Care Access Centre
65 Lorne Ave. East, Stratford, ON N5A 6S4
Tel: 519-273-2222; *Fax:* 519-273-2139
Toll-Free: 1-800-269-3683
info-stratford@sw.ccac-ont.ca
www.ccac-ont.ca

Sandra Coleman, Executive Director, South West CCAC

Sudbury: Centre de santé communautaire de Sudbury
19 Frood Rd., Sudbury, ON P3C 4Y9
Tél: 705-670-2274; *Téléc:* 705-670-2277
gelinasf@csc.sudbury.com
www.csc.sudbury.com

France Gélinas, Executive Director

Sudbury: Manitoulin-Sudbury CCAC
1760 Regent St. South, Sudbury, ON P3E 3Z8
Tel: 705-522-3461; *Fax:* 705-522-8018
Toll-Free: 800-461-2919
info@ms.ccac-ont.ca
www.ms.ccac-ont.ca

Nancy Mongeon, Executive Director

Thunder Bay: CCAC of The District of Thunder Bay
#200, 1159 Alloy Dr., Thunder Bay, ON P7B 6M8
Tel: 807-345-7339; *Fax:* 807-345-8868
Toll-Free: 800-626-5406
www.tb.ccac-ont.ca

Tuija Puiras, Executive Director

Thunder Bay: NorWest Community Health Centre - Thunder Bay Site
525 Simpson St., Thunder Bay, ON P7C 3J6
Tel: 807-622-8235; *Fax:* 807-622-7637
execdirector@norwestchc.org
www.norwestchc.org/thunder_bay.htm

Wendy Talbot, Executive Director

Timmins: Cochrane District CCAC
#101, 330 Second Ave., Timmins, ON P4N 8A4
Tel: 705-267-7766; *Fax:* 705-267-7795
Toll-Free: 888-668-2222
inquiries-cdccac@cochrane.ccac-ont.ca
www.cdccac.com

Joy Galloway, Executive Director

Timmins: Misiway Milopemahtesewin Community Health Centre
130 Wilson Ave., Timmins, ON P4N 2S9
Tel: 705-264-2200; *Fax:* 705-264-2243
misiwayoa@vianet.ca
www.misiway.ca

Cah-Ling Lew, Executive Director

Tobermory: Grey Bruce Health Services Tobermory Clinic
7275 Hwy. 6, Tobermory, ON NOH 270
Tel: 519-793-3445
www.gbhs.on.ca/tobermory.php
Note: Specialties: Family health; Community care; Minor day surgery; Mental health counselling. Number of Employees: 4 physicians + 1 nurse practitioner + 1 social worker + several clinic nurses

Toronto: Access Alliance Multicultural Community Health Centre
#500, 340 College St., Toronto, ON M5T 3A9
Tel: 416-324-8677; *Fax:* 416-324-9074
mail@accessalliance.ca
www.accessalliance.ca
Note: Provides community health services to refugees & immigrants
Axelle Janczur, Executive Director

Toronto: Anishnawbe Health Toronto
225 Queen St. East, Toronto, ON M5A 1S4
Tel: 416-360-0486; *Fax:* 416-365-1083
www.aht.ca
Year Founded: 1984
Note: An accredited community health centre, utilizing traditional healing approaches. A range of services is available, including fetal alcohol spectrum disorder services, diabetic care, HIV testing, mental health services & psychiatry, counselling,

naturopathy, chiropody, women's services, massage therapy, & dental services. Other centres located at: 179 Gerrard St. E., 416-920-2605; and 22 Vaughan Rd., 416-657-0379. Mental Health Crisis Management Service: 416-891-8606.
Joe Hester, Executive Director

Toronto: Anne Johnston Health Station
2398 Yonge St., Toronto, ON M4P 2H4
Tel: 416-486-8666; *Fax:* 416-486-8660

Catherine Brookman, Executive Director

Toronto: Bernard Betel Centre for Creative Living
1003 Steeles Ave. West, Toronto, ON M2R 3T6
Tel: 416-225-2112; *Fax:* 416-225-2097
reception@betelcentre.org
www.betelcentre.org
Note: provide education, recreation, arts, fitness and health services
Esta Wall, Executive Director

Toronto: Black Creek Community Health Centre
#5, 2202 Jane St., Toronto, ON M3M 1A4
Tel: 416-249-8000; *Fax:* 416-249-4594
patrizia@bcchc.com
www.bcchc.com

Cary Milner, Executive Director

Toronto: CCAC Central - Sheppard Site
#700, 45 Sheppard Ave. East, Toronto, ON M2N 5W9
Tel: 416-222-2241
info@central.ccac-ont.ca
www.ccac-ont.ca

Vikram Gulati, Board Chair

Toronto: CCAC Central East - Scarborough Branch Office
1940 Eglinton Ave. East, 3rd Fl., Toronto, ON M1L 4R1
Tel: 416-750-2444; *Fax:* 416-750-4117
Toll-Free: 1-866-779-1931
www.ccac-ont.ca

William N. Botshka, Board Chair

Toronto: CCAC Toronto Central
#305, 250 Dundas St. West, Toronto, ON M5T 2Z5
Tel: 416-506-9888; *Fax:* 416-506-0374
Toll-Free: 1-866-243-0061
toronto_ccac@toronto.ccac-ont.ca
www.ccac-ont.ca

Judith Hayward, Board Chair

Toronto: CCAC Toronto Central - Leaside Park Drive Site-East York
Former Name: East York Access Centre
#1, 1 Leaside Park Dr., Toronto, ON M4H 1R1
Tel: 416-423-3559; *Fax:* 416-423-9800
toronto_ccac@toronto.ccac-ont.ca
www.ccac-ont.ca

Judith Hayward, Executive Director

Toronto: Central Toronto Community Health Centres Queen West Community Health Centre
168 Bathurst St., Toronto, ON M5V 2R4
Tel: 416-703-8482; *Fax:* 416-703-8479
info@ctchc.com
www.ctchc.com
Note: Medical services (with specialized services for the homeless), psychiatric & mental health services, individual & group counselling, harm reduction program (safer sex, safer drug use, Hepatitis C & HIV prevention), needle exchange, diabetes education program, chiropody, perinatal nursing, dental clinic.
Hal DeLair, Executive Director

Toronto: Central Toronto Community Health Centres Shout Clinic
467 Jarvis St., Toronto, ON M4Y 2G8
Tel: 416-927-8553; *Fax:* 416-927-9365
info@ctchc.com
www.ctchc.com

Year Founded: 1992
Note: Walk-in medical clinic providing comprehensive health care services to homeless & street involved youth, 16-24 years of age.
Hal DeLair, Executive Director

Toronto: Centre francophone de Toronto
Ancien nom: Centre médico-social communautaire
22 College St., 1st Fl., Toronto, ON M5G 1K3
Tél: 416-922-2672; *Téléc:* 416-922-6624
jg@cmsctoronto.org

Jean-Gilles Pelletier, Executive Director

Toronto: Davenport Perth Neighbourhood Centre
1900 Davenport Rd., Toronto, ON M6N 1B7
Tel: 416-658-6812; *Fax:* 416-656-1264

Keith McNair, Executive Director

Toronto: East End Community Health Centre
343 Coxwell Ave., Toronto, ON M4L 3B5
Tel: 416-778-5858; *Fax:* 416-778-5855

Joyce Kalsen, Executive Director

Toronto: Flemingdon Health Centre
10 Gateway Blvd., Toronto, ON M3C 3A1
Tel: 416-429-4991; *Fax:* 416-422-3573
fhcinfo@fhc-chc.com

Peter Yue, Executive Director

Toronto: Four Villages Community Health Centre
1700 Bloor St. West, Toronto, ON M6P 4C3
Tel: 416-604-3361; *Fax:* 416-604-3367

Almerinda Rebelo, Executive Director

Toronto: Lawrence Heights Community Health Centre
12 Flemington Rd., Toronto, ON M6A 2N4
Tel: 416-787-1661; *Fax:* 416-787-3761
achohen@lhchc.com
www.lhchc.com

Andrea Cohen, Executive Director

Toronto: Parkdale Community Health Centre
1229 Queen St. West, Toronto, ON M6K 1L2
Tel: 416-537-2455; *Fax:* 416-537-5133
Note: Specialties: Service in several languages; Primary care; Educational programs, such as pre- and post-natal classes; Support groups; Counselling; Mental health support; HIV testing
Simone Hammond, Executive Director

Toronto: Regent Park Community Health Centre
465 Dundas St. East, Toronto, ON M5A 2B2
Tel: 416-364-2261; *Fax:* 416-364-0822
rpchc@regentparkchc.org
www.regentparkchc.org

Year Founded: 1973
Note: Emphasis on an integrated approach: health promotion, disease prevention, social services. A community-founded & operated facility, with a focus on comprehensive, accessible care. Services in English, Cantonese, Mandarin, Vietnames, Somali & Spanish. The Pathways to Education Program for youth at risk, created & first implemented in Regent Park, has been adopted by communities across Canada
Carolyn Acker, Executive Director

Toronto: South Riverdale Community Health Centre
955 Queen St. East, Toronto, ON M4M 3P3
Tel: 416-461-1925; *Fax:* 416-461-3578
srchc@srchc.com

Lynne Raskin, Executive Director

Toronto: Stonegate Community Health Centre
150 Berry Rd., Toronto, ON M8Y 1W3
Tel: 416-231-7070; *Fax:* 416-231-2663
info@stonegatechc.org
www.stonegatechc.org
Note: Specialties: Asthma care program research; Pre & post natal programs; Early years programs; Women's programs; Seniors' programs; Housing support & case management
Lucia Furgivele, Executive Director

Toronto: Toronto East General Hospital Family Health Centre
840 Coxwell Ave., Toronto, ON M4C 5T2
Tel: 416-469-6464; *Fax:* 416-469-6164
ptrep@tegh.on.ca (Patients); community@tegh.on.ca (Community)
www.tegh.on.ca

Year Founded: 2002
Note: Specialties: Low-risk obstetrics; Psychotherapy; Telephone health advisory service

Toronto: West Hill Community Services
3545 Kingston Rd., Toronto, ON M1M 1R6
Tel: 416-284-5931; *Fax:* 416-724-5205
westhill@westhill-cs.on.ca
www.westhill-cs.on.ca

Pat Jensen, Executive Director

Toronto: Women's Health in Women's Hands
#500, 2 Carlton St., Toronto, ON M5B 1J3
Tel: 416-593-7655; *Fax:* 416-593-5867
TTY: 416-593-5835
whiwh@web.net
www.whiwh.com

Notisha Massaquoi, Executive Director

Tweed: Gateway Community Health Centre
PO Box 99, 41 McClellan St., Tweed, ON K0K 3J0
Tel: 613-478-1211; *Fax:* 613-478-6692

Jeanne Goodhand, Executive Director

West Lorne: West Elgin Community Health Centre
PO Box 761, 168 Main St., West Lorne, ON N0L 2P0
Tel: 519-768-1715; *Fax:* 519-768-2548
info@wechc.on.ca
www.wechc.on.ca
Note: Provides health services and community programs to residents of the western Elgin area

Whitby: CCAC Central East - Whitby Head Office
Former Name: Durham Access to Care
Whitby Corporate Centre, 209 Dundas St. East, 5th Fl., Whitby, ON L1N 7H8
Tel: 905-430-3308; *Fax:* 905-430-3297
Toll-Free: 1-800-263-3877
www.ccac-ont.ca

William N. Botshka, Board Chair

Windsor: CCAC Windsor/Essex
5415 Tecumseh Rd. East, 2nd Fl., Windsor, ON N8T 1C5
Tel: 519-258-8211; *Fax:* 519-258-2004
ccac.reception@we.ccac-ont.ca
www.we.ccac-ont.ca

Mary Wilson, Executive Director

Windsor: Sandwich Community Health Centre
PO Box 7391, 749 Felix Ave., Windsor, ON N9C 4E9
Tel: 519-258-6002; *Fax:* 519-528-3693
mailbox@sandwichchc.org
www.sandwichchc.org
Year Founded: 1982

Windsor: Teen Health Centre
Head Office, 1585 Ouellette Ave., Windsor, ON N8X 1K5
Tel: 519-253-8481; *Fax:* 519-253-4362
www.teenhealthcentre.com
Note: Specialties: Counselling; Primary care; Special Additions, a prenatal program; Diabetes In Action, a community based diabetes program; Street Health Homeless Initiative Program, a program to serve homeless or at-risk persons in Windsor & Essex County
Sheila Gordon, Executive Director

Woodstock: CCAC Oxford County
1147 Dundas St., Woodstock, ON N4S 8W3
Tel: 519-539-1284; *Fax:* 519-539-0065
Toll-Free: 1-800-561-5490
info-woodstock@sw.ccac-ont.ca
www.ccac-ont.ca

Sandra Coleman, Executive Director, South West CCAC

Special Treatment Centres

Barrie: Royal Victoria Hospital of Barrie Community Care Centre for Substance Abuse
70 Wellington St. West, Barrie, ON L4N 1K4
Tel: 705-728-4226; *Fax:* 705-728-7308
www.rvh.on.ca

Number of Beds: 17 beds
Note: Intoxification management, withdrawal management, assessments, family education, discharge planning
Jack Vandenberg, Director

Brantford: Lansdowne Children's Centre
39 Mount Pleasant St., Brantford, ON N3T 1S7
Tel: 519-753-3153; *Fax:* 519-753-5927
lansdowne.children@sympatico.ca

Martin McIntyre, Director

***Cambridge:* KidsAbility - Centre for Child Development**
Cambridge Site
Former Name: Rotary Children's Centre
c/o Chaplin Family YMCA, 250 Hespeler Rd., Cambridge, ON N1R 3H3
Tel: 519-621-7580; *Fax:* 519-621-4651
www.kidsability.ca
Year Founded: 1957
Note: Specialty: Services for children & young adults with physical, developmental, & communication disabilities

***Chatham:* Prism Centre for Audiology & Children's Rehabilitation**
Former Name: Kent County Children's Treatment Centre
355 Lark St., Chatham, ON N7L 5B2
Tel: 519-354-0520; *Fax:* 519-354-7355
http://www.prismcentre.com/
Mary Anne McLean, Executive Director
Donna Litwin-Makey, Executive Director
519-354-0520 ext.228, dlitwinmakey@prismcentre.com

***Cornwall:* Cornwall Withdrawal Management Centre**
35 Second St. East, Cornwall, ON K6H 1Y2
Tel: 613-938-8506; *Fax:* 613-938-2867
Number of Beds: 16 beds
Note: detoxification hospital
Christine Penney, Manager

***Fergus:* KidsAbility - Centre for Child Development**
Fergus Site
Former Name: Rotary Children's Centre
160 St. David St. South, Fergus, ON N1M 2L3
Tel: 519-787-2612; *Fax:* 519-843-7597
www.kidsability.ca
Year Founded: 1957
Note: Specialty: Services for children & young adults with physical, developmental, & communication disabilities

***Guelph:* KidsAbility - Centre for Child Development**
Guelph Site
Former Name: Rotary Children's Centre
c/o West End Community Centre, 21 Imperial Rd. South, Guelph, ON N1K 1X3
Tel: 519-780-0186; *Fax:* 519-780-0470
www.kidsability.ca
Year Founded: 1957
Note: Specialty: Services for children & young adults with physical, developmental, & communication disabilities

***Hamilton:* Hamilton Regional Cancer Centre**
699 Concession St., Hamilton, ON L8V 5C2
Tel: 905-387-9495; *Fax:* 905-575-6323
www.hrcc.on.ca
Dr. George Browman, CEO

***Kingston:* Cancer Centre of Southeastern Ontario**
25 King St. West, Kingston, ON K7L 5P9
Tel: 613-544-2630; *Fax:* 613-544-9708
Toll-Free: 800-567-5722
www.krcc.on.ca

***Kingston:* Child Development Centre**
c/o Hotel Dieu Hospital, 166 Brock St., Kingston, ON K7L 5G2
Tel: 613-544-3400; *Fax:* 613-545-3557
www.hoteldieu.com/cdcopen.html
Robin L. Jones, Director

***Kingston:* Hotel Dieu Hospital Kingston Detoxification Centre**
240 Brock St., Kingston, ON K7L 5G2
Tel: 613-549-6461; *Fax:* 613-546-4254
www.hoteldieu.com
Note: detoxification hospital
Gerry Gregory, Director

***Kitchener:* Waterloo Regional Withdrawal Management Centre**
52 Glasgow St., Kitchener, ON N2G 1N6
Tel: 519-749-4300; *Fax:* 519-749-4328
Number of Beds: 21 beds

***London:* London Health Sciences Centre**
London Regional Cancer Program
PO Box 5165, 790 Commissioners Rd. East, London, ON N6A 4L6
Tel: 519-685-8600
LRCPEducation@lhsc.on.ca (Patient education)
www.lhsc.on.ca
Note: Specialties: Inpatient & outpatient cancer care; Radiation therapy; Chemotherapy; Syooirt services, such as social work & diet & nutrition counselling
Dr. Michael Sherar, Vice-President

***London:* Thames Valley Children's Centre**
779 Baseline Rd. East, London, ON N6C 5Y6
Tel: 519-685-8680; *Fax:* 519-685-8689
tvcc@tvcc.on.ca; innovations@tvcc.on.ca (Innovative products/books)
www.tvcc.on.ca
Year Founded: 1949
Note: Specialties: Rehabilitation services for children with physical disabilities, developmental delays, & communication disorders; Assessment & diagnosis services; Autism intervention program; Intensive behavioural intervention; Physiotherapy; Occupational therapy; Research; School support program.
Number of Employees: 350+ + 500 volunteers + 55 students
John A. LaPorta, Exec. Director/CEO

***Mississauga:* Erinoak Kids**
2277 South Millway, Mississauga, ON L5L 2M5
Tel: 905-820-7111; *Fax:* 905-820-1333
Note: Outpatient services only
Diana Thomson, Executive Director

***Mount Brydges:* Southwest Middlesex Health Centre**
22262 Mill Rd., RR#5, Mount Brydges, ON N0L 1W0
Tel: 519-264-2800
A. Lamont, Administrator

***Orillia:* Huronia Regional Centre**
PO Box 1000, 700 Memorial Ave., Orillia, ON L3V 6L2
Number of Beds: 584 beds
Note: rehabilitation hospital
James Duncan, Administrator

***Oshawa:* Grandview Children's Centre**
Former Name: Grandview Rehabilitation & Treatment Centre of Dur
600 Townline Rd. South, Oshawa, ON L1H 7K6
Tel: 905-728-1673; *Fax:* 905-728-2961
Toll-Free: 800-304-6180
www.grtc.ca
Vicky Earle, Executive Director

***Ottawa:* The Morgentaler Clinic**
Ottawa Site
65 Bank St., Ottawa, ON K1P 5N2
Tel: 613-567-8300; *Fax:* 613-567-9128
info@yenott.com
www.morgentaler.ca
Note: Specialty: Abortion services; Counselling

***Ottawa:* The Ottawa Children's Treatment Centre (OCTC)**
Le Centre de traitement pour enfants d'Ottawa
395 Smyth Rd., Ottawa, ON K1H 8L2
Tel: 613-737-0871; *Fax:* 613-523-5167
Toll-Free: 800-565-4839
www.octc.ca
Note: From several locations in Ottawa & area, The Centre provides specialized care for children with multiple physical, developmental & behavioural needs. Services in English & French
Kathleen Stokely, Executive Director

***Ottawa:* The Ottawa Hospital (TRC) Rehabilitation Centre**
505 Smyth Rd., Ottawa, ON K1H 8M2
Tel: 613-737-7350
TTY: 613-526-1132
patientrelations@ottawahospital.on.ca
www.ottawahospital.on.ca
Note: Specialties: Rehabilitation of persons with a disabling physical illness or injury; Prosthetics & orthotics; Physiotherapy; Occupational therapy; Respiratory therapy; Speech-language pathology; Psychological services; Vocational rehabilitation counselling; Social work; Research
Cathy Danbrook, CEO

***Ottawa:* Ottawa Regional Cancer Centre**
General Campus, 501 Smyth Rd., Ottawa, ON K1H 1C4
Tel: 613-737-7700
patientlibrary@ottawahospital.on.ca
www.ottawahospital.on.ca/sc/cancer/index-e.asp
Note: Specialties: Screening; Early Detection; Diagnosis; Treatment; Supportive Care; Palliative Care; Research
Dr. William K. Evans, CEO

***Ottawa:* Sisters of Charity of Ottawa Health Services Detoxification Centre**
62 Bruyère St., Ottawa, ON K1N 5C5
Tel: 613-241-1525; *Fax:* 613-241-2172
Virginia Hamilton, Director

***Peterborough:* Five Counties Children's Centre**
872 Dutton Rd., Peterborough, ON K9H 7G1
Tel: 705-748-2221; *Fax:* 705-748-3526
Toll-Free: 888-779-9916
info@fivecounties.on.ca
www.fivecounties.on.ca
Note: children with special needs 0-19 years of age
Diane Pick, CEO

***Sarnia:* Pathways Health Centre for Children**
1240 Murphy Rd., Sarnia, ON N7S 2Y6
Tel: 519-542-3471; *Fax:* 519-542-4115
info@pathwayscentre.org
www.pathwayscentre.org
Note: children's treatment centre
Jenny Greensmith, Executive Director

***Sault Ste Marie:* Children's Rehabiliation Centre - Algoma**
74 Johnson Ave., Sault Ste Marie, ON P6C 2V5
Tel: 705-759-1131; *Fax:* 705-759-0783
Note: outpatient health services centre
Donna Morrison, Executive Director

***Sault Ste Marie:* Sault Ste. Marie Detoxification Unit**
911 Queen St. East, Sault Ste Marie, ON P6A 2B6
Tel: 705-942-1872; *Fax:* 705-759-6369
Number of Beds: 15 beds
Note: detox centre
Raimo Viitala, Manager

***St Agatha:* kidsLINK (NDSA)**
PO Box 190, 1855 Notre Dame Dr., St Agatha, ON N0B 2L0
Tel: 519-746-5437; *Fax:* 519-746-3055
Number of Beds: 26 beds
Note: Children's mental health residential & day treatment services; outpatient services, respite, prevention & early intervention for children & families
Sonia Pouyat, CEO

***St Catharines:* Hôtel Dieu Shaver Health & Rehabilitation Centre**
Affiliated with: Hamilton Niagara Haldimand Brant Local Health Integration Network
Former Name: Hôtel-Dieu Health Sciences Hospital - Niagara
541 Glenridge Ave., St Catharines, ON L2T 4C2
Tel: 905-685-1381; *Fax:* 905-687-3232
info@hoteldieushaver.org
www.hoteldieushaver.org
Number of Beds: 124 beds
Note: Complex Continuing Care & Rehabilitation
Jane Rufrano, CEO

***St Catharines:* Niagara Peninsula Children's Centre**
567 Glenridge Ave., St Catharines, ON L2T 4C2
Tel: 905-688-3550; *Fax:* 905-688-1055
Toll-Free: 800-896-5496
info@npcc.on.ca
www.npcc.on.ca
Note: children's rehabilitation centre
John TeBrake, Executive Director

***St Catharines:* St Catharines Detoxification (Men's) Unit**
10 Adams St., St Catharines, ON L2R 2V8
Tel: 905-682-7211; *Fax:* 905-687-9768
Number of Beds: 22 beds
Note: men's detox
Norma Medulun, Director

***St Catharines:* St Catharines Detoxification (Women's) Unit**
6 Adams St., St Catharines, ON L2R 2V8
Tel: 905-687-9721; *Fax:* 905-687-9768
Number of Beds: 14 beds
Norma Medulun, Director

Sudbury: Children's Treatment Centre
c/o Laurentian Hospital, 1204 St Jerome St., Sudbury, ON P3A 2V9
Tel: 705-560-8000; *Fax:* 705-560-4273
Note: outpatient, community-based rehabilitation centre
Sally Spence, Coordinator
Pat Tessier, Environmental Services

Sudbury: Women's Withdrawal Management Service
336 Pine St., Sudbury, ON P3C 1X8
Tel: 705-671-7167; *Fax:* 705-675-5730
Number of Beds: 13 beds
Note: non-medical withdrawal management service
Lise Chamberland, Manager

Thunder Bay: George Jeffrey Children's Treatment Centre
507 North Lillie St., Thunder Bay, ON P7C 4V8
Tel: 807-623-4381; *Fax:* 807-623-6626
www.georgejeffrey.com
Note: special needs children
Eiji Tsubouchi, CEO

Timmins: Cochrane Temiskaming Children's Treatment Centre
#1, 733 Ross Ave. East, Timmins, ON P4N 8S8
Tel: 705-264-4700; *Fax:* 705-268-3585
Toll-Free: 800-575-3210
Mary MacKay, Executive Director

Toronto: Bloorview Kids Rehab
Bloorview Site
Former Name: Bloorview Children's Hospital
150 Kilgour Road, Toronto, ON M4G 1R8
Tel: 416-425-6220; *Fax:* 416-425-6591
Toll-Free: 1-800-363-2440
info@bloorview.ca
www.bloorview.ca
Number of Beds: 75
Note: pediatric rehabilitation & continuing care complex
Valerie McMurty, President/CEO

Toronto: Bob Rumball Centre for the Deaf
2395 Bayview Ave., Toronto, ON M2L 1A2
Tel: 416-449-9651; *Fax:* 416-449-8881
TTY: 416-449-2728
info@bobrumball.org
www.bobrumball.org
Number of Beds: 56 beds
Note: long-term care facility for the deaf
Rev. Bob Rumball, Executive Director
Robert Ray, Director, Physical Plant

Toronto: Bridgepoint Hospital
Former Name: The Riverdale Hospital
14 St. Matthews Rd., Toronto, ON M4M 2B5
Tel: 416-461-8252; *Fax:* 416-461-5696
www.bridgepointhealth.ca
Number of Beds: 547 beds
Note: chronic care & rehabilitation hospital
Marian Walsh, President/CEO
Bill Grant, Director, Engineering
416/461-2190
Joseph Mancuso, Director, Environmental Services & Facilities Planning
Robert Carman, Chair

Toronto: Cabbagetown Women's Clinic
302 Gerrard St. East, Toronto, ON M5A 2G7
Tel: 416-323-0642; *Fax:* 416-323-3099
Toll-Free: 800-399-1592
www.cabbagetownwomensclinic.com
Year Founded: 1989
Note: Licensed as and Independent Health facility funded by the Ontario Min. of Health & Long Term Care, the clinic provides medical services to women seeking a legal & safe abortion.

Toronto: Casey House Hospice
9 Huntley St., Toronto, ON M4Y 2K8
Tel: 416-962-7600; *Fax:* 416-962-5147
info@caseyhouse.on.ca
www.caseyhouse.com
Number of Beds: 13 beds; 120 home care clients
Note: hospice; home care office
Catherine Adam, Interim CEO

Toronto: Centre for Addiction & Mental Health ARF Site
Former Name: Addiction Research Foundation
33 Russell St., Toronto, ON M5S 2S1
Tel: 416-595-6000; *Fax:* 416-595-9997
Toll-Free: 800-463-6273
webmaster@camh.net
www.camh.net
Number of Beds: 614 beds
Note: drug rehabilitation centre
Dr. Paul Garfinkel, President; CEO

Toronto: Centre for Addiction & Mental Health Brentcliffe Rd. Site
175 Brentcliffe Rd., Toronto, ON M4G 3Z1
Tel: 416-425-8501
Number of Beds: 47 beds

Toronto: Centre for Addiction & Mental Health (Corporate Office)
33 Russell St., Toronto, ON M5S 2S1
Tel: 416-595-6878
webmaster@camh.net
www.camh.net
Number of Beds: 614 beds
Note: addiction treatment
Dr. Paul Garfinkel, President/CEO

Toronto: Choice in Health Clinic
#301, 1678 Bloor St. West, Toronto, ON M4X 1W3
Tel: 416-975-9300; *Fax:* 416-975-0314
www.choiceinhealth.ca
Note: abortion clinic
Michelle Joseph, Executive Director

Toronto: Eye Bank of Canada Ontario Division
c/o Dept. of Ophthalmology, University of Toronto, 1 Spadina Cres., Toronto, ON M5S 2J5
Tel: 416-978-7355; *Fax:* 416-978-1522
eye.bank@utoronto.ca
www.eyebank.utoronto.ca
Dr. David Rootman, Medical Director
Dr. William Dixon, Medical Co-director

Toronto: Marvelle Koffler Breast Centre
J. & W. Lebovic Health Complex, Mount Sinai Hospit, 600 University Ave., 12th Fl., Toronto, ON M5G 1X5
Tel: 416-586-8799
www.mountsinai.on.ca/care/mkbc
Year Founded: 1995
Note: Specialties: Outpatient facility for breast health & disease; Mammography / Breast imaging; Pathology; Surgery; Psychiatry; Nutrition; Boutique addressing the needs of women who have experienced breast cancer; Palliative medicine
Dr. P. Goodwin, Director

Toronto: The Morgentaler Clinic
727 Hillsdale Ave. East, Toronto, ON M4S 1V4
Tel: 416-932-0446; *Fax:* 416-932-0837
Toll-Free: 800-556-6835
mclinic@passport.ca
www.morgentaler.ca
Note: Specialties: Abortion services; Counselling; Contraceptive education; Testing for sexually transmitted infections
Dr. Henry Morgentaler, Director

Toronto: Runnymede Healthcare Centre
625 Runnymede Rd., Toronto, ON M6P 3A3
Tel: 416-762-7316; *Fax:* 416-762-3836
www.runnymedehc.ca
Year Founded: 1945
Note: Specialties: Complex continuing care for persons with long-term disorders, such as neurological disorders; Occupational therapy; Physiotherapy; Speech-language pathology; Social work
Normand A. Allaire, President; CEO

Toronto: St. John's Rehabilitation Hospital
285 Cummer Ave., Toronto, ON M2M 2G1
Tel: 416-226-6780; *Fax:* 416-226-6265
info@stjohnsrehab.com
www.stjohnsrehab.com
Number of Beds: 160 beds
Note: Ontario's only hospital dedicated to specialized rehabilitation services & care: burn injuries, organ transplant rehabilitation, cancer, cardiovascular surgery, strokes & other neurological conditions, traumatic injuries & complex medical conditions. Teaching site for the University of Toronto & a leading research facility. A multicultural & multifaith environment dedicated to the values of care of the Sisters of St. John the Divine
Malcolm Moffat, President; CEO
Joyce Bailey, Board Chair

Toronto: St. Michael's Hospital Detoxification Centre
314 Adelaide St. East, Toronto, ON M5A 1N1
Tel: 416-864-5078; *Fax:* 416-864-5146
Number of Beds: 22 beds
Note: detoxification hospital
John Rutledge, Director

Toronto: Sunnybrook Health Sciences Centre - Holland Orthopaedic & Arthritic Centre
43 Wellesley St. East, Toronto, ON M4Y 1H1
Tel: 416-967-8500; *Fax:* 416-967-8521
www.sunnybrook.ca
Note: Care for complex injuries of the musculoskeletal system, with a focus on traumatic injury management, joint reconstruction & replacement, surgery, sports & activity-related injury management, rehabilitation, rheumatology. The Clinic has a second location at the main Sunnybrook site, 2075 Bayview Ave., Toronto
Dr. Barry A. McLellan, President/CEO

Toronto: Sunnybrook Health Sciences Centre - The Odette Cancer Centre
2075 Bayview Ave., Toronto, ON M4N 3M5
Tel: 416-480-5000; *Fax:* 416-217-1338
www.sunnybrook.ca
Note: Comprehensive cancer care, multidisciplinary, evidence-based approach; research, education & community outreach
Dr. Barry A. McLellan, President/CEO

Toronto: Toronto East General Hospital Withdrawal Management Centre
985 Danforth Ave., Toronto, ON M4J 1M1
Tel: 416-461-2010; *Fax:* 416-461-1164
ptrep@tegh.on.ca (Patients); community@tegh.on.ca (Community)
www.tegh.on.ca
Number of Beds: 22 beds
Note: Specialties: Crisis intervention for adult males; Physical care for males in acute states of intoxication; Withdrawal from alcohol & other addictive substances; Addictions assessments; Counselling; Rehabilitation services; Education on substance abuse to family members
D. Smith, Manager

Toronto: Toronto Rehabilitation Institute
Also Known As: Toronto Rehab
550 University Ave., Toronto, ON M5G 2A2
Tel: 416-597-3422; *Fax:* 416-597-1977
communications@torontorehab.on.ca
www.torontorehab.com
Number of Beds: 541 beds
Note: Rehabilitation & complex continuing care; includes Hillcrest Centre; Lakeside Long-Term Care Centre; Lyndhurst Centre; E.W. Bickle Centre; Rumsey Centre, & University Centre
Mark Rochon, President/CEO

Toronto: Toronto Western Hospital - Addiction Outpatient/Aftercare Clinic
399 Bathurst St., Toronto, ON M5T 2S8
Tel: 416-603-5735; *Fax:* 0
Note: Assessment & referral, individual & group therapy, counseling, psychiatric consultation, education. Services in English, French, Portuguese, Polish

Toronto: University Health Network - Princess Margaret Hospital
610 University Ave., Toronto, ON M5G 2M9
Tel: 416-946-2000
uhn.info@uhn.on.ca
www.uhn.ca/PMH/
Year Founded: 1952
Number of Beds: 130 inpatient beds
Note: A teaching hospital of the University of Toronto, PMH is a global leader in the fight against cancer & one of the top cancer treatment & research centres in the world. Specialties include: surgical oncology, chemotherapy, psychosocial oncology, radiation therapy, bone marrow transplantation, radiation oncology, hematology, & medical imaging. The Ontario Cancer Institute comprises the research wing of the hospital. Staff: 139+ oncologists, 400 RN's, 1,178 support staff
Sarah Downey, Executive Director; Site Lead

Toronto: West End Creche Child & Family Clinic
197 Euclid Ave., Toronto, ON M6J 2J8
Tel: 416-868-1827; *Fax:* 416-868-1827
Tony Diniz, Executive Director

Toronto: West Park Healthcare Centre
Former Name: West Park Hospital
82 Buttonwood Ave., Toronto, ON M6M 2J5
Tel: 416-243-3600; *Fax:* 416-243-8947
feedback@westpark.org
www.westpark.org
Number of Beds: 477 beds
Note: rehabilitation & chronic care facility
Anne-Marie Malek, President/CEO
Mike Bonnah, Director, Facilities & Materials Management

Waterloo: KidsAbility - Centre for Child Development
Former Name: Rotary Children's Centre
500 Hallmark Dr., Waterloo, ON N2K 3P5
Tel: 519-886-8886; *Fax:* 519-886-7292
Toll-Free: 888.372.2259
www.kidsability.ca
Year Founded: 1957
Note: Specialties: Services for children & young adults with physical, developmental, & communication disabilities; Autism intervention; Occupational therapy; Physiotherapy; Speech-language therapy; Augmentative communication; Therapeutic recreation; Social work. Number of Employees: 200 + 300 volunteers
Stephen Swatridge, Executive Director

Windsor: Children's Rehabilitation Centre of Essex County
3945 Matchette Rd., Windsor, ON N9C 4C2
Tel: 519-252-7281; *Fax:* 519-252-5873
info@childrensrehab.com
www.childrensrehab.com
Elaine M. Whitmore, CEO

Windsor: Windsor Regional Hospital Withdrawal Management
393 Mill St., Windsor, ON N9C 2R3
Tel: 519-257-5225; *Fax:* 519-257-5175
Number of Beds: 20 beds
Note: detoxification hospital
William Marcotte, Director, Operations

Nursing Homes

Ailsa Craig: Craigholme Nursing Home
221 Main St. East, RR#1, Ailsa Craig, ON N0M 1A0
Tel: 519-293-3215; *Fax:* 519-293-3941
www.craigwielgardens.on.ca
Number of Beds: 83 beds
Heather Beauregard, Adm.

Alexandria: Community Nursing Home
PO Box 300, 92 Centre St., Alexandria, ON K0C 1A0
Tel: 613-525-2022; *Fax:* 613-525-2023
Number of Beds: 70 beds
Terry A. Dubé

Almonte: Almonte Country Haven
333 Country St., Almonte, ON K0A 1A0
Tel: 613-256-3095; *Fax:* 613-256-3096
rgourlie@omniway.ca
www.omni-way.com/ourhomes/almonte.htm
Number of Beds: 82 beds
Rick Gourlie, Administrator

Almonte: Fairview Manor
PO Box 1360, 95 Spring St., Almonte, ON K0A 1A0
Tel: 613-256-3113; *Fax:* 613-256-5780
Number of Beds: 100 beds
Helen James, Director, Housekeeping
Linda Chaplin, Administrator

Aurora: Willows Estate
13837 Yonge St., Aurora, ON L4G 3G8
Tel: 905-727-0128; *Fax:* 905-841-0454
www.omni-way.com
Number of Beds: 84 beds
Note: Specialties: Long-term care; Care for persons with Alzheimer's disease & dementia; Life enrichment program
Susan Bean, Administrator
Ray Strevez, Supervisor, Environmental Services

Aylmer: Chateau Gardens Nursing Home
465 Talbot St. West, Aylmer, ON N5H 1K8
Tel: 519-773-3423; *Fax:* 519-765-2573
www.chateaugardens.com
Number of Beds: 60 beds
Mary Vergeer, Administrator

Aylmer: Terrace Lodge
475 Talbot St. East, 49462 Talbot Line, Aylmer, ON N5H 3A5
Tel: 519-773-9205; *Fax:* 519-765-2627
www.elginhomes.ca
Number of Beds: 100 beds
Note: Specialties: Long-term care; Secure unit; Physiotherapy; Activity program; Adult day program, including a specialized program for Alzheimer's patients; Respite care; Palliative care
Helen Notte, Administrator

Bancroft: Hastings Centennial Manor
PO Box 758, 1 Manor Lane, Bancroft, ON K0L 1C0
Tel: 613-332-2070; *Fax:* 613-332-2837
Number of Beds: 110 beds
B. White, Supervisor, Maintenance
Claudette Dignard-Remillard, Administrator

Barrie: Coleman Care Centre
140 Cundles Rd. West, RR#2, Barrie, ON L4M 4S4
Tel: 705-726-8691; *Fax:* 705-726-5085
Number of Beds: 112 beds
Ralph Spracklin, Maintenance
Françoise Bouchard, Administrator

Barrie: Grove Park Home for Senior Citizens
234 Cook St., Barrie, ON L4M 4H5
Tel: 705-726-1003; *Fax:* 705-726-1076
www.groveparkhome.on.ca
Number of Beds: 143 beds
Robert Dixon, Director, Physical Plant
Terry Codling, Administrator

Barrie: Leisureworld Caregiving Centre - Barrie
130 Owen St., Barrie, ON L4M 3H7
Tel: 705-726-8621; *Fax:* 705-726-0821
adm.barrie@leisureworld.ca
www.leisureworld.ca/barrie.html
Number of Beds: 57 beds
Mary LaChapelle, Administrator

Barrys Bay: Valley Manor Nursing Home
PO Box 880, 88 Mintha St., Barrys Bay, ON K0J 1B0
Tel: 613-756-2643; *Fax:* 613-756-7601
www.valleymanor.org
Number of Beds: 90 beds
Note: Adult Day Program
Ron Coulas, Director, Physical Plant
Linda Shulist, Administrator

Beamsville: Albright Manor
5035 Mountain St., Beamsville, ON L0R 1B2
Tel: 905-563-8252; *Fax:* 905-563-5223
Number of Beds: 231 beds
John E. Buma, CEO

Beeton: Simcoe Manor Home for the Aged
PO Box 100, Beeton, ON L0G 1A0
Tel: 905-729-2267; *Fax:* 905-729-4350
Number of Beds: 126 beds
Earl Gray, Supervisor

Belleville: Bellmont Long-Term Care Facility
Former Name: Montgomery Lodge Nursing Home.
250 Bridge St. West, Belleville, ON K8P 5N3
Tel: 613-968-8835; *Fax:* 613-968-3207
Number of Beds: 128 beds
David Clegg, Administrator

Belleville: Belmont Long Term Care Facility
250 Bridge St. West, Belleville, ON K8P 1B6
Tel: 613-968-4434; *Fax:* 613-968-3207
Number of Beds: 60 beds
James A. Clegg, Administrator

Belleville: Hastings Manor
PO Box 458, 476 Dundas St. West, Belleville, ON K8N 5B2
Tel: 613-968-6467; *Fax:* 613-967-0128
info@hastingsmanorfoundation.ca
www.hastingsmanorfoundation.ca
Year Founded: 1908
Number of Beds: 253 beds
Claudette Dignard-Remillard, Administrator

Belleville: Westgate Lodge
37 Wilkie St., Belleville, ON K8P 4E4
Tel: 613-966-1323; *Fax:* 613-966-5126
admin@westgatelodge.ca
Number of Beds: 88 beds
Elizabeth McGrath, Administrator

Bobcaygeon: Pinecrest Nursing Home
3418 County Rd. 36, RR#2, Bobcaygeon, ON K0M 1A0
Tel: 705-738-2366; *Fax:* 705-738-9414
Number of Beds: 65 beds
Note: Specialties: Activation program
Maryliz Mitchell, Administrator

Bolton: King Nursing Home
49 Sterne St., Bolton, ON L7E 5T1
Tel: 905-857-4117; *Fax:* 905-857-5181
kingnh@on.aibn.com
Year Founded: 1966
Number of Beds: 86 beds
Janice L. King, Administrator

Bolton: Vera M. Davis Community Care Centre
80 Allan Dr., Bolton, ON L7E 1P7
Tel: 905-857-0975; *Fax:* 905-857-7872
Number of Beds: 64 beds
Wendy Beattie, Administrator

Bradford: Bradford Place Nursing Home
2656 6th Line, RR#1, Bradford, ON L3Z 2A4
Tel: 905-952-2270; *Fax:* 905-775-0263
olivia.schmitz@specialty-care.com
www.specialty-care.com
Number of Beds: 150 beds
Olivia Schmitz, Administrator
olivia.schmitz@specialty-care.com

Brampton: Extendicare - Brampton
7891 McLaughlin Rd., Brampton, ON L6Y 5H8
Tel: 905-459-4904; *Fax:* 905-459-5625
cnh_brampton@extendicare.com
www.extendicarecanada.com/brampton/
Number of Beds: 150 beds

Brampton: Leisureworld Caregiving Centre - Brampton Meadows
215 Sunny Meadows Blvd., Brampton, ON L6R 3B5
Tel: 905-458-7604
adm.bm@leisureworld.ca
www.leisureworld.ca/brampton_meadows.html
Number of Beds: 160 beds
Angie Heinze, Administrator

Brampton: Leisureworld Caregiving Centre - Brampton Woods
9257 Goreway Dr., Brampton, ON L6T 3Y7
Tel: 905-799-7502
susan.wendt@leisureworld.ca
www.leisureworld.ca/brampton_woods.html
Number of Beds: 160 beds
Susan Wendt, Administrator

Brampton: Peel Manor
525 Main St. North, Brampton, ON L6X 1N9
Tel: 905-453-4140; *Fax:* 905-453-9140
Number of Beds: 177 beds
Note: Long-term care centre
Carolyn Clubine, Administrator

Brantford: Hardy Terrace Long Term Care
612 Mount Pleasant Rd., RR#2, Brantford, ON N3T 5L5
Tel: 519-484-2431; *Fax:* 519-484-2590
Number of Beds: 69 beds
Lloyd Smith, Administrator

Brantford: Leisureworld Caregiving Centre - Brantford
389 West St., Brantford, ON N3R 3V9
Tel: 519-759-4666; *Fax:* 519-759-0200
adm.brantford@leisureworld.ca
www.leisureworld.ca/brantford.html
Number of Beds: 120 permanent, 2 short stay beds
Christy Whiddet, Director of Care
Barbara Naykalyk-Hunt, Administrator

Brockville: St. Lawrence Lodge
PO Box 1130, 1803 Prescott Rd. East, Brockville, ON K6V 5W2
Tel: 613-345-0255; *Fax:* 613-345-1029
info@stll.org
www.stll.org
Number of Beds: 240 beds
Note: Long-term care home
Gary Blair, Purchasing Agent
William R. Luker, Administrator

Brockville: Sherwood Park Manor
1814 Hwy. 2 East, Brockville, ON K6V 5T1
Tel: 613-342-5531; *Fax:* 613-342-3767
Number of Beds: 107 beds
Joan Bennett, Administrator
J. Vanderwal, Director, Physical Plant

Brunner: Country Meadows Retirement & Living Centre
Ana St., Lot 16, Brunner, ON N0K 1C0
Tel: 519-595-8903; *Fax:* 519-595-8272
brunner@perth.net
Number of Beds: 43 beds
Elinor Morley, Administrator

Brussels: Huronlea Home for the Aged
820 Turnberry St. South, Brussels, ON N0G 1H0
Tel: 519-887-9267; *Fax:* 519-482-5263
Number of Beds: 64 beds; 2 respite beds
Barb Springhall, Administrator

Burlington: Cama Woodlands Nursing Home
159 Panin Rd., Burlington, ON L7P 5A6
Tel: 905-681-6441; *Fax:* 905-681-2678
a.lawlor@bellnet.ca
www.camawoodlands.com
Number of Beds: 64 beds
Allene Lawlor, Administrator

Burlington: Maple Villa Long Term Care Centre
441 Maple Ave., Burlington, ON L7S 1L8
Tel: 905-639-2264; *Fax:* 905-639-3034
maplevilla@maplevilla.ca
www.maplevilla.ca
Number of Beds: 93 beds
Barbara Goetz, Administrator

Cambridge: Fairview Mennonite Home
515 Langs Dr., Cambridge, ON N3H 5E4
Tel: 519-653-5719; *Fax:* 519-650-1242
Number of Beds: 84 beds
Earl Gerber, Director, Maintenance
T. Kennel, Exec. Dir.

Cambridge: Golden Years Nursing Home
PO Box 3277, 704 Eagle St. North, Cambridge, ON N3H 4T3
Tel: 519-653-5493; *Fax:* 519-650-1495
nancy@goldenyearscambridge.com
www.goldenyearscambridge.com
Number of Beds: 88 beds
Nancy Kauffman-Lambert, Administrator

Campbellford: Burnbrae Gardens
320 Burnbrae Road East, RR#3, Campbellford, ON K0L 1L0
Tel: 705-653-4100; *Fax:* 705-653-2598
scymbaluk@omniway.com
www.onmi-way.com/ourhomes/burnbrae.htm
Number of Beds: 43 beds
Susan Cymbaluk, Administrator/Director of Care
scymbaluk@omniway.com
Rosie Coppens, Office Manager

Cannifton: E.J. McQuigge Lodge
PO Box 68, Black Diamond Rd. & Hwy. 37, Cannifton, ON K0K 1K0
Tel: 613-966-7717; *Fax:* 613-966-7646
agarland@mcquiggelodge.com
www.mcquiggelodge.com
Number of Beds: 56 beds
Anita Garland, Administrator
agarland@mcquiggelodge.com

Cannington: Bon-Air Nursing Home
131 Laidlaw St. South, Cannington, ON L0E 1E0
Tel: 705-432-2385; *Fax:* 705-432-3331
bonair@chartwellreit.ca
Number of Beds: 55 units
Lynne Disik, Administrator

Chapleau: Bignucolo Residence
PO Box 757, 6 Broomhead Rd., Chapleau, ON P0M 1K0
Tel: 705-864-1520; *Fax:* 705-864-0449
Year Founded: 1998
Number of Beds: 25 beds
Note: Specialties: Long-term care; Chronic care; Respite care; Pet therapy

Chatham: St. Andrews Residence
99 Park St., Chatham, ON N7M 3R5
Tel: 519-354-8103; *Fax:* 519-351-2407
info@standrewsresidence.com
www.standrewsresidence.com
Number of Beds: 95 beds
W.L. Alexander, Administrator/CEO

Chatham: Victoria Residence
190 Stanley Ave., Chatham, ON N7M 3J9
Tel: 519-354-0610; *Fax:* 519-354-7741
Number of Beds: 90 beds
Note: home for the aged
Patricia Cuncic, Administrator

Chesley: Elgin Abbey Nursing & Retirement Home
PO Box 7, 380 First Ave. North, Chesley, ON N0G 1L0
Tel: 519-363-3195; *Fax:* 519-363-0375
elginabb@log.on.ca
Number of Beds: 41 beds; 27 long-term-care, 14 retirement home
Jennifer Soper, Program Manager
Tracee Givens, Administrator

Clinton: Huronview Home for the Aged
77722A London Rd. Hwy 4 S, RR#5, Clinton, ON N0M 1L0
Tel: 519-482-3451
Number of Beds: 119 beds
Barb Springall, Administrator

Cobourg: Extendicare - Cobourg
130 New Densmore Rd., Cobourg, ON K9A 5W2
Tel: 905-372-0377; *Fax:* 905-372-0477
cnh_cobourg@extendicare.com
www.extendicarecanada.com
Number of Beds: 69 beds

Collingwood: Collingwood Nursing Home Limited
250 Campbell St., Collingwood, ON L9Y 4J9
Tel: 705-445-3991; *Fax:* 705-445-5060
cnh@collingwoodnursinghome.com
www.collingwoodnursinghome.com
Number of Beds: 60 beds
Peter Zober, Administrator

Corbeil: Nipissing Manor Nursing Care Centre
1202 Hwy. 94, RR#1, Corbeil, ON P0H 1K0
Tel: 705-752-1100; *Fax:* 705-752-2570
Number of Beds: 143 beds
W.E. Graham, Administrator

Cornwall: Glen-Stor-Dun Lodge
1900 Montréal Rd., Cornwall, ON K6H 7L1
Tel: 613-933-3384; *Fax:* 613-933-7214
www.glenstordunlodge.com
Number of Beds: 132 beds
D. Seller, Director, Housekeeping/Physical Plant
Donna Derouchie, Administrator

Cornwall: Parisien Manor
439 Second St. East, Cornwall, ON K6H 1Z2
Tel: 613-933-2592; *Fax:* 613-933-3839
www.parisienmanor.ca
Year Founded: 1982
Note: Specialties: Long-term care; Activation programs; Counselling; Social services; Dental services; Music therapy; Physiotherapy; Occupational therapy; Foot care
Norman Quenneville, Administrator

Cornwall: St. Joseph's Villa (Cornwall)
14 York St., Cornwall, ON K6J 5T2
Tel: 613-933-6040; *Fax:* 613-933-9429
executiveoffices@stjosephscentre.ca
www.stjosephscentre.ca
Number of Beds: 150 beds
Jeanette Despatie, Executive Director
Allan Greg, Director, Physical Plant

Cornwall Island: Tsi ion kwa nonh so:te
Former Name: Akwesasne Adult Care Facility
RR#3, Cornwall Island, ON K6H 5R7
Tel: 613-932-1409; *Fax:* 613-932-8845
Number of Beds: 30 beds
Note: Specialties: Geriatric residential health care; Water therapy; Palliative care
Bonnie Cole, Administrator

Creemore: Creedan Valley Nursing Home
PO Box 309, 143 Mary St., Creemore, ON L0M 1G0
Tel: 705-466-3437; *Fax:* 705-466-3063
Number of Beds: 96 beds
Debbie Fleming, Administrator

Creemore: Leisureworld Caregiving Centre - Creedan Valley
143 Mary St., Creemore, ON L0M 1G0
Tel: 705-466-3437
adm.creedan@leisureworld.ca
www.leisureworld.ca/creedan.html
Number of Beds: 95 beds
Paula Rentner, Administrator

Deep River: North Renfrew Long-Term Care Centre
PO Box 1988, 47 Ridge Rd., Deep River, ON K0J 1P0
Tel: 613-584-1900; *Fax:* 613-584-9183
nrltcsin@magma.ca
www.magma.ca/~nrltcsin
Number of Beds: 20 long-term care; 9 supportive care; 1 respite
Ann Aikens, Administrator

Delhi: Delhi Long Term Care Centre
750 Gibraltar St., Delhi, ON N4B 3B3
Tel: 519-582-3400; *Fax:* 519-582-0300
delhinh@kwic.com
Number of Beds: 60 beds
Janet Krolouski, Administrator

Deseronto: Friendly Manor Nursing Home
PO Box 305, Hwy. 2, Deseronto, ON K0K 1X0
Tel: 613-396-3438; *Fax:* 613-396-2729
judy_manor@hotmail.com
Number of Beds: 60 beds
Judith Norlock, Manager

Elmira: Leisureworld Caregiving Centre - Elmira
120 Barnswallow Dr., Elmira, ON N3B 2Y9
Tel: 519-669-5777
angie.heinz@leisureworld.ca
www.leisureworld.ca/elmira.html
Number of Beds: 92 permanent, 2 short stay beds
Cathy Holland, Administrator

Elora: Wellington County Terrace Home for the Aged
PO Box 70, Wellington Dr., Elora, ON N0B 1S0
Tel: 519-846-5359; *Fax:* 519-846-9192
Number of Beds: 176 beds
Peter M. Barnes, Administrator
R. Granger, Purchasing Director
Don Giles, Director, Housekeeping

Englehart: Northview Nursing Home
PO Box 1139, 77 River Rd., Englehart, ON P0J 1H0
Tel: 705-544-8191; *Fax:* 705-544-8255
northview@ntl.sympatico.ca
Number of Beds: 48 beds
Ruth Sulis, Administrator/DOC
A. Saunders, Director, Physical Plant

Espanola: Espanola Nursing Home
799 Queensway Ave., Espanola, ON P5E 1R3
Tel: 705-869-1420; *Fax:* 705-869-2608
Number of Beds: 30 beds
Paul L. Davies, Administrator
Diane Mokohonuk, Environmental Manager

Essex: Iler Lodge
Former Name: Essex Health Care Centre
111 Iler Ave., Essex, ON N8M 1T6
Tel: 519-776-9482; *Fax:* 519-776-4292
ilerlodge@reveraliving.com
www.reveraliving.com/homes/exr/
Number of Beds: 104 beds
Cheryl Labute, Administrator

Forest: North Lambton Rest Home
PO Box 640, 39 Morris St., Forest, ON N0N 1J0
Tel: 519-786-2151; *Fax:* 519-786-2156
Number of Beds: 87 beds
Jeffrey J. Harvey, Assistant Administrator
George Tomlinson, Environmental Services Supervisor

Fort Erie: Crescent Park Lodge
4 Hagey Ave., Fort Erie, ON L2A 5M5
Tel: 905-871-8330; *Fax:* 905-871-9212
Number of Beds: 68 beds
Rose Turner, Administrator

Gananoque: Carveth Care Centre
375 James St., Gananoque, ON K7G 2Z1
Tel: 613-382-4752; *Fax:* 613-382-8514
Number of Beds: 94 beds
Tim Gibson, Vice-President, Administration & Finance
Ray Gentile, Supervisor, Plant Maintenance

Georgetown: Bennett Health Care Centre
1 Princess Anne Dr., Georgetown, ON L7G 2B8
Tel: 905-873-0115; *Fax:* 905-873-1403
info@bennetthealthcarecentre.ca
www.bennetthealthcarecentre.ca
Number of Beds: 66 beds
Mark Ewer, Administrator

Gloucester: Extendicare - Laurier Manor
1715 Montréal Rd., Gloucester, ON K1J 6N4
Tel: 613-741-5122; *Fax:* 613-741-8432
Number of Beds: 240 beds
Norm Slatter, Administrator

Goderich: Maitland Manor
290 South St., Goderich, ON N7A 4G6
Tel: 519-524-7324; *Fax:* 519-524-8739
maitland@reveraliving.com
www.reveraliving.com

Number of Beds: 91 beds
Note: Specialties: Long-term care; Restorative care programs; Foot care; Specialized skin & wound care program; Physiotherapy; Music therapy; Respite care
Angie Dunn, Acting Administrator

Gravenhurst: Leisureworld Caregiving Centre - Muskoka
200 Kelly Dr., Gravenhurst, ON P1P 1P3
Tel: 705-687-3444; *Fax:* 705-687-9094
marion.barton@leisureworld.ca
www.leisureworld.ca/muskoka.html
Year Founded: 1999
Number of Beds: 180 long-term care, 2 short term beds, 28 retirement suites
Marion Barton, Administrator
Denise Ward, Director, Care

Grimsby: Kilean Lodge
83 Main St. East, Grimsby, ON L3M 1N6
Tel: 905-945-9243; *Fax:* 905-945-1126
kileanlodge@reveraliving.com
www.reveraliving.com/homes/70
Number of Beds: 50 beds
Sonja Jonescu, Executive Director

Grimsby: Shalom Manor
12 Bartlett Ave., Grimsby, ON L3M 4N5
Tel: 905-945-9631; *Fax:* 905-945-1211
info@shalommanor.ca
www.shalommanor.ca
Year Founded: 1966
Number of Beds: 144 beds
Note: Home for the aged affiliated with the Christian Reformed Church
Chris Rynberk, CEO
Rita Fluit, Director, Nursing
Yettie Termorshuizen, Director, Environmental Services

Guelph: Eden House Nursing Home
Affiliated with: Waterloo Wellington Local Health Integration Network
Country Rd. 29, RR#2, Guelph, ON N1H 6H8
Tel: 519-856-4622; *Fax:* 519-856-1274
admin@edenhousecarehome.ca
www.edenhousecarehome.ca
Number of Beds: 58 nursing home, 21 retirement home
John Bouwmeester, Administrator

Guelph: Lapointe-Fisher Nursing Home
271 Metcalfe St., Guelph, ON N1E 4Y8
Tel: 519-821-9030; *Fax:* 519-821-6021
guelph@lapointefisher.ca
guelph.lapointefisher.ca
Number of Beds: 92 beds
Tom Hudson, Administrator
Reg Carreor, Environmental Services Supervisor

Haileybury: Extendicare - Tri-Town
PO Box 999, 143 Bruce St., Haileybury, ON P0J 1K0
Tel: 705-672-2151; *Fax:* 705-672-5348
gjulien@extendicare.com
Number of Beds: 60 beds
Ghislaine Julien, Administrator

Haliburton: Extendicare - Haliburton
PO Box 780, 167 Park St., Haliburton, ON K0M 1S0
Tel: 705-457-1722; *Fax:* 705-457-3914
cnh_halibruton@extendicare.com
www.extendicarecanada.com/haliburton/
Number of Beds: 60 beds
Jane Rosenberg, Administrator
Doug Holmes, Maintenance Supervisor

Halton Hills: Extendicare - Halton Hills
9 Lindsay Court, Halton Hills, ON L7G 6G9
Tel: 905-702-8760; *Fax:* 905-702-7430
www.extendicare.com
Number of Beds: 130 beds
André Spekkens, Administrator

Hamilton: Arbour Creek Long Term Care Centre
2717 King St. East, Hamilton, ON L8G 1J3
Tel: 905-573-4900
info.arbourcreek@thomashealthcare.com
Number of Beds: 128 beds
Shirley Thomas Weir

Hamilton: Extendicare - Hamilton
90 Chedmac Dr., Hamilton, ON L9C 7S6
Tel: 905-318-4472; *Fax:* 905-318-1162
cnh_hamilton@extendicare.com
www.extendicarecanada.com/hamilton/
Number of Beds: 160 beds

Hamilton: Hamilton Continuing Care
125 Wentworth St. South, Hamilton, ON L8N 2Z1
Tel: 905-527-1482; *Fax:* 905-527-0679
lorraine_preston_orchard@hotmail.com
Number of Beds: 64 beds
Lorraine Preston-Orchard, Administrator

Hamilton: Macassa Lodge
701 Upper Sherman Ave., Hamilton, ON L8V 3M7
Tel: 905-546-2800; *Fax:* 905-546-4989
saphsweb@hamilton.ca
www.hamilton.ca/phcs/macassa
Number of Beds: 270 beds
Note: Specialties: Long term care; Adult day program; Social work
Mark Ewer, Administrator

Hamilton: Parkview Nursing Centre
545 King St. West, Hamilton, ON L8P 1C1
Tel: 905-525-5903; *Fax:* 905-525-8717
www.parkviewnursingcentre.com
Number of Beds: 126 beds
Andrea Pohl, Administrator
Tom Sachade, Manager, Maintenance/Plysical Plant

Hamilton: Victoria Nursing Home
176 Victoria Ave. North, Hamilton, ON L8L 5G1
Tel: 905-527-9111; *Fax:* 905-526-1871
www.victoriagardens.ca
Number of Beds: 76 beds
Ranka Stipancic, Administrator

Hanover: Hanover Care Centre
700 - 19 Ave., Hanover, ON N4N 3S6
Tel: 519-364-3700; *Fax:* 519-364-7194
hcc@bmts.com
Number of Beds: 41 beds
Dennis Laver, Director, Physical Plant
Bill Garcia, Administrator

Hearst: Foyer des Pionniers
PO Box 1538, 1317 Edward St., Hearst, ON P0L 1N0
Tel: 705-372-2820; *Fax:* 705-372-2826
Number of Beds: 61 beds
Joëlle Lacroix, Director of Care

Ingersoll: Leisureworld Caregiving Centre - Oxford
263 Wonham St. South, Ingersoll, ON N5C 3P6
Tel: 519-485-3920
adm.oxford@leisureworld.ca
www.leisureworld.ca
Year Founded: 1975
Number of Beds: 80 long-term care beds
Note: Specialties: Restorative care; Physiotherapy program; Pet therapy; Palliative care
Carolee Milliner, Administrator
Ted Cripps, Environmental Services Supervisor

Iroquois Falls: South Centennial Manor
240 Fyfe St., Iroquois Falls, ON P0K 1E0
Tel: 705-258-3836; *Fax:* 705-258-3694
Number of Beds: 68 beds
Dan O'Mara, CEO
Richard Hadley, Director, Physical Plant

Kapuskasing: Extendicare - Kapuskasing
PO Box 460, 45 Ontario St., Kapuskasing, ON P5N 2Y5
Tel: 705-335-8337; *Fax:* 705-337-6051
cnh_kapuskasing@extendicare.com
www.extendicarecanada.com/kapuskasing/
Number of Beds: 60 beds
Jacynthe Ouellette, Administrator

Kapuskasing: North Centennial Manor
2 Kimberley Dr., Kapuskasing, ON P5N 1L5
Tel: 705-335-6125; *Fax:* 705-337-1091
Number of Beds: 71 beds
Note: non-profit charitable home for the aged
Gil M. Dionne, Administrator
Jean-Claude Lauzon, Supervisor, Plant Maintenance

Kemptville: Bayfield Manor Nursing & Retirement Home
PO Box 300, 100 Elvira St., Kemptville, ON K0G 1J0
Tel: 613-258-7484; *Fax:* 613-258-3838
bayfield@bayfieldmanor.on.ca
www.bayfieldmanor.on.ca
Number of Beds: 66 bed nursing home + 46 suite retirement home
Michael J. Hall, Administrator

Kenora: Birchwood Terrace Central Park Lodge
PO Box 2630, 237 Lakeview Drive, R.R. #1, Kenora, ON P9N 3X8
Tel: 807-468-9532; *Fax:* 807-468-4060
birchwoodterrace@reveraliving.com
Number of Beds: 94 beds
Soili Helppi, Executive Director
soili.helppi@reveraliving.com

Kenora: Pinecrest Home for the Aged
1220 Valley Dr., Kenora, ON P9N 2W7
Tel: 807-468-3165; *Fax:* 807-468-6346
Kevin L. Queen, Administrator

King City: King City Lodge Nursing Home
146 Fog Rd., King City, ON L7B 1A3
Tel: 905-833-5037; *Fax:* 905-833-5925
www.kingcitylodge.com
Number of Beds: 36 beds
Kelly Graham, Administrator; Director, Nursing

Kingston: Extendicare - Kingston
309 Queen Mary Rd., Kingston, ON K7M 6P4
Tel: 613-549-5010; *Fax:* 613-549-7347
cnh_kingston@extendicare.com
www.extendicarecanada.com/kingston/
Number of Beds: 150 beds
Marilyn C. Benn, Administrator

Kingston: Rideaucrest Home
175 Rideau St., Kingston, ON K7K 3H6
Tel: 613-530-2818; *Fax:* 613-531-9107
Number of Beds: 170 beds
Note: municipal home for the aged
John D. Smith, Administrator

Kirkland Lake: Extendicare - Kirkland Lake
PO Box 3900, 155 Government Rd. East, Kirkland Lake, ON P2N 3P4
Tel: 705-567-3268; *Fax:* 705-567-4638
cnh_kirklandlake@extendicare.com
www.extendicarecanada.com/kirklandlake/
Number of Beds: 100 beds
Susan Enouy, Administrator

Kirkland Lake: Teck Pioneer Residence
145A Government Rd. East, Kirkland Lake, ON P2N 3P4
Tel: 705-567-3264
www.teckpioneerresidence.com
Year Founded: 1965
Note: Specialties: Nursing services for long-term care residents; Dementia care; Activity program; Restorative care
Nancy Allick, Administrator
Donna LeGros, Director, Nursing
Phil Sullivan, Environmental Services Supervisor

Kitchener: A.R. Goudie Eventide Home (Salvation Army)
369 Frederick St., Kitchener, ON N2H 2P1
Tel: 519-744-5182; *Fax:* 519-744-3887
info@argoudieeventide.ca
www.argoudieeventide.ca
Number of Beds: 80 beds
Mr. Gary Butt, Executive Director
gbutt@argoudieeventide.ca
Ms. Anabela Henriques, Manager, Resident Care Services
ahenriques@argoudieeventide.ca
Alison Westman, Manager, Dietary & Environmental Services
awestman@argoudieeventide.ca

Kitchener: Forest Heights Long Term Care Centre
60 Westheights Dr., Kitchener, ON N2N 2A8
Tel: 519-576-3320; *Fax:* 519-745-3227
Number of Beds: 240 beds
Michelle Vermeeren, Administrator

Kitchener: Trinity Village Care Centre (TVCC)
2727 Kingsway Dr., Kitchener, ON N2C 1A7
Tel: 519-893-6320; *Fax:* 519-893-3432
cverleyen@trinityvillage.com
www.trinityvillage.com
Number of Beds: 150 residential capacity
Note: Specialties: Eden Alternative Philosophy of Care; Long-term care; Therapeutic services; Recreation programming; Palliative care
Debby Riepert, Administrator
Elizabeth Barnes, Supervisor, Environmental Health

Kitchener: Village of Winston Park
695 Blockline Rd., Kitchener, ON N2E 3K1
Tel: 519-576-2430; *Fax:* 519-576-8990
info@winstonpark.net
www.winstonpark.net

Number of Beds: 271 beds
Michael Schmidt, Administrator

L'Orignal: Résidence Champlain
Former Name: CHS pleasant Rest Inc; Pleasant Rest Nursing Home
428 Front Rd. Wesst, L'Orignal, ON K0B 1K0
Tel: 613-675-4617; *Fax:* 613-675-1374
champlain@chartwellreit.ca
www.chartwellreit.ca

Number of Beds: 60 beds
Jacinthe Loiselle, Administrator

Lakefield: Extendicare - Lakefield
19 Fraser St., Lakefield, ON K0L 2H0
Tel: 705-652-7112; *Fax:* 705-652-7733
cnh_lakefield@extendicare.com
www.extendicarecanada.com/lakefield/
Number of Beds: 100 beds

Leamington: Leamington Nursing Home
24 Franklin Rd., Leamington, ON N8H 4B7
Tel: 519-326-3289; *Fax:* 519-326-0102
Number of Beds: 120 beds
Roxanne Belli, Administrator

Leamington: Leamington United Mennonite Home
35 Pickwick Dr., Leamington, ON N8H 2P2
Tel: 519-326-6109; *Fax:* 519-326-3595
Number of Beds: 82 beds
Linda Tiessen, Administrator

Leamington: Sun Parlor Home for Senior Citizens
175 Talbot St. East, Leamington, ON N8H 1L9
Tel: 519-326-5731; *Fax:* 519-326-8952
www.countyofessex.on.ca/countyservices/sunparlor_home.asp
Year Founded: 1900
Number of Beds: 206 beds
Note: Specialties: Long-term care; Mental health services; Physiotherapy; Restorative care programs; Speech therapy; Occupational therapy; Audiology screening; Life enrichment services
Bill MacDonald, Administrator

Lindsay: Extendicare - Kawartha Lakes
125 Colborne St. East, Lindsay, ON K9V 4R3
Tel: 705-878-5392; *Fax:* 705-878-7910
cnh_kawarthalakes@extendicare.com
www.extendicarecanada.com/lindsaykawartha/
Number of Beds: 64 beds

Lions Head: Golden Dawn Nursing Home
PO Box 129, 80 Main St., Lions Head, ON N0H 1W0
Tel: 519-793-3433; *Fax:* 519-793-4503
Number of Beds: 45 beds
Frank Walker, Administrator
Bruce Haksins, Maintenance Supervisor

Little Current: Manitoulin Centennial Manor
PO Box 460, 70 Robinson St. West, Little Current, ON P0P 1K0
Tel: 705-368-2710; *Fax:* 705-368-2694
Number of Beds: 60 beds
Cathy Deacon, Administrator; Director, Residential Services

London: Chateau Gardens (Queens) Nursing Home
518 Queens Ave., London, ON N6B 1Y7
Tel: 519-434-2727; *Fax:* 519-679-3482
Number of Beds: 63 beds
Donna Heffron, Administrator

London: Chelsey Park (Oxford) Nursing Home
310 Oxford St. West, London, ON N6H 4N6
Tel: 519-432-1855; *Fax:* 519-679-7324
www.chelseypark.com
Number of Beds: 243 beds
Note: retirement community
Rhonda Roberts, Administrator

London: Extendicare - London
860 Waterloo St., London, ON N6A 3W6
Tel: 519-433-6658; *Fax:* 519-642-1711
cnh_london@extendicare.com
Number of Beds: 170 beds
Charles Marczinski, Administrator
John Plachta, Supervisor, Maintenance

London: McCormick Home
2022 Kains Rd., London, ON N6K 0A8
Tel: 519-432-2648; *Fax:* 519-645-6982
www.mccormickhome.on.ca
Number of Beds: 160 beds
Note: Specialties: Long-term care; Ddementia care; Alzheimer outreach services day program; Social work

Michael P. Boucher, Executive Director
Roy Langille, Director, Physical Operations

Long Sault: Woodland Villa
30 Mille Roches Rd., Long Sault, ON K0C 1P0
Tel: 613-534-2276; *Fax:* 613-534-8559
mrasenberg@omniway.ca
www.omni-way.com/ourhomes/woodland.htm
Number of Beds: 112 beds
Michael Rasenberg, Administrator

Markdale: Grey Gables Home for the Aged
Former Name: Grey Owen Lodge
PO Box 380, 206 Toronto St. South, Markdale, ON N0C 1H0
Tel: 519-986-3010; *Fax:* 519-986-4644
sperson@greycounty.ca
Number of Beds: 66 beds
Shirley Person, Administrator

Markham: Markhaven, Home for Seniors
54 Parkway Ave., Markham, ON L3P 2G4
Tel: 905-294-2233; *Fax:* 905-294-6521
markhaven@markhaven.ca
www.markhaven.ca
Note: Specialties: Medical care; Nursing care; Physiotherapy; Special needs activities. Number of Employees: 149
Don Jennings, Maintenance Supervisor
Noreen Kallai, Executive Director

Maryhill: Twin Oaks of Maryhill Inc.
1360 Maryhill Rd., Maryhill, ON N0B 2B0
Tel: 519-648-2117
www.twinoaksmaryhill.com
Number of Beds: 31 beds
Note: Specialties: Secured area
Ralph Link, Administrator

Mattawa: Algonquin Nursing Home
PO Box 270, 231 Tenth St., Mattawa, ON P0H 1V0
Tel: 705-744-2202; *Fax:* 705-744-2787
Toll-Free: 800-579-4284
vala@anh.ca
www.anh.ca
Number of Beds: 72 beds
Leonard Simpson, Maintenance
Zena Monestime, Administrator

Meaford: Meaford Long Term Care Centre
135 William St., Meaford, ON N4L 1T4
Tel: 519-538-1010; *Fax:* 519-538-5699
businessoffice@meafordlongtermcare.com
www.meafordlongtermcare.com
Number of Beds: 77 beds
Note: Specialties; Restorative care program; Psychogeriatric outreach; Life enrichment programs; Services of a wound care specialist; Services of a pain specialist; Palliative care
Doris Bilitz, Administrator
Randy Turner, Environmental Services

Merrickville: Hilltop Manor
1005 St Lawrence St., Merrickville, ON K0G 1N0
Tel: 613-269-4707; *Fax:* 613-269-3534
elizabeth@hilltopmanor.ca
www.hilltopmanor.ca
Number of Beds: 89 beds

Merrickville: Hilltop Manor Nursing Home Ltd.
PO Box 430, 1005 St. Lawrence St., Merrickville, ON K0G 1N0
Tel: 613-269-4707; *Fax:* 613-269-3534
hilltop@alphainter.net
Number of Beds: 60 beds
Bernard Bouchard, Administrator
Wayne Pierce, Environmental Supervisor

Metcalfe: Township of Osgoode Care Centre
7650 Snake Island Rd., Metcalfe, ON K0A 2P0
Tel: 613-821-1034; *Fax:* 613-821-0388
osgoodecare@virtualwave.com
Number of Beds: 55 units
Note: Specialties: Long-term nursing care; Organized leisure activities
Murray B. Munro, Administrator
Deborah Nixon, Director, Nursing
Blaine Wright, General Service Supervisor

Milverton: Knollcrest Lodge
50 William St., Milverton, ON N0K 1M0
Tel: 519-595-8121; *Fax:* 519-595-8199
srae@knollcrestlodge.com
Number of Beds: 77 beds
Susan Rae, Administrator

Minden: Hyland Crest Senior Citizens' Home
PO Box 30, 6 McPherson St., Minden, ON K0M 2K0
Tel: 705-286-2140; *Fax:* 705-286-6384
hylandcrest@interhop.net
Number of Beds: 62 beds
Foster Loucks, Administrator
Peter Fearrey, Maintenance Supervisor
Peter Fearrey, Director, Environmental Services

Mississauga: Carmel Heights Seniors' Residence
Former Name: Carmel Heights Home for the Aged
1720 Sherwood Forest Circle, Mississauga, ON L5K 1R1
Tel: 905-822-5298; *Fax:* 905-822-7386
carmelheights@rogers.com
www.carmelheights.ca
Number of Beds: 48 beds
Note: home for the aged residential care
Sr. M. Veronica, Administrator

Mississauga: Chelsey Park (Streetsville) Nursing Home
1742 Bristol Rd. West, Mississauga, ON L5M 1X9
Tel: 905-826-3045; *Fax:* 905-826-9978
www.diversicare.ca
Number of Beds: 118 beds
Wendy Shelley, Administrator
George Holland, Coordinator, Environmental Services

Mississauga: Chelsey Park Nursing Home
2250 Hurontario St., Mississauga, ON L5B 1M8
Tel: 905-270-0411; *Fax:* 905-270-1749
Number of Beds: 237 beds
Dr. Alice Grzesiak, Administrator

Mississauga: Extendicare - Mississauga
855 John Watt Blvd., Mississauga, ON L5W 1G2
Tel: 905-696-0719
cnh_mississauga@extendicare.com
Number of Beds: 140 beds

Mississauga: Mississauga Lifecare Centre
55 The Queensway West, Mississauga, ON L5B 1B5
Tel: 905-270-0170; *Fax:* 905-270-8465
Number of Beds: 26 respite; 166 long-term care
Ina Reynolds, Administrator
Bill Cody, Director, Maintenance

Mississauga: Mississauga Long Term Care Facility
Former Name: Mississauga Nursing Home Inc.
26 Peter St. North, Mississauga, ON L5H 2G7
Tel: 905-278-2213
www.mltcfacility.com
Number of Beds: 55 beds
Novak Bajin, Administrator

Mississauga: Sheridan Villa
2460 Truscott Dr., Mississauga, ON L5J 3Z8
Tel: 905-791-8668; *Fax:* 905-823-7971
Number of Beds: 236 beds
Inga Mazuryk, Administrator
John Squire, Environmental Services

Mississauga: Tyndall Nursing Home Ltd.
1060 Eglinton Ave. East, Mississauga, ON L4W 1K3
Tel: 905-624-1511; *Fax:* 905-629-9346
info@tyndallnursinghome.com
www.tyndallestates.net
Number of Beds: 151 residents
Note: Specialties: Long-term care; Restorative feeding program
B.D. Jolly, Administrator
Alisea Vernon, Health; Safety Committee

Mitchell: Mitchell Nursing Home Ltd.
Affiliated with: Ritz Lutheran Villa
184 Napier St., Mitchell, ON N0K 1N0
Tel: 519-348-8861; *Fax:* 519-348-4214
Year Founded: 1969
Number of Beds: 48 beds
Cathy Wight, Administrator

New Hamburg: Nithview Home and Seniors Village
200-218 Boullee St., New Hamburg, ON N0B 2G0
Tel: 519-662-2280; *Fax:* 519-662-1090
Year Founded: 1972
Number of Beds: 96 beds
Note: Mennonite nursing home
Brent Martin, Administrator

Newcastle: Fosterbrooke Long Term Care Facility
330 King St. West, Newcastle, ON L1B 1G9
Tel: 905-987-4702; *Fax:* 905-987-3621
fosterbrooke@cplreit.com
Number of Beds: 88 beds
Barbara Tomaszewski, Acting Administrator

***Newcastle:* Fosterbrooke Long Term Care Facility**
330 King St. West, Newcastle, ON L1B 1G9
Tel: 905-987-4702; *Fax:* 905-987-3621
Number of Beds: 88 beds
Christine Nidd, Administrator

***Newmarket:* Central Care Corporation - Mackenzie Place**
52 George St., Newmarket, ON L3Y 4V3
Tel: 905-853-3242; *Fax:* 905-895-5139
www.cplcanada.com
Number of Beds: 93 beds
Anne Deelstra, Administrator

***Newmarket:* Eagle Terrace**
329 Eagle St., Newmarket, ON L3Y 1K3
Tel: 905-895-5187; *Fax:* 905-895-2645
eagleterrace@cplreit.com
Number of Beds: 70 beds
Michael Griffin, Administrator
Elizabeth Laur, Director

***Newmarket:* Eagle Terrace**
329 Eagle St., Newmarket, ON L3Y 1K3
Tel: 905-895-5187; *Fax:* 905-895-2645
eagleterrace@reveraliving.com
retirementresidencesreit.com/homes/07/
Number of Beds: 70 beds
Michael Griffin, Administrator

***Newmarket:* Maple Health Centre - York Region Long-Term Care & Seniors Branch**
194 Eagle St., Newmarket, ON L3Y 1J6
Tel: 905-895-3628; *Fax:* 905-895-5843
Number of Beds: 100 beds
Lynn Parsons, Assistant Administrator; Director, Care

***Newmarket:* Newmarket Health Centre-York Region Long-Term Care & Seniors Branch**
194 Eagle St., Newmarket, ON L3Y 1J6
Tel: 905-895-3628; *Fax:* 905-895-5843
Number of Beds: 132 beds
Marlene Parsons, Assistant Administrator; Director, Care

***Niagara Falls:* Oakwood Park Lodge**
6747 Oakwood Dr., Niagara Falls, ON L2E 7E3
Tel: 905-356-8732; *Fax:* 905-356-2122
oakwoodparklodge@cogeco.net
www.conmedhealth.com
Year Founded: 1975
Number of Beds: 153 beds
Paul Taylor, Administrator

***Niagara Falls:* The Salvation Army Honorable Ray & Helen Lawson Eventide Home**
5050 Jepson St., Niagara Falls, ON L2E 1K5
Tel: 905-356-1221; *Fax:* 905-356-9609
info@niagaraeventide.ca
www.niagaraeventide.ca
Note: Specialties: Long-term care for senior; Activity program
Maj. Grace Herber, Administrator
Harold Barwes, Head, Maintenance

***Niagara Falls:* Valley Park Lodge**
6400 Valley Way, Niagara Falls, ON L2E 7E3
Tel: 905-358-3277; *Fax:* 905-358-3012
Number of Beds: 65 beds
Jennifer Kennedy, Administrator
Ron Jones, Maintenance Supervisor

***North Bay:* Leisureworld Caregiving Centre - North Bay**
401 William St., North Bay, ON P1A 1X5
Tel: 705-476-2602; *Fax:* 705-476-1624
ruth.gauthier@leisureworld.ca
www.leisureworld.ca/northbay.html
Number of Beds: 147 suites, 1 short stay bed; 6 convalescent care
Ruth Gauthier, Administrator
Carol Passmore, Director, Nursing

***Northbrook:* Pine Meadow Nursing Home**
PO Box 100, 124 Lloyd St., Northbrook, ON K0H 2G0
Tel: 613-336-9120; *Fax:* 613-336-9144
Year Founded: 1993
Number of Beds: 60 beds
Note: Specialties: Residential nursing care for seniors
Kim Harvey, Administrator

***Norwich:* Norvilla Nursing Home**
11 Elgin St. East, Norwich, ON N0J 1P0
Tel: 519-863-2717; *Fax:* 519-863-3955
Number of Beds: 40 beds

***Ohsweken:* Iroquois Lodge**
PO Box 309, 1755 Chiefswood Rd, Ohsweken, ON N0A 1M0
Tel: 519-445-2224; *Fax:* 519-445-4180
iroquoislodge@on.aibn.com
Number of Beds: 50 beds
Wanda Green, Administrator
Patti Powless, Nursing Supervisor

***Orillia:* Oak Terrace**
291 Mississauga St. West, Orillia, ON L3V 3B9
Tel: 705-325-2289; *Fax:* 705-325-7178
oakterrace@reveraliving.com
Note: Specialties: Foot care; Physiotherapy programs; Restorative care programs; Dental services; Music therapy; Pet therapy
Marianne Williams, Administrator

***Orleans:* St. Louis Residence**
879, ch Parc Hiawatha, Orleans, ON K1C 2Z6
Tel: 613-562-6262; *Fax:* 613-683-5001
rslinfo@bruyere.org
Number of Beds: 198 beds
Note: charitable home for the aged
Hélène Tassé, Administrator

***Oshawa:* Extendicare - Oshawa**
82 Park Rd. North, Oshawa, ON L1J 4L1
Tel: 905-579-0011; *Fax:* 905-579-1733
www.extendicare.com
Number of Beds: 175 beds
Linda Grills, Administrator

***Ottawa:* Extendicare - Medex**
1865 Baseline Rd., Ottawa, ON K2C 3K6
Tel: 613-225-5650; *Fax:* 613-225-0960
cnh_medex@extendicare.com
Number of Beds: 193 beds
William Smith, Administrator
T. de Kemp, Supervisor, Maintenance

***Ottawa:* Extendicare - New Orchard Lodge**
99 New Orchard Ave., Ottawa, ON K2B 5E6
Tel: 613-820-2110; *Fax:* 613-820-6380
cnh_neworchardlodge@extendicare.com
Number of Beds: 111 beds
Susan Reed, Administrator
William Kirk, Director, Phyical Plant

***Ottawa:* Extendicare - Starwood**
114 Starwood Rd., Ottawa, ON K2G 3N5
Tel: 613-224-3960
Number of Beds: 192 beds

***Ottawa:* Extendicare - West End Villa**
2179 Elmira Dr., Ottawa, ON K2C 3S1
Tel: 613-829-3501; *Fax:* 613-829-3504
cnh_westendvilla@extendicare.com
Number of Beds: 240 beds
Note: nursing home
Lynda Welch, Administrator

***Ottawa:* Glebe Centre Inc.**
Former Name: Bronson Place
950 Bank St., Ottawa, ON K1S 5G6
Tel: 613-238-2727; *Fax:* 613-238-4759
info@glebecentre.ca
www.glebecentre.ca
Janice Bridgewater, Senior Centre Director
jbridgewater@glebecentre.ca

***Ottawa:* Island Lodge**
1 Porter's Island, Ottawa, ON K1N 5M2
Tel: 613-789-5100; *Fax:* 613-789-3704
Number of Beds: 165 beds
Diane Officer, Executive Director
Ray Duffy, Environmental Services

***Ottawa:* Perley & Rideau Veterans' Health Centre**
1750 Russell Rd., Ottawa, ON K1G 5Z6
Tel: 613-526-7170; *Fax:* 613-526-7172
www.prvhc.com
Year Founded: 1995
Number of Beds: 450 residential capacity
Note: Specialties: Geriatric care; Recreation services; Dementia programming; Respite care for people in the mid-stages of dementia; Convalescent care
Greg Fougère, Executive Director
Bob Paré, Manager, Plant Services
Kerry Kelly, Manager, Housekeeping Linen Servs. & Materials Managemen

***Ottawa:* Villa Marconi**
1026 Baseline Rd., Ottawa, ON K2C 0A6
Tel: 613-727-6201; *Fax:* 613-727-9352
villamarconi@villamarconi.com
www.villamarconi.com
Number of Beds: 125 beds
Walter Cibischino, President

***Owen Sound:* Lee Manor**
875 - 6 St. East, Owen Sound, ON N4K 5W5
Tel: 519-376-4420; *Fax:* 519-371-5406
www.greycounty.on.ca
Number of Beds: 150 beds
Note: Municipal home for aged
Marjorie McNeil, Administrator

***Parkhill:* Chateau Gardens Parkhill**
PO Box 129, 250 Tain St., Parkhill, ON N0M 2K0
Tel: 519-294-6342; *Fax:* 519-294-0107
Number of Beds: 59 beds
Brenda Nethercott, Administrator

***Parry Sound:* Belvedere Heights**
21 Belvedere Ave., Parry Sound, ON P2A 2A2
Tel: 705-746-5871; *Fax:* 705-774-7300
bh@zeuter.com
www.belvedereheights.com
Number of Beds: 101 beds
Bev Preuss, CEO

***Pembroke:* Miramichi Lodge**
725 Pembrooke St. W, Pembroke, ON K8A 8S9
Tel: 613-735-0175; *Fax:* 613-735-8061
Number of Beds: 166 beds
Shelley Sheedy, Administrator

***Perth:* Lanark Lodge**
115 Christie Lake Rd., Perth, ON K7H 3C6
Tel: 613-267-4225; *Fax:* 613-264-2668
lanarklodge@county.lanark.on.ca
Number of Beds: 163 beds
Whynn Turner, Administrator

***Perth:* Perth Community Care Centre**
101 Christie Lake Rd., RR#4, Perth, ON K7H 3C6
Tel: 613-267-2506; *Fax:* 613-267-7060
adm.perth@diversicare.ca
www.diversicare.ca
Number of Beds: 121 residential capacity
Note: Specialties: Long-term care; Activity program; Restorative care program; Physiotherapy
Joyce Firlotte, Administrator

***Peterborough:* Extendicare - Peterborough**
80 Alexander Ave., Peterborough, ON K9J 6B4
Tel: 705-743-7552; *Fax:* 705-742-9664
Number of Beds: 172 beds
Margaret Lazure, Administrator

***Peterborough:* St. Joseph's at Fleming**
Former Name: Marycrest Home of the Aged; Anson House
659 Brealey Dr., Peterborough, ON K9K 2R8
Tel: 705-743-4744; *Fax:* 705-743-7532
www.stjosephsatfleming.com
Year Founded: 2004
Debra Cooper Burger, Administrator

***Petrolia:* Fiddick's Nursing Home**
PO Box 340, 437 First Ave., Petrolia, ON N0N 1R0
Tel: 519-882-0370; *Fax:* 519-882-0375
fiddicks@xcelco.on.ca
Number of Beds: 128 beds
Michael Fiddick, Administrator
Todd Fiddick, Supervisor, Plant Maintenance

***Picton:* H.J. MacFarland Memorial Home**
603 Hwy 49, RR#2, Picton, ON K0K 2T0
Tel: 613-476-2138; *Fax:* 613-476-6952
egervais@pecounty.on.ca
Number of Beds: 84 beds
Ellen Gervais, Administrator
egervais@pecounty.on.ca

***Picton:* Kentwood Park**
PO Box 1298, 2 Ontario St., Picton, ON K0K 2T0
Tel: 613-476-5671; *Fax:* 613-476-3986
www.omni-way.com/ourhomes/kentwood.htm
Number of Beds: 48 beds
Tina Cole, Administrator/Nursing Administrative Services Manager
tcole@omniway.ca

***Picton:* Picton Manor Nursing Home**
9 Hill St. West, Picton, ON K0K 2T0
Tel: 613-476-6140; *Fax:* 613-476-5240
www.pictonmanor.com
Number of Beds: 78 beds
Note: Specialties: Nursing care; Restorative care; Activity program; Life enrichment progran; Palliative care
Norma Bongard, Administrator

***Picton:* West Lake Terrace**
PO Box 2229, R.R. #1, 1673 County Rd. #12, Picton, ON K0K 2T0
Tel: 613-393-2055; *Fax:* 613-393-2057
Number of Beds: 47 beds
Mary Lynn Lester, Administrator

***Plantagenet:* Pinecrest Nursing Home Ltd.**
PO Box 250, 101 Parent St., RR#1, Plantagenet, ON K0B 1L0
Tel: 613-673-4835; *Fax:* 613-673-2675
Note: Specialties: Long-term care; Activity program
Marcel Parent, Administrator

***Port Dover:* Dover Cliffs Long Term Care Centre, Port Dover**
Former Name: Versa-Care Centre, Port Dover
PO Box 430, 501 St. George St., Port Dover, ON N0A 1N0
Tel: 519-583-1422; *Fax:* 519-583-3197
pailinelyne@cplodges.com
www.cplcanada.com
Number of Beds: 70 beds
Pauline Lyne, Executive Director
Shelly Desgagne, Office Manager
shellydesgagne@cplodges.com

***Port Hope:* Community Nursing Home**
20 Hope St. South, Port Hope, ON L1A 2M8
Tel: 905-885-6367; *Fax:* 905-885-6368
Number of Beds: 97 beds
Nancy Jordan, Administrator

***Port Hope:* Extendicare - Port Hope**
360 Croft St., Port Hope, ON L1A 4K8
Tel: 905-885-1266; *Fax:* 905-885-5328
cnh_porthope@extendicare.com
www.extendicare.com
Number of Beds: 128 beds

***Port Perry:* Community Nursing Home**
PO Box 660, 15941 Simcoe St. North, Port Perry, ON L9L 1A6
Tel: 905-985-3205; *Fax:* 905-985-3721
Number of Beds: 107 beds
Kim Mitchell, Administrator

***Powassan:* Eastholme Home for the Aged**
PO Box 400, 62 Big Bend Ave., Powassan, ON P0H 1Z0
Tel: 705-724-2005; *Fax:* 705-724-5429
easthome@onlink.net
www.eastholme.ca
Number of Beds: 104 beds
Steven Piekarski, Administrator
Stephen Pierarski, Administrator

***Prescott:* Wellington House**
PO Box 401, 990 Edward St. North, Prescott, ON K0E 1T0
Tel: 613-925-2834; *Fax:* 613-925-5425
Number of Beds: 60 beds
Note: Long-term care facility
Bernadette Timco, Administrator
Diana Gaudet, Supervisor, Environmental Services

***Puslinch:* Morriston Park Nursing Home Inc.**
7363 Calfass Rd., RR#2, Puslinch, ON N0B 2J0
Tel: 519-822-9179; *Fax:* 519-822-4459
Number of Beds: 28 beds
Alfred Urfey, Administrator

***Red Lake:* Northwood Lodge**
PO Box 420, Hwy 105, Red Lake, ON P0V 2M0
Tel: 807-727-2323; *Fax:* 807-727-3546
northwood.lodge@kenoradistricthomes.ca
Number of Beds: 32 beds
Note: home for the aged
Doris Coghill, Administrator

***Renfrew:* Bonnechere Manor**
470 Albert St., Renfrew, ON K7V 4L5
Tel: 613-432-4873; *Fax:* 613-432-7138
Year Founded: 1958
Number of Beds: 177 beds
Shayne Hoelke, Admintstrator

***Renfrew:* Groves Park Lodge Long Term Care Facility**
Former Name: Groves Park Lodge Nursing Home
470 Raglan St. North, Renfrew, ON K7V 1P5
Tel: 613-432-5823; *Fax:* 613-432-5287
carrol.haywood@gemhealth.com
www.gemhealth.com/gem_health_care_group_groves_park.html
Number of Beds: 75 beds
Carrol Haywood, Administrator

***Richmond Hill:* Leisureworld Caregiving Centre - Richmond Hill**
170 Red Maple Rd., Richmond Hill, ON L4B 4T8
Tel: 905-731-2273
jodi.macisaac@leisureworld.ca
www.leisureworld.ca/richmondhill.html
Number of Beds: 160 beds
Jodi MacIsaac, Administrator

***Richmond Hill:* Mariann Home**
9915 Yonge St., Richmond Hill, ON L4C 1V1
Tel: 905-884-9276; *Fax:* 905-884-1800
mariann.home@rogers.com
Number of Beds: 64 beds
Note: Specialties: Peritoneal dialysis; Care for seniors with cognitive or psychiatric impairment; Palliative care. Number of employees: 80
Sr. Mary William Verhoeven, Administrator

***Rockland:* St. Joseph Nursing Home**
1615 Laurier St., Rockland, ON K4K 1C8
Tel: 613-446-5126; *Fax:* 613-446-1516
Number of Beds: 64 beds
Ginette Whittingham, Administrator

***Sarnia:* Vision Nursing Home**
229 Wellington St., Sarnia, ON N7T 1G9
Tel: 519-336-6551; *Fax:* 519-336-5878
recpt@vision74.com
Number of Beds: 108 permanent beds, 2 respite
Note: Christian-based nursing home
Bernard Bax, Administrator
Neil Whittle, Supervisor, Maintenance

***Sault Ste Marie:* Extendicare - Tendercare**
770 Great Northern Rd., Sault Ste Marie, ON P6A 5K7
Tel: 705-949-3611; *Fax:* 705-945-6303
cnh_tendercare@extendicare.com
Number of Beds: 120 beds
Janice Dupuis, Administrator

***Sault Ste Marie:* Extendicare - Van Daele**
39 Van Daele St., Sault Ste Marie, ON P6B 4V3
Tel: 705-949-7934; *Fax:* 705-945-0968
cnh_vandaele@extendicare.com
Number of Beds: 150 beds
Janice Hodgson, Administrator

***Sault Ste Marie:* F.J. Davey Home**
860 Great Northern Rd., Sault Ste Marie, ON P6A 5K7
Tel: 705-942-2204; *Fax:* 705-942-2234
Number of Beds: 184 beds
Peter J. MacLean, Administrator

***Sault Ste Marie:* Mauno Kaihla Koti**
723 North St., Sault Ste Marie, ON P6B 6G8
Tel: 705-945-9987; *Fax:* 705-945-1217
Number of Beds: 60 beds
Lewis Massad, Executive Director

***Scarborough:* Kennedy Lodge Nursing Home**
1400 Kennedy Rd., Scarborough, ON M1P 4V6
Tel: 416-752-8282; *Fax:* 416-752-0645
kennedylodge@reveraliving.com
Number of Beds: 289 beds
Note: long term care facility
Donna Michaels, Administrator

***Schumacher:* Extendicare - Timmins**
Affiliated with: North East Local Health Integration Network
PO Box 817, 15 Hollinger Lane, Schumacher, ON P0N 1G0
Tel: 705-360-1913; *Fax:* 705-268-3975
cnh_timmins@extendicare.com
Number of Beds: 121 beds
Claude Roy, Administrator

***Selby:* Village Green Long Term Care Facility**
PO Box 94, Selby, ON K0K 2Z0
Tel: 613-388-2693; *Fax:* 613-388-2694
Number of Beds: 66 beds
Linda Pierce, Administrator

***Simcoe:* Cedarwood Village**
500 Queensway West, Simcoe, ON N3Y 4R4
Tel: 519-426-8305; *Fax:* 519-426-2511
cedarwood@kwic.com
Number of Beds: 91 beds
Tanna Day, Administrator

***Simcoe:* Norfolk Hospital Nursing Home (NHNH)**
365 West St., Simcoe, ON N3Y 1T7
Tel: 519-426-0130; *Fax:* 519-429-6988
residents@ngh.on.ca (Residents' e-mail)
www.ngh.on.ca
Year Founded: 1975
Number of Beds: 80 beds
Note: Specialties: Long-term nursing care; Activation program; Wound care; Physiotherapy; Occupational therapy; Speech Therapy; Restorative care; Pet therapy; Social work; Psychogeriatics; Palliative care
William C. Lewis, Executive Director
J.J. Knott, Director, Physical Plant

***Sioux Lookout:* William A. (Bill) George Extended Care Facility**
75 Fifth Ave., Sioux Lookout, ON P8T 1K9
Tel: 807-737-1364; *Fax:* 807-737-2449
Number of Beds: 20 beds
Debra Harris, Executive Director
Ed Patterson, Environmental Services

***Smiths Falls:* Broadview Nursing Centre**
210 Brockville St., Smiths Falls, ON K7A 3Z4
Tel: 613-283-1845; *Fax:* 613-283-7073
bnc@on.aibn.com
Number of Beds: 75 beds
Sandra Sheridan, Director of Care

***St Catharines:* Extendicare - St. Catharines**
283 Pelham Rd., St Catharines, ON L2S 1X7
Tel: 905-688-3311; *Fax:* 905-688-5774
cnh_stcatharines@extendicare.com
Number of Beds: 152 beds
Jane Freeman, Acting Administrator

***St Catharines:* Heidehof Home for the Aged**
600 Lake St., St Catharines, ON L2N 4J4
Tel: 905-935-3344; *Fax:* 905-935-0081
www.heidehof.com
Number of Beds: 106 beds
Elena Caddis, Administrator
ecaddis@heidehof.com
Erika Ledwez, Manager, Resident & Community Relations
eledwez@heidehof.com

***St Catharines:* Tabor Manor**
1 Tabor Dr., St Catharines, ON L2N 1V9
Tel: 905-934-2548
office@tabormanor.net
www.tabormanor.net/site
Number of Beds: 82 residential capacity
Note: Specialties: Accommodation & nursing care to senior citizens, especially those of the Mennonite constituency in Niagara; Activity program; Foot care
Ben Wohlgemut, Administrator
Tony Carrière, Director, Physical Plant

***St Catharines:* West Park Health Centre**
103 Pelham Rd., St Catharines, ON L2S 1S9
Tel: 905-688-1031; *Fax:* 905-688-9646
Number of Beds: 93 beds
Natalie Foster, Administrator

***St Jacobs:* Derbecker's Heritage House Ltd.**
54 Eby St., St Jacobs, ON N0B 2N0
Tel: 519-664-2921; *Fax:* 519-664-2380
Number of Beds: 72 beds
Pamela Derbecker, Administrator

***Stoney Creek:* Pine Villa Nursing Home**
490 Hwy. #8, Stoney Creek, ON L8G 1G6
Tel: 905-662-5033
info.pinevilla@thomashealthcare.com
www.thomashealthcare.com
Year Founded: 1967
Number of Beds: 38 beds
Note: Specialties: Nursing care; Enhanced restorative care program; Physiotherapy; Foot care; Massage therapy; Activity program
Conrad Thomas, Administrator

***Stouffville:* Green Gables Manor Inc.**
9th Line Rd., RR#2, Stouffville, ON L4A 7X3
Tel: 905-640-1310; *Fax:* 905-640-2231
Number of Beds: 69 beds
Gerald Harquail, President

Stouffville: Parkview Home for the Aged
123 Weldon Rd., Stouffville, ON L4A 0G8
Tel: 905-640-1911; *Fax:* 905-640-4051
admin@parkviewhome.ca
www.parkviewhome.ca
Number of Beds: 109 beds
Note: Long-term care facility
Wallace Kribs, Home Administrator
Michael MacDonald, Director, Environmental Services

Stratford: Hillside Manor
5066 Perth East Line 34, RR#5, Stratford, ON N5A 6S6
Tel: 519-393-5132; *Fax:* 519-393-5130
hillsidemanor@reveraliving.com
www.reveraliving.com/homes/19/
Number of Beds: 90 beds
Sylvie Ledermueller, Administrator
Mary Anne Weller, Director of Care

Stratford: PeopleCare Stratford
198 Mornington St., Stratford, ON N5A 5G3
Tel: 519-271-4440; *Fax:* 519-271-4446
www.peoplecare.ca
Year Founded: 1980
Number of Beds: 60 residents
Note: Specialties: Long-term care; Activity program; Restorative care
Patricia Kelly, Administrator

Stratford: Spruce Lodge Senior Citizens Residence
643 West Gore St., Stratford, ON N5A 1L4
Tel: 519-271-4090; *Fax:* 519-271-5862
Number of Beds: 128 beds
Peter L. Bolland, Administrator

Strathroy: Strathmere Lodge
PO Box 5000, 599 Albert St., Strathroy, ON N7G 3J3
Tel: 519-245-2520; *Fax:* 519-245-5711
www.county.middlesex.on.ca/strathmerelodge
Year Founded: 1880
Note: Specialties: Special care area for Alzheimer residents; Respite care & short stays
Larry Hills, Administrator
Terry Meservia, Supervisor, Maintenance

Sturgeon Falls: Au Château Home for the Aged
100 Michaud St., PO Bag 110, Sturgeon Falls, ON P2B 2Z4
Tel: 705-753-1550; *Fax:* 705-753-3135
Number of Beds: 162 beds
Wayne M. Foisey, Administrator
Simone Brazeau, Coordinator, Environmental Services

Sudbury: Extendicare - Falconbridge
281 Falconbridge Rd., Sudbury, ON P3A 5K4
Tel: 705-566-7980; *Fax:* 705-566-2997
cnh_falconbridge@extendicare.com
www.extendicarecanada.com/sudburyfalconbridge/
Number of Beds: 234 beds
James Foreman, Administrator
J. Kovacs, Director, Physical Plant

Sudbury: Extendicare - York
333 York St., Sudbury, ON P3E 5J3
Tel: 705-674-4221; *Fax:* 705-674-4281
cnh_york@extendicare.com
Number of Beds: 288 beds
Nancy Foreman, Administrator

Tavistock: Bonnie Brae Health Care Centre
PO Box 489, 55 Woodstock St. North, Tavistock, ON N0B 2R0
Tel: 519-655-2420; *Fax:* 519-655-3432
bonniebrae@reveraliving.com
www.reveraliving.com/homes/51
Number of Beds: 80 beds
Joyce Penney, Administrator
joycepenney@reveraliving.com

Tecumseh: Banwell Gardens
3000 Banwell Rd., Tecumseh, ON N8N 2M4
Tel: 519-735-3204; *Fax:* 519-735-1836
vctecumseh@cplreit.com
Number of Beds: 142 beds
Sharell Polk, Administrator
James Ashton, Manager, Environmental Services

Tecumseh: Brouillette Manor
11900 Brouillette Ct., Tecumseh, ON N8N 4X8
Tel: 519-735-9810; *Fax:* 519-735-8569
Number of Beds: 60 beds
Nancy Comiskey, Administrator

Tecumseh: Extendicare - Tecumseh
2475 St. Alphonse St., Tecumseh, ON N8N 2X2
Tel: 519-739-2998
Number of Beds: 128 beds

Thessalon: Algoma Manor
135 Dawson St., Thessalon, ON P0R 1L0
Tel: 705-842-2840; *Fax:* 705-842-2650
csmith@adhfa.org
www.adsab.on.ca/algomamanor/index.htm
Number of Beds: 106 beds
Peter MacLean, Administrator
Mark Heller, Coordinator, Environmental Services

Thornbury: Errinrung Residence
Former Name: Errinrung Nursing & Retirement Home
PO Box 69, 67 Bruce St., Thornbury, ON N0H 2P0
Tel: 519-599-2737; *Fax:* 519-599-3410
Number of Beds: 74 beds
Note: Total Employees: 38 f-t; 30 p-t
Yvonne Taylor, Director of Retirement Home
Deb Hughson, Director of Care

Thunder Bay: Bethammi Nursing Home, St. Joseph's Heritage
63 Carrie St., Thunder Bay, ON P7A 4J2
Tel: 807-768-4400; *Fax:* 807-768-8820
Number of Beds: 110 beds
Carl White, President
Victor Carlson, Director, Environmental Services

Thunder Bay: Dawson Court Home for the Aged
523 North Algoma St., Thunder Bay, ON P7A 5C2
Tel: 807-684-2926; *Fax:* 807-345-8854
Number of Beds: 150 beds
Michael Kennedy, Administrator
mkennedy@thunderbay.ca

Thunder Bay: Grandview Lodge/Thunder Bay
200 Lillie St. North, Thunder Bay, ON P7C 5Y2
Tel: 807-625-2923; *Fax:* 807-623-4075
Number of Beds: 150 beds
Wendy Kirkpatrick

Thunder Bay: Pioneer Ridge
750 Tungsten St., Thunder Bay, ON P7B 6R1
Tel: 807-684-3910; *Fax:* 807-684-3916
www.thunderbay.ca
Number of Beds: 150 beds
Note: Specialties: Long-term nursing care for older persons; Restorative care; Rehabilitation; Units for persons with cognitive challenges, Alzheimer's disease, & other dementias; Secure therapeutic parks; Life enrichment program
Joyce Greene, Administrator

Tillsonburg: Maple Manor Nursing Home
73 Bidwell St., Tillsonburg, ON N4G 3T8
Tel: 519-842-3563; *Fax:* 519-842-3038
Number of Beds: 102 beds
George Kaniuk, Administrator

Timmins: Golden Manor Home for the Aged
481 Melrose Blvd., Timmins, ON P4N 5H3
Tel: 705-360-2664; *Fax:* 705-360-2683
golden_manor@timmins.ca
Number of Beds: 174 beds
Heather Bozzer, Administrator
Claude Bruneau, Supervisor, Maintenance

Toronto: Apotex Centre - Jewish Home for the Aged
3560 Bathurst St., Toronto, ON M6A 2E1
Tel: 416-785-2500; *Fax:* 416-785-2464
Number of Beds: 372 beds

Toronto: Barton Place Long Term Care Facility
914 Bathurst St., Toronto, ON M5R 3G5
Tel: 416-533-9473; *Fax:* 416-538-2685
www.bartonplace.ca
Number of Beds: 130 beds
Réjane Jones, Administrator

Toronto: Bendale Acres
2920 Lawrence Ave. East, Toronto, ON M1P 2T8
Tel: 416-397-7000; *Fax:* 416-397-7067
Number of Beds: 302 beds
Margaret Aerola, Administrator
Richard Doberstein, Supervisor, Maintenance
Russ Persons, Manager, Building Services

Toronto: Casa Verde Health Centre
3595 Keele St., Toronto, ON M3J 1M7
Tel: 416-633-3431; *Fax:* 416-633-6736
Number of Beds: 252 beds
Haren Kapadia, Administrator

Toronto: Castleview Wychwood Towers
351 Christie St., Toronto, ON M6G 3C3
Tel: 416-392-5700; *Fax:* 416-392-4157
Number of Beds: 490 beds
Vija Mallia, Administrator
Steven Hughes, Manager, Building Services

Toronto: Cheltenham Nursing Home
5935 Bathurst St., Toronto, ON M2R 1Y8
Tel: 416-223-4050; *Fax:* 416-223-4159
Number of Beds: 170 beds
Marlene Van Ham, Administrator

Toronto: Christie Gardens
600 Melita Cres., Toronto, ON M6G 3Z4
Tel: 416-530-1330; *Fax:* 416-530-1686
cbelmore@christiegardens.org
www.christiegardens.org
Number of Beds: 88 beds
Catherine Belmore, Administrator

Toronto: Craiglee Nursing Home
102 Craiglee Dr., Toronto, ON M1N 2M7
Tel: 416-264-2260
Number of Beds: 94 beds
Doris McDougall, Administrator

Toronto: Cummer Lodge Home for the Aged
205 Cummer Ave., Toronto, ON M2M 2E8
Tel: 416-392-9500; *Fax:* 416-392-9499
Number of Beds: 391 beds
Leah Walters, Administrator
George Abiad, Manager, Building Services

Toronto: Drs. Paul & John Rekai Centre
Also Known As: Rekai Centre
345 Sherbourne St., Toronto, ON M5A 2S3
Tel: 416-964-1599; *Fax:* 416-969-3907
Number of Beds: 129 beds
Linda Joyal, Director of Resident Programs

Toronto: Ehatare Nursing Home
40 Old Kingston Rd., Toronto, ON M1E 3J5
Tel: 416-284-0828; *Fax:* 416-284-5595
ehatare@on.aibn.com
Number of Beds: 32 beds
Ruth McFarlane, Administrator
Enno Pflug, Director, Physical Plant

Toronto: Extendicare - Bayview
550 Cummer Ave., Toronto, ON M2K 2M2
Tel: 416-226-1331; *Fax:* 416-226-2745
cnh_bayview@extendicare.com
www.extendicarecanada.com/willowdale/
Number of Beds: 203 beds
Susan Schendel, Administrator

Toronto: Extendicare - Guildwood
60 Guildwood Pkwy., Toronto, ON M1E 1N9
Tel: 416-266-7711; *Fax:* 416-269-5123
cnh_guildwood@extendicare.com
www.extendicarecanada.com/westhill/
Number of Beds: 169 beds
Dwayne Wyrwas, Administrator

Toronto: Extendicare - Rouge Valley
551 Conlins Rd., Toronto, ON M1B 5S1
Tel: 416-282-6768
www.extendicare.com
Number of Beds: 192 beds

Toronto: Extendicare - Scarborough
3830 Lawrence Ave. East, Toronto, ON M1G 1R6
Tel: 416-439-1243; *Fax:* 416-439-4818
www.extendicare.com
Number of Beds: 155 beds

Toronto: Fairview Nursing Home
14 Cross St., Toronto, ON M6J 1S8
Tel: 416-534-8829; *Fax:* 416-538-1658
Number of Beds: 108 beds
Herbert Chambers, Administrator

Toronto: Fudger House
439 Sherbourne St., Toronto, ON M4X 1K6
Tel: 416-392-5252; *Fax:* 416-392-4174
Number of Beds: 249 beds
Lorraine Siu, Administrator
Derek Bloomfield, Coordinator, Environmental Services

Toronto: Garden Court Nursing Home
1 Sand Beach Rd., Toronto, ON M8V 2W2
Tel: 416-259-6172; *Fax:* 416-259-7925

Number of Beds: 45 beds
Dean Davey, Administrator
P. Collins, Supervisor, Plant Maintenance

Toronto: Hellenic Care for Seniors
33 Winona Dr., Toronto, ON M6G 3Z7
Tel: 416-654-3904; *Fax:* 416-654-1080
hcare@hellenichome.org
www.hellenichome.org
Number of Beds: 81 beds
Dorothy Godbold, Administrator

Toronto: Heritage Nursing Home
1195 Queen St. East, Toronto, ON M4M 1L6
Tel: 416-461-8185; *Fax:* 416-461-5472
administrator@heritagenursinghome.com
www.heritagenursinghome.com
Number of Beds: 201 beds
Note: Specialties: Long-term nursing care; Supervision & security for residents with Alzheimer's Disease or dementia; Restorative care, including physiotherapy; Activation & recreation program; Chinese programs
Melba Graham, Administrator

Toronto: Highbourne Lifecare Centre
420 The East Mall, Toronto, ON M9B 3Z9
Tel: 416-621-8000; *Fax:* 416-621-8003
www.ourhomeyourhome.eycan.com
Number of Beds: 250 beds
Evelyn McDonald, Administrator

Toronto: Ivan Franko Ukrainian Home (Etobicoke)
767 Royal York Rd., Toronto, ON M8Y 2T3
Tel: 416-239-7364
Number of Beds: 85 beds
Maria Kiebalo, Administrator

Toronto: Kipling Acres
2233 Kipling Ave., Toronto, ON M9W 4L3
Tel: 416-392-2300; *Fax:* 416-392-3360
Year Founded: 1959
Number of Beds: 337 beds
Lianne Neumann, Administrator
lneumann@toronto.ca

Toronto: Lakeshore Lodge
3197 Lakeshore Blvd. West, Toronto, ON M8V 3X5
Tel: 416-392-9400; *Fax:* 416-392-9401
hfa-ll@toronto.ca
www.toronto.ca/homesfortheaged/lakeshore.htm
Number of Beds: 150 beds
Robert Price, Administrator

Toronto: Leisureworld Caregiving Centre - Ellesmere
1000 Ellesmere Rd., Toronto, ON M1P 5G2
Tel: 416-291-0222
adm.ellesmere@leisureworld.ca
www.leisureworld.ca/ellesmere.html
Number of Beds: 224 beds
Michael Aikins, Administrator

Toronto: Leisureworld Caregiving Centre - Etobicoke
70 Humberline Dr., Toronto, ON M9W 7H3
Tel: 416-213-7300
lora.palmer@leisureworld.ca
www.leisureworld.ca/etobicoke.html
Number of Beds: 160 beds
Lora Palmer, Administrator
Caterina Ierino, Director of Care

Toronto: Leisureworld Caregiving Centre - Lawrence
2005 Lawrence Ave. West, Toronto, ON M9N 3V4
Tel: 416-243-8879
adm.lawrence@leisureworld.ca
www.leisureworld.ca/lawrence.html
Year Founded: 2002
Number of Beds: 224 beds; 2 respite
Gary Bowers, Administrator
Amo Nandlall, Director of Care

Toronto: Leisureworld Caregiving Centre - Norfinch
22 Norfinch Dr., Toronto, ON M3N 1X1
Tel: 416-623-1120; *Fax:* 416-623-1121
anne.deelstramcnara@leisureworld.ca
www.leisureworld.ca/norfinch.html
Year Founded: 2003
Number of Beds: 160 beds
Anne Deelstra McNamara, Administrator
Jane Pristach, Director of Nursing

Toronto: Leisureworld Caregiving Centre - O'Connor
1800 O'Connor Dr., Toronto, ON M4A 1W7
Tel: 416-285-2000
jeanette.sanichar@leisureworld.ca
www.leisureworld.ca/oc_gate.html
Year Founded: 2001
Number of Beds: 318 beds
Jeanette Sanichar, Administrator
Stacey Gamble, Assistant Director of Nursing

Toronto: Leisureworld Caregiving Centre - Rockcliffe
Former Name: Rockcliffe Long Term Care Facility
3015 Lawrence Ave. East, Toronto, ON M1P 2V7
Tel: 416-264-3201; *Fax:* 416-264-2914
adm.rockcliffe@leisureworld.ca
www.leisureworld.ca/rockcliffe.html
Year Founded: 1972
Number of Beds: 204 beds
Andrea E. Boswell, Administrator
Nelson Urbe, Maintenance Technician

Toronto: Leisureworld Caregiving Centre - St. George
225 St. George St., Toronto, ON M5R 2M2
Tel: 416-967-3985; *Fax:* 416-967-3951
jane.noble@leisureworld.ca
www.leisureworld.ca/stgeorge.html
Number of Beds: 238 beds
Barbara Beecroft, Director of Nursing
Jane Noble, Administrator

Toronto: Leisureworld Caregiving Centre - Scarborough
130 Midland Ave., Toronto, ON M1N 4B2
Tel: 416-264-2301; *Fax:* 416-264-3704
terry.teare@leisureworld.ca
www.leisureworld.ca/scarborough.html
Number of Beds: 299 long-term care, 53 retirement beds
Note: Retirement beds in adjoining Midland Gardens
Terry Teare, Administrator
Kathy Metcalfe, Director of Care

Toronto: Lincoln Place Nursing Home
429 Walmer Rd., Toronto, ON M5P 2X9
Tel: 416-967-6949; *Fax:* 416-928-1965
Number of Beds: 248 beds
Celeste Blocker, Administrator
Kim Weece, Director, Environmental Services

Toronto: Mon Sheong Home for the Aged
36 D'Arcy St., Toronto, ON M5T 1J7
Tel: 416-977-3762; *Fax:* 416-977-3231
msf@monsheong.org
www.monsheong.org
Number of Beds: 105 beds
Ricky Kwan, Administrator
Joseph Wong, Supervisor, Housekeeping/Maintenance

Toronto: North Park Nursing Home
450 Rustic Rd., Toronto, ON M6L 1W9
Tel: 416-247-0531; *Fax:* 416-247-6159
northparknursinghome@rogers.com
Number of Beds: 75 beds
Alayne Twaddle, Director, Residential Care

Toronto: Norwood Nursing Home Ltd.
122 Tyndall Ave., Toronto, ON M6K 2E2
Tel: 416-535-3011
administration@norwoodcare.ca
Year Founded: 1957
Number of Beds: 60 beds
Note: Specialties: Long-term care; Rehabilitative care; Palliative care room
Dr. Horst Sebald, Administrator

Toronto: Thompson House
1 Overland Dr., Toronto, ON M3C 2C3
Tel: 416-447-7244; *Fax:* 416-447-6364
info@betterlivinghealth.org
www.betterlivinghealth.org
Number of Beds: 136 beds
Note: Specialties: Long-term care; Nursing care; Physiotherapy; Rehabilitative services; Recreation program; Restorative care; Social work; Palliative care
Bernita Borgh, Vice-President, Residential Services

Toronto: True Davidson Acres
200 Dawes Rd., Toronto, ON M4C 5M8
Tel: 416-397-0400
Year Founded: 1973
Note: Specialties: Nursing care; Rehabilitation; Recreation program; Music & art therapy

Sylvia Moreland, Administrator

Toronto: Ukrainian Canadian Care Centre
60 Richview Rd., Toronto, ON M9A 5E4
Tel: 416-243-7653; *Fax:* 416-243-7452
www.stdemetrius.ca
Number of Beds: 152 beds
Note: Specialties: Long-term care; Therapeutic recreation; Social work
Sandy Lomaszewycz, Executive Director
Natalie Popowich, Coordinator, Environmental Services

Toronto: Wesburn Manor
400 The West Mall, Toronto, ON M9C 5S1
Tel: 416-394-3600; *Fax:* 416-394-3606
Number of Beds: 192 beds
Elaine Russell, Administrator

Toronto: The Wexford Residence Inc.
1860 Lawrence Ave. East, Toronto, ON M1R 5B1
Tel: 416-752-8877; *Fax:* 416-752-8414
Toll-Free: 1-877-807-0810
information@thewexford.org
www.thewexford.org
Year Founded: 1978
Number of Beds: 166 long-term care residents
Note: Specialties: Long-term care & apartment accommodation for seniors; Secure units for persons with cognitive impairments; Physiotherapy; Podiatry; Life enrichment therapy
Nicholas J. Manherz, Executive Director
Alan Pitts, Coordinator, Environmental Services

Toronto: Yee Hong Centre for Geriatric Care
2311 McNicoll Ave., Toronto, ON M1V 5L3
Tel: 416-321-6333; *Fax:* 416-321-6313
centre@yeehong.com
www.yeehong.com
Number of Beds: 250 beds
Florence Wong, CEO

Toronto: Yorkview Lifecare Centre
2045 Finch Ave. West, Toronto, ON M3N 1M9
Tel: 416-745-0811; *Fax:* 416-745-0568
Number of Beds: 276 beds
Marce Fulford, Administrator

Trenton: Trent Valley Lodge
195 Bay St., Trenton, ON K8V 1H9
Tel: 613-392-9235; *Fax:* 613-392-0688
tvl@bellnet.ca
Year Founded: 1970
Number of Beds: 70 beds
Note: Specialties: Restorative care; Activation services; Long-term stroke care
Bill Weaver, Administrator

Trout Creek: Lady Isabelle Nursing Home
PO Box 10, 102 Corkery St., Trout Creek, ON P0H 2L0
Tel: 705-723-5232; *Fax:* 705-723-5794
main@ladyisabelle.ca
www.ladyisabelle.ca
Number of Beds: 66 beds
Sadie Newman, Administrator
George Newman, Manager, Physical Plant/Material Management

Unionville: Bethany Lodge
23 Second St., Unionville, ON L3R 2C2
Tel: 905-477-3838; *Fax:* 905-477-2888
www.bethanylodge.org
Number of Beds: 128 beds
Basil Tambakis, Administrator

Vineland: United Mennonite Home (UMH)
Former Name: United Mennonite Home for the Aged
4024 Twenty-Third St., Vineland, ON L0R 2C0
Tel: 905-562-7385; *Fax:* 905-562-3711
thehome@umh.ca
www.umh.ca
Year Founded: 1955
Number of Beds: 128 beds
Note: Specialties: Activity program; Physiotherapy; Pet therapy
Art Sieb, Administrator

Virgil: Heritage Place
1743 Four Mile Creek Rd., Virgil, ON L0S 1T0
Tel: 905-468-1111
Number of Beds: 36 beds
Tim Siemens, CEO

***Walkerton:* Brucelea Haven**
PO Box 1600, 41 McGivern St. West, Walkerton, ON N0G 2V0
Tel: 519-881-1570; *Fax:* 519-881-0231
bcgil@brucecounty.on.ca
www.brucecounty.on.ca/bruceleahaven.php
Year Founded: 1898
Number of Beds: 144 beds
Elanor McEwen, Administrator
Lesley Borth, Director of Care

***Wardsville:* Babcock Community Care Centre**
Former Name: Babcock Nursing Home
196 Wellington St., Wardsville, ON N0L 2N0
Tel: 519-693-4415; *Fax:* 519-693-4876
jbabcock@mnsi.net
www.babcockonline.com
Number of Beds: 60 beds
J.C. Babcock, Administrator/Owner

***Warkworth:* Community Nursing Home**
PO Box 68, 97 Mill St., Warkworth, ON K0K 3K0
Tel: 705-924-2311; *Fax:* 705-924-1711
cnhwarakworth@communitylifecare.on.ca
Number of Beds: 60 beds
Myrna Ogden, Administrator
Linda Black, Environmental Contact

***Waterdown:* Alexander Place**
329 Parkside Dr., Waterdown, ON L0K 2H0
Tel: 905-689-2662
alexanderplace@jarlette.com
www.hamiltonltc.org/facilities/alexander.htm
Number of Beds: 128 beds

***Waterloo:* Parkwood Mennonite Home Inc.**
726 New Hampshire St., Waterloo, ON N2K 4M1
Tel: 519-885-4810; *Fax:* 519-885-6720
info@parkwoodmennonitehome.com
www.fairviewmennonitehomes.com/parkwood
Number of Beds: 96 beds
Gloria Dirks, Administrator
John McCutchen, Manager, Environmental Services

***Welland:* Foyer Richelieu Welland Inc.**
655 Tanguay Ave., Welland, ON L3B 6A1
Tel: 905-734-1400; *Fax:* 905-734-1386
Number of Beds: 61 beds
Dr. André Tremblay, Administrator

***Welland:* Woodlands of Sunset**
Affiliated with: Hamilton Niagara Haldimand Brant Local Health Integration Network
920 Pelham St., Welland, ON L3C 1Y5
Tel: 905-892-3845; *Fax:* 905-892-5882
www.regional.niagara.on.ca
Number of Beds: 120 beds
Tom Hunter, Administrator
G. Meek, Manager, Purchasing

***Whitby:* Fairview Lodge**
PO Box 300, 632 Dundas St. West, Whitby, ON L1N 5S3
Tel: 905-668-5851; *Fax:* 905-668-8934
Number of Beds: 198 beds
Laura MacDermaid, Administrator

***Wiarton:* Gateway Haven**
PO Box 10, 671 Frank St., Wiarton, ON N0H 2T0
Tel: 519-534-1113; *Fax:* 519-534-4733
bcgwh@brucecounty.on.ca
Number of Beds: 100 beds
Bob Moreton, Administrator
Doug Buckland, Environmental Services

***Wikwemikong:* Wikwemikong Nursing Home**
PO Box 114, 2281 Wikwemikong Way, Wikwemikong, ON P0P 2J0
Tel: 705-859-3107; *Fax:* 705-859-2245
Number of Beds: 60 beds
Mark Manitowabi, Administrator
David Fox, Manager, Purchasing

***Winchester:* Dundas Manor Nursing Home**
PO Box 970, 533 Clarence St., Winchester, ON K0C 2K0
Tel: 613-774-2293; *Fax:* 613-774-4015
dunman@istar.ca
Number of Beds: 98 beds
Note: seniors home
Jill M. Alguire, Administrator
Daniel Dorey, Maintenance Supervisor

***Windsor:* Chateau Park Nursing Home**
2990B Riverside Dr. West, Windsor, ON N9C 1A2
Tel: 519-254-4341; *Fax:* 519-254-7931
Number of Beds: 59 beds
Mary Butler, Administrator

***Windsor:* Extendicare - Southwood Lakes**
1255 North Talbot Rd., Windsor, ON N9G 3A4
Tel: 519-945-7249
cnh_southwoodlakes@extendicare.com
Number of Beds: 150 beds

***Windsor:* Malden Park Continuing Care Centre**
1453 Prince Rd., Windsor, ON N9C 3Z4
Tel: 519-257-5451; *Fax:* 519-257-5444
TTY: 519-257-5106
Number of Beds: 145 beds
Note: Long-term Care Facility
Al Grundner, Administrator

***Windsor:* Villa Maria Home for the Aged**
2856 Riverside Dr. West, Windsor, ON N9C 1A2
Tel: 519-254-3763; *Fax:* 519-254-7657
Number of Beds: 120 beds
Note: home for the aged
Ken Deane, President/CEO

***Woodbridge:* Pine Grove Lodge**
8403 Islington Ave. West, Woodbridge, ON L4L 1X3
Tel: 905-850-3605
pinegrovelodge@chartwellreit.ca
www.chartwellreit.ca
Year Founded: 1959
Number of Beds: 40 suites
Note: Specialties; Long-term care; Medication administration; Wellness monitoring; Cultural & activity program, catering to Italian & Canadian cultures; Recreation therapy; Occupational therapy; Physiotherapy; Podiatry; Respite care

***Woodslee:* Country Village Health Care Centre**
County Rd. 8, RR#2, Woodslee, ON N0R 1V0
Tel: 519-839-4812; *Fax:* 519-839-4813
Number of Beds: 104 beds
Jane Brooks Keller, Administrator
Doug Ferguson, Manager, Maintenance

***Zurich:* Blue Water Rest Home**
37792 Zurich-Hensall Road, RR 3, Zurich, ON N0M 2T0
Tel: 519-236-4373; *Fax:* 519-236-7685
bluewaterhome@hay.net
Number of Beds: 65 beds
Martha Craig, Administrator

Long Term/Retirement Care

Long Term Care Facilities

***Alliston:* Good Samaritan Nursing Home**
481 Victoria St. East, Alliston, ON L9R 1J8
Tel: 705-435-5722; *Fax:* 705-435-0235
gsnh@csolve.net
Number of Beds: 64 beds
Don Stymeist, Supervisor, Physical Plant
Lynda Weaver, Administrator

***Amherstburg:* Richmond Terrace**
89 Rankin Ave., Amherstburg, ON N9V 1E7
Tel: 519-736-5571; *Fax:* 519-736-2995
www.richmondterrace.ca
Number of Beds: 115 beds
Victoria Iler, Administrator
viler@richmondterrace.ca

***Ancaster:* The Willowgrove Long Term Care Residence**
Affiliated with: Chartwell Seniors Housing REIT
1217 Old Mohawk Rd., Ancaster, ON L9K 1P6
Tel: 905-304-6781
willowgroveltc@chartwellreit.ca
www.chartwellreit.ca
Number of Beds: 168 units
Stephen Suske, CEO, Chartwell Seniors Housing REIT

***Athens:* Maple View Lodge**
PO Box 100, 746 County Rd. 42 E, Athens, ON K0E 1B0
Tel: 613-924-2696; *Fax:* 613-924-2123
Number of Beds: 60 beds
Note: home for the aged
Faye Barkley, Acting Administrator

***Aurora:* Aurora Resthaven**
32 Mill St., Aurora, ON L4G 2R9
Tel: 905-727-1939; *Fax:* 905-727-6299
aurororesthaven@chartwellreit.ca
www.chartwellreit.ca/home_locations/aurora_rest.htm
Number of Beds: 176 beds
Sheila Hoinkes, Administrator

***Aurora:* Blue Hills Child & Family Service**
402 Bloomington Rd. West, Aurora, ON L4G 3G8
Tel: 905-773-4323; *Fax:* 905-773-8133
Toll-Free: 1-866-536-4323
gendeliv@bluehillschildandfamily.ca
www.bluehillschildandfamily.ca
Number of Beds: 9 beds
Note: children's mental health centre; special care home; outpatient services; family therapy
Sylvia Pivko, Executive Director
spivko@bluehillschildandfamily.ca

***Aylmer:* Chateau Gardens Aylmer**
465 Talbot St. West, Aylmer, ON N5H 1K8
Tel: 519-773-3423; *Fax:* 519-765-2573
aylmer@chateaugardens.com
www.chateaugardens.com
Number of Beds: 60 beds
Mary Vergeer, Administrator

***Barrie:* Heritage Place**
20 Brooks St., Barrie, ON L4N 7X2
Tel: 705-728-2389; *Fax:* 705-728-6049
www.ioof.com/?page_id=13
Doreen M. Saunders, CEO
dsaunders@ioof.com

***Barrie:* I.O.O.F. Senior Citizen Homes Inc.**
Heritage Place, 10 Brooks St., Barrie, ON L4N 5L3
Tel: 705-728-2364; *Fax:* 705-728-6024
Number of Beds: 155 beds long-term care; 80 units supportive housing; 20 uni
Note: long-term care & seniors housing
Doreen M. Saunders, CEO

***Barrie:* Victoria Village Manor**
78 Ross St., Barrie, ON L4N 1G3
Tel: 705-728-3456; *Fax:* 705-728-4057
www.victoriavillage.ca
Number of Beds: 128 long-term care beds, 57 life-lease housing units

***Beaverton:* Lakeview Manor**
133 Main St. West, Beaverton, ON L0K 1A0
Tel: 705-426-7388; *Fax:* 705-426-4218
pearle.perez@region.durhamon.ca
Number of Beds: 149 beds
Note: home for the aged
Pearle Perez, Administrator
Warren Manning, Manager, Support Services

***Belleville:* Plainfield Community Homes**
9 Millennium Pkwy., Belleville, ON K8N 4Z5
Tel: 613-969-7407; *Fax:* 613-969-7775
Number of Beds: 80 beds
Note: community residences for those with developmental disabilites
John B. Klassen, Executive Director

***Blind River:* Golden Birches Terrace**
525 Causley St., Blind River, ON P0R 1B0
Tel: 705-356-2265; *Fax:* 705-356-1220
Number of Beds: 42 beds
Gaston Lavigne, CEO

***Bracebridge:* The Pines**
98 Pine St., Bracebridge, ON P1L 1N5
Tel: 705-645-4488; *Fax:* 705-645-6857
www.muskoka.on.ca/community/the_pines.htm
Number of Beds: 160 beds
Note: Long term care residence
Janice Fox, Administrator
jfox@muskoka.on.ca

***Bradford:* Specialty Care Bradford Valley**
2656 Line 6, Bradford, ON L3Z 3H5
Tel: 905-952-2270; *Fax:* 905-775-0263
olivia.schmitz@specialty-care.com
www.specialty-care.com
Olivia Schmitz, Administrator

***Brampton:* Leisureworld Caregiving Centre - Tullamore**
133 Kennedy Rd. South, Brampton, ON L6W 3G3
Tel: 905-459-2324
adm.tullamore@leisureworld.ca
www.leisureworld.ca
Year Founded: 1965
Number of Beds: 159 beds
Note: Specialties: Long-term care; Restorative care; Occupational therapy; Physiotherapy; Care for persons with Alzheimer's disease; Respite care; Pet therapy; Palliative care

Wendy Shelley, Administrator

Brampton: Rosedale Retirement Residence
12 William St., Brampton, ON L6V 1L2
Tel: 905-454-3788; *Fax:* 905-846-0447
Number of Beds: 12 beds
Rose Hamilton, Administrator

Brampton: Specialty Care Woodhall Park
10260 Kennedy Rd. North, Brampton, ON L6T 3S1
Tel: 905-495-4695; *Fax:* 905-495-4693
david.wilson@specialty-care.com
www.specialty-care.com
Number of Beds: 147 beds
David Wilson, Administrator

Brantford: Brantwood Residential Development Centre
25 Bell Lane, Brantford, ON N3T 1E1
Tel: 519-753-2658; *Fax:* 519-753-5639
info@brantwood.ca
www.brantwood.ca
Number of Beds: 67 beds
Dianne Belliveau, Executive Director

Brantford: John Noble Home
97 Mount Pleasant St., Brantford, ON N3T 1T5
Tel: 519-756-2920; *Fax:* 519-754-1521
jnhuser@on.aibn.com
www.jnh.ca
Number of Beds: 156 beds
Eleanor Maslin, Administrator

Brantford: St. Joseph's Lifecare Centre
Former Name: St. Joseph's Hospital
99 Wayne Gretzky Pkwy., Brantford, ON N3S 6T6
Tel: 519-751-7096; *Fax:* 519-753-7996
www.sjlc.ca
Romeo Cercone, Administrator

Brighton: Maplewood
PO Box 249, 12 Maplewood Ave., Brighton, ON K0K 1H0
Tel: 613-475-2442; *Fax:* 613-475-4445
Number of Beds: 49 beds
Note: Long-term care residence
Arlene Lawlor, Administrator; Director, Nursing

Burlington: Billings Court Manor
3700 Billings Court, Burlington, ON L7N 3N6
Tel: 905-333-4006; *Fax:* 905-333-4416
Toll-Free: 888-274-6445
Number of Beds: 160 units
Ann Chartier, Administrator

Burlington: Participation House - Hamilton & District
1022 Waterdown Rd., Burlington, ON L7T 1N3
Tel: 905-527-7949; *Fax:* 905-333-8711
info@participationhouse.hamilton.on.ca
www.participationhouse.hamilton.on.ca
Number of Beds: 39 beds
Note: Provides services designed to enhance the quality of life of adults with disabilities
Cindy Kinnon, Executive Director

Caledon: Charlestown Residential School
19646 Kennedy Rd., RR#1, Caledon, ON L0N 1C0
Tel: 519-941-8472; *Fax:* 519-941-0824
Number of Beds: 20 beds
Note: special care home, group home, treatment centre (behaviour)
Wayne Dunster, Executive Director

Chatham: Copper Terrace Long Term Care Facility
91 Tecumseh Rd., Chatham, ON N7M 1B3
Tel: 519-354-5442; *Fax:* 519-354-0362
www.copperterrace.ca
Number of Beds: 151 beds
Kathy Morningstar, Administrator
kmorningstar@ckha.on.ca

Chatham: Meadow Park Care Centre - Chatham
110 Sandys St., Chatham, ON N7L 4X3
Tel: 519-351-1330; *Fax:* 519-351-7933
www.jarlette.com
Number of Beds: 97 beds
Anne Marie Rumble, Administrator
amrumble@jarlette.com
Joanne Wytinck, Director of Care
jwytinck@jarlette.com

Chatham: Riverview Gardens
Former Name: Thamesview Lodge
519 King St. West, Chatham, ON N7M 1G8
Tel: 519-352-4823; *Fax:* 519-352-2891
CKseniors@chatham-kent.ca
www.chatham-kent.ca
Number of Beds: 320 beds
Colleen Wilson, Director, Senior Services
Donna Cottingham, Manager, Resident Care Services

Chatsworth: Country Lane Long Term Care Centre
RR#3, Chatsworth, ON N0H 1G0
Tel: 519-794-2244; *Fax:* 519-794-2597
countrylane@reveraliving.com
www.reveraliving.com
Number of Beds: 34 beds
Lynn Jamieson, Administrator

Chesley: Parkview Manor
98 - 3rd St. SE, Chesley, ON N0G 1L0
Tel: 519-363-2416; *Fax:* 519-363-2171
parkviewmanor@reveraliving.com
www.reveraliving.com
Number of Beds: 34 beds
Carole Woods, Administrator

Clarence Creek: Centre d'accueil Roger-Séguin
435 Lemay St., Clarence Creek, ON K0A 1N0
Tel: 613-488-2053; *Fax:* 613-488-2274
Number of Beds: 110 beds
Note: charitable
Charles Lefebvre, Administrator

Cobourg: Golden Plough Lodge
983 Burnham St., Cobourg, ON K9A 5J6
Tel: 905-372-8759; *Fax:* 905-372-8525
hassanja@county.northumberland.on.ca
Number of Beds: 162 beds
John Hassan, Administrator

Cochrane: Villa Minto
PO Box 280, 241 - 8 St., Cochrane, ON P0L 1C0
Tel: 705-272-7200; *Fax:* 705-272-4155
Number of Beds: 33 beds
Note: Villa Minto is an independent LTC facility housed in the chronic care wing of The Lady Minto Hospital
Dan O'Mara, Administrator

Cornwall: Sandfield Place
Also Known As: 458422 Ontario Limited
220 Emma St., Cornwall, ON K6J 5V8
Tel: 613-933-6972; *Fax:* 613-938-2261
sandfield@bellnet.ca
www.sandfieldplace.ca
Number of Beds: 53 long term care beds, 34 retirement beds
Note: Long term care & retirement living
Bill Kinnear, Administrator
bill,kinnear@bellnet.ca

Delaware: Middlesex Terrace
2094 Gideon Dr., R.R.#1, Delaware, ON N0L 1E0
Tel: 519-652-3483; *Fax:* 519-652-8733
www.middlesexterrace.ca
Number of Beds: 105 beds
Tanya Pol, Administrator
tpol@middlesexterrace.ca

Dundas: St. Joseph's Villa (Dundas)
Affiliated with: Hamilton Niagara Haldimand Brant Local Health Integration Network
56 Governor's Rd., Dundas, ON L9H 5G7
Tel: 905-627-3541; *Fax:* 905-628-0825
pokrafka@sjv.on.ca
www.sjv.on.ca
Number of Beds: 378 beds
Paul O'Krafka, Executive Director
Jerry Vajsar, Supervisor, Maintenance

Dundas: Wentworth Lodge
41 South St. West, Dundas, ON L9H 4C4
Tel: 905-546-2618; *Fax:* 905-546-2854
saphsweb@hamilton.ca
www.hamilton.ca/phcs/wentworth
Number of Beds: 160 beds
Note: home for the aged
Lynda Secord, Administrator

Dunnville: Grandview Lodge
657 Lock St. West, Dunnville, ON N1A 1V9
Tel: 905-774-7547; *Fax:* 905-774-1440
grandview@haldimandcounty.on.ca
www.haldimandcounty.on.ca
Number of Beds: 128 beds
Joanne McGuire, Administrator

Harold Winger, Supervisor, Maintenance

Durham: Rockwood Terrace
PO Box 660, 575 Sadler St. East, Durham, ON N0G 1R0
Tel: 519-369-6035; *Fax:* 519-369-6736
www.greycounty.ca
Number of Beds: 100 beds
Note: Long term care
Karen Kraus, Administrator
kkraus@greycounty.ca

Elmira: Chateau Gardens (Elmira) Nursing Home
11 Herbert St., Elmira, ON N3B 2B8
Tel: 519-669-2921; *Fax:* 519-669-3027
Number of Beds: 48 beds
Joan Norris, Administrator
Allison Westman, Environmental Services Supervisor

Elmvale: Sara-Vista Long Term Care Facility
27 Simcoe St., Elmvale, ON L0L 1P0
Tel: 705-322-2182; *Fax:* 705-322-8326
saravista@reveraliving.com
www.reveraliving.com
Number of Beds: 60 beds
Karen Jones, Administrator

Fort Erie: Gilmore Lodge
50 Gilmore Rd., Fort Erie, ON L2A 2M1
Tel: 905-871-6160; *Fax:* 905-871-0435
Number of Beds: 79 beds
Bev Goodman, Administrator

Fort Erie: Maple Park Lodge
6 Hagey Ave., Fort Erie, ON L2A 5M5
Tel: 905-994-0224; *Fax:* 905-994-8628
Number of Beds: 96 units
Note: Nursing home

Fort Frances: Rainycrest Home for the Aged
550 Osborne St., Fort Frances, ON P9A 3T2
Tel: 807-274-9858; *Fax:* 807-274-7368
Number of Beds: 147 beds
Note: home for the aged
Jill Colquhoun, Administrator
Allan Johnstone, Coordinator, Environmental Services

Glenburnie: Fairmount Home for the Aged
2069 Battersea Rd., RR#1, Glenburnie, ON K0H 1S0
Tel: 613-546-4264; *Fax:* 613-546-0489
jshillington@frontenaccounty.ca
www.frontenaccounty.ca/?q=fairmount_home
Number of Beds: 128 beds
Note: home for the aged
Julie Shillington, Administrator

Gore Bay: Manitoulin Lodge
3 Main St., Gore Bay, ON P0P 1H0
Tel: 705-282-2007; *Fax:* 705-282-3422
www.jarlette.com
Number of Beds: 61 beds
Lorna Fogg, Administrator
lfogg@jarlette.com

Grimsby: Deer Park Villa
150 Central Ave., Grimsby, ON L3M 4Z3
Tel: 905-945-4164; *Fax:* 905-945-1239
Toll-Free: 877-945-4764
kim.eros@regional.niagara.on.ca
Number of Beds: 39 beds
Kim Eros, Administrator/Director of Resident Care
kim.eros@regional.niagara.on.ca

Guelph: The Elliott Community
170 Metcalfe St., Guelph, ON N1E 4Y3
Tel: 519-822-0491; *Fax:* 519-822-5658
info@elliottcommunity.org
www.elliottcommunity.org
Number of Beds: 270 beds
Note: Retirement suites & long term care
Trevor Lee, CEO

Haileybury: Temiskaming Lodge
100 Bruce St., Haileybury, ON P0J 1K0
Tel: 705-672-2123; *Fax:* 705-672-5734
www.jarlette.com
Number of Beds: 82 beds
Francine Gosselin, Administrator
fgosselin@jarlette.com

Hamilton: Grace Villa Hamilton
45 Lockton Cres., Hamilton, ON L8V 4V5
Tel: 905-387-4812; *Fax:* 905-387-4814
jzomer@gracevilla.ca
www.gracevilla.ca

Number of Beds: 184 beds
JoAnn Zomer, Administrator
jzomer@gracevilla.ca

Hamilton: Idlewyld Manor
449 Sanatorium Rd., Hamilton, ON L9C 2A7
Tel: 905-574-2000; *Fax:* 905-574-0482
office@idlewyldmanor.com
www.idlewyldmanor.com

Number of Beds: 101 beds
Robert J. Malloy, Executive Director

Hamilton: St. Elizabeth Villa
391 Rymal Rd. West, Hamilton, ON L9B 1V2
Tel: 905-388-9691; *Fax:* 905-388-9953
stelizabeth.villa@bellnet.ca
www.stelizabethhomesociety.org

Note: assisted living
Sr. Maria Szucs, Administrator

Hamilton: St. Peter's Residence at Chedoke
125 Redfern Ave., Hamilton, ON L9C 7W9
Tel: 905-777-3837; *Fax:* 905-383-1099
residence@stpetes.ca
www.stpetes.ca

Number of Beds: 210 beds
Donna Cripps, President/CEO

Hamilton: Shalom Village
70 Macklin St. North, Hamilton, ON L8S 3S1
Tel: 905-529-1613; *Fax:* 905-529-7542
info@shalomvillage.on.ca
www.shalomvillage.on.ca

Number of Beds: 60 beds
Note: Long term care & assisted living, day program; kosher meals provided; Jewish & ecumenical services. Shalom Village Too with 64 beds & 30 apartments is located adjacent
Patricia Morden, Chief Executive Coach

Hamilton: Townsview Lifecare Centre
39 Mary St., Hamilton, ON L8R 3L8
Tel: 905-523-6427; *Fax:* 905-528-0610
eyi_townsview_complex@extendicare.com
www.hamiltonltc.org

Number of Beds: 219 beds
Andrew Adamyk, Administrator
aadamyk@extendicare.com

Hamilton: The Wellington
1430 Upper Wellington St., Hamilton, ON L9A 5H3
Tel: 905-385-2111; *Fax:* 905-385-2110
www.thewellington.ca

Number of Beds: 102 long term care beds, 80 retirement beds
Note: Long term care & retirement community
Tanya Macdonald, Administrator
Doretta Skidmore, Contact, Residence Information
dskidmore@thewellington.ca

Huntsville: Muskoka Landing
65 Rogers Cove Dr., Huntsville, ON P1H 2L9
Tel: 705-788-7713; *Fax:* 705-788-1424
www.jarlette.com

Number of Beds: 94 long-term care beds
Bill Thurlow, Administrator
bthurlow@jarlette.com

Jacksons Point: Cedar Lane Lodge
895 Lake Dr. East, Jacksons Point, ON L0E 1L0
Tel: 905-722-8928

Number of Beds: 17 beds
Note: supported independant living
Jeff Smith, Administrator

Jasper: Rosebridge Manor
131 Roses Bridge Rd., RR#2, Jasper, ON K0G 1G0
Tel: 613-283-5471; *Fax:* 613-283-9012
www.omniway.com

Number of Beds: 78 beds
Dorothy Broeders-Morin, Administrator
dmorin@omniway.ca
Gary Foster, Director, Housekeeping/Physical Plant

Kincardine: Trillium Court Seniors Community
550 Phillip Pl., Kincardine, ON N2Z 3A6
Tel: 519-396-4400; *Fax:* 519-366-9092
trillium@reveraliving.com
www.reveraliving.com

Number of Beds: 40 beds + 60 retirement suites
Note: Independent & assisted living, retirement lodge, long-term care, respite & convalescent options
Pam Campbell, Administrator
M. Furnvale, Supervisor, Environmental Services

Kingston: Providence Care - St. Mary's of the Lake Hospital Site
340 Union St., Kingston, ON K7L 5A2
Tel: 613-544-5220; *Fax:* 613-544-8558
bonuttim@providencecare.ca
www.pccchealth.org

Number of Beds: 144 beds
Note: Acute care, complex continuing care, geriatric medicine, rehabilitation, palliative care, respite care
Michele Bonutti, Site Administrator/CFO

Kingston: Providence Manor
275 Sydenham St., Kingston, ON K7K 1G7
Tel: 613-549-4164; *Fax:* 613-549-7472
nowlans@providencecare.ca
www.pccchealth.org

Number of Beds: 243 beds
Note: Long-term care
Shelagh Nowlan, Site Administrator

Kingston: Specialty Care Trillium Centre
800 Edgar St., Kingston, ON K7M 8S4
Tel: 613-547-0040; *Fax:* 613-547-3734
jennifer.powley@specialty-care.com
www.specialty-care.com

Number of Beds: 234 units
Note: Comprehensive long-term care services. Trillium Ridge Retirement Community located adjacent
Jennifer Powley, Administrator

Kitchener: Lanark Heights Long-Term Care
46 Lanark Cres., Kitchener, ON N2N 2Z8
Tel: 519-743-4200; *Fax:* 519-743-4225
info@lanarkcare.com
www.lanarkcare.com

Number of Beds: 107 units

Kitchener: Sunnyside Home
247 Franklin St. North, Kitchener, ON N2A 1Y5
Tel: 519-893-8482; *Fax:* 519-893-4450
www.region.waterloo.on.ca

Number of Beds: 251 residential capacity
Note: Specialty: Long-term care
Gail Carlin, Administrator
Wendy Reid, Chair, Health & Safety Committee
Reg Weber, Supervisor, Maintenance

Kitchener: The Westmount Long Term Care Residence
Affiliated with: Chartwell Seniors Housing REIT
200 David Bergey Dr., Kitchener, ON N2E 3Y4
Tel: 519-570-2115; *Fax:* 519-579-9770
westmountltc@chartwellreit.ca
www.chartwellreit.ca

Number of Beds: 160 units
Stephen Suske, CEO, Chartwell Seniors Housing REIT

Komoka: Country Terrace Long Term Care Home
Affiliated with: South West Local Health Integration Network
Former Name: Country Terrace Nursing Home
10072 Oxbow Dr., RR#3, Komoka, ON N0L 1R0
Tel: 519-657-2955; *Fax:* 519-657-8516
mraithby@countryterrace.ca
www.countryterrace.ca

Number of Beds: 120 beds
Mary Raithby, Executive Director

L'Orignal: Résidence Champlain
Affiliated with: Chartwell Seniors Housing REIT
428 Front Rd. West, L'Orignal, ON K0B 1K0
Tel: 613-675-4617
champlain@chartwellreit.ca
www.chartwellreit.ca

Number of Beds: 60 beds
Stephen Suske, CEO, Chartwell Seniors Housing REIT

Lancaster: Chateau Gardens (Lancaster)
PO Box 429, 105 Military Rd. North, Lancaster, ON K0C 1N0
Tel: 613-347-3016; *Fax:* 613-347-1680
Number of Beds: 60 beds
Ron Gingrich, Administrator

Limoges: Résidence Limoges
131-133 Ottawa St., Limoges, ON K0A 2M0
Tél: 613-443-5303; *Téléc:* 613-443-1943
Nombre de lits: 25 lits
François Grégoire, Administrateur

Limoges: St. Viateur Nursing Home
1003 Limoges Rd. South, Limoges, ON K0A 2M0
Tel: 613-443-5751; *Fax:* 613-443-5950
Number of Beds: 64 beds

Richard R. Marleau, Administrator

Lindsay: Chimo Youth & Family Services, Inc.
#3, 2 Kent St. West, Lindsay, ON K9V 2Y1
Tel: 705-324-3300; *Fax:* 705-324-3304
Number of Beds: 16 beds
Note: children's residential mental health residence
Margaret Rose Jackson, Executive Director

Lindsay: Frost Manor
225 Mary St. West, Lindsay, ON K9V 5K3
Tel: 705-324-8333; *Fax:* 705-878-5840
www.omni-way.com

Number of Beds: 62 beds
Linda Burr, Administrator

London: Anago Resources Inc.
371 Princess Ave., London, ON N6B 2A7
Tel: 519-435-1099; *Fax:* 519-435-0062
info@anago.on.ca
www.anago.on.ca

Number of Beds: 63 beds
Note: young offenders; developmental handicap group home; child & family intervention treatment
Mandy L. Bennett, Executive Director

London: Chateau Gardens London
2000 Blackwater Rd., London, ON N5X 4K6
Tel: 519-434-2727

Number of Beds: 95 beds

London: Chelsey Park Retirement Community
310 Oxford St. West, London, ON N6H 4N6
Tel: 519-432-1855
www.chelseypark.com

Number of Beds: 247 beds

London: Dearness Services
710 Southdale Rd., London, ON N6E 1R8
Tel: 519-661-0400; *Fax:* 519-661-0446
Number of Beds: 348 beds
L. Hignett, Administrator

London: Longworth Long Term Care
590 Longworth Rd., London, ON N6K 4X9
Tel: 519-472-6424; *Fax:* 519-472-8852
info@longworthcare.com
www.longworthcare.com

Number of Beds: 160 beds
Note: Specialties: Long term care; Restorative care program; Massage therapy; Physiotherapy; Family & personal counseling services

London: Meadow Park Care Centre & Retirement Lodge - London
1210 Southdale Rd. East, London, ON N6E 1B4
Tel: 519-686-0484; *Fax:* 519-686-9932
www.jarlette.com
Note: Long term care facility & retirement lodge
Terri Daly, Administrator, Care Centre
tdaly@jarlette.com
Michelle Gatt, General Manager, Retirement Lodge
mgatt@jarlette.com

London: St. Joseph's Health Care, London Mount Hope Centre for Long Term Care
21 Grosvenor St., London, ON N6A 1Y1
Tel: 519-646-6000; *Fax:* 519-646-6054
Communications.Department@sjhc.london.on.ca
www.sjhc.london.on.ca

Number of Beds: 390 beds
Jane Boudreau-Bailey, Director

Markham: The Woodhaven Long Term Care Residence
Affiliated with: Chartwell Seniors Housing REIT
380 Church St., Markham, ON L6B 1E1
Tel: 905-472-3320
woodhavenltc@chartwellreit.ca
www.chartwellreit.ca

Number of Beds: 192 units
Stephen Suske, CEO, Chartwell Seniors Housing REIT

Maxville: Maxville Manor
80 Mechanic St. West, Maxville, ON K0C 1T0
Tel: 613-527-2170; *Fax:* 613-527-3103
www.maxvillemanor.ca

Year Founded: 1968
Number of Beds: 120 beds + 2 respite beds
Note: Specialties: Long-term care services; Therapy services; The Seniors' Centre, providing outreach services to persons in the community with physical disabilities & special needs; Adult day program; Seniors' clinics, such as hearing, optometry, & foot care. Number of Employees: 130

R.E.C. Munro, Executive Director
Sally Bennett, Director, Nursing
Neil McCormick, Director, Environmental Services

Midland: Hillcrest Village Care Centre
Former Name: St. Andrew's Centennial Manor
255 Russell St., Midland, ON L4R 5L6
Tel: 705-526-3781; *Fax:* 705-526-5656
information@hvcc.ca
www.hvcc.ca
Number of Beds: 100 beds
Walter Ens, Administrator

Milton: Allendale
185 Ontario St. South, Milton, ON L9T 2M4
Tel: 905-878-4141; *Fax:* 905-878-8797
Toll-Free: 866-442-5866
johnstoi@halton.ca
www.halton.ca/scs/seniors/ltc/allendale.htm
Number of Beds: 300 beds
Ingrid Johnston, Administrator

Milton: Mount Nemo Christian Nursing Home
4486 Guelph Line, RR#2, Milton, ON L9T 2X6
Tel: 905-335-3636; *Fax:* 905-335-3699
mountnemonursinghome@cogeco.net
www.mountnemochristiannh.on.ca
Number of Beds: 60 beds
Note: long term care home
Lynette Royeppen, Administrator

Mississauga: Cawthra Gardens
590 Lolita Gardens, Mississauga, ON L5A 4N8
Tel: 905-306-9984
Number of Beds: 192 beds

Mississauga: Chelsey Park Mississauga Long-Term Care Facility
2250 Hurontario St., Mississauga, ON L5B 1M8
Tel: 905-270-0411
Number of Beds: 237 beds

Mississauga: Chelsey Park Streetsville Long-Term Care Facility
1742 Bristol Rd. West, Mississauga, ON L5M 1X9
Tel: 905-826-3045

Mississauga: Heritage House Retirement Home
73 King St. West, Mississauga, ON L5B 1H1
Tel: 905-279-4800; *Fax:* 905-615-8141
theheritagehouse@rogers.com
www.heritagehouseonline.com
Note: Specialties: Physiotherapy; Occupational therapy; Specialized rehabilitative care; Recovery from surgery; Cardiac care program; Orthopedic care; Acitvity program; Respite or short stays
Janice MacInnis, Administrator
Angus MacInnis, Administrator

Mississauga: Specialty Care Mississauga Road
4350 Mississauga Rd., Mississauga, ON L5M 7C8
Tel: 905-812-1175; *Fax:* 905-812-1173
gayle.stuart@specialty-care.com
www.specialty-care.com
Number of Beds: 160 beds
Gayle Stuart, Administrator

Mississauga: Villa Forum
175 Forum Dr., Mississauga, ON L4Z 4E5
Tel: 905-501-1443; *Fax:* 905-501-0094
Number of Beds: 160 units
Note: Long-term care facility

Mississauga: The Wenleigh Long Term Care Residence
Affiliated with: Chartwell Seniors Housing REIT
2065 Leanne Blvd., Mississauga, ON L5K 2L6
Tel: 905-822-4663
wenleighltc@chartwellreit.ca
www.chartwellreit.ca
Number of Beds: 161 units
Stephen Suske, CEO, Chartwell Seniors Housing REIT

Mitchell: Ritz Lutheran Villa
Rd. 164 - 4118A, RR#5, Mitchell, ON N0K 1N0
Tel: 519-348-8612; *Fax:* 519-348-4420
info@ritzlutheranvilla.com
www.ritzlutheranvilla.com
Number of Beds: 83 beds
Note: charitable home for the aged, retirement community with rental apartments & life lease town homes
Brent E. Nafziger, Administrator
Randy Satchell, Building Services Supervisor

Napanee: The John M. Parrott Centre
Former Name: Lenadco Home
309 Bridge St. West, Napanee, ON K7R 2G4
Tel: 613-354-3306; *Fax:* 613-354-7387
bsmith@lennox-addington.on.ca
www.lennox-addington.on.ca
Number of Beds: 168 beds
Note: Long term care
Brian Smith, Director

Nepean: Carleton Lodge
55 Lodge Rd., Nepean, ON K2C 3H1
Tel: 613-825-3763; *Fax:* 613-825-0245
hanora.mcgrath@ottawa.ca
Number of Beds: 160 beds
Hanora McGrath, Administrator

Newmarket: Southlake Residential Care Village
640 Grace St., Newmarket, ON L3Y 2L1
Tel: 905-895-7661; *Fax:* 905-895-9806
www.southlakeregional.org/southlakeresidentialcarevillage.html
Year Founded: 2004
Number of Beds: 192 beds
Note: Number of staff: 200
Terry Collins, Executive Director
tcollins@extendicare.com

Niagara Falls: Bella Senior Care Residence
8720 Willoughby Dr., Niagara Falls, ON L2G 7X3
Tel: 905-295-2727
info@bellaseniorcare.com
www.bellaseniorcare.com
Number of Beds: 160 units

Niagara on the Lake: Chateau Gardens - Niagara
PO Box 985, 120 Wellington St., Niagara on the Lake, ON L0S 1J0
Tel: 905-468-2111; *Fax:* 905-468-4463
niagara@chateaugardens.com
www.chateaugardens.com
Number of Beds: 124 beds
Susan Norton, Administrator

Niagara on the Lake: Upper Canada Lodge
272 Wellington St., Niagara on the Lake, ON L0S 1J0
Tel: 905-468-4208; *Fax:* 905-468-0520
uppercanada@niagararegion.ca
Year Founded: 1988
Number of Beds: 80 beds
Colleen Johnson, Administrator
Dave Shedden, Supervisor, Maintenance

North Bay: Cassellholme
400 Olive St., North Bay, ON P1B 6J4
Tel: 705-474-4250; *Fax:* 705-474-6129
bethcamph@on.aibn.com
www.cassellholme.on.ca
Number of Beds: 240 beds
Note: home for the aged
Beth Campbell, Administrator

Oakville: The Waterford Long Term Care Residence
Affiliated with: Chartwell Seniors Housing REIT
2140 Baronwood Dr., Oakville, ON L6M 4V6
Year Founded: 2003
Number of Beds: 168 units
Stephen Suske, CEO, Chartwell Seniors Housing REIT

Oakville: Wyndham Manor
291 Reynolds St., Oakville, ON L6J 3L5
Tel: 905-849-7766
Number of Beds: 128 beds

Orillia: The Leacock Care Centre
25 Museum Dr., Orillia, ON L3V 7T9
Tel: 705-325-9181; *Fax:* 705-325-5179
www.jarlette.com
Number of Beds: 145 long-term care beds
Marilyn Hauser, Administrator
mhauser@jarlette.com

Orleans: Kingsway Arms at St. Joseph Manor
1510 St. Joseph Blvd., Orleans, ON K1C 7L1
Tel: 613-830-4000; *Fax:* 613-830-7607
manoirstjoseph@on.aibn.com
www.kingswayarms.com/stjoseph.php
Number of Beds: 80 beds
Jeannine Zacconi, Director of Care

Orleans: Madonna Long Term Care Facility
1541 St. Joseph Blvd., Orleans, ON K1C 1S9
Tel: 613-824-2040
sallibhai@chartwellreit.ca
www.chartwellreit.ca
Note: Specialties: Restorative care; Palliative care

Orleans: Résidence Saint-Louis
879, ch Hiawatha Park, Orleans, ON K1C 2Z6
Tél: 613-824-1720; *Téléc:* 613-824-8064
rslinfo@scohs.on.ca
www.scohs.on.ca
Nombre de lits: 198 lits
Note: Établissement francophone de soins de longue durée
Jean Bartkowiak, Président-directeur général, Service de santé SCO Health Service

Oshawa: Hillsdale Estates
590 Oshawa Blvd. North, Oshawa, ON L1G 5T9
Tel: 905-579-1777; *Fax:* 905-579-3911
Year Founded: 2003
Number of Beds: 435 beds
Len Cserhati, Administrator
Linda Doherty, Director, Resident Care

Oshawa: Thorntonview
186 Thornton Rd. South, Oshawa, ON L1J 5Y2
Tel: 905-576-5181; *Fax:* 905-576-0078
thorntonview@reveraliving.com
www.reveraliving.com
Number of Beds: 154 beds
Note: Long-term care, palliative care, services for physically challenged adults
Arlene Inkster, Administrator

Oshawa: The Wynfield Long Term Care Residence
451 Woodmount Dr., Oshawa, ON L1G 8E3
Tel: 905-571-0065; *Fax:* 905-579-4902
wynfieldltc@chartwellreit.ca
www.chartwellreit.ca
Number of Beds: 172 beds
Katherine Jackson, Administrator
Stephen Suske, CEO, Chartwell Seniors Housing REIT

Ottawa: Carlingview Manor
2330 Carling Ave., Ottawa, ON K2B 7H1
Tel: 613-820-9328; *Fax:* 613-820-9774
carlingviewmanor@cplodges.com
Number of Beds: 320 beds
Lori Norris, Administrator

Ottawa: Hillel Lodge
Also Known As: The Bess & Moe Greenberg Family Hillel Lodge
10 Nadolny Sachs Private, Ottawa, ON K2A 4G7
Tel: 613-728-3900; *Fax:* 613-728-6550
Number of Beds: 100 beds
Stephen Schneiderman, Executive Director

Ottawa: Hillel Lodge (The Bess & Moe Greenberg Family)
10 Nadolny Sachs Pvt., Ottawa, ON K2A 4G7
Tel: 613-728-3900; *Fax:* 613-728-6550
sss@hillel-ltc.com
Number of Beds: 100 beds
Note: Charitable home for the aged
Stephen Schneiderman, Executive Director

Ottawa: St. Patrick's Home of Ottawa Inc.
2865 Riverside Dr., Ottawa, ON K1V 8N5
Tel: 613-731-4660; *Fax:* 613-731-4056
here@stpats.ca
www.stpats.ca
Number of Beds: 202 beds
Note: home for the aged
Sr. Mona Martin, Executive Director

Ottawa: The Salvation Army Ottawa Booth Centre
Former Name: Metropole & Salvage Depot
171 George St., Ottawa, ON K1N 5W5
Tel: 613-241-1573; *Fax:* 613-241-2818
www.ottawaboothcentre.org
Year Founded: 1908
Note: Specialties: Anchorage Program, an addiction treatment program; Street outreach
Carson Durdle, Executive Director

Ottawa: Wymering Manor Ltd.
845 Kirkwood Ave., Ottawa, ON K1Z 5Y1
Tel: 613-722-8811; *Fax:* 613-722-0795
Number of Beds: 28 beds
Note: long-term psychiatric care home for women
Mary Calerone, Manager

Owen Sound: Versa-Care Summit Place
850 - 4th St. East, Owen Sound, ON N4K 6A3
Tel: 519-376-3212; *Fax:* 519-371-0923
summitplace@reveraliving.com
www.reveraliving.com

Number of Beds: 159 beds
Renate Cowan, Executive Director
renate.cowan@reveraliving.com

Palmerston: Royal Terrace
600 Whites Rd., Palmerston, ON N0G 2P0
Tel: 519-343-2611; *Fax:* 519-343-2860
royalter@wightman.ca
www.royalterracepalmerston.ca
Number of Beds: 121 beds
Note: Long-term & residential care
Kash Ramchandani, Administrator

Paris: Park Lane Terrace
295 Grand River St. North, Paris, ON N3L 2N9
Tel: 519-442-2753; *Fax:* 519-442-6176
www.parklaneterrace.ca
Number of Beds: 132 beds
Debora Saville, Administrator
dsaville@parklaneterrace.ca

Parry Sound: Lakeland Long Term Care Facility
6 Albert St., Parry Sound, ON P2A 3A4
Tel: 705-746-9667; *Fax:* 0
Toll-Free: 1-866-959-9005
swhite@lakelandltc.ca
www.chartwellreit.ca or www.wpshc.com
Note: Located within the West Parry Sound Health Centre complex
Norman Maciver, CEO

Pembroke: Marianhill
600 Cecelia St., Pembroke, ON K8A 7Z3
Tel: 613-735-6838; *Fax:* 613-732-3934
www.marianhill.ca
Number of Beds: 200 beds
Note: Catholic long-term and chronic care facility
Terry McBurney, Executive Director

Penetanguishene: Georgian Manor
7 Harriett St., Penetanguishene, ON L9M 1K8
Tel: 705-549-3166; *Fax:* 705-549-6062
djackson@county.simcoe.on.ca
Number of Beds: 107 beds
Note: home for the aged
Jane Sinclair, Senior Administrator

Penetanguishene: Ruth Haarer Home for Special Care
Former Name: Ruth Haarer Residence
PO Box 1067, 2 Water St., Penetanguishene, ON L9M 1V6
Tel: 705-549-7296
Number of Beds: 18 beds
Ruth Haarer, Administrator

Peterborough: Fairhaven Home
881 Dutton Rd., Peterborough, ON K9H 7S4
Tel: 705-743-4265; *Fax:* 705-743-6292
Number of Beds: 253 beds
Note: home for the aged
Deborah Hammons, Executive Director

Peterborough: Riverview Manor
1155 Water St., Peterborough, ON K9H 3P8
Tel: 705-748-6706; *Fax:* 705-748-5407
magreco@omniway.ca
www.omni-way.com
Number of Beds: 124 beds
Sue Matwey, Administrator

Peterborough: Springdale Country Manor
2698 Clifford Line, Peterborough, ON K9J 6X6
Tel: 705-742-8811; *Fax:* 705-742-8812
www.omni-way.com/ourhomes/springdale.htm
Number of Beds: 65 beds
Maureen Imamovic, Administrator
mimamovic@omniway.ca

Petrolia: Lambton Meadowview Villa
3958 Petrolia Line, RR#4, Petrolia, ON N0N 1R0
Tel: 519-882-1470; *Fax:* 519-882-1633
Number of Beds: 123 beds, 2 short stay beds
Note: home for the aged
Marlene Jackson, Acting Resident Manager

Port Colborne: Northland Manor
Northland Pointe, 2 Fielder Ave., Port Colborne, ON L3K 6G4
Tel: 905-835-9335; *Fax:* 905-835-6518
northland@niagararegion.ca
Number of Beds: 150 beds
Note: Long-term care facility
Maureen Shantz, Administrator

Port Stanley: Extendicare - Port Stanley
4551 East Rd., Port Stanley, ON N5L 1J6
Tel: 519-782-3339; *Fax:* 519-782-4756
cnh_portstanley@extendicare.com
www.extendicare.com
Number of Beds: 60 beds
Bahime Charania, Administrator; Director, Nursing

Ridgetown: The Village Retirement Residence
9 Myrtle St., Ridgetown, ON N0P 2C0
Tel: 519-674-5427; *Fax:* 519-674-2422
thevillageretirementresidence@reveraliving.com
www.reveraliving.com
Number of Beds: 160 beds
Donna Kingelin

Rockland: St. Joseph Long-Term Care Facility
1615 Laurier St., Rockland, ON K4K 1C8
Tel: 613-446-5126
Number of Beds: 64 units

Sarnia: Sumac Lodge
1464 Blackwell Rd., Sarnia, ON N7S 5M4
Tel: 519-542-3421; *Fax:* 519-542-3604
sumaclodge@reveraliving.com
www.reveraliving.com
Number of Beds: 100 beds
Ann Currie, Executive Director
ann.currie@reveraliving.com

Sarnia: Twin Lakes Terrace
Affiliated with: Steeves & Rozema Group
1310 Murphy Rd., Sarnia, ON N7S 6K5
Tel: 519-542-2939; *Fax:* 519-542-0879
kim_vandam@srgroup.ca
www.srgroup.ca
Number of Beds: 56 beds; 60 long-term care beds
Note: Independent & assisted living, convalescent & respite options
Kim Van Dam, Managing Director

Sarsfield: Sarsfield Colonial Home
PO Box 130, 2861 Colonial Rd., Sarsfield, ON K0A 3E0
Tel: 613-835-2977; *Fax:* 613-835-2982
Number of Beds: 46 beds
Chantal Crispin, Administrator
chantalcrispin@rogers.com

Shelburne: Dufferin Oaks Home for Senior Citizens
151 Centre St., Shelburne, ON L0N 1S4
Tel: 519-925-2140; *Fax:* 519-925-5067
duffoaks@dufferincounty.on.ca
www.dufferincounty.on.ca
Number of Beds: 160 beds
Note: non-profit municipal long-term care facility
Brenda Urbanski, Administrator
Gerald Black, Supervisor, Maintenance

Simcoe: Norview Lodge
PO Box 604, 44 Rob Blake Way, Simcoe, ON N3Y 4L8
Tel: 519-426-0902; *Fax:* 519-426-9867
www.norfolkcounty.on.ca
Number of Beds: 179 beds
Note: home for the aged
Kim Jenereaux, Administrator
Brian Koncir, Supervisor, Maintenance

St Catharines: Henley House Limited
20 Earnest St., St Catharines, ON L2N 7T2
Tel: 905-937-9703
www.chartwellreit.ca
Number of Beds: 160 beds
Note: Specialties: Long-term nursing & personal care; Therapeutic programs; Physiotherapy; Restorative care; Palliative care

St Catharines: Linhaven
403 Ontario St., St Catharines, ON L2N 1L5
Tel: 905-934-3364; *Fax:* 905-934-6975
Number of Beds: 248 beds
Note: Specialties: Long term care; Alzheimer's disease, memory loss, & related dementias; Respite services; Adult day service
Dan Oettinger, Administrator

St Catharines: Niagara Ina Grafton Gage Home
413 Linwell Rd., St Catharines, ON L2M 7Y2
Tel: 905-935-6822; *Fax:* 905-935-6847
poneill@niggv.on.ca
www.niggv.on.ca
Number of Beds: 40 beds
Note: supportive housing for seniors
Patrick O'Neill, CEO

St Thomas: Barton Residence
31 Southwick St., St Thomas, ON N5R 3R7
Tel: 519-633-3413
Number of Beds: 16 lits
Sheila Barton, Proprietor

St Thomas: Kettle Creek Residence
Former Name: Kettle Creek Gardens
58 St. George St., St Thomas, ON N5P 2L1
Tel: 519-633-7647; *Fax:* 519-633-9312
kettlecreek@execulink.com
Note: HSC needs
Dana Lawrence, Administrator

St Thomas: Valleyview Home for the Aged
350 Burwell Rd., St Thomas, ON N5P 0A3
Tel: 519-631-1030; *Fax:* 519-631-3462
mccarroll@valleyview.st-thomas.on.ca
Number of Beds: 136 beds
Note: home for the aged
Michael Carroll, Administrator

St. Thomas: Elgin Manor Home for the Aged
39232 Fingal Line, St. Thomas, ON N5P 3S5
Tel: 519-631-0620; *Fax:* 519-631-2307
www.elginhomes.ca
Number of Beds: 90 beds
Pat Vendevenne, Director, Homes & Senior Services
pvandevenne@elgin-county.on.ca

Stittsville: Specialty Care Granite Ridge
5501 Abbott St., Stittsville, ON K2S 2C5
Tel: 613-836-0331; *Fax:* 613-241-1986
norm.slatter@specialty-care.com
www.specialty-care.com
Number of Beds: 224 beds
Norm Slatter, Administrator

Stoney Creek: Clarion Nursing Home
337 Hwy. 8, Stoney Creek, ON L8G 1E7
Tel: 905-664-2281; *Fax:* 905-664-2966
info@clarionnursinghome.on.ca
www.clarionnursinghome.on.ca
Number of Beds: 100 beds
Michael Janjic, Administrator

Stoney Creek: Heritage Green Nursing Home
353 Isaac Brock Dr., Stoney Creek, ON L8J 2J3
Tel: 905-573-7177; *Fax:* 905-573-7151
hgnh@bellnet.ca
www.hamiltonltc.org/facilities/heritage.htm
Number of Beds: 167 beds
Rosemary Okimi, Administrator
Reg Charles, Manager, Maintenance

Stoney Creek: Stoney Creek Lifecare Centre
199 Glover Rd., Stoney Creek, ON L8E 5J2
Tel: 905-643-1795
eyi_stoneycreek_lc@extendicare.com
www.hamiltonltc.org
Number of Beds: 45 beds
Stephanie Zajczenko-Opdam, Administrator
sopdam@extendicare.com

Stouffville: Specialty Care Bloomington Cove
13621 Ninth Line, Stouffville, ON L4A 7X3
Tel: 905-640-1310; *Fax:* 905-640-0995
bernard.boreland@specialty-care.com
www.specialty-care.com
Number of Beds: 112 beds
Bernard Boreland, Administrator

Stratford: L'Arche Stratford
PO Box 522 Main Street, Stratford, ON N5A 6T7
Tel: 519-271-9751; *Fax:* 519-271-1861
info@larche.stratford.on.ca
www.larche.ca/en/communities/stratford/
Number of Beds: 24 beds

Stratford: Greenwood Court
90 Greenwood Dr., Stratford, ON N5A 7W5
Tel: 519-273-4662; *Fax:* 519-273-1458
Number of Beds: 45 beds
Fred Zehr, Administrator

Thunder Bay: Harper Residence
42 Lake St., Thunder Bay, ON P7B 2V6
Tel: 807-345-7625; *Fax:* 807-346-8733
harper@tbaytel.net
Number of Beds: 10 beds
Note: Group home
Sheila Harper

***Thunder Bay:* OPTIONS Northwest Personal Support Services**
95 Cumberland St. North, Thunder Bay, ON P7A 4M1
Tel: 807-344-4994; *Fax:* 807-346-5811
www.optionsnorthwest.com
Year Founded: 1965
Note: Specialty: Personal & residential support for persons with developmental challenges, physical disabilities, chronic behaviour problems, & mental health challenges; Counselling; Support groups
Bernard Travis, Executive Director

***Thunder Bay:* Roseview Manor**
Former Name: Central Park Lodge
99 Shuniah St., Thunder Bay, ON P7A 2Z2
Tel: 807-344-6929; *Fax:* 807-344-7132
roseviewmanor@reveraliving.com
www.reveraliving.com
Number of Beds: 157 beds
Gail Gallant, Executive Director

***Tilbury:* Tilbury Manor Long-Term Care Home**
PO Box 160, 16 Fort St., Tilbury, ON N0P 2L0
Tel: 519-682-0243; *Fax:* 519-682-2358
adm.tilbury@diversicare.ca
www.diversicare.ca
Number of Beds: 75 beds
Jennifer Middleton, Administrator

***Toronto:* Altamont Long-Term Care Facility**
92 Island Rd., Toronto, ON M1C 2P5
Tel: 416-284-4781; *Fax:* 416-284-3634
adm.altamont@diversicare.ca
Number of Beds: 159 beds

***Toronto:* Baycrest Centre for Geriatric Care**
3560 Bathurst St., Toronto, ON M6A 2E1
Tel: 416-785-2500; *Fax:* 416-785-2464
www.baycrest.org
Number of Beds: 300 beds
Note: group home

***Toronto:* Carefree Lodge**
306 Finch Ave. East, Toronto, ON M2N 4S5
Tel: 416-397-1500; *Fax:* 416-397-1501
Number of Beds: 126 beds
Note: home for the aged
Debbie Araujo, Administrator

***Toronto:* Central Park Lodge West Side**
1145 Albion Rd., Toronto, ON M9V 4J7
Tel: 416-745-4800; *Fax:* 416-745-0445
westside@reveraliving.com
www.reveraliving.com
Number of Beds: 290 beds
Soo Wong, Administrator
S. Amadeo, Supervisor, Environmental Services

***Toronto:* Cheltenham Long-Term Care Facility**
5935 Bathurst St., Toronto, ON M2R 1Y8
Tel: 416-223-4050
Number of Beds: 170 beds

***Toronto:* Chester Village**
717 Broadview Ave., Toronto, ON M4K 2P5
Tel: 416-466-2173; *Fax:* 416-466-6781
Number of Beds: 174 beds
Note: home for the aged
Henriette Koning, CEO
Richard Dreja, Director, Physical Plant

***Toronto:* Copernicus Lodge**
66 Roncesvalles Ave., Toronto, ON M6R 3A7
Tel: 416-536-7122; *Fax:* 416-536-8242
Number of Beds: 108 beds
Note: home for the aged
Gisela Styka, Executive Director

***Toronto:* Dom Lipa Nursing Home & Seniors Centre**
52 Neilson Dr., Toronto, ON M9C 1V7
Tel: 416-621-3820; *Fax:* 416-621-9773
info@domlipa.ca; t.macdermid@domlipa.ca
www.domlipa.ca
Number of Beds: 66 nursing home, 30 retirement beds
Theresa MacDermid, Administrator

***Toronto:* The Gibson Long Term Care Centre**
Affiliated with: Chartwell Seniors Housing REIT
Former Name: Extendicare - North York
1925 Steeles Ave. East, Toronto, ON M2H 2H3
Tel: 416-493-4666; *Fax:* 416-493-4886
gibsonltc@chartwellreit.ca
www.chartwellreit.ca
Number of Beds: 202 beds
Stephen Suske, CEO, Chartwell Seniors Housing REIT

***Toronto:* Ina Grafton Gage Home (Toronto)**
2 O'Connor Dr., Toronto, ON M4K 2K1
Tel: 416-422-4890; *Fax:* 416-422-1613
info@iggh.org
www.iggh.org
Number of Beds: 110 beds
Gordon Blowes, Administrator
Hernando Zorilla, Director, Physical Plant

***Toronto:* Kingsway Arms at McCowan**
2881 Eglinton Ave. East, Toronto, ON M4G 2K3
Tel: 416-266-4445; *Fax:* 416-264-8377
mccowan.kams@rogers.com
www.kingswayarms.com/mccowan.php
Gina Cook, Executive Director
Tim Valyear, Director, Marketing
marketingoffice.kams@rogers.com

***Toronto:* Lakeside Long-Term Care Centre**
150 Dunn Ave., Toronto, ON M6K 2R6
Tel: 416-533-2828
www.torontorehab.com/patient/longterm/index.htm
Number of Beds: 128 Beds

***Toronto:* Maynard Nursing Home**
28 Halton St., Toronto, ON M6J 1R3
Tel: 416-533-5198; *Fax:* 416-533-3531
www.maynardnursinghome.com
Year Founded: 1961
Number of Beds: 77 beds
Note: Specialties: Service to residents of Portuguese origin; Recreational & social activities
Rosemary Mifsud, Administrator

***Toronto:* Nisbet Lodge**
740 Pape Ave., Toronto, ON M4K 3S7
Tel: 416-469-1105; *Fax:* 416-469-2996
info@nisbetlodge.com
www.nisbetlodge.com
Number of Beds: 103 beds
Note: Christian long-term care home
Glen Moorhouse, Executive Director

***Toronto:* North York General Hospital - Seniors' Health Centre**
2 Buchan Ct., Toronto, ON M2J 5A3
Tel: 416-756-0066; *Fax:* 416-495-9738
www.nygh.on.ca
Number of Beds: 192 beds
Note: Long term care facility, ambulatory geriatric services
Bonnie Adamson, CEO

***Toronto:* The O'Neill Centre**
33 Christie St., Toronto, ON M6G 3B1
Tel: 416-536-1116; *Fax:* 416-536-6941
adminassist@oneillcentre.ca
www.oneillcentre.ca
Number of Beds: 172 beds
Note: Resident care & retirement living
Christine Dalglish, Administrator

***Toronto:* Oakdale Child & Family Service Ltd.**
291 Chisholm Ave., Toronto, ON M4C 4W5
Tel: 416-699-5600; *Fax:* 416-699-6547
tor-oakdale@on.aibn.com
www.oakdaleservices.com
Note: Specialties: Long & short term care for children with special needs; Teaching independence in life skills, social & community awareness, & appropriate communication methods
Lisa Bache, Administrator

***Toronto:* Providence Healthcare**
Former Name: Providence Centre Home for the Aged, Chronic Care
3276 St. Clair Ave. East, Toronto, ON M1L 1W1
Tel: 416-285-3666; *Fax:* 416-285-3758
info@providence.on.ca
www.providence.on.ca
Number of Beds: 288 long-term care, 347 hospital beds
Note: Comprised of Providence Hospital, the Cardinal Ambrozic Houses of Providence, & Providence Community Centre; long-term care, rehabilitation & complex continuing care, community clinics, Alzheimer Day Program, caregiver support services, Tamil Caregiver Project. Focus is on the mission & values of the founding Sisters of St. Joseph
Neil McEvoy, President/CEO
Josie Walsh, Vice President, Programs; Chief Nurse Executive
Dr. Peter Nord, Vice President, Medical Affairs; Chief of Staff

***Toronto:* La Salle Manor**
61 Fairfax Cres., Toronto, ON M1L 1Z7
Tel: 416-752-3932; *Fax:* 416-752-4047
Number of Beds: 28 beds
Note: supportive housing
Br. Francis McCrea, Administrator

***Toronto:* Shepherd Lodge**
3760 Sheppard Ave. East, Toronto, ON M1T 3K9
Tel: 416-609-5700; *Fax:* 416-609-8329
info@shepherdvillage.org
www.shepherdvillage.org
Year Founded: 1961
Number of Beds: 252 beds
Brock Hall, Vice President, Client Care Services

***Toronto:* Suomi-Koti Toronto**
Also Known As: Toronto Finnish Cdn Srs Centre & Nursing Home
795 Eglinton Ave. East, Toronto, ON M4G 4E4
Tel: 416-425-4134; *Fax:* 416-425-6319
seniorscentre@suomikoti.ca
www.suomikoti.ca
Number of Beds: 88 apartment units, 34 nursing beds
Juha Mynttinen, Administrator
Leila Carnegie, Director of Care

***Toronto:* Villa Colombo Homes for the Aged Inc.**
40 Playfair Ave., Toronto, ON M6B 2P9
Tel: 416-789-2113; *Fax:* 416-789-5435
general@villacolombo.on.ca
www.villacharities.com
Number of Beds: 391 beds
Pat Stoddart, Administrator
Mac Brett, Director, Housekeeping/Maintenance

***Toronto:* West Park Long-Term Care Centre**
82 Buttonwood Ave., Toronto, ON M6M 2J5
Tel: 416-243-3600; *Fax:* 416-243-8947
feedback@westpark.org
www.westpark.org
Note: Rehabilitation, complex continuing care, and long-term care facility

***Toronto:* The Westbury Long Term Care Centre**
495 The West Mall, Toronto, ON M9C 5S3
Tel: 416-622-7094
westburyltc@chartwellreit.ca
www.chartwellreit.ca
Note: Specialties: Nursing & personal care; Restorative care; Social, recreational, & physical activity programs; Specialized neighbourhood for persons with dementia; Palliative care

***Trenton:* Crown Ridge Place Nursing Home**
106 Crown St., Trenton, ON K8V 6R3
Tel: 613-392-1289; *Fax:* 613-392-6360
gfreeman@crownridgehealth.ca
Number of Beds: 84 beds
Greg Freeman, Administrator

***Unionville:* Union Villa**
Unionville Home Society, 4300 Hwy. #7 East, Unionville, ON L3R 1L8
Tel: 905-477-2839
customerservice@uhs.on.ca
www.uhs.on.ca/uhs_unionvilla.php
Year Founded: 1970
Number of Beds: 160 residential capacity
Note: Specialties: Long-term nursing care; Activation program; Therapeutic mental & physical stimulation; Respite care; Day guest program
Graham Constantine, President/CEO

***Val Caron:* Elizabeth Centre**
Centre Elizabeth
2100 Main St., Val Caron, ON P3N 1S7
Tel: 705-897-7695; *Fax:* 705-897-0181
www.jarlette.com
Number of Beds: 128 beds
Shelly Murphy, Administrator
smurphy@jarlette.com

***Vanier:* Centre d'accueil Champlain**
275 Perrier Ave., Vanier, ON K1L 5C6
Tel: 613-746-3543; *Fax:* 613-746-5572
Number of Beds: 160 beds
Note: home for the aged
Pierre Arsenault, Administrator

***Wallaceburg:* Fairfield Park**
1934 Dufferin Ave., Wallaceburg, ON N8A 4M2
Tel: 519-627-1663; *Fax:* 519-627-9920
Number of Beds: 99 beds
Tracey Maxim, Administrator

Shona Outridge, Director of Operations

Watford: **Watford Quality Care Centre**
PO Box 400, 344 Victoria St., Watford, ON N0M 2S0
Tel: 519-876-2928; *Fax:* 519-876-3930
www.watfordqualitycare.ca

Number of Beds: 62 beds
Lynne-Anne Gallaway, Administrator
lgallaway@watfordqualitycare.ca

Windsor: **Huron Lodge**
1881 Cabana Rd. W, Windsor, ON N9G 1C7
Tel: 519-253-6060; *Fax:* 519-977-8027
www.citywindsor.ca/000278.asp

Number of Beds: 256 beds
Note: Number of Employees: 160
Lucie B. Lombardo, Administrator
Linda Larsh, Manager, Environmental Services

Windsor: **Regency Park Nursing Home**
567 Victoria Ave., Windsor, ON N9A 4N1
Tel: 519-254-1141; *Fax:* 519-254-3759
Number of Beds: 72 beds
Annemarie White, Administrator

Woodbridge: **Friuli Long-Term Care**
40 Friuli Ct., Woodbridge, ON
Tel: 416-443-0409
Number of Beds: 168 beds

Woodbridge: **Kristus Darzs Latvian Home**
11290 Pine Valley Dr., Woodbridge, ON L4L 1A6
Tel: 905-832-3300; *Fax:* 905-832-2029
kristusdarzs@kdlatvianhome.com
www.kdlatvianhome.com

Number of Beds: 100 beds
Jolanta Linde, Director of Operations

Woodstock: **Woodingford Lodge**
PO Box 308, 423 Devonshire Ave., Woodstock, ON N4S 7X9
Tel: 519-539-1245; *Fax:* 519-539-8937
www.county.oxford.on.ca
Number of Beds: 228 beds
Beth Martin, Administrator

Nursing Homes

Ajax: **Ballycliffe Lodge Ltd.**
70 Station Rd., Ajax, ON L1S 1R9
Tel: 905-683-7321; *Fax:* 905-427-5846
ballycliffelodge@chartwellreit.ca
www.chartwellreit.ca
Number of Beds: 100 beds; 65 retirement lodge beds
Christine Langton, Administrator

Amherstview: **Helen Henderson Care Centre**
343 Amherst Dr., Amherstview, ON K7N 1X3
Tel: 613-384-4585; *Fax:* 613-384-9407
Number of Beds: 70 retirement home beds; 102 nursing home beds
Larry Gibson, Administrator

Arnprior: **The Grove Arnprior & District Nursing Home**
275 Ida St. North, Arnprior, ON K7S 3M7
Tel: 613-623-6547; *Fax:* 613-623-4554
arnprior.hospital@arnprior.com
www.arnpriorhospital.com

Number of Beds: 60 beds
Marlene McRoberts, Chair
David Moore, Vice Chair

Arthur: **Caressant Care Nursing and Retirement Homes Limited**
Caressant Care Arthur
PO Box 700, 215 Eliza St., Arthur, ON N0G 1A0
Tel: 519-848-3795; *Fax:* 519-848-2273
www.caressantcare.com

Number of Beds: 80 beds
Lara Riehl, Administrator

Blenheim: **Blenheim Community Village**
PO Box 220, 10 Mary Ave., Blenheim, ON N0P 1A0
Tel: 519-676-8119; *Fax:* 519-676-0610
blenheim@reveraliving.com
www.reveraliving.com/homes/bl

Number of Beds: 101 beds
Note: nursing home & retirement lodge
Barbara Ferren, Executive Director

Bobcaygeon: **Specialty Care Case Manor**
Former Name: Case Manor Nursing Home
28 Boyd St., Bobcaygeon, ON K0M 1A0
Tel: 705-738-2374; *Fax:* 705-738-3821
margaret.misetic@specialty-care.com
www.specialty-care.com

Number of Beds: 96 beds
Margaret Misetic, Administrator

Bourget: **Caressant Care Nursing and Retirement Homes Limited**
Caressant Care Bourget
PO Box 99, 2279 Laval St., Bourget, ON K0A 1E0
Tel: 613-487-2331; *Fax:* 613-487-3464
www.caressantcare.com

Number of Beds: 50 beds
Louise Dion, Administrator

Bowmanville: **Marnwood Life Care Centre**
26 Elgin St., Bowmanville, ON L1C 3C8
Tel: 905-623-5731; *Fax:* 905-623-4497
Number of Beds: 60 beds
Note: Specialties: Social work; Physiotherapy
Tracey Werheid, Administrator

Bowmanville: **Strathaven Life Care Centre**
264 King St. East, Bowmanville, ON L1C 1P9
Tel: 905-623-2553; *Fax:* 905-623-1374
eyi_strathaven_lc@extendicare.com
www.ourhomeyourhome.eycan.com

Number of Beds: 199 beds
Patrick Brown, Administrator
pjbrown@extendicare.com

Brampton: **Holland Christian Homes Inc.**
Former Name: Faith Manor Nursing Home
7900 McLaughlin Rd. South, Brampton, ON L6V 3N2
Tel: 905-459-3333; *Fax:* 905-459-8667
fronre@hch.ca
www.hch.ca

Number of Beds: 120 beds
Note: Dutch Heritage
John Kalverda, Executive Director
johnka@hch.ca
Peter Dykstra, Administrator, Grace Manor
petedy@hch.ca

Brantford: **Versa-Care Centre - Brantford**
425 Park Rd. North, Brantford, ON N3R 7G5
Tel: 519-759-1040; *Fax:* 519-759-5343
vcbrantford@reveraliving.com
www.reveraliving.com

Number of Beds: 167 beds
Debbie Bonney, Administrator

Burlington: **The Brant Centre Long Term Care Residence**
Affiliated with: Chartwell Seniors Housing REIT
1230 Northshore Blvd. East, Burlington, ON L7S 1C5
Tel: 905-639-2848; *Fax:* 0
brantcentreltc@chartwellreit.ca
www.chartwellreit.ca

Year Founded: 2003
Number of Beds: 175 beds
Adam Banks, Administrator
Barbara Murphy, Director of Care
Stephen Suske, CEO, Chartwell Seniors Housing REIT

Cambridge: **Caressant Care Nursing and Retirement Homes Limited**
Cambridge Country Manor
3680 Speedsville Rd., Cambridge, ON N3H 4R6
Tel: 519-650-0100; *Fax:* 519-650-1697
Number of Beds: 79 beds
Brenda Nadeau, Administrator

Cambridge: **Riverbend Place Retirement Community**
650 Coronation Blvd., Cambridge, ON N1R 7S6
Tel: 519-740-3820; *Fax:* 519-740-0961
riverbendplace@reveraliving.com
www.reveraliving.com
Number of Beds: 146 beds
Note: Assisted living & independent living programs; short term, respite & convalescent options; community includes nursing home, retirement lodge, apartments
Margaret Dykeman, Administrator

Cambridge: **Saint Luke's Place**
1624 Franklin Blvd., Cambridge, ON N3C 3P4
Tel: 519-658-5183; *Fax:* 519-658-2991
www.saintlukesplace.ca

Number of Beds: 150 beds
Note: home for the aged; provides long term care, retirement home & apartments
Bev Preuss, Administrator

Carleton Place: **Stoneridge Manor**
256 High St., Carleton Place, ON K7C 1X1
Tel: 613-257-4355; *Fax:* 613-253-2190
stoneridgemanor@reveraliving.com
www.reveraliving.com

Number of Beds: 60 beds
Michelle Ferguson, Administrator
michelle.ferguson@reveraliving.com

Cobden: **Caressant Care Nursing and Retirement Homes Limited**
Caressant Care Cobden
12 Wren Dr., Cobden, ON K0J 1K0
Tel: 613-646-2109; *Fax:* 613-646-2182
www.caressantcare.com

Year Founded: 2000
Number of Beds: 60 beds
Linda Tracey, Administrator

Cobourg: **Streamway Villa Nursing Home**
19 James St. West, Cobourg, ON K9A 2J8
Tel: 905-372-0163; *Fax:* 905-372-0581
www.omni-way.com

Number of Beds: 59 beds
Robin Holland, Administrator
rholland@omniway.ca

Collingwood: **Bay Haven Nursing Home Inc.**
499 Hume St., Collingwood, ON L9Y 4H8
Tel: 705-445-6501; *Fax:* 705-445-6506
bayhaven@georgian.net
www.bayhaven.com

Number of Beds: 60 beds
Karen Milligan, Administrator

Collingwood: **Sunset Manor & Village**
49 Raglan St., Collingwood, ON L9Y 4X1
Tel: 705-445-4499; *Fax:* 705-445-9742
www.county.simcoe.on.ca/healthsocialservices/longtermcare/sunsetmanor/
Year Founded: 1968
Number of Beds: 148 beds
Note: Nursing & convalescent home
Erin Evans, Site Administrator; Director, Resident Care

Cornwall: **Versa-Care - Cornwall**
201 - 11 St. East, Cornwall, ON K6H 2Y6
Tel: 613-933-7420; *Fax:* 613-933-2759
vccornwall@reveraliving.com
www.reveraliving.com

Number of Beds: 118 beds
Donna Derouchie, Administrator

Courtland: **Caressant Care Nursing and Retirement Homes Limited**
Caressant Care Courtland
Former Name: Sacred Heart Villa
PO Box 279, 4850 County Rd. 59, Courtland, ON N0J 1E0
Tel: 519-688-0710; *Fax:* 519-688-0052
Number of Beds: 54 beds
Linda Hare, Administrator
Gilbert Dooms, Supervisor, Maintenance

Embrun: **St. Jacques Nursing Home**
Foyer St-Jacques
PO Box 870, 915 Notre Dame St., Embrun, ON K0A 1W0
Tel: 613-443-3442; *Fax:* 613-443-1716
info@stjacques.ca
www.stjacques.ca

Number of Beds: 60 beds
Ginette Beaudin, Administrator
gbeaudin@stjacques.ca

Exeter: **Exeter Villa Nursing & Retirement Home**
Affiliated with: ATK Care Inc.
155 John St. East, Exeter, ON N0M 1S1
Tel: 519-235-1581; *Fax:* 519-235-3219
exevilla@cabletv.on.ca
www.atkcareinc.ca/exeterservices
Number of Beds: 57 nursing care beds, 66 retirement beds
Nancy Tweddle, Administrator

Fergus: **Caressant Care Nursing and Retirement Homes Limited**
Caressant Care Fergus
450 Queen St. East, Fergus, ON N1M 2Y7
Tel: 519-843-2400
www.caressantcare.com

Year Founded: 1986
Number of Beds: 87 beds
Shannon Brinkman, Administrator
Marion Douglas, Director, Nursing

Fordwich: **Fordwich Village Nursing Home**
Affiliated with: ATK Care Inc.
3063 Adelaide St., Fordwich, ON N0G 1V0
Tel: 519-335-3168; *Fax:* 519-335-3825
fordwichadmin@tnt21.com
www.atkcareinc.ca/fordwhichservices

Number of Beds: 33 beds
Note: Long term care facility
Catherine Weber, Administrator

Hagersville: **Norcliffe LifeCare Centre**
85 Main St. North, Hagersville, ON N0A 1H0
Tel: 905-768-1641; *Fax:* 905-768-1685
Number of Beds: 60 units
Note: Retirement home
Marilyn Tone, Acting Administrator

Hamilton: **St. Olga's Lifecare Centre**
570 King St. West, Hamilton, ON L8P 1C2
Tel: 905-522-8572; *Fax:* 905-522-1553
eyi_st.olgas_LC@extendicare.com
www.hamiltonltc.org/facilities/st_olgas.htm

Number of Beds: 93 beds
Judy Peck, Administrator
jpeck@extendicare.com

Hamilton: **Versa-Care Centre - Hamilton**
330 Main St. East, Hamilton, ON L8N 3T9
Tel: 905-523-7134; *Fax:* 905-523-7137
vchamilton@reveraliving.com
www.reveraliving.com

Number of Beds: 128 beds
Walter Sguazzin, Administrator

Harriston: **Caressant Care Nursing and Retirement Homes Limited**
Caressant Care Harriston
PO Box 520, 24 Louise St., Harriston, ON N0G 1Z0
Tel: 519-338-3700; *Fax:* 519-338-2744
www.caressantcare.com

Number of Beds: 89 beds
Note: Long term care facility, with secure unit for residents with dementia, & adjacent retirement home.
Mary-Therese Haid, Administrator
Eleanor MacEwen, Infection Control

Hawkesbury: **Résidence Prescott et Russell**
Prescott & Russell Residence
1020, boul Cartier, Hawkesbury, ON K6A 1W7
Tél: 613-632-2755; *Téléc:* 613-632-4056
www.prescott-russell.on.ca

Nombre de lits: 146 lits
Note: Maison de soins de longue durée. Employés: 171
Louise Lalonde, Administratrice
François Martineau, Directeur des soins infirmiers
Danielle Duval, Coordonnatrice, Admissions; Services financiers

Hensall: **Queensway Nursing & Retirement Home**
PO Box 369, 100 Queen St. East, Hensall, ON N0M 1X0
Tel: 519-262-2830; *Fax:* 519-262-3403
queensway.admin@tcc.on.ca

Number of Beds: 60 beds nursing home & 57 beds retirement home
Note: retirement home
Kathy Holdsworth, Administrator

Huntsville: **Fairvern Nursing Home Inc.**
Affiliated with: Muskoka Algonquin Healthcare
14 Mill St., Huntsville, ON P1H 2A4
Tel: 705-789-4476; *Fax:* 705-789-1371
fairvernmail@mahc.ca
www.mahc.ca & www.fairvernnursinghome.ca

Number of Beds: 76 beds
Barry Lockhart, CEO
Christopher Thomas, Chair

Keswick: **Specialty Care Cedarvale Lodge**
121 Morton Dr., Keswick, ON L4P 2M5
Tel: 905-476-2656; *Fax:* 905-476-5689
www.specialty-care.com

Number of Beds: 100 beds
Note: Nursing home with 40-bed retirement home attached
Donna Taylor, Administrator
donna.taylor@specialty-care.com

Kitchener: **Forest Heights Long Term Care Centre**
60 Westheights Dr., Kitchener, ON N2N 2A8
Tel: 519-576-3320; *Fax:* 519-745-3227
Number of Beds: 240 beds

Michelle Vermeeren, Administrator
Dolly LaBelle, Health; Safety Committee
Lynne Jones, Purchasing Agent

Listowel: **Caressant Care Nursing and Retirement Homes Limited**
Caressant Care Listowel
710 Reserve Ave., Listowel, ON N4W 2L1
Tel: 519-291-1041; *Fax:* 519-291-5420
www.caressantcare.com

Number of Beds: 52 beds
Lara Martinez, Administrator

London: **Versa-Care Elmwood Place**
Former Name: Elmwood Place
46 Elmwood Pl. West, London, ON N6J 1J2
Tel: 519-433-7259; *Fax:* 519-660-0158
elmwoodpl@reveraliving.com
www.reveraliving.com/homes/lo/

Number of Beds: 97 beds
Lorell Jones, Administrator

Marmora: **Caressant Care Nursing and Retirement Homes Limited**
Caressant Care Marmora
58 Bursthall St., Marmora, ON K0K 2M0
Tel: 613-472-3130; *Fax:* 613-472-5388
www.caressantcare.com

Number of Beds: 84 beds
Linda Merkley, Administrator

Matheson: **Rosedale Centre**
507 - 8th Ave., Matheson, ON P0K 1N0
Year Founded: 1989
Number of Beds: 20 beds
Note: Specialty: Long term nursing & supportive care; Foot care; Therapy; Number of Employees: 72 (Bingham Memorial Hospital & adjoined Rosedale Centre)
Daniel O'Mara, Chief Executive Officer
705-273-2424, ext. 2, mailto:micsceo@puc.net

Mount Forest: **Saugeen Valley Nursing Centre Ltd.**
465 Dublin St., Mount Forest, ON N0G 2L3
Tel: 519-323-2140; *Fax:* 519-323-3540
svnc@wightman.ca

Number of Beds: 87 beds
Note: Nursing & respite care
Andrea Parsons, Administrator

Norwood: **Pleasant Meadow Manor**
Affiliated with: OMNI
99 Alma St., Norwood, ON K0L 2V0
Tel: 705-639-5308; *Fax:* 705-639-5309
www.omni-way.com/ourhomes/pleasant.htm

Number of Beds: 61 beds
Note: Long term care
Fraser Wilson, CEO
Sandra Brow, Administrator; Director of Care, Care

Orangeville: **Avalon Care Centre & Retirement Lodge**
355 Broadway Ave., Orangeville, ON L9W 3Y3
Tel: 519-941-3351; *Fax:* 519-941-9532
www.jarlette.com

Number of Beds: 137 long term care beds, 77 retirement lodge beds
Note: Long term care centre & retirement residence
Chan Sooklal, Administrator, Care Centre
csooklal@jarlette.com
Debbie Rydall, General Manager, Retirement Lodge
drydall@jarlette.com

Orillia: **Trillium Manor Home for the Aged**
12 Grace Ave., Orillia, ON L3V 2K2
Tel: 705-325-1504; *Fax:* 705-325-7661
Year Founded: 1969
Number of Beds: 122 beds
Janice McQuaig, Site Administrator
Jane Sinclair, General Manager, Health & Cultural Services

Ottawa: **La Villa Marguerite**
75 Bruyere St., Ottawa, ON K1N 5C8
Tel: 613-562-4262; *Fax:* 613-562-4223
villa-marguerite@scohs.on.ca
www.scohs.on.ca

Number of Beds: 71 beds
Note: Long-term care
Jean Bartkowiak, President/CEO, Service de santé SCO Health Service

Owen Sound: **Versa-Care Georgian Heights**
1115 - 10 St. East, Owen Sound, ON N4K 6B1
Tel: 519-371-1441; *Fax:* 519-371-1092
georgianheights@reveraliving.com
www.reveraliving.com

Number of Beds: 40 beds
Joanne Porter, Administrator

Owen Sound: **Versa-Care Maple View**
1029 - 4th Ave. West, Owen Sound, ON N4K 4W1
Tel: 519-376-2522; *Fax:* 519-376-3110
mapleview@reveraliving.com
www.reveraliving.com

Number of Beds: 29 beds
Andrea Hodgkins, Acting Administrator

Paris: **Telfer Place Retirement Residence**
245 Grand River St. North, Paris, ON N3L 3V8
Tel: 519-442-4411; *Fax:* 519-442-6724
telferplaceretirementresidence@reveraliving.com
www.reveraliving.com

Number of Beds: 45 beds
Note: Independent living program; retirement lodge, apartments; long-term care; convalescent & respite options
Kathy Le Gresley, Administrator
Henry Filetstra, Supervisor, Maintenance

Picton: **Versa-Care Hallowell House**
PO Box 800, RR#1, Picton, ON K0K 2T0
Tel: 613-476-4444; *Fax:* 613-476-1566
hallowellhouse@reveraliving.com
www.reveraliving.com

Number of Beds: 97 beds
Janice F. Wilkes, Administrator
Carl Markland, Supervisor, Maintenance

Port Hope: **Regency Manor Retirement & Nursing Home**
66 Dorset St. East, Port Hope, ON L1A 1E3
Tel: 905-885-4558; *Fax:* 905-885-7386
regencymanor@bellnet.ca

Number of Beds: 101 beds
Charlene Smith, Administrator

Sarnia: **Trillium Villa**
1221 Michigan Ave., Sarnia, ON N7S 3Y3
Tel: 519-542-5529; *Fax:* 519-542-5953
trillium_villa@snr.on.ca
www.ltc.snr.on.ca

Year Founded: 1970
Number of Beds: 152 beds
Joyce Haneca, Administrator

Sault Ste Marie: **Great Northern Retirement Home**
760 Great Northern Rd., Sault Ste Marie, ON P6A 5K7
Tel: 705-945-9405; *Fax:* 705-945-6303
Number of Beds: 120 retirement, 34 interim nursing home beds
Nadia Longo, Administrator

Seaforth: **Seaforth Manor Nursing Home**
100 James St., Seaforth, ON N0K 1W0
Tel: 519-527-0030; *Fax:* 519-527-2862
seaforth.admin@tcc.on.ca

Number of Beds: 118 beds
Note: Nursing & retirement home
Catherine Schalk, Administrator

Shelburne: **Shelburne Residence**
200 Robert St., Shelburne, ON L0N 1S1
Tel: 519-925-3746; *Fax:* 519-925-1476
shelburne.admin@bellnet.ca

Number of Beds: 60 nursing beds, 28 retirement rooms
Note: Combined nursing home & retirement facility
Mike Dickin, Administrator

St Catharines: **Tufford Nursing Home**
312 Queenston St., St Catharines, ON L2P 2X4
Tel: 905-682-0503
www.hamptontufford.com

Year Founded: 1960
Number of Beds: 64 residential capacity
Note: Specialties: Long-term nursing care; Social work; Physiotherapy; Podiatry; Activation program; Palliative care

St Catharines: **Versa-Care Centre - St. Catharines**
168 Scott St., St Catharines, ON L2N 1H2
Tel: 905-934-3321; *Fax:* 905-934-9011
vcstcatharines@reveraliving.com
www.reveraliving.com

Number of Beds: 200 beds
Sandra A. Fredericks, Administrator

***St Marys:* Kingsway Lodge**
310 Queen St. East, RR #6, St Marys, ON N4X 1C8
Tel: 519-284-2921; *Fax:* 519-284-4468
info@kingswaylodge.com
www.kingswaylodge.com
Number of Beds: 89 beds, 52 units
Scott A. Mackay, Administrator
smackay@on.aibn.com

***St Marys:* Wildwood Care Centre Inc.**
PO Box 2200, 100 Ann St., St Marys, ON N4X 1A1
Tel: 519-284-3628; *Fax:* 519-284-0575
www.wildwoodcarecentre.com
Number of Beds: 82 beds
Lynn Walsh, Administrator

***St Thomas:* Caressant Care Nursing and Retirement Homes Limited**
Caressant Care St. Thomas - Mary Bucke St. Facility
4 Mary Bucke St., St Thomas, ON N5R 5J6
Tel: 519-633-3164; *Fax:* 519-631-8362
www.caressantcare.com
Number of Beds: 60 beds
Ann Starswell, Administrator

***St. Thomas:* Caressant Care Nursing and Retirement Homes Limited**
Caressant Care St. Thomas - Bonnie Place Facility
15 Bonnie Pl., St. Thomas, ON N5R 5T8
Tel: 519-633-6493; *Fax:* 519-633-9329
www.caressantcare.com
Number of Beds: 182 beds
Note: Long term care facility, with secure unit for residents with dementia.
Vicki Martinez, Administrator

***Stayner:* Stayner Nursing Home**
PO Box 350, 244 Main St. East, Stayner, ON L0M 1S0
Tel: 705-428-3614; *Fax:* 705-428-0537
Number of Beds: 49 beds
Lorraine Baker, Administrator

***Stirling:* Stirling Manor Nursing Home**
PO Box 220, 218 Edward St., Stirling, ON K0K 3E0
Tel: 613-395-2596; *Fax:* 613-395-0930
www.stirling-rawdon.com
Number of Beds: 75 beds
Judith Norlock, Administrator
judy_manor@hotmail.com
Linda Phillips, Acting Director, Nursing
Cheryl Campbell, Office Manager

***Strathroy:* Sprucedale Care Centre Inc.**
96 Kittridge Ave. East, Strathroy, ON N7G 2A8
Tel: 519-245-2808; *Fax:* 519-245-1767
Number of Beds: 62 beds
Darren Micallef, Administrator
darren@sprucedale.ca

***Sutton:* River Glen Haven Nursing Home**
Affiliated with: ATK Care Inc.
160 High St., Sutton, ON L0E 1R0
Tel: 905-722-3631; *Fax:* 905-722-8638
rghadmin@bellnet.ca
www.atkcareinc.ca/suttonservices.htm
Number of Beds: 109 beds
Note: Long term & secured care
Karen Ryan, Administrator

***Tavistock:* Caressant Care Nursing and Retirement Homes Limited**
The Maples Home for Seniors
94 William St., Tavistock, ON N0B 2R0
Tel: 519-655-2344; *Fax:* 519-655-2162
Number of Beds: 43 beds
Lois Riehl, Administrator

***Thunder Bay:* Pinewood Court**
2625 East Walsh St., Thunder Bay, ON P7E 2E5
Tel: 807-577-1127; *Fax:* 0
pinewoodcourt@reveraliving.com
www.reveraliving.com
Number of Beds: 75 beds
Note: Long term care
Cheryl Grant, Administrator
Ron Campbell, Director, Environmental Services

***Thunder Bay:* Versa-Care Centre - Thunder Bay**
135 South Vickers St., Thunder Bay, ON P7E 1J2
Tel: 807-623-9511; *Fax:* 807-623-6992
vcthunderbay@reveraliving.com
www.reveraliving.com
Number of Beds: 161 beds
Joanne Lent, Executive Director

***Toronto:* St. Clair O'Connor Community Nursing Home**
2701 St. Clair Ave. East, Toronto, ON M4B 3M3
Tel: 416-757-8757; *Fax:* 416-751-7315
Number of Beds: 25 beds
Susan Gallant, Administrator
s.gallant@scoc.ca

***Toronto:* Seven Oaks**
9 Neilson Rd., Toronto, ON M1E 5E1
Tel: 416-392-3500; *Fax:* 416-392-3579
www.toronto.ca/ltc/sevenoaks.htm/
Year Founded: 1989
Number of Beds: 249 beds
Note: Services for long term care, including adult day programs, services to the Armenian & Tamil communities, & an on-site child care centre
Karen Wallace, Administrator

***Toronto:* Tendercare Living Centre**
1020 McNicoll Ave., Toronto, ON M1W 2J6
Tel: 416-499-2020; *Fax:* 416-499-3379
peggyli@tendercare.ca
www.tendercare.ca
Number of Beds: 254 beds
Note: Nursing home & retirement community
Francis Martis, Administrator

***Toronto:* Tony Stacey Centre for Veterans Care**
59 Lawson Rd., Toronto, ON M1C 2J1
Tel: 416-284-9235; *Fax:* 416-284-7169
info@tonystaceycentre.ca
www.tonystaceycentre.ca
Year Founded: 1977
Number of Beds: 100 beds
Catherine Hilge, Administrator
chilge@bellnet.ca

***Toronto:* Versa-Care Centre - Rexdale**
95 Humber College Blvd., Toronto, ON M9V 5B5
Tel: 416-746-7466; *Fax:* 416-740-5812
vcrexdale@reveraliving.com
www.reveraliving.com
Number of Beds: 94 beds
Andrew Shinder, Administrator
Glen Elliott, Director, Physical Plant

***Toronto:* White Eagle Residence**
Affiliated with: Chartwell Seniors Housing REIT
138 Dowling Ave., Toronto, ON M6K 3A6
Tel: 416-533-7935; *Fax:* 416-533-5154
whiteeagleresidence@chartwellreit.ca
www.chartwellreit.ca
Number of Beds: 56 beds
Stephen Suske, CEO, Chartwell Seniors Housing REIT

***Uxbridge:* ReachView Village**
Former Name: Versa-Care Centre, Uxbridge
130 Reach St., Uxbridge, ON L9P 1L3
Tel: 905-852-5281; *Fax:* 905-852-0117
reachviewvillage@reveraliving.com
www.reveraliving.com
Number of Beds: 100 beds

***Waterloo:* Pinehaven Nursing Home & Retirement Residence**
229 Lexington Rd., Waterloo, ON N2K 2E1
Tel: 519-885-0255; *Fax:* 519-885-4216
jross@thecaringnetwork.ca
www.pinehaven.ca
Number of Beds: 85 beds
Note: Specialty: long term care
Joanne Ross, Administrator

***Whitby:* Sunnycrest Nursing Home**
1635 Dundas St. East, Whitby, ON L1N 2K9
Tel: 905-576-0111; *Fax:* 905-576-4712
info@sunnycrest.ca
www.sunnycrest.ca
Number of Beds: 136 beds
Jane Smith, Administrator
jsmith@sunnycrest.ca

***Windsor:* Riverside Place**
3181 Meadowbrook Lane, Windsor, ON N8T 0A4
Tel: 519-974-0148; *Fax:* 519-974-7305
riversideplace@reveraliving.com
www.reveraliving.com

***Windsor:* Versa-Care Windsor Place**
350 Dougall Ave., Windsor, ON N9A 4P4
Tel: 519-256-7868; *Fax:* 519-256-1991
vcwindsorplace@reveraliving.com
www.reveraliving
Number of Beds: 244 beds
Bonnie Spry, Administrator

***Woodbridge:* Devonshire Pine Grove Inc.**
c/o Pine Grove Lodge, 8403 Islington Ave. North, Woodbridge, ON L4L 1X3
Tel: 905-850-3605; *Fax:* 905-850-3832
smrpinelodge@rogers.com
chartwellcare.com
Number of Beds: 100 nursing home beds & 40 retirement residence suites
Sonia Ryerson, Administrator

***Woodstock:* Caressant Care Nursing and Retirement Homes Limited**
Caressant Care Woodstock
81 Fyfe Ave., Woodstock, ON N4S 8Y3
Tel: 519-539-6461; *Fax:* 519-539-7467
www.caressantcare.com
Number of Beds: 240 beds
Judy Peck, Administrator

Retirement Residences

***Amherstburg:* Victoria Street Manor**
184 Victoria St. South, Amherstburg, ON N9V 2K5
Tel: 519-736-2525; *Fax:* 519-736-8587
www.countyofessex.on.ca
Number of Beds: 14 beds
Note: Specialties: Residential care for seniors; Medication administration
Della Dyck, Manager

***Amherstview:* Briargate Retirement Living Centre**
4567 Bath Rd., Amherstview, ON K7N 1A8
Tel: 613-384-9333; *Fax:* 613-384-4443
briargate@reveraliving.com
Number of Beds: 95 beds
Leanne Weir, Executive Director

***Ancaster:* Carrington Place Retirement Residence**
75 Dunham Dr., Ancaster, ON L9G 1X7
Tel: 905-648-0343; *Fax:* 905-648-9581

***Ancaster:* Highgate Retirement Residence**
325 Fiddlers Green Rd., Ancaster, ON L9G 1W9
Tel: 905-648-8399; *Fax:* 905-648-3350
Number of Beds: 40 beds
Clare Aiken, Administrator

***Arnprior:* Arnprior Villa Retirement Residence**
15 Arthur St., Arnprior, ON K7S 1A1
Tel: 613-623-0414; *Fax:* 613-623-0947
arnprior@reveraliving.com
www.reveraliving.com
Number of Beds: 81 beds
Becky Hollingsworth, Executive Director

***Aurora:* Aurora Retirement Centre**
145 Murray Dr., Aurora, ON L4G 2C7
Tel: 905-841-2777; *Fax:* 905-841-1562
auroraretirement@chartwellreit.ca
www.chartwellreit.ca/home_locations/aurora_ret.htm
Number of Beds: 58 units
Avril Davies, Administrator

***Aurora:* Park Place Manor**
15055 Yonge St., Aurora, ON L4G 6T4
Tel: 905-727-2952; *Fax:* 905-727-5435
parkplacemanor@chartwellreit.ca
www.chartwellreit.ca
Number of Beds: 93 suites
Note: Specialties: Recreational activities; Wellness monitoring; Foot care; Respite, trial, seasonal, & convalescent stay
John Jeffs, Administrator

***Barrie:* Barrie Manor**
340 Blake St., Barrie, ON L4M 1L3
Tel: 705-722-3611; *Fax:* 705-722-4530
barriemanor@home.com
www.simcoecounty.net/barriemanor.htm
Number of Beds: 113 beds
Sylvia Ward, Administrator

Barrie: Mulcaster Mews
130 Mulcaster St., Barrie, ON L4M 3M9
Tel: 705-725-9119; *Fax:* 705-725-8848
enquires@mulcastermews.ca
www.geocities.com/mulcastermews
Number of Beds: 52 beds
Maggie Rae, Administrator

Barrie: Roberta Place
489 Essa Rd., Barrie, ON L4N 9E4
Tel: 705-728-2900; *Fax:* 705-728-8535
www.jarlette.com
Number of Beds: 138 bed retirement lodge, 139 long term care beds
Note: Roberta Place long term care facility is located at 503 Essa Rd.
Carolyn McLeod, Administrator
cmcleod@jarlette.com
Sandra Fernandez, General Manager, Retirement Lodge
sfernandez@jarlette.com

Barrie: Simcoe Terrace Retirement Centre
44 Donald St., Barrie, ON L4N 1E3
Tel: 705-722-5750; *Fax:* 705-722-7041
info@simcoeterrace.com
www.simcoeterrace.com
Number of Beds: 98 beds
Anne Ollikainen, Administrator

Barrie: Woods Park Care Centre
110 Lillian Cres., Barrie, ON L4N 5H7
Tel: 705-739-6881; *Fax:* 705-739-0638
cathy.cotton@specialty-care.com
Number of Beds: 67 units
Note: nursing home/retirement home
Cathy Cotton, Administrator

Beachburg: Country Haven Retirement Home
1387 Beachburg Rd., RR#1, Beachburg, ON K0J 1C0
Tel: 613-582-7021; *Fax:* 613-582-7075
chrh@nrtco.net
www.countryhavenretirementhome.com
Number of Beds: 75 beds
R. Legault, Manager

Belleville: Bayview Retirement Home
435 Dundas St. West, Belleville, ON K8P 1B6
Tel: 613-966-6268; *Fax:* 613-966-6675
bayview@chartwellreit.ca
www.chartwellreit.ca
Number of Beds: 60 beds
Patricia Tooze, Administrator

Belleville: The Richmond Retirement Residence
175 North Front St., Belleville, ON K8P 4Y8
Tel: 613-966-4407
www.richmondretirement.ca
Note: Specialties: Medication management; Wellness program; Social & therapeutic programs; Respite stays
Andrea E. McLister, Administrator

Bracebridge: Bracebridge Villa Retirement Lodge
690 Hwy. 118 West, Bracebridge, ON P1L 1W8
Tel: 705-645-6364; *Fax:* 705-645-1684
interest@bracebridgevilla.ca
www.bracebridgevilla.ca
Number of Beds: 82 units
Corrine Hall, Manager

Bracebridge: James Street Place
148 James St., Bracebridge, ON P1L 1S7
Tel: 705-645-1431; *Fax:* 705-645-5415
jamesstreet@chartwellreit.ca
www.chartwellreit.ca/home_locations/james_street.htm
Number of Beds: 73 suites
Rosalid Taylor, Administrator

Brampton: Woodhall Park Retirement Village
10250 Kennedy Rd., RR#4, Brampton, ON L6T 3S1
Tel: 905-846-1441
postmaster@woodhallpark.ca
www.woodhallpark.ca
Number of Beds: 80 suites
Andrew Post, Administrator

Brantford: Amber Lea Place
Affiliated with: Mundi Holdings Ltd.
384 St. Paul Ave., Brantford, ON N3R 4N4
Tel: 519-754-0000; *Fax:* 519-759-1401
info@amberleaplace.com
www.amberleaplace.com
Number of Beds: 50 beds
Dev Mundi, Administrator

Brantford: Charlotte Villa Retirement Residence
120 Darling St., Brantford, ON N3T 5W6
Tel: 519-759-5250; *Fax:* 519-759-8403
charlotte@reveraliving.com
www.reveraliving.com
Number of Beds: 80 beds
Note: Independent & assisted living, secured living for dementia care
Carol Sterkenburg, Administrator/Care Coordinator

Brantford: Tranquility Place
PO Box 3000, 436 Powerline Rd., Brantford, ON N3T 6G5
Tel: 519-759-2222
www.allegroresidences.ca
Year Founded: 1988
Note: Specialties: Physiotherapy; Foot care clinic; Physical activities
Paul Rade, General Manager

Brighton: Applefest Lodge
PO Box 850, 120 Elizabeth St., Brighton, ON K0K 1H0
Tel: 613-475-3510; *Fax:* 613-475-3431
info@applefestlodge.ca
www.applefestlodge.ca
Number of Beds: 50 beds
Marilyn McLeod, Manager
interest@applefestlodge.com

Brockville: Bridlewood Manor
1026 Bridlewood Dr., Brockville, ON K6V 7J8
Tel: 613-345-2477; *Fax:* 613-345-4188
bridlewood@reveraliving.com
www.reveraliving.com/homes/207
Number of Beds: 67 units
Dennis Daoust, Executive Director

Brockville: Rosedale Retirement Centre
Affiliated with: Chartwell Seniors Housing REIT
1813 County Rd. 2E, RR#1, Brockville, ON K6V 5T1
Tel: 613-342-0200; *Fax:* 613-342-8729
rosedale@chartwellreit.ca
www.chartwellreit.ca
Number of Beds: 69 suites
Stephen Suske, CEO, Chartwell Seniors Housing REIT

Burlington: Appleby Place
500 Appleby Line, Burlington, ON L7L 5Z6
Tel: 905-333-1611; *Fax:* 905-333-0596
applebyplace@lrc.ca
www.reveraliving.com/homes/8001/
Number of Beds: 90 units
Mary Turnbull, General Manager

Burlington: Bethany Residence
2387 Industrial St., Burlington, ON L7P 3A1
Tel: 905-335-3463; *Fax:* 905-335-1202
Number of Beds: 121 beds
Sheri Levy-Abraham, Manager

Burlington: Brantwood Lifecare Centre
802 Hager Ave., Burlington, ON L7S 1X2
Tel: 905-637-3481; *Fax:* 905-637-7514
www.ourhomeyourhome.eycan.com
Number of Beds: 178 beds
Kevin Baglole, Administrator
kbaglole@extendicare.com

Burlington: Christopher Court Retirement Home
392 Pearl St., Burlington, ON L7R 2M9
Tel: 905-639-4055; *Fax:* 905-639-9171
reynolds@residencesallegro.com
www.residencesallegro.com
Number of Beds: 50 beds
Lorie Tokola, General Manager

Burlington: Christopher Terrace Retirement Home
3131 New St., Burlington, ON L7N 3P8
Tel: 905-632-5072; *Fax:* 905-632-5074
Number of Beds: 80 beds
Laurie Johnston, Manager

Burlington: Lakeshore Place Retirement Residence
5314 Lakeshore Rd., Burlington, ON L7L 6L8
Tel: 905-333-0009; *Fax:* 905-333-3103
info@caregard.ca
www.lakeshoreplace.ca/lakeshore.htm
Number of Beds: 156 beds (residential care, assisted & daily living)
Note: assisted living retirement residence
Nancy Fischer, Administrator

Burlington: Park Avenue Manor
924 Park Ave. West, Burlington, ON L7T 1N7
Tel: 905-333-3323
parkavenuegm@cogeco.net
www.chartwellreit.ca
Number of Beds: 69 suites
Note: Specialties: Recreational activities; Medication administration; Wellness monitoring; Respite care; Convalescent, seasonal, & trial stays
Carrie T. Campbell, General Manager

Cambridge: Avonlea Place
611 Dunbar Rd., Cambridge, ON N3H 2T4
Tel: 519-650-1102; *Fax:* 519-650-3382
avonleaplace@rogers.com
Number of Beds: 32 beds
Jason Rumph

Cambridge: Queen's Square Terrace
Affiliated with: Chartwell Seniors Housing REIT
10 Melville St. North, Cambridge, ON N1S 1H5
Tel: 519-621-2777; *Fax:* 519-622-1299
queenssquare@chartwellreit.ca
www.chartwellreit.ca
Number of Beds: 80 suites
Stephen Suske, CEO, Chartwell Seniors Housing REIT

Carleton Place: Carleton Place Manor
6 Arthur St., Carleton Place, ON K7C 4S4
Tel: 613-253-7360; *Fax:* 613-253-5048
Number of Beds: 115 rooms
Corrie Berryman, Executive Director

Chatham: Maple City Retirement Residence
97 McFarlane Ave., Chatham, ON N7L 4V6
Tel: 519-354-7111; *Fax:* 519-351-5780
adm.maplecity@diversicare.ca
www.diversicare.ca
Number of Beds: 75 beds
Hilda Michielsen, Administrator

Chatham: Residence on The Thames
Affiliated with: Steeves & Rozema Group
850 Grand Ave. West, Chatham, ON N7L 5H5
Tel: 519-351-7220; *Fax:* 519-436-0360
crystal_houle@srgroup.ca
www.srgroup.ca
Number of Beds: 75 beds
Note: Independent living
Liddy Krieger, Executive Director
Crystal Houle, Office Manager

Codrington: Dorland House Retirement Residence
387 Goodrich Rd., Codrington, ON K0K 1R0
Tel: 613-475-4846; *Fax:* 613-475-4961
dorlandhouse@sympatico.ca
www.orca-homes.com
Number of Beds: 28 beds
Joan Dorland, Administrator

Cornwall: Chateau Cornwall
41 Amelia St., Cornwall, ON K6H 7E5
Tel: 613-937-4700; *Fax:* 613-932-6407
chateaucornwall@chartwellreit.ca
Number of Beds: 105 suites
Denis Carr, Manager

Delhi: Delrose Retirement Residence
725 Gibraltar St., Delhi, ON N4B 3C7
Tel: 519-582-4072; *Fax:* 519-582-2273
Number of Beds: 53 beds
Annemarie Barker, Administrator

Dresden: Park Street Place Retirement Residence
650 Park St., Dresden, ON N0P 1M0
Tel: 519-683-4474; *Fax:* 519-683-4555
www.diversicare.ca
Year Founded: 1987
Note: Specialties: Foot care; Physiotherapy; Medication management; Recreational activities; Respite & convalescent stays
Hilda Michielsen, Administrator

Dundas: The Georgian Retirement Residence
Affiliated with: Chartwell Seniors Housing REIT
255 Governor's Rd., Dundas, ON L9H 3K4
Tel: 905-627-8444; *Fax:* 905-627-9820
georgian@chartwellreit.ca
www.chartwellreit.ca
Number of Beds: 60 suites
Stephen Suske, CEO, Chartwell Seniors Housing REIT

Fort Erie: Garrison Place Retirement Residence
373 Garrison Rd., Fort Erie, ON L2A 1N1
Tel: 905-871-6410; *Fax:* 905-871-5422
garrisonplace@reveraliving.com
www.reveraliving.com
Number of Beds: 80 beds
Note: Secured living for dementia care residents; respite & convalescent options
Judy Gibson, Manager

Georgetown: Mountainview Residence
222 Mountainview Rd. North, Georgetown, ON L7G 3R2
Tel: 905-877-1800; *Fax:* 905-873-9083
info@mountainviewresidence.com
www.mountainviewresidence.com
Number of Beds: 82 suites
Christopher Summer, Manager

Gloucester: Camilla Gardens
1119 Bathgate Dr., Gloucester, ON K1J 9N4
Tel: 613-747-7000; *Fax:* 613-747-1804
camillagardens@bellnet.ca
www.camillaresidence.yp.ca
Number of Beds: 54 beds
Lyne Bellefeuille, Administrator

Gloucester: Elmsmere Retirement Residence
889 Elmsmere St., Gloucester, ON K1J 8G4
Tel: 613-745-2409; *Fax:* 613-745-4955
elmsmereplace@reveraliving.com
Number of Beds: 57 units
Pierre Lefebvre, Manager

Gloucester: Ogilvie Villa
1345 Ogilvie Rd., Gloucester, ON K1J 7P5
Tel: 613-742-6524; *Fax:* 613-742-7380
ogilvie@reveraliving.com
www.reveraliving.com
Year Founded: 1995
Number of Beds: 64 residential capacity
Note: Specialties: Recreation program; Short term stays
Bob Lemay, Manager

Goderich: Goderich Place Retirement Residence
30 Balvina Dr. East, Goderich, ON N7A 4L5
Tel: 519-524-4243; *Fax:* 519-524-8173
goderichplace@on.aibn.com
Number of Beds: 68 beds
Valerie Posadas, Administrator

Goderich: Maple Grove Lodge
45 Nelson St. East, Goderich, ON N7A 1R7
Tel: 519-524-8610
Number of Beds: 25 beds
Note: Nursing home

Gravenhurst: Gravenhurst Manor
300 Muskoka Rd. North, Gravenhurst, ON P1P 1N8
Tel: 705-687-3356; *Fax:* 705-687-5685
gravenhurstmanor@chartwellreit.ca
www.chartwellreit.ca/home_locations/gravenhurst.htm
Number of Beds: 50 suites
Gay Pengilly, Administrator

Grimsby: Maplecrest Village Retirement Residence
85 Main St. East, Grimsby, ON L3M 1N6
Tel: 905-945-7044; *Fax:* 905-945-6187
maplecrest@reveraliving.com
Number of Beds: 80 beds
Leanne Dabbs, Administrator

Guelph: College Place Retirement Residence
Former Name: Meadowcroft Place Retirement Centre
166 College Ave. West, Guelph, ON N1G 1S4
Tel: 519-822-0090; *Fax:* 519-822-2310
college@reveraliving.com
www.reveraliving.com
Number of Beds: 57 residential capacity
Note: Specialties: Assisted living program; Podiatry services; Recreation program; Short term stays
Alice Johnstone, Executive Director

Guelph: Norfolk Manor
128 Norfolk St., Guelph, ON N1H 4J8
Tel: 519-837-1100; *Fax:* 519-836-4003
david@norfolkmanor.ca
www.norfolkmanor.ca
Number of Beds: 67 beds
David Ing, Manager

Guelph: Stone Lodge Retirement Residence
165 Cole Rd., Guelph, ON N1G 4N9
Tel: 519-767-0880; *Fax:* 519-767-1690
stonelodge@reveraliving.com
www.reveraliving.com
Number of Beds: 130 units
Note: Independent & assisted living; convalescent & respite options
E. Lyn Fisher, Administrator

Guelph: Village of Riverside Glen
60 Woodlawn Rd. East, Guelph, ON N1H 8M8
Tel: 519-822-5272; *Fax:* 519-822-5520
www.oakwoodretirement.com/riverside.html
Number of Beds: 196 beds
Michell Vermeeren, Manager

Hamilton: Atrium Villa
467 Main St. East, Hamilton, ON L8M 1K1
Tel: 905-521-4442; *Fax:* 905-521-8247
atriumvilla@chartwellreit.ca
chartwellreit.ca/home_locations/atrium_villa.htm
Number of Beds: 67 units
Margaret Coulter, Manager

Hamilton: Central Park Lodges - Hamilton
35 Arkledun Ave., Hamilton, ON L8N 2H5
Tel: 905-522-2471; *Fax:* 905-570-0032
Number of Beds: 76 beds
Carol Sterkenburg, Administrator

Hamilton: Good Shepherd Centre
PO Box 1003, 135 Mary St., Hamilton, ON L8N 3R1
Tel: 905-528-9109; *Fax:* 905-546-1743
Number of Beds: 24 beds
Richard McPhee, Executive Director

Hamilton: Proctor Manor Retirement Home
Former Name: Proctor Manor Nursing Home
81 Proctor Blvd., Hamilton, ON L8M 2M5
Tel: 905-545-2427; *Fax:* 905-547-7195
Number of Beds: 23 beds
Joyce Carey, Manager

Hamilton: Stinson Manor
112 Stinson St., Hamilton, ON L8N 1S5
Tel: 905-521-9112; *Fax:* 905-521-9106

Hamilton: Townsview Retirement Residence
52 Catherine St. North, Hamilton, ON L8R 1J1
Tel: 905-527-1200
www.ourhomeyourhomecanada.ca
Number of Beds: 57 residential capacity
Note: Specialties: Personal nursing care; Catheter care; Colostomy care; Diabetes care; Oxygen care; Wellness program; Medication administration; Activity program
Derrick Bernardo, Administrator

Hanover: The Village Seniors Community
101 Tenth St., Hanover, ON N4N 1M9
Tel: 519-364-4320; *Fax:* 519-364-6953
thevillageseniors'community@reveraliving.com
www.reveraliving.com
Number of Beds: 70 long-term, 95 retirement beds, 100 seniors' apartments
Karen Kraus, Administrator

Harrow: Harrowood Seniors Community
Former Name: Harrowood Rest Home
1 Pollard Dr., Harrow, ON N0R 1G0
Tel: 519-738-2286; *Fax:* 519-738-2700
Number of Beds: 105 beds
Note: seniors community
Carol Chisholm, Administrator

Hawkesbury: Place Mont Roc
100 Industrial Blvd., Hawkesbury, ON K6A 3M8
Tel: 613-632-2900
pmr@hawk.igs.net
Number of Beds: 95 beds
Heather Sheffield, Administrator

Huntsville: Rogers Cove Retirement Residence
Affiliated with: Chartwell Seniors Housing REIT
4 Coveside Dr., Huntsville, ON P1H 2J9
Tel: 705-789-1600; *Fax:* 705-789-8781
rogerscove@chartwellreit.ca
www.chartwellreit.ca
Number of Beds: 55 suites
Stephen Suske, CEO, Chartwell Seniors Housing REIT

Ingersoll: Oxford Manor Retirement Home
276 Oxford St., Ingersoll, ON N5G 2W1
Tel: 519-485-0350; *Fax:* 519-485-7254
oxfordmanor@chartwellreit.ca
www.chartwellreit.ca
Number of Beds: 46 units
Note: Specialties: Activity program; Medication administration; Wellness monitoring; Respite care; Trial stays
Diance Nant, Administrator

Kanata: Chartwell House Kanata
20 Shirley's Brook Dr., Kanata, ON K2K 2W8
Tel: 613-591-8939; *Fax:* 613-591-1933
Number of Beds: 84 beds
Johanne Laframboise, General Manager
jlaframboise@chartwellreit.ca
Lisa Giles, Community Relations Manager
lgiles@chartwellreit.ca

Kanata: Fairfield Manor Retirement Home
17 Lombardo Dr., Kanata, ON K2L 4E8
Tel: 613-592-5772; *Fax:* 613-592-8928
info@fairfieldmanor.ca
www.fairfieldmanor.ca
Number of Beds: 46 Beds
Lisa Knopp, Administrator

Kanata: Kanata Retirement Residence
145 Castlefrank Rd. South, Kanata, ON K2L 3X9
Tel: 613-831-3333; *Fax:* 613-831-0153
kanataplace@reveraliving.com
Number of Beds: 66 units
Robyn Bosik, Executive Director

Kanata: Walden Retirement Residence
27 Weaver Cres., Kanata, ON K2K 2Z8
Tel: 613-591-3991; *Fax:* 613-591-9647
Number of Beds: 93 beds
Heidi Eichenberger, General Manager

Kincardine: Malcolm Place
PO Box 100, 255 Durham St., Kincardine, ON N2Z 2Y6
Tel: 519-396-5800; *Fax:* 519-396-5236
home@malcolmplace.on.ca
www.malcolmplace.ca
Number of Beds: 41 beds
Note: Retirement Residence
Dorinda Bowers, Administrator

Kingston: The Rosewood
833 Sutton Mills Ct., Kingston, ON K7P 2N9
Tel: 613-384-7131; *Fax:* 613-634-3247
debbie.helferty@specialty-care.com
www.speciality-care.com
Number of Beds: 70 units
Note: Independent living
Debbie Helferty, General Manager

Kingston: St. Lawrence Place
181 Ontario St., Kingston, ON K7L 5M1
Tel: 613-544-5900; *Fax:* 613-544-9971
st.lawrence@reveraliving.com
www.reveraliving.com
Number of Beds: 71 units
Margaret Bennett, Executive Director

Kingston: Trillium Ridge Retirement Community
800 Edgar St., Kingston, ON K7M 8S4
Tel: 613-547-0040; *Fax:* 613-547-3734
taimi.post@specialty-care.com
www.specialty-care.com
Note: Independent living. Specialty Care Trillium Centre long-term care residence located adjacent
Taimi Post, Director, Marketing & Resident Services

Kingsville: Kings Manor Residence
31 Pearl St. West, Kingsville, ON N9Y 1V3
Tel: 519-733-5378; *Fax:* 519-733-8552
mmayhew@mnsi.net
Number of Beds: 9 beds
Marie Mayhew, Manager

Kitchener: Bankside Terrace
71 Bankside Dr., Kitchener, ON N2N 3L1
Tel: 519-749-9999; *Fax:* 519-749-1947
bankside@chartwellreit.ca
www.chartwellreit.ca/home_locations/bankside_terrace.htm
Number of Beds: 86 units
Brad Lawrence, Manager

Kitchener: Conestoga Lodge Retirement Residence
55 Hugo Cres., Kitchener, ON N2M 5J1
Tel: 519-576-2140; *Fax:* 519-576-1790
www.conestogalodge.com

Number of Beds: 88 beds
Betty Cushing, Manager

Kitchener: Conestoga Towers - Trillium Retirement Apartments
221 Queen St. South, Kitchener, ON N2G 1W5
Tel: 519-578-9280; *Fax:* 519-578-9626

Number of Beds: 36 beds
Barbara Sutcliffe, Administrator

Kitchener: Fergus Place Retirement Residence
Former Name: Meadowcroft Place
164 Fergus Ave., Kitchener, ON N2A 2H2
Tel: 519-894-9600; *Fax:* 519-894-3383
fergus@reveraliving.com
www.reveraliving.com

Number of Beds: 76 residential capacity
Note: Specialty: Short term stays
Jane Hagelberg, Administrator

Kitchener: Lafontaine Terrace
169 Borden Ave. North, Kitchener, ON N2H 3J5
Tel: 519-576-2800; *Fax:* 519-742-4242
lafontaine@on.aibn.com

Jeff Edwards, Administrator

Kitchener: Lanark Place Retirement Residence
44 Lanark Cres., Kitchener, ON N2N 2Z8
Tel: 519-743-0121; *Fax:* 519-743-8901
info@lanarkcare.com
www.lanarkcare.com

Number of Beds: 107 units
Nancy Douglas, Manager

Kitchener: Victoria Place Retirement Residence
290 Queen St. South, Kitchener, ON N2G 1W3
Tel: 519-576-1300; *Fax:* 519-744-7097
victoriaplace@reveraliving.com
www.reveraliving.com

Number of Beds: 73 beds
Note: Independent & assisted living
Deb Gemmell, Executive Director

Leamington: Erie Glen Manor Retirement Residence
119 Robson Rd., Leamington, ON N8H 3V4
Tel: 519-322-2384; *Fax:* 519-322-1411

Number of Beds: 81 beds
Shelley Gould, Administrator

Leamington: Leamington Lodge Residential Care Centre Ltd.
PO Box 353, 24 Russell St., Leamington, ON N8H 3W3
Tel: 519-326-3591; *Fax:* 519-326-8787
Number of Beds: 40 beds
Jane Lee, Administrator

London: Ashwood Manor Ltd.
79 David St., London, ON N6P 1B4
Tel: 519-652-9006; *Fax:* 519-652-2592
info@ashwoodmanor.com
www.ashwoodmanor.com

Number of Beds: 72 units
Kathleen Hobden, Administrator

London: Central Park Lodge - London
279 Horton St., London, ON N6B 1L3
Tel: 519-434-4544; *Fax:* 519-673-4971
cplondon@reveraliving.com
www.reveraliving.com

Number of Beds: 87 units
Note: Assisted living
Susan O'Neill, Administrator

London: Horizon Place Retirement Residence
Former Name: Meadowcroft Place
760 Horizon Dr., London, ON N6H 5G3
Tel: 519-641-6330; *Fax:* 519-641-0570
horizon@reveraliving.com
www.reveraliving.com

Number of Beds: 84 residential capacity
Note: Specialties: Assisted living program; Recreation therapy; Podiatry; Short term stays
Marilyn Weekley, Manager

London: Kensington Village
1340 Huron St., London, ON N5V 3R3
Tel: 519-455-3910; *Fax:* 519-455-1570
sbrooks@kensingtonvillage.org
www.kensingtonvillage.org

Year Founded: 1984
Number of Beds: 139 suites
Peter Schlegel, Administrator
519/455-3910 ext.290, pschlegel@kensingtonvillage.org
Wendy Harrison, Director, Retirement Care
519/455-3910 ext.248, wharrison@kensingtonvillage.org

London: Longworth Retirement Residence
600 Longworth Rd., London, ON N6K 4X9
Tel: 519-472-1115; *Fax:* 519-472-1134
info@longworthcare.com
www.longworthcare.com

Number of Beds: 126 suites
Note: Specialty: Retirement / assisted living; Physiotherapy; Massage therapy; Reiki; Reflexology

London: Waverley Mansion Retirement Residence
10 Grand Ave., London, ON N5C 1K9
Tel: 519-667-1381; *Fax:* 519-667-9601
gm.waverley@diversicare.ca
www.diversicare.ca

Year Founded: 1987
Number of Beds: 65 beds
Note: Specialties: Supported care services for older adults; Medication administration & supervision; Physiotherapy; Foot care; Recreational program; Respite care; Convalescent stays
Suzi McArthur, Administrator

Midland: King Place Retirement Residence
750 King St., Midland, ON L4R 4K5
Tel: 705-526-0514; *Fax:* 705-526-8769
kingplace@reveraliving.com
www.reveraliving.com

Number of Beds: 80 beds
Note: Independent & assisted living; secured living for dementia care residents; respite & convalescent options
Sharon Penrose, Manager

Midland: The Villa Care Centre & Retirement Lodge
689 Yonge St., Midland, ON L4R 2E1
Tel: 705-526-4238; *Fax:* 705-526-5080
www.jarlette.com

Number of Beds: 158 beds
Edith Robitaille, Administrator
erobitaille@jarlette.com
Tanya Wilfling, General Manager
twilfling@jarlette.com
Michelle Lloyd, Customer Service Coordinator
mlloyd@jarlette.com

Mississauga: Beechwood Place
1500 Rathburn Rd. East, Mississauga, ON L4W 4L7
Tel: 905-238-0800; *Fax:* 905-238-4926
beechwoodplace@lrc.ca

Number of Beds: 137 suites
Deborah Rushton, Executive Director
Julie Shuster, Director of Marketing

Mississauga: Bough Beeches Place Retirement Residence
Former Name: Meadowcroft Place
1130 Bough Beeches Blvd., Mississauga, ON L4W 4G3
Tel: 905-625-2022; *Fax:* 905-238-3052
boughbeeches@reveraliving.com
www.reveraliving.com

Year Founded: 1984
Number of Beds: 109 residential capacity
Note: Specialties: Assisted living program; Secured living program, for persons with dementia & Alzheimers disease; Short term stays; Fitness program; Podiatry services
Karen Douglas, Administrator

Mississauga: Erin Mills Lodge
2132 Dundas St. West, Mississauga, ON L5K 2K7
Tel: 905-823-6700; *Fax:* 905-823-2410
info@erinmillscare.com
www.erinmillscare.com

Number of Beds: 141 retirement units, 86 long-term care beds
Mary Whalen, Administrator

Mississauga: King Gardens Retirement Residence
85 King St. East, Mississauga, ON L5A 4G6
Tel: 905-566-4545; *Fax:* 905-566-0327
kinggardens@reveraliving.com
www.reveraliving.com/homes/226

Number of Beds: 147 beds
Agnes Kupny, Executive Director

Morrisburg: Hartford Retirement Centre
3 Fifth St. West, Morrisburg, ON K0C 1X0
Tel: 613-543-3984; *Fax:* 613-543-4262
hartford@chartwellreit.ca
www.chartwellreit.ca

Number of Beds: 67 suites
Lynn Hill, Administrator

Mount Forest: Birmingham Lodge
356A Birmingham St. East, Mount Forest, ON N0G 2L2
Tel: 519-323-4019; *Fax:* 519-323-3005
www.diversicare.ca

Number of Beds: 95 units
Ilonka van Willigen, Administrator

Napanee: The Riverine Independent & Retirement Living
328 Dundas St. West, Napanee, ON K7R 4B5
Tel: 613-354-8188; *Fax:* 613-354-8186
Toll-Free: 866-387-2217

Number of Beds: 42 beds
Note: Specialties: Medication administration; Social & recreational program
Greg Freeman, Manager

Nepean: Riverpark Place Retirement Residence
1 Corkstown Rd., Nepean, ON K2H 1B6
Tel: 613-828-8882; *Fax:* 613-828-8908
info@caregard.ca
www.riverparkplace.ca

Number of Beds: 173 beds (residential care, assisted & daily living)
Cathy Arthurs-Hall, Administrator

Nepean: Stillwater Creek Retirement Community
18 Robertson Rd., Nepean, ON K2H 1C6
Tel: 613-828-7575; *Fax:* 613-828-7524
info@caregard.ca
www.stillwatercreek.ca

Year Founded: 2001
Number of Beds: 204 units
Note: Specialties: Independent living; Assisted living; Recreation programs
Mike Traub, Administrator

Newmarket: Alexander Muir Retirement Residence
197 Prospect St., Newmarket, ON L3Y 3T7
Tel: 905-836-8399; *Fax:* 905-836-9322
mayers@residencesallegro.com
www.residencesallegro.com/en/

Number of Beds: 96 units
Michael Ayers, General Manager

Niagara Falls: Cavendish Manor Retirement Residence
5781 Dunn St., Niagara Falls, ON L2G 2N9
Tel: 905-354-2733; *Fax:* 905-354-4164
www.cavendishmanor.com

Number of Beds: 69 units
Janice Amos, Manager

Niagara Falls: Chippawa Place
4118 Main St., Niagara Falls, ON L2G 6C2
Tel: 905-295-6744; *Fax:* 905-295-6306

Number of Beds: 26 beds
Mark Budic, Administrator
Susan Budic, Administrator

Niagara Falls: Lundy Manor Retirement Residence
7860 Lundy's Lane, Niagara Falls, ON L2H 1H1
Tel: 905-356-1511; *Fax:* 905-356-1736
lundy@reveraliving.com
www.reveraliving.com

Number of Beds: 95 capacity
Note: Specialties: Assisted living program; Short term stays; Podiatry services
Art Derbernardi, Manager

Niagara Falls: Willoughby Manor
Affiliated with: Chartwell Seniors Housing REIT
3584 Bridgewater St., Niagara Falls, ON L2G 6H1
Tel: 905-295-6288; *Fax:* 905-295-4767
willoughbymanor@chartwellreit.ca
www.chartwellreit.ca

Number of Beds: 52 suites
Note: Retirement residence, with convalescent, respite & seasonal stay options
Stephen Suske, CEO, Chartwell Seniors Housing REIT

North Bay: Barclay House Retirement Residence
Affiliated with: Chartwell Seniors Housing REIT
600 Chippewa St. West, North Bay, ON P1B 9E7
Tel: 705-476-6585; *Fax:* 705-476-6542
barclay@chartwellreit.ca
www.chartwellreit.ca

Number of Beds: 64 suites
Stephen Suske, CEO, Chartwell Seniors Housing REIT

Norwood: Maple View Retirement Centre
90 Victoria St., RR#2, Norwood, ON K0L 2V0
Tel: 705-639-5374; *Fax:* 705-639-1793

Number of Beds: 60 beds

Kim Ward, Administrator

Oakville: Churchill Place
345 Church St., Oakville, ON L6J 7G4
Tel: 905-338-3311; *Fax:* 905-338-7117
churchillplace@lrc.ca
www.reveraliving.com
Number of Beds: 69 suites
Note: Independent living, convalescent & respite options
Carole Huppenthal, General Manager

Oakville: The Kensington
25 Lakeshore Rd. West, Oakville, ON L6K 3X8
Tel: 905-844-4000; *Fax:* 905-842-9229
thekensingtonon@lrc.ca
www.reveraliving.com
Number of Beds: 120 suites
Note: Independent living
Judy Martin, General Manager

Oakville: Oakville Senior Citizens Residence
#2220, 2222 Lakeshore Rd. West, Oakville, ON L6L 5G5
Tel: 905-827-4139; *Fax:* 905-827-8047
oscr@oakvilleseniors.com
www.oakvilleseniors.com
Number of Beds: 164 apartment tower units + 172 residential tower rooms

Oakville: Trafalgar Lodge Retirement Residence
299 Randall St., Oakville, ON L6J 6B4
Tel: 905-842-8408; *Fax:* 905-842-8410
trafalgar@reveraliving.com
www.reveraliving.com
Number of Beds: 75 units
Note: Independent & assisted living; convalescent & respite options
Eileen Brajovic, Executive Director

Orangeville: Lord Dufferin Centre
32 First St., Orangeville, ON L9W 2E1
Tel: 519-941-8433; *Fax:* 519-941-2615
www.lorddufferincentre.ca
Number of Beds: 78 private suites
Note: Specialties: Physiotherapy; Foot care
Donna Holwell, Manager

Orillia: Atrium Retirement Residence
230 Coldwater Rd. West, Orillia, ON L3V 3M2
Tel: 705-325-7300; *Fax:* 705-325-9078
atrium@chartwellreit.ca
chartwellreit.ca/home_locations/atrium.htm
Number of Beds: 50 units
Miriam Leduc, Manager

Orillia: Birchmere Retirement Residence
234 Bay St., Orillia, ON L3V 3W8
Tel: 705-326-8520; *Fax:* 705-326-5273
birchmere@on.aibn.com
Number of Beds: 77 beds
Jackie Payne, Administrator

Orillia: Champlain Manor
65 Fittons Rd. West, Orillia, ON L3V 3V2
Tel: 705-326-8597; *Fax:* 705-326-9831
champlainmanor@on.aibn.com
www.retireorillia.com
Number of Beds: 65 beds
Jackie Payne, Administrator

Oshawa: Cedarcroft Place (Oshawa)
649 King St. East, Oshawa, ON L1H 8P9
Tel: 905-723-9490
cedarcroft-oshawa@cplodges.com
Number of Beds: 102 units
Marjorie Beattie, Administrator

Ottawa: Amica at Bearbrook Court
2645 Innes Rd., Ottawa, ON K1B 3J7
Tel: 613-837-8720; *Fax:* 613-837-8107
bearbrook@amica.ca
www.amica.ca/bearbrook/
Number of Beds: 122 suites
Luke Goulette, General Manager

Ottawa: Billings Lodge
1180 Bélanger Ave., Ottawa, ON K1H 8A2
Tel: 613-737-7877; *Fax:* 613-737-7886
Number of Beds: 100 beds
Alain Brunet, Administrator

Ottawa: Blackburn Lodge Seniors Residence Inc.
2412 Cléroux Cres., Ottawa, ON K1W 1A3
Tel: 613-837-7467; *Fax:* 613-837-0250
agraham@blackburnlodge.com
www.blackburnlodge.com
Number of Beds: 53 beds
Alyson Graham, Assistant Manager
David Porter, Manager

Ottawa: Central Park Lodges - Ottawa 1
2374 Carling Ave., Ottawa, ON K2B 7G5
Tel: 613-820-7333; *Fax:* 613-820-6815
ottawa1@reveraliving.com
www.reveraliving.com
Number of Beds: 135 units
Note: Independent & assisted living, respite & convalescent options. Central Park Lodge Ottawa 2 located at 2370 Carling Ave.
Ray Hould, General Manager

Ottawa: Colonel By Retirement Residence
43 Aylmer St., Ottawa, ON K1S 4R5
Tel: 613-730-2002
colonelby@cplodges.com
Number of Beds: 122 units

Ottawa: The Edinburgh Retirement Residence
10 Vaughan St., Ottawa, ON K1M 2H6
Tel: 613-747-2233; *Fax:* 613-747-6741
edinburgh@reveraliving.com
www.reveraliving.com
Number of Beds: 66 beds
Note: Independent & assisted living programs
Mary Albota, Administrator

Ottawa: Hunt Club Manor
1351 Hunt Club Rd., Ottawa, ON K1V 1A6
Tel: 613-733-4776; *Fax:* 613-733-0496
huntclubmanor@reveraliving.com
www.retirementresidences.com/homes/8018/
Number of Beds: 78 beds
Tracy Fowers, General Manager

Ottawa: Manoir Gallien
162 Murray St., Ottawa, ON K1N 5M8
Tel: 613-241-1331; *Fax:* 613-241-2693
info@manoirgalleon.com
Number of Beds: 75 units
Note: Senior's residence
Sandra Sullivan, Administrator

Ottawa: New Edinburgh Square
420 Mackay St., Ottawa, ON K1M 2C4
Tel: 613-744-0901; *Fax:* 613-742-3039
newedinburghsquare@chartwellreit.ca
www.chartwellreit.ca
Number of Beds: 111 suites
Jacqueline Brown, General Manager

Ottawa: Parklane Residence
1095 Merivale Rd., Ottawa, ON K1Z 6A9
Tel: 613-725-1064; *Fax:* 613-728-3533
Number of Beds: 107 beds
Note: Retirement residence
Claude Desforges, Manager

Ottawa: Presland Residence
198 Presland Rd., Ottawa, ON K1K 2B8
Tel: 613-745-0089
Serge Grégoire, Administrator

Ottawa: Rideau Place On-The-River
Affiliated with: Chartwell Seniors Housing REIT
550 Wilbrod St., Ottawa, ON K1N 9M3
Tel: 613-234-6003; *Fax:* 613-234-9498
rideauplace@chartwellreit.ca
www.chartwellreit.ca; www.rideauplace.com
Number of Beds: 98 suites
Note: Retirement residence; short-term respite & convalescent care
Stephen Suske, CEO, Chartwell Seniors Housing REIT
Brian Kimberley, Marketing Manager

Ottawa: Rothwell Heights Retirement Residence
1735 Montréal Rd., Ottawa, ON K1J 6N4
Tel: 613-744-2322
Number of Beds: 114 units
Anita Hurtubise, Administrator

Ottawa: Sandy Hill Retirement Residence
353 Friel St., Ottawa, ON K1N 7W7
Tel: 613-234-3838; *Fax:* 613-234-5472
sandyhill@reveraliving.com
www.reveraliving.com
Number of Beds: 71 beds
Note: Independent & assisting living programs; respite, convalescent options
Mélanie Lefebvre, Executive Director

Ottawa: Sterling Place Retirement Residence
2716 Richmond Rd., Ottawa, ON K2B 8M3
Tel: 613-829-6527; *Fax:* 613-829-6201
sterling@reveraliving.com
www.reveraliving.com
Number of Beds: 116 beds
Note: Independent & assisted living programs; dementia care; respite & convalescent options
Rosemary Rowley, Manager

Ottawa: Stittsville Retirement Community
1354 Stittsville Main St., Ottawa, ON K2S 1V4
Tel: 613-836-2216; *Fax:* 613-836-1903
stittville@reveraliving.com
www.reveraliving.com
Number of Beds: 75 beds
Note: Independent living
Pat Leishman, Manager

Ottawa: Thorncliffe Place Retirement Home
1 Thorncliffe Pl., Ottawa, ON K2H 9N9
Tel: 613-596-3853; *Fax:* 613-596-6225
info@thorncliffeplace.com
www.thorncliffeplace.com
Year Founded: 1989
Number of Beds: 81 suites
Note: Specialties: Activity program; Supervision of medications; Memory support; Elderobics; Convalescent stays
Don Francis, Administrator

Ottawa: Watford House Residence
75 Powell Ave., Ottawa, ON K1S 1Z9
Tel: 613-230-7423; *Fax:* 613-230-9194
Number of Beds: 22 beds
Anatoli Brouchkov, Administrator

Owen Sound: Central Place
855 - 3 Ave. East, Owen Sound, ON N4K 2K6
Tel: 519-371-1968; *Fax:* 519-371-5357
Number of Beds: 90 beds
John Landen, President

Owen Sound: Hannah Walker Place
832 - 2 Ave. West, Owen Sound, ON N4K 4M5
Tel: 519-371-1664; *Fax:* 519-371-5286
Number of Beds: 57 beds
John F. Landen, President

Owen Sound: John Joseph Place
854 - 2 Ave. West, Owen Sound, ON N4K 4M5
Tel: 519-371-3240; *Fax:* 519-371-6441
Number of Beds: 45 beds
Linda Crigger, Facility Manager

Pakenham: Country View Lodge
4676 Darks Side Rd., Pakenham, ON K0A 2X0
Tel: 613-624-5714; *Fax:* 613-624-5715
info@countryviewlodge.ca
www.countryviewlodge.ca
Number of Beds: 34 beds
Note: retirement home with assisted living/nursing service
Abdullah Al Hussain, Administrator

Paris: Penmarvian Retirement Home
185 Grand River St. North, Paris, ON N3L 2N2
Tel: 519-442-7140; *Fax:* 519-442-7156
info@penmarvian.com
www.penmarvian.com
Year Founded: 1980
Number of Beds: 38 beds
Note: Specialties: Nursing care; Activity program
Maria Toncic, Administrator

Perth: Rideau Ferry Country Home
1333, Rideau Ferry Rd., RR#5, Perth, ON K7H 3C7
Tel: 613-267-6213; *Fax:* 613-267-6261
Number of Beds: 45 units
Note: Offers both retirement residences and assisted daily living services
Mary Ross, Administrator

Peterborough: Empress Gardens Retirement Residence
131 Charlotte St., Peterborough, ON K9J 2T6
Tel: 705-876-1314; *Fax:* 705-876-1908
thegardens@aoninc.com
www.gardensofpeterborough.ca
Number of Beds: 88 beds
Joanne Stone, Executive Director

Peterborough: Peterborough Manor
1039 Water St., Peterborough, ON K9H 3P5
Tel: 705-748-5343; *Fax:* 705-876-4741
peterboroughmanor@chartwellreit.ca
www.chartwellreit.ca
Number of Beds: 101 suites
Note: Specialties: Medication administration; Wellness monitoring; Assistance to persons with oxygen, catheters, & ostomies; Activity program; Podiatry; Respite care; Convalescent stays
Martha Creally, Administrator

Peterborough: Princess Gardens Retirement Residence
100 Charlotte St., Peterborough, ON L9J 7L4
Tel: 705-750-1234; *Fax:* 705-750-0711
Toll-Free: 1-866-741-6036
www.princessgardens.ca
Number of Beds: 132 beds
Note: Independent retirement amenities; assisted living/enriched care options; respite & convalescent care
Juris Taurins, Manager

Pickering: Community Nursing Home
1955 Valley Farm Rd., Pickering, ON L1V 1X6
Tel: 905-831-2522; *Fax:* 905-420-6030
jbrantonwallace@clmi.ca
Number of Beds: 233 long-term care beds, 61 retirement suites
Joan Branton Wallace, Administrator

Port Hope: Port Hope Villa
65 Ward St., Port Hope, ON L1A 1L8
Tel: 905-885-2915; *Fax:* 905-885-2921
ldukes@communitylifecare.on.ca
Number of Beds: 33 beds
Leslie Dukes, Administrator

Port Hope: The Tower of Port Hope Retirement Residence
Affiliated with: Chartwell Seniors Housing REIT
164 Peter St., Port Hope, ON L1A 1C6
Tel: 905-885-7261; *Fax:* 905-885-1519
towerofporthope@chartwellreit.ca
www.chartwellreit.ca
Number of Beds: 44 suites
Stephen Suske, CEO, Chartwell Seniors Housing REIT
Julie Inglis, Administrator

Port Perry: West Shore Village
293 Perry St., Port Perry, ON L9L 1S6
Tel: 905-985-8660; *Fax:* 905-985-1881
Toll-Free: 1-800-248-0848
info@westshorevillage.ca
www.westshorevillage.ca
Number of Beds: 71 suites
Note: Specialties: Supported living for seniors; Foot care; Reflexology; Massage therapy; Recreational program; Respite care
Karen Arbuckle, Manager

Renfrew: Quail Creek Retirement Centre
450 Albert St., Renfrew, ON K7V 4K4
Tel: 613-432-9502; *Fax:* 613-432-9533
quailcreek@chartwellreit.ca
www.chartwellreit.ca
Number of Beds: 58 beds
Bev Powell, Administrator

Richmond: Richmond Lodge Ltd.
PO Box 1030, 6197 Perth St., Richmond, ON K0A 2Z0
Tel: 613-838-5016; *Fax:* 613-838-5017
info@richmondlodge.ca
www.richmondlodge.ca
Number of Beds: 42 beds
Note: Retirement residence
Claudette Richel, Administrator

Richmond Hill: Brookside/Hilltop Retirement Residence
980 Elgin Mills Rd. East, Richmond Hill, ON L4S 1M4
Tel: 905-884-9248; *Fax:* 905-884-9745
brooksideplace@reveraliving.com
www.retirementresidences.com/homes/208
Number of Beds: 140 units
Sandra Fernandez, Executive Director

Rockland: Résidence Jardins Bellerive
2950 Laurier St., Rockland, ON K4K 1T3
Tel: 613-446-7122; *Fax:* 613-446-7343
Number of Beds: 80 Units
Youri Brouchkov, Administrator

Rockland: Résidence Simon Inc.
845, rue St-Jean, Rockland, ON K4K 1K5
Tél: 613-446-7023; *Téléc:* 613-446-4867
Nombre de lits: 46 lits
Albert Bourdeau, Propriétaire

Sarnia: Marshall Gowland Manor
749 Devine St., Sarnia, ON N7T 1X3
Tel: 519-336-3720; *Fax:* 519-336-3734
www.lambtononline.com
Year Founded: 2004
Number of Beds: 126 beds
Note: Specialties: Long-term care; Day programs
Jackie Miller, Resident Manager

Sarnia: Residence on The St. Clair
Affiliated with: Steeves & Rozema Group
170 Front St. South, Sarnia, ON N7T 2M5
Tel: 519-336-1455; *Fax:* 519-336-8966
cathy_mcintosh@srgroup.ca
www.srgroup.ca
Number of Beds: 73 beds
Note: Independent living, convalescent & respite options
Cathy McIntosh, Managing Director

Sarnia: Rosewood Manor
Affiliated with: Steeves & Rozema Group
711 Indian Rd. North, Sarnia, ON N7T 7Z5
Tel: 519-332-8877; *Fax:* 519-332-5047
heather_taylor@srgroup.ca
www.srgroup.ca
Number of Beds: 55 beds
Note: Independent & assisted living
Heather Taylor, Executive Director

Sault Ste Marie: Pathways Retirement Residence
Former Name: Pathways Seniors Residence
375 Trunk Rd., Sault Ste Marie, ON P6A 6T5
Tel: 705-759-1079; *Fax:* 705-759-1211
info@pathwaysret.com
www.pathwaysret.com
Number of Beds: 133 beds
Elaine Robertson, Administrator

Sault Ste Marie: Windsor Park Retirement Residence
617 Queen St. East, Sault Ste Marie, ON P6A 2A6
Tel: 705-949-2273; *Fax:* 705-949-2279
Number of Beds: 75 beds
Nat Cicchelli, Administrator

Seaforth: Maplewood Manor
13 Church St., Seaforth, ON N0K 1W0
Tel: 519-527-1440

Simcoe: Heritage Lodge
182 Norfolk St. South, Simcoe, ON N3Y 2W4
Tel: 519-428-0930; *Fax:* 519-428-9103
Annemarie Barker, Administrator

Smiths Falls: Willowdale Retirement Centre
Affiliated with: Chartwell Seniors Housing REIT
9 Armstrong Dr., Smiths Falls, ON K7A 5H7
Tel: 613-283-0691; *Fax:* 613-283-0350
willowdale@chartwellreit.ca
www.chartwellreit.ca
Number of Beds: 59 suites
Stephen Suske, CEO, Chartwell Seniors Housing REIT

St Catharines: The Loyalist Retirement Residence
190 King St., St Catharines, ON L2R 3J7
Tel: 905-641-4422; *Fax:* 905-641-4989
loyalist@reveraliving.com
www.retirementresidences.com
Number of Beds: 118 residential capacity
Note: Specialties: Assisted living; Nursing supervision; Medication administration; Podiatry services; Recreation & fitness program; Respite care; Convalescent stays
Lydia Tarasiuk, Administrator

St Catharines: Mount Carmel Home
78 Yates St., St Catharines, ON L2R 5R9
Tel: 905-685-9155
Year Founded: 1920
Number of Beds: 69 beds
Note: seniors residence
M. Anne, Administrator

St Catharines: Tufford Manor Retirement Home
312 Queenston Rd., St Catharines, ON L2P 2X4
Tel: 905-682-0411; *Fax:* 905-682-2770
www.hamptontufford.com
Note: Specialties: Short term stays Medication administration
Mike Walter, Administrator
Maria Soares, Director, Housekeeping/Maintenance

St Thomas: Metcalfe Gardens Retirement Residence
45 Metcalfe St., St Thomas, ON N5R 5Y1
Tel: 519-631-9393; *Fax:* 519-631-2563
www.diversicare.ca
Year Founded: 1988
Number of Beds: 97 suites
Note: Specialties: Foot care; Physiotherapy; Recreation programs; Respite care
Deborah Geerlinks, Administrator

St. Joachim: St. Joachim Manor
2718 County Rd. 42, St. Joachim, ON N0R 1S0
Tel: 519-728-1215; *Fax:* 519-728-0113
Number of Beds: 23 beds
Zlatko Horvat, Owner
Nada Horvat, Owner

Stoney Creek: Stoney Creek Retirement Residence
199 Glover Rd., Stoney Creek, ON L8E 5J2
Tel: 905-643-1795; *Fax:* 905-643-1085
www.ourhomeyourhomecanada.ca
Year Founded: 1994
Number of Beds: 39 units
Note: Specialties: Activity program; Catheter care; Colostomy care; Oxygen care; Diabetes care; Medication administration; Wellness program
Genny Lourenco, Retirement Manager

Stratford: Anne Hathaway Residence
Former Name: The Griffin Residence
480 Downie St., Stratford, ON N5A 7Y5
Tel: 519-275-2125; *Fax:* 519-275-2126
annehathaway@chartwellreit.ca
Number of Beds: 68 beds
Dianne Roth, Administrator

Stratford: Cedarcroft Place Retirement Home
260 Church St., Stratford, ON N5A 2R6
Tel: 519-275-0030; *Fax:* 519-273-0373
cedarcroft-stratford@cplodges.com
Number of Beds: 110 units
Daniel Vito, Administrator

Sudbury: Hillside Park Retirement Residence
82 Ignatius St., Sudbury, ON P3C 5G3
Tel: 705-675-1999; *Fax:* 705-675-8233
Number of Beds: 69 beds
Anil Pabani, Administrator

Sudbury: Westmount Retirement Residence
Affiliated with: Chartwell Seniors Housing REIT
599 William Ave., Sudbury, ON P3A 5W3
Tel: 705-566-6221; *Fax:* 705-566-0808
westmount@chartwellreit.ca
www.chartwellreit.ca
Number of Beds: 84 suites
Stephen Suske, CEO, Chartwell Seniors Housing REIT

Temiskaming Shores: Northdale Manor
PO Box 370, 142-130 Lakeshore Rd., Temiskaming Shores, ON P0J 1P0
Tel: 705-647-6541; *Fax:* 705-647-8284
nordale@ntl.sympatico.ca
www.northdalemanor.ca
Number of Beds: 70 suites
Note: Retirement home
Jan Edwards, Administrator

Thornhill: Glynnwood Retirement Residence
7700 Bayview Ave., Thornhill, ON L3T 5W1
Tel: 905-881-9475; *Fax:* 905-881-9490
glynnwood@on.aibn.com
Number of Beds: 143 units
Paul Mitchell, Administrator

Thorold: Chestnut Court Retirement Home
10 Ormond St. North, Thorold, ON L2V 1Y7
Tel: 905-227-5550; *Fax:* 905-227-5575
info@chestnuthome.com
www.chestnuthome.com
Number of Beds: 50 beds

Elizabeth Dumoulin, Administrator

Tilbury: Hudson Manor
PO Box 1150, 36 Lawson St., Tilbury, ON N0P 2L0
Tel: 519-682-3366; *Fax:* 519-682-0688
douellette.hm@diversicare.ca
Number of Beds: 50 beds
Debbie Ouellette, Administrator

Tillsonburg: Tillsonburg Retirement Centre
Affiliated with: Chartwell Seniors Housing REIT
183 Rolph St., Tillsonburg, ON N4G 3Y9
Tel: 519-688-0347; *Fax:* 519-688-2471
tillsonburgretirement@chartwellreit.ca
www.chartwellreit.ca
Number of Beds: 51 suites
Stephen Suske, CEO, Chartwell Seniors Housing REIT

Timmins: Chateau Georgian Retirement Residence
455 Cedar St. North, Timmins, ON P4N 8K4
Tel: 705-267-7935
chateaugeorgian@chartwellreit.ca
www.chartwellreit.ca
Number of Beds: 63 suites
Note: Specialties: Wellness monitoring; Physical therapy; Recreation therapy; Podiatry; Respite care; Convalescent stays
Lynn Budd, Manager

Toronto: The Annex Retirement Residence
123 Spadina Rd., Toronto, ON M5R 2T1
Tel: 416-961-6446; *Fax:* 416-961-3299
theannex@reveraliving.com
www.reveraliving.com
Number of Beds: 102 beds
Note: Independent & assisted living, secured living for dementia care
Maria Silva, General Manager

Toronto: The Balmoral Club
155 Balmoral Ave., Toronto, ON M4V 1J5
Tel: 416-927-0055; *Fax:* 416-927-0925
balmoralclub@amica.ca
www.amica.ca
Number of Beds: 66 beds
Monica Byrne, Administrator

Toronto: Baycrest Centre for Geriatric Care
Terraces of Baycrest
55 Ameer Ave., Toronto, ON M6A 2Z1
Tel: 416-785-2500; *Fax:* 416-785-2496
mjacobson@baycrest.org
www.baycrest.org
Info Line: 416-785-2379
Number of Beds: 199 Apartments
Note: supportive living
Sheila Smyth, Director

Toronto: Baycrest Centre for Geriatric Care
3560 Bathurst St., Toronto, ON M6A 2E1
Tel: 416-785-2500; *Fax:* 416-785-2464
swherbert@baycrest.org
www.baycrest.org
Number of Beds: 300 beds
Stephen W. Herbert, President/CEO

Toronto: Beach Arms Retirement Residence
505 Kingston Rd., Toronto, ON M4L 1V5
Tel: 416-698-0414; *Fax:* 416-698-9839
info@beacharms.com
www.beacharms.com
Number of Beds: 80 beds
Susan Turner, Administrator

Toronto: Belmont House
55 Belmont St., Toronto, ON M5R 1R1
Tel: 416-964-9231; *Fax:* 416-964-1448
information@belmonthouse.com
www.belmonthouse.com
Number of Beds: 55 apartments, 26 retirement suites; 140 long-term care beds
Note: Total employees: 28
Maria Elias, Chief Executive Officer
melias@belmonthouse.com

Toronto: Centennial Park Place Retirement Residence
Former Name: Meadowcroft Place Retirement Residence
25 Centennial Park Rd., Toronto, ON M9C 5H1
Tel: 416-621-2139; *Fax:* 416-621-9801
centennial@reveraliving.com
www.reveraliving.com
Number of Beds: 48 residential capacity
Note: Specialty: Podiatry services; Fitness program
Naida McKechnie, Manager

Toronto: Central Park Lodges - Queens Drive 1
265 Queens Dr., Toronto, ON M6L 3C6
Tel: 416-241-1113; *Fax:* 416-241-1801
queensdr2@reveraliving.com
www.reveraliving.com
Number of Beds: 113 beds
Note: Independent & assisted living, respite & convalescent options. Central Park Lodge Queens Drive 2 located at 303 Queens Drive
Brenda MacCallum, General Manager

Toronto: Central Park Lodges - Queens Drive 2
303 Queens Dr., Toronto, ON M6L 3C1
Tel: 416-241-1113; *Fax:* 416-241-1801
queensdr2@reveraliving.com
www.reveraliving.com
Number of Beds: 156 units
Note: Independent & assisted living. Central Park Lodge Queens Drive 1 located at 265 Queens Drive
L. Kabot, Administrator

Toronto: Don Mills Seniors' Apartments
1055-1057 Don Mills Rd., Toronto, ON M3C 1W9
Tel: 416-445-7555; *Fax:* 416-445-0417
donmillsseniorsapts@lrc.ca
www.reveraliving.com/homes/8005/
Number of Beds: 143 suites
Erik Smith, General Manager

Toronto: Donway Place
8 The Donway East, Toronto, ON M3C 3R7
Tel: 416-445-7555; *Fax:* 416-445-0417
donway.place@lrc.ca
www.reveraliving.com/homes/8006/
Number of Beds: 245 suites
Erik Smith, Administrator

Toronto: Eden Manor
251 St George St., Toronto, ON M5R 2M2
Tel: 416-515-1136; *Fax:* 416-515-1137
edenmanor@bellnet.ca
www.edenmanor.ca
Number of Beds: 25 beds
W. Boggs, Administrator

Toronto: Fellowship Towers
877 Yonge St., Toronto, ON M4W 3M2
Tel: 416-923-8887; *Fax:* 416-923-1343
inquiries@fellowshiptowers.com
www.fellowshiptowers.com
Number of Beds: 284 beds
Marilyn Burton, Administrator
mburton@fellowshiptowers.com

Toronto: Forest Hill Place
645 Castlefield Ave., Toronto, ON M5N 3A5
Tel: 416-785-1511; *Fax:* 416-785-6228
fh.mkg@lrc.ca
www.lrc.ca
Number of Beds: 125 suites

Toronto: Glebe Manor Retirement Residence
17 Glebe Rd. West, Toronto, ON M5P 1C8
Tel: 416-485-1150; *Fax:* 416-485-6378
J.T. Whitebread, Administrator

Toronto: Grenadier Retirement Residence
2100 Bloor St. West, Toronto, ON M6S 1M7
Tel: 416-769-2885; *Fax:* 416-769-7238
www.thegrenadier.com
Note: Specialties: Physiotherapy; Wellness program; Activity program; Medication administration; Short-term stays
Dwight Mountney, Administrator

Toronto: Harold & Grace Baker Centre
1 Northwestern Ave., Toronto, ON M6M 2J7
Tel: 416-654-2889; *Fax:* 416-654-0217
bakercentre@reveraliving.com
www.reveraliving.com
Number of Beds: 233 beds
Milena Sujer, Administrator
Owen Shaw, Manager, Environmental Services

Toronto: Hazelton Place
111 Avenue Rd., Toronto, ON M5R 3J8
Tel: 416-928-0111; *Fax:* 416-928-0118
www.hazeltonplace.ca
Number of Beds: 130 units
Lillian Russell, General Manager

Toronto: Lansing Retirement Residence
10 Senlac Rd., Toronto, ON M2N 6P8
Tel: 416-250-7029; *Fax:* 416-250-7853
Number of Beds: 110 beds
Jill Estioko, Manager

Toronto: Leaside Retirement Residence
10 William Morgan Dr., Toronto, ON M4H 1E7
Tel: 416-425-3722; *Fax:* 416-425-3946
leaside@reveraliving.com
www.reveraliving.com
Number of Beds: 211 beds
Note: Secured living for dementia care
P. Lemdal, General Manager

Toronto: Livingston Lodge Retirement Residence
65 Livingston Rd., Toronto, ON M1E 1L1
Tel: 416-264-4348; *Fax:* 416-264-4340
www.residencesallegro.com
Number of Beds: 103 capacity
Note: Specialities: Physiotherapy; Foot care
Janet Iwaszozenko, Executive Director

Toronto: McNicoll Manor
1020 McNicoll Ave., Toronto, ON M1W 2J6
Tel: 416-499-3313; *Fax:* 416-499-3379
www.tendercare.ca
Note: Specialties: Physiotherapy
Maureen McAlaster, Coordinator

Toronto: New Horizons Tower
1140 Bloor St. West, Toronto, ON M6H 4E6
Tel: 416-536-6111; *Fax:* 416-536-6748
welcome@newhorizonstower.com
www.newhorizonstower.com
Number of Beds: 197 beds
Note: Christian nursing home
Ian C. Logan, Administrator

Toronto: Pine Villa Retirement Residence
1035 Eglinton Ave. West, Toronto, ON M6C 2C8
Tel: 416-787-5626; *Fax:* 416-787-3441
pinevilla@reveraliving.com
www.reveraliving.com
Number of Beds: 71 units
Note: Specialties: Medication administration; Assistance for residents who require oxygen, catheters, & ostomies; Physiotherapy; Podiatry; Recreation therapy
Sharon Rosenblum, Executive Director

Toronto: Rayoak Place Retirement Residence
Also Known As: Meadowcroft Place
1340 York Mills Rd., Toronto, ON M3A 3R1
Tel: 416-391-0633; *Fax:* 416-391-3320
rayoakplace@reveraliving.com
www.reveraliving.com
Number of Beds: 66 beds
Note: Independent & assisted living
Linda Mullins, Manager

Toronto: Shepherd Terrace Retirement Suites
3758 Sheppard Ave. East, Toronto, ON M1T 3K9
Tel: 416-609-5700; *Fax:* 416-293-6229
www.shepherdvillage.org
Number of Beds: 144 units, including 112 assisted living suites
Brock Hall, Administrator

Toronto: Spencer House
36 Spencer Rd., Toronto, ON M6K 2J6
Tel: 416-531-5737; *Fax:* 416-531-4722
dsquires@leisureworld.ca
www.leisureworld.ca
Number of Beds: 120 long-term care; 58 retirement beds
Donald Squires, Administrator

Toronto: Terrace Gardens Retirement Residence
3705 Bathurst St., Toronto, ON M6A 2E8
Tel: 416-789-7670; *Fax:* 416-789-3372
terrace@reveraliving.com
www.reveraliving.com
Note: Jewish retirement residence; independent & assisted living, secured living for dementia care, convalescent & respite options; COR supervised, mashgiach on site

Utterson: Rowanwood Retirement Residence
81 Rowanwood Rd., Utterson, ON P0B 1M0
Tel: 705-789-6424; *Fax:* 705-789-1821
rowanwood@cplodges.com
Number of Beds: 86 beds
Gail Sargeant, Manager

Vankleek Hill: Heritage Lodge Retirement Residence
Former Name: Vankleek Residence
48 Wall St., Vankleek Hill, ON K0B 1R0
Tel: 613-678-2690; *Fax:* 613-678-6760
vankleek@reveraliving.com

Number of Beds: 72 beds
Sandra McCormick, Executive Director

Varry's Bay: Water Tower Lodge
9 Stafford St., Varry's Bay, ON K0J 1B0
Tel: 613-756-9086
watertowerlodge@nrtco.net
www.watertowerlodge.com

Number of Beds: 44 units

Vineland: The Orchards Retirement Residence
Heritage Village, 3421 Frederick Ave., Vineland, ON L0R 2C0
Tel: 905-562-7357; *Fax:* 905-562-3051
Toll-Free: 800-263-4957
www.residencesallegro.com

Year Founded: 1999
Note: Specialties: Medication management; Personal care assistance; Activities program; Physiotherapy; Respite & convalescence care
Bonnie Magwood, Administrator

Walkerton: Maple Court Villa
5 Fourth St., Walkerton, ON N0G 2V0
Tel: 519-881-2233; *Fax:* 519-881-0336
maplecourt@chartwellreit.ca

Number of Beds: 47 Suites
Note: Nursing home
JoAnn Todd, Administrator

Waterloo: Lutherwood
Luther Village on the Park
139 Father David Bauer Dr., Waterloo, ON N2L 6L1
Tel: 519-747-4413
www.luthervillage.org

Note: Specialties: Assisted living

Waterloo: Terrace on the Square
Affiliated with: Chartwell Seniors Housing REIT
100 Caroline St. South, Waterloo, ON N2L 1X5
Tel: 519-749-2888; *Fax:* 519-749-1674
terraceonthesquare@chartwellreit.ca
www.chartwellreit.ca

Number of Beds: 88 suites
Stephen Suske, CEO, Chartwell Seniors Housing REIT

Windsor: Central Park Lodge - Windsor
3387 Riverside Dr. East, Windsor, ON N8Y 1A8
Tel: 519-948-5293; *Fax:* 519-948-7513
windsor@reveraliving.com
www.reveraliving.com

Number of Beds: 141 units
Note: Independent & assisted living, secured living for dementia care, respite & convalescent options
Jean Piccinato, General Manager
Marc St. Pierre, Manager, Physical Plant

Windsor: Devonshire Seniors' Residence
901 Riverside Dr. West, Windsor, ON N9A 7J6
Tel: 519-252-2273; *Fax:* 519-252-2324
Toll-Free: 877-521-5686
info@devonshireseniors.com
www.orca-homes.com

Number of Beds: 259 beds
Sharon Woodward, General Manager

Wingham: Braemar Retirement Centre
719 Josephine St. North, Wingham, ON N0G 2W0
Tel: 519-357-3430; *Fax:* 519-357-2303
Toll-Free: 1-888-817-5828
info@braemar-rc.com
www.braemar-rc.com

Number of Beds: 25 beds
Archie Macgowan, Administrator
519/357-3430 ext.224, macgowana@hurontel.on.ca
M.C. MacGowan, President/CEO
519/357-3430 ext.235, mcmacgowan@braemar-rc.com

Mental Health Facilities

Mental Health Hospitals/Facilities

Aurora: Southdown Institute
1335 St. John's Rd. East, Aurora, ON L4G 3G8
Tel: 905-727-4214; *Fax:* 905-727-4214
administration@southdown.on.ca; assessment@southdown.on.ca
www.southdown.on.ca

Number of Beds: 44 beds
Note: Specialties: Residential & outpatient psychological treatment to clergy & religious; Psychodynamic group therapy; Individual & group addiction counselling; 12-step groups; Specialized group treatment for persons who have violated sexual boundaries; Art therapy; Health education
Dr. Raymond Dlugos, CEO

Blenheim: Southwestern Regional Centre
RR#1, Blenheim, ON N0P 1A0
Tel: 519-676-6001; *Fax:* 519-676-5836

Number of Beds: 496 beds
Poul Christensen, Administrator

Brockville: Brockville Mental Health Centre
Former Name: Brockville Psychiatric Hospital
PO Box 1050, 1804 Hwy. 2 East, Brockville, ON K6V 5W7
Tel: 613-345-1461; *Fax:* 613-342-6194
www.rohcg.on.ca

Number of Beds: 200 beds
George Weber, President/CEO

Fergus: Community Mental Health Clinic
234 St. Patrick St. East, Fergus, ON N1M 1M6
Tel: 519-843-6191; *Fax:* 519-265-7723

Dr. V. Lediett, Executive Director

Guelph: Homewood Health Centre
150 Delhi St., Guelph, ON N1E 6K9
Tel: 519-824-1010; *Fax:* 519-824-8751
www.homewood.org/healthcentre/main.php

Year Founded: 1883
Number of Beds: 312 beds
Note: Number of Employees: 650; Specialty: Behavioural, addiction & psychiatric services
W. Sheppard, Director, Environmental Services
Dr. Edgardo L. Pérez, CEO; Chief of Staff

Hamilton: St. Joseph's Centre for Mountain Health Services
PO Box 585, 100 - 5 St. West, Hamilton, ON L8N 3K7
Tel: 905-388-2511; *Fax:* 905-575-6038
www.stjosham.on.ca

Number of Beds: 165 beds
Darlene Barnes, Vice-President
Al Manente, Director, Plant Services
Zenek J. Dybka, Assistant, Hospital Services

Kingston: Ongwanada Hospital
191 Portsmouth Ave., Kingston, ON K7M 8A6
Tel: 613-548-4417; *Fax:* 613-548-8135
www.ongwanada.com

Year Founded: 1948
Number of Beds: 227 beds
Note: Specialties: Support for persons with developmental disabilities; Day support; Medical services; Vocational & life skills training; Occupational therapy; Physiotherapy; Hydrotherapy; Snoezelen rRoom; Community behavioural services; Respite care; Research. Number of employees: 494
Robert W. Seaby, Executive Director

Kingston: Providence Care - Mental Health Services
Former Name: Kingston Psychiatric Hospital
PO Box 603, 752 King St., Kingston, ON K7L 4X3
Tel: 613-546-1101; *Fax:* 613-548-5588
prowsea@providencecare.ca
www.pccchealth.org

Number of Beds: 198 beds
Note: Adult Treatment & Rehabilitation, Geriatric Psychiatry, Forensic Psychiatry
Allen Prowse, Vice President, Mental Health; Administrator

London: Child & Parent Resource Institute
600 Sanatorium Rd., London, ON N6H 3W7
Tel: 519-858-2774; *Fax:* 519-858-3913

Number of Beds: 75 beds
Anne Stark, Administrator

London: Regional Mental Healthcare, London
Affiliated with: St. Joseph's Health Care, London
PO Box 5532 B, 850 Highbury Ave., London, ON N6A 4H1
Tel: 519-455-5110; *Fax:* 519-455-9986
Communications.Department@sjhc.london.on.ca
www.sjhc.london.on.ca

Number of Beds: 385 beds

North Bay: Northeast Mental Health Centre
Former Name: North Bay Psychiatric Hospital
PO Box 3010, 4700 Hwy. 11 North, North Bay, ON P1B 8L1
Tel: 705-474-1200; *Fax:* 705-472-1694
www.nemhc.on.ca

W. Duguette, Chief Engineer/Maintenance Supervisor

Oakville: Central West Specialized Developmental Services
Former Name: Oaklands Regional Centre
53 Bond St., Oakville, ON L6K 1L8
Tel: 905-844-7864; *Fax:* 905-844-3545
sbadali@cwsds.ca

Year Founded: 2006
Note: Specialties: Care & support to persons with multiple developmental disabilities; Basic life skill development; Psychiatry; Behaviour therapy; Occupational therapy; Speech therapy; Respite care
Jim Preston, Director

Ottawa: Royal Ottawa Health Care Group
1145 Carling Ave., Ottawa, ON K1Z 7K4
Tel: 613-722-6521; *Fax:* 613-722-4577
www.rohcg.on.ca

Number of Beds: 199 beds (Royal Ottawa Hospital)
Bruce Swan, CEO
Jerry Rogers, Director, Environmental Services

Penetanguishene: Penetanguishene Mental Health Centre
500 Church St., Penetanguishene, ON L9M 1G3
Tel: 705-549-3181; *Fax:* 705-549-1549
www.mhcva.on.ca

W. Gregoire, Manager, Plant Services

St Thomas: Regional Mental Health Care, St. Thomas
Affiliated with: St. Joseph's Health Care, London
PO Box 2004, 467 Sunset Dr., St Thomas, ON N5P 3V9
Tel: 519-631-8510; *Fax:* 519-633-0852
Communications.Department@sjhc.london.on.ca
www.sjhc.london.on.ca

Number of Beds: 145 beds

Sudbury: Northeast Mental Health Centre
Sudbury Campus
680 Kirkwood Dr., Sudbury, ON P3E 1X3
Tel: 705-675-9193; *Fax:* 705-675-6817
dchateauvert@nemhc.on.ca
www.nemhc.on.ca

Number of Beds: 12 children's beds
Robert Cunningham, CEO

Sudbury: Sudbury Regional Hospital - Kirkwood Site
Hôpital régional de Sudbury - Emplacement Kirkwood
680 Kirkwood Dr., Sudbury, ON P3E 1X3
Tel: 705-675-9193; *Toll-Free:* 1-866-469-0822
communications@hrsrh.on.ca
www.hrsrh.on.ca

Note: Acute inpatient psychiatry services
Vickie Kaminiski, CEO
Chris McKibbon, Chief of Staff

Thunder Bay: Lakehead Psychiatric Hospital
PO Box 2930, 580 Algoma St. North, Thunder Bay, ON P7B 5G4
Tel: 807-343-4300; *Fax:* 807-343-4387
Toll-Free: 800-209-9034
www.sjcg.net/services/mentalhealth/lph/

Dawn Eccles, Coordinator, Environmental Services

Toronto: Bellwood Health Services Inc.
1020 McNicoll Ave., Toronto, ON M1W 2J6
Tel: 416-495-0926; *Fax:* 416-495-7943
Toll-Free: 800-387-6198
info@bellwood.ca
www.bellwood.ca

Note: Specialties: Treatment & education for persons who struggle with addictions, such as alcohol & drugs, eating disorders, post traumatic stress disorder, problem gambling, & problematic sexual behaviour; Assessment; Withdrawal management services; Residential treatment program for persons with alcohol addiction; 12-step education & support groups; Life skills coaching; Stress management; Group therapy; Nutritional education & counselling
M. Linda Bell, Chief Executive Officer
Laura Bhoi, President
Janet Lansche, Vice-President, Finance & Administration
Susan McGrail, Director, Clinical Services
Dr. Mark Weiss, Medical Director
Mani Alcaide, Manager, Nursing
Michael Hartmann, Manager, Continuing Care & Volunteer Services
Penny Lawson, Manager, Family Services & Special Programs

***Toronto:* Thistletown Regional Centre for Children & Adolescents**
51 Panorama Ct., Toronto, ON M9V 4L8
Tel: 416-326-0600; *Fax:* 416-326-9078
Note: Specialties: Counselling for children & youth up to 19 years of age; Family assessment & therapy; Treatment & education for youth with autism & developmental disorders; Sexual abuse treatment & family education; Home support; Outpatient services
Dr. Gail Gonda, Administrator

***Toronto:* Toronto East General Hospital (COS) Community Outreach Services**
#203, 177 Danforth Ave., Toronto, ON M4K 1N2
Tel: 416-461-2000; *Fax:* 416-461-2222
ptrep@tegh.on.ca (Patients); community@tegh.on.ca (Community)
www.tegh.on.ca
Note: Specialties: Community based mental health services; Counselling to adults; Supported housing; Psychiatric treatment; Psycho-social rehabilitation; Family support program; Community & school outreach program

***Whitby:* Whitby Mental Health Centre**
700 Gordon St., Whitby, ON L1N 5S9
Tel: 905-668-5881; *Fax:* 905-430-4032
Toll-Free: 1-800-341-6323
communications@wmhc.ca
www.whitbymentalhealthcentre.ca
Note: Specialized, tertiary mental health care on an inpatien/outpatient basis. Residences in Stouffville, Oshawa; community service sites in Newmarket, Georgina, Maple, Uxbridge, Port Perry, Bowmanville, Lindsay & Whitby. Number of staff: 1,200
Glenna Raymond, President/CEO

Special Care Homes

***Aurora:* Kerry's Place Autism Services**
#190, 34 Berczy St., Aurora, ON L4G 1W9
Tel: 905-841-6611; *Fax:* 905-841-1461
www.kerrysplace.com
Year Founded: 1974
Note: autistic adults home
Dr. Glenn Rampton, Executive Director
grampton@kerrysplace.org

***Belleville:* Cheshire Homes - Hastings-Prince Edward**
246 John St., Belleville, ON K8N 3G1
Tel: 613-966-2941; *Fax:* 613-966-2461
cheshirehomes@on.aibn.com
T. Wylie-Meyers, Director

***Brantford:* Participation House Brantford**
PO Box 2048, 10 Bell Lane, Brantford, ON N3T 5W5
Tel: 519-756-1430; *Fax:* 519-756-0795
www.participationhousebrantford.org
Number of Beds: 30 beds
Note: Non-for-profit organization serving the needs of adults with physical disabilities
Steve Leighfield, Executive Director

***Campbellford:* Wingfield**
RR#3, Campbellford, ON K0L 1L0
Tel: 705-653-3127
wingfieldhome@sympatico.ca
www.wingfieldhome.com
Number of Beds: 24 beds
Note: private home for developmentally handicapped adults
W. Klompmaker, Administrator
J. Shelley, Administrator

***Cochrane:* Cochrane Community Living**
PO Box 2330, Cochrane, ON P0L 1C0
Tel: 705-272-5365; *Fax:* 705-272-4983
iccl@msicafe.com
Number of Beds: 12 beds in 3 facilities
Mac Hiltz, Interim Executive Director

***Collingwood:* Canford House**
695 St. Marie St., Collingwood, ON L9Y 3L4
Tel: 705-445-5203; *Fax:* 705-445-7357
Number of Beds: 32 beds
Wayne Canning, Administrator

***Cornwall:* Mains Ouvertes/Open Hands**
123 Pick St., Cornwall, ON K6J 3P5
Tel: 613-933-0012; *Fax:* 613-932-5134
Number of Beds: 27 beds
Gerry Miller, Executive Director

***Dryden:* Patricia Gardens Care Home**
#100, 35 Van Horne Ave., Dryden, ON P8N 3B4
Tel: 807-223-5278

***Gravenhurst:* Val-Glo Home for Special Care**
Doe Lake Rd., RR#3, Gravenhurst, ON P1P 1R3
Tel: 705-687-6285
Number of Beds: 14 beds
Dianne Rivers, Administrator

***Hamilton:* Lynwood Hall Child & Family Centre**
526 Upper Paradise Rd., Hamilton, ON L9C 5E3
Tel: 905-389-1361; *Fax:* 905-389-8765
www.lynwoodhall.com
Note: Specialties: Mental health services, including day treatment, home-based services, & residential services
Alex Thomson, Executive Director

***Hanmer:* Kingsley Residential Home**
PO Box 118, 36 Oscar St., Hanmer, ON P3P 1X6
Tel: 705-969-5538
Number of Beds: 6 beds
Jeannine Kingsley, Proprietor

***Hanover:* HARC Inc.**
521 - 11th Ave., Hanover, ON N4N 2J3
Tel: 519-364-6100; *Fax:* 519-364-7488
harcinc@bmts.com
Number of Beds: 15 beds
Charlie Caudle, Executive Director

***Holland Landing:* Cedar Lane Residential Home Inc.**
19704 Holland Landing Rd., Holland Landing, ON L9N 1M8
Tel: 905-836-4272

***Keswick:* Pipe & Slipper Home**
2926 Old Homestead Rd., Keswick, ON L4P 3E9
Tel: 905-476-3601

***Kilworthy:* Trentview House**
1647 Kilworthy Rd., RR#1, Kilworthy, ON P0E 1G0
Tel: 705-689-5685; *Fax:* 705-689-5844
trentviewhouse@encode.com
Year Founded: 1979
Number of Beds: 25 beds
Note: Specialties: Services for adults with mental health disabilities

***Kirkfield:* Silver Hills Residential Home**
PO Box 63, Kirkfield, ON K0M 2B0
Tel: 705-438-3556; *Fax:* 705-438-3556
Number of Beds: 12 beds
Barbara Brown, Administrator

***Kitchener:* Beattie Residential Home**
251 Queen St. South, Kitchener, ON N2G 1W4
Tel: 519-743-0047
Number of Beds: 20 beds
Kathy Beattie, Administrator

***Kitchener:* Smith Residential Home**
226 Queen St. South, Kitchener, ON N2P 2P7
Tel: 519-743-5117
jvos@sunbeamlodge.com
Number of Beds: 26 beds
Pat Smith, Executive Director

***Kitchener:* Sunbeam Lodge**
389 Pinnacle Dr., Kitchener, ON N2G 3W5
Tel: 519-896-6718
teena@sunbeamlodge.com
www.sunbeamlodge.com
Number of Beds: 22 beds
Note: Specialties: Lont-term residential care & treatment for children with special needs; Day program; Physiotherapy treatment; Kinesiology; Communications programs; Independent living skills program. Number of Employees: 9 Registered Nurses & Registered Practical Nurses + 2 Kinessiologists + 1 Program Coordinator + 21 Child Care Attendants + 1 Dietician + 2 Housekeepers + 1 Executive Secretary
John Vos, Administrator
Shabnam Vos, Administrator

***Kitchener:* Sunbeam Residential Development Centre**
2749 Kingsway Dr., Kitchener, ON N2C 1A7
Tel: 519-893-6200; *Fax:* 519-893-9034
postmaster@sunbeamcentre.com
www.sunbeamcentre.com
Year Founded: 1956
Note: Specialties: Care for individuals with diverse & complex developmental challenges; Long-term & short-term support; Activation; Sensory stimulation
Dr. Shaune Lawton, Executive Director

***Lindsay:* Keast Residence**
RR#6, Lindsay, ON K9V 4R6
Tel: 705-328-0631
Number of Beds: 12 beds
M. Keast, Administrator

***Lucan:* Crest Support Services**
13570 Elginfield Rd., RR#1, Lucan, ON N0M 2J0
Tel: 519-227-6766; *Fax:* 519-227-6768
www.crestsupportservices.ca
Note: Specialties: Services for adults with mental health or developmental disabilities; Accommodation services; Operation of three small businesses to provide training & employment opportunities
David Ragobar, Executive Director
david@thecrestcentre.com

***Markham:* Participation House**
9 Butternut Lane, Markham, ON L3P 3M1
Tel: 905-294-0944; *Fax:* 905-294-7834
postmaster@participationhouse.net
www.participationhouse.net
Number of Beds: 52 beds
Note: Provides services designed to enhance the qualify of life of people with disabilities
Sharon M. Lawlor, Executive Director

***Nepean:* Total Communication Environment (TCE)**
#5, 203 Colonnade Rd. South, Nepean, ON K2E 7K3
Tel: 613-228-0999; *Fax:* 613-228-1402
TTY: 613-228-8669
tceadmin@tceottawa.org; tcehr@tceottawa.org (Human Resources)
www.tceottawa.org
Year Founded: 1979
Note: Specialties: Services for adults with multiple disabilities & special communication needs; Respite care; Day services; Outreach to long-term care homes
Karen Anderson, Executive Director

***Newmarket:* Brigitta's Residential Home Inc.**
128 Arden Ave., Newmarket, ON L3Y 4H6
Tel: 905-895-5890
Number of Beds: 22 beds
Brigitta Miller, Administrator

***Newmarket:* Brookside Lodge**
542 Wellington St., Newmarket, ON L3Y 2C6
Tel: 905-853-7342
Number of Beds: 29 beds
Dave Sedore, Proprietor

***Newmarket:* Brown's Residential Home**
399 Queen St., Newmarket, ON L3Y 2G9
Tel: 905-898-1955

***Newmarket:* Heritage Lodge**
508 College St., Newmarket, ON L3Y 1C6
Tel: 905-853-1587; *Fax:* 905-764-1360
johngas@learned.com
Number of Beds: 21 beds
John Gaspar, Director

***Newmarket:* Lakeview Place Home for Special Care**
#223, 16715-12 Yonge St., Newmarket, ON L3X 1X4
Tel: 905-898-1015; *Fax:* 905-898-6414
info@tshyr.ca
www.tshyr.ca
Number of Beds: 19 beds
Monica Auerbach, Executive Director

***Newmarket:* Parkview Manor**
683 Gorham St., Newmarket, ON L3Y 1L5
Tel: 905-895-9064; *Fax:* 905-895-9064
parkview@caringplaces.com
www.caringplaces.com
Number of Beds: 23 beds
Note: Home for special care
John Gaspar, Director

***North Bay:* North Bay & District Association for Community Living**
161 Main St. East, North Bay, ON P1B 1A9
Tel: 705-476-3288; *Fax:* 705-476-4788
www.nbdacl.org
Number of Beds: 35 beds
Rheal Thorn, Executive Director

Orangeville: Dufferin Association for Community Living
#10, 29 Centennial Rd., Orangeville, ON L9W 1R1
Tel: 519-941-8971; *Fax:* 519-941-9121
Number of Beds: 44 beds
Starr Olsen, Executive Director

Ottawa: Roberts/Smart Centre
1199 Carling Ave., Ottawa, ON K1Z 8N8
Tel: 613-728-1946; *Fax:* 613-728-4986
Toll-Free: 800-279-9941
info@rsc-crs.com
www.robertssmartcentre.com
Number of Beds: 47 beds
Cameron Macleod, Executive Director

Owen Sound: Kent Residential Home
Former Name: Tucker's Residential Home
1065 - 9 Ave. West, Owen Sound, ON N4K 5R8
Tel: 519-371-5029; *Fax:* 519-371-3237
kenthome@bellnet.ca
Number of Beds: 18 beds
Note: residential home for people with mental illness
Yvonne Kent

Oxford Mills: Old Mill Guest Home
PO Box 218, 12 Bridge St., Oxford Mills, ON K0G 1S0
Tel: 613-258-3366; *Fax:* 613-258-3130
Number of Beds: 22 beds
Note: Specialties: Residential services for post-psychiatric patients; Social programs

Peterborough: Community Living Peterborough
223 Aylmer St., Peterborough, ON K9J 3K3
Tel: 705-743-2411; *Fax:* 705-743-3722
Number of Beds: 32 beds
Dianne M. Austin, Manager

Peterborough: Kinark Child & Family Services
380 Armour Rd., Peterborough, ON K9H 7L7
Tel: 705-742-3803; *Fax:* 705-743-4144
kinzz@sympatico.ca
Number of Beds: 12 beds
Note: children's mental health centre
Alan Vallillee, Area Program Director

Petrolia: Lambton County Developmental Services
Former Name: Lambton County Association for Mentally Handicappe
PO Box 1210, 339 Centre St., Petrolia, ON N0N 1R0
Tel: 519-882-0933; *Fax:* 519-882-3386
administration@lcds.on.ca
www.lcds.on.ca
Number of Beds: 68 beds
Note: Provides services to persons with intellectual disabilities
Don Seymour, Executive Director

Powassan: Eide's Residential Home
495 Main St., Powassan, ON P0H 1Z0
Tel: 705-724-2748

Saint-Pascal-Baylon: St. Pascal Residential Home
2454 du Lac Rd., RR#1, Saint-Pascal-Baylon, ON K0A 3N0
Tel: 613-488-2626

St Catharines: Montebello Place
Former Name: Horvath Residence
1 Montebello Pl., St Catharines, ON L2R 6B5
Tel: 905-984-6506; *Fax:* 905-984-6504
Year Founded: 1973
Number of Beds: 15 beds
Sharon Okum, Co-Owner
David Okum, Co-Owner

St Thomas: Tara Hall Residential Care Home
38 Chester St., St Thomas, ON N5R 1V2
Tel: 519-631-4937; *Fax:* 519-631-1526
tarahall@rogers.com
Year Founded: 1988
Number of Beds: 36 beds
Note: Specialties: Assisted living for adults with an intellectual disability, brain injury, or mental illness
James Akey, Manager

Thunder Bay: Marcinowsky Residential Home
601 Alice Ave., RR#14, Thunder Bay, ON P7G 1X1
Tel: 807-767-6199
Number of Beds: 10 beds
Stephanie Marcinowsky, Administrator/Owner

Toronto: Community Head Injury Resource Services of Toronto
62 Finch Ave. West, Toronto, ON M2N 7G1
Tel: 416-240-8000; *Fax:* 416-240-1149
hedyc@chirs.com
www.chirs.com/CHIRS/
Number of Beds: 27 beds
Hedy Chandler, Executive Director

Toronto: Griffin Centre
24 Silverview Dr., Toronto, ON M2M 2B3
Tel: 416-222-1153; *Fax:* 416-222-1321
contact@griffin-centre.org
www.griffin-centre.org
Number of Beds: 10 beds
Laurie Dart, Executive Director

Toronto: Hincks-Dellcrest Treatment Centre
440 Jarvis St., Toronto, ON M4Y 2H4
Tel: 416-924-1164; *Fax:* 416-924-8208
info@hincksdellcrest.org
www.hincksdellcrest.org
Note: Children's mental health
John Spekkens, Executive Director

Toronto: Salvation Army Broadview Village
1132 Broadview Ave., Toronto, ON M4K 2S5
Tel: 416-425-1052; *Fax:* 416-425-6579
Number of Beds: 61 beds
Note: Facility for adults with developmental disabilities
Capt. Glenda Davis, Director

Toronto: Youthdale Treatment Centres Ltd.
227 Victoria St., Toronto, ON M5B 1T8
Tel: 416-368-4896; *Fax:* 416-368-3192
Number of Beds: 70 beds
Dan Hagler, Executive Director

Vars: Pine Rest Residence
PO Box 109, 5876 Bearbrook Rd., Vars, ON K0A 3H0
Tel: 613-835-2849; *Fax:* 613-835-9335
Number of Beds: 33 residential capacity
Note: Specialties: Residential care for persons with developmental disabilities, psychiatric disabilities, or those who suffer from alcoholism; Medication supervision; Respite care
Raymond Meloche, Administrator

Vars: Résidence Ste-Marie
Ste-Marie Residence
PO Box 73, 5855, ch Buckland, Vars, ON K0H 3H0
Tel: 613-835-2525
Number of Beds: 40 lits
Note: Spécialisée à la prestation des soins aux personnes atteintes de maladie mentale grave; soins infirmiers, activités hebdomadaires
Gaétan Brisson, Propriétaire
Suzanne Brisson, Propriétaire

Vineland: Amber Lodge
4024 Martin Rd., RR#1, Vineland, ON L0R 2C0
Tel: 905-562-7272; *Fax:* 905-892-9700
William Ram, Administrator/Owner

Vineland: Bethesda Home for the Mentally Handicapped Inc.
PO Box 1000, Vineland, ON L0R 2C0
Tel: 905-562-4184; *Fax:* 905-562-4621
Number of Beds: 42 beds
Donald Boese, Executive Director

Waterloo: Lutherwood
Administrative Office, 139 Father David Bauer Dr., Waterloo, ON N2L 6L1
Tel: 519-884-7755; *Fax:* 519-884-9071
admin@lutherwood.ca
www.lutherwood.ca
Note: Specialties: Mental health services for children & families, including assessment, a youth shelter, housing support services, residential treatment, family crisis & prevention counselling, a community services program, & school-based interventions; Senior services, including independent & supported living resources
John Colangeli, CEO

Waterloo: Lutherwood Children's Mental Health Services
285 Benjamin Rd., Waterloo, ON N2J 3Z4
Tel: 519-884-1470; *Fax:* 519-886-8479
www.lutherwood.ca
Number of Beds: 6 beds (Bridgelands program); 10 beds (Woodlands program)
Note: Specialties: Day treatment program; Residential treatment program; Group & individual skills training; Individual & family counselling; Home support; Community integration; Crisis support

Waterloo: Underhill Residential Home
127 Erb St. West, Waterloo, ON N2L 1T7
Tel: 519-884-7160; *Fax:* 519-884-5936
Note: Specialties: Residential & personal care services for seniors & persons with mental health concerns

Prince Edward Island

Government Departments in Charge

PRINCE EDWARD ISLAND: Department of Community Services, Seniors & Labour
Jones Bldg., PO Box 2000, 11 Kent St., 2nd Fl., Charlottetown, PE C1A 7N8
Tel: 902-620-3777; *Fax:* 902-368-4740
Toll-Free: 1-866-594-3777
www.gov.pe.ca/sss

Hon. Janice Sherry, Minister, Community Services, Seniors & Labour
902-368-4930, Fax: 902-368-4974, jasherry@gov.pe.ca
Sharon Cameron, Deputy Minister
902-368-6520, Fax: 902-368-4740, secameron@gov.pe.ca
Rona M. Brown, Director, Child & Family Services
902-368-5396, Fax: 902-368-4258, rmbrown@gov.pe.ca
W. Lorne Clow, Director, Corporate & Financial Services
902-368-6109, Fax: 902-894-0242, wlclow@gov.pe.ca
Bob D. Creed, Director, Social Programs
902-368-6446, Fax: 902-620-3553, bdcreed@gov.pe.ca
Faye M. Martin, Director, Pharmacy, Housing, Dentistry & Seniors
902-569-0545, Fax: 902-894-0242, fmmartin@gov.pe.ca
Laura Steeves, Communications Officer
902-620-3409, Fax: 902-894-0242

PRINCE EDWARD ISLAND: Department of Health & Wellness
PO Box 2000, 16 Garfield St., 1st Fl., Charlottetown, PE C1A 7N8
Tel: 902-368-6130; *Fax:* 902-368-6136
www.gov.pe.ca/health

Hon. Carolyn Bertram, Minister, Health & Wellness
902-368-5250, Fax: 902-368-4121, cibertran@gov.pe.ca
Tracey Cutcliffe, Deputy Minister
902-368-5290, Fax: 902-368-4121, tdcutcliffe@gov.pe.ca
Kevin Barnes, Director, Policy & Administration
902-368-4865, Fax: 902-368-4224, kcbarnes@gov.pe.ca
Thelma Johnston, Director, Vital Statistics
902-838-0884, Fax: 902-838-0883
Dr. Mark Triantafillou, Director, Mental Health
902-368-5411, Fax: 902-620-3077
Autumn Tremere, Communications Officer
902-368-5610, Fax: 902-368-4224, agtremere@gov.pe.ca

Regional Health Authorities

Alberton: West Prince Health Region
PO Box 10, Alberton, PE C0B 1B0
Tel: 902-853-8660; *Fax:* 902-853-8658
pajost@ihis.org
Number of Beds: 40 acute care, 72 long-term care beds
Phil Jost, CEO

Charlottetown: Health PEI
PO Box 2000, Charlottetown, PE C1A 7N8
Tel: 902-368-6130; *Fax:* 902-368-6136
healthinput@gov.pe.ca
www.oneislandhealthsystem.ca
Year Founded: 2010
Note: Population Served: 140,985. Area Covered: The Province of Prince Edward Island
Leo Steven, Chair
Keith Dewar, President; Chief Executive Officer
Rick Adams, Executive Director, Queen Elizabeth Hospital
Deborah Bradley, Executive Director, Community Hospitals & Primary Health Care
Arlene Gallant-Bernard, Executive Director, Prince County Hospital
Terry Keefe, Executive Director, Financial Services
Pamela Trainor, Executive Director, Corporate Development & Innovation
Dale Vandenborre, Executive Director, Health Information Management
Cecil Villard, Executive Director, Home Based &Long Term Care
Dr. Richard Wedge, Executive Director, Medical Affairs
Darlene Gillis, Manager, Communications
902-368-6172, dgillis@gov.pe.ca

***Charlottetown:* Provincial Health Services Authority**
PO Box 6600, Charlottetown, PE C1A 8T5
Tel: 902-894-0141; *Fax:* 902-894-0138
Year Founded: 2002
Note: Responsible for planning & delivering specialized acute & secondary health care services
Keith Dewar, CEO

***Charlottetown:* Queens Health Region**
Former Name: Queens Region Health Authority
PO Box 2000, 161 St. Peters Rd., Charlottetown, PE C1A 7N8
Tel: 902-368-6160; *Fax:* 902-368-6169
Note: Child & family services, community services, continuing care, social support
Susan Howard, CEO
Sylvia Poirier, Chair

***Montague:* Kings Health Region**
PO Box 3000, 35 Douses Rd., Montague, PE C0A 1R0
Tel: 902-838-0945; *Fax:* 902-838-0940
Betty Fraser, CEO

***Summerside:* East Prince Health Board**
243 Harbour Dr., Summerside, PE C1N 3G6
Tel: 902-888-8028; *Fax:* 902-888-8458
Katherine Kelly, CEO

Hospitals

Hospitals - General

***Alberton:* Western Hospital Corporation**
PO Box 10, Alberton, PE C0B 1B0
Tel: 902-853-8650; *Fax:* 902-853-8651
mgbolger@ihis.org
Number of Beds: 25 beds
Marlene Bolger, Administrator

***Charlottetown:* Queen Elizabeth Hospital Inc.**
PO Box 6600, 60 Riverside Dr., Charlottetown, PE C1A 8T5
Tel: 902-894-2111; *Fax:* 902-894-2416
TTY: 902-894-2204
www.gov.pe.ca
Number of Beds: 274 beds
Note: Acute care hospital, with burn care services, coronary care, psychiatry, physiotherapy, occupational therapy, orthpedic & specialized gynecological surgery, eye surgery, plastic surgery, neonatal intensive care, cancer care, diagnostic imaging
Rick Adams, Executive Director
Kelly Rayner, Director, Hospital Services

***Montague:* King's County Memorial Hospital**
409 McIntyre Ave., Montague, PE C0A 1R0
Tel: 902-838-0777; *Fax:* 902-838-0770
njfallis@ihis.org
Number of Beds: 30 beds
Jean Fallis, Administrator
njfallis@ihis.org

***O'Leary:* Community Hospital O'Leary**
PO Box 160, 14 MacKinnon Dr., O'Leary, PE C0B 1V0
Tel: 902-859-8700; *Fax:* 902-859-8774
Year Founded: 1957
Number of Beds: 13 acute care beds + 24 long-term care beds + 1 respite bed
Note: Specialties: Acute care; Immunization program; Lifeline emergency response system; Long-term care (Phone: 902-859-8750, Fax: 902-859-8756); Respite care
Phil Jost, CEO

***Souris:* Souris Hospital**
PO Box 640, 17 Knights Ave., Souris, PE C0A 2B0
Tel: 902-687-7150; *Fax:* 902-687-7175
www.gov.pe.ca/health/index.php3?number=1020338&lang=E#SHContact
Number of Beds: 17 beds
Note: An acute care, rural facility with services including ambulatory care, x-ray, physiotherapy, occupational therapy, pharmacy, nutrition counseling, private dental clinic, provincial & seniors housing program, immunization program
Betty Fraser, CEO, KHR
Terry Campbell, Site Administrator

***Summerside:* Prince County Hospital**
PO Box 3000, 65 Roy Boates Ave., Summerside, PE C1N 2A9
Tel: 902-432-2500; *Fax:* 902-438-4511
gmmartin@ihis.org
www.pchcare.com
Number of Beds: 102 beds
Note: Specialties: Emergency, surgery, internal medicine, obstetrics, pediatrics, psychiatry, radiology, rehabilitation, oncology
Arlene Gallant-Bernard, Executive Director

***Tyne Valley:* Stewart Memorial Hospital**
PO Box 10, Tyne Valley, PE C0B 2C0
Tel: 902-831-7900; *Fax:* 902-831-7901
Number of Beds: 23 beds
Note: Specialties: Acute care; Long-term care, Respite care; Palliative care
Aleah MacLennan, Nursing Coordinator

Community Health Centres

Community Health Care Centres

***Charlottetown:* Home Care Support**
PO Box 2000, 115 Murchison Lane., Charlottetown, PE C1A 7N5
Tel: 902-368-4790; *Fax:* 902-368-4858
Nora McCabe

***Montague:* Home Care Support**
PO Box 820, Montague, PE C0A 1R0
Tel: 902-838-0950; *Fax:* 902-838-0774
Sandy MacLean, Home Care Nursing Supervisor

***O'Leary:* Home Care Support**
PO Box 160, O'Leary, PE C0B 1V0
Tel: 902-859-8730; *Fax:* 902-859-8701
Paula Caulien

Special Treatment Centres

***Charlottetown:* Euston Street Group Home**
190 Euston St., Charlottetown, PE C1A 1W8
Tel: 902-566-2964
Note: adolescent group home
Donnie Campbell, Manager

***Charlottetown:* Maple Street Group Home**
14 Vail Dr., Charlottetown, PE C1A 2L5
Tel: 902-368-1699
Number of Beds: 12 beds; one 72-hour emergency care bed
Note: adolescent group home
Donnie Campbell, Manager

***Charlottetown:* Provincial Addictions Treatment Facility**
PO Box 2000, Charlottetown, PE C1A 7N8
Tel: 902-368-4120; *Fax:* 902-368-6229
Toll-Free: 1-888-299-8399
www.gov.pe.ca/hirc
Number of Beds: 41 beds
Note: To provide safe, medically supervised detoxification
Jim Good, Family Counselor

***Charlottetown:* Provincial Adolescent Group Home**
PO Box 2000, 185 Beach Grove Rd., Charlottetown, PE C1E 1Z7
Tel: 902-368-6420; *Fax:* 902-368-6428
mamacmillan@ihis.org
Number of Beds: 9 beds; 1 emergency 72-hour bed
Note: adolescent residential treatment
John MacMillan, Manager, Adolescent Services

Nursing Homes

***Alberton:* Maplewood Manor**
PO Box 400, 400 Church St., Alberton, PE C0B 1B0
Tel: 902-853-8610; *Fax:* 902-853-8616
Number of Beds: 47 beds
Note: government-run
Phil Jost, CEO

***Charlottetown:* Beach Grove Home**
200 Beach Grove Rd., Charlottetown, PE C1E 1L3
Tel: 902-368-6750; *Fax:* 902-368-6764
Number of Beds: 131 beds
Note: government-run
Cecil Villard, Director

***Charlottetown:* Garden Home**
310 North River Rd., Charlottetown, PE C1A 3M4
Tel: 902-892-4131; *Fax:* 902-892-7326
Number of Beds: 112 beds
Note: private
Kirk DeBoer, Administrator

***Charlottetown:* Lennox Nursing Home**
140 Water St., Charlottetown, PE C1A 1A7
Tel: 902-894-4968; *Fax:* 902-368-2004
Number of Beds: 25 beds
Note: private
Tamara Casford, Administrator

***Charlottetown:* MacMillan Lodge Ltd.**
PO Box 1861, 230 Richmond St., Charlottetown, PE C1A 1J5
Tel: 902-894-7173; *Fax:* 902-894-3818
Year Founded: 1999
Claudette MacMillan, Owner/Operator

***Charlottetown:* Park West Lodge**
22 Richmond St., Charlottetown, PE C1A 1H4
Tel: 902-566-2260; *Fax:* 902-894-7818
Kevin Gauthier

***Charlottetown:* PEI Atlantic Baptist Homes Inc.**
16 Centennial Dr., Charlottetown, PE C1A 5C5
Tel: 902-566-5975; *Fax:* 902-368-3760
altbaptist@eastlink.ca
Number of Beds: 101 beds
Note: Specialty: Long-term care by an interdisciplinary team
Enid Dollar, Administrator

***Charlottetown:* The Prince Edward Home**
5 Brighton Rd., Charlottetown, PE C1A 8T6
Tel: 902-368-5946; *Fax:* 902-368-5646
Number of Beds: 131 beds
Note: Palliative care, convalescent, respite care; long-term care; day program for seniors; meals-on-wheels program
Don Gorveatt, Director

***Montague:* Riverview Manor**
PO Box 820, 82 Main St. South, Montague, PE C0A 1R0
Tel: 902-838-0772; *Fax:* 902-838-0774
jlfraser@ihis.org
Number of Beds: 50 beds
Note: Long-term & palliative care
Judy Fraser, Administrator

***Souris:* Colville Manor**
PO Box 640, 44 Chapel Ave., Souris, PE C0A 2B0
Tel: 902-687-7090; *Fax:* 902-687-7103
Number of Beds: 51 beds
Note: government-run
Marilyn Barrett, Acting Director, Acute & Continuing Care

***Summerside:* Summerset Manor**
205 Lefurgey Ave., Summerside, PE C1N 2L9
Tel: 902-888-8310; *Fax:* 902-888-8338
Number of Beds: 82 beds
Note: Specialties: Long-term care; Operation of the Chapman Centre, a day program that provides therapeutic services to seniors who live in their own home; Physiotherapy; Occupational therapy; Foot care; Respite care
Faye Feener, Manager

***Summerside:* Wedgewood Manor**
310 Brophy St., Summerside, PE C1N 5N4
Tel: 902-888-8340; *Fax:* 902-888-8369
Faye Feener, Manager

Long Term/Retirement Care

Long Term Care Facilities

***Alberton:* Rev. W.J. Phillips Residence**
Alberton, PE C0B 1B0
Tel: 902-853-3109; *Fax:* 902-853-2485
www.phillipsresidence.com
Number of Beds: 14 beds; 14 independent living units
Note: community care & beds
Garth MacKinnon

***Belfast:* Dr. John Gillis Memorial Lodge**
Eldon Belfast PO, Belfast, PE C0A 1A0
Tel: 902-659-2337; *Fax:* 902-659-2865
douglas@gillislodge.com
Number of Beds: 62 beds
Douglas MacKenzie

***Charlottetown:* Andrews of Charlottetown**
73 Malpeque Rd., Charlottetown, PE C1A 7J9
Tel: 902-368-2790; *Fax:* 902-894-3464
info@andrewsofpei.com
andrewsofpei.com/andrews_of_charlottetown.php
Number of Beds: 72 beds
Note: community care beds

***Charlottetown:* Champion Lodge**
48 Green St., Charlottetown, PE C1A 2E8
Tel: 902-894-8968; *Fax:* 902-894-3878
Number of Beds: 8 beds

Colleen MacDonald

***Charlottetown:* Charlotte Residence**
39 All Souls Lane, Charlottetown, PE C1A 1P9
Tel: 902-894-8134
Number of Beds: 26 beds
Joyce Pickles, Administrator

***Charlottetown:* Corrigan Home**
22 Hemlock Ct., Charlottetown, PE C1A 8E3
Tel: 902-894-9686; *Fax:* 902-894-3686
Number of Beds: 28 beds
Note: community care beds

***Charlottetown:* Corrigan Lodge**
8 Ellis Rd., Charlottetown, PE C1A 8N4
Tel: 902-894-5858
Number of Beds: 16 beds
Note: community care beds

***Charlottetown:* Elm Crest Lodge**
267 Richmond St., Charlottetown, PE C1A 1J7
Tel: 902-566-5996; *Fax:* 902-368-8382
Number of Beds: 14 beds
Note: community care beds

***Charlottetown:* Langille House**
214 Kent St., Charlottetown, PE C1A 1P2
Tel: 902-628-8228; *Fax:* 902-628-6656
Number of Beds: 33 beds
Note: community care beds
Shirley Keenan

***Charlottetown:* McQuaid Lodge**
36 Kent St., Charlottetown, PE C1A 1M8
Tel: 902-892-0791
Gerard Arsenault

***Charlottetown:* Old Rose Lodge**
319 Queen St., Charlottetown, PE C1A 4C4
Tel: 902-368-8313
theoldroselodge@pei.aibn.com
Helen Roberts

***Charlottetown:* Stamper Residence**
29 Fitzroy St., Charlottetown, PE C1A 1R2
Tel: 902-894-3815
Number of Beds: 20 beds
Joyce Pickles, Administrator

***Charlottetown:* Tenderwood Lodge Inc.**
15 Hawthorne Ave., Charlottetown, PE C1A 5X8
Tel: 902-566-5174

***Charlottetown:* Whisperwood Villa**
160 St. Peters Rd., Charlottetown, PE C1A 5P8
Tel: 902-566-5556; *Fax:* 902-566-5222
Number of Beds: 88 beds + 36 nursing home beds
Note: community care facility; private nursing home
Ray Brow, Administrator

***Crapaud:* South Shore Villa**
PO Box 111, 159 Sherwood Forest Dr., Crapaud, PE C0A 1J0
Tel: 902-658-2228; *Fax:* 902-658-2576
Number of Beds: 52 beds
Note: Parent ID changed only, 08/10 — Not a complete update
Lynn Dawson

***Georgetown:* Carroll's Lodge**
PO Box 133, 110 Gordon St., Georgetown, PE C0A 1L0
Tel: 902-652-2369
Number of Beds: 7 beds
Barb Carroll

***Hunter River:* Rosewood Residence**
PO Box 97, 4260 Hopedale Rd., Route 13, Hunter River, PE C0A 1N0
Tel: 902-964-2436; *Fax:* 902-964-2436
info@rosewoodresidence.ca
www.rosewoodresidence.ca
Number of Beds: 41 beds
Note: community care beds
Lori E. Weeks, Director

***Kensington:* Clinton View Lodge**
RR#6, Kensington, PE C0B 1M0
Tel: 902-866-2276; *Fax:* 902-886-2073
Number of Beds: 43 beds (25 nursing home beds)
Note: private nursing home; community care facility
Tracy Perrin

***Kensington:* MacEwen Mews Seniors Residence**
RR#6, Kensington, PE C0B 1M0
Tel: 902-836-4678

***Lower Montague:* Shady Rest Convalescent Home**
RR#2, Lower Montague, PE C0A 1R0
Tel: 902-838-4298; *Fax:* 902-838-4298
Number of Beds: 37 beds
Note: community care beds
Jackie MacKay, Owner/Operator

***Miscouche:* Miscouche Villa**
PO Box 40, 20 Lady Slipper Dr., Miscouche, PE C0B 1T0
Tel: 902-436-1946; *Fax:* 902-436-3215
johnd@pei.sympatico.ca
Number of Beds: 35 beds
Note: community care beds
Barbara Perry, Manager

***Montague:* MacKinnon Pines Community Care Facility**
PO Box 298, 505 Campbellton St., Montague, PE C0A 1R0
Tel: 902-838-2656; *Fax:* 902-838-3542

***Montague:* Queens Gardens**
394 Queens Rd., Montague, PE C0A 1R0
Tel: 902-838-8440
Number of Beds: 7 beds

***New Glasgow:* River View Home**
RR#2, New Glasgow, PE C0A 1N0
Tel: 902-964-2795; *Fax:* 902-621-0453
Number of Beds: 20 beds
Note: community care beds for seniors & the mentally challenged
Kathy Dutton, Proprietor
Martin Dutton

***O'Leary:* Lady Slipper Villa**
PO Box 40, 490 Main St., O'Leary, PE C0B 1V0
Tel: 902-859-3544; *Fax:* 902-859-3255
info@ladyslippervilla.com
ladyslippervilla.com
Number of Beds: 47 beds
Note: community care beds
Karen Cook, Administrator

***Souris:* Bayview Lodge**
22 Washington St., Souris, PE C0A 2B0
Tel: 902-687-3122; *Fax:* 902-687-3512
Number of Beds: 32 beds
Note: community care beds
Gerard Arsenault

***Summerside:* Andrews of Summerside**
317 Pope Rd., Summerside, PE C1N 6G4
Tel: 902-436-0859; *Fax:* 902-436-1565
info@andrewsofpei.com
www.andrewsofpei.com/andrews_of_summerside.php
Number of Beds: 58 beds
Note: community care facility
Erroll Andrews, Administrator

***Summerside:* MacDonald's Community Care Home Inc.**
197 Cambridge St., Summerside, PE C1N 1N1
Tel: 902-436-7359

***Tignish:* Tignish Seniors Home Care Cooperative Limited**
116 MacLeod Lane, Tignish, PE C0B 2B0
Tel: 902-882-4663
Year Founded: 2002
Note: Specialty: Assisted living
Leslie VanHee, Administrator

***Tyne Valley:* Murphy's Country Lodge**
Tyne Valley, PE C0B 2C0
Tel: 902-831-2213; *Fax:* 902-831-2309
Number of Beds: 11 beds
Note: community care beds
Earlene Murphy

***Wellington:* Chez Nous**
PO Box 88, 64 Sunset Dr., Wellington, PE C0B 2E0
Tel: 902-854-3426; *Fax:* 902-854-3055
cheznous@isn.net
Number of Beds: 25 beds
Note: community care beds
Antoine Richard

Mental Health Facilities

Mental Health Hospitals/Facilities

***Charlottetown:* Hillsborough Hospital & Special Care Centre**
PO Box 1929, 115 Murchison Lane, Charlottetown, PE C1A 7N5
Tel: 902-368-5400; *Fax:* 902-368-5467
www.gov.pe.ca/health
Number of Beds: 75 beds
Note: Specialties: Psychiatry; Medical services for persons with acute or long-term mental illnesses or mental handicaps, & psychogeriatric patients; Day services for former patients; Assessment; Behavioural management
Cecil Villard, Administrator
Don Hughes, Director, Environmental Services

***Charlottetown:* Sherwood Home**
PO Box 1929, Charlottetown, PE C1A 7N8
Tel: 902-368-4141; *Fax:* 902-368-4931
Number of Beds: 14 beds
Elaine Blanchard, Administrator

Québec

Département gouvernemental responsable

QUÉBEC: Ministère de la Santé et des services sociaux
1075, ch Ste-Foy, Québec, QC G1S 2M1
Tél: 418-266-8900; *Téléc:* 418-644-4574
Ligne sans frais: 800-707-3380
info@msss.gouv.qc.ca
www.msss.gouv.qc.ca

Agences de développement de réseaux locaux de service de santé et de services sociaux

***Baie-Comeau:* Agence de la santé et des services sociaux de la Côte-Nord**
691, rue Jalbert, Baie-Comeau, QC G5C 2A1
Tél: 418-589-9845; *Téléc:* 418-295-2703
www.agencesante09.gouv.qc.ca
Nicole Demers, Présidente-directrice générale

***Chibougamau:* Centre régional de la santé et des services sociaux de la Baie-James**
Ancien nom: Régie régionale de la santé et des services sociau
312, 3e rue, Chibougamau, QC G8P 1N5
Tél: 418-748-3575; *Téléc:* 418-748-2021
Diane Laboissonnière, Présidente-directrice-gen. (intérim)

***Chicoutimi:* Agence de la santé et des services sociaux du Saguenay-Lac-St-Jean**
930, rue Jacques-Cartier est, Chicoutimi, QC G7H 7K9
Tél: 418-545-4980; *Téléc:* 418-545-8791
info@santesaglac.gouv.qc.ca
www.santesaglac.gouv.qc.ca
Martine Couture, Présidente-directrice générale

***Chisasibi:* Conseil cri de la santé et des services sociaux de la Baie-James**
CP 250, Chisasibi, QC J0M 1E0
Tél: 819-855-2844; *Téléc:* 819-855-2098
Joanne Bezzubetz, Directrice générale

***Gaspé:* Agence de la santé et des services sociaux de la Gaspésie-Iles-de-la-Madeleine**
144, boul Gaspé, Gaspé, QC G4X 1A9
Tél: 418-368-2349; *Téléc:* 418-368-4942
agence11@ssss.gouv.qc.ca
www.agencessgim.ca
Pierre Michaud, Président-directeur général

***Gatineau:* Agence de la santé et des services sociaux de l'Outaouais**
Également connu sous le nom de: Santé Outaouais
104, rue Lois, Gatineau, QC J8Y 3R7
Tél: 819-770-7747; *Téléc:* 819-770-3891
www.santeoutaouais.qc.ca
Roch Martel, Président-directeur général

Joliette: **Agence de la santé et des services sociaux de Lanaudière**
245, rue du Curé-Majeau, Joliette, QC J6E 8S8
Tél: 450-759-1157; *Téléc:* 450-759-0023
chetu@ssss.gouv.qc.ca
www.santelanaudiere.qc.ca

Jean-François Foisy, Président-directeur général

Kuujjuaq: **Régie régionale de la santé et des services sociaux du Nunavik**
CP 900, Kuujjuaq, QC J0M 1C0
Tél: 819-964-2222; *Téléc:* 819-964-2888
information_rrsss17@ssss.gouv.qc.ca
www.rrsss17.gouv.qc.ca

Gilles Boulet, Dir. gen. (intérim)

Laval: **Agence de la santé et des services sociaux de Laval**
Tour A, 800, boul Chomedey, 2e étage, Laval, QC H7N 3Y4
Tél: 450-978-2000; *Téléc:* 450-978-2100
regie-laval@ssss.gouv.qc.ca
www.sssslaval.gouv.qc.ca

Claude Desjardins, Président-directeur général (intérim)

Longueuil: **Agence de la santé et des services sociaux de la Montérégie**
1255, rue Beauregard, Longueuil, QC J4K 2M3
Tél: 450-928-6777; *Téléc:* 450-679-6443
agencemonteregie@ssss.gouv.qc.ca
www.santemonteregie.qc.ca/agence

Luc Boileau, Président-directeur général

Montréal: **Agence de la santé et des services sociaux de Montréal**
3725, rue St-Denis, Montréal, QC H2X 3L9
Tél: 514-286-6500; *Téléc:* 514-286-5669
www.santemontreal.qc.ca

David Levine, Président-directeur général

Québec: **Agence de la santé et des services sociaux de la Capitale-Nationale**
555, boul Wilfrid-Hamel est, Québec, QC G1M 3X7
Tél: 418-525-1500; *Téléc:* 418-529-4463
03rrsss@ssss.gouv.qc.ca
www.rrsss03.gouv.qc.ca

Michel Fontaine, Président-directeur général

Rimouski: **Agence de la santé et des services sociaux du Bas-St-Laurent**
#115, 288, rue Pierre-Saindon, Rimouski, QC G5L 9A8
Tél: 418-724-5231; *Téléc:* 418-723-1597
www.agencesssbsl.gouv.qc.ca
Note: L'Agence regroupe des établissements de santé et de services sociaux des régions suivantes: Kamouraska, Rivière-du-Loup, Témiscouata, Les Basques, Rimouski-Neigette, La Mitis, La Matapédia, et Matane.
Claude Lévesque, Président-directeur général

Rouyn-Noranda: **Agence de la santé et des services sociaux de l'Abitibi-Témiscamingue**
1, 9e rue, Rouyn-Noranda, QC J9X 2A9
Tél: 819-764-3264; *Téléc:* 819-797-1947
www.sante-abitibi-temiscamingue.gouv.qc.ca

Lise St-Amour, Présidente-Directrice générale

Saint-Jérôme: **Agence de la santé et des services sociaux des Laurentides**
#210, 1000, rue Labelle, Saint-Jérôme, QC J7Z 5N6
Tél: 450-436-8622; *Téléc:* 450-432-8712
information.rr15@ssss.gouv.qc.ca
www.rrsss15.gouv.qc.ca

Micheline Vallières-Joly, Présidente-directrice générale
Miriam David, Responsable des achats en commun

Sainte-Marie: **Agence de la santé et des services sociaux de Chaudière-Appalaches**
363, rte Cameron, Sainte-Marie, QC G6E 3E2
Tél: 418-386-3363; *Téléc:* 418-389-1500
reception.rr12@ssss.gouv.qc.ca
www.agencesss12.gouv.qc.ca

Marc Tanguay, Président-directeur général

Sherbrooke: **Agence de la santé et des services sociaux de l'Estrie**
#300, 300, rue King est, Sherbrooke, QC J1G 1B1
Tél: 819-566-7861; *Téléc:* 819-569-8894
information.agence05@ssss.gouv.qc.ca
www.santeestrie.qc.ca

Michel Baron, Président-directeur général

Trois-Rivières: **Agence de la santé et des services sociaux de la Mauricie et du Centre-du-Québec**
550, rue Bonaventure, Trois-Rivières, QC G9A 2B5
Tél: 819-693-3636; *Téléc:* 819-373-1627
commissaires.plaintes04@ssss.gouv.qc.ca
www.agencesss04.qc.ca

Michèle Laroche, Présidente-directrice générale

Centres hospitaliers

Amos: **Centre de santé et de services sociaux Les Eskers de l'Abitibi**
Affiliée à: Agence de la santé et des services sociaux de l'Abitibi-Témiscamingue
622, 4e rue ouest, Amos, QC J9T 2S2
Tél: 819-732-3341; *Téléc:* 819-732-7054
www.sante-abitibi-temiscamingue.gouv.qc.ca
Nombre de lits: 96 lits hospitaliers; 103 lits de soins de longue durée
Note: Le CSSS regroupe le Centre hospitalier Hôtel-Dieu d'Amos, un centre d'hébergement, et 4 points de service CLSC.
Michel Michaud, Directeur général
michel_michaud@ssss.gouv.qc.ca
Jean McGuire, Président, Conseil d'administration

Amqui: **Centre de santé et de services sociaux de La Matapédia**
Affiliée à: Agence de la santé et des services sociaux du Bas-St-Laurent
135, av Gaétan-Archambault, Amqui, QC G5J 2K5
Tél: 418-629-2211; *Téléc:* 418-629-4498
www.csssmatapedia.qc.ca; www.chamqui.qc.com
Nombre de lits: 40 lits hospitaliers; 96 lits de soins de longue durée
Note: Le CSSS regroupe l'Hôpital d'Amqui, le centre d'hébergement Marie-Anne Ouellet, et 3 points de service CLSC (Causapscal,Sayabec, et St-Moïse).
Alain Paquet, Directeur général

Baie-Saint-Paul: **Centre de santé et de services sociaux de Charlevoix**
Affiliée à: Agence de la santé et des services sociaux de la Capitale-Nationale
a/s Hôpital de Baie-Saint-Paul, 74, rue Ambroise-Fafard, Baie-Saint-Paul, QC G3Z 2J6
Tél: 418-435-5150
www.cssscharlevoix.qc.ca
Note: Le CSSS de Charlevoix regroupe 2 hôpitaux (Baie-Saint-Paul, et La Malbaie); 5 points de service CLSC; 4 centres d'hébergement; et 8 points de service CRDI.
Micheline Tremblay, Directrice générale
micheline.tremblay@ssss.gouv.qc.ca

Candiac: **Centre de santé et de services sociaux Jardins-Roussillon**
Affiliée à: Agence de la santé et des services sociaux de la Montérégie
90, boul Marie-Victorin, Candiac, QC J5R 1C1
Tél: 450-659-7661; *Téléc:* 450-444-6260
www.santemonteregie.qc.ca/jardins-roussillon
Note: Le CSSS regroupe l'Hôpital Anna-Laberge, 3 centres d'hébergement, et 3 points de service CLSC.
Paul Moreau, Directeur général

Dolbeau-Mistassini: **CSSS Maria-Chapdelaine**
Affiliée à: Agence de la santé et des services sociaux du Saguenay-Lac-St-Jean
2000, boul Sacré-Coeur, Dolbeau-Mistassini, QC G8L 2R5
Tél: 418-276-1234; *Téléc:* 418-276-4355
www.csssmariachapdelaine.com
Nombre de lits: 59 lits hospitaliers; 119 lits de soins de longue durée
Note: Centre administratif du CSSS, et l'Hôpital de Dolbeau-Mistassini. Le CSSS regroupe 2 centres d'hébergement (L'Oasis, et Centre d'hébergement Normandin), 2 points de service CLSC (Normandin, et Les Jardins du Monastère), et l'Hôpital.
Normand Brassard, Directeur général

Drummondville: **Centre de santé et de services sociaux Drummond**
Affiliée à: Agence de la santé et des services sociaux de la Mauricie et du Centre-du-Québec
570, rue Heriot, Drummondville, QC J2B 1C1
Tél: 819-478-6464
csssdrummond@ssss.gouv.qc.ca
www.csssdrummond.qc.ca

Year Founded: 2004
Nombre de lits: 191 lits hospitaliers; 474 lits de soins de longue durée
Note: Le CSSS regroupe l'Hôpital Sainte-Croix, le CLSC Drummond, 3 centres d'hébergement, et 5 autres points de service; il est affilié à l'Université de Sherbrooke pour les activités d'enseignement médical.
Nagui Habashi, Directeur général

La Sarre: **Centre de santé et de services sociaux des Aurores-Boréales**
Affiliée à: Agence de la santé et des services sociaux de l'Abitibi-Témiscamingue
679, 2e Rue est, La Sarre, QC J9Z 2X7
Tél: 819-333-2311; *Téléc:* 819-333-4316
www.sante-abitibi-temiscamingue.gouv.qc.ca
Nombre de lits: 71 lits hospitaliers (courte durée); 182 lits de soins de longue durée
Note: Le CSSS regroupe un centre de soins de courte durée (La Sarre), 3 centres d'hébergement (La Sarre, Macamic, et Palmarolle), et 6 points de service CLSC (Beaucanton, Duparquet, Dupuy, Gallichan, Normétal, et Taschereau).
Paul Fortin, Directeur général
paul_fortin@ssss.gouv.qc.ca
Ghislain Godbout, Président, Conseil d'administration

Lac-Mégantic: **CSSS du Granit**
Affiliée à: Agence de la santé et des services sociaux de l'Estrie
3569, rue Laval, Lac-Mégantic, QC G6B 1A5
Tél: 819-583-0330; *Téléc:* 819-583-5239
Ligne sans frais: 800-827-2572
info.granit@ssss.gouv.qc.ca
www.csssgranit.qc.ca
Nombre de lits: 35 lits hospitaliers; 122 lits de soins de longue durée (3 points de service)
Note: Le CSSS regroupe un centre hospitalier, 2 centres et 1 unité d'hébergement, 2 centres de jour, et 4 points de services CLSC.
Pierre Latulippe, Directeur général

Lachute: **Centre de santé et de services sociaux d'Argenteuil**
Affiliée à: Agence de la santé et des services sociaux des Laurentides
145, av de la Providence, Lachute, QC J8H 4C7
Tél: 450-562-3761; *Téléc:* 450-566-3316
www.csssargenteuil.qc.ca
Nombre de lits: 49 lits hospitaliers; 131 lits de soins de longue durée
Note: Le CSSS offre des services de santé physique et services aux personnes en perte d'autonomie; point de service de Grenville: 93, rue des Érables, 819-242-0778.
Raymond Roberge, Directeur général

Laval: **Centre de santé et de services sociaux de Laval**
Affiliée à: Agence de la santé et des services sociaux de Laval
1515, boul Chomedey, Laval, QC H7V 3Y7
Tél: 450-978-8300
www.cssslaval.qc.ca
Nombre de lits: 532 lits hospitaliers; 777 lits de soins de longue durée
Note: Le CSSS, le plus gros au Québec, regroupe l'Hôpital de la Cité-de-la-Santé, 5 centres d'hébergement, et 7 points de service CLSC; services hospitaliers de courte durée; services ambulatoires; services d'hébergement et de soins de longue durée; services de première ligne.
Luc Lepage, Directeur général
Alain Goudreau, Directeur, Services professionnels et hospitaliers/Affaires mé
Lucie Gagnon, Directrice, Soins infirmiers

Longueuil: **Centre de santé et de services sociaux Pierre-Boucher**
Affiliée à: Agence de la santé et des services sociaux de la Montérégie
1333, boul Jacques-Cartier est, Longueuil, QC J4M 2A5
Tél: 450-468-8111
www.santemonteregie.qc.ca/cssspierreboucher
Nombre de lits: 340 lits hospitaliers; 916 lits de soins de longue durée
Note: Le CSSS regroupe l'Hôpital Pierre-Boucher, 7 points de

service CLSC, 7 centres d'hébergement, et un centre d'hébergement privé non conventionné.
Caroline Barbir, Directrice générale

Magog: Centre de santé et de services sociaux de Memphrémagog
Affiliée à: Agence de la santé et des services sociaux de l'Estrie
50, rue Saint-Patrice est, Magog, QC J1X 3X3
Tél: 819-843-2572; *Téléc:* 819-868-3240
Ligne sans frais: 800-268-2572
csssm.santeestrie.qc.ca
Nombre de lits: 36 lits hospitaliers; 132 lits de soins de longue durée
Note: Le CSSS regroupe l'Hôpital de Memphrémagog, et 2 points de service CLSC; soins de longue durée, et services aux personnes en perte d'autonomie.
Monique Corbeil, Directrice générale
Jules Racine, Coordonnateur, Services techniques

Matane: Centre de santé et de services sociaux de Matane
333, rue Thibault, Matane, QC G4W 2W5
Tél: 418-562-3135; *Téléc:* 418-562-9374
www.agence.sssbsl.gouv.qc.ca
Nombre de lits: 45 lits hospitaliers; 152 lits de soins de longue durée
Note: Le CSSS regroupe l'Hôpital de Matane, le centre d'hébergement de Matane, et 3 points de service CLSC.
Nicole Morin, Directrice générale

Mont-Laurier: Centre de santé et de services sociaux d'Antoine-Labelle
Affiliée à: Agence de la santé et des services sociaux des Laurentides
515, boul Dr Albiny-Paquette, Mont-Laurier, QC J9L 1K8
Tél: 819-623-6127; *Téléc:* 819-623-9451
www.cssssal.org
Year Founded: 2004
Nombre de lits: 473 lits
Note: Le CSSS regroupe l'Hôpital de Mont-Laurier, le Centre de services de Rivière-Rouge, le Centre d'hébergement Sainte-Anne, et 3 points de service CLSC.
Jean-Pierre Urbain, Directeur général

Montréal: CSSS de Saint-Léonard et Saint-Michel
Affiliée à: Agence de la santé et des services sociaux de Montréal
3130, rue Jarry est, Montréal, QC H1Z 4N8
Tél: 514-722-3000
csss-stleonardstmichel.qc.ca
Note: Centre administratif du CSSS; 3 centres d'hébergement: Quatre-Temps, Quatre-Saisons, et Saint-Michel; 2 CLSCs: Saint-Léonard, et Saint-Michel.
Suzanne Hébert, Directrice générale

Montréal: CSSS Jeanne-Mance
Affiliée à: Agence de la santé et des services sociaux de Montréal
155, boul Saint-Joseph est, Montréal, QC H2T 1H4
Tél: 514-842-7180; *Téléc:* 514-380-5152
www.csssjeannemance.ca
Note: Le CSSS Jeanne-Mance regroupe 5 CLSCs: Faubourgs/Parthenais, Faubourgs/Sanguinet, Faubourgs/Visitation, Plateau-Mont-Royal, et Saint-Louis-du-Parc; 7 CHSLDs: Armand-Lavergne, Bruchési, Centre-Ville-de-Montréal, Manoire-de-l'Age-d'Or, Émilie-Gamelin, Ernest-Routhier, et Jean-De La Lande; et 1 clinique de médecine familiale: Notre-Dame.
Ron Rayside, Président du Conseil d'administration
Sylvie Simard, Directrice générale intérimaire

Notre-Dame-du-Lac: Centre de santé et de services sociaux de Témiscouata
Affiliée à: Agence de la santé et des services sociaux du Bas-St-Laurent
58, rue de l'Église, Notre-Dame-du-Lac, QC G0L 1X0
Tél: 418-899-6751; *Téléc:* 418-899-2809
marie.noelle.bosse.cssstemis@ssss.gouv.qc.ca
www.cssstemiscouata.com
Nombre de lits: 35 lits hospitaliers (courte durée); 111 lits de soins de longue durée
Note: Le CSSS regroupe l'Hôpital de Notre-Dame-du-Lac, 5 points de service CLSC, 3 centres d'hébergement, et 9 autres points de service.
Camil Dion, Directeur général

Rimouski: Centre régional de santé et de services sociaux de Rimouski-Neigette
Affiliée à: Agence de la santé et des services sociaux du Bas-St-Laurent
150, av Rouleau, Rimouski, QC G5L 5T1
Tél: 418-723-7851; *Téléc:* 418-724-8632
courrierweb.crsssr@ssss.gouv.qc.ca
www.chrr.qc.ca
Nombre de lits: 255 lits hospitaliers; 246 lits de soins de longue durée
Note: Le CSSS regroupe l'Hôpital régional de Rimouski, le centre d'hébergement de Rimouski, et 4 points de service CLSC; soins généraux et spécialisés (néonatalogie, psychiatrie, santé physique).
Raymond Coulombe, Directeur général

Rivière-du-Loup: Centre de santé et de services sociaux de Rivière-du-Loup
Affiliée à: Agence de la santé et des services sociaux du Bas-St-Laurent
75, rue St-Henri, Rivière-du-Loup, QC G5R 2A4
Tél: 418-868-1010; *Téléc:* 418-868-1035
www.csssriviereduloup.qc.ca
Nombre de lits: 145 lits hospitaliers; 207 lits de soins de longue durée
Note: Le CSSS regroupe le Centre hospitalier régional du Grand-Portage, 3 centres d'hébergement, et 3 points de service CLSC.
Raymond April, Directeur général
Alyre Bois, Président, Conseil d'administration
Julie Roy, Secrétaire

Roberval: Centre de santé et de services sociaux Domaine-du-Roy
Affiliée à: Agence de la santé et des services sociaux du Saguenay-Lac-St-Jean
450, rue Brassard, Roberval, QC G8H 1B9
Tél: 418-275-0110; *Téléc:* 418-275-6202
hdr@ssss.gouv.qc.ca; info@cmdp-roberval.com
www.cmdp-roberval.com
Nombre de lits: 135 lits hospitaliers; 201 lits de soins de longue durée; 15 lits traitement spécialisés
Note: Le CSSS regroupe l'hôpital (Hôtel-Dieu de Roberval), le CLSC et le centre de réadaptation en alcoolisme et autres toxicomanies (Pavillon Gérard-Tremblay), et le Centre d'hébergement Roberval; 2 autres points de service CLSC; et 2 autres centres d'hébergement.
Jacques Dubois, Directeur général

Rouyn-Noranda: Centre de santé et de services sociaux de Rouyn-Noranda
Affiliée à: Agence de la santé et des services sociaux de l'Abitibi-Témiscamingue
4, 9e Rue, Rouyn-Noranda, QC J9X 2B2
Tél: 819-764-5131; *Téléc:* 819-764-2948
diane_cote@ssss.gouv.qc.ca
www.sante-abitibi-temiscamingue.gouv.qc.ca; www.csssrn.qc.ca
Nombre de lits: 123 lits hospitaliers; 172 lits de soins de longue durée
Note: Le CSSS regroupe l'Hôpital de Rouyn-Noranda, le Centre d'hébergement Rouyn-Noranda, le Centre d'hébergement Ressource du Sourire, et 8 points de service CLSC.
Huguette Lemay, Directrice générale
Luc Blanchette, Président, Conseil d'administration
Martine Humbert, Directrice, Santé physique

Saint-Hyacinthe: Centre de santé et de services sociaux Richelieu-Yamaska
Affiliée à: Agence de la santé et des services sociaux de la Montérégie
2750, boul Laframboise, Saint-Hyacinthe, QC J2S 4Y8
Tél: 450-771-3333; *Téléc:* 450-771-3748
info@lesommetavotreportee.qc.ca
www.lesommetavotreportee.qc.ca;
www.santemonteregie.qc.ca/richelieu-yamaska
Note: Centre administratif du CSSS; Hôpital Honoré-Mercier; 3 points de service CLSC: des Maskoutains (Saint-Hyacinthe), MRC-d'Acton, et des Patriotes (Beloeil); 5 centres d'hébergement: Andrée-Perrault, l'Hôtel-Dieu-de-Saint-Hyacinthe, MRC-d'Acton, Marguerite-Adam, et Montarville; 1 clinique de médecine familiale.
Daniel Castonguay, Directeur général

Saint-Jean-sur-Richelieu: CSSS Haut-Richelieu-Rouville
Affiliée à: Agence de la santé et des services sociaux de la Montérégie
978, boul du Séminaire nord, Saint-Jean-sur-Richelieu, QC J3A 1E5
Tél: 450-358-2572; *Téléc:* 450-349-4115
www.santemonteregie.qc.ca/haut-richelieu-rouville
Note: 15 installations, y compris L'Hôpital du Haut-Richelieu; 4 points de service CLSC; 6 centres d'hébergement; une clinique jeunesse; et services de consultation externe (psychiatrie, réadaptation pédiatrique, clinique d'évaluation TED).
Christine Lessard, Directrice générale

Saint-Pascal: Centre de santé et de services sociaux de Kamouraska
575, av Martin, Saint-Pascal, QC G0L 3Y0
Tél: 418-856-7000; *Téléc:* 418-492-1793
www.agencesssbsl.gouv.qc.ca
Nombre de lits: 49 lits hospitaliers; 181 lits de soins de longue durée
Note: Le CSSS regroupe le Centre Notre-Dame-de-Fatima (centre hospitalier), 3 centres d'hébergement, et 3 points de service CLSC.
Michel Beaulieu, Directeur général

Sainte-Agathe-des-Monts: Centre de santé et de services sociaux des Sommets
Affiliée à: Agence de la santé et des services sociaux des Laurentides
Pavillon administratif Jacques-Duquette, 234, rue Saint-Vincent, Sainte-Agathe-des-Monts, QC J8C 2B8
Tél: 819-324-4000; *Téléc:* 819-324-4010
www.csss-sommets.com
Nombre de lits: 104 lits hospitaliers; 219 lits de soins de longue durée
Note: Le CSSS regroupe un hôpital, 3 centres d'hébergement, et 3 points de service CLSC.
Jacques Morin, Président, Conseil d'administration

Sainte-Thérèse: Centre de santé et de services sociaux de Thérèse-De Blainville
Affiliée à: Agence de la santé et des services sociaux des Laurentides
125, rue Duquet, Sainte-Thérèse, QC J7E 0A5
Tél: 450-430-4553
www.cssstheresedeblainville.qc.ca
Nombre de lits: 377 lits de soins de longue durée
Note: Le CSSS regroupe un centre de services médicaux, 2 centres d'hébergement, un centre de prélèvement, et un point de service à Sainte-Anne-des-Plaines.
André Poirier, Directeur général

Sherbrooke: CSSS-Institut universitaire de gériatrie de Sherbrooke
Affiliée à: Agence de la santé et des services sociaux de l'Estrie
375, rue Argyll, Sherbrooke, QC J1J 3H5
Tél: 819-780-2220
www.csss-iugs.ca
Info Line: 811
Nombre de lits: 64 lits hospitaliers; 765 lits de soins de longue durée
Note: Centre de la direction générale du CSSS, et l'Hôpital et Centre d'hébergement Argyll; le CSSS regroupe 4 centres d'hébergement: Argyll, D'Youville, St-Joseph, et St-Vincent; 2 hôpitaux: Argyll, et D'Youville; 5 points de service CLSC; et un centre de maternité; 2 500 employé(e)s.
Carol Fillion, Directeur général
Michel Levesque, Directeur, Soins infirmiers
Suzanne Gosselin, Directrice, Services professionnels et du partenariat médical
Marie Trousdell, Directrice, Services et programmes aux personnes âgées ou en pe

Témiscaming: Centre de santé et de services sociaux de Témiscaming-et-de-Kipawa
Affiliée à: Agence de la santé et des services sociaux de l'Abitibi-Témiscamingue
CP 760, 180, rue Anvik, Témiscaming, QC J0Z 3R0
Tél: 819-627-3385; *Téléc:* 819-327-3629
www.temiscaming.et/csss;
www.sante-abitibi-temiscamingue.gouv.qc.ca
Nombre de lits: 6 lits hospitaliers; 14 lits de soins de longue durée
Note: Le CSSS regroupe un hôpital, un centre d'hébergement, et un point de service CLSC.
Jean-Philippe Legault, Directeur général
jean-philippe_legault@ssss.gouv.qc.c

***Trois-Pistoles:* Centre de santé et de services sociaux des Basques**
Affiliée à: Agence de la santé et des services sociaux du Bas-St-Laurent
550, rue Notre-Dame est, Trois-Pistoles, QC G0L 4K0
Tél: 418-851-3700; *Téléc:* 418-851-2934
www.agencesssbsl.gouv.qc.ca
Nombre de lits: 60 lits hospitaliers; 26 lits de soins de longue durée
Note: Le CSSS regroupe le Centre hospitalier de Trois-Pistoles, le centre d'hébergement Villa Dubé, et un point de service CLSC.
Line Moisan, Directrice générale
Roberto Dionne, Président, Conseil d'administration

***Trois-Rivières:* Centre de santé et de services sociaux de Trois-Rivières**
Affiliée à: Agence de la santé et des services sociaux de la Mauricie et du Centre-du-Québec
155, rue Toupin, Trois-Rivières, QC G8T 3Z8
Tél: 819-370-2100; *Téléc:* 819-379-9644
www.cssstr.qc.ca
Nombre de lits: 10 lits hospitaliers; 660 lits de soins de longue durée
Note: Le CSSS regroupe le Centre Cloutier-du Rivage (hôpital); le Centre de services ambulatoires de gériatrie; les points de service CLSC de l'Horloge, Les Forges, Marguerite-Bourgeois, et Ste-Geneviève; Résidence Cooke, Résidence Joseph-Denys, le Centre St-Joseph et Résidence La Providence, et Résidence Louis-Denoncourt.
Jacques Longval, Directeur général

***Val-d'Or:* Centre de santé et de services sociaux de la Vallée-de-l'Or**
Affiliée à: Agence de la santé et des services sociaux de l'Abitibi-Témiscamingue
725, 6e rue, Val-d'Or, QC J9P 3Y1
Tél: 819-825-6711; *Téléc:* 819-825-7909
marie-clair_côté@ssss.gouv.qc.ca
www.sante-abitibi-temiscamingue.gouv.qc.ca; www.csssvo.qc.ca
Nombre de lits: 145 lits hospitaliers; 185 lits de soins de longue durée
Note: Le CSSS regroupe l'Hôpital et le CLSC de Val-d'Or, 2 autres points de service CLSC, 2 centres d'hébergement, et l'Hôpital psychiatrique de Malartic.
Jérôme Lamont, Directeur général
André Tessier, Directeur intérimaire, Services hospitaliers

***Victoriaville:* Centre de santé et de services sociaux d'Arthabaska-et-de-l'Érable**
Affiliée à: Agence de la santé et des services sociaux de la Mauricie et du Centre-du-Québec
5, rue des Hospitalières, Victoriaville, QC G6P 6N2
Tél: 819-357-2030; *Téléc:* 819-357-4314
www.csssae.qc.ca
Nombre de lits: 199 lits hospitaliers; 451 lits de soins de longue durée
Note: Le CSSS regroupe l'Hôtel-Dieu d'Arthabaska, 4 points de service CLSC, et 8 centres d'hébergement.
Marcel Dubois, Président, Conseil d'administration

***Ville-Marie:* Centre de santé et de services sociaux du Lac-Témiscamingue**
Affiliée à: Agence de la santé et des services sociaux de l'Abitibi-Témiscamingue
22, rue Notre-Dame nord, Ville-Marie, QC J9V 1W8
Tél: 819-622-2773; *Téléc:* 819-629-3257
www.sante-abitibi-temiscamingue.gouv.qc.ca; www.cssslt.qc.ca
Nombre de lits: 31 lits hospitaliers; 69 lits de soins de longue durée
Note: Le CSSS regroupe un hôpital (Pavillon Sainte-Famille), un centre d'hébergement (Pavillon Duhamel), et 8 points de service CLSC.
Jacynthe Bérubé, Directrice générale
jacynthe_berube@ssss.gouv.qc.ca

***Windsor:* Centre de santé et de services sociaux du Val-Saint-François**
Affiliée à: Agence de la santé et des services sociaux de l'Estrie
79, rue Allen, Windsor, QC J1S 2P8
Tél: 819-542-2777; *Téléc:* 819-845-5521
vsf,santeestrie.qc.ca
Nombre de lits: 135 lits de soins de longue durée
Note: Le CSSS regroupe 3 points de service CLSC (Urgence mineure de Windsor, Richmond, et Valcourt); et 3 centres d'hébergement (Windsor, Richmond, et Valcourt).
Pierre Lalande, Directeur général

***Maria:* Centre de santé et de services sociaux de la Baie-des-Chaleurs**
Affiliée à: Agence de la santé et des services sociaux de la Gaspésie-Iles-de-la-Madeleine
419, boul Perron, Maria, QC G0C 1Y0
Tél: 418-759-3443; *Téléc:* 418-759-5063
Ligne sans frais: 888-311-3451
csssbc@csssbc.qc.ca
www.csssbc.qc.ca
Nombre de lits: 77 lits hospitaliers; 214 lits de soins de longue durée
Note: Le CSSS regroupe l'Hôpital de Maria; 3 centres d'hébergement (Maria, New Carlisle, et Matapédia); 5 points de service CLSC (Malauze de Matapédia, Saint-Omer, Pointe-à-la-Croix, Paspébiac, et Caplan); et un centre de médecine familiale.
Bernard Nadeau, Directeur général

Centres de traitments spécialisés

***Mont-Joli:* Centre de santé et de services sociaux de La Mitis**
800, av du Sanatorium, Mont-Joli, QC G5H 3L6
Tél: 418-775-7261; *Téléc:* 418-775-8551
www.centremitissien.net
Nombre de lits: 24 lits; 175 lits de soins de longue durée
Note: Le CSSS regroupe un centre de santé, un centre d'hébergement, un point de service CLSC, un centre de réadaptation en déficience physique, et la Maison des naissances Colette-Julien.
Isabelle Malo, Directrice générale
cmssc_dg@centremitissien.net

Hôpitaux

Centres hospitaliers

***Alma:* Centre de santé et de services sociaux de Lac-Saint-Jean-Est**
Affiliée à: Agence de la santé et des services sociaux du Saguenay-Lac-St-Jean
Ancien nom: Centre le Jeannois
300, boul Champlain sud, Alma, QC G8B 3N8
Tél: 418-669-2000; *Téléc:* 418-668-9695
Nombre de lits: 260 lits
Bertin Riverin, Directeur général

***Amos:* Centre hospitalier Hôtel-Dieu d'Amos CSSS Les Eskers de l'Abitibi**
622, 4e rue ouest, Amos, QC J9T 2S2
Tél: 819-732-3341; *Téléc:* 819-732-7054
www.sante-abitibi-temiscamingue.gouv.qc.ca
Nombre de lits: 96 lits
Note: Services diagnostiques; urgence et traumatologie; othopédie; rhumatologie; ophtalmologie; chirurgie plastique/reconstructive/maxillo-faciale; gynécologie; obstétrique; gériatrie; physiotherapie; réadaptation cardio-respiratoire.
Michel Michaud, Directeur général, CSSS Les Eskers de l'Abitibi
michel_michaud@ssss.gouv.qc.ca

***Asbestos:* Centre de santé et de services sociaux des sources**
Affiliée à: Agence de la santé et des services sociaux de l'Estrie
Ancien nom: Centre de santé de la MRC d'Asbestos
475, 3e av, Asbestos, QC J1T 1X6
Tél: 819-879-7151; *Téléc:* 819-879-7433
Nombre de lits: 17 lits, 88 lits longue durée
Mario Morand, Directeur général

***Baie-Comeau:* Centre de santé et de services sociaux de Manicouagan**
Affiliée à: Agence de la santé et des services sociaux de la Côte-Nord
635, boul Joliet, Baie-Comeau, QC G5C 1P1
Tél: 418-589-3701; *Téléc:* 418-589-9654
Ligne sans frais: 877-484-3701
jean_marc_arsenault@ssss.gouv.qc.ca
Nombre de lits: 106 lits
Daniel Côté, Directeur général

***Baie-Saint-Paul:* Hôpital de Baie-Saint-Paul CSSS de Charlevoix**
Affiliée à: Agence de la santé et des services sociaux de la Capitale-Nationale
74, rue Ambroise-Fafard, Baie-Saint-Paul, QC G3Z 2J6
Tél: 418-435-5150
www.cssscharlevoix.qc.ca
Nombre de lits: 40 lits hospitaliers; 56 lits de soins de longue durée
Note: Services: anesthésie, chirurgie, gériatrie, psychiatrie, radiologie, ophtalmologie, urologie; soins généraux et spécialisés; urgence.
Micheline Tremblay, Directrice générale, CSSS de Charlevoix
micheline.tremblay@ssss.gouv.qc.ca

***Beauceville:* Centre de santé et de services sociaux de Beauce**
Centre administratif
Affiliée à: Agence de la santé et des services sociaux de Chaudière-Appalaches
253, 108e rue, Beauceville, QC G5X 2Z3
Tél: 418-228-2031; *Téléc:* 418-227-3825
csssbeauce@ssss.gouv.qc.ca
www.csssbeauce.qc.ca
Nombre de lits: 117 lits en santé physique; 25 lits en santé mentale
Note: Installations: Centre hospitalier Beauce-Etchemin (Saint-Georges); les CLSCs: Saint-Joseph, Beauceville, La Guadeloupe, Saint-Georges, & Saint-Gédéon; les Centres d'hébergement: Beauceville, Saint-Georges (ouest), & Saint-Georges (est).

***Beaupré:* Hôpital Sainte-Anne-de-Beaupré CSSS de Québec-Nord**
Affiliée à: Agence de la santé et des services sociaux de la Capitale-Nationale
11000, rue des Montagnards, Beaupré, QC G0A 1E0
Tél: 418-827-3738
www.csssqn.qc.ca
Nombre de lits: 172 lits
Note: Services infirmiers, médicaux, et psychosociaux.
Lucie Lacroix, Directrice générale, CSSS de Québec-Nord

***Bedford:* Centre hospitalier de Bedford**
Affiliée à: Agence de la santé et des services sociaux de la Montérégie
CP 1140, 34, rue St-Joseph, Bedford, QC J0J 1A0
Tél: 450-248-3339
Nombre de lits: 42 lits

***Chandler:* Centre de santé et de services sociaux du Rocher-Percé**
Centre hospitalier de Chandler
Affiliée à: Agence de la santé et des services sociaux de la Gaspésie-Iles-de-la-Madeleine
Également connu sous le nom de: Hôpital de Chandler
CP 3300, 451, rue Mgr Ross est, Chandler, QC G0C 1K0
Tél: 418-689-2261; *Téléc:* 418-689-5945
www.agencesssgim.ca
Nombre de lits: 113 lits
Note: Soins hospitaliers; soins de longue durée; a fusionné avec le CLSC-CHSLD Pabok en 2004.
Chantal Duguay, Directrice générale

***Châteauguay:* Hôpital Anna-Laberge CSSS Jardins-Roussillon**
Affiliée à: Agence de la santé et des services sociaux de la Montérégie
200, boul Brisebois, Châteauguay, QC J6K 4W8
Tél: 450-699-2425; *Ligne sans frais:* 800-700-0621
www.santemonteregie.qc.ca/jardins-roussillons
Nombre de lits: 226 lits hospitaliers
Paul Moreau, Directeur général, CSSS Jardins-Roussillon

***Chibougamau:* Centre régional de santé et services sociaux Baie-James**
Affiliée à: Centre régional de la santé et des services sociaux de la Baie-James
312, 3e rue, Chibougamau, QC G8P 1N5
Tél: 418-748-3575; *Téléc:* 418-748-6391
Nombre de lits: 32
Diane Laboissonnière, Directrice générale

***Chicoutimi:* Centre de santé et de services sociaux de Chicoutimi**
Affiliée à: Agence de la santé et des services sociaux du Saguenay-Lac-St-Jean
CP 5006, 305, av Saint-Vallier, Chicoutimi, QC G7H 5H6
Tél: 418-541-1000; *Téléc:* 418-541-1144
Nombre de lits: 432 lits hospitaliers, 275 lits longue durée
Richard Lemieux, Directeur général

***Coaticook:* Centre de santé et de services sociaux de la MRC de Coaticook**
Affiliée à: Agence de la santé et des services sociaux de l'Estrie
Ancien nom: Centre de santé de la MRC de Coaticook
138, rue Jeanne-Mance, Coaticook, QC J1A 1W3
Tél: 819-849-9102; *Téléc:* 819-849-6735
rlavigne.coaticook@ssss.gouv.qc.ca

Pierre-André Rainville, Directeur général

Côte Saint-Luc: Hôpital Mont-Sinai
Affiliée à: Agence de la santé et des services sociaux de Montréal
5690, boul Cavendish, Côte Saint-Luc, QC H4W 1S7
Tél: 514-369-2222; Téléc: 514-369-2225
www.sinaimontreal.ca

Nombre de lits: 57 lits
Joseph Rothbart, Directeur général

Coteau-du-Lac: Centre de santé et de services sociaux du Suroit
341, ch du Fleuve, Coteau-du-Lac, QC J0P 1B0
Tél: 450-371-9925; Téléc: 450-377-1372

Nombre de lits: 391 lits
François Rabeau, Directeur général

Donnacona: Centre hospitalier Portneuf
250, boul Gaudreau, Donnacona, QC G3M 1L7
Tél: 418-285-3025; Téléc: 418-285-3508
lucie_gagnon@ssss.gouv.qc.ca

Nombre de lits: 369 lits
Lucie Gagnon, Directrice générale
Philippe Leboeuf, Président du conseil d'administration

Drummondville: Hôpital Sainte-Croix
CSSS Drummond
Affiliée à: Agence de la santé et des services sociaux de la Mauricie et du Centre-du-Québec
570, rue Heriot, Drummondville, QC J2B 1C1
Tél: 819-478-6464
csssdrummond@ssss.gouv.qc.ca
www.csssdrummond.qc.ca

Nombre de lits: 191 lits
Note: Anatomopathologie, chirurgie générale, gynécologie-obstétrique, pédiatrie, médecine familiale/interne/nucléaire, ophtalmologie, orthopédie, psychiatrie, radiologie, urologie.
Nagui Habashi, Directeur général, CSSS Drummond

Fermont: Centre de santé et de services sociaux de l'Hématite
Affiliée à: Agence de la santé et des services sociaux de la Côte-Nord
CP 550, 1, rue Aquilon, Fermont, QC G0G 1J0
Tél: 418-287-5461; Téléc: 418-287-5281

Nombre de lits: 5 lits
Normand Ducharme, Directeur général

Gaspé: Centre de santé et de services sociaux de la Côte-de-Gaspé
Hôpital Hôtel-Dieu
Affiliée à: Agence de la santé et des services sociaux de la Gaspésie-Iles-de-la-Madeleine
215, boul de York ouest, Gaspé, QC G4X 2W2
Tél: 418-368-3301; Téléc: 418-368-7150
www.cssscotedegaspe.ca

Nombre de lits: 56 lits hospitaliers
Jean-Pierre Tremblay, Directeur général

Gatineau: Centre de santé et de services sociaux de Gatineau
Affiliée à: Agence de la santé et de services sociaux de l'Outaouais
Également connu sous le nom de: CSSS de Gatineau
Centre administratif, 257, rue Laurier, Gatineau, QC J8X 3W8
Tél: 819-966-6420
www.csssgatineau.qc.ca

Year Founded: 2004
Nombre de lits: 508 lits
Note: Le CSSS de Gatineau regroupe les hôpitaux de Gatineau et de Hull, 8 sites de CLSC, 4 centres d'hébergement, la Maison de naissance de l'Outaouais, 3 hôpitaux de jours gériatriques, et un centre de médicine familiale; 425 médecins; 8 sages-femmes; 5 000 employé(e)s.
André O. Rodier, Directeur général
819-966-6560

Gatineau: CSSS de Papineau - Centre administratif
Affiliée à: Agence de la santé et de services sociaux de l'Outaouais
578, rue MacLaren est, Gatineau, QC J8L 2W1
Tél: 819-986-3359; Téléc: 819-986-5671
csss_papineau@ssss.gouv.qc.ca
www.cssspapineau.qc.ca

Gilles Clavel, Directeur général (par intérim)

Gatineau: CSSS de Papineau - Hôpital de Papineau
Affiliée à: Agence de la santé et de services sociaux de l'Outaouais
155, rue Maclaren est, Gatineau, QC J8L 0C2
Tél: 819-986-3341; Téléc: 819-986-4000
csss_papineau@ssss.gouv.qc.ca
www.cssspapineau.qc.ca

Nombre de lits: 63 lits hospitaliers; 55 lits soins longue durée
Gilles Clavel, Directeur général (par intérim), CSSS de Papineau

Gatineau: Hôpital de Gatineau
CSSS de Gatineau
Affiliée à: Agence de la santé et de services sociaux de l'Outaouais
909, boul de La Vérendrye, Gatineau, QC J8P 7H2
Tél: 819-966-6100
www.csssgatineau.qc.ca

Nombre de lits: 243 lits
André O. Rodier, Directeur général, CSSS de Gatineau
819-966-6560
Dr. André Moreau, Directeur, Services professionnels/Affaires médicales
819-966-6104
Gilles Coulombe, Directeur, Soins infirmiers/Pratiques professionnelles
819-966-6540

Gatineau: Hôpital de Hull
CSSS de Gatineau
Affiliée à: Agence de la santé et de services sociaux de l'Outaouais
116, boul Lionel-Émond, Gatineau, QC J8Y 1W7
Tél: 819-966-6200; Téléc: 819-966-6306
www.csssgatineau.qc.ca

Nombre de lits: 265 lits
André O. Rodier, Directeur général, CSSS de Gatineau
819-966-6560

Granby: Centre de santé et de services sociaux de la Haute Yamaska
Affiliée à: Agence de la santé et des services sociaux de la Montérégie
205, boul Leclerc Ouest, Granby, QC J2G 1T7
Tél: 450-375-8000; Téléc: 450-375-8032

Nombre de lits: 303 lits
Claude Vézina, Directeur général

Greenfield Park: Hôpital Charles LeMoyne
Affiliée à: Agence de la santé et des services sociaux de la Montérégie
3120, boul Taschereau, Greenfield Park, QC J4V 2H1
Tél: 450-466-5000; Téléc: 450-466-8887
www.santemonteregie.qc.ca/hclm

Nombre de lits: 571 lits
Note: L'Hôpital est le centre hospitalier régional et universitaire de la Montéregie; affilié à l'Université de Sherbrooke; soins et services de court durée en santé physique, santé mentale, réadaptation; recherche; enseignement universitaire.
Yvan Gendron, Directeur général
Dr. Alphonse Montminy, Directeur, Services professionnels et hospitaliers
Ginette Brunelle, Directrice, Soins infirmiers

Hâvre-Saint-Pierre: Centre de santé et de services sociaux de La Minganie
Affiliée à: Agence de la santé et des services sociaux de la Côte-Nord
1035, Promenade des Anciens, Hâvre-Saint-Pierre, QC G0G 1P0
Tél: 418-538-2212; Téléc: 418-538-2365

Nombre de lits: 13 lits hospitaliers, 60 lits longue durée
Danièle Limoges, Directrice générale
Richard Thibeault, Contremaître

Joliette: Les entreprises Symel inc.
Affiliée à: Agences de développement de réseaux locaux de services de santé et de services sociaux
600, rue Saint-Louis, Joliette, QC J6E 9C9
Tél: 450-756-4282; Téléc: 450-755-4959

Nombre de lits: 28 lits
Cynthia Lapointe, Directrice générale

Jonquière: Centre de santé et de services sociaux de Jonquière
Affiliée à: Agence de la santé et des services sociaux du Saguenay-Lac-St-Jean
Ancien nom: Centre hospitalier Jonquière
2230, rue de l'Hôpital, Jonquière, QC G7X 4H6
Tél: 418-695-7700; Téléc: 418-695-7729
info@carrefoursante.qc.ca
www.carrefoursante.qc.ca

Nombre de lits: 70 lits hospitaliers, 299 lits de longue durée
Note: Centre hospitalier, centre local de services communautaires, centre d'hébergement, centre de réadaptation (alcoolisme/toxicomanie; déficience physique).
Lucille Dauphin, Directrice générale

Kahnawake: Conseil des Mohawks de Kahnawake
CP 720, Kahnawake, QC J0L 1B0
Tél: 450-638-3930; Téléc: 450-638-4634

Nombre de lits: 10 lits hospitaliers, 33 lits longue durée
Suzanne Horn, Directrice générale

La Baie: Centre de santé et de services sociaux Cléophas-Claveau
Affiliée à: Agence de la santé et des services sociaux du Saguenay-Lac-St-Jean
CP 38, 1000, rue Docteur-Desgagné, La Baie, QC G7B 3P9
Tél: 418-544-3381; Téléc: 418-544-0770
www.santesaglac.gouv.qc.ca

Nombre de lits: 25 lits hospitaliers, 114 lits de longue durée
Note: Centre hospitalier: Hôpital de La Baie; centre local de services communautaires; et centres d'hébergement: Foyer de Bagotville, Foyer Saint-Joseph de la Baie.
Martine Nepton, Directrice générale

La Malbaie: Hôpital de La Malbaie
CSSS de Charlevoix
Affiliée à: Agence de la santé et des services sociaux de la Capitale-Nationale
Également connu sous le nom de: Centre hospitalier de St-Joseph de La Malbaie
CP 340, 303, rue St-Étienne, La Malbaie, QC G5A 1T1
Tél: 418-665-1700
www.cssscharlevoix.qc.ca

Nombre de lits: 56 lits hospitaliers
Micheline Tremblay, Directrice générale, CSSS de Charlevoix
micheline.tremblay@ssss.gouv.qc.ca

La Tuque: Centre de santé et de services sociaux du Haut-Saint-Maurice
Affiliée à: Agence de la santé et des services sociaux de la Mauricie et du Centre-du-Québec
885, boul Ducharme, La Tuque, QC G9X 3C1
Tél: 819-523-4581; Téléc: 819-523-7992

Nombre de lits: 82 lits
Michèle Ouellet, Directrice générale (intérim)

LaSalle: Centre hospitalier de LaSalle
Affiliée à: Agence de la santé et des services sociaux de Montréal
Également connu sous le nom de: l'Hôpital de LaSalle
8585, Terrasse Champlain, LaSalle, QC H8P 1C1
Tél: 514-362-8000
www.santemontreal.qc.ca
Nombre de lits: 110 lits hospitaliers, 123 lits longue durée

Lac-Etchemin: Centre de santé et de services sociaux des Etchemins
Centre administratif
Affiliée à: Agence de la santé et des services sociaux de Chaudière-Appalaches
331, place du Sanatorium, Lac-Etchemin, QC G0R 1S0
Tél: 418-625-3101; Téléc: 418-625-3109
csssetchemins@ssss.gouv.qc.ca
www.cssetchemins.qc.ca

Nombre de lits: 206 lits
Note: Installations: l'Hôpital; le CLSC Saint-Prosper, et Centre d'hébergement Pavillon de l'Hospitalité; pour la clientèle en santé mentale: L'Équinoxe, L'Intemporel, & L'Intermédiare; pour la clientèle en déficience physique: Résidence Le Tremplin; & L'Atelier du Lac (réadaptation travail socioprofessionnel).
France Laplante Theberge, Directrice générale (intérim)

Laval: Hôpital de la Cité-de-la-Santé
CSSS de Laval
1755, boul René-Laennec, Laval, QC H7M 3L9
Tél: 450-668-1010
www.cssslaval.qc.ca

Nombre de lits: 414 lits hospitaliers; 38 lits de psychiatrie
Luc Lepage, Directeur général, CSSS de Laval
Alain Goudreau, Directeur, Services professionnels et hospitaliers/Affaires mé

Laval: Jewish Rehabilitation Hospital
Hôpital juif de réadaptation
Affiliée à: Agence de la santé et de services sociaux de Laval
3205, Place Alton-Goldbloom, Laval, QC H7V 1R2
Tél: 450-688-9550; Téléc: 450-688-3673
www.hjr-jrh.qc.ca

Year Founded: 1962
Nombre de lits: 120
André Ibghy, Executive Director
450/688-9550 ext.201, Fax: 450/688-4401,
aibghy_hjr@ssss.gouv.qc.ca

***Laval:* Santé Courville inc.**
Affiliée à: Agence de la santé et de services sociaux de Laval
5200, 80e rue, Laval, QC H7R 5T6
Tél: 450-627-7990; *Téléc:* 450-627-7993
Nombre de lits: 120 lits
Christine Durocher, Directrice générale

***Les Escoumins:* Centre de santé et de services sociaux de la Haute-Côte-Nord**
Affiliée à: Agence de la santé et des services sociaux de la Côte-Nord
CP 1000, 4, rue de l'Hôpital, Les Escoumins, QC G0T 1K0
Tél: 418-233-2931; *Téléc:* 418-233-2608
Nombre de lits: 20 lits hospitaliers, 76 lits longue durée
Micheline Anctil, Directrice générale
Katleen Dion, Directeur, soins infirmiers

***Lévis:* Hôtel-Dieu de Lévis**
Centre administratif
Affiliée à: Agence de la santé et des services sociaux de Chaudière-Appalaches
143, rue Wolfe, Lévis, QC G6V 3Z1
Tél: 418-835-7121; *Téléc:* 418-835-7143
info@hdl.qc.ca
www.hdl.qc.ca
Nombre de lits: 343 lits
Hervé Moysan, Directeur général
Robert Amyot, Directeur, Services techniques
Diana Lancup, Responsable des services sanitaires et lingerie

***Longueuil:* Hôpital Pierre-Boucher**
CSSS Pierre-Boucher
1333, boul Jacques-Cartier est, Longueuil, QC J4M 2A5
Tél: 450-468-8111
www.santemonteregie.qc.ca/cssspierreboucher
Nombre de lits: 340 lits
Note: Urgence; soins intensifs; soins palliatifs; services médicaux; chirurgie; psychiatrie.
Caroline Barbir, Directrice générale, CSSS Pierre-Boucher

***Loretteville:* Centre hospitalier Chauveau**
Affiliée à: Agence de la santé et des services sociaux de la Capitale-Nationale
29, rue de l'Hôpital, Loretteville, QC G2A 2T7
Tél: 418-842-3651; *Téléc:* 418-842-8931
Nombre de lits: 154 lits + service ambulatoire
Reynald Gagnon, Directeur général

***Louiseville:* Centre de santé et de services sociaux de Maskinongé**
41, boul Comtois, Louiseville, QC J5V 2H8
Tél: 819-228-2731; *Téléc:* 819-228-2973
yves_martin@ssss.gouv.qc.ca
Nombre de lits: 151 lits
Yves Martin, Directeur général

***Lourdes-de-Blanc-Sablon:* Centre de santé et de services sociaux de la Basse-Côte-Nord**
Affiliée à: Agence de la santé et des services sociaux de la Côte-Nord
CP 130, 1070, boul Dr Camille Marcoux, Lourdes-de-Blanc-Sablon, QC G0G 1W0
Tél: 418-461-2144; *Téléc:* 418-461-2731
Nombre de lits: 22 lits hospitaliers, 28 lits longue durée
André Racine, Directeur général (intérim)

***Maniwaki:* CSSS de la Vallée-de-La-Gatineau**
Affiliée à: Agence de la santé et de services sociaux de l'Outaouais
309, boul Desjardins, Maniwaki, QC J9E 2E7
Tél: 819-449-2300; *Téléc:* 819-449-6137
www.csvg.qc.ca
Nombre de lits: 40 lits hospitaliers, 101 lits longue durée
Michel Leger, Directeur général

***Mansfield et Pontefract:* Centre de santé et de services sociaux du Pontiac**
Affiliée à: Agence de la santé et de services sociaux de l'Outaouais
CP 430, 160, ch de la Chute, Mansfield et Pontefract, QC J0X 1V0
Tél: 819-683-3000; *Téléc:* 819-683-3682
Ligne sans frais: 800-567-9625
www.santepontiac.qc.ca
Nombre de lits: 39 lits hospitaliers, 115 lits longue durée
Richard Grimard, Directeur général

***Maria:* Hôpital de Maria**
CSSS de la Baie-des-Chaleurs
Affiliée à: Agence de la santé et des services sociaux de la Gaspésie-Iles-de-la-Madeleine
419, boul Perron, Maria, QC G0C 1Y0
Tél: 418-759-3443; *Téléc:* 418-759-5063
csssbc@csssbc.qc.ca
www.csssbc.qc.ca
Nombre de lits: 77 lits
Note: Unité de médecine familiale Baie-des-Chaleurs: 418-759-1336, poste 2811.
Bernard Nadeau, Directeur général, CSSS de la Baie-des-Chaleurs

***Mont-Laurier:* Hôpital de Mont-Laurier**
CSSS d'Antoine-Labelle
Affiliée à: Agence de la santé et des services sociaux des Laurentides
2561, ch de la Lièvre sud, Mont-Laurier, QC J9L 3G3
Tél: 819-623-1234; *Téléc:* 819-440-4376
Nombre de lits: 62 lits
Jean-Pierre Urbain, Directeur général, CSSS d'Antoine-Labelle

***Montmagny:* Centre de santé et de services sociaux de Montmagny-L'Islet**
Centre administratif
Affiliée à: Agence de la santé et des services sociaux de Chaudière-Appalaches
350, boul Taché ouest, Montmagny, QC G5V 3R8
Tél: 418-248-0630; *Téléc:* 418-248-6838
www.csssml.qc.ca
Nombre de lits: 71 lits hospitaliers
Note: Installations: Hôtel-Dieu de Montmagny (l'hôpital); les CLSCs: Saint-Jean Port-Joli, Saint-Pamphile, Saint-Fabien-de-Panet, Montmagny, & l'Isle-aux-Grues; les Centres d'hébergement: Sainte-Perpétue, Saint-Eugène, Cap-Saint-Ignace, Saint-Fabien-de-Panet, Saint-Jean Port-Joli, & Montmagny.
Marie-Claude Ouellet, Directeur général

***Montréal:* Centre de santé et de services sociaux du coeur de l'île**
Affiliée à: Agence de la santé et des services sociaux de Montréal
1385, rue Jean-Talon est, Montréal, QC H2E 1S6
Tél: 514-495-6754; *Téléc:* 514-495-6734
www.hopitaljean-talon.qc.ca
Nombre de lits: 320 lits
Francine Lortie, Directrice générale

***Montréal:* Centre de santé et de services sociaux du Sud-Ouest-Verdun**
Affiliée à: Agence de la santé et des services sociaux de Montréal
Ancien nom: CSSS de Verdun/C. St-Paul, St-Henri et P. St-Charl
6161, rue Laurendeau, Montréal, QC H4E 3X6
Tél: 514-766-0546; *Téléc:* 514-732-5107
Nombre de lits: 1,309 lits
Danielle McCann, Directrice générale

***Montréal:* Centre hospitalier de l'Université de Montréal**
Affiliée à: Agence de la santé et des services sociaux de Montréal
3840, rue St-Urbain, Montréal, QC H2W 1T8
Tél: 514-890-8000; *Téléc:* 514-412-7224
Nombre de lits: 1217 lits hospitaliers, 170 lits longue durée
Denis R. Roy, Directeur général

***Montréal:* Centre hospitalier de St. Mary**
Affiliée à: Agence de la santé et des services sociaux de Montréal
3830, av Lacombe, Montréal, QC H3T 1M5
Tél: 514-345-3511; *Téléc:* 514-345-3836
www.smhc.qc.ca
Nombre de lits: 251 lits hospitaliers, 65 lits longue durée
Arvind K. Joshi, Directeur général

***Montréal:* Centre hospitalier Fleury**
Affiliée à: Agence de la santé et des services sociaux de Montréal
2180, rue Fleury est, Montréal, QC H2B 1K3
Tél: 514-381-9311; *Téléc:* 514-383-5086
bruno.lheureux.chfleury@ssss.gouv.qc.ca
Nombre de lits: 149 lits hospitaliers, 25 lits longue durée
Dr. Bruno J. L'Heureux, Directeur général associé

***Montréal:* Centre hospitalier Jacques-Viger**
Affiliée à: Agence de la santé et des services sociaux de Montréal
1051, rue St-Hubert, Montréal, QC H2L 3Y5
Tél: 514-842-7181
Nombre de lits: 447 lits

***Montréal:* Centre hospitalier Richardson/Centre Henri Bradet**
Affiliée à: Agence de la santé et des services sociaux de Montréal
5425, rue Bessborough, Montréal, QC H4V 2S7
Tél: 514-483-1380; *Téléc:* 514-483-4596
Nombre de lits: 42 lits hospitaliers, 125 lits longue durée
Francine Dupuis, Directrice générale (par intérim)

***Montréal:* Centre hospitalier universitaire Sainte-Justine**
Affiliée à: Agence de la santé et des services sociaux de Montréal
3175, ch de la Côte Ste-Catherine, Montréal, QC H3T 1C5
Tél: 514-345-4931; *Téléc:* 514-345-4808
Nombre de lits: 434 lits hospitaliers, 55 lits longue durée
Khiem Dao, Directeur général

***Montréal:* Centre universitaire de santé McGill - Hôpital neurologique de Montréal**
Montréal Neurological Hospital
Affiliée à: Agence de la santé et des services sociaux de Montréal
3801, University, Montréal, QC H3A 2B4
Tél: 514-934-1934; *Téléc:* 514-398-3338
www.muhc.mcgill.ca
Nombre de lits: 1,193 lits, 173 lits longue durée
Arthur T. Porter, Directeur général
Jean Pierre Bertrand, Directeur, Services techniques
Stephen Black, Manager, Environmental Services

***Montréal:* Hôpital Catherine Booth de l'Armée du Salut**
Affiliée à: Agence de la santé et des services sociaux de Montréal
4375, av Montclair, Montréal, QC H4B 2J5
Tél: 514-481-0431; *Téléc:* 514-481-0029
s.bourdeau@ssss.gouv.qc.ca
Nombre de lits: 84 lits
Note: réadaptation
Edith Verstege, Directrice générale (intérim)

***Montréal:* Hôpital de réadaptation Lindsay**
Affiliée à: Agence de la santé et des services sociaux de Montréal
6363, ch Hudson, Montréal, QC H3S 1M9
Tél: 514-737-3661; *Téléc:* 514-737-0592
hrl@ssss.gouv.qc.ca
www.hopital-lindsay.qc.ca
Nombre de lits: 155 lits
Note: hôpital spécialisé de courte-durée
Réjean Plante, Directeur général

***Montréal:* Hôpital du Sacré-Coeur de Montréal**
Affiliée à: Agence de la santé et des services sociaux de Montréal
5400, boul Gouin ouest, Montréal, QC H4J 1C5
Tél: 514-338-2222; *Téléc:* 514-338-2384
www.crhsc.umontreal.ca/hscm/
Nombre de lits: 554 lits hospitaliers
Note: outpatient services & trauma centre
Michel Larivière, Directeur général
Julien Ricard, Chef de service de la salubrité
514/338-2214

***Montréal:* Hôpital général de Montréal**
The Montréal General Hospital
Affiliée à: Agence de la santé et des services sociaux de Montréal
1650, av Cedar, Montréal, QC H3G 1A4
Tél: 514-934-1934; *Téléc:* 514-934-8200
www.muhc.ca
Nombre de lits: 417 beds
Arthur T. Porter, Directeur général

***Montréal:* Hôpital général juif Sir Mortimer B. Davis**
Sir Mortimer B. Davis Jewish General Hospital
Affiliée à: Agence de la santé et des services sociaux de Montréal
3755, ch Côte Ste-Catherine, Montréal, QC H3T 1E2
Tél: 514-340-8222; *Téléc:* 514-340-7510
Nombre de lits: 571 lits hospitaliers, 100 lits longue durée
Henri Elbaz, Directeur général
Jacques Benzaquen, Directeur, Services techniques

***Montréal:* Hôpital Maisonneuve-Rosemont**
Affiliée à: Agence de la santé et des services sociaux de Montréal
5415, boul de l'Assomption, Montréal, QC H1T 2M4
Tél: 514-252-3400; *Téléc:* 514-252-3408
www.maisonneuve-rosemont.org
Nombre de lits: 617 lits hospitaliers, 183 lits longue durée
Carole Deschambeault, Directrice générale

***Montréal:* Hôpital Santa Cabrini**
Affiliée à: Agence de la santé et des services sociaux de Montréal
5655, rue St-Zotique est, Montréal, QC H1T 1P7
Tél: 514-252-6000; *Téléc:* 514-252-6453
Nombre de lits: 141 lits hospitaliers
Irène Giannetti, Directrice générale

***Montréal:* Hopital Shriners pour enfants (Quebec) inc.**
Affiliée à: Agence de la santé et des services sociaux de Montréal
1529, av Cedar, Montréal, QC H3G 1A6
Tél: 514-842-4464; *Téléc:* 514-842-7553
Nombre de lits: 40 lits
Maureen Brennan, Directrice générale

***Montréal:* Institut de cardiologie de Montréal**
Affiliée à: Agence de la santé et des services sociaux de Montréal
5000, rue Bélanger est, Montréal, QC H1T 1C8
Tél: 514-376-3330; *Téléc:* 514-593-2540
www.icm-mhi.org
Nombre de lits: 153 lits
Robert Busilacchi, Directeur général

***Montréal:* Institut Philippe Pinel de Montréal**
Affiliée à: Agence de la santé et des services sociaux de Montréal
10905, boul Henri-Bourassa est, Montréal, QC H1C 1H1
Tél: 514-648-8461; *Téléc:* 514-494-4406
www.pinel.qc.ca/
Nombre de lits: 295 lits
Paul-André Lafleur, Directeur général
Paul-Emile Trudeau, Directeur, Services techniques

***Montréal:* Institut universitaire de gériatrie de Montréal**
Affiliée à: Agence de la santé et des services sociaux de Montréal
4565, ch Queen Mary, Montréal, QC H3W 1W5
Tél: 514-340-1424; *Téléc:* 514-340-3500
Nombre de lits: 379 lits
Céline Crowe, Directrice générale (intérim)

***Nicolet:* Centre de santé et de services sociaux de Bécancour-Nicolet-Yamaska**
Affiliée à: Agence de la santé et des services sociaux de la Mauricie et du Centre-du-Québec
Ancien nom: Centre de santé Nicolet-Yamaska
675, rue St-Jean-Baptiste, Nicolet, QC J3T 1S4
Tél: 819-293-2071; *Téléc:* 819-293-6160
Nombre de lits: 10 lits de courte durée gériatrique, 303 lits longue durée
Raynald Beaupré, Directeur général
André Melançon, Chef, Services techniques

***Ormstown:* Hôpital Barrie Memorial**
Affiliée à: Agence de la santé et des services sociaux de la Montérégie
Centre de santé et de services sociaux du Haut-Sai, CP 200, 28, rue Gale, Ormstown, QC J0S 1K0
Tél: 450-829-2321; *Téléc:* 450-829-3582
Nombre de lits: 49 lits hospitaliers
Francine Lortie, Directrice générale
francine.lotrie@rrsss16.gouv.qc.ca

***Pointe-Claire:* Hôpital général du Lakeshore**
Affiliée à: Agence de la santé et des services sociaux de la Montérégie
160, ch Stillview, Pointe-Claire, QC H9R 2Y2
Tél: 514-630-2225; *Téléc:* 514-630-3302
Nombre de lits: 227 lits hospitaliers, 30 lits longue durée
Luc Lepage, Directeur général

***Québec:* Centre de santé et de services sociaux de Québec-Nord**
7150, boul Cloutier, Québec, QC G1H 5V5
Tél: 418-651-2572; *Téléc:* 418-628-8668
Nombre de lits: 959 lits
Lucie Lacroix, Directrice générale

***Québec:* Le Centre de santé et de services sociaux de Québec-Nord (CSSSQN)**
2915, av. du Bourg-Royal, 4e étage, Québec, QC G1C 3S2
Tél: 418-661-5666; *Téléc:* 418-780-8726
Nombre de lits: 18 lits hospitaliers, 144 lits longue durée
Reynald Gagnon, Directeur général

***Québec:* Centre hospitalier affilié universitaire de Québec**
Hôpital de l'Enfant-Jésus - Hôpital du Saint-Sacrement
Affiliée à: Agence de la santé et des services sociaux de la Capitale-Nationale
1401, 18e rue, Québec, QC G1J 1Z4
Tél: 418-649-0252; *Téléc:* 418-649-5557
www.cha.quebec.qc.ca
Nombre de lits: 668 lits
Marie Girard, Directeur général

***Québec:* Centre hospitalier universitaire de Québec (CHUQ)**
Affiliée à: Agence de la santé et des services sociaux de la Capitale-Nationale
11, Côte du Palais, Québec, QC G1R 2J6
Tél: 418-525-4444; *Téléc:* 418-691-5205
Nombre de lits: 187 lits hospitaliers; 946 lits (courte durée et pouponnière); 100 lits (hébergement et soins de longue durée); 54 lits (néonatalogie)
René Rouleau, Directeur général

***Québec:* Hôpital Jeffery Hale**
Affiliée à: Agence de la santé et des services sociaux de la Capitale-Nationale
1250, ch Ste-Foy, Québec, QC G1S 2M6
Tél: 418-683-4471; *Téléc:* 418-683-8980
dg.jhale@sympatico.ca
Nombre de lits: 12 lits hospitaliers, 100 lits longue durée
Louis Hanrahan, Directeur général
Réné Corriveau, Coordonnateur, services techniques

***Rimouski:* Hôpital régional de Rimouski**
CSSS de Rimouski-Neigette
150, av Rouleau, Rimouski, QC G5L 5T1
Tél: 418-723-7851; *Téléc:* 418-724-8632
courrierweb.crsssr@ssss.gouv.qc.ca
www.chrr.qc.ca
Nombre de lits: 255 lits
Raymond Coulombe, Directeur général, CSSS de Rimouski-Neigette

***Rivière-Rouge:* Centre de services de Rivière-Rouge**
CSSS d'Antoine-Labelle
1525, rue L'Annonciation nord, Rivière-Rouge, QC J0T 1T0
Tél: 819-275-2118; *Téléc:* 819-275-2464
www.csssal.org
Jean-Pierre Urbain, Directeur général, CSSS d'Antoine-Labelle

***Roberval:* Hôtel-Dieu de Roberval/Centre d'hébergement Roberval**
CSSS Domaine-du-Roy
450, rue Brassard, Roberval, QC G8H 1B9
Tél: 418-275-0110; *Téléc:* 418-275-6202
hdr@ssss.gouv.qc.ca
www.cmdp-roberval.com
Nombre de lits: 135 lits hospitaliers; 100 lits de soins de longue durée
Note: L'hôpital offre service d'urgence, médecine générale/interne/nucléaire, ophtalmologie, obstétrique, orthopédie, pédiatrie, chirurgie, psychiatrie, urologie, réadaptation physique.
Jacques Dubois, Directeur général, CSSS Domaine-du-Roy

***Saint-Charles-Borromée:* Centre de santé et de services sociaux du Nord de Lanaudière**
Affiliée à: Agences de développement de réseaux locaux de services de santé et de services sociaux
1000, boul Sainte-Anne, Saint-Charles-Borromée, QC J6E 6J2
Tél: 450-759-8222; *Téléc:* 450-759-7969
Nombre de lits: 996 lits
Note: Centre hospitalier à vocations multiples
Caroline Barbir, Directrice générale

***Saint-Eustache:* CSSS du Lac-des-Deux-Montagnes**
Affiliée à: Agence de la santé et des services sociaux des Laurentides
520, boul Arthur-Sauvé, Saint-Eustache, QC J7R 5B1
Tél: 450-473-6811; *Téléc:* 450-473-6966
www.moncsss.com
Year Founded: 2004
Nombre de lits: 221 lits hospitaliers; 258 lits d'hébergement/SLD
Note: Réseau local de services de santé et de services sociaux; 4 installations: CH de Saint-Benoît, CH de Saint-Eustache, CLSC Jean-Olivier-Chénier, et Hôpital de Saint-Eustache; 2 400 employés/employées et médecins, et 180 bénévoles.
Roch Martel, Directeur général

***Saint-Eustache:* Manoir Saint-Eustache**
Affiliée à: Agence de la santé et des services sociaux des Laurentides
CP 850, 55, rue Chenier, Saint-Eustache, QC J7R 4Y8
Tél: 450-472-0013; *Téléc:* 450-472-3104
Nombre de lits: 194 lits

***Saint-Hyacinthe:* Hôpital Honoré-Mercier**
CSSS Richelieu-Yamaska
Affiliée à: Agence de la santé et des services sociaux de la Montérégie
2750, boul Laframboise, Saint-Hyacinthe, QC J2S 4Y8
Tél: 450-771-3333; *Téléc:* 450-771-3748
info@lesommetavotreportee.qc.ca
www.lesommetavotreportee.qc.ca;
www.santemonteregie.qc.ca/richelieu-yamaska
Nombre de lits: 273 lits
Note: Centre mère-enfant-famille; Pédiatrie; Soins intensifs; Chirurgie.
Daniel Castonguay, Directeur général, CSSS Richelieu-Yamaska
Dr. Diane Poirier, Directrice, Affaires médicales
Carmen Messier, Directrice, Soins infirmiers/Pratiques professionnelles

***Saint-Jean-sur-Richelieu:* Hôpital du Haut-Richelieu**
CSSS Haut-Richelieu-Rouville
Affiliée à: Agence de la santé et des services sociaux de la Montérégie
978, boul du Séminaire nord, Saint-Jean-sur-Richelieu, QC J3A 1B7
Tél: 450-359-5000; *Téléc:* 450-359-5251
Nombre de lits: 307 lits
Note: L'Hôpital, et le centre administratif du CSSS Haut-Richelieu-Rouville.
Christine Lessard, Directrice générale, CSSS Haut-Richelieu-Rouville
Dr. Krystyna Pecko, Directrice générale adjointe/Directrice des affaires mé

***Saint-Marc-des-Carrières:* Centre de santé et de services sociaux de Portneuf**
Affiliée à: Agence de la santé et des services sociaux de la Capitale-Nationale
CP 400, 1045, boul Bona-Dussault, Saint-Marc-des-Carrières, QC G0A 4B0
Tél: 418-285-3025; *Téléc:* 418-285-3508
Nombre de lits: 14 lits hospitaliers, 347 lits longue durée
Note: hébergement et soins de longue durée: Centre d'hébergement Donnaconna, Centre d'hébergement Saint-Casimir, Centre d'hébergement Saint-Marc-des-Carrières, Centre d'hébergement Saint-Raymond, Centre hospitalier Portneuf
Lucie Gagnon, Directrice générale

***Saint-Romuald:* Centre de santé et de services sociaux du Grand Littoral**
Centre administratif
Affiliée à: Agence de la santé et des services sociaux de Chaudière-Appalaches
975, rue de la Concorde, Saint-Romuald, QC G6W 8A7
Tél: 418-380-8991; *Téléc:* 418-832-9041
info-directiongenerale-csssgrandlittoral@ssss.gouv.qc.ca
www.csssgrandlittoral.qc.ca
Note: Installations: CLSC & Unité de médecine familiale Saint-Romuald; les autres CLSCs: Saint-Lazare, Sainte-Marie, Laurier-Station, Lévis, & Centre Paul-Gilbert; les Centres d'hébergement: Saint-Gervais, Saint-Raphaël, Saint-Anselme, Sainte-Claire, Lévis, Hébergement Ilot Desjardins, Résidence Louis Édouard-Couture, Saint-Apollinaire, Saint-Flavien, Sainte-Croix, Saint-Sylvestre, Sainte-Marie, Saint-Isidore, & Sainte-Hénédine.

***Saint-Tite:* Centre de santé et de services sociaux de la Vallée-de-la-Batiscan**
CP 430, 750, rue du Couvent, Saint-Tite, QC G0X 3H0
Tél: 418-365-7555; *Téléc:* 418-365-6009
Nombre de lits: 171 lits
Alain Lampron, Directeur général

***Sainte-Adèle:* Centre de santé et de services sociaux des Pays-d'en-Haut**
Affiliée à: Agence de la santé et des services sociaux des Laurentides
1390, boul de Sainte-Adèle, Sainte-Adèle, QC J8B 2N5
Tél: 450-229-6601; *Téléc:* 450-229-7220

Nombre de lits: 91 lits
Jacqueline Gagnon, Directrice générale

Sainte-Anne-de-Bellevue: Hôpital Sainte-Anne
Affiliée à: Agence de la santé et des services sociaux de Montréal
Le ministère des affaires des anciens combattants, 305, boul des Anciens-Combattants, Sainte-Anne-de-Bellevue, QC H9X 1Y9
Tél: 514-457-3440; *Ligne sans frais:* 800-361-9287
steanne@vac-acc.gc.ca
www.vac-acc.gc.ca
Nombre de lits: 590 lits
Rachel Corneille-Gravel, Directrice générale

Salaberry-de-Valleyfield: Centre de santé et de services sociaux du Suroît
Affiliée à: Agence de la santé et des services sociaux de la Montérégie
150, rue St-Thomas, Salaberry-de-Valleyfield, QC J6T 6C1
Tél: 450-371-9920
www.chsuroit.qc.ca
Nombre de lits: 384 lits
François Rabeau, Directeur général

Sept-Iles: Centre de santé et de services sociaux de Sept-Iles
Affiliée à: Agence de la santé et des services sociaux de la Côte-Nord
45, rue Père Divet, Sept-Iles, QC G4R 3N7
Tél: 418-962-9761; *Téléc:* 418-962-2701
Nombre de lits: 117 lits hospitaliers, 96 lits longue durée
Jean-René Blouin, Directeur général
Claude Lantaigne, Chef, Services d'entretien sanitaire

Shawinigan: Centre de santé et de services sociaux de l'énergie
Affiliée à: Agence de la santé et des services sociaux de la Mauricie et du Centre-du-Québec
1705, av Georges, Shawinigan, QC G9N 2N1
Tél: 819-536-7500; *Téléc:* 819-536-7658
Nombre de lits: 404 lits
Guy Lemieux, Directeur général

Shawinigan-Sud: Hôpital du Centre-de-la Mauricie
Affiliée à: Agence de la santé et des services sociaux de la Mauricie et du Centre-du-Québec
50, 119e rue, Shawinigan-Sud, QC G9P 5K1
Tél: 819-536-7500
Nombre de lits: 178 lits hospitaliers, 45 lits longue durée

Shawville: Centre hospitalier du Pontiac
Affiliée à: Agence de la santé et de services sociaux de l'Outaouais
200, rue Argue, Shawville, QC J0X 2Y0
Tél: 819-647-2211; *Téléc:* 819-647-2409
santepontiac.qc.ca/
Nombre de lits: 71 lits
Richard Grimard, Directeur général
Jacques Boissonneault, Chef de service, Biologie médicale

Sherbrooke: Centre hospitalier universitaire de Sherbrooke
555, rue Murray, Sherbrooke, QC J1G 2K8
Tél: 819-346-1110; *Téléc:* 819-822-6789
www.chus.qc.ca
Nombre de lits: 682 lits
Patricia Gauthier, Directrice générale

Sorel-Tracy: Centre de santé et de services sociaux de Sorel-Tracy
Affiliée à: Agence de la santé et des services sociaux de la Montérégie
400, av Hôtel-Dieu, Sorel-Tracy, QC J3P 1N5
Tél: 450-746-5555; *Téléc:* 450-746-4897
Nombre de lits: 260 lits
Benoît Marchessault, Directeur général

Ste-Anne-des-Monts: Centre de santé et de services sociaux de la Haute-Gaspésie
Hôpital des Monts
Affiliée à: Agence de la santé et des services sociaux de la Gaspésie-Iles-de-la-Madeleine
Également connu sous le nom de: Hôpital de Sainte-Anne-des-Monts
50, rue du Belvédère, Ste-Anne-des-Monts, QC G4V 1X4
Tél: 418-763-2261; *Téléc:* 418-763-7460
www.agencesssgim.ca; www.cssshautegaspesie.qc.ca
Year Founded: 1972
Nombre de lits: 35 lits hospitaliers
Robert Deschênes, Directeur général
Pierre Roger, Directeur, Services techniques

René Ouellet, Chef, Entretien ménager, buanderie, lingerie

Terrebonne: Centre de santé et de services sociaux du Sud de Lanaudière
Affiliée à: Agences de développement de réseaux locaux de services de santé et de services sociaux
911, montée des Pionniers, Terrebonne, QC J6V 2H2
Tél: 450-654-7525; *Téléc:* 450-470-2640
Nombre de lits: 347 lits
Michel Bouffard, Directeur général

Terrebonne: Centre hospitalier Pierre-Le Gardeur
Affiliée à: Agences de développement de réseaux locaux de services de santé et de services sociaux
911, montée des Pionniers, Terrebonne, QC J6V 2H2
Tél: 450-654-7525
www.chpierrelegardeur.ca
Nombre de lits: 273 lits

Thetford Mines: Centre de santé et de services sociaux de la région de Thetford
Centre administratif
Affiliée à: Agence de la santé et des services sociaux de Chaudière-Appalaches
1717, rue Notre-Dame est, Thetford Mines, QC G6G 2V4
Tél: 418-338-7777; *Téléc:* 418-335-7616
chra@ssss.gouv.qc.ca
www.centresantethetford.ca
Nombre de lits: 336 lits
Note: Installations: l'Hôpital; les CLSCs: Thetford Mines, Adstock, Disraeli, & East Broughton; les Centres d'hébergement: Denis-Marcotte, Lac-Noir, Marc-André-Jacques, St-Joseph, René-Lavoie, & Valin.
François Chauvette, Directeur des activités, CLSC
Denis Martin, Directeur de l'hébergement
Normand Baker, Directeur général, CSSSRT

Trois-Pistoles: Centre hospitalier Trois-Pistoles
CSSS des Basques
550, rue Notre-Dame est, Trois-Pistoles, QC G0L 4K0
Tél: 418-851-1111; *Téléc:* 418-851-2934
www.agencesssbsl.gouv.qc.ca
Nombre de lits: 60 lits
Line Moisan, Directrice générale, CSSS des Basques

Trois-Rivières: Centre St-Joseph/Résidence La Providence
CSSS de Trois-Rivières
Affiliée à: Agence de la santé et des services sociaux de la Mauricie et du Centre-du-Québec
731, rue Sainte-Julie, Trois-Rivières, QC G9A 1Y1
Tél: 819-370-2100
www.cssstr.qc.ca
Nombre de lits: 198 lits hospitaliers; 100 lits de soins de longue durée
Note: Centre St-Joseph: services hospitaliers; Résidence La Providence: hébergement 819-370-2200, poste 43104.
Jacques Longval, Directeur général, CSSS de Trois-Rivières

Verdun: Hôpital Douglas
Affiliée à: Agence de la santé et des services sociaux de Montréal
6875, boul Lasalle, Verdun, QC H4H 1R3
Tél: 514-761-6131; *Téléc:* 514-761-4816
dredea@douglas.mcgill.ca
Nombre de lits: 210 lits hospitaliers, 192 lits longue durée
Note: mental hospital affiliated with McGill University; also community services, outpatient services, housing, social rehabilitation, specialized services (eating disorders, alcoholism & drug abuse, schizophrenia, aging, dementia & Alzheimer dementia)
Jacques Hendlisz, Directeur général

Verdun: Pavillon Manoir
Affiliée à: Agence de la santé et des services sociaux de Montréal
Ancien nom: CHSLD Champlain - Manoir de Verdun
5500, boul Lasalle, Verdun, QC H4H 1N9
Tél: 514-769-8801
Nombre de lits: 220 lits

Victoriaville: Hôtel-Dieu d'Arthabaska
CSSS d'Arthabaska-et-de-l'Érable
Affiliée à: Agence de la santé et des services sociaux de la Mauricie et du Centre-du-Québec
5, rue des Hospitalières, Victoriaville, QC G6P 6N2
Tél: 819-357-2030; *Téléc:* 819-357-7406
www.csssae.qc.ca
Nombre de lits: 199 lits
Marcel Dubois, Président, Conseil d'administration, CSSS d'Arthabaska-et-de-l

Wakefield: Centre de santé et de services sociaux des Collines
Affiliated with: Agence de la santé et des services sociaux de l'Outaouais
Also Known As: CSSS des Collines
PO Box 160 Wakefield, 101, ch Burnside, Wakefield, QC J0X 3G0
Tel: 819-459-1112; *Fax:* 819-459-1894
Toll-Free: 877-459-1112
www.santedescollines.qc.ca
Number of Beds: 16 lits hospitaliers; 10 lits de soins de longue durée
Note: Le CSSS: l'Hôpital Mémorial de Wakefield (services bilingues); Centre d'hébergement La Pêche; le CLSC des Collines et ses 4 points de services de Cantley, Chelsea, La Pêche, et Val-des-Monts; 18 médecins et 8 médecins conseils; 275 employés/employées.
Pierre Rochon, Directeur général

Weedon: Centre de santé et de services sociaux du Haut-St-François
Affiliée à: Agence de la santé et des services sociaux de l'Estrie
Ancien nom: CLSC-CHSLD du Haut-St-François
460, 2e av, Weedon, QC J0B 3J0
Tél: 819-877-3434; *Téléc:* 819-877-3714
Nombre de lits: 108 lits
Louisette Gosselin, Directrice générale

Hôpitaux privés

Kahnawake: Kateri Memorial Hospital Centre
CSSS Jardins-Roussillon
Centre hospitalier Kateri Memorial
Affiliated with: Agence de la santé et des services sociaux de la Montérégie
Also Known As: Tehsakotitsén:tha
PO Box 10, Kahnawake, QC J0L 1B0
Tel: 450-638-3930; *Fax:* 450-638-4634
admin@kmhc.ca
www.kmhc.ca; www.santemonteregie.qc.ca/jardins-roussillon
Number of Beds: 43 beds/lits
Note: Family medicine, home care, community health, infection prevention and control, nutrition services, occupational therapy, physiotherapy, speech therapy, social services.
Susan Horne, Executive Director

Montréal: Centre métropolitain de Chirurgie Plastique Inc.
Affiliée à: Agence de la santé et des services sociaux de Montréal
999, rue de Salaberry, Montréal, QC H3L 1L2
Tél: 514-332-7091; *Téléc:* 514-332-7095
Nombre de lits: 17 lits
Pierre Brassard, Directeur général

Montréal: Hôpital Marie-Clarac
Affiliée à: Agence de la santé et des services sociaux de Montréal
3530, boul Gouin est, Montréal, QC H1H 1B7
Tél: 514-321-8800; *Téléc:* 514-321-9626
www.hopitalmarie-clarac.qc.ca/
Nombre de lits: 204 lits
Sr. Pierre-Anne Mandato, Directrice générale

Montréal: Hôpital Shriners pour enfants (Québec) inc.
Shriners Hospital for Children
Affiliée à: Agence de la santé et des services sociaux de Montréal
1529, av Cedar, Montréal, QC H3G 1A6
Tél: 514-842-4464; *Téléc:* 514-842-7553
Nombre de lits: 40 lits
Maureen Brennan, Directrice générale
John Krisa, Superviseur, Installations matériels

Sillery: La Maison Michel Sarrazin
Affiliée à: Agence de la santé et des services sociaux de la Capitale-Nationale
2101, ch St-Louis, Sillery, QC G1T 2P5
Tél: 418-688-0878; *Téléc:* 418-681-8636
info@michel-sarrazin.ca
www.michel-sarrazin.ca
Nombre de lits: 15 lits
Michel L'Heureux, Directeur général

Centres locaux des services communautaires (CLSC)

Alma: **CLSC Le Norois**
Affiliée à: Agence de la santé et des services sociaux du Saguenay-Lac-St-Jean
Édifice complexe J.-Gagnon, 100, rue Saint-Joseph sud, Alma, QC G8B 7A6
Tél: 418-668-4563; *Téléc:* 418-668-6462
monette.desbiens@ssss.gouv.qc.ca
Bertin Riverin, Directeur général

Aupaluk: **Dispensaire d'Aupaluk**
Aupaluk, QC J0M 1X0
Tél: 819-491-9090; *Téléc:* 819-491-7020
clsc.aupaluk@ssss.gouv.qc.ca
Nombre de lits: 1 lit
Madge Pomerleau, Directrice générale

Barachois: **CLSC Mer et Montagnes**
Point de service Barachois
Affiliée à: Agence de la santé et des services sociaux de la Gaspésie-Iles-de-la-Madeleine
1070, rte 132, Barachois, QC G0C 1A0
Tél: 418-645-2572; *Téléc:* 418-645-2106
www.csssscotedegaspe.ca
Note: CSSS Côte-de-Gaspé.

Bassin: **Centre de santé et de services sociaux des Iles**
CLSC de Bassin
Affiliée à: Agence de la santé et des services sociaux de la Gaspésie-Iles-de-la-Madeleine
CP 57, 702, ch du Bassin, Bassin, QC G4T 0C8
Tél: 418-937-2572; *Téléc:* 418-937-5381
www.agencesssgim.ca; www.csssdesiles.qc.ca

Beloeil: **CLSC La Vallée des Patriotes**
Affiliée à: Agence de la santé et des services sociaux de la Montérégie
347, rue Duvernay, Beloeil, QC J3G 5S8
Tél: 514-536-2572
Nombre de lits: 225 lits

Berthierville: **CLSC d'Autray**
Affiliée à: Agences de développement de réseaux locaux de services de santé et de services sociaux
761, rue Notre-Dame, Berthierville, QC J0K 1A0
Tél: 450-836-7011
Nombre de lits: 237 lits
Norman Blackburn, Directeur général

Boucherville: **CLSC des Seigneuries de Boucherville**
CSSS Pierre-Boucher
Affiliée à: Agence de la santé et des services sociaux de la Montérégie
160, boul De Montarville, Boucherville, QC J4B 6S2
Tél: 450-655-3630; *Téléc:* 450-655-8530
www.santemonteregie.qc.ca/cssspierreboucher
Caroline Barbir, Directrice générale, CSSS Pierre-Boucher

Brossard: **Centre de santé et de services sociaux Champlain**
Affiliée à: Agence de la santé et des services sociaux de la Montérégie
Complexe Taschereau, #100, 5811, boul Taschereau, Brossard, QC J4Z 1A5
Tél: 450-445-4452; *Téléc:* 450-445-5535
Suzanne Beauchamp, Directrice générale

Candiac: **CLSC Kateri**
CSSS Jardins-Roussillon
Affiliée à: Agence de la santé et des services sociaux de la Montérégie
90, boul Marie-Victorin, Candiac, QC J5R 1C1
Tél: 450-659-7661; *Téléc:* 450-444-6260
www.santemonteregie.qc.ca/jardins-roussillon
Nombre de lits: 340 lits
Paul Moreau, Directeur général, CSSS Jardins-Roussillon

Cantley: **Centre de santé et de services sociaux des Collines - CLSC Cantley**
Affiliated with: Agence de la santé et de services sociaux de l'Outaouais
Also Known As: CSSS-CLSC des Collines
850, Montée de la Source, Cantley, QC J8V 3H4
Tel: 819-459-1112; *Fax:* 819-827-5818
Toll-Free: 877-459-1112
www.santedescollines.qc.ca
Pierre Rochon, Directeur général, CSSS des Collines

Cap-Chat: **Centre de santé et de services sociaux de la Haute-Gaspésie**
CLSC de Cap-Chat
Affiliée à: Agence de la santé et des services sociaux de la Gaspésie-Iles-de-la-Madeleine
49, rue Notre-Dame, Cap-Chat, QC G0E 1E0
Tél: 418-786-5594; *Téléc:* 418-786-2638
www.agencesssgim.ca; www.cssshautegaspesie.qc.ca
Robert Deschênes, Directeur général

Cap-aux-Meules: **Centre de santé et de services sociaux des Iles**
CLSC de Cap-aux-Meules
Affiliée à: Agence de la santé et des services sociaux de la Gaspésie-Iles-de-la-Madeleine
420, ch Principal, Cap-aux-Meules, QC G4T 1S1
Tél: 418-986-2572; *Téléc:* 418-986-4911
www.agencesssgim.ca; www.csssdesiles.qc.ca

Caplan: **CLSC de Caplan**
CSSS de la Baie-des-Chaleurs
Affiliée à: Agence de la santé et des services sociaux de la Gaspésie-Iles-de-la-Madeleine
96, rte 132, Caplan, QC G0C 1H0
Tél: 418-388-2572; *Téléc:* 418-388-2645
csssbc@csssbc.qc.ca
www.csssbc.qc.ca
Bernard Nadeau, Directeur général, CSSS de la Baie-des-Chaleurs

Châteauguay: **CLSC Châteauguay**
CSSS Jardins-Roussillon
Affiliée à: Agence de la santé et des services sociaux de la Montérégie
101, rue Lauzon, Châteauguay, QC J6K 1C7
Tél: 450-699-3333; *Téléc:* 450-691-6202
www.santemonteregie.qc.ca/jardins-roussillon
Paul Moreau, Directeur général, CSSS Jardins-Roussillon

Chertsey: **CLSC de Matawinie**
Affiliée à: Agences de développement de réseaux locaux de services de santé et de services sociaux
485, rue Dupuis, Chertsey, QC J0K 3K0
Tél: 450-882-2488

Chicoutimi: **Centre de santé et de services sociaux de Chicoutimi**
CP 5006, 305, St Vallier, Chicoutimi, QC G7H 5H6
Tél: 418-541-1000; *Téléc:* 418-541-1144
Dr. Richard Lehieux, Directeur général

Côte Saint-Luc: **Centre local de services communautaires René-Cassin**
Affiliée à: Agence de la santé et des services sociaux de Montréal
#600, 5800, boul Cavendish, Côte Saint-Luc, QC H4W 2T5
Tél: 514-488-9163; *Téléc:* 514-485-1612
dkobernick@ssss.gouv.qc.ca
www.geronto.org
Note: local health & social service centre
Joëlle Khalfa, Directeur général

Côte Saint-Luc: **Hôpital Mont-Sinai**
Affiliée à: Agence de la santé et des services sociaux de Montréal
5690, boul Cavendish, Côte Saint-Luc, QC H4W 1S7
Tél: 514-369-2222; *Téléc:* 514-369-2225
Nombre de lits: 57 lits
Joseph Rothbart, Directeur général

Drummondville: **CLSC Drummond**
CSSS Drummond
Affiliée à: Agence de la santé et des services sociaux de la Mauricie et du Centre-du-Québec
350, rue Saint-Jean, Drummondville, QC J2B 5L4
Tél: 819-474-2572
csssdrummond@ssss.gouv.qc.ca
www.csssdrummond.qc.ca
Note: Santé au travail: 819-474-8428
Nagui Habashi, Directeur général, CSSS Drummond

Forestville: **Centre de santé et de services sociaux de la Haute-Côte-Nord - Pavillon Forestvi**
Affiliée à: Agence de la santé et des services sociaux de la Côte-Nord
CP 790, 2, 7e rue, Forestville, QC G0T 1E0
Tél: 418-587-2212; *Téléc:* 418-587-2865
Nombre de lits: 20 lits
Micheline Anctil, Directrice générale

Gascons: **CLSC de Gascons**
Affiliée à: Agence de la santé et des services sociaux de la Gaspésie-Iles-de-la-Madeleine
CP 28, 63, rte 132, Gascons, QC G0C 1P0
Tél: 418-396-2572; *Téléc:* 418-396-2367
www.agencesssgim.ca
Note: CSSS du Rocher-Percé.

Gaspé: **CLSC Mer et Montagnes**
Point de service Gaspé
Affiliée à: Agence de la santé et des services sociaux de la Gaspésie-Iles-de-la-Madeleine
CP 6397, 205, boul de York ouest, 2e étage, Gaspé, QC G4X 2R8
Tél: 418-368-2572; *Téléc:* 418-368-1532
www.cssscotedegaspe.ca
Note: CSSS Côte-de-Gaspé.

Gatineau: **CLSC de Gatineau - Point de service de la Gappe**
CSSS de Gatineau
Affiliée à: Agence de la santé et de services sociaux de l'Outaouais
777, boul de la Gappe, Gatineau, QC J8T 8R2
Tél: 819-966-6550; *Téléc:* 819-966-6552
www.csssgatineau.qc.ca
Note: Services généraux santé; soins infirmiers et ambulatoires; consulation médicale pour les clientèles vulnérables.
André O. Rodier, Directeur général, CSSS de Gatineau
Micheline Malette, Directrice, Services généraux/Santé publique
819-966-6510

Gatineau: **CLSC de Gatineau - Point de service Gatineau**
CSSS de Gatineau
Affiliée à: Agence de la santé et de services sociaux de l'Outaouais
80, av Gatineau, Gatineau, QC J8T 4J3
Tél: 819-966-6550; *Téléc:* 819-966-6572
www.csssgatineau.qc.ca
Note: Centre local de services communautaires.
André O. Rodier, Directeur général, CSSS de Gatineau

Gatineau: **CLSC de Gatineau - Point de service LeGuerrier**
CSSS de Gatineau
Affiliée à: Agence de la santé et de services sociaux de l'Outaouais
425, rue LeGuerrier, Gatineau, QC J9H 6N8
Tél: 819-966-6540; *Téléc:* 819-966-6541
www.csssdegatineau.qc.ca
André O. Rodier, Directeur général, CSSS de Gatineau
819-966-6560
Micheline Malette, Directrice, Services généraux/Santé publique

Gatineau: **CLSC Vallée-de-la-Lievre**
Affiliée à: Agence de la santé et de services sociaux de l'Outaouais
578, rue Maclaren est, Gatineau, QC J8L 2W1
Tél: 819-986-3359; *Téléc:* 819-986-5671
csss_papineau@ssss.gouv.qc.ca
www.cssspapineau.qc.ca
Gilles Clavel, Directeur général (par intérim), CSSS de Papineau

***Grande-Entrée:* Centre de santé et de services sociaux des Iles**
CLSC d'Old Harry
Affiliée à: Agence de la santé et des services sociaux de la Gaspésie-Iles-de-la-Madeleine
CP 2, site 5, rte 199, Grande-Entrée, QC G4T 7B3
Tél: 418-985-2572; *Téléc:* 418-985-2862
www.agencesssgim.ca; www.csssdesiles.qc.ca

Germain Chevarie, Directeur général

***Grande-Vallée:* CLSC Mer et Montagnes**
Point de service Grande-Vallée
Affiliée à: Agence de la santé et des services sociaux de la Gaspésie-Iles-de-la-Madeleine
71, rue St-François-Xavier est, Grande-Vallée, QC G0E 1K0
Tél: 418-393-2572; *Téléc:* 418-393-2952
www.csssscotedegaspe.ca
Note: CSSS Côte-de-Gaspé.

***Grosse-Ile:* Centre des santé et de services des Iles**
CLSC de l'Est
Affiliée à: Agence de la santé et des services sociaux de la Gaspésie-Iles-de-la-Madeleine
773, ch Principal, Grosse-Ile, QC G4T 6B5
Tél: 418-985-2572; *Téléc:* 418-985-2862
www.agencesssgim.ca; www.csssdesiles.qc.ca

***Huntingdon:* CLSC Huntingdon**
Affiliée à: Agence de la santé et des services sociaux de la Montérégie
#200, 10, rue King, Huntingdon, QC J0S 1H0
Tél: 450-264-6108; *Téléc:* 450-264-6801

Guy Deschenes, Directeur général

***Ile d'Entrée:* Centre de santé et de services sociaux des Iles**
CLSC de l'Ile d'Entrée
Affiliée à: Agence de la santé et des services sociaux de la Gaspésie-Iles-de-la-Madeleine
Ile d'Entrée, QC G4T 1Z1
Tél: 418-986-4299; *Téléc:* 418-986-4094
www.agencesssgim.ca; www.csssdesiles.qc.ca

***Joliette:* CLSC de Joliette**
380, boul Base-de-Roc, Joliette, QC J6E 9J6
Tél: 450-755-2111; *Téléc:* 450-755-4896

Jean-François Foisy, Directeur général adjoint

***Jonquière:* CLSC de la Jonquière**
Affiliée à: Agence de la santé et des services sociaux du Saguenay-Lac-St-Jean
CP 580, 3667, boul Harvey, Jonquière, QC G7X 7W4
Tél: 418-695-2572

Lucille Dumont, Directrice générale

***Kawawachikamach:* CLSC Naskapi**
Affiliée à: Agence de la santé et des services sociaux de la Côte-Nord
CP 5154, 9, rue Naskapi, Kawawachikamach, QC G0G 2Z0
Tél: 418-585-2897; *Téléc:* 418-585-3126
Ligne sans frais: 866-585-2110

Luc Guènette, Directeur général (intérim)

***Kipawa:* Health Centre of Eagle Village**
3 Ogima, Eagle Village First Nation, Kipawa, QC J0Z 2H0
Tél: 819-627-9060; *Téléc:* 819-627-1885
davem@eaglevillagefirstnation.ca
www.eaglevillagefirstnation.ca

David McLaren, Health Director
davidm@eaglevillagefirstnation.ca

***Kuujjuaq:* Centre de santé Tulattavik de l'Ungava**
Affiliated with: Régie régionale de la santé et des services sociaux du Nunavik
PO Box 149, Kuujjuaq, QC J0M 1C0
Tel: 819-964-2905; *Fax:* 819-964-6353
information_rrsss17@ssss.gouv.qc.ca
www.rrsss17.gouv.qc.ca; www.ungava.info
Number of Beds: 15 lits hospitaliers; 10 lits de soins de longue durée
Note: Urgence; soins médicaux; soins infirmiers; maternité; radiologie; pharmacie; électrocardiographie; laboratoire; physiothérapie.

Madge Pomerleau, Directrice générale
madge.pomerleau@ssss.gouv.qc.ca

***La Malbaie:* CLSC de La Malbaie**
CSSS de Charlevoix
535, boul de Comporté, La Malbaie, QC G5A 1S8
Tél: 418-665-6413
www.cssscharlevoix.qc.ca

Micheline Tremblay, Directrice générale, CSSS de Charlevoix
micheline.tremblay@ssss.gouv.qc.ca

***La Tuque:* CLSC du Haunt Saint-Maurice**
350, av Brown, La Tuque, QC G9X 2W4
Tél: 819-523-6171; *Téléc:* 819-523-6176

Guy Lemieux, Directeur général

***LaSalle:* CLSC de LaSalle**
Affiliée à: Agence de la santé et des services sociaux de Montréal
8550, boul Newman, LaSalle, QC H8N 1Y5
Tél: 514-364-2572; *Téléc:* 514-364-6365
www.santemontreal.qc.ca

Jean-Paul Bouchard, Directeur général

***Lachine:* Centre de santé et de services sociaux de Dorval-Lachine-LaSalle**
Centre administratif
Affiliée à: Agence de la santé et des services sociaux de Montréal
1900, rue Notre-Dame, Lachine, QC H8S 2G2
Tél: 514-364-2572
www.santemontreal.qc.ca
Note: Installations: l'Hôpital de LaSalle (110 lits de courte durée, 123 lits de longue durée); les CLSCs: LaSalle, & Dorval-Lachine; les Centres d'hébergement: LaSalle (202 lits), Dorval (111 lits), Lachine (200 lits), & Nazaire-Piché (Lachine; 100 lits).
Jean-Paul Bouchard, Directeur général

***Lachine:* CLSC de Dorval-Lachine**
Affiliée à: Agence de la santé et des services sociaux de Montréal
1900, rue Notre-Dame, Lachine, QC H8S 2G2
Tél: 514-639-0650; *Téléc:* 514-639-0666
www.santemontreal.qc.ca
Note: Services de santé; services sociaux curatifs et préventifs.
Paul Perreault, Directeur général

***Lachute:* Centre de santé et de services sociaux d'Argenteuil**
145, av de la Providence, Lachute, QC J8H 4C7
Tél: 450-562-3761; *Téléc:* 450-566-3316
Nombre de lits: 49 lits
Jocelyn Ouellet, Directeur général

***Laval:* CLSC des Mille-Iles**
CSSS de Laval
4731, boul Levesque est, Laval, QC H7C 1M9
Tél: 450-661-2572; *Téléc:* 450-661-6177
www.cssslaval.qc.ca
Note: Les autres points de service CLSC: Marigot (2 sites), Mille-Iles (304, boul Cartier ouest), Ruisseau-Papineau (2 sites), et Sainte-Rose.
Luc Lepage, Directeur général, CSSS de Laval

***Longueuil:* CLSC de Longueuil-Ouest**
CSSS Pierre-Boucher
Affiliée à: Agence de la santé et des services sociaux de la Montérégie
201, boul Curé-Poirier, Longueuil, QC J4J 2G4
Tél: 450-651-9830; *Téléc:* 450-651-4606
www.santemonteregie.qc.ca/cssspierreboucher

Caroline Barbir, Directrice générale, CSSS Pierre-Boucher

***Longueuil:* CLSC Simonne-Monet-Chartrand**
CSSS Pierre-Boucher
Affiliée à: Agence de la santé et des services sociaux de la Montérégie
1303, boul Jacques-Cartier est, Longueuil, QC J4M 2Y8
Tél: 450-463-2850; *Téléc:* 450-646-7552
www.santemonteregie.qc.ca/cssspierreboucher

Caroline Barbir, Directrice générale, CSSS Pierre-Boucher

***Low:* CLSC Low - Centre de Santé Vallée-de-la-Gatineau**
Affiliée à: Agence de la santé et de services sociaux de l'Outaouais
CP 130, 334, rte 105, Low, QC J0X 2C0
Tél: 819-422-3548; *Téléc:* 819-422-3568

André Marcoux, Directeur général

***Marsoui:* Centre de santé et de services sociaux de la Haute-Gaspésie**
CLSC de Marsoui
Affiliée à: Agence de la santé et des services sociaux de la Gaspésie-Iles-de-la-Madeleine
CP 154, 1, rue du Quai, Marsoui, QC G0E 1S0
Tél: 418-288-5511; *Téléc:* 418-288-2572
www.agencesssgim.ca; www.cssshautegaspesie.qc.ca

***Matapédia:* CLSC Malauze de Matapédia/Centre d'hébergement de Matapédia**
CSSS de la Baie-des-Chaleurs
Affiliée à: Agence de la santé et des services sociaux de la Gaspésie-Iles-de-la-Madeleine
14, rue Perron est, Matapédia, QC G0J 1V0
Tél: 418-865-2221; *Téléc:* 418-865-2317
csssbc@csssbc.qc.ca
www.csssbc.qc.ca
Note: Services sociaux; programme petite enfance; clinique de vaccination et dépistage; programme de santé mentale; services aux personnes handicapées; soutien à domicile; service dentaire. Le centre d'hébergement est situé au deuxième étage du CLSC.
Bernard Nadeau, Directeur général, CSSS de la Baie-des-Chaleurs

***Mont-Laurier:* CLSC des Hautes-Laurentides**
Affiliée à: Agence de la santé et des services sociaux des Laurentides
515, boul Albiny-Paquette, Mont-Laurier, QC J9L 1K8
Tél: 819-623-1228

***Mont-Louis:* Centre de santé et de services sociaux de la Haute-Gaspésie**
CLSC de Mont-Louis
Affiliée à: Agence de la santé et des services sociaux de la Gaspésie-Iles-de-la-Madeleine
CP 100, 19, 1er av ouest, Mont-Louis, QC G0E 1T0
Tél: 418-797-2744; *Téléc:* 418-797-5173
www.agencesssgim.ca; www.cssshautegaspesie.qc.ca

***Montréal:* Centre de santé et de services sociaux Cavendish**
Affiliée à: Agence de la santé et des services sociaux de Montréal
5425, av Bessborough, Montréal, QC H4V 2S7
Tél: 514-483-1380; *Téléc:* 514-483-4596
www.santemontreal.qc.ca
Nombre de lits: 125 lits
Note: Installations: l'Hôpital Richardson (125 lits); les CLSCs: Notre-Dame-de-Grâce-Montréal-Ouest, & René-Cassin (Côte St-Luc); le Centre d'hébergement Henri-Bradet.
Francine Dupuis, Directrice générale

***Montréal:* Centre de santé et de services sociaux d'Ahuntsic et Montréal-Nord**
Affiliée à: Agence de la santé et des services sociaux de Montréal
1725, boul Gouin est, Montréal, QC H2C 3H6
Tél: 514-384-2000; *Téléc:* 514-384-4245
www.santemontreal.qc.ca
Note: Installations: l'Hôpital Fleury (194 lits); les CLSCs: Ahuntsic, & Montréal-Nord; les Centres d'hébergement: Paul-Lizotte, Laurendeau, Légaré, & Louvain.
Mac Fortin, Directeur général

***Montréal:* Centre de santé et de services sociaux d'Ahuntsic et Montréal-Nord (Hôpital Fleu**
Affiliée à: Agence de la santé et des services sociaux de Montréal
2180 est, rue Fleury, Montréal, QC H2BH2C 3H6
Tél: 514-381-9311; *Téléc:* 514-383-5249

Bruno L'Heureux, Directeur exécutif, Hôpital Fleury et Services professionnels et hospit

***Montréal:* Centre de santé et de services sociaux de la Montagne**
Affiliée à: Agence de la santé et des services sociaux de Montréal
5700, ch de la Côte-des-Neiges, Montréal, QC H3T 2A8
Tél: 514-731-8531; *Téléc:* 514-731-9600
www.santemontreal.qc.ca
Note: Installations: les CLSCs: Côte-des-Neiges (Outremont), Métro, & Parc-Extension; Maison de naissance

Côte-des-Neiges; Programme régional d'acceuil & d'intégration des demandeurs d'asile.
Marc Sougavinski, Dir. gen.

Montréal: Centre de santé et de services sociaux de la Pointe-de-l'Ile
Affiliée à: Agence de la santé et des services sociaux de Montréal
9503, rue Sherbrooke est, Montréal, QC H1L 6P2
Tél: 514-356-2572; *Téléc:* 514-356-2571
Andre Gagnière, Directeur général

Montréal: Centre de santé et de services sociaux du coeur-de-l'île
Affiliée à: Agence de la santé et des services sociaux de Montréal
Ancien nom: CSSS de la Petite Patrie et Villeray
1385, rue Jean-Talon est, Montréal, QC H2E 1S6
Tél: 514-495-6754; *Téléc:* 514-495-6734
Nombre de lits: 320 lits
Manon Boily, Directrice générale

Montréal: Centre de santé et de services sociaux du Sud-Ouest-Verdun
Affiliée à: Agence de la santé et des services sociaux de Montréal
6161, rue Laurendeau, Montréal, QC H4E 3X6
Tél: 514-766-0546; *Téléc:* 514-732-5107
www.csssudouestverdun.qc.ca
Nombre de lits: 1550 lits (permanent, temporaire, courte durée, gériatrique)
Danielle McCann, Directeur général

Montréal: Centre de santé et de services sociaux Lucille-Teasdale
Affiliée à: Agence de la santé et des services sociaux de Montréal
3095, rue Sherbrooke est, Montréal, QC H1W 1B2
Tél: 514-523-1173; *Téléc:* 514-528-2706
Nombre de lits: 1,223 lits
Gary Furlong, Directeur général

Montréal: Centre local de services communautaires Métro
Affiliée à: Agence de la santé et des services sociaux de Montréal
#500, 1801, boul de Maisonneuve ouest, Montréal, QC H3H 1J9
Tél: 514-934-0354; *Téléc:* 514-934-3776
Gary Furlong, Directeur général

Montréal: Centre local de services communautaires Saint-Henri
Affiliée à: Agence de la santé et des services sociaux de Montréal
3833, rue Notre-Dame ouest, Montréal, QC H4C 1P8
Tél: 514-933-7541; *Téléc:* 514-933-1740
Louis-Paul Thauvette, Directeur général

Montréal: Clinique communautaire de Pointe St-Charles
Affiliée à: Agence de la santé et des services sociaux de Montréal
500, av Ash, Montréal, QC H3K 2R4
Tél: 514-937-9251; *Téléc:* 514-937-3492
Clermont Racine, Directeur général

Montréal: CLSC Ahuntsic
Affiliée à: Agence de la santé et des services sociaux de Montréal
1165, boul Henri-Bourassa est, Montréal, QC H2C 3K2
Tél: 514-381-4221
Daniel Corbeil, Directeur général

Montréal: CLSC Côte-des-Neiges
Affiliée à: Agence de la santé et des services sociaux de Montréal
5700, ch de la Côte-des-Neiges, Montréal, QC H3T 2A8
Tél: 514-731-8531; *Téléc:* 514-731-9600
www.santemontreal.qc.ca; www.clsccote-des-neiges.qc.ca
Marc Sougavinski, Directeur général

Montréal: CLSC de Bordeaux-Cartierville
Affiliée à: Agence de la santé et des services sociaux de Montréal
11822, av du Bois-de-Boulogne, Montréal, QC H3M 2X6
Tél: 514-331-2572; *Téléc:* 514-331-5827
www.santemontreal.qc.ca

Montréal: CLSC de Rosemont du CSSS Lucille-Teasdale
Affiliée à: Agence de la santé et des services sociaux de Montréal
3311, boul Saint-Joseph est, Montréal, QC H1X 1W3
Tél: 514-524-3541; *Téléc:* 514-524-2624
www.santemontreal.qc.ca/csss/teasdale
Nombre de lits: 1215 lits dans le CSSS
Gary Furlong, Directeur général du CSSS

Montréal: CLSC des Faubourgs - Visitation CSSS Jeanne-Mance
Affiliée à: Agence de la santé et des services sociaux de Montréal
1705, rue de la Visitation, Montréal, QC H2L 3C3
Tél: 514-527-2361; *Téléc:* 514-598-7754
www.csssjeannemance.ca
Ron Rayside, Président du Conseil d'administration, CSSS Jeanne-Mance
Sylvie Simard, Directrice générale intérimaire, CSSS Jeanne-Mance

Montréal: CLSC du Plateau Mont-Royal
Affiliée à: Agence de la santé et des services sociaux de Montréal
4689, av Papineau, Montréal, QC H2H 1V4
Tél: 514-521-7663; *Téléc:* 514-521-1886
www.clsc-du-plateau-mt-royal.qc.ca
Nicole Corbin, Directrice générale

Montréal: CLSC du Plateau Mont-Royal
Affiliée à: Agence de la santé et des services sociaux de Montréal
4689, av Papineau, Montréal, QC H2H 1V4
Tél: 514-521-0645

Montréal: CLSC Hochelaga-Maisonneuve
Affiliée à: Agence de la santé et des services sociaux de Montréal
4201, rue Ontario est, Montréal, QC H1V 1K2
Tél: 514-253-2181; *Téléc:* 514-253-1239
jean.pierre.perreault@ssss.gouv.qc.ca
www.clsc-hochelaga-maisonneuve.qc.ca
André Desilets, Directeur général

Montréal: CLSC la Petite Patrie
Affiliée à: Agence de la santé et des services sociaux de Montréal
6520, rue de Saint-Vallier, Montréal, QC H2S 2P7
Tél: 514-273-4508; *Téléc:* 514-272-6278

Montréal: CLSC Mercier-Est/Anjou
Affiliée à: Agence de la santé et des services sociaux de Montréal
9403, rue Sherbooke est, Montréal, QC H1L 6P2
Tél: 514-356-2572; *Téléc:* 514-356-2571
meadg@microtec.net
André Lemelin, Directeur général

Montréal: CLSC Notre-Dame-de-Grâce/Montréal-Ouest
Affiliée à: Agence de la santé et des services sociaux de Montréal
2525, boul Cavendish, Montréal, QC H4B 2Y4
Tél: 514-485-1670; *Téléc:* 514-485-6406
clscndg@clsc-ndg.qc.ca
clsc-ndg.qc.ca
Terry Kaufman, Directeur général

Montréal: CLSC Parc Extension
Affiliée à: Agence de la santé et des services sociaux de Montréal
445, rue Jean-Talon ouest, Montréal, QC H3N 1R1
Tél: 514-273-9591; *Téléc:* 514-273-8954

Montréal: CLSC Pointe-aux-Trembles/Montréal-Est
Affiliée à: Agence de la santé et des services sociaux de Montréal
13926, rue Notre-Dame est, Montréal, QC H1A 1T5
Tél: 514-642-4050; *Téléc:* 514-498-7505

Montréal: CLSC Rivière-des-Prairies
Affiliée à: Agence de la santé et des services sociaux de Montréal
CSSS de la Pointe-de-l'Ile, 8655, boul Perras, Montréal, QC H1E 4M7
Tél: 514-494-4924; *Téléc:* 514-494-8182
Gaétan Mercure, Directeur général

Montréal: CLSC Saint-Louis-du-Parc CSSS Jeanne-Mance
Affiliée à: Agence de la santé et des services sociaux de Montréal
#100, 15, av du Mont-Royal ouest, Montréal, QC H2T 2R9
Tél: 514-286-9657; *Téléc:* 514-286-9706
www.csssjeannemance.ca
Ron Rayside, Président du Conseil d'administration, CSSS Jeanne-Mance
Sylvie Simard, Directrice générale intérimaire, CSSS Jeanne-Mance

Montréal: CLSC Saint-Michel
Affiliée à: Agence de la santé et des services sociaux de Montréal
7950, boul Saint-Michel, Montréal, QC H1Z 3E1
Tél: 514-374-8223; *Téléc:* 514-374-9180
Manon Boily, Directrice générale

Montréal: CLSC Villeray
Affiliée à: Agence de la santé et des services sociaux de Montréal
1425, rue Jarry est, Montréal, QC H2E 1A7
Tél: 514-376-4141
Nicole Clouâtre, Directrice générale

Montréal: CLSC-CHSLD Olivier-Guimond
Affiliée à: Agence de la santé et des services sociaux de Montréal
Ancien nom: CLSC Olivier-Guimond
5810, rue Sherbrooke est, Montréal, QC H1N 1B2
Tél: 514-255-2365; *Téléc:* 514-255-1443
Alain Lemay, Directeur général (intérim)

Montréal: Santé au travail
#430, 75, rue de Port-Royal, Montréal, QC H3L 3T1
Tél: 514-858-2460; *Téléc:* 514-858-6568

Montréal-Nord: CLSC Montréal-nord
Affiliée à: Agence de la santé et des services sociaux de Montréal
11441, boul Lacordaire, Montréal-Nord, QC H1G 4J9
Tél: 514-327-0400; *Téléc:* 514-327-1275
Pierre Latry, Directeur général

Murdochville: CLSC Mer et Montagnes Point de service Murdochville
Affiliée à: Agence de la santé et des services sociaux de la Gaspésie-Iles-de-la-Madeleine
600, rue Dr William-May, Murdochville, QC G0E 1W0
Tél: 418-784-2572; *Téléc:* 418-784-3629
www.cssscotedegaspe.ca
Note: CSSS Côte-de-Gaspé.

New Carlisle: Centre de santé Le Rivage Le CLSC
Affiliée à: Agence de la santé et des services sociaux de la Gaspésie-Iles-de-la-Madeleine
CP 208, 96, rte 132, New Carlisle, QC G0C 1H0
Tél: 418-388-2572; *Téléc:* 418-388-2645

Paspébiac: **CLSC de Paspébiac**
CSSS de la Baie-des-Chaleurs
Affiliée à: Agence de la santé et des services sociaux de la Gaspésie-Iles-de-la-Madeleine
273, boul Gérard-D.-Lévesque ouest, Paspébiac, QC G0C 2K0
Tél: 418-752-2572; *Téléc:* 418-752-6734
csssbc@csssbc.qc.ca
www.csssbc.qc.ca

Bernard Nadeau, Directeur général, CSSS de la Baie-des-Chaleurs

Percé: **CLSC de Percé**
Affiliée à: Agence de la santé et des services sociaux de la Gaspésie-Iles-de-la-Madeleine
CP 269, 98, rte 132, Percé, QC G0C 2L0
Tél: 418-782-2572; *Téléc:* 418-782-5501
www.agencesssgim.ca
Note: CSSS du Rocher-Percé.

Pierrefonds: **Centre de santé et de services sociaux de l'Ouest-de-l'Ile**
West Island Health and Social Services Centre
Affiliée à: Agence de la santé et des services sociaux de Montréal
13800, boul Gouin ouest, Pierrefonds, QC H8Z 3H6
Tél: 514-626-2572; *Téléc:* 514-626-6514
www.santemontreal.qc.ca
Note: Installations: l'Hôpital général du Lakeshore; les CLSCs: Pierrefonds, Lac-Saint-Louis (Pointe-Claire); et le Centre d'hébergement Denis-Benjamin-Viger (L'Ile-Bizard).
Luc LePage, Dir. gen.

Plessisville: **CLSC-CHSLD de l'Érable**
CSSS d'Arthabaska-et-de-l'Érable
Affiliée à: Agence de la santé et des services sociaux de la Mauricie et du Centre-du-Québec
1331, rue Saint-Calixte, Plessisville, QC G6L 1P4
Tél: 819-362-6301; *Téléc:* 819-362-6300
www.csssae.qc.ca
Nombre de lits: 40 lits de soins de longue durée
Note: CLSC de l'Érable, et l'Unité de soins longue durée de l'Érable.
Marcel Dubois, Président, Conseil d'administration, CSSS d'Arthabaska-et-de-l

Pohénégamook: **CLSC de Pohénégamook**
CSSS de Témiscouata
Affiliée à: Agence de la santé et des services sociaux du Bas-St-Laurent
1922, rue St-Vallier, Pohénégamook, QC G0L 2T0
Tél: 418-859-2450; *Téléc:* 418-859-1285
www.csssstemiscouata.com
Nombre de lits: 25 lits
Camil Dion, Directeur général, CSSS de Témiscouata

Pointe-Claire: **CLSC Lac St-Louis**
Affiliée à: Agence de la santé et des services sociaux de Montréal
180, av Cartier, Pointe-Claire, QC H9S 4S1
Tél: 514-697-4110; *Téléc:* 514-697-6341
rbresnen@ssss.gouv.qc.ca

Ruth Bresnen, Directrice générale adjointe interimaire

Pointe-à-la-Croix: **CLSC de Pointe-à-la-Croix**
CSSS de la Baie-des-Chaleurs
Affiliée à: Agence de la santé et des services sociaux de la Gaspésie-Iles-de-la-Madeleine
48, boul Interprovincial, Pointe-à-la-Croix, QC G0C 1L0
Tél: 418-788-5454; *Téléc:* 418-788-2510
csssbc@csssbc.qc.ca
www.csssbc.qc.ca

Bernard Nadeau, Directeur général, CSSS de la Baie-des-Chaleurs

Port-Cartier: **Centre de santé et de services sociaux de Port-Cartier**
Affiliée à: Agence de la santé et des services sociaux de la Côte-Nord
3, rue de Shelter Bay, Port-Cartier, QC G5B 2W9
Tél: 418-766-2572; *Téléc:* 418-766-5229

Daniel Camire, Directeur général

Puvirnituq: **Centre de santé Inuulitsivik**
Affiliated with: Régie régionale de la santé et des services sociaux du Nunavik
ch Baie d'Hudson, Puvirnituq, QC J0M 1P0
Tel: 819-988-2957; *Fax:* 819-988-2796
inuulitsivik@ssss.gouv.qc.ca
www.inuulitsivik.ca
Number of Beds: 17 lits hospitaliers; 8 lits de soins de longue durée
Note: Soins médicaux, soins dentaires; sages-femmes; services en santé mentale; télémedicine; laboratoire; points de service: Akulivik, Inukjuak, Ivujivik, Kuujjuarapik, Puvirnituq, Salluit et Umiujuaq.
Jane Beaudoin, Directrice générale

Quaqtaq: **Dispensaire de Quaqtaq**
Affiliée à: Régie régionale de la santé et des services sociaux du Nunavik
General Delivery, Quaqtaq, QC J0M 1J0
Tél: 819-492-9977; *Téléc:* 819-492-9004
clsc.quaqtaq@ssss.gouv.qc.ca

Madge Pomerleau, Directrice générale

Québec: **Centre de santé et de services sociaux de la vieille-capitale**
Affiliée à: Agence de la santé et des services sociaux de la Capitale-Nationale
1, av du Sacré-Coeur, Québec, QC G1N 2W1
Tél: 418-529-4777; *Téléc:* 418-691-0711

Sylvain Gagnon, Directeur général

Québec: **CLSC Haute-Ville**
Affiliée à: Agence de la santé et des services sociaux de la Capitale-Nationale
55, ch Ste-Foy, Québec, QC G1R 1S9
Tél: 418-641-2572; *Téléc:* 418-691-0711

Gaétan Garon, Directeur général

Québec: **CLSC Haute-Ville-des-Rivières**
1720, boul Père-Lelièvre, Québec, QC G1M 3J6
Tél: 418-688-9212

Richelieu: **CLSC du Richelieu**
Affiliée à: Agence de la santé et des services sociaux de la Montérégie
700, rue Martel, Richelieu, QC J3L 5R6
Tél: 450-658-7561; *Téléc:* 450-460-3544

Danielle McCann, Directrice générale

Richmond: **CLSC de Richmond**
CSSS du Val-Saint-François
110, rue Barlow, Richmond, QC J0B 2H0
Tél: 819-542-2777; *Téléc:* 819-826-3867
vsf.santeestrie.qc.ca

Pierre Lalande, Directeur général, CSSS du Val-Saint-François

Rimouski: **CLSC Rimouski-Neigette**
CSSS de Rimouski-Neigette
Affiliée à: Agence de la santé et des services sociaux du Bas-St-Laurent
165, rue des Gouverneurs, Rimouski, QC G5L 7R2
Tél: 418-724-7204; *Téléc:* 418-724-5494
courrierweb.crsssr@ssss.gouv.qc.ca
www.chrr.qc.ca
Note: 3 autres points de service: Saint-Fabien, Saint-Marcellin, et Saint-Narcisse
Raymond Coulombe, Directeur général, CSSS de Rimouski-Neigette

Rivière-au-Renard: **CLSC Mer et Montagnes**
Point de service Rivière-au-Renard
Affiliée à: Agence de la santé et des services sociaux de la Gaspésie-Iles-de-la-Madeleine
154, boul Renard est, Rivière-au-Renard, QC G4X 5R5
Tél: 418-269-2572; *Téléc:* 418-269-5294
www.cssscotedegaspe.ca
Nombre de lits: 3 lits
Note: CSSS Côte-de-Gaspé.
Jean-Pierre Tremblay, Directeur général

Rivière-du-Loup: **CLSC de Rivière-du-Loup**
CSSS de Rivière-du-Loup
Affiliée à: Agence de la santé et des services sociaux du Bas-St-Laurent
22, rue Saint-Laurent, Rivière-du-Loup, QC G5R 4W5
Tél: 418-867-2642; *Téléc:* 418-867-4713
www.csssriviereduloup.qc.ca

Raymond April, Directeur général, CSSS Rivière-du-Loup

Rouyn-Noranda: **CLSC - l'Hôpital de Rouyn-Noranda**
CSSS de Rouyn-Noranda
Affiliée à: Agence de la santé et des services sociaux de l'Abitibi-Témiscamingue
3, 9e rue, Rouyn-Noranda, QC J9X 2A9
Tél: 819-764-5131; *Téléc:* 819-764-2948
www.sante-abitibi-temiscamingue.gouv.qc.ca; www.csssrn.qc.ca
Note: Point de service CLSC, et consultations externes CHSGS.
Huguette Lemay, Directrice générale, CSSS de Rouyn-Noranda

Saint-André-Avellin: **CLSC et Centre d'hébergement Petite-Nation**
Affiliée à: Agence de la santé et de services sociaux de l'Outaouais
14, rue Saint-André, Saint-André-Avellin, QC J0V 1W0
Tél: 819-983-7341; *Téléc:* 819-983-7812
clsc-chsld_petite-nation@ssss.gouv.qc.ca
www.cssspapineau.qc.ca; www.santeautravail.net

Gilles Clavel, Directeur général (par intérim), CSSS de Papineau

Saint-Esprit: **CLSC Montcalm**
Affiliée à: Agences de développement de réseaux locaux de services de santé et de services sociaux
102, rue St-Isidore, Saint-Esprit, QC J0K 2L0
Tél: 450-839-3676; *Téléc:* 450-839-7811

Paul-Yvon de Billy, Directeur général

Saint-Eustache: **Centre de santé et de services sociaux Deux-Montagnes et Sud de Mirabel**
CLSC Jean-Olivier-Chenier
Affiliée à: Agence de la santé et des services sociaux des Laurentides
29, ch Oka, Saint-Eustache, QC J7R 1K6
Tél: 450-491-1233; *Téléc:* 450-491-3424
www.monclsc.com

Christiane Arbour, Directrice générale

Saint-Félicien: **Centre local de services communautaires des Prés-Bleus**
Affiliée à: Agence de la santé et des services sociaux du Saguenay-Lac-St-Jean
CP 10, 1228, boul Sacre-Coeur, Saint-Félicien, QC G8K 2R2
Tél: 418-679-5270; *Téléc:* 418-679-3510

Jean-Guy Lamothe, Directeur général (par intérim)

Saint-Hubert: **CLSC Saint-Hubert**
Affiliée à: Agence de la santé et des services sociaux de la Montérégie
6800, boul Cousineau, Saint-Hubert, QC J3Y 8Z4
Tél: 450-443-7400; *Téléc:* 450-676-4645
16_clsc_sainthubert@rrsss16.gouv.qc.ca

Suzanne Beauchamp, Directrice générale

Saint-Jean-sur-Richelieu: **CLSC de la Vallée-des-Forts**
CSSS Haut-Richelieu-Rouville
978, boul du Séminaire nord, Saint-Jean-sur-Richelieu, QC J3A 1E5
Tél: 450-358-2572; *Téléc:* 450-349-0724
www.santemonteregie.qc.ca/haut-richelieu-rouville

Christine Lessard, Directrice générale, CSSS Haut-Richelieu-Rouville

Saint-Jérome: **CLSC Arthur-Buies**
Affiliée à: Agence de la santé et des services sociaux des Laurentides
430, rue Labelle, Saint-Jérome, QC J7Z 5L3
Tél: 450-431-2221

Saint-Léonard: **CLSC de Saint-Léonard**
CSSS de Saint-Léonard et Saint-Michel
Affiliée à: Agence de la santé et des services sociaux de Montréal
5540, rue Jarry est, Saint-Léonard, QC H1P 1T9
Tél: 514-328-3460
csss-stleonardstmichel.qc.ca

Suzanne Hébert, Directrice générale, CSSS de Saint-Léonard et Saint-Michel

Saint-Ludger: **CSSS du Granit - CLSC Saint-Ludger**
Affiliée à: Agence de la santé et des services sociaux de l'Estrie
210-A, rue La Salle, Saint-Ludger, QC G0M 1W0
Tél: 819-548-0330; *Téléc:* 819-548-5553
www.csssgranit.qc.ca

Pierre Latulippe, Directeur général, CSSS du Granit

Saint-Omer: **CLSC de Saint-Omer**
CSSS de la Baie-des-Chaleurs
Affiliée à: Agence de la santé et des services sociaux de la Gaspésie-Iles-de-la-Madeleine
107, rte 132 ouest, Saint-Omer, QC G0C 2Z0
Tél: 418-364-7064; *Téléc:* 418-364-7119
csssbc@csssbc.qc.ca
www.csssbc.qc.ca

Bernard Nadeau, Directeur général, CSSS de la Baie-des-Chaleurs

Saint-Paulin: **CLSC de St-Paulin**
2841, rue Laflèche, Saint-Paulin, QC J0K 3G0
Tél: 819-268-2572; *Téléc:* 819-268-2505

Saint-Rémi: **CLSC Jardin-du-Québec**
CSSS Jardins-Roussillon
2, rue Sainte-Famille, Saint-Rémi, QC J0L 2L0
Tél: 450-454-4671; *Téléc:* 450-454-4538
www.santemonteregie.qc.ca/jardins-roussillon

Paul Moreau, Directeur général, CSSS Jardins-Roussillon

Sainte-Geneviève-de-Batis: **CLSC des Chenaux**
Affiliée à: Agence de la santé et des services sociaux de la Mauricie et du Centre-du-Québec
90, rte Rivière-à-Veillette, RR#4, Sainte-Geneviève-de-Batis, QC G0X 2R0
Tél: 418-362-2727

Gaétan Lebel, Directeur général

Salaberry-de-Valleyfield: **CLSC Seigneurie de Beauharnois**
Affiliée à: Agence de la santé et des services sociaux de la Montérégie
#200, 71, rue Maden, Salaberry-de-Valleyfield, QC J6S 3V4
Tél: 514-371-0143; *Téléc:* 514-371-7682

François Rabeau, Directeur général

Sherbrooke: **CLSC de Sherbrooke - Point de service 50 rue Camirand**
CSSS-Institut universitaire de gériatrie de Sherbrooke
Affiliée à: Agence de la santé et des services sociaux de l'Estrie
50, rue Camirand, Sherbrooke, QC J1H 4J5
Tél: 819-780-2222
www.csss-iugs.ca
Note: Autres points de service: 95, rue Camirand; 356, rue King ouest; 1200, rue King est; et 8, rue Speid.
Carol Fillion, Directeur général, CSSS-Institut universitaire de gériatrie de Sherbro

Sorel-Tracy: **Hôpital Richelieu/CLSC du Havre**
Affiliée à: Agence de la santé et des services sociaux de la Montérégie
30, rue Ferland, Sorel-Tracy, QC J3P 3C7
Tél: 450-743-5569; *Téléc:* 450-743-1803

Ginette Rhealt, Manager

Ste-Anne-des-Monts: **Centre de santé et de services sociaux de la Haute-Gaspésie**
CLSC de Ste-Anne-des-Monts
Affiliée à: Agence de la santé et des services sociaux de la Gaspésie-Iles-de-la-Madeleine
52, rue Belvédère, Ste-Anne-des-Monts, QC G4V 1X4
Tél: 418-763-7771; *Téléc:* 418-763-7176
www.agencesssgim.ca; www.cssshautegaspesie.qc.ca

Terrebonne: **CLSC Lamater**
Affiliée à: Agences de développement de réseaux locaux de services de santé et de services sociaux
1317, boul des Seigneurs, Terrebonne, QC J6W 5B1
Tél: 450-471-2881

François Lamarre, Directeur général

Trois-Rivières: **Centre de service Les Forges**
Affiliée à: Agence de la santé et des services sociaux de la Mauricie et du Centre-du-Québec
500, rue Saint-Georges, Trois-Rivières, QC G9A 2K8
Tél: 819-379-7131; *Téléc:* 819-373-7726

Gilles Tétu, Directeur général

Val-Bélair: **CLSC de la Jacques-Cartier**
Affiliée à: Agence de la santé et des services sociaux de la Capitale-Nationale
1465, rue de l'Etna, Val-Bélair, QC G3K 2S2
Tél: 418-843-2572; *Téléc:* 418-842-4662

Reynald Gagnon, Directeur général

Vaudreuil-Dorion: **Centre de santé et de services sociaux de Vaudreuil-Soulanges**
Affiliée à: Agence de la santé et des services sociaux de la Montérégie
490, boul Harwood, Vaudreuil-Dorion, QC J7V 7H4
Tél: 450-455-6171; *Téléc:* 450-455-9086

Diane Boileau Seperich, Directrice générale

Victoriaville: **CLSC Suzor-Côté**
CSSS d'Arthabaska-et-de-l'Érable
Affiliée à: Agence de la santé et des services sociaux de la Mauricie et du Centre-du-Québec
100, rue de l'Ermitage, Victoriaville, QC G6P 9N2
Tél: 819-758-7281
www.csssae.qc.ca

Marcel Dubois, Président, Conseil d'administration, CSSS d'Arthabaska-et-de-l

Centres de traitments spécialisés

Amos: **Centre Normand**
621, rue Harricana, Amos, QC J9T 2P9
Tél: 819-732-8241; *Téléc:* 819-727-2210
www.sante-abitibi-temiscamingue.gouv.qc.ca; www.centrenormand.org

Nombre de lits: 10 lits
Note: Offre des services de réadaptation aux personnes qui présentent une dépendance - à l'alcool, drogues illicites, médicaments, jeu; services de support psychosocial.
Pierre Michel Guay, Directeur général
pierremichel_guay@ssss.gouv.qc.ca

Amos: **CRDI Abitibi-Témiscamingue Clair-Foyer**
841, 3e rue ouest, Amos, QC J9T 2T4
Tél: 819-732-6511; *Téléc:* 819-732-0922
www.sante-abitibi-temiscamingue.gouv.qc.ca
Nombre de lits: 31 lits
Note: Centre de réadaptation (déficience intellectuelle); services de support.
Denis Plourde, Directeur général
danplo@ssss.gouv.qc.ca

Baie-Comeau: **Centre de protection et de réadaptation de la Côte-Nord**
Affiliée à: Agence de la santé et des services sociaux de la Côte-Nord
835, boul Joliet, Baie-Comeau, QC G5C 1P5
Tél: 418-589-9927; *Téléc:* 418-589-4304
Note: et centre jeunesse
Claude Montigny, Directeur général

Baie-Comeau: **Centre de protection et de réadaptation de la Côte-Nord**
836, boul Joliet, Baie-Comeau, QC G5C 1P5
Tél: 418-589-9927; *Téléc:* 418-589-4304
Nombre de lits: 225 lits
Claude Montigny, Directeur général

Beauceville: **Centre de réadaptation en alcoolisme et toxicomanie de Chaudière-Appalaches**
Affiliée à: Agence de la santé et des services sociaux de Chaudière-Appalaches
253, rte 108, Beauceville, QC G5X 2Z3
Tél: 418-774-3304; *Téléc:* 418-774-4423
alto_beauce@ssss.gouv.qc.ca
www.agencesss12.gouv.qc.ca

Nombre de lits: 14 lits
Huguette Giroux, Directrice générale

Beauport: **Centre de réadaptation Ubald-Villeneuve**
Ancien nom: Centre de réadaptation en toxicomanie de Québec
2525, ch de la Canardière, 2e étage, Beauport, QC G1J 2G3
Tél: 418-663-5008; *Téléc:* 418-663-6575

Nombre de lits: 22 lits
Note: toxicomanie
Dominique Paquette, Directrice générale

Bonaventure: **Centre de réadaptation de la Gaspésie**
Point de service MRC de Bonaventure
Affiliée à: Agence de la santé et des services sociaux de la Gaspésie-Iles-de-la-Madeleine
CP 667, 238, av Port-Royal, Bonaventure, QC G0C 1E0
Tél: 418-534-4243; *Téléc:* 418-534-2411
www.agencesssgim.ca
Note: Déficiences physiques et intellectuelles.

Bonaventure: **Centre jeunesse Gaspésie/Les Iles**
Point de service Unité La Balise
Affiliée à: Agence de la santé et des services sociaux de la Gaspésie-Iles-de-la-Madeleine
CP 308, 193, av Port Royal, Bonaventure, QC G0C 1E0
Tél: 418-534-3283; *Téléc:* 418-534-4024
www.agencesssgim.ca

Nombre de lits: 12 lits
Note: Pour mésadaptées socio-affectifs.

Bonaventure: **Centre jeunesse Gaspésie/Les Iles**
Point de service Succursale Bonaventure-Avignon
Affiliée à: Agence de la santé et des services sociaux de la Gaspésie-Iles-de-la-Madeleine
CP 308, 106, av Port-Royal, Bonaventure, QC G0C 1E0
Tél: 418-534-2272; *Téléc:* 418-534-4278
www.agencesssgim.ca

Cap-aux-Meules: **Centre jeunesse Gaspésie/Les Iles**
Point de service Succursale des Iles
Affiliée à: Agence de la santé et des services sociaux de la Gaspésie-Iles-de-la-Madeleine
CP 268, 539-2, ch Principal, Cap-aux-Meules, QC G4T 1E7
Tél: 418-986-2230; *Téléc:* 418-986-5445
www.agencesssgim.ca

Carleton: **Centre de réadaptation de la Gaspésie**
Point de service MRC d'Avignon - Carleton
Affiliée à: Agence de la santé et des services sociaux de la Gaspésie-Iles-de-la-Madeleine
CP 26, 314, boul Perron ouest, Carleton, QC G0C 1J0
Tél: 418-364-6037; *Téléc:* 418-364-7040
www.agencesssgim.ca
Note: Déficience intellectuelle.

Chandler: **Centre de réadaptation de la Gaspésie**
Point de service MRC du Rocher-Percé
Affiliée à: Agence de la santé et des services sociaux de la Gaspésie-Iles-de-la-Madeleine
CP 2168, 328, boul René-Lévesque ouest, Chandler, QC G0C 1K0
Tél: 418-689-4286; *Téléc:* 418-689-7155
www.agencesssgim.ca
Note: Déficiences physiques et intellectuelles.

Chandler: **Centre jeunesse Gaspésie/Les Iles**
Point de service Succursale Rocher-Percé
Affiliée à: Agence de la santé et des services sociaux de la Gaspésie-Iles-de-la-Madeleine
CP 280, 105, rue Commerciale ouest, Chandler, QC G0C 1K0
Tél: 418-689-2286; *Téléc:* 418-689-4643
www.agencesssgim.ca

Charlesbourg: **Centre de réadaptation La Maisonnée**
855, boul Louis XIV, Charlesbourg, QC G1H 1A6
Tél: 418-628-0662; *Téléc:* 418-628-5440
celine.auclair@ssss.gouv.qc.ca

Nombre de lits: 11 lits
Note: centre de réadaptation
Lucie Lacroix, Directrice générale

Chicoutimi: Le Centre jeunesse du Saguenay-Lac-Saint-Jean
520, rue Jacques-Cartier est, Chicoutimi, QC G7H 8A2
Tél: 418-549-4853; *Téléc:* 418-693-0768
Ligne sans frais: 800-463-9188
www.cjsaglac.qc.ca
Nombre de lits: 116 lits
Note: centre de réadaptation
Daniele Riverin, Directrice générale

Fatima: Centre de réadaptation de la Gaspésie Point de service MRC des Iles-de-la-Madeleine
Affiliée à: Agence de la santé et des services sociaux de la Gaspésie-Iles-de-la-Madeleine
CP 549, 695, ch des Caps, Fatima, QC G4T 2S9
Tél: 418-986-4870; *Téléc:* 418-986-2623
www.agencesssgim.ca
Note: Déficience physique.

Gaspé: Centre de réadaptation de la Gaspésie Point de service MRC de La Côte-de-Gaspé
Affiliée à: Agence de la santé et des services sociaux de la Gaspésie-Iles-de-la-Madeleine
CP 6320, 150, rue Mgr Ross, aile 550, Gaspé, QC G4X 2R8
Tél: 418-368-2306; *Téléc:* 418-368-7761
www.agencesssgim.ca
Note: Déficiences physiques et intellectuelles.

Gaspé: Centre jeunesse Gaspésie/Les Iles Point de service Unité La Vigie
Affiliée à: Agence de la santé et des services sociaux de la Gaspésie-Iles-de-la-Madeleine
418, montée Wakeham, Gaspé, QC G4X 2V7
Tél: 418-368-1803; *Téléc:* 418-368-8744
www.agencesssgim.ca
Nombre de lits: 14 places
Note: Centre de réadaptation.

Gaspé: Centre jeunesse Gaspésie/Les Iles
Affiliée à: Agence de la santé et des services sociaux de la Gaspésie-Iles-de-la-Madeleine
#100, 205, boul de York ouest, Gaspé, QC G4X 2V7
Tél: 418-368-1803; *Téléc:* 418-368-5478
www.agencesssgim.ca
Nombre de lits: 55 lits

Gaspé: Centre jeunesse Gaspésie/Les Iles Point de service Unité La Rade
Affiliée à: Agence de la santé et des services sociaux de la Gaspésie-Iles-de-la-Madeleine
#100, 205, boul de York ouest, Gaspé, QC G4X 2V7
Tél: 418-368-1803; *Téléc:* 418-368-6303
www.agencesssgim.ca

Gaspé: Centre jeunesse Gaspésie/Les Iles Point de service Succursale Côte-de-Gaspé
Affiliée à: Agence de la santé et des services sociaux de la Gaspésie-Iles-de-la-Madeleine
#100, 205, boul de York ouest, Gaspé, QC G4X 2V7
Tél: 418-368-3381; *Téléc:* 418-368-5101
www.agencesssgim.ca

Gatineau: Centre Jellinek
Ancien nom: Pavillon Jelinek
25, rue Saint-François, Gatineau, QC J9A 1B1
Tél: 819-776-5584; *Téléc:* 819-776-0255
Ligne sans frais: 866-776-5585
jellinek@jellinek.org
www.jellinek.org
Nombre de lits: 33 places
Note: centre de réadaptation des drogues, de l'alcool ou du jeu
Raymond Rochon, Directeur général

Gatineau: Centre régional de réadaptation La Ressource
135, boul Saint-Raymond, Gatineau, QC J8Y 6X7
Tél: 819-777-6261; *Téléc:* 819-777-0701
Nombre de lits: 37 lits
Note: centre de réadaptation (déficience auditive, visuelle, & motrice)
Jean-Pierre Blais, Directeur général

Gatineau: Les Centres jeunesse de l'Outaouais
105, boul Sacré-Coeur, Gatineau, QC J8X 1C5
Tél: 819-771-6631
Nombre de lits: 149 lits
Note: centre jeunesse, protection
Gilles Clavel, Directeur général

Gatineau: Pavillon du Parc inc.
768, boul St-Joseph, Gatineau, QC J8Y 4B8
Tél: 819-684-1022; *Téléc:* 819-684-1023
info@pavillonduparc.qc.ca
www.pavillonduparc.qc.ca
Nombre de lits: 92 lits
Note: centre de réadaptation
Thierry Boyer, Directeur général

Joliette: Centre de réadaptation La Myriade
339, boul Base-de-Roc, Joliette, QC J6E 5P3
Tél: 450-753-9600; *Téléc:* 450-753-1930
Nombre de lits: 38 lits
Robert Lasalle, Directeur général

Joliette: Les Centres jeunesse de Lanaudière
260, rue Lavaltrie sud, Joliette, QC J6E 5X7
Tél: 450-756-4555; *Téléc:* 450-756-0814
Nombre de lits: 135 lits
Pierre Racette, Directeur général

Jonquière: Centre de santé et de services sociaux de Jonquière
2230, rue de l'Hôpital, Jonquière, QC G7X 4H6
Tél: 418-695-7700; *Téléc:* 418-695-7729
Nombre de lits: 40 lits
Lucie Dauphin, Directrice générale

Kuujjuaq: Centre de santé Tulattavik de l'Ungava
CP 149, Kuujjuaq, Kuujjuaq, QC J0M 1C0
Tél: 819-964-2905; *Téléc:* 819-964-2653
Nombre de lits: 23 lits
Madge Pomerleau, Directrice générale

Lachine: Centre de réadaptation de l'Ouest de Montréal
Affiliée à: Agence de la santé et des services sociaux de Montréal
8000, rue Notre-Dame, Lachine, QC H8R 1H2
Tél: 514-363-3025; *Téléc:* 514-364-5997
Nombre de lits: 186 lits
Note: centre de réadaptation en déficience intellectuelle
John Aung-Thwin, Directeur général

Lachine: Centre de réadaptation Lisette-Dupras
8000, rue Notre-Dame, Lachine, QC H8R 1H2
Tél: 514-364-2280; *Téléc:* 514-364-0608
www.lisette-dupras.ca.
Nombre de lits: 524 lits
Note: centre de réadaptation
John Aung-Thwin, Directeur général

Laval: Centre Jeunesse de Laval
308, boul Cartier ouest, Laval, QC H7N 2J2
Tél: 450-975-4150; *Téléc:* 450-975-4276
Nombre de lits: 269 lits
Note: Centre de la protection de la jeunesse/centre de réadaptation
Pierre Patenaude, Directeur général

Laval: CRDI Normand-Laramée
304, boul Cartier ouest, 2e étage, Laval, QC H7N 2J2
Tél: 450-972-2099; *Téléc:* 450-972-2020
Nombre de lits: 95 lits
Note: centre de réadaptation
Claude Belley, Directeur général

Lennoxville: Centre d'accueil Dixville inc.
CP 150, 155, rue Belvidere, Lennoxville, QC J1M 1Z4
Tél: 819-821-2928; *Téléc:* 819-821-2920
Nombre de lits: 100 lits
Note: centre de réadaptation
Francine Caron, Directrice générale

Lennoxville: Centre Notre-Dame de l'Enfant (Sherbrooke) Inc.
CP 150, 155, rue Belvidere, Lennoxville, QC J1M 1Z4
Tél: 819-821-2928; *Téléc:* 819-821-2920
Nombre de lits: 178 lits
Note: centre de réadaptation en déficience intellectuelle
Francine Caron, Directrice générale

Lévis: Centre de réadaptation en déficience intellectuelle de Chaudière-Appalaches Centre administratif
Affiliée à: Agence de la santé et des services sociaux de Chaudière-Appalaches
55, rue du Mont-Marie, Lévis, QC G6V 0B8
Tél: 418-833-3218; *Téléc:* 418-833-9849
Ligne sans frais: 866-333-3218
crdi@chaudiere.appalaches@ssss.gouv.qc.ca
www.crditedca.com
Nombre de lits: 674 lits
Dominique Paquette, Directeur général

Lévis: Les Centres jeunesse Chaudière-Appalaches Centre administratif
#300, 100, rue Monseigneur-Bourget, Lévis, QC G6V 2Y9
Tél: 418-837-9331; *Téléc:* 418-838-8860
www.cj12.qc.ca
Nombre de lits: 146 lits
Note: Services de la protection de la jeunesse; service aux jeunes contrevenants; service d'adoption; services de réadaptation. Installations: Lévis, Saint-Romuald, Montmagny, Sainte-Marie, Saint-Joseph, Saint-Georges & Thetford Mines.
Pierre Morin, Directeur général

Longueuil: Centre de réadaptation en déficience intellectuelle Montérégie-est
1255, rue Beauregard, Longueuil, QC J4K 2M3
Tél: 450-679-6511; *Téléc:* 450-928-3655
16_crdime_information@ssss.gouv.qc.ca
www.crdime.qc.ca
Nombre de lits: 1157 lits
Johanne Gauthier, Directrice générale

Longueuil: Centre jeunesse de la Montérégie
25, boul Lafayette, Longueuil, QC J4K 5C8
Tél: 450-928-5125; *Téléc:* 450-679-3731
Nombre de lits: 398 lits
Camil Picard, Directeur général

Mont-Laurier: Centre de santé et de services sociaux d'Antoine-Labelle
515, boul Albiny-Paquette, Mont-Laurier, QC J9L 1K8
Tél: 819-623-6127; *Téléc:* 819-623-9451
Nombre de lits: 138 lits
Pierre Gfeller, Directeur général

Mont-Royal: Centre Miriam
8160, ch Royden, Mont-Royal, QC H4P 2T2
Tél: 514-345-0210; *Téléc:* 514-345-8965
www.centremiriam.ca
Nombre de lits: 241 lits
Note: centre de réadaptation
Jean-Pierre Aumont, Directeur général (intérim)

Montréal: Association montréalaise pour les aveugles
Montréal Association for the Blind
7000, rue Sherbrooke ouest, Montréal, QC H4B 1R3
Tél: 514-489-8201; *Téléc:* 514-489-3477
mabinfo@mab.ca
www.mab.ca
Nombre de lits: 8 lits
Note: centre de réadaptation (déficience visuelle) et CHSLD
Paul Gareau, Directeur général

Montréal: Atelier le Fil d'Ariane inc.
#100, 4837, rue Boyer, Montréal, QC H2J 3E6
Tél: 514-842-5592; *Téléc:* 514-842-8343
lisette.clauveau.ariane@ssss.gouv.qc.ca
www.atelierlefildariane.org
Nombre de lits: 20 places
Note: Un atelier de travail pour des adultes ayant des limitations fonctionnelles sur le plan intellectuel; l'atelier favorise l'intégration sociale & communautaire & l'autonomie personnelle & professionnelle des artisans.
Lisette Claveau, Directrice générale

Montréal: Centre d'accueil le programme de Portage inc.
865, carré Richmond, Montréal, QC H3J 1V8
Tél: 514-939-0202; *Téléc:* 514-939-3929
Nombre de lits: 231 lits
Note: centre de réadaptation des drogues
Peter Vamos, Directeur général

Montréal: Centre de réadaptation Constance-Lethbridge
Affiliée à: Agence de la santé et des services sociaux de Montréal
7005, boul de Maisonneuve ouest, Montréal, QC H4B 1T3
Tél: 514-487-1770; *Téléc:* 514-487-5494
Note: déficience motrice
Ghislaine Prata, Directrice générale

Montréal: Centre Dollard-Cormier
950, rue de Louvain est, Montréal, QC H2M 2E8
Tél: 514-385-0046; *Téléc:* 514-385-5728
www.centredollardcormier.qc.ca
Nombre de lits: 55 lits
Madeleine Roy, Directrice générale

Montréal: Centre hospitalier universitaire Sainte-Justine
3175, ch de la Côte Sainte-Catherine, Montréal, QC H3T 1C5
Tél: 514-345-4931; *Téléc:* 514-345-4808
Nombre de lits: 55 lits
Khiem Dao, Directeur général

Montréal: Centre jeunesse de Montréal - Institut universitaire
4675, rue Bélanger, Montréal, QC H1T 1C2
Tél: 514-593-3979; *Téléc:* 514-593-3982
institut.universitaire@cjm-iu.qc.ca
www.centrejeunessedemontreal.qc.ca
Nombre de lits: 826 admissions
Note: services psychosociaux et de réadaptation
Jean-Pierre Duplantie, Directeur général

Montréal: La Corporation du centre de réadaptation Lucie-Bruneau
Affiliée à: Agence de la santé et des services sociaux de Montréal
2275, av Laurier est, Montréal, QC H2H 2N8
Tél: 514-527-4521; *Téléc:* 514-527-0979
Nombre de lits: 50 lits
Note: centre de réadaptation (déficience motrice)
Alain Lefebvre, Directeur général

Montréal: CSSS de Bordeaux-Cartierville-Saint Laurent
Centre administratif
Affiliée à: Agence de la santé et des services sociaux de Montréal
555, boul Gouin ouest, Montréal, QC H3L 1K5
Tél: 514-331-3020; *Téléc:* 514-331-0874
www.santemontreal.qc.ca
Note: Installations: les CLSCs: Bordeaux-Cartierville, & Saint-Laurent; les Centres d'hébergement: Notre-Dame-de-la-Merci, Saint-Joseph-de-la-Providence, Saint-Laurent, & Cartierville.
Daniel Corbeil, Directeur général

Montréal: Hôpital de réadaptation Villa Medica
Affiliée à: Agence de la santé et des services sociaux de Montréal
225, rue Sherbrooke est, Montréal, QC H2X 1C9
Tél: 514-288-8201
www.villamedica.ca
Nombre de lits: 150 lits
Note: centre hospitalier de réadaptation
Michel Duchesne, Directeur général

Montréal: L'institut de réadaptation de Montréal
Affiliée à: Agence de la santé et des services sociaux de Montréal
6300, av Darlington, Montréal, QC H3S 2J4
Tél: 514-340-2085; *Téléc:* 514-340-2091
www.irm.qc.ca
Nombre de lits: 102 lits
Note: centre de réadaptation
Jacques R. Nolet, Directeur général

Montréal: Institut Raymond-Dewar
Affiliée à: Agence de la santé et des services sociaux de Montréal
3600, rue Berri, Montréal, QC H2L 4G9
Tél: 514-284-2581; *Téléc:* 514-284-5086
ird@raymond-dewar.gouv.qc.ca
www.raymond-dewar.qc.ca
Note: centre de réadaptation (déficience auditive et de la parole et du language)
Pierre-Paul Lachapelle, Directeur général

Montréal: Maison Elisabeth
2131, av de Marlowe, Montréal, QC H4A 3L4
Tél: 514-482-2488; *Fax:* 514-482-9467
Nombre de lits: 18 lits
Linda Schachtler, Directrice générale

Montréal: The Morgentaler Clinic
Montreal Site
Clinique Morgentaler
#710, 30, boul St Joseph est, Montréal, QC H2T 1G9
Tel: 514-844-4844; *Fax:* 514-844-7883
Toll-Free: 888-401-4844
cliniquem@bellnet.ca
www.morgentalermontreal.ca
Year Founded: 1968
Note: Specialties: Pregnancy termination services; Post-abortion service

Montréal: Services de réadaptation L'Intégrale
Ancien nom: Centre de réadaptation l'Intégrale
#110, 75, rue de Port-Royal est, Montréal, QC H3L 3T1
Tél: 514-387-1234; *Téléc:* 514-387-5013
www.integrale.org
Nombre de lits: 31 lits
Jean-Pierre Aumont, Directeur général

Puvirnituq: Centre de santé Inuulitsivik
ch Baie d'Hudson, Puvirnituq, QC J0M 1P0
Tél: 819-988-2957; *Téléc:* 819-988-2796
Nombre de lits: 8

Québec: Centre de réadaptation en déficience intellectuelle de Québec
110, rue de Courcelette, Québec, QC G1N 4T4
Tél: 418-683-2511; *Téléc:* 418-683-9735
Nombre de lits: 530 lits
Renaud Cloutier, Directeur général (intérim)

Québec: Institut de réadaptation en déficience physique de Québec
Affiliée à: Agence de la santé et des services sociaux de la Capitale-Nationale
525, boul Wilfrid Hamel, Québec, QC G1M 2S8
Tél: 418-529-9141; *Téléc:* 418-529-7318
communications@irdpq.qc.ca
www.irdpq.qc.ca
Nombre de lits: 165 lits
Note: centre de réadaptation (déficience physique)
Richard Brousseau, Directeur général

Restigouche: Centre jeunesse Gaspésie/Les Iles Point de service Unité Gignu
Affiliée à: Agence de la santé et des services sociaux de la Gaspésie-Iles-de-la-Madeleine
CP 193, 4, ch Pacific, Restigouche, QC G0C 2R0
Tél: 418-788-5605; *Téléc:* 418-788-2751
www.agencesssgim.ca

Rimouski: Centre de réadaptation en déficience intellectuelle du Bas St-Laurent
Ancien nom: Centre de réadaptation intellectuelle du Bas St-La
274, rue Potvin, Rimouski, QC G5L 7P5
Tél: 418-723-4425; *Téléc:* 418-722-6113
Nombre de lits: 348 lits
Guylaine Côté, Directrice générale

Rimouski: Centre jeunesse du Bas-St-Laurent
CP 3500, 287, rue Pierre-Saindon, 3e étage, Rimouski, QC G5L 8V5
Tél: 418-723-1255; *Téléc:* 418-722-0620
www.agencesssbsl.gouv.qc.ca
Nombre de lits: 73 lits
Marie-Sylvie Bêche, Directrice générale

Roberval: Centre de réadaptation en déficience intellectuelle du Saguenay-Lac-Saint-Jean
835, rue Roland, Roberval, QC G8H 3J5
Tél: 418-275-1360; *Téléc:* 418-275-6595
Nombre de lits: 617 lits
Note: Centre de réadaptation pour personnes présentant une déficience intellectuelle
Laurent Bouillon, Directeur général

Roberval: CLSC-CRAT de Roberval
CSSS Domaine-du-Roy
Pavillon Gérard-Tremblay, 400, av Bergeron, aile A, Roberval, QC G8H 1K8
Tél: 418-275-0634; *Téléc:* 418-275-0423
hdr@ssss.gouv.qc.ca
www.cmdp-roberval.com
Nombre de lits: CRAT: 15 lits
Note: Le CLSC offre des services de santé et Info-Santé (811), services sociaux généraux, et services spécifiques; le CRAT offre des services d'adaptation ou réadaptation en alcoolisme et autres toxicomanies.
Jacques Dubois, Directeur général, CSSS Domaine-du-Roy

Rouyn-Noranda: Centre de réadaptation La Maison
CP 1055, 100, ch Docteur-Lemay, Rouyn-Noranda, QC J9X 5C8
Tél: 819-762-6592; *Téléc:* 819-762-2049
www.sante-abitibi-temiscamingue.gouv.qc.ca; www.crlm.qc.ca
Nombre de lits: 55 lits
Note: Centre de réadaptation (déficience physique, troubles envahissants du développement).
Line St-Amour, Directrice générale
Line_St-Amour@ssss.gouv.qc.ca

Saint-Jean-sur-Richelieu: Les services de réadaptation du Sud-Ouest et du Renfort
#105, 315, rue MacDonald, Saint-Jean-sur-Richelieu, QC J3B 8J3
Tél: 450-348-6121; *Téléc:* 450-348-8440
Nombre de lits: 581 lits
Gilles Bertrand, Directeur général

Saint-Jérome: Centre du Florès
500, boul des Laurentides, Saint-Jérome, QC J7Z 4M2
Tél: 450-569-2970; *Téléc:* 450-569-2961
Ligne sans frais: 877-569-2970
Nombre de lits: 0
Note: centre de réadaptation
Cathy Lévesque, Attachée de direction
cathy_levesque@ssss.gouv.qc.ca
Lucie Leduc, Directrice générale

Saint-Jérome: Centre jeunesse des Laurentides
#241, 500, boul des Laurentides, Saint-Jérome, QC J7Z 4M2
Tél: 450-436-7607; *Téléc:* 450-436-4811
Nombre de lits: 160 lits
Bernard Fortin, Directeur général

Saint-Jérome: Pavillon Ste-Marie inc.
Affiliée à: Agence de la santé et des services sociaux des Laurentides
45, rue du Pavillon, Saint-Jérome, QC J7Y 3R6
Tél: 450-438-3583; *Téléc:* 450-438-7481
Nombre de lits: 100 lits
Francyne Jolicoeur, Directrice générale

Saint-Philippe: Pavillon Foster
CP 119, 6, rue Foucreault, Saint-Philippe, QC J0L 2K0
Tél: 450-659-8911; *Téléc:* 450-659-7173
www.pavillonfoster.org
Nombre de lits: 20 lits
Note: alcohol/drug rehabilitation
John Topp, Directeur général

Saint-Romuald: Centre de réadaptation en déficience physique Chaudière-Appalaches
Affiliée à: Agence de la santé et des services sociaux de Chaudière-Appalaches
2055, boul de la Rive-Sud, Saint-Romuald, QC G6W 2S5
Tél: 418-834-5888; *Téléc:* 418-834-0018
www.rrss12.gouv.qc.ca
Nombre de lits: 48 lits
Note: Programmes: Déficience auditive, Déficience du langage, Déficience motrice (enfant, adulte), Clinique de sclérose en plaques, Programme d'évaluation & de réadaptation en conduite automobile, Neurotraumatisme, Dépistage du traumatisme craniocérébral léger, Programme intensif de gestion autonome de la douleur, et Programme de suppléance à la communication. Points de service: Beauce-Etchemin (Beauceville), Montmagny-L'Islet (Montmagny), l'Amiante (Thetford Mines), et Littoral (Charny).

Sept-Iles: Bande indienne des montagnes de Sept-Iles/Maliotenam
1089, rue Dequen, Sept-Iles, QC G4R 4L9
Tél: 418-962-0222; *Téléc:* 418-968-0935
Nombre de lits: 29 lits
Jean-Marie Caron, Directeur général

Sherbrooke: Centre de réadaptation Estrie inc.
Affiliée à: Agence de la santé et des services sociaux de l'Estrie
1930, rue King ouest, Sherbrooke, QC J1J 2E2
Tél: 819-346-8411; *Téléc:* 819-564-7670
Nombre de lits: 117 lits
Note: centre de réadaptation (déficience motrice)
Lucie Dumas, Directrice générale

Sherbrooke: Centre Jean-Patrice Chaisson/Maison St-Georges
Affiliée à: Agence de la santé et des services sociaux de l'Estrie
1930, rue King ouest, Sherbrooke, QC J1J 2E2
Tél: 819-821-2500; *Téléc:* 819-563-8322
Nombre de lits: 45 lits
Note: centre de réadaptation des drogues
Denis Bougie, Directeur général

Sherbrooke: Centre jeunesse de l'Estrie
594, boul Queen nord, Sherbrooke, QC J1H 3R7
Tél: 819-564-7100; *Téléc:* 819-564-7109
Nombre de lits: 121 lits
Note: centre jeunesse
Carol Fillion, Directrice générale (intérim)

Sherbrooke: **Villa Marie-Claire inc.**
470, rue Victoria, Sherbrooke, QC J1H 3J2
Tél: 819-563-1622; *Téléc:* 819-563-6990
Nombre de lits: 15 lits
Louisette Breton, Directrice générale

St-Léonard: **Centre de réadaptation en déficience intellectuelle Gabrielle Major**
Affiliée à: Agence de la santé et des services sociaux de Montréal
Ancien nom: Centre d'accueil Charleroi.
6455, rue Jean Talon est, 6e étage, St-Léonard, QC H1S 3E8
Tél: 514-259-2245; *Téléc:* 514-259-5906
Nombre de lits: 221 lits
Ginette Bissonnette, Directrice générale (intérim)

Ste-Anne-des-Monts: **Centre de réadaptation de la Gaspésie**
Affiliée à: Agence de la santé et des services sociaux de la Gaspésie-Iles-de-la-Madeleine
CP 370, 230, rte du Parc, Ste-Anne-des-Monts, QC G4V 2C4
Tél: 418-763-3325; *Téléc:* 418-763-5631
www.agencesssgim.ca
Nombre de lits: 131 lits
Jacques Tremblay, Directeur général

Ste-Anne-des-Monts: **Centre de réadaptation de la Gaspésie**
Point de service MRC de la Haute-Gaspésie
Affiliée à: Agence de la santé et des services sociaux de la Gaspésie-Iles-de-la-Madeleine
230, rte du Parc, Ste-Anne-des-Monts, QC G4V 2C4
Tél: 418-763-3325; *Téléc:* 418-763-5631
www.agencesssgim.ca
Note: Déficiences physiques et intellectuelles.

Ste-Anne-des-Monts: **Centre de santé et de services sociaux de la Haute-Gaspésie**
Centre de réadaptation L'Escale
Affiliée à: Agence de la santé et des services sociaux de la Gaspésie-Iles-de-la-Madeleine
50, rue Belvédère, Ste-Anne-des-Monts, QC G4V 1X4
Tél: 418-763-5000; *Téléc:* 418-763-9024
www.agencesssgim.ca; www.csssshautegaspesie.qc.ca
Note: Pour personnes toxicomanes. Le Centre se relocalisera en 2010. Les nouvelles installations seront adjacentes à l'Hôpital des Monts.

Ste-Anne-des-Monts: **Centre jeunesse Gaspésie/Les Iles**
Point de service Succursale Haute-Gaspésie
Affiliée à: Agence de la santé et des services sociaux de la Gaspésie-Iles-de-la-Madeleine
#EB-132, 230, rte du Parc, Ste-Anne-des-Monts, QC G4V 2C4
Tél: 418-763-2251; *Téléc:* 418-763-2538
www.agencesssgim.ca

Ste-Anne-des-Monts: **Hôpital des Monts**
Centre de réadaptation L'Escale
Affiliée à: Agence de la santé et des services sociaux de la Gaspésie-Iles-de-la-Madeleine
50 rue Belvedere, Ste-Anne-des-Monts, QC G4V 1X4
Tél: 418-763-5000; *Téléc:* 418-763-9024
www.agencesssgim.ca; www.csssshautegaspesie.qc.ca
Note: Pour personnes toxicomanes. Le Centre relocalisera en 2010. Les nouvelles installations seront adjacentes à l'Hôpital des Monts.

Trois-Rivières: **Centre de réadaptation Interval**
Affiliée à: Agence de la santé et des services sociaux de la Mauricie et du Centre-du-Québec
20, rue Notre-Dame est, Trois-Rivières, QC G8T 9J1
Tél: 819-693-0041; *Téléc:* 819-693-0045
www.centreinterval.qc.ca
Nombre de lits: 40 lits
Note: centre de réadaptation (déficience motrice)
Serge Lemieux, Directeur général

Trois-Rivières: **Centre de services en déficience intellectuelle Mauricie-Centre-du-Québec**
Affiliée à: Agence de la santé et des services sociaux de la Mauricie et du Centre-du-Québec
3255, rue Foucher, Trois-Rivières, QC G8Z 1M6
Tél: 819-379-6868; *Téléc:* 819-379-5155
Nombre de lits: 523 lits
Michel Boutet, Directeur général

Trois-Rivières: **Le Centre jeunesse de la Mauricie et Centre-du-Québec**
1455, boul du Carmel, Trois-Rivières, QC G8Z 3R7
Tél: 819-378-5481; *Téléc:* 819-378-6857
Nombre de lits: 142 lits
Note: centre de réadaptation
Richard Desrochers, Directeur général

Trois-Rivières: **Domremy Mauricie-Centre-du-Québec**
440, rue des Forges, Trois-Rivières, QC G9A 2H5
Tél: 819-374-4744; *Téléc:* 819-374-4502
Nombre de lits: 30 lits
Note: centre de réadaptation des drogues
Pierre Bourassa, Directeur général

Val-d'Or: **Centre jeunesse de l'Abitibi-Témiscamingue**
700, boul Forest, Val-d'Or, QC J9P 2L3
Tél: 819-825-0002; *Téléc:* 819-825-5132
Nombre de lits: 57 lits
Regean Bergeron, Directrice générale

Verdun: **Havre-Jeunesse**
4360, boul Lasalle, Verdun, QC H4G 2A8
Tél: 514-769-5050; *Téléc:* 514-769-3510
Nombre de lits: 15 lits
Wallace B. Johnson, Directeur général

Wemotaci: **Conseil de la Nation Atikamekw**
Wemotaci, QC G0X 3R0
Tél: 418-523-6153; *Téléc:* 418-676-8965
Nombre de lits: 9
Clément St-Cyr, Directeur général

Westmount: **Centre de jeunesse Mont Saint-Patrick Inc.**
5, Weredale Park, Westmount, QC H3Z 1Y5
Tél: 514-989-1885
Nombre de lits: 9 lits
Note: centre de réadaptation (déficience visuelle)
Michael Udy, Directeur général

Westmount: **Les Centres de jeunesse Shawbridge**
5 Weredale Park, Westmount, QC H3Z 1Y5
Tél: 514-989-1885
Nombre de lits: 138 lits
Note: centre de réadaptation (déficience motrice)
Michael Udy, Directeur général

Westmount: **Les centres de la jeunesse et de la famille Saint-Georges**
Ancien nom: Centre d'accueil Horizons de la Jeunesse
5, Weredale Park, Westmount, QC H3Z 1Y5
Tél: 514-932-7161
Nombre de lits: 243 lits
Note: centre de réadaptation (déficience motrice) + déficience sensorielle
Michael Udy, Directeur général

Centres d'accueil et d'hébergement

Buckingham: **Centre d'accueil de Buckingham**
Affiliée à: Agence de la santé et de services sociaux de l'Outaouais
111, rue Lucerne, Buckingham, QC J8L 2M4
Tél: 819-986-1043; *Téléc:* 819-986-9602
Nombre de lits: 79 lits
Jacques Prud'Homme, Directeur général

Dorval: **Le Strathmore**
2400, ch Herron, Dorval, QC H9S 5W3
Tél: 514-631-7288; *Téléc:* 514-631-9208
lestrathmore@chartwellreit.ca
www.chartwellreit.ca/home_locations/lestrathmore.htm
Nombre de lits: 70 lits
Barbara Lee, Directrice générale

Gatineau: **Résidence Ste-Marie**
156, boul Lorrain, Gatineau, QC J8P 2G2
Tél: 819-663-5736; *Téléc:* 819-643-1358
Nombre de lits: 23 lits
Palmyra Séguin, Directrice générale

Granby: **Centre Howard Enr.**
237, boul Montcalm, Granby, QC J2G 5C2
Tél: 514-372-7678
Nombre de lits: 66 lits
Marcel Rémillard, Directeur général

Grandes-Bergeronnes: **Centre de santé et de services sociaux de la Haute-Côte-Nord - Pavillon Bergeron**
Affiliée à: Agence de la santé et des services sociaux de la Côte-Nord
CP 68, 450, rue de la Mer, Grandes-Bergeronnes, QC G0T 1G0
Tél: 418-232-6224; *Téléc:* 418-232-6771
Nombre de lits: 32 lits
Micheline Anctil, Directeur général

Ham-Nord: **Foyer Saints-Anges de Ham-Nord inc.**
Affiliée à: Agence de la santé et des services sociaux de la Mauricie et du Centre-du-Québec
CP 269, 493, rue Principale, Ham-Nord, QC G0P 1A0
Tél: 819-344-2940; *Téléc:* 819-344-2584
Nombre de lits: 38 lits
Alain Lavertu, Directeur général

Iberville: **Pavillon Iberville Enr.**
135, 8e av, Iberville, QC J2X 1K8
Tél: 514-346-9292
Nombre de lits: 15 lits
Rachèle Dorval, Propriétaire

Joliette: **Centre d'accueil Saint-Eusèbe**
Affiliée à: Agences de développement de réseaux locaux de services de santé et de services sociaux
585, boul Manseau, Joliette, QC J6E 3E5
Tél: 450-759-8222; *Téléc:* 450-759-1579
Nombre de lits: 159 lits
Jean-Claude Berlinguet, Directeur général

Montréal: **Centre d'accueil Judith Jasmin**
Affiliée à: Agence de la santé et des services sociaux de Montréal
8850, rue Bisaillon, Montréal, QC H1K 4N2
Tél: 514-354-5990; *Téléc:* 514-354-4916
Nombre de lits: 75 lits

Montréal: **Centre de coordination des services Dandurand**
Affiliée à: Agence de la santé et des services sociaux de Montréal
3958, rue Dandurand, 3e étage, Montréal, QC H1X 1P7
Tél: 514-723-2003; *Téléc:* 514-729-9697

Montréal: **Centre hospitalier Gériatrique Maimonides**
Affiliée à: Agence de la santé et des services sociaux de Montréal
5795, av Caldwell, Montréal, QC H4W 1W3
Tél: 514-483-2121; *Téléc:* 514-483-1561
maimonides@ssss.gouv.qc.ca
Nombre de lits: 387 lits
Barbra Gold, Directrice générale

Montréal: **Résidence Pie IX**
Affiliée à: Agence de la santé et des services sociaux de Montréal
4090, rue Martial, Montréal, QC H1H 1X4
Tél: 514-327-2333; *Téléc:* 514-327-3276
Nombre de lits: 42 lits
Note: Centre de réadaptation
Serge Beauchamp, Directeur général

Montréal-Nord: **Pavillon de la Détente 1993 Enr.**
6880, boul Gouin est, Montréal-Nord, QC H1G 6L8
Tél: 514-321-5107; *Téléc:* 514-328-8987
Nombre de lits: 55 lits
Irène Sirois, Administratrice

Pierrefonds: **Manoir Ile de l'Ouest**
Affiliée à: Agence de la santé et des services sociaux de Montréal
17725, boul Pierrefonds, Pierrefonds, QC H9J 3L1
Tél: 514-620-9850; *Téléc:* 514-620-3196
Nombre de lits: 63 lits
Heather Karakas, Directrice générale

Rawdon: **Heather Hospital Inc.**
Hôpital Heather inc.
Affiliée à: Agences de développement de réseaux locaux de services de santé et de services sociaux
3462, 3e av, Rawdon, QC J0K 1S0
Tél: 450-834-2512; *Téléc:* 450-834-5798
Nombre de lits: 85 lits
Paul Arbec, Directeur général

Roberval: **Résidence des Érables**
992, boul Saint-Joseph, Roberval, QC G8H 2L9
Tél: 418-275-4376

Nombre de lits: 23 lits
Note: déficience intellectuelle

Saint-Benoît-Labre: Pavillon Baillargeon inc.
357, rte 271, Saint-Benoît-Labre, QC G0M 1P0
Tél: 418-228-9141; *Téléc:* 418-226-3772
Nombre de lits: 35 places
Richard Busque, Directeur général

Saint-Eustache: Domaine des Trois Pignons
112, 25e av, Saint-Eustache, QC J7P 2V2
Tél: 450-473-5961; *Téléc:* 450-491-1847
Nombre de lits: 92 lits
Suzanne Clavet, Directrice générale

Saint-Fabien: Pavillon St-Fabien
CP 520, 142, 1re rue, Saint-Fabien, QC G0L 2Z0
Tél: 418-869-2709
Nombre de lits: 27 lits
Sylvain Paquet, Directeur général

Saint-Pierre-de-l'Ile-d'O: Centre d'hébergement Alphonse-Bonenfant
Affiliée à: Agence de la santé et des services sociaux de la Capitale-Nationale
1199, ch Royal, Saint-Pierre-de-l'Ile-d'O, QC G0A 4E0
Tél: 418-828-9114; *Téléc:* 418-828-1127
Nombre de lits: 50 lits
Aline Prémont, Directeur général

Saint-Zacharie: Résidence l'Eden
668, 12e av, Saint-Zacharie, QC G0M 2C0
Tél: 418-593-5200; *Téléc:* 418-593-5200
Year Founded: 1964
Nombre de lits: 30 lits
Linda L. Lacroix

Sainte-Geneviève: Château sur le Lac
Affiliée à: Agence de la santé et des services sociaux de Montréal
16289, boul Gouin ouest, Sainte-Geneviève, QC H9H 1E2
Tél: 514-620-9794; *Téléc:* 514-696-3196
Nombre de lits: 50 lits
B.S. Kachra, Directeur général

Verdun: Manoir des Floralies Verdun
Affiliée à: Agence de la santé et des services sociaux de Montréal
1050, rue Gordon, Verdun, QC H4G 2S2
Tél: 514-766-2858; *Téléc:* 514-766-8701
Nombre de lits: 103 lits
Louise Fontaine, Directrice générale

Victoriaville: Pavillon Familial des Bois-Francs inc.
21, rue Marchand, Victoriaville, QC G6P 4J5
Tél: 819-752-9920

Centres d'hébergement et des soins de longue durée (CHSLD)

Acton Vale: Centre d'hébergement de la MRC-d'Acton
CSSS Richelieu-Yamaska
Affiliée à: Agence de la santé et des services sociaux de la Montérégie
1268, rue Ricard, Acton Vale, QC J0H 1A0
Tél: 450-546-3234; *Téléc:* 450-546-4811
info@lesommetavotreportee.qc.ca
www.lesommetavotreportee.qc.ca;
www.santemonteregie.qc.ca/richelieu-yamaska
Nombre de lits: 81 lits
Daniel Castonguay, Directeur général, CSSS Richelieu-Yamaska
Réjeanne Boudreau, Directrice du Programme hébergement-milieu de vie, CSSS Richelieu-Yamaska

Akwesasne: Conseil Mohawk d'Akwesasne
CP 40, Akwesasne, QC H0M 1A0
Tél: 613-575-2507
Nombre de lits: 30 lits
Bonnie Cole, Directrice générale

Anjou: CHSLD Le Royer
Affiliée à: Agence de la santé et des services sociaux de Montréal
7351, rue Jean-Desprez, Anjou, QC H1K 5A6
Tél: 514-493-9397; *Téléc:* 514-493-9103
Nombre de lits: 96 lits
Guy Joly, Directeur général

Baie-Saint-Paul: Centre d'accueil Pierre-Dupré
CP 1779, 10, rue Boivin, Baie-Saint-Paul, QC G3Z 1B0
Tél: 418-435-5562; *Téléc:* 418-435-4049

Nombre de lits: 60 lits
Robert Vallières, Directeur général

Beaconsfield: Manoir Beaconsfield
Affiliée à: Agence de la santé et des services sociaux de Montréal
34, av Woodland, Beaconsfield, QC H9W 4V9
Tél: 514-694-2000; *Téléc:* 514-694-5000
Nombre de lits: 23 lits
Annie Maffre, Directrice générale

Beauharnois: Centre d'accueil le Vaisseau d'Or
55, rue Saint-André, Beauharnois, QC J6N 3G7
Tél: 450-429-6403; *Téléc:* 450-429-6602
Nombre de lits: 88 lits
Lise Bélisle-Bélanger, Directrice générale

Beauport: Centre d'hébergement du Fargy
Affiliée à: Agence de la santé et des services sociaux de la Capitale-Nationale
700, boul des Chutes, Beauport, QC G1E 2B7
Tél: 418-663-9934
Nombre de lits: 60 lits, 4 lits d'hébergement temporaires

Beauport: Centre d'hébergement Saint-Augustin.
Affiliée à: Agence de la santé et des services sociaux de la Capitale-Nationale
2135, rue Terrasse-Cadieux, Beauport, QC G1C 1Z2
Tél: 418-667-3910
www.cha.quebec.qc.ca
Nombre de lits: 34 lits de gériatrie

Beauport: Centre de santé Orléans (Yvonne Sylvain)
3365, rue Guimont, Beauport, QC G1E 2H1
Tél: 418-663-8171; *Téléc:* 418-663-0602
Nombre de lits: 116 lits
Lucie Lacroix, Directrice général

Beloeil: Centre d'hébergement Champlain-Beloeil
Affiliée à: Agence de la santé et des services sociaux de la Montérégie
221, rue Brunelle, Beloeil, QC J3G 2M9
Tél: 514-467-3356
Nombre de lits: 53 lits

Beloeil: Centre d'hébergement Marguerite-Adam
CSSS Richelieu-Yamaska
Affiliée à: Agence de la santé et des services sociaux de la Montérégie
425, rue Hubert, Beloeil, QC J3G 2T1
Tél: 450-467-1631; *Téléc:* 450-467-4210
info@lesommetavotreportee.qc.ca
www.lesommetavotreportee.qc.ca;
www.santemonteregie.qc.ca/richelieu-yamaska
Nombre de lits: 70 lits
Daniel Castonguay, Directeur général, CSSS Richelieu-Yamaska
Réjeanne Boudreau, Directrice du Programme hébergement-milieu de vie, CSSS Richelieu-Yamaska

Berthierville: CHSLD Le Château inc.
1231, rue Dr Olivier-M.-Gendron, Berthierville, QC J0K 1A0
Tél: 450-836-6241; *Téléc:* 450-836-4013
Nombre de lits: 64 lits
Guy Ducharme, Directeur général

Boucherville: Centre d'hébergement Jeanne-Crevier
CSSS Pierre-Boucher
151, rue De Muy, Boucherville, QC J4B 4W7
Tél: 450-641-0595; *Téléc:* 450-641-3082
www.santemonteregie.qc.ca/cssspierreboucher
Nombre de lits: 93 lits
Caroline Barbir, Directrice générale, CSSS Pierre-Boucher

Bromptonville: Centre Brompton
Affiliée à: Agence de la santé et des services sociaux de l'Estrie
15, rue de la Croix sud, Bromptonville, QC J0B 1H0
Tél: 819-846-2708; *Téléc:* 819-846-4328

Brossard: Centre d'accueil Marcelle Ferron inc.
Affiliée à: Agence de la santé et des services sociaux de la Montérégie
8600, boul Marie Victorin, Brossard, QC J4X 1A1
Tél: 450-923-1430; *Téléc:* 450-923-1805
camf@dsuper.net
Nombre de lits: 175 lits
Zefferino Guiducci, Directeur général

Brossard: CHSLD Vigi Brossard
Affiliée à: Vigi Santé Ltée
5955, boul Grande-Allée, Brossard, QC J4Z 3G4
Tél: 450-656-8500; *Téléc:* 450-656-8586
www.vigisante.com
Nombre de lits: 66 lits
Note: Agence/région administrative: Agence de la santé et des services sociaux de Montérégie.

Cap-aux-Meules: Centre hospitalier de l'Archipel CHSLD Villa Plaisance
Affiliée à: Agence de la santé et des services sociaux de la Gaspésie-Iles-de-la-Madeleine
596, ch Principal, Cap-aux-Meules, QC G4T 1G1
Tél: 418-986-3658
www.agencesssgim.ca; www.csssdesiles.qc.ca
Nombre de lits: 50 lits
Note: CSSS des Iles.
Germain Chevarie, Directeur général

Chambly: Manoir Soleil inc.
125, rue Daigneault, Chambly, QC J3L 1G7
Tél: 450-658-4441; *Téléc:* 450-658-6521
Nombre de lits: 68 lits
Nancy Gaudet, Directrice générale

Chandler: Centre de santé et de services sociaux du Rocher-Percé
CLSC-CHSLD Pabok
Affiliée à: Agence de la santé et des services sociaux de la Gaspésie-Iles-de-la-Madeleine
Également connu sous le nom de: CLSC de Chandler
CP 1090, 633, av Daignault, Chandler, QC G0C 1K0
Tél: 418-689-2572; *Téléc:* 418-689-4707
www.agencesssgim.ca
Nombre de lits: 62 lits
Note: A fusionné avec le Centre hospitalier de Chandler en 2004.
Chantal Duguay, Directrice générale

Chandler: CLSC-CHSLD Pabok
Point de service Le CHSLD - Villa Pabos
Affiliée à: Agence de la santé et des services sociaux de la Gaspésie-Iles-de-la-Madeleine
Également connu sous le nom de: CLSC de Chandler
75, rue des Cèdres, Chandler, QC G0C 1K0
Tél: 418-689-6621; *Téléc:* 418-689-4860
www.agencesssgim.ca
Note: CSSS du Rocher-Percé.

Charlesbourg: Centre d'hébergement de Charlesbourg
Affiliée à: Agence de la santé et des services sociaux de la Capitale-Nationale
7150, boul Cloutier, Charlesbourg, QC G1H 5V5
Tél: 418-628-0456; *Téléc:* 418-622-8676
Nombre de lits: 64 lits
Note: Hébergement permanent, centre de jour

Charlesbourg: Centre d'hébergement St-Jean-Eudes
6000, 3e av ouest, Charlesbourg, QC G1H 7J5
Tél: 418-627-1124; *Téléc:* 418-627-4995
Nombre de lits: 141 lits
Clémence Boucher, Directrice générale

Charlesbourg: Centre d'hébergement St-Joseph inc.
Affiliée à: Agence de la santé et des services sociaux de la Capitale-Nationale
1430, av Notre-Dame, Charlesbourg, QC G2N 1S1
Tél: 418-849-1891; *Téléc:* 418-849-1892
Nombre de lits: 30 lits
Yvonnette Côté-Létourneau, Directrice générale

Châteauguay: Centre d'hébergement Champlain Châteauguay
CSSS Jardins-Roussillon
Affiliée à: Agence de la santé et des services sociaux de la Montérégie
210, rue Salaberry sud, Châteauguay, QC J6K 3M9
Tél: 450-632-4451; *Téléc:* 450-699-1696
www.santemonteregie.qc.ca/jardins-roussillon
Nombre de lits: 96 lits
Paul Moreau, Directeur général, CSSS Jardins-Roussillon

Chicoutimi: Centre d'hébergement Mgr-Victor-Tremblay
Affiliée à: Agence de la santé et des services sociaux du Saguenay-Lac-St-Jean
1236, rue D'Angoulême, Chicoutimi, QC G7H 6P9
Tél: 418-698-3911

Nombre de lits: 50 lits

Chicoutimi: CHSLD de Chicoutimi
904, rue Jacques-Cartier est, Chicoutimi, QC G7H 2A9
Tél: 418-698-3900; *Téléc:* 418-543-6285
Nombre de lits: 104 lits
Benoît Duplessis, Directeur général

Chicoutimi: Foyer St-François inc.
912, rue Jacques-Cartier est, Chicoutimi, QC G7H 2A9
Tél: 418-549-3727; *Téléc:* 418-543-2038
sonia.bergeron@ssss.gouv.qc.ca
Nombre de lits: 64 lits
Sonia Bergeron, Directrice générale

Clermont: Foyer de Clermont inc.
Affiliée à: Agence de la santé et des services sociaux de la Capitale-Nationale
CP 520, 6, rue du Foyer, Clermont, QC G4A 1G8
Tél: 418-439-4684
Nombre de lits: 42 lits

Cleveland: Foyer Wales
506, rte 243, Cleveland, QC J0B 2H0
Tél: 819-826-3266; *Téléc:* 819-826-2549
Nombre de lits: 222 lits
Simms Stuart, Directeur général

Contrecoeur: CLSC-CHSLD de Contrecoeur
CSSS Pierre-Boucher
Affiliée à: Agence de la santé et des services sociaux de la Montérégie
4700, rte Marie-Victorin, Contrecoeur, QC J0L 1C0
Tél: 450-587-5025; *Téléc:* 450-587-8411
www.santemonteregie.qc.ca/cssspierreboucher
Nombre de lits: 52 lits
Note: Centre d'hébergement, et le point de service CLSC des Seigneuries de Contrecoeur (450-652-2917).
Caroline Barbir, Directrice générale, CSSS Pierre-Boucher

Côte Saint-Luc: Centre d'hébergement Waldorf inc.
7400, ch de la Côte-Saint-Luc, Côte Saint-Luc, QC H4W 3J4
Tél: 514-369-1000; *Téléc:* 514-489-3968
lewaldorf@reveraliving.com
www.reveraliving.com
Nombre de lits: 20 lits
Aileen Rabinovitch, Directrice générale

Côte Saint-Luc: Centre hospitalier gériatrique Maimonides
Affiliée à: Agence de la santé et des services sociaux de Montréal
5795, av Caldwell, Côte Saint-Luc, QC H4W 1W3
Tél: 514-483-2121
Nombre de lits: 387 lits
Barbra Gold, Directrice générale

Côte Saint-Luc: Les résidences montréalaises de l'église unie pour personnes agées
5790, av Parkhaven, Côte Saint-Luc, QC H4W 1Y1
Tél: 514-482-0590; *Téléc:* 514-482-2643
Nombre de lits: 216 beds
Annette Rudy, Dir. gen.

Coteau-du-Lac: Pavillon Laura Ferguson
CP 909, 60, ch du Fleuve, Coteau-du-Lac, QC J0P 1B0
Tél: 514-267-3379
Nombre de lits: 15 places
Paul-Henri Boutin, Directeur général

Cowansville: Centre de santé et de services sociaux La Pommeraie
950, rue Principale, Cowansville, QC J2K 1K3
Tél: 450-266-5522
Nombre de lits: 251 lits
Diane Daigle, Directrice générale

Cowansville: Résidence Manoir Beaumont (1988) Inc.
430, rue Beaumont, Cowansville, QC J2K 1W1
Tél: 514-263-6235; *Téléc:* 514-263-8598
Nombre de lits: 36 lits
Note: Hébergement et soins de longue durée
Monique Fréchette, Directrice générale

Deux-Montagnes: CHSLD Vigi Deux-Montagnes inc.
Affiliée à: Vigi Santé Ltée
580, 20e av, Deux-Montagnes, QC J7R 7E9
Tél: 450-473-5111; *Téléc:* 450-491-4686
www.vigisante.com
Nombre de lits: 76 lits
Note: Agence/région administrative: Agence de la santé et des services sociaux des Laurentides.
Robert Fournier, Directeur général

Disraéli: Résidence René-Lavoie
Affiliée à: Agence de la santé et des services sociaux de Chaudière-Appalaches
CP 698, 260, av Champlain, Disraéli, QC G0N 1E0
Tél: 418-449-2020; *Téléc:* 418-449-4006
csssrt@ssss.gouv.qc.ca
www.centresantethetford.ca/sante-quebec/
Nombre de lits: 47 lits

Dolbeau: Pavillon Maison du Bel Age
2020, rue Provencher, Dolbeau, QC G8L 3E6
Tél: 418-276-1866; *Téléc:* 418-276-1866
Nombre de lits: 53 places
Note: Maison d'hébergement pour personnes agées autonomes
Gisèle Laroche, Directrice générale

Dollard-des-Ormeaux: Vigi Santé Ltée
197, rue Thornhill, Dollard-des-Ormeaux, QC H9B 3H8
Tél: 514-684-0930; *Téléc:* 514-684-0179
www.vigisante.com
Nombre de lits: 1,500 lits
Note: Propriétaire et administrateur de 15 centres d'hébergement, présente dans plusieurs régions du Québec. Le siège du CHSLD Vigi Dollard-des-Ormeaux, avec 160 lits.
Vincenzo Simonetta, Directeur général

Dorval: Centre d'hébergement Chartwell inc.
2400, ch Herron, Dorval, QC H9S 5W3
Tél: 514-631-7288; *Téléc:* 514-631-9208
Nombre de lits: 325 lits
Claudette Cloutier, Directrice générale

Drummondville: Centre d'hébergement Frederick-George-Heriot
CSSS Drummond
75, rue St-Georges, Drummondville, QC J2C 4G6
Tél: 819-477-0544
csssdrummond@ssss.gouv.qc.ca
www.csssdrummond.qc.ca
Nombre de lits: 354 lits
Nagui Habashi, Directeur général, CSSS Drummond
Lyse Garant, Directrice du Programme, Personnes en perte d'autonomie

Farnham: Foyers Farnham inc.
Affiliée à: Agence de la santé et des services sociaux de la Montérégie
800, rue Saint-Paul nord, Farnham, QC J2N 2K6
Tél: 450-293-3168; *Téléc:* 450-293-7878
Nombre de lits: 61 lits

Gaspé: CHSLD Mgr Ross
Affiliée à: Agence de la santé et des services sociaux de la Gaspésie-Iles-de-la-Madeleine
150, rue Mgr Ross, Gaspé, QC G4X 2S7
Tél: 418-368-3301; *Téléc:* 418-368-6730
www.cssscotedegaspe.ca
Nombre de lits: 129 lits
Note: CSSS Côte-de-Gaspé.

Gatineau: CHSLD de Hull - Centre d'hébergement Foyer du Bonheur
CSSS de Gatineau
Affiliée à: Agence de la santé et de services sociaux de l'Outaouais
125, boul Lionel-Émond, Gatineau, QC J8Y 5S8
Tél: 819-966-6410; *Téléc:* 819-966-6414
www.csssgatineau.qc.ca; www.santeoutaouais.qc.ca
Nombre de lits: 263 lits
Nancy Bergeron, Directrice adjointe en hébergement, Soutien à l'autonomie
819-966-6440

Gatineau: CHSLD de Hull - Centre d'hébergement La Pietà
CSSS de Gatineau
Affiliée à: Agence de la santé et de services sociaux de l'Outaouais
273, rue Laurier, Gatineau, QC J8X 3W8
Tél: 819-966-6420; *Téléc:* 819-966-6421
www.csssgatineau.qc.ca; www.santeoutaouais.qc.ca
Nombre de lits: 158 lits
Nancy Bergeron, Directrice adjointe en hébergement, Soutien à l'autonomie
819-966-6440

Gatineau: CLSC-CHSLD de Gatineau - Centre d'hébergement Maison Bon Séjour
CSSS de Gatineau
Affiliée à: Agence de la santé et de services sociaux de l'Outaouais
134, rue Jean-René Monette, Gatineau, QC J8P 7C3
Tél: 819-966-6450; *Téléc:* 819-966-6453
www.csssgatineau.qc.ca
Nombre de lits: 100 lits
Nancy Bergeron, Directrice adjointe en hébergement, Soutien à l'autonomie
819-966-6440

Gracefield: CHSLD Gracefield
Affiliée à: Agence de la santé et de services sociaux de l'Outaouais
CP 317, 1, rue du Foyer, Gracefield, QC J0X 1W0
Tél: 819-463-2100; *Téléc:* 819-463-4721
Nombre de lits: 31 lits
Bruno Larivière, Coordonateur, Hébergement

Granby: Centre Villa Bonheur
Affiliée à: Agence de la santé et des services sociaux de la Montérégie
71, rue Court, Granby, QC J2G 4Y7
Tél: 450-776-5222; *Téléc:* 450-372-7617
Nombre de lits: 108 lits

Grand-Mère: CHSLD du Centre Mauricie
Affiliée à: Agence de la santé et des services sociaux de la Mauricie et du Centre-du-Québec
1650, 6e av, Grand-Mère, QC G9T 2K4
Tél: 819-533-2500; *Téléc:* 819-538-7640
Nombre de lits: 406 lits
Guy D'Anjou, Directeur général

Huntingdon: Centre hospitalier du Comté de Huntingdon
CP 6000, 198, rue Châteaugauy, Huntingdon, QC J0S 1H0
Tél: 450-264-6111; *Téléc:* 450-264-4923
Nombre de lits: 60 lits
Guy Deschenes, Directeur général

Ile-Bizard: Centre d'accueil Denis-Benjamin Viger
Affiliée à: Agence de la santé et des services sociaux de Montréal
3292, rue Cherrier, Ile-Bizard, QC H9C 1E4
Tél: 514-620-6310; *Téléc:* 514-620-6553
Nombre de lits: 125 lits

Ile-Perrot: Centre d'accueil Laurent-Bergevin
Affiliée à: Agence de la santé et des services sociaux de la Montérégie
200, boul Perrot, Ile-Perrot, QC J7V 7M7
Tél: 514-453-5860; *Téléc:* 514-453-8939
Nombre de lits: 82 lits

Irlande: Pavillon Morisset Huppé Inc.
CP 2060, 290, rte 165, Irlande, QC G6H 2N7
Tél: 418-428-3568; *Téléc:* 418-428-3021
lucy.morisset.info@globetrotter.net
Nombre de lits: 14 places
Note: Pavillon d'hébergement pour adultes handicapés physiques intellectuels lourds
Lucie Morisset-Huppé, Directrice générale

Jonquière: Centre d'hébergement Georges-Hébert
Affiliée à: Agence de la santé et des services sociaux du Saguenay-Lac-St-Jean
2841, rue Faraday, Jonquière, QC G7S 5C8
Tél: 418-695-7727; *Téléc:* 418-695-7737
wpp01.msss.gouv.gc.ca
Nombre de lits: 75 lits

Jonquière: Centre d'hébergement Sainte-Marie
2184, rue Perrier, Jonquière, QC G7X 9C9
Tél: 418-695-7800; *Téléc:* 418-695-7738
Nombre de lits: 66 lits
Note: Hébergement permanent et temporaire

Jonquière: Pavillon Arvida
Affiliée à: Agence de la santé et des services sociaux du Saguenay-Lac-St-Jean
CP 1200, 1841, rue Deschênes, Jonquière, QC G7S 4K6
Tél: 418-548-8231; *Téléc:* 418-548-6875
Nombre de lits: 60 lits

La Baie: Foyer de Bagotville
Affiliée à: Agence de la santé et des services sociaux du Saguenay-Lac-St-Jean
562, rue Victoria, La Baie, QC G7B 3M6
Tél: 418-544-2853; *Téléc:* 418-544-6012
Nombre de lits: 33 lits

La Baie: **Foyer St-Joseph de La Baie inc.**
Affiliée à: Agence de la santé et des services sociaux du Saguenay-Lac-St-Jean
1893, rue Alexis-Simard, La Baie, QC G7B 2K9
Tél: 418-544-2865; *Téléc:* 418-544-8936
Nombre de lits: 48 lits

La Guadeloupe: **Pavillon Notre-Dame**
CP 490, 437, 15e rue ouest, La Guadeloupe, QC G0M 1G0
Tél: 418-459-3476; *Téléc:* 418-459-6428
Nombre de lits: 50 lits
Richard Busque, Directeur général

LaSalle: **Centre d'hébergement de LaSalle**
Affiliée à: Agence de la santé et des services sociaux de Montréal
8686, rue Centrale, LaSalle, QC H8P 3N4
Tél: 514-364-6700
www.santemontreal.qc.ca
Nombre de lits: 202 lits
Léonard Vincent, Directeur général

LaSalle: **Hôpital Ste-Thérèse inc.**
Affiliée à: Agence de la santé et des services sociaux de Montréal
9307, boul LaSalle, LaSalle, QC H8R 2M7
Tél: 514-366-3556; *Téléc:* 514-367-3718
Nombre de lits: 47 lits

Labelle: **CHSLD de Labelle**
CSSS des Sommets
CP 38, 50, rue de l'Église, Labelle, QC J0T 1H0
Tél: 819-686-2372; *Téléc:* 819-686-1950
www.csss-sommets
Nombre de lits: 46 lits
Jacques Morin, Président, Conseil d'administration, CSSS des Sommets

Lac-Bouchette: **Centre d'hébergement de Lac-Bouchette inc.**
CSSS Domaine-du-Roy
Édifice Foyer de Lac-Bouchette, CP 39, 99, rte de l'Ermitage, Lac-Bouchette, QC G0W 1V0
Tél: 418-348-6313; *Téléc:* 418-348-6342
Nombre de lits: 14 lits
Jacques Dubois, Directeur général, CSSS Domaine-du-Roy

Lac-Mégantic: **CSSS du Granit - CHSLD/Centre de jour Lac-Mégantic**
Affiliée à: Agence de la santé et des services sociaux de l'Estrie
3675, rue du Foyer, Lac-Mégantic, QC G6B 2K2
Tél: 819-583-0330; *Téléc:* 819-583-0900
Nombre de lits: 46 lits
Pierre Latulippe, Directeur général, CSSS du Granit

Lac-au-Saumon: **Centre d'hébergement Marie-Anne Ouellet**
CSSS de La Matapédia
6, rue Turbide, Lac-au-Saumon, QC G0J 1M0
Tél: 418-778-5816; *Téléc:* 418-778-3391
www.csssmatapedia.qc.ca
Nombre de lits: 96 lits
Alain Paquet, Directeur général, CSSS de La Matapédia

Lachenaie: **Centre hospitalier Pierre-Le Gardeur**
911, montée des Pionniers, Lachenaie, QC J6V 2H2
Tél: 450-654-7525
communications-chlg@chpierrelegardeur.ca
www.chpierrelegardeur.ca/
Nombre de lits: 20 lits
Gisèle Boyer, Directrice générale

Lachine: **Centre d'hébergement de Lachine**
Affiliée à: Agence de la santé et des services sociaux de Montréal
650, place d'Accueil, Lachine, QC H8S 3Z5
Tél: 514-634-7161
www.santemontreal.qc.ca
Nombre de lits: 217 lits

Lachine: **CHSLD Nazaire-Piché**
Affiliée à: Agence de la santé et des services sociaux de Montréal
150, 15e av, Lachine, QC H8S 3L9
Tél: 514-637-1780
www.santemontreal.qc.ca
Nombre de lits: 100 lits
Marie-Hélène Girard, Directrice générale

Lambton: **CSSS du Granit - CLSC/CHSLD de Lambton**
Également connu sous le nom de: La Maison Paternelle
310-A, rue Principale, Lambton, QC G0M 1H0
Tél: 418-486-7441; *Téléc:* 418-486-2172
www.csssgrant.qc.ca
Nombre de lits: 32 lits
Note: Le point de service Lambton regroupe un centre local de services communautaire (CLSC), un centre d'hébergement, et un centre de jour.
Pierre Latulippe, Directeur général, CSSS du Granit

Laval: **Centre d'hébergement de la Rive Prodimax inc.**
Affiliée à: Agence de la santé et de services sociaux de Laval
4605, boul Sainte-Rose, Laval, QC H7R 5S9
Tél: 450-627-5599; *Téléc:* 450-627-5107
www.sssslaval.gouv.qc.ca
Nombre de lits: 79 lits
Note: Centre privé non-conventionné.
Jacques Le Guern, Directeur général

Laval: **Centre d'hébergement de la Villa-des-Tilleuls inc.**
Affiliée à: Agence de la santé et de services sociaux de Laval
5590, boul des Laurentides, Laval, QC H7K 2K2
Tél: 450-628-0322; *Téléc:* 450-622-3674
msss.gouv.qc.ca; www,sssslaval.gouv.qc.ca
Nombre de lits: 68 lits
Note: Centre privé non-conventioné.
Réginald Ratle, Directeur général

Laval: **Centre d'hébergement l'Eden de Laval inc**
Affiliée à: Agence de la santé et de services sociaux de Laval
8528, boul Lévesque est, Laval, QC H7A 1W6
Tél: 450-665-6283
msss.qc.ca; www.sssslaval.gouv.qc.ca
Nombre de lits: 43 lits
Note: Centre privé non-conventioné.
Alain Fafard, Directeur général

Laval: **Centre d'hébergement St-François inc.**
4105, Montée Masson, Laval, QC H7B 1B6
Tél: 450-666-6541; *Téléc:* 450-666-1601
Nombre de lits: 53 lits
Marie-Christine Moulin, Directrice générale

Laval: **CHSLD Saint-Jude inc.**
Affiliée à: Agence de la santé et des services sociaux de Laval
4410, boul St-Martin ouest, Laval, QC H7T 1C3
Tél: 450-687-7714; *Téléc:* 450-682-0330
Nombre de lits: 204 lits
Daniel Leclair, Directeur général

Laval: **Manoir St-Patrice inc.**
3615, boul Perron, Laval, QC H7V 1P4
Tél: 450-681-1621; *Téléc:* 450-681-6120
Nombre de lits: 132 lits
Ann Carey, Directrice générale

Laval: **La Résidence du Bonheur**
Affiliée à: Agence de la santé et de services sociaux de Laval
5855, rue Boulard, Laval, QC H7B 1A3
Tél: 450-666-1567; *Téléc:* 450-666-6387
info@residencedubonheur.com
www.residencedubonheur.com; www.sssslaval.gouv.qc.ca
Nombre de lits: 50 lits
Note: Centre privé non-conventionné.
John Pakis, Directeur général
john.pakis@residencedubonheur.com

Laval: **Résidence Riviera inc.**
2999, boul Notre-Dame, Laval, QC H7V 4C4
Tél: 450-682-0111; *Téléc:* 450-682-0154
www.chsldresidenceriviera.com
Nombre de lits: 128 lits
Jean Nadon, Directeur général
Michel Samson, Directeur, Services techniques

Lévis: **Centre d'accueil Saint-Joseph de Lévis inc**
Affiliée à: Agence de la santé et des services sociaux de Chaudière-Appalaches
107, rue Saint-Louis, Lévis, QC G6V 6R9
Tél: 418-833-3414; *Téléc:* 418-833-3417

Lévis: **Centre d'accueil Saint-Joseph de Lévis inc.**
107, rue Saint-Louis, Lévis, QC G6V 4G9
Tél: 418-833-3414; *Téléc:* 418-833-3417
www.casaintjosephdelevis.qc.ca
Nombre de lits: 158 lits
Gervais Morissette, Directeur général

Lévis: **CLSC-CHSLD de la MRC Desjardins**
15, rue de l'Arsenal, Lévis, QC G6V 4P6
Tél: 418-835-3400
Nombre de lits: 95 lits
Renée Lachance-Auger, Directrice générale

Lévis: **Pavillon Bellevue inc.**
Affiliée à: Agence de la santé et des services sociaux de Chaudière-Appalaches
99, rue Monseigneur-Bourget, Lévis, QC G6V 9V2
Tél: 418-833-3490; *Téléc:* 418-833-6874
Nombre de lits: 50 lits
Claude Talbot, Directeur général

Lévis: **Villa Mon Domaine inc.**
Affiliée à: Agence de la santé et des services sociaux de Chaudière-Appalaches
109, av Mont-Marie, Lévis, QC G6V 8B4
Tél: 418-837-6408; *Téléc:* 418-837-2626
Nombre de lits: 57 lits
Jean-Noël Begin, Directeur général

Longueuil: **Centre d'accueil St-Laurent inc.**
CSSS Pierre-Boucher
480, rue LeMoyne ouest, Longueuil, QC J4H 1X1
Tél: 450-670-5480; *Téléc:* 450-670-9874
www.santemonteregie.qc.ca/cssspierreboucher
Nombre de lits: 32 lits
Note: CHSLD privé non conventionné
Caroline Barbir, Directrice générale, CSSS Pierre-Boucher

Longueuil: **CHSLD de Mgr-Coderre**
CSSS Pierre-Boucher
Affiliée à: Agence de la santé et des services sociaux de la Montérégie
2761, rue Beauvais, Longueuil, QC J4M 2A4
Tél: 450-448-3607; *Téléc:* 450-448-4322
www.santemonteregie.qc.ca/cssspierreboucher
Nombre de lits: 154 lits
Caroline Barbir, Directrice générale, CSSS Pierre-Boucher

Longueuil: **CHSLD du Chevalier-De Lévis**
CSSS Pierre-Boucher
Ancien nom: CHSLD de Longueuil
40, rue Lévis, Longueuil, QC J4H 1S5
Tél: 450-670-5391; *Téléc:* 450-670-7292
www.santemonteregie.qc.ca/cssspierreboucher
Nombre de lits: 142 lits
Caroline Barbir, Directrice générale, CSSS Pierre-Boucher

Longueuil: **CHSLD René-Lévesque**
CSSS Pierre-Boucher
1901, rue Claude, Longueuil, QC J4G 1Y5
Tél: 450-651-4609; *Téléc:* 450-670-7731
www.santemonteregie.qc.ca/cssspierreboucher
Nombre de lits: 224 lits
Caroline Barbir, Directrice générale, CSSS Pierre-Boucher

Loretteville: **Foyer de Loretteville inc.**
Affiliée à: Agence de la santé et des services sociaux de la Capitale-Nationale
165, rue Lessard, Loretteville, QC G2B 2V9
Tél: 418-842-9191; *Téléc:* 418-842-4472
Nombre de lits: 74 lits

Lyster: **Centre d'hébergement des Quatre-Vents**
CSSS d'Arthabaska-et-de-l'Érable
Affiliée à: Agence de la santé et des services sociaux de la Mauricie et du Centre-du-Québec
Ancien nom: Foyer de Lyster
2180, rue Bécancour, Lyster, QC G0S 1V0
Tél: 819-389-5923; *Téléc:* 819-389-5969
Nombre de lits: 26 lits
Marcel Dubois, Président, Conseil d'administration, CSSS d'Arthabaska-et-de-l

Magog: **Gestion SGH Inc.**
Ancien nom: Résidence Ste-Marguerite Marie
64, rue St-Pierre, Magog, QC J1X 3A2
Tél: 819-843-0202; *Téléc:* 819-843-9518
Nombre de lits: 27 lits
Carine Thuin, Directeur général

Malartic: **Centre d'hébergement Saint-Martin de Malartic**
CSSS de la Vallée-de-l'Or
Affiliée à: Agence de la santé et des services sociaux de l'Abitibi-Témiscamingue
CP 639, 701, rue de la Paix, Malartic, QC J0Y 1Z0
Tél: 819-757-3663; *Téléc:* 819-757-3309
www.sante-abitibi-temiscamingue.gouv.qc.ca; www.csssvo.qc.ca
Nombre de lits: 57 lits
Note: Centre d'hébergement/centre de jour.
Jérôme Lamont, Directeur général, CSSS de la Vallée-de-l'Or
Marie Cloutier, Directrice, Programme personnes en perte d'autonomie

Maria: **Centre d'hébergement de Maria**
CSSS de la Baie-des-Chaleurs
Affiliée à: Agence de la santé et des services sociaux de la Gaspésie-Iles-de-la-Madeleine
Ancien nom: Résidence Saint-Joseph
491, boul Perron, Maria, QC G0C 1Y0
Tél: 418-759-3458; *Téléc:* 418-759-5103
csssbc@csssbc.qc.ca
www.csssbc.qc.ca
Nombre de lits: 91 lits
Bernard Nadeau, Directeur général, CSSS de la Baie-des-Chaleurs

Marieville: **Centre d'hébergement Sainte-Croix**
CSSS Haut-Richelieu-Rouville
Affiliée à: Agence de la santé et des services sociaux de la Montérégie
300, rue Docteur-Poulin, Marieville, QC J3M 1L7
Tél: 450-460-4475; *Téléc:* 450-460-4104
www.santemonteregie.qc.ca/haut-richelieu-rouville
Nombre de lits: 128 lits
Note: Hébergement permanent et temporaire, centre de jour, réadaptation fonctionnelle intensive.
Lucie Tétreault, Directrice, Personnes en perte d'autonomie liée au vieillisemen

Matane: **Centre d'hébergement de Matane**
CSSS de Mataine
Affiliée à: Agence de la santé et des services sociaux du Bas-St-Laurent
150, av Saint-Jérôme, Matane, QC G4W 3A2
Tél: 418-562-4154; *Téléc:* 418-562-9281
www.agencesssbsl.gouv.qc.ca
Nombre de lits: 106 lits
Nicole Morin, Directrice générale, CSSS de Matane

Métabetchouan-Lac-a-la-Cr: **Pavillon de Métabetchouan et point de service sud (CLSC)**
Affiliée à: Agence de la santé et des services sociaux du Saguenay-Lac-St-Jean
1895, rte 169, Métabetchouan-Lac-a-la-Cr, QC G8G 1B4
Tél: 418-349-2861; *Téléc:* 418-349-8774
Nombre de lits: 168 lits

Mirabel: **Centre de santé et de services sociaux Deux-Montagnes et Sud de Mirabel**
Centre d'accueil de St-Benoît
9100, rue Dumouchel, Mirabel, QC J7N 5A1
Tél: 450-258-2481; *Téléc:* 450-258-4980
Nombre de lits: 75 lits
Christiane Arbour, Directrice générale

Mont-Joli: **CHSLD de La Mitis**
CSSS de La Mitis
Affiliée à: Agence de la santé et des services sociaux du Bas-St-Laurent
800, av du Sanatorium, Mont-Joli, QC G5H 3L6
Tél: 418-775-7261; *Téléc:* 418-775-1241
www.centremitissien.net
Nombre de lits: 175 lits
Isabelle Malo, Directrice générale, CSSS de La Mitis
cmssc_dg@centremitissien.net

Mont-Laurier: **CHSLD Sainte-Anne**
CSSS d'Antoine-Labelle
Affiliée à: Agence de la santé et des services sociaux des Laurentides
Ancien nom: CHSLD Sainte-Anne et Côme Cartier
411, rue de la Madone, Mont-Laurier, QC J9L 1S1
Tél: 819-623-5940; *Téléc:* 819-623-7347
www.csssal.org
Nombre de lits: 128 lits
Jean-Pierre Urbaine, Directeur général, CSSS d'Antoine-Labelle
Jean-Pierre St-Louis, Coordonnateur des unités de vie, CHSA

Mont-Royal: **CHSLD Vigi Mont-Royal**
Affiliée à: Vigi Santé Ltée
275, av Brittany, Mont-Royal, QC H3P 3C2
Tél: 514-739-5593; *Téléc:* 514-733-7973
www.vigisante.com
Nombre de lits: 273 lits
Note: Agence/région administrative: Agence de la santé et des services sociaux de Montréal.
Vincent Simonetta, Directeur général

Montréal: **Centre Biermans**
Affiliée à: Agence de la santé et des services sociaux de Montréal
Ancien nom: CHSLD Biermans-Triest
7905, rue Sherbrooke est, Montréal, QC H1L 1A4
Tél: 514-351-9891; *Téléc:* 514-351-1556
Nombre de lits: 197 lits
Note: centre de réadaptation

Montréal: **Centre d'accueil Father Dowd**
Father Dowd Home
Affiliée à: Agence de la santé et des services sociaux de Montréal
6565, ch Hudson, Montréal, QC H3S 2T7
Tél: 514-341-1007; *Téléc:* 514-341-8988
Nombre de lits: 134 lits
Carole McDonough, Directrice générale

Montréal: **Centre d'accueil Heritage Inc.**
5716, ch de la Côte-Saint-Antoine, Montréal, QC H4A 1R9
Tél: 514-484-2645
Nombre de lits: 16 lits
Ron Marolia, Directeur général

Montréal: **Centre d'accueil Louis Riel**
Affiliée à: Agence de la santé et des services sociaux de Montréal
2120, rue Augustin-Cantin, Montréal, QC H3K 3G3
Tél: 514-931-2263; *Téléc:* 514-931-2299
Nombre de lits: 100 lits
Germain Harvey, Directeur général

Montréal: **Centre d'hébergement Armand-Lavergne**
CSSS Jeanne-Mance
Affiliée à: Agence de la santé et des services sociaux de Montréal
3500, rue Chapleau, Montréal, QC H2K 4N3
Tél: 514-527-8921
www.csssjeannemance.ca; www.santemontreal.qc.ca
Nombre de lits: 182 lits
Note: Centre de jour; centre d'hébergement permanent.
Ron Rayside, Président du Conseil d'administration, CSSS Jeanne-Mance
Sylvie Simard, Directrice générale intérimaire, CSSS Jeanne-Mance

Montréal: **Centre d'hébergement de Louvain**
Affiliée à: Agence de la santé et des services sociaux de Montréal
9600, rue St-Denis, Montréal, QC H2M 1P2
Tél: 514-381-7256; *Téléc:* 514-381-6486
Nombre de lits: 155 lits
Richard Jean, Directeur général

Montréal: **Centre d'hébergement de Saint-Michel**
CSSS de Saint-Léonard et Saint-Michel
3130, rue Jarry est, Montréal, QC H1Z 4N8
Tél: 514-722-3000
csss-stleonardstmichel.qc.ca
Nombre de lits: 192 lits
Note: Centre administratif du CSSS, et centre d'hébergement.
Suzanne Hébert, Directrice générale, CSSS de Saint-Léonard et Saint-Michel
Johanne Maître, Directrice de l'hébergement, CSSS de Saint-Léonard et Saint-Michel

Montréal: **Centre d'hébergement des Quatre-Temps**
CSSS de Saint-Léonard et Saint-Michel
Affiliée à: Agence de la santé et des services sociaux de Montréal
Ancien nom: CHSLD les Havres
7400, boul Saint-Michel, Montréal, QC H2A 2Z8
Tél: 514-270-9271; *Téléc:* 514-270-6779
csss-stleonardstmichel.qc.ca
Nombre de lits: 192 lits
Suzanne Hébert, Directrice générale, CSSS de Saint-Léonard et Saint-Michel
Johanne Maître, Directrice de l'hébergement, CSSS de Saint-Léonard et Saint-Michel

Montréal: **Centre d'hébergement Légaré**
Affiliée à: Agence de la santé et des services sociaux de Montréal
1615, av Émile-Journault, Montréal, QC H2M 2G3
Tél: 514-384-5490
www.santemontreal.qc.ca
Nombre de lits: 105 lits
Daniel Corbeil, Directeur général

Montréal: **Centre d'hebergement Marie-Rollet**
Affiliée à: Agence de la santé et des services sociaux de Montréal
5003, rue Saint-Zotique est, Montréal, QC H1T 1N6
Tél: 514-729-5281; *Téléc:* 514-593-5568
Nombre de lits: 110 lits
Note: Hébergement et soins de longue durée
Renée Pettigrew, Directrice

Montréal: **Centre de soins prolongés Grace Dart**
Affiliée à: Agence de la santé et des services sociaux de Montréal
5155, rue Ste-Catherine est, Montréal, QC H1V 2A5
Tél: 514-255-2833; *Téléc:* 514-255-6275
Nombre de lits: 381 lits
Léon Gilbert, Directeur général (intérim)

Montréal: **Centre Le Cardinal inc.**
Affiliée à: Agence de la santé et des services sociaux de Montréal
12900, rue Notre-Dame est, Montréal, QC H1A 1R9
Tél: 514-645-2766; *Téléc:* 514-640-6267
Nombre de lits: 204 lits
Léonard Chevarie, Directeur général

Montréal: **CHSLD Bourget inc.**
Affiliée à: Agence de la santé et des services sociaux de Montréal
11570, rue Notre-Dame est, Montréal, QC H1B 2X4
Tél: 514-645-1673; *Téléc:* 514-645-1673
Nombre de lits: 112 lits
Note: Un établissement privé.
Diane Girard, Directrice générale

Montréal: **CHSLD Centre-Ville-de-Montréal**
CSSS Jeanne-Mance
Affiliée à: Agence de la santé et des services sociaux de Montréal
66, boul René-Lévesque est, Montréal, QC H2X 1N3
Tél: 514-861-9331; *Téléc:* 514-861-8385
Nombre de lits: 196 lits
Ron Rayside, Président du Conseil d'administration, CSSS Jeanne-Mance
Sylvie Simard, Directrice générale intérimaire, CSSS Jeanne-Mance

Montréal: **Les CHSLD de mon quartier**
Affiliée à: Agence de la santé et des services sociaux de Montréal
Ancien nom: gentre-hospitalier -Centre d'accueil Gouin-Rosemon
7445, rue Hochelaga, Montréal, QC H1N 3V2
Tél: 514-251-6000; *Téléc:* 514-251-9826
Nombre de lits: 351 lits
France Mailhot, Directrice générale

Montréal: **CHSLD de St-Andrew, de Father-Dowd et de St-Margaret**
50 av Hillside, Montréal, QC H3Z 1V9
Tél: 514-932-3630; *Téléc:* 514-932-4379
Nombre de lits: 300 lits
Note: Résidence Father Dowd: 134 lits, 6565 ch Hudson; Résidence St-Andres: 70 lits, 3350 boul Cavendish; Résidence St-Margaret: 96 lits, 50 av Hillside.
Carole McDonough, Directeur général

Montréal: **CHSLD du Manoir-de-l'Age-d'Or**
CSSS Jeanne-Mance
3430, rue Jeanne-Mance, Montréal, QC H2X 2J9
Tél: 514-842-1147; *Téléc:* 514-842-1146
www.csssjeannemance.ca
Nombre de lits: 189 lits
Ron Rayside, Président du Conseil d'administration, CSSS Jeanne-Mance
Sylvie Simard, Directrice générale intérimaire, CSSS Jeanne-Mance

***Montréal:* CHSLD Émilie-Gamelin**
CSSS Jeanne-Mance
Affiliée à: Agence de la santé et des services sociaux de Montréal
1440, rue Dufresne, Montréal, QC H2K 3J3
Tél: 514-527-8921; *Téléc:* 514-527-3587
www.csssjeannemance.ca
Nombre de lits: 184 lits
Ron Rayside, Président du Conseil d'administration, CSSS Jeanne-Mance
Sylvie Simard, Directrice générale intérimaire, CSSS Jeanne-Mance

***Montréal:* CHSLD Jean XXIII inc.**
Affiliée à: Agence de la santé et des services sociaux de Montréal
6900, 15e av, Montréal, QC H1X 2V9
Tél: 514-725-2190; *Téléc:* 514-728-5901
Nombre de lits: 24 lits
Marie-Claire Lamontagne, Directrice générale

***Montréal:* CHSLD Jeanne-LeBer**
Affiliée à: Agence de la santé et des services sociaux de Montréal
7445, rue Hochelaga, Montréal, QC H1N 3V2
Tél: 514-251-6000
Nombre de lits: 351 lits

***Montréal:* CHSLD juif de Montréal**
Affiliée à: Agence de la santé et des services sociaux de Montréal
5725, av Victoria, Montréal, QC H3W 3H6
Tél: 514-738-4500; *Téléc:* 514-738-2611
Nombre de lits: 160 beds
Barbara Gold, Dir. gén. (intérim)

***Montréal:* CHSLD les Cèdres**
95, boul Gouin est, Montréal, QC H3L 1A6
Tél: 514-389-1023; *Téléc:* 514-389-0581
cedars@istar.ca
Nombre de lits: 22 lits
Diane Chaunt, Directrice générale

***Montréal:* CHSLD Manoir Fleury inc.**
Affiliée à: Agence de la santé et des services sociaux de Montréal
2145, rue Fleury est, Montréal, QC H2B 1J8
Tél: 514-388-1553; *Téléc:* 514-388-4161
Nombre de lits: 25 lits
Rose Renzo, Directrice générale

***Montréal:* CHSLD Marie-Claret inc.**
Affiliée à: Vigi Santé Ltée
3345, boul Henri-Bourassa est, Montréal, QC H1H 1H6
Tél: 514-322-4380; *Téléc:* 514-326-8811
www.vigisante.com
Nombre de lits: 78 lits
Note: Agence/région administrative: Agence de la santé et des services sociaux de Montréal.
Jean-Guy Laplante, Directeur général

***Montréal:* CHSLD Paul Gouin**
Affiliée à: Agence de la santé et des services sociaux de Montréal
5900, rue St-Vallier, Montréal, QC H2S 2P3
Tél: 514-273-3681; *Téléc:* 514-273-7645
Nombre de lits: 100 lits

***Montréal:* CHSLD Providence Notre-Dame-de-Lourdes**
Affiliée à: Agence de la santé et des services sociaux de Montréal
1870, boul Pie-IX, Montréal, QC H1V 2C6
Tél: 514-527-4595; *Téléc:* 514-527-4475
Nombre de lits: 162 lits
Robert St-Pierre, Directeur général

***Montréal:* Foyer Rousselot**
Affiliée à: Agence de la santé et des services sociaux de Montréal
5655, rue Sherbrooke est, Montréal, QC H1N 1A4
Tél: 514-254-9421; *Téléc:* 514-254-3967
Nombre de lits: 157 lits
Robert Boucher, Directeur général

***Montréal:* Groupe Champlain inc.**
Affiliée à: Groupe Santé Sedna inc.
7150, rue Marie-Victorin, Montréal, QC H1G 2J5
Tél: 514-324-2044; *Téléc:* 514-324-5900
www.groupechamplain.qc.ca
Year Founded: 1966
Nombre de lits: 1443 lits
Note: 15 établissements
André Brunelle, Directeur général

***Montréal:* L'Hôpital Chinois de Montréal (1963)**
Affiliée à: Agence de la santé et des services sociaux de Montréal
189, av Viger est, Montréal, QC H2X 3Y9
Tél: 514-871-0961; *Téléc:* 514-871-0966
Nombre de lits: 128 lits
Anthony Shao, Directeur général

***Montréal:* Institut Canadien-Polonais du Bien-Etre inc.**
Affiliée à: Agence de la santé et des services sociaux de Montréal
5655, rue Bélanger, Montréal, QC H1T 1G2
Tél: 514-259-2551; *Téléc:* 514-259-9948
Nombre de lits: 126 lits
Anna Brychcy, Directrice générale

***Montréal:* Manoir Cartierville**
Affiliée à: Agence de la santé et des services sociaux de Montréal
12235, rue Grenet, Montréal, QC H4J 2N9
Tél: 514-337-7300; *Téléc:* 514-337-4188
manoircartierville@ssss.gouv.qc.ca
Nombre de lits: 285 lits
Eveline Lyrette, Directrice générale

***Montréal:* Petites Soeurs des Pauvres - Ma Maison St-Joseph**
Affiliée à: Agence de la santé et des services sociaux de Montréal
5605, rue Beaubien est, Montréal, QC H1T 1X4
Tél: 514-254-4991; *Téléc:* 514-257-1742
Nombre de lits: 80 lits
Sr. Cécile de L'Enfant-Jésus, Directrice générale

***Montréal:* Résidence Berthiaume-du Tremblay**
Affiliée à: Agence de la santé et des services sociaux de Montréal
1635, boul Gouin est, Montréal, QC H2C 1C2
Tél: 514-381-1841; *Téléc:* 514-381-1090
www.berthiaume-du-tremblay.com
Nombre de lits: 246 lits
Nicole Ouellet, Directrice générale

***Montréal:* La Résidence Fulford**
Affiliée à: Agence de la santé et des services sociaux de Montréal
1221, rue Guy, Montréal, QC H3H 2K8
Tél: 514-935-5933; *Téléc:* 514-933-3773
Nombre de lits: 6 lits
Note: residence for women
Laurie Kirkpatrick, Directrice générale

***Montréal:* Résidence Rive Soleil inc.**
Affiliée à: Agence de la santé et des services sociaux de Montréal
15150, rue Notre-Dame est, Montréal, QC H1A 1W6
Tél: 514-642-5509; *Téléc:* 514-642-8320
Nombre de lits: 50 lits
Christiane Chaussé, Directrice général

***Montréal:* Résidence Sainte-Claire inc.**
Affiliée à: Agence de la santé et des services sociaux de Montréal
8950, rue Sainte-Claire est, Montréal, QC H1L 1Z1
Tél: 514-351-3877; *Téléc:* 514-352-5956
Nombre de lits: 38 lits
Yvan Daniel, Directeur général

***Montréal:* Résidence St-Jacques**
Affiliée à: Agence de la santé et des services sociaux de Montréal
8712, rue St-Hubert, Montréal, QC H2M 1Y5
Tél: 514-389-5800; *Téléc:* 514-389-8399
Year Founded: 1989
Nombre de lits: 25 lits
Paulette Théodore, Directrice générale

***Montréal:* Résidence Yvon-Brunet**
Affiliée à: Agence de la santé et des services sociaux de Montréal
6250, av Newman, Montréal, QC H4E 4K4
Tél: 514-765-8000; *Téléc:* 514-765-8064
Year Founded: 1982
Nombre de lits: 185 lits
Daniel Chartrand, Directeur du programme hébergement
Danielle McCann, Directrice générale
danielle.mccann@ssss.gouv.qc.ca

***Montréal:* Résidences Mance-Décary (CHSLD)**
Affiliée à: Agence de la santé et des services sociaux de Montréal
1800, rue St-Jacques, Montréal, QC H3J 2R5
Tél: 514-935-4681; *Téléc:* 514-935-6189
Nombre de lits: 580 lits
André Paquette, Directeur général

***Montréal-Nord:* CHSLD Gouin inc.**
Affiliée à: Groupe Champlain inc.
4445, boul Henri-Bourassa est, Montréal-Nord, QC H1H 5M4
Tél: 514-324-2044
www.groupechamplain.qc.ca
Nombre de lits: 93 lits
Note: Agence/région administrative: Agence de la santé et des services sociaux de Montréal.
André Brunelle, Directeur général

***Montréal-Nord:* Résidence Angelica inc.**
Affiliée à: Agence de la santé et des services sociaux de Montréal
3435, boul Gouin est, Montréal-Nord, QC H1H 1B1
Tél: 514-324-6110; *Téléc:* 514-324-9332
Nombre de lits: 400 lits
Sr. Anne-Marie Marolo, Directrice générale

***Montréal-Nord:* Villa Belle Rive inc.**
Affiliée à: Agence de la santé et des services sociaux de Montréal
5320, boul Gouin est, Montréal-Nord, QC H1G 1B4
Tél: 514-321-1367; *Téléc:* 514-322-4211
Nombre de lits: 27 lits
Louis-René Lanctôt, Directeur général

***New Carlisle:* Centre d'hébergement de New Carlisle**
CSSS de la Baie-des-Chaleurs
Affiliée à: Agence de la santé et des services sociaux de la Gaspésie-Iles-de-la-Madeleine
108, rue Principale, New Carlisle, QC G0C 1Z0
Tél: 418-752-3386; *Téléc:* 418-752-6483
csssbc@csssbc.qc.ca
www.csssbc.qc.ca
Nombre de lits: 75 lits
Bernard Nadeau, Directeur général, CSSS de la Baie-des-Chaleurs

***Normandin:* CLSC-CHSLD de Normandin**
CSSS Maria Chapdelaine
Affiliée à: Agence de la santé et des services sociaux du Saguenay-Lac-St-Jean
1205, rue St-Cyrille, Normandin, QC G8M 4K1
Tél: 418-274-1234; *Téléc:* 418-274-6970
www.csssmariachapdelaine.com
Nombre de lits: 35 lits de soins de longue durée
Note: Centre d'hébergement; point de service CLSC; centre de jour.
Normand Brassard, Directeur général, CSSS Maria Chapdelaine

***North Hatley:* Connaught Home**
77 Main St., North Hatley, QC J0B 2C0
Tél: 819-842-2164; *Téléc:* 819-842-2667
massawippi@videotron.ca
Nombre de lits: 41 lits
Richard F. Tracy, Executive Director

***North Hatley:* La Maison Blanche de North Hatley inc.**
CP 298, 977, rue Massawippi, North Hatley, QC J0B 2C0
Tél: 819-842-2478; *Téléc:* 819-842-2470
Nombre de lits: 60 lits
Serge Croteau, Directeur général

***Notre-Dame-du-Bon-Conseil:* CLSC-CHSLD L'Accueil Bon-Conseil**
CSSS Drummond
Affiliée à: Agence de la santé et des services sociaux de la Mauricie et du Centre-du-Québec
91, rue Saint-Thomas, Notre-Dame-du-Bon-Conseil, QC J0C 1A0
Tél: 819-336-2122
csssdrummond@ssss.gouv.qc.ca
www.csssdrummond.qc.ca
Nombre de lits: 52 lits
Note: Centre d'hébergement; le point de service CLSC: 819-474-2572.
Nagui Habashi, Directeur général, CSSS Drummond

***Notre-Dame-du-Nord:* CHSLD des premières nations du Timiskaming**
CSSS du Lac-Témiscamingue
Affiliée à: Agence de la santé et des services sociaux de l'Abitibi-Témiscamingue
20, av Algonquin, Notre-Dame-du-Nord, QC J0Z 3B0
Tél: 819-723-2225; *Téléc:* 819-723-2112
www.sante-abitibi-temiscamingue.gouv.qc.ca; wpp01.msss.gouv.qc.ca
Nombre de lits: 20 lits
Note: Établissement privé non conventionné
Estelle St-Cyr Perreault, Directrice générale

***Oka:* Manoir Oka inc.**
Affiliée à: Agence de la santé et des services sociaux des Laurentides
CP 567, 2083, ch Oka, Oka, QC J0N 1E0
Tél: 450-479-6447; *Téléc:* 450-479-6447
Nombre de lits: 34 lits
Robert Fournier, Directeur général

***Pierrefonds:* Manoir Pierrefonds inc. - 9130-9377QC.inc.**
Affiliée à: Agence de la santé et des services sociaux de Montréal
18465, boul Gouin ouest, Pierrefonds, QC H9K 1A6
Tél: 514-626-6651; *Téléc:* 514-626-6415
Nombre de lits: 183 unités
Lorraine Lincourt, Directrice générale

***Pierreville:* Foyer Lucien Shooner inc.**
Affiliée à: Agence de la santé et des services sociaux de la Mauricie et du Centre-du-Québec
CP 220, 50, rue Lt-Gouv.-Paul-Comtois, Pierreville, QC J0G 1J0
Tél: 450-568-2712; *Téléc:* 450-568-3658
Nombre de lits: 38 lits
Marcel Nolet, Directeur général

***Plessisville:* Foyer des Bois-Francs**
Affiliée à: Agence de la santé et des services sociaux de la Mauricie et du Centre-du-Québec
1450, av Trudelle, Plessisville, QC G6L 3K4
Tél: 819-362-3558; *Téléc:* 819-362-9266
Nombre de lits: 40 lits
Michel Lauzon, Directeur général

***Pointe-Claire:* CHSLD Bayview inc.**
Affiliée à: Agence de la santé et des services sociaux de Montréal
Également connu sous le nom de: Centre Bayview
27, ch Lakeshore, Pointe-Claire, QC H9S 4H1
Tél: 514-695-9384; *Téléc:* 514-695-5723
www.chsldbayview.com
Nombre de lits: 128 lits
Note: Un établissement privé de soins de longue durée.
George Guillon, Directeur général

***Princeville:* Centre d'hébergement de Saint-Eusèbe**
CSSS d'Arthabaska-et-de-l'Érable
Affiliée à: Agence de la santé et des services sociaux de la Mauricie et du Centre-du-Québec
Également connu sous le nom de: Foyer St-Eusèbe
CP 610, 435, rue Saint-Jacques, Princeville, QC G6L 5C5
Tél: 819-364-2355; *Téléc:* 819-364-7824
www.csssae.qc.ca
Nombre de lits: 26 lits
Marcel Dubois, Président, Conseil d'administration, CSSS d'Arthabaska-et-de-l

***Québec:* Centre d'accueil Nazareth inc.**
Affiliée à: Agence de la santé et des services sociaux de la Capitale-Nationale
715, rue des Glacis, Québec, QC G1R 3P8
Tél: 418-694-0492; *Téléc:* 418-694-9452
Nombre de lits: 75 lits
Louise Gaudreault, Directrice générale

***Québec:* Centre d'hébergement Saint-Antoine**
Affiliée à: Agence de la santé et des services sociaux de la Capitale-Nationale
1451, boul Père-Lelièvre, Québec, QC G1M 1N8
Tél: 418-683-2516; *Téléc:* 418-683-4031
www.csssvc.qc.ca
Nombre de lits: 284 lits
Note: Hébergement et soins de longue durée
Gerard Roy, Directeur général

***Québec:* Centre hospitalier Nôtre-Dame du Chemin inc.**
510, ch Ste-Foy, Québec, QC G1S 2J5
Tél: 418-681-7882; *Téléc:* 418-681-5387
Nombre de lits: 50 lits
Antoine Pichette, Directeur général

***Québec:* Centre hospitalier St-François inc**
1604, 1e av, Québec, QC G1L 3L6
Tél: 418-524-6033; *Téléc:* 418-524-9542
Nombre de lits: 29 lits
Yvan Girard, Directeur général

***Québec:* Centre hospitalier St-Sacrement ltée**
Affiliée à: Agence de la santé et des services sociaux de la Capitale-Nationale
1165, ch Ste-Foy, Québec, QC G1S 2M8
Tél: 418-527-4836; *Téléc:* 418-527-1743
stephan.pichette@ssss.gouv.qc.ca
Nombre de lits: 63 lits
Stéphan Pichette, Directeur général

***Québec:* CLSC-CHSLD Basse-Ville - Limoilou - Vanier**
Affiliée à: Agence de la santé et des services sociaux de la Capitale-Nationale
260, boul Langelier, Québec, QC G1K 5N1
Tél: 418-529-0931; *Téléc:* 418-521-5801
msss.gouv.qc.ca
Nombre de lits: 99 lits
André Métivier, Directeur général

***Québec:* La Corporation Notre-Dame de Bon-Secours**
990, rue Gérard-Morisset, Québec, QC G1S 1X6
Tél: 418-681-4637
Nombre de lits: 20 lits
Michel Bilodrau, Directeur général

***Québec:* Foyer Ste-Marie-des-Anges Résidence**
2390, boul Masson, Québec, QC G1P 1J4
Tél: 418-871-5365
www.cmafhaiti.org/foyer.htm
Nombre de lits: 14 chambres
Note: Pour personnes retraitées autonomes et en perte d'autonomie
Gisèle Boivin, Directrice générale

***Québec:* Habitation Grande-Allée**
1175, av Turnbull, Québec, QC G1R 5L5
Tél: 418-522-3979; *Téléc:* 418-522-7870
Nombre de lits: 30 lits
Lyse Gauthier, Directrice générale

***Québec:* Hôpital Ste-Monique inc.**
4805, boul Wilfrid Hamel, Québec, QC G1P 2J7
Tél: 418-871-8701; *Téléc:* 418-871-0105
Nombre de lits: 58 lits
Andrée Begin, Directrice générale
Edith Tassé, Directrice, Soins infirmiers et du personnel

***Québec:* Résidence Louis-Hebert**
Affiliée à: Agence de la santé et des services sociaux de la Capitale-Nationale
1550, rue Pointe-aux-Lièvres nord, Québec, QC G1L 4M8
Tél: 418-529-5511; *Téléc:* 418-524-1143
Nombre de lits: 52 lits
Richard Rousseau, Directeur général par intérim

***Rawdon:* CHSLD Heather I**
Également connu sous le nom de: Manoir Heather/Heather Lodge
3931, ch Lakeshore, Rawdon, QC J0K 1S0
Tél: 450-834-3070; *Téléc:* 450-834-5805
info@manoirheather.com
www.manoirheather.com
Nombre de lits: 76 lits
Note: CHSLD Heather II: 3462, 3e av, Rawdon, QC J0K 1S0, 450-834-2512.
Paul Arbec, Directeur général

***Rawdon:* Monsieur Rémy Landry**
Affiliée à: Agences de développement de réseaux locaux de services de santé et de services sociaux
Ancien nom: Centre d'Accueil Bouleaux Argentés
3567, rue Church, Rawdon, QC J0K 1S0
Tél: 450-834-2794; *Téléc:* 450-834-8286
Nombre de lits: 16 lits
Rémy Landry, Directeur général

***Richmond:* Centre d'hébergement de Richmond**
CSSS du Val-Saint-François
Affiliée à: Agence de la santé et des services sociaux de l'Estrie
980, rue McGauran, Richmond, QC J0B 2H0
Tél: 819-542-2777; *Téléc:* 819-826-5724
vsf.santeestrie.qc.ca
Nombre de lits: 54 lits
Pierre Lalande, Directeur général, CSSS du Val-Saint-François

***Richmond:* Wales Home**
Foyer Wales
Affiliée à: Agence de la santé et des services sociaux de l'Estrie
506, rte 243 nord, Richmond, QC J0B 2H0
Tél: 819-826-3266; *Téléc:* 819-826-2549
www.waleshome.ca
Nombre de lits: 190 lits
Stuart Simms, Directeur général

***Rimouski:* Centre d'hébergement de Rimouski**
CSSS de Rimouski-Neigette
Affiliée à: Agence de la santé et des services sociaux du Bas-St-Laurent
645, boul Saint-Germain ouest, Rimouski, QC G5L 3S2
Tél: 418-724-4111; *Téléc:* 418-724-0604
courrierweb.crsssr@ssss.gouv.qc.ca
www.chrr.qc.ca
Nombre de lits: 246 lits
Raymond Coulombe, Directeur général, CSSS de Rimouski-Neigette

***Rimouski:* Foyer Ste-Bernadette inc.**
280, av Belzile, Rimouski, QC G5L 8K7
Tél: 418-723-0040; *Téléc:* 418-723-0615
Nombre de lits: 24 lits
Claude Talbot, Directeur général

***Rimouski:* Manoir de Caroline inc.**
280, rue Belzile, Rimouski, QC G5L 8K7
Tél: 418-723-0611; *Téléc:* 418-723-0615
Nombre de lits: 85 lits
Claude Talbot, Directeur général

***Rivière-Bleue:* Centre d'hébergement Rivière-Bleue**
CSSS de Témiscouata
Affiliée à: Agence de la santé et des services sociaux du Bas-St-Laurent
45, rue du Foyer sud, Rivière-Bleue, QC G0L 2B0
Tél: 418-893-5511; *Téléc:* 418-893-7151
www.cssstemiscouata.com
Nombre de lits: 44 lits
Monique Dumas, Directrice, Services des personnes en perte d'autonomie, CSSS d

***Rivière-Ouelle:* Centre Thérèse-Martin**
CSSS de Kamouraska
Affiliée à: Agence de la santé et des services sociaux du Bas-St-Laurent
100, ch de la Petite-Anse, Rivière-Ouelle, QC G0L 2C0
Tél: 418-856-7000; *Téléc:* 418-856-4381
www.agencesssbsl.gouv.qc.ca
Nombre de lits: 48 lits
Michel Beaulieu, Directeur général, CSSS de Kamouraska

***Rivière-du-Loup:* Centre d'hébergement Saint-Joseph**
CSSS de Rivière-du-Loup
Affiliée à: Agence de la santé et des services sociaux du Bas-St-Laurent
28, rue Joly, Rivière-du-Loup, QC G5R 3H2
Tél: 418-862-6385; *Téléc:* 418-862-1986
www.cssrivieredulup.qc.ca
Nombre de lits: 145 lits
Note: Hébergement permanent et centre de jour.
Raymond April, Directeur général, CSSS de Rivière-du-Loup

***Rouyn-Noranda:* Centre d'hébergement de Rouyn-Noranda**
CSSS de Rouyn-Noranda
Affiliée à: Agence de la santé et des services sociaux de l'Abitibi-Témiscamingue
Ancien nom: Maison Pie XII
512, av Richard, Rouyn-Noranda, QC J9X 4M1
Tél: 819-762-0908; *Téléc:* 819-764-5036
www.sante-abitibi-temiscamingue.gouv.qc.ca; www.csssrn.qc.ca
Nombre de lits: 157 lits
Note: Centre d'hébergement, centre de jour, hôpital de jour.
Huguette Lemay, Directrice générale, CSSS de Rouyn-Noranda
Annie Audet, Directrice, Programme des personnes en perte d'autonomie

***Saint-Alexandre-de-Kamour:* Centre Villa Maria**
CSSS de Kamouraska
Affiliée à: Agence de la santé et des services sociaux du Bas-St-Laurent
404, av du Foyer, Saint-Alexandre-de-Kamour, QC G0L 2G0
Tél: 418-856-7000; *Téléc:* 418-495-2829
Nombre de lits: 46 lits

Michel Beaulieu, Directeur général, CSSS de Kamouraska

Saint-Antoine-sur-Richeli: Accueil du Rivage inc.
1008, ch du Rivage, Saint-Antoine-sur-Richeli, QC J0L 1R0
Tél: 450-787-3436; *Téléc:* 450-787-1156
communication.csssry@rrsss16.gouv.qc.ca
www.santemonteregie.qc.ca
Nombre de lits: 36 lits
Jean Bergeron, Directeur général

Saint-Antonin: Centre d'hébergement de Saint-Antonin
CSSS de Rivière-du-Loup
Affiliée à: Agence de la santé et des services sociaux du Bas-St-Laurent
CP 430, 286, rue Principale, Saint-Antonin, QC G0L 2J0
Tél: 418-862-7993; *Téléc:* 418-862-5278
www.csssriviereduloup.qc.ca
Nombre de lits: 42 lits
Raymond April, Directeur général, CSSS de Rivière-du-Loup

Saint-Augustin-de-Desmaur: Jardins du Haut Saint-Laurent (1992) inc.
4770, rue Saint-Felix, Saint-Augustin-de-Desmaur, QC G3A 1B1
Tél: 418-872-4936; *Téléc:* 418-872-4245
jhsl1990@hardins-hsl.com
www.jardins-hsl.com
Nombre de lits: 140 lits
Nathalie Côté, Directrice générale

Saint-Bernard-de-Lacolle: Florence Groulx inc.
7, rang Saint-Louis, Saint-Bernard-de-Lacolle, QC J0J 1V0
Tél: 450-246-3879; *Téléc:* 450-246-4111
Nombre de lits: 50 lits
Daniel Gaudette, Directeur général

Saint-Bruno-de-Montarvill: Centre d'hébergement de Montarville
CSSS Richelieu-Yamaska
Affiliée à: Agence de la santé et des services sociaux de la Montérégie
265, boul Seigneurial ouest, Saint-Bruno-de-Montarvill, QC J3V 2H4
Tél: 450-461-2650; *Téléc:* 450-461-2968
info@lesommetavotreportee.qc.ca
www.lesommetavotreportee.qc.ca;
www.santemonteregie.qc.ca/richelieu-yamaska
Nombre de lits: 155 lits
Daniel Castonguay, Directeur général, CSSS Richelieu-Yamaska
Réjeanne Boudreau, Directrice du Programme hébergement-milieu de vie, CSSS Richelieu-Yamaska

Saint-Casimir: Centre d'hébergement Saint-Casimir
Affiliée à: Agence de la santé et des services sociaux de la Capitale-Nationale
CP 10, 605, rue Fleury, Saint-Casimir, QC G0A 3L0
Tél: 418-339-2861; *Téléc:* 418-339-2875
Nombre de lits: 64 lits
Fernand Morasse, Directeur général

Saint-Célestin: Centre Saint-Célestin
Affiliée à: Agence de la santé et des services sociaux de la Mauricie et du Centre-du-Québec
CP 90, 475, rue Houde, Saint-Célestin, QC J0C 1G0
Tél: 819-229-3617; *Téléc:* 819-229-1165
Nombre de lits: 52 lits
Marcel Nolet, Directeur général

Saint-Constant: Centre d'hébergement Jean-Louis-Lapierre
CSSS Jardins-Roussillon
199, rue St-Pierre, Saint-Constant, QC J5A 2N8
Tél: 450-632-4451; *Téléc:* 450-632-2004
www.santemonteregie.qc.ca/jardins-roussillon
Nombre de lits: 76 lits
Paul Moreau, Directeur général, CSSS Jardins-Roussillon

Saint-Cyprien: Centre d'hébergement de Saint-Cyprien
101-C, rue Collin, Saint-Cyprien, QC G0L 2P0
Tél: 418-963-2272
www.csssriviereduloup.qc.ca
Nombre de lits: 20 lits
Raymond April, Directeur général, CSSS de Rivière-du-Loup

Saint-Eustache: Société en commandite centre d'accueil l'Ermitage
112, 25e av, Saint-Eustache, QC J7P 2V2
Tél: 450-473-5961; *Téléc:* 450-491-1847
Nombre de lits: 78 lits
Kevin Shemie, Directeur général

Saint-Félicien: Centre d'hébergement de Saint-Félicien
CSSS Domaine-du-Roy
Affiliée à: Agence de la santé et des services sociaux du Saguenay-Lac-St-Jean
Édifice Foyer de la Paix, 1229, boul Sacré-Coeur, Saint-Félicien, QC G8K 1A5
Tél: 418-679-1585; *Téléc:* 418-679-2376
hdr@ssss.gouv.qc.ca
www.cmdp-roberval.com
Nombre de lits: 46 lits
Note: Hébergement permanent et temporaire; centre de jour.
Jacques Dubois, Directeur général, CSSS Domaine-du-Roy

Saint-Gabriel-de-Brandon: Centre d'accueil Desy
Affiliée à: Agences de développement de réseaux locaux de services de santé et de services sociaux
CP 840, 90, rue Maskinonge, Saint-Gabriel-de-Brandon, QC J0K 2N0
Tél: 450-835-4712; *Téléc:* 450-835-7606
Nombre de lits: 54 lits
Jacques Morin, Comptable

Saint-Georges: Centre hospitalier de l'Assomption
Affiliée à: Agence de la santé et des services sociaux de Chaudière-Appalaches
16750, boul Lacroix, Saint-Georges, QC G5Y 2G4
Tél: 416-228-2041; *Téléc:* 416-226-4117

Saint-Georges-de-Beauce: CHSLD L'Assomption
Affiliée à: Groupe Champlain inc.
16750, boul Lacroix, Saint-Georges-de-Beauce, QC G5Y 2G4
Tél: 418-228-2041; *Téléc:* 418-228-9366
www.groupechamplain.qc.ca
Nombre de lits: 96 lits
Note: Agence/région administrative: Agence de la santé et des services sociaux de Lanaudière.

Saint-Hubert: Centre Henriette Céré
Affiliée à: Agence de la santé et des services sociaux de la Montérégie
6435, ch de Chambly, Saint-Hubert, QC J3Y 3R6
Tél: 514-678-3291; *Téléc:* 514-443-1360
Nombre de lits: 99 lits
Jean-Denis Godbout, Directeur général

Saint-Hubert: Centre hospitalier Rive-sud inc.
5300, ch Chambly, Saint-Hubert, QC J3Y 3N7
Tél: 450-445-0123; *Téléc:* 450-445-1175
Nombre de lits: 34 lits
André Brunelle, Directeur général

Saint-Hubert: Pavillon Résidence Saint-Hubert
5160, montée Saint-Hubert, Saint-Hubert, QC J3Y 1V7
Tél: 450-676-8411
Nombre de lits: 38
Note: ressource intermédiaire en santé mentale

Saint-Hubert: Pavillon St-Hubert
3823, rue Grand Boulevard, Saint-Hubert, QC J4T 2M3
Tél: 450-445-3598; *Téléc:* 450-462-3767

Saint-Hyacinthe: Centre d'hébergement Andrée-Perrault
CSSS Richelieu-Yamaska
Affiliée à: Agence de la santé et des services sociaux de la Montérégie
1955, av Pratte, Saint-Hyacinthe, QC J2S 7W5
Tél: 514-771-4536; *Téléc:* 450-771-5499
info@lesommetavotreportee.qc.ca
www.lesommetavotreportee.qc.ca;
www.santemonteregie.qc.ca/richelieu-yamaska
Nombre de lits: 70 lits
Daniel Castonguay, Directeur général, CSSS Richelieu-Yamaska
Réjeanne Boudreau, Directrice du Programme hébergement-milieu de vie, CSSS Richelieu-Yamaska

Saint-Hyacinthe: CHSLD Résidence Bourg-Joli inc.
Affiliée à: Agence de la santé et des services sociaux de la Montérégie
2915, boul Laframboise, Saint-Hyacinthe, QC J2S 4Z3
Tél: 450-773-4197; *Téléc:* 450-773-6545
Nombre de lits: 24 lits
Marc Breton, Directeur général

Saint-Jean-sur-Richelieu: Centre d'hébergement Georges-Phaneuf
CSSS Haut-Richelieu-Rouville
Affiliée à: Agence de la santé et des services sociaux de la Montérégie
230, rue Jacques-Cartier nord, Saint-Jean-sur-Richelieu, QC J3B 6T4
Tél: 450-346-1133; *Téléc:* 450-346-2199
www.santemonteregie.qc.ca/haut-richelieu-rouville
Nombre de lits: 124 lits
Lucie Tétreault, Directrice, Personnes en perte d'autonomie liée au vieillissement

Saint-Jean-sur-Richelieu: Centre d'hébergement Gertrude-Lafrance
CSSS Haut-Richelieu-Rouville
Affiliée à: Agence de la santé et des services sociaux de la Montérégie
150, boul Saint-Luc, Saint-Jean-sur-Richelieu, QC J3A 1G2
Tél: 450-349-5555; *Téléc:* 450-348-7693
www.santemonteregie.qc.ca/haut-richelieu-rouville
Nombre de lits: 174 lits
Lucie Tétreault, Directrice, Personnes en perte d'autonomie liée au vieillissement

Saint-Jérome: L'Auberge St-Jérôme Inc.
Affiliée à: Agence de la santé et des services sociaux des Laurentides
66, rue Danis, Saint-Jérome, QC J7Y 2R3
Tél: 514-436-3131
Nombre de lits: 92 lits

Saint-Jérome: CHSLD de la Rivière du Nord
Affiliée à: Agence de la santé et des services sociaux des Laurentides
531, rue Laviolette, Saint-Jérome, QC J7Y 2T8
Tél: 450-436-3061; *Téléc:* 450-436-8328
Nombre de lits: 305 lits
Note: Centres d'hébergement: Youville, l'Auberge, et Lucien G. Rolland.
Jean-Pierre Perreault, Directeur général

Saint-Lambert: CHSLD de la MRC de Champlain
831, av Notre-Dame, Saint-Lambert, QC J4R 1S1
Tél: 450-672-3320; *Téléc:* 450-672-3370
andree.ouellette@rrsss16.gouv.qc.ca
Nombre de lits: 313 lits
Gisèle Lacoste, Directrice générale
Real Guilbert, Directeur, Services techniques

Saint-Lambert: Résidence du Parc
33, av Argyle, Saint-Lambert, QC J4P 3P5
Tél: 450-878-3081; *Téléc:* 450-465-4369
residenceduparc@reveraliving.com
www.reveraliving.com
Nombre de lits: 105 lits
Denyse Saey, Directrice générale

Saint-Laurent: Les Cèdres - Centre d'accueil pour personnes âgées
#200, 1275, boul de la Côte-Vertu, Saint-Laurent, QC H4L 4V2
Tél: 514-389-1023; *Téléc:* 514-389-0581
Nombre de lits: 25 lits
Rose Khoury, Directrice générale

Saint-Laurent: Centre d'hébergement St-Vincent-Marie inc.
Affiliée à: Agence de la santé et des services sociaux de Montréal
1175, boul de la Côte-Vertu, Saint-Laurent, QC H4L 5J1
Tél: 514-744-1175
Nombre de lits: 66 lits
Danny Macdonald, Directeur général

Saint-Laurent: CHSLD-CLSC Saint-Laurent
Affiliée à: Agence de la santé et des services sociaux de Montréal
1055, av Ste-Croix, Saint-Laurent, QC H4L 3Z2
Tél: 514-748-6400; *Téléc:* 514-748-6449
Nombre de lits: 154 lits

Saint-Liguori: Foyer Saint-Liguori
Affiliée à: Agences de développement de réseaux locaux de services de santé et de services sociaux
771, rue Principale, Saint-Liguori, QC J0K 2X0
Tél: 450-753-7062; *Téléc:* 450-753-3208
Nombre de lits: 48 lits
Paul-Yvon de Billy, Directeur général

***Saint-Louis-du-Ha!-Ha!:* Centre d'hébergement St-Louis**
CSSS de Témiscouata
Affiliée à: Agence de la santé et des services sociaux du Bas-St-Laurent
25, rue Saint-Philippe, Saint-Louis-du-Ha!-Ha!, QC G0L 3S0
Tél: 418-854-2631; *Téléc:* 418-854-0430
www.cssstemiscouata.com
Nombre de lits: 43 lits
Monique Dumas, Directrice, Services des personnes en perte d'autonomie, CSSS d

***Saint-Michel-de-Bellechas:* CHSLD Vigi Notre-Dame de Lourdes**
Affiliée à: Vigi Santé Ltée
CP 10, 80, rue Principale, Saint-Michel-de-Bellechas, QC G0R 3S0
Tél: 418-884-2811; *Téléc:* 418-884-3714
www.vigisante.com
Nombre de lits: 40 lits
Note: Agence/région administrative: Agence de la santé et des services sociaux de Chaudière-Appalaches.
Vincent Simonetta, Directeur général
Michelle Harvey, Directeur adjointe, Services techniques

***Saint-Michel-des-Saints:* Centre d'accueil Brassard**
Affiliée à: Agences de développement de réseaux locaux de services de santé et de services sociaux
CP 309, 390, rue Brassard, Saint-Michel-des-Saints, QC J0K 3B0
Tél: 514-833-6331; *Téléc:* 514-833-6093
Nombre de lits: 35 lits
Jean-Jacques Lamarche, Directeur général par intérim

***Saint-Michel-du-Squatec:* CHSLD de Squatec**
CSSS de Témiscouata
Ancien nom: Domaine du Sommet
10, rue Saint-André, Saint-Michel-du-Squatec, QC G0L 4H0
Tél: 418-855-2442; *Téléc:* 418-855-2357
www.cssstemiscouata.com
Nombre de lits: 24 lits
Monique Dumas, Directrice, Services des personnes en perte d'autonomie, CSSS d

***Saint-Narcisse:* Centre multiservice - Centre d'accueil de St-Narcisse**
Affiliée à: Agence de la santé et des services sociaux de la Mauricie et du Centre-du-Québec
361, rue du College, Saint-Narcisse, QC G0X 2Y0
Tél: 418-328-3351; *Téléc:* 418-328-4140
Nombre de lits: 31 lits
Gilles Cossette, Directeur général

***Saint-Pacôme:* Centre d'Anjou**
CSSS de Kamouraska
Affiliée à: Agence de la santé et des services sociaux du Bas-St-Laurent
127, rue Galarneau, Saint-Pacôme, QC G0L 3X0
Tél: 418-856-7000; *Téléc:* 418-852-3230
www.agencesssbsl.gouv.qc.ca
Nombre de lits: 60 lits
Michel Beaulieu, Directeur général, CSSS de Kamouraska

***Saint-Pierre-les-Becquets:* Centre d'hébergement Romain-Becquet**
Affiliée à: Agence de la santé et des services sociaux de la Mauricie et du Centre-du-Québec
255, rte Marie-Victorin, Saint-Pierre-les-Becquets, QC G0X 2Z0
Tél: 819-263-2245; *Téléc:* 819-263-2636
Nombre de lits: 35 lits
Note: Hébergement permanent et temporaire
Jacqueline Côté, Chef, Administration

***Saint-Raymond:* Centre hébergement Saint-Raymond**
Affiliée à: Agence de la santé et des services sociaux de la Capitale-Nationale
324, rue Saint-Joseph, Saint-Raymond, QC G3L 1J7
Tél: 418-337-4611; *Téléc:* 418-337-4808
Nombre de lits: 64 lits
Fernand Morasse, Directeur général

***Saint-Rémi:* Centre d'hébergement de Saint-Rémi**
CSSS Jardins-Roussillon
Affiliée à: Agence de la santé et des services sociaux de la Montérégie
CP 820, 110, rue du Collège, Saint-Rémi, QC J0L 2L0
Tél: 450-454-4694; *Téléc:* 450-454-3614
www.santemonteregie.qc.ca/jardins-roussillon
Nombre de lits: 58 lits
Paul Moreau, Directeur général, CSSS Jardins-Roussillon

***Saint-Romuald:* CHSLD Chanoine-Audet inc.**
Affiliée à: Groupe Champlain inc.
2155, ch du Sault, Saint-Romuald, QC G6W 2K7
Tél: 418-834-5322; *Téléc:* 418-834-5754
www.groupechamplain.qc.ca
Nombre de lits: 96 lits
Note: Agence/région administrative: Agence de la santé et des services sociaux de Chaudière-Appalaches.
Julie Gendreau, Directeur général

***Saint-Siméon:* CLSC-CHSLD de Saint-Siméon**
CSSS de Charlevoix
Affiliée à: Agence de la santé et des services sociaux de la Capitale-Nationale
CP 7, 371, rue Saint-Laurent, Saint-Siméon, QC G0T 1X0
Tél: 418-638-2414
www.cssscharlevoix.qc.ca
Nombre de lits: 18 lits
Note: Centre local de services communautaires (418-638-2369); centre d'hébergement et centre de jour.
Micheline Tremblay, Directrice générale, CSSS de Charlevoix
micheline.tremblay@ssss.gouv.qc.ca

***Saint-Timothée:* La Maison des Aîne(e)s**
Affiliée à: Agence de la santé et des services sociaux de la Montérégie
1, rue des Aînes, Saint-Timothée, QC J6S 6M8
Tél: 450-377-3925; *Téléc:* 450-377-3490
Nombre de lits: 38 lits
Denis Charland, Directeur général

***Saint-Tite:* Centre multiservice Foyer Mgr Paquin**
Affiliée à: Agence de la santé et des services sociaux de la Mauricie et du Centre-du-Québec
CP 400, 580, rue du Couvent, Saint-Tite, QC G0X 3H0
Tél: 418-365-5107; *Téléc:* 418-365-7914
Nombre de lits: 55 lits
Gilles Cossette, Directeur général

***Sainte-Anne-de-la-Pérade:* Centre multiservice Foyer de la Pérade**
Affiliée à: Agence de la santé et des services sociaux de la Mauricie et du Centre-du-Québec
CP 217, 60, rue de la Fabrique, Sainte-Anne-de-la-Pérade, QC G0X 2J0
Tél: 418-325-2313; *Téléc:* 418-325-3233
Nombre de lits: 42 lits
Gilles Cossette, Directeur général

***Sainte-Cécile:* Pavillon Ste-Cécile**
4581, rue Principale, Sainte-Cécile, QC G0Y 1J0
Tél: 819-583-0400; *Téléc:* 819-583-0983
Nombre de lits: 15 lits
Alain Hinse, Directeur général

***Sainte-Foy:* Résidence Paul Triquet**
Affiliée à: Agence de la santé et des services sociaux de la Capitale-Nationale; CHUQ
Également connu sous le nom de: La Maison Paul-Triquet
789, rue de Belmont, Sainte-Foy, QC G1V 4V2
Tél: 418-657-6890; *Téléc:* 418-657-6894
maisonpaultriquet@mail.chuq.qc.ca
www.chuq.qc.ca/maisonpaultriquet
Year Founded: 1987
Nombre de lits: 64 lits
Note: Centre d'hébergement de soins de longue durée pour anciens combattants
René Rouleau, Directeur général

***Sainte-Sophie:* Centre d'hébergement Jaclo Inc.**
CP 129, 2319, rue Sainte-Marie, Sainte-Sophie, QC J0R 1S0
Tél: 450-436-5627; *Téléc:* 450-436-6663
Nombre de lits: 31 lits
Claude Brière, Directeur général

***Sainte-Thérèse:* Centre d'hébergement Drapeau-Deschambault**
CSSS de Thérèse-De Blainville
Affiliée à: Agence de la santé et des services sociaux des Laurentides
100, rue du Chanoine Lionel-Groulx, Sainte-Thérèse, QC J7E 5E1
Tél: 450-437-4267; *Téléc:* 450-437-0788
www.cssstheresedeblainville.qc.ca
Nombre de lits: 223 lits
André Poirier, Directeur général, CSSS de Thérèse-De Blainville

***Sainte-Thérèse:* CHSLD Boise Ste-Thérèse Inc.**
179, Place Fabien-Drapeau, Sainte-Thérèse, QC J7E 5W6
Tél: 450-430-6767; *Téléc:* 450-430-6965
boisesteterese@darkshell.com
Nombre de lits: 41 CHSLD privé; 60 autonomes
Stephanie Drolet, Directrice générale

***Saint-Éphrem-de-Beauce:* Résidence St-Éphrem inc.**
CP 310, 1, rue Plante, Saint-Éphrem-de-Beauce, QC G0M 1R0
Tél: 418-484-2121; *Téléc:* 418-484-2144
restep@telstep.net
Nombre de lits: 40 lits
Lynda Roy, Directrice générale

***Salaberry-de-Valleyfield:* Les Centres du Haut St-Laurent (CHSLD) Valleyfield**
Affiliée à: Agence de la santé et des services sociaux de la Montérégie
80, rue de Marche, Salaberry-de-Valleyfield, QC J6T 1P5
Tél: 450-373-4013; *Téléc:* 450-373-0325
chsl@rocler.qc.ca
www.rocler.qc.ca/chsl
Nombre de lits: 177 lits
Claude Chayer, Directeur général

***Shawinigan:* CHSLD Vigi Les Chutes**
Affiliée à: Vigi Santé Ltée
5000, av Albert-Tessier, Shawinigan, QC G9N 8P9
Tél: 819-539-5408; *Téléc:* 819-539-5400
www.vigisante.com
Nombre de lits: 64 lits
Note: Agence/région administrative: Agence de la santé et des services sociaux de la Mauricie.
Vincent Simonetta, Directeur général

***Shawville:* Pavillon Pontiac**
Affiliée à: Agence de la santé et de services sociaux de l'Outaouais
Ancien nom: CHSLD Shawville
CP 2001, 290, rue Marion, Shawville, QC J0X 2Y0
Tél: 819-647-5755; *Téléc:* 819-647-2453
Nombre de lits: 50 lits
Joan Brown, Manager

***Sherbrooke:* Centre d'hébergement St-Joseph**
CSSS-Institut universitaire de gériatrie de Sherbrooke
Affiliée à: Agence de la santé et des services sociaux de l'Estrie
611, boul Queen-Victoria nord, Sherbrooke, QC J1H 3R6
Tél: 819-780-2222
www.csss-iugs.ca
Nombre de lits: 144 lits
Carol Fillion, Directeur général, CSSS-Institut universitaire de gériatrie de Sherbro

***Sherbrooke:* CHSLD Vigi Shermont inc.**
Affiliée à: Vigi Santé Ltée
3220, 12e av nord, Sherbrooke, QC J1H 5H3
Tél: 819-820-8900; *Téléc:* 819-820-8902
www.vigisante.com
Nombre de lits: 52 lits
Note: Agence/région administrative: Agence de la santé et des services sociaux de l'Estrie.
Jean Sevigny, Directeur général

***Sherbrooke:* Les Dominicaines des saints anges gardiens**
Ancien nom: Mont St-Dominique
361, rue Moore, Sherbrooke, QC J1H 1C1
Tél: 819-346-5512; *Téléc:* 819-563-5023
Nombre de lits: 50 lits
Nevenka Skrindar, Directrice générale

***Sillery:* Pavillon Saint-Dominique**
1045, boul René-Lévesque ouest, Sillery, QC G1S 1V3
Tél: 418-681-3561; *Téléc:* 418-687-9196
info@pavstdom.org
www.pavstdom.org
Nombre de lits: 152 lits
Jeannine Nadeau, Directrice générale

***Sillery:* Saint Brigid's Home Inc.**
Affiliée à: Agence de la santé et des services sociaux de la Capitale-Nationale
1645, ch Saint-Louis, Sillery, QC G1S 4M3
Tél: 418-681-4687; *Téléc:* 418-527-6862
Nombre de lits: 162 lits
Louis Hanrahan, Directeur général

***Sorel-Tracy:* CHSLD du Bas-Richelieu**
151, rue George, Sorel-Tracy, QC J3P 1C8
Tél: 450-746-5555; *Téléc:* 450-746-4897
Nombre de lits: 261 lits
René Legault, Directeur général (intérim)

Sorel-Tracy: **Foyer Richelieu**
Affiliée à: Agence de la santé et des services sociaux de la Montérégie
40, rue de Ramesay, Sorel-Tracy, QC J3P 3Y7
Tél: 514-742-5936; *Téléc:* 514-742-1613
Nombre de lits: 60 lits
Jacques Blais, Directeur général

Sorel-Tracy: **Hôpital Richelieu/CLSC Du Havre**
Affiliée à: Agence de la santé et des services sociaux de la Montérégie
30, rue Ferland, Sorel-Tracy, QC J3P 3C7
Tél: 514-743-5569; *Téléc:* 514-743-1803
Nombre de lits: 18 lits
Jacques Blais, Directeur général
Jeanine Larosée, Chef, Entretient sanitaire

Sorel-Tracy: **Résidence Sorel-Tracy inc.**
4025, rue Frontenac, Sorel-Tracy, QC J3R 4G8
Tél: 450-742-9428; *Téléc:* 450-742-9668
Nombre de lits: 64 lits
Julie Bien-Aimé, Directrice générale

St-Charles-de-Bellechasse: **Résidence Charles Couillard Inc.**
20, av St-Georges, St-Charles-de-Bellechasse, QC G0R 2T0
Tél: 418-887-6455; *Téléc:* 418-887-1316
Nombre de lits: 35 lits
Gerard Dion, Directeur général

St-Georges: **Centre hospitalier de l'Assomption Inc.**
16750, boul Lacroix, St-Georges, QC G5Y 2G4
Tél: 418-228-2041; *Téléc:* 418-228-9366
Nombre de lits: 96 lits
Gérard Gendreau, Directeur général

St-Jovite: **CLSC-CHSLD des Trois Vallées - Résidence St-Jovite**
CP 910, 925, rue Ouimet, St-Jovite, QC J0T 2H0
Tél: 819-425-2793; *Téléc:* 819-425-8857
Nombre de lits: 69 lits
Christine Lessard, Directrice générale

St-Sauveur-des-Monts: **CHSLD Villa du Vieux Sapin Inc.**
Ancien nom: Les Residences Desjardins
55, rue Hochar, St-Sauveur-des-Monts, QC J0R 1R6
Tél: 450-227-2241; *Téléc:* 450-227-6186
Nombre de lits: 34 lits
Colette Desjardins, Directrice générale

Ste-Cécile-de-Masham: **CLSC-CHSLD des Collines**
9, ch Passe-Partout, Ste-Cécile-de-Masham, QC J0X 2W0
Tél: 819-456-1112; *Téléc:* 819-456-4531
Ligne sans frais: 877-459-1112
www.santedescollines.qc.ca
Nombre de lits: Centre d'hébergement La Pêche: 32 lits.
Note: Y compris le Centre d'hébergement La Pêche et le CLSC Masham.
Pierre Rochon, Directeur général, CSSS des Collines
Jean-Paul Racine, Président, Conseil d'administration

Ste-Marguerite-du-Lac-Mas: **Manoir de la Pointe Bleue (1978)**
Affiliée à: Agence de la santé et des services sociaux des Laurentides
428, rue du Baron-Louis-Empain, Ste-Marguerite-du-Lac-Mas, QC J0T 1L0
Tél: 450-228-2503; *Téléc:* 450-228-3312
Nombre de lits: 91 lits
Jacqueline Gagnon, Directrice générale

Sutton: **Foyer Sutton**
Affiliée à: Agence de la santé et des services sociaux de la Montérégie
CP 719, 50, rue Western, Sutton, QC J0E 2K0
Tél: 514-538-3332; *Téléc:* 514-538-0514
Nombre de lits: 74 lits
Michel Asselin, Directeur général

Terrebonne: **CHSLD de La Côte Boisée inc.**
4300, rue d'Angora, Terrebonne, QC J6X 4P1
Tél: 450-471-5877; *Téléc:* 450-471-7511
Nombre de lits: 140 lits
Gerald Asselin, Directeur général

Thetford Mines: **Résidence La Rosée d'Or**
736, boul Ouellet ouest, Thetford Mines, QC G6G 4X5
Tél: 418-335-7681; *Téléc:* 418-338-3774
Nombre de lits: 9 lits
Laurent Chartier

Trois-Rivières: **Résidence Cooke**
CSSS de Trois-Rivières
Affiliée à: Agence de santé et des services sociaux de la Mauricie et du Centre-du-Québec
3450, rue Ste-Marguerite, Trois-Rivières, QC G8Z 1X3
Tél: 819-375-7713
www.cssstr.qc.ca
Nombre de lits: 190 lits
Jacques Longval, Directeur général, CSSS de Trois-Rivières

Trois-Rivières: **Résidence Joseph-Denys**
CSSS de Trois-Rivières
Affiliée à: Agence de la santé et des services sociaux de la Mauricie et du Centre-du-Québec
1274, rue Laviolette, Trois-Rivières, QC G9A 1W4
Tél: 819-378-4837; *Téléc:* 819-374-6697
www.cssstr.qc.ca
Nombre de lits: 119 lits
Note: Hébergement permanent et temporaire.
Jacques Longval, Directeur général, CSSS de Trois-Rivières

Trois-Rivières: **Résidence Louis-Denoncourt**
CSSS de Trois-Rivières
Affiliée à: Agence de la santé et des services sociaux de la Mauricie et du Centre-du-Québec
435, rue Saint-Roch, Trois-Rivières, QC G9A 2L9
Tél: 819-376-2566; *Téléc:* 819-376-5620
www.cssstr.qc.ca
Nombre de lits: 75 lits
Note: Hébergement permanent
Jacques Longval, Directeur général, CSSS de Trois-Rivières

Upton: **Domaine du Bel Age**
CP 89, 906, rue Lanoie, Upton, QC J0H 2E0
Tél: 514-549-4405
Nombre de lits: 9 lits
Jacqueline Gosslin, Directrice générale

Vanier: **Résidence Christ-Roi**
Affiliée à: Agence de la santé et des services sociaux de la Capitale-Nationale
300, boul Wilfrid-Hamel, Vanier, QC G1M 2R9
Tél: 418-682-1711; *Téléc:* 418-682-1770
Nombre de lits: 142 lits
Note: Hébergement permanent/soins de longue durée, hôpital de jour, hébergement temporaire, consultations externes
Gaétan Garon, Directeur général
Lucien Jobin, Directeur, Services techniques
Francine Smith, Chef du service d'entretien sanitaire

Varennes: **CHSLD du Littoral**
Ancien nom: Foyer Lajemmerais
60, rue d'Youville, Varennes, QC J3X 1T6
Tél: 450-652-2995; *Téléc:* 450-652-4755
Nombre de lits: 261 lits
Bernard Lamy, Directeur général (par intérim)

Vaudreuil-Dorion: **2863-9839 Québec inc.**
Affiliée à: Agence de la santé et des services sociaux de la Montérégie
170, rue Boileau, Vaudreuil-Dorion, QC J7V 8A3
Tél: 450-424-6458
Nombre de lits: 51 lits
Denis Charland, Directeur général

Vaudreuil-Dorion: **Le Regroupement des CHSLD des Trois Rives**
Affiliée à: Agence de la santé et des services sociaux de la Montérégie
408, av St-Charles, Vaudreuil-Dorion, QC J7V 7M9
Tél: 450-453-5860; *Téléc:* 450-455-1998
Nombre de lits: 341 lits
Lise Bélisle, Directeur général

Verdun: **Centre d'accueil Real Morel**
Affiliée à: Agence de la santé et des services sociaux de Montréal
3500, rue Wellington, Verdun, QC H4G 1T3
Tél: 514-761-5874; *Téléc:* 514-761-7264
Nombre de lits: 148 lits

Victoriaville: **Centre d'hébergement du Chêne**
CSSS d'Arthabaska-et-de-l'Érable
Affiliée à: Agence de la santé et des services sociaux de la Mauricie et du Centre-du-Québec
61, rue de l'Ermitage, Victoriaville, QC G6P 6X4
Tél: 819-758-7511; *Téléc:* 819-758-2398
www.csssae.qc.ca
Nombre de lits: 122 lits
Note: Les autres centres d'hébergement: Quatre-Vents, Saint-Eusèbe, Sacré-Coeur, Étoiles-d'Or, et Roseau.
Marcel Dubois, Président, Conseil d'administration, CSSS d'Arthabaska-et-de-l

Waterloo: **Centre de Waterloo**
Affiliée à: Agence de la santé et des services sociaux de la Montérégie
5300, av Courville, Waterloo, QC J0E 2N0
Tél: 450-539-5512; *Téléc:* 450-375-5655
Nombre de lits: 41 lits longue durée

Waterloo: **Centre gériatrique Courville**
Affiliée à: Agence de la santé et des services sociaux de la Montérégie
CP 580, 5305, av Courville, Waterloo, QC J0E 2N0
Tél: 450-539-1821; *Téléc:* 450-539-1937
ecourville@belage.qc.ca
Nombre de lits: 52 lits
Evelyn Courville, Directrice générale

Waterville: **Foyer de Waterville**
265, rue Compton est, Waterville, QC J0B 3H0
Tél: 819-837-2454; *Téléc:* 819-837-2916
Nombre de lits: 20 lits
Jeannette Delage, Directrice générale

Weedon: **Site Foyer de Weedon**
Affiliée à: Agence de la santé et des services sociaux de l'Estrie
245, rue Saint-Janvier, Weedon, QC J0B 3J0
Tél: 819-877-2500; *Téléc:* 819-877-3089
Nombre de lits: 53 lits
Colette Maynard, Directrice, Soins Infirmiers

Westmount: **Centre d'accueil St-Margaret**
St. Margaret's Home
50, av Hillside, Westmount, QC H3Z 1V9
Tél: 514-932-3630; *Téléc:* 514-932-4379
Nombre de lits: 96 lits
Carole McDonough, Directeur général

Westmount: **Chateau Westmount inc.**
Affiliée à: Agence de la santé et des services sociaux de Montréal
4860, boul de Maisonneuve ouest, Westmount, QC H3Z 3G2
Tél: 514-369-3000; *Téléc:* 514-369-0014
info@chateauwestmount.ca
Nombre de lits: 112 lits
Ginette Villeneuve, Directrice générale

Wotton: **Le Centre d'accueil de Wotton**
Affiliée à: Agence de la santé et des services sociaux de l'Estrie
CP 270, 666, rue Saint-Jean, Wotton, QC J0A 1N0
Tél: 819-828-2251; *Téléc:* 819-828-3555
Nombre de lits: 23 lits
Mario Morand, Directeur général

Centres d'accueil et d'hébergement

La Doré: **Ressource intermédiaire de La Doré**
CSSS Domaine-du-Roy
Également connu sous le nom de: Résidence La Doré
CP 190, 4921, rue des Peupliers, La Doré, QC G0W 2J0
Tél: 418-256-3851; *Téléc:* 418-256-3608
hdr@ssss.gouv.qc.ca
www.cmdp-roberval.com
Nombre de lits: 21 lits
Guy Dufour, Directeur général

Laval: **Centre d'hébergement de Sainte-Dorothée**
CSSS de Laval
350, boul Samson ouest, Laval, QC H7X 1J4
Tél: 514-689-0933; *Téléc:* 514-689-3147
Nombre de lits: 277 lits
Note: Les autres centres d'hébergement: Fernand-Larocque, Idola-Saint-Jean, La Pinière, et Rose-de-Lima.
Luc Lepage, Directeur général, CSSS de Laval

Baie-d'Urfé: **Maxwell Residence**
678, rue Surrey, Baie-d'Urfé, QC H9X 3S1
Tel: 514-457-3111; *Fax:* 514-457-7909
www.maxwellresidence.com
Note: Specialties: Fitness center & health programs
R.W. Maxwell, Administrator

Laval: Les Loggias et Villa Val des Arbres Chartwell Seniors Housing REIT
Affiliated with: Agence de la santé et de services sociaux de Laval
3245, boul St-Martin est, Laval, QC H7E 4T6
Tel: 450-661-0911; *Fax:* 450-661-9820
info@villavaldesarbres.com
www.chartwellreit.ca; www.villavaldesarbres.com
Note: Centre privé non-conventionné; 163 unités, 48 appartements, 115 chambres.
Denis Lagueux, Président, Chartwell-Québec

Hôpitaux psychiatriques et assistance communautaire

Beauport: Centre hospitalier Robert Giffard
Affiliée à: Agence de la santé et des services sociaux de la Capitale-Nationale
2601, rue de la Canardière, Beauport, QC G1J 2G3
Tél: 418-663-5321; *Téléc:* 418-663-9774
www.rgiffard.qc.ca
Nombre de lits: 503 lits
Michel Gervais, Directeur général

Fatima: Centre de réadaptation en déficience intellectuelle-TED
Affiliée à: Agence de la santé et des services sociaux de la Gaspésie-Iles-de-la-Madeleine
695, ch des Caps, Fatima, QC G4T 2S9
Tél: 418-986-3590; *Téléc:* 418-986-5778
www.agencesssgim.ca; www.csssdesiles.qc.ca

Gatineau: Centre hospitalier Pierre-Janet
Affiliée à: Agence de la santé et de services sociaux de l'Outaouais
20, rue Pharand, Gatineau, QC J9A 1K7
Tél: 819-771-7761; *Téléc:* 819-771-2908
www.pierre-janet.qc.ca/bienvenue.htm
Nombre de lits: 87 lits
Pierre Gagnon, Directeur général
Michel Thivierge, Chef, Services techniques
819/776-8096

Malartic: Hôpital psychiatrique de Malartic CSSS de la Vallée-de-l'Or
Affiliée à: Agence de la santé et des services sociaux de l'Abitibi-Témiscamingue
CP 800, 1141, rue Royale, Malartic, QC J0Y 1Z0
Tél: 819-757-4342; *Téléc:* 819-757-4330
www.sante-abitibi-temiscamingue-gouv.qc.ca; www.csssvo.qc.ca
Nombre de lits: 34 lits
Note: Services de santé mentale et psychiatrie; soins aigus; soins de longue durée.
Jérôme Lamont, Directeur général, CSSS de la Vallée-de-l'Or
Alain Beaucage, Directeur, Programme santé mentale/psychiatrie

Montréal: Hôpital Louis-H. Lafontaine
Affiliée à: Agence de la santé et des services sociaux de Montréal
7401, rue Hochelaga, Montréal, QC H1N 3M5
Tél: 514-251-4000; *Téléc:* 514-251-0856
www.hlhl.qc.ca
Nombre de lits: 606 lits
André Lemieux, Directeur général

Montréal: Hôpital Rivière-des-Prairies
Affiliée à: Agence de la santé et des services sociaux de Montréal
7070, boul Perras, Montréal, QC H1E 1A4
Tél: 514-323-7260; *Téléc:* 514-323-8622
www.hrdp.qc.ca
Nombre de lits: 125 lits
Michel Lapointe, Directeur général

Québec: Centre de réadaptation en déficience intellectuelle de Québec
Affiliée à: Agence de la santé et des services sociaux de la Capitale-Nationale
110, rue de Courcelette, Québec, QC G1M 2S8
Tél: 418-529-9141; *Téléc:* 418-529-7318
Renaud Turmel, Directeur général (intérim)

Saint-Wenceslas: Centre l'Aubier inc.
CP 27, 1170, rue Sainte-Thérèse, Saint-Wenceslas, QC G0Z 1J0
Tél: 819-224-7669
Nombre de lits: 50 lits
Francine P. Lampron, Directrice générale

Saskatchewan

Government Departments in Charge

SASKATCHEWAN: Saskatchewan Health
T.C. Douglas Building, 3475 Albert St., Regina, SK S4S 6X6
Tel: 306-787-0146; *Fax:* 306-787-8310
info@health.gov.sk.ca
www.health.gov.sk.ca
Note: Establishes policy & standards, provides funding, supports regional health authorities, & ensures the provision of essential health services. Branches: acute & emergency services, communications, community care branch, Deputy Minister's Office, drug plan & extended benefits, financial services, Health Information Solutions Centre, health registration & vital statistics, human resources, medical services, policy & planning branch, population health, primary health services, regional accountability, regional policy, Saskatchewan Disease Control Laboratory, & workforce planning
Ernie Craig, Senior Information Consultant

Regional Health Authorities

Black Lake: Athabasca Health Authority
PO Box 124, Black Lake, SK S0J 0H0
Tel: 306-439-2200; *Fax:* 306-439-2211
vrobillard@athabascahealth.ca
www.athabascahealth.ca
Note: Provides health care services to the First Nations communities of Black Lake, & Fond du Lac; Stony Rapids; Uranium City; & Camsell Portage.
Georgina Macdonald, CEO

Buffalo Narrows: Keewatin Yatthé Regional Health Authority
Metis Society Bldg., PO Box 40, Pederson Ave., Buffalo Narrows, SK S0M 0J0
Tel: 306-235-2220; *Fax:* 306-235-2229
Toll-Free: 866-274-8506
richard.petit@kyrha.sk.ca
www.kyrha.sk.ca
Number of Beds: 58 beds
Carol Gillis, CEO

La Ronge: Mamawetan Churchill River Health Region
PO Box 6000, La Ronge, SK S0J 1L0
Tel: 306-425-2422; *Fax:* 306-425-5513
information@mcrrha.sk.ca
www.mcrrha.sk.ca
Note: Regional health authority serving over 22,000 people
Kathy Chisholm, CEO

Moose Jaw: Five Hills Health Region
455 Fairford St. East, Moose Jaw, SK S6H 1H3
Tel: 306-694-0296; *Fax:* 306-694-0282
Toll-Free: 1-888-425-1111
inquiries@fhhr.ca
www.fhhr.ca
Note: Facilities: In-patient acute care hospitals in Assiniboia, Central Butte, Gravelbourg, & Moose Jaw; Health & wellness centres in Craik, Kincaid, Lafleche, Rockglen, Mossbank, & Willow Bunch. Number of Employees: 1,700. Population Served: 55,246. Area Served: South-central Saskatchewan
Cheryl Craig, Chief Executive Officer
Velma Geddes, Chair
Craig Beesley, Executive Director, Strategy & Communications
306-694-0300

North Battleford: Prairie North Health Region
1092 - 107 St., North Battleford, SK S9A 1Z1
Tel: 306-446-6606; *Fax:* 306-446-4114
cora.r@pnrha.ca
www.pnrha.ca
David Fan, CEO

Prince Albert: Prince Albert Parkland Health Region
PO Box 5700, 2345 - 10 Ave. West, Prince Albert, SK S6V 7V6
Tel: 306-765-6100; *Fax:* 306-763-6096
Toll-Free: 800-922-1834
kholmgren@paphr.sk.ca
www.paphr.sk.ca
Cecile Hunt, CEO

Regina: Regina Qu'Appelle Health Region
2180 - 23 Ave., Regina, SK S4S 0A5
Tel: 306-766-5279; *Fax:* 306-766-5222
Toll-Free: 888-354-8111
publicaffairs@rqhealth.ca
www.rqhealth.ca
Number of Beds: 1,504 beds
Note: Offers health services and programs to over 245,000 people across 120 communities
Dwight Nelson, President; CEO

Rosetown: Heartland Regional Health Authority
PO Box 2110, 100 Hwy. #4 South, Rosetown, SK S0L 2V0
Tel: 306-882-4111; *Fax:* 306-882-1389
heartland@hrha.sk.ca
www.hrha.sk.ca
Number of Beds: 499 long term care beds; 67 acute care; 50 other
Note: Facilities in 16 communities, including a district hospital in Kindersley. Services include primary & acute health care, emergency services, telehealth, public health, dental health, counselling, addictions services, occupation therapy, speech & language therapy, nutrition.
Ken Wersch, CEO/President

Saskatoon: Saskatoon Regional Health Authority
Saskatoon Square, 410 - 22nd St. East, 3rd Fl., Saskatoon, SK S7K 5T6
Tel: 306-655-3300; *Fax:* 306-655-3394
general.inquiries@saskatoonhealthregion.ca
www.saskatoonhealthregion.ca
Number of Beds: 830 beds
Note: Provides health services to over 290,000 people across over 100 communitures
Maura Davies, CEO/President

Swift Current: Cypress Health Region
429 - 4th Ave. NE, Swift Current, SK S9H 2J9
Tel: 306-778-5100; *Fax:* 306-773-9513
Toll-Free: 1-888-461-7443
info@cypressrha.ca
www.cypresshealth.ca
Note: Facilities: 20 hospitals, long term care facilities, & health centres. Number of Employees: 1,650. Population Served: 44,000. Area Served: Southwest Saskatchewan
Tyler Bragg, Chair
Dr. Ivo Radevski, Senior Medical Officer
Beth Adashynski, Executive Director, Quality & Privacy
Larry Allsen, Executive Director, Finance
Bryce Martin, Executive Director, Communications
Brenda Schwan, Executive Director, Human Resources
Beth Vachon, Executive Director, Community Health Services
Kim Kruse, Director, Executive & Board Support

Tisdale: Kelsey Trail Regional Health Authority
PO Box 1780, 901 - 108 Ave. Wet, Tisdale, SK S0E 1T0
Tel: 306-873-3898; *Fax:* 306-873-3224
ddobson@kthr@shin.sk.ca
www.kelseytrailhealth.ca
Number of Beds: 61 beds
Joe Kirwan, Interim President; CEO

Weyburn: Sun Country Health Region
PO Box 2003, Weyburn, SK S4H 2Z9
Tel: 306-842-8718; *Fax:* 306-842-8738
info@schr.sk.ca
www.suncountry.sk.ca
Number of Beds: 461 beds
Calvin Tant, CEO

Yorkton: Sunrise Regional Health Authority
270 Bradbrooke Dr., Yorkton, SK S3N 2K6
Tel: 306-786-0103; *Fax:* 306-786-0122
www.sunrisehealthregion.sk.ca
Number of Beds: 561 beds
Joe Kirwan, CEO

Hospitals

Hospitals - General

Arcola: Arcola Health Centre
Affiliated with: Sun Country Regional Health Authority
PO Box 419, 607 Prairie Ave., Arcola, SK S0C 0G0
Tel: 306-455-2771; *Fax:* 306-455-2397
www.suncountry.sk.ca
Note: Hospital Specialties: Emergency; Inpatient services

***Assiniboia:* Assiniboia Union Hospital**
Affiliated with: Five Hills Regional Health Authority
501 - 6 Ave., Assiniboia, SK S0H 0B0
Tel: 306-642-3351
www.fhhr.ca
Number of Beds: 12 acute care beds; 4 respite / palliative care beds
Note: Hospital specialties: Emergency service; Acute care; Laboratory service; Respite care; Palliative care

***Balcarres:* Balcarres Integrated Care Centre (BICC)**
Affiliated with: Regina Qu'Appelle Health Region
PO Box 340, 100 South Elgin St., Balcarres, SK S0G 0C0
Tel: 306-334-2634; *Fax:* 306-334-2674
www.rqhealth.ca
Year Founded: 1999
Number of Beds: 9 acute care beds; 42 long term beds; 2 respite beds
Note: Hospital Specialties: Emergency services; Acute care; Physiotherapy; Diabetes education; Mental health & drug & alcohol counselling; Respite services; Day care services; Home care nursing; Long term care Number of Employees: 90
Lorraine Mazerall, Facility Manager
lorraine.mazerall@rqhealth.ca
Elaine Stefanick, Coordinator, Care

***Big River:* Big River Health Centre**
Affiliated with: Prince Albert Parkland Regional Health Authority
PO Box 100, 220 - 1st Ave. North, Big River, SK S0J 0E0
Tel: 306-469-2220
www.paphr.sk.ca
Number of Beds: 9 acute care beds; 28 long term care beds; 2 respite care beds; 1 palliative care bed
Note: Specialties: Emergency services; Acute care; Laboratory services; Public health services; Physiotherapy; Occupational therapy; Long term care; Home care; Respite care; Palliative care

***Biggar:* Biggar Union Hospital**
Affiliated with: Heartland Regional Health Authority
PO Box 130, 501 - 1 Ave. West, Biggar, SK S0K 0M0
Tel: 306-948-3323; *Fax:* 306-948-2011
www.hrha.sk.ca
Number of Beds: 13 acute care beds, 2 other
Note: Acute care.
Marian Fritz, Facility Manager

***Broadview:* Broadview Hospital**
Affiliated with: Regina Qu'Appelle Health Region
PO Box 100, 901 Nina St., Broadview, SK S0G 0K0
Tel: 306-696-2441; *Fax:* 306-696-2611
www.rqhealth.ca
Number of Beds: 16 acute care beds
Note: Hospital Specialties: Emergency services; Diagnostic services; Ambulatory care; Native liaison work; Respite care; Palliative care
Jacqui Fawcett-Kennett, Manager
jacqui.fawcett-kennett@rqhealth.ca

***Canora:* Canora Hospital**
Affiliated with: Sunrise Regional Health Authority
PO Box 749, 1219 Main St., Canora, SK S0A 0L0
Tel: 306-563-5621; *Fax:* 306-563-5571
www.sunrisehealthregion.sk.ca
Year Founded: 1968
Number of Beds: 16 acute care beds; 10 long term care beds; 2 respite beds
Note: Hospital Specialties: Emergency services; Laboratory services; Radiology; Acute care; Occupational therapy; Respite care; Long term care
Karen Kraynick, Administrator

***Central Butte:* Central Butte Regency Hospital**
Affiliated with: Five Hills Regional Health Authority
PO Box 40, Central Butte, SK S0H 0T0
Tel: 306-796-2190
inquiries@fhhr.ca
www.fhhr.ca
Number of Beds: 5 acute care beds; 22 residents at special care home
Note: Hospital Specialties: Acute care; Special care home

***Davidson:* Davidson & District Health Centre**
Affiliated with: Heartland Regional Health Authority
PO Box 758, 900 Government Rd., Davidson, SK S0G 1A0
Tel: 306-567-2801; *Fax:* 306-567-2073
www.hrha.sk.ca;
www.townofdavidson.com/services/healthservices.php
Number of Beds: 30 long term care beds, 2 acute care, 6 other
Note: Acute care, long term care.
Cathy Hinther, Care Team Manager

***Esterhazy:* St. Anthony's Hospital**
Affiliated with: Sunrise Regional Health Authority
PO Box 280, 216 Ancona St., Esterhazy, SK S0A 0X0
Tel: 306-745-3973; *Fax:* 306-745-3245
www.sunrisehealthregion.sk.ca/default.aspx?page=15
Year Founded: 1940
Number of Beds: 22 acute care beds
Note: Emergency & outpatient services, visiting primary care services & dietition, x-ray
Mr. Joe Kirwan, CEO, SRHA
306-786-0103, Fax: 306-786-0122
Ms. Sharon Tropin, Director, Communication, SRHA
306- 786-0144
Ms. Carol Unchulenko, Facility Administrator
carol.unchulenko@shr.sk.ca

***Estevan:* St. Joseph's Hospital**
Affiliated with: Sun Country Regional Health Authority
PO Box 5000, 1174 Nicholson Rd., Estevan, SK S4A 2V6
Tel: 306-637-2400; *Fax:* 306-637-2490
Number of Beds: 93 beds
Darwin Giem, Executive Director
Emile Wilvers, Maintenance Manager
306/634-0418

***Fort Qu'Appelle:* All Nations Healing Hospital (ANHH)**
Affiliated with: Regina Qu'Appelle Health Region
PO Box 300, 450 - 8th St., Fort Qu'Appelle, SK S0G 1S0
Tel: 306-332-5611; *Fax:* 306-332-5033
gboehme@fhqtc.com (Director of ANHH & Health Services)
www.fortquappelle.com/anhh.html
Number of Beds: 13 acute care beds + 1 palliative care bed
Note: Hospital Specialties: First Nations health services; Acute care; Emergency services; Women's health (306-332-2673); Mental health; Diabetes education; Nutrition education; Number of Employees: 100
Lorna Breitkreuz, Director, Client Services
306-332-2440, lbreitkreuz@fhqtc.com

***Gravelbourg:* St. Joseph's Hospital/Foyer d'Youville**
Affiliated with: Five Hills Regional Health Authority
PO Box 50, 216 Bettez St., Gravelbourg, SK S0H 1X0
Tel: 306-648-3185; *Fax:* 306-648-3440
thinks_stjoes@sasktel.net
www.stjosephshospital-gravelbourg.com
Number of Beds: 9 hospital beds, 50 nursing home beds

***Hafford:* Hafford Hospital & Special Care Centre**
Affiliated with: Prince Albert Parkland Regional Health Authority
PO Box 130, 213 South Ave. East, Hafford, SK S0J 1A0
Tel: 306-549-4266; *Fax:* 306-549-4660
Number of Beds: 18 beds
Linda E. Fendelet, Director of Care

***Herbert:* Herbert Morse Hospital**
Affiliated with: Cypress Regional Health Authority
PO Box 220, 303 Brownlee St., Herbert, SK S0H 2A0
Tel: 306-784-2202; *Fax:* 306-784-3452

***Hudson Bay:* Hudson Bay Health Care Facility**
Affiliated with: Kelsey Trail Regional Health Authority
PO Box 940, 614 Prince St., Hudson Bay, SK S0E 0Y0
Tel: 306-865-2219; *Fax:* 306-865-2429
Number of Beds: 15 beds
Note: integrated facility with acute, long-term care & respite & daycare
Sharon Wood, Director, Health Services

***Humboldt:* Humboldt District Hospital**
Affiliated with: Saskatoon Regional Health Authority
Former Name: St. Elizabeth's Hospital
PO Box 10, 1210 - 9 St. North, Humboldt, SK S0K 2A0
Tel: 306-682-2603; *Fax:* 306-682-4046
www.saskatoonhealthregion.ca/your_health/ch_humbolt.htm
Number of Beds: 42 beds
Rick Schindel, Executive Director

***Ile-a-la-Crosse:* St. Joseph's Hospital**
Affiliated with: Keewatin Yatthé Regional Health Authority
PO Bag 500, Ile-a-la-Crosse, SK S0M 1C0
Tel: 306-833-2016; *Fax:* 306-833-2556
Number of Beds: 31 beds, including 12 longterm care beds
Lorraine Roy, Administrator

***Indian Head:* Indian Head Union Hospital**
Affiliated with: Regina Qu'Appelle Health Region
PO Box 340, 300 Hospital St., Indian Head, SK S0G 2K0
Tel: 306-695-2272; *Fax:* 306-695-2525
Number of Beds: 15 beds
Peter Fell, Supervisor, Plant Maintenance
Karen Earnshaw, Manager

***Kamsack:* Kamsack Hospital/Kamsack Nursing Home**
Affiliated with: Sunrise Regional Health Authority
PO Box 429, 341 Stewart St., Kamsack, SK S0A 1S0
Tel: 306-542-2635; *Fax:* 306-542-4360
Number of Beds: 20 acute care, 63 long-term care, 2 respite beds
Chris Meyer, Hospital Administrator

***Kelvington:* Kelvington Hospital**
Affiliated with: Kelsey Trail Regional Health Authority
PO Box 70, 512 - 1 Ave. South, Kelvington, SK S0A 1W0
Tel: 306-327-4711; *Fax:* 306-327-5115
Number of Beds: 18 beds
Denise Geck, Director, Health Services

***Kerrobert:* Kerrobert Integrated Health Care Facility**
Affiliated with: Heartland Health Region
PO Box 320, 635 Alberta Ave., Kerrobert, SK S0L 1R0
Tel: 306-834-2646; *Fax:* 306-834-1007
www.hrha.sk.ca
Number of Beds: 26 long term care beds, 24 acute/program/long term care
Note: Long term care facility + health centre.
Fenton Yeo, Facility Manager
B. Roszell, Supervisor, Physical Plant

***Kindersley:* Kindersley Integrated Health Care Facility**
Affiliated with: Heartland Regional Health Authority
1003 - 1 St. West, Kindersley, SK S0L 1S2
Tel: 306-463-2611; *Fax:* 306-463-4550
www.hrha.sk.ca
Number of Beds: 21 acute care beds, 5 other; 80 long term care beds
Note: Long term care; acute care.
Wanda Desrosiers, Facility Manager
Harvey Penner, Chief Engineer

***Kipling:* Kipling Memorial Health Centre**
Affiliated with: Sun Country Health Region
PO Box 420, 803 - 1 St., Kipling, SK S0G 2S0
Tel: 306-736-2552; *Fax:* 306-736-8407
Number of Beds: 14 beds
Colleen Easton, Manager, Health Services
A. Gall, Supervisor, Physical Plant

***La Loche:* La Loche Health Centre**
Affiliated with: Keewatin Yatthé Regional Health Authority
Bag 1, La Loche, SK S0M 1G0
Tel: 306-822-6333; *Fax:* 306-822-2112
Toll-Free: 888-688-7072
Number of Beds: 27 beds
Mary Bradstreet-Metali, Director, Primary Care

***Lanigan:* Lanigan Hospital**
Affiliated with: Saskatoon Regional Health Authority
PO Box 609, 306 Downing Dr., Lanigan, SK S0K 2M0
Tel: 306-365-1400; *Fax:* 306-365-3354
www.saskatoonhealthregion.ca/your_health/ch_lanigan.htm
Number of Beds: 10 beds
Janet Lees, Manager

***Leader:* Leader Hospital**
Affiliated with: Cypress Regional Health Authority
423 Main St. East, Leader, SK S0N 1H0
Tel: 306-628-3845; *Fax:* 306-628-3320
www.cypresshealth.ca/leader.htm
Number of Beds: 24

***Lestock:* St. Joseph's Integrated Care Centre**
Affiliated with: Regina Qu'Appelle Health Region
PO Box 280, 505 Westmoor St., Lestock, SK S0A 2G0
Tel: 306-274-2215; *Fax:* 306-274-2045
Number of Beds: 16 beds
F. Ricci, Manager, Plant Maintenance
Kate Beattie, Manager

***Lloydminster:* Lloydminster Hospital**
Affiliated with: Prairie North Health Region
3820 - 43 Ave., Lloydminster, SK S9V 1Y5
Tel: 306-820-6000; *Fax:* 306-825-6516

Number of Beds: 58 acute care beds
Note: Hospital Specialties: Cancer treatment & Care-Alberta Community Cancer Centres; Hemodialysis - Northern Alberta Renal Program; Surgical services & recovery; Obstetrics; Paediatrics; Special care unit. Number of Employees: 664
Lois Sonnega, Director, Acute Care

Loon Lake: **Loon Lake Hospital & Special Care Home**
Affiliated with: Prairie North Health Region
PO Box 69, 510 - 2nd Ave., Loon Lake, SK S0M 1L0
Tel: 306-837-2114; *Fax:* 306-837-2268

Neal Sylvestre, Director, Rural Health Facilities

Maidstone: **Maidstone Health Complex**
Affiliated with: Prairie North Health Region
PO Box 160, 214 - 5th Ave. East, Maidstone, SK S0M 1M0
Tel: 306-893-2622; *Fax:* 306-893-2922
Number of Beds: 11 acute beds + 24 long-term care beds + 2 respite beds
Note: Specialties: Community health services, including home care & counselling; Acute care; Long-term care wing; Respite care; Palliative care
Emily Hardy, Facility Manager

Maple Creek: **Maple Creek Hospital**
Affiliated with: Cypress Regional Health Authority
PO Box 1330, Hwy. 21 South, Maple Creek, SK S0N 1N0
Tel: 306-662-2611; *Fax:* 306-662-3210
www.cypresshealth.ca/maplecreek.htm
Number of Beds: 20

Meadow Lake: **Northwest Health Facility**
Affiliated with: Prairie North Health Region
Also Known As: Meadow Lake Hospital
#2, 711 Centre St., Meadow Lake, SK S9X 1E6
Tel: 306-236-1500; *Fax:* 306-236-3244
Note: Specialty: Acute care; Diagnostic imaging
Debbie Carey, Director, Acute Care Services

Melfort: **Melfort Hospital**
Affiliated with: Kelsey Trail Regional Health Authority
PO Box 1480, 510 Broadway Ave., Melfort, SK S0E 1A0
Tel: 306-752-8700; *Fax:* 306-752-8711
www.kelseytrailhealth.ca
Note: Specialties: Acute care; General Surgery; Radiology services; Chemotherapy; Mental health & addiction services; Diabetes & Heart Health Centre; Palliative care
Judy Blair, Director, Health Services

Melville: **St. Peter's Hospital**
Affiliated with: Sunrise Regional Health Authority
PO Box 1810, 200 Heritage Dr., Melville, SK S0A 2P0
Tel: 306-728-5407; *Fax:* 306-728-4870
www.sunrisehealthregion.sk.ca/default.aspx?page=21
Year Founded: 1942
Number of Beds: 30 acute care beds
Note: Emergency services, obstetrics, general surgery, outpatient services, physiotherapy, social work, Lifeline Response Centre, chemotherapy outreach program, pharmacy
Mr. Joe Kirwan, CEO, SRHA
306-786-0103, Fax: 306-786-0122
Ms. Sharon Tropin, Director, Communications, SRHA
306- 786-0144
Ms. Kim Bucsis, Site Manager
Fax: 306-728-1859, kim.bucsis@shr.sk.ca

Moose Jaw: **Moose Jaw Union Hospital**
Affiliated with: Five Hills Regional Health Authority
455 Fairford St. East, Moose Jaw, SK S6H 1H3
Tel: 306-694-0200; *Fax:* 306-694-5596
Number of Beds: 120 beds
Dan Florizone, CEO
John Borody, President; CEO

Moosomin: **Southeast Integrated Care Centre - Moosomin**
Affiliated with: Regina Qu'Appelle Health Region
Former Name: Moosomin Union Hospital
PO Box 1, 320 Gertie St., Moosomin, SK S0G 3N0
Tel: 306-435-3303; *Fax:* 306-435-3211
Number of Beds: 27 in-patient; 58 long-term
Dan Ireland, Supervisor, Physical Plant
Sharon Ann Wood, Manager

Nipawin: **Nipawin Hospital**
Affiliated with: Kelsey Trail Regional Health Authority
PO Box 389, 800 - 6 St. East, Nipawin, SK S0E 1E0
Tel: 306-862-4643; *Fax:* 306-862-9310
Number of Beds: 36 beds
Marg Currie, Director, Health Services

North Battleford: **Battlefords Union Hospital**
Affiliated with: Prairie North Health Region
1092 - 107 St., North Battleford, SK S9A 1Z1
Tel: 306-446-6600; *Fax:* 306-446-6561
www.pnrha.ca
Number of Beds: 200 beds
Note: Hospital specialties: Emergency services; Acute care; Day patient clinic
Shelly Horsman, Nurse Manager
Shelly.Horsman@pnrha.ca
Sharon Jaindl, Health Information Services
Sharon.Jaindl@pnrha.ca
Pam Nyholt, Supervisor, Laboratory
Pam.Nyholt@pnrha.ca

Outlook: **Outlook & District Health Centre**
Affiliated with: Heartland Regional Health Authority
PO Box 309, 609 Pangman St., Outlook, SK S0L 2N0
Tel: 306-867-8676; *Fax:* 306-867-9449
Year Founded: 2008
Number of Beds: 11 acute care beds + 45 continuing care beds
Note: Specialties: Acute care; Diagnostic services; Therapies; Community health; Public health inspecitions; Mental health services; Home care; Long-term care; Respite care; Adult day care; Palliative care
Thelma McPherson, Facility Manager

Porcupine Plain: **Porcupine Carragana Hospital**
Affiliated with: Kelsey Trail Regional Health Authority
PO Box 70, Windsor Ave., Porcupine Plain, SK S0E 1H0
Tel: 306-278-2211; *Fax:* 306-278-3088
Number of Beds: 13 beds
Christine Pohl, Director, Heatlh Services
Keith Butler, Supervisor, Physical Plant

Preeceville: **Preeceville & District Integrated Health Centre**
Affiliated with: Sunrise Regional Health Authority
Former Name: Preeceville Hospital; Preeceville & District Integ
PO Box 469, 712 - 7 St. NE, Preeceville, SK S0A 3B0
Tel: 306-547-2102; *Fax:* 306-547-2223
Number of Beds: 10 acute care, 38 long-term care beds
Note: Doctors' medical clinic, acute & long-term care
G. Jolson, Director, Physical Plant
Joanne Bodnar, Nurse Administrator

Prince Albert: **Victoria Hospital**
Affiliated with: Prince Albert Parkland Regional Health Authority
1200 - 24 St. West, Prince Albert, SK S6V 5T4
Tel: 306-764-1551; *Fax:* 306-763-5322
Number of Beds: 147 beds
Tom Graham, Director, Housekeeping
John Piggott, Director, Operations

Redvers: **Redvers Health Centre**
Affiliated with: Sun Country Regional Health Authority
PO Box 30, 18 Eichhorst St., Redvers, SK S0C 2H0
Tel: 306-452-3553; *Fax:* 306-452-3556
Number of Beds: 12 beds
Myrna Petersen, Manager, Health Services
Joe Chicione, Maintenance

Regina: **Pasqua Hospital**
Affiliated with: Regina Qu'Appelle Health Region
4101 Dewdney Ave., Regina, SK S4T 1A5
Tel: 306-766-2222; *Fax:* 306-766-2745
Number of Beds: 179 beds
Dwight Nelson, President; CEO
Darrell Tunstead, Director, Property Management Services
306/766-2314

Regina: **Regina General Hospital**
Affiliated with: Regina Qu'Appelle Health Region
1440 - 14 Ave., Regina, SK S4P 0W5
Tel: 306-766-4444; *Fax:* 306-766-4723
Number of Beds: 404 beds
Note: Offers full-range acute care services; home to the Wasakaw Pisim Native Health Centre, Sleep Disorders Centre, and 50-bed mental health facility
Dwight Nelson, President; CEO
Darrell Tunstead, Director, Property Management Services
306/766-2314,

Rosetown: **Rosetown & District Health Centre**
Affiliated with: Heartland Health Region
PO Box 850, Hwy. 4 North, Rosetown, SK S0L 2V0
Tel: 306-882-2672; *Fax:* 306-882-3335
Year Founded: 1964
Number of Beds: 22 beds
Gail Adamowski, Facility Manager

Rosthern: **Rosthern Hospital**
Affiliated with: Saskatoon Regional Health Authority
PO Box 309, 2016 - 2 St., Rosthern, SK S0K 3R0
Tel: 306-232-4811; *Fax:* 306-232-4887
Year Founded: 1950
Number of Beds: 30 beds
Note: Acute care facility with six physicians on-staff, plus 60 employees
Henry Zacharias, Supervisor
Robert Hogel, Administrator

Saskatoon: **Royal University Hospital**
Affiliated with: Saskatoon Regional Health Authority
103 Hospital Dr., Saskatoon, SK S7N 0W8
Tel: 306-655-1000; *Fax:* 306-655-1037
Year Founded: 1955
Number of Beds: 377 beds
Jim Fergusson, President
Dr. Clarence Clotter, MHO; General Manager, Public Health Services
306/655-4338, Fax: 306/655-4414

Saskatoon: **St. Paul's Hospital**
Affiliated with: Saskatoon Regional Health Authority
1702 - 20 St. West, Saskatoon, SK S7M 0Z9
Tel: 306-655-5800; *Fax:* 306-655-5555
www.stpaulshospital.org
Number of Beds: 213 beds
Brenda FizGerald, CEO
Jerri Taman, Manager, Housekeeping
David Loveridge, Manager, Powerhouse

Saskatoon: **Saskatoon City Hospital**
Affiliated with: Saskatoon Regional Health Authority
701 Queen St., Saskatoon, SK S7K 0M7
Tel: 306-655-8000; *Fax:* 306-655-8269
Year Founded: 1909
Number of Beds: 280 beds
John Malcolm, President
Richard Rodda, Vice-President, Support Services & Operations

Shellbrook: **Shellbrook & District Hospital**
Affiliated with: Prince Albert Parkland Regional Health Authority
PO Box 70, 211 - 2nd Ave. W, Shellbrook, SK S0J 2E0
Tel: 306-747-2603; *Fax:* 306-747-3004
Number of Beds: 20 beds
Mansford Kennedy, Supervisor, Physical Plant
Clifford E. Skange, Administrator

Spiritwood: **Spiritwood & District Health Complex**
Affiliated with: Prince Albert Parkland Regional Health Authority
PO Box 159, 400 - 1 St. East, Spiritwood, SK S0J 2M0
Tel: 306-883-2133; *Fax:* 306-883-4446
Toll-Free: 800-887-6251
Number of Beds: 36 beds
Ms. Cecile Hunt, CEO, PAPRHA
306-765-6405, Fax: 306-765-6401
Ms. Carroll Joyes, Director, Long Term Care, PAPRHA
Mr. Doug Dahl, Communication Officer, PAPRHA
306-765-6409

Swift Current: **Cypress Regional Hospital**
Affiliated with: Cypress Regional Health Authority
Former Name: Swift Current Regional Hospital
2004 Saskatchewan Dr., Swift Current, SK S9H 5M8
Tel: 306-778-9400; *Fax:* 306-773-9431
http://www.cypressrha.ca/facilities_sc_page.htm
Year Founded: 1951
Note: Services include intensive care, long-term care, palliative care, inpatient and outpatient surgery, renal dialysis, pediatric care, CT scans, obstetrics/gynecology, midwifery and general medical care.
Ms. Beth Vachon, interim CEO, CRHA
Mr. Bryce Martin, Executive Director, Communications, CRHA

Tisdale: **Tisdale Hospital**
Affiliated with: Kelsey Trail Regional Health Authority
PO Box 1630, 2010 - 110th Ave. West, Tisdale, SK S0E 1T0
Tel: 306-873-2621; *Fax:* 306-873-5994
www.kelseytrailhealth.ca
Note: Specialties: Acute care; Diabetes & Heart Health Centre; Hemodialysis satellite unit; Mental health & addiction services; Home care; Palliative care
Anne Haley-Callaghan, Manager, Community Health

***Unity:* Unity & District Health Centre**
Former Name: Unity Hospital
PO Box 741, Hwy. 14 North, Unity, SK S0K 4L0
Tel: 306-228-2666; *Fax:* 306-228-2292
Year Founded: 2001
Note: Specialties: Acute care; Diagnostic services; Maternity services; Community health services; Public health nursing; Mental health services; Counselling; Physiotherapy; Occupational therapy; Home care; Long-term care; Respite care; Palliative care
Kim Halter, Facility Manager
Randy Scherr, Supervisor, Plant Maintenance

***Uranium City:* Uranium City Health Centre**
Affiliated with: Athabasca Health Authority
PO Box 360, Baska Rd., Uranium City, SK S0J 2W0
Tel: 306-498-2412; *Fax:* 306-498-2577

***Wadena:* Wadena Hospital**
Affiliated with: Saskatoon Regional Health Authority
PO Box 10, 533 - 5 St. NE, Wadena, SK S0A 4J0
Tel: 306-338-2515; *Fax:* 306-338-2720
Year Founded: 1989
Number of Beds: 18 beds
Note: Provides acute, respite, and long-term care
Dayle Maryniak, Site Manager

***Wakaw:* Wakaw Hospital**
Affiliated with: Saskatoon Regional Health Authority
PO Box 309, 301 - 1 St. North, Wakaw, SK S0K 4P0
Tel: 306-233-4611; *Fax:* 306-233-5990
Number of Beds: 22 beds
Note: Acute care facility
Pat Taciuk, Manager

***Watrous:* Watrous Hospital**
Affiliated with: Saskatoon Regional Health Authority
PO Box 130, 702 - 4 St. East, Watrous, SK S0K 4T0
Tel: 306-946-1200; *Fax:* 306-946-2369
Number of Beds: 14 beds
J. Reichert, Supervisor, Physical Plant
Wendy Crouch, Manager

***Wawota:* Wawota Memorial Health Centre**
Affiliated with: Sun Country Regional Health Authority
PO Box 60, 609 Choo Foo Cres., Wawota, SK S0G 5A0
Tel: 306-739-2244; *Fax:* 306-739-2479
Number of Beds: 6 beds
Laurel Charles, Manager, Health Services

***Weyburn:* Weyburn General Hospital**
Affiliated with: Sun Country Regional Health Authority
PO Box 2003, 201 - 1 Ave. NE, Weyburn, SK S4H 2Z9
Tel: 306-842-8400; *Fax:* 306-842-0737
Number of Beds: 50 beds
Lee Spencer, CEO
Gene Schmidt, Director, Materials Management
Don Rose, Director, Physical Plant

***Wolseley:* Wolseley Memorial Union Hospital**
Affiliated with: Regina Qu'Appelle Health Region
PO Box 458, 801 Ouimet St., Wolseley, SK S0G 5H0
Tel: 306-698-2213; *Fax:* 306-698-2988
Number of Beds: 15 beds
Jeanette Switzer, Facilities Manager

***Wynyard:* Wynyard Integrated Facility**
Affiliated with: Saskatoon Regional Health Authority
PO Box 670, 400 - 1st St. West, Wynyard, SK S0A 4T0
Tel: 306-554-6126; *Fax:* 306-554-2765
Number of Beds: 58 beds
J. Skilinick, Supervisor, Physical Plant
Lara Prystai, Manager, Client Services

***Yorkton:* Yorkton Regional Health Centre**
Affiliated with: Sunrise Regional Health Authority
270 Bradbrooke Dr., Yorkton, SK S3N 2K6
Tel: 306-782-2401; *Fax:* 306-786-6295
www.shr.sk.ca/default.aspx?page=27
Number of Beds: 87 beds; 6 ICU; 12 Pediatrics; 15 maternity; 21 surgery
Donna Milbrandt, Director, Client Services

Federal Hospitals

***Saskatoon:* Regional Psychiatric Centre (Prairies)**
c/o Correctional Service Canada, 2520 Central Ave., Saskatoon, SK S7K 3X5
Tel: 306-975-5400; *Fax:* 306-975-6024
Number of Beds: 210 beds
Peter Guenter, Executive Director

Community Health Centres

Community Health Care Centres

***Arborfield:* Arborfield & District Health Care Centre**
Affiliated with: Kelsey Trail Regional Health Authority
PO Box 160, 5 Ave., Arborfield, SK S0E 0A0
Tel: 306-769-8757; *Fax:* 306-769-8759
Number of Beds: 36 beds
Sharon Frisky, Director, Health Services

***Beauval:* Beauval Health Centre**
Affiliated with: Keewatin Yatthé Regional Health Authority
PO Box 68, Beauval, SK S0M 0G0
Tel: 306-288-4800; *Fax:* 306-288-2225
Robin Wallace, Nurse, Primary Care

***Beechy:* Beechy Health Centre**
Affiliated with: Heartland Regional Health Authority
PO Box 68, 226 1st Ave. North, Beechy, SK S0L 0C0
Tel: 306-859-2118; *Fax:* 306-859-2206
www.hrha.sk.ca; www.beechysask.ca/healthcare.htm
Note: Primary health care, lab/radiology services, visiting community health services: public health, counselling, occupational health, nutrition.
Donna Sutherland, Primary Health

***Bengough:* Bengough Health Centre**
Affiliated with: Sun Country Health Region
PO Box 399, 400 - 2 St. West, Bengough, SK S0C 0K0
Tel: 306-268-2048; *Fax:* 306-268-4339
bhc@sk.sympatico.ca
Number of Beds: 28 long-term care beds, 1 palliative, 1 respite, 2 observato
Madonna L. Unterresner, Community Health Services Manager

***Birch Hills:* Birch Hills Medical Centre**
Affiliated with: Prince Albert Parkland Regional Health Authority
PO Box 578, 7 Wilson St., Birch Hills, SK S0J 0G0
Tel: 306-749-3331; *Fax:* 306-749-2440
Karl Humeniuk, CEO

***Black Lake:* Athabasca Health Facility**
Affiliated with: Athabasca Health Authority
PO Box 124, Black Lake, SK S0J 0H0
Tel: 306-439-2200; *Fax:* 306-439-2210
Year Founded: 2003
Number of Beds: 14 beds
Note: Located on the Chicken Indian Reserve. Services include acute care, birthing services, long term care, emergency & ambulatory care, public health, mental health, addictions therapy, traditional healing, radiology & lab services.

***Borden:* Borden Community Health Centre**
Affiliated with: Saskatoon Regional Health Authority
PO Box 90, Borden, SK S0K 0N0
Tel: 306-997-2110; *Fax:* 306-997-2114
Monica Kohlhammer, Administrator

***Buffalo Narrows:* Buffalo Narrows Health Centre**
Affiliated with: Keewatin Yatthé Regional Health Authority
PO Box 40, Buffalo Narrows, SK S0M 0J0
Tel: 306-235-5800; *Fax:* 306-235-4500
Kate Cote, Nurse, Primary Care

***Cabri:* Prairie Health Care Centre**
Affiliated with: Cypress Regional Health Authority
PO Box 79, 517 - 1 St. North, Cabri, SK S0N 0J0
Tel: 306-587-2623; *Fax:* 306-587-2751
Number of Beds: 22 beds
Dean Scott, Supervisor, Maintenance

***Carrot River:* Carrot River Health Centre**
Affiliated with: Kelsey Trail Regional Health Authority
PO Box 10, 4101 - 1 Ave. West, Carrot River, SK S0E 0L0
Tel: 306-768-2725; *Fax:* 306-768-3233
Number of Beds: 38 beds
Bessie Lefebvre, Director, Health Services

***Climax:* Border Health Centre**
Affiliated with: Cypress Regional Health Authority
PO Box 60, 301 - 1 St. West, Climax, SK S0N 0N0
Tel: 306-293-2222; *Fax:* 306-293-2860
www.cypresshealth.ca/climax
Number of Beds: 4 beds

***Coronach:* Coronach Health Centre**
Affiliated with: Sun Country Health Region
PO Box 150, 240 South Ave. East, Coronach, SK S0H 0Z0
Tel: 306-267-2022; *Fax:* 306-267-2324
Number of Beds: 15 beds
Judy Ludtke, Manager, Community Health Services
306/267-2123

***Craik:* Craik & District Health Centre**
Affiliated with: Five Hills Regional Health Authority
PO Box 208, 620 Mary St., Craik, SK S0G 0V0
Tel: 306-734-2288; *Fax:* 306-734-2248
Number of Beds: 16 beds

***Creighton:* Creighton Health Centre**
Affiliated with: Mamawetan Churchill River Health Region
PO Box 219, Creighton, SK S0P 0A0
Tel: 306-688-8620; *Fax:* 306-688-8629

***Cudworth:* Cudworth Nursing Home/Health Centre**
Affiliated with: Saskatoon Regional Health Authority
PO Box 190, 607 - 4 Ave., Cudworth, SK S0K 1B0
Tel: 306-256-3423; *Fax:* 306-256-3343
Number of Beds: 32 beds
Rose Normand, Site Manager

***Cumberland House:* Cumberland House Health Centre**
Affiliated with: Kelsey Trail Regional Health Authority
PO Box 8, 2 Ave., Cumberland House, SK S0E 0S0
Tel: 306-888-2244; *Fax:* 306-884-2269

***Cupar:* Cupar Health Centre**
Affiliated with: Regina Qu'Appelle Health Region
PO Box 100, Cupar, SK S0G 0Y0
Tel: 306-723-4300; *Fax:* 306-723-4416
Betty Smith, Acting Manager

***Cut Knife:* Cut Knife Health Complex**
Affiliated with: Prairie North Health Region
PO Box 220, Cut Knife, SK S0M 0N0
Tel: 306-398-4718; *Fax:* 306-398-2206
Number of Beds: 33 beds
Note: attached Special Care Home
Louise Blais, Facility Manager

***Delisle:* Delisle Community Health & Social Centre**
Affiliated with: Saskatoon Regional Health Authority
305 First St. West, Delisle, SK S0L 0P0
Tel: 306-493-2810; *Fax:* 306-493-2812
M. Shostal, CEO

***Dinsmore:* Dinsmore Health Care Centre**
Affiliated with: Heartland Regional Health Authority
PO Box 219, 1 St. East, Dinsmore, SK S0L 0T0
Tel: 306-846-2222; *Fax:* 306-846-2225
Number of Beds: 18 long term care beds, 4 other
Note: Long term care; visiting care services include physiotherapy, occupational therapy, mental health consultation, nutrition, child health.
Anne Rankin, Facility Manager
Jim Cheyne, Supervisor, Plant Maintenance

***Dodsland:* Dodsland Clinic**
Former Name: Dodsland Health Centre
4 Ave., Dodsland, SK S0L 0V0
Tel: 306-356-2172
Note: community-owned clinic

***Eastend:* Eastend Wolf Willow Health Centre**
Affiliated with: Cypress Regional Health Authority
PO Box 490, 555 Redcoat Dr., Eastend, SK S0N 0T0
Tel: 306-295-3534; *Fax:* 306-295-3223
Number of Beds: 24 beds

Eatonia: **Eatonia Health Centre**
Affiliated with: Heartland Regional Health Authority
205 - 2nd Ave. West, Eatonia, SK S0L 0Y0
Tel: 306-967-2591; *Fax:* 306-967-2373
www.hrha.sk.ca; www.townofeatonia.com/services/healthcare.html
Note: Physician services; wellness program; lab/radiology; home care services; emergency services; occupational therapy; pharmacy deliveries.
Faye Hofer, Facility Manager

Edam: **Lady Minto Health Care Center**
Affiliated with: Prairie North Health Region
PO Box 330, Edam, SK S0M 0V0
Tel: 306-397-2222; *Fax:* 306-397-2225
caroll.s@pnrha.ca
Number of Beds: 2 convalescent, 3 respite, 1 palliative, 14 long-term care b
Note: integrated facility
Caroll Spence, Facility Manager

Elrose: **Elrose Health Centre**
Affiliated with: Heartland Regional Health Authority
PO Box 100, 505 Main St., Elrose, SK S0L 0Z0
Tel: 306-378-2882; *Fax:* 306-378-2812
www.hrha.sk.ca
Number of Beds: 30 long term care beds, 3 other
Note: Long term care; respite/palliative & convalescent.
Wendy Smith, Care Team Manager

Eston: **Eston Health Centre**
Affiliated with: Heartland Regional Health Authority
PO Box 667, 800 Main St., Eston, SK S0L 1A0
Tel: 306-962-3667; *Fax:* 306-962-3900
www.hrha.sk.ca
Number of Beds: 32 long term care beds, 4 other
Ruth Miller, Facility Manager, Care
R. Hartsook, Supervisor, Plant Maintenance

Fillmore: **Fillmore Union Health Centre**
Affiliated with: Sun Country Health Region
Former Name: Fillmore Health Centre
PO Box 246, 100 Main St., Fillmore, SK S0G 1N0
Tel: 306-722-3315; *Fax:* 306-722-3877
Number of Beds: 25 beds
Reg Fisher, Manager, Physical Plant Maintenance
Linda Wilson, Director, Community Services

Foam Lake: **Foam Lake Health Centre**
Affiliated with: Sunrise Regional Health Authority
PO Box 190, 715 Saskatchewan Ave. East, Foam Lake, SK S0A 1A0
Tel: 306-272-3325; *Fax:* 306-272-4449
Brianna Arneson, Manager, Health Services

Gainsborough: **Gainsborough & Area Health Centre**
Affiliated with: Sun Country Health Region
PO Box 420, 312 Stephens St., Gainsborough, SK S0G 1S0
Tel: 306-685-2277; *Fax:* 306-685-4636
Number of Beds: 19 beds
R. Spencer, Supervisor, Physical Plant
Laurie Cole, Administrator

Goodsoil: **L. Gervais Memorial Health Centre**
Affiliated with: Prairie North Health Region
PO Box 100, Main St., Goodsoil, SK S0M 1A0
Tel: 306-238-2100; *Fax:* 306-238-4449
Number of Beds: 18 beds
Note: health centre with a nursing home & attached special care home
Louise Roth, Facility Manager

Grenfell: **Grenfell Health Centre**
Affiliated with: Regina Qu'Appelle Health Region
PO Box 243, 721 Stella St., Grenfell, SK S0G 2B0
Tel: 306-697-2853; *Fax:* 306-697-3459
Diana Lerner, Manager

Gull Lake: **Gull Lake Special Care Centre**
Affiliated with: Cypress Regional Health Authority
PO Box 539, 751 Grey St., Gull Lake, SK S0N 1A0
Tel: 306-672-4700; *Fax:* 306-672-4133
Number of Beds: 37 beds

Hodgeville: **Hodgeville Health Centre**
Affiliated with: Cypress Regional Health Authority
PO Box 232, 105 Main St., Hodgeville, SK S0H 2B0
Tel: 306-677-2292; *Fax:* 306-677-2584

Imperial: **Long Lake Valley Integrated Facility**
Affiliated with: Regina Qu'Appelle Health Region
PO Box 180, Imperial, SK S0G 2J0
Tel: 306-963-2210; *Fax:* 306-963-2518
publicaffairs@rqhealth.ca (Regina Qu'Appelle Health Region)
Year Founded: 1992
Number of Beds: 15 long term care beds; 3 respite or palliative beds
Note: Specialties: Short-term & long-term care; Respite & day care services; Well baby clinics; Foot Care clinics; Outreach programs; Education programs
Wanda Gustafson, Administrator

Invermay: **Invermay Health Centre/Gateway Lodge**
Affiliated with: Sunrise Regional Health Authority
PO Box 160, 303 - 4 Ave. North, Invermay, SK S0A 1M0
Tel: 306-593-2133; *Fax:* 306-593-4566
Number of Beds: 26 beds
Oney Pollock, Manager, Health Services

Ituna: **Ituna Pioneer Health Care Centre**
Affiliated with: Sunrise Regional Health Authority
PO Box 130, 320 - 5 Ave. East, Ituna, SK S0A 1N0
Tel: 306-795-2622; *Fax:* 306-795-3592
Number of Beds: 38 beds
Shelley Cherney, Administrator, Health Services

Kincaid: **Kincaid Health Centre**
Affiliated with: Five Hills Regional Health Authority
PO Box 179, Municipal Rd., Kincaid, SK S0H 2J0
Tel: 306-264-3233; *Fax:* 306-264-3878
Pat Williamson, Sec.-Treas.

Kinistino: **Kinistino Health Centre**
Affiliated with: Prince Albert Parkland Regional Health Authority
111 Meyers Ave., Kinistino, SK S0J 1H0
Tel: 306-864-2292
Number of Beds: 10 beds

Kyle: **Kyle & District Health Centre**
Affiliated with: Heartland Health Region
PO Box 70, 208 - 3 Ave. East, Kyle, SK S0L 1T0
Tel: 306-375-2251; *Fax:* 306-375-2422
Number of Beds: 19 beds
Wendy Gunderson, Facility Manager

La Ronge: **La Ronge Health Centre**
Affiliated with: Mamawetan Churchill River Health Region
PO Box 6000, 227 Backlund St., La Ronge, SK S0J 1L0
Tel: 306-425-2422; *Fax:* 306-425-5432
information@mcrrha.sk.ca
www.mcrrha.sk.ca
Number of Beds: 18 acute, 14 longterm, 8 detox, 8 pediatric, 2 respite
Kathy Chisholm, CEO

Lafleche: **LaFleche & District Health Centre**
Affiliated with: Five Hills Regional Health Authority
PO Box 159, 315 Main St., Lafleche, SK S0H 2K0
Tel: 306-472-5230; *Fax:* 306-472-5405
Number of Beds: 16 beds

Lampman: **Lampman Community Health Centre**
Affiliated with: Sun Country Health Region
PO Box 100, 309 - 2 Ave. East, Lampman, SK S0C 1N0
Tel: 306-487-2561; *Fax:* 306-487-3103
Number of Beds: 22 beds
Bernadette Wright, Community Coordinator
G. Neumier, Manager, Plant Maintenance

Langenburg: **Langenburg Health Centre**
Affiliated with: Sunrise Regional Health Authority
200 Heritage Dr., Langenburg, SK S0A 2A0
Tel: 306-743-2661; *Fax:* 306-743-5025
Number of Beds: 48 beds

Leoville: **Evergreen Health Centre**
Affiliated with: Prince Albert Parkland Regional Health Authority
PO Box 160, 238 - 2nd St., Leoville, SK S0J 1N0
Tel: 306-984-2136; *Fax:* 306-984-2046
Number of Beds: 17 beds
Note: Nursing home
Terri Kirushelniski, Director of Care

Leroy: **Leroy Community Health & Social Centre**
Affiliated with: Saskatoon Regional Health Authority
PO Box 7, 211 - 1 Ave. NE, Leroy, SK S0K 2P0
Tel: 306-286-3347; *Fax:* 306-286-3888

Lloydminster: **Lloydminster & District Co-operative Health Services Ltd.**
PO Box 530, Lloydminster, SK S9V 0Y6
Tel: 306-825-4427

Lucky Lake: **Lucky Lake Health Centre**
Affiliated with: Heartland Health Region
First Ave., Lucky Lake, SK S0L 1Z0
Tel: 306-858-2133; *Fax:* 306-858-2312
Bruce Iverarity, Maintenance
Betty Ann Trumbley, Facility Manager

Macklin: **St. Joseph's Health Centre**
Affiliated with: Heartland Health Region
PO Box 190, Hwy. 31 North, Macklin, SK S0L 2C0
Tel: 306-753-2115; *Fax:* 306-753-2181
Number of Beds: 3 acute care; 23 long term care
Fenton Yeo, Executive Director

Maryfield: **Maryfield Health Centre**
Affiliated with: Sun Country Regional Health Authority
PO Box 164, 233 Main St., Maryfield, SK S0G 3K0
Tel: 306-646-2133; *Fax:* 306-646-2088

Midale: **Mainprize Manor & Health Centre**
Affiliated with: Sun Country Health Region
PO Box 239, 206 South St., Midale, SK S0C 1S0
Tel: 306-458-2300; *Fax:* 306-458-2764
Note: Specialties: Doctor clinics; Outpatient service; Day respite care; Long-term care
Bernadette Wright, Director, Community Services

Montmartre: **Montmartre Health Centre**
Affiliated with: Regina Qu'Appelle Health Region
PO Box 206, 237 - 2 Ave. East, Montmartre, SK S0G 3M0
Tel: 306-424-2222; *Fax:* 306-424-2227
Number of Beds: 16 beds
Marg Hayes, Facility Manager

Mossbank: **Mossbank Health Centre**
Affiliated with: Five Hills Regional Health Authority
General Delivery, Mossbank, SK S0H 3G0
Tel: 306-354-2300; *Fax:* 306-354-2819

Neilburg: **Manitou Health Centre**
Affiliated with: Prairie North Health Region
PO Box 190, 105 - 2nd Ave. W, Neilburg, SK S0M 2C0
Tel: 306-823-4262; *Fax:* 306-823-4590
Louise Blais, Coordinator, Health Services

Neudorf: **Neudorf Health & Social Centre**
420 Main St., Neudorf, SK S0A 2T0
Tel: 306-748-2566; *Fax:* 306-748-2868
Note: Senior centre

Nokomis: **Nokomis Health Centre (Puffer Special Care Home Corp.).**
Affiliated with: Saskatoon Regional Health Authority
PO Box 98, 103 - 2 Ave. East, Nokomis, SK S0G 3R0
Tel: 306-528-2114; *Fax:* 306-528-4655
Number of Beds: 17 beds
Wendy Renwick, Manager, Client Services

Oxbow: **Galloway Health Centre**
Affiliated with: Sun Country Health Region
PO Box 268, 917 Tupper St., Oxbow, SK S0C 2B0
Tel: 306-483-2956; *Fax:* 306-483-5178
Number of Beds: 14 beds
Bill Cannon, Community Coordinator

Pangman: **Pangman Health Centre**
Affiliated with: Sun Country Regional Health Authority
PO Box 90, 211 Keeler St., Pangman, SK S0C 2C0
Tel: 306-442-2044; *Fax:* 306-442-4227
www.suncountry.sk.ca
Note: Specialties: Rehabilitation services; Public health inspection; Mental health services; Diabetes program; Ambulance services; Home care; Palliative care
Pat Kessler, Community Health Services Manager

Paradise Hill: **Paradise Hill Health Centre**
Affiliated with: Prairie North Health Region
PO Box 179, 1st Ave., Paradise Hill, SK S0M 2G0
Tel: 306-344-2255; *Fax:* 306-344-2277
www.pnrha.ca

Neal Sylvestre, Director, Rural Facilities

Pinehouse: Pinehouse Health Centre
Affiliated with: Mamawetan Churchill River Health Region
PO Box 70, Pinehouse, SK S0J 2B0
Tel: 306-884-5670; *Fax:* 306-884-5689
www.mcrrha.sk.ca
Note: Specialties: Public health; Health education; Primary care; Addiction services; Mental health services; Home care services

Ponteix: Ponteix Health Centre
Affiliated with: Cypress Health Region
PO Box 600, 428 - 2 Ave., Ponteix, SK S0N 1Z0
Tel: 306-625-3382; *Fax:* 306-625-3764
Toll-Free: 1-877-800-0002
www.cypresshealth.ca/ponteix.htm/
Note: Specialties: Radiology, Laboratory Services, Home Care, Nutrition, Mental Health, Baby Clinic, Public Health, Foyer St. Joseph Nursing Home, Ambulance Service

Prince Albert: Prince Albert Co-Operative Health Centre
Affiliated with: Prince Albert Parkland Regional Health Authority
110 - 8 St. East, Prince Albert, SK S6V 0V7
Tel: 306-763-6464; *Fax:* 306-763-2101
E. Calder, Administrator

Quill Lake: Quill Lake Community Health & Social Centre
Affiliated with: Saskatoon Regional Health Authority
PO Box 126, 50 Main St., Quill Lake, SK S0A 3E0
Tel: 306-383-2266; *Fax:* 306-383-2290

Radville: Radville Marian Health Centre
Affiliated with: Sun Country Health Region
217 Warren St., Radville, SK S0C 2G0
Tel: 306-869-2224; *Fax:* 306-869-2653
Number of Beds: 51 beds
Robert Shaw, Administrator

Raymore: Raymore Community Health & Social Centre
Affiliated with: Regina Qu'Appelle Health Region
PO Box 134, 806 - 2 Ave., Raymore, SK S0A 3J0
Tel: 306-746-2231; *Fax:* 306-746-4639
Year Founded: 1981
Andrea Sebastian, Contact

Regina: Al Ritchie Health Action Centre
Affiliated with: Regina Qu'Appelle Health Region
325 Victoria Ave., Regina, SK S4N 0P5
Tel: 306-766-7660; *Fax:* 306-766-7409
www.rqhealth.ca
Note: Provides GED exam support services, skills registry, job search support, prenatal nutrition advice, community computer, Dad's Group, family crafts, quit smoking program, seniors' potluck lunch, community kitchen, foot care, primary care nurse (by appt), food bank referrals, video lending library.
D. Lemon, Supervisor

Regina: Four Directions Community Health Centre
Affiliated with: Regina Qu'Appelle Health Region
3510 - 5 Ave., Regina, SK S4T 0M2
Tel: 306-766-7540; *Fax:* 306-766-7534
Sharon Banning, Supervisor

Rockglen: Grasslands Health Centre
Affiliated with: Five Hills Regional Health Authority
PO Box 219, 1006 Hwy. 2, Rockglen, SK S0H 3R0
Tel: 306-476-2030; *Fax:* 306-476-2534
Number of Beds: 17 beds

Rose Valley: Rose Valley Health Centre
Affiliated with: Kelsey Trail Regional Health Authority
PO Box 310, 119 McCallum St., Rose Valley, SK S0E 1M0
Tel: 306-322-2115; *Fax:* 306-322-2037
Judy Moen, Community Health Manager

Sandy Bay: Sandy Bay Health Centre
Affiliated with: Mamawetan Churchill River Health Region
PO Box 39, Sandy Bay, SK S0P 0G0
Tel: 306-754-5400; *Fax:* 306-754-5429
Note: Provides Primary Care, Public Health, Health Education, Telehealth, and Home Care services

Saskatoon: Community Health Services (Saskatoon) Association Ltd.
Affiliated with: Saskatoon Regional Health Authority
455 - 2 Ave. North, Saskatoon, SK S7K 2C2
Tel: 306-664-4241; *Fax:* 306-644-4120

Smeaton: Smeaton & District Health Centre
Affiliated with: Kelsey Trail Regional Health Authority
PO Box 158, Smeaton, SK S0J 2J0
Tel: 306-426-2051; *Fax:* 306-426-2229
Margo Marshall, Community Coordinator

Southey: Southey Health Action Centre
Affiliated with: Regina Qu'Appelle Health Region
PO Box 519, Southey, SK S0G 4P0
Tel: 306-726-2239; *Fax:* 306-726-4472
southeyhealth@sasktel.net
www.rqhealth.ca
Rosemary Flaman, Contact

Spalding: Spalding Community Health Centre
Affiliated with: Saskatoon Regional Health Authority
PO Box 220, 133 Centre St., Spalding, SK S0K 4C0
Tel: 306-872-2011; *Fax:* 306-872-2186
Jan Berger, Manager

St Walburg: St Walburg Health Complex
Affiliated with: Prairie North Health Region
PO Box 339, St Walburg, SK S0M 2T0
Tel: 306-248-6719; *Fax:* 306-248-3413
Number of Beds: 31 beds
Note: attached special care home
Chris Thiele, Facility Manager

Strasbourg: Strasbourg & District Health Centre
Affiliated with: Saskatoon Regional Health Authority
303 Edward St., Strasbourg, SK S0G 4V0
Tel: 306-725-3220; *Fax:* 306-725-4060
www.townofstrasbourg.ca
Year Founded: 1974
Note: Specialties: Physiotherapy; Counselling; Public health services
Tracy Hastings, Manager

Turtleford: Riverside Health Complex
Affiliated with: Prairie North Health Region
PO Box 10, 1 St. South, Hwy. 303, Turtleford, SK S0M 2Y0
Tel: 306-845-2195; *Fax:* 306-845-2772
www.pnrha.ca
Number of Beds: 31 beds
Note: Attached special care home
Neal Sylvestre, Director, Rural Health Facilities

Vanguard: Vanguard Health Care Centre
Affiliated with: Cypress Regional Health Authority
PO Box 190, Division St., Vanguard, SK S0N 2V0
Tel: 306-582-2044; *Fax:* 306-582-4833
Note: Weekly clinic, nurse practitioner on staff, lab & x-ray services twice a week, visiting health professionals
Dr. Suresh Kassett, Family Physician

Weyakwin: Weyakwin Health Centre
Affiliated with: Mamawetan Churchill River Health Region
General Delivery, Weyakwin, SK S0J 1W0
Tel: 306-663-6100; *Fax:* 306-663-6165

Whitewood: Whitewood Community Health Centre
Affiliated with: Regina Qu'Appelle Health Region
PO Box 669, 921 Gambetta St., Whitewood, SK S0G 5C0
Tel: 306-735-2688; *Fax:* 306-735-2512
Number of Beds: 30 beds
Muriel Beutler, Manager

Wilkie: Wilkie & District Health Centre/Poplar Courts
Affiliated with: Heartland Regional Health Authority
PO Box 459, 304 - 7 Ave. East, Wilkie, SK S0K 4W0
Tel: 306-843-2644; *Fax:* 306-843-3222
Number of Beds: 4 acute care, 37 long-term care beds
Carrien Glassford, Care Team Manager

Willow Bunch: Willow Bunch Wellness Centre
Affiliated with: Five Hills Regional Health Authority
PO Box 6, 17 - 3 St. East, Willow Bunch, SK S0H 4K0
Tel: 306-473-2310; *Fax:* 306-473-2677

Wynyard: Community Health Services Association
Affiliated with: Saskatoon Regional Health Authority
PO Box 1539, 315 Bosworth St., Wynyard, SK S0A 4T0
Tel: 306-554-3363; *Fax:* 306-554-2994
Sharon Armstrong

Nursing Stations

Stony Rapids: Black Lake Nursing Station
General Delivery, Stony Rapids, SK S0J 2R0
Tel: 306-284-2124; *Fax:* 306-264-2090

Special Treatment Centres

Melville: Saul Cohen Family Resource Centre
Affiliated with: Sunrise Regional Health Authority
PO Box 164, 720 Manitoba St., Melville, SK S0A 2P0
Tel: 306-728-2629; *Fax:* 306-728-5569
saulcohencentre@hotmail.com
www.geocities.com/HotSprings/Resort/9900/
Note: Outpatient counseling & support individuals & families affected by addictions
Sherry Shumay

North Battleford: Saskatchewan Hospital
Affiliated with: Prairie North Health Region
PO Box 39, North Battleford, SK S9A 2X8
Tel: 306-446-6800; *Fax:* 306-445-5392
Number of Beds: 156 beds
Note: psychiatric rehabilitation hospital
Linda Shynkaruk, Director

Regina: Wascana Rehabilitation Centre
Affiliated with: Regina Qu'Appelle Health Region
2180 - 23 Ave., Regina, SK S4S 0A5
Tel: 306-766-5100; *Fax:* 306-766-5244
Number of Beds: 307 inpatient
Note: rehabilitation centre, long term care centre
Dwight Nelson, President; CEO

Nursing Homes

Assiniboia: Assiniboia Pioneer Lodge
Affiliated with: Five Hills Regional Health Authority
PO Box 1120, 800 - 1 St. West, Assiniboia, SK S0H 0B0
Tel: 306-642-3311; *Fax:* 306-642-3099
Number of Beds: 128 beds
Jim Larson, Administrator

Assiniboia: Ross Payant Centennial Home
Affiliated with: Five Hills Regional Health Authority
Former Name: Ross Payant Centennial Home
PO Box 1120, 300 Jubilee Place, Assiniboia, SK S0H 0B0
Tel: 306-642-3330; *Fax:* 306-642-3243
Number of Beds: 38 beds

Big River: Lakewood Lodge
PO Box 760, Big River, SK S0J 0E0
Tel: 306-469-2333; *Fax:* 306-469-2193
Number of Beds: 29 beds
Helen Donald, Director, Care

Biggar: Diamond Lodge Co. Ltd.
Affiliated with: Heartland Regional Health Authority
PO Box 340, 402 - 2 St. West, Biggar, SK S0K 0M0
Tel: 306-948-3385; *Fax:* 306-948-5421
Number of Beds: 60 beds
Jo Angelopoulos, Facility Manager

Birch Hills: Birchview Nursing Home
Affiliated with: Prince Albert Parkland Regional Health Authority
Former Name: Birchview Lodge
PO Box 578, 7 Wilson St., Birch Hills, SK S0J 1J0
Tel: 306-749-2288; *Fax:* 306-749-2440
Number of Beds: 30 beds

Broadview: Broadview & District Centennial Lodge Inc.
Affiliated with: Regina Qu'Appelle Health Region
PO Box 670, 310 Calgary St., Broadview, SK S0G 0K0
Tel: 306-696-2459; *Fax:* 306-696-2577
Number of Beds: 36 beds
Linda Zinkhan, Manager

Canwood: Whispering Pine Place Inc.
Affiliated with: Prince Albert Parkland Regional Health Authority
PO Box 418, 300 - 1st Ave., Canwood, SK S0J 0K0
Tel: 306-468-2900; *Fax:* 306-468-2199
Number of Beds: 30 beds
Brenda Person, Administrator

***Carlyle:* Moose Mountain Lodge**
Affiliated with: Sun Country Health Region
PO Box 729, 6 St. West, Carlyle, SK S0C 0R0
Tel: 306-453-2434; *Fax:* 306-453-2726
Number of Beds: 52 beds
Joanne Hollingshead, Manager
Harold Smith, Maintenance

***Carnduff:* Sunset Haven**
Affiliated with: Sun Country Health Region
PO Box 250, 415 Spencer St., Carnduff, SK S0C 0S0
Tel: 306-482-3424; *Fax:* 306-482-5233
www.suncountry.sk.ca
Note: Specialties: Long-term care; Home care; Palliative care
Cathy Stephenson, Sec.-Treas.
Shirley Wright, Director of Care

***Central Butte:* Central Butte Regency Hospital**
Affiliated with: Five Hills Regional Health Authority
PO Box 430, Central Butte, SK S0H 0T0
Tel: 306-796-4338; *Fax:* 306-796-4407
Number of Beds: 22 beds
Debbie Bauck, Program Coordinator

***Cupar:* Cupar & District Nursing Home Inc.**
Affiliated with: Regina Qu'Appelle Health Region
PO Box 310, 213 Mills St., Cupar, SK S0G 0Y0
Tel: 306-723-4228; *Fax:* 306-723-4248
Number of Beds: 48 beds
Betty Smith, Interim Administrator

***Duck Lake:* Duck Lake & District Nursing Home Inc. Goodwill Manor**
Affiliated with: Saskatoon Regional Health Authority
PO Box 370, Victoria Ave., Duck Lake, SK S0K 1J0
Tel: 306-467-4440; *Fax:* 306-467-2220
Number of Beds: 30 beds
Jean-Marie Allard, Facility Coordinator

***Estevan:* Estevan Regional Nursing Home**
Affiliated with: Sun Country Health Region
PO Box 5000, 1921 Wallock Rd., Estevan, SK S4A 2V6
Tel: 306-634-2689; *Fax:* 306-634-7906
Number of Beds: 76 beds
Brenda Rabman, Administrator

***Eston:* Jubilee Lodge Inc.**
Affiliated with: Heartland Health Region
822 Main St., Eston, SK S0L 1A0
Tel: 306-962-3667; *Fax:* 306-962-3900
ruth.miller@hrha.sk.ca
www.hrha.sk.ca
Number of Beds: 37 beds
Ruth Miller, Administrator
W. Turner, Director, Physical Plant

***Foam Lake:* Foam Lake Jubilee Home**
Affiliated with: Sunrise Regional Health Authority
PO Box 460, 421 Alberta Ave. East, Foam Lake, SK S0A 1A0
Tel: 306-272-4141; *Fax:* 306-272-4973
Number of Beds: 51 beds
Arlene Scratton, Manager, Health Services

***Fort Qu'appelle:* Echo Lodge**
Affiliated with: Regina Qu'Appelle Health Region
PO Box 1790, 560 Broadway St. West, Fort Qu'appelle, SK S0G 1S0
Tel: 306-332-4300; *Fax:* 306-332-5708
Number of Beds: 51 beds
Darlene Demoskoff

***Grenfell:* Grenfell & District Pioneer Home**
Affiliated with: Regina Qu'Appelle Health Region
PO Box 760, 710 Regina Ave., Grenfell, SK S0G 2B0
Tel: 306-697-2842; *Fax:* 306-697-2280
Number of Beds: 34 beds
Diana Lerner, Manager
Rick Gerhardt, Maintenance

***Indian Head:* Golden Prairie Home**
Affiliated with: Regina Qu'Appelle Health Region
PO Box 250, 916 Eden St., Indian Head, SK S0G 2K0
Tel: 306-695-3636; *Fax:* 306-695-2698
Number of Beds: 38 beds
Karen Earnshaw, Manager

***Kelvington:* Kelvindell Lodge**
Affiliated with: Kelsey Trail Regional Health Authority
PO Box 280, 701 - 6 Ave. West, Kelvington, SK S0A 1W0
Tel: 306-327-5151; *Fax:* 306-327-4504
Number of Beds: 46 beds
Shelley Rutherford, Asst. Manager, Community Health
Kevin O'Neil, Maintenance

***Kerrobert:* Buena Vista Lodge**
Affiliated with: Heartland Regional Health Authority
645 Columbia Ave., Kerrobert, SK S0L 1R0
Tel: 306-834-2646; *Fax:* 306-834-1007
Number of Beds: 28 beds
Fenton Yeo, Facility Manager
L. Menssa, Director, Physical Plant

***Kindersley:* Heritage Manor**
Affiliated with: Heartland Health Region
1003 - 1st St. West, Kindersley, SK S0L 1S2
Tel: 306-463-2611; *Fax:* 306-465-4550
Number of Beds: 80 beds
Wanda Desrosiers, Facility Manager
Peter Whiteman, Director, Physical Plant

***Kinistino:* Jubilee Lodge**
Affiliated with: Prince Albert Parkland Regional Health Authority
PO Box 370, 410 Myers Ave., Kinistino, SK S0J 1H0
Tel: 306-864-2851; *Fax:* 306-864-2440
Number of Beds: 36 beds
Carol Pryznyk, Administrator

***Kipling:* Willowdale Lodge**
Affiliated with: Sun Country Health Region
PO Box 537, 128 - 4 St. South, Kipling, SK S0G 2S0
Tel: 306-736-2218; *Fax:* 306-736-2986
Number of Beds: 28 beds
Kelly Bru, Facility Manager
Linus Blacstock, Maintenance

***Langham:* Langham Senior Citizens Home**
Affiliated with: Saskatoon Regional Health Authority
PO Box 287, 140 Main St., Langham, SK S0K 2L0
Tel: 306-283-4210; *Fax:* 306-283-4212
Number of Beds: 17 beds
Margaret Balzer, Administrator

***Leader:* Western Senior Citizens Home**
Affiliated with: Cypress Regional Health Authority
PO Box 69, 400 - 1 St. West, Leader, SK S0N 1H0
Tel: 306-628-3565; *Fax:* 306-628-3733
Number of Beds: 36 beds
Note: Level 3 & 4

***Leask:* Wheatland Lodge Inc.**
Affiliated with: Prince Albert Parkland Regional Health Authority
PO Box 130, Hwy. 40, Leask, SK S0J 1M0
Tel: 306-466-4949; *Fax:* 306-466-2209
Number of Beds: 30 beds
Darlene Batty, Director, Care

***Lumsden:* Lumsden & District Heritage Home Inc.**
Affiliated with: Regina Qu'Appelle Health Region
PO Box 479, 10 Aspen Bay, Lumsden, SK S0G 3C0
Tel: 306-731-2247; *Fax:* 306731-3307
heritagehome@rqhealth.ca
Number of Beds: 30 long-term care beds
Note: Specialties: Assisted living services for seniors; Adult day support program
Wilf Frey, Maintenance
Shirley Wright, Executive Director

***Maple Creek:* Cypress Lodge Nursing Home**
Affiliated with: Cypress Regional Health Authority
Former Name: Cypress Lodge Corp
PO Box 878, Hwy. 21 South, Maple Creek, SK S0N 1N0
Tel: 306-662-2671; *Fax:* 306-662-2501
Number of Beds: 48 beds

***Melfort:* Nirvana Pioneer Villa**
PO Box 1480, Melfort, SK S0E 1A0
Tel: 306-752-8827; *Fax:* 306-752-8822
Sandy Weseen, Coordinator, Care

***Melfort:* Parkland Place**
Affiliated with: Kelsey Trail Regional Health Authority
Former Name: Parkland Care Centre
PO Box 2260, 402 Bemister Ave. East, Melfort, SK S0E 1A0
Tel: 306-752-1777; *Fax:* 306-752-1776
www.kelseytrailhealth.ca
Number of Beds: 103 long-term care beds; 2 respite beds
Note: Specialty: Acquired brain injury program
Melanie Woods, Coordinator, Care

***Melville:* St. Paul Lutheran Home**
Affiliated with: Sunrise Regional Health Authority
PO Box 1390, 100 Heritage Dr., Melville, SK S0A 2P0
Tel: 306-728-7340; *Fax:* 306-728-5471
Number of Beds: 143 beds
Note: Long-term care facility affiliated with the Evangelical Lutheran Church in Canada
Gord Wyatt, Director, Long-term Care

***Moose Jaw:* Extendicare - Moose Jaw**
Affiliated with: Five Hills Regional Health Authority
1151 Coteau St. West, Moose Jaw, SK S6H 5G5
Tel: 306-693-5191; *Fax:* 306-692-1770
cnh_moosejaw@extendicare.com
Number of Beds: 127 beds

***Moose Jaw:* Providence Place**
Affiliated with: Five Hills Regional Health Authority
100 - 2nd Ave. NE, Moose Jaw, SK S6H 1B8
Tel: 306-694-8081; *Fax:* 306-694-8804
rmul@fhhr.ca
Number of Beds: 188 beds
Note: Geriatric long-term care, assessment & rehabilitation
Raymond E. Mullire

***Moosomin:* Eastern Saskatchewan Pioneer Lodge Nursing Home**
Affiliated with: Regina Qu'Appelle Health Region
405 Windover Ave., Bag #3, Moosomin, SK S0G 3N0
Tel: 306-435-2100; *Fax:* 306-435-4295
Number of Beds: 57 beds
Sharon Ann Wood, Interim Manager

***Nipawin:* Pineview Lodge**
Affiliated with: Kelsey Trail Regional Health Authority
PO Box 2105, 400 - 6th Ave. East, Nipawin, SK S0E 1E0
Tel: 306-862-9828; *Fax:* 306-862-2400
www.kelseytrailhealth.ca
Number of Beds: 96 beds
Note: Specialties: Long-term care; Dementia care unit; Day care services; Respite care

***North Battleford:* River Heights Lodge**
Affiliated with: Prairie North Health Region
2001 - 99 St., North Battleford, SK S9A 0S3
Tel: 306-446-6950; *Fax:* 306-445-6032
Number of Beds: 106 beds
Note: Special care home
Kelly Day, Facility Manager

***Ponteix:* Foyer St-Joseph Nursing Home**
Affiliated with: Cypress Regional Health Authority
PO Box 450, 428 - 2 Ave., Ponteix, SK S0N 1Z0
Tel: 306-625-3366; *Fax:* 306-625-3918
Number of Beds: 33 beds
Larry Piché, Director, Physical Plant

***Porcupine Plain:* Red Deer Nursing Home**
Affiliated with: Kelsey Trail Regional Health Authority
PO Box 70, 330 Oak St., Porcupine Plain, SK S0E 1H0
Tel: 306-278-2469; *Fax:* 306-278-3088
Number of Beds: 36 long-term care beds; 2 respite beds
Chris Pohl, Community Health Manager

***Preeceville:* Preeceville Lions Housing Corp. Ltd.**
Affiliated with: Sunrise Regional Health Authority
PO Box 348, 26 - 3 Ave. NW, Preeceville, SK S0A 3B0
Tel: 306-547-3112; *Fax:* 306-547-3215
Number of Beds: 28 beds; 1 respite
N. Babiuk, Physical Plant
Joanne Bodnar, Manager, Health Services

***Redvers:* Redvers Centennial Haven**
Affiliated with: Sun Country Health Region
PO Box 399, 18 Eichhorst St., Redvers, SK S0C 2H0
Tel: 306-452-3331; *Fax:* 306-452-3556
Number of Beds: 24 beds
Myrna Peterson, Manager, Health Services

***Regina:* Extendicare - Elmview**
Affiliated with: Regina Qu'Appelle Health Region
4125 Rae St., Regina, SK S4S 3A5
Tel: 306-586-1787; *Fax:* 306-585-0255
Number of Beds: 62 beds
Cathy Hauck, Administrator

***Regina:* Extendicare - Parkside**
Affiliated with: Regina Qu'Appelle Health Region
4540 Rae St., Regina, SK S4S 3B4
Tel: 306-586-0220; *Fax:* 306-585-0622
Number of Beds: 228 beds

Lloyd Wood, Maintenance Supervisor
Dona Jones, Administrator

Regina: Extendicare - Sunset
Affiliated with: Regina Qu'Appelle Health Region
260 Sunset Dr., Regina, SK S4S 2S3
Tel: 306-586-3355; Fax: 306-584-8082
Number of Beds: 152 beds
Sandra Callan, Administrator

Regina: Qu'Appelle House
Affiliated with: Regina Qu'Appelle Health Region
1425 College Ave., Regina, SK S4P 1B4
Tel: 306-522-0335; Fax: 306-522-4800
Number of Beds: 34 beds
Diane Serban, Executive Director

Regina: Regina Lutheran Home
Affiliated with: Regina Qu'Appelle Health Region
1925 - 5 Ave. North, Regina, SK S4R 7W1
Tel: 306-543-4055; Fax: 306-543-4094
Number of Beds: 91 beds
Note: Nursing home
Glenn Knapp, Director, Maintenance
Allan Hoffman, Executive Director

Regina: Regina Pioneer Village Ltd.
Affiliated with: Regina Qu'Appelle Health Region
430 Pioneer Dr., Regina, SK S4T 6L8
Tel: 306-757-5646; Fax: 306-757-5001
Number of Beds: 390 beds
Arnold Evancio, Manager, Maintenance
Dick Chinn, CEO

Regina: Santa Maria Senior Citizens Home
Affiliated with: Regina Qu'Appelle Health Region
4215 Regina Ave., Regina, SK S4S 0J5
Tel: 306-766-7100; Fax: 306-766-7115
Number of Beds: 147 beds
Bill Wilson, Manager, Maintenance
Beverly Olineck, Administrator

Rosetown: Wheatbelt Centennial Lodge Inc.
Affiliated with: Heartland Regional Health Authority
PO Box 250, 301 Centennial Dr., Rosetown, SK S0L 2V0
Tel: 306-882-5210; Fax: 306-882-6696
Number of Beds: 28 beds
B. Madden, Director, Physical Plant
Gail Adamowski, Facility Manager

Rosthern: Mennonite Nursing Home Inc.
Affiliated with: Saskatoon Regional Health Authority
PO Box 370, Hwy. 11 South, Rosthern, SK S0K 3R0
Tel: 306-232-4861; Fax: 306-232-5611
www.saskatoonhealthregion.ca
Year Founded: 1963
Note: Specialties: Long-term care; Adult Day Program
Joan Lemauviel, CEO

Saltcoats: Lakeside Manor Care Home Inc.
Affiliated with: Sunrise Regional Health Authority
PO Box 340, 101 Crescent Lake Rd., Saltcoats, SK S0A 3R0
Tel: 306-744-2305; Fax: 306-744-2414
Number of Beds: 28 beds, 2 respite
Shirley Pachal, Facility Manager

Saskatoon: Jubilee Residences Inc. (Porteous)
Affiliated with: Saskatoon Regional Health Authority
833 Ave. P North, Saskatoon, SK S7L 2W5
Tel: 306-382-2626; Fax: 306-382-2633
yvonne.morgan@saskatoonhealthregion.ca
www.jubileeresicences.ca/
Number of Beds: 95 beds
Yvonne Morgan, Administrator
306/382-2626 ext.222, Fax: 306/382-2633

Saskatoon: Jubilee Residences Inc. (Stensrud)
Affiliated with: Saskatoon Regional Health Authority
2202 McEown Ave., Saskatoon, SK S7L 3L6
Tel: 306-373-5580; Fax: 306-477-0308
handerson@jubilee.sk.ca
Number of Beds: 95 beds
Heather Anderson, Administrator

Saskatoon: Oliver Lodge Special Care Home
Affiliated with: Saskatoon Regional Health Authority
1405 Faulkner Cres., Saskatoon, SK S7L 3R5
Tel: 306-382-4111; Fax: 306-382-9822
Year Founded: 1949
Number of Beds: 139 beds
Note: Specialties: Specialized services for persons with dementia; Day program for seniors; Respite care
Morley Mitchell, Administrator

Saskatoon: Parkridge Centre
Affiliated with: Saskatoon Regional Health Authority
110 Gropper Cres., Saskatoon, SK S7M 5N9
Tel: 306-655-3800; Fax: 306-655-3801
www.parkridgequalityoflife.com
Number of Beds: 217 beds
Karen Knelsen, Resident Care Services
Dale Gagnon, Manager, Plant Operation

Saskatoon: St. Ann's Senior Citizens Village Corp.
Affiliated with: Saskatoon Regional Health Authority
2910 Louise St., Saskatoon, SK S7J 3L8
Tel: 306-374-8900; Fax: 306-477-2623
Number of Beds: 80 beds
Note: Affiliated with the Catholic Health Ministry of Saskatchewan
R.A. Sveinbjornson, Administrator

Saskatoon: St. Joseph's Home
Affiliated with: Saskatoon Regional Health Authority
33 Valens Dr., Saskatoon, SK S7L 3S2
Tel: 306-382-6306; Fax: 306-384-0140
Number of Beds: 85 beds
Sr. Theodosia, Administrator

Saskatoon: Saskatoon Convalescent Home
Affiliated with: Saskatoon Regional Health Authority
101 - 31 St. West, Saskatoon, SK S7L 0P6
Tel: 306-244-7155; Fax: 306-244-2066
www.saskatoonconvalescenthome.com
Number of Beds: 59 beds
Patricia Jarvis, Administrator

Saskatoon: Sherbrooke Community Centre
Affiliated with: Saskatoon Regional Health Authority
401 Acadia Dr., Saskatoon, SK S7H 2E7
Tel: 306-655-3600; Fax: 306-655-3727
www.sherbrookecommunitycentre.ca
Number of Beds: 270 beds
Note: Long-term care home. Also provides a Community Day Program for 100 local residents
Bruce Pyett, Director, Maintenance
Suellen Beatty, CEO

Saskatoon: Sunnyside Adventist Care Centre
Affiliated with: Saskatoon Regional Health Authority
Former Name: Sunnyside Nursing Home
2200 St. Henry Ave., Saskatoon, SK S7M 0P5
Tel: 306-653-1267; Fax: 306-653-7223
admin@sunnysidecare.ca
www.sunnysidecare.ca
Year Founded: 1964
Note: Specialties: Nursing care; Physiotherapy; Activity program; Palliative care
Collin Akre, Administrator

Spiritwood: Idylwild Lodge
PO Box 159, Spiritwood, SK S0J 2M0
Tel: 306-883-2267; Fax: 306-883-3121
Number of Beds: 35 beds
Carroll Joyes, Director, Care
Louis Willick, Director, Maintenance

Stoughton: Newhope Pioneer Lodge Inc.
Affiliated with: Sun Country Health Region
PO Box 38, 123 Government Rd. North, Stoughton, SK S0G 4T0
Tel: 306-457-2552; Fax: 306-457-3732
Number of Beds: 30 beds
Linda Wilson, Director, Community Services

Swift Current: Palliser Regional Care Centre
Affiliated with: Cypress Regional Health Authority
440 Central Ave. South, Swift Current, SK S9H 3G6
Tel: 306-778-5160
www.cypresshealth.ca
Number of Beds: 94 beds

Swift Current: Prairie Pioneers Lodge
Affiliated with: Cypress Regional Health Authority
302 Central Ave. South, Swift Current, SK S9H 3G3
Tel: 306-778-5192; Fax: 306-773-1635
Number of Beds: 41 beds

Swift Current: Swift Current Care Centre (SCCC)
Affiliated with: Cypress Regional Health Authority
700 Aberdeen St. SE, Swift Current, SK S9H 3E3
Tel: 306-773-9371; Fax: 306-773-1353
www.cypresshealth.ca
Number of Beds: 63 beds
Note: Specialties: Nursing care from Registered Nurses, Registered Psychiatric Nurses, & Licensed Practical Nurses; Social work; Activity program; Respite care program

Tisdale: Newmarket Manor
Affiliated with: Kelsey Trail Regional Health Authority
PO Box 2620, 2001 Newmarket Dr., Tisdale, SK S0E 1T0
Tel: 306-873-5828; Fax: 306-873-4822
Number of Beds: 40 beds
Ann Boxall, Director, Care

Tisdale: Sasko Park Lodge
Affiliated with: Kelsey Trail Regional Health Authority
PO Box 1330, 806 - 97 Ave., Tisdale, SK S0E 1T0
Tel: 306-873-4585; Fax: 306-873-2404
Number of Beds: 33 beds, 15 suites
Ann Boxall, Director, Care

Turtleford: Riverside Health Complex Integrated Facility
Former Name: Turtle River Nusing Home
PO Box 10, 1st St. S, Turtleford, SK S0M 2Y0
Tel: 306-845-2195; Fax: 306-845-2772
Number of Beds: 27 beds
Patrick Blais, Coordinator, Health Services

Wakaw: Lakeview Pioneer Lodge Inc.
Affiliated with: Saskatoon Regional Health Authority
PO Box 189, 400 First St. North, Wakaw, SK S0K 4P0
Tel: 306-233-4621; Fax: 306-233-5225
Number of Beds: 46 beds
Gracie Kungle, Administrator

Waldheim: Menno Homes of Saskatchewan Inc.
PO Box 130, Waldheim, SK S0K 4R0
Tel: 306-945-2070; Fax: 306-945-4641
menno.homes@sasktel.net
Year Founded: 1963
Number of Beds: 105 residential capacity
Note: Number of Employees: 105
Marlin J. Roth, Executive Director

Watrous: Manitou Lodge
Affiliated with: Saskatoon Regional Health Authority
PO Box 130, 404 - 1 St., Watrous, SK S0K 4T0
Tel: 306-946-3718; Fax: 306-946-2296
Number of Beds: 35 beds
Debbie Okrainetz, Manager, Client Services

Wawota: Deer View Lodge
Affiliated with: Sun Country Health Region
PO Box 240, 201 Wilfred St., Wawota, SK S0G 5A0
Tel: 306-739-2400; Fax: 306-739-2802
Number of Beds: 34 beds

Wolseley: Lakeside Home
Affiliated with: Regina Qu'Appelle Health Region
PO Box 10, 710 Quimet, Wolseley, SK S0G 5H0
Tel: 306-698-2573; Fax: 306-698-2975
Number of Beds: 78 beds
Ruth Platt, Purchasing Agent
Jim Bonner, Maintenance Supervisor
Maggie Petrychyn, Manager

Yorkton: Yorkton & District Nursing Home Corporation
Affiliated with: Sunrise Regional Health Authority
200 Bradbrooke Dr., Yorkton, SK S3N 2K5
Tel: 306-786-0800; Fax: 306-786-0808
www.sunrisehealthregion.sk.ca
Number of Beds: 243 beds
Lynn Wrishko, Manager, Health Services
Brenda Walsh, Manager, Health Services

Long Term/Retirement Care

Nursing Homes

Moose Jaw: Pioneer Housing Lodge & Village
Affiliated with: Five Hills Regional Health Authority
1000 Albert St., Moose Jaw, SK S6H 2Y2
Tel: 306-693-4616

Personal Care Homes

Avonlea: Coteau Range Manor
Affiliated with: Five Hills Regional Health Authority
PO Box 239, 210 New Warren Pl., Avonlea, SK S0H 0C0
Tel: 306-868-2033
Number of Beds: 40 beds

Bangor: Morris Lodge Society Inc.
PO Box 54, Lots 4-12, Block 6, Main St., Bangor, SK S0A 0E0
Tel: 306-728-5322; *Fax:* 306-728-2048
Number of Beds: 20 beds

Beechy: Beechy Community Care Home
205 Railway Ave., Beechy, SK S0L 0C0
Tel: 306-859-4470
Number of Beds: 10 beds
Noël Taylor, Genevieve Fleuter

Biggar: Beaulah's Care Home
320 - 2 Ave. East, Biggar, SK S0K 0M0
Tel: 306-948-5648; *Fax:* 306-948-2860
Number of Beds: 10 beds
Beaulah Oystryk

Codette: Serenity Lane
Affiliated with: Kelsey Trail Regional Health Authority
PO Box 152, Codette, SK S0E 0P0
Tel: 306-862-2579
Number of Beds: 10 beds
Debbie Karlee

Eatonia: Eatonia Oasis Living Inc.
Former Name: Eatonia Personal Care Home
PO Box 217, 205, 2nd Ave. W, Eatonia, SK S0L 0Y0
Tel: 306-967-2447; *Fax:* 306-967-2373
eatoniaoasisliving.com
Number of Beds: 23 beds
Lorraine Bews, Chairperson

Estevan: Creighton Lodge
1028 Hillcrest Dr., Estevan, SK S4A 1Y7
Tel: 306-634-4154

Herbert: Herbert Heritage Manor
PO Box 10, Herbert, SK S0H 2A0
Tel: 306-784-3167; *Fax:* 306-784-3564
hhm@sasktel.net
Number of Beds: 40 beds
Note: personal care home level 1 & 2
Brian D. Penner, Administrator

Kamsack: Eaglestone Lodge Personal Care Home Inc.
PO Box 1330, Kamsack, SK S0A 1S0
Tel: 306-542-2620; *Fax:* 306-542-4342
Number of Beds: 42 beds
Kim Fullawka, Manager; Director, Care

Lanigan: Central Parkland Lodge
Affiliated with: Saskatoon Regional Health Authority
PO Box 609, 36 Downing Dr. East, Lanigan, SK S0K 2M0
Tel: 306-365-1400; *Fax:* 306-365-3354
Number of Beds: 35 beds
Darla Washington, Manager, Client Services

Moose Jaw: Capilano Court
Affiliated with: Five Hills Regional Health Authority
1236 - 3rd Ave. NW, Moose Jaw, SK S6H 3V3
Tel: 306-693-4518

Moose Jaw: Chez Nous
Affiliated with: Five Hills Regional Health Authority
1101 Grafton Ave., Moose Jaw, SK S6H 3S4
Tel: 306-693-4371; *Fax:* 306-693-5300
Number of Beds: 60 beds

Moose Jaw: Evergreen's Personal Care Home
Affiliated with: Five Hills Regional Health Authority
1033 Main St. North, Moose Jaw, SK S6H 0X1
Tel: 306-692-7410
Number of Beds: 10 beds
Leland Agar
Lois Agar

Moose Jaw: Ina Grafton Gage Home
Affiliated with: Five Hills Regional Health Authority
200 Iroquois St. East, Moose Jaw, SK S6H 4T3
Tel: 306-692-4882; *Fax:* 306-692-3433
Brenda Deobald, Administrator; Director, Care

Moose Jaw: Oxford Place Inc.
Affiliated with: Five Hills Regional Health Authority
1007 Main St. North, Moose Jaw, SK S6H 0X1
Tel: 306-692-2837; *Fax:* 306-692-3837
oxfordplace@sasktel.net

Moose Jaw: Valley View Centre
PO Box 1300, Moose Jaw, SK S6H 4R2
Tel: 306-694-3000; *Fax:* 306-694-3003
Number of Beds: 348 beds
Terry Hardy, Director

Oxbow: Bow Valley Villa Corp.
319 Wylie Ave., Oxbow, SK S0C 2B0
Tel: 306-483-2744; *Fax:* 306-483-2915

Pangman: Deep South Personal Care Home
Affiliated with: Sun Country Regional Health Authority
PO Box 150, 211 Keeler St., Pangman, SK S0C 2C0
Tel: 306-442-2043; *Fax:* 306-442-4261
dspch@sasktel.net
Connie Lozinsky, Administrator

Ponteix: Rolling Hills Villa Ltd.
PO Box 148, 332 - 2 St. West, Ponteix, SK S0N 1Z0
Tel: 306-625-3511

Prince Albert: Hillside Care Home
Affiliated with: Prince Albert Parkland Regional Health Authority
231 - 21 St. East, Prince Albert, SK S6V 1L9
Tel: 306-764-5039
Number of Beds: 10 beds
Angie Kopera, Owner
Nettie Mitchell, Owner

Prince Albert: Nelson Care Home Ltd.
Affiliated with: Prince Albert Parkland Regional Health Authority
1336 - 7th St. East, Prince Albert, SK S6V 0V1
Tel: 306-922-9506

Rosthern: Rosthern Mennonite Home for the Aged
PO Box 790, 510 - 4 Ave., Rosthern, SK S0K 3R0
Tel: 306-232-4822
Number of Beds: 20 beds
Jacob Loewen, Chair

Saskatoon: Arbor Villa Care Home
Affiliated with: Saskatoon Regional Health Authority
315 Kenderdine Rd., Saskatoon, SK S7N 3S9
Tel: 306-249-3317
Number of Beds: 13 beds

Saskatoon: Ashton Care Home
Affiliated with: Saskatoon Regional Health Authority
438 Ave. Y North, Saskatoon, SK S7L 3L2
Tel: 306-382-8975; *Fax:* 306-283-4142
Number of Beds: 10 beds
Bernice Obnokon

Saskatoon: Balicanta Personal Care Home
Affiliated with: Saskatoon Regional Health Authority
510 Spencer Cres., Saskatoon, SK S7K 7T4
Tel: 306-934-5903
Number of Beds: 12 beds
Marino Balicanta

Saskatoon: Bergman's Private Home Care
Affiliated with: Saskatoon Regional Health Authority
333 LaRonge Rd., Saskatoon, SK S7K 4S1
Tel: 306-934-2031; *Fax:* 306-934-2031

Saskatoon: Betty Sandulak's Personal Care Home
Affiliated with: Saskatoon Regional Health Authority
Former Name: Betty's Private Care Home
122 Adilman Dr., Saskatoon, SK S7K 7S5
Tel: 306-931-7859
Number of Beds: 10 beds

Saskatoon: Fairhaven Personal Care Home
Affiliated with: Saskatoon Regional Health Authority
139 Olmstead Rd., Saskatoon, SK S7M 4L9
Tel: 306-382-7800

Saskatoon: M & M Private Care Home
Affiliated with: Saskatoon Regional Health Authority
518/520 Russell Rd., Saskatoon, SK S7K 6L6
Tel: 306-242-6501; *Fax:* 306-934-8027
Number of Beds: 12 beds
Note: Specialties: Diabetic care; Respite care
Marionela Cabello

Saskatoon: Marg's Care Home Ltd.
Affiliated with: Saskatoon Regional Health Authority
310 Adilman Dr., Saskatoon, SK S7K 7K5
Tel: 306-975-1189

Shellbrook: T.L.C. Personal Care Home
308 - 3rd Ave. East, Shellbrook, SK S0J 2E0
Tel: 306-747-3123
Year Founded: 1997

Speers: Oasis Personal Care Home
Affiliated with: Prince Albert Parkland Regional Health Authority
PO Box 26, Speers, SK S0M 2V0
Tel: 306-246-2067; *Fax:* 306-246-2028
info@oasiscarehome.ca
www.oasiscarehome.ca
Year Founded: 1993
Delbert Miller, Co-Owner; Operator
Sheila Miller, Co-Owner; Operator

St Louis: Regnier Personal Care Home Inc.
457 River Rd., St Louis, SK S0J 2C0
Tel: 306-422-8223
Lynn Regnier

Theodore: Theodore Health Centre
Affiliated with: Sunrise Regional Health Authority
PO Box 70, 615 Anderson Ave., Theodore, SK S0A 4C0
Tel: 306-647-2115; *Fax:* 306-647-2238
www.sunrisehealthregion.sk.ca
Number of Beds: 20 beds
Note: Specialties: Long-term care; Nursing services; Phlebotomy service; Respite care; Palliative care
Donna Gawryliuk, Head Nurse

Wadena: Pleasant View Care Home
Affiliated with: Saskatoon Regional Health Authority
PO Box 10, 533 - 5 St. NE, Wadena, SK S0A 4J0
Tel: 306-338-2412; *Fax:* 306-338-2720
Number of Beds: 46 beds
Bayle Maryniak, Site Manager

Watson: Quill Plains Centennial Lodge/Watson Health Complex
Affiliated with: Saskatoon Regional Health Authority
PO Box 220, 402 - 2 St. NE, Watson, SK S0K 4V0
Tel: 306-287-3791; *Fax:* 306-287-3386
Number of Beds: 54 beds

Weyburn: Crocus Plains Villa Ltd.
Affiliated with: Sun Country Regional Health Authority
1135 Park Ave., Weyburn, SK S4H 0K6
Tel: 306-842-0616
Carole Krieger, President

Weyburn: Parkway Lodge Personal Care Home
Affiliated with: Sun Country Regional Health Authority
420 - 8 Ave. SE, Weyburn, SK S4H 3N2
Tel: 306-842-7868

Weyburn: Tatagwa View
Affiliated with: Sun Country Regional Health Authority
Former Name: Souris Valley Extended Care Centre
PO Box 2003, 808 Souris Valley Rd., Weyburn, SK S4H 2Z9
Tel: 306-842-8398; *Fax:* 306-842-8341
www.suncountry.sk.ca
Year Founded: 2005
Number of Beds: 123 beds
Note: Specialties: Long-term care; Mental health services (10 beds); Acquired brain injury services; Diabetes program; Rehabilitation services; Day care centre; Palliative care
Marnell Cornish, Administrator

Special Care Homes

Saskatoon: LutherCare Communities
Affiliated with: Saskatoon Regional Health Authority
Former Name: Lutheran Sunset Home
Main Corporate Office, 1212 Osler St., Saskatoon, SK S7N 0T9
Tel: 306-664-0300; *Fax:* 306-664-0311
luthercare@shaw.ca
www.luthercare.com
Year Founded: 1955
Note: Specialties: Group living for young adults; Community day

programs for adults; Home support; Intermediate care; Seniors' housing; Long-term nursing care
Bernard McCallion, CEO

Saskatoon: LutherCare Communities Luther Seniors' Centre
1800 Alexandra Ave., Saskatoon, SK S7K 3C7
Tel: 306-664-0366; Fax: 306-664-0395
lsc@luthercare.com
www.luthercare.com
Year Founded: 1985
Note: Specialties: Day program for adults with irreversible dementia; Social services; Nursing; Personal care; Sensory stimulation

Saskatoon: LutherCare Communities Luther Special Care Home
1212 Osler St., Saskatoon, SK S7N 0T9
Tel: 306-664-0300
luthercare@shaw.ca
www.luthercare.com
Year Founded: 1955
Number of Beds: 129 beds, including 49 special needs beds & 2 respite beds
Note: Specialties: Secure special needs unit for residents with cognitive impairment; Nursing care; Physio, occupational, & recreational therapy; Community day program for seniors at risk; Respite care

Mental Health Facilities

Mental Health Hospitals/Facilities

Weyburn: Community Health Services
PO Box 2003, Weyburn, SK S4H 2Z9
Tel: 306-842-8718; Fax: 306-842-8738
DSchultz@schd.sk.ca
Number of Beds: 10 beds
Note: community health centre
Joan Panteluk, Manager, Community Health Services

Special Care Homes

Arborfield: Arborfield Special Care Lodge
Affiliated with: Kelsey Trail Regional Health Authority
PO Box 160, Arborfield, SK S0E 0A0
Tel: 306-769-8757; Fax: 306-769-8759
Number of Beds: 36 beds
Sharon Frisky, Community Coordinator

Battleford: Battlefords District Care Centre
Affiliated with: Prairie North Health Region
PO Box 69, 1308 Winnipeg St., Battleford, SK S0M 0E0
Tel: 306-446-6900; Fax: 306-937-2258
hccc@bathd.sk.ca
Number of Beds: 124 beds
Carol Dyck, Facility Manager

Canora: Canora Gateway Lodge
Affiliated with: Sunrise Regional Health Authority
PO Box 1387, 212 Centre Ave. East, Canora, SK S0A 0L0
Tel: 306-563-5685; Fax: 306-563-5711
Number of Beds: 78 beds
Oney Pollock, Manager, Health Services

Carrot River: Pasquia Special Care Home
Affiliated with: Kelsey Trail Regional Health Authority
PO Box 250, 4101 - 1 Ave West, Carrot River, SK S0E 0L0
Tel: 306-862-2725; Fax: 306-768-3233
Number of Beds: 35 long-term care beds
Andrew Will

Dalmeny: Spruce Manor Special Care Home
Affiliated with: Saskatoon Regional Health Authority
PO Box 190, 701 First St., Dalmeny, SK S0K 1E0
Tel: 306-254-2101; Fax: 306-254-2178
Number of Beds: 36 beds
Tom Nicholls, Administrator
Jonathan Redekop, Maintenance

Esterhazy: Centennial Special Care Home
Affiliated with: Sunrise Regional Health Authority
PO Box 310, 300 James St., Esterhazy, SK S0A 0X0
Tel: 306-745-6444; Fax: 306-745-2741
Number of Beds: 46 beds
Doreen Strong, Manager, Health Services

Herbert: Herbert Nursing Home Inc.
Affiliated with: Cypress Regional Health Authority
PO Box 520, 405 Herbert Ave., Herbert, SK S0H 2A0
Tel: 306-784-2466; Fax: 306-784-2449
Number of Beds: 55 beds
Gordon Milton, Administrator
Lyle Zacharias, Director, Plant Maintenance

Humboldt: St. Mary's Villa
Affiliated with: Saskatoon Regional Health Authority
PO Box 1360, 1109 - 13 St. North, Humboldt, SK S0K 2A0
Tel: 306-682-2628; Fax: 306-682-3211
Number of Beds: 101 beds
Jan Berger, Site Manager

Langenberg: Centennial Special Care Home
Affiliated with: Sunrise Regional Health Authority
PO Box 9, 200 Heritage Dr, Langenberg, SK S0A 2A0
Tel: 306-743-2232; Fax: 306-743-5025
Number of Beds: 48 beds

Lloydminster: Jubilee Home
Affiliated with: Prairie North Health Region
3902 - 45 Ave., Lloydminster, SK S9V 1Z1
Tel: 306-820-5950; Fax: 306-825-9869
www.pacha.ca
Number of Beds: 50 beds
Bobbie Stevenson, Facility Manager

Mankota: Prairie View Health Centre
Affiliated with: Cypress Regional Health Authority
PO Box 390, 241 - 1 Ave., Mankota, SK S0H 2W0
Tel: 306-628-3565; Fax: 306-628-3733
Number of Beds: 20 beds

Meadow Lake: Northland Pioneers Lodge Inc.
Affiliated with: Prairie North Health Region
515 - 3 St. West, Meadow Lake, SK S9X 1L1
Tel: 306-236-1500; Fax: 306-236-3244
Number of Beds: 55 beds
Shelley Wasyliw, Facility Manager

Melville: Centennial Special Care Home
PO Box 1390, 200 Heritage Rd., Melville, SK S0A 2P0
Tel: 306-743-2232; Fax: 306-743-5025

Middle Lake: Bethany Pioneer Village Inc.
Affiliated with: Saskatoon Regional Health Authority
PO Box 8, Middle Lake, SK S0K 2X0
Tel: 306-367-2033; Fax: 306-367-2155
Number of Beds: 36 beds
Glenn McDougall, Administrator

Moosomin: Eastern Saskatchewan Pioneer Lodge
Affiliated with: Regina Qu'Appelle Health Region
506 Windover Ave., Bag 3, Moosomin, SK S0G 3N0
Tel: 306-435-2326; Fax: 306-435-3335
Number of Beds: 57 beds
Sharon Ann Wood

Nipawin: Nipawin District Nursing Home
Affiliated with: Kelsey Trail Regional Health Authority
PO Box 2105, 400 - 6th Ave. East, Nipawin, SK S0E 1E0
Tel: 306-862-9828; Fax: 306-862-2400
Number of Beds: 96 beds

North Battleford: Société Joseph Breton Inc. (Villa Pascal)
Affiliated with: Prairie North Health Region
1301 - 113 St., North Battleford, SK S9A 3K1
Tel: 306-445-8465; Fax: 306-445-5117
Number of Beds: 40 beds
Thérèse Michaud, Administrator

Prince Albert: Herb Bassett Home
Affiliated with: Prince Albert Parkland Regional Health Authority
1220 - 25 St. West, Prince Albert, SK S6V 7P7
Tel: 306-765-6000; Fax: 306-765-6207
Number of Beds: 144 beds
John Piggott

Prince Albert: Mont St. Joseph Home Inc.
Affiliated with: Prince Albert Parkland Regional Health Authority
777 - 28 St. East, Prince Albert, SK S6V 8C2
Tel: 306-953-4500; Fax: 306-953-4550
Number of Beds: 120 beds
Note: Special care home
Brian Martin, Executive Director

Raymore: Silver Heights Special Care Home
Affiliated with: Regina Qu'Appelle Health Region
PO Box 549, 402 McLean St., Raymore, SK S0A 3J0
Tel: 306-746-5744; Fax: 306-746-5747
Number of Beds: 31 beds
Kate Beattie, Facility Manager

Regina: Salvation Army William Booth Special Care Home
Affiliated with: Regina Qu'Appelle Health Region
50 Angus Rd., Regina, SK S4R 8P6
Tel: 306-543-0655; Fax: 306-543-1292
Number of Beds: 83 beds
Capt. Graham Brown, Executive Director

Saskatoon: Circle Drive Special Care Home Inc.
Affiliated with: Saskatoon Regional Health Authority
PO Box 60020, 3055 Preston Ave. South, Saskatoon, SK S7T 1C3
Tel: 306-955-4800; Fax: 306-955-2376
Number of Beds: 50 beds
Blair MacPherson, Supervisor, Physical Plant
Leonard Enns, Administrator

Saskatoon: Convent of Sion
Affiliated with: Saskatoon Regional Health Authority
#114, 3104 Louise Pl., Saskatoon, SK S7J 5J8
Tel: 306-373-0335
macdonaldkay@shaw.ca
Number of Beds: 6 beds
Sr. Kay MacDonald, Director

Saskatoon: Extendicare - Preston
Affiliated with: Saskatoon Regional Health Authority
2225 Preston Ave., Saskatoon, SK S7J 2E7
Tel: 306-374-2242; Fax: 306-373-2203
Number of Beds: 82 beds
Patricia Amos, Administrator

Saskatoon: Senior Sisters of Sion Residence
Affiliated with: Saskatoon Regional Health Authority
333 Acadia Dr., Saskatoon, SK S7H 3V5
Tel: 306-374-9566; Fax: 306-374-6648
kaymac@sasktel.net
Number of Beds: 27 beds
Sr. Katherine MacDonald, Director

Saskatoon: Ursuline Sisters of St Angela's Convent (St Angela's)
Affiliated with: Saskatoon Regional Health Authority
1212 College Dr., Saskatoon, SK S7N 0W4
Tel: 306-242-5566; Fax: 306-975-7046
Number of Beds: 5 beds

Strasbourg: Last Mountain Pioneer Home
Affiliated with: Saskatoon Regional Health Authority
PO Box 549, 700 Prospect Ave., Strasbourg, SK S0G 4V0
Tel: 306-725-3342; Fax: 306-725-3404
cfuessel.lshd@shin.sk.ca
Number of Beds: 43 beds
Connie Fuessel, Manager

Warman: Warman Mennonite Special Care Home
Affiliated with: Saskatoon Regional Health Authority
PO Box 100, 201 - 3 Ave. North, Warman, SK S0K 4S0
Tel: 306-933-2011; Fax: 306-933-2782
Number of Beds: 31 beds
John Friesen, Administrator

Weyburn: Weyburn Special Care Home
Affiliated with: Sun Country Health Region
PO Box 2003, 704 - 5 St. NE, Weyburn, SK S4H 2Z9
Tel: 306-842-4455; Fax: 306-842-3084
Number of Beds: 90 beds

Yukon Territory

Government Departments in Charge

YUKON TERRITORY: Health & Social Services
PO Box 2703, Whitehorse, YT Y1A 2C6
Tel: 867-667-5770; Fax: 867-667-3096
www.hss.gov.yk.ca

Hospitals

Hospitals - General

Watson Lake: Watson Lake Hospital
PO Box 500, Watson Lake, YT Y0A 1C0
Tel: 867-536-4444; Fax: 867-536-7302
Number of Beds: 10 beds
Note: Number of staff: 1 nurse-in-charge, 7 additional nurses
Sue Rudd, Nurse in Charge

Whitehorse: **Whitehorse General Hospital**
5 Hospital Rd., Whitehorse, YT Y1A 3H7
Tel: 867-393-8700; *Fax:* 867-393-8771
www.whitehorsehospital.ca

Number of Beds: 49 beds
Ron Browne, CEO

Community Health Centres

Community Health Care Centres

Beaver Creek: **Beaver Creek Health Centre**
General Delivery, Beaver Creek, YT Y0B 1A0
Tel: 867-862-4444; *Fax:* 867-862-7909

Carcross: **Carcross Health Centre**
General Delivery, Carcross, YT Y0A 1B0
Tel: 867-821-4444; *Fax:* 867-821-3909
hc.carcross@gov.yk.ca

Carmacks: **Carmacks Health Centre**
PO Box 230, Carmacks, YT Y0B 1C0
Tel: 867-863-4444; *Fax:* 867-863-6612
carmacks.nic@gov.yk.ca

Number of Beds: 2 beds
Jocelyn Rhode, Acting Nurse Practitioner in Charge

Dawson: **Dawson City Health Centre**
PO Box 10, Dawson, YT Y0B 1G0
Tel: 867-993-4444; *Fax:* 867-993-5811

Destruction Bay: **Destruction Bay Health Centre**
General Delivery, Destruction Bay, YT Y0B 1H0
Tel: 867-841-4444; *Fax:* 867-841-5274

Faro: **Faro Health Centre**
PO Box 99, Faro, YT Y0B 1K0
Tel: 867-994-4444; *Fax:* 867-994-3457

Haines Junction: **Haines Junction Health Centre**
PO Box 5334, Haines Junction, YT Y0B 1L0
Tel: 867-634-4444; *Fax:* 867-634-2733

Mayo: **Mayo Nursing Station**
PO Box 98, Mayo, YT Y0B 1M0
Tel: 867-996-4444; *Fax:* 867-996-2018
hc.mayo@gov.yk.ca

Note: Specialties: Public health services; Health promotion services; Home care services. Number of Employees: 1 doctor + 3 community nurse practitioners

Old Crow: **Old Crow Health Centre**
General Delivery, Old Crow, YT Y0B 1N0
Tel: 867-996-4444; *Fax:* 867-966-3614
www.oldcrow.ca/nursing

Year Founded: 1960
Note: Specialties: Nursing care; Health promotion; Home & community care

Pelly Crossing: **Pelly Crossing Health Centre**
General Delivery, Pelly Crossing, YT Y0B 1P0
Tel: 867-537-4444; *Fax:* 867-537-3611
hc.pelly-crossing@gov.yk.ca

Ross River: **Ross River Health Centre**
General Delivery, Ross River, YT Y0B 1S0
Tel: 867-969-4444; *Fax:* 867-969-2014

Teslin: **Teslin Health Centre**
General Delivery, Teslin, YT Y0A 1B0
Tel: 867-390-4444

Note: Specialties: Public health services; Health promotion; Clinical care by community nurses; Home care

Watson Lake: **Watson Lake Health Centre**
PO Box 500, Watson Lake, YT Y0A 1C0
Tel: 867-536-7483; *Fax:* 867-536-7011

Sue Rudd

Long Term/Retirement Care

Long Term Care Facilities

Dawson City: **McDonald Lodge for Seniors**
PO Box 310, 636 - 5th Ave., Dawson City, YT Y0B 1G0
Tel: 867-993-5345; *Fax:* 867-993-5849
Toll-Free: 1-800-661-0408

Number of Beds: 11 residential beds, including 2 respite beds
Note: 0pecialties: Residential care for seniors & physically challenged persons who require moderate assistance; Recreational & therapeutic activities; Respite care; Home support services; Palliative care
Adeline Griffin-Viney, Manager

Whitehorse: **Copper Ridge Place**
60 Lazulite Dr., Whitehorse, YT Y1A 6S9
Tel: 867-393-7500; *Fax:* 867-393-7510
bev.oyler@gov.yk.ca

Number of Beds: 96 beds

Whitehorse: **Norman D. Macaulay Lodge**
2 Klondike Rd., Whitehorse, YT Y1A 3L5
Tel: 867-667-5955; *Fax:* 867-393-6237
bev.oyler@gov.yk.ca

Number of Beds: 44 beds

SECTION 11
LAW FIRMS

Major Law Firms

Aird & Berlis LLP
#1800, Brookfield Place, CP 754, 181 Bay St., Toronto, ON M5J 2T9 Canada
Tel: 416-863-1500; *Fax:* 416-863-1515
www.airdberlis.com
www.facebook.com/pages/Aird-Berlis/116517495028459,
twitter.com/AirdBerlis,
www.linkedin.com/company/aird-&-berlis-llp
Profile: 1 Offices, 130 Lawyers, Founded in: 1919
Legal services in the areas of Banking Law, Corporate & Commercial Law, Corporate Finance, Insolvency & Restructuring, Litigation, Real Estate Law, and Tax Law
Senior and Managing Partners
Leo F. Longo, Senior Partner
416-865-7778
llongo@airdberlis.com
Eldon Bennett, Managing Partner
416-865-7704
ebennett@airdberlis.com
Jack Bernstein, Senior Partner
416-865-7766
jbernstein@airdberlis.com

Bennett Jones LLP - Calgary
#4500, Bankers Hall East Tower, 855 - 2nd St. SW, Calgary, AB T2P 4K7
Tel: 403-298-3100; *Fax:* 403-265-7219
www.bennettjones.ca
twitter.com/BennettJonesLaw
Profile: 6 Offices, 351 Lawyers, Founded in: 1922
Senior and Managing Partners
Perry Spitznagel, Q.C., Vice-Chair & Managing Partner
403-298-3153
spitznagelp@bennettjones.ca

Blaney McMurtry LLP
#1500, 2 Queen St. East, Toronto, ON M5C 3G5
Tel: 416-593-1221; *Fax:* 416-593-5437
info@blaney.com
www.blaney.com
Profile: 1 Offices, 125 Lawyers, Founded in: 1954
Senior and Managing Partners
D. Barry Prentice, Senior Partner
416-593-3953
Michael J. Penman, Senior Partner
416-593-3966
Crawford W. Spratt, Senior Partner
416-593-3965
cspratt@blaney.com
Michael J. Bennett, Managing Partner
416-593-3905
mbennett@blaney.com

Burnet, Duckworth & Palmer LLP
#2400, 525 - 8th Ave. SW, Calgary, AB T2P 1G1
Tel: 403-260-0100; *Fax:* 403-260-0332
counsel@bdplaw.com
www.bdplaw.com
Profile: 1 Offices, 135 Lawyers, Founded in: 1915
Corporate; Commercial; Taxation; Real Estate; Securities
Senior and Managing Partners
Gary R. Bugeaud, Managing Partner
403-260-0155
grb@bdplaw.com
Harry S. Campbell, Q.C., Senior Partner; Vice-Chair
403-260-0281
hsc@bdplaw

Cain Lamarre Casgrain Wells - Val-d'Or
#202, 855, 3e av, Val-d'Or, QC J9P 1T2
Tél: 819-825-4153; *Téléc:* 819-825-9769
info@clcw.ca
www.clcw.qc.ca
Profile: 16 Offices, 160 Lawyers, Founded in: 1999
Senior and Managing Partners

Cassels Brock & Blackwell LLP
#2100, Scotia Plaza, 40 King St. West, Toronto, ON M5H 3C2
Tel: 416-869-5300; *Fax:* 416-360-8877
www.casselsbrock.com
Profile: 1 Offices, 200 Lawyers, Founded in: 1888
Full-service law firm, with an emphasis on tax and business law, both domestic and international
Senior and Managing Partners
David R. Peterson, P.C., Q.C., Senior Partner
416-869-5451
dpeterson@casselsbrock.com
H. Donald Guthrie, Q.C., Senior Consulting Partner
416-869-5334
hdguthrie@casselsbrock.com

Davies Ward Phillips & Vineberg LLP
1 First Canadian Place, 44th Fl., Toronto, ON M5X 1B1
Tel: 416-863-0900; *Fax:* 416-863-0871
www.dwpv.com
twitter.com/_Davies_
Profile: 3 Offices, 240 Lawyers, Founded in: 1961
Business transactions & business operations including acquisitions, divestitures, financing, securities, real estate & land development
Senior and Managing Partners
Carol Hansell, Senior Partner
416-863-5592
chansell@dwpv.com
George N. Addy, Senior Partner
416-863-5588
gaddy@dwpv.com
Robert T. Bauer, Senior Partner
416-863-5552
rbauer@dwpv.com
William M. Ainley, Senior Partner
416-863-5509
wainley@dwpv.com
D. Shawn McReynolds, Managing Partner
416-863-5538
smcreynolds@dwpv.com
Kevin J. Thomson, Senior Partner
416-863-5590
kthomson@dwpv.com

Davis LLP - Vancouver
#2800, Park Place, 666 Burrard St., Vancouver, BC V6C 2Z7
Tel: 604-687-9444; *Fax:* 604-687-1612
www.davis.ca
Profile: 8 Offices, 240 Lawyers, Founded in: 1892
As a full-service law firm, Davis LLP provides a comprehensive range of legal services to clients around the world, through offices across Canada & in Japan. The firm has 88 partners worldwide, & 134 other lawyers around the world. Business can be conducted in English, French, Japanese, Spanish, Mandarin, Cantonese, Korean, German, Italian, Dutch, Estonian, & Polish. Established in Vancouver in 1892, the firm has more than 220 lawyers working in integrated practice groups that focus on client service & specialization. Davis strives to help clients achieve their business objectives & resolve business problems quickly & effectively. The firm is strong in all the traditional areas of legal practice. Across the firm, lawyers continuously cultivate commercial & government relationships to both facilitate the conduct of business & to identify new business opportunities for clients. Davis & its lawyers are recognized as leaders in numerous domestic & international ratings publications.
Senior and Managing Partners
Donald W. Campbell, Senior Strategy Advisor
604-643-2991
dcampbell@davis.ca
Linda I. Parsons, Q.C., Senior Partner
604-643-6445
lparsons@davis.ca
Dale G. Sanderson, Q.C., Senior Partner
604-643-6330
dsanderson@davis.ca
Brian F. Hiebert, Managing Partner
604-643-2917
bhiebert@davis.ca
D. Ross Clark, Q.C., Senior Partner
604-643-2911
drclark@davis.ca
W. Ross Ellison, Q.C., Senior Partner
604-643-2918
rellison@davis.ca
Stuart B. Morrow, Senior Partner
604-643-2948
sbmorrow@davis.ca
Timothy G. Duholke, FCA, Senior Tax Advisor
604-643-6400
tduholke@davis.ca
Kathryn I. Denhoff, Senior Partner
604-643-2995
kdenhoff@davis.ca

Fasken Martineau - Toronto
#2400, Bay Adelaide Centre, P.O. Box 20, 333 Bay St., Toronto, ON M5H 2T6
Tel: 416-366-8381; *Fax:* 416-364-7813
Toll-Free: 800-268-8424
toronto@fasken.com
www.fasken.com
www.facebook.com/group.php?gid=154446131283771,
twitter.com/faskenmartineau,
www.linkedin.com/company/fasken-martineau-dumoulin
Profile: 9 Offices, 675 Lawyers, Founded in: 1863
Fasken Marineau provides legal services to the full array of participants in the financial services industry; our clients include leading Canadian & foreign banks, life & property & casualty insurance companies, loan & trust companies, cooperatives & credit unions, finance companies, insurance agents & brokers & other financial services providers; we pride ourselves on knowing each client's business & the current issues & trends affecting them; we work closely with our clients across the breadth of their transactional investment & other activities & in their relations with Canadian regulators; our group regularly provides advice regarding mergers & acquisitions, financings, restructurings, the establishment of financial services businesses, the development & distribution of financial services products & all manner of regulatory issues with both federal & provincial regulators
Senior and Managing Partners
Tony Baldanza, Senior Partner
416-865-4352
abaldanza@fasken.com
John A. Campion, Senior Partner
416-865-4357
jcampion@fasken.com
David N. Corbett, Managing Partner, Firm
416-868-3504
dcorbett@fasken.com
Martin K. Denyes, Managing Partner, Ontario
416-868-3489
mdenyes@fasken.com
Samuel R. Rickett, Senior Partner
416-868-3436
srickett@fasken.com
Stephen Erlichman, Senior Partner
416-865-4552
serlichman@fasken.com
Jeff Kaufman, Senior Partner
416-868-3417
jkaufman@fasken.com

Fraser Milner Casgrain LLP - Toronto
#400, Toronto-Dominion Centre, 77 King St. West, Toronto, ON M5K 0A1
Tel: 416-863-4421; *Fax:* 416-863-4592
www.fmc-law.com
twitter.com/FMC_LAW
Profile: 6 Offices, 500 Lawyers, Founded in: 1839
The firm provides legal services in the following areas: Business Immigration; Competition/Antitrust/Foreign Investment Review; Corporate & Commercial Law; Corporate Governance; Employment & Labour Law; Financial Services; Franchising; Insolvency & Restructuring; Intellectual Property Law; International Trade Law; Mergers & Acquisitions; Pensions & Benefits Law; Private Equity & Venture Capital; Public-Private Partnerships; Real Estate Law; Corporate Finance & Securities; Tax Law; and Wealth Management
Senior and Managing Partners
Thomas J. Hunter, Senior Partner
416-863-4555
tom.hunter@fmc-law.com
Michael N. (Mike) Kaplan, Managing Partner
416-863-4421
mike.kaplan@fmc-law.com
Ronald A. Goldenberg, Senior Partner
416-863-4724
ronald.goldenberg@fmc-law.com
Frank E. P. Bowman, Senior Partner
416-367-6820
frank.bowman@fmc-law.com

Goodmans LLP
#3400, Bay Adelaide Centre, 333 Bay St., Toronto, ON M5H 2S7
Tel: 416-979-2211; *Fax:* 416-979-1234
info@goodmans.ca
www.goodmans.ca
Profile: 2 Offices, 200 Lawyers, Founded in: 1917
Goodmans is a leading Canadian law firm, well-recognized across Canada & internationally for its excellence & market leadership in large-scale corporate transactions. Goodmans is a full-service business law firm that offers clients a wide range of services & expertise in all of the major business law areas, including: Broadcasting, Telecommunications & New Media; Commercial Real Estate; Corporate & Commercial Law; Corporate Restructuring; Corporate Finance & Securities; Litigation; Mergers & Acquisitions; Municipal, Planning & Property Tax Law; Pensions; Trusts & Estates & Tax. With over 200 lawyers, Goodmans provides a complete spectrum of legal advice & representation to domestic & foreign business clients ranging from emerging technology companies to financial institutions & conglomerates
Senior and Managing Partners
Bryon Sonberg, Managing Director

Heenan Blaikie S.E.N.C.R.L/SRL
#2500, 1250, boul René-Lévesque ouest, Montréal, QC H3B 4Y1
Tel: 514-846-1212; *Fax:* 514-846-3427
www.heenanblaikie.com
Profile: 11 Offices, 550 Lawyers, Founded in: 1973
Heenan Blaikie LLP business law practitioners provide a full range of services to some of Canada's largest corporations & financial institutions, as well as to many smaller, growth-oriented companies in all types of transactions & corporate governance issues: mergers & acquisitions, international & domestic joint ventures, reorganizations, regulatory matters, venture capital investment, financing arrangements with commercial & private lenders, directors' & officers' liabilities, trademark & copyright matters; software licensing & outsourcing contracts
Senior and Managing Partners
Guy Tremblay, National Co-Managing Partner
514-846-2271
gtremblay@heenan.ca

Lavery, de Billy - Montréal
#4000, 1, Place Ville-Marie, Montréal, QC H3B 4M4
Tel: 514-871-1522; *Fax:* 514-871-8977
info@lavery.qc.ca
www.laverydebilly.com
Profile: 3 Offices, 175 Lawyers, Founded in: 1913
Senior and Managing Partners

Macleod Dixon LLP
#3700, Canterra Tower, 400 Third Ave. SW, Calgary, AB T2P 4H2
Tel: 403-267-8222; *Fax:* 403-264-5973
danielle.gill@macleoddixon.com
www.macleoddixon.com
Profile: 7 Offices, 300 Lawyers, Founded in: 1912
Senior and Managing Partners
W. (Bill) H. Tuer, Managing Partner
403-267-8385
bill.tuer@macleoddixon.com

MacPherson Leslie & Tyerman LLP - Regina
#1500, Hill Centre I, 1874 Scarth St., Regina, SK S4P 4E9
Tel: 306-347-8000; *Fax:* 306-352-5250
www.mlt.com
Profile: 4 Offices, 115 Lawyers, Founded in: 1920
Client-centered & business-oriented law firm; experience extends from the more traditional practice areas of business law (such as corporate finance, mergers & acquisitions, tax, insolvency, commercial litigation) to other rapidly developing areas
Senior and Managing Partners
Donald K. Wilson, Q.C., Managing Partner
306-347-8437
dwilson@mlt.com

McCarthy Tétrault LLP - Toronto
#5300, Toronto-Dominion Bank Tower, Box 48, Toronto, ON M5K 1E6
Tel: 416-362-1812; *Fax:* 416-868-0673
Toll-Free: 877-244-7711
info@mccarthy.ca; tschier@mccarthy.ca (Media contact)
www.mccarthy.ca
Profile: 6 Offices, 616 Lawyers, Founded in: 1855
One of our largest practice areas is in corporate finance, where we represent public issuers & underwriters in corporate finance matters involving the preparation of prospectuses & other offering documents for public & private offerings; we have extensive experience in dealing with mergers & acquisitions & corporate reorganizations; our practice has involved us in many significant takeovers, as well as the development & implementation of defensive strategies in hostile bid situations to improve shareholder values
Senior and Managing Partners
James M. Farley, Q.C., Senior Counsel
416-601-7840
jfarley@mccarthy.ca
Thomas B. Akin, Senior Partner
416-601-7934
takin@mccarthy.ca

McMillan LLP - Toronto
#4400, BCE Place, Bay Wellington Tower, 181 Bay St., Toronto, ON M5J 2T3
Tel: 416-865-7000; *Fax:* 416-865-7048
Toll-Free: 888-622-4624
info@mcmillan.ca
www.mcmillan.ca
Profile: 5 Offices, 395 Lawyers, Founded in: 1903
Senior and Managing Partners
John W. Craig, Senior Partner
416-865-7128
john.craig@mcmillan.ca
Graham W.S. Scott, Q.C., Senior Partner
416-865-7247
graham.scott@mcmillan.ca
John A. Paterson, Senior Partner
416-865-7021
john.paterson@mcmillan.ca
Michael P. Whitcombe, Senior Partner
416-865-7126
michael.whitcombe@mcmillan.ca

Miller Thomson LLP - Toronto
#5800, Scotia Plaza, P.O. Box 1011, 40 King St. West, Toronto, ON M5H 3S1
Tel: 416-595-8500; *Fax:* 416-595-8695
Toll-Free: 888-762-5559
toronto@millerthomson.com
www.millerthomson.com
twitter.com/millerthomson,
www.linkedin.com/company/Miller-Thomson-LLP
Profile: 11 Offices, 470 Lawyers, Founded in: 1957
Bankruptcy; Corporate Commercial; E-Commerce; Estates/Pensions; Financial Services; Franchising; Insolvency & Insurance; Mergers & Acquisitions; Securities; Tax Law
Senior and Managing Partners
Clifford Goldlist, Senior Partner
416-601-4117
cgoldlist@millerthomson.com
Jeffrey C. Carhart, Senior Partner
416-595-8615
jcarhart@millerthomson.com
Barbara R.C. Doherty, Senior Partner
416-595-8621
bdoherty@millerthomson.com

Norton Rose OR LLP - Montréal
#2500, 1 Place Ville Marie, Montréal, QC H3B 1R1
Tél: 514-847-4747; *Téléc:* 514-286-5474
montreal@nortonrose.com
www.nortonrose.com
Profile: 5 Offices, 450 Lawyers, Founded in: 1879
Asset-based Lending; Banking & Financial Products; Corporate & Commercial Law; Insolvency & Restructuring; Mergers & Acquisitions; Projects & Project Finance; Securities; Tax
Senior and Managing Partners
Brian Mulroney, P.C., C.C., LL.D., Senior Partner
514-847-4779
brian.mulroney@nortonrose.com
Claude Brunet, Senior Partner
514-847-4726
claude.brunet@nortonrose.com
Jean Piette, Senior Partner
514-847-4584
jean.piette@nortonrose.com
Jean-Pierre Colpron, Senior Partner
514-847-4880
jean-pierre.colpron@nortonrose.com
David R. Collier, Senior Partner
514-847-4539
david.collier@nortonrose.com
Marc S. Benoît, Senior Partner
514-847-6049
marc.benoit@nortonrose.com
Kevin P. Murphy, Senior Partner
514-847-4293
kevin.murphy@nortonrose.com
Pierre Pronovost, Senior Partner
514-847-4485
pierre.pronovost@nortonrose.com
Martin Rochette, Senior Partner
514-847-4430
martin.rochette@nortonrose.com
Michel G. Sylvestre, Senior Partner
514-847-4460
michel.sylvestre@nortonrose.com
Gilles Touchette, Senior Partner
514-847-4532
gilles.touchette@nortonrose.com
Danièle Boutet, Senior Partner
514-847-4527
daniele.boutet@nortonrose.com
Michel G. Carle, Senior Partner
514-847-4501
michel.carle@nortonrose.com
Mario M. Caron, Senior Partner
514-847-4525
mario.caron@nortonrose.com
Christine A. Carron, Senior Partner
514-847-4404
christine.carron@nortonrose.com
Jules Charette, Senior Partner
514-847-4450
jules.charette@nortonrose.com
Robert P. Charlton, Senior Partner
514-847-4459
robert.charlton@nortonrose.com
Christian J. Beaudry, Senior Partner
514-847-4416
christian.beaudry@nortonrose.com
John A. Coleman, Managing Partner
514-847-4503
john.coleman@nortonrose.com
R. Luc Beaulieu, Senior Partner
514-847-4428
luc.beaulieu@nortonrose.com
Marc Duquette, Senior Partner
514-847-4508
marc.duquette@nortonrose.com
François Fontaine, Senior Partner
514-847-4413
francois.fontaine@nortonrose.com
L. Yves Fortier, C.C., Q.C., Senior Partner
514-847-4740
yves.fortier@nortonrose.com
Lise Bergeron, Senior Partner
514-847-4506
lise.bergeron@nortonrose.com
Jean G. Bertrand, Managing Partner
514-847-4401
jean.bertrand@nortonrose.com
Pierre Hébert, Senior Partner
514-847-4474
pierre.hebert@nortonrose.com
William Hesler, Q.C., Senior Partner
514-847-4510
william.hesler@nortonrose.com
Olivier F. Kott, Senior Partner
514-847-4445
olivier.kott@nortonrose.com
Pierre Bienvenu, Senior Partner
514-847-4452
pierre.bienvenu@nortonrose.com
Louise Laplante, Senior Partner
514-847-4433
louise.laplante@nortonrose.com
Hélène Lefebvre, Senior Partner
514-847-4457
helene.lefebvre@nortonrose.com
Francis R. Legault, Senior Partner
514-847-4495
francis.legault@nortonrose.com

Osler, Hoskin & Harcourt LLP - Toronto
#6100, P.O. Box 50, One First Canadian Place, Toronto, ON M5X 1B8
Tel: 416-362-2111; *Fax:* 416-862-6666
counsel@osler.com
www.osler.com
Profile: 5 Offices, 500 Lawyers,
Advises many of Canada's corporate leaders as well as U.S. & international parties with extensive interests in Canada; third-party research confirms the firm's preeminent position in the marketplace; with over 500 lawyers based in Toronto, Montréal, Ottawa, Calgary & New York, our critical mass of experience with the largest domestic & cross-border business combinations enables us to exercise acknowledged strengths in mergers & acquisitions, tax, competition & litigation, & leverage our specialty expertise in fields like commercial property & infrastructure projects, IP & IT, among many others
Senior and Managing Partners
Lyndon A.J. Barnes, Senior Partner
416-862-6679
lbarnes@osler.com
Andrew H. Kingissepp, Senior Partner
416-862-6507
akingissepp@osler.com
Dale R. Ponder, Managing Partner
416-862-6500
dponder@osler.com
Terrence R. Burgoyne, Senior Partner
416-862-6601
tburgoyne@osler.com
Judith E. Harris, Senior Partner
416-862-4609
jharris@osler.com
Harvey Kirsh, Senior Partner
416-862-6844
hkirsh@osler.com

Stewart McKelvey - Halifax
#900, Purdy's Wharf Tower One, P.O. Box 997, Stn. Central, 1959 Upper Water St., Halifax, NS B3J 2X2
Tel: 902-420-3200; *Fax:* 902-420-1417
halifax@stewartmckelvey.com
www.stewartmckelvey.com

Profile: 6 Offices, 220 Lawyers, Founded in: 1867
Senior and Managing Partners
Richard F. Southcott, Regional Managing Partner
902-420-3304
rsouthcott@stewartmckelvey.com
John M. Rogers, Q.C., Managing Partner/CEO
902-420-3340
jrogers@stewartmckelvey.com

Stikeman Elliott LLP - Toronto
#5300, Commerce Court West, 199 Bay St., Toronto, ON M5L 1B9
Tel: 416-869-5500; *Fax:* 416-947-0866
Toll-Free: 877-973-5500
www.stikeman.com
Profile: 8 Offices, 500 Lawyers, Founded in: 1952
As a full-service business law firm, we advise on a wide range of matters including securities, structured financial products, investment activity, mergers & acquisitions, joint ventures, public-private partnerships & government advisory mandates; our particular strength lies in developing innovative, workable solutions to complex legal concerns; our success in building an international profile is reflected in our consistent inclusion in international "league tables" in such areas as project finance, privatizations & international securities transactions
Senior and Managing Partners
Roderick F. Barrett, Managing Partner
416-869-5524
rbarrett@stikeman.com
William J. Braithwaite, Senior Partner
416-869-5654
wbraithwaite@stikeman.com
Kathryn I. Chalmers, Senior Partner
416-869-5544
kchalmers@stikeman.com
Richard E. Clark, Senior Partner
416-869-5546
rclark@stikeman.com
Rocco M. Delfino, Senior Partner
416-869-5512
rdelfino@stikeman.com
Brenda Hebert, Senior Partner
416-869-5578
bhebert@stikeman.com
W. Brian Rose, Senior Partner
416-869-5685
brose@stikeman.com
Wayne E. Shaw, Senior Partner
416-869-5520
wshaw@stikeman.com
Marvin Yontef, Senior Partner
416-869-5530
myontef@stikeman.com
James C. Davis, Senior Partner
416-869-5539
jdavis@stikeman.com
Kathleen G. Ward, Senior Partner
416-869-5617
kward@stikeman.com

Torys LLP
#3000, Toronto-Dominion Centre, P.O. Box 270, 79 Wellington St. West, Toronto, ON M5K 1N2
Tel: 416-865-0040; *Fax:* 416-865-7380
www.torys.com
twitter.com/toryslip, www.linkedin.com/company/torys-llp
Profile: 3 Offices, 276 Lawyers, Founded in: 1941
Torys LLP is an international business law firm with offices in Toronto, New York and Calgary. Torys is known for its seamless cross-border services in a range of areas, including mergers and acquisitions; corporate and capital markets; litigation and dispute resolution; restructuring and insolvency; taxation; competition and antitrust; environmental, health and safety; debt finance and lending; project development and finance; managed assets; private equity and venture capital; financial institutions; pension and employment; intellectual property; technology, media and telecom; life sciences; real estate; infrastructure and energy; climate change and emissions trading; and personal client services.
Senior and Managing Partners
Les M. Viner, Managing Partner
416-865-8107
lviner@torys.com

Provincial Law Firms

Alberta

***Airdrie*: Warnock & Rathgeber - *2**
225 First Ave. NW, Airdrie, AB T4B 2M8
Tel: 403-948-0009; *Fax:* 403-948-6740
office@wrlawyers.ca
www.wrlawyers.ca

***Banff*: Karras Rathbone - *2**
P.O. Box 899, Stn. Main, 205 Bear St., Banff, AB T1L 1A9
Tel: 403-762-2770; *Fax:* 403-762-5961
karalaw@telus.net

***Barrhead*: Driessen Law Office - *1**
P.O. Box 4220, Stn. Main, 5017 - 50 Ave., Barrhead, AB T7N 1A2
Tel: 780-674-2276; *Fax:* 780-674-4592
solutions@driessenlaw.ca

***Blairmore*: Valerie J. Danielson Law Office - *1**
P.O. Box 1620, 13143 - 20th Ave., Blairmore, AB T0K 0E0
Tel: 403-562-2132; *Fax:* 403-562-2700
valeriejdanielson@shaw.ca

***Bonnyville*: Allan Wayne Fraser, Professional Corporation - *1**
CP 6710, Stn. Main, 4816 - 50 Ave., Bonnyville, AB T9N 2H2
Tel: 780-826-3355; *Fax:* 780-826-6132
awfraser@telusplanet.net

***Bonnyville*: Wood & Wiebe - *2**
#101, CP 8060, Stn. Main, 4811 - 50 Ave., Bonnyville, AB T9N 2J3
Tel: 780-826-5767; *Fax:* 780-826-4654
woodwieb@telusplanet.net

***Brooks*: Bell Law Office - *1**
CP 670, Stn. Main, Brooks, AB T1R 1B6
Tel: 403-362-3447; *Fax:* 403-362-4379
dhb@telus.net

***Brooks*: Susan E. Robertson - *1**
411B Third Ave. West, Brooks, AB T1R 0B2
Tel: 403-362-4064; *Fax:* 403-362-4024

***Calgary*: Laurie Allen & Associates, Barristers, Solicitors, Mediators - *5**
#800, 355 - 4 Ave. SW, Calgary, AB T2P 0J1
Tel: 403-266-5556; *Fax:* 403-266-5427
mail@laurieallen.com
www.laurieallen.com

***Calgary*: Robert J.E. Allen Law Office - *1**
#206, 4600 Crowchild Trail NW, Calgary, AB T3A 2L6
Tel: 403-216-5522; *Fax:* 403-216-5524
admin@calgarylawyer.net

***Calgary*: Anderson Law Firm - *1**
14 Strathridge Grove SW, Calgary, AB T3H 4M1
Tel: 403-253-4597; *Fax:* 403-253-4599
latitude@telus.net

***Calgary*: Linda A. Anderson - *1**
#16, 2439 - 54 Ave. SW, Calgary, AB T3E 1M4
Tel: 403-243-6400; *Fax:* 403-243-0126
linda@lindaandersonlaw.com

***Calgary*: Arkell Damen Hoffman, Barristers, Solicitors, & Notaries - *3**
109 - 14 Ave. SE, Calgary, AB T2G 1C6
Tel: 403-531-4151; *Fax:* 403-531-4153
info@adh-law.com

***Calgary*: Theodore L. Babie - *1**
615 - 36 St. NE, Calgary, AB T2A 4W3
Tel: 403-273-3673; *Fax:* 403-273-0931

***Calgary*: Deborah L. Barron - *1**
#303, Mayfair Place, 6707 Elbow Drive SW, Calgary, AB T2V 0E5
Tel: 403-238-0000; *Fax:* 403-238-2255
dbarron@deborahbarronlaw.com
www.deborahbarronlaw.com

***Calgary*: Batting, Der, Barristers & Solicitors - *1**
#2410, 645 - 7 Ave. SW, Calgary, AB T2P 4G8
Tel: 403-263-4949; *Fax:* 403-261-8977
rbatting@telus.net; debhaigh@telus.net
www.rbattinglaw.com

***Calgary*: Alan V.M. Beattie, Q.C. - *1**
3621 - 1A St. SW, Calgary, AB T2S 1R4
Tel: 403-245-5255; *Fax:* 403-228-0254
beattiea@shaw.ca

***Calgary*: Gary E. Bilyk Professional Corporation - *1**
#602, 706 - 7 Ave. SW, Calgary, AB T2P 0Z1
Tel: 403-266-2810; *Fax:* 403-264-1151
gebilyklawyer@shaw.ca

***Calgary*: Blumell & Hartney - *2**
#203, 2411 - 4 St. NW, Calgary, AB T2M 2Z8
Tel: 403-282-4544; *Fax:* 403-284-4535
b.blumell@shawbiz.ca; m.hartney@shaw.ca

***Calgary*: Michael J. Bondar, Professional Corporation - *1**
#1840, 801 - 6 Ave. SW, Calgary, AB T2P 3W2
Tel: 403-266-5511; *Fax:* 403-237-6620
mjbondar@shaw.ca

***Calgary*: Borden Ladner Gervais LLP - Calgary - *111**
Centennial Place, East Tower, #1900, 520 - 3rd Ave. SW, Calgary, AB T2P 0R3
Tel: 403-232-9500; *Fax:* 403-266-1395
info@blg.com
www.blg.com

***Calgary*: Bruni & Company - *2**
707 - 15th Ave. SW, Calgary, AB T2R 0R8
Tel: 403-266-5664; *Fax:* 403-262-6343
brunicorp@shaw.ca

***Calgary*: Lisa M. Burgis - *1**
#2410, 645 - 7 Ave. SW, Calgary, AB T2P 4G8
Tel: 403-213-2999; *Fax:* 403-261-8977
lburgis@telus.net

***Calgary*: Burstall Winger LLP - *26**
#1600, Dome Tower, 333 - 7th Ave. SW, Calgary, AB T2P 2Z1
Tel: 403-264-1915; *Fax:* 403-266-6016
info@burstall.com
www.burstall.com

***Calgary*: Butlin Oke Roberts & Nobles - *5**
#100, 1501 - 1 St. SW, Calgary, AB T2R 0W1
Tel: 403-543-7750; *Fax:* 403-543-7759

***Calgary*: Richard Cairns, Q.C. - *1**
#210, The Burns Bldg., 237 - 8 Ave. SE, Calgary, AB T2G 5C3
Tel: 403-205-3155; *Fax:* 403-546-0034
counsel@echambers.ca
www.echambers.ca

***Calgary*: Calgary Legal Guidance**
#100, 840 - 7th Ave. SW, Calgary, AB T2P 3G2
Tel: 403-234-9266; *Fax:* 403-234-9299
clg@clg.ab.ca
www.clg.ab.ca

***Calgary*: Cameron Horne Law Office LLP, Barristers & Solicitors - *2**
#820, 10201 Southport Rd. SW, Calgary, AB T2W 4X9
Tel: 403-531-2700; *Fax:* 403-531-2707
sandy@cameronhorne.ca; geoff@cameronhorne.ca
www.cameronhorne.ca

***Calgary*: Campbell O'Hara - *6**
#1160, 1122 - 4th St. SW, Calgary, AB T2R 1M1
Tel: 403-294-0030; *Fax:* 403-229-2977

***Calgary*: Caron & Partners LLP, Barristers & Solicitors - *16**
#2100, Scotia Centre, 700 - 2 St. SW, 21st Fl., Calgary, AB T2P 2W1
Tel: 403-262-3000; *Fax:* 403-237-0111
legalservices@caronpartners.com
www.caronpartners.com

***Calgary*: Carscallen Leitch LLP - *29**
#1500, 407 - 2 St. SW, Calgary, AB T2P 2Y3
Tel: 403-262-3775; *Fax:* 403-262-2952
info@cllawyers.com
www.cllawyers.com

***Calgary*: Castle & Associates, Barristers & Solicitors - *7**
#302, 221 - 10th Ave. SE, Calgary, AB T2G 0V9
Tel: 403-265-3403; *Fax:* 403-269-3217
mailbox@castleandassociates.ca
www.castleandassociates.ca

***Calgary*: Checkland & Company - *4**
#1100, 444 - 5th Ave. SW, Calgary, AB T2P 2T8
Tel: 403-233-9101; *Fax:* 403-233-9135

** indicates number of lawyers*

Calgary: Clark & Associates - *2
#203, 136 - 17 Ave. NE, Calgary, AB T2E 1L6
Tel: 403-520-2011; Fax: 403-230-3509
bclark@clarkandassociates.ca
www.clarkandassociates.ca

Calgary: Clark Dymond McCaffery O'Brien-Kelly - *3
#300, 1122 - 4 St. SW, Calgary, AB T2R 1M1
Tel: 403-265-7070; Fax: 403-232-6750
lawcdmg@telusplanet.net

Calgary: James K. Conley - *1
#210, The Burns Bldg., 237 - 8th Ave. SE, Calgary, AB T2G 5C3
Tel: 403-290-0994; Fax: 403-265-7680
jkconley@telus.net

Calgary: Timothy J. Corcoran - *1
#701, 4656 Westwinds Dr. NE, Calgary, AB T3J 3Z5
Tel: 403-263-6000; Fax: 403-280-7666
alberta@lawyer.com

Calgary: Cornerstone Law Group LLP - *2
#420, 10655 Southport Rd. SW, Calgary, AB T2W 4Y1
Tel: 403-296-1700; Fax: 403-258-0020
tom@cornerstonelaw.ca; jordan@cornerstonelaw.ca
www.cornerstonelaw.ca

Calgary: Craig Law LLP - *3
3408 - 114 Ave. SE, Calgary, AB T2Z 3V6
Tel: 403-297-0130; Fax: 403-297-0133

Calgary: Cuming & Gillespie - *2
#1130, 396 - 11th Ave. SW, Calgary, AB T2R 0C5
Tel: 403-571-0555; Fax: 403-232-8818
Toll-Free: 800-682-2480
james@cglaw.ca
www.cglaw.ca

Calgary: D'Souza & Associates - *3
#202, 811 Manning Rd. NE, Calgary, AB T2E 7L4
Tel: 403-531-9520; Fax: 403-272-6586

Calgary: Daniel J. Aberle Professional Corporation - *1
#305, 602 - 11 Ave. SW, Calgary, AB T2R 1J8
Tel: 403-229-1129; Fax: 403-245-9660

Calgary: Gary A. Daniels - *1
#200, 209 - 19 St. NW, Calgary, AB T2N 2H9
Tel: 403-297-0800; Fax: 403-283-7000
garyadaniels@shaw.ca

Calgary: Dartnell & Lutz - *2
#840, 840 - 6 Ave. SW, Calgary, AB T2P 3E5
Tel: 403-264-8484; Fax: 403-263-9110
dartnell-lutz@shaw.ca

Calgary: Davison Worden Mather LLP - *6
#1710, 540 - 5 Ave. SW, Calgary, AB T2P 0M2
Tel: 403-262-7745; Fax: 403-262-7011
www.dwmlaw.ca

Calgary: Dawe Law Office - *3
#200, 1409 Edmonton Trail NE, Calgary, AB T2E 3K8
Tel: 403-277-3100; Fax: 403-230-5855
info@dawelawoffice.com

Calgary: Demiantschuk, Lequier, Burke & Hoffinger - *10
#1200, 1015 - 4th St. SW, Calgary, AB T2R 1J4
Tel: 403-252-9937; Fax: 403-263-8529
assistance@legalsolutions.ca
www.legalsolutions.ca

Calgary: Balfour Q.H. Der, Q.C. - *1
#2410, 645 - 7 Ave. SW, Calgary, AB T2P 4G8
Tel: 403-234-8824; Fax: 403-261-8977
bqhder@telus.net

Calgary: Dixon Law Firm - *2
#1020, Canadian Centre, 833 - 4 Ave. SW, Calgary, AB T2P 3T5
Tel: 403-297-9480; Fax: 403-266-1487

Calgary: Docken & Company - *3
#900, 800 - 6th Ave. SW, Calgary, AB T2P 3G3
Tel: 403-269-3612; Fax: 403-269-8246
info@docken.com
www.docken.com

Calgary: Dunphy Best Blocksom LLP, Barristers & Solicitors - *20
#2100, 777 - 8th Ave. SW, Calgary, AB T2P 3R5
Tel: 403-265-7777; Fax: 403-269-8911
info@dbblaw.com
www.dbblaw.com

Calgary: Edy, Dalton - *6
#800, 1015 - 4 St. SW, Calgary, AB T2R 1J4
Tel: 403-263-3200; Fax: 403-263-3202
reception@edydalton.com; sjdalton@edydalton.com
www.edydalton.com

Calgary: Ellert Law - *2
#510, 706 - 7 Ave. SW, Calgary, AB T2P 0Z1
Tel: 403-269-3315; Fax: 403-269-3329
dale.ellert@ellertlaw.com

Calgary: P. Robert Enns - *1
#222, 1100 - 8 Ave. SW, Calgary, AB T2P 3T9
Tel: 403-262-6588; Fax: 403-262-6590
prenns@shaw.ca

Calgary: Everard Kubitz & Mueller - *3
#308, 2116 - 27 Ave. NE, Calgary, AB T2E 7A6
Tel: 403-250-7100; Fax: 403-291-5473
lawyers@ekmlawyers.com

Calgary: Faber Bickman Leon - *7
#350, 603 - 7 Ave. SW, Calgary, AB T2P 2T5
Tel: 403-263-1540; Fax: 403-269-2653
lfaber@fbllaw.ca; dbickman@fbllaw.ca; lleon@fbllaw.ca
www.fbllaw.ca

Calgary: Fagan & Chow - *2
#375, 926 - 5th Ave. SW, Calgary, AB T2P 0N7
Tel: 403-517-1777; Fax: 403-517-1776
davidg_chow@yahoo.ca
www.patrickfagan.com

Calgary: Felesky Flynn LLP - *33
#5000, Suncor Energy, 150 - 6th Ave. SW, Calgary, AB T2P 3Y7
Tel: 403-260-3300; Fax: 403-263-9649
felesky@felesky.com
www.felesky.com

Calgary: P.L. Fiess - *1
#312, 602 - 11 Ave. SW, Calgary, AB T2R 1J8
Tel: 403-266-0033; Fax: 403-261-4958
phillfeiss@hotmail.com

Calgary: Fleishman-Hillard Canada Inc. - *1
#1000, 1122 - 4th St. SW, Calgary, AB T2R 1M1
Tel: 403-266-4710; Fax: 403-269-5346
bryan.thomas@fleishman.ca
www.fleishman.ca

Calgary: Fleming LLP, Barristers & Solicitors - *10
#900, 926 - 5th Ave. SW, Calgary, AB T2P 0N7
Tel: 403-266-5550; Fax: 403-265-6910
Toll-Free: 877-566-5550
www.flemingllp.com

Calgary: Fric, Lowenstein & Co. LLP - *4
#310, 2891 Sunridge Way, Calgary, AB T1Y 7K7
Tel: 403-291-2594; Fax: 403-291-2668
friclow@telusplanet.net

Calgary: Gaetano & Associates - *1
327 Kincora Heights NW, Calgary, AB T3R 1N3
Tel: 403-730-3474; Fax: 403-730-3471
jdgaetano@shaw.ca

Calgary: German Fong Albus, Barristers & Solicitors - *3
#418, Hewlett Packard Bldg., 715 - 5 Ave. SW, Calgary, AB T2P 2X6
Tel: 403-263-7880; Fax: 403-237-7075
mjfong@gfal-law.com; sfalbus@gfal-law.com
www.gfal-law.com

Calgary: Global Public Affairs
#460, 800 - 6th Ave. SW, Calgary, AB T2P 3G3
Tel: 403-264-3800; Fax: 403-264-3808
kanderson@globalpublic.com
www.globalpublicaffairs.ca

Calgary: The Law Firm of W. Donald Goodfellow, Q.C. - *3
#715, 999 - 8th St. SW, Calgary, AB T2R 1J5
Tel: 403-228-7102; Fax: 403-228-7199
wdonald@goodfellowqc.com; pbiggar@goodfellowqc.com
www.goodfellowqc.com

Calgary: Gorman, Gorman, Burns & Watson - *2
#500, 1135 - 17 Ave. SW, Calgary, AB T2T 0B6
Tel: 403-244-5515; Fax: 403-244-5605

Calgary: David M. Gottlieb, Law Office - *1
#8, 5602 - 4 St. NW, Calgary, AB T2K 1B2
Tel: 403-275-4881; Fax: 403-274-0367
gottlieb.david@telusplanet.net

Calgary: Gowling Lafleur Henderson LLP - Calgary - *112
#1400, Scotia Centre, 700 - 2nd St. SW, Calgary, AB T2P 4V5
Tel: 403-298-1000; Fax: 403-263-9193
kenneth.warren@gowlings.com
www.gowlings.com

Calgary: A.F.W. Grenon - *1
#200, 1210 - 11th Ave. SW, Calgary, AB T3C 0M4
Tel: 403-571-4450; Fax: 403-571-4444

Calgary: Hadley & Davis - *2
#311, 1711 - 4 St. SW, Calgary, AB T2S 1V8
Tel: 403-264-1234; Fax: 403-264-0999
info@hadleydavis.com
www.hadleydavis.com

Calgary: Bryan F. Hagel - *1
#23, 2451 Dieppe Ave. SW, Calgary, AB T3E 7K1
Tel: 403-243-8360; Fax: 403-287-3008
bryanfhagel@yahoo.ca

Calgary: Hansen & Company - *2
538 - 9 Ave. SE, Calgary, AB T2G 0S1
Tel: 403-261-6890; Fax: 403-263-1632
Toll-Free: 800-523-6162
info@hansen-company.com
www.hansen-company.com

Calgary: Larry S. Heald - *1
#300, 840 - 6 Ave. SW, Calgary, AB T2P 3E5
Tel: 403-266-2131; Fax: 403-261-6862
heald@shaw.ca

Calgary: Stephen Graham Heinz - *1
#2900, 350 - 7 Ave. SW, Calgary, AB T2P 3N9
Tel: 403-262-4462; Fax: 403-265-4496
stephen.heinz@3web.net

Calgary: Hill & Knowlton Canada
#540, 202 - 6th Ave. SW, Calgary, AB T2P 2R9
Tel: 403-299-9380; Fax: 403-299-9389
peter.hunt@hillandknowlton.ca (Peter Hunt, General Manager)
www.hillandknowlton.ca

Calgary: Michael M. Jamison - *1
2503 - 22 St. SW, Calgary, AB T2T 5G3
Tel: 403-217-1250; Fax: 403-287-1968
mmjlaw2@shaw.ca

Calgary: Jensen Shawa Solomon Duguid Hawkes LLP - *20
#800, Lancaster Bldg., 304 - 8 Ave. SW, Calgary, AB T2P 1C2
Tel: 403-571-1520; Fax: 403-571-1528
inquiries@jssbarristers.ca
www.jssbarristers.ca

Calgary: Jivraj Knight & Pritchett, Barristers & Solicitors - *3
#1000, 444 - 5 Ave. SW, Calgary, AB T2P 2T8
Tel: 403-261-0017; Fax: 403-266-6030
mailbox@jkp-law.com; knight@JKP-Law.com; jivraj@JKP-Law.com
www.jkp-law.com

Calgary: Kelly & Kelly - *4
#220, 3505 - 32nd St. NE, Calgary, AB T1Y 5Y9
Tel: 403-266-6296; Fax: 403-264-2954
kellykp@telusplanet.net; tjolliff@telusplanet.net

Calgary: Robert D. Kerr - *1
#300, 840 - 6 Ave. SW, Calgary, AB T2P 3E5
Tel: 403-265-1331; Fax: 403-265-1332
bkerr@shaw.ca

Calgary: Jack A. King, Q.C. - *1
10 Forest Grove Pl. SE, Calgary, AB T2A 7G6
Tel: 403-235-4600

Calgary: George R. Klatt - *1
#400, Centre 70, 7015 Macleod Trail SW, Calgary, AB T2H 2K6
Tel: 403-255-3033; Fax: 403-255-0403

* indicates number of lawyers

***Calgary*: Kuefler & Company - *3**
#012, 601 - 10th Ave. SW, Calgary, AB T2R 0B2
Tel: 403-237-0123; *Fax:* 403-237-0128
quinn.kuefler@kueflerlaw.com

***Calgary*: Laird, Armstrong, Barristers & Solicitors - *4**
#870, 234 - 5149 Country Hills Blvd. NW, Calgary, AB T3A 5K8
Tel: 403-233-0050; *Fax:* 403-266-1238
inquiries@lairdarmstrong.com
www.lairdarmstrong.com

***Calgary*: Catherine G. Langlois - *1**
#2410, 645 - 7 Ave. SW, Calgary, AB T2P 4G8
Tel: 403-531-9300; *Fax:* 403-261-8977
civillaw@telus.net

***Calgary*: Lauzon Law Office - *1**
#218, 5403 Crowchild Trail NW, Calgary, AB T3B 4Z1
Tel: 403-288-7601; *Fax:* 403-288-3689

***Calgary*: Laven & Company, Legal Counsel - *3**
#900, McFarlane Tower, 700 - 4th Ave. SW, Calgary, AB T2P 3J4
Tel: 403-263-2444; *Fax:* 403-265-1792
www.lavenco.com

***Calgary*: Lee & Kong - *2**
#330, 1324 - 17 Ave. SW, Calgary, AB T2T 5S8
Tel: 403-233-9432; *Fax:* 403-237-9614
leekong@canada.com

***Calgary*: Corinna Lee - *1**
509 - 20th Ave. SW, Calgary, AB T2S 0E7
Tel: 403-228-2238; *Fax:* 403-228-5550

***Calgary*: Lehan, Menzies, Walters & Abdi - *6**
9937 Fairmount Dr. SE, Calgary, AB T2J 0S2
Tel: 403-261-4010; *Fax:* 403-261-4040

***Calgary*: Lenhardt Law Office - *1**
#301, 888 - 7 Ave. SW, Calgary, AB T2P 3J3
Tel: 403-237-6970; *Fax:* 403-237-6974

***Calgary*: Lirenman, Peterson - *3**
#300, Notre Dame Place, 255 - 17 Ave. SW, Calgary, AB T2S 2T8
Tel: 403-245-0111; *Fax:* 403-245-0115

***Calgary*: Lord Russell - *6**
410 - 6th St. SW, Calgary, AB T2P 1X2
Tel: 403-262-7722; *Fax:* 403-262-5991
simonl@telus.net; vicruss@telus.net

***Calgary*: Low, Glenn & Card - *6**
#120, 3636 - 23 St. NE, Calgary, AB T2E 8Z5
Tel: 403-291-2532; *Fax:* 403-291-2534
lawyer@lgc-law.com

***Calgary*: Machida Mack Shewchuk Meagher LLP - *6**
#1300, 707 - 7th Ave. SW, Calgary, AB T2P 3H6
Tel: 403-221-8333; *Fax:* 403-221-8339
nmachida@mmsmlawyers.com

***Calgary*: Birjinder P.S. Mangat**
#217, 3825 - 34 St. NE, Calgary, AB T1Y 6Z8
Tel: 403-735-6088; *Fax:* 403-735-6089
bmangat@cadvision.com

***Calgary*: Masuch, Albert LLP - *9**
#209, 10836 - 24 St. SE, Calgary, AB T2Z 4C9
Tel: 403-543-1100; *Fax:* 403-543-1111
www.manlaw.com

***Calgary*: McCaffery Mudry Pritchard LLP, Barristers & Solicitors - *7**
#2200, 736 - 6 Ave. SW, Calgary, AB T2P 3T7
Tel: 403-260-1400; *Fax:* 403-260-1444
postmaster@mccafferylaw.ca
www.mccafferylaw.ca

***Calgary*: McConnell MacInnes - *7**
1245 - 70 Ave. SE, Calgary, AB T2H 2X8
Tel: 403-278-7001; *Fax:* 403-271-2826
kfm@mcmaclaw.com; jrm@mcmaclaw.com

***Calgary*: McGown Johnson - *4**
#120, 7260 - 12th St. SE, Calgary, AB T2H 2S5
Tel: 403-255-5114; *Fax:* 403-258-3840

***Calgary*: McKenna Law Office - *1**
1505 - 5 St. SW, Calgary, AB T2R 1P2
Tel: 403-716-2092; *Fax:* 403-234-7911
paul@mckennalegal.com

***Calgary*: McKinnon Carstairs - *2**
#525, First Alberta Place, 777 - 8 Ave. SW, Calgary, AB T2P 3R5
Tel: 403-261-8822; *Fax:* 403-261-4892
rlmckinnon@mckinnoncarstairs.com

***Calgary*: McLeod & Company LLP - *37**
14505 Bannister Rd. SE, 3rd Fl., Calgary, AB T2X 3J3
Tel: 403-278-9411; *Fax:* 403-271-1769
pnbreen@mcleod-law.com; tmcarswell@mcleod-law.com
www.mcleod-law.com

***Calgary*: McManus & Hubler - *2**
63 Rockcliff Landing NW, Calgary, AB T3G 5Z5
Tel: 403-208-6099; *Fax:* 403-208-6018
Toll-Free: 877-423-6054
sean@mcmanus-hubler.ca
www.mcmanus-hubler.ca

***Calgary*: Anne E. McTavish - *1**
7410E - 5th St. SE, Calgary, AB T2H 2L9
Tel: 403-252-4965; *Fax:* 403-253-7743
anne.mctavish@telusplanet.net

***Calgary*: Miles, Davison LLP - *24**
#1600, Bow Valley Square II, 205 - 5th Ave. SW, Calgary, AB T2P 2V7
Tel: 403-298-0333; *Fax:* 403-263-6840
thefirm@milesdavison.com
www.milesdavison.com

***Calgary*: Millar Smith & Associates, Barristers, Solicitors, Notaries - *1**
#300, 1130 Kensington Rd. NW, Calgary, AB T2N 3P3
Tel: 403-283-1925; *Fax:* 403-270-8033
millar.associates@shaw.ca
www.wes-law.com

***Calgary*: Milne, Davis & Young - *2**
#850, 933 - 17th Ave. SW, Calgary, AB T2T 5R6
Tel: 403-229-3000; *Fax:* 403-229-3282
milnedavisyoung@shaw.ca

***Calgary*: Moore Wittman Phillips - *6**
#850, 1015 - 4 St. SW, Calgary, AB T2R 1J4
Tel: 403-269-8500; *Fax:* 403-269-8515
mwp@nucleus.com

***Calgary*: Maureen Morgan - *1**
#206, P.O. Box 73001, Stn. RPO Woodbine, 2525 Woodview Dr. SW, Calgary, AB T2W 6E4
Tel: 403-233-2215; *Fax:* 403-264-1328
maureenmorgan96@hotmail.com

***Calgary*: Richard W. Muenz - *1**
#2410, 645 - 7 Ave. SW, Calgary, AB T2P 4G8
Tel: 403-543-6666; *Fax:* 403-261-8977
rwmuenz@telus.net

***Calgary*: Munro & Wood, Barristers & Solicitors - *2**
#500, 2424 - 4 St. SW, Calgary, AB T2S 2T4
Tel: 403-299-9285; *Fax:* 403-228-1389
katewood@telus.net
www.munrowood.ca

***Calgary*: Murray & Company - *1**
#104, 2003 - 14 St. NW, Calgary, AB T2M 3N4
Tel: 403-297-9850; *Fax:* 403-297-9855
murraywg@shaw.ca

***Calgary*: North Hill Law Office - *1**
P.O. Box 32053, Stn. RPO Bankview, 2619 - 14 St. SW, Calgary, AB T2T 5X6
Tel: 403-282-1515; *Fax:* 403-220-1575
oldmanncuba@hotmail.com

***Calgary*: O'Brien, Devlin, Markey & Macleod, Barristers & Solicitors - *3**
#1310, Watermark Tower, 530 - 8th Ave. SW, Calgary, AB T2P 3S8
Tel: 403-265-5616; *Fax:* 403-264-8146
nobrien@obriendevlin.com; bdevlin@obriendevlin.com
www.obriendevlin.com

***Calgary*: Olson Lemons LLP, Barristers & Solicitors - *6**
744 - 4 Ave. SW, 10th Fl., Calgary, AB T2P 3T4
Tel: 403-974-3400; *Fax:* 403-974-3427
hr@olsonlemons.com (Human Resources)
www.olsonlemons.com

***Calgary*: Ouellette, Rice - *2**
#425, 630 - 6 Ave. SW, Calgary, AB T2P 0S8
Tel: 403-263-3855; *Fax:* 403-265-5855
oullette-rice@telusplanet.net

***Calgary*: Parlee McLaws LLP - *82**
#3400, Suncor Energy Centre, 150 - 6th Ave. SW, Calgary, AB T2P 3Y7
Tel: 403-294-7000; *Fax:* 403-265-8263
lawyers@parlee.com
www.parlee.com

***Calgary*: Peterson, Shields, & Galbraith - *6**
#204, 755 Lake Bonavista Dr. SE, Calgary, AB T2J 0N3
Tel: 403-271-9710; *Fax:* 403-271-3942
info@petersonshields.com; rmp@petersonshields.com

***Calgary*: Phipps Law Office - *1**
#303, 8180 MacLeod Trail SE, Calgary, AB T2H 2B8
Tel: 403-531-0182; *Fax:* 403-531-0180

***Calgary*: Pittman MacIsaac & Roy - *4**
#2600, West Tower, Sun Life Plaza, 144 - 4th Ave. SW, Calgary, AB T2P 3N4
Tel: 403-237-6566; *Fax:* 403-237-6594
www.pmrlaw.ca

***Calgary*: Pomerance & Company - *3**
#1430, 1122 - 4th St. SW, Calgary, AB T2R 1M1
Tel: 403-278-5840; *Fax:* 403-271-6929
Toll-Free: 866-278-5840
pomeranc@telus.net
www.pomerancelaw.ca

***Calgary*: Lawrence S. Portigal - *1**
6638 Bow Cres. NW, Calgary, AB T3B 2B9
Tel: 403-286-6380; *Fax:* 403-286-6821
lportig@yahoo.com

***Calgary*: PricewaterhouseCoopers LLP - *3**
#3100, Petro-Canada Centre, 111 - 5th Ave. SW, Calgary, AB T2P 0M9
Tel: 403-509-7500; *Fax:* 403-781-1825
www.pwc.com/ca

***Calgary*: ProVenture Law LLP - *4**
#2, Mount Royal Village, 880 - 16th Ave. SW, Calgary, AB T2R 1J9
Tel: 403-294-5710; *Fax:* 403-262-4860
www.proventurelaw.com

***Calgary*: Purdy & Purdy - *2**
#801, 1015 - 4th St. SW, Calgary, AB T2R 1J4
Tel: 403-777-4850; *Fax:* 403-777-4855

***Calgary*: Radke & Associates - *2**
#205, 5917 - 1A St. SW, Calgary, AB T2H 0G4
Tel: 403-252-4466; *Fax:* 403-258-0695
radkelaw@telus.net; lisakerwin@radkeandassociates.com
www.radkeandassociates.com

***Calgary*: Rae & Company, Barristers, Solicitors, Notaries Public - *3**
#2910, 715 - 5 Ave. SW, Calgary, AB T2P 2X6
Tel: 403-264-8389; *Fax:* 403-264-8399
mfandrick@raeandcompany.com;
jmlemieux@raeandcompany.com
www.raeandcompany.com

***Calgary*: Reich Nichol - *2**
#226, 4935 - 40 Ave. NW, Calgary, AB T3A 2N1
Tel: 403-288-6500; *Fax:* 403-288-6510
jimreich@telusplanet.net; blake.nichol@telus.net

***Calgary*: Riccio Law - *2**
#100, 4103B Centre St. North, Calgary, AB T2E 2Y6
Tel: 403-289-3131; *Fax:* 403-289-2396
ariccio@shaw.ca; jsymonds@shawcable.com
www.nvo.com/riccio

***Calgary*: Rogers & Company, Barristers & Solicitors**
#200, 815 - 10 Ave. SW, Calgary, AB T2R 0B4
Tel: 403-263-6805; *Fax:* 403-263-6800

***Calgary*: Ross, Hepner - *4**
921 - 18 Ave. SW, Calgary, AB T2T 0H2
Tel: 403-244-6800; *Fax:* 403-265-2455
rosslk@shaw.ca; hepnera@telusplanet.net

***Calgary*: A. Charles Ruff - *1**
#202, 1409 Edmonton Trail NE, Calgary, AB T2E 3K8
Tel: 403-230-0999; *Fax:* 403-230-0991
chasruff@shaw.ca

***Calgary*: Salmon & Company - *2**
#1100, 707 - 7 Ave. SW, Calgary, AB T2P 3H6
Tel: 403-231-2705; *Fax:* 403-705-1214
david@salmonco.ca

** indicates number of lawyers*

***Calgary*: Schwartzberg Law Office - *1**
3923 - 17 Ave. SW, Calgary, AB T3E 0C3
Tel: 403-232-1302; *Fax:* 403-249-6655
schwartzberglaw@shawcable.com

***Calgary*: Scott Venturo LLP - *22**
#203, Eau Claire Market, 200 Barclay Parade SW, Calgary, AB T2P 4R5
Tel: 403-261-9043; *Fax:* 403-265-4632
Toll-Free: 877-505-5651
www.scottventuro.com

***Calgary*: Sefcik & Company - *1**
#212, 20 Sunpark Plaza SE, Calgary, AB T2X 3T2
Tel: 403-258-1124; *Fax:* 403-640-1220

***Calgary*: William J. Shachnowich - *1**
1700 Varsity Estates Dr. NW, Calgary, AB T3B 2W9
Tel: 403-269-1313; *Fax:* 403-210-0106
shachnow@telus.net

***Calgary*: Shea Nerland Calnan LLP - *16**
#2800, 715 - 5th Ave. SW, Calgary, AB T2P 2X6
Tel: 403-299-9600; *Fax:* 403-299-9601
snc@snclaw.com
www.snclaw.com

***Calgary*: Shennette Leuschner McKay - *7**
#710, 909 - 11th Ave. SW, Calgary, AB T2R 1L7
Tel: 403-269-8282; *Fax:* 403-269-8295
louise@slmfamilylaw.ca; hlmckay@slmfamilylaw.ca

***Calgary*: Smith & Smith - *2**
#503, 1300 - 8 St. SW, Calgary, AB T2R 1B2
Tel: 403-229-1727; *Fax:* 403-229-1730

***Calgary*: Smith Law Office - *1**
348 - 14 St. NW, Calgary, AB T2N 1Z7
Tel: 403-283-8018; *Fax:* 403-270-3065
j.smith@smithlawoffice.ca

***Calgary*: Smith Mack Lamarsh - *3**
#450, United Place, 808 - 4 Ave. SW, Calgary, AB T2P 3E8
Tel: 403-234-7779; *Fax:* 403-263-7897
cmsmith@telusplanet.net; slamarsh@telusplanet.net

***Calgary*: W. Murray Smith - *1**
348 - 14 St. NW, Calgary, AB T2N 1Z7
Tel: 403-283-8018; *Fax:* 403-270-3065

***Calgary*: Sparrow Law Office - *1**
#10, 628 - 12 Ave. SW, Calgary, AB T2R 0H6
Tel: 403-234-9722; *Fax:* 403-237-8748
sparrow@nucleus.com

***Calgary*: Spier Harben - *11**
#1400, Iveagh House, 707 - 7th St. SW, Calgary, AB T2P 3H6
Tel: 403-263-5130; *Fax:* 403-264-9600
asattin@spierharben.com

***Calgary*: Stephens Holman Devraj - *2**
412 - 16th Ave. NE, Calgary, AB T2E 1K2
Tel: 403-265-6400; *Fax:* 403-262-9294
rishmad@shdlawyers.ca
www.shdlawyers.ca

***Calgary*: Stewart & McCullough - *4**
#307, 1228 Kensington Rd. NW, Calgary, AB T2N 3P7
Tel: 403-270-2641; *Fax:* 403-670-7025
martin.meronek@shaw.ca

***Calgary*: Peter A. Stone - *1**
1923 - 5th St. SW, Calgary, AB T2S 2B2
Tel: 403-283-8460; *Fax:* 403-283-8461
pstone@telusplanet.net

***Calgary*: Stones Carbert Waite Wells LLP - *14**
#2000, Encor Place, 645 - 7th Ave. SW, Calgary, AB T2P 4G8
Tel: 403-263-5656; *Fax:* 403-263-5553
info@scwlawyers.com
www.scwlawyers.com

***Calgary*: Story Law Office - *1**
#240, 3015 - 12 St. NE, Calgary, AB T2E 7J2
Tel: 403-250-1918; *Fax:* 403-250-3287

***Calgary*: Sugimoto & Company - *5**
#204, 2635 - 37 Ave. NE, Calgary, AB T1Y 5Z6
Tel: 403-291-4650; *Fax:* 403-291-4099
sugimoto@sugimotolaw.com

***Calgary*: Nancy A. Swanby - *1**
#700, One Executive Place, 1816 Crowchild Trail NW, Calgary, AB T2M 3Y7
Tel: 403-520-5455; *Fax:* 403-220-1389
nancy@swanby.com

***Calgary*: Szabo & Company, Barristers & Solicitors**
#400, 1111 - 11th Ave. SW, Calgary, AB T2R 0G5
Tel: 403-229-1111; *Fax:* 403-245-0569
Toll-Free: 866-229-0717
info@szaboco.com
www.szaboco.com

***Calgary*: Michael J. Tadman - *1**
#10, 628 - 12 Ave. SW, Calgary, AB T2R 0H6
Tel: 403-234-9722; *Fax:* 403-237-8748
tadman@nucleus.com

***Calgary*: M.S. Takada - *1**
#200, 604 - 1 St. SW, Calgary, AB T2P 1M7
Tel: 403-234-9477; *Fax:* 403-261-1839

***Calgary*: Taylor Conway - *2**
#440, 7220 Fisher St. SE, Calgary, AB T2H 2H8
Tel: 403-259-4028; *Fax:* 403-640-0103

***Calgary*: Thackray Burgess - *34**
#1900, 736 - 6 Ave. SW, Calgary, AB T2P 3T7
Tel: 403-531-4700; *Fax:* 403-531-4720

***Calgary*: Thompson, Ball & McMahon - *2**
#534, 11012 Macleod Trail SE, Calgary, AB T2J 6A5
Tel: 403-271-5050; *Fax:* 403-271-5298
thompsonball@telus.net; jpmcm@telus.net

***Calgary*: Thornborough, Smeltz - *4**
#630, Southcentre Executive Tower, 11012 Macleod Trail SE, Calgary, AB T2J 6A5
Tel: 403-271-3221; *Fax:* 403-271-6684
tammy@thornsmeltz.com

***Calgary*: TingleMerrett LLP, Barristers & Solicitors - *12**
#1250, Standard Life Bldg., 639 - 5th Ave. SW, Calgary, AB T2P 0M9
Tel: 403-571-8000; *Fax:* 403-571-8008
cmerrett@tinglemerrett.com; dallison@tinglemerrett.com
www.tinglemerrett.com

***Calgary*: Richard T. Tumanon - *1**
#301, 5555 Falsbridge Dr. NE, Calgary, AB T3J 3E8
Tel: 403-262-3841; *Fax:* 403-269-7173

***Calgary*: Van Harten Foster Iovinellis - *6**
#1206, 734 - 7 Ave. SW, Calgary, AB T2P 3P8
Tel: 403-269-3655; *Fax:* 403-237-5109
hmvh@shaw.ca; vofi@shaw.ca; roadlawyers@shaw.ca

***Calgary*: Vickers & Associates - *3**
#600, 805 - 10th Ave. SW, Calgary, AB T2R 0B4
Tel: 403-269-9400; *Fax:* 403-266-2447
hvickers@vickerassoc.com; dhendrix@vickersassoc.com

***Calgary*: Vinci, Phillips - *2**
1509 - 26 Ave. SW, Calgary, AB T2T 1C4
Tel: 403-265-4323; *Fax:* 403-262-8087

***Calgary*: Walsh Wilkins Creighton LLP - *18**
#2800, 801 - 6 Ave. SW, Calgary, AB T2P 4A3
Tel: 403-267-8400; *Fax:* 403-264-9400
mail@wwclawyers.com
www.wwclawyers.com

***Calgary*: Samuel D.C. Wan - *1**
191 Edgepark Way NW, Calgary, AB T3A 4T2
Tel: 403-973-0678

***Calgary*: Peter M. Ward - *1**
#300, 400 - 5th Ave. SW, Calgary, AB T2P 0L6
Tel: 403-263-1158; *Fax:* 403-264-9218

***Calgary*: Warren Tettensor Amantea LLP - *12**
1413 - 2nd St. SW, Calgary, AB T2R 0W7
Tel: 403-228-7007; *Fax:* 403-244-1948
info@warren.ab.ca
www.warren.ab.ca

***Calgary*: Peggy A. Wedderburn - *1**
#16, 2439 - 54th Ave. SW, Calgary, AB T3E 1M4
Tel: 403-242-8081; *Fax:* 403-246-2055
pwedderburn@shaw.ca

***Calgary*: West End Legal Centre - *1**
1705 - 10th Ave. SW, Calgary, AB T3C 0K1
Tel: 403-249-5297; *Fax:* 403-249-5001
welc@telusplanet.net

***Calgary*: White & Company - *2**
#204, 3716 - 61 Ave. SE, Calgary, AB T2C 1Z4
Tel: 403-236-2110; *Fax:* 403-279-4842

***Calgary*: Wilson Laycraft - *10**
#1601, 333 - 11th Ave. SW, Calgary, AB T2R 1L9
Tel: 403-290-1601; *Fax:* 403-290-0828
reception@wilcraft.com
www.wilcraft.com

***Calgary*: Dawn M. Wilson - *1**
44 Bow Village Cres. NW, Calgary, AB T3B 4X2
Tel: 403-247-9090; *Fax:* 403-247-9090

***Calgary*: Wise Walden Barkauskas - *5**
#600, 700 - 4 Ave. SW, Calgary, AB T2P 3J4
Tel: 403-263-6601; *Fax:* 403-269-6785
jdwise@divorceinc.com; mewalden@divorceinc.com
www.wisedivorce.com; www.divorceinc.com

***Calgary*: Stephen R. Wojcik - *1**
604 - 1 St. SW, 2nd Fl., Calgary, AB T2P 1M7
Tel: 403-547-4415; *Fax:* 403-208-0717
wojicks@shaw.ca

***Calgary*: Wolch, Hursh, deWit & Watts - *4**
#1500, 633 - 6 Ave. SW, Calgary, AB T2P 2Y5
Tel: 403-265-6500; *Fax:* 403-263-1111
hersh@wolch.com; lhursh@shawcable.com;
wtdewit@shawcable.com

***Calgary*: Wolfman & Company - *2**
#700, 640 - 8th Ave. SW, Calgary, AB T2P 1G7
Tel: 403-263-6710; *Fax:* 403-266-1896
info@wolfmanlaw.com

***Calgary*: David I. Wolfman - *1**
328 Pumphill Gardens SW, Calgary, AB T2V 4M7
Tel: 403-266-4433; *Fax:* 403-266-4433
thewolfmans@telus.net

***Calgary*: Yanko & Popovic Law Firm - *2**
#302, 325 - 25 St. SE, Calgary, AB T2A 7H8
Tel: 403-262-0262; *Fax:* 403-204-0284

***Calgary*: Youth Criminal Defence Office - *9**
#600, 444 - 5 Ave. SW, Calgary, AB T2P 2T8
Tel: 403-297-4400; *Fax:* 403-297-4201
sfellger@ycdo.ca

***Calgary*: Zenith Hookenson LLP**
#218, Mayfair Place, 6707 Elbow Dr. SW, Calgary, AB T2V 0E4
Tel: 403-259-5041; *Fax:* 403-258-0719

***Calgary*: Jeffrey C. Zhang - *1**
#512, 206 - 7 Ave. SW, Calgary, AB T2P 0W7
Tel: 403-465-5632; *Fax:* 403-265-1645

***Calgary*: Zinner & Sara - *2**
#145, 1935 - 32 Ave. NE, Calgary, AB T2E 7C8
Tel: 403-262-7363; *Fax:* 403-233-0392

***Camrose*: Andreassen Borth, Barristers, Solicitors, Notaries, Mediators - *4**
#200, 4870 - 51 St., Camrose, AB T4V 1S1
Tel: 780-672-3181; *Fax:* 780-672-0682
aob@telusplanet.net
www.andreassenolsonborth.com

***Camrose*: Farnham West Stolee LLP - *3**
5016 - 52 St., Camrose, AB T4V 1V7
Tel: 780-679-0444; *Fax:* 780-679-0958
camlaw@telusplanet.net

***Camrose*: Fielding & Company LLP - *4**
#100, 4918 - 51 St., Camrose, AB T4V 1S3
Tel: 780-672-8851; *Fax:* 780-672-4707
lawyers@camroselaw.com
www.camroselaw.com

***Camrose*: Knaut, Johnson - *2**
4925 - 51 St., Camrose, AB T4V 1S4
Tel: 780-672-5561; *Fax:* 780-672-5565

***Canmore*: Canmore Legal Services - *1**
909A Railway Ave., Canmore, AB T1W 1P3
Tel: 403-678-9818; *Fax:* 403-609-2333
johnschneider@shaw.ca

***Canmore*: Tannis J. Naylor - *1**
826B - 10th St., Canmore, AB T1W 2A7
Tel: 403-678-5777; *Fax:* 403-678-5679
t_naylor@telus.net

***Canmore*: Peter Perren - *1**
726 - 10 St., Canmore, AB T1W 2A6
Tel: 403-678-6988; *Fax:* 403-678-5952
pperren@telusplanet.net

** indicates number of lawyers*

Canmore: Rencz & Docking - *2
#225, 1001 - 6th Ave., Canmore, AB T1W 3L8
Tel: 403-678-5823; *Fax*: 403-678-4890
www.canmorelawyer.com

Carstairs: Stiles & Naqi - *2
P.O. Box 790, 209 - 10th Ave. South, Carstairs, AB T0M 0N0
Tel: 403-337-3357; *Fax*: 403-337-3359

Chestermere: Karl H.H. Trobst - *1
368 West Chestermere Dr., Chestermere, AB T1X 1B3
Tel: 403-272-1056
karltrobst@hotmail.com

Coaldale: Leonard D. Fast - *1
P.O. Box 1360, Stn. Main, 1709 - 20 Ave., Coaldale, AB T1M 1N2
Tel: 403-345-4415; *Fax*: 403-345-2719
lfastlaw@telusplanet.net

Coaldale: Lammi Law - *1
P.O. Box 1329, Stn. Main, 1910 - 18 St., Coaldale, AB T1M 1N1
Tel: 403-345-3922; *Fax*: 403-345-2172
lammilaw@telusplanet.net

Cochrane: Fercho & Associates - *1
#14, 205 - 1 St. East, Cochrane, AB T4C 1X6
Tel: 403-932-4477; *Fax*: 403-932-4084
rfercho@lawyers.com

Cochrane: Franchi - Rothecker Law Office - *1
629 - 2 St. West, Cochrane, AB T4C 1Z7
Tel: 403-932-3843; *Fax*: 403-932-3108
reception@rotheckerlaw.ca

Cochrane: Mabbott & Company, Barristers & Solicitors - *4
#5, 201 Grand Blvd., Cochrane, AB T4C 2G4
Tel: 403-932-3066; *Fax*: 403-932-3076
reception@mabbott.ca
www.mabbott.ca

Cold Lake: Todd & Drake LLP - *4
P.O. Box 908, 4807 - 51 St., Cold Lake, AB T9M 1P2
Tel: 780-594-7151; *Fax*: 780-594-7155
Toll-Free: 877-594-7151
rmtodd@tdlaw.ca; ldrake@tdlaw.ca
www.tdlaw.cawww.facebook.com/pages/Todd-Drake-LLP/168339593224163, www.twitter.com/toddrakellp

Coronation: E. Roger Spady - *1
P.O. Box 328, 5015 Victoria Ave., Coronation, AB T0C 1C0
Tel: 403-578-3131; *Fax*: 403-578-2660

Daysland: Patricia E. Spencer - *1
P.O. Box 372, 5037 - 46 St., Daysland, AB T0B 1A0
Tel: 780-374-2199; *Fax*: 780-374-2259
spinner7@telus.net

Didsbury: Brian M. Forestell - *1
P.O. Box 625, 1701 - 20th Ave., Didsbury, AB T0M 0W0
Tel: 403-335-8491; *Fax*: 403-335-8589
briandid@telusplanet.net

Didsbury: Roy D. Shellnutt - *1
P.O. Box 898, 2021 - 19th Ave., Didsbury, AB T0M 0W0
Tel: 403-335-2145; *Fax*: 403-335-3185
shellnutlaw@hotmail.com

Drumheller: Ross, Todd & Company - *3
P.O. Box 970, 98 - 3 Ave. West, Drumheller, AB T0J 0Y0
Tel: 403-823-5186; *Fax*: 403-823-6407
reception@drumhellerlaw.com;
sharon.clark@drumhellerlaw.com

Drumheller: Schumacher, Gough & Company - *2
P.O. Box 2800, 196 - 3rd Ave. West, Drumheller, AB T0J 0Y0
Tel: 403-823-2424; *Fax*: 403-823-6984
Toll-Free: 866-923-2424
sgp_law@telus.net; sgp_harry@telus.net

Edmonton: Abbey Hunter Davison - *4
9636 - 102A Ave., Edmonton, AB T5H 0G5
Tel: 780-421-8585; *Fax*: 780-425-0472
dhabbey@shaw.ca

Edmonton: David R. Abbey - *1
#780, TransAlta Place, 10150 - 100 St. NW, Edmonton, AB T5J 0P6
Tel: 780-423-2793; *Fax*: 780-423-2750
dabbey@telus.net

Edmonton: Abells Regan - *2
#950, Canadian Western Bank Place, 10303 Jasper Ave. NW, Edmonton, AB T5J 3N6
Tel: 780-442-4420; *Fax*: 780-424-9370
rsabells@abellsregan.com; emregan@abellsregan.com

Edmonton: Ackroyd LLP Barristers & Solicitors - *17
#1500, First Edmonton Place, 10665 Jasper Ave., Edmonton, AB T5J 3S9
Tel: 780-423-8905; *Fax*: 780-423-8946
aprd@ackroydlaw.com
www.ackroydlaw.com

Edmonton: Jack N. Agrios, Q.C., LL.B, O.C. - *1
#1325, Manulife Place, 10180 - 101 St., Edmonton, AB T5J 3S4
Tel: 780-696-6915; *Fax*: 780-969-6901
jack@jackagrios.com

Edmonton: Andrew, March & Oake - *9
#300, 10020 - 101A Ave. NW, Edmonton, AB T5J 3G2
Tel: 780-429-3391; *Fax*: 780-424-8483

Edmonton: Ares Law - *1
LeMarchand Tower, 11507 - 100 Ave., Edmonton, AB T5K 2R2
Tel: 780-488-1951; *Fax*: 780-482-6048

Edmonton: Attia, Reeves, Tensfeldt, Snow - *9
#200, 10525 Jasper Ave. NW, Edmonton, AB T5J 1Z4
Tel: 780-424-3334; *Fax*: 780-424-4252

Edmonton: Baker Purdon Caskenette - *2
10263 - 178 St., Edmonton, AB T5S 1M3
Tel: 780-489-5566; *Fax*: 780-486-7735
bpurdon@planet.eon.net

Edmonton: Barry Elgert Peddie - *3
10432 Jasper Ave. NW, Edmonton, AB T5J 1Z3
Tel: 780-429-3005; *Fax*: 780-425-8931
kpeddie@beplaw.ca

Edmonton: Dennis E. Bayrak - *1
#800, 10310 Jasper Ave. NW, Edmonton, AB T5J 2W4
Tel: 780-426-4884; *Fax*: 780-425-9358
bayrak@telus.net

Edmonton: Beresh Cunningham Aloneissi O'Neill Hurley - *10
#300, MacLean Block, Box 300, 10110 - 107 St., Edmonton, AB T5J 1J4
Tel: 780-421-4766; *Fax*: 780-429-0346
Toll-Free: 877-277-4766
bdc@bdc.ca

Edmonton: Helmut Berndt - *1
#1780, 10020 - 101A Ave. NW, Edmonton, AB T5J 3G2
Tel: 780-439-6643; *Fax*: 780-439-6696

Edmonton: Bhalla Law Offices - *1
9360 - 34 Ave., Edmonton, AB T6E 5X8
Tel: 780-450-6155; *Fax*: 780-490-0116
rajiv@bhallalawoffice.com

Edmonton: Biamonte Cairo & Shortreed LLP - *13
#1600, 10025 - 102A Ave., Edmonton, AB T5J 2Z2
Tel: 780-425-5800; *Fax*: 780-426-1600
Toll-Free: 888-425-2620
biamonte@biamonte.com

Edmonton: Bishop & McKenzie LLP - *29
#2500, 10104 - 103 Ave., Edmonton, AB T5J 1V3
Tel: 780-426-5550; *Fax*: 780-426-1305
edmonton@bishopmckenzie.com
www.bishopmckenzie.com

Edmonton: Bitner & Associates Law Offices - *1
6932 Roper Rd. NW, Edmonton, AB T6B 3H9
Tel: 780-461-6633; *Fax*: 780-461-9239
www.bitnerlaw.com

Edmonton: Kerry A. Bjarnason - *1
#600, 9707 - 110 St., Edmonton, AB T5K 2L9
Tel: 780-433-4547; *Fax*: 780-482-6613
kbjarnason@telusplanet.net

Edmonton: Bosecke & Song LLP - *3
#306, 9945 - 50th St., Edmonton, AB T6A 0L4
Tel: 780-469-0494; *Fax*: 780-469-4181
firm@edmontonlaw.ca
www.edmontonlaw.ca

Edmonton: Braithwaite Boyle - *5
Braithwaite Boyle Bldg., 11816 - 124 St. NW, Edmonton, AB T5L 0M3
Tel: 780-451-9191; *Fax*: 780-451-9198
Toll-Free: 800-661-4902
ken.braithwaite@accidentinjurylawyer.com
www.accidentinjurylawyer.com

Edmonton: Braul McEvoy & Gee - *3
#2170, Sun Life Place, 10123 - 99 St., Edmonton, AB T5J 3H1
Tel: 780-423-2481; *Fax*: 780-423-2474
lawyers@braullaw.ab.ca

Edmonton: Broda & Company - *1
13723 - 93 St., Edmonton, AB T5E 5V6
Tel: 780-456-9330; *Fax*: 780-456-9339

Edmonton: Brosseau & Associates - *2
#1955, Commerce Place, 10155 - 102 St. NW, Edmonton, AB T5J 4G8
Tel: 780-426-4000; *Fax*: 780-424-4616

Edmonton: Brownlee LLP - *59
#2200, Commerce Place, 10155 - 102 St., Edmonton, AB T5J 4G8
Tel: 780-497-4800; *Fax*: 780-424-3254
e-mail@brownleelaw.com
www.brownleelaw.com

Edmonton: Bryan & Company LLP - *38
#2600, Manulife Place, Box 2600, 10180 - 101 St., Edmonton, AB T5J 3Y2
Tel: 780-423-5730; *Fax*: 780-428-6324
Toll-Free: 800-357-9265
info@bryanco.com; djcorrigan@bryanco.com (Advocacy)
www.bryanco.com

Edmonton: Cameron & Cameron - *3
#390, 10187 - 104 St., Edmonton, AB T5J 0Z9
Tel: 780-423-5300; *Fax*: 780-423-5333
cnclaw@telusplanet.net

Edmonton: Campbell & Company - *5
#100, 4208 - 97 St. NW, Edmonton, AB T6E 5Z9
Tel: 780-434-6565; *Fax*: 780-434-1692

Edmonton: Campbell & Van Doesburg - *2
#300, 10230 - 142 St., Edmonton, AB T5N 3Y6
Tel: 780-451-2661; *Fax*: 780-452-1051
charles@campbellvandoesburg.com

Edmonton: A.F. Campbell - *1
#2410, Oxford Tower, 10235 - 101 St. NW, Edmonton, AB T5J 3G1
Tel: 780-428-8882; *Fax*: 780-421-0818
pgl31416@telusplanet.ca

Edmonton: J.K.J. Campbell
#208, Whitemud Business Park, 4245 - 97 St. NW, Edmonton, AB T6E 5Y7
Tel: 780-434-8777; *Fax*: 780-436-6357
johncam@telusplanet.net

Edmonton: Canadian Corporate Consultants Ltd. - *1
#1202, 10109 - 106 St., Edmonton, AB T5J 3L7
Tel: 780-429-4488; *Fax*: 780-425-3575
cancorpavi@compusmart.ab.ca
www.cancorp.com

Edmonton: Carr & Company - *3
#1296, 10665 Jasper Ave., Edmonton, AB T5J 3S9
Tel: 780-425-5959; *Fax*: 780-423-4728
mail@carrlaw.com
www.carrlaw.com

Edmonton: Chadi & Company - *7
#1901, 10060 Jasper Ave. NW, Edmonton, AB T5J 3R8
Tel: 780-429-2300; *Fax*: 780-441-9876

Edmonton: Chamberlain Hutchison - *3
#155, 10403 - 122 St. NW, Edmonton, AB T5N 4C1
Tel: 780-423-3661; *Fax*: 780-426-1293
ajclaw@telus.net

Edmonton: K.J. Chapman - *1
#208, 10080 Jasper Ave. NW, Edmonton, AB T5J 1V9
Tel: 780-420-0505; *Fax*: 780-420-1256
ken@cambridgestrategies.com

Edmonton: Chatwin Cox & Michalyshyn - *6
#1000, 10060 Jasper Ave. NW, Edmonton, AB T5J 3R8
Tel: 780-421-7667; *Fax*: 780-424-7231
lawyers@chatwin.ab.ca

** indicates number of lawyers*

Edmonton: **Chomicki Baril Mah LLP - *19**
#1201, TD Tower, 10088 - 102 Ave., Edmonton, AB T5J 4K2
Tel: 780-423-3441; *Fax:* 780-420-1763
office_admin@cbmllp.com
www.cbmllp.com

Edmonton: **Chopra, Chopra & Chopra - *1**
#517, 12111 - 51 St., Edmonton, AB T6H 6A3
Tel: 780-429-4961; *Fax:* 780-426-3512
manichopra.msn@attcanada.net

Edmonton: **Michael H. Clancy - *1**
9844 - 106 St. NW, Edmonton, AB T5K 1B8
Tel: 780-424-9014; *Fax:* 780-424-9023
Toll-Free: 800-647-7723

Edmonton: **Cleall Barristers Solicitors - *12**
#2500, Commerce Place, 10155 - 102nd St., Edmonton, AB T5J 4G8
Tel: 780-425-2500; *Fax:* 780-425-1222
main@cleall.ca
www.cleall.ca

Edmonton: **Cochard Johnson - *2**
#607, Royal Bank Bldg., 10117 Jasper Ave., Edmonton, AB T5J 1W8
Tel: 780-429-9929; *Fax:* 780-429-9981

Edmonton: **Coley, Hennessy & Cassis - *3**
#212, 3132 Parsons Rd., Edmonton, AB T6N 1L6
Tel: 780-468-2551; *Fax:* 780-466-8006
chc@connect.ab.ca

Edmonton: **Combe & Kent - *2**
#800, 10310 Jasper Ave. NW, Edmonton, AB T5J 2W4
Tel: 780-425-4666; *Fax:* 780-425-9358

Edmonton: **Coulter & Power - *2**
#2200, Metropolitan Pl., 10303 Jasper Ave., Edmonton, AB T5J 3N6
Tel: 780-413-2300; *Fax:* 780-420-0049

Edmonton: **C.D. Cousineau - *1**
#215, 11098 - 156 St. SW, Edmonton, AB T5P 4M8
Tel: 780-455-0485; *Fax:* 780-447-5853

Edmonton: **Cox Trofimuk Campbell - *4**
#2400, 10303 Jasper Ave., Edmonton, AB T5J 3T8
Tel: 780-422-6242; *Fax:* 780-428-1137

Edmonton: **Ted R. Croll - *1**
#1300, 10665 Jasper Ave., Edmonton, AB T5J 3S9
Tel: 780-420-9903; *Fax:* 780-424-3631
trcroll@shaw.ca

Edmonton: **Cummings Andrews Mackay LLP - *8**
#500, 10150 - 100 St. NW, Edmonton, AB T5J 0P6
Tel: 780-428-8222; *Fax:* 780-426-2670
Toll-Free: 800-565-5745
cam@cummings.ab.ca
www.cummings.ab.ca

Edmonton: **Brock I. Dagenais - *1**
#1405, TD Tower, 10088 - 102 Ave., Edmonton, AB T5J 2Z1
Tel: 780-424-8519; *Fax:* 780-425-0931
brock.dagenais@gmail.com

Edmonton: **Davidson Gregory Danyliuk - *3**
110 Place, 10008 - 110 St., Edmonton, AB T5K 1J6
Tel: 780-482-5496; *Fax:* 780-482-1930
Toll-Free: 866-887-8868
crimlaw@telusplanet.net

Edmonton: **Dawson, Stevens, Duckett & Shaigec - *10**
#300, Anderson Dawson Bldg., 9924 - 106 St., Edmonton, AB T5K 1C4
Tel: 780-424-9058; *Fax:* 780-425-0172
Toll-Free: 800-661-3176
www.dsscrimlaw.com

Edmonton: **de Villars Jones - *5**
#300, Noble Bldg., 8540 - 109 St., Edmonton, AB T6G 1E6
Tel: 780-433-9000; *Fax:* 780-433-9780
adev@sagecounsel.com

Edmonton: **Dean Duckett Carlson - *9**
#700, 10104 - 103 Ave. NW, Edmonton, AB T5J 0H8
Tel: 780-423-3366; *Fax:* 780-423-0505
office@deanduckett.com
www.deanduckett.com

Edmonton: **Gary A. Dlin - *1**
7904 Gateway Blvd., Edmonton, AB T6E 6C3
Tel: 780-438-4972; *Fax:* 780-435-1037

Edmonton: **Doherty Schuldhaus - *2**
#219, 6203 - 28 Ave., Edmonton, AB T6L 6K3
Tel: 780-450-1106; *Fax:* 780-461-8612

Edmonton: **Duncan & Craig LLP, Lawyers & Mediators - *46**
#2800, Scotia Place, 10060 Jasper Ave., Edmonton, AB T5J 3V9
Tel: 780-428-6036; *Fax:* 780-428-9683
Toll-Free: 800-782-9409
edmonton@dcllp.com
www.dcllp.com

Edmonton: **Durocher Simpson - *6**
Old Strathcona Law Office, 7904 Gateway Blvd., Edmonton, AB T6E 6C3
Tel: 780-420-6850; *Fax:* 780-425-9185
mail@dursim.com
www.dursim.com

Edmonton: **E.L. Eccleston - *1**
235 North Town Mall, Edmonton, AB T5E 6C1
Tel: 780-478-6635; *Fax:* 780-476-8587
eccl@telusplanet.net

Edmonton: **David C. Elliott - *1**
9724 - 101A St. NW, Edmonton, AB T5K 2R6
Tel: 780-425-7337; *Fax:* 780-425-5710
words@davidelliott.ca

Edmonton: **Embury & McFayden - *1**
#602, Centre 104, 5241 Calgary Trail NW, Edmonton, AB T6H 5G8
Tel: 780-439-7302; *Fax:* 780-433-6510
emburymc@telus.net

Edmonton: **Emery Jamieson LLP - *26**
#1700, Oxford Tower, 10235 - 101st St., Edmonton, AB T5J 3G1
Tel: 780-426-5220; *Fax:* 780-420-6277
Toll-Free: 866-212-5220
general@emeryjamieson.com
www.emeryjamieson.com

Edmonton: **Environmental Law Centre (ELC) - *4**
#800, 10025 - 106 St., Edmonton, AB T5J 1G4
Tel: 780-424-5099; *Fax:* 780-424-5133
Toll-Free: 800-661-4238
elc@elc.ab.ca
www.elc.ab.ca

Edmonton: **Ewasiuk & Associates - *1**
#311, 8925 - 51 Ave. SE, Edmonton, AB T6E 5J3
Tel: 780-465-1155; *Fax:* 780-465-2507
ealaw@telusplanet.net

Edmonton: **Feehan Law Office - *2**
#1740, Sun Life Place, 10123 - 99 St., Edmonton, AB T5J 3H1
Tel: 780-424-6425; *Fax:* 780-424-6477

Edmonton: **Field Law - Edmonton - *59**
#2000, Oxford Tower, 10235 - 101st St., Edmonton, AB T5J 3G1
Tel: 780-423-3003; *Fax:* 780-428-9329
Toll-Free: 800-222-6479
wbrown@fieldlaw.com; lturner@fieldlaw.com
www.fieldlaw.com

Edmonton: **Fix & Smith - *2**
10277 - 97 St. NW, Edmonton, AB T5J 0L9
Tel: 780-424-2245; *Fax:* 780-423-0425

Edmonton: **Fleming & Gubbins - *2**
9636 - 102A ave. NW, Edmonton, AB T5H 0G5
Tel: 780-424-9505; *Fax:* 780-425-0472

Edmonton: **Frieser Robinson MacKay - *6**
Freiser Robinson MacKay Building, 10410 - 81 Ave., Edmonton, AB T6E 1X5
Tel: 780-429-1717; *Fax:* 780-421-8335
Toll-Free: 877-302-1717
inquiries@frmlaw.com
www.frmlaw.com

Edmonton: **Galbraith Empson - *2**
#1750, 10123 - 99 St., Edmonton, AB T5J 3H1
Tel: 780-424-9558; *Fax:* 780-424-5852
galson@shaw.ca

Edmonton: **Galbraith Law - *1**
17318 - 106 Ave., Edmonton, AB T5S 1H9
Tel: 780-483-6111; *Fax:* 780-483-6411
Toll-Free: 866-483-6111
stan@galbraith.ab.ca
www.galbraith.ab.ca

Edmonton: **Richard Gariepy - *1**
10039 - 117 St., Edmonton, AB T5K 1W7
Tel: 780-482-7370; *Fax:* 780-482-2553

Edmonton: **Gawlinski & Parkatti, Barristers & Solicitors - *2**
#Sun Life Pl., #990, 10123 - 99th St., Edmonton, AB T5J 3H1
Tel: 780-428-6645; *Fax:* 780-428-6649
sjgawlinski@gp-law.ca; dtparkatti@gp-law.ca
www.gp-law.ca

Edmonton: **Blair M. Geiger - *1**
7904 Gateway Blvd. NW, Edmonton, AB T6E 6C3
Tel: 780-438-4972; *Fax:* 780-436-7771
bgeiger@telusplanet.net

Edmonton: **Dale Gibson Consulting Barrister - *1**
11018 - 125 St. NW, Edmonton, AB T5M 0M1
Tel: 780-452-9530; *Fax:* 780-453-5872
giblaw@telusplanet.net

Edmonton: **R.D. Gillespie - *1**
#300, 10209 - 97 St., Edmonton, AB T5J 0L6
Tel: 780-424-3255; *Fax:* 780-429-2615
robert.gillespie@interbaun.com

Edmonton: **Gledhill Larocque - *5**
#300, 10209 - 97 St., Edmonton, AB T5J 0L6
Tel: 780-425-3511; *Fax:* 780-426-5919

Edmonton: **Goldford Law Office - *2**
#200, 10735 - 107th St., Edmonton, AB T5H 0W6
Tel: 780-482-1000; *Fax:* 780-482-0963
hgoldford@goldfordlaw.com

Edmonton: **Gunn Prithipaul & Hatch - *5**
#100, 9924 - 106th St. NW, Edmonton, AB T5K 1C4
Tel: 780-488-4460; *Fax:* 780-488-4783
info@gplegal.ca
www.gplegal.ca

Edmonton: **Hajduk Gibbs LLP, Barristers & Solicitors - *4**
#202, Platinum Place Bldg., 10120 - 118 St. NW, 2nd Fl., Edmonton, AB T5K 1Y4
Tel: 780-428-4258; *Fax:* 780-425-9439
Toll-Free: 800-749-9989
info@hajdukandgibbs.com
www.hajdukandgibbs.com

Edmonton: **Hall & Van Campenhout - *2**
12026 - 102 Ave. NW, Edmonton, AB T5K 0R9
Tel: 780-482-5732; *Fax:* 780-482-5736

Edmonton: **Hansma Bristow & Finlay LLP, Barristers, Solicitors & Notaries Public - *7**
13815 - 127 St. NW, 2nd Fl., Edmonton, AB T6V 1A8
Tel: 780-456-3661; *Fax:* 780-457-9381
info@hblaw.ca; hansma@hblaw.ca; r.finlay@hblaw.ca

Edmonton: **Hardman Law Office - *1**
18067 - 107 Ave., Edmonton, AB T5S 1K3
Tel: 780-484-2041; *Fax:* 780-484-8950
hardman@compusmart.ab.ca

Edmonton: **R. Allan Harris Professional Corp. - *1**
#1090, The Phipps-McKinnon Bldg., 10020 - 101A Ave., Edmonton, AB T5J 3G2
Tel: 780-421-1641; *Fax:* 780-421-1936

Edmonton: **Haymour Kalil - *1**
#2031, Scotia Place 2, 10060 Jasper Ave. NW, Edmonton, AB T5J 3R8
Tel: 780-425-5700; *Fax:* 780-429-4573
haymour@telusplanet.net

Edmonton: **Christopher R. Head - *1**
#2400, 10303 Jasper Ave., Edmonton, AB T5J 3T8
Tel: 780-422-6242; *Fax:* 780-428-1137
Toll-Free: 877-797-6242
chead@danet.com

Edmonton: **H.J.D. Henderson - *1**
10938 - 124 St., Edmonton, AB T5M 0H5
Tel: 780-451-2769; *Fax:* 780-451-3534
hamish.henderson@telus.net

** indicates number of lawyers*

Edmonton: **Hendrickson Gower Massing & Olivieri LLP - *8**
#2250, Scotia 1, 10060 Jasper Ave., Edmonton, AB T5J 3R8
Tel: 780-421-8816; *Fax:* 780-424-5864
Toll-Free: 800-421-8816
www.hgmolaw.com

Edmonton: **Henning Byrne - *7**
#1450, Standard Life Centre, 10405 Jasper Ave. NW, Edmonton, AB T5J 3N4
Tel: 780-421-1707; *Fax:* 780-425-9438
Toll-Free: 888-702-1707
general@henningbyrne.com
www.henningbyrne.com

Edmonton: **Heritage Law Offices - *5**
#108, 284 - 109 St., Edmonton, AB T6J 6B7
Tel: 780-436-0011; *Fax:* 780-436-7000

Edmonton: **B.J. Herring - *1**
10402 - 155 St., Edmonton, AB T5P 2M3
Tel: 780-469-2609

Edmonton: **Leroy N. Hiller - *1**
#1720, Sun Life Place, 10123 - 99th St., Edmonton, AB T5J 3H1
Tel: 780-424-6660; *Fax:* 780-426-2980
lnhiller@telusplanet.net

Edmonton: **John Hinton - *1**
5508 - 141 St. NW, Edmonton, AB T6H 4A2
Tel: 780-434-4710; *Fax:* 780-437-4281

Edmonton: **Hladun & Company - *4**
#300, 10711 - 102 St., Edmonton, AB T5H 2T8
Tel: 780-423-1888; *Fax:* 780-424-0934
inquiries@hladun.com

Edmonton: **Terry E. Hofmann - *1**
P.O. Box 51070, Stn. Highlands, 6525 - 118 Ave., Edmonton, AB T5W 5G5
Tel: 780-448-3885; *Fax:* 780-448-5840

Edmonton: **Douglas B. Holman - *1**
#700, 10150 - 100 St. NW, Edmonton, AB T5J 0P6
Tel: 780-429-3644; *Fax:* 780-429-3685

Edmonton: **William K. Horwitz - *1**
#140, 17010 - 103 Ave., Edmonton, AB T5S 1K7
Tel: 780-486-3100; *Fax:* 780-489-9671

Edmonton: **Stanley V.T. Hum - *1**
#1003, 10010 - 106 St. SW, Edmonton, AB T5J 3L8
Tel: 780-453-8988; *Fax:* 780-424-7379
stan_hum@hotmail.com

Edmonton: **Hustwick Payne - *9**
#600, Capital Pl., 9707 - 110 St. NW, Edmonton, AB T5K 2L9
Tel: 780-482-6555; *Fax:* 780-482-6613
reception@hhplegal.com
www.hplegal.ca

Edmonton: **Implementation & Advisory Group Ltd. - *2**
#1400, Baker Centre, 10025 - 106 St., Edmonton, AB T5J 1G4
Tel: 780-482-5577; *Fax:* 780-482-5939
robin.bobocel@iag.ca

Edmonton: **Jiwaji Law Office - *2**
#204, 2603 Hewes Way NW, Edmonton, AB T6L 6W6
Tel: 780-448-0467; *Fax:* 780-448-3962
moosaj@telus.net

Edmonton: **John Stadnyk Law Office, Barristers & Solicitors - *1**
#300, 14925 - 111 Ave., Edmonton, AB T0A 0M0
Tel: 780-414-0222; *Fax:* 780-414-0002
Toll-Free: 877-414-0222
www.stadnyklaw.com
john@stadnyklaw.com

Edmonton: **John Todd Holdings Ltd. - *1**
#102, 10178 - 117 St., Edmonton, AB T5K 2X9
Tel: 780-906-1759
bremertodd@shaw.ca

Edmonton: **Jomha, Skrobot LLP - *3**
#2260, 10123 - 99th St. NW, Edmonton, AB T5J 3H1
Tel: 780-424-0688; *Fax:* 780-424-0695
jomhalaw@telusplanet.net

Edmonton: **Kennedy Agrios - *5**
#1325, 10180 - 101 St. NW, Edmonton, AB T5J 3S4
Tel: 780-969-6900; *Fax:* 780-969-6901

Edmonton: **Kirwin LLP - *7**
#200, 10339 - 124 St. NW, Edmonton, AB T5N 3W1
Tel: 780-448-7401; *Fax:* 780-453-3281
mail@kirwinllp.com

Edmonton: **Robert A. Kiss - *1**
17393 - 108 Ave, Edmonton, AB T5S 1G2
Tel: 780-447-7205; *Fax:* 780-481-6258

Edmonton: **Kolthammer, Batchelor & Laidlaw LLP - *4**
#208, 11062 - 156 St. NW, Edmonton, AB T5P 4M8
Tel: 780-489-5003; *Fax:* 780-486-2107
kolthamm@telusplanet.net

Edmonton: **I. Samuel Kravinchuk - *1**
#800, 10310 Jasper Ave. NW, Edmonton, AB T5J 2W4
Tel: 780-426-4884; *Fax:* 780-425-9359

Edmonton: **Katherine A. Kubica - *1**
1910 Sun Life Place, 10123 - 99 St., Edmonton, AB T5J 3H1
Tel: 780-425-8000; *Fax:* 780-425-8488

Edmonton: **Kuckertz Law Office - *2**
#202, 8003 - 102 St., Edmonton, AB T6E 4A2
Tel: 780-432-9308; *Fax:* 780-439-9950
h.kuckertz@kuckertzlaw.com

Edmonton: **Kulasa Campbell - *3**
#100, 10703 - 181 St. NW, Edmonton, AB T5S 1N3
Tel: 780-484-0665; *Fax:* 780-486-7282
tkulasa@connect.ab.ca

Edmonton: **Larbalestier Stewart - *2**
#2400, 10303 Jasper Ave., Edmonton, AB T5J 3T8
Tel: 780-422-6242; *Fax:* 780-428-1137
Toll-Free: 877-797-6242
lastlaw@larbalestierstewart.com

Edmonton: **Laurier Law Office - *3**
8623 - 149 St., Edmonton, AB T5R 1B3
Tel: 780-486-0207; *Fax:* 780-483-0848

Edmonton: **Keith M. Leslie - *1**
1612 - 89 St. NW, Edmonton, AB T6K 2A9
Tel: 780-463-4019; *Fax:* 780-468-2976
kleslie@agt.net

Edmonton: **Linton Law Office - *1**
#200, 10426 - 81 Ave. NW, Edmonton, AB T6E 1X5
Tel: 780-415-5540; *Fax:* 780-415-5541
kathy.linton@lintonlawoffice.com

Edmonton: **Philip G. Lister Professional Corporation - *1**
#2410, Oxford Tower, 10235 - 101 St., Edmonton, AB T5J 3G1
Tel: 780-422-6114; *Fax:* 780-421-0818
phil@listerlaw.com

Edmonton: **Julie C. Lloyd - *1**
#950, 10303 Jasper Ave. NW, Edmonton, AB T5J 3N6
Tel: 780-442-4417; *Fax:* 780-424-9370
jclloyd@telusplanet.net

Edmonton: **Peter T.K. Loong - *1**
10704 - 108 St., 2nd Fl., Edmonton, AB T5H 3A3
Tel: 780-424-3200; *Fax:* 780-424-2369
peterloonglaw@telusplanet.net

Edmonton: **Lyons Albert & Cook - *2**
#306, 10328 - 81 Ave. NW, Edmonton, AB T6E 1X2
Tel: 780-437-0743; *Fax:* 780-438-6695
laclaw@telusplanet.net

Edmonton: **Reginald S. MacDonald - *1**
#301, 10171 Saskatchewan Dr. NW, Edmonton, AB T6E 4R5
Tel: 780-439-7000; *Fax:* 780-439-7248

Edmonton: **J.D. MacEachern - *1**
#910, CN Tower, 10004 - 104 Ave. NW, Edmonton, AB T5J 0K1
Tel: 780-428-1079; *Fax:* 780-429-6121
maceac@shaw.ca

Edmonton: **Mah & Company - *2**
#1013, TD Tower, 10088 - 102 Ave., Edmonton, AB T5J 2Z1
Tel: 780-428-3888; *Fax:* 780-425-8383

Edmonton: **Malhotra & Company - *1**
#315, 10909 Jasper Ave., Edmonton, AB T5J 3L9
Tel: 780-423-5792; *Fax:* 780-426-0081

Edmonton: **James W. Mandick Professional Corporation - *1**
#1850, 10123 - 99 St. NW, Edmonton, AB T5J 3H1
Tel: 780-423-3311; *Fax:* 780-423-3321
jmandick@wmlaw.ca

Edmonton: **M.B. Marcovitch - *1**
#1300, 10665 Jasper Ave. NW, Edmonton, AB T5J 3S9
Tel: 780-453-4390; *Fax:* 780-424-3631

Edmonton: **Matheson & Company LLP - *6**
10410 - 81 Ave., Edmonton, AB T6E 1X5
Tel: 780-433-5881; *Fax:* 780-432-9453
general@mathesonlaw.com

Edmonton: **McGee Richard - *3**
#1155, Weber Centre, 5555 Calgary Trail NW, Edmonton, AB T6H 5P9
Tel: 780-437-2240; *Fax:* 780-438-5788
trichard@mcgeerichard.com
www.mcgeerichard.com

Edmonton: **McKay-Carey & Company - *1**
#1900, 10123 - 99 St. NW, Edmonton, AB T5J 3H1
Tel: 780-424-0222; *Fax:* 780-421-0834

Edmonton: **McKee & Company - *2**
#281, 11717 - 42 St. NW, Edmonton, AB T5W 4V8
Tel: 780-471-1100; *Fax:* 780-471-1150
mckee.co@shaw.ca

Edmonton: **Mckenzie House Law Group - *2**
#8603, 104 St. NW, Edmonton, AB T6E 4G6
Tel: 780-424-3558; *Fax:* 780-424-5515

Edmonton: **McLennan Ross LLP - *46**
#600, West Chambers, 12220 Stony Plain Rd., Edmonton, AB T5N 3Y4
Tel: 780-482-9200; *Fax:* 780-482-9100
Toll-Free: 800-567-9200
info@mross.com
www.mross.com

Edmonton: **McMenemy & Tilleard. - *2**
#700, 10150 - 100 St. NW, Edmonton, AB T5J 0P6
Tel: 780-429-3644; *Fax:* 780-429-3685

Edmonton: **R. McPhail - *1**
#150, 12225 - 105 Ave., Edmonton, AB T5N 0Y3
Tel: 780-482-5947; *Fax:* 780-482-2429

Edmonton: **McPike Johnston Barristers & Solicitors - *2**
11914 - 129 Ave., Edmonton, AB T5E 0N3
Tel: 780-455-6678; *Fax:* 780-453-1093
mcpike@4lawyer.ca

Edmonton: **Ingrid E. Meier - *1**
9718 - 92 St., Edmonton, AB T6C 3S4
Tel: 780-436-5954; *Fax:* 780-401-3204
lawyer@meier.ca

Edmonton: **Ron J. Meleshko - *1**
15412 - 55 St. NW, Edmonton, AB T5Y 2S4
Tel: 780-414-0298

Edmonton: **Melnyk & Co. - *3**
#200, 9939 Jasper Ave., Edmonton, AB T5J 2W8
Tel: 780-428-8900; *Fax:* 780-429-8889
melnykco@telusplanet.net

Edmonton: **Joseph J. Michaels - *1**
#1985 Sun Life Place, 10123 - 99 St. NW, Edmonton, AB T5J 3H1
Tel: 780-424-0354

Edmonton: **Miller Boileau Family Law Group - *3**
11835 - 102nd Ave. NW, Edmonton, AB T5K 0R6
Tel: 780-482-2888; *Fax:* 780-482-4600
mail@millerboileau.com
www.millerboileau.com

Edmonton: **Mintz & Chow - *6**
#400, 10357 - 109 St. NW, Edmonton, AB T5J 1N3
Tel: 780-425-2041; *Fax:* 780-425-2195
mincho@telusplanet.net

Edmonton: **W. Robert Mitchell - *1**
#405, 10408 - 124 St., Edmonton, AB T5N 1R5
Tel: 780-482-5791; *Fax:* 780-488-0965

Edmonton: **Murray, Chilibeck & Horne - *3**
10605 - 172nd St. NW, Edmonton, AB T5S 1P1
Tel: 780-484-2323; *Fax:* 780-486-4289

** indicates number of lawyers*

Edmonton: Alann J. Nazarevich - *1
9803 - 31 Ave., Edmonton, AB T6N 1C5
Tel: 780-430-0363; *Fax*: 780-430-0984

Edmonton: Neuman Thompson - *6
#200, 12220 Stony Plain Rd. NW, Edmonton, AB T5N 3Y4
Tel: 780-482-7645; *Fax*: 780-488-0026

Edmonton: Kenneth Ng - *1
3234 Parsons Rd.W, Edmonton, AB T6N 1M2
Tel: 780-988-9188; *Fax*: 780-496-9717

Edmonton: Nicholl & Akers - *7
#200, 10187 - 104 St. NW, Edmonton, AB T5J 0Z9
Tel: 780-429-2771; *Fax*: 780-425-1665

Edmonton: Nickerson Roberts Holinski & Mercer - *9
#100, 7712 - 104 St., Edmonton, AB T6E 4C5
Tel: 780-428-0041; *Fax*: 780-425-0272
reception@nrhmlaw.com
www.nrhmlaw.com

Edmonton: Gregory O'Laughlin - *1
#300, 10209 - 97 St. NW, Edmonton, AB T5J 0L6
Tel: 780-424-9059; *Fax*: 780-429-2615

Edmonton: Ronald J. Obirek - *1
#240, 6005 - 103 St. NW, Edmonton, AB T6H 2H3
Tel: 780-496-9046; *Fax*: 780-436-9669
rjobirek@telusplanet.net

Edmonton: Ogilvie LLP - *26
#1400, 10303 Jasper Ave., Edmonton, AB T5J 3N6
Tel: 780-421-1818; *Fax*: 780-429-4453
info@ogilvielaw.com
www.ogilvielaw.com

Edmonton: Kelly R. Palmer - *1
#1800, 10250 - 101 St. NW, Edmonton, AB T5J 3P4
Tel: 780-448-9275; *Fax*: 780-423-0163

Edmonton: Phillip G. Parker - *1
10704 - 108 St., 2nd Fl., Edmonton, AB T5H 3A3
Tel: 780-424-3200; *Fax*: 780-424-2369

Edmonton: Patrick & Patrick - *1
#800, 10310 Jasper Ave. NW, Edmonton, AB T5J 2W4
Tel: 780-426-4884; *Fax*: 780-425-9358

Edmonton: Patrick Dolphin Professional Corporation - *1
10621 - 124 St. NW, Edmonton, AB T5N 1S5
Tel: 780-423-4081; *Fax*: 780-425-5247

Edmonton: Penonzek Murray - *2
#147, 10403 - 122 St. NW, Edmonton, AB T5N 4C1
Tel: 780-482-1199; *Fax*: 780-482-1883
k.penonzek@shawbiz.ca

Edmonton: Patrick J. Phelan - *1
#1550, Sun Life Pl., 10123 - 99 St., Edmonton, AB T5J 3H1
Tel: 780-424-7730; *Fax*: 780-428-4484
patrick.phelan@telus.net

Edmonton: Roy A. Philion - *1
#880, 10020 - 101 Ave. NW, Edmonton, AB T5J 3G2
Tel: 780-423-2977; *Fax*: 780-424-8098

Edmonton: Ronald W. Poitras - *1
#300, 10209 - 97 St., Edmonton, AB T5J 0L6
Tel: 780-424-3270; *Fax*: 780-429-2615

Edmonton: Polack, Meindersma, Liddell - *3
#300, High Park Corner, 14925 - 111 Ave., Edmonton, AB T5M 2P6
Tel: 780-486-0926; *Fax*: 780-444-1393

Edmonton: Pringle & Associates - *7
#300, Transalta Place, 10150 - 100 St. NW, Edmonton, AB T5J 0P6
Tel: 780-424-8866; *Fax*: 780-426-1470
www.pringleandassociates.com

Edmonton: Prismatic Group Inc. - *1
#205, 3132 Parsons Rd., Edmonton, AB T6N 1L6
Tel: 780-495-0200; *Fax*: 780-439-2369
bill.donahue@prismatic.ca

Edmonton: Pundit & Chotalia - *2
#1506, Edmonton City Centre, 10025 - 102A Ave., Edmonton, AB T5J 2Z2
Tel: 780-421-0861; *Fax*: 780-425-6048
shirish@chotalia.com

Edmonton: Rand Kiss Turner - *3
#1600, 10020 - 101A Ave. NW, Edmonton, AB T5J 3G2
Tel: 780-423-1984; *Fax*: 780-423-1969

Edmonton: M. Naeem Rauf
#300, 10209 - 97 St., Edmonton, AB T5J 0L6
Tel: 780-453-4399; *Fax*: 780-429-2615

Edmonton: Peter E. Recto - *1
6423 - 154th Avenue, Edmonton, AB T5Y 2N7
Tel: 780-423-1283; *Fax*: 780-473-8324
recto2001@hotmail.com

Edmonton: H.M. Reich - *1
#1550, Sun Life Place, 10123 - 99 St., Edmonton, AB T5J 3H1
Tel: 780-424-7732; *Fax*: 780-428-4484
reichlaw@telus.net

Edmonton: Reynolds, Mirth, Richards & Farmer LLP - *36
#3200, Manulife Place, 10180 - 101 St., Edmonton, AB T5J 3W8
Tel: 780-425-9510; *Fax*: 780-429-3044
Toll-Free: 800-661-7673
mail@rmrf.com
www.rmrf.com

Edmonton: Richard D. Rennick Professional Corporation - *1
#2200, 10123 - 99 St. NW, Edmonton, AB T5J 3H1
Tel: 780-426-5510; *Fax*: 780-420-1645
lawfirm@rennicklaw.ca

Edmonton: Richards Hunter - *4
#1270, 5555 Calgary Trail NW, Edmonton, AB T6H 5P9
Tel: 780-436-8554; *Fax*: 780-436-8566
main@wortonhunter.com

Edmonton: Ritchie Mill Law Office - *5
#102, 10171 Saskatchewan Dr. NW, Edmonton, AB T6E 4R5
Tel: 780-431-1444; *Fax*: 780-431-1499
Toll-Free: 888-333-8818
office@rmlo.com

Edmonton: James A. Robertson - *1
#300, Wentworth, 10209 - 97 St. NW, Edmonton, AB T5J 0L6
Tel: 780-423-1680; *Fax*: 780-421-7304
jamesrob@shaw.ca

Edmonton: Terry J. Romaniuk - *1
9743 - 89 Ave. NW, Edmonton, AB T6E 2S1
Tel: 780-433-8127

Edmonton: David W. Ross - *1
8623 - 149 St., Edmonton, AB T5R 1B3
Tel: 780-425-1965; *Fax*: 780-483-0848
dwross@bigfoot.com

Edmonton: James D. Ross - *1
#1003, Highfield Place, 10010 - 106 St., Edmonton, AB T5J 3L8
Tel: 780-482-3144; *Fax*: 780-424-7379

Edmonton: Samy F. Salloum - *1
1341 Carter Crest Rd., Edmonton, AB T6R 2L6
Tel: 780-426-7777; *Fax*: 780-426-7778

Edmonton: Savaryn & Savaryn - *1
P.O. Box 45083, Stn. Landsdowne, Edmonton, AB T6H 5Y1
Tel: 780-422-7548
savaryn@telusplanet.net

Edmonton: Savich Law Office - *1
#200, 10350 - 172 St., Edmonton, AB T5S 1G9
Tel: 780-486-7300; *Fax*: 780-489-0682
don@savichlaw.ca
www.savichlaw.ca

Edmonton: B.M. Schloss - *1
#800, Sun Life Place, 10123 - 99 St. NW, Edmonton, AB T5J 3H1
Tel: 780-448-9300; *Fax*: 780-489-9982
bschloss@schloss.ca

Edmonton: Schwab, Schwab & Schwab - *3
9908 - 106 St., Edmonton, AB T5K 1C4
Tel: 780-426-6715; *Fax*: 780-426-2301
schwab@telusplanet.net

Edmonton: D.L. Schwartz - *1
#324, 10909 Jasper Ave. NW, Edmonton, AB T5J 3L9
Tel: 780-424-0259; *Fax*: 780-424-0299
thebigkahuna@interbaun.com

Edmonton: Sharek Logan & van Leenen LLP - *8
#701, Tower 2, Scotia Place, 10060 Jasper Ave. NW, Edmonton, AB T5J 3R8
Tel: 780-413-3100; *Fax*: 780-413-3152
www.sharekco.com

Edmonton: G.P. Shewchuk - *1
#310, 8944 - 182 St. NW, Edmonton, AB T5T 2E3
Tel: 780-481-1299; *Fax*: 780-481-1674

Edmonton: William Shim
#2000B, Sun Life Place, 10123 - 99 St. NW, Edmonton, AB T5J 3H1
Tel: 780-423-8060; *Fax*: 780-425-4201

Edmonton: Shores Belzil Jardine - *9
#1800, 10250 - 101 St. NW, Edmonton, AB T5J 3P4
Tel: 780-448-9275; *Fax*: 780-423-0163
louis@shoresbelzil.com
www.shoresbelzil.com

Edmonton: Shtabsky & Tussman LLP - *7
#1400, 10025 - 102A Ave., Edmonton, AB T5J 2Z2
Tel: 780-429-4671; *Fax*: 780-424-3580
st400@stlaw.com
www.stlaw.com

Edmonton: W.J. Shymko - *1
#200, 10105 - 108 Ave., Edmonton, AB T5H 1A7
Tel: 780-425-6414; *Fax*: 780-425-6416

Edmonton: Simons & Stephens - *2
#710, 10055 - 106 St. NW, Edmonton, AB T5J 2Y2
Tel: 780-482-1536; *Fax*: 780-488-1914
nsimons@telus.net

Edmonton: Larry A. Sitko - *1
#201, 12907 - 97 St. NW, Edmonton, AB T5E 4C2
Tel: 780-476-7686; *Fax*: 780-476-7688

Edmonton: Snyder & Associates LLP - *11
#2500, 10123 - 99 St., Edmonton, AB T5J 3H1
Tel: 780-426-4133; *Fax*: 780-424-1588
Toll-Free: 877-426-4148
www.snyder.ca

Edmonton: Stewart Law Offices - *2
11724 - 103 Ave. NW, Edmonton, AB T5K 0S7
Tel: 780-482-3800; *Fax*: 780-482-5600
stwlaw@telusplanet.net

Edmonton: Stillman LLP - *6
#300, 10335 - 172 St., Edmonton, AB T5S 1K9
Tel: 780-484-4445; *Fax*: 780-484-4184
Toll-Free: 888-258-2529
lawyers@stillmanllp.com

Edmonton: Strategic Results Consulting Inc. - *1
13703 - 101A Ave., Edmonton, AB T5N 0K9
Tel: 780-994-9184

Edmonton: André A. Szaszkiewicz - *1
#202, 1289 - 91 St., Edmonton, AB T6X 1H1
Tel: 780-452-2000; *Fax*: 780-455-7229
andresz@telusplanet.net

Edmonton: Tarrabain & Company - *9
#2150, Tower One, Scotia Place, 10060 Jasper Ave., Edmonton, AB T5J 3R8
Tel: 780-429-1010; *Fax*: 780-429-0101
lawyers@tarrabain.com
www.tarrabain.com

Edmonton: Christopher G. Taskey - *1
8603 - 104th St. NW, Edmonton, AB T6E 4G6
Tel: 780-424-3558; *Fax*: 780-423-5515
ctaskey@shawbiz.ca

Edmonton: Taylor & Jewell - *2
#215, Millbourner Mall, 38 Ave. NW, Edmonton, AB T6K 3L6
Tel: 780-450-5761; *Fax*: 780-468-4524

Edmonton: R.I. Tennant - *1
#712, 10010 - 106 St., Edmonton, AB T5J 3L8
Tel: 780-425-2289

Edmonton: Sylvia O. Tensfeldt - *1
#200, 10525 Jasper Ave. NW, Edmonton, AB T5J 1Z4
Tel: 780-424-3334; *Fax*: 780-424-4252

Edmonton: Thom Law Office - *1
8506 - 104 St., Edmonton, AB T6E 4G4
Tel: 780-434-5870; *Fax*: 780-436-8420
len@thomlaw.com
www.thomlaw.com

** indicates number of lawyers*

Edmonton: Tkachuk & Patterson - *2
#1260, First Edmonton Place, 10665 Jasper Ave. NW, Edmonton, AB T5J 3S9
Tel: 780-428-1593; *Fax:* 780-426-6679
tkalaw@alberta.com

Edmonton: George Turcin - *1
15819 Stony Plain Rd., Edmonton, AB T5P 3Z7
Tel: 780-452-3208; *Fax:* 780-447-5410

Edmonton: Helen S. Tymoczko - *1
#106, 10108 - 125 St., Edmonton, AB T5N 4B6
Tel: 780-472-1758; *Fax:* 780-476-4085

Edmonton: M. Brent Tyson - *1
#300, 10209 - 97th St. NW, Edmonton, AB T5J 0L6
Tel: 780-488-3333; *Fax:* 780-429-2615
brent@tysonlaw.ca
www.tysonlaw.ca

Edmonton: Venkatraman Purewal & Pillay - *4
#303, 9811 - 34 Ave., Edmonton, AB T6E 5X9
Tel: 780-436-7060; *Fax:* 780-436-7064
lawyers@vplaw.ca

Edmonton: Wachowich & Company - *4
#555, 10310 Jasper Ave. NW, Edmonton, AB T5J 2W4
Tel: 780-429-0555; *Fax:* 780-425-4795
mail@wachowich.com
www.wachowich.com

Edmonton: Welsh & Company - *1
#888, 4445 Calgary Trail South, Edmonton, AB T6H 5R7
Tel: 780-438-3500; *Fax:* 780-438-3129

Edmonton: Uwe Welz - *1
7904 - 103 St., Edmonton, AB T6E 6C3
Tel: 780-432-7711; *Fax:* 780-439-1177
uwpc@telusplanet.net

Edmonton: Westwood Consultants - *1
#1206, 5328 Calgary Trial South, Edmonton, AB T6H 4J8
Tel: 780-437-7990
coultier.denise@ic.gc.ca

Edmonton: Wheatley Sadownik - *4
#2000, 10123 - 99 St., Edmonton, AB T5J 3H1
Tel: 780-423-6671; *Fax:* 780-420-6327
mail@wheatleysadownik.com
www.wheatleysadownik.com

Edmonton: Willis Bokenfohr Thorsrud - *3
#410, ATB Place, 9888 Jasper Ave., Edmonton, AB T5J 5C6
Tel: 780-452-2764; *Fax:* 780-452-3247

Edmonton: Witten LLP, Barristers & Solicitors - *42
#2500, Canadian Western Bank Place, 10303 Jasper Ave., Edmonton, AB T5J 3N6
Tel: 780-428-0501; *Fax:* 780-429-2559
lawyers@wittenlaw.com
www.wittenlaw.com

Edmonton: Collin Wong - *1
10704 - 108 St., 2nd Fl., Edmonton, AB T5H 3A3
Tel: 780-488-7003; *Fax:* 780-488-1593
cwongpf@compusmart.ab.ca

Edmonton: Peter S. Wong - *1
#204, Kingsdale Professional Centre, 9644 - 54 Ave., Edmonton, AB T6E 5V1
Tel: 780-430-1070; *Fax:* 780-430-1773
pwong@sequiter.com

Edmonton: Wood Law Office - *2
#304, 10209 - 97 St. NW, Edmonton, AB T5J 0L6
Tel: 780-482-3291; *Fax:* 780-452-1821
laurieiwood@gmail.com

Edmonton: Hu Eliot Young Law Office - *1
8520 - 104 St. NW, Edmonton, AB T6E 4G4
Tel: 780-425-8400; *Fax:* 780-424-3777
heyoung@telusplanet.net

Edmonton: Ronald J. Young - *1
#204, 10265 - 107 St., Edmonton, AB T5J 5G2
Tel: 780-424-3311; *Fax:* 780-425-9609

Edmonton: A.R. Zariwny - *1
#200, 10351 - 82 Ave. NW, Edmonton, AB T6E 1Z9
Tel: 780-433-5999; *Fax:* 780-439-6456
zlo@oanet.com

Edson: Robert W. Anderson - *1
P.O. Box 6748, 202B - 50 St., Edson, AB T7E 1V1
Tel: 780-723-3245; *Fax:* 780-723-5443
rwandlaw@telus.net

Edson: Dennis C. Calvert - *1
P.O. Box 6658, Stn. Main, 107 - 50 St., Edson, AB T7E 1V1
Tel: 780-723-6047; *Fax:* 780-723-3602

Fairview: H.A. Byers - *1
P.O. Box 2200, Fairview, AB T0H 1L0
Tel: 780-835-4100; *Fax:* 780-835-4171

Fort MacLeod: Vallance & Co. - *1
P.O. Box 757, 249 Main St., Fort MacLeod, AB T0L 0Z0
Tel: 403-553-4484; *Fax:* 403-553-3444
Toll-Free: 866-553-4484
vallance@shockwave.com

Fort McMurray: Campbell & Cooper - *4
#212, 9714 Main St., Fort McMurray, AB T9H 1T6
Tel: 780-791-7787; *Fax:* 780-791-0750
laywers@mcmurraylaw.com

Fort McMurray: Gorsalitz Law Office - *1
9912 Manning Ave., Fort McMurray, AB T9H 2B9
Tel: 780-791-4115; *Fax:* 780-743-0040

Fort McMurray: Samuel N. Mason - *1
#104, 10012 Franklin Ave., Fort McMurray, AB T9H 2K6
Tel: 780-743-5002; *Fax:* 780-743-4150

Fort McMurray: Wolff Taitinger - *2
10019R Franklin Ave., Fort McMurray, AB T9H 2K7
Tel: 780-790-9040; *Fax:* 780-743-1813
main@wolftaitlaw.com

Fort Saskatchewan: Fotty & Torok-Both - *4
10509 - 100 Ave., Fort Saskatchewan, AB T8L 1Z5
Tel: 780-998-4841; *Fax:* 780-998-4821

Fort Saskatchewan: Jenkins & Jenkins - *2
#200, 9906 - 102 St., Fort Saskatchewan, AB T8L 2C3
Tel: 780-998-4200; *Fax:* 780-998-4370
cjenkins@jenkins-law.com

Grande Cache: Harry Arnesen - *1
P.O. Box 385, 2502 Pine Plaza, Grande Cache, AB T0E 0Y0
Tel: 780-827-2458; *Fax:* 780-827-3734

Grande Prairie: Dobko & Wheaton - *4
10022 - 102 Ave., Grande Prairie, AB T8V 0Z7
Tel: 780-539-6200; *Fax:* 780-532-9052
Toll-Free: 866-539-6200
www.dwlaw.ca

Grande Prairie: Gurevitch Headon & Associates - *3
9931 - 106 Ave., Grande Prairie, AB T8V 1J4
Tel: 780-539-3710; *Fax:* 780-532-2788
Toll-Free: 866-720-3710
gplaw@telus.net
www.grandeprairielaw.ca

Grande Prairie: Howey Law Office - *1
201 Professional Bldg., 9905 - 101 Ave., Grande Prairie, AB T8V 0X7
Tel: 780-539-0690; *Fax:* 780-539-3813

Grande Prairie: Kay, McVey, Smith & Carlstrom LLP - *11
#600, Windsor Ct., 9835 - 101st Ave., Grande Prairie, AB T8V 5V4
Tel: 780-532-7771; *Fax:* 780-532-1158
Toll-Free: 888-531-7771
ksms@kayship.com
www.kayship.com

Grande Prairie: Lewis & Chrenek - *5
#108, 9824 - 97 Ave., Grande Prairie, AB T8V 7K2
Tel: 780-539-6800; *Fax:* 780-539-7975
lewchr@telusplanet.net

Grande Prairie: Robert S. Pollick Professional Corporation, Barristers & Solicito - *1
#200, 10006 - 101 Ave., Grande Prairie, AB T8V 0Y1
Tel: 780-538-8290; *Fax:* 780-538-4515
enniski@telusplanet.net

Grande Prairie: Walisser Shavers LLP - *2
#202, 10027 - 101 Ave., Grande Prairie, AB T8V 0X9
Tel: 780-532-0315; *Fax:* 780-532-3369
loganw@telusplanet.net

Hanna: Ross, Todd & Company - *3
P.O. Box 1330, 124 - 2 Ave. West, Hanna, AB T0J 1P0
Tel: 403-854-4431; *Fax:* 403-854-2561
reception@drumhellerlaw.com

High Prairie: Harry J. Jong - *2
P.O. Box 1379, High Prairie, AB T0G 1E0
Tel: 780-523-4554; *Fax:* 780-523-5550
hjlaw@cablecomet.com

High River: A. George Dearing Professional Corp. - *1
#103, 14 - 2 Ave. SE, High River, AB T1V 2B8
Tel: 403-652-2771; *Fax:* 403-652-2699
info@ageorgedearing.ca
www.ageorgedearing.ca

Hinton: Johnson McClelland Murdoch - *4
213 Pembina Ave., Hinton, AB T7V 2B3
Tel: 780-865-2222; *Fax:* 780-865-8857
lawyer@jmmlaw.ca

Hinton: Woods & Robson - *2
110 Brewster Dr., Hinton, AB T7V 1B4
Tel: 780-865-3086; *Fax:* 780-865-7149
woodsrob@telusplanet.net

Hobbema: J. Wilton Littlechild, Q.C. - *1
P.O. Box 370, Hobbema, AB T0C 1N0
Tel: 780-585-3038; *Fax:* 780-585-2025
jwlittle@incentre.net

Innisfail: Tulloch Law Office - *1
P.O. Box 6099, 5030 - 50 St., Innisfail, AB T4G 1S7
Tel: 403-227-5591; *Fax:* 403-227-1230
carolyntulloch@telus.net

Lac La Biche: John W. Kozina - *1
P.O. Box 1439, 10130 Alberta Ave., Lac La Biche, AB T0A 2C0
Tel: 780-623-4818; *Fax:* 780-623-2933

Lac La Biche: Thomas R. Maccagno
P.O. Box 1270, 10120 - 101 Ave., Lac La Biche, AB T0A 2C0
Tel: 780-623-4177; *Fax:* 780-623-2266

Leduc: James K. Arends - *1
#206, 5904A - 50 St., Leduc, AB T9E 6J5
Tel: 780-986-1443; *Fax:* 780-980-5385
jarends@shaw.ca

Leduc: Elgert & Company - *1
5206 - 50 St., Leduc, AB T9E 6Z6
Tel: 780-986-3487; *Fax:* 780-986-2040
herbelgert@shaw.ca

Leduc: Jackie, Handerek & Forester, Barristers & Solicitors - *6
4710 - 50th St., Leduc, AB T9E 6W2
Tel: 780-986-5081; *Fax:* 780-986-8807
jhf@leduclawyers.ab.ca
www.leduclawyers.ab.ca

Leduc: E. Kahlke - *1
5102 - 50 Ave., Leduc, AB T9E 6V4
Tel: 780-986-8427; *Fax:* 780-986-3108

Leduc: Zalapski & Pahl - *4
#1, 5304 - 50 St., Leduc, AB T9E 6Z6
Tel: 780-986-8428; *Fax:* 780-986-2552

Lethbridge: Douglas N. Alger - *1
#203, 434 - 7 St. South, Lethbridge, AB T1J 2G7
Tel: 403-380-6005; *Fax:* 403-380-6088
alger@algerlaw.com
www.algerlaw.com

Lethbridge: Claudia R. Connolly - *3
#202, 506 - 4 Ave. South, Lethbridge, AB T1J 0N5
Tel: 403-329-8188; *Fax:* 403-328-7079

Lethbridge: Davidson & Williams LLP - *11
P.O. Box 518, 501 - 4 St. South, Lethbridge, AB T1J 4X2
Tel: 403-328-1766; *Fax:* 403-320-5434
lethbridge@davidsonandwilliams.com
www.davidsonandwilliams.com

Lethbridge: Frank de Walle - *1
323 - 7 St. South, Lethbridge, AB T1J 2G4
Tel: 403-328-8800; *Fax:* 403-328-8502
dewalle@telusplanet.net

Lethbridge: Dimnik & Company - *4
334 - 12 St. South, Lethbridge, AB T1J 2R1
Tel: 403-320-9800; *Fax:* 403-320-9124
info@lethbridgelawyers.com
www.lethbridgelawyers.com

Lethbridge: Dodic Toone Maclean - *4
416B Stafford Dr. South, Lethbridge, AB T1J 2L2
Tel: 403-329-1330; *Fax:* 403-329-1311

** indicates number of lawyers*

***Lethbridge*: Huckvale Wilde Harvie MacLennan LLP - *7**
P.O. Box 1028, 410 - 6th St. South, Lethbridge, AB T1J 4A2
Tel: 403-328-8856; *Fax:* 403-380-4050
mad@huckvale.ca

***Lethbridge*: R.F. Llewellyn - *1**
#202, 1921 Mayor Magrath Dr. South, Lethbridge, AB T1K 2R8
Tel: 403-329-0222; *Fax:* 403-329-8489

***Lethbridge*: MacLachlan McNab Hembroff - *6**
1003 - 4th Ave. South, Lethbridge, AB T1J 0P7
Tel: 403-381-4966; *Fax:* 403-329-9300
mmh@mmhlawyers.com
www.mmhlawyers.com

***Lethbridge*: William F. Malcolm Professional Corporation - *1**
406 Stafford Dr. South, Lethbridge, AB T1J 2L2
Tel: 403-329-0001; *Fax:* 403-329-0868

***Lethbridge*: Millar & Keith LLP - *2**
200 - 3rd St. South, Lethbridge, AB T1J 1Y7
Tel: 403-327-5716; *Fax:* 403-329-4063
mtklaw@telusplanet.net

***Lethbridge*: Milne Pritchard Law Office - *2**
#807, 400 - 4 Ave. South, Lethbridge, AB T1J 4E1
Tel: 403-329-1133; *Fax:* 403-329-0395
www.milnepritchard.com

***Lethbridge*: Harold N. Moodie - *1**
P.O. Box 9, Stn. Main, 212 - 5 St. South, 2nd Fl., Lethbridge, AB T1J 3Y3
Tel: 403-328-0005; *Fax:* 403-329-0945

***Lethbridge*: Peterson & Purvis LLP - *8**
P.O. Box 1165, 537 - 7th St. South, Lethbridge, AB T1J 4A4
Tel: 403-328-9667; *Fax:* 403-320-1393
p-plaw@telusplanet.net

***Lethbridge*: Pollock & Company - *3**
#200, 434 - 7th St. South, Lethbridge, AB T1J 4K1
Tel: 403-329-6900; *Fax:* 403-327-9790
Toll-Free: 800-262-4857
dlplaw@lawpollock.com
www.lawpollock.com

***Lethbridge*: Rhonda Ruston, Q.C. - *1**
501 - 4 St. South, Lethbridge, AB T1J 4K2
Tel: 403-328-4483; *Fax:* 403-206-7435
rkruston@telusplanet.net

***Lethbridge*: Shapiro & Company - *1**
#200, 427 - 5 St. South., Lethbridge, AB T1J 2B6
Tel: 403-328-9300; *Fax:* 403-328-9307
shapco@telusplanet.net

***Lethbridge*: Stringam Denecky LLP Law Office - *15**
314 - 3 St. South, Lethbridge, AB T1Y 1J9
Tel: 403-328-5577; *Fax:* 403-327-1141
results@stringam.ca; sdenecky@stringam.ca
www.stringam.cawww.facebook.com/stringamdenecky,
www.linkedin.com/company/stringam-denecky-llp

***Lloydminster*: Kindrachuk Dobson - *1**
Stafford Building, 5014 - 48 St., 2nd fl., Lloydminster, AB T9V 0H8
Tel: 780-875-6600; *Fax:* 780-875-6601
info@kindrachukdobson.com

***Lloydminster*: Kirzinger, Wells - *2**
#203, 5101 - 48 St., Lloydminster, AB T9V 0H9
Tel: 780-875-8400; *Fax:* 780-875-8499

***Lloydminster*: Knight Law Office - *1**
4912 - 50th Ave., Lloydminster, AB S9V 1K5
Tel: 780-875-9555; *Fax:* 780-875-9557
bknight@silvercrest.ca

***Lloydminster*: Lonsdale Law Office - *1**
P.O. Box 1248, 5117 - 48 St., Lloydminster, AB S9V 1G1
Tel: 780-875-5185; *Fax:* 780-875-6547
lonsdalelaw@lgl.cc
www.lgl.cc

***Medicine Hat*: Biddell Law Office - *3**
735 - 2 St. SE, Medicine Hat, AB T1A 0E2
Tel: 403-527-7737; *Fax:* 403-528-8907
kbiddell@monarch.net

***Medicine Hat*: Gordon, Smith & Company - *3**
P.O. Box 490, 378 - 1 St. SE, Medicine Hat, AB T1A 7G2
Tel: 403-527-5506; *Fax:* 403-527-0577
gsco@shockware.com

***Medicine Hat*: William L. Haynes - *1**
#108, 1235 Southview Dr. SE, Medicine Hat, AB T1B 4K3
Tel: 403-528-8883; *Fax:* 403-526-7698
bill@hayneslaw.net

***Medicine Hat*: Hill & Hill - *2**
#6, 3151 Dunmore Rd. SE, Medicine Hat, AB T1B 2H2
Tel: 403-527-1544; *Fax:* 403-526-2551

***Medicine Hat*: Leis, Wiese & Company - *3**
#1, 1364 Southview Dr. SE, Medicine Hat, AB T1B 4E7
Tel: 403-527-7766; *Fax:* 403-527-7788

***Medicine Hat*: MacLean Wiedemann - *3**
525 - 2 St. SE, Medicine Hat, AB T1A 0C5
Tel: 403-527-3343; *Fax:* 403-526-0473

***Medicine Hat*: Niblock & Company - *6**
P.O. Box 609, Stn. Main, 420 Macleaod Trail SE, Medicine Hat, AB T1A 7G5
Tel: 403-526-2806; *Fax:* 403-526-2356

***Medicine Hat*: Pritchard & Company LLP - *7**
#204, P.O. Box 100, 430 - 6th Ave. SE, Medicine Hat, AB T1A 7E8
Tel: 403-527-4411; *Fax:* 403-527-9806
lawyers@pritchardandcompany.com
www.pritchardandcompany.com

***Medicine Hat*: D.G. Schindel - *1**
#1, 3295 Dunmore Rd. SE, Medicine Hat, AB T1B 3R2
Tel: 403-529-5548; *Fax:* 403-529-2694
daryl@millerlaw.ca

***Medicine Hat*: Sihvon Carter Fisher & Berger LLP - *8**
499 - 1st St. SE, Medicine Hat, AB T1A 0A7
Tel: 403-526-2600; *Fax:* 403-526-3217
scfb@scfb.ca
www.scfb.ca

***Nanton*: Laurie M. Gordon - *1**
P.O. Box 586, 2213 - 20th St., Nanton, AB T0L 1R0
Tel: 403-646-6111; *Fax:* 403-646-6112
lmgordon@telusplanet.net

***Nanton*: Robert G. Roddie, Q.C. - *1**
P.O. Box 100, 2113 - 20 St., Nanton, AB T0L 1R0
Tel: 403-646-2211; *Fax:* 403-646-3159
rodmclaw@telusplanet.net

***Okotoks*: Diane Luttmer Professional Corporation - *1**
P.O. Box 267, Okotoks, AB T1S 1A5
Tel: 403-938-8296; *Fax:* 403-938-8286
dluttmer@platinum.ca

***Okotoks*: Charles A. Dixon - *1**
P.O. Box 1169, 51 Riverside Gate, Okotoks, AB T1S 1B2
Tel: 403-938-8131; *Fax:* 403-938-6365

***Okotoks*: Edward D. Simper - *1**
P.O. Box 1117, Stn. Main, 84 Elizabeth St., Okotoks, AB T1S 1B2
Tel: 403-938-2101; *Fax:* 403-938-6020
simpered@fclc.com

***Olds*: R. Brent Carlyle**
P.O. Box 3755, 4911 - 51 Ave., Olds, AB T4H 1P5
Tel: 403-556-7762; *Fax:* 403-556-8859
brentc@reveal.ca

***Olds*: Alvin F. Ganser - *1**
P.O. Box 4040, 4834 - 50 St., Olds, AB T4H 1P7
Tel: 403-556-8481; *Fax:* 403-556-3830

***Olds*: Martinson & Harder - *3**
#1, 5401 - 49 Ave., Olds, AB T4H 1G3
Tel: 403-556-8955; *Fax:* 403-556-8895
contact@martinsonharder.com

***Parksville*: Evans & Company - *1**
P.O. Box 40, Stn. Main, 182 Memorial Ave., Parksville, AB V2P 2G3
Tel: 250-248-5748; *Fax:* 250-248-5758
evansandco@telus.net

***Peace River*: Mathieu Hryniuk LLP - *7**
P.O. Box 6210, 10012 - 101 St., Peace River, AB T8S 1S2
Tel: 780-624-2565; *Fax:* 780-624-5766
Toll-Free: 800-661-1962
mh@mhllp.ca
mhllp.ca

***Peace River*: Thietke, Murphy & Harcourt - *5**
P.O. Box 6778, 9910 - 97 Ave., Peace River, AB T8S 1S5
Tel: 780-624-1122; *Fax:* 780-624-4443
Toll-Free: 800-353-6270

***Pincher Creek*: Jasman & Evans - *1**
P.O. Box 2530, 985 East Ave., Pincher Creek, AB T0K 1W0
Tel: 403-627-2877; *Fax:* 403-627-4495
jasman_evans@shaw.ca

***Ponoka*: Noble & Kidd - *1**
P.O. Box 4278, 5024 - 51 Ave., Ponoka, AB T4J 1R7
Tel: 403-783-3325; *Fax:* 403-783-5080
noblekid@telus.net

***Ponoka*: Richard D. Wyrozub - *1**
P.O. Box 4338, Stn. Main, Ponoka, AB T4J 1R7
Tel: 403-783-5521; *Fax:* 403-783-2012

***Priddis*: Rath & Company - *7**
RR#1, Box 44, Site 8, Priddis, AB T0L 1W0
Tel: 403-931-4047; *Fax:* 403-931-4048
rathco@telus.net

***Red Deer*: Brian Adair - *1**
#207, 4909 - 48 St., Red Deer, AB T4N 1S8
Tel: 403-342-1777; *Fax:* 403-341-4775

***Red Deer*: Susan K. Allison - *1**
4919 - 48 St., 2nd Floor, Red Deer, AB T4N 1S8
Tel: 403-340-3136; *Fax:* 403-343-7016

***Red Deer*: Duhamel Manning Feehan Warrender Glass LLP - *13**
5233 - 49 Ave., Red Deer, AB T4N 6G5
Tel: 403-343-0812; *Fax:* 403-340-3545
altalaw@reddeeraltalaw.com
www.reddeeraltalaw.com

***Red Deer*: Dunkle McBeath - *2**
5004 - 48 Ave., Red Deer, AB T4N 3T6
Tel: 403-347-5522; *Fax:* 403-347-5632
dkm_law@telusplanet.net

***Red Deer*: Flanagan Sully - *2**
#202, 4825 - 47 St., Red Deer, AB T4N 1R3
Tel: 403-342-7715; *Fax:* 403-347-5955
fslaw@telusplanet.net

***Red Deer*: C.E. Forgues - *1**
7891 - 50 Ave., Red Deer, AB T4P 2S4
Tel: 403-342-7044; *Fax:* 403-342-7055

***Red Deer*: Gerig Hamilton Neeland - *5**
#501, 4901 - 48 St., Red Deer, AB T4N 6M4
Tel: 403-343-2444; *Fax:* 403-343-6522
info@ghnh.net

***Red Deer*: Donald A. Gross - *1**
#274, 4919 - 59 St., Red Deer, AB T4N 6C9
Tel: 403-343-3715; *Fax:* 403-343-7435

***Red Deer*: Johnston Ming Manning LLP - *13**
Royal Bank Bldg., 4943 - 50th St., 3rd & 4th Fl., Red Deer, AB T4N 1Y1
Tel: 403-346-5591; *Fax:* 403-346-5599
info@jmmlawrd.ca
www.johnstonmingmanning.com

***Red Deer*: Lee & Short - *4**
4801 - 49 St., Red Deer, AB T4N 1T8
Tel: 403-343-1212; *Fax:* 403-341-3066
galbrecht@leeshort.com

***Red Deer*: Brian S. MacNairn - *1**
#201, 5008 Ross St., Red Deer, AB T4N 1Y3
Tel: 403-347-2700; *Fax:* 403-346-5825
macnairn@telusplanet.net

***Red Deer*: P.E.B. MacSween - *1**
4824 - 51 St., Red Deer, AB T4N 2A5
Tel: 403-342-5595; *Fax:* 403-342-7519

***Red Deer*: Peter C. McElhaney - *1**
#201, 4702 - 49th Ave., Red Deer, AB T4N 6L5
Tel: 403-346-2026; *Fax:* 403-309-1969

** indicates number of lawyers*

***Red Deer*: Gerald W. Neufeld - *1**
#209, 4815 Gaetz Ave., Red Deer, AB T4N 4A5
Tel: 403-343-2202; *Fax:* 403-343-2203
gneufeld@telusplanet.net

***Red Deer*: Patrick A. Penny - *1**
#290, 4819C - 48 Ave., Red Deer, AB T4N 3T2
Tel: 403-342-9595; *Fax:* 403-346-9778

***Red Deer*: Schnell Hardy Jones LLP - *8**
#504, 4909 - 49th St., Red Deer, AB T4N 1V1
Tel: 403-342-7400; *Fax:* 403-340-0520
Toll-Free: 800-342-7405
lawyers@schnell-law.com
www.schnell-law.com

***Red Deer*: Sisson Warren Sinclair - *9**
#600, First Red Deer Place, 4911 - 51 St., Red Deer, AB T4N 6V4
Tel: 403-343-3320; *Fax:* 403-343-6069
email@swslawyers.com

***Red Deer*: William D. Weiswasser - *1**
#104, 4808 Ross St., Red Deer, AB T4N 1X5
Tel: 403-343-0317; *Fax:* 403-343-0318
mediate@agt.net

***Redwater*: D.L. McCallum - *1**
P.O. Box 396, Redwater, AB T0A 2W0
Tel: 780-942-3040; *Fax:* 780-942-2003
Toll-Free: 800-390-2257

***Rimbey*: David R. Pfau - *1**
P.O. Box 1009, 5001 - 50th Ave., Rimbey, AB T0C 2J0
Tel: 403-843-2296; *Fax:* 403-843-2344

***Rocky Mountain House*: Peter Crossley Law Office - *1**
P.O. Box 1108, 4616 - 47 Ave., Rocky Mountain House, AB T4T 1A8
Tel: 403-845-2828; *Fax:* 403-845-4630

***Rocky Mountain House*: Dunsford & Scott - *3**
P.O. Box 370, 5135 - 48 Ave., Rocky Mountain House, AB T4T 1A3
Tel: 403-845-7112; *Fax:* 403-845-4670
reception@dunsfordandscott.com

***Rocky Mountain House*: Woollard Hopkins & Company - *2**
5133 - 49 St., Rocky Mountain House, AB T4T 1B8
Tel: 403-845-2545; *Fax:* 403-845-2285
wooll@woollardhopkins.com

***Sherwood Park*: Stanley H. King - *1**
77 Chippewa Rd., Sherwood Park, AB T8A 6J7
Tel: 780-910-7475; *Fax:* 780-416-4891
stan@westana.com

***Sherwood Park*: Wayne LeDrew - *1**
#16, 140 Athabascan Ave., Sherwood Park, AB T8A 4E3
Tel: 780-467-3014; *Fax:* 780-464-8504
wledrew@telusplanet.net

***Sherwood Park*: Nigro & Company - *1**
282 Kaska Rd., Sherwood Park, AB T8A 4G7
Tel: 780-467-9559; *Fax:* 780-467-0720

***Sherwood Park*: Thomas E. Spratlin - *1**
#14B, 363 Sioux Rd., Sherwood Park, AB T8A 4W7
Tel: 780-464-5404; *Fax:* 780-417-1759
spratlin@telus.net

***Slave Lake*: Allan G. McMillan - *1**
#2, 221 - 3 Ave. NW, Slave Lake, AB T0G 2A1
Tel: 780-849-2227; *Fax:* 780-849-2143
mcmillan@telusplanet.net

***Slave Lake*: Twinn Barristers & Solicitors - *1**
P.O. Box 1460, 810 Caribou Trail NE, Slave Lake, AB T0G 2A0
Tel: 780-849-4319; *Fax:* 780-805-3274
ctwinn@twinnlaw.com

***Spruce Grove*: Ayers & Company - *2**
#210, P.O. Box 4372, Stn. Main, 215 McLeod Ave., Spruce Grove, AB T7X 3B5
Tel: 780-962-9500; *Fax:* 780-962-9535

***Spruce Grove*: N.L.A. (Loretta) Edlund - *1**
#35, 54023 SH 779, Spruce Grove, AB T7X 3V5
Tel: 780-968-1668; *Fax:* 780-968-1667
nlaedlund@gmail.com

***Spruce Grove*: Randall C. Heil - *1**
#201, Cumbria Centre, 93 McLeod Ave., Spruce Grove, AB T7X 2Z9
Tel: 780-962-9700; *Fax:* 780-962-9329
rheil@telus.net

***Spruce Grove*: Robert A. Joly - *1**
#4, 20 McLeod Ave., Spruce Grove, AB T7X 3Y1
Tel: 780-962-4447; *Fax:* 780-962-3638
bbjoly@shaw.ca

***Spruce Grove*: Robinson & Company - *2**
P.O. Box 4113, 16 Westgrove Dr., Spruce Grove, AB T7X 3B3
Tel: 780-962-0660; *Fax:* 780-962-0622
brbnsn@telusplanet.net

***St Albert*: Goldsman, Ritzen, Shadlyn - *5**
#609, Grandin Park Tower, 22 Sir Winston Churchill Ave., St Albert, AB T8N 1B4
Tel: 780-458-0500; *Fax:* 780-459-2472

***St Albert*: K. June Koska Professional Corporation - *1**
40 Berrymore Dr., St Albert, AB T8N 6B8
Tel: 780-460-1721; *Fax:* 780-460-1334

***St Albert*: Vaughn H. Myers - *1**
#201, Mission Hill Plaza, 398 St. Albert Rd., St Albert, AB T8N 5J9
Tel: 780-460-2505; *Fax:* 780-459-5088

***St Albert*: Oddleifson & Kaup - *2**
#118, 7 St. Anne St., St Albert, AB T8N 2X4
Tel: 780-459-2220; *Fax:* 780-459-0621

***St Albert*: Quantz Law Group - *3**
#220, 8 Perron St., St Albert, AB T8N 1E4
Tel: 780-458-7690; *Fax:* 780-458-5510
info@quantzlaw.com
www.quantzlaw.com

***St Albert*: Thomas A. Rowand Professional Corp. - *1**
#208, Summit Centre, 200 Boudreau Rd., St Albert, AB T8N 6B9
Tel: 780-458-9440; *Fax:* 780-458-9442
trowand@telusplanet.net

***St Albert*: Wallace Law Office - *1**
#3, 30 Rayborn Cres., St Albert, AB T8N 5B7
Tel: 780-458-7717; *Fax:* 780-460-1818
kdwl@telusplanet.net

***St Albert*: Weary & Company - *2**
#400, 30 Green Grove Dr., St Albert, AB T8N 5H6
Tel: 780-459-5596; *Fax:* 780-459-6572

***St Albert*: William Glabb Law Office - *1**
#601, Grandin Park Tower, 22 Sir Winston Churchill Ave., St Albert, AB T8N 1B4
Tel: 780-459-2200; *Fax:* 780-459-2281
wmglabblawoffice@shaw.ca
www.williamglabblawoffice.com

***St Paul*: Lamoureux & Lawrence - *4**
4713 - 50th St., St Paul, AB T0A 3A4
Tel: 780-645-5202; *Fax:* 780-645-6507
law@stpaul-law.ca

***Stony Plain*: Birdsell Grant LLP - *8**
#102, 5300 - 50 St., Stony Plain, AB T7Z 1T8
Tel: 780-963-8181; *Fax:* 780-963-9618
info@birdsell.ca

***Stony Plain*: M.P. Stone - *1**
#300, P.O. Box 56, Stn. Main, RR#3, Stony Plain, AB T7Z 1X3

***Strathmore*: Getz & Associates - *2**
P.O. Box 2370, 225A Wheatland Trail, Strathmore, AB T1P 1K3
Tel: 403-934-2500; *Fax:* 403-934-2794
johng@getzlaw.ca

***Strathmore*: R.E.J. Jarvis - *2**
#110, 304 - 3 Ave., Strathmore, AB T1P 1Z1
Tel: 403-934-5000; *Fax:* 403-934-4853
rejarvis@shaw.ca

***Sylvan Lake*: Brian C. Flanagan - *1**
#203, 5043 - 50A St., Sylvan Lake, AB T4S 1R1
Tel: 403-887-5441; *Fax:* 403-887-3010
burflan@telusplanet.net

***Sylvan Lake*: Deborah M. Hanly - *1**
P.O. Box 9113, Stn. Main, 20 Woodland Cres., Sylvan Lake, AB T4S 1S6
Tel: 403-887-4410; *Fax:* 403-887-4416
Toll-Free: 877-887-7789
tax-law@shaw.ca

***Sylvan Lake*: Vanden Brink Law Office - *1**
P.O. Box 9613, Stn. Main, Sylvan Lake, AB T4S 1S8
Tel: 403-885-2222; *Fax:* 403-885-2226
benbrink@direcway.com

***Taber*: Baldry Sugden, LLP - *3**
5401 - 50 Ave., Taber, AB T1G 1V2
Tel: 403-223-3585; *Fax:* 403-223-1732
balsug@telusplanet.net

***Three Hills*: Norman L. Tainsh Prof. Corp. - *1**
P.O. Box 1234, 205 Main St., Three Hills, AB T0M 2A0
Tel: 403-443-2200; *Fax:* 403-443-2025
Toll-Free: 888-939-2200
ntainsh@tainsh.ca

***Turner Valley*: Beverly A.B. Broadhurst - *1**
#2, P.O. Box 501, 101 Sunset Blvd. SW, Turner Valley, AB T0L 2A0
Tel: 403-933-3255; *Fax:* 403-933-4104

***Vermilion*: Reynolds & Flemke - *2**
#11, 5125 - 50 Ave., Vermilion, AB T9X 1A8
Tel: 780-853-5339; *Fax:* 780-853-4200

***Vermilion*: Wheat Law Office - *2**
5042 - 49 Ave., Vermilion, AB T9X 1B7
Tel: 780-853-4707; *Fax:* 780-853-4499
wheatlaw@telusplanet.net

***Wainwright*: Peter Van Winssen - *1**
1013 - 5 Ave., Wainwright, AB T9W 1L6
Tel: 780-842-5140; *Fax:* 780-842-3830

***Westlock*: Tims & Company - *2**
#2, P.O. Box 490, 9831 - 107th St., Westlock, AB T7P 1R9
Tel: 780-349-5366; *Fax:* 780-349-6510

***Wetaskiwin*: Deckert Allen Cymbaluk Genest - *4**
#301, P.O. Box 6060, 5201 - 51st Ave., Wetaskiwin, AB T9A 2E8
Tel: 780-352-3301; *Fax:* 780-352-5976

***Wetaskiwin*: McDonald Street Law Office - *1**
4408 - 51 St., Wetaskiwin, AB T9A 1K5
Tel: 780-352-0369; *Fax:* 780-352-0393

***Wetaskiwin*: Schumacher & Associates - *4**
5118 - 50 Ave., Wetaskiwin, AB T9A 0S6
Tel: 780-352-6691; *Fax:* 780-352-0599
schumacher@incentre.net

***Whitecourt*: McConnell Law Office - *1**
P.O. Box 1795, Stn. Main, 5115 Highway St., Whitecourt, AB T7S 1P5
Tel: 780-778-4945; *Fax:* 780-778-3851

British Columbia

***100 Mile House*: Centennial Law Corporation - *3**
P.O. Box 819, 100 Mile House, BC V0K 2E0
Tel: 250-395-3881; *Fax:* 250-395-2644
centenniallaw@bcinternet.net

***100 Mile House*: George J. Wool - *1**
5741 Simon Lake Rd., 100 Mile House, BC V0K 2E1
Tel: 250-791-9295; *Fax:* 250-791-9228
gwool@bcinternet.net

***Abbotsford*: Joshua M. Bach - *1**
#506, 2700 McCallum Rd., Abbotsford, BC V2S 6X9
Tel: 800-506-6304

***Abbotsford*: Kenneth R. Beatch - *1**
2459 Pauline St., Abbotsford, BC V2S 3S1
Tel: 604-853-9555; *Fax:* 604-859-3361
ken@drugdefence.com
www.drugdefence.com

***Abbotsford*: Bronson, Jones & Company - *5**
#300, 2890 Garden St., Abbotsford, BC V2T 4W7
Tel: 604-852-5100; *Fax:* 604-850-2164

***Abbotsford*: Fast Welwood & Wiens - *4**
#305, 2692 Clearbrook Rd., Abbotsford, BC V2T 2Y8
Tel: 604-850-6640; *Fax:* 604-857-1833
info@faswel.com

** indicates number of lawyers*

***Abbotsford*: Larry W. Goddard - *1**
#105, 2955 Gladwin Rd., Abbotsford, BC V2T 5T4
Tel: 604-853-3535; *Fax:* 604-853-9033

***Abbotsford*: Linley Welwood LLP - *7**
#305, 2692 Clearbrook Rd., Abbotsford, BC V2T 2Y8
Tel: 604-850-6640; *Fax:* 604-850-6616
www.linleywelwood.com

***Abbotsford*: Marcotte Law Office - *1**
#1, 33775 Essendene Ave., Abbotsford, BC V2S 2H1
Tel: 604-855-6688; *Fax:* 604-855-6515

***Abbotsford*: Palmer Gillen - *2**
#1, 33775 Essendene Ave., Abbotsford, BC V2S 2H1
Tel: 604-859-3887; *Fax:* 604-859-3883
www.abbotsfordlawyers.com

***Abbotsford*: Robertson, Downe & Mullally - *20**
33695 South Fraser Way, Abbotsford, BC V2S 2C1
Tel: 604-853-0774; *Fax:* 604-852-3829
Toll-Free: 888-853-0774
info@rdmlawyers
www.rdmlawyers.com

***Abbotsford*: Lloyd H. Wilson - *1**
2644 Montrose Ave., Abbotsford, BC V2S 3T6
Tel: 604-853-3355; *Fax:* 604-853-2644
lloydhwilson_company@hotmail.com

***Armstrong*: Blakely & Co. - *1**
#201, P.O. Box 357, 2595 Pleasant Valley Blvd., Armstrong, BC V0E 1B0
Tel: 250-546-3188; *Fax:* 250-546-2677
blakely@junction.net

***Armstrong*: Culos & Company - *1**
P.O. Box 70, 2553 Pleasant Valley Blvd., Armstrong, BC V0E 1B0
Tel: 250-546-2448; *Fax:* 250-546-2621
robculos@telus.net

***Brentwood Bay*: Sandra E. Jenko - *1**
#112, 7088 West Saanich, Brentwood Bay, BC V8M 1P9
Tel: 250-652-5151

***Burnaby*: Bergen Legal Services - *1**
5816 Sherban Ct., Burnaby, BC V5B 4P2
Tel: 604-291-9291; *Fax:* 604-291-9335

***Burnaby*: W.E. Bergmann - *1**
4550 East Hastings St., Burnaby, BC V5C 2K4
Tel: 604-298-8211; *Fax:* 604-298-8216

***Burnaby*: Cobbett & Cotton - *7**
4259 East Hastings St., Burnaby, BC V5C 2J5
Tel: 604-299-6251; *Fax:* 604-299-6627
mail@cobett-cotton.com

***Burnaby*: Edwards, Edwards & Edwards - *3**
#510, 5021 Kingsway, Burnaby, BC V5H 4A5
Tel: 604-433-2445; *Fax:* 604-433-8209

***Burnaby*: James K. Fitzsimmons - *1**
#200, 6960 Royal Oak Ave., Burnaby, BC V5J 4J2
Tel: 604-298-8939; *Fax:* 604-298-8956

***Burnaby*: Robert A. Foran - *1**
#275, c/o UMA Group Ltd., 3001 Wayburne Dr., Burnaby, BC V5G 4W3
Tel: 604-631-6232; *Fax:* 604-685-1035
bob.foran@uma.aecom.com
www.umagroup.com

***Burnaby*: James K. Fraser Law Corporation - *1**
#200, 4603 Kingsway, Burnaby, BC V5H 4M4
Tel: 604-433-0010; *Fax:* 604-435-0269
jkf@jkf.ca

***Burnaby*: Greenbank Murdoch & Company - *2**
#2109, 4710 Kingsway, Burnaby, BC V5H 4M2
Tel: 604-437-6611; *Fax:* 604-437-3065
info@bmgm.com

***Burnaby*: Hawthorne, Piggott & Company - *7**
#208, 1899 Willingdon Ave., Burnaby, BC V5C 5T1
Tel: 604-299-8371; *Fax:* 604-299-1523
lawyers@hawthornelaw.com

***Burnaby*: Hwang & Company - *3**
#333, 4501 North Rd., Burnaby, BC V3N 4R7
Tel: 604-421-3669; *Fax:* 604-421-6339
mh@korcanlaw.com

***Burnaby*: O'Neill, Rozenberg - *2**
#201, 4547 Hastings St., Burnaby, BC V5C 2K3
Tel: 604-294-8311; *Fax:* 604-294-5278
Toll-Free: 800-354-1888

***Burnaby*: Pihl & Company - *1**
#205, 5481 Kingsway, Burnaby, BC V5H 2G1
Tel: 604-437-8837; *Fax:* 604-437-3529

***Burnaby*: Russell Kuhl & Co. - *2**
#220, 4411 Hastings St., Burnaby, BC V5C 2K1
Tel: 604-298-1038; *Fax:* 604-298-1037
russellradio@telus.net; mail@jeffkuhl.com

***Burnaby*: Sellens & Associates - *3**
#330, 9940 Lougheed Hwy., Burnaby, BC V3J 1N3
Tel: 604-421-0716; *Fax:* 604-421-7692

***Burnaby*: Starr & Company - *2**
#205, 5481 Kingsway, Burnaby, BC V5H 2G1
Tel: 604-435-5588; *Fax:* 604-435-5588
gbstarr@telus.net

***Burnaby*: Warren, Eder - *2**
#216, 3989 Henning Dr., Burnaby, BC V5C 6P8
Tel: 604-687-0134; *Fax:* 604-687-5176
Toll-Free: 800-461-3455
warren&eder@shawbiz.ca

***Burnaby*: Maureen J. Wesley - *1**
4270 McGill St., Burnaby, BC V5C 1M9
Tel: 604-298-6555; *Fax:* 604-298-6540

***Burnaby*: Patricia Yaremovich - *1**
#105, 6540 East Hastings St., Burnaby, BC V5B 4Z5
Tel: 604-320-0688; *Fax:* 604-320-0007
pyaremovich@shaw.ca

***Campbell River*: Graham & Frame - *2**
#301, 1100 Island Hwy., Campbell River, BC V9W 8C6
Tel: 250-286-6691; *Fax:* 250-286-1191
fisherrk@telus.net

***Campbell River*: Claire I. Moglove - *1**
#201, 909 Island Hwy., Campbell River, BC V9W 2C2
Tel: 250-286-9946; *Fax:* 250-286-0052
cmaglove@island.net

***Campbell River*: Shook, Wickham, Bishop & Field - *9**
906 Island Hwy., Campbell River, BC V9W 2C3
Tel: 250-287-8355; *Fax:* 250-287-8112
info@crlawyers.ca
www.crlawyers.ca

***Campbell River*: Karen D. Stevan - *1**
475 Evergreen Rd., Campbell River, BC V9W 3R6
Tel: 250-286-3308; *Fax:* 250-286-3387
kdstevan@yahoo.ca

***Campbell River*: Tees Kiddle Spencer - *4**
#200, 1260 Shoppers Row, Campbell River, BC V9W 2C8
Tel: 250-287-7755; *Fax:* 250-287-3999
Toll-Free: 800-224-7755
tks@tkslaw.com
www.tkslaw.com

***Castlegar*: Polonicoff & Perehudoff - *2**
1115 - 3 St., Castlegar, BC V1N 2A1
Tel: 250-365-3343; *Fax:* 250-365-6307
polper@netidea.com

***Castlegar*: Wyllie & Co. - *1**
1418 Columbia Ave., Castlegar, BC V1N 3K3
Tel: 250-365-8451; *Fax:* 250-365-3488
wyllielaw@telus.net
www.macisaacgroup.com

***Chemainus*: Mary Lynn Bancroft - *1**
Box 168, 9834 Croft St., Chemainus, BC V0R 1K0
Tel: 250-246-4771; *Fax:* 250-246-2547
mbancroft@shaw.ca

***Chilliwack*: Kaye Thome Toews & Hansford - *7**
CP 372, 9202 Young Rd., Chilliwack, BC V2P 6J4
Tel: 604-792-1977; *Fax:* 604-792-7077
Toll-Free: 888-792-1977
ktc@ktclawoffice.com
www.ktthlawyers.com

***Clearbrook*: Kuzminski Neufeld Rebane, Valley Law Group - *3**
#201, 2890 Garden St., Clearbrook, BC V2T 4W7
Tel: 604-853-5401; *Fax:* 604-853-8358

***Clearwater*: John Kurta - *1**
P.O. Box 5171, 32 East Old North Thompson Hwy., Clearwater, BC V0E 1N0
Tel: 250-674-2126; *Fax:* 250-674-3493

***Comox*: Schaffrick & Sutton - *2**
1984 Comox Ave., Comox, BC V9M 3M7
Tel: 250-339-3363; *Fax:* 250-339-3315
Toll-Free: 877-778-8866

***Coquitlam*: David Boulding - *1**
#206, 2922 Glen Dr., Coquitlam, BC V3B 2P7
Tel: 604-945-2043; *Fax:* 604-945-2063
dmboulding@shaw.ca

***Coquitlam*: Drysdale Bacon McStravick - *7**
#211, 1015 Austin Ave., Coquitlam, BC V3K 3N9
Tel: 604-939-8321; *Fax:* 604-939-7584
inquiries@dbmlaw.ca
www.dbmlaw.ca

***Coquitlam*: Spagnuolo & Company Real Estate Lawyers - *10**
#300, 906 Roderick Ave., Coquitlam, BC V3K 1R1
Tel: 604-527-4242; *Fax:* 604-527-8976
Toll-Free: 888-873-2829
info@bcrealestatelawyers.com
www.bcrealestatelawyers.com

***Coquitlam*: Spraggs & Company - *1**
#202, 1030 Westwood St., Coquitlam, BC V3C 4E4
Tel: 604-464-3333

***Coquitlam*: Taylor Bardal - *3**
#220, 1024 Ridgeway Ave., Coquitlam, BC V3J 1S5
Tel: 604-931-3477; *Fax:* 604-931-1277

***Coquitlam*: Judy Wong - *1**
#205, 3030 Lincoln Ave., Coquitlam, BC V3B 6B4
Tel: 604-945-6982; *Fax:* 604-945-6819

***Coquitlam*: Zipp & Company - *2**
820 Henderson Ave., Coquitlam, BC V3K 1P2
Tel: 604-936-7743

***Courtenay*: James E. Dow - *1**
#7, 625 Cliffe Ave., Courtenay, BC V9N 2J6
Tel: 250-338-7701; *Fax:* 250-338-6641
jamesdow@shaw.ca

***Courtenay*: Ives Burger, Barristers & Solicitors - *3**
505 - 5 St., Courtenay, BC V9N 1K2
Tel: 250-334-2416; *Fax:* 250-334-3198
info@ivesburgerlaw.com
www.ivesburgerlaw.com

***Courtenay*: C.H.L. Morris - *1**
949 Fitzgerald Ave., Courtenay, BC V9N 2R6
Tel: 250-338-5311; *Fax:* 250-338-1818
crispinmorris@shaw.ca

***Courtenay*: Roy William Pouss - *1**
243 - 4th St., Courtenay, BC V9N 1G7
Tel: 250-334-3188; *Fax:* 250-334-3174

***Courtenay*: Swift Datoo Law Corporation - *8**
#201, 467 Cumberland Rd., Courtenay, BC V9N 2C5
Tel: 250-334-4461; *Fax:* 250-334-2335
Toll-Free: 877-334-4461
lawyers@swiftdatoo.com
www.swiftdatoo.com

***Cranbrook*: Patrick J. Dearden - *1**
#201, 129 - 10th Ave. South, Cranbrook, BC V1C 2N1
Tel: 250-426-7431; *Fax:* 250-426-3746

***Cranbrook*: Kelle M. Maag Law Corporation - *1**
20 - 11th Ave. South, Cranbrook, BC V1C 2P1
Tel: 250-426-5508; *Fax:* 250-426-1904

***Cranbrook*: Murielle A. Matthews - *1**
801B Baker St., Cranbrook, BC V1C 1A3
Tel: 250-426-0601; *Fax:* 250-426-0642

***Cranbrook*: Miles, Daroux, Zimmer & Sheard - *4**
45 - 8th Ave. South, Cranbrook, BC V1C 2K4
Tel: 250-489-3350; *Fax:* 250-489-2235
s.daroux@shaw.ca

***Cranbrook*: Rella & Paolini - *2**
#6, 10 Ave. South, 2nd Fl., Cranbrook, BC V1C 2M8
Tel: 250-426-8981; *Fax:* 250-426-8987
Toll-Free: 866-426-8981
rellaco@shaw.ca

** indicates number of lawyers*

Cranbrook: Robertson & Co. - *1
#200, 135 - 10 Ave. South, Cranbrook, BC V1C 2N1
Tel: 250-489-4346; *Fax:* 250-489-1899
robertson@cranbrooklaw.com
www.cranbrooklaw.com

Cranbrook: Steidl, Kambeitz - *2
#201, 907 Baker St., Cranbrook, BC V1C 1A4
Tel: 250-426-7211; *Fax:* 250-426-6100
sk@steidlco.com

Cranbrook: Darrel C. Symington - *1
123 - 12th Ave. South, Cranbrook, BC V1C 2S2
Tel: 250-489-2800; *Fax:* 250-489-1173
dsymington@cyberllink.ca

Dawson Creek: Higson Apps - *3
#201, 1136 - 103 Ave., Dawson Creek, BC V1G 2G7
Tel: 250-782-9134; *Fax:* 250-782-9135
Toll-Free: 888-782-9134
rapps@plenerthigson.com

Dawson Creek: Mitchell Schuller - *3
#2, 933 - 103 Ave., Dawson Creek, BC V1G 2G4
Tel: 250-782-8155; *Fax:* 250-782-4525
mitchellschuller@shawcable.com

Delta: James M. Antifay Law Corporation - *1
#212, 7313 - 120 St., Delta, BC V4C 6P5
Tel: 604-572-8333; *Fax:* 604-572-6744
jantifay@allstream.net
www.antifayjamesm.supersites.ca

Delta: James Broad - *1
9337 - 120 St., Delta, BC V4C 6R8
Tel: 604-585-3422; *Fax:* 604-585-3613

Delta: Buckley Hogan - *3
9453 - 120 St., Delta, BC V4C 6S2
Tel: 604-588-0431; *Fax:* 604-588-0062
lawyers@buckho.com

Delta: Delta Legal Office - *1
#211, 7313 - 120 St., Delta, BC V4C 6P5
Tel: 604-599-1188; *Fax:* 604-599-1975
iggibson@deltalegal.com

Delta: Danielle D. Deschamps-Carlson - *3
#201, 5155 Trunk Rd., Delta, BC V4K 1W4
Tel: 604-940-8182; *Fax:* 604-940-9892
info@severidelawgroup.com

Delta: Lehal & Company - *1
#200, 6905 - 120th St., Delta, BC V4E 2A8
Tel: 604-596-1321; *Fax:* 604-596-1320

Delta: Leung, Arthur-Leung - *1
5110 Ladner Trunk Rd., Delta, BC V4K 1W3
Tel: 604-940-8888; *Fax:* 604-946-6628

Delta: David C. McPhillips - *1
4924 - 2A Ave., Delta, BC V4M 3V1
Tel: 604-943-6750; *Fax:* 604-943-6350

Delta: Stasiuk & Rose - *2
#203, 1205 - 56 St., Delta, BC V4L 2A6
Tel: 604-943-8272; *Fax:* 604-943-8416
r.stasiuk@stasiuk-rose.com

Delta: TNT Lawyers - *3
7929 - 120 St., Delta, BC V4C 6P6
Tel: 604-502-5615; *Fax:* 604-591-8722
Toll-Free: 800-750-5122
info@icbcinjurylawyers.ca
www.icbcinjurylawyers.ca

Delta: Dell C. Valair - *1
10 - 5900 Ferry Rd., Delta, BC V4K 5C3
Tel: 604-940-3318; *Fax:* 604-940-3324
dell@lightspeed.ca

Delta (Tsawwassen): Millichamp & Company - *1
#210, 1530 - 56 St., Delta (Tsawwassen), BC V4L 2A8
Tel: 604-943-7401; *Fax:* 604-943-7402
millichamplawco@gmail.com

Duncan: Donald S. Allan - *1
#204, 225 Canada Ave., Duncan, BC V9L 1T6
Tel: 250-748-2340; *Fax:* 250-748-2343
d.s.allan@shaw.ca

Duncan: Coleman Fraser Parcells - *4
#202, 58 Station St., Duncan, BC V9L 1M4
Tel: 250-748-1013; *Fax:* 250-743-8318
Toll-Free: 888-748-1013

Duncan: Desjardins & Arndt - *2
466 TransCanada Highway, Duncan, BC V9L 3R6
Tel: 250-748-5253; *Fax:* 250-746-1511
vincedesjardins@shaw.ca

Duncan: Robert W. Nelford - *1
3250 Hillwood Rd., Duncan, BC V9L 5K6
Tel: 250-746-8555; *Fax:* 250-748-1957
robertn@com-net.com

Duncan: Orchard & Company - *5
321 St. Julian St., Duncan, BC V9L 3S5
Tel: 250-746-5899; *Fax:* 250-746-7182
admin@orchardandco.ca
www.orchardandco.ca

Duncan: Ridgway & Company - *5
#200, 44 Queens Rd., Duncan, BC V9L 2W4
Tel: 250-746-7121; *Fax:* 250-746-4070
info@ridgco.com
www.ridgco.com

Duncan: Taylor Granitto - *4
466 Trans Canada Hwy., Duncan, BC V9L 3R6
Tel: 250-748-4444; *Fax:* 250-748-5920
Toll-Free: 800-665-5414
dtaylor@taylor-co.com
www.taylor-co.com

Duncan: J.B. Whittaker - *1
Stn. Main, 7334 Waltons Mountain Rd., RR#1, Duncan, BC V9L 5W8
Tel: 250-748-6674

Fernie: R.W. Bentley - *1
P.O. Box 2038, Fernie, BC V0B 1M0
Tel: 250-423-9241; *Fax:* 250-423-6440
bentleylaw@elkvalley.net

Fort St John: Earmme & Associates - *3
10740 - 101st Ave., Fort St John, BC V1J 2B4
Tel: 250-785-6961; *Fax:* 250-785-6967

Fort St John: Rodney J. Strandberg Law Corp. - *1
#320, 9900 - 100 Ave., Fort St John, BC V1J 5S7
Tel: 250-787-7760; *Fax:* 250-787-7752
strandberglaw@telus.net

Garibaldi Highlands: Brian N. Hughes - *1
#201, P.O. Box 557, 1364 Pemberton Ave., Garibaldi Highlands, BC V0N 1T0
Tel: 604-892-5114; *Fax:* 604-892-0114

Gibsons: Peter J. Holden - *1
995 Grandview Rd., RR#10, Gibsons, BC V0N 1V3
Tel: 604-630-3913; *Fax:* 604-630-3914

Gibsons: J. Wayne Rowe - *1
758 School Rd., Gibsons, BC V0N 1V0
Tel: 604-886-2029; *Fax:* 604-886-9191

Gibsons: Leanne L. Turnbull - *1
523 Central Ave., RR#1, Gibsons, BC V0N 1V1
Tel: 604-886-7666; *Fax:* 604-886-7636
leeturnbull@dccnet.com

Hope: Kennedy, Jensen - *2
CP 1719, 400 Park St., Hope, BC V0X 1L0
Tel: 604-869-9981; *Fax:* 604-869-7640
www.kennedyjensen.com

Hornby Island: Sally Campbell - *1
4505 Roburn Rd., Hornby Island, BC V0R 1Z0
Tel: 250-335-2272; *Fax:* 250-335-0895
scampbel@island.net
www.island.net/~scampbell

Hornby Island: Sue M. Kelly - *1
P.O. Box 14, Stn. Anderson, Hornby Island, BC V0R 1Z0
Tel: 250-335-0735; *Fax:* 250-335-0732
smkelly@telus.net

Invermere: Kluge, Boyd - *2
P.O. Box 2647, 906 - 8 Ave., Invermere, BC V0A 1K0
Tel: 250-342-4447; *Fax:* 250-342-3298
barnim@telus.net

Kamloops: Bilkey, Quinn - *7
#301, 186 Victoria St., Kamloops, BC V2C 5R3
Tel: 250-374-6661; *Fax:* 250-828-2836
info@bilkeyquinn.com
www.bilkeyquinn.com

Kamloops: George Coutlee & Co. - *1
1270 Salish Rd., Kamloops, BC V2H 1K1
Tel: 250-372-9922; *Fax:* 250-372-1114

Kamloops: Cundari & Company Law Corporation - *4
#810, 175 - 2 Ave., Kamloops, BC V2C 5W1
Tel: 250-372-3368; *Fax:* 250-372-5554
cundari@cundarilaw.com
www.cundarilaw.com

Kamloops: Fulton & Company LLP, Lawyers & Trade-Mark Agents - *26
#300, 350 Lansdowne St., Kamloops, BC V2C 1Y1
Tel: 250-372-5542; *Fax:* 250-851-2300
law@fultonco.com
www.fultonco.com

Kamloops: Gibraltar Law Group - *3
#102, 418 St. Paul St., Kamloops, BC V2C 2J6
Tel: 250-374-3737; *Fax:* 250-374-0035
Toll-Free: 877-374-3737
mail@gibraltarlawgroup.com
www.gibraltarlawgroup.com

Kamloops: Gillespie Renkema Barnett Broadway LLP - *1
#200, 121 St. Paul St., Kamloops, BC V2C 3K8
Tel: 250-374-4463; *Fax:* 250-374-5250

Kamloops: HMZ Law - *5
#600, 175 Second Ave., Kamloops, BC V2C 5W1
Tel: 250-372-1221; *Fax:* 250-372-8339
Toll-Free: 800-558-1933
hmz@hmzlaw.com
www.hmzlaw.com

Kamloops: Jensen Carroll Watt - *7
#300, Old Firehall #1, 125 - 4 Ave., Kamloops, BC V2C 3N3
Tel: 250-372-8811; *Fax:* 250-828-6697
Toll-Free: 800-949-3362
jmc@jmc.bc.ca

Kamloops: Kahle & Co. Law Corporation - *1
243A Seymour St., Kamloops, BC V2C 2E7
Tel: 250-828-8666; *Fax:* 250-828-0048
Toll-Free: 888-529-1937
kahleco@telus.net
www.kahleco.com

Kamloops: Mary MacGregor Law Corporation - *1
975 Victoria St., Kamloops, BC V2C 2C1
Tel: 250-828-0282; *Fax:* 250-828-0287
mary.macgregor@mmlc.ca
www.marymacgregor.ca

Kamloops: Mair Jensen Blair Lawyers LLP - *15
#700, 275 Lansdowne St., Kamloops, BC V2C 6H6
Tel: 250-374-3161; *Fax:* 250-374-6992
info@mjblaw.com
www.mjblaw.com

Kamloops: David A. McMillan - *1
#401, 286 St. Paul St., Kamloops, BC V2C 6G4
Tel: 250-828-0702; *Fax:* 250-828-0703
dmlawoff@telus.net

Kamloops: Morelli Chertkow LLP, Lawyers - *11
#300, 180 Seymour St., Kamloops, BC V2C 2E3
Tel: 250-374-3344; *Fax:* 250-374-1144
Toll-Free: 888-374-3350
info@morellichertkow.com
www.morellichertkow.com

Kamloops: Craig Nixon Law Corp. - *1
#880, 175 - 2nd Ave., Kamloops, BC V2C 5W1
Tel: 250-374-1555; *Fax:* 250-374-9992
onlc@direct.ca

Kamloops: Oien, Church - *2
#212, 220 - 4th Ave., Kamloops, BC V2C 3N6
Tel: 250-851-8323; *Fax:* 250-851-8373
Toll-Free: 888-857-8323
oienchurch@telus.net

Kamloops: Stanford & Company - *1
#212, 220 - 4th Ave., Kamloops, BC V2C 3N5
Tel: 250-851-8582; *Fax:* 250-851-8583
michelle_stanford@telus.net

Kamloops: Taylor Epp & Dolder - *3
#300, 153 Seymour St., Kamloops, BC V2C 2C8
Tel: 250-374-3456; *Fax:* 250-828-6808
taylor_epp_dolder@telus.net

Kamloops: Wozniak & Walker - *2
533 Nicola St., Kamloops, BC V2C 2P9
Tel: 250-374-6226; *Fax:* 250-374-4485

** indicates number of lawyers*

***Kaslo*: T.R. Humphries - *1**
P.O. Box 636, Kaslo, BC V0G 1M0
Tel: 250-353-2292; *Fax:* 250-353-7430
Trhlaw@telus.net

***Kelowna*: Bearisto Sabey - *3**
#201, 401 Glenmore Rd., Kelowna, BC V1V 1Z6
Tel: 250-762-6111; *Fax:* 250-762-6480
Toll-Free: 866-268-6383
lawyers@sabeyrule.ca

***Kelowna*: Burgess & Company - *2**
#202, 3528 Scott Rd., Kelowna, BC V1W 3H6
Tel: 250-861-5533; *Fax:* 250-861-4442
dblaw@shawcable.com

***Kelowna*: Christiansen, Drummond - *2**
#207, 389 Queensway Ave., Kelowna, BC V1Y 8E6
Tel: 250-862-2332; *Fax:* 250-862-2353
cnklaw@telus.net

***Kelowna*: Doak Shirreff LLP - *14**
#200, Chancery Place, 537 Leon Ave., Kelowna, BC V1Y 2A9
Tel: 250-763-4323; *Fax:* 250-763-4780
Toll-Free: 800-661-4959
thefirm@doakshirreff.com
www.doakshirreff.com

***Kelowna*: Fraser Murray Huck - *3**
#200, 1449 St Paul St., Kelowna, BC V1Y 7S5
Tel: 250-868-8306; *Fax:* 250-868-8301
cfraser@frasermurraylaw.com

***Kelowna*: Glazier Polley - *4**
1674 Bertram St., 2nd Fl., Kelowna, BC V1Y 9G4
Tel: 250-763-3343; *Fax:* 250-763-9524

***Kelowna*: Gordon & Company - *2**
#102, 1433 St. Paul St., Kelowna, BC V1Y 2E4
Tel: 250-860-9997; *Fax:* 250-860-9937
gordonco@uniserve.com

***Kelowna*: Laura J. Gosset - *1**
#214, 440 Cascia Dr., Kelowna, BC V1W 4Y4
Tel: 250-764-8434; *Fax:* 250-764-1817
lauragosset@shaw.ca

***Kelowna*: Wade D. Jenson - *1**
#200, 369 Queensway Ave., Kelowna, BC V1Y 8E6
Tel: 250-868-2239; *Fax:* 250-861-5079

***Kelowna*: Martin Johnson Law Corporation - *2**
830 Bernard Ave., Kelowna, BC V1Y 6P5
Tel: 250-868-2848; *Fax:* 250-868-3080
Toll-Free: 877-868-2848
office@heritagelawgroup.com
www.heritagelawgroup.com

***Kelowna*: Roberta L. Jordan - *1**
#16, 4524 Eldorado Ct., Kelowna, BC V1W 1G3
Tel: 250-764-0888; *Fax:* 250-764-0680

***Kelowna*: Robert O. Levin - *2**
#607, 1708 Dolphin Ave., Kelowna, BC V1Y 9S4
Tel: 250-868-2101; *Fax:* 250-868-2414
robert@rlevin.com

***Kelowna*: M. Gail Miller - *1**
#904, 1708 Dolphin Ave., Kelowna, BC V1Y 9S4
Tel: 250-763-6767; *Fax:* 250-763-0980

***Kelowna*: Petraroia Langford Rush LLP - *5**
#800, 1708 Dolphin Ave., Kelowna, BC V1Y 9S4
Tel: 250-861-5332; *Fax:* 250-861-8772
info@plrllp.comm
www.plerlaw.com

***Kelowna*: Pihl & Associates Law Corporation - *6**
#300, 1465 Ellis St., Kelowna, BC V1Y 2A3
Tel: 250-762-5434; *Fax:* 250-762-5450
lawyers@pihl.bc.ca
www.okanaganlawyers.com

***Kelowna*: Porter Ramsay LLP - *9**
#200, 1465 Ellis St., Kelowna, BC V1Y 2A3
Tel: 250-763-7646; *Fax:* 250-762-9960
Toll-Free: 888-933-4411
lawyers@porterramsay.com
www.porterramsay.com

***Kelowna*: Pushor Mitchell LLP, Lawyers & Trade-Mark Agents - *31**
1665 Ellis St., 3rd Fl., Kelowna, BC V1Y 2B3
Tel: 250-762-2108; *Fax:* 250-762-9115
Toll-Free: 800-558-1155
lawyers@pushormitchell.com
www.pushormitchell.com

***Kelowna*: Schlosser & Co. - *1**
3017 Tutt St., Kelowna, BC V1Y 2H4
Tel: 250-763-1393

***Kelowna*: Daniel E. Spelliscy - *1**
715 Sutherland Ave., Kelowna, BC V1Y 5X4
Tel: 250-862-9586; *Fax:* 250-862-2677
dspelliscy@yahoo.com

***Kelowna*: Thomas Butler LLP - *4**
#700, 1708 Dolphin Ave., Kelowna, BC V1Y 9S4
Tel: 250-763-0200; *Fax:* 250-762-8848
www.thomasbutlerllp.com

***Kelowna*: Tinker, Churchill, Wallis - *3**
1573 Ellis St., Kelowna, BC V1Y 2A7
Tel: 250-763-7333; *Fax:* 250-763-5507
reception@tinkerchurchill.com
www.bevchurchillfamilylawyer.com

***Kelowna*: Douglas W. Welder - *1**
#200, 586 Leon Ave., Kelowna, BC V1Y 6J6
Tel: 250-868-8228; *Fax:* 250-868-8232
welder@okanagan.net

***Kelowna*: Marc R.B. Whittemore - *1**
830 Bernard Ave., Kelowna, BC V1Y 6P5
Tel: 250-868-2202; *Fax:* 250-868-2270
marc@whittemorelawcorporation.com

***Kelowna*: Robert J. Wotherspoon - *1**
2730 Cordova Way, Kelowna, BC V1Z 2N3
Tel: 250-769-5342

***Kimberley*: Walford & Associates Law Corp. - *1**
290 Wallinger Ave., Kimberley, BC V1A 1Z1
Tel: 250-427-0111; *Fax:* 250-427-0555
Toll-Free: 866-427-0111
randall@resortlaw.com
www.resortlaw.com

***Kitimat*: Wozney & Company - *2**
366 City Centre, Kitimat, BC V8C 1T6
Tel: 250-632-7151; *Fax:* 250-632-7100
rwozney@telus.net

***Ladysmith*: Robson, O'Connor - *2**
P.O. Box 1890, 22 High St., Ladysmith, BC V9G 1B4
Tel: 250-245-7141; *Fax:* 250-245-2921
Toll-Free: 800-641-1311
robcon@shawcable.com

***Langley*: Bryenton, Rosberg & Company - *4**
#300, 20689 Fraser Hwy., Langley, BC V3A 4G4
Tel: 604-530-7135; *Fax:* 604-530-7118
bryros@telus.net

***Langley*: Campbell, Burton & McMullan LLP - *11**
#200, 4769 - 222 St., Langley, BC V2Z 3C1
Tel: 604-533-3821; *Fax:* 604-533-5521
info@cbmlawyers.com
www.cbmlawyers.com

***Langley*: Darnell & Company Lawyers - *2**
#202, 6351 - 197 St., Langley, BC V2Y 1X8
Tel: 604-532-9119; *Fax:* 604-532-9127
www.langleylaw.ca

***Langley*: Fleming, Olson & Taneda - *3**
4038 - 200B St., Langley, BC V3A 1N9
Tel: 604-533-3411; *Fax:* 604-533-8749
fotlawyers@aol.com

***Langley*: Carl D. Holm - *1**
#102, 20475 Douglas Cres., Langley, BC V3A 4B6
Tel: 604-533-1401; *Fax:* 604-533-2024

***Langley*: Jarvis McGee - *4**
#130, 5769 - 201A St., Langley, BC V3A 8H9
Tel: 604-530-8319; *Fax:* 604-530-8319
www.icbccases.com or www.jarvismcgee.com

***Langley*: J. Michael Le Dressay & Associates - *2**
20570 - 56th Ave., Langley, BC V3A 3Z1
Tel: 604-530-2191; *Fax:* 604-530-6282
jmledressay@stargate.ca

***Langley*: MacDonald, Boyle & Jeffery - *1**
20450 Fraser Hwy., Langley, BC V3A 4G2
Tel: 604-530-3141; *Fax:* 604-530-9573

***Langley*: Peter Minten Personal Law Corporation - *1**
20570 - 56 Ave., Langley, BC V3A 3Z1
Tel: 604-530-2191; *Fax:* 604-530-6282
pminten@stargate.ca

***Langley*: Waterstone Law Group LLP - *9**
#304, 20338 - 65th Ave., Langley, BC V2Y 2X3
Tel: 604-533-2300; *Fax:* 604-533-2387
Toll-Free: 800-880-1667
info@waterstonelaw.com
www.waterstonelaw.com

***Lantzville*: Kristin Rongve - *1**
7180 Lantzville Rd., Lantzville, BC V0R 2H0
Tel: 250-390-3157; *Fax:* 250-390-4857

***Lillooet*: R. Kendel Kaser - *1**
P.O. Box 1449, 416 Main St., Lillooet, BC V0K 1V0
Tel: 250-256-7519; *Fax:* 250-256-7554

***Madeira Park*: Michael C. Crowe - *1**
P.O. Box 310, 12874 Madeira Park Rd., Madeira Park, BC V0N 2H0
Tel: 604-883-9875; *Fax:* 604-883-9873
m_crowe@sunshine.net

***Maple Ridge*: Vernon & Thompson Law Group - *4**
22311 - 119 Ave., Maple Ridge, BC V2X 2Z2
Tel: 604-463-6281; *Fax:* 604-463-7497
law@vernon-thompson.com

***Matsqui Village*: John Andrew Miner - *1**
CP 219, 34033 Lougheed Hwy., Matsqui Village, BC V2V 5X8
Tel: 604-826-3930; *Fax:* 604-826-4172

***Mill Bay*: Hicks & Co. - *2**
#24, Mill Bay Shopping Centre, P.O. Box 83, 2720 Mill Bay Rd., Mill Bay, BC V0R 2P0
Tel: 250-743-3756; *Fax:* 250-743-3756

***Mission*: Jarrett & Company - *1**
9701 Dewdney Trunk Rd., Mission, BC V2V 7G5
Tel: 604-826-5582

***Mission*: MacDonald Klassen Law Office - *1**
#2, 7331 James St., Mission, BC V2V 3V5
Tel: 604-820-1059; *Fax:* 604-820-1080
Toll-Free: 866-820-1059
macdonald_klassen_law@telus.net

***Mission*: Taylor, Tait, Ruley & Company - *6**
33066 First Ave., Mission, BC V2V 1G3
Tel: 604-826-1266; *Fax:* 604-826-4288
info@taylortait.com
www.taylortait.com

***Nanaimo*: David C. Brown - *1**
#106, 360 Selby St., Nanaimo, BC V9R 2R5
Tel: 250-741-8201; *Fax:* 250-741-8202
david-brown@shaw.ca

***Nanaimo*: Carlson & Company - *3**
669 Terminal Ave. North, Nanaimo, BC V9S 4K1
Tel: 250-753-7582; *Fax:* 250-753-7583
lawyers@carlson-law.com

***Nanaimo*: Fabris McIver Hornquist & Radcliffe - *4**
CP 778, 40 Cavan St., Nanaimo, BC V9R 5M2
Tel: 250-753-6661; *Fax:* 250-753-6648

***Nanaimo*: Hamilton Waterman Kaine - *2**
70 Prideaux St., Nanaimo, BC V9R 2M5
Tel: 250-755-1783; *Fax:* 250-755-1780
debra@hwklaw.ca

***Nanaimo*: Heath & Company - *7**
#200, 1808 Bowen Rd., Nanaimo, BC V9S 5W4
Tel: 250-753-2202; *Fax:* 250-753-3949
Toll-Free: 866-753-2202
consult@nanaimolaw.com
www.nanaimolaw.com

***Nanaimo*: A. Peter Hertzberg - *1**
#206, 75 Front St., Nanaimo, BC V9R 5H9
Tel: 250-753-1891; *Fax:* 250-753-1892
Toll-Free: 866-753-1891
hertzberglaw@telus.net

** indicates number of lawyers*

***Nanaimo*: Hobbs Hargrave - *2**
301 Franklyn St., Nanaimo, BC V9R 2X5
Tel: 250-753-3477; *Fax:* 250-753-7927
bhobbs@hobbslaw.com
www.hobbslaw.com

***Nanaimo*: Johnston Franklin - *4**
#210, 3260 Norwell Dr., Nanaimo, BC V9T 1X5
Tel: 250-756-3823; *Fax:* 250-756-6188
Toll-Free: 888-343-0782
lawyers@johnstonfranklin.ca
www.johnstonfranklin.ca

***Nanaimo*: Gary R. Korpan - *1**
3598 Hammond Bay Rd., Nanaimo, BC V9T 1E9
Tel: 250-758-9445; *Fax:* 250-754-8263
gkorpan@island.net

***Nanaimo*: Manning & Kirkhope - *2**
430 Wentworth St., Nanaimo, BC V9R 3E1
Tel: 250-753-6766; *Fax:* 250-753-0080
Toll-Free: 877-753-6766
office@mannkirk.com
www.mannkirk.com

***Nanaimo*: Merrill, Long & Co. - *2**
201 Milton St., Nanaimo, BC V9R 2K5
Tel: 250-754-4441; *Fax:* 250-754-4286
ranlaw@telus.net
www.merrilllong.com

***Nanaimo*: Mont & Walker Law Corporation - *4**
201 Selby St., Nanaimo, BC V9R 2R2
Tel: 250-753-6435; *Fax:* 250-753-5285
mont@islandlaw.ca
www.islandlaw.ca

***Nanaimo*: Petley-Jones & Co. Law Corp. - *1**
5732 Hammond Bay Rd., Nanaimo, BC V9T 5N2
Tel: 250-758-7370; *Fax:* 250-758-8703
info@petley-jones.net
www.petley-jones.net

***Nanaimo*: Ramsay Lampman Rhodes - *16**
111 Wallace St., Nanaimo, BC V9R 5B2
Tel: 250-754-3321; *Fax:* 250-754-1148
Toll-Free: 800-263-3321
info@rlr-law.com
www.rlr-law.com

***Nanaimo*: Robert N. Stacey Law Corp. - *1**
#10, 321 Wesley St., Nanaimo, BC V9R 2T5
Tel: 250-753-0844; *Fax:* 250-753-0877
rnstacey@telus.net
www.bcdivorceonline.com

***Nanaimo*: Elisabeth Strain**
#103, 360 Selby St., Nanaimo, BC V9R 2R5
Tel: 250-753-0860; *Fax:* 250-753-0861
elisabeth@strain.ca
www.strain.ca

***Nanaimo*: Victor Svacek - *1**
#206, 75 Front St., Nanaimo, BC V9R 5H9
Tel: 250-753-1891; *Fax:* 250-753-1892
Toll-Free: 866-753-1891
svaceklaw@telus.net

***Nanaimo*: Vining, Senini - *6**
P.O. Box 190, Stn. Main, 30 Front St., Nanaimo, BC V9R 5K9
Tel: 250-754-1234; *Fax:* 250-754-8080

***Nanaimo*: Eric L. Williams - *1**
55 Front St., Nanaimo, BC V9R 5H9
Tel: 250-741-1100; *Fax:* 250-741-1094
Toll-Free: 888-959-1100
eric.williams@telus.net

***Nanaimo*: C.D. Wilson & Associates - *1**
630 Terminal Ave. N., Nanaimo, BC V9S 4K2
Tel: 250-741-1400; *Fax:* 250-741-1441
nanaimo@cdwilson.bc.ca

***Nelson*: Susan Kurtz - *1**
407 Nelson Ave., Nelson, BC V1L 2N1
Tel: 250-354-1881; *Fax:* 250-354-1808

***Nelson*: Nasmyth, Morrow & Bogusz - *2**
#105, 465 Ward St., Nelson, BC V1L 1S7
Tel: 250-352-3171; *Fax:* 250-352-1777
nmgb@telus.net

***Nelson*: Stacey, Trillo & Company - *2**
#1, 405 Baker St., Nelson, BC V1L 4H7
Tel: 250-352-3125; *Fax:* 250-352-3145
greg@stacey-trillo.com
www.stacey-trillo.com

***Nelson*: Terry Napora Law Office - *1**
608 Baker St., Nelson, BC V1L 4J4
Tel: 250-352-3321; *Fax:* 250-354-4547
Toll-Free: 800-579-5338
tnapora@napwood.ca

***Nelson*: Susan E. Wallach - *1**
#4, 577 Baker St., Nelson, BC V1L 4J1
Tel: 250-352-6124; *Fax:* 250-352-3460

***New Westminster*: Gordon J. Bondoreff - *1**
#202, 713 Columbia St., New Westminster, BC V3M 1B2
Tel: 604-526-4491; *Fax:* 604-526-5979
gbondoreff@telus.net

***New Westminster*: Dickey, Browning, Ray, Soga, Dunne - *5**
#203, 668 Carnarvon St., New Westminster, BC V3M 5Y6
Tel: 604-526-4525; *Fax:* 604-526-8595
info@triallawyers.ca
www.triallawyers.ca

***New Westminster*: Raymond E. Drabik Law Corp. - *1**
#217, 713 Columbia St., New Westminster, BC V3M 1B2
Tel: 604-526-4875; *Fax:* 604-526-4879
red_law@telus.net

***New Westminster*: Goodwin & Mark - *6**
#217, 713 Columbia St., New Westminster, BC V3M 1B2
Tel: 604-522-9884; *Fax:* 604-526-8044
gm@goodmark.ca
www.goodmark.ca

***New Westminster*: Angela S. Kerslake - *1**
131 - 8th St., New Westminster, BC V3M 3P6
Tel: 604-520-6276; *Fax:* 604-520-5765

***New Westminster*: Kinman Mulholland - *2**
#400, 628 Sixth Ave., New Westminster, BC V3M 6Z1
Tel: 604-526-1805; *Fax:* 604-526-8056
info@kamlawyers.com
www.kamlawyers.com

***New Westminster*: Scarborough, Herman, Harvey & Bluekens - *4**
900 Quayside Dr., 10th Fl., New Westminster, BC V3M 6G1
Tel: 604-521-2223; *Fax:* 604-521-7772
sbluekens@shh.bc.ca

***North Saanich*: Barbara J. Yates - *1**
430 Wain Rd., North Saanich, BC V8L 5P9
Tel: 250-656-0979; *Fax:* 250-656-4333

***North Vancouver*: Ardagh Hunter - *2**
#300, 1401 Lonsdale Ave., North Vancouver, BC V7M 2H9
Tel: 604-986-4366; *Fax:* 604-986-9286
account@ahtlaw.com

***North Vancouver*: Begin & Company - *1**
#302, 140 West 15th St., North Vancouver, BC V7M 1R6
Tel: 604-987-5297; *Fax:* 604-980-6322
beginandco@shaw.ca

***North Vancouver*: Trevors R. Bjurman - *1**
#205, 1433 Lonsdale Ave., North Vancouver, BC V7M 2H9
Tel: 604-983-3728; *Fax:* 604-983-0148
bjurman@smartt.com

***North Vancouver*: Oren E. Breitman - *1**
1503 Dovercourt Rd., North Vancouver, BC V7K 1K6
Tel: 604-218-9480; *Fax:* 604-984-0502
orenb@shaw.ca

***North Vancouver*: Forrest, Gray, Lewis & Gillett - *1**
#201, 145 - 15th St. East, North Vancouver, BC V7L 2P7
Tel: 604-988-5244; *Fax:* 604-988-0093
fglg@dowco.com

***North Vancouver*: Charlotte C. Gregory - *1**
205 St. Patrick's Ave., North Vancouver, BC V7L 3N3
Tel: 604-983-2886; *Fax:* 604-983-2886
cgregory@istar.ca

***North Vancouver*: M. Hollander - *1**
#320, 145 West 17 St., North Vancouver, BC V7M 1V5
Tel: 604-986-4354; *Fax:* 604-986-9183
marjon@intergate.ca

***North Vancouver*: Jabour, Sudeyko - *1**
#603, 145 East 13th St., North Vancouver, BC V7L 2L4
Tel: 604-986-8600; *Fax:* 604-986-4872
Toll-Free: 877-860-7575
dsudeyko@telus.net
www.jaboursudeyko.com

***North Vancouver*: Robert W. Johnson - *1**
#300, 1401 Lonsdale Ave., North Vancouver, BC V7M 2H9
Tel: 604-984-0305; *Fax:* 604-984-0304
robert.johnson@ahtlaw.com

***North Vancouver*: E.B. Kroon - *1**
#100, 132 East 14 St., North Vancouver, BC V7L 2N3
Tel: 604-980-7021; *Fax:* 604-980-7426

***North Vancouver*: Lakes & Whyte LLP - *6**
#200, 879 Marine Dr., North Vancouver, BC V7P 1R7
Tel: 604-984-3646; *Fax:* 604-984-8573
Toll-Free: 800-488-7788
info@lakeswhyte.com
www.lakeswhyte.com

***North Vancouver*: Lee T. Lau Law Corp. - *1**
365 Lynn Ave., North Vancouver, BC V7J 2C4
Tel: 604-988-5222; *Fax:* 604-988-5356
lau@leelau.net
www.leelau.net

***North Vancouver*: Lynn Valley Law - *1**
#40, 1199 Lynn Valley Rd., North Vancouver, BC V7J 3H2
Tel: 604-985-8000; *Fax:* 604-985-5999
admin@lynnlaw.ca
www.lynnlaw.ca

***North Vancouver*: North Shore Law LLP - *15**
171 West Esplanade, 6th Floor, North Vancouver, BC V7M 3J9
Tel: 604-980-8571; *Fax:* 604-980-4019
Toll-Free: 877-980-8571
inquiries@northshorelaw.com
www.northshorelaw.com

***North Vancouver*: Ron Perrick Law Corp. - *2**
#480, 145 West 17 St., North Vancouver, BC V7M 1V5
Tel: 604-984-9521; *Fax:* 604-984-9104

***North Vancouver*: Poyner Baxter LLP - *3**
#408, 145 Chadwick Ct., North Vancouver, BC V7M 3K1
Tel: 604-988-6321; *Fax:* 604-988-3632
info@poynerbaxter.com
www.poynerbaxter.com

***North Vancouver*: Ratcliff & Company LLP - *27**
#500, East Tower, 221 West Esplanade, North Vancouver, BC V7M 3J3
Tel: 604-988-5201; *Fax:* 604-988-1452
admin@ratcliff.com
www.ratcliff.com

***North Vancouver*: Robert C. Reid - *1**
#233, 1433 Lonsdale Ave., North Vancouver, BC V7M 2H9
Tel: 604-984-4357; *Fax:* 604-984-4326
robertcreid@hotmail.com

***North Vancouver*: D.A. Roper - *1**
334 West 15th St., North Vancouver, BC V7M 1S5
Tel: 604-986-0488; *Fax:* 604-984-3463
roperlaw@shawbiz.ca

***North Vancouver*: Thomas Immigration Law Group - *2**
1885 Marine Dr., North Vancouver, BC V7P 1V5
Tel: 604-988-0795; *Fax:* 604-988-0718
office@executive-visa.com
www.executive-visa.com

***Oliver*: Gordon & Young - *3**
P.O. Box 1800, 36011 - 97th St., Oliver, BC V0H 1T0
Tel: 250-498-4941; *Fax:* 250-498-4100

***Osoyoos*: Gordon & Company - *2**
#202, 8309 Main St., Osoyoos, BC V0H 1V0
Tel: 250-495-6508; *Fax:* 250-495-6404
gordonco@telus.net
www.sunnyosoyoos.com/webpages/gordon_company.htm

***Parksville*: Davis & Avis - *2**
#201, CP 1600, 156 Morison Ave., Parksville, BC V9P 2H5
Tel: 250-248-5731; *Fax:* 250-248-5730
law@davis-avis.com
www.davis-avis.com

** indicates number of lawyers*

***Parksville*: John A. Hossack & Company - *1**
CP 1486, 311 McKinnon St., Parksville, BC V9P 2H4
Tel: 250-248-9241; *Fax:* 250-248-8375
john@hossack-law.com
www.hossack-law.com

***Parksville*: Patricia E. Lebedovich - *1**
P.O. Box 214, Parksville, BC V9P 2G4
Toll-Free: 866-711-3084
lebedovich@shaw.ca

***Peachland*: John E. Humphries Law Corporation - *1**
5848B Beach Ave., Peachland, BC V0H 1X7
Tel: 250-767-2221; *Fax:* 250-767-3477
johnehumphrieslaw@hotmail.com

***Penticton*: Boyle & Company - *10**
#3201, 100 Front St., Penticton, BC V2A 1H1
Tel: 250-492-6100; *Fax:* 250-492-4877
Toll-Free: 800-665-8244
www.boyleco.bc.ca

***Penticton*: Gilchrist & Company - *4**
#101, 123 Martin St., Penticton, BC V2A 7X6
Tel: 250-492-3033; *Fax:* 250-492-6162
info@gilchristlaw.com
www.gilchristlaw.com

***Penticton*: Kathryn J. Ginther - *1**
#301, 301 Main St., Penticton, BC V2A 5B7
Tel: 250-487-4355; *Fax:* 250-487-4356
kjg@kgintherlaw.com

***Penticton*: Halbauer & Company - *1**
#104, 2504 Skana Lake Road, Penticton, BC V2A 6G1
Tel: 250-492-7225; *Fax:* 250-492-7395
www.pentictonlawyers.com

***Penticton*: Thomas A. Kampman - *1**
409 Ellis St., Penticton, BC V2A 4M1
Tel: 250-493-6786; *Fax:* 250-493-3964
tom@kampmanoliverkeene.com

***Penticton*: Zaseybida, Bonga - *2**
#101, 100 Nanaimo Ave. East, Penticton, BC V2A 1M4
Tel: 250-492-2244; *Fax:* 250-492-0090
zaseybida-bonga@telus.net

***Pitt Meadows*: Becker & Company Law Offices - *1**
#230, 19150 Lougheed Hwy., Pitt Meadows, BC V3Y 2H6
Tel: 604-465-9993; *Fax:* 604-465-0066
info@becker-company.com
www.becker-company.com

***Port Alberni*: Badovinac, Scoffield & Mosley - *3**
3290 - 3 Ave., Port Alberni, BC V9Y 4E1
Tel: 250-724-1275; *Fax:* 250-724-7200
bsm@albernilaw.com
www.albernilaw.com

***Port Alberni*: Beckingham & Co. - *2**
5029 Argyle St., Port Alberni, BC V9Y 1V5
Tel: 250-724-0111; *Fax:* 250-724-4422
beck@port.island.net

***Port Coquitlam*: John K. Bledsoe - *1**
2239B McAllister Ave., Port Coquitlam, BC V3C 2A9
Tel: 604-941-6162; *Fax:* 604-941-4369

***Port Coquitlam*: Darychuk Deane-Cloutier - *2**
#310, 2755 Lougheed Hwy., Port Coquitlam, BC V3B 5Y9
Tel: 604-464-2644; *Fax:* 604-464-2533

***Port Coquitlam*: Payne & Associates - *1**
#105, 1465 Salisbury Ave., Port Coquitlam, BC V3B 6J3
Tel: 604-944-4115; *Fax:* 604-944-4120

***Port Coquitlam*: Larry W. Pippard - *1**
#2, 3397 Hastings St., Port Coquitlam, BC V3B 4M8
Tel: 604-464-5615
larrywpippard@shaw.ca

***Port Coquitlam*: Henry Sarava - *1**
#2300, 2850 Shaughnessy St., Port Coquitlam, BC V3C 6K5
Tel: 604-944-2114; *Fax:* 604-552-7709
henrysarava@hotmail.com
www.lawyers.com/saravacriminaldefence

***Port Coquitlam*: Smyth & Co. - *4**
#330, 2755 Lougheed Hwy., Port Coquitlam, BC V3B 5Y9
Tel: 604-942-6560; *Fax:* 604-942-1347

***Port Hardy*: Nowosad & Company - *1**
CP 1289, 8700 Market St., Port Hardy, BC V0N 2P0
Tel: 250-949-6031; *Fax:* 250-949-2633
info@macisaacgroup.com
www.macisaacgroup.com

***Port Moody*: Burke Tomchenko Morrison - *5**
#301, 2502 St. Johns St., Port Moody, BC V3H 2B4
Tel: 604-937-1166; *Fax:* 604-937-5577
firm@btmlawyers.com
www.btmlawyers.com

***Port Moody*: Morrison Voss - *2**
2225 Clarke St., Port Moody, BC V3H 1Y6
Tel: 604-937-4757; *Fax:* 604-937-4714
Toll-Free: 866-944-8888
jsvoss@morrisonvoss.com

***Powell River*: Garling Ostensen - *1**
4581 Marine Ave., Powell River, BC V8A 2K7
Tel: 604-485-2818; *Fax:* 604-485-7161
garost@powellriverlawyers.com

***Powell River*: James Garrett-Rempel - *1**
4766 Michigan Ave., Powell River, BC V8A 2S9
Tel: 604-485-9898; *Fax:* 604-485-9850
jgrlaw@shaw.ca
www.garrett-rempel.com

***Powell River*: F. Gregory Reif - *1**
#201, 4801 Joyce Ave., Powell River, BC V8A 3B7
Tel: 604-485-2056; *Fax:* 604-485-2196
gregreif@telus.net

***Powell River*: Whyard Villani - *3**
4448A Marine Ave., Powell River, BC V8A 2K2
Tel: 604-485-6188; *Fax:* 604-485-6923
info@whyardvillani.com
www.whyardvillani.com

***Prince George*: Coller Levine, Barristers & Solicitors - *2**
1140 - 3rd Ave., Prince George, BC V2L 3E5
Tel: 250-960-2169; *Fax:* 250-960-2196
coller@collerlevine.ca
www.collerlevine.ca

***Prince George*: John A. Davis - *1**
#1, 1515 - 2 Ave., Prince George, BC V2L 3B8
Tel: 250-564-5544; *Fax:* 250-562-9427
jdlaw@shawcable.com

***Prince George*: Dick Byl Law Corporation - *8**
#900, 550 Victoria St., Prince George, BC V2L 2K1
Tel: 250-564-3400; *Fax:* 250-564-7873
Toll-Free: 800-835-0088
dbyl@dbylaw.com
www.dbylaw.com

***Prince George*: Fatt & Elson, Barristers & Solicitors - *2**
#503, 1488 - 4th Ave., Prince George, BC V2L 4Y2
Tel: 250-564-1334; *Fax:* 250-564-4266
Toll-Free: 888-564-1334
lawyers@fattandelson.com

***Prince George*: Fletcher Repstock - *5**
440 Brunswick St., Prince George, BC V2L 2B6
Tel: 250-564-1313; *Fax:* 250-563-4362
Toll-Free: 877-690-1110
repstock@netbistro.com

***Prince George*: Richard C. Gibbs - *1**
1134 - 3rd Ave., Prince George, BC V2L 3E5
Tel: 250-564-6460; *Fax:* 250-562-0671
rcgibbs@telus.net

***Prince George*: Heather Sadler Jenkins LLP - *16**
#700, Royal Bank Bldg., P.O. Box 4500, 550 Victoria St., Prince George, BC V2L 2K1
Tel: 250-565-8000; *Fax:* 250-565-8001
Toll-Free: 866-565-8777
hsj@hsjlawyers.com
www.hsjlawyers.com

***Prince George*: Hope Heinrich, Barristers & Solicitors - *9**
1598 - 6th Ave., Prince George, BC V2L 5G7
Tel: 250-563-0681; *Fax:* 250-562-3761
Toll-Free: 800-663-8230

***Prince George*: Richard B. Krehbiel - *1**
6932 View Pl., Prince George, BC V2K 4C6
Tel: 250-962-5843; *Fax:* 250-962-5842
rkrehbie@pgweb.com

***Prince George*: Leverman & Company - *1**
Courtyard Lane, 1057 - 3rd Ave., Prince George, BC V2L 3E3
Tel: 250-564-1212; *Fax:* 250-756-1588

***Prince George*: Ronald W. Madill - *1**
1033 - 3rd Ave., Prince George, BC V2L 3E3
Tel: 250-562-5000; *Fax:* 250-562-5105

***Prince George*: J.A. Mooney - *1**
1033 - 3rd Ave., Prince George, BC V2L 3B3
Tel: 250-562-3324; *Fax:* 250-562-9444
jim@jamesmooney.com

***Prince George*: Traxler Haines - *6**
#614, 1488 - 4 Ave., Prince George, BC V2L 4Y2
Tel: 250-563-7741; *Fax:* 250-563-2953

***Prince George*: Tyo Law Corp. - *1**
#304, 1488 - 4 Ave., Prince George, BC V2L 4Y2
Tel: 250-564-9757; *Fax:* 250-564-9734
Toll-Free: 877-365-4093
tyolaw@shaw.ca

***Prince George*: Weatherly & Brown - *2**
925 Vancouver St., Prince George, BC V2L 2P6
Tel: 250-563-8110; *Fax:* 250-563-1466

***Prince George*: Wilbur & Company - *1**
1057 - 3rd Ave., Prince George, BC V2L 3E3
Tel: 250-564-1444; *Fax:* 250-563-2842
dwilbur@shaw.ca

***Prince George*: Wilson King LLP - *10**
#1000, 299 Victoria St., Prince George, BC V2L 5B8
Tel: 250-960-3200; *Fax:* 250-562-7777
Toll-Free: 800-365-4566
www.wilsonking.com

***Prince Rupert*: Marina C-K Kan - *1**
P.O. Box 722, Prince Rupert, BC V8J 3S1
Tel: 250-624-6060; *Fax:* 250-624-6451

***Prince Rupert*: Narbonne Law Office - *1**
P.O. Box 256, Prince Rupert, BC V8J 3P6
Tel: 250-624-4899; *Fax:* 250-624-3046
www.narbonnelawoffice.com

***Prince Rupert*: Irene G. Peters Law Corp. - *2**
#304, 1488 - 14 Ave., Prince Rupert, BC V2L 4Y2
Tel: 250-627-7771; *Fax:* 250-624-2191

***Prince Rupert*: Punnett & Johnston - *2**
#7, 222 - 3rd Ave. West, Prince Rupert, BC V8J 1L1
Tel: 250-624-2106; *Fax:* 250-627-8805
pj@citytel.net

***Prince Rupert*: Silversides, Merrick & McLean - *4**
P.O. Box 188, 217 - 3rd Ave. West, Prince Rupert, BC V8J 3P7
Tel: 250-624-2116; *Fax:* 250-627-7786
reception@silverco.ca

***Qualicum Beach*: Marshall & Lamperson - *2**
CP 879, 710 Memorial Ave., Qualicum Beach, BC V9K 1T2
Tel: 250-752-5615; *Fax:* 250-752-2055
doug@qualicumlaw.ca

***Qualicum Beach*: Rodway & Perry - *2**
#1, CP 138, 699 Beach Rd., Qualicum Beach, BC V9K 1S7
Tel: 250-752-9526; *Fax:* 250-752-9521
rodwayandperry@shaw.ca
www.macisaacgroup.com

***Qualicum Beach*: Walker & Wilson, Barristers & Solicitors - *2**
#2, 707 Primrose St., Qualicum Beach, BC V9K 2K1
Tel: 250-752-6951; *Fax:* 250-752-6022
kwalker@qblaw.ca
www.qblaw.ca

***Quesnel*: John B. Schmitz - *1**
633 Clark St., Quesnel, BC V2J 1L3
Tel: 250-992-6793; *Fax:* 250-992-6795

***Revelstoke*: Bernard C. Lavallée - *1**
P.O. Box 244, 109 Connaught Ave., Revelstoke, BC V0E 2S0
Tel: 250-837-5168; *Fax:* 250-837-5178
bcl59lawyer@rctvonline.net

***Revelstoke*: Robert A. Lundberg Law Corporation - *1**
119 Campbell Ave., Revelstoke, BC V0E 2S0
Tel: 250-837-5196; *Fax:* 250-837-4746
robertlundberg@rctvonline.net

** indicates number of lawyers*

***Richmond*: Ash, O'Donnell, Hibbert - *4**
#1, 11575 Bridgeport Rd., Richmond, BC V6X 1T5
Tel: 604-273-9111; *Fax:* 604-273-1117
aohlaw2007@gmail.com
www.ashodonnellhibbert.ca

***Richmond*: David G. Baker, Barrister - *1**
#210, 7340 Westminster Hwy., Richmond, BC V6X 1A1
Tel: 604-244-7587; *Fax:* 604-303-6922
davegbaker@yahoo.ca
www.davidgbaker.ca

***Richmond*: Berger & Company - *2**
#130, 8400 Granville Ave., Richmond, BC V6Y 1P6
Tel: 604-273-9959; *Fax:* 604-273-9910
eberger@telus.net
www.berger-and-company.com

***Richmond*: David W. Blinkhorn - *1**
#230, 7360 Westminster Hwy., Richmond, BC V6X 1A1
Tel: 604-244-7880; *Fax:* 604-244-9611

***Richmond*: V.N. Carvalho - *1**
13811 Gilbert Rd., Richmond, BC V7E 2H8
Tel: 604-274-5636; *Fax:* 604- -
vncarvalho@shaw.ca

***Richmond*: S.R. Chamberlain, Barrister & Solicitor - *2**
#1, 7100 River Rd., Richmond, BC V6X 1X5
Tel: 604-244-0646; *Fax:* 604-244-0617
mail@src-law.com

***Richmond*: Robert J. Charlton - *1**
#816, 6081 No. 3 Rd., Richmond, BC V6Y 2B2
Tel: 604-214-7818; *Fax:* 604-214-7819
rjc@rjcharlton.com
www.rjcharlton.com

***Richmond*: Chouinard & Company - *2**
#816, 6081 No. 3 Rd., Richmond, BC V6Y 2B2
Tel: 604-214-7818; *Fax:* 604-214-7819
Toll-Free: 877-685-8999
ray@chouinardlaw.com
www.chouinardlaw.com

***Richmond*: Cohen, Buchan, Edwards - *9**
#208, 4940 No. 3 Rd., Richmond, BC V6X 3A5
Tel: 604-273-6411; *Fax:* 604-273-4512
gary@cbelaw.com
www.cbelaw.com

***Richmond*: John C. Fairburn**
#305, 5811 Cooney Rd., Richmond, BC V6X 3M1
Tel: 604-279-8283; *Fax:* 604-279-8243
fairburnlaw@execcentre.com

***Richmond*: Fast & Company, Barristers & Solicitors - *2**
#5080, 8171 Ackroyd Rd., Richmond, BC V6X 3K1
Tel: 604-273-6424; *Fax:* 604-273-2290
mlfast@fastandco.ca
www.fastandco.ca

***Richmond*: Forbes & Boyle - *3**
#215, 8171 Cook Rd., Richmond, BC V6Y 3T8
Tel: 604-273-7575; *Fax:* 604-273-8475
info@forbesboyle.ca

***Richmond*: Douglas B. Graves - *1**
#317, 8055 Anderson Rd., Richmond, BC V6Y 1S2
Tel: 604-276-0069

***Richmond*: Henderson Livingston Stewart LLP - *4**
Old Steveston Courthouse, 12011 - 3rd Ave., Richmond, BC V7E 3K1
Tel: 604-241-2855; *Fax:* 604-241-2866
office@hlslawyers.com
www.steveston.bc.ca

***Richmond*: Bernard Hoodekoff - *1**
#206, 5811 Cooney Rd., Richmond, BC V6X 3M1
Tel: 604-278-8451; *Fax:* 604-278-8453

***Richmond*: Humphry Paterson - *2**
#205, 8171 Park Rd., Richmond, BC V6Y 1S9
Tel: 604-278-3031; *Fax:* 604-278-3021
humpat@telus.net

***Richmond*: INC Business Lawyers - *2**
#1201, 11871 Horseshoe Way, Richmond, BC V7A 5H5
Tel: 604-272-6960; *Fax:* 604-272-6959
Toll-Free: 888-272-7771
info@incorporate.ca
www.incorporate.ca

***Richmond*: Jang Cheung Lee Chu Law Corporation - *7**
#700, London Plaza, 5951 No. 3 Rd., Richmond, BC V6X 2E3
Tel: 604-276-8300; *Fax:* 604-276-8309
office@jclclawcorp.com
www.jclclawcorp.com

***Richmond*: Kahn Zack Ehrlich Lithwick - *10**
#270, 10711 Cambie Rd., Richmond, BC V6X 3G5
Tel: 604-270-9571; *Fax:* 604-270-8282
Toll-Free: 888-529-6368
general@kzellaw.com
www.kzellaw.com

***Richmond*: Nancy L. Kinsman, Barrister & Solicitor - *1**
#315, 8171 Cook Rd., Richmond, BC V6Y 3T8
Tel: 604-273-4664; *Fax:* 604-273-7442
nkinsman@familylawbc.ca
www.familylawbc.ca

***Richmond*: Kenneth B. Krag - *1**
#228, 8055 Anderson Rd., Richmond, BC V6Y 1S2
Tel: 604-270-8702; *Fax:* 604-270-6708

***Richmond*: Theodore Kuchta - *1**
8480 Rosebank Cres., Richmond, BC V7A 2K6
Tel: 604-274-4513; *Fax:* 604-276-2800
tedkuch@aol.com

***Richmond*: Susan Label - *1**
#250, 11590 Cambie Rd., Richmond, BC V6X 3Z5
Tel: 604-273-6448; *Fax:* 604-273-6998
www.susanlabel.com

***Richmond*: Morley A. Levitt - *1**
#120, 11181 Voyageur Way, Richmond, BC V6X 3N9
Tel: 604-270-9611; *Fax:* 604-270-4588
info@protectmyestate.ca
www.protectmyestate.ca

***Richmond*: Lim & Company - *5**
#320, 7480 Westminster Hwy., Richmond, BC V6X 1A1
Tel: 604-303-0788; *Fax:* 604-303-0789
info@lim-and-company-law.com
www.lim-and-company-lawyers.com

***Richmond*: V. Brent Louie, Personal Law Corporation - *1**
#203, 2680 Shell Rd., Richmond, BC V6X 4C9
Tel: 604-270-8708; *Fax:* 604-270-8735
vblouie@shaw.ca

***Richmond*: Peter Li & Company - *2**
#110, 4400 Hazelbridge Way, Richmond, BC V6X 3R8
Tel: 604-273-6308; *Fax:* 604-273-6393
peterliandco@yahoo.com

***Richmond*: Phillips Paul - *2**
#215, 4800 No. 3 Rd., Richmond, BC V6X 3A6
Tel: 604-273-5297; *Fax:* 604-273-1643
philpaul@direct.ca

***Richmond*: Rees-Thomas & Company - *3**
#5080, 8171 Ackroyd Rd., Richmond, BC V6X 3K1
Tel: 604-279-9300; *Fax:* 604-273-2290
info@reesthomas.com

***Richmond*: Scardina & Co. - *1**
#215, 4800 No. 3 Rd., Richmond, BC V6X 3A6
Tel: 604-273-5558; *Fax:* 604-273-5550

***Richmond*: Spry Hawkins Micner - *1**
#440, VanCity Tower, 5900 No. 3 Rd., Richmond, BC V6X 3P7
Tel: 604-233-7001; *Fax:* 604-233-7017
annette@willpowerlaw.com
www.willpowerlaw.com

***Richmond*: Bruce A. Thompson Law Corp. - *1**
#215, Churchill Centre, 2nd Fl., 8171 Cook Rd., Richmond, BC V6Y 3T8
Tel: 604-270-7773; *Fax:* 604-273-8475

***Richmond*: Wong & Tsang - *4**
#310, 8120 Granville Ave., Richmond, BC V6Y 1P3
Tel: 604-279-9023; *Fax:* 604-279-9025

***Richmond*: Mary E.B. Wood - *1**
#724, 6081 - No. 3 Rd., Richmond, BC V6Y 2B2
Tel: 604-273-5547; *Fax:* 604-273-3044
mebwood@telus.net
www.marywoodlawyer.com

***Roberts Creek*: Lynn Chapman - *1**
1947 Crystal Cr., Roberts Creek, BC V0N 2W1
Tel: 604-885-0356; *Fax:* 604-885-0358
lchapman@dccnet.com

***Saanichton*: C.J. Kip Wilson - *1**
#6, 7855 East Saanich Rd., Saanichton, BC V8M 2B4
Tel: 250-544-0727; *Fax:* 250-544-0728
kipwilson@home.com

***Salmon Arm*: Brooke, Jackson, Downs - *4**
Centennial Building, CP 67, 51 - 3rd St. NE, Salmon Arm, BC V1E 4N2
Tel: 250-832-9311; *Fax:* 250-832-3801
bjdlaw@sunwave.net
www.bjdlaw.com

***Salmon Arm*: Derek McManus Law Corporation - *1**
CP 57, 450 Lakeshore Dr. NE, Salmon Arm, BC V1E 4N2
Tel: 250-833-4720; *Fax:* 250-832-4787
corp@salmonarmlaw.com
www.salmonarmlaw.com

***Salmon Arm*: Seale Law Corp. - *1**
CP 3248, 450 Lakeshore Dr. NE, Salmon Arm, BC V1E 4S1
Tel: 250-832-9301; *Fax:* 250-832-9300

***Salmon Arm*: Sivertz Kiehlbauch - *3**
#320, P.O. Box 190, 351 Hudson Ave. NE, Salmon Arm, BC V1E 4N3
Tel: 250-832-8031; *Fax:* 250-832-6177

***Salmon Arm*: Verdurmen & Company - *1**
CP 826, 450 Lakeshore Dr. NE, Salmon Arm, BC V1E 4N9
Tel: 250-833-0914; *Fax:* 250-833-0924
vlex@telus.net
www.macisaacgroup.com

***Salt Spring Island*: Fisher, Murphy & Woodward - *1**
#1, 105 Rainbow Rd., Salt Spring Island, BC V8K 2V5
Tel: 250-537-5505; *Fax:* 250-537-5099
www.saltspringlawfirm.comwww.facebook.com/pages/Fisher-Murphy-Woodward-Lawyers/253823191300084

***Salt Spring Island*: J. Anthony McEwen - *1**
1860 Fulford-Ganges Rd., Salt Spring Island, BC V8K 2A5
Tel: 250-653-4979; *Fax:* 250-653-9212

***Salt Spring Island*: James Pasuta - *1**
P.O. Box 414, Stn. Ganges, 560 Fulford-Ganges Rd., Salt Spring Island, BC V8K 2W1
Tel: 250-537-9995; *Fax:* 250-537-9975

***Sechelt*: William C. Prowse - *1**
6866 Island View Rd., Sechelt, BC V0N 3A8
Tel: 604-740-0303; *Fax:* 604-740-0306
transmed@telus.net

***Sechelt*: Robinson & Co. Law Office - *1**
P.O. Box 920, Sechelt, BC V0N 3A0
Tel: 604-885-7541; *Fax:* 604-885-7561
robco@telus.net

***Sidney*: Alice E. Finall - *1**
2412B Beacon Ave., 2nd Fl., Sidney, BC V8L 1X4
Tel: 250-656-6668; *Fax:* 250-656-9366
final@telus.net

***Sidney*: Henley & Walden - *4**
#201, 2377 Bevan Ave., Sidney, BC V8L 4M9
Tel: 250-656-7231; *Fax:* 250-656-0937
Toll-Free: 800-656-7231
inquiries@henleywalden.com
www.henleywalden.com

***Sidney*: McKimm & Lott - *7**
9830 - 4th St., Sidney, BC V8L 2Z3
Tel: 250-656-3961; *Fax:* 250-655-3329
reception@mclott.com
www.mclott.com

***Smithers*: Perry & Company - *4**
CP 790, 1081 Main St., Smithers, BC V0J 2N0
Tel: 250-847-4341; *Fax:* 250-847-5634
www.perryco.ca

***Smithers*: G. Ronald Toews, Q.C. - *1**
P.O. Box 970, 3835 - 10th Ave., Smithers, BC V0J 2N0
Tel: 250-847-2187; *Fax:* 250-847-2183
grt@buckley.net

** indicates number of lawyers*

Sooke: Hallgren & Faulkner - *2
P.O. Box 939, 104-6739 West Coast Rd., Sooke, BC V9Z 1H9
Tel: 250-642-5271; *Fax*: 250-642-6006
Toll-Free: 800-358-5271
info@hallgrenfaulkner.ca

Squamish: Race & Company - *6
#201, CP 1850, 1365 Pemberton Ave., Squamish, BC V0N 3G0
Tel: 604-892-5254; *Fax*: 604-892-5461
d.race@racesq.com
www.raceandcompany.com

Summerland: Bell, Jacoe & Company, Barristers & Solicitors - *2
P.O. Box 520, 13211 Victoria Rd. North, Summerland, BC V0H 1Z0
Tel: 250-494-6621; *Fax*: 250-494-8055
Toll-Free: 800-663-0392
belljacoe@shaw.ca
www.bell-jacoe.com

Surrey: Alan J. Benson - *1
#106, 15585 - 24 Ave., Surrey, BC V4A 2J4
Tel: 604-538-4911; *Fax*: 604-538-5754

Surrey: Roger S. Bhatti - *1
#203, 8556 - 120th St., Surrey, BC V3W 3N5
Tel: 604-590-1177; *Fax*: 604-596-8800
rblaw@intergate.ca

Surrey: Spencer A. Bowers - *1
8893 - 160 St., Surrey, BC V4N 2X8
Tel: 604-951-9224; *Fax*: 604-951-9224
sabowers@axionet.com

Surrey: Brawn, Karras & Sanderson - *3
#340, 5620 - 152nd St., Surrey, BC V3A 3K2
Tel: 604-588-5344; *Fax*: 604-588-2331
infodesk@bkslaw.com
www.bkslaw.com

Surrey: Caissie & Company - *1
#205, 15127 - 100 Ave., Surrey, BC V3R 0N9
Tel: 604-586-7200; *Fax*: 604-583-5870
info@calaw.bc.ca
www.calaw.bc.ca

Surrey: James L. Davidson & Company - *3
#403, P.O. Box 271, 16033 - 108 Ave., Surrey, BC V4N 1P2
Tel: 604-951-2990; *Fax*: 604-951-2991
jld@look.ca

Surrey: Paul E. Del Rossi - *1
#1012, 7445 - 132nd St., Surrey, BC V3W 1J8
Tel: 604-590-5600; *Fax*: 604-590-5626
Toll-Free: 866-990-5600
pdelrossi@sternandalbert.com

Surrey: G. Egolf - *1
14135 - 60 Ave., Surrey, BC V3X 2N2
Tel: 604-594-4166

Surrey: Fritz Shirreff & Vickers - *4
#201, 15127 - 100th Ave., Surrey, BC V3R 0N9
Tel: 604-582-5157; *Fax*: 604-582-5167
info@fsvlawyers.com
www.fsvlawyers.com

Surrey: Greig, Wilson & Rasmussen LLP - *5
#300, Guildford Landmark Bldg., 15127 - 100th Ave., Surrey, BC V3R 0N9
Tel: 604-583-7917; *Fax*: 604-583-7139
info@gwrlawyers.com
www.gwrlawyers.com

Surrey: Guildford Law Group - *3
#200, 10330 - 152 St., Surrey, BC V3R 4G8
Tel: 604-585-1196; *Fax*: 604-585-3293
www.guildfordlaw.com

Surrey: Hamilton Duncan Armstrong & Stewart Law Corporation - North Surrey - *20
#1450, Station Tower Gateway, 13401 - 108th Ave., Surrey, BC V3T 5T3
Tel: 604-581-4677; *Fax*: 604-581-5947
info@hdas.com
www.hdas.com

Surrey: Hamilton Duncan Armstrong & Stewart Law Corporation - South Surrey - *19
#210, Rodeo Square, 5620 - 152nd St., Surrey, BC V3S 3K2
Tel: 604-575-8088; *Fax*: 604-575-8118
info@hdas.com
www.hdas.com

Surrey: Sharen Janeson - *1
#456, 15355 - 24 Ave., Surrey, BC V4A 2H9
Tel: 604-536-6884; *Fax*: 604-618-9500
sjaneson@shaw.ca

Surrey: Kaminsky & Company - *4
#220, 7525 King George Blvd., Surrey, BC V3W 5A8
Tel: 604-591-7877; *Fax*: 604-591-1978
inbox@kaminskyco.com
www.kaminskyco.com

Surrey: Kane, Shannon & Weiler - *21
#220, 7565 - 132nd St., Surrey, BC V3W 1K5
Tel: 604-591-7321; *Fax*: 604-591-7149
info@ksw.bc.ca
www.ksw.bc.ca

Surrey: Kereluk & Company - *1
#125, 15225 - 104 Ave., Surrey, BC V3R 6Y8
Tel: 604-589-3278; *Fax*: 604-589-8473
mail@kereluklaw.com
www.kereluklaw.com

Surrey: James R. Kitsul - *1
19395 Langley Bypass, Surrey, BC V3S 6K1
Tel: 604-539-2610; *Fax*: 604-534-3811
kitsul@supersave.ca

Surrey: William D. MacLeod Law Corp. - *1
#205A, York Business Centre, 12830 - 80 Ave., Surrey, BC V3W 3A8
Tel: 604-572-7200; *Fax*: 604-572-7213

Surrey: MacMillan, Tucker, & Mackay - *3
5690 - 176A St., Surrey, BC V3S 4H1
Tel: 604-574-7431; *Fax*: 604-574-3021

Surrey: Maier & Co. - *1
#310, 10524 King George Hwy., Surrey, BC V3S 2X2
Tel: 604-582-5951; *Fax*: 604-588-0779
maier@telus.net

Surrey: Manthorpe Law Offices - *1
#102, 15399 - 102A Ave., Surrey, BC V3R 7K1
Tel: 604-582-7743; *Fax*: 604-582-7753

Surrey: A.L. McAndrew - *1
#240, 13711 - 72 Ave., Surrey, BC V3W 2P2
Tel: 604-591-2288; *Fax*: 604-591-7366

Surrey: Cameron C. McLeod - *1
#310, 10524 King George Hwy, Surrey, BC V3T 2X2
Tel: 604-583-6318; *Fax*: 604-588-0779
mcleodlaw@dccnet.com

Surrey: McQuarrie Hunter LLP - *26
#200, 13889 - 104th Ave., Surrey, BC V3T 1W8
Tel: 604-581-0461; *Fax*: 604-581-7110
www.mcquarrie.com

Surrey: Allan D. McRae - *1
#309, 1656 Martin Dr., Surrey, BC V4A 6E7
Tel: 604-538-1511

Surrey: Murchison Thomson & Clarke LLP - *23
#101, Surrey Central Business Park, 7565 - 132 St., Surrey, BC V3W 1K5
Tel: 604-590-8855; *Fax*: 604-590-2000
info@murchisonthomson.com
www.murchisonthomson.com

Surrey: Nyack & Persad - *2
#201, 9380 - 120 St., Surrey, BC V3V 4B9
Tel: 604-588-9933; *Fax*: 604-588-2731
nyackpersad@hotmail.com

Surrey: Michael G. Parent, Law Corporation - *1
#203, 15225 - 104 Ave., Surrey, BC V3R 6Y8
Tel: 604-589-6437; *Fax*: 604-589-7238

Surrey: Peterson Stark Scott - *11
#300, 10355 - 136A Street, Surrey, BC V3T 5R3
Tel: 604-588-9321; *Fax*: 604-589-5391
Toll-Free: 800-555-3288
sry@psslaw.ca
www.psslaw.ca

Surrey: Donald F. Porter - *1
#203, 8318 - 120 St., Surrey, BC V3W 3N4
Tel: 604-594-5155; *Fax*: 604-594-1304
dfporter@allstream.net

Surrey: Richards & Richards - *3
10325 - 150 St., Surrey, BC V3R 4B1
Tel: 604-588-6844; *Fax*: 604-588-8800
richard.george@richardslaw.com

Surrey: E.R. Swedahl - *1
#11, 15243 - 91 Ave., Surrey, BC V3R 8P8
Tel: 604-581-3232; *Fax*: 604-589-3741

Surrey: Taylor, Bjorge & Company - *2
#205, 1676 Martin Dr., Surrey, BC V4A 6E7
Tel: 604-536-1117; *Fax*: 604-536-0445

Surrey: Gordon G. Walters - *1
12321 Beecher St., Surrey, BC V4A 3A7
Tel: 604-596-3300; *Fax*: 604-535-7350

Surrey: P. Barry Whaites - *1
#200, 5746 - 176A St., Surrey, BC V3S 4H2
Tel: 604-574-0770; *Fax*: 604-574-0107

Terrace: Crampton Personal Law Corporation - *2
4623 Park Ave., Terrace, BC V8G 1V5
Tel: 250-635-6330; *Fax*: 250-635-4795
Toll-Free: 800-667-0080
Gordon_Crampton@telus.net; bryan_crampton@telus.net

Terrace: Talstra & Company - *3
#101, 3219 Eby St., Terrace, BC V8G 4R3
Tel: 250-638-1137; *Fax*: 250-638-1306
Toll-Free: 877-998-4222

Terrace: Warner Bandstra Brown - *5
#200, 4630 Lazelle Ave., Terrace, BC V8G 1S6
Tel: 250-635-2622; *Fax*: 250-635-4998

Trail: Ghilarducci & Cromarty - *2
1309 Bay Ave., Trail, BC V1R 4A7
Tel: 250-368-6455; *Fax*: 250-368-6107

Trail: McEwan Harrison & Co. - *5
1432 Bay Ave., Trail, BC V1R 4B1
Tel: 250-368-8211; *Fax*: 250-368-9401
www.mcewanharrison.com

Trail: Westcott Simpkin & Co. - *1
1402 Bay Ave., Trail, BC V1R 4B1
Tel: 250-358-9171; *Fax*: 250-368-3369
westcottlaw@shawbiz.ca

Ucluelet: James P. Roth - *1
CP 909, 1566 Peninsula Rd., Ucluelet, BC V0R 3A0
Tel: 250-726-4307; *Fax*: 250-726-2180
info@macisaacgroup.com
www.macisaacgroup.com

Vancouver: Aaron, Gordon & Daykin - *6
#600, 815 Hornby St., Vancouver, BC V6Z 2E6
Tel: 604-689-7571; *Fax*: 604-685-8563
reception@agdlaw.ca
www.agdlaw.ca

Vancouver: Access Law Group - *7
#1700, 1185 Georgia St. West, Vancouver, BC V6E 4E6
Tel: 604-689-8000; *Fax*: 604-689-8835
reception@accesslaw.ca
www.accesslaw.ca

Vancouver: Jack A. Adelaar - *1
#1702, 808 Nelson St., Vancouver, BC V6Z 2H2
Tel: 604-687-8840; *Fax*: 604-687-8370
jadelaar@telus.net

Vancouver: Adrian & Company - *2
5660 Yew St., Vancouver, BC V6M 3Y3
Tel: 604-266-7811; *Fax*: 604-266-5869

Vancouver: Alexander Holburn Beaudin & Lang, LLP - *75
#2700, P.O. Box 10057, 700 West Georgia St., Vancouver, BC V7Y 1B8
Tel: 604-484-1700; *Fax*: 604-484-9700
Toll-Free: 877-688-1351
info@ahbl.ca
www.ahbl.ca

Vancouver: William J. Alexander Law Corporation - *1
#167, 1917 - 4th Ave. West, Vancouver, BC V6J 1M7
Tel: 604-831-3743; *Fax*: 604-831-6273

Vancouver: Allan & Lougheed - *2
1622 - 7th Ave. West, 2nd Fl., Vancouver, BC V6J 1S5
Tel: 604-733-2411; *Fax*: 604-736-6225
aandllaw@telus.net

Vancouver: Altridge & Company - *1
#741, 1489 Marine Dr., Vancouver, BC V7T 1B8
Tel: 604-688-3557; *Fax*: 604-688-0535
pga@altridge.com
www.altridge.com

** indicates number of lawyers*

Vancouver: **Alvin Hui Law Corp. - *1**
1606 Hornby St., Vancouver, BC V6Z 2T4
Tel: 604-732-3898; *Fax:* 604-739-2821
ahlc@telus.net

Vancouver: **Paul Andersen - *2**
1662 - 8th Ave. West, Vancouver, BC V6J 4R8
Tel: 604-734-8411; *Fax:* 604-734-8511
andersen_paul@telus.net

Vancouver: **Brian W. Anderson Law Corporation - *1**
835 Granville St., 2nd Fl., Vancouver, BC V6Z 1K7
Tel: 604-684-5367

Vancouver: **Jane Anderson - *1**
#1782, 808 Nelson St., Vancouver, BC V6Z 2H2
Tel: 604-488-1162; *Fax:* 604-488-0666
janeanderso@telus.net

Vancouver: **Anfield Sujir Kennedy & Durno - *6**
#1600, Pacific Centre, P.O. Box 10068, 609 Granville St., Vancouver, BC V7Y 1C3
Tel: 604-669-1322; *Fax:* 604-669-3877
mailbox@askdlaw.com

Vancouver: **Armstrong Simpson - *4**
#2080, 777 Hornby St., Vancouver, BC V6Z 1S4
Tel: 604-683-7361; *Fax:* 604-662-3231

Vancouver: **Aydin Bird - *4**
#530, North Office Tower, 650 - 41 Ave. West, Vancouver, BC V5Z 2M9
Tel: 604-266-5828; *Fax:* 604-266-3929
aydin@aydinco.com
www.aydinco.com

Vancouver: **Baker & Baker - *3**
808 Nelson St., 17th Fl., Vancouver, BC V6Z 2H2
Tel: 604-642-0107; *Fax:* 604-681-3504
info@bakerbaker.ca
www.bakerbaker.ca

Vancouver: **Barbeau, Evans, Goldstein - *4**
#280, 666 Burrard St., Vancouver, BC V6C 2X8
Tel: 604-688-4900; *Fax:* 604-688-0649
info@beg-law.com
www.beg-law.com

Vancouver: **Gail Barnes - *1**
149 Main St., Vancouver, BC V6A 2S5
Tel: 604-684-1124; *Fax:* 604-684-1122
egray@sprint.ca

Vancouver: **Barrigar Intellectual Property Law - *5**
#202, 543 Seymour St., Vancouver, BC V6C 1X8
Tel: 604-689-9255; *Fax:* 604-689-9265
email@barrigar.com
www.barrigar.com

Vancouver: **Basham Thompson & Liu - *7**
#2550, Granville Sq., 200 Granville St., Vancouver, BC V6C 1S4
Tel: 604-601-3863; *Fax:* 604-681-8632

Vancouver: **Beach Avenue Barristers, A Law Corporation - *3**
#150, 1008 Beach Avenue, Vancouver, BC V6E 1T7
Tel: 604-629-0429; *Fax:* 604-689-4451

Vancouver: **Beck, Robinson & Company - *4**
#700, 686 West Broadway, Vancouver, BC V5Z 1G1
Tel: 604-874-0204; *Fax:* 604-874-0820
lawyers@beckrobinson.com
www.beckrobinson.com

Vancouver: **P.J. Beirne**
157 Alexander St., 3rd Fl., Vancouver, BC V6A 1B8
Tel: 604-683-4311; *Fax:* 604-683-4317

Vancouver: **David R. Bellamy - *1**
#101, 1012 Beach Ave., Vancouver, BC V6E 1T7
Tel: 604-662-8900; *Fax:* 604-662-8902
dbellamy@bellamy.bc.ca

Vancouver: **Robert W. Bellows - *1**
#620, 1385 West 8 Ave., Vancouver, BC V6H 3V9
Tel: 604-736-5500; *Fax:* 604-736-5522
rbellows@telus.net

Vancouver: **Bennett, Parkes - *2**
#460, 2609 Granville St., Vancouver, BC V6H 3H3
Tel: 604-734-6838; *Fax:* 604-738-6789

Vancouver: **Bernard & Partners - *15**
#1500, 570 Granville St., Vancouver, BC V6C 3P1
Tel: 604-681-1700; *Fax:* 604-681-1788
tuytel@bernardpartners.com
www.bernardpartners.com

Vancouver: **Shoni Lee Bernard - *1**
5052 Victoria Dr., Vancouver, BC V5P 3T8
Tel: 604-473-9330; *Fax:* 604-323-0093

Vancouver: **Beruschi & Company - *2**
#501, 905 West Pender St., Vancouver, BC V6C 1L6
Tel: 604-669-3116; *Fax:* 604-669-5886
admin@beruschi.com

Vancouver: **Raymond J. Bianchin - *1**
#410, 2609 Granville St., Vancouver, BC V6H 3H3
Tel: 604-683-8111; *Fax:* 604-685-0194

Vancouver: **Birnie & Company - *2**
#2433, Three Bentall Centre, P.O. Box 49116, Stn. Bentall, 595 Burrard St., Vancouver, BC V7X 1G4
Tel: 604-688-4511; *Fax:* 604-688-0511
dbirnie@birnieco.com

Vancouver: **Pamela S. Boles - *1**
#210, 970 Burrard St., Vancouver, BC V6Z 2R4
Tel: 604-688-5001; *Fax:* 604-685-5006

Vancouver: **Bolton & Muldoon - *4**
#360, 1122 Mainland St., Vancouver, BC V6B 5L1
Tel: 604-687-7078; *Fax:* 604-687-3022

Vancouver: **Boughton Law Corporation - *50**
#700, P.O. Box 49290, 595 Burrard St., Vancouver, BC V7X 1S8
Tel: 604-687-6789; *Fax:* 604-683-5317
lawyers@boughton.ca
www.boughton.ca

Vancouver: **Joyce W. Bradley - *1**
P.O. Box 45565, Stn. Westside, Vancouver, BC V6S 2N5
Tel: 604-732-3886; *Fax:* 604-732-3781
jwbmediate@telus.net

Vancouver: **W. Anita Braha - *1**
P.O. Box 65986, Stn. F, Vancouver, BC V5N 5L4
Tel: 604-251-2526; *Fax:* 604-251-2606

Vancouver: **H.K. Brown - *1**
#1504, 100 West Pender St., 15th Fl., Vancouver, BC V6B 1R8
Tel: 604-684-1021; *Fax:* 604-688-6243
henrykbrownlawcorporation@telus.net

Vancouver: **Peter W. Brown Law Corp. - *2**
2081 - 37 Ave. West, Vancouver, BC V6M 1N7
Tel: 604-261-0300; *Fax:* 604-261-0312
peterwbrown@owblawcorp.com

Vancouver: **J.G. Buchanan - *1**
#788, 601 West Broadway, Vancouver, BC V5Z 4C2
Tel: 604-876-0343; *Fax:* 604-876-9035

Vancouver: **Bull, Housser & Tupper LLP - *100**
#3000, Royal Centre, P.O. Box 11130, 1055 West Georgia St., Vancouver, BC V6E 3R3
Tel: 604-687-6575; *Fax:* 604-641-4949
Toll-Free: 888-687-6575
mailbox@bht.com
www.bht.com

Vancouver: **Susan P. Burak, Lawyer, Mediator & Collaborative Lawyer - *1**
1622 - 7th Ave West, 2nd Fl., Vancouver, BC V6J 1S5
Tel: 604-733-2411; *Fax:* 604-736-6225
ajzburak@shaw.ca

Vancouver: **Burke & Jones - *2**
687 - 20th Ave. East, Vancouver, BC V5V 1M9
Tel: 604-879-6365; *Fax:* 604-879-6367
acb@burkeandjones.com

Vancouver: **Burns, Fitzpatrick, Rogers & Schwartz - *8**
#1400, 510 Burrard St., Vancouver, BC V6C 3A8
Tel: 604-685-0121; *Fax:* 604-685-2104
bfrs@bfrs.ca
www.bfrs.ca

Vancouver: **Burrard Communications Inc. - *1**
#200, 409 Granville St., Vancouver, BC V6C 1T2
Tel: 604-619-1980; *Fax:* 604-689-0477

Vancouver: **Bradley M. Caldwell - *1**
#401, 815 Hornby St., Vancouver, BC V6Z 2E6
Tel: 604-689-8894; *Fax:* 604-689-5739

Vancouver: **Cawkell Brodie Glaister LLP - *4**
#1260, 1188 Georgia St. West, Vancouver, BC V6E 4A2
Tel: 604-684-3323; *Fax:* 604-684-3350
info@cawkell.org
www.cawkell.com

Vancouver: **Chalke & Company - *1**
708-1155 W. Pender St., Vancouver, BC V6E 2P4
Tel: 604-980-4855; *Fax:* 604-980-6469

Vancouver: **Chan Yue & Lee - *1**
#212, 475 Main St., Vancouver, BC V6A 2T7
Tel: 604-687-4576; *Fax:* 604-683-3258
canyua@intergate.ca

Vancouver: **Chen & Leung - *9**
#728, North Tower, Oakridge Centre, 650 - 41st Ave. West, Vancouver, BC V5Z 2M9
Tel: 604-264-8331; *Fax:* 604-264-8387
info@cllawyers.ca
www.cllawyers.ca

Vancouver: **Chow & Company - *1**
378 Smithe St., Vancouver, BC V6B 1T7
Tel: 604-669-0268; *Fax:* 604-669-9863
n-chow@telus.net

Vancouver: **Gregory T. Chu - *1**
#650, 1188 West Georgia St., Vancouver, BC V6E 4A2
Tel: 604-628-5005; *Fax:* 604-987-9939
gtchu@telus.net

Vancouver: **Clark Wilson LLP - *80**
#800, 885 Georgia St. West, Vancouver, BC V6C 3H1
Tel: 604-687-5700; *Fax:* 604-687-6314
agb@cwilson.com
www.cwilson.com

Vancouver: **Cobb St. Pierre - *6**
#308, 425 Carrall St., Vancouver, BC V6B 6E3
Tel: 604-602-9770; *Fax:* 604-684-9690
info@acquit.ca

Vancouver: **Cochran Bradshaw - *3**
439 Helmcken St., Vancouver, BC V6B 2E6
Tel: 604-681-9200; *Fax:* 604-681-8339
cochranlaw@telus.net

Vancouver: **Morley E. Cofman Law Corporation - *1**
#1500, 701 West Georgia St., Vancouver, BC V7Y 1C6
Tel: 604-696-6674; *Fax:* 604-801-5911
mcofman@shaw.ca

Vancouver: **Leonard M. Cohen - *1**
#570, 999 West Broadway, Vancouver, BC V5Z 1K5
Tel: 604-731-8118

Vancouver: **Brian Coleman Q.C. - *1**
#380, 425 Carrall St., Vancouver, BC V6B 6E3
Tel: 604-683-5821; *Fax:* 604-683-9354
coleman@telus.net

Vancouver: **Guy J. Collette - *1**
#605, 1080 Howe St., Vancouver, BC V6Z 2T1
Tel: 604-662-7777; *Fax:* 604-669-4053
guy@collettelaw.com
www.collettelaw.com

Vancouver: **Collins & Cullen - *2**
#750, 999 West Broadway, Vancouver, BC V5Z 1K5
Tel: 604-730-2678; *Fax:* 604-730-2628

Vancouver: **James Comparelli - *2**
#704, 510 West Hastings St., Vancouver, BC V6B 1L8
Tel: 604-683-6888; *Fax:* 604-683-4497
james@comparelli.com
www.comparelli.com

Vancouver: **Carla Courtenay Law Office - *1**
#501, 815 Hornby St., Vancouver, BC V6Z 2E6
Tel: 604-682-2200; *Fax:* 604-682-2246
lilias@cclaw.bc.ca
www.cclaw.bc.ca

Vancouver: **Coutts Weiler & Pulver - *8**
#1485, P.O. Box 253, 555 Burrard St., Vancouver, BC V7X 1M9
Tel: 604-682-1866; *Fax:* 604-682-6947
info@cwplaw.ca
www.cwplaw.ca

** indicates number of lawyers*

Vancouver: Raffaele Crescenzo - *1
#206, 1651 Commercial Dr., Vancouver, BC V5L 3Y3
Tel: 604-255-9030; *Fax*: 604-255-9075

Vancouver: F.S. Crestani - *1
5052 Victoria Dr., Vancouver, BC V5P 3T8
Tel: 604-251-1168; *Fax*: 604-253-7726

Vancouver: Kenneth Cristall - *1
#610, P.O. Box 12110, 808 Nelson St., Vancouver, BC V6Z 2H2
Tel: 604-654-2250; *Fax*: 604-682-8879

Vancouver: Harry Crosby - *1
5052 Victoria Dr., Vancouver, BC V5P 3T8
Tel: 604-321-6922; *Fax*: 604-323-0093

Vancouver: Crossin Coristine Woodall - *5
#660, 220 Cambie St., Vancouver, BC V6B 2M9
Tel: 604-689-3242; *Fax*: 604-689-3292

Vancouver: Cruickshank Huinink Zukerman - *3
#250, 1122 Mainland St., Vancouver, BC V6B 5L1
Tel: 604-688-3933; *Fax*: 604-681-6677

Vancouver: Cummings Law Corporation - *1
#320, 650 West 41st Ave., Vancouver, BC V5Z 2M9
Tel: 604-264-7038; *Fax*: 604-264-7039
info@cummingslawcorp.com

Vancouver: Barbara J. Curran
#407, 825 Granville St., Vancouver, BC V6Z 1K9
Tel: 604-689-4501; *Fax*: 604-689-5572
bjcurran@telus.net

Vancouver: Cuttler & Company
CP 12184, Stn. Nelson Square, #1811, 808 Nelson St., Vancouver, BC V6Z 2H2
Tel: 604-673-4225; *Fax*: 604-633-1838

Vancouver: D. Brad Henry Law Corporation - *1
#1900, 1177 West Hastings Street, Vancouver, BC V6E 2K3
Tel: 604-718-6892; *Fax*: 604-718-6873

Vancouver: Aspha J. Dada & Co. - *2
2479 Kingsway, Vancouver, BC V5R 5G8
Tel: 604-433-3300; *Fax*: 604-436-3937
info-ajd@telus.net

Vancouver: Dallas & Company - *2
852 Seymour St., Vancouver, BC V6B 3L6
Tel: 604-681-6171; *Fax*: 604-683-1000
dallas&co@telus.net

Vancouver: A. Kenneth Dangerfield - *1
#1000, P.O. Box 49290, Stn. Bentall, 595 Burrard St., Vancouver, BC V7X 1S8
Tel: 604-687-6789; *Fax*: 604-683-5317
kdangerfield@boughton.ca

Vancouver: Greg Delbigio
#1720, 355 Burrard St., Vancouver, BC V6C 2G8
Tel: 604-687-9831; *Fax*: 604-687-7089
greg_delbigio@telus.net

Vancouver: A.J. DeMeulemeester - *1
#202, 119 Pender St. West, Vancouver, BC V6B 1S5
Tel: 604-685-6610; *Fax*: 604-682-5687

Vancouver: Derpak, White & Company - *3
#901, 1788 Broadway West, Vancouver, BC V6J 1Y1
Tel: 604-736-9791; *Fax*: 604-736-7197
derpakwhite@telus.net

Vancouver: Directis Consulting Group Ltd. - *1
#720, 999 Broadway West, Vancouver, BC V5Z 1K5
Tel: 604-730-2668
sue@directis.ca

Vancouver: J.W. Dobbin - *1
123 Main St., Vancouver, BC V6A 2S5
Tel: 604-669-6045; *Fax*: 604-669-6041
jwd@jwdobbin.com

Vancouver: David H. Doig & Associates - *2
#1450, 1188 Georgia St. West, Vancouver, BC V6E 4A2
Tel: 604-687-8874; *Fax*: 604-687-8134
ddoig@daviddoig.com

Vancouver: Dolden Wallace Folick LLP - *17
888 Dunsmuir St., 10th Fl., Vancouver, BC V6C 3K4
Tel: 604-689-3222; *Fax*: 604-689-3777
info@dolden.com
www.dolden.com

Vancouver: Donaldson Jetté - *4
#490, 1090 Hornby St., Vancouver, BC V6B 2W9
Tel: 604-681-5232; *Fax*: 604-681-1331
hrusso@donaldsonjette.ca

Vancouver: Donna L. Kydd Law Corporation - *1
#250, 1501 West Broadway, Vancouver, BC V6J 4Z6
Tel: 604-732-5031; *Fax*: 604-732-5071
dlkydd@kyddlaw.ca; sthomas@kyddlaw.ca
www.kyddlaw.ca

Vancouver: Donovan & Company - *9
73 Water St., 6th Fl., Vancouver, BC V6B 1A1
Tel: 604-688-4272; *Fax*: 604-688-4282
allan_donovan@aboriginal-law.com
www.aboriginal-law.com

Vancouver: Emil M. Doricic - *1
195 Alexander St., 2nd Fl., Vancouver, BC V6A 1B8
Tel: 604-688-8338; *Fax*: 604-688-8356

Vancouver: Le Dressay & Company - *1
#103, 1525 - 8th Ave. West, Vancouver, BC V6J 1T5
Tel: 604-739-0017; *Fax*: 604-739-0041
dan@ledressay.com

Vancouver: DuMoulin Boskovich LLP - *16
#1800, Manulife Place, Box 52, 1095 West Pender St., Vancouver, BC V6E 2M6
Tel: 604-669-5500; *Fax*: 604-688-8491
Toll-Free: 800-288-9893
info@dubo.com
www.dubo.comwww.linkedin.com/company/2293070?trk=tyah

Vancouver: Dunnaway, Jackson & Associates - *2
#1205, 808 Nelson St., Vancouver, BC V6Z 2H2
Tel: 604-682-0007; *Fax*: 604-682-8711

Vancouver: Earnscliffe BC Inc. - *2
#617, 1030 West Georgia St., Vancouver, BC V6E 2Y3
Tel: 604-678-2900; *Fax*: 604-678-2904
mdrummond@earnscliffe.ca

Vancouver: Edwards, Kenny & Bray LLP - *27
#1900, The Grosvenor Bldg., 1040 West Georgia St., Vancouver, BC V6E 4H3
Tel: 604-689-1811; *Fax*: 604-689-5177
inquiry@ekb.com
www.ekb.com

Vancouver: Ellis, Nauss & Jones - *2
#600, 1665 West Broadway, Vancouver, BC V6J 1X1
Tel: 604-731-9276; *Fax*: 604-734-0206

Vancouver: Ellis, Roadburg - *2
#200, 853 Richards St., Vancouver, BC V6B 3B4
Tel: 604-669-7131; *Fax*: 604-669-7684

Vancouver: Embarkation Law Group - *6
#600, P.O. Box 26, 609 West Hastings St., 6th Fl., Vancouver, BC V6B 4W4
Tel: 604-662-7404; *Fax*: 604-662-7466
Toll-Free: 888-662-7404
info@elgcanada.com
www.elgcanada.com

Vancouver: Dick W. Eng Law Corp. - *1
#701, 601 Broadway West, Vancouver, BC V5Z 4C2
Tel: 604-877-0880; *Fax*: 604-877-0330
dick.eng@telus.net

Vancouver: Robert J. Falconer, Q.C. - *1
#400, 409 Granville St., Vancouver, BC V6C 1T2
Tel: 604-683-5674; *Fax*: 604-682-8417
robert.falconer@axion.net

Vancouver: Fan & Co. - *3
#601, 609 Gore Ave., Vancouver, BC V6A 2Z8
Tel: 604-683-0471; *Fax*: 604-683-8748
hfan@telus.net

Vancouver: Farris, Vaughan, Wills & Murphy LLP - *87
700 West Georgia St., 25th Floor, Vancouver, BC V7Y 1B3
Tel: 604-684-9151; *Fax*: 604-661-9349
info@farris.com
www.farris.com

Vancouver: Fayers & Company - *2
#380, 5740 Cambie St., Vancouver, BC V5Z 3A6
Tel: 604-325-1246; *Fax*: 604-325-1261

Vancouver: Larry C. Flader - *1
4244 Doncaster Way, Vancouver, BC V6S 2L6
Tel: 604-224-7225

Vancouver: Robert S. Fleming - *1
#107, 5605 Hampton Pl., Vancouver, BC V6T 2H2
Tel: 604-682-1659; *Fax*: 604-633-1838
rsfleming@telus.net

Vancouver: Constance C. Fogal - *1
3570 Hull St., Vancouver, BC V5N 4R9
Tel: 604-872-2128

Vancouver: Fraser & Company - *9
#1200, 999 Hastings St. West, Vancouver, BC V6C 2W2
Tel: 604-669-5244; *Fax*: 604-669-5791
securities@fraserlaw.com

Vancouver: Gordon J. Fretwell Law Corp. - *1
#1780, 400 Burrard St., Vancouver, BC V6C 3A6
Tel: 604-689-1280; *Fax*: 604-689-1288
law@fretwell.ca
www.fretwell.ca

Vancouver: Friesen & Epp - *4
5660 Yew St., Vancouver, BC V6M 3Y3
Tel: 604-264-8386; *Fax*: 604-264-8815
erwinepp@stargate.ca

Vancouver: Ganapathi & Company - *2
#302, 1224 Hamilton St., Vancouver, BC V6B 2S8
Tel: 604-689-9222; *Fax*: 604-689-4888
Toll-Free: 866-689-9222
nathan@ganapathico.com; info@ganapathico.com
www.ganapathico.com

Vancouver: Alnoor R.S. Gangji - *1
#788, 601 West Broadway, Vancouver, BC V5Z 4C2
Tel: 604-708-3783; *Fax*: 604-876-9035
aglawyer@dowco.com

Vancouver: Donald R. Gardner - *1
#402, 195 Alexander St., Vancouver, BC V6A 1N8
Tel: 604-687-1766; *Fax*: 604-687-0181
barristerfromsmu@hotmail.com

Vancouver: Robert G. Gateman - *1
#202, 1112 Brougton St., Vancouver, BC V6G 2A8
Tel: 604-687-4911
gateman@interchange.bc.ca

Vancouver: Gayle D. Gavin - *1
4168 - 11th Ave., Vancouver, BC V6R 2L6
Tel: 604-222-2827

Vancouver: Getz Prince Wells LLP - *8
#1810, 1111 West Georgia St., Vancouver, BC V6E 4M3
Tel: 604-685-6367; *Fax*: 604-685-9798
admin@getzpw.com
www.getzpw.com

Vancouver: Gibbons Fowler Nathanson - *6
#440, The Marine Building, 355 Burrard St., Vancouver, BC V6C 2G8
Tel: 604-684-0778; *Fax*: 604-684-0799
reception@gibbonsfowler.com
www.gibbonsfowler.com

Vancouver: Kenneth Glasner Q.C. Law Corp. - *1
#1414, P.O. Box 12158, 808 Nelson St., Vancouver, BC V6Z 2H2
Tel: 604-683-4181; *Fax*: 604-683-0226
glasnerqc@telus.net

Vancouver: Global Trade Resources - *1
#609, 1009 Expo Blvd., Vancouver, BC V6Z 2V9
Tel: 604-306-7475; *Fax*: 604-682-7477
irehmanji@novuscom.net

Vancouver: Goldman Zimmer Bray - *3
#950, 1111 Melville St., Vancouver, BC V6E 3V6
Tel: 604-682-6181; *Fax*: 604-683-5723
ngoldman@goldmath.com

Vancouver: C.H.J. Gordon - *1
#115, 2025 - 1st Ave. West, Vancouver, BC V6J 1H1
Tel: 604-730-8838

Vancouver: P.D. Gornall - *1
#1820, 355 Burrard St., Vancouver, BC V6C 2G8
Tel: 604-681-7932; *Fax*: 604-775-8555
pdg@telus.net

Vancouver: GR Strategies Inc. - *1
#602, 134 Abbott St., Vancouver, BC V6B 2K4
Tel: 604-685-6303
cg@grstrategies.com

** indicates number of lawyers*

Vancouver: **Granger & Co. - *2**
#1400, 777 Hornby St., Vancouver, BC V6Z 1S4
Tel: 604-685-1900; *Fax:* 604-685-2034

Vancouver: **Murray H. Grant - *1**
#2020, P.O. Box 11547, 650 West Georgia St., Vancouver, BC V6B 4N7
Tel: 604-683-9621; *Fax:* 604-683-5084

Vancouver: **Granville Law Group - *2**
#200, 835 Granville St., Vancouver, BC V6Z 1K7
Tel: 604-669-6580; *Fax:* 604-688-7291

Vancouver: **Grossman & Stanley, Business Lawyers - *4**
#800, Box 55, 1090 West Georgia St., Vancouver, BC V6E 3V7
Tel: 604-683-7454; *Fax:* 604-683-8602
info@grossmanstanley.com
www.grossmanstanley.com

Vancouver: **Gudmundseth Mickelson LLP - *6**
#2525, 1075 West Georgia St., Vancouver, BC V6E 3C9
Tel: 604-685-6272; *Fax:* 604-685-8434
info@lawgm.com

Vancouver: **W.F. Guinn - *1**
671G Market Hill, Vancouver, BC V5Z 4B5
Tel: 604-872-6658; *Fax:* 604-876-3304

Vancouver: **Guy & Company - *1**
#100, 190 Alexander St., Vancouver, BC V6A 1B5
Tel: 604-681-6164; *Fax:* 604-681-7420
guy_and_company@telus.net

Vancouver: **Hara & Company - *2**
#301, 460 Nanaimo St., Vancouver, BC V5L 4W3
Tel: 604-255-4800; *Fax:* 604-255-8111
haraco@telus.net

Vancouver: **Harper Grey LLP - *53**
#3200, Vancouver Centre, 650 West Georgia St., Vancouver, BC V6B 4P7
Tel: 604-687-0411; *Fax:* 604-669-9385
info@harpergrey.com
www.harpergrey.com

Vancouver: **Harris & Brun - *6**
555 West Georgia St., Vancouver, BC V6B 1Z5
Tel: 604-683-2466; *Fax:* 604-683-4541

Vancouver: **Harris & Company LLP - *33**
Bentall 5, 550 Burrard St., 14th Floor, Vancouver, BC V6C 2B5
Tel: 604-684-6633; *Fax:* 604-684-6632
info@harrisco.com
www.harrisco.com

Vancouver: **Heddema & Partners LLP - *4**
#2800, P.O. Box 49279, Stn. Bentall Centre, 1055 Dunsmuir St., Vancouver, BC V7X 1P4
Tel: 604-669-4416; *Fax:* 604-681-4184
lawyers@heddemalaw.ca

Vancouver: **John E. Helsing - *1**
#347, 1275 West 6th Ave., Vancouver, BC V6H 1A6
Tel: 604-739-7731; *Fax:* 604-738-7134

Vancouver: **Hemsworth, Schmidt - *2**
#430, 580 Hornby St., Vancouver, BC V6C 3B6
Tel: 604-687-4456; *Fax:* 604-687-0586

Vancouver: **Hobbs Giroday - *3**
#908, 938 Howe St., Vancouver, BC V6Z 1N9
Tel: 604-669-6609; *Fax:* 604-669-6612
www.hobbsgiroday.com

Vancouver: **Hogan & Company - *1**
#900, 850 Hastings St. West, Vancouver, BC V6C 1E1
Tel: 604-687-8806; *Fax:* 604-687-7089

Vancouver: **Holmes & Company - *2**
#1880, 1066 Hastings St. West, Vancouver, BC V6E 3X1
Tel: 604-688-7861; *Fax:* 604-688-0426
sdh@holmescompany.com
www.holmescompany.comwww.linkedin.com/company/holmes-and-company

Vancouver: **Holmes & King - *4**
#1300, 1111 Georgia St. West, Vancouver, BC V6E 4M3
Tel: 604-681-1310; *Fax:* 604-681-1307
lawyers@mhklaw.com

Vancouver: **Hoogbruin & Company - *1**
#650, 1188 West Georgia St., Vancouver, BC V6E 4A2
Tel: 604-609-3783; *Fax:* 604-682-8348

Vancouver: **Hordo & Bennett - *8**
#1801, Nelson Sq., P.O. Box 12146, 808 Nelson St., Vancouver, BC V6Z 2H2
Tel: 604-682-5250; *Fax:* 604-682-7872
general@hrb.bc.ca

Vancouver: **Peter J. Hull - *1**
869 West 20 Ave., Vancouver, BC V5Z 1Y3
Tel: 604-874-0200

Vancouver: **Wayne Hum & Co. - *1**
#1608, 1166 Alberni St., Vancouver, BC V6E 3Z3
Tel: 604-687-6806; *Fax:* 604-687-6809

Vancouver: **Forrest C. Hume - *1**
#700, 1080 Howe St., Vancouver, BC V6Z 2T1
Tel: 604-488-1499; *Fax:* 604-488-1489
fchume@humelawcorp.com

Vancouver: **Hunter Litigation Chambers - *19**
#2100, 1040 West Georgia St., Vancouver, BC V6E 4H1
Tel: 604-891-2400; *Fax:* 604-647-4554
www.litigationchambers.com

Vancouver: **F.M. Irvine - *1**
4447, West 5th Ave., Vancouver, BC V6R 1S4
Tel: 604-224-5125; *Fax:* 604-224-5128
sirvine@interchange.ubc.ca

Vancouver: **Alex Irwin Law Corp. - *1**
#2620, Royal Centre, 1055 West Georgia St., Vancouver, BC V6E 3R5
Tel: 604-664-3720; *Fax:* 604-689-2806
alex@iwjlaw.com
www.iwjlaw.com

Vancouver: **Vahan A. Ishkanian - *1**
#1100, 1200 - 73rd Ave. West, Vancouver, BC V6P 6G5
Tel: 604-267-3033; *Fax:* 604-264-6133
vishkanian@pepito.ca

Vancouver: **Bridget M. Jacob - *1**
#1500, 701 West Georgia St., Vancouver, BC V7Y 1C6
Tel: 604-738-1080; *Fax:* 604-738-1088
Toll-Free: 888-738-1082
bmjacob@telus.net

Vancouver: **Donald Jang - *1**
#701, 601 West Broadway, Vancouver, BC V5Z 4C2
Tel: 604-877-0880; *Fax:* 604-877-0330

Vancouver: **Jeffery & Calder - *4**
#601, 815 Hornby St., Vancouver, BC V6Z 2E6
Tel: 604-669-5534; *Fax:* 604-669-7563
contact@jefferycalder.com
www.jefferycalder.com

Vancouver: **Jenkins Marzban Logan LLP - *17**
#900, Nelson Square, 808 Nelson St., Vancouver, BC V6Z 2H2
Tel: 604-681-6564; *Fax:* 604-681-0766
info@jml.ca
www.jml.ca

Vancouver: **J. Douglas Jevning - *1**
#1503, 100 West Pender St., Vancouver, BC V6B 1R8
Tel: 604-688-7414; *Fax:* 604-688-6243
doug_jevning@telus.net

Vancouver: **Josephson Angus Barristers - *3**
#906, Cathedral Place, 925 West Georgia St., Vancouver, BC V6C 3L2
Tel: 604-684-9887; *Fax:* 604-684-3221
contacts@jabarristers.ca
www.jabarristers.ca

Vancouver: **Steven B. Jung - *1**
#701, 601 West Broadway, Vancouver, BC V5Z 4C2
Tel: 604-877-2684; *Fax:* 604-877-0330
stevenjung@telus.net

Vancouver: **R.N. Jussa - *1**
#204, 4676 Main St., Vancouver, BC V5V 3R7
Tel: 604-872-8191; *Fax:* 604-872-8217

Vancouver: **Michael A. Kale Law Office - *1**
#1301, 808 Nelson St., Vancouver, BC V6Z 2H2
Tel: 604-685-8877; *Fax:* 604-685-3259
mkale@stevenskale.com

Vancouver: **Kaplan & Waddell - *3**
#102, 2590 Granville St., Vancouver, BC V6H 3H1
Tel: 604-736-8021; *Fax:* 604-736-3845

Vancouver: **Katz & Company - *1**
#1018, Nelson Square, P.O. Box 12135, 808 Nelson St., Vancouver, BC V6Z 2H2
Tel: 604-669-6226; *Fax:* 604-669-6752

Vancouver: **Peter M. Kendall - *1**
#850, 475 West Georgia St., Vancouver, BC V6B 4M9
Tel: 604-685-3512; *Fax:* 604-681-9142

Vancouver: **C. Robert Kennedy - *1**
#206, 190 Alexander St., Vancouver, BC V6A 1B5
Tel: 604-684-3927; *Fax:* 604-684-3228

Vancouver: **Kerfoot & Company - *4**
#300, 5687 Yew St., Vancouver, BC V6M 3Y2
Tel: 604-263-2565; *Fax:* 604-263-2737
bbk@kerfootandco.com
www.kerfootandco.com

Vancouver: **Khanna & Co. - *1**
#1540, 1100 Melville St., Vancouver, BC V6E 4A6
Tel: 604-605-5500; *Fax:* 604-689-5596

Vancouver: **Killam Cordell Murray - *4**
#2000, 401 Georgia St. West, Vancouver, BC V6B 5A1
Tel: 604-622-5252; *Fax:* 604-622-5244
sgc@killamcordel.com

Vancouver: **William N. King - *1**
#400, United Kingdom Bldg., 409 Granville St., Vancouver, BC V6C 1T2
Tel: 604-682-1245; *Fax:* 604-682-8417
janice.s@shaw.ca

Vancouver: **Klein, Lyons - *9**
#1100, 1333 Broadway West, Vancouver, BC V6H 4C1
Tel: 604-874-7171; *Fax:* 604-874-7180
info@kleinlyons.com
www.kleinlyons.com

Vancouver: **KM Technical Services - *1**
#PH 21, 2175 - 3 Ave. West, Vancouver, BC V6K 1L2
Tel: 250-247-9577
konrad.mauch@shaw.ca

Vancouver: **Koffman Kalef LLP - *22**
885 West Georgia St., 19th Fl., Vancouver, BC V6C 3H4
Tel: 604-891-3688; *Fax:* 604-891-3788
info@kkbl.com
www.kkbl.com

Vancouver: **Dimitri A. Kontou - *1**
#1550, 355 Burrard St., Vancouver, BC V6G 2C8
Tel: 604-662-7244; *Fax:* 604-687-3097
dkontou@telus.net

Vancouver: **Gordon Kopelow - *1**
#302, 1110 Hamilton St., Vancouver, BC V6B 2S2
Tel: 604-684-0096; *Fax:* 604-684-0048
gjkopelow@telus.net

Vancouver: **Kornfeld & Company - *2**
#310, 698 Seymour St., Vancouver, BC V6B 3K6
Tel: 604-689-3838; *Fax:* 604-689-0526

Vancouver: **Kornfeld Mackoff Silber LLP - *16**
#1100, Bentall Centre, CP 11, 505 Burrard St., Vancouver, BC V7X 1M5
Tel: 604-331-8300; *Fax:* 604-683-0570
Toll-Free: 866-331-8999
spertschi@kmslawyers.com
www.kmslawyers.com

Vancouver: **Ron Y. Kornfeld - *1**
1622 7th Ave. West, 2nd Fl., Vancouver, BC V6J 1S5
Tel: 604-733-2448; *Fax:* 604-736-5131
rykornfeld@telus.net

Vancouver: **Yoke Lam - *1**
#328, 88 East Pender St., Vancouver, BC V6A 1T1
Tel: 604-689-1123; *Fax:* 604-689-2003

Vancouver: **Lando & Company - *6**
#2010, Royal Centre, P.O. Box 11140, 1055 Georgia St. West, Vancouver, BC V6E 3P3
Tel: 604-682-6821; *Fax:* 604-662-8293
info@lando.ca
www.lando.ca

Vancouver: **Georgialee A. Lee & Associates - *4**
#1201, P.O. Box 12163, 808 Nelson St., Vancouver, BC V6Z 2H2
Tel: 604-669-2030; *Fax:* 604-669-2038

** indicates number of lawyers*

***Vancouver*: Stan N. Lanyon - *1**
#650, 475 Georgia St. West, Vancouver, BC V6B 4M9
Tel: 604-608-6108; *Fax:* 604-683-3846
stan.lanyon@arboffices.com

***Vancouver*: Laughton & Company - *2**
#1090, 1090 Georgia St. West, Vancouver, BC V6E 3V7
Tel: 604-683-6665; *Fax:* 604-683-6622

***Vancouver*: Law Office of David J. MacFarlane, Barrister & Solicitor**
#490, 99 West Broadway, Vancouver, BC V5Z 1K5
Tel: 604-732-7481; *Fax:* 604-732-3205
macper@telus.net

***Vancouver*: Lawson Lundell LLP - Vancouver - *100**
#1600, Cathedral Place, 925 West Georgia St., Vancouver, BC V6C 3L2
Tel: 604-685-3456; *Fax:* 604-669-1620
genmail@lawsonlundell.com
www.lawsonlundell.com

***Vancouver*: Laxton & Company - *3**
1285 West Pender St., 10th Fl., Vancouver, BC V6E 4B1
Tel: 604-682-3871; *Fax:* 604-682-3704

***Vancouver*: Valmon J. LeBlanc - *1**
#1400, 1125 Howe St., Vancouver, BC V6Z 2K8
Tel: 604-687-0909; *Fax:* 604-688-0933

***Vancouver*: Lecovin & Company - *2**
#560, P.O. Box 193, 1125 Howe St., Vancouver, BC V6Z 2K8
Tel: 604-687-1721; *Fax:* 604-687-1799
lecovin@intergate.ca

***Vancouver*: Lee & Company - *2**
#203, 856 Homer St., Vancouver, BC V6B 2W5
Tel: 604-687-1212; *Fax:* 604-669-6868

***Vancouver*: Jack L. Lee - *1**
127 East Pender St., 3rd Fl., Vancouver, BC V6A 1T6
Tel: 604-683-7241; *Fax:* 604-683-3279

***Vancouver*: Judith C. Lee - *1**
Sun Tower, 100 West Pender St., 10th Fl., Vancouver, BC V6B 1R8
Tel: 604-688-7972; *Fax:* 604-683-3886
judithlee@shaw.ca

***Vancouver*: Lesperance Mendes - *7**
#410, 900 Howe St., Vancouver, BC V6Z 2M4
Tel: 604-685-3567; *Fax:* 604-685-7505
kmw@lmlaw.ca
www.lmlaw.ca

***Vancouver*: Lew & Lee - *3**
#108, 329 Main St., Vancouver, BC V6A 2S9
Tel: 604-685-8331; *Fax:* 604-685-8334

***Vancouver*: Chuck Lew - *1**
#1010, 207 Hastings St. West, Vancouver, BC V6B 1H7
Tel: 604-688-3601; *Fax:* 604-688-7866
lewlaw@uniserve.com

***Vancouver*: H.H. Lew & Company - *1**
22 - 10th Ave. West, Vancouver, BC V5Y 1R6
Tel: 604-879-3151; *Fax:* 604-879-3707
hhlew@shaw.ca

***Vancouver*: Lex Pacifica Law Corporation - *1**
#1000, 543 Granville St., Vancouver, BC V6C 1X8
Tel: 604-689-1024; *Fax:* 604-689-1028
johnshevchuk@lexpacifica.com

***Vancouver*: Rhona M. Lichtenwald - *1**
#620, 1385 West 8 Ave., Vancouver, BC V6H 3V9
Tel: 604-739-4655; *Fax:* 604-739-9976
rhona@collaborativelawyer.ca
www.collaborativelawyer.ca

***Vancouver*: Carey Linde Personal Law Corporation - *2**
#605, 1080 Howe St., Vancouver, BC V6Z 2T1
Tel: 604-684-7794; *Fax:* 604-682-1243
lawyer@divorce-for-men.com
www.divorce-for-men.com

***Vancouver*: Lindsay Kenney LLP - *55**
#1800, 401 West Georgia St., Vancouver, BC V6B 5A1
Tel: 604-687-1323; *Fax:* 604-687-2347
Toll-Free: 866-687-1323
info@lklaw.ca
www.lklaw.ca

***Vancouver*: Lipetz & Company - *1**
#202, 2902 West Broadway, Vancouver, BC V6K 2G8
Tel: 604-733-5611; *Fax:* 604-738-5611

***Vancouver*: Keith A. Lo - *2**
#338, 237 Keefer St., Vancouver, BC V6A 1X6
Tel: 604-687-4315; *Fax:* 604-681-2289

***Vancouver*: Logan & Company**
#1500, 1030 Georgia St. West, Vancouver, BC V6E 2Y3
Tel: 604-682-8521; *Fax:* 604-682-8753

***Vancouver*: Loh & Company - *4**
#708, North Tower, 650 - 41st Ave. West, Vancouver, BC V5Z 2M9
Tel: 604-261-1234; *Fax:* 604-261-1222
general@lohandco.com

***Vancouver*: R.H. Long & Co. - *1**
865 - 46th Ave. West, Vancouver, BC V5Z 2R4
Tel: 604-876-0492; *Fax:* 604-876-3219
rhlong@shaw.ca

***Vancouver*: Tim Louis & Company - *1**
#208, 175 East Broadway, Vancouver, BC V5T 1W2
Tel: 604-732-7678; *Fax:* 604-732-7579
timlouis@timlouislaw.com
www.timlouislaw.com

***Vancouver*: Lowe & Company - *6**
#900, 777 West Broadway, Vancouver, BC V5Z 4J7
Tel: 604-875-9338; *Fax:* 604-875-1325
info@canadavisalaw.com
www.canadavisalaw.com

***Vancouver*: Phillip R. Lundrie - *2**
#3, 2597 Hastings St. East, 2nd Fl., Vancouver, BC V5K 1Z2
Tel: 604-257-3588; *Fax:* 604-257-3511
plundrie@aol.com

***Vancouver*: Lyons Hamilton - *4**
#404, 815 Hornby St., Vancouver, BC V6Z 2E6
Tel: 604-684-6718; *Fax:* 604-684-2501
lyonsco@mdi.ca

***Vancouver*: Macaulay McColl LLP - *9**
#1575, P.O. Box 11635, 650 West Georgia St., Vancouver, BC V6B 4N9
Tel: 604-687-9811; *Fax:* 604-687-8716
Toll-Free: 800-233-4405
lawyers@macaulay.com
www.macaulay.com

***Vancouver*: Macdonald Fahey**
#1900, 1177 West Hastings Street, Vancouver, BC V6E 2K3
Tel: 604-718-6869; *Fax:* 604-629-2175

***Vancouver*: MacKenzie Fujisawa LLP - *20**
#1600, 1095 West Pender St., Vancouver, BC V6E 2M6
Tel: 604-689-3281; *Fax:* 604-685-6494
lawyers@maclaw.bc.ca
www.mackenziefujisawa.com

***Vancouver*: MacKinlay Woodson Diebel - *2**
#1170, 1040 West Georgia St., Vancouver, BC V6E 4H1
Tel: 604-669-1511; *Fax:* 604-669-1566
corp@woodsonlaw.bc.ca

***Vancouver*: M. Diane MacKinnon - *1**
#728, 650 - 41st Ave. West, Vancouver, BC V5Z 2M9
Tel: 604-263-7891; *Fax:* 604-263-5781
mdmac@telus.net

***Vancouver*: MacLean Family Law Group - *4**
#3103, 1077 Cordova St. West, Vancouver, BC V6C 2C6
Tel: 604-602-9000; *Fax:* 604-682-0556
info@bcfamilylaw.ca

***Vancouver*: MacLeod & Company - *2**
#1900, 777 Hornby St., Vancouver, BC V6Z 1S4
Tel: 604-687-6731; *Fax:* 604-682-2534
bmacleod@macleodlaw.com
www.macleodlaw.com

***Vancouver*: Morag M.J. MacLeod - *1**
#800, 555 West Georgia St., Vancouver, BC V6B 1Z6
Tel: 604-430-8444; *Fax:* 604-430-1164
celtlaw@telus.net

***Vancouver*: Maitland & Company - *5**
#700, 625 Howe St., Vancouver, BC V6C 2T6
Tel: 604-681-7474; *Fax:* 604-681-3896
Toll-Free: 877-681-7474
maitco@maitland.com
www.maitland.com/Newindex

***Vancouver*: Mark R. Epstein Law Corporation - *2**
#1900, 1177 West Hastings Street, Vancouver, BC V6E 2K3
Tel: 604-685-4321; *Fax:* 604-685-7901

***Vancouver*: Maxwell Bulmer Hopman - *4**
900 Helmcken St., Vancouver, BC V6Z 1B3
Tel: 604-669-4912; *Fax:* 604-662-3975

***Vancouver*: Joanne S. McClusky - *1**
#810, 675 Hastings St. West, Vancouver, BC V6B 1N2
Tel: 604-689-4010; *Fax:* 604-684-2349
jmcclusky@telus.net

***Vancouver*: McCrea & Associates - *4**
#102, 1012 Beach Ave., Vancouver, BC V6E 1T7
Tel: 604-662-8200; *Fax:* 604-662-8225
lawyers@mccrealaw.ca
www.mccrealaw.ca

***Vancouver*: McCullough O'Connor Irwin LLP - *14**
#2610, Oceanic Plaza, 1066 West Hastings St., Vancouver, BC V6E 3X1
Tel: 604-687-7077; *Fax:* 604-687-7099
moimail@moisolicitors.com
www.moisolicitors.com

***Vancouver*: Ruth E. McIntyre - *1**
#1520, 355 Burrard St., Vancouver, BC V6C 2G8
Tel: 604-688-5185; *Fax:* 604-688-5186
www.rmcintyre.com

***Vancouver*: McKenzie & Company - *2**
891 Helmcken St., Vancouver, BC V6Z 1B1
Tel: 604-687-7811; *Fax:* 604-685-4358

***Vancouver*: McLachlan Brown Anderson - *9**
938 Howe St., 10th Fl., Vancouver, BC V6Z 1N9
Tel: 604-331-6000; *Fax:* 604-331-6008

***Vancouver*: Bruce E. McLeod - *1**
#1120, 1040 West Georgia St., Vancouver, BC V6E 4H1
Tel: 604-682-3133; *Fax:* 604-682-3161
bmcleod1@telus.net

***Vancouver*: McNeney & McNeney - *5**
#300, 195 Alexander St., Vancouver, BC V6A 1N8
Tel: 604-867-1766; *Fax:* 604-687-0181
Toll-Free: 800-535-6565
bikerlaw@kwik.net

***Vancouver*: Richard A. McPhee - *1**
#1025, 1185 West Georgia St., Vancouver, BC V6E 4E6
Tel: 604-682-0926; *Fax:* 604-688-8615
vml@pro.net

***Vancouver*: Megan Ellis & Company - *2**
#700, 555 Georgia St. West, Vancouver, BC V6B 1Z6
Tel: 604-683-7144; *Fax:* 604-683-0207

***Vancouver*: Brian E. Mickelson - *1**
100 West Pender St., 2nd Fl., Vancouver, BC V6B 1R8
Tel: 604-688-8588; *Fax:* 604-681-0652

***Vancouver*: John L. Mickelson - *2**
#302, 1110 Hamilton St., Vancouver, BC V6B 2S2
Tel: 604-684-0040; *Fax:* 604-684-0048
dajones@telus.net

***Vancouver*: Michael Mines - *1**
#1550, 355 Burrard St., Vancouver, BC V6C 2G8
Tel: 604-688-1460; *Fax:* 604-687-3097

***Vancouver*: MMK Consulting Inc. - *1**
#1202, 1130 Pender St. West, Vancouver, BC V6E 4A4
Tel: 604-484-4622; *Fax:* 604-738-2801
gmair@mmkconsulting.com

***Vancouver*: Morris & Co. - *2**
#460, 850 West Hastings St., Vancouver, BC V6C 1E1
Tel: 604-685-5175; *Fax:* 604-669-2744

***Vancouver*: Don Morrison - *2**
#1109, 207 West Hastings St., Vancouver, BC V6B 1H7
Tel: 604-685-7097; *Fax:* 604-662-7511
don.morrison@telus.net
www.donmorrisonlaw.com

***Vancouver*: Mortimer & Rose - *2**
#920, 777 Hornby St., Vancouver, BC V6Z 1S4
Tel: 604-669-0440; *Fax:* 604-669-0228

***Vancouver*: Murdy & McAllister - *7**
#1155, Two Bentall Centre, P.O. Box 49059, Stn. Bentall, 555 Burrard St., Vancouver, BC V7X 1C4
Tel: 604-689-5263; *Fax:* 604-689-9029

** indicates number of lawyers*

Vancouver: Murphy, McComb, Witten - *2
#208, 2800 - 1st Ave. East, Vancouver, BC V5M 4N9
Tel: 604-255-9018; *Fax:* 604-255-8588
info@mmw.bc.ca

Vancouver: Murray Jamieson - *6
#200, 1152 Mainland St., Vancouver, BC V6B 4X2
Tel: 604-688-0777; *Fax:* 604-688-9700
www.murrayjamieson.com

Vancouver: James B. Myers Law Corporation
#740, 475 West Georgia St., Vancouver, BC V6B 4M9
Tel: 604-682-2670; *Fax:* 604-682-2348

Vancouver: Myers, Waddell, McMurdo & Karp - *10
195 Alexander St., 5th Fl., Vancouver, BC V6A 1B8
Tel: 604-688-8331; *Fax:* 604-688-8350
Toll-Free: 888-244-9995
lm@myersco.ca
www.myersco.ca or www.vancouverdefencelawyer.com

Vancouver: Nathanson, Schachter & Thompson LLP - *8
#750, 900 Howe St., Vancouver, BC V6Z 2M4
Tel: 604-662-8840; *Fax:* 604-684-1598
info@nst.bc.ca
www.nst.bc.ca

Vancouver: National Public Relations - *2
#350, 355 Burrard St., Vancouver, BC V6C 2G8
Tel: 604-684-6655; *Fax:* 604-684-6981

Vancouver: Nelson & Vanderkruyk - *3
#440, 355 Burrard St., Vancouver, BC V6C 2G8
Tel: 604-684-1311; *Fax:* 604-684-6402
nelsonvanderkruyk@nvlaw.ca

Vancouver: B.J. Nelson - *1
#103, 1012 Beach Ave., Vancouver, BC V6E 1T7
Tel: 604-685-7317; *Fax:* 604-682-3965

Vancouver: Ng Ariss Fong - *3
#219, P.O. Box 160, 900 Howe St., Vancouver, BC V6Z 2M4
Tel: 604-331-1155; *Fax:* 604-677-5410
general@ngariss.com
www.ngariss.com

Vancouver: Kimball R. Nichols - *1
1591 Bowser Ave., Vancouver, BC V7P 2Y4
Tel: 604-682-0541; *Fax:* 604-924-5541

Vancouver: K.F. Nordlinger, Q.C. & Associates - *4
#109, 1008 Beach Ave., Vancouver, BC V6E 1T7
Tel: 604-689-5134; *Fax:* 604-689-5323
katherine@nordlinger.net

Vancouver: Northwest Law Group - *6
#1880, 1055 West Georgia St., Vancouver, BC V6E 3P3
Tel: 604-687-5792; *Fax:* 604-687-6650

Vancouver: Norton Stewart Business Lawyers - *5
#1600, P.O. Box 11104, 1055 West Georgia St., Vancouver, BC V6E 3P3
Tel: 604-687-0555; *Fax:* 604-689-1248

Vancouver: Oland & Company - *2
#2020, Vancouver Centre, P.O. Box 11547, 650 West Georgia St., Vancouver, BC V6B 4N7
Tel: 604-683-9621; *Fax:* 604-669-4556
shiplaw@aboland.com

Vancouver: Glen Orris Q.C. Law Corporation - *1
#500, 815 Hornby St., Vancouver, BC V6Z 2E6
Tel: 604-669-6711; *Fax:* 604-669-5180
glen@orrislawcorp.com

Vancouver: Osten & Osten - *1
#356, P.O. Box 11113, 5740 Cambie St., Vancouver, BC V6E 3A6
Tel: 604-683-9104; *Fax:* 604-688-0034

Vancouver: Owen Bird Law Corporation - *33
#2900, Three Bentall Centre, CP 49130, 595 Burrard St., Vancouver, BC V7X 1J5
Tel: 604-688-0401; *Fax:* 604-688-2827
inquiries@owenbird.com
www.owenbird.com

Vancouver: Oyen Wiggs Green & Mutala LLP, Intellectual Property Lawyers - *16
#480, The Station, 601 West Cordova St., Vancouver, BC V6B 1G1
Tel: 604-669-3432; *Fax:* 604-681-4081
Toll-Free: 866-475-2922
mail@patentable.com
www.patentable.com

Vancouver: Paine Edmonds LLP - *15
#1100, 510 Burrard St., Vancouver, BC V6C 3A8
Tel: 604-683-1211; *Fax:* 604-681-5084
Toll-Free: 800-669-8599
law@paine-edmonds.com
www.paine-edmonds.com

Vancouver: Palkowski & Company Law Corp. - *3
#703, 938 Howe St., Vancouver, BC V6Z 1N9
Tel: 604-331-4422; *Fax:* 604-331-4466
rjlegal@palkowski.com
www.palkowski.com

Vancouver: Pape Salter Teillet - *3
#460, 220 Cambie St., Vancouver, BC V6B 2M9
Tel: 604-681-3002; *Fax:* 604-681-3050
admin@pstlaw.ca

Vancouver: Al Paquette - *1
#5, 8431 Granville St., Vancouver, BC V6P 4Z9
Tel: 604-261-3211; *Fax:* 604-261-5382

Vancouver: Peck & Company - *1
#610, 744 Hastings St. West, Vancouver, BC V6C 1A5
Tel: 604-669-0208; *Fax:* 604-669-0616

Vancouver: D.B. Phelps - *1
#1200, 805 Broadway West, Vancouver, BC V5Z 1K1
Tel: 604-736-3722; *Fax:* 604-736-3725

Vancouver: Pierce Law Group - *1
#850, 475 Georgia St. West, Vancouver, BC V6B 4M9
Tel: 604-681-4434; *Fax:* 604-681-9142
contact@bcdisabilitylaw.com

Vancouver: Vincent E. Pigeon - *1
#410, 688 Hastings St. West, Vancouver, BC V6B 1P1
Tel: 604-684-2889; *Fax:* 604-685-2900
vpigeon@telus.net
www.vincentpigeonlawter.com

Vancouver: Sarah B. Pollard - *1
#400, 1681 Chestnut St., Vancouver, BC V6J 4M6
Tel: 604-732-5667; *Fax:* 604-732-1262
lawoffice@sprint.ca

Vancouver: Susan L. Polsky Shamash - *1
#150, 4600 Jacombs Rd., Vancouver, BC V6V 3B1
Tel: 604-664-7800; *Fax:* 604-664-7898
Toll-Free: 800-663-2782

Vancouver: Lianne Potter Law Corporation - *1
#218, 470 Granville St., Vancouver, BC V6C 1V5
Tel: 604-688-0042; *Fax:* 604-688-0062
lpotter@lwp-lawcorp.com

Vancouver: Poulsen & Co. - *4
#1800, 999 West Hastings St., Vancouver, BC V6C 2W2
Tel: 604-681-0123; *Fax:* 604-683-1375
pchapman@poulsenlaw.com
www.poulsenlaw.com

Vancouver: Quinlan Abrioux - *14
#1510, TD Tower, P.O. Box 10031, Stn. Pacific Centre, 700 West Georgia St., Vancouver, BC V7Y 1A1
Tel: 604-687-3711; *Fax:* 604-687-3741
www.qalaw.com

Vancouver: Quorum Business Lawyers - *7
#1450, 1075 West Georgia St., Vancouver, BC V6E 3C9
Tel: 604-682-0701; *Fax:* 604-682-7359
www.quorumlaw.com

Vancouver: Radelet & Company - *2
#1330, 1075 Georgia St. West, Vancouver, BC V6E 3C9
Tel: 604-689-0878; *Fax:* 604-689-1386
james@radelet.com

Vancouver: Richard Raibmon - *1
#1535, Nelson Sq., P.O. Box 12134, 808 Nelson St., Vancouver, BC V6Z 2H2
Tel: 604-688-8551; *Fax:* 604-687-1799
rlrlaw@uniserve.com

Vancouver: Rankin, Bond - *2
#200, 157 Alexander St., Vancouver, BC V6A 1B8
Tel: 604-682-3621; *Fax:* 604-682-3919

Vancouver: Rao, McKercher & Company - *2
#908, 510 Burrard St., Vancouver, BC V6C 3A8
Tel: 604-664-7474; *Fax:* 604-664-7477

Vancouver: Gayle M. Raphanel - *1
#501, 815 Hornby St., Vancouver, BC V6Z 2E6
Tel: 604-682-2200; *Fax:* 604-682-2246
gmr@dowco.com

Vancouver: Richards Buell Sutton LLP - *37
#700, 401 West Georgia St., Vancouver, BC V6B 5A1
Tel: 604-682-3664; *Fax:* 604-688-3830
info@rbs.ca
www.rbs.ca

Vancouver: Ritchie Sandford - *2
#1300, 355 Burrard St., Vancouver, BC V6C 2G8
Tel: 604-684-0778; *Fax:* 604-684-0799

Vancouver: Roberts & Stahl - *5
#500, 220 Cambie St., Vancouver, BC V6B 2M9
Tel: 604-684-6377; *Fax:* 604-684-6387
cbarthe@robertsstahl.com
www.robertsstahl.com

Vancouver: Daniel J. Rogers - *1
#1210, 1140 Pender St. West, Vancouver, BC V6E 4G1
Tel: 604-681-5600; *Fax:* 604-681-1475
dan@shorttco.com

Vancouver: Roper Greyell LLP, Employment & Labour Lawyers - *24
#800, Park Place, 666 Burrard St., Vancouver, BC V6C 3P3
Tel: 604-806-0922; *Fax:* 604-806-0933
info@ropergreyell.com
www.greyell.com

Vancouver: Rosenberg & Rosenberg - *3
671D Market Hill, Vancouver, BC V5Z 4B5
Tel: 604-879-4505; *Fax:* 604-879-4934
rosenberg_law@telus.net

Vancouver: Rosenbloom & Aldridge - *3
#440, 355 Burrard St., Vancouver, BC V6C 2G8
Tel: 604-605-5555; *Fax:* 604-684-6402
rosenbloom_aldridge@telus.net

Vancouver: J.H. Rosner - *1
#770, 475 Georgia St. West, Vancouver, BC V6B 4M9
Tel: 604-687-6638; *Fax:* 604-682-2481
roslaw@telus.net

Vancouver: R.D. Ross Q.C. - *1
4741 West 2 Ave., Vancouver, BC V6T 1C1
Tel: 604-228-9701; *Fax:* 604-228-9055

Vancouver: Howard Rubin Law Corp. - *1
405E - 4 St., Vancouver, BC V7L 1J4
Tel: 604-984-2030; *Fax:* 604-988-0068
howard@howard-rubin.com

Vancouver: Morrie Sacks Law Corporation - *1
#207, 1525 - 8th Ave. West, Vancouver, BC V6T 1T5
Tel: 604-685-7629; *Fax:* 604-685-7630
morrie@collaborativedivorce.ca
www.nocourtdivorce.ca

Vancouver: Salley Bowes Harwardt Law Corp. - *4
#1750, 1185 Georgia St. West, Vancouver, BC V6E 4E6
Tel: 604-688-0788; *Fax:* 604-688-0778
info@sbh.bc.ca
www.sbh.bc.ca

Vancouver: Gary M. Salloum - *1
286 - 21st Ave. West, Vancouver, BC V5Y 2E5

Vancouver: Gregory L. Samuels - *1
#585, 1385 - 8th Ave., Vancouver, BC V6H 3V9
Tel: 604-742-4242; *Fax:* 604-742-4243
gls@borderlaw.com

Vancouver: Charles A. Sandberg - *1
#108, 2786 - 16 Ave. West, Vancouver, BC V6K 4M1
Tel: 604-734-7768; *Fax:* 604-733-1229

Vancouver: Michael D. Sanders - *1
811 Drake St., Vancouver, BC V6Z 1C1
Tel: 604-669-5005; *Fax:* 604-669-1334

** indicates number of lawyers*

***Vancouver*: Sangra, Moller - *6**
#1000, Cathedral Place, 925 Georgia St. West, Vancouver, BC V6C 3L2
Tel: 604-662-8808; *Fax:* 604-669-8803
info@sangramoller.com
www.sangramoller.com

***Vancouver*: Catherine A. Sas - *1**
#501, 134 Abbott St., Vancouver, BC V6B 2K4
Tel: 604-689-5444; *Fax:* 604-689-5666
Toll-Free: 888-689-5445
casas@axionet.com
www.canadian-visa-lawyer.com

***Vancouver*: P.N. Scarisbrick - *1**
234 Abbott St., Vancouver, BC V6B 2K8
Tel: 604-688-0495; *Fax:* 604-688-0201

***Vancouver*: Scarlett Manson Angus - *4**
#1200, 777 Hornby St., Vancouver, BC V6Z 1S4
Tel: 604-684-4777; *Fax:* 604-684-7773
lawfirm@smalaw.com

***Vancouver*: Antya Schrack - *1**
#116, 970 Burrard St., Vancouver, BC V6Z 2R4
Tel: 604-682-2078; *Fax:* 604-682-6697
schrack@telus.net
www.immigrate-to-canada.ca

***Vancouver*: Schroeder & Company - *3**
#1119, 808 Nelson St., Vancouver, BC V6Z 2H2
Tel: 604-688-6737; *Fax:* 604-688-0271
fschroeder@schroeder.bc.ca

***Vancouver*: Schuman Daltrop Basran & Robin - *4**
900 Helmcken St., Vancouver, BC V6Z 1B3
Tel: 604-669-4912; *Fax:* 604-669-4911

***Vancouver*: David A. Schwartz - *1**
#600, 890 West Pender St., Vancouver, BC V6C 1J9
Tel: 604-687-0811; *Fax:* 604-687-1327
Toll-Free: 855-687-0811
schwartzdav@gmail.com
www.davidschwartzsecuritieslaw.com

***Vancouver*: A.P. Serka, Q.C. - *1**
#788, 601 West Broadway, Vancouver, BC V5Z 4C2
Tel: 604-876-8761; *Fax:* 604-876-9035

***Vancouver*: Shandro Dixon Edgson - *6**
#400, 999 Hastings St. West, Vancouver, BC V6C 2W2
Tel: 604-689-0400; *Fax:* 604-685-2009
law@sdelawyers.com

***Vancouver*: Shapiro Hankinson & Knutson**
Two Bental Centre, #700, 555 Burrard St., Vancouver, BC V7X 1M8
Tel: 604-684-0727; *Fax:* 604-684-7094

***Vancouver*: Murray H. Shapiro - *1**
694 West 19th Ave., Vancouver, BC V5Z 1X1
Tel: 604-879-6777; *Fax:* 604-879-6728

***Vancouver*: Shapray, Cramer & Associates - *4**
#670, World Trade Centre, 999 Canada Pl., Vancouver, BC V6C 3E1
Tel: 604-681-0900; *Fax:* 604-681-0920

***Vancouver*: S.S. Shelton - *1**
3469 Commercial St., Vancouver, BC V5N 4E8
Tel: 604-251-2144; *Fax:* 604-251-2781

***Vancouver*: George Shimizu - *1**
#718, P.O. Box 50959, 808 Nelson St., Vancouver, BC V6Z 2H2
Tel: 604-685-4467; *Fax:* 604-685-4408
geoshimizu@telus.net

***Vancouver*: Silbernagel & Company - *2**
#700, 595 Howe St., Vancouver, BC V6C 2T5
Tel: 604-687-9621; *Fax:* 604-687-5960
stephen@silbernagellaw.com

***Vancouver*: Simon Wener - *2**
#620, 1385 - 8 Ave. West, Vancouver, BC V6H 3V9
Tel: 604-736-5500; *Fax:* 604-736-5522
info@simonwener.com
www.simonwener.com

***Vancouver*: Singleton Urquhart LLP - *35**
#1200, 925 Georgia St. West, Vancouver, BC V6C 3L2
Tel: 604-682-7474; *Fax:* 604-682-1283
su@singleton.com
www.singleton.com

***Vancouver*: Sisett & Co. - *2**
#603, 601 West Broadway, Vancouver, BC V5Z 4C2
Tel: 604-879-8811; *Fax:* 604-879-7346
Toll-Free: 800-446-5879
sisett@sisettlaw.com
www.sisettlaw.com

***Vancouver*: SJE Consulting Ltd. - *1**
6311 Adera St., Vancouver, BC V6M 3J7
Tel: 877-753-2678; *Fax:* 877-753-2679
sjeconsulting@telus.net

***Vancouver*: Skorah Doyle - *2**
#2100, 200 Granville St., Vancouver, BC V6C 1S4
Tel: 604-602-8501; *Fax:* 604-608-1660

***Vancouver*: Smart & Williams - *3**
#1190, 840 Howe St., Vancouver, BC V6Z 2L2
Tel: 604-687-6278; *Fax:* 604-687-6298
vlang@smartwilliams.com

***Vancouver*: Smith & Hughes - *2**
#102, 4088 Cambie St., Vancouver, BC V5Z 2X8
Tel: 604-683-4176; *Fax:* 604-683-2621
rhughes@smithhughes.com
www.smith-hughes.com

***Vancouver*: South Fraser Law Group - *4**
#200, 6330 Fraser St., Vancouver, BC V5W 3A4
Tel: 604-321-3232; *Fax:* 604-325-0093
lawyers@southfraserlaw.com
www.southfraserlaw.com

***Vancouver*: Michael P.S. Spearing - *1**
#501, 1949 Beach Ave., Vancouver, BC V6G 1Z2
Tel: 604-681-0699
michaelspearing@telus.net

***Vancouver*: Specht & Pryer - *4**
Oceanic Plaza, 1066 West Hastings St., 20th Fl., Vancouver, BC V6E 3X2
Tel: 604-736-0883; *Fax:* 604-736-0118
staff@spechtandpryer.com

***Vancouver*: Spring Brammall - *1**
2774 Granville St., Vancouver, BC V6H 3J3
Tel: 604-732-3881; *Fax:* 604-732-3883

***Vancouver*: Stamp of Approval - *1**
5914 Elm St., Vancouver, BC V6N 1A9
Tel: 604-266-0020
stampofapproval@telus.net

***Vancouver*: Stephens & Holman - *6**
#500, 1200 - 33 St. West, Vancouver, BC V6P 6Z6
Tel: 604-730-4100; *Fax:* 604-736-2867
simon.holman@stephenandhelman.com
www.stephensandholman.com

***Vancouver*: John S. Stowe - *1**
#301, 134 Abbott St., Vancouver, BC V6B 2K4
Tel: 604-684-1665; *Fax:* 604-687-3097
john_stowe@bc.sympatico.ca

***Vancouver*: Sugden, McFee & Roos - *9**
#700, The Landing, 375 Water St., Vancouver, BC V6B 5N3
Tel: 604-687-7700; *Fax:* 604-687-5596
www.smrlaw.ca

***Vancouver*: Sutherland & Company - *1**
#1620, 401 Georgia St. West, Vancouver, BC V6B 5A1
Tel: 604-688-0047; *Fax:* 604-688-8880

***Vancouver*: David F. Sutherland & Associates - *1**
1710 Dunbar St., Vancouver, BC V6R 3L8
Tel: 604-737-8711; *Fax:* 604-737-8655
dfs@dfsutherland.com

***Vancouver*: Tao & Company - *2**
#860, 999 West Broadway, Vancouver, BC V5Z 1K5
Tel: 604-730-8219; *Fax:* 604-730-2553

***Vancouver*: Taylor & Blair - *2**
#270, 1385 - 8th Ave. West, Vancouver, BC V6H 3V9
Tel: 604-737-6900; *Fax:* 604-737-6901

***Vancouver*: Taylor & Company - *2**
#218, 470 Granville St., Vancouver, BC V6C 1V5
Tel: 604-662-8373; *Fax:* 604-662-8321
wtaylor@twlaw.ca

***Vancouver*: Taylor Jordan Chafetz - *8**
#1010, 777 Hornby St., Vancouver, BC V6Z 1S4
Tel: 604-683-2223; *Fax:* 604-683-2798
tsaumure@tjclaw.com
www.tjclaw.com

***Vancouver*: Colin Taylor Law Corporation**
#502, 888 Bute St., Vancouver, BC V6E 1Y5
Tel: 604-798-8775; *Fax:* 604-608-6117
colintaylor@telus.net

***Vancouver*: G.J. Te Hennepe - *1**
#203, 4545 West 10th Ave., Vancouver, BC V6R 4N2
Tel: 604-228-1433; *Fax:* 604-228-9822
tehennepe@telus.net

***Vancouver*: Isaac Thau - *1**
#101, 1012 Beach Ave., Vancouver, BC V6E 1T7
Tel: 604-685-4220; *Fax:* 604-685-0400
lthau@orbitinc.net

***Vancouver*: Eric P. Thiessen - *1**
#702, 756 Great Northern Way, Vancouver, BC V5T 1E4
Tel: 604-876-6220; *Fax:* 604-876-6253

***Vancouver*: Thomas, Rondeau - *7**
#300, 576 Seymour St., Vancouver, BC V6b 3K1
Tel: 604-688-6775; *Fax:* 604-688-6995
cthomas@thomasrondeau.com
www.thomasrondeau.com

***Vancouver*: Thompson & Elliott - *4**
1285 West Broadway, 8th Fl., Vancouver, BC V6H 3X8
Tel: 604-731-1161; *Fax:* 604-731-6527

***Vancouver*: Bonnie L. Thorpe - *1**
6909 Cambie St., Vancouver, BC V6P 3H1
Tel: 604-325-0020; *Fax:* 604-325-0020

***Vancouver*: Timothy J. Vondette Law Corporation - *1**
#506, 1128 Hornby St., Vancouver, BC V6Z 2L4
Tel: 604-669-6990; *Fax:* 604-669-6944
tvondette@aol.com

***Vancouver*: Anthony G.V. Tobin - *1**
#816, 938 Howe St., Vancouver, BC V6Z 1N9
Tel: 604-331-1591; *Fax:* 604-688-8120
agvtobin@endisputes.com
www.endisputes.com

***Vancouver*: Toews & Company - *2**
#1488, 777 Hornby St., Vancouver, BC V6Z 1S4
Tel: 604-601-5365; *Fax:* 604-681-3019
info@toewsco.net

***Vancouver*: Tupper, Jonsson & Yeadon - *6**
#1710, 1177 Hastings St. West, Vancouver, BC V6E 2L3
Tel: 604-683-9262; *Fax:* 604-681-0139
tupjon@globalserve.net

***Vancouver*: La Van & Company - *3**
#704, 1478 West Hastings St., Vancouver, BC V6G 3J6
Tel: 604-669-1411; *Fax:* 604-669-9080
jack@lavanco.com

***Vancouver*: Winfred A. van der Sande - *1**
2774 Granville St., Vancouver, BC V6H 3J3
Tel: 604-739-7989; *Fax:* 604-732-3883

***Vancouver*: C.J. Van Twest - *1**
#405, 1160 Burrard St., Vancouver, BC V6Z 2E8
Tel: 604-683-8874; *Fax:* 604-683-8841
twest@interchange.ubc.ca

***Vancouver*: Varty & Company - *2**
#900, 555 Burrard St., Vancouver, BC V7X 1M8
Tel: 604-684-5356; *Fax:* 604-443-5001
www.vartylaw.ca

***Vancouver*: Vector Corporate Finance Lawyers - *3**
#1040, 999 West Hastings St., Vancouver, BC V6C 2W2
Tel: 604-683-1102; *Fax:* 604-683-2643
www.vectorlaw.com

***Vancouver*: Vermette & Co. - *2**
#230, P.O. Box 40, 200 Granville St., Vancouver, BC V6C 1S4
Tel: 604-331-0381; *Fax:* 604-331-0382
ip@vermetteco.com
www.vermetteco.com

***Vancouver*: Von Dehn & Company - *3**
#700, 595 Howe St., Vancouver, BC V6C 2T5
Tel: 604-688-4541; *Fax:* 604-687-5960
vondehnco@telus.net

***Vancouver*: T. Wing Wai - *1**
#205, 475 Main St., Vancouver, BC V6A 2T7
Tel: 604-688-2291; *Fax:* 604-688-8983

** indicates number of lawyers*

Vancouver: **Walker & Company - *1**
#1500, 1030 West Georgia St., Vancouver, BC V6E 2Y3
Tel: 604-682-1147; *Fax:* 604-681-7705
agwalker@telus.net

Vancouver: **Gregory A. Wasko - *1**
1306 Bidwell St., #D, Vancouver, BC V6G 2L1
Tel: 604-662-3038

Vancouver: **Watson Goepel Maledy LLP - *36**
#1700, 1075 West Georgia St., Vancouver, BC V6E 3C9
Tel: 604-688-1301; *Fax:* 604-688-8193
wgm@wgmlaw.com
www.wgmlaw.com

Vancouver: **Elizabeth E. Watson - *1**
#4412, 349 Georgia St. West, Vancouver, BC V6B 3Z8
Tel: 604-877-1412; *Fax:* 604-877-0134
ewatson@telus.net

Vancouver: **Richard H. Watts Law Corporation - *1**
1776 - 29th Av. West, Vancouver, BC V6J 2Z5
Tel: 604-682-2671; *Fax:* 604-648-8142

Vancouver: **Webster Hudson & Akerly LLP - *14**
#510, 1040 West Georgia St., Vancouver, BC V6E 4H1
Tel: 604-682-3488; *Fax:* 604-682-3438
www.wha.bc.ca

Vancouver: **Western Policy Consultants Inc. (WPC Inc.) - *1**
#1450, Pacific Centre, P.O. Box 10015, 700 West Georgia St., Vancouver, BC V7Y 1A1
Tel: 604-684-2228; *Fax:* 604-683-6345
western@telus.net

Vancouver: **K.S. Westlake - *1**
#1720, 355 Burrard St., Vancouver, BC V6C 2G8
Tel: 604-687-9831; *Fax:* 604-687-7089
kenwestlake@telus.net

Vancouver: **Westpoint Law Group - *1**
#1900, 1177 West Hastings Street, Vancouver, BC V6E 2K3
Tel: 604-718-6886; *Fax:* 604-629-1882

Vancouver: **Wilcox & Company Law Corporation - *3**
#1910, 777 Hornby St., Vancouver, BC V6Z 1S4
Tel: 604-687-1374; *Fax:* 604-687-2731
dwilcox@wilcoxlawcorp.com

Vancouver: **Ron J. Wilinofsky - *1**
#202, 1275 - 6th Ave. West, Vancouver, BC V6H 1A6
Tel: 604-736-6818; *Fax:* 604-688-5032

Vancouver: **Williamson Giesen Murray - *2**
#200, 1290 Homer St., Vancouver, BC V6B 2Y5
Tel: 604-681-1004; *Fax:* 604-684-1199
www.wgmlaw.ca

Vancouver: **P.J. Wilson - *1**
#400, 744 West Hastings St., Vancouver, BC V6C 1A5
Tel: 604-684-4751; *Fax:* 604-684-8319

Vancouver: **Andrew J. Winstanley - *1**
#410, 688 Hastings St. West, Vancouver, BC V6B 1P1
Tel: 604-682-2939; *Fax:* 604-682-2241
ajwinstanley@teleus.net

Vancouver: **Stephen K. Winter Law Corp. - *1**
#910, 808 Hastings St. West, Vancouver, BC V6C 2X4
Tel: 604-682-3733; *Fax:* 604-688-5590
swinters@uniserve.com

Vancouver: **David J. Wizinsky - *1**
#450, 800 Pender St. West, Vancouver, BC V6C 2V6
Tel: 604-805-6114; *Fax:* 604-689-5528
wiz@uniserve.com

Vancouver: **WLG ET Al. Consulting Ltd. - *1**
#103, 2515 Burrard St., Vancouver, BC V6J 3J6
wlg@pacificcoast.net

Vancouver: **George Wong & Company - *1**
155 East Pender St., Vancouver, BC V6A 1T6
Tel: 604-687-6166; *Fax:* 604-687-8002
gwco@telus.net

Vancouver: **P.L. Wong - *1**
#407, 1541 West Broadway, Vancouver, BC V6J 1W7
Tel: 604-731-5301; *Fax:* 604-731-1266

Vancouver: **W.G. Wong - *1**
145 Keefer St., 2nd Fl., Vancouver, BC V6A 1X3
Tel: 604-685-9361; *Fax:* 604-684-1299
wwong@radiant.net

Vancouver: **Robert Wood & Company - *2**
#100, 2501 Spruce St., Vancouver, BC V6N 2P8
Tel: 604-731-1200; *Fax:* 604-266-0119
rwood@dawsonwood.com

Vancouver: **A.K. Wooster - *1**
#570, 999 West Broadway, Vancouver, BC V5Z 1K5
Tel: 604-684-1204; *Fax:* 604-684-1206
akwoods@aol.com

Vancouver: **D.W.H. Yerxa - *1**
#1200, 805 West Broadway, Vancouver, BC V5Z 1K1
Tel: 604-873-5225

Vancouver: **Young & Noble - *1**
#1119, 808 Nelson St., Vancouver, BC V6Z 2H2
Tel: 604-669-9755; *Fax:* 604-921-4817
john.noble@youngnoble.com

Vancouver: **Young, Anderson - *19**
#1616, Nelson Square, CP 12147, 808 Nelson St., Vancouver, BC V6Z 2H2
Tel: 604-689-7400; *Fax:* 604-689-3444
Toll-Free: 800-665-3540
reception@younganderson.ca
www.younganderson.ca

Vancouver: **David L. Youngson - *1**
#10, 1656 - 11th Ave. West, Vancouver, BC V6J 2B9
Tel: 604-266-6588; *Fax:* 604-266-6393
saluspopuli@shaw.ca

Vancouver: **Xiao Zheng - *1**
#450, 1040 West Georgia St., Vancouver, BC V6E 4H1
Tel: 604-608-0387; *Fax:* 604-608-0385
zheng@axionet.com

Vancouver: **Deborah Lynn Zutter - *1**
609 West Hastings, 6th Fl., Vancouver, BC V6B 4W4
Tel: 604-219-2259; *Fax:* 604-662-7466
dzutter@telus.net
www.debzutter.com

Vanderhoof: **Steven F. Peleshok - *1**
P.O. Box 1128, 2608 Burrard Ave., Vanderhoof, BC V0J 3A0
Tel: 250-567-9277; *Fax:* 250-567-2657

Vernon: **Allan Francis Pringle LLP - *6**
3009B - 28 St., Vernon, BC V1T 4Z7
Tel: 250-542-1177; *Fax:* 250-542-1105
office@afp-law.ca
www.afp-law.ca

Vernon: **Cancade Crosby - *2**
2608 - 48 Ave., Vernon, BC V1T 8K8
Tel: 250-549-1999; *Fax:* 250-558-3910
Toll-Free: 877-646-1999
cancadelaw@hotmail.com

Vernon: **Danyliu & Company - *1**
9055 Binns Rd., Vernon, BC V1B 3B7
Tel: 250-549-3111; *Fax:* 250-549-4135
Toll-Free: 888-549-3186
danyliu@shaw.ca

Vernon: **Kenneth R. Fiddes - *1**
#2, 2908 - 31 Ave., Vernon, BC V1T 2G4
Tel: 250-542-5391; *Fax:* 250-542-4199
fiddes@shaw.ca

Vernon: **Alan M. Gaudette - *1**
#9, 11341 Kidston Rd., Vernon, BC V1B 1Z4
Tel: 250-545-3132; *Fax:* 250-545-1617
amgaudette@shaw.ca

Vernon: **Kern & Company Law Corp. - *1**
#3, 2908 - 32 St., Vernon, BC V1T 5M1
Tel: 250-549-2184; *Fax:* 250-549-2207
kernlaw@junction.net

Vernon: **Kidston & Company - *4**
#200, 3005 - 30th St., Vernon, BC V1T 2M1
Tel: 250-545-0711; *Fax:* 250-545-4776
tmm@kidston.ca
www.kidston.ca

Vernon: **John S. Maguire Barrister & Solicitor - *1**
3018 - 29 St., Vernon, BC V1T 5A7
Tel: 250-545-6054; *Fax:* 250-545-7227
jsmag@sigmag.com

Vernon: **Nixon Wenger - *19**
3201 - 30 Ave., 4th Fl., Vernon, BC V1T 2C6
Tel: 250-542-5353; *Fax:* 250-542-7273
Toll-Free: 800-243-5353
nw@nixonwenger.com
www.nixonwenger.com

Vernon: **Robert Moffat Law Corp. - *1**
2912 - 29th St., Vernon, BC V1T 5A6
Tel: 250-542-1312; *Fax:* 250-542-2788
Toll-Free: 800-371-0181
moffatvernon@shawcable.com

Vernon: **Steiner & Company - *1**
3107A - 31 Ave., Vernon, BC V1T 2G9
Tel: 250-545-1371; *Fax:* 250-542-5630
Toll-Free: 800-661-2600

Victoria: **Acheson Whitley - *5**
535 Yates St., 4th Fl., Victoria, BC V8W 2Z6
Tel: 250-384-6262; *Fax:* 250-384-5353
Toll-Free: 877-275-8766
info@achesonwhitley.com
www.achesonwhitley.com

Victoria: **Robert D. Adair - *1**
#201, 4430 Chatterton Way, Victoria, BC V8X 5J2
Tel: 250-479-9367; *Fax:* 250-479-8316
adair@adairlaw.ca

Victoria: **Anniko, Hunter - *2**
#201, 300 Gorge Rd. West, Victoria, BC V9A 1M8
Tel: 250-385-1233; *Fax:* 250-385-4078
ah@annikohunter-law.com

Victoria: **Jacqueline Beltgens - *1**
3929 Woodhaven Terrace, Victoria, BC V8N 1S7
Tel: 250-385-3909
jbeltgens@pinc.com

Victoria: **Berge, Hart & Cassels - *3**
1207 Quadra St., Victoria, BC V8W 2K8
Tel: 250-388-9477; *Fax:* 250-388-9470
admin@bergehart.ca

Victoria: **Christopher Brennan - *1**
1027 Pandora Ave., Victoria, BC V8V 3P6
Tel: 250-388-9024; *Fax:* 250-388-9060
chrisbrennan@shaw.ca

Victoria: **Cardinal Law - *7**
736 Broughton St., Victoria, BC V8W 1E1
Tel: 250-386-8707; *Fax:* 250-386-3265
Toll-Free: 800-459-9499
info@cardlaw.com
www.cardlaw.com

Victoria: **Carr Buchan & Co. - *5**
520 Comerford St., Victoria, BC V9A 6K8
Tel: 250-388-7571; *Fax:* 250-388-7327
Toll-Free: 888-313-7571
carrbuchan@esquimaltlaw.com; fhughes@esquimaltlaw.com

Victoria: **Clapp & Company - *1**
4599 Chatterton Way, Victoria, BC V8X 4Y7
Tel: 250-479-1422; *Fax:* 250-479-1667

Victoria: **Clay & Company. Lawyers & Mediators - *6**
837 Burdett Ave., Main Fl., Victoria, BC V8W 1B3
Tel: 250-386-2261; *Fax:* 250-389-1336
Toll-Free: 877-688-9634
lawyers@clay.bc.ca
www.clay.bc.ca

Victoria: **Gary E. Coad Law Corp. - *1**
#8, 2727 Quadra St., Victoria, BC V8T 4E5
Tel: 250-388-9003; *Fax:* 250-388-3577
coad@islandnet.com

Victoria: **Considine & Company, Barristers & Solicitors - *1**
30 Dallas Rd., Victoria, BC V8V 0A2
Tel: 250-381-7788; *Fax:* 250-381-1042
www.considinelaw.com

Victoria: **Cook Roberts LLP - *20**
1175 Douglas St., 7th Fl., Victoria, BC V8W 2E1
Tel: 250-385-1411; *Fax:* 250-413-3300
lawmark@cookroberts.bc.ca
www.cookroberts.bc.ca

Victoria: **Cox, Taylor - *9**
Burnes House, 26 Bastion Sq., 3rd Fl., Victoria, BC V8W 1H9
Tel: 250-388-4457; *Fax:* 250-382-4236
mailbox@coxtaylor.bc.ca

** indicates number of lawyers*

***Victoria*: Crease Harman & Company - *14**
#800, 1070 Douglas St., Victoria, BC V8W 2S8
Tel: 250-388-5421; *Fax:* 250-388-4294
creaseharman@creaseharman.com
www.creaseharman.com

***Victoria*: Dinning Hunter Lambert & Jackson - Victoria Head Office - *15**
1202 Fort St., Victoria, BC V8V 3L2
Tel: 250-381-2151; *Fax:* 250-386-2123
Toll-Free: 800-246-5457
info@dinninghunter.com
www.dinninghunter.com

***Victoria*: Jeremy S.G. Donaldson - *1**
2555 Sinclair Rd., Victoria, BC V8N 1B8
Tel: 250-721-5759; *Fax:* 250-721-5475

***Victoria*: Easdon & Company - *1**
#500, 645 Fort St., Victoria, BC V8W 1G2
Tel: 250-386-3544; *Fax:* 250-380-7299
easdonlaw@pacificcoast.net

***Victoria*: Michael W. Egan - *1**
#104C, 3550 Saanich Rd., Victoria, BC V8X 1X2
Tel: 250-382-3426; *Fax:* 250-382-3427

***Victoria*: Frank A.V. Falzon Law Corporation - *1**
#200, 3561 Shelbourne St., Victoria, BC V8P 4G8
Tel: 250-384-3995; *Fax:* 250-384-4924
favf@islandnet.com

***Victoria*: P.S. Finnegan - *1**
#6, 1140 Fort St., Victoria, BC V8V 3K8
Tel: 250-384-4252; *Fax:* 250-384-4252
psfinnegan@shaw.ca

***Victoria*: Firestone & Tyhurst - *2**
#301, 919 Fort St., Victoria, BC V8V 3K3
Tel: 250-386-1112; *Fax:* 250-386-1124

***Victoria*: Joseph Gereluk Law Office - *1**
#401, 1011 Fort St., Victoria, BC V8V 3K5
Tel: 250-380-1423; *Fax:* 250-380-0920

***Victoria*: Larry P. Gilbert - *1**
479 Sturdee St., Victoria, BC V9A 6R2
Tel: 250-478-8881; *Fax:* 250-478-8801

***Victoria*: Peter Golden - *1**
#218, 852 Fort St.., Victoria, BC V8W 1H8
Tel: 250-361-3131; *Fax:* 250-361-9161

***Victoria*: Goult & Company - *1**
2185 Theatre Lane, Victoria, BC V8R 6T1
Tel: 250-595-1621; *Fax:* 250-595-5888
goultco@shaw.ca

***Victoria*: Green & Helme - *4**
1161 Fort St., Victoria, BC V8V 3K9
Tel: 250-361-9600; *Fax:* 250-361-9181
greenandhelme@greenclaus.com

***Victoria*: Lenore B. Harlton - *1**
#105, 230 Menzie St., Victoria, BC V8V 2G7
Tel: 250-382-5161; *Fax:* 250-382-5160

***Victoria*: Hatter, Thompson, Shumka & McDonagh - *4**
#201, 919 Fort St., Victoria, BC V8V 3K3
Tel: 250-388-4931; *Fax:* 250-386-8088
Toll-Free: 800-667-0705

***Victoria*: James I. Heller - *1**
#7, 547 Herald St., Victoria, BC V8W 1S5
Tel: 250-360-1040; *Fax:* 250-188-8824
jimheller@shaw.ca

***Victoria*: Holmes & Isherwood - *1**
1190 Fort St., Victoria, BC V8V 3K8
Tel: 250-383-7157; *Fax:* 250-383-1535

***Victoria*: Horne Coupar - *8**
Royal Trust Building, 612 View St., 3rd Fl., Victoria, BC V8W 1J5
Tel: 250-388-6631; *Fax:* 250-388-5974
Toll-Free: 866-467-2490
answers@hc-law.com
www.hc-law.com

***Victoria*: Raymond T. Horne - *1**
#46, 530 Marsett Pl., Victoria, BC V8Z 7J2
Tel: 250-658-6756
rhorne@istar.ca

***Victoria*: Hutchison Oss-Cech Marlatt, Barristers & Solicitors - *5**
#1, 505 Fisgard St., Victoria, BC V8W 1R3
Tel: 250-360-2500
info@hom-law.com
www.hom-law.com

***Victoria*: Jawl & Bundon - *8**
1007 Fort St., 4th Fl., Victoria, BC V8V 3K5
Tel: 250-385-5787; *Fax:* 250-385-4364
info@jawlandbundon.com

***Victoria*: W.S. Johnson Law Corp. - *1**
#309, 895 Fort St., Victoria, BC V8W 1H7
Tel: 250-382-2404; *Fax:* 250-382-2426

***Victoria*: Jones Emery Hargreaves Swan - *12**
#1212, 1175 Douglas St., Victoria, BC V8W 2E1
Tel: 250-382-7222; *Fax:* 250-382-5436
lawyers@jonesemery.com

***Victoria*: Alice Shun Yee Lo - *1**
#401, 1011 Fort St., Victoria, BC V8V 3K5
Tel: 250-380-1423; *Fax:* 250-380-0920
alicelo@telus.net

***Victoria*: Susan J. Loney Law Office - *1**
1006 Russell St., Victoria, BC V9A 3X9
Tel: 250-384-1804; *Fax:* 250-384-1805
loneylaw@shaw.ca

***Victoria*: Lovett Westmacott - *2**
#417, 645 Fort St., Victoria, BC V8W 1G2
Tel: 250-480-7481; *Fax:* 250-480-7455
admin@lwpubliclaw.ca

***Victoria*: MacIsaac & Company - *6**
CP 933, 1117 Wharf St., 3rd Fl., Victoria, BC V8W 1T7
Tel: 250-381-5353; *Fax:* 250-380-7272
Toll-Free: 800-663-6299
info@macisaacgroup.com
www.macisaacgroup.com

***Victoria*: MacIsaac & MacIsaac - *4**
2227 Sooke Rd., Victoria, BC V9B 1W8
Tel: 250-478-1131; *Fax:* 250-478-3106
mac@macisaaclaw.ca

***Victoria*: MacMinn & Company - *5**
846 Broughton St., Victoria, BC V8W 1E4
Tel: 250-381-6444; *Fax:* 250-381-7857

***Victoria*: Maguire & Company - *1**
1727 Jefferson Ave., Victoria, BC V8N 2B3
Tel: 250-370-0300; *Fax:* 250-370-0302
magco@telus.net

***Victoria*: David A. Main - *1**
#330, 702 Fort St., Victoria, BC V8W 1H2
Tel: 250-383-4541; *Fax:* 250-382-5160

***Victoria*: Marshall Allen & Massey - *4**
1519 Amelia St., Victoria, BC V8W 2K1
Tel: 250-920-0144; *Fax:* 250-920-0177

***Victoria*: McConnan, Bion, O'Connor & Peterson - *14**
#420, 880 Douglas St., Victoria, BC V8W 2B7
Tel: 250-385-1383; *Fax:* 250-385-2841
Toll-Free: 888-385-1383
info@mcbop.com
www.mcbop.com

***Victoria*: McCullough Parsons Blazina - *10**
#200, 1011 Fort St., Victoria, BC V8V 3K5
Tel: 250-480-1529; *Fax:* 250-480-4910
Toll-Free: 800-360-6488
info@mpblawyers.com
mpblawyers.com

***Victoria*: McMicken & Bennett - *2**
303 - 1111 Blanshard St., Victoria, BC V8W 2H7
Tel: 250-385-9555; *Fax:* 250-385-9841
lawyer@mcmickenbennett.bc.ca

***Victoria*: Milton, Johnson - *2**
#204, 947 Fort St., Victoria, BC V8V 3K3
Tel: 250-385-5523; *Fax:* 250-385-7420

***Victoria*: Robert Moore-Stewart - *1**
#616, 620 View St., Victoria, BC V8W 1J6
Tel: 250-380-1887; *Fax:* 250-380-9134
rmoorest@telus.net

***Victoria*: Jane B. Morley - *1**
#417, 645 Fort St., Victoria, BC V8W 1G2
Tel: 250-480-7487; *Fax:* 250-480-7488
jbmorley@mrlaw.ca

***Victoria*: Catherine Morris - *1**
Lampion Pacific Law Corporation, Victoria, BC
www.lampion.bc.ca

***Victoria*: David Mulroney & Company - *6**
#701, 1803 Douglas St., Victoria, BC V8T 5C3
Tel: 250-389-6022; *Fax:* 250-389-6033

***Victoria*: Neighbourhood Law Centre - *1**
207 Menzies St., Victoria, BC V8V 2G6
Tel: 250-383-5012; *Fax:* 250-385-1174
amicus@islandnet.com
www.islandnet.com/~amicus

***Victoria*: John M. Orr Law Office - *1**
#102, 2358 The Esplanade, Victoria, BC V8P 3K7
Tel: 250-595-8675; *Fax:* 250-595-7421
orrlaw@shaw.ca

***Victoria*: Pearlman Lindholm - *14**
#201, 19 Dallas Rd., Victoria, BC V8V 5A6
Tel: 250-388-4433; *Fax:* 250-388-5856
nphilpott@pearlmanlindholm.com
www.pearlmanlindholm.com

***Victoria*: Purves, Hickford - *3**
#203, 1028 Fort St., Victoria, BC V8V 3K4
Tel: 250-361-1645; *Fax:* 250-386-6609
ph_h@shaw.ca

***Victoria*: Quadra Legal Centre - *3**
#101, 2750 Quadra St., Victoria, BC V8T 4E8
Tel: 250-380-1566; *Fax:* 250-380-3090

***Victoria*: Randall & Company - *3**
#103, 1006 Fort St., Victoria, BC V8V 3K4
Tel: 250-382-9282; *Fax:* 250-382-0366
randall@randallco.com

***Victoria*: Nichola Reid & Company - *2**
#214, 284 Helmcken Rd., Victoria, BC V9B 1T2
Tel: 250-744-1844; *Fax:* 250-744-1890

***Victoria*: Marlene Russo - *1**
#110, 1175 Cook St., Victoria, BC V8V 4A1
Tel: 250-380-0076; *Fax:* 250-380-0092
marlene_russo@telus.net

***Victoria*: Salmond, Ashurst - *3**
1620 Cedar Hill Cross Rd., Victoria, BC V8P 2P6
Tel: 250-477-4143; *Fax:* 250-477-4451
derekgsalmon@ashurst.com

***Victoria*: Sihota & Starkey - *1**
1248 Esquimalt Rd., Victoria, BC V9A 3N8
Tel: 250-381-5111; *Fax:* 250-381-3947
crisstarkey@pacificcoast.net

***Victoria*: Skillings & Company - *1**
#B, 777 Blanshard St., Victoria, BC V8W 2G9
Tel: 250-388-5136; *Fax:* 250-388-5195
skillco@shawcable.com

***Victoria*: Smith Hutchison Law Corporation - *2**
#202, 1640 Oak Bay Ave., Victoria, BC V8W 1E5
Tel: 250-388-6666; *Fax:* 250-389-0400
mhutchqc@bclawfirm.com
www.bclawfirm.com

***Victoria*: Stevenson, Doell & Company - *4**
999 Fort St., Victoria, BC V8V 3K3
Tel: 250-388-7881; *Fax:* 250-388-7324

***Victoria*: Stevenson, Luchies & Legh - *6**
#300, 848 Courtney St., Victoria, BC V8W 1C4
Tel: 250-381-4040; *Fax:* 250-414-5180
Toll-Free: 888-381-8555
lawyers@sll.ca
www.sll.ca

***Victoria*: Straith & Company - *3**
#704, 880 Douglas St., Victoria, BC V8W 2B7
Tel: 250-386-1434; *Fax:* 250-386-1421
Toll-Free: 877-636-1434
inquiries@straithlaw.ca

***Victoria*: Christine A. Stretton - *1**
#204, 947 Fort St., Victoria, BC V8V 3K3
Tel: 250-388-5333; *Fax:* 250-382-8644
castretton@pacificcoast.net

** indicates number of lawyers*

Victoria: **Diane E. Tourell - *1**
#520, 645 Fort St., Victoria, BC V8W 1G2
Tel: 250-384-1443; *Fax:* 250-360-1778
detourell@qswireless.com

Victoria: **Dalmar F. Tracy - *1**
#206, 1005 Cook St., Victoria, BC V8V 3Z6
Tel: 250-384-5331; *Fax:* 250-384-5206

Victoria: **Jill K. Turner - *1**
#101, 4475 Viewmount Ave., Victoria, BC V8Z 6L8
Tel: 250-360-0983; *Fax:* 250-658-1949
jill@turnelegal.com

Victoria: **Turnham Woodland, Barristers & Solicitors - *4**
1002 Wharf St., Victoria, BC V8W 1T4
Tel: 250-385-1122; *Fax:* 250-385-6522
hturnham@turnwood.bc.ca
www.turnhamwoodland.ca

Victoria: **Aaltje van Grootheest - *1**
4054 Knibbs Green, Victoria, BC V8Z 6Y7
Tel: 250-479-4692; *Fax:* 250-479-5162
avglaw@telus.net

Victoria: **Velletta & Company - *7**
#302, 852 Fort St., Victoria, BC V8W 1H8
Tel: 250-383-9104; *Fax:* 250-383-1922
Toll-Free: 866-383-9104
mail@victorialaw.bc.ca
www.victorialaw.bc.ca

Victoria: **Waddell Raponi Lawyers - *5**
1002 Wharf St., Victoria, BC V8W 1T4
Tel: 250-385-4311; *Fax:* 250-385-2012
www.waddellraponi.com

Victoria: **Peter I. Waldmann - *1**
1982 Forrester St., Victoria, BC V8R 3H1
Tel: 250-381-3113; *Fax:* 250-381-3122
Toll-Free: 877-381-3113
waldmann@shaw.ca

Victoria: **Wilson Marshall - *5**
#200, 911 Yates St., Victoria, BC V8V 4X3
Tel: 250-385-8741; *Fax:* 250-385-0433
Toll-Free: 877-385-8741
reception@wilsonmarshall.com

Victoria: **Wong & Doerksen - *2**
1618 Government St., Victoria, BC V8W 1Z3
Tel: 250-381-7799; *Fax:* 250-386-7799
kdoerksen@wongdoerksen.com

Victoria: **Woodward & Company - *14**
844 Courtney St., 2nd Fl., Victoria, BC V8W 1C4
Tel: 250-383-2356; *Fax:* 250-380-6560
reception@woodwardandcompany.com
www.woodwardandcompany.com

Victoria: **Wendy K. Zimmerman - *1**
1006 Russell St., Victoria, BC V9A 3K9
Tel: 250-384-1804; *Fax:* 250-384-1805
Toll-Free: 800-313-9581
wendy@vicwestlaw.ca
www.vicwestlaw.ca

West Vancouver: **Alan Stewart Andree, Esq. - *1**
#21, 285 - 17th St., West Vancouver, BC V7V 3S6
Tel: 604-922-6999; *Fax:* 604-922-6912
stewart@alansr.com

West Vancouver: **Brister, Yeager Law Corporation - *2**
#202, 1555 Marine Dr., West Vancouver, BC V7V 1N9
Tel: 604-921-1295; *Fax:* 604-921-1297
ryeager@dimissal.ca
www.dismissal.ca

West Vancouver: **Christopher B. Chu - *1**
#200, 100 Park Royal South, West Vancouver, BC V7T 1A2
Tel: 604-925-5898; *Fax:* 604-648-8361
cbchu@mail.com

West Vancouver: **David T. Forsyth - *1**
#1110, 100 Park Royal South, West Vancouver, BC V7T 1A2
Tel: 604-925-0045; *Fax:* 604-926-7782
dforsyth33@shaw.ca

West Vancouver: **Wm. Randall Fowle - *3**
#1003, 100 Park Royal South, West Vancouver, BC V7T 1A2
Tel: 604-922-6310; *Fax:* 604-922-6302
Toll-Free: 800-663-8996
fowle@axion.net

West Vancouver: **G.C. Geraghty - *1**
#200, 100 Park Royal South, West Vancouver, BC V7T 1A2
Tel: 604-921-9221; *Fax:* 604-921-9125
geraghty@gglawcorp.com
www.gglawcorp.com

West Vancouver: **Goluboff & Mazzei, Barristers & Solicitors - *3**
#201, 585 - 16th St., West Vancouver, BC V7V 3R8
Tel: 604-925-6900; *Fax:* 604-926-7817
rgoluboff@goluboffmazzei.com
www.goluboffmazzei.com

West Vancouver: **James C. Hutchinson - *1**
#200, 100 Park Royal, West Vancouver, BC V7T 1A2
Tel: 604-926-2876; *Fax:* 604-926-2836

West Vancouver: **Ketchum Communications Ltd. - *1**
3230 Mathers Ave., West Vancouver, BC V7T 2W6
Tel: 604-922-5204; *Fax:* 604-922-9774

West Vancouver: **Myrle L. Lawrence, Law Corporation - *1**
#203, 815 Main St., West Vancouver, BC V7T 2Z3
Tel: 604-925-9260; *Fax:* 604-925-9261
mlawrence@veritaslaw.ca

West Vancouver: **McCrea & Company - *1**
#101, 2221 Folkestone Way, West Vancouver, BC V7S 2Y6
Tel: 604-926-4524; *Fax:* 604-926-0222

West Vancouver: **McLean Armstrong - *6**
#300, 1497 Marine Dr., West Vancouver, BC V7T 1B8
Tel: 604-925-0672; *Fax:* 604-925-8984
info@mcleanarmstrong.com
www.mcleanarmstrong.com

West Vancouver: **E. Michael McMahon - *1**
#204, 2408 Haywood Ave., West Vancouver, BC V7V 1Y1
Tel: 604-926-1076; *Fax:* 604-926-1023
www.taxlitigate.com

West Vancouver: **John Moonen & Associates Ltd. - *1**
6475 Fox St., West Vancouver, BC V7W 2C3
Tel: 604-921-6433; *Fax:* 604-921-6433
johnmoonen@telus.net

West Vancouver: **Ryan & Associates - *1**
1220 Esquimalt Ave., West Vancouver, BC V7T 1K3
Tel: 604-926-3815; *Fax:* 604-926-3971
peterryan@telus.net

West Vancouver: **David H. Stoller - *1**
#801, 100 Park Royal S., West Vancouver, BC V7T 1A2
Tel: 604-922-4702; *Fax:* 604-922-0374
stoller@fireplug.net

West Vancouver: **Ann Marie Sweeney - *1**
#104, 1590 Bellevue Ave., West Vancouver, BC V7V 1A7
Tel: 604-922-0131; *Fax:* 604-922-0171

Westbank: **Bassett & Company - *5**
#260, 2300 Carrington Rd., Westbank, BC V4T 2N6
Tel: 250-768-5152; *Fax:* 250-768-3003
info@okanaganlaw.com
www.okanaganlaw.com

Whistler: **Mountain Law Corporation - *1**
#200, 1410 Alpha Lake Rd., Whistler, BC V0N 1B1
Tel: 604-938-4947; *Fax:* 604-938-0471
shrimpco@direct.ca
www.mountainlaw.com

Whistler: **Ian D. Reith - *1**
#14, 4227 Village Stroll, RR#4, Whistler, BC V0N 1B4
Tel: 604-932-6501; *Fax:* 604-932-5615

Whistler: **Taylor & Company Law Corporation - *1**
Black Tusk Village, 60 Rock Ridge, Whistler, BC V0N 1B1
Tel: 604-938-4840

Whistler: **Whistler Law Offices - *1**
#209, 4368 Main St., Whistler, BC V0N 1B1
Tel: 604-938-1763; *Fax:* 604-938-1764
Toll-Free: 877-938-1763
www.whistlerlawoffices.com

White Rock: **Cleveland & Doan - *3**
1321 Johnston Rd., White Rock, BC V4B 3Z3
Tel: 604-536-5002; *Fax:* 604-536-7002
lawyers@cleveland-doan.com
www.cleveland-doan.com

White Rock: **E.G. Mark - *1**
15252 Thrift Ave., White Rock, BC V4B 2L2
Tel: 604-542-0202; *Fax:* 604-542-0203

White Rock: **Medland & Company - *1**
14582 - 18th Ave., White Rock, BC V4A 5V5
Tel: 604-230-8476; *Fax:* 604-535-4145
medlandco@shaw.ca

White Rock: **Joseph M. Prodor - *1**
15260 Thrift Ave., White Rock, BC V4B 2L1
Tel: 604-536-4676; *Toll-Free:* 877-577-6367
jprodor@axionet.com

Williams Lake: **Alan P. Czepil - *1**
#202, 366 Yorston St., Williams Lake, BC V2G 4J5
Tel: 250-398-7001; *Fax:* 250-398-5651
czepl@telus.net

Williams Lake: **Vanderburgh & Company - *3**
#5, 123 Borland St., Williams Lake, BC V2G 1R1
Tel: 250-392-7161; *Fax:* 250-392-7060
aev@cariboolaw.com
www.cariboolaw.com

Winlaw: **Kenyon McGee - *1**
P.O. Box 11, 5612 Hwy. 6, Winlaw, BC V0G 2J0
Tel: 250-226-7615; *Fax:* 250-226-7818
kmlaw@netidea.com

Manitoba

Beausejour: **Bellan Wasylin & Associates - *5**
P.O. Box 520, 527 Park Ave., Beausejour, MB R0E 0C0
Tel: 204-268-2000; *Fax:* 204-268-3519

Beausejour: **Middleton & Middleton - *1**
P.O. Box 1150, 527 Park Ave., Beausejour, MB R0E 0C0
Tel: 204-268-4566; *Fax:* 204-268-4572
Toll-Free: 866-222-3259
wcmiddle@mb.sympatico.ca

Brandon: **Burgess Law Office - *1**
724 - 18th St., Brandon, MB R7A 5B5
Tel: 204-725-7070; *Fax:* 204-727-5995
burgesslaw@mts.net

Brandon: **Henry N. Carroll Q.C. - *3**
1331 Princess Ave., Brandon, MB R7A 0R4
Tel: 204-727-2266; *Fax:* 204-727-0548

Brandon: **Terri E. Deller Law Office - *1**
801 Princess Ave., Brandon, MB R7A 0P5
Tel: 204-726-0128
dellerlaw@westman.wave.ca

Brandon: **Donald Legal Services - *2**
#6, 940 Princess Ave., Brandon, MB R7A 0P6
Tel: 204-729-4900; *Fax:* 204-728-4477
ld@donaldlegal.com; rlonstrup@donaldlegal.com

Brandon: **Hunt, Miller & Co. LLP - *7**
148 - 8 St., Brandon, MB R7A 3X1
Tel: 204-727-8491; *Fax:* 204-727-4350
hmc@westman.wave.ca

Brandon: **Meighen, Haddad & Company - *15**
P.O. Box 22105, 110 - 11 St., Brandon, MB R7A 6Y9
Tel: 204-727-8461; *Fax:* 204-726-1948
mail@mhlaw.ca
www.mhlaw.ca

Brandon: **Paterson Patterson Wyman & Abel**
#1, Carriage House, 1040 Princess Ave., Brandon, MB R7A 0P8
Tel: 204-727-2424; *Fax:* 204-728-4670
patersons@mts.net
www.patersons.ca

Brandon: **James W. Potter - *1**
1202 Princess Ave., Brandon, MB R7A 0R3
Tel: 204-727-6431; *Fax:* 204-727-2818

Brandon: **Roy, Johnston & Company - *8**
363 - 10 St., Brandon, MB R7A 4E9
Tel: 204-727-0761; *Fax:* 204-726-1339
royjohnstonco@westman.wave.ca

Carman: **Brown & Associates - *2**
71 Main St. South, Carman, MB R0G 0J0
Tel: 204-745-2028; *Fax:* 204-745-3513
lawyers@brownlawoffice.org
www.brownlawoffice.org

** indicates number of lawyers*

Carman: Lee & Lee - *2
5 Centre Ave. West, Carman, MB R0G 0J0
Tel: 204-745-6751; *Fax:* 204-745-3481

Dauphin: Dawson Law Office - *1
34 - 1 Ave. NW, Dauphin, MB R7N 1G7
Tel: 204-638-4101; *Fax:* 204-638-8541

Dauphin: Hawkins & Sanderson - *1
20 - 2nd Ave. NW, Dauphin, MB R7N 1H2
Tel: 204-638-4121; *Fax:* 204-638-5942

Dauphin: Irwin Law Office - *2
122 Main St. North, Dauphin, MB R7N 1C2
Tel: 204-638-9249; *Fax:* 204-638-3647
irwinlaw@mts.net

Dauphin: Johnston & Company - *7
P.O. Box 551, 18 - 3 Ave. NW, Dauphin, MB R7N 2V4
Tel: 204-638-3211; *Fax:* 204-638-9646
irwinlaw@mts.net

Dauphin: Johnston & Company - *5
P.O. Box 551, 18 - 3rd Ave. NW, Dauphin, MB R7N 2V4
Tel: 204-638-3211; *Fax:* 204-638-9646
jandco@mb.sympatico.ca

Dauphin: Parkland Community Law Centre - *4
31 - 3rd Ave. NE, Dauphin, MB R7N 0Y5
Tel: 204-622-7000; *Fax:* 204-622-7029
Toll-Free: 800-810-6977

Deloraine: Sheldon Lanchbery - *1
P.O. Box 489, Deloraine, MB R0M 0M0
Tel: 204-747-2082; *Fax:* 204-747-2180
slanchbery@escape.ca

Erickson: Platt Law Office - *1
Erickson Professional Centre, P.O. Box 70, 36 Main St., Erickson, MB R0J 1P0
Tel: 204-636-7838; *Fax:* 204-636-7861
ajp@plattlegal.ca
www.plattlegal.ca

Flin Flon: Ginnell, Bauman, Watt - *2
P.O. Box 697, 47 Main St., Flin Flon, MB R8A 1N5
Tel: 204-687-3431; *Fax:* 204-687-5219

Killarney: Val Duke Barrister & Solicitor - *1
P.O. Box 99, Killarney, MB R0K 1G0
Tel: 204-523-4464; *Fax:* 204-523-5676
valdukelawoffice@mts.net

Manitou: Selby Law Office - *2
P.O. Box 279, 351 Main St., Manitou, MB R0G 1G0
Tel: 204-242-2801; *Fax:* 204-242-2723
selbylaw@mts.net

Minnedosa: Sims & Company - *2
P.O. Box 460, 76 Main St. South, Minnedosa, MB R0J 1E0
Tel: 204-867-2717; *Fax:* 204-867-2434
minnedosa@simsco.mb.ca
www.simsco.mb.ca

Morden: Hoeschen & Sloane
326 Stephen St., Morden, MB R6M 1T5
Tel: 204-822-4463; *Fax:* 204-822-6416
hslaw@mts.net

Neepawa: Taylor Law Office - *2
P.O. Box 309, 269 Hamilton St, Neepawa, MB R0J 1H0
Tel: 204-476-2336; *Fax:* 204-476-5783
taylaw@mymts.net

Portage la Prairie: Greenberg & Greenberg - *2
P.O. Box 157, 231 Saskatchewan Ave. East, Portage la Prairie, MB R1N 3B2
Tel: 204-857-6878; *Fax:* 204-857-3011
greenlaw@mts.net

Portage la Prairie: Miller Pressey Selinger - *1
P.O. Box 368, 103 Saskatchewan Ave. East, Portage la Prairie, MB R1N 3B7
Tel: 204-857-3436; *Fax:* 204-857-9238
mpslaw@mts.net

Roblin: Marcel J.J.R. Gregoire - *1
P.O. Box 1630, 158 Main St., Roblin, MB R0L 1P0
Tel: 204-937-2117; *Fax:* 204-937-4576
mgreg@mb.sympatico.ca

Russell: Mason D. Jardine - *1
P.O. Box 1270, 346 Main St., Russell, MB R0J 1W0
Tel: 204-773-2165; *Fax:* 204-773-2920
mjardine@escape.ca

Selkirk: W. Douglas Kitchen - *1
1202 River Rd., Selkirk, MB R1A 2E1
Tel: 204-482-8929

Selkirk: Kohaykewych & Associates - *1
413 Main St., Selkirk, MB R1A 1V2
Tel: 204-482-7925; *Fax:* 204-482-7099
kohaykewych@mts.net

Selkirk: David L. Moore & Assoc. - *2
407 Main St., Selkirk, MB R1A 1T9
Tel: 204-482-3921; *Fax:* 204-482-5564
Toll-Free: 877-482-3921
d.moore.law@mts.net

Souris: Forrest & Forrest - *1
P.O. Box 276, 4 Crescent Ave., Souris, MB R0K 2C0
Tel: 204-483-2171; *Fax:* 204-483-3389
fforrest@mts.net

Steinbach: Loewen Henderson Banman Legault LLP - *4
#200, 250 Main St., Steinbach, MB R5G 1Y8
Tel: 204-326-6454; *Fax:* 204-326-6917

Steinbach: Smith Neufeld Jodoin - *14
P.O. Box 1267, Steinbach, MB R5G 1M9
Tel: 204-326-3442; *Fax:* 204-326-2154
lawyers@snj.mb.ca
www.snj.mb.ca

Stonewall: Grantham Law Offices - *1
Westside Plaza, P.O. Box 1400, #1, 333 Main St., Stonewall, MB R0C 2Z0
Tel: 204-467-5527; *Fax:* 204-467-5550

Swan River: Burnside & Company - *2
P.O. Box 340, 509 Main St. East, Swan River, MB R0L 1Z0
Tel: 204-734-3485; *Fax:* 204-734-2872
ggb@burnsideferris.com

Swan River: Palsson Law Office - *2
P.O. Box 1238, 114 - 5th Ave. North, Swan River, MB R0L 1Z0
Tel: 204-734-4528; *Fax:* 204-734-5085

Teulon: Steven R. Shinnie - *1
P.O. Box 149, 34 Main St., Teulon, MB R0C 3B0
Tel: 204-886-3959; *Fax:* 204-886-3962

The Pas: Bjornsson & Wight Law Office - *2
#3, P.O. Box 1769, 314 Edwards Ave., The Pas, MB R9A 1L5
Tel: 204-627-1200; *Fax:* 204-627-1210
dblwlaw@mailme.ca

The Pas: Mirwaldt & Gray - *3
P.O. Box 2280, 272 - 2nd St. West, The Pas, MB R9A 1M1
Tel: 204-623-7845; *Fax:* 204-623-5353
mirwgray@mail.mts.net

The Pas: Watkins Law Office - *1
P.O. Box 1349, Stn. Main, 114 - 3rd St., The Pas, MB R9A 1L3
Tel: 204-623-6472; *Fax:* 204-623-6486

Thompson: Mayer, Dearman & Pellizzaro - *3
7 Selkirk Ave., Thompson, MB R8N 0M4
Tel: 204-677-2393; *Fax:* 204-778-8125

Thompson: McDonald, Huberdeau - *3
Westwood Mall, 436 Thompson Dr. North, Thompson, MB R8N 0C6
Tel: 204-677-2366; *Fax:* 204-677-3249

Thompson: Ronald J. Nadeau Law Office - *1
76 Severn Cres., Thompson, MB R8N 1M6
Tel: 204-677-4807; *Fax:* 204-778-6559

Virden: McNeill Harasymchuk McConnell - *3
P.O. Box 520, 243 Raglan St. S, Virden, MB R0M 2C0
Tel: 204-748-1220; *Fax:* 204-748-3007

Winkler: Hoeschen & Stewart
#6, 720 Norquay Dr., Winkler, MB R6W 4A6
Tel: 204-325-4233; *Fax:* 204-325-9889
hslaw@mts.net

Winnipeg: 6327435 Canada Ltd - *1
#203, 897 Corydon Ave., Winnipeg, MB R3M 0W7
Tel: 204-453-1965; *Fax:* 204-475-5247

Winnipeg: Abrams George Tweed Wawrykow - *4
#4, 549 Regent Ave. West, Winnipeg, MB R2C 1R9
Tel: 204-949-3080; *Fax:* 204-949-3089
btweed@atwlaw.ca

Winnipeg: Agrawal Law Office - *1
#B, 83 Sherbrook St., Winnipeg, MB R3C 2B2
Tel: 204-779-7265; *Fax:* 204-779-6334

Winnipeg: Aikins, MacAulay & Thorvaldson LLP - *90
#30th Floor, 360 Main St., Winnipeg, MB R3C 4G1
Tel: 204-957-0050; *Fax:* 204-957-0840
amt@aikins.com
www.aikins.com

Winnipeg: Alexander Law Office - *1
387 Broadway Ave., Winnipeg, MB R3C 0V5
Tel: 204-943-1677; *Fax:* 204-949-9232
dalaw_101@hotmail.com

Winnipeg: Antymniuk & Antymniuk - *3
#11, 1500 Dakota St., Winnipeg, MB R2N 3Y7
Tel: 204-254-3511; *Fax:* 204-257-5139

Winnipeg: Scott Armstrong Law Office - *1
64 Silver Springs Bay, Winnipeg, MB R2K 4L4
Tel: 204-663-8772; *Fax:* 204-663-8432
armstrong.scott@usa.net

Winnipeg: Asper Foundation - *1
#1504, 201 Portage Ave., Winnipeg, MB R3B 3K6
Tel: 204-989-5538; *Fax:* 204-989-5536
mlevy@aspergroup.com

Winnipeg: Assiniboia Law Group - *1
3651 Roblin Blvd., Winnipeg, MB R3R 0E2
Tel: 204-949-3240; *Fax:* 204-949-3249
jbarber@shawbiz.ca

Winnipeg: Bernstein & Hirsch - *3
#508, 283 Portage Ave., Winnipeg, MB R3B 2B5
Tel: 204-942-0706; *Fax:* 204-957-1345

Winnipeg: Booth, Dennehy LLP - *15
387 Broadway Ave., Winnipeg, MB R3C 0V5
Tel: 204-957-1717; *Fax:* 204-943-6199
general@dek-law.com

Winnipeg: Broadway Law Group - *6
#300, 326 Broadway Ave., Winnipeg, MB R3C 0S5
Tel: 204-984-9420; *Fax:* 204-947-2757

Winnipeg: Brodsky & Company - *3
#1212, 363 Broadway Ave., Winnipeg, MB R3C 3N9
Tel: 204-940-4433; *Fax:* 204-940-4435

Winnipeg: Bradley J. Brooks - *1
P.O. Box 27009, 360 Main St., Winnipeg, MB R3C 4T3
Tel: 204-992-4700; *Fax:* 204-992-2462
Toll-Free: 888-259-4700
bbrooks@cite-on-site.ca

Winnipeg: Bueti, Baumstark - *2
#206, 897 Corydon Ave., Winnipeg, MB R3M 0W7
Tel: 204-475-3570; *Fax:* 204-453-0136

Winnipeg: Campbell Marr - *13
10 Donald St., Winnipeg, MB R3C 1L5
Tel: 204-942-3311; *Fax:* 204-943-7997
dimarr@campbellmarr.com
www.campbellmarr.com

Winnipeg: Canwest Direction Ltd. - *2
#1504, 201 Portage Ave., Winnipeg, MB R3B 8K6
Tel: 204-989-5525; *Fax:* 204-989-5536
gasper@aspergroup.com

Winnipeg: Michael Capozzi - *1
45 Wharton Blvd., Winnipeg, MB R2Y 0S9
Tel: 204-832-4807; *Fax:* 204-895-2336

Winnipeg: Cassidy Ramsay - *7
385 St. Mary Ave., 2nd Fl., Winnipeg, MB R3C 0N1
Tel: 204-943-7454; *Fax:* 204-943-9563
kwan@cassidyramsay.com

Winnipeg: Champagne Law Office - *1
390 Provencher Blvd., Unit F, Winnipeg, MB R2H 0H1
Tel: 204-956-1199; *Fax:* 204-956-5333

Winnipeg: Chapman Goddard Kagan - *8
1864 Portage Ave., Winnipeg, MB R3J 0H2
Tel: 204-888-7973; *Fax:* 204-832-3461
Toll-Free: 800-665-6119
info@cgklaw.ca
www.cgklaw.ca

** indicates number of lawyers*

Winnipeg: **Jack M. Chapman & Associates - *1**
#246, 2026 Corydon Ave., #162, Winnipeg, MB R3P 0N5
Tel: 204-942-9994; *Fax:* 204-885-7420
ve4ae@aol.com

Winnipeg: **Cherniack Smith - *7**
#200, 100 Osborne St., Winnipeg, MB R3L 1Y5
Tel: 204-452-4000; *Fax:* 204-477-1856

Winnipeg: **S. Cohan - *1**
#607, 386 Broadway, Winnipeg, MB R3C 3R6
Tel: 204-944-1413; *Fax:* 204-943-5102

Winnipeg: **Phillip F.B. Cramer Law Office - *1**
390 York St., Winnipeg, MB R3C 0P3
Tel: 204-987-0070; *Fax:* 204-987-0076
pfcramer@mts.net

Winnipeg: **D'Arcy & Deacon LLP - *34**
330 St. Mary Ave., 12th Fl., Winnipeg, MB R3C 4E1
Tel: 204-942-2271; *Fax:* 204-943-4242
inquiries@darcydeacon.com
www.darcydeacon.com

Winnipeg: **Deeley, Fabbri, Sellen - *15**
#903, 386 Broadway, Winnipeg, MB R3C 3R6
Tel: 204-949-1710; *Fax:* 204-956-4457
info@dfslaw.ca
www.dfslaw.ca

Winnipeg: **Dowhan & Dowhan - *2**
61 Albert St., Winnipeg, MB R3B 1G3
Tel: 204-942-4235; *Fax:* 204-956-4560

Winnipeg: **Duboff Edwards Haight & Schachter - *10**
#1900, 155 Carlton St., Winnipeg, MB R3C 3H8
Tel: 204-942-3361; *Fax:* 204-942-3362
duboff@dehslaw.com

Winnipeg: **Edmond & Associates - *4**
#204, 1120 Grant Ave., Winnipeg, MB R3M 2A6
Tel: 204-452-5314; *Fax:* 204-452-5989
gedmond@edmond.ca

Winnipeg: **Einarson & Einarson - *3**
#1105, 444 St. Mary Ave., Winnipeg, MB R3C 3T1
Tel: 204-942-2419

Winnipeg: **Fredrick D. & Associates Inc. - *1**
#830, 167 Lombard Ave., Winnipeg, MB R3C 0B3
Tel: 204-453-8065; *Fax:* 204-475-2067
fmantey@fdanda.com

Winnipeg: **David Friesen Q.C. & Associates - *1**
#711, 213 Notre Dame Ave., Winnipeg, MB R3B 1N3
Tel: 204-942-2171

Winnipeg: **Richard S. Fulham - *1**
1900 Portage Ave., Winnipeg, MB R3J 0H9
Tel: 204-957-1413; *Fax:* 204-957-1858

Winnipeg: **Funk & Strell - *2**
#1400, 1 Lombard Pl., Winnipeg, MB R3B 0X3
Tel: 204-957-5600; *Fax:* 204-949-1043
funk@mts.net

Winnipeg: **Zachary I. Garber - *1**
385 St. Mary Ave., 2nd Fl., Winnipeg, MB R3C 0N1
Tel: 204-943-7454; *Fax:* 204-943-9563

Winnipeg: **J. David George & Associates - *2**
108 Regent Ave. East, Winnipeg, MB R2C 0C1
Tel: 204-982-7503; *Fax:* 204-222-4761
david-dg@shaw.ca

Winnipeg: **Martin D. Glazer - *1**
#506, 294 Portage Ave., Winnipeg, MB R3C 0B9
Tel: 204-942-6560; *Fax:* 204-942-2696
mglazlaw@mts.net

Winnipeg: **Martin Gutnik - *1**
#307, 1661 Portage Ave., Winnipeg, MB R3J 3T7
Tel: 204-786-8924; *Fax:* 204-786-8525
martin@gutnik.com
www.gutnik.com

Winnipeg: **Habing Law - *3**
2643 Portage Ave., Winnipeg, MB R3J 0P9
Tel: 204-832-8322; *Fax:* 204-832-3906
ron@habinglaw.com

Winnipeg: **Hogue, ALain J. Law Office - *1**
194 Provencher Blvd., Winnipeg, MB R2H 0G3
Tél: 204-237-9600; *Téléc:* 204-233-2689

Winnipeg: **Hook & Smith - *4**
#201, 3111 Portage Ave., Winnipeg, MB R3K 0W4
Tel: 204-885-4520; *Fax:* 204-837-9846
general@hookandsmith.com

Winnipeg: **Inkster Christie Hughes LLP, Barristers & Solicitors - *13**
#700, 444 St. Mary Ave., Winnipeg, MB R3C 3T1
Tel: 204-947-6801
info@inksterchristie.ca
www.inksterchristie.ca

Winnipeg: **Frederick Innis - *1**
8 Ruskin Row, Winnipeg, MB R3M 2R6
Tel: 204-231-9600
innis@shaw.ca

Winnipeg: **Marion Ironquil Meadmore - *1**
1187 Fleet Ave., Winnipeg, MB R3M 1K9
Tel: 204-947-1509

Winnipeg: **Karasevich Windsor Jenion Hedley LLP - *4**
#440, 5 Donald St. South, Winnipeg, MB R3L 2T4
Tel: 204-477-0285; *Fax:* 204-453-8876
jgk@escape.ca

Winnipeg: **D.R. Knight Law Office - *5**
#202, 900 Harrow St. East, Winnipeg, MB R3M 3Y7
Tel: 204-948-0400; *Fax:* 204-948-0401
don.knight@knightlaw.ca

Winnipeg: **Krawchuk & Company - *2**
#2250, 360 Main St., Winnipeg, MB R3C 3Z3
Tel: 204-943-4561; *Fax:* 204-947-5724
krawchukandco@mts.net

Winnipeg: **Frank Lawrence - *1**
#202, 1382 Henderson Hwy., Winnipeg, MB R2G 1M8
Tel: 204-338-9705

Winnipeg: **Victoria E. Lehman Law Offices - *1**
412 Wardlaw Ave., Winnipeg, MB R3L 0L7
Tel: 204-453-6416; *Fax:* 204-477-1379

Winnipeg: **Levene, Tadman, Gutkin, Golub LLP - *16**
#700, 330 St. Mary Ave., Winnipeg, MB R3C 3Z5
Tel: 204-957-0520; *Fax:* 204-957-1696
www.lt.mb.ca

Winnipeg: **Liffman Soronow - *2**
#210, 400 St. Mary Ave., Winnipeg, MB R3C 4K5
Tel: 204-925-6070; *Fax:* 204-944-0513
hal@escape.ca

Winnipeg: **Loewen & Martens, Barristers & Solicitors - *5**
1101 Henderson Hwy., Winnipeg, MB R2G 1L4
Tel: 204-338-9364; *Fax:* 204-338-8379
lmlaw@shawbiz.ca

Winnipeg: **MacInnes, Burbidge - *2**
#500, 177 Lombard Ave., Winnipeg, MB R3B 0W5
Tel: 204-942-5256; *Fax:* 204-942-5259

Winnipeg: **Hilary C. Maxim - *1**
212B Regent Ave. West, Winnipeg, MB R2C 1R2
Tel: 204-224-2600; *Fax:* 204-222-2824

Winnipeg: **McDonald Law Office - *1**
258 Tache Ave., Winnipeg, MB R2H 1Z9
Tel: 204-927-3900; *Fax:* 204-927-3909
Toll-Free: 800-393-1110
info@mcdonaldlaw.ca
www.mcdonaldlaw.ca

Winnipeg: **McJannet Rich - *5**
#1710, Newport Centre, 330 Portage Ave., Winnipeg, MB R3C 0C4
Tel: 204-957-0951; *Fax:* 204-989-0688

Winnipeg: **McMahon Consulting - *1**
418 Cordova St., Winnipeg, MB R3N 1A6
Tel: 204-489-0756; *Fax:* 204-487-4724
mcmahon@mts.net

Winnipeg: **McRoberts Law Office LLP - *13**
#200, Madison Square, 1630 Ness Ave., Winnipeg, MB R3J 3X1
Tel: 204-944-7907; *Fax:* 204-772-1684
consult@mcrobertslawoffice.com
www.mcrobertslawoffice.com

Winnipeg: **Michaels & Stern - *2**
#300, 326 Broadway Ave., Winnipeg, MB R3C 0S5
Tel: 204-989-5500; *Fax:* 204-989-5508
michaelsandstern@mts.net

Winnipeg: **Peter J. Moss - *5**
1002 Pembina Hwy., Winnipeg, MB R3T 1Z5
Tel: 204-284-3221; *Fax:* 204-284-7960
mosslaw@shaw.ca

Winnipeg: **Murray & Kovnats - *2**
#100, 1600 Ness Ave., Winnipeg, MB R3J 3W7
Tel: 204-957-1700; *Fax:* 204-942-2325
brmk1@aol.com

Winnipeg: **Mutchmor, Violago, Overall, Grimes - *3**
390 York Ave., Winnipeg, MB R3C 0P3
Tel: 204-989-1300; *Fax:* 204-989-1301

Winnipeg: **Myers Weinberg LLP - *25**
#724, Cargill Bldg., 240 Graham Ave., Winnipeg, MB R3C 0J7
Tel: 204-942-0501; *Fax:* 204-956-0625
info@myersfirm.com

Winnipeg: **Stanley S. Nozick - *1**
#605, 386 Broadway, Winnipeg, MB R3C 3R6
Tel: 204-944-8227; *Fax:* 204-944-9246
snozick@escape.ca

Winnipeg: **Orle, Davidson, Giesbrecht, Bargen - *10**
280 Stradbrook Ave., Winnipeg, MB R3L 0J6
Tel: 204-989-2760; *Fax:* 204-989-2774
general@odgb.mb.ca
www.odgb.mb.ca

Winnipeg: **Murray S. Palay - *1**
#703, 161 Portage Ave. East, Winnipeg, MB R3B 0Y4
Tel: 204-944-2491; *Fax:* 204-944-8046
mpalay@quadasset.com

Winnipeg: **Pam Smith & Company - *4**
#1210, 363 Broadway, Winnipeg, MB R3C 3N9
Tel: 204-982-4414; *Fax:* 204-943-2573
smsmgmt@mts.net

Winnipeg: **Parashin Law Office - *1**
404 McGregor St., Winnipeg, MB R2W 4X5
Tel: 204-582-3558

Winnipeg: **PDB Communications - *1**
72 Humboldt Ave., Winnipeg, MB R2M 0M1
Tel: 204-237-9879; *Fax:* 204-237-9879
pdesaulniers@shaw.ca

Winnipeg: **Perlov Stewart LLP - *5**
#610, One Lombard Place, Winnipeg, MB R3B 3G5
Tel: 204-944-9295; *Fax:* 204-956-4270
www.pslfirm.ca

Winnipeg: **Phillips, Aiello - *10**
668 Corydon Ave., Winnipeg, MB R3M 0X7
Tel: 204-949-7700; *Fax:* 204-452-0922
Toll-Free: 866-949-7701
phillipsaiello@phillipsaiello.ca

Winnipeg: **Pitblado LLP - *57**
#2500, Commodity Exchange Tower, 360 Main St., Winnipeg, MB R3C 4H6
Tel: 204-956-0560; *Fax:* 204-957-0227
firm@pitblado.com
www.pitblado.com

Winnipeg: **Pollock & Company - *5**
#1120, 363 Broadway, Winnipeg, MB R3C 3N9
Tel: 204-956-0450; *Fax:* 204-947-0109
mail@pollockandcompany.com

Winnipeg: **Gordon C. Pollock - *1**
#1401, 180 Tuxedo Ave., Winnipeg, MB R3P 2A6
Tel: 204-489-4945; *Fax:* 204-489-5071
gpollock7@shaw.ca

Winnipeg: **Posner & Trachtenberg - *2**
#710, 491 Portage Ave., Winnipeg, MB R3B 2E4
Tel: 204-940-9602; *Fax:* 204-944-8878

Winnipeg: **Jay C. Prober - *1**
#208, 387 Broadway Ave., Winnipeg, MB R3C 0V5
Tel: 204-957-1205; *Fax:* 204-943-6199

Winnipeg: **Pullan Kammerloch Frohlinger - *10**
#300, 240 Kennedy St., Winnipeg, MB R3C 1T1
Tel: 204-956-0490; *Fax:* 204-947-3747
firm@pkf-law.com
www.pkflawyers.com

** indicates number of lawyers*

Winnipeg: Radchuk & Company - *1
10 Salvia Bay, Winnipeg, MB R2V 2L8
Tel: 204-338-8880; *Fax:* 204-334-5241

Winnipeg: Arlene S. Ratuski - *1
#201, 1215 Henderson Hwy., Winnipeg, MB R2G 1L8
Tel: 204-334-4994; *Fax:* 204-339-6449

Winnipeg: Rénald Rémillard - *1
123 Lawndale Ave., Winnipeg, MB R2H 1T2
Tel: 204-237-1818; *Fax:* 204-233-0245
rremillard@ustboniface.mb.ca

Winnipeg: Edward Rice - *1
#301, 63 Albert St., Winnipeg, MB R3B 1G4
Tel: 204-944-1905; *Fax:* 204-947-5895
ricelaw@mts.net

Winnipeg: Russell Ridd - *1
405 Broadway, 6th Fl., Winnipeg, MB R3C 3L6
Tel: 204-945-2871; *Fax:* 204-945-1260
rridd@gov.mb.ca

Winnipeg: Robertson Shypit Soble Wood - *5
#202, 1555 St. Mary's Rd., Winnipeg, MB R2M 5L9
Tel: 204-257-6061; *Fax:* 204-254-7183

Winnipeg: James F.C. Rose - *1
582 Bruce Ave., Winnipeg, MB R3J 0W5
Tel: 204-889-3885; *Fax:* 204-889-3885
Toll-Free: 800-414-8091
jamesrose@shaw.ca
www.members.shaw.ca/jamesrose/baddebt.htm

Winnipeg: Rosenbaum & Company - *4
#201, 2211 McPhillips St., Winnipeg, MB R2V 3M5
Tel: 204-338-4663; *Fax:* 204-338-4667

Winnipeg: Sheldon Rosenstock - *1
848 Waterloo St., Winnipeg, MB R3N 0T6
Tel: 204-488-4121; *Fax:* 204-488-1869
rosensto@shaw.ca
www.rosenstockimmigration.com

Winnipeg: Rutledge Law Office - *2
#310, 3025 Portage Ave., Winnipeg, MB R3K 2E2
Tel: 204-987-7575; *Fax:* 204-837-3638
rutlaw@mts.net

Winnipeg: Mario J. Santos - *1
#206, 819 Sargent Ave., Winnipeg, MB R3E 0B9
Tel: 204-783-0554; *Fax:* 204-772-4231

Winnipeg: Shewchuk & Associates - *2
2645 Portage Ave., Winnipeg, MB R3J 0P9
Tel: 204-889-4595

Winnipeg: Sinclair & Associates - *2
#231, 1120 Grant Ave., Winnipeg, MB R3M 2A6
Tel: 204-474-2468; *Fax:* 204-474-2535
sgilchrist@sinclairassociates.ca

Winnipeg: Slusky & Slusky - *1
#1028, 363 Broadway, Winnipeg, MB R3C 3N9
Tel: 204-943-5455; *Fax:* 204-942-4301

Winnipeg: Soronow Law Office
#210, 400 St. Mary Ave., Winnipeg, MB R3C 4K5
Tel: 204-925-6074; *Fax:* 204-944-0513
sgs@mts.net

Winnipeg: J.S. Sukhan - *1
1158 Clarence Ave., Winnipeg, MB R3T 1S9
Tel: 204-284-0728

Winnipeg: Tacium, Vincent, Orlikow - *1
#200, 99A Scurfield Blvd., Winnipeg, MB R3Y 1G4
Tel: 204-989-8767; *Fax:* 204-989-8765
resolveconflict@mb.aibn.com

Winnipeg: Tapper Cuddy LLP - *23
#1000, 330 St. Mary Ave., Winnipeg, MB R3C 3Z5
Tel: 204-944-8777; *Fax:* 204-947-2593
tc@tcwpg.com
www.tcwpg.com

Winnipeg: Taylor McCaffrey LLP - *62
400 St. Mary Ave., 9th Fl., Winnipeg, MB R3C 4K5
Tel: 204-949-1312; *Fax:* 204-957-0945
www.tmlawyers.com

Winnipeg: Tepley Law Office - *1
#401, 460 Main St., Winnipeg, MB R3B 1B6
Tel: 204-942-7218

Winnipeg: Teskey Legal & ADR Services - *1
1905 One Evergreen Pl., Winnipeg, MB R3L 0E9
Tel: 204-943-8395; *Fax:* 204-943-1288
teskey@mb.sympatico.ca

Winnipeg: Thompson Dorfman Sweatman LLP - *68
#2200, CanWest Global Place, 201 Portage Ave., Winnipeg, MB R3B 3L3
Tel: 204-957-1930; *Fax:* 204-934-0570
tds@tdslaw.com
www.tdslaw.com

Winnipeg: John F. Thullner - *1
#102, 2200 McPhillips St., Winnipeg, MB R2V 3P4
Tel: 204-694-0161

Winnipeg: Tupper & Adams - *8
200 Portage Ave., 4th Fl., Winnipeg, MB R3C 3X2
Tel: 204-942-0161; *Fax:* 204-943-2385
general@tupper-adams.mb.ca
www.tupper-adams.mb.ca

Winnipeg: W.R. Van Walleghem - *1
#206, 1120 Grant Ave., Winnipeg, MB R3M 2A6
Tel: 204-477-0210; *Fax:* 204-452-9746

Winnipeg: Walsh & Company - *3
426 Portage Ave., Winnipeg, MB R3C 0C9
Tel: 204-947-2282; *Fax:* 204-943-0211
paulwalsh@walshandco.com

Winnipeg: Warkentin & Calver - *1
3651 Roblin Blvd., Winnipeg, MB R3R 0E2
Tel: 204-949-3230; *Fax:* 204-949-3249
pcalver@warkcal.ca
www.warkcal.ca

Winnipeg: E. Waskiw - *1
441 Perth Ave., Winnipeg, MB R2V 0T9
Tel: 204-334-7372

Winnipeg: Arthur M. Werier - *1
905 Corydon Ave., Winnipeg, MB R3M 0W8
Tel: 204-475-7923

Winnipeg: Wilder Wilder & Langtry - *8
#1500, Richardson Bldg., 1 Lombard Pl., Winnipeg, MB R3B 0X3
Tel: 204-947-1456; *Fax:* 204-957-1368
Toll-Free: 888-470-0847
admin@wilderwilder.com
www.wilderwilder.com

Winnipeg: Zaifman Associates - *4
191 Lombard Ave., 5th Fl., Winnipeg, MB R3B 0X1
Tel: 204-944-8888; *Fax:* 204-956-2909
zaifman@zaifmanlaw.com
www.pureimmigration.com

Winnipeg: Saheel, Zaman Law Corporation - *4
#1130, 363 Broadway, Winnipeg, MB R3C 3N9
Tel: 204-943-9922; *Fax:* 204-975-1802
szaman@szamanlaw.com

Winnipeg: Daria Zyla - *1
1230 Hector Bay West, Winnipeg, MB R3M 3R9
Tel: 204-452-5626; *Fax:* 204-475-7979

New Brunswick

Atholville: Roger G. Gauvin - *1
65 Fairview St., Atholville, NB E3N 4N3
Tel: 506-753-4545; *Fax:* 506-753-2006

Bathurst: Chiasson & Roy - *3
#203, Stn. Main, 216 Main St., Bathurst, NB E2A 3Z2
Tel: 506-548-3375; *Fax:* 506-548-4264

Bathurst: John Douglas Hazen - *1
132 Main St., Bathurst, NB E2A 1A4
Tel: 506-545-9220; *Fax:* 506-545-9224

Bathurst: Robichaud, Theriault, Riordon, Arseneault - *5
#300, Keystone Place, P.O. Box 506, 270 Douglas Ave., Bathurst, NB E2A 3Z4
Tel: 506-548-8822; *Fax:* 506-548-5297

Bouctouche: Yvon J.G. LeBlanc - *2
25, boul Irving, Bouctouche, NB E4S 3J5
Tel: 506-743-2427; *Fax:* 506-743-8314
lebbell@nbnet.nb.ca

Bouctouche: Mark Robere - *1
#2, 6, rue Station, Bouctouche, NB E4S 3X1
Tel: 506-743-2262; *Fax:* 506-743-9014
roberem@nbnet.nb.ca

Campbellton: J.Yvon Arseneau C.P. Inc. - *3
P.O. Box 520, Stn. Main, 112 Roseberry St., Campbellton, NB E3N 3G9
Tel: 506-753-3000; *Fax:* 506-753-2393
jyarseneau@nb.aibn.com

Campbellton: Terrance H. Delaney, Q.C. - *2
#206, P.O. Box 490, 123 Water St., Campbellton, NB E3N 3G9
Tel: 506-753-7618; *Fax:* 506-759-7315
terra1@nb.sympatico.ca

Caraquet: Alie A. LeBouthillier - *1
CP 5661, 295, boul St-Pierre ouest, Caraquet, NB E1W 1B7
Tél: 506-727-3484; *Téléc:* 506-727-3484
alie@nb.aira.com

Chipman: Nicholas D. DiCarlo
P.O. Box 489, Stn. Main, 131 Main St., Chipman, NB E4A 3N6
Tel: 506-339-6688; *Fax:* 506-339-5598
ndicarlo@nbaibn.com

Chipman: Sharon R. Lockwood - *1
28 Northrup Dr., Chipman, NB E4A 2P7
Tel: 506-339-6632; *Fax:* 506-339-5130
sharon.lockwood@nb.aibn.com

Dalhousie: Dubé & Associate - *2
P.O. Box 1900, 390 William St., Dalhousie, NB E0K 1B0
Tel: 506-684-5661; *Fax:* 506-684-5011

Dieppe: Martin J. Aubin - *1
250 Acadie Ave., Dieppe, NB E1A 1G5
Tel: 506-856-6083; *Fax:* 506-853-0110

Dieppe: Thompson & Thompson - *2
379 Champlain St., Dieppe, NB E1A 1P2
Tel: 506-859-7794; *Fax:* 506-859-1297

Edmundston: Roger D. Poitras - *1
87, ch Canada, Edmundston, NB E3V 1V6
Tél: 506-739-7335; *Téléc:* 506-735-4139

Fredericton: Cleveland J. Allaby - *1
#200, 480 Queen St., Fredericton, NB E3B 1B6
Tel: 506-459-9737; *Fax:* 506-452-8962
allabycj@nbnet.nb.ca

Fredericton: Atkinson & Atkinson - *1
P.O. Box 700, 108 Queen St., Fredericton, NB E3B 5B4
Tel: 506-451-7777; *Fax:* 506-451-1029
fealaw@nb.aibn.com

Fredericton: Carol H.Y. Boxill - *1
P.O. Box 1321, Stn. A, 57 Carleton St., Fredericton, NB E3B 5E3
Tel: 506-454-5108; *Fax:* 506-450-3880
aa623@fan.nb.ca

Fredericton: Le Cabinet Bertrand Law - *1
#402, 850 Prospect St., Fredericton, NB E3B 9M5
Tel: 506-450-3325; *Fax:* 506-450-6333
bertran2@nbnet.nb.ca

Fredericton: B.H. Campbell - *1
P.O. Box 295, Stn. A, 334 Saint John St., Fredericton, NB E3B 4B6
Tel: 506-458-8140; *Fax:* 506-450-6186
bhclaw@nb.aibn.com

Fredericton: Leycester D. D'Arcy - *1
P.O. Box 93, Stn. A, Fredericton, NB E3B 4Y2
Tel: 506-454-2552

Fredericton: Dean & McMath - *2
406 Regent St., Fredericton, NB E3B 3X7
Tel: 506-458-8555; *Fax:* 506-444-0920
dwmcmath@deanmcmath.ca

Fredericton: DLB Consulting Inc. - *1
#310, 590 Queen St., Fredericton, NB E3B 7H9
Tel: 506-459-4546
dlbcons@rogers.com

Fredericton: Eddy & Downs - *2
#210, P.O. Box 1205, Stn. A, 65 Regent St., Fredericton, NB E3B 5C8
Tel: 506-443-9700; *Fax:* 506-443-9710

** indicates number of lawyers*

***Fredericton*: Gaffney & Burke - *2**
466 Bowlen St., Fredericton, NB E3A 2T4
Tel: 506-458-8124; *Fax:* 506-458-2652
gaffneyburke@nb.aibn.com

***Fredericton*: Gordon F. Gregory Law Office - *1**
#2, 110 Queen St., Fredericton, NB E3B 1A5
Tel: 506-458-8060; *Fax:* 506-459-8288

***Fredericton*: Hughes, Yeamans, Campbell - *2**
P.O. Box 295, 551 Charlotte St., Fredericton, NB E3B 4Y9
Tel: 506-458-8140; *Fax:* 506-450-6186

***Fredericton*: Kenny & Murray - *5**
P.O. Box 1572, Stn. A, 228 Brunswick St., Fredericton, NB E3B 5G2
Tel: 506-458-1108; *Fax:* 506-458-2645
kenny@nbnet.nb.ca

***Fredericton*: Matthews McCrea Elliott - *7**
197 Main St., Fredericton, NB E3A 1E1
Tel: 506-458-5959; *Fax:* 506-460-5934
office@matthewsmccreaelliott.com
www.matthewsmccreaelliott.com

***Fredericton*: Charles S. McAllister - *1**
68 London Ct., Fredericton, NB E3B 6K9
Tel: 506-454-6852

***Fredericton*: Daniel W. McCormack - *1**
P.O. Box 1356, Stn. A, 259 Brunswick St., Fredericton, NB E3B 5S3
Tel: 506-459-3331; *Fax:* 506-457-6332

***Fredericton*: McNally & Smart - *2**
P.O. Box 3152, Stn. LCD 1, 819 Union St., Fredericton, NB E3A 5G9
Tel: 506-472-4872; *Fax:* 506-472-9844

***Fredericton*: Mockler Peters Oley Rouse - *7**
P.O. Box 547, Stn. A., 839 Aberdeen St., Fredericton, NB E3B 5A6
Tel: 506-444-6589; *Fax:* 506-444-6550
www.mpor.ca

***Fredericton*: J. Shawn O'Toole - *1**
#201, 346 Queen St., Fredericton, NB E3B 1B2
Tel: 506-458-8833; *Fax:* 506-454-1999

***Fredericton*: Mark C. Paul-Elias - *1**
#5, Pepper Creek Plaza, 336, Rte. 10, Richibucto Rd., Fredericton, NB E3A 7E1
Tel: 506-458-1880; *Fax:* 506-458-9868
peppercreek@brunnet.net

***Fredericton*: Pink Larkin - *4**
#210, 1133 Regent St., Fredericton, NB E3B 3Z2
Tel: 506-458-1989; *Fax:* 506-458-1127
www.pinklarkin.com

***Fredericton*: Gerald R. Pugh - *1**
57 Carleton St., 4th Fl., Fredericton, NB E3B 3T2
Tel: 506-450-2666; *Fax:* 506-457-4295
drwp@nb.aibn.com

***Fredericton*: Yerxa, Stephenson - *3**
#208, P.O. Box 175, Stn. A, 403 Regent St., Fredericton, NB E3B 4Y9
Tel: 506-459-1450; *Fax:* 506-459-2301
lawoffice@yerstep.com
www.yerstep.com

***Grand Falls*: Duffie, DesChênes - *2**
Box 7336, 346 Chapel St., Grand Falls, NB E3Z 2M4
Tel: 506-473-2221; *Fax:* 506-473-3253
peduffie@nbnet.nb.ca

***Grand Falls*: Godbout, Ouellette - *2**
698 E.H. Daigle Blvd., Grand Falls, NB E3Z 2S1
Tel: 506-473-6272; *Fax:* 506-473-6065
godouel@nbnet.nb.ca

***Grand Falls*: Gilles A. Pichette, Q.C. - *1**
P.O. Box 7128, 257 Broadway, Grand Falls, NB E3Z 2K1
Tel: 506-473-4776; *Fax:* 506-473-6493
gillespichette@nb.aibn.com

***Grand Falls*: Peter Seheult - *1**
#7248, 275 Sheriff St., Grand Falls, NB E3Z 3A1
Tel: 506-473-2164; *Fax:* 506-473-5543
seheult@nbnet.nb.ca

***Hampton*: Veniot Law Office - *1**
71 Randall Dr., Hampton, NB E5N 6A4
Tel: 506-832-3418; *Fax:* 506-832-3755

***Lamèque*: Roger A. Noël - *2**
CP 2038, Stn. Main, 5120E, rte 113, Lamèque, NB E8T 3N4
Tél: 506-344-2217; *Téléc:* 506-344-5380
info@eteudelegalenoel.com

***Memramcook*: Jacques Gauthier - *1**
835, rue Principale, Memramcook, NB E4K 2R9
Tél: 506-758-9002; *Téléc:* 506-758-2400
acadian22@hotmail.com

***Minto*: Mario DiCarlo - *1**
255 Main St., Minto, NB E4B 3R8
Tel: 506-327-3777; *Fax:* 506-327-6080
mariodicarlo@bellaliant.net

***Minto*: Sheila R. Thorne - *1**
24 Queen St., Minto, NB E4B 3P2
Tel: 506-327-6120

***Miramichi*: Rosemary Losier - *1**
P.O. Box 112, Stn. Main, 173 Wellington St., Miramichi, NB E1N 3A5
Tel: 506-773-6817

***Miramichi*: Maynes, Mahoney & Tremblay - *4**
P.O. Box 518, 1723 Water St., Miramichi, NB E1N 3A8
Tel: 506-778-8336; *Fax:* 506-778-2103

***Moncton*: Michel C. Arsenault - *1**
1255 Main St., Moncton, NB E1C 1H9
Tel: 506-857-8008; *Fax:* 506-857-8885
mcalaw@nb.aibn.com

***Moncton*: Bingham Robinson McLennan Ehrhardt & Teed - *18**
#300, Heritage Court, 95 Foundry St., Moncton, NB E1C 5H7
Tel: 506-857-8856; *Fax:* 506-857-2017

***Moncton*: Robert N. Charman - *1**
170 Highfield St., Moncton, NB E1C 5P2
Tel: 506-854-8656; *Fax:* 506-854-8684
rcharman@nbnet.nb.ca

***Moncton*: Corporate Communications Limited - *1**
844 Main St., Moncton, NB E1C 1G2
Tel: 506-855-1771; *Fax:* 506-859-1691
mrobichaud@cclgroup.ca

***Moncton*: Delehanty Rinzler Druckham - *3**
#101, P.O. Box 1083, 720 Main St., Moncton, NB E1C 8P6
Tel: 506-857-3030; *Fax:* 506-857-0085
www.drdlaw.ca

***Moncton*: Forbes Roth Basque - *7**
P.O. Box 480, Moncton, NB E1C 8L9
Tel: 506-857-4880; *Fax:* 506-857-0151

***Moncton*: Fowler & Fowler - *2**
69 Waterloo St., Moncton, NB E1C 0E1
Tel: 506-857-8811; *Fax:* 506-857-9297

***Moncton*: John D. Hughes**
P.O. Box 29072, 98 Bonaccord St., Moncton, NB E1G 4R3
Tel: 506-382-9072

***Moncton*: LeBlanc Boucher Rodger Bourque - *3**
740 Main St., Moncton, NB E1C 1E6
Tel: 506-858-0110; *Fax:* 506-858-9497
lbrb@nbnet.nb.ca

***Moncton*: LeBlanc Boudreau Maillet - *6**
#200, 735 Main St., Moncton, NB E1C 1E5
Tel: 506-858-5666; *Fax:* 506-858-5570
leblord@nbnet.nb.ca

***Moncton*: LeBlanc, Martin, Sweet & Cormier - *5**
P.O. Box 1285, 51 Highfield St., Moncton, NB E1C 8P9
Tel: 506-859-1212; *Fax:* 506-859-7309

***Moncton*: Susan D. LeBlanc - *1**
76 Albert St., Moncton, NB E1C 1B1
Tel: 506-859-4402; *Fax:* 506-859-9195

***Moncton*: Letcher & Murray - *3**
76 Albert St., Moncton, NB E1C 1B1
Tel: 506-857-2070; *Fax:* 506-859-9195

***Moncton*: Lise Lorrain - *1**
P.O. Box 25117, RPO Mountain Rd., Moncton, NB E1C 9M9
Tel: 506-855-6084; *Fax:* 506-389-3867
llorrain@nbnet.nb.ca

***Moncton*: Maxwell - Matheson - *2**
Assumption Place, 770 Main St., 10th Fl., Moncton, NB E1C 1E7
Tel: 506-857-8470; *Fax:* 506-857-4031

***Moncton*: Mitchell Law Office - *1**
89 Church St., Moncton, NB E1C 4Z4
Tel: 506-853-1105; *Fax:* 506-853-9348

***Moncton*: Murphy Collette Murphy - *7**
250 Lutz St., Moncton, NB E1C 5G3
Tel: 506-856-8560; *Fax:* 506-856-8579
manager@murco.nb.ca
www.murco.nb.ca

***Moncton*: Murphy, Murphy & Mollins - *3**
89 Church St., Moncton, NB E1C 4Z4
Tel: 506-857-9120; *Fax:* 506-857-9129
mmmlaw@nb.aibn.com

***Moncton*: Alan D. Schelew - *1**
#100, P.O. Box 182, 803 Main St., Moncton, NB E1C 8K9
Tel: 506-857-2272; *Fax:* 506-857-2276
schelew@nb.aibn.com
www.monctonlawyer.com

***Oromocto*: Blair W. McKay - *1**
#3, 291 Restigouche Rd., Oromocto, NB E2V 2H2
Tel: 506-446-3000; *Fax:* 506-446-9010

***Perth-Andover*: Mark C. Johnson - *1**
P.O. Box 3066, 1143 West Riverside Dr., Perth-Andover, NB E7H 5G5
Tel: 506-273-6818; *Fax:* 506-273-6590
mjlaw@nb.aibn.com

***Perth-Andover*: Stewart C. Paul, Law Office - *1**
P.O. Box 2981, Stn. Main, Perth-Andover, NB E7H 5M2
Tel: 506-273-4445; *Fax:* 506-273-4491

***Petit-Rocher*: Robert M. Boudreau - *1**
561 rue Principale, Petit-Rocher, NB E8J 1J4
Tél: 506-783-4246; *Téléc:* 506-783-2354
rboudro@nbnet.nb.ca

***Richibucto*: Joseph Robichaud**
#1, 9406 Main St., Richibucto, NB E4W 4E1
Tel: 506-523-4442; *Fax:* 506-523-4819

***Riverview*: McAllister & Grew - *3**
704A Coverdale Rd., Riverview, NB E1B 3L1
Tel: 506-853-3040; *Fax:* 506-859-9588
hgrew@nbnet.nb.ca

***Riverview*: Wilbur & Wilbur - *2**
706B Coverdale Rd., Riverview, NB E1B 3L1
Tel: 506-387-7715; *Fax:* 506-387-5875
swilbur@wilburandwilbur.com
www.wilburandwilbur.com

***Sackville*: Meldrum Law - *2**
7 Bridge St., Sackville, NB E4L 3N6
Tel: 506-536-3870; *Fax:* 506-536-2131
Toll-Free: 866-792-1416
meldrumk@nbnet.nb.ca

***Sackville*: Ove B. Samuelsen - *1**
1 Squire St., Sackville, NB E4L 4K8
Tel: 506-536-0511; *Fax:* 506-536-1169
ovesam@nbnet.nb.ca

***Saint John*: Michael D. Bamford**
#420, 40 Charlotte St., Saint John, NB E2L 2H6
Tel: 506-634-8130; *Fax:* 506-633-0389

***Saint John*: Barry Spalding - Saint John Office - *20**
#710, Mercantine Centre, P.O. Box 6010, Stn. A, 55 Union Street, Saint John, NB E2L 4R5
Tel: 506-633-4226; *Fax:* 506-633-4206
Toll-Free: 888-743-4226
info@barryspalding.com
www.barryspalding.com

***Saint John*: Boyle, Dennis - *1**
345 Lancaster Ave. West, Saint John, NB E2M 2L3
Tel: 506-634-7575; *Fax:* 506-634-8237

***Saint John*: Clark Drummie - *22**
P.O. Box 6850, 40 Wellington Row, Saint John, NB E2L 4S3
Tel: 506-633-3800; *Fax:* 506-633-3811
cd@clarkdrummie.ca
www.clarkdrummie.ca

***Saint John*: Correia & Collins - *3**
1 Market Sq., Stn. A, Saint John, NB E2L 4S4
Tel: 506-648-1700; *Fax:* 506-648-1701
www.correiaandcollins.com

** indicates number of lawyers*

Saint John: **Allen G. Doyle Law Office - *1**
45 Canterbury St., Saint John, NB E2L 2C6
Tel: 506-633-4198; *Fax:* 506-633-1645
a.g.doyle@nb.aibn.com

Saint John: **Lynda D. Farrell - *4**
City Hall, P.O. Box 1971, Stn. Main, 15 Market Sq., 8th Fl., Saint John, NB E2L 4L1
Tel: 506-658-2860; *Fax:* 506-658-2802

Saint John: **Gilbert McGloan Gillis - *15**
P.O. Box 7174, 22 King St., Saint John, NB E2L 1G3
Tel: 506-634-3600; *Fax:* 506-634-3612
Toll-Free: 888-246-4529
gmg@gmglaw.com
www.gmglaw.com

Saint John: **Gorman Nason - *10**
P.O. Box 7286, Stn. A, 121 Germain St., Saint John, NB E2L 4S6
Tel: 506-634-8600; *Fax:* 506-634-8685
info@GormanNason.com
www.gormannason.com

Saint John: **John M. Henderson - *1**
#410, 40 Charlotte St., Saint John, NB E2L 2H6
Tel: 506-652-5502; *Fax:* 506-634-1795
jmhlaw@nbnet.nb.ca

Saint John: **Frank J. Hogan - *1**
491 Bay St. West, Saint John, NB E2M 7L3
Tel: 506-635-1462; *Fax:* 506-672-4545
hoganfj@nbnet.nb.ca

Saint John: **Mary Ann G. Holland - *1**
P.O. Box 7041, Stn. Brunswick, 120 Prince William St., Saint John, NB E2L 4S4
Tel: 506-652-3774; *Fax:* 506-633-0581
lawyer@nbnet.nb.ca

Saint John: **W. Rodney Macdonald - *1**
108 Prince William St., Saint John, NB E2L 2B3
Tel: 506-632-8999; *Fax:* 506-634-1532

Saint John: **A. Wilber MacLeod Q.C. - *1**
108 Prince William St., Saint John, NB E2L 2B3
Tel: 506-632-8999

Saint John: **Elizabeth T. McLeod, QC - *1**
#5C, Brunswick Sq., P.O. Box 20045, 28 King St., Saint John, NB E2L 5B2
Tel: 506-632-4048; *Fax:* 506-652-6594

Saint John: **Mosher Chedore**
#300, 33 Charlotte St., 3rd Fl., Saint John, NB E2L 2H3
Tel: 506-634-1600; *Fax:* 506-634-0740
lawfirm@nb.sympatico.ca

Saint John: **Richard A. Northrup - *1**
#420, 40 Charlotte St., Saint John, NB E2L 2H6
Tel: 506-634-8134; *Fax:* 506-693-3473
nbrick@nb.aibn.com

Saint John: **Riley, John G. - *1**
#410, 40 Charlotte St., Saint John, NB E2L 2H6
Tel: 506-634-1188; *Fax:* 506-634-1795
jgrileylaw@nb.aibn.com

Saint John: **Sherwood & Flanagan - *2**
10 Peel St., Saint John, NB E2L 3G9
Tel: 506-634-0001; *Fax:* 506-634-0456
mary-eileen@sherwoodandflanagan.com

Saint John: **Teed & Teed, Barristers & Solicitors - *1**
P.O. Box 6639, Stn. A, 127 Prince William St., Saint John, NB E2L 4S1
Tel: 506-634-7320; *Fax:* 506-634-7423
info@teedandteed.com
www.teedandteed.com

Saint John: **Whelly & Kelly - *4**
122 Carleton St., Saint John, NB E2L 2Z7
Tel: 506-634-1193; *Fax:* 506-693-9040
partner@nb.aibn.com

Saint John: **Patrick R. Wilbur - *1**
#410, P.O. Box 6601, Stn. Brunswick, 40 Charlotte St., Saint John, NB E2L 4S1
Tel: 506-632-6001; *Fax:* 506-633-6031
prwilburlaw@nb.aibn.com

Saint John: **Theodore E. Wilson - *1**
10 Prince Edward St., Saint John, NB E2L 4M5
Tel: 506-633-8788; *Fax:* 506-632-2023

Shediac: **Michel C. Leger - *2**
CP 1900, 5, rue Mill, Shediac, NB E4P 2H8
Tél: 506-532-0100; *Téléc:* 506-532-6332
mike0100@nbnet.nb.ca

Shippagan: **Godin, Lizotte, Robichaud, Guignard - *4**
246, boul J.D.Gauthier, Shippagan, NB E8S 1P9
Tél: 506-336-0400; *Téléc:* 506-336-0409
glrg@nbnet.nb.ca

Shippagan: **Theriault, Larocque, Boudreau - *3**
P.O. Box 160, 283 J.D. Gauthier Blvd., Shippagan, NB E8S 1N6
Tel: 506-336-4726; *Fax:* 506-336-1159
tla@nbnet.nb.ca

St Andrews: **David A. Bartlett - *1**
239 Water St., St Andrews, NB E5B 1B3
Tel: 506-529-9000; *Fax:* 506-529-9003
bartllaw@nb.aibn.com

St George: **Peter A. Johnston Law Office - *2**
4 Main St., St George, NB E5C 3J1
Tel: 506-755-3376; *Fax:* 506-755-8044
larjon@nbnet.nb.ca

St. Stephen: **Ronald W. Sutherland - *1**
71 King St., St. Stephen, NB E3L 2C4
Tel: 506-466-5330; *Fax:* 506-466-3692

Sussex: **D. James Garrish - *1**
#1, 480 Main St., Sussex, NB E4S 2S4
Tel: 506-433-4234; *Fax:* 506-432-1814
gersmi@nbnet.nb.ca

Sussex: **Palmer & Palmer - *2**
17 Queen St., Sussex, NB E4E 2A4
Tel: 506-433-2168; *Fax:* 506-433-4740

Sussex: **Purnell & Fulton - *1**
30 Church Ave., Sussex, NB E4E 1Y7
Tel: 506-433-4215; *Fax:* 506-433-4216
lawyers@nbnet.nb.ca

Tracadie-Sheila: **Doiron, Lebouthillier, Boudreau, Allain - *4**
CP 3010, Stn. Bureau, 3674, rue Principale, Tracadie-Sheila, NB E1X 1G5
Tél: 506-395-0044; *Téléc:* 506-395-0050
dllb@nbnet.nb.ca

Woodstock: **McCue Brewer Dickinson - *3**
179 Broadway St., Woodstock, NB E7M 1B7
Tel: 506-325-2835; *Fax:* 506-328-6248
mblaw@nbnet.nb.ca

Woodstock: **Stephen L. Wilson - *1**
#1, 733 Main St., Woodstock, NB E7M 2E6
Tel: 506-325-1100; *Fax:* 506-328-4873
stepwil@nbnet.nb.ca

Newfoundland & Labrador

Bay Roberts: **Moores, Andrews, Collins - *3**
P.O. Box 806, Bay Roberts, NL A0A 1G0
Tel: 709-786-7114; *Fax:* 709-786-6952
mac@mac-law.ca

Bay Roberts: **Morrow & Morrow - *2**
P.O. Box 870, 344 Conception Bay Hwy., Bay Roberts, NL A0A 1G0
Tel: 709-786-9207; *Fax:* 709-786-9507
morrow@nf.aibn.com

Carbonear: **J. William Finn - *1**
66 Powell Dr., Carbonear, NL A1Y 1A5
Tel: 709-596-5143; *Fax:* 709-596-3208

Channel-Port-aux-Basques: **Marks & Parsons - *4**
#3, P.O. Box 640, 9 Barhaven Dr., Channel-Port-aux-Basques, NL A0M 1C0
Tel: 709-695-7341; *Fax:* 709-695-3944
b.marks@mplaw.com

Clarenville: **Hughes & Brannan Law Offices - *2**
357 Memorial Dr., Clarenville, NL A5A 1R8
Tel: 709-466-3106; *Fax:* 709-466-3107
hughes.brannan@nfld.net

Conception Bay South: **Robert R. Regular - *2**
#110, Villa Nova Plaza, 120 Conception Bay Hwy., Conception Bay South, NL A1W 3A6
Tel: 709-834-2132; *Fax:* 709-834-3025
rregular@robertregularlaw.com

Corner Brook: **Monaghan, Murphy & Watton - *4**
Mercantile Trust Bldg., Box 815, Stn. Main, 17 West St., Corner Brook, NL A2H 6H9
Tel: 709-634-3231; *Fax:* 709-634-8889
contacts@monmar.nf.net

Corner Brook: **Poole Althouse, Barristers & Solicitors - *10**
Western Trust Bldg., P.O. Box 812, 49 - 51 Park St., Corner Brook, NL A2H 6H7
Tel: 709-634-3136; *Fax:* 709-634-8247
Toll-Free: 877-634-3136
info@pa-law.ca
www.poolealthouse.ca

Corner Brook: **Watton, Graham, Law Office - *1**
Noton Bldg., P.O. Box 188, 133 Riverside Dr., Corner Brook, NL A2H 6C7
Tel: 709-639-7490; *Fax:* 709-634-7229
watton@nf.aibn.com

Gander: **Easton Hillier Lawrence Preston - *8**
Polaris Bldg., 61 Elizabeth Dr., Gander, NL A1V 1G4
Tel: 709-256-4006; *Fax:* 709-651-2850
Toll-Free: 800-256-4006
info@ganderlawyers.com
www.ganderlawyers.com

Happy Valley-Goose Bay: **Olthuis Kleer Townshend - *1**
15 King Cres., Happy Valley-Goose Bay, NL A0P 1E0
linnes@oktlaw.com

Labrador City: **Miller & Hearn - *2**
P.O. Box 129, Stn. Main, Labrador City, NL A2V 2K3
Tel: 709-944-3666; *Fax:* 709-944-5494
miller&hearn@crrstv.net

Mount Pearl: **Budden, Morris - *5**
184 Park Ave., Mount Pearl, NL A1N 1K8
Tel: 709-747-0077; *Fax:* 709-747-0104
lawyers@buddenmorris.com
www.buddenmorris.com

Paradise: **Aylward, Chislett & Whitten - *3**
#200, 1655 Topsail Road, Paradise, NL A1L 1V1
Tel: 709-722-6000; *Fax:* 709-726-1225
contact@acwlaw.ca
www.acwlaw.ca

Paradise: **Susan L. Fisher - *1**
15 Deborah Lynn Hts., Paradise, NL A1L 3E6
Tel: 709-773-1806; *Fax:* 709-773-1807
susanfisher@nl.rogers.com

Springdale: **Shawn C.A. Colbourne Law Office - *1**
P.O. Box 69, 8 Juniper Rd., Springdale, NL A0J 1T0
Tel: 709-673-3693; *Fax:* 709-673-3991
colbourne.5@nf.sympatico.ca

St. John's: **Benson Myles - *21**
#900, Atlantic Place, P.O. Box 1538, 215 Water St., St. John's, NL A1C 5N8
Tel: 709-579-2081; *Fax:* 709-579-2647
info@bensonmyles.com
www.bensonmyles.com

St. John's: **Browne, Fitzgerald, Morgan, Avis - *6**
Terrace on the Square, Level II, P.O. Box 23135, RPO Churchill Sq., St. John's, NL A1B 4J9
Tel: 709-724-3800; *Fax:* 709-754-3800

St. John's: **Bruce & Company - *1**
11 Church Hill, St. John's, NL A1C 3Z7
Tel: 709-738-0006; *Fax:* 709-738-0375
bruceco@nf.sympatico.ca

St. John's: **Cox and Palmer - St. John's - *43**
#1000, Scotia Centre, 235 Water St., St. John's, NL A1C 1B6
Tel: 709-738-7800; *Fax:* 709-738-7999
stjohns@coxandpalmer.com
www.coxandpalmer.com

St. John's: **Crosbie, Ches Barristers - *5**
169 Water St., St. John's, NL A1C 1B1
Tel: 709-579-4000; *Fax:* 709-579-9671
Toll-Free: 888-579-3262
ccb@chescrosbie.nf.net

St. John's: **Michael W. Dodd & Associates - *2**
#301, P.O. Box 578, Stn. C, 291 Water St., St. John's, NL A1C 5K8
Tel: 709-754-4098; *Fax:* 709-754-3223
mdodd@mdoddlaw.com

** indicates number of lawyers*

***St. John's*: Duffy & Associates**
#102, 95 Bonaventure Ave., St. John's, NL A1B 2X5
Tel: 709-757-8285; *Fax:* 709-757-8284

***St. John's*: Christopher English - *1**
3 Pine Bud Pl., St. John's, NL A1B 1N1
Tel: 709-754-4855; *Fax:* 709-737-2164
cenglish@mun.ca

***St. John's*: Ernst & Young LLP - *2**
139 Water St., 7th Fl., St. John's, NL A1C 1B2
Tel: 709-726-2840; *Fax:* 709-726-0345
www.ey.com

***St. John's*: Fraize Law Offices - *2**
P.O. Box 5217, St. John's, NL A1C 5W1
Tel: 709-726-7978; *Fax:* 709-726-8201
tfraize@fraizelawoffices.nf.net

***St. John's*: French, Noseworthy & Associates - *5**
#122, Elizabeth Towers, 100 Elizabeth Ave., St. John's, NL A1B 1S1
Tel: 709-754-1800; *Fax:* 709-754-2701
jbfrench@nf.aibn.com

***St. John's*: L. Power Consulting Inc. - *1**
59 Hayward Ave., St. John's, NL A1C 3W6
Tel: 709-682-3543; *Fax:* 709-726-4849
leopower@nf.sympatico.ca

***St. John's*: Lewis, Day - *2**
#A, 84 Airport Rd., 1st Fl., St. John's, NL A1A 4Y3
Tel: 709-753-2545; *Fax:* 709-753-2266
Toll-Free: 877-553-2545
kellyhall@lewisday.ca, admin@lewisday.ca
www.lewisday.com

***St. John's*: Lewis, Sinnott, Shortall, Hurley - *4**
#300, TD Place, P.O. Box 884, Stn. C, 140 Water St., St. John's, NL A1C 5L7
Tel: 709-753-7810; *Fax:* 709-738-2965
lssh@nf.aibn.com

***St. John's*: Martin Whalen Hennebury Stamp - *11**
P.O. Box 5910, 15 Church Hill, St. John's, NL A1C 5X4
Tel: 709-754-1400; *Fax:* 709-754-0915
info@mwhslaw.com
www.mwhslaw.com

***St. John's*: John W. McGrath - *2**
18 Argyle St., St. John's, NL A1A 1V3
Tel: 709-726-5250; *Fax:* 709-738-0614
jwmcgrath@nf.aibn.com

***St. John's*: Noonan, Oakley - *2**
P.O. Box 5303, St. John's, NL A1C 5W1
Tel: 709-726-9598; *Fax:* 709-726-9614
joakley@nfld.net

***St. John's*: Earle O'Dea - *15**
P.O. Box 5955, 323 Duckworth St., St. John's, NL A1C 5X4
Tel: 709-726-3524; *Fax:* 709-726-9600
odeaearle@odeaearle.nf.ca
www.odeaearle.nf.ca

***St. John's*: Ottenheimer Baker - *19**
Baine Johnson Centre, P.O. Box 5457, 10 Fort William Pl., St. John's, NL A1C 5W4
Tel: 709-722-7584; *Fax:* 709-722-9210
info@ottenheimerbaker.com
www.ottenheimerbaker.com

***St. John's*: Ottenheimer Boone - *2**
8 Albany St., St. John's, NL A1E 3C5
Tel: 709-579-8890; *Fax:* 709-579-1647

***St. John's*: Roebothan, McKay & Marshall - *13**
P.O. Box 5236, 209 Duckworth St., St. John's, NL A1C 5W1
Tel: 709-753-5805; *Fax:* 709-753-5221
Toll-Free: 800-563-5563
wrmm@wrmm.nf.net

***St. John's*: Keith Rose**
18 Argyle St., St. John's, NL A1A 1V3
Tel: 709-738-2190; *Fax:* 709-738-0614

***St. John's*: Strategic Growth & Relations Management - *1**
11 Calgary St., St. John's, NL A1A 3W1
Tel: 709-743-2427; *Fax:* 709-754-3467
gregmercer@nl.rogers.com

***St. John's*: Graham A. Wells - *1**
P.O. Box 26111, Stn. LeMarchant, 10 Freshwater Rd., St. John's, NL A1C 5T9
Tel: 709-739-7768; *Fax:* 709-739-4434

***Stephenville*: Fred R. Stagg, Barrister & Solicitor - *1**
28 Main St., Stephenville, NL A2N 2Z4
Tel: 709-643-5651; *Fax:* 709-643-5369
fstagg@frs-law.com

Northwest Territories

***Hay River*: MacDonald & Associates - *3**
#5, 6 Courtoreille St., Hay River, NT X0E 1G2
Tel: 867-874-6727; *Fax:* 867-874-6828
dmacdonald@nt.sympatico.ca

***Hay River*: Stephen M. Shabala - *1**
#205, 31 Capital Dr., Hay River, NT X0E 1G2
Tel: 867-874-3365; *Fax:* 867-874-6955

***Yellowknife*: Denroche & Associates - *3**
P.O. Box 2910, Stn. Main, 5107 - 53rd. St., Yellowknife, NT X1A 2R2
Tel: 867-920-4151; *Fax:* 867-920-4252
reception@denrochelaw.ca
www.denrochelaw.ca

***Yellowknife*: Peter C. Fuglsang & Associates - *1**
P.O. Box 2459, Stn. Main, 4912 - 49 St., Yellowknife, NT X1A 2P8
Tel: 867-920-4344; *Fax:* 867-873-3386

***Yellowknife*: Keenan Bengts Law Office - *2**
P.O. Box 262, 5018 - 47th St., Yellowknife, NT X1A 2N2
Tel: 867-873-8631; *Fax:* 867-920-2511
kbengtslaw@theedge.ca

***Yellowknife*: Marshall & Company - *1**
P.O. Box 1236, Stn. Main, 5125 - 48 St., Yellowknife, NT X1A 2N9
Tel: 867-873-4969; *Fax:* 867-873-6567
mmarshall@marshall.yk.com
www.marshall.yk.com

***Yellowknife*: Peterson, Stang & Malakoe - *7**
P.O. Box 939, 4902 - 49 St., Yellowknife, NT X1A 2N7
Tel: 867-669-8450; *Fax:* 867-873-6543
lawyers@norlaw.nt.ca
www.norlaw.nt.ca

***Yellowknife*: Phillips & Wright - *2**
#1008, 4920 - 52nd St., Yellowknife, NT X1A 3T1
Tel: 867-873-3335; *Fax:* 867-873-2773

***Yellowknife*: Wallbridge & Associates - *3**
P.O. Box 383, 5016 - 47th St., Yellowknife, NT X1A 2N3
Tel: 867-920-4000; *Fax:* 867-920-7389
garth@wallbridgelaw.net

Nova Scotia

***Amherst*: Beaton, Blaikie, Nurse & Farrell - *3**
P.O. Box 295, Amherst, NS B4H 3Z2
Tel: 902-667-0515; *Fax:* 902-667-6161
bblaw@ns.sympatico.ca

***Amherst*: Fairbanks Law Office - *1**
P.O. Box 103, Amherst, NS B4H 3Y6
Tel: 902-667-7579; *Fax:* 902-667-0644
william.fairbanks@ns.aliantzinc.ca
www.fairbankslawoffice.com

***Amherst*: Hicks, LeMoine - *3**
P.O. Box 279, 15 Princess St., Amherst, NS B4H 3Z2
Tel: 902-667-7214; *Fax:* 902-667-5886
info@hickslemoine.ca
www.hickslemoine.ca

***Amherst*: Jerry Langille, Inc. - *1**
P.O. Box 548, 55 Church St., Amherst, NS B4H 4A1
Tel: 902-667-3856; *Fax:* 902-667-0104
jerry@jlilaw.com

***Annapolis Royal*: Armstrong & Armstrong - *1**
P.O. Box 575, Annapolis Royal, NS B0S 1A0
Tel: 902-532-2155; *Fax:* 902-532-7211
armstrong@ns.aliantzinc.ca

***Annapolis Royal*: Patricia L. Reardon - *1**
P.O. Box 366, 234 St. George St., Annapolis Royal, NS B0S 1A0
Tel: 902-532-7904; *Fax:* 902-532-7775
preardon@auracom.com

***Antigonish*: Daniel J. MacIsaac - *1**
P.O. Box 1478, Stn. Main, 30 Church St., Antigonish, NS B2G 2L7
Tel: 902-863-5398; *Fax:* 902-863-9440

***Antigonish*: MacPherson MacNeil Macdonald - *2**
188 Main St., Antigonish, NS B2G 2B9
Tel: 902-863-2925; *Fax:* 902-863-2925
mthree@eastlink.com

***Antigonish*: William F. Meehan, Q.C. - *1**
P.O. Box 1803, Stn. Main, 195 Main St., Antigonish, NS B2G 2M5
Tel: 902-863-3136; *Fax:* 902-863-6270
wmeehan@hotmail.com

***Arichat*: Ivo R. Winter - *1**
P.O. Box 180, 14 Bay St., Arichat, NS B0E 1A0
Tel: 902-226-3711; *Fax:* 902-226-1837
ivowinter@ns.sympatico.ca

***Baddeck*: Daniel T.L. Chiasson - *1**
P.O. Box 567, 137 Upper Twinning St., Baddeck, NS B0E 1B0
Tel: 902-295-1245; *Fax:* 902-295-2610
dan.baddeck@ns.sympatico.ca

***Barrington*: G. David Eldridge - *1**
P.O. Box 157, 2459 Hwy. 3, Barrington, NS B0W 1E0
Tel: 902-637-2878; *Fax:* 902-637-2025
eldridgeqc@eastlink.ca

***Bedford*: Cameron Rhindress - *1**
1394 Bedford Hwy., Bedford, NS B4A 1E2
Tel: 902-835-7444; *Fax:* 902-835-3819
crhindross@accesscable.net

***Bedford*: David J. Cook - *2**
#216, 1496 Bedford Hwy., Bedford, NS B4A 1E5
Tel: 902-835-8355; *Fax:* 902-835-1301
tchambers@accesswave.ca

***Bedford*: Gillis Associates, Barristers & Solicitors - *2**
#310, Sun Tower, 1550 Bedford Hwy., Bedford, NS B4A 1E6
Tel: 902-835-6174; *Fax:* 902-835-1486
Toll-Free: 866-277-3863
admin@gillisassociates.ca
www.gillisassociates.ca

***Bedford*: Kent & Barrett - *2**
#404, 1550 Bedford Hwy., Bedford, NS B4A 1E6
Tel: 902-835-1011; *Fax:* 902-835-4565

***Bedford*: Melnick, Doll, Condran - *3**
#302, 1160 Bedford Hwy., Bedford, NS B4A 1C1
Tel: 902-835-2300; *Fax:* 902-835-2303
melnick.doll.condran@ns.sympatico.ca

***Bedford*: Pressé Mason, Barristers & Solicitors - *4**
1254 Bedford Hwy., Bedford, NS B4A 1C6
Tel: 902-832-1175; *Fax:* 902-832-1856
Toll-Free: 800-630-2254
lawyers@pressemason.ns.ca
www.pressemasonlaw.ca

***Berwick*: Astek Legal Services - *1**
3799 Welsford St., Berwick, NS B0P 1E0
Tel: 902-538-3916; *Fax:* 902-538-3632
astek1@ns.sympatico.ca

***Berwick*: Stewart & Turner - *2**
P.O. Box 208, 196 Cottage St., Berwick, NS B0P 1E0
Tel: 902-538-3123; *Fax:* 902-538-7933

***Berwick*: Waterbury Newton - *2**
P.O. Box 475, 188 Commercial St., Berwick, NS B0P 1E0
Tel: 902-538-3168; *Fax:* 902-538-8680
reception@wnns.ca
www.nslawyers.com

***Bridgewater*: Conrad & Feindel - *3**
70 Dufferin St., Bridgewater, NS B4V 2G3
Tel: 902-543-4655; *Fax:* 902-543-6853
conradfeindel@eastlink.ca

***Bridgewater*: J. Patrick Morris - *1**
344 King St., Bridgewater, NS B4V 1A9
Tel: 902-543-6661; *Fax:* 902-543-6639
morris@eastlink.ca

***Bridgewater*: Power, Dempsey, Cooper & Leefe - *5**
84 Dufferin St., Bridgewater, NS B4V 2G3
Tel: 902-543-7815; *Fax:* 902-543-3196
pdclaw@ns.sympatico.ca

** indicates number of lawyers*

Bridgewater: The Law Offices of Timothy A. Reid - *1
176 Aberdeen Rd., Bridgewater, NS B4V 2S9
Tel: 902-543-1303; *Fax:* 902-543-3243
tareid@ns.sympatico.ca

Bridgewater: Romneylaw Inc. - *2
P.O. Box 368, 136 Aberdeen Rd., Bridgewater, NS B4V 2W9
Tel: 902-543-4444; *Fax:* 902-543-0232
romneylaw1@eastlink.ca

Bridgewater: Taylor & Silver - *2
82 Aberdeen Rd., Bridgewater, NS B4V 2S6
Tel: 902-543-0068; *Fax:* 902-543-7243

Canning: Cornwallis Legal Services - *1
P.O. Box 69, 765 Canard St., Lower Canard, Canning, NS B0P 1H0
Tel: 902-582-3372; *Fax:* 902-582-3201

Chester: Cassidy Nearing Berryman
27 Pleasant St., Chester, NS B0J 1J0
Tel: 902-275-3032; *Fax:* 902-423-2485
cassidy@cnb.ca

Chester: Welland & Associates - *1
P.O. Box 504, Chester, NS B0J 1J0
Tel: 902-275-4792; *Fax:* 902-275-4414
welland@ns.sympatico.ca

Cheticamp: Réjean Aucoin - *1
P.O. Box 328, Cheticamp, NS B0E 1H0
Tel: 902-224-1450; *Fax:* 902-224-2224
rejean.aucoin@ns.sympatico.ca

Cheticamp: C&E Management Consulting - *1
P.O. Box 972, Cheticamp, NS B0E 1H0
Tel: 902-224-1662
chester.muise@ns.sympatico.ca

Cheticamp: Carmel A. Lavigne - *1
P.O. Box 579, 15595 Cabot Trail, Cheticamp, NS B0E 1H0
Tel: 902-224-2551; *Fax:* 902-224-2555
clavigne@ns.sympatico.ca

Dartmouth: Bailey & Associates - *6
#800, 46 Portland St., Dartmouth, NS B2Y 1H4
Tel: 902-465-4888; *Fax:* 902-465-4844
appointments@baileylawyers.com
www.baileylawyers.com

Dartmouth: Boyne Clarke - *39
#700, Belmont House, P.O. Box 876, 33 Alderney Dr., Dartmouth, NS B2Y 3Z5
Tel: 902-469-9500; *Fax:* 902-463-7500
Toll-Free: 800-207-6589
info@boyneclarke.ns.ca
www.boyneclarke.ns.ca

Dartmouth: Burton Ronald W. Lawyers - *1
169 Main St., Dartmouth, NS B2X 1S1
Tel: 902-434-4492; *Fax:* 902-434-5485
burtonl@ns.sympatico.ca

Dartmouth: Casey Rodgers Chisholm Penny - *6
#203, 175 Main St., Dartmouth, NS B2X 1S1
Tel: 902-434-6181; *Fax:* 902-434-7737
www.crcplaw.com

Dartmouth: Corporate Strategic Consulting - *1
60 Bellbrook Cres., Dartmouth, NS B2W 6S2
Tel: 902-434-3998; *Fax:* 902-434-8933
richie.mann@ns.sympatico.ca

Dartmouth: David A. Grant - *1
63 Tacoma Dr., Dartmouth, NS B2W 3E7
Tel: 902-463-6300; *Fax:* 902-435-7910
davidgrant@ns.sympatico.ca

Dartmouth: Heritage House Law Office - *5
92 Ochterloney St., Dartmouth, NS B2Y 1C5
Tel: 902-465-6669; *Fax:* 902-466-4412
helenf@heritagelaw.ca; cheryla@heritgelaw.ca

Dartmouth: Landry McGillivray, Barristers, Solicitors, Notaries - *10
#300, Quaker Landing, P.O. Box 1200, Stn. Main, 33 Ochterloney St., Dartmouth, NS B2Y 4B8
Tel: 902-463-8800; *Fax:* 902-463-0590
slg@landrymcgillivray.ns.ca
www.landrymcgillivray.ca

Dartmouth: Langille & Associates - *1
#201, P.O. Box 767, 56 Portland St., Dartmouth, NS B2Y 3Z3
Tel: 902-463-5200; *Fax:* 902-465-5200
ken.langille@ns.aliantzinc.ca

Dartmouth: Owen & Morrison - *3
#604, Queen Sq., 45 Alderney Dr., Dartmouth, NS B2Y 2N6
Tel: 902-463-8100; *Fax:* 902-465-2581

Dartmouth: Lester Pyne - *1
194 Caledonia Rd., Dartmouth, NS B2X 1L4
Tel: 902-434-6167; *Fax:* 902-434-5448

Dartmouth: RAMentor - *1
6 Wyndholme Ave., Dartmouth, NS B2Y 1T3
Tel: 902-464-9628; *Fax:* 902-461-1350
rmackay1@ns.sympatico.ca

Dartmouth: Sealy Cornish - *4
#200, Box 300, 56 Portland St., Dartmouth, NS B2Y 1H2
Tel: 902-466-2500; *Fax:* 902-463-0500
sealycornish@scolaw.ns.ca

Dartmouth: True North Public Affairs - *1
22 Crestwood Pl., Dartmouth, NS B2V 2P5
Tel: 902-440-2634
cbidgood@ns.sympatico.ca

Dartmouth: Weldon McInnis - *7
118 Ochterloney St., Dartmouth, NS B2Y 1C7
Tel: 902-469-2421; *Fax:* 902-463-4452
Toll-Free: 800-757-2421
office@weldonmcinnis.ca
www.weldonmcinnis.ca

Dartmouth: Wolfson, Schelew, Zatzman - *3
#500, Bank of Commerce Bldg., P.O. Box 2308, 73 Tacoma Dr., Dartmouth, NS B2W 3Y4
Tel: 902-435-7000; *Fax:* 902-435-4085
Toll-Free: 888-990-5263
wszlaw@wsz.ns.ca
www.atyp.com/wsz

Digby: Brian E. McConnell - *1
P.O. Box 1239, 3 Birch St., Digby, NS B0V 1A0
Tel: 902-245-5856; *Fax:* 902-245-6800
bmcconnell@ns.aliantzinc.ca

Digby: James L. Outhouse Q.C. - *1
P.O. Box 1567, 78 Water St., Digby, NS B0V 1A0
Tel: 902-245-2551; *Fax:* 902-245-6622
jamesouthouse@ns.aliantzinc.ca

Elmsdale: Quigley's Law Office - *1
P.O. Box 653, 214 Hwy. 214, Elmsdale, NS B2S 1J7
Tel: 902-883-2757; *Fax:* 902-883-4401
kquigleylaw@aol.com

Enfield: Blackburn English - *3
287 Hwy. 2, Enfield, NS B2T 1C9
Tel: 902-883-2264; *Fax:* 902-883-8744
blackburn.english@ns.sympatico.ca

Fall River: Miller Campbell & Associates
3301 Hwy. 2, Unit A, Fall River, NS B2T 1J2
Tel: 902-860-0030; *Fax:* 902-865-8262
pbmiller@millercampbell.com

Glace Bay: Crosby, Burke & Macrury
P.O. Box 86, Stn. Main, 38 Union St., Glace Bay, NS B1A 5V1
Tel: 902-849-3971; *Fax:* 902-849-7009

Glace Bay: McIntyre, Gillis & O'Leary - *2
P.O. Box 187, Stn. Main, 65 Minto St., Glace Bay, NS B1A 5V2
Tel: 902-849-6507; *Fax:* 902-849-0555
gblaw@auracom.com

Glace Bay: David H. Raniseth - *1
P.O. Box 249, 34 McKeen St., Glace Bay, NS B1A 5B9
Tel: 902-849-0960; *Fax:* 902-849-6512

Glen Haven: Prospectus Associates Inc. - *1
19 Foxberry Hill, Glen Haven, NS B3Z 2V7
Tel: 902-823-1275; *Fax:* 902-823-1295

Greenwood: David A. Proudfoot Barrister & Solicitor - *1
P.O. Box 100, 811 Central Ave., Greenwood, NS B0P 1N0
Tel: 902-765-3301; *Fax:* 902-765-6493
amplaw2@ns.sympatico.ca

Guysborough: Campbell & MacKeen - *2
P.O. Box 200, 146 Main St., Guysborough, NS B0H 1N0
Tel: 902-533-2644; *Fax:* 902-533-3526

Halifax: Frederick Angus - *1
#935, 5991 Spring Garden Rd., Halifax, NS B3H 1Y6
Tel: 902-420-9595; *Fax:* 902-423-8040
fred.angus@ns.sympatico.ca

Halifax: Richard G. Arab - *1
7147 Abbott Dr., Halifax, NS B3J 1L1
Tel: 902-420-9355; *Fax:* 902-444-3441
rarab@hfx.eastlink.ca

Halifax: Ashworth Dennis - *4
#200, P.O. Box 307, 5162 Duke St., Halifax, NS B3J 2N7
Tel: 902-429-8590; *Fax:* 902-423-2968
bmtlaw@bmtlaw.ns.ca

Halifax: Auld Allen - *2
1452 Dresden Row, Halifax, NS B3J 3T5
Tel: 902-492-3633; *Fax:* 902-492-3655
auld@auldallen.ns.ca
www.auldallen.ns.ca

Halifax: Barss, Hare & Turner - *1
#137, Roy Bldg., Stn. Central, 1657 Barrington St., Halifax, NS B3J 2A1
Tel: 902-423-1249

Halifax: Beaton Derrick - *2
1345 Hollis St., Halifax, NS B3J 1T8
Tel: 902-474-7482; *Fax:* 902-474-8115

Halifax: Beveridge, MacPherson & Duncan - *3
P.O. Box 547, Stn. Central, 1684 Barrington St., 4th Fl., Halifax, NS B3J 2R7
Tel: 902-423-9143; *Fax:* 902-422-7837

Halifax: Marven C. Block, Q.C. - *1
#305, Coburg Pl., 6389 Coburg Rd., Halifax, NS B3H 2A5
Tel: 902-425-5077; *Fax:* 902-429-5198
lomar@istar.ca

Halifax: Blois, Nickerson & Bryson - *17
#500, P.O. Box 2147, 1568 Hollis St., Halifax, NS B3J 3B7
Tel: 902-425-6000; *Fax:* 902-429-7347
info@bloisnickerson.com
www.bloisnickerson.com

Halifax: Burchell Hayman Parish - *23
#1800, 1801 Hollis St., Halifax, NS B3J 3N4
Tel: 902-423-6361; *Fax:* 902-420-9326
firm@burchells.ca
www.burchells.ca

Halifax: Evangeline Cain-Grant - *1
6156 Quinpool Rd., Halifax, NS B3L 1A3
Tel: 902-422-3500; *Fax:* 902-422-9660

Halifax: Cantini Law Group
#1301, 2000 Barrington St., Halifax, NS B3J 3K1
Tel: 902-420-9577; *Fax:* 902-423-0887

Halifax: CFN Consultants - *1
#2001, Purdy's Wharf Tower II, 1969 Upper Water St., Halifax, NS B3J 3R7
Tel: 902-491-4279; *Fax:* 902-429-5237
rlesperance@cfncon.com

Halifax: Christie Cuffari Law Office - *1
#310, 1657 Barrington St., Halifax, NS B3J 2A1
Tel: 902-422-2297; *Fax:* 902-422-2162
cclo@ca.inter.net

Halifax: The Law Office of Peter Claman, Q.C. - *1
#1503, P.O. Box 68, 1959 Upper Water St., Halifax, NS B3J 2L4
Tel: 902-492-4000; *Fax:* 902-492-4001

Halifax: Coady Filliter - *7
#208, 880 Spring Garden Rd., Halifax, NS B3H 1Y1
Tel: 902-429-6264; *Fax:* 902-423-3044
wroy@coadyfilliter.com

Halifax: Cooper & McDonald - *6
Old Auction House, 1669 Granville St., Halifax, NS B3J 1X2
Tel: 902-429-2191; *Fax:* 902-425-3217

Halifax: Corporate Communications Limited - *2
2695 Dutch Village Rd., Halifax, NS B3L 4V2
Tel: 902-421-1777; *Fax:* 902-453-5221

Halifax: Cragg & Weir - *3
6452 Quinpool Rd., Halifax, NS B3L 1A8
Tel: 902-422-1776; *Fax:* 902-429-0016
bob.cragg@ns.sympatico.ca

Halifax: Crowe Dillon Robinson - *8
#2000, 7075 Bayers Rd., Halifax, NS B3L 2C1
Tel: 902-453-1732; *Fax:* 902-454-9948

** indicates number of lawyers*

***Halifax*: Gilles J. Deveau - *1**
P.O. Box 163, Stn. Central, Halifax, NS B3J 2M4
Tel: 902-454-8105; *Fax:* 902-454-4551
gilles.deveau@ns.sympatico.ca

***Halifax*: Gerald Doucet Consulting Inc. - *1**
6970 Armview Ave., Halifax, NS B3H 2M4
Tel: 902-420-0254; *Fax:* 902-425-8492

***Halifax*: Kevin P. Downie, Barrister & Solicitor - *1**
#1402, P.O. Box 580, Stn. M, 5121 Sackville St., Halifax, NS B3J 2R7
Tel: 902-425-7233; *Fax:* 902-425-2252
kpdownie@ns.aliantzinc.ca

***Halifax*: Sally B. Faught - *1**
#1307, 2000 Barrington St., Halifax, NS B3J 3K1
Tel: 902-423-8200; *Fax:* 902-423-3100
sbf.gdl@ns.sympatico.ca

***Halifax*: Michael F. Feindel - *1**
Nolan Davis Bldg., P.O. Box 22162, Stn. Bayers, 7020 Mumford Rd., Halifax, NS B3L 4T7
Tel: 902-455-7730; *Fax:* 902-455-7739

***Halifax*: Garson, Knox & MacDonald - *3**
1741 Brunswick St., Halifax, NS B3J 3X8
Tel: 902-425-0222; *Fax:* 902-423-4690

***Halifax*: Gilbert L. Gaudet - *1**
6156 Quinpool Rd., Halifax, NS B3L 1A3
Tel: 902-422-1243

***Halifax*: Simon L. Gaum, Q.C. - *1**
#206, Tower One, Halifax Shopping Centre, 7001 Mumford Rd., Halifax, NS B3L 4N9
Tel: 902-423-6391; *Fax:* 902-455-0974

***Halifax*: Gavras McClure - *2**
#300, Vogue Bldg., 1649 Barrington St., Halifax, NS B3J 1Z9
Tel: 902-423-5711; *Fax:* 902-431-9444
jgavras@hfx.eastlink.ca

***Halifax*: Goldberg Thompson - *8**
#400, Sentry Place, 1559 Brunswick St., Halifax, NS B3J 2G1
Tel: 902-421-1161; *Fax:* 902-425-0266
inquiries@uncommonlaw.com
www.goldbergthompson.com

***Halifax*: Harvey Hebert & Manthorne - *5**
#501, 1819 Granville St., Halifax, NS B3J 1X8
Tel: 902-492-0614; *Fax:* 902-492-0634
Toll-Free: 877-492-0614
general@harveyhebert.com

***Halifax*: Beatrice A. Havlovic - *1**
1459 Brenton St., Halifax, NS B3J 3S7
Tel: 902-423-8100; *Fax:* 902-423-6011
bhavlovic@linguanet.ca

***Halifax*: Haynes Group of Lawyers, Inc. - *4**
#200, 1718 Argyle St., Halifax, NS B3J 3N6
Tel: 902-422-8400; *Fax:* 902-422-4465
Toll-Free: 888-880-7774
info@hayneslaw.ca
www.hayneslaw.ca

***Halifax*: Walter E. Hopkins - *1**
#105, 276 Bedford Hwy., Halifax, NS B3M 2K6
Tel: 902-445-2984; *Fax:* 902-445-4333

***Halifax*: Glen E. Jefferson - *1**
40 Gateway Rd., Halifax, NS B3M 1M9
Tel: 902-443-2039; *Fax:* 902-443-6721

***Halifax*: MacDonald Elliott Legal Services - *2**
#343, 7071 Bayers Rd., Halifax, NS B3L 2C2
Tel: 902-454-9827; *Fax:* 902-454-7630
macdonaldlegal@hfx.eastlink.ca

***Halifax*: MacDonald Law Office, Paton & Paton - *1**
12 Robert Allen Dr., Halifax, NS B3M 3G8
Tel: 902-457-5111; *Fax:* 902-457-5113
act@istar.com

***Halifax*: Kenneth A. MacInnis & Associates - *3**
#340, 1801 Hollis St., Halifax, NS B3J 3N4
Tel: 902-421-1817; *Fax:* 902-423-8504

***Halifax*: McGinty McCleave - *3**
#705, Park Lane, Box 227, 5657 Spring Garden Rd., Halifax, NS B3J 3R4
Tel: 902-422-5881; *Fax:* 902-422-5882
mcginty.mccleave@ns.aliantzinc.ca

***Halifax*: Medjuck & Medjuck - *2**
#700, Summit Place, P.O. Box 1074, 1601 Lower Water St., Halifax, NS B3J 2X1
Tel: 902-429-4061; *Fax:* 902-422-7639
medjuck@ns.sympatico.ca

***Halifax*: Merrick Jamieson Sterns Washington & Mahody - *7**
#503, 5475 Spring Garden Rd., Halifax, NS B3J 3T2
Tel: 902-429-3123; *Fax:* 902-429-3522

***Halifax*: Metcalf & Company - *6**
Benjamin Wier House, 1459 Hollis St., Halifax, NS B3J 1V1
Tel: 902-420-1990; *Fax:* 902-429-1171
metcalf&company@metcalf.ns.ca
www.metcalf.ns.ca

***Halifax*: Moore & Associates - *4**
P.O. Box 1537, Stn. Central, 1475 Hollis St., Halifax, NS B3J 2Y3
Tel: 902-420-1066; *Fax:* 902-420-1938
mcm.ma@ns.sympatico.ca

***Halifax*: Morris & Bureau - *3**
#307, 6080 Young St., Halifax, NS B3K 5L2
Tel: 902-454-8070; *Fax:* 902-454-7070

***Halifax*: Andrew Munro - *1**
#501, 5162 Duke St., Halifax, NS B3J 1N7
Tel: 902-492-3310; *Fax:* 902-492-0013
amunro@eastlink.ca

***Halifax*: John P. Nisbet - *1**
142 Main Ave., Halifax, NS B3M 1B2
Tel: 902-445-3736

***Halifax*: Noseworthy, Di Costanzo, Diab - *3**
6470 Chebucto Rd., Halifax, NS B3L 1L4
Tel: 902-444-4747; *Fax:* 902-444-4301

***Halifax*: Clyde A. Paul & Associates - *4**
349 Herring Cove Rd., Halifax, NS B3R 1V9
Tel: 902-477-2518; *Fax:* 902-479-1482
capaul@ns.sympatico.ca

***Halifax*: Pink, Joel E. Q.C., & Associates, Barristers & Solicitors - *3**
#300, 1583 Hollis St., Halifax, NS B3H 2P8
Tel: 902-492-0550; *Fax:* 902-492-0570
www.criminaldefence.com

***Halifax*: Quackenbush, Thomson & Robbins - *5**
2571 Windsor St., Halifax, NS B3K 5C4
Tel: 902-492-1655; *Fax:* 902-492-1697
qtr@qtrlaw.com

***Halifax*: Ritch Durnford, Lawyers - *16**
#1200, CIBC Bldg., 1809 Barrington St., Halifax, NS B3J 3K8
Tel: 902-429-3400; *Fax:* 902-422-4713
info@ritchdurnford.com; library@ritchdurnford.com
www.ritchdurnford.com

***Halifax*: Joseph S. Roza - *1**
#210, 6021 Young St., Halifax, NS B3K 2A1
Tel: 902-425-5111; *Fax:* 902-425-5112
j.roza@ns.sympatico.ca
www.josephroza.com

***Halifax*: Scaravelli & Associates - *5**
#2030, 1801 Hollis St., Halifax, NS B3J 3N4
Tel: 902-429-4104; *Fax:* 902-423-4009
Toll-Free: 877-429-4104

***Halifax*: Singleton & Associates - *2**
2579 Windsor St., Halifax, NS B3K 5C4
Tel: 902-492-7000; *Fax:* 902-492-4309
tsingleton@singleton.ns.ca

***Halifax*: Stockton, Maxwell & Elliott - *3**
6309 Chebucto Rd., Halifax, NS B3L 1K9
Tel: 902-422-6055; *Fax:* 902-429-7655

***Halifax*: Wagner & Associates - *5**
1869 Upper Water St., Halifax, NS B3J 1S9
Tel: 902-425-7330; *Fax:* 902-422-1233
Toll-Free: 800-465-8794
seriousinjury@wagnerlaw.ca
www.wagnerandassociates.com

***Halifax*: Walker's Law Office Inc. - *1**
6221 Jubilee Rd., Halifax, NS B3H 2G3
Tel: 902-425-5297; *Fax:* 902-425-5095
catherinewalker@eastlink.ca

***Halifax*: Walker, Dunlop - *6**
PO Box 36057, RPO Spring Garden, Halifax, NS B3J 3J1
Tel: 902-423-8121; *Fax:* 902-429-0621
walker.dunlop@ns.sympatico.ca

***Halifax*: Wickwire Holm - *22**
#2100, P.O. Box 1054, 1801 Hollis St., Halifax, NS B3J 2X6
Tel: 902-429-4111; *Fax:* 902-429-8215
Toll-Free: 866-429-4111
wh@wickwireholm.com
www.wickwireholm.com

***Halifax*: Warren K. Zimmer - *1**
#200, P.O. Box 786, 5162 Duke St., Halifax, NS B3J 2V2
Tel: 902-429-7787; *Fax:* 902-429-7788
wkzimmer@istar.ca

***Halifax*: Diane K. Zwicker - *1**
1561 Vernon St., Halifax, NS B3H 3M8
Tel: 902-425-2193
dzwicker@sprint.ca

***Kentville*: Forse, Nathanson - *2**
P.O. Box 655, 325 Main St., Kentville, NS B4N 3X7
Tel: 902-678-1616; *Fax:* 902-678-1615
Toll-Free: 800-667-3879

***Kentville*: Donald C. Fraser - *1**
P.O. Box 668, Stn. Main, 35R Webster St., Kentville, NS B4N 3X9
Tel: 902-678-4006; *Fax:* 902-678-2999
fraser.law@ns.aliantzinc.ca

***Kentville*: Manning & Associates - *1**
27 Cornwallis St., Kentville, NS B4N 2E2
Tel: 902-679-1600; *Fax:* 902-679-5122
chris.manning@manningassociates.ca

***Kentville*: Muttarts Law Firm - *7**
P.O. Box 515, 20 Cornwallis St., Kentville, NS B4N 3X3
Tel: 902-678-2157; *Fax:* 902-678-9455
mtdc_law@mtdc.ns.ca
www.mtdc.ns.ca

***Kentville*: Tayllor MacLellan Cochrane - *1**
50 Cornwallis St., Kentville, NS B4N 2E4
Tel: 902-678-6156; *Fax:* 902-678-6010
Toll-Free: 888-486-2529
lawfirm@tmclaw.com
www.tmclaw.com

***Liverpool*: Allen C. Fownes - *1**
#188, P.O. Box 1739, 190 Main St., Liverpool, NS B0T 1K0
Tel: 902-354-2744; *Fax:* 902-354-2746
acfownes@novascotialaw.com
www.novascotialaw.com

***Liverpool*: Tutty & DiPersio - *2**
#167, P.O. Box 760, 171 Main St., Liverpool, NS B0T 1K0
Tel: 902-354-5756; *Fax:* 902-354-7395

***Lower Sackville*: David F. Farwell - *1**
#206, Vogue Optical Plaza, 405 Sackville Dr., Lower Sackville, NS B4C 2R9
Tel: 902-865-5537; *Fax:* 902-865-4354
davidfarwell@ns.sympatico.ca

***Lower Sackville*: Robert W. Newman & Associates - *1**
85 Sackville Cross Rd., Lower Sackville, NS B4C 2M2
Tel: 902-864-2722; *Fax:* 902-864-3164
robert.newman@ns.sympatico.ca

***Lower Sackville*: Richardson's Law Office - *2**
#100A, 800 Sackville Dr., Lower Sackville, NS B4E 1R8
Tel: 902-864-2300; *Fax:* 902-864-4410
Toll-Free: 877-304-2300
richardson@novalawyer.com
www.novalawyer.com

***Lunenburg*: Burke & Macdonald - *2**
P.O. Box 549, 28 King St., Lunenburg, NS B0J 2C0
Tel: 902-634-8354; *Fax:* 902-634-4226

***Martock*: Foxcreek Consulting Services - *1**
383 Windsor Backroad, RR#1, Martock, NS B0N 2T0
Tel: 902-497-1691
foxcreek@ns.sympatico.ca

***Middleton*: Cole Sawler - *2**
P.O. Box 400, 264 Main St., Middleton, NS B0S 1P0
Tel: 902-825-6288; *Fax:* 902-825-4340
officemanager@colesawlerlaw.ca
www.colesawlerlaw.ca

** indicates number of lawyers*

***Middleton*: C. Hanson Dowell Q.C. - *1**
P.O. Box 910, 250 Main St., Middleton, NS B0S 1P0
Tel: 902-825-3059; *Fax:* 902-825-3154
lawdow@ns.sympatico.ca

***Middleton*: Durland, Gillis & Schumacher, Associates - *2**
P.O. Box 700, 74 Commercial St., Middleton, NS B0S 1P0
Tel: 902-825-3415; *Fax:* 902-825-2522

***Musquodoboit Harbour*: Eastern Shore Law Centre - *1**
P.O. Box 357, 1653 Ostrea Lake Rd., Musquodoboit Harbour, NS B0J 2L0
Tel: 902-889-3796; *Fax:* 902-889-3735
easternshorelaw@aol.com
www.easternshorelaw.com

***New Glasgow*: R.A. Balmanoukian - *1**
137 McColl St., New Glasgow, NS B2H 4Z6
Tel: 902-755-3393; *Fax:* 902-755-6373
blackacre@north.nsis.com

***New Glasgow*: Goodman MacDonald & Patterson - *3**
P.O. Box 697, Stn. Main, 47 Riverside Dr., New Glasgow, NS B2H 5G2
Tel: 902-752-5090; *Fax:* 902-755-3545

***New Glasgow*: MacIntosh, MacDonnell & MacDonald - *10**
#260, Aberdeen Business Centre, P.O. Box 368, Stn. Main, 610 East River Rd., 2nd Fl., New Glasgow, NS B2H 5E5
Tel: 902-752-8441; *Fax:* 902-752-7810
Toll-Free: 888-752-8441
office@macmacmac.ns.ca

***New Waterford*: Charles Broderick - *1**
P.O. Box 151, 3316 Plummer Ave., New Waterford, NS B1H 4K4
Tel: 902-862-6471; *Fax:* 902-862-9513
cblaw@istar.ca

***New Waterford*: M. Sweeney Hinchey - *1**
3383 Plummer Ave., New Waterford, NS B1H 1Z1
Tel: 902-862-2368; *Fax:* 902-862-9581
hinchems@yahoo.com

***North Sydney*: M. Mora B. Maclennan - *1**
33 Archibald Ave., North Sydney, NS B2A 2W6
Tel: 902-794-2060; *Fax:* 902-794-3558

***North Sydney*: Michael A. Tobin - *1**
P.O. Box 1925, Stn. Main, 254 Commercial St., North Sydney, NS B2A 3S9
Tel: 902-794-8803; *Fax:* 902-794-9869
miketobinlaw@syd.eastlink.ca

***Pictou*: MacLean & MacDonald - *2**
P.O. Box 730, 90 Coleraine St., Pictou, NS B0K 1H0
Tel: 902-485-4347; *Fax:* 902-485-8887
law@macleanmacdonald.com

***Pictou*: Scanlan Graham Scanlan - *2**
P.O. Box 1720, 94 Water St., Pictou, NS B0K 1H0
Tel: 902-485-4313; *Fax:* 902-485-5083
sgslaw@ns.sympatico.ca

***Port Hawkesbury*: Pickup & MacDowell - *2**
#2, 308 Philpott St., Port Hawkesbury, NS B9A 2B8
Tel: 902-625-2500; *Fax:* 902-625-0500
pkpmd@auracom.com

***Port Hood*: Francis X. Moloney - *1**
P.O. Box 122, 351 Main St., Port Hood, NS B0E 2W0
Tel: 902-787-3113; *Fax:* 902-787-3105

***Pubnico*: d'Entremont & Boudreau - *2**
P.O. Box 118, Pubnico, NS B0W 2W0
Tel: 902-762-3119; *Fax:* 902-762-3124
rjboudreau@klis.com

***Shelburne*: Celia J. Melanson, Barristor & Solicitor, Inc. - *1**
P.O. Box 562, 171 Water St., Shelburne, NS B0T 1W0
Tel: 902-875-4188; *Fax:* 902-875-1316
celia.melanson@ns.sympatico.ca
www.celiamelanson.com

***Shelburne*: Donald R. Miller - *1**
6767 Shore Rd. RR#3, Shelburne, NS B0T 1W0
Tel: 902-637-2527; *Fax:* 902-637-2165

***Shelburne*: Johanne L. Tournier - *1**
Shelburne Industrial Park, Site 3, Comp. 4, RR#2, Shelburne, NS B0T 1W0
Tel: 902-875-4753; *Fax:* 902-875-3783
jasmith77@juno.com

***Sherbrooke*: Robin W. Archibald - *1**
P.O. Box 176, Sherbrooke, NS B0J 3C0
Tel: 902-522-2067; *Fax:* 902-522-2299
robinlaw@auracom.com

***Shubenacadie*: Carruthers & MacDonell Law Office Inc. - *3**
Chubenacadie Professional Centre, P.O. Box 280, #204, 5 Mill Village Rd., Shubenacadie, NS B0N 2H0
Tel: 902-758-2591; *Fax:* 902-758-4022

***Stellarton*: Hector J. MacIsaac - *1**
P.O. Box 849, 253 Foord St., Stellarton, NS B0K 1S0
Tel: 902-752-5143; *Fax:* 902-928-1299

***Stellarton*: R.E. O'Blenis - *1**
P.O. Box 1500, 179 Foord St., Stellarton, NS B0K 1S0
Tel: 902-752-1575

***Stellarton*: Skoke & Company**
P.O. Box 850, Foord St., Stellarton, NS B0K 1S0
Tel: 902-755-5711; *Fax:* 902-752-6561

***Sydney*: Anderson, Nathanson - *1**
P.O. Box 79, Stn. Pier Post., 797 Victoria Rd., Sydney, NS B1N 3B1
Tel: 902-849-5110; *Fax:* 902-849-6110
andnat@andersonnathanson.com

***Sydney*: Cusack Law Office - *1**
205 Charlotte St., Sydney, NS B1P 1C4
Tel: 902-564-8396; *Fax:* 902-564-0030
cusacklaw@ns.sympatico.ca

***Sydney*: Vincent A. Gillis - *1**
P.O. Box 847, Stn. A, 321 Townsend St., Sydney, NS B1P 6J1
Tel: 902-562-3222; *Fax:* 902-539-4199
vagillislaw@ns.sympatico.ca

***Sydney*: Khattar & Khattar - *6**
P.O. Box 387, 378 Charlotte St., Sydney, NS B1P 6H2
Tel: 902-539-9696; *Fax:* 902-562-7147
Toll-Free: 888-542-8827
elaine@khattar.ca

***Sydney*: John G. Khattar - *1**
P.O. Box 1626, 463 Prince St., Sydney, NS B1P 5L6
Tel: 902-564-6611; *Fax:* 902-564-8805
jkhatter@syd.eastlink.ca

***Sydney*: Lorway MacEachern - *4**
112 Charlotte St., Sydney, NS B1P 1B9
Tel: 902-539-4447; *Fax:* 902-564-9844
northlaw@cbnet.ns.ca

***Sydney*: MacDonald & MacLennan - *1**
P.O. Box 1148, 275 Charlotte St., Sydney, NS B1P 6J7
Tel: 902-564-4429; *Fax:* 902-539-2303

***Sydney*: H.F. MacIntyre & Associates - *2**
P.O. Box 788, Stn. A, 245 Charlotte St., Sydney, NS B1P 6J1
Tel: 902-562-4224; *Fax:* 902-562-0606
macintyre.assoc@ns.sympatico.ca

***Sydney*: Hugh R. McLeod - *1**
P.O. Box 306, 275 Charlotte St., Sydney, NS B1P 6H2
Tel: 902-539-2261; *Fax:* 902-539-3386
hugh.mcleod@ns.sympatico.ca

***Sydney*: John W. Morgan - *1**
29 Riverdale Dr., Sydney, NS B1R 1P2
Tel: 902-539-2800; *Fax:* 902-563-5585
jwmorgan@cbrm.ns.ca

***Sydney*: Ralph W. Ripley Barrister & Solicitor Inc. - *1**
#202, P.O. Box 7, 295 Charlotte St., Sydney, NS B1P 6G9
Tel: 902-564-4446; *Fax:* 902-539-7765
rripley@ns.aliantzinc.ca

***Sydney*: M. Joseph Rizzetto - *1**
#206, 275 Charlotte St., 2nd Fl., Sydney, NS B1P 1C6
Tel: 902-562-6262; *Fax:* 902-539-3567
info@rizzetto.ns.ca

***Sydney*: Rudderham Chernin Law Office Inc. - *2**
500 George St., Sydney, NS B1P 1K6
Tel: 902-567-0250; *Fax:* 902-567-0252
info@rclaw.ns.ca

***Truro*: Archibald Lederman - *2**
P.O. Box 1100, Stn. Main, 43 Walker St., Truro, NS B2N 5G9
Tel: 902-895-0524; *Fax:* 902-893-7608
plederman@archibaldlederman.ca

***Truro*: Burchell, MacDougall - *18**
P.O. Box 1128, 710 Prince St., Truro, NS B2N 5H1
Tel: 902-895-1561; *Fax:* 902-895-7709
Toll-Free: 800-565-1200
truro@burchellmacdougall.com
www.burchellmacdougall.com

***Truro*: David F. Curtis Q.C. - *1**
#202, P.O. Box 458, 640 Prince St., Truro, NS B2N 1G4
Tel: 902-895-0528; *Fax:* 902-893-1158
dcurtislaw@ns.aliantzinc.ca

***Truro*: Melinda J. MacLean, Q.C. - *1**
P.O. Box 126, Stn. Main, 188 Queen St., Truro, NS B2N 5B6
Tel: 902-895-2866; *Fax:* 902-893-1455

***Truro*: McLellan, Richards & Bégin - *2**
P.O. Box 1064, 779 Prince St., Truro, NS B2N 5G9
Tel: 902-895-4417; *Fax:* 902-897-9890
Toll-Free: 866-600-0011
www.truro-law.com

***Truro*: Gerard P. Scanlan - *1**
P.O. Box 1228, Stn. Main, 640 Prince St., Truro, NS B2N 5N2
Tel: 902-895-9249; *Fax:* 902-893-3078
scanpayn@tru.eastlink.ca

***Truro*: Yuill Chisholm Killawee - *2**
541 Prince St., Truro, NS B2N 1E8
Tel: 902-893-0243; *Fax:* 902-897-0282

***Upper Tantallon*: Smith-Camp & Associates - *1**
#203, 5209 St. Margaret's Bay Rd., Upper Tantallon, NS B3Z 1E3
Tel: 902-826-2193; *Fax:* 902-826-1043
smithcamplaw@hotmail.com

***Waverley*: David Chown Consulting - *1**
P.O. Box 5095, Waverley, NS B2R 1S2
Tel: 902-860-1104; *Fax:* 902-860-2655
david.chown@ns.sympatico.ca

***Westville*: S. Charles Facey, Q.C. - *1**
P.O. Box 610, 1912 Drummond Rd., Westville, NS B0K 2A0
Tel: 902-396-4191; *Fax:* 902-396-3606
charles.facey@ns.sympatico.ca

***Windsor*: Adams & Company - *2**
P.O. Box 2379, 189 Gerrish St., Windsor, NS B0N 2T0
Tel: 902-798-8384; *Fax:* 902-798-0432
hadams.adamsco@ns.sympatico.ca

***Windsor*: How Lawrence White Bowes - *3**
P.O. Box 3177, 98 Gerrish St., Windsor, NS B0N 2T0
Tel: 902-798-5997; *Fax:* 902-798-8925
jjwhite@scotialaw.com; dbowes@scotialaw.com
www.scotialaw.com

***Windsor*: Nelson Law - *2**
P.O. Box 2018, 258 King St., Windsor, NS B0N 2T0
Tel: 902-798-5797; *Fax:* 902-798-2332
nelson.law@ns.sympatico.ca

***Windsor*: John D. Romans - *1**
P.O. Box 1024, 140 King St., Windsor, NS B0N 2T0
Tel: 902-798-8311

***Wolfville*: Kimball Brogan Law Office - *4**
121 Front St., Wolfville, NS B4P 1A6
Tel: 902-542-5757; *Fax:* 902-542-5759
Toll-Free: 800-294-7851
info@kimballbrogan.ca
www.kimballbrogan.ca

***Wolfville*: Dianne E. Thompson-Sheppard, Q.C. - *1**
80 Kent Ave., Wolfville, NS B4P 1V1
Tel: 902-542-2388; *Fax:* 902-542-0794
paddles@ns.sympatico.ca

***Yarmouth*: R.K. Murray Judge - *1**
28 Ellis Ave., Yarmouth, NS B5A 2X2
Tel: 902-742-0383; *Fax:* 902-742-2300

Nunavut

***Iqaluit*: Chandler & Cooper - *2**
P.O. Box 2021, Iqaluit, NU X0A 0H0
Tel: 867-979-3505; *Fax:* 867-979-3506
norhtlaw@nunanet.com

** indicates number of lawyers*

Iqaluit: McIsaac, Penner - *3
Maliiganik Tukisiiniakvik Society, P.O. Box 29, Iqaluit, NU X0A 0H0
Tel: 867-979-5377; *Fax:* 867-979-4346

Ontario

Ajax: William E. Foden - *2
572 Kingston Rd. West, Ajax, ON L1T 3A2
Tel: 905-428-8200; *Fax:* 905-428-8666
foden@on.aibn.com

Ajax: Glover & Associates, Barristers, Solicitors, Notaries
562 Kingston Rd. West, Ajax, ON L1T 3A2
Tel: 905-619-3700; *Fax:* 905-619-0022
info@gloverlaw.ca
www.gloverlaw.ca

Ajax: Greening & Bucknam - *1
#202, 50 Commercial Ave., Ajax, ON L1S 2H5
Tel: 905-683-7037; *Fax:* 905-683-7627
bucknam@rogers.com

Ajax: Graham F. Pinos, Q.C. - *1
31 Leah Cres., Ajax, ON L1T 3J2
Tel: 416-428-6838; *Fax:* 416-428-0212
graham.pinos@rogers.com

Ajax: Reilly D'Heureux Lanzi LLP - *4
Pickering Village, 555 Kingston Rd. West, 2nd Fl., Ajax, ON L1S 6M1
Tel: 905-427-4077; *Fax:* 905-427-4042
mpreilly@reillylegal.com
www.reillylegal.com

Ajax: Singh, Tucciarone - *2
#206, 158 Harwood Ave. South, Ajax, ON L1S 2H6
Tel: 905-683-1042; *Fax:* 905-683-7794
Toll-Free: 800-801-4602
singh-tucciarone@on.aibn.com

Ajax: Juanita Wislesky - *1
#202, 15 Harwood Rd. Ave. South, Ajax, ON L1S 2B9
Tel: 905-686-1686
juanita_wislesky@yahoo.ca

Ajax: George D. Wright - *1
543 Kingston Rd. West, Ajax, ON L1S 6M1
Tel: 905-427-7200; *Fax:* 905-427-2999

Alexandria: Jean-Marc Lefebvre, Q.C. - *2
P.O. Box 519, 32 Main St. North, Alexandria, ON K0C 1A0
Tel: 613-525-1358; *Fax:* 613-525-3411
lefebvre@bellnet.ca

Alexandria: Nelligan O'Brien Payne - *46
139 Main St. South, Alexandria, ON K0C 1A0
Tel: 613-525-2396; *Fax:* 613-525-2752
Toll-Free: 888-565-9912
info@nelligan.ca
www.nelligan.ca

Allenford: Richard R. Evans - *1
P.O. Box 14, 7771 Hwy. 21, Allenford, ON N0H 1A0
Tel: 519-934-2875; *Fax:* 519-934-1460
rrevans@bmts.com

Alliston: John W. Clarke - *1
#3, P.O. Box 408, Stn. Main, 103 Victoria St. West, Alliston, ON L9R 1V6
Tel: 705-435-4301; *Fax:* 705-435-3407

Alliston: Mary L. Galbraith - *1
22 Church St. South, Alliston, ON L9R 1V9
Tel: 705-435-4324; *Fax:* 705-435-2628

Alliston: Gilmore & Gilmore - *2
P.O. Box 250, 458 Victoria St. East, Alliston, ON L9R 1V5
Tel: 705-435-4339; *Fax:* 705-435-6520
Toll-Free: 877-855-3425
info@gilmoreandgilmore.com
www.gilmoreandgilmore.com

Alliston: James W. Smith - *1
P.O. Box 730, Stn. Main, 8 Victoria St. East, Alliston, ON L9R 1V9
Tel: 705-435-0160; *Fax:* 705-435-5049
jsmithl@bellnet.ca

Almonte: L.G. William Chapman - *1
P.O. Box 362, 77 Little Bridge St., Almonte, ON K0A 1A0
Tel: 613-256-3072; *Fax:* 613-256-5164
lgwilliamchapman@bellnet.ca
www.lgwilliamchapman.com

Almonte: Elizabeth A. Swarbrick - *4
#107, P.O. Box 639, 83 Little Bridge St., Almonte, ON K0A 1A0
Tel: 613-256-9811; *Fax:* 613-256-9814
elizabeth@familyfocusedlaw.com
www.familyfocusedlaw.com

Almonte: Evelyn Wheeler - *1
P.O. Box 1540, 38 Mill St., Almonte, ON K0A 1A0
Tel: 613-256-4148; *Fax:* 613-256-4708
www.evelynwheeler.com

Amherstburg: Baker Busch - *2
41 Sandwich St. South, Amherstburg, ON N9V 1Z5
Tel: 519-736-2154; *Fax:* 519-736-2466

Amherstburg: Robert D. McKerrow - *1
57 Richmond St., Amherstburg, ON N9V 1G1
Tel: 519-736-8555; *Fax:* 519-736-1413
rkrow@bellnet.ca

Amherstview: William E.M. Vince - *1
6 Speers Blvd., #G, Amherstview, ON K7N 1Z6
Tel: 613-389-6727; *Fax:* 613-389-6256
wvince@cogeco.ca

Ancaster: G. Kevin Eggleton - *1
#110, 911 Golf Links Rd., Ancaster, ON L9K 1H9
Tel: 905-304-5297; *Fax:* 905-304-7711

Ancaster: Randy L. Levinson - *1
58 Cumming Ct., Ancaster, ON L9G 1V3
Tel: 905-648-7239; *Fax:* 905-648-4437
randy@randylevinson.com
www.randylevinson.com

Ancaster: Saija Enterprises Inc. - *1
96 Chatterson Dr., Ancaster, ON L9G 3X2
Tel: 905-648-5973; *Fax:* 905-648-9198
nirudesai100@hotmail.com

Ancaster: Wynne, Dingwall & Pringle - *3
Stn. Ancaster, 231 Wilson St. East, #B, Ancaster, ON L9G 2B8
Tel: 905-648-1851; *Fax:* 905-648-1715
www.ancasterlaw.com

Angus: Gordon R. MacKenzie Professional Corporation - *1
P.O. Box 600, Unit A, 189 Mill St., Angus, ON L0M 1B2
Tel: 705-424-1331; *Fax:* 705-424-6441
gmackenzie@on.aibn.com
www.yourlocallawyer.com

Arnprior: M. Martha Coady - *1
32 John St. North, Arnprior, ON K7S 2N2
Tel: 613-623-7327; *Fax:* 613-623-8506

Arnprior: Pamela R. LeMay - *1
64 McGonigal St. West, Arnprior, ON K7S 1M1
Tel: 613-623-7705; *Fax:* 613-623-2189
plemay@lemaylaw.ca

Arnprior: C.P. Merla - *1
#4, 75 Elgin St. West, Arnprior, ON K7S 3T9
Tel: 613-623-6593; *Fax:* 613-623-8947

Aurora: Gordon F. Allan - *1
12 St. John's Sideroad East, Aurora, ON L4G 3G8
Tel: 905-895-3425; *Fax:* 905-726-3098

Aurora: Boland Howe Barristers LLP - *5
130 Industrial Pkwy. North, Aurora, ON L4G 4C3
Tel: 905-841-5717; *Fax:* 905-841-7128
info@bolandhowe.com
www.bolandhowe.com

Aurora: Di Cecco, Jones - *2
#205, 15171 Yonge St., Aurora, ON L4G 1M1
Tel: 905-751-1517; *Fax:* 905-751-1518
dicecco.jones@diceccojones.com

Aurora: Laurion Law Office - *1
41 Wellington St. East, Aurora, ON L4G 1H6
Tel: 905-841-2222; *Fax:* 905-841-3388
jlaurion@laurionlaw.com

Aurora: Barry W. Switzer - *1
P.O. Box 246, 15187 Yonge St., Aurora, ON L4G 1L8
Tel: 905-727-9488; *Fax:* 905-841-8647

Aurora: Thomas McPherson & Associates - *2
P.O. Box 338, 15220 Yonge St., Aurora, ON L4G 3H4
Tel: 905-727-3151; *Fax:* 905-841-2164
mcpherson@auroralaw.net
www.mcphersonassoc.yp.ca

Aylmer: Doyle & Prendergast - *2
10 Sydenham St. East, Aylmer, ON N5H 1L2
Tel: 519-773-3105; *Fax:* 519-765-1728

Aylmer: Gloin, Hall & Shields - *4
139 Talbot St. East, Aylmer, ON N5H 1H3
Tel: 519-773-9221; *Fax:* 519-765-1885
ghsaylaw@amtelecom.net

Bancroft: Glenna M. Ireland - *1
P.O. Box 1361, 11 Fairway Blvd., Bancroft, ON K0L 1C0
Tel: 613-332-0406; *Fax:* 613-332-0609

Bancroft: L.C. Plater - *1
P.O. Box 1150, 129 Hastings St. North, Bancroft, ON K0L 1C0
Tel: 613-332-1605; *Fax:* 613-332-2619

Bancroft: Robert C. Henderson & Associates - *2
P.O. Box 225, 51 Hastings St. North, Bancroft, ON K0L 1C0
Tel: 613-332-0500; *Fax:* 613-332-5733
rchenderson@bellnet.ca

Barrie: Nancy Lee Allison - *1
P.O. Box 308, 285 Grove Street East, Barrie, ON L4M 2R2
Tel: 705-737-5702; *Fax:* 705-737-1614
nlalliso@csolve.net

Barrie: John G. Alousis - *1
76 Mulcaster St., Barrie, ON L4M 3M4
Tel: 705-735-0065; *Fax:* 705-735-0277
john@alousislaw.com
www.alousislaw.com

Barrie: Peter D. Archibald - *1
P.O. Box 907, 59 Collier St., Barrie, ON L4M 4Y6
Tel: 705-726-4511; *Fax:* 705-726-0613
pda@bconnex.net

Barrie: Brian Bond
25 Poyntz St., Barrie, ON L4M 3N8
Tel: 705-734-1550; *Fax:* 705-734-0306
bwb@bondlaw.ca

Barrie: Susan Joyce Brenner - *1
130 Collier St., Barrie, ON L4M 1H3
Tel: 705-734-1801; *Fax:* 705-734-2324

Barrie: Thomas Bryson - *1
11 Sophia St. West, Barrie, ON L4N 1H9
Tel: 705-728-2232; *Fax:* 705-728-7525
tbrysonlaw@bellnet.ca

Barrie: Burgar, Rowe - *18
P.O. Box 758, 90 Mulcaster St., Barrie, ON L4M 4Y5
Tel: 705-721-3377; *Fax:* 705-721-4025
burgarrowe@burgarrowe.com
www.burgarrowe.com

Barrie: Peter C. Card - *1
111 Toronto St., Barrie, ON L4N 1V1
Tel: 705-739-9111; *Fax:* 705-739-8111

Barrie: Carroll Heyd Chown - *5
#20, P.O. Box 548, 556 Bryne Dr., Barrie, ON L4M 4T7
Tel: 705-722-4400; *Fax:* 705-722-0704
admin@chcbarristers.com

Barrie: Cowan & Carter - *1
P.O. Box 722, 107 Collier St., Barrie, ON L4M 4Y5
Tel: 705-728-4521; *Fax:* 705-728-8744

Barrie: Craig Boswell McDermot - *4
158 Dunlop St. East, Barrie, ON L4M 1B1
Tel: 705-734-2911; *Fax:* 705-734-2047

Barrie: Cugelman & Eisen - *2
#201, 28 Owen St., Barrie, ON L4M 3G7
Tel: 705-721-1888; *Fax:* 705-721-7755
cugelman@cugelmaneisen.com
www.cugelmaneisen.com

Barrie: Alfred W.J. Dick - *1
80 Worsley St., Barrie, ON L4M 1L8
Tel: 705-728-9006; *Fax:* 705-728-9876

Barrie: Julianne Ecclestone - *1
80 Worsley St., Barrie, ON L4M 1L8
Tel: 705-725-8050; *Fax:* 705-722-0189

** indicates number of lawyers*

Barrie: Brian G. Galbraith - *4
124 Dunlop St. West, Barrie, ON L4N 1B1
Tel: 705-727-4242; Fax: 705-727-4240
Brian@GalbraithFamilyLaw.com
www.galbraithfamilylaw.com

Barrie: Graham Wilson & Green, Barristers & Solicitors, Notaries, Mediators - *12
#107, 190 Cundles Rd. East, Barrie, ON L4M 4S5
Tel: 705-737-1811; Fax: 705-737-5390
gwg@gwg.on.ca
www.gwg.on.ca

Barrie: Klaus N. Jacoby - *1
P.O. Box 350, 34 Clapperton St., Barrie, ON L4M 4T5
Tel: 705-726-0238; Fax: 705-726-9197
jaco@jacobylaw.ca

Barrie: Mark A. Kelly - *1
43 Worsley St., Barrie, ON L4M 1L7
Tel: 705-739-6955; Fax: 705-739-6956
markkelly@bellnet.ca

Barrie: Peter Lamprey - *1
78 Worsley St., Barrie, ON L4M 1L8
Tel: 705-722-1114; Fax: 705-720-1155
peter@plamprey.com
www.plamprey.com

Barrie: Christine D. Lunn - *1
118 Collier St., Barrie, ON L4M 1H4
Tel: 705-739-0929; Fax: 705-725-7977

Barrie: McLellan Associates - The Law Store - *1
510 Bayfield St., Barrie, ON L4M 4S5
Tel: 705-726-7765; Fax: 705-726-8071

Barrie: J. Marvin Menzies - *1
#104, P.O. Box 1175, Stn. Main, 89 Dunlop St. East, Barrie, ON L4M 5E2
Tel: 705-722-5432; Fax: 705-722-0218
marvinmenzies@on.aibn.com

Barrie: R. John Mitchell - *1
P.O. Box 1, 40 Clapperton St., Barrie, ON L4M 4S9
Tel: 705-726-8855; Fax: 705-721-0782

Barrie: Murray/Ralston - *3
119 Collier St., Barrie, ON L4M 1H5
Tel: 705-737-3229; Fax: 705-737-5380
admin@murraytalston.com
www.murrayralston.com

Barrie: Gerald E. Norman - *1
P.O. Box 732, 99 Bayfield St., Barrie, ON L4M 4Y5
Tel: 705-726-2772; Fax: 705-734-1942
geraldnorman@normanlawoffice.ca
www.normanlawoffice.ca

Barrie: Oatley, Vigmond, Personal Injury Lawyers LLP - *14
151 Ferris Lane, Barrie, ON L4M 6C1
Tel: 705-726-9021; Fax: 705-726-2132
Toll-Free: 888-662-2481
info@oatleyvigmond.com
www.oatleyvigmond.com

Barrie: Owen, Harris-Lowe - *4
P.O. Box 848, 26 Owen St., Barrie, ON L4M 4Y6
Tel: 705-726-1181; Fax: 705-726-1463
odlaw@owendickey.com
www.owendickey.com

Barrie: Michael E. Reed - *1
105 Collier St., Barrie, ON L4M 1H2
Tel: 705-726-4300; Fax: 705-725-7910
michael@michaelreedlaw.com
www.michaelreedlaw.com

Barrie: Catherine A. Rogers - *1
78 Mulcaster St., Barrie, ON L4M 3M4
Tel: 705-734-2800; Fax: 705-734-2807

Barrie: Charles F. Ruttan - *1
23 Owen St., Barrie, ON L4M 3G8
Tel: 705-737-0688; Fax: 705-722-4749
chuckruttan@ruttanlaw.ca

Barrie: Mark Scharf - *1
103 Collier St., Barrie, ON L4M 1H2
Tel: 705-728-0555; Fax: 705-722-3741

Barrie: Dennis Tascona Barrister & Solicitor - *1
130 Collier St, Barrie, ON L4M 1H4
Tel: 705-734-1801; Fax: 705-734-2324
dennistascona@bellnet.ca

Barrie: Joseph N. Tascona - *1
84 Worsley St., Barrie, ON L4M 1L8
Tel: 705-725-1769; Fax: 705-725-1772

Barrie: Eric C. Taves - *1
P.O. Box 295, 86 Worsley St., Barrie, ON L4M 4T2
Tel: 705-728-4770; Fax: 705-728-7642
etaves@etaves-law.com
www.etaves-law.com

Barrie: George W. Taylor, Q.C. - *1
46 Kempenfelt Dr., Barrie, ON L4M 1B9
Tel: 705-728-8352

Beamsville: M.G. Vandeyar - *1
#7, Lincoln Kingsway Plaza, P.O. Box 489, 5041 King St., Beamsville, ON L0R 1B0
Tel: 905-563-8818; Fax: 905-563-7750

Beaverton: Woodcock & Tomlinson - *1
P.O. Box 512, 402 Simcoe St., Beaverton, ON L0K 1A0
Tel: 705-426-7317; Fax: 705-426-5740

Belle River: J.L. Deziel - *1
P.O. Box 909, 531 Notre Dame, Belle River, ON N0R 1A0
Tel: 519-728-2000; Fax: 519-728-4599
Toll-Free: 800-501-3494
jldeziel@cogeco.net

Belleville: Wendy J. Elliott - *1
187B North Front St., Belleville, ON K8P 3C1
Tel: 613-966-0394; Fax: 613-966-1307
wjelliott@hotmail.com

Belleville: Graydon & Hurley - *2
112 Front St., Belleville, ON K8N 2Y7
Tel: 613-966-4614; Fax: 613-966-6182

Belleville: Edward J. Kafka - *3
P.O. Box 243, 309 Front St., Belleville, ON K8N 5A2
Tel: 613-968-3416; Fax: 613-968-3417
elkafka.barr@bellnet.ca

Belleville: Richard R. Ketcheson - *1
#200, 199 Front St., Belleville, ON K8N 5H5
Tel: 613-966-1123; Fax: 613-966-0478

Belleville: O'Flynn Weese LLP - *10
65 Bridge St. East, Belleville, ON K8N 1L8
Tel: 613-966-5222; Fax: 613-966-7991
info@owtlaw.com
www.owtlaw.com

Belleville: Procter Professional Corporation - *4
#204, P.O. Box 700, 365 Front St. North, Belleville, ON K8N 5B3
Tel: 613-962-2584; Fax: 613-962-0968
wprocter@procterlaw.ca

Belleville: Reynolds O'Brien LLP - *8
P.O. Box 1327, 183 Front St., Belleville, ON K8N 5J1
Tel: 613-966-3031; Fax: 613-966-2390
mail@reynoldsobrien.com
www.reynoldsobrien.com

Belleville: Peter A. Robertson - *1
#101, 3 Applewood Dr., Belleville, ON K8P 4E3
Tel: 613-969-9611; Fax: 613-969-9775
Toll-Free: 800-561-6385
probertson@cogeco.net
www.cdncounsel.com

Belleville: C. Roderick Rolston - *1
#202, 175 Front St., Belleville, ON K8N 2Y9
Tel: 613-962-9154; Fax: 613-962-8109
Toll-Free: 800-361-4437
rrolston@reach.net

Belleville: Templeman Menninga LLP - *24
#200, P.O. Box 234, 205 Dundas St. East, Belleville, ON K8N 5A2
Tel: 613-966-2620; Fax: 613-966-2866
info@tmlegal.com
www.tmlegal.ca

Belleville: Berend Van Huizen - *1
210 Church St., Belleville, ON K8N 3C3
Tel: 613-962-8645; Fax: 613-962-7689
berend@berendvanhuizenlaw.com
www.berendvanhuizenlaw.com

Blenheim: Kerr & Wood - *1
P.O. Box 1150, 15 George St., Blenheim, ON N0P 1A0
Tel: 519-676-5465; Fax: 519-676-3918
kerrwood@ciaccess.com

Blyth: John C. Myers - *1
P.O. Box 280, 439 Queen St. North, Blyth, ON N0M 1H0
Tel: 519-523-9148; Fax: 519-523-9148

Bobcaygeon: Robert J. Walker - *1
P.O. Box 243, 4 King St. West, Bobcaygeon, ON K0M 1A0
Tel: 705-738-3588; Fax: 705-738-4252

Bolton: Jean P. Carberry - *1
34 Queen St., Bolton, ON L4E 1B3
Tel: 905-857-2332; Fax: 905-857-2367
jpclaw@jpclaw.ca

Bolton: W. Ross Milliken - *1
P.O. Box 225, 49 Queen St. North, Bolton, ON L7E 5T2
Tel: 905-857-2835; Fax: 905-857-0097
ross.milliken@boltonlaw.ca
www.rossmilliken.com

Bolton: Neiman, Callegari - *2
#H3, 18 King St. East, Bolton, ON L7E 1E8
Tel: 905-857-0095; Fax: 905-857-0488
info@neimancallegari.ca
www.neimancallegari.ca

Bolton: Mark E. Penfold - *2
P.O. Box 225, 49 Queen St. North, Bolton, ON L7E 5T2
Tel: 905-857-2835; Fax: 905-857-0091
Toll-Free: 800-954-4054
mark.penfold@boltonlaw.ca

Bowmanville: William Brown - *1
P.O. Box 1, 71 Mearns Court, Bowmanville, ON L1C 4N4
Tel: 905-623-3305; Fax: 905-623-3287

Bowmanville: Mervyn B. Kelly - *1
42 Prince St., Bowmanville, ON L1C 1G6
Tel: 905-623-4444
merv@claringtonlawyers.com
www.claringtonlawyers.com

Bracebridge: Ronald G. Burk - *1
32 Wharf Rd., Bracebridge, ON P1L 2A7
Tel: 705-645-3007; Fax: 705-645-3998
rgburklaw@on.aibn.com

Bracebridge: Brian G. Jacques - *1
#103, P.O. Box 1227, 145 Ontario Street, Bracebridge, ON P1L 2A7
Tel: 705-645-8743; Fax: 705-645-8895
brianjacqueslaw@bellnet.ca

Bracebridge: Lee, Roche & Kelly - *4
P.O. Box 990, 6 Dominion St., Bracebridge, ON P1L 1V2
Tel: 705-645-2286; Fax: 705-645-5541
Toll-Free: 866-331-1100
nickroche@lrklaw.ca

Bracebridge: Penelope A. Lithgow - *1
58B Ontario St., Bracebridge, ON P1L 2A6
Tel: 705-645-8118

Bracebridge: Brian E. Slocum - *1
63 Quebec St., Bracebridge, ON P1L 2A4
Tel: 705-645-2900; Fax: 705-645-2549
slocum@slocumlaw.com

Bracebridge: Judith L. Stephenson - *1
58 Ontario St., Bracebridge, ON P1L 2A6
Tel: 705-645-5251; Fax: 705-645-9193

Bracebridge: Sugg, Fitton & Taylor LLP - *2
5 Chancery Lane 1, Bracebridge, ON P1L 2E3
Tel: 705-645-5211; Fax: 705-645-8021
chancerylane@cogeco.net

Bracebridge: Bruce McLeod Thompson - *1
3 Dominion Street, Bracebridge, ON P1L 2E6
Tel: 705-646-1000; Fax: 705-646-9510
Toll-Free: 800-661-8080

Bracebridge: Peter N. Ward - *1
P.O. Box 10009, Stn. Main, 47 Quebec St., Bracebridge, ON P1L 1W6
Tel: 705-645-1338

Bracebridge: Wyjad Fleming Associates - *2
P.O. Box 177, 39 Dominion St., Bracebridge, ON P1L 1T6
Tel: 705-645-8787; Fax: 705-645-3390
bracebridge@wylaw.ca
www.wylaw.ca

* indicates number of lawyers

***Bradford*: Evans & Evans - *2**
P.O. Box 190, 21 Holland St. West, Bradford, ON L3Z 2A8
Tel: 905-775-3381; *Fax:* 905-775-8835
law@evansevans.ca

***Bradford*: Gaska & Ballantyne-Gaska - *2**
P.O. Box 1677, Stn. Main, 60 Barrie St., Bradford, ON L3Z 2B9
Tel: 905-775-0015; *Fax:* 905-775-7772
ballantyne.gaska@rogers.com

***Bradford*: E. Pauline Taylor - *1**
76 Holland St. West, Bradford, ON L3Z 2B6
Tel: 905-775-9606; *Fax:* 905-775-0692

***Brampton*: Linda B. Alexander - *1**
#201, 197 County Court Blvd., Brampton, ON L6W 4P6
Tel: 905-450-7757; *Fax:* 905-455-9190
email@lindaalexander.com
lindaalexander.com

***Brampton*: Bowyer, Greenslade, Webster, Allison LLP, Barristers, Solicitors - *3**
#600, 24 Queen St. East, Brampton, ON L6V 1A3
Tel: 905-451-1300; *Fax:* 905-451-4451

***Brampton*: Edmond O'Donoghue Brown - *1**
#100, 205 County Court Blvd., Brampton, ON L6W 4R6
Tel: 905-454-4141; *Fax:* 905-454-4463
edbrown@bellnet.ca

***Brampton*: Connon & Iacobelli - *2**
#403, 201 County Court Blvd., Brampton, ON L6W 4L2
Tel: 905-454-3070; *Fax:* 905-454-2964
connon-iacobelli@on.aibn.com

***Brampton*: D.R. Cook & Company - *3**
#1, 20 Regan Rd., Brampton, ON L7A 1C3
Tel: 905-840-7650; *Fax:* 905-840-7749

***Brampton*: Dale, Streiman & Kurz - *6**
480 Main St. North, Brampton, ON L6V 1P8
Tel: 905-455-7300; *Fax:* 905-455-5848
Toll-Free: 866-219-8109
mail@dsklaw.com
www.dsklaw.com

***Brampton*: Dalzell & Waite - *2**
#19, 1 Bartley Bull Pkwy., Brampton, ON L6W 3T7
Tel: 905-454-2288; *Fax:* 905-454-2297

***Brampton*: Davis Webb LLP - *7**
#800, 24 Queen St. East, Brampton, ON L6V 1A3
Tel: 905-451-6714; *Fax:* 905-454-1876
info@daviswebb.ca
www.daviswebb.com

***Brampton*: Fader Furlan Moss LLP - *7**
#200, 134 Queen St. East, Brampton, ON L6V 1B2
Tel: 905-459-6160; *Fax:* 905-459-4606
Toll-Free: 877-468-8494
www.faderfurlanmoss.com

***Brampton*: Folites Legal Professional Coporation - *2**
#1, 14 Nelson St. West, Brampton, ON L6X 1B7
Tel: 905-457-2118; *Fax:* 905-457-3707
ronefolkes@folkeslaw.ca
www.folkeslaw.com

***Brampton*: Pina Grella - *1**
#101, 8501 Mississauga Rd., Brampton, ON L6Y 5G8
Tel: 905-453-6000; *Fax:* 905-453-6016
pina@grellalaw.com

***Brampton*: Hillier & Hillier - *1**
165 Main St. North, Brampton, ON L6X 1N1
Tel: 905-453-8636; *Fax:* 905-453-6267
ava@avahillier.ca

***Brampton*: Stephen A. Holmes - *1**
180 Queen St. West, Brampton, ON L6X 1A8
Tel: 905-796-3030; *Fax:* 905-796-2157
sholmes@on.aibn.com
www.stephenholmeslawoffice.com

***Brampton*: Hope & Henderson Law Office - *2**
253 Main St. North, Brampton, ON L6X 1N3
Tel: 905-451-7700; *Fax:* 905-451-6620
henlaw@sympatico.ca

***Brampton*: John H. Kalina - *1**
#304, 197 County Court Blvd., Brampton, ON L6W 4P6
Tel: 905-456-8055; *Fax:* 905-487-9613
Toll-Free: 866-503-7354
hjkalina@lawyer4u.ca
www.lawyer4u.ca

***Brampton*: Kania Lawyers - *7**
223 Main St. North, Brampton, ON L6X 1N2
Tel: 905-451-3222; *Fax:* 905-451-1267
Toll-Free: 877-485-2642
www.kanialawyers.com

***Brampton*: Lawrence, Lawrence, Stevenson - *14**
43 Queen St. West, Brampton, ON L6Y 1L9
Tel: 905-451-3040; *Fax:* 905-451-5058
lls@lawrences.com
www.lawrences.com

***Brampton*: D.R. Lent - *1**
38 Queen St. West, Brampton, ON L6X 1A1
Tel: 905-457-4215; *Fax:* 905-457-6454

***Brampton*: R.J. Linton - *1**
21 John St., Brampton, ON L6W 1Z1
Tel: 905-453-3145; *Fax:* 905-454-2270

***Brampton*: D.F. Logan Law Office - *1**
#201, 45 Bramalea Rd., Brampton, ON L6T 2W4
Tel: 905-791-0375; *Fax:* 905-791-6549

***Brampton*: Alison R. Mackay - *1**
#400, 201 County Court Blvd., Brampton, ON L6W 4L2
Tel: 905-455-6000; *Fax:* 905-456-1209
mackaya@rogers.com
www.alisonmackay.yp.ca

***Brampton*: Holmes A. Matheson - *1**
#301, 134 Queen St. East, Brampton, ON L6V 1B2
Tel: 905-451-6504; *Fax:* 905-451-0288
hamatheson@on.aibn.com

***Brampton*: McCabe, Filkin & Garvie - *5**
#320, Plaza II, 350 Rutherford Rd. South, Brampton, ON L6W 4P7
Tel: 905-452-7400; *Fax:* 905-452-6444
mfa@mccabefilkin.com

***Brampton*: McClelland Law, A Professional Corporation, Lawyers - *2**
202 Main St. North, Brampton, ON L6V 1P1
Tel: 905-793-3026; *Fax:* 905-793-2446
info@mcclellandlaw.com
www.mcclellandlaw.com

***Brampton*: W. John McCulligh - *1**
#301, 197 County Court Blvd., Brampton, ON L6W 4P6
Tel: 905-459-1545; *Fax:* 905-459-2826
wmcculligh@bellnet.ca

***Brampton*: Kotak Nainesh - *1**
#405, City South Plaza, 7700 Hurontario St., Brampton, ON L6Y 4M3
Tel: 905-459-6464; *Fax:* 905-459-0550

***Brampton*: North Peel & Dufferin Community Legal Services - *4**
#601, 24 Queen St. East, Brampton, ON L6V 1A3
Tel: 905-455-0160; *Fax:* 905-455-0832
Toll-Free: 866-455-0160

***Brampton*: Laszlo Pandy - *1**
26 Bramsteele Rd., Brampton, ON L6W 1B3
Tel: 905-457-0977; *Fax:* 905-457-8108

***Brampton*: Prouse, Dash & Crouch - *11**
50 Queen St. West, Brampton, ON L6X 4H3
Tel: 905-451-6610; *Fax:* 905-451-1549
Toll-Free: 877-217-4732
pdc@pdclawyers.ca
www.prousedash.ca

***Brampton*: Richardson, Schnall & Sanderson - *1**
#402, 134 Queen St. East, Brampton, ON L6V 1B2
Tel: 905-451-1593; *Fax:* 905-451-3132

***Brampton*: Simmons, Da Silva & Sinton - *11**
#200, 201 County Court Blvd., Brampton, ON L6W 4L2
Tel: 905-457-1660; *Fax:* 905-457-5641
www.sdslawfirm.com

***Brampton*: Mark E. Skursky - *1**
#101, 2 Fisherman Dr., Brampton, ON L7A 1B5
Tel: 905-840-0001; *Fax:* 905-840-0002
skurskylawoffice@on.aibn.com

***Brampton*: George Paul Smith - *1**
280 Main St. North, Brampton, ON L6V 1P6
Tel: 905-457-9791; *Fax:* 905-457-9798
gpsmith@pathcom.com
www.peelbarristers.com

***Brampton*: Victor E. Szumlanski - *1**
9610 McLaughlin Rd. North, Brampton, ON L6X 0B8
Tel: 905-456-1673; *Fax:* 905-456-1201

***Brampton*: Alan Wainwright - *1**
#102, 197 County Court Blvd., Brampton, ON L6W 4P6
Tel: 905-453-9520; *Fax:* 905-450-7842
awainwright@bellnet.ca
www.peelbarristers.com/wainwright

***Brampton*: Cynthia K. Waite - *3**
#102, 197 County Court Blvd., Brampton, ON L6W 4P6
Tel: 905-450-3800; *Fax:* 905-450-8376
cyndy@wjfamilylaw.com

***Brampton*: Michael J. Walsh - *1**
280 Main St. North, Brampton, ON L6V 1P6
Tel: 905-453-4105; *Fax:* 905-457-3075
walaw@on.aibn.com

***Brampton*: J.T. Wiley - *1**
#100, 205 County Court Blvd., Brampton, ON L6W 4R6
Tel: 905-454-5600; *Fax:* 905-454-4463

***Brantford*: Douglas C. Ainsworth - *1**
Stn. Main, 120B Market St., Brantford, ON N3T 3A1
Tel: 519-756-4220; *Fax:* 519-756-3462

***Brantford*: Boddy, Ryerson - *6**
#101, P.O. Box 1265, 172 Dalhousie St., Brantford, ON N3T 5T3
Tel: 519-753-8417; *Fax:* 519-753-7421

***Brantford*: Donald C. Calder - *1**
40 Nelson St., Brantford, ON N3T 2M8
Tel: 519-759-1910; *Fax:* 519-759-2881

***Brantford*: S. Frost - *1**
101 Wellington St., Brantford, ON N3T 2M1
Tel: 519-753-4113

***Brantford*: Guiler Law Office - *1**
36 King St., Brantford, ON N3T 3C5
Tel: 519-751-4517; *Fax:* 519-751-4725
guilerlaw@kwic.com

***Brantford*: Sandra J. Harris - *1**
#202, 50 King St., Brantford, ON N3T 3C7
Tel: 519-756-0350; *Fax:* 519-756-6611
sjharrison@on.aibn.com

***Brantford*: Hospodar, Davies & Goold - *3**
120 Market St., Brantford, ON N3T 3A1
Tel: 519-759-0082; *Fax:* 519-759-8490

***Brantford*: M. John Jakub - *1**
45 Peel St., Brantford, ON N3S 5L7
Tel: 519-754-0495; *Fax:* 519-754-1882
johnjakub@rogers.com

***Brantford*: Lefebvre & Lefebvre LLP - *7**
P.O. Box 488, 75 Chatham St., Brantford, ON N3T 5N9
Tel: 519-756-3350; *Fax:* 519-756-4727
info@lefebvrelawyers.ca
www.lefebvrelawyers.ca

***Brantford*: Miller, Miller & Maltby - *2**
11 Nelson St., Brantford, ON N3T 2M6
Tel: 519-753-4118; *Fax:* 519-753-2596

***Brantford*: Reeves & Buck LLP - *3**
#B101, 325 West St., Brantford, ON N3R 3V6
Tel: 519-759-0900; *Fax:* 519-759-7702
firm@reevesbuck.ca
www.reevesbuck.ca

***Brantford*: Carmelo N. Runco - *1**
107 Wellington St, Brantford, ON N3T 2M1
Tel: 519-754-0405

***Brantford*: Newton Staats - *3**
P.O. Box 1417, 188 Mohawk St., Brantford, ON N3S 2X2
Tel: 519-756-5217; *Fax:* 519-756-4783
staatsnewton@on.aibn.com

***Brantford*: Trepanier Verity - *6**
P.O. Box 144, Stn. Main, 63 Charlotte St., Brantford, ON N3T 2W6
Tel: 519-756-8700; *Fax:* 519-756-5454
info@trepanierverity.com

** indicates number of lawyers*

***Brantford*: Underwood, Ion & Johnson LLP - *2**
P.O. Box 1536, 442 Grey St., Unit B, Brantford, ON N3T 5V6
Tel: 519-759-0920; *Fax:* 519-759-2122
dennis@uijlaw.com

***Brantford*: Paul Vandervet - *1**
P.O. Box 1495, 107 Wellington St., Brantford, ON N3T 5V6
Tel: 519-759-4240; *Fax:* 519-759-4863
vandervet@bellnet.ca

***Brantford*: Wayne P. Vipond - *1**
#103, 49 Henderson Ave., Brantford, ON N3R 4V8
Tel: 519-751-0240; *Fax:* 519-751-0251
wvipond@bellnet.ca

***Brantford*: Waterous, Holden, Amey, Hitchon LLP - *19**
P.O. Box 1510, 20 Wellington St., Brantford, ON N3T 5V6
Tel: 519-759-6220; *Fax:* 519-759-8360
law@waterousholden.com
www.waterousholden.com

***Brantford*: Michael R. White - *1**
#103, North Brantford Professional Centre, 525 Park Rd. North, Brantford, ON N3R 7K8
Tel: 519-752-9004; *Fax:* 519-752-0449

***Brantford*: Wyatt, Purcell, Stillman & Karkkainen - *3**
P.O. Box 1115, Stn. Main, 442 Grey St., Brantford, ON N3S 7N3
Tel: 519-756-5800; *Fax:* 519-756-3861
wyattpurcell@wyatturcell.com

***Brigden*: W.E. Tennyson - *1**
P.O. Box 232, 3015 Brigden Rd., Brigden, ON N0N 1B0
Tel: 519-864-1189; *Fax:* 519-864-1966
tennysonlaw@bellnet.ca

***Brighton*: Ben A. Ring - *1**
P.O. Box 1600, 13 Young St., Brighton, ON K0K 1H0
Tel: 613-475-3444; *Fax:* 613-475-3447

***Brighton*: Thompson Law Office - *1**
67 Main St., Brighton, ON K0K 1H0
Tel: 613-475-1175; *Fax:* 613-475-4012
thomsonlaw@bellnet.ca

***Brighton*: Weaver & Curtis - *2**
P.O. Box 1660, 25 Main St., Brighton, ON K0K 1H0
Tel: 613-475-4645; *Fax:* 613-475-4646

***Brockville*: Barr & O'Brien - *2**
#206, 9 Broad St., Brockville, ON K6V 6Z4
Tel: 613-498-0800; *Fax:* 613-498-0001
Toll-Free: 800-673-3429
www.barrobrien.com

***Brockville*: Michael P. Bird - *1**
#304, 9 Broad St., Brockville, ON K6V 6Z4
Tel: 613-342-1183; *Fax:* 613-342-0887
mpbird@ripnet.com

***Brockville*: Fitzpatrick & Culic - *1**
21 Pine St., Brockville, ON K6V 1E9
Tel: 613-342-6693; *Fax:* 613-342-8449
culiclaw@ripnet.com

***Brockville*: R.W. Flood - *1**
13 Hartley St., Brockville, ON K6V 3N2
Tel: 613-345-0087; *Fax:* 613-342-5294

***Brockville*: Fraser & Bickerton - *1**
#100, P.O. Box 692, 36 Broad St., Brockville, ON K6V 5V8
Tel: 613-345-3377; *Fax:* 613-345-3372
www.fraserbickerton.ca

***Brockville*: David A. Hain - *1**
P.O. Box 757, 58 King St. East, Brockville, ON K6V 5W1
Tel: 613-342-5577; *Fax:* 613-342-1773
david@hainlaw.com
www.hainlaw.com

***Brockville*: Hammond Osborne - *2**
#207, 9 Broad St., Brockville, ON K6V 6Z4
Tel: 613-498-0944; *Fax:* 613-498-0946
Toll-Free: 877-498-0944
rob@hammondosborne.ca
www.hammondosborne.ca

***Brockville*: Henderson Johnston Fournier - *2**
Equity Bldg., 61 King St. East, Brockville, ON K6V 5V4
Tel: 613-345-5613; *Fax:* 613-345-6473
info@hendersonjohnstonfournier.com
www.hendersonjohnstonfournier.com

***Brockville*: John M. Johnston - *1**
P.O. Box 81, 2 Court House Ave., Brockville, ON K6V 4T1
Tel: 613-345-5335; *Fax:* 613-345-4496
jjohnsto@ripnet.com

***Brockville*: John H. Macintosh, Q.C. - *1**
P.O. Box 451, 2 Court House Ave., Brockville, ON K6V 5V6
Tel: 613-345-5653; *Fax:* 613-345-6022
jmacintosh@ripnet.com

***Brockville*: Michael J. O'Shaughnessy - *1**
P.O. Box 2121, Stn. Main, 21 Court House Ave., Brockville, ON K6V 6N5
Tel: 613-342-4491; *Fax:* 613-342-6405
mike@courthouse.ca
www.michaeloshaughnessy.ca

***Brockville*: Harry R. Preston - *1**
#201, P.O. Box 1814, Stn. Main, 68 King St. West, Brockville, ON K6V 3P9
Tel: 613-342-1866; *Fax:* 613-342-1634
preslaw@bellnet.ca

***Brockville*: Wilson Evely - *1**
P.O. Box 1, 3 Court Terrace, Brockville, ON K6V 4T4
Tel: 613-345-1907; *Fax:* 613-345-4604
wilson-evely@bellnet.ca

***Brooklin*: Mason Bennett Johncox - *3**
79 Baldwin St., Brooklin, ON L1M 1A4
Tel: 905-620-4499; *Fax:* 905-620-7738
inquiries@whitbylawyers.com
www.whitbylawyers.com

***Bruce Mines*: Peterson & Peterson**
P.O. Box 100, 76 Taylor St., Bruce Mines, ON P0R 1C0
Tel: 705-785-3491; *Fax:* 705-785-3768
la~ryd.peterson@sympatico.ca

***Burlington*: Cleaver Crawford LLP - *2**
2019 Caroline St., Burlington, ON L7R 1L1
Tel: 905-634-5581; *Fax:* 905-634-1563
eldon.hunt@cleavercrawford.ca

***Burlington*: Dunlop & Associates - *3**
3556 Commerce Ct., Burlington, ON L7N 3L7
Tel: 905-681-3311; *Fax:* 905-681-3565
info@dunloplaw.com
www.dunloplaw.com

***Burlington*: Feltmate Delibato Heagle LLP - *14**
#200, 3600 Billings Ct., Burlington, ON L7N 3N6
Tel: 905-639-8881; *Fax:* 905-639-8017
www.fdhlawyers.com

***Burlington*: Forbes Law Office - *1**
#2, 3455 Harvester Rd., Burlington, ON L7N 3P2
Tel: 905-333-1622; *Fax:* 905-333-1624
robf@forbeslaw.ca

***Burlington*: Green Germann - *3**
P.O. Box 400, 411 Guelph Line, Burlington, ON L7R 3Y3
Tel: 905-639-1222; *Fax:* 905-632-6977
info@greengermann.ca
www.greengermann.ca

***Burlington*: Haber & Associates, Lawyers - *6**
3370 South Service Rd., 2nd Fl., Burlington, ON L7N 3M6
Tel: 905-639-8894; *Fax:* 905-639-0459
sharon@haber-lawyer.com
www.haber-lawyer.com

***Burlington*: Catherine A. Haber - *1**
3370 South Service Rd., 2nd Fl., Burlington, ON L7N 3M6
Tel: 905-333-4421; *Fax:* 905-333-0575
cahaber@allstream.net
www.haberlaw.goldbook.ca

***Burlington*: Hastings, Charlebois - *2**
3513 Mainway Dr., Burlington, ON L7M 1A9
Tel: 905-332-1888; *Fax:* 905-332-0021
mail@hclawyers.ca

***Burlington*: John Hicks Law Office - *1**
#7, 541 Brant St., Burlington, ON L7R 2G6
Tel: 905-681-3131; *Fax:* 905-333-6688
john.hicks@bellnet.ca

***Burlington*: Hofbauer Associates - *3**
#205, 1455 Lakeshore Rd. North, Burlington, ON L7S 2J1
Tel: 905-634-0040; *Fax:* 905-349-0809
info@capatents.com
www.capatents.com

***Burlington*: Richard R. Kosterski - *1**
394 Guelph Line, Burlington, ON L7R 3L4
Tel: 905-637-8249; *Fax:* 905-637-6015
richard@kosterskilaw.ca

***Burlington*: Martin & Hillyer Associates - *8**
2122 Old Lakeshore Rd., Burlington, ON L7R 1A3
Tel: 905-637-5641; *Fax:* 905-637-5404
info@lakeshorelaw.com
www.martinandhillyer.com

***Burlington*: Muir & Unmat - *2**
468 Elizabeth St., Burlington, ON L7R 2M2
Tel: 905-634-8030; *Fax:* 905-333-4613

***Burlington*: J. Douglas Redfearn - *1**
#220, 3385 Harvester Rd., Burlington, ON L7N 3N2
Tel: 905-333-5322; *Fax:* 905-333-9835
redfearn@familylawassociates.ca
www.familylawassociates.ca

***Burlington*: Robert J. Redhead Ltd. - *1**
616 Holly Hill Cres., Burlington, ON L7L 3Z7
Tel: 905-631-7573; *Fax:* 905-631-6708
info@redheadlimited.com
www.redheadlimited

***Burlington*: Simpson & Rich - *1**
#12, 460 Brant St., Burlington, ON L7R 4B6
Tel: 905-681-1521; *Fax:* 905-333-5075
gdrlaw@worldchat.com

***Burlington*: SimpsonWigle LAW LLP - *27**
#501, Sims Square Bldg., 390 Brant St., Burlington, ON L7R 4J4
Tel: 905-639-1052; *Fax:* 905-333-3960
Toll-Free: 800-434-4414
info@simpsonwigle.com
www.simpsonwigle.com

***Burlington*: Thomas R. Sutherland Q.C. - *1**
3310 South Service Road, Burlington, ON L7N 3M6
Tel: 905-634-5521; *Fax:* 905-631-7914

***Burlington*: Harold Kim Taylor - *1**
3380 South Service Road, Burlington, ON L7N 3J5
Tel: 905-681-6400; *Fax:* 905-681-6510

***Burlington*: Thatcher & Wands - *2**
1457 Ontario St., Burlington, ON L7S 1G6
Tel: 905-681-0444; *Fax:* 905-681-2937
office@thatcherandwands.com
www.thatcherandwands.com

***Burlington*: Elizabeth A. Urban - *1**
3365 Harvester Rd., Main Level, Burlington, ON L7N 3N2
Tel: 905-333-6640; *Fax:* 905-681-6510

***Burlington*: Wright Law Office - *1**
452 Locust Street, Burlington, ON L7S 1V1
Tel: 905-633-7738
thompsonlaw@bellnet.ca

***Caledon East*: George W. Jenney - *1**
15891 Airport Rd., Caledon East, ON L7C 1J3
Tel: 905-584-9300; *Fax:* 905-584-9233

***Caledonia*: Arrell Law LLP - *3**
2 Caithness St. West, Caledonia, ON N3W 2J2
Tel: 905-765-5414; *Fax:* 905-765-5144
www.arrellplacelaw.com

***Caledonia*: Benedict & Ferguson - *2**
322 Argyle St. South, Caledonia, ON N3W 1K8
Tel: 905-765-4004; *Fax:* 905-765-3001

***Caledonia*: L.S. Humenik - *1**
P.O. Box 2112, 19 Argyle St. North, Caledonia, ON N3W 1B6
Tel: 905-765-3162; *Fax:* 905-765-4313
larman@mountaincable.net

***Callander*: George D. Olah - *1**
492 Main Street, Callander, ON P0H 1H0
Tel: 705-752-1323; *Fax:* 705-752-1283
georgeolah@bellnet.ca

***Cambridge*: Brownell & Reier - *2**
32 Grand Ave. South, Cambridge, ON N2S 2L6
Tel: 519-623-2311; *Fax:* 519-623-6957
info@brownellandreier.ca
www.brownellandreier.ca

** indicates number of lawyers*

Cambridge: Copp & Cosman - *2
#409, Cambridge Place, P.O. Box 1729, Stn. Galt, 73 Water St. North, Cambridge, ON N1R 7G8
Tel: 519-623-4799; *Fax:* 519-623-7154
cosman@coppcosman.com

Cambridge: Teresa L. Fairborn - *1
135 Argyle St. South, Cambridge, ON N3H 1P8
Tel: 519-653-1460; *Fax:* 519-653-4169
teresa@fairbornllb.com

Cambridge: Gary E.J. Hauser - *1
1666 King St. East, Cambridge, ON N3H 3R7
Tel: 519-653-1521; *Fax:* 519-650-1466
ghauser@golden.net

Cambridge: George R. Ingram - *1
#206, P.O. Box 1447, 99 Main St., Cambridge, ON N1R 1W1
Tel: 519-621-9000; *Fax:* 519-621-9009
gringram@sentex.net

Cambridge: Rein Kao - *1
24 Queens Square, Cambridge, ON N1S 1H6
Tel: 519-624-8722; *Toll-Free:* 888-559-2726

Cambridge: David A. Kinder - *1
546 Grand Ridge Dr., Cambridge, ON N1S 4Y9
Tel: 519-740-6676; *Fax:* 519-623-8545
kinder@sympatico.ca

Cambridge: William Korz, Q.C. - *1
927 King Street, Cambridge, ON N3H 5M3
Tel: 519-653-7174; *Fax:* 519-653-5222
wmkorz@execulink.com

Cambridge: George E. Loker - *1
P.O. Box 1723, Stn. Galt, 108 Myers Rd., Cambridge, ON N1R 2Z8
Tel: 519-621-4300; *Fax:* 519-621-4300
eloker@golden.net

Cambridge: Paul M. Mann Professional Corp. - *1
25 George St. South, Cambridge, ON N1S 2N3
Tel: 519-623-0700; *Fax:* 519-622-4091
info@paulmann.ca
www.paulmann.ca

Cambridge: McDonald Ross - *2
9 Brant Rd. South, Cambridge, ON N1S 2W4
Tel: 519-622-0499; *Fax:* 519-740-6368
jwm@mcdonaldross.com

Cambridge: Jane A. McKenzie - *1
Netus Business Centre, 19 Thorne St., Cambridge, ON N2H 4W1
Tel: 519-745-7614; *Fax:* 519-745-9778
jane.mckenzie@execulink.com
www.cambridgefamilylaw.com

Cambridge: McSevney Law Offices - *2
708 Duke St., Cambridge, ON N3H 3T6
Tel: 519-653-3217; *Fax:* 519-653-3702
www.mcsevneylaw.com

Cambridge: Pavey, Law & Witteveen LLP - *5
P.O. Box 1707, Stn. Galt, 19 Cambridge St., Cambridge, ON N1R 3R8
Tel: 519-621-7260; *Fax:* 519-621-1304
info@paveylaw.com
www.paveylaw.com

Cambridge: Pettitt, Schwarz - *2
#403, 73 Water St. North, Cambridge, ON N1R 7L6
Tel: 519-621-2450; *Fax:* 519-621-5750
bob@pettittschwarz.com
www.pettittschwarz.com

Cambridge: Linda L. Ratcliffe - *1
927 King St. East, Cambridge, ON N3H 3P4
Tel: 519-650-0763; *Fax:* 519-653-5222

Cambridge: Henry R. Shields - *1
2 Water St. North, Cambridge, ON N1R 3B1
Tel: 519-622-2150; *Fax:* 519-623-0997
henryshields@on.aibn.com

Cambridge: J. Craig Wilson - *1
P.O. Box 1297, 2 Water St. North, Cambridge, ON N1R 3B1
Tel: 519-622-0192

Cambridge: W.C. Wraight - *1
P.O. Box 22103, 15 Main St., Cambridge, ON N1R 8E3
Tel: 519-623-3330; *Fax:* 519-621-0136

Campbellford: Paul D.H. Burgess - *1
P.O. Box 1540, 64 Front St. North, Campbellford, ON K0L 1L0
Tel: 705-653-5555; *Fax:* 705-653-5557
burgess-law@heydon.com

Campbellville: Robert B. Burgess, Q.C. - *1
P.O. Box 86, 8220 MacArthur Dr., Campbellville, ON L0P 1B0
Tel: 905-854-2790; *Fax:* 905-854-1968
rbburgess@sympatico.ca

Campbellville: Justenvironment - *1
15 Timber Run Crt., Campbellville, ON L0P 1B0
Tel: 905-659-4732; *Fax:* 905-659-4733
mrudolph@justenvironment.com
www.justenvironment.com

Carleton Place: Kenneth J. Bennett - *1
32 Beckwith Street, Carleton Place, ON K7C 2T2
Tel: 613-257-1655; *Fax:* 613-257-8837

Carleton Place: P.D. Courtice - *1
P.O. Box 29, 164 Bridge St., Carleton Place, ON K7C 2V7
Tel: 613-257-5001; *Fax:* 613-257-8797
pdclaw@on.aibn.com

Carleton Place: N. Alan Jones - *1
92 Bridge St., Carleton Place, ON K7C 2V3
Tel: 613-257-3811; *Fax:* 613-253-0479
ajones@bellnet.ca

Carp: Nutrisphere - *1
118 Grey Fox Dr., Carp, ON K0A 1L0
Tel: 613-256-4091; *Fax:* 613-256-4091
helyn.mac@sympatico.ca

Casselman: Benoit & Benoit - *1
#661, CP 650, 661, rue Principale, Casselman, ON K0A 1M0
Tél: 613-764-3694; *Téléc:* 613-764-3198
cbrisson@bellnet.ca

Casselman: Mireille C. LaViolette - *1
CP 179, 719, rue Principale, Casselman, ON K0A 1M0
Tél: 613-764-3747; *Téléc:* 613-764-1000
info@mireillelaviolette.com
www.mireillelaviolette.com

Chapleau: Weaver, Simmons LLP - *27
Civic Centre, P.O. Box 329, Pine St., Chapleau, ON P0M 1K0
Tel: 705-864-1505
thefirm@weaversimmons.com
www.weaversimmons.com

Chatham: James E.S. Allin - *1
186 Wellington Street West, Chatham, ON N7M 2G6
Tel: 519-352-6540; *Fax:* 519-352-9097
jallin@ciaccess.com

Chatham: Benoit, Van Raay, Spisani, Fuerth & Quaglia - *5
P.O. Box 1087, Stn. Main, 124 Thames St., Chatham, ON N7L 2Y8
Tel: 519-352-8580; *Fax:* 519-352-4114

Chatham: Mark M. MacKew - *1
237 Wellington St. West, Chatham, ON N7M 1J9
Tel: 519-354-0407; *Fax:* 519-354-3250
mark@mackewlaw.com
www.mackewlaw.com

Chatham: Stanley G. Mayes - *1
16 Victoria Ave., Chatham, ON N7L 2Z6
Tel: 519-436-1040; *Fax:* 519-436-2442
mail@mayeslawfirm.ca
www.mayeslawfirm.ca

Chatham: Gudrun Mueller-Wilm - *1
P.O. Box 554, Stn. C, 6 Harvey St., Chatham, ON N7M 1L6
Tel: 519-358-1822; *Fax:* 519-358-7406

Chatham: F. Vaughn Pugh - *1
190 Wellington St. West, Chatham, ON N7M 1J6
Tel: 519-354-4360
fvpugh@on.aibn.com

Chatham: John B. Trinca - *1
P.O. Box 428, 75 Thames St., Chatham, ON N7L 1S4
Tel: 519-352-7750; *Fax:* 519-352-4159
jtrinca@mnsi.net

Chatham: Paul D. Watson - *1
P.O. Box 661, 213 King St., 2nd Fl., Chatham, ON N7M 1E6
Tel: 519-351-7721; *Fax:* 519-351-7726
pdwoffice@cogeco.net

Chelmsford: Gerard E. Guimond
P.O. Box 2225, 3527 Errington Ave. North, Chelmsford, ON P0M 1L0
Tel: 705-855-4511; *Fax:* 705-855-5631

Chesley: McClelland Law Office - *1
159 - 1st Ave. South, Chesley, ON N0G 1L0
Tel: 519-363-3293; *Fax:* 519-363-2315

Chesley: Ross C. McLean - *2
P.O. Box 118, 27 1st Ave. South, Chesley, ON N0G 1L0
Tel: 519-363-3190; *Fax:* 519-363-2213
rossmclean@bmts.com

Chesterville: Cass, Grenkie - *4
P.O. Box 700, 13 Ralph St., Chesterville, ON K0C 1H0
Tel: 613-448-2735; *Fax:* 613-448-1395
cassgrenkie@gglrlaw.ca

Clinton: Philip B. Cornish - *1
35 Ontario St., Clinton, ON N0M 1L0
Tel: 519-482-1434; *Fax:* 519-482-1481

Clinton: D. Gerald Hiltz - *1
P.O. Box 1087, 52 Huron St., Clinton, ON N0M 1L0
Tel: 519-482-3414; *Fax:* 519-482-7525

Coboconk: Tyler P. Higgins
P.O. Box 219, 6654 Hwy. 35, Coboconk, ON K0M 1K0
Tel: 705-454-2625

Cobourg: John D. Carroll - *1
P.O. Box 475, 35 King St. East, Cobourg, ON K9A 1K6
Tel: 905-372-5424; *Fax:* 905-372-1943
shazam@eagle.ca

Cobourg: Rodger F. Cooper - *1
#102, 253 Division St., Cobourg, ON K9A 3P9
Tel: 905-372-8728; *Fax:* 905-372-0720
Toll-Free: 888-251-1945
cooper@eagle.ca

Cobourg: Ember Leigh Hamilton - *1
161 Sutherland Crescent, Cobourg, ON K9A 5L6
Tel: 905-373-0589; *Fax:* 905-373-0928
ember@eagle.com

Cobourg: Hustler & Kay - *2
301 Division St., Cobourg, ON K9A 3R2
Tel: 905-372-1991; *Fax:* 905-372-1995
gkay@on.aibn.com

Cobourg: Irvine & Irvine - *1
24 Covert St., Cobourg, ON K9A 2L6
Tel: 905-372-5449; *Fax:* 905-372-1707
rirvine@eagle.ca

Cobourg: SMM Law Professional Corp. - *3
#205, The Fleming Bldg., 1005 Elgin St., Cobourg, ON K9A 5J4
Tel: 905-372-3395; *Fax:* 905-372-1695
smmlaw@smmlaw.com
www.smmlaw.com

Cobourg: Anne Marie Steger - *1
P.O. Box 9, 256 George St., Cobourg, ON K9A 3L6
Tel: 905-372-2217; *Fax:* 905-372-1783
anne.marie@bellnet.ca

Cobourg: William J. Taggart - *1
35 King St. East, Cobourg, ON K9A 1K6
Tel: 905-372-8700; *Fax:* 905-372-1943

Colborne: J.A. Carter - *1
P.O. Box 699, 26 King St. East, Colborne, ON K9A 1K7
Tel: 905-355-3322; *Fax:* 905-355-3104
Toll-Free: 877-399-3322
jcarter@bellnet.ca

Collingwood: Baulke Augaitis Stahr LLP - *4
P.O. Box 100, 150 Hurontario St., Collingwood, ON L9Y 3Z4
Tel: 705-445-4930; *Fax:* 705-445-1871
Toll-Free: 866-230-9993
info@collingwoodlaw.com
www.collingwoodlaw.com

Collingwood: Besse, Merrifield & Cowan LLP - *3
47 Hurontario St., Collingwood, ON L9Y 2L7
Tel: 705-446-2000; *Fax:* 705-446-1044
Toll-Free: 888-879-3052
besse@blclawoffices.com
www.bmclawoffices.com

* *indicates number of lawyers*

Collingwood: Christie/Cummings - *3
325 Hume St., Collingwood, ON L9Y 1W4
Tel: 705-444-3650; Fax: 705-444-0024
maccummings@christiecummings.com

Collingwood: Compenso Communications Inc - *1
#3, 115 Hurontario Street, Collingwood, ON L9Y 2L9
Tel: 705-445-8540; Fax: 705-445-2681
info@compenso.ca
www.compenso.ca

Collingwood: Brian Greasley - *1
P.O. Box 490, 33 Ste. Marie St., Collingwood, ON L9Y 3J9
Tel: 705-429-5199; Fax: 705-445-2269

Collingwood: Larry E. Lant - *1
P.O. Box 248, Stn. Main, 217 Minnesota St., Collingwood, ON L9Y 3S4
Tel: 705-445-2886; Fax: 705-444-5837
lantlaw@on.aibn.com

Collingwood: Neathery & Mumford - *2
#4, 450 Hume St., Collingwood, ON L9Y 1W6
Tel: 705-444-6051; Fax: 705-444-0969

Concord: Bisceglia & Associates - *4
#200, 7941 Jane St., Concord, ON L4K 4L6
Tel: 905-695-5200; Fax: 905-695-5201
www.lawtoronto.com

Concord: Talal Chehab
#208, 3100 Steeles Ave. West, Concord, ON L4K 3R1
Tel: 905-738-2463; Fax: 905-738-4901

Concord: John G. Chris - *1
8700 Dufferin St., Concord, ON L4K 4S6
Tel: 416-661-5989; Fax: 905-669-0444
postmaster@jgc-law.com
www.jgc-law.com

Concord: D'Ambrosio Law Office - *1
#300, 3100 Steeles Ave. West, Concord, ON L4K 3R1
Tel: 905-761-7400; Fax: 905-738-4901
romeo36@colosseum.com

Concord: John De Matteis - *1
#300, 3100 Steeles Ave. West, Concord, ON L4K 3R1
Tel: 905-738-4900; Fax: 905-738-4901

Concord: Patrick Di Monte - *1
#211, 3100 Steeles Ave. West, Concord, ON L4K 3R1
Tel: 905-738-2101; Fax: 905-738-1168
patdimonte@on.aibn.com

Concord: Louis M. Fried - *1
#212, 2180 Steeles Ave. West, Concord, ON L4K 2Z5
Tel: 905-738-0180; Fax: 905-738-6203
Toll-Free: 866-306-3286
louismfried@on.aibn.com

Concord: Thomas F. Kowal - *1
#300, 3100 Steeles Ave. West, Concord, ON L4K 3R1
Tel: 905-738-5755; Fax: 905-738-4901
tkowal@allstream.net

Concord: Okell & Weisman - *2
#407, 1600 Steeles Ave. West, Concord, ON L4K 4M2
Tel: 905-761-8711; Fax: 905-761-8633

Concord: Norman S. Panzica - *1
A, 9100 Jane St., Concord, ON L4K 4L8
Tel: 905-738-1078; Fax: 905-738-0528
npanzica@rogers.com
www.normanpanzica.com

Concord: Piersanti & Company - *5
#10, 445 Edgeley Blvd., Concord, ON L4K 4G1
Tel: 905-738-2176; Fax: 905-738-5182
piersanti@look.com

Concord: Alan G. Silverstein - *2
#318, 1600 Steeles Ave. West, Concord, ON L4K 4M2
Tel: 905-761-1600; Fax: 905-761-0948
alan.silverstein@rogers.com

Cornwall: Adams, Sherwood, Swabey & Follon - *4
305 - 2 St. East, Cornwall, ON K6H 1Y8
Tel: 613-938-3330; Fax: 613-938-7885
adams@adamssherwood.ca
www.adamssherwoof.ca

Cornwall: Bergeron Filion - *2
103 Sydney St., Cornwall, ON K6H 3H1
Tel: 613-932-2911; Fax: 613-932-2356
bobbergeron@pppoe.ca

Cornwall: Tilton T. Donihee - *1
132 2nd Street East, Cornwall, ON K6H 1Y4
Tel: 613-933-0792; Fax: 613-938-7632
tdoniee@gta.igs.net

Cornwall: Giovanniello, Bellefeuille - *2
340 - 2nd St. East, Cornwall, ON K6H 1Y9
Tel: 613-938-0294; Fax: 613-932-2374
law@gblawfirm.ca
www.gblawfirm.ca

Cornwall: Guindon, MacLean & Castle - *3
50 - 2 St. East, Cornwall, ON K6H 1Y3
Tel: 613-933-3931; Fax: 613-933-6123
info@g-m-c.on.ca

Cornwall: Law Office of Diane M. Lahaie - *1
28 - 7 St. West, Cornwall, ON K6J 2X9
Tel: 613-936-8833; Fax: 613-936-6717

Cornwall: Anne Marie Levesque - *1
110 Sydney St., Cornwall, ON K6H 3H2
Tel: 613-932-7654; Fax: 613-938-1692
amlevesque@sympatico.ca

Cornwall: Ian D. Paul - *1
5 Third St. East, Cornwall, ON K2H 2L6
Tel: 613-933-9455; Fax: 613-933-7566
ipaul@on.aibn.com

Cornwall: D. Randolph Ross - *1
120 Sydney St., Cornwall, ON K6H 3H2
Tel: 613-932-2044; Fax: 613-937-0993
drross@mail2.glen-net.ca

Cornwall: Donald J. White - *1
700 Montreal Rd., Cornwall, ON K6H 1C4
Tel: 613-933-6443; Fax: 613-933-6453
nwhite10@cogeco.ca

Cornwall: Wilson, Poirier, Byrne - *2
132 - 2nd St. West, Cornwall, ON K6J 1G5
Tel: 613-938-2224; Fax: 613-938-8005
apoirier@bellnet.ca; tombyrne@bellnet.ca

Deep River: Thomas E. Roche - *1
P.O. Box 1240, 27 Champlain St., Deep River, ON K0J 1P0
Tel: 613-584-3392; Fax: 613-584-4922
rochdaki@bellnet.ca

Delhi: John R. Hanselman - *1
138 Eagle St., Delhi, ON N4B 1S5
Tel: 519-582-0770; Fax: 519-582-1876

Dresden: Timothy D. Mathany - *1
P.O. Box 568, 347 St. George St. South, Dresden, ON N0P 1M0
Tel: 519-683-6219; Fax: 519-683-6548

Dryden: Beamish MacKinnon - *5
P.O. Box 86, 100 Claybanks Rd., Dryden, ON P8N 2Y7
Tel: 807-223-7478; Fax: 807-223-6402
beamishmackinnon@beamacklaw.ca

Dryden: McAuley & Partners - *4
P.O. Box 159, 4 Whyte Ave., Dryden, ON P8N 2Y8
Tel: 807-223-2254; Fax: 807-223-3794
www.mcauleylaw.com

Dryden: Vermeer & Van Walleghem - *2
P.O. Box 938, Stn. Main, 65 King St., 2nd Fl., Dryden, ON P8N 2Z5
Tel: 807-223-3311; Fax: 807-223-4133
lawweb@vermeerlaw.com
www.vermeerlaw.com

Dundalk: John L. Ferris - *1
360 Main St. East, Dundalk, ON N0C 1B0
Tel: 519-923-2031; Fax: 519-923-5131

Dundas: David S. Lesperance - *1
#202, 84 King St. West, Dundas, ON L9H 1T9
Tel: 905-627-3037; Fax: 905-627-9868
dsl@globalrelocate.com
www.globalrelocate.com

Dunnville: G. Donald Chambers - *1
110 Lock St. East, Dunnville, ON N1A 1J7
Tel: 905-744-7485; Fax: 905-774-7486

Dunrobin: Goodfellow Agricola Consultants Inc. - *1
2005 - 6th Line Rd. RR#1, Dunrobin, ON K0A 1T0
Tel: 613-832-0865
randal@goodfellowagricola.com
www.goodfellowagricola.com

Dutton: Martin Joldersma - *1
P.O. Box 279, 159 Main Street, Dutton, ON N0L 1J0
Tel: 519-762-2882; Fax: 519-762-2880
martinjoldersma@on.aibn.com

Elliot Lake: Kearns Law Office - *1
15 Manitoba Rd., Elliot Lake, ON P5A 2A6
Tel: 705-848-3601; Fax: 705-848-8416
Toll-Free: 800-268-7733
kearn1@bellnet.ca

Elmira: Cynthia M. Rudavsky - *1
9 Church St. West, Elmira, ON N3B 1M2
Tel: 519-669-2200; Fax: 519-669-4349
rudavsky@sentex.net

Elmira: Woods, Clemens & Fletcher Professional Corporation - *4
P.O. Box 216, 9 Memorial Ave., Elmira, ON N3B 2R1
Tel: 519-669-5101; Fax: 519-669-5618
lawoffice@woodsclemens.ca

Elora: J.E. Morris - *1
149 Geddes Street, Elora, ON N0B 1S0
Tel: 519-846-5366; Fax: 519-846-8170
john@johnmorrislaw.ca

Elora: Gregory A. Oakes - *1
155 Geddes St., Elora, ON N0B 1S0
Tel: 519-846-5555; Fax: 519-846-5554

Embrun: Campbell & Sabourin LLP/SRL - *2
#1, 165 Bay St., Embrun, ON K0A 1W1
Tel: 613-443-5683; Fax: 613-443-3285
info@campbellaw.on.ca
www.campbellaw.on.ca

Embrun: Jean G. Martel - *1
800, rue Notre Dame, Embrun, ON K0A 1W1
Tel: 613-443-3267; Fax: 613-443-3857
martelj@rogers.com

Essex: Hickey, Bryne - *2
14 Centre St., Essex, ON N8M 1N9
Tel: 519-776-7349; Fax: 519-776-8161
byrnelaw@bellnet.ca

Essex: Jim Renick Law Office - *1
14 Wilson Ave., Essex, ON N8M 2L7
Tel: 519-776-9020; Fax: 519-776-9027
info@walstedtrenick.com

Etobicoke: John H. Bailey - *1
#901, 701 Evans Ave., Etobicoke, ON M9C 1A3
Tel: 416-622-2725; Fax: 416-622-8952
jhblaw@aol.com

Etobicoke: Birks, Langdon & Elliott - *2
#329, 4195 Dundas St. West, Etobicoke, ON M8X 1Y4
Tel: 416-239-3431; Fax: 416-239-8259

Etobicoke: Christie & Associates - *4
750 Scarlett Road, Etobicoke, ON M9P 2V1
Tel: 416-249-8300; Fax: 416-249-1480

Etobicoke: P.G. Derry - *1
1 Eva Road, Etobicoke, ON M9C 4Z5
Tel: 416-868-6483; Fax: 416-364-1697

Exeter: Little Masson & Reid - *2
71 Main St. North, Exeter, ON N0M 1S0
Tel: 519-235-0670; Fax: 519-235-1603

Exeter: Raymond & McLean - *1
P.O. Box 100, 387 Main St. South, Exeter, ON N0M 1S0
Tel: 519-235-2234; Fax: 519-235-2671
raymclea@quadro.net

Fenelon Falls: David J. Gowanlock - *1
P.O. Box 607, 16 May St., Fenelon Falls, ON K0M 1N0
Tel: 705-887-2582; Fax: 705-887-1871

Fenelon Falls: John D. Walden
57 Lindsay St., Fenelon Falls, ON K0M 1N0
Tel: 705-887-2941

Fergus: Leigh G. Fishleigh - *1
169 St. Andrew St. West, Fergus, ON N1M 1N6
Tel: 519-843-7100; Fax: 519-843-3038
leigh.fishleigh@bellnet.ca

Fergus: Grant & Acheson - *4
P.O. Box 128, 265 Bridge St., Fergus, ON N1M 2W7
Tel: 519-843-1960; Fax: 519-843-6888
www.grant-acheson.com

* indicates number of lawyers

***Fonthill*: Jill Anthony - *4**
P.O. Box 743, 10 Hwy. 20 East, Fonthill, ON L0S 1E0
Tel: 905-892-2621; *Fax:* 905-892-1022
janthony@jillanthony.com
www.jillanthony.com

***Fort Erie*: Hagan & McDowell - *2**
P.O. Box 68, 29 Jarvis St., Fort Erie, ON L2A 5M6
Tel: 905-871-4440; *Fax:* 905-871-9266
rmcdowell@computan.com

***Fort Erie*: D.J. Jacobi - *1**
P.O. Box 1028, 1321 Garrison Rd., Fort Erie, ON L2A 1P3
Tel: 905-871-4244

***Fort Frances*: Clare Allan Brunetta - *1**
P.O. Box 656, 420 Victoria Ave., Fort Frances, ON P9A 3M9
Tel: 807-274-9809; *Fax:* 807-274-8760
cbrunetta@nwonet.net

***Fort Frances*: Lawrence A. Eustace - *1**
510 Portage Ave., Fort Frances, ON P9A 2A3
Tel: 807-274-3247; *Fax:* 807-274-6447
larry@eustace-law.com

***Fort Frances*: J. Rod McLeod - *1**
Site 206 - 10, 1455 Idylwild Drive, Fort Frances, ON P9A 3M6
Tel: 807-274-2832; *Fax:* 807-274-7968
rod@mcleodlawoffice.com

***Fort Frances*: Lawrence G. Phillips - *1**
237 Church St., Fort Frances, ON P9A 1C7
Tel: 807-274-8525; *Fax:* 807-274-5758
phillaw19@hotmail.com

***Fort Frances*: Donald A. Taylor - *1**
504 Armit Ave., Fort Frances, ON P9A 2H7
Tel: 807-274-7811; *Fax:* 807-274-8485
dalaw@shaw.ca

***Gananoque*: Michael R. Eyolfson - *1**
#5, 140 Garden St., Gananoque, ON K7G 1H9
Tel: 613-382-7772; *Fax:* 613-382-3030
elfson@sprint.ca

***Gananoque*: Steacy & Delaney - *1**
Stn. Main, 110 Stone St., Gananoque, ON K7G 2A1
Tel: 613-382-2137; *Fax:* 613-382-7794
l.stacey@ganlaw.com
www.gananoque.com/steacyanddelaney

***Georgetown*: Clinton D. Banbury - *1**
#2, 211 Guelph St., Georgetown, ON L7G 5B5
Tel: 905-877-5252; *Fax:* 905-877-4100
cbanbury@banburylaw.com

***Georgetown*: Jeffrey L. Eason - *1**
P.O. Box 159, Stn. Main, 116 Guelph St., Georgetown, ON L7G 4T1
Tel: 905-877-6961; *Fax:* 905-877-9725
jeffreyleason@bellnet.ca

***Georgetown*: Helson Kogon Ashbee Schaljo & Associates LLP - *5**
132 Mill St., Georgetown, ON L7G 2C6
Tel: 905-877-5206; *Fax:* 905-877-3948
helsonkogon.general@cogeco.net

***Georgetown*: W. Glen How & Associates**
P.O. Box 40, Georgetown, ON L7G 4T1
Tel: 905-873-4545; *Fax:* 905-873-4522
wghow@wghow.ca

***Georgetown*: R.T. Howitt, Q.C. - *1**
#301, 83 Mill St., Georgetown, ON M9C 1X6
Tel: 905-877-5139; *Fax:* 905-877-1155

***Georgetown*: William H. Manderson - *1**
#1004, 83 Mill Street, Georgetown, ON L7G 5E9
Tel: 905-873-0121
billmanderson@on.aibn.com

***Georgetown*: R. Paul Millman - *1**
116 Guelph St., Georgetown, ON L7G 4A3
Tel: 905-873-9481; *Fax:* 905-873-9483
rpmlaw@on.aibn.com

***Georgetown*: Sopinka & Kort - *2**
145 Mill St., Georgetown, ON L7G 2C2
Tel: 905-877-0196; *Fax:* 905-877-0604
wsopinka@sopinka-kort.com

***Glencoe*: Gary R. Merritt - *1**
P.O. Box 309, 213 Main St., Glencoe, ON N0L 1M0
Tel: 519-287-3432; *Fax:* 519-287-2498
merritt@bellnet.ca

***Gloucester*: John Lutes Consulting Inc. - *1**
1135 St. Germain Cr., Gloucester, ON K1C 2L7
Tel: 613-830-0203; *Fax:* 613-830-0250

***Gloucester*: MacQuarrie Whyte Killoran - *3**
#208, 1980 Ogilvie Rd., Gloucester, ON K1J 9L3
Tel: 613-748-1600; *Fax:* 613-748-0800
info@mwklaw.ca
www.ottawaorleanslawyers.com; www.mwklaw.ca

***Goderich*: Mary E. Cull - *1**
50 East St., Goderich, ON N7A 1N3
Tel: 519-524-1115; *Fax:* 519-524-1116

***Goderich*: Donnelly & Murphy - *7**
18 Court House Square, Goderich, ON N7A 3Y7
Tel: 519-524-2154; *Fax:* 519-524-8550
admin@dmlaw.on.ca

***Goderich*: Timothy G. Macdonald - *1**
1 Nelson St. East, Goderich, ON N7A 1R7
Tel: 519-524-1120; *Fax:* 519-524-2576

***Goderich*: Norman B. Pickell - *1**
58 South Street, Goderich, ON N7A 3L5
Tel: 519-524-8335; *Fax:* 519-524-1530
pickell@normanpickell.com
www.normanpickell.com

***Goderich*: Troyan & Fincher - *2**
44 North St., Goderich, ON N7A 2T4
Tel: 519-524-2115; *Fax:* 519-524-4481
troyanfincher@cabletv.on.ca

***Gore Bay*: Terence E. Land, Barrister & Solicitor - *1**
P.O. Box 90, 4 Eleanor St., Gore Bay, ON P0P 1H0
Tel: 705-282-2710; *Fax:* 705-282-2205

***Gore Bay*: James E. Weppler - *1**
P.O. Box 222, 65 Meredith St., Gore Bay, ON P0P 1H0
Tel: 705-282-3354; *Fax:* 705-282-3211

***Grand Bend*: Michael G. Forrester - *1**
General Delivery, 82 Ontario St. South, Grand Bend, ON N0M 1T0
Tel: 519-238-5297; *Fax:* 519-238-5234

***Gravenhurst*: Stuart & Cruickshank - *2**
P.O. Box 1270, 195 Church St., Gravenhurst, ON P1P 1V4
Tel: 705-687-3441; *Fax:* 705-687-5405
s.c@bellnet.ca

***Gravenhurst*: Lyle A. Sullivan - *1**
225 Muskoka Rd. South, Gravenhurst, ON P1P 1H6
Tel: 705-687-2219; *Fax:* 705-687-7951
lyleasullivan@bellnet.ca

***Grimsby*: Donald C. Loney - *1**
55 Main St. East, Grimsby, ON L3M 1R3
Tel: 905-945-9271; *Fax:* 905-945-3066
Toll-Free: 800-363-5073
sml@on.aibn.com

***Grimsby*: George Krusell - *1**
260 Main St. East, Grimsby, ON L3M 1P8
Tel: 905-945-2300; *Fax:* 905-945-8529

***Grimsby*: Lovett & Cunningham - *2**
P.O. Box 100, 66 Main St. East, Grimsby, ON L3M 4G1
Tel: 905-945-2269; *Fax:* 905-945-6652

***Grimsby*: Palios & Associates - *1**
#1, 11 Ontario, Grimsby, ON L3M 3G8
Tel: 905-945-6007; *Fax:* 905-945-6670
npalios@palioslaw.com

***Guelph*: AlanCo Inc. - *1**
#42, 1550 Gordon St., Guelph, ON N1L 1C7
Tel: 519-546-3960
frank.johansen@alanco.ca

***Guelph*: Lynn Archbold - *1**
27 Cork St., Guelph, ON N1H 2W9
Tel: 519-763-4748; *Fax:* 519-763-4207
lynnarchbold@bellnet.ca

***Guelph*: Dason Law Office - *1**
367 Woolwich St., Guelph, ON N1H 3W4
Tel: 519-824-2020; *Fax:* 519-824-2023

***Guelph*: Charles R. Davidson**
172 Woolwich St., Guelph, ON N1H 3V5
Tel: 519-767-6637; *Fax:* 519-826-5212
charles@crdavidson.ca

***Guelph*: Guy D.E. Farb - *1**
22 Paisley St., Guelph, ON N1H 2N6
Tel: 519-763-6644; *Fax:* 519-763-8091
lawguy@execulink.comwww.linkedin.com/pub/guy-farb/18/559/986

***Guelph*: Siobhan Ann Hanley - *1**
98 Surrey St. East, Guelph, ON N1H 3P9
Tel: 519-824-2586; *Fax:* 519-824-6661
shanley@bellnet.ca

***Guelph*: INAC Services Limited - *1**
232 Dublin St. North, Guelph, ON N1H 4P3
Tel: 519-766-1395; *Fax:* 519-766-1348
dreynolds@inacservices.com
www.inacservices.com

***Guelph*: Jackman & Rowles - *2**
P.O. Box 37, Stn. Main, 17 Cork St. West, Guelph, ON N1H 2W9
Tel: 519-824-4883; *Fax:* 519-821-2910
mmjr@on.aibn.com

***Guelph*: Philip B. Langlotz - *1**
35C Spring St., Guelph, ON N1E 1Z9
Tel: 519-837-3609
langlotz@golden.net

***Guelph*: Maiocco & DiGravio - *2**
230 Speedvale Ave. West, Guelph, ON N1H 1C4
Tel: 519-836-2710; *Fax:* 519-836-7312

***Guelph*: McElderry, Morris - *5**
P.O. Box 875, 84 Woolwich St., Guelph, ON N1H 3T9
Tel: 519-822-8150; *Fax:* 519-822-1921

***Guelph*: Bryna D. McLeod - *1**
221 Woolwich St., Guelph, ON N1H 3V4
Tel: 519-767-2141; *Fax:* 519-763-2204
www.brynamcleod.com

***Guelph*: Charles Milne & Company Inc. - *1**
68 Bridle Path, RR#3, Guelph, ON N1H 6H9
Tel: 519-767-9062; *Fax:* 519-767-9428
charles@sgci.com

***Guelph*: Moon Heath LLP - *3**
P.O. Box 180, Stn. Main, 164 Norfolk St., Guelph, ON N1H 6J9
Tel: 519-824-2540; *Fax:* 519-763-6785
info@moonheath.com
www.moonheath.com

***Guelph*: Nicholson & Doney - *3**
P.O. Box 1505, 137 Norfolk St., Guelph, ON N1H 6N9
Tel: 519-837-3000; *Fax:* 519-837-1758
Toll-Free: 888-839-1898
ron@nicholsondoney.ca
www.nicholsondoney.ca

***Guelph*: Judith C. Sidlofsky Stoffman - *1**
#226, 2 Quebec St., Guelph, ON N1H 2T3
Tel: 519-822-8226; *Fax:* 519-822-8227

***Guelph*: SmithValeriote Law Firm LLP - *21**
#100, P.O. Box 1240, Stn. Main, 105 Silvercreek Pkwy. North, Guelph, ON N1H 6N6
Tel: 519-837-2100; *Fax:* 519-837-1617
info@smithvaleriote.com
www.smithvaleriote.com

***Guelph*: Sorbara, Schumacher, McCann LLP - *18**
457 Woolwish Street, Guelph, ON N1H 3X6
Tel: 519-836-1510; *Fax:* 519-836-9215
firm@sorbaralaw.com
www.sorbaralaw.com

***Guelph*: Vorvis, Anderson, Gray, Armstrong LLP - *4**
353 Elizabeth Street, Guelph, ON N1H 2X9
Tel: 519-824-7400; *Fax:* 519-824-7521
vaga@vaga.ca
www.vaga.ca

***Guelph*: Waldrum & Associates - *1**
29 Honeysuckle Dr., Guelph, ON N1G 4X7
Tel: 613-822-6330
butch@thewaldrums.com

***Hagersville*: James R. Baxter - *1**
P.O. Box 490, 19 King St. West, Hagersville, ON N0A 1H0
Tel: 905-768-3363; *Fax:* 905-768-1550
jrbaxter@mountaincable.net

** indicates number of lawyers*

***Haileybury*: Byck Law Office - *1**
439 Ferguson Ave., Haileybury, ON P0J 1K0
Tel: 705-672-2600; *Fax:* 705-672-2779
temlaw@nt.net
www.temlaw.com

***Haliburton*: R.G. Selbie - *1**
P.O. Box 186, Haliburton, ON K0M 1S0
Tel: 705-457-2435; *Fax:* 705-457-3074

***Halton Hills*: Steven C. Foster - *2**
#201, 232 Guelph St., Halton Hills, ON L7G 4B1
Tel: 905-873-0204; *Fax:* 905-873-4962
sfoster@arnold-foster.com

***Hamilton*: John S. Abrams - *1**
#300, 69 John St. South, Hamilton, ON L8N 2B9
Tel: 905-522-3600; *Fax:* 905-529-1570
jabrams@bellnet.ca

***Hamilton*: Agro, Zaffiro - *19**
P.O. Box 2069, Stn. LCD 1, 1 James St. South, Hamilton, ON L8N 3G6
Tel: 905-527-6877; *Fax:* 905-527-6843
mail@agrozaffiro.com
www.agrozaffiro.com

***Hamilton*: Deborah Lee Barfknecht - *1**
#601, 25 Main St. West, Hamilton, ON L8P 1H1
Tel: 905-521-1898; *Fax:* 905-521-0486

***Hamilton*: R.B. Barrs - *1**
#204, 640 Upper James St., Hamilton, ON L9C 2Z2
Tel: 905-387-9212; *Fax:* 905-387-6109

***Hamilton*: Bartolini, Berlingieri, Barrafato; Fortino LLP - *5**
#101, 154 Main St. East, Hamilton, ON L8N 1G9
Tel: 905-577-6833; *Fax:* 905-577-6839
lawfirm@bbb-lawyers.on.ca

***Hamilton*: John A. Bland - *1**
#801, Union Gas Bldg., 20 Hughson St. South, Hamilton, ON L8N 2A1
Tel: 905-524-3533; *Fax:* 905-524-5142

***Hamilton*: Peter Borkovich - *1**
46 Jackson St. East, Hamilton, ON L8N 1L1
Tel: 905-527-0990; *Fax:* 905-521-1976

***Hamilton*: Brock Howard Bedford - *1**
166 John St. South, Hamilton, ON L8N 2C4
Tel: 905-527-3867; *Fax:* 905-527-3860

***Hamilton*: Burns, Vasan & Associates - *6**
#305, 21 King St. West, Hamilton, ON L8P 4W9
Tel: 905-522-1381; *Fax:* 905-522-0855
douglasburns@bvlvlaw.ca

***Hamilton*: Camporese & Associates - *2**
#805, Commerce Place, 1 King St. West, Hamilton, ON L8P 1A4
Tel: 905-522-7068; *Fax:* 905-522-5734

***Hamilton*: K.K. Channan - *1**
947 Main St. East, Hamilton, ON L8M 1M9
Tel: 905-544-9411; *Fax:* 905-544-6155
kkchannan@sympatico.ca
www.kkchannan.yp.ca

***Hamilton*: Gary Chertkoff, Q.C. - *1**
#412, 20 Jackson St. West, Hamilton, ON L8P 1L2
Tel: 905-522-2439; *Fax:* 905-522-9198

***Hamilton*: Child, Chaimovitz - *2**
#250, 100 Main St. East, Hamilton, ON L8N 3W4
Tel: 905-526-7030; *Fax:* 905-526-0682
info@childchaimovitz.ca

***Hamilton*: Michael P. Clarke - *1**
#1400, 25 Main St. West, Hamilton, ON L8P 1H1
Tel: 905-527-4399; *Fax:* 905-521-0210
michaelpclarke@bellnet.ca

***Hamilton*: Clyde Halford - *1**
336 Sanatorium Rd., Hamilton, ON L9C 2A4
Tel: 905-388-0973; *Fax:* 905-388-2797

***Hamilton*: Confente, Garcea - *2**
#340, 69 John St. South, Hamilton, ON L8N 2B9
Tel: 905-529-9999; *Fax:* 905-529-1160

***Hamilton*: Connor, Connor, Guyer & Araiche - *2**
#210, 1104 Fennell Ave. East, Hamilton, ON L8T 1R9
Tel: 905-385-3229; *Fax:* 905-385-6182
ccga@mountaincable.net

***Hamilton*: Earl R. Cranfield Q.C. - *1**
#608, 20 Hughson St. South, Hamilton, ON L8N 2A1
Tel: 905-528-0089; *Fax:* 905-528-7692
ecranfield@nas.net

***Hamilton*: Janis P. Criger - *1**
#700, 25 Main St. West, Hamilton, ON L8P 1H1
Tel: 905-525-4639; *Fax:* 905-525-2103
jpcriger@crigerlaw.com
www.craiglaw.ca

***Hamilton*: Cummins Seto - *3**
65 Walnut St. South, Hamilton, ON L8N 2L2
Tel: 905-528-5150; *Fax:* 905-528-1150
www.cumminsseto.com

***Hamilton*: Stephen F. De Wetter - *1**
#1215, 25 Main St. West, Hamilton, ON L8P 1H1
Tel: 905-521-8878; *Fax:* 905-577-0229
dewetterlaw@gmail.com

***Hamilton*: DiCenzo & Associates - *2**
#41, 1070 Stone Church Rd. East, Hamilton, ON L8W 3K8
Tel: 905-574-3300; *Fax:* 905-574-1766
adicenzo@weblaw.ca

***Hamilton*: Dudzic, Barristers & Solicitors - *2**
#1014, P.O. Box 988, Stn. LCD1, 105 Main St. East, Hamilton, ON L8N 3R1
Tel: 905-528-4251; *Fax:* 905-528-5325
dudziclaw@dudziclaw.com

***Hamilton*: Duxbury Law Professional Corporation Barristers & Solicitors - *2**
#1500, 1 King St. West, Hamilton, ON L8P 1A4
Tel: 905-570-1242; *Fax:* 905-570-1955
brian@duxburylaw.ca

***Hamilton*: Paul H. Ennis, Q.C - *1**
#502, 105 Main St. East, Hamilton, ON L8N 1G6
Tel: 905-525-9335; *Fax:* 905-525-9988

***Hamilton*: Evans Sweeny Bordin LLP, Lawyers & Advocates - *7**
#1201, 1 King St. West, Hamilton, ON L8P 1A4
Tel: 905-523-5666; *Fax:* 905-523-8098
jfe@esblawyers.com
www.esblawyers.com

***Hamilton*: Evans, Philp - *23**
P.O. Box 930, Stn. A, Hamilton, ON L8N 3P9
Tel: 905-525-1200; *Fax:* 905-525-7897
info@evansphilp.com
www.evansphilp.com

***Hamilton*: Foreman Rosenblatt & Lewis - *3**
425 York Blvd., Hamilton, ON L8R 3M3
Tel: 905-525-3570; *Fax:* 905-523-0363
ylcinfo@yorklawcentre.com

***Hamilton*: Frankel Law Offices - *1**
#1001, 105 Main St. East, Hamilton, ON L8N 1G6
Tel: 905-522-3972; *Fax:* 905-528-2767
stephan@frankelaw.ca
www.frankelaw.ca

***Hamilton*: Genesee & Clarke - *3**
#2225, 25 Main St. West, Hamilton, ON L8P 1H1
Tel: 905-527-6666; *Fax:* 905-522-7085
frank@geneseeclarke.com

***Hamilton*: Gerald Swaye & Associates Professional Corporation - *7**
#901, 105 Main St. East, Hamilton, ON L8N 1G6
Tel: 905-524-2861; *Fax:* 905-524-2313
gswaye@swaye.ca
www.swaye.ca

***Hamilton*: Robbie D. Gordon - *1**
P.O. Box 490, 488 Ferguson Ave., Hamilton, ON L8L 4Z5
Tel: 705-672-3338; *Fax:* 705-672-2451

***Hamilton*: Guyatt, Grasznbeek & Millikin - *1**
#401, 20 Jackson St. West, Hamilton, ON L8P 1L2
Tel: 905-528-8369; *Fax:* 905-528-8066
keith.millikin@bellnet.ca

***Hamilton*: Harper, Jaskot - *5**
#200, 1 James St. South, Hamilton, ON L8P 4R5
Tel: 905-522-3517; *Fax:* 905-522-3555
Toll-Free: 800-522-3517
www.jaskotfamilylaw.ca

***Hamilton*: Harvey Katz & Associates, Barristers, Solicitors, & Notaries Public - *3**
14 Hess St. South, Hamilton, ON L8P 3M8
Tel: 905-523-1442; *Fax:* 905-525-3817
harvey@hjklaw.on.ca
www.hjklaw.on.ca

***Hamilton*: Michael E. Hinchey - *1**
203 MacNab St. South, Hamilton, ON L8P 3C8
Tel: 905-525-1630; *Fax:* 905-527-3686

***Hamilton*: Inch Hammond Professional Corporation - *10**
#1500, 1 King St. West, Hamilton, ON L8P 4X8
Tel: 905-525-4481; *Fax:* 905-525-0031
ies@inchlaw.com

***Hamilton*: Brian J. Inglis - *1**
#803, 20 Hughson St. South, Hamilton, ON L8N 2A1
Tel: 905-527-6727; *Fax:* 905-527-6310
inglislaw@interlynx.net

***Hamilton*: Jaskula, Sherk - *2**
#915, 25 Main St., Hamilton, ON L8P 1H1
Tel: 905-577-1040; *Fax:* 905-577-7775
csherk@jaskulasherk.com

***Hamilton*: George E. Johnson - *1**
19 Augusta St., Hamilton, ON L8N 1P6
Tel: 905-523-7333; *Fax:* 905-523-1311

***Hamilton*: Kathryn A. Junger - *1**
19 Augusta St., Hamilton, ON L8N 1P6
Tel: 905-523-7333; *Fax:* 905-523-1311

***Hamilton*: H.E. Katz - *1**
15 Bold St., Hamilton, ON L8P 1T3
Tel: 905-522-0040; *Fax:* 905-522-2981
call@howardkatzlaw.com

***Hamilton*: Michael W. Kelly - *1**
#101, 154 Main St. East, Hamilton, ON L8N 1G9
Tel: 905-546-1920; *Fax:* 905-546-8471
mikelly@bellnet.ca

***Hamilton*: Mary Elizabeth Kneeland Barrister & Solicitor - *1**
131 John St. South, Ground Level, Hamilton, ON L8N 2C3
Tel: 905-572-7737; *Fax:* 905-529-8819
an261@hwcn.org

***Hamilton*: John O. Krawchenko - *1**
175 Hunter Street East, Hamilton, ON L8N 4E7
Tel: 905-546-0525; *Fax:* 905-546-0596

***Hamilton*: Landeg, Spitale - *2**
#806, 20 Hughson St. South, Hamilton, ON L8N 2A1
Tel: 905-529-7462; *Fax:* 905-528-6787

***Hamilton*: Lazier Hickey Langs O'Neal - *10**
25 Main St. West, 15th Fl., Hamilton, ON L8P 1H1
Tel: 905-525-3652; *Fax:* 905-525-6278
lawfirm@lazierhickey.com
www.lazierhickey.com

***Hamilton*: Lees & Lees - *1**
#2225, 25 Main St. West, Hamilton, ON L8P 1H1
Tel: 905-523-7830; *Fax:* 905-523-4677
leeslaw@leesandlees.ca

***Hamilton*: W.J.I. Malcolm - *1**
#709, 20 Hughson St. South, Hamilton, ON L8N 2A1
Tel: 905-528-4291; *Fax:* 905-528-4292

***Hamilton*: McArthur, Vereschagin & Brown LLP - *4**
195 James St. South, Hamilton, ON L8P 3A8
Tel: 905-527-6900; *Fax:* 905-527-5177
sam@labourlaw.com

***Hamilton*: Anthony E. McCusker - *2**
#101, 200 Aberdeen Avenue, Hamilton, ON L8P 2P9
Tel: 905-523-0593; *Fax:* 905-522-0988
Toll-Free: 877-523-3909
mccusker@on.aibn.com

***Hamilton*: McHugh Mowat Whitmore Ionico MacPherson LLP - *6**
337 Queenston Rd., Hamilton, ON L8K 1H7
Tel: 905-549-4676; *Fax:* 905-549-5819
www.mmwimlawfirm.ca

***Hamilton*: McLelland & Dean - *1**
1 King St. West, 7th Fl., Hamilton, ON L8P 1A4
Tel: 905-546-0393; *Fax:* 905-527-6286

* *indicates number of lawyers*

***Hamilton*: McQuesten Legal & Community Services - *3**
1440 Main St. East, Hamilton, ON L8K 6M3
Tel: 905-545-0442; *Fax:* 905-545-2645

***Hamilton*: Millar, Alexander - *2**
#830, 120 King St. West, Hamilton, ON L8P 4V2
Tel: 905-528-1186

***Hamilton*: Milligan Gresko Brown Vitulli Limberis LLP, Barristers & Solicitors - *4**
#1060, 120 King St. West, Hamilton, ON L8P 4V2
Tel: 905-522-7700; *Fax:* 905-528-6543
gjg@mgblawyers.ca
www.mgbvllaw.com

***Hamilton*: E.Y. Morwick - *1**
97 John St. South, Hamilton, ON L8N 2C2
Tel: 905-529-2343; *Fax:* 905-528-0070

***Hamilton*: Nolan Law Offices - *3**
1 King St. West, 7th Fl., Hamilton, ON L8P 1A4
Tel: 905-522-9261; *Fax:* 905-525-5836
info@nolanlaw.ca
www.nolalnaw.ca

***Hamilton*: J.Z. Olenski - *1**
#200, 845 Upper James St., Hamilton, ON L9C 3A3
Tel: 905-387-3922; *Fax:* 905-387-0291
johnlenski@netscape.net

***Hamilton*: George J. Parker - *1**
142 James St. South, Lower Level, Hamilton, ON L8P 3A2
Tel: 905-523-5636; *Fax:* 905-523-4910

***Hamilton*: A. Pazaratz - *1**
117 Hunter St. East, Hamilton, ON L8N 1M5
Tel: 905-523-5850; *Fax:* 905-528-0722

***Hamilton*: Michael S. Puskas - *1**
46 Jackson St. East, Hamilton, ON L8N 1L1
Tel: 905-527-4495; *Fax:* 905-527-4496
michael.puskas@bellnet.ca

***Hamilton*: Daniel P. Randazzo - *1**
44 Hughson St. South, Hamilton, ON L8N 2A7
Tel: 905-777-1773; *Fax:* 905-777-1774
randazzo@netinc.ca

***Hamilton*: Geoffrey M. Read - *1**
172 Main St. East, Hamilton, ON L8N 1G9
Tel: 905-684-3187; *Fax:* 905-522-6677

***Hamilton*: Robinson, McCallum, McKerracher, Graham - *1**
#300, 69 John St. South, Hamilton, ON L8N 2B9
Tel: 905-528-1435; *Fax:* 905-529-1570
m.graham@on.aibn.com

***Hamilton*: Rory J. Cornale - *1**
#301, 4 Hughson St. South, Hamilton, ON L8N 3Z1
Tel: 905-521-9989; *Fax:* 905-525-7737
rory.cornale@derubeis-chetcuti.com

***Hamilton*: Ross & McBride - *30**
P.O. Box 907, Stn. LCD1, 1 King St. West, Hamilton, ON L8N 3P6
Tel: 905-526-9800; *Fax:* 905-526-0732
www.rossmcbride.com

***Hamilton*: Ross & McBride LLP - *37**
Commerce Place, P.O. Box 907, 1 King Street West, 10th Fl., Hamilton, ON L8N 3P6
Tel: 905-526-9800; *Fax:* 905-526-0732
contact@rossmcbride.com
www.rossmcbride.com

***Hamilton*: Michael N. Rubenstein - *1**
#200, 242 James St. South, Hamilton, ON L8P 3B3
Tel: 905-525-9636; *Fax:* 905-521-0690
smerz@primus.ca

***Hamilton*: L.I. Sapiano - *1**
#1500, 105 Main St. East, Hamilton, ON L8N 1G6
Tel: 905-523-1665; *Fax:* 905-523-4436
lsapiano@gta.igs.net

***Hamilton*: Scarfone Hawkins LLP - *19**
P.O. Box 926, Stn. Depot 1, 1 James St. South, 14th Fl., Hamilton, ON L8N 3P9
Tel: 905-523-1333; *Fax:* 905-523-5878
info@shlaw.ca
www.scarfonehawkinsllp.com

***Hamilton*: Monica U.M. Scholz - *1**
184 Jackson St. East, Hamilton, ON L8N 1L4
Tel: 905-577-6070; *Fax:* 905-577-6051

***Hamilton*: Schreiber & Smurlick - *1**
1219 Main St. East, Hamilton, ON L8K 1A5
Tel: 905-545-1107

***Hamilton*: Simpson & Watson - *3**
950 King St. West, Hamilton, ON L8S 1K8
Tel: 905-527-1174; *Fax:* 905-577-0661
davidsimpson@simpsonwatson.com
www.simpsonwatson.com

***Hamilton*: Smith & Smith - *1**
1416 King St. East, Hamilton, ON L8M 1H8
Tel: 905-544-6034

***Hamilton*: F.P. Sondola - *1**
#205, 124 James St. South, Hamilton, ON L8P 2Z4
Tel: 905-523-1970; *Fax:* 905-523-1971

***Hamilton*: Shelley M. Stanzlik - *1**
120 Jackson St. East, Hamilton, ON L8N 1L3
Tel: 905-777-1155; *Fax:* 905-777-1142
rgee@icom.ca

***Hamilton*: Jay Warren State - *1**
P.O. Box 907, Stn. LCD 1, 1 King St. West, Hamilton, ON L8N 3P6
Tel: 905-572-5818; *Fax:* 905-526-0732
jstate@rossmcbride.com

***Hamilton*: J.J. Steadman - *1**
124 MacNab St. South, Hamilton, ON L8P 3C3
Tel: 905-529-6400; *Fax:* 905-521-1924

***Hamilton*: Sullivan, Festeryga, Lawlor & Arrell - *17**
1 James St. South, 11th Fl., Hamilton, ON L8P 4R5
Tel: 905-528-7963; *Fax:* 905-577-0077
general@sullivanfesteryga.com
www.sullivanfesteryga.com

***Hamilton*: Szpiech, Ellis, Skibinski, Shipton - *4**
414 Main St. East, Hamilton, ON L8N 1J9
Tel: 905-524-2454; *Fax:* 905-523-1733
sess@on.aibn.com

***Hamilton*: Edward Tharen - *1**
1243 Barton St. East, Hamilton, ON L8H 2V8
Tel: 905-547-1618; *Fax:* 905-549-5654

***Hamilton*: Thoman Soule LLP, Lawyers - *6**
P.O. Box 187, Stn. LCD 1, 46 Jackson St. East, Hamilton, ON L8N 3C5
Tel: 905-529-8195; *Fax:* 905-529-7906
info@thomansoule.com
www.thomansoule.com

***Hamilton*: Tkach & Tokiwa - *1**
#71, Mountain Plaza Mall, 651 Upper James St., Hamilton, ON L9C 5R8
Tel: 905-383-3545; *Fax:* 905-574-3020
tkachlaw@mountaincable.net

***Hamilton*: Turkstra Mazza Associates - *6**
15 Bold St., Hamilton, ON L8P 1T3
Tel: 905-529-3476; *Fax:* 905-529-3663

***Hamilton*: Jennifer M. Vandenberg - *1**
172 Main St. East, Hamilton, ON L8N 1G9
Tel: 905-572-6611; *Fax:* 905-572-9440
jvandenberg@cogeco.ca

***Hamilton*: Wasserman & Associates - *1**
#6, 105 Main St. East, Hamilton, ON L8N 1G6
Tel: 905-522-4242; *Fax:* 905-521-0052

***Hamilton*: Gary Leonard Waxman - *1**
#234, 845 Upper James St., Hamilton, ON L9C 3A3
Tel: 905-388-0585; *Fax:* 905-575-1613
waxman@mountaincable.net

***Hamilton*: Weisz, Rocchi & Scholes - *6**
#200, Effort Trust Bldg., 242 Main St. East, Hamilton, ON L8N 1H5
Tel: 905-523-1842; *Fax:* 905-523-4011
info@wrs.on.ca
www.wrs.on.ca

***Hamilton*: Nicholas R. White - *1**
120 Jackson St. East, Hamilton, ON L8N 1L3
Tel: 905-521-8901; *Fax:* 905-521-9564
nwhite@netaccess.on.ca

***Hamilton*: Yachetti, Lanza & Restivo - *6**
#100, 154 Main St. East, Hamilton, ON L8N 1G9
Tel: 905-528-7534; *Fax:* 905-528-5275
info@ylrlawyers.com
www.ylrlawyers.com

***Hanover*: Kenneth P. Duffy - *1**
414 - 10 St., Hanover, ON N4N 1P6
Tel: 519-364-1440; *Fax:* 519-364-6023
kduffy@wightman.ca

***Hanover*: Robert W. Garcia Professional Corporation - *2**
P.O. Box 37, Hanover, ON N4N 3C3
Tel: 519-364-3643; *Fax:* 519-364-6594
rgarcia@garcia-law.com

***Hanover*: Halpin & McMeeken, Barristers & Solicitors - *1**
478 Tenth St., Hanover, ON N4N 1R4
Tel: 519-364-5505; *Fax:* 519-364-0165
kevin@hanoverlaw.ca
www.hanoverlaw.ca

***Harrow*: Golden & Golden - *1**
P.O. Box 279, 13 King St. West, Harrow, ON N0R 1G0
Tel: 519-738-4111; *Fax:* 519-738-3470

***Harrow*: Karl G. Melinz - *1**
P.O. Box 880, 41A Centre St. West, Harrow, ON N0R 1G0
Tel: 519-738-2232; *Fax:* 519-738-9080
kgmelinz@mmsi.net

***Hawkesbury*: Gerald E. Langlois & Associates - *2**
471 McGill St., Hawkesbury, ON K6A 1R1
Tel: 613-632-8600; *Fax:* 613-632-5274
langlois@hawk.igs.net

***Hawkesbury*: Julien & Cormier Professional Corporation - *2**
132 Race St., Hawkesbury, ON K6A 1V2
Tel: 613-632-0148; *Fax:* 613-632-1810

***Hawkesbury*: Lachapelle Law Office - *1**
444 McGill St., Hawkesbury, ON K6A 1R2
Tel: 613-632-7032; *Fax:* 613-632-5472
lachapellelawoffice@bellnet.ca

***Hawkesbury*: Pilon Professional Corporation - *1**
280 Main St. West, Hawkesbury, ON K6A 2H7
Tel: 613-632-0103; *Fax:* 613-632-2800
pilons@bellnet.ca

***Hawkesbury*: Woods Parisien - *2**
#200, 115 Main St. East, Hawkesbury, ON K6A 1A1
Tel: 613-632-8557; *Fax:* 613-632-8559
parisien@on.aibn.com

***Hillsburgh*: Robert P. Harper - *1**
P.O. Box 10, 115 Main St., Hillsburgh, ON N0B 1Z0
Tel: 519-855-4961; *Fax:* 519-855-4029
robertharper@bellnet.ca

***Huntsville*: James S. Anderson**
#5, 133 Hwy. 60, Huntsville, ON P1H 1C2
Tel: 705-789-8823; *Fax:* 705-789-1272
jamesanderson@sympatico.ca

***Huntsville*: A.B. Cochran - *1**
#5, 133 Hwy. 60, Huntsville, ON P1H 1C2
Tel: 705-789-5538; *Fax:* 705-789-1272
acochran@vianet.ca

***Huntsville*: G.A. Smith - *1**
#1, 3 Fairy Ave., Huntsville, ON P1H 1G7
Tel: 705-789-8829; *Fax:* 705-789-2984
glensmith@bellnet.ca

***Ingersoll*: Nesbitt Coulter LLP - *1**
183 Thames St. South, Ingersoll, ON N5C 2T6
Tel: 519-485-5651; *Fax:* 519-485-6582
mborndahl@nesbittlaw.com

***Innisfil*: D. Anne Cheney - *1**
P.O. Box 7074, 1984 Wilkinson St., Innisfil, ON L9S 1A8
Tel: 705-734-9644; *Fax:* 705-734-0333

***Innisfil*: Patrick A. Duco - *1**
2093 Lilac Dr., #B, Innisfil, ON L9S 1Z1
Tel: 705-436-1020; *Fax:* 705-436-1027

***Innisfil*: Gibson & Adams LLP - *4**
8000 Yonge St., Innisfil, ON L9S 1L5
Tel: 705-436-1701; *Fax:* 705-436-1710
ganda@gibsonandadams.ca

** indicates number of lawyers*

***Iroquois Falls*: J. Kenneth Alexander - *1**
P.O. Box 290, Stn. A, 283 Main St., Iroquois Falls, ON P0K 1G0
Tel: 705-232-4309; *Fax:* 705-232-5274

***Iroquois Falls*: Susan T. McGrath - *1**
P.O. Box 700, Iroquois Falls, ON P0K 1G0
Tel: 705-232-4055; *Fax:* 705-232-6301
mcgrath@nt.net

***Jarvis*: W.E. Kelly - *1**
P.O. Box 430, 32 Main St. North, Jarvis, ON N0A 1J0
Tel: 519-587-4561; *Fax:* 519-587-5052

***Kanata*: Alan Pratt Law Office - *2**
#201, 105 Schneider Rd., Kanata, ON K2K 1Y3
Tel: 613-254-5415; *Fax:* 613-254-9859

***Kanata*: B.L. Smith & Associates - *1**
57 Hodgson Ct., Kanata, ON K2K 2T4
Tel: 613-599-4614; *Fax:* 613-599-4614

***Kanata*: LaBarge Weinstein - *16**
#800, 515 Legget Dr., Kanata, ON K2K 3G4
Tel: 613-599-9600; *Fax:* 613-599-0018
info@lwlaw.com
www.lwlaw.com

***Kanata*: PwM Consulting - *1**
#344, 300 Earl Grey Dr., Kanata, ON K2T 1C1
Tel: 613-839-1555; *Fax:* 613-839-2555
peterm@pwmconsulting.com

***Kanata*: J. Jacques Robert**
486 Hazeldean Rd., Kanata, ON K2L 1V4
Tel: 613-860-1377; *Fax:* 613-837-7664

***Kapuskasing*: Bourgeault Brunelle Dumais Boucher - *4**
P.O. Box 446, 7 Cain Ave., Kapuskasing, ON P5N 1S8
Tel: 705-335-6121; *Fax:* 705-335-8127

***Kapuskasing*: J.M. Michel Majerovich - *1**
28 Kolb Ave., Kapuskasing, ON P5N 1G1
Tel: 705-335-5051; *Fax:* 705-337-5051

***Kapuskasing*: Perras Mongenais - *2**
10B Circle St., Kapuskasing, ON P5N 1T3
Tel: 705-335-3939; *Fax:* 705-335-3960

***Kapuskasing*: Guy A. Wainwright - *1**
19 Cain Ave., Kapuskasing, ON P5N 1T2
Tel: 705-335-8501; *Fax:* 705-337-1474
gwainrt@ntl.sympatico.ca

***Kenora*: Carten Law Office - *2**
#201, P.O. Box 2050, Stn. Main, 344 Second St. South, Kenora, ON P9N 3X8
Tel: 807-468-3036; *Fax:* 807-468-7576
cartenlaw@gokenora.com

***Kenora*: David James Elliott - *1**
Stone House, 225 Main St. South, Kenora, ON P9N 1T3
Tel: 807-468-3355; *Fax:* 807-468-7858

***Kenora*: Gibson & Wexler - *2**
P.O. Box 2450, 111 Main St. South, Kenora, ON P9N 3X8
Tel: 807-468-3061; *Fax:* 807-468-7940

***Kenora*: Hook, Seller & Lundin - *4**
#204, Bannister Centre, 301 - 1 Ave. South, Kenora, ON P9N 1W2
Tel: 807-468-9831; *Fax:* 807-468-8384
jthook@hsllawyers.com
www.hsllawyers.com

***Kenora*: Barbara E. Minshall - *1**
105 Main St., Kenora, ON P9N 1T1
Tel: 807-468-3038; *Fax:* 807-468-8122
bminshall@voyageur.ca

***Kenora*: Shewchuk, MacDonell, Ormiston, Richardt & Fregeau LLP - *6**
P.O. Box 1970, 214 Main St. South, Kenora, ON P9N 1T2
Tel: 807-468-9828; *Fax:* 807-468-5504
www.kenoralaw.com

***Keswick*: Iain T. Donnell - *1**
183 Simcoe Ave., Keswick, ON L4P 2H6
Tel: 905-476-9100; *Fax:* 905-476-2027

***Keswick*: R.E. Pollock - *1**
#300, 449 The Queensway South, Keswick, ON L4P 2C9
Tel: 905-476-0021; *Fax:* 905-476-0134

***Kincardine*: Marshall & Mahood - *2**
313 Lambton St., Kincardine, ON N2Z 2Y8
Tel: 519-396-8144; *Fax:* 519-396-9446
marshall.mahood@tn2.com

***Kincardine*: William S. Mathers - *1**
226 Queen St., Kincardine, ON N2Z 2S5
Tel: 519-396-4147; *Fax:* 519-396-1872
wwmlawyer@bmts.com

***Kingston*: Wm. J.F. Bishop - *2**
P.O. Box 1403, 338 Montreal St., Kingston, ON K7L 5C6
Tel: 613-544-0644; *Fax:* 613-544-2197
bill.bishop@on.aibn.com

***Kingston*: Black, Lloyd, Caron - *2**
P.O. Box 247, 249 Brock St., Kingston, ON K7L 4V8
Tel: 613-546-3286; *Fax:* 613-549-1193
blcm@adan.kingston.net

***Kingston*: Caldwell & Moore - *2**
260 Barrie St., Kingston, ON K7L 3K7
Tel: 613-545-1860; *Fax:* 613-545-1862
caldwell-moore@cogeco.ca

***Kingston*: Jack W. Chong - *1**
P.O. Box 1382, Stn. Main, 273 King St. East, Kingston, ON K7L 5C6
Tel: 613-549-1225; *Fax:* 613-549-3882

***Kingston*: Robert K. Cooper - *1**
11 Carruthers St., Kingston, ON K7L 1L9
Tel: 613-544-3634

***Kingston*: Cunningham, Swan, Carty, Little & Bonham LLP - *24**
#201, City Place II, 1473 John Counter Blvd., Kingston, ON K7M 8Z6
Tel: 613-544-0211; *Fax:* 613-542-9814
info@cswan.com
www.cswan.com

***Kingston*: Ecclestone & Ecclestone LLP - *2**
1046 Gardiners Rd., Kingston, ON K7P 1R7
Tel: 613-384-0735; *Fax:* 613-384-0731
email@ecclaw.net
www.ecclaw.net

***Kingston*: Elizabeth I Ollson - *1**
1770 Bath Rd., Kingston, ON K7M 4Y2
Tel: 613-384-8122; *Fax:* 613-384-7056
eollson@kos.net

***Kingston*: John R. Gale - *1**
238 Wellington St., 1st Fl., Kingston, ON K7K 2Y8
Tel: 613-546-4283; *Fax:* 613-546-9861
info@galeforlaw.ca
www.galeforlaw.ca

***Kingston*: Wayne C. Gay & Associate - *2**
P.O. Box 370, Stn. Main, 275 Ontario St., Kingston, ON K7L 4W2
Tel: 613-549-4300; *Fax:* 613-549-6948
waynegay@waynegay.com

***Kingston*: Good & Elliott Hawkins LLP - *3**
P.O. Box 1253, Stn. Main, 153 Brock St., Kingston, ON K7L 4Y8
Tel: 613-544-1330; *Fax:* 613-547-4538

***Kingston*: Wayne R.J. Headrick - *1**
1770 Bath Rd., Kingston, ON K7M 4Y2
Tel: 613-384-4403; *Fax:* 613-384-7056
wheadrik@kos.net

***Kingston*: Hickey & Hickey - *2**
P.O. Box 110, 93 Clarence St., Kingston, ON K7L 4V6
Tel: 613-548-3191; *Fax:* 613-548-8195
hickeym@on.aibn.com

***Kingston*: Mary Ann Higgs - *1**
#206, P.O. Box 700, 275 Ontario St., Kingston, ON K7L 4X1
Tel: 613-548-7399; *Fax:* 613-548-1862
maryannhiggs@on.aibn.com

***Kingston*: Jack Soule Consulting - *1**
60 Riverside Dr., Kingston, ON K7L 4V1
Tel: 613-541-0013; *Fax:* 613-541-0112
jack@soule.ca

***Kingston*: Jacob Macpherson Menard - *2**
#102, 780 Midpark Dr., Kingston, ON K7M 7P6
Tel: 613-389-1999; *Fax:* 613-384-8777
macpherson@kingston-lawyers.ca

***Kingston*: R. Wayne Keeler - *1**
11 Drayton Ave., Kingston, ON K7K 4X5
Tel: 613-531-4600; *Fax:* 613-547-4577
keelerw@kos.net

***Kingston*: Wayne T. King - *1**
#203, P.O. Box 221, 303 Bagot St., Kingston, ON K7L 4V8
Tel: 613-547-6481; *Fax:* 613-547-9025
wayne.tking@bellnet.ca

***Kingston*: R. Graham Lord - *1**
1770 Bath Rd., Kingston, ON K7M 4Y2
Tel: 613-384-4403; *Fax:* 613-384-7056
rglord@kingston.net

***Kingston*: J. Bruce MacNaughton - *1**
P.O. Box 1621, 45 Johnson St., Kingston, ON K7L 5C8
Tel: 613-546-9990; *Fax:* 613-546-6176
bruce@macnaughton.law.com

***Kingston*: Mary-Jo Maur - *1**
#1, 151 Wellington St., Kingston, ON K7L 3E1
Tel: 613-530-2665; *Fax:* 613-530-2241
mary-jo.maur@bellnet.ca

***Kingston*: M.A. McCue - *1**
#201A, 837 Princess St., Kingston, ON K7L 1G8
Tel: 613-542-3700; *Fax:* 613-542-5700
mamccue@kingston.net

***Kingston*: G.Y. McDiarmid - *1**
P.O. Box 1010, Stn. Main, 3 Rideau St., Kingston, ON K7L 4X8
Tel: 613-546-3274; *Fax:* 613-546-1493
gmcdiarmid@on.aibn.com

***Kingston*: Morley Law Office - *1**
211 Division St., Kingston, ON K7K 3Z2
Tel: 613-542-2192; *Fax:* 613-542-2393
info@lesmorley.com
www.lesmorley.com

***Kingston*: Fergus J. (Chip) O'Connor - *1**
P.O. Box 1959, 104 Johnson St., Kingston, ON K7L 5J7
Tel: 613-546-5581; *Fax:* 613-546-5540
oconnor@kos.net

***Kingston*: Philip M. Osanic - *1**
817 Blackburn Mews, Kingston, ON K7P 2N6
Tel: 613-634-4440; *Fax:* 613-634-4443

***Kingston*: J. Yvonne Pelley - *1**
817 Blackburn Mews, Kingston, ON K7P 2N6
Tel: 613-634-4440; *Fax:* 613-634-4443
jypelley@on.aibn.com

***Kingston*: Racioppo Zuber Coetzee Dionne LLP**
#201, 574 Princess St., Kingston, ON K7L 1C9
Tel: 613-544-1482; *Fax:* 613-546-3633

***Kingston*: Jennifer L. Sims - *1**
#201, 303 Bagot St., Kingston, ON K7K 5W7
Tel: 613-530-2230; *Fax:* 613-530-2231

***Kingston*: Douglas M. Slack - *1**
#1, 817 Blackburn Mews, Kingston, ON K7P 2N6
Tel: 613-384-7260; *Fax:* 613-384-7262
dm.slack@utoronto.ca

***Kingston*: Britton C. Smith - *1**
P.O. Box 1376, Stn. Main, 74 Johnson St., Kingston, ON K7L 5C6
Tel: 613-547-3798; *Fax:* 613-547-6814

***Kingston*: Letitia M. Steele - *1**
P.O. Box 29013, Stn. Portsmouth, Kingston, ON K7M 8W6
Tel: 613-542-1795; *Fax:* 613-542-2471

***Kingston*: Tepper Law Office - *1**
P.O. Box 1265, Stn. Main, 461 Princess St., Kingston, ON K7L 4Y8
Tel: 613-546-1169; *Fax:* 613-546-6992
gtepper@kingston.net

***Kingston*: A.F. Thomson - *1**
232 Brock St., Kingston, ON K7L 1S4
Tel: 613-549-5111; *Fax:* 613-549-4074
thomson@kingston.net

***Kingston*: Thomas W. Troughton - *1**
#103, P.O. Box 668, Stn. Main, 780 Midpark Dr., Kingston, ON K7L 4X1
Tel: 613-634-0302; *Fax:* 613-384-8777
troughton@frontenaclaw.on.ca

** indicates number of lawyers*

Kingston: **Trousdale & Trousdale - *2**
#200, 184 Wellington St., Kingston, ON K7L 3E4
Tel: 613-546-2231; *Fax:* 613-546-9001

Kingston: **Willoughby MacLeod Warkentin LLP - *2**
734 Arlington Park Place, Kingston, ON K7M 8H9
Tel: 613-384-5678; *Fax:* 613-384-6025
info@macleodlaw.net

Kingsville: **Dunnion & Dunmore - *1**
59 Main St. East, Kingsville, ON N9Y 1A1
Tel: 519-733-6573; *Fax:* 519-733-3172
pdunmore@cogeco.net

Kirkland Lake: **Judith L. Munn - *1**
P.O. Box 970, 11 Station Rd. South, Kirkland Lake, ON P2N 3L2
Tel: 705-567-9224; *Fax:* 705-567-9227
judmunn@ntl.aibn.com

Kirkland Lake: **G. Shorrock - *1**
P.O. Box 490, Kirkland Lake, ON P2N 3J5
Tel: 705-567-5213; *Fax:* 705-567-3987
shorlaw@ntl.sympatico.ca

Kitchener: **Derek K. Babcock - *1**
28 Weber St. West, Kitchener, ON N2H 3Z2
Tel: 519-742-3570; *Fax:* 519-576-7451
dbabcock@on.aibn.com

Kitchener: **Thomas L. Brock - *1**
17 Irvin St., Kitchener, ON N2H 1K6
Tel: 519-742-1270; *Fax:* 519-742-6973

Kitchener: **Chris Lawyers - *1**
194 Weber St. East, Kitchener, ON N2H 1E4
Tel: 519-570-4400; *Fax:* 519-570-4242
Toll-Free: 888-570-9697
contactus@chrislawyers.com
www.chrislawyers.com

Kitchener: **J. Mark Coffey - *1**
#705, Corporation Square, 30 Duke St. West, Kitchener, ON N2H 3W5
Tel: 519-742-5100; *Fax:* 519-742-5229

Kitchener: **H.J. Cox - *1**
#610, 50 Queen St. North, Kitchener, ON N2H 6P4
Tel: 519-744-6551; *Fax:* 519-744-9885
hjcox@golden.net

Kitchener: **N.A. Crawford - *1**
1444 King St. East, Kitchener, ON N2G 2N7
Tel: 519-743-3615; *Fax:* 519-743-2212

Kitchener: **Dietrich Law Office - *2**
141 Duke St. East, Kitchener, ON N2H 1A6
Tel: 519-749-0770; *Fax:* 519-749-0288
george.deitrich@sympatico.ca

Kitchener: **Farhood, Boehler & Associates - *2**
#510, 101 Frederick St., Kitchener, ON N2H 6R2
Tel: 519-744-9949; *Fax:* 519-744-7974

Kitchener: **Timothy C. Flannery - *1**
82 Weber St. East, Kitchener, ON N2H 1C7
Tel: 519-578-8017; *Fax:* 519-578-8327
flannery@golden.net

Kitchener: **George C. Amos - *1**
276 Frederick St., Kitchener, ON N2H 2N4
Tel: 519-576-8480; *Fax:* 519-579-3042
george@amoslaw.ca

Kitchener: **Giffen LLP - *12**
#500, Commerce House, P.O. Box 2396, 50 Queen St. North, Kitchener, ON N2H 6M3
Tel: 519-578-4150; *Fax:* 519-578-8740
Toll-Free: 866-688-4150
info@giffenlawyers.com
www.giffenlawyers.com

Kitchener: **R. Haalboom, Q.C. - *1**
7 Duke St. West, Kitchener, ON N2H 6N7
Tel: 519-579-2920; *Fax:* 519-576-0471
richard@haalboom.ca

Kitchener: **R.J. Hare - *1**
741 King St. West, Kitchener, ON N2G 1E3
Tel: 519-576-6710

Kitchener: **Richard H.F. Herold - *1**
53 Roy St., Kitchener, ON N2H 4B4
Tel: 519-749-0555; *Fax:* 519-741-9041

Kitchener: **Hertzberger & Associates, Barristers & Solicitors - *2**
Penthouse, Corporation Square, 30 Duke St. West, Kitchener, ON N2H 3W5
Tel: 519-570-1944; *Fax:* 519-570-0989
reception@hertzbergerlaw.com
www.hertzbergerlaw.com

Kitchener: **J.T. Jansen - *1**
46 Brembel St., Kitchener, ON N2B 3T8
Tel: 519-741-1911; *Fax:* 519-741-5945
timjansen@bellnet.ca

Kitchener: **Kay Professional Corporation - *4**
177 Victoria St. North, Kitchener, ON N2H 5C5
Tel: 519-579-1220; *Fax:* 519-743-8063
law@kaylaw.ca
www.kaylaw.ca

Kitchener: **Kelly & Co. - *3**
#903, 50 Queen St. North, Kitchener, ON N2H 6P4
Tel: 519-579-3360; *Fax:* 519-579-2556
bkelly@kellylaw.com
www.kellylaw.com

Kitchener: **Kokila D. Khanna**
#900, 50 Queen St. North, Kitchener, ON N2H 6P4
Tel: 516-571-1542; *Fax:* 516-571-0945

Kitchener: **Sheldon Kosky - *1**
71 Weber St. East, Kitchener, ON N2H 1C6
Tel: 519-578-1480; *Fax:* 519-579-2537

Kitchener: **Stephanie A. Krug - *1**
17 Irvin St., Kitchener, ON N2H 1K6
Tel: 519-743-1603; *Fax:* 519-742-6973
stephaniekrug@aol.com

Kitchener: **R.G.R. Lawrence, Q.C. - *1**
18 Irvin St., Kitchener, ON N2H 1K8
Tel: 519-742-4443; *Fax:* 519-578-4201

Kitchener: **Ludwig, Lichtenheldt & Eby - *3**
P.O. Box 1463, Stn. C, 97 Frederick St., Kitchener, ON N2G 4H6
Tel: 519-579-3000; *Fax:* 519-579-5660

Kitchener: **Madorin, Snyder LLP - *16**
P.O. Box 1234, Stn. C, 55 King St. West, Kitchener, ON N2G 4G9
Tel: 519-744-4491; *Fax:* 519-741-8060
reception@kw-law.com
www.kw-law.com

Kitchener: **Richard Marchak - *1**
#9, 300 Victoria St. North, Kitchener, ON N2H 6R9
Tel: 519-570-3635; *Fax:* 519-570-0104

Kitchener: **Tracy L.M. Miller - *1**
#203, 7 Duke St. West, Kitchener, ON N2H 6N7
Tel: 519-745-1912; *Fax:* 519-745-1987

Kitchener: **Mollison, McCormick - *6**
P.O. Box 2307, Stn. B, 71 Weber St. East, Kitchener, ON N2H 6L2
Tel: 519-579-1040; *Fax:* 519-579-2537
mmollison@mollisonlaw.com

Kitchener: **Morrison Reist - *2**
279 Queen St. South, Kitchener, ON N2G 1W4
Tel: 519-576-5351; *Fax:* 519-576-5411
Toll-Free: 800-354-5723
law@morrisonreist.com
www.morrisonreist.com

Kitchener: **Morscher & Morscher - *1**
85 Margaret Ave. North, Kitchener, ON N2J 3R2
Tel: 519-749-8100; *Fax:* 519-749-8141

Kitchener: **Jacqueline Mulvey - *1**
293 Frederick St., Kitchener, ON N2H 2N6
Tel: 519-744-3704; *Fax:* 519-744-3662
jmulvey@golden.net

Kitchener: **Mark T. Nowak - *1**
370 Frederick St., Kitchener, ON N2H 2P3
Tel: 519-746-8340; *Fax:* 519-746-8144
marknowak@bellnet.ca

Kitchener: **John E. Opolko - *1**
372 Queen St. South, Kitchener, ON N2G 1W7
Tel: 519-743-2670; *Fax:* 519-743-2670

Kitchener: **Wayne G. Rabley - *1**
234 Frederick St., Kitchener, ON N2H 2M8
Tel: 519-570-1010; *Fax:* 519-570-4458

Kitchener: **B.H. Ritter - *1**
17 Irvin St., Kitchener, ON N2H 1K6
Tel: 519-744-1169; *Fax:* 519-742-6973
britter1@aol.com

Kitchener: **Roetsch & Schaffer - *2**
284 Frederick St., Kitchener, ON N2H 2N4
Tel: 519-576-5310; *Fax:* 519-576-2797

Kitchener: **John D. E. Shannon - *1**
30 Spetz St., Kitchener, ON N2H 1K1
Tel: 519-743-3654; *Fax:* 519-578-9521
jdeslaw@bellnet.ca

Kitchener: **Sloane & Pinchen - *2**
#301, 824 King St. North, Kitchener, ON N2G 1G1
Tel: 519-578-3094; *Fax:* 519-578-3682
craig@sloanepinchen.com; david@sloanepinchen.com

Kitchener: **Smith, Hunt, Buck - *2**
P.O. Box 2008, Stn. C, Kitchener, ON N2H 6L1
Tel: 519-579-3400; *Fax:* 519-741-9041
office@smithhuntbuck.com

Kitchener: **Smyth, Hobson - *1**
#206, 7 Duke St. West, Kitchener, ON N2H 6N7
Tel: 519-578-9400; *Fax:* 519-578-7482

Kitchener: **Carolyn R. Thomas & Associate - *1**
#900, 50 Queen St. North, Kitchener, ON N2H 6P4
Tel: 519-576-4459; *Fax:* 519-576-9349
carolyn@carolynrthomas.ca
www.carolynrthomas.ca

Kitchener: **Teresa Tummillo-Goy - *1**
228 Frederick St., Kitchener, ON N2H 2M8
Tel: 519-888-9440; *Fax:* 519-888-9750
teresa@ttglaw.ca

Kitchener: **Voll & Santos - *2**
30 Spetz St., Kitchener, ON N2H 1K1
Tel: 519-578-3400; *Fax:* 519-578-9521

Kitchener: **Walters Gubler - *2**
#604, 30 Duke St. West, Kitchener, ON N2H 3W5
Tel: 519-578-8010; *Fax:* 519-578-9395
inquiries@wglaw.org

Kitchener: **Wildeboer Dellelce LLP - *2**
#401, 72 Victoria St. South, Kitchener, ON N2G 4Y9
Tel: 519-741-8708; *Fax:* 519-741-9576
www.wildlaw.ca

Kitchener: **Colleen J. Winn - *1**
604 Charles St. East, Kitchener, ON N2G 2R5
Tel: 519-743-3981; *Fax:* 519-743-3647

Kitchener: **Stephen C. Woodworth - *1**
#9, 300 Victoria St. North, Kitchener, ON N2H 6R9
Tel: 519-570-0033; *Fax:* 519-570-0104

Kitchener: **W.R. Zalman - *1**
#102, 684 Belmont Ave. West, Kitchener, ON N2M 1N6
Tel: 519-579-6170; *Fax:* 519-579-6171

Kleinburg: **Black & Associates - *3**
#1, 10472 Islington Ave., Kleinburg, ON L0J 1C0
Tel: 905-939-8050; *Fax:* 905-939-8025
blackm@bellnet.ca
www.blackandassociates.ca

L'Orignal: **Rodrigue Landriault - *1**
P.O. Box 315, L'Orignal, ON K0B 1K0
Tel: 613-675-4526; *Fax:* 613-235-7442

L'Orignal: **Tolhurst & Miller - *4**
1030 King St., L'Orignal, ON K0B 1K0
Tel: 613-675-4512; *Fax:* 613-675-1103
Toll-Free: 866-752-8277
www.tolhurstandmiller.on.ca

Lakefield: **Baker & Cole - *2**
8 Bridge St., Lakefield, ON K0L 2H0
Tel: 705-652-8161; *Fax:* 705-652-7088
thomas.cole@nexicom.net

Lakefield: **G.A. Booth - *1**
P.O. Box 116, 34 Bridge St., Lakefield, ON K0L 2H0
Tel: 705-652-3378; *Fax:* 705-652-6823
gary@boothlawoffice.org

Lancaster: **Paul D. Syrduk - *1**
P.O. Box 9, 10 Oak St., Lancaster, ON K0C 1N0
Tel: 613-347-2423; *Fax:* 613-347-7118
syruduk@glen-net.ca

** indicates number of lawyers*

Leamington: Owen Spettigue Professional Corporation - *1
P.O. Box 327, 57 Talbot St. East, Leamington, ON N8H 3W3
Tel: 519-326-2687; Fax: 519-326-1344
cowenspettiguelaw@bellnet.ca

Leamington: Reid, Collins, Ricci, Enns & Rollier - *5
60 Talbot St. West, Leamington, ON N8H 1M4
Tel: 519-326-3237; Fax: 519-326-8139
rrcre@mnsi.net

Lefaivre: Hydroplane Services Mergus Inc. - *1
2575 Conc. 2, Lefaivre, ON K0B 1J0
Tel: 613-676-2510
jferrary@hotmail.com

Lindsay: Brent Walmsley - *1
#220, Kent Place Mall, 189 Kent St. West, Lindsay, ON K9V 5G6
Tel: 705-878-8131; Fax: 705-878-4642

Lindsay: Cornell, Mortlock & Sillberg - *1
P.O. Box 536, Stn. Main, 272 Kent St. West, Lindsay, ON K9V 4S5
Tel: 705-324-4312; Fax: 705-324-7525

Lindsay: J.W. Evans - *1
P.O. Box 427, Stn. Main, 219 Kent St. West, Lindsay, ON K9V 4S5
Tel: 705-324-3207; Fax: 705-328-1128

Lindsay: Evans, Whitford, Nagel Associates - *3
18 York St. South, Lindsay, ON K9V 3A2
Tel: 705-328-2727; Fax: 705-328-2770

Lindsay: Frost, Frost & Gorwill - *1
#217, 189 Kent St. West, Lindsay, ON K9V 5G6
Tel: 705-324-2193; Fax: 705-324-9879

Lindsay: Carol E. Jamieson - *1
18 Cambridge St. North, Lindsay, ON K9V 4C3
Tel: 705-878-8864; Fax: 705-878-1813
caroljamieson@cogeco.ca

Lindsay: Timothy W. Johnston - *1
#218, The Kent Place Mall, 189 Kent St. West, Lindsay, ON K9V 5G6
Tel: 705-328-2393; Fax: 705-328-2428

Lindsay: J. Scott McLeod - *1
#7, 1 William St. South, Lindsay, ON K9V 3A3
Tel: 705-324-6711; Fax: 705-324-5723

Lindsay: Scott & Scott - *1
#219, P.O. Box 660, 189 Kent St. West, Lindsay, ON K9V 4S5
Tel: 705-324-5181; Fax: 705-324-8077

Lindsay: Leonard S. Siegel - *1
P.O. Box 997, 11 Adelaide St. North, Lindsay, ON K9V 5N4
Tel: 705-878-7990; Fax: 705-878-7992
lsiegel@kawarthalaw.ca

Listowel: Pratt & Pratt - *1
P.O. Box 10, 280 Inkerman St. West, Listowel, ON N4W 3H2
Tel: 519-291-3612; Fax: 519-291-3613
dwpratt@prattlawoffice.ca

London: Ambrogio & Ambrogio - *2
#611, 200 Queens Ave., London, ON N6A 1J3
Tel: 519-438-7219; Fax: 519-438-5919

London: Anissimoff Professional Corporation - *3
#201, Richmond North Office Centre, 235 North Centre Rd., London, ON N5X 4E7
Tel: 519-673-5591; Fax: 519-673-6784
serge@anissimoff.on.ca

London: Karl Arvai Professional Corp. - *4
#1508, 140 Fullarton St., London, ON N6A 5P2
Tel: 519-672-0911; Fax: 519-642-1272
k.arvai@karlarvai.com

London: Daniel S.J. Bangarth - *1
#209, 1069 Wellington Rd. South, London, ON N6E 2H6
Tel: 519-472-2340; Fax: 519-657-8173
darlene.howard@sympatico.ca

London: Brenda D. Barr - *1
257 Piccadilly St., London, ON N6A 1S3
Tel: 519-672-5953; Fax: 519-672-8736
brenda@barrfamilylaw.com

London: Bates Law Office - *1
#1, 151 Pine Valley Blvd., London, ON N6K 3T6
Tel: 519-472-0330; Fax: 519-472-1814
tabates@rogers.com

London: Joanne G. Beasley & Associates - *2
593 Talbot St., London, ON N6A 2T2
Tel: 519-642-1520; Fax: 519-673-3868
info@beasleylawoffice.com

London: Beechie, Madison, Sawchuk LLP - *3
439 Waterloo St., London, ON N6B 2P1
Tel: 519-673-1070; Fax: 519-439-4363

London: Behr Law Firm - *3
#1105, 383 Richmond St., London, ON N6M 3C4
Tel: 519-438-4530; Fax: 519-679-6576

London: Belanger, Cassino, Coulston & Gallagher - *4
#153, 759 Hyde Park Rd., London, ON N6H 3S2
Tel: 519-472-6310; Fax: 519-657-5189

London: G.P. Belch
P.O. Box 5035, Stn. B, 300 Dufferin Ave., London, ON N6A 4L9
Tel: 519-661-4708; Fax: 519-661-5530
gbelch@london.ca

London: Belecky & Belecky - *2
95 Dufferin Ave., London, ON N6A 1K3
Tel: 519-673-5630; Fax: 519-667-4836
aj@belecky.ca; jf@belecky.ca

London: Brown, Beattie, O'Donovan LLP - *24
City Centre Tower, 380 Wellington St., 16th Fl., London, ON N6A 5B5
Tel: 519-679-0400; Fax: 519-679-6350
bboinfo@bbo.on.ca
www.bbo.on.ca

London: Mervin F. Burgard, Q.C. - *1
#203, 219 Oxford St. West, London, ON N6H 1S5
Tel: 519-679-9900; Fax: 519-679-8546

London: Campbell M. Dockstader - *1
36 Chapple Hill Rd., London, ON N6G 2H3
Tel: 519-657-4080; Fax: 519-657-2516

London: Carlyle Peterson - *5
#216, 700 Richmond St., London, ON N6A 5C7
Tel: 519-432-0632; Fax: 519-432-0634
cp@cplaw.com

London: Rano Channan - *1
68 Tamarack Cres., London, ON N6K 3J7

London: Luigi E. Circelli - *1
557 Talbot St., London, ON N6A 2S9
Tel: 519-673-1850; Fax: 519-673-4966
lcircelli@bellnet.ca

London: Cohen Highley LLP - *22
One London Pl., 255 Queens Ave., 11th Fl., London, ON N6A 5R8
Tel: 519-672-9330; Fax: 519-672-5960
hall@cohenhighley.com
www.cohenhighley.com

London: Russell W. Cornett - *1
499 McGarrell Dr., London, ON N6G 5K7
Tel: 519-675-0926
russellwcornett@hotmail.com

London: Cram & Associates - *4
#514, 200 Queens Ave., London, ON N6A 1J3
Tel: 519-673-1670; Fax: 519-439-5011
www.cramassociates.comwww.facebook.com/pages/Cram-Associates/219463871414493, twitter.com/CramAssociates

London: Crossan Ferguson Olanski LLP - *3
629 Wellington St., London, ON N6A 3R8
Tel: 519-858-2222; Fax: 519-858-2323
Toll-Free: 877-772-2424
diana@strictlybusiness.ca

London: Current Consulting - *1
767 Redoak Place, London, ON N6H 5R8
Tel: 519-601-4545
terrydooner@alumni.uwaterloo.ca

London: William L. Dewar - *1
479 Talbot St., London, ON N6A 2S4
Tel: 519-672-1830; Fax: 519-661-0095
wildew@on.aibn.com

London: Ronald W. Dickie - *1
#3237, 450 Talbot St., London, ON N6A 4K3
Tel: 519-679-9660; Fax: 519-667-3362
rwdickielaw@on.aibn.com

London: Kenneth Duggan - *1
#203, 111 Waterloo St., London, ON N6B 2M4
Tel: 519-672-5360; Fax: 519-433-6975
kvduggan@bellnet.ca

London: Excalibur Communications - *1
1653 Kathryn Dr., London, ON N6G 2R7
Tel: 519-439-1140; Fax: 519-439-3112
mary@excaliburcommunications.ca

London: Foster, Townsend, Graham & Associates - *15
551 Waterloo St., London, ON N6B 2R1
Tel: 519-672-5272; Fax: 519-672-9313
Toll-Free: 888-354-0448
firm@ftgalaw.com
www.ftgalaw.com

London: Frauts, Dobbie - *3
585 Talbot St., London, ON N6A 2T2
Tel: 519-679-4000; Fax: 519-679-7700
info@frautsdobbie.ca

London: Fryday, Murphy, Brown - *2
#201, 145 Wharncliffe Rd. South, London, ON N6J 2K4
Tel: 519-679-8800; Fax: 519-673-3632
kfryday@londonlawyers.com

London: David G. Fysh - *1
520 Springbank Dr., London, ON N6J 1G8
Tel: 519-472-3974; Fax: 519-472-3756
david@davidfysh.com
www.davidfysh.com

London: Giffen & Partners - *4
465 Waterloo St., London, ON N6B 2P4
Tel: 519-679-4700; Fax: 519-432-8003
office@giffens.com

London: Gordon B. Good - *1
#710, 171 Queens Ave., London, ON N6A 5J7
Tel: 519-433-4663; Fax: 519-679-8080
gordongood@goodlawoffice.com

London: J.G. Harding - *1
635 Wellington St., London, ON N6A 3R8
Tel: 519-439-0641; Fax: 519-439-0643
j.harding@bmts.com

London: Harrison Pensa LLP - *51
P.O. Box 3237, 450 Talbot St., London, ON N6A 4K3
Tel: 519-679-9660; Fax: 519-667-3362
info@harrisonpensa.com
www.harrisonpensa.com

London: Antin Jaremchuk - *1
100 Fullarton St., London, ON N6A 1K1
Tel: 519-432-2417; Fax: 519-663-1165
jaremchuk@sympatico.ca

London: Michael J. Lamb - *1
#102, 101 Cherryhill Blvd., London, ON N6H 4S4
Tel: 519-645-1104; Fax: 519-645-1107
lamblaw@on.aibn.com

London: Therese D.P. Landry Law Office - *1
#319, 148 York St., London, ON N6A 1A9
Tel: 519-438-4111

London: Paul F. Lepine - *1
570 Queens Ave., London, ON N6B 1Y8
Tel: 519-432-4155; Fax: 519-432-6861
pflepine@mnsi.net

London: Lerners LLP - *64
P.O. Box 2335, 80 Dufferin Ave., London, ON N6A 4G4
Tel: 519-672-4510; Fax: 519-672-2044
lerner.london@lerners.ca
www.lerners.ca

London: V. Libis - *1
93 Dufferin Ave., London, ON N6A 1K3
Tel: 519-434-6821; Fax: 519-434-9515
valdis.libis@odyssey.on.ca

London: John R. Lisowski - *1
607 Queens Ave., London, ON N6B 1Y9
Tel: 519-679-5000; Fax: 519-673-1717

London: Little & Jarrett - *5
P.O. Box 2757, 412 King St., London, ON N6A 4H4
Tel: 519-672-8121; Fax: 519-432-0784

** indicates number of lawyers*

***London*: Little, Inglis & Price - *4**
148 Wortley Rd., London, ON N6C 3P5
Tel: 519-672-5415; *Fax:* 519-672-3906
admin@lip.on.ca

***London*: Lockyer Spence LLP - *1**
#600, 465 Richmond St., London, ON N6A 5P4
Tel: 519-675-1058; *Fax:* 519-675-1086

***London*: Michael F. Loebach - *2**
#508, 171 Queens Ave., London, ON N6A 5J7
Tel: 519-439-3031; *Fax:* 519-439-3540
info@mloebachlaw.com

***London*: MacKewn, Winder, Kirwin LLP - *4**
#300, 376 Richmond St., London, ON N6A 3C7
Tel: 519-672-2040; *Fax:* 519-672-6583
mwk@mwk.on.ca

***London*: Nancy Z. Magguilli - *1**
PO Box 29002, RPO Westmount Mall, London, ON N6K 4L9
Tel: 519-641-6255; *Fax:* 519-641-6255

***London*: Edward J. Mann - *1**
#605, 137 Dundas St., London, ON N6A 1E9
Tel: 519-672-8707; *Fax:* 519-660-4678
ejmann@on.aibn.com

***London*: McKenzie Lake Lawyers LLP - *35**
300 Dundas St., London, ON N6B 1T6
Tel: 519-672-5666; *Fax:* 519-672-2674
info@mckenzielake.com
www.mckenzielake.com

***London*: McNamara, Pizzale - *3**
#220, 200 Queens Ave., London, ON N6A 1J3
Tel: 519-434-2174; *Fax:* 519-642-7654
mcpizz@execulink.com

***London*: Menear Worrad & Associates - *6**
100 Fullarton St., London, ON N6A 1K1
Tel: 519-672-7370; *Fax:* 519-663-1165
info@menearlaw.com
www.menearlaw.com

***London*: Brian K. Morris - *1**
#36, 14 Cadeau Terrace, London, ON N6K 4X5
Tel: 519-461-4684
brian.morris@sympatico.ca

***London*: Armand Morrow - *1**
42 Hampton Cres., London, ON N6H 2N8
Tel: 519-471-7607; *Fax:* 519-471-9121

***London*: Frederick A. Mueller - *1**
141 Wortley Rd., London, ON N6C 3P4
Tel: 519-673-1300; *Fax:* 519-673-1728
fred_mueller@rogers.com

***London*: Barry F. Nelligan - *1**
#202, 145 Wharncliffe Rd. South, London, ON N6J 2K4
Tel: 519-438-1709; *Fax:* 519-438-1700

***London*: Nicholson, Smith - *5**
295 Central Ave., London, ON N6B 2C9
Tel: 519-679-3366; *Fax:* 519-679-0958

***London*: Suhas T. Nimkar - *1**
151 York St., London, ON N6A 1A8
Fax: 519-474-9578
Toll-Free: 866-551-5255
suhasnimkar@aol.com

***London*: Michael R. Nyhof**
380 Queens Ave., London, ON N6B 1X6
Tel: 519-642-4015; *Fax:* 519-642-4034
michaelnyhof@on.aibn.com

***London*: James R. O'Donnell - *1**
#16, 440 Wellington St., London, ON N6A 3P2
Tel: 519-673-0600; *Fax:* 519-439-3468
james@jamesodonnell.ca

***London*: Patton Cormier & Associates - *4**
#1512, 140 Fullarton St., London, ON N6A 5P2
Tel: 519-432-8282; *Fax:* 519-432-7285
apatton@pattoncormier.ca

***London*: Payne Group International Inc. (PGi2) - *1**
145 Wakefield Cres., London, ON N5X 1Z6
Tel: 519-859-7442
rpayne@PGi2.com

***London*: Judith M. Potter - *1**
54 Hunt Club Dr., London, ON N6H 3Y3
Tel: 519-432-8811; *Fax:* 519-663-1165
jpotter@start.ca

***London*: Peter J. Quigley - *1**
924 Oxford East, London, ON N5Y 3J9
Tel: 519-453-3393; *Fax:* 519-453-3341

***London*: S. Michael Robertson - *1**
#105, 186 Albert St., London, ON N6A 1M1
Tel: 519-660-1147; *Fax:* 519-660-0840
smrobertson.lawyer@bellnet.ca

***London*: Siskind, Cromarty, Ivey & Dowler LLP - *65**
P.O. Box 2520, 680 Waterloo St., London, ON N6A 3V8
Tel: 519-672-2121; *Fax:* 519-672-6065
Toll-Free: 877-672-2121
info@siskinds.com
www.siskinds.com

***London*: Stambler & Mills - *1**
#1511, 148 Fullarton St., London, ON N6A 5P3
Tel: 519-672-6240; *Fax:* 519-433-9593

***London*: Szemenyei Kerwin MacKenzie LLP**
P.O. Box 482, Stn. Lambeth, 2479 Main St., London, ON N6P 1R1
Tel: 519-652-1616; *Fax:* 519-652-1622

***London*: L. Kent Thomas - *1**
11 Stanley St., London, ON N6C 1A9
Tel: 519-438-4181; *Fax:* 519-433-5557

***London*: Thomson Mahoney Dobson Delorey - *6**
#200, 145 Wharncliffe Rd., London, ON N6J 2K4
Tel: 519-673-1151; *Fax:* 519-673-3632
tmdd@londonlawyers.com

***London*: Underhill Joles - *1**
607 Princess Ave., London, ON N6B 2C1
Tel: 519-432-4644; *Fax:* 519-438-3936

***London*: Despina S. Valassis - *1**
579 Talbot St., London, ON N6A 2T2
Tel: 519-439-2768

***London*: Walker & Wood - *1**
60 Barons Ct., London, ON N6C 5J3
Tel: 519-672-3500; *Fax:* 519-672-2420
walkerwood@rogers.com

***London*: Watson Jacobs McCreary - *1**
#14, 380 Adelaide St. North, London, ON N6B 3P6
Tel: 519-663-2296; *Fax:* 519-663-1034
mklug@bellnet.ca

***London*: Holly A. Watson - *1**
380 Queens Ave., London, ON N6B 1X6
Tel: 519-642-4015; *Fax:* 519-642-4034
hollywatson@on.aibn.com

***London*: Kenneth J. Williams - *1**
902 Adelaide St. North, London, ON N5Y 2M5
Tel: 519-641-2200; *Fax:* 519-641-7995
kwilliams@kenwlaw.ca

***London*: David Winninger - *1**
557 Talbot St., London, ON N6A 2S9
Tel: 519-858-3152; *Fax:* 519-858-3182

***Madoc*: Karen J. Yarrow - *1**
P.O. Box 670, 91 St. Lawrence St. East, Madoc, ON K0K 2K0
Tel: 613-473-2802; *Fax:* 613-473-4472
kyarrow@lks.net

***Manotick*: Saxony Canadian Consulting Corp. - *1**
1224 Rideau Bend Cres., Manotick, ON K4M 1A8
Tel: 613-692-2355; *Fax:* 613-692-7798
rfmacrae@yahoo.ca

***Manotick*: Glen F. Schruder**
1050 Hill St., Manotick, ON K4M 1J2
Tel: 613-692-2379

***Manotick*: Wilson Law Partners LLP - *3**
P.O. Box 429, 5542 Main St., Manotick, ON K4M 1A4
Tel: 613-692-3547; *Fax:* 613-692-0826
andrew@wilsonlawpartners.com
www.wilsonlawpartners.com

***Maple*: Judith Holzman Law Offices - *1**
2126 Major Mackenzie Dr., Maple, ON L6A 1P7
Tel: 905-303-1070; *Fax:* 905-303-4364
Toll-Free: 866-233-0945
judith@jhlawoffices.com

***Maple*: M.D. Newman - *1**
62 Lancer Dr., Maple, ON L6A 1C9
Tel: 905-832-5602; *Fax:* 905-832-5446
mdnewman@rogers.com

***Markdale*: Dunlop, Johnson & Pust - *2**
P.O. Box 433, 21 Main St. East, Markdale, ON N0C 1H0
Tel: 519-986-2100; *Fax:* 519-986-2904
johnslaw@on.aibn.com; pustlaw@on.aibn.com

***Markdale*: Harris, Willis - *1**
P.O. Box 466, 45 Main St. West, Markdale, ON N0C 1H0
Tel: 519-986-2740; *Fax:* 519-986-4205
ewillis@bmts.com

***Markdale*: Rodney T. O'Halloran - *1**
P.O. Box 522, RR#7, Markdale, ON N0C 1H0
Tel: 519-986-1428; *Fax:* 519-986-1471

***Markham*: Elliot Berlin - *1**
#101, 16 Esna Park Dr., Markham, ON L3R 5X1
Tel: 905-470-9444; *Fax:* 905-470-9449
eberlin@sympatico.ca

***Markham*: Bigioni Barristers & Solicitors - *2**
#201, 6060 Hwy. 7 East, Markham, ON L3P 3A9
Tel: 905-294-5222; *Fax:* 905-294-1607
bigionibarristers@on.aibn.com

***Markham*: Marvin B. Bongard - *1**
P.O. Box 509, 10 Washington St., Markham, ON L3P 3R2
Tel: 905-294-7555; *Fax:* 905-294-8360
marvin@mbongard.com

***Markham*: Burstein & Greenglass LLP - *4**
#200, Royal Bank Bldg., 7481 Woodbine Ave., Markham, ON L3R 2W1
Tel: 905-475-1266; *Fax:* 905-475-7851
office@bglaw.ca

***Markham*: Timothy M. Carter - *1**
58 Pennock Cres., Markham, ON L3R 3M4
Tel: 905-479-8802; *Fax:* 905-479-4137
timcarter@sympatico.ca
www.employmentlawissues.com/bio_tim.phpwww.linkedin.com/profile/view?id=4098996

***Markham*: Cattanach Hindson Sutton VanVeldhuizen - *7**
52 Main St. North, Markham, ON L3P 1X5
Tel: 905-294-0666; *Fax:* 905-294-5688

***Markham*: CG Management & Communications Inc. - *2**
#200, 175 Commerce Valley Dr. West, Markham, ON L3T 7P6
Tel: 905-709-4424; *Fax:* 905-709-2664
ekim@cggroup.com

***Markham*: Anna Chung - *2**
#209, 80 Acadia Ave., Markham, ON L3R 9V1
Tel: 905-940-6802; *Fax:* 905-940-6804
Toll-Free: 877-213-2284

***Markham*: Ernest Dicker, Q.C. - *1**
10 Fairway Heights Cres., Markham, ON L3T 1K2
Tel: 905-889-5556; *Fax:* 905-889-3306

***Markham*: John Gamble - *1**
60 McPherson St., Markham, ON L3R 3V6
Tel: 905-944-1754; *Fax:* 905-944-1753

***Markham*: Sydney Gangbar, Q.C. - *1**
#303, 80 Tiverton Ct., Markham, ON L3R 0G4
Tel: 905-470-0272; *Fax:* 905-470-8365
sydneygangbar@rogers.com

***Markham*: E. Alan Garbe - *1**
7507 Kennedy Rd., Markham, ON L3R 0L8
Tel: 905-415-9100; *Fax:* 905-479-3625
eagarbe@garbe-law.com

***Markham*: Paul Gollom - *1**
7507 Kennedy Rd., Markham, ON L3R 0L8
Tel: 905-881-6200; *Fax:* 905-883-8381
pgollom@look.ca

***Markham*: Jozefacki, Fielding - *2**
#200, 4961 Hwy. 7 East, Markham, ON L3R 1N1
Tel: 905-940-3141; *Fax:* 905-940-3139
jozefackilaw@hotmail.com

***Markham*: Barry M. Kaufman - *1**
#308, 3950 - 14th Ave., Markham, ON L3R 0A9
Tel: 905-477-8848; *Fax:* 905-477-8489
barrykaufman@rogers.com

** indicates number of lawyers*

***Markham*: Alan J. Luftspring - *1**
#236, 7181 Woodbine Ave., Markham, ON L3R 1A3
Tel: 905-479-1200; *Fax:* 905-479-9769
alanluftspring@rogers.com
www.gtalawyer.com

***Markham*: Irene L. Matthews - *1**
#104, 7225 Woodbine Ave., Markham, ON L3R 1A3
Tel: 905-475-9716; *Fax:* 905-475-9142

***Markham*: Mingay & Vereshchak - *3**
81 Main St. North, Markham, ON L3P 1X7
Tel: 905-294-0550; *Fax:* 905-294-9141
info@mvlaw.net

***Markham*: G. Arthur Moad - *1**
#206, 5762 Hwy. 7, Markham, ON L3P 1A8
Tel: 905-294-6446; *Fax:* 905-294-4436
gamoad@on.aibn.com

***Markham*: R. Parnes - *1**
Markham Industrial Park, P.O. Box 3249, 4701 Hwy. 7., Markham, ON L3R 6G6
Tel: 905-477-5151; *Fax:* 905-477-6778

***Markham*: Theodore B. Rotenberg Barrister - *1**
#303, 80 Tiverton Ct., Markham, ON L3R 0G4
Tel: 905-479-3331; *Fax:* 905-479-5017
general@rogerlaw.com

***Markham*: Alan R. Smith - *1**
#207, 2800 - 14th Ave., Markham, ON L3R 0E4
Tel: 905-415-8858; *Fax:* 905-940-1285
alansmithlaw@on.aibn.com

***Markham*: Paul F. Smith - *1**
#202, 5762 Hwy. 7, Markham, ON L3P 1A8
Tel: 905-294-9955; *Fax:* 905-294-4004

***Markham*: A. Melvin Sokolsky - *1**
#3, 200 Riviera Dr., Markham, ON L3R 5M1
Tel: 905-944-9427; *Fax:* 905-479-7025

***Markham*: E. Bruce Solomon - *1**
7507 Kennedy Rd., Markham, ON L3R 0L8
Tel: 905-479-1900; *Fax:* 905-479-9793
ebs@markhamlaw.ca

***Markham*: D.M. Starzynski, Q.C. - *1**
#205, 16th Ave. Shopping Centre, 9275 Hwy. 48 North, Markham, ON L6E 1A3
Tel: 905-294-3891; *Fax:* 905-471-2550
Toll-Free: 877-411-0902
starzynski@sympatico.ca

***Markham*: Howard J. Stern - *1**
#308, 3621 Hwy. 7 East, Markham, ON L2R 0G6
Tel: 416-410-7880; *Fax:* 416-410-7880

***Markham*: Thomas & Pelman**
4701 Hwy. 7 East, Markham, ON L3R 1M7
Tel: 905-477-2233; *Fax:* 905-477-7668
thomasandpelman@thomasandpelman.com

***Markham*: Wilson, Vukelich LLP - *18**
#710, 60 Columbia Way, Markham, ON L3R 0C9
Tel: 905-940-8700; *Fax:* 905-940-8785
Toll-Free: 866-508-8700
information@wvllp.ca
www.wvllp.ca

***Markham*: Shirley Yee**
#200, 80 Acadia Ave., Markham, ON L3R 9V1
Tel: 905-940-6800; *Fax:* 905-305-7630
shirleyyeelaw@hotmail.com

***Markham*: Jack Zwicker - *1**
#306, 7100 Woodbine Ave., Markham, ON L3R 5J2
Tel: 905-470-2544; *Fax:* 905-470-2571
jackzwicker@rogers.com

***Marmora*: A.L. Philpot - *1**
P.O. Box 430, 65 Forsyth St., Marmora, ON K0K 2M0
Tel: 613-472-2245; *Fax:* 613-472-3310
bcomeau@countrylawyer.on.ca
www.countrylawyer.on.ca

***Matheson*: J.A. Barber - *1**
P.O. Box 189, 362 MacDougall St., Matheson, ON P0K 1N0
Tel: 705-273-2151; *Fax:* 705-273-2144

***Meaford*: Carol A. Allen - *1**
P.O. Box 3272, 54 Sykes St. South, Meaford, ON N4L 1A5
Tel: 519-538-9929; *Fax:* 519-538-9931
Toll-Free: 877-538-9929
carolallen@rogers.com

***Meaford*: Kopperud Hamilton - *1**
76 Sykes St. North, Meaford, ON N4L 1R2
Tel: 519-538-2044; *Fax:* 519-538-5323
Toll-Free: 877-593-1938
kopperudlaw@bmts.com
www.bluemountainlawyers.com

***Meaford*: Scheifele, Erskine & Renken - *4**
P.O. Box 3395, 39 Nelson St. West, Meaford, ON N4L 1A5
Tel: 519-538-2510; *Fax:* 519-538-1843
info@meafordlawyers.com

***Merrickville*: Douglas Coupar & Associates - *1**
RR#4, Merrickville, ON K0G 1N0
Tel: 613-269-3232; *Fax:* 613-269-3773

***Metcalfe*: Gary M. Chayko - *1**
P.O. Box 579, Metcalfe, ON K2P 1L5
Tel: 613-230-7260; *Fax:* 613-230-2163
gchayko@netscape.net

***Midland*: Chin & Orr Professional Corporation - *4**
382 King St., Midland, ON L4R 3M9
Tel: 705-526-5529; *Fax:* 705-526-3071
Toll-Free: 877-526-5529
law@chinandorr.com

***Midland*: Deacon Taws - *2**
476 Elizabeth St., Midland, ON L4R 1Z8
Tel: 705-526-3791; *Fax:* 705-526-2688
admin@deacontaws.com
www.deacontaws.com

***Midland*: Ferguson Barristers - *6**
531 King St., Midland, ON L4R 3N6
Tel: 705-526-1471; *Fax:* 705-526-1067
Toll-Free: 800-563-6348
www.facebook.com/group.php?gid=143074919075604
www.fergusonbarristers.cawww.twitter.com/fergusonlaw

***Midland*: Hacker Gignac Rice LLP - *13**
518 Yonge St., Midland, ON L4R 2C5
Tel: 705-526-2231; *Fax:* 705-526-0313
Toll-Free: 800-205-4052
hgr@hgr.ca
www.hgr.ca

***Midland*: Mark Kowalsky - *1**
P.O. Box 280, 8970 County Rd. #93, Midland, ON L4R 4K8
Tel: 705-526-1336; *Fax:* 705-526-8499

***Midland*: Prost Associates - *2**
P.O. Box 96, 323 Midland Ave., Midland, ON L4R 4K6
Tel: 705-526-9328; *Fax:* 705-526-1209
info@prostlaw.com
www.prostlwa.com

***Midland*: Wanda L. Warren & Associate - *2**
512 Dominion Ave., Midland, ON L4R 1P8
Tel: 705-528-1665; *Fax:* 705-526-3238
Toll-Free: 800-838-8706

***Milton*: Ingrid Hibbard - *1**
539 Moorelands Cres., Milton, ON L9T 4B2
Tel: 905-875-3828; *Fax:* 905-875-3829
ihibbard@pelangio.com

***Milton*: Hutchinson, Thompson, Henderson & Mott - *2**
264 Main St., Milton, ON L9T 1P2
Tel: 905-878-2841; *Fax:* 905-878-3937
lawoffice@lawmilton.com

***Milton*: D.I. Malcolm - *1**
6439 Hwy. 25 South, RR#1, Milton, ON L9T 2X5
Tel: 905-876-3033; *Fax:* 905-876-3448

***Milverton*: W. Stirling Kenny Law Office - *1**
11 Main St. North, Milverton, ON N0K 1M0
Tel: 519-595-8171; *Fax:* 519-271-7397

***Minden*: Donald J. Lange - *1**
Comp. 50, RR#2, Minden, ON K0M 2K0
Tel: 705-489-4974; *Fax:* 705-489-4975
donaldlange@donaldlange.com
www.donaldlange.com

***Mississauga*: Esther O. Abraham Law Office - *1**
#110A, 377 Burnhamthorpe Rd. East, Mississauga, ON L5A 3Y1
Tel: 905-270-3755; *Fax:* 905-270-3844
esther@dlaw.ca
www.dlaw.ca

***Mississauga*: Affiliated Customs Brokers Ltd. - *1**
6470 Northam Dr., Mississauga, ON L4V 1H9
Tel: 905-676-3936; *Fax:* 905-672-5335

***Mississauga*: David A. Aiken - *1**
#200, 39 Lake Shore Rd. East, Mississauga, ON L5G 1C9
Tel: 905-602-5230; *Fax:* 905-871-8507
d.aiken.law@davidaaiken.com

***Mississauga*: J. Paul Bannon - *2**
#360, 33 City Centre Dr., Mississauga, ON L5B 2N5
Tel: 905-272-3412

***Mississauga*: Richard S. Barrett - *1**
1498 Lewisham Dr., Mississauga, ON L5J 3R4
Tel: 905-823-1487; *Fax:* 905-823-2529
lawyer@rogers.com
www.the-friendly-lawyer.com

***Mississauga*: N. Bartels - *1**
#304, 470 Hensall Circle, Mississauga, ON L5A 1X7
Tel: 905-276-8286

***Mississauga*: Paula L. Bateman, Barrister & Solicitor - *2**
6505 Mississauga Rd., #C, Mississauga, ON L5N 1A6
Tel: 905-567-4440; *Fax:* 905-821-1572

***Mississauga*: Stephen I. Beck - *1**
295 Matheson Blvd. East, Mississauga, ON L4Z 1X8
Tel: 905-568-8351; *Fax:* 905-568-9772
sbecklaw@on.aibn.com

***Mississauga*: Richard T. Bennett - *2**
82 Queen St. South., Mississauga, ON L5M 1K6
Tel: 905-826-1453; *Fax:* 905-826-7185
richardbennett@sprint.ca

***Mississauga*: Eugene J. Bhattacharya - *1**
295 Matheson Blvd. East, Mississauga, ON L4Z 1X8
Tel: 905-507-3796; *Fax:* 905-507-6011

***Mississauga*: Binsky Whittle - *1**
#200, 2345 Stanfield Rd., Mississauga, ON L4Y 3R3
Tel: 905-270-8811; *Fax:* 905-270-2977
www.binskywhittle.com

***Mississauga*: George F. Brant - *1**
62 Queen St. South, Mississauga, ON L5M 1K4
Tel: 905-826-2511; *Fax:* 905-286-1335
gbrant@attglobal.net

***Mississauga*: Brian Chan Barrister, Solicitor & Notary Public - *1**
#42, 145 Traders Blvd. East, Mississauga, ON L4Z 3L3
Tel: 905-712-2888; *Fax:* 905-712-3838

***Mississauga*: Michael J. Bukovac - *1**
1325 Burnhamthorpe Rd. East, Mississauga, ON L4Y 3V8
Tel: 905-238-1411; *Fax:* 905-629-9277
michaelbukovac@on.aibn.com

***Mississauga*: Burych Lawyers - *3**
#204, 89 Queensway West, Mississauga, ON L5B 2V2
Tel: 905-896-8600; *Fax:* 905-896-9757
burychlawyers@bellnet.ca

***Mississauga*: Campbell Partners LLP - *4**
2624 Dunwin Dr., Mississauga, ON L5L 3T5
Tel: 905-828-2247; *Fax:* 905-828-4311
info@campbelllawyers.net
www.campbelllawyers.net

***Mississauga*: Larry R. Plener - *2**
2564 Confederation Pkwy., Mississauga, ON L4Z 1S1
Tel: 905-897-8611; *Fax:* 905-897-8807
lplener@sympatico.ca

***Mississauga*: Carey McCallum & Nimjee - *1**
1325 Burnhamthorpe Rd. East, Mississauga, ON L4Y 3V8
Tel: 905-624-6817; *Fax:* 905-624-0522

***Mississauga*: Thomas Carey - *1**
1325 Burnhamthorpe Rd. East, Mississauga, ON L4Y 3V8
Tel: 905-624-1149; *Fax:* 905-624-0522
tomcarey@bellnet.ca

***Mississauga*: J.C. Chapman - *1**
2572 Stanfield Rd., Mississauga, ON L4Y 1S2
Tel: 905-270-7034; *Fax:* 905-270-1001
jcchapman@on.aibn.com

***Mississauga*: Richard C. Chojnacki - *1**
#301, 29 Tannery St., Mississauga, ON L5N 1V1
Tel: 905-821-3644; *Fax:* 905-821-8355

* *indicates number of lawyers*

***Mississauga*: L.R. Cutler - *1**
#1201, 90 Burnhamthorpe Rd. West, Mississauga, ON L5B 3C3
Tel: 905-276-5200; *Fax:* 905-276-2193

***Mississauga*: Wieslawa Dabrowska - *1**
#405, 4310 Sherwoodtowne Blvd., Mississauga, ON L4Z 4C4
Tel: 905-281-0308; *Fax:* 905-281-3552
viesiad@istar.ca

***Mississauga*: Daigle & Hancock LLP - *4**
51 Village Centre Pl., Mississauga, ON L4Z 1V9
Tel: 905-273-3339; *Fax:* 905-273-5672
Toll-Free: 877-273-3339
lawyers@daiglehancock.com
www.daiglehancock.com

***Mississauga*: Arthur H. David - *1**
#6 & 12, 2145 Dunwin Dr., Mississauga, ON L5L 4L9
Tel: 905-828-2300; *Fax:* 905-828-4602
a.david@bellnet.ca

***Mississauga*: Douglas M. Davidson - *1**
#200, 1552 Dundas St. West, Mississauga, ON L5C 1E4
Tel: 905-279-3330; *Fax:* 905-279-2735

***Mississauga*: Day + Borg LLP - *2**
93 Queen St. South, Mississauga, ON L5M 1K7
Tel: 905-826-5670; *Fax:* 905-826-5673
www.dayborg.com

***Mississauga*: DeRusha Law Firm - *4**
#1, 1015 Matheson Blvd. East, Mississauga, ON L4W 3A4
Tel: 905-625-2874; *Fax:* 905-625-0614
info@derushalawfirm.com
www.derushalawfirm.com

***Mississauga*: Dicarlo, Wong & Pugliese Associates - *2**
#204, 1090 Dundas St. East, Mississauga, ON L4Y 2B8
Tel: 905-272-0303; *Fax:* 905-272-0081

***Mississauga*: Eades Law Office - *1**
7229 Pacific Circle, Mississauga, ON L5T 1S9
Tel: 905-795-4040; *Fax:* 905-564-2315

***Mississauga*: Richard Alan Fellman - *1**
#100, 46 Village Centre Pl., Mississauga, ON L4Z 1V9
Tel: 905-275-2231; *Fax:* 905-275-8323
rfellman@on.aibn.com

***Mississauga*: Michael J. Fisher - *1**
#4, 265 Queen St. South, Mississauga, ON L5M 1L9
Tel: 905-812-9700; *Fax:* 905-812-0770
mjfisher@globalserve.net

***Mississauga*: David A. Fram - *1**
810 Meadow Wood Road, Mississauga, ON L5J 2S6
Tel: 905-916-0130; *Fax:* 905-916-1600
david@davidfram.com
www.davidfram.com

***Mississauga*: Garvey & Garvey LLP - *3**
972 Clarkson Rd. South, Mississauga, ON L5J 2V7
Tel: 905-823-4400; *Fax:* 905-823-5153

***Mississauga*: Fabio Gazzola, Barrister & Solicitor - *1**
#6, 2145 Dunwin Dr., Mississauga, ON L5L 4L9
Tel: 905-820-1277; *Fax:* 905-828-4602
gazzolaf@bellnet.ca

***Mississauga*: J.M.P. Ghalioungui - *1**
#11, 4040 Creditview Rd.., Mississauga, ON L5C 3Y8
Tel: 905-820-4442; *Fax:* 905-820-4442

***Mississauga*: John L.Z. Gora - *1**
893 Beechwood Ave., Mississauga, ON L5G 4E3
Tel: 905-278-7678; *Fax:* 905-271-5568

***Mississauga*: Harris & Harris LLP - *8**
#300, 2355 Skymark Ave., Mississauga, ON L4W 4Y6
Tel: 905-629-7800; *Fax:* 905-629-4350
info@harrisandharris.com
www.harrisandharris.com

***Mississauga*: Jane Harvey Associates**
Square One Shopping Centre, 100 City Centre Dr., Mississauga, ON L5B 2C9
Tel: 905-272-2266; *Fax:* 905-270-2876
janehlaw@magma.ca
www.janeharveylawyers.com

***Mississauga*: Wm. G. Jeffery - *1**
#301, 8 Stavebank Rd. North, Mississauga, ON L5G 2T4
Tel: 905-278-7271; *Fax:* 905-278-7514

***Mississauga*: Kain & Ball - *3**
#240, 1900 Dundas St. West, Mississauga, ON L5K 1P9
Tel: 905-855-4888; *Fax:* 905-855-3760
kainandball@on.aibn.com

***Mississauga*: Keel Cottrelle LLP - *6**
#104, 100 Matheson Blvd. East, Mississauga, ON L4Z 2G7
Tel: 905-890-7700
kkozak@keelcottrelle.on.ca

***Mississauga*: Julian B. Keller - *1**
#301, 25 Watline Ave., Mississauga, ON L4Z 2Z1
Tel: 905-890-2211; *Fax:* 905-890-2246
juliankeller@rogers.com

***Mississauga*: Sami N. Kerba - *1**
1093 Lakeshore Rd. East, Mississauga, ON L5E 1E8
Tel: 905-274-6073; *Fax:* 905-274-9876
samikerba@nskerba.com

***Mississauga*: Keyser Mason Ball LLP, Barristers & Solicitors - *24**
#1600, 4 Robert Speck Pkwy., Mississauga, ON L4Z 1S1
Tel: 905-276-9111; *Fax:* 905-276-2298
kmb@kmblaw.com
www.kmblaw.com

***Mississauga*: Klein Law, Barristers, Mediators, Notaries - *3**
#38, 1100 Central Pkwy. West, Mississauga, ON L5C 4E5
Tel: 905-272-2540; *Fax:* 905-272-2100
contact@kleinlaw.ca
www.kleinlaw.ca

***Mississauga*: Kostyniuk & Bruggeman - *3**
#213, 1515 Matheson Blvd. East, Mississauga, ON L4W 2P5
Tel: 905-602-5551; *Fax:* 905-602-9775
rkostyniuk@rogers.com

***Mississauga*: S. Lenard Kotylo**
#1, P.O. Box 1067, Stn. B, 1105 Crestlawn Dr., Mississauga, ON L4Y 3W4
Tel: 905-282-0918

***Mississauga*: Kozlowski & Company - *1**
5065 Foresthill Drive, Mississauga, ON L5M 5A7
Tel: 905-542-7070; *Fax:* 905-542-3434

***Mississauga*: Malicki & Malicki - *1**
3020 Kirwin Ave., Mississauga, ON L5A 2K6
Tel: 905-279-6250; *Fax:* 905-279-3878
marek@malicki.ca

***Mississauga*: Marks & Ciraco - *2**
#303, 4310 Sherwoodtowne Blvd., Mississauga, ON L4Z 4C4
Tel: 905-712-8300; *Fax:* 905-712-8559
www.marksandciraco.com

***Mississauga*: Martin C. Schulz - *1**
#500, 201 City Centre Dr., Mississauga, ON L5B 2T4
Tel: 905-897-2200; *Fax:* 905-897-1517
mschulz@bellnet.ca

***Mississauga*: Cindy McGoldrick - *1**
#103, 2691 Credit Valley Rd., Mississauga, ON L5M 7A1
Tel: 905-608-9967; *Fax:* 905-608-8206
cindy@cindymcgoldrick.com

***Mississauga*: Robert D. McIntyre, Q.C. - *1**
#410, 30 Eglinton Ave. West, Mississauga, ON L5B 3E7
Tel: 905-366-9700; *Fax:* 905-366-9707
rdm@ontlaw.com
www.ontlaw.com

***Mississauga*: Ronald F. Mossman - *1**
#300, 34 Village Centre Pl., Mississauga, ON L4Z 1V9
Tel: 905-848-4020; *Fax:* 905-848-4026
ronmossman@rmossman.com

***Mississauga*: D.M. Nathwani - *1**
#129, 1250 Mississauga Valley Blvd., Mississauga, ON L5A 3R6
Tel: 905-273-7887

***Mississauga*: R. Geoffrey Newbury - *1**
#106, 150 Lakeshore Rd. West, Mississauga, ON L5H 3R2
Tel: 905-271-9600; *Fax:* 905-271-1638
newbury@mandamus.org

***Mississauga*: Niebler, Liebeck**
1469 Indian Grove, Mississauga, ON L5H 2S5
Tel: 905-271-3232; *Fax:* 905-271-3677
niebler@on.aibn.com

***Mississauga*: O'Connor Zanardo - *2**
4275 Village Centre Ct., Top Fl., Mississauga, ON L4Z 1V3
Tel: 905-896-4370; *Fax:* 905-896-4926

***Mississauga*: O.J. Osmak - *1**
#126, Central Parkway Mall, 377 Burnhamthorpe Rd. East, Mississauga, ON L5A 3Y1
Tel: 905-277-0229; *Fax:* 905-277-4966
osmak@on.aibn.com

***Mississauga*: Ovenden & Ovenden - *2**
#204, 130 Dundas St. East, Mississauga, ON L5A 3V8
Tel: 905-270-8544; *Fax:* 905-273-7386

***Mississauga*: Pallett Valo LLP - *27**
#1600, 90 Burnhamthorpe Rd. West, Mississauga, ON L5B 3C3
Tel: 905-273-3300; *Fax:* 905-273-6920
Toll-Free: 800-323-3781
marketing@pallettvalo.com
www.pallettvalo.com

***Mississauga*: Petrillo Law Offices - *2**
#201, 2600 Skymark Ave., Unit 1, Mississauga, ON L4W 5B2
Tel: 905-949-9433; *Fax:* 905-949-1153
info@petrillolaw.com
www.petrillolaw.com

***Mississauga*: F. Polla - *1**
#100, 3643 Cawthra Rd., Mississauga, ON L5A 2Y4
Tel: 905-566-8640

***Mississauga*: Rawding, Lindsay - *2**
#201, 3415 Dixie Rd., Mississauga, ON L4Y 2B1
Tel: 905-625-4442; *Fax:* 905-624-0184

***Mississauga*: Terry D. Richardson - *1**
18 Mississauga Rd. North, Mississauga, ON L5H 2H4
Tel: 905-891-0011; *Fax:* 905-891-1410

***Mississauga*: Ridout & Maybee LLP, Intellectural Property & Technology Law Firm - *2**
#308, 1 City Centre Dr., Mississauga, ON L5B 1M2
Tel: 905-276-2300; *Fax:* 905-276-7687
mail@ridoutmaybee.com

***Mississauga*: J. Saltzman**
#15, 7205 Goreway Dr., Mississauga, ON L4T 2T9
Tel: 905-671-1178; *Fax:* 905-671-8030
jerry_westwood@hotmail.com

***Mississauga*: Edgar R. Schink - *1**
#405, 130 Dundas St. East, Mississauga, ON L5A 3V8
Tel: 905-270-8882; *Fax:* 905-270-7665

***Mississauga*: Allan Shulman - *1**
2225 Erin Mills Pkwy., Mississauga, ON L5K 1T9
Tel: 905-822-3563; *Fax:* 905-822-6342
ashulman@on.aibn.com

***Mississauga*: John F. Silvester - *1**
#544, 33 City Centre Dr., Mississauga, ON L5B 2N5
Tel: 905-275-2588; *Fax:* 905-275-0714

***Mississauga*: Singh Lyn Ragonetti Bindal LLP - *3**
#52, 2355 Derry Rd. East, Mississauga, ON L5S 1V6
Tel: 905-293-9800; *Fax:* 905-293-9801
info@lawyers4u.ca

***Mississauga*: Speigel Nichols Fox LLP - *7**
#400, 30 Eglinton Ave. West, Mississauga, ON L5R 3E7
Tel: 905-366-9700; *Fax:* 905-366-9707
www.ontlaw.com

***Mississauga*: Tannahill, Lockhart & Clark Law LLP - *3**
#10, 5805 Whittle Rd., Mississauga, ON L4Z 2J1
Tel: 905-502-5770; *Fax:* 905-502-5009
www.tlcl.ca

***Mississauga*: Thompson, MacColl & Stacy - *9**
#5, 1020 Matheson Blvd. East, Mississauga, ON L4W 4J9
Tel: 905-625-5591; *Fax:* 905-238-3313

***Mississauga*: Brian M. Watson - *1**
#105, 3034 Palston Rd., Mississauga, ON L4Y 2Z6
Tel: 905-272-0942; *Fax:* 905-272-1682
watsonlaw@sympatico.ca

***Mississauga*: Annette Wilson - *1**
#203, 1325 Eglinton Ave. East, Mississauga, ON L4W 4L9
Tel: 905-602-1989; *Fax:* 905-602-8491

* *indicates number of lawyers*

***Mississauga*: Michael Woods - *1**
#203, 120 Traders Blvd. East, Mississauga, ON L4Z 2H7
Tel: 905-568-3810; *Fax:* 905-568-1206
michaelwoods@on.aibn.com

***Mississauga*: Richard M. Woodside - *1**
2479 Burnford Trail, Mississauga, ON L5M 5E4
Tel: 905-567-4562

***Mississauga*: Janice E. Younker - *1**
1370 Hurontario St., Mississauga, ON L5G 3H4
Tel: 905-271-2784; *Fax:* 905-271-5960
younkerlaw@the-wire.com

***Mitchell*: Botsford Professional Corporation - *1**
P.O. Box 850, 24 Ontario Rd., Mitchell, ON N0K 1N0
Tel: 519-348-4731; *Fax:* 519-348-4107
blair@botsfordlaw.com

***Mitchell*: William E. Wilson - *1**
102 Ontario Rd., Mitchell, ON N0K 1N0
Tel: 519-348-8488; *Fax:* 519-348-4226
wewilson@ezlink.ca

***Monotick*: Alan C. Macleod - *1**
P.O. Box 1158, 5576 Dickinson St., Monotick, ON K4M 1A9
Tel: 613-692-4180; *Fax:* 613-692-0073

***Moosonee*: Keewaytinok Native Legal Services - *2**
P.O. Box 218, 40 Revillon Rd. North, Moosonee, ON P0L 1Y0
Tel: 705-336-2981; *Fax:* 705-336-2577
lantzp@lao.on.ca; khangkd@lao.on.ca
www.keewaytinok.org

***Morrisburg*: Gorrell, Grenkie, Leroy & Rémillard - *2**
P.O. Box 820, Stn. Morrisburg, 67 Main St., Morrisburg, ON K0C 1X0
Tel: 613-543-2922; *Fax:* 613-543-4228
info@yourlawfirm.ca
www.yourlawfirm.ca

***Morrisburg*: McInnis, MacEwen, Horner & Pietersma - *2**
P.O. Box 733, Morrisburg, ON K0C 1X0
Tel: 613-543-2946; *Fax:* 613-543-3867

***Mount Albert*: 2037770 Ontario Inc. - *1**
90 Shannon Rd., Mount Albert, ON L0G 1M0
Tel: 905-473-3418; *Fax:* 905-473-6846
rciano@campaignresearch.ca

***Mount Forest*: Deverell & Lemaich LLP - *2**
P.O. Box 460, Stn. Mount Forest, 166 Main St. South, Mount Forest, ON N0G 2L0
Tel: 519-323-1600; *Fax:* 519-323-3877
info@northwellington-law.ca

***Mount Forest*: Fallis, Fallis & McMillan - *2**
150 Main St. South, Mount Forest, ON N0G 2L0
Tel: 519-323-2800; *Fax:* 519-323-4115
ffmlaw@wightman.ca

***Napanee*: C. F. Doreleyers - *2**
P.O. Box 398, Stn. Main, 35 Dundas St. East, Napanee, ON K7R 3P5
Tel: 613-354-3375; *Fax:* 613-354-5641

***Nepean*: Michael G. Carey - *1**
84 Centrepointe Dr., Nepean, ON K2G 6B1
Tel: 613-723-4774; *Fax:* 613-723-2377
careylawoffice@bellnet.ca

***Nepean*: Charman Broadcasting Policy Inc. - *1**
47 Elke Dr., Nepean, ON K2J 2B9
Tel: 613-825-2770; *Fax:* 613-825-7034
wcharman@rogers.com

***Nepean*: Chiarelli Cramer Witteveen - *3**
Centrepointe Chambers, 92 Centrepointe Dr., Nepean, ON K2G 6B1
Tel: 613-723-9100; *Fax:* 613-723-9105
ccw@centrepointelaw.com

***Nepean*: Clermont Clausi Gardiner & Associates - *5**
1447 Woodroffe Ave., Nepean, ON K2G 1W1
Tel: 613-225-0037; *Fax:* 613-225-0921

***Nepean*: E. Max Cohen, Q.C. - *1**
24 Kitimat Cres., Nepean, ON K2H 7G5
Tel: 613-828-5855; *Fax:* 613-237-0510

***Nepean*: Doraty & Ferris**
28 Northside Rd., Nepean, ON K2H 5Z3
Tel: 613-829-7171; *Fax:* 613-829-0244
inquiries@doratyferris.com

***Nepean*: JL Consulting - *1**
142F Valley Stream Dr., Nepean, ON K2H 9C6
Tel: 613-721-8904; *Fax:* 613-721-8918

***Nepean*: Landry, Vanier - *1**
90 Centrepointe Dr., Nepean, ON K2G 6B1
Tel: 613-226-3336; *Fax:* 613-226-8767
vanier@vanierlaw.on.ca

***Nepean*: MacKay & Sanderson - *2**
#201, 1580 Merivale Rd., Nepean, ON K2G 4B5
Tel: 613-238-6180; *Fax:* 613-238-3288

***Nepean*: Michael E. Mastronardi - *1**
12 Apache Cres., Nepean, ON K2E 6H7
Tel: 613-858-9158
dmastr1213@rogers.com

***Nepean*: P3 Strategic Alliance Inc. - *1**
106 Starwood Rd., Nepean, ON K2G 1Z7
Fax: 905-476-8977
Toll-Free: 888-791-7834
cpitt@rogers.com

***Nepean*: Stephen A. Ritchie - *1**
92 Centrepointe Dr., Nepean, ON K2G 6B1
Tel: 613-224-6674; *Fax:* 613-723-9105
aritchie@allstream.net

***Nepean*: Skorupinski Enterprises - *1**
2 Ararat Ct., Nepean, ON K2H 8R9
Tel: 613-828-5969; *Fax:* 613-828-8987
sskorupinski@rogers.com

***Nepean*: Jo-Anne E. Ward - *1**
17 Scout St., Nepean, ON K2C 4B9
Tel: 613-729-7667

***New Liskeard*: Ramsay Law Office - *2**
P.O. Box 160, 18 Armstrong St., New Liskeard, ON P0J 1P0
Tel: 705-647-4010; *Fax:* 705-647-4341
Toll-Free: 800-837-6648
ramsaypr@nt.net
www.nt.net/~ramsaypr

***Newcastle*: Valentine Lovekin - *1**
35 King St., Newcastle, ON L1B 1H2
Tel: 905-987-3500; *Fax:* 905-987-3503
lovekin@lovekinlaw.com

***Newcastle*: Walters, Dizenbach, Ferguson - *3**
29 King Ave. East, Newcastle, ON L1B 1H3
Tel: 905-987-4735; *Fax:* 905-987-1061

***Newmarket*: Paul H. Caroline - *1**
#300, 16775 Yonge St., Newmarket, ON L3Y 8J4
Tel: 905-836-4018; *Fax:* 905-836-4020

***Newmarket*: Dunsmuir Advocates - *2**
P.O. Box 2003, Stn. Main, 17070 Yonge St., Newmarket, ON L3Y 6W4
Tel: 905-895-7741; *Fax:* 905-853-5851
www.dunsmuiradvocates.com

***Newmarket*: Mark Henry - *1**
105 Eagle St., Newmarket, ON L3Y 1J2
Tel: 905-898-2686; *Fax:* 905-898-3957

***Newmarket*: Hill Hunter Losell Law Firm LLP - *7**
#200, P.O. Box 324, Stn. Main, 17360 Yonge St., Newmarket, ON L3Y 4X7
Tel: 905-895-1007; *Fax:* 905-895-4064

***Newmarket*: Neal J. Kearney - *1**
#207, 1091 Gorham St., Newmarket, ON L3Y 8X7
Tel: 905-898-3012; *Fax:* 905-853-9894
kearneylaw@on.aibn.com

***Newmarket*: David Lakie - *1**
105 Eagle St., Newmarket, ON L3Y 1J2
Tel: 905-898-2686; *Fax:* 905-898-3957

***Newmarket*: Debra L. McNairn - *1**
#222, 465 Davis Dr., Newmarket, ON L3Y 7T9
Tel: 905-836-1371; *Fax:* 905-898-2050

***Newmarket*: Derrick McNamara - *1**
24 Hillview Dr., Newmarket, ON L3Y 4H9
Tel: 905-954-0593; *Fax:* 905-954-1827

***Newmarket*: Paul E. Montgomery - *1**
#300, 16775 Yonge St., Newmarket, ON L3Y 8J4
Tel: 905-836-4018; *Fax:* 905-836-4020
paulmontgomery@rogers.com

***Newmarket*: Murphy & Lewis - *2**
572 Davis Dr., Newmarket, ON L3Y 2P4
Tel: 905-836-4750; *Fax:* 905-836-6691
Toll-Free: 800-262-2659

***Newmarket*: Ramm Consultants Inc. - *1**
2944 Vivian Rd., Newmarket, ON L3Y 4W1
Tel: 905-715-7513
tramm@rammconsultants.com

***Newmarket*: A. Schneider - *1**
291 Davis Dr., Newmarket, ON L3Y 2N6
Tel: 905-898-1342; *Fax:* 905-898-1344

***Newmarket*: Steinberg, Bruce & Paterson - *3**
#109, 1091 Gorham St., Newmarket, ON L3Y 7V1
Tel: 905-830-9940; *Fax:* 905-830-9246

***Newmarket*: Stiver Vale - *7**
195 Main St. South, Newmarket, ON L3Y 3Y9
Tel: 905-895-4571; *Fax:* 905-853-2958

***Niagara Falls*: Broderick & Partners - *7**
P.O. Box 897, 4625 Ontario Ave., Niagara Falls, ON L2E 6V6
Tel: 905-356-2621; *Fax:* 905-356-6904

***Niagara Falls*: David P. Czifra - *1**
P.O. Box 868, 4786 Queen St., Niagara Falls, ON L2E 6V6
Tel: 905-357-6633; *Fax:* 905-356-3635
czifra@vaxxine.com

***Niagara Falls*: Charles A. Galloway - *1**
5146 Victoria Ave., Niagara Falls, ON L2E 4E3
Tel: 905-356-2512; *Fax:* 905-356-2513

***Niagara Falls*: Margaret A. Hoy - *1**
P.O. Box 868, 4786 Queen St., Niagara Falls, ON L2E 6V6
Tel: 905-354-4414; *Fax:* 905-354-1272

***Niagara Falls*: D. Ceri Hugill - *1**
6304 Stonefield Park, Niagara Falls, ON L2J 4K1
Tel: 905-708-9529; *Fax:* 905-353-1790
resolver@cogeco.ca

***Niagara Falls*: S. James Knight, Q.C. - *1**
4683 Queen St., Niagara Falls, ON L2E 2L9
Tel: 905-356-1524; *Fax:* 905-357-9686

***Niagara Falls*: Patricia Lucas - *1**
4056 Dorchester Rd., Niagara Falls, ON L2E 6M9
Tel: 905-357-4510; *Fax:* 905-357-9757

***Niagara Falls*: Martin Sheppard Fraser LLP - *13**
P.O. Box 900, 4701 St. Clair Ave., 2nd Fl., Niagara Falls, ON L2E 6V7
Tel: 905-354-1611; *Fax:* 905-354-5540
Toll-Free: 800-263-2502
lawyers@martinshep.com
www.martinshep.com

***Niagara Falls*: D.J. McDonald - *1**
P.O. Box 726, Stn. Main, 4683 Queen St., Niagara Falls, ON L2E 6V5
Tel: 905-356-1524; *Fax:* 905-357-9686
danielmcdonald@bellnet.ca

***Niagara Falls*: McKay, Heath - *2**
#102, 4701 St. Clair Ave., Niagara Falls, ON L2E 3S9
Tel: 905-357-0660; *Fax:* 905-357-5680

***Niagara Falls*: G.F. McNab, Q.C. - *1**
4056 Dorchester Rd., Niagara Falls, ON L2E 6M9
Tel: 905-357-4510; *Fax:* 905-357-9757
mcnablucas@on.aibn.com

***Niagara Falls*: N. Minov - *1**
2455 Lepp Ave., Niagara Falls, ON L2J 2B9
Tel: 905-356-4420; *Fax:* 905-356-0333

***Niagara Falls*: James Rocca - *1**
4056 Dorchester Rd., Niagara Falls, ON L2E 6M9
Tel: 905-357-3730; *Fax:* 905-356-6185
jamesrocca@bellnet.com

***Niagara Falls*: Sharpe, Beresh & Gnys - *4**
Elgin Block, 4673 Ontario Ave., 3rd Fl., Niagara Falls, ON L2E 3R1
Tel: 905-357-5555; *Fax:* 905-357-5760
sharpe@sbglawfirm.com

***Niagara Falls*: Brian N. Sinclair, Q.C. - *1**
6617 Drummond Rd., Niagara Falls, ON L2G 4N4
Tel: 905-356-7755; *Fax:* 905-356-7772
evah@on.aibn.com

** indicates number of lawyers*

***Niagara Falls*: William Slovak, Q.C. - *1**
5627 Main St., Niagara Falls, ON L2G 5Z3
Tel: 905-374-6000; *Fax:* 905-374-9410
Toll-Free: 877-231-0011
mjs5627@hotmail.com

***Niagara Falls*: Malcolm A.F. Stockton - *1**
P.O. Box 868, Stn. Main, 4786 Queen St., Niagara Falls, ON L2E 6V6
Tel: 905-357-3500; *Fax:* 905-356-3635
stockton@iaw.com
www.iaw.com/~stockton

***Niagara Falls*: Guy Ungaro - *1**
#101, 3486 Portage Rd., Niagara Falls, ON L2J 2K4
Tel: 905-357-5310; *Fax:* 905-357-9677
guyungaro@hotmail.com

***Niagara Falls*: Brian C. Wilcox - *1**
6617 Drummond Rd., Niagara Falls, ON L2G 4N4
Tel: 905-358-0782; *Fax:* 905-356-7772
Toll-Free: 877-220-7211
brian@bcwlawoffice.com
www.bcwlawoffice.com

***Niagara on the Lake*: Richard J.W. Andrews - *1**
#201, 111A Garrison Village Dr., Niagara on the Lake, ON L0S 1J0
Tel: 905-468-0081; *Fax:* 905-468-0087
rjwandrews@on.aibn.com
www.adamsheritage.com/lawyer/

***Niagara on the Lake*: W.R. King - *1**
P.O. Box 900, 431 Mississauga St., Niagara on the Lake, ON L0S 1J0
Tel: 905-468-3272; *Fax:* 905-468-5441
kinglaw@bellnet.ca

***North Augusta*: Emerson Communications Inc. - *1**
12931 Land O'Nod, RR#3, North Augusta, ON K0G 1R0
Tel: 613-290-7905; *Fax:* 613-269-4866
eostiguy@magma.ca

***North Bay*: Birnie Law Firm - *1**
P.O. Box 100, Stn. Main, 116 McIntyre St. West, North Bay, ON P1B 8G8
Tel: 705-497-1900; *Fax:* 705-497-1700
m.c.b@birnielawfirm.ca

***North Bay*: Bowness & Murray - *2**
348 Fraser St., North Bay, ON P1B 3W7
Tel: 705-474-9680; *Fax:* 705-474-4218

***North Bay*: Clements, Barrister & Solicitor - *1**
477 Sherbrooke St., North Bay, ON P1B 2C2
Tel: 705-472-4890; *Fax:* 705-472-9612

***North Bay*: Colvin & Colvin Professional Corporation - *2**
P.O. Box 657, Stn. Main, 577 Main St. West, North Bay, ON P1B 8J5
Tel: 705-476-5161; *Fax:* 705-476-9902
Toll-Free: 877-268-8566
colvinlaw@cogeco.net

***North Bay*: Gorman Barristers - *1**
Thompson Building, 101 McIntyre St. West, North Bay, ON P1B 2Y5
Tel: 705-476-0500; *Fax:* 705-476-8054

***North Bay*: M. Lucie Laperriere - *1**
325 Ski Club Rd., North Bay, ON P1B 7R3
Tel: 705-495-8554; *Fax:* 705-495-6274
lr-law@efni.com

***North Bay*: Larmer Law Office - *1**
335 Main St. West, North Bay, ON P1B 2T9
Tel: 705-476-5544; *Fax:* 705-476-0118
glarmer@larmer.ca

***North Bay*: Lucenti, Orlando & Ellies Professional Corporation - *4**
P.O. Box 358, 373 Main St. West, North Bay, ON P1B 8H5
Tel: 705-472-9500; *Fax:* 705-472-4814
info@loellp.ca

***North Bay*: Robert J. Martyn**
374 Fraser St., North Bay, ON P1B 3W7
Tel: 705-476-7080; *Fax:* 705-476-8084

***North Bay*: James R. McIntosh - *1**
325 Main St. West, North Bay, ON P1B 2T9
Tel: 705-476-2500; *Fax:* 705-476-9347
maclaw@efni.com

***North Bay*: McLachlan Froud LLP - *2**
#202, 373 Main St. West, North Bay, ON P1B 2T9
Tel: 705-476-6333; *Fax:* 705-476-4397
hughmclachlan@sympatico.ca; jeffrey.froud@sympatico.ca

***North Bay*: Joe Sinicrope - *1**
495 Main St. West, North Bay, ON P1B 2V3
Tel: 705-495-1334; *Fax:* 705-495-7990
joesinicrope@neilnet.com

***North Bay*: Wallace Klein Partners in Law LLP - *7**
P.O. Box 37, 225 McIntyre St. West, North Bay, ON P1B 8G8
Tel: 705-474-2920; *Fax:* 705-474-1758
info@partnersinlaw.net

***North York*: Tilda M. Roll - *1**
#600, 1120 Finch Ave. West, North York, ON M3J 3H7
Tel: 416-665-6888; *Fax:* 416-665-8225
tmroll@aggsrlawyers.ca

***Oakville*: Douglas D. Baggs - *1**
P.O. Box 100, Stn. Main, 233 Robinson St., Oakville, ON L6J 4Z5
Tel: 905-842-8600; *Fax:* 905-842-8242
doug@dougbaggs.com
dougbaggs.com

***Oakville*: Stephen B. Collinson - *1**
457 Kerr St., Oakville, ON L6K 3C2
Tel: 905-842-1600; *Fax:* 905-842-2775

***Oakville*: John G. Cox - *1**
297 Church St., Oakville, ON L6J 1N9
Tel: 905-842-3211; *Fax:* 905-842-3765

***Oakville*: Diane F. Daly - *1**
#301, 165 Cross Ave., Oakville, ON L6J 0A9
Tel: 905-844-5883; *Fax:* 905-844-9765
dianedaly@dalylaw.ca
www.oakvillelaw.ca

***Oakville*: Richard B. Day - *1**
164 Trafalgar Rd., Oakville, ON L6J 3G6
Tel: 905-844-8581; *Fax:* 905-842-6166
rick@daylaw.ca

***Oakville*: J.B. Gardner - *1**
P.O. Box 249, 228 Lakeshore Rd. East, Oakville, ON L6J 5A2
Tel: 905-844-3218; *Fax:* 905-844-3699
jbg@quixnet.net

***Oakville*: Stuart W. Henderson - *1**
P.O. Box 249, 228 Lakeshore Rd. East, Oakville, ON L6J 5A2
Tel: 905-844-3218; *Fax:* 905-844-3699
swhenderson@on.aibn.com

***Oakville*: Brian W. King, Q.C. - *1**
#34, Hopedale Mall, 1515 Rebecca St., Oakville, ON L6L 5G8
Tel: 905-827-0808; *Fax:* 905-827-8380
bking@briankinglaw.com
www.briankinglaw.com

***Oakville*: Patrick M. Kirby - *1**
1373 Secord Ave., Oakville, ON L6L 2K9
Tel: 905-825-5277; *Fax:* 905-825-3178

***Oakville*: Law Offices of Charles W. Pley, Canada & USA Immigration Lawyers - *1**
#102, 2660 Sherwood Heights Dr., Oakville, ON L6J 7Y8
Tel: 905-829-2100; *Fax:* 905-829-2100
info@pleylaw.com
www.pleylaw.com

***Oakville*: Lush, Bowker Aird - *4**
P.O. Box 734, 261 Lakeshore Rd. East, Oakville, ON L6J 1H9
Tel: 905-844-0381; *Fax:* 905-849-4540
Toll-Free: 877-844-0381
lawyers@lushbowkeraird.on.ca

***Oakville*: Thomas H. Marshall, Q.C., Barristers & Solicitors - *3**
#205, 1540 Cornwall Rd., Oakville, ON L6J 7W5
Tel: 905-844-0464; *Fax:* 905-844-3983
sanderson@oakvillefamilylawyer.ca
www.oakvillefamilylawyer.ca

***Oakville*: Terri L. McCarthy - *1**
#3A, 418 North Service Rd. East, Oakville, ON L6H 5R2
Tel: 905-842-4223; *Fax:* 905-842-7401
tlm.law@on.aibn.com

***Oakville*: David L. McKenzie - *1**
#211, 277 Lakeshore Rd. East, Oakville, ON L6J 6J3
Tel: 905-845-7591; *Fax:* 905-845-8876

***Oakville*: Kathryn S. Naumetz, Law Office - *1**
263 Church St., Oakville, ON L6J 1N7
Tel: 905-845-2241; *Fax:* 905-845-0193

***Oakville*: Keith D. Nelson - *1**
#205, North (Rear) Entrance, 243 North Service Rd. West, Oakville, ON L6M 3E5
Tel: 905-338-8481; *Fax:* 905-338-0748
kdnelson@nelsonlawyer.com
www.nelsonlawyer.com

***Oakville*: O'Connor MacLeod Hanna LLP - *21**
700 Kerr St., Oakville, ON L6K 3W5
Tel: 905-842-8030; *Fax:* 905-842-2460
info@omh.ca
www.omh.ca

***Oakville*: P. William Perras, Jr. - *1**
#210, 1540 Cornwall Rd., Oakville, ON L6J 7W5
Tel: 905-827-2700; *Fax:* 905-827-2766
billperras@on.aibn.com

***Oakville*: David J. Pilo - *1**
#301, 88 Dunn St., Oakville, ON L6J 3C7
Tel: 905-338-2002; *Fax:* 905-338-3810
dpilo@on.aibn.com

***Oakville*: Policy Alliance Inc. - *1**
2030 Merchants Gate, Oakville, ON L6M 2Z8
Tel: 905-842-5910; *Fax:* 905-842-9885
youngt.policyalliance@cogeco.ca

***Oakville*: Ryrie, Kerr, Davidson - *2**
P.O. Box 100, Stn. Main, 233 Robinson St., Oakville, ON L6J 4Z5
Tel: 905-842-8600; *Fax:* 905-842-4774

***Oakville*: Shanahan, Martin A - *1**
#200, 2620 Bristol Circle, Oakville, ON L6H 6Z7
Tel: 905-829-2700

***Oakville*: Karen A. Thompson - *1**
#100, 251 North Service Rd. West, Oakville, ON L6M 3E7
Tel: 905-338-7941; *Fax:* 905-844-9765
karens@karenthompsonlaw.ca
www.karenthompsonlaw.ca

***Oakville*: Helen M. Thomson - *1**
#1160, 1011 Upper Middle Rd. East, Oakville, ON L6H 5Z9
Tel: 416-410-8895; *Fax:* 416-410-8895

***Oakville*: Townsend & Associates - *2**
#10, 1525 Cornwall Rd., Oakville, ON L6J 0B2
Tel: 905-829-8600; *Fax:* 905-829-2035
lyn.townsend@ltownsend.ca

***Orangeville*: Mullin, Thwaites & Ward LLP - *4**
25 First St., Orangeville, ON L9W 2Z5
Tel: 519-941-4559; *Fax:* 519-941-4806
psprouleward@mtwlawoffice.com
www.mtwlawoffice.com

***Orangeville*: Parkinson & Parkinson - *1**
145 Broadway St., Orangeville, ON L9W 1K2
Tel: 519-941-3627; *Fax:* 519-941-3444
pp@parkinsonparkinson.ca

***Orangeville*: Peterson & Peterson**
P.O. Box 1607, 18 Lawton St., Orangeville, ON L9W 4X4
Tel: 705-356-9877; *Fax:* 705-356-7498
larryd.peterson@sympatico.ca

***Orangeville*: L. Anne Welwood - *1**
14 Zina St., Orangeville, ON L9W 1E1
Tel: 519-941-9710; *Fax:* 519-941-9244
aweldwood@welwoodlaw.com

***Orangeville*: Stephen F. White, Barrister & Solicitor - *1**
30 Mill St., Orangeville, ON L9W 2M3
Tel: 519-941-9440; *Fax:* 519-941-3803

***Orillia*: H. Robert Barlow, Q.C. - *1**
Stn. Main, 5 McLean Cr., RR#1, Orillia, ON L3V 6H1
Tel: 705-326-6881; *Fax:* 705-326-3063

***Orillia*: Crawford, McKenzie, McLean, Anderson & Duncan LLP - *7**
P.O. Box 520, Stn. Orillia, 40 Coldwater St. East, Orillia, ON L3V 6K4
Tel: 705-325-2753; *Fax:* 705-325-4913
mclaw@mclaw.ca

** indicates number of lawyers*

***Orillia*: Allan French - *1**
#201, P.O. Box 998, 6 West St. North, Orillia, ON L3V 6K8
Tel: 705-327-6671; *Fax:* 705-327-9084
afl@afrenchlawyer.ca

***Orillia*: Brian D. Kinnear - *1**
#108, P.O. Box 656, 17 Colborne St. East, Orillia, ON L3V 6K7
Tel: 705-323-9386; *Fax:* 705-323-9388
bkinnearlaw@on.aibn.com

***Orillia*: Lisa Welch Madden Law Firm - *1**
22 Matchedash St. N, Orillia, ON L3V 6K2
Tel: 705-325-6439; *Fax:* 705-325-7058
madden@lwmlaw.com

***Orillia*: Allan C. Parslow - *1**
212 John St., Orillia, ON L3V 3H7
Tel: 705-329-2223; *Fax:* 705-329-0433

***Orillia*: Russell Christie LLP - *7**
P.O. Box 158, 505 Memorial Ave., Orillia, ON L3V 6J3
Tel: 705-325-1326; *Fax:* 705-327-1811
rcmkw@russellchristie.com

***Orleans*: Brisebois & Webster - *2**
#103, 1803 St. Joseph Blvd., Orleans, ON K1C 6E7
Tel: 613-837-1140; *Fax:* 613-837-1689
briseboiswebster@hotmail.com

***Orleans*: Dust Evans Grandmaitre Professional Corporation - *5**
2589 St. Joseph Blvd., Orleans, ON K1C 1G4
Tel: 613-837-1010; *Fax:* 613-837-9670
Toll-Free: 800-379-6668
info@dustevans.com
www.dustevans.com

***Orleans*: G. Decker Consulting Services - *1**
1168 Bordeau Grove, Orleans, ON K1C 2M7
Tel: 613-824-7672
gdecker@magma.ca

***Orleans*: Galarneau & Associates Professional Corp. - *4**
2831 St. Joseph Blvd., Orleans, ON K1C 1G6
Tel: 613-830-7111; *Fax:* 613-830-7108
bjg@galarneauassoc.com
www.galarneauassoc.com

***Orleans*: J & L Associates - *1**
1863 Des Epinettes Ave., Orleans, ON K1C 6N5
Tel: 613-355-9545
gordonsharpe@aol.com

***Orleans*: Michael M. Johnson & Associates Inc. - *1**
1647 Sunview Dr., Orleans, ON K1C 5C6
Tel: 613-824-3232; *Fax:* 613-841-6686
mmjohnson@sympatico.ca

***Orleans*: Brian Kelly Consulting - *1**
1596 St. Georges St., Orleans, ON K1E 2M9
Tel: 613-841-1395

***Orleans*: W.E. Robert Little & Associates Inc. - *1**
6158 Voyageur Dr., Orleans, ON K1C 2W3

***Orleans*: Marc Nadon - *1**
#101, 3009 St. Joseph Blvd., Orleans, ON K1E 1E1
Tel: 613-837-4437; *Fax:* 613-837-4204
info@marcnadon.ca

***Orleans*: On The Hill Consulting - *1**
611 Merkley Dr., Orleans, ON K4A 1S3
Tel: 613-875-1795
phillips@telus.blackberry.ca

***Orleans*: Donald Partsch - *1**
1718 Des Sapins Gardens, Orleans, ON K1C 8E4
Tel: 613-837-3655
donald.partsch@sympatico.ca

***Orleans*: Phillipe Henault Enterprises Inc. - *1**
1204 St-Moritz Ct., Orleans, ON K1C 2B3
Tel: 613-824-2184; *Fax:* 613-824-9534

***Orleans*: Sicotte Professional Corp. - *5**
3009 St. Joseph Blvd., Orleans, ON K1E 1E1
Tel: 613-837-7408; *Fax:* 613-837-8015
admin@sicotte.ca

***Orleans*: Roger P. Trudel - *1**
2828 St. Joseph Blvd., Orleans, ON K1C 1G7
Tel: 613-837-2641; *Fax:* 613-830-5613
roger.trudel@on.aibn.com

***Orono*: W.K. Lycett, Q.C. - *1**
P.O. Box 87, 5301 Main St., Orono, ON L0B 1M0
Tel: 905-983-5007; *Fax:* 905-983-9022
wklycett@look.ca

***Oshawa*: Aleksandr G. Bolotenko - *1**
#978, Stn. A, 225 King St. East, Oshawa, ON L1H 7H2
Tel: 905-433-1176; *Fax:* 905-433-0283
agblaw.com

***Oshawa*: Boychyn & Boychyn - *1**
#1E, 57 Simcoe St. South, Oshawa, ON L1H 4G4
Tel: 905-576-2670; *Fax:* 905-576-0915
dboychyn@rogers.com

***Oshawa*: Julie Clark - *1**
P.O. Box 365, Stn. A, 32 Elgin St. East, Oshawa, ON L1H 7L5
Tel: 905-434-6411; *Fax:* 905-571-6114

***Oshawa*: Catherine Cornwall-Taylor - *1**
32 Elgin St. East, Oshawa, ON L1J 1T1
Tel: 905-434-6411; *Fax:* 905-571-6114

***Oshawa*: Creighton Victor Alexander Hayward Morison & Hall LLP - *5**
P.O. Box 26010, 235 King St. East, Oshawa, ON L1H 8R4
Tel: 905-723-3446; *Fax:* 905-432-2323
inquire@durhamlawyers.ca
www.durhamlawyers.ca

***Oshawa*: Diamond, Fischman & Pushman - *2**
P.O. Box 26008, Stn. 206, 179 King St. East, Oshawa, ON L1H 8R4
Tel: 905-723-5243; *Fax:* 905-436-6041
office@dflplaw.com

***Oshawa*: Elliott & Hughes - *2**
106 Stevenson Rd. South, Oshawa, ON L1J 5M1
Tel: 905-571-1774; *Fax:* 905-571-7706
Toll-Free: 877-272-5220

***Oshawa*: Diane M. England - *1**
167 Simcoe St. North, Oshawa, ON L1G 4S8
Tel: 905-721-1277; *Fax:* 905-721-1217
mail@dianeengland.com

***Oshawa*: Farquharson & Adamson - *1**
74 Simcoe St. South, Oshawa, ON L1H 4G6
Tel: 905-404-1947; *Fax:* 905-404-9050

***Oshawa*: Shan K. Jain, Q.C. - *1**
#2, 215 Simcoe St. North, Oshawa, ON L1G 4T1
Tel: 905-432-7787; *Fax:* 905-432-2343
jainc@sprint.ca

***Oshawa*: Kelly Greenway Bruce - *8**
P.O. Box 886, 114 King St. East, Oshawa, ON L1H 7N1
Tel: 905-723-2278; *Fax:* 905-432-2663
mail@oshawalawyers.com
www.oshawalawyers.com

***Oshawa*: Kitchen Kitchen Simeson McFarlane - *7**
P.O. Box 428, 86 Simcoe St. South, Oshawa, ON L1H 7L5
Tel: 905-579-5302; *Fax:* 905-579-6073
Toll-Free: 888-669-6446
mail@kksm.com

***Oshawa*: K.L. Lancaster - *1**
9 Ontario St., Oshawa, ON L1G 4Y9
Tel: 905-571-3901; *Fax:* 905-571-4241

***Oshawa*: Laskowsky & Laskowsky - *1**
73 Centre St. South, Oshawa, ON L1H 4A1
Tel: 905-579-0777; *Fax:* 905-576-9918

***Oshawa*: Mack, Kisbee & Greer - *3**
146 Simcoe St. North, Oshawa, ON L1G 4S7
Tel: 905-571-1400; *Fax:* 905-571-0735

***Oshawa*: Marks & Marks - *1**
#304, 17 King St. East, Oshawa, ON L1H 1A8
Tel: 905-728-5151; *Fax:* 905-433-4018

***Oshawa*: Richard J. Mazar Professional Corp. - *1**
#210, 419 King St. West, Oshawa, ON L1J 2K5
Tel: 905-571-2558; *Fax:* 905-571-3548
mazar@mazarlaw.com

***Oshawa*: Elaine M.F. McCallum - *1**
P.O. Box 1098, Stn. B, 174 Athol St. East, Oshawa, ON L1J 5Y9
Tel: 905-579-8866; *Fax:* 905-579-8913
Toll-Free: 888-579-5252
elainemfmccallum@on.aibn.com

***Oshawa*: Sharon A. Moote - *1**
#210, 200 Bond St. West, Oshawa, ON L1J 2L7
Tel: 905-432-7880; *Fax:* 905-432-7674

***Oshawa*: Joseph Neal - *1**
142 Simcoe St. North, Oshawa, ON L1G 4S7
Tel: 905-436-9015; *Fax:* 905-436-6098
jneal@oshawalawyers.ca

***Oshawa*: Josef Neubauer - *1**
106 Stevenson Rd. South, Oshawa, ON L1J 5M1
Tel: 905-433-1991; *Fax:* 905-433-7038

***Oshawa*: O'Brien, Balka & Elrick, Barristers & Solicitors - *6**
219 King St. East, Oshawa, ON L1H 1C5
Tel: 905-576-3402; *Fax:* 905-576-3915
Toll-Free: 866-245-5063
obe@oshawalaw.com
www.oshawalaw.com

***Oshawa*: Margot Poepjes - *1**
#217, 650 King St. East, Oshawa, ON L1H 1G5
Tel: 905-433-4020; *Fax:* 905-433-7028

***Oshawa*: Scott & Olver LLP - *3**
#4, 39 Bond St. East, Oshawa, ON L1G 1B2
Tel: 905-579-9400; *Fax:* 905-579-7400
scottolver@scottandolver.ca

***Oshawa*: Sosna & Burch - *3**
#8, 500 King St. West, Oshawa, ON L1J 2K9
Tel: 905-440-4759; *Fax:* 905-440-4764
sosna-burch@sosnaburch.com

***Oshawa*: Frank H.M. Stolwyk - *1**
57 Simcoe St. South, Unit 1-F, Oshawa, ON L1H 4G4
Tel: 905-576-8100; *Fax:* 905-579-6762
franks4950@aol.com

***Oshawa*: Strike, Salmers & Furlong - *3**
P.O. Box 2096, Stn. A, 55 William St. East, Oshawa, ON L1H 7V4
Tel: 905-723-1101; *Fax:* 905-723-1157
allanfurlong@ssf-oshawa.com

***Oshawa*: Ronald L. Swartz - *1**
231 Simcoe St. North, Oshawa, ON L1G 4T1
Tel: 905-576-3392; *Fax:* 905-576-3397
rlswatrz@interlinks.net

***Oshawa*: David B. Thomas - *1**
28B Albert St., Oshawa, ON L1H 8S5
Tel: 905-576-5666; *Fax:* 905-576-5289

***Oshawa*: Martin Tweyman - *1**
#101, 19 Celina St., Oshawa, ON L1H 4M9
Tel: 905-571-1500; *Fax:* 905-571-7528
martin.tweyman.oshawa@bellnet.ca

***Oshawa*: Ronald F. Worboy - *1**
153 Simcoe St. North, Oshawa, ON L1G 4S6
Tel: 905-723-2288; *Fax:* 905-576-1355

***Oshawa*: Yanch & Yanch - *1**
#1D, P.O. Box 154, 57 Simcoe St. South, Oshawa, ON L1H 7L1
Tel: 905-728-9495; *Fax:* 905-721-8044
yanchfirm@hotmail.com

***Ottawa*: 1323666 Ontario Inc. - *1**
431 Roxborough Ave., Ottawa, ON K1M 0L3
Tel: 613-746-8849; *Fax:* 613-745-8950
echiasson@rogers.com

***Ottawa*: Douglas R. Adams - *1**
#1502, 222 Queen St., Ottawa, ON K1P 5V9
Tel: 613-238-8076; *Fax:* 613-238-5519

***Ottawa*: Addelman & Baum - *2**
#800, 85 Albert St., Ottawa, ON K1P 6A4
Tel: 613-237-2673; *Fax:* 613-237-8146
douglasmbaum@rogers.com

***Ottawa*: Ahmad-Yousuf & Assoc. - *3**
#100, 180 Metcalfe St., Ottawa, ON K2P 1P5
Tel: 613-236-1111; *Fax:* 613-232-7763

***Ottawa*: AML Associates Inc. - *1**
10 Archer Sq., Ottawa, ON K1V 9Y8
Tel: 613-738-2000; *Fax:* 613-738-2358
ae.dumas@sympatico.ca

***Ottawa*: Anders, Young, Strong & Jonah - *4**
#401, 1580 Merivale Rd., Ottawa, ON K2G 4B5
Tel: 613-224-1621; *Fax:* 613-224-8827

** indicates number of lawyers*

Ottawa: **Andrews Robichaud - *6**
#500, 1306 Wellington St., Ottawa, ON K1Y 3B2
Tel: 613-237-1512; *Fax:* 613-237-9580
info@andrewsrobichaud.com
www.andrewsrobichaud.com

Ottawa: **APCO Worldwide (Canada) - *2**
#703, 255 Albert St., Ottawa, ON K1P 6A9
Tel: 613-565-4242; *Fax:* 613-565-1937

Ottawa: **ASMI Advance Systems Marketing International Inc. - *1**
#402, 222 Queen St., Ottawa, ON K1P 5V9
Tel: 613-565-4704; *Fax:* 613-565-4767
deborahdexter@asmi.ca

Ottawa: **Association House - *1**
#1110, 130 Albert St., Ottawa, ON K1P 5G4
Tel: 613-567-3080; *Fax:* 613-232-7148

Ottawa: **Association House - *1**
#1860, 45 O'Connor St., Ottawa, ON K1P 1A4
Tel: 613-567-3638; *Fax:* 613-232-7148
gmcintosh@associationhouse.com

Ottawa: **Augustine Bater Polowin LLP - *7**
#1100, 141 Laurier Ave. West, Ottawa, ON K1P 5J3
Tel: 613-569-9500; *Fax:* 613-569-9522
info@abplaw.com

Ottawa: **Axion - *1**
#200, 196 Bradford St., Ottawa, ON K2B 5Z4
Tel: 613-290-5572; *Fax:* 613-726-8938
lsavard@axionplus.biz

Ottawa: **Robert G. Bales - *1**
#200, 504 Kent St., Ottawa, ON K2P 2B9
Tel: 613-567-0674; *Fax:* 613-236-4064

Ottawa: **Gary R. Barnes - *3**
#500, 200 Elgin St., Ottawa, ON K2P 1L5
Tel: 613-225-2529; *Fax:* 613-225-3930
barnesgary@rogers.com

Ottawa: **Beament Green - *6**
979 Wellington Ave., Ottawa, ON K1Y 2X7
Tel: 613-241-3400; *Fax:* 613-241-8555
info@beament.com
www.beament.com

Ottawa: **Bélanger Guy & Assoc. Inc. - *1**
#602, 250 City Centre Ave., Ottawa, ON K1R 6K7
Tel: 613-230-7175; *Fax:* 613-230-3799
bga@bga-inc.com

Ottawa: **Jean Belanger - *1**
2230 Quinton St., Ottawa, ON K1H 6V3
Tel: 613-731-6362; *Fax:* 613-731-6199

Ottawa: **Bell, Baker LLP - *12**
#500, 116 Lisgar St., Ottawa, ON K2P 0C2
Tel: 613-237-3444; *Fax:* 613-237-1413

Ottawa: **Bell, Unger, Riley, Morris - *4**
24 Bayswater Ave., Ottawa, ON K1Y 2E4
Tel: 613-235-1266; *Fax:* 613-230-2727
rkriley@ottwaimmigration.com

Ottawa: **Binavince & Associates Professional Corporation - *4**
116 Lisgar St., 6th Fl., Ottawa, ON K2P 0C2
Tel: 613-236-2199; *Fax:* 613-236-3136
lawyers@binavince.com
www.binavince.com

Ottawa: **John E. Bogue - *1**
#802, 200 Elgin St., Ottawa, ON K2P 1L5
Tel: 613-234-4901; *Fax:* 613-236-8906

Ottawa: **Bosada & Associates - *1**
#222, 280 Metcalfe St., Ottawa, ON K2P 1R7
Tel: 613-563-1001; *Fax:* 613-563-1031
richard@bosada.ca

Ottawa: **Bradley, Hiscock, McCracken - *5**
1581 Greenbank Rd., Ottawa, ON K2J 4Y6
Tel: 613-825-4585; *Fax:* 613-825-5101
bhlaw@bhlaw.ca

Ottawa: **Alan S.J. Brass - *1**
#1002, 200 Elgin St., Ottawa, ON K2P 1L5
Tel: 613-238-5757; *Fax:* 613-688-1212

Ottawa: **Brazeau Seller LLP - *17**
#750, 55 Metcalfe St., Ottawa, ON K1P 6L5
Tel: 613-237-4000; *Fax:* 613-237-4001
www.brazeauseller.com

Ottawa: **C.P. Brett - *1**
70 Gloucester St., Ottawa, ON K2P 0A2
Tel: 613-230-2907; *Fax:* 613-235-4430
cpbrett@attglobal.net

Ottawa: **Thomas W. Brooker - *1**
#208, 1400 Clyde Ave., Ottawa, ON K2G 3J2
Tel: 613-226-3265; *Fax:* 613-224-8943
tom@brookerlawoffice.ca

Ottawa: **Bulger, Young - *3**
1493 Merivale Rd., Lower Level, Ottawa, ON K2E 5P3
Tel: 613-728-5881; *Fax:* 613-728-6158

Ottawa: **Burton Katsepontes - *2**
#200, 283 Dalhousie St., Ottawa, ON K1N 7E5
Tel: 613-239-3064; *Fax:* 613-237-9181
npklaw@corpweb.net

Ottawa: **Donald J. Byrne - *1**
#26, 1568 Carling Ave., Ottawa, ON K1Z 7M4
Tel: 613-722-5292; *Fax:* 613-729-6732
dbyrne@primus.ca

Ottawa: **Callan-Honeywell LLP - *2**
418 Preston St., Ottawa, ON K1S 4N2
Tel: 613-729-2460; *Fax:* 613-729-1710
www.callanhoneywell.ca

Ottawa: **Canadian Diamond Consultants Inc. - *1**
2895 Old Montréal Rd., Ottawa, ON K4C 1G2
Tel: 613-833-5499; *Fax:* 613-833-2488
c.d.c@rogers.com

Ottawa: **Caparim International - *1**
37 Linden Terrace, Ottawa, ON K1S 1Z1
Tel: 613-563-3292; *Fax:* 613-563-2676

Ottawa: **CapelleKane Immigration Lawyers Professional Corporation - *2**
#300, 311 Richmond Rd., Ottawa, ON K1Z 6X3
Tel: 613-230-7070; *Fax:* 613-230-9444
contact@capellekane.com
www.capellekane.com

Ottawa: **Carraigtyr Consulting & Associates - *1**
799 Colson Ave., Ottawa, ON K1G 1R6
Tel: 613-260-2222; *Fax:* 613-260-2222
james100@rogers.com

Ottawa: **Carroll & Wallace - *3**
#502, 66 Slater St., Ottawa, ON K1P 5H1
Tel: 613-236-5494; *Fax:* 613-232-7322
cwmlaw@cyberus.ca

Ottawa: **Robert M. Chartrand - *1**
#101, 745B Montréal Rd., Ottawa, ON K1K 0T1
Tel: 613-745-9446; *Fax:* 613-745-0800

Ottawa: **Edward Y.W. Cheung - *1**
#22, 5340 Canotek Rd., Ottawa, ON K1J 9C8
Tel: 613-748-9898; *Fax:* 613-748-1114
yw61@aol.com

Ottawa: **Paul-Emile Chiasson - *1**
#600, 116 Lisgar St., Ottawa, ON K2P 0C2
Tel: 613-230-8800; *Fax:* 613-236-3136
pechiasson@sympatico.ca

Ottawa: **Civica Inc. - *1**
45 O'Connor St., Ottawa, ON K1P 1A4
Tel: 613-232-0969; *Fax:* 613-447-2730
cwilson@civica.ca

Ottawa: **Cogitare - *1**
2294 Courtice Ave., Ottawa, ON K1H 7G8
Tél: 613-733-6165; *Téléc:* 613-733-1105
bhubert@cogiscene.com

Ottawa: **Conlin & McAlpin - *2**
1678 Bank St., Ottawa, ON K1V 7Y6
Tel: 613-737-4140; *Fax:* 613-737-7903
pconlin@conlinlaw.com

Ottawa: **Rosalind Conway & Associate - *2**
#320, 185 Somerset St. West, Ottawa, ON K2P 0J2
Tel: 613-594-0300; *Fax:* 613-594-8111
rosalind.conway@magma.ca

Ottawa: **Cooligan/Ryan LLP - *10**
#1100, 200 Elgin St., Ottawa, ON K2P 1L5
Tel: 613-236-0735; *Fax:* 613-238-3501
mail@colliganryan.com

Ottawa: **Cordwood International Inc. - *1**
25 MacNabb Pl., Ottawa, ON K1L 8J5
Tel: 613-741-1615; *Fax:* 613-741-9388
ted.gibson@sympatico.ca

Ottawa: **Corporated Communications Limited - *1**
#202, 335 Maclaren St., Ottawa, ON K2P 0M5
Tel: 613-324-2928; *Fax:* 613-235-9694
rfrelich.ccl@cclgroup.ca

Ottawa: **Crestview Public Affairs Inc. - *1**
#1510, 85 Albert St., Ottawa, ON K1P 6A4
Tel: 613-232-0462
peter.naglik@crestviewpublicaffairs.com

Ottawa: **DAI Inc. - *1**
#300, 67A Sparks St., Ottawa, ON K1P 5A5
Tel: 613-238-6317; *Fax:* 613-238-0007
ataylor@daigroup.ca

Ottawa: **Deloitte & Touche - *2**
100 Queen St., Ottawa, ON K1P 5T8
Tel: 613-751-5242; *Fax:* 613-236-2328
ruroberts@deloitte.ca

Ottawa: **T.M. Denton Consultants - *1**
37 Heney St., Ottawa, ON K1N 5V6
Tel: 613-789-5397; *Fax:* 613-789-5398
tmdenton@ftn.net

Ottawa: **Dickie & Lyman Lawyers LLP - *2**
#440, 55 Metcalfe St., Ottawa, ON K1P 6L5
Tel: 613-235-0101; *Fax:* 613-238-0101
jcarter@dickieandlyman.com

Ottawa: **DioGuardi Tax Law - *3**
#600, 100 Gloucester St., Ottawa, ON K2P 0A4
Tel: 613-237-2222; *Fax:* 613-237-9463
Toll-Free: 877-829-7902
pd@dioguarditaxlaw.com
www.taxrx.ca

Ottawa: **Doucet McBride LLP - *12**
#100, 85 Plymouth St., Ottawa, ON K1S 3E2
Tel: 613-233-4474; *Fax:* 613-233-8868
lawyers@doucetmcbride.com
www.doucetmcbride.com

Ottawa: **Fred Doucet Consulting International Inc. (FDCI) - *3**
#372, 440 Laurier Ave. West, Ottawa, ON K1R 7X6
Tel: 613-782-2217; *Fax:* 613-782-2221
fdoucet@rogers.com

Ottawa: **Doyle Salewski Inc. - *2**
404 Bank St., Ottawa, ON K2P 1Y5
Tel: 613-569-4444; *Fax:* 613-569-1116

Ottawa: **Drache LLP - *5**
222 Somerset St. West, Ottawa, ON K2P 2G3
Tel: 613-233-2675; *Fax:* 613-233-6752

Ottawa: **Dubuc/Osland - *3**
#706, 350 Sparks St., Ottawa, ON K1R 7S8
Tel: 613-236-3360; *Fax:* 613-236-3771

Ottawa: **Daniel F. Dunlap - *1**
#5, 371A Richmond Rd., Ottawa, ON K2A 0E7
Tel: 613-722-7788; *Fax:* 613-722-8909
ddunlap@dunlaplaw.ca

Ottawa: **Earnscliffe Strategy Group Inc. - *6**
#300, 46 Elgin St., Ottawa, ON K1P 5K6
Tel: 613-563-4455; *Fax:* 613-236-6173

Ottawa: **Michael D. Edelson & Associates - *5**
#600, 200 Elgin St., Ottawa, ON K2P 1L5
Tel: 613-237-2290; *Fax:* 613-237-0071
mail@edelsonlaw.ca
www.edelsonlaw.ca

Ottawa: **J.J. Mark Edwards - *1**
96 Helena St., Ottawa, ON K1Y 3N1
Tel: 613-722-2613; *Fax:* 613-722-9484
medwards@edwardslaw.ca

** indicates number of lawyers*

Ottawa: Emond Harnden - *25
707 Bank St., Ottawa, ON K1S 3V1
Tel: 613-563-7660; Fax: 613-563-8001
Toll-Free: 888-563-7660
info@ehlaw.ca
www.ehlaw.ca

Ottawa: Bruce Engel Barrister & Solicitor - *2
70 Gloucester St., 1st Fl., Ottawa, ON K2P 0A2
Tel: 613-235-6324; Fax: 613-235-7442
bruce.engel@rogers.com

Ottawa: Everson Public Affairs - *1
13 Morris St., Ottawa, ON K1S 4A6
Tel: 613-233-0573; Fax: 613-233-3655
sexton@sympatico.ca

Ottawa: Fanaian's Law Office - *1
30 States Way, Ottawa, ON K2P 0Z6
Tel: 613-567-0833
fanaian@hotmail.com

Ottawa: Farber & Robillard - *2
330 Churchill Ave. North, Ottawa, ON K1Z 5B9
Tel: 613-722-9418; Fax: 613-722-5981

Ottawa: Pablo G.A. Fernandez-Davila - *1
162 Laurier Ave. West, Ottawa, ON K1P 5J4
Tel: 613-565-8686; Fax: 613-565-8989
info@fernandez-davila.com

Ottawa: Finlayson & Singlehurst - *3
70 Gloucester St., 4th Fl., Ottawa, ON K2P 0A2
Tel: 613-232-0227; Fax: 613-232-0542
fands@attglobal.net

Ottawa: Ann L. Flint - *1
#203, 190 Somerset St. West, Ottawa, ON K2P 0J4
Tel: 613-594-5461; Fax: 613-594-5468

Ottawa: George Flumian - *1
222 Argyle Ave., Ottawa, ON K2P 1B9
Tel: 613-236-8321; Fax: 613-230-6597

Ottawa: Fortey & Arbique - *2
#210, 1335 Carling Ave., Ottawa, ON K1Z 8N8
Tel: 613-725-0303; Fax: 613-725-1292
info@forteyarbique.com

Ottawa: Francopol Inc. - *1
1364 Ogden St., Ottawa, ON K1J 8C4
Tel: 613-796-5363; Fax: 613-235-2323
jctrottier@francopol.ca

Ottawa: Steven A. Fried - *1
303 Waverly St., Ottawa, ON K2P 0V9
Tel: 613-233-4420; Fax: 613-288-1554
sfried@stevenfried.com

Ottawa: Susan Gahrns Law Office - *1
116 Lisgar St., 6th Fl., Ottawa, ON K2P 0C2
Tel: 613-235-6299; Fax: 613-235-4704
law@gahrns.com

Ottawa: Goldberg Wiseman Stroud & Hollingsworth LLP, Barristers & Solicitors - *4
486 Gladstone Ave., Ottawa, ON K1R 5N8
Tel: 613-237-4922; Fax: 613-237-2920
info@gwshlaw.com
www.gsklaw.com

Ottawa: Donald R. Good - *2
Merivale Depot, P.O. Box 5118, Ottawa, ON K2C 3H4
Tel: 613-228-9676; Fax: 613-228-7404
Toll-Free: 800-661-8837
farmlaw@on.aibn.com

Ottawa: Donald J. Gormley - *1
#204, 190 Somerset St. West, Ottawa, ON K2P 0J4
Tel: 613-237-7726; Fax: 613-237-1977
donald.gormley@sympatico.ca

Ottawa: Goss, McCorriston, Stel - *3
#203, 2430 Bank St., Ottawa, ON K1V 0T7
Tel: 613-738-0023; Fax: 613-738-1294

Ottawa: Government Policy Research Associates Inc. - *1
#107, 408 Queen St., Ottawa, ON K1R 5A7
Tel: 613-235-5360; Fax: 613-235-5866

Ottawa: Government Strategies Corp. (GSC) - *1
#200, 134 Sparks St., Ottawa, ON K1P 5B6
Tel: 613-230-6311; Fax: 613-230-1258

Ottawa: Mary Granskou Consulting - *1
101 Clearview Ave., Ottawa, ON K1Y 2L1
Tel: 613-722-6800
granskou@magma.ca

Ottawa: Grant & Dawn - *4
226 MacLaren St., Ottawa, ON K2P 0L6
Tel: 613-235-2212; Fax: 613-235-5294

Ottawa: Geoffrey Grenville-Wood - *1
43 Florence St., Ottawa, ON K2P 0W6
Tel: 613-232-2688; Fax: 613-232-2680
geoffrey@grenvillewood.com

Ottawa: Grey, Clark, Shih & Associates Ltd. - *3
#901, 100 Sparks St., Ottawa, ON K1P 5B7
Tel: 613-238-7743; Fax: 613-238-0368

Ottawa: Gribbis Enterprises Ltd. - *1
20 Ellisson Way, Ottawa, ON K1G 4P6
Tel: 613-738-1632; Fax: 613-248-0110
jim.gribben@sympatico.ca

Ottawa: GS Government Consulting Services - *1
26 Maple Stand Way, Ottawa, ON K2G 6P4
Tel: 613-823-8079; Fax: 613-825-8592
gshields@magma.ca

Ottawa: David R. Habib - *1
18 Honeyood Ct., Ottawa, ON K1V 1Y4
Tel: 613-822-4100; Fax: 613-822-1698
habiblaw@rogers.com

Ottawa: John H. Hale Barrister & Solicitor
#203, 185 Somerset St., Ottawa, ON K2P 0J2
Tel: 613-230-4253; Fax: 613-230-6996

Ottawa: Brendan Hawley & Associates - *1
29 Taj Ct., Ottawa, ON K1G 5K7
brendan.hawley@sympatico.ca

Ottawa: Hewitt, Hewitt, Nesbitt, Reid - *7
#604, Fuller Bldg., 75 Albert St., Ottawa, ON K1P 5E7
Tel: 613-563-0202; Fax: 613-563-0445
info@hewitts-law.com

Ottawa: High Park Group - *1
#421, 130 Albert St., Ottawa, ON K1G 5P4
Tel: 613-234-3039
pnaglik@highparkgroup.com

Ottawa: Hillwatch Inc.
#200, 334 Maclaren St., Ottawa, ON K2P 0M6
Tel: 613-238-8700; Fax: 613-234-9823
admin@hillwatch.com
www.hillwatch.com

Ottawa: Susan Hodgson - *1
#307, 150 Isabella St., Ottawa, ON K1S 1V7
Tel: 613-237-0505; Fax: 613-567-3559
susan@hodgsonlaw.ca

Ottawa: Honey/MacMillan - *3
146 Richmond Rd., Ottawa, ON K1Z 6W2
Tel: 613-722-2493; Fax: 613-722-2773
honeymac@rogers.com

Ottawa: Humphreys Public Affairs Group Inc. - *2
#1620, 130 Albert St., Ottawa, ON K1P 5G4
Tel: 613-230-3155; Fax: 613-236-2556

Ottawa: ICG Defence Consultants Inc.
275 Slater St., Ottawa, ON K1P 5H9
Tel: 613-233-0848

Ottawa: Impact Public Affairs - *4
#910, 50 O'Connor St., Ottawa, ON K1P 6L2
Tel: 613-233-8906; Fax: 613-230-2669

Ottawa: Industry Government Relations Group (IGRG) - *4
#1502, 85 Albert St., Ottawa, ON K1P 6A4
Tel: 613-232-1421; Fax: 613-232-9554

Ottawa: Inter/Sect Alliance Inc. - *1
#100, 408 Queen St., Ottawa, ON K1R 5A7
Tel: 613-235-5385; Fax: 613-235-5866
isa@intersectalliance.ca

Ottawa: Intervistas Consulting Inc. - *1
#901, 50 O'Connor St., Ottawa, ON K1P 6L2
Tel: 613-783-3448; Fax: 613-782-2428
sam_barone@intervistas.com

Ottawa: Irh & Associates - *1
2388 Wyndale Cres., Ottawa, ON K1H 7A6
Tel: 613-737-4636; Fax: 613-233-9527
lhuneault@livingstonintl.com

Ottawa: Don Jarvis Consultants - *1
#202, 408 Queen St., Ottawa, ON K1R 5A7
Tel: 613-238-7809; Fax: 613-235-5866
djc@intersectalliance.ca

Ottawa: Karam Greenspon - *4
301 Elgin St., Ottawa, ON K2P 2N9
Tel: 613-232-9911; Fax: 613-232-5979

Ottawa: Kelly Santini LLP - *12
#2300, 66 Slater St., Ottawa, ON K1P 5H1
Tel: 613-238-6321; Fax: 613-233-4553

Ottawa: J.K. Kerr, Q.C. - *1
#404, 71 Bank St., Ottawa, ON K1P 5N2
Tel: 613-232-7902; Fax: 613-563-8067

Ottawa: Kiedrowski & Associates - *1
74 Iona St., Ottawa, ON K1Y 3L8
Tel: 613-724-3857; Fax: 613-724-3891
john.kiedrowski@sympatico.ca

Ottawa: KPMG - *1
#2000, 160 Elgin St., Ottawa, ON K2P 2P8
Tel: 613-212-2832; Fax: 613-212-2896
www.kpmg.ca

Ottawa: Laird, Sheena - *2
#110, 261 Cooper St., Ottawa, ON K2P 0G3
Tel: 613-232-3575; Fax: 613-232-6622
asselin7@bellnet.ca
www.asselinlaird.com

Ottawa: Langevin Morris LLP - *14
190 O'Connor St., 9th Fl., Ottawa, ON K2P 2R3
Tel: 613-230-5787; Fax: 613-230-8563
general@langevinmorris.com
www.langevinmorris.com

Ottawa: Laveaux, Franck
#215, 1725 St-Laurent Blvd., Ottawa, ON K1G 3V4
Tel: 613-523-0307; Fax: 613-523-0377
lex@laveaux.com
www.laveaux.com

Ottawa: LDL International Inc. - *1
#203, 320 Crichton St., Ottawa, ON K1M 1W5
Tel: 613-746-6273; Fax: 613-746-1338
ldlintl@sympatico.ca

Ottawa: Leadmark Consulting Group - *1
#1300, 155 Queen St., Ottawa, ON K1P 6L1
Tel: 613-232-2400; Fax: 613-232-2404
pauladdy@leadmarkconsulting.com

Ottawa: Louise M.S. LeBlanc - *1
29 Terrace Dr., Ottawa, ON K2H 9N3
Tel: 613-596-4256; Fax: 613-596-4235
lmsleblanc@sympatico.ca

Ottawa: Lois M. Leslie - *1
233 Bradford St., Ottawa, ON K2B 5Z5
Tel: 613-829-0108

Ottawa: Lightstone, Lyon
#420, 875 Carling Ave., Ottawa, ON K1S 5P1
Tel: 613-729-2460; Fax: 613-729-1710
lyon@lightcall.ca

Ottawa: Logres - *1
#11, 244 Charlotte St., Ottawa, ON K1N 8L3
Tel: 613-851-1712
cbyers@logresconsulting.com

Ottawa: Low, Murchison, LLP - *17
#200, 441 Maclaren St., Ottawa, ON K2P 2H3
Tel: 613-236-9442; Fax: 613-236-7942
lawyer@lowmurchison.com
www.lowmurchison.com

Ottawa: Macdonald, Affleck - *2
#104, 169 Lisgar St., Ottawa, ON K2P 0C3
Tel: 613-236-8712; Fax: 613-236-5145

Ottawa: MacKay & Sanderson - *2
#201, 1580 Merivale Rd., Ottawa, ON K2G 4B5
Tel: 613-238-6180; Fax: 613-238-3288

Ottawa: MacKinnon & Phillips - *8
#802, 200 Elgin St., Ottawa, ON K2P 1L5
Tel: 613-236-0662; Fax: 613-236-8906

* indicates number of lawyers

Ottawa: Maclaren, Corlett - *8
#1625, 50 O'Connor St., Ottawa, ON K1P 6L2
Tel: 613-233-1146; *Fax*: 613-233-7190
mail@macorlaw.com
www.macorlaw.com

Ottawa: G. Carey MacLellan - *1
#1, 200 Cooper St., Ottawa, ON K2P 0G1
Tel: 613-232-9364; *Fax*: 613-230-3551

Ottawa: Carol Macleod & Associates Inc. - *1
#5, 156 St. Patrick St., Ottawa, ON K1N 5J8
Tel: 613-562-3938; *Fax*: 613-562-3865
contact@carolmacleod.com

Ottawa: Mann & Partners LLP - *10
#612, 1600 Scott St., Ottawa, ON K1Y 4N7
Tel: 613-722-1500; *Fax*: 613-722-7677
www.mannlawyers.com

Ottawa: Howard Mann - *1
424 Hamilton Ave. South, Ottawa, ON K1Y 1E3
Tél: 613-729-0621; *Téléc*: 613-729-0306
hmann@ottawa.net

Ottawa: Marcus McNamara & Wilson - *4
#305, 185 Somerset St. West, Ottawa, ON K2P 0J2
Tel: 613-233-4083; *Fax*: 613-233-3132
marpar@sympatico.ca

Ottawa: Marks & Marks LLP - *1
#201, 190 Somerset St. West, Ottawa, ON K2P 0J4
Tel: 613-230-2123; *Fax*: 613-230-5707

Ottawa: Leonard Max, Q.C.
#201, 357 Preston St., Ottawa, ON K1S 4M8
Tel: 613-269-3872; *Fax*: 613-269-3581

Ottawa: Sean J. May - *1
#309, 185 Somerset St. West, Ottawa, ON K2P 0J2
Tel: 613-230-6524; *Fax*: 613-230-2705
smay@mayandkonyer.com

Ottawa: Mazerolle & Lemay - *6
#202, 1173 Cyrville Rd., Ottawa, ON K1J 7S6
Tel: 613-746-5700; *Fax*: 613-746-1783
www.mazerollelemay.com

Ottawa: MBM Intellectual Property Law LLP
270 Albert St., 14th Fl., Ottawa, ON K1P 5G8
Tel: 613-567-0762; *Fax*: 613-563-7671
mbm@mbm.com
www.mbm.com

Ottawa: McCann Law Offices - *4
#605, 200 Elgin St., Ottawa, ON K2P 1L5
Tel: 613-236-1410; *Fax*: 613-563-1367

Ottawa: McCloskey McCloskey - *2
#202, 5307 Canotek Rd., Ottawa, ON K1J 9M2
Tel: 613-745-0395; *Fax*: 613-745-8007
law@mccloskey.net

Ottawa: McDonald & Quinn - *1
#1, 1480 Woodward Ave., Ottawa, ON K1Z 7W6
Tel: 613-729-1005; *Fax*: 613-729-1176

Ottawa: McFadden, Fincham - *4
#606, 225 Metcalfe St., Ottawa, ON K2P 1P9
Tel: 613-234-1907; *Fax*: 613-234-5233
mail@mcfaddenfincham.com
www.mcfaddenfincham.com

Ottawa: McGuinty Law Offices Professional Corporation - *3
1192 Rockingham Ave., Ottawa, ON K1H 8A7
Tel: 613-526-3858; *Fax*: 613-526-3187
reception@mcguintylaw.ca
www.mcguintylaw.com

Ottawa: Gordon C. McKechnie - *2
c/o Canadian Bank Note Company, 145 Richmond Rd., Ottawa, ON K1Z 1A1
Tel: 613-722-3421; *Fax*: 613-722-3334

Ottawa: McLaughlin-Moses Strategic Advisory Services - *1
#310, 81 Metcalfe St., Ottawa, ON K1P 6K7
Tel: 416-721-7401
rmclaughlin@chapmaninc.ca

Ottawa: Robert F. Meagher - *1
#502, 66 Slater St., Ottawa, ON K1P 5H1
Tel: 613-563-4278; *Fax*: 613-232-7322

Ottawa: Menzies & Coulson - *7
111 Sherwood Dr., Ottawa, ON K1Y 3V1
Tel: 613-722-1313; *Fax*: 613-722-4712
Toll-Free: 888-722-1313
menzies@menziescoulson.com

Ottawa: John E. Merner - *3
136 Lewis St., Ottawa, ON K2P 0S7
Tel: 613-567-6093; *Fax*: 613-567-7164

Ottawa: Merovitz Potechin LLP - *8
#301, 200 Catherine St., Ottawa, ON K2P 2K9
Tel: 613-563-7544; *Fax*: 613-563-4577
mplaw@mpottawa.com

Ottawa: Mile26 Strategy - *1
#A, 40 Clarendon Ave., Ottawa, ON K1Y 0P2
Tel: 613-878-6784
carlaventin@hotmail.com

Ottawa: Eric A. Milligan - *1
#400, 45 Rideau St., Ottawa, ON K1N 5W8
Tel: 613-562-4077; *Fax*: 613-562-4102
milligan@delsysresearch.com

Ottawa: Miltons IP Professional Corporation - *6
#700, 225 Metcalfe St., Ottawa, ON K2P 1P9
Tel: 613-567-7824; *Fax*: 613-567-4689
Toll-Free: 866-297-1179
info@miltonsip.com
www.miltonsip.com

Ottawa: Richard Minard - *1
58 Clegg St., Ottawa, ON K1S 0H8
Tel: 613-237-6874; *Fax*: 613-234-1728
rminard@on.aibn.com

Ottawa: Mirsky, Pascoe - *3
#300, 39 Robertson Rd., Ottawa, ON K2H 8R2
Tel: 613-828-2120; *Fax*: 613-596-0881

Ottawa: MM Inc. - *1
#310, 81 Metcalfe St., Ottawa, ON K1P 6K7
Tel: 416-300-1322
judithmoses@rogers.com

Ottawa: Moffat & Co., Macera & Jarzyna - *24
Stn. D, 427 Laurier Ave. West, 12th Fl., Ottawa, ON K1R 7Y2
Tel: 613-238-8173; *Fax*: 613-235-2508
mail@macerajarzyna.com
www.macerajarzyna.com

Ottawa: Monachus Consulting - *1
19 Elm St., Ottawa, ON K1R 6M9
Tel: 613-233-7175; *Fax*: 613-563-9277
afchambers@monachus.com

Ottawa: Christopher A. Moore Professional Corporation - *1
63 Robert St., Ottawa, ON K2P 1G5
Tel: 613-230-9448; *Fax*: 613-230-3624
chalmo@istar.ca

Ottawa: More & McLeod - *1
#212, 2249 Carling Ave., Ottawa, ON K2B 7E9
Tel: 613-820-7888; *Fax*: 613-820-3044
morelaw@bellnet.ca

Ottawa: Mount Clark Yemensky - *3
#208, 1400 Clyde Ave., Ottawa, ON K2G 3J2
Tel: 613-226-8817; *Fax*: 613-224-8943

Ottawa: Kevin Murphy - *1
#500, 200 Elgin St., Ottawa, ON K2P 1L5
Tel: 613-567-8248; *Fax*: 613-236-6958

Ottawa: Robert Elmo Murray - *1
5 Kitimat Cres., Ottawa, ON K2H 7G4
Tel: 613-829-6773; *Fax*: 613-567-3559

Ottawa: S.A. Murray Consulting Inc. (SAMCI) - *2
336 MacLean St., Ottawa, ON K2P 0M6
Tel: 613-236-3383; *Fax*: 613-236-4184

Ottawa: Kenneth J. Naftel - *1
#307, 150 Isabella St., Ottawa, ON K1S 1V7
Tel: 613-237-0505; *Fax*: 613-567-3559
ken@kennaftel.ca

Ottawa: Nelligan O'Brien Payne - *42
#1500, 50 O'Connor, Ottawa, ON K1P 6L2
Tel: 613-238-8080; *Fax*: 613-238-2098
info@nelligan.ca
www.nelligan.ca

Ottawa: Nicol & Lazier - *2
#400, 331 Cooper St., Ottawa, ON K2P 0G5
Tel: 613-232-4241; *Fax*: 613-236-9325

Ottawa: Niebergall & Grabowski - *2
#200, 200 Elgin St., Ottawa, ON K2P 1L5
Tel: 613-232-8508; *Fax*: 613-232-9654
paulniebergall@rogers.com

Ottawa: Wanda Noel Barrister & Solicitor - *1
171 Lanark Ave., Ottawa, ON K1Z 1C1
Tel: 613-729-6322; *Fax*: 613-729-7441
wanda.noel@sympatico.ca

Ottawa: Claire B. O'Connor - *1
#101, 745B Montréal Rd., Ottawa, ON K1K 0T1
Tel: 613-745-9446; *Fax*: 613-745-0800
cboc@bellnet.ca

Ottawa: Michael B. Oliveira - *1
#402, 280 Metcalfe St., Ottawa, ON K2P 1R7
Tel: 613-567-1016; *Fax*: 613-567-9126
moliveira@sprint.ca

Ottawa: Eugene L. Oscapella - *1
70 MacDonald St., Ottawa, ON K2P 1H6
Tel: 613-238-5909; *Fax*: 613-238-2891
eugene@oscapella.ca

Ottawa: Joy C. Overtveld - *1
284 Wellington St., Ottawa, ON K1A 0H8
Tel: 613-941-6805; *Fax*: 613-957-4019
overtvel@magma.ca
www.magma.ca/~overtvel/

Ottawa: P3 Collaborations - *1
36 Sai Cres., Ottawa, ON K1G 5N8
Tel: 613-739-9971
bcavan@p3collaborations.com

Ottawa: Paradis, Jones, Horwitz, Bowles Associates - *4
#900, 200 Elgin St., Ottawa, ON K2P 1L5
Tel: 613-238-5074; *Fax*: 613-230-3250

Ottawa: Parallax Public Affairs Inc. - *1
#1110, 130 Albert St., Ottawa, ON K1P 5G4
Tel: 613-230-5939; *Fax*: 613-232-7148

Ottawa: Parent, Carr - *2
116 Lisgar St. 6th Fl., Ottawa, ON K2P 0C2
Tel: 613-567-1431; *Fax*: 613-567-1433

Ottawa: Parliamentary Group/Groupe Parlementaire - *3
#400, 200 Elgin St., Ottawa, ON K2P 1L5
Tel: 613-860-0043
patrick.gagnon@parlgroup.com

Ottawa: Margaret J. Parlor - *1
307 Greenview Ave., Ottawa, ON K2B 6A8
Tel: 613-828-3726

Ottawa: Francis K. Peddle - *1
168 Henderson Ave., Ottawa, ON K1N 7P6
Tel: 613-232-1740; *Fax*: 613-232-0407
ftpeddle@bellnet.ca

Ottawa: Kimberley A. Pegg - *3
#1, 200 Cooper St., Ottawa, ON K2P 0G1
Tel: 613-232-9331; *Fax*: 613-230-3551

Ottawa: Stephen M. Pender - *2
116 Lisgar St., Ottawa, ON K2P 0C2
Tel: 613-569-0104; *Fax*: 613-235-4704
pender-leef@on.aibn.com

Ottawa: Perley-Robertson, Hill & McDougall LLP - *36
#1400, 340 Albert St., Ottawa, ON K1R 0A5
Tel: 613-238-2022; *Fax*: 613-238-8775
Toll-Free: 800-268-8292
lawyers@perlaw.ca
www.perlaw.ca

Ottawa: Pfeiffer & Associates - *1
157 McLeod St., Ottawa, ON K2P 0Z6
Tel: 613-238-4115; *Fax*: 613-563-8273
amy@pfeifferlaw.ca
www.pfeifferlaw.ca

Ottawa: Piazza, Brooks - *2
#202, 309 Cooper St., Ottawa, ON K2P 0G5
Tel: 613-238-2244; *Fax*: 613-238-3382
ph@piazzalaw.com

** indicates number of lawyers*

***Ottawa*: Pinnacle Public Affairs - *1**
#1203, 275 Slater St., Ottawa, ON K1P 5H9
Tel: 613-594-8484
titch@pinnaclepublicaffairs.com

***Ottawa*: Plant Quinn Thiele - *7**
#700, 200 Elgin St., Ottawa, ON K2P 1L5
Tel: 613-563-1131; *Fax:* 613-230-8297
mquinn@pqtlaw.com
www.pqtlaw.com

***Ottawa*: Plaskacz & Associates - *1**
114 Crichton St., Ottawa, ON K1M 1V9
Tel: 613-244-6084
plaskacz@plaskacz.com
www.plaskacz.com

***Ottawa*: Policy Insights Inc. - *3**
#402, 222 Queen St., Ottawa, ON K1P 5V9
Tel: 613-563-8078; *Fax:* 613-563-4284
info@policyinsights.com
www.policyinsights.com

***Ottawa*: Denis J. A. Pommainville - *1**
302 St. Patrick St., Ottawa, ON K1N 5K5
Tel: 613-241-7335; *Fax:* 613-241-5012
pommainville@bellnet.ca

***Ottawa*: Protocol Plus Inc. - *1**
10 Allendale Private, Ottawa, ON K2P 2G3
Tel: 613-795-4254
raj@pearson-shoyama.ca

***Ottawa*: Prystupa Law Office - *2**
#203, 1419 Carling Ave., Ottawa, ON K1Z 7L6
Tel: 613-729-4669; *Fax:* 613-729-7768
admin@prystupalaw.ca
www.prystupalaw.ca

***Ottawa*: Public Affairs Counsel - *1**
177 Powell Ave., Ottawa, ON K1S 2A2
Tel: 613-292-0326; *Fax:* 613-235-9790
isabel.metcalfe@sympatico.ca

***Ottawa*: Public Affairs Strategy Group - *3**
#406, 350 Sparks St., Ottawa, ON K1R 7S8
Tel: 613-594-0202; *Fax:* 613-233-5880
info@pasq.net
www.delta-media.com/meet/pasg-e.html

***Ottawa*: Public Knowledge Canada - *1**
855 Explorer Lane, Ottawa, ON K1C 2S3
Tel: 613-834-8403
garth.williams@publicknowledge.ca

***Ottawa*: Helene Bruce Puccini - *1**
#307, 150 Isabella St., Ottawa, ON K1S 1V7
Tel: 613-230-6295; *Fax:* 613-567-3559
helene@puccini.ca

***Ottawa*: PvF Consulting - *1**
176 Holmwood Ave., Ottawa, ON K1S 2P4
Tel: 613-233-1633; *Fax:* 613-233-3889
phil@pvfconsulting.com

***Ottawa*: Radnoff, Pearl LLP - *12**
100 Gloucester St., Ottawa, ON K2P 0A4
Tel: 613-594-8844; *Fax:* 613-594-9092
www.radnoffpearl.com

***Ottawa*: Ranger & Associés - *1**
#1000, 141 Laurier Ave. West, Ottawa, ON K1P 5J3
Tel: 613-234-2255; *Fax:* 613-234-2301

***Ottawa*: Rasmussen Starr Ruddy LLP - *11**
#660, 660 Carling Ave., Ottawa, ON K1Z 1G3
Tel: 613-232-1830; *Fax:* 613-232-2499
mail@rsrlaw.ca
www.rsrlaw.ca

***Ottawa*: Raven, Cameron, Ballantyne, Yazbeck LLP - *10**
1600 - 220 Laurier Ave. West, Ottawa, ON K1P 5Z9
Tel: 613-567-2901; *Fax:* 613-567-2921
info@ravenlaw.com
www.ravenlaw.com

***Ottawa*: Rawson Group Initiatives Inc. - *2**
#300, 222 Argyle Ave., Ottawa, ON K2P 1B9
Tel: 613-236-7960; *Fax:* 613-230-6597

***Ottawa*: Karen Ann Reid - *1**
#503, 200 Elgin St., Ottawa, ON K2P 1L5
Tel: 613-238-8777; *Fax:* 613-238-4824
kareid@istop.com

***Ottawa*: Rick & Associates - *3**
#109, 591 March Rd., Ottawa, ON K2K 2M5
Tel: 613-592-0088; *Fax:* 613-592-3322
info@rickassociates.com
www.rickassociates.com

***Ottawa*: Frank I. Ritchie - *1**
2253 Alta Vista Dr., Ottawa, ON K1H 7L9
Tel: 613-731-8288

***Ottawa*: Larry A. Roine - *1**
#200, 2650 Queensview Dr., Ottawa, ON K2B 8H6
Tel: 613-820-8888; *Fax:* 613-820-8818

***Ottawa*: Terrence M. Romanow - *1**
2038 Black Friars Rd., Ottawa, ON K2A 3K8
Tel: 613-722-8224; *Fax:* 613-722-0908

***Ottawa*: Rothwell Group Inc. - *3**
#820, 45 O'Connor St., Ottawa, ON K1P 1A4
Tel: 613-567-6775; *Fax:* 613-567-6803

***Ottawa*: Ryk Oliver Corporation - *1**
1130 Castle Hill Cres., Ottawa, ON K2C 2A8
Tel: 613-723-2816; *Fax:* 613-723-5525
vaneyk@rogers.com

***Ottawa*: Suzanne Sabourin - *1**
1633 Schouten Dr., Ottawa, ON K1E 2H9
Tel: 613-837-8546
suzannesabourin_220@hotmail.com

***Ottawa*: Sack Goldblatt Mitchell - *5**
#500, 30 Metcalfe St., Ottawa, ON K1P 5L4
Tel: 613-235-5327; *Fax:* 613-235-3041
mailbox@eglaw.com
www.sgmlaw.com

***Ottawa*: Macey Schwartz - *1**
#1006, 75 Albert St., Ottawa, ON K1P 5E7
Tel: 613-236-1872; *Fax:* 613-236-8639
macey@bellnet.ca

***Ottawa*: Scott & Coulson - *2**
#420, 1335 Carling Ave., Ottawa, ON K1Z 8N8
Tel: 613-725-3723; *Fax:* 613-729-8613

***Ottawa*: Segal, Talarico, Habib, Molot LLP - *6**
#200, 2650 Queensview Dr., Ottawa, ON K2B 8H6
Tel: 613-820-8888; *Fax:* 613-820-8818
www.legal-team.com

***Ottawa*: Sevigny Law Office - *2**
#1620, 344 Slater St., Ottawa, ON K1R 7Y3
Tel: 613-751-4459; *Fax:* 613-751-4471
info@sevignylaw.com

***Ottawa*: Shapiro, Cohen - *6**
P.O. Box 3440, Stn. D, 112 Kent St., Ottawa, ON K1P 6P1
Tel: 613-232-5300; *Fax:* 613-563-9231
Toll-Free: 800-563-9390

***Ottawa*: Sheppard & Claude - *2**
#200, 745A Montreal Rd., Ottawa, ON K1K 0T1
Tel: 613-748-3333; *Fax:* 613-748-1599
aclaude@sheppardclaude.ca

***Ottawa*: Shields & Hunt - *6**
68 Chamberlain Ave., Ottawa, ON K1S 1V9
Tel: 613-230-3232; *Fax:* 613-230-1664
gjones@shields-hunt.com
www.shields-hunt.com

***Ottawa*: Paula M. Smith - *1**
450 Laurier Ave. East, Ottawa, ON K1N 6R3
Tel: 613-565-0490

***Ottawa*: Soloway, Wright LLP - *21**
#900, 427 Laurier Ave. West, Ottawa, ON K1R 7Y2
Tel: 613-236-0111; *Fax:* 613-238-8507
Toll-Free: 800-207-5880
info@solowaywright.com
www.solowaywright.com

***Ottawa*: Wayne A. Stacey & Associates Ltd. - *1**
2145 Hubbard Cres., Ottawa, ON K1J 6L3
Tel: 613-745-9151
wstacey@stacey.ca

***Ottawa*: Steinberg Thompson d'Artois Rockman Summers - *5**
#1000, 150 Metcalfe St., Ottawa, ON K2P 1P1
Tel: 613-594-5996; *Fax:* 613-230-4161

***Ottawa*: Stewart/Associates - *2**
#402, 200 Elgin St., Ottawa, ON K2P 1L5
Tel: 613-235-0453; *Fax:* 613-235-3304
stewartasso@travel-net.com

***Ottawa*: Jennifer A. Stiell - *1**
#307, 150 Isabella St., Ottawa, ON K1S 1V7
Tel: 613-237-0505; *Fax:* 613-567-3559
jstiell@cyberus.ca

***Ottawa*: Strategex Consultants Inc. - *1**
#211, 24 York St., Ottawa, ON K1N 1K2
Tel: 613-562-3686; *Fax:* 613-562-3688

***Ottawa*: Strategic Partners Group - *1**
#420, 1145 Hunt Club Rd., Ottawa, ON K1V 0Y3
Tel: 613-249-0611; *Fax:* 613-249-0421
mcuconato@rogers.blackberry.net

***Ottawa*: The Strategy Project - *1**
38 Melgund Ave., Ottawa, ON K1S 2S2
Tel: 613-567-9592; *Fax:* 613-567-9561
jim@strategyproject.ca

***Ottawa*: StrategyCorp Ottawa Inc. - *4**
#550, 100 Queen St., Ottawa, ON K1P 1J9
Tel: 613-231-2630; *Fax:* 613-231-4113
marsha@strategycorp.com

***Ottawa*: Summa Strategies Canada Inc. - *11**
#1000, 100 Sparks St., Ottawa, ON K1P 5B7
Tel: 613-235-1400; *Fax:* 613-235-1444
www.summa.ca

***Ottawa*: Anna E. Sundin - *1**
276 Sunnyside Ave., Ottawa, ON K1S 0R8
Tel: 613-445-3183; *Fax:* 613-730-7484
asundin@storm.ca

***Ottawa*: Sussex Strategy Group - *1**
#200, 440 Laurier West, Ottawa, ON K1R 7X6
Tel: 613-782-2320; *Fax:* 613-782-2228
fiacono@sussex-strategy.com
www.sussex-strategy.com

***Ottawa*: Michael W. Swinwood - *1**
346 Waverly Street, Ottawa, ON KP2 0W5
Tel: 613-563-7474; *Fax:* 613-256-8115
shagar@cyberus.ca

***Ottawa*: Tactix Government Consulting Inc. - *7**
#880, 45 O'Connor St., Ottawa, ON K1P 1A4
Tel: 613-566-7053; *Fax:* 613-566-2026
www.tactix.ca

***Ottawa*: Christopher C.C. Tan - *1**
70 Gloucester St., Ottawa, ON K2P 0A2
Tel: 613-235-2308; *Fax:* 613-235-6933

***Ottawa*: Temple Scott Associates Inc. - *2**
#201, 8 York St., Ottawa, ON K1N 5S6
Tel: 613-241-6000; *Fax:* 613-241-6001
www.tsa.ca

***Ottawa*: Thomas & Partners - *3**
#360, 30 Metcalfe St., Ottawa, ON K1P 5L4
Tel: 613-232-7522; *Fax:* 613-232-7525
ottawa@thomasandpartners.com
www.thomasandpartners.com

***Ottawa*: Tierney Stauffer - *11**
#510, 1600 Carling Ave., Ottawa, ON K1Z 0A1
Tel: 613-728-8057; *Fax:* 613-728-9866
www.tierneystauffer.com

***Ottawa*: TL Maville & Associates Inc. - *1**
P.O. Box 5011, Ottawa, ON K2C 3H3
Tel: 613-727-0533; *Fax:* 613-727-1556
tom.maville@sympatico.ca

***Ottawa*: Tunney, McMurray - *2**
#806, 200 Elgin St., Ottawa, ON K2P 1L5
Tel: 613-235-5660; *Fax:* 613-235-0805
tmbarry@rogers.com

***Ottawa*: Gilad Vered - *1**
1801 Woodward Dr., Ottawa, ON K2C 0R3
Tel: 613-226-2000; *Fax:* 613-225-0391
gvered@arnon.ca

***Ottawa*: Victor Ages Vallance LLP, Barristers & Solicitors - *8**
112 Lisgar St., Ottawa, ON K2P 0C2
Tel: 613-238-1333; *Fax:* 613-238-8949
rfurtado@vavlawyers.com
www.vavlawyers.com

** indicates number of lawyers*

***Ottawa*: Vincent Dagenais Gibson LLP/S.R.L. - *11**
#600, 325 Dalhousie St., Ottawa, ON K1N 7G2
Tel: 613-241-2701; *Fax:* 613-241-2599
susan.emmett@vdgjustice.ca

***Ottawa*: Ian H. Warren - *1**
#2000, 150 Metcalfe St., Ottawa, ON K2P 1P1
Tel: 613-565-3813; *Fax:* 613-234-0418
jacklaw@storm.ca

***Ottawa*: Wellington Strategy Group Inc. - *3**
#1005, 350 Sparks St., Ottawa, ON K1R 7S8
Tel: 613-594-0001; *Fax:* 613-594-8777

***Ottawa*: Robert A. Whillans - *1**
540 Courtenay Ave., Ottawa, ON K2A 3B3
Tel: 613-238-1515; *Fax:* 613-238-1323

***Ottawa*: Williams McEnery - *8**
169 Gilmour St., Ottawa, ON K2P 0N8
Tel: 613-237-0520; *Fax:* 613-237-3163
www.williamsmcenery.com

***Ottawa*: David M. Wray - *1**
#310, P.O. Box 2760, Stn. D, 151 Slater St., Ottawa, ON K1P 5W8
Tel: 613-233-1322; *Fax:* 613-230-5168
dwray@wray-canada.com

***Owen Sound*: Neil J. Arnold - *1**
935 - 2nd Ave. West, Owen Sound, ON N4K 4M8
Tel: 519-372-2218; *Fax:* 519-372-2599
neiljarnold@bmts.com

***Owen Sound*: Ian C. Boddy - *1**
195 - 9th St. West, Owen Sound, ON N4K 3N5
Tel: 519-372-9886; *Fax:* 519-372-1091
ianboddy@bellnet.ca

***Owen Sound*: Herbert E. Boyce - *1**
#103, Dominion Place, P.O. Box 968, 887 Third Ave. East, Owen Sound, ON N4K 6H6
Tel: 519-371-4160; *Fax:* 519-371-1604

***Owen Sound*: Chander G. Chaddah - *1**
P.O. Box 965, 712 - 2 Ave. East, Owen Sound, ON N4K 6H6
Tel: 519-376-4343; *Fax:* 519-376-2547
www.cf-law.on.ca

***Owen Sound*: Andrew E. Drury - *1**
#5B, 945 - 3 Ave. East, Owen Sound, ON N4K 2K8
Tel: 519-372-1850; *Fax:* 519-372-1602

***Owen Sound*: D.A. Grace - *1**
P.O. Box 952, Stn. Main, 949 - 2 Ave. West, Owen Sound, ON N4K 4M8
Tel: 519-371-9370; *Fax:* 519-371-5747
dougrace@bmts.com

***Owen Sound*: Greenfield & Barrie - *2**
P.O. Box 665, 142 - 10 St. West, Owen Sound, ON N4K 5R4
Tel: 519-376-4930; *Fax:* 519-376-4010
gblaw@btms.com

***Owen Sound*: Kirby, Robinson, Treslan & Conlan - *6**
P.O. Box 730, 930 -1 Ave. West, Owen Sound, ON N4K 5W9
Tel: 519-376-7450; *Fax:* 519-376-8288
info@owensoundlawyers.com

***Owen Sound*: Catherine A. Laing - *1**
P.O. Box 664, 935 - 2 Ave. West, Owen Sound, ON N4K 5R4
Tel: 519-371-2202; *Fax:* 519-376-4683
calaing@bellnet.ca

***Owen Sound*: Alan E. Marsh - *1**
#102, P.O. Box 581, 345 - 8 St. East, Owen Sound, ON N4K 5R1
Tel: 519-371-8373; *Fax:* 519-371-8971
aemarsh@bmts.com

***Owen Sound*: Middlebro' & Stevens LLP - *6**
P.O. Box 100, 1030 - 2 Ave. East, Owen Sound, ON N4K 5P1
Tel: 519-376-8730; *Fax:* 519-376-7135
ms@mslaw.ca
www.mslaw.ca

***Owen Sound*: Murray & Thomson - *2**
P.O. Box 1060, 912 - 2 Ave. West, Owen Sound, ON N4K 6K6
Tel: 519-376-6350; *Fax:* 519-376-0835
message@mtlaw.ca
www.mtlaw.ca

***Owen Sound*: Scott C. Vining - *1**
1199, 1st Avenue East, Owen Sound, ON N4K 2E2
Tel: 519-371-6210; *Fax:* 519-371-6238
vininglaw@brucetelecom.com

***Parry Sound*: Larry W. Douglas - *1**
22 Miller St., Parry Sound, ON P2A 1S8
Tel: 705-746-9471; *Fax:* 705-746-9606

***Parry Sound*: David A. Holmes - *1**
2 William St., Parry Sound, ON P2A 1V1
Tel: 705-746-4223; *Fax:* 705-746-6368
daholmes@cogeco.ca

***Parry Sound*: Lisa M. Lund Barrister & Solicitor - *1**
34 Mary St., Parry Sound, ON P2A 1E4
Tel: 705-746-4215; *Fax:* 705-746-5357
lisa.lund@lisalund.ca

***Parry Sound*: A. Wayne Piddington - *2**
97 James St., Parry Sound, ON P2A 1T7
Tel: 705-746-9365; *Fax:* 705-746-7159
newmanps@vianet.ca

***Parry Sound*: Powell, Cunningham, Grandy - *1**
88 James St., Parry Sound, ON P2A 1T9
Tel: 705-746-4207; *Fax:* 705-746-2945
pcg@cogeco.net

***Parry Sound*: D. Andrew Thomson - *1**
10 William St., Parry Sound, ON P2A 1V1
Tel: 705-746-5838; *Fax:* 705-746-4351
athomson@dathomsonbarrister.ca

***Pembroke*: Blair Jones Professional Corporation - *1**
1064 Pembroke St. West, Pembroke, ON K8A 5R4
Tel: 613-735-8226; *Fax:* 613-735-8474
jonesIaw@magma.ca

***Pembroke*: Adrian R. Cleaver - *1**
P.O. Box 1147, 156 MacKay St., Pembroke, ON K8A 6Y6
Tel: 613-732-1377; *Fax:* 613-732-3889
acleaver@nrtco.net

***Pembroke*: B. Lynne Felhaber - *1**
#100, 77 Mary St., Pembroke, ON K8A 5V4
Tel: 613-735-6866; *Fax:* 613-735-6641

***Pembroke*: Glen Price, Lawyers - *2**
P.O. Box 697, Stn. Main, 141A Lake St., Pembroke, ON K8A 6X9
Tel: 613-732-2883; *Fax:* 613-732-3436
Toll-Free: 877-732-2884
glenpricelawyer.com

***Pembroke*: Huckabone, O'Brien, Instance. Bradley, Lyle - *6**
P.O. Box 487, 284 Pembroke St. East, Pembroke, ON K8A 6X7
Tel: 613-735-2341; *Fax:* 613-735-0920
admin@hsolawyers.com
www.hsolawyers.com

***Pembroke*: Johnson, Fraser & March - *3**
P.O. Box 366, Stn. Main, 259 Pembroke St. East, Pembroke, ON K8A 6X6
Tel: 613-735-0624; *Fax:* 613-735-0625
jfmlawyers@nrtco.net

***Pembroke*: R.B. Leach - *1**
224 Pembroke St. West, Pembroke, ON K8A 5N2
Tel: 613-732-4903; *Fax:* 613-732-0867

***Pembroke*: Quintal & Christinck - *2**
P.O. Box 205, 238 Pembroke St. East, Pembroke, ON K8A 3J7
Tel: 613-735-5777; *Fax:* 613-735-5935
quintal@nrtco.net

***Pembroke*: Roy C. Reiche - *1**
203 Nelson St., Pembroke, ON K8A 3N1
Tel: 613-735-2313; *Fax:* 613-735-2013

***Perth*: Greg W. Anderson - *1**
10 Market Sq., Perth, ON K7H 1V7
Tel: 613-267-9898; *Fax:* 613-267-2741
greg@greganderson.ca
www.greganderson.ca

***Perth*: James M. Bond - *2**
10 Market Sq., Perth, ON K7H 1V7
Tel: 613-267-1212; *Fax:* 613-267-7059
jim.bond@jamesmbond.ca
www.bondhughes.ca

***Perth*: John J.S. Chalmers - *1**
P.O. Box 2, Stn. Main, RR#3, Perth, ON K7H 3C5
Tel: 613-264-1505; *Fax:* 613-264-9259

***Perth*: Michael P. Reid - *1**
#202, Code's Mill, 53 Herriott St., Perth, ON K7H 1T5
Tel: 613-267-7280; *Fax:* 613-267-7285
mike@reidlaw.ca
www.reidlaw.ca

***Perth*: Rubino & Chaplin - *1**
P.O. Box 338, 10A Gore St. West, Perth, ON K7H 3E4
Tel: 613-267-5227; *Fax:* 613-267-3951
admin@rubinoandchaplin.ca

***Perth*: Kenneth W. Smith - *1**
P.O. Box 157, 27 Foster St., Perth, ON K7H 3E3
Tel: 613-267-5910; *Fax:* 613-264-0789
kenwsmith@on.aibn.com
www.kennethwsmith.com

***Perth*: Woodwark & Stevens - *2**
8 Gore St. West, Perth, ON K7H 2L6
Tel: 613-264-8080; *Fax:* 613-264-8084
info@woodwarkstevens.com
www.woodwarkstevens.com

***Peterborough*: Gary E. Ainsworth - *1**
#101, P.O. Box 1358, Stn. Main, 294 Rink St., Peterborough, ON K9J 7H6
Tel: 705-749-0628; *Fax:* 705-749-0633
gea@ainslaw.com
www.ainslaw.com

***Peterborough*: Richard Aitken - *1**
P.O. Box 2126, Stn. Main, 364 Water St., Peterborough, ON K9J 7Y4
Tel: 705-742-0440; *Fax:* 705-742-0889
raitkens@cgocable.net

***Peterborough*: R.W. Beninger - *1**
#205, P.O. Box 426, 261 George St. North, Peterborough, ON K9J 6Z3
Tel: 705-743-0065; *Fax:* 705-742-1867

***Peterborough*: W. Jelle Bosch - *1**
#203, P.O. Box 2364, 130 Hunter St. West, Peterborough, ON K9J 7Y8
Tel: 705-741-3630; *Fax:* 705-741-6339

***Peterborough*: John S. Crook - *1**
#5, P.O. Box 1539, Stn. Main, 261 George St. North, Peterborough, ON K9J 7H7
Tel: 705-742-5415; *Fax:* 705-742-1867

***Peterborough*: H. Girvin Devitt - *1**
P.O. Box 1449, Stn. Main, 858 Chemong Rd., Peterborough, ON K9J 7H6
Tel: 705-742-5471
devitt@nexicom.net

***Peterborough*: Douglas F. Walker Professional Corporation - *2**
243 Hunter St. W., Peterborough, ON K9H 2L4
Tel: 705-748-3012; *Fax:* 705-748-2746
www.dfwalker.com

***Peterborough*: Dunn & Dunn - *1**
469 Water St., Peterborough, ON K9H 3M2
Tel: 705-743-6460; *Fax:* 705-748-2675

***Peterborough*: Michael J. Dwyer - *1**
359 Aylmer St. North, Peterborough, ON K9J 7A5
Tel: 705-743-4221; *Fax:* 705-743-2187
mdwyer@bellnet.ca

***Peterborough*: Farquharson Daly - *1**
161 Hunter St. West, Peterborough, ON K9H 2L1
Tel: 705-742-9241; *Fax:* 705-741-1601

***Peterborough*: T.G. Gain - *1**
273 Water St., Peterborough, ON K9H 3P1
Tel: 705-749-6633; *Fax:* 705-749-9765
leygain@on.aibn.com

***Peterborough*: P. Douglas Galvin - *1**
#1, P.O. Box 1118, Stn. Main, 182 McDonnel St., Peterborough, ON K9J 7H4
Tel: 705-743-7500; *Fax:* 705-743-2336

***Peterborough*: Gowland, Boriss - *4**
P.O. Box 1629, 371 Reid St., Peterborough, ON K9H 4G4
Tel: 705-743-7252; *Fax:* 705-743-1850

** indicates number of lawyers*

Peterborough: Joan M. Guerin - *1
#4, P.O. Box 1420, Stn. Main, 193 Simcoe St., Peterborough, ON K9J 7H6
Tel: 705-743-9087; *Fax:* 705-743-8528

Peterborough: William F. Hampton - *1
219 Sherbrooke St., Peterborough, ON K9J 2N2
Tel: 705-876-6900; *Fax:* 705-876-6922

Peterborough: Harrison Law Office - *1
P.O. Box 1916, 306 Stewart St., Peterborough, ON K9J 7X7
Tel: 705-741-5233; *Fax:* 705-741-2463
spharrison@trytel.net

Peterborough: James S. Hauraney - *1
305 Reid St., Peterborough, ON K9J 3R2
Tel: 705-748-2333; *Fax:* 705-748-2618

Peterborough: A. John Hodgins - *1
677 Brown Line, Peterborough, ON K9J 6X6
Tel: 416-251-9390; *Fax:* 416-251-0449
ajhodgins@hodginslaw.net

Peterborough: Howell Fleming LLP - *10
P.O. Box 148, 415 Water St., Peterborough, ON K9J 6Y5
Tel: 705-745-1361; *Fax:* 705-745-6220
lkulatungam@howellfleming.com
www.howellfleming.com

Peterborough: Rod E. Johnston - *1
P.O. Box 29, 521 George St. North, Peterborough, ON K9J 6Y5
Tel: 705-748-2244; *Fax:* 705-748-2540
info@rodjohnstonlaw.com

Peterborough: E.J. Jordan - *1
P.O. Box 958, 359 Aylmer St. North, Peterborough, ON K9J 7A5
Tel: 705-743-4221; *Fax:* 705-743-2187

Peterborough: Lech, Lightbody & O'Brien - *2
116 Hunter St. West, Peterborough, ON K9H 2K6
Tel: 705-742-3844; *Fax:* 705-742-0121
maryruth@hunterstreetlaw.com

Peterborough: Lillico Bazuk Kent Galloway - *4
P.O. Box 568, 163 Hunter St. West, Peterborough, ON K9J 6Z6
Tel: 705-743-3577; *Fax:* 705-743-0013
lbkg@lbkglaw.com

Peterborough: Linda Willcox Whetung Professional Corporation - *1
521 George St. North, Peterborough, ON K9J 6Y5
Tel: 705-743-6470; *Fax:* 705-743-3128
linda@lindawhetung.com

Peterborough: Lockington Lawless Fitzpatrick - *11
P.O. Box 1146, 332 Aylmer St. North, Peterborough, ON K9J 7H4
Tel: 705-742-1674; *Fax:* 705-742-4677
info@locklaw.ca

Peterborough: J.M. Longworth - *1
P.O. Box 1747, Stn. Main, 310 Rubidge St., Peterborough, ON K9J 7X6
Tel: 705-749-0100; *Fax:* 705-742-8718

Peterborough: John E. McGarrity - *1
Stn. Main, 343 Stewart St., Peterborough, ON K9H 4A7
Tel: 705-743-1822; *Fax:* 705-743-4870
mcgarrity@trytel.net

Peterborough: McGillen Keay - *3
#202, P.O. Box 1718, 140 King St., Peterborough, ON K9J 7X6
Tel: 705-748-2241; *Fax:* 705-748-9125
www.mcgillenkeay.com

Peterborough: McMichael, Davidson - *1
64 Hunter St. West, Peterborough, ON K9H 2K4
Tel: 705-745-0571; *Fax:* 705-745-0411
lawoffice@mcmichaeldavidson.com

Peterborough: Moldaver & McFadden - *2
121 George St. North, Peterborough, ON K9J 7H6
Tel: 705-743-1801; *Fax:* 705-743-0397

Peterborough: Christopher M. Spear - *1
430 Sheridan St., Peterborough, ON K9H 3J9
Tel: 705-741-2144; *Fax:* 705-741-2712

Peterborough: Robert A. Stocker - *1
174 Wallis Dr., Peterborough, ON K9J 6C3
Tel: 705-745-5786
raslaw@cogeco.ca

Peterborough: Richard J. Taylor - *1
P.O. Box 1963, Stn. Main, 306 Stewart St., Peterborough, ON K9J 7X7
Tel: 705-876-7791; *Fax:* 705-876-9280
taylorlaw@trytel.net

Peterborough: G.H. Usher - *1
P.O. Box 327, 359 Aylmer St. North, Peterborough, ON K9J 6Z3
Tel: 705-743-4221; *Fax:* 705-743-8692

Peterborough: J. Ross Whittington - *1
P.O. Box 327, 359 Aylmer St. North, Peterborough, ON K9J 6Z3
Tel: 705-743-4221; *Fax:* 705-743-8692

Petrolia: Robert B. Gray - *1
#3, 4495 Petrolia Line, Petrolia, ON N0N 1R0
Tel: 519-882-0132; *Fax:* 519-336-3289

Petrolia: Wallace B. Lang - *1
P.O. Box 700, 4245 Petrolia Lane, Petrolia, ON N0N 1R0
Tel: 519-882-0770; *Fax:* 519-882-3144

Pickering: G.W. Edmiston - *1
1281 Commerce St., Pickering, ON L1W 1C7
Tel: 905-839-8270

Pickering: Alan Fisher - *1
#824, 1880 Valley Farm Rd., Pickering, ON L1V 6B3
Tel: 905-839-7248

Pickering: J. Paul Fletcher - *1
P.O. Box 667, Stn. Main, Pickering, ON L1V 3T3
Tel: 905-922-2027
jpaulfletcherlaw@aol.com

Pickering: Brian R. Hawke - *1
1 Evelyn Ave., Pickering, ON L1V 1N3
Tel: 905-509-5267; *Fax:* 905-509-5270
bhawke@on.aibn.com

Pickering: John G. Howes - *1
#800, 1315 Pickering Pkwy., Pickering, ON L1V 7G5
Tel: 905-420-8628; *Fax:* 905-420-1073
Toll-Free: 800-373-6641
john@howeslaw.com

Pickering: Sherwood, Hunt - *2
364 Kingston Rd., Pickering, ON L1V 1A2
Tel: 905-509-5500; *Fax:* 905-509-0070

Pickering: Harvey Storm - *1
#8B, 1400 Bayly St., Pickering, ON L1W 3R2
Tel: 905-839-5121; *Fax:* 905-420-4062
Toll-Free: 888-876-5529
harvey@harveystorm.com
www.harveystorm.com

Pickering: Murray Stroud - *1
356 Kingston Rd., Pickering, ON L1V 1A2
Tel: 905-509-1353; *Fax:* 905-509-2370
mstroud@stroudlaw.ca
www.stroudlaw.ca

Pickering: Tim Vanular Lawyers Professional Corporation - *2
#C10-C11, Brock North Plaza, 2200 Brock Rd. North, Pickering, ON L1X 2R2
Tel: 905-427-4886; *Fax:* 905-427-5542
Toll-Free: 800-243-4151
vanular@vanulaw.com
www.vanulaw.comhttp://www.facebook.com/pages/Tim-Vanular-Lawyers-Professional-Corporation/, www.twitter.com/Vanulaw, http://ca.linkedin.com/pub/tim-vanular/33/546/a93

Pickering: G.R. Wakefield - *1
1 Evelyn Ave., Pickering, ON L1V 1N3
Tel: 905-509-5267; *Fax:* 905-509-5270
grwakefield@rogers.com

Pickering: Walker, Head - *8
#800, Corporate Centre, 1315 Pickering Pkwy., Pickering, ON L1V 7G5
Tel: 905-839-4484; *Fax:* 905-420-1073
wlkhd@walkerhead.com
www.walkerhead.com

Pickering: J. Robert Wood & Associates - *1
#419, 1400 The Esplanade North, Pickering, ON L1V 6V2
Tel: 905-837-9425; *Fax:* 905-837-9168
jrwood@rogers.com

Picton: Bruce F. Campbell - *1
P.O. Box 1260, 194 Main St., Picton, ON K0K 2T0
Tel: 613-476-2366; *Fax:* 613-476-9821
bcampbl@kos.net

Picton: William M. Martin - *1
P.O. Box 2160, 316 Main St., Picton, ON K0K 2T0
Tel: 613-476-2116; *Fax:* 613-476-8143

Picton: Shelagh M. Mathers - *1
#4, 6 Talbot St., Picton, ON K0K 2T0
Tel: 613-476-2733; *Fax:* 613-476-6064
matherslaw@kos.net

Picton: Donald T. Mowat - *1
P.O. Box 2290, 165 Main St., Picton, ON K0K 2T0
Tel: 613-476-3261; *Fax:* 613-476-4417

Picton: Walmsley & Walmsley - *1
P.O. Box 1500, 340 Main St., Picton, ON K0K 2T0
Tel: 613-476-5516; *Fax:* 613-476-5725
walaw@kos.net

Picton: Jack H. Ward - *1
P.O. Box 530, 51 Mary St., Picton, ON K0K 2T0
Tel: 613-476-3640; *Fax:* 613-476-3435

Point Edward: Fleck & Daigneault - *3
#102, 704 Mara St., Point Edward, ON N7V 1X4
Tel: 519-337-5288; *Fax:* 519-337-5674
pascale@xcelco.on.ca

Point Edward: Peter Westfall - *1
#104, 805 Christina St. North, Point Edward, Point Edward, ON N7V 1X6
Tel: 519-344-1155; *Fax:* 519-344-1842
pwestfall@bellnet.ca

Port Colborne: Brian N. Lambie - *1
109 Adelaide St., Port Colborne, ON L3K 2W4
Tel: 905-835-8455; *Fax:* 905-835-5966

Port Colborne: Robt. H.H. Reilly - *1
P.O. Box 127, Port Colborne, ON L3K 5V8
Tel: 905-835-1141; *Fax:* 905-835-2185

Port Colborne: John D. Tuck - *1
P.O. Box 334, 84 West St., Port Colborne, ON L3K 5W1
Tel: 905-834-4525; *Fax:* 905-834-3254
pclaw@bellnet.ca

Port Colborne: Wilson, Opatovsky - *2
P.O. Box 99, 190 Elm St., Port Colborne, ON L3K 5V7
Tel: 905-835-1163; *Fax:* 905-835-2171
Toll-Free: 888-288-8338

Port Elgin: George D. Gruetzner - *1
P.O. Box 10, 667 Goderich St., Port Elgin, ON N0H 2C0
Tel: 519-832-2482; *Fax:* 519-389-4617

Port Perry: Michael L. Fowler - *2
175 North St., Port Perry, ON L9L 1B7
Tel: 905-985-8411; *Fax:* 905-985-0029
mfowler@fowlerlaw.ca

Prescott: Richard M. Tobin - *1
257 King St. West, PO Box 760, Prescott, ON K0E 1T0
Tel: 613-925-2853; *Fax:* 613-925-5741

Rama: Nahwegahbow, Corbiere - *3
P.O. Box 46, 7410 Benson Side Rd., Rama, ON L0K 1T0
Tel: 705-325-0520; *Fax:* 705-325-7204
mail@nncfirm.ca

Renfrew: Sharon L. Anderson-Olmstead - *1
117 Raglan St. South, Renfrew, ON K7V 1P8
Tel: 613-432-5898; *Fax:* 613-432-5899
sharon_anderson@bellnet.ca

Renfrew: Chown & Smith - *2
297 Raglan St. South, Renfrew, ON K7V 1R6
Tel: 613-432-3669; *Fax:* 613-432-2874
admin@chownandsmith.com
www.chownandsmith.com

Renfrew: Lawrence E. Gallagher - *1
33 Renfrew Ave. East, Renfrew, ON K7V 2W6
Tel: 613-432-8537; *Fax:* 613-432-8538
legallagher@nrtco.net

Renfrew: Joseph D. Legris Professional Corp. - *1
248 Argyle St. South, Renfrew, ON K7V 1T7
Tel: 613-432-3689; *Fax:* 613-432-3936
jlegris@legrislaw.com
www.legrislaw.com

** indicates number of lawyers*

***Renfrew*: McNab, Stewart & Prince - *2**
117 Raglan St. South, Renfrew, ON K7V 1P8
Tel: 613-432-5844; *Fax:* 613-432-7832
dstewart@mcnablaw.com; tprince@mcnablaw.com
www.mcnablaw.com

***Richmond Hill*: Ronald A. Balinsky - *1**
96 Arnold Cres., Richmond Hill, ON L4C 3R8
Tel: 905-884-8161; *Fax:* 905-884-3155
rbalinsky@balinskylawfirm.com

***Richmond Hill*: Peter D. Bouroukis - *1**
#411, 15 Wertheim Ct., Richmond Hill, ON L4B 3H7
Tel: 905-771-7030; *Fax:* 905-771-7027
pbouroukis@rogers.com

***Richmond Hill*: Jay Chauhan - *1**
#309, 330 Hwy. 7 East, Richmond Hill, ON L4B 3P8
Tel: 905-771-1235; *Fax:* 905-771-1237
jayadvocate@yahoo.ca
www.jaychauhan.com

***Richmond Hill*: Annie A. Cheng - *1**
#221A, 550 Hwy. 7 East, Richmond Hill, ON L4B 3Z4
Tel: 905-709-9988; *Fax:* 905-709-1885
aacheng@solutionsinlaw.ca

***Richmond Hill*: James H. Chow - *1**
#512, 330 Hwy. 7 East, Richmond Hill, ON L4B 3P8
Tel: 905-881-3363

***Richmond Hill*: Corinne M. Rivers - *1**
#104, 13311 Yonge St., Richmond Hill, ON L4E 3L6
Tel: 905-773-9911; *Fax:* 905-773-9927
corrine@cmrlaw.cawww.linkedin.com/pub/corinne-rivers/4/b44/6
5

***Richmond Hill*: Terry G. Hawtin - *1**
#301, 650 Hwy. 7 East, Richmond Hill, ON L4B 2N7
Tel: 905-709-9020; *Fax:* 905-709-4721
hawtin@hawtinlaw.ca

***Richmond Hill*: Anthea Koon - *1**
#206, 15 Wertheim Ct., Richmond Hill, ON L4B 3H7
Tel: 905-889-0698; *Fax:* 905-889-8390
antheakoon@rogers.com

***Richmond Hill*: Alla Koren - *1**
12 Rollinghill Rd., Richmond Hill, ON L4E 4C1
Tel: 905-780-1500; *Fax:* 905-780-0070
akoren@rogers.com

***Richmond Hill*: John J. Lawlor Q.C. - *1**
#102, 10211 Yonge St., Richmond Hill, ON L4C 3B3
Tel: 905-884-9133; *Fax:* 905-884-9507
johnlawlor@on.aibn.com

***Richmond Hill*: Garry E. Levine - *1**
16 O'Connor Cres., Richmond Hill, ON L4C 7P3
Tel: 905-709-9444; *Fax:* 905-770-3782
glevine@rogers.com

***Richmond Hill*: Shirley K.T. Lo - *1**
#PH 10, 330 Hwy. 7 East, Richmond Hill, ON L4B 3P8
Tel: 905-707-5707; *Fax:* 905-707-5752
kshirleylo@hotmail.com

***Richmond Hill*: L.A. Lombardi & Co. Ltd. - *1**
#200, 66 West Beaver Creek, Richmond Hill, ON L4B 1G5
Tel: 416-924-9559; *Fax:* 416-924-7974

***Richmond Hill*: Malach & Fidler - *11**
#6, 30 Wertheim Ct., Richmond Hill, ON L4B 1B9
Tel: 905-889-1667; *Fax:* 905-889-1139
mf@netcom.ca

***Richmond Hill*: Parker Garber & Chesney - *1**
250 West Beaver Creek Rd., Richmond Hill, ON L4B 1C7
Tel: 905-764-0404; *Fax:* 905-764-0320

***Richmond Hill*: Paul Harte Professional Corporation, Barristers & Solicitors - *1**
#301, 1595 Sixteenth Ave., Richmond Hill, ON L4B 3N9
Tel: 905-709-7405; *Fax:* 905-763-2167
Toll-Free: 888-441-3341
pharte@hartelaw.com; mdamiano@hartelaw.com
www.hartelaw.com

***Richmond Hill*: Rohmer & Fenn - *3**
#503, Park Place Corporate Centre, 15 Wertheim Ct., Richmond Hill, ON L4B 3H7
Tel: 905-763-6690; *Fax:* 905-763-6699
firm@rohmerfenn.com

***Richmond Hill*: Barry Seltzer - *1**
#204, 9140 Leslie St., Richmond Hill, ON L4B 0A9
Tel: 905-475-9001; *Fax:* 905-475-9004
barry@barryseltzer.com

***Richmond Hill*: Virgilio, Vumbaca - *2**
#500, 1 Pearce St. West, Richmond Hill, ON L4B 3K3
Tel: 905-882-8666; *Fax:* 905-882-1082
jvirgilio@virgiliolaw.com

***Richmond Hill*: Gordon E. Watkin - *1**
#212A, Hillcrest Mall, 9350 Yonge St., Richmond Hill, ON L4C 5G2
Tel: 905-884-3778; *Fax:* 905-884-2655

***Ridgetown*: Edward T. Little - *1**
P.O. Box 700, 64 Main St. East, Ridgetown, ON N0P 2C0
Tel: 519-674-5436; *Fax:* 519-674-3352
etlittle@bellnet.ca

***Ridgetown*: Daniel B. Nicol - *1**
P.O. Box 700, 64 Main St. East, Ridgetown, ON N0P 2C0
Tel: 519-674-3372; *Fax:* 519-674-3352
dbnicol@pppoe.ca

***Ridgeway*: Community Legal Services of Niagara South - *1**
P.O. Box 430, 266 Ridge Rd., Ridgeway, ON L0S 1N0
Tel: 905-894-4775; *Fax:* 905-894-6101

***Ripley*: Crawford, Mill & Davies**
P.O. Box 100, 38 Queen St., Ripley, ON N0G 2R0
Tel: 519-395-2633; *Fax:* 519-395-4947
cmdripley@hurontel.ca

***Rockwood*: Douglas S. Black - *1**
P.O. Box 95, 118 Main St. South, Rockwood, ON N0B 2K0
Tel: 519-856-4555; *Fax:* 519-856-4680
dblacklaw@bellnet.ca

***Rockwood*: Judith P. Ryan**
P.O. Box 550, Rockwood, ON N0B 2K0
Tel: 519-856-2223; *Fax:* 519-856-2047
jpmryan@aol.com

***Sarnia*: Paul R. Beaudet - *1**
P.O. Box 2162, 251 Exmouth St., Sarnia, ON N7T 7L7
Tel: 519-337-1529; *Fax:* 519-336-2569
beaudet@ebtech.net
www.sarnia.com/beaudet

***Sarnia*: Terry L. Brandon - *1**
1069 London Rd., Sarnia, ON N7S 1P2
Tel: 519-337-4634; *Fax:* 519-337-5586
terrybrandon@sympatico.ca

***Sarnia*: Roderick Brown, Q.C. - *1**
555 Exmouth St., Sarnia, ON N7T 5P6
Tel: 519-336-7880; *Fax:* 519-336-6584
re_brown2927@hotmail.com

***Sarnia*: James J. Carpeneto - *1**
316 Christina St. North, Sarnia, ON N7T 5V5
Tel: 519-336-6955; *Fax:* 519-336-8401

***Sarnia*: W.M. Dawson, Q.C. - *1**
#201, 805 Christina St. North, Sarnia, ON N7V 1X6
Tel: 519-337-2321; *Fax:* 519-337-2466

***Sarnia*: Elliott & Porter - *2**
#101, St. Clair Corporate Centre, 265 Front St. North, Sarnia, ON N7T 7X1
Tel: 519-336-4600; *Fax:* 519-336-4640

***Sarnia*: George Murray Shipley Bell, LLP - *9**
P.O. Box 2196, 2 Ferry Dock Hill, Sarnia, ON N7T 7L8
Tel: 519-336-8770; *Fax:* 519-336-1811

***Sarnia*: Gray, Bruce, Cimetta (Cablo Cimetta Professional Corporation) - *4**
P.O. Box 2259, 1166 London Rd., Sarnia, ON N7T 7L7
Tel: 519-336-9700; *Fax:* 519-336-3289

***Sarnia*: C. Ed Gresham**
#203, 805 Christina St. North, Sarnia, ON N7V 1X6
Tel: 519-337-9224; *Fax:* 519-337-7440

***Sarnia*: David G. Hockin - *1**
#101, 265 Front St. North, Sarnia, ON N7T 7X1
Tel: 519-336-4357; *Fax:* 519-336-4367
lawyer@ebtech.net

***Sarnia*: Pamela J. McLeod - *1**
1350 L'Heritage Dr., Sarnia, ON N7S 6H8
Tel: 519-542-7714; *Fax:* 519-542-5577
mcleodlaw@ebtech.net

***Sarnia*: Robbins, Henderson & Davis - *4**
#201, 208 North Christina St., Sarnia, ON N7V 1X6
Tel: 519-344-5265; *Fax:* 519-344-1558

***Sarnia*: Raymond A. Whitnall - *1**
345 Christina St. North, Sarnia, ON N7T 5V6
Tel: 519-336-9460; *Fax:* 519-336-8366

***Sarnia*: Wyrzykowski & Robb - *2**
P.O. Box 2200, Stn. Main, Sarnia, ON N7T 7L7
Tel: 519-336-6118; *Fax:* 519-336-9550
orw@ebtech.net

***Sault Ste Marie*: Aiello, Pawelek - *2**
#102, 123 March St., Sault Ste Marie, ON P6A 2Z5
Tel: 705-946-8590; *Fax:* 705-946-8589

***Sault Ste Marie*: Allemano & Fitzgerald - *2**
P.O. Box 10, Sault Ste Marie, ON P6A 5L2
Tel: 705-942-0142; *Fax:* 705-942-7188

***Sault Ste Marie*: Bisceglia Dumanski Rasaiah LLP - *3**
747 Queen St. East, 2nd Fl., Sault Ste Marie, ON P6A 2A8
Tel: 705-942-5856; *Fax:* 705-942-6493
bdlawfirm@bellnet.ca
www.bdlawfirm.ca

***Sault Ste Marie*: Kenneth R. Davies**
525 Wellington St. East, Sault Ste Marie, ON P6A 2M4
Tel: 705-256-7839; *Fax:* 705-942-8271

***Sault Ste Marie*: Ferranti & Chorney - *2**
189 East St., Sault Ste Marie, ON P6A 3C8
Tel: 705-949-6200; *Fax:* 705-949-6208

***Sault Ste Marie*: Hamilton, Nixon - *2**
P.O. Box 249, 67 Elgin St., Sault Ste Marie, ON P6A 5L8
Tel: 705-759-8498; *Fax:* 705-759-8781

***Sault Ste Marie*: Laidlaw, Paciocco, Melville - *3**
#604, 421 Bay St., Sault Ste Marie, ON P6A 1X3
Tel: 705-949-7790; *Fax:* 705-949-5816
paciocco@vianet.ca

***Sault Ste Marie*: O. Kennedy Lawson - *1**
#104, 473 Queen St. East, Sault Ste Marie, ON P6A 1Z5
Tel: 705-759-5030; *Fax:* 705-942-5309

***Sault Ste Marie*: Mathews, Dinsdale & Clark LLP**
#301, 369 Queen St., Sault Ste Marie, ON P6A 1Z4
Tel: 705-253-3711; *Fax:* 705-253-1102
vchiappella@mathewsdinsdale.com

***Sault Ste Marie*: Eric D. McCooeye - *1**
348 Albert St. East, Sault Ste Marie, ON P6A 2J6
Tel: 705-945-8868; *Fax:* 705-945-9051
smccooeye@shaw.ca

***Sault Ste Marie*: O'Neill Cresswell DeLorenzi Mendes - *6**
116 Spring St., Sault Ste Marie, ON P6A 3A1
Tel: 705-949-6901; *Fax:* 705-949-0618
info@saultlawyers.com
www.saultlawyers.com

***Sault Ste Marie*: Orazietti, Kwolek, Walz - *4**
128 March St., Sault Ste Marie, ON P6A 2Z3
Tel: 705-256-5601; *Fax:* 705-945-9427
soolaw@soonet.com

***Sault Ste Marie*: R.C. Peres, Q.C. - *1**
#104, 212 Queen St. East, Sault Ste Marie, ON P6A 5X8
Tel: 705-949-9411; *Fax:* 705-949-3759

***Sault Ste Marie*: William R. Scott - *1**
#202, 629A Queen St. East, Sault Ste Marie, ON P6A 2A6
Tel: 705-949-4333; *Fax:* 705-945-0958
wmrscottlaw@yahoo.com

***Sault Ste Marie*: Carol A. Shamess - *1**
181 March St., Sault Ste Marie, ON P6A 2Z6
Tel: 705-942-2580; *Fax:* 705-942-5048

***Sault Ste Marie*: Jack Squire - *1**
191 Northern Ave. East, Sault Ste Marie, ON P6B 4H8
Tel: 705-949-0162; *Fax:* 705-541-9616

***Sault Ste Marie*: T. Frederick Baxter, Barrister & Solicitor - *1**
494 Albert St. East, Sault Ste Marie, ON P6A 2K2
Tel: 705-759-0948; *Fax:* 705-759-2042

** indicates number of lawyers*

***Sault Ste Marie*: Walker, Thompson - *1**
#506, P.O. Box 428, 123 March St., Sault Ste Marie, ON P6A 5M1
Tel: 705-949-7806; *Fax:* 705-759-0457
walkerlaw@sympatico.ca

***Sault Ste Marie*: Willson, Carter - *2**
494 Albert St. East, Sault Ste Marie, ON P6A 2K2
Tel: 705-942-2000; *Fax:* 705-942-6511

***Sault Ste Marie*: Wishart Law Firm LLP - *6**
#500, 390 Bay St., Sault Ste Marie, ON P6A 1X2
Tel: 705-949-6700; *Fax:* 705-949-2465
wishart@wishartlaw.com
www.wishartlaw.com

***Scarborough*: Antflyck, Mazin Aulis LLP - *3**
1501 Ellesmere Rd., Scarborough, ON M1P 4T6
Tel: 416-431-1500; *Fax:* 416-431-1912
antflyckmazin@on.aibn.com

***Scarborough*: Stanley Baker - *1**
#700, 55 Town Centre Ct., Scarborough, ON M1P 4X4
Tel: 416-296-1794; *Fax:* 416-296-1259
stanleybaker@rogers.com

***Scarborough*: Andrea E.K. Chun - *1**
#700, One Corporate Plaza, 2075 Kennedy Rd., Scarborough, ON M1T 3V3
Tel: 416-754-3060; *Fax:* 416-754-3321
andreachun@bellnet.ca

***Schomberg*: Clarke G. Smith - *1**
#10, Brownsville Junction Plaza, 17250 Hwy. 27, Schomberg, ON L0G 1T0
Tel: 905-939-2344; *Fax:* 905-727-7096
cgsmith@rogers.com

***Seaforth*: Devereaux Murray LLP - *2**
P.O. Box 220, 77 Main St. South, Seaforth, ON N0K 1W0
Tel: 519-527-0850; *Fax:* 519-527-2324
c4thlaw@devereauxmurray.ca

***Seeleys Bay*: D.J. Atkinson - *1**
RR#1, Seeleys Bay, ON K0H 2N0
Tel: 613-382-2692

***Shelburne*: Courtney H. Foster**
P.O. Box 11, RR#4, Shelburne, ON L0N 1S8
Tel: 519-925-5854; *Fax:* 519-925-3159

***Shelburne*: Timmerman & Haskell - *2**
P.O. Box 216, 305 Owen Sound St., Shelburne, ON L0N 1S0
Tel: 519-925-2608; *Fax:* 519-925-2268

***Simcoe*: Brimage, Tyrrell, Van Severen & Homeniuk - *10**
21 Norfolk St. North, Simcoe, ON N3Y 4L1
Tel: 519-426-5840; *Fax:* 519-426-7515
law@brimage.com
www.brimage.com

***Simcoe*: Cline, Backus, Nightingale & McArthur, LLP - *8**
P.O. Box 528, Stn. Main, 39 Colborne St. North, Simcoe, ON N3Y 4N5
Tel: 519-426-6763; *Fax:* 519-426-2055
cbnmlaw@kwic.com
www.clinebackus.com

***Simcoe*: Cobb & Jones LLP - *7**
P.O. Box 548, 23 Argyle St., Simcoe, ON N3Y 4N5
Tel: 519-428-0170; *Fax:* 519-428-3105
cobblaw@cobbjones.ca
www.cobbjones.ca

***Simcoe*: William Mark Dresser - *1**
P.O. Box 103, Simcoe, ON N3Y 4K8
Tel: 519-426-8118; *Fax:* 519-426-8962
lawmark@sympatico.ca

***Simcoe*: Sheppard, MacIntosh, Lados & Nunn LLP - *4**
P.O. Box 677, 58 Peel St., Simcoe, ON N3Y 4T2
Tel: 519-426-1382; *Fax:* 519-426-1392
lawyers@sheppardmacintosh.com
www.sheppardmacintosh.com

***Simcoe*: Smelko Law Office - *1**
25 Norfolk St. North, Simcoe, ON N3Y 3N6
Tel: 519-426-1711; *Fax:* 519-426-7863
Toll-Free: 866-684-8527
smelkolaw@on.aibn.com

***Sioux Lookout*: Kevin W. Romyn - *1**
P.O. Box 99, 69 Queen St., Sioux Lookout, ON P8T 1A1
Tel: 807-737-2562; *Fax:* 807-737-2571
romynlaw@gosiouxlookout.com

***Smiths Falls*: G.W. Fournier - *1**
P.O. Box 752, 35 Daniel St., Smiths Falls, ON K7A 4W6
Tel: 613-283-8818; *Fax:* 613-283-8951

***Smiths Falls*: Howard Ryan Kelford Knott & Dixon, Barristers & Solicitors - *5**
2 Main St. East, Smiths Falls, ON K7A 1A2
Tel: 613-283-6772; *Fax:* 613-283-8840
Toll-Free: 888-852-5175
lthompson@smithsfallslaw.ca
www.smithsfallslaw.ca

***Smiths Falls*: Kirkland, Murphy & Kennedy Professional Corporation - *3**
P.O. Box 220, 15 Russell St. East, Smiths Falls, ON K7A 4T1
Tel: 613-283-0515; *Fax:* 613-283-8557
reception@smithsfallslawyers.com

***Smiths Falls*: Ross Cliffen & Morrison - *3**
P.O. Box 804, 30 Russell St. East, Smiths Falls, ON K7A 4W6
Tel: 613-283-7331; *Fax:* 613-283-6792
rosslaw@ripnet.com
www.rossandcliffen.com

***Southampton*: Robert E. Forsyth - *1**
P.O. Box 420, 243 High St., Southampton, ON N0H 2L0
Tel: 519-797-3223; *Fax:* 519-797-3192
forsyth3@bmts.com

***St Catharines*: W.J. Garry Bracken - *1**
50 Dunvegan Rd., St Catharines, ON L2P 1H6
Tel: 905-988-9389; *Fax:* 905-685-1753
bracklaw@cogeco.ca

***St Catharines*: Chown, Cairns LLP - *17**
P.O. Box 760, 80 King St., St Catharines, ON L2R 6Y8
Tel: 905-688-4500; *Fax:* 905-688-0015
lawyers@chowlaw.com
www.chownlaw.com

***St Catharines*: Coy, Barch - *1**
46 Ontario St., St Catharines, ON L2R 5J4
Tel: 905-641-1146; *Fax:* 905-641-1148

***St Catharines*: Crossingham, Brady - *2**
P.O. Box 307, 63 Ontario St., St Catharines, ON L2R 6V2
Tel: 905-641-1621; *Fax:* 905-685-1461
cbm@vaxxine.com

***St Catharines*: Daniel & Partners LLP - *9**
Dominion Bldg., P.O. Box 24022, 39 Queen St., St Catharines, ON L2R 7P7
Tel: 905-688-9411; *Fax:* 905-688-5747
Toll-Free: 800-263-3650
lawyers@niagaralaw.ca

***St Catharines*: Mark F. Dedinsky - *1**
154 James St., 2nd Fl., St Catharines, ON L2R 5C5
Tel: 905-688-6275; *Fax:* 905-682-0264

***St Catharines*: Forster, Lewandowski & Cords - *2**
P.O. Box 1180, Stn. Main, 82 Lake St., St Catharines, ON L2R 7A7
Tel: 905-688-9110; *Fax:* 905-688-0901
Toll-Free: 866-715-9380
f.l.c@on.aibn.com

***St Catharines*: Ralph H. Frayne - *1**
9 Raymond St., St Catharines, ON L2R 2S9
Tel: 905-684-1147; *Fax:* 905-684-7147

***St Catharines*: Erik Grinbergs**
37 Church St., St Catharines, ON L2R 3B7
Tel: 905-688-9800; *Fax:* 905-684-0009
grinberg@vaxxine.com

***St Catharines*: John B. Hanna - *1**
P.O. Box 24044, Stn. Main, St Catharines, ON L2R 7P7
Tel: 905-687-9347; *Fax:* 905-687-3939

***St Catharines*: Heelis, Williams, Little & Almas LLP, Barristers & Solicitors - *6**
P.O. Box 1056, 14 Church St., St Catharines, ON L2R 7A3
Tel: 905-687-8200; *Fax:* 905-684-4844
rwilliam@14churchstlawoffice.com
www.14churchstlawoffice.com

***St Catharines*: Lancaster, Brooks & Welch LLP - *17**
P.O. Box 790, 80 King St., St Catharines, ON L2R 6Z1
Tel: 905-641-1551; *Fax:* 905-641-1830
www.lbwlawyers.com

***St Catharines*: Legal Aid**
#302, P.O. Box 954, 110 James St., St Catharines, ON L2R 6Z4
Tel: 905-685-1012; *Fax:* 905-685-7202

***St Catharines*: Frank M. Marotta - *1**
21 Duke St., St Catharines, ON L2R 5W1
Tel: 905-688-5401; *Fax:* 905-688-6204
fmarotta@vaxxine.com

***St Catharines*: Martens, Lingard LLP - *7**
195 King St., St Catharines, ON L2R 3J6
Tel: 905-687-6551; *Fax:* 905-687-6553
lawyers@martenslingard.ca

***St Catharines*: Paula McPherson - *1**
51 Hillcrest Ave., St Catharines, ON L2R 4Y3
Tel: 905-641-3457
resolve@sympatico.ca

***St Catharines*: Tracy J. Middleton Collini - *1**
234 Vine St., St Catharines, ON L2M 4T1
Tel: 905-937-9229; *Fax:* 905-937-9228
collinilaw@msn.com

***St Catharines*: O'Neill & Radford - *1**
154 James St., St Catharines, ON L2R 7A3
Tel: 905-641-2633; *Fax:* 905-682-0264
bmradford@bellnet.ca

***St Catharines*: Ian G. Pearson - *1**
154 James St., 2nd Fl., St Catharines, ON L2R 5C5
Tel: 905-682-7882; *Fax:* 905-682-0264
ipearson@bellnet.ca

***St Catharines*: Sullivan, Mahoney LLP - *27**
P.O. Box 1360, 40 Queen St., St Catharines, ON L2R 6Z2
Tel: 905-688-6655; *Fax:* 905-688-5814
lawyers@sullivan-mahoney.com
www.sullivan-mahoney.com

***St Catharines*: Virginia L. Workman - *1**
#1004, 1 St. Paul, St Catharines, ON L2R 7L2
Tel: 905-704-0804; *Fax:* 905-704-4464
virginiaworkman@bellnet.ca

***St Marys*: William J. Galloway - *1**
P.O. Box 897, Stn. Main, 172 Queen St. East, St Marys, ON N4X 1B6
Tel: 519-284-2112; *Fax:* 519-284-3081

***St Thomas*: Jerome A. Collins - *1**
36 Hincks St., St Thomas, ON N5R 3N6
Tel: 519-633-3973; *Fax:* 519-633-7916

***St Thomas*: W.J. Glover, Law Office - *1**
P.O. Box 575, Stn. Main, 458 Talbot St., St Thomas, ON N5P 3V6
Tel: 519-633-2300; *Fax:* 519-633-0964
gloverlawyer@aol.com

***St Thomas*: Gunn & Associates - *5**
108 Centre St., St Thomas, ON N5R 2Z7
Tel: 519-631-0700; *Fax:* 519-631-1468
lawyers@gunn.on.ca
www.gunn.on.ca

***St Thomas*: Arnold B. Walker - *1**
4 Elgin St., St Thomas, ON N5R 3L6
Tel: 519-633-3273; *Fax:* 519-633-8585

***Stoney Creek*: Cicchi & Giangregorio - *2**
1-99 Hwy. 8, Stoney Creek, ON L8G 1C1
Tel: 905-664-6645; *Fax:* 905-664-6952

***Stoney Creek*: Coombs & Lutz - *1**
6 Lake Ave. South, Stoney Creek, ON L8G 1P3
Tel: 905-664-6341; *Fax:* 905-664-8966
lutz@bellnet.ca

***Stoney Creek*: Mary J. MacKinnon - *2**
860 Queenston Rd., Stoney Creek, ON L8G 4A8
Tel: 905-662-0046; *Fax:* 905-662-3339
info@mackinnonlaw.com
www.mackinnonlaw.com

***Stoney Creek*: Murray R. Mazza - *1**
426 Hwy. 8, Stoney Creek, ON L8G 1G2
Tel: 905-561-1444
idseast@cogeco.net

** indicates number of lawyers*

***Stoney Creek*: O'Brien & Skrtich - *1**
26 King St. East, Stoney Creek, ON L8G 1J8
Tel: 905-662-2855; *Fax:* 905-662-8881

***Stoney Creek*: Mari-Anne Saunders - *1**
#303, 800 Queenston Rd., Stoney Creek, ON L8G 1A7
Tel: 905-664-6683; *Fax:* 905-664-4876

***Stouffville*: Button, Armstrong & Ness - *3**
P.O. Box 220, Stn. Main, 6361 Main St., Stouffville, ON L4A 7Z5
Tel: 905-640-3530; *Fax:* 905-640-7027
banlaw@rogers.com

***Stratford*: John W. Buechler - *1**
488 Erie St., Stratford, ON N5A 2N6
Tel: 519-271-3520; *Fax:* 519-271-0097

***Stratford*: Michael F. Fair - *1**
24 Downie St., 2nd Fl., Stratford, ON N5A 6W3
Tel: 519-271-2912; *Fax:* 519-271-2732

***Stratford*: MBK Law LLP - *4**
42 Waterloo St., Stratford, ON N5A 4A7
Tel: 519-273-2734; *Fax:* 519-273-2713
info@mbklaw.ca

***Stratford*: Mountain Mitchell LLP - *7**
P.O. Box 846, 56 Albert St., Stratford, ON N5A 6W3
Tel: 519-271-6770; *Fax:* 519-271-9261
main@mountainmitchell.com
www.mountainmitchell.com

***Stratford*: Skinner, Dunphy & Bantle LLP - *4**
P.O. Box 542, 1 Ontario St., Stratford, ON N5A 6T7
Tel: 519-271-7330; *Fax:* 519-271-1762
thefirm@stratfordlaw.com

***Stratford*: L. Ray Waller - *1**
#103, P.O. Box 813, Stn. Main, 386 Cambria St., Stratford, ON N5A 6W1
Tel: 519-271-4420; *Fax:* 519-271-7833

***Strathroy*: Robert J. Dack - *1**
16 Front St. East, Strathroy, ON N7G 1Y4
Tel: 519-245-0370; *Fax:* 519-245-0523

***Strathroy*: Jones, Gibbons & Reis - *2**
39 Front St. West, Strathroy, ON N7G 1X5
Tel: 519-245-1110; *Fax:* 519-245-5859
jmr@webgate.net

***Strathroy*: Quinlan & Somerville - *2**
18 Front St. East, Strathroy, ON N7G 1Y4
Tel: 519-245-0342; *Fax:* 519-245-0108
lawyers@quinlansomerville.com

***Strathroy*: H.P. Ramkelawan - *1**
P.O. Box 254, Stn. Main, RR#5, Strathroy, ON N7G 3J2
Tel: 519-245-6074

***Strathroy*: George E. Sinker - *2**
53 Front St. West, Strathroy, ON N7G 1X6
Tel: 519-245-1144; *Fax:* 519-245-6090
gsinker@bellnet.ca

***Sudbury*: Michael G. Barnett - *1**
264 Elm St., Sudbury, ON P3C 1V4
Tel: 705-674-3210; *Fax:* 705-674-1265

***Sudbury*: William G. Beach - *1**
224 Applegrove St., Sudbury, ON P3C 1N3
Tel: 705-675-5685; *Fax:* 705-675-6601

***Sudbury*: Beckett, Huneault - *2**
135 Applegrove St., Sudbury, ON P3C 1N2
Tel: 705-673-9551; *Fax:* 705-673-0476

***Sudbury*: Gerald D. Brouillette - *1**
235 Elm St., Sudbury, ON P3C 1T8
Tel: 705-674-2822; *Fax:* 705-674-2975
gerry.brouillette@sympatico.ca

***Sudbury*: Conroy Trebb Scott Hurtubise LLP, Barristers, Solicitors - *6**
164 Elm St., Sudbury, ON P3C 1T7
Tel: 705-674-6441; *Fax:* 705-673-9567
Toll-Free: 800-627-1825
info@sudburylegal.com
www.sudburylegal.com

***Sudbury*: DeDiana, Eloranta & Longstreet - *1**
219 Pine St., Sudbury, ON P3C 1X4
Tel: 705-674-4289; *Fax:* 705-671-1047

***Sudbury*: Desmarais, Keenan LLP - *10**
#201, 62 Frood Rd., Sudbury, ON P3C 4Z3
Tel: 705-675-7521; *Fax:* 705-675-7390
Toll-Free: 800-290-5465
www.desmaraiskeenan.com

***Sudbury*: Hugh A. Doig, Q.C. - *1**
296 Larch St., Sudbury, ON P3B 1M2
Tel: 705-674-4213; *Fax:* 705-671-1652
doig@on.aibn.com

***Sudbury*: Robert L. Fabbro - *1**
#1, 54 Elgin St., Sudbury, ON P3E 3N2
Tel: 705-675-6620; *Fax:* 705-675-6655
robertfabbro@on.aibn.com

***Sudbury*: Brian N. Howe - *1**
235 Elm St. West, Sudbury, ON P3C 1T8
Tel: 705-674-8317; *Fax:* 705-674-2952

***Sudbury*: Elizabeth Kari - *1**
293 Elm St., 2nd Fl., Sudbury, ON P3C 1V6
Tel: 705-670-2770; *Fax:* 705-670-9172
ekari@cyberbeach.net

***Sudbury*: Donald Kuyek - *1**
229 Elm St. West, Sudbury, ON P3C 1T8
Tel: 705-675-1227; *Fax:* 705-675-5350
Toll-Free: 877-414-0311

***Sudbury*: Lacroix, Forest LLP/s.r.l. - *10**
Place Balmoral, 36 Elgin St., Sudbury, ON P3C 5B4
Tel: 705-674-1976; *Fax:* 705-674-6978
office@sudburylaw.com
www.sudburylaw.com

***Sudbury*: J. Robert LeBlanc - *1**
125 Durham St., 2nd Fl., Sudbury, ON P3E 3M9
Tel: 705-674-5858; *Fax:* 705-674-9137
bleblanc@cyberbeach.net

***Sudbury*: Patricia L. Meehan - *1**
293 Elm St. West, Sudbury, ON P3C 1V6
Tel: 705-674-2272; *Fax:* 705-674-5238
patricia.meehan@sympatico.ca

***Sudbury*: Mensour & Mensour - *2**
#101, 238 Elm St., Sudbury, ON P3C 1V3
Tel: 705-673-6787; *Fax:* 705-673-1418

***Sudbury*: Miller, Maki - *14**
176 Elm St., Sudbury, ON P3C 1T7
Tel: 705-675-7503; *Fax:* 705-675-8669
oharam@millermaki.com

***Sudbury*: Paquette & Renzini - *3**
#200, 1188 St. Jerome St., Sudbury, ON P3A 2V9
Tel: 705-560-2121; *Fax:* 705-560-8072
mail@paquette-renzini.ca

***Sudbury*: Parisé Law Office - *2**
58 Lisgar St., 2nd Fl., Sudbury, ON P3E 3L7
Tel: 705-674-4042; *Fax:* 705-674-4242
pariselaw@unitz.ca

***Sudbury*: Glenn E.J. Sandberg**
#200, 144 Elm St. West, Sudbury, ON P3C 1T7
Tel: 705-671-9922; *Fax:* 705-671-2107

***Sudbury*: Norman G. Stoner - *1**
#202, 124 Cedar St., Sudbury, ON P3E 1B4
Tel: 705-675-8307; *Fax:* 705-675-7245
ngslaw@bellnet.ca

***Sudbury*: Stanley J. Thomas - *1**
111 Durham St., Sudbury, ON P3E 3M9
Tel: 705-674-8306; *Fax:* 705-675-8466

***Sudbury*: Law Office of Serge F. Treherne - *1**
P.O. Box 1269, 144 Elm St. West, Sudbury, ON P3C 1T7
Tel: 705-670-9689; *Fax:* 705-670-9141
Toll-Free: 877-550-5616

***Sudbury*: Violette Law Offices - *1**
#1, 11 Elgin St., Sudbury, ON P3C 5B6
Tel: 705-674-1300; *Fax:* 705-671-1044
Toll-Free: 866-991-1300
office@violettelaw.com

***Sudbury*: Wilkins & Wilkins - *2**
P.O. Box 490, Stn. B, 176 Elm St., Sudbury, ON P3E 4P6
Tel: 705-675-1200

***Sundridge*: Michael A. Hardy & Associates - *2**
P.O. Box 1060, 105 Main St. East, Sundridge, ON P0A 1Z0
Tel: 705-384-5770; *Fax:* 705-384-5771
sunlaw@bellnet.ca

***Sutton*: Patrick J. Fahey Law Office - *2**
P.O. Box 487, 100 High St., Sutton, ON L0E 1R0
Tel: 905-722-3771; *Fax:* 905-722-9852
pat.pjf@rogers.com

***Thornhill*: Augustine M. Arrigo, Q.C. - *1**
48 Guardsman Rd., Thornhill, ON L3T 6L4
Tel: 905-889-6131

***Thornhill*: Leslie (Masood) Brown**
#225B, Commerce Gate, 505 Hwy. 7 East, Thornhill, ON L3T 7T1
Tel: 905-731-5083; *Fax:* 905-731-4078
les@torontolegalservices.ca

***Thornhill*: Edward L. Burlew - *1**
16 John St., Thornhill, ON L3T 1X8
Tel: 905-882-2422; *Fax:* 905-882-2431
Toll-Free: 888-486-5677

***Thornhill*: Law Office of Cosimo A. Crupi Barrister & Solicitor - *1**
#302, 305 Renfrew Dr., Thornhill, ON L3R 9S7
Tel: 905-415-8900; *Fax:* 905-415-8902
cacrupi@crupilaw.ca
www.crupilaw.ca

***Thornhill*: Iain Stewart Cunningham - *1**
20 Cypress Point Ct., Thornhill, ON L3T 1V7
Tel: 905-764-7376; *Fax:* 905-707-5818

***Thornhill*: Stephen R. Dyment - *1**
#216, 2900 Steeles Ave. East, Thornhill, ON L3T 4X1
Tel: 905-882-1277; *Fax:* 905-882-8536

***Thornhill*: Fish & Associates Professional Corporation - *2**
7951 Yonge St., Thornhill, ON L3T 2C4
Tel: 905-881-1500; *Fax:* 905-881-6535
bfish@fishlaw.ca
www.familyfight.com

***Thornhill*: A.M. Flisfeder - *1**
45 Janesville Rd., Thornhill, ON L4J 6Z9
Tel: 416-469-0375; *Fax:* 416-469-0375

***Thornhill*: Gregory J. Gaglione - *1**
#202, 7368 Yonge St., Thornhill, ON L4J 8H9
Tel: 416-882-0066; *Fax:* 416-882-2550

***Thornhill*: Elana P. Glass - *1**
149 Langtry Pl., Thornhill, ON L4J 8L6
Tel: 416-587-5680

***Thornhill*: Barry S. Greenberg - *1**
7626A Yonge St., Thornhill, ON L4J 1V9
Tel: 905-886-9535; *Fax:* 905-886-9540
bsgreenberg@rogers.com

***Thornhill*: Perry H. Gruenberger - *1**
#220, 8500 Leslie St., Thornhill, ON L3T 7M8
Tel: 905-764-6411; *Fax:* 905-886-6034

***Thornhill*: Seymour Iseman - *1**
#216, 2900 Steeles Ave. East, Thornhill, ON L3T 4X1
Tel: 905-881-8800; *Fax:* 905-881-7391
siseman@allstream.net

***Thornhill*: Lexim - *1**
79 Sanibel Cres., Thornhill, ON L4J 8K7
Tel: 647-295-8683
jcooper@cjpac.ca

***Thornhill*: Arthur Lundy - *1**
#402, 300 John St., Thornhill, ON L3T 5W4
Tel: 905-886-3110; *Fax:* 905-886-0989

***Thornhill*: Carolyn L. MacDonald - *1**
14 Morgan Ave., Thornhill, ON L3T 1R1
Tel: 905-707-7723; *Fax:* 905-707-5818

***Thornhill*: Janet MacDougall - *1**
#202, 8108 Yonge St., Thornhill, ON L4J 1W4
Tel: 905-886-4907; *Fax:* 905-886-8070

***Thornhill*: R.G. Merritt - *1**
#205, 7089 Yonge St., Thornhill, ON L3T 2A7
Tel: 905-889-3430; *Fax:* 905-889-7290
rgmerritt@home.com

** indicates number of lawyers*

***Thornhill*: D. Todd Morganstein - *1**
#110, 8111 Yonge St., Thornhill, ON L3T 4V9
Tel: 905-881-8289; *Fax:* 905-881-2696

***Thornhill*: Roselyn Pecus - *1**
#310, 1 Promenade Circle, Thornhill, ON L4J 4P8
Tel: 905-709-8105; *Fax:* 905-709-8180

***Thornhill*: Tania Perlin**
#B10-137, 800 Steeles Ave. West, Thornhill, ON L4J 7L2
Tel: 416-225-5424; *Fax:* 416-225-3611

***Thornhill*: Raphael Barristers - *4**
#202, 1137 Centre St., Thornhill, ON L4J 3M6
Tel: 416-594-1812; *Fax:* 416-594-0868
Toll-Free: 877-217-1812
info@raphaelpersonalinjurylawyers.com
www.raphaelpersonalinjurylawyers.com

***Thornhill*: Thomas H. Riesz - *1**
#218, 180 Steeles Ave. West, Thornhill, ON L4J 2L1
Tel: 905-881-5609; *Fax:* 905-881-9859

***Thornhill*: Erwin S. Seltzer - *1**
9 MacArthur Dr., Thornhill, ON L4J 7T6
Tel: 905-731-7131

***Thornhill*: Ben Weinstein - *1**
#203, 1 Clark Ave. West, Thornhill, ON L4J 7Y6
Tel: 905-889-5364; *Fax:* 905-889-3231

***Thornhill*: Judith M. Wolf - *1**
#260, 1054 Centre St., Thornhill, ON L4J 8E5
Tel: 905-731-3372; *Fax:* 905-731-7913

***Thorold*: Jurmain Law Office - *2**
8A Clairmont St., Thorold, ON L2V 1R1
Tel: 905-227-2829; *Fax:* 905-227-9206
info@jurmainlaw.com
www.jurmainlaw.com

***Thorold*: John J. Simon - *1**
P.O. Box 505, Stn. Thorold, 7 Front St. North, Thorold, ON L2V 4W1
Tel: 905-227-9191; *Fax:* 905-227-7234
john_smith@hotmail.com

***Thorold*: Young, McNamara - *2**
18 Albert St. East, Thorold, ON L2V 1P1
Tel: 905-227-3777; *Fax:* 905-227-5988

***Thunder Bay*: Atwood Labine Arnone McCartney LLP - *7**
501 Donald St. East, Thunder Bay, ON P7E 6N6
Tel: 807-623-4342; *Fax:* 807-623-2098
asl@asl-law.com
www.alamlaw.ca

***Thunder Bay*: Marc L. Bode, Barrister & Solicitor - *1**
#816, 34 Cumberland St. North, Thunder Bay, ON P7A 4L3
Tel: 807-344-9444; *Fax:* 807-344-3420
marcbode@thaytel.net

***Thunder Bay*: David S. Bruzzese - *1**
#320, Marina Park Centre, 180 Park Ave., Thunder Bay, ON P7B 6J4
Tel: 807-344-1020; *Fax:* 807-344-1433
dsb.law@shawlink.ca

***Thunder Bay*: Buset & Partners LLP - *15**
1121 Barton St., Thunder Bay, ON P7B 5N3
Tel: 807-623-2500; *Fax:* 807-622-7808
Toll-Free: 866-532-8738
law@buset-partners.com
www.buset-partners.com

***Thunder Bay*: Carrel+Partners LLP - *13**
1136 Alloy Dr., Thunder Bay, ON P7B 6M9
Tel: 807-346-3000; *Fax:* 807-346-3600
Toll-Free: 800-263-0578
info@carrel.com
www.carrel.com

***Thunder Bay*: Cheadles LLP - *8**
#2000, P.O. Box 10429, 715 Hewitson St., Thunder Bay, ON P7B 6T8
Tel: 807-622-6821; *Fax:* 807-623-3892

***Thunder Bay*: Christie Potestio Freitag - *3**
#203, 920 Tungsten St., Thunder Bay, ON P7B 5Z6
Tel: 807-344-6651; *Fax:* 807-345-1105
potestio@chrpot.on.ca

***Thunder Bay*: Donald R. Colborne - *1**
Site 14, Comp 67, RR#13, Thunder Bay, ON P7B 5E4
Tel: 807-344-6628; *Fax:* 807-983-3079
colborne@microage-tb.com

***Thunder Bay*: Richard W. Courtis - *1**
#101, 1151 Barton St., Thunder Bay, ON P7B 5N3
Tel: 807-623-3000; *Fax:* 807-623-1251
Toll-Free: 877-266-6646
courtis@hotmail.com

***Thunder Bay*: Cupello & Company - *4**
#104, 105 South May St., Thunder Bay, ON P7E 1B1
Tel: 807-622-8201; *Fax:* 807-622-3755
Toll-Free: 888-223-0739
law@cupello-company.com

***Thunder Bay*: Erickson & Partners - *8**
291 South Court St., Thunder Bay, ON P7B 2Y1
Tel: 807-345-1213; *Fax:* 807-345-2526
Toll-Free: 800-465-3912

***Thunder Bay*: Filipovic, Brothers & Conway - *5**
#20, Tomlinson Block, 8A North Cumberland St., Thunder Bay, ON P7A 4L1
Tel: 807-343-9090; *Fax:* 807-345-1397
Toll-Free: 800-760-8694

***Thunder Bay*: Dennis A. Forbes & Associates - *1**
155 Rupert St., Thunder Bay, ON P7B 3X2
Tel: 807-345-1250; *Fax:* 807-345-1250
dennis@dennisforbes.com

***Thunder Bay*: Peter Heerema - *1**
44 Algoma St. South, Thunder Bay, ON P7B 3A9
Tel: 807-346-4053; *Fax:* 807-346-8714
peter.heerema@tbaytel.net

***Thunder Bay*: Illingworth & Illingworth - *2**
#201, 1151 Barton St., Thunder Bay, ON P7B 5N3
Tel: 807-623-7222; *Fax:* 807-622-5297
lawyers@tbaytel.net

***Thunder Bay*: Lac des Mille Lacs First Nation - *1**
#328, 1100 Memorial Ave., Thunder Bay, ON P7B 4A3
Tel: 807-622-9835; *Fax:* 807-622-9866
ldmlfn@tbaytel.net

***Thunder Bay*: Rick E. Lauder - *1**
217 Van Norman St., Thunder Bay, ON P7A 4B6
Tel: 807-683-4444; *Fax:* 807-345-0337
rick.lauder@shawbiz.ca
www.ricklauder.shawbiz.ca

***Thunder Bay*: William L. Lees & Associates Ltd. - *1**
491 Richmond St., Thunder Bay, ON P7A 1R2
Tel: 807-683-6946; *Fax:* 807-683-5089
wllees@shaw.ca

***Thunder Bay*: Martin Scrimshaw Scott - *4**
Cumberland Park, 1 Cumberland St. South, Thunder Bay, ON P7B 2T1
Tel: 807-345-3600; *Fax:* 807-344-8152
msslaw@tbaytel.net

***Thunder Bay*: Thomas C. Mitton - *1**
123 South Brodie St., Thunder Bay, ON P7E 1B8
Tel: 807-623-4320; *Fax:* 807-622-8038
tcmitton@tbaytel.net

***Thunder Bay*: Peter Mrowiec - *1**
#816, 34 Cumberland St. North, Thunder Bay, ON P7A 4L3
Tel: 807-344-0099; *Fax:* 807-344-3420
pmlaw@tbaytel.net

***Thunder Bay*: Robert D. Mullen - *1**
395 Fort William Rd., Thunder Bay, ON P7B 2Z3
Tel: 807-344-5848; *Fax:* 807-344-5877
rmullen@shawbiz.ca

***Thunder Bay*: Petrone Hornak Garofalo Mauro - *9**
76 Algoma St. North, Thunder Bay, ON P7A 4Z4
Tel: 807-344-9191; *Fax:* 807-345-8391
Toll-Free: 800-465-3988

***Thunder Bay*: A.D. Stewart - *1**
#112, 105 May St. North, Thunder Bay, ON P7C 3N9
Tel: 807-623-7852; *Fax:* 807-623-0014
astewart@807-city.on.ca

***Thunder Bay*: Frank Valente - *1**
#5-8A, 8 Cumberland St. North, Thunder Bay, ON P7A 4L1
Tel: 807-345-5225; *Fax:* 807-345-8400

***Thunder Bay*: Vauthier, Paivalainen - *1**
275 Bay St., Thunder Bay, ON P7B 1R7
Tel: 807-343-9394; *Fax:* 807-344-1562

***Thunder Bay*: Thomas G. Watkinson - *1**
123 Brodie St. South, Thunder Bay, ON P7E 1B8
Tel: 807-624-5605; *Fax:* 807-623-6096

***Thunder Bay*: Weiler, Maloney, Nelson - *11**
#201, 1001 William St., Thunder Bay, ON P7B 6M1
Tel: 807-623-1111; *Fax:* 807-623-4947
weilers@wmnlaw.com
www.weilers.ca

***Tilbury*: R.M. Jutras - *1**
P.O. Box 417, 50 Queen St. South, Tilbury, ON N0P 2L0
Tel: 519-682-3100; *Fax:* 519-682-3622

***Tilbury*: Taylor & Delrue - *3**
P.O. Box 459, 40 Queen St. South, Tilbury, ON N0P 2L0
Tel: 519-682-0164; *Fax:* 519-682-2777
taydel@cogeco.net

***Tillsonburg*: James G. Battin - *1**
25 Bidwell St., Tillsonburg, ON N4G 3T4
Tel: 519-688-9033; *Fax:* 519-688-9036
bidlaw@kwic.com

***Tillsonburg*: Gibson, Linton, Toth, Campbell & Bennett - *3**
P.O. Box 5, Stn. Main, 36 Broadway, Tillsonburg, ON N4G 4H3
Tel: 519-842-3658; *Fax:* 519-842-5001
gltcb@kwic.com

***Tillsonburg*: Groom & Szorenyi - *1**
36 Broadway, Tillsonburg, ON N4G 4H3
Tel: 519-842-4205; *Fax:* 519-842-4261

***Tillsonburg*: Jenkins & Gilvesy - *2**
P.O. Box 280, Stn. Main, 107 Broadway Street, Tillsonburg, ON N4G 4H5
Tel: 519-842-9017; *Fax:* 519-842-3394
http://www.linkedin.com/pub/lisa-gilvesy/9/622/65a

***Tillsonburg*: Mandryk, Stewart & Morgan - *3**
65 Bidwell St., Tillsonburg, ON N4G 3T8
Tel: 519-842-4228; *Fax:* 519-842-7659
mhlaw@oxford.net

***Timmins*: Sydney Brooks - *1**
81 Balsam St. South, Timmins, ON P4N 2C9
Tel: 705-264-5341; *Fax:* 705-264-2550

***Timmins*: Carlesso Barazzutti - *2**
#204, Scotiabank Bldg., 3 Pine St. South, Timmins, ON P4N 2J9
Tel: 705-264-1374; *Fax:* 705-264-1450

***Timmins*: Suzanne Desrosiers - *1**
92 Spruce St. North, Timmins, ON P4N 6M8
Tel: 705-268-6492; *Fax:* 705-264-1940
sdesrosiers@peroonainternet.com

***Timmins*: Evans, Bragagnolo & Sullivan - *8**
120 Pine St. South, Timmins, ON P4N 2K4
Tel: 705-264-1285; *Fax:* 705-264-7424
ebslawyers@ebslawyers.com

***Timmins*: J.P. Huot - *1**
P.O. Box 1065, 36 Maple St. South, Timmins, ON P4N 7H9
Tel: 705-267-6464; *Fax:* 705-264-3260

***Timmins*: Petersen Consulting - *1**
136 Cedar St. South, Timmins, ON P4N 2G8
Tel: 705-264-5323; *Fax:* 705-268-0300
pcmanage@nt.net

***Timmins*: Racicot, Maisonneuve, Labelle, Cooper - *6**
15 Balsam St. South, Timmins, ON P4N 2C7
Tel: 705-264-2385; *Fax:* 705-268-3949
mlclaw@ntl.sympatico.ca

***Timmins*: Riopelle Griener Professional Corporation - *8**
#202, 85 Pine St. South, Timmins, ON P4N 2K1
Tel: 705-264-9591; *Fax:* 705-264-1393
Toll-Free: 866-624-1614
www.rglaw.cahttp://www.facebook.com/#!/RiopelleGriener

** indicates number of lawyers*

Toronto: Aaron & Aaron - *1
#1400, 10 King St. East, Toronto, ON M5C 1C3
Tel: 416-364-9366; Fax: 416-364-3818
bob@aaron.ca
www.aaron.ca

Toronto: G.J. Abols - *1
#8866, 700 Bay St., Toronto, ON M5G 1Z6
Tel: 416-598-8866; Fax: 416-971-7656

Toronto: Abrams & Krochak, Professional Corporation - *2
#402, 250 Merton St., Toronto, ON M4S 1B1
Tel: 416-482-3387; Fax: 416-482-0647
askus@akcanada.com
www.abramsandkrochak.comwww.facebook.com/AKCanada, twitter.com/AbramsKrochak

Toronto: Adair Morse LLP - *19
#1800, 1 Queen St. East, Toronto, ON M5C 2W5
Tel: 416-863-1230; Fax: 416-863-1241
info@adairmorse.com
www.adairmorse.com

Toronto: G. Chalmers Adams - *1
#100, 1255 Yonge St., Toronto, ON M4T 1W6
Tel: 416-929-7232; Fax: 416-929-7225
info@gcadams.on.ca

Toronto: Adler Bytensky - *6
#1708, 5000 Yonge St., Toronto, ON M2N 7E9
Tel: 416-365-3151; Fax: 416-365-0866
www.crimlawcanada.com

Toronto: Advocacy Centre for the Elderly - *5
#701, 2 Carlton St., Toronto, ON M5B 1J3
Tel: 416-598-2656; Fax: 416-598-7924
www.advocacycentreelderly.org

Toronto: Advocate Placement Ltd. - *4
#200, 1200 Bay St., Toronto, ON M5R 2A5
Tel: 416-927-9222; Fax: 416-927-8772
Toll-Free: 800-461-1275
resume@advocateplacement.com
www.advocateplacement.com

Toronto: Affleck Greene McMurty LLP - *13
#200, 365 Bay St., Toronto, ON M5H 2V1
Tel: 416-360-2800; Fax: 416-360-5960
info@agmlawyers.com
www.agmlawyers.com

Toronto: Agnew, Gladstone LLP - *2
215 Carlton St., Toronto, ON M5A 2K9
Tel: 416-964-0021; Fax: 416-964-0744
yagnew@agnewgladstone.com
www.agnewgladstone.com

Toronto: Claudio R. Aiello - *1
#900, 920 Yonge St., Toronto, ON M4W 3C7
Tel: 416-969-9900; Fax: 416-969-9060
claudio@aiellolaw.ca

Toronto: Irving J. Aiken - *1
#1105, 65 Queen St. West, Toronto, ON M5H 2M5
Tel: 416-947-0199; Fax: 416-947-0379

Toronto: Jerome T. Albert
921 Manning Ave., Toronto, ON M6G 2X5
Tel: 416-535-3173

Toronto: Alloway & Associates - *3
290 Lawrence Ave. West, Toronto, ON M5M 1B3
Tel: 416-971-9293; Fax: 416-971-9349
email@alloway.net
www.alloway.net

Toronto: Alpert Law Firm - *2
#900, 1 St. Clair Ave. East, Toronto, ON M4T 2V7
Tel: 416-923-0809; Fax: 416-923-1549
halpert@alpertlawfirm.ca
www.alpertlawfirm.ca

Toronto: Harriet Altman - *1
68 Garnier Court, Toronto, ON M2M 4C9
Tel: 416-224-5240; Fax: 416-224-0360
Toll-Free: 877-224-5229

Toronto: Sheldon L. Altman - *1
264B Adelaide St. East, Toronto, ON M5A 1N1
Tel: 416-929-1313; Fax: 416-929-1316
altmansheldon@aol.com
www.sheldonaltman.com

Toronto: Altwerger, Baker, Weinberg - *3
#2901, P.O. Box 2450, 2300 Yonge St., Toronto, ON M4P 1E4
Tel: 416-480-1662; Fax: 416-480-0017
stevea@lexpertor.com

Toronto: Jaikrishin R. Ambwani - *1
#330, 100 Cowdray Ct., Toronto, ON M1S 5C8
Tel: 416-754-4404; Fax: 416-754-7746
jack@jackambwani.com
www.jackambwani.com

Toronto: Julie Evelyn Amourgis - *1
#800, 439 University Ave., Toronto, ON M5G 1Y8
Tel: 416-504-5844; Fax: 416-369-1723

Toronto: Anderson Bourdon Burgess
#116, 295 The West Mall, Toronto, ON M9C 4Z4
Tel: 416-621-9644; Fax: 416-621-9668
anderson@andersonbb.com
www.andersonbb.com

Toronto: Dwight Anderson - *1
1709 Bloor St. West, Toronto, ON M6P 4E5
Tel: 416-769-3522; Fax: 416-769-2302
dwightanderson@rogers.com

Toronto: Joan Anderson - *1
#702, 100 Alexander St., Toronto, ON M4Y 1B9
Tel: 416-929-9909; Fax: 416-929-2367
anderson.j@sympatico.ca

Toronto: Andriessen & Associates - *4
#900, 701 Evans Ave., Toronto, ON M9C 1A3
Tel: 416-620-7020; Fax: 416-620-1398
info@andriessen.ca
www.andriessen.ca

Toronto: Philip Anisman Barrister & Solicitor - *1
#1704, 80 Richmond St. West, Toronto, ON M5H 2A4
Tel: 416-363-4200; Fax: 416-363-6200

Toronto: Dennis Apostolides - *1
867 Danforth Ave., Toronto, ON M4J 1L7
Tel: 416-463-1147; Fax: 416-463-1762
apostolides@rogers.com

Toronto: Jerry Applebaum - *1
36 Covington Rd., Toronto, ON M6A 1G1
Tel: 416-785-1140

Toronto: Aprile Law - *1
#1510, North York City Centre, 5140 Yonge St., Toronto, ON M2N 6L7
Tel: 416-218-5268; Fax: 866-544-5268
info@aprilelaw.com

Toronto: Armel, Gray LLP - *5
#500, 390 Bay St., Toronto, ON M5H 2Y2
Tel: 416-362-1400; Fax: 416-362-1404

Toronto: D.W. Arn - *1
380 Bathurst St., Toronto, ON M5T 2S6
Tel: 416-603-3658; Fax: 416-603-1144

Toronto: Aronovitch Macaulay Rollo LLP - *21
251 King St. East, Toronto, ON M5A 1K2
Tel: 416-369-9393; Fax: 416-369-0665
info@amrlaw.ca
www.amrlaw.com

Toronto: Ara P. Arzumanian - *1
#2200, 181 University Ave., Toronto, ON M5H 3M7
Tel: 416-777-1400; Fax: 416-777-1999
ara@businessandtechlaw.com
www.businessandtechlaw.com

Toronto: Harvey Ash - *1
#900, 5799 Yonge St., Toronto, ON M2M 3V3
Tel: 416-250-0080; Fax: 416-225-1124
harveyash@lawyer.ca

Toronto: William Ash - *1
#801, 55 Eglinton Ave. East, Toronto, ON M4P 1G8
Tel: 416-486-8751; Fax: 416-486-8789
willash@bellnet.ca

Toronto: Ashbourne & Caskey - *1
2077 Lawrence Ave. West, Toronto, ON M9N 1H7
Tel: 416-247-6677; Fax: 416-247-3519

Toronto: Atherton Barristers - *1
#1604, 55 University Ave., Toronto, ON M5J 2H7
Tel: 416-365-1030; Fax: 416-946-1619
Toll-Free: 866-237-1030
bcatherton@ablaw.com
www.athertonbarristers.com

Toronto: S.J. AvRuskin - *1
66 Charles St. East., Toronto, ON M4Y 2R3
Tel: 416-922-4147; Fax: 416-922-8022

Toronto: Aylesworth LLP - *33
Ernst & Young Tower, TD Centre, P.O. Box 124, 222 Bay St., 18th Fl., Toronto, ON M5K 1H1
Tel: 416-777-0101; Fax: 416-865-1398
ekay@aylaw.com
www.aylesworth.com

Toronto: Denise Badley - *1
#2, 2069 Danforth Ave., 2nd Fl., Toronto, ON M4C 1J8
Tel: 416-690-6195; Fax: 416-690-6271
dbadleylaw@rogers.com

Toronto: J. Waldo Baerg - *1
#506, 372 Bay St., Toronto, ON M5H 2W9
Tel: 416-366-3705; Fax: 416-366-0157
waldobaerg@on.aibn.com

Toronto: Baker & Company - *4
#3300, 130 Adelaide St. West, Toronto, ON M5H 3P5
Tel: 416-777-0100; Fax: 416-366-3992
info@bakerlawyers.com
www.bakerlawyers.com

Toronto: Baker & McKenzie LLP - *51
#2100, Brookfield Place, P.O. Box 874, 181 Bay St., Toronto, ON M5J 2T3
Tel: 416-863-1221; Fax: 416-863-6275
www.bakernet.com

Toronto: Baker Schneider Ruggiero LLP - *8
#1000, 120 Adelaide St. West, Toronto, ON M5H 3V1
Tel: 416-363-2211; Fax: 416-363-0645

Toronto: Gordon R. Baker, Q.C. - *1
#1440, Exchange Tower, P.O. Box 426, 130 King St. West, Toronto, ON M5X 1E3
Tel: 416-365-7203; Fax: 416-365-7204
gord@gordbaker.com
www.gordbaker.com

Toronto: J. Anthony Baker - *1
500 Danforth Ave., Toronto, ON M4K 1P6
Tel: 416-463-4411; Fax: 416-463-4562
baker@tonybakerlaw.com
www.tonybakerlaw.com

Toronto: Ahmad N. Baksh - *1
#307, 1280 Finch Ave. West, Toronto, ON M3J 3K6
Tel: 416-667-1922; Fax: 416-667-0304
anbaksh@bellnet.ca

Toronto: John M. Banfill Q.C. - *1
#300, 133 Berkeley St., Toronto, ON M5A 2X1
Tel: 416-365-0019; Fax: 416-365-0022
jmbanfill@bellnet.ca

Toronto: Banks & Starkman - *2
#310, 200 Ronson Dr., Toronto, ON M9W 5Z9
Tel: 416-243-3394; Fax: 416-243-9692
lbanks@banksandstarkman.com
www.banksandstarkman.com

Toronto: J.R. Barrs - *1
23 Bedford Road, Toronto, ON M5R 2J9
Tel: 416-366-6466; Fax: 416-364-2308

Toronto: Jacqueline R. Bart - *1
#2200, Law Chambers, ING Tower, 181 University Ave., Toronto, ON M5H 3M7
Tel: 416-601-1346; Fax: 416-601-1357
jbart@canadianrelocationlaw.com
www.canadianrelocationlaw.com

Toronto: Basman, Smith - *19
111 Richmond St. West, 8th Floor, Toronto, ON M5H 2G4
Tel: 416-365-0300; Fax: 416-365-9276
Toll-Free: 877-262-0001
info@basmansmith.com
www.basmansmith.com

Toronto: Bastedo, Stewart, Smith
#1800, 180 Dundas St. West, Toronto, ON M5G 1Z8
Tel: 416-595-1916; Fax: 416-596-7538

Toronto: Batcher, Wasserman & Associates - *2
#500, 718 Wilson Ave., Toronto, ON M3K 1E2
Tel: 416-635-6300; Fax: 416-635-6376
Toll-Free: 877-813-0820

** indicates number of lawyers*

Toronto: Bates Barristers - *4
34 King Street East, 12th Floor, Toronto, ON M5C 2X8
Tel: 416-869-9898; Fax: 416-869-9405
info@batesbarristers.com
www.batesbarristers.com

Toronto: Beard, Winter - *47
#701, 130 Adelaide St. West, Toronto, ON M5H 2K4
Tel: 416-593-5555; Fax: 416-593-7760
info@beardwinter.com
www.beardwinter.com

Toronto: Beber & Associates - *2
#2900, 390 Bay St., Toronto, ON M5H 2Y2
Tel: 416-867-2280; Fax: 416-869-0321
www.beber.ca

Toronto: Sandra Bebris - *1
#300, 1370 Don Mills Rd., Toronto, ON M3B 3N7
Tel: 416-510-1324; Fax: 416-441-0591
bebris@pathcom.com

Toronto: Steven Bellissimo - *1
#1200, 439 University Ave., Toronto, ON M5G 1Y8
Tel: 416-362-6437; Fax: 416-972-9940
steve@sblaw.ca

Toronto: Bellmore & Moore - *5
#1600, 393 University Ave., Toronto, ON M5G 1E6
Tel: 416-581-1818; Fax: 416-581-1279
www.bellmoreandmoore.com

Toronto: Belmont, Fine & Associates - *2
#601, 1120 Finch Ave. West, Toronto, ON M3J 3H7
Tel: 416-661-2066; Fax: 416-661-2116
belmontfine@yahoo.com
www.belmontfine.com

Toronto: Bennett & Company - *2
#1500, 151 Yonge Street, Toronto, ON M5C 2W7
Tel: 416-363-8688; Fax: 416-363-8083
bennett@ican.net
www.bennettonbankruptcy.ca

Toronto: Bennett Best Burn LLP - *12
#1700, 150 York St., Toronto, ON M5H 3S5
Tel: 416-362-3400; Fax: 416-362-2211
info@bbburn.com
www.bbburn.com

Toronto: Benson Percival Brown - *17
#800, 250 Dundas St. West, Toronto, ON M5T 2Z6
Tel: 416-977-9777; Fax: 416-977-1241
www.bensonpercival.com

Toronto: Bereskin & Parr - *55
Scotia Plaza, 40 King St. West, 40th Fl., Toronto, ON M5H 3Y2
Tel: 416-364-7311; Fax: 416-361-1398
Toll-Free: 888-364-7311
info@bereskinparr.com
www.bereskinparr.com

Toronto: Bergel & Edson - *7
#501, 1018 Finch Ave. West, Toronto, ON M3J 3L5
Tel: 416-663-2211; Fax: 416-663-2348
Toll-Free: 866-492-3743
www.bergeledson.com

Toronto: Max Berger Professional Law Corporation - *2
#207, 1033 Bay St., Toronto, ON M5S 3A5
Tel: 416-969-9263; Fax: 416-969-9098
max@maxberger.ca
www.maxberger.ca

Toronto: Berkow, Cohen LLP - *6
#400, 141 Adelaide St. West, Toronto, ON M5H 3L5
Tel: 416-364-4900; Fax: 416-364-3865
jberkow@berkowcohen.com
www.berkowcohen.com

Toronto: Bradley F. Berns - *1
#902, 505 Consumers Rd., Toronto, ON M2J 4V8
Tel: 416-490-6456; Fax: 416-490-6439

Toronto: Bersenas Jacobsen Chouest Thomson Blackburn LLP - *10
#201, 33 Yonge St., Toronto, ON M5E 1G4
Tel: 416-982-3800; Fax: 416-982-3801
info@lexcanada.com
www.lexcanada.com

Toronto: Myer Betel - *1
7 Farrington Dr., Toronto, ON M2L 2B4
Tel: 416-447-4333; Fax: 416-447-3773
mbctel@rogers.com

Toronto: Lynn Bevan Professional Corporation - *1
60 Oriole Rd., Toronto, ON M4V 2G1
Tel: 416-955-0400; Fax: 416-955-0410
lbevan@lynnbevan.com
www.lynnbevan.com

Toronto: Bhatia, Minipreet - *1
#405, 3601 Victoria Park Ave., Toronto, ON M1W 3Y3
Tel: 416-493-1727; Fax: 416-756-3663

Toronto: Bigelow, Hendy - *4
#200, 789 Don Mills Rd., Toronto, ON M3C 1T5
Tel: 416-429-3110; Fax: 416-429-3057
www.bigelowhendy.com

Toronto: Birchall Northey - *2
533 College Street, Toronto, ON M6G 1A8
Tel: 416-860-1212; Fax: 416-860-1827
admin@birchallnorthey.com
www.birchallnorthey.com

Toronto: Peter Bird - *1
31 Prince Arthur Dr., Toronto, ON M5R 1B2
Tel: 416-929-9408; Fax: 416-960-5456
peterbird@on.aibn.com

Toronto: Birenbaum & Bernstein - *2
#104, 2801 Keele St., Toronto, ON M37 2G6
Tel: 416-633-3720; Fax: 416-633-4546

Toronto: Birenbaum, Steinberg, Landau, Savin & Colraine LLP - *9
#1000, 33 Bloor St. East, Toronto, ON M4W 3H1
Tel: 416-961-4100; Fax: 416-961-2531
birenbaum@bslsc.com
www.bslsc.com

Toronto: Donald H. Bitter, Q.C. - *1
#407, 600 Church St., Toronto, ON M4Y 2E7
Tel: 416-360-4357; Fax: 416-463-8259
notguilty@rogers.com

Toronto: Black, Sutherland LLP - *11
#3425, P.O. Box 34, 130 Adelaide St. West, Toronto, ON M5H 3P5
Tel: 416-361-1500; Fax: 416-361-1674
Toll-Free: 866-902-7557
info@blacksutherland.com
www.blacksutherland.com

Toronto: Harry Blaier - *1
#1800, Madison Centre, 4950 Yonge St., Toronto, ON M2N 6K1
Tel: 416-224-0200; Fax: 416-224-0758
hblaier@torlaw.com

Toronto: Edith M. Blake - *1
75 The Donway West, Toronto, ON M3C 2E9
Tel: 416-445-0310; Fax: 416-445-0316

Toronto: Jonathan A. Bliss - *1
370 Bloor St. East, Toronto, ON M4W 3M6
Tel: 416-927-9000; Fax: 416-927-9069
jonbliss@sympatico.ca

Toronto: Bloom & Lanys - *1
#100, 250 Roehampton Ave., Toronto, ON M4P 1R9
Tel: 416-486-9913; Fax: 416-485-6054
Toll-Free: 877-835-7658
barb@bloom-lanys.com

Toronto: Joseph L. Bloomenfeld - *1
#2110, 120 Adelaide St. West, Toronto, ON M5H 2C9
Tel: 416-363-7315; Fax: 416-363-7697

Toronto: Blouin, Dunn LLP - *8
#1800, 155 University Ave., Toronto, ON M5H 3B7
Tel: 416-365-7888; Fax: 416-365-7988
info@blouindunn.com
www.blouindunn.com

Toronto: Bluestein & Pearlstein LLP - *3
#1100, 121 King St. West, Toronto, ON M5H 3T9
Tel: 416-363-8844; Fax: 416-363-8807

Toronto: Blumberg Segal LLP - *6
#1202, 390 Bay St., Toronto, ON M5H 2Y2
Tel: 416-361-1982; Fax: 416-363-8451
info@blumbergs.ca
www.blumbergs.ca

Toronto: Carla L. Bocci - *1
#1917, 25 Adelaide St. East, Toronto, ON M5C 3A1
Tel: 416-365-2961; Fax: 416-365-1859

Toronto: Bodnaruk & Capone - *2
#416, P.O. Box 49, 370 King St. West, Toronto, ON M5V 1J9
Tel: 416-593-7000; Fax: 416-593-5359

Toronto: Bogart Robertson & Chu - *4
#1608, 141 Adelaide St. West, Toronto, ON M5H 3L5
Tel: 416-601-1991; Fax: 416-601-0006
contact@brclaw.com

Toronto: G.H. Bomza - *1
#2303, 180 Dundas St. West, Toronto, ON M5G 1Z8
Tel: 416-598-2244; Fax: 416-598-3830
rosehallmgmt@bellnet.ca

Toronto: Sharon G.H. Bond - *1
#100, 110 Eglinton Ave. West, Toronto, ON M4R 1A3
Tel: 416-483-5354; Fax: 416-483-5360
sghb@sharonbondlaw.com

Toronto: Ira E. Book - *1
#200, 85 Scarsdale Rd., Toronto, ON M3B 2R2
Tel: 416-447-2665; Fax: 416-447-0066
ira@irabook.com

Toronto: Norman H.R. Borski, Q.C. - *1
#201, 2256B Bloor St. West, Toronto, ON M6S 1N6
Tel: 416-766-2441

Toronto: Y.R. Botiuk, Q.C. - *2
#212, 2323 Bloor St. West, Toronto, ON M6S 4W1
Tel: 416-763-4333; Fax: 416-763-0613

Toronto: Bougadis, Chang LLP - *3
#600, 360 Bay St., Toronto, ON M5H 2V6
Tel: 416-703-2402; Fax: 416-703-2406
office@bcbarristers.com
www.bcbarristers.com

Toronto: T. Sam Boutzouvis - *1
#501, 326 Richmond St. West, Toronto, ON M5V 1V3
Tel: 416-591-0111

Toronto: Mary E.E. Boyce - *1
69 Elm St., Toronto, ON M5G 1H2
Tel: 416-591-7588; Fax: 416-971-9092

Toronto: Boyle & Co. LLP, Solicitors - *5
#1900, 25 Adelaide St. East, Toronto, ON M5C 3A1
Tel: 416-867-8800; Fax: 416-867-8833
www.boyleco.com

Toronto: P.G. Bradley - *1
1051 Tapscott Rd., Toronto, ON M1X 1A1
Tel: 416-298-0066; Fax: 416-299-8008
patrick@runnymede-dev.com

Toronto: L.A. Braithwaite, C.M., O.Ont., Q.C. - *1
250 Wincott Dr., Toronto, ON M9R 2R5
Tel: 416-249-2288; Fax: 416-249-2280

Toronto: Brannan Meiklejohn Barristers - *2
262 Avenue Rd., Toronto, ON M4V 2G7
Tel: 416-926-3797; Fax: 416-926-3712

Toronto: Brans, Lehun, Baldwin - *8
#2401, 120 Adelaide St. West, Toronto, ON M5H 1T1
Tel: 416-601-1040; Fax: 416-601-0655
info@blbcdnlaw.com

Toronto: G.K.C. Braund, Q.C. - *1
#204, 3333 Bayview Ave., Toronto, ON M2K 1G4
Tel: 416-223-0862; Fax: 416-223-4073

Toronto: Brauti Thorning LLP - *8
#1800, 151 Yonge St., Toronto, ON M5C 2W7
Tel: 416-362-4567; Fax: 416-362-8410
www.btlegal.ca

Toronto: Philip E. Brent - *1
#1160, 36 Toronto St., Toronto, ON M5C 2C5
Tel: 416-203-1449; Fax: 416-203-1772
brentayr@allstream.net

Toronto: Bresver, Grossman, Scheininger & Chapman - *5
#2900, 390 Bay St., Toronto, ON M5H 2Y2
Tel: 416-869-0366; Fax: 416-869-0321

Toronto: Daniel J. Brodsky - *1
11 Prince Arthur Ave., Toronto, ON M5R 1B2
Tel: 416-964-2618; Fax: 416-964-8305
brodsky@interlog.com

** indicates number of lawyers*

***Toronto*: Brown & Burnes - *6**
#1400, 390 Bay St., Toronto, ON M5H 2Y2
Tel: 416-366-7927; *Fax:* 416-363-9602
info@brownburnes.com
www.brownburnes.com

***Toronto*: Brown & Cohen Communications & Public Affairs Inc. - *2**
321 Brooke Ave., Toronto, ON M5M 2L4
Tel: 416-484-1132; *Fax:* 416-783-8177
info@brown-cohen.com
www.brown-cohen.com

***Toronto*: Brown & Korte Barristers - *12**
130 Adelaide St. West, 31st Fl., Toronto, ON M5H 3P5
Tel: 416-869-0123; *Fax:* 416-869-0271
lawyers@brownandkorte.ca
www.brownandkorte.com

***Toronto*: Kenneth J. Brown - *1**
45 Mogul Dr., Toronto, ON M2H 2M8
Tel: 416-499-8005; *Fax:* 416-499-8048
k.j.brown@sympatico.ca

***Toronto*: M.H. Brown - *1**
38 Berwick Ave., Toronto, ON M5P 1H1
Tel: 416-487-5122; *Fax:* 416-487-5168
mel@browngroup.net

***Toronto*: Brown, Peck & Lubelsky - *4**
5287 Yonge St., Toronto, ON M2N 5R3
Tel: 416-223-8811; *Fax:* 416-223-8485

***Toronto*: G.J. Bruner - *1**
167 Danforth Ave., Toronto, ON M4K 1N2
Tel: 416-461-0983; *Fax:* 416-462-3347

***Toronto*: Anthony G. Bryant - *1**
#1706, 51 York Mills Road, Toronto, ON M2P 1B6
Tel: 416-927-7441; *Fax:* 416-413-0230
tbryant@istar.ca

***Toronto*: Frederic L. Buckland - *1**
1199 The Queensway, Toronto, ON M8Z 1R7
Tel: 416-236-0906; *Fax:* 416-236-1365
buckland@interlog.com

***Toronto*: Buie Cohen LLP - *2**
#205, 250 Merton St., Toronto, ON M4S 1B1
Tel: 416-869-3400; *Fax:* 416-703-6522
cmbuie@buiecohen.com

***Toronto*: J.J. Burke - *1**
#302, 2405 Lakeshore Blvd. West, Toronto, ON M8V 1C6
Tel: 416-252-9101
jjburke@bellnet.ca

***Toronto*: Harry R. Burkman - *1**
#2810, P.O. Box 129, 1 First Canadian Pl., Toronto, ON M5X 1A4
Tel: 416-364-3831; *Fax:* 416-364-3832
hburkman@burkman.com
www.burkman.com

***Toronto*: Burnett & Jacobson - *3**
48 St. Clair Ave. West, Toronto, ON M4V 3C9
Tel: 416-922-8710; *Fax:* 416-964-5840

***Toronto*: Burstein, Unger - *2**
P.O. Box 180, 127 John St., Toronto, ON M5V 2E2
Tel: 416-204-1825; *Fax:* 416-204-1849
paul@127john.com

***Toronto*: Bernard Burton - *1**
#410, 120 Carlton St., Toronto, ON M5A 4K2
Tel: 416-922-1263; *Fax:* 416-922-1963
bernardburton@chmlegal.com

***Toronto*: Bury & Tarka - *2**
#1515, 390 Bay St., Toronto, ON M5H 2Y2
Tel: 416-363-9966; *Fax:* 416-363-4499

***Toronto*: Bussin & Bussin - *3**
#1822, 181 University Ave., Toronto, ON M5H 3M7
Tel: 416-364-4925; *Fax:* 416-868-1818
bruce@bussinlaw.com

***Toronto*: Paul Calarco - *1**
#1500, 700 Bay Street, Toronto, ON M5G 1Z6
Tel: 416-598-1948; *Fax:* 416-596-7629
pcalarco@on.aibn.com
www.paulcalarco.com

***Toronto*: CaleyWray - *10**
#1205, 111 Richmond St. West, Toronto, ON M5H 2G4
Tel: 416-366-3763; *Fax:* 416-366-3293
mail@caleywray.com
www.caleywray.com

***Toronto*: Campbell Strategies Inc. - *3**
95 Wellington St. West, Toronto, ON M5J 2N7
Tel: 416-368-7353; *Fax:* 416-368-9848
info@campbelstrategies.com
www.campbellstrategies.com

***Toronto*: John R. Campbell, Q.C. - *2**
5 Douglas Crescent, Toronto, ON M4W 2E6
Tel: 416-924-9066; *Fax:* 416-961-0510
hkljrc@pathcom.com

***Toronto*: G.H. Cancilla - *1**
#506, 372 Bay St., Toronto, ON M5H 2W9
Tel: 416-366-9504; *Fax:* 416-628-6628
ghc@cancillaw.com

***Toronto*: John Cannings, Barristers - *5**
#400, 425 University Ave., Toronto, ON M5G 1T6
Tel: 416-591-0703; *Fax:* 416-591-0710
info@jcannings.com
www.jcannings.com/

***Toronto*: Ruth Canton - *1**
2489 Bloor St. West, Toronto, ON M6S 1R6
Tel: 416-769-5759; *Fax:* 416-769-3132
Toll-Free: 888-838-7432

***Toronto*: Rochelle F. Cantor - *1**
180 Spadina Rd., Toronto, ON M5R 2T8
Tel: 416-861-1625; *Fax:* 416-861-1466

***Toronto*: Capp, Shupak - *5**
#1703, 2 St. Clair Ave. West, Toronto, ON M4V 1L5
Tel: 416-944-2313; *Fax:* 416-323-0697
shupak@cappshupak.com
www.marilynshupak.com

***Toronto*: Cappell Parker LLP, Barristers & Solicitors - *2**
#1200, Toronto-Dominion Centre, 95 Wellington St. West, Toronto, ON M5J 2Z9
Tel: 416-367-0900; *Fax:* 416-367-0901
fecappell@cappell.com
www.cappell.com

***Toronto*: Cappellacci DaRoza LLP - *2**
#500, 462 Wellington St. West, Toronto, ON M5V 1E3
Tel: 416-955-9500; *Fax:* 416-955-9503
ecappellacci@capplaw.ca
www.capplaw.ca

***Toronto*: Caramanna, Friedberg LLP - *5**
#405, Lucliff Place, P.O. Box 144, 700 Bay St., Toronto, ON M5G 1Z6
Tel: 416-924-5969; *Fax:* 416-924-9973
info@cflaw.ca
www.cflaw.ca

***Toronto*: Michael W. Caroline - *1**
#803, Waterpark Place, 10 Bay St., Toronto, ON M5J 2R8
Tel: 416-203-2250; *Fax:* 416-203-2280
mwc@michaelcaroline.com
www.michaelcaroline.com

***Toronto*: John S.H. Carriere - *1**
#600, 330 Bay St., Toronto, ON M5H 2S8
Tel: 416-363-5594; *Fax:* 416-363-8492
johncarriere@bellnet.ca

***Toronto*: C. Anthony Carroll - *1**
#1807, 8 King St. East, Toronto, ON M5C 1B5
Tel: 416-361-0522; *Fax:* 416-361-0248
carrollt@istar.ca

***Toronto*: Carson, Gross, Christie, Knudsen - *5**
#600, 10 Carlson Ct., Toronto, ON M9W 6L2
Tel: 416-361-0900; *Fax:* 416-361-3459
info@cgck.com

***Toronto*: G.M. Cass - *1**
#302, 1200 Sheppard Ave. East, Toronto, ON M2K 2S5
Tel: 416-767-2277; *Fax:* 416-491-0273
www.garrycass.com

***Toronto*: Ceresney, Weisberg Associates - *2**
#202, 4651 Sheppard Ave. East, Toronto, ON M1S 3V4
Tel: 416-291-7701; *Fax:* 416-291-1766

***Toronto*: Chaitons LLP - *20**
185 Sheppard Ave. West, Toronto, ON M2N 1M9
Tel: 416-222-8888; *Fax:* 416-222-8402
info@chaitons.com
www.chaiton.com

***Toronto*: Chang & Boos - *5**
#1100, 77 Bloor St. West, Toronto, ON M5S 1M2
Tel: 416-362-6632; *Fax:* 416-362-1125
hchang@americanlaw.com
www.americanlaw.com

***Toronto*: Evan Chang - *1**
#203, 1315 Lawrence Ave. East, Toronto, ON M3A 3R3
Tel: 416-449-1214; *Fax:* 416-449-9396
evan.c@sympatico.ca

***Toronto*: Peter P. Chang - *1**
#2300, 2025 Sheppard Ave. East, Toronto, ON M2J 1V6
Tel: 416-497-1575; *Fax:* 416-497-2261
peterchang@rogers.com

***Toronto*: Beverly C. Chapin-Hill - *1**
16 Neville Park Blvd., Toronto, ON M4E 3P6
Tel: 416-690-1832; *Fax:* 416-698-6041
bev@chapinandchapin.ca
www.chapinandchapin.com

***Toronto*: Chapnick & Associates - *4**
228 Carlton St., Toronto, ON M5A 2L1
Tel: 416-968-2160; *Fax:* 416-975-9338
www.chapnickassociates.com

***Toronto*: Chappell, Bushell, Stewart LLP - *8**
#3310, 20 Queen St. West, Toronto, ON M5H 3R3
Tel: 416-351-0005; *Fax:* 416-351-0002
info@cbslaw.to
www.chappellbushellstewart.com

***Toronto*: Office of the Children's Lawyer - *23**
393 University Ave., 14th Fl., Toronto, ON M5G 1W9
Tel: 416-314-8000; *Fax:* 416-314-8050
www.attorneygeneral.jus.gov.on.ca/english/family/ocl/

***Toronto*: Ronald W. Chisholm, Q.C. - *1**
#510, 330 University Ave., Toronto, ON M5G 1R7
Tel: 416-586-0777; *Fax:* 416-586-0267

***Toronto*: Chitiz Pathak LLP - *15**
#1600, 320 Bay St. Ave., Toronto, ON M5H 4A6
Tel: 416-368-6200; *Fax:* 416-368-0300
info@chitizpathak.com
www.chitizpathak.com

***Toronto*: Christopher E. Chop - *1**
#2000, 1 Queen St. East, Toronto, ON M5C 2W5
Tel: 416-601-4159; *Fax:* 416-601-0206
choplaw@gmail.com

***Toronto*: Christies - *8**
#301, Confederation Sq., 20 Richmond St. East, Toronto, ON M5C 2R9
Tel: 416-367-0680; *Fax:* 416-367-0429
information@christie-lawyers.com
www.christie-lawyers.com

***Toronto*: B.N. Christoff - *1**
#304, 3335 Yonge St., Toronto, ON M4N 2M1
Tel: 416-482-0990; *Fax:* 416-482-6511

***Toronto*: Cipollone & Cipollone Barristers - *1**
#2100, 130 Adelaide St. West, Toronto, ON M5H 3P5
Tel: 416-368-5366; *Fax:* 416-368-5361

***Toronto*: Dino J. Cirone - *1**
#2, 2084 Danforth Ave., Toronto, ON M4C 1J9
Tel: 416-423-8515; *Fax:* 416-423-4971

***Toronto*: Civicworks Consulting Group Inc. - *1**
246 Sandringham Dr., Toronto, ON M3H 1G3
Tel: 416-587-7053; *Fax:* 416-636-0134
bobbywalman@rogers.com

***Toronto*: S.G. Clapp - *1**
18 Erskine Ave., Toronto, ON M4P 1Y2
Tel: 416-484-4840; *Fax:* 416-484-0821
stanleyclapp@on.aibn.com

***Toronto*: Deta J. Clark - *1**
#402, 5075 Yonge St., Toronto, ON M2N 6C6
Tel: 416-733-3135

***Toronto*: Clark, Farb, Fiksel - *6**
188 Avenue Rd., Toronto, ON M5J 2J1
Tel: 416-599-7761; *Fax:* 416-324-4220
www.cfflaw.com

** indicates number of lawyers*

***Toronto*: Clarke, Freeman, Miller & Ryan - *1**
1863 Danforth Ave., Toronto, ON M4C 1J3
Tel: 416-698-9323; *Fax:* 416-698-9110

***Toronto*: Clean 16 Environmental Technologies Corp. - *1**
#6134, 2100 Bloor St. West, Toronto, ON M6S 5A5
Tel: 416-352-1973; *Fax:* 416-352-1973
info@clean16.com

***Toronto*: L. Peter Clyne - *1**
#1709, 5650 Yonge St., Toronto, ON M2M 4G3
Tel: 416-922-0864; *Fax:* 416-922-6856
clynelaw@on.aibn.com

***Toronto*: Robert G. Coates - *1**
#307, 120 Carlton St., Toronto, ON M5A 4K2
Tel: 416-925-6490; *Fax:* 416-925-4492
robert@rgcoates.com
www.rgcoates.com

***Toronto*: Cohen & Associate - *2**
#801, 1 St. Clair Ave. East, Toronto, ON M4T 2V7
Tel: 416-323-0907; *Fax:* 416-324-8053
cohen@bellnet.ca

***Toronto*: M.V. Cohen - *1**
111 Richmond Street West, Toronto, ON M5H 2G4
Tel: 416-363-8366
mvcohen2002@yahoo.ca

***Toronto*: Cohen, Sabsay LLP - *4**
#500, 350 Bay St., Toronto, ON M5H 2S6
Tel: 416-364-7436; *Fax:* 416-364-0083
cohen@cohensabsay.com
www.cohensabsay.com

***Toronto*: David Cohn - *1**
#301, 481 University Ave., Toronto, ON M5G 2E9
Tel: 416-777-1100; *Fax:* 416-364-2308

***Toronto*: John Collins - *1**
#400, 357 Bay St., Toronto, ON M5H 2R7
Tel: 416-364-9006; *Fax:* 416-862-7911
john.collins@on.aibn.com

***Toronto*: Connected Insight - *1**
123 Jefferson Ave., Toronto, ON M6K 3E4
Tel: 416-203-8222
hal@connectedinsight.ca
www.connectedinsight.ca

***Toronto*: Conway Davis Gryski - *5**
#601, 130 Adelaide St. West, Toronto, ON M5H 3P5
Tel: 416-214-4554; *Fax:* 416-214-9915
Toll-Free: 877-559-4554
contactus@cdglaw.net
www.conwaydavisgryski.com

***Toronto*: Conway Kleinman Kornhauser LLP - *3**
#1102, 390 Bay St., Toronto, ON M5H 2Y2
Tel: 416-368-5400; *Fax:* 416-368-5454

***Toronto*: Wayne Cook Consulting - *1**
82 Inniscross Cres., Toronto, ON M1V 2S9
Tel: 416-609-0372; *Fax:* 416-609-1953

***Toronto*: Cooper & Cooper - *1**
#208, 133 Richmond St. West, Toronto, ON M5H 2L3
Tel: 416-362-6459; *Fax:* 416-362-3139

***Toronto*: Allen M. Cooper - *1**
#101, 15 Elm St., Toronto, ON M5G 1H1
Tel: 416-977-8070; *Fax:* 416-977-8151

***Toronto*: Daniel Cooper Law Office - *1**
193 Heath St. West, Toronto, ON M4V 1V3
Tel: 416-925-3772; *Fax:* 416-925-3457
daniel@dcooper.com

***Toronto*: Kirk J. Cooper - *1**
#308, 120 Carlton St., Toronto, ON M5A 4K2
Tel: 416-923-4277; *Fax:* 416-923-4144
kirkcooperlaw@rogers.com
www.kirkcooperlaw.com

***Toronto*: Cooper, Kleinman - *2**
3 Rowanwood Ave., Toronto, ON M4W 1Y5
Tel: 416-867-1400; *Fax:* 416-867-1873
gwcooper@cooperkleinman.ca

***Toronto*: Morris Cooper - *1**
99 Yorkville Ave., Toronto, ON M5R 3K5
Tel: 416-961-2626; *Fax:* 416-961-4000
cooper@cooperlaw.ca

***Toronto*: Robert A. Cooper - *1**
#208, 4211 Yonge St., Toronto, ON M2P 2A9
Tel: 416-222-8115; *Fax:* 416-222-8505

***Toronto*: Copeland Duncan - *2**
31 Prince Arthur Ave., Toronto, ON M5R 1B2
Tel: 416-964-8126; *Fax:* 416-960-5456
paulcope9@yahoo.com

***Toronto*: Jack Copelovici - *1**
#204, 1220 Sheppard Ave. East, Toronto, ON M2K 2S5
Tel: 416-494-0910; *Fax:* 416-494-5480
jack@copel-law.com

***Toronto*: Barry S. Corbin - *1**
#2000, 393 University Ave., Toronto, ON M5G 1E6
Tel: 416-593-4200; *Fax:* 416-593-1352
barry.corbin@corbinestateslaw.com
www.corbinestateslaw.com

***Toronto*: Costa Law Firm - *5**
1015 Bloor St. West, Toronto, ON M6H 1M1
Tel: 416-535-6329; *Fax:* 416-535-4735
davidcosta@bell.blackberry.net
www.costalawfirm.ca

***Toronto*: Fernando D. Costa - *1**
#200, 1112 Dundas St. West, Toronto, ON M6J 1X2
Tel: 416-534-6357; *Fax:* 416-534-6219
fd.costa@bellnet.ca

***Toronto*: Costigan Horgan - *2**
#410, 120 Carlton St., Toronto, ON M5A 4K2
Tel: 416-922-8611; *Fax:* 416-922-1963
acostigan@chmlegal.com

***Toronto*: Counsel Public Affairs Inc - *5**
#1606, 95 St. Clair West, Toronto, ON M4V 1N6
Tel: 416-920-0716; *Fax:* 416-352-6069
reception@counselpa.com
www.counselpa.com

***Toronto*: D.B. Cousins - *1**
#203, 425 University Ave., Toronto, ON M5G 1T6
Tel: 416-977-8871; *Fax:* 416-599-8075
david.b.cousins@bellnet.ca

***Toronto*: Coutts, Crane, Ingram - *7**
#700, 480 University Ave., Toronto, ON M5G 1V2
Tel: 416-977-0956; *Fax:* 416-977-5331
info@couttscrane.com
www.couttscrane.com

***Toronto*: Cowan & Cremer - *2**
#216, 214 King Street West, Toronto, ON M5H 3S6
Tel: 416-322-3671; *Fax:* 416-971-5520
cowancremer@sympatico.ca
www.cowancremer.com

***Toronto*: Ronald Cowitz - *1**
#308, 344 Bloor St. West, Toronto, ON M5S 3A7
Tel: 416-944-9594

***Toronto*: Christopher G. Cox - *1**
#209, 1711 McCowan Rd., Toronto, ON M1S 2Y3
Tel: 416-447-4274; *Fax:* 416-823-3215
cgcoxlaw@hotmail.com

***Toronto*: Cozen O'Connor - *8**
#2000, 1 Queen St. East, Toronto, ON M5C 2W5
Tel: 416-361-3200; *Fax:* 416-361-1405

***Toronto*: F.H. Cremer - *1**
#201, 1593 Wilson Ave., Toronto, ON M3L 1A5
Tel: 416-244-5575; *Fax:* 416-247-3844

***Toronto*: Crewe & Marks - *2**
74 Riverdale Ave., Toronto, ON M4K 1C3
Tel: 416-967-9933; *Fax:* 416-967-9933
nsc@riv.com

***Toronto*: Frank D. Crewe - *2**
#500, 70 Bond St., Toronto, ON M5B 1X3
Tel: 416-362-2202; *Fax:* 416-363-9135

***Toronto*: Howard Crosner - *1**
#1400, 10 King St. East, Toronto, ON M5C 1C3
Tel: 416-947-0455; *Fax:* 416-364-3818
crosner77@eol.ca
www.crosner.com

***Toronto*: Leroy A. Crosse - *1**
#203, 705 Lawrence Ave. West, Toronto, ON M6A 1B4
Tel: 416-785-8338; *Fax:* 416-785-9369

***Toronto*: Paul J. Crowe - *1**
#220, 4950 Yonge St., Toronto, ON M2N 6K1
Tel: 416-733-0255; *Fax:* 416-221-9965
Toll-Free: 877-649-9999
pauljcrowe@hotmail.com

***Toronto*: Crum-Ewing & Poliacik - *2**
56 Sheppard Ave. West, Toronto, ON M2N 1M2
Tel: 416-733-9292; *Fax:* 416-733-9654
poliacik@ceplaw.ca

***Toronto*: Cummings Cooper Schusheim & Berliner LLP - *6**
#408, 4110 Yonge St., Toronto, ON M2P 2B5
Tel: 416-512-9500; *Fax:* 416-512-9501
info@ccsb-law.com
www.ccsb-law.com

***Toronto*: Gino A.J. Cundari - *1**
1179 St. Clair Ave. West, Toronto, ON M6E 1B5
Tel: 416-654-9000; *Fax:* 416-654-6688

***Toronto*: Peter Cusimano, Barrister & Solicitor - *1**
#100, 332 Sheppard Ave. East, Toronto, ON M2N 3B4
Tel: 416-222-0588; *Fax:* 416-222-0239
lawyer@cusimano.com
www.cusimano.com

***Toronto*: J. Jerome Cusmariu - *1**
1310 Dundas St. West, Toronto, ON M6J 1Y1
Tel: 416-533-1173; *Fax:* 416-533-0761
jcusmariu@on.aibn.com

***Toronto*: E.H. Cutler - *1**
#18A, 156 Duncan Mill Rd., Toronto, ON M3B 3N2
Tel: 416-449-4962; *Fax:* 416-449-5107
ernestcutler@bellnet.ca

***Toronto*: Andrew M. Czernik - *1**
#605, 920 Yonge St., Toronto, ON M4W 3C7
Tel: 416-920-4994; *Fax:* 416-920-5885
aczernik@on.aibn.com

***Toronto*: Czuma, Ritter - *2**
410 - 120 Carlton St., Toronto, ON M5A 4K2
Tel: 416-599-5799; *Fax:* 416-599-9981
michael@michaelczuma.com
www.michaelczuma.com

***Toronto*: E.L. D'Alimonte - *1**
#203, 1111 Albion Rd., Toronto, ON M9V 1A9
Tel: 416-741-5373

***Toronto*: Anthony D'Avella - *1**
#306, 4920 Dundas St. West, Toronto, ON M9A 1B7
Tel: 416-234-2198; *Fax:* 416-234-5142
anton.davella@on.aibn.com

***Toronto*: Dale & Lessmann LLP - *14**
#2100, 181 University Ave., Toronto, ON M5H 3M7
Tel: 416-863-1010; *Fax:* 416-863-1009
info@dalelessmann.com
www.dalelessmann.com

***Toronto*: Daniel F. Daly - *1**
#206, 20 Holly St., Toronto, ON M4S 3B1
Tel: 416-485-6700; *Fax:* 416-485-6711

***Toronto*: Damery & Mamak - *2**
101 Roncesvalles Ave., Toronto, ON M6R 2K9
Tel: 416-532-3349; *Fax:* 416-533-2967

***Toronto*: Danson, Recht, Voudouris LLP - *5**
#2000, 700 Bay St., Toronto, ON M5G 1Z6
Tel: 416-929-2200; *Fax:* 416-929-2192
www.drv-law.com

***Toronto*: Danson, Zucker & Connelly - *3**
#500, 70 Bond St., Toronto, ON M5B 1X3
Tel: 416-863-9955; *Fax:* 416-863-4896

***Toronto*: Daoust Vukovich LLP - *20**
#3000, 20 Queen St. West, Toronto, ON M5H 3R3
Tel: 416-597-6888; *Fax:* 416-597-8897
general@dv-law.com
www.dv-lew.com

***Toronto*: James Daris - *1**
#101, 8 Irwin Ave., Toronto, ON M4Y 1K9
Tel: 416-465-4973; *Fax:* 416-465-6042

***Toronto*: David Charles Barristers Professional Corp. - *4**
#800, 1200 Bay St., Toronto, ON M5R 2A5
Tel: 416-923-7407; *Fax:* 416-923-6070

** indicates number of lawyers*

Toronto: Davies Howe Partners - *10
99 Spadina Ave., 5th Fl., Toronto, ON M5V 3P8
Tel: 416-977-7088; *Fax:* 416-977-8931
info@davieshowe.com
www.davieshowe.com

Toronto: Davies McLean Zweig Associates - *3
1035 McNicoll Ave., Toronto, ON M1W 3W6
Tel: 416-756-7500; *Fax:* 416-512-1212

Toronto: Davis & Turk - *2
#340, 1100 Sheppard Ave. West, Toronto, ON M3K 2B4
Tel: 416-630-5511; *Fax:* 416-630-7724

Toronto: Marie Davison - *1
327 Eglinton Ave. East, Toronto, ON M4P 1L7
Tel: 416-486-9701; *Fax:* 416-483-1397

Toronto: De Faria & De Faria - *2
872 Dundas St. West, Toronto, ON M6J 1V7
Tel: 416-603-4440; *Fax:* 416-603-4441

Toronto: De Ponte & Scalisi - *2
#600, 155 Rexdale Blvd., Toronto, ON M9W 5Z8
Tel: 416-746-7829; *Fax:* 416-746-9335

Toronto: J.N. De Sommer - *1
112 Adelaide St. East, Toronto, ON M5C 1K9
Tel: 416-341-7077; *Fax:* 416-368-2918
jndesommer@rbs.rogers.com

Toronto: Tilaka de Zoysa - *1
#207, 2131 Lawrence Ave. East, Toronto, ON M1R 5G4
Tel: 416-752-2253; *Fax:* 416-752-6356

Toronto: Deacon, Spears, Fedson & Montizambert - *7
#2900, 2300 Yonge St., Toronto, ON M4P 1E4
Tel: 416-489-5677; *Fax:* 416-489-7794
info@condolaw.to
www.condolaw.to

Toronto: Deeth Williams Wall LLP - *19
#400, 150 York St., Toronto, ON M5H 3S5
Tel: 416-941-9440; *Fax:* 416-941-9443
info@dww.com
www.dww.com

Toronto: DelZotto, Zorzi LLP - *12
4810 Dufferin St., #D, Toronto, ON M3H 5S8
Tel: 416-665-5555; *Fax:* 416-665-9653
info@dzlaw.com
www.dzlaw.com

Toronto: A.M. Dempsey, Q.C. - *1
533 Queen St. East, Toronto, ON M5A 1V1
Tel: 416-364-6755; *Fax:* 416-364-7049

Toronto: Richard G.J. Desrocher - *1
20 Leamington Ave., Toronto, ON M8Z 2W4
Tel: 416-236-5679; *Fax:* 416-236-7370

Toronto: Donald W. Devenney - *1
#1106, 66 Spadina Rd., Toronto, ON M5R 2T4
Tel: 416-964-2687

Toronto: Deverett Law Offices - *2
163 Willowdale Ave., Toronto, ON M2N 4Y7
Tel: 416-222-6789; *Fax:* 416-222-7605
info@deverettlaw.com
www.deverettlaw.com

Toronto: Jane H. Devlin - *1
#701, 100 Adelaide St. West, Toronto, ON M5H 1S3
Tel: 416-366-3091; *Fax:* 416-366-0879
arbserv@istar.ca

Toronto: Devon Government Relations - *5
#903, 1200 Bay St., Toronto, ON M5R 2A5
Tel: 416-504-5151; *Fax:* 416-504-5655
rirwin@devongroup.ca
www.devongroup.ca

Toronto: Devry, Smith & Frank - *27
#100, 95 Barber Greene Rd., Toronto, ON M3C 3E9
Tel: 416-449-1400; *Fax:* 416-449-7071
info@devrylaw.ca
www.devrylaw.ca

Toronto: Iqbal I. Dewji - *1
#810, 255 Duncan Mill Road, Toronto, ON M3B 2H9
Tel: 416-449-9600; *Fax:* 416-449-9348
iimd@rogers.com

Toronto: Philip J. Di Iorio Professional Corporation - *2
821 The Queensway, Toronto, ON M8Z 1N6
Tel: 416-253-1223; *Fax:* 416-253-0186

Toronto: Diamond & Diamond - *8
#400, 700 Lawrence Ave. West, Toronto, ON M6A 3B4
Tel: 416-256-1600; *Fax:* 416-256-0100

Toronto: Michael R. Diamond - *1
#200, 111 Eglinton Ave. East, Toronto, ON M4P 1H4
Tel: 416-482-2666; *Fax:* 416-482-4165
sndicator@sympatico.ca

Toronto: Dickson MacGregor Appell LLP - *9
#306, 10 Alcorn Ave., Toronto, ON M4V 3A9
Tel: 416-927-0891; *Fax:* 416-927-0385
ellis@dicksonlawyers.com
www.dicksonlawyers.com

Toronto: Dimock Stratton LLP - *17
P.O. Box 102, 20 Queen St. West, 32nd Fl., Toronto, ON M5H 3R3
Tel: 416-971-7202; *Fax:* 416-971-6638
firm@dimock.com
www.dimock.com

Toronto: Dion, Durrell & Associates - *2
#2900, 250 Yonge St., Toronto, ON M5B 2L7
Tel: 416-408-2626; *Fax:* 416-408-3721
information@dion-durrell.com
www.dion-durrell.com

Toronto: H.J. Doan Barrister & Solicitor - *1
18 Wild Briarway, Toronto, ON M2J 2L2
Tel: 416-491-2700; *Fax:* 416-502-9373

Toronto: Doane Phillips Yonge LLP - *3
#300, 53 Jarvis St., Toronto, ON M5C 2H2
Tel: 416-366-3777; *Fax:* 416-366-9197

Toronto: C.H. Dolman, Q.C. - *1
#102, 10 Milner Business Ct., Toronto, ON M1B 3C6
Tel: 416-754-8177; *Fax:* 416-754-8337
cdolman@rogers.com

Toronto: Leonard Domino & Associates - *10
#1800, 130 King St. West, Toronto, ON M5X 1E3
Tel: 416-860-6244; *Fax:* 416-537-2545
info@leonarddomino.com
www.leonarddomino.com

Toronto: Brian P. Donnelly - *1
#1509, 180 Dundas St. West, Toronto, ON M5G 1Z8
Tel: 416-597-2191; *Fax:* 416-597-9808

Toronto: J. Brian Donnelly - *1
#201, 1165A St. Clair Ave. West, Toronto, ON M6E 1B2
Tel: 416-653-0311; *Fax:* 416-653-6653
jbd@jbdonnelly.com

Toronto: Dotsikas Hawtin Lawyers - *2
#502, 1235 Bay St., Toronto, ON M5R 3K4
Tel: 416-925-1601; *Fax:* 416-925-4571
peter@dotsikaslaw.com

Toronto: Downtown Legal Services - *5
655 Spadina Ave., Toronto, ON M5S 2H9
Tel: 416-934-4535; *Fax:* 416-934-4536
law.dls@utoronto.ca
www.dls.utoronto.ca

Toronto: William C. Draimin - *1
#101, 45 St. Clair Ave. West, Toronto, ON M4V 1K9
Tel: 416-920-4605; *Fax:* 416-960-0698
wdraimin@draiminlaw.com

Toronto: Dranoff & Huddart - *2
#314, 1033 Bay St., Toronto, ON M5S 3A5
Tel: 416-925-4500; *Fax:* 416-925-5197
info@dranoffhuddart.com
www.dranoffhuddart.com

Toronto: J. Blair Drummie - *1
326 Richmond St. West, Toronto, ON M5V 1X2
Tel: 416-921-0915; *Fax:* 416-925-6181

Toronto: Du Markowitz LLP - *3
#2000, Madison Centre, 4950 Yonge St., Toronto, ON M2N 6K1
Tel: 416-590-1900; *Fax:* 416-590-1600
info@dumarkowitz.com
www.dumarkowitz.com

Toronto: John Duncan & Associates - *3
#701, The Fashion Bldg., 130 Spadina Ave., Toronto, ON M5V 2L4
Tel: 416-593-2513; *Fax:* 416-593-2514
info@duncanmorin.com
www.duncanmorin.com

Toronto: Thomas S. Dungey - *1
46 Fairview Blvd., Toronto, ON M4K 1L9
Tel: 416-469-3088; *Fax:* 416-469-6739
tsdungey@rogers.com

Toronto: Lloyd T. Duong - *1
2377 Dundas St. West, Toronto, ON M6P 1W7
Tel: 416-535-3463

Toronto: Norman L. Durbin - *1
2530 Jane St., Toronto, ON M3L 1S1
Tel: 416-743-2345; *Fax:* 416-743-0645

Toronto: Dutton Brock LLP - *31
#1700, 438 University Ave., Toronto, ON M5G 2L9
Tel: 416-593-4411; *Fax:* 416-593-5922
info@duttonbrock.com
www.duttonbrock.com

Toronto: Diana C. Dzwiekowski - *1
260 Willard Ave., Toronto, ON M6S 3R2
Tel: 416-762-7251; *Fax:* 416-762-7252

Toronto: East Toronto Community Legal Services - *4
1320 Gerrard St. East, Toronto, ON M4L 3X1
Tel: 416-461-8102; *Fax:* 416-461-7497

Toronto: Eccleston LLP - *6
#3820, Toronto Dominion Centre, Box 230, 66 Wellington St. West, Toronto, ON M5K 1J3
Tel: 416-504-2722; *Fax:* 416-504-2686
www.ecclestonllp.com

Toronto: Ecclestone, Hamer, Poisson & Neuwald & Freeman - *5
#900, 372 Bay St., Toronto, ON M5C 1J3
Tel: 416-365-7135; *Fax:* 416-365-2189
ecclchyk@idirect.com

Toronto: John M. Edgar - *1
2901 Bloor St. West, Toronto, ON M8X 1B3
Tel: 416-231-3261; *Fax:* 416-231-8352

Toronto: George Edmonds, Q.C. - *1
#700, 2 St. Clair Ave. West, Toronto, ON M4V 1L5
Tel: 416-955-0947; *Fax:* 416-863-3997
edmonds@interlog.com

Toronto: Egan LLP - *14
TD Centre, Ernst & Young Tower, P.O. Box 197, Stn. TD Centre, 222 Bay St., Toronto, ON M5K 1J7
Tel: 416-943-2400; *Fax:* 416-943-2735
www.ey.com/CA/; www.eganllp.com

Toronto: Elston Watt LLP - *4
#2310, Bay-Wellington Tower, BCE Place, P.O. Box 792, 181 Bay St., Toronto, ON M5J 2T3
Tel: 416-977-9811; *Fax:* 416-977-9850
mail@elstonwatt.com

Toronto: Mitch Engel - *1
#502, 1235 Bay St., Toronto, ON M5R 3K4
Tel: 416-944-8882; *Fax:* 416-925-4571
m.engel@rogers.com

Toronto: Enterprise Canada - *19
#1202, 595 Bay St., Toronto, ON M5G 2C2
Tel: 416-586-1474; *Fax:* 416-586-1480
mmartin@enterprisecanada.com

Toronto: Environics Communications Inc. - *2
#900, 33 Bloor St. East, Toronto, ON M4W 3H1
Tel: 416-969-2702; *Fax:* 416-920-1822
communicate@environicspr.com
eci.environics.net

Toronto: Epstein Cole LLP - *25
#2200, 393 University Ave., Toronto, ON M5G 1E6
Tel: 416-862-9888; *Fax:* 416-862-2142
www.epsteincole.com

Toronto: Norman Epstein - *1
281 Eglinton Ave. East, Toronto, ON M4P 1L3
Tel: 416-225-5577; *Fax:* 416-483-5541

** indicates number of lawyers*

Toronto: Eric Lewis & Associates
116 Parliament Street, Toronto, ON M5A 2Y8
Tel: 416-367-1918; *Fax:* 416-362-1918
lewis_smyth@hotmail.com

Toronto: J.A. Ermacora - *1
75 Lowther Ave., Toronto, ON M5R 1C9
Tel: 416-961-5500; *Fax:* 416-961-9905
jermac@sympatico.ca

Toronto: Charles A. Eyton-Jones - *1
1238 Kingston Rd., Toronto, ON M1N 1P3
Tel: 416-691-4529; *Fax:* 416-691-2563
info@eyton-jones.ca
www.eyton-jones.ca

Toronto: Fabian & Kaye - *2
#103, 1210 Sheppard Ave. East, Toronto, ON M2K 1E3
Tel: 416-491-6411; *Fax:* 416-491-2219

Toronto: Fair & Siegel
#1002, 250 Heath St. West, Toronto, ON M5P 3L4
Tel: 416-948-1652; *Fax:* 416-483-9228
msiegel@rogers.com

Toronto: Falconer Charney - *7
8 Prince Arthur Ave., Toronto, ON M5R 1A9
Tel: 416-964-3408; *Fax:* 416-929-8179
falconercharney@fcbarristers.com
www.fcbarristers.com

Toronto: Ricardo G. Federico - *1
#900, 920 Yonge St., Toronto, ON M4W 3C7
Tel: 416-928-1458; *Fax:* 416-322-3684

Toronto: Frederick S. Fedorsen - *2
551 Gerrard St. East, Toronto, ON M4M 1X7
Tel: 416-463-6666; *Fax:* 416-463-8259
fred@fedorsennorth.com

Toronto: Jodi L. Feldman - *1
#303, 21 St. Clair Ave. East, Toronto, ON M4T 1L9
Tel: 416-922-3233; *Fax:* 416-922-3234

Toronto: Jane L. Ferguson - *1
#250, 1027 Yonge St., Toronto, ON M4W 2K9
Tel: 416-920-7533; *Fax:* 416-923-5576
jlferg@bellnet.ca

Toronto: Fernandes Hearn LLP - *9
#700, 155 University Ave., Toronto, ON M5H 3B7
Tel: 416-203-9500; *Fax:* 416-203-9444
info@fernandeshearn.com
www.fernandeshearn.com

Toronto: Field, Brown - *3
5140 Yonge Street, Toronto, ON M7A 2K2
Tel: 416-595-1111; *Fax:* 416-595-7312

Toronto: Gerald Fields - *1
#1800, P.O. Box 427, 130 King St. West, Toronto, ON M5X 1J8
Tel: 416-862-8000; *Fax:* 416-862-8001
Toll-Free: 888-268-6735
gfields@cornerstonegroup.com

Toronto: Filion Wakely Thorup Angeletti LLP - *26
#2601, P.O. Box 32, 150 King St. West, Toronto, ON M5H 4B6
Tel: 416-408-3221; *Fax:* 416-408-4814
toronto@filion.on.ca
www.filion.on.ca

Toronto: Filmlegals Entertainment Law Service - *1
7 Langley Ave., Toronto, ON M4K 1B4
Tel: 416-466-1487; *Fax:* 416-466-2548
mkrys@filmlegals.com
www.filmlegals.com

Toronto: Andrew Fine - *1
#306, 1000 Finch Ave. West, Toronto, ON M3J 2V5
Tel: 416-785-9499

Toronto: Finkelstein & Associates - *1
P.O. Box 23016, 437 Spadina Rd., Toronto, ON M5P 2W3
Tel: 416-487-2353; *Fax:* 416-487-1245

Toronto: Fireman Wolfe LLP - *7
#415, P.O. Box 19, 55 St. Clair Ave. West, Toronto, ON M4V 2Y7
Tel: 416-967-9100; *Fax:* 416-967-1200
www.firemanlawyers.com

Toronto: Fisch & Antonette - *1
419 College St., Toronto, ON M5T 1T1
Tel: 416-920-6312; *Fax:* 416-920-1780
josephyfisch@hotmail.com

Toronto: Joseph Y. Fisch - *2
#1, 394 College St., Toronto, ON M5T 1S7
Tel: 416-920-6312; *Fax:* 416-920-1780
josephyfisch@hotmail.com

Toronto: Barry B. Fisher - *1
#2000, 393 University Ave., Toronto, ON M5G 1E6
Tel: 416-585-2330; *Fax:* 416-585-2105
barryfisher@rogers.com

Toronto: R.A. Fisher - *1
#309, 95 Barber Greene Rd., Toronto, ON M3C 3E9
Tel: 416-449-3004; *Fax:* 416-441-6898
royfisher@hotmail.com

Toronto: Donald R. Fiske - *1
#665, West Tower, Clarica Centre, 3300 Bloor St. West, Toronto, ON M8X 2X8
Tel: 416-234-2177; *Fax:* 416-234-9039
fiske@bellnet.ca

Toronto: Fleischer & Kochberg - *1
#203, 77 Finch Ave. West, Toronto, ON M2N 2H5
Tel: 416-223-8102; *Fax:* 416-223-9502
thefirm@relo-law.com
www.relo-law.com

Toronto: Fleming, Breen - *2
370 Bloor St. East, Toronto, ON M4W 3M6
Tel: 416-927-9000; *Fax:* 416-927-9069
richard@defender.ca

Toronto: Fleming, White & Burgess - *2
#1000, 2 Bloor St. West, Toronto, ON M4W 3E2
Tel: 416-961-2868; *Fax:* 416-961-2964
flemingwhite@bellnet.ca

Toronto: Fleury, Comery LLP - *4
#104, 215 Morrish Rd., Toronto, ON M1C 1E9
Tel: 416-282-5754; *Fax:* 416-282-9906
thefirm@fleurcom.on.ca
www.fleurcom.on.ca

Toronto: Ronald Flom - *2
#712, 2345 Yonge St., Toronto, ON M4P 2E5
Tel: 416-482-2777; *Fax:* 416-482-2599

Toronto: Fogler, Rubinoff LLP - *105
#1200, Toronto-Dominion Centre, 95 Wellington St. West, Toronto, ON M5J 2Z9
Tel: 416-864-9700; *Fax:* 416-941-8852
Toll-Free: 866-861-9700
thefirm@foglers.com
www.foglers.com

Toronto: Forget & Matthews LLP, Barristers - *10
#402, 214 King St. West, Toronto, ON M5H 3S6
Tel: 416-593-5400; *Fax:* 416-595-5400
infolaw@fmlaw.ca
www.fmlaw.ca

Toronto: R. Brian Foster Q.C. - *1
#1, 16 Four Seasons Pl., Toronto, ON M9B 6E5
Tel: 416-695-2700; *Fax:* 416-695-3687
brianfoster@bellnet.ca

Toronto: Fournie Mickleborough LLP - *4
#701, 90 Adelaide St. West, Toronto, ON M5H 3V9
Tel: 416-366-3999; *Fax:* 416-366-2860
rcm@companylawyers.com
www.companylawyers.com

Toronto: Kevin Fox, Barrister & Solicitor - *1
174 Davenport Rd., Toronto, ON M5R 1J2
Tel: 416-323-3252; *Fax:* 416-929-6885
kfox@davenportlaw.cawww.linkedin.com/pub/kevin-fox/17/97b/5 77

Toronto: Walter Fox - *3
#312, 100 Richmond St. West, Toronto, ON M5H 3K6
Tel: 416-363-9238; *Fax:* 416-363-9230
fox@sympatico.ca

Toronto: Franco, Lento - *1
#504, 3200 Dufferin St., Toronto, ON M3K 2A7
Tel: 416-398-4044; *Fax:* 416-398-7396
ldlaw@total.net

Toronto: Fraser, Simms and Reid - *1
#2, 15 John St., Toronto, ON M9N 1J2
Tel: 416-241-0111; *Fax:* 416-241-1911

Toronto: Harvey Freedman - *3
#100, 79 Shuter St., Toronto, ON M5B 1B3
Tel: 416-363-1737; *Fax:* 416-861-9919
hfreedman@freedmans.ca

Toronto: Joel P. Freedman - *1
#200, 3200 Dufferin St., Toronto, ON M6A 2T3
Tel: 416-248-6231; *Fax:* 416-241-0080
jpfreedman@freedmanlaw.com

Toronto: Norman J. Freedman, Q.C.
#2150, 121 King St. West, Toronto, ON M5H 3T9
Tel: 416-815-7767; *Fax:* 416-815-7722

Toronto: Randall R. Friedland - *1
#1301, 2200 Yonge St., Toronto, ON M4S 2C6
Tel: 416-932-4969; *Fax:* 416-932-0541
friedland@jodlaw.com

Toronto: J. Friedman, Q.C. - *1
#202, 30 St. Clair Ave. West, Toronto, ON M4V 3A1
Tel: 416-515-0575; *Fax:* 416-515-0454
jack.friedman@bellnet.ca

Toronto: David G. Friend, Q.C. - *1
#202, 3459 Sheppard Ave. East, Toronto, ON M1T 3K5
Tel: 416-754-0333; *Fax:* 416-292-0473
dfriend@bellnet.ca

Toronto: Fritz & Associates
44 Upjohn Road, Toronto, ON M3B 2W1
Tel: 416-441-6747; *Fax:* 416-447-8588

Toronto: Fryer Levitt - *1
#2, 421 Eglinton Ave. West, Toronto, ON M5N 1A4
Tel: 416-323-1377; *Fax:* 416-323-9355
jelevitt@fryerlevitt.com
www.fryerlevitt.com

Toronto: Harry Frymer - *1
#320, 100 Richmond St. West, Toronto, ON M5H 3K6
Tel: 416-869-1073; *Fax:* 416-869-1840

Toronto: Derrick Fulton Barrister & Solicitor - *1
#1515, 390 Bay St., Toronto, ON M5H 2Y2
Tel: 416-594-3338; *Fax:* 416-860-1474
dmfulton@istar.ca
home.istar.ca/~dmfulton/

Toronto: Fyshe McMahon LLP - *9
#2000, 393 University Ave., Toronto, ON M5G 1E6
Tel: 416-977-1525; *Fax:* 416-977-1526

Toronto: F.A. Gabriel - *1
#203, 425 University Ave., Toronto, ON M5G 1T6
Tel: 416-593-6621; *Fax:* 416-599-8075
fgabriel@bellnet.ca

Toronto: Gaertner Tobin LLP - *9
#400, 144 Front St. West, Toronto, ON M5J 2L7
Tel: 416-599-7700; *Fax:* 416-599-7800
mkent@gtllp.com
www.gtllp.com

Toronto: Laurie A. Galway - *1
27 Prince Arthur Ave., Toronto, ON M5R 1B2
Tel: 416-413-9466; *Fax:* 416-960-1498
lauriegalway@27princearthur.com

Toronto: Douglas Gordon Garbig, A Professional Corporation - *1
#3101, P.O. Box 52, 401 Bay St., Toronto, ON M5H 2Y4
Tel: 416-862-7822; *Fax:* 416-862-2568
garbig@garbig.com

Toronto: Gardiner Miller Arnold LLP - *6
#1202, 390 Bay St., Toronto, ON M5H 2Y2
Tel: 416-363-2614; *Fax:* 416-363-8451
gmainfo@gmalaw.ca
www.gmalaw.ca

Toronto: Gardiner, Roberts LLP - *67
#3100, Scotia Plaza, 40 King St. West, Toronto, ON M5H 3Y2
Tel: 416-865-6600; *Fax:* 416-865-6636
www.gardiner-roberts.com

Toronto: Garfin Zeidenberg LLP - *13
#800, Yonge Norton Centre, 5255 Yonge St., Toronto, ON M2N 6P4
Tel: 416-512-8000; *Fax:* 416-512-9992
Toll-Free: 877-529-9910
gzinfo@gzlegal.com
www.gzlegal.com

** indicates number of lawyers*

Toronto: Susan W. Garfin - *1
#2000, 393 University Ave., Toronto, ON M5G 1E6
Tel: 416-599-9933; *Fax:* 416-599-5497
garfin@rogers.com

Toronto: Garfinkle, Biderman - *19
#801, Dundee Place, 1 Adelaide St. East, Toronto, ON M5C 2V9
Tel: 416-869-1234; *Fax:* 416-869-0547
www.garfinkle.com

Toronto: Gasee, Cohen & Youngman, Barrister & Solicitor - *6
#200, 65 Queen St. West, Toronto, ON M5H 2M5
Tel: 416-363-3351; *Fax:* 416-363-0252
info@gcylaw.com
www.gcylaw.com

Toronto: Leon Gavendo - *1
#2000, Law Chambers, University Centre, 393 University Ave., Toronto, ON M5G 1E6
Tel: 416-585-3109; *Fax:* 416-585-9668
lgavendo@on.aibn.com

Toronto: L.B. Geffen - *1
#205, 2907 Kennedy Rd., Toronto, ON M1V 1S8
Tel: 416-292-6688; *Fax:* 416-292-6649
lgeffen@idirect.com

Toronto: Gelfand & Co. - *2
519 King St. West, Toronto, ON M5V 1K4
Tel: 416-929-4949; *Fax:* 416-929-1996
Toll-Free: 877-286-4296
lgelfand@gelfandandco.com

Toronto: Geller & Minster - *3
2 Keewatin Ave., Toronto, ON M4P 1Z8
Tel: 416-480-2200; *Fax:* 416-480-2693
geller@bellnet.ca

Toronto: Genest Murray LLP - *6
#700, 130 Adelaide St. West, Toronto, ON M5H 4C1
Tel: 416-368-8600; *Fax:* 416-360-2625
www.genestmurray.ca

Toronto: Basil L. Georgieff - *1
3543A St. Clair Ave. East, Toronto, ON M1K 1L6
Tel: 416-464-6888; *Fax:* 416-267-1452
basgeo@msn.com

Toronto: Lorne Gershuny - *1
1577 Bloor St. West, Toronto, ON M6P 1A6
Tel: 416-539-0989; *Fax:* 416-536-3618
lgershuny@hotmail.com

Toronto: Gertler & Associates - *2
5341 Dundas St. West, Toronto, ON M9B 1B1
Tel: 416-410-8613; *Fax:* 416-231-9492
www.gertlerandassociates.com

Toronto: Henry J. Gertner
4 Finch Ave. West, Toronto, ON M2N 6L1
Tel: 416-225-5992; *Fax:* 416-225-7611
gertnerlaw@bellnet.ca

Toronto: Ghose Law Office - *2
#308, 1620 Albion Rd., Toronto, ON M9V 4B4
Tel: 416-744-1480; *Fax:* 416-744-9855
gmreception@bellnet.ca
www.gmlawoffice.ca

Toronto: Giffels Associates Limited - *1
30 International Blvd., Toronto, ON M9W 5P3
Tel: 461-675-5950; *Fax:* 461-675-4620
Toll-Free: 800-567-8918
stephen.obrien@giffels.com
www.giffels.com

Toronto: Gilbert & Yallen - *3
204 St. George St., 3rd Fl., Toronto, ON M5R 2N5
Tel: 416-927-0001; *Fax:* 416-927-0930

Toronto: Gilbert's LLP - *12
The Flatiron Building, 49 Wellington St. East, Toronto, ON M5E 1C9
Tel: 416-703-1100; *Fax:* 416-703-7422
tim@gilbertslaw.ca
www.gilbertslaw.ca

Toronto: Gilbert, Wright & Kirby LLP - *9
#2302, P.O. Box 103, 401 Bay St., Toronto, ON M5H 2Y4
Tel: 416-363-3100; *Fax:* 416-363-1379
info@gwklaw.com
www.gwklaw.com

Toronto: Gilbertson Davis Emerson LLP - *8
#2020, 20 Queen St. West, Toronto, ON M5H 3R3
Tel: 416-979-2020; *Fax:* 416-979-1285
office@gilbertsondavis.com
www.gilbertsondavis.com

Toronto: John D. Gilfillan, Q.C. - *1
#1200, 8 King St. East, Toronto, ON M5C 1B5
Tel: 416-861-1881; *Fax:* 416-861-1737
gilfillan@interware.net

Toronto: Gillespie Consulting - *1
100 Beech Ave., Toronto, ON M4E 3H6
Tel: 416-699-8786; *Fax:* 416-699-8786
gusgillespie@rogers.com

Toronto: Leslie M. Giroday - *1
190 Sixth St., Toronto, ON M8V 3A5
Tel: 416-255-1063; *Fax:* 416-251-8699
lmgiroday@sympatico.ca

Toronto: Glaholt LLP - *9
#800, 141 Adelaide St. West, Toronto, ON M5H 3L5
Tel: 416-368-8280; *Fax:* 416-368-3467
Toll-Free: 866-452-4658
bb@glaholt.com
www.glaholt.com

Toronto: Earl Glasner - *1
#320, 100 Richmond St. West, Toronto, ON M5H 3K6
Tel: 416-869-1076
earlglasner@rogers.com

Toronto: Alan A. Glass - *1
#500, 1000 Finch Ave. West, Toronto, ON M3J 2V5
Tel: 416-667-9796; *Fax:* 416-667-8048

Toronto: Glass, Murray, Bianchi - *4
50 Richmond St. East, 5th Fl., Toronto, ON M5C 1N7
Tel: 416-363-9295; *Fax:* 416-363-7659
lglass@glassassoc.com

Toronto: Louis Glatt - *1
2354 Danforth Ave., Toronto, ON M4C 1K7
Tel: 416-422-2107; *Fax:* 416-422-2606

Toronto: Global Ventures - *1
E3 - 296 Mill Rd., Toronto, ON M9C 4X8
Tel: 416-569-9306; *Fax:* 416-620-7768
consultrussi@aol.com

Toronto: Glober & Cohen, Associates - *3
114 Scollard St., Toronto, ON M5R 1G2
Tel: 416-324-9994; *Fax:* 416-324-0966

Toronto: Gluckstein & Associates LLP - *7
#301, P.O. Box 53, 595 Bay St., Toronto, ON M5G 2C2
Tel: 416-408-4252; *Fax:* 416-408-4235
Toll-Free: 866-308-7722
info@gluckstein.com
www.gluckstein.com

Toronto: Godfrey & Corcoran - *1
#702, 55 Queen St. East, Toronto, ON M5C 1R6
Tel: 416-363-0484; *Fax:* 416-363-0485
ccorcoran@idirect.com

Toronto: Sydney L. Goldenberg - *1
125 Highbourne Rd., Toronto, ON M5P 2J5
Tel: 416-482-3206; *Fax:* 416-482-8619

Toronto: Goldhar & Nemoy - *2
#214, 120 Carlton St., Toronto, ON M5A 4K2
Tel: 416-928-1488; *Fax:* 416-924-7166

Toronto: Avra Goldhar - *1
27 Abbeywood Trail, Toronto, ON M3B 3B4
Tel: 416-444-4378; *Fax:* 416-444-5721
agoldhar@rogers.com

Toronto: H.A. Goldkind - *1
#320, 100 Richmond St. West, Toronto, ON M5H 3K6
Tel: 416-366-5280

Toronto: Goldman Sloan Nash & Haber LLP - *25
#1600, 480 University Avenue, Toronto, ON M5G 1V6
Tel: 416-597-9922; *Fax:* 416-597-3370
welcome@gsnh.com
www.gsnh.com

Toronto: Jeffrey L. Goldman - *1
#500, 425 University Ave., Toronto, ON M5G 1T6
Tel: 416-597-9223; *Fax:* 416-977-5200
jglaw@aol.com

Toronto: Jeffrey W. Goldman - *1
#300, 3500 Dufferin St., Toronto, ON M3K 1N2
Tel: 416-787-1818; *Fax:* 416-787-1810
jeffreygoldman@goldmanlawoffice.com

Toronto: R.M. Goldman - *1
#301, 481 Univeristy Ave., Toronto, ON M5G 2E9
Tel: 416-977-8008; *Fax:* 416-364-2308
rgoldman@defender.ca

Toronto: Goldman, Spring, Kichler & Sanders - *7
#700, 40 Sheppard Ave. West, Toronto, ON M2N 6K9
Tel: 416-225-9400; *Fax:* 416-225-4805

Toronto: Goldstein & Grubner LLP - *2
#212, 3459 Sheppard Ave. East, Toronto, ON M1T 3K5
Tel: 416-292-0414; *Fax:* 416-292-4508
k.goldstein@rogers.com; igrubner@rogers.com
www.gglawyers.ca

Toronto: H.S. Goldstein - *1
#1202, P.O. Box 159, 4950 Yonge St., Toronto, ON M2N 6K1
Tel: 416-223-0600

Toronto: Goldstein, Rosen & Rassos LLP - *2
#102, 1648 Victoria Park Ave., Toronto, ON M1R 1P7
Tel: 416-757-4156; *Fax:* 416-757-9318
trassos@grrlaw.ca

Toronto: Golish & Golish - *2
21 Fairholme Avenue, Toronto, ON M6B 2W4
Tel: 416-789-2438; *Fax:* 416-789-2438

Toronto: David Gomes - *1
112 Adelaide St. East, Toronto, ON M5C 1K9
Tel: 416-361-0906; *Fax:* 416-368-2918
dgomes0604@rogers.com

Toronto: Goodman, Solomon & Gold - *3
#1500, 439 University Ave., Toronto, ON M5G 1Y8
Tel: 416-595-5555; *Fax:* 416-595-7020

Toronto: Stanley Goodman, Q.C. - *1
#1800, 4950 Yonge St., Toronto, ON M2N 6K1
Tel: 416-224-0224; *Fax:* 416-224-0758
stangoodman@torlaw.com

Toronto: Martin Z. Goose - *1
#504, 555 Burnhamthorpe Rd., Toronto, ON M9C 2Y3
Tel: 416-239-4811; *Fax:* 416-239-1707
martingoose@bellnet.ca

Toronto: Nathan Gotlieb - *1
#1800, Madison Centre, 4950 Yonge St., Toronto, ON M2N 6K1
Tel: 416-224-0200; *Fax:* 416-224-0758
ngotlieb@torlaw.com

Toronto: G.L. Gottlieb, Q.C. - *1
#309, 600 Bay St., Toronto, ON M5G 1M6
Tel: 416-977-3835; *Fax:* 416-977-3807
glgqc@interlog.com
www.glgqc.com

Toronto: Max A. Gould - *1
#1000, 30 St. Clair Ave. West, Toronto, ON M4V 3A1
Tel: 416-964-0290; *Fax:* 416-964-7102

Toronto: Michael J. Gould - *1
75 Bannatyne Dr., Toronto, ON M2L 2P2
Tel: 416-510-3030

Toronto: Graham Tobe - *1
#202, 1 Yorkdale Rd., Toronto, ON M6A 3A1
Tel: 416-256-1555; *Fax:* 416-256-0918

Toronto: D.J. Grant - *1
#412, 1220 Sheppard Ave. East, Toronto, ON M2K 2S5
Tel: 416-490-9206; *Fax:* 416-490-9949

Toronto: Deryk A. Gravesande - *1
2 Carlton Street, Toronto, ON M5B 1J3
Tel: 416-206-1110

Toronto: Green & Chercover - *15
30 St. Clair Ave. West, 10th Fl., Toronto, ON M4V 3A1
Tel: 416-968-3333; *Fax:* 416-968-0325
inquiry@greenchercover.ca
www.greenchercover.ca

Toronto: Green & Spiegel - *12
#2800, 390 Bay St., Toronto, ON M5H 2Y2
Tel: 416-862-7880; *Fax:* 416-862-1698

** indicates number of lawyers*

Toronto: David J. Green - *1
#1, 399 Spadina Ave., Toronto, ON M5T 2G6
Tel: 416-979-2333; *Fax:* 416-597-8966

Toronto: Weldon F. Green, Q.C. - *1
P.O. Box 151, 6 Portneuf Ct., Toronto, ON M5A 4E4
Tel: 416-364-4465; *Fax:* 416-364-3657
wfgreenco@on.aibn.com

Toronto: Donald M. Greenbaum, Q.C. - *1
5075 Yonge St., Toronto, ON M2N 6C6
Tel: 416-631-7504; *Fax:* 416-631-9895
baum@globility.com

Toronto: Greenberg & Levine - *2
2223 Kennedy Rd., Toronto, ON M1T 3G5
Tel: 416-292-6500; *Fax:* 416-292-6559
reception@greenbergandlevine.com
www.greenbergandlevine.com

Toronto: Greenberg, Jack - *1
#204, 181 Eglinton Ave. East, Toronto, ON M4P 1J4
Tel: 416-485-8833; *Fax:* 416-485-3246
jackgreenberg@greenberglawyers.ca

Toronto: Greenspan, White - *7
144 King St. East, Toronto, ON M5C 1G8
Tel: 416-366-3961; *Fax:* 416-366-7994
www.greenspanwhite.com

Toronto: Greenwoods Barristers & Solicitors - *2
#100, 3500 Dufferin St., Toronto, ON M3K 1N2
Tel: 416-638-4100; *Fax:* 416-638-3529
Toll-Free: 866-578-4100
agreenwd@greenwoodslaw.com
www.greenwoodslaw.com

Toronto: E.J. Gresik - *1
101 Scollard St., Toronto, ON M5R 1G4
Tel: 416-924-0781; *Fax:* 416-960-9650

Toronto: C. Grimanis - *1
799 Carlaw Avenue, Toronto, ON M4K 3E4
Tel: 416-469-1176; *Fax:* 416-469-4252

Toronto: Groia & Company Professional Corporation - *7
365 Bay St., 11th Fl., Toronto, ON M5H 2V1
Tel: 416-203-2115; *Fax:* 416-203-9231
postmaster@groiaco.com
www.groiaco.com

Toronto: Bernard Gropper - *1
#300, 261 Davenport Rd., Toronto, ON M5R 1K3
Tel: 416-962-3000; *Fax:* 416-487-3002
bgropper@gropperlaw.com

Toronto: C.H. Grosberg - *1
#205, 2907 Kennedy Rd., Toronto, ON M1V 1S8
Tel: 416-752-9745; *Fax:* 416-292-6649

Toronto: Grosso McCarthy Inc. - *2
P.O. Box 45, 200 Front Street West, 23rd Floor, Toronto, ON M5V 3K2
Tel: 416-362-6141; *Fax:* 416-362-6145
fgrosso@grossomccarthy.com
www.grossomccarthy.com

Toronto: Derek T. Ground - *1
16 Oakview Avenue, Toronto, ON M6P 3J2
Tel: 416-604-3434; *Fax:* 416-604-3596
derek.ground@sympatico.ca

Toronto: Grundy Cass Professional Corporation - *3
#2310, Bay Wellington Tower, P.O. Box 792, 181 Bay St., Toronto, ON M5J 2T3
Tel: 416-849-8003; *Fax:* 416-849-8004

Toronto: Guberman Garson Immigration Lawyers - *5
#1920, 130 Adelaide St. West, Toronto, ON M5H 3P5
Tel: 416-363-1234; *Fax:* 416-363-8760
immlaw@ggilaw.com
www.ggilaw.com

Toronto: J.M. Guoba - *2
#211, 2425 Eglinton Ave. East, Toronto, ON M1K 5G8
Tel: 416-759-4500; *Fax:* 416-759-4510

Toronto: Peter F. Haber - *1
325 Mutual St., Toronto, ON M4Y 1X6
Tel: 416-961-0265; *Fax:* 416-961-1860
Toll-Free: 888-841-1104
peterhaber@rogers.com

Toronto: Lawrence Hadbavny - *1
Law Society of Upper Canada, 130 Queen St. West, Toronto, ON M5H 2N6
Tel: 416-947-3906; *Fax:* 416-644-4880
lhadbavn@lsuc.on.ca

Toronto: Michael P. Haddad - *2
208 Carlton St., Toronto, ON M5A 2L1
Tel: 416-926-8151; *Fax:* 416-927-9005
mhaddad@istar.ca

Toronto: Hahn & Maian - *2
664 Mount Pleasant Rd., Toronto, ON M4S 2N3
Tel: 416-486-9445; *Fax:* 416-486-1174
johnhahn@idirect.com

Toronto: Kenneth A. Hahn - *1
1078 Kipling Ave., Toronto, ON M9B 3M2
Tel: 416-231-3353; *Fax:* 416-231-6773

Toronto: Miles M. Halberstadt, Q.C. - *1
#200, 379 Dundas St. East, Toronto, ON M5A 2A6
Tel: 416-944-0441; *Fax:* 416-944-8330
mileshalberstadt@hotmail.com

Toronto: Hall Webber LLP Entertainment & New Media Law - *4
#400, 1200 Bay St., Toronto, ON M5R 2A5
Tel: 416-920-3849; *Fax:* 416-920-8373
mail@ent-law.com
www.ent-law.com

Toronto: David F. Halpenny - *1
#403, 111 Peter St., Toronto, ON M5V 2H1
Tel: 416-867-9208; *Fax:* 416-867-9139

Toronto: Allan S. Halpert - *2
37 Maitland St., Toronto, ON M4Y 1C8
Tel: 416-968-7733; *Fax:* 416-968-7192
allan@halpertlaw.com

Toronto: Munyonzwe Hamalengwa
#18A, 100 Westmore Dr., Toronto, ON M9V 5C3
Tel: 416-644-1106; *Fax:* 416-644-1126
mhamalengwa@sympatico.ca
www.munyonzwehamalengwa.ca

Toronto: Harvey L. Hamburg - *1
#215, 120 Carlton St., Toronto, ON M5A 4K2
Tel: 416-968-9054; *Fax:* 416-968-9023
hhamburg@sympatico.ca

Toronto: Michael A. Handler - *1
2950 Keele St., Toronto, ON M3M 2H2
Tel: 416-638-0680; *Fax:* 416-398-3007

Toronto: Hans & Hans - *1
17 Wembley Rd., Toronto, ON M6C 2E8
Tel: 416-960-5445; *Fax:* 416-924-7541
hansoff10@rogers.com

Toronto: Zakaul Haque - *1
#205, 1058A Albion Rd., Toronto, ON M9V 1A7
Tel: 416-743-6302; *Fax:* 416-743-4783

Toronto: George M. Harasymowycz - *1
#200, 2311 Bloor St. West, Toronto, ON M6S 1P1
Tel: 416-766-2472; *Fax:* 416-766-3297
george@haraslaw.com

Toronto: Murray P. Harrington - *1
285 Pitfield Rd., Toronto, ON M1S 1Z2
Tel: 416-299-0477; *Fax:* 416-299-7570

Toronto: David E. Harris - *1
#1900, 439 University Ave., Toronto, ON M5G 1Y8
Tel: 416-585-9329; *Fax:* 416-408-2372
delih@inforamp.net

Toronto: Ricki D. Harris - *2
#1800, 4950 Yonge St., Toronto, ON M2N 6K1
Tel: 416-224-0200; *Fax:* 416-224-0758
rdharris@torlaw.com

Toronto: Klaus Hartmann - *1
391 Willowdale Ave., Toronto, ON M2N 5A8
Tel: 416-590-0311; *Fax:* 416-590-0312

Toronto: Douglas G. Hatch - *1
#619, 4211 Yonge St., Toronto, ON M2P 2A9
Tel: 416-512-7521; *Fax:* 416-512-1946
dhatch@rogers.com

Toronto: Peter L. Hatch - *1
31 Prince Arthur Ave., Toronto, ON M5R 1B2
Tel: 416-972-6962; *Fax:* 416-960-5456

Toronto: Frederick Simon Hawa - *1
2267 Lakeshore Blvd. West, Toronto, ON M8V 3X2
Tel: 416-252-5190
fredhawa@sympatico.ca

Toronto: John Hay & Associates - *1
#1207, 4003 Bayview Ave., Toronto, ON M2M 3Z8
Tel: 416-226-2049; *Fax:* 416-494-5586
john.hay@sympatico.ca

Toronto: Hazzard & Hore - *7
#1002, 141 Adelaide St. West, Toronto, ON M5H 3L5
Tel: 416-868-0074; *Fax:* 416-868-1468
info@hazardandhore.com
www.hazzardandhore.com

Toronto: Heather McGeorge C.A., LL.B - *1
#1510, North York City Centre, 5140 Yonge St., Toronto, ON M2N 6L7
Tel: 416-218-5251
mcgeorge.heather@gmail.com

Toronto: Marian D. Hebb - *2
250 Merton Street, Toronto, ON M4S 1B1
Tel: 416-971-6618; *Fax:* 416-971-4144
mhebb@sympatico.ca

Toronto: Stephen H. Hebscher - *1
#1800, 4950 Yonge St., Toronto, ON M2N 6K1
Tel: 416-550-6554; *Fax:* 416-224-0758
crimlaw@torlaw.com

Toronto: E.S. Heiber - *1
#200, 70 Bond St., Toronto, ON M5B 1X3
Tel: 416-362-2768; *Fax:* 416-865-5328
esheiber@hvllp.com

Toronto: Heifetz, Crozier, Law - *5
#600, 10 King St. East, Toronto, ON M5C 1C3
Tel: 416-863-1717; *Fax:* 416-368-3133
dcrozier@hclaw.com
www.hclaw.com

Toronto: Julian Heller & Associates - *3
#1905, 120 Adelaide St. West, Toronto, ON M5H 1T1
Tel: 416-364-2404; *Fax:* 416-364-0793
jheller@hellerandassociates.on.ca

Toronto: Heller, Rubel - *9
#1902, 120 Adelaide St. West, Toronto, ON M5H 1T1
Tel: 416-863-9311; *Fax:* 416-863-9465
mshore@hellerrubel.com

Toronto: Hicks Morley Hamilton Stewart Storie LLP - *84
TD Tower, TD Centre, Box 371, P.O. Box 371, Stn. TD Centre, 66 Wellington St., 30th Fl., Toronto, ON M5K 1K8
Tel: 416-362-1011; *Fax:* 416-362-9680
www.hicksmorley.com

Toronto: High Park Advocacy Group - *5
303 Jane St., Toronto, ON M6S 3Z3
Tel: 416-535-2815; *Fax:* 416-531-4769
tegan@highparkgroup.com
www.highparkgroup.com

Toronto: John L. Hill - *1
127 Bishop Ave., Toronto, ON M2M 1Z6
Tel: 416-226-3221; *Fax:* 416-226-3222
conlaw@pathcom.com

Toronto: Hiltz Szigeti LLP - *2
#906, 94 Cumberland St., Toronto, ON M5R 1A3
Tel: 416-968-6575; *Fax:* 416-968-3424
lawyers@hslaw.ca

Toronto: David Himelfarb - *1
#1400, 111 Richmond St. West, Toronto, ON M5H 2G4
Tel: 416-365-0303; *Fax:* 416-365-9276

Toronto: Hinkson Sachak Mcleod
#301, 366 Bay St., Toronto, ON M5H 4B2
Tel: 416-368-3476; *Fax:* 416-363-9917
shinkson@hinksonlaw.com

Toronto: Hitchman & Sprigings - *6
#5704, 40 King St. West, Toronto, ON M5H 3Y2
Tel: 416-777-2270; *Fax:* 416-777-2271
mail@hitchman.com
www.hitchman.com

** indicates number of lawyers*

Toronto: Hodder Barristers - *6
#2200, DBRS Tower, Adelaide Place, 181 University Ave., Toronto, ON M5H 3M7
Tel: 416-601-4818; *Fax:* 416-947-0909
info@hodderbarristers.com
www.torontolawyerlawfirm.com

Toronto: Hodgson Russ LLP - *3
#2309, P.O. Box 30, 150 King St. West, Toronto, ON M5H 1J9
Tel: 416-595-5100; *Fax:* 416-595-5021
info@hodgsonruss.com
www.hodgsonruss.com

Toronto: Hoffman, Sillery, Buckstein & Chuback - *3
#200, 1810 Avenue Rd., Toronto, ON M5M 3Z2
Tel: 416-787-1161; *Fax:* 416-787-3894

Toronto: Gerri C. Holder - *1
#901, 701 Evans Ave., Toronto, ON M9C 1A3
Tel: 416-626-3069; *Fax:* 416-622-8952
gholder@rogers.com

Toronto: Christopher Holoboff - *1
#500, 27 Queen St. East, Toronto, ON M5C 2M6
Tel: 416-868-0878; *Fax:* 416-868-0879
choloboff@aol.com

Toronto: Hooey, Remus - *6
#400, 1 University Ave., 4th Floor, Toronto, ON M5J 2P1
Tel: 416-362-4000; *Fax:* 416-362-3646
hrlaw@hooeyremus.com
www.hooeyremus.com

Toronto: E.R. Hornstein - *1
19 Relmore Rd., Toronto, ON M5P 2Y4
Tel: 416-901-7949

Toronto: Houser, Henry & Syron - *6
#2000, 145 King St. West, Toronto, ON M5H 2B6
Tel: 416-362-3411; *Fax:* 416-362-3757
inquiries@houserhenry.com
www.houserhenry.com

Toronto: Howie, Sacks & Henry LLP - *12
#2800, P.O. Box 4, 401 Bay St., Toronto, ON M5H 2Y4
Tel: 416-361-5990; *Fax:* 416-361-0083
Toll-Free: 877-474-5997
hsh@hshlawyers.com
www.hshlawyers.com

Toronto: John A. Howlett - *1
36 Toronto Street, Toronto, ON M5C 2C5
Tel: 416-941-9444; *Fax:* 416-913-1444
jhowlett@bellnet.ca

Toronto: John P. Howorun - *1
#1702, 360 Bay St., Toronto, ON M5H 2V6
Tel: 416-363-9355; *Fax:* 416-363-6371

Toronto: Hrycyna, Pothemont - *2
#200, 1081 Bloor St. West, Toronto, ON M6H 1M5
Tel: 416-532-8006; *Fax:* 416-532-2666
taras.hycyna@bellnet.ca

Toronto: Hughes, Amys LLP - *28
#200, 48 Yonge St., Toronto, ON M5E 1G6
Tel: 416-367-1608; *Fax:* 416-367-8821
Toll-Free: 800-565-1713
info@hughesamys.com
www.hughesamys.com

Toronto: Hughes, Dorsch, Garland, Coles LLP - *5
#400, 365 Bay St., Toronto, ON M5H 2V1
Tel: 416-868-1300; *Fax:* 416-861-1147

Toronto: Edward F. Hung - *2
#319, 1033 Bay St., Toronto, ON M5S 3A5
Tel: 416-926-8777; *Fax:* 416-926-1799
edhung@best-litigate.com
www.lawyersintoronto.com

Toronto: Susanne L. Hunter - *1
31 Prince Arthur Ave., Toronto, ON M5R 1B2
Tel: 416-975-0388; *Fax:* 416-960-5456

Toronto: Peter D. Hutcheon - *1
372 Bay St., Toronto, ON M5H 2W9
Tel: 416-515-2049; *Fax:* 416-929-3204
peter@tantech.com

Toronto: P.N.J. Hutchinson - *1
#302, P.O. Box 68, 70 Dixfield Dr., Toronto, ON M9C 4J4
Tel: 416-621-4430

Toronto: David L. Hynes - *1
#2200, 181 University Ave., Toronto, ON M5H 3M7
Tel: 416-601-9299; *Fax:* 416-601-9311
dlh@davidlhynes.com

Toronto: Nick Iannazzo, Barrister & Solicitor - *1
#500, 425 University Ave., Toronto, ON M5G 1T6
Tel: 416-598-2002; *Fax:* 416-598-8183
niannazzo@on.aibn.com

Toronto: ICF Consulting Canada Inc. - *1
#808, 277 Wellington St. West, Toronto, ON M5V 3E4
Tel: 416-341-0990; *Fax:* 416-341-0383
info@icfi.com
www.icfi.com

Toronto: Iler, Campbell - *8
#700, 890 Yonge St., Toronto, ON M4W 3P4
Tel: 416-598-0103; *Fax:* 416-598-3484
www.ilercampbell.com

Toronto: International Project & Protocol Services Inc. - *1
307 St. Clements Ave., Toronto, ON M4R 1H3
Tel: 416-481-7623
ipps@rogers.com
www.ipps.net

Toronto: IR Counsel Inc. - *1
417 Guildwood Pkwy., Toronto, ON M1E 1R3
Tel: 416-822-3130; *Fax:* 416-822-3132
bsmith@ironline.ca

Toronto: Joan M. Irwin - *1
#2200, P.O. Box 154, 4950 Yonge St., Toronto, ON M2N 6K1
Tel: 416-733-1992; *Fax:* 416-222-0021

Toronto: Alvin Isenberg - *2
#804, 5075 Yonge St., Toronto, ON M2N 6C6
Tel: 416-225-5136; *Fax:* 416-225-6877
info@shumanlaw.ca
www.shumanlaw.ca

Toronto: Israel Foulon LLP - *3
#200, 30A Hazleton Ave., Toronto, ON M5R 2E2
Tel: 416-640-1550; *Fax:* 416-640-1555
inquiries@israelfoulon.com
israelfoulon.com

Toronto: Cydney G. Israel - *1
61 Saint Nicholas St., Toronto, ON M4Y 1W6
Tel: 416-962-6188; *Fax:* 416-925-0162

Toronto: Jackman, Waldman & Associates - *6
281 Eglinton Ave. East, Toronto, ON M4P 1L3
Tel: 416-482-6501; *Fax:* 416-489-9618

Toronto: Carol E.F. Jackson - *1
#900, 60 Yonge St., Toronto, ON M5E 1H5
Tel: 416-363-3292; *Fax:* 416-868-6381

Toronto: Jacobson & Jacobson - *2
#222, 3089 Bathurst St., Toronto, ON M6A 2A4
Tel: 416-787-0611; *Fax:* 416-787-4873

Toronto: James, Siddall & Derzko - *4
#1305, 55 Queen St. East, Toronto, ON M5C 1R6
Tel: 416-860-0166; *Fax:* 416-860-0041

Toronto: Elham Jamshidi - *1
277 Richmond Street, Toronto, ON M5V 1X1
Tel: 416-586-0220

Toronto: Jane Finch Community Legal Services - *3
#409, 1315 Finch Ave. West, Toronto, ON M3J 2G6
Tel: 416-398-0677; *Fax:* 416-398-7172
www.janefinchcommunitylegalservices.ca

Toronto: Janssen & Associates - *2
89 Scollard St., Toronto, ON M5R 1G4
Tel: 416-929-1103; *Fax:* 416-929-9610

Toronto: Dale F. Jean-Pierre - *1
#700, 55 Town Centre Crt., Toronto, ON M1P 4X4
Tel: 416-290-0560; *Fax:* 416-290-1259

Toronto: Jeffery, Robertson, Watson & Pendrith - *2
#1812, 2 Carlton St., Toronto, ON M5B 1J3
Tel: 416-977-7700; *Fax:* 416-977-8570
nwatson@sympatico.ca

Toronto: The Jeffrey Group Ltd. - *1
#506, 133 Richmond St. West, Toronto, ON M5H 2L3
Tel: 416-361-1475
pjeffrey@thejeffreygroup.com

Toronto: John A. Johnson - *1
697 The Queensway, Toronto, ON M8V 1L2
Tel: 416-503-4418

Toronto: Daphne Johnston - *1
#2000, 393 University Ave., Toronto, ON M5G 1E6
Tel: 416-599-9635; *Fax:* 416-599-6043
Toll-Free: 800-364-5793
daphnejohnston@rogers.com

Toronto: Jones, Rogers LLP - *5
#1600, 155 University Ave., Toronto, ON M5H 3B7
Tel: 416-361-0626; *Fax:* 416-361-6303
law@jonesrogers.ca

Toronto: Joseph G. LoPresti, Barrister & Solicitor - *1
#1510, North York City Centre, 5140 Yonge St., Toronto, ON M2N 6L7
Tel: 416-218-5271; *Fax:* 416-250-7008
joseph@loprestilaw.ca
www.loprestilaw.ca

Toronto: Mary K.E. Joseph - *1
113 Riverdale Ave., Toronto, ON M4K 1C2
Tel: 416-363-8048; *Fax:* 416-406-0038
mary@maryjoseph.ca

Toronto: Ron Jourard - *1
#504, 3200 Dufferin St., Toronto, ON M6A 3B2
Tel: 416-398-6685; *Fax:* 416-398-7396
Toll-Free: 888-257-0002
jourard@defencelaw.com
www.defencelaw.com

Toronto: Robert W. Judge - *1
44 Fairview Blvd., Toronto, ON M4K 1L9
Tel: 416-466-7007; *Fax:* 416-466-7050

Toronto: Steven W. Junger - *1
#14, 620 Supertest Rd., Toronto, ON M3J 2M8
Tel: 416-787-7247; *Fax:* 416-787-3021
s.junger@sympatico.ca

Toronto: Juriansz & Li - *3
#1709, North American Life Centre, 5650 Yonge St., Toronto, ON M2M 4G3
Tel: 416-226-2342; *Fax:* 416-222-6874

Toronto: Justice for Children & Youth - *6
#1203, 415 Yonge St., Toronto, ON M5S 2T9
Tel: 416-920-1633; *Fax:* 416-920-5855
Toll-Free: 866-999-5329
info@jfcy.org
www.jfcy.org

Toronto: Kacaba & Associates - *2
#440, 100 Richmond St. West, Toronto, ON M5H 3K6
Tel: 416-361-1777; *Fax:* 416-361-1776

Toronto: Kagan, Shastri - *6
188 Avenue Rd., Toronto, ON M5R 2J1
Tel: 416-368-2100; *Fax:* 416-368-8206

Toronto: The Kalen Group - *1
262 Avenue Rd., Toronto, ON M4V 2G7
Tel: 416-929-7781; *Fax:* 416-929-7784
kalen@mrgeenjeans.ca

Toronto: Speros Kanellos - *1
#202, 211 Consumers Rd., Toronto, ON M2J 4G8
Tel: 416-493-3100; *Fax:* 416-493-4377

Toronto: Chan Yeung Kang - *1
#210, 280 Sheppard Ave. East, Toronto, ON M2N 3B1
Tel: 416-221-1417; *Fax:* 416-221-1732
cykanglaw@hotmail.com

Toronto: William Kaplan - *1
#200, 70 Bond St., Toronto, ON M5B 1X3
Tel: 416-865-5341; *Fax:* 416-360-5746
william@williamkaplan.com
www.williamkaplan.com

Toronto: Kapoor Barristers - *2
#210, 20 Adelaide St. East, Toronto, ON M5C 2T6
Tel: 416-363-2700; *Fax:* 416-368-6811
info@kapoorbarristers.com
www.kapoorbarristers.com

Toronto: Kappel Ludlow LLP - *2
#1400, 439 University Ave., Toronto, ON M5G 1Y8
Tel: 416-408-4565; *Fax:* 416-408-4569
info@kappelludlow.com
www.kappelludlow.com

** indicates number of lawyers*

Toronto: **Karta Strategy - *1**
#609, 45 Carlton St., Toronto, ON M5B 2H9
Tel: 416-506-0609
kchopra@kartastrategy.com

Toronto: **Joseph H. Kary - *1**
90A Isabella St., Toronto, ON M4Y 1N4
Tel: 416-929-9656; *Fax*: 416-363-2473

Toronto: **Sheldon L. Kasman & Associate - *2**
#201, 1622 Eglinton Ave. West, Toronto, ON M6E 2G8
Tel: 416-789-1888; *Fax*: 416-789-5928
law@kasman.com
www.kasman.com

Toronto: **Garen Kassabian - *1**
#203, 8 Sampson Mews, Toronto, ON M3C 0H5
Tel: 416-443-9494; *Fax*: 416-443-0575
garen@bellnet.ca

Toronto: **Kavanagh Bateman & Baek LLP - *4**
#550, 141 Adelaide St. West, Toronto, ON M5H 3L5
Tel: 416-304-0600; *Fax*: 416-304-0669

Toronto: **J.M. Kavanagh, Q.C. - *1**
#340, 100 Cowdray Ct., Toronto, ON M1S 5C8
Tel: 416-265-3560; *Fax*: 416-265-1944

Toronto: **Robert C. Kay - *1**
161 Bay Street, Toronto, ON M5J 2S1
Tel: 416-362-9999

Toronto: **D.H. Kayfetz - *1**
99 South Dr., Toronto, ON M4W 1R7
Tel: 416-364-8131; *Fax*: 416-964-9009

Toronto: **Keith & Kramer - *2**
#404, 1200 Bay St., Toronto, ON M5R 2A5
Tel: 416-922-4417; *Fax*: 416-922-9328
tkeith@interlog.com

Toronto: **Christina H. Kelk - *1**
94 South Dr., Toronto, ON M4W 1R6
Tel: 416-966-1266; *Fax*: 416-966-2670
kelk@sympatico.ca

Toronto: **Kelly & Lacy - *4**
144 King St. East, 3rd Fl., Toronto, ON M5C 1G8
Tel: 416-362-3681; *Fax*: 416-366-1762
jennings@144king.com

Toronto: **Kelly ADR Services - *1**
#200, 112 Adelaide St. East, Toronto, ON M5C 1K9
Tel: 416-362-8555; *Fax*: 416-362-8825
kjkelly@adrchambers.com

Toronto: **H. Michael Kelly, Q.C. - *1**
#200, 112 Adelaide St. East, Toronto, ON M5C 1K9
Tel: 416-960-3781; *Toll-Free*: 800-856-5154

Toronto: **Evan N. Kenley - *1**
#301, 1352 Bathurst St., Toronto, ON M5K 3H7
Tel: 416-932-1148; *Fax*: 416-932-1108

Toronto: **M.L. Kerbel - *1**
#1001, 65 Queen St. West, Toronto, ON M5H 2M5
Tel: 416-364-9532
mlkerbel@sympatico.ca

Toronto: **Shayne G. Kert - *1**
370 Bloor St. East, Toronto, ON M4W 3M6
Tel: 416-863-0141; *Fax*: 416-927-9069

Toronto: **Kestenberg Siegal Lipkus - *8**
65 Granby St., Toronto, ON M5B 1H8
Tel: 416-597-0000; *Fax*: 416-597-6567
postmaster@ksllaw.com
www.ksllaw.com

Toronto: **El-Farouk A. Khaki - *1**
315 Mutual St., Toronto, ON M4Y 1X6
Tel: 416-925-7227; *Fax*: 416-925-2450
elfin925@rogers.com

Toronto: **R.S. Kimel - *1**
444 Adelaide St. West, Toronto, ON M5V 1S7
Tel: 416-703-1877; *Fax*: 416-504-9216

Toronto: **King & King - *1**
#2, 823 Millwood Rd., Toronto, ON M4G 1W3
Tel: 416-368-4678; *Fax*: 416-368-7234
aek@kingandking.net

Toronto: **Kirkland Capital Corporation - *1**
#105, 120 Rosedale Valley Rd., Toronto, ON M4W 1P8
Tel: 416-921-9992; *Fax*: 416-921-9998
info@kirklandcapital.com

Toronto: **Don P. Kirsh - *1**
#207, 3500 Dufferin St., Toronto, ON M3K 1N2
Tel: 416-630-6136; *Fax*: 416-630-6135
dkirsh@bellnet.ca
www.donkirsh.ca

Toronto: **Sheila Kirsh - *1**
#1812, 181 University Ave., Toronto, ON M5H 3M7
Tel: 416-367-1765; *Fax*: 416-594-0868
sheila@kirsh-law.com
www.kirsh-law.com

Toronto: **Howard Joshua Kirshenbaum - *1**
#17, 1140 Sheppard Ave. West, Toronto, ON M3K 2A2
Tel: 416-865-5339; *Fax*: 416-777-9255
kirshenbaum@msn.com

Toronto: **Klaiman, Edmonds - *3**
#1000, 60 Yonge St., Toronto, ON M5E 1H5
Tel: 416-867-9600; *Fax*: 416-867-9783
reception@klaimanedmonds.com
www.klaimanedmonds.com

Toronto: **Judi E. Klein - *1**
#104, 2552 Finch Ave. West, Toronto, ON M9M 2G3
Tel: 416-749-7747; *Fax*: 416-749-9190
judi-klein@look.ca
www.judieklein.supersites.ca

Toronto: **Paula Knopf Arbitrations Ltd. - *1**
4 Biggar Ave., Toronto, ON M6H 2N4
Tel: 416-652-1516; *Fax*: 416-652-2632
pkopf@allstream.net

Toronto: **Joel B. Kohm - *1**
#601, 18 Wynford Dr., Toronto, ON M3C 3S2
Tel: 416-510-1435; *Fax*: 416-510-0081
joel.kohm@rogers.com

Toronto: **Marc Koplowitz Associates - *2**
#2900, 390 Bay St., Toronto, ON M5H 2Y2
Tel: 416-368-1100; *Fax*: 416-368-1998
marc@koplaw.com

Toronto: **Kopolovic, Strigberger - *1**
#300, 69 Elm St., Toronto, ON M5G 1H2
Tel: 416-971-7272; *Fax*: 416-971-9092

Toronto: **Korman & Company - *3**
721 Queen St. East, Toronto, ON M4M 1H1
Tel: 416-465-4232; *Fax*: 416-465-6912
info@kormancompany.com
www.kormancompany.com

Toronto: **Koroloff & Huckins - *2**
#304, 1110 Sheppard Ave. East, Toronto, ON M2K 2W2
Tel: 416-229-6226; *Fax*: 416-229-6517

Toronto: **Koskie Minsky - *36**
#900, P.O. Box 52, 20 Queen St. West, Toronto, ON M5H 3R3
Tel: 416-977-8353; *Fax*: 416-977-3316
www.koskieminsky.com

Toronto: **Kostyniuk & Greenside - *11**
#300, 5468 Dundas St. West, Toronto, ON M9B 6E3
Tel: 416-762-8238; *Fax*: 416-762-5042
www.kostyniukandgreenside.com

Toronto: **Kotler Law Firm - *1**
#617, 1 Eglinton Ave. East, Toronto, ON M4P 3A1
Tel: 416-932-4949; *Fax*: 416-487-2992
hgk@koterlaw.ca

Toronto: **Irwin Koziebrocki - *1**
#400, 100 Richmond St. West, Toronto, ON M5H 3K6
Tel: 416-364-7292; *Fax*: 416-364-7473
thekozman@aol.com

Toronto: **Neil L. Kozloff - *1**
#1900, 439 University Ave., Toronto, ON M5G 1Y8
Tel: 416-408-1114; *Fax*: 416-408-2372

Toronto: **Alex Krakowitz - *1**
#2200, P.O. Box 75, 1 Dundas St. West, Toronto, ON M5G 1Z3
Tel: 416-598-4626; *Fax*: 416-599-8341
Toll-Free: 800-410-1013
alex.krakowitz@lawpro.ca

Toronto: **Kramer Henderson Sidlofsky LLP - *5**
#2100, 120 Adelaide St. West, Toronto, ON M5H 1T1
Tel: 416-601-6820; *Fax*: 416-601-0712
info@kramerhenderson.com
www.kramerhenderson.com

Toronto: **Krauss, Weinryb - *2**
#1540, 5140 Yonge St., Toronto, ON M2N 6L7
Tel: 416-222-4446; *Fax*: 416-222-9788

Toronto: **Gerald Kroll, Q.C. - *1**
#1800, 4950 Yonge St., Toronto, ON M2N 6K1
Tel: 416-224-0200; *Fax*: 416-224-0758
kroll@torlaw.com

Toronto: **Kuretzky Vassos - *9**
#1404, 151 Yonge St., Toronto, ON M5C 2W7
Tel: 416-865-0504; *Fax*: 416-865-9567
info@kuretzkyvassos.com
www.kuretzkyvassos.com

Toronto: **Helen Kurgatnikov Miller, Barrister & Solicitor - *1**
#914, 1110 Finch Ave. West, Toronto, ON M3J 2T2
Tel: 416-665-4343

Toronto: **Kvas Miller Everitt - *3**
#3100, 3300 Bloor St. West, Toronto, ON M8X 2X3
Tel: 416-921-6558; *Fax*: 416-923-0760
kme@idirect.com
www.kmelawyers.com

Toronto: **Grace F. Kwan - *1**
90A Isabella St., 3rd Fl., Toronto, ON M4Y 1N4
Tel: 416-968-2014; *Fax*: 416-968-2054
gkwan@295.ca

Toronto: **Wolfgang H. Kyser - *1**
#310, 401 Queen's Quay West, Toronto, ON M5V 2Y2
Tel: 416-863-1053; *Fax*: 416-861-0191

Toronto: **Stephen M. Labow - *1**
#610, 480 University Ave., Toronto, ON M5G 1V2
Tel: 416-947-1172; *Fax*: 416-596-0808
stephen@labow.ca

Toronto: **Lackman, Firestone Law Offices - *2**
#511, 4576 Yonge Street, Toronto, ON M2N 6N4
Tel: 416-364-0020; *Fax*: 416-364-0389

Toronto: **Lafontaine & Associates - *3**
#506, 330 University Ave., Toronto, ON M5G 1R7
Tel: 416-204-1835; *Fax*: 416-204-1849
greg@127john.com

Toronto: **Laishley Reed LLP - *6**
#2000, 3 Church St., Toronto, ON M5E 1M2
Tel: 416-981-9401; *Fax*: 416-981-0060
info@laishleyreed.com
www.laishleyreed.com

Toronto: **Tikam K. Lalla - *1**
1203 Bloor St. West, Toronto, ON M6H 1N4
Tel: 416-532-2801; *Fax*: 416-532-4942

Toronto: **D. Wayne Lalonde - *1**
#2000, The Law Chambers, 393 University Ave., 20th Fl., Toronto, ON M5G 1E6
Tel: 416-585-2868; *Fax*: 416-593-4446
dwaynelalonde@lawchambers.com
www.lawchambers.com

Toronto: **Mary L.F. Lam - *2**
40 Binscarth Road, Toronto, ON M4W 1Y1
Tel: 416-383-0266; *Fax*: 416-383-0299
mary.lam@rogers.com

Toronto: **Jack S. Lambert - *1**
79 Edith Dr., Toronto, ON M4R 1Z1
Tel: 416-226-6333; *Fax*: 416-226-6344
jacklamlaw@rogers.com

Toronto: **Garry E.J. Lamourie - *1**
#2104, 180 Dundas St. West, Toronto, ON M5G 1Z8
Tel: 416-597-9828; *Fax*: 416-597-9808

Toronto: **C. Robert Langdon, Q.C. - *1**
140 Dinnick Cres., Toronto, ON M4N 1L8
Tel: 416-483-2887; *Fax*: 416-484-4306
c.robert.langdon@sympatico.ca

Toronto: **Douglas G. Lash - *1**
145 Glengrove Ave., Toronto, ON M4R 1P1
Tel: 416-932-2399; *Fax*: 416-932-9306
dlash@zebulongroup.com

** indicates number of lawyers*

Toronto: **Wayne S. Laski - *1**
#1800, 4950 Yonge St., Toronto, ON M2N 6K1
Tel: 416-224-0200; *Fax:* 416-224-0758
wlaski@wlaski.com

Toronto: **Sam Laufer - *1**
#3902, 44 Charles St. West, Toronto, ON M4Y 1R8
Tel: 416-922-9455; *Fax:* 416-923-8870
legitlaw@yahoo.com.au

Toronto: **John V. Lawer, Q.C. - *1**
#306, 40 St. Clair Ave. East, Toronto, ON M4T 1M9
Tel: 416-922-0737; *Fax:* 416-922-1896
johnv@johnvlawer.on.ca

Toronto: **Lax O'Sullivan Scott Lisus LLP - *16**
#1920, 145 King St. West, Toronto, ON M5H 1J8
Tel: 416-598-1744; *Fax:* 416-598-3730
www.counsel-toronto.com

Toronto: **Laxton Glass LLP - *11**
#200, 390 Bay St., Toronto, ON M5H 2Y2
Tel: 416-363-2353; *Fax:* 416-363-7112

Toronto: **Sheldon S. Lazarovitz - *1**
31 Westgate Blvd., Toronto, ON M3H 1N8
Tel: 416-638-6080; *Fax:* 416-638-6246
lazarovitz@rogers.com

Toronto: **Timothy J. Leach - *1**
#309, 658 Danforth Ave., Toronto, ON M4J 5B9
Tel: 416-868-0265; *Fax:* 416-868-0478

Toronto: **John Y.C. Lee - *1**
#418, 4002 Sheppard Ave. East, Toronto, ON M1S 1S6
Tel: 416-299-8900; *Fax:* 416-299-8232

Toronto: **Julia Yuen-Nam Lee - *1**
825 Gerrard St. East, Toronto, ON M4M 1Y2
Tel: 416-466-6888

Toronto: **Paul Lee & Associates - *7**
20 Maitland St., Toronto, ON M4Y 1C5
Tel: 416-961-2707; *Fax:* 416-961-5575
office@paullee.ca

Toronto: **J.C. Lemire - *1**
#500, 70 Bond St., Toronto, ON M5B 1X3
Tel: 416-363-1097; *Fax:* 416-863-4896

Toronto: **Lenczner Slaght Royce Smith Griffin LLP - *45**
#2600, 130 Adelaide St., West, Toronto, ON M5H 3P5
Tel: 416-865-9500; *Fax:* 416-865-9010
info@litigate.com
www.litigate.com

Toronto: **George J. Leon - *1**
29 Berwick Ave., Toronto, ON M5P 1G9
Tel: 416-487-1385; *Fax:* 416-485-0437
gleon@idirect.com

Toronto: **Thomas J. Leroy - *1**
#304, 375 University Ave., Toronto, ON M5G 2G1
Tel: 416-979-2352; *Fax:* 416-979-8562
leroyt@lao.on.ca

Toronto: **Gérard Lévesque - *1**
184 Lake Promenade, Toronto, ON M8W 1A8
Tel: 416-253-0129; *Fax:* 416-253-4737

Toronto: **Levine Associates - *3**
#1400, 10 King St. East, Toronto, ON M5C 1C3
Tel: 416-364-2345; *Fax:* 416-364-3818
shelleylevine@levlaw.com

Toronto: **Lorne Levine - *1**
#305, 55 Eglinton Ave. East, Toronto, ON M4P 1G8
Tel: 416-483-1251; *Fax:* 416-483-1257

Toronto: **Levine, Sherkin, Boussidan - *4**
#300, 23 Lesmill Rd., Toronto, ON M3B 3P6
Tel: 416-224-2400; *Fax:* 416-224-2408
www.lsblaw.com

Toronto: **Levinson & Associates - *1**
#610, 480 University Ave., Toronto, ON M5G 1V2
Tel: 416-591-8484; *Fax:* 416-596-0808
levinson@levadvocate.net
www.levadvocate.net

Toronto: **Levitan Lawyers - *1**
22 Soho St., Toronto, ON M5T 1Z7
Tel: 416-368-4600; *Fax:* 416-368-1166

Toronto: **Sherry Levitan - *1**
#403, 1 Yorkdale Rd., Toronto, ON M6A 3A1
Tel: 416-784-1222; *Fax:* 416-784-0777
slevitan@bellnet.ca

Toronto: **Shirley E. Levitan - *1**
69 Elm St., Toronto, ON M5G 1H2
Tel: 416-585-2626; *Fax:* 416-971-9092
shilev@idirect.com

Toronto: **Levitt, Lightman, Dewar & Graham LLP - *3**
#1, 16 Four Seasons Pl., Toronto, ON M9B 6E5
Tel: 416-620-0362; *Fax:* 416-620-5158
flevitt@lldg.ca

Toronto: **Alan D. Levy - *1**
75 Robert St., Toronto, ON M5S 2K4
Tel: 416-929-8282; *Fax:* 416-929-9895
alan@alanlevy.ca
www.alanlevy.ca

Toronto: **E.J. Levy, Q.C. - *1**
#400, 100 Richmond St. West, Toronto, ON M5H 3K6
Tel: 416-364-7292; *Fax:* 416-364-7473

Toronto: **Lewis & Associates - *5**
41 Madison Ave., Toronto, ON M5R 2S2
Tel: 416-924-2227; *Fax:* 416-924-9993
lewisassociates@eol.ca

Toronto: **Andrew C. Lewis - *1**
#208, 90 Eglinton Ave. East, Toronto, ON M4P 2Y3
Tel: 416-322-7010; *Fax:* 416-483-2737
lewisac@bellnet.ca

Toronto: **Joseph E. Lewis - *1**
#202, 327 Eglinton Ave. East, Toronto, ON M4P 1L7
Tel: 416-486-0084; *Fax:* 416-486-7363

Toronto: **Raymond W.M. Li - *1**
#8, 4158 Kingston Rd., Toronto, ON M1E 2M6
Tel: 416-977-7773

Toronto: **Susan M.C. Libanio - *1**
#617, 1 Summerhill Rd., Toronto, ON M8V 1R9
Tel: 416-533-6002; *Fax:* 416-533-6097
smel@rogers.com

Toronto: **P. Yoel Lichtblau - *1**
499 Wilson Heights Blvd., Toronto, ON M3H 2V7
Tel: 416-633-2465; *Fax:* 416-398-3369
ylichtblau@rogers.com

Toronto: **Lindenberg & Lindenberg - *2**
#100, 287 Eglinton Ave. East, Toronto, ON M4P 1L3
Tel: 416-484-8177; *Fax:* 416-322-0807

Toronto: **Link Strategies INc. - *1**
#910, P.O. Box 28, 1 Toronto St., Toronto, ON M5C 2V6
Tel: 416-368-0323; *Fax:* 416-368-6068
kgallagher@linkstrategies.ca

Toronto: **John Liss - *1**
207 Brunswick Ave., Toronto, ON M5S 2M4
Tel: 416-968-2558; *Fax:* 416-961-7906

Toronto: **John A.G. Lister - *1**
167 Danforth Ave., Toronto, ON M4K 1N2
Tel: 416-461-0983; *Fax:* 416-462-3347
jaglister@on.aibn.com

Toronto: **Nadia Liva - *1**
15 Bedford Rd., Toronto, ON M5R 2J7
Tel: 416-598-0106; *Fax:* 416-868-0273
nadialiva@15bedford.com

Toronto: **H. David Locke - *1**
#200, 37 Prince Arthur Ave., Toronto, ON M5R 1B2
Tel: 416-601-1525; *Fax:* 416-601-0392

Toronto: **Paula V. Locke - *1**
#200, 37 Prince Arthur Ave., Toronto, ON M5R 1B2
Tel: 416-601-1525; *Fax:* 416-601-0392

Toronto: **Lofranco Chagpar Barristers - *6**
#1300, 5255 Yonge St., Toronto, ON M2N 6P4
Tel: 416-223-8333; *Fax:* 416-223-3404
info@lofrancobarristers.com

Toronto: **Gerald P. Logan - *1**
317 Grace St., Toronto, ON M6G 3A7
Tel: 416-535-8920; *Fax:* 416-537-6550

Toronto: **Joachim M. Loh - *1**
#10, 3880 Midland Ave., Toronto, ON M1V 5K4
Tel: 416-609-8289; *Fax:* 416-609-8857
jmloh@jmlohlaw.com

Toronto: **Lomer, Frost - Barristers - *2**
#1515, 180 Dundas St. West, Toronto, ON M5G 1Z8
Tel: 416-923-1900; *Fax:* 416-847-2564

Toronto: **Loopstra Nixon LLP - *18**
#600, Woodbine Place, 135 Queens Plate Dr., Toronto, ON M9W 6V7
Tel: 416-746-4710; *Fax:* 416-746-8319
TheStraightAnswer@loonix.com
www.loopstranixon.com

Toronto: **Francisco B. Luna - *1**
#1704, 2 Carlton St., Toronto, ON M5B 1J3
Tel: 416-977-3287; *Fax:* 416-977-1950
f.luna@on.aibn.com

Toronto: **Karen D. Lundy - *1**
#2150, 1 Queen St. East, Toronto, ON M5C 2W5
Tel: 416-866-8858; *Fax:* 416-364-3866
karen.lundy@waldin.ca

Toronto: **Lawrence M. Lychowyd - *1**
236A Bain Ave., Toronto, ON M4K 1G3
Tel: 416-466-8063; *Fax:* 416-694-3367
larrythelawyer@sympatico.ca
www.larrythelawyer.ca

Toronto: **Michael M. Lynch, Q.C. - *1**
#414, Richmond Tower, 100 Richmond St. West, Toronto, ON M5H 3K6
Tel: 416-972-9828; *Fax:* 416-964-0823

Toronto: **Bryan A. MacBride - *1**
#612, 55 Lombard, Toronto, ON M5C 2R7
Tel: 416-601-9222; *Fax:* 416-601-9223
bamc@rogers.com

Toronto: **J.M. Macchione - *1**
#2000, 77 Bloor St. West, Toronto, ON M5S 1M2
Tel: 416-966-8373; *Fax:* 416-923-3654
janice.macchione@realstar.ca

Toronto: **MacDonald & Partners LLP - *12**
90 Adelaide St. West, 3rd Fl., Toronto, ON M5H 3V9
Tel: 416-971-4802; *Fax:* 416-971-9584
famlaw@mpllp.com
www.macdonaldpartners.com

Toronto: **MacDonald Group - *1**
4 Swanwick Ave., Toronto, ON M4E 1Z1
Tel: 416-937-6646

Toronto: **Mary-Douglass MacDonald - *1**
122 Prince George Dr., Toronto, ON M9B 2Y2
Tel: 416-231-4899; *Fax:* 416-231-7306
mdmacdonald@rogers.com

Toronto: **W.A. MacDonald Associates Inc. - *1**
#3720, BCE Place, P.O. Box 621, 161 Bay St., Toronto, ON M5J 2S1
Tel: 416-865-7091; *Fax:* 416-865-7934

Toronto: **Mary E. MacInnes - *1**
25 McGlashan Ct., Toronto, ON M5M 4M6
Tel: 416-487-8210

Toronto: **Carolyn A. MacLean - *1**
#102, 40 Isabella St., Toronto, ON M4Y 1N1
Tel: 416-925-4008; *Fax:* 416-920-0367

Toronto: **Theresa M. MacLean - *1**
#202, 40 Isabella St., Toronto, ON M4Y 1N1
Tel: 416-964-9224; *Fax:* 416-920-0367

Toronto: **Doug MacLeod, Barristor & Solicitor - *1**
#1700, 22 St Clair Ave. East, Toronto, ON M4T 2S3
Tel: 416-977-9894; *Fax:* 416-977-7337
doug@dougmacleod.com
www.dougmacleod.com

Toronto: **Paul A. MacLeod - *1**
32 Elm St., Toronto, ON L3M 1H3
Tel: 905-945-9659; *Fax:* 905-945-0838
office@macleod-barr.com

Toronto: **MacMaster, Poolman Law Office - *1**
#203, 150 Eglinton Ave. East, Toronto, ON M4P 1E8
Tel: 416-250-8387; *Fax:* 416-250-6233
info@macmasterpoolman.com
www.macmasterpoolman.com

** indicates number of lawyers*

Toronto: MacMillan Rooke Boeckle - *5
#3005, P.O. Box 96, 401 Bay St., Toronto, ON M5H 2Y4
Tel: 416-360-1194; Fax: 416-360-8469
Toll-Free: 800-661-7606
info@macmillanrooke.com

Toronto: S.G.R. MacMillan - *1
#2110, 120 Adelaide St. West, Toronto, ON M5H 1T1
Tel: 416-363-0100; Toll-Free: 877-363-0100
mail@sgrm.com
www.sgrm.com

Toronto: Dan Malamet - *1
10 Audubon Ct., Toronto, ON M2N 1T9
Tel: 416-865-6952; Fax: 416-863-6275
dan.malamet@bakernet.com

Toronto: T.R. Anthony Malcolm - *1
#601, 8 King St. East, Toronto, ON M5C 1B5
Tel: 416-864-1608; Fax: 416-864-1549
tram@tramalcolm.com

Toronto: Malo, Pilley & Lehman - *3
1067 Bloor St. West, Toronto, ON M6H 1M5
Tel: 416-534-3555; Fax: 416-534-7625

Toronto: Mancia & Mancia - *1
#601, 80 Richmond St. West, Toronto, ON M5H 2A4
Tel: 416-363-7422; Fax: 416-363-4975
cmancia@bellnet.ca

Toronto: Harvey Mandel - *1
#203, 55 Queen St. East, Toronto, ON M5C 1R6
Tel: 416-364-7717; Fax: 416-364-4813

Toronto: Pierre F. Marchildon - *1
#308, Dundas-Lambton Centre, 4195 Dundas St. West, Toronto, ON M8X 1Y4
Tel: 416-236-0686; Fax: 416-236-0650
Toll-Free: 866-236-0686
pfmlaw@on.aibn.com

Toronto: Marcos Associates - *2
1718 Dundas St. West, Toronto, ON M6K 1V5
Tel: 416-537-3151; Fax: 416-537-3153
emarcos@on.aibn.com

Toronto: Paul E. Marcus
York University, West Office Bldg., 4700 Keele St., Toronto, ON M3J 1P3
Tel: 416-650-8025; Fax: 416-650-8032
marcusp@yorkfoundation.yorku.ca
www.yorku.ca/foundation

Toronto: June A. Maresca - *1
#400, 2490 Bloor St. West, Toronto, ON M6S 1R4
Tel: 416-762-8617; Fax: 416-760-7338
jmaresca@on.aibn.com

Toronto: Marin, Evans & Bell - *2
#500, 200 Adelaide St. West, Toronto, ON M5H 1W7
Tel: 416-408-2177; Fax: 416-408-1718

Toronto: Charles C. Mark, Q.C. - *1
#2010, P.O. Box 28, 401 Bay St., Toronto, ON M5H 2Y4
Tel: 416-869-0929; Fax: 416-869-9118
ccmark@on.aibn.com

Toronto: Markes Lawyers - *12
#506, 1090 Don Mills Rd., Toronto, ON M3C 3R6
Tel: 416-350-3500; Fax: 416-350-3510
amarkes@markeslawyers.com
www.markeslawyers.com

Toronto: Markle, May, Phibbs - *8
#300, 500 Sheppard Ave. East, Toronto, ON M2N 6H7
Tel: 416-593-4385; Fax: 416-593-4478

Toronto: H. David Marks, Q.C. - *1
#2150, 1 Queen St. East, Toronto, ON M5C 2W5
Tel: 416-863-1550; Fax: 416-863-9670
david.marks@waldin.ca

Toronto: Larry M. Marshall - *1
#1017, 250 Consumers Rd., Toronto, ON M2J 4V6
Tel: 416-497-2526; Fax: 416-497-3143
lmarshal@idirect.com

Toronto: E.E. Marszewski - *1
13 Maple Ave., Toronto, ON M4W 2T5
Tel: 416-927-1820; Fax: 416-967-4549
marszewski@aol.com

Toronto: Calvin Martin, Q.C. - *1
600 Church St., Toronto, ON M4Y 2E7
Tel: 416-922-5854; Fax: 416-944-0285
dvc14@calvinmartinqc.com
www.calvinmartinqc.com

Toronto: Malcolm M. Martin - *1
#310, 49 The Donway West, Toronto, ON M3C 3M9
Tel: 416-449-4111; Fax: 416-449-7879
mmartin@malcolmmartin.com

Toronto: Martinello & Associates - *3
#208, United Centre, 255 Duncan Mill Rd., Toronto, ON M3B 3H9
Tel: 416-510-8866; Fax: 416-449-9977
martinello@on.aibn.com

Toronto: Alexander Martynowicz - *1
#300, 940 The East Mall, Toronto, ON M9B 6J7
Tel: 416-622-9222; Fax: 416-622-0333

Toronto: Ville K. Masalin - *1
#309, 191 Eglinton Ave. East, Toronto, ON M4P 1K1
Tel: 416-484-9347; Fax: 416-484-9027

Toronto: Masters & Masters - *2
#440, 65 Queen St. West, Toronto, ON M5H 2M5
Tel: 416-361-1399; Fax: 416-361-6181
masterslaw@sympatico.ca
www.masterslaw.com

Toronto: Gaetano P. Matteazzi - *1
#100, 25 Morrow Ave., Toronto, ON M6R 2H9
Tel: 416-534-8881; Fax: 416-516-5305

Toronto: Mark O. Mattson - *1
17 Fenwood Heights, Toronto, ON M1M 2V6
Tel: 416-265-6548

Toronto: McBride Wallace Laurent & Cord LLP - *7
#200, 5464 Dundas St. West, Toronto, ON M9B 1B4
Tel: 416-231-6555; Fax: 416-231-6630

Toronto: McCague, Peacock, Borlack, McInnis & Lloyd LLP - *24
#2700, The Exchange Tower, P.O. Box 136, Stn. 1st, 130 King St. West, Toronto, ON M5X 1C7
Tel: 416-860-0001; Fax: 416-860-0003
general@mwph.com

Toronto: D.V. McCarthy - *1
#302, 885 Progress Ave., Toronto, ON M1H 3G3
Tel: 416-289-9620; Fax: 416-439-9553

Toronto: Robert L. McClelland - *1
#313, 2498 Yonge St., Toronto, ON M4P 2H8
Tel: 416-481-7360; Fax: 416-574-0429
ronmcc@ca.inter.net

Toronto: McComb Dockrill - *2
#2707, T-D Bank Tower, Toronto-Dominion Centre, P.O. Box 17, Stn. T-D Centre, Toronto, ON M5K 1A1
Tel: 416-366-1881; Fax: 416-366-0608
mccombdockrill@on.aibn.com

Toronto: John D. McCrie - *1
#9, 15 Belfield Rd., Toronto, ON M9W 1E8
Tel: 416-243-9501; Fax: 416-243-2990
johndmccrie@on.aibn.com

Toronto: David J. McGhee - *1
390 Bay St., 30th Fl., Toronto, ON M5H 2Y2
Tel: 416-362-9736; Fax: 416-362-9435
djmcghee@on.aibn.com

Toronto: McGowan & Co. - *3
#1400, 10 Bay St., Toronto, ON M5J 2R8
Tel: 416-350-2481; Fax: 416-363-1875

Toronto: David R. McGregor - *1
#316, 18 Wynford Dr., Toronto, ON M3C 3S2
Tel: 416-485-1123; Fax: 416-485-8742
dmseus@yahoo.ca

Toronto: McIlroy & McIlroy Inc. - *1
203 Riverside Dr., Toronto, ON M6S 4A8
Tel: 416-777-0447; Fax: 416-777-0436
www.mcilroy.com

Toronto: McInnis, Nicoll - *2
#507, 330 Bay St., Toronto, ON M5H 2S8
Tel: 416-362-1354; Fax: 416-362-1465

Toronto: McIver & McIver - *2
#700, 1 Richmond St. West, Toronto, ON M5H 3W4
Tel: 416-864-9000; Fax: 416-864-9190

Toronto: Michael A. McKee - *1
9 Elmlea Rd., Toronto, ON M9P 2M6
Tel: 416-928-6611; Fax: 416-928-9515
mckeelawoffice@yahoo.ca

Toronto: McLean & Kerr LLP - *23
#2800, 130 Adelaide St. West, Toronto, ON M5H 3P5
Tel: 416-364-5371; Fax: 416-366-8571
mail@mcleankerr.com
www.mcleankerr.com

Toronto: Reginald M. McLean - *1
1035 McNicoll Ave., Toronto, ON M1W 3W6
Tel: 416-512-1200; Fax: 416-512-1212
maclaw@bellnet.ca

Toronto: McMaster, McIntyre & Smyth LLP, Barristers & Solicitors - *5
2777 Dundas St. West, Toronto, ON M6P 1Y4
Tel: 416-769-4188; Fax: 416-769-4147
Toll-Free: 888-769-4188
mail@mmslawyers.com
www.mmslawyers.com

Toronto: McPhadden, Samac, Merner, Barry - *4
#300, 8 King St. East, Toronto, ON M5C 1B5
Tel: 416-363-5195; Fax: 416-363-7485
reception@msmb.ca
www.msmb.ca

Toronto: Deborah L. Meldazy - *1
426 Davenport Rd., Toronto, ON M4V 1B5
Tel: 416-929-8524; Fax: 416-929-4042
dmeldazy@sympatico.ca

Toronto: Menzies, von Bogen - *2
1071B Bloor St. West, Toronto, ON M6H 1M5
Tel: 416-532-2833; Fax: 416-532-6553
Toll-Free: 877-218-0084
menzies2@on.aibn.com

Toronto: Paul Mergler - *1
1199 The Queensway, Toronto, ON M8Z 1R7
Tel: 416-232-9589; Fax: 416-232-9522
pabkon@interlog.com

Toronto: E.H. Merifield - *1
#2200, 4950 Yonge St., Toronto, ON M2N 6K1
Tel: 416-218-8381; Fax: 416-218-8384

Toronto: Clarke A. Merritt - *2
#3300, Box 33, 20 Queen St. West, Toronto, ON M5H 3R3
Tel: 416-971-3306; Fax: 416-971-4849
cmerrittl@aol.com

Toronto: Michael G. McLachlan - *1
#103, 30 St. Clair Ave. West, Toronto, ON M4V 3A1
Tel: 416-596-7077; Fax: 416-596-7629
mgmlaw1@gmail.com
www.mgmlaw.ca

Toronto: David M. Midanik - *1
34 Shaflesbury Ave., Toronto, ON M4T 1A1
Tel: 416-967-1603; Fax: 416-967-1604
david@midaniklawoffice.com
www.midaniklawoffice.com

Toronto: Yaroslav Mikitchook - *1
#509, 80 Richmond St. West, Toronto, ON M5H 2A4
Tel: 416-361-1668; Fax: 416-361-6140

Toronto: Jack A. Mikolajko - *1
#506, P.O. Box 31, 2333 Dundas St. West, Toronto, ON M9R 3A6
Tel: 416-538-8493; Fax: 416-538-2274
jmikolajko@bellnet.ca

Toronto: Millar Kreklewetz LLP - *4
24 Duncan St., 3rd Fl., Toronto, ON M5V 2B8
Tel: 416-864-6200; Fax: 416-864-6201
mkmail@taxandtradelaw.com
www.taxandtradelaw.com

Toronto: Miller & Miller - *2
1577 Bloor St. West, Toronto, ON M6P 1A6
Tel: 416-536-1159; Fax: 416-536-3618

Toronto: Glen M.A. Miller - *1
#211, 3850 Finch Ave. East, Toronto, ON M1T 3T6
Tel: 416-299-6785; Fax: 416-299-6204

Toronto: Helen Miller - *1
#914, 1110 Finch Ave. West, Toronto, ON M3J 2T2
Tel: 416-665-4343; Fax: 416-665-0110

** indicates number of lawyers*

Toronto: Keith R. Millikin - *1
#310, 200 Ronson Dr., Toronto, ON M9W 5Z9
Tel: 416-243-3394; Fax: 416-243-9692
kmillikin@banksandstarkman.com

Toronto: Mills & Mills LLP - *25
#700, 2 St. Clair Ave. West, Toronto, ON M4V 1L5
Tel: 416-863-0125; Fax: 416-863-3997
mills@millsandmills.ca
www.millsandmills.ca

Toronto: Douglas J. Millstone - *1
#309, 2100 Ellesmere Rd., Toronto, ON M1H 3B7
Tel: 416-289-7996; Fax: 416-289-7998
Toll-Free: 888-437-7996
dmilldtone@bellnet.ca
www.dmillstonelaw.com

Toronto: Minden Gross Grafstein & Greenstein LLP - *50
#2200, 145 King St. West, Toronto, ON M5H 4G2
Tel: 416-362-3711; Fax: 416-864-9223
dcarty@mindengross.com
www.mindengross.com

Toronto: Paul Minz - *1
#1, 3520 Pharmacy Ave., Toronto, ON M1W 2T8
Tel: 416-499-9350; Fax: 416-499-1463

Toronto: Mircheff & Mircheff - *1
#2B, 3030 Midland Ave., Toronto, ON M1S 5C9
Tel: 416-321-2885; Fax: 416-321-3345
mircheff@on.aibn.com

Toronto: Misir, Patterson - *4
880 St. Clair Ave. West, Toronto, ON M6C 1C5
Tel: 416-653-8600; Fax: 416-653-9639

Toronto: Miskin Flancman & Frisch - *2
1286 Kennedy Rd., Toronto, ON M1P 2L5
Tel: 416-752-2221; Fax: 416-752-8434
Toll-Free: 877-468-1120
miskflan@hotmail.com

Toronto: Mitchell, Bardyn & Zalucky LLP - *13
#200, 3029 Bloor St. West, Toronto, ON M8X 1C5
Tel: 416-234-9111; Fax: 416-234-9114
info@mbzlaw.com

Toronto: Heather Mitchell - *1
#300, 165 Avenue Rd., Toronto, ON M5R 3S4
Tel: 416-927-6565; Fax: 416-975-3999
hhmitchell@heathermitchelllaw.com

Toronto: M.J. Mitchell, Q.C. - *1
#403, 1 Yorkdale Rd., Toronto, ON M6A 3A1
Tel: 416-362-0901; Fax: 416-781-3110
purlex@bellnet.ca

Toronto: M.S. Mogil - *1
#610, 4211 Yonge St., Toronto, ON M2P 2A9
Tel: 416-590-7999; Fax: 416-590-9998

Toronto: Sai@#d Mohammedally - *1
#B3, 45 Overlea Blvd., Toronto, ON M4H 1C3
Tel: 416-425-7695; Fax: 416-425-7596
saidmoha@bellnet.ca

Toronto: Bernard J. Monaghan - *1
#4084, 3080 Yonge St., Toronto, ON M4N 3N1
Tel: 416-486-9919; Fax: 416-486-1885

Toronto: Barbara Morgan - *1
#216, 4195 Dundas St. West, Toronto, ON M8X 1Y4
Tel: 416-234-8248; Fax: 416-234-8252

Toronto: Morris & Morris LLP - *7
#920, 390 Bay St., Toronto, ON M5H 2Y2
Tel: 416-366-2291; Fax: 416-366-5988

Toronto: D.S. Morris - *1
129 John St., Toronto, ON M5V 2E2
Tel: 416-977-4799; Fax: 416-977-4472

Toronto: L.J. Morris - *1
101 Scollard St., Toronto, ON M5R 1G4
Tel: 416-924-0711; Fax: 416-960-9650

Toronto: Morrison Brown Sosnovitch - *12
#910, P.O. Box 28, 1 Toronto St., Toronto, ON M5C 2V6
Tel: 416-368-0600; Fax: 416-368-6068
bizlaw@businesslawyers.com
www.businesslawyers.com

Toronto: S.S. Moskowitz - *1
740 Spadina Ave., Toronto, ON M5S 2J2
Tel: 416-961-8864; Fax: 416-961-7654

Toronto: Mostyn & Mostyn - *4
845 St. Clair Ave. West, 4th Fl., Toronto, ON M6C 1C3
Tel: 416-653-3819; Fax: 416-653-3891
info@mostyn.ca
www.mostyn.ca

Toronto: Anthony Moustacalis - *1
#1000, 121 Richmond St. West, Toronto, ON M5H 2K1
Tel: 416-363-2656; Fax: 416-363-4920

Toronto: Henry Moyal - *1
North American Centre, 8 Finch Ave. West, Toronto, ON M2N 6L1
Tel: 416-733-3193; Fax: 416-250-1818
Toll-Free: 888-847-2078
canada@moyal.com
www.moyal.com

Toronto: Matthew Moyal - *1
North American Centre, 8 Finch Ave. West, Toronto, ON M2N 6L1
Tel: 416-733-0330; Fax: 416-250-1818
moyal@idirect.com

Toronto: Mulholland Consulting - *1
#401, 790 Bay St., Toronto, ON M5G 1N8
Tel: 416-596-2719; Fax: 416-596-2700
emulholland@rightplay.com

Toronto: Katrina L. Mulligan - *1
#600, 1000 Finch Ave. West, Toronto, ON M3J 2V5
Tel: 416-518-1288; Fax: 416-650-1980
katrinamulligan@sympatico.ca

Toronto: Murray & Gregory - *2
160 John St., 3rd Fl., Toronto, ON M5V 2E5
Tel: 416-598-1643; Fax: 416-598-9520

Toronto: Elizabeth J. Nadeau - *1
#600, 1000 Finch Ave. West, Toronto, ON M3J 2V5
Tel: 416-650-1011; Fax: 416-650-1980

Toronto: J. Naumovich
#101, 813 Broadview Ave., Toronto, ON M4K 2P8
Tel: 416-466-2119; Fax: 416-466-2581

Toronto: Navigator Ltd. - *2
British Colonial Bldg., 8 Wellington St. East, 3rd Fl., Toronto, ON M5E 1C5
Tel: 416-640-1579; Fax: 416-642-6435
jratchford@navltd.com

Toronto: W.E.M. Naylor - *1
#203, 637 College St., Toronto, ON M6G 1B5
Tel: 416-532-9940; Fax: 416-532-9983
naylor-william@on.aibn.com

Toronto: Neal and Smith - *2
#300, 3443 Finch Ave. East, Toronto, ON M1W 2S1
Tel: 416-494-4545; Fax: 416-494-4660
nealsmith@bellnet.ca
www.nealandsmith.com

Toronto: Neil Craig Associates - *1
5 Brule Cres., Toronto, ON M6S 4H8
Tel: 416-604-3326; Fax: 416-604-2268

Toronto: Neinstein & Associates LLP - *8
#700, 1200 Bay St., Toronto, ON M5R 2A5
Tel: 416-920-4242; Fax: 416-923-8358
Toll-Free: 866-920-4242
www.neinstein.com

Toronto: C. Ann Nelson - *1
#400, 2490 Bloor St. West, Toronto, ON M6S 1R4
Tel: 416-760-7076; Fax: 416-760-7338

Toronto: Theodore Nemetz - *1
#801, 1 St. Clair Ave. East, Toronto, ON M4T 2V7
Tel: 416-961-6560; Fax: 416-964-2494
nemetz@bellnet.ca

Toronto: Newman Weinstock - *1
#201, 3625 Dufferin St., Toronto, ON M3K 1Z2
Tel: 416-630-3220; Fax: 416-630-7632
rawein@on.aibn.com

Toronto: Alexandra Ngan - *1
#306, 1033 Bay St., Toronto, ON M5S 3A5
Tel: 416-925-3333; Fax: 416-925-3339

Toronto: Metz L. Ngan - *1
#209, 155 Gordon Baker Rd., Toronto, ON M2H 3N7
Tel: 416-502-9232; Fax: 416-502-3061
metznga@ipoline.com

Toronto: Peter J. Ngan - *1
#207, 738 Sheppard Ave. East, Toronto, ON M2K 1C4
Tel: 416-298-1828; Fax: 416-298-2186
pjngan@yahoo.ca
www.peterngan.com

Toronto: Trang T. Nguyen - *1
#12, 3875 Keele St., Toronto, ON M3J 3H5
Tel: 416-638-9422; Fax: 416-398-8358

Toronto: Cynthia A. Nicholas - *1
17 Annis Rd., Toronto, ON M1M 2Y8
Tel: 416-264-2875; Fax: 416-264-2330

Toronto: Alexander R. Nicol - *1
175 Rumsey Rd., Toronto, ON M4G 1P4
Tel: 416-467-7652; Fax: 416-425-4217

Toronto: Howard Nightingale - *1
#302, 4580 Dufferin St., Toronto, ON M3H 5Y2
Tel: 416-663-4423; Fax: 416-663-4424
Toll-Free: 877-224-8225
info@howardnightingale.com
www.howardnightingale.com

Toronto: Noik & Associates - *4
#400, 3410 Sheppard Ave. East, Toronto, ON M1T 3K4
Tel: 416-754-1020; Fax: 416-754-1784
bnoik@noik.com

Toronto: O'Donohue & O'Donohue - *3
#210, 330 Bay St., Toronto, ON M5H 2S8
Tel: 416-361-3231; Fax: 416-361-3472
mail@odonohue.ca

Toronto: O'Neill, Browning, Pineau - *2
#302, 372 Bay St., Toronto, ON M5H 2W9
Tel: 416-868-0544; Fax: 416-868-0724
browninglaw@rigers

Toronto: O'Reilly, Moll - *1
300 Main St., Toronto, ON M4C 4X5
Tel: 416-690-3324; Fax: 416-690-3330

Toronto: Oiye, Henderson - *2
#1812, 2 Carlton St., Toronto, ON M5B 1J3
Tel: 416-977-7700; Fax: 416-977-8570
alex@oiyehenderson.com

Toronto: Olch, Torgov, Cohen LLP - *2
#901, 111 Richmond St. West, Toronto, ON M5H 2G4
Tel: 416-363-8366; Fax: 416-363-0783
otc@otclaw.ca

Toronto: Orbach, Katzman & Herschorn - *3
#1001, 317 Adelaide St. West, Toronto, ON M5V 1P9
Tel: 416-967-6777; Fax: 416-967-1506
sender@okhlaw.ca

Toronto: Mark M. Orkin, Q.C. - *1
#1401, 111 Richmond St. West, Toronto, ON M5H 2G4
Tel: 416-363-4108; Fax: 416-365-9276
mmorkin@look.ca

Toronto: Ormston, Bellissimo, Younan - *5
#900, 1000 Finch Ave. West, Toronto, ON M3J 2V5
Tel: 416-787-6505; Fax: 416-787-0455

Toronto: Samuel Osak - *1
6 Bitteroot Rd., Toronto, ON M3H 4J4
Tel: 416-630-1041; Fax: 416-630-1043
sosak@sympatico.ca

Toronto: M.A. Osborne - *1
#201, 100 Sheppard Ave. West, Toronto, ON M2N 1M6
Tel: 416-225-1145; Fax: 416-225-0832

Toronto: Oster Wolfman LLP - *4
#200, 133 Berkeley St., Toronto, ON M5A 2X1
Tel: 416-365-7163; Fax: 416-365-1270
kow@kow.on.ca

Toronto: Otis & Korman - *2
41 Madison Ave., Toronto, ON M5R 2S2
Tel: 416-979-0670; Fax: 416-979-3778
korman@istar.ca

Toronto: Samy Ouanounou - *1
#352, 1111 Finch Ave. West, Toronto, ON M3J 2E5
Tel: 416-222-3434; Fax: 416-222-3629
solaw@on.aibn.com

* indicates number of lawyers

Toronto: Outerbridge Miller Sefton - *3
#920, 4 King St. West, Toronto, ON M5H 1B6
Tel: 416-360-6182; *Fax:* 416-360-7729
info@omslaw.com
www.omslaw.com

Toronto: Owens, Wright - *12
#300, 20 Holly St., Toronto, ON M4S 3B1
Tel: 416-486-9800; *Fax:* 416-486-3309
owenswright@owenswright.com

Toronto: Pace Law Firm - *12
295 The West Mall, 6th Fl., Toronto, ON M9C 4Z4
Tel: 416-236-3060; *Fax:* 416-236-1809
Toll-Free: 877-236-3060
lawyers@pacelawfirm.com
www.pacelawfirm.com

Toronto: Pacey & Partners - *4
#1610, 1 Queen St. East, Toronto, ON M5C 2W5
Tel: 416-868-0612; *Fax:* 416-868-3022

Toronto: Susanne I. Palmer - *1
57 Huntley St., Toronto, ON M4Y 2L2
Tel: 416-924-0023
partnering@sympatico.ca

Toronto: Demetrius Pantazis - *1
#204, 1315 Lawrence Ave. East, Toronto, ON M3A 3R3
Tel: 416-469-5355; *Fax:* 416-469-8136
dpantazis@on.aibn.com

Toronto: Pape Barristers Professional Corporation - *4
#1910, P.O. Box 69, 1 Queen St. East, Toronto, ON M5C 2W5
Tel: 416-364-8765; *Fax:* 416-364-8855
pjp@papebarristers.com

Toronto: Papernick & Papernick - *1
60 Purdon Dr., Toronto, ON M3H 4X1
Tel: 416-633-0043; *Fax:* 416-633-9488

Toronto: Allan Papernick, Q.C. - *1
#203, 1200 Eglinton Ave. East, Toronto, ON M3C 1H9
Tel: 416-445-1273; *Fax:* 416-445-1678
apapernick@bellnet.ca

Toronto: Ado Park Q.C. - *1
#604, 357 Bay St., Toronto, ON M5H 2T7
Tel: 416-363-4451; *Fax:* 416-363-9256

Toronto: Parkdale Community Legal Services - *6
1266 Queen St. West, Toronto, ON M6K 1L3
Tel: 416-531-2411; *Fax:* 416-531-0885
mailbox@parkdalelegal.org
www.parkdalelegal.org

Toronto: Mary Lou Parker - *1
#800, 2 St. Clair Ave. East, Toronto, ON M4T 2T5
Tel: 416-920-4708; *Fax:* 416-920-3819
mlparker@tor.axxent.ca

Toronto: Paterson, MacDougall LLP, Barristers, Solicitors - *13
#900, P.O. Box 100, 1 Queen St. East, Toronto, ON M5C 2W5
Tel: 416-366-9607; *Fax:* 416-366-3743
bmacdoug@pmlaw.com
www.pmlaw.com

Toronto: Philip Patterson - *1
#305, 1033 Bay St., Toronto, ON M5S 3A5
Tel: 416-968-9188; *Fax:* 416-925-2860
ppaterson@on.aibn.com

Toronto: Paul & Paul - *2
39 Hayden St., Toronto, ON M4Y 2P2
Tel: 416-968-1777; *Fax:* 416-968-1211
npaul@bellnet.ca

Toronto: J.G. Paul - *1
#5, 1778 Bloor St. West, Toronto, ON M6P 3K4
Tel: 416-767-9919; *Fax:* 416-767-6272

Toronto: Murray E. Payne - *1
3329 Bloor St. West, Toronto, ON M8X 1E7
Tel: 416-232-1242; *Fax:* 416-231-1280

Toronto: Peace, Burns, Halkiw & Manning LLP - *2
#100, 25 Morrow Ave., Toronto, ON M6R 2H9
Tel: 416-533-1025; *Fax:* 416-516-5305

Toronto: Peirce, McNeely Associates - *3
25 Lesmill Rd., Toronto, ON M3B 2T3
Tel: 416-449-2060; *Fax:* 416-449-2068

Toronto: Michael Pelensky - *1
#300, 2 Toronto St., Toronto, ON M5C 2B6
Tel: 416-863-1300; *Fax:* 416-863-4942

Toronto: Penman Vona Professional Corporation, Barristers & Solicitors - *2
#307A, 4195 Dundas St. West, Toronto, ON M8X 1Y4
Tel: 416-231-5696; *Fax:* 416-231-5697
gvona@penman.cawww.facebook.com/people/George-Vona/547477354, www.linkedin.com/pub/george-vona/5/243/7b4

Toronto: Glenn B. Peppiatt - *1
939 Mt. Pleasant Rd., Toronto, ON M4P 2L7
Tel: 416-323-3232; *Fax:* 416-323-9350
peplaw@rogers.com

Toronto: Perks & Hanson - *2
#901, 130 Adelaide St. West, Toronto, ON M5H 3P5
Tel: 416-362-3366; *Fax:* 416-362-3174
perks@perksandhanson.com

Toronto: James Perly Consulting Inc. - *1
#1406, 168 King St. East, Toronto, ON M5A 4S4
Tel: 416-855-9130
jperly@jamesperly.com

Toronto: Peters & Kestelman - *1
245 Coxwell Ave., Toronto, ON M4L 3B4
Tel: 416-465-3561; *Fax:* 416-465-3563

Toronto: Petropoulos & Rapos - *1
#305, 1920 Ellesmere Rd., Toronto, ON M1H 2V6
Tel: 416-431-5870; *Fax:* 416-289-4144
jami1@bellnet.ca

Toronto: V. Walter Petryshyn - *1
1247 Dundas St. West, Toronto, ON M6J 1X6
Tel: 416-534-8431; *Fax:* 416-531-2455

Toronto: PGC Consultants Inc. - *1
426 Sumach St., Toronto, ON M4X 1V5
Tel: 416-515-9312; *Fax:* 416-515-8884
peterchubb@rogers.com

Toronto: Phillips & Phillips - *1
#2200, 181 University Ave., Toronto, ON M5H 3M7
Tel: 416-601-6802; *Fax:* 416-601-9590
brucenorth@phillipsandphillipslaw.com

Toronto: Douglas N. Phillips - *1
13 Reno Dr., Toronto, ON M1K 2V5
Tel: 416-757-3445; *Fax:* 416-759-8036
dnplaw@rogers.com

Toronto: Picov & Kleinberg - *2
#100, 110 Eglinton Ave. West, Toronto, ON M4R 1A3
Tel: 416-488-2100; *Fax:* 416-488-2794
kpicov@bellnet.ca

Toronto: L.A. Piller - *1
#2200, 181 University Ave., Toronto, ON M5H 3M7
Tel: 416-601-1622; *Fax:* 416-363-7239
lpiller@pillerross.com
www.pillerross.com

Toronto: Jillian M. Pivnick - *1
#410, 350 Lonsdale Rd., Toronto, ON M5P 1R6
Tel: 416-484-6306

Toronto: D.V. Pledge, Barrister & Solicitor - *1
#203, 1013 Wilson Ave., Toronto, ON M3K 1G1
Tel: 416-630-8702; *Fax:* 416-630-8714
donnav.pledge@bellnet.ca
www.dvpledge.ca

Toronto: Harry Poch Environmental Lawyer - *1
20 Beaverhall Dr., Toronto, ON M2L 2C7
Tel: 416-444-7971; *Fax:* 416-444-8971
harrypoch@rogers.com

Toronto: Policy Concepts - *1
21 St. Clair Ave. East, Toronto, ON M4T 1L9
Tel: 416-922-6156; *Fax:* 416-922-4295
policyconcepts@on.aibn.com

Toronto: Stephen P. Ponesse - *1
#3000, 390 Bay St., Toronto, ON M5H 2Y2
Tel: 416-361-3582; *Fax:* 416-368-7217
stephenponesse@on.aibn.com

Toronto: Porjes Walsh - *3
#2200, 181 University Ave., Toronto, ON M5H 3M7
Tel: 416-601-0002; *Fax:* 416-363-1660
dawn.mcconnell@sympatico.ca

Toronto: Portland Group - *1
#518, 1001 Bay St., Toronto, ON M5S 3A6
Tel: 416-413-9206
trobson@rogers.com

Toronto: Don Poscente - *1
683 Mt. Pleasant Rd., Toronto, ON M4T 1A8
Tel: 416-410-3333

Toronto: E.G. Posen - *1
101 Brookview Dr., Toronto, ON M6A 2K5
Tel: 416-782-5344
posen@pathcom.com

Toronto: Joseph M. Posen - *1
517 Glengarry Ave., Toronto, ON M5M 1G2
Tel: 416-783-2494
jposen@home.com

Toronto: Posesorski, Gary M. - *1
5 Wembley Rd., Toronto, ON M6C 2E8
Tel: 416-780-9655; *Fax:* 416-783-4574

Toronto: Wietse G. Posthumus - *1
#2700, West Tower, 55 Avenue Rd., Toronto, ON M5R 3L2
Tel: 416-929-3030; *Fax:* 416-961-9898

Toronto: Potts, Weisberg & Musil - *3
#206, 90 Eglinton Ave. East, Toronto, ON M4P 2Y3
Tel: 416-485-7366; *Fax:* 416-485-7368
pwmlaw@interlog.com

Toronto: Powell Weir, Barristers & Solicitors - *2
#506, 50 Gervais Dr., Toronto, ON M3C 1Z3
Tel: 416-441-6840; *Fax:* 416-441-0330
powlaw@interlog.com
www.powellweir.com

Toronto: Preisman, Kotnala - *2
#302, 885 Progress Ave., Toronto, ON M1H 3G3
Tel: 416-439-9559; *Fax:* 416-439-9553

Toronto: C.G. Preobrazenski - *1
#414, The Richmond Tower, 100 Richmond St. West, Toronto, ON M5H 3K6
Tel: 416-964-1717; *Fax:* 416-964-0823
marie@interware.com

Toronto: Stephen Price & Associates - *1
#1708, 5000 Yonge St., Toronto, ON M2N 7E9
Tel: 416-365-0766; *Fax:* 416-365-0866

Toronto: Prime Strategies Group Inc. - *1
#220, 156 Front St. West, Toronto, ON M5J 2L6
Tel: 416-313-3031
vic@primestrat.com

Toronto: D.R. Proctor, Q.C. - *1
#8A, 1921 Eglinton Ave. East, Toronto, ON M1L 2L6
Tel: 416-751-3958; *Fax:* 416-751-3770

Toronto: V.E. Purcell, Q.C. - *1
6 Silverdale Cres., Toronto, ON M3A 3H1
Tel: 416-445-7600; *Fax:* 416-425-4310

Toronto: R.G. Pyne - *1
3329 Bloor St. West, Toronto, ON M8X 1E7
Tel: 416-231-3339; *Fax:* 416-231-1280

Toronto: Quadra Consulting Group - *1
26 Dalhousie St., Toronto, ON M5B 2A5
Tel: 416-364-0073; *Fax:* 416-362-7542
pmeyer@quadraconsultinggroup.com

Toronto: Quirk, McGillicuddy & Sutton - *1
1604 Dufferin St., Toronto, ON M6H 3L7
Tel: 416-652-3543; *Fax:* 416-652-2730
fran@qmsutton.ca

Toronto: R2B Strategies - *1
145 Briar Hill Ave., Toronto, ON M4R 1H8
Tel: 416-435-8833; *Fax:* 416-481-3266
suk.yiu@utoronto.ca

Toronto: Rachlin & Wolfson LLP - *10
#1500, 390 Bay St., Toronto, ON M5H 2Y2
Tel: 416-367-0202; *Fax:* 416-367-1820
enquiry@rachlinlaw.com
www.rachlinlaw.com

Toronto: Danuta H. Radomski - *1
351 Castlefield Ave., Toronto, ON M5N 1L4
Tel: 416-322-6134; *Fax:* 416-489-1462
dradomski@on.aibn.com

** indicates number of lawyers*

Toronto: Ralph S Caswell - *1
#1908, 150 York St., Toronto, ON M5H 3S5
Tel: 416-542-5400; Fax: 416-597-1479
caswell@barexpress.net

Toronto: R. Sam Ramlall - *1
#700, 5799 Yonge St., Toronto, ON M2M 3V3
Tel: 416-512-6465; Fax: 416-512-6042
rsamramlall@bellnet.ca

Toronto: Rawana & Rawana Barristers & Solicitors - *2
11721 Sheppard Ave. East, 2nd Fl., Toronto, ON M1B 1G3
Tel: 416-281-8505; Fax: 416-286-4353

Toronto: Rayson & Associates - *4
#302, 3845 Bathurst St., Toronto, ON M3H 3N2
Tel: 416-630-5600; Fax: 416-630-5906
erayson@rayson.ca

Toronto: John L. Razulis - *1
#219, 534 Lawrence Ave., Toronto, ON M6A 1A2
Tel: 416-787-1918; Fax: 416-787-7161
counsel@lawfulwork.ca
www.lawfulwork.ca

Toronto: John H. Reble - *1
277 Glengrove Ave. West, Toronto, ON M5N 1W3
Tel: 416-485-9123
jreble@istar.ca

Toronto: The Refugee Law Office - *4
#206, 375 University Ave., Toronto, ON M5G 2G1
Tel: 416-977-8111; Fax: 416-977-5567
rlo@lao.on.ca

Toronto: Regan Desjardins LLP - *10
#1502, P.O. Box 2069, 20 Eglinton Ave. West, Toronto, ON M4R 1K8
Tel: 416-601-1000; Fax: 416-601-9255
reception@rkdlaw.com
www.regandesjardins.com

Toronto: T.S. Reiber Professional Corporation - *1
#211, 1110 Sheppard Ave. East, Toronto, ON M2K 2W2
Tel: 416-927-9841; Fax: 416-975-1531
terry@reiber.ca

Toronto: Reid, McLean & Scott - *1
2938 Danforth Ave., Toronto, ON M4C 1M5
Tel: 416-699-1131; Fax: 416-699-1958

Toronto: Mary P. Reilly - *2
701 Coxwell Ave., Toronto, ON M4C 3C1
Tel: 416-461-7553; Fax: 416-461-2679

Toronto: Reingold & Reingold - *1
#4068, P.O. Box 17, 3080 Yonge St., Toronto, ON M4N 3N1
Tel: 416-483-3364; Fax: 416-440-1942
jrqc58@bellnet.ca

Toronto: A.C.J. Reisler - *1
161 Bridgeland Ave., Toronto, ON M6A 1Z1
Tel: 416-781-4002; Fax: 416-781-7797
areisler@wastecogroup.com

Toronto: Stanley Reisman - *1
#308, 360 Bloor St. West, Toronto, ON M5S 1X1
Tel: 416-961-8864; Fax: 416-961-7654

Toronto: Reiter, Nemetz - *2
#451, 1111 Finch Ave. West, Toronto, ON M3J 2E5
Tel: 416-665-1458; Fax: 416-665-0895

Toronto: Rekai Frankel LLP - *6
33 Bloor St. East, 16th Fl., Toronto, ON M4W 3H1
Tel: 416-960-8876; Fax: 416-924-2371
eleanor@mobilitylaw.com
www.mobilitylaw.com

Toronto: David J.M. Rendeiro
#200, 1201 Dundas St. West, Toronto, ON M6J 1X3
Tel: 416-588-8000; Fax: 416-588-8002

Toronto: Reznick, Parsons - *2
#1917, 25 Adelaide St. East, Toronto, ON M5C 3A1
Tel: 416-863-6026; Fax: 416-863-9334

Toronto: Lewis J. Richardson - *1
#2000, 393 University Ave., Toronto, ON M5G 1E6
Tel: 416-599-1226; Fax: 416-962-9997

Toronto: Richman & Richman - *1
#404, 255 Duncan Mill Rd., Toronto, ON M3B 3H9
Tel: 416-510-1575; Fax: 416-510-1580
richman.richman@on.aibn.com

Toronto: Nina S. Richmond - *1
148 Brookdale Ave., Toronto, ON M5M 1P5
Tel: 416-489-4191; Fax: 416-489-5822
nina.richmond@rogers.com

Toronto: D.S. Rickerd, Q.C. - *1
21 Elm Ave., Toronto, ON M4W 1M9
Tel: 416-929-5177; Fax: 416-921-8322
drickerd@yorku.ca

Toronto: Ricketts, Harris LLP - *12
#816, Guardian of Canada Tower, 181 University Ave., Toronto, ON M5H 2X7
Tel: 416-364-6211; Fax: 416-364-1697
mail@rickettsharris.com
www.rickettsharris.com

Toronto: Gerald Rifkin - *1
#500, 1000 Finch Ave. West, Toronto, ON M3J 2V5
Tel: 416-667-9796; Fax: 416-667-8048

Toronto: Riley, McGivney - *3
#2300, 439 University Ave., Toronto, ON M5G 1Y8
Tel: 416-364-7611; Fax: 416-596-7562
mailbox@rileymclaw.ca

Toronto: Riverdale Law Group - *3
257 Danforth Ave., Toronto, ON M4K 1N2
Tel: 416-466-6264; Fax: 416-466-8465

Toronto: Riverdale Mediation - *2
257 Danforth Ave., Toronto, ON M4K 1N2
Tel: 416-466-6264; Fax: 416-466-8465
www.riverdalemediation.com

Toronto: Roach, Schwartz & Associates, Barristers & Solicitors - *7
688 St. Clair Ave. West, Toronto, ON M6C 1B1
Tel: 416-657-1465; Fax: 416-657-1511
www.roachschwartz.com

Toronto: Robbins & Associates - *3
#510, 481 University Ave., Toronto, ON M5G 2E9
Tel: 416-360-6530; Fax: 416-360-1056

Toronto: William H. Roberts - *1
#201, 34 Southport St., Toronto, ON M6S 3N3
Tel: 416-769-3162; Fax: 416-762-8972

Toronto: Robertson & Keith - *1
3464 Kingston Rd., Toronto, ON M1M 1R5
Tel: 416-261-1220; Fax: 416-261-1716

Toronto: Robins, Appleby & Taub LLP - *20
#2600, 120 Adelaide St. West, Toronto, ON M5H 1T1
Tel: 416-868-1080; Fax: 416-868-0306
www.robinsapplebyandtaub.com

Toronto: James L. Robinson - *1
2424 Bloor St. West, 2nd Fl., Toronto, ON M6S 1P9
Tel: 416-601-1411; Fax: 416-769-5365

Toronto: Lawlor Rochester - *1
#800, 141 Adelaide St. West, Toronto, ON M5H 3L5
Tel: 416-366-2267; Fax: 416-368-3467
bb@glaholt.com
www.glaholt.com

Toronto: Rogers & Rowland - *1
#400, 1235 Bay St., Toronto, ON M5R 3K4
Tel: 416-364-2333; Fax: 416-864-0271
mail@rogersrowland.com

Toronto: Rogers Law Office - *1
#3B, 4 Deer Park Cres., Toronto, ON M4V 2C3
Tel: 416-363-6626; Fax: 416-363-6628
file@rlo.ca
www.rlo.ca

Toronto: Rogers, Moore - *18
#1900, 181 University Ave., Toronto, ON M5H 3M7
Tel: 416-594-4500; Fax: 416-594-9100
rogersmoore@rogersmoore.com
www.rogersmoore.com

Toronto: Nelson Roland - *1
333 Adelaide St. West, 3rd Fl., Toronto, ON M5V 1R5
Tel: 416-351-1591; Fax: 416-340-9250
nroland@allstream.net

Toronto: Norman W. Ronka, Law Office of - *1
946 College St., Toronto, ON M6H 1A5
Tel: 416-969-0917; Fax: 416-905-8221

Toronto: Law Office of Christopher J. Roper - *1
#3300, The Cadillac Fairview Tower, 20 Queen St. West, Toronto, ON M5H 3R3
Tel: 416-368-6788; Fax: 416-368-5705
cjroper@interhop.net

Toronto: Rose & Rose - *2
#100, 1200 Sheppard Ave. East, Toronto, ON M2K 2S5
Tel: 416-590-9990; Fax: 416-590-9991

Toronto: Rose, Persiko, Rakowsky, Melvin LLP - *2
#600, 390 Bay St., Toronto, ON M5H 2Y2
Tel: 416-868-1900; Fax: 416-868-1708

Toronto: Rosen & Company - *5
#500, 350 Bay St., Toronto, ON M5H 2S6
Tel: 416-205-9700; Fax: 416-205-9970
johnrosen@rosenlaw.ca
www.rosenlaw.ca

Toronto: Allan C. Rosen - *1
#904, 27 Queen St. East, Toronto, ON M5C 2M6
Tel: 416-363-1601; Fax: 416-363-5620
acrosenlaw@rogers.com

Toronto: Solomon L. Rosen - *1
#1, 2933 Dufferin St., Toronto, ON M6B 3S7
Tel: 416-789-7133; Fax: 416-782-3507

Toronto: Elliot F. Rosenberg - *1
#201, 4949 Bathurst St., Toronto, ON M2R 1Y1
Tel: 416-512-7373; Fax: 416-512-7374
tlpress@patncom.com

Toronto: Irving Rosenberg - *1
#507, 1000 Finch Ave. West, Toronto, ON M3J 2V5
Tel: 416-398-0102; Fax: 416-398-0103
irose@on.aibn.com

Toronto: Rosenblatt Associates - *2
208 Adelaide St. West, 2nd Fl., Toronto, ON M5H 1W7
Tel: 416-644-4000; Fax: 416-861-1215
david@immigrate.net
www.immigrate.net

Toronto: Stanley Rosenfarb - *1
#800, 2001 Sheppard Ave. East, Toronto, ON M2J 4Z8
Tel: 416-494-4899; Fax: 416-494-3024
stan@srlaw.com

Toronto: Larry H. Ross - *1
#200, 609 Bloor St. West, Toronto, ON M6G 1K5
Tel: 416-535-6211; Fax: 416-535-7698

Toronto: R.M. Ross - *1
181 University Ave., 22nd Fl., Toronto, ON M5H 3M7
Tel: 416-601-1563; Fax: 416-363-7239
rross@pillerross.com

Toronto: A.M. Rossman - *1
#216, 801 York Mills Rd., Toronto, ON M3B 1X7
Tel: 416-444-2201; Fax: 416-444-0571

Toronto: Cecil L. Rotenberg - *3
#900, 1000 Finch Ave. West, Toronto, ON M3J 2V5
Tel: 416-449-8866; Fax: 416-510-9090
immigration@clrqc.com
www.clrqc.com

Toronto: I. Robert Rotenberg - *1
#1100, 11 King St. West, Toronto, ON M5H 4C7
Tel: 416-591-9100; Fax: 416-591-9008
rotenberg@sympatico.ca

Toronto: Frank L. Roth - *1
#500, 70 Bond St., Toronto, ON M5B 1X3
Tel: 416-963-8776; Fax: 416-863-4896
flr@bondlaw.net

Toronto: Neal H. Roth - *1
#401, 60 St. Clair Ave. East, Toronto, ON M4T 1N5
Tel: 416-351-7706; Fax: 416-351-7684
nealroth@on.aibn.com
www.nealroth.com

Toronto: Rothman & Rothman - *1
#638, 121 Richmond St. West, Toronto, ON M5H 2K1
Tel: 416-367-9901; Fax: 416-367-9979
rothman@sympatico.ca

Toronto: Nancy-Gay Rotstein - *1
#202, 40 Holly St., Toronto, ON M4S 3C3
Tel: 416-488-0800; Fax: 416-488-8350
nrotstein@municipal.ca

* indicates number of lawyers

Toronto: Roy Elliott Kim O'Connor LLP - *11
#1400, 10 Bay St., Toronto, ON M5J 2R8
Tel: 416-362-1989; Fax: 416-362-6204
info@reko.ca
www.reko.ca

Toronto: Rubenstein, Siegel - *2
#402, 1200 Sheppard Ave. East, Toronto, ON M2K 2S5
Tel: 416-499-5252; Fax: 416-499-2290

Toronto: Barry Rubinoff - *1
488 Huron St., Toronto, ON M5R 2R3
Tel: 416-966-4884; Fax: 416-966-6768

Toronto: Ruby & Edwardh - *7
11 Prince Arthur Ave., Toronto, ON M5R 1B2
Tel: 416-964-9664; Fax: 416-964-8305

Toronto: Ruderman, Shaw - *2
#1820, P.O. Box 2037, 20 Eglinton Ave. West, Toronto, ON M4R 1K8
Tel: 416-484-8558; Fax: 416-484-6918
info@rudermanshaw.com

Toronto: Victor E. Rudinskas - *1
27 John St., 2nd Fl., Toronto, ON M9N 1J4
Tel: 416-240-0594; Fax: 416-248-5922
Toll-Free: 877-888-8390
vrudinskas@trebnet.com

Toronto: George A. Rudnik - *1
#1901, 260 Queens Quay West, Toronto, ON M5J 2N3
Tel: 416-927-7788; Fax: 416-925-9963

Toronto: Rueter Scargall Bennett LLP - *7
#4220, Box 226, 161 Bay St., Toronto, ON M5J 2S1
Tel: 416-869-9090; Fax: 416-869-3411

Toronto: Martin K.I. Rumack - *1
#202, 2 St. Clair Ave. East, Toronto, ON M4T 2T5
Tel: 416-961-3441; Fax: 416-961-1045
martin@martinrumack.com
www.martinrumack.com

Toronto: Brian A. Rumanek - *1
#204, 200 Evans Ave., Toronto, ON M8Z 1J7
Tel: 416-252-9115; Fax: 416-253-0494
thelawman@rogers.com

Toronto: Richard E. Rusek - *1
1623 Bloor St. West, Toronto, ON M6P 1A6
Tel: 416-533-8563

Toronto: Rush, G.C.
2970 Lake Shore Blvd. West, Toronto, ON M8V 1J7
Tel: 416-251-2291

Toronto: C.H. Rutherford - *1
#500, 1000 Finch Ave. West, Toronto, ON M3J 2V5
Tel: 416-667-9796

Toronto: Rebecca J. Rutherford - *1
#308, 100 Richmond St. West, Toronto, ON M5H 3K6
Tel: 416-598-3928; Fax: 416-947-1236

Toronto: Ryder, Wright, Blair & Holmes LLP - *7
333 Adelaide St. West, 3rd Fl., Toronto, ON M5V 1R5
Tel: 416-340-9070; Fax: 416-340-9250

Toronto: Rye & Partners - *3
#1200, 65 Queen St. West, Toronto, ON M5H 2M5
Tel: 416-362-4901; Fax: 416-362-8291
partners@ryeandpartners.com
www.ryeandpartners.com

Toronto: Nadir Sachak - *1
#301, 366 Bay St., Toronto, ON M5H 4B2
Tel: 416-363-7172; Fax: 416-363-9917
Toll-Free: 877-878-7206

Toronto: Howard Saginur - *1
#1510, 5140 Yonge St., Toronto, ON M2N 6L7
Tel: 416-512-1912; Fax: 416-512-1989
howard@saginur.com
www.saginur.com

Toronto: F.G. Salehmohamed - *1
#202, 747 Don Mills Rd., Toronto, ON M3C 1T2
Tel: 416-421-7000; Fax: 416-421-5388

Toronto: M. Saltman Arbitrations Ltd. - *1
#107, 100 Adelaide St. West, Toronto, ON M5H 2G4
Tel: 416-366-3091; Fax: 416-366-0879
arbserve@aol.com

Toronto: Samis & Company - *9
400 University Ave., 16 Fl., Toronto, ON M5G 1S5
Tel: 416-365-0000; Fax: 416-365-9993
info@samislaw.com
www.samislaw.com

Toronto: Sanderson Entertainment Law - *2
#201, 326 Richmond St. West, Toronto, ON M5V 1X2
Tel: 416-971-6616; Fax: 416-971-4144
info@sandersonlaw.ca
www.sandersonlaw.ca

Toronto: Sandler, Gordon - *2
#260, 1027 Yonge St., Toronto, ON M4W 2K9
Tel: 416-971-5102; Fax: 416-971-5305

Toronto: Shil K. Sanwalka, Q.C. - *1
#602, 18 Wynford Dr., Toronto, ON M3C 3S2
Tel: 416-449-7755; Fax: 416-449-6969
skslaw@sanwalka.org

Toronto: Umberto Sapone - *2
#201, P.O. Box 17, 3200 Dufferin St., Toronto, ON M6A 3B2
Tel: 416-789-2689; Fax: 416-789-0454

Toronto: Dianne Saxe, Ph.D. - *3
248 Russell Hill Rd., Toronto, ON M4V 2T2
Tel: 416-962-5882; Fax: 416-962-8817
admin@envirolaw.com
www.envirolaw.comhttp://www.linkedin.com/in/envirolaw

Toronto: J.F. Scandiffio - *1
533 Queen St. East, Toronto, ON M5A 1V1
Tel: 416-364-6755; Fax: 416-364-7049

Toronto: P.M. Scandiffio, Q.C. - *1
#308, 344 Bloor St. West, Toronto, ON M5S 3A7
Tel: 416-515-1660; Fax: 416-515-1526

Toronto: John J.M. Scarfe - *1
27 Prince Arthurs Ave., Toronto, ON M5R 1B2
Tel: 416-410-4060; Fax: 416-960-1498
jscarfe@torontocriminallawyer.ca

Toronto: Scher & De Angelis Professional Corp. - *2
#210, 69 Bloor St. East, Toronto, ON M4W 1A9
Tel: 416-515-9686; Fax: 416-961-2534
scherde@interlog.com
www.interlog.com/~scherde

Toronto: Lionel H. Schipper, Q.C. - *1
#1010, 22 St. Clair Ave. East, Toronto, ON M4T 2S3
Tel: 416-923-7755; Fax: 416-961-7011

Toronto: Simon Schneiderman - *1
#1807, 8 King St. East, Toronto, ON M5C 1B5
Tel: 416-361-0680; Fax: 416-361-0248
clophie@aol.com

Toronto: Schnurr Kirsh Schnurr Oelbaum Tator LLP - *7
#1700, 65 Queen St., Toronto, ON M5H 2M5
Tel: 416-860-1057; Fax: 416-367-2502
www.estatelitigation.net

Toronto: Cecil Schwartz - *1
#2108, Madison Centre, P.O. Box 130, 4950 Yonge St., Toronto, ON M2N 6K1
Tel: 416-250-0083; Fax: 416-512-8275
cecil@cecilschwartz.com

Toronto: Scott & Oleskiw - *2
#235, 215 Spadina Ave., Toronto, ON M5T 2C7
Tel: 416-591-9229; Fax: 416-591-9200
admin@scottoleskiw.com

Toronto: B.M. Scully Barrister & Solicitor - *1
31 Prince Arthur Ave., Toronto, ON M5R 1B2
Tel: 416-968-2456; Fax: 416-960-5456

Toronto: Peter B. Scully - *1
42 Heath St. West., Toronto, ON M4V 1T3
Tel: 416-929-2909; Fax: 416-929-2909
scullylaw@sympatico.ca

Toronto: seclaw.ca - *1
75 Lowther Ave., Toronto, ON MR 1C9
Tel: 416-535-0297; Fax: 416-535-0088
caspar@seclaw.ca

Toronto: Gary L. Segal - *1
#1000, 60 St. Clair Ave. West, Toronto, ON M4T 1N5
Tel: 416-967-5400; Fax: 416-967-7877
immigration@garysegal.com

Toronto: Sennecke, Alexander Christian Erich
#2401, 120 Adelaide St. West, Toronto, ON M5H 1T1
Tel: 416-410-2113; Fax: 416-410-9423
asennecke@sennecke.com

Toronto: Seon Gutstadt Lash LLP - *6
#1800, 4950 Yonge St., Toronto, ON M2N 6K1
Tel: 416-224-0224; Fax: 416-224-0758
boblash@torlaw.com
www.torlaw.com

Toronto: Sera Associates - *2
#1800, 4950 Yonge St., Toronto, ON M2N 6K1
Tel: 416-222-7668; Fax: 416-224-0758

Toronto: Frederick J. Shanahan - *1
#414, 100 Richmond St. West, Toronto, ON M5H 3K6
Tel: 416-972-6449; Fax: 416-964-0823
f_shanny@hotmail.com

Toronto: Lawrence N. Shapiro - *1
#800, 2001 Sheppard Ave. East, Toronto, ON M2J 4Z8
Tel: 416-494-4899; Fax: 416-494-3024
lshapiro@tpg.to

Toronto: David Share Associates - *4
3442 Yonge St., Toronto, ON M4N 2M9
Tel: 416-488-9000; Fax: 416-488-9004
dshare@sharelawyers.com
www.sharelawyers.com

Toronto: Sharma & Sharma - *2
942 Gerrard St. East, Toronto, ON M4M 1Z2
Tel: 416-461-0467; Fax: 416-461-5817

Toronto: Chet Sharma - *1
#7, 1658 Victoria Park Ave., Toronto, ON M1R 1P7
Tel: 416-285-1550; Fax: 416-285-1698
chetsharma@aol.com

Toronto: Shearman & Sterling LLP - *15
#4405, Commerce Court West, P.O. Box 247, 199 Bay St., Toronto, ON M5L 1E8
Tel: 416-360-8484; Fax: 416-360-2958
www.shearman.com

Toronto: Shekter, Dychtenberg LLP - *5
#2900, 390 Bay St., Toronto, ON M5H 2Y2
Tel: 416-941-9995; Fax: 416-869-0321
richard@shekter.com

Toronto: Shell Lawyers - *3
#401, 672 Dupont St., Toronto, ON M6G 1Z6
Tel: 416-539-0226; Fax: 416-539-0565
brian@shelllawyers.ca
www.shelllawyers.ca

Toronto: Shelton Associates - *2
#810, 439 University Ave., Toronto, ON M5G 1Y8
Tel: 416-977-8888; Fax: 416-977-1964

Toronto: Sheppard Shalinksy Brown - *3
488 Huron St., Toronto, ON M5R 2R3
Tel: 416-966-6885; Fax: 416-966-6837
Ysheppard@sfmlaw.com

Toronto: Sheridan, Ippolito & Associates - *2
#506, 2 Jane St., Toronto, ON M6S 4W3
Tel: 416-763-3399; Fax: 416-763-3443
info@sheridanippolito.com
www.sheridanippolito.com

Toronto: Sherman, Brown, Dryer, Karol, Gold, Lebow - *1
#900, 5075 Yonge St., Toronto, ON M2N 6C6
Tel: 416-224-9800; Fax: 416-222-3091
cory@sanda.ca

Toronto: S.L. Sherman - *1
2645 Eglinton Ave. East, Toronto, ON M1K 2S2
Tel: 416-261-7161; Fax: 416-261-7163

Toronto: Sherrard Kuzz LLP - *8
#1500, 155 University Ave., Toronto, ON M5H 3B7
Tel: 416-603-0700; Fax: 416-603-6035
info@sherrardkuzz.com
www.sherrardkuzz.com

Toronto: Shibley Righton LLP - *32
#700, 250 University Ave., Toronto, ON M5H 3E5
Tel: 416-214-5200; Fax: 416-214-5400
Toll-Free: 877-214-5200
torontoinfo@shibleyrighton.com
www.shibleyrighton.com

** indicates number of lawyers*

***Toronto*: Alvin J. Shidlowski - *1**
#1100, 20 Dundas St. West, Toronto, ON M5G 2G8
Tel: 416-591-9100; *Fax:* 416-591-9008
ajs7@rogers.com

***Toronto*: Shields O'Donnell MacKillop LLP - *11**
65 Queen St. West, 181th Fl., Toronto, ON M5H 2M5
Tel: 416-304-6400; *Fax:* 416-304-6406
info@djmlaw.ca
www.djmlaw.ca

***Toronto*: Bernard S. Shier - *1**
219 Carlton St., Toronto, ON M5A 2L2
Tel: 416-923-8997; *Fax:* 416-923-8380

***Toronto*: Stanley I. Shier, Q.C. - *1**
65 Queen St. West, 17th Fl., Toronto, ON M5H 2M5
Tel: 416-366-9591; *Fax:* 416-366-2107
stanleyshier@shierlaw.com

***Toronto*: O.B. Shime, Q.C. - *1**
#200, 70 Bond St., Toronto, ON M5B 1X3
Tel: 416-366-8009; *Fax:* 416-365-7702
disputeservices@bellnet.ca

***Toronto*: Shamim Shivji - *1**
#400, 144 Front St. West, Toronto, ON M5J 2L7
Tel: 416-599-5469
sshivji@interlog.com

***Toronto*: E.I. Shoihet - *1**
9 Cortleigh Blvd., Toronto, ON M4R 1K5
Tel: 416-863-9594

***Toronto*: Geary B. Shorser - *1**
#2000, 393 University Ave., Toronto, ON M5G 1E6
Tel: 416-977-7749; *Fax:* 416-593-1352

***Toronto*: Ian C. Shoub - *1**
1000 Finch Ave. West, 4th Fl., Toronto, ON M3J 2V5
Tel: 416-661-0990; *Fax:* 416-663-3236
ishoub@on.aibn.com

***Toronto*: Robert Shour - *1**
#2000, 393 University Ave., Toronto, ON M5G 1E6
Tel: 416-977-4492; *Fax:* 416-977-4971
ralshour@on.aibn.com

***Toronto*: Louis D. Silver, Q.C. - *1**
15 Silvergrove Rd., Toronto, ON M2L 2N5
Tel: 416-445-2795; *Fax:* 416-445-7243
louisdsilverqc@rogers.com

***Toronto*: Martin I. Silver - *1**
#403, 1 Yorkdale Rd., Toronto, ON M6A 3A1
Tel: 416-781-5224; *Fax:* 416-781-3110
trilex@interlog.com

***Toronto*: Sheldon N. Silverman - *1**
#638, 121 Richmond St. West, Toronto, ON M5H 2K1
Tel: 416-363-6295; *Fax:* 416-363-3047
ssilverman@sympatico.ca
www.sheldonsilverman.com

***Toronto*: Sim & McBurney - *10**
330 University Ave., 6th Fl., Toronto, ON M5G 1R7
Tel: 416-595-1155; *Fax:* 416-595-1163

***Toronto*: Sim, Hughes, Ashton & McKay LLP - *9**
330 University Ave., 6th Fl., Toronto, ON M5G 1R7
Tel: 416-595-1155; *Fax:* 416-595-1163
mailsim@sim-mcburney.com
www.sim-mcburney.com

***Toronto*: Monty M. Simmonds, Q.C. - *1**
#1000, 2 St. Clair Ave. West, Toronto, ON M4V 1L5
Tel: 416-967-6706; *Fax:* 416-967-9483
services@medshire.com

***Toronto*: Michael S. Simrod - *1**
#500, 1000 Finch Ave. West, Toronto, ON M3J 2V5
Tel: 416-667-0980
msimrod@rogers.com

***Toronto*: Isaac Singer - *1**
2424 Bloor St. West, Toronto, ON M6S 1P9
Tel: 416-766-1135; *Fax:* 416-769-5365
isinger@bellnet.ca

***Toronto*: Singer, Keyfetz, Crackower & Saltzman - *2**
532 Eglinton Ave. East, Toronto, ON M4P 1N6
Tel: 416-488-6900; *Fax:* 416-488-7530

***Toronto*: Singer, Kwinter LLP - *8**
#214, Polo Centre, 1033 Bay St., Toronto, ON M5S 3A5
Tel: 416-961-2882; *Fax:* 416-961-6760
Toll-Free: 866-285-6927
info@singerkwinter.com
www.singerkwinter.com

***Toronto*: Michael S. Singer - *1**
#200, 4211 Yonge St., Toronto, ON M2P 2A9
Tel: 416-224-8383; *Fax:* 416-224-2408
michael.s.singer@gmail.com

***Toronto*: Yaso Sinnadurai - *1**
#202, 2100 Ellesmere Rd., Toronto, ON M1H 3B7
Tel: 416-265-3456; *Fax:* 416-265-2770

***Toronto*: Regina Sinukoff Barrister & Solicitor - *1**
#507, 1000 Finch Ave. West, Toronto, ON M3J 2V5
Tel: 416-739-7272; *Fax:* 416-739-7770
rsinukoff@on.aibn.com

***Toronto*: Steven H. Sinukoff - *1**
#240, 118 Eglinton Ave. West, Toronto, ON M4R 2G4
Tel: 416-489-7997; *Fax:* 416-256-9244
stevensinukoff@bellnet.ca

***Toronto*: Michael Sitzer - *1**
255 Lesmill Rd., Toronto, ON M3B 2V1
Tel: 416-391-2500; *Fax:* 416-391-3165
msitzer@sitzergroup.com

***Toronto*: Skadden, Arps, Slate, Meagher & Flom LLP - *9**
#1750, P.O. Box 258, Stn. T-D Centre, 222 Bay St., Toronto, ON M5K 1J5
Tel: 416-777-4700; *Fax:* 416-777-4747

***Toronto*: Skapinker & Shapiro LLP - *2**
#904, 180 Bloor St., Toronto, ON M5S 2V6
Tel: 416-214-1500; *Fax:* 416-214-0658
divorcelawyer@bellnet.ca
www.ontariofamilylaw.com

***Toronto*: Stewart Floyd Sklar - *1**
#5, 1267A St. Clair Ave. West, 2nd Fl., Toronto, ON M6E 1B8
Tel: 416-654-6111; *Fax:* 416-654-6100

***Toronto*: S.H. Skolnik - *1**
#318, 4002 Sheppard Ave. East, Toronto, ON M1S 4R5
Tel: 416-297-7300; *Fax:* 416-298-7142

***Toronto*: Steven Allen Skurka - *2**
#205, 970 Lawrence Ave. West, Toronto, ON M6A 3B6
Tel: 416-787-6529; *Fax:* 416-787-7788
sskurka@sslawyers.com

***Toronto*: Slater & Wells - *2**
644 Evans Ave., Toronto, ON M8W 2W6
Tel: 416-259-4293; *Fax:* 416-259-1286

***Toronto*: Paul Slocombe - *1**
387A Jane St., Toronto, ON M6S 3Z3
Tel: 416-762-0725; *Fax:* 416-762-6350

***Toronto*: Andrea M. Smart - *1**
8 Rolston Ave., Toronto, ON M5A 3Z2
Tel: 416-961-8829; *Fax:* 416-961-8829

***Toronto*: Cindy L. Smith**
#2104, 180 Dundas St. West, Toronto, ON M5G 1Z8
Tel: 416-408-0008; *Fax:* 416-597-9808

***Toronto*: K.D. Smith - *1**
#500, 70 Bond St., Toronto, ON M5B 1X3
Tel: 416-361-0232; *Fax:* 416-863-4896

***Toronto*: Raymond I. Smith - *1**
#1507, 8 King St. East., Toronto, ON M5C 1B5
Tel: 416-861-8695; *Fax:* 416-861-9074
raylaw@on.aibn.com

***Toronto*: Stanley Smither - *1**
#B1, 309 Mt. Pleasant Rd., Toronto, ON M4T 2C2
Tel: 416-485-7511; *Fax:* 416-488-9028

***Toronto*: D.B. Snider - *1**
978 Kingston Rd., Toronto, ON M4E 1S9
Tel: 416-699-0424; *Fax:* 416-699-0285

***Toronto*: Kenneth E. Snider - *1**
#309, 2100 Ellesmere Rd., Toronto, ON M1H 3B7
Tel: 416-438-4515; *Fax:* 416-289-7998
ksnider@bellnet.ca

***Toronto*: Irving Snitman - *1**
554 Annette St., Toronto, ON M6S 2C2
Tel: 416-767-0805; *Fax:* 416-767-4619
irv@irvingsnitman.com

***Toronto*: Solnik & Solnik Professional Corp. - *2**
2991 Dundas St. West, Toronto, ON M6P 1Z4
Tel: 416-767-7506; *Fax:* 416-767-4738
manny@solnikandsolnik.com
www.solnikandsolnik.com

***Toronto*: Solomon, Grosberg LLP - *6**
#1704, 55 University Ave., Toronto, ON M5J 2H7
Tel: 416-366-7828; *Fax:* 416-366-3513
lawyers@solgro.com

***Toronto*: J.J. Somjen - *2**
#810, 1240 Bay St., Toronto, ON M5R 2A7
Tel: 416-922-8083; *Fax:* 416-922-4234
somjen@somjen.com

***Toronto*: Larry S. Sonenberg - *1**
1123 Albion Rd., Toronto, ON M9V 1A9
Tel: 416-749-6000; *Fax:* 416-749-6004
Toll-Free: 877-388-5962
lssonenberg@on.aibn.com

***Toronto*: Sosa & Associates - *1**
#600, 161 Eglinton Ave. East, Toronto, ON M4P 1J5
Tel: 416-480-2324; *Fax:* 416-480-2923

***Toronto*: Sotos LLP - *12**
#1250, 180 Dundas St. West, Toronto, ON M5G 1Z8
Tel: 416-977-0007; *Fax:* 416-977-0717
info@sotosllp.com
www.sotosllp.com

***Toronto*: Spencer Law Firm - *1**
#300, 162 Cumberland St., Toronto, ON M5R 3N5
Tel: 416-967-1571; *Fax:* 416-966-1161

***Toronto*: Barry A. Spiegel - *1**
#1202, 390 Bay St., Toronto, ON M5H 2Y2
Tel: 416-865-0330; *Fax:* 416-363-8451
barry@spieglaw.com

***Toronto*: Belva Spiel - *1**
#402, 1670 Bayview Ave., Toronto, ON M4G 3C2
Tel: 416-486-1688; *Fax:* 416-486-2274

***Toronto*: Michael Spiro - *1**
#207, 3625 Dufferin St., Toronto, ON M3K 1Z2
Tel: 416-630-1370; *Fax:* 416-633-2229

***Toronto*: Harvey Spring - *1**
#488, 22 College St., Toronto, ON M5G 1K2
Tel: 416-967-0800; *Fax:* 416-967-2783
harveyspring@bellnet.ca

***Toronto*: C.A. Stafford - *1**
1036 Coxwell Ave., Toronto, ON M4C 3G5
Tel: 416-421-3211

***Toronto*: Jerome Stanleigh - *1**
#100, 20 York Mills Rd., Toronto, ON M2P 2C2
Tel: 416-924-0151; *Fax:* 416-924-2887
jerome@stanleigh.com

***Toronto*: James Stefoff - *1**
#1505, 80 Richmond St. West, Toronto, ON M5H 2A4
Tel: 416-366-7984

***Toronto*: Maxwell Steidman, Q.C. - *1**
#201, 1013 Wilson Ave., Toronto, ON M3K 1G1
Tel: 416-366-7661; *Fax:* 416-360-6868

***Toronto*: Larry C. Stein - *1**
#203, 2 Tippett Rd., Toronto, ON M3H 2V2
Tel: 416-636-8100; *Fax:* 416-636-6545

***Toronto*: Lorisa Stein - *1**
#800, 150 York St., Toronto, ON M5H 3S5
Tel: 416-596-8081
lorisa@idirect.com
www.lorisastein.com

***Toronto*: Steinberg Morton Frymer - *14**
#1100, 5255 Yonge St., Toronto, ON M2N 6P4
Tel: 416-225-2777; *Fax:* 416-225-7112
smf@smflaw.com
www.smflaw.com

***Toronto*: James A. Stephenson, Q.C. - *1**
3 Daleberry Pl., Toronto, ON M3B 2A5
Tel: 416-383-1488

** indicates number of lawyers*

Toronto: Stern & Landesman - *3
#1724, 390 Bay St., Toronto, ON M5H 2Y2
Tel: 416-869-3422; Fax: 416-869-3449

Toronto: Gary A. Stern - *1
1938 Avenue Rd., Toronto, ON M5M 4A2
Tel: 416-780-0199; Fax: 416-780-0155
Toll-Free: 800-678-6705
gastern@torlaw.com

Toronto: Steven M. Fishbayn Barrister & Solicitor - *1
100 Richmond St. West, Toronto, ON M5H 3K6
Tel: 416-361-9555; Fax: 416-862-7602

Toronto: Deborah L. Stewart - *1
106 Glencairn Ave., Toronto, ON M4R 1M9
Tel: 416-226-9340; Fax: 416-226-5341

Toronto: Stikeman Keeley Spiegel Pasternack LLP - *4
220 Bay St., 7th Fl., Toronto, ON M5J 2W4
Tel: 416-367-1930; Fax: 416-365-1813
info@stikeman.to
www.stikeman.to

Toronto: Stitt Feld Handy Group - *6
112 Adelaide St. East, Toronto, ON M5C 1K9
Tel: 416-307-0000; Fax: 416-307-0011
Toll-Free: 800-318-9741
contact@adr.ca
www.sfhgroup.com

Toronto: Stockwoods LLP - *12
#2512, 150 King St. West, Toronto, ON M5H 1J9
Tel: 416-593-7200; Fax: 416-593-9345
www.stockwoods.ca

Toronto: Stone & Osborne - *2
#201, 100 Sheppard Ave. West, Toronto, ON M2N 1M6
Tel: 416-225-1145; Fax: 416-225-0832

Toronto: Stone & Wenus - *2
330 Broadview Ave., Toronto, ON M4M 2G9
Tel: 416-469-4125; Fax: 416-469-2877

Toronto: David S. Strashin - *1
#702, 55 Eglinton Ave. East, Toronto, ON M4P 1G8
Tel: 416-482-8171; Fax: 416-485-4174

Toronto: Michael Strathman - *1
219 Carlton St., Toronto, ON M5A 2L2
Tel: 416-922-2424; Fax: 416-923-8380
michael@strathmanlaw.ca

Toronto: Stringer, Brisbin, Humphrey Management Lawyers - *11
#1100, 110 Yonge St., Toronto, ON M5C 1T4
Tel: 416-862-1616; Fax: 416-363-7358
Toll-Free: 866-821-7306
chumphrey@sbhlawyers.com
www.sbhlawyers.com

Toronto: John F. Stroz, Q.C. - *1
2275 Dundas St. West, Toronto, ON M6R 1X6
Tel: 416-536-2131; Fax: 416-536-5451

Toronto: John S. Struthers - *1
#501, 205 Richmond St. West, Toronto, ON M5V 1V3
Tel: 416-361-9609; Fax: 416-361-9443
jss@istar.ca

Toronto: J.A.F. Struyk - *1
1144 Queen St. East, Toronto, ON M4M 1L1
Tel: 416-463-1188; Fax: 416-463-9020
strike@tcn.net

Toronto: Robert P. Sullivan - *1
#1807, 8 King St. East, Toronto, ON M5C 1B5
Tel: 416-361-0390; Fax: 416-361-0248
rpsullivan@on.aibn.com

Toronto: S. Suppa - *1
#10, 927 The Queensway, Toronto, ON M8Z 5Z7
Tel: 416-252-5688; Fax: 416-252-4511

Toronto: Suter Law
102 Annette St., Toronto, ON M6P 1N6
Tel: 416-760-0529; Fax: 416-769-0529

Toronto: Ian Sutherland Barrister & Solicitor - *1
554 Annette St., Toronto, ON M6S 2C2
Tel: 416-763-0787; Fax: 416-763-0563
ian@sutherland.com
www.iansutherland.com

Toronto: Ralph A. Sutton - *1
#1800, 4950 Yonge St., Toronto, ON M2N 6K1
Tel: 416-224-0200; Fax: 416-224-0758
rsutton@torlaw.com

Toronto: Swadron Associates - *6
115 Berkeley St., Toronto, ON M5A 2W8
Tel: 416-362-1234; Fax: 416-362-1232
mail@swadron.com
www.swadron.com

Toronto: Kenneth P. Swan - *1
#500, 70 Bond St., Toronto, ON M5B 1X3
Tel: 416-368-5279; Fax: 416-363-9135
kpswan@bondlaw.net

Toronto: Swanick & Associates - *5
#101, 225 Duncan Mill Rd., Toronto, ON M3B 3K9
Tel: 416-510-1888; Fax: 416-510-1945

Toronto: H.A. Swartz - *2
#106, 1120 Finch Ave. West, Toronto, ON M3J 3H7
Tel: 416-665-0600; Fax: 416-665-2848

Toronto: Lori M. Swartz
#2200, P.O. Box 75, 1 Dundas St. West, Toronto, ON M5G 1Z3
Tel: 416-598-5899; Fax: 416-599-8341
Toll-Free: 800-410-1013
lori.swartz@lawpro.ca

Toronto: Eric J. Swetsky - *1
25 Sylvan Valley Way, Toronto, ON M5M 4M4
Tel: 416-787-4376; Fax: 416-787-3538
www.advertisinglawyer.ca

Toronto: Mimi Tang - *1
#202, 1210 Sheppard Ave. East, Toronto, ON M2K 1E3
Tel: 416-491-2929; Fax: 416-491-0990

Toronto: Tanner & Guiney - *1
#3425, Box 34, 130 Adelaide St. West, Toronto, ON M5H 3P5
Tel: 416-862-7745; Fax: 416-862-7874
rgtanner@tannerguiney.com
www.tannerguiney.com

Toronto: Tatham, Pearson - *3
5524 Lawrence Ave. East, Toronto, ON M1C 3B2
Tel: 416-284-4749; Fax: 416-284-3086
Toll-Free: 800-970-5670
info@tathampearson.com

Toronto: Stanley Taube - *1
#503, 33 Jackes Ave., Toronto, ON M4T 1E2
Tel: 416-513-1233

Toronto: Taveroff & Associates - *2
#900, 2 Sheppard Ave. East, Toronto, ON M2N 5Y7
Tel: 416-221-9343; Fax: 416-221-8928

Toronto: Fred Tayar & Associates, Professional Corporation - *3
#900, 20 Queen St. West, Toronto, ON M5H 3R3
Tel: 416-363-1800; Fax: 416-363-3356
fred@fredtayar.com

Toronto: Teeger Schiller Inc. - *1
304 Richview Ave., Toronto, ON M5P 3G5
Tel: 416-480-0832; Fax: 416-480-0962
eschiller@teegerschiller.com

Toronto: Nicole J. Tellier - *2
#200, 390 Dupont St., Toronto, ON M5R 1V9
Tel: 416-926-9669; Fax: 416-926-9079
ntellier@tellierlaw.com

Toronto: Stephen Thom - *1
#500, 70 Bond St., Toronto, ON M5B 1X3
Tel: 416-364-3371; Fax: 416-863-4896

Toronto: Thomson, Rogers - *33
#3100, 390 Bay St., Toronto, ON M5H 1W2
Tel: 416-868-3100; Fax: 416-868-3134
Toll-Free: 888-223-0448
info@thomsonrogers.com
www.thomsonrogers.com

Toronto: Ian Thornhill - *1
#406, 255 Duncan Mill Rd., Toronto, ON M3B 3H9
Tel: 416-224-2004; Fax: 416-224-2101
ithornhilllaw@rogers.com

Toronto: Thornton Grout Finnigan LLP - *23
#3200, Toronto-Dominion Centre, P.O. Box 329, 100 Wellington St. West, Toronto, ON M5K 1K7
Tel: 416-304-1616; Fax: 416-304-1313
info@tgf.ca
www.tgf.ca

Toronto: Thorsteinssons LLP Tax Lawyers - *20
BCE Place, P.O. Box 786, 181 Bay St., 33rd Fl., Toronto, ON M5J 2T3
Tel: 416-864-0829; Fax: 416-864-1106
Toll-Free: 888-666-9998
managingpartner@thor.ca
www.thor.ca

Toronto: Lorne B. Tick - *1
36 Elkpath Ave., Toronto, ON M2L 2W1
Tel: 416-444-9146; Fax: 416-444-9146
ltick@rogers.com

Toronto: Tikal's - *1
178 St. George St., Toronto, ON M5R 2M7
Tel: 416-968-7070; Fax: 416-968-1876

Toronto: Philip Tinianov - *1
#1800, 4950 Yonge St., Toronto, ON M2N 6K1
Tel: 416-363-0866; Fax: 416-224-0758
ptinianov@torlaw.com

Toronto: M.K. Titherington - *1
46 Northcliffe Blvd., Toronto, ON M6H 3H2
Tel: 416-656-6465

Toronto: Tkatch & Associates - *2
#488, 22 College St., Toronto, ON M5G 1K2
Tel: 416-968-0333; Fax: 416-968-0232
tkatchlaw@aol.com

Toronto: Norman W. Tomas - *1
954A Royal York Rd., Toronto, ON M8X 2E5
Tel: 416-233-5567; Fax: 416-233-9779
ntomas@bellnet.ca

Toronto: James Tomlinson - *1
#218A, 85 Ellesmere Rd., Toronto, ON M1R 4B9
Tel: 416-447-0476; Fax: 416-447-8611

Toronto: Mary Tomlinson - *1
123 Glenrose Ave., Toronto, ON M4T 1K7

Toronto: Toomath & Associates - *1
133 Berkeley St., 3rd Fl., Toronto, ON M5A 2X1
Tel: 416-869-0900; Fax: 416-366-4711

Toronto: Torkin Manes LLP - *76
#1500, 151 Yonge St., Toronto, ON M5C 2W7
Tel: 416-863-1188; Fax: 416-863-0305
Toll-Free: 800-665-1555
info@torkinmanes.com
www.torkinmanes.com

Toronto: Paul G. Torrie - *2
45 Saint Nicholas St., Toronto, ON M4Y 1W6
Tel: 416-964-9530; Fax: 416-925-8122
paul@global-adr.com

Toronto: Tough & Podrebarac LLP - *4
#300, 166 Pearl St., Toronto, ON M5H 1L3
Tel: 416-348-7500; Fax: 416-348-7505

Toronto: Traub Moldaver - *5
#1801, 4 King St. West, Toronto, ON M5H 1B6
Tel: 416-214-6500; Fax: 416-214-7275
Toll-Free: 877-727-6500

Toronto: Philip J. Traversy - *1
#900, 2 Sheppard Ave. East, Toronto, ON M2N 5Y7
Tel: 416-221-9343; Fax: 416-221-8928
p.traversy@rogers.com

Toronto: T.J. Treloar - *1
#401, 302 The East Mall, Toronto, ON M9B 6C7
Tel: 416-232-2919; Fax: 416-232-9201

Toronto: Quoc Toan Trinh - *1
1577 Bloor St. West, Toronto, ON M6P 1A6
Tel: 416-533-8987; Fax: 416-536-3618
trinhqtoan@on.aibn.com

Toronto: William M. Trudell - *2
15 Bedford Rd., Toronto, ON M5R 2J7
Tel: 416-598-2019; Fax: 416-868-0273
wtrudell@15bedford.com

** indicates number of lawyers*

***Toronto*: Constantine Tsantis - *1**
69 Elm St., Toronto, ON M5G 1H2
Tel: 416-599-6689; *Fax:* 416-971-9092

***Toronto*: Maureen L. Tucker - *1**
43 Madawaska Ave., Toronto, ON M2M 2R1
Tel: 416-221-5122; *Fax:* 416-226-9737
Toll-Free: 877-580-2049
mltlaw@on.aibn.com

***Toronto*: Helen R. Turner - *1**
#1505, 80 Richmond St. West, Toronto, ON M5H 2A4
Tel: 416-366-7985; *Fax:* 416-366-4670

***Toronto*: Howard Ungerman - *1**
37 Maitland St., Toronto, ON M4Y 1C8
Tel: 416-924-4111; *Fax:* 416-924-4112

***Toronto*: Urquhart, Urquhart, Aiken & Medcof - *1**
#1505, 5140 Yonge St., Toronto, ON M2N 6L7
Tel: 416-595-1111; *Fax:* 416-595-7312
fieldbrown@bellnet.ca

***Toronto*: S. Van Duffelen - *1**
#100, 700 University Ave., Toronto, ON M5G 1Z5
Tel: 416-598-5667; *Fax:* 416-946-1180
vanduffelenlaw@on.aibn.com

***Toronto*: Michael B. Vaughan Q.C.**
#3100, 130 Adelaide St. West, Toronto, ON M5H 3P5
Tel: 416-363-9611; *Fax:* 416-363-9672
mbv@idirect.com

***Toronto*: Veritas Communications Inc. - *1**
#704, 161 Eglinton Ave. East, Toronto, ON M4P 1J5
Tel: 416-482-2248; *Fax:* 416-482-2292

***Toronto*: David R. Vine - *1**
#1604, 80 Richmond St. West, Toronto, ON M5H 2A4
Tel: 416-863-9341; *Fax:* 416-863-9342

***Toronto*: Mark H. Viner - *1**
541 Old Orchard Grove, Toronto, ON M5M 2G8
Tel: 416-785-7469; *Fax:* 416-785-1581
mviner@pathcom.com

***Toronto*: Julia M. Viva - *1**
58 Plymbridge Rd., Toronto, ON M2P 1A3
Tel: 416-488-7222; *Fax:* 416-489-6258

***Toronto*: James D. Vlasis - *1**
#240, 118 Eglinton Ave. West, Toronto, ON M4R 2G4
Tel: 416-920-3447; *Fax:* 416-920-3448
jamesvlasis@vlasislaw.com

***Toronto*: Wagman, Sherkin - *2**
#200, 756A Queen St. East, Toronto, ON M4M 1H4
Tel: 416-465-1102; *Fax:* 416-465-3941
charles_wagman@wagmansherkin.ca

***Toronto*: Waldin, de Kenedy - *3**
#2150, 1 Queen St. East, Toronto, ON M5C 2W5
Tel: 416-364-6761; *Fax:* 416-364-3866
waldin@waldin.ca

***Toronto*: Walker Poole Nixon LLP - *6**
#515, 5160 Yonge St., Toronto, ON M2N 6L9
Tel: 416-225-5160; *Fax:* 416-225-0072
info@wpnlaw.com
www.wpnlaw.com

***Toronto*: Bruce E. Walker - *2**
#205, 65 Wellesley St. East, Toronto, ON M4Y 1G7
Tel: 416-961-7451; *Fax:* 416-961-5966
bwalker@bwalkerlaw.com
www.bwalkerlaw.com

***Toronto*: Walker, Ellis - *2**
390 Bay St., 30th Fl., Toronto, ON M5H 1W2
Tel: 416-363-2144; *Fax:* 416-363-1541

***Toronto*: J.H.G. Wallace - *1**
551 Gerrard St. East, Toronto, ON M4M 1X7
Tel: 416-463-6666; *Fax:* 416-463-8259

***Toronto*: Walsh McLuskie Doyle - *4**
#2308, 180 Dundas St. West, Toronto, ON M5G 1Z8
Tel: 416-598-8177; *Fax:* 416-598-5466
firm@wmdlaw.net

***Toronto*: Walton Advocates - *5**
30 Hazelton Ave., Toronto, ON M5R 2E2
Tel: 416-489-3171; *Fax:* 416-489-9973

***Toronto*: Walton, Brigham & Kelly - *2**
301 Donlands Ave., Toronto, ON M4J 3R8
Tel: 416-425-4300; *Fax:* 416-425-4310
tkelly@bellnet.ca

***Toronto*: Wappel, Toome, Babits, Laar & Bell LLP - *6**
#1801, 400 University Ave., Toronto, ON M5G 1S5
Tel: 416-598-1333; *Fax:* 416-598-5024

***Toronto*: Warren Bergman Associates - *2**
2925 Bathrust St., Toronto, ON M6S 3B1
Tel: 416-763-4183; *Fax:* 416-763-1310
Toll-Free: 877-763-4183
dwarren@warrenbergman.com

***Toronto*: Howard E. Warren - *1**
#802, 2 Sheppard Ave. East, Toronto, ON M2N 5Y7
Tel: 416-598-4777; *Fax:* 416-598-4316
hwarren@askhoward.com

***Toronto*: Robert D. Warren**
15 Bedford Rd., Toronto, ON M5R 2J7
Tel: 416-368-5393; *Fax:* 416-905-7736

***Toronto*: Wasser Resources Inc. - *1**
42 Arlstan Dr., Toronto, ON M3H 4V9
Tel: 416-638-1645
bwasser@sympatico.ca

***Toronto*: M.O. Watson - *1**
27 Whitehorn Cres., Toronto, ON M2J 3B1
Tel: 416-493-8541; *Fax:* 416-493-9042
barwat@rogers.com

***Toronto*: Weatherhead, Weatherhead - *2**
#500, 27 Queen St. East, Toronto, ON M5C 2M6
Tel: 416-362-1369; *Fax:* 416-362-5013
weatherhead@bellnet.ca

***Toronto*: J.H. Webster - *2**
2600 Danforth Ave., Toronto, ON M4C 1L3
Tel: 416-699-9644; *Fax:* 416-699-8905

***Toronto*: John David Webster, Q.C. - *1**
290 Lytton Blvd., Toronto, ON M5N 1R6
Tel: 416-489-6255

***Toronto*: John Weingust, Q.C. - *1**
Penthouse, 481 University Ave., 10th Fl., Toronto, ON M5G 2E9
Tel: 416-977-7786; *Fax:* 416-340-0064

***Toronto*: F. Sheldon Weinles - *1**
104 Caribou Rd., Toronto, ON M5N 2A9
Tel: 416-780-1330; *Fax:* 416-780-1331

***Toronto*: Joyce R. Weinman - *1**
#300, 20 Holly St., Toronto, ON M4S 3B1
Tel: 416-848-1019; *Fax:* 416-486-3309
joyce@jwdental.com
www.jwdental.com

***Toronto*: Gilbert Weinstock - *1**
#401, 1850 Victoria Park Ave., Toronto, ON M1R 1T1
Tel: 416-759-1354; *Fax:* 416-759-3256
gilbertweinstock@gmail.com

***Toronto*: WeirFoulds LLP - *78**
#1600, Exchange Tower, P.O. Box 480, 130 King St. West, Toronto, ON M5X 1J5
Tel: 416-365-1110; *Fax:* 416-365-1876
firm@weirfoulds.com
www.weirfoulds.com

***Toronto*: John Weisdorf, Q.C. - *1**
#1000, 121 Richmond St. West, Toronto, ON M5H 2K1
Tel: 416-861-1000; *Fax:* 416-861-8166

***Toronto*: Irwin Wenus - *1**
27 Acton Ave., Toronto, ON M3H 4G6
Tel: 416-633-5830

***Toronto*: Stephen Werbowyj Professional Corporation**
1199 The Queensway, Toronto, ON M8Z 1R2
Tel: 416-233-9461; *Fax:* 416-233-1524
werbowyj@bellnet.ca

***Toronto*: Ian D. Werker - *1**
#2000, 393 University Ave., Toronto, ON M5G 1E6
Tel: 416-593-7552; *Fax:* 416-593-0668
ian@werkerlaw.com

***Toronto*: West Scarborough Community Legal Services - *4**
#201, 2425 Eglinton Ave. East, Toronto, ON M1K 5G8
Tel: 416-285-4460; *Fax:* 416-285-1070

***Toronto*: Lawrence C. Wesson, Barrister & Solicitor - *1**
#710, 40 Sheppard Ave. West, Toronto, ON M2N 6K9
Tel: 416-225-7625; *Fax:* 416-225-1665

***Toronto*: Grace Westcott, Barrister & Solicitor - *1**
133 Laother Ave., Toronto, ON M5R 1E4
Tel: 416-489-2738; *Fax:* 416-489-1918
gw@westcottlaw.com

***Toronto*: Lionel B. White, Q.C. - *1**
65 Duggan Ave., Toronto, ON M4V 1Y1
Tel: 416-364-1127; *Fax:* 416-364-6903
lex.white@rogers.com

***Toronto*: Robin J. Wigdor - *1**
#901, 159 Frederick St., Toronto, ON M5A 4P1
Tel: 416-504-7237
robin@wigdor.com
www.wigdor.com/robin/

***Toronto*: Willard & Devitt - *1**
155 Roncesvalles Ave., Toronto, ON M6R 2L3
Tel: 416-531-1136; *Fax:* 416-531-4096
robert@robertbeaumont.ca

***Toronto*: W.M. Sharpe - *3**
#307, 40 Wynford Dr., Toronto, ON M3C 1J5
Tel: 416-482-5321; *Fax:* 416-322-2083
wmsharpe@shippinglaw.ca
www.yachtsales.com/sharpe

***Toronto*: Paul T. Willis - *1**
#308, 120 Carlton St., Toronto, ON M5A 4K2
Tel: 416-926-9806; *Fax:* 416-926-9737
paul.t.willis@on.aibn.com

***Toronto*: Willms & Shier Environmental Lawyers LLP - *11**
#900., 4 King St. West, Toronto, ON M5H 1B6
Tel: 416-863-0711; *Fax:* 416-863-1938
info@willmsshier.com
www.willmsshier.com

***Toronto*: Willowdale Community Legal Services - *2**
#106, 245 Fairview Mall Dr., Toronto, ON M2J 4T1
Tel: 416-492-2437; *Fax:* 416-492-6281

***Toronto*: Willson Lewis LLP, Barristers & Solicitors - *5**
#200, 1183 King St. West, Toronto, ON M6K 3C5
Tel: 416-534-9504; *Fax:* 416-534-9503
cwillson@willsonlewis.com
www.willsonlewis.com

***Toronto*: David S. Wilson - *1**
#2000, 393 University Ave., Toronto, ON M5G 1E6
Tel: 416-943-1223; *Fax:* 416-943-1049
dswilson@davidswilsonlaw.com

***Toronto*: Matthew F. Wilton & Associate**
127 John St., Toronto, ON M5V 2E2
Tel: 416-860-9889; *Fax:* 416-204-1849

***Toronto*: Norman H. Winter - *1**
#801, 1 St. Clair Ave. East, Toronto, ON M4T 2V7
Tel: 416-964-0325; *Fax:* 416-964-2494
nw@nwinlaw.com

***Toronto*: Wise & Associates Professional Corporation - *3**
#201, 40 Scollard St., Toronto, ON M5R 3S1
Tel: 416-866-4144; *Fax:* 416-866-7946
roy.wise@wiseandassociates.com

***Toronto*: G.R. Wise - *1**
3329 Bloor St. West, Toronto, ON M8X 1E7
Tel: 416-231-7399; *Fax:* 416-231-1280

***Toronto*: Gary L. Wiseman - *1**
#1800, 4950 Yonge St., Toronto, ON M2N 6K1
Tel: 416-224-0200; *Fax:* 416-224-0758
gwiseman@idirect.com

***Toronto*: L. Patricia Wong - *1**
#108, 14 Prince Arthur Ave., Toronto, ON M5R 1A9
Tel: 416-972-6957; *Fax:* 416-972-6427
werzy@planeteer.com

** indicates number of lawyers*

Toronto: Newton Wong & Associates - *2
#307, 1033 Bay St., Toronto, ON M5S 3A5
Tel: 416-971-9118; *Fax:* 416-971-7210

Toronto: Wing H. Wong - *1
#202, 4433 Sheppard Ave. East, Toronto, ON M1S 1V3
Tel: 416-298-6767; *Fax:* 416-298-3844

Toronto: Cynthia J. Woods - *1
#301, 2490 Bloor St. West, Toronto, ON M6S 1R4
Tel: 416-763-3065; *Fax:* 416-763-6876
info@woodslaw.ca
www.woodslaw.ca

Toronto: Woolgar VanWiechen Ketcheson Ducoffe LLP - *9
#401, 70 The Esplanade, Toronto, ON M5E 1R2
Tel: 416-867-1666; *Fax:* 416-867-1434
www.woolvan.com

Toronto: George A. Wootten, Q.C. - *1
#901, 701 Evans Ave., Toronto, ON M9C 1A3
Tel: 416-621-7470; *Fax:* 416-621-6838

Toronto: Wright & Associates - *5
897 Kipling Ave., Toronto, ON M8Z 5H3
Tel: 416-236-7905; *Fax:* 416-236-5644
wright.associates@wnalaw.com

Toronto: K.E. Wright - *1
#1001, 65 Queen St. West, Toronto, ON M5H 2M5
Tel: 416-364-1157

Toronto: Peter J. Wuebbolt - *1
1554A Bloor St. West, Toronto, ON M6P 1A4
Tel: 416-516-4621; *Fax:* 416-516-1679

Toronto: Sara Wunch - *1
#1600, 480 University Ave., Toronto, ON M5T 1V6
Tel: 416-595-7001; *Fax:* 416-595-5663

Toronto: Nicholas A. Xynnis - *1
#400, 100 Richmond St. West, Toronto, ON M5H 3K6
Tel: 416-862-1010; *Fax:* 416-862-7602

Toronto: Arthur Yallen
204 St. George St., Toronto, ON M5R 2N5
Tel: 416-927-0001; *Fax:* 416-927-0930

Toronto: John Yaremko, Q.C. - *1
1 Connable Dr., Toronto, ON M5R 1Z7
Tel: 416-921-7158

Toronto: Francesca E. Yaskiel - *1
#903, 121 Richmond St. West, Toronto, ON M5H 2K1
Tel: 416-847-0847; *Fax:* 416-363-0263

Toronto: Gerald B. Yasskin - *1
#402, 1183 Finch Ave. West, Toronto, ON M3J 2G2
Tel: 416-667-0982; *Fax:* 416-665-4291

Toronto: Yee & Lee - *2
#109, 40 Wynford Dr., Toronto, ON M3C 1J5
Tel: 416-977-0091; *Fax:* 416-977-6335

Toronto: David P. Yerzy - *1
#108, 14 Prince Arthur Ave., Toronto, ON M5R 1A9
Tel: 416-972-6957; *Fax:* 416-972-6427
73203.2004@compuserve.com

Toronto: Hyun Soo Yi - *1
#204, 640 Bloor St. West, Toronto, ON M6G 1K9
Tel: 416-534-7711; *Fax:* 416-534-7714

Toronto: Theodore C. Yoannou - *1
#600, 1000 Finch Ave. West, Toronto, ON M3J 2V5
Tel: 416-650-1011; *Fax:* 416-650-1980
tedyoannou@hotmail.com

Toronto: York Community Services
1651 Keele St., Toronto, ON M6M 3W2
Tel: 416-653-5400; *Fax:* 416-653-8049
franklim@lao.on.ca

Toronto: Joseph R. Young - *1
#200, 20 Cumberland St., Toronto, ON M4W 1J5
Tel: 416-969-8887; *Fax:* 416-969-8866
jryoung@globalmigration.com

Toronto: D.R. Zadorozny - *1
#216, 4195 Dundas St. West, Toronto, ON M8X 1Y4
Tel: 416-239-2333; *Fax:* 416-239-1752
Toll-Free: 866-396-7251
drz@drzlaw.com

Toronto: Silvie Zakuta - *1
112 Adelaide St. East, Toronto, ON M5C 1K9
Tel: 416-923-1656; *Fax:* 416-368-2918
szakuta@aol.com

Toronto: Zaldin & Fine - *3
#1012, 111 Richmond St. West, Toronto, ON M5H 2G4
Tel: 416-868-1431; *Fax:* 416-868-6381
zalfin@ca.inter.net

Toronto: Lawrence Zaldin - *1
#424, 3600 Yonge St., Toronto, ON M4N 3R8
Tel: 416-488-1766; *Fax:* 416-488-3555
lzaldin@sympatico.ca

Toronto: Zammit Semple LLP - *4
#601, 130 Bloor St. West, Toronto, ON M5S 1N5
Tel: 416-923-2601; *Fax:* 416-923-1391

Toronto: C. Zapf - *1
2424 Bloor St. West, 2nd Fl., Toronto, ON M6S 1P9
Tel: 416-766-4208; *Fax:* 416-769-5365

Toronto: M. David Zbarsky - *1
#1001, 85 Thorncliffe Park Dr., Toronto, ON M4H 1L6
Tel: 416-421-6252; *Fax:* 416-467-6780

Toronto: Zeldin, Collin - *1
23 Bedford Rd., Toronto, ON M5R 2J9
Tel: 416-964-7914; *Fax:* 416-964-8067
collin@zecol.com

Toronto: David L. Zifkin - *1
90A Isabella St., 1st Fl., Toronto, ON M4Y 1N4
Tel: 416-927-7720; *Fax:* 416-964-9348
dzifkin@zifkin.com
www.zifkin.com

Toronto: R. Zisman
#307, 120 Carlton St., Toronto, ON M5A 4K2
Tel: 416-925-6490; *Fax:* 416-925-4492
rzisman@rgcoates.com

Toronto: Howard G. Zweig - *1
1035 McNicoll Ave., Toronto, ON M1W 3W6
Tel: 416-512-1201; *Fax:* 416-512-1212
zweiglaw@bellnet.ca

Toronton: M.M. Jemmott, Q.C. - *1
344 Dupont Street, Torontom, ON M5R 1V9
Tel: 416-975-0787
marvajemmott@bellnet.ca

Tottenham: Feehely, Gastaldi - *4
P.O. Box 370, 5 Mill St. East, Tottenham, ON L0G 1W0
Tel: 905-936-4262; *Fax:* 905-936-5102
fg@feehelygastaldi.com

Tottenham: Smith & Associates - *2
P.O. Box 970, 23 Queen St. South, Tottenham, ON L0G 1W0
Tel: 905-936-4221; *Fax:* 905-936-4223

Trenton: Bonn Law Office - *4
80 Division St., Trenton, ON K8V 5S5
Tel: 613-392-9207; *Fax:* 613-392-6367
georgebonn@bonnlaw.com

Trenton: Fleming Garrett Sioui - *5
P.O. Box 397, Stn. Main, 21 Quinte St., Trenton, ON K8V 5R6
Tel: 613-965-6430; *Fax:* 613-965-6400
fgs@reach.net

Tweed: L.G. Bryan - *1
P.O. Box 669, 325 Victoria St. North, Tweed, ON K0K 3J0
Tel: 613-478-6100; *Fax:* 613-478-3485
lbryan@intranet.ca

Tweed: Bart F. Lackie - *1
2718 Mallbank Rd., RR#4, Tweed, ON K0K 3J0
Tel: 613-478-9940; *Fax:* 613-478-6061
bart@linesat.com

Unionville: Susan M. Ambrose - *1
105 Main St., Unionville, ON L3R 2G1
Tel: 905-477-0624; *Fax:* 905-477-5846
inquiries@lawgals.com

Unionville: Janet L. Gillespie - *1
178 Main St., Unionville, ON L3R 2G9
Tel: 905-479-6352; *Fax:* 905-479-1991
jlgillespie@rogers.com

Unionville: Minken & Associates Professional Corporation - *5
#200, 190 Main St., Unionville, ON L3R 2G9
Tel: 905-477-7011; *Fax:* 905-477-7010
Toll-Free: 866-477-7011
admin@minken.com
www.minken.com; www.employmentlawissues.ca

Unionville: M.T.P. Wood - *1
10050 Warden Ave., Unionville, ON L6C 1N3
Tel: 905-887-5999; *Fax:* 905-887-5826

Uxbridge: Bailey & Sedore - *2
11 Brock St. East, Uxbridge, ON L9P 1M4
Tel: 905-852-3363; *Fax:* 905-852-3480

Uxbridge: Paul D. Fox - *1
6749 Concession 6, RR#1, Uxbridge, ON L9P 1R1
Tel: 905-852-4560; *Fax:* 905-852-4435
paulfox@bellnet.ca

Uxbridge: Randall B. Hoban - *1
20 Bascom St., Uxbridge, ON L9P 1J3
Tel: 905-852-3666

Uxbridge: P.D. Turner, Q.C. - *1
P.O. Box 760, 63 Albert St., Uxbridge, ON L9P 1E5
Tel: 905-852-6196; *Fax:* 905-852-6197
doug@pdturner.com

Uxbridge: Wilson Associates - *2
22 Brock St. East, Uxbridge, ON L9P 1P1
Tel: 905-852-3353; *Fax:* 905-852-5120
lawyers@uxbridgelaw.com
www.uxbridgelaw.com

Vanier: Equinox affaires publiques - *1
C.P. 79163 RPO Vanier, Vanier, ON K1L 1A1
Tel: 819-613-2882; *Fax:* 888-237-4765
Toll-Free: 877-640-7933
info@equinoxinc.ca
www.equinoxinc.ca

Vaughan: Bianchi, Presta - *9
#300, 9100 Jane St., Vaughan, ON L4K 0A4
Tel: 905-738-1078; *Fax:* 905-738-0528
www.bianchipresta.com

Vaughan: Bratty & Partners LLP - *14
#200, 7501 Keele St., Vaughan, ON L4K 1Y2
Tel: 905-760-2600; *Fax:* 905-760-2900
info@bratty.com
www.bratty.com

Vaughan: Drudi, Alexiou, Kuchar LLP - *4
#307, 7050 Weston Rd., Vaughan, ON L4L 8G7
Tel: 905-850-6116; *Fax:* 905-850-9146

Vaughan: Fine & Deo - *7
#300, 3100 Steeles Ave. West, Vaughan, ON L4K 3R1
Tel: 905-760-1800; *Fax:* 905-760-0050
Toll-Free: 888-346-3336
info@finedeo.com

Vaughan: Gambin RDQ LLP - *7
#400, 3901 Hwy. 7, Vaughan, ON L4L 8L5
Tel: 905-264-7800; *Fax:* 905-264-7808

Vaughan: Enzo Salvatori - *1
#4, 161 Pennsylvania Ave., Vaughan, ON L4K 1C3
Tel: 416-745-1777; *Fax:* 416-745-2220

Vaughan: Shiner Kent LLP - *3
#203, 3800 Steeles Ave. West, Vaughan, ON L4L 4G9
Tel: 905-798-2929; *Fax:* 905-850-3397

Vermilion Bay: Shirley D. Gauthier - *1
P.O. Box 490, Stn. Main, Vermilion Bay, ON P0V 2V0
Tel: 807-938-7984; *Fax:* 807-227-2902

Walkerton: D.A. Farr - *1
P.O. Box 518, 229 Durham St. East, Walkerton, ON N0G 2V0
Tel: 519-881-1611; *Fax:* 519-881-1733
dfarr@wightman.ca

Walkerton: Magwood, Van De Vyvere, Thompson, & Grove-McClement LLP - *4
#8280, P.O. Box 880, 215 Durham St., Walkerton, ON N0G 2V0
Tel: 519-881-3230; *Fax:* 519-881-3595
wmvt@bmts.com

Wallaceburg: Carscallen, Reinhart, Mathany, Maslak
P.O. Box 409, Stn. Main, 619 James St., Wallaceburg, ON N8A 4X1
Tel: 519-627-2261; *Fax:* 519-627-1030

** indicates number of lawyers*

Wallaceburg: **Hyde, Hyde & McGregor - *2**
233 Creek St., Wallaceburg, ON N8A 4C3
Tel: 519-627-2081; *Fax:* 519-627-1615

Wasaga Beach: **Maurice Loton - *1**
P.O. Box 500, 802 Mosley St., Wasaga Beach, ON L9Z 2H4
Tel: 705-429-4332; *Fax:* 705-429-4683

Wasaga Beach: **McNeill Law Office - *1**
P.O. Box 550, 1014 Mosley St., Wasaga Beach, ON L9Z 1A5
Tel: 705-429-1776; *Fax:* 705-429-7095

Waterdown: **A.S. Lonn - *1**
#23, 35 Main St. North, Waterdown, ON L0R 2H0
Tel: 905-689-6060; *Fax:* 905-689-9578
allan.lonn@on.aibn.com

Waterford: **A. M. Lee Gaunt - *1**
P.O. Box 580, Stn. Port Dover, 46 Main St. South, Waterford, ON N0A 1N0
Tel: 519-583-1411; *Fax:* 519-583-1110
leegaunt@kwic.com

Waterford: **Birnie & Gaunt - *2**
P.O. Box 429, 70 Alice St., Waterford, ON N0E 1Y0
Tel: 519-443-8676; *Fax:* 519-443-5596

Waterford: **C.A. Brennan - *1**
P.O. Box 1229, 19 Main St. South, Waterford, ON N0E 1Y0
Tel: 905-443-8643; *Fax:* 905-443-4489
neilbrennan@bellnet.ca

Waterloo: **Amy, Appleby & Brennan - *3**
372 Erb St. West, Waterloo, ON N2L 1W6
Tel: 519-884-7330; *Fax:* 519-884-7390
aab-lawoffice@rogers.com

Waterloo: **Richard C. Biggs - *1**
500 Dutton Dr., Waterloo, ON N2L 4C6
Tel: 519-886-1678; *Fax:* 519-886-1791
biggslaw@bellnet.ca

Waterloo: **Chris & Volpini - *2**
375 University Ave. East, Waterloo, ON N2K 3M7
Tel: 519-888-0999; *Fax:* 519-888-0995
cvlaw@chrisvolpinilawyers.com

Waterloo: **Dueck, Sauer, Jutzi & Noll LLP - *8**
403 Albert St., Waterloo, ON N2L 3V2
Tel: 519-884-2620; *Fax:* 519-884-0254
tedd@dsjnlaw.com
www.dsjnlaw.com

Waterloo: **W. Marlene Fitzpatrick - *1**
420 Weber St. North, Waterloo, ON N2L 4E7
Tel: 519-725-9500; *Fax:* 519-725-2379
marlenefitzpatrick@on.aibn.com

Waterloo: **Haney, Haney & Kendall - *5**
P.O. Box 185, 41 Erb St. East, Waterloo, ON N2J 3Z9
Tel: 519-747-1010; *Fax:* 519-747-9323
hhk@haneylaw.com

Waterloo: **Fred J. Heimbecker - *1**
295 Weber St. North, Waterloo, ON N2J 3H8
Tel: 519-886-1750; *Fax:* 519-886-0503
heim@bellnet.ca

Waterloo: **William C. Hoskinson - *1**
P.O. Box 22103, 50 Westmount Rd. North, Waterloo, ON N2L 6J7
Tel: 519-571-1022; *Fax:* 519-743-0490

Waterloo: **John E. Lang - *1**
21 Post Horn Place, Waterloo, ON N2L 5E8
Tel: 519-578-3330; *Fax:* 519-578-3337
johnelang@rogers.com

Waterloo: **Kominek, Gladstone - *1**
#311, 55 Erb St. East., Waterloo, ON N2J 4K8
Tel: 519-886-1050; *Fax:* 519-747-9565
glynne.gladstone2@sympatico.ca

Waterloo: **Eric M. Kraushaar - *1**
#5, 620 Davenport Rd., Waterloo, ON N2V 2C2
Tel: 519-886-0088; *Fax:* 519-746-1122
eric@churchill-homes.com

Waterloo: **Paul W. Lang, Q.C. - *1**
347 Beechlawn Dr., Waterloo, ON N2L 5L8
Tel: 519-884-3382; *Fax:* 519-884-1073

Waterloo: **Levesque & Deane - *2**
#5B, 490 Dutton Dr., Waterloo, ON N2L 6H7
Tel: 519-725-2929; *Fax:* 519-725-2920
debbie@kwlegal.com

Waterloo: **Lowes, Salmon & Gadbois - *3**
500 Dutton Dr., Waterloo, ON N2L 4C6
Tel: 519-884-0800; *Fax:* 519-884-1026
Toll-Free: 877-258-2575
tlowes@watlaw.ca
www.watlaw.ca

Waterloo: **Joe Mattes Barrister, Solicitor & Trademark Agent - *1**
#200, 24 Dupont St. East, Waterloo, ON N2J 2G9
Tel: 519-884-5600; *Fax:* 519-884-9963
joe@matteslaw.com

Waterloo: **P.M. Miller - *1**
15 Westmount Rd. South, Waterloo, ON N2L 2K2
Tel: 519-884-1332; *Fax:* 519-884-1161

Waterloo: **Oldfield, Greaves, D'Agostino & Billo - *6**
P.O. Box 16580, 172 King St. South, Waterloo, ON N2J 4X8
Tel: 519-576-7200; *Fax:* 519-576-0131
watlaw@watlaw.com

Waterloo: **Petker & Associates - *3**
295 Weber St. North, Waterloo, ON N2J 3H8
Tel: 519-886-1204; *Fax:* 519-886-5674

Waterloo: **James E. Pitcher - *1**
420 Weber St. North, Waterloo, ON N2J 4A7
Tel: 519-725-9444; *Fax:* 519-725-2379

Waterloo: **Shortt, Hanbidge, Richardson & Welch - *4**
P.O. Box 550, Stn. Waterloo, 7 Union St. East, Waterloo, ON N2J 4B8
Tel: 519-579-5600; *Fax:* 519-579-2725
shs@shslaw.com

Waterloo: **Sloan Strype LLP - *2**
P.O. Box 547, 92 Erb St. East, Waterloo, ON N2J 4B8
Tel: 519-886-1590; *Fax:* 519-886-8545
jsloan@sloanstrypelaw.com
www.sloanstrypelaw.com

Waterloo: **Edward Roy Tschirhart - *1**
291 Faraday Ct., Waterloo, ON N2L 6A4
Tel: 519-880-1374; *Fax:* 519-880-8853
e.tschirhart@sympatico.ca

Waterloo: **Barbara Wallace - *1**
326 Conservation Dr., Waterloo, ON N2V 1V3
Tel: 519-888-0599

Waterloo: **Weir & Fedy - *2**
#105, 109 Erb St. West, Waterloo, ON N2L 1T4
Tel: 519-883-1844; *Fax:* 519-883-1845
jweir@weirfedy.com

Waterloo: **White, Duncan & Linton LLP - *6**
P.O. Box 457, 45 Erb St. East, Waterloo, ON N2J 4B5
Tel: 519-886-3340; *Fax:* 519-886-8651

Waterloo: **Whitney Consulting - *1**
145 Avondale Ave. South, Waterloo, ON N2L 2C5
Tel: 519-342-7457
joe@whitneyconsulting.ca

Watford: **Wallace B. Lang - *1**
5290 Nauvoo Rd., Watford, ON N0M 2S0
Tel: 519-876-2742; *Fax:* 519-876-2073

Welland: **George C.M. Banks - *1**
P.O. Box 127, Stn. Main, 191 Division St., Welland, ON L3B 5P2
Tel: 905-735-1770; *Fax:* 905-735-7031
george.banks@bellnet.ca

Welland: **Vince Bellantino - *1**
8 East Main St., Welland, ON L3B 3W3
Tel: 905-788-3881; *Fax:* 905-788-3885

Welland: **Blackadder Green Marion Halinda & Wood LLP - *5**
P.O. Box 580, 136 East Main St., Welland, ON L3B 5R3
Tel: 905-735-3620; *Fax:* 905-735-1577

Welland: **Flett Beccario, Barristers & Solicitors - *8**
P.O. Box 340, Stn. Main, 190 Division St., Welland, ON L3B 5P9
Tel: 905-732-4481; *Fax:* 905-732-2020
flett@flettbeccario.com
www.flettbeccario.com

Welland: **William V. Frith - *1**
#301, P.O. Box 757, Stn. Main, 76 Division St., Welland, ON L3B 5R5
Tel: 905-735-7582; *Fax:* 905-735-0093
w_firth@iaw.com

Welland: **Houghton, Sloniowski & Stengel - *3**
170 Division St., Welland, ON L3B 4A2
Tel: 905-734-4577; *Fax:* 905-732-3765
Toll-Free: 888-483-9770

Welland: **Rodney J. Kajan - *1**
#102, P.O. Box 130, 60 King St., Welland, ON L3B 5P2
Tel: 905-732-1352; *Fax:* 905-732-0531

Welland: **Kormos & Evans Law Office - *1**
14 Niagara St., Welland, ON L3C 1H9
Tel: 905-732-4424; *Fax:* 905-732-7574
markevans@on.aibn.com
www.markevanslaw.com

Welland: **Anthony W. Pylypuk - *1**
P.O. Box 605, 80 King St., Welland, ON L3B 5R4
Tel: 905-735-2300; *Fax:* 905-735-9230
awpylypuk@pylypuk.com

Welland: **Solugik Public Affairs - *1**
563 Leonard Ave., Welland, ON L3C 3A9
Tel: 905-735-4302; *Fax:* 905-735-0162
andyroy@sympatico.ca

Welland: **Swayze & Swayze - *1**
P.O. Box 667, Stn. Main, 131 Division St., Welland, ON L3B 5R4
Tel: 905-734-4553; *Fax:* 905-734-8015
swayze@bellnet.ca

Welland: **Talmage & DiFiore - *2**
P.O. Box 97, 221 Division St., Welland, ON L3B 5P2
Tel: 905-732-4477; *Fax:* 905-732-4718
talstradi@iaw.on.ca

Welland: **Douglas R. Thomas - *1**
P.O. Box 564, Stn. Main, 9 Main St. East, Welland, ON L3B 5R3
Tel: 905-732-5529; *Fax:* 905-732-2211
thomform@iaw.on.ca

Westport: **Barker Willson Professional Corporation - *3**
P.O. Box 309, 30 Main St., Westport, ON K0G 1X0
Tel: 613-273-3166; *Fax:* 613-273-3676
bwoffice@barkerwillson.com
www.barkerwillson.com

Wheatley: **J.H. Eaton - *1**
26 Erie St. South, Wheatley, ON N0P 2P0
Tel: 519-825-7032; *Fax:* 519-825-9570
joyce.eaton@3web.net

Whitby: **Donna C. Babbs Family Law Professional Corporation - *1**
P.O. Box 358, Stn. Main, 117 King St., Whitby, ON L1N 5S4
Tel: 905-668-7704; *Fax:* 905-665-9229

Whitby: **Michael F. Boland - *1**
114 Green St., Whitby, ON L1N 4C8
Tel: 905-668-2606

Whitby: **David J. Gillespie - *1**
P.O. Box 208, Stn. Main, 214 Dundas St. East, 2nd Fl., Whitby, ON L1N 5S1
Tel: 905-666-2221; *Fax:* 905-666-2344

Whitby: **Stacy Howell**
#208, 420 Green St., Whitby, ON L1N 8R1
Tel: 905-668-7747; *Fax:* 905-668-7787
showell@bellnet.ca

Whitby: **Jenkins & Newman - *3**
106 Colborne St. East, Whitby, ON L1N 1V8
Tel: 905-666-8588; *Fax:* 905-666-4873

Whitby: **Johnston, Montgomery, Barristers & Solicitors - *2**
201 Byron St. South, Whitby, ON L1N 4P7
Tel: 905-666-2252; *Fax:* 905-430-0878
lphillips@lawwhitby.com
www.lawhitby.com

Whitby: **Michaels & Michaels - *1**
#201, 1450 Hopkins St., Whitby, ON L1N 2C3
Tel: 905-665-7711; *Fax:* 905-430-9100
michaels_michaels@on.aibn.com

Whitby: **Rosenberg, Pringle - *2**
#214, 185 Brock St. North, Whitby, ON L1N 4H3
Tel: 905-665-9594; *Fax:* 905-665-7124

** indicates number of lawyers*

Whitby: Edward P. Schein - *1
107 Kent St., Whitby, ON L1N 4Y1
Tel: 905-666-1266; Fax: 905-668-2023

Whitby: Schneider, Howard - *1
107 Kent St., Whitby, ON L1N 4Y1
Tel: 905-668-1677; Fax: 905-668-2023

Whitby: Siksay & Fraser - *2
618 Athol St., Whitby, ON L1N 3Z8
Tel: 905-666-4772; Fax: 905-666-3233

Whitby: B.P. Stelmach - *1
#5, 11 Stanely Ct., Whitby, ON L1N 8P9
Tel: 905-430-6611; Fax: 905-430-6828
stelmach@bellnet.ca

Whitby: Debra J. Sweetman - *1
340 Byron St. South, Whitby, ON L1N 4P8
Tel: 905-666-8166; Fax: 905-666-8163
Toll-Free: 800-428-6944
debrajsweetman@aol.com

Whitby: Thomson Law Firm - *1
P.O. Box 358, Stn. Main, 117 King St., Whitby, ON L1N 5S4
Tel: 905-668-7704; Fax: 905-668-1268

Wiarton: Peter Pegg - *1
P.O. Box 569, 647 Berford St., Wiarton, ON N0H 2T0
Tel: 519-534-2011; Fax: 519-534-4494

Winchester: David J. Barnhart - *1
P.O. Box 730, 489 Main St., Winchester, ON K0C 2K0
Tel: 613-774-2808; Fax: 613-774-5731

Windsor: Ballance & Melville - *2
#100, 251 Goyeau St., Windsor, ON N9A 6V2
Tel: 519-255-1414; Fax: 519-255-7404
dawnmelville@bellnet.ca

Windsor: Barat, Farlam, Millson - *5
#510, 251 Goyeau St., Windsor, ON N9A 6V2
Tel: 519-258-2424; Fax: 519-258-2451
bfm@bellnet.ca

Windsor: Bartlet & Richardes LLP - *13
#1000, Canada Bldg., 374 Ouellette Ave., Windsor, ON N9A 1A9
Tel: 519-253-7461; Fax: 519-253-2321
mail@bartlet.com
www.bartlet.com

Windsor: Belowus Easton English - *3
100 Ouellette Ave., 7th Fl., Windsor, ON N9A 6T3
Tel: 519-973-1900; Fax: 519-973-0225

Windsor: T. James Bennett - *1
661 Champlain Dr., Windsor, ON N9E 1M6
Tel: 519-250-4397

Windsor: Anita M. Berecz - *1
#304, 267 Pelissier St., Windsor, ON N9A 5N8
Tel: 519-258-8306; Fax: 519-258-4184
amberecz law@bellnet.ca

Windsor: Bondy, Riley, Koski - *2
#310, 176 University Ave. West, Windsor, ON N9A 5P1
Tel: 519-258-1641; Fax: 519-258-1725
info@bondyriley.com

Windsor: A.J. Bradie - *2
691 Ouellette Ave., Windsor, ON N9A 4J4
Tel: 519-255-1542; Fax: 519-255-9888
obrodie@mnsi.net

Windsor: Danny Branoff - *1
912 Wyandotte St. East, Windsor, ON N9A 3J8
Tel: 519-258-4244; Fax: 519-258-4247

Windsor: Mario Carnevale Law Office - *2
2488 McDougall Ave., Windsor, ON N8X 3N7
Tel: 519-969-8855; Fax: 519-969-0085

Windsor: Maria Carroccia - *1
#602, Canada Bldg., 374 Ouellette Ave., Windsor, ON N9A 1A8
Tel: 519-258-0905; Fax: 519-258-8755
Toll-Free: 888-959-9917

Windsor: F. Michael Cervi - *1
#400, 1500 Ouellette Ave., Windsor, ON N8X 1K7
Tel: 519-258-9494; Fax: 519-258-9985

Windsor: Chodola Reynolds Binder - *5
720 Walker Rd., Windsor, ON N8Y 2N3
Tel: 519-254-6433; Fax: 519-254-7990
info@crblaw.cawww.facebook.com/pages/Windsor-Lawyers/130689596945631,
www.linkedin.com/company/chodola-reynolds-binder

Windsor: Clarks - *8
#1200, Canada Bldg., 374 Ouellette Ave., Windsor, ON N9A 1A8
Tel: 519-254-4990; Fax: 519-254-2294
info@clarkslaw.com
www.clarkslaw.com

Windsor: Robert J. Comartin - *1
350 Devonshire Rd., Windsor, ON N8Y 2L4
Tel: 519-253-7050; Fax: 519-253-7049

Windsor: Corrent & Macri - *5
#201, 2485 Ouellette Ave., Windsor, ON N8X 1L5
Tel: 519-255-7332; Fax: 519-255-9123
mail@correntmacri.com

Windsor: Culmone Law, Barrister, Solicitor, Notary Public - *1
410 Giles Blvd. East, Windsor, ON N9A 4C6
Tel: 519-258-3632; Fax: 519-977-1199
floro@culmonelaw.com
www.culmonelaw.com

Windsor: David Deluzio Law Firm - *1
#200, 52 Chatham St. West, Windsor, ON N9A 5M6
Tel: 519-256-1994; Fax: 519-256-7233

Windsor: Robert M. DiPietro - *1
#302, 380 Ouellette Ave., Windsor, ON N9A 6X5
Tel: 519-258-8248; Fax: 519-255-7685

Windsor: Jon Dobrowolski - *1
#309, Westcourt Place, 251 Goyeau St., Windsor, ON N9A 6V2
Tel: 519-258-0034; Fax: 519-258-9133

Windsor: Donaldson, Donaldson, Greenaway - *5
547 Devonshire Rd., Windsor, ON N8Y 2L6
Tel: 519-255-7333; Fax: 519-255-7173
ddglaw@on.aibn.com

Windsor: Ducharme Fox LLP - *13
800 University Ave. West, Windsor, ON N9A 5R9
Tel: 519-259-1800; Fax: 519-259-1830
admin@ducharmefox.com

Windsor: Fazio & Associates - *4
333 Wyandotte St. East, Windsor, ON N9A 3H7
Tel: 519-258-5030; Fax: 519-971-9051

Windsor: Julie Fodor - *1
642 Windermere Rd., Windsor, ON N8Y 3E1
Tel: 519-256-8238; Fax: 519-258-5780
jfoder.law@bellnet.ca

Windsor: Gatti Law Professional Corporation - *2
#400, 267 Pelissier St., Windsor, ON N9A 4K4
Tel: 519-258-1010; Fax: 519-258-0163
arg@argatti.com

Windsor: Goldstein DeBiase Manzocco, The Personal Injury Law Firm - *5
#900, 176 University Ave. West, Windsor, ON N9A 5P1
Tel: 519-253-5242; Fax: 519-253-0218
gdm@thepersonalinjurylawfirm.net
www.thepersonalinjurylawfirm.net

Windsor: Goulin & Patrick - *2
500 Windsor Ave., Windsor, ON N9A 6Y5
Tel: 519-258-8073; Fax: 519-977-0694
goulinpa@wincom.net

Windsor: Anthony J. Grassi - *1
#322, 13300 Tecumseh Rd. East, Windsor, ON N8N 4R8
Tel: 519-739-1559
anthonygrassi@bellnet.ca

Windsor: Greg Monforton and Partners - *7
#1300, 100 Ouellette Ave., Windsor, ON N9A 6T3
Tel: 519-258-6490; Fax: 519-258-4104
Toll-Free: 800-663-1145
www.gregmonforton.com

Windsor: Neil M. Guttman
#100, 215 Eugenie St. West, Windsor, ON N8X 2X7
Tel: 519-250-0130; Fax: 519-250-1772

Windsor: Jason P. Howie - *1
350 Devonshire Rd., Windsor, ON N8Y 2L4
Tel: 519-973-1500; Fax: 519-973-9905
jason@jasonpaulhowie.com

Windsor: Kamin, Fisher, Burnett, Ziriada & Robertson - *5
#200, 176 University Ave. West, Windsor, ON N9A 5P1
Tel: 519-252-1123; Fax: 519-977-6503
info@kaminlaw.ca

Windsor: Katzman, Wylupek - *5
1427 Ouellette Ave., Windsor, ON N8X 1K1
Tel: 519-254-6324; Fax: 519-254-6774
www.katzman-wylupek.com

Windsor: Kerr & Kerr - *1
#309, 251 Goyeau St., Windsor, ON N9A 2V2
Tel: 519-252-2211; Fax: 519-252-0132
Toll-Free: 888-772-9552
akerr@kerr-kerr.com

Windsor: Kirwin Partners LLP, Lawyers - *10
423 Pelissier St., Windsor, ON N9A 4L2
Tel: 519-255-9840; Fax: 519-255-1413
www.kirwinpartners.com

Windsor: Christos Kyrtsakas - *1
5655 Tecumseh Rd. East, Windsor, ON N8T 1C8
Tel: 519-974-6303; Fax: 519-974-8644

Windsor: Lisa S. Labute - *1
#407, 251 Goyeau St., Windsor, ON N9A 6V2
Tel: 519-252-6822; Fax: 519-252-2638
lslabute@mnsi.net

Windsor: Legal Assistance of Windsor - *3
85 Pitt St. East, Windsor, ON N9A 2V3
Tel: 519-256-7831; Fax: 519-256-1387
www.uwindsor.ca/legalassistanceofwindsor

Windsor: Maleyko, D'hondt - *3
#260, 2109 Ottawa St., Windsor, ON N8Y 1R8
Tel: 519-258-8220; Fax: 519-258-7788

Windsor: A.R. Mariotti - *1
#202, 176 University Ave. West, Windsor, ON N9A 5P1
Tel: 519-258-1931; Fax: 519-973-7575
arm.law@sympatico.ca

Windsor: Brenda A. McGinty - *1
518 Victoria Ave., Windsor, ON N9A 4M8
Tel: 519-255-1535; Fax: 519-255-1719

Windsor: McTague Law Firm LLP - *21
455 Pelissier St., Windsor, ON N9A 6Z9
Tel: 519-255-4300; Fax: 519-255-4360
info@mctaguelaw.com
www.mctaguelaw.com

Windsor: McWilliams & McWilliams - *1
#710, 100 Ouellette Ave., Windsor, ON N9A 6T3
Tel: 519-258-1100; Fax: 519-258-7384
mjmcwilliams@winlaw.ca

Windsor: Tullio Meconi - *1
349 Wyandotte St. East, Windsor, ON N9A 3H7
Tel: 519-252-7274

Windsor: Donald D. Merritt - *1
#103, 525 Windsor Ave., Windsor, ON N9A 1J4
Tel: 519-258-8060; Fax: 519-258-9877

Windsor: Miller Canfield Paddock & Stone LLP - *21
#300, P.O. Box 1390, 443 Ouellette Ave., Windsor, ON N9A 6R4
Tel: 519-977-1555; Fax: 519-977-1566
www.millercanfield.com

Windsor: S. Frank Miller - *1
518 Victoria Ave., Windsor, ON N9A 4M8
Tel: 519-258-3044; Fax: 519-255-1719
frankmilleratlaw@earthlink.net

Windsor: Joana G. Miskinis - *1
518 Victoria Ave., Windsor, ON N9A 4M8
Tel: 519-254-3757; Fax: 519-255-1719

Windsor: Mousseau DeLuca McPherson Prince LLP - *11
#500, 251 Goyeau, Windsor, ON N9A 6V2
Tel: 519-258-0615; Fax: 519-258-6833
lawyers@mousseaulaw.com

* indicates number of lawyers

Windsor: **Michael P. O'Hearn - *1**
#A-1, P.O. Box 1212, Stn. A, 75 Riverside Dr. East, Windsor, ON N9A 6P8
Tel: 519-255-1250; *Fax:* 519-971-9607
mike.ohearn@sympatico.ca

Windsor: **John G. Ohler - *2**
101 Tecumseh Rd. West, Windsor, ON N8X 1E8
Tel: 519-256-5496; *Fax:* 519-256-1492
ohlerlawfirm@bellnet.ca

Windsor: **James W. Oxley**
1854 Kildare Rd., Windsor, ON N8W 2W7
Tel: 519-258-7211

Windsor: **D.R. Revait - *1**
#209, Royal Windsor Terrace, 380 Pelissier, Windsor, ON N9A 6W8
Tel: 519-258-7030; *Fax:* 519-258-2629
derek.revait@bellnet.ca

Windsor: **Salem & McCullough - *2**
2828 Howard Ave., Windsor, ON N8X 3Y3
Tel: 519-966-3633; *Fax:* 519-972-7788

Windsor: **Daniel W. Scott - *1**
#302, 380 Ouellette Ave., Windsor, ON N9A 6X5
Tel: 519-258-8248

Windsor: **Stephen L. Shanfield - *1**
#333, 880 Ouellette Ave., Windsor, ON N9A 1C7
Tel: 519-258-3338; *Fax:* 519-258-3335
ssh@mnsi.net
www.shanfieldlaw.com

Windsor: **Brian Sherwell - *1**
827 Pillette Rd., Windsor, ON N8Y 3B4
Tel: 519-945-1109; *Fax:* 519-948-0003

Windsor: **Shulgan Martini Marusic LLP - *7**
2491 Ouellette Ave., Windsor, ON N8X 1L5
Tel: 519-969-1817; *Fax:* 519-969-9655
info@smmbarristers.com

Windsor: **Sorensen, Baker - *2**
1600 Wyandotte St. East, Windsor, ON N8Y 1C7
Tel: 519-256-3111; *Fax:* 519-256-5468

Windsor: **R. Craig Stevenson - *1**
#18A, 25 Amy Croft Dr., Windsor, ON N9K 1C7
Tel: 519-735-0777; *Fax:* 519-735-2999
rcslaw@mnsi.net
www.rcraigstevensonlawoffice.com

Windsor: **Stipic Arpino - *3**
1574 Ouellette Ave., Windsor, ON N8X 1K7
Tel: 519-258-3201; *Fax:* 519-258-2665
msa@mnsi.net

Windsor: **Tamara Stomp & Associate - *2**
721 Walker Rd., Windsor, ON N8Y 2N2
Tel: 519-948-9778; *Fax:* 519-948-9773
stomp@mnsi.net

Windsor: **Sutts, Strosberg LLP - *20**
#600, Westcourt Place, 251 Goyeau St., Windsor, ON N9A 6V4
Tel: 519-258-9333; *Fax:* 519-186-6613
www.strosbergco.com

Windsor: **Michael V. Watters - *1**
P.O. Box 7292, Stn. Sandwich, Windsor, ON N9C 3Z1
Tel: 519-253-6877; *Fax:* 519-253-9277

Windsor: **G.V. Wortley - *1**
2490 Talbot Rd., Windsor, ON N9H 1A6
Tel: 519-967-9410; *Fax:* 519-967-9431
wortley@jet2.net

Windsor: **Martin Wunder, Q.C. - *1**
#908, 100 Ouellette Ave., Windsor, ON N9A 6T3
Tel: 519-252-1121

Woodbridge: **Gary A. Beaulne - *2**
#401, 3700 Steeles Ave. West, Woodbridge, ON L4L 8K8
Tel: 905-850-5060; *Fax:* 905-850-5066
Toll-Free: 866-850-5006
garyabeaulne@hotmail.com

Woodbridge: **F. Borgatti - *1**
7135 Islington Ave., 2nd Fl., Woodbridge, ON L4L 1V9
Tel: 905-851-2883; *Fax:* 905-851-2887

Woodbridge: **Bortolussi & Associates, Barristers & Solicitors - *3**
#3, 100 Strada Dr., Woodbridge, ON L4L 5V7
Tel: 905-856-1816; *Fax:* 905-856-6682

Woodbridge: **Roger Bourque - *1**
#300, 3800 Steeles Ave. West, Woodbridge, ON L4L 4G9
Tel: 905-856-7101; *Fax:* 905-856-1524
rogerbourque@bellnet.ca

Woodbridge: **Capo, Sgro, Dilena, Hemsworth, Mendicino - *7**
#400, 7050 Weston Rd., Woodbridge, ON L4L 8G7
Tel: 905-850-7000; *Fax:* 905-850-7050

Woodbridge: **Ralph Ciccia - *1**
#400, 7050 Weston Rd., Woodbridge, ON L4L 8G7
Tel: 905-850-6408; *Fax:* 905-850-7050
rciccia@ciccia.ca

Woodbridge: **Cosman, Gray LLP - *3**
#104, 8 Director Ct., Woodbridge, ON L4L 3Z5
Tel: 905-850-3110; *Fax:* 905-850-3123
mark.cosman@cosmangray.com

Woodbridge: **D'Alimonte Law - *1**
#27, 4300 Steeles Ave. West, Woodbridge, ON L4L 4C2
Tel: 905-264-1553; *Fax:* 905-264-5450
jdalimonte@bellnet.ca

Woodbridge: **Sean L.K. Daley - *1**
#200, 4000 Steeles Ave. West, Woodbridge, ON L4L 4V9
Tel: 905-850-2002; *Fax:* 905-850-2007

Woodbridge: **M. DiPaolo - *1**
#400, 7050 Weston Rd., Woodbridge, ON L4L 8G7
Tel: 905-850-7575; *Fax:* 905-850-7050
mdipaolo@di-paolo.ca

Woodbridge: **Anthony Gagliese - *1**
#12, 5875 Hwy.#7, Woodbridge, ON L4L 8Z7
Tel: 905-264-1449; *Fax:* 905-264-3944
tony@sum-itclub.com

Woodbridge: **John Lo Faso - *1**
#600, 3700 Steeles Ave. West, Woodbridge, ON L4L 8K8
Tel: 905-856-3700; *Fax:* 905-850-9969
johnlofaso@westonlaw.ca

Woodbridge: **Mancini Associates LLP - *3**
#505, 7050 Weston Rd., Woodbridge, ON L4L 8G7
Tel: 905-851-7717; *Fax:* 905-851-7718

Woodbridge: **Massimo Panicali - *1**
#4, 253 Jevlan Dr., Woodbridge, ON L4L 7Z6
Tel: 905-850-2642; *Fax:* 905-850-8544
mass.pan-demonium@on.aibn.com

Woodbridge: **Paradiso & Associates - *1**
#504, 216 Chrislea Rd., Woodbridge, ON L4L 8S5
Tel: 905-850-6006; *Fax:* 905-850-5616
Toll-Free: 800-429-735
mail@paradisolaw.com
www.paradisolaw.com

Woodbridge: **Piccin, Bottos - *5**
#201, 4370 Steeles Ave. West, Woodbridge, ON L4L 4Y4
Tel: 905-850-0155; *Fax:* 905-850-0498

Woodbridge: **Claudio Polsinelli - *1**
#600, 3700 Steeles Ave. West, Woodbridge, ON L4L 8K8
Tel: 905-856-3700; *Fax:* 905-856-1213
claudio@westonlaw.ca

Woodbridge: **Rigobon, Carli - *3**
#401, 3700 Steeles Ave. West, Woodbridge, ON L4L 8K8
Tel: 905-850-5060; *Fax:* 905-850-5066
michael@rigoboncarli.com
www.rigoboncarli.com

Woodbridge: **Felix Rocca - *1**
#302, 7050 Weston Rd., Woodbridge, ON L4L 8G7
Tel: 905-851-7747; *Fax:* 905-851-7834
felixrocca@rogers.com

Woodbridge: **Jack Rosati - *1**
#206, 4550 Hwy. 7, Woodbridge, ON L4L 4Y6
Tel: 905-264-7566; *Fax:* 905-264-4054

Woodbridge: **Rovazzi, Pallotta - *4**
#901, 3700 Steeles Ave. West, Woodbridge, ON L4L 8K8
Tel: 905-850-2468; *Fax:* 905-850-4066
m.rovazzi@rplaw.ca

Woodbridge: **Devi D. Sharma - *1**
#625, 7050 Weston Rd., Woodbridge, ON L4L 8G7
Tel: 905-856-6404; *Fax:* 905-856-6264

Woodbridge: **Stabile Professional Corporation - *2**
#905, 3700 Steeles Ave. West, Woodbridge, ON L4L 8K8
Tel: 905-851-6711; *Fax:* 905-851-5773
vista@stablaw.com

Woodbridge: **Tanzola & Sorbara - *5**
#101, 10 Director Ct., Woodbridge, ON L4L 7E8
Tel: 905-265-2252; *Fax:* 905-265-0667

Woodbridge: **Turner, Brooks - *1**
#15, 4220 Steeles Ave. West, Woodbridge, ON L4L 3S8
Tel: 905-851-7110; *Fax:* 905-851-4229
sturner.barrister@bellnet.ca

Woodbridge: **P.M. Valenti - *1**
#300, West Bldg., 3800 Steeles Ave., Woodbridge, ON L4L 4G9
Tel: 905-850-8550; *Fax:* 905-850-9998

Woodstock: **George H. Bishop - *1**
32 Metcalf St., Woodstock, ON N4S 3E7
Tel: 519-539-8559; *Fax:* 519-539-2401
angie-bishoplaw@rogers.com

Woodstock: **Debra A. Brown - *1**
94 Graham St., Woodstock, ON N4S 6J7
Tel: 519-539-9870; *Fax:* 519-539-9248
debra@dabrownlaw.com

Woodstock: **Peter H. Kratzmann - *1**
48 Vansittart Ave., Woodstock, ON N4S 6E2
Tel: 519-537-2221; *Fax:* 519-537-5150
phklaw@primus.ca

Woodstock: **Gordon Lemon - *3**
P.O. Box 336, 487 Princess St., Woodstock, ON N4S 7X6
Tel: 519-537-6629; *Fax:* 519-539-2459
info@beattylaw.on.ca

Woodstock: **Gary D. McQuaid - *1**
380 Hunter St., Woodstock, ON N4S 4G2
Tel: 519-539-1310

Woodstock: **White Coad LLP - *3**
P.O. Box 1059, 5 Wellington St. North, Woodstock, ON N4S 6P1
Tel: 519-421-1500; *Fax:* 519-539-6926
rcoad@whitecoad.com
www.whitecoad.com

Woodstock: **R.B. Wolyniuk - *3**
P.O. Box 1233, 19 Riddell St., Woodstock, ON N4S 8R2
Tel: 519-539-7431; *Fax:* 519-539-4975

Prince Edward Island

Alberton: **J. Allan Shaw, Law Corporation - *1**
P.O. Box 40, 479 Church St., Alberton, PE C0B 1B0
Tel: 902-853-3313; *Fax:* 902-853-3753

Charlottetown: **Campbell Lea - *9**
P.O. Box 429, 15 Queen St., Charlottetown, PE C1A 7K7
Tel: 902-566-3400; *Fax:* 902-566-9266
office@campbelllea.com
www.campbelllea.com

Charlottetown: **Carr, Stevenson & MacKay - *9**
Peake House, P.O. Box 522, 50 Water St., Charlottetown, PE C1A 7L1
Tel: 902-892-4156; *Fax:* 902-566-1377
csm@csmlaw.com
www.csmlaw.com/

Charlottetown: **Kenneth A. Clark Law Office - *1**
#21, P.O. Box 2831, Stn. Central, 25 Queen St., Charlottetown, PE C1A 8C4
Tel: 902-566-9996; *Fax:* 902-566-9997

Charlottetown: **Diamond & Associates - *3**
P.O. Box 39, Stn. Central, 224 Queen St., Charlottetown, PE C1A 7K2
Tel: 902-892-1200; *Fax:* 902-892-4848
diamond@isn.net

Charlottetown: **Foster Hennessey MacKenzie - *3**
P.O. Box 38, Stn. Central, 129 Water St., Charlottetown, PE C1A 7K2
Tel: 902-892-3406; *Fax:* 902-368-8239

** indicates number of lawyers*

Charlottetown: Peter C. Ghiz - *1
120 Prince St., Charlottetown, PE C1A 4R4
Tel: 902-628-6300; *Fax:* 902-628-6399
Toll-Free: 800-399-3221
peterghiz@peterghizlawyer.com

Charlottetown: Macnutt & Dumont - *4
P.O. Box 965, 57 Water St., Charlottetown, PE C1A 7M4
Tel: 902-894-5003; *Fax:* 902-368-3782
info@macnuttdumont.ca

Charlottetown: Matheson & Murray - *8
#202, Queen Square, 119 Queen St., Charlottetown, PE C1A 4B3 Canada
Tel: 902-894-7051; *Fax:* 902-368-3762
info@mathesonandmurray.com
www.mathesonandmurray.com

Charlottetown: McInnes Cooper - *7
#620, BDC Pl., 119 Kent St., Charlottetown, PE C1A 1N3
Tel: 902-368-8473; *Fax:* 902-368-8346
mcctn@mcinnescooper.com
www.mcinnescooper.com

Charlottetown: Philip Mullally Q.C. - *1
P.O. Box 2560, Stn. Central, 51 University Ave., Charlottetown, PE C1A 8C2
Tel: 902-892-5452; *Fax:* 902-892-7013
pmullally@philipmullallylawoffice.com

Charlottetown: Paul J.D. Mullin Q.C. - *1
P.O. Box 604, Stn. Central, 14 Great George St., Charlottetown, PE C1A 7L3
Tel: 902-368-3221; *Fax:* 902-894-7491
mullinlaw@pei.aibn.com

Charlottetown: Brenda J. Picard - *1
PEI Legal Aid, P.O. Box 2000, Stn. Central, 40 Great George St., Charlottetown, PE C1A 7N8
Tel: 902-368-6043; *Fax:* 902-368-6122
bjpicard@gov.pe.ca

Charlottetown: Elizabeth S. Reagh Q.C. - *1
17 West St., Charlottetown, PE C1A 3S3
Tel: 902-892-7667; *Fax:* 902-368-8629
reagh@isn.net

Montague: Alfred K. Fraser, Q.C. - *2
P.O. Box 516, 554 Main St. North, Montague, PE C0A 1R0
Tel: 902-838-2041; *Fax:* 902-838-2754
pearle@akfraserlaw.com

Mount Stewart: Marlene R. Clarke Q.C. - *1
P.O. Box 63, Mount Stewart, PE C0A 1T0
Tel: 902-676-2954; *Fax:* 902-676-2954

Stratford: Randy Price Consulting Ltd. - *1
31 Brandy Lane, Stratford, PE C1B 1M8
Tel: 902-566-2195; *Fax:* 902-566-2195
randy.price@pei.sympatico.ca

Summerside: Kathleen Loo Craig - *1
P.O. Box 11, Stn. Main, Summerside, PE C1N 4P6
Tel: 902-887-2900; *Fax:* 902-887-2100

Summerside: David R. Hammond Q.C. - *1
740A Water St. East, Summerside, PE C1N 5X1
Tel: 902-436-4267; *Fax:* 902-436-4268
dhammond@pei.aibn.com

Summerside: Lyle & McCabe - *2
P.O. Box 300, 290 Water St., Summerside, PE C1N 4Y8
Tel: 902-436-4296; *Fax:* 902-436-4072
www.lylemccabelawoffice.com

Summerside: Stephen D.G. McKnight - *1
P.O. Box 1570, Stn. Main, 494 Granville St., Summerside, PE C1N 4K4
Tel: 902-436-4851; *Fax:* 902-436-5063
stephen@keyandmcknight.com

Summerside: Robert McNeill - *1
251 Water St., Summerside, PE C1N 1B5
Tel: 902-436-4847; *Fax:* 902-436-8183

Québec

Alma: Les Avocats Mario Bouchard Inc. - *3
2340, au du Pont sud, RR#1, Alma, QC G8B 5V2
Tél: 418-668-7677; *Téléc:* 418-668-0539
mariob46@cgocable.ca
www.mariobouchard.com

Alma: Larouche, Lalancette, Pilote & Bouchard - *7
723, ch du Pont-Taché nord, Alma, QC G8B 5B7
Tél: 418-662-6475; *Téléc:* 418-662-9239
www.llpb.ca

Amos: Ayotte Martineau McGuire Boyer - *2
39A, av 1re ouest, Amos, QC J9T 1T7
Tél: 819-732-5258; *Téléc:* 819-732-0394

Amos: Bigué, avocats - *6
91, Première ave ouest, Amos, QC J9T 1T7
Tél: 819-732-8911; *Téléc:* 819-732-1470

Amos: Geoffroy, Matte, Kélada & Associés - *4
4, rue Principale, Amos, QC J9T 2K6
Tél: 819-732-1698; *Téléc:* 819-732-7513
geoffroy.matte@sympatico.ca

Anjou: M.L. Anne Boutin - *1
#2220, 7999, boul les Galeries d'Anjou, Anjou, QC H1M 1W9
Tél: 514-353-4411; *Téléc:* 514-353-4553
boutina@cadillacfairview.com

Asbestos: Denis Beaubien - *1
601, boul Simoneau, Asbestos, QC J1T 4G7
Tél: 819-879-7177; *Téléc:* 819-879-2962
denis.beaubien@cgocable.ca

Baie-Comeau: Wullaert, Bachir, Tremblay, Bibeau et Trudeau - *4
279, boul LaSalle, Baie-Comeau, QC G4Z 1T2
Tél: 418-294-8793; *Téléc:* 418-294-8258

Baie-Saint-Paul: Gagné Letarte - *16
#205A, 11, rue St-Jean-Baptiste, Baie-Saint-Paul, QC G3Z 1M1
Tél: 418-435-6890; *Téléc:* 418-435-3082
www.gagneletarte.qc.ca

Beauport: Blouin & Associés - *3
1217, av Royal, Beauport, QC G1E 2B2
Tél: 418-663-2931; *Téléc:* 418-663-3792
blouin@blouinetassocies.com
www.blouinetassocies.com

Beloeil: Bastien, Morand, Blanchette - *6
201, boul Laurier, Beloeil, QC J3G 4G8
Tél: 450-467-5849; *Téléc:* 450-467-3152
Ligne sans frais: 877-467-5849
rbastien@avocatsbmb.com

Beloeil: Doré, Tourigny, Fiset & Associés - *5
#314, 535, boul Sir-Wilfrid Laurier, Beloeil, QC J3G 5E9
Tél: 450-446-8474; *Téléc:* 450-467-7134

Berthierville: André Sylvestre
1300, rue Notre Dame, Berthierville, QC J0K 1A0
Tél: 450-836-6213; *Téléc:* 450-836-7712
andre_sylvestre@bellnet.ca

Boischatel: JBRP & Associés Inc. - *1
CP 141, 112 Montmorency, Boischatel, QC G0A 1H0
Tél: 418-822-2904; *Téléc:* 418-822-4192

Boucherville: Lecompte Deguire Avocats - *2
1019, rue de la Ventrouze, Boucherville, QC J4B 5V3
Tél: 450-641-0065; *Téléc:* 450-641-3721
lecomptedeguire@videotron.ca

Bromont: Communications Anie Perrault - *1
207, rue Martin, Bromont, QC J2L 3B3
Tél: 450-263-3728; *Téléc:* 450-263-3731
anie@commap.ca

Brossard: Pierre Chenail & associés inc. - *1
9195, Croissant Rollin, Brossard, QC J4X 2P7
pierre.chenail@videotron.ca

Brossard: Louis Hargreaves, Avocat - *1
5480, croissant Beaumanoir, Brossard, QC J4Z 2G4
Tél: 450-462-3142; *Téléc:* 450-462-5881
louishargreaves@hotmail.com

Buckingham: Denis Montreuil - *1
143, rue Joseph, Buckingham, QC J8L 1G3
Tél: 819-986-2701

Cabano: Annick Bédard - *1
CP 370, 14, rue Pelletier, Cabano, QC G0L 1E0
Tél: 418-854-2206; *Téléc:* 418-854-0072

Chandler: Gaul & Associes - *1
CP 757, Chandler, QC G0C 1K0
Tél: 418-689-2241

Chibougamau: Larouche & Girard, Avocats - *3
127, rue des Forces armées, Chibougamau, QC G8P 3A1
Tel: 418-748-6468; *Fax:* 418-748-2323
larouchegirard@lino.com

Chicoutimi: Martin Côté, Avocat - *1
CP 1475, Stn. Racine, 106, rue Garon, Chicoutimi, QC G7H 3C1
Tél: 418-543-3111; *Téléc:* 418-543-0753

Chicoutimi: Girard Allard Guimond Avocats - *3
#202, 200, rue Racine est, Chicoutimi, QC G7H 1S1
Tél: 418-543-0725; *Téléc:* 418-543-1765
girardallardguimond@bellnet.ca

Châteauguay: Marie-Andrée Mallette - *1
272, boul St-Jean-Baptiste, Châteauguay, QC J6K 3C2
Tél: 450-699-9499; *Téléc:* 450-699-9710
marieandreemallette@videotron.ca

Cowansville: Claude Boulet - *1
#330, 104, rue du Sud, Cowansville, QC J2K 2X2
Tél: 450-263-0061; *Téléc:* 450-263-9468
c.boulet@endirect.qc.ca

Cowansville: Dontigny & Morin - *2
436, rue du Sud, Cowansville, QC J2K 2X7
Tél: 450-263-5458; *Téléc:* 450-263-7376

Deschambault: Bernatchez Associés - Avocats - *1
209, ch du Roy, Deschambault, QC G0A 1S0
Tél: 418-286-2287; *Téléc:* 418-286-6453
www.avoc.ca

Dolbeau-Mistassini: Bouchard Voyer Boily - *3
1273, boul Wallberg, Dolbeau-Mistassini, QC G8L 1H3
Tél: 418-276-2234; *Téléc:* 418-276-3582
bvb@bellnet.ca

Dolbeau-Mistassini: Simard, Boivin, Lemieux - *4
112, av de l'Église, Dolbeau-Mistassini, QC G8L 4W4
Tél: 418-276-2570; *Téléc:* 418-276-8797
Ligne sans frais: 877-276-2570
blh@blh.ca
www.sblavocats.com

Donnacona: Claude Dussault - *1
299, rue Notre-Dame, Donnacona, QC G3M 1H1

Dorval: Amaron, Viberg & Pecho - *3
#200, 280, av Dorval, Dorval, QC H9S 3H4
Tél: 514-636-4992; *Téléc:* 514-636-8122

Dorval: Francine Gagnon - *1
545A, prom Lakeshore, Dorval, QC H9S 2B1
Tél: 514-631-6429; *Téléc:* 514-631-5606

Drummondville: Paul Biron, Avocat - *1
#202, 150, rue Marchand, Drummondville, QC J2C 4N1
Tél: 819-477-8741; *Téléc:* 819-477-7166

Drummondville: Roger Blais Avocat Inc - *2
215, rue Lindsay, Drummondville, QC J2C 1N8
Tél: 819-477-2235; *Téléc:* 819-477-8674
blaisavocats@bellnet.ca

Drummondville: Boudreau, Méthot, Tourigny - *2
83, rue St-Damase, Drummondville, QC J2B 6E5
Tél: 819-477-3517; *Téléc:* 819-477-0700

Drummondville: FBL - *1
1325, boul Lemire, Drummondville, QC J2C 7X9
Tél: 819-477-1234; *Téléc:* 819-474-4757
benoit.laflamme@fbl.com

Drummondville: Hinse, Tousignant et Associés - *3
360, rue Marchand, Drummondville, QC J2C 4N9
Tél: 819-477-3424; *Téléc:* 819-477-7728
Ligne sans frais: 888-488-3424
hinsetousignant@bellnet.ca
www.hinsetousignantavocats.com

Drummondville: Jutras et Associés - *5
449, rue Hériot, Drummondville, QC J2B 1B4
Tél: 819-477-6321; *Téléc:* 819-474-5691
info@jutras.qc.ca
www.jutras.qc.ca

Gatineau: Jean-Paul Aubry - *1
175, rue Champlain, Gatineau, QC J8X 3R3
Tél: 819-771-8645; *Téléc:* 819-771-9338

Gatineau: Christine M. Auger - *1
177, rue Gamelin, Gatineau, QC J8Y 1W1
Tél: 819-770-4022; *Téléc:* 819-770-9729

** indicates number of lawyers*

Gatineau: Beaudry, Bertrand Avocats - *10
Maison du Citoyen, 25, rue Laurier, 4e étage, Gatineau, QC J8X 4C8
Tel: 819-770-4880; Fax: 819-595-4979
avocats@beaudry-bertrand.com

Gatineau: Robert Bélanger, Avocat - *1
307, boul Saint-Joseph, Gatineau, QC J8Y 3Y6
Tél: 819-771-6679; Téléc: 819-771-9675
robert.belanger.avocat@sympatico.ca

Gatineau: Françoise Boivin - *1
#104, 160, boul de l'Hôpital, Gatineau, QC J8T 8J1
Tél: 819-243-7293; Téléc: 819-243-5913
francoiseboivin@videotron.ca

Gatineau: Boucher & Associés - *2
768, boul Saint-Joseph, Gatineau, QC J8Y 4B8
Tél: 819-568-0041; Téléc: 819-568-4569

Gatineau: Dufour, Isabelle, Leduc, Bouthillette, Lapointe, Beaulieu - *9
#301, 200, rue Montcalm, Gatineau, QC J8Y 3B5
Tel: 819-778-1870; Fax: 819-778-8860
dilblb@dilblb.com

Gatineau: Pierre Fontaine - *1
25, rue Bernier, Gatineau, QC J8Z 1E7
Tél: 819-771-6578

Gatineau: Gaudreau - *2
167, rue Notre-Dame-de-l'Ile, Gatineau, QC J8X 3T3
Tél: 819-770-7928; Téléc: 819-770-1424
bergeron.gaudreau@qc.aira.com

Gatineau: André Gingras, Avocat - *1
30, rue Maricourt, Gatineau, QC J29 1R9
Tel: 819-595-4748; Fax: 819-772-4193
mariannamerica@videotron.ca

Gatineau: Alain Gourd Communications Inc. - *1
22, ch Cochrane, Gatineau, QC J9H 2G2
Tél: 819-664-4487; Téléc: 819-684-0322
alain@gourdcommunications.com

Gatineau: Kehoe, Blais, Major - Avocats - *3
#200, 344, boul Maloney est, Gatineau, QC J8P 7A6
Tél: 819-663-2439; Téléc: 819-663-4816
kbm@bellnet.ca

Gatineau: Lapointe, Cayen - *3
#200, 370, boul Gréber, Gatineau, QC J8T 5R6
Tél: 819-568-0663; Téléc: 819-568-0226
lapointecayen@videotron.ca

Gatineau: Letellier & Associés - *7
#127, 139, boul de l'Hôpital, Gatineau, QC J8T 8A3
Tél: 819-243-1336; Téléc: 819-243-9425
info@letellier.com
www.letellier.com

Gatineau: E. Wayne Lora - *2
175, rue Champlain, Gatineau, QC J8X 3R3
Tél: 819-778-6511; Téléc: 819-770-5703
wlora@mac.com

Gatineau: Pharand Joyal - *5
166, rue Wellington, Gatineau, QC J8X 2J4
Tél: 819-771-7781; Téléc: 819-771-0608
pharand.joyal@qc.aira.com

Gatineau: Ste-Marie & Lacombe - *2
175, rue Champlain, Gatineau, QC J8X 3R3
Tél: 819-770-7800; Téléc: 819-770-5703

Gatineau: Sarrazin & Charlebois - *2
162, rue Wellington, Gatineau, QC J8X 2J4
Tél: 819-770-4888; Téléc: 819-770-0712
sarrazin-charlebois@videotron.ca

Gatineau: Stratégies corporatives Houle - *1
#200, 81, Jean-Proulx St., Gatineau, QC J8Z 1W2
Tél: 819-771-6213; Téléc: 819-771-3858
fhoule@strategieshoule.com

Gatineau: Tobaccostat Canada - *1
141 Frank-Robinson Ave., Gatineau, QC J9H 4A9
Tel: 819-684-0244; Fax: 819-684-9979
lmartial@magma.ca

Gatineau: Pierre Verreault - *1
1-9, St-Dominique, Gatineau, QC J9A 1A1
Tél: 819-772-7757
verreault@hotmail.com

Gracefield: Louise Major - *1
40, rue Principale, Gracefield, QC J0X 1W0
Tél: 819-463-3477; Téléc: 819-463-4603
lmajor@notarius.net

Granby: Gaudet Galipeau Parcel - Avocats - *5
18, rue Court, Granby, QC J2G 4Y5
Tél: 450-777-1070; Téléc: 450-777-5960
gaudav@bellnet.ca

Granby: Daniel Laflamme - *1
#200, 328, rue Principale, Granby, QC J2G 2W4
Tél: 450-372-3545

Granby: Gilles Viens - *1
380, rue St-Jacques, Granby, QC J2G 3N6
Tél: 450-777-1312; Téléc: 450-777-8659
viensg@qc.aira.com

Hampstead: Judith Lifshitz - *1
30, ch Belsize, Hampstead, QC H3X 3J8
Tél: 514-488-8561; Téléc: 514-488-0121

Joliette: Asselin & Asselin - Avocats - *4
569, rue Archambault, Joliette, QC J6E 2W7
Tél: 450-755-5050; Téléc: 450-755-5111

Joliette: Boulard & Richer - Avocates - *2
198, rue St-Joseph, Joliette, QC J6E 5C6
Tél: 450-753-8360; Téléc: 450-753-8359

Joliette: Ferland & Bélair - *3
#150, 430, rue de Lanaudière, Joliette, QC J6E 7X1
Tél: 450-759-7412; Téléc: 450-759-5366
Ligne sans frais: 888-759-7412
avocats@ferlandbelair.ca

Joliette: Alain Généreux Avocat - *1
400, rue Baby, Joliette, QC J6E 2W1
Tél: 450-752-6655; Téléc: 450-752-1098
alaingenereux@citenet.net

Joliette: Claudette Vincelette - *1
125, rue Beaudry nord, Joliette, QC J6E 6A4
Tél: 450-759-3958; Téléc: 450-756-2933
vincelet@primus.ca

Jonquière: Turcotte Fortin Cantin Marceau & Gagnon - *6
CP 2040, Stn. Kenogami, 2106 Sainte-Famille, Jonquière, QC G7X 7X6
Tél: 418-547-2108; Téléc: 418-547-9519
tfcmg@bellnet.ca

Kahnawake: JTNE - *1
P.O. Box 355, Kahnawake, QC J0L 1B0
Tel: 514-946-4785
joe@mohawk.ca

Kahnawake: Mohawk Council of Kahnawake Legal Services - *4
CP 720, Kahnawake, QC J0L 1B0
Tél: 450-632-7500; Téléc: 450-638-3663
legal@mck.ca
www.kahnawake.com

L'Ile Perrot: Aumais Chartrand - Avocats - *6
#12, 100, boul Don Quichotte, L'Ile Perrot, QC J7V 6L7
Tél: 514-425-2233; Téléc: 514-453-0977
aumaischartrand@bellnet.ca
www.aumaischartrand.com

La Malbaie: Marie-Claude Dallaire - *1
#220, CP 237, 251, rue John-Nairne, La Malbaie, QC G5A 1T7
Tél: 418-665-6417; Téléc: 418-665-6174
marieclaude.dallaire@ccjg.qc.ca

Lac-Beauport: Alain Baccigalupo - *1
27, ch le Tour du Lac, Lac-Beauport, QC G0A 2C0
Tél: 418-849-0396; Téléc: 418-656-7861

Lac-Mégantic: Daniel Drouin - *1
4927, rue Laval, Lac-Mégantic, QC G6B 1E2
Tél: 819-583-0787; Téléc: 819-583-4631
ddrouin@notarius.net

Lac-Mégantic: Monty, Coulombe
5109 rue Frontenac, Lac-Mégantic, QC G6B 1H2
Tél: 819-583-3833; Téléc: 819-583-5673

Lac-Simon: Sylvie Savoie - *1
Lac-Simon, QC J5A 2G9
Tél: 819-428-9366

Lachine: Communications Da Vinci - *1
605, 36e av, Lachine, QC H8T 3L1
Tel: 514-713-3683
pierre.leger@sympatico.ca

Lachine: Laurier, Cêré & Couturier - *3
356, 90e av, Lachine, QC H8R 2Z7
Tél: 514-363-0220; Téléc: 514-363-9495
laurierj@videotron.ca

Lachine: Louise Saint-Amour - *1
#3, 1375, rue Notre-Dame, Lachine, QC H8S 2C9
Tél: 514-634-8243; Téléc: 514-634-3044
saintamourlouise@yahoo.ca

Lachute: William M.C. Steeves - *1
18, boul de la Providence, Lachute, QC J8H 3K9
Tél: 450-562-2465; Téléc: 450-562-2467

Lasalle: Pascal Pillarella - *1
#202, 7925, boul Newman, Lasalle, QC H8N 2N9
Tél: 514-364-3100; Téléc: 514-364-1604

Laval: 9122-9203 Québec Inc. - *1
200, J.-J.-Joubert Pl., Laval, QC H7G 4H6
Tél: 514-862-0682; Téléc: 514-450-6698
eithier.michel@sympatico.ca

Laval: Alepin Gauthier, Avocats - *13
#601, 3080, boul Le Carrefour, Laval, QC H7T 2R5
Tél: 450-681-3080; Téléc: 450-681-1476
info@alepin.com
www.alepin.com

Laval: Allaire & Associés - *17
#202, CP 422, Stn. St-Martin, 1333, boul Chomedey, Laval, QC H7V 3Z4
Tél: 450-978-5866; Téléc: 450-978-5871

Laval: Jean L. Beauchamp - *1
405, rue Santerre, Laval, QC H7H 2X6
Tél: 450-628-6330; Téléc: 450-628-6389
jlbeauchamp@videotron.ca

Laval: Bélanger, Garceau - *2
#309, 400, boul St-Martin ouest, Laval, QC H7M 3Y8
Tél: 450-669-1313; Téléc: 450-669-1122
belangergarceau@videotron.ca

Laval: Bertrand, Guerard & Bleau - *3
134, boul. des Laurentides, Laval, QC H7G 2T3
Tél: 450-663-0851

Laval: François Bordeleau - *1
60, rue Alexandre, Laval, QC H7G 3K9
Ligne sans frais: 877-975-2060

Laval: France Cormier - *1
3682, rue Isabelle, Laval, QC H7P 4Z6
Tel: 450-622-7616; Fax: 450-622-5254
francecormier@videotron.ca

Laval: Dagenais, Poupart - *5
#650, 2550, boul Daniel-Johnson, Laval, QC H7T 2L1
Tél: 450-978-2442; Téléc: 450-973-4010

Laval: Robert Dupuis - *1
509, rue Lartigue, Laval, QC H7N 3T6
Tél: 450-663-5280; Téléc: 450-663-5281
Ligne sans frais: 866-663-5280
merobertdupuis_avocat@msn.com

Laval: Fournier, Diamond - *2
#1102, 2500, boul Daniel-Johnson, Laval, QC H7T 2P6
Tél: 450-682-7011; Téléc: 450-686-8566

Laval: Michel B. Fournier - *1
#204, 4150, boul St-Martin ouest, Laval, QC H7T 1C1
Tél: 450-686-2600; Téléc: 450-681-3642
mb.fournier@sympatico.ca

Laval: GTDS Inc. - *1
#320, Place Lunebourg, 1200 Chomedey Blvd., Laval, QC H7V 3Z3
Tél: 514-993-8220; Téléc: 514-450-6883
marc.delahaut@gtdsinc.com

Laval: Lamarche, Pierre - *1
237A, boul des Prairies, Laval, QC H7N 2T8
Tél: 450-667-9802; Téléc: 450-667-5740
plamarche@g1bonavocat.com
www.g1bonavocat.com

* indicates number of lawyers

Laval: **Jean Mignault - *1**
#2020, 400 Armand-Frapier, Laval, QC H7V 4B4
Tél: 514-332-4110; *Téléc:* 514-334-6043
jean.mignault@2020.net

Laval: **Pierre Morin Conseil - *1**
#213, 3221, autorte 440 ouest, Laval, QC H7P 5P2
Tél: 450-680-1126; *Téléc:* 450-680-1889
pmorin@gpim.org

Laval: **Turcotte, Nolet - *5**
#470, 500, boul St. Martin ouest, Laval, QC H7M 3Y2
Tél: 450-901-0151; *Téléc:* 450-901-0152
turcotte.nolet@qc.aira.com

Longueuil: **Raymond Allard - *1**
1150, boul Marie-Victorin, Longueuil, QC J4G 2M4
Tél: 450-442-8600; *Téléc:* 450-463-1043
rallard@strsm.qc.ca

Longueuil: **Archambault, Desjardins & Godin - *11**
1251, rue Beauregard, Longueuil, QC J4K 2M3
Tél: 450-674-4906; *Téléc:* 450-651-8644

Longueuil: **Bernard, Brassard - Avocats - *13**
#200, 101, boul Roland-Therrien, Longueuil, QC J4H 4B9
Tél: 450-670-7900; *Téléc:* 450-670-0673
Ligne sans frais: 888-670-7900
commitment@bernard-brassard.com
www.bernard-brassard.com

Longueuil: **Jacques Boissonnault - *1**
630, ch de Chambly, Longueuil, QC J4H 3L8
Tél: 514-831-3052; *Téléc:* 514-450-6512
Ligne sans frais: 866-462-3192
avocat.jb@videotron.ca

Longueuil: **Dubois et Associés - *3**
#97, 45, Place Charles-Lemoyne, Longueuil, QC J4K 5G5
Tél: 450-646-2613; *Téléc:* 450-646-4225
duboisetassocies@videotron.ca

Longueuil: **Monique Fortier - *2**
#95, 45, Place Charles Lemoyne, Longueuil, QC J4K 5G5
Tél: 450-651-4418

Lorraine: **André J. Courtemanche - *1**
107, boul Val D'Ajol, Lorraine, QC J6Z 4G4
Tél: 450-582-4242; *Téléc:* 450-965-6958
acourtemanche@muridal.ca

Lévis: **Lagueux Roy Gosselin - *4**
CP 1247, Stn. Lévis, 67, Côte-du-Passage, Lévis, QC G6V 6R8
Tél: 418-833-0311; *Téléc:* 418-833-1749
glmotaires@notarius.net

Lévis: **Pelletier D'Amours - *7**
CP 3500, 6300, boul de la Rive sud, Lévis, QC G6V 6P9
Tél: 418-835-4944; *Téléc:* 418-835-8847
Ligne sans frais: 800-314-4944

Magog: **Yves Messier - *1**
#100, 155 Principale ouest, Magog, QC J1X 2A7
Tél: 819-868-0714; *Fax:* 819-868-0746
yavocat@videotron.ca
www.quebeclegal.com

Matane: **Deschenes & Doiron, Avocats, s.e.n.c. - *2**
352, av St-Jérôme, Matane, QC G4W 3B1
Tél: 418-562-2097; *Téléc:* 418-562-2926
dedoiron@globetrotter.qc.ca

Mont-Joli: **Yvan Pelletier - *1**
CP 333, Stn. BureauChef, 1555, boul Jacques-Cartier, Mont-Joli, QC G5H 3L2
Tél: 418-775-4306

Mont-Laurier: **Roger Rancourt, Avocat - *1**
673, Carré Laurier, Mont-Laurier, QC J9L 2W4
Tél: 819-623-4485

Mont-Laurier: **Simard, Deschênes et Barrette - *4**
445, rue du Pont, Mont-Laurier, QC J9L 2R8
Tél: 819-623-4259; *Téléc:* 819-623-9628

Mont-Royal: **Consultations Delaney Inc. - *1**
101, av Dresden, Mont-Royal, QC H3P 3K1
Tél: 514-733-7754; *Téléc:* 514-733-0586
delaneyf@sympatico.ca

Montmagny: **Robert Daveluy, Q.C. - *1**
#22, 46, rue St-Jean-Baptiste est, Montmagny, QC G5V 1J8
Tél: 418-248-1072

Montmagny: **Marcel Guimont - *2**
CP 482, 25, rue du Palais-de-Justice, Montmagny, QC G5V 3S9
Tél: 418-248-1530; *Téléc:* 418-248-4157

Montpellier: **Nouveau Re g'Art Inc. - *1**
39, ch de la Baie-de-l'Ours, Montpellier, QC J0V 1M0
Tél: 819-428-1459; *Fax:* 819-428-1461
mlalonde@nouveauregart.com

Montréal: **Adessky Lesage - *2**
#525, 4150, rue Ste-Catherine ouest, Montréal, QC H3Z 2Y5
Tél: 514-288-8070; *Téléc:* 514-288-8655
general@adesskylesage.com

Montréal: **L'Agence Goodwin - *3**
#200, 839, rue Sherbrooke est, Montréal, QC H2L 1K6
Tél: 514-598-5252; *Téléc:* 514-598-1878
artistes@goodwin.agent.ca
www.agencegoodwin.com

Montréal: **Joseph W. Allen - *1**
#203, 6855, av de l'Epée, Montréal, QC H3N 2C7
Tél: 514-274-9393; *Téléc:* 514-274-5614
jwallenimmlaw@bellnet.ca

Montréal: **Amar & Associés - *3**
#1700, 770 Sherbrooke St., Montréal, QC H3B 1G1
Tél: 514-878-1532; *Téléc:* 514-878-4761
michael@amar.ca

Montréal: **Claude F. Archambault - Avocat - *3**
50, rue Le Royer ouest, Montréal, QC H2Y 1W7
Tél: 514-845-4234; *Téléc:* 514-845-4236
www.claudefarchambault.pj.ca

Montréal: **Arsenault, Lemieux - *2**
2328, rue Ontario est, Montréal, QC H2K 1W1
Tél: 514-527-8903; *Téléc:* 514-527-1410
arsenault.lemieux@qc.aira.com

Montréal: **Andrew Barbacki - *1**
#2920, 500, place d'Armes, Montréal, QC H2Y 2W2
Tél: 514-397-1752; *Téléc:* 514-847-1212

Montréal: **Baron Abrams - *9**
#200, 4141, rue Sherbrooke ouest, Montréal, QC H3Z 1B8
Tél: 514-935-7783; *Téléc:* 514-989-1811
info@baronabrams.com

Montréal: **Barsalou Lawson - *10**
#1500, 2000, av McGill College, Montréal, QC H3A 3H3
Tel: 514-982-3355; *Fax:* 514-982-2550
www.barsalou.ca

Montréal: **Howard A. Barza - *1**
#450, 2015, rue Peel, Montréal, QC H3A 1T8
Tél: 514-288-9322; *Téléc:* 514-288-2562

Montréal: **Bastien & Champagne - *2**
#100, 6621, rue Sherbrooke est, Montréal, QC H1N 1C7
Tél: 514-253-0876; *Téléc:* 514-253-2578

Montréal: **Jacques Bazinet - *1**
4276, rue Fabre, Montréal, QC H2J 3T6
Tél: 514-527-1702; *Téléc:* 514-597-1352

Montréal: **BCF LLP - *61**
1100, boul René-Lévesque ouest, 25e étage, Montréal, QC H3B 5C9
Tél: 514-397-8500; *Téléc:* 514-397-8515
info@bcf.ca
www.bcf.ca

Montréal: **Beaudry Dessurealt - *3**
#304, 480, boul St-Laurent, Montréal, QC H2Y 3Y7
Tél: 514-282-0727; *Téléc:* 514-282-9363

Montréal: **Diane Bélanger, Avocate - *2**
178, Jean-Talon est, Montréal, QC H2R 1S7
Tél: 514-597-9807; *Téléc:* 514-490-1807

Montréal: **Bélanger, Sauvé - *73**
#1700, 1, Place Ville Marie, Montréal, QC H3B 2C1
Tél: 514-878-3081; *Fax:* 514-878-3053
info@belangersauve.com
www.belangersauve.com

Montréal: **Peter J. Bellan - *1**
#1A, 5130, rue Charleroi, Montréal, QC H1G 2Z8
Tél: 514-955-0691; *Téléc:* 514-322-5069

Montréal: **Edouard J. Belliardo - *1**
#701, 4, rue Notre-Dame est, Montréal, QC H2Y 1B8
Tél: 514-845-6253; *Téléc:* 514-845-8056

Montréal: **Nicole Benchimol - *1**
#1200, 2015, rue Peel, Montréal, QC H3A 1T8
Tél: 514-844-1515; *Téléc:* 514-845-4472

Montréal: **Bérard Avocats - *2**
417, rue des Seigneurs, 2e étage, Montréal, QC H3J 1X7
Tél: 514-934-1760; *Téléc:* 514-934-1212

Montréal: **Berger & Winston - *2**
#1150, 615, boul René-Lévesque ouest, Montréal, QC H3B 1P5
Tél: 514-288-4177; *Téléc:* 514-876-1090
martin@bergerandwinston.com

Montréal: **Jean Bernier - *1**
560, boul St Joseph est, Montréal, QC H2J 1J9
Tél: 514-849-2301; *Téléc:* 514-849-2309

Montréal: **Elaine Bissonnette - *1**
3892, rue Monselet, Montréal, QC H1H 2C1
Tel: 514-323-8770; *Fax:* 514-323-8700
ebissonnette@sympatico.ca
www.avocatebissonnette.com

Montréal: **Marc Bissonnette - *1**
#301, 4, rue Notre-Dame est, Montréal, QC H2Y 1B7
Tél: 514-871-8250; *Téléc:* 514-871-2892
marc.bissonnette@sympatico.ca

Montréal: **Harry Blank - *1**
#1416, 1255, rue University, Montréal, QC H3B 3X1
Tél: 514-866-1125; *Téléc:* 514-866-6898
hablank@videotron.ca

Montréal: **Harry J.F. Bloomfield - *1**
#1720, 1080, Côte du Beaver Hall Hill, Montréal, QC H2Z 1S8
Tél: 514-871-9571; *Téléc:* 514-397-0816
hbloomfield@fieldbloom.com
www.bloomfieldandassociates.ca

Montréal: **Sonia, Bogdaniec - *1**
#47, 450, rue St-Gabriel, Montréal, QC H2Y 2Z9
Tél: 514-942-0471

Montréal: **Rika Bohbot - *1**
#1511, 555, rue Chabanel ouest, Montréal, QC H2N 2J2
Tél: 514-385-3000; *Téléc:* 514-385-6625

Montréal: **Boucher Harper - *7**
#610, 630, rue Sherbrooke ouest, Montréal, QC H3A 1E4
Tél: 514-878-1900; *Téléc:* 514-878-3679

Montréal: **Pierre-Paul Boucher - *1**
7568, rue St-Denis, Montréal, QC H2R 2E6
Tél: 514-495-8900; *Téléc:* 514-495-8367

Montréal: **François Bourdon - *1**
2308, rue Sherbrooke est, Montréal, QC H2K 1E5
Tél: 514-526-0821; *Téléc:* 514-521-5397

Montréal: **Jacques Bourgault - *1**
7575, rue des Ecores, Montréal, QC H2E 2W5
Tél: 514-987-4534; *Téléc:* 514-522-8222

Montréal: **Boyer, Gariépy - *4**
#200, 417, rue St-Nicolas, Montréal, QC H2Y 2P4
Tél: 514-287-9585; *Téléc:* 514-844-5243
boga@bellnet.ca

Montréal: **Diane Brais - *1**
#700, 240, rue St-Jacques ouest, Montréal, QC H2Y 1L9
Tél: 514-985-5454; *Téléc:* 514-985-5433
braislaw@qc.aibn.com

Montréal: **Braman Barbacki Moreau - *8**
#1300, 2001, av McGille College, Montréal, QC H3A 1G1
Tél: 514-286-1144; *Téléc:* 514-288-4773
bbminfo@bbmlex.com

Montréal: **Sarto Brisebois - *2**
#710, 10, rue St-Jacques, Montréal, QC H2Y 1L3
Tél: 514-849-9444; *Téléc:* 514-849-0119

Montréal: **Brisset Bishop -Avocats - *6**
#2020, 2020, rue University, Montréal, QC H3A 2A5
Tél: 514-393-3700; *Fax:* 514-393-1211
general@brissetbishop.com
www.brissetbishop.com

Montréal: **Yvan Brodeur - *1**
#401, 31, rue St-Jacques, Montréal, QC H2Y 1K9
Tél: 514-849-5659; *Téléc:* 514-849-3633

Montréal: **P.R. Brosseau**
#D90, 1321, rue Sherbrooke ouest, Montréal, QC H3G 1J4
Tél: 514-842-6066

** indicates number of lawyers*

Montréal: Jacques Brunet - *1
#103, 3714, rue Ontario est, Montréal, QC H1W 1R9
Tél: 514-524-6638

Montréal: Rebecca Butovsky - *1
3562, av de Vendome, Montréal, QC H4A 3M7
Tél: 514-484-2942

Montréal: Cabinet de Relations Publiques National Inc. - *3
#800, 2001, av McGill College, Montréal, QC H3A 1G1
Tél: 514-843-7171; Fax: 514-843-6976
info@mtl.national.ca
www.national.ca

Montréal: Daniel Caisse - *3
33, St-Jacques, 4e étage, Montréal, QC H2Y 1L3
Tél: 514-288-2250
caisseetrichard@qc.aira.com

Montréal: Diane G. Cameron - *1
#206, 4700, av Bonavista, Montréal, QC H3W 2C5
Tél: 514-483-2619; Téléc: 514-483-3616

Montréal: Campbell, Cohen, Leveille - *4
#1802, 2, Place Alexis Nihon, 3500, boul de Maisonneuve ouest, Montréal, QC H3Z 3C1
Tél: 514-937-9445; Téléc: 514-937-2618

Montréal: Capital Hill Group/Groupe Capital Hill - *1
#C-23, 1100, de la Gauchetière ouest, Montréal, QC H3B 2S2
Tél: 514-844-5530; Téléc: 514-844-5165
info@capitalhill.ca

Montréal: Andre Carbonneau - *1
2567, rue Ontario est, Montréal, QC H2K 1W6
Tél: 514-528-2626; Téléc: 514-528-2615
acarbonn@sprynet.com

Montréal: Pauline Cazelais, Q.C. - *1
2339, Terrasse Guindon, Montréal, QC H1H 1L7
Tél: 514-522-5427

Montréal: Cerundolo & Maiorino - *2
1807, rue Jean-Talon est, Montréal, QC H1E 1T4
Tél: 514-376-0335; Téléc: 514-376-6334

Montréal: Morris Chaikelson - *1
4950, av Ponsard, Montréal, QC H3W 2A5
Tél: 514-482-1896; Téléc: 514-482-0359
chaimor@videotron.ca

Montréal: Chalifoux, Montpetit, Vaillancourt & Associés - *12
#200, 28, rue Notre-Dame est, Montréal, QC H2Y 1B9
Tél: 514-842-1006; Téléc: 514-842-1811

Montréal: François Chapados - *1
#2400, 1010, rue Sherbrooke ouest, Montréal, QC H3A 2T2
Tél: 514-844-2234; Téléc: 514-844-2087

Montréal: Charbonneau & Archambault - *2
#2420, 500, place d'Armes, Montréal, QC H2Y 2W2
Tél: 514-842-0754

Montréal: Charness, Charness & Charness - *3
#1100, 440, boul René-Lévesque ouest, Montréal, QC H2Z 1V7
Tel: 514-878-1808; Fax: 514-871-1149
char3law@bellnet.ca

Montréal: Maurice Chevalier - *1
#1407, 3555, rue Berri, Montréal, QC H2L 4G4
Tél: 514-845-5551

Montréal: Choquette Beaupré Rheaume - *4
#200, 5316, av du Parc, Montréal, QC H2V 4G7
Tél: 514-270-3192; Téléc: 514-270-8876

Montréal: Colby, Monet, Demers, Delage & Crevier - *16
#2900, Tour McGill College, 1501, av McGill College, Montréal, QC H3A 3M8
Tel: 514-284-3663; Fax: 514-284-1961
cmddc@colby-monet.com
www.colby-monet.com

Montréal: Gabrielle Collu - *1
3646, av Laval, Montréal, QC H2X 3C9
Tél: 514-844-7338; Téléc: 514-849-9689
collug@videotron.ca

Montréal: Lulu Cornellier - *1
#2821, 1, Place Ville Marie, Montréal, QC H3B 4R4
Tél: 514-842-1822; Téléc: 514-842-0052
lulucor@videotron.ca

Montréal: Benoit Côté - *1
1252, rue Beaubien est, Montréal, QC H2S 1T9
Tél: 514-272-5755
benoit.cote@bellnet.ca

Montréal: Couzin Taylor LLP - *3
CP 4550, Stn. B, Montréal, QC H3B 5J3
Tél: 514-879-6600; Téléc: 514-879-2666
marcel.guilbault@ca.ey.com

Montréal: Cyr, Hamel, Bégin - *3
#300, 13301, rue Sherbrooke est, Montréal, QC H1A 1C2
Tél: 514-642-2676; Téléc: 514-642-1663
jacquescyr@vocat.com
www.chbavocats.ca

Montréal: Daigneault, avocats inc. - *4
#400, Place D'Youville, 353, rue Saint-Nicolas, Montréal, QC H2Y 2P1
Tél: 514-985-2929; Téléc: 514-985-0595
Ligne sans frais: 888-228-5834
enviro@daigneaultinc.com
www.daigneaultinc.com

Montréal: Jean-Louis Daunais - *1
#100, 10550, rue Iberville, Montréal, QC H2B 2V1
Tél: 514-385-1601

Montréal: Davies Ward Phillips & Vineberg S.E.N.C.R.L., s.r.l. - *242
1501, av McGill College, 26e étage, Montréal, QC H3A 3N9
Tél: 514-841-6400; Téléc: 514-841-6499
Ligne sans frais: 888-841-6400
jfournier@dwpv.com
www.dwpv.com

Montréal: De Grandpré Chait SENCRL-LLP - *62
#2900, 1000, rue de la Gauchetière ouest, Montréal, QC H3B 4W5
Tel: 514-878-4311; Fax: 514-878-4333
info@degrandpre.com
www.degrandpre.com

Montréal: Claude de la Madeleine - *1
3600, boul Henri-Bourassa est, Montréal, QC H1H 1J4
Tél: 514-323-2112

Montréal: Charles Derome - *1
5064, av du Parc, Montréal, QC H2V 4G1
Tél: 514-271-4700; Téléc: 514-271-4708
charles.derome@videotron.net

Montréal: Claude Des Marais - *1
1206, boul St. Joseph, Montréal, QC H2J 1L6
Tél: 514-521-0047

Montréal: Suzanne Deschamps - *1
1555, rue Peel, 14e étage, Montréal, QC H3A 3L8
Tél: 514-872-6215; Téléc: 514-872-6225
sdeschamps@ville.montreal.qc.ca

Montréal: Desjardins, Lapointe, Mousseau, Bélanger - *9
#2185, 600, rue de la Gauchetière ouest, Montréal, QC H3B 4L8
Tél: 514-875-5404; Téléc: 514-875-5647
notaire@dlmb.ca
www.dlmb.ca

Montréal: Robert Desjardins - *1
4515, rue Notre-Dame ouest, Montréal, QC H4C 1S3
Tél: 514-932-0819

Montréal: Desrosiers, Turcotte, Vanclair, Massicotte - *6
#503, 480, boul St. Laurent, Montréal, QC H2Y 3Y7
Tél: 514-387-9284; Téléc: 514-397-9922

Montréal: Donato Di Tullio - *1
7647, boul Gouin est, Montréal, QC H1E 1A7
Tél: 514-648-1048; Téléc: 514-648-3288
ditullio@odyssee.net

Montréal: Doyon Izzi Nivoix - *6
#501, 6455, rue Jean-Talon est, Montréal, QC H1S 3E8
Tél: 514-253-3338; Téléc: 514-251-0560
info@dinlex.com

Montréal: Druker Zilbert Schwartz - *5
#605, 1255, carré Phillips, Montréal, QC H3B 3G5
Tél: 514-871-1300; Téléc: 514-871-1304

Montréal: Mario Du Mesnil - *2
1595, rue St-Hubert, 4e étage, Montréal, QC H2L 3Z2
Tél: 514-526-6625; Téléc: 514-524-4341

Montréal: Duceppe, Théoret & Associés - *3
1595, rue St-Hubert, 4e étage, Montréal, QC H2L 3Z2
Tél: 514-526-6621; Téléc: 514-524-4341

Montréal: Dugas & Legros - *2
P.O. Box 1000, Stn. M, 4545, av Pierre-de-Coubertin, Montréal, QC H1V 3R2
Tel: 514-252-3137; Fax: 514-253-7156
juridique@loisirquebec.qc.ca

Montréal: Emile J. Fattal - *1
#705, 1134, rue Ste-Catherine ouest, Montréal, QC H3B 1H4
Tél: 514-861-4545; Téléc: 514-874-1639
occidental@europe.com

Montréal: Jon M. Feldman - *1
#1500, 1 Westmount Sq., Montréal, QC H3Z 2P9
Tel: 514-935-6222
jfeldman@jlaw.ca

Montréal: Filteau & Belleau - *2
#301, 28, rue Notre-Dame est, Montréal, QC H2Y 1B9
Tél: 514-843-7877; Téléc: 514-499-1889

Montréal: Finkelberg, Light - *1
#1200, 1, Westmount Sq., Montréal, QC H3Z 2P9
Tel: 514-932-7392; Fax: 514-932-0990
plight@sympatico.ca

Montréal: Fishman Flanz Meland Paquin SENCRL/LLP - *11
#4100, 1250, boul René-Lévesque ouest, Montréal, QC H3B 4W8
Tel: 514-932-4100; Fax: 514-932-4170
info@ffmp.ca
www.ffmp.ca

Montréal: C.A. Fitzwilliam - *1
#2821, 1, Place Ville Marie, Montréal, QC H3B 4R4
Tél: 514-940-5353
cf@fitzwilliamlegal.com

Montréal: Frankel & Spina - *2
#401, 60, rue St-Jacques, Montréal, QC H2Y 1L5
Tél: 514-849-3544; Téléc: 514-849-4457
plvspina@frankelspina.ca

Montréal: Franklin & Franklin - *2
#545, 4141, rue Sherbrooke ouest, Montréal, QC H3Z 1B8
Tél: 514-935-3576; Téléc: 514-935-6862
info@franklinlegal.com

Montréal: Fridhandler & Goldberg - *2
#1700, 700, rue Sherbrooke ouest, Montréal, QC H3A 1G1
Tel: 514-288-7929; Fax: 514-844-7290
bfridhandler@bellnet.ca

Montréal: Frumkin, Feldman & Glazman - *3
#2270, Place du Canada, 1010, rue de la Gauchetière ouest, Montréal, QC H3B 2N2
Tél: 514-861-2812; Téléc: 514-861-6062

Montréal: Jean-Rene Gagnon - *1
#200, 606, rue Cathcart, Montréal, QC H3B 1K9
Tél: 514-393-9500; Téléc: 514-393-9324
ljalbert@gga-mtl.ca

Montréal: Garceau Pasquin Pagé Viens - *15
204, Place d'Youville, Montréal, QC H2Y 2B4
Tél: 514-845-5171; Téléc: 514-845-5578
lesavocats@procassur.com

Montréal: Gariepy, Marcoux, Richard, DuBois - *9
#2420, 500, place d'Armes, Montréal, QC H2Y 2W2
Tél: 514-845-3533; Téléc: 514-845-9522
gmrd@gmrd.com

Montréal: Gasco Goodhue - *15
#2100, 1080, côte du Beaver Hall, Montréal, QC H2Z 1S8
Tél: 514-397-0066; Téléc: 514-397-0393
lawyers@gasco.qc.ca
www.gasco.qc.ca

Montréal: Ulrich Gautier - *1
#2350, 500, place D'Armes, Montréal, QC H2Y 2W2
Tél: 514-288-3344; Téléc: 514-288-3344
ugautier@videotron.ca

Montréal: Gendron, Carpentier, S.E.N.C - *2
#300, 615, boul René-Lévesque ouest, Montréal, QC H3B 1P5
Tél: 514-395-4527; Téléc: 514-395-6031
cargen@bellnet.ca

** indicates number of lawyers*

Montréal: Gervais & Gervais - *1
#2100, 500, place d'Armes, Montréal, QC H2Y 2W2
Tél: 514-288-4241; *Téléc*: 514-849-9984

Montréal: GGA Communications Inc. - *1
#200, 606, rue Cathcart, Montréal, QC H3B 1K9
Tél: 514-393-9500; *Téléc*: 514-393-9324
www.ggacom.com

Montréal: Gingras Ouellet - *2
4141, av Pierre-de-Coubertin, Montréal, QC H1V 3N7
Tél: 514-252-4638; *Téléc*: 514-252-6906

Montréal: Goldwater, Dubé, Family Law - *4
#2310, 3500, de Maisonneuve ouest, Montréal, QC H3Z 3C1
Tél: 514-861-4367; *Téléc*: 514-861-7601
inquiries@goldwaterdube.com
www.goldwaterdube.com

Montréal: Gottlieb & Pearson - *9
#1920, 2020, rue University, Montréal, QC H3A 2A5
Tél: 514-288-1744; *Téléc*: 514-288-6629
thibault@gottliebpearson.com

Montréal: Gouveia, Gouveia - *3
#1704, 507, Place d'Armes, Montréal, QC H2Y 2W8
Tél: 514-844-0116; *Téléc*: 514-844-9053

Montréal: Elizabeth Greene - *1
#650, 4141, rue Sherbrooke ouest, Montréal, QC H3Z 1B8
Tél: 514-934-4852; *Téléc*: 514-935-3559

Montréal: Gross, Pinsky - *11
2, Place Alexis Nihon, 3500, boul de Maisonneuve ouest, Montréal, QC H3Z 3C1
Tel: 514-934-1333; *Fax*: 514-933-0810
gropin@grosspinsky.com

Montréal: Gurman, Crevier Inc. - *2
#700, 125, rue Chabanel ouest, Montréal, QC H2N 1E4
Tél: 514-858-1118; *Téléc*: 514-858-1121
agurman@gurman-crevier.com

Montréal: Hadjis & Hadjis - *2
#707, 1117, rue Ste-Catherine ouest, Montréal, QC H3B 1H9
Tél: 514-849-3526; *Téléc*: 514-849-1595

Montréal: Martine Hamel - *1
#300, 13301, rue Sherbrooke est, Montréal, QC H1A 1C2
Tél: 514-642-4473; *Téléc*: 514-642-1663

Montréal: Hamilton, Cooper, Ashkenazy - *3
#401, 4226, boul St-Jean, Montréal, QC H9G 1X5
Tél: 514-626-0266; *Téléc*: 514-626-0011
info@hcalaw.ca

Montréal: Handelman, Handelman & Schiller - *3
#1610, 1255, rue Université, Montréal, QC H3B 3X3
Tél: 514-866-5071; *Téléc*: 514-866-4210
re@hhslaw.ca

Montréal: Hanna Glasz & Sher - *5
#1750, 770, rue Sherbrooke ouest, Montréal, QC H3A 1G1
Tél: 514-284-9551; *Téléc*: 514-284-3419
briansher@qc.aibn.com

Montréal: Hébert, Downs, Lepage, Soulière & Carette - *6
#2830, 500, place d'Armes, Montréal, QC H2Y 2W2
Tél: 514-284-2351; *Téléc*: 514-284-2354
edowns@hdavocates.com
www.hdavocats.com

Montréal: Brent K. Hussey - *1
#200, 280, av Droval, Montréal, QC H9S 3H4
Tél: 514-636-4992; *Téléc*: 514-636-8122
bkhussey@videotron.ca

Montréal: Hutchins Caron & Associates, Barristers & Solicitors - *5
#700, 485 rue McGill, Montréal, QC H2Y 2H4
Tel: 514-849-2403; *Fax*: 514-849-4907
Toll-Free: 877-849-2403
admin@hutchinslegal.ca
www.hutchinslegal.ca

Montréal: Michel A. Iacono, BA, BCL, LL.M. Avocat-Barrister & Solicitor - *1
#2000, 300, rue Léo-Pariseau, Montréal, QC H2X 4B3
Tél: 514-288-1414

Montréal: I.H. Kaufman - *1
#711, 1117, rue Ste-Catherine ouest, Montréal, QC H3B 1H9
Tél: 514-282-7401; *Téléc*: 514-282-9209

Montréal: Kierans & Guay - *2
#440, 606, rue Cathcart, Montréal, QC H3B 1K9
Tel: 514-866-3394; *Fax*: 514-866-3398

Montréal: Kliger & Kliger - *2
#808, 1255, carré Phillips, Montréal, QC H3B 3G1
Tél: 514-281-1720; *Téléc*: 514-281-0678

Montréal: Kounadis Perreault - *3
#2000, 300, av Leo-Pariseau, Montréal, QC H2X 4B3
Tél: 514-844-8631; *Téléc*: 514-844-6691

Montréal: Kugler Kandestin - *7
#2101, 1, Place Ville-Marie, Montréal, QC H3B 2C6
Tél: 514-878-2861; *Téléc*: 514-875-8424
info@kugler-kandestin.com
www.kugler-kandestin.com

Montréal: Lucien Lachapelle - *1
5971, rue St-Hubert, Montréal, QC H2S 2L8
Tél: 514-277-2164

Montréal: Gaetan Lagarde - *2
#201, 1554, boul Mont-Royal est, Montréal, QC H2J 1Z2
Tél: 514-521-2442; *Téléc*: 514-525-5561
gaela@videotron.ca

Montréal: Lamarre Perron Lambert Vincent - *6
#200, 480, boul St-Laurent, Montréal, QC H2Y 3Y7
Tél: 514-798-1515; *Téléc*: 514-798-5599

Montréal: Raymond Landry - *1
#404, 505 boul René-Lévesque ouest, Montréal, QC H2Z 1Y7
Tel: 514-908-2171; *Fax*: 514-940-7044
rlandry@ca.inter.net

Montréal: Lapointe Rosenstein Marchand Melançon - *70
#1400, 1250, boul René-Lévesque ouest, Montréal, QC H3B 5E9
Tel: 514-925-6300; *Fax*: 514-925-9001
Toll-Free: 800-728-6228
www.lrmm.com

Montréal: LaTraverse Avocats - *4
#1510, 1010, rue Sherbrooke ouest, Montréal, QC H3A 2R7
Tél: 514-938-1313; *Téléc*: 514-938-3691
latraverse@latraverse.ca
www.latraverse.ca

Montréal: Lazare & Altschuler - *2
#2210, 1010, rue Sherbrooke ouest, Montréal, QC H3A 2R7
Tél: 514-878-3341; *Téléc*: 514-878-3314
lazare@lazalt.com

Montréal: Micheline Lebrun-Sylvestre - *1
#305, 10500, boul de l'Acadie, Montréal, QC H4N 2V4

Montréal: John E. Lechter - *1
#202, 2015, rue Drummond, Montréal, QC H3G 1W7
Tel: 514-845-4287; *Fax*: 514-845-1803

Montréal: Léger Robic Richard, S.E.N.C.R.L. - *23
Centre CDP Capital, Bloc E, 8e étage, 1001, Square-Victoria, Montréal, QC H2Z 2B7
Tél: 514-987-6242; *Téléc*: 514-845-7874
info@robic.com
www.robic.ca

Montréal: Liebman & Associés
#1500, 1, carré Westmount, Montréal, QC H3Z 2P9
Tél: 514-846-0666; *Téléc*: 514-935-2314
info@liebman.org
www.liebman.org

Montréal: Lord & Associes - *6
#210, 1010, rue Ste-Catherine est, Montréal, QC H2L 2G3
Tél: 514-864-7313; *Téléc*: 514-864-7329

Montréal: Robert Loulou - *1
#1, 7924, rue St-Denis, Montréal, QC H2R 2G1
Tél: 514-388-3511; *Téléc*: 514-388-3211

Montréal: Lozeau Gonthier Masse Richard - *8
#1900, 1010, rue de la Gauchetière ouest, Montréal, QC H3B 2N2
Tél: 514-981-5600; *Téléc*: 514-981-5601
lgmr@ican.net

Montréal: Mannella & Associés - *3
3055, boul de l'Assomption, Montréal, QC H1N 2H1
Tel: 514-899-5375; *Fax*: 514-899-0476
mannella@qc.aira.com

Montréal: Marchi, Bellemare - *5
#200, 400, ave McGill, Montréal, QC H2Y 2G1
Tél: 514-288-5753; *Téléc*: 514-284-6606
marchibellemare.com

Montréal: Mario-Olivier Massie
5400, boul Gouin ouest, Montréal, QC H4J 1C5
Tel: 514-338-2303; *Fax*: 514-338-3153

Montréal: Maynard & Zaor - *3
#1101, 507, Place d'Armes, Montréal, QC H2Y 2W8
Tél: 514-288-1101; *Téléc*: 514-499-8548

Montréal: McConomy, Narvey, Green - *3
#1500, 1255, rue University, Montréal, QC H3B 3X2
Tél: 514-866-4466; *Téléc*: 514-866-4467

Montréal: McGilton Johnston Hodess - *3
#1210, 2045, rue Stanley, Montréal, QC H3A 2V4
Tél: 514-842-1714; *Téléc*: 514-842-1718

Montréal: Melançon, Marceau, Grenier & Sciortino - *15
#300, 1717, boul René-Lévesque est, Montréal, QC H2L 4T3
Tél: 514-525-3414; *Téléc*: 514-525-2803
www.mmgs.qc.ca

Montréal: Jean Mercier - *1
#203, 4059, rue Hochelaga, Montréal, QC H1W 1K4
Tél: 514-252-0888

Montréal: Miller & Khazzam - *2
#525, 4150, Ste-Catherine ouest, Montréal, QC H3Z 2Y5
Tél: 514-875-8040; *Téléc*: 514-875-8044

Montréal: Miller, Adel & Associés - *3
#1210, 507, Place d'Armes, Montréal, QC H2Y 2W8
Tél: 514-845-4151; *Téléc*: 514-845-0306
aadel@adellaw.net

Montréal: Miratech Consulting Group - *1
555, boul René-Lévesque ouest, Montréal, QC H2Z 1B1
Tél: 514-393-1378; *Téléc*: 514-284-1385
pducharme@marcon.qc.ca

Montréal: Moisan Lasalle Perreault - *2
#280, 450, rue Sherbrooke est, Montréal, QC H2L 1J8
Tél: 514-844-3077; *Téléc*: 514-844-1018
raymondelasalle@qc.aira.com

Montréal: Mondor, Rougeau, Lambert, Le Borgne - *6
#200, 402, rue Notre-Dame est, Montréal, QC H2Y 1C8
Tél: 514-840-9119; *Téléc*: 514-840-0177

Montréal: Monette Barakett, Avocats S.E.N.C. - *25
#2100, 1010, rue de la Gauchetière ouest, Montréal, QC H3B 2R8
Tél: 514-878-9381; *Téléc*: 514-878-3957
monette@monette-barakett.com
www.monette-barakett.com

Montréal: Carmelo Morabito - *1
#3001, 5095, rue Jean-Talon est, Montréal, QC H1S 3G4
Tél: 514-727-0332; *Téléc*: 514-727-9315
carmorab@total.net

Montréal: Myszka & Tepner - *2
#204, 4781, av Van Horne, Montréal, QC H3W 1J1
Tél: 514-737-4069

Montréal: R.E. Notkin & Assoc. Inc. - *1
4814 Cedar Cres., Montréal, QC H3W 2H9
Tel: 514-738-4271
rnotkin@post.harvard.edu

Montréal: Nudleman Lamontagne - *2
#458, 1981, ave McGill College, Montréal, QC H3A 2W9
Tél: 514-866-6674; *Téléc*: 514-866-9822
info@nlglegal.ca

Montréal: O'Reilly & Associés - *4
#1007, 1155, rue University, Montréal, QC H3B 3A7
Tél: 514-871-8117; *Téléc*: 514-871-9177

Montréal: Octane - *1
417, rue Saint-Pierre, Montréal, QC H2Y 2M4
laucoin@octane-strategie.com

Montréal: Oligny & Jacques - *2
#107, 1394, du Mont-Royal est, Montréal, QC H2J 1Y7
Tél: 514-871-2240; *Téléc*: 514-871-0874
oligny@generation.net

* indicates number of lawyers

***Montréal*: Pateras & Iezzoni - *5**
#2314, 500, place d'Armes, Montréal, QC H2Y 2W2
Tél: 514-284-0860; *Téléc:* 514-843-7990
fgill@pateras-iezzoni.com

***Montréal*: Pearl & Associates - *3**
1170, Place du Frère André, 4e étage, Montréal, QC H3B 3C6
Tél: 514-861-1170; *Téléc:* 514-861-0850
Ligne sans frais: 866-710-1170
lawyers@pearlandassociates.com

***Montréal*: John J. Pepper, Q.C & Associates - *1**
#2500, 1155, boul René-Lévesque ouest, Montréal, QC H3B 2K4
Tél: 514-875-6565; *Téléc:* 514-843-8415

***Montréal*: Gregoire Perron & Assocjes - *1**
84, rue Notre-Dame ouest, 5e étage, Montréal, QC H2Y 1S6
Tel: 514-285-6441; *Fax:* 514-285-8589
Toll-Free: 888-285-6441
gperron@videotron.ca

***Montréal*: Frederick R. Phillips - *1**
5511, place Bradford, Montréal, QC H3W 2M6
Tél: 514-733-8469

***Montréal*: Phillips, Friedman, Kotler - *18**
#900, Place du Canada, 1010, rue de la Gauchetière ouest, Montréal, QC H3B 2P8
Tél: 514-878-3371; *Téléc:* 514-878-3691
info@pfklaw.com
www.pfklaw.com/

***Montréal*: Marcel Plante - *1**
6984, rue St-Denis, Montréal, QC H2S 2S4
Tél: 514-272-8217

***Montréal*: Polak, Therrien, Turcotte - *1**
#1500, 1, carré Westmount, Montréal, QC H3Z 2P9
Tél: 514-935-6226; *Téléc:* 514-935-2314

***Montréal*: Polisuk Lord - *2**
#2650, 1155, boul René-Lévesque ouest, Montréal, QC H3B 4S5
Tél: 514-861-8546; *Téléc:* 514-861-1298
rwlord@polisuklord.com

***Montréal*: Pollack, Kravitz & Teitelbaum - *3**
#1810, 1, carre Westmount, Montréal, QC H3Z 2P9
Tél: 514-905-1373; *Téléc:* 514-905-1377

***Montréal*: Pragmatis Inc. - *1**
730, boul Georges-Vanier, Montréal, QC H3J 2T3
Tel: 514-941-7125; *Fax:* 514-227-5430
mpoirier@pragmatis.biz

***Montréal*: Propre Compte - *1**
#1120, 555, boul René-Lévesque ouest, Montréal, QC H2Z 1B1
Tél: 514-874-1910; *Téléc:* 514-874-0953
jules.pleau@sympatico.ca

***Montréal*: Jacques Ranger - *1**
5694, av Laurendeau, Montréal, QC H4E 3W4
Tél: 514-766-0756

***Montréal*: Robinson Sheppard Shapiro LLP - *71**
#4600, 800, Place Victoria, Montréal, QC H4Z 1H6
Tel: 514-878-2631; *Fax:* 514-878-1865
info@rsslex.com
www.rsslex.com

***Montréal*: Rousseau, Gaudry - *3**
12675, rue Sherbrooke est, 2e étage, Montréal, QC H1A 3W7
Tél: 514-875-8243; *Téléc:* 514-875-9903
Ligne sans frais: 888-875-8243
rrousseau@rousseaugaudry.com
www.rousseaugaudry.com

***Montréal*: Leonard I. Sabloff & Associates - *1**
6600, route Trans-Canada, Montréal, QC H9R 4S2
Tel: 514-426-4626; *Fax:* 514-426-3977
sabloff@hotmail.com

***Montréal*: Johanne St. Pierre - *1**
#101, 1395, rue Fleury est, Montréal, QC H2C 1R7

***Montréal*: Jean Saulnier - *1**
7190, rue St-Denis, Montréal, QC H2R 2E2
Tél: 514-273-1525

***Montréal*: Bernard K. Schneider - *1**
#3, 6175, av d'Esplanade, Montréal, QC H2T 3A2
Tél: 514-277-6540; *Téléc:* 514-277-6554

***Montréal*: Anthony N. Schratz - *1**
#400, 630, rue Sherbrooke ouest, Montréal, QC H3A 1E4
Tél: 514-289-9362; *Téléc:* 514-289-9312
aschratz@bellnet.ca

***Montréal*: Seal Seidman G.P. - *4**
#1050, 2015, rue Drummond, Montréal, QC H3G 1W7
Tél: 514-842-8861; *Téléc:* 514-288-1708
lseidman@sealseidman.qc.ca

***Montréal*: Laizer Sirota - *1**
#305, 10, rue St-Jacques, Montréal, QC H2Y 1L3
Tél: 514-844-1123; *Téléc:* 514-844-4071

***Montréal*: Ian M. Solloway**
#1700, 700, rue Sherbrooke ouest, Montréal, QC H3A 1G1
Tel: 514-282-9144; *Fax:* 514-844-7290
sollow@videotron.ca

***Montréal*: Charles Louis Spector**
#1250, 505, boul René-Levesque ouest, Montréal, QC H2Z 1Y7
Tel: 514-878-2556; *Fax:* 514-954-5077

***Montréal*: Spiegel Sohmer Inc.**
#1203, 5, place Ville Marie, Montréal, QC H3B 2G2
Tél: 514-875-2100; *Téléc:* 514-875-8237
www.spiegelsohmer.com

***Montréal*: Arthur H. Steckler - *1**
#120, 5115, av de Gaspé, Montréal, QC H2T 3B7
Tél: 514-273-8891; *Téléc:* 514-273-1576

***Montréal*: Stein Monast, S.E.N.C.R.L.**
#2400, Tour de la Banque Nationale, 600, rue de la Gauchetière ouest, Montréal, QC H3B 4L8
Tél: 514-878-9411; *Téléc:* 514-878-4800
Ligne sans frais: 800-670-0102
www.desjardinsducharme.ca

***Montréal*: Stern & Blumer - *2**
#1825, CP 983, 300, av Leo-Pariseau, Montréal, QC H2W 2N1
Tél: 514-842-1133; *Téléc:* 514-842-3105

***Montréal*: Sternthal Katznelson Montigny - *9**
#1020, Place du Canada, 1010, rue de la Gauchetière ouest, Montréal, QC H3B 2N2
Tél: 514-878-1011; *Téléc:* 514-878-9195
info@skm.ca
www.skm.ca

***Montréal*: Sumbulian, Mark, Avocat / Advocate - *1**
#1610, 1350, rue Sherbrooke ouest, Montréal, QC H3G 1J1
Tél: 514-281-1955; *Téléc:* 514-281-1956
sumbulian@bellnet.ca

***Montréal*: Talbot & Avocats - *2**
4519, rue St-Denis, Montréal, QC H2J 2L4
Tél: 514-849-2930; *Téléc:* 514-982-0716
liber-t@vigie.net

***Montréal*: Tassé & Vescio - *2**
2421, rue Allard, Montréal, QC H4E 2L3
Tél: 514-769-9654; *Téléc:* 514-769-7363

***Montréal*: Tiger Goldman - *2**
#716, 1010, rue Sherbrooke ouest, Montréal, QC H3A 2R7
Tél: 514-284-8401; *Téléc:* 514-284-8408

***Montréal*: Harvey Toulch - *1**
#406, 1117, rue Ste-Catherine ouest, Montréal, QC H3B 1H9
Tél: 514-849-1289; *Téléc:* 514-849-3101
hm@info-internet.net

***Montréal*: Robert Toupin - *1**
1344, rue Jean-Talon est, Montréal, QC H2E 1S1
Tél: 514-278-5400; *Téléc:* 514-278-7584

***Montréal*: Trudel Nadeau Avocats S.E.N.C.R.L. - *20**
#2500, Place du Parc, 300, av Léo-Pariseau, Montréal, QC H2X 4B7
Tél: 514-849-5754; *Téléc:* 514-499-0312
info@trudelnadeau.com
www.trudelnadeau.com

***Montréal*: Tucci & Associés - *4**
201, rue St-Zotique est, Montréal, QC H2S 1L2
Tél: 514-271-0650; *Téléc:* 514-270-2164
tucci@tucci.ca
www.tucci.ca

***Montréal*: Peter H. Turner - *1**
256, rue Devon, Montréal, QC H3R 1B9
Tél: 514-731-3544; *Téléc:* 514-737-3770

***Montréal*: Unterberg, Carisse, Labelle, Dessureault, Lebeau & Petit - *4**
#700, 1980, rue Sherbrooke ouest, Montréal, QC H3H 1E8
Tél: 514-934-0841; *Téléc:* 514-937-6547
contact@utlnet.com

***Montréal*: Woods & Partners - *16**
#1700, 2000, rue McGill College, Montréal, QC H3A 3H3
Tel: 514-982-4545; *Fax:* 514-284-2046
general@woods.qc.ca
www.litigationboutique.com

***Montréal*: Zimmerman, Blitt - *2**
#410, 345, av Victoria, Montréal, QC H3Z 2N2
Tél: 514-483-2444; *Téléc:* 514-483-2477

***New Carlisle*: Grenier, Grenier, Grenier - *3**
CP 519, New Carlisle, QC G0C 1Z0
Tél: 418-752-3308; *Téléc:* 418-752-6935
grenier1@globetrotter.qc.ca

***New Carlisle*: St-Onge & Assels - *2**
CP 727, 100A, boul Gérard-D.-Levesque, New Carlisle, QC G0C 1Z0
Tél: 418-752-3351; *Téléc:* 418-752-2740
stonge_assels@globetrotter.net

***Paspébiac*: Gilles Moulin - *1**
CP 880, Paspébiac, QC G0C 2K0
Tél: 418-752-2244

***Pierrefonds*: Mark Anthony Ciarallo - *1**
4838, rue Oka, Pierrefonds, QC H9K 1H6
Tél: 514-696-7931; *Téléc:* 514-696-0548

***Pointe-Claire*: Stanley Gelfand - *1**
#306, 189, boul Hymus, Pointe-Claire, QC H9R 1E9
Tél: 514-695-4542; *Téléc:* 514-695-7975

***Québec*: Beaumont, Provencal, Breton - *5**
1756, rue Notre-Dame, Québec, QC G2E 3C5
Tél: 418-871-2955; *Téléc:* 418-871-7352

***Québec*: Beauvais, Truchon Avocats - *28**
#200, CP 1000, 79, boul René-Lévesque est, Québec, QC G1R 4T4
Tél: 418-692-4180; *Téléc:* 418-692-5321
www.beauvaistruchon.com

***Québec*: Bedard, Herman - *2**
#206, 51, rue des Jardins, Québec, QC G1R 4L6
Tél: 418-692-2425; *Téléc:* 418-692-2528

***Québec*: Bélanger, Murray, Richard & Associés - *7**
#520, 400, boul Jean-Lesage, Québec, QC G1K 8W1
Tél: 418-522-7000; *Téléc:* 418-522-8212
bmravocats@webnet.qc.ca

***Québec*: André Bernatchez - *1**
#220, 157, rue des Chênes ouest, Québec, QC G1L 1K6
Tél: 418-628-4575

***Québec*: Maurice Bernatchez - *1**
#2, 1460, av de la Verendrye, Québec, QC G1J 4V8
Tél: 418-667-7830

***Québec*: Yvan Bilodeau - *1**
#180, 801, ch St-Louis, Québec, QC G1S 1C1
Tél: 418-686-4875; *Téléc:* 418-686-6160

***Québec*: Boily Morency - *4**
#230, 70, rue Dalhousie, Québec, QC G1K 4B2
Tel: 418-694-0704; *Fax:* 418-694-2140
bomo@videotron.ca

***Québec*: Bouchard Pagé Tremblay, S.E.N.C. - Avocats - *8**
6580, 1e av, Québec, QC G1H 2W4
Tél: 418-622-6699; *Téléc:* 418-628-1912
bouchardpagetremblay@oricom.ca
www.bouchardpagetremblay.com

***Québec*: Robert Bouchard - *1**
#103, 30, av St-Denis, Québec, QC G1R 4B6
Tél: 418-694-4096; *Téléc:* 418-841-3690
rbouchard@groupeconscientia.com

***Québec*: Roland Cote - *1**
1445, rue Maine, Québec, QC G1G 2J6

***Québec*: Dussault Lemieux Larochelle sencrl - *14**
#450, 2795, boul Laurier, Québec, QC G1V 4M7
Tél: 418-657-2424; *Téléc:* 418-657-1793
avocats@dllavocats.com

** indicates number of lawyers*

Québec: **Gagnon, Girard, Julian et Matte - *7**
#301, 1535, ch Ste-Foy, Québec, QC G1S 2P1
Tél: 418-681-0037; *Téléc*: 418-681-0539
ggjm@qc.aira.com

Québec: **La Société d'Avocats Garneau, Verdon, Michaud, Samson - *10**
67, rue Ste-Ursule, Québec, QC G1R 4E7
Tél: 418-692-3010; *Téléc*: 418-692-1742
gvm@qc.aira.com

Québec: **Giasson et Associés - *29**
#551, 2, rue des Jardins, Québec, QC G1R 4S9
Tél: 418-641-6156; *Téléc*: 418-641-6353
serge.giasson@ville.quebec.qc.ca

Québec: **Gosselin, Bussières, Bedard, Ouellet - *4**
#315, 400, boul Jean-Lesage, Québec, QC G1K 8W1
Tél: 418-529-9968; *Téléc*: 418-524-5243

Québec: **Grondin, Poudrier, Bernier - *36**
#900, 500, Grande Allée est, Québec, QC G1R 2J7
Tél: 418-683-3000; *Téléc*: 418-683-8784
Ligne sans frais: 800-463-5172
gpb@grondinpoudrier.com
www.grondinpoudrier.com

Québec: **Hodran Consultants Inc. - *1**
#305, 4, Jardins Merici, Québec, QC G1S 4M4
Tél: 514-571-2940
gcardin@genomecanada.ca

Québec: **Joli-Cour Lacasse Avocats - *26**
#600, 1134, Grande Allée Ouest, Québec, QC G1S 1E5
Tél: 418-681-7007; *Téléc*: 418-681-7100
communications@jolicoeurlacasse.com
www.jolicoeurlacasse.com

Québec: **Langlois Kronström Desjardins - *81**
#300, 801, Grande Allée ouest, Québec, QC G1S 1C1
Tel: 418-650-7000; *Fax*: 418-650-7075
Toll-Free: 888-650-7001
info@lkd.ca
www.langloiskronstromdesjardins.com

Québec: **Micheline Anne Montreuil - *1**
1050, rue François-Blondeau, Québec, QC G1H 2H2
Tél: 418-621-5032; *Téléc*: 418-621-5092
micheline@micheline.ca
www.micheline.ca

Québec: **Morency Avocats - *31**
#400, 3075, ch des Quatre-Bourgeois, Québec, QC G1W 4X5
Tél: 418-651-9900; *Téléc*: 418-651-5184
avocats@morencyavocats.com
www.morencyavocats.com

Québec: **O'Brien, Avocats - *10**
#600, 140, Grande Allée est, Québec, QC G1R 5M8
Tél: 418-648-1511; *Téléc*: 418-648-9335
obrien@obrienavocats.qc.ca

Québec: **Siskinds Desmeules Avocats - *5**
#320, 43, rue Buade, Québec, QC G1R 4A2
Tél: 418-694-2009; *Téléc*: 418-694-0281
claude.desmeules@siskindsdesmeules.com

Québec: **Tremblay, Bois, Mignault & Lemay - *34**
#200, 1195, av Lavigerie, Québec, QC G1V 4N3
Tél: 418-658-9966; *Téléc*: 418-658-6100
Ligne sans frais: 800-807-9966
avocats@tremblaybois.qc.ca
www.tremblaybois.qc.ca

Repentigny: **Duval, Brochu, Tremblay & Associées - *2**
#201, 275B, rue Paradis, Repentigny, QC J6A 8H2
Tél: 450-581-2777; *Téléc*: 450-585-7565

Rimouski: **Jean Blouin - *1**
216, av de la Cathedrale, Rimouski, QC G5L 5J2

Rimouski: **Norman Dumais - *1**
#200, CP 998, Stn. Bureau-Chef, 97, rue St-Germain ouest, Rimouski, QC G5L 7E1
Tél: 418-723-3179; *Téléc*: 418-723-3195
dumais.avocat@globetrotter.net

Rimouski: **Laprise, Lacroix & Associes - *4**
#R0901, 9, rue Jules-A. Brillant, Rimouski, QC G5L 7E4
Tél: 418-722-5587; *Téléc*: 418-722-5949
raymond.lacroix@telus.com

Rivière-du-Loup: **Aide Juridique - *3**
#203, 37, rue de la Cour, Rivière-du-Loup, QC G5R 1J1
Tél: 418-862-1522; *Téléc*: 418-862-4528
bajrdl@ccjbslg.qc.ca

Rivière-du-Loup: **Belzile & Associés - *3**
#1027, 2, rue de la Cour, Rivière-du-Loup, QC G5R 4C3
Tél: 418-862-9460; *Téléc*: 418-862-9939

Rivière-du-Loup: **Rioux Bossé Massé Moreau - *6**
CP 487, 12, rue de la Cour, Rivière-du-Loup, QC G5R 3Z1
Tél: 418-862-3565; *Téléc*: 418-862-4408
rbmm@qc.aira.com
www.rbmm.qc.ca

Rosemère: **Indev Inc. - *1**
88, rue Jack-Rice, Rosemère, QC J7A 4Z1
Tél: 514-875-5475; *Téléc*: 514-875-5475
yves.lasnier@in-dev.ca

Rouyn-Noranda: **Denis Harvey - *1**
53, du Terminus ouest, Rouyn-Noranda, QC J9X 2P4
Tél: 819-262-2301; *Téléc*: 819-765-0653
dharvey@ccjat.gc.ca

Saint-Félicien: **Sandra Bouchard, Avocate - *1**
1082, rue Saint-Christophe, Saint-Félicien, QC G8K 1Z2
Tél: 418-679-5566; *Téléc*: 418-630-2111
sandbouc@destination.ca

Saint-Georges: **Raymond Lessard - *1**
12285, av 1re, Saint-Georges, QC G5Y 2E2

Saint-Hyacinthe: **Claude L. Bédard Avocat - *1**
1782, rue Girouard ouest, Saint-Hyacinthe, QC J2S 3A1
Tél: 450-774-2749; *Téléc*: 450-774-9533
claude.bedard@sympatico.ca

Saint-Hyacinthe: **Brodeur, Boileau - *3**
1700, rue Girouard ouest, Saint-Hyacinthe, QC J2S 3A1
Tél: 450-773-8566; *Téléc*: 450-778-3749

Saint-Hyacinthe: **Sylvestre & Associés Avocats S.E.N.C. - *9**
#236, 1600, rue Girouard ouest, Saint-Hyacinthe, QC J2S 2Z8
Tél: 450-773-8445; *Téléc*: 450-773-2112
etude@avocatssylvestre.ca

Saint-Jean-Port-Joli: **Les Avocats Blanchet Gaudreault - *2**
512, route de l'Eglise, Saint-Jean-Port-Joli, QC G0R 3G0
Tél: 418-598-7004; *Téléc*: 418-598-7390
blanchet.gaudreault@globetrotter.net

Saint-Jean-sur-Richelieu: **Bérubé & Pion, SENCRL - *3**
#225, 145, boul St-Joseph, Saint-Jean-sur-Richelieu, QC J3B 1W5
Tél: 450-359-7171; *Téléc*: 450-359-9957

Saint-Jean-sur-Richelieu: **Paul Barry Gingras - *2**
229, rue Jacques-Cartier nord, Saint-Jean-sur-Richelieu, QC J3B 6T3
Tél: 450-347-0433; *Téléc*: 450-346-0099
gingras@qc.aira.com

Saint-Jean-sur-Richelieu: **Lachance & Morin - *2**
108, rue St-Charles, Saint-Jean-sur-Richelieu, QC J3B 2C1
Tél: 450-346-4464

Saint-Jean-sur-Richelieu: **Claude Lauzon - *1**
160, rue Longueuil, Saint-Jean-sur-Richelieu, QC J3B 6P1
Tél: 450-347-2344; *Téléc*: 450-347-4132

Saint-Joseph-de-Beauce: **Cliche, Laflamme & Loubier - *6**
CP 160, 109, rue Verreault, Saint-Joseph-de-Beauce, QC G0S 2V0
Tél: 418-397-5264; *Téléc*: 418-397-5269
cliclafl@globetrotter.qc.ca

Saint-Joseph-de-Beauce: **Giroux & Binette - *2**
#100, 700, av Robert-Cliche, Saint-Joseph-de-Beauce, QC G0S 2V0
Tél: 418-397-7288; *Téléc*: 418-397-7283

Saint-Jérôme: **CRBI - *1**
461, de la Seigneurie, Saint-Jérôme, QC J5L 2K5
Tél: 450-530-7548
crbi@videotron.ca

Saint-Jérôme: **Lalonde Geraghty Riendeau Lapierre - *8**
44, rue De Martigny ouest, Saint-Jérôme, QC J7Z 2E9
Tél: 450-436-8022; *Téléc*: 450-436-5185
lalondegeraghty@lgrl.ca
www.lgrl.ca

Saint-Jérôme: **Prévost Fortin D'Aoust - *30**
#400, 55, rue Castonguay, Saint-Jérôme, QC J7Y 2H9
Tel: 450-436-8244; *Fax*: 450-436-9735
info@pfdlex.com
www.pfdlex.com

Saint-Lambert: **André Demers - *1**
439, av Notre-Dame, Saint-Lambert, QC J4P 2K5
Tél: 514-875-2007; *Téléc*: 514-466-7315

Saint-Lambert: **Paul Joffe - *1**
360, av Putney, Saint-Lambert, QC J4P 3B6
Tél: 450-465-3654; *Téléc*: 450-465-5730
p.joffe@sympatico.ca

Saint-Lambert: **Lagacé & Legault International Inc. - *3**
#200, 2015, rue Victoria, Saint-Lambert, QC J4S 1H1
Tel: 450-923-9381; *Fax*: 450-466-3919
clagace@lagacelegault.com

Saint-Lambert: **William Sullivan - *1**
147, ch Tiffin, Saint-Lambert, QC J4P 3E8
Tél: 514-397-1504; *Téléc*: 514-397-1505
wslaw@qc.aibn.com

Saint-Laurent: **Belanger, Fiore - *2**
#300, 685, boul Décarie, Saint-Laurent, QC H4L 5G4
Tél: 514-744-0825; *Téléc*: 514-744-9861
belanger.annie@videotron.ca; fiore.carole@vl.videotron.ca

Saint-Laurent: **Gaston E. Bouchard - *1**
1015, rue Champigny, Saint-Laurent, QC H4L 4P3
Tél: 514-744-0918; *Téléc*: 514-345-4718

Saint-Laurent: **Kravitz & Kravitz - *3**
#350, 750, boul Marcel-Laurin, Saint-Laurent, QC H4M 2M4
Tél: 514-748-2889; *Téléc*: 514-748-5191
kravitz@centra.ca

Saint-Laurent: **SpeechGadgets Inc. - *1**
1466, rue MacDonald, Saint-Laurent, QC H4L 2A7
Tel: 514-817-9312; *Fax*: 514-744-1592
ted.hill@videotron.ca

Saint-Sauveur: **Jay Plante & Associates - *1**
300, ch de L'Ancienne Érablière, Saint-Sauveur, QC J0R 1R2
Tel: 514-261-8619; *Fax*: 514-450-2278
jay_plante@sympatico.ca

Sainte-Anne-du-Lac: **Harmac du Lac Inc. - *1**
23, ch de L'Oseille, Sainte-Anne-du-Lac, QC J0R 1B0
Tél: 450-224-0289; *Téléc*: 450-224-0290
harmacdulac@sympatico.ca

Sainte-Foy: **Claude Berlinguette - *1**
1429, rue du Nordet, Sainte-Foy, QC G2G 2C2
Tél: 418-871-1478

Sainte-Foy: **David Stratégies Marketing - *1**
2796, rue de Poitiers, Sainte-Foy, QC G1W 2B8
Tél: 418-651-6967; *Téléc*: 418-694-9795
andredavid@oricom.ca

Sainte-Julie: **Roland Boyer - *1**
69, av Mont Bruno, RR#3, Sainte-Julie, QC J3E 3A1
Tél: 450-649-3772; *Téléc*: 450-649-0101
rolandboyer@yahoo.com

Sainte-Marie: **Sylvain, Parent, Gobeil - *4**
CP 40, 225, rue du College, Sainte-Marie, QC G6E 3B4
Tél: 418-387-2727; *Téléc*: 418-387-7070
spgs@globetrotter.net

Sainte-Thérèse: **Marc H. Lamoreux - *1**
44, ch Cote St-Louis ouest, Sainte-Thérèse, QC J7E 2H7
Tél: 514-979-5918

Salaberry-de-Valleyfield: **Les Avocats Rancourt, Legault & St-Onge - *6**
175, rue Salaberry, Salaberry-de-Valleyfield, QC J6T 2J1
Tél: 450-371-2221; *Téléc*: 450-371-2094
courrier@rancourtlegault.com
www.rancourtlegault.com

** indicates number of lawyers*

Sept-Iles: Besnier, Dion & Rondeau - *6
865, boul Laure, Sept-Iles, QC G4R 1Y6
Tél: 418-962-9775; Téléc: 418-968-6806
besnier.avocats@cgocable.ca

Sept-Iles: Desrosiers & Associés - *3
#201, 440, av Brochu, Sept-Iles, QC G4R 2W8
Tél: 418-962-7392; Téléc: 418-962-6100
desricar@globetrotter.qc.ca

Shawinigan: Pierre Dugré - *1
305, 7e rue, Shawinigan, QC G9N 1C6
Tél: 819-537-8902; Téléc: 819-537-0267
Ligne sans frais: 877-744-0090
pierredugre@cgocable.ca

Sherbrooke: Claude R. Beauchamp - *1
#101, 380, rue King ouest, Sherbrooke, QC J1H 1R4
Tél: 819-563-7733; Téléc: 819-563-7734

Sherbrooke: Pierre Belhumeur - *1
#101, 380, rue King ouest, Sherbrooke, QC J1H 1R4
Tél: 819-566-1676; Téléc: 819-563-7734
pilul@interlinx.qc.ca

Sherbrooke: François Bouchard, Avocat - *1
#610, 455, rue King ouest, Sherbrooke, QC J1H 6E9
Tél: 819-563-4898; Téléc: 819-563-5837
fbouchard@essagal.ca

Sherbrooke: Gerard G. Boudreau - *1
2571, boul Portland, Sherbrooke, QC J1J 1V6
Tél: 819-562-0848; Téléc: 819-569-3580

Sherbrooke: Linda Boulanger - *1
#3, 30, rue Vaudry, Sherbrooke, QC J1M 1B2
Tél: 819-820-2661; Téléc: 819-820-8330
lindaboulangeravocate@yahoo.ca

Sherbrooke: Jean-Claude Boutin - *1
#100, 75, rue Wellington nord, Sherbrooke, QC J1H 5A9
Tél: 819-569-9933; Téléc: 819-822-0041

Sherbrooke: Delorme, LeBel, Bureau, s.e.n.c. - *7
#100, 2355, rue King ouest, Sherbrooke, QC J1J 2G6
Tél: 819-566-6222; Téléc: 819-566-4221
dlb@dlbavocats.com

Sherbrooke: Drouin Lemieux - *2
18, rue Wellington nord, Sherbrooke, QC J1H 5B7
Tél: 819-566-3939
drouinlemieux@qc.aira.com

Sherbrooke: Fontaine, Panneton & Associes - *8
#220, 2050, rue King ouest, Sherbrooke, QC J1J 2E8
Tél: 819-564-1222; Téléc: 819-822-2180
louis.panneton1@qc.aira.com

Sherbrooke: Gérin Custeau Francoeur - *3
100, rue Richmond, Sherbrooke, QC J1H 6E1
Tél: 819-348-0274

Sherbrooke: Guenin Cormier Gallant Morin
759, rue King est, Sherbrooke, QC J1G 1C6
Tel: 819-565-1808; Fax: 819-565-2729
gcgm@globetrotter.net

Sherbrooke: Hackett, Campbell, Bouchard - *4
80, rue Peel, Sherbrooke, QC J1H 4K1
Tél: 819-565-7885; Téléc: 819-566-0888
info@hcblegal.com

Sherbrooke: Plastiques st Composites Pierre Larivière Inc. - *1
1690, rue White, Sherbrooke, QC J1J 1Z4
Tel: 819-822-6569; Fax: 819-566-2016
pcpl@videotron.ca

Sillery: Affaires gouvernementales et publiques - *1
1303, rue Maguire, Sillery, QC G1T 1Z2
Tél: 418-682-3157; Téléc: 418-681-4338
lemieuxa@total.net

Sillery: Hickson, Martin, Blanchard - *3
1170, ch St-Louis, Sillery, QC G1S 1E5
Tél: 418-681-9671; Téléc: 418-527-6938
hickson.martin.blanchard@qc.aira.com

Sorel: Ally & Ally - *1
53, rue George, Sorel, QC J3P 1B9
Tél: 450-743-7979; Téléc: 450-743-9821

Sorel: Carole Lepage - *1
96, rue George, Sorel, QC J3P 1C3
Tél: 450-742-3766; Téléc: 450-742-1133
avocate@carolelepage.qc.ca

St-Georges-de-Beauce: Jérôme Poirier - *1
11720, 1re av, St-Georges-de-Beauce, QC G5Y 2C8
Tél: 418-228-3123; Téléc: 418-228-0494
jerome.poirier@globetrotter.net

St-Léonard: DiPace, Mercadente - *6
#202, 5450, rue Jarry est, St-Léonard, QC H1P 1T9
Tél: 514-326-3300; Téléc: 514-326-4706
mercadante@videotron.net

St-Romuald-d'Etchemin: Huguette Gagnon - *1
CP 2096, St-Romuald-d'Etchemin, QC G6W 5M3
Tél: 418-839-2045; Téléc: 418-839-2061
gagnonh@videotron.ca

Ste-Thérèse-De-Blainville: Brazeau, Grégoire & Cliche - *3
72, rue Blainville ouest, Ste-Thérèse-De-Blainville, QC J7E 1X3
Tél: 514-430-1530; Téléc: 514-430-3607

Trois-Rivières: Roger Bellemare, Avocat - *2
5540, rue Decelles, Trois-Rivières, QC G8Y 6Y8
Tél: 819-376-7918; Téléc: 819-376-1425

Trois-Rivières: Biron, Spain & Associés - *3
CP 444, 154, rue Radisson, Trois-Rivières, QC G9A 5G4
Tél: 819-375-4187; Téléc: 819-375-7395

Trois-Rivières: Braun & Bélisle - *2
#4, 1185, rue Hart, Trois-Rivières, QC G9A 4S4
Tél: 819-691-1390; Téléc: 819-378-7344

Trois-Rivières: Godin, Boucher, Brunet, DuPlessis - *4
CP 1474, Stn. Chef, 190, rue Bonaventure, Trois-Rivières, QC G9A 5L6
Tél: 819-379-5225; Téléc: 819-379-4545
godindenysp@qc.aira.com

Trois-Rivières: Louis Hénaire - *1
983, rue Hart, Trois-Rivières, QC G9A 4S3
Tél: 819-379-3355; Téléc: 819-379-1227

Val-Bélair: J. Michel Bouchard - *1
1805, av Industrielle, Val-Bélair, QC G3K 1L8
Tél: 418-842-0996

Val-d'Or: Cossette & DuFour - *1
795, 3e av, Val-d'Or, QC J9P 1S8
Tél: 819-825-2787; Téléc: 819-874-4160

Valleyfield: Droiun, Gingras, Robert & Toulouse - *4
#200A, 30, av de Centenaire, Valleyfield, QC J6S 5X4
Tél: 450-370-3064; Téléc: 450-370-3068
ccjers.valleyfield@sympatico.ca

Valleyfield: Vachon, Martin & Besner - *3
72, rue Montcalm, Valleyfield, QC J6T 2C9
Tél: 514-371-7771; Téléc: 514-371-2438
vachon@rocler.qc.ca

Varennes: Desjardins, Lessard - *2
#203, 1950, boul René Gaultier, Varennes, QC J3X 1P5
Tél: 450-652-1830; Téléc: 450-652-3484

Verdun: Robert Beaudet - *2
5331, rue Bannantyne, Verdun, QC H4H 1E8
Tél: 514-769-8527; Téléc: 514-769-7466

Verdun: Robert Church - *1
82, boul William, Verdun, QC H3E 1R6
Tel: 514-765-8903; Fax: 514-765-3472

Victoriaville: Caron, Garneau, Bellavance - *3
268, boul Bois Francs nord, Victoriaville, QC G6P 1G5
Tél: 819-758-8251; Téléc: 819-752-4520
avocatscg@bellnet.ca

Westmount: Aster & Aster - *2
#410, 345, av Victoria, Westmount, QC H3Z 2N2
Tel: 514-483-2445; Fax: 514-483-0009
asterma@asterlaw.com
www.asterlaw.com

Westmount: Robert Berger - *1
4269, rue Ste-Catherine ouest, Westmount, QC H3Z 1P7
Tél: 514-847-3667; Téléc: 514-847-0011
rberger@lexingtonrealties.ca

Westmount: Luisa Biasutti - *1
#410, 4115, rue Sherbrooke ouest, Westmount, QC H3Z 1K9
Tél: 514-933-3838; Téléc: 514-933-2668
biasutti@groupeteq.com

Westmount: Paul B. Cohen - *1
#809, 4000, boul de Maisonneuve ouest, Westmount, QC H3Z 1J9
Tel: 514-931-3691; Fax: 514-931-3637
paulcohen@bellnet.ca

Westmount: A. Barry Coleman - *1
#660, 4141, rue Sherbrooke ouest, Westmount, QC H3Z 1B8
Tél: 514-935-5030; Téléc: 514-935-3559

Westmount: Crestohl & Associates - *1
#1200, 1, Carré Westmount, Westmount, QC H3Z 2P4
Tél: 514-932-7392; Téléc: 514-932-0990

Westmount: David & Touchette - *2
#1800, 1 Westmount Sq., Westmount, QC H3Z 2P9
Tél: 514-871-8174; Téléc: 514-871-8052
mdavid@davidtouchette.com
www.davidtouchette.com

Westmount: M. Diamond & Associates Inc. - *3
#400, 345, av Victoria, Westmount, QC H3Z 2N2
Tél: 514-483-2303; Téléc: 514-483-2373

Westmount: André R. Dorais Avocats - *3
#2000, 1, carré Westmount, Westmount, QC H3Z 2P9
Tél: 514-938-0808; Téléc: 514-938-8888
adorais@ardavocats.com

Westmount: Me Linda Hammerschmid - *4
#1290, 1 Westmount Sq., Westmount, QC H3Z 2P9
Tel: 514-846-1013; Fax: 514-846-1803

Westmount: Irving Mitchell Kalichman SENCRL/LLP Avocats Advocates - *8
4119, rue Sherbrooke ouest, Westmount, QC H3Z 1A7
Tel: 514-935-4460; Fax: 514-935-2999

Westmount: Stein & Stein - *4
4101, rue Sherbrooke ouest, Westmount, QC H3Z 1A7
Tel: 514-866-9806; Fax: 514-875-8218
law@steinandstein.com
www.steinandstein.com

Westmount: Rosalie Szewczuk - *1
4420, rue Ste-Catherine ouest, Westmount, QC H3Z 1R2
Tel: 514-933-4453; Fax: 514-934-3134
rosiesz@videotron.ca

Saskatchewan

Alameda: Cundall, Baumgartner & Co.
115 Fifth St., Alameda, SK S0C 0A0
Tel: 306-489-2216; Fax: 306-489-4602

Assiniboia: Lewans & Ford - *2
P.O. Box 759, 228 Centre St., Assiniboia, SK S0H 0B0
Tel: 306-642-3543; Fax: 306-642-5777

Assiniboia: Marlin Law Office - *1
P.O. Box 1088, 200 Centre St., Assiniboia, SK S0H 0B0
Tel: 306-642-3933; Fax: 306-642-5399
gmarlin@sk.sympatico.ca

Assiniboia: Mountain & Mountain - *2
P.O. Box 459, 101 - 4 Ave. West, Assiniboia, SK S0H 0B0
Tel: 306-642-3866; Fax: 306-642-5848
lee.mountain@sasktel.net
mounl.sasktelwebsite.net/

Biggar: Busse Law Professional Corporation - *2
Credit Union Bldg., P.O. Box 669, 302 Main St., Biggar, SK S0K 0M0
Tel: 306-948-3346; Fax: 306-948-3366
busselaw@sasktel.net
www.busselaw.net

Broadview: Gary G. Moore - *1
P.O. Box 610, 616 Main St., Broadview, SK S0G 0K0
Tel: 306-696-2454; Fax: 306-696-3105

Brownlee: Frederick R.C. Rawlings - *1
P.O. Box 70, Brownlee, SK S0H 0M0
Tel: 306-759-2621

Canora: Rosowsky, Campbell & Seidle - *1
P.O. Box 309, 115 - 2 Ave. West, Canora, SK S0A 0L0
Tel: 306-563-4250
ros.cam@sk.sympatico.ca

Davidson: Dellene S. Church - *1
P.O. Box 724, 200 Garfield St., Davidson, SK S0G 1A0
Tel: 306-567-5554; Fax: 306-567-2831
dsc-law@sasktel.net

* indicates number of lawyers

***Estevan*: Kohaly & Elash - *2**
P.O. Box 580, 1312 - 4th St., Estevan, SK S4A 0X2
Tel: 306-634-3631; *Fax:* 306-634-6901
paulelash@kemlaw.sk.ca

***Estevan*: Komarnicki Trobert - *2**
#305, P.O. Box 725, 1133 - 4 St., Estevan, SK S4A 2A6
Tel: 306-634-2616; *Fax:* 306-634-9881
ktlaw@sasktel.net

***Estevan*: Orlowski Law Office - *2**
1215 - 5th St., Estevan, SK S4A 0Z5
Tel: 306-634-3353; *Fax:* 306-634-7714
orlowski.law@sasktel.net

***Eston*: Hughes Law Office - *1**
P.O. Box 729, 305 Main St. South, Eston, SK S0L 1A0
Tel: 306-962-4111; *Fax:* 306-962-3302
hugheseston@hotmail.com

***Fort Qu'appelle*: Halford Law Office - *1**
122 Boundary Avenue North, Fort Qu'appelle, SK S0G 1S0
Tel: 306-332-5661; *Fax:* 306-332-4293

***Gravelbourg*: Anderson & Company - *2**
P.O. Box 1016, 209 Main St, Gravelbourg, SK S0H 1X0
Tel: 306-648-2582; *Fax:* 306-648-2501

***Humboldt*: Behiel, Will & Biemans - *4**
P.O. Box 878, 602 - 9 St., Humboldt, SK S0K 2A0
Tel: 306-682-2642; *Fax:* 306-682-5165
office_bmwlaw@sasktel.net
www.behielwill.com

***Indian Head*: KMP Law - *2**
523 Grand Ave., Indian Head, SK S0G 2K0
Tel: 306-695-2704
kmplaw.com

***Kindersley*: Ard Law Office - *1**
P.O. Box 1898, 111 1 Avenue West, Kindersley, SK S0L 1S0
Tel: 306-463-2626; *Fax:* 306-463-4917
ard.law@sasktel.net

***Kindersley*: Sheppard & Millar - *2**
P.O. Box 1510, 113 - 1 Ave. East., Kindersley, SK S0L 1S0
Tel: 306-463-4647; *Fax:* 306-463-6133

***La Ronge*: Buckle Law Office - *1**
#1B, 1603 Bedford Dr., La Ronge, SK S0J 1L0
Tel: 306-425-5959; *Fax:* 306-425-2840

***Langenburg*: Layh & Associates - *2**
Welke House, P.O. Box 250, 216 Road Ave. East, Langenburg, SK S0A 2A0
Tel: 306-743-5520; *Fax:* 306-743-5589
info@layhlaw.com
www.layhlaw.com

***Lloydminster*: Clements & Smith - *3**
#212, P.O. Box 440, Stn. Main, 5704 - 44 St., Lloydminster, SK S9V 0Y4
Tel: 780-875-7999; *Fax:* 780-875-1020
clements@bordercity.com

***Lloydminster*: Fox Wakefield - *2**
P.O. Box 50, 5105 - 49 St., Lloydminster, SK S9V 0Y6
Tel: 780-875-9105; *Fax:* 780-875-6748

***Meadow Lake*: Francis & Company - *2**
P.O. Box 310, 822 - 9th Ave. West, Meadow Lake, SK S9X 1Y3
Tel: 306-236-5540; *Fax:* 306-236-5571
info@franciscolaw.ca
www.franciscolaw.ca

***Meadow Lake*: Gerald R. Perkins - *1**
#2, 132 Centre St., Meadow Lake, SK S9X 1Z7
Tel: 306-236-4040; *Fax:* 306-236-4878
perkinslawoffice@sasktel.net

***Melfort*: Annand Law Office - *2**
P.O. Box 69, 208 Main St., Melfort, SK S0E 1A0
Tel: 306-752-2707; *Fax:* 306-752-4484
info@annandlawoffice.com
www.annandlawoffice.com

***Melfort*: Kapoor Selnes Klimm - *3**
417 Main St., Melfort, SK S0E 1A0
Tel: 306-752-5777; *Fax:* 306-752-2712

***Melfort*: Ronald Price-Jones - *1**
P.O. Box 129, #3 Hwy. East, Melfort, SK S0E 1A0
Tel: 306-752-5701; *Fax:* 306-752-2444
ronp-j@sasktel.net

***Melville*: Bell, Kreklewich & Company - *3**
P.O. Box 2000, 147 - 3 Ave. East, Melville, SK S0A 2P0
Tel: 306-728-5468; *Fax:* 306-728-4444
bell.kreklewich_bkc@sasktel.net

***Melville*: Schmidt Law Office - *1**
P.O. Box 160, 126 - 2nd Ave., Melville, SK S0A 2P0
Tel: 306-728-5481; *Fax:* 306-728-4201
s.lo@sasktel.net

***Moose Jaw*: Murray D. Acton - *1**
330 Main St. North, Moose Jaw, SK S6H 3J9
Tel: 306-694-0052; *Fax:* 306-691-0445
actonlaw@shaw.ca

***Moose Jaw*: Ron G. Bader - *1**
53 Stadecona St. West, Moose Jaw, SK S6H 1Z2
Tel: 306-691-5858; *Fax:* 306-691-5822
Toll-Free: 800-845-4748
ron@rgblaw.com

***Moose Jaw*: Curran & Fielding - *2**
#108, 54 Ominica St. West, Moose Jaw, SK S6H 1W9
Tel: 306-693-7181; *Fax:* 306-691-0187

***Moose Jaw*: Grayson & Company - *7**
P.O. Box 908, 350 Langdon Cres., Moose Jaw, SK S6H 4P6
Tel: 306-693-6176; *Fax:* 306-693-1515
grayson@sasknet.net

***Moose Jaw*: Terrance Ocrane Law Office - *1**
#1, 53 Stadacona St. West, Moose Jaw, SK S6H 1Z2
Tel: 306-694-4922; *Fax:* 306-692-6386
ocranelawoffice@sasktel.net

***Moose Jaw*: B.A. Walper-Bossence Q.C. - *1**
84 Athabasca St. W, Moose Jaw, SK S6H 2B5
Tel: 306-693-7288; *Fax:* 306-692-6760
brendawalperlaw@shaw.ca
www.walperlaw.ca

***Moose Jaw*: Wheatley Law Firm - *1**
1357 Queen Crescent, Moose Jaw, SK S6H 7K7
Tel: 306-692-0113; *Fax:* 306-693-3230

***Moose Jaw*: Whittaker, Craik, MacLowich & Hughes - *2**
P.O. Box 1178, 109 Ominica St. West, Moose Jaw, SK S6H 4P9
Tel: 306-694-4677; *Fax:* 306-694-5747

***Moosomin*: Osman, Gordon & Co. - *6**
P.O. Box 280, 626 Carleton St., Moosomin, SK S0G 3N0
Tel: 306-435-3851; *Fax:* 306-435-3962

***Nipawin*: Carson Law Office - *1**
P.O. Box 1983, Nipawin, SK S0E 1E0
Tel: 306-862-5554

***Nipawin*: Eremko & Eremko - *1**
P.O. Box 250, Nipawin, SK S0E 1E0
Tel: 306-862-4477

***Nipawin*: Taylor & Co. - *3**
P.O. Box 850, 117 - 1 Ave. East, Nipawin, SK S0E 1E0
Tel: 306-873-1865
j.taylor_lawoffice@sasktel.net

***North Battleford*: Cawood Walker Demmans Baldwin - *4**
#201, P.O. Box 905, 1291 - 102 St., North Battleford, SK S9A 2Z3
Tel: 306-445-6177; *Fax:* 306-445-7076
cawood.et.al@sasktel.net

***North Battleford*: David Conroy - *1**
#101, 1351 - 101 St., North Battleford, SK S9A 0Z9
Tel: 306-445-3613; *Fax:* 306-445-9088
conroylaw@sasktel.net

***North Battleford*: Jones & Hudec - *6**
P.O. Box 1179, 10211 - 12 Ave., North Battleford, SK S9A 3K2
Tel: 306-446-2211; *Fax:* 306-446-3022
jhlaw@sasktel.net
www.joneshudec.com

***North Battleford*: Marusia A. Kobrynsky - *1**
10817 Meighen Cres., North Battleford, SK S9A 3L2
Tel: 306-445-8369; *Fax:* 306-446-3022
mkobrynsky@sasktel.net

***North Battleford*: Lindgren, Blais, Frank & Illingworth - *4**
P.O. Box 940, 1301 - 101 St., North Battleford, SK S9A 2Z3
Tel: 306-445-2421; *Fax:* 306-445-2313
mlbfh@sasktel.net
www.lbfilaw.com

***North Battleford*: Migneault Greenwood - *4**
1391 101st Street, North Battleford, SK S9A 2Y8
Tel: 306-445-4436; *Fax:* 306-445-6444
kevan@mglawoffice.com

***Preeceville*: Peet Law Firm - *1**
P.O. Box 1210, 17 First Ave. NW, Preeceville, SK S0A 3B0
Tel: 306-547-5590

***Prince Albert*: Balon Krishan - *3**
1335B - 2nd Ave. West, Prince Albert, SK S6V 5B2
Tel: 306-922-5151; *Fax:* 306-763-1755
bkm.law@sasktel.net

***Prince Albert*: Ron Cherkewich - *1**
#3, 27 - 11 St. West, Prince Albert, SK S6V 3A8
Tel: 306-764-1537; *Fax:* 306-763-0505
ron.cya@sasktel.net

***Prince Albert*: Eggum, Abrametz, Eggum - *4**
#101, 88 - 13th St. East, Prince Albert, SK S6V 1C6
Tel: 306-763-7441; *Fax:* 306-764-2882
klleggum@inet2000.com; petervabrametz@inet2000.com

***Prince Albert*: Holash Logue McCullagh Law Office - *3**
1102 - 1 Ave. West, Prince Albert, SK S6V 4Y6
Tel: 306-764-4244; *Fax:* 306-764-4949

***Prince Albert*: Kirkby Law Office - *1**
#102, 1061 Central Ave., Prince Albert, SK S6V 4V4
Tel: 306-764-4673; *Fax:* 306-922-0434
kirkbylaw@sasktel.net

***Prince Albert*: Loewen & Klassen Law Office - *2**
1100 1st Avenue East, Prince Albert, SK S6V 2A7
Tel: 306-922-0212; *Fax:* 306-922-2422

***Prince Albert*: Sanderson Balicki Parchomchuk - *8**
110 - 11 St. East, Prince Albert, SK S6V 1A1
Tel: 306-764-2222; *Fax:* 306-764-2221
www.sbplaw.ca

***Prince Albert*: Stephens Law Office - *1**
#3, 27 - 11th St. West, Prince Albert, SK S6V 3A8
Tel: 306-764-3456; *Fax:* 306-922-3772
www.stephenslaw.ca

***Prince Albert*: West, Siwak - *2**
1109 Central Ave., Prince Albert, SK S6V 4V7
Tel: 306-763-7467; *Fax:* 306-763-7469
west.siwak@sasktel.net

***Prince Albert*: Wilcox Zuk Law Office - *6**
20 - 12 St. West, Prince Albert, SK S6V 3B3
Tel: 306-922-4700; *Fax:* 306-922-0633
princealbert@mwzlaw.com

***Prince Albert*: Zatlyn Law Office - *5**
#231, 1061 Central Ave., Prince Albert, SK S6V 7N7
Tel: 306-922-1444; *Fax:* 306-922-5848
zatlyn@sasktel.net

***Regina*: Anderson Law Firm Professional Corporation - *1**
#1400, 2002 Victoria Ave., Regina, SK S4P 0R7
Tel: 306-789-8868; *Fax:* 306-789-3366

***Regina*: Beke Law Firm - *1**
#200, 2040 McIntyre St., Regina, SK S4P 2R6
Tel: 306-569-9964
bekelaw@sasktel.net

***Regina*: Bertram Scrivens MacLeod - *6**
#1730, Avord Tower, 2002 Victoria Ave., Regina, SK S4P 0R7
Tel: 306-525-2737; *Fax:* 306-565-3244
office@bertramlaw.ca
www.bsmlaw.ca

***Regina*: Dahlem Findlay - *1**
2100 Smith St., Regina, SK S4P 2P2
Tel: 306-522-3631; *Fax:* 306-565-2616
don.findlay@sasktel.net
www.donfindlay.ca

***Regina*: Duchin, Bayda & Kroczynski - *4**
2515 Victoria Ave., Regina, SK S4P 0T2
Tel: 306-359-3131; *Fax:* 306-359-3372

** indicates number of lawyers*

***Regina*: Gates & Company - *5**
3132 Avonhurst Dr., Regina, SK S4R 3J7
Tel: 306-949-5544; *Fax:* 306-775-2995
office@gateslaw.ca

***Regina*: Elaine Germain - *1**
2269 Hamilton St., Regina, SK S4P 2E7
Tel: 306-525-8311; *Fax:* 306-565-2766

***Regina*: Gerrand Rath Johnson - *13**
#700, Toronto Dominion Bank Bldg., 1914 Hamilton St., Regina, SK S4P 3N6
Tel: 306-522-3030; *Fax:* 306-522-3555
grj@grj.ca
www.grj.ca

***Regina*: Griffin Toews Maddigan Brabant - *6**
1530 Angus St., Regina, SK S4T 1Z1
Tel: 306-525-6125; *Fax:* 306-525-5226
griffin.toews@sasktel.net

***Regina*: Cindy M. Haynes Law Office - *1**
4126 Wascana Ridge, Regina, SK S4V 2S1
Tel: 306-789-2242; *Fax:* 306-789-4950
cindym.haynes@cableregina.com

***Regina*: Jaques Law Office - *1**
1542 Albert St., Regina, SK S4P 2S4
Tel: 306-359-3041; *Fax:* 306-525-4173
jaques@hierlaw.com
www.hierlaw.com

***Regina*: Kanuka Thuringer LLP, Barristers & Solicitors - *24**
#1400, 2500 Victoria Ave., Regina, SK S4P 3X2
Tel: 306-525-7200; *Fax:* 306-359-0590
firm@kanukathuringer.com
www.kanukathuringer.com

***Regina*: KMP Law - *5**
2600 Victoria Ave., Regina, SK S4T 1K2
Tel: 306-761-6200; *Fax:* 306-761-6222
kmplaw.com

***Regina*: Kowalishen Law Firm - *1**
1954 Angus St., Regina, SK S4T 1Z6
Tel: 306-525-2385; *Fax:* 306-525-2386
kowalishenlaw@hotmail.com

***Regina*: MacKay & McLean - *3**
2042 Cornwall St., Regina, SK S4P 2K5
Tel: 306-569-1301; *Fax:* 306-569-8560
dgmackay@sasktel.net
www.mackaymclean.com/index

***Regina*: MacLean Keith - *4**
Nicol Ct., 2398 Scarth St., Regina, SK S4P 2J7
Tel: 306-757-1611; *Fax:* 306-757-0712

***Regina*: McCrank Stewart LLP - *11**
#401, 1916 Dewdney Ave., Regina, SK S4R 1G9
Tel: 306-525-2191; *Fax:* 306-757-8138
www.msj.ca

***Regina*: McDougall Gauley - *33**
1500 - 1881 Scarth St., Regina, SK S4P 4K9
Tel: 306-757-1641; *Fax:* 306-359-0785
mramsay@mcdougallgauley.com
www.mcdougallgauley.com

***Regina*: Merchant Law Group LLP - Regina - *50**
#100, Saskatchewan Drive Plaza, 2401 Saskatchewan Dr., Regina, SK S4P 4H8
Tel: 306-359-7777; *Fax:* 306-522-3299
Toll-Free: 888-567-7777
merchant@merchantlaw.com
www.merchantlaw.com

***Regina*: Morgan, Khaladkar & Skinner - *2**
2510 - 13 Ave., Regina, SK S4P 0W2
Tel: 306-525-9191; *Fax:* 306-525-0006

***Regina*: Noble, Johnston & Associates - *4**
1143 Lakewood Ct. North, Regina, SK S4X 3S3
Tel: 306-949-5616; *Fax:* 306-775-2234
info@noblejohnston.com
www.noblejohnston.com

***Regina*: Olive, Waller, Zinkhan & Waller - *18**
#1000, 2002 Victoria Ave., Regina, SK S4P 0R7
Tel: 306-359-1888; *Fax:* 306-352-0771
owzw@owzw.com
www.owzw.com

***Regina*: Phillips & Co. - *3**
Holdane House, 2100 Scarth St., Regina, SK S4P 2H6
Tel: 306-569-0811; *Fax:* 306-565-3434
phillips.co@sasktel.net

***Regina*: Ann Phillips - *1**
#205, 2022 Cornwall St., Regina, SK S4P 2K5
Tel: 306-791-2626; *Fax:* 306-352-2020
annphillips@attglobal.net

***Regina*: Reimer & Canham - *2**
116 Albert St., Regina, SK S4R 2N2
Tel: 306-791-2503; *Fax:* 306-543-9655

***Regina*: Sheppard, Braun, Muma - *2**
#204, 3988 Albert St., Regina, SK S4S 3R1
Tel: 306-586-6020; *Fax:* 306-586-8525
sbmlaw@sasktel.net

***Regina*: Silversides & Cox - *2**
180 Saskatchewan Pl., 1870 Albert St., Regina, SK S4P 4B7
Tel: 306-337-4560; *Fax:* 306-337-4568

***Regina*: James Sirounis Law Office**
#100, 1150 Albert St., Regina, SK S4R 2R1
Tel: 306-569-7711

***Regina*: Walker, Singer & McCannell - *3**
1872 Angus St., Regina, SK S4T 1Z4
Tel: 306-352-8109; *Fax:* 306-352-7339

***Regina*: Willows Tulloch - *1**
533 Victoria Avenue, Regina, SK S4N 0P4
Tel: 306-924-8600; *Fax:* 306-924-8601
ntulloch@accesscom.ca

***Regina*: Garrett Wilson Q.C. - *1**
2237 Smith St., Regina, SK S4P 2P5
Tel: 306-352-1641; *Fax:* 306-525-8884

***Rosetown*: Aseltine Skelton & Turner - *2**
P.O. Box 1120, 314 Main St., Rosetown, SK S0L 2V0
Tel: 306-882-4244; *Fax:* 306-882-3969

***Saskatoon*: A.S.K. Law - *3**
#210, 75 - 24th St. East, Saskatoon, SK S7K 0K3
Tel: 306-933-3933; *Fax:* 306-933-9505
www.asklaw.ca

***Saskatoon*: Agnew & Company - *3**
279 - 3rd Avenue North, Saskatoon, SK S7K 2H8
Tel: 306-244-7966; *Fax:* 306-244-8010
agnewco@sasktel.net

***Saskatoon*: Balfour Moss - *5**
#600, Princeton Tower, 123 - 2nd Ave. South, Saskatoon, SK S7K 7E6
Tel: 306-665-7844; *Fax:* 306-652-1586
balfourmoss.saskatoon@balfourmoss.com
www.balfourmoss.com

***Saskatoon*: Bodnar Campbell - *2**
#400, 245 - 3 Ave. South, Saskatoon, SK S7K 1M4
Tel: 306-664-3314; *Fax:* 306-664-3354
mbodnarlaw@sasktel.net

***Saskatoon*: Brayford Shapiro - *2**
311 - 21 St. East., Saskatoon, SK S7K 0C1
Tel: 306-244-5656; *Fax:* 306-244-5644
www.shapirolaw.ca

***Saskatoon*: Brent & Greenhorn - *2**
3026 Taylor St. East, Saskatoon, SK S7H 4J2
Tel: 306-955-9544; *Fax:* 306-955-2656
bandg@sasktel.net
www.lynnegreenhorn.com

***Saskatoon*: Burlingham Cuelenaere Legal Prof. Corp. - *4**
1043 - 8 St. East, Saskatoon, SK S7H 0S2
Tel: 306-343-9581; *Fax:* 306-343-1947
burlinghamcuelenaere@sasktel.net

***Saskatoon*: William J. Campbell - *1**
#100, 220 - 3 Ave. South, Saskatoon, SK S7K 1M1
Tel: 306-664-3314; *Fax:* 306-664-3354
wjcampbell@sasktel.net

***Saskatoon*: Cuelenaere, Kendall, Katzman & Watson - *15**
#500, Standard Life Bldg., 128 - 4th Ave. South, Saskatoon, SK S7K 1M8
Tel: 306-653-5000; *Fax:* 306-652-4171
admin@cuelenaere.com
www.cuelenaere.com

***Saskatoon*: Dufour Scott Phelps & Mason - *5**
#400, 135 - 21st St. East, Saskatoon, SK S7K 0B4
Tel: 306-244-2201; *Fax:* 306-244-2420
www.dufourlaw.com

***Saskatoon*: Halyk Kennedy Knox - *3**
321 - 6 Ave. North, Saskatoon, SK S7K 2S3
Tel: 306-665-3434; *Fax:* 306-652-1915
halyk@sasktel.net

***Saskatoon*: Marvin W. Henderson - *1**
1219 - 8th St. East, Saskatoon, SK S7H 0S5
Tel: 306-652-1234; *Fax:* 306-652-1235
mwhlaw@sasktel.net

***Saskatoon*: Hnatyshyn Gough - *5**
#601, 402 - 21st St. East, Saskatoon, SK S7K 0C3
Tel: 306-653-5150; *Fax:* 306-652-5859
hglaw@hglaw.ca
www.hglaw.ca

***Saskatoon*: Kloppenburg & Kloppenburg - *2**
#603, Princeton Tower, 123 - 2nd Ave. South, Saskatoon, SK S7K 7E6
Tel: 306-665-7600; *Fax:* 306-665-7800
juristen@kloppenburg.ca
www.kloppenburg.ca

***Saskatoon*: KMP Law - *3**
#505, 333 - 3 Ave. North, Saskatoon, SK S7K 2M2
Tel: 306-652-8833; *Fax:* 306-652-3333
kmplaw.com

***Saskatoon*: Koskie Helms - *2**
#3, 501 Gray Ave., Saskatoon, SK S7N 2H8
Tel: 306-242-8478; *Fax:* 306-653-2120
firm@koskie.com
www.koskie.com

***Saskatoon*: Leland Kimpinski LLP - *7**
#800, 230 - 22nd St. East, Saskatoon, SK S7K 0E9
Tel: 306-244-6686; *Fax:* 306-653-7008
info@lelandlaw.ca
www.lelandlaw.ca

***Saskatoon*: MacDermid Lamarsh - *7**
301 - 3rd Ave. South, Saskatoon, SK S7K 1M6
Tel: 306-652-9422; *Fax:* 306-242-1554
macmarsh@macmarsh.com
www.macdermidlamarsh.com

***Saskatoon*: MacLean Keith - *2**
#1300, 410 - 22 St. East, Saskatoon, SK S7K 5T6
Tel: 306-664-9200; *Fax:* 306-664-1960
maxleankeith@sk.sympatico.ca

***Saskatoon*: Louis E. Martel - *1**
811 Bayview Cres., Saskatoon, SK S7V 1B7
Tel: 306-652-6830; *Fax:* 306-652-6836
martellawoffice@sasktel.net
www.martellawoffice.ca

***Saskatoon*: Mathiason, Valkenburg - *1**
#705, 230 - 22nd St. East, Saskatoon, SK S7K 0E9
Tel: 306-242-1202; *Fax:* 306-244-4423
mvm@sasktel.net

***Saskatoon*: McKercher LLP - *59**
374 Third Ave. South, Saskatoon, SK S7K 1M5
Tel: 306-653-2000; *Fax:* 306-653-2669
info@mckercher.ca
www.mckercher.ca

***Saskatoon*: Donald R. Morgan - *1**
#810, 410 - 22nd St. East, Saskatoon, SK S7K 5T6
Tel: 306-665-2666; *Fax:* 306-652-6646
morgan@donmorgan.ca

***Saskatoon*: Nussbaum & Company - *2**
#204, 2102 - 8 St. East, Saskatoon, SK S7H 0V1
Tel: 306-955-8890; *Fax:* 306-955-1293
nussbaum@sasktel.net

***Saskatoon*: Piche & Company - *1**
204-611 University Dr., Saskatoon, SK S7N 3Z1
Tel: 306-955-7667; *Fax:* 306-955-7727
Toll-Free: 866-234-3444
pichelaw@sasktel.net

***Saskatoon*: Plaxton Gillies Barristers & Solicitors - *2**
#200, 402 - 21 St. East, Saskatoon, SK S7K 0C3
Tel: 306-653-1500; *Fax:* 306-664-6659
contactus@plaxtonlaw.com

** indicates number of lawyers*

***Saskatoon*: Quon Ferguson - *2**
#704, 224 - 4th Ave. South, Saskatoon, SK S7K 5M5
Tel: 306-665-8828; *Fax:* 306-665-8835

***Saskatoon*: Rask & Company - *6**
#300, 402 - 21st St. East, Saskatoon, SK S7K 0C3
Tel: 306-242-2500; *Fax:* 306-242-2538
kim@rasklaw.com
www.rasklaw.com

***Saskatoon*: Robertson Stromberg Pedersen LLP - *21**
#600, Canada Building, 105 - 21st St. East, Saskatoon, SK S7K 0B3
Tel: 306-652-7575; *Fax:* 306-652-2445
Toll-Free: 800-667-0070
www.thinkrsplaw.com

***Saskatoon*: Roe & Company - *6**
#313, 220 - 3 Ave. South, Saskatoon, SK S7K 1M1
Tel: 306-244-9865; *Fax:* 306-934-6827
smurray@sasktel.net
http://www.roeandcompany.ca/

***Saskatoon*: Rozdilsky, Baniak - *2**
#301, 220 - 3rd Ave. South, Saskatoon, SK S7K 1M1
Tel: 306-477-5408; *Fax:* 306-664-9992

***Saskatoon*: Scharfstein Gibbings Walen & Fisher LLP - *12**
#500, Scotiabank Bldg., 111 - 2 Ave. South, Saskatoon, SK S7K 1K6
Tel: 306-653-2838; *Fax:* 306-652-4747
lawyers@scharfsteinlaw.com
www.scharfsteinlaw.com

***Saskatoon*: Scott & Fehr Law Office - *4**
211 - 33rd St. West, Saskatoon, SK S7L 0V2
Tel: 306-955-6822; *Fax:* 306-955-6823
office@scottfehr.com

***Saskatoon*: Sonnenschein Law Office - *1**
Lincoln's Inn, 313 - 20th St. East, Saskatoon, SK S7K 0A9
Tel: 306-652-4730; *Fax:* 306-653-5760
sonnenschein@sasktel.net

***Saskatoon*: Stevenson Hood Thornton Beaubier LLP - *14**
#500, 123 - 2nd Ave. South, Saskatoon, SK S7K 7E6
Tel: 306-244-0132; *Fax:* 306-653-1118
info@shtb-law.com
www.shtb-law.com

***Saskatoon*: Stooshinoff Law Office - *2**
#300, 416 - 21st St. East, Saskatoon, SK S7K 0C2
Tel: 306-653-9000; *Fax:* 306-653-5284
stooshinoff.law@sasktel.net

***Saskatoon*: Wallace Meschishnick Clackson Zawada - *16**
#901, 119 - 4th Ave. South, Saskatoon, SK S7K 5X2
Tel: 306-933-0004; *Fax:* 306-933-2006
info@wmcz.com
www.wmcz.com

***Saskatoon*: Steven J. Wilson - *1**
2120 York Ave., Saskatoon, SK S7J 1H8
Tel: 306-956-3345; *Fax:* 306-955-1699

***Shaunavon*: Coralie O. Geving - *1**
23 - 3 Ave. East, Shaunavon, SK S0N 2M0
Tel: 306-297-2205; *Fax:* 306-297-2411

***Swift Current*: Anderson & Company - *6**
P.O. Box 610, 51 - 1st Ave. NW, Swift Current, SK S9H 3W4
Tel: 306-773-2891; *Fax:* 306-778-3364
anderson.company@sasktel.net

***Swift Current*: Holland Law Office - *1**
P.O. Box 97, 262 - 2 Ave. NE, Swift Current, SK S9H 3V5
Tel: 306-773-0661; *Fax:* 306-773-9630

***Swift Current*: MacBean Tessem - *6**
Box 550, P.O. Box 550, 151 First Ave. NE, Swift Current, SK S9H 2B1
Tel: 306-773-9343; *Fax:* 306-778-3828
macbeantessem@macbeantessem.com
www.macbeantessem.com

***Swift Current*: McLaughlin, Forrester, Heinrichs - *3**
#9, P.O. Box 100, 244 - 1 Ave. NE, Swift Current, SK S9H 2B4
Tel: 306-773-7205; *Fax:* 306-773-9715
mfh.law@sasktel.net

***Turtleford*: D.S. Wooff - *1**
P.O. Box 99, Turtleford, SK S0M 2Y0
Tel: 306-845-2599

***Unity*: Hepting Neil & Jeanson - *3**
P.O. Box 600, 206 - 2nd Ave. West, Unity, SK S0K 4L0
Tel: 306-228-2631; *Fax:* 306-228-4449
hepting.neil@sasktel.net

***Wadena*: Marquette Law Firm - *1**
P.O. Box 699, 234 Main St. North, Wadena, SK S0A 4J0
Tel: 306-338-2554; *Fax:* 306-338-3131

***Weyburn*: NSWB Law Firm - *7**
P.O. Box 8, 319 Souris Ave. NE, Weyburn, SK S4H 2J8
Tel: 306-842-4654; *Fax:* 306-842-0522
law@nswb.com
www.nswb.com

***Wynyard*: Klebeck Law Office - *1**
P.O. Box 1120, 115 Ave. B East, Wynyard, SK S0A 4T0
Tel: 306-554-2523; *Fax:* 306-554-2099
klebeck.law.office@sasktel.net

***Wynyard*: Paulson & Ferraton - *1**
P.O. Box 460, 106 Main St., Wynyard, SK S0A 4T0
Tel: 306-554-2134; *Fax:* 306-554-2342
paulson.ferraton@sasktel.net

***Yorkton*: Stanatinos, Leland & Campbell LLP - *9**
P.O. Box 188, 36 - 4 Ave. North, Yorkton, SK S3N 2V7
Tel: 306-783-8541; *Fax:* 306-786-7484

***Yorkton*: Tourney, Dellow - *2**
#2, 16 - 3rd Ave. North, Yorkton, SK S3N 1B9
Tel: 306-782-2211; *Fax:* 306-782-2213
tourneydellow@sasktel.net

Yukon Territory

***Whitehorse*: Austring, Fendrick, Fairman & Parkkari - *8**
The Drury Bldg., 3081 - 3rd Ave., Whitehorse, YT Y1A 4Z7
Tel: 867-668-4405; *Fax:* 867-668-3710
Toll-Free: 800-661-0533
info@lawyukon.com
www.lawyukon.com

***Whitehorse*: Lackowicz & Hoffman - *6**
#300, 204 Black St., Whitehorse, YT Y1A 2M9
Tel: 867-668-5252; *Fax:* 867-668-5251
lackowicz.shier@yukonlaw.com

***Whitehorse*: Macdonald & Company - *3**
#200, 204 Lambert St., Whitehorse, YT Y1A 3T2
Tel: 867-667-7885; *Fax:* 867-667-7600
gmacdonald@anton.yk.ca

** indicates number of lawyers*

SECTION 12
LIBRARIES

Library & Archives Canada: 1509

Government Departments in Charge of Libraries: 1509

Library listings are arranged by province. Each province includes the following categories:

Regional Systems

Public Libraries

Archives

Library & Archives Canada
395 Wellington St., Ottawa ON K1A 0N4
613/996-5115; Fax: 613/995-6274
URL: www.collectionscanada.ca
Librarian & Archivist of Canada, Daniel J. Caron

Canadian Book Exchange Centre (CBEC): 613/952-8902; Fax: 613/954-9891; Email: cbeccel@lacbac.gc.ca; URL: www.collectionscanada.ca/cbeccel/; Symbol: OONL; OOA-Chief, Bill Murphy

Canadian Cataloguing in Publications Program (CIP): 819/994-6881; Fax: 819/997-7517; Email: cip@lacbac.gc.ca; URL:www.collectionscanada.ca/cip; Symbol: OONL; OOA-CIP Coordinator, Luc Simard

Canadian ISBN/ISMN Agency: 819/994-6872; Fax: 819/997-7517; Email: isbn@lac-bac.gc.ca; URL:www.collectionscanada.ca/isbn; Symbol: OONL; OOA

Database Networks (Union Catalogue): 819/997-7990; Fax: 819/994-4388; Email: union.catalogue@lacbac.gc.ca; URL: www.collectionscanada.ca/6/21/; Symbol: OONL; OOA-Chief, Emilie Lowenberg

Jacob M. Lowy Collection: 613/995-7960; Fax: 613/943-1112; Email: lowy@lac-bac.gc.ca; URL:www.collectionscanada.ca/6/26/s26-400-e.html; Symbol: OONL-Curator, Cheryl Jaffee

Legal Deposit: 819/997-9565; Fax: 819/953-8508; Email: legal.deposit@lac-bac.gc.ca; URL: www.collectionscanada.ca/6/25/index-e.html; Symbol: OONL; OOA-Chief, John Stegenga

Reference & Genealogy Division: 613/996-5115; Fax:613/995-6274; Email: reference@lac-bac.gc.ca; URL: www.collectionscanada.ca/services/005-220-e.html; www.genealogy.gc.ca/index_e.html; Symbol: OONL; OOA-Director, Antonio Lechasseur

Government Departments in Charge of Libraries

ALBERTA: Alberta Community Development, Community & Citizenship Services, Libraries, Community & Voluntary Sector Services Branch, Libraries Section, #803, Standard Life Centre, 10405 Jasper Ave., Edmonton, AB T5J 4R7, 780/427-6315; Fax: 780/415-8594, Email: libraries@gov.ab.ca, URL: www.cd.gov.ab.ca - Director, Punch Jackson

BRITISH COLUMBIA: Ministry of Education, Public Library Services Branch, 65 Humbold St., 5th Fl., PO Box 9831, Stn Prov Govt, Victoria BC V8V 4W8, 250/356-1791; Fax: 250/953-3225; Toll Free: 800-663-7051, Email: plsb@gov.bc.ca, URL: www.bced.gov.bc.ca/pls - Director of Library Services, Maureen Wood

MANITOBA: Culture, Heritage & Tourism Public Library Services Branch, #200, 1525 - 1st St. South, Brandon MB R7A 7A1, 204/726-6590, Fax: 204/726-6868, Email: pls@gov.mb.ca, URL: www.gov.mb.ca/chc/maplin - Director, Maureen Cubberley

NEW BRUNSWICK: New Brunswick Public Library Service, Place 2000, Provincial Office, 250 King St., Fredericton NB E3B 9M9, 506/453-2354, Fax: 506/444-4064, Email: sylvie.nadeau@gnb.ca, URL: www.gnb.ca/003/index-e.asp - Executive Director, Sylvie Nadeau

NEWFOUNDLAND & LABRADOR: Provincial Information & Library Resources Board, 48 St. George's Ave., Stephenville NL A2N 1K9, 709/643-0900, Fax: 709/643-0925, Email: shawntetford@nlpubliclibraries.ca, URL: www.nlpubliclibraries.ca - Executive Director, Shawn Tetford

NORTHWEST TERRITORIES: Northwest Territories Public Library Services, 75 Woodland Dr., Hay River NT X0E 1G1, 867/874-6531, Fax: 867/874-3321, Toll Free: 866-297-0232, Email: alison_hopkins@gov.nt.ca, URL: www.nwtpls.gov.nt.ca -Territorial Librarian, Alison Hopkins

NOVA SCOTIA: Nova Scotia Provincial Library, 770 Kempt Rd., Halifax NS B3K 4X8, 902/ 424-2457, Fax: 902/424-0633, Email: admin@nshpl.library.ns.ca, URL: www.library.ns.ca - Provincial Librarian, Jennifer Evans

NUNAVUT: Nunavut Public Library Services, PO Box 270, Baker Lake NU X0C 0A0, 867/793-3327, Fax: 867/793-3332, URL: www.gov.nu.ca/cley/home/english/libraries.html - Manager, Library Services, Petra Mauerhoff

ONTARIO: Ministry of Culture, Heritage & Libraries Branch, 400 University Ave., 4th Fl., Toronto ON M7A 2R9, 416/314-7342: Fax: 416/314-7635, Email: suzanne.roweknight@mcl.gov.on.ca; rita.scagnetti@mcl.gov.on.ca, URL: www.culture.gov.on.ca/english/culdiv/library - Manager of Libraries: Suzanne Rowe-Knight, Director, Heritage & Libraries Branch: Rita Scagnetti

PRINCE EDWARD ISLAND: Provincial Library Service, 89 Redhead Rd., PO Box 7500, Morell PE C0A 1S0, 902/961-7320, Fax: 902/961-7322, Email: ajgroen@gov.pe.ca, URL: www.library.pe.ca - Provincial Librarian, Allan J. Groen

QUÉBEC: Ministère de la Culture et des Communications, Lecture et Livre, Bibliothèques - Direction de la coordination et du soutien à la gestion des programmes, Édifice Guy-Frégault, 225, Grande Allée est, Bloc C, RC, Québec QC G1R 5G5, 418/380-2304, Télécopieur: 418/380-2324, Courriel: jacques.morrier@mcc.gouv.qc.ca, URL: www.mcc.gouv.qc.ca - Responsable: Jacques Morrier

SASKATCHEWAN: Provincial Library, 1945 Hamilton St., 8th Fl., Regina SK S4P 2C8, 306/787-2976, Fax: 306/787-2029, Email: jcampbell@library.gov.sk.ca, URL: www.learning.gov.sk.ca/branches/prov_library/index.shtml - Provincial Librarian: Joylene Campbell

YUKON: Yukon Public Libraries, Public Library Services, Government of Yukon, Community Libraries, PO Box 2703, Whitehorse YT Y1A 2C6, 867/667-5239, Fax: 867/393-6333, Toll Free (in Yukon): 800-661-0408, local 5239, Email: whitehorse.library@gov.yk.ca, URL: www.community.gov.yk.ca/libraries - Manager: Julie Ourom

Alberta

Regional Systems

Chinook Arch Regional Library System
2902 - 7th Ave. North, Lethbridge AB T1H 5C6
Tel: 403-380-1500; *Fax:* 403-380-3550
arch@chinookarch.ab.ca
www.chinookarch.ab.ca

Maggie Macdonald, CEO
mmacdonald@chinookarch.ab.ca
Anna Linnville, Manager, Public Services
alinnville@chinookarch.ab.ca
Tom Moffatt, Manager, Information Technology
tmoffatt@chinookarch.ab.ca
Mary Ann Harms, Head, Acquisitions
mharms@chinookarch.ab.ca

Marigold Library System
710 - 2nd St., Strathmore AB T1P 1K4
Tel: 403-934-5334; *Fax:* 403-934-5331
admin@marigold.ab.ca
www.marigold.ab.ca

Rowena Lunn, Director
rfl@marigold.ab.ca
Linda Williams, Consultant/Library Services
lindaw@marigold.ab.ca
Karen Labuik, Assistant Director
klabuik@marigold.ab.ca
Steven Pattison, Automation & Network Services
stevenp@marigold.ab.ca

Northern Lights Library System
5615 - 48 St., Elk Point AB T0A 1A0
Tel: 780-724-2596; *Fax:* 780-724-2597
Toll-Free: 800-561-0387
info@nlls.ab.ca
www.nlls.ab.ca

Mircea Panciuk, Director
director@nlls.ab.ca
780-724-2596 ext. 236

Parkland Regional Library System
5404 - 56th Ave., Lacombe AB T4L 1G1
Tel: 403-782-3850; *Fax:* 403-782-4650
rsheppard@prl.ab.ca
www.prl.ab.ca

Ronald Sheppard, Director
Mary Jane Bilsland, Consultant

Peace Library System
8301 - 110 St., Grande Prairie AB T8W 6T2
Tel: 780-538-4656; *Fax:* 780-539-5285
Toll-Free: 800-422-6875
peacelib@peacelibrarysystem.ab.ca
www.peacelibrarysystem.ab.ca

Linda Duplessis, Director
ldupless@peacelibrarysystem.ab.ca
Carol Downing, Technical Services Manager
cdowning@peacelibrarysystem.ab.ca
780-538-4656
Padmini Ramaswamy, Network Administrator
pramaswa@peacelibrarysystem.ab.ca

Shortgrass Library System
2375 - 10th Ave. SW, Medicine Hat AB T1A 8G2
Tel: 403-529-0550; *Fax:* 403-528-2473
director@shortgrass.ca
www.shortgrass.ca

Petra Mauerhoff, CEO & Director
petra@shortgrass.ca
Robert Batchelder, Assistant Director, Technical Services
bob@shortgrass.ca
Peggy Curthoys, Acquisitions Officer
peggy@shortgrass.ca

Yellowhead Regional Library
433 King St., Spruce Grove AB T7X 2Y1
Tel: 780-962-2003; *Fax:* 780-962-2770
yrlquery@yrl.ab.ca
www.yrl.ab.ca

Clive Maishment, Director
Kevin Dodds, Assistant Director
kdodds@yrl.ab.ca
Wendy Sears-Ilnicki, Manager, Bibliographic Services
wsears@yrl.ab.ca
Robert Zylstra, Manager, Technology Services
rzylstra@yrl.ab.ca

Public Libraries

Acadia Valley: Acadia Municipal Library
Warren Peers School, PO Box 6, Acadia Valley AB T0J 0A0
Tel: 403-972-3744; *Fax:* 403-972-2000
aavalibrary@marigold.ab.ca
www.marigold.ab.ca/about/memberlibs/acadia.html

Maxine Booker, Chair
Brandi Peacock, Manager
Debbie Neilson, Library Assistant

Acme: Acme Municipal Library
610 Walsh Ave., Acme AB T0M 0A0
Tel: 403-546-3879; *Fax:* 403-546-2248
aamlibrary@marigold.ab.ca
www.marigold.ab.ca/about/memberlibs/acme.html

Colleen Herrara, Library Manager
aamlibrary@marigold.ab.ca

Airdrie: Airdrie Public Library
#111, 304 Main St. South, Airdrie AB T4B 3C3
Tel: 403-948-0600; *Fax:* 403-912-4002
info@airdriepubliclibrary.ca
www.airdriepubliclibrary.ca

Janine Jevne, Director
janine.jevne@airdriepubliclibrary.ca

Alberta Beach: Alberta Beach Public Library
4811 - 50th Ave., Alberta Beach AB T0E 0A0
Tel: 780-924-3491; *Fax:* 780-924-3491
www.albertabeachlibrary.ca

Sylvia McGinley, Chair
Joanne Hilger, Secretary
Deb Hawkins-Stewart, Treasurer

Alder Flats: Alder Flats Public Library
Hwy. 13, Alder Flats AB T0C 0A0
Tel: 780-388-3881; *Fax:* 780-388-3887
Other Numbers: 780-514-7639 (Off Hours); 780-388-0049 (Summer)
afpl@wrps.ab.ca
www.alderflatslibrary.ab.ca

Judy Miners, Library Director
780-388-3881

Alix: Alix Public Library
4928 - 50th St., Alix AB T0C 0B0
Tel: 403-747-3233
alixpublic@libs.prl.ab.ca
alixpublic.prl.ab.ca

Beth Richardson, Librarian

Alliance: Alliance Community Library
101 - 1st Ave. East, Alliance AB T0B 0A0
Tel: 780-879-3733
alliancelibrary@libs.prl.ab.ca
alliance.prl.ab.ca/index.htm

Tracy Rombough, Libary Manager
aplen7@telusplanet.net

Amisk: Amisk Municipal Library
5005 - 50 St., Amisk AB T0B 0B0
Tel: 780-628-5457
amiskpubliclibrary@libs.prl.ab.ca
http://amisklibrary.prl.ab.ca/

Carmen Toma, Library Manager

***Andrew:* Andrew Municipal Public Library**
5021 - 50 St., Andrew AB T0B 0C0
Tel: 780-365-3501; *Fax:* 780-365-3734
public@mcsnet.ca
www.andrewschool.ca
Denise Dorland, Library Technician II
780-365-3501 ext. 4

***Arrowwood:* Arrowwood Municipal Library**
22 Main St., Arrowwood AB T0L 0B0
Tel: 403-534-3932; *Fax:* 403-534-3932
Toll-Free: 866-941-4177
help@arrowwoodlibrary.ca
www.arrowwoodlibrary.ca/client/arrowwood
Dorothy Way, Library Manager

***Ashmont:* Ashmont Community Library**
Ashmont School, Main St., Ashmont AB T0A 0C0
Tel: 780-726-3877; *Fax:* 780-726-3777
www.ashmontlibrary.ab.ca
Karen Duperron, Librarian

***Athabasca:* Alice B. Donahue Library & Archives**
4716 - 48th St., Athabasca AB T9S 2B6
Tel: 780-675-2735
www.athabascalibrary.ab.ca
Cynthia Graefe, Library Manager & Resource Sharing Contact
librarian@athabascalibrary.ab.ca

***Banff:* Banff Public Library**
101 Bear St., Banff AB T1L 1H3
Tel: 403-762-2661; *Fax:* 403-762-3805
banff_library@telusplanet.net
www.banfflibrary.ab.ca
Holly Nguyen, Librarian
Susanne Repstock, Assistant Librarian

***Barnwell:* Barnwell Municipal Library**
490 Cottonwood St., Barnwell AB T0K 0B0
Tel: 403-223-3626; *Toll-Free:* 866-941-4177
libbar@barnwelllibrary.ca
www.barnwelllibrary.ca/client/barnwell
Cindy Evanson, Library Manager
cevanson@barnwelllibrary.ca
403-223-3626

***Barrhead:* Barrhead Public Library**
5103 - 53 Ave., Barrhead AB T7N 1N9
Tel: 780-674-8519; *Fax:* 780-674-8520
plibrary@barrheadpubliclibrary.ca
www.barrheadpubliclibrary.ca
Elaine Dickie, Library Director

***Bashaw:* Bashaw Municipal Library**
5112 - 52nd St., Bashaw AB T0B 0H0
Tel: 780-372-4055; *Fax:* 780-372-4055
bashawlibrary@libs.prl.ab.ca
bashawlibrary.prl.ab.ca/
Cindy Hunter, Library Manager
780-372-4055

***Bassano:* Bassano Memorial Library**
522 - 2nd Ave., Bassano AB T0J 0B0
Tel: 403-641-4065
bmlcapic@eidnet.org
www.shortgrass-lib.ab.ca/bml

***Bawlf:* David Knipe Memorial Library**
203 Hanson St., PO Box 116, Bawlf AB T0B 0J0
Tel: 780-373-3882; *Fax:* 780-373-3882
bawlflibrary@libs.prl.ab.ca
bawlflibrary.prl.ab.ca
Fern Reinke, Library Manager

***Bear Canyon:* Bear Point Community Library**
PO Box 43, Bear Canyon AB T0H 0B0
Tel: 780-595-3771; *Fax:* 780-595-3762
librarian@bearpointlibrary.ab.ca
www.bearpointlibrary.ab.ca
Tannis Bigam, Librarian

***Beaumont:* Bibliothèque de Beaumont Library**
5700 - 49th St., Beaumont AB T4X 1S7
Tel: 780-929-2665; *Fax:* 780-929-1291
www.beaumontlibrary.com
Martin Walters, Library Manager
martin@beaumontlibrary.com
Andrea Ciochetti, Program Coordinator
andrea@beaumontlibray.com

***Beaverlodge:* Beaverlodge RCMP Centennial Library**
406 - 10th St., Beaverlodge AB T0H 0C0
Tel: 780-354-2569; *Fax:* 780-354-3078
abarlibrary@telusplanet.net
www.beaverlodgelibrary.ab.ca
Shelly Longson, Library Manager

***Beiseker:* Beiseker Municipal Library**
Old Railway Station, 601 - 1st Ave., Beiseker AB T0M 0G0
Tel: 403-947-3230; *Fax:* 403-947-2146
abemlibrary@marigold.ab.ca
www.beisekerlibrary.com
Tracy Bell, Library Manager

***Bellevue:* Bellevue Municipal Library**
2802 - 222nd St., Bellevue AB T0K 0C0
Tel: 403-564-5201; *Fax:* 403-564-5201
libbel@chinookarch.ab.ca
Doreen Glavin, Librarian
403-564-5201

***Bentley:* Bentley Municipal Library**
5014 - 49 Ave., Bentley AB T0C 0J0
Tel: 403-748-4626; *Fax:* 403-748-4627
bentleylibrary@libs.prl.ab.ca
bentleylibrary.prl.ab.ca
Tina Whitfield, Library Manager

***Berwyn:* Berwyn W.I. Municipal Library**
5105 - 51st St., Berwyn AB T0H 0E0
Tel: 780-338-3616; *Fax:* 780-338-3616
librarian@berwynlibrary.ab.ca
Kim Byard, Library Manager

***Big Valley:* Big Valley Municipal Library**
29 - 1st Ave. South, Big Valley AB T0J 0G0
Tel: 403-876-2642; *Fax:* 403-876-2401
bigvalleylibrary@prl.ab.ca
bvlibrary.prl.ab.ca
Janice E. Hermus, Librarian

***Black Diamond:* Sheep River Community Library**
301 Center Ave., Black Diamond AB T0L 0H0
Tel: 403-933-3278; *Fax:* 403-933-3278
abdsrclibrary@marigold.ab.ca
Muhammad Zia-Ul-Haque, Librarian
Eleanor Chinnick, Senior Librarian
Nadine Russell, Library Clerk

***Blackfalds:* Blackfalds Public Library**
5018 Waghorn St., Blackfalds AB T0M 0J0
Tel: 403-885-2343; *Fax:* 403-885-4353
Other Numbers: 403-885-6251 program room
library@blackfaldslibrary.com
www.blackfaldslibrary.com
Carley Binder, Librarian

***Blairmore:* Crowsnest Pass Municipal Library - Blairmore**
2114 - 127 St., Blairmore AB T0K 0E0
Tel: 403-562-8393; *Fax:* 403-562-8397
libbla@chinookarch.ab.ca
Judy Bradley, Librarian

***Blue Ridge:* Blue Ridge Community Library**
24A Main St., Blue Ridge AB T0E 0B0
Tel: 780-648-7323; *Fax:* 780-648-2348
www.yrl.ab.ca/about/lib/abrc.html
Mary Anne Lehman, Chair
Susan Curtis, Librarian
sucurtis@telusplanet.net

***Bodo:* Bodo Public Library**
PO Box 93, Bodo AB T0B 0M0
Tel: 780-753-6079; *Fax:* 780-753-8195
bodolibrary@libs.prl.ab.ca
www.prl.ab.ca/ABOD
Roxanna Wotschell, Library Manager

***Bon Accord:* Bon Accord Public Library**
PO Box 749, Bon Accord AB T0A 0K0
Tel: 780-921-2540; *Fax:* 780-921-2580
www.bonaccordlibrary.ab.ca
Dyvonna Inkster, Chair
Gayle Boyd, Library Manager
Joyce Curtis-Bonardi, Contact, Interlibrary Loans
Anita van der Leek, Contact, Programs

***Bonnyville:* Bonnyville Municipal Library**
4804 - 49th Ave., Bonnyville AB T9N 2J3
Tel: 780-826-3071; *Fax:* 780-826-2058
librarian@bonnyvillelibrary.ab.ca
www.bonnyvillelibrary.ab.ca
Ina Smith, Library Director

Linda Smiley, Assistant Library Manager
Colleen Schoeninger, Programmer
Brigitte Stewart, Contact, Circulation & Interlibrary Loan

***Bow Island:* Bow Island Municipal Library**
510 Centre St., Bow Island AB T0K 0G0
Tel: 403-545-2828; *Fax:* 403-545-6642
bowlib@shortgrass.ca
www.shortgrass.ca/bowisland/
Susan Andersen, Library Manager

***Bowden:* Bowden Public Library**
1700 - 23rd St., Bowden AB T0M 0K0
Tel: 403-224-3688; *Fax:* 403-224-2244
bowdenlibrary@libs.prl.ab.ca
www.town.bowden.ab.ca/library.html
Roy Middleton, President
Diane Berggren, Library Manager
Benita Dalton, Library Manager's Assistant

***Boyle:* Boyle Public Library**
5002 - 3 St., Boyle AB T0A 0M0
Tel: 780-689-4161; *Fax:* 780-689-5660
librarian@boylepublib.ab.ca
www.boylepublib.ab.ca
Katherine Bulmer, Library Manager

***Breton:* Breton Public Library**
4916 - 50th Ave., Breton AB T0C 0P0
Tel: 780-696-3740; *Fax:* 780-696-3590
bretonlibrary@yrl.ab.ca
www.bretonlibrary.ab.ca
Diane Shave, Library Director

***Brocket:* Oldman River Cultural Centre Library**
PO Box 70, Brocket AB T0K 0H0
Tel: 403-965-3939; *Fax:* 403-965-2289
Reg Crow Shoe, Director

***Brooks:* Berry Creek Community School Library**
RR#2, Brooks AB T1R 1E2
Tel: 403-566-3743; *Fax:* 403-566-3736
acclibrary@marigold.ab.ca
www.marigold.ab.ca/about/memberlibs/berrycreek.html
Susan Conners, Library Manager

***Brooks:* Brooks Public Library**
420 - 1st Ave. West, Brooks AB T1R 1B9
Tel: 403-362-2947; *Fax:* 403-362-8111
brolib@shortgrass.ca
www.shortgrass-lib.ab.ca/bpl
Dino Champlone, Head Librarian
Shannon Vossepoel, Library Manager

***Brownfield:* Brownfield Community Library**
PO Box 63, Brownfield AB T0C 0R0
Tel: 403-578-2247; *Fax:* 403-578-4208
brownfieldlibrary@libs.prl.ab.ca
www.prl.ab.ca/ABROW
Pat Martin, Chair
Darvy Gilbertson, Librarian
Margo McPhail, Librarian Assistant

***Brownvale:* Brownvale Community Library**
PO Box 178, Brownvale AB T0H 0L0
Tel: 780-597-2250
Maureen Osowetski, Library Manager

***Bruderheim:* Metro Kalyn Community Library**
5017 - 49th St., Bruderheim AB T0B 0S0
Tel: 780-796-3032; *Fax:* 780-796-3032
librarian@bruderheimpl.ab.ca
www.bruderheimpl.ab.ca
Diana Mack, Community Librarian

***Cadogan:* Cadogan Public Library**
304 - 2nd St., General Delivery, Cadogan AB T0B 0T0
Tel: 780-753-6933; *Fax:* 780-753-3155
cadoganlibrary@libs.prl.ab.ca
Deb Prediger, Library Manager

***Calgary:* Alberta Association of College Librarians Newsletter**
SAIT, 1301 - 16th Ave. NW, Calgary AB T2M 0L4
Tel: 780-497-5141
dave.weber@sait.ca
www.nait.ca/libresources/aacl/news.htm
Dave Weber, Editor

***Calgary:* Calgary Public Library**
616 MacLeod Trail SE, Calgary AB T2G 2M2
Tel: 403-260-2600
dear.library@calgarypubliclibrary.com
calgarypubliclibrary.com
Gerry Meek, CEO

Ellen Humphrey, Assistant Director, Customer Services
Paul Lane, Assistant Director, Strategic Services
Scott Stanley, Senior Manager, Information Technology
Anne Sawa, Senior Manager, Support Services
Grant Kaiser, Senior Manager, Marketing & Development
Joye Hardman, Manager, Technical Services, Collections & Electronic Resources
Cathy Freer-Leszcynski, Manager, Community Services
Gerry Burger-Martindale, Customer Service Manager, Central Library
Evette Berry, Customer Service Manager, Circulation

***Calgary:* Letter of the LAA**
80 Baker Cres. NW, Calgary AB T2L 1R4
Tel: 403-284-5818; *Fax:* 403-282-6646
christine.sheppard@shaw.ca
www.laa.ab.ca
Christine Sheppard, Editor

***Calmar:* Calmar Public Library**
4705 - 50th Ave., PO Box 238, Calmar AB T0C 0V0
Tel: 780-985-3472; *Fax:* 780-985-2859
calmarlibrary@yrl.ab.ca
www.calmarpubliclibrary.ca
Carol Nystrom, Library Director
Susannah Kotyk, Library Assistant

***Camrose:* Camrose Public Library**
4710 - 50th Ave., Camrose AB T4V 0R8
Tel: 780-672-4214; *Fax:* 780-672-9165
cpldir@libs.prl.ab.ca
www.library.camrose.ab.ca
Donna Watson, Chair
Jo-Anne Cooper, Director, Library Services
Cheryl Hamel, Manager, Administrative Services

***Canmore:* Canmore Public Library**
950 - 8 Ave., Canmore AB T1W 2T1
Tel: 403-678-2468; *Fax:* 403-678-2165
info@canmorelibrary.ab.ca
www.canmorelibrary.ab.ca
Don Pickard, Chair

***Carbon:* Carbon Municipal Library**
Community Centre, PO Box 70, Carbon AB T0M 0L0
Tel: 403-572-3440
acarmlibrary@marigold.ab.ca
Steve Nedoshytko, Chair
Jay-Lynn Boutin, Library Manager

***Cardston:* Jim & Mary Kearl Library**
25 - 3rd Ave. West, Cardston AB T0K 0K0
Tel: 403-653-4775; *Fax:* 403-653-4716
libcard@chinookarch.ab.ca
Donna Beazer, Library Manager
dbeazer@cardstonlibrary.ca
403-653-4707

***Carmangay:* Carmangay & District Municipal Library**
414 Grand Ave., Carmangay AB T0L 0N0
Tel: 403-643-3777; *Fax:* 403-643-3777
help@carmangaylibrary.ca
www.carmangaylibrary.ca/client/carmangay
Marian Schibbelhute, Library Manager

***Caroline:* Caroline Municipal Library Board**
5023 - 50 Ave., Caroline AB T0M 0M0
Tel: 403-722-4060; *Fax:* 403-722-4070
carolinelibrary@libs.prl.ab.ca
carolinelibrary.prl.ab.ca
Iris Stevens, Chair
Rita Collins, Library Co-Manager
Allison Hewitt, Library Co-Manager

***Carstairs:* Carstairs Public Library**
1402 Scarlett Ranch Rd., Carstairs AB T0M 0N0
Tel: 403-337-3943; *Fax:* 403-337-3943
carstairs@libs.prl.ab.ca
www.carstairspublic.prl.ab.ca
Anne Strilchuk, Librarian
Joanne Merrick, Assistant

***Castor:* Castor Public Library**
5103 - 51 St., Castor AB T0C 0X0
Tel: 403-882-3999
castorlibrary@libs.prl.ab.ca
www.prl.ab.ca/ACAST
Wendy Bozek, Library Manager

***Cereal:* Cereal & District Municipal Library**
415 Main St., Cereal AB T0J 0N0
Tel: 403-326-3883
acermlibrary@marigold.ab.ca
Denise Reider, Library Manager

***Champion:* Champion Municipal Library**
2 Ave. South, Champion AB T0L 0R0
Tel: 403-897-3099; *Fax:* 403-897-3098
help@championlibrary.ca
www.championlibrary.ca
Patty Abel, Librarian
Claudette Simons, Staff

***Chauvin:* Chauvin Municipal Library**
5200 - 4th Ave. North, Chauvin AB T0B 0V0
Tel: 780-858-3744; *Fax:* 780-858-2392

***Claresholm:* Claresholm Municipal Library**
211 - 49 Ave. West, Claresholm AB T0L 0T0
Tel: 403-625-4168; *Fax:* 403-625-2939
libcla@chinookarch.ab.ca
Kathy Davies, Library Manager
kdavies@chinookarch.ab.ca
Anita Stone, Library Staff
Pat Cormier, Library Staff
Karen Uhl, Library Staff

***Cleardale:* Menno Simons Public Library**
PO Bag 100, Cleardale AB T0H 3Y0
Tel: 780-685-3623; *Fax:* 780-685-3665
gulas@prsd.ab.ca
Sylvia Gula, Librarian

***Clive:* Clive Public Library**
Clive Village Office, 5115 - 50 St., Clive AB T0C 0Y0
Tel: 403-784-3131; *Fax:* 403-784-3131
clivelibrary@libs.prl.ab.ca
www.clivepublib.prl.ab.ca
Sue Giesbrecht, Chair
Sandra Ward, Librarian
Dawna Rodney, Assistant Librarian

***Coaldale:* Coaldale Public Library**
2014 - 18 St., Coaldale AB T1M 1E9
Tel: 403-345-1340; *Fax:* 403-345-1342
help@coaldalelibrary.ca
www.coaldalelibrary.ca
Jane Franz, Librarian

***Cochrane:* Nan Boothby Memorial Library**
405 Railway St. West, Cochrane AB T4C 2E2
Tel: 403-932-4353; *Fax:* 403-932-4385
nanboothby@home.com
www.cochranepubliclibrary.ca
Adrian Dalwood, Librarian

***Cold Lake:* Cold Lake Public Library**
5513B - 48 Ave., Cold Lake AB T9M 1X9
Tel: 780-594-8828; *Fax:* 780-594-7787
ill@library.coldlake.ab.ca (Resource sharing)
www.library.coldlake.ab.ca
Kellie Bellew Martin, Chair
Mary Anne Penner, Library Director
director@library.coldlake.ab.ca
Cynthia Sloychuk, Contact, Resource Sharing
780-594-7425

***Consort:* Consort Municipal Library**
Consort School, PO Box 456, Consort AB T0C 1B0
Tel: 403-577-2501; *Fax:* 403-577-2112
aconmlibrary@marigold.ab.ca
Lisa Myers-Sortland, Chair
Marian Walsh, Library Manager

***Coronation:* Coronation Memorial Library**
5001 Royal St., PO Box 453, Coronation AB T0C 1C0
Tel: 403-578-3445
coronationlibrary@libs.prl.ab.ca
Val Cornell, Chair
Margo McPhail, Librarian
Azusa Watson, Assistant Librarian

***Coutts:* Coutts Municipal Library**
218 - 1st Ave. South, Coutts AB T0K 0N0
Tel: 403-344-3804; *Fax:* 403-344-3815
Sharon Wollersheim, Librarian
sharon.wollersheim@horizon.ab.ca

***Cremona:* Cremona Municipal Library**
Village of Cremona Municipal Bldg., 205 - 1 St. East, Cremona AB T0M 0R0
Tel: 403-637-3100
cremonalibrary@libs.prl.ab.ca
www.prl.ab.ca
Sandra Herbert, Library Manager

***La Crete:* La Crete Community Library**
10001 - 99 Ave., La Crete AB T0H 2H0
Tel: 780-928-3166; *Fax:* 780-928-3166
helenw@fvsd.ab.ca
Helen Wiebe, Librarian
helenw@fvsd.ab.ca
Tammy Schellenberg, Library Assistant
tammysc@fvsd.ab.ca
Sharon Fehr, Library Assistant
sharonf@fvsd.ab.ca
Helen Neustacter, Library Assistant
helenn@fvsd.ab.ca

***Crossfield:* Crossfield Municipal Library**
1026 Chisholm Ave., Crossfield AB T0M 0S0
Tel: 403-946-4232; *Fax:* 403-946-4212
admin@crossfieldlibrary.org
www.crossfieldlibrary.org
Social Media: twitter.com/#!/CrossfieldLib; www.facebook.com/group.php?gid=156681641025114
Lorea Horton, Library Manager

***Czar:* Czar Municipal Library**
PO Box 127, Czar AB T0B 0Z0
Tel: 780-857-3740; *Fax:* 780-857-2224
czarlibrary@libs.prl.ab.ca
Jackie Almberg, Library Manager

***Darwell:* Darwell Public Library**
Darwell Community Hall, 54225B Hwy. 765, Darwell AB T0E 0L0
Tel: 780-892-3746; *Fax:* 780-892-3743
www.darwellpubliclibrary.ab.ca
Diana Richardson, Library Director

***Daysland:* Daysland Public Library**
5130 - 50th St., Daysland AB T0B 1A0
Tel: 780-679-7263
dayslandlibrary@libs.prl.ab.ca
www.prl.ab.ca
Mickey Miller, Library Manager

***Debolt:* Debolt Public Library**
PO Box 480, Debolt AB T0H 1B0
Tel: 780-957-3770
librarian@deboltlibrary.ab.ca
Yvonne McIntyre, Library Manager

***Delburne:* Delburne Municipal Library**
2210 Main St., Delburne AB T0M 0V0
Tel: 403-749-3848; *Fax:* 403-749-3848
delburnelibrary@libs.prl.ab.ca
delburnelibrary.prl.ab.ca/
Relda Chambers, Librarian

***Delia:* Delia Municipal Library**
Delia School, Delia AB T0J 0W0
Tel: 403-364-3777; *Fax:* 403-364-3805
admlibrary@marigold.ab.ca
Barb Marshall, Chair
Leah Hunter, Library Manager

***Derwent:* Derwent Municipal Library**
PO Box 210, Derwent AB T0B 1C0
Tel: 780-741-3744; *Fax:* 780-741-3792
Leona Bielech, Librarian

***Devon:* Devon Public Library**
Devon Shopping Center, #101, 17 Athabasca Ave., Devon AB T9G 1G5
Tel: 780-987-3720
www.devonpubliclibrary.ca
Barry Fildes, Chair
Audrey Benjamin, Library Director
Linda Garez, Library Assistant
Holly Gilmour, Coordinator, Programs

***Didsbury:* Didsbury Municipal Library**
2033 - 19 Ave., Didsbury AB T0M 0W0
Tel: 403-335-3142; *Fax:* 403-335-3141
didsburylibrary@libs.prl.ab.ca
dml.prl.ab.ca
Inez Kosinski, Librarian
403-335-3142

***Donalda:* Donalda Municipal Library**
5001 Main St., Donalda AB T0B 1H0
Tel: 403-883-2345; *Fax:* 403-883-2022
donaldalibrary@libs.prl.ab.ca
donaldalibrary.prl.ab.ca
Susan Dahl, Library Manager

Drayton Valley: Drayton Valley Municipal Library
5120 - 52 St., Drayton Valley AB T7A 1R7
Tel: 780-514-2228; Fax: 780-514-2532
dvml@incentre.net
www.draytonvalleylibrary.ca
Social Media: www.twitter.com/#!/dvlibrary
Lyndara Cowper-Smith, Chair
Sandy Faunt, Assistant Librarian

Drumheller: Drumheller Public Library
224 Centre St., Drumheller AB T0J 0Y0
Tel: 403-823-5382; Fax: 403-823-3651
drumlib@magtech.ca
www.drumhellerlibrary.ca
Linde Turner, Head Librarian
Debbie Laplante, Head, Technical Services

Duchess: Duchess Public Library
PO Box 88, Duchess AB T0J 0Z0
Tel: 403-378-4369; Fax: 403-378-4369
manager@duchesspubliclibrary.ca
www.duchesspubliclibrary.ca
Shannon Vanderloh, Library Manager
Donna Billingsley, President

Duffield: Duffield Community Library
1 Main St., Duffield AB T0E 0N0
Tel: 780-892-2644; Fax: 780-892-3344
www.duffieldcommunitylibrary.ab.ca
Sandy Cornell, Chair
Brenda Baron, Community Librarian
bbaron@psd70.ab.ca

Duffield: Keephills Community Library
RR#1, Duffield AB T0E 0N0
Tel: 780-731-0000; Fax: 780-731-2433
Other Numbers: 780-731-3965
www.keephillslibrary.ab.ca
Debbie Ramsay, Library Director
dramsay@psd70.ab.ca

Eaglesham: Eaglesham Public Library
PO Box 206, Eaglesham AB T0H 1H0
Tel: 780-359-3792; Fax: 780-359-3745
www.eagleshamlibrary.ab.ca/
Norma Bolster, Contact

Eckville: Eckville Public Library
PO Box 492, Eckville AB T0M 0X0
Tel: 403-746-3240; Fax: 403-746-2900
eckvillelibrary@libs.prl.ab.ca
www.prl.ab.ca/AECK
Judith Thompson, Library Manager

Edberg: Edberg Municipal Library
48 First Ave. West, PO Box 93, Edberg AB T0B 1J0
Tel: 780-678-5606; Fax: 780-678-5606
edberglibrary@libs.prl.ab.ca
www.edberglibrary.prl.ab.ca/index.html
Colleen Wack, Library Manager
Paulina Klevgaard, Library Assistant
Colin Wack, Library Assistant

Edgerton: Edgerton Public Library
5037 - 50 Ave., Box 180, Edgerton AB T0B 1K0
Tel: 780-755-2666; Fax: 780-755-2667
www.edgertonlibrary.ab.ca
Mary Ann Sparks, Librarian
780-758-2666

Edmonton: The AALT Technician: Journal of the Alberta Association of Library Technicians
PO Box 700, Edmonton AB T5J 2L4
Toll-Free: 866-350-2258
journal@aalt.org
www.aalt.org/about/journal/index.html
Crystal Friars, Editor

Edmonton: Edmonton Public Library
7 Sir Winston Churchill Sq., Edmonton AB T5J 2V4
Tel: 780-496-7000; Fax: 780-496-1885
Other Numbers: Customer Service: 780-496-7070
webmaster@epl.ca
www.epl.ca
Linda C. Cook, Chief Executive Officer
lcook@epl.ca
780-496-7050
Pilar Martinez, Executive Director, Public Services
pmartinez@epl.ca
780-496-5522
Joanne Griener, Executive Director, Management Services
jgriener@epl.ca
780-496-6822
Virginia Clevette, Manager, Centre for Reading & the Arts
780-496-7062
Mary Jane Bilsland, Manager, Information Services Division
780-442-6280
Kathleen Pine, Manager, Children's Division
780-496-7040

Edson: Edson Public Library
4726 - 8th Ave., Edson AB T7E 1S8
Tel: 780-723-6691; Fax: 780-723-9728
www.edsonlibrary.ca
JoAnn Hooper, Library Manager
jhooper@edsonlibrary.ca
Ann Steffes, Chair
Gerrie Clery, Archives Clerk
archives@edsonlibrary.org

Elk Point: Elk Point Public Library
5123 - 50 Ave., Elk Point AB T0A 1A0
Tel: 780-724-3737; Fax: 780-724-3739
www.elkpointlibrary.ab.ca
Daphne Schnurer, Librarian

Elnora: Elnora Public Library
210 Main St., Elnora AB T0M 0Y0
Tel: 403-773-3966; Fax: 403-773-3922
elnoralibrary@libs.prl.ab.ca
elnoralibrary.prl.ab.ca/
Social Media: www.facebook.com/group.php?gid=62017158360
Wanda Strandquist, Library Manager
Tanis Westersund, Chair

Empress: Empress Municipal Library
PO Box 188, Empress AB T0J 1E0
Tel: 403-565-3936; Fax: 403-565-2010
aemlibrary@marigold.ab.ca
Charl Vincent, Library Manager

Enchant: Enchant Community Library
PO Box 3000, Enchant AB T0K 0V0
Tel: 403-739-3835; Fax: 403-739-2585
libenc@enchantlibrary.ca
www.enchantlibrary.ca/
Sharon Hagen, Librarian

Entwistle: Entwistle Municipal Library
PO Box 323, Entwistle AB T0E 0S0
Tel: 780-727-3811; Fax: 780-727-2440
kgibb@psd70.ab.ca
Karen Gibb, Librarian

Evansburg: Evansburg & District Municipal Library
PO Box 339, Evansburg AB T0E 0T0
Tel: 780-727-2030; Fax: 780-727-2060
www.evansburglibrary.ab.ca
Heather Nutbrown, Library Manager
Linda Mackoway, Library Director

Exshaw: Bighorn Library
2 Heart Mt. Dr., Exshaw AB T0L 2C0
Tel: 403-673-3571; Fax: 403-673-3571
aexclibrary@marigold.ab.ca
Rose Reid, Librarian

Fairview: Fairview Public Library
PO Box 248, Fairview AB T0H 1L0
Tel: 780-835-2613; Fax: 780-835-2613
librarian@fairviewlibrary.ab.ca
www.fairviewlibrary.ab.ca/
Chris Burkholder, Librarian
librarian@fairviewlibrary.ab.ca
780-835-2613

Falher: Bibliothèque Dentinger/ Dentinger Library
CP 60, Falher AB T0H 1M0
Tél: 780-837-2776; Téléc: 780-837-8755
www.peacelibrarysystem.ab.ca/Falher.html
Maureen Carter, Responsable

Fawcett: M. Alice Frose Library
PO Box 150, Fawcett AB T0G 0Y0
Tel: 780-954-3827; Fax: 780-954-3934
mmeyn@phrd.ab.ca
www.fawcettlibrary.ab.ca
Marie Meyn, Library Clerk

Flatbush: Flatbush Community Library
General Delivery, Flatbush AB T0G 0Z0
Tel: 780-681-3756; Fax: 780-681-3940
librarian@flatbushlibrary.ab.ca
www.flatbushlibrary.ab.ca
Rose Herdman, Librarian

Foremost: Foremost Municipal Library
103 - 1st Ave., Foremost AB T0K 0X0
Tel: 403-867-3855
forlib@shortgrass-lib.ab.ca
www.shortgrass-lib.ab.ca/foremost/
Joanne Harty, Library Manager

Forestburg: Forestburg Municipal Library
4901 - 50th St., Forestburg AB T0B 1N0
Tel: 780-582-4110; Fax: 780-582-4127
forestburglibrary@libs.prl.ab.ca
www.forestburg.ca/home/community_services/library
Judy Oberg, Librarian

Fort Assiniboine: Fort Assiniboine Public Library
Fort Assiniboine School, 35 State Ave., Fort Assiniboine AB T0G 1A0
Tel: 780-584-2227; Fax: 780-674-8575
www.fortassiniboinelibrary.ab.ca
Irene Olson, Board Chair
Louise Davison, Library Manager
ldavison@phrd.ab.ca
Doreen Lee, Library Clerk

Fort MacLeod: Fort MacLeod Municipal Library
PO Box 1479, Fort MacLeod AB T0L 0Z0
Tel: 403-553-3880; Fax: 403-553-2643
Sharon Edwards, Librarian

Fort McMurray: Fort McMurray Public Library
151 MacDonald Dr., Fort McMurray AB T9H 5C5
Tel: 780-743-7800; Fax: 780-743-5952
fmpl.ca
Craig Shufelt, Director
Mark Anthony, Manager, Technical Services
780-743-7810
Angela Gallant, Manager, Circulation Services
780-792-5137
Carolyn Murray, Marketing Manager
780-743-7807
Sara House, Manager, Adult Services
780-743-7036
Sharon Roberts, Manager, Children's Services
780-792-5136

Fort Saskatchewan: Fort Saskatchewan Public Library
10011 - 102 St., Fort Saskatchewan AB T8L 2C5
Tel: 780-998-4275; Fax: 780-992-3255
fsasklib@fspl.ca
www.fspl.ca
Debbie Saranchuk, Chair
Angela Kublik, Director
akublik@fspl.ca

Fort Vermilion: Fort Vermilion Community Library
5103 River Rd., Fort Vermilion AB T0H 1N0
Tel: 780-927-4279; Fax: 780-927-4746
afvclibrary@platinum.ca
www.fvclibrary.com
Debbie Bucckert, Library Manager

Fox Creek: Fox Creek Municipal - School Library
501 - 8 St., Fox Creek AB T0H 1P0
Tel: 780-622-2343; Fax: 780-622-4160
foxcreeklibrary@yahoo.com
www.foxcreeklibrary.ca
Leslie Ann Sharkey, Head Librarian
Kerrianne Pasula, Librarian
Nicole Tyson, Library Technician

Galahad: Galahad Municipal Library
PO Box 25, Galahad AB T0B 1R0
Tel: 780-583-3917; Fax: 780-583-3957
gallib@libs.prl.ab.ca
galahadpublic.prl.ab.ca/
Lori Wegenast, Librarian
Eden McDonald-Yale, Assistant

Gem: Gem Jubilee Library
PO Box 6, Gem AB T0J 1M0
Tel: 403-641-3245

La Glace: La Glace Community Library
9924 - 97 Ave., La Glace AB T0H 2J0
Tel: 780-568-4696; Fax: 780-568-4707
librarian@laglacelibrary.ab.ca
www.laglacelibrary.ab.ca
Evelyn Siebert, Library Head

Gleichen: **Gleichen & District Library Society**
404 Main St., Gleichen AB T0J 1N0
Tel: 403-734-2390; *Fax:* 403-734-2390
agmlibrary@marigold.ab.ca
www.marigold.ab.ca/about/memberlibs/gleichen.html
Amanda Gendron, President
Faydra Beard, Library Manager

Glenwood: **Glenwood Municipal Library**
PO Box 1156, Glenwood AB T0K 2R0
Tel: 403-626-3660; *Fax:* 403-626-3660
help@glenwoodlibrary.ca
www.glenwoodlibrary.ca
Melissa Lybbert, Library Manager

Grande Cache: **Grande Cache Municipal Library**
10601 Shand Ave., Grande Cache AB T0E 0Y0
Tel: 780-827-2081; *Fax:* 780-827-3112
www.grandecachelibrary.ab.ca
Laurel A. Kelsch, Library Director
laurkels@gyrd.ab.ca

Grande Prairie: **Grande Prairie Public Library**
#101, 9839 - 103 Ave., Grande Prairie AB T8V 6M7
Tel: 780-532-3580; *Fax:* 780-538-4983
gplib@gppl.ab.ca
www.gppl.ab.ca
Laurie Harrison, Library Director
lharrison@gppl.ab.ca
780-357-7463
Pam Chislett, Deputy Director
pchislett@gppl.ab.ca
Laura Reilly, Child Services Manager
lreilly@gppl.ab.ca
780-357-7454
Belinda Blackbourn, Technical Services Manager
bblackbourn@gppl.ab.ca
780-357-7460
Joan Taylor, Customer Services Manager
jtaylor@gppl.ab.ca
780-357-7452

Granum: **Granum Public Library**
310 Railway Ave., Granum AB T0L 1A0
Tel: 403-687-3912; *Fax:* 403-687-3912
help@granumpubliclibrary.ca
www.granumpubliclibrary.ca

Grassland: **Grassland Public Library**
Hwy. 63, Grassland AB T0A 1V0
Tel: 780-525-3733; *Fax:* 780-525-3750
librarian@grasslandlibrary.ab.ca
www.grasslandlibrary.ab.ca
Lori Zachkewich, Library Manager

Grassy Lake: **Grassy Lake Public Library**
PO Box 690, Grassy Lake AB T0K 0Z0
Tel: 403-655-2232; *Fax:* 403-655-2259
help@grassylakelibrary.ca
www.grassylakelibrary.ca

Grimshaw: **Grimshaw Municipal Library**
5007 - 47 Ave., Grimshaw AB T0H 1W0
Tel: 780-332-4553; *Fax:* 780-332-1250
www.grimshawlibrary.ab.ca
Linda Chmilar, Library Manager
lchmilar@grimshawlibrary.ab.ca
Vanessa Cowie, Assistant Librarian
ordering@grimshawlibrary.ab.ca

Gunn: **Rich Valley Public Library**
RR#1, Gunn AB T0E 1A0
Tel: 780-967-3525
rvpublib@yrl.ab.ca
www.richvalleylibrary.ab.ca
Betti-Ann Laporte, Librarian

Hanna: **Hanna Municipal Library**
202 - 1st Ave. West, Hanna AB T0J 1P0
Tel: 403-854-3865; *Fax:* 403-854-2772
library@hanna.ca
www.hanna.ca/library
Mary McKay, Library Director
C. Kelndorfer, ILL

Hardisty: **Hardisty & District Public Library**
5027 - 50 St., Hardisty AB T0B 1V0
Tel: 780-888-3947; *Fax:* 780-888-3947
hardistylibrary@libs.prl.ab.ca
hardistylib.prl.ab.ca
Billi-Jo Wildeboer, Library Manager

Hay Lakes: **Hay Lakes Municipal Library**
106 Main St., Hay Lakes AB T0B 1W0
Tel: 780-878-2665
haylakescontact@prl.ab.ca
haylakeslibrary.prl.ab.ca
Belinda Wegner, Library Manager
Tanya Reist, Chair

Hays: **Hays Public Library**
PO Box 36, Hays AB T0K 1B0
Tel: 403-725-3744; *Fax:* 403-725-3744
help@hayslibrary.ca
www.hayslibrary.ca
Diane Wickenheiser, Library Manager

Heinsburg: **Heinsburg Community Library**
General Delivery, Heinsburg AB T0A 1X0
Tel: 780-943-3913; *Fax:* 780-943-3773
heinsburglibrary@netscape.net
www.heinsburgcapsite.8k.com
Kelly Hovdestad, Library Clerk
kelly_hovdestad@sperd.ca
Rayma Isaac, Library Clerk

Heisler: **Heisler Municipal Library**
100 Haultain Ave., Heisler AB T0B 2A0
Tel: 780-889-3999; *Fax:* 780-889-3999
heislerlibrary@libs.prl.ab.ca
www.prl.ab.ca/AHEI
Marvis Zimmer, Library Manager
Lorie Zimmer, Librarian

High Level: **High Level Municipal Library**
10601 - 103 St., High Level AB T0H 1Z0
Tel: 780-926-2097; *Fax:* 780-926-4268
librarian@highlevellibrary.ab.ca
www.highlevellibrary.ab.ca
Jennilyn Boire, Library Director

High Prairie: **High Prairie Municipal Library**
4723 - 53 Ave., High Prairie AB T0G 1E0
Tel: 780-523-3838; *Fax:* 780-523-3838
librarian@highprairielibrary.ab.ca
www.highprairielibrary.ab.ca
Janet Lemay, Library Manager
Angie Caughlin, Assistant Librarian (Interlibrary Loans)
Tracy Roberts, Assistant Librarian (Programming)

High River: **High River Centennial Library**
909 - 1st St. West, High River AB T1V 1A5
Tel: 403-652-2917; *Fax:* 403-652-7203
ahrm@marigold.ab.ca
http://www.marigold.ab.ca/content/member-library-directory
Deb Gardiner, Librarian

Hines Creek: **Hines Creek Municipal Library**
PO Box 750, Hines Creek AB T0H 2A0
Tel: 780-494-3879; *Fax:* 780-494-3605
librarian@hinescreeklibrary.ab.ca
hinescreeklibrary.ab.ca
Sharon Nazarko, Librarian
librarian@hinescreeklibrary.ab.ca
780-494-3879

Hinton: **Hinton Municipal Library**
803 Switzer Dr., Hinton AB T7V 1V1
Tel: 780-865-2363; *Fax:* 780-865-4292
Other Numbers: info hotline: 780/865-6050
hettwild@hintonlibrary.org
www.hintonlibrary.org
Hetty Wilderdijk, Director, Library Arts & Culture
780-865-6051

Holden: **Holden Municipal Library**
4912 - 50 St., Holden AB T0B 2C0
Tel: 780-688-3838; *Fax:* 780-688-3838
librarian@holdenlibrary.ab.ca
www.holdenlibrary.ab.ca
Julianne Foster, Chair
Annette Chrystian, Library Clerk

Hughenden: **Hughenden Public Library**
PO Box 36, Hughenden AB T0B 2E0
Tel: 780-856-2435; *Fax:* 780-856-2435
hughendenlibrary@libs.prl.ab.ca
Patricia Mackie, Library Manager
hughendenlibrary@libs.prl.ab.ca
Keith Degenhardt, Co-Chair
Lori Knutson, Co-Chair
Ann Fontaine, Secretary
Kevin Lowes, Treasurer

Hussar: **Hussar Municipal Library**
102 - 2 St. NW, Hussar AB T0J 1S0
Tel: 403-787-3788; *Fax:* 403-787-3922
ahumlibrary@marigold.ab.ca
www.marigold.ab.ca/about/memberlibs/hussar.html
Gay V. Harms, Library Manager

Hythe: **Hythe Public Library**
10013 - 100 St., Hythe AB T0H 2C0
Tel: 780-356-3014; *Fax:* 780-356-2009
staff@hythelibrary.ab.ca
www.hythelibrary.ab.ca
Karen Bass, Library Manager

Innisfail: **Innisfail Public Library**
4949 - 49th St., Innisfail AB T4G 1A5
Tel: 403-227-4407; *Fax:* 403-227-3122
innisfail@libs.prl.ab.ca
ipl.prl.ab.ca
Colleen Hayden, Librarian
chayden@libs.prl.ab.ca

Irma: **Irma Community Library**
5012 - 51st Ave., Irma AB T0B 2H0
Tel: 780-754-3746; *Fax:* 780-754-3802
www.irmalibrary.ca
Leah Larson, Library Manager
leah.larson@btps.ca

Irricana: **Irricana Municipal Library**
302 - 2 St., Irricana Sports Complex, Irricana AB T0M 1B0
Tel: 403-935-4818; *Fax:* 403-935-4270
ailibrary@marigold.ab.ca
www.marigold.ab.ca/about/memberlibs/irricana.html
Laura Blanton, Library Manager

Irvine: **Irvine Library**
78 South Railway St., Irvine AB T0J 1V0
Tel: 403-834-3758
Joan L. Côté, Chair
403-834-3820
Sherley Beleay, Acquistitions Librarian

Jarvie: **Jarvie Public Library**
PO Box 193, Jarvie AB T0G 1H0
Tel: 780-943-3935; *Fax:* 780-349-5291
elea@mcsnet.ca
www.westlocklibrary.ca/content/jarvie-public-library
Kim Klein, Librarian
kklein@phrd.ab.ca

Keg River: **Keg River Community Library**
PO Box 3, Keg River AB T0H 2G0
Tel: 780-981-2128; *Fax:* 780-981-2262
www.kegriverlibrary.ab.ca
Janice Freeman, Library Manager
Susan MacDougall, Library Staff
Betty Hasenack, Library Staff
Faye Van Oers Papirny, Library Staff

Killam: **Killam Community Library**
5017 - 49th Ave., Killam AB T0B 2L0
Tel: 780-385-3032; *Fax:* 780-385-3698
killamlibrary@libs.prl.ab.ca
Karen Auburn, Librarian
780-376-2197

Kinuso: **Kinuso Municipal Library**
PO Box 60, Kinuso AB T0G 1K0
Tel: 780-775-3694; *Fax:* 780-775-3650
librarian@kinusolibrary.ab.ca
Susan Moody, Librarian

Kitscoty: **Kitscoty Municipal Library**
4910 - 51 St., Kitscoty AB T0B 2P0
Tel: 780-846-2822; *Fax:* 780-846-2215
www.kitscotypubliclibrary.ab.ca/Home
Peggy Davies, Librarian

Lac La Biche: **Stuart MacPherson Library**
McArthur Place, Lower Level, 10307 - 100 St., Lac La Biche AB T0A 2C0
Tel: 780-623-7467; *Fax:* 780-623-7499
headlibrarian@stuartmacphersonlibrary.ca
Maureen Penn, Librarian

Lacombe: **Lacombe Public Library**
#101, 5214 - 50 Ave., Lacombe AB T4L 0B6
Tel: 403-782-3433; *Fax:* 403-782-3329
christinap@libs.prl.ab.ca
www.lacombelibrary.org
Christina Petrisor, Head Librarian
christinap@libs.prl.ab.ca

Lafond: **Lafond Public Library**
PO Box 20, Lafond AB T0A 2G0
Tel: 780-645-2432; *Fax:* 780-645-2432
www.town.stpaul.ab.ca/places/Lafond-Public-Library_7216
Romona Logozar, Librarian

Lamont: **Lamont Municipal Library**
PO Box 180, Lamont AB T0B 2R0
Tel: 780-895-2228; *Fax:* 780-895-2600
www.lamont.ca
Joanne Flaman, Public Librarian
Rose Konsorada, School Librarian

Leduc: **Leduc Public Library**
2 Alexandra Park, Leduc AB T9E 4C4
Tel: 780-986-2637; *Fax:* 780-986-3462
www.leduclibrary.ca
Social Media: http://twitter/#!/LeducLibrary
Christine Brown, Head Librarian
cbrown@library.leduc.ab.ca
Angela Binnie, Information Services Coordinator
abinnie@library.leduc.ab.ca

Lethbridge: **Lethbridge Public Library**
810 - 5th Ave. South, Lethbridge AB T1J 4C4
Tel: 403-380-7310; *Fax:* 403-329-1478
lpl@lethbridgepubliclibrary.ca
www.lethbridgepubliclibrary.ca
Elizabeth Rossnagel, Director
lrossnagel@lethbridgepubliclibrary.ca
403-380-7340
Todd Gnissios, Associate Director: Branches & Outreach
tgnissios@lethbridgepubliclibrary.ca
703-320-4187
Linda McElravy, Associate Director: Public Services
lmcelravy@lethbridgepubliclibrary.ca
403-380-7312

Linden: **Linden Municipal Library**
215 - 1st. SE, Linden AB T0M 1J0
Tel: 403-546-3757; *Fax:* 403-546-4220
almlibrary@marigold.ab.ca
www.marigold.ab.ca/about/memberlibs/linden.html
Debbie Martin, Librarian
Danielle Malsbury, Assistant

Lloydminster: **Lloydminster Public Library**
5010 - 49th St., Lloydminster AB T9V 0K2
Tel: 780-875-0850; *Fax:* 780-875-6523
info@lloydminster.info
www.lloydminster.info
Ronald Gillies, Head Librarian
hlib@lloydminster.info
Michele Duczek, Reference Librarian
mducek@lloydminster.info
780-875-0877

Lomond: **Lomond Community Library**
PO Box 290, Lomond AB T0L 1G0
Tel: 403-792-3934; *Fax:* 403-792-3934
liblom@chinookarch.ab.ca
Mary McNamara, Librarian
liblom@chinookarch.ab.ca
403-792-3934

Longview: **Longview Municipal Library**
128 Morrison Place, Longview AB T0L 1H0
Tel: 403-558-3927; *Fax:* 403-558-3927
alomlibrary@marigold.ab.ca
Joan Maxwell, Library Manager

Lougheed: **Lougheed Public Library**
5004 - 50 St., Lougheed AB T0B 2V0
Tel: 780-386-2498; *Fax:* 780-386-2136
lougheedlibrary@libs.prl.ab.ca
Lorraine Greenlee, Librarian
780-888-1278

Magrath: **Magrath Public Library**
6N - 1 St. W., Magrath AB T0K 1J0
Tel: 403-758-6498; *Fax:* 403-758-6442
www.magrathlibrary.ca
Charlotte Lester, Librarian
clester@magrathlibrary.ca

Manning: **Manning Municipal Library**
311 - 4th Ave. SE, Manning AB T0H 2M0
Tel: 780-836-3054; *Fax:* 780-836-3054
librarian@manninglibrary.ab.ca
www.manninglibrary.ab.ca
Lesley Spry-Shandro, Head Librarian
780-836-3054
M.J. Lissack, Library Clerk, Genealogy
780-836-3054
Lori Jackson, Library Clerk, Programming
780-836-3054

Mannville: **Mannville Municipal Library**
5029, 50 St. - PO Box 186, Mannville AB T0B 2W0
Tel: 780-763-3611; *Fax:* 780-763-3611
librarian@mannvillelibrary.ab.ca
www.mannvillelibrary.ab.ca
Theresa Myroniuk, Library Head

Marwayne: **Marwayne Public Library**
105 - 2nd St. South, Marwayne AB T0B 2X0
Tel: 780-847-3930; *Fax:* 780-847-3796
librarian@marwaynelibrary.ab.ca
www.marwaynelibrary.ab.ca
Riley Sleeman, Collections/Education Co-ordinator

Mayerthorpe: **Mayerthorpe Public Library**
4909 - 52nd St., Mayerthorpe AB T0E 1N0
Tel: 780-786-2404; *Fax:* 780-786-4590
mayep@telusplanet.net
www.mayerthorpelibrary.ab.ca
Eleanor Mitchell, Librarian

McLennan: **McLennan Municipal Library**
19 - 1st Ave. NW, McLennan AB T0H 2L0
Tel: 780-324-3767; *Fax:* 780-324-2288
librarian@mclennanlibrary.ab.ca
Carole Laboucan, Librarian

Medicine Hat: **Medicine Hat Public Library**
414 First St. SE, Medicine Hat AB T1A 0A8
Tel: 403-502-8527; *Fax:* 403-502-8529
library@medicinehat.ca
www.shortgrass-lib.ab.ca/mhpl
Rachel Sarjeant-Jenkins, Chief Librarian
403-502-8528
Sheila Drummond, Head, Reference Services
403-502-8531
Carol Ann Cross-Roen, Head, Children's Services
403-502-8532
Hilary Munro, Head, Adult Services
403-502-8533
Annette ziegler, Manager, Circulation Services
403-502-8539

Milk River: **Milk River Municipal Library**
321 - 3rd Ave. NE, Milk River AB T0K 1M0
Tel: 403-647-3793
mkrlib@chinookarch.ab.ca
www.chinookarch.ab.ca/chinookarch/
Lynn Bouldry, Librarian
lbouldry@milkriverlibrary.ca

Millarville: **Millarville Community Library**
Box 59, Millarville AB T0L 1K0
Tel: 403-931-3919; *Fax:* 403-931-2475
amclibrary@marigold.ab.ca
Norma Dawson, Librarian

Millet: **Millet Public Library**
PO Box 30, Millet AB T0C 1Z0
Tel: 780-387-5222
millet@yrl.ab.ca
www.milletlibrary.ca
Kristin Litke, Library Manager

Milo: **Milo Municipal Library**
#220-1st St. South, Milo AB T0L 1L0
Tel: 403-599-3850; *Fax:* 403-599-3850
help@milolibrary.ca
eps.chinookarch.ca/rooms/portal/page/21975_Milo
Joanne Monner, Head Librarian

Mirror: **Mirror Public Library**
5202 - 50 Ave., Mirror AB T0B 3C0
Tel: 403-788-3044
mirrorlibrary@gmail.com
Heather Beamish, Librarian

Morrin: **Morrin Municipal Library**
Main St., PO Box 284, Morrin AB T0J 2B0
Tel: 403-772-3922; *Fax:* 403-772-3707
amomlibrary@marigold.ab.ca
M'liss Edwards, Library Manager

Myrnam: **Myrnam Community Library**
New Myrnam School, 5105 - 50 St., Myrnam AB T0B 3K0
Tel: 780-366-3801; *Fax:* 780-366-2332
librarian@myrnamlibrary.ab.ca
www.myrnamlibrary.ab.ca
Ann Godziuk, Librarian
librarian@myrnamlibrary.ab.ca
780-366-3801

Nampa: **Nampa Municipal Library**
PO Box 509, Nampa AB T0H 2R0
Tel: 780-322-3805; *Fax:* 780-322-3955
nlibrary@nampalibrary.ab.ca
Cathy Rasmussen, Librarian

Nanton: **Nanton Municipal Library/Thelma Fanning Memorial Library**
1907 - 21 Ave., Nanton AB T0L 1R0
Tel: 403-646-5535; *Fax:* 403-646-2653
nantlibr@chinookarch.ab.ca
Judi McMasters, Library Manager
jmcmasters@chinookarch.ab.ca
Mary Durant, Library Assistant
nantlibr@chinookarch.ab.ca

Neerlandia: **Neerlandia Public Library**
PO Box 10, Neerlandia AB T0G 1R0
Tel: 780-674-5384; *Fax:* 780-674-2927
solthuis@phrd.ab.ca
Sandra Olthuis, Librarian
Dagmar Visser, Librarian

New Sarepta: **New Sarepta Community Library**
c/o New Sarepta Community High School, 5150 Center St., PO Box 147, New Sarepta AB T0B 3M0
Tel: 780-941-2432; *Fax:* 780-941-2224
newsareptalibrary@yrl.ab.ca
www.newsareptalibrary.ca
Willow Schnell, Library Director
Pearl Gregor, Chair

Newbrook: **Newbrook Public Library**
Main St., PO Box 208, Newbrook AB T0A 2P0
Tel: 780-576-3772; *Fax:* 780-576-2115
librarian@newbrooklibrary.ab.ca
www.newbrooklibrary.ab.ca
Rose Alexander, Library Manager

Niton Junction: **Green Grove Public Library**
53521A Range Rd. 130, Niton Junction AB T0E 1S0
Tel: 780-795-2474; *Fax:* 780-795-3933
www.greengrovelibrary.ab.ca
Toni Ice, Library Manager
toniice@gyrd.ab.ca
Lida Saulnier, Chair

Nordegg: **Nordegg Public Library**
General Delivery, Nordegg AB T0M 2H0
Tel: 403-721-2339
nordegglibrary@libs.prl.ab.ca
Heather Clement, Librarian

Okotoks: **Okotoks Public Library**
7 Riverside Dr. West, Okotoks AB T1S 1A6
Tel: 403-938-2220; *Fax:* 403-938-4317
assistant@okotokslibrary.ca
www.okotokslibrary.ca
Tessa Nettleton, Director
okotokslibrary@okotoks.net
403-938-2220
Mary Weir, Administrative Assistant
Caleigh Haworth, Assistant Librarian

Olds: **Olds & District Municipal Library**
5217 - 52 St., Olds AB T4H 1H7
Tel: 403-556-6460; *Fax:* 403-556-6692
oml2@libs.prl.ab.ca
oml.prl.ab.ca
Lesley Winfield, Head Librarian
oml2libs.prl.ab.ca
403-556-6460

Onoway: **Onoway Public Library**
4808 - 51 St., Onoway AB T0E 1V0
Tel: 780-967-2445; *Fax:* 780-967-2445
onowaylibrary@yrl.ab.ca
www.onowaylibrary.ab.ca
Kelly Huxley, Librarian
onowaylibrary@yrl.ab.ca
Lucy Strobl, Chair

Oyen: **Oyen Municipal Library**
105 - 3rd Ave. West, Oyen AB T0J 2J0
Tel: 403-664-3580; *Fax:* 403-664-2520
aoymlibrary@marigold.ab.ca
Tricia Fischbuch, Librarian

Paradise Valley: **Three Cities Municipal Library**
PO Box 60, Paradise Valley AB T0B 3R0
Tel: 780-745-2277; *Fax:* 780-745-2641
sbabcock@paradisevalleylibrary.ab.ca
Sandra Babcock, Librarian
780-745-2541

***Peace River:* Peace River Municipal Library**
9807 - 97 Ave., Peace River AB T8S 1H6
Tel: 780-624-4076; *Fax:* 780-624-4086
www.prmlibrary.ab.ca
Jennifer Straub, Acting Chair

***Penhold:* Penhold & District Public Library**
1013 Aberdeen St., Penhold AB T0M 1R0
Tel: 403-886-2636; *Fax:* 403-886-2638
penholdlibrary@libs.prl.ab.ca
penholdlibrary.prl.ab.ca
Myra Binnendyk, Head of Library
Karen Thomson, Assistant Librarian

***Picture Butte:* Picture Butte Municipal Library**
120 - 4th St. South, Picture Butte AB T0K 1V0
Tel: 403-732-4141
lbexte@picturebuttelibrary.ca
Linda Bexte, Library Manager

***Pincher Creek:* Pincher Creek Municipal Library**
899 Main St., Pincher Creek AB T0K 1W0
Tel: 403-627-3813; *Fax:* 403-627-2847
help@pinchercreeklibrary.ca
Janice Day, Acting Librarian
403-627-3813
Geraldine Mansen, Assistant Librarian
help@pinchercreeklibrary.ca

***Plamondon:* Plamondon Municipal Library**
PO Box 630, Plamondon AB T0A 2T0
Tel: 780-798-3852; *Fax:* 780-798-3860
headlibrarian@stuartmacphersonlibrary.ca
www.plamondonlibrary.ab.ca
Maureen Penn, Director, Library Services
Pam Lien, School Librarian

***Ponoka:* Ponoka Jubilee Library**
5110 - 48 Ave., Ponoka AB T4J 1J3
Tel: 403-783-3843; *Fax:* 403-783-3973
jubilee@rttinc.com
Norma-Jean Colquhoun, Librarian

***Provost:* Provost Municipal Library**
PO Box 449, Provost AB T0B 3S0
Tel: 780-753-2801
provostlibrary@libs.prl.ab.ca
Colleen Vaughn, Library Supervisor

***Radway:* Radway Public Library**
PO Box 220, 4915-50th Street, Radway AB T0A 2V0
Tel: 780-736-3548; *Fax:* 780-736-3858
librarian@radwaylibrary.ab.ca
www.radwaylibrary.ab.ca
Terrie-Lynne Rosa, Librarian
Sharon Krawchuk, Chair, County of Thorhild No. 7 Library Board

***Rainbow Lake:* Rainbow Lake Municipal Library**
1 Atco Rd., Rainbow Lake AB T0H 2Y0
Tel: 780-956-3656; *Fax:* 780-956-3858
librarian@rainbowlakelibrary.ab.ca
Cheryl Edwards, Librarian
Mark Levy, Librarian

***Rainier:* Alcoma Public Library**
c/o Alcoma School, General Delivery, Rainier AB T0J 2M0
Tel: 403-362-3741; *Fax:* 403-362-8897
aplcapic@eidnet.org
www.shortgrass-lib.ab.ca/acl

***Ralston:* Graham Community Library**
R35 Dugway Dr., Community Centre, Ralston AB T0J 2N0
Tel: 403-544-3670; *Fax:* 403-544-3814
grahamlib@yahoo.ca
www.grahamcommunitylibrary.ca
Stefanie Schranz, Librarian Manager
grahamlib@yahoo.ca

***Raymond:* Raymond Public Library**
15 Broadway South, Raymond AB T0K 2S0
Tel: 403-752-4785; *Fax:* 403-752-4785
rlibrary@chinookarch.ab.ca
Faye Geddes, Librarian

***Red Deer:* Red Deer Public Library**
4818 - 49th St., Red Deer AB T4N 1T9
Tel: 403-346-4576
Other Numbers: 403-346-4688 (Children's department)
www.rdpl.org
Mike Todd, Chair
miket@aipins.ca
Dean Frey, Director
dfrey@rdpl.org
403-342-9102
Cory Stier, Assistant Director
403-342-9124
Donna Alberts, Librarian, Youth Services & Circulation
403-342-9114
Cynthia Belanger, Librarian, Adult Services
403-342-9104
Tatiana Poliakevitch, Librarian, Community Development
403-755-1130
Jen Waters, Librarian, Teen Services
403-755-1146
Celia Jaipaul, Coordinator, Family Literacy
403-755-1158
Lois Prostebby, Coordinator, Adult Literacy
403-346-2533
Kareena Fulton, Supervisor, Circulation
403-342-9108
Trish Klein, Supervisor, Readers' Services
403-342-9110

***Redcliff:* Redcliff Public Library**
131 Main St. South, Redcliff AB T0J 2P0
Tel: 403-548-3335
redlib@shortgrass-lib.ab.ca
www.shortgrass.ca/rpl/
Reita Wilson, Library Manager
403-548-3335
Margot Peskor, Head Library Clerk
Sharon Tattersall, Library Clerk
Madeleine Littlechilds, Casual Library Clerk
Christine Bindr, Casual Library Clerk

***Redwater:* Redwater Public Library**
4915 - 48th St., Redwater AB T0A 2W0
Tel: 780-942-3464; *Fax:* 780-942-2013
director@redwaterlibrary.ab.ca
www.redwaterlibrary.ab.ca
Judy Dewald, Director of Library Services
director@redwaterlibrary.ab.ca
Linda Kuzik, Library Clerk
ill@redwaterlibrary.ab.ca

***Rimbey:* Rimbey Municipal Library**
4938 - 50 Ave., Rimbey AB T0C 2J0
Tel: 403-843-2841; *Fax:* 403-843-2841
rimbeylibrarian@libs.prl.ab.ca
rimbeylibrary.prl.ab.ca
Jean Keetch, Librarian
Shannon Kiss, Library Assistant

***Rochester:* Rochester Community Library**
PO Box 309, Rochester AB T0G 1Z0
Tel: 780-698-3970; *Fax:* 780-698-2290
tammy.morey@aspenview.org
www.rochesterlibrary.ab.ca
Tammy Morey, Librarian

***Rocky Mountain House:* Rocky Mountain House Public Library**
4922 - 52 St., Rocky Mountain House AB T4T 1B1
Tel: 403-845-2042; *Fax:* 403-845-5633
armh@telusplanet.net
rmhlibrary.prl.ab.ca
Karen Paquette, Library Manager

***Rockyford:* Rockyford Municipal & District Library**
PO Box 277, Rockyford AB T0J 2R0
Tel: 403-533-3964
armlibrary@marigold.ab.ca
Frances Garriott, Head Librarian

***Rolling Hills:* Rolling Hills Public Library**
302 - 4th St., Rolling Hills AB T0J 2S0
Tel: 403-964-2186; *Fax:* 403-964-3659
rhlcapic@eidnet.org
Johnene Amulung, Library Volunteer

***Rosemary:* Rosemary Community Library**
Rosemary Academic School, Block 6, Dahlia St., PO, Box 210, Rosemary AB T0J 2W0
Tel: 403-378-4493; *Fax:* 403-378-4388
www.shortgrass-lib.ab.ca/rml
Petra Mauerhoff, Chief Executive Officer
petra@shortgrass.ca
Bob Batchelder, Assistant Director, Technical Services
bob@shortgrass.ca

***Rumsey:* Rumsey Community Library**
PO Box 113, Rumsey AB T0J 2Y0
Tel: 403-368-3939; *Fax:* 403-368-2207
arumlibrary@marigold.ab.ca
Patty Steen, Librarian

***Rycroft:* Rycroft Municipal Library**
PO Box 248, Rycroft AB T0H 3A0
Tel: 780-765-3973; *Fax:* 780-765-2002
Kimberley Bawkowy, Librarian

***Ryley:* McPherson Public Library**
PO Box 139, Ryley AB T0B 4A0
Tel: 780-663-3999; *Fax:* 780-663-3909
librarian@mcphersonlibrary.ab.ca
www.mcphersonlibrary.ab.ca
Andrea Mendoza, Chair
Sherry Presley, Librarian

***St Albert:* St Albert Public Library**
5 St Anne St., St Albert AB T8N 3Z9
Tel: 780-459-1530; *Fax:* 780-458-5772
sapl@sapl.ab.ca
www.sapl.ab.ca
Pamela Forsyth, Director
pforsyth@sapl.ab.ca
780-459-1681
Peter Bailey, Head of Public Services
pbailey@sapl.ab.ca
780-459-1686
Pat Fader, Head of Technical Services
pfader@sapl.ab.ca
780-459-1684
Barbara Moreau, Children's Department Coordinator
bmoreau@sapl.ab.ca
780-459-1536
Wanda German, Circulation Services Manager
wgerman@sapl.ab.ca
780-459-1537

***St Isidore:* St Isidore Community Library/ Bibliothèque de St Isidore**
PO Box 1168, St Isidore AB T0H 3B0
Tel: 780-624-8182; *Fax:* 780-624-9182
marielavoie@bibliothequestisidore.ab.ca
Marie Lavoie, Chair & Librarian

***St Paul:* St Paul Municipal Library**
4802 - 53 St., St Paul AB T0A 3A0
Tel: 780-645-4904; *Fax:* 780-645-5198
librarian@stpaullibrary.ab.ca
www.stpaullibrary.ab.ca

***Sangudo:* Sangudo Public Library**
PO Box 524, Sangudo AB T0E 2A0
Tel: 780-785-3431; *Fax:* 780-785-3179
www.sangudolibrary.ca
Cassandra Boll, Library Manager

***Seba Beach:* Seba Beach Public Library**
PO Box 159, Seba Beach AB T0E 2B0
Tel: 780-797-3940; *Fax:* 780-797-3800
www.sebabeachlibrary.ab.ca
Judy Mott, Library Manager

***Sedgewick:* Sedgewick Municipal Library**
5011 - 51 Ave., Sedgewick AB T0B 4C0
Tel: 780-384-3003; *Fax:* 780-384-3003
sedgewicklibrary@libs.prl.ab.ca
sedgpublib.prl.ab.ca
Judy Ferrier, Librarian

***Sexsmith:* Sexsmith Shannon Library**
9917 - 99 Ave., Sexsmith AB T0H 3C0
Tel: 780-568-4333; *Fax:* 780-568-4333
librarian@shannonlibrary.ab.ca
www.shannonlibrary.ab.ca
Sheryl Pelletier, Library Manager

***Sherwood Park:* Strathcona County Library**
#300, 2020 Sherwood Dr., Sherwood Park AB T8A 5P7
Tel: 780-449-5801; *Fax:* 780-467-6861
ssiga@sclibrary.ab.ca
www.sclibrary.ab.ca
Sharon Siga, Library Director
ssiga@sclibrary.ab.ca
780-449-5814
Heide Blackmore, Supervisor, Adult Services
hblackmore@sclibrary.ab.ca
780-449-5810
Sharon Nuttycombe, Supervisor, Technical Services & Systems
snuttycombe@sclibrary.ab.ca
780-449-5811
Donna Riehl, Supervisor, Youth Services
driehl@sclibrary.ab.ca
780-449-5809
Cathy Nielsen, Supervisor, Circulation Services
cnielsen@sclibrary.ab.ca
780-449-5806

Slave Lake: **Slave Lake Municipal Library**
320 - 2nd St. NE, Slave Lake AB T0G 2A0
Tel: 780-849-5250; *Fax:* 780-849-3275
librarian@slavelakelibrary.ab.ca
www.slavelakelibrary.ab.ca
Lori Herdzik, Librarian

Smith: **Smith Community Library**
924 - 9th St., Smith AB T0G 2B0
Tel: 780-829-2389; *Fax:* 780-829-2389
librarian@smithlibrary.ab.ca
www.smithlibrary.ab.ca
Mary Hastie, Librarian
780-829-3882

Smoky Lake: **Smoky Lake Municipal Public Library**
5010 - 50th St., Smoky Lake AB T0A 3C0
Tel: 780-656-4212; *Fax:* 780-656-4212
librarian@smokylakelibrary.ab.ca
www.smokylakelibrary.ab.ca
Melody Kaban, Library Manager

Spirit River: **Spirit River Municipal Library**
4812 - 44th Ave., Spirit River AB T0H 3G0
Tel: 780-864-4038; *Fax:* 780-864-3006
tracy@spiritriverlibrary.ab.ca
Tracy Skoworodko, Librarian
Judy Brown, Chair

Spruce Grove: **Spruce Grove Public Library**
35 - 5th Ave., Spruce Grove AB T7X 2C5
Tel: 780-962-4423; *Fax:* 780-962-4826
library@sprucegrovelibrary.org
www.sprucegrovelibrary.org
Tammy Svenningsen
tammy@sprucegrovelibrary.org

Standard: **Standard Municipal Library**
822 The Broadway, Standard AB T0J 3G0
Tel: 403-644-3995
astmlibrary@marigold.ab.ca
www.marigold.ab.ca/
Sharon Duffala, Librarian

Stavely: **Stavely Municipal Library**
4823 - 49th St., Stavely AB T0L 1Z0
Tel: 403-549-2190; *Fax:* 403-549-2190
help@stavelylibrary.ca
Jean Cochlan, Librarian

Stettler: **Stettler Public Library**
6202 - 44th Ave., Stettler AB T0C 2L1
Tel: 403-742-2292; *Fax:* 403-742-5481
spl@libs.prl.ab.ca
spl.prl.ab.ca
Social Media: www.facebook.com/group.php?gid=2492499282
Deborah Cryderman, Library Manager
Crystal Friars, Assistant Manager

Stirling: **Stirling Municipal Library**
229 - 4th Ave., Stirling AB T0K 2E0
Tel: 403-756-3665
libstir@chinookarch.ab.ca
Charlene Fletcher, Director, Library Services
libstir@chinookarch.ab.ca
Sheila Cooper-Bikman, Assistant
Shawna Hogenson, Assistant Librarian

Stony Plain: **Stony Plain Public Library**
#112, 4613 - 52nd Ave., Stony Plain AB T7Z 1E7
Tel: 780-963-5440; *Fax:* 780-963-1746
info@stonyplainlibrary.org
www.stonyplainlibrary.org
Linda Naccarato, Director
lindan@stonyplainlibrary.org
780-968-5709
Robert Jacobsen, Assistant Director
robertj@stonyplainlibrary.org
780-963-5440

Strathmore: **Strathmore Municipal Library**
85 Lakeside Blvd., Strathmore AB T1P 1A1
Tel: 403-934-5440; *Fax:* 403-934-1908
asmlibmgr@marigold.ab.ca
Margie Lavoie, Librarian

Sundre: **Sundre Municipal Library**
#2, 310 Centre St. N, Sundre AB T0M 1X0
Tel: 403-638-4000; *Fax:* 403-638-5755
sundrelibrary@libs.prl.ab.ca
www.sundre.prl.ab.ca
Michael Baird, Library Director
403-638-4000

Swan Hills: **Swan Hills Public Library**
5536 Main St., Swan Hills AB T0G 2C0
Tel: 780-333-4505; *Fax:* 780-333-4551
nkeough@yrl.ab.ca
www.swanhillslibrary.ab.ca
Nancy Keough, Head Librarian

Sylvan Lake: **Sylvan Lake Public Library**
4715 - 50 Ave., Sylvan Lake AB T4S 1C5
Tel: 403-887-2130; *Fax:* 403-887-0537
sylvan.library@shawbiz.ca
sylvanlibrary.prl.ab.ca/sylvan.htm
Barbara Bulat, Director
barbara.bulat@shawbiz.ca
403-887-2130

Taber: **Taber Public Library**
5415 - 50 Ave., Taber AB T1G 1V2
Tel: 403-223-4343; *Fax:* 403-223-4314
help@taberlibrary.ca
Helen Jury, Head Librarian
403-223-4343
Diane Zelenka, Librarian

Thorhild: **Thorhild & District Municipal Library**
210 - 7 Ave., Thorhild AB T0A 3J0
Tel: 780-398-3502; *Fax:* 780-398-2100
librarian@thorhildlibrary.ab.ca
thorhildlibrary.ab.ca
Rose Alexander, Library Manager

Thorsby: **Thorsby Municipal Library**
PO Box 319, Thorsby AB T0C 2P0
Tel: 780-789-3808; *Fax:* 780-789-3805
www.thorsbymunicipallibrary.ab.ca
Louise Normandeau, Library Director

Three Hills: **Three Hills Municipal Library**
122 - 3rd Ave. South, Three Hills AB T0M 2A0
Tel: 403-443-2360
athmlibrary@marigold.ab.ca
www.3hillslibrary.com
Wendy Cuffe, Head Librarian
Susan Hamm, Assistant Librarian

Tilley: **Tilley Public Library**
PO Box 177, Tilley AB T0J 3K0
Tel: 403-377-2233; *Fax:* 403-377-2097
tillib@shortgrass.ca
Brenda Arnold, Librarian
brendaa@grasslands.ab.ca
Dianne Voroney, Chair

Tofield: **Tofield Municipal Library**
5407 - 50 St., Tofield AB T0B 4J0
Tel: 780-662-3838; *Fax:* 780-662-3929
librarian@tofieldlibrary.ca
library.tofieldalberta.ca
Connie Forst, Library Manager

Tomahawk: **Tomahawk Public Library**
PO Box 69, Tomahawk AB T0E 2H0
Tel: 780-339-3935; *Fax:* 780-339-2121
Chris Goerz, Librarian
Monika Cappis, Chair, Parkland County Library Board

Trochu: **Trochu Municipal Library**
317 Main St., Trochu AB T0M 2C0
Tel: 403-442-2458
atrmlibrary@marigold.ab.ca
Sherie Campbell, Librarian

Two Hills: **Alice Melnyk Public Library**
5009 Diefenbaker (50th) Ave., Two Hills AB T0B 4K0
Tel: 780-657-3553; *Fax:* 780-657-3553
www.twohillslibrary.ab.ca
Elizabeth Wells, Library Manager & Resource Sharing Contact
librarian@twohillslibrary.ab.ca

Valhalla Centre: **Valhalla Community Library**
PO Box 68, Valhalla Centre AB T0H 3M0
Tel: 780-356-3834; *Fax:* 780-356-3834
librarian@valhallalibrary.ab.ca
Gail Perry, Librarian
780-356-2382

Valleyview: **Valleyview Municipal Library**
4804 - 50 Ave., Valleyview AB T0H 3N0
Tel: 780-524-3033; *Fax:* 780-524-4563
www.valleyviewlibrary.ab.ca
Susanne Tremblay, Library Coordinator

Vauxhall: **Vauxhall Public Library**
314 - 2nd Ave. North, Vauxhall AB T0K 2K0
Tel: 403-654-2370; *Fax:* 403-654-2370
libvau@chinookarch.ab.ca
Carol Bell, Librarian
403-654-2037

Vegreville: **Vegreville Public Library**
4709 - 50 St., Vegreville AB T9C 1L2
Tel: 780-632-3491; *Fax:* 780-603-2338
library@vegreville.com
www.vegrevillelibrary.ab.ca
Amber Zary, Director
780-632-3491
Jennie Barlott, Assistant Librarian

Vermilion: **Vermilion Public Library**
5001 - 49th Ave., Vermilion AB T9X 1B8
Tel: 780-853-4288; *Fax:* 780-853-1783
admin@vermilionpubliclibrary.ca
www.vermilionpubliclibrary.ca
Donna Jones, Library Manager

Veteran: **Veteran Municipal Library**
PO Box 527, Veteran AB T0C 2S0
Tel: 403-575-3915; *Fax:* 403-575-3870
Nicole Larson, Librarian
Linda Schetzsle, Chair

Viking: **Viking Municipal Library**
4920, 53 Ave., Viking AB T0B 4N0
Tel: 780-336-4992; *Fax:* 780-336-4992
librarian@vikinglibrary.ab.ca
www.vikinglibrary.ab.ca
Marayann Wolosinka, Librarian
Gina-Lee Hinton, Staff

Vimy: **Vimy Community/School Library**
PO Box 29, Vimy AB T0G 2J0
Tel: 780-961-3014; *Fax:* 780-961-2094
Pauline Despins, Librarian

Vulcan: **Vulcan Municipal Library**
303 Centre St., Vulcan AB T0L 2B0
Tel: 403-485-2571; *Fax:* 403-485-2571
help@vulcanlibrary.ca
eps.chinookarch.ca/rooms/portal/page/22161_Vulcan
Linda Lambert, Librarian
Cathie McNiven, Assistant Librarian
cmcniven@chinookarch.ab.ca

Wabamun: **Wabamun Public Library**
5132 - 53 Ave., Wabamun AB T0E 2K0
Tel: 780-892-2713; *Fax:* 780-892-7294
bettyl@wabamunlibrary.ca
www.wabamunlibrary.ca
Betty Lalonde, Head Librarian

Wainwright: **Wainwright Public Library**
921 - 3rd Ave., Wainwright AB T9W 1C5
Tel: 780-842-2673; *Fax:* 780-842-2340
librarian@wainwrightlibrary.ab.ca
www.wainwrightlibrary.ab.ca
Jodi Dahlgren, Librarian

Wandering River: **Wandering River Women's Institute Community Library**
PO Box 8, Wandering River AB T0A 3M0
Tel: 780-771-3939; *Fax:* 780-774-2117
librarian@wanderingriverlibrary.ab.ca
Gerda Rebkowich, Chairperson

Warburg: **Warburg Public Library**
PO Box 299, Warburg AB T0C 2T0
Tel: 780-848-2391; *Fax:* 780-848-2296
warburglibrary@yrl.ab.ca
Gail O'Neil, Library Manager

Warner: **Warner Memorial Municipal Library**
206 - 3rd Ave., Warner AB T0K 2L0
Tel: 403-642-3988; *Fax:* 403-642-3988
help@warnerlibrary.ca
www.warnerlibrary.ca
Andrea Tapp, Librarian
Jillian Hounssine, Substitute Librarian

Waskatenau: **Anne Chorney Public Library**
5125 - 51 St., Waskatenau AB T0A 3P0
Tel: 780-358-2777; *Fax:* 780-358-2777
librarian@waskatenaulibrary.ab.ca
www.waskatenaulibrary.ab.ca
Goedele Kerckhof, Library Manager

Water Valley: **Water Valley Public Library**
PO Box 250, Water Valley AB T0M 2E0
Tel: 403-637-3899
watervalleylibrary@libs.prl.ab.ca
www.watervalleycommunity.ca/library.html
Jaymee Shea, Librarian

Westlock: **Westlock Municipal Library**
#1, 10007 - 100 Ave., Westlock AB T7P 2H5
Tel: 780-349-3060; *Fax:* 780-349-5291
info@westlocklibrary.ca
www.westlocklibrary.ca/
Social Media: http://twitter.com/#!/westlocklibrary
Doug Whistance-Smith, Director
dwhistance@westlocklibrary.ca
780-349-3060

Wetaskiwin: **Wetaskiwin Public Library**
5002 - 51st Ave., Wetaskiwin AB T9A 0V1
Tel: 780-361-4446; *Fax:* 780-352-3266
library@wetaskiwin.ca
Manisha Khetarpal, Manager, Library Services
mkhetarpal@wetaskiwin.ca
Rachelle Kuzyk, Manager, Administrative Services
rkuzyk@wetaskiwin.ca

Whitecourt: **Whitecourt & District Public Library**
5201 - 49 St., Whitecourt AB T7S 1N3
Tel: 780-778-2900; *Fax:* 780-778-2827
www.whitecourtlibrary.ab.ca
Thyra Verbaas, Librarian
Lila Wells, Assistant Librarian

Wildwood: **Wildwood Public Library**
5112 - 50th St., Wildwood AB T0E 2M0
Tel: 780-325-3882; *Fax:* 780-325-3920
www.wildwoodlibrary.ab.ca
Terrie Stone, Library Manager

Winfield: **Winfield Community Library**
PO Box 360, Winfield AB T0C 2X0
Tel: 780-682-2423; *Fax:* 780-682-2490
winfieldlibrary@yrl.ab.ca
Pat Thoreson, Librarian
Maureen Webster, Staff

Worsley: **Worsley & District Library**
216 Alberta Ave., Worsley AB T0H 3W0
Tel: 780-685-3842; *Fax:* 780-685-3766
www.worsleylibrary.ab.ca
Colleen Rook, Librarian
Bonnie Bigam, Chair
780-685-2427

Wrentham: **Wrentham Library**
PO Box 111, Wrentham AB T0K 2P0
Tel: 403-222-2485; *Fax:* 403-222-2101
libwren@chinookarch.ab.ca
Alice Cook, Library Supervisor

Youngstown: **Youngstown Municipal Library**
Main St., PO Box 39, Youngstown AB T0J 3P0
Tel: 403-779-3864; *Fax:* 403-779-3864
aymlibrary@marigold.ab.ca
Annette Lupuliak, Librarian

Zama City: **Zama Community Library**
PO Box 14, Zama City AB T0H 4E0
Tel: 780-683-2888; *Fax:* 780-683-2889
www.zamacity.ca
Janet Forrest, Librarian

Archives

Banff: **Alpine Club of Canada**
PO Box 160, Banff AB T1L 1A3
Tel: 403-762-2291; *Fax:* 403-762-2339
archives@whyte.org
Ruth Oltmann, Librarian, Alpine Club

Banff: **Banff Centre for Continuing Education**
107 Tunnel Mountain Dr., Banff AB T1L 1H5
Tel: 403-762-6265; *Fax:* 403-762-6266
library@banffcentre.ca
www.banffcentre.ca/library
James Rout, Managing Librarian
james_rout@banffcentre.ca
403-762-6658
Jane Parkinson, Archivist
jane_parkinson@banffcentre.ca
403-762-6440
Vincent Schillaci-Ventura, Music Librarian
vincent_schillaci-ventura@banffcentre.ca
406-762-6266

Banff: **Whyte Museum of the Canadian Rockies**
PO Box 160, Banff AB T1L 1A3
Tel: 403-762-2291; *Fax:* 403-762-2339
archives@whyte.org
whyte.org
Elizabeth Kundert-Cameron, Librarian
403-762-2291 ext. 332

Brooks: **Eastern Irrigation District**
550 Industrial Rd., Brooks AB T1R 1B2
Tel: 403-362-1400; *Fax:* 403-362-6206
archive@eid.ab.ca
www.eid.ab.ca/general_information.htm
Darlene Fisher, Records Manager Specialist
403-362-1439

Calgary: **Calgary Highlanders Museum & Archives**
4520 Crowchild Trail SW, Calgary AB T3E 1T8
Tel: 403-974-2855
Mike Henry, Archvist

Calgary: **Calgary Police Service**
316 - 7th Ave. SE, Calgary AB T2G 4Z1
Tel: 403-206-4566
pol11014@calgarypolice.ca
www.youthlinkcalgary.com
Janet Pieschel, Executive Director
Gail Niinimaa, Administrator

Calgary: **The City of Calgary**
Admin Bldg., 313 - 7th Ave. SE, Main Fl., Calgary AB T2P 2M5
Tel: 403-268-8180; *Fax:* 403-268-6731
archives@calgary.ca
www.calgary.ca
Carol Berrington, Corporate Records Coordinator
carol.berrington@calgary.ca
403-268-5804

Calgary: **Glenbow - Alberta Institute/Glenbow Museum**
130 - 9th Ave. SE, Calgary AB T2G 0P3
Tel: 403-268-4204; *Fax:* 403-232-6569
glenbow@glenbow.org
www.glenbow.org
Douglas E. Cass, Director, Library & Archives
dcass@glenbow.org
403-268-4203
Lindsay Moir, Senior Librarian

Calgary: **Heritage Park Society**
1900 Heritage Dr. SW, Calgary AB T2V 2X3
Tel: 403-268-8500; *Fax:* 403-268-8501
reception@heritagepark.ab.ca
www.heritagepark.ca
Sylvia Harnden, Curator
403-268-8536

Calgary: **Legal Archives Society of Alberta**
#510, 919 - 11th Ave. SW, Calgary AB T2R 1P3
Tel: 403-244-5510; *Fax:* 403-541-9102
legalarc@legalarchivessociety.ab.ca
www.legalarchivessociety.ab.ca
Graham Price, President
legalarc@legalarchivessociety.ab.ca
Brenda McCafferty, Archivist
Tanya Barber, Administrative/Archival Assistant

Calgary: **Lord Strathcona's Horse Regimental Museum**
4520 Crowchild Trail SW, Calgary AB T2T 5J4
Tel: 403-974-2854; *Fax:* 403-974-2858
archives@strathconas.ca
www.strathconas.ca
Lee Ramsden, Archivist
403-974-2854

Calgary: **Naval Museum of Alberta**
1820 - 24 St. SW, Calgary AB T2T 0G6
Tel: 403-242-0002; *Fax:* 403-240-1966
bhconnolly@rogers.com
Bruce Connolly, Assistant Curator

Calgary: **Sisters Faithful Companions of Jesus**
219 - 19th Ave. SW, Calgary AB T2S 0C8
Tel: 403-228-3623; *Fax:* 403-541-9297
shc@fcjsisters.ca
www.fcjsisters.org
Elizabeth Fitzgerald, Archivist

Cardston: **Cardston & District Historical Society**
89 - 3rd Ave. West, Cardston AB T0K 0K0
Tel: 403-653-4726
H. Dale Lowry, Director

Edmonton: **Canadian Moravian Archives**
2304 - 38 St., Edmonton AB T6L 4K9
Tel: 780-440-3050; *Fax:* 780-463-2143
William G. Brese, President
wbrese@interbaun.com

Edmonton: **City of Edmonton Archives**
10440 - 108 Ave., Edmonton AB T5H 3Z9
Tel: 780-496-8711; *Fax:* 780-496-8732
cms.archives@edmonton.ca
www.edmonton.ca/archives
Kim Christie-Milley, Reference Archivist

Edmonton: **Edmonton Public Schools**
10425 - 99th Ave., Edmonton AB T5K 0E5
Tel: 780-422-1970; *Fax:* 780-426-0192
archives@epsb.ca
archives.epsb.net
Catherine D. Luck, Supervisor
catherine.luck@epsb.ca

Edmonton: **Provincial Archives of Alberta**
8555 Roper Rd., Edmonton AB T6E 5W1
Tel: 780-427-1750; *Fax:* 780-427-4646
paa@gov.ab.ca
www.archivesalberta.org/walls/paa.htm
Jonathan Davidson, Reference Archivist, Library & Access Services
jonathan.davidson@gov.ab.ca
780-427-1056
Irene Jendzjowsky, Manager, Private Records, Library & Reference Srvs & FOIP
irene.jendzjowsky@gov.ab.ca
Dennis Hyduk, Head, Technical Services
dennis.hyduk@gov.ab.ca
780-427-0236

Edmonton: **Ukrainian Canadian Archives & Museum of Alberta**
9543 - 110th Ave., Edmonton AB T5H 1H3
Tel: 780-424-7580; *Fax:* 780-420-0562
ucama@shaw.ca
www.ucama.com
Alexander Makar, Director

Jasper: **Jasper-Yellowhead Museum & Archives**
PO Box 42, Jasper AB T0E 1E0
Tel: 780-852-3013; *Fax:* 780-852-3240
archives@jaspermuseum.org
www.jaspermuseum.org
Meghan Power, Archivist

Lethbridge: **Sir Alexander Galt Museum & Archives**
502 - 1st St. South, Lethbridge AB T1J 1Y4
Tel: 403-329-7302; *Fax:* 403-329-4958
Toll-Free: 866-320-3898
archives@galtmuseum.com
www.galtmuseum.com/index.htm
Greg Ellis, City Archivist

Medicine Hat: **Esplanade Arts & Heritage Centre**
401 - 1st St. SE, Medicine Hat AB T1A 8W2
Tel: 403-502-8582; *Fax:* 403-502-8589
phipype@medicinehat.ca
www.esplanade.ca/archives/archives.html
Philip Pype, Archivist
403-502-8585

Millet: **Millet & District Historical Society**
c/o Millet & District Museum & Archives Room,, 5120 - 50 St., Millet AB T0C 1Z0
Tel: 780-387-5558; *Fax:* 780-387-5548
info@milletmuseum.ca
home.cablerocket.com/~milletmuseum
Tracey Leavitt, Museum/Archives Coordinator
Jean Scott, Volunteer/Museum & Archives Manager

Morley: **Nakoda Institute**
PO Box 120, Morley AB T0L 1N0
Tel: 403-881-3949; *Fax:* 403-881-4250
Ian Getty, Contact

Olds: **Mountain View Museum - Olds Historical Society**
PO Box 3882, Olds AB T4H 1P6
Tel: 403-556-8464
mvmuseum@oldsmuseum.ca
www.oldsmuseum.ca
Geraldine Wiper, Archivist
J. Kearney, Staff

***Red Deer:* Red Deer & District Archives**
4525 - 47A Ave., Red Deer AB T4N 6Z6
Tel: 403-309-8403; *Fax:* 403-340-8728
archives@reddeer.ca
Michael Dawe, City Archivist
Garth Clarke, Archivist
403-309-8403

***St Albert Place:* Musée Héritage Museum**
5 St Anne St., St Albert Place AB T8N 3Z9
Tel: 780-459-1528
museum@artsheritage.ca
http://museeheritagemuseum.blogspot.com/
Ann Ramsden, Director of Heritage

***Stony Plain:* The Multicultural Heritage Centre**
5411 - 51 St., Stony Plain AB T7Z 1X7
Tel: 780-963-2777; *Fax:* 780-963-0233
margit@multicentre.org
www.multicentre.org
Margit Knupp, Historical Resources Coordinator
margit@multicentre.org
780-963-2777

***Taber:* Taber & District Museum Society**
4702 - 50th St., Taber AB T1G 2B6
Tel: 403-223-5708; *Fax:* 403-223-0529
timchin@telusplanet.net
Karen Ingram, Manager

***Wetaskiwin:* City of Wetaskiwin**
4904 - 51 St., Wetaskiwin AB T9A 1L2
Tel: 780-361-4423; *Fax:* 780-352-0930
archives@wetaskiwin.ca
www2.wetaskiwin.ca/Archives/
Carolyn Hill, Archivist
archives@wetaskiwin.ca

British Columbia

Regional Systems

Cariboo Regional District Library
180 - 3rd Ave. North, #A, Williams Lake BC V2G 2A4
Tel: 250-392-3630; *Toll-Free:* 800-665-1636
wlake@cariboord.bc.ca
www.cln.bc.ca
Colleen Swift, Manager, Library Services
cswift@cariboord.bc.ca

Fraser Valley Regional Library
34589 Delair Rd., Abbotsford BC V2S 5Y1
Tel: 604-859-7141; *Fax:* 604-852-5701
Toll-Free: 888-668-4141
www.fvrl.bc.ca
Peter Fassbender, Chair
Maureen Woods, Chief Executive Officer
maureen.woods@fvrl.bc.ca
Rob O'Brennan, Director, Public Services
robert.obrennan@fvrl.bc.ca
Mary O'Callaghan, Director, Corporate Services & Manager, Marketing & Communications
mary.ocallaghan@fvrl.bc.ca
Scott Hargrove, Senior Manager, Information Technology
scott.hargrove@fvrl.bc.ca
Sher O'Hara, Senior Manager, Products & Services
sher.ohara@fvrl.bc.ca
Vickie Klemetson, Supervisor, Outreach Services
vickie.klemetson@fvrl.bc.ca
Sharyle Peters, Personnel Officer
sharyle.peters@fvrl.bc.ca

Okanagan Regional Library Headquarters
1430 KLO Rd., Kelowna BC V1W 3P6
Tel: 250-860-4033; *Fax:* 250-861-8696
Other Numbers: 250-860-4652 (Telecirc for account access)
www.orl.bc.ca
Ted Bacigalupo, Chair
Lesley Dieno, Executive Director
ldieno@orl.bc.ca
Barb Drake, Manager, Human Resources
bdrake@orl.bc.ca

Peace River Associated Libraries
c/o Hudson's Hope Public Library, 30 Dudley Dr., Hudson's Hope BC V0C 1V0
Tel: 250-783-9414; *Fax:* 250-783-9414
hh.ill@pris.bc.ca
www.pris.bc.ca/pral/main.htm
Mariann Field Hill, Chair

Public Library InterLINK
7252 Kingsway, Lower Level, Burnaby BC V5E 1G3
Tel: 604-517-8441; *Fax:* 604-517-8410
info@interlinklibraries.ca
www.interlinklibraries.ca
Rita Avigdor, Manager of Operations
rita.avigdor@interlinklibraries.ca
Colleen Smith, Audiobook Coordinator
colleen.smith@interlinklibraries.ca
604-517-8441

Thompson-Nicola Regional District Library System
#300, 465 Victoria St., Kamloops BC V2C 2A9
Tel: 250-374-8866; *Fax:* 250-374-8355
postmaster@tnrdlib.bc.ca
www.tnrdlib.bc.ca
Kevin Kierans, Director of Libraries
kkierans@tnrdlib.bc.ca

Vancouver Island Regional Library
6250 Hammond Bay Rd., Nanaimo BC V9T 6M9
Tel: 250-758-4697; *Fax:* 250-758-2482
info@virl.bc.ca
www.virl.bc.ca
Rosemary Bonanno, Executive Director
Elizabeth Pack, Director of Public Services
epack@virl.bc.ca
250-729-2304
Martin Gavin, Director of Support Services
mgavin@virl.bc.ca
250-729-2305
Fiona Anderson, Director of Systems & Technical Services
fanderson@virl.bc.ca
250-729-2311
Adrian Maas, Director of Finance
amaas@virl.bc.ca
250-729-2319
Harold Kamikawaji, Director of Human Resources
hkamikawaji@virl.bc.ca
250-729-2306

Public Libraries

***Alert Bay:* Alert Bay Public Library**
118 Fir St., Alert Bay BC V0N 1A0
Tel: 250-974-5721; *Fax:* 250-974-5026
abplb@island.net
www.alertbay.com/library/
Sheila Jolliffe, Community Librarian

***Atlin:* Atlin Library**
Courthouse Bldg., 2nd St., Atlin BC V0W 1A0
Linda Brown, Contact

***Bowen Island:* Bowen Island Public Library**
430 Bowen Trunk Rd., Bowen Island BC V0N 1G0
Tel: 604-947-9788; *Fax:* 604-947-9788
info@bowenlibrary.ca
www.bowenlibrary.ca
Tina Nielsen, Librarian
tnielsen@bowenlibrary.ca

***Burnaby:* Burnaby Public Library**
6100 Willingdon Ave., Burnaby BC V5H 4N5
Tel: 604-436-5427; *Fax:* 604-436-2961
Other Numbers: 604-293-0034 Telecirc
bpl@bpl.bc.ca
www.bpl.bc.ca
Social Media: twitter.com/#!/burnabypl; www.facebook.com/burnabypubliclibrary
Edel Toner-Rogala, Chief Librarian
604-436-5427
Deb Thomas, Deputy Chief Librarian
thomasd@bpl.bc.ca
Karen Steele, Librarian, Technical Services
karen.steele@bpl.bc.ca
604-436-5424
John Davenport, Librarian, Technical Services
jdavenpo@bpl.bc.ca
604-436-5435
Miriam Moses, System Supervisor/Librarian
mmoses@bpl.bc.ca
604-436-5437

***Burnaby:* Rare Bird**
c/o Anne Grainger, 7464 Rosewood St., Burnaby BC V5E 2G5
Tel: 604-990-0507
www.cablelan.net/frose/CLABCnews.html

***Burns Lake:* Burns Lake Public Library**
585 Government St., Burns Lake BC V0J 1E0
Tel: 250-692-3192; *Fax:* 250-692-7488
libraryn@burnslakelibrary.com
burnslake.bclibrary.ca
Linda L. Palmer, Head Librarian
Elaine Wiebe, Library Director
elaine@burnslakelibrary.com
Tenille Woskett, Assistant Director
tenille@burnslakelibrary.com

***Castlegar:* Castlegar & District Public Library**
1005 - 3rd St., Castlegar BC V1N 2A2
Tel: 250-365-6611; *Fax:* 250-365-7765
info@castlegarlibrary.com
www.castlegarlibrary.com
Heather Maisel, Library Director
director@castlegarlibrary.com
250-365-7751
Julie Kalesnikoff, Librarian
julie@castlegarlibrary.com
Cheryl Babakaiff, Office Manager
cheryl@castlegarlibrary.com
Corinne Shortridge, Computer Technician
corinne@castlegarlibrary.com

***Chetwynd:* Chetwynd Public Library**
5012 - 46th St., Chetwynd BC V0C 1J0
Tel: 250-788-2559; *Fax:* 250-788-2186
fasleson@pris.bc.ca
www.chetwyndpubliclibrary.com
Fay Asleson, Librarian
Jennifer Gosse, Chair

***Coquitlam:* Coquitlam Public Library**
575 Poirier St., Coquitlam BC V3J 6A9
Tel: 604-937-4144; *Fax:* 604-937-4145
director@library.coquitlam.bc.ca
www.library.coquitlam.bc.ca
Rhian Piprell, Director
rpiprell@library.coquitlam.bc.ca
604-937-4132
Kathleen Wyatt, Information Services Coordinator
kwayatt@library.coquitlam.bc.ca
604-937-4147
Jocelan Litton, Head, Technical Services
jlitton@library.coquitlam.bc.ca
604-937-4150
Nancy Collins, Systems Supervisor
systems@library.coquitlam.bc.ca
604-937-4151

***Cranbrook:* Cranbrook Public Library**
1212 2nd St. N, Cranbrook BC V1C 4T6
Tel: 250-426-4063; *Fax:* 250-426-2098
staff@cranbrookpubliclibrary.ca
www.cranbrookpubliclibrary.ca
Ursula Brigl, Library Director
ubrigl@cranbrookpubliclibrary.ca
250-426-4063 ext. 101

***Crawford Bay:* Eastshore Community Library (Reading Centre)**
16234 King St., Crawford Bay BC V0B 1E0
Tel: 250-227-6960

***Dawson Creek:* Dawson Creek Municipal Public Library**
1001 McKellar Ave., Dawson Creek BC V1G 4W7
Tel: 250-782-4661; *Fax:* 250-782-4667
dclib@pris.ca
dawsoncreek.bclibrary.ca
Jenny Snyder, Head Librarian

***Dease Lake:* Dease Lake Reading Centre**
PO Box 237, Dease Lake BC V0C 1L0
Tel: 250-771-3636
Carolyn Moore, Librarian

***Edgewater:* Edgewater Reading Centre**
PO Box 129, Edgewater BC V0A 1E0
Tel: 250-347-9558

***Edgewood:* Inonoaklin Valley Reading Centre**
409 Monashee Ave., Edgewood BC V0G 1J0
Tel: 250-269-7212; *Fax:* 250-269-7633
sbampton@hotmail.com
Susan Bampton, Librarian
sbampton@hotmail.com
Kathy Watson, Chair

Elkford: Elkford Public Library
816 Michel Rd., Elkford BC V0B 1H0
Tel: 250-865-2912; Fax: 250-865-2460
elklib1@yahoo.ca
www.elkfordlibrary.org
Diane Andrews, Head Librarian
elklib1@yahoo.ca
Rosalie Atherton, Library Clerk

Fauquier: Fauquier Reading Centre
519 Willow St., Fauquier BC V0G 1K0
Tel: 250-269-7348
Frank Poirier, Librarian
Karen Watson, Chair
karen.watson@canada.com
250-236-7390

Fernie: Fernie Heritage Library
492 - 3rd Ave., Fernie BC V0B 1M0
Tel: 250-423-4458; Fax: 250-423-7906
library@elkvalley.net
www.ferniehertiagelibrary.com
Emma Dressler, Librarian

Fort Nelson: Fort Nelson Public Library
Town Square, 5315 - 50th Ave. South, Fort Nelson BC V0C 1R0
Tel: 250-774-6777; Fax: 250-774-6777
fnpl@fortnelson.bclibrary.ca
www.fortnelson.bclibrary.ca
Ramona Allan, Chair
Nola Newman, Community Librarian
Sylvia Bramhill, Assistant Librarian, Interlibrary Loans
Joan Davidson, Assistant Librarian
Linda Novotny, Assistant Librarian, Technical Support

Fort St James: Fort St James Public Library
425 Manson St., Fort St James BC V0J 1P0
Tel: 250-996-7431; Fax: 250-996-7484
fortlib@fsjames.com
fortstjames.bclibrary.ca
Diana Uhrich, Librarian
Jo-Anne Schemenauer, Assistant Librarian
Flora Arias Molina, Library Aide

Fort St John: Fort St John Public Library
10015 - 100th Ave., Fort St John BC V1J 1Y7
Tel: 250-785-3731; Fax: 250-785-7982
fsjlibrary@fsjlibrary.ca
fortstjohn.bclibrary.ca
Kimberly Partanen, Head

Fraser Lake: Fraser Lake Public Library
228 Endako Ave., Fraser Lake BC V0J 1S0
Tel: 250-699-8888; Fax: 250-699-8899
fllibrarian@bcgroup.net
fraserlake.bclibrary.ca/
Audrey Fennema, Chief Librarian
Anne Mowry, Library Assistant
Hazel Thomas, Library Assistant

Fruitvale: Beaver Valley Public Library
1847 - 1st St., Fruitvale BC V0G 1L0
Tel: 250-367-7114; Fax: 250-367-7130
bvpublic@telus.net
beavervalley.bclibrary.ca
Marie Onyett, Head Librarian

Gibsons: Gibsons District Public Library
470 South Fletcher Rd., Gibsons BC V0N 1V0
Tel: 604-886-2130; Fax: 604-886-2689
www.gibsons.bclibrary.ca
Ms Michelle Southam, Chief Librarian
michelle.southam@gdpl.scrd.bc.ca
Pat Swadden, Assistant Librarian

Grand Forks: Grand Forks & District Public Library
7342 - 5th St., Grand Forks BC V0H 1H0
Tel: 250-442-3944; Fax: 250-442-2645
grandforks.bclibrary.ca
Heather Buzzell, Library Director
Amanda Deverson, Library Assistant

Granisle: Granisle Public Library
#2 Village Sq., McDonald Ave., Granisle BC V0J 1W0
Tel: 250-697-2713
library@granisle.net
granisle.bclibrary.ca
Sherry Smith, Chief Librarian

Grasmere: Grasmere Reading Centre
PO Box 75, Grasmere BC V0B 1R0
Tel: 250-887-3412; Fax: 250-887-3274
Bonnie Crosson, Head of Library

Greenwood: Greenwood Public Library
346 South Copper St., Greenwood BC V0H 1J0
Tel: 250-445-6111; Fax: 250-445-6111
greenlib@shaw.ca
greenwood.bclibrary.ca
Judy Foucher, Community Librarian
Clare Folvik, Assistant Librarian

Hazelton: Hazelton District Public Library
4255 Government St., Hazelton BC V0J 1Y0
Tel: 250-842-5961; Fax: 250-842-2176
hazlib@bulkley.net
www.hazeltonlibrary.bc.ca
Eve Hope, Librarian

Houston: Houston Public Library
3150 - 14th St., Houston BC V0J 1Z0
Tel: 250-845-2256; Fax: 250-845-2088
library.houston.ca
Toni McKilligan, Chief Librarian
Erna Vander Heide, Children's Librarian
Dana Giesbrecht, Library Assistant
Gail Conroy, Library Assistant

Invermere: Invermere Public Library
201 - 7th Ave., Invermere BC V0A 1K0
Tel: 250-342-6416; Fax: 250-342-6416
invlibrary@cyberlink.bc.ca
invermere.bclibrary.ca
Elizabeth Robinson, Head Librarian

Kimberley: Kimberley Public Library
115 Spokane St., Kimberley BC V1A 2E5
Tel: 250-427-3112; Fax: 250-427-7157
staff@kimberleylibrary.net
kimberley.bclibrary.ca
Karin von Wittgenstein, Director

Kitwanga: Gitanyow Independent School Reading Centre
PO Box 369, Kitwanga BC V0J 2A0
Tel: 250-849-5528; Fax: 250-849-5870
Other Numbers: 250-849-5384 administration
Bernadette McLean, Chair

Lions Bay: Lions Bay Library (Reading Centre)
400 Centre Rd., Lions Bay BC V0N 2E0
Tel: 604-921-6944

Mackenzie: Mackenzie Public Library
400 Skeena Dr., Mackenzie BC V0J 2C0
Tel: 250-997-6343; Fax: 250-997-5792
macklib@mackbc.com
mackenzie.bclibrary.ca
Wanda Davis, Librarian

Madeira Park: Pender Harbour Reading Centre
12952 Madeira Park Rd., Madeira Park BC V0N 2H0
Tel: 604-883-2983

McBride: McBride & District Public Library
241 Dominion St., McBride BC V0J 2E0
Tel: 250-569-2411; Fax: 250-569-2411
library@mcbridebc.org
www.mcbridebc.org/library
Margaret Griffiths, Community Librarian

Midway: Midway Public Library
612 - 6th Ave., Midway BC V0H 1M0
Tel: 250-449-2620; Fax: 250-449-2389
info@midwaylibrary.bc.ca
midway.bclibrary.ca
Stephanie Boltz, Librarian
info@midwaylibrary.bc.ca

Nelson: Nelson Municipal Library
602 Stanley St., Nelson BC V1L 1N4
Tel: 250-352-6333; Fax: 250-354-1799
jstockdale@nelson.ca
nelson.bclibrary.ca
June Stockdale, Chief Librarian
Martha Scott, Assistant 3-Cataloguing
Nancy Radonich, Youth Services
Maureen Stoll, Assistant 2, Office Manager

New Denver: New Denver Reading Centre
PO Box 38, New Denver BC V0G 1S0
Tel: 250-358-2221
Agnes Emary, Chair

New Westminster: New Westminster Public Library
716 - 6th Ave., New Westminster BC V3M 2B3
Tel: 604-527-4660; Fax: 604-527-4674
listener@nwpl.ca
www.nwpl.ca
Julie Spurrell, Chief Librarian
spurrell@nwpl.ca
604-527-4675
Susan Buss, Interim Head, Reference Services
sbuss@nwpl.ca
604-527-4661
Marie McKee, Head of Technical Services
mmckee@nwpl.ca
604-527-4671
Ellen Heaney, Head of Children's Services
eheaney@nwpl.ca
604-527-4678

North Vancouver: North Vancouver City Library
120 West 14th St., North Vancouver BC V7M 1N9
Tel: 604-998-3450; Fax: 604-983-3624
nvcl@cnv.org
www.cnv.org/nvcl
Jane Watkins, Chief Librarian
jwatkins@cnb.org
604-990-4226
Wai-Lin Chee, Deputy Chief Librarian
wchee@cnv.org
604-990-4222

North Vancouver: North Vancouver District Public Library
1277 Lynn Valley Rd., North Vancouver BC V7J 2A1
Tel: 604-990-5800; Fax: 604-984-7600
www.nvdpl.ca
Areef Abraham, Chair
scoularh@nvdpl.ca
Heather Scoular, Director, Library Services
scoularh@nvdpl.ca
604-990-5800 ext. 8103
Michael DeKoven, Manager, Support Services
dekovenm@nvdpl.ca
604-990-5800 ext. 8120
Corinne McConchie, Manager, Technical Services
mcconchiec@nvdpl.ca
604-990-5800 ext. 8113
Delores Weightman, Manager, Office & Human Resources
604-990-5800 ext. 8102
Heather Goodwin, Librarian, Home Service
604-990-5800 ext. 8124

Pender Island: Pender Island Public Library
4407 Bedwell Harbour Rd., Pender Island BC V0N 2M0
Tel: 250-629-3722; Fax: 250-629-3788
pender.bclibrary.ca
Liz Testemale, Librarian
bpi.ill@gulfislands.com

Penticton: Penticton Public Library
785 Main St, Penticton BC V2A 5E3
Tel: 250-770-7781
Other Numbers: InfoDesk: 250-770-7782; Kids' Library: 250-777-7783
library@summer.com
www.library.penticton.bc.ca
Larry R. Little, Chief Librarian
Karen Kellerman, Public Services Librarian
Shelley Murphy, Systems Librarian
Julia Cox, Youth Services Librarian

Port Coquitlam: Archives Association of British Columbia Newsletter
#249, 34A - 2755 Lougheed Hwy., Port Coquitlam BC V3B 5Y9
aabc.ca/newslett.htm
Leah Pearse, Newsletter Committee Chair
leah.pearse@gmail.com

Port Moody: Port Moody Public Library
100 Newport Dr., Port Moody BC V3H 5C3
Tel: 604-469-4575; Fax: 604-469-4576
askthelibrary@cityofportmoody.com
library.portmoody.ca
Heather Scoular, Library Director
heather.scoular@cityofportmoody.com

Pouce Coupe: Pouce Coupe Public Library
5000 - 49 Ave., Pouce Coupe BC V0C 2C0
Tel: 250-786-5765
bpoc.ill@pris.bc.ca
www.poucecoupe.bclibrary.ca
Courtenay Johnston, Community Librarian
Patricia McDonald, Assistant Librarian

Powell River: Powell River Municipal Library
4411 Michigan Ave., Powell River BC V8A 2S3
Tel: 604-485-4796; Fax: 604-485-5320
powellriverlibrary@shaw.ca
www.powellriverlibrary.ca
Stephanie Hall, Head Librarian

Prince George: Prince George Public Library
887 Dominion St., Prince George BC V2L 5L1
Tel: 250-563-9251; Fax: 250-563-0892
www.lib.pg.bc.ca
Social Media: www.facebook.com/pglibrary
Allan Wilson, Chief Librarian
Marc Saunders, Manager, Public Services
Marjorie Tunney, Manager, Administrative Services

Prince Rupert: Prince Rupert Public Library
101 - 6th Ave. West, Prince Rupert BC V8J 1Y9
Tel: 250-627-1345; Fax: 250-627-7743
info@princerupertlibrary.ca
www.princerupertlibrary.ca
Denise St. Arnaud, Chief Librarian
chieflib@citytel.net

Radium Hot Springs: Radium Hot Springs Public Library
4863 Stanley St., Radium Hot Springs BC V0A 1M0
Tel: 250-347-2434
radiumpubliclibrary@hotmail.com

Richmond: Richmond Public Library
#100, 7700 Minoru Gate, Richmond BC V6Y 1R9
Tel: 604-231-6422
Other Numbers: 604-231-6413 (Reference Desk)
www.yourlibrary.ca
Gregory Buss, Chief Librarian
greg.buss@yourlibrary.ca
604-231-6418

Riondel: Riondel Reading Centre
PO Box 29, Riondel BC V0B 2B0
Tel: 250-225-3570
Muriel Paquette, Chair

Roberts Creek: Roberts Creek Community Library
General Delivery, Roberts Creek BC V0N 2W0
Tel: 604-886-2130

Rossland: Rossland Public Library
2180 Columbia Ave., Rossland BC V0G 1Y0
Tel: 250-362-7611; Fax: 250-362-7138
rosslib@telus.net
rosslib.kics.bc.ca
Indira Wickremasinghe, Head Librarian
Lynn Amann, Children's Librarian & Assistant Librarian

Sechelt: Sechelt Public Library
5797 Cowrie St., Sechelt BC V0N 3A0
Tel: 604-885-3260; Fax: 604-885-5183
info@sechelt.bclibrary.ca
www.sechelt.bclibrary.ca
Iris Loewen, Chief Librarian
iris.loewen@sechelt.bclibrary.ca
Rose Toenders, Assistant Librarian
rose.toenders@sechelt.bclibrary.ca

Smithers: Smithers Public Library
3817 Alfred Ave., Smithers BC V0J 2N0
Tel: 250-847-3043; Fax: 250-847-1533
info@smitherslibrary.ca
www.smitherslibrary.ca
Iva Allen, Library Director

Stewart: Stewart Public Library
824 Main St., Stewart BC V0T 1W0
Tel: 250-636-2380; Fax: 250-636-2380
bsp_ill@mountainharbour.ca
www.stewart.bclibrary.ca
Galina Dyrant, Librarian
Anne Jefferson, Chair

Surrey: Surrey Public Library
10350 University Dr., Surrey BC V3T 4B8
Tel: 604-598-7300; Fax: 604-598-7310
bsur@surrey.ca
www.surreylibraries.ca
Social Media: www.facebook.com/surreylibraries
Beth Barlow, Chief Librarian
babarlow@surrey.ca
604-598-7304
Melanie Houlden, Deputy Chief Librarian
mghoulden@surrey.ca
604-598-7305
Michael Ho, Manager, Administrative Services
mho@surrey.ca
604-598-7303
Stephanie Kurmey, Librarian, Collections Services
slkurmey@surrey.ca
604-598-7383

Taylor: Taylor Public Library
10008 - 104 Ave., Taylor BC V0C 2K0
Tel: 250-789-9878; Fax: 250-789-3543
library@districtoftaylor.com
taylor.bclibrary.ca
Social Media:
www.facebook.com/group.php?gid=113819095313441
Sherry Murphy, Librarian

Trail: Trail & District Public Library
1051 Victoria St., Trail BC V1R 3T3
Tel: 250-364-1731; Fax: 250-364-2176
director@traillibrary.com
www.traillibrary.com
Helen Graham, Director
director@traillibrary.com

Tumbler Ridge: Tumbler Ridge Public Library
340 Front St., Tumbler Ridge BC V0C 2W0
Tel: 250-242-4778; Fax: 250-242-4707
mburton@tumblerridgelibrary.org
www.tumblerridge.bclibrary.ca
Michele Burton, Library Manager
Sharon Bray, Children's Services
sbray@tumblerridgelibrary.org
Kristen Holmlund, Technical Services
kholmlund@tumblerridgelibrary.org
Bintang Howard, Admin. Assistant
bhoward@tumblerridgelibrary.org

Valemount: Valemount Public Library
1090A Main St., Valemount BC V0E 2Z0
Tel: 250-566-4367; Fax: 250-566-4278
library@valemount.ca
valemount.bclibrary.ca
Wendy Cinnamon, Chief Librarian
Elli Haag, Assistant Librarian/Interlibrary Loan Librarian
Hollie Blanchette, Technology
Giovanna Gislimberti, Clerk

Vancouver: BCLA Reporter
#150, 900 Howe St., Vancouver BC V6Z 2M4
Tel: 604-683-5354; Fax: 604-609-0707
office@bcla.bc.ca
www.bcla.bc.ca
Ted Benson, Editor

Vancouver: The Bookmark
c/o BC Teachers' Federation, #100, 550 West 6th Ave., Vancouver BC V5Z 4P2
Tel: 604-871-2283
www.bctf.ca/BCTLA/bookmark.html
Heather Daly, Editor
Carolyn Cutt, Reviews Editor
Valerie Pollock, Reviews Editor

Vancouver: Isaac Waldman Jewish Public Library
950 West 41st Ave., Jewish Community Centre of Greater Vancouver, Vancouver BC V5Z 2N7
Tel: 604-257-5111; Fax: 604-257-5119
library@jccgv.bc.ca
www.jcclibrary.ca
Karen Corrin, Librarian
Kelly Rae, Library Technician

Vancouver: Teacher Librarian: the Journal for School Library Professionals K-12
#343, 100 - 1001 West Broadway, Vancouver BC V6H 4E4
Tel: 604-925-0266; Fax: 604-925-0566
admin@teacherlibrarian.com
www.teacherlibrarian.com
Ken Haycock, Editor

Vancouver: Vancouver Public Library
350 West Georgia St., Vancouver BC V6B 6B1
Tel: 604-331-4000; Fax: 604-331-4080
TDD: 6043313606
Other Numbers: Central Branch: 604-331-3603
info@vpl.ca
www.vpl.vancouver.bc.ca
Sandra Singh, City Librarian
Sandra.Singh@vpl.ca
604—33-1-40
Olivia Craster, Division Head, Acquistions
olivicra@vpl.ca
604-331-4033
Sandra Singh, Director, Systems & Special Projects
sandrsin@vpl.ca
604-331-4070
Shelagh Flaherty, Director, Central Library & Reference Services
shelafla@vpl.ca
604-331-4001
Corinne Durston, Director, Branch Libraries West & Technical Services
corindur@vpl.ca
604-331-4009
Diana Guinn, Director, Branch Libraries East & Outreach Services
dianagui@vpl.ca
604-331-4009
Jean Kavanagh, Manager, Marketing & Communications
jkavanagh@vpl.va
604-331-3895
Kate Russell, Special Collections Librarian
katherus@vpl.ca
604-331-3721

Vancouver: Yaacing
#150, 900 Howe St., Vancouver BC V6Z 2M4
Tel: 604-683-5354; Fax: 604-609-0707
office@bcla.bc.ca
www.bcla.bc.ca/yaacs
Phillippa Brown, Editor

Vanderhoof: Vanderhoof Public Library
PO Bag 6000, Vanderhoof BC V0J 3A0
Tel: 250-567-4060; Fax: 250-567-4458
vhpl@telus.net
www.vanderhoofpubliclibrary.com
Jane Gray, Librarian

Victoria: Greater Victoria Public Library
735 Broughton St., Victoria BC V8W 3H2
Tel: 250-384-5222; Fax: 250-385-5971
TDD: 2504130364
www.gvpl.ca
Lee Teal, Interim CEO
lteal@gvpl.ca
250-413-0353
Lynne Jordan, Deputy CEO/Director of Strategic Development
jjordan@gvpl.ca
250-413-0354
Daniel Phillips, Manager, IT Solutions
dphillips@gvpl.ca
250-413-0357

Victoria: View Royal Public Library
45B View Royal Ave., Victoria BC V9B 1A6
Tel: 250-479-2723; Fax: 250-479-2723
vivr.ill@shaw.ca
members.shaw.ca/vivr.ill
Jim Powell, Chair

West Vancouver: West Vancouver Memorial Library
1950 Marine Dr., West Vancouver BC V7V 1J8
Tel: 604-925-7400; Fax: 604-925-5933
Other Numbers: Art Gallery: 604-925-7407
info@westvanlibrary.ca
www.westvanlibrary.ca
Social Media: www.twitter.com/westvanlibrary; www.facebook.com/WestVancouverMemorialLibrary
Jenny Benedict, Director, Library Services
jbenedict@westvanlibrary.ca
604-925-7424
Deb Hutchison Koep, Deputy Director & Head, Technology & Technical Services
dkoep@westvanlibrary.ca
604-925-7443
Cheryl McGregor, Head, Information Services
cmcgregor@westvanlibrary.ca
604-925-7439
Ellen Scoretz, Head, Circulation
escoretz@westvanlibrary.ca
604-925-7430
Lauren Henderson, Manager, Operations
lhenderson@westvanlibrary.ca
604-925-7431

Whistler: Whistler Public Library
4329 Main St., Whistler BC V0N 1B4
Tel: 604-935-8433; Fax: 604-935-8434
info@whistlerlibrary.ca
www.whistlerlibrary.ca
Lauren Stara, Library Director
lstara@whistlerlibrary.ca
604-935-8438
Suzanne Thomas, Library Technician
sthomas@whistlerlibrary.ca
604-935-8433 ext. 8722

Beverly Newell, Community Librarian
bnewell@whistlerlibrary.ca
Danusia Smit, Circulation Manager
604-935-8433 ext. 8729
Nadine White, Public Services Librarian
604-935-8433 ext. 8725

Archives

Abbotsford: Matsqui-Sumas-Abbotsford Museum Archives
1B, 32320 George Ferguson Way, Abbotsford BC V2T 6N4
Tel: 604-853-0313; *Fax:* 866-373-2771
prcoordinator.msamuseum@shawbiz.ca
www.abbotsford.net/msamuseum
Social Media:
www.facebook.com/profile.php?id=100001845282384
Dorothy Van der Ree, Executive Director
Christina Reid, Collections Manager
collectionsmanager@shawbiz.ca

Alert Bay: U'Mista Cultural Centre
Front St., PO Box 253, Alert Bay BC V0N 1A0
Tel: 250-974-5403; *Fax:* 250-974-5499
info@umista.ca
umista.org
Andrea Sanborn, Contact

Ashcroft: Ashcroft Museum
402 Brink St., Ashcroft BC V0K 1A0
Tel: 250-453-9232; *Fax:* 250-453-9664
Kathy Paulos, Curator
250-453-9232

Barkerville: Barkerville Historic Town
PO Box 19, Barkerville BC V0K 1B0
Tel: 604-994-3302
W.G. Quackenbush, Curator
bill.quackenbush@bakrerville.ca
888-994-3332 ext. 25
Duane Abel, Curatorial Assistant
duane.abel@barkerville.ca
888-994-3332 ext. 26

Bella Bella: Heiltsuk Cultural Education Centre
PO Box 880, Bella Bella BC V0T 1Z0
Tel: 250-957-2626; *Fax:* 250-957-2780
hcec04@yahoo.com
www.hcec.ca
Jennifer Carpenter, Director
jgcarp@hcec.ca
Terri Reid, Resource Centre Assistant
treid@hcec.ca

Burnaby: Japanese Canadian National Museum
6688 Southoaks Cres., Burnaby BC V5E 4M7
Tel: 604-777-7000; *Fax:* 604-777-7001
jcnm@nikkeiplace.org
www.jcnm.ca
Timothy Savage, Archivist
tsavage@nikkeiplace.org

Campbell River: Campbell River Museum & Archives
470 Ocean Island Hwy., Campbell River BC V9W 4Z9
Tel: 250-287-3103; *Fax:* 250-286-0109
general.inquiries@crmuseum.ca
www.crmuseum.ca
Linda Hogarth, Curator & Education Manager
linda.hogarth@crmuseum.ca

Chilliwack: Chilliwack Archives
9291 Corbould St., Chilliwack BC V2P 4A6
Tel: 604-795-9255; *Fax:* 604-795-5291
www.chilliwackmuseum.ca
Social Media: twitter.com/#!/Chwkmusandarch
Ron Denman, Director
604-795-5210
Kelly Harms, Archivist

Cranbrook: Canadian Museum of Rail Travel - Cranbrook Archives, Museum Landmark Foundation
57 Van Horne St. South, Cranbrook BC V1C 4H9
Tel: 604-489-3918; *Fax:* 250-486-5744
mail@trainsdeluxe.com
www.trainsdeluxe.com
Garry Anderson, Executive Director/Archivist
mail@trainsdeluxe.com
250-489-3918

Cumberland: Cumberland Museum & Archives
2680 Dunsmuir Ave., PO Box 258, Cumberland BC V0R 1S0
Tel: 250-336-2445; *Fax:* 250-336-2321
barb@cumberlandmuseum.ca
www.cumberlandmuseum.ca
Barbara Lemky, Contact

Delta: Delta Museum & Archives
4858 Delta St., Delta BC V4K 2T8
Tel: 604-946-9322; *Fax:* 604-946-5791
Kathy Bossort, Archivist

Delta: Parent Finders of Canada
19 English Bluff Rd., Delta BC V4M 2M4
Tel: 604-948-1069; *Fax:* 604-948-2036
jvanstone@dccnet.com
www.parentfinders.org
Joan E. Vanstone, National Director
jvanstone@dccnet.com
604-948-1069

Duncan: Cowichan Valley Museum & Archives
Duncan Train Station, Canada Ave., PO Box 1014, Duncan BC V9L 3Y2
Tel: 250-746-6612; *Fax:* 250-746-6612
cvmuseum.archives@shaw.ca
cowichanvalleymuseum.bc.ca
Kathryn Gagnon, Contact

Fort Langley: Langley Centennial Museum & National Exhibition Centre
9135 King St., Fort Langley BC V1M 2S2
Tel: 604-532-3536; *Fax:* 604-888-7291
information@langleymuseum.org
www.langleymuseum.org
Peter Tulumello, Manager, Cultural Services
Kobi Christian, Curator, Arts & Heritage
Jeff Chenatte, Educator, Arts & Heritage

Fort St John: North Peace Historical Society
9323 - 100th St., Fort St John BC V1J 4N4
Tel: 250-787-0430; *Fax:* 250-787-0405
fsjnpmuseum@solarwinds.com
collections.ic.gc.ca/north_peace/
Garth A. Sager, Museum Manager

Fort Steele: Fort Steele Heritage Town
9851 Hwy. 93/95, Fort Steele BC V0B 1N0
Tel: 250-417-6000; *Fax:* 250-489-2624
Info@FortSteele.bc.ca
www.fortsteele.bc.ca
Kristin Schachtel, Head

Harrison Mills: Kilby Store & Farm
215 Kilby Rd., Harrison Mills BC V0M 1L0
Tel: 604-796-9576; *Fax:* 604-796-9592
info@kilby.ca
www.kilby.ca
Bob Parliament, Area Manager
604-796-3859

Hazelton: 'Ksan Historical Village & Museum
PO Box 326, Hazelton BC V0J 1Y0
Tel: 250-842-5544; *Fax:* 250-842-6533
Toll-Free: 877-842-5518
ksan@ksan.org
www.ksan.org
Laurel Smith Wilson, Executive Director
kwan@ksan.org
250-842-5544

Kamloops: Kamloops Museum & Archives
207 Seymour St., Kamloops BC V2C 2E7
Tel: 250-828-3576; *Fax:* 250-828-3760
museum@kamloops.ca
www.kamloops.ca/museum/index.shtml
Elisabeth Duckworth

Kamloops: Secwepemc Cultural Education Society
#311, 355 Yellowhead Hwy., Kamloops BC V2H 1H1
Tel: 250-828-9749; *Fax:* 250-372-8833
www.secwepemc.org/museum/archives
Daniel Saul, Museum Manager
dsaul@kib.ca

Kaslo: Kootenay Lake Archives
312 - 4th St., Kaslo BC V0G 1M0
Tel: 250-353-9633
archives@klhs.bc.ca
www.klhs.bc.ca/archives.htm
Elizabeth Scarlett, Archivist

Kelowna: Kelowna Public Archives
470 Queensway Ave., Kelowna BC V1Y 6S7
Tel: 250-763-2417; *Fax:* 250-763-5722
archives@kelownamuseums.ca
www.kelownamuseums.ca/kelowna-public-archives.html
Donna Johnson, Archivist
Tara Hurley, Archivist

Kitimat: Kitimat Centennial Museum
293 City Centre, Kitimat BC V8C 1T6
Tel: 250-632-8950; *Fax:* 250-632-7429
kitimatmuseum@telus.net
www.kitimatmuseum.ca
Louise Avery, Curator

Lake Cowichan: Kaatza Historical Society
125 South Shore Rd., Lake Cowichan BC V0R 2G0
Tel: 250-749-6142; *Fax:* 250-749-3900
www.kaatzamuseum.ca
Barbara Simkins, Curator/Manager
Barbara Simkins, Curator

Maple Ridge: Corporation of the District of Maple Ridge
11995 Haney Pl., Maple Ridge BC V2X 6A9
Tel: 604-463-5221; *Fax:* 604-467-7329
Irene Gauld, Contact

Merritt: Nicola Valley Museum & Archives
2201 Coldwater Ave., Merritt BC V1K 1B8
Tel: 250-378-4145; *Fax:* 250-378-4145
nvma@uniserve.com
www.nicolavalleymuseum.org
Barb Watson, Office Administrator
nvma@uniserve.com
250-378-4145
Jo Atkinson, Assistant Administrator
nvma@uniserve.com

Mission: Mission Community Archives
33215 - 2nd Ave., Mission BC V2V 4L1
Tel: 604-820-2621
mca@missionarchives.com
www.missionarchives.com
Valerie Billesberger, Archivist/Records Manager
604-820-2621

Nakusp: Arrow Lakes Historical Society
92B - 7th Ave. NW, Nakusp BC V0G 1R0
Tel: 250-265-0110; *Fax:* 250-265-0110
alhs@netidea.com
Rosemarie Parent, President
miltrose@telus.net
250-265-3323
Joyce McQuair, Director
250-265-4370

Nanaimo: Nanaimo District Museum
100 Museum Way, Nanaimo BC V9R 5S8
Tel: 250-753-1821; *Fax:* 250-740-0125
info@nanaimomuseum.ca
www.nanaimomuseum.ca
David Hill-Turner, Curator

Nelson: Nelson & District Museum, Art Gallery, Archives & Historical Society
502 Vernon St., Nelson BC V1L 4E7
Tel: 250-352-9813; *Fax:* 250-352-9810
www.touchstonesnelson.ca/archives/index.php
Shawn F. Lamb, Collections Manager and Archivist
collections@touchstonesnelson.ca

Nelson: Roman Catholic Diocese of Nelson
402 West Richards St., Nelson BC V1L 3K3
Tel: 250-352-6921; *Fax:* 250-352-1737
nelson.diocese@telus.net
www.diocese.nelson.bc.ca
R.J. (Ron) Welwood, Contact
r-fwelwood@shaw.ca

New Westminster: New Westminster Museum/Archives
302 Royal Ave., New Westminster BC V3L 1H7
Tel: 604-527-4640; *Fax:* 604-527-4641
bdykes@newwestcity.ca
www.nwpr.bc.ca
Barry Dykes, Archivist
bdykes@newwestcity.ca
604-527-4642
Colin Stevens, Manager
cstevens@newwestcity.ca
604-527-4639
Cynthia Bronaugh, Staff
cbronaugh@newwestcity.ca

***North Vancouver:* North Vancouver Museum & Archives**
3203 Institute Rd., North Vancouver BC V7K 3E5
Tel: 604-990-3700; *Fax:* 604-987-5688
nvmac@dnv.org
www.dnv.org/nvma
Janet Turner, Archivist
turnerj@dnv.org
Daien Ide, Reference Historian
ided@dnv.org

***Penticton:* Penticton (R.N. Atkinson) Museum & Archives**
785 Main St., Penticton BC V2A 5E3
Tel: 250-490-2451; *Fax:* 250-492-0440
museum@city.penticton.bc.ca
penticton.ca/museum/default.asp
Peter Ord, Director & Curator
museum@city.penticton.bc.ca
250-490-2451

***Port Alberni:* Alberni District Historical Society**
4255 Wallace St., Port Alberni BC V9Y 3Y6
Tel: 250-723-2181; *Fax:* 250-723-1035
aadhs1@gmail.com
Judy Carlson, Volunteer Archivist
aadhs1@gmail.com

***Port Clements:* Port Clements Historical Society**
PO Box 417, Port Clements BC V0T 1R0
Tel: 250-557-4576

***Prince George:* Exploration Place**
333 Becott Pl., Prince George BC V2L 4V7
Tel: 250-562-1612; *Fax:* 250-562-6395
Toll-Free: 866-562-1612
archive@theexplorationplace.com
www.theexplorationplace.com
Bob Campbell, Manager, Curatorial Services
bob@theexplorationplace.com
250-562-1612 ext. 230
Kristina Stark, Assistant Curator
kristina@theexplorationplace.com
250-562-1612

***Prince Rupert:* Prince Rupert City & Regional Archives**
100 - 1st Ave, East, Prince Rupert BC V8J 1A6
Tel: 250-624-3326; *Fax:* 250-624-3706
archives@citytel.net
www.princerupertlibrary.ca/archives/
Jean Eiers-Page, Archivist

***Quesnel:* Quesnel & District Museum & Archives**
705 Carson Ave., Quesnel BC V2J 2B6
Tel: 250-992-9580; *Fax:* 250-992-9680
ehunter@city.quesnel.bc.ca
www.quesnelmuseum.ca
Elizabeth Hunter, Curator
ehunter@city.quesnel.bc.ca

***Revelstoke:* Revelstoke Museum & Archives**
PO Box 1908, Revelstoke BC V0E 2S0
Tel: 250-837-3067; *Fax:* 250-837-3094
revelstokemuseum@telus.net
www.revelstokemuseum.ca
Cathy English, Curator
250-837-3067

***Richmond:* City of Richmond Archives**
7700 Minoru Gate, Richmond BC V6Y 1R9
Tel: 604-247-8305; *Fax:* 604-231-6464
archives@richmond.ca
www.richmond.ca/cityhall/archives/about/about.htm
Lynne Waller, Archivist
lwaller@richmond.ca
604-231-6430

***Sooke:* Sooke Region Museum & Visitor Centre**
2070 Phillips Rd., Sooke BC V9Z 0Y3
Tel: 250-642-6351; *Fax:* 250-642-7089
Toll-Free: 866-888-4748
info@sookeregionmuseum.com
www.sookeregionmuseum.com
Joyce Linell, Contact

***Summerland:* Summerland Museum & Heritage Society**
PO Box 1491, Summerland BC V0H 1Z0
Tel: 250-494-9395; *Fax:* 250-494-9326
info@summerlandmuseum.org
www.summerlandmuseum.org
Sherril Foster, Curator

***Surrey:* City of Surrey Archives**
6022 - 176th St., Surrey BC V3S 4E8
Tel: 604-502-6459; *Fax:* 604-502-6457
rgallagher@surrey.ca
Bev Sommer, Manager of Heritage Services
bsommer@surrey.ca
604-502-6460
R Gallagher, Reference Specialist
rgallagher@surrey.ca
604-502-6459

***Trail:* Trail City Archives**
1394 Pine Ave., Trail BC V1R 4E6
Tel: 250-364-0829; *Fax:* 250-364-0830
history@trail.ca
www.trailhistory.com
Jamie Forbes, Corporate Administrator
jforbes@trail.ca
250-364-0800
Sarah Benson, Director
sbenson@trail.ca
250-364-0829

***Vancouver:* British Columbia Sports Hall of Fame & Museum**
Gate A, BC Place Stadium, Beatty & Robson Sts., Vancouver BC V6B 4Y8
Tel: 604-687-5520; *Fax:* 604-687-5510
www.bcsportshalloffame.com
Jason Beck, Curator
jason.beck@bssportshalloffame.com
604-687-5520

***Vancouver:* City of Vancouver Archives**
1150 Chestnut St., Vancouver BC V6J 3J9
Tel: 604-736-8561; *Fax:* 604-736-0626
archives@vancouver.ca
www.vancouver.ca/archives
Leslie Mobbs, City Archivist & Director, Records & Archives Division
leslie.mobbs@vancouver.ca

***Vancouver:* Institute of Indigenous Government / Union of BC Indian Chiefs**
342 Water St., 5th Fl., Vancouver BC V6B 1B6
Tel: 604-684-0231; *Fax:* 604-684-5726
library@ubcic.bc.ca
www.ubcic.bc.ca/department/library.htm
Kim Lawson, Archivist/Librarian
library@ubcic.bc.ca
604-684-0241
Jennifer Cole, Head, Technical Services/Acquisitions
library@ubcic.bc.ca
604-684-0241

***Vancouver:* Jewish Historical Society of BC**
#206, 950 West 41st Ave., Vancouver BC V5Z 2N7
Tel: 604-257-5199
www.jewishmuseum.ca
Diane Rodgers, Archivist

***Vancouver:* Roman Catholic Archdiocese of Vancouver**
150 Robson St., Vancouver BC V6B 2A7
Tel: 604-683-0281; *Fax:* 604-683-4288
www.rcav.org/archives
Anthea Seles, Records Manager/Archivist
aseles@rcav.bc.ca
604-683-0281 ext. 302

***Vancouver:* Satellite Video Exchange Society**
1965 Main St., Vancouver BC V5T 3C1
Tel: 604-872-8449; *Fax:* 604-876-1185
videoout@telus.net
www.videoinstudios.com
Lauren Howes, Distribution Coordinator

***Vancouver:* Vancouver Ballet Society**
677 Davie St., 6th Fl., Vancouver BC V6B 2G6
Tel: 604-681-1425
www.vancouverballetsociety.ca/Archives.html
Leslie Nadon, Administrator
vbs@telus.net
Maureen Allen, Library & Archives Chair

***Vancouver:* Vancouver Holocaust Education Centre**
#50, 950 West 41st Ave., Vancouver BC V5Z 2N7
Tel: 604-264-0499; *Fax:* 604-264-0497
library@vhec.org
www.vhec.org
Roberta Kremer, Executive Director
rkremer@vhec.org
John Welfly, Librarian
library@vhec.org
Cedar Morton, Administrator
admin@vhec.org

***Vernon:* Greater Vernon Museum & Archives**
3009 - 32nd Ave., Vernon BC V1T 2L8
Tel: 250-542-3142; *Fax:* 250-542-5358
archives@vernonmuseum.ca
www.vernonmuseum.ca
Barbara Bell, Archivist

***Victoria:* City of Victoria Archives**
8 Centenial Sq., Victoria BC V8W 1P7
Tel: 250-361-0375; *Fax:* 250-361-0394
archives@victoria.ca
www.victoria.ca/archives/archives.shtml
Trevor Livelton, Archivist
Carey Palliser, Archives Assistant
archives@victoria.ca

***Victoria:* Esquimalt Municipal Archives**
1149-A Esquimalt Rd., Victoria BC V9A 3N6
Tel: 250-412-8540; *Fax:* 250-412-8541
parkerd@esquimalt.ca
Dave Parker, Archivist
parkerd@esquimalt.ca

***Victoria:* Roman Catholic Diocese of Victoria**
#1, 4044 Nelthorpe St., Victoria BC V8X 2A1
Tel: 250-479-1331; *Fax:* 250-479-5423
chancery@rcdvictoria.org
www.rcdvictoria.org
Michael Lapierre, Vicar-General
Wim Kalkman, Assistant

***Victoria:* Saanich Municipal Archives**
3100 Tillicum Rd., Victoria BC V9A 6T2
Tel: 250-475-1775; *Fax:* 250-388-7819
caroline.duncan@saanich.ca
www.saanicharchives.ca
Caroline Duncan, Municipal Archivist
caroline.duncan@saanich.ca
250-475-1775
Evelyn Wolfe, Archival Research Assistant
evelyn.wolfe@saanich.ca
250-475-1775 ext. 3479

***Victoria:* Sisters of St Ann**
1550 Begbie St., Victoria BC V8R 1K8
Tel: 250-592-0685; *Fax:* 250-592-0234
archives@ssabc.ca
Michaeleen King, Archivist

***West Vancouver:* West Vancouver Archives**
680 - 17th St., West Vancouver BC V7V 3T2
Tel: 604-925-7298
archives@westvancouver.ca
www.wvma.net
Shaunna Moore, District Archivist
smoore@westvancouver.ca
604-925-7298

***White Rock:* White Rock Museum & Archives**
14970 Marine Dr., White Rock BC V4B 1C4
Tel: 604-541-2222; *Fax:* 604-541-2223
whiterockmuseum@telus.net
Hugh Ellenwood, Community Historian

Manitoba

Regional Systems

Border Regional Library
312 - 7th Ave., Virden MB R0M 2C0
Tel: 204-748-3862; *Fax:* 204-748-3862
brlibrary.cimnet.ca
Linda Grant-Braybrook, Librarian

Evergreen Regional Library
65 First Ave., Gimli MB R0C 1B0
Tel: 204-642-7912; *Fax:* 204-642-8319
exec@mts.net
www.townofarborg.com/library.default.asp
Valerie Eyolfson, Head Librarian
exec@mts.net
204-642-7912
Karen Gottfried, Assistant Librarian
exec@mts.net
204-642-7912
Sandyie Reykdal, Clerk Librarian
exec@mts.net
204-642-7912

Lac du Bonnet Regional Library
PO Box 216, Lac du Bonnet MB R0E 1A0
Tel: 204-345-2653; *Fax:* 204-345-6827
mldb@mts.net

Vickie Short, Head Librarian
Janice Hoffman, Assistant Librarian
Lisa Rand, Assistant Librarian
Pat Loeppry, Library Clerk

Lakeland Regional Library
318 Williams Ave., Killarney MB R0K 1G0
Tel: 204-523-4949
lrl@mts.net
www.lakelandregionallibrary.ca

Gloria Kinsley, Librarian

Parkland Regional Library
504 Main St. North, Dauphin MB R7N 1C9
Tel: 204-638-6410; *Fax:* 204-638-9483
prlhq@parklandlib.mb.ca
www.parklandlib.mb.ca

Glenn Butchart, Director
gbutchart@parklandlib.mb.ca

South Central Regional Library
160 Main St., Winkler MB R6W 4B4
Tel: 204-325-7174; *Fax:* 204-331-1847
headlib@scrlibrary.mb.ca
www.scrlibrary.mb.ca

Mary Toma, Head Librarian
headlib@srclibrary.mb.ca
204-325-5864
Esther Penner, Head of Technical Services
techserv@scrlibrary.mb.ca

Southwestern Manitoba Regional Library
149 Main St., Melita MB R0M 1L0
Tel: 204-522-3923
swmblib@mail.techplus.com
www.mts.net/~swmblib/

Valorie Wray, Librarian
Jamie Dickinson, Assistant Librarian
Norma Rae Tilbury, Secretary-Treasurer
Vicki Miner, Branch Librarian
204-634-2215
Trish Ratcliffe, Branch Librarian

Western Manitoba Regional Library/ Brandon Public Library
#1, 710 Rosser Ave., Brandon MB R7A 0K9
Tel: 204-727-6648; *Fax:* 204-727-4447
brandon@wmrl.ca
www.wmrl.ca

Kathy Thornborough, Chief Librarian
Shelley Mortensen, Assistant Librarian

Public Libraries

Baldur: **Regional Municipality of Argyle Public Library**
627 Elizabeth St. East, Baldur MB R0K 0B0
Tel: 204-535-2314; *Fax:* 204-535-2242
rmargyle@gmail.com

Cheri McLaren

Beausejour: **Brokenhead River Regional Library**
427 Park Ave., Beausejour MB R0E 0C0
Tel: 204-268-7570; *Fax:* 204-268-7570
brrlibr@MTS.net
www.efree.mb.ca/brrl/home.html

Debbie Winnicki, Head Librarian

Boissevain: **Boissevain & Morton Regional Library**
436 South Railway St., Boissevain MB R0K 0E0
Tel: 204-534-6478; *Fax:* 204-534-3710
mbom@mts.net
www.bmlibrary.ca

Brandon: **Public Library Services newsletter / Le Bulletin d'information des services de bibliothèques publiques**
#200, 1525 First St. South, Brandon MB R7A 7A1
Tel: 204-726-6590
pls@gov.mb.ca
maplin.gov.mb.ca/cgi-bin/about.cgi

La Broquerie: **Bibliothèque Saint-Joachim Library**
29, Normandeau Bay, La Broquerie MB R0A 0W0
Tel: 204-424-9533; *Fax:* 204-424-5610
bstjl@bsjl.ca
www.bsjl.ca

Yolande Tétrault, Présidente, Conseil d'administration
Rolande Durand, Bibliothécaire
204-424-9533

Carman: **Boyne Regional Library**
15 - 1st Ave. SW, Carman MB R0G 0J0
Tel: 204-745-3504
boynereg@mts.net

Sandra Yeo, Head Librarian
204-745-3504

Cartwright: **Cartwright Branch Library**
483 North Railway St., Cartwright MB R0K 0L0
Tel: 204-529-2261
cartlib@mts.net
www.lakelandregionallibrary.ca

Andrea Trembath, Branch Librarian

Churchill: **Churchill Public Library**
Town Centre Complex, PO Box 730, Churchill MB R0B 0E0
Tel: 204-675-2731; *Fax:* 204-675-2934

Bonnie Allen, Librarian

Deloraine: **Bren Del Win Centennial Library**
311 North Railway Ave. West, PO Box 584, Deloraine MB R0M 0M0
Tel: 204-747-2415; *Fax:* 204-747-3446
bdwlib@mts.net

Helen Schoenbaert, Chair
Lorraine Stovin, Librarian

Eriksdale: **Eriksdale Public Library**
PO Box 219, Eriksdale MB R0C 0W0
Tel: 204-739-2668; *Fax:* 204-739-2668
epl1@mts.net

Rita L. Cushnie, Librarian
epl1@mts.net

Flin Flon: **Flin Flon Public Library**
58 Main St., Flin Flon MB R8A 1J8
Tel: 204-687-3397; *Fax:* 204-687-4233
ffpl@mts.net
www.flinflonpubliclibrary.ca

Phyllis Stadnick, Library Administrator
ffpladmin@mts.net
204-687-3397

Gillam: **Bette Winner Public Library**
PO Box 400, Gillam MB R0B 0L0
Tel: 204-652-2617; *Fax:* 204-652-2617
bwinner@gillamnet.com
Social Media:
www.facebook.com/group.php?gid=160167924017586

Ricci Bangle, Head Librarian

Headingley: **Headingley Public Library**
49 Alboro St., Headingley MB R4J 1A3
Tel: 204-888-5410; *Fax:* 204-831-7207
hml@mts.net
www.headingleylibrary.ca

Joan Spice, Head Librarian

Holland: **Victoria Municipal Library**
PO Box 371, Holland MB R0G 0X0
Tel: 204-526-2011
victlib@goinet.ca

Ivan Bruneay, Chair

Ile-des-Chênes: **Bibliothèque Ritchot - Ile-des-Chênes**
École Gabrielle-Roy, CP 581, Ile-des-Chênes MB R0A 0T0
Tél: 204-878-2147; *Téléc:* 204-878-3495
ritchot@atrium.ca
www.richot.com/libraries.htm

Louise Durand, Bibliothécaire

Lundar: **Pauline Johnson Library**
23 Main St., Lundar MB R0C 1Y0
Tel: 204-762-5367
mlpj@mts.net

Kristin Jobling, Assistant Librarian

Lynn Lake: **Lynn Lake Centennial Library**
PO Box 1127, Lynn Lake MB R0B 0W0
Tel: 204-356-8222

Margaret Thomson, Librarian

MacGregor: **North Norfolk MacGregor Regional Library**
35 Hampton St. East, MacGregor MB R0H 0R0
Tel: 204-685-2796; *Fax:* 204-685-2478
maclib@mts.net

Antoinette Blankvoort, Head Librarian
Bernice Albers, Assistant Librarian
204-685-2294

Minnedosa: **Minnedosa Regional Library**
45 - 1st Ave. SE, Minnedosa MB R0J 1E0
Tel: 204-867-2585; *Fax:* 204-867-6140
mmr@mts.net

Linda Cook, Librarian
Lisa Bilcowski, Assistant Librarian

Morris: **Valley Regional Library**
141 Main St. South, Morris MB R0G 1K0
Tel: 204-746-2136
valleylib@mts.net
www.town.morris.mb.ca/library.html

Dinne DeKezel, Librarian
204-746-2136
Diane Ali, Assistant Librarian
Jane Stevenson, Head Volunteer
Meredith Loewen, Volunteer
Rikki Bergstresser, Student Librarian

Norway House: **Ayamiscikawikamik Public Library**
General Delivery, Norway House MB R0B 1B0
Tel: 204-359-6047; *Fax:* 204-359-6262
sam@yahoo.ca

Violet Ouellette, Librarian

Notre-Dame-de-Lourdes: **Bibliothèque Père Champagne/ Père Champagne Library**
44, rue Rodgers, CP 399, Notre-Dame-de-Lourdes MB R0G 1M0
Tel: 204-248-2386
ndbiblio@yahoo.ca

Gisèle Théroux, Responsable

The Pas: **The Pas Regional Library**
53 Edwards Ave., The Pas MB R9A 1R2
Tel: 204-623-2023; *Fax:* 204-623-4594
library@mts.net
www.thepasregionallibrary.com

Carol Ham, Library Administrator

Pilot Mound: **Pilot Mound Library**
219 Broadway Ave. West, Pilot Mound MB R0G 1P0
Tel: 204-825-2035; *Fax:* 204-825-2784
pmlibrary@mts.net
www.pilotmoundlibrary.ca

Allison MacAulay, Librarian

Pinawa: **Pinawa Public Library**
Community Centre, Vanier Ave., Pinawa MB R0E 1L0
Tel: 204-753-2496; *Fax:* 204-753-2770
email@pinawapubliclibrary.com
www.pinawapubliclibrary.com

Marg Stokes, Head Librarian
plibrary@sdwhiteshell.mb.ca
204-753-2496
Audrey Miller, Library Assistant
plibrary@sdwhiteshell.mb.ca
204-753-2496
Donna Schofield, Library Assistant
plibrary@sdwhiteshell.mb.ca
204-753-2496

Portage la Prairie: **Portage la Prairie Regional Library**
40B Royal Rd. North, Portage la Prairie MB R1N 1V1
Tel: 204-857-4271; *Fax:* 204-239-4387
portlib@portagelibrary.com

Percy Gregoire-Voskamp, Head Librarian
pvoskamp@portagelibrary.com

Rapid City: **Rapid City Regional Library**
PO Box 8, Rapid City MB R0K 1W0
Tel: 204-826-2732
rcreglib@mts.net

Shirley Martin, Head Librarian

Reston: **Reston District Library**
220 - 4th St., Reston MB R0M 1X0
Tel: 204-877-3673
restonlb@yahoo.ca

Rivers: **Prairie Crocus Regional Library**
137 Main St., Rivers MB R0K 1X0
Tel: 204-328-7613
pcrl@mts.net
www.prairiecrocuslibrary.ca

Dora M. Irvine, Librarian

Rossburn: **Rossburn Regional Library**
53 Main St. North, Rossburn MB R0J 1V0
Tel: 204-859-2687; *Fax:* 204-859-2687
rrl@mts.net

Stephanie Parkinson, Librarian/Book-Keeper
rrl@mts.net

Ivy Blake, Library Assistant
rrl@mts.net

***Russell:* Russell & District Regional Library**
339 Main St., Russell MB R0J 1W0
Tel: 204-773-3127
ruslib@mts.net
Louise Sidoryk, Library Technician

***Saint-Claude:* Bibliothèque Saint-Claude/ St. Claude Library**
50 - 1st St., Saint-Claude MB R0G 1Z0
Tel: 204-379-2524
stclib@mts.net
Lynn Gobin, Librarian

***St. Georges:* Bibliothèque Allard Library**
104086 PTH 11, St. Georges MB R0E 1V0
Tel: 204-367-8443; *Fax:* 204-367-1780
info@allardlibrary.com
www.allardlibrary.com
Social Media:
www.facebook.com/group.php?gid=144949018850811
Diane Dubé, Citizen Rep RM of Alexander - Chairperson

***St Jean Baptiste:* Bibliothèque Montcalm Library**
113B - 2nd Ave., St Jean Baptiste MB R0G 2B0
Tel: 204-758-3137; *Fax:* 204-758-3574
biblio@atrium.ca
www.rmofmontcalm.com/bibliothequemontcalmlibrary
Diane Bérard, Bibliothécaire
dmtberard@hotmail.com

***St Pierre Jolys:* Jolys Regional Library/ Bibliothèque régionale Jolys**
505 Hébert Ave., St Pierre Jolys MB R0A 1V0
Tel: 204-433-7729
stplibrary@jrlibrary.mb.ca
www.jrlibrary.mb.ca
Janet Banfield, CEO

***Selkirk:* Red River North Regional Library**
303 Main St., Selkirk MB R1A 1S7
Tel: 204-482-3522; *Fax:* 204-482-6166
library@ssarl.org
www.ssarl.org
Ken Kuryliw, Director, Library Services
kkuryliw@ssarl.org
Lorraine Smith, Technical Services Coordinator
lsmith@ssarl.org
Katherine Anderson, Public Services & Information Technology Coordinator
kanderson@ssarl.org

***Shilo:* Shilo Community Library**
Bldg. T 100, Notre Dame & French, Box 177, Shilo MB R0K 2A0
Tel: 204-765-2590
shilocommunitylibrary@yahoo.ca
Social Media: www.facebook.com/group.php?gid=7280251236

***Snow Lake:* Snow Lake Community Library**
Joseph H. Kerr School, 201 Cherry Ave., Snow Lake MB R0B 1M0
Tel: 204-358-2322; *Fax:* 204-358-2116
www.snowlake.com
Vivian Bennett, Librarian
204-358-2833

***Somerset:* Somerset Library/ Bibliothèque Somerset**
289 Carlton Ave., Somerset MB R0G 2L0
Tel: 204-744-2170
somlib@mts.net
Lucille Labossiere, Librarian
204-744-2860

***Souris:* Glenwood & Souris Regional Library**
#18, 114 - 2nd St. South, Souris MB R0K 2C0
Tel: 204-483-2757
gsrl@mts.net
Margaret Greaves, Library Supervisor
Cindy Minary, Assistant Librarian

***Ste Rose du Lac:* Ste Rose Regional Library**
General Delivery, Ste Rose du Lac MB R0L 1S0
Tel: 204-447-2527
sroselib@mts.net
www.steroseregionallibrary.info
Elaine Chaput, Head Librarian
Sonia Houde, Assistant Librarian
Tara Dubord, Technical Services

***Ste-Anne-des-Chênes:* Bibliothèque Ste-Anne Library**
16, rue de l'Eglise, Ste-Anne-des-Chênes MB R5H 1H8
Tél: 204-422-9958; *Téléc:* 204-422-9958
steannelib@steannemb.ca
bibliosteannelib.8m.com/cac_en.html
Monica Ball, Bibliothécaire
Clément Charrière, Président
Norbert Ritchot, Secrétaire
steannelib@steannemb.ca
Mimi Pattyn, Trésorière
steannelib@steannemb.ca

***Steinbach:* Jake Epp Library**
255 Elmdale St., Steinbach MB R6G 1N6
Tel: 204-326-6841; *Fax:* 204-326-6859
jakeepplibrary@yahoo.com
www.jakeepplibrary.com
Loraine Trudeau, Head Librarian
jakeepplibrary@yahoo.com
204-326-6841

***Stonewall:* South Interlake Regional Library**
419 Main St., Stonewall MB R0C 2Z0
Tel: 204-467-8415; *Fax:* 204-467-9809
sirl@mts.net
www.sirlibrary.com
Darlene Dallman, Chief Administation Officer
sirl@mts.net
204-467-5767

***Swan River:* North-West Regional Library**
610 - 1st St. North, Swan River MB R0L 1Z0
Tel: 204-734-3880; *Fax:* 204-734-3880
nwrl@mts.net
www.swanriverlibrary.ca
June McKenzie, Head Librarian

***Thompson:* Thompson Public Library**
81 Thompson Dr. North, Thompson MB R8N 0C3
Tel: 204-677-3717; *Fax:* 204-778-5844
info@thompsonlibrary.com
www.thompsonlibrary.com
Cheryl Davies, Administrator
admin@thompsonlibrary.com

***Winnipeg:* AMA Newsletter**
PO Box 26005, Stn. Maryland, Winnipeg MB R3G 3R3
Tel: 204-942-3491; *Fax:* 204-942-3492
ama1@mts.net
www.mbarchives.mb.ca
Carole Pelchat, Chair

***Winnipeg:* MFL Occupational Health Centre**
#102, 275 Broadway, Winnipeg MB R3C 4M6
Tel: 204-949-0811; *Fax:* 204-956-0848
Toll-Free: 888-843-1229
mflohc@mflohc.mb.ca
www.mflohc.mb.ca/mflohc_folder/information_&_resources.html
Tiffany Pau, Library Coordinator
204-949-7909

***Winnipeg:* MLA Newsline**
#606, 100 Arthur St., Winnipeg MB R3B 1H3
Tel: 204-943-4567; *Fax:* 204-942-1555
mla@uwinnipeg.ca
www.mla.mb.ca
Liane Patterson, Director, Communications & Publications

***Winnipeg:* Winnipeg Public Library**
251 Donald St., Winnipeg MB R3C 3P5
Tel: 204-986-6472; *Fax:* 204-942-5671
TDD: 2049863485
wpl.city.winnipeg.mb.ca/library/
Rick Walker, Manager of Library Services
rwalker@winnipeg.ca
Vera Andrysiak, Central Services Coordinator
vandrysiak@winnipeg.ca
204-986-6458
Betty Parry, Support Services Coordinator
bparry@winnipeg.ca
204-986-5002
Kathleen Williams, Outreach Services Coordinator
kwilliam@winnipeg.ca
204-986-4255
Bruno Legal, Marketing Coordinator
blegal@winnipeg.ca
204-986-4334
Carol Mahe, Branch Services Coordinator
cmahe@winnipeg.ca
204-986-6473

Archives

***Boissevain:* Boissevain Community Archives**
436 South Railway St., Boissevain MB R0K 0E0
Tel: 204-534-6478; *Fax:* 204-534-3710
mbom@mts.net
www.boissevain.ca/archives_library/archives_resources.html
Michelle Scott, Archivist

***Brandon:* City of Brandon**
410 - 9th St., Brandon MB R7A 6A2
Tel: 204-729-2289; *Fax:* 204-729-8244
www.city.brandon.mb.ca
Donna Phillips, Classification Clerk

***Brandon:* Magnacca Research Centre**
122 - 18th St., Brandon MB R7A 5A4
Tel: 204-727-1722; *Fax:* 204-727-1722
dalymuseum@wcgwave.ca
www.dalyhousemuseum.ca/archives.htm
Social Media: http://twitter.com/#!/DalyHouseMuseum;
www.facebook.com/dalyhouse
Eileen Trott, Archivist

***Brandon:* 26th Field Regiment RCA/12th Manitoba Dragoons Museum**
1116 Victoria Ave., Brandon MB R7A 1B2
Tel: 204-728-2559; *Fax:* 204-725-1766
museum@12mbdragoons.com
www.12mbdragoons.com
Ross Neale, Curator
museum@12mbdragoons.com
Gord Sim, Secretary
museum@12mbdragoons.com

***Carberry:* Carberry Plains Archives**
115 Main St., Carberry MB R0K 0H0
Tel: 204-834-6614; *Fax:* 204-834-6604
cparchives@mts.net
www.mts.net/~archives/
Penny Shaw, Archivist
cparchives@mts.net

***Churchill:* Diocese of Churchill Hudson Bay**
Eskimo Museum, 242 La Verendrye Ave., Churchill MB R0B 0E0
Tel: 204-675-2030; *Fax:* 204-675-2140
Lorraine Brandson, Curator

***Flin Flon:* Flin Flon Community Archives**
58 Main St., Flin Flon MB R8A 1J8
Tel: 204-687-3397; *Fax:* 204-687-4233
ffpl@mts.net
Phyllis Stadnick, Administrator

***Killarney:* J.A.V. David Museum**
414 Williams Ave., Killarney MB R0K 1G0
Tel: 204-523-7325
Donna Wilkins, Archivist

***Leaf Rapids:* Leaf Rapids Community Archives**
PO Box 190, Leaf Rapids MB R0B 1W0
Tel: 204-473-2742; *Fax:* 204-473-2566
Lisa Everton, Archivist
lrpl@mts.net
204-473-2742

***MacGregor:* North Norfolk MacGregor Archives**
PO Box 435, MacGregor MB R0H 0R0
Tel: 204-685-2805
Lorraine Chant, Contact

***Shilo:* Royal Canadian Artillery Museum**
Canadian Forces Base Shilo, Shilo MB R0K 2A0
Tel: 204-765-3000; *Fax:* 204-765-5289
rcamuseum@techplus.ca
Rick Sanderson, Director

***Steinbach:* Mennonite Heritage Village**
231 PTH 12 North, Steinbach MB R5G 1T8
Tel: 204-326-9661; *Fax:* 204-326-5046
Toll-Free: 800-280-8741
info@mhv.ca
www.mhv.ca
Social Media:
www.facebook.com/pages/Mennonite-Heritage-Village/107997272562045
Roland Sawatzky, Senior Curator
rolands@mhv.ca
204-326-9661

***Thompson:* Heritage North Museum**
162 Princeton Dr., Thompson MB R8N 2A4
Tel: 204-677-2216; *Fax:* 204-677-8953
hnmuseum@mts.net
www.thompson.heritage.north.museum/600archives.htm
Paul Legault, Contact

***Winnipeg:* Archevêché de St-Boniface**
151 de la Cathédrale Ave., Winnipeg MB R2H 0H6
Tél: 204-237-9851; *Téléc:* 204-231-2652
Yolande Comeau, Secrétaire de la chancelerie

***Winnipeg:* Archives des Soeurs Grises, St Boniface/ Grey Nun Archives, St-Boniface**
151 Despins St., Winnipeg MB R2H 0L7
Tél: 204-237-8941; *Téléc:* 204-237-3466
Carole Boily, Archiviste
cboily@sgm.mb.ca

***Winnipeg:* Archives of Manitoba/ Archives du Manitoba**
#130, 200 Vaughan St., Winnipeg MB R3C 1T5
Tel: 204-945-3971; *Fax:* 204-948-2008
Toll-Free: 800-617-3588
archives@gov.mb.ca
www.gov.mb.ca/chc/archives/
Gordon Dodds, Archivist of Manitoba
204-945-6140

***Winnipeg:* Centre for Mennonite Brethren Studies**
1310 Taylor Ave., Winnipeg MB R3M 3Z6
Tel: 204-669-6575; *Fax:* 204-654-1865
Toll-Free: 888-669-6575
kreddig@mbconf.ca
www.mbconf.ca/mbstudies/index.en.html
Ken Reddig, Director
kreddig@mbconf.ca
Conrad Stoesz, Archivist
cstoesz@mbconf.ca

***Winnipeg:* City of Winnipeg**
380 William Ave., Winnipeg MB R3A 0J1
Tel: 204-986-5325; *Fax:* 204-986-7133
www.winnipeg.ca/clerks/docs/archives/archives.stm
Gerry Berkowski, City Records Manager & Archivist

***Winnipeg:* Costume Museum of Canada**
109 Pacific Ave., Winnipeg MB R3B 0M1
Tel: 204-989-0072; *Fax:* 204-989-0074
Social Media:
www.facebook.com/pages/Costume-Museum-of-Canada/948974 56640
Brenda Hamer, Collections Coordinator

***Winnipeg:* Fire Fighters Historical Society of Winnipeg**
56 Maple St., Winnipeg MB R3B 0Y8
Tel: 204-942-4817; *Fax:* 204-885-1306
firemuseum@gatewest.net
www.winnipegfiremuseum.ca
Barbara Kuryluk, Curator
kuryluk@gatewest.net
204-942-4817
Ted Kuryluk, President
204-888-8021
Terry Brisley, Vice-President
204-222-5045
William Mitchell, Director
204-256-1007

***Winnipeg:* Fort Garry Horse Museum & Archives**
551 Machray Ave., Winnipeg MB R2W 1A8
Tel: 204-586-6298; *Fax:* 204-582-0370
www.fortgarryhorse.ca
Larry Lajeunesse, Museum Chairman
204-582-0370
Gordon Crossley, Museum Director

***Winnipeg:* Grand Lodge of Manitoba Archives**
420 Corydon Ave., Winnipeg MB R3L 0N8
Tel: 204-832-6062; *Fax:* 204-284-3527
rkiv@mts.net
www.mbgrandlodge.com/masonic-resource-center/archives
Allan G. Brock, Grand Archivist
rkiv@mts.net

***Winnipeg:* Jewish Heritage Centre of Western Canada**
#C116, 123 Doncaster St., Winnipeg MB R3N 2B2
Tel: 204-477-7461; *Fax:* 204-477-7465
jhc@jhcwc.org
www.jhcwc.org/archives.htm
Vanesa Harari, Archivist
vharari@jhcwc.org

***Winnipeg:* Manitoba Gay/Lesbian Archive**
#1, 222 Osborne St. South, Winnipeg MB R3C 1Z3
Tel: 204-284-5208; *Fax:* 204-478-1160
Toll-Free: 888-399-0005
Other Numbers: Other phone: 204/474-0212
info@rainbowresourcecentre.org
www.rainbowresourcecentre.org
Lindsay Butt, Librarian
info@rainbowresourcecentre.org
204-284-5208

***Winnipeg:* Manitoba Museum**
190 Rupert Ave., Winnipeg MB R3B 0N2
Tel: 204-988-0662; *Fax:* 204-942-3679
csteffan@manitobamuseum.ca
www.manitobamuseum.ca
Patricia Henry, Library Technician

***Winnipeg:* Mennonite Heritage Centre**
600 Shaftesbury Blvd., Winnipeg MB R3P 0M4
Tel: 204-888-6781; *Fax:* 204-831-5675
Toll-Free: 866-888-6785
archives@mennonitechurch.ca
www.mennonitechurch.ca/programs/archives/
Alf Redekopp, Director
aredekopp@mennonitechurch.ca
Connie Wiebe, Archives Secretary
cwiebe@mennonitechurch.ca
Conrad Stoesz, Archivist
cstoesz@mennonitechurch.ca

***Winnipeg:* Sisters of Our Lady of the Missions/ Religieuses de Notre Dame des Missions**
St Edward's Convent, Provincial Office, 800 Adele Ave, Winnipeg MB R3E 0K6
Tel: 204-774-5067
www.rndm.org/

***Winnipeg:* Soeurs Missionnaires Oblates du Sacré-Coeur et de Marie Immaculée/ Missionary Oblate Sisters of the Sacred Heart & of Mary Immaculate**
Missionary Oblate Sisters of Saint Boniface, #111, 420 rue DesMeuronsulneau, Winnipeg MB R2H 2N9
Tél: 204-233-7287; *Téléc:* 204-235-7418
generaladministration@missionaryoblatesisters.
www.missionaryoblatesisters.ca
Thérèse Bilodeau, Archiviste

***Winnipeg:* Transcona Historical Museum**
141 Regent Ave. West, Winnipeg MB R2C 1R1
Tel: 204-222-0423
www.transconamuseum.mb.ca

***Winnipeg:* Ukrainian Catholic Church Archeparchy of Winnipeg**
233 Scotia St., Winnipeg MB R2V 1V7
Tel: 204-338-7801; *Fax:* 204-339-4006
nataliacurator@yahoo.ca
www.archeparchy.ca
Gloria Romaniuk, Archivist
Natalia Radawetz, Museum Curator

***Winnipeg:* Western Canada Aviation Museum**
Hangar T-2, 958 Ferry Rd., Winnipeg MB R3H 0Y8
Tel: 204-786-5503; *Fax:* 204-775-4761
info@wcam.mb.ca
www.wcam.mb.ca
Brian Watson, Coordinator
John C. Bonner, Head, Reference

New Brunswick

Regional Systems

AWK Library Regional Office/ Région de bibliothèques AWK
#201, 644 Main St., Moncton NB E1C 1E2
Tel: 506-869-6032; *Fax:* 506-869-6022
annette.selmes@gnb.ca
www.gnb.ca
Tina Bourgeois, Regional Director
tina.bourgeois@gnb.ca
Nadine Goguen, Acting Assistant Regional Director
nadine.goguen2@gnb.ca
Robin Illsley, Acting Public Services Librarian
robin.illsley@gnb.ca
Catherine Vienneau, Acting Technical Services Librarian
catherine.vienneau@gnb.ca

Chaleur Library Region/ Région de bibliothèques Chaleur
113A Roseberry St., Campbellton NB E3N 2G6
Tel: 506-789-6599; *Fax:* 506-789-7318
tina.bourgeois@gnb.ca
www1.gnb.ca
Sarah Kilfoil, Regional Director
sarah.kilfoil@gnb.ca
Vacant, Assistant Regional Director
Vacant, Public Services Librarian
Georgette Lavail, Techinical Services Librarian
georgette.lavail@gnb.ca
506-789-7327
Debbie Mann, Administrative Assistant
debbie.mann@gnb.ca
506-789-7325
Shirley Savoie, Regional Office Secretary
shirley.savoie@gnb.ca
506-789-6599

Fundy Library Regional Office/ Région de bibliothèques de Fundy
1 Market Sq., Saint John NB E2L 4Z6
Tel: 506-643-7222; *Fax:* 506-643-7225
lucy.harrigan@gnb.ca
www.gnb.ca
Ian A. Wilson, Regional Director
ian.wilson@gnb.ca
506-643-7242
Alexandra Brooks, Assistant Regional Director
Alexandra.brooks@gnb.ca
506-643-7233
Jean Cunningham, Public Services Librarian
jean.cunningham@gnb.ca
506-643-7230
Gayle DuJohn, Regional Office Secretary
gayle.dujohn@gnb.ca
506-643-7222
Lucy Harrigan, Administrative Assistant
lucy.harrigan@gnb.ca
506-643-7235
Carole May, Administrative Assistant
carole.may@gnb.ca
506-643-7235
Joel Goudreau, Technical Support Analyst
joel.goudreau@gng.ca
506-643-2924
Vacant, Technical Services Librarian
506-643-7226
Pamela Galbraith, Library Assistant, Technical Services
pam.galbraith@gnb.ca
506-643-7245
Melanie Hatfield, Library Assistant, Technical Services
melanie.hatfield@gnb.ca
506-643-7245
Mary Melanson, Library Clerk, Technical Services
mary.melanson@gnb.ca
506-643-7244
Karen Merritt, Library Clerk, Technical Services
karen.merritt@gnb.ca
506-643-7244

Haut-Saint-Jean Library Regional Office/ Région de bibliothèques Haut-Saint-Jean
540 Principale St., Saint-Basile NB E7C 1J5
Tel: 506-263-3423; *Fax:* 506-263-3425
www.gnb.ca
Johanne Jacob, Regional Director
johanne.jacob@gnb.ca
Patrick Provencher, Assistant Regional Director
patrick.provencher@gnb.ca
Pauline Grondin, Regional Office Secretary
pauline.grondin@gnb.ca

York Library Region/ Région de bibliothèques York
4 Carleton St., Fredericton NB E3B 5P4
Tel: 506-453-5380; *Fax:* 506-457-4878
www.gnb.ca
Jill Foster, Regional Director
jill.foster@gnb.ca
Bill Mitchell, Assistant Regional Director
bill.mitchell@gnb.ca
506-457-7271
Joyce Newman, Librarian, Technical Services
joyce.newman@gnb.ca
506-444-2606

Public Libraries

Atholville: **Bibliothèque publique d'Atholville/ Atholville Public Library**
275, rue Notre-Dame, Atholville NB E3N 4T1
Tél: 506-789-2914; *Téléc:* 506-789-2056
biblioda@gnb.ca
www1.gnb.ca

Bas-Caraquet: **Bibliothèque publique de Bas-Caraquet/ Bas-Caraquet Public Library**
8185-2, rue St-Paul, Bas-Caraquet NB E1W 6C4
Tél: 506-726-2775; *Téléc:* 506-726-2770
bibliobc@gnb.ca
www1.gnb.ca

Bathurst: **Bibliothèque publique Smurfit-Stone/ Smurfit-Stone Public Library**
#1, 150, rue St. George, Bathurst NB E2A 1B5
Tél: 506-548-0706; *Téléc:* 506-548-0708
bibliocn@gnb.ca
www1.gnb.ca

Beresford: **Bibliothèque publique Mgr-Robichaud/ Mgr. Robichaud Public Library**
#3, 855, rue Principale, Beresford NB E8K 1T3
Tél: 506-542-2704; *Téléc:* 506-542-2714
bibliomr@gnb.ca
www1.gnb.ca

Boiestown: **Boiestown Community - School Library**
Upper Miramichi Regional High School, #1, 3466 Rte. 625, Boiestown NB E6A 1C8
Tel: 506-369-2022; *Fax:* 506-369-2023
boiestown.library@gnb.ca
www.gnb.ca

Bouctouche: **Bibliothèque publique Gérald-Leblanc/ Gérald Leblanc Public Library**
#100, 84, boul Irving, Bouctouche NB E4S 3L4
Tél: 506-743-7263; *Téléc:* 506-743-7263
bibliopb@gnb.ca
www1.gnb.ca

Campbellton: **Bookmobile**
113A Roseberry St., Campbellton NB E3N 2G6
Tel: 506-789-6599; *Fax:* 506-789-7318
chaleurbm@gnb.ca
www1.gnb.ca

Campbellton: **Campbellton Centennial Library/ Bibliothèque du Centenaire de Campbellton**
2 Aberdeen St., Campbellton NB E3N 2J4
Tel: 506-753-5253; *Fax:* 506-753-3803
bibliocc@gov.nb.ca
www1.gnb.ca

Caraquet: **Bibliothèque publique Mgr-Paquet/ Mgr. Paquet Public Library**
10A, du rue Colisée, Caraquet NB E1W 1A5
Tél: 506-726-2681; *Téléc:* 506-726-2685
bibliock@gnb.ca
www1.gnb.ca

Chipman: **Chipman Public Library**
8 King St., Chipman NB E4A 2H3
Tel: 506-339-5852; *Fax:* 506-339-9804
chipman.publiclibrary@gnb.ca
www.gnb.ca

Dalhousie: **Bibliothèque du centenaire de Dalhousie/ Dalhousie Centennial Library**
403, rue Adelaide, Dalhousie NB E8C 1B6
Tél: 506-684-7370; *Téléc:* 506-684-7374
bibliocd@gnb.ca
www1.gnb.ca

Dieppe: **Bibliothèque publique de Dieppe/ Dieppe Public Library**
333, av Acadie, Dieppe NB E1A 1G9
Tél: 506-877-7945; *Téléc:* 506-877-7910
bibliopd@gnb.ca
www.gnb.ca

Doaktown: **Doaktown Community - School Library**
Doaktown Consolidated High School, 430 Main St., Doaktown NB E9C 1E8
Tel: 506-365-2018; *Fax:* 506-365-2019
dtcslib@gnb.ca
www.gnb.ca

Dorchester: **Dorchester Public Library**
3516 Cape Rd., Dorchester NB E4K 2X5
Tel: 506-379-3032
DorchPL@gnb.ca
www1.gnb.ca

Edmundston: **Mgr. W.J. Conway Public Library/ Bibliothèque publique Mgr-W.-J. Conway**
33, Irène St., Edmundston NB E3V 1B7
Tel: 506-735-4713; *Fax:* 506-737-6848
biblioed@gnb.ca
www.gnb.ca

Florenceville: **Andrew & Laura McCain Public Library/ Bibliothèque publique Andrew-et-Laura-McCain**
8 McCain St., Florenceville NB E7L 3H6
Tel: 506-392-5294; *Fax:* 506-392-8108
florenpl@gnb.ca
www.gnb.ca

Fredericton: **Dr. Marguerite Michaud Library/ Bibliothèque Dr Marguerite Michaud**
Centre communautaire Sainte-Anne, 715 Priestman St., Fredericton NB E3B 5W7
Tél: 506-453-7100; *Téléc:* 506-453-3958
BiblioDMM@gnb.ca
www.franco-fredericton.com/bibliomm

Fredericton: **Fredericton - Nashwaaksis Public - School Library**
324 Fulton Ave., Fredericton NB E3A 5J4
Tel: 506-453-3241; *Fax:* 506-444-4129
nashwaaksis.library@gnb.ca
www.gnb.ca

Fredericton: **Fredericton Public Library**
12 Carleton St., Fredericton NB E3B 5P4
Tel: 506-460-2800; *Fax:* 506-460-2801
FtonPub@gnb.ca
www.gnb.ca

Fredericton: **York Bookmobile**
4 Carleton St., Fredericton NB E3B 5P4
Tel: 506-453-5380; *Fax:* 506-457-4878
york.bookmobile@gnb.ca
www.gnb.ca

Grand Falls: **Grand Falls Public Library/ Bibliothèque publique de Grand-Sault**
Town Hall, #201, 131 Pleasant St., Grand Falls NB E3Z 1G6
Tel: 506-475-7781; *Fax:* 506-475-7783
gfplib@gnb.ca
www.gnb.ca

Grand Manan: **Grand Manan Library**
1144 Rte. 776, Grand Manan NB E5G 4E8
Tel: 506-662-7099; *Fax:* 506-662-7094
GrandMananLibrary@gnb.ca
www1.gnb.ca/0003/library.asp?Code=FG

Hartland: **Dr. Walter Chestnut Public Library/ Bibliothèque publique Dr-Walter-Chestnut**
#1, 395 Main St., Hartland NB E7P 2N3
Tel: 506-375-4876; *Fax:* 506-375-6816
hartlandl@gnb.ca
www.gnb.ca

Harvey: **Harvey Community Library**
Harvey High School, 2055 Rte. 3, Harvey NB E6K 3W9
Tel: 506-366-2206; *Fax:* 506-366-2210
harvey.library@gnb.ca
www.gnb.ca

Hillsborough: **Hillsborough Public Library**
#2, 2849 Main St., Hillsborough NB E4H 2X7
Tel: 506-734-3722; *Fax:* 506-734-3711
Hillsborough.publiclibrary@gnb.ca
www1.gnb.ca

Kedgwick: **Kedgwick Public Library/ Bibliothèque publique de Kedgwick**
116 Notre-Dame St., #P, Kedgwick NB E8B 1H8
Tel: 506-284-2757; *Fax:* 506-284-4557
bibliopk@gnb.ca
www.gnb.ca

Lamèque: **Bibliothèque publique de Lamèque/ Lamèque Public Library**
46, rue du Pêcheur nord, Lamèque NB E8T 1J3
Tél: 506-344-3262; *Téléc:* 506-344-3263
bibliopl@gnb.ca
www1.gnb.ca

McAdam: **McAdam Public Library**
Municipal Bldg., 146 Saunders Rd., McAdam NB E6J 1L2
Tel: 506-784-1403; *Fax:* 506-784-1402
mcadam.library@gnb.ca
www.gnb.ca

Memramcook: **Bibliothèque publique de Memramcook/ Memramcook Public Library**
#1, 540, rue Centrale, Memramcook NB E4K 3S6
Tél: 506-758-4029; *Téléc:* 506-758-4030
bibliopm@gnb.ca
www1.gnb.ca

Minto: **Minto Public Library**
Municipal Bldg., #2, 420 Pleasant Dr., Minto NB E4B 2T3
Tel: 506-327-3220; *Fax:* 506-327-3041
minto.publiclibrary@gnb.ca
www.gnb.ca

Miramichi: **Miramichi - Médiathèque Père-Louis-Lamontagne**
Centre communautaire Carrefour Beausoleil, 300 Beaverbrook Rd., Miramichi NB E1V 1A1
Tél: 506-627-4084; *Téléc:* 506-627-4592
mediathequeP@gnb.ca
www.mpll.nb.ca

Miramichi: **Miramichi - Newcastle Public Library**
100 Fountain Head Lane, Miramichi NB E1V 4A1
Tel: 506-623-2450; *Fax:* 506-623-2335
Npublib@gnb.ca
www.gnb.ca

Mirimichi: **Miramichi - Chatham Public Library**
24 King St., Mirimichi NB E1N 2N1
Tel: 506-773-6274; *Fax:* 506-773-6963
chathmpl@gnb.ca
www.gnb.ca

Moncton: **Moncton Public Library/ Bibliothèque publique de Moncton**
#101, 644 Main St., Moncton NB E1C 1E2
Tel: 506-869-6000; *Fax:* 506-869-6040
mplib@gnb.ca
www.monctonpubliclibrary.ca

Nackawic: **Nackawic Public - School Library/ Bibliothèque publique-scolaire de Nackawic**
30 Landegger Dr., Nackawic NB E6G 1E9
Tel: 506-572-2136; *Fax:* 506-575-2336
nackawic.library@gnb.ca
www.gnb.ca

Oromocto: **Oromocto Public Library**
54 Miramichi Rd., Oromocto NB E2V 1S2
Tel: 506-357-3329; *Fax:* 506-357-5161
oromocto.publiclibrary@gnb.ca
www.gnb.ca

Perth-Andover: **Perth-Andover Public Library/ Bibliothèque publique de Perth-Andover**
642 East Riverside Dr., Perth-Andover NB E7H 1Z6
Tel: 506-273-2843; *Fax:* 506-273-1913
paplib@gnb.ca
www.gnb.ca

Petitcodiac: **Petitcodiac Public Library**
#101, 6 Kay St., Petitcodiac NB E4Z 4K6
Tel: 506-756-3144; *Fax:* 506-756-3142
Petitcodiac.PublicLibrary@gnb.ca
www1.gnb.ca/publiclibraries

Petit-Rocher: **Bibliothèque publique de Petit-Rocher/ Petit-Rocher Public Library**
#110, 702, rue Principale, Petit-Rocher NB E8J 1V1
Tél: 506-542-2744; *Téléc:* 506-542-2745
bibliopr@gnb.ca
www1.gnb.ca

Plaster Rock: **Plaster Rock Public - School Library/ Bibliothèque publique-scolaire de Plaster Rock**
290A Main St., Plaster Rock NB E7G 2C6
Tel: 506-356-6018; *Fax:* 506-356-6019
prplib@gnb.ca
www.gnb.ca

Port Elgin: **Port Elgin Public Library**
1 Station St., Port Elgin NB E4M 1C6
Tel: 506-538-2118; *Fax:* 506-538-2126
PortEPL@gnb.ca
www1.gnb.ca

Quispamsis: **Kennebecasis Public Library**
1 Landing Ct., Quispamsis NB E2E 4R2
Tel: 506-849-5314; *Fax:* 506-849-5318
info@kvlibrary.org
www.kvlibrary.org

Richibucto: **Bibliothèque publique de Richibucto/ Richibucto Public Library**
9376, rue Main, Richibucto NB E4W 4C9
Tél: 506-523-7851; *Téléc:* 506-523-7851
bibliori@gnb.ca
www1.gnb.ca

Richibucto: **Subheadquarters**
9239 Main St., Richibucto NB E4W 5P5
Tel: 506-523-7666; *Fax:* 506-523-7648
imelda.collette@gnb.ca
www1.gnb.ca

Riverview: **Riverview Public Library**
34 Honour House Ct., Riverview NB E1B 3Y9
Tel: 506-387-2108; *Fax:* 506-387-4970
riverview.publiclibrary@gnb.ca
www.townofriverview.ca/web?service=vpage/2947

Sackville: **Sackville Public Library**
66 Main St., Sackville NB E4L 4A7
Tel: 506-364-4915; *Fax:* 506-364-4915
spublib@gnb.ca
www.geocities.com/sacklib/SKLIB.html

Saint John: **Le Cormoran Library**
67 Ragged Point Rd., Saint John NB E2K 5C3
Tel: 506-658-4610; *Fax:* 506-658-3984
BiblioLC@gnb.ca

Saint John: **Saint John Free Public Library, East Branch**
#2, 545 Westmorland Pl., Saint John NB E2J 2G5
Tel: 506-643-7250; *Fax:* 506-696-5354
EastBranch.PublicLibrary@gnb.ca

Saint John: **Saint John Free Public Library, Main Branch**
1 Market Sq., Saint John NB E2L 4Z6
Tel: 506-643-7220; *Fax:* 506-643-7225
sjfpl@gnb.ca
www.gnb.ca/0003/regions/saint_john_main_branch.asp

Saint John: **Saint John Free Public Library, West Branch**
621 Fairville Blvd., Saint John NB E2M 4X5
Tel: 506-643-7260; *Fax:* 506-672-1752
westbranch.publiclibrary@gnb.ca

St Andrews: **Ross Memorial Library**
110 King St., St Andrews NB E5B 1Y6
Tel: 506-529-5125; *Fax:* 506-529-5129
standrpl@gnb.ca
www.rossmemlibrary.org

Saint-Antoine: **Bibliothèque publique de Saint-Antoine/ Saint-Antoine Public Library**
11, av Jeanne d'Arc, Saint-Antoine NB E4V 1H2
Tél: 506-525-4028; *Téléc:* 506-525-4199
bibliosa@gnb.ca
www1.gnb.ca

Saint-Basile: **Haut Saint-Jean-Bookmobile**
540 Principale St., Saint-Basile NB E7C 1J5
Tel: 506-263-3426; *Fax:* 506-263-3437
bibliobus-hsj@gnb.ca
www.gnb.ca

Saint-François-de-Madawaska: **Mgr. Plourde Public Library/ Bibliothèque publique Mgr-Plourde**
15 Bellevue St., Saint-François-de-Madawaska NB E7A 1A4
Tel: 506-992-6052; *Fax:* 506-992-6047
stfplib@gnb.ca
www.gnb.ca

Saint-Léonard: **Dr. Lorne J. Violette Public Library/ Bibliothèque publique Dr.-Lorne-J.-Violette**
180 St-Jean St., Saint-Léonard NB E7E 2B9
Tel: 506-423-3025; *Fax:* 506-423-3026
stlplib@gnb.ca
www.gnb.ca

Saint-Quentin: **La Moisson Public Library/ Bibliothèque publique La Moisson de Saint-Quentin**
Municipal Bldg., 206 Canada St., Saint-Quentin NB E8A 1H1
Tel: 506-235-1955; *Fax:* 506-235-1957
bibliolm@gnb.ca
www.bibliothequesaint-quentin.com

St Stephen: **St Croix Public Library**
11 King St., St Stephen NB E3L 2C1
Tel: 506-466-7529; *Fax:* 506-466-7574
ststeppl@gnb.ca
www.gnb.ca/publiclibraries

Salisbury: **Salisbury Public Library**
3215 Main St., Salisbury NB E4J 2K7
Tel: 506-372-3240; *Fax:* 506-372-3261
salisbury.publiclibrary@gnb.ca
www1.gnb.ca

Shediac: **Bibliothèque publique de Shediac/ Shediac Public Library**
#100, 290, rue Main, Shediac NB E4P 2E3
Tél: 506-532-7014; *Téléc:* 506-532-8400
bibliosh@gnb.ca
www1.gnb.ca

Shippagan: **Bibliothèque publique Laval-Goupil/ Laval-Goupil Public Library**
128, rue Mgr-Chiasson, Shippagan NB E8S 1X7
Tél: 506-336-3920; *Téléc:* 506-336-3921
bibliops@gnb.ca
www1.gnb.ca

Stanley: **Stanley Community Library**
#2, 28 Bridge St., Stanley NB E6B 1B2
Tel: 506-367-2492; *Fax:* 506-367-2764
stanley.library@gnb.ca
www.gnb.ca

Sussex: **Sussex Regional Library**
46 Magnolia Ave., Sussex NB E4E 2H2
Tel: 506-432-4585; *Fax:* 506-432-4583
sussexpl@gnb.ca

Tracadie-Sheila: **Bibliothèque publique de Tracadie-Sheila/ Tracadie-Sheila Public Library**
3620, rue Principale, Tracadie-Sheila NB E1X 1C9
Tél: 506-394-4005; *Téléc:* 506-394-4009
bibliots@gnb.ca
www1.gnb.ca

Welshpool: **Campobello Public Library**
3 Welshpool St., Welshpool NB E5E 1G3
Tel: 506-752-7082; *Fax:* 506-752-7083
Social Media: www.facebook.com/group.php?gid=16314039207

Woodstock: **L.P. Fisher Public Library/ Bibliothèque publique L.-P.-Fisher**
679 Main St., Woodstock NB E7M 2E1
Tel: 506-325-4777; *Fax:* 506-325-4811
lpfisher.library@gnb.ca
www.gnb.ca

Archives

Bathurst: **Herman J. Good, VC, Canadian Legion**
575 St Peters Ave., Bathurst NB E2A 2Y5
Tel: 506-546-3135; *Fax:* 506-546-1011
Michael White, Curator
506-546-4751

Bouctouche: **Musée de Kent**
150, ch du Couvent, Bouctouche NB E4S 3C1
Tél: 506-743-5005
admin@museedekent.ca
www.museedekent.ca/
Pierre Cormier, Directeur

Caraquet: **Fédération des caisses populaires acadiennes**
295, boul St-Pierre ouest, Caraquet NB E1W 1A4
Tél: 506-726-4000; *Téléc:* 506-726-4001
edna.blanchard@acadie.com
Edna Blanchard, Commis aux archives
edna.blanchard@acadie.com

Dalhousie: **Restigouche Regional Museum**
115 George St., Dalhousie NB E8C 1R6
Tel: 506-684-7490; *Fax:* 506-684-7613
gurrm@nbnet.nb.ca
Bill Clarke, Contact

Edmundston: **Centre de documentation et d'études Madawaskayennes**
165, boul Hébert, Edmundston NB E3V 2S8
Tél: 506-737-5058; *Téléc:* 506-737-5373
mtheriau@umce.ca
www.umce.ca/biblio/cdem/
Guy Lefrançois, Responsable
glefranc@umce.ca

Fredericton: **Provincial Archives of New Brunswick/ Archives provinciales du Nouveau-Brunswick**
University of New Brunswick, Bonar Law-Bennett Bldg., 23 Dineen Dr., Fredericton NB E3B 5H1
Tel: 506-453-2122; *Fax:* 506-453-3288
provincial.archives@gnb.ca
www.gnb.ca/Archives
Marion Beyea, Director & Archivist
Marion.Beyea@gnb.ca
506-444-4021
Dean Lund, Manager, Conservation
Dean.Lund@gnb.ca
506-444-6724
Dale R. Cogswell, Manager, Government Records
Dale.Cogswell@gnb.ca
506-457-3512
Fred Farrell, Manager, Photographs, Public Sector
Fred.Farrell@gnb.ca
506-444-4146

Grand Falls: **Grand Falls Museum/ Musée de Grand-Sault**
#100, 68 Madawaska Rd., Grand Falls NB E3Y 1C6
Tel: 506-473-5265
Anne Rideout Côté, President, Grand Falls Historical Society

Grand Manan: **Grand Manan Museum**
1141 Rte. 776, Grand Manan NB E5G 4E9
Tel: 506-662-3424
gmadmin@grandmananmuseum.ca
www.grandmananmuseum.ca
Ava Sturgeon, Archivist
ava@nb.sympatico.ca

Hampton: **King's County Museum**
27 Centennial Rd., Hampton NB E5N 6N3
Tel: 506-832-6009; *Fax:* 506-832-6409
kingscm@nbnet.nb.ca
personal.nbnet.nb.ca/kingscm
A. Faye Pearson, Museum Director
506-832-6009

Miramichi: **St Michael's Museum & Genealogical Centre**
10 Howard St., Miramichi NB E1N 3A7
Tel: 506-778-5152; *Fax:* 506-778-5156
mmuseum@nbnet.nb.ca
www.saintmichaelsmuseum.com
Theresa Flynn, Head Librarian

Saint John: **New Brunswick Museum**
277 Douglas Ave., Saint John NB E2K 1E5
Tel: 506-643-2322; *Fax:* 506-643-2360
Toll-Free: 888-268-9595
archives@nbm-mnb.ca
www.nbm-mnb.ca
Felicity Osepchook, Head
506-643-2324

Saint John: **Roman Catholic Diocese of Saint John**
1 Bayard Dr., Saint John NB E2L 3L5
Tel: 506-653-6807; *Fax:* 506-653-6812
archives@dioceseofsaintjohn.org
Mary McDevitt, Archivist

Saint John: **Saint John Jewish Historical Museum**
29 Wellington Row, Saint John NB E2L 3H4
Tel: 506-633-1833; *Fax:* 506-642-9926
sjjhm@nbnet.nb.ca
personal.nbnet.nb.ca/sjjhm
Katherine Biggs-Craft, Head

St Andrews: **Charlotte County Archives**
123 Frederick St., St Andrews NB E5B 1Z1
Tel: 506-529-4248; *Fax:* 506-529-4248
contact@ccarchives.ca
www.ccarchives.ca

Shippagan: **Société historique Nicolas-Denys**
Université de Moncton, Campus de Shippagan, 218, boul J.-D.-Gauthier, Shippagan NB E8S 1P6
Tél: 506-336-3461; *Téléc:* 506-336-3434
shnd@umcs.ca
www2.umoncton.ca/cfdocs/cea/reseau/centre9.html
Philippe Basque, Président
Nathalie Lanteigne, Responsable

Woodstock: **Carleton County Historical Society**
128 Connell St., Woodstock NB E7M 1L5
Tel: 506-328-9706; *Fax:* 506-328-2942
cchs@nb.aibn.com
www.cchs-nb.ca

Newfoundland & Labrador

Regional Systems

Newfoundland & Labrador Public Libraries - Central Division
6 Bell Pl., Gander NL A1V 1X2
Tel: 709-651-5356; *Fax:* 709-256-2194
Patricia Parsons, Central Division Manager
pparsons@nlpl.ca
709-651-5351
Michelle Stuckless, Librarian

Newfoundland & Labrador Public Libraries - West Newfoundland-Labrador Division
5 Union St., Corner Brook NL A2H 5M7
Tel: 709-634-7333; *Fax:* 709-634-7313
schilcote@nlpl.ca
www.nlpl.ca
Sanford Chilcote, Manager
schilcote@nlpl.ca
709-634-7333

Provincial Information & Library Resources Board - Eastern Division
Arts & Culture Centre, St. John's NL A1B 3A3
Tel: 709-737-3508; *Fax:* 709-737-3571
johnwhite@nlpl.ca
www.nlpl.ca
John White, Division Manager
johnwhite@nlpubliclibraries.ca
709-737-3508

Public Libraries

***L'Anse au Loup:* Labrador South Public Library**
L'Anse au Loup NL A0K 3L0
Tel: 709-927-5542
podell@nlpl.ca
www.nlpl.ca
Pauline O'Dell, Library Technician

***Arnold's Cove:* Arnold's Cove Public Library**
5 Highliner Dr., Arnold's Cove NL A0B 1A0
Tel: 709-463-8707
gsmith@nlpl.ca
www.nlpl.ca
Gwen Smith, Librarian

***Baie Verte:* Baie Verte Public Library**
PO Box 178, Baie Verte NL A0K 1B0
Tel: 709-532-8361
ecooper@nlpl.ca
www.nlpl.ca
Eileen Cooper, Library Technician

***Bay Roberts:* Bay Roberts Public Library**
76 Cross Rd., Bay Roberts NL A0A 1G0
Tel: 709-786-9629
mclarke@nlpl.ca
www.nlpl.ca
Marilyn Clarke, Librarian

***Bell Island:* Bell Island Public Library**
Provincial Government Bldg., 20 Bennett St., Bell Island NL A0A 4H0
Tel: 709-488-2413
www.nlpl.ca
John White, Manager, Easter Division
johnwhite@nlpl.ca
709-737-3508
Lois Clarke, Library Technician
lclarke@nlpl.ca

***Bishop's Falls:* Bishop's Falls Public Library**
PO Box 329, Bishop's Falls NL A0H 1C0
Tel: 709-258-6244
cstanley@nlpl.ca
www.nlpl.ca
Cora Stanley, Librarian

***Bonavista:* Bonavista Memorial Public Library**
PO Box 400, Bonavista NL A0C 1B0
Tel: 709-468-2185
bwilton@nlpl.ca
www.nlpl.ca
Brenda Wilton, Librarian

***Botwood:* Botwood Kinsmen Public Library**
240 Water St., Botwood NL A0H 1E0
Tel: 709-257-2091
pcoates@nlpl.ca
www.nlpl.ca
Phyllis Coates, Library Technician

***Brigus:* Brigus Public Library**
General Delivery, Brigus NL A0A 1K0
Tel: 709-528-3156
epercey@nlpl.ca
www.nlpl.ca
Elsie Percey, Library Technician

***Buchans:* Buchans Public Library**
Lakeside Academy, Buchans Hwy., Lakeside Academy, Buchans NL A0H 1G0
Tel: 709-672-3859
dpennell@nlpl.ca
www.nlpl.ca
Dawn Pennell, Librarian

***Burgeo:* Burgeo Public Library**
PO Box 370, Burgeo NL A0M 1A0
Tel: 709-886-2673
fmacdonald@nlpl.ca
www.nlpl.ca.ca
Freda MacDonald, Library Technician

***Burin:* Burin Public Library**
PO Box 219, Burin NL A0E 1G0
Tel: 709-891-1924
ppeddle@nlpl.ca
www.nlpl.ca
Patricia Peddle, Librarian

***Cape St George:* Cape St George Public Library**
879 Oceanview Dr., Cape St George NL A0N 1T1
Tel: 709-644-2852; *Fax:* 709-664-2852
ecornect@nlpl.ca
www.nlpl.ca
Elizabeth Cornect, Library Technician

***Carbonear:* Carbonear Public Library**
PO Box 928, Carbonear NL A1Y 1C4
Tel: 709-596-3382
msnow@nlpl.ca
www.nlpl.ca
Maureen Snow, Librarian

***Carmanville:* Carmanville Public Library**
Phoenix Academy, 95-97 Main St., PO Box 105, Carmanville NL A0G 1N0
Tel: 709-534-2370
kbutt@nlpl.ca
www.nlpl.ca
Kay Butt, Librarian

***Cartwright:* Cartwright Public Library**
PO Box 330, Cartwright NL A0K 1V0
Tel: 709-938-7219
hclark@nlpl.ca
www.nlpl.ca
Hilda Clark, Library Technician

***Catalina:* Catalina (Joseph E. Clouter) Public Library**
PO Box 69, Catalina NL A0C 1J0
Tel: 709-469-3045
kjohnson@nlpl.ca
www.nlpl.ca
Kimberley Johnson, Librarian

***Centreville:* Intertown Public Library**
c/o Centreville Academy, 2 Memory Lane, PO Box 100, Centreville NL A0G 4P0
Tel: 709-678-2700
vrogers@nlpl.ca
www.nlpl.ca
Veronica Rogers, Librarian

***Change Islands:* Change Islands Public Library**
c/o A.R. Scammell Academy, Main St. North, PO Box 129, Change Islands NL A0G 1R0
Tel: 709-621-5566
choffe@nlpl.ca
www.nlpl.ca
Christine Hoffe, Librarian

***Channel-Port-aux-Basques:* Port aux Basques Public Library**
PO Box 790, Channel-Port-aux-Basques NL A0M 1C0
Tel: 709-695-3471; *Fax:* 709-695-3471
bingram@nlpl.ca
www.nlpl.ca
Brenda Ingram, Library Technician

***Churchill Falls:* Churchill Falls Public Library**
PO Box 160, Churchill Falls NL A0R 1A0
Tel: 709-925-3281; *Fax:* 709-925-3487
cyoung@nlpl.ca
www.nlpl.ca
Social Media:
www.facebook.com/group.php?gid=169595486419342
Loretta Bryant, Library Technician

***Clarenville:* Clarenville Public Library**
98 Manitoba Dr., Clarenville NL A5A 1K7
Tel: 709-466-7634
tmaclean@nlpl.ca
www.nlpl.ca
Tanya MacLean, Librarian

***Conception Bay South:* Conception Bay South Public Library**
110 Conception Bay Hwy., Conception Bay South NL A1W 3A5
Tel: 709-834-4241
brideout@nlpl.ca
www.nlpl.ca
Bertha Rideout, Library Technician

***Cormack:* Cormack Public Library**
280A Veterans Dr., Cormack NL A8A 2R4
Tel: 709-635-7022; *Fax:* 709-635-7022
mmorris@nlpl.ca
www.nlpl.ca
Marie Morris, Library Technician

***Corner Brook:* Corner Brook Public Library**
Sir Richard Squires Bldg., Mt Bernard Ave., Corner Brook NL A2H 6J8
Tel: 709-634-0013; *Fax:* 709-634-0200
mfeaver@nlpl.ca
www.cornerbrooklibrary.org
Melissa Feaver, Librarian
mfeaver@nlpl.ca

***Cow Head:* Cow Head Public Library**
PO Box 130, Cow Head NL A0K 2A0
Tel: 709-243-2467
nshears@nlpl.ca
www.nlpl.ca
Nora Shears, Library Technician

***Daniels Harbour:* Daniels Harbour Public Library**
15 Church Lane, Daniels Harbour NL A0K 2C0
Tel: 709-898-2283
shumber@nlpl.ca
www.nlpl.ca
Sharon Humber, Library Technician

***Deer Lake:* Deer Lake Public Library**
4 Poplar Rd., Deer Lake NL A8A 1Z4
Tel: 709-635-3671; *Fax:* 709-635-3671
wcramm@nlpl.ca
www.nlpl.ca
Worneta Cramm, Library Technician
Loretta Wight, Library Assistant
Tina Rose, Library Assistant

***Doyles:* Codroy Valley Public Library**
General Delivery, Doyles NL A0N 1J0
Tel: 709-955-3158; *Fax:* 709-955-2620
jgillis@nlpl.ca
www.nlpl.ca
Judy Gillis, Library Technician

***Fogo:* Fogo Island Public Library**
Fogo NL A0G 2B0
Tel: 709-266-2210; *Fax:* 709-266-2384
mfoley@nlpl.ca
www.nlpl.ca
Marion Foley, Library Technician

***Fortune:* Fortune Public Library**
PO Box 400, Fortune NL A0E 1P0
Tel: 709-832-0232
fherridge@nlpl.ca
www.nlpl.ca
Fay Herridge, Library Technician

***Fox Harbour PB:* Fox Harbour Public Library**
PO Box 74, Fox Harbour PB NL A0B 1V0
Tel: 709-227-2135
cmurray@nlpl.ca
www.nlpl.ca
Catherine Murray, Library Technician

***Gambo:* Gambo Public Library**
6 Centennial Rd., Gambo NL A0G 1T0
Tel: 709-674-5052
scollins@nlpl.ca
www.nlpl.ca
Sylvia Collins, Library Technician

***Gander:* Gander Public & Resource Library**
6 Bell Pl., Gander NL A1V 1X2
Tel: 709-651-5356
mstuckless@nlpl.ca
www.nlpl.ca
Michelle Stuckless, Library Technician

***Garnish:* Garnish (Greta Hollett) Memorial Library**
PO Box 40, Garnish NL A0E 1T0
Tel: 709-826-2371
lnolan@nlpl.ca
www.nlpl.ca
Linda Nolan, Library Technician

***Gaultois:* Gaultois Public Library**
PO Box 100, Gaultois NL A0H 1N0
Tel: 709-841-3311
www.nlpl.ca

***Glenwood:* Glenwood Public Library**
26 Main St., Glenwood NL A0G 2K0
Tel: 709-679-5700
kgillingham@nlpl.ca
www.nlpl.ca
Kelly Gillingham, Librarian

***Glovertown:* Alexander Bay Public Library**
Glovertown Academy, Penney's Brook Rd., Glovertown NL A0G 2L0
Tel: 709-533-6688
rsweetapple@nlpl.ca
www.nlpl.ca
Rose Sweetapple, Librarian

***Grand Bank:* Grand Bank Public Library**
PO Box 1000, Grand Bank NL A0E 1W0
Tel: 709-832-0310
jfox@nlpl.ca
www.nlpl.ca
Jane Fox, Library Technician

***Grand Falls-Windsor:* Harmsworth Public Library**
Gordon Pinsent Centre for the Arts, 1 Cromer Ave., Grand Falls-Windsor NL A2A 1W9
Tel: 709-489-2303; *Fax:* 709-489-9328
mcrant@nlpl.ca
www.nlpl.ca
Madonna Crant, Librarian

***Greenspond:* Greenspond Memorial Library**
PO Box 70, Greenspond NL A0G 2N0
Tel: 709-269-3434
cblackwood@nlpl.ca
www.nlpl.ca
Cindy Blackwood, Librarian

***Happy Valley-Goose Bay:* Melville Public Library**
Elizabeth Goudie Bldg., 141 Hamilton River Rd., Happy Valley-Goose Bay NL A0P 1E0
Tel: 709-896-8045
hskoglund@nlpl.ca
www.nlpl.ca
Hyra Skoglund, Library Tecnician

***Harbour Breton:* Harbour Breton Public Library**
PO Box 569, Harbour Breton NL A0H 1P0
Tel: 709-885-2165
vbennett@nlpl.ca
www.nlpl.ca
Vivian Bennett, Library Technician

***Harbour Grace:* Harbour Grace Public Library**
PO Box 40, Harbour Grace NL A0A 2M0
Tel: 709-596-3894
dquinn@nlpl.ca
www.nlpl.ca
Doreen Quinn, Library Technician

***Hare Bay:* Hare Bay/Dover Public Library**
Jane Collins Academy, 22 Anstey's Rd., Hare Bay NL A0G 2P0
Tel: 709-537-2391; *Fax:* 709-537-2374
rcollins@nlpl.ca
www.nlpl.ca
Robin Collins, Librarian

***Harry's Harbour:* Harry's Harbour Public Library**
PO Box 65, Harry's Harbour NL A0J 1E0
Tel: 709-624-5464
eking@nlpl.ca
www.nlpl.ca
Ellen King, Librarian

***Hermitage:* Hermitage Public Library**
John Watkins Academy, PO Box 159, Hermitage NL A0H 1S0
Tel: 709-883-2421
bwillmott@nlpl.ca
www.nlpl.ca
Bernice Willmott, Library Technician

***Holyrood:* Holyrood Public Library**
PO Box 263, Holyrood NL A0A 2R0
Tel: 709-229-7852
dcarr@nlpl.ca
www.nlpl.ca
Dianne Carr, Library Technician

***Kings Point:* Tilley Memorial Public Library**
PO Box 100, Kings Point NL A0J 1J0
Tel: 709-268-2282
pbowers@nlpl.ca
www.nlpl.ca
Patsy Bowers, Library Technician

***Labrador City:* Margaret Butt Memorial Public Library**
306 Hudson Dr., Labrador City NL A2V 1L5
Tel: 709-944-2190; *Fax:* 709-944-3674
tandrews@nlpl.ca
www.nlpl.ca
Trudy Andrews, Library Technician

***Lark Harbour:* Lark Harbour (Blow-Me-Down) Public/School Library**
PO Box 120, Lark Harbour NL A0L 1H0
Tel: 709-681-2147; *Fax:* 709-681-2147
lsheppard@nlpl.ca
www.nlpl.ca
Lesley Sheppard, Library Technician

***Lewisporte:* Lewisporte Public Library**
PO Box 1179, Lewisporte NL A0G 3A0
Tel: 709-535-2519
jsnow@nlpl.ca
www.nlpl.ca
Judy Snow, Librarian

***Lourdes:* Lourdes Public/School Library**
82 Main St., Lourdes NL A0N 1R0
Tel: 709-642-5388
pwoodrow@nlpl.ca
www.nlpl.ca
Patricia Woodrow, Library Technician

***Lumsden:* Lumsden Public Library**
Lumsden School Complex, PO Box 119, Lumsden NL A0G 3E0
Tel: 709-530-2617
kstagg@nlpl.ca
www.nlpl.ca
Kay Stagg, Librarian

***Marystown:* Marystown Public Library**
PO Box 1270, Marystown NL A0E 2M0
Tel: 709-279-1507
pmayo@nlpl.ca
www.nlpl.ca
Patricia Mayo, Library Technician

***Mount Pearl:* Mount Pearl (Ross King) Memorial Public Library**
65 Olympic Dr., Mount Pearl NL A1N 5H6
Tel: 709-368-3603
ygillard@nlpl.ca
www.nlpl.ca
Yvonne Gillard, Library Technician

***Musgrave Harbour:* John B. Wheeler Public Library**
PO Box 130, Musgrave Harbour NL A0G 3J0
Tel: 709-655-2730
eabbott@nlpl.ca
www.nlpl.ca
Eunice Abbott, Library Technician

***Norris Arm:* Norris Arm Public Library**
65 Norris Ave., PO Box 100, Norris Arm NL A0G 3M0
Tel: 709-653-2531
lrowsell@nlpl.ca
www.nlpl.ca
Leona Rowsell, Librarian

***Norris Point:* Norris Point Public Library**
PO Box 129, Norris Point NL A0K 3V0
Tel: 709-458-3368
jsamms@nlpl.ca
www.nlpl.ca
Judy Samms, Library Technician

***North West River:* North West River Library & CAP Site**
PO Box 410, North West River NL A0P 1M0
Tel: 709-497-8705; *Fax:* 709-497-8705
nwrvollibrary@hotmail.com
northwestriverlibrary.weebly.com
Social Media:
www.facebook.com/group.php?gid=122067064513337
Wendy Mitchell, Librarian

***Old Perlican:* Old Perlican Public Library**
PO Box 265, Old Perlican NL A0A 3G0
Tel: 709-587-2028
etuttle@nlpl.ca
www.nlpl.ca
Elizabeth Tuttle, Library Technician

***Pasadena:* Pasadena Public Library**
16 - 10th Ave., Pasadena NL A0L 1K0
Tel: 709-686-2792
amenchion@nlpl.ca
www.nlpl.ca
Angela Menchion, Library Technician

***Placentia:* Placentia Public Library**
PO Box 119, Placentia NL A0B 2Y0
Tel: 709-227-3621
dbowering@nlpl.ca
www.nlpl.ca
Doris Bowring, Library Technician

***Point Leamington:* Point Leamington Public Library**
PO Box 78, Point Leamington NL A0H 1Z0
Tel: 709-484-3541
bwarford@nlpl.ca
www.nlpl.ca
Beverley Warford, Librarian

***Port au Port:* Port au Port Public Library**
PO Box 220, Port au Port NL A0N 1T0
Tel: 709-648-2472; *Fax:* 709-648-9512
jclarke@nlpl.ca
www.nlpl.ca
Janice Clarke, Library Technician
Wanda Martin, Staff

***Port Saunders:* Port Saunders (Ingornachoix) Public Library**
PO Box 59, Port Saunders NL A0K 4H0
Tel: 709-861-3690
ebiggin@nlpl.ca
www.nlpl.ca
Evelyn Biggin, Library Technician

***Pouch Cove:* Pouch Cove Public Library**
PO Box 40, Pouch Cove NL A0A 3L0
Tel: 709-335-2652
lbragg@nlpl.ca
www.nlpl.ca
Laura Bragg, Library Technician
Laura Noseworthy, Library Technician

***Pouch Cove:* Resource Links**
PO Box 9, Pouch Cove NL A0A 3L0
Tel: 709-335-2394; *Fax:* 709-335-2978
resourcelinks@nfld.com
www.resourcelinks.ca
Victoria Pennell, Editor

***Ramea:* Ramea Public Library**
PO Box 59, Ramea NL A0N 2J0
Tel: 709-625-2344
flushman@nlpl.ca
www.nlpl.ca
Frances Lushman, Library Technician

***Robert's Arm:* Robert's Arm Public Library**
PO Box 119, Robert's Arm NL A0J 1R0
Tel: 709-652-3100
hsuley@nlpl.ca
www.nlpl.ca
Helen Suley, Librarian

***Rocky Harbour:* Rocky Harbour Public Library**
PO Box 40, Rocky Harbour NL A0K 4N0
Tel: 709-458-2900
jsamms@nlpl.ca
www.nlpl.ca
Judy Samms, Library Technician

***St Alban's:* St Alban's Public Library**
PO Box 70, St Alban's NL A0H 2E0
Tel: 709-538-3034
www.nlpl.ca
Kerri-Ann Snook, Librarian

***St Anthony:* St Anthony Public Library**
PO Box 129, St Anthony NL A0K 4S0
Tel: 709-454-3025
jelliott@nlpl.ca
www.nlpl.ca
Jocelyn Elliott, Library Technician

***St Bride's:* Cape Shore Public Library**
General Delivery, St Bride's NL A0B 2Z0
Tel: 709-337-2360
jnash@nlpl.ca
www.nlpl.ca
Jacqueline Nash, Library Technician

***St Fintans:* St Fintan's (Bay St George South) Public/School Library**
PO Box 70, St Fintans NL A0N 1Y0
Tel: 709-645-2186; *Fax:* 709-645-2780
amacinnis@nlpl.ca
www.nlpl.ca
Anita MacInnis, Library Technician

***St George's:* St George's Public Library**
PO Box 249, St George's NL A0N 1Z0
Tel: 709-647-3808; *Fax:* 709-647-3108
jdowney@nlpl.ca
www.nlpl.ca
Joan Downey, Library Technician

***St. John's:* ANLA Bulletin**
RPO Churchill Sq., PO Box 23155, St. John's NL A1B 4J9
Tel: 709-726-2867; *Fax:* 709-729-0578
anla@nf.sympatico.ca
www.anla.nf.ca
Jessie Chisholm, Editor

***St. John's:* APLA Bulletin**
Queen Elizabeth II Library, Memorial University, St. John's NL A1B 3Y1
Tel: 709-737-2080; *Fax:* 709-737-2153
igibson@mun.ca
www.apla.ca/bulletin
Ian Gibson, Editor
Jane Duffy, Editor
jane.duffy@dal.ca

***St. John's:* St John's Public Libraries**
Arts & Culture Centre, 125 Allendale Rd., St. John's NL A1B 3A3
Tel: 709-737-2133; *Fax:* 709-737-2660
reference@nlpl.ca
www.nlpl.ca
Michelle Walters, Manager
michellewalters@nlpublicl ibraries.ca
709-737-3946

***St Lawrence:* St Lawrence Public Library**
PO Box 366, St Lawrence NL A0E 2V0
Tel: 709-873-2650
vlockyer@nlpl.ca
www.nlpl.ca
Vicki Etechegary-Lockyer, Library Technician

***St Lunaire-Griquet:* St Lunaire-Griquet Public Library**
General Delivery, St Lunaire-Griquet NL A0K 2X0
Tel: 709-623-2904
mbussey@nlpl.ca
www.nlpl.ca
Mae Bussey, Library Technician

***La Scie:* La Scie Public Library**
PO Box 285, La Scie NL A0K 3M0
Tel: 709-675-2004
ktilley@nlpl.ca
www.nlpl.ca
Karen Tilley, Library Technician

***Seal Cove WB:* Seal Cove Public Library**
PO Box 70, Seal Cove WB NL A0K 5E0
Tel: 709-531-2505
kpinksen@nlpl.ca
www.nlpl.ca
Karen Pinksen, Librarian

***Sop's Arm:* Sop's Arm Public Library**
Main St., General Delivery, Sop's Arm NL A0K 5K0
Tel: 709-482-2225
dwhite@nlpl.ca
www.nlpl.ca
Diane White, Library Technician

***Southern Harbour:* Southern Harbour Public Library**
PO Box 167, Southern Harbour NL A0B 3H0
Tel: 709-463-8814
bwhiffen@nlpl.ca
www.nlpl.ca
Bride Whiffen, Library Technician

***Springdale:* Springdale Public Library**
Indian River High School, PO Box 1414, Springdale NL A0J 1T0
Tel: 709-673-4169
jhamilton@nlpl.ca
www.nlpl.ca
Judy Hamilton, Librarian

***Stephenville:* Newfoundland & Labrador Public Libraries**
48 St George's Ave., Stephenville NL A2N 1K9
Tel: 709-643-0900; *Fax:* 709-643-0925
illstaff@nlpl.ca
www.nlpl.ca
Shawn Tetford, Executive Director
stetford@nlpl.ca
709-643-0902
Charles Cameron, Director, Regional Services
ccameron@nlpl.ca
709-643-0922
Andrew Hunt, Director, Financial Services
ahunt@nlpl.ca
709-643-0904
John White, Eastern Divisional Manager
johnwhite@nlpl.ca
709-737-3508
Newman George, Director, Information Technology
ngeorge@nlpl.ca
709-643-0911
Patricia Parsons, Central Divisional Manager
pparsons@nlpl.ca
709-651-5351
Michelle Walters, St. John's Manager
mwalters@nlpl.ca
709-737-3946

***Stephenville:* Stephenville (Kindale) Public Library**
45 Carolina Ave., Stephenville NL A2N 3P8
Tel: 709-643-4262; *Fax:* 709-643-5781
mwhite@nlpl.ca
www.nlpl.ca
Monica White, Library Technician

***Stephenville Crossing:* Stephenville Crossing Public Library**
PO Box 610, Stephenville Crossing NL A0N 2C0
Tel: 709-646-2173; *Fax:* 709-646-2065
jdowney@nlpl.ca
www.nlpl.ca
Joan Downey, Library Technician

***Summerford:* Summerford Public Library**
1 Main St., Summerford NL A0G 4E0
Tel: 709-629-3244
mboyd@nlpl.ca
www.nlpl.ca
Mavis Boyd, Librarian

***Torbay:* Torbay Public Library**
1288A Torbay Rd., Torbay NL A1K 1B2
Tel: 709-437-6571
mdeibel@nlpl.ca
www.nlpl.ca
Marcia Deibel, Library Technician

***Trepassey:* Trepassey Public Library**
PO Box 183, Trepassey NL A0A 4B0
Tel: 709-438-2224
pmccormack@nlpl.ca
www.nlpl.ca
Patricia McCormack, Library Technician

***Twillingate:* Twillingate Public Library**
PO Box 338, Twillingate NL A0G 4M0
Tel: 709-884-2353
dhayward@nlpl.ca
www.nlpl.ca
Deborah Hayward, Librarian

***Victoria:* Victoria Memorial Public Library**
PO Box 190, Victoria NL A0A 4G0
Tel: 709-596-3682
scolbourne@nlpl.ca
www.nlpl.ca
Shona Colbourne, Library Technician

***Wabush:* Wabush Public Library**
PO Box 179, Wabush NL A0R 1B0
Tel: 709-282-3479; *Fax:* 709-282-3479
pstrickland@nlpl.ca
www.nlpl.ca
Paulette Strickland, Library Technician

***Wesleyville:* Wesleyville Public Library**
Lester Pearson High School, PO Box 70, Wesleyville NL A0G 4R0
Tel: 709-536-5777
bhounsell@nlpl.ca
www.nlpl.ca
Beverley Hounsell, Librarian

***Whitbourne:* Whitbourne Public Library**
PO Box 400, Whitbourne NL A0B 3K0
Tel: 709-759-2461
gsomerton@nlpl.ca
www.nlpl.ca
Gloria Somerton, Library Technician

***Winterton:* Winterton Public Library**
PO Box 119, Winterton NL A0B 3M0
Tel: 709-583-2119
bpitcher@nlpl.ca
www.nlpl.ca
Betty Pitcher, Library Technician

***Woody Point:* Woody Point (Edgar L. Roberts Memorial) Library**
PO Box 179, Woody Point NL A0K 1P0
Tel: 709-453-2556
mharris@nlpl.ca
www.nlpl.ca
Michelle Harris, Library Technician

Archives

***Bonavista:* Bonavista Historical Society**
102 Church St., Bonavista NL A0C 1B0
Tel: 709-468-2880
www.anla.nf.ca/bvista.htm
Gordon Bradley, President

***Botwood:* Botwood Heritage Society Archive**
PO Box 490, Botwood NL A0H 1E0
Tel: 709-257-2071; *Fax:* 709-257-3330
Everett Elliott, Contact

***Happy Valley-Goose Bay:* Them Days Labrador Archives**
3 Courte Manche St., Happy Valley-Goose Bay NL A0P 1E0
Tel: 709-896-8531; *Fax:* 709-896-4970
them.days@nf.aibn.com
www.themdays.com
Aimee Chaulk, Editor
Josie Lethbridge, Administrator

***Harbour Grace:* Conception Bay Museum**
PO Box 298, Harbour Grace NL A0A 2M0
Tel: 709-596-0506
www.hrgrace.ca/museum.html
Peggy Fahey, Curator

***Musgrave Harbour:* Fisherman's Museum**
4 Marine Dr., PO Box 159, Musgrave Harbour NL A0G 3J0
Tel: 709-655-2162
Sophie Mercer, Town Clerk
709-655-2119

***St. John's:* City of St John's Archives**
495 Water St., 3rd Fl., St. John's NL A1C 5M2
Tel: 709-576-8167; *Fax:* 709-576-8254
archives@stjohns.ca
www.stjohns.ca/cityservices/archives/index.jsp
Helen Miller, Archivist

***St. John's:* Congregation of Sisters of Mercy of Newfoundland**
Waterford Bridge Rd., St. John's NL A1C 5P5
Tel: 709-726-7320; *Fax:* 709-726-4414
archives@sistersofmercynf.org
www.sistersofmercynf.org
Elizabeth Davis, Congregational Leader

***St. John's:* Newfoundland Historical Society/ Archival & Library Collection**
Colonial Bldg., Military Rd., PO Box 23154,, Churchill Sq., St. John's NL A1B 4J9
Tel: 709-722-3191; *Fax:* 709-729-0578
nhs@nf.aibn.com
www.infonet.st-johns.nf.ca/providers/nfldhist
Allan Byrne, Office Manager

***St. John's:* Presentation Congregation Archives**
Cathedral Sq., Presentation Convent, PO Box 758, St. John's NL A1C 5L4
Tel: 709-753-7291; *Fax:* 709-753-1578
prescong@nf.aibn.com
Mary Perpetua Kennedy, Archivist
perpetuakennedy@hotmail.com
Patricia Whittle, Assistant Archivist
bozowhittle@yahoo.com

***St. John's:* Provincial Archives of Newfoundland & Labrador**
9 Bonaventure Ave., St. John's NL A1C 5P9
Tel: 709-757-8030; *Fax:* 709-757-8031
archives@therooms.ca
www.therooms.ca/archives/
Greg Walsh, Director/Provincial Archivist
709-757-8032
R. Calvin Best, Head, Client Services
709-757-8034
Heather Locke, Archives Technician
709-757-8034

***St. John's:* Queen's College**
#3000, 210 Prince Philip Dr., St. John's NL A1B 3R6
Tel: 709-753-0116; *Fax:* 709-753-1214
Toll-Free: 877-753-0116
queens@mun.ca
www.mun.ca/queens
John Mellis, Contact

***St. John's:* Roman Catholic Archdiocese of St John's**
200 Military Rd., St. John's NL A1C 5N5
Tel: 709-726-3660; *Fax:* 709-739-6458
ldohey@nf.aibn.com
www.stjohnsarchdiocese.nf.ca/archives.asp
Larry Dohey, Archivist
ldohey@nf.aibn.com

***St. John's:* Sport Archives of Newfoundland and Labrador**
The Rooms Provincial Archives, Rm. 18 Colonial Bldg., Military Rd., St. John's NL A1B 4J6
Tel: 709-729-0591
sanl@mail.gov.nl.ca
www.tcr.gov.nl.ca/panl/sanl/
Linda Murphy, Volunteer Archivist

***Trinity TB:* Trinity Historical Society Archives**
Lester-Garland House, West St., 3rd Fl., PO Box 8, Trinity TB NL A0C 2S0
Tel: 709-464-3599; *Fax:* 709-464-3599
info@trinityhistoricalsociety.com
www.trinityhistoricalsociety.com
Clarence Dewling, Archivist
Deon Bailey, IT Specialist
info@trinityhistoricalsociety.com
709-464-3599

***Wesleyville:* Bonavista North Regional Museum & Gallery**
PO Box 257, Wesleyville NL A0G 4R0
Tel: 709-536-2110; *Fax:* 709-536-3039
museum@nf.aibn.com
Duke Kelloway, Chair
Janet Davis, Secretary-Treasurer

Northwest Territories

Regional Systems

NWT Public Library Services
75 Woodland Dr., Hay River NT X0E 1G1
Tel: 867-874-6531; *Fax:* 867-874-3321
kevin_lafferty@gov.nt.ca
www.nwtpls.gov.nt.ca
Alison Hopkins, Territorial Librarian
alison_hopkins@gov.nt.ca
867-874-3531
Brian Dawson, Head, Technical Services
brian_dawson@gov.nt.ca
867-874-6531

Public Libraries

***Fort Simpson:* John Tsetso Memorial Library**
PO Box 258, Fort Simpson NT X0E 0N0
Tel: 867-695-3276; *Fax:* 867-695-3276
si_library@gov.nt.ca
www.ece.gov.nt.ca/Public_Library_Services/CommunityLibraries.h
Lorraine Ocko, Librarian
867-695-3275

***Fort Smith:* Mary Kaeser Library**
170 McDougal Rd., Fort Smith NT X0E 0P0
Tel: 867-872-2296; *Fax:* 867-872-5303
mkl@gov.nt.ca
Jeri Miltenberger, Local Librarian
jeri_miltenberger@gov.nt.ca

***Hay River:* Hay River Dene Reserve Community Library**
Chief Sunrise Education Centre, PO Box 3055, Hay River NT X0E 1G4
Tel: 867-874-2128; *Fax:* 867-874-3678
Other Numbers: 867-874-6444
Barbara Berlinguette, Contact
Kevin Lafferty, Interlibrary Loans Clerk
kevin_lafferty@gov.nt.ca

***Hay River:* Northwest Territories Centennial Library**
75 Woodland Dr., Hay River NT X0E 1G1
Tel: 867-874-6486; *Fax:* 867-874-3834
www.nwtpls.gov.nt.ca
Christine Gyapay, Local Librarian
christine_gyapay@gov.nt.ca

***Inuvik:* Inuvik Centennial Library**
100 MacKenzie Rd., Inuvik NT X0E 0T0
Tel: 867-777-8620; *Fax:* 867-777-8621
IK_Library@gov.nt.ca
www.inuvik.ca/townhall/library.html
Beverly Garven, Head Librarian

***Norman Wells:* Norman Wells Community Library**
PO Box 97, Norman Wells NT X0E 0V0
Tel: 867-587-2956; *Fax:* 867-587-2193
normanwells_library@gov.nt.ca
Lori Shapansky, Local Librarian

***Tulita:* Tulita Community Library**
General Delivery, Tulita NT X0E 0K0
Tel: 867-588-4471; *Fax:* 867-588-4908
Darlene Etchinelle, Librarian

***Yellowknife:* Yellowknife Public Library**
Centre Square Mall, 5022 - 49th St., 2nd Fl., Yellowknife NT X1A 3R8
Tel: 867-920-5642; *Fax:* 867-920-5671
library@yellowknife.ca
www.yellowknife.ca
Deborah Bruser, Library Manager
dbruser@yellowknife.ca
867-669-3401
Kris Solowy, Library Technician
ksolowy@yellowknife.ca
867-669-3402
Jennifer Knowlan, Public Service Librarian
jknowlan@yellowknife.ca
867-920-5642

Archives

***Fort Smith:* Northern Life Museum National Exhibition Centre**
110 King St., Fort Smith NT X0E 0P0
Tel: 867-872-2859; *Fax:* 867-872-5808
nlmnec@auroranet.nt.ca
www.nwtresearch.com/canoe/museum.htm
Kevin Brunt, Curator of Collections
curator@auroranet.net.ca
Laurie Young, Manager

***Yellowknife:* Northwest Territories Dept. of Education, Culture & Employment**
Prince of Wales Northern Heritage Centre, PO Box, 1320, Yellowknife NT X1A 2L9
Tel: 867-873-7698; *Fax:* 867-873-0660
nwtarchives@ece.learnnet.nt.ca
www.pwnhc.ca
D. Richard Valpy, Territorial Archivist
richard_valpy@ece.learnnet.nt.ca
867-873-7657

Nova Scotia

Regional Systems

Annapolis Valley Regional Library
26 Bay Rd., Bridgetown NS B0S 1C0
Tel: 902-665-2995; *Fax:* 902-665-4899
Toll-Free: 866-922-0229
www.valleylibrary.ca
Shirley Pineo, Chair
Frances Newman, Regional Librarian
Charlotte Janes, Head, Systems & Administration

Cape Breton Regional Library
50 Falmouth St., Sydney NS B1P 6X9
Tel: 402-562-3279; *Fax:* 902-564-0765
Other Numbers: 902-562-3279 (Bookmobile services)
inssc@nssc.library.ns.ca
www.cbrl.ca
Rod MacArthur, Chair
Faye MacDougall, Regional Librarian
fmacdoug@nssc.library.ns.ca
Ian R. MacIntosh, Deputy Regional Librarian & Collections Librarian
imacinto@nssc.library.ns.ca
Theresa MacDonald, Librarian, Technical Services
tmacdona@nssc.library.ns.ca
Clare MacKillop, Supervisor, Cape Breton County Branch Libraries
cmackill@nssc.library.ns.ca
Erin Phillips, Supervisor, Victoria County Library Services
ephillip@nssc.library.ns.ca
Rosalie Gillis, Coordinator, Community Support
rgillis@nssc.library.ns.ca
Tara MacNeil, Coordinator, Programs
tmacneil@nssc.library.ns.ca

Colchester-East Hants Public Library
754 Prince St., Truro NS B2N 1G9
Tel: 902-895-0235; *Fax:* 902-895-7149
Toll-Free: 888-632-9088
anstc@nstc.library.ns.ca
cehlibrary.ednet.ns.ca
Janet D. Pelley, Library Director
jpelley@nstc.library.ns.ca
Lesley Brann, Administrator, Adult & Outreach Services
lbrann@nstc.library.ns.ca
Bill Morgan, Administrator, Automated & Technical Services
bmorgan@nstc.library.ns.ca
M. Lynda Marsh, Administrator, Youth Services
lmarsh@nstc.library.ns.ca
Sandra Phillips, Reference Services Librarian
sphillip@nstc.library.ns.ca
Alexandra Care, Electronic Services Librarian
acare@nstc.library.ns.ca

Eastern Counties Regional Library
390 Murray St., Mulgrave NS B0E 2G0
Tel: 902-747-2597; *Fax:* 902-747-2500
info@nsme.library.ns.ca
www.ecrl.library.ns.ca
Shirley McNamara, Chair
Petra Mauerhoff, Chief Librarian
pmauerhoff@nsme.library.ns.ca
Lesley Carruthers, Manager, Outreach Services
lcarruth@nsme.library.ns.ca
Mary Landry, Manager, Public Services & Reference & French Services Librarian
mlandry@nsme.library.ns.ca

Patricia McCormick, Manager, Systems & Technical Services
pmccormi@nsme.library.ns.ca
Mildred Carrigan, Library Assistant, Inter-Library Loans
mcarriga@nsme.library.ns.ca
Lana Hadley, Accounts Administrator
bookkeep@nsme.library.ns.ca

Halifax Public Libraries
60 Alderney Dr., Dartmouth NS B2Y 4P8
Tel: 902-490-5744; *Fax:* 902-490-5889
Other Numbers: 902-490-5753 (Accounts); 903-490-5710 (Research)
www.halifaxpubliclibraries.ca

Leo McKenna, Chair
Judith Hare, Chief Executive Officer
Susan McLean, Deputy CEO & Director, Public Services
Francisca Goldsmith, Director, Branch Services
Bruce Gorman, Director, Information Technology & Collection Management
Al LeBlanc, Director, Finance & Facilities
Cathy Maddigan, Director, Human Resources
Paula Saulnier, Director, Corporate Research & Development
Darlene Beck, Regional Manager, Reference Services
Karen Dahl, Regional Manager, Youth Services
Heather MacKenzie, Regional Manager, Services to Older Adults
Sarah Wenning, Regional Manager, Reader's Services
Kevin Crick, Manager, Information Technology
Denis Cunningham, Manager, Communications & Marketing
Tracey Jones, Manager, Literacy, ESL, & Diversity Services
Debbie LeBel, Manager, Collection Development

Pictou-Antigonish Regional Library
PO Box 276, New Glasgow NS B2H 5E3
Fax: 902-755-6775
Toll-Free: 866-779-7761
estackho@nsngp.library.ns.ca
www.parl.ns.ca

Eric Stackhouse, Chief Librarian, Systems Librarian, & Board Secretary
Fred Popowich, Deputy Chief & Technical Services Librarian
Kristel Fleuren-Hunter, Children's Services Librarian
Trecia Schell, Community Services Librarian
Fern MacDonald, Manager, User Services
Melanie Pauls, Coordinator, Community Access to Technology

Western Counties Regional Library
405 Main St., Yarmouth NS B5A 1G3
Tel: 902-742-2486; *Fax:* 902-742-6920
insy@nsy.library.ns.ca (Interlibrary loans)
www.westerncounties.ca

Gary Archibald, Chair
ansy@nsy.library.ns.ca
Trudy Amirault, Regional Library Director
tamiraul@nsy.library.ns.ca
Joanne Head, Deputy Director
jhead@nsy.library.ns.ca
Richard Beharriell, Coordinator, Library Services
rbeharriell@nsy.library.ns.ca
Erin Comeau, Coordinator, Library Services
ecomeau@nsy.library.ns.ca
Deborah Duke Little, Coordinator, Library Services
dlittle@nsy.library.ns.ca
Yvonne LeBlanc, Manager, Office
ansy@nsy.library.ns.ca
Ian White, Manager, Public Relations
iwhite@nsy.library.ns.ca
Scott MacMullen, Supervisor, Maintenance, Buildings & Vehicles & System Administrator
smacmull@nsy.library.ns.ca
Carol Surette, Bookkeeper
csurette@nsy.library.ns.ca

Public Libraries

***Amherst:* Cumberland Regional Library**
PO Box 220, Amherst NS B4H 3Z2
Tel: 902-667-2135; *Fax:* 902-667-1360
crl@nsamc.library.ns.ca
www.crl.library.ns.ca

Robert Angel, Chair
Beth Clinton, Chief Librarian & Board Secretary
Denise Corey, Deputy Chief Librarian

***Halifax:* Épilogue**
c/o Faculty of Management, Dalhousie University, Halifax NS B3H 3J5
Tel: 902-494-3656; *Fax:* 902-494-2451
Bertrum H. MacDonald, Editor

***Halifax:* Occasional Papers Series**
c/o Faculty of Management, Dalhousie University, Halifax NS B3H 3J5
Tel: 902-494-3656; *Fax:* 902-494-2451
sim@dal.ca
www.sim.management.dal.ca/Research_and_Publications/Descripti

Fiona Black, Editor
fiona.black@dal.ca

***Halifax:* Y-A Hotline**
c/o Faculty of Management, Dalhousie University, Halifax NS B3H 3J5
Tel: 902-494-3656; *Fax:* 902-494-2451
howardv@dal.ca
www.mgmt.dal.ca/slis/Publications/YAHotline.html
Vivian Howard, Editor

***Hebbville:* South Shore Regional Library**
Bldg. 15442, Hwy. #3, PO Box 34, Hebbville NS B4V 2W3
Tel: 902-543-2548; *Fax:* 902-543-8191
Toll-Free: 877-455-2548
info@southshorepubliclibraries.ca
www.southshorepubliclibraries.ca

Cheryl Stenström, Chief Librarian
Jeff Mercer, Branch/Extension/Systems Librarian
Cathy MacDonald, Mobile Branch/Technical Services Librarian

Archives

***Amherst:* Cumberland County Museum & Archives**
150 Church St., Amherst NS B4H 3C4
Tel: 902-667-2561; *Fax:* 902-667-0996
ccmuseum@ns.aliantzinc.ca
www.cumberlandcountymuseum.com
Social Media: www.facebook.com/group.php?gid=148688355199338
Shirley Nickerson, Manager/Curator

***Annapolis Royal:* Historic Restoration Society of Annapolis County**
136 St. George St., Annapolis Royal NS B0S 1A0
Tel: 902-532-7754; *Fax:* 902-532-0700
Ryan Scranton, Executive Director
scrantrg@gov.ns.ca

***Antigonish:* Antigonish Heritage Museum**
20 East Main St., Antigonish NS B2G 2E9
Tel: 902-863-6160
www.parl.ns.ca/aheritage
Jocelyn Gillis, Manager

***Baddeck:* Alexander Graham Bell National Historic Site/ Lieu Historique National Alexander Graham Bell**
559 Chebucto St., Baddeck NS B0E 1B0
Tel: 902-295-2069; *Fax:* 902-295-3496
TDD: 9022951512
aynsley.macfarlane@pc.gc.ca
bell.uccb.ns.ca
Aynsley MacFarlane, Site Manager

***Barrington:* Cape Sable Historical Society Centre**
2402 Hwy. 3, Barrington NS B0W 1E0
Tel: 902-637-2185
barmuseumcomplex@eastlink.ca
www.capesablehistoricalsociety.com/

Brenda Maxwell, Archives Manager
maxwelbm@gov.ns.ca

***Barss Corners:* Parkdale-Maplewood Community Museum**
3005 Barss Corner Rd., Barss Corners NS B0R 1A0
Tel: 902-644-2893; *Fax:* 902-644-3422
Other Numbers: Off-season: 902-644-2375
p-mcm@hotmail.com
parkdale.ednet.ns.ca

Barbara Gail Wentzell, Curator
p-mcm@hotmail.com
Donna Arenburg, Museum Assistant
donna_arenburg@hotmail.com

***Bridgetown:* Bridgetown & Area Historical Society**
12 Queen St., PO Box 645, Bridgetown NS B0S 1C0
Tel: 902-665-4530
www.jameshousemuseum.com
Frances Nixon, Museum Administrator

***Bridgewater:* DesBrisay Museum**
130 Jubilee Rd., Bridgewater NS B4V 3X9
Tel: 902-543-4033; *Fax:* 902-543-4713
museum@bridgewater.ca
www.desbrisaymuseum.ca
Social Media: www.facebook.com/pages/DesBrisay-Museum/190907454254694

Linda Bedford, Curator
lbedford@bridgewater.ca

***Canso:* Canso Historical Society**
c/o Whitman House Museum, 1297 Union St., Canso NS B0H 1H0
Tel: 902-366-2170; *Fax:* 902-366-3093
cansotouristbureau@ns.sympatico.ca

***Centreville:* Archelaus Smith Museum**
915 Hwy. 330, Centreville NS B0W 1P0
Tel: 902-745-2642
blancherossoconnell@hotmail.com
www.archelaus.org/index.html

Charla Strang, Treasurer
902-745-0428
Blanche O'Connell, President
blancherossoconnell@hotmail.com
902-745-2642
Willamae Ross, Secretary
902-745-3343

***Church Point:* St Mary's Museum/ Le Musée Sainte Marie**
PO Box 28, 1713 Hwy 1, Church Point NS B0W 1M0
Tel: 902-769-2378; *Fax:* 902-769-0048
http://www.museeeglisesaintemariemuseum.ca
Blanche Forrest, Secretary, Museum Committee

***Dartmouth:* Black Cultural Centre for Nova Scotia**
1149 Main St., Dartmouth NS B2Z 1A8
Tel: 902-434-6223; *Fax:* 902-434-2306
Toll-Free: 800-465-0767
mail@bccns.com
www.bccns.com

Henry Bishop, Chief Curator
Russell Grosse, Museum Assistant

***Dartmouth:* Cole Harbour Rural Heritage Society**
471 Poplar Dr., Dartmouth NS B2W 4L2
Tel: 905-434-0222
farm.museum@ns.aliantzinc.ca
coleharbourfarmmuseum.ca

***Dartmouth:* Dartmouth Heritage Museum**
Evergreen House, 26 Newcastle St., Dartmouth NS B2Y 3M5
Tel: 902-464-2300; *Fax:* 902-464-8210
dhmuseum@ednet.ns.ca
www.dartmouthheritagemuseum.ns.ca
Anita Price, Curator

***Halifax:* Canadian Broadcasting Corporation (Halifax)/ Société Radio-Canada (Halifax)**
PO Box 3000, Halifax NS B3J 3E9
Tel: 902-420-4160; *Fax:* 902-420-4281
doug.kirby@cbc.ca
www.novascotia.cbc.ca

Doug Kirby, Media Library Coordinator
doug_kirby@cbc.ca
902-420-4160
Gordon Warren, Media Librarian
gordon.warren@cbc.ca
902-420-4186

***Halifax:* Nova Scotia Archives & Records Management**
6016 University Ave., Halifax NS B3H 1W4
Tel: 902-424-6060; *Fax:* 902-424-0628
nsarm@gov.ns.ca
www.gov.ns.ca/nsarm
W. Brian Speirs, Provincial Archivist

***Halifax:* Nova Scotia Sport Hall of Fame**
#446, 1800 Argyle St., Halifax NS B3J 3N8
Tel: 902-421-1266; *Fax:* 902-425-1148
sporthalloffame@eastlink.ca
www.novascotiasporthalloffame.com

Bill Robinson, Executive Director
billr@eastlink.ca
Shane Mailman, Facility & Communications Manager
sporthalloffame@eastlink.ca

Halifax: **Pier 21**
1055 Marginal Rd., Halifax NS B3H 4P6
Tel: 902-425-7770; *Fax:* 902-423-4045
library@pier21.ca
www.pier21.ca
Carrie-Ann Smith, Research Librarian

Halifax: **The Shambhala Archives**
1084 Tower Rd., Halifax NS B3H 2Y5
Tel: 902-420-1118; *Fax:* 902-423-2750
archives@shambhala.org
www.shambhala.org/archives

Halifax: **Sisters of Charity of St. Vincent de Paul - Halifax**
Sisters of Charity Centre, 215 Seton Rd., Halifax NS B3M 0C9
Tel: 902-406-8136; *Fax:* 902-457-3506
archives@schalifax.ca
www.schalifax.ca
Patti Bannister, Congregational Archivist

Liverpool: **The Thomas Raddall Research Centre**
109 Main St., Liverpool NS B0T 1K0
Tel: 902-354-4058; *Fax:* 902-354-2050
rafusela@gov.ns.ca
queensmuseum.netfirms.com/archives.html
Linda Rafuse, Director

Middleton: **Macdonald Museum**
21 School St., Middleton NS B0S 1P0
Tel: 902-825-6116; *Fax:* 902-825-0531
macdonald.museum@ns.sympatico.ca
www.macdonaldmuseum.ca
Alison Brathwaite, Librarian & Curatorial Assistant

Parrsboro: **Parrsborough Shore Historical Society**
PO Box 98, Parrsboro NS B0M 1S0
Tel: 902-254-2899
Susan Clarke, Manager
ottawa.house@ns.sympatico.ca
Conrad Byers, Genealogist
June Wagestaff, Assistant Manager

Pictou: **Hector Exhibit Centre**
86 Haliburton Rd., Pictou NS B0K 1H0
Tel: 902-485-4563; *Fax:* 902-485-5213
pcghs@gov.ns.ca
www.rootsweb.com/~nspcghs/
Marlene Chisholm, Researcher
marlene.chisholm@ns.sympatico.ca

Port Hastings: **Port Hastings Historical Museum & Archives**
9 Church St., Port Hastings NS B9A 1N5
Tel: 902-625-1295
gutofcanso@ns.sympatico.ca
Beryl MacDonald-MacLeod, Curator
Dernie Gillis, Historical Society President

Shearwater: **Shearwater Aviation Museum**
12 Wing Shearwater, PO Box 5000, Stn Main, Shearwater NS B0J 3A0
Tel: 902-720-2165; *Fax:* 902-720-2037
info@shearwateraviationmuseum.ns.ca
www.shearwateraviationmuseum.ns.ca
Social Media: http://twitter.com/#!/YAWmuseum;
www.facebook.com/shearwateraviationmuseum
Christine Dunphy, Librarian/Archivist
902-720-2165

Shelburne: **Shelburne County Museum**
20 Dock St., Shelburne NS B0T 1W0
Tel: 902-875-3219; *Fax:* 902-875-4141
shelburne.museum@ns.sympatico.ca
www.historicshelburne.com
Finn Bower, Curator
Betty Stoddard, Assistant Curator

Truro: **Colchester Historical Society Museum and Archives**
29 Young St., Truro NS B2N 3W3
Tel: 902-895-6284; *Fax:* 902-895-9530
colchesterarchives@ns.aliantzinc.ca
http://colchesterhistoreum.ca/
Nan D. Harvey, Archivist
Penny Lighthall, Curator

Tusket: **Argyle Township Court House Archives**
8162 Hwy. 3, PO Box 101, Tusket NS B0W 3M0
Tel: 902-648-2493; *Fax:* 902-648-2537
pcrowell@argylecourthouse.com
www.argylecourthouse.com
Peter Crowell, Municipal Records Manager & Archivist
pcrowell@argylecourthouse.com

Windsor: **West Hants Historical Society**
281 King St., Windsor NS B0N 2T0
Tel: 902-798-4706; *Fax:* 902-798-8535
whhs@glinx.com
www.glinx.com/users/whhs
Lilla Siderius, Head

Yarmouth: **Yarmouth County Museum Research Library & Archives**
22 Collins St., Yarmouth NS B5A 3C8
Tel: 902-742-5539; *Fax:* 902-749-1120
ycarchives@eastlink.ca
yarmouthcountymuseum.ednet.ns.ca
Jamie Serran, Archivist

Nunavut

Regional Systems

Nunavut Public Library Services
PO Box 270, Baker Lake NU X0C 0A0
Tel: 867-793-3327; *Fax:* 867-793-3332
Robin Brown, Acting Manager, Library Policy
rbrown2@gov.nu.ca
867-793-3327
Derek Yap, Electronic Services Librarian
Taryl Gula, Community Services Librarian
Lucy Niego, Secretary/Clerk

Public Libraries

Arviat: **Donald Suluk Library**
PO Bag 4000, Arviat NU X0C 0E0
Tel: 867-857-2579; *Fax:* 867-857-4048
www.publiclibraries.nu.ca/communities.html
Diane Sigurdson, Local Librarian

Baker Lake: **Thomas Tapatai Library**
PO Box 150, Baker Lake NU X0C 0A0
Tel: 867-793-4657; *Fax:* 867-793-4659
ttlbaker@yahoo.ca
Sally Aaruaq, Local Librarian

Cambridge Bay: **May Hakongak Community Library**
PO Box 2160, Cambridge Bay NU X0B 0C0
Tel: 867-983-2163; *Fax:* 867-983-3397
cfirlotte@publiclibraries.nu.ca
www.kitikmeotheritage.ca/exhibits.htm
Carmen Firlotte, Local Librarian
cfirlotte@publiclibraries.nu.ca

Clyde River: **Clyde River Community Library**
c/o Ilisaqsivik Family Resource Centre, Ilisaqsivik Society, PO Box 150, Clyde River NU X0A 0E0
Tel: 867-924-6565; *Fax:* 867-924-6570
www.ilisaqsivik.ca
Raygee Atsiqtaq, Local Librarian
ratsiqtaq@publiclibraries.nu.ca

Igloolik: **Igloolik Amitturmiut Library**
PO Box 30, Igloolik NU X0A 0L0
Tel: 867-934-8812; *Fax:* 867-934-8779
nubnp@gov.nu.ca
Nancy Kadlutsika, Local Librarian
nkadlutsiak@publiclibraries.nu.ca

Iqaluit: **Iqaluit Centennial Library**
Unikkaarvik Bldg., PO Bag 189A, Iqaluit NU X0A 0H0
Tel: 867-979-5400; *Fax:* 867-979-1373
nuic@gov.nu.ca
www.publiclibraries.nu.ca/communities.html
Madeleine Cornthwaite, Librarian
mcornthwaite@gov.nu.ca

Kugluktuk: **Kugluktuk Community Library**
PO Box 190, Kugluktuk NU X0B 0E0
Tel: 867-982-4406; *Fax:* 867-982-3404
jongahak@publiclibraries.nu.ca
Jennifer Ongahak, Local Librarian
jongahak@publiclibraries.nu.ca

Nanisivik: **Nanisivik Community Library**
PO Box 115, Nanisivik NU X0A 0X0
Tel: 867-436-7445; *Fax:* 867-436-7235
Ley Cheverie, Librarian
867-436-7445

Pangnirtung: **Qimiruvik Library**
Angmarlik Centre, PO Box 403, Pangnirtung NU X0A 0R0
Tel: 867-473-8678; *Fax:* 867-473-8685
lnauyuq@publiclibraries.nu.ca
Lorna Nauyuq, Local Librarian
867-473-8678

Pond Inlet: **Rebecca P. Idlout Library**
Bldg. 215, Pond Inlet NU X0A 0S0
Tel: 867-899-8972; *Fax:* 867-899-8175
pondinletlibrary@yahoo.ca
Ezrah Kasarnak, Librarian

Rankin Inlet: **John Ayaruaq Library**
PO Bag 002, Rankin Inlet NU X0C 0G0
Tel: 867-645-8081; *Fax:* 867-645-8082
ftheytaz@publiclibraries.nu.ca
Fabienne Theyez, Local Librarian
library@artic.ca
867-645-8081

Archives

Iqaluit: **Nunatta Sunakkutangit Museum**
Bldg. 212, PO Box 1900, Iqaluit NU X0A 0H0
Tel: 867-979-5537; *Fax:* 867-979-4533
Brian Lunger, Manager/Curator
museum@nunanet.com

Iqaluit: **Nunavut Dept. of Culture, Language, Elders & Youth**
Bldg. 917, 2nd Fl. PO Box 1000, Stn 800, Iqaluit NU X0A 0H0
Tel: 867-975-5500; *Fax:* 867-975-5504
www.cley.gov.nu.ca/en/archive.aspx
Edward Atkinson, Territorial Archivist & Historian

Ontario

Regional Systems

Ontario Library Service North/ Service des bibliothèques de l'Ontario nord
334 Regent St., Sudbury ON P3C 4E2
Tel: 705-675-6467; *Fax:* 705-675-2285
Toll-Free: 800-461-6348
www.olsn.ca
Leanne Clendening, CEO
lclendening@olsn.ca
705-675-6467 ext. 209
Lorraine Leblanc, Deputy CEO
lleblanc@olsn.ca
705-675-6467 ext. 231

Southern Ontario Library Service (SOLS)
#902, 111 Peter St., Toronto ON M5H 2H1
Tel: 416-961-1669; *Fax:* 416-961-5122
Toll-Free: 800-387-5765
www.sols.org
Laurey Gillies, CEO
lgillies@sols.org
Daryl Novak, Director, Operations
dnovak@sols.org

Public Libraries

Addison: **Elizabethtown/Kitley Twp Public Library**
6544 New Dublin Rd., RR#2, Addison ON K0E 1A0
Tel: 613-345-7480; *Fax:* 613-345-7235
Toll-Free: 800-492-3175
mail@elizabethtown-kitley.on.ca
www.elizabethtown-kitley.on.ca/library.htm
Ruth Blanchard, Librarian

Ajax: **Ajax Public Library**
55 Harwood Ave. South, Ajax ON L1S 2H8
Tel: 905-683-4000; *Fax:* 905-683-6960
libraryinfo@townofajax.com
www.townofajax.com/library
Geoffrey Nie, Chief Librarian
geoff.nie@townofajax.com
905-683-4000 ext. 8825
Dan Gioiosa, Support Services Manager
dan.gioiosa@townofajax.com
905-683-4000 ext. 8824
Cindy Kimber, Branch Service Coordinator
cindy.kimber@townofajax.com
905-683-4000 ext. 8902
Cindy Poon, Public Service Manager
cindy.poon@townofajax.com
905-683-4000 ext. 8801

***Alban:* French River Public Library/ Bibliothèque publique de la Rivière-des-français**
796 Chemin/Hwy 64, Alban ON P0M 1A0
Tel: 705-857-1771; *Fax:* 705-857-1392
anceo@on.aibn.com
www.frenchriverlibrary.ca
Suzanne Duval, Librarian
anceo@on.aibn.com
705-898-2965

***Alliston:* New Tecumseth Public Library**
17 Victoria St. East, Alliston ON L9R 1T3
Tel: 705-435-0250; *Fax:* 705-435-0750
www.ntpl.ca
Paula Coutts, CEO
pcoutts@ntpl.ca
Margaret Doucette, Administrative Assistant

***Almonte:* Mississippi Mills Public Library**
155 High St., Almonte ON K0A 1A0
Tel: 613-256-1037
pnelson@mississippimills.ca
www.mississippimills.com/library
Peter Nelson, Chief Librarian
Monica Blackburn, Contact, ILL & Children's Services

***Angus:* Essa Centennial Library**
18 King St., Angus ON L0M 1B2
Tel: 705-424-6531; *Fax:* 705-424-5512
essalib@essa.library.on.ca
www.essa.library.on.ca
Janine Harris-Wheatley, CEO
ceoadmin@essa.library.on.ca
705-424-2679
Shaun Fox, Coordinator of Public Service
Angie Wishart, Coordinator of Support Services

***Apsley:* North Kawartha Public Library**
175 Burleigh St., PO Box 335, Apsley ON K0L 1A0
Tel: 705-656-4333; *Fax:* 705-656-2538
info@northkawarthalibrary.com
www.northkawarthalibrary.com
Shannon Hunter, CEO
s.hunter@northkawartha.on.ca
Debbie Hall, Librarian
d.hall@northkawarthalibrary.com
Susan Suhr, Technical Services Coordinator
s.suhr@northkawarthalibrary.com

***Arnprior:* Arnprior Public Library**
21 Madawaska St., Arnprior ON K7S 1R6
Tel: 613-623-2279; *Fax:* 613-623-0281
library@arncap.com
www.arncap.com/library/index.htm
Neil Salminen, Chair
Susan Robert, Chief Librarian
Karen DeLuca, Children's & Teen Services Librarian
Betty Robertson, Interlibrary Loan Contact

***Astorville:* East Ferris Public Library/ Bibliothèque publique d'East Ferris**
1257 Village Rd., PO Box 160, Astorville ON P0H 1B0
Tel: 705-752-2042; *Fax:* 705-752-2042
efpl@onlink.net
www.olsn.ca/east_ferrispl
Christine Joly, Co-Chair
Norma McQuoid, Co-Chair
Jennifer Laporte, Chief Executive Officer
Connie Lortie, Library Assistant

***Athens:* Township of Athens Public Library**
5 Central St., Athens ON K0E 1B0
Tel: 613-924-2048
athenspl@bellnet.ca
Freda Schaafsma, Head Librarian
613-924-9036
Hennie Janssens, Children's Librarian

***Atikokan:* Atikokan Public Library**
Civic Centre, Atikokan ON P0T 1C0
Tel: 807-597-4406; *Fax:* 807-597-1514
jlewis@aplibrary.org
www.aplibrary.org
Jonathan Lewis, CEO/Librarian
jlewis@aplibrary.org
807-594-4406
Tracey Sinclair, Head of Children's Services
tsinclair@nwconx.net

***Aurora:* Aurora Public Library**
15145 Yonge St., Aurora ON L4G 1M1
Tel: 905-727-9493; *Fax:* 905-727-9374
Other Numbers: Telecirc 905-727-0314
www.library.aurora.on.ca
Louise Procter Maio, CEO
lproctermaio@library.aurora.on.ca
905-727-9494 ext. 221

***Bala:* Wahta Mohawks Public Library**
2664, Muskoka Rd. #38, Bala ON P0C 1A0
Tel: 705-756-2354; *Fax:* 705-756-2376
www.wahta.ca/programs.htm
Shirley Sahanatien, CEO

***Bancroft:* Bancroft Public Library**
14 Flint St., Bancroft ON K0L 1C0
Tel: 613-332-3380; *Fax:* 613-332-5473
bancroftlibrary@bellnet.ca
www.bancroftpubliclibrary.ca
Kimberly McMunn, CEO

***Barrie:* Barrie Public Library**
60 Worsley St., Barrie ON L4M 1L6
Tel: 705-728-1010; *Fax:* 705-728-4322
barlib@barrie.ca
www.library.barrie.on.ca
Al Davis, Director of Library Services
adavis@barrie.ca
705-728-1010 ext. 7500
Khuan Seow, Manager, Information Technology
kseow@barrie.ca
705-728-1010 ext. 7010
Shonna Froebel, Manager, Adult Information Services
sfroebel@barrie.ca
705-728-1010 ext. 7007
Jane Salmon, Manager, Children's & Youth Services
jsalmon@barrie.ca
705-728-1010 ext. 7017
Heather Betz, Business Officer
hbetz@barrie.ca
705-728-1010 ext. 7006

***Barry's Bay:* Barry's Bay & Area Public Library**
19474 Opeongo Line, Barry's Bay ON K0J 1B0
Tel: 613-756-2000; *Fax:* 613-756-2000
bblibry@bellnet.ca
library.barrys-bay.ca
Angela E. Lorbetskie, Librarian

***Baysville:* Lake of Bays Public Library**
Community Centre, 10 University Ave., Baysville ON P0B 1A0
Tel: 705-767-2361; *Fax:* 705-767-2361
www.lakeofbayslibrary.ca
David Johnstone, Chair
lakeofbaysboard@vianet.ca
Linda Lacroix, Chief Executive Officer
linla@vianet.on.ca

***Beamsville:* Lincoln Public Library**
4996 Beam St., Beamsville ON L0R 1B0
Tel: 905-563-7014; *Fax:* 905-563-1810
info@lincoln.library.on.ca
www.lincoln.library.on.ca
Jill Nicholson, CEO
nicholson@lincoln.library.on.ca

***Bear Island:* Temagami First Nation Public Library/ Bibliothèque publique de Tribu Temagami**
General Delivery, Bear Island ON P0H 1C0
Tel: 705-237-8876; *Fax:* 705-237-8959
www.temagamifirstnation.ca/
Virginia Mackenzie, CEO
705-237-8876

***Bearskin Lake:* Bearskin Lake Public Library/ Bibliotheque Publique de Bearskin**
Bearskin Lake ON P0V 1E0
Tel: 807-363-2518; *Fax:* 807-363-1066
Robert Mickenack, Councillor

***Beaverton:* Brock Township Public Libraries**
401 Simcoe St., PO Box 310, Beaverton ON L0K 1A0
Tel: 705-426-9283; *Fax:* 705-426-9353
info@brocklibraries.ca
www.brocklibraries.ca
Karen Enss, Chair
karenenss@brocklibraries.ca
705-432-3241
Rona O'Banion, Chief Executive Officer
ronaobanion@brocklibraries.ca
Cheryl Dillon, Coordinator, Systems
cheryldillon@brocklibraries.ca
Cheryl Jabour, Children's Librarian
cheryljabour@brocklibraries.ca

***Belleville:* Belleville Public Library**
254 Pinnacle St., Belleville ON K8N 3A1
Tel: 613-968-6731; *Fax:* 613-968-6841
Other Numbers: Telecirc: 613-968-4708
www.bellevillelibrary.com
Lesley Bell, CEO
lbell@bellevillelibrary.com
613-968-6731 ext. 2222
Trevor Pross, Manager, Public & Virtual Services
tpross@bellevillelibrary.com
613-968-6731 ext. 2241
Fanny Tom, Head of Circulation
ftom@bellevillelibrary.com
613-968-6731 ext. 2243
Soyoung Lee, Children's Librarian
slee@bellevillelibrary.com
613-968-6731 ext. 2246
Susan Holland, Gallery Curator
gallery@bellevillelibrary.com
613-986-6731 ext. 2239

***Birch Island:* Whitefish River First Nation Public Library**
46 Bay of Islands Rd., Birch Island ON P0P 1A0
Tel: 705-285-0028; *Fax:* 705-285-4532
whitefishriverfirstnationlibrary@hotmail.com
www.whitefishriver.ca/admin/public_library.htm
Gregor Jocko, CEO/Librarian
705-285-0028

***Blenheim:* Caldwell First Nation Library**
RR#2, 10297 Talbot Rd., Blenheim ON N0P 1A0
Tel: 519-676-5499
Larry Johnson, Chief

***Blind River:* Blind River Public Library/ Bibliothèque de Blind River**
8 Woodward Ave., Blind River ON P0R 1B0
Tel: 705-356-7616
brpl@onlink.net
www.onlink.net/~brpl

***Blind River:* Mississauga First Nation Library**
148 Village Rd., Blind River ON P0R 1B0
Tel: 705-356-5335; *Fax:* 705-356-4206
mfnlibrary@onlink.net
www.onlink.net/~mfnlib/library.htm
Sherry Caibaiosai, Librarian

***Bonfield:* Bonfield Public Library**
365 Hwy. 531, Bonfield ON P0H 1E0
Tel: 705-776-2396; *Fax:* 705-776-1154
bpl@ontera.net
www.ontera.net/~bpl
Greg Boxwell, Chair

***Borden:* Borden Public & Military Library/ Bibliothèque publique et militaire de Borden**
Bldg. E-102, 41 Kapyong Rd., Borden ON L0M 1C0
Tel: 705-424-1200
www.borden.forces.gc.ca/998/89/46/52-eng.asp
Donald Allen, Chief Librarian

***Bowmanville:* Clarington Public Library**
163 Church St., Bowmanville ON L1C 1T7
Tel: 905-623-7322
Other Numbers: 905-623-7322, ext. 731 (Interlibrary loans)
info@clarington-library.on.ca
www.clarington-library.on.ca
Edith Hopkins, Chief Executive Officer
Linda Del Grande, Manager, Support Services
Darlene McCann, Coordinator, Circulation
Linda Del Grande, Manager, Branch Services
ldelgrande@clarington-library.on.ca
905-326-7322 ext. 721
Judy Pell, Manager, Administrative Services
Allan Hewitt, Chair
Tammy Johnson, Marketing & Partnerships Librarian
tjohnson@clarington-library.on.ca
905-623-7322 ext. 775
Trevor Pross, Coordinator, Children's Services
tpross@clarington-library.on.ca
905-623-7322 ext. 732

***Bracebridge:* Bracebridge Public Library**
94 Manitoba St., Bracebridge ON P1L 2B5
Tel: 705-645-4171; *Fax:* 705-645-6551
bracelib@vianet.on.ca
www.bracebridge.library.on.ca

Cathryn Rodney, CEO/Chief Librarian
crodney@vianet.ca

Bradford: Bradford West Gwillimbury Public Library
100 Holland Ct., Bradford ON L3Z 2A7
Tel: 905-775-3328; *Fax:* 905-775-1236
bwgmailbox@bradford.library.on.ca
www.bradford.library.on.ca
Gary Lamb, Chair
Liz Fenwick, Chief Executive Officer

Brampton: Brampton Library
65 Queen St. East, Brampton ON L6W 3L6
Tel: 905-793-4636
info@bramlib.on.ca
www.bramlib.on.ca
Adele Kostiak, Chief Executive Officer
akostiak@bramlib.on.ca
905-793-4636 ext. 4311
Lesley Bates, Manager, Corporate Services & Planning
lbates@bramlib.on.ca
905-793-4636 ext. 4361
Judy Hyland, Manager, Information Services
jhyland@bramlib.on.ca
905-793-4636 ext. 4368
Arthur Sykes, Manager, Library Systems
asykes@bramlib.on.ca
905-793-4636 ext. 4107
Sherri Bain, Coordinator, Children's Services
sbain@bramlib.on.ca
905-793-4636 ext. 4325

Brantford: Brantford Public Library
173 Colborne St., Brantford ON N3T 2G8
Tel: 519-756-2220; *Fax:* 519-756-4979
info@brantford.library.on.ca
http://brantford.library.on.ca
Social Media: http://twitter.com/#!/BtfdLibrary;
www.facebook.com/group.php?gid=112507975464133
Penny MacKenzie, Chair
penny_mackenzie@hotmail.com
519-753-9887
Rose Vespa, Chief Executive Officer
rvespa@brantford.library.on.ca

Bridgenorth: Smith-Ennismore-Lakefield Public Library
826 Ward St., Bridgenorth ON K0L 1H0
Tel: 705-292-5065; *Fax:* 705-292-6695
www.mypubliclibrary.ca
Joan MacDonald, Librarian
jmacdonald@mypubliclibrary.ca

Brighton: Brighton Public Library
35 Alice St., Brighton ON K0K 1H0
Tel: 613-475-2511; *Fax:* 613-475-3453
brightonpl@gmail.com
www.brighton.library.on.ca
Peter Gysbers, Chair
Maureen Venton, Library Chief Executive Officer
Sharon Bugg, Assistant Librarian
Jeni Dyment, Contact, Children's Library

Britt: Britt Public Library
841 Riverside Dr., Britt ON P0G 1A0
Tel: 705-383-2292; *Fax:* 705-383-0077
britt.lib@hotmail.com
www.olsn.ca/BrittPL
Barbara Wohleber, Chief Executive Officer

Britt: Magnetawan First Nation Public Library/ Bibliothèque publique de Prèmiere Nation de Magnetawan
Box 15, RR#1, Britt ON P0G 1A0
Tel: 705-383-2477; *Fax:* 705-383-2566
mfnlibrary@hotmail.com
Wanda Noganosh, Librarian

Brockville: Augusta Township Public Library
4500 County Rd. 15, RR#2, Brockville ON K6V 5T2
Tel: 613-926-2449; *Fax:* 613-926-0440
augusta@augustalibrary.com
www.augustalibrary.com
Jacquie Kelly, Chair
Angie Knights, Librarian
Linda Parrott, Librarian

Brockville: Brockville Public Library
23 Buell St., Brockville ON K6V 5T7
Tel: 613-342-3936; *Fax:* 613-342-9598
info@brockvillelibrary.ca
www.brockvillelibrary.ca
Margaret Wicklum, Chair
Margaret Williams, Chief Executive Officer & Chief Librarian
margaret@brockvillelibrary.ca
613-342-3936 ext. 22
Cindy Fischer, Manager, Office
cindy@brockvillelibrary.ca
613-342-3936 ext. 23
Amanda Robinson, Manager, Access Services
amanda@brockvillelibrary.ca
613-342-3936 ext. 24
Margie Bentley, Contact, Local History Files
margie@brockvillelibrary.ca
613-342-3936 ext. 21
Lisa Cirka, Contact, Children's Services & Young Adult Services
lisa@brockvillelibrary.ca
613-342-3936 ext. 21
Laura Julien, Contact, Interlibrary Loan & Book Club Service
613-342-3936 ext. 28
Dena Kreissler, Contact, Shut-In Services
dena@brockvillelibrary.ca
613-342-3936 ext. 21

Bruce Mines: Bruce Mines & Plummer Additional Union Public Library
33 Desbarats St., Bruce Mines ON P0R 1C0
Tel: 705-785-3370; *Fax:* 705-785-3370
bmpa@ontera.net
www.bruceminesandplummerlibrary.ca
Lorelee Gordon, CEO/Librarian
Jackie Bloye, Clerk

Buckhorn: Galway-Cavendish & Harvey Twp Public Library
5 George St., Buckhorn ON K0L 1J0
Tel: 705-657-3695; *Fax:* 705-657-3695
www.galwaycavendishharveylibrary.ca/
Social Media: www.facebook.com/group.php?gid=30135419972
Maria Bradburn, CEO
Mary Syvret, Assistant Librarian
Gloria Curry, Library Assistant

Burks Falls: Burks Falls, Armour & Ryerson Union Public Library
39 Copeland St., Burks Falls ON P0A 1C0
Tel: 705-382-3327; *Fax:* 705-382-3327
bflib1@surenet.net
www.surenet.net/~bflib1
Sandy Henshall, CEO

Burlington: Burlington Public Library
2331 New St., Burlington ON L7R 1J4
Tel: 905-639-3611; *Fax:* 905-681-7277
askalibrarian@bpl.on.ca
www.bpl.on.ca
Maureen Barry, CEO
barrym@bpl.on.ca
905-639-3611 ext. 100
Andrea Gordon, Interim Director, Service Development
gordona@bpl.on.ca
905-639-3611 ext. 101
Rick Craig, Director, Finance & Facilities
craigr@bpl.on.ca
905-639-3611 ext. 102
Linda Dobson, Director, Human Resources
dobsonl@bpl.on.ca
905-693-3611 ext. 163

Burlington: The Courier
c/o AIC Investment Services Inc., 1375 Kerns Rd., Burlington ON L7R 4X8
Tel: 905-331-4242; *Fax:* 905-331-4309
sblundell@aic.com
www.sla.org/chapter/ctor/newsletter/courierinfo.asp
Elizabeth Malak-McMullan, Editor
Heather Postill, Editor

Calabogie: Greater Madawaska Public Library
4984 Calabogie Rd., Calabogie ON K0J 1H0
Tel: 613-752-2317; *Fax:* 613-752-2617
mjhale@bellnet.ca
www.townshipofgreatermadawaska.com/library.htm
Mary-Joan Hale, CEO/Librarian
mjhale@bellnet.ca
613-752-2317

Caledon East: Caledon Public Library
6500 Old Church Rd., Caledon East ON L7C 0H3
Tel: 905-584-1456; *Fax:* 905-584-1374
www.caledon.library.on.ca
Bill Manson, Chief Executive Officer
bmanson@caledon.library.on.ca
519-927-5662
Gillian Booth-Moyle, Contact, Technical Services
gboothmoyle@caledon.library.on.ca
905-584-1456 ext. 224
Mary Maw, Contact, Communications & Programming
mmaw@caledon.library.on.ca
905-857-1431 ext. 228
Kelley Potter, Contact, Juvenile & Young Adult Services
kpotter@caledon.library.on.ca
905-857-1431 ext. 238
Mojgan Schmalenberg, Contact, Technology Services
mschmale@caledon.library.on.ca
905-857-1431 ext. 237
Sharon Wilson, Contact, Westside Branches
swilson@caledon.library.on.ca
905-584-1456 ext. 222

Callander: Callander Public Library
30 Catherine St., Callander ON P0H 1H0
Tel: 705-752-2544; *Fax:* 705-752-2819
apeden@ontera.net
www.mycallander.ca/library/library-home/
Alison Peden, CEO
705-752-2544

Calstock: Constance Lake First Nation Public Library
2 Musko St., PO Box 5000, Calstock ON P0L 1B0
Tel: 705-463-1199; *Fax:* 705-463-2077
suthliz@clfn.on.ca
Lizzie Sutherland, CEO
suthliz@clfn.on.ca

Cambridge: Cambridge Libraries & Galleries
1 North Sq., Cambridge ON N1S 2K6
Tel: 519-621-0460; *Fax:* 519-621-2080
www.cambridgelibraries.ca
Marilyn Scott, Board Chair
Greg Hayton, CEO
ghayton@cambridgelibraries.ca
Mary Misner, Gallery Director
mmisner@cambridgegalleries.ca
Cathy Kiedrowski, Head, Information Services
ckiedrowski@cambridgelibraries.ca
519-621-0460 ext. 118
Nancy Ryan, Volunteer Coordinator
519-621-0460 ext. 121
Lucie Martel, Librarian

Campbellford: Trent Hills Public Library
98 Bridge St. East, Campbellford ON K0L 1L0
Tel: 705-653-3611; *Fax:* 705-653-4611
trenthillslibrary@trenthills.ca
www.trenthillslibrary.ca
Donna Wilson, CEO

Carleton Place: Carleton Place Public Library
101 Beckwith St., Carleton Place ON K7C 2T3
Tel: 613-257-2702
carletonlibdsl@vianet.ca
www.carletonplace.ca
Janet Baril, Librarian

Cartier: Cartier Public Library/ Bibliothèque publique de Cartier
Lansdowne St., PO Box 1000, Cartier ON P0M 1J0
Tel: 705-965-2481
Joanne Ederer, Chief Executive Officer

Casselman: Bibliothèque publique de Casselman/ Casselman Public Library
675, rue Dollard, Casselman ON K0A 1M0
Tél: 613-764-5505; *Téléc:* 613-764-5507
bibliotheque@bibliocasselman.ca
www.bibliocasselman.ca
Aline Gareau, Bibliothécaire

Castleton: Township of Cramahe Public Library
Town Hall, 1780 Percy St., Castleton ON K0K 1M0
Tel: 905-344-7320; *Fax:* 905-344-7320
Sue La Berge, CEO

Chapleau: Chapleau Public Library
20 Pine St. East, Chapleau ON P0M 1K0
Tel: 705-864-0852; *Fax:* 705-864-0295
plchapleau@post.library.on.ca
www.chapleaucapsite.zoomshare.com
Maureen Travis, Chief Librarian
Gisele Robitaille, Assistant Librarian
Cassandra Comte, Assistant Librarian

***Chatham:* Chatham-Kent Public Library**
120 Queen St., Chatham ON N7M 2G6
Tel: 519-354-2940; *Fax:* 519-354-2602
CKlibrary@chatham-kent.ca
www.chatham-kent.ca/community+services/library
Diane Daly, Chair
cklibraryboard@chatham-kent.ca
Kathryn D. Goodhue, Director, Library Services
kathryng@chatham-kent.ca

***Christian Island:* Beausoleil First Nation Library**
80 Kate Kegwin St., Christian Island ON L0K 1C0
Tel: 705-247-2255; *Fax:* 705-247-2239
bfnlibrary@hotmail.com
Kathy Peters, Librarian

***Clinton:* Huron County Library**
77722B London Rd., RR#5, Clinton ON N0M 1L0
Tel: 519-482-5457; *Fax:* 519-482-7820
libraryadmin@huroncounty.ca
www.huroncounty.ca/library
Dorothy Kelly, Chair
Beth Ross, County Librarian
Meighan Wark, Branch Services Librarian
mwark@huroncounty.ca
Natalie Vander Burgt, Teen Program Coordinator

***Cobalt:* Cobalt Public Library/ Bibliothèque publique du Cobalt**
30 Lang St., Cobalt ON P0J 1C0
Tel: 705-679-8120; *Fax:* 705-679-8120
cobaltlibrary@ontera.net
cobaltlibrary.com
Margaret Leaper, Chief Executive Officer

***Cobden:* Township of Whitewater Region**
12 Wren Dr., Cobden ON K0J 1K0
Tel: 613-646-7592
www.whitewaterregion.ca/departments/library.htm
Heather Steege, Librarian
coblib@nrtco.net
613-646-7592

***Cobourg:* Cobourg Public Library**
200 Ontario St., Cobourg ON K9A 5P4
Tel: 905-372-9271; *Fax:* 905-372-4538
info@cobourg.library.on.ca
www.cobourg.library.on.ca
Social Media: www.twitter.com/cobourgPL
Charmaine Lindsay, CEO
clindsay@cobourg.library.on.ca
905-372-9271 ext. 6200
Bonnie Symons, Manager, Public Services
Heather Viscount, Manager, Access Services

***Cochrane:* Cochrane Public Library/ Bibliothèque publique Cochrane**
178 - 4th Ave., Cochrane ON P0L 1C0
Tel: 705-272-4178; *Fax:* 705-272-4165
library@town.cochrane.on.ca
www.olsn.ca/cochrane
Social Media:
www.facebook.com/group.php?gid=194354363915161
Christina Blazecka, Chief Executive Officer
Carole-Ann Churcher, Assitant Chief Executive Officer / Interlibrary Loans

***Coe Hill:* Wollaston & Limerick Public Library**
2149 Hwy. 620, Coe Hill ON K0L 1P0
Tel: 613-337-5183; *Fax:* 613-337-5183
coehilllibrary@bellnet.ca
www.wolaston-limericklibrary.ca
Bonnie Weise, Head Librarian

***Coldwater:* Coldwater Memorial Public Library**
31 Coldwater Rd., Coldwater ON L0K 1E0
Tel: 705-686-3601; *Fax:* 705-686-3741
library@coldwater.library.on.ca
www.coldwater.library.on.ca
Adah Silk, Chair

***Collingwood:* Collingwood Public Library**
100 Second St., Collingwood ON L9Y 1E5
Tel: 705-445-1571
clib@collingwoodpubliclibrary.ca
www.collingwoodpubliclibrary.ca
Donna Mansfield, Chair
Kerri M. Robinson, Director, Library Services

***Cornwall:* Akwesasne Library & Museum**
c/o Mohawk Council of Akwesasne, PO Box 579, Cornwall ON K6H 5T3
Tel: 518-358-2240; *Fax:* 518-358-2649
Other Numbers: 613-575-2250
info@akwesasneculturalcenter.org
www.akwesasneculturalcenter.org
Glory Cole, Director
coleg@northnet.org
Bernadine Boots, ILL/Reference

***Cornwall:* Cornwall Public Library (Ontario)/ Bibliothèque publique de Cornwall**
45 Second St. East, PO Box 939, Cornwall ON K6H 5V1
Tel: 613-932-4796; *Fax:* 613-932-2715
generalmail@library.cornwall.on.ca
www.library.cornwall.on.ca
Jacqueline Houde, Chair
Dawn Kiddell, CEO & Chief Librarian
dkiddell@cornwall.library.on.ca
Abigail MacLean, Head, Administration
amaclean@library.cornwall.on.ca
Stephanie McMartin, Head, Information Systems & Technical Services
smcmartin@library.cornwall.on.ca
Daphne Morris, Head, Adult Services
dfmorris@library.cornwall.on.ca
Brenda Wilson, Head, Young Adults & Children's Services
bjwilson@library.cornwall.on.ca
Pierre Dufour, Contact, Programming & Public Relations
pdufour@library.cornwall.on.ca

***Cornwall:* Stormont, Dundas & Glengarry County Library/ Bibliothèque des comtés unis Stormont, Dundas et Glengarry**
26 Pitt St., Cornwall ON K6J 3P2
Tel: 613-936-8777; *Fax:* 613-936-2532
generalinfo@sdglibrary.ca
www.sdglibrary.ca
Bill McGimpsey, Chair
Pamela Haley, Manager, Library Services
phaley@sdglibrary.ca
613-936-8777 ext. 226
Karen Franklin, Service Delivery Librarian
kfranklin@sdglibrary.ca
613-936-8777 ext. 211
Bernice Gauthier, Technical Services Coordinator, Acquisitions & Cataloguing
bgauthier@sdglibrary.ca
613-936-8777
Maureen Stephens, Technical Services Coordinator, Interlibrary Loan
mstephens@sdglibrary.ca
613-936-8777

***Curve Lake:* Curve Lake First Nation Public Library**
22 Winooleeda St., Curve Lake ON K0L 1R0
Tel: 705-657-3217; *Fax:* 705-657-8708
www.curvelakefn.com/library.htm
Susie V. Taylor, CEO
705-657-8045 ext. 217
Patricia Taylor, Librarian
705-657-3217

***Cutler:* Serpent River First Nation Public Library**
49 Village Rd., Cutler ON P0P 1B0
Tel: 705-844-2009; *Fax:* 705-844-2736
ljones.srfn@ontera.net
Patricia Squires, Librarian

***Deep River:* Deep River Public Library**
55 Ridge Rd., Deep River ON K0J 1P0
Tel: 613-584-4244
www.deepriverlibrary.ca
Tom Wiwcharuk, Chief Executive Officer

***Deep River:* Laurentian Hills Public Library**
34465 Hwy. 17, RR#1, Deep River ON K0J 1P0
Tel: 613-584-2714; *Fax:* 613-584-9145
library@town.laurentianhills.on.ca
town.laurentianhills.on.ca/Library/
Maureen L. Bakewell, Librarian

***Deseronto:* Deseronto Public Library**
358 Main St., Deseronto ON K0K 1X0
Tel: 613-396-2744; *Fax:* 613-396-3466
deserontopubliclibrary@yahoo.ca
www.deserontopubliclibrary.ca
Don Simpson, Chair
Frances Smith, CEO & Librarian
Ruth Sager, Librarian Assistant

***Deseronto:* Kanhiote/Tyendinaga Territory Public Library**
1644 York Rd., RR#1, Deseronto ON K0K 1X0
Tel: 613-967-6264; *Fax:* 613-396-3627
karenl@tyendinaga.net
www.tyendinaga.net/volunteer/kanhiote
Karen Lewis, CEO
karenl@tyendinaga.net

***Devlin:* Naicatchewenin Indian Band Library**
Rainy Lake Indian Reserve, RR#1, Devlin ON P0W 1C0
Tel: 807-486-3407; *Fax:* 807-486-3704
Darlene Smith, Librarian

***Dobie:* Dobie Public Library**
92 McPherson St., Dobie ON P0K 1B0
Tel: 705-568-8951; *Fax:* 705-568-8951
publib@nt.net
Dianne Quinn, CEO

***Dokis:* Dokis First Nation Public Library**
129 Loop St., Dokis ON P0M 2K0
Tel: 705-763-2511; *Fax:* 705-763-2765
dokislibrary@hotmail.com
Angeline Dokis, Librarian
dokislibrary@hotmail.com

***Dorion:* Dorion Public Library**
170 Dorion Loop Rd., Dorion ON P0T 1K0
Tel: 807-857-2318; *Fax:* 807-857-2203
dorlib@tbaytel.net
www.dorionpubliclibrary.ca
Betty Chambers, Head Librarian
Claudia Hubbard, Assistant
Lee Harris, Assistant
Valerie Modin, Chair

***Douglas:* Admaston-Bromley Public Library**
PO Box 130, Hwy. 60, Douglas ON K0J 1S0
Tel: 613-649-2576; *Fax:* 613-649-2676
info@admastonbromleylibrary.com
www.admastonbromleylibrary.com
Anne English, Head Librarian

***Douro:* Douro-Dummer Public Library/ Bibiothèque publique de Douro-Dummer**
435 - 4th Line, General Delivery, Douro ON K0L 1S0
Tel: 705-652-8599
library@dourodummer.on.ca
http://www.dourodummer.on.ca/library/
Edna Latone, Librarian
Walter Myles, Chair

***Dryden:* Dryden Public Library**
36 Van Horne Ave., Dryden ON P8N 2A7
Tel: 807-223-1475; *Fax:* 807-223-4312
library@dryden.ca
www.dryden.ca/city_services/library
Sandra Weitzel, CEO
Kim Vares, Chair
Joanne Bunney, Vice-Chair

***Dubreuilville:* Bibliothèque publique de Dubreuilville/ Dubreuilville Public Library**
120 Magpie St., Dubreuilville ON P0S 1B0
Tél: 705-884-1435; *Téléc:* 705-884-1437
Ligne sans frais: 877-637-8010
dpl@dubreuilville.ca
Brigitte Tremblay, Directrice

***Dunchurch:* Whitestone Hagerman Memorial Public Library**
2206 Hwy. 124, Dunchurch ON P0A 1G0
Tel: 705-389-3311; *Fax:* 705-389-3311
whitestonelibrary@vianet.ca
www.dunchurchlibrary.org
Lori Guillemette, Library Administrator

***Dundalk:* Southgate Public Library**
90 Main St. East, Dundalk ON N0C 1B0
Tel: 519-923-3248
southgatepl@bmts.com
www.southgate-library.com
Dianne Dean, CEO
southgatepl@bmts.com

***Dunnville:* Haldimand County Public Library**
111 Broad St. East, Dunnville ON N1A 1E8
Tel: 905-774-7595; *Fax:* 905-774-4294
djackson@haldimandcounty.on.ca
www.haldimandcounty.on.ca
Debra Jackson, CEO
djackson@haldimandcounty.on.ca
905-318-3272 ext. 15

Paul Diette, Deputy CEO
pdiette@haldimandcounty.on.ca
905-318-3272 ext. 11

***Durham:* West Grey Library System**
240 Garafraxa St. North, Durham ON N0G 1R0
Tel: 519-369-2107; *Fax:* 519-369-9966
westgreylibrary@yahoo.ca
www.westgreylibraries.com
Marlaine Elvidge, Chief Executive Officer, West Grey Library System
Sharon Davis, Senior Assistant Librarian
Christine Morrow, Senior Assistant Librarian

***Eabamet Lake:* Fort Hope First Nation Public Library**
PO Box 297, Eabamet Lake ON P0T 1L0
Tel: 807-242-8421; *Fax:* 807-242-1592

***Ear Falls:* Ear Falls Public Library**
50 Balsam Ave., Ear Falls ON P0V 1T0
Tel: 807-222-3209; *Fax:* 807-222-3432
efpl@shaw.ca
www.olsn.ca/earfallspl
Becky Bergman, Librarian
Monique Barrow, Casual Call-in

***Earlton:* Township of Armstrong Public Library/ Bibliothèque publique Canton Earlton**
35 - 10th St., Earlton ON P0J 1E0
Tel: 705-563-2717; *Fax:* 705-563-2093
earltonlibrary@ntl.sympatico.ca
Chantal Lavergne, CEO
earltonlibrary@ntl.sympatico.ca
Bernice Lockhart, Assistant Librarian
blockhart@ntl.sympatico.ca

***Eganville:* Bonnechere Union Public Library**
74A Maple St., Eganville ON K0J 1T0
Tel: 613-628-2400; *Fax:* 613-628-5377
info@bonnechereupl.com
www.bonnechereupl.com
Jennifer Coleman-Davidson, CEO/CFO
ceo@bonnechereupl.com

***Elgin:* Rideau Lakes Public Library**
26 Halladay St., PO Box 189, Elgin ON K0G 1E0
Tel: 613-359-5334; *Fax:* 613-359-5418
elginlibrary@ripnet.com
www.rideaulakeslibrary.ca
Rita Purcell, Library Chair
purcell.rita@sympatico.ca

***Elk Lake:* Elk Lake Public Library**
PO Box 218, Elk Lake ON P0J 1G0
Tel: 705-678-2340; *Fax:* 705-678-2340
elklake@ontera.net
Peggy Verrier, CEO
elklake@ontera.net
705-678-2340
Heidi Foley, Assistant Librarian

***Elliot Lake:* Elliot Lake Public Library**
Algo Centre Mall, 151 Ontario Ave., Elliot Lake ON P5A 2T2
Tel: 705-461-7204; *Fax:* 705-461-9464
www.elliotlakelibrary.com
Pat McGurk, Interim CEO
705-461-7204 ext. 2801

***Embrun:* Bibliothèque publique du Canton de Russell/ Russell Township Public Library**
#2, 717 Notre-Dame St., Embrun ON K0A 1W1
Tel: 613-443-3636; *Fax:* 613-443-0668
mylibrary@russellbiblio.com
www.russellbiblio.com
Claire Dionne, Directrice générale
claire.dionne@russellbiblio.com
Joanne Yelle, Responsable, Services technique
joanne.yelle@russellbiblio.com

***Emo:* Emo Public Library**
Jessie St., PO Box 490, Emo ON P0W 1E0
Tel: 807-482-2575; *Fax:* 807-482-2575
emolib@bellnet.ca
www.twspemo.on.ca
Shirley Sheppard, Librarian
Kathy Leek, Assistant Librarian & Electronic Data Assistant

***Emsdale:* Perry Twp (Emsdale) Public Library**
25 Joseph St., Emsdale ON P0A 1J0
Tel: 705-636-5454; *Fax:* 705-636-5454
perrylib@ontera.net
www.olsn.ca/library/perry/index.htm
Patricia Aitchison, Head Librarian
705-636-5454

***Englehart:* Englehart Public Library/ Bibliothèque publique d'Englehart**
#809, 71 - 4th Ave., Englehart ON P0J 1H0
Tel: 705-544-2100; *Fax:* 705-544-2238
techepl@ontera.net
www.englehartpubliclibrary.ca
Munroe Burton, Chair
Sharon Williams, Librarian/CEO
Nicole Robichaud, Assistant Manager
David Van Schip, Computer Technician

***Espanola:* Espanola Public Library**
245 Avery Dr., Espanola ON P5E 1S4
Tel: 705-869-2940; *Fax:* 705-869-6463
library@town.espanola.on.ca
www.espanola.library.on.ca
Charles Grayson, Chief Librarian

***Essex:* Essex County Library**
#101, 360 Fairview Ave. West, Essex ON N8M 1Y3
Tel: 519-776-5241; *Fax:* 519-776-6851
www.essexcountylibrary.ca
William (Bill) Varga, Chair
Edward R. George, Chief Librarian
egeorge@essexcountylibrary.ca
Patricia Knight, Contact, Systems

***Fauquier:* Bibliothèque publique de Fauquier-Strickland/ Fauquier-Strickland Public Library**
25, rue Grzela, Fauquier ON P0L 1G0
Tél: 705-339-2521; *Téléc:* 705-339-2421
biblioff@vianet.ca
www.olsn.ca
Jocelyne Ratté, Directrice générale
Claude Tremblay Blais, Aide-bibliothécaire

***Fergus:* Wellington County Library**
552 Wellington Rd. 18, RR#1, Fergus ON N1M 2W3
Tel: 519-846-0918; *Fax:* 519-846-2066
www.county.wellington.on.ca
Murray McCabe, Chief Librarian
murraym@wellington.ca
519-846-0918 ext. 6224
Janice Coles, Assistant Chief Librarian
janicec@wellington.ca
519-846-0918 ext. 229
Janice Ellison, Contact, Administration
janicee@wellington.ca
519-846-0918 ext. 6227
Elaine Salter, Contact, Cataloguing
elaines@wellington.ca
519-846-0918 ext. 223
Deanna Stevens, Contact, Interlibrary Loan
deannas@wellington.ca
519-846-0918 ext. 225

***Flesherton:* Grey Highlands Public Library**
10 Elizabeth St., Flesherton ON N0C 1E0
Tel: 519-924-2241; *Fax:* 519-924-2562
flepub@bmts.com
www.greyhighlandspubliclibrary.com/index.htm
Wilda Allen, CEO/Chief Librarian
pallen@bmts.com

***Flinton:* Addington-Highlands Public Library**
927 Flinton Rd., Flinton ON K0H 1P0
Tel: 613-333-1091
FlintonLibraryCAP@addingtonhighlandspubliclibr
www.addingtonhighlandspubliclibrary.ca
June Phillips, CEO & Head Librarian
Bonnie Leoen, Part-time Librarian

***Fonthill:* Pelham Public Library**
43 Pelham Town Sq., Fonthill ON L0S 1E0
Tel: 905-892-6443; *Fax:* 905-892-3392
pelhampl@post.library.on.ca
www.pelhamlibrary.on.ca
Stephanie Stowe, CEO
905-892-6443
June Bowslaugh, Assistant Librarian
Brigitte Armour, Interlibrary Loans

***Forest:* Chippewas of Kettle & Stony Point Library**
RR#2, 6218 Indian Lane, Forest ON N0N 1J0
Tel: 519-786-2955; *Fax:* 519-786-6904
ksplibrary@xcelco.on.ca
Beverly Bresette, CEO
bevb@xcelco.ca

***Fort Erie:* Fort Erie Public Library**
136 Gilmore Rd., Fort Erie ON L2A 2M1
Tel: 905-871-2546; *Fax:* 905-871-2191
www.forterie.library.on.ca
Maria Brigantino, CEO
mbrigantino@forterie.library.on.ca
905-871-2546 ext. 303
Marsha Hunt, Information Services Librarian
mhunt@forterie.library.on.ca
905-871-2546 ext. 304
Michael Schell, Systems Administrator
mschell@forterie.library.on.ca
905-871-2546 ext. 301
Joel Nash, Public Services Coordinator
jnash@forterie.library.on.ca

***Fort Frances:* Fort Frances Public Library**
363 Church St., Fort Frances ON P9A 1C9
Tel: 807-274-9879; *Fax:* 807-274-4496
msedgwick@fort-frances.com
library.fort-frances.com
Margaret Sedgwick, Librarian

***Gananoque:* Gananoque Public Library**
100 Park St., Gananoque ON K7G 2Y5
Tel: 613-382-2436
gplp@bellnet.ca
John Love, Librarian

***Garden River:* Garden River First Nation Public Library**
14 Syrette Lake Rd., Garden River ON P6A 5K9
Tel: 705-946-3933; *Fax:* 705-945-1415
Irene Gray, CEO
irene.gray@gardenriver.ca

***Garden Village:* Nipissing First Nation Public Library**
36 Semo Rd., Garden Village ON P2B 3K2
Tel: 705-753-2050; *Fax:* 705-753-0571
glennab@nfn.ca
Glenna Beaucage, CEO

***Georgetown:* Halton Hills Public Library**
9 Church St., Georgetown ON L7G 2A3
Tel: 905-873-2681; *Fax:* 905-873-6118
www.library.hhpl.on.ca
Jane Diamanti, Director
diamantij@hhpl.on.ca
905-873-2681 ext. 2501
Geoffrey Cannon, Manager of Public Services
cannong@hhpl.on.ca
905-873-2681 ext. 2513
Walter Lewis, Manager of Library Systems & Technical Services
lewisw@hhpl.on.ca
905-873-2681 ext. 2506

***Geraldton:* Greenstone Public Library**
405 Second St. West, Geraldton ON P0T 1M0
Tel: 807-854-2421; *Fax:* 807-854-2421
greenstonepl@hotmail.com
www.olsn.ca/greenstone/
Mari Mannisto, CEO
greenstonepl@hotmail.com

***Gilmour:* Tudor & Cashel Baverstock Memorial Public Library**
371 Weslemkoon Lake Rd., Gilmour ON K0L 1W0
Tel: 613-474-1096; *Fax:* 613-474-0664
www.tudorandcashel.com
Mary Hawkins, CEO/Librarian
Barb Sanderson, Assistant Librarian

***Gogama:* Gogama Public Library/ Bibliothèque publique de Gogama**
Low Ave., PO Box 238, Gogama ON P0M 1W0
Tel: 705-894-2448
glibrary@onlink.net
Sue Primeau, Volunteer Head Librarian

***Gogama:* Mattagami First Nation Public Library**
PO Box 99, Gogama ON P0M 1W0
Tel: 705-894-2003; *Fax:* 705-894-2386
mjnms@hotmail.com
www.olsn.ca
Patsy Mckay, CEO
msh@onlink.net
705-894-2003

***Golden Lake:* Algonquins of Pikwakanagan Library**
c/o 1657A Mishomis Inamo, Golden Lake ON K0J 1X0
Tel: 613-625-2402
library@pikwakanagan.ca
Estelle Amikons, CEO

***Gore Bay:* Gore Bay Union Public Library**
15 Water St., Gore Bay ON P0P 1H0
Tel: 705-282-2221; *Fax:* 705-282-2221
gorebaylibrary@gorebaycable.com
Johanna Allison, CEO
gblibrary@onlink.net

***Grafton:* Alnwick - Haldimand Public Libraries**
10836 County Rd. #2, Grafton ON K0K 2G0
Tel: 905-349-2822
hallibhq@eagle.ca
www.alnwickhaldimand.ca
Carol Dempsey, Chief Executive Officer

***Grand Valley:* Grand Valley Public Library**
4 Amaranth St. East, Grand Valley ON L0N 1G0
Tel: 519-928-5622; *Fax:* 519-928-2586
grandvalleylibrary@primus.ca
www.grandvalley.org
Shann Leighton, CEO
shannleighton@primus.ca

***Gravenhurst:* Gravenhurst Public Library**
180 Sharpe St. West, Gravenhurst ON P1P 1J1
Tel: 705-687-3382; *Fax:* 705-687-7016
illo@gravenhurst.ca
www.gravenhurst.ca/library
Edward Reece, CEO
ereece@gravenhurst.ca
Robena Kirton, Chief Librarian

***Grimsby:* Grimsby Public Library**
18 Carnegie Lane, Grimsby ON L3M 1Y1
Tel: 905-945-5142; *Fax:* 905-945-4442
Barry Church, Chief Librarian

***Guelph:* Guelph Public Library**
100 Norfolk St., Guelph ON N1H 4J6
Tel: 519-824-6220
www.library.guelph.on.ca
Randall Wilson, Chair
Norman C. McLeod, Chief Executive Officer
Glenda Duffin, Contact, Extension Services
Kerry Hannah, Contact, Children's Services
Steven Kraft, Contact, Adult Information Services
Colleen Lipp, Contact, Adult Circulation Services
Gordon Lipp, Contact, Library Systems
Laurel Marsolais, Contact, Interlibrary Loans

***Hagersville:* Mississaugas of the New Credit First Nation Public Library**
2789 Missisauga Rd., RR#6, Hagersville ON N0A 1H0
Tel: 905-768-5686; *Fax:* 905-768-4592
www.newcreditfirstnation.com
Cynthia Jamieson, Executive Director
cjamieson@newcreditfirstnation.com

***Haileybury:* Temiskaming Shores Public Library**
545 Lakeshore Rd., Haileybury ON P0J 1K0
Tel: 705-672-3707; *Fax:* 705-672-5966
haillib@ontera.net
www.temisklibrary.com
Roger Oblin, Chair
Rebecca Hunt, Library CEO & Haileybury Branch Librarian

***Haliburton:* Haliburton County Public Library**
78 Maple Ave., Haliburton ON K0M 1S0
Tel: 705-457-2241; *Fax:* 705-457-9586
info@haliburtonlibrary.ca
www.haliburtonlibrary.ca
Social Media:
www.facebook.com/group.php?gid=216747128340069
Nancy McLuskey, Chair
Bessie Sullivan, Chief Executive Officer
705-457-2241
Susan Robinson, Community Partnerships & Administration
705-457-2241
Sherrill Sherwood, Collection Development & Marketing
705-457-2241

***Hamilton:* Hamilton Public Library**
55 York Blvd., Hamilton ON L8R 3K1
Tel: 905-546-3200; *Fax:* 905-546-3202
TDD: 9055463474
askhpl@hpl.ca
www.hpl.ca
Ken Roberts, Chief Librarian
kroberts@hpl.ca
905-546-3215
Robin Hewitt, Director, Finance & Facilities
rhewitt@hpl.ca
905-546-3200 ext. 3226
Lisa DuPelle, Director, Human Resources
ldupelle@hpl.ca
905-546-3200 ext. 3290
Beth Hovius, Director, Public Service & Collection Development
bhovius@hpl.ca
905-546-3200 ext. 3285
Maureen Sawa, Director, Public Service & Community Development
msawa@hpl.ca
905-546-3200 ext. 3213
Sue Beattie, Manager, Circulation, Book Mobiles
Darcy Glidden, Manager, Adult Services, Local History & Archives

***Hanover:* Hanover Public Library**
451 - 10th Ave., Hanover ON N4N 2P1
Tel: 519-364-1420; *Fax:* 519-364-1747
hanpub@hanover.ca
Social Media:
www.facebook.com/group.php?gid=216793488339895
Agnes Rivers-Moore, Chief Librarian
arm@hanover.ca

***Havelock:* Havelock-Belmont-Methuen Twp Public Library**
13 Quebec St., Havelock ON K0L 1Z0
Tel: 705-778-2621; *Fax:* 705-778-2621
habellib@nexicom.net
www.hbmlibrary.on.ca
Sandra Harris, Head Librarian/CEO
habellib@nexicom.net

***Hawkesbury:* Bibliothèque publique de Hawkesbury/ Hawkesbury Public Library**
550 Higginson St., Hawkesbury ON K6A 1H1
Tél: 613-632-0106; *Téléc:* 613-636-2097
info@bibliotheque.hawkesbury.on.ca
www.bibliotheque.hawkesbury.on.ca
Lynn Belle-Isle, Directrice générale

***Hearst:* Bibliothèque publique de Hearst/ Hearst Public Library**
801 George St., Hearst ON P0L 1N0
Tel: 705-372-2843; *Fax:* 705-372-2833
hearstpl@ontera.net
www.bibliohearst.on.ca
Francine Daigle, Director, Library Services
Julie Portelance, Library Services Technician

***Hilton Beach:* Hilton Union Public Library**
3048 Marks St., Hilton Beach ON P0R 1G0
Tel: 705-246-2557
diane.gerhart@sympatico.ca
Diane Gerhart, Librarian
diane.gerhart@sympatico.ca

***Holland Landing:* East Gwillimbury Public Library**
19513 Yonge St., Holland Landing ON L9N 1L8
Tel: 905-836-6492; *Fax:* 905-836-6499
infoegpl@primus.ca
www.eastgwillimbury.ca/library
Greg Gulas, CEO
ggulas@primus.ca
905-836-6492

***Hornepayne:* Hornepayne Township Public Library**
200 Front St., Hornepayne ON P0M 1Z0
Tel: 807-868-2332; *Fax:* 807-868-3111
lkahara@ontera.net
Lynda Kahara, CEO

***Huntsville:* Huntsville Public Library**
7 Minerva St., Huntsville ON P1H 1W4
Tel: 705-789-5232
library@huntsvillelibrary.net
www.huntsvillelibrary.net
Ana Mackenzie, Chief Librarian

***Ignace:* Ignace Public Library**
36 Main St., Ignace ON P0T 1T0
Tel: 807-934-2280; *Fax:* 807-934-6452
ipl-catherine@nwconx.net
www.olsn.ca/ignace
Pam Greenwood, Contact

***Innisfil:* Innisfil Public Library**
967 Innisfil Beach Rd., Innisfil ON L9S 1V3
Tel: 705-431-7410
lakeshore@innisfil.library.on.ca
www.innisfil.library.on.ca
Susan Downs, Chief Librarian & CEO
sdowns@innisfil.library.on.ca
Jayne Asselstine, Deputy Chief Librarian
Marilyn Pillar, Manager, Lakeshore Branch

***Iron Bridge:* Huron Shores Public Library**
10 John St., Iron Bridge ON P0R 1H0
Tel: 705-843-2192; *Fax:* 705-843-2035
huronshores@onlink.net
www.olsn.ca/huronshores
Terri Beharriell, CEO/Librarian
Tim McDougall, CAP Chair

***Iroquois Falls:* Bibliothèque publique d'Iroquois Falls Public Library**
725 Synagogue St., Iroquois Falls ON P0K 1G0
Tel: 705-232-5722; *Fax:* 705-232-7166
ifpl@ontera.net
www.olsn.ca/iroquoisfallsp/
Lina Tremblay-Joseph, CEO
Diane Gagnon, Assistant Librarian
Carole Rioux, Clerk

***Kagawong:* Billings Twp Public Library**
18 Upper St., Kagawong ON P0P 1J0
Tel: 705-282-2944
billings@xplornet.com
Beth Gordon, CEO

***Kakabeka Falls:* Conmee Public Library**
Conmee Community Centre, 19 Holland Rd. West, RR#1, Kakabeka Falls ON P0T 1W0
Tel: 807-475-5229
conmeelibrary@msn.com
www.conmee.com/library.html
Selly Pajamaki, Chief Executive Officer
spajamaki@aidsthunderbay.org

***Kapuskasing:* Kapuskasing Public Library/ Bibliothèque publique de Kapuskasing**
24 Mundy Ave., Kapuskasing ON P5N 1P9
Tel: 705-335-3363; *Fax:* 705-335-2464
kaplibrary@ntl.sympatico.ca
Social Media:
www.facebook.com/pages/Kapuskasing-Public-Library/1232403 94393542
Cecile Langlois, Librarian

***Kearney:* Kearney & Area Public Library**
8 Main St., Kearney ON P0A 1M0
Tel: 705-636-5849; *Fax:* 705-636-7060
kearneylibrary@hotmail.com
www.olsn.ca/kearney
Brandi Nolan, CEO/Librarian

***Keene:* Otonabee-South Monaghan Public Library**
3252 County Rd. 2, Keene ON K0L 2G0
Tel: 705-295-6814
keene_library@nexicom.net
www.otosoumon.library.on.ca
Carolanne Nadeau, CEO

***Kemptville:* North Grenville Public Library**
669 South Gower Dr., Kemptville ON K0G 1J0
Tel: 613-258-4711; *Fax:* 613-258-4134
info@ngpl.ca
www.ngpl.ca
Susan Higgins, Manager, Library Services
shiggins@ripnet.com
Patricia Evans, Head, Interlibrary Loan Dept.
pevans@ripnet.com

***Kenora:* City of Kenora Public Library**
24 Main St. South, Kenora ON P9N 1S7
Tel: 807-467-2081; *Fax:* 807-467-2085
maeisler@kenora.ca
www.kenorapubliclibrary.org
Erin Roussin, Head Librarian
eroussin@kenora.ca
Lori Jackson, Head of Reference
ljackson@kenora.ca
Cathy Peacock, Assistant Librarian
cpeacock@kenora.ca
Marg Eisler, Online Contact, Interlibrary Loan
maeisler@kenora.ca
Kelly Wald, Adult Services
kwald@kenora.ca
Crystal Alcock, Childrens Services
cralcock@kenora.ca
Lee Spicer, Technical Services
lspicer@kenora.ca
Pat Kornas, Circulation
pkornas@kenora.ca

***Keswick:* Georgina Public Libraries**
90 Wexford Dr., Keswick ON L4P 3P7
Tel: 905-476-7233; *Fax:* 905-476-8724
www.georgina-library.com

Mary Baxter, CEO/Director, Library Services
mbaxter@georgina.ca
905-476-7233 ext. 101

***Killaloe:* Killaloe & District Public Library**
1 John St., Killaloe ON K0J 2A0
Tel: 613-757-2211; *Fax:* 613-757-3634
killaloelibrary@maskcom.ca
www.killaloe-hagarty-richards.ca/library/default.htm
Nicole Zummach, Librarian/CEO
Pat Foran, Library Clerk
Norma Graham, Librarian

***King City:* King Township Public Library**
1970 King Rd., King City ON L7B 1A6
Tel: 905-833-5101; *Fax:* 905-833-0824
www.king-library.on.ca
Murray McCabe, CEO & Chief Librarian
m.mccabe@king-library.on.ca
Sharon Bentley, Deputy Chief Librarian
s.bentley@king-library.on.ca
905-939-2102
Kelley England, Manager, Children's & Young Adult Services
k.england@king-library.on.ca
Adele Reid, Manager, King City & Library Budgets
a.reid@king-library.on.ca

***Kingfisher Lake:* Kingfisher Lake First Nation Public Library**
General Delivery, Kingfisher Lake ON P0V 1Z0
Tel: 807-532-0067

***Kingston:* Canadian Law Library Review / Bibliothèques de droit canadiennes**
#310, 4 Cataraqui St., Kingston ON K7L 5C8
Tel: 613-531-9339; *Fax:* 613-531-0626
office@callacbd.ca
www.callacbd.ca/cll-jour.html
Lenore Rapkin, Editor

***Kingston:* Kingston Frontenac Public Library**
130 Johnson St., Kingston ON K7L 1X8
Tel: 613-549-8888; *Fax:* 613-549-8476
www.kfpl.ca
Claudette Richardson, Chair
Deborah Defoe, Chief Librarian & CEO
Doug Brown, Manager, Facilities
Patricia Enright, Manager, Children's Services & Rural Branches
John Feenstra, Manager, Projects & Financial Services
Barb Love, Manager, Adult Services
Shelagh Quigley, Manager, Human Resources
Lester Webb, Manager, Systems & Technical Services

***Kirkland Lake:* Teck Centennial Library**
10 Kirkland St. East, Kirkland Lake ON P2N 1P1
Tel: 705-567-7966; *Fax:* 705-568-6303
library@tkl.ca
www.olsn.ca/kirklandlakepl/
Cheryl Lafreniere, Chief Librarian

***Kitchener:* Kitchener Public Library**
85 Queen St. North, Kitchener ON N2H 2H1
Tel: 519-743-0271; *Fax:* 519-743-1261
askus@kpl.org
www.kpl.org
Sonia Lewis, CEO
sonia.lewis@kpl.org
Cheryl Kaar, Bibliographic Services Coordinator
Lesa Balch, Senior Manager, Service Development

***Lanark:* Lanark Highlands Public Library**
75 George St., Lanark ON K0G 1K0
Tel: 613-259-3068
lanarklib@perth.igs.net
www.lanarkhighlands.ca/MunicipalServices/Library.htm
Wanda Proulx, CEO

***Lansdowne:* Leeds & the Thousand Islands Public Library**
1B Jessie St., Lansdowne ON K0E 1L0
Tel: 613-659-3885; *Fax:* 613-659-4192
leedsti@ltipl.net
www.ltipl.net
Linda Chadwick, Librarian

***Larder Lake:* Larder Lake Public Library/ Bibliothèque publique de Larder Lake**
29 Godfrey St., Larder Lake ON P0K 1L0
Tel: 705-643-2222; *Fax:* 705-643-2222
llpublib@onlink.net
Patricia Bodick, Library Technician/CEO
Sonia Jensen, Library Assistant

***Latchford:* Latchford Public Library**
66 Main St., Latchford ON P0J 1N0
Tel: 705-676-2030
lpl@ontera.net
Edith Robillard, CEO
Jacki Perry, Children's Services
Perry Livingston, ILL
Georgina Garreau, Reference Services

***Limoges:* Bibliothèque publique de la municipalité de la Nation**
205, ch Limoges, Limoges ON K0A 2M0
Tél: 613-443-1630; *Téléc:* 613-443-9643
biblioinfo@nationmun.ca
www.nationmunbiblio.ca
Mèdia social: twitter.com/#!/BiblioLaNation;
www.facebook.com/group.php?gid=109251539103571
Jeanne Leroux, Directrice générale
jeanneleroux@nationmun.ca
613-524-2252
Micheline Bergevin, Bibliotechnicienne Services techniques
mbergevin@nationmun.ca
Christine Lepage, Commis de bibliothèque
clepage@nationmun.ca

***Lindsay:* City of Kawartha Lakes Public Library**
190 Kent St. West, Lindsay ON K9V 2Y6
Tel: 705-324-9411; *Fax:* 705-878-1859
Toll-Free: 888-822-2225
libraryadministration@city.kawarthalakes.on.ca
www.city.kawarthalakes.on.ca/residents/library-services
Barbara Truax, Chair
Kevin Williams, Chief Executive Office
kwilliams@city.kawarthalakes.on.ca
Linda Kent, Chief Librarian
lkent@city.kawarthalakes.on.ca

***Listowel:* North Perth Public Library**
260 Main St. West, Listowel ON N4W 1A1
Tel: 519-291-4621; *Fax:* 519-291-2235
npl@northperth.library.on.ca
www.northperth.library.on.ca
Sheila Durand, CEO
sdurand@northperth.library.on.ca

***Little Current:* Aundeck Omni Kaning First Nation Public Library**
13 Hill St., Little Current ON P0P 1K0
Tel: 705-368-3696; *Fax:* 705-368-3563
aokpubliclibrary@hotmail.com
Norma McGraw, Librarian
705-368-3696

***Little Current:* Northeastern Manitoulin & the Islands Public Library**
50 Meredith St. West, Little Current ON P0P 1K0
Tel: 705-368-2444; *Fax:* 705-368-0708
nemilib@vianet.on.ca
www.nemilib.vianet.ca
Judith Kift, Librarian & CEO
Brittany Morphet, CAP Youth Worker

***London:* London Public Library**
251 Dundas St., London ON N6A 6H9
Tel: 519-661-4600; *Fax:* 519-663-9013
Other Numbers: TDD 519-432-8835
info@lpl.london.on.ca
www.londonpubliclibrary.ca
Susanna Hubbard Krimmer, CEO
519-661-5143
Margaret Mitchell, Director, Quality Improvement
margaret.mitchell@lpl.london.on.ca
519-661-5134
Anne Baker, Director, Human Resources & Organizational Effectiveness
519-661-5114
Lindsay Sage, Director, Marketing & Development
519-661-6403
Tom Travers, Director, Information Technology Services
tom.travers@lpl.london.on.ca
519-661-5100 ext. 6475

***M'Chigeeng:* M'Chigeeng First Nation Public Library**
18 Lakeview Dr., M'Chigeeng ON P0P 1G0
Tel: 705-377-5540; *Fax:* 705-377-5080
bookwormsandy@yahoo.com
Sandra Bayer, CEO
705-377-5540

***MacTier:* Township of Georgian Bay Public Library**
2 Muskoka Rd., MacTier ON P0C 1H0
Tel: 705-375-5430; *Fax:* 705-375-5430
mactier1@interhop.net
www.olsn.ca/georgianbaypl/
Barbara Swyers, CEO
Gail Demkiw, Branch Contact

***Madoc:* Madoc Public Library**
20 Davidson St., Madoc ON K0K 2K0
Tel: 613-473-4456
madoc_public_library@bellnet.ca
www.madocpubliclibrary.com
Susan Smith, CEO
susansmith@bellnet.ca

***Magnetawan:* Magnetawan Public Library**
4304 North Sparks St., Magnetawan ON P0A 1P0
Tel: 705-387-4411; *Fax:* 705-387-0636
magcap@ontera.net
www.magnetawanlibrary.ca
Bonnie Davidson, CEO/Librarian
Lorinda Makoviczki, Assistant Librarian

***Manitouwadge:* Manitouwadge Public Library**
Community Centre, Manitouwadge ON P0T 2C0
Tel: 807-826-3913; *Fax:* 807-826-4640
library-man@nwconx.net
Janis Lamothe, Librarian/CEO

***Manitowaning:* Assiginack Public Library**
25 Spragge St., Manitowaning ON P0P 1N0
Tel: 705-859-2110; *Fax:* 705-859-3010
aplgoodtomes@email.com
www.assiginacklibrary.org
Debbie Robinson, CEO/Librarian

***Marathon:* Marathon Public Library**
22 Peninsula Rd., Marathon ON P0T 2E0
Tel: 807-229-0740; *Fax:* 807-229-3336
tneedham@tbaytel.net
Tamara Needham, Librarian

***Markham:* Markham Public Library**
6031 Highway 7, Markham ON L3P 3A7
Tel: 905-513-7977; *Fax:* 905-471-6015
comments@markham.library.on.ca
www.markhampubliclibrary.ca
Social Media:
www.facebook.com/group.php?gid=132151853488105
Catherine Biss, CEO
cbiss@markham.library.on.ca
Larry Pogue, Director, Administration & Operational Support
lpogue@markham.library.on.ca

***Markstay:* Markstay-Warren Public Library/ Bibliothèque publique de Markstay-Warren**
7 Pioneer St. East, Markstay ON P0M 2W0
Tel: 705-507-2612
www.olsn.ca/markstay-warrenpl

***Marmora:* Marmora & Lake Public Library**
37 Forsyth St., Marmora ON K0K 2M0
Tel: 613-472-3122
marmoralibrary@gmail.com
www.marmora.info/library
Sheryl Price, CEO

***Massey:* Sables Spanish River Public Library Board**
Massey & Township Public Library, 185 Grove St., Massey ON P0P 1P0
Tel: 705-865-2641; *Fax:* 705-865-2641
infomasseylibrary@gmail.com
www.masseylibrary.com
Elizabeth Gamble, CEO & Treasurer
Ruth DeClerck, Assistant Librarian

***Massey:* Sagamok Anishnawbek Public Library**
PO Box 610, Massey ON P0P 1P0
Tel: 705-865-2970; *Fax:* 705-865-3411
Colleen Eshkakogan, Librarian

***Matheson:* Black River-Matheson Public Library**
PO Box 450, Matheson ON P0K 1N0
Tel: 705-273-2760; *Fax:* 705-273-1755
brmlibrary@hotmail.com
www.blackriver-matheson.com
Karen Ukrainetz, CEO/Librarian

***Mattawa:* Mattawa (John Dixon) Public Library**
370 Pine St., Mattawa ON P0H 1V0
Tel: 705-744-5550; *Fax:* 705-744-1714
mplibrary@efni.com
users.efni.com/~mplibrary/

Lise Moore Asselin, CEO
Lynne Pellerin, Reference & Technical Services
Nicole Leblanc, Interlibrary Loans

***Maynooth:* Hastings Highlands Public Library**
33011 Hwy 62 North, Maynooth ON K0L 2S0
Tel: 613-338-2262; *Fax:* 613-338-3292
info@hastingshighlandspubliclibrary.ca
www.hastingshighlandspubliclibrary.ca
Julie Andrews-Jotham, CEO/Librarian

***McKellar:* McKellar Twp Public Library**
701 Hwy. 124, McKellar ON P0G 1C0
Tel: 705-389-2611; *Fax:* 705-389-2611
mckellarlib@vianet.ca
www.mckellarpubliclibrary.ca
Joan Ward, Librarian
jward@post.library.on.ca
Terri Short, Staff
asterken@post.library.on.ca

***Meaford:* Meaford Public Library**
15 Trowbridge St. West, Meaford ON N4L 1V4
Tel: 519-538-1060; *Fax:* 519-538-1808
info@meafordlibrary.on.ca
www.meafordlibrary.on.ca
Rita Orr, CEO
rita@meaford.com
Michael Crowley, Children's Coordinator
Lynne Fascinato, Contact, Interlibrary Loan
David Port, Chair

***Merrickville:* Merrickville Public Library**
446 Main St. East, Merrickville ON K0G 1N0
Tel: 613-269-3326
merrickville_ill@bellnet.ca
www.village.merrickville-wolford.on.ca/mpl/library.htm
Mary Kate Laphen, Librarian

***Midhurst:* Simcoe County Library Co-Operative**
County Administration Centre, 1110 Hwy. 26, Midhurst ON L0L 1X0
Tel: 705-726-9300; *Fax:* 705-726-3991
gayle.hall@simcoe.ca
www.geocities.com/Athens/Forum/9021/
Gayle Hall, Chief Librarian
gayle.hall@simcoe.ca
705-726-4300 ext. 1258

***Midhurst:* Springwater Township Public Library**
12 Finlay Mill Rd., Midhurst ON L0L 1X0
Tel: 705-737-5650; *Fax:* 705-737-3594
midhurst.library@springwater.ca
www.springwater.ca/thingstodo/libraries
Lynn Patkau, Chief Librarian

***Midland:* Midland Public Library**
320 King St., Midland ON L4R 3M6
Tel: 705-526-4216; *Fax:* 705-526-1474
midlibrary@town.midland.on.ca
www.midlandlibrary.com
Bill Molesworth, Chief Librarian
bmolesworth@town.midland.on.ca
Gail Griffith, Head, Adult Services
Betty Fullerton, Head, Technical Services
Bonnie Reynolds, Head, Children's Services

***Millbrook:* Cavan Monaghan Libraries**
1 Dufferin St., Millbrook ON L0A 1G0
Tel: 705-932-2919; *Fax:* 705-932-4019
www.cavanmonaghanlibraries.ca
Margot Loucks, Chief Executive Librarian & Librarian

***Milton:* Milton Public Library**
45 Bruce St., Milton ON L9T 2L5
Tel: 905-875-2665; *Fax:* 905-875-4324
TDD: 9058751550
www.mpl.on.ca
Leslie Fitch, CEO
leslie.fitch@mpl.on.ca
905-875-2665 ext. 3252
Melanie Southern, Information Services
melanie.Southern@mpl.on.ca
905-875-2665 ext. 3265

***Milverton:* Perth East Public Library**
27 Main St. South, Milverton ON N0K 1M0
Tel: 519-595-8395; *Fax:* 519-595-2943
pel@pcin.on.ca
www.pertheast.library.on.ca
Patti Henhoeffer, CEO
phenhoeffer@pcin.on.ca

***Mindemoya:* Central Manitoulin Public Libraries**
6020 King St., Mindemoya ON P0P 1S0
Tel: 705-377-5334; *Fax:* 705-377-5585
bookworm@amtelecom.net
Claire Cline, CEO/Chief Librarian
Mel Delange, Library Assistant
Evelyn Taylor, Library Assistant

***Mine Centre:* Seine River First Nation Public Library**
PO Box 129, Mine Centre ON P0W 1H0
Tel: 807-599-2870; *Fax:* 807-599-2871
Glenda Potson, Librarian
gpotson@fort-frances.lakeheadu.ca
Susan Johnson, Head, Reference

***Mississauga:* Mississauga Library System**
301 Burnhamthorpe Rd. West, Mississauga ON L5B 3Y3
Tel: 905-615-3500; *Fax:* 905-615-3625
library.info@mississauga.ca
www.mississauga.ca/portal/residents/library
Don Mills, Director of Library Services
don.mills@mississauga.ca
905-615-3200 ext. 3601
Anne Yuen, Head, Acquisitions & Bibliographic Services
anne.yuen@mississauga.ca
905-615-3642

***Mitchell:* West Perth Public Library**
105 St. Andrew St., Mitchell ON N0K 1N0
Tel: 519-348-9234; *Fax:* 519-348-4540
wpl@pcin.on.ca
www.westperth.library.on.ca
Caroline Shewburg, Librarian

***Mobert:* Pic Mobert First Nation Public Library**
General Delivery, Mobert ON P0M 2J0
Tel: 807-822-1594; *Fax:* 807-822-1578
principal@picmobert.ca

***Moonbeam:* Bibliothèque publique de Moonbeam/ Moonbeam Public Library**
53, av St-Aubin, Moonbeam ON P0L 1V0
Tel: 705-367-2462; *Fax:* 705-367-2120
biblio@moonbeam.ca
biblio.moonbeam.ca
Gisèle Belisle, Directrice-Responsable
Angèle Albert, Directrice adjointe

***Morson:* Big Grassy First Nation Public Library**
PO Box 453, Morson ON P0W 1J0
Tel: 807-488-5916; *Fax:* 807-488-5345
bglibrary@bgfn.on.ca
www.bgfn.on.ca/library.htm
Kitty Gale, Librarian

***Muncey:* Chippewas of the Thames**
RR#1, 328 Chippewa Rd., Muncey ON N0L 1Y0
Tel: 519-289-2176; *Fax:* 519-289-2230
Arlene Elm, Librarian

***Muncey:* Munsee-Delaware First Nation Public Library**
RR#1, Muncey ON N0L 1Y0
Tel: 519-289-5396; *Fax:* 519-289-5156
Rose Snake, CEO

***Murillo:* Oliver Paipoonge Public Library**
1 Baxendale Rd., Murillo ON P0T 2G0
Tel: 807-935-2729
www.olsn.ca/OliverPaipoonge
Maxine McCulloch, CEO
mmcculloch@post.library.on.ca

***Napanee:* Lennox & Addington County Library**
97 Thomas St. East, Napanee ON K7R 4B9
Tel: 613-354-4883; *Fax:* 613-354-3112
www.lennox-addington.on.ca
Mary Anne Evans, Director, Information Services
mevans@lennox-addington.on.ca
Susan Dalton, Manager, Information Services
sdalton@lennox-addington.on.ca

***Naughton:* Whitefish Lake First Nation Public Library**
c/o Band Offices, 25 Reserve Rd., Naughton ON P0M 2M0
Tel: 705-692-1102; *Fax:* 705-692-5010
library@wlfn.com
www.wlfn.com
Mary Fraser, Librarian

***Nepean:* Nepean Public Library/ Bibliothèque publique de Nepean**
101 Centrepointe Dr., Nepean ON K2G 5K7
Tel: 613-727-6637; *Fax:* 613-727-6677
www.biblioottawalibrary.ca/explore/branches/nc_e.cfm
George Skarzynski, Executive Director
george.skarzynski@library.on.ca
613-727-6637
Peter Loades, Head, Information Services
613-727-6659
Doris Rankin, Coordinator, Automated & Tech Services
613-727-6647
Fay Foster, Manager, Collections Development
613-727-6647

***Nestor Falls:* Ojibways of Onigaming First Nation Public Library**
School Rd., Nestor Falls ON P0X 1K0
Tel: 807-484-2612; *Fax:* 807-484-2352
onigamingfn@yahoo.com
Geraldine Kelly, CEO

***Newmarket:* Newmarket Public Library**
438 Park Ave., Newmarket ON L3Y 1W1
Tel: 905-953-5110; npl@newmarketpl.ca; *Fax:* 905-953-5104
www.newmarketpl.ca
Social Media: http://twitter.com/#!/newmarktlibrary; www.facebook.com/pages/Newmarket-Public-Library/247080242075
Todd Kyle, CEO
tkyle@newmarketpl.ca
Linda Peppiatt, Deputy CEO
lpeppiatt@newmarketpl.ca
905-953-5110 ext. 4740
Heather Halliday, Head of Adult Services
hhalliday@newmarketpl.ca
905-953-5110 ext. 4800
Susan Hoffman, Head of Children's Services
shoffman@newmarketpl.ca
905-953-5110 ext. 4680
Jennifer Leveridge, Community Services Librarian
jleveridge@newmarketpl.ca
905-953-5110 ext. 4710
Simon Chong, Systems Manager
schong@newmarketpl.ca
905-953-5110 ext. 4840

***Niagara Falls:* Niagara Falls Public Library**
4848 Victoria Ave., Niagara Falls ON L2E 4C5
Tel: 905-356-8080; *Fax:* 905-356-7004
nfpl@nflibrary.ca
www.nflibrary.ca
Joseph Longo, Chief Librarian
jlongo@nflibrary.ca
Andrew Porteus, Head, Reference & Information
aporteus@nflibrary.ca
Janet Martin, Head, Technical Services
jmartin@nflibrary.ca
Jan Leak, Systems Administrator
jmleak@nflibrary.ca

***Niagara on the Lake:* Niagara Historical Research Centre**
c/o Niagara on the Lake Public Library, 10, Anderson Lane, Niagara on the Lake ON L0S 1J0
Tel: 905-468-2023; *Fax:* 905-468-3334
historylinda@yahoo.ca
vaxxine.com/fa/notlpl/
Greg Smith, CEO
Linda Gula, Head of Reference
historylinda@yahoo.ca
905-468-2023

***Niagara on the Lake:* Niagara on the Lake Public Library**
10 Anderson Lane, Niagara on the Lake ON L0S 1J0
Tel: 905-468-2023; *Fax:* 905-468-3334
www.notlpubliclibrary.org
J. Crux, CEO
jcrux@notl.org
Debbie Smith, Assistant Library Manager
debbiesmith@notl.org
L. Tait, Library Assistant
ltait@notl.org

***Nipigon:* Nipigon Public Library**
25 Third St., Nipigon ON P0T 2J0
Tel: 807-887-3142; *Fax:* 807-887-3142
niplib@nwconx.net
www.nwconx.net/~niplib/nnpl.html
Sumiye Sugawara, Library Technician/CEO

***Nobel:* Shawanaga First Nation Public Library**
2 Church St., Nobel ON P0G 1G0
Tel: 705-366-2526; *Fax:* 705-366-2740
csousa_20@hotmail.com
Chelsie Sousa, CEO
csousa_20@hotmail.com

***North Bay:* North Bay Public Library**
271 Worthington St. East, North Bay ON P1B 1H1
Tel: 705-474-4830
library@cityofnorthbay.ca
www.cityofnorthbay.ca/library
Paul Walker, CEO
Rebecca Larocque, Head, Reference, AV & Systems
Judith Bouman, Head, Technical & Adult Services
Robert Boisvert, Head, French Services
Nora Elliott-Coutts, Deputy CEO & Head, Children's Services

***Norwood:* Asphodel-Norwood Public Library**
2363 County Rd. 45, Norwood ON K0L 2V0
Tel: 705-639-2228
norwest@asphodelnorwood.com
www.anpl.org

***Oakville:* Oakville Public Library**
120 Navy St., Oakville ON L6J 2Z4
Tel: 905-815-2042; *Fax:* 905-815-2024
Other Numbers: Information Oakville 905-815-2046
interloan@oakville.ca
www.opl.on.ca
Lori Sims, CEO
lsims@oakville.ca
Gail Richardson, Acting Director, Online Services
grichardson@oakville.ca
Charlotte Meissner, Director, Corporate Services
cmeissner@oakville.ca
Janice Kullas, Director, Service Planning & Development
jkullas@oakville.ca

***Ohsweken:* Six Nations Public Library**
PO Box 149, Ohsweken ON N0A 1M0
Tel: 519-445-2954; *Fax:* 519-445-2873
info@snpl.ca
www.snpl.ca
Sabrina Saunders, Director, Library Services
saunders@snpl.ca
519-445-2954

***Opasatika:* La Bibliothèque d'Opasatika/ Opasatika Public Library**
6, rue St. Antione, CP 100, Opasatika ON P0L 1Z0
Tél: 705-369-3421; *Téléc:* 705-369-2002
twpopas@ntl.sympatico.ca
www.geocities.com/bibliotheque_opasatika/
Diane Lambert, Bibliothécaire
librairi@ntl.sympatico.ca
705-369-3346

***Orangeville:* Orangeville Public Library**
1 Mill St., Orangeville ON L9W 2M2
Tel: 519-941-0610; *Fax:* 519-941-4698
info@orangeville.ca
www.orangeville.library.on.ca
Cindy Weir, CEO
cweir@orangeville.ca
519-941-0610 ext. 222

***Orillia:* Orillia Public Library**
500 Gill St., Orillia ON L3V 4L1
Tel: 705-325-2338; *Fax:* 705-327-1744
info@orilliapubliclibrary.ca
www.orilliapubliclibrary.ca/
Suzanne Campbell, Interim CEO
scampbell@orilliapubliclibrary.ca
Kelli Absalom, Director, Information Services
kabsalom@orilliapubliclibrary.ca
David Rowe, Director, Technical Services
drowe@orilliapubliclibrary.ca
Suzanne Campbell, Director, Children Services
scampbell@orilliapubliclibrary.ca

***Orillia:* Ramara Public Library**
5482 Hwy. 12 South, Orillia ON L3V 6H7
Tel: 705-325-5776; *Fax:* 705-325-8176
info@ramarapubliclibrary.org
www.ramarapubliclibrary.org
Janet Banfield, CEO

***Oshawa:* Oshawa Public Library**
65 Bagot St., Oshawa ON L1H 1N2
Tel: 905-579-6111; *Fax:* 905-433-8107
khaley@oshawalibrary.on.ca
www.oshawalibrary.on.ca
Ian Heckford, CEO
iheckford@oshawalibrary.on.ca
905-579-6111 ext. 212
Ellen Stroud, Manager, Branch Services
estroud@oshawalibrary.on.ca
905-579-6111 ext. 254
Rick Ficek, Manager, Information & Adult Services
rficek@oshawalibrary.on.ca
Anne Donnellan, Manager, Technical Services
adonnellan@oshawalibrary.on.ca
905-579-6111 ext. 224
Robert Merry, Manager, Corporate Services
rmerry@oshwawlibrary.on.ca
905-579-6111 ext. 214
Karen Haley, Executive Assistant
khaley@oshawalibrary.on.ca
905-579-6111 ext. 213

***Oshawa:* United Way - Oshawa, Whitby, Clarington, Brock & Scugog**
345 Simcoe St. South, Oshawa ON L1H 4J2
Tel: 905-436-7377; *Fax:* 905-436-6414
Toll-Free: 866-436-6910
informdurham@bellnet.ca
www.informdurham.com
Cathy Gowland, Manager, Information Services

***Ottawa:* ACA Bulletin**
PO Box 2596, Stn D, Ottawa ON K1P 5W6
Tel: 613-234-6977; *Fax:* 613-234-8500
aca@archivists.ca
archivists.ca/publications/bulletin.aspx
Larry Dohey, Editor
ldohey@nf.aibn.com

***Ottawa:* Archivaria**
PO Box 2596, Stn. D, Ottawa ON K1P 5W6
Tel: 613-234-6977; *Fax:* 613-234-8500
aca@archivists.ca
archivists.ca/publications/archivaria.aspx
Catherine Bailey, Editor

***Ottawa:* Bulletin**
Communications, Library & Archives Canada, 395 Wellington St., Ottawa ON K1A 0N4
Tel: 613-995-7969; *Fax:* 613-991-9871
publications@lac-bac.gc.ca
www.collectionscanada.ca/publications/bulletin/index-e.html
Jean-Marie Brière, Editor
Rhonda Wilson, Editor

***Ottawa:* CAML Review**
c/o Music Division, 395 Wellington St., Ottawa ON K1A 0N4
Tel: 613-996-7519; *Fax:* 613-952-2895
dmaley@laurentian.ca
www.yorku.ca/caml
Desmond Maley, Editor
Denise Prince, Editor

***Ottawa:* Feliciter**
#400, 1150 Morrison Dr., Ottawa ON K2H 8S9
Tel: 613-232-9625; *Fax:* 613-563-9895
jgreen@cla.ca
www.cla.ca/AM/Template.cfm?Section=Feliciter1
Mary-Lu Brennan, Convenor, Member Communications Advisory Committee

***Ottawa:* Impact**
#400, 1150 Morrison Dr., Ottawa ON K2H 8S9
Tel: 613-232-9625; *Fax:* 613-563-9895
Victoria Pennell, Editor

***Ottawa:* Ottawa Public Library/ Bibliothèque publique d'Ottawa**
120 Metcalfe St., Ottawa ON K1P 5M2
Tel: 613-580-2945; *Fax:* 613-567-8815
Other Numbers: Info Service: 613-580-2940
www.biblioottawalibrary.ca
Barbara Clubb, City Librarian and CEO
barbara.clubb@biblioottawalibrary.ca
Monique E. Désormeaux, Division Manager, Service Excellence
monique.desormeaux@biblioottawalibrary.ca
Elaine Condos, Division Manager, System Wide Services & Innovation
elaine.condos@biblioottawalibrary.ca
Danielle McDonald, Division Manager, Facilities & Business Services
danielle.mcdonald@biblioottawalibrary.ca
Jane Venus, Acrting Manager, Adult & Information Services
jane.venus@biblioottawalibrary.ca
Matthew Pritz, Manager, Business Services
Matthew.Pritz@ottawa.ca
Jane Venus, Manager, Children's & Teen Services
jane.venus@biblioottawalibrary.ca
Diana Pepall, Manager, Collection Development
diana.pepall@biblioottawalibrary.ca
Maureen McEvoy, Manager, Communications & Community Relations
maureen.mcevoy@biblioottawalibrary.ca
Jennifer Stirling, Manager, Digital Services
Jennifer.Stirling@biblioottawalibrary.ca
Nelly Beylouni-Zamat, Acting Manager, Diversity & Accessibility Services
Nelly.Beylouni-Zamat@biblioottawalibrary.ca
Craig Ginther, Manager, Innovation & Continuous Improvement
craig.ginther@biblioottawalibrary.ca
Richard Stark, Manager, Library Facilities, Planning & Development
richard.stark@biblioottawalibrary.ca
Line Gravelle, Manager, Main Library & Borrower Services
Line.Gravelle@biblioottawalibrary.ca
Anna Mould, Manager, Staff Development & Service Excellence
Anna.Mould@ottawa.ca
Donna Clark, Manager, Strategic Coordination
Donna.Clark@biblioottawalibrary.ca

***Ottawa:* School Libraries in Canada**
c/o Derrick Grose, Lisgar Collegiate Institute Library, 29 Lisgar St., Ottawa ON K2P 0B9
Fax: 613-235-7497
sliceditor@gmail.com
www.clatoolbox.ca/casl/slic/
Derrick Grose, Editor
613-239-2696
Mack D. Male, Technical Editor

***Owen Sound:* Owen Sound & North Grey Union Public Library**
824 - 1st Ave. West, Owen Sound ON N4K 4K4
Tel: 519-376-6623; *Fax:* 519-376-7170
library@owensound.library.on.ca
www.owensound.library.on.ca
Judy Armstrong, Library Director/CEO
jbarms@owensound.library.on.ca
519-376-6623 ext. 201
Richard Sulkers, Deputy Chief Librarian
rsulkers@owensound.library.on.ca
519-376-6623 ext. 210
Christine Carmichael, Technical Services & Systems Manager
carmichc@owensound.library.on.ca
519-376-6623 ext. 203
Beth Hall, Administrative & Public Services Manager
bhall@owensound.library.on.ca
519-376-6623 ext. 205
Nadia Danyluk, Children & Youth Services Librarian
ndanyluk@owensound.library.on.ca
519-376-6623 ext. 202
Tim Nicholls Harrison, Adult & Community Learning Services Manager
tnicholls-harrison@owensoundd.library.on.ca
519-376-6623 ext. 243

***Paris:* County of Brant Public Library**
12 William St., Paris ON N3L 1K7
Tel: 519-442-2433; *Fax:* 519-442-7582
www.brant.library.on.ca
Gay Kozak Selby, Chief Librarian
gay.kozakselby@brant.ca

***Parry Sound:* Parry Sound Public Library**
29 Mary St., Parry Sound ON P2A 1E3
Tel: 705-746-9601; *Fax:* 705-746-9601
pspl@vianet.ca
www.pspl.on.ca
Social Media:
www.facebook.com/group.php?gid=346576685525
Selena Martin, Assistant Librarian

***Parry Sound:* Seguin Township Public Library**
15 Humphrey Dr., Parry Sound ON P2A 2W8
Tel: 705-732-4526; *Fax:* 705-732-4526
humphreylibrary@cogeco.net
www.olsn.ca/seguin/index.html
Patricia Coles, Chief Executive Officer
pcoles@cogeco.net
Ruth Smith, Branch Head

***Parry Sound:* Wasauksing First Nation Public Library**
1508 Geewadin Rd., Parry Sound ON P2A 2X4
Tel: 705-746-2531; *Fax:* 705-746-5984
Carol M. Pegahmagabow, CEO

Pawitik: **Naotkamegwanning First Nation Public Library**
General Delivery, Pawitik ON P0X 1L0
Tel: 807-226-5710; *Fax:* 807-226-1066
nfnpl2010@live.ca
Janelle Crow, Chief Executive Officer

Pelee Island: **Pelee Island Public Library**
1073 West Shore Rd., Pelee Island ON N0R 1M0
Tel: 519-724-2028
Lynn Tiessen, Chair
Debbie Crawford, Librian
Eileen Perusek, Library Technician Volunteer

Pembroke: **Pembroke Public Library**
237 Victoria St., Pembroke ON K8A 4K5
Tel: 613-732-8844; *Fax:* 613-732-1116
askus@pembroke.library.on.ca
www.pembroke.library.on.ca
Margaret Mau, CEO

Penetanguishene: **Penetanguishene Public Library**
24 Simcoe St., Penetanguishene ON L9M 1R6
Tel: 705-549-7164; *Fax:* 705-549-3932
rmarchand@penetanguishene.library.on.ca
www.penetanguishene.library.on.ca
Rosemary Marchand, CEO
Cynthia Coté, Head, Public & Technical Services
ccote@penetanguishene.library.on.ca

Perth: **Perth Union Library**
30 Herriott St., Perth ON K7H 1T2
Tel: 613-267-1224; *Fax:* 613-267-7899
perthlibrary@vianet.ca
www.perthunionlibrary.ca
Elizabeth Goldman, CEO/Head Librarian
egoldman@perthunionlibrary.ca
Susan Synder, Children's, Interlibrary Loan

Petawawa: **Petawawa Public Library**
16 Civic Centre Rd., Petawawa ON K8H 3H5
Tel: 613-687-2227; *Fax:* 613-687-2527
info@petawawapubliclibrary.ca
www.petawawapubliclibrary.ca
C.M. Goldsmith, Librarian

Peterborough: **Library Lines**
520 Weller St., Peterborough ON K9H 2N6
Tel: 705-743-5998
gwjwthexton@nexicom.net
www.churchlibraries.ca/publications.htm
June Wilson Thexton, Editor

Peterborough: **Peterborough Public Library**
345 Aylmer St. North, Peterborough ON K9H 3V7
Tel: 705-745-5382; *Fax:* 705-745-8958
comments@city.peterborough.on.ca
www.peterborough.library.on.ca
Becky Rogers, CEO
brogers@city.peterborough.on.ca
705-745-5382 ext. 2380
Laura Gardner, Collection Development Librarian
lgardner@city.peterborough.on.ca
705-745-5382 ext. 2361
Marisa Giuliani, Access Services Librarian
mgiuliani@city.peterborough.on.ca
705-745-5382 ext. 2351
Betty-Kay Murray, Children's Librarian
bmurray@city.peterborough.on.ca
705-745-5382 ext. 2370
Karen Bisschop, Information Services Librarian
kbisschop@peterborough.on.ca
705-745-5382 ext. 2352

Philipsburg: **Region of Waterloo Library**
2017 Nafziger Rd., RR#2, Philipsburg ON N3A 3H4
Tel: 519-575-4590; *Fax:* 519-634-5371
libhq@region.waterloo.on.ca
www.rwl.library.on.ca
Lucille Bish, Director, Community Services
blucille@region.waterloo.on.ca
Katherine Seredynska, Manager, Public Services
skath@region.waterloo.on.ca
Kae Elgie, Manager, Information Services
ekae@region.waterloo.on.ca

Pickering: **Pickering Public Library**
1 The Esplanade, Pickering ON L1V 6K7
Tel: 905-831-6265; *Fax:* 905-831-6927
Toll-Free: 888-831-6266
TDD: 9058312789
help@picnet.org
www.picnet.org
Cathy Grant, CEO
Valerie Ridgeway, Deputy CEO
valerier@picnet.org
905-831-6265 ext. 6251
Elaine Bird, Director of Support Services
elaineb@picnet.org
905-831-6265 ext. 6224
Colleen Bolin, Manager of Branch Services
colleenb@picnet.org
905-831-6265 ext. 6003
Kathy Williams, Director of Public Services
kathyw@picnet.org
905-831-6265 ext. 6251

Picton: **County of Prince Edward Public Library**
208 Main St., Picton ON K0K 2T0
Tel: 613-476-5962; *Fax:* 613-476-3325
frdesk@peclibrary.org
www.peclibrary.org
Barbara Sweet, CEO
Dianne Cranshaw, Assistant CEO & Contact, Interlibrary Loan
613-399-2023
Krista Richardson, Manager, Archives
613-399-2023
Kate Konkin, Coordinator, Seniors Programs
613-476-5962
Eric Pierce, Coordinator, Information Technology & Computer Training
613-476-5962
Liz Zylstra, Coordinator, Youth Programs
613-476-5962
Christine Renaud, Branch Manager
613-476-5962

Port Carling: **Township of Muskoka Lakes Library Board**
69 Joseph St., Port Carling ON P0B 1J0
Tel: 705-765-5650; *Fax:* 705-765-0422
pclib@muskoka.com
www.muskoka.com/library
Elizabeth H. Glen, CEO/Librarian
pclib@muskoka.com
705-765-5650
Cathy Duck, Library Staff
Barb Neibert, Library Staff
Lorna Macfarlane, Library Staff
Mari Carson, Library Staff
Randy Thomson, Library Staff
Cynthia Michaud, Library Staff

Port Colborne: **Port Colborne Public Library**
310 King St., Port Colborne ON L3K 4H1
Tel: 905-834-6512; *Fax:* 905-835-5775
www.portcolbornelibrary.org
Jennifer R. Parry, Director of Library Services
Derek Miller, Chair
Robert Heil, CEO

Port Elgin: **Bruce County Public Library**
1243 McKenzie Rd., Port Elgin ON N0H 2C6
Tel: 519-832-6935; *Fax:* 519-832-9000
bruce2@brucecounty.on.ca
library.brucecounty.on.ca
Marzio Apolloni, CEO
mapolloni@brucecounty.on.ca
Shirley Morningstar, Contact, Children's Services
L. Wieler, Contact, Collection Development
Jo-Ann Alexander, Contact, Audiovisual
Dan Blacklock, Contact, ILLO
Chris Wood, Contact, Technical Services

Port Hope: **Port Hope Public Library**
31 Queen St., Port Hope ON L1A 2Y8
Tel: 905-885-4712; *Fax:* 905-885-4181
library@porthope.ca
www.phpl.ca
Barbara Stephenson, Chief Librarian
bstephenson@porthpe.ca
Alison Houston, Assistant Librarian
ahouston@porthope.ca

Port Loring: **Port Loring & District (Argyle) Public Library**
11767 Hwy. 522, Port Loring ON P0H 1Y0
Tel: 705-475-2316; *Fax:* 705-757-3284
ArgyleCommunityLibrary@hotmail.com
Patti O'Handley, Chief Executive Officer

Port McNicoll: **Tay Township Public Libraries**
715 - 4th Ave., Port McNicoll ON L0K 1R0
Tel: 705-534-3511; *Fax:* 705-534-3511
pmlibrary@tay.township.on.ca
www.tay.library.on.ca
Heather Walker, Head Librarian
hwalker@tay.township.on.ca
705-534-3511
Allison Thompson, CEO
athompson@tay.township.on.ca
705-534-7248 ext. 240
Robert Coryell, Chair
dcoryell@rogers.com

Port Perry: **Mississaugas of Scugog Island First Nation Library**
22600 Island Rd., Port Perry ON L9L 1B6
Tel: 905-985-1826; *Fax:* 905-985-7958
library@scugogfirstnation.com
Joan Wood, Librarian
jwood@scugogfirstnation.com
905-985-1826 ext. 222

Port Perry: **Scugog Memorial Public Library**
231 Water St., Port Perry ON L9L 1A8
Tel: 905-985-7686; *Fax:* 905-985-7210
info@scugoglibrary.ca
www.scugoglibrary.ca
Amy Caughlin, CEO
acaughlin@scugoglibrary.ca
Wendy Tang, Head, Reference

Port Rowan: **Port Rowan Public Library**
1034 Main St., Port Rowan ON N0E 1M0
Tel: 519-586-3201; *Fax:* 519-586-3297
norfolk.library@norfolkcounty.ca
www.ncpl.ca
Marsha Johnstone, Librarian

Powassan: **Powassan & District Union Public Library**
324 Clark St., Powassan ON P0H 1Z0
Tel: 705-724-3618; *Fax:* 705-724-5525
hmcdonnell@ontera.net
powlib.www2.onlink.net
Helen McDonnell, CEO
hmcdonnell@post.library.on.ca

Prescott: **Prescott Public Library**
360 Dibble St. West, Prescott ON K0E 1T0
Tel: 613-925-4340; *Fax:* 613-925-0100
library@prescott.ca
www.prescott.ca/library/index.asp
Jane McGuire, Chief Librarian/CEO
Susen Kaylo Raas, Assistant Librarian
Linda Doris, Library Assistant
Roxanne Brown, Library Assistant

Rainy River: **Rainy River Public Library**
202 - 4th St., Rainy River ON P0W 1L0
Tel: 807-852-3375; *Fax:* 807-852-3375
librr@tbaytel.net
my.tbaytel.net/librr/
Sheila McIntosh, Librarian/CEO
Corey Dyck, Assistant Librarian
librr@nwconx.net

Rama: **Chippewas of Rama First Nation Public Library**
6147 Rama Rd., Rama ON L3V 6H6
Tel: 705-325-3611; *Fax:* 705-325-2801
sherryl@ramafirstnation.ca
Sarah Cunningham, Libary Coordinator
sarahc@ramafirstnation.ca
705-325-3611 ext. 1405
Shelley Snache, Children's Services
shelley.snache@mnjikaning.ca
705-325-3611 ext. 1437

Red Lake: **Red Lake Public Library**
117 Howey St., Red Lake ON P0V 2M0
Tel: 807-727-2230; *Fax:* 807-727-2230
rllib212@yahoo.com
www.nwconx.net/~rllib
Arlene Johnson, CEO

Red Rock: **Red Rock Public Library**
42 Salls St., Red Rock ON P0T 2P0
Tel: 807-886-2558; *Fax:* 807-886-2558
rrocklib@gmail.com
www.nextlibrary.com/redrock
Sandra Parker, Librarian

Redbridge: **Phelps Public Library**
42 Old Mill Rd., RR#1, Redbridge ON P0H 2A0
Tel: 705-663-2720
Beverly Reynolds, Librarian

Renfrew: **Renfrew Public Library**
13 Railway Ave. East, Renfrew ON K7V 3A9
Tel: 613-432-8151; *Fax:* 613-432-7680
renlib@renfrew.library.on.ca
www.renfrew.library.on.ca
Bettijane O'Neill, Chief Librarian
Susan Klinck, Head, Children Services

Richards Landing: **St Joseph Twp Public Library**
PO Box 9, Richards Landing ON P0R 1J0
Tel: 705-246-2353; *Fax:* 705-246-2353
sjtlibrary@ontera.net
stjosephisland.net
Sharon Thomas, Librarian/Treasurer/CEO

Richmond Hill: **Richmond Hill Public Library**
1 Atkinson St., Richmond Hill ON L4C 0H5
Tel: 905-884-9288; *Fax:* 905-884-6544
www.rhpl.richmondhill.on.ca
Social Media: www.facebook.com/rhpl.news
Jane Horrocks, CEO
Catherine Charles, Corporate Relations Officer
ccharles@rhpl.ca
905-770-0310 ext. 300

Rockland: **Bibliothèque publique de Clarence-Rockland/ Clarence-Rockland Public Library**
1560, rue Laurier, Rockland ON K4K 1P7
Tél: 613-446-5680; *Téléc:* 613-446-1518
biblioinfo@biblibclarence-rockland.ca
Daniel Noel, Directeur général
Michèle Chrétien, Responsable

Roseneath: **Alderville Learning Centre & Library**
11696 Second Line Rd., Roseneath ON K0K 2X0
Tel: 905-352-2488; *Fax:* 905-352-1080
Other Numbers: 905-352-2793 (Learning Centre)
aldervillelearningcentre@eagle.ca
www.aldervillelearningcentre.com
Dona Wigmore, Librarian

St Catharines: **St Catharines Public Library**
54 Church St., St Catharines ON L2R 7K2
Tel: 905-688-6103; *Fax:* 905-688-6292
admin@stcatharines.library.on.ca
www.stcatharines.library.on.ca
Lilita Stripnieks, CEO
lstripnieks@stcatharines.library.on.ca
905-688-6103 ext. 235
Jack Foster, Business Administrator
David Bott, Manager, IT & Networks
John Dunn, Manager, Automated System & Technical Services
Diane Andrusko, Manager, Adult Information Services
Ann McKenzie, Manager, Children's & Community Services
Anna Chiota, Manager, Branch Services
Anne Penfold, Manager, Circulation

St Charles: **St. Charles Public Library**
22 Ste. Anne St., St Charles ON P0M 2W0
Tel: 705-867-5332; *Fax:* 705-867-2511
stcharles-library@yahoo.ca
cap-pac.8m.com
Nicole Lafontaine, Chief Librarian
stcharles-library@yahoo.ca
705-867-5332
Carol Vaillant, Assistant Librarian

Saint-Isidore: **Bibliothèque publique de la municipalité de La Nation**
25, rue de L'Arena, Saint-Isidore ON K0C 2B0
Tel: 613-524-2252; *Fax:* 613-524-2545
biblioinfo@nationmun.ca
www.nationmunbiblio.ca
Social Media:
www.facebook.com/group.php?gid=109251539103571
Jeanne Leroux, Directrice général
jeanneleroux@nationmun.ca
613-524-2252

St Marys: **St Marys Public Library**
15 Church St. North, St Marys ON N4X 1B4
Tel: 519-284-3346; *Fax:* 519-284-2630
libraryinfo@stmaryspubliclibrary.ca
www.townofstmarys.com/public-library/
Social Media: http://twitter.com/#!/stmaryspl;
www.facebook.com/group.php?gid=33345900699
Yunmi Hwang, Librarian/CEO
yhwang@town.stmarys.on.ca
Jan McClelland, Library Technician
jmcclelland@town.stmarys.on.ca
Julie Robson, Library Clerk

St. Thomas: **Elgin County Library**
450 Sunset Dr., St. Thomas ON N5R 5V1
Tel: 519-631-1460; *Fax:* 519-631-9209
sloponen@elgin-county.on.ca
www.library.elgin-county.on.ca
Sandi Loponen, Library Coordinator
sloponen@elgin-county.on.ca
Dalene Van Zyl, Reference Resource Person
dvanzyl@elgin-county.on.ca
Susan Morrell, Reference Resource Person
smorrell@elgin-county.on.ca

St Thomas: **St Thomas Public Library**
153 Curtis St., St Thomas ON N5P 3Z7
Tel: 519-631-6050; *Fax:* 519-631-1987
rdenham@st-thomas.library.on.ca
www.st-thomas.library.on.ca
Rudi Denham, CEO
Paul Blower, Head, Reference/Adult Services
pblower@st-thomas.library.on.ca
Heather Robinson, Head, Children & Teens Services
hrobinson@st-thomas.library.on.ca

Sandy Lake: **Deer Lake Indian Band Library**
c/o Band Offices via Favourable Lake PO, Sandy Lake ON P0V 1V0
L. Stoney, Librarian

Saugeen: **Saugeen First Nation Library**
812 French Bay Rd., Saugeen ON N0H 2L0
Tel: 519-797-5986; *Fax:* 519-797-5987
sfnlibrary@bmts.com
Theresa Gill, CEO

Sault Ste Marie: **Batchewana First Nation**
236 Frontenac St., RR#4, Sault Ste Marie ON P6A 5K9
Tel: 705-759-0914; *Fax:* 705-759-9171
Toll-Free: 877-236-2632
mcdonagh@batchewana.ca
www.batchewana.ca
Darlene Syrette, Librarian

Sault Ste Marie: **Prince Township Library/ Bibliothèque publique du Canton Prince**
3042 Second Line, RR#6, Sault Ste Marie ON P6A 6K4
Tel: 705-779-3653; *Fax:* 705-779-2725
ptpl@twp.prince.on.ca
www.twp.prince.on.ca
Marguerite LaHaye, CEO
ptpl@twp-rince.on.ca
705-779-3653

Sault Ste Marie: **Sault Ste Marie Public Library**
50 East St., Sault Ste Marie ON P6A 3C3
Tel: 705-759-5236
Other Numbers: 705-759-5242 (Admin.); 705-759-5231 (Account info.)
www.ssmpl.ca
Christopher Rous, Chair
Elizabeth Rossnagel, Director, Public Libraries
e.rossnagel@cityssm.on.ca
Mark Jones, Acting Head, Technical Services & Circulation
m.jones@cityssm.on.ca
Roxanne Rissanen, Acting Head, Public Services
r.rissanen@cityssm.on.ca
Matthew MacDonald, Children's Librarian
m.macdonald@cityssm.on.ca
Julie Ringrose, Adult Services Librarian
j.ringrose@cityssm.on.ca

Savant Lake: **Savant Lake Community Library**
General Delivery, Savant Lake ON P0V 2S0
Tel: 807-584-2242; *Fax:* 807-584-2272
Barbara Smith, Principal

Schreiber: **Schreiber Public Library**
314 Scotia St., Schreiber ON P0T 2S0
Tel: 807-824-2477; *Fax:* 807-824-2996
schlib@nwconx.net
www.schreiberlibrary.ca
Donna Mikeluk, Head Librarian
schlib@nwconx.net
807-824-2477
Sue Currie, Assistant Librarian
807-824-2477

Shannonville: **Tyendinaga Township Public Library**
852 Melrose Rd., RR#1, Shannonville ON K0K 3A0
Tel: 613-967-0606; *Fax:* 613-396-2080
librarian@ttpl.ca
www.ttpl.ca
Frances Smith, Librarian/CEO

Sheguiandah: **Sheguiandah First Nation Public Library**
142 O'Ogemah Miilcan Rd., Sheguiandah ON P0P 1W0
Tel: 705-368-2198; *Fax:* 705-368-3697
sheg1stnationpl@yahoo.com
Tammi Assinewai, Librarian

Shelburne: **Shelburne Public Library**
PO Box 127, Shelburne ON L0N 1S0
Tel: 519-925-2168; *Fax:* 519-925-2168
spl1@bellnet.ca
Mary Lynne Armstrong, CEO

Sheshegwaning: **Sheshegwaning Public Library**
1125 Sheshegwaning St., Sheshegwaning ON P0P 1X0
Tel: 705-283-3014; *Fax:* 705-283-4038
debracada@hotmail.com
www.olsn.ca/sheshegwaning
Debra Cada, CEO
debracada@hotmail.com

Shoal Lake: **Iskutewisakaggun #39 First Nation Community Public Library**
PO Box 5, Kejick Post Office, Shoal Lake ON P0X 1E0
Tel: 807-733-3621; *Fax:* 807-733-3635
i_ross38@hotmail.com
Irene Ross, CEO
i_ross38@hotmail.com

Simcoe: **Norfolk County Public Library**
46 Colborne St. South, Simcoe ON N3Y 4H3
Tel: 519-426-3506; *Fax:* 519-426-0657
library@norfolkcounty.on.ca
www.norfolk.library.on.ca
Bill Hett, CEO
Janet Cowan, Administrative Assistant

Sioux Lookout: **Sioux Lookout Public Library**
21 5th Ave., Sioux Lookout ON P8T 1B3
Tel: 807-737-3660; *Fax:* 807-737-4046
info@slpl.on.ca
www.slpl.on.ca
Wendy MacDonald, CEO/Chief Librarian
slpl@nwconw.net
807-737-3660

Sioux Narrows: **Sioux Narrows Public Library**
Sioux Narrows Public School, PO Box 119, Sioux Narrows ON P0X 1N0
Tel: 807-226-5204; *Fax:* 807-226-5712
library@kmts.ca
Alice Motlong, Head Librarian
807-226-5204

Smiths Falls: **Smiths Falls Public Library**
81 Beckwith St. North, Smiths Falls ON K7A 2B9
Tel: 613-283-2911; *Fax:* 613-283-9834
smithsfallslibrary@vianet.ca
Karen Schecter, Chief Librarian
Elizabeth Lavender, Head, Reference
Debra Kuehl, Children's Librarian

Smithville: **West Lincoln Public Library**
Town Hall Complex, 318 Canboro St., Smithville ON L0R 2A0
Tel: 905-957-3756
westlincolnlibrary.tripod.com

Smooth Rock Falls: **Smooth Rock Falls Public Library/ Bibliothèque publique de Smooth Rock Falls**
120 Ross Rd., Smooth Rock Falls ON P0L 2B0
Tel: 705-338-2318; *Fax:* 705-338-2330
smooth@ntl.sympatico.ca
Lise Gagnon, CEO
Lynne Pelletier, Contact, ILL & Children's Services

South River: **South River-Machar Union Library**
22 Marie St., PO Box 190, South River ON P0A 1X0
Tel: 705-386-0222; *Fax:* 705-386-0222
osrmlibrary@hotmail.com
www.oisn.ca/srmupl
Jan Heinonen, CEO
osrmlibrary@hotmail.com
Jo-Ann Long, Assistant Librarian
osrmlibrary@hotmail.com

Southwold: **Oneida Community Library**
2315 Keystone Pl., Southwold ON N0L 2G0
Tel: 519-652-3977
Corey Nicholas, CEO

***Spanish:* Spanish Public Library/ Bibliothèque publique du Spanish**
8 Trunk Rd., Spanish ON P0P 2A0
Tel: 705-844-2555; *Fax:* 705-844-2555
library@town.spanish.on.ca
www.town.spanish.on.ca/pages/library.asp
Hanne Sauvé, Chief Librarian
library@town.spanish.on.ca
705-844-2555
Jannifer MacPhail, Front Desk

***Spencerville:* Edwardsburgh / Cardinal Public Library**
5 Henderson St., Spencerville ON K0E 1X0
Tel: 613-658-5575
cardinallibrary@bellnet.ca
www.cardinallibrary.ca
Marva Sothmann, Head Librarian
Kathy Colwell, Library Assistant
Beth Johnson, Library Assistant

***Stayner:* Clearview Public Library**
201 Huron St., Stayner ON L0M 1S0
Tel: 705-428-3595
jlachapelle@clearview.ca
www.clearview.library.on.ca
Social Media:
www.facebook.com/group.php?gid=285803031750
Joyce Smith, Chair
Jennifer LaChappelle, Chief Executive Officer

***Stirling:* Stirling-Rawdon Public Library**
43 Front St., Stirling ON K0K 3E0
Tel: 613-395-2837
sue@stirlinglibrary.com
www.stirlinglibrary.com/
Sue Winfield, CEO/Head Librarian
Theresa Brennan, Assistant Librarian
Jaye Bannon, Children's Librarian

***Stonecliffe:* Head, Clara & Maria Township Public Library**
15 Township Hall Rd., Stonecliffe ON K0J 2K0
Tel: 613-586-2526; *Fax:* 613-586-2596
hcmlibra@xplornet.com
Gayle Watters, CEO

***Stouffville:* Whitchurch-Stouffville Public Library**
30 Burkholder St., Stouffville ON L4A 4K1
Tel: 905-642-7323; *Fax:* 905-640-1384
Toll-Free: 888-603-4292
cnordheimerjames@whitchurch-library.on.ca
www.whitchurch-library.on.ca
Carolyn Nordheimer James, CEO
cnordheimer@whitchurch-library.on.ca
905-642-7323 ext. 223
Catherine Sword, Coordinator, Public Services
csword@whitchurch-library.on.ca
905-642-7323 ext. 224
Anne Houle, Coordinator, Children & Youth Services
ahoule@whitchurch-library.on.ca
905-642-7323 ext. 228
Marcia Jackson-Friginette, Coordinator, Technical Services
mfriginette@whitchurch-library.on.ca
905-642-7323 ext. 222

***Stratford:* Stratford Public Library**
19 St Andrew St., Stratford ON N5A 1A2
Tel: 519-271-0220; *Fax:* 519-271-3843
spl@pcin.on.ca
www.stratford.library.on.ca
Sam Coghlan, CEO

***Strathroy:* Middlesex County Library**
34B Frank St., Strathroy ON N7G 2R4
Tel: 519-245-8237; *Fax:* 519-245-8238
www.middlesex.library.on.ca
Lindsay Brock, Reference Librarian
519-245-1290
Patti Wallace, Children's Librarian
519-245-8237 ext. 27
Carol Roberts, Branch Coordinator
croberts@county.middlesex.on.ca
519-245-8237 ext. 22
Stan MacKenzie, Library Technician, Interlibrary Loans
519-245-8237 ext. 26
Pamela Warzecha, Library Technician, Special Services
519-245-8237 ext. 21

***Stratton:* Stratton Community Library**
11605 Hwy. 11, Stratton ON P0W 1N0
Tel: 807-483-5455; *Fax:* 807-483-5882
morley@nwonet.net
Anna H.M. Boily, Clerk-Treasurer

***Sturgeon Falls:* West Nipissing Public Library/ Bibliothèque publique de Nipissing Ouest**
#107, 225 Holditch St., Sturgeon Falls ON P2B 1T1
Tel: 705-753-2620; *Fax:* 705-753-2131
mail@wnpl.ca
www.wnpl.ca
Carole Marion, Chief Executive Officer
cmarion@wnpl.ca

***Sudbury:* Greater Sudbury Public Library/ Bibliothèque publique du grand Sudbury**
74 Mackenzie St., Sudbury ON P3C 4X8
Tel: 705-673-1155; *Fax:* 705-673-6145
www.sudbury.library.on.ca
Social Media: www.facebook.com/group.php?gid=19877797824
Martin Lajeunesse, Chair
(Roy) Hannu Piironen, Vice-Chair

***Sundridge:* Sundridge-Strong Union Public Library**
110 Main St., Sundridge ON P0A 1Z0
Tel: 705-384-7311; *Fax:* 705-384-7311
sslibrary@hotmail.com
www.olsn.ca/sundridgestronglibrary
Denise Rogers, Librarian

***Sutton West:* Chippewas of Georgina Island First Nation Public Library**
Joseph Snake Rd., RR#2, Sutton West ON L0E 1R0
Tel: 705-437-4328; *Fax:* 705-437-4597
Karen Foster, CEO
karenfoster@knet.ca
705-437-4327
Lynn Mooney, Literacy Coordinator
705-437-4327

***Tehkummah:* Tehkummah Township Public Library**
Municipal Offices Bldg., RR#1, Tehkummah ON P0P 2C0
Tel: 705-859-3301; *Fax:* 705-859-2605
tehklib@yahoo.ca
Judy McDermid, Librarian

***Temagami:* Temagami Public Library**
Welcome Centre, 7 Lakeshore Dr., Temagami ON P0H 2H0
Tel: 705-569-2945; *Fax:* 705-569-2834
library@temagami.ca
www.temagami.ca/htm/library.htm
Shelley Rowland, CEO/Librarian

***Terrace Bay:* Terrace Bay Public Library**
13 Selkirk Ave., Terrace Bay ON P0T 2W0
Tel: 807-825-3315; *Fax:* 807-825-1249
terracebaypl@hotmail.com
terracebay.library.on.ca
Social Media:
www.facebook.com/group.php?gid=116263591747005
Mary Deschatelets, CEO
807—82-5-33 ext. 234
Jean Fenton, Assistant Librarian
807—82-5-33 ext. 222

***Thamesville:* Delaware Nation Public Library**
RR#3, Thamesville ON N0P 2K0
Tel: 519-692-3411; *Fax:* 519-692-5522
Other Numbers: Alternate tel: 519/692-3936
dkstonefi@yahoo.ca
Darryl Stonefish, CEO

***Thessalon:* Thessalon First Nation Public Library**
RR#2, PO Box 9, Thessalon ON P0R 1L0
Tel: 705-842-1258; *Fax:* 705-842-2332
thessalonfirstnationlibrary@hotmail.com
Julie Bisaillon, Chief Executive Officer
bisaillon_julie@hotmail.com

***Thessalon:* Thessalon Union Public Library**
187 Main St., Thessalon ON P0R 1L0
Tel: 705-842-2306; *Fax:* 705-842-5690
library@thesslibcap.com
www.thesslibcap.com
Social Media:
www.facebook.com/group.php?gid=104998919541074
Sandra McKee, CEO/Librarian
Sharon Couvillon, Contact, Technical Services

***Thornbury:* The Blue Mountains Public Library**
PO Box 580, Thornbury ON N0H 2P0
Tel: 519-599-3681; *Fax:* 519-599-7951
info@thebluemountainslibrary.ca
www.thebluemountainslibrary.ca
Carol Cooley, CEO
ccooley@thebluemountainslibrary.ca
Laurel Moss, Coordinator, Technical Services
lmoss@thebluemountainslibrary.ca
Jennifer Perks, Coordinator, Children & Youth Services
jperks@thebluemountainslibrary.ca
Donna St. Jacques, Coordinator, Desk Services
dstjacques@thebluemountainslibrary.ca

***Thorold:* Thorold Public Library**
14 Ormond St. North, Thorold ON L2V 1Y8
Tel: 905-227-2581; *Fax:* 905-227-2311
thoroldpubliclibrary@cogeco.net
www.thoroldpubliclibrary.ca
Patricia Bronson, CEO
pbronson@cogeco.net
905-227-2581
Tony Vandermaas, Chair
Cheryl Bowman, Contact, Audiovisual, ILLO, Reference & Technical Services

***Thunder Bay:* Thunder Bay Public Library**
285 Red River Rd., Thunder Bay ON P7B 1A9
Tel: 807-345-8275; *Fax:* 807-344-5119
Other Numbers: 807-624-4200 (Reference); 807-344-7138 (Renewals)
adults@tbpl.ca (Adult services)
www.tbpl.ca
George Saarinen, Chair
gsaarinen@tbpl.ca
Gina La Force, Chief Librarian
glaforce@tbpl.ca
807-684-6802
Tina Tucker, Director, Community Development
ttucker@tbpl.ca
807-684-6813
Yvonne Wodell, Director, Human Resources
ywodell@tbpl.ca
807-684-6806
Joanna Aegard, Head, Virtual Library Services
jaegard@tbpl.ca
807-684-6819
Stephen Hurrell, Head, Automated Support Systems
shurrell@tbpl.ca
807-684-6807
Angela Meady, Head, Children's & Youth Services
ameady@tbpl.ca
807-684-6810
Barb Philp, Head, Adult Services
bphilp@tbpl.ca
807-684-6811
Sylvia Renaud, Head, Technical Services
srenaud@tbpl.ca
807-684-6808
Jesse Roberts, Head, Reference Services
jroberts@tbpl.ca
807-624-4203

***Tillsonburg:* Tillsonburg Public Library**
2 Library Lane, Tillsonburg ON N4G 4S7
Tel: 519-842-5571; *Fax:* 519-842-2941
publiclibrary@tillsonburg.ca
Matthew Scholtz, Librarian
mscholtz@web.ocl.net

***Timmins:* Timmins Public Library/ Bibliothèque municipale de Timmins**
320 Second Ave., Timmins ON P4N 8A4
Tel: 705-360-2623; *Fax:* 705-360-2688
tpl_2@timmins.ca
tpl.timmins.ca
Judith Heinzen, CEO
tpl_4@timmins.ca
705-360-8520
Elaine De Bonis, Assistant Director
elaine.debonis@timmins.ca
705-360-8517
Teresa Woodrow, Head, Support Services
teresa.woodrow@timmins.ca
705-360-8523
Chantal Benson, Head, Technical Support & Services
chantal.benson@timmins.ca
705-360-8518

***Toronto:* ACCESS**
#303, 100 Lombard St., Toronto ON M5C 1M3
Tel: 416-363-3388; *Fax:* 416-941-9581
Toll-Free: 866-873-9867
Other Numbers: Toll Free Fax: 1-800-387-1181
info@accessola.com
www.accessola.com
Larry Moore, Editor

***Toronto:* The Bibliographical Society of Canada Bulletin / La Société bibliographique du canada. Bulletin**
c/o Anne McGaughey, PO Box 575, Stn. P, Toronto ON M5S 2T1
Tel: 416-487-6729
mcgaughe@yorku.ca
www.library.utoronto.ca/bsc
Patricia Belier, Editor

***Toronto:* Cross Cultural Communication Centre**
2909 Dundas St. West, Toronto ON M6P 1Z1
Tel: 416-760-7855; *Fax:* 416-760-7911
Carmen Alcalde, Librarian
Beverly Lawrence, Assistant Librarian

***Toronto:* Informed**
c/o Claude T. Bissell Bldg., 140 St George St., Toronto ON M5S 3G6
Tel: 416-978-3034; *Fax:* 416-978-5762
alumni@fis.utoronto.ca
www.fis.utoronto.ca/people/fisaa/FISnewsletter/
Judy Donnelly, Editor
Sara Figueiredo, Editor

***Toronto:* Jewish Public Library of Toronto**
4600 Bathurst St., 4th Fl., Toronto ON M2R 3V3
Tel: 416-635-2996
jewishpubliclibrary@ujafed.org
Susan Jackson, Executive Director, Latner Centre for Jewish Knowledge & Heritage
416-635-2996

***Toronto:* Off the Record**
#301, 258 Adelaide St. East, Toronto ON M5A 1N1
Tel: 416-533-9592; *Fax:* 416-533-1481
aao@aao-archivists.ca
http://aao-archivists.ca/news/off-the-record
Shelley Respondek, Director
director2@aao-archivists.ca

***Toronto:* Papers of the Bibliographical Society of Canada / Cahiers de la Société bibliographique du canada**
42 Belmont St., Toronto ON M5R 1P8
Tel: 416-487-6729
slatham@gbrownc.on.ca
www.library.utoronto.ca/bsc/paperseng.html
Sheila Latham, Editor
Jeannine Green, Review Editor (English)
Basil Stuart-Stubbs, Chair, Publications Committee

***Toronto:* Shelf Life**
789 Yonge St., Toronto ON M4W 2G8
Tel: 416-393-7215
www.torontopubliclibrary.ca/new_she_index.jsp
Nancy Marshall, Library Board Contact

***Toronto:* The Teaching Librarian**
#303, 100 Lombard St., Toronto ON M5C 1M3
Tel: 416-363-3388; *Fax:* 416-941-9581
Toll-Free: 866-873-9867
membership@accessola.com
www.accessola.com/osla/about/magazine.htm

***Toronto:* Toronto Public Library**
789 Yonge St., Toronto ON M4W 2G8
Tel: 416-393-7000; *Fax:* 416-393-7083
TDD: 4163937100
www.torontopubliclibrary.ca
Linda MacKenzie, Director, Research & Reference Libraries
lmackenzie@torontopubliclibrary.ca
416-393-7133
Ron Dyck, Director, Information Technology & Facilities
rdyck@torontopubliclibrary.ca
416-393-7130
Katherine Palmer, Director, Planning & Policy
kpalmer@torontopubliclibrary.ca
416-395-5602
Linda Hazzan, Director, Marketing & Communications
lhazzan@torontopubliclibrary.ca
416-393-7214
Anne Bailey, Director, Branch Libraries
abailey@torontopubliclibrary.ca
416-397-5944
Vickery Bowles, Director, Collections Management
vbowles@torontopubliclibrary.ca
416-395-5506
Dan Keon, Director, Human Resources
dkeon@torontopubliclibrary.ca
416-395-5850
Heather Rumball, President/Director of Development, Toronto Public Library Foundation
hrumball@torontopubliclibrary.ca
416-393-7134

***Trenton:* Quinte West Public Library**
7 Creswell Dr., Trenton ON K8V 6X5
Tel: 613-394-3381; *Fax:* 613-394-2079
Other Numbers: 613-394-3381, ext. 3322 (Circulation services)
info.qwpl@city.quintewest.on.ca
www.library.quintewest.com
Craig Desjardins, Chair
Rita Turtle, Chief Exectuive Officer
rturtle.qwpl@city.quintewest.on.ca
613-394-3381 ext. 3315
Robert Amesse, Coordinator, Adult Information & Reference
ramesse.qwpl@city.quintewest.on.ca
613-394-3381 ext. 3325
Rosemary Kirby, Contact, Children's Information & Reference
rkirby.qwpl@city.quintewest.on.ca
613-394-3381 ext. 3311
Linda Lafond, Contact, Interlibrary Loan Information
illo.qwpl@city.quintewest.on.ca
613-394-3381 ext. 3316
Kim Vivian, Contact, Homeward Bound
kvivian.qwpl@city.quintewest.on.ca
613-394-3381 ext. 3325

***Tweed:* Municipality of Tweed Public Library**
255 Metcalf St., Tweed ON K0K 3J0
Tel: 613-478-1066; *Fax:* 613-478-6457
tweedlibrary@vianet.ca
tweedlibrary.ca
Catherine Anderson, CEO

***Uxbridge:* Uxbridge Twp Public Library**
9 Toronto St. South, Uxbridge ON L9P 1P3
Tel: 905-852-9747
uxlib@powergate.ca
www.uxlib.com
Alexandra Hartmann, Chief Librarian
Steve LeMottee, Interim Head of Reference
Pam Noble, Head, Children's Services

***Val Rita:* Val Rita-Harty Public Library/ Bibliothèque municipale de Val Rita-Harty**
106, rue Gouvernement, Val Rita ON P0L 2G0
Tel: 705-335-8700; *Fax:* 705-335-8700
bibliovalrita@hotmail.com
www.valharty.ca
Cecile Lamontagne, Présidente du conseil bibliothèque

***Vankleek Hill:* Champlain Township Public Library/ Bibliothèque Champlain**
94 Main St. East, PO Box 520, Vankleek Hill ON K0B 1R0
Tel: 613-678-2216; *Fax:* 613-678-2216
library@champlaintwplibrary.ca
www.champlaintwplibrary.ca
Lise Béliveau, Chair
Lynda Poyser, CEO & Head Librarian
lpoyser@champlaintwplibrary.ca
Diane Bourgault, Circulation Clerk & Library Assistant
dianeb@champlaintwplibrary.ca
Margaret MacMillan, Circulation Clerk & Library Assistant
marg@champlaintwplibrary.ca
Cynthia Martin, Circulation Clerk & Library Assistant
cynthia@champlaintwplibrary.ca

***Vaughan:* Vaughan Public Libraries**
900 Clark Ave. West, Vaughan ON L4J 8C1
Tel: 905-653-7323; *Fax:* 905-709-1530
www.vaughanpl.info
Social Media: twitter.com/#!/vaughanpl;
www.facebook.com/pages/Vaughan-Public-Libraries/133050006764886
Margie Singleton, Chief Executive Officer
margie.singleton@vaughan.ca
905-653-7323 ext. 4101
Aleksandra Dowiat Vine, Director, Planning & Communication
aleksandra.dowiat-vine@vaughan.ca
905-653-7323 ext. 4120
Marilyn Guy, Director, Operations
marilyn.guy@vaughan.ca
905-653-7323 ext. 4114
Sandy Vander Werff, Director, Finance
sandy.vanderwerff@vaughan.ca
905-653-7323 ext. 4104
Terri Watman, Director, Service Delivery
terri.watman@vaughan.ca
905-653-7323 ext. 4124

***Virginiatown:* McGarry Twp Public Library/ Bibliothèque publique de McGarry**
1 - 27 St., Virginiatown ON P0K 1X0
Tel: 705-634-2312; *Fax:* 705-634-2312
mcgarry@onlink.net
www.mcgarrypubliclibrary.8m.com/main_en.html
Leah Collins, CEO/Librarian

***Wainfleet:* Wainfleet Twp Public Library**
19M9 Park St., PO Box 118, Wainfleet ON L0S 1V0
Tel: 905-899-1277; *Fax:* 905-899-2495
www.wainfleetlibrary.ca
Lorrie Atkinson, CEO
latkinson@wainfleetlibrary.ca
Leanne Good, Library Programmer
lgood@wainfleetlibrary.ca
Cheryl Davis-Catchpaw, Administrative Assistant/Library Clerk
cdavis-catchpaw@wainfleetlibrary.ca
Dariusz Zelichowski, IT/Systems Specialist
wainweb@township.wainfleet.org

***Wallaceburg:* Bkejwanong First Nation Public Library**
RR#3, Wallaceburg ON N8A 4K9
Tel: 519-627-7034; *Fax:* 519-627-7035
bkejlib@mail.com
Lynda Lou Classens, Librarian/CEO
library@wifn.org
519-627-7034

***Wasaga Beach:* Wasaga Beach Public Library**
120 Glenwood Dr., Wasaga Beach ON L9Z 2K5
Tel: 705-429-5481; *Fax:* 705-429-5481
wblibrary@georgian.net
www.wasagabeach.library.on.ca
Jackie Beaudin, CEO

***Waterloo:* Waterloo Public Library**
35 Albert St., Waterloo ON N2L 5E2
Tel: 519-886-1310; *Fax:* 519-886-7936
TDD: 18667863942
cbrown@wpl.ca
www.wpl.ca
Cathy Matyas, Chief Librarian
cmatyas@wpl.ca
519-886-1310 ext. 123
Gloria Van Eek-Meijers, Information Services Manager
gvaneek@wpl.ca
519-886-1310 ext. 125
Sheila Mehes, Technical Services Manager
smehes@wpl.ca
519-886-1310 ext. 116
Ellen Jones, Systems Manager
ejones@wpl.ca
519-889-1310 ext. 132
Lynda Gale, Public Services/Deputy Chief Librarian
lgale@wpl.ca
519-886-1310 ext. 122

***Wawa:* Wawa Public Library**
40 Broadway Ave., Wawa ON P0S 1K0
Tel: 705-856-2062; *Fax:* 705-856-1488
mtpl@wawa.cc
www.mtpl.on.ca
Jayne Griffith, Head Librarian
jgriffith@wawa.cc
Barb McCullough, Assistant Librarizn

***Weagamow Lake:* North Caribou First Nation Public Library**
PO Box 158, Weagamow Lake ON P0V 2Y0
Tel: 807-469-1288; *Fax:* 807-469-1132
beatricekanate@knet.ca
Beatrice Kanate, CEO

***Welland:* Welland Public Library**
50 The Boardwalk, Welland ON L3B 6J1
Tel: 905-734-6210; *Fax:* 905-734-8955
ref@welland.library.on.ca
www.welland.library.on.ca
Social Media:
www.facebook.com/group.php?gid=346692018392
Janet C. Booth, CEO & Secretary-Treasurer
jbooth@welland.library.on.ca
Douglas Abbott, Coordinator, Information Services
dabbott@welland.library.on.ca
Stephen Hanns, Manager, Public Services
shanns@welland.library.on.ca
Barbara Murphy, Manager, Support Services
bmurphy@welland.library.on.ca
Daniella Liebregts, Coordinator, Children's & Youth Services
dliebreghts@welland.library.on.ca

***Wendover:* Bibliothèque publique du Canton d'Alfred et Plantagenet/ Alfred & Plantagenet Public Library**
3104 av du Quai, Wendover ON K0A 3K0
Tél: 613-673-2923
bibliowend@yahoo.ca
www.alfred-platagenet.com/en/Libraries_42.html
Catherine Bélisle, Directrice
Anne St-Pierre, Aide

***Westport:* Westport Public Library**
3 Spring St., Westport ON K0G 1X0
Tel: 613-273-3223; *Fax:* 613-273-3223
library@rideau.net
Pamela Stuffles, Librarian

***Whitby:* Whitby Public Library**
405 Dundas St. West, Whitby ON L1N 6A1
Tel: 905-668-6531; *Fax:* 905-668-7445
admin@whitbylibrary.on.ca
www.whitbylibrary.on.ca
Ian Ross, Chief Librarian
Rhonda Jessup, Public Services Manager
Elaine Yatulis Dobbin, Manager, Technical Services & Systems
Michelle Frenette, Manager, Support Services

***White River:* White River Public Library**
123 Superior St., White River ON P0M 3G0
Tel: 807-822-1113
wrlib@nwconx.net
www.whiteriverlibrary.com
Jan Ramage, CEO

***Whitedog:* Wabaseemoong First Nation Public Library**
General Delivery, Whitedog ON P0X 1P0
Tel: 807-927-2000

***Whitney:* South Algonquin Public Library**
PO Box 208, Whitney ON K0J 2M0
Tel: 613-637-5471; *Fax:* 613-637-5471
whitlib@northcom.net
www.olsn.ca/southalgonquin
Charlene Alexander, CEO
613-637-5471
Cynthia Haskin, Branch Library
madlib@northcom.net
613-637-1099

***Wiarton:* Ninda Kikaendjigae Wigammik First Nation Public Library**
RR#5, Wiarton ON N0H 2T0
Tel: 519-534-1508; *Fax:* 519-534-2130
Daphne Johnston, CEO/Librarian
daphnejohnston@nawashfn.ca
Ralph Akiwenzie, Chair

***Wikwemikong:* Wikwemikong First Nation Public Library**
34A Henry St., Wikwemikong ON P0P 2J0
Tel: 705-859-2692; *Fax:* 705-859-3851
wikylibrary@hotmail.com
www.olsn.ca/wpl
Sheri Mishibinijima, Librarian
smish@amtelecom.net

***Windsor:* Windsor Public Library**
850 Ouellette Ave., Windsor ON N9A 4M9
Tel: 519-255-6770; *Fax:* 519-255-7207
TDD: 519255-7207
wpl@city.windsor.on.ca
www.windsorpubliclibrary.com
Nancy Peel, Manager
npeel@windsorpubliclibrary.com
519-255-6770
Jean Foster, Acting CEO
jfoster@windsorpubliclibrary.com

***Woodstock:* Oxford County Library**
Oxford County Administration Bldg., 21 Reeve St., Woodstock ON N4S 7Y3
Tel: 519-539-9800; *Fax:* 519-485-4028
www.ocl.net
Don McKay, Chair
Lisa Miettinen, Chief Executive Officer & Chief Librarian
lmiettinen@ocl.net
Cristina McLaren, Librarian, Branch Services
cmclaren@ocl.net
Susan Gillespie, Cataloguer
sgillespie@ocl.net

***Woodstock:* Woodstock Public Library**
445 Hunter St., Woodstock ON N4S 4G7
Tel: 519-539-4801; *Fax:* 519-539-5246
gbaumbach@woodstock.library.on.ca
www.woodstock.library.on.ca
Gary Baumbach, Chief Librarian
gbaumbach@woodstock.library.on.ca
Susan Start, Head of Information Services
Darlene Pretty, Head of Children's Services
Trudy Groothuis, Head of Circulation Services

***Wyoming:* Lambton County Library Headquarters**
787 Broadway St., Wyoming ON N0N 1T0
Tel: 519-845-3324; *Fax:* 519-845-0700
Toll-Free: 866-324-6912
Other Numbers: 519-845-3324, ext. 428 (Home Library Service)
library.headquarters@county-lambton.on.ca
www.lclmg.org
Robert Tremain, General Manager
robert.tremain@county-lambton.on.ca
519-845-0801 ext. 5236

Archives

***Ameliasburgh:* Quinte Educational Museum & Archives**
13 Coleman St. Group Box 14, Ameliasburgh ON K0K 1A0
Tel: 613-966-5501
info@qema1978.com
www.qema1978.com/
Dan Rainey, President
danrainey@qema1978.com

***Amherstburg:* Marsh Collection Society**
235A Dalhousie St., Amherstburg ON N9V 1W6
Tel: 519-736-9191; *Fax:* 519-736-7166
mcschin@mnsi.net
www.mnsi.net/~mcschin
Jennifer MacLeod, Archivist
mcschin@mnsi.net
519-736-9191

***Amherstburg:* North American Black Historical Museum**
277 King St., Amherstburg ON N9V 2C7
Tel: 519-736-5433; *Toll-Free:* 800-713-6336
nabhm@mnsi.net
www.blackhistoricalmuseum.com
Elise Harding-Davis, Curator/Administrator

***Aylmer:* Aylmer & District Museum Association**
14 East St., Aylmer ON N5H 1W2
Tel: 519-773-9723; *Fax:* 519-773-9723
aylmermuseum@amtelecom.net
www.amtelecom.net/~aymlermuseum/
Pat Zimmer, Curator

***Bayfield:* Bayfield Archives Room**
20 Main St. North, Bayfield ON N0M 1G0
Tel: 519-565-2376
bayarchives@tcc.on.ca
www.bayfieldhistorical.ca
Elaine Sturgeon, Archivist
519-565-2376

***Beachville:* County of Oxford Archives**
12 Vine St., Beachville ON N0J 1A0
Tel: 519-539-9800; *Fax:* 519-423-1964
archives@oxfordcounty.ca
www.oxfordcounty.ca/archives
Mary Gladwin, Archivist
mgladwin@oxfordcounty.ca
519-426-1928 ext. 210
Liz Mayville, Assistant Archivist
519-423-1928 ext. 209

***Brampton:* Region of Peel Archives**
Peel Heritage Complex, 9 Wellington St. East, Brampton ON L6W 1Y1
Tel: 905-791-4055; *Fax:* 905-451-4931
diane.allengame@peelregion.ca
www.region.peel.on.ca/heritage/archives.htm
Diane Allengame, Collections Registrar/Regional Archivist
diane.allengame@peelregion.ca
905-791-4055

***Brantford:* Brant Museum Archives**
57 Charlotte St., Brantford ON N3T 2W6
Tel: 519-752-2483; *Fax:* 519-752-1931
information@brantmuseum.ca
brantmuseum.ca
Joan Kanigan-Fairen, Executive Director

***Bridgenorth:* Smith Ennismore Historical Society**
826 Ward St., Bridgenorth ON K0L 1H0
Tel: 705-292-9430; *Fax:* 705-742-4136
sehs.on.ca
Bernice Harris, Contact
m.bharris@cogeco.ca
Jim Northey, Contact
sehs@sehs.on.cao.ca

***Brockville:* Brockville Museum**
5 Henry St., Brockville ON K6V 6M4
Tel: 613-342-4397; *Fax:* 613-342-7345
info@brockvillemuseum.com
www.brockvillemuseum.com
Bonnie Burke, Curator/Director
bburke@brockville.com
613-342-4397

***Burlington:* Joseph Brant Museum**
1240 North Shore Blvd. East, Burlington ON L7S 1C5
Tel: 905-634-3556; *Fax:* 905-634-4498
Toll-Free: 888-748-5386
jbm@on.aibn.com
Barbara E. Teatero, Director
Paul Stone, Curator

***Cambridge:* Cambridge Archives**
46 Dickson St., 2nd Fl., Cambridge ON N1R 1T7
Tel: 519-740-4680; *Fax:* 519-623-0058
archives@cambridge.ca
www.cambridge.ca/city_clerk/city_archives
Jim Quantrell, Archivist
quantrellj@city.cambridge.on.ca
519-740-4680 ext. 4610

***Cannington:* Cannington & Area Historical Society**
PO Box 196, Cannington ON L0E 1E0
Tel: 705-432-2430; *Fax:* 705-432-2909

***Chatham:* Chatham-Kent Museum**
75 William St. North, Chatham ON N7M 4L4
Tel: 519-360-1998; *Fax:* 519-354-4170
CKccc@chatham-kent.ca
Stephanie Suitor, Curator
stephanies@chatham-kent.ca

***Combermere:* Madonna House Archives**
2888 Dafoe Rd. RR#2, Combermere ON K0J 1L0
Tel: 613-756-1766; *Fax:* 613-756-0211
archives@madonnahouse.org
www.madonnahouse.org
Mary Rowland, Contact

***Delhi:* Delhi Tobacco Museum & Heritage Centre**
200 Talbot Rd., Delhi ON N4B 2A2
Tel: 519-582-0278; *Fax:* 519-582-0122
tobacco.museum@norfolkcounty.ca
Judy A. Livingstone, Curator/Director
Tanya Zajac, Assistant Curator

***Fergus:* Wellington County Museum & Archives**
0536 Wellington Rd. 18, RR#1, Fergus ON N1M 2W3
Tel: 519-846-0916; *Fax:* 519-846-9630
karen@wcm.on.ca
www.wcm.on.ca
Bonnie Callen, Museum Administrator
Karen Wagner, Archivist

***Fort Frances:* Fort Frances Museum & Cultural Centre**
259 Scott St., Fort Frances ON P9A 1G8
Tel: 807-274-7891; *Fax:* 807-274-4103
phawley@fort-frances.com
www.fort-frances.com/museum
Pam Hawley, Director-Curator

***Georgetown:* Esquesing Historical Society**
9 Church St., Georgetown ON L7G 2A3
Tel: 905-877-9510
mrowe6@cogeco.ca
www.esquesinghistoricalsociety.ca
Stephen Blake, President, Esquesing Historical Society
Mark Rowe, Archivist
mrowe6@cogeco.ca
905-877-9510

***Goderich:* Huron County Museum Archives**
110 North St., Goderich ON N7A 2T8
Tel: 519-524-2686; *Fax:* 519-524-1922
www.huroncounty.ca/museum
Beth Ross, Director
bross@huroncounty.ca
519-524-2686

Patricia Hamilton, Assistant Curator
phamilton@huroncounty.ca
519-524-2686

***Gravenhurst:* Gravenhurst Archives**
Gravenhurst Public Library, 180 Sharpe St. West, Gravenhurst ON P1P 1J1
Tel: 705-687-3382; *Fax:* 705-687-7016
rkirton@gravenhurst.ca
Marion Fry, Volunteer Archivist

***Guelph:* Guelph Museums**
6 Dublin St. South, Guelph ON N1H 4L5
Tel: 519-836-1221; *Fax:* 519-836-5280
museum@guelph.ca
www.guelph.ca/museum
Bev Dietrich, Curator
519-836-1221 ext. 224
Kathleen Wall, Assistant Curator
519-836-1221 ext. 225

***Haliburton:* Haliburton Highlands Museum**
PO Box 389, Haliburton ON K0M 1S0
Tel: 705-457-2760
info@haliburtonhighlandsmuseum.com
www.haliburtonhighlands.com/museum
Thomas Ballantine, Director
Stephen Hill, Curator

***Hamilton:* Canadian Baptist Archives/ Archives baptistes canadiennes**
c/o McMaster Divinity College, 1280 Main St. West, Hamilton ON L8S 4K1
Tel: 905-525-9140; *Fax:* 905-577-4782
cbarch@mcmaster.ca
www.macdiv.ca/students/baptistarchives.php
Gordon Heath, Director
gheath@mcmaster.ca
905-525-9140 ext. 26409
Melissa Richer, Archivist
cbarch@mcmaster.ca
905-525-9140 ext. 23511
Matt Lowe, Archivist
cbarch@mcmaster.ca
905-525-9140 ext. 23511

***Kenora:* Lake of the Woods Museum**
300 Main St. South, Kenora ON P9N 3X5
Tel: 807-467-2105; *Fax:* 807-467-2109
museum@kmts.ca
www.lakeofthewoodsmuseum.ca
Lori Nelson, Director
Riley Sleeman, Collections/Education Coordinator
Wendy Midgard, Finance/Temp. Ex. Coordinator

***Kingston:* Fort Henry**
PO Box 213, Kingston ON K7L 4V8
Tel: 613-542-7388; *Fax:* 613-542-3054
getaway@parks.on.ca
www.forthenry.com
Ron Ridley, Curator
ron.ridley@forthenry.com

***Kingston:* The International Hockey Hall of Fame & Museum**
277 York St., Kingston ON K7K 1R7
Tel: 613-544-2355; *Fax:* 613-544-2844
info@ihhof.com
www.ihhof.com
Mark Potter, President

***Kingston:* Marine Museum of the Great Lakes at Kingston**
55 Ontario St., Kingston ON K7L 2Y2
Tel: 613-542-2261; *Fax:* 613-542-0043
marmus@marmuseum.ca
www.marmuseum.ca
Maurice Smith, Curator Emeritus

***Kingston:* Religious Hospitallers of St. Joseph, St Joseph Province**
16 Manitou Cres. East, Kingston ON K7N 1B2
Tel: 613-389-0275; *Fax:* 613-384-6978
reg.archives@bellnet.ca
Rodney Carter, Archivist

***Kingston:* Roman Catholic Archdiocese of Kingston**
390 Palace Rd., Kingston ON K7L 4T3
Tel: 613-548-4461; *Fax:* 613-548-4744
www.romancatholic.kingston.on.ca/index.html

***Kingston:* Sisters of Providence of St. Vincent de Paul**
1200 Princess St., Kingston ON K7M 3C9
Tel: 613-544-4525; *Fax:* 613-531-9805
archives@providence.ca
Gayle Desarmia, Head, Information & Heritage Services
archives@providence.ca
613-544-4525

***Kitchener:* Doon Heritage Crossroads**
10 Huron Rd., Kitchener ON N2P 2R7
Tel: 519-748-1914; *Fax:* 519-748-0009
TDD: 5197480537
hliz@region.waterloo.on.ca
www.region.waterloo.on.ca/doon/
Elizabeth Hardin, Registrar/Researcher
hliz@region.waterloo.on.ca

***Kitchener:* Schneider Corporation**
321 Courtland Ave. East, Kitchener ON N2G 2W1
Tel: 519-741-5000
Karen Trussler, Communication Editor/Archivist

***Kleinburg:* McMichael Canadian Art Collection/ Collection McMichael d'Art Canadien**
10365 Islington Ave., Kleinburg ON L0J 1C0
Tel: 905-893-1121; *Fax:* 905-893-2588
lmorita@mcmichael.com
Linda Morita, Librarian/Archivist
lmorita@mcmichael.com

***London:* Museum London**
421 Ridout St. North, London ON N6A 5H4
Tel: 519-661-0333; *Fax:* 519-661-2559
jcewan@museumlondon.ca
www.museumlondon.ca/
Janette Cousins Ewan, Art Registrar

***London:* The Royal Canadian Regiment Museum**
Wolseley Barracks, 750 Elizabeth St., London ON N5Y 4T7
Tel: 519-660-5102; *Fax:* 519-660-5344
breede.c@forces.gc.ca
thercr.ca
Claus Breede, Curator
519-660-5102

***Midland:* Huronia Museum**
549 Little Lake Park, Midland ON L4R 4P4
Tel: 705-526-2844; *Fax:* 705-527-6622
director@huroniamuseum.com
www.huroniamuseum.com
Jamie Hunter, Curator
Nicole Henderson, Collections Manager

***Milton:* Halton Region Museum**
5181 Kelso Rd., Milton ON L9T 2X7
Tel: 905-875-2200; *Fax:* 905-876-4322
Toll-Free: 866-442-5866
museum@halton.ca
www.region.halton.on.ca/museum
Linda Twitchell, Curator
Michele Finn, Information Coordinator
905-875-2200

***Minesing:* Simcoe County Archives**
1149 Hwy. 26, RR#2, Minesing ON L0L 1Y2
Tel: 705-726-9331; *Fax:* 705-725-5341
archives@simcoe.ca
www.county.simcoe.on.ca/cultureinformation/archives/
Bruce Beacock, County Archivist

***Mississauga:* Pentecostal Assemblies of Canada**
2450 Milltower Ct., Mississauga ON L5N 5Z6
Tel: 905-542-7400; *Fax:* 905-542-7313
archives@paoc.org
www.paoc.org/about/archives
Marilyn Stroud, Assistant Archivist
mstroud@paoc.org
905-842-7400 ext. 5282

***Morrisburg:* Upper Canada Village**
13740 County Rd. 2, Morrisburg ON K0C 1X0
Tel: 613-543-3704; *Fax:* 613-543-4098
www.uppercanadavillage.com
Jan Omond, Contact
Bruce Henbest, Contact

***Napanee:* Lennox & Addington County Museum & Archives**
97 Thomas St. East, Napanee ON K7R 4B9
Tel: 613-354-3027; *Fax:* 613-354-1005
archives@lennox-addington.on.ca
lennox-addington.on.ca
Jane Foster, Manager
613-354-3027
Shelley Respondek, Archivist
613-354-3027

***Niagara on the Lake:* Shaw Festival Theatre Foundation Library**
PO Box 774, Niagara on the Lake ON L0S 1J0
Tel: 905-468-7140; *Fax:* 905-468-5438
www.shawfest.com
Nancy Butler, Head
Carol Gray, Library Assistant
Sandra Woodruff, Library Assistant

***North Bay:* Nipissing Archives**
Discovery North Bay, 100 Ferguson St., North Bay ON P1B 1W8
Tel: 705-476-2323; *Fax:* 705-476-9300
info@heritagenorthbay.com
www.city.north-bay.on.ca/museum
Jennifer Bell, Director
education@heritagenorthbay.com

***Norwich:* Norwich & District Historical Society**
91 Stover St. North, RR#3, Norwich ON N0J 1P0
Tel: 519-863-3638; *Fax:* 519-863-2343
norwichdhs@execulink.com
www.norwichdhs.ca
Mary Beth Start, Curator/Archivist
Janet Hilliker, Archivist
archives@norwichdhs.ca

***Oil Springs:* Oil Museum of Canada**
2324 Kelly Rd., Oil Springs ON N0N 1P0
Tel: 519-834-2840; *Fax:* 519-834-2840
oil.museum@county-lambton.on.ca
www.lclmg.org/lclmg/Museums/tabid/53/Default.aspx
Connie Bell, Manager
connie.bell@county-lambton.on.ca

***Orillia:* Mariposa Folk Foundation**
37 Mississauga St. W, Orillia ON L3V 3A5
Tel: 705-329-2333; *Fax:* 705-329-4099
www.mariposafolk.com
Paulette Kirkey, President

***Orillia:* Stephen Leacock Museum/Archives**
50 Museum Dr., Orillia ON L3V 7T9
Tel: 705-329-1908; *Fax:* 705-326-5578
leacock@transdata.ca
www.leacockmuseum.com
Craig Metcalf, Director

***Orono:* Clarke Museum & Archives**
7086 Old Kirby School Rd., RR#1, Orono ON L0B 1M0
Tel: 905-983-9243

***Oshawa:* Oshawa Community Museum & Archives**
1450 Simcoe St. South, Lakeview Park, Oshawa ON L1H 8S8
Tel: 905-436-7624; *Fax:* 905-436-7625
archivist@oshawamuseum.org
www.oshawamuseum.org/archives.html
Amber Nowak, Contact

***Oshawa:* Robert McLaughlin Gallery**
Civic Centre, 72 Queen St., Oshawa ON L1H 3Z3
Tel: 905-576-3000; *Fax:* 905-576-9774
communications@rmg.on.ca
www.rmg.on.ca
Barb Duff, Library Services Coordinator
bduff@rmg.on.ca
905-576-3000 ext. 102
Sonya Jones, Curatorial Assistant, Bouckley Photography Collection
sjones@rmg.on.ca
905-576-3000 ext. 110

***Ottawa:* Archives Deschâtelets**
175, rue Main, Ottawa ON K1S 1C3
Tel: 613-237-0580; *Fax:* 613-232-4064
ardescha@yahoo.ca

***Ottawa:* Bytown Railway Society**
PO Box 141, Stn A, Ottawa ON K1N 8V1
Tel: 613-745-1201
info@bytownrailwaysociety.ca
www.bytownrailwaysociety.ca
Paul Bown, Archivist

***Ottawa:* C. Robert Craig Memorial Library**
Ottawa City Archives, 110 Laurier Ave. West, Ottawa ON K1P 1J1
Tel: 613-580-2424; *Fax:* 613-580-2614
KennethHealy@cs.com
www.ovar.ca/CraigLibrary/craiglib.htm
Dave Knowles, President & Librarian
knowles@istar.ca
613-722-4473

***Ottawa:* Canadian Institute of Geomatics/ Association canadienne des sciences géomatiques**
#400, 1390 Prince of Wales Dr., Ottawa ON K2C 3N6
Tel: 613-224-9851; *Fax:* 613-224-9577
editgeo@magma.ca
www.cig-acsg.ca
Carol Railer, Production & Advertising Manager
Harold Jones, Staff

***Ottawa:* Canadian Intergovernmental Conference Secretariat/ Secrétariat des conférences intergouvernementales Canadiennes**
222 Queen St., 10th Fl., Ottawa ON K1P 5V9
Tel: 613-995-4310; *Fax:* 613-947-4336
info@scics.gc.ca
www.scics.gc.ca
Jane Dubé, Head, Information Management

***Ottawa:* Canadian Museum of Nature/ Musée canadien de la nature**
PO Box 3443, Stn D, Ottawa ON K1P 6P4
Tel: 613-364-4042; *Fax:* 613-364-4026
cmnlib@mus-nature.ca
www.nature.ca
Patrice Stevenson, Librarian
pstevenson@mus-nature.ca
613-364-4045
Ted Sypniewski, Serials & Acquisitions Officer
613-566-4734
Chantal Dussault, Archivist
cdussault@mus-nature.ca
613-364-4047
Mike Wayne, Circulation & ILL
613-364-4042

***Ottawa:* Canadian Ski Museum/ Le Musée canadien du ski**
1960 Scott St., Ottawa ON K1Z 8L8
Tel: 613-722-3584; *Fax:* 613-722-2914
info@skimuseum.ca
www.skimuseum.ca

***Ottawa:* Canadian Women's Movement Archives/ Archives canadiennes du mouvement des femmes**
Morisset Library, University of Ottawa, #603, 65 University Pvt, Ottawa ON K1N 6N5
Tel: 613-562-5910; *Fax:* 613-562-5133
arcs@uottawa.ca
www.biblio.uottawa.ca/
Lucie Desjardins, Archivist
lucie.desjardins@uottawa.ca
Jacqueline Petre-Pleacoff, Archival Technician
jacqueline.petre@uottawa.ca

***Ottawa:* Centre de recherche en histoire religieuse du Canada/ Research Centre in Religious History of Canada**
223 Main St., Ottawa ON K1S 1C4
Tél: 613-236-1393; *Téléc:* 613-782-3005
crh-rc-rhc@ustpaul.ca
www.ustpaul.ca/RCRHC/index_e.asp
Pierre Hurtubise, Directeur

***Ottawa:* City of Ottawa Archives/ Archives municipales d'Ottawa**
Bytown Pavilion, 111 Sussex Dr., 1st Fl., Ottawa ON K1N 1J1
Tel: 613-580-2424; *Fax:* 613-580-2614
archives@ottawa.ca
ottawa.ca/residents/heritage/archives/index_en.html
David Bullock, City Archivist
david.bullock@ottawa.ca
613-580-2424 ext. 13787

***Ottawa:* Friends of Library & Archives Canada**
395 Wellington St., Ottawa ON K1A 0N4
Tel: 613-992-8304; *Fax:* 613-943-2343
friends.amis@lac-bac.gc.ca
www.collectionscanada.ca/friends/index-e.html
Ron Cohan, President

***Ottawa:* National Archival Appraisal Board/ Conseil national d'évaluation des archives**
c/o CCA, #501, 130 Albert St., Ottawa ON K1P 5G4
Tel: 613-565-1222; *Fax:* 613-565-5445
info@naab.ca
www.naab.ca
Louise Pilon, Administrator
lpilon@archives.ca

***Ottawa:* Oblats de Marie Immaculée**
175 Main St., Ottawa ON K1S 1C3
Tél: 613-237-0580; *Téléc:* 613-237-4064
ardescha@yahoo.ca
Andre Dubois, Archiviste
ardescha@yahoo.ca
Gérard Landreville, Autre personnel
Luc Fortin, Autre personnel

***Ottawa:* Ottawa Jewish Archives**
21 Nadolny Sachs Private Lane, Ottawa ON K2A 1R9
Tel: 613-798-4696; *Fax:* 613-798-4695
archives@jewishottawa.com
www.jewsihottawa.com
Social Media: www.facebook.com/JFedOttawa
Laurie Dougherty, Archivist
ldougherty@jewishottawa.com

***Ottawa:* Roman Catholic Archdiocese of Ottawa/ Corporation Episcopale Catholique Romaine d'Ottawa**
1247 Kilborn Pl., Ottawa ON K1H 6K9
Tel: 613-738-5025; *Fax:* 613-738-0130
archottawa.ca
Eugene Margeson, Archivist
emargeson@archottawa.ca

***Ottawa:* The Royal College of Physicians & Surgeons of Canada**
774 Echo Dr., Ottawa ON K1S 5N8
Tel: 613-730-8177; *Fax:* 613-730-2410
Toll-Free: 800-668-3740
barbara.woodward@rcpsc.edu
rcpsc.medical.org/membership/roddick_e.php

***Ottawa:* Scouts Canada**
1345 Baseline Rd., Ottawa ON K2C 0A7
Tel: 613-224-5131; *Fax:* 613-224-3571
Toll-Free: 888-726-8876
mailbox@scouts.ca
www.scouts.ca

***Ottawa:* Soeurs du Sacré-Coeur de Jésus, Saint-Hubert**
15 Oblate Ave., Ottawa ON K1S 0E6
Tél: 613-237-6607
Hélène Beaulieu, Responsable

***Owen Sound:* Grey Roots Museum & Archives**
102599 Grey Rd. 18, RR#4, Owen Sound ON N4K 5N6
Tel: 519-376-3690; *Fax:* 519-376-4654
Toll-Free: 877-473-9766
info@greyroots.com
www.greyroots.com/collections-research
Karin Noble, Archivist
karin.noble@greyroots.com
Kate Jackson, Assistant Archivist
kate.jackson@greyroots.com

***Pembroke:* Grey Sisters of the Immaculate Conception**
Marguerite Centre, 700 MacKay St., Pembroke ON K8A 1G6
Tel: 613-732-9916; *Fax:* 613-735-2048
jacquie@margueritecentre.com
Jacquelyn Wolgemuth, Head Librarian

***Perth:* The Perth Museum & Archives**
11 Gore St. East, Perth ON K7H 1H4
Tel: 613-267-1947; *Fax:* 613-267-5635
perthmuseum@town.perth.on.ca
www.perthcanada.com
Susan McNichol, Curator
perthmuseum@town.perth.on.ca
Debbie Sproule, Assistant Curator
perthmuseum@town.perth.on.ca

***Peterborough:* Peterborough Centennial Museum & Archives**
Armour Hill, 300 Hunter St. East, Peterborough ON K9H 2L8
Tel: 705-743-5180; *Fax:* 705-743-2614
mcharles@city.peterborough.on.ca
www.pcma.ca/archives_about.htm
Mary Charles, City Archivist

***Picton:* County of Prince Edward Archives**
44 Union St., Picton ON K0K 2T0
Tel: 613-476-6100
archives@pecounty.on.ca
www.pecounty.on.ca/archives.html
Pamela Noxon, Chair
613-393-2204

***Prescott:* Grenville County Historical Society**
500 Railway Ave., Prescott ON K0E 1T0
Tel: 613-925-0489
gchs@ripnet.com
web.ripnet.com/~gchs
Bonnie Gaylord, Research Chair

***St Catharines:* Ontario Genealogical Society**
PO Box 2224, St Catharines ON L2M 7R8
nbogs@becon.org
www.ogs.on.ca/niagara/default.htm
Cheryl Bowman, Contact
bowcarr@hotmail.com
905-685-6900

***St Catharines:* St Catharines Museum at Lock 3**
1932 Welland Canals Pkwy., St Catharines ON L2R 7K6
Tel: 905-984-8880; *Fax:* 905-984-6910
museum@stcatharines.ca
www.stcatharines.ca
Kathleen Powell, Curator
905-984-8880 ext. 250

***Sault Ste Marie:* Sault Ste Marie & 49th Field Regiment RCA Historical Society**
690 Queen St. East, Sault Ste Marie ON P6A 2A4
Tel: 705-256-7278; *Fax:* 705-759-3058
heritage@saultmuseum.com
www.saultmuseum.com
Kim Forbes, Director/Curator

***Simcoe:* Norfolk Heritage Centre**
109 Norfolk St. South, Simcoe ON N3Y 2W3
Tel: 519-426-1583; *Fax:* 519-426-1584
office@norfolklore.com
www.norfolklore.com
William R. Yeager, Curator
curator@norfolklore.com
519-426-1583
Scott Gillies, Manager
marketing@norfolklore.com
519-426-1583

***Southampton:* Bruce County Museum & Cultural Centre**
33 Victoria St. North, Southampton ON N0H 2L0
Tel: 519-797-2080; *Fax:* 519-797-2191
Toll-Free: 866-318-8889
archives@brucecounty.on.ca
www.brucemuseum.ca
Barbara Ribey, Director/Curator
bribey@brucecounty.on.ca
David Sharron, Archivist
dsharron@brucecounty.on.ca
Ann-Marie Collins, Archival Assistant
acollins@brucecounty.on.ca
Vicky Cooper, Collections Registrar
vcooper@brucecounty.on.ca

***Stratford:* The Stratford Shakespeare Festival Archives**
423 Brunswick St., Stratford ON N5A 7Z8
Tel: 519-271-0055; *Fax:* 519-271-1040
jedmonds@stratfordshakespearefestival.com
www.stratfordshakespearefestival.com
Jane Edmonds, Archives Manager
jedmonds@stratfordfestival.ca
Ellen Charendoff, Archives Co-ordinator
charendoff@stratfordshakespearefestival.com
519-271-0055 ext. 4310
Christine Schindler, Archives Co-ordinator
cschindler@stratfordshakespearefestival.com
519-271-0055 ext. 4328

***Stratford:* Stratford-Perth Archives**
24 St Andrew St., Stratford ON N5A 1A3
Tel: 519-271-0531; *Fax:* 519-273-5746
sparchives@perthcounty.ca
www.perthcounty.ca
Betty Jo Belton, Archivist
519-271-0531 ext. 256

***Teeterville:* Teeterville Pioneer Museum**
194 Teeter St., Teeterville ON N0E 1S0
Tel: 519-582-0278; *Fax:* 519-582-0122
Other Numbers: Summer phone: 519/443-4400
teeterville.museum@norfolkcounty.on.ca
Judy A. Livingstone, Curator/Director
Tanya Zajac, Assistant Curator

***Thunder Bay:* City of Thunder Bay**
235 Vickers St. North, Thunder Bay ON P7E 1J5
Tel: 807-625-2270; *Fax:* 807-622-4212
mszybalski@thunderbay.ca
www.thunderbay.ca/City_Government/City_Records_and_Archives.ht
Matt Szybalski, Manager, Corporate Records & Archivist
mszybalski@thunderbay.ca
807-625-3390

***Thunder Bay:* Northwestern Ontario Sports Hall of Fame**
219 May St. South, Thunder Bay ON P7E 1B5
Tel: 807-622-2852; *Fax:* 807-622-2736
nwosport@tbaytel.net
www.nwosportshalloffame.com
Kathryn Dwyer, Curator
807-622-2852
Diane Imrie, Executive Director

***Thunder Bay:* Thunder Bay Historical Museum**
425 Donald St. East, Thunder Bay ON P7E 5V1
Tel: 807-623-0801; *Fax:* 807-622-6880
info@thunderbaymuseum.com
www.thunderbaymuseum.com
Thorold Tronrud, Curator
807-623-0801

***Toronto:* Archives of Ontario**
134 Ian Macdonald Blvd., Toronto ON M7A 2C5
Tel: 416-327-1600; *Fax:* 416-327-1999
Toll-Free: 800-668-9933
reference@ontario.ca
www.archives.gov.on.ca
Miriam McTiernan, Archivist of Ontario
miriam.mctiernan@ontario.ca
416-327-1602
Michael Johnson, Director, Archives Management & Information Storage
michael.johnson1@ontario.ca
416-327-1577

***Toronto:* Art Gallery of Ontario/ Musée des beaux-arts de l'Ontario**
317 Dundas St. West, Toronto ON M5T 1G4
Tel: 416-979-6642; *Fax:* 416-979-6602
library_archives@ago.net
www.ago.net
Karen McKenzie, Chief Librarian
karen_mckenzie@ago.net
416-979-6660
L.R. Pfaff, Deputy Librarian & Head, Reader Services
larry_pfaff@ago.net
416-979-6660
Don Rance, Librarian, Information Systems
donald_rance@ago.net
416-979-6660

***Toronto:* Arts & Letters Club**
14 Elm St., Toronto ON M5G 1G7
Tel: 416-597-0223
info@artsandlettersclub.ca
www.artsandlettersclub.ca
Margaret Spence, Chair, Library Committee
Scott James, Club Archives Contact

***Toronto:* Bergendal Collection of Mediaeval Manuscripts**
15 Duncan St., Toronto ON M5H 3P9
Tel: 416-925-8044; *Fax:* 416-925-3631
bergendalcoll@sympatico.ca
www3.sympatico.ca/bergendalcoll
Joseph Pope, Curator
joepope@sympatico.ca
416-925-8044
Donald Taylor, Head of Technical Services
416-591-8801
Annabel Cary, Head, Systems
416-593-5542

***Toronto:* Brothers of the Christian Schools Archives**
131 Farnham Ave., Toronto ON M4V 1H7
Tel: 416-929-7878; *Fax:* 416-929-1277
wfarrell@rogers.com
Walter Farrell, F.S.C., Archivist
wfarrell@rogers.com

***Toronto:* Burgee Data Archives**
117 Airdrie Rd., Toronto ON M4G 1M6
Tel: 416-423-9979; *Fax:* 416-423-9979
peter.edwards@etel.tdsb.on.ca
Peter B. Edwards, Director

***Toronto:* The Canadian Children's Book Centre**
#101, 40 Orchard View Blvd., Toronto ON M4R 1B9
Tel: 416-975-0010; *Fax:* 416-975-8970
info@bookcentre.ca
www.bookcentre.ca
Naseem Hrab, Librarian
naseem@bookcentre.ca

***Toronto:* Canadian Lesbian & Gay Archives**
50 Charles St East, Toronto ON M4Y 2N6
Tel: 416-777-2755
queeries@clga.ca
www.clga.ca/archives/
Mary MacDonald, President

***Toronto:* Canadian Opera Company/ La compagnie d'opéra canadienne**
227 Front St. East, Toronto ON M5A 1E8
Tel: 416-306-2328; *Fax:* 416-363-5584
birthej@coc.ca
Birthe Joergensen, Archivist

***Toronto:* Canadian Royal Heritage Trust**
#206A, 3050 Yonge St., Toronto ON M4N 2K4
Tel: 416-482-4909; *Fax:* 416-544-8082
kg3library@crht.ca
www.crht.ca/
Claudia Willetts, Librarian
kg3library@crht.ca
416-482-4909

***Toronto:* City of Toronto Archives**
255 Spadina Rd., Toronto ON M5R 2V3
Tel: 416-397-0778; *Fax:* 416-392-9685
archives@toronto.ca
www.toronto.ca/archives
Daphne Gaby Donaldson, Director of Corporate Records & Archives
ddonald@toronto.ca
416-392-9673
Andrea Aitken, Reference & Standards Officer
aaitken@toronto.ca
416-397-7975

***Toronto:* College of Physicians & Surgeons of Ontario**
80 College St., Toronto ON M5G 2E2
Tel: 416-967-2600; *Fax:* 416-961-3330
Toll-Free: 800-268-7096
rma@cpso.on.ca
www.cpso.on.ca
Joseph Travers, Contact
416-967-2600 ext. 227

***Toronto:* Etobicoke Historical Society**
c/o Montgomery's Inn, 4709 Dundas St. West, Toronto ON M9A 1A8
dorans@idirect.com
www.etobicokehistorical.com
Gregory Wowchuk, President
dorans@idirect.com
Robert Given, Historian

***Toronto:* Exhibition Place**
2 Manitoba Dr., Toronto ON M6K 3C3
Tel: 416-263-3658; *Fax:* 416-263-3681
LCobon@explace.on.ca
www.explace.on.ca
Linda Cobon, Manager, Records & Archives

***Toronto:* The Film Reference Library**
2 Carlton St., East Mezzanine, Toronto ON M5B 1J3
Tel: 416-967-1517; *Fax:* 416-967-0628
www.filmreferencelibrary.ca
Sylvia Frank, Director
Eve Goldin, Library Manager
egoldin@tiffg.ca

***Toronto:* General Archives of the Basilian Fathers**
95 St Joseph St., Toronto ON M5S 2R9
Tel: 416-921-7861; *Fax:* 416-921-8357
archives@basilian.org
www.basilian.org
James E. Rent, CSB, Archivist

***Toronto:* Heritage Scarborough**
24 Collins Rd., Toronto ON M1C 1C3
Tel: 416-396-6930
Richard Schofield, Heritage Consultant & Scarborough Archivist

***Toronto:* Hockey Hall of Fame**
BCE Place, 30 Yonge St., Toronto ON M5E 1X8
Tel: 416-360-7735; *Fax:* 416-360-1316
acquisitions@hhof.com
www.hhof.com/html/rc00.shtml
Miragh Addis, Archivist & Collections Registrar
maddis@hhof.com
Craig Campbell, Manager, Resource Centre & Archives
Tyler Wolosewich, Coordinator, Archival Services

***Toronto:* Holy Blossom Temple**
1950 Bathurst St., Toronto ON M5P 3K9
Tel: 416-789-3291
www.holyblossom.org
David Hart, Archivist
Sheila Smolkin, Archivist

***Toronto:* Institute of the Blessed Virgin Mary in North America (Loretto Sisters)**
101 Mason Blvd., Toronto ON M5M 3E2
Tel: 416-487-5543; *Fax:* 416-485-9884
ibvmadm@rogers.com
www.ibvm.ca/
Juliana Dusel, IBVM, Archivist

***Toronto:* Jesuits in English Canada**
1325 Bay St., Toronto ON M5R 2C4
Tel: 416-962-4500; *Fax:* 416-962-4501
Jacques Monet, Archivist

***Toronto:* Montgomery's Inn Museum**
4709 Dundas St. West, Toronto ON M9A 1A8
Tel: 416-394-8113; *Fax:* 416-394-6027
rreid@toronto.ca
Randall Reid, Programmes Officer
416-394-6025

***Toronto:* National Ballet of Canada/ Ballet national du Canada**
470 Queens Quay West, Toronto ON M5V 3K4
Tel: 416-345-9686; *Fax:* 416-345-8323
anevile@national.ballet.ca
www.national.ballet.ca/thecompany/archives/
Adrienne Nevile, Archives Coordinator

***Toronto:* Ontario Genealogical Society**
#102, 40 Orchard View Blvd., Toronto ON M4R 1B9
Tel: 416-489-0734; *Fax:* 416-489-9803
lchester@ogs.on.ca
www.ogs.on.ca
L.A. Chester, Chair
V. Lynham, Technician

***Toronto:* The Ontario Jewish Archives**
4600 Bathurst St., Toronto ON M2R 3V2
Tel: 416-635-2883; *Fax:* 416-635-1408
ojal@ujafed.org
www.ontariojewisharchives.org
Ellen Scheinberg, Director
escheinberg@ujafed.org
416-635-2883
Carolyn Harris, Archivist
charris@ujafed.org

***Toronto:* The Presbyterian Church in Canada**
50 Wynford Dr., Toronto ON M3C 1J7
Tel: 416-441-1111; *Fax:* 416-441-2825
Toll-Free: 800-619-7301
karnold@presbyterian.ca
www.presbyterianarchives.ca
Kim Arnold, Archivist/Records Administrator
karnold@presbyterian.ca
Bob Anger, Assistant Archivist
bangar@presbyterian.ca

***Toronto:* Queen's Own Rifles of Canada Regimental Museum**
c/o Casa Loma, 1 Austin Terrace, Toronto ON M5R 1X8
Tel: 416-923-1171; *Fax:* 416-923-5734
info@casaloma.org
P. Sigmundson, Curator

***Toronto:* Queen's York Rangers (1st American Regiment) Museum**
CFA Fort York, 660 Fleet St. West, Toronto ON M5V 1A9
Tel: 416-203-4600
rhq@qyrang.ca
www.qyrang.ca

Diane Kruger, Curator
rhq@qyrang.org

Toronto: Roman Catholic Archdiocese of Toronto
#505, 1155 Yonge St., Toronto ON M4T 1W2
Tel: 416-934-3400; Fax: 416-934-3444
archives@archtoronto.org
www.archtoronto.org/archives
Marc Lerman, Diocesan Archivist
416-934-3400 ext. 505

Toronto: The Royal Canadian Yacht Club
141 St George St., Toronto ON M5R 2L8
Tel: 416-967-7245; Fax: 416-967-5710
heritage@rcyc.ca
www.rcyc.ca
Diane Blake, Staff Archivist
416-967-7245 ext. 351
Albert Mallon, Honourary Historian

Toronto: St John's Convent
233 Cummer Ave., Toronto ON M2M 2E8
Tel: 416-226-2201; Fax: 416-222-4442
convent@ssjd.ca
www.ssjd.ca/convent.html
Joyce Bodley, Librarian
416-226-2201 ext. 309
Margaret Ruth Steele, Assistant
416-226-2201 ext. 309

Toronto: St John's Rehabilitation Hospital Archives
c/o Administration, 285 Cummer Ave., Toronto ON M2M 2G1
Tel: 416-226-6780; Fax: 416-226-6265
info@stjohnsrehab.com
www.stjohnsrehab.com/

Toronto: The Salvation Army
26 Howden Rd., Toronto ON M1R 3E4
Tel: 416-285-4344; Fax: 416-285-7763
heritage_centre@can.salvationarmy.org
www.salvationist.ca/heritage
John E. Carew, Director
john_carew@can.salvationarmy.org

Toronto: Scarboro Mission Society
2685 Kingston Rd., Toronto ON M1M 1M4
Tel: 416-261-7135; Fax: 416-261-0820
Toll-Free: 800-260-4815
info@scarboromissions.ca
www.scarboromissions.ca
John Carten, Councillor
jcarten@scarboromissions.ca

Toronto: Scarborough Historical Society
6282 Kingston Rd., Toronto ON M1C 1K9
Tel: 416-995-6930; Fax: 416-282-9482
www.scarboroughhistorical.com/archives
Richard Schofield, Archivist

Toronto: Sculptors Society of Canada/ La Société des sculpteurs du Canada
500 Church St., Toronto ON M4Y 2C8
Tel: 647-435-5858
gallery@cansculpt.org
www.cansculpt.org
Karen Stoskopf Harding, Archivist

Toronto: Sisters of St Joseph of Toronto
3377 Bayview Ave., Toronto ON M2M 3S4
Tel: 416-222-1101; Fax: 416-222-9816
lwicks@csj-to.ca
www.csj-to.ca
Linda Wicks, Archivist

Toronto: Sisters Servants of Mary Immaculate
5 Austin Terrace, Toronto ON M5R 1Y1
Tel: 416-924-7422; Fax: 416-928-9261
ssmi.org@rogers.com
www.ssmi.org
Frances Byblow, Contact

Toronto: Tartu Institute
300 Bloor St. W, Toronto ON M5B 1W4
Tel: 416-925-9405; Fax: 416-925-2295
rweiler7@cogeco.ca
Roland Weller, Archivist
rweller7@cogeco.ca
905-627-3856

Toronto: Todmorden Mills Heritage Museum & Art Centre
850 Coxwell Ave., Toronto ON M4C 5R1
Tel: 416-396-2819
todmorden@toronto.ca
Rita Russell, Acting Curator
416-396-2819

Toronto: Toronto Port Authority
60 Harbour St., Toronto ON M5J 1B7
Tel: 416-863-2011; Fax: 416-863-4830
www.torontoport.com/corporate_archives.asp?id=37

Toronto: Toronto Symphony Orchestra
60 Simcoe St., Toronto ON M5J 2H5
Tel: 416-593-0976; Fax: 416-593-6788
gcorrin@tso.ca
John Dunn, Volunteer Archivist
Gary Corrin

Toronto: United Church of Canada Archives
3250 Bloor St. West, Toronto ON M8X 2Y4
Tel: 416-231-5931; Fax: 416-231-3103
archives@united-church.ca
www.united-church.ca
Sharon P. Larade, Chief Archivist

Toronto: Upper Canada College Archives
200 Lonsdale Rd., Toronto ON M4V 1W6
Tel: 416-488-1125; Fax: 416-484-8613
mspence@ucc.on.ca
www.ucc.on.ca/podium/default.aspx?t=6617
Marian Spence, Archivist

Toronto: Weston Historical Society
1901 Weston Rd., Toronto ON M9N 3P1
Tel: 416-249-6663
westonhistoricalsociety@rogers.com
www.welcometoweston.ca/whs
Eva Ferguson, Project Manager
416-487-0049 ext. 10

Toronto: York Pioneer & Historical Society
2482 Yonge St., Toronto ON M4P 2H5
Tel: 416-483-0907
mrsh638@aol.com
John Marshall, Archivist
416-961-4420

Tweed: Tweed & Area Heritage Centre
40 Victoria St. North, Tweed ON K0K 3J0
Tel: 613-478-3989; Fax: 613-478-6457
tweedheritageinfo@on.aibn.com
Evan Morton, Curator
613-478-3989

Uxbridge: Uxbridge Historical Centre
7239 Concession 6, Uxbridge ON L9P 1R2
Tel: 905-852-5854; Fax: 905-852-5854
museum@town.uxbridge.on.ca
www.uxlib.com/museum
Allan McGillivray, Curator
museum@town.uxbridge.on.ca
905-852-5854

Vaughan: City of Vaughan Archives
10401 Dufferin St., Vaughan ON L6A 1S2
Tel: 905-832-2281
archives@city.vaughan.on.ca
www.city.vaughan.on.ca/culture_recreation/archives/index.cfm

Vernon: Osgoode Township Historical Society
7814 Lawrence St., Vernon ON K0A 3J0
Tel: 613-821-4062
oths@magma.ca
www.magma.ca/~oths/
James Stevenson, Curator/Archivist
oths@magma.ca

Waterford: The Waterford & Townsend Historical Society
Spruce Row Museum, 159 Nichol St., Waterford ON N0E 1Y0
Tel: 519-443-4211; Fax: 519-443-5640
sprucerow.museum@norfolkcounty.on.ca
Glen Bell, Contact

Waterloo: Evangelical Lutheran Church in Canada
#1502, 6 Willow St., Waterloo ON N2J 4S3
Tel: 519-884-1970
erichrwschultz@aol.com
www.easternsynod.org
Erich R.W. Schultz, Archivist
erichrwschultz@aol.com

Waterloo: Mennonite Archives of Ontario
Conrad Grebel University College, 140 Westmount, Rd. North, Waterloo ON N2L 3G6
Tel: 519-885-0220; Fax: 519-885-0014
marchive@uwaterloo.ca
grebel.uwaterloo.ca/mao/index.html
Sam Steiner, Librarian & Archivist
steiner@library.uwaterloo.ca

Whitby: Town of Whitby Archives
Whitby Public Library, 405 Dundas St., Whitby ON L1N 6A1
Tel: 905-668-6531; Fax: 905-668-7445
b.winter@sympatico.ca
Brian Winter, Archivist

Williamstown: Glengarry Historical Society
Bethune-Thompson House, 19730 John St., Williamstown ON K0C 2J0
Tel: 613-347-3006
David G. Anderson, Contact
anderson@glen-net.ca

Windsor: Assumption University Archives
400 Huron Church Rd., Windsor ON N9C 2J9
Tel: 519-973-7033; Fax: 519-973-7089
cbertrand@assumptionu.ca
www.assumptionu.ca

Windsor: Serbian Heritage Museum
6770 Tecumseh Rd. East, Windsor ON N8T 1E6
Tel: 519-944-4884; Fax: 519-974-3963
members.tripod.com/swo_heritage/serbian.htm
Deanna Pavlov, Curator

Windsor: Windsor's Community Museum/ Le Musée communautaire de Windsor
254 Pitt St. West, Windsor ON N9A 5L5
Tel: 519-253-1812; Fax: 519-253-0919
wmuseum@city.windsor.on.ca
www.windsorpubliclibrary.com/branches/museum/hours.php

Prince Edward Island

Regional Systems

Prince Edward Island Public Library Service
89 Red Head Rd., Morell PE C0A 1S0
Tel: 902-961-7320; Fax: 902-961-7322
plshq@gov.pe.ca
www.library.pe.ca
Kathleen Eaton, Provincial Librarian
keeaton@gov.pe.ca
Gary Ramsay, Reference Librarian
gwramsay@gov.pe.ca
902-368-4643
Liam O'Hare, Systems Librarian
lfohare@gov.pe.ca
902-961-7322
Barbara Kissick, Youth Services Librarian
bjkissick@gov.pe.ca
902-368-4641
Nichola Cleaveland, Government Services Librarian
nacleave@gov.pe.ca
902-398-4653

Public Libraries

Abram-Village: Bibliothèque publique d'Abram-Village
a/s École Évangéline, RR#3, Abram-Village PE C0B 2E0
Tél: 902-854-7268; Téléc: 902-854-2981
abram@gov.pe.ca
www.library.pe.ca

Alberton: Alberton Public Library
460 Main St., PO Box 449, Alberton PE C0B 1B0
Tel: 902-853-3049
alberton@gov.pe.ca
www.library.pe.ca

Borden: Borden-Carleton Public Library
244 Borden Ave., Borden PE C0B 1X0
Tel: 902-437-6492
borden-carleton@gov.pe.ca
www.library.pe.ca

Breadalbane: Breadalbane Public Library
4023 Dixon Rd., Breadalbane PE C0A 1E0
Tel: 902-964-2520
breadalbane@gov.pe.ca
www.library.pe.ca

Charlottetown: Bibliothèque Dr. J. Edmond Arsenault
5 rue Acadienne Hillsborough Pkwy., Charlottetown PE C1C 1M2
Tél: 902-368-6092
carrefour@gov.pe.ca
www.library.pe.ca

Charlottetown: Confederation Centre Public Library
PO Box 7000, Charlottetown PE C1A 8G8
Tel: 902-368-4642; Fax: 902-368-4652
ccpl@gov.pe.ca
www.library.pe.ca

Cornwall: Cornwall Public Library (PEI)
39 Lowther Dr., Cornwall PE C0A 1H0
Tel: 902-629-8415
cornwall@gov.pe.ca
www.library.pe.ca

Crapaud: Crapaud Public Library
20424 Trans Canada Hwy., Crapaud PE C0A 1J0
Tel: 902-658-2297
crapaud@gov.pe.ca
www.library.pe.ca

Georgetown: Georgetown Genevieve Soloman Memorial Library
36 Kent St., Georgetown PE C0A 1L0
Tel: 902-652-2832
georgetown@gov.pe.ca
www.library.pe.ca

Hunter River: Hunter River Public Library
19816 Rte. 2, Hunter River PE C0A 1N0
Tel: 902-964-2800
hunter_river@gov.pe.ca
www.library.pe.ca

Kensington: Kensington Public Library
55 Victoria St., Kensington PE C0B 1M0
Tel: 902-836-3721
kensington@gov.pe.ca
www.library.pe.ca

Kinkora: Kinkora Public Library
45 Anderson St., Kinkora PE C0B 1N0
Tel: 902-887-2172
kinkora@gov.pe.ca
www.library.pe.ca

Montague: Montague Public Library
273 Queen's Rd., Montague PE C0A 1R0
Tel: 902-838-2928
montague@gov.pe.ca
www.library.pe.ca

Morell: Morell Public Library
89 Red Head Rd., Morell PE C0A 1S0
Tel: 902-961-3389
morell@gov.pe.ca
www.library.pe.ca

Mount Stewart: Mount Stewart Public Library
104 Main St., Mount Stewart PE C0A 1T0
Tel: 902-676-2050
mtstewart@gov.pe.ca
www.library.pe.ca

Murray Harbour: Murray Harbour Public Library
1381 Main St., Murray Harbour PE C0A 1V0
Tel: 902-962-3875
murray_harbour@gov.pe.ca
www.library.pe.ca

Murray River: Murray River Leona Giddings Memorial Library
1066 McInnis Rd., Murray River PE C0A 1V0
Tel: 902-962-2667
murray_river@gov.pe.ca
www.library.pe.ca

O'Leary: O'Leary Public Library
18 Community St., O'Leary PE C0B 1V0
Tel: 902-859-8788
www.library.pe.ca

St. Peters: St. Peters Public Library
1968 Cardigan Rd., St. Peters PE C0A 2A0
Tel: 902-961-3415
www.library.pe.ca

Souris: Souris Public Library
75 Main St., Souris PE C0A 2B0
Tel: 902-687-2157; Fax: 902-687-4426
souris@gov.pe.ca
www.library.pe.ca

Stratford: Stratford Public Library (PEI)
57 Bunbury Rd., Stratford PE C1B 1T8
Tel: 902-569-7441
stratford@edu.pe.ca
www.library.pe.ca

Summerside: Bibliothèque J.-Henri-Blanchard
5, av Maris Stella, Summerside PE C1N 3Y5
Tél: 902-432-2748; Téléc: 902-888-1686
blanchard@gov.pe.ca
www.library.pe.ca

Summerside: School Library Advocate
c/o Wendy Doucette, Elm St. School, 256 Elm St., Summerside PE C1N 3V5
Tel: 902-368-6085
wodoucette@edu.pe.ca
www.edu.pe.ca/peitla/sla.htm
Wendy Doucette, President

Summerside: Summerside Rotary Library
192 Water St., Summerside PE C1N 1B1
Tel: 902-436-7323; Fax: 902-888-8055
summerside@gov.pe.ca
www.library.pe.ca

Tignish: Tignish Public Library
103 School St., Tignish PE C0B 2B0
Tel: 902-882-7363
tignish@gov.pe.ca
www.library.pe.ca

Tyne Valley: Tyne Valley Public Library
19 Allen Rd., Tyne Valley PE C0B 2C0
Tel: 902-831-2928
tyne_valley@gov.pe.ca
www.library.pe.ca

Archives

Charlottetown: Prince Edward Island Public Archives & Records Office
Hon. George Coles Bldg., 4th Fl., 175 Richmond St., PO Box 1000, Charlottetown PE C1A 7M4
Tel: 902-368-4290; Fax: 902-368-6327
archives@gov.pe.ca
www.gov.pe.ca/cca/index.php3?number=1004626&lang=E
Jill MacMicken Wilson, Provincial Archivist
jswilson@gov.pe.ca
902-368-4351
Ann-Marie McIsaac, Provincial Records Manager
902-368-6093

Québec

Regional Systems

Réseau BIBLIO de l'Abitibi-Témiscamingue-Nord-du-Québec
20, av Québec, Rouyn-Noranda QC J9X 2E6
Tél: 819-762-4305; Téléc: 819-762-5309
info@reseaubiblioatnq.qc.ca
www.reseaubiblioduquebec.qc.ca/portail/index.aspx?page=2&RID=1
Louis Dallaire, Directeur général
louis.dallaire@reseaubiblioatnq.qc.ca
Louise Julien, Responsable, Traitment documentaire
louise.julien@crsbpat.qc.ca
Lidia Turgeon, Responsable, Services administratifs
lidia.turgeon@crsbpat.qc.ca
Chantal Baril, Responsable, Soutien professionnel
chantal.baril@crsbpat.qc.ca

Réseau BIBLIO de l'Estrie
4155, rue Brodeur, Sherbrooke QC J1L 1K4
Tél: 819-565-9744; Téléc: 819-565-9157
crsbpe@reseaubiblioestrie.qc.ca
www.reseaubiblioestrie.qc.ca
Joelle Thivierge, Directrice générale
jthivierge@reseaubiblioestrie.qc.ca
819-565-9744 ext. 102
France Lachance, Service à la clientele
flachance@reseaubiblioestrie.qc.ca
819-565-9744 ext. 103
Françoise Desprès, Prêt entre bibliothèques
fdespres@reseaubiblioestrie.qc.ca
819-565-9744 ext. 105

Réseau BIBLIO de l'Outaouais
2295, rue Saint-Louis, Gatineau QC J8T 5L8
Tél: 819-561-6008; Téléc: 819-561-6767
biblio@crsbpo.qc.ca
www.reseaubiblioduquebec.qc.ca/portail/index.aspx?page=2&RID=8
Sylvie Thibault, Directrice générale
sylvie.thibault@crsbpo.qc.ca
Claudette Deschênes, Agente de bureau
claudette.deschênes@crsbpo.qc.ca
Jonathan Careau, Coordonnateur du soutien technique aux bibliothèques
jonathan.careau@crsbpo.qc.ca

Réseau BIBLIO de la Capitale-Nationale et de la Chaudière-Appalaches
3189, rue Albert-Demers, Charny QC G6X 3A1
Tél: 418-832-6166; Téléc: 418-832-6168
Ligne sans frais: 866-446-6166
info@reseaubibliocnca.qc.ca
www.reseaubiblioduquebec.qc.ca/portail/index.aspx?page=2&RID=9
Isabelle Poirier, Directrice générale
ipoirier@reseaubibliocnca.qc.ca
Daniel Jubinville, Technicienne en documentation
djubinville@reseaubibliocnca.qc.ca
Marc Hébert, Agent culturel
mhebert@reseaubibliocnca.qc.ca

Réseau BIBLIO de la Côte-Nord
59, rue Napoléon, Sept-Iles QC G4R 5C5
Tél: 418-962-1020; Téléc: 418-962-5124
biblio@reseaubibliocn.qc.ca
www.reseaubiblioduquebec.qc.ca/portail/index.aspx?page=2&RID=3
Jean-Roch Gagnon, Directeur général
jrgagnon@reseaubibliocn.qc.ca
Chantal Hould, Responsable, Services techniques
chantalh@reseaubibliocn.qc.ca

Réseau BIBLIO de la Gaspésie-Iles-de-la-Madeleine
31, rue des Écoliers, Cap-Chat QC G0J 1E0
Tél: 418-786-5597; Téléc: 418-786-2024
info@reseaubibliogim.qc.ca
www.reseaubiblioduquebec.qc.ca/portail/index.aspx?page=2&RID=4
Aurélien Bisson, Directeur général
aurelien.bisson@reseaubibliogim.qc.ca
Monique Demers, Bibliothécaire, soutien aux bibliothèques affiliées
monique.demers@reseaubibliogim.qc.ca
Carole Bernatchez, Technicienne en documentation
carole.bernatchez@reseaubibliogim.qc.ca

Réseau BIBLIO de la Montérégie
275, rue Conrad-Pelletier, La Prairie QC J5R 4V1
Tél: 450-444-5433; Téléc: 450-659-3364
crsaide@reseaubibliomonteregie.qc.ca
www.reseaubibliomonteregie.qc.ca
Jacqueline Labelle, Directrice générale
jlabelle@reseaubibliomonteregie.qc.ca
Josée Audet, Directrice, Services techniques
josee.audet@reseaubibliomonteregie.qc.ca
Annie Bonneyville, Conseillère aux bibliothèques affiliées

Réseau BIBLIO des Laurentides
29, rue Brissette, Sainte-Agathe-des-Monts QC J8C 3L1
Tél: 819-326-6440; Téléc: 819-326-0885
info@crsbpl.qc.ca
www.reseaubiblioduquebec.qc.ca/portail/index.aspx?page=2&RID=5
JoAnne Turnbull, Directrice générale
jturnbull@crsbpl.qc.ca
Julie Filion, Directrice, Soutien aux bibliothèques
jfilion@crsbpl.qc.ca
Norbert Morveau, Directeur, Soutien informatique
nmorneau@crsbpl.qc.ca
Claire Dufresne, Bibliothécaire

Réseau BIBLIO du Bas-Saint-Laurent
465, rue St-Pierre, Rivière-du-Loup QC G5R 4T6
Tél: 418-867-1682; Téléc: 418-867-3434
crsbp@crsbp.net
www.reseaubibliobsl.qc.ca
Jacques Côté, Directeur général
jacques.cote@crsbp.net
Josée Brulotte, Bibliothécaire, directrice soutien au réseau
josee.brulotte@crsbp.net

Réseau BIBLIO du Centre-du-Québec, de Lanaudière et de la Mauricie
3125, rue Girard, Trois-Rivières QC G8Z 2M4
Tél: 819-375-9623; Téléc: 819-375-0132
Ligne sans frais: 877-324-2546
crsbp@reseaubibliocqlm.qc.ca
www.reseaubibliocqlm.qc.ca
Hélène Arseneau, Directrice générale
helene.arseneau@reseaubibliocqlm.qc.ca
Michelle Vallée, Directrice, Services aux bibliothèques
michelle.vallee@reseaubibliocqlm.qc.ca
Valérie Simard, Directrice, Service techniques coopératifs
valerie.simard@reseaubibliocqlm.qc.ca

Lauren Duchemin, Directrice, Services administratifs
lauren.duchemin@reseaubibliocqlm.qc.ca
Francine Allen, Responsable, Choix et traitement
francine.allen@reseaubibliocqlm.qc.ca

Public Libraries

Acton Vale: **Bibliothèque Acton Vale**
1093A, rue Saint-André, Acton Vale QC J0H 1A0
Tél: 450-546-2703; *Téléc:* 450-642-1165
acton.vale@reseaubibliomonteregie.qc.ca
Sophia Bédard, Responsable

Aguanish: **Bibliothèque d'Aguanish**
106, rue Jacques-Cartier, Aguanish QC G0G 1A0
Tél: 418-533-2323; *Téléc:* 418-533-2012
aguanib@globetrotter.net
www.reseaubiblioduquebec.qc.ca
Normande Blais, Responsable
418-533-2352

Albanel: **Bibliothèque publique d'Albanel**
153A, Principale, Albanel QC G8M 3J3
Tél: 613-279-5762
albanel@reseaubibliosIsj.qc.ca
Marguerite Dubeau, Responsable
613-279-5800
Hélène Theberge, Assistante
613-279-3381

Albertville: **Bibliothèque d'Albertville**
1058, rue Principale, Albertville QC G0J 1A0
Tél: 418-756-6015
biblio.albert@crsbp.net
www.reseaubiblioduquebec.qc.ca
Danielle Berger, Responsable

Alma: **Bibliothèque municipale d'Alma**
500, rue Collard ouest, Alma QC G8B 1N2
Tél: 418-669-5140; *Téléc:* 418-669-5089
martin.bouchard@alma.biblio.qc.ca
www.ville.alma.qc.ca/mini_site.php?idMini=175
Martin Bouchard, Responsable
Guylaine Simard, Technicienne en documentation

Alma: **Bibliothèque publique de Delisle**
221, rue des Bruyères, Alma QC G8E 1J9
Tél: 418-668-2697
delisle@reseaubibliosIsj.qc.ca
Ghislain Girard, Responsable
418-480-3396

Alma: **Bibliothèque publique de Saint-Coeur-de-Marie**
5791, av du Pont nord, Alma QC G8E 1X1
Tél: 418-347-3729; *Téléc:* 418-347-3697
stcoeur@reseaubibliosIsj.qc.ca
www.reseaubiblioduquebec.qc.ca/portail/index.aspx?page=3&BI D=5
Martine Gobeil, Responsable
Sylvie Larouche, Adjointe
Joanne Duperre, Secrétaire
Julie Dallaire, Trésorière

Amherst: **Bibliothèque de Saint-Rémi**
124, rue St-Louis, Amherst QC J0T 2L0
Tél: 819-687-3372; *Téléc:* 819-687-8430
stremi@crsbpl.qc.ca
www.reseaubiblioduquebec.qc.ca
Hélène Dion, Responsable

Amqui: **Bibliothèque Madeleine-Gagnon**
24, promenade de l'Hôtel de Ville, Amqui QC G5J 3E1
Tél: 418-629-4242; *Téléc:* 418-629-4090
bibliotheque@ville.amqui.qc.ca
Marie Côté, Responsable

Ange-Gardien: **Bibliothèque municipale d'Ange-Gardien**
249, rue Saint-Joseph, Ange-Gardien QC J0E 1E0
Tél: 450-293-3987
ange.gardien@reseaubibliomonteregie.qc.ca
www.reseaubiblioduquebec.qc.ca/portail/index.aspx?page=3&BI D=6
Sylvie Raymond, Responsable
Lynda Soucy, Responsable, Collection locale
Sylvie Raymond, Responsable, Animation et promotion

Angliers: **Bibliothèque d'Angliers**
14, rue Baie Miller, Angliers QC J0Z 1A0
Tél: 819-949-4351; *Téléc:* 819-949-4321
angliers@reseaubibliatnq.qc.ca
www.reseaubiblioduquebec.qc.ca
Manon Corbin, Responsable

Magalie Corbin-Boivin, Bénévole
Lyna Pine, Bénévole
Amélya Urrutiaguer, Bénévole

L'Anse-Saint-Jean: **Bibliothèque publique de L'Anse-St-Jean**
3, rue du Couvent, L'Anse-Saint-Jean QC G0V 1J0
Tél: 418-549-7196
anse@reseaubibliosIsj.qc.ca
www.reseaubiblioduquebec.qc.ca
Germaine Boudreault, Responsable
Marie Thibeault, Adjointe

Armagh: **Bibliothèque municipale d'Armagh**
9, rue de la Salle, Armagh QC G0R 1A0
Tél: 418-466-3004; *Téléc:* 418-466-2409
armabib@globetrotter.qc.ca
www.reseaubiblioduquebec.qc.ca/armagh
Sylvie Chabot, Responsable

Arntfield: **Bibliothèque de Arntfield**
15, rue Fugère, Arntfield QC J0Z 1B0
Tél: 819-279-2241; *Téléc:* 819-279-2481
arntfield@reseaubibliatnq.qc.ca
www.reseaubiblioduquebec.qc.ca
Jeannine Drouin, Responsable
819-279-2329

Arundel: **Bibliothèque d'Arundel/ Arundel Library**
2, rue du Village, Arundel QC J0T 1A0
Tél: 819-687-8246; *Téléc:* 819-687-8760
arundel@crsbpl.qc.ca
www.reseaubiblioduquebec.qc.ca
Fran Jones, Responsable

Asbestos: **Bibliothèque municipale d'Asbestos**
351, boul Saint-Luc, Asbestos QC J1T 2W4
Tél: 819-879-4363; *Téléc:* 819-879-0608
bibliasbestos@ville.asbestos.qc.ca
www.ville.asbestos.qc.ca/biblio/index.html
Julie Fontaine, Responsable

L'Ascension: **Bibliothèque de l'Ascension**
4, rue Principale ouest, L'Ascension QC J0T 1W0
Tél: 819-275-1546; *Téléc:* 819-275-1546
bibliotheque@municipalite-lascension.qc.ca
www.reseaubiblioduquebec.qc.ca/l'ascension
Monique Turpin, Responsable
Danielle Tremblay, Adjointe

L'Ascension: **Bibliothèque publique de L'Ascension**
900, 4e av est, L'Ascension QC G0W 1Y0
Tél: 418-347-3482; *Téléc:* 418-347-4253
ascens@reseaubibliosIsj.qc.ca
www.reseaubiblioduquebec.qc.ca/portail/index.aspx?page=3&BI D=5
Diane Tremblay, Coordonnatrice

L'Assomption: **Bibliothèque Christian-Roy**
375, rue St-Pierre, L'Assomption QC J5W 2B6
Tél: 450-589-5671; *Téléc:* 450-589-6882
bibliotheque@ville.lassomption.qc.ca
www.ville.lassomption.qc.ca/cbiblio.html
Marjolaine Bertrand, Bibliothécaire
450-589-5671 ext. 237

L'Assomption: **Les Bibliothèques publiques de Laval-Laurentides-Lanaudière**
399, rue Dorval, L'Assomption QC J5W 1A1
Tél: 450-589-5671; *Téléc:* 450-589-6882
bibliotheque@ville.lassomption.qc.ca
www.bplll.qc.ca
Stéphane Legault, Président
bibliotheque@ville.lassomption.qc.ca
450-589-5671 ext. 237

Aston-Jonction: **Bibliothèque d'Aston-Jonction**
210, rue Lemire, Aston-Jonction QC G0Z 1A0
Téléc: 819-226-3459
biblio070@reseaubibliocqlm.qc.ca
www.reseaubiblioduquebec.qc.ca
Léa Houle, Responsable
Jeanne-d'Arc Béliveau, Bénévole
Monique Doucet, Bénévole

Auclair: **Bibliothèque Auclair**
777, rue du Clocher, Auclair QC G0L 1A0
Tél: 418-899-0417
biblio.auclair@crsbp.net
www.reseaubiblioduquebec.qc.ca
Cécile Castonguay, Responsable

Aumond: **Bibliothèque de Aumond**
679, rue Principale, Aumond QC J0W 1W0
Tél: 819-449-4006; *Téléc:* 819-449-7448
Diane Guénette, Responsable

La Baie: **Bibliothèque de La Baie**
1911, 6e av, La Baie QC G7B 1S1
Tél: 418-698-5350; *Téléc:* 418-697-5087
webbiblio@ville.saguenay.qc.ca
www.ville.saguenay.qc.ca
Anne Lebel, Chef de division, Bibliothèques de Saguenay
anne.lebel@ville.saguenay.qc.ca
Céline Verreault, Responsable, Bibliothèques de l'arrond. de La Baie
celine.verreault@ville.saguenay.qc.ca
Virginie Beaudoin, Responsable de l'Animation
virginie.beaudoin@ville.saguenay.qc.ca

Baie-Comeau: **Bibliothèque municipale Alice-Lane**
6, av Radisson, Baie-Comeau QC G4Z 1W4
Tél: 418-296-8304; *Téléc:* 418-296-8328
vbc@ville.baie-comeau.qc.ca
Yvon Grondin, Superviseur responsable
ygrondin@ville.baie-comeau.qc.ca
418-396-8361

Baie-des-Sables: **Bibliothèque de Baie-des-Sables**
20, rue du Couvent, Baie-des-Sables QC G0J 1C0
Tél: 418-772-6704
biblio.sables@crsbp.net
www.reseaubiblioduquebec.qc.ca
Monique Roy, Responsable

Baie-du-Febvre: **Bibliothèque de Baie-du-Febvre**
23, rue de l'Église, Baie-du-Febvre QC J0G 1A0
Tél: 450-783-6484; *Téléc:* 450-783-2235
biblio032@reseaubibliocqlm.qc.ca
www.reseaubiblioduquebec.qc.ca
Lise Laforce, Responsable

Baie-Sainte-Catherine: **Bibliothèque municipale de Baie-Sainte-Catherine**
308, rue Leclerc, Baie-Sainte-Catherine QC G0T 1A0
Tél: 418-237-4241; *Téléc:* 418-237-4223
www.reseaubiblioduquebec.qc.ca/baie-sainte-catherine
Patricia Ouellet, Responsable

Baie-Saint-Paul: **Bibliothèque René-Richard**
9, rue Forget, Baie-Saint-Paul QC G3Z 1T4
Tél: 418-435-5858; *Téléc:* 418-435-0010
bibliobsp@charlevoix.net
www.baiestpaul.com/bibliotheque/
Denise Ouellet, Responsable
Hélène Simard, Adjointe

Baie-Trinité: **Bibliothèque de Baie-Trinité**
3, rue St-Joseph, Baie-Trinité QC G0H 1A0
Tél: 418-939-2231; *Téléc:* 418-939-2616
www.reseaubiblioduquebec.qc.ca
Ghislaine Harvey, Responsable
ghislhar@hotmail.com
418-939-2535

Barraute: **Bibliothèque Barraute**
600, 1re Rue, Barraute QC J0Y 1A0
Tél: 819-734-6762; *Téléc:* 819-734-6762
barraute@reseaubibliatnq.qc.ca
Claire Voyer, Responsable

Bassin: **Bibliothèque de L'Ile-du-Havre-Aubert**
#104, 280, ch de Bassin, Bassin QC G4T 0B5
Tél: 418-937-2279; *Téléc:* 418-937-5558
bibliohavre@munIles.ca
www.reseaubiblioduquebec.qc.ca
Christiane Turbide, Responsable

Batiscan: **Bibliothèque municipale de Batiscan**
791-2, place de la Solidarité, Batiscan QC G0X 1A0
Tél: 819-840-0600; *Téléc:* 819-362-3174
biblio025@reseaubibliocqlm.qc.ca
www.reseaubiblioduquebec.qc.ca
Caroline Pelletier, Responsable
Agathe Deschesnes, Adjointe

Béarn: **Bibliothèque de Béarn**
38, rue Principale nord, Béarn QC J0Z 1G0
Tél: 819-726-2251; *Téléc:* 819-726-2121
bearn@reseaubibliatnq.qc.ca
www.reseaubiblioduquebec.qc.ca
Linda Gaudet, Responsable

Beaucanton: **Bibliothèque Beaucanton**
2709, boul McDuff, #C, Beaucanton QC J0Z 1H0
Tél: 819-941-2686; *Téléc:* 819-941-2686
beaucanton@reseaubiblioatnq.qc.ca
www.reseaubiblioduquebec.qc.ca
Célyne Beauchamp, Responsable

Beauceville: **Bibliothèque Madeleine-Doyon**
100, Place de l'Église, Beauceville QC G5X 1X3
Tél: 418-774-2466; *Téléc:* 418-774-2499
biblio@ville.beauceville.qc.ca
www.reseaubiblioduquebec.qc.ca/beauceville
Marie-Andrée Giroux, Responsable
Brigitte Veilleux, Adjointe

Beauharnois: **Bibliothèque Dominique-Julien**
#100, 600, rue Ellice, Beauharnois QC J6N 3P7
Tél: 450-429-3546; *Téléc:* 450-429-3820
Marielle Vinet, Responsable

Beaulac-Garthby: **Bibliothèque de Saints-Martyrs-Canadiens**
13, ch du Village, Beaulac-Garthby QC G0Y 1B0
Tél: 819-344-5171
biblio157@reseaubibliocqlm.qc.ca
www.reseaubiblioduquebec.qc.ca
Pierre L. Ramsay, Responsable
Thérèse Lemay, Bénévole

Beaumont: **Bibliothèque Luc-Lacourcière**
64, ch du Domaine, Beaumont QC G0R 1C0
Tél: 418-837-2658; *Téléc:* 418-837-2658
bibl.l.lacourciere@videotron.ca
www.reseaubiblioduquebec.qc.ca/beaumont/
Nicole Maheu, Responsable

Beaupré: **Bibliothèque La Plume d'oie**
11298, rue de La Salle, Beaupré QC G0A 1E0
Tél: 418-827-8483; *Téléc:* 418-827-3818
bibliotheque@ville.beaupre.qc.ca
www.reseaubiblioduquebec.qc.ca/beaupre/
Charlotte Bouchard, Responsable

Bécancour: **Bibliothèque publique de Bécancour**
1295, av Nicolas-Perrot, Bécancour QC G9H 1A1
Tél: 819-294-4455

Bedford: **Bibliothèque Léon-Maurice-Côté**
52, rue Du Pont, Bedford QC J0J 1A0
Tél: 450-248-4625
bedford@reseaubibliomonteregie.qc.ca
Renée Dallaire, Responsable
Estelle Messier, Co-responsable
Andrée Beaudoin, Responsable, PIB

Bégin: **Bibliothèque publique de Bégin**
120B, rue Tremblay, Bégin QC G0V 1B0
Tél: 418-672-4503
begin@reseaubiblioslsj.qc.ca
Marie-Joseph Thérriault, Responsable

Belcourt: **Bibliothèque de Belcourt**
219, rue Communautaire, Belcourt QC J0Y 2M0
Tél: 819-737-8894; *Téléc:* 819-737-4084
belcourt@reseaubiblioatnq.qc.ca
www.reseaubiblioduquebec.qc.ca
Christine Labbée, Responsable

Bellecombe: **Bibliothèque de Bellecombe**
1161, rte des Pionniers, Bellecombe QC J0Z 1K0
Tél: 819-797-8302; *Téléc:* 819-797-6585
bellecombe@reseaubiblioatnq.qc.ca
www.reseaubiblioduquebec.qc.ca
Gaétane Morrissette, Responsable

Belleterre: **Bibliothèque de Belleterre**
265, 1e av, Belleterre QC J0Z 1L0
Tél: 819-722-2052; *Téléc:* 819-722-2527
belleterre@reseaubiblioatnq.qc.ca
www.reseaubiblioduquebec.qc.ca
Claudette Rioux Gauthier, Responsable
Joanne Pichette, Bénévole
Julienne Boyer, Bénévole
Rosianne Gauthier, Bénévole
Noëlla Giroux, Bénévole
Murielle Larivière, Bénévole
Céline Phillipps Gauthier, Bénévole
Shirley Rivard, Bénévole
Jacqueline Savard, Bénévole
Lise Valiquette, Bénévole

Beloeil: **Bibliothèque municipale de Beloeil**
620, rue Richelieu, Beloeil QC J3G 5E8
Tél: 450-467-7872; *Téléc:* 450-467-3257
biblio@ville.beloeil.qc.ca
Johanne Guèvremont, Directrice
biblio@ville.beloeil.qc.ca
450-467-7872
Hélène Fournier, Technicienne en documentation

Berthier-sur-Mer: **Bibliothèque Camille-Roy**
5, rue du Couvent, Berthier-sur-Mer QC G0R 1E0
Tél: 418-259-2353; *Téléc:* 418-259-2038
biblcamr@globetrotter.qc.ca
www.reseaubiblioduquebec.qc.ca
Jocelyne Guimont, Responsable
418-259-2622

Le Bic: **Bibliothèque de Le Bic**
149, rue Sainte-Cécile, Le Bic QC G0L 1B0
Tél: 418-736-5325
biblio.lebic@crsbp.net
www.reseaubiblioduquebec.qc.ca
Martine Fournier, Bibliothécaire

Biencourt: **Bibliothèque de Biencourt**
#1, 2, rue Saint-Marc, Biencourt QC G0K 1T0
Tél: 418-499-2423
biblio.biencourt@crsbp.net
www.reseaubiblioduquebec.qc.ca
Marthe Aubry Leduc, Responsable

Blainville: **Bibliothèque municipale de Blainville**
1000, ch du Plan-Bouchard, Blainville QC J7C 3S9
Tél: 450-434-5370; *Téléc:* 450-434-5378
bibliotheque@ville.blainville.qc.ca
www.ville.blainville.qc.ca
Patrick Toupin, Directeur, Loisirs et développement communautaire

Blue Sea: **Bibliothèque Blue Sea**
2, ch Blue Sea, Blue Sea QC J0X 1C0
Tél: 819-463-2261; *Téléc:* 819-463-4345
admbluesea@crsbpo.qc.ca
www.reseaubiblioduquebec.qc.ca/bluesea
Isabelle Gauthier, Responsable

Boisbriand: **Bibliothèque municipale de Boisbriand**
901, boul. de la Grande-Allée, Boisbriand QC J7G 1W6
Tél: 450-435-7466; *Téléc:* 450-435-0627
slegault@ville.boisbriand.qc.ca
Stéphane Legault, Directeur

Bois-Franc: **Bibliothèque de Bois-Franc**
466, rte 105, Bois-Franc QC J9E 3A9
Tél: 819-441-0645; *Téléc:* 819-449-4407
admboisfranc@crsbpo.qc.ca
www.reseaubiblioduquebec.qc.ca/BoisFranc
Francine Marenger, Bibliothécaire

Bonaventure: **Bibliothèque Françoise-Bujold**
95A, av Port-Royal, Bonaventure QC G0C 1E0
Tél: 418-534-4238; *Téléc:* 418-534-4336
bonapret@globetrotter.net
Thérèse Arsenault, Responsable

Boucherville: **Bibliothèque Montarville-Boucher-De la Bruère**
501, ch du Lac, Boucherville QC J4B 6V6
Tél: 450-449-8650; *Téléc:* 450-449-6865
bibliotheque@ville.boucherville.qc.ca
www.ville.boucherville.qc.ca
Sylvie Provost, Directrice
Brigitte Arsenault, Responsable, Services techniques

Bouchette: **Bibliothèque de Bouchette**
36, rue Principale, Bouchette QC J0X 1E0
Tél: 819-465-2555; *Téléc:* 819-465-2318
admbouchette@crsbpo.qc.ca
www.reseaubiblioduquebec.qc.ca/Bouchette
Pierre Carrière, Responsable

Boulanger: **Bibliothèque publique de Sainte-Jeanne-d'Arc**
400, rue Verreault, Boulanger QC G0W 1E0
Tél: 418-276-1189
jeanne@reseaubiblioslsj.qc.ca
www.reseaubiblioduquebec.qc.ca
Madelaine Tremblay, Responsable

Brébeuf: **Bibliothèque de Brébeuf**
#2, 217, rte 323, Brébeuf QC J0T 1B0
Tél: 819-425-9833; *Téléc:* 819-425-6611
brebeuf@crsbpl.qc.ca
www.reseaubiblioduquebe.qc.ca
Ginette Bernard, Responsable

Brigham: **Bibliothèque municipale de Brigham**
118, av des Cèdres, Brigham QC J2K 4J4
Tél: 450-266-0500
brigham@reseaubibliomonteregie.qc.ca
Céline Vaillancourt, Responsable
rbcv@endirect.qc.ca
450-263-6677

Bristol: **Bibliothèque de Bristol/ Bristol Library**
32, ch Aylmer, Bristol QC J0X 1G0
Tél: 819-647-5555; *Téléc:* 819-647-2424
admbristol@crsbpo.qc.ca
www.reseaubiblioduquebec.qc.ca/Bristol
Kelly Dowe, Responsable

Brossard: **Bibliothèque de Brossard (Georgette-Lepage)**
7850, av San-Francisco, Brossard QC J4X 2A4
Tél: 450-923-6350; *Téléc:* 450-923-7042
bibliotheque@ville.brossard.qc.ca
www.ville.brossard.qc.ca/biblio
Suzanne Payette, Directrice
suzanne.payette@ville.brossard.qc.ca
Brigitte Gagnon, Chef de division, Services au public
brigitte.gagnon@ville.brossard.qc.ca

Brownsburg-Chatham: **Bibliothèque de Brownsburg-Chatham**
200, rue MacVicar, Brownsburg-Chatham QC J8G 2Z6
Tél: 450-533-5355
biblio@brownsburgchatham.ca
www.reseaubiblioduquebec.qc.ca
Brigitte Bowen, Responsable

Bryson: **Bibliothèque de Bryson**
833, rue Principale, Bryson QC J0X 1H0
Tél: 819-648-2543; *Téléc:* 819-648-5297
admbryson@crsbpo.qc.ca
www.reseaubiblioduquebec.qc.ca/Bryson
Charlotte Miljour, Responsable

Buckingham: **Bibliothèque municipale de Buckingham**
181, rue Joseph, Buckingham QC J8L 1G6
Tél: 819-595-7461
Lise Robitaille, Responsable
819-986-4211
Carole Larocque, Technicienne en documentation
819-986-4214

Buckland: **Bibliothèque Biblio Buck**
4340, rue Principale, Buckland QC G0R 1G0
Tél: 418-789-3119; *Téléc:* 418-789-3119
www.reseaubiblioduquebec.qc.ca/buckland
Claude Gignac, Responsable
Diane Laflamme, Adjointe
Lise Hudon, Responsable de l'animation

Cabano: **Bibliothèque Cabano**
14A, du Vieux Chemin, Cabano QC G0L 1E0
Tél: 418-845-5568; *Téléc:* 418-854-0118
biblio.cabano@crsbp.net
Huguette Nadeau, Responsable
biblio.cabano@crsbp.net
418-854-5568 ext. 200

Cacouna: **Bibliothèque de Cacouna**
420, rue du Couvent, Cacouna QC G0L 1G0
Tél: 418-860-2651
biblio.cacouna@crsbp.net
www3.sympatico.ca/bibkakou
Louise Létourneau, Responsable

Cadillac: **Bibliothèque Cadillac**
15, 1ère av est, Cadillac QC J0Y 1C0
Tél: 819-759-3606; *Téléc:* 819-759-3607
cadillac@reseaubiblioatnq.qc.ca
www.crsbpat.qc.ca/cadillac/
Rita Maranda, Responsable

Calixa-Lavallée: **Bibliothèque municipale de Calixa-Lavallée**
771, rang Beauce, Calixa-Lavallée QC J0L 1A0
Tél: 450-583-5417
calixa.lavallee@reseaubibliomonteregie.qc.ca
www.reseaubiblioduquebec.qc.ca
Nicole Jacques, Responsable

Campbell's Bay: **Bibliothèque de Campbell's Bay/Litchfield**
4, rue Patterson, Campbell's Bay QC J0X 1K0
Tél: 819-648-5676; *Téléc:* 819-648-2045
admcampbell@crsbpo.qc.ca
www.reseaubiblioduquebec.qc.ca/CampbellsBay
Lucille Lacourse, Responsable

Candiac: **Bibliothèque municipale de Candiac**
59, ch Haendel, Candiac QC J5R 1R7
Tél: 450-635-6032; *Téléc:* 450-635-0900
biblio@ville.candiac.qc.ca
www.ville.candiac.qc.ca
Patricia Lemieux, Responsable

Cantley: **Bibliothèque municipale de Cantley**
8, ch River, Cantley QC J8V 2Z9
Tél: 819-827-3434; *Téléc:* 819-827-4328
biblio@bibliocantley.qc.ca
www.bibliocantley.qc.ca
Bibiane Rondeau, Coordonnatrice

Cap-aux-Meules: **Bibliothèque de Cap-aux-Meules**
#3, 315, ch Principal, Cap-aux-Meules QC G4T 1E2
Tél: 418-986-6821; *Téléc:* 418-986-5446
bibliocamiles@hotmail.com
Suzanne Chevrier, Responsable

Cap-Chat: **Bibliothèque La ruche littéraire**
27, des Écoliers, Cap-Chat QC G0J 1E0
Tél: 418-786-2068
bbocchat@globetrotter.qc.ca
Carmeline Langlais, Responsable
418-786-2149

Cap-d'Espoir: **Bibliothèque de Cap-d'Espoir**
52, rue du Curé-Poirier, Cap-d'Espoir QC G0C 1G0
Tél: 418-782-2921; *Téléc:* 418-782-2590
bbocesp@ville.perce.qc.ca
www.reseaubiblioduquebec.qc.ca
Marie-Lise Rail, Responsable

Caplan: **Bibliothèque Jeanne-Ferlatte**
17, boul Perron est, Caplan QC G0C 1H0
Tél: 418-388-2545; *Téléc:* 418-388-2429
bibliocaplan@hotmail.com
Colette Bertrand, Responsable

Cap-Saint-Ignace: **Bibliothèque Léo-Pol-Morin**
100, Place de l'Église, Cap-Saint-Ignace QC G0R 1H0
Tél: 418-246-3037; *Téléc:* 418-246-5663
biblicap@globetrotter.qc.ca
www.reseaubiblioduquebec.qc.ca/cap-saint-ignace
Lyne Gobeil, Responsable
Lyne Richard, Adjointé

Cap-Santé: **Bibliothèque municipale de Cap-Santé**
15, rue Marie-Fitzbach, Cap-Santé QC G0A 1L0
Tél: 418-285-6891; *Téléc:* 418-285-0009
capsante@globetrotter.qc.ca
www.reseaubiblioduquebec.qc.ca/cap-sante
Francine Germain, Responsable
418-285-2374

Capucins: **Bibliothèque de Capucins**
294, rte du Village, Capucins QC G0J 1H0
Tél: 418-786-2013
bbocapu@globetrotter.net
www.reseaubiblioduquebec.qc.ca
Jeannine Harrisson, Responsable

Carleton-sur-Mer: **Bibliothèque Gabrielle-Bernard-Dubé**
774, boul Perron, Carleton-sur-Mer QC G0C 1J0
Tél: 418-364-7103
livre1@globetrotter.net
Julie Poulin, Responsable

Causapscal: **Bibliothèque de Causapscal**
3, Place de la Fabrique, Causapscal QC G0J 1J0
Tél: 418-756-3522
biblio.causap@crsbp.net
www.reseaubiblioduquebec.qc.ca
Thérèse Audit, Responsable

Les Cèdres: **Bibliothèque municipale de Les Cèdres**
1060, ch du Fleuve, Les Cèdres QC J7T 1A1
Tél: 450-452-4363
cedres@reseaubibliomonteregie.qc.ca
www.reseaubiblioduquebec.qc.ca
Odette Marois, Responsable
omarois@ville.lescedres.qc.ca

Chambly: **Bibliothèque municipale de Chambly**
1691, rue Bourgogne, Chambly QC J3L 1Y8
Tél: 450-658-2711; *Téléc:* 450-447-4525
biblio@ville.chambly.qc.ca
www.ville.chambly.qc.ca/biblio
Carole Mainville-Bériault, Directrice
cmberiault@ville.chambly.qc.ca
450-658-0674

Chambord: **Bibliothèque publique de Chambord**
72-1, boul de la Montagne, Chambord QC G0W 1G0
Tél: 418-342-6274
chambord@reseaubiblioslsj.qc.ca
Andrée Chiasson, Responsable
Kathy Lemay, Responsable

Champlain: **Bibliothèque de Champlain**
963, rue Notre-Dame, Champlain QC G0X 1C0
Tél: 819-840-0407; *Téléc:* 819-295-3032
biblio005@reseaubiblioclqm.qc.ca
www.reseaubiblioduquebec.qc.ca
Isabelle Vézina, Responsable

Chandler: **Bibliothèque municipale-scolaire de Chandler**
131, boul René-Lévesque, Chandler QC G0C 1K0
Tél: 418-689-3808; *Téléc:* 418-689-3639
giselec@globetrotter.net
Gisele Cyr, Directeur

Chapais: **Bibliothèque publique de Chapais**
28, 1e av, Chapais QC G0W 1H0
Tél: 418-745-3244
chapais@reseaubiblioslsj.qc.ca
www.reseaubiblioduquebec.qc.ca
Line Lambert, Responsable

Charette: **Bibliothèque de Charette (Armance-Samson)**
390, rue Saint-Édouard, Charette QC G0X 1E0
Tél: 819-221-2095
biblio023@reseaubiblioclqm.qc.ca
www.reseaubiblioduquebec.qc.ca
Louise Gélinas, Responsable

Charlemagne: **Bibliothèque Camille-Laurin de Charlemagne**
84, rue du Sacré-Coeur, Charlemagne QC J5Z 1W8
Tél: 450-581-7243; *Téléc:* 450-581-0597
biblio@ville.charlemagne.qc.ca
www.ville.charlemagne.qc.ca/biblio.htm
Christine Arel, Responsable
biblio@ville.charlemagne.qc.ca
450-581-7243 ext. 36
Julie Savoie, Technicienne en documentation
450-581-7243 ext. 34
Lise Boissonneault, Commis
450-581-7243 ext. 23
Karine Carufel, Commis
450-581-7243 ext. 23

Châteauguay: **Bibliothèque municipale de Châteauguay**
25, boul Maple, Châteauguay QC J6J 3P7
Tél: 450-698-3080; *Téléc:* 450-698-3077
biblio@ville.chateauguay.qc.ca
www.ville.chateauguay.qc.ca
Céline Lussier, Chef, Division bibliothèque
celine-lussier@ville.chateauguay.qc.ca
450-698-3095
Véronique Marcotte, Bibliothécaire, Référence
veronique.marcotte@ville.chateauguay.qc.ca
450-698-3094
Marie-France Martel, Technicienne en documentation
450-698-3086
Michel St-Onge, Technicien en documentation
450-698-3087
Jocelyne Brunet, Technicienne en documentation
450-698-3084

Chazel: **Bibliothèque municipale de Chazel**
343, rue Principale, Chazel QC J0Z 1N0
Tél: 819-333-3262
chazel.ao.ca
Hélène Charrois, Coordonnatrice

Chelsea: **Bibliothèque de Chelsea/ Chelsea Library**
100, ch Old Chelsea, Chelsea QC J9B 1C1
Tél: 819-827-4019
bibliotheque@chelsea.ca
www.chelsea.ca
Béatrice O'Byrne, Bibliothécaire

Chelsea: **Bibliothèque de Chelsea, succursale Farm Point/ Chelsea Library, Farm Point Branch**
331, ch de la Rivière, Chelsea QC J9B 2M6
Tél: 819-459-3158; *Téléc:* 819-827-2642
bibliotheque@chelsea.ca
www.chelsea.ca
Christine Léger, Responsable

Chénéville: **Bibliothèque Chénéville/Lac-Simon**
77, rue Hôtel-de-Ville, Chénéville QC J0V 1E0
Tél: 819-428-3583; *Téléc:* 819-428-4838
www.reseaubiblioduquebec.qc.ca/Cheneville
Madeleine Tremblay, Responsable

Chertsey: **Bibliothèque de Chertsey**
333, av de l'Amitié, Chertsey QC J0K 3K0
Tél: 450-882-4738
mpicard@municipalite.chertsey.qc.ca
www.reseaubiblioduquebec.qc.ca
Monique Picard, Responsable
mpicard@municipalite.chertsey.qc.ca

Chester-Est: **Bibliothèque de Chester-Est**
3456, rue Principale, Chester-Est QC G0P 1H0
Tél: 819-382-2862
Other Numbers: Hôtel de ville: 819-382-2650
biblio148@reseaubiblioclqm.qc.ca
Émilie Brown-Pothitos, Responsable

Chesterville: **Bibliothèque de Chesterville**
474, rue de l'Acceuil, Chesterville QC G0P 1J0
Tél: 819-382-2997
biblio146@reseaubiblioclqm.qc.ca
www.reseaubiblioduquebec.qc.ca
Louise Lefebvre, Responsable

Chevery: **Bibliothèque de Chevery**
CP 92, Chevery QC G0G 1G0
Tél: 418-787-2244; *Téléc:* 418-787-2241
www.reseaubiblioduquebec.qc.ca
Ana Osborne, Responsable

Chibougamau: **Bibliothèque municipale de Chibougamau**
601, 3e rue, Chibougamau QC G8P 3A2
Tél: 418-748-2497; *Téléc:* 418-748-2980
bibliotheque@ville.chibougamau.qc.ca
www.ville.chibougamau.qc.ca
Lise Matte, Bibliotechnicienne
lisematte@ville.chibougamau.qc.ca
418-748-2497

Chicoutimi: **Bibliothèque de Chicoutimi**
155, rue Racine est, Chicoutimi QC G7H 1R5
Tél: 418-698-5350; *Téléc:* 418-698-5359
webbiblio@ville.saguenay.qc.ca
www.ville.saguenay.qc.ca
Anne Lebel, Chef de division, Bibliothèques de Saguenay
anne.lebel@ville.saguenay.qc.ca
Claude Dumais, Responsable, Bibliothèques de l'arrond. de Chicoutimi
claude.dumais@ville.saguenay.qc.ca
Isabelle Nepton, Responsable de l'Animation
isabelle.nepton@ville.saguenay.qc.ca

Chicoutimi: **Bibliothèque de Rivière-du-Moulin**
1410, rue des Cèdres, Chicoutimi QC G8A 2E6
Tél: 418-698-3226
webbiblio@ville.saguenay.qc.ca
www.ville.saguenay.qc.ca
Anne Lebel, Chef de division, Bibliothèques de Saguenay
anne.lebel@ville.saguenay.qc.ca
Claude Dumais, Responsable, Bibliothèques de l'arrond. de Chicoutimi
claude.dumais@ville.saguenay.qc.ca
Ginette Tremblay, Responsable de la bibliothèque

Chute-aux-Outardes: **Bibliothèque de Chute-aux-Outardes**
4, rue de l'École, Chute-aux-Outardes QC G0H 1C0
Tél: 418-567-2535; *Téléc:* 418-567-4478
bibliotheque.desjardins@csestuaire.qc.ca
www.reseaubiblioduquebec.qc.ca
Manon Finn, Responsable

Chute-Saint-Philippe: **Bibliothèque de Chute-Saint-Philippe**
592, ch du Progrès, Chute-Saint-Philippe QC J0W 1A0
Tél: 819-585-3397; *Téléc:* 819-585-4949
bibliotheque@chute-saint-philippe.ca
www.reseaubiblioduquebec.qc.ca/chute-saint-philippe
Françoise St-Amour, Responsable

Clarenceville: **Bibliothèque municipale de Saint-Georges-de-Clarenceville**
1340, ch Middle, Clarenceville QC J0J 1B0
Tél: 450-294-3200
clarenceville@reseaubibliomonteregie.qc.ca
Nestor Rassart, Responsable
Ginette Fournel, Responsable, PIB

Cléricy: **Bibliothèque de Cléricy**
931, rue du Souvenir, Cléricy QC J0Z 1P0
Tél: 819-637-2131; *Téléc:* 819-637-2133
clericy@reseaubiblioatnq.qc.ca
www.reseaubiblioduquebe.qc.ca
Lise Robin Boucher, Responsable

Clermont: **Bibliothèque municipale de Clermont**
11, rue Jean Talon, Clermont QC G4A 1A4
Tél: 418-439-2903; *Téléc:* 418-439-4889
bibiloc@cite.net
www.reseaubiblioduquebec.qc.ca/clermont
Ginette Simard, Responsable

Clerval: **Bibliothèque de Clerval**
579, rue du Village, Clerval QC J0Z 1R0
Tél: 819-783-2640; *Téléc:* 819-783-2640
clerval@crsbpat.qc.ca
www.crsbpat.qc.ca/clerval
Germaine Thibault-Riopel, Responsable

Cloridorme: **Bibliothèque de Cloridorme**
472, rte 132, Cloridorme QC G0E 1G0
Tél: 418-395-2609; *Téléc:* 418-395-2228
munclori@globetrotter.qc.ca
www.reseaubiblioduquebec.qc.ca
Marie Dufresne, Responsable

Cloutier: **Bibliothèque de Cloutier**
531, rte 391 sud, Cloutier QC J0Z 1S0
Tél: 819-797-8613; *Téléc:* 819-797-1299
cloutier@reseaubiblioatnq.qc.ca
www.reseaubiblioduquebec.qc.ca
Rachel Jutras, Responsable

Coaticook: **Bibliothèque Françoise-Maurice**
34, rue Main est, Coaticook QC J1A 1N2
Tél: 819-849-4013; *Téléc:* 819-849-0479
biblcoat@bibliotheque.coaticook.qc.ca
www.bibliotheque.coaticook.qc.ca
Patrick Falardeau, Directeur, Conseil d'administration

Colombier: **Bibliothèque de Colombier**
570, rue Principale, Colombier QC G0H 1P0
Tél: 418-565-3013; *Téléc:* 418-565-3289
bibliocolombier@hotmail.com
Isabelle Maltais, Responsable

La Conception: **Bibliothèque de La Conception**
1373, boul du Centenaire, La Conception QC J0T 1M0
Tél: 819-686-3016; *Téléc:* 819-686-5808
biblio69@crsbpl.qc.ca
www.reseaubiblioduquebec.qc.ca
Manuela Brassard-Erba, Responsable

La Corne: **Bibliothèque de La Corne**
380A, rte 111, La Corne QC J0Y 1R0
Tél: 819-799-2365; *Téléc:* 819-799-3571
lacorne@reseaubiblioatnq.qc.ca
www.reseaubiblioduquebec.qc.ca
Paméla Dumais, Responsable

Coteau-du-Lac: **Bibliothèque Jules-Fournier**
3, rue du Parc, Coteau-du-Lac QC J0P 1B0
Tél: 450-763-2763; *Téléc:* 450-763-2495
bibliotheque@coteau-du-lac.com
Louise Laventure, Régisseur
louiselaventure@coteau-du-lac.ca
Sylvie Cloutier, Préposée au prêt

Les Coteaux: **Bibliothèque municipale Des Coteaux**
65, rte 338, Les Coteaux QC J7X 1A2
Tél: 450-267-1414; *Téléc:* 450-267-3532
coteaux@reseaubibliomonteregie.qc.ca
Lucie Hamel, Responsable
Carole Labelle, Adjointe

Cowansville: **Bibliothèque Gabrielle-Giroux-Bertrand**
171, rue Principale, Cowansville QC J2K 3L9
Tél: 450-263-4071; *Téléc:* 450-263-7477
biblio129@reseaubibliomonteregie.qc.ca
www.reseaubiblioduquebec.qc.ca; www.cowansville.org
Brigitte Messier, Responsable

Crabtree: **Bibliothèque de Crabtree**
59, 16e rue, Crabtree QC J0K 1B0
Tél: 450-754-4332
biblio114@reseaubibliocqlm.qc.ca
www.reseaubiblioduquebec.qc.ca
Marjolaine Bertrand, Responsable
450-754-4332

Dalmas: **Bibliothèque publique de St-Augustin**
710, rue Principale, Dalmas QC G0W 1K0
Tél: 418-374-1084
augustin@reseaubiblioslsj.qc.ca
Rosette Savard, Responsable

Dalquier: **Bibliothèque Saint-Félix-de-Dalquier**
20, rue Principale nord, Dalquier QC J0Y 1G0
Tél: 819-732-2424
Francine Briand, Responsable
819-732-2424

Danville: **Bibliothèque municipale de Danville**
Hôtel de Ville, Danville QC J0A 1A0
Tél: 819-839-3236; *Téléc:* 819-839-2918
biblio053@reseaubiblioestrie.qc.ca
www.reseaubiblioduquebec.qc.ca
Daniel Hinse, Responsable

Daveluyville: **Bibliothèque de Daveluyville**
436, 5e Rue, Daveluyville QC G0Z 1C0
Tél: 819-367-3645; *Téléc:* 819-367-3550
biblio057@reseaubibliocqlm.qc.ca
www.reseaubiblioduquebec.qc.ca
Jacqueline B. Pépin, Responsable

Dégelis: **Bibliothèque Élisabeth-Turgeon**
663, 6e rue ouest, Dégelis QC G5T 1Y3
Tél: 418-853-2380
biblio.degelis@crsbp.net
www.reseaubiblioduquebec.qc.ca
Gertrude Leclerc, Responsable

Delson: **Bibliothèque municipale de Delson**
1, 1e av, Delson QC J5B 1M9
Tél: 450-632-1050
delson@reseaubibliomonteregie.qc.ca
Lyne Croussette, Responsable

Desbiens: **Bibliothèque publique de Desbiens**
1058, rue Marcellin, local 2, Desbiens QC G0W 1N0
Tél: 418-346-5739
desbiens@reseaubiblioslsj.qc.ca
www.reseaubiblioduquebec.qc.ca/portail/index.aspx?page=3&BID=5
Régine Brassard, Responsable

Deschaillons-sur-St-Laurent: **Bibliothèque de Deschaillons-sur-Saint-Laurent**
1042A, rue Marie-Victorin, Deschaillons-sur-St-Laurent QC G0S 1G0
Tél: 819-292-2483; *Téléc:* 819-292-3194
biblio101@reseaubibliocqlm.qc.ca
www.reseaubiblioduquebec.qc.ca
Odette Gilbert, Responsable

Deschambault-Grondines: **Bibliothèque Du Bord de l'Eau**
115, rue de l'Église, Deschambault-Grondines QC G0A 1S0
Tél: 418-286-6938; *Téléc:* 418-286-6511
bibdesch@globetrotter.qc.ca
www.reseaubiblioduquebec.qc.ca/deschambault/
Jacqueline Gignac, Responsable
Marlène Gariépy, Adjointe
418-286-6491
Marie-Claude Gauthier, Responsable, Extranet
418-286-6491
Madeleine Bouillé, Responsable, Animation
Diane Genest, Responsable, Échanges
Isabelle Petit, Responsable, Collection locale

Destor: **Bibliothèque Destor**
951B, ch du Parc, Destor QC J9X 5A3
Tél: 819-637-2279; *Téléc:* 819-637-5512
destor@reseaubiblioatnq.qc.ca
Rita Tremblay, Responsable
Guylaine Pelletier, Adjointe

Deux-Montagnes: **Bibliothèque de Deux-Montagnes/ Deux-Montagnes Libary**
200, rue Henri-Dunant, Deux-Montagnes QC J7R 4W6
Tél: 450-473-2702; *Téléc:* 450-473-2816
jchaput@ville.deux-montagnes.qc.ca
www.ville.deux-montagnes.qc.ca/bibliotheque/
Johanne Chaput, Responsable, Activités culturelles
450-473-2702
Mireille Brodeur, Commis
Louise St-Laurent, Technicienne en documentation
Marie Grandmont, Commis
Guylaine Lemire, Technicienne en documentation
Lyne Carroll, Commis
Nathalie Morin, Commis

Dolbeau-Mistassini: **Bibliothèque de Dolbeau-Mistassini**
175, 4e av, Dolbeau-Mistassini QC G8L 1W6
Tél: 418-276-1317; *Téléc:* 418-276-8188
www.dolbeau.biblio.qc.ca
Pauline Lapointe, Responsable
lapointe@biblio-dolbeau.qc.ca
Liette Caron, Technicienne en documentation
lcaron@ville.dolbeau-mistassini.qc.ca
Annie Lamontagne, Technicienne en documentation
alamontagne@ville.dolbeau-mistassini.qc.ca

La Doré: **Bibliothèque publique de la Doré**
4450, des Peupliers, La Doré QC G8J 1E5
Tél: 418-256-3992; *Téléc:* 418-256-3992
www.reseaubiblioduquebec.qc.ca/portail/index.aspx?page=3&BID=5
Colombe Tremblay, Responsable

Dosquet: **Bibliothèque La Bouquinerie/Dosquet**
1, rue Viger, Dosquet QC G0S 1H0
Tél: 418-728-3994; *Téléc:* 418-728-3338
www.reseaubiblioduquebec.qc.ca/dosquet
France Laflamme, Responsable
Lise Martineau, Responsable, PIB
Gaétan Labbé, Responsable, Échanges
Édith Gosselin, Responsable, Collection locale

Drummondville: **Bibliothèque municipale Côme-Saint-Germain**
545, rue des Écoles, Drummondville QC J2B 1J6
Tél: 819-478-6573; *Téléc:* 819-478-0399
biblio@ville.drummondville.qc.ca
www.ville.drummondville.qc.ca
Joceline-Andrée Turcotte, Chef de division
jturcotte@ville.drummondville.qc.ca
819-478-6588
Michel LeBlanc, Technicien en documentation
819-474-8841
Suzanne Pelletier, Technicienne en documentation
spelletier@ville.drummondville.qc.ca
819-474-8882
Natalie Bissonnette, Bibliothécaire
nbissonnette@ville.drummondville.qc.ca

Duhamel: **Bibliothèque Duhamel**
1899, rue Principale, Duhamel QC J0V 1G0
Tél: 819-428-7100; *Téléc:* 819-428-1941
admduhamel@crsbpo.qc.ca
www.reseaubiblioduquebec.qc.ca/Duhamel/
Roselyne Bernard, Responsable
Marylou Bermard, Bénévole
Pearl Fillion, Bénévole

Dunham: **Bibliothèque municipale de Dunham/ Dunham Municipal Library**
3638, rue Principale, Dunham QC J0E 1M0
Tél: 450-295-2621
dunham@reseaubibliomonteregie.qc.ca
www.reseaubiblioduquebec.qc.ca
Marie Bonneville, Responsable

Duparquet: **Bibliothèque Duparquet**
54, rue Principale, Duparquet QC J0Z 1W0
Tél: 819-948-2455; *Téléc:* 819-948-2266
duparquet@reseaubiblioatnq.qc.ca
www.crsbpat.qc.ca/duparquet/
Lise Baron, Responsable

Dupuy: **Bibliothèque de Dupuy**
63, av du Chemin de Fer, Dupuy QC J0Z 1X0
Tél: 819-783-2147; *Téléc:* 819-783-2147
dupuy@reseaubiblioatnq.qc.ca
www.reseaubiblioduquebec.qc.ca
Huguette Huot, Responsable

Durham-Sud: **Bibliothèque de Durham-Sud**
77, rue de l'Église, Durham-Sud QC J0H 2C0
Tél: 819-858-1156; *Téléc:* 819-858-2044
biblio153@reseaubibliocqlm.qc.ca
Jacques Boyer, Responsable

East Broughton: **Bibliothèque La Bouquinerie/East Broughton/Sacré-Coeur-de-Jésus**
372A, av du Collège, East Broughton QC G0N 1G0
Tél: 418-427-4900; *Téléc:* 418-427-3514
bouquinerie@eastbroughton.com
www.reseaubiblioduquebec.qc.ca/eastbroughton/
Lynda Laplante, Responsable

Les Éboulements: **Bibliothèque Félix-Antoine-Savard**
248B, rue du Village, Les Éboulements QC G0A 2M0
Tél: 418-489-2990; *Téléc:* 418-635-2520
bibliotheque@leseboulements.com
www.reseaubiblioduquebec.qc.ca/leseboulements/
Philippe Naud, Responsable

Entrelacs: **Bibliothèque d'Entrelacs**
2351, ch Entrelacs, Entrelacs QC J0T 2E0
Tél: 450-228-3931; *Téléc:* 450-228-4866
biblient@entrelacs.com
www.entrelacs.com/biblio_frame.htm
Suzanne Larivière, Responsable

L'Épiphanie: **Bibliothèque de L'Épiphanie**
83, rue Amireault, L'Épiphanie QC J5X 1A1
Tél: 450-588-4470
biblio061@reseaubibliocqlm.qc.ca
www.reseaubiblioduquebec.qc.ca
Nathalie L'Espérance, Responsable

Les Escoumins: **Bibliothèque municipale des Escoumins**
12, rue Boily, Les Escoumins QC G0T 1K0
Tél: 418-233-3097; *Téléc:* 418-233-3273
escobiblio@globetrotter.qc.ca
Odile Boisvert, Responsable

Esprit-Saint: **Bibliothèque d'Esprit-Saint**
121, rue Principale, Esprit-Saint QC G0K 1A0
Tél: 418-779-2716
biblio.esprit@crsbp.net
www.reseaubiblioduquebec.qc.ca
Sylvie Boucher, Responsable

L'Étang-du-Nord: **Bibliothèque de l'Étang-du-Nord**
1589, ch Étang-du-Nord, L'Étang-du-Nord QC G4T 3C1
Tél: 418-986-3321; *Téléc:* 418-986-6231
georgettenoelchev@hotmail.com
Georgette Chevarie, Responsable

Fabre: **Bibliothèque Le Coquelicot**
620, av de l'Église, Fabre QC J0Z 1Z0
Tél: 819-634-2745; *Téléc:* 819-634-2646
fabre@reseaubiblioatnq.qc.ca
www.reseaubiblioduquebec.qc.ca
Jacinthe Breton Desrochers, Responsable

Farnham: **Bibliothèque de Farnham inc.**
479, rue de l'Hôtel de Ville, Farnham QC J2N 2H3
Tél: 450-293-3375; *Téléc:* 450-293-2989
bibliofarnham@bellnet.ca
bibliofarnham.ca
Dino Coudé, Responsable

Fassett: **Bibliothèque Fassett/Notre-Dame-de-Bonsecours**
19, rue Gendron, Fassett QC J0V 1H0
Tél: 819-423-6943; *Téléc:* 819-423-5388
admfassett@crsbpo.qc.ca
www.reseaubiblioduquebec.qc.ca/Fassett/
Nathalie Frenière, Responsable
Gabrielle Lefaivre, Bénévole

Fatima: **Bibliothèque de Fatima**
#2, 730, ch des Caps, Fatima QC G4T 2T3
Tél: 418-986-4736
biblio.fatima@hotmail.com
www.reseaubiblioduquebec.qc.ca
Thérèse Harvie, Responsable

Ferland-et-Boilleau: **Bibliothèque publique de Ferland-Boileau**
466, rte 381, Ferland-et-Boilleau QC G0V 1H0
Tél: 418-676-2547; *Téléc:* 418-676-2506
ferland@reseaubibliosIsj.qc.ca
www.reseaubiblioduquebec.qc.ca
Isabelle Lavoie, Responsable

Ferme-Neuve: **Bibliothèque de Ferme-Neuve**
144, 12e rue, Ferme-Neuve QC J0W 1C0
Tél: 819-587-3102; *Téléc:* 819-587-4820
bibfn@tlb.sympatico.ca
www.reseaubiblioduquebec.qc.ca
Andrée Quevillon, Responsable

Fermont: **Bibliothèque publique de Fermont**
130, Le Carrefour, Fermont QC G0G 1J0
Tél: 418-287-3227; *Téléc:* 418-287-3274
biblio.fermont@sympatico.ca
www3.sympatico.ca/biblio.fermont
Aline Martel, Technicienne en documentation
bibliofermont@diffusionfermont.ca
418-287-3227

Forestville: **Bibliothèque municipale de Forestville**
10, 10e rue, Forestville QC G0T 1E0
Tél: 418-587-4483; *Téléc:* 418-587-2458
biblioforestville@globetrotter.net
www.reseaubiblioduquebec.qc.ca
Roger Dumont, Responsable

Fort-Coulonge: **Bibliothèque de Fort-Coulonge**
134, rue Principale, Fort-Coulonge QC J0X 1V0
Tél: 819-683-3421; *Téléc:* 819-683-3627
biblio.fc@fortcoulonge.qc.ca
www.fortcoulonge.qc.ca
Pierrette Lafrenière, Responsable

Fortierville: **Bibliothèque de Fortierville**
198A, rue de la Fabrique, Fortierville QC G0S 1J0
Tél: 819-287-4309; *Téléc:* 819-287-5922
biblio015@reseaubibliocqlm.qc.ca
Denise Lemay, Responsable
Diane Perreault, Bénévole
Adrienne Nault, Bénévole

Fossambault-sur-le-Lac: **Bibliothèque municipale de Fossambault-sur-le-Lac (La Source)**
145, boul Gingras, Fossambault-sur-le-Lac QC G0A 3M0
Tél: 418-875-3133; *Téléc:* 418-875-3544
fossam@coopcscf.com
www.fossambault-sur-le-lac.com
Monique Blouin, Responsable
418-875-2876

Franquelin: **Bibliothèque municipale de Franquelin**
27, rue des Érables, Franquelin QC G0H 1E0
Tél: 418-294-6170; *Téléc:* 418-296-6946
www.reseaubiblioduquebec.qc.ca
Steeve Grenier, Responsable

Fugèreville: **Bibliothèque de Fugèreville**
33A, rue Principale, Fugèreville QC J0Z 2A0
Tél: 819-748-2276; *Téléc:* 819-748-2422
fugereville@reseaubiblioatnq.qc.ca
www.reseaubiblioduquebec.qc.ca
Gaétane Falardeau, Responsable

Gallichan: **Bibliothèque La Gallithèque**
207, ch de la Rivière ouest, Gallichan QC J0Z 2B0
Tél: 819-787-6301
gallichan@mrcao.qc.ca
gallichan.ao.ca
Brigitte Rivard, Responsable

Gallix: **Bibliothèque municipale de Gallix**
524, av Lapierre, Gallix QC G0G 1L0
Tél: 418-766-3264
www.reseaubiblioduquebec.qc.ca
Lyne Porlier, Responsable

Gaspé: **Bibliothèque Alma-Bourget-Costisella**
10, côte Cartier, Gaspé QC G4X 1V2
Tél: 418-368-2104; *Téléc:* 418-368-8532
biblio.gaspe@globetrotter.net
Adrienne Bisson, Responsable

Gaspé: **Bibliothèque de Cap-aux-Os**
1826, boul Forillon, Gaspé QC G4X 6L4
Tél: 418-368-2104; *Téléc:* 418-368-6810
www.reseaubiblioduquebec.qc.ca
Rita Beaudin, Responsable

Gaspé: **Bibliothèque de Douglastown**
28, rue St-Patrick, Gaspé QC G4X 2Y2
Tél: 418-368-2104; *Téléc:* 418-368-0284
www.reseaubiblioduquebec.qc.ca
Maria Griffith, Responsable

Gaspé: **Bibliothèque de L'Anse-au-Griffon**
465, boul du Griffon, Gaspé QC G4X 6A3
Tél: 418-368-2104; *Téléc:* 418-368-6837
bboaag@globetrotter.qc.ca
www.reseaubiblioduquebec.qc.ca
Camille Malouin, Responsable

Gaspé: **Bibliothèque de L'Anse-à-Valleau**
9, rue Mathurin, Gaspé QC G4X 4A8
Tél: 418-368-2104
www.reseaubiblioduquebec.qc.ca
Priscillia Poirier, Responsable
priscillia.poirier@globetrotter.qc.ca

Gaspé: **Bibliothèque de Petit-Cap**
439, boul Petit-Cap, Gaspé QC G4X 4L1
Tél: 418-368-2104
bibliopetitcap@globetrotter.net
www.reseaubiblioduquebec.qc.ca
Philomène Cloutier, Responsable

Gaspé: **Bibliothèque de Saint-Majorique**
3-1, Montée de Corte-Réal, Gaspé QC G4X 6R7
Tél: 418-368-2104
biblio.stmajorique@globetrotter.net
www.reseaubiblioduquebec.qc.ca
Gracia Cabot, Responsable

Gatineau: **Bibliothèque municipale de Gatineau**
#317, 144, boul de l'Hôpital, Gatineau QC J8T 7S7
Tél: 819-595-7460; *Téléc:* 819-243-2399
Ligne sans frais: 800-299-2002
bibliotheque@gatineau.ca
www.ville.gatineau.qc.ca/gatineau/bibliotheque.htm
Carole Laguë, Chef de division
lague.carole@gatineau.qc.ca
819-243-2548

Gethsémani: **Bibliothèque de La Romaine**
École Marie-Sarah, Poste Restante, Gethsémani QC G0G 1M0
Tél: 418-787-2241
www.reseaubiblioduquebec.qc.ca

Girardville: **Bibliothèque publique de Girardville**
180, rue Principale, Girardville QC G0W 1R0
Tél: 418-258-3222; *Téléc:* 418-258-3473
girardv@reseaubibliosIsj.qc.ca
Francine Lambert, Responsable
418-258-3222
Carolle Lalancette, Co-responsable

Godbout: **Bibliothèque municipale de Godbout**
102B, rue Alexandre, Godbout QC G0H 1G0
Tél: 418-568-7702; *Téléc:* 418-568-7356
biblio.godbout@hotmail.com
www.reseaubiblioduquebec.qc.ca
Caroline Morin, Responsable
curbymorin@globetrotter.net
418-568-7420

Gracefield: **Bibliothèque de Gracefield**
3, rue de la Polyvalente, Gracefield QC J0X 1W0
Tél: 819-463-1180; *Téléc:* 819-463-4236
admgracefield@crsbpo.qc.ca
www.reseaubiblioduquebec.qc.ca/Gracefield
Denise Pelletier Rochon, Responsable

Granby: **Bibliothèque Paul-O.-Trépanier**
11, rue Dufferin, Granby QC J2G 2T8
Tél: 450-776-8320; *Téléc:* 450-776-8313
Other Numbers: Horaire (btc vocale): (450) 776-8310
bibliotheque@ville.granby.qc.ca
www.biblio.ville.granby.qc.ca/bibliotheque/
Linda Laberge, Responsable
llaberge@ville.granby.qc.ca
Lyne Plourde, Bénévole

Grande-Entrée: **Bibliothèque de Grande-Entrée**
214, rte 199, Grande-Entrée QC G4T 7A4
Tél: 418-985-2288; *Téléc:* 418-985-2149
biblioge@muniles.ca
www.reseaubiblioduquebec.qc.ca
Raoul Cyr, Responsable

Grande-Rivière: **Bibliothèque La Détente/Grande-Rivière**
210, rue du Carrefour, Grande-Rivière QC G0C 1V0
Tél: 418-385-3833; *Téléc:* 418-385-2290
geber@globetrotter.qc.ca
Marie-Paule Berger, Responsable

Grandes-Bergeronnes: **Bibliothèque Les Bergeronnes**
514, rue du Boisé, Grandes-Bergeronnes QC G0T 1G0
Tél: 418-232-1134; *Téléc:* 418-232-6602
Ninon Marty, Responsable

Grandes-Piles: **Bibliothèque de Grandes-Piles**
650, 4e av, Grandes-Piles QC G0X 1H0
Tél: 819-533-3697; *Téléc:* 819-538-6947
biblio030@reseaubibliocqlm.qc.ca
www.reseaubiblioduquebec.qc.ca
Line Blanchard, Responsable

Grande-Vallée: **Bibliothèque de Grande-Vallée**
3, rue St-François-Xavier est, Grande-Vallée QC G0E 1K0
Tél: 418-393-2166; *Téléc:* 418-393-2274
bbogrval@globetrotter.net
www.reseaubiblioduquebec.qc.ca
Gaétanne Normand, Responsable
normandg@hotmail.com

Grand-Mère: **Bibliothèque Hélène-B. Beauséjour**
650, 8e rue, Grand-Mère QC G9T 6K1
Tél: 819-538-5555
bibliotheque@ville.shawinigan.qc.ca
www.shawinigan.ca
Charlotte Lecours, Responsable des bibliothèques
819-536-7211 ext. 501

Grand-Remous: **Bibliothèque de Grand-Remous**
1508, rte Transcanadienne, Grand-Remous QC J0W 1E0
Tél: 819-438-2168; *Téléc:* 418-438-2364
admgrandremous@crsbpo.qc.ca
www.reseaubiblioduquebec.qc.ca/Grand-Remous
Lise Fraser, Responsable

Greenfield Park: **Bibliothèque de Greenfield Park**
225, rue Empire, Greenfield Park QC J4V 1T9
Tél: 450-463-7140; *Téléc:* 450-466-8112
www.longueuil.ca/bibliotheques/
Lise Lafleur, Responsable
lise.lafleur@ville.longueuil.qc.ca
Nicole Brabant, Responsable, PIB

Grenville: **Bibliothèque de Grenville**
18, rue Tri-Jean, Grenville QC J0V 1J0
Tél: 819-242-2585; *Téléc:* 819-242-5891
biblio@grenville.ca
www.reseaubiblioduquebec.qc.ca/grenville
Céline Joly, Responsable
Hélène Joly, Bénévole au comptoir de prêts

Grenville-sur-la-Rouge: **Bibliothèque de Calumet**
130, rue Principale, Grenville-sur-la-Rouge QC J0V 1B0
Tél: 819-242-8088; *Téléc:* 819-242-1232
biblio5@crsbpl.qc.ca
www.reseaubiblioduquebec.qc.ca
Judy Smith, Responsable

Grenville-sur-la-Rouge: **Bibliothèque de Pointe-au-Chêne**
2714, rte 148, Grenville-sur-la-Rouge QC J0V 1B0
Tél: 819-242-0298
biblio12@crsbpl.qc.ca
www.reseaubiblioduquebec.qc.ca
Johanne Nantel, Responsable

Grondines: **Bibliothèque L'Ardoise**
525, ch Sir-Lomer-Gouin, Grondines QC G0A 1W0
Tél: 418-268-8359; *Téléc:* 418-268-5553
bibligron@csportneuf.qc.ca
www.reseaubiblioduquebec.qc.ca/grondines/
Guylaine Rivard, Responsable
Michelle Trottier, Adjointe

Gros-Morne: **Bibliothèque de Gros-Morne**
1, rue de l'Église ouest, Gros-Morne QC G0E 1L0
Tél: 418-797-2610
www.reseaubiblioduquebec.qc.ca
Albertine Laflamme, Responsable

Grosse-Ile: **Bibliothèque de Grosse-Ile**
448, ch Principal, Grosse-Ile QC G4T 6A8
Tél: 418-986-2885; *Téléc:* 418-985-2955
Natasha Joncas, Responsable

Guérin: **Bibliothèque de Guérin**
516A, rue St-Gabriel, Guérin QC J0Z 2E0
Tél: 819-784-7024; *Téléc:* 819-784-7026
guerin@reseaubiblioatnq.qc.ca
www.reseaubiblioduquebec.qc.ca
Sylvie Laverdière, Responsable

Guyenne: **Bibliothèque de Guyenne**
1255-F, rang 5, Guyenne QC J0Y 1L0
Tél: 819-732-9128; *Téléc:* 819-732-0904
guyenne@reseaubiblioatnq.qc.ca
www.reseaubiblioduquebec.qc.ca
Francine Simard, Responsable

Ham-Nord: **Bibliothèque de Ham-Nord**
474, rue Principale, Ham-Nord QC G0P 1A0
Tél: 819-344-2805; *Téléc:* 819-344-2805
biblio150@reseaubibliocqlm.qc.ca
www.reseaubiblioduquebec.qc.ca
Joanne Lacasse, Responsable

Harrington Harbour: **Bibliothèque de Harrington Harbour**
CP 7, Harrington Harbour QC G0G 1N0
Tél: 418-787-2244; *Téléc:* 418-787-2241
bibliohh@globetrotter.net
www.reseaubiblioduquebec.qc.ca
Judi Ransom, Responsable

Havre-aux-Maisons: **Bibliothèque de Havre-aux-Maisons**
37, ch Central, Havre-aux-Maisons QC G4T 5H1
Tél: 418-969-2100
biblioham@muniles.ca
www.reseaubiblioduquebec.qc.ca
Marcel Thériault, Responsable

Havre-Saint-Pierre: **Bibliothèque municipale de Havre-St-Pierre**
1045, rue Dulcinée, Havre-Saint-Pierre QC G0G 1P0
Tél: 418-538-3301; *Téléc:* 418-538-3439
biblio.havrest-pierre@globetrotter.net
www.reseaubiblioduquebec.qc.ca
Nicole Cormier, Responsable

Hemmingford: **Bibliothèque municipale d'Hemmingford/ Hemmingford Community Library**
552, av Goyette, Hemmingford QC J0L 1H0
Tél: 450-247-0010
hemmingford@reseaubibliomonteregie.qc.ca
www.reseaubiblioduquebec.qc.ca
Elizabeth Nicholls, Responsable

Henryville: **Bibliothèque municipale d'Henryville**
#104, 854, rue St-Jean-Baptiste, Henryville QC J0J 1E0
Tél: 450-299-1165
henryville@reseaubibliomonteregie.qc.ca
www.reseaubiblioduquebec.qc.ca
Mathieu Fortin, Responsable

Hérouxville: **Bibliothèque de Hérouxville**
1060, rue Saint-Pierre, Hérouxville QC G0X 1J0
Tél: 418-365-7337; *Téléc:* 418-365-7041
biblio090@reseaubibliocqlm.qc.ca
www.reseaubiblioduquebec.qc.ca
Julie L'Heureux, Responsable

Honfleur: **Bibliothèque La Livrothèque**
320, rue Saint-Jean, Honfleur QC G0R 1N0
Tél: 418-885-8212; *Téléc:* 418-885-9195
livro@globetrotter.qc.ca
www.reseaubiblioduquebec.qc.ca/honfleur/
Isabelle Roussy, Responsable
Nathalie Beaudoin, Adjointe
Lyne Fournier, Responsable, Collection locale
Nicole Morin, Responsable, PIB

Hope Town: **Bibliothèque de Hope Town**
224, rte 132, Hope Town QC G0C 2K0
Tél: 418-752-3848; *Téléc:* 418-752-2434
hopelibrary@globetrotter.net
www.reseaubiblioduquebec.qc.ca
Lynda McWhirter, Responsable

Huberdeau: **Bibliothèque d'Huberdeau**
101, rue Du Pont, Huberdeau QC J0T 1G0
Tél: 819-687-1164; *Téléc:* 819-687-8808
huberdeau@crsbpl.qc.ca
www.reseaubiblioduquebec.qc.ca
Suzanne Fortin, Responsable
Brenda Gaudreault, Bénévole
Bernard Dervillez, Bénévole
Huguette Deslauriers, Bénévole

Huntingdon: **Little Green Library/ La Petite Bibliothèque Verte**
6 Hunter St., Huntingdon QC J0S 1H0
Tel: 450-264-4872
Laura Smith, President
Ola Proudfoot, Cataloguer
Mary Quinnel, Head, Acquisitions (English)
Evelyne Latreille, Head, Acquisitions (French)

Ile-du-Grand-Calumet: **Bibliothèque Ile-du-Grand-Calumet**
2, rue Brizard, Ile-du-Grand-Calumet QC J0X 1J0
Tél: 819-648-5966; *Téléc:* 819-648-2659
admcalumet@crsbpo.qc.ca
www.reseaubiblioduquebec.qc.ca/Grand-Calument/
Chantal Corriveau, Responsable

Inverness: **Bibliothèque de Inverness (L'Inverthèque)**
1801, rue Dublin, Inverness QC G0S 1K0
Tél: 418-453-2867; *Téléc:* 418-453-2554
biblio145@reseaubibliocqlm.qc.ca
www.reseaubiblioduquebec.qc.ca
Hélène Laplante, Responsable

L'Isle-aux-Coudres: **Bibliothèque 'Pour la suite du monde'**
1026, ch des Coudriers, L'Isle-aux-Coudres QC G0A 3J0
Tél: 418-438-2602; *Téléc:* 418-438-2750
iacsdm@charlevoix.net
www.reseaubiblioduquebec.qc.ca/coudres
Claudine Hovington, Responsable
418-438-2602

L'Isle-aux-Grues: **Bibliothèque La Rose des Vents/L'Isle-aux-Grues**
107, ch de la Volière, L'Isle-aux-Grues QC G0R 1P0
Tél: 418-248-8060; *Téléc:* 418-248-4680
Lisette Painchaud, Responsable
418-248-4687

L'Islet: **Bibliothèque Jean-Paul-Bourque/L'Islet-sur-Mer**
16, rte des Pionniers est, L'Islet QC G0R 2B0
Tél: 418-247-7576; *Téléc:* 418-247-5009
www.reseaubiblioduquebec.qc.ca/l'islet-sur-mer/
Jacqueline C. Kirouac, Responsable
Hélène St-Pierre, Adjointe

L'Islet: **Bibliothèque Léon-Laberge**
#1, 284, boul Nilus-Leclerc, L'Islet QC G0R 2C0
Tél: 418-247-5345; *Téléc:* 418-247-5085
bleonl@globetrotter.qc.ca
www.reseaubiblioduquebec.qc.ca/l'islet/
Madeleine Gagnon, Responsable
Johanne Dessureault, Responsable, Animation

L'Isle-Verte: **Bibliothèque de Notre-Dame-des-Sept-Douleurs**
ch de l'Ile, L'Isle-Verte QC G0L 1K0
Tél: 418-898-3451
biblio.douleurs@crsbp.net
www.reseaubiblioduquebec.qc.ca
Maryse Dickner, Responsable

Issoudun: **Bibliothèque La Rêverie/Notre-Dame-de-Sacré-Coeur-d'Issoudun**
268, rue Principale, Issoudun QC G0S 1L0
Tél: 418-728-9061; *Téléc:* 418-728-2303
www.reseaubiblioduquebec.qc.ca/issoudun
Carole Couture, Responsable
Rosaline Croteau, Responsable, PIB

Jonquière: **Bibliothèque d'Arvida**
2850, Place Davis, Jonquière QC G7X 7W7
Tél: 418-698-5350; *Téléc:* 418-699-6046
webbiblio@ville.saguenay.qc.ca
www.ville.saguenay.qc.ca
Anne Lebel, Chef de division, Bibliothèques de Saguenay
anne.lebel@ville.saguenay.qc.ca
Luc Lepage, Responsable, Bibliothèques de l'arrond. de Jonquière
luc.lepage@ville.saguenay.qc.ca
Monique Laprise, Responsable de l'Animation
monique.laprise@ville.saguenay.qc.ca

Jonquière: **Bibliothèque de Kénogami**
3750, boul du Royaume, Jonquière QC G7X 9S4
Tél: 418-698-5350
webbiblio@ville.saguenay.qc.ca
www.ville.saguenay.qc.ca
Anne Lebel, Chef de division, Bibliothèques de Saguenay
anne.lebel@ville.saguenay.qc.ca
Luc Lepage, Responsable, Bibliothèques de l'arrond. de Jonquière
luc.lepage@ville.saguenay.qc.ca
Monique Laprise, Responsable de l'Animation
monique.laprise@ville.saguenay.qc.ca

***Jonquière:* Bibliothèque St-Michel**
3885, boul Harvey, Jonquière QC G7X 9B1
Tél: 418-698-5350
webbiblio@ville.saguenay.qc.ca
www.ville.saguenay.qc.ca
Anne Lebel, Chef de division, Bibliothèques de Saguenay
anne.lebel@ville.saguenay.qc.ca
Luc Lepage, Responsable, Bibliothèques de l'arrond. de Jonquière
luc.lepage@ville.saguenay.qc.ca
Monique Laprise, Responsable de l'Animation
monique.laprise@ville.saguenay.qc.ca

***Kégaska:* Bibliothèque municipale de Kégaska**
Poste Restante, Kégaska QC G0G 1S0
Tél: 418-787-2244; *Téléc:* 418-787-2241
www.reseaubiblioduquebec.qc.ca

***Kiamika:* Bibliothèque de Kiamika**
3, ch Valiquette, Kiamika QC J0W 1G0
Tél: 819-585-3225; *Téléc:* 819-585-3992
kiamika@sympatico.ca
Nanette Sirois, Responsable

***Kingsey Falls:* Bibliothèque de Kingsey Falls**
13, rue Caron, Kingsey Falls QC J0A 1B0
Tél: 819-363-3818
biblio040@reseaubibliocqlm.qc.ca
Suzanne Boulet, Responsable

***Kinnear's Mills:* Bibliothèque La Boukinnerie**
120, rue des Églises, Kinnear's Mills QC G0N 1K0
Tél: 418-424-0082; *Téléc:* 418-424-3015
biblikin@gabskycom.com
www.reseaubiblioduquebec.qc.ca
Michelle Bernier-Pageau, Responsable
Gaétane Malo, Responsable des PIB

***Knowlton:* Bibliothèque Commémorative Pettes/ Pettes Memorial Library**
276, ch Knowlton, Knowlton QC J0E 1V0
Tél: 450-243-6128; *Téléc:* 450-243-5272
pettes.ca

***Labelle:* Bibliothèque de Labelle**
7393, boul du Curé-Labelle, Labelle QC J0T 1H0
Tél: 819-681-3371; *Téléc:* 819-686-3820
labelle@crsbpl.qc.ca
www.reseaubiblioduquebec.qc.ca
Nathalie Robson, Responsable
labelle@crspbl.qc.ca

***Labrecque:* Bibliothèque publique de Labrecque**
3425, rue Ambroise, Labrecque QC G0W 2S0
Tél: 418-481-1618; *Téléc:* 418-481-2022
labrecque@reseaubiblioslsj.qc.ca
www.reseaubiblioduquebec.qc.ca/portail/index.aspx?page=3&BID=5
Denise Villeneuve, Responsable
418-481-1327
Christine Jean, Bénévole
418-481-1377
Audrey Néron, Bénévole
418-481-1465

***Lac-a-la-Croix:* Bibliothèque publique de Lac-à-la-Croix**
#002, 335, de Rouillac, Lac-a-la-Croix QC G8G 2B5
Tél: 418-349-8133
lac.croix@reseaubiblioslsj.qc.ca
Guylaine Dufour, Responsable

***Lac-à-la-Tortue:* Bibliothèque de Lac-à-la-Tortue**
1082, 37e av, Lac-à-la-Tortue QC G0X 1L0
Tél: 819-538-5882
bibliotheque@ville.shawinigan.qc.ca
www.shawinigan.ca
Charlotte Lecours, Responsable des bibliothèques

***Lac-au-Saumon:* Bibliothèque Bertrand-Leblanc**
20, Place de la Municipalité, Lac-au-Saumon QC G0J 1M0
Tél: 418-778-3008
biblio.saumon@crsbp.net
www.reseaubiblioduquebec.qc.ca
France Lee, Responsable

***Lac-aux-Sables:* Bibliothèque de Lac-aux-Sables**
820, rue Saint-Alphonse, Lac-aux-Sables QC G0X 1M0
Tél: 418-336-3238; *Téléc:* 418-336-2500
biblio045@reseaubibliocqlm.qc.ca
www.reseaubiblioduquebec.qc.ca
Louise Veillette, Responsable

***Lac-Beauport:* Bibliothèque L'Écrin**
46, ch du Village, Lac-Beauport QC G0A 2C0
Tél: 418-849-6133; *Téléc:* 418-849-0361
ecrin@ccapcable.com
www.reseaubiblioduquebec.qc.ca/lac-beauport
Claudette Robillard, Responsable
Jocelyne Bradett, Adjointe
Claudette Baker, Adjointe

***Lac-Bouchette:* Bibliothèque publique de Lac-Bouchette**
#110, 258, rue Principale, Lac-Bouchette QC G0W 1V0
Tél: 418-348-9302
lac.bouchett@reseaubiblioslsj.qc.ca
www.reseaubiblioduquebec.qc.ca/portail/index.aspx?page=3&BID=5
Lucie Paradis, Responsable

***Lac-Cayamant:* Bibliothèque municipale de Cayamant**
5, ch Lachapelle, Lac-Cayamant QC J0X 1Y0
Tél: 819-463-4171; *Téléc:* 819-463-4020
admcayamant@crsbpo.qc.ca
www.reseaubiblioduquebec.qc.ca/Cayamant
Suzanne Vallières, Responsable

***Lac-des-Aigles:* Bibliothèque Lac-des-Aigles**
75A, rue Principale, Lac-des-Aigles QC G0K 1V0
Tél: 418-779-2300
biblio.aigles@crsbp.net
Lise Leblanc, Responsable
418-779-2330

***Lac-des-Écorces:* Bibliothèque de Lac-des-Écorces**
570, boul St-François, Lac-des-Écorces QC J0W 1H0
Tél: 819-585-2555
bibliolde@lacdesecorces.ca
www.reseaubiblioduquebec.qc.ca
Nicole Thériault, Responsable
Karolle Thériault, Adjointe

***Lac-des-Iles:* Bibliothèque de Saint-Aimé-du-Lac-des-Iles**
877, ch Diotte, Lac-des-Iles QC J0W 1J0
Tél: 819-597-4174; *Téléc:* 819-597-2554
biblio59@crsbpl.qc.ca
www.reseaubiblioduquebec.qc.ca
Pierrette D. Pilotte, Responsable

***Lac-des-Loups:* Bibliothèque Lac-des-Loups (La Pêche)**
275, rue Pontbriand, Lac-des-Loups QC J0X 3K0
Tél: 819-456-3222; *Téléc:* 819-456-4534
admlac-des-loups@crsbpo.qc.ca
www.reseaubiblioduquebec.qc.ca/Lac-Des-Loups
Michelle Archambault, Responsable

***Lac-des-Plages:* Bibliothèque Lac-des-Plages**
2053, ch Tour-du-Lac, Lac-des-Plages QC J0T 1K0
Tél: 819-426-2391; *Téléc:* 819-426-2085
admdesplages@crsbpo.qc.ca
www.reseaubiblioduquebec.qc.ca/Lac-Des-Plages
Micheline Tessier, Responsable

***Lac-des-Seize-Iles:* Bibliothèque de Lac-des-Seize-Iles**
47, de l'Église, Lac-des-Seize-Iles QC J0T 2M0
Tél: 450-226-9942
biblio@xplornet.com
www.reseaubiblioduquebec.qc.ca/lac-des-seize-iles
Anne Bates, Responsable
Lucille Pelletier, Adjointe

***Lac-du-Cerf:* Bibliothèque de Lac-du-Cerf**
15, rue Émard, Lac-du-Cerf QC J0W 1S0
Tél: 819-597-2249; *Téléc:* 819-597-4163
biblio@lac-du-cerf.ca
www.reseaubiblioduquebec.qc.ca
Francine Boismenu-St-Louis, Responsable

***Lac-Édouard:* Bibliothèque de Lac-Édouard**
195, rue Principale, Lac-Édouard QC G0X 3N0
Tél: 819-653-2238; *Téléc:* 819-653-2238
biblo024@reseaubibliocqlm.qc.ca
www.reseaubiblioduquebec.qc.ca
Sonia Cloutier, Responsable

***Lac-Etchemin:* Bibliothèque L'Élan**
208A, 2e av, Lac-Etchemin QC G0R 1S0
Tél: 418-625-5325; *Téléc:* 418-625-3175
biblio@sogetel.net
www.reseaubiblioduquebec.qc.ca/lac-etchemin/
Jacques Gagnon, Responsable
Germaine Godbout, Responsable, PIB
418-625-7796
Lorraine Gilbert, Responsable, Collection locale
418-625-4707
Jacek Kuczynski, Responsable, Informatique
418-625-3699

***Lachute:* Bibliothèque Jean-Marc-Belzile**
378, rue Principale, Lachute QC J8H 1Y2
Tél: 450-562-3781; *Téléc:* 450-562-1431
biblio@ville.lachute.qc.ca
Émilie Paquin, Chef de service de la bibliothèque et des activités culturelles
epaquin@ville.lachute.qc.ca
450-562-3781 ext. 255

***Lac-Kénogami:* Bibliothèque de Lac-Kénogami**
3000, ch de l'Église, Lac-Kénogami QC G7X 7V6
Tél: 418-695-4717; *Téléc:* 418-547-6158
webbiblio@ville.saguenay.qc.ca
www.ville.saguenay.qc.ca
Caroline Tremblay, Responsable
Monique Laprise, Responsable, l'Animation
monique.laprise@ville.saguenay.qc.ca
Luc Lepage, Responsable, Bibliothèques de l'arrond. de Jonquière
luc.lepage@ville.saguenay.qc.ca
Anne Lebel, Chef de division, Bibliothèques de Saguenay
anne.lebel@ville.saguenay.qc.ca

***Lac-Mégantic:* Bibliothèque municipale de Lac-Mégantic**
5086, rue Frontenac, Lac-Mégantic QC G6B 1H3
Tél: 819-583-0876; *Téléc:* 819-583-0878
www.bibliomegantic.qc.ca
Daniel Lavoie, Directeur/Bibliothécaire
direction@bibliomegantic.qc.ca
Nancy Giroux, Technicienne en documentation
nancy@bibliomegantic.qc.ca
Annie Trudel, Technicienne en documentation
annie@bibliomegantic.qc.ca
Denise Grenier, Préposée à la saisie de données
denise@bibliomegantic.qc.ca
Natalie Rosa, Commis au comptoir, Entretien

***Lacolle:* Bibliothèque municipale de Lacolle**
3, rue de Collège, Lacolle QC J0J 1J0
Tél: 450-515-8050
www.lacolle.com/services.html
Linda Corbière, Responsable

***Lac-Saguay:* Bibliothèque de Lac-Saguay**
257A, rte 117, Lac-Saguay QC J0W 1L0
Tél: 819-278-3972; *Téléc:* 819-278-0260
info@lacsaguay.qc.ca
www.reseaubiblioduquebec.qc.ca
Micheline Bouliane, Responsable
Denise Lachance, Adjointe

***Lac-Sainte-Marie:* Bibliothèque municipale de Lac-Sainte-Marie**
8, rue Laramée, Lac-Sainte-Marie QC J0X 1Z0
Tél: 819-467-3779; *Téléc:* 819-467-4826
admstemarie@crsbpo.qc.ca
www.reseaubiblioduquebec.qc.ca/Lac-Ste-Marie
Marie-Paule Bertrand, Bibliothécaire

***Lac-Saint-Paul:* Bibliothèque de Lac-Saint-Paul**
384, rue Principale, Lac-Saint-Paul QC J0W 1K0
Tél: 819-587-4283; *Téléc:* 819-587-4892
biblio52@crsbpl.qc.ca
www.reseaubiblioduquebec.qc.ca/lac-saint-paul
Charlaine Miller, Responsable
819-587-4379

***Lac-Supérieur:* Bibliothèque de Lac-Supérieur**
1277, ch du Lac-Supérieur, Lac-Supérieur QC J0T 1J0
Tél: 819-681-3370; *Téléc:* 819-688-3010
biblio@muni.lacsuperieur.qc.ca
www.reseaubiblioduquebec.qc.ca
Thérèse Gaucher, Responsable

***Laforce:* Bibliothèque Laforce**
703, rue Principale, Laforce QC J0Z 2J0
Tél: 819-722-2461; *Téléc:* 819-722-2462
laforce@reseaubiblioatnq.qc.ca
Lise Bray, Responsable

***Lamarche:* Bibliothèque publique de Lamarche**
102, rue Principale, Lamarche QC G0W 1X0
Tél: 418-481-2713
lamarche@reseaubiblioslsj.qc.ca
www.reseaubiblioduquebec.qc.ca
Rose Perron-Tremblay, Responsable

Landrienne: **Bibliothèque Landrienne**
158, rue Principale est, Landrienne QC J0Y 1V0
Tél: 819-732-4357; *Téléc:* 819-732-3866
landrienne@reseaubiblioatnq.qc.ca
Linda Perron, Responsable

Lanoraie: **Bibliothèque de Lanoraie (Ginette-Rivard-Tremblay)**
#100, 12, rue Louis-Joseph-Doucet, Lanoraie QC J0K 1E0
Tél: 450-887-1100; *Téléc:* 450-836-5229
biblio060@reseaubibliocqlm.qc.ca
Jacques Gagné, Responsable

Larouche: **Bibliothèque publique de Larouche**
709, rue Gauthier, Larouche QC G0W 1Z0
Tél: 418-695-2201
larouche@reseaubiblioslsj.qc.ca
www.reseaubiblioduquebec.qc.ca/portail/index.aspx?page=3&BID=5
Lucette Douillard, Directrice

Laterrière: **Bibliothèque de Laterrière**
6167, rue Notre-Dame, Laterrière QC G7N 1A1
Tél: 418-698-5350; *Téléc:* 418-678-2647
webbiblio@ville.saguenay.qc.ca
www.ville.saguenay.qc.ca
Anne Lebel, Chef de division, Bibliothèques de Saguenay
anne.lebel@ville.saguenay.qc.ca
Claude Dumais, Responsable, Bibliothèques de l'arrond. de Chicoutimi
claude.dumais@ville.saguenay.qc.ca
Lise Tremblay, Responsable de la bibliothèque

Laurier-Station: **Bibliothèque Wilfrid Laurier**
147, rue Saint-Denis, Laurier-Station QC G0S 1N0
Tél: 418-728-5939
bwlaurier@globetrotter.net
www.reseaubiblioduquebec.qc.ca
Nancy Dubois, Responsable
Normande Bergeron, Responsable, Échanges
Mélissa Bouchard, Adjointe

Laurierville: **Bibliothèque de Laurierville**
148A, rue Grenier, Laurierville QC G0S 1P0
Tél: 819-365-4913; *Téléc:* 819-365-4936
biblio122@reseaubibliocqlm.qc.ca
Aline Desrochers, Responsable

Laval: **Bibliothèques de Laval. Service de la vie communautaire, de la culture et des communications**
1535, boul Chomedey, Laval QC H7V 3Z4
Tél: 450-662-4343; *Téléc:* 450-978-5833
adm-biblio@ville.laval.qc.ca
www.ville.laval.qc.ca
Paul Lemay, Dir. Serv. de vie communautaire, culture et communications
p.lemay@ville.laval.qc.ca
Jean-François Roulier, Chef de division
j-f.roulier@ville.laval.qc.ca
450-978-6888 ext. 5848
Ghislaine Bélanger, Chef de division
450-978-6888 ext. 5982

Lavaltrie: **Bibliothèque de Lavaltrie**
241, Saint-Antoine-Nord, Lavaltrie QC J5T 2G7
Tél: 450-586-2921; *Téléc:* 450-586-0124
biblio011@reseaubibliocqlm.qc.ca
Brigitte Richer, Directrice
Lise Pigeon, Adjointe
Manon Beauchamp, Coordonnatrice, Accès Internet

Laverlochère: **Bibliothèque de Laverlochère**
3, rue Principale sud, Laverlochère QC J0Z 2P0
Tél: 819-765-2549; *Téléc:* 819-765-2089
laverlochere@reseaubiblioatnq.qc.ca
www.reseaubiblioduquebec.qc.ca
Maryse Gervais, Responsable

Lebel-sur-Quévillon: **Bibliothèque Lebel-sur-Quévillon**
500, Place Quévillon, Lebel-sur-Quévillon QC J0Y 1X0
Tél: 819-755-4826; *Téléc:* 819-755-8124
lebel@reseaubiblioatnq.qc.ca
Mona Savard, Responsable

Leclercville: **Bibliothèque Aux Rayons d'Or**
166, rue de l'Église, Leclercville QC G0S 2K0
Jeannine Beaudet, Responsable
Francine B. Demers, Responsable des statistiques, Secrétaire

Lefebvre: **Bibliothèque de Lefebvre**
193, 10e rang, Lefebvre QC J0H 2C0
Tél: 819-394-3354; *Téléc:* 819-394-2782
biblio081@reseaubibliocqlm.qc.ca
www.reseaubiblioduquebec.qc.ca
France Gagnon Noël, Responsable

Lejeune: **Bibliothèque de Lejeune**
69, rue de la Grande-Coulée, Lejeune QC G0L 1S0
Tél: 418-855-2428
biblio.lejeune@crsbp.net
www.reseaubiblioduquebec.qc.ca
Pauline Gilbert, Responsable

Lemieux: **Bibliothèque de Lemieux**
526, rue de l'Eglise, Lemieux QC G0X 1S0
Tél: 819-283-2506
biblio138@reseaubibliocqlm.qc.ca
www.reseaubiblioduquebec.qc.ca
Lucie Blanchette, Responsable

Lennoxville: **Bibliothèque publique de Lennoxville/ Lennoxville Public Library**
101, rue Queen, Lennoxville QC J1M 1J7
Tél: 819-562-4949; *Téléc:* 819-563-3705
bibliolen@gmail.com
www.lennoxvillelibrary.ca
Barbara Gosselin, Responsable

Longue-Pointe-de-Mingan: **Bibliothèque de Longue-Pointe-de-Mingan**
878, ch du Roi, Longue-Pointe-de-Mingan QC G0G 1V0
Tél: 418-949-2053; *Téléc:* 418-949-2166
Andrée Legault, Responsable

Longueuil: **Bibliothèques publiques de Longueuil**
1100, rue Beauregard, Longueuil QC J4K 2L1
Tél: 450-463-7180; *Téléc:* 450-646-8874
www.longueuil.ca/bibliotheques/
Micheline Perreault, Chef du Service des bibliothèques
micheline.perreault@ville.longueuil.qc.ca
450-463-7100 ext. 7244
Marjolaine Millette, Chef des opérations, service au public et marketing
marjolaine.millette@ville.longueuil.qc.ca
450-463-7100 ext. 3160
Martin Dubois, Chef des opérations, services techniques et technologie
martin.dubois@ville.longueuil.qc.ca
450-463-7100 ext. 2479

Lorraine: **Bibliothèque municipale de Lorraine**
31, boul de Gaulle, Lorraine QC J6Z 3W9
Tél: 450-621-1071
bibliotheque@ville.lorraine.qc.ca
www.ville.lorraine.qc.ca
Paulette Gouroff, Directrice
450-621-1071

Lorrainville: **Bibliothèque Lorrainville**
2, rue St-Jean-Baptiste est, Lorrainville QC J0Z 2R0
Tél: 819-625-2464; *Téléc:* 819-625-2380
lorrainville@reseaubiblioatnq.qc.ca
www.lorrainville.ca
Alain Guimond, Responsable

Lotbinière: **Bibliothèque 'Au fil des pages'**
30, rue Joly, local 100, Lotbinière QC G0S 1S0
Tél: 418-796-2912; *Téléc:* 418-796-2198
www.reseaubiblioduquebec.qc.ca/lotbiniere
Lucille Beaudet, Responsable
Gisèle Bouchard, Responsable, PEB
Diane Cadoret, Responsable, Échanges
Denise Chrétien, Responsable, Collection locale
Hélène Gagnon, Responsable, Statistiques
Ginette Auger, Responsable, Extranet

Lourdes-de-Blanc-Sablon: **Bibliothèque de Blanc-Sablon**
20, rue Mgr Scheffer, Lourdes-de-Blanc-Sablon QC G0G 1W0
Tél: 418-461-2030; *Téléc:* 418-461-2529
www.reseaubiblioduquebec.qc.ca
Vincent Joncas, Responsable

Low: **Bibliothèque municipale de Low**
4A, ch D'Amour, Low QC J0X 2C0
Tél: 819-422-3218; *Téléc:* 819-422-3796
admlow@crsbpo.qc.ca
www.reseaubiblioduquebec.qc.ca/Low
Lise Legros, Responsable

Luskville-Pontiac: **Bibliothèque de Luskville**
2024, rte 148, Luskville-Pontiac QC J0X 2G0
Tél: 819-455-2370; *Téléc:* 819-455-9756
admluskville@crsbpo.qc.ca
www.reseaubiblioduquebec.qc.ca/Luskville
Louise Ramsay, Responsable

Lyster: **Bibliothèque de Lyster (Graziella-Ouellet)**
2375, rue Bécancour, Lyster QC G0S 1V0
Tél: 819-389-5787; *Téléc:* 819-389-5981
biblio144@reseaubibliocqlm.qc.ca
Pierrette Fradette, Responsable

Macamic: **Bibliothèque de Colombourg**
705, Rang 2-3 ouest, Macamic QC J0Z 2S0
Tél: 819-333-5783; *Téléc:* 819-333-1075
colombourg@reseaubiblioatnq.qc.ca
www.reseaubiblioduquebec.qc.ca
Noëlla Royer, Responsable
Katy Ducharme, Bénévole
Julie Mongrain, Bénévole
Suzanne Paré, Bénévole

Macamic: **Bibliothèque de Macamic**
34A, 6e av ouest, Macamic QC J0Z 2S0
Tél: 819-782-4604; *Téléc:* 819-782-4464
macamic@reseaubiblioatnq.qc.ca
www.reseaubiblioduquebec.qc.ca
Ginette Labbé, Responsable

La Macaza: **Bibliothèque de La Macaza**
53, rue des Pionniers, La Macaza QC J0T 1R0
Tél: 819-275-2077; *Téléc:* 819-275-2337
biblio-lamacaza@bellnet.ca
www.reseaubiblioduquebec.qc.ca
Nicole Ayotte, Responsable
nicoleayotte1@hotmail.com
Ghislaine Plouffe, Adjointe

Madeleine-Centre: **Bibliothèque Jacques-Ferron**
104, rue Principale, Madeleine-Centre QC G0E 1P0
Tél: 418-393-3269; *Téléc:* 418-393-2869
bbostema@globetrotter.qc.ca
Carole Giroux, Responsable

Magog: **Bibliothèque municipale d'Omerville**
65, rue St-Jacques ouest, Magog QC J1X 4H4
Tél: 819-868-6679
biblio078@reseaubiblioestrie.qc.ca
www.reseaubiblioduquebec.qc.ca
Monique Saint-Onge, Responsable

Magog: **Bibliothèque municipale Memphrémagog**
61, rue Merry nord, Magog QC J1X 2E7
Tél: 819-843-1330; *Téléc:* 819-843-1594
biblio@ville.magog.qc.ca
www.ville.magog.qc.ca
Diane Boulé, Responsable/Bibliothécaire
dianeb@abacom.com
Luc Grenier, Technicien en documentation
lukg@abacom.com

Malartic: **Bibliothèque Malartic**
621, De la Paix, Malartic QC J0Y 1Z0
Tél: 819-757-4449; *Téléc:* 819-757-3084
malartic@reseaubiblioatnq.qc.ca
Maurice Bélanger, Responsable

La Malbaie: **Bibliothèque Laure-Conan**
395, rue St-Etienne, La Malbaie QC G5A 1S8
Tél: 418-665-6027; *Téléc:* 418-665-6481
bibli.malbaie@qc.aira.com
ville.lamalbaie.qc.ca/fr/bibliotheques/
Marie-Claire Fortin, Directrice

La Malbaie: **Bibliothèque municipale de Cap-à-l'Aigle**
768, rue Saint-Raphaël, La Malbaie QC G5A 2P2
Tél: 418-665-7596; *Téléc:* 418-665-7597
Louise Belley, Responsable
Marie-Claire Tremblay, Responsable, Échanges

Manawan: **Bibliothèque de Manawan**
470, rue Otapi, Manawan QC J0K 1M0
Tél: 819-971-1379; *Téléc:* 819-971-1266
biblio067@reseaubibliocqlm.qc.ca
Janette Ottawa, Responsable

Mandeville: **Bibliothèque municipale de Mandeville**
162A, rue Desjardins, Mandeville QC J0K 1L0
Tél: 514-835-2055
bibliomandeville@intermonde.net
municipalite.mandeville.qc.ca
Monique Bessette, Coordonnatrice

***Maniwaki:* Bibliothèque de Maniwaki/Déléage/Egan-Sud**
14, rue Comeau, Maniwaki QC J9E 2R8
Tél: 819-449-2738; *Téléc:* 819-449-7626
admmaniwaki@crsbpo.qc.ca
www.reseaubiblioduquebec.qc.ca/Maniwaki/
Colette Archambault, Responsable
Jacqueline Martin, Adjointe

***Manseau:* Bibliothèque de Manseau**
200A, rue Roux, Manseau QC G0X 1V0
Tél: 819-356-2450; *Téléc:* 819-356-2721
biblio084@reseaubibliocqlm.qc.ca
www.reseaubiblioduquebec.qc.ca
Denise Bernier, Responsable

***Mansfield:* Bibliothèque Mansfield-et-Pontefract**
314, rue Principale, Mansfield QC J0X 1V0
Tél: 819-683-3491; *Téléc:* 819-683-3590
admmansfield@crsbpo.qc.ca
www.reseaubiblioduquebec.cq.ca/Mansfield/
Martine Laroche, Responsable

***Maria:* Bibliothèque Noël-Audet**
475, rue des Chardonnerets, Maria QC G0C 1Y0
Tél: 418-759-3832; *Téléc:* 418-759-5035
bbomaria@globetrotter.qc.ca
www.reseaubiblioduquebec.qc.ca
Sylvie Boudreau, Responsable

***Marieville:* Bibliothèque Commémorative Desautels**
1801, rue du Pont, Marieville QC J3M 1J7
Tél: 450-460-4444; *Téléc:* 450-460-3526
biblio126@reseaubibliomonteregie.qc.ca
www.ville.marieville.qc.ca/bibliotheque/
Daniel Lalonde, Responsable
d.lalonde@ville.marieville.qc.ca

***Marsoui:* Bibliothèque de Marsoui**
2, rue des Écoliers, Marsoui QC G0E 1S0
Tél: 418-288-5508
michelle.cote@globetrotter.net
www.reseaubiblioduquebec.qc.ca
Michelle Côté, Responsable

***Mascouche:* Bibliothèque municipale de Mascouche**
3015, ave des Ancêtres, Mascouche QC J7K 1X6
Tél: 450-474-4159; *Téléc:* 450-474-3410
biblio@ville.mascouche.qc.ca
www.ville.mascouche.qc.ca
Sarah Germain, Bibliothécaire professionnelle

***Mashteuiatsh:* Bibliothèque publique de Mashteuiatsh**
507, rue Uapileu, Mashteuiatsh QC G0W 2H0
Tél: 418-275-2473; *Téléc:* 418-275-0097
masht@reseaubiblioslsj.qc.ca
www.reseaubiblioduquebec.qc.ca/portail/index.aspx?page=3&BID=5
Johane Langlais, Responsable
Johane Langlais, Bibliotechnicienne

***Maskinongé:* Bibliothèque de Maskinongé**
11, rue Marcel, Maskinongé QC J0K 1N0
Tél: 819-227-4656
biblio059@reseaubibliocqlm.qc.ca
www.reseaubiblioduquebec.qc.ca
Andrée Livernoche, Responsable

***Massueville:* Bibliothèque municipale de Massueville/St-Aimé**
846A, rue de l'Église, Massueville QC J0G 1K0
Tél: 450-788-3120
aime@reseaubibliomonteregie.qc.ca
www.reseaubiblioduquebec.qc.ca
Claire Berger, Responsable

***Matane:* Bibliothèque municipale de Matane (Fonds de Solidarité FTQ)**
Complexe culturel Joseph-Rouleau, #2, 520, av Saint-Jérôme, Matane QC G4W 3B5
Tél: 418-562-9233; *Téléc:* 418-566-2064
biblio@ville.matane.qc.ca
www.ville.matane.qc.ca/bibliotheque_municipale.html
Lise Whittom Grenier, Responsable
l.grenier@ville.matane.qc.ca

***Matapédia:* Bibliothèque de Matapédia**
5, rue Hôtel-de-Ville, Matapédia QC G0J 1V0
Tél: 418-865-2917; *Téléc:* 418-865-2828
bbomatap@globetrotter.net
www.reseaubiblioduquebec.qc.ca
Julie Michaud, Responsable
418-865-2135

***Les Méchins:* Bibliothèque municipale de Les Méchins**
164, rue Principale, Les Méchins QC G0J 1T0
Tél: 418-729-1346
biblio.lesmechins@mrcdematane.qc.ca
www.lesmechins.com
Louise Farand, Responsable
418-729-1346

***Mercier:* Bibliothèque municipale de Mercier**
16, rue du Parc, Mercier QC J6R 1E5
Tél: 450-692-6780; *Téléc:* 450-691-6529
danielmorin@bibliothequedemercier.qc.ca
Daniel Morin, Responsable
daniel.morin@bibliothequedemercier.qc.ca

***Messines:* Bibliothèque de Messines**
3, ch de la Ferme, Messines QC J0X 2J0
Tél: 819-465-2637; *Téléc:* 819-465-2943
admmessines@crsbpo.qc.ca
www.reseaubiblioduquebec.qc.ca/Messines
Claire Lacroix, Responsable

***Métabetchouan-Lac-à-la-Croi:* Bibliothèque publique de Métabetchouan**
87, rue Saint-André, Métabetchouan-Lac-à-la-Croi QC G8G 1Z2
Tél: 418-349-8495
metabet@reseaubiblioslsj.qc.ca
www.reseaubiblioduquebec.qc.ca
Hélène Lachance, Responsable
418-349-3517

***Middle Bay:* Bibliothèque de Middle Bay**
Middle Bay QC G0G 1Z0
Tél: 418-379-2911; *Téléc:* 418-379-2959
Louise Buckle, Responsable

***La Minerve:* Bibliothèque de La Minerve**
8, rue Mailloux, La Minerve QC J0T 1S0
Tél: 819-274-2313; *Téléc:* 819-274-2031
laminerve@crsbpl.qc.ca
www.reseaubiblioduquebec.qc.ca
Marcelle Grégoire, Responsable

***Mirabel:* Bibliothèque municipale de Mirabel**
17710, rue du Val-d'Espoir, Mirabel QC J7J 1A1
Tél: 450-475-2082; *Téléc:* 450-430-2868
www.ville.mirabel.qc.ca/bibliotheque.asp
France Genest, Chef bibliothécaire
f.genest@ville.mirabel.qc.ca
Carole Gaudet, Technicienne en documentation
c.gaudet@ville.mirabel.qc.ca
Sylvie Labelle, Secrétaire
s.labelle@ville.mirabel.qc.ca
Fanny Laberge, Technicienne en documentation
f.laberge@ville.mirabel.qc.ca
Diane Girouard, Technicienne en documentation
d.girouard@ville.mirabel.qc.ca

***Moisie:* Bibliothèque de Moisie**
250, ch des Forges, Moisie QC G0G 2B0
Tél: 418-927-2279
www.reseaubiblioduquebec.qc.ca/moisie
Nancy Malenfant, Personne-ressource

***Montbeillard:* Bibliothèque Montbeillard**
551, rue du Village, Montbeillard QC J0Z 2X0
Tél: 819-797-7110; *Téléc:* 819-797-2390
montbeillard@reseaubiblioatnq.qc.ca
Diane St-Onge, Responsable

***Mont-Brun:* Bibliothèque Mont-Brun**
955, rue Principale, Mont-Brun QC J0Z 2Y0
Tél: 819-637-7101; *Téléc:* 819-637-2374
montbrun@reseaubiblioatnq.qc.ca
www.crsbpat.qc.ca/montbrun/
Noëlla Thibault, Responsable
Gisèle Guilbert Rodrigue, Bénévole

***Montcalm:* Bibliothèque de Montcalm**
30, rte du Lac-Rond Nord, Montcalm QC J0T 2V0
Tél: 819-687-2575; *Téléc:* 819-687-2374
biblio@municipalite.montcalm.qc.ca
www.reseaubiblioduquebec.qc.ca/montcalm
Pierre Nadeau, Responsable

***Mont-Carmel:* Bibliothèque Odile-Boucher**
22, rue de la Fabrique, Mont-Carmel QC G0L 1W0
Tél: 418-498-3500
biblio.carmel@crsbp.net
Denise Chamberland, Responsable
418-498-3492

***Montcerf-Lytton:* Bibliothèque Montcerf-Lytton**
16, rue Principale nord, 2e étage, Montcerf-Lytton QC J0W 1N0
Tél: 819-449-2065; *Téléc:* 819-449-7310
admmontcerf@crsbpo.qc.ca
www.reseaubiblioduquebec.qc.ca/Montcerf/
Christine Ménard, Responsable

***Montebello:* Bibliothèque de Montebello**
240A, rue Bonsecours, Montebello QC J0V 1L0
Tél: 819-423-6213; *Téléc:* 819-423-5703
admmontebello@crsbpo.qc.ca
www.reseaubiblioduquebec.qc.ca/Montebello/
Mariette Côté, Responsable

***Mont-Joli:* Bibliothèque Jean-Louis-Desrosiers**
1477, boul Jacques-Cartier, Mont-Joli QC G5H 2V5
Tél: 418-775-4106; *Téléc:* 418-775-4037
julie.belanger@ville.mont-joli.qc.ca
Julie Bélanger, Responsable

***Mont-Laurier:* Bibliothèque de Des Ruisseaux**
1269, boul Des Ruisseaux, Mont-Laurier QC J9L 3G6
Tél: 819-623-6748; *Téléc:* 819-623-6810
desruisseaux@crsbpl.qc.ca
www.reseaubiblioduquebec.qc.ca
Louise Paquette, Responsable

***Mont-Laurier:* Bibliothèque de Mont-Laurier**
385, rue Du Pont, Mont-Laurier QC J9L 2R5
Tél: 819-623-1833; *Téléc:* 819-623-7079
bibliotheque.mont-laurier@tlb.sympatico.ca
www.reseaubiblioduquebec.qc.ca
Edith Whear, Responsable

***Mont-Laurier:* Bibliothèque de Val-Limoges**
3620, ch Val-Limoges, Mont-Laurier QC J9L 3G6
Tél: 819-623-9124
vallimoges@crsbpl.qc.ca
www.reseaubiblioduquebec.qc.ca
Louise Paquette, Responsable

***Mont-Louis:* La Bibliothèque Liratou de Mont-Louis**
1, 1e av ouest, Mont-Louis QC G0E 1T0
Tél: 418-797-2310; *Téléc:* 418-797-2928
www.reseaubiblioduquebec.qc.ca
Annie-France Létourneau, Responsable

***Montpellier:* Bibliothèque de Montpellier**
4B, rue du Bosquet, Montpellier QC J0V 1M0
Tél: 819-428-3663; *Téléc:* 819-428-1221
admmontpellier@crsbpo.qc.ca
www.reseaubiblioduquebec.qc.ca/Montpellier/
Claudette Riopel, Responsable

***Montréal:* ABQLA Bulletin**
CP 1095, Montréal QC H9S 4H9
Tél: 514-697-0146
abqla@abqla.qc.ca
www.abqla.qc.ca/bulletin.html
Meg Sinclair, Editor

***Montréal:* ARGUS**
#103, 353, rue St-Nicolas, Montréal QC H2Y 2P1
Tél: 514-845-3327; *Téléc:* 514-845-1618
admin@cbpq.qc.ca
URL: www.cbpq.qc.ca
Robert Garon, Directeur

***Montréal:* Atwater Library/ Bibliothèque Atwater**
1200, av Atwater, Montréal QC H3Z 1X4
Tel: 514-935-7344; *Fax:* 514-935-1960
info@atwaterlibrary.ca
www.atwaterlibrary.ca
Lynn Verge, Executive Director
lverge@atwaterlibrary.ca
514-935-7344
Rani Yoganathan, Acquisitions Manager
ryoganathan@atwaterlibrary.ca
Gail O'Hagan, Circulation Desk Manager
goohagan@atwaterlibrary.ca

***Montréal:* La bibliographie du Québec**
2275, rue Holt, Montréal QC H2G 3H1
Tél: 514-873-1100; *Téléc:* 514-873-4310
bibliographie@banq.qc.ca

***Montréal:* Bibliothèque Reginald J.P. Dawson**
1967, boul Graham, Montréal QC H3R 1G9
Tél: 514-734-2966; *Téléc:* 514-734-3089
denis.chouinard@ville.mont-royal.qc.ca
www.ville.mont-royal.qc.ca/index.php?id=112

Denis Chouinard, Chef de division
denis.chouinard@ville.mont-royal.qc.ca
514-734-2966

Montréal: Corpo Clip
#103, 353, rue St-Nicolas, Montréal QC H2Y 2P1
Tél: 514-845-3327; *Téléc:* 514-845-1618
info@cbpq.qc.ca
www.cbpq.qc.ca
Michel Claveau, Éditeur

Montréal: Documentation et bibliothèques
#202, 3414, av du Parc, Montréal QC H2X 2H5
Tél: 514-281-5012; *Téléc:* 514-281-8219
Gilles Deschatelets, Éditeur

Montréal: En direct de l'EBSI
CP 6128, Succ Centre-Ville, Montréal QC H3C 3J7
Tél: 514-343-2244; *Téléc:* 514-343-5753
ebsiinfo@ebsi.umontreal.ca
www.fas.umontreal.ca/EBSI

Montréal: The Fraser-Hickson Institute/ Institut Fraser-Hickson
4855, av Kensington, Montréal QC H3X 3S6
Tel: 514-489-5301; *Fax:* 514-489-5302
webmaster@fraserhickson.qc.ca
www.fraserhickson.qc.ca
Frances Ackerman, Librarian

Montréal: Jewish Public Library (Montréal)/ La Bibliothèque publique juive (Montréal)
1, carré Cummings Sq., 5151, Côte Ste-Catherine Rd., Montréal QC H3W 1M6
Tel: 514-345-2627; *Fax:* 514-345-6477
info@jplmontreal.org
www.jewishpubliclibrary.org
Eva Raby, Executive Director
Kathy Diamond, Reference Librarian
Eddie Paul, Head, Bibliographic & Information Services
Allan Oberman, Head of Information & Administrative Services
Shannon Hodge, Archivist
archives@jplmontreal.org
514-345-2027

Montréal: Nouvelles de l'ASTED
#202, 3414, av du Parc, Montréal QC H2X 2H5
Tél: 514-281-5012; *Téléc:* 514-281-8219
info@asted.org
www.asted.org

Montréal: A rayons ouverts
475, boul de Maisonneuve est, Montréal QC H2L 5C4
Tél: 514-873-1101; *Téléc:* 514-873-9312
info@bnquebec.ca
www.banq.qc.ca

Montréal: Réseau des bibliothèques publiques de Montréal
801, rue Brennan (Pavillon Prince), 5e étage, Montréal QC H2C 0G4
Tél: 514-872-5923; *Téléc:* 514-872-4911
www.ville.montreal.qc.ca/biblio
Louise Guillemette-Labory, Directrice-associée
lglabory@ville.montreal.qc.ca
Luc Jodoin, Chef de division, Planification et développement réseau
Michel Claveau, Chef de division, Activités regroupées
Monique Khouzam, Chef de division, Programme et services aux arrondissements

Mont-Saint-Hilaire: Bibliothèque Armand-Cardinal
150, rue du Centre Civique, Mont-Saint-Hilaire QC J3H 3M8
Tél: 450-467-2854; *Téléc:* 450-446-5879
bibliotheque@villemsh.ca
www.ville.mont-saint-hilaire.qc.ca
Francine Ledoux-Nadeau, Bibliothécaire
francine.ledoux.nadeau@ville.mont-saint-hila

Mont-Saint-Michel: Bibliothèque de Mont-Saint-Michel
94, rue de l'Église, Mont-Saint-Michel QC J0W 1P0
Tél: 819-587-3093
biblio55@lino.com
www.reseaubiblioduquebec.qc.ca
Lucette Castonguay, Responsable

Mont-Saint-Pierre: Bibliothèque Kevin Pouliot-Bernatchez
102, rue Cloutier, Mont-Saint-Pierre QC G0E 1V0
Tél: 418-797-2898; *Téléc:* 418-797-2307
bbomtsp@globetrotter.net
Karine Sergerie, Responsable

Mont-Tremblant: Bibliothèque Samuel-Ouimet
1147, rue de St-Jovite, Mont-Tremblant QC J8E 1V1
Tél: 819-425-8614; *Téléc:* 819-425-1391
biblio.samuel-o@villedemont-tremblant.qc.ca
www.reseaubiblioduquebec.qc.ca
Gabriel Lemelin, Responsable

Morin-Heights: Bibliothèque de Morin-Heights
823, ch du Village, Morin-Heights QC J0R 1H0
Tél: 450-226-3232; *Téléc:* 450-226-8786
bibliomh@cgocable.ca
www.reseaubiblioduquebec.qc.ca
Audrey Gibeault, Responsable

La Motte: Bibliothèque de La Motte
349, ch St-Luc, La Motte QC J0Y 1T0
Tél: 819-732-0505; *Téléc:* 819-727-4248
lamotte@reseaubiblioatnq.qc.ca
www.reseaubiblioduquebec.qc.ca
Nicole Richard, Responsable

Murdochville: Bibliothèque de Murdochville
635, 5e rue, Murdochville QC G0E 1W0
Tél: 418-784-2866; *Téléc:* 418-784-2607
bbomurd@globetrotter.net
www.reseaubiblioduquebec.qc.ca
Sonia Dunn, Responsable

Mutton Bay: Bibliothèque municipale de Mutton Bay
École St-Lawrence, PR, Mutton Bay QC G0G 2C0
Tél: 418-733-2263; *Téléc:* 418-773-2696
Darlene Gallichon, Responsable

Namur: Bibliothèque Namur/ Namur Library
331, rue Hôtel-de-Ville, Namur QC J0V 1N0
Tél: 819-426-2457; *Téléc:* 819-426-3074
admnamur@crsbpo.qc.ca
www.reseaubiblioduquebec.qc.ca/Namur/
Tammie Leggett, Responsable

Napierville: Bibliothèque municipale de Napierville
290, rue St-Alexandre, Napierville QC J0J 1L0
Tél: 450-245-0030; *Téléc:* 450-245-3777
napierville@reseaubibliomonteregie.qc.ca
www.reseaubiblioduquebec.qc.ca
Viviane Leroux, Responsable

Natashquan: Bibliothèque de Natashquan
29, ch d'en Haut, Natashquan QC G0G 2E0
Tél: 418-726-3362; *Téléc:* 418-726-3698
natashb@globetrotter.net
www.reseaubiblioduquebec.qc.ca
Cindy Carbonneau, Responsable

Nédélec: Bibliothèque de Nédélec
68, rue Principale, Nédélec QC J0Z 2Z0
Tél: 819-784-2297; *Téléc:* 819-784-2126
nedelec@reseaubiblioatnq.qc.ca
www.reseaubiblioduquebec.qc.ca
Jacqueline Aylwin, Responsable

Neuville: Bibliothèque Félicité-Angers
760, rte 138, Neuville QC G0A 2R0
Tél: 418-876-2023; *Téléc:* 418-876-3349
f.-angers@videotron.ca
www.reseaubiblioduquebec.qc.ca/neuville
Diane Forgues-Michaud, Responsable

New Richmond: Bibliothèque du Vieux-Couvent
99, Place Suzanne-Guité, New Richmond QC G0C 2B0
Tél: 418-392-7070; *Téléc:* 418-392-5331
biblio@villenewrichmond.com
www.reseaubiblioduquebec.qc.ca
Chantal Cormier, Responsable

Newport: Bibliothèque de Newport
208, rte 132, Newport QC G0C 2A0
Tél: 418-777-2523; *Téléc:* 418-689-3639
bbonewpt@globetrotter.qc.ca
www.reseaubiblioduquebec.qc.ca
Dolores Bouchard, Responsable

Nicolet: Bibliothèque de Nicolet
116, rue Evariste-Lecompte, Nicolet QC J3T 1E6
Tél: 819-293-6007; *Téléc:* 819-293-6767
biblio072@reseaubibliocqlm.qc.ca
www.reseaubiblioduquebec.qc.ca
Serge Rousseau, Responsable

Nominingue: Bibliothèque de Nominingue
2112, ch du Tour du Lac, Nominingue QC J0W 1R0
Tél: 819-278-3384; *Téléc:* 819-278-4967
biblio51@crsbpl.qc.ca
www.reseaubiblioduquebec.qc.ca/nominingue
Nicole Jorg, Responsable

Normandin: Bibliothèque municipale de Normandin
1156, rue Valois, Normandin QC G8M 3Z8
Tél: 418-274-2241; *Téléc:* 418-274-2241
bibliotheque@ville.normandin.qc.ca
www.normandin.biblio.qc.ca/
Thérèse Cloutier, Présidente
Bruno Forget, Responsable
bibliotheque@ville.normandin.qc.ca

Normétal: Bibliothèque Normétal
36A, rue Principale, Normétal QC J0Z 3A0
Tél: 819-788-2505; *Téléc:* 819-788-2730
normetal@reseaubiblioatnq.qc.ca
www.crsbpat.qc.ca/normetal/
Annie Lamoureux, Responsable

North Hatley: Bibliothèque de North Hatley/ North Hatley Library
165, rue Main, North Hatley QC J0B 2C0
Tél: 819-842-2110
biblio@nhlibrary.qc.ca
www.nhlibrary.qc.ca
Susan Gwyn, Responsable

Notre-Dame-de-Ham: Bibliothèque de Notre-Dame-de-Ham
25, rue de l'Église, Notre-Dame-de-Ham QC G0P 1C0
Tél: 819-344-5010
biblio149@reseaubibliocqlm.qc.ca
France McSween, Responsable

Notre-Dame-de-la-Merci: Bibliothèque de Notre-Dame-de-la-Merci
1900, Montée de la Réserve, Notre-Dame-de-la-Merci QC J0T 2A0
Tél: 819-424-2152; *Téléc:* 819-424-7347
biblio42@crsbpl.qc.ca
www.reseaubiblioduquebec.qc.ca
Célina Riopel, Responsable

Notre-Dame-de-la-Paix: Bibliothèque Notre-Dame-de-la-Paix
10, rue Saint-Jean-Baptiste, Notre-Dame-de-la-Paix QC J0V 1P0
Tél: 819-522-6610; *Téléc:* 819-522-6710
admpaix@crsbpo.qc.ca
www.reseaubiblioduquebec.qc.ca/Notre-Dame-de-la-Paix
Suzon Côté, Responsable

Notre-Dame-de-la-Salette: Bibliothèque de Notre-Dame-de-la-Salette
68, rue des Saules, Notre-Dame-de-la-Salette QC J0X 2L0
Tél: 819-766-2872; *Téléc:* 819-766-2983
admsalette@crsbpo.qc.ca
www.reseaubiblioduquebec.qc.ca/Notre-Dame-de-la-Salette
Christine Rose Boucher, Responsable

Notre-Dame-de-Lorette: Bibliothèque publique de Notre-Dame-de-Lorette
Couvent Maria-Goretti, 22, rue Principale, Notre-Dame-de-Lorette QC G0W 1B0
Tél: 418-276-3941
ndlorette@reseaubiblioslsj.qc.ca
www.reseaubiblioduquebec.qc.ca/portail/index.aspx?page=3&BID=5
Georgette Bouchard, Responsable

Notre-Dame-de-Lourdes: Bibliothèque Notre-Dame-de-Lourdes
3971, rue Principale, Notre-Dame-de-Lourdes QC J0K 1K0
Tél: 450-759-7864
bibliondl@intermonde.net
www.notredamedelourdes.ca/services-biblio.asp
Johanne Vincent, Responsable

Notre-Dame-de-Montauban: Bibliothèque de Notre-Dame-de-Montauban
421, rue Principale, Notre-Dame-de-Montauban QC G0X 1W0
Tél: 418-336-2353
biblio058@reseaubibliocqlm.qc.ca
www.reseaubiblioduquebec.qc.ca
Denise Villemure, Responsable

Notre-Dame-de-Pontmain: Bibliothèque de Notre-Dame-de-Pontmain
15, rue Notre-Dame, Notre-Dame-de-Pontmain QC J0W 1S0
Tél: 819-597-2382
bibliotheque@munpontmain.qc.ca
www.reseaubiblioduquebec.qc.ca
Francine Leclair, Responsable

Notre-Dame-de-Portneuf: **Bibliothèque La Découverte/Notre-Dame-de-Portneuf**
500A, rue Notre-Dame, Notre-Dame-de-Portneuf QC G0A 2Z0
Tél: 418-286-4452; *Téléc:* 418-286-8150
bibliodecouv@globetrotte.net
www.reseaubiblioduquebec.qc.ca/portneuf
Johanne Savard, Responsable
johannesavard@hotmail.ca
418-286-3509

Notre-Dame-des-Monts: **Bibliothèque La Girouette**
87, rue Notre-Dame, Notre-Dame-des-Monts QC G0T 1L0
Téléc: 418-439-0883
www.reseaubiblioduquebec.qc.ca/monts/
Marie-Paule Boudreault, Responsable
Johanne Tremblay, Responsable, Échanges
Michel Turcotte, Responsable de l'animation

Notre-Dame-des-Pins: **Bibliothèque Le Signet/Notre-Dame-des-Pins**
2755, 1e av, Notre-Dame-des-Pins QC G0M 1K0
Tél: 418-774-9454
www.reseaubiblioduquebec.qc.ca/pins/
Lyette Roy, Responsable
Claire Maranda, Adjointe
Denise Bégin, Responsable, PIB

Notre-Dame-du-Bon-Conseil: **Bibliothèque de Notre-Dame-du-Bon-Conseil**
541, rue Notre-Dame, Notre-Dame-du-Bon-Conseil QC J0C 1A0
Tél: 819-336-2967
biblio096@reseaubibliocqlm.qc.ca
www.reseaubiblioduquebec.qc.ca
Véronique Montesinos, Responsable

Notre-Dame-du-Lac: **Bibliothèque Notre-Dame-du-Lac**
681, rue Commerciale, Notre-Dame-du-Lac QC G0L 1X0
Tél: 418-899-6004
biblio.ndlac@crsbp.net
Judith Pellerin, Responsable
418-899-6045

Notre-Dame-du-Laus: **Bibliothèque de Notre-Dame-du-Laus**
4, rue de l'Église, Notre-Dame-du-Laus QC J0X 2M0
Tél: 819-767-2772
biblio057@crsbpl.qc.ca
www.reseaubiblioduquebec.qc.ca
Francine Boisvert, Responsable

Notre-Dame-du-Nord: **Bibliothèque Notre-Dame-du-Nord**
15, rue Desjardins, Notre-Dame-du-Nord QC J0Z 3B0
Tél: 819-723-2695; *Téléc:* 819-723-2483
nord@reseaubiblioatnq.qc.ca
Carmen Laliberté, Responsable

Notre-Dame-du-Portage: **Bibliothèque de Notre-Dame-du-Portage**
539, rte du Fleuve, Notre-Dame-du-Portage QC G0L 1Y0
Tél: 418-862-9163
biblio.portage@crsbp.net
www.reseaubiblioduquebec.qc.ca
Jacinthe Leblanc, Responsable

Nouvelle: **Bibliothèque de Nouvelle**
470, rue Francoeur, Nouvelle QC G0C 2E0
Tél: 418-794-2253; *Téléc:* 418-794-2254
bbonouv@globetrotter.net
www.reseaubiblioduquebec.qc.ca
Louise Leblanc, Responsable

Noyan: **Bibliothèque municipale de Noyan/ Noyan Public Library**
1312, ch de la Petite-France, Noyan QC J0J 1B0
Tél: 450-294-2175
noyan@reseaubibliomonteregie.qc.ca
Claude Jeunehomme, Responsable

Obedjiwan: **Bibliothèque d'Obedjiwan**
92, rue Tcikatnaw, Obedjiwan QC G0W 3B0
Tél: 819-974-1221; *Téléc:* 819-974-1224
biblio065@reseaubibliocqlm.qc.ca
www.reseaubiblioduquebec.qc.ca
Rachelle Chachai, Responsable

Odanak: **Bibliothèque de Odanak**
58, rue Waban-Aki, Odanak QC J0G 1H0
Tél: 514-568-0107; *Téléc:* 514-568-0107
biblio139@reseaubibliocqlm.qc.ca
www.reseaubiblioduquebec.qc.ca/Portail/index.aspx?page=3&BID=1
Marie-Chantal Bouchard, Responsable

Old Fort Bay: **Bibliothèque de Old Fort**
Old Fort Bay QC G0G 2G0
Tél: 418-379-2911; *Téléc:* 418-379-2959
René Fequet, Responsable

Ormstown: **Bibliothèque municipale d'Ormstown**
85, rue Roy, Ormstown QC J0S 1K0
Tél: 450-829-3249
ormstown@reseaubibliomonteregie.qc.ca
Madeleine Robidoux, Responsable

Otter Lake: **Bibliothèque Otter Lake**
340, av Martineau, Otter Lake QC J0X 2P0
Tél: 819-453-7344; *Téléc:* 819-453-7311
admotterlake@crsbpo.qc.ca
www.reseaubiblioduquebec.qc.ca/OtterLake/
Esther Dubeau, Responsable

Packington: **Bibliothèque Packington**
115, rue Soucy, Packington QC G0L 1Z0
Tél: 418-853-5362; *Téléc:* 418-853-6427
biblio.packing@crsbp.net
Denis Moreau, Responsable

Padoue: **Bibliothèque de Padoue**
215, rue Beaulieu, Padoue QC G0J 1X0
Tél: 418-775-8188
biblio.padoue@crsbp.net
Cécile Ouellet Caron, Responsable

Palmarolle: **Bibliothèque Palmarolle**
115, rue Principale, Palmarolle QC J0Z 3C0
Tél: 819-787-3459; *Téléc:* 819-787-2412
palmarolle@reseaubiblioatnq.qc.ca
Ghislaine Bégin, Responsable

Papineauville: **Bibliothèque de Papineauville**
294, rue Papineau, Papineauville QC J0V 1R0
Tél: 819-427-5511
admpapineau@crsbpo.qc.ca
www.reseaubiblioduquebec.qc.ca/Papineauville
Suzanne Gauthier, Responsable

Parisville: **Bibliothèque de Parisville**
1260, rue St-Jacques, Parisville QC G0S 1X0
Tél: 819-292-2644; *Téléc:* 819-292-2214
biblio103@reseaubibliocqlm.qc.ca
Jeannine Boucher, Responsable

Paspébiac: **Bibliothèque de Paspébiac**
95, boul Gérard-D.-Levesque Ouest, Paspébiac QC G0C 2K0
Tél: 418-752-2277; *Téléc:* 418-752-6747
pretpas@globetrotter.qc.ca
www.reseaubiblioduquebec.qc.ca
Noula Castilloux, Responsable

Percé: **Bibliothèque de Percé**
137, rte 132, Percé QC G0C 2L0
Tél: 418-782-5305; *Téléc:* 418-782-5487
bboperce@ville.perce.qc.ca
www.reseaubiblioduquebec.qc.ca
Pierrette Cloutier, Responsable

Péribonka: **Bibliothèque publique de Péribonka**
296A, Édouard-Niquet, Péribonka QC G0W 2G0
Tél: 418-374-2890; *Téléc:* 418-374-2491
peribonk@reseaubiblioslsj.qc.ca
www.reseaubiblioduquebec.qc.ca/portail/index.aspx?page=3&BID=5
Cynthia Gauthier, Responsable
418-374-2831
Line Fortin, Acquisitions
Chantale Néron, Acquisitions
Johane Hudon, Retards

Petite-Rivière-St-François: **Bibliothèque Gabrielle-Roy/Petite-Rivière-Saint-François**
1069, rue Principale, Petite-Rivière-St-François QC G0A 2L0
Tél: 418-632-5895; *Téléc:* 418-632-5886
biblioprsf@hotmail.com
www.reseaubiblioduquebec.qc.ca/petite-riviere
Suzanne Lapointe, Responsable
Viviane Guay, Adjointe
Esther Bouchard, Responsable, Échanges/Collection locale
Martine Lavoie, Responsable, Animation

Petite-Vallée: **Bibliothèque de Petite-Vallée**
45, rue Principale, Petite-Vallée QC G0E 1Y0
Tél: 418-393-2949; *Téléc:* 418-393-2949
bibliopv@globetrotter.net
www.reseaubiblioduquebec.qc.ca
Lorraine Lachance, Responsable

Petit-Saguenay: **Bibliothèque publique de Petit-Saguenay**
50, rue Tremblay, Petit-Saguenay QC G0V 1N0
Tél: 418-272-3083
petitsag@reseaubiblioslsj.qc.ca
www.reseaubiblioduquebec.qc.ca/portail/index.aspx?page=3&BID=5
Aurore Gagné, Responsable

Pierreville: **Bibliothèque de Notre-Dame-de-Pierreville**
48, rue Principale, Pierreville QC J0G 1J0
Tél: 450-568-2087
biblio142@reseaubibliocqlm.qc.ca
www.reseaubiblioduquebec.qc.ca
Maryse Boisvert, Responsable
450-568-2090
Dominique Boisvert, Bénévole
450-568-6788

Pierreville: **Bibliothèque de Pierreville (Jean-Luc-Précourt)**
26, rue Ally, Pierreville QC J0G 1J0
Tél: 450-568-3500; *Téléc:* 450-568-0689
biblio051@reseaubibliocqlm.qc.ca
www.reseaubiblioduquebec.qc.ca
Chantale Bellamy, Responsable

Pike River: **Bibliothèque Saint-Pierre-de-Véronne-à-Pike-River**
548, rte 202, Pike River QC J0J 1P0
Tél: 450-248-7689; *Téléc:* 450-248-2120
pike.river@reseaubibliomonteregie.qc.ca
www.pikeriver.com/_pikeriver/biblio.htm
Stéphane Dulude, Bénévole

Pincourt: **Bibliothèque de Pincourt/ Pincourt Library**
225, boul Pincourt, Pincourt QC J7V 9T2
Tél: 514-425-1104; *Téléc:* 514-425-6668
www.villepincourt.qc.ca
Sylvie de Repentigny, Régisseure
Mireille Péladeau, Technicienne en documentation

Plaisance: **Bibliothèque de Plaisance**
281, rue Desjardins, Plaisance QC J0V 1S0
Tél: 819-427-1189; *Téléc:* 819-427-5015
admplaisance@crsbpo.qc.ca
www.reseaubiblioduquebec.qc.ca/Plaisance
Martine Prud'homme, Responsable

Plessisville: **Bibliothèque municipale de la Ville de Plessisville**
1800, rue Saint-Calixte, Plessisville QC G6L 1R6
Tél: 819-362-6628; *Téléc:* 819-362-6421
bibliotheque@ville.plessisville.qc.ca
www.ville.plessisville.qc.ca/fr/content/heures_biblio.aspx
Suzanne Bédard, Responsable
sbedard@ville.plessisville.qc.ca
819-362-6628

La Pocatière: **Bibliothèque municipale de La Pocatière**
#4, 900, 6e av, La Pocatière QC G0R 1Z0
Tél: 418-856-3459
biblio.pocati@crsbp.net
www.reseaubiblioduquebec.qc.ca
Sylvie Dionne, Responsable

Pointe-à-la-Croix: **Bibliothèque de La Petite-Rochelle**
44A, rue Lasalle, Pointe-à-la-Croix QC G0C 1L0
Tél: 418-788-1305
biblio.41@hotmail.com
www.reseaubiblioduquebec.qc.ca
Lise P. Young, Responsable

Pointe-aux-Outardes: **Bibliothèque de Pointe-aux-Outardes**
481, ch Principale, Pointe-aux-Outardes QC G0H 1H0
Tél: 418-567-9529; *Téléc:* 418-567-4409
biblipao@globetrotter.net
Guylaine Chouinard, Responsable

Pointe-Calumet: **Bibliothèque La Sablière**
190, 41e Av, Pointe-Calumet QC J0N 1G2
Tél: 450-473-6991; *Téléc:* 450-473-6571
www.reseaubiblioduquebec.qc.ca

Brigitte Lessard, Responsable
b.lessard@municipalite.point-calumet.qc.ca
Louise Charron, Adjointe

***Pointe-des-Cascades:* Bibliothèque Adrienne Demontigny-Clément**
52, ch du Fleuve, Pointe-des-Cascades QC J0P 1M0
Tél: 450-455-5310
pointe.cascades@reseaubibliomonteregie.qc.ca
Camille St-Marseille, Responsable
Johane Séguin Poirier, Adjointe

***Pointe-Lebel:* Bibliothèque de Pointe-Lebel**
255, rue Granier, Pointe-Lebel QC G0H 1N0
Tél: 418-589-2424; *Téléc:* 418-589-6154
www.reseaubiblioduquebec.qc.ca/pointe-lebel
Lise Therrien, Responsable
418-589-2424

***Pont-Rouge:* Bibliothèque Auguste-Honoré-Gosselin**
41, rue du Collège, Pont-Rouge QC G3H 3A4
Tél: 418-873-4067; *Téléc:* 418-873-4141
bibliopontrouge@hotmail.com
www.reseaubiblioduquebec.qc.ca/pont-rouge
Denyse Simard, Responsable
Gilberte Gallant, Responsable des PIB
Odile Germain, Responsable, Échanges
Murielle Darveau, Responsable, Activités culturelles
Réjeanne Brousseau, Responsable, Collection locale
Yves Germain, Responsable, Statistiques

***Port-Cartier:* Bibliothèque municipale de Port-Cartier (Le Manuscrit)**
21, rue des Cèdres, Port-Cartier QC G5B 2W5
Tél: 418-766-3366; *Téléc:* 418-766-3561
bportcar@globetrotter.qc.ca
www.villeport-cartier.com
Stéphan Harvey, Régisseur culturel
418-766-3854
Chantal Maltais, Bibliotechnicienne

***Port-Menier:* Bibliothèque municipale de l'Ile d'Anticosti**
38, ch des Forestiers, Port-Menier QC G0G 2Y0
Tél: 418-535-0381
biblioanticosti@xplornet.com
Wendy Tremblay, Responsable
418-535-0250

***Portneuf-sur-Mer:* Bibliothèque de Portneuf-sur-Mer**
170, rue Principale, Portneuf-sur-Mer QC G0T 1P0
Tél: 418-238-5303; *Téléc:* 418-238-5319
annie.morin@bellnet.ca
Annie Morin, Sec.-trés., Portneuf-sur-Mer
Christine Olivier, Responsable

***Poularies:* Bibliothèque Poularies**
990, rue Principale, Poularies QC J0Z 3E0
Tél: 819-782-5159; *Téléc:* 819-782-5063
poularies@reseaubiblioatnq.qc.ca
Sophie Dallaire, Responsable

***La Prairie:* Bibliothèque Léo-Lecavalier**
500, rue Saint-Laurent, La Prairie QC J5R 5X2
Tél: 450-444-6710; *Téléc:* 450-444-6708
biblio@ville.laprairie.qc.ca
www.ville.laprairie.qc.ca/bibliotheque/acces.asp
Brigitte Tremblay, Responsable

***Préissac Nord:* Bibliothèque de Préissac-des-Rapides**
6, rue Des Rapides, Préissac Nord QC J0Y 2E0
Tél: 819-732-4938; *Téléc:* 819-732-4909
preissacn@reseaubiblioatnq.qc.ca
www.reseaubiblioduquebec.qc.ca
Huguette Béland, Responsable

***Préissac Sud:* Bibliothèque de Preissac Sud**
186, av du Lac, Préissac Sud QC J0Y 2E0
Tél: 819-759-4138; *Téléc:* 819-759-4138
preissacs@reseaubiblioatnq.qc.ca
www.reseaubiblioduquebec.qc.ca
Yolande P. Gagné, Responsable
Pierre Duquette, Responsable Prêt-PEB
Huguette Saucier, Responsable, Prêt-périodiques
Ghislaine Perreault, Responsable, Prêt-PEB

***Prévost:* Bibliothèque Jean-Charles-Des Roches**
2945, boul du Curé-Labelle, Prévost QC J0R 1T0
Tél: 450-224-5231; *Téléc:* 450-224-3024
prevost@crsbpl.qc.ca
www.reseaubiblioduquebec.qc.ca
Christian Schryburt, Responsable

***Price:* Bibliothèque de Price**
1, rue du Centre, Price QC G0J 1Z0
Tél: 418-775-5596
biblio.price@crsbp.net
www.reseaubiblioduquebec.qc.ca
Lise Roy, Responsable

***Princeville:* Bibliothèque de Princeville (Madeleine-Bélanger)**
140, rue Saint-Jean-Baptiste sud, Princeville QC G6L 5A5
Tél: 819-364-5071
biblio079@reseaubibliocqlm.qc.ca
Madeleine Beaudoin, Responsable

***Proulxville:* Bibliothèque de Saint-Séverin**
1986, Place du Centre, Proulxville QC G0X 2B0
Tél: 418-365-5844; *Téléc:* 418-365-7544
biblio008@reseaubibliocqlm.qc.ca
www.reseaubiblioduquebec.qc.ca
Sylvie Brouillette, Responsable

***Québec:* Archives: La revue de l'Association des archivistes du Québec**
CP 423, Québec QC G1R 4R2
Tél: 418-652-2357; *Téléc:* 418-646-0868
infoaaq@archivistes.qc.ca
www.archivistes.qc.ca/revuearchives/revuearchives.html

***Québec:* Bulletin de la Bibliothèque de l'Assemblée nationale**
Édifice Pamphile-Le May, 1035, rue des Parlementaires, Québec QC G1A 1A3
Tél: 418-643-7596; *Téléc:* 418-641-2636
bulletin@assnat.qc.ca
www.assnat.qc.ca/fra/Bibliotheque/publications/Bulletin
Carmen Gosselin, Éditeur

***Québec:* La chronique**
CP 423, Québec QC G1R 4R2
Tél: 418-652-2357; *Téléc:* 418-646-0868
infoaaq@archivistes.qc.ca
www.archivistes.qc.ca

***Québec:* Réseau des bibliothèques de la Ville de Québec**
350, rue Saint-Joseph est, Québec QC G1K 3B2
Tél: 418-641-6789; *Téléc:* 418-641-6787
www.bibliothequesdequebec.qc.ca
Marie Goyette, Directrice
Louis Roberge, Responsable, Référence
Louis Frémont, Responsable, Multimédia
Martine Lacasse, Responsable, Jeunesse-famille/Place des enfants
Éric Therrien, Responsable, Public adulte

***Quyon:* Quyon Library**
12, rue Saint-John, Quyon QC J0X 2V0
Tél: 819-458-1227; *Téléc:* 819-458-9756
admquyon@crsbpo.qc.ca
www.reseaubiblioduquebec.qc.ca/Quyon
Bernadette Milks, Coordonnateur

***Ragueneau:* Bibliothèque municipale Amaury-Tremblay**
13, rue des Loisirs, Ragueneau QC G0H 1S0
Tél: 418-567-8453; *Téléc:* 418-567-2344
www.reseaubiblioduquebec.qc.ca
Édith Martel, Responsable

***Ravignan:* Bibliothèque Liratu**
108A, rue de l'Église, Ravignan QC G0R 2L0
Téléc: 418-267-5930
www.reseaubiblioduquebec.qc.ca/saint-louis-de-gonzague/
Yollande Rancourt-Bilodeau, Responsable

***Rawdon:* Bibliothèque de Rawdon (Alice-Quintal)**
3643, rue Queen, Rawdon QC J0X 1S0
Tél: 450-834-2596
biblio076@reseaubibliocqlm.qc.ca
www.reseaubiblioduquebec.qc.ca
Renée Lalonde, Responsable

***La Reine:* Bibliothèque La Reine**
1, 3e av ouest, La Reine QC J0Z 2L0
Tél: 819-947-5271; *Téléc:* 819-947-5271
lareine@reseaubiblioatnq.qc.ca
Angèle Thouin, Responsable
Jeannine Blais, Bénévole
Pierrette East, Bénévole

***Rémigny:* Bibliothèque de Rémigny**
1304, ch de l'Église, Rémigny QC J0Z 3H0
Tél: 819-761-2331; *Téléc:* 819-761-2421
remigny@reseaubiblioatnq.qc.ca
www.reseaubiblioduquebec.qc.ca
Jocelyne Savignac, Responsable

***Repentigny:* Bibliothèque municipale de Repentigny**
1, Place d'Evry, Repentigny QC J6A 8H7
Tél: 450-470-3420; *Téléc:* 450-470-3079
bibliotheque@ville.repentigny.qc.ca
www.ville.repentigny.qc.ca/bibliotheque
Chantal Brodeur, Chef de division
brodeurc@ville.repentigny.qc.ca
450-470-3001 ext. 3427
Christine Lemieux, Adjointe
lemieuxc@ville.repentigny.qc.ca
450-470-3001 ext. 3343

***Richelieu:* Bibliothèque municipale Simonne-Monet-Chartrand**
200, boul Richelieu, Richelieu QC J3L 3R4
Tél: 450-658-1157
richelieu@reseaubibliomonteregie.qc.ca
www.villederichelieu.org
Claude Monast, Responsable
Manon Auclair, Responsable, Échanges et Animation

***Richmond:* Bibliothèque municipale de Richmond-Cleveland**
820, rue Gouin, Richmond QC J0B 2H0
Tél: 819-826-5814; *Téléc:* 819-826-5547
bibliothequercm@ville.richmond.qc.ca
www.ville.richmond.qc.ca
Suzanne Nault, Responsable

***Rigaud:* Bibliothèque municipale de Rigaud**
102, St Pierre, Rigaud QC J0P 1P0
Tél: 450-451-8841; *Téléc:* 450-451-8845
biblio@ville.rigaud.qc.ca
www.ville.rigaud.qc.ca/
Isabelle Guérard, Coordonnatrice
biblio@ville.rigaud.qc.ca
450-451-8841
Anne-Marie Fournier, Commis

***Rimouski:* Bibliothèque de Sainte-Blandine**
22, rue Lévesque, Rimouski QC G5N 5S6
Tél: 418-735-5055
biblio.blandine@crsbp.net
www.reseaubiblioduquebec.qc.ca
Nicole Testa, Responsable

***Rimouski:* Bibliothèque Lisette-Morin**
110, rue de l'Évêché, Rimouski QC G5L 7C7
Tél: 418-724-3164
bibliotheque.lisette-morin@ville.rimouski.qc.c
www.ville.rimouski.qc.ca/citoyens/bibliotheques/lisettemorin.a
Nicole Gagnon, Responsable

***Rimouski:* Bibliothèque Pointe-au-Père**
315, av Thomas-Dionne, Rimouski QC G5M 1M7
Tél: 418-722-4748
biblio.pere@crsbp.net
Ginette Ménard, Responsable

***Ripon:* Bibliothèque de Ripon**
31, rue Coursol, Ripon QC J0V 1V0
Tél: 819-983-2000; *Téléc:* 819-983-1327
admripon@crsbpo.qc.ca
www.reseaubiblioduquebec.qc.ca/Ripon
Céline Derouin, Responsable

***Rivière-à-Claude:* Bibliothèque de Rivière-à-Claude**
520, rue Principale est, Rivière-à-Claude QC G0E 1Z0
Tél: 418-797-2455
mcrioux@globetrotter.net
www.reseaubiblioduquebec.qc.ca
Marie-Claude Rioux, Responsable

***Rivière-au-Tonnerre:* Bibliothèque de Rivière-au-Tonnerre**
473, rue Jacques-Cartier, Rivière-au-Tonnerre QC G0G 2L0
Tél: 418-465-2255; *Téléc:* 418-465-2956
crsbp@globetrotter.net
Marie-Josée Lapierre, Responsable

***Rivière-du-Loup:* Bibliothèque municipale Françoise-Bédard**
67, rue du Rocher, Rivière-du-Loup QC G5R 1J8
Tél: 418-862-4252; *Téléc:* 418-862-3478
yves.savard@ville.riviere-du-loup.qc.ca
www.ville.riviere-du-loup.qc.ca/biblio

Sylvie Michaud, Directrice
sylvie.michaud@ville.riviere-du-loup.qc.ca
Claudine Gamache, Animatrice
Aline Bourgoin, Responsable, services techniques

***Rivière-Éternité:* Bibliothèque publique de Rivière Eternité**
404, rue Principale, Rivière-Éternité QC G0V 1P0
Tél: 418-272-1052
eternite@reseaubiblioslsj.qc.ca
Lucie Gagné, Responsable

***Rivière-Héva:* Bibliothèque Rivière-Héva**
15A, rue du Parc, Rivière-Héva QC J0Y 2H0
Tél: 819-735-2306; *Téléc:* 819-735-4251
www.reseaubiblioduquebec.qc.ca/portail/index.aspx?page=3&BiD=8
Nicole Turcotte, Responsable
Claire Julien, Bénévole

***Rivière-Pentecôte:* Bibliothèque de Rivière-Pentecôte**
4344, rue Jacques-Cartier, Rivière-Pentecôte QC G0H 1R0
Tél: 418-799-2143; *Téléc:* 418-799-2263
www.reseaubiblioduquebec.qc.ca
Hélène Jean, Responsable

***Rivière-Rouge:* Bibliothèque de Sainte-Véronique**
2167, boul Fernand-Lafontaine, Rivière-Rouge QC J0T 1T0
Tél: 819-275-3759; *Téléc:* 819-275-3759
bibliovero@riviere-rouge.ca
www.reseaubiblioduquebec.qc.ca
Claire Cochet, Responsable
Nicole Lefebvre, Bénévole
Rita Radermaker, Bénévole
Denise Ranger, Bénévole
Suzanne Ranger-Dubé, Bénévole

***Roberval:* Bibliothèque Georges-Henri-Lévesque**
829, boul St-Joseph, Roberval QC G8H 2L6
Tél: 418-275-2333; *Téléc:* 418-275-7045
jaudette@ville.roberval.qc.ca
www.roberval.biblio.qc.ca
Jacques Audette, Responsable
Lise Morin, Secrétaire

***Rock Forest:* Bibliothèque du secteur de Rock Forest**
968, rue du Haut-Bois sud, Rock Forest QC J1N 2C8
Tél: 819-823-8676; *Téléc:* 819-823-8345
bibliotheque.rockforest@ville.sherbrooke.qc.ca
www.ville.sherbrooke.qc.ca

***Rollet:* Bibliothèque Rollet**
761, rue Principale, Rollet QC J0Z 3J0
Tél: 819-797-7110; *Téléc:* 819-493-1210
rollet@reseaubiblioatnq.qc.ca
www.crsbpat.qc.ca/rollet/
Liliane Monderie, Responsable

***Rosemère:* Bibliothèque municipale H J Hemens de Rosemère**
339, rue Grande-Côte, Rosemère QC J7A 1K2
Tél: 450-621-6132; *Téléc:* 450-621-6131
biblio@ville.rosemere.qc.ca
ville.rosemere.qc.ca/biblio
Marc Bineault, Bibliothécaire - Chef de service
mbineault@ville.rosemere.qc.ca
514-621-6132
Ginette Corbeil Rivet, Responsable, Services techniques et référence

***Rougemont:* Bibliothèque municipale de Rougemont**
839, rue Principale, Rougemont QC J0L 1M0
Tél: 450-469-3213
rougemont@reseaubibliomonteregie.qc.ca
Simone Tétrault, Responsable
450-469-3452
Francine Chalifoux, Bénévole

***Rouyn-Noranda:* Bibliothèque de Beaudry**
6884, boul Témiscamingue, Rouyn-Noranda QC J9Y 1N1
Tél: 819-797-2543; *Téléc:* 819-797-2108
beaudry@reseaubiblioatnq.qc.ca
Marguerite Petit, Responsable

***Rouyn-Noranda:* Bibliothèque municipale de Rouyn-Noranda**
201, av Dallaire, Rouyn-Noranda QC J9X 4T5
Tél: 819-762-0944; *Téléc:* 819-797-7136
info@biblrn.qc.ca
www.biblrn.qc.ca
Joël Lacoursière, Directeur général
joel.lacoursiere@biblrn.qc.ca
Ginette Montigny, Responsable, Services techniques
ginette.montigny@biblrn.qc.ca

***Rouyn-Noranda:* L'échange**
20, av Québec, Rouyn-Noranda QC J9X 2E6
Tél: 819-762-4305; *Téléc:* 819-762-5309
info@crsbpat.qc.ca
www.reseaubiblioatnq.qc
Rosianne Avoine, Éditeur

***Roxton Pond:* Bibliothèque municipale de Roxton Pond**
905, rue Saint-Jean, Roxton Pond QC J0E 1Z0
Tél: 450-372-6991
roxton.pond@reseaubibliomonteregie.qc.ca
www.reseaubiblioduquebec.qc.ca
Diane Blanchard, Responsable

***Sabrevois:* Bibliothèque municipale de Sainte-Anne-de-Sabrevois**
1218, rte 133, Sabrevois QC J0J 2G0
Tél: 450-346-0899
sabrevois@reseaubibliomonteregie.qc.ca
Guylaine Marchand, Responsable

***Sacré-Coeur-Saguenay:* Bibliothèque de Sacré-Coeur**
89-A, Principale nord, Sacré-Coeur-Saguenay QC G0T 1Y0
Tél: 418-236-4621; *Téléc:* 418-236-9144
www.reseaubiblioduquebec.qc.ca
Vanessa Deschênes, Responsable
vandeschenes@hotmail.com

***Saint-Adelphe:* Bibliothèque de Saint-Adelphe (Roger-Fontaine)**
150, rue Baillargeon, Saint-Adelphe QC G0X 2G0
Tél: 418-322-6634; *Téléc:* 418-322-5434
biblio004@reseaubibliocqlm.qc.ca
www.reseaubiblioduquebec.qc.ca
Lyne Deshaies, Responsable

***Saint-Adolphe-d'Howard:* Bibliothèque de Saint-Adolphe-d'Howard**
1881, ch du Village, Saint-Adolphe-d'Howard QC J0T 2B0
Tél: 819-327-2117; *Téléc:* 819-327-2282
biblio24@crsbpl.qc.ca
www.reseaubiblioduquebec.qc.ca
Vickie Vandal, Responsable

***Saint-Aimé-des-Lacs:* Bibliothèque La Plume d'Or**
123B, rue Principale, Saint-Aimé-des-Lacs QC G0T 1S0
Tél: 418-439-2229
www.reseaubiblioduquebec.qc.ca/lacs
Hélène Perron, Responsable
Monique Gravel, Adjointe/Responsable Animation/Extranet

***Saint-Alban:* Bibliothèque Biblio-Chut!/Saint-Alban**
179, rue Principale, Saint-Alban QC G0A 3B0
Tél: 418-268-3557; *Téléc:* 418-268-5073
www.reseaubiblioduquebec.qc.ca/saint-alban
Monette Perreault, Responsable
Lise Pleau, Adjointe

***Saint-Alexis-de-Matapédia:* Bibliothèque de Saint-Alexis-de-Matapédia**
190, rue Principale, Saint-Alexis-de-Matapédia QC G0J 2E0
Tél: 418-299-2520; *Téléc:* 418-299-3011
Rachel Lebrun, Responsable

***Saint-Alexis-de-Montcalm:* Bibliothèque de Saint-Alexis**
232, rue Principale, Saint-Alexis-de-Montcalm QC J0K 1T0
Tél: 450-839-7277; *Téléc:* 450-831-2108
biblio110@reseaubibliocqlm.qc.ca
France Parent, Responsable

***Saint-Alexis-des-Monts:* Bibliothèque de Saint-Alexis-des-Monts (Léopold-Bellemare)**
105, rue Hôtel-de-Ville, Saint-Alexis-des-Monts QC J0K 1V0
Tél: 819-265-3598
biblio028@reseaubibliocqlm.qc.ca
Danielle Gagnon, Responsable

***Saint-Alphonse-de-Caplan:* Bibliothèque de A B C du savoir**
134A, rue Principale ouest, Saint-Alphonse-de-Caplan QC G0C 2V0
Tél: 418-388-5577; *Téléc:* 418-388-2435
bbostal@globetrotter.net
www.reseaubiblioduquebec.qc.ca
Roselyn Onraet, Responsable

***Saint-Alphonse-de-Granby:* Bibliothèque municipale de Saint-Alphonse-de-Granby**
360, rue Principale, Saint-Alphonse-de-Granby QC J0E 2A0
Tél: 450-375-7229; *Téléc:* 450-375-4570
alphonse@reseaubibliomonteregie.qc.ca
Julie Fortin, Responsable
Annie Lessard, Responsable, Animation/Administration

***Saint-Alphonse-Rodriguez:* Bibliothèque de Saint-Alphonse-Rodriguez (Docteur-Jacques-Olivier)**
20, rue de la Plage, Saint-Alphonse-Rodriguez QC J0K 1W0
Tél: 450-883-2264; *Téléc:* 450-883-3959
biblio062@reseaubibliocqlm.qc.ca
Lina Laforest, Responsable

***Saint-Amable:* Maison de la culture Jacqueline Gemme**
446, rue Daniel, Saint-Amable QC J0L 1N0
Tél: 450-649-1524
amable@reseaubibliomonteregie.qc.ca
www.reseaubiblioduquebec.qc.ca
France Therrien, Responsable

***Saint-Ambroise:* Bibliothèque publique de Saint-Ambroise**
156, rue Gaudreault, Saint-Ambroise QC G7P 2J9
Tél: 418-672-2253
stambr@reseaubiblioslsj.qc.ca
www.reseaubiblioduquebec.qc.ca
Carole Gagné, Responsable

***Saint-André-Avellin:* Bibliothèque de Saint-André-Avellin**
532, rue Charles-Auguste Montreuil, Saint-André-Avellin QC J0V 1W0
Tél: 819-983-2840; *Téléc:* 819-983-2344
admavellin@crsbpo.qc.ca
www.reseaubiblioduquebec.qc.ca/St-Andre-Avellin
Adéodat Bernard, Responsable

***Saint-André-d'Argenteuil:* Bibliothèque 'Au fil des mots'**
1, rte des Seigneurs, Saint-André-d'Argenteuil QC J0V 1X0
Tél: 450-537-2022
Andréanne Legault, Responsable

***Saint-André-de-Kamouraska:* Bibliothèque de Saint-André**
126, rue Principale, Saint-André-de-Kamouraska QC G0L 2H0
Tél: 418-493-2150
biblio.andre@crsbp.net
www.reseaubiblioduquebec.qc.ca
Micheline Saint-André, Responsable

***Saint-André-de-Restigouche:* Bibliothèque de Saint-André-de-Restigouche**
163, rue Principale, Saint-André-de-Restigouche QC G0J 1G0
Tél: 418-865-2234; *Téléc:* 418-865-1393
TDD: 4188651393
m.st.and.restigouche@globetrotter.net
www.reseaubiblioduquebec.qc.ca
Blandine Parent, Responsable

***Saint-Anicet:* Bibliothèque municipale de Saint-Anicet**
1547, rte 132, Saint-Anicet QC J0S 1M0
Tél: 450-264-9431; *Téléc:* 450-264-3544
anicet@reseaubibliomonteregie.qc.ca
Carmen Bourgoyne, Responsable

***Saint-Antoine-de-Tilly:* Bibliothèque La Corne de brume**
943, rte de L'Église, Saint-Antoine-de-Tilly QC G0S 2C0
Tél: 418-886-2603
www.reseaubiblioduquebec.qc.ca/tilly
Hughes Lansac, Responsable
Jean-Marc Dumas, Adjoint
Reine Bourassa, Responsable, PIB
Louise Bernier, Responsable, Échanges

***Saint-Antoine-sur-Richelieu:* Bibliothèque Hélène-Dupuis-Marion**
#2, 1060, rue du Moulin Payet, Saint-Antoine-sur-Richelieu QC J0L 1R0
Tél: 450-787-3140; *Téléc:* 450-787-2852
antoine@reseaubibliomonteregie.qc.ca
Nicole Villiard, Responsable

***Saint-Antonin:* Bibliothèque Paradis du Livre**
261, rue Principale, Saint-Antonin QC G0L 2J0
Tél: 418-867-2353; *Téléc:* 418-862-3268
biblio.antonin@crsbp.net
Hélène Léveillé, Responsable

***Saint-Apollinaire:* Bibliothèque Au Jardin des livres/Saint-Apollinaire**
#102, 94, rue Principale, Saint-Apollinaire QC G0S 2E0
Tél: 418-881-2447; *Téléc:* 418-881-4152
bibliotheque@st-apollinaire.com
www.reseaubiblioduquebec.qc.ca/saint-apollinaire
Denise Olivier, Responsable
Francine Leclerc, Adjointe au responsable
Francine Rousseau, Secrétaire-relationniste
Karine Bernier, Trésorière

***Saint-Arsène:* Bibliothèque Saint-Arsène**
49, rue de l'Église, Saint-Arsène QC G0L 2K0
Tél: 418-867-2205
biblio.arsene@crsbp.net
Suzanne Michaud, Responsable

***Saint-Athanase:* Bibliothèque Saint-Athanase**
6081, ch de l'Église, Saint-Athanase QC G0L 2L0
Tél: 418-859-1143
biblio.athanase@crsbp.net
Diane Dumont, Responsable

***Saint-Aubert:* Bibliothèque Charles-E.-Harpe**
14, rue des Loisirs, Saint-Aubert QC G0R 2R0
Tél: 418-598-3623; *Téléc:* 418-598-3369
bibliaub@videotron.qc.ca
www.reseaubiblioduquebec.qc.ca/saint-aubert/
Céline Bélanger, Responsable

***Saint-Augustin-de-Desmaures:* Bibliothèque Alain-Grandbois**
160, rue Jean-Juneau, Saint-Augustin-de-Desmaures QC G3A 2P1
Tél: 418-878-5473; *Téléc:* 418-878-1300
bibliotheque.alain-grandbois@ville.st-augustin
www.ville.st-augustin.qc.ca/biblio
Martine Lirette, Directrice de la bibliothèque
Martine.Lirette@ville.st-augustin.qc.ca

***Saint-Augustin-Saguenay:* Bibliothèque de Saint-Augustin**
École de Saint-Augustin, 710, rue Principale, Saint-Augustin-Saguenay QC G0W 1K0
Tél: 418-374-1084; *Téléc:* 418-947-2533
augustin@reseaubibliosIsj.qc.ca
www.reseaubiblioduquebec.qc.ca
Pauline Fortin, Responsable

***Saint-Barthélemy:* Bibliothèque de Saint-Barthélemy**
1980, rue Bonin, Local 105, Saint-Barthélemy QC J0K 1X0
Tél: 450-885-3511; *Téléc:* 450-885-2165
biblio046@reseaubibliocqlm.qc.ca
Louise Belhumeur, Responsable

***Saint-Basile:* Bibliothèque Au fil des mots/Saint-Basile**
41, rue Caron, Saint-Basile QC G0A 3G0
Tél: 418-329-2858; *Téléc:* 418-329-3743
biblio@saintbasile.qc.ca
www.reseaubiblioduquebec.qc.ca/saint-basile
Lise Bélanger, Responsable
Juliette Bourgoin, Adjointe
Josée Marcotte, Responsable, PIB
Denise Hardy, Responsable, Échanges

***Saint-Basile-le-Grand:* Bibliothèque Roland Leblanc**
40, rue Savaria, Saint-Basile-le-Grand QC J3N 1L8
Tél: 450-461-8085; *Téléc:* 450-461-8089
bibliotheque@ville.saint-basile-le-grand.qc.ca
www.bibliothequesaintbasile.qc.ca
France Goyette, Directrice

***Saint-Benjamin:* Bibliothèque La Détente/Saint-Benjamin**
440, rue du Collège, Saint-Benjamin QC G0M 1N0
Tél: 418-594-8189; *Téléc:* 418-594-6068
www.reseaubiblioduquebec.qc.ca/saint-benjamin
Régine Perras, Responsable
418-594-5635

***Saint-Benoît-Labre:* Bibliothèque L'Envolume**
216, rte 271, Saint-Benoît-Labre QC G0M 1P0
Tél: 418-228-9250; *Téléc:* 418-228-0518
biblstbe@globetrotter.qc.ca
www.reseaubiblioduquebec.qc.ca/saint-benoit-labre/
Josette Labbé, Responsable
Suzanne Legroulx, Responsable, Échanges/Animation

Carmen Quirion, Responsable, PIB

***Saint-Bernard:* Bibliothèque Liratout/Saint-Bernard**
540, rue Vaillancourt, Saint-Bernard QC G0S 2G0
Tél: 418-475-4669; *Téléc:* 418-475-4602
bibliost-bernard@nouvellebeauce.com
www.reseaubiblioduquebec.qc.ca/saint-bernard
Carolle Larochelle, Responsable

***Saint-Bernard-de-Michaudvil:* Bibliothèque municipale de Saint-Bernard-de-Michaudville**
390, rue Principale, Saint-Bernard-de-Michaudvil QC J0H 1C0
Tél: 450-792-3190; *Téléc:* 450-792-3591
bernard.sud@reseaubibliomonteregie.qc.ca
Marie-Sylvie Lavallée, Responsable

***Saint-Blaise-sur-Richelieu:* Bibliothèque municipale de Saint-Blaise-sur-Richelieu**
#6, 795, rue des Loisirs, Saint-Blaise-sur-Richelieu QC J0J 1W0
Tél: 450-291-5944; *Téléc:* 450-291-5095
blaise@reseaubibliomonteregie.qc.ca
Laure Desrochers, Responsable

***Saint-Bonaventure:* Bibliothèque de Saint-Bonaventure**
110, rue Cyr, Saint-Bonaventure QC J0C 1C0
Tél: 819-396-1676; *Téléc:* 819-396-2335
biblio120@reseaubibliocqlm.qc.ca
www.reseaubiblioduquebec.qc.ca
Gisèle Corbin, Responsable
819-396-1676

***Saint-Bruno:* Bibliothèque publique de Saint-Bruno**
550, rue des 4H, Saint-Bruno QC G0W 2L0
Tél: 418-343-2007
stbruno@reseaubiblioslsj.qc.ca
www.reseaubiblioduquebec.qc.ca/portail/index.aspx?page=3&BID=5
Denise Martel, Responsable
418-343-3488

***Saint-Bruno-de-Guigues:* Bibliothèque de Saint-Bruno-de-Guigues**
23B, rue Principale nord, Saint-Bruno-de-Guigues QC J0Z 2G0
Tél: 819-728-2910; *Téléc:* 819-728-2404
guigues@reseaubiblioatnq.qc.ca
www.reseaubiblioduquebec.qc.ca
Louise Gagnon, Responsable

***Saint-Bruno-de-Kamouraska:* Bibliothèque des Brulots**
6, rue Du Couvent, Saint-Bruno-de-Kamouraska QC G0L 2M0
Tél: 418-492-5281
biblio.bruno@crsbp.net
www.reseaubiblioduquebec.qc.ca
Ginette Beaulieu, Responsable

***Saint-Bruno-de-Montarville:* Bibliothèque municipale de Saint-Bruno-de-Montarville**
82, boul Seigneurial ouest, Saint-Bruno-de-Montarville QC J3V 5N7
Tél: 450-645-2950; *Téléc:* 450-441-8485
bibliotheque@stbruno.ca
Jean-Marc Lynch, Bibliothécaire en chef
jean-marc.lynch@ville.stbruno.qc.ca
450-653-2443 ext. 2850

***Saint-Calixte:* Bibliothèque de Saint-Calixte**
6250, rue Hôtel-de-Ville, Saint-Calixte QC J0K 1Z0
Tél: 450-222-2782; *Téléc:* 450-222-2789
biblio@mscalixte.qc.ca
www.reseaubiblioduquebec.qc.ca/saint-calixte
Madeleine Vézina, Responsable
Gisèle D'Amours, Adjointe

***Saint-Casimir:* Bibliothèque Jean-Charles-Magnan**
510, boul de la Montagne, Saint-Casimir QC G0A 3L0
Tél: 418-339-2909; *Téléc:* 418-339-3105
jcmagnan@csportneuf.qc.ca
www.reseaubiblioduquebec.qc.ca/saint-casimir/
Ange-Aimée Asselin, Responsable
Nicole Tessier, Responsable, PIB

***Saint-Célestin:* Bibliothèque de Saint-Célestin (Claude-Bouchard)**
450B, rue Marquis, Saint-Célestin QC J0C 1G0
Tél: 819-229-3403
biblio130@reseaubibliocqlm.qc.ca
www.reseaubiblioduquebec.qc.ca
Nicole Cameron, Responsable

***Saint-Charles-de Bourget:* Bibliothèque publique de Saint-Charles-de-Bourget**
362, rue Principale, Saint-Charles-de Bourget QC G0V 1G0
Tél: 418-672-1082; *Téléc:* 418-672-4403
stcharle@reseaubiblioslsj.qc.ca
www.reseaubiblioduquebec.qc.ca
Isabelle Néron, Responsable
418-672-1082
Joanne Vallière, Bénévole
Natalie Harvey, Bénévole
Louise Breton, Bénévole
Claire Chayer, Bénévole
Isabelle Forgues, Bénévole

***Saint-Charles-de-Drummond:* Club de Lecture Centre Réal-Rochefort/Saint-Charles-de-Drummond**
565, rue Victorin, Saint-Charles-de-Drummond QC J2C 1C1
Tél: 819-477-2326; *Téléc:* 819-477-0697
ccsc@ville.drummondville.qc.ca
Guyslaine Dion-Daneault, Responsable

***Saint-Charles-Garnier:* Bibliothèque de Saint-Charles-Garnier**
38, de Saint-Charles-Garnier, Saint-Charles-Garnier QC G0K 1K0
Tél: 418-798-4305
biblio.garnier@crsbp.net
www.reseaubiblioduquebec.qc.ca
Brigitte Gagnon, Responsable

***Saint-Clément:* Bibliothèque de Saint-Clément**
25A, rue Saint-Pierre, Saint-Clément QC G0L 2N0
Tél: 418-963-2258; *Téléc:* 418-963-2619
biblio.clement@crsbp.net
www.reseaubiblioduquebec.qc.ca
Thérèse Saint-Pierre, Responsable

***Saint-Cléophas:* Bibliothèque de Saint-Cléophas**
356, rue Principale, Saint-Cléophas QC G0J 3N0
Tél: 418-536-3215
biblio.cleophas@crsbp.net
www.reseaubiblioduquebec.qc.ca
Gina Poirier, Responsable
418-536-3031
Linda Hudon, Bénévole

***Saint-Cléophas-de-Brandon:* Bibliothèque de Saint-Cléophas-de-Brandon**
750, rue Principale, Saint-Cléophas-de-Brandon QC J0K 2A0
Tél: 450-889-5683; *Téléc:* 450-889-8007
biblio107@reseaubibliocqlm.qc.ca
www.reseaubiblioduquebec.qc.ca
Marie-Line Gingras, Responsable

***Saint-Clet:* Bibliothèque municipale de Saint-Clet**
25, rue Piché, Saint-Clet QC J0P 1S0
Tél: 450-465-3175
clet@reseaubibliomonteregie.qc.ca
www.reseaubiblioduquebec.qc.ca
Brigitte Lalonde, Responsable

***Saint-Colomban:* Bibliothèque de Saint-Colomban**
347, montée de l'Église, Saint-Colomban QC J5K 1B1
Tél: 450-436-1453; *Téléc:* 450-432-1863
biblio@st-colomban.qc.ca
www.reseaubiblioduquebec.qc.ca
Média social:
www.facebook.com/group.php?gid=133415300034333
Lucie Jubinville, Directrice

***Saint-Côme:* Bibliothèque de Saint-Côme**
1677, 55e rue, Saint-Côme QC J0K 2B0
Tél: 450-883-3911; *Téléc:* 450-883-6431
biblio054@reseaubibliocqlm.qc.ca
Josée Blanchard, Responsable

***Saint-Côme-Linière:* Bibliothèque municipale de Saint-Côme-Linière**
1375, 18e rue, Saint-Côme-Linière QC G0M 1J0
Tél: 418-685-3825; *Téléc:* 418-685-2566
bibliostcome@hotmail.com
www.reseaubiblioduquebec.qc.ca/saint-come
Chantal Poulin, Responsable
Laurette Thompson, Adjointe

***Saint-Constant:* Bibliothèque municipale de Saint-Constant**
85, Mtée Saint-Régis, Saint-Constant QC J5A 1X8
Tél: 450-638-2010; *Téléc:* 450-632-9399
bibliotheque@ville.saint-constant.qc.ca
www.ville.saint-constant.qc.ca/Citoyens/bibliotheque.asp
Nathalie Groulx, Responsable

***Saint-Cuthbert:* Bibliothèque de Saint-Cuthbert**
1891, rue Principale, Saint-Cuthbert QC J0K 2C0
Tél: 450-836-4852; *Téléc:* 450-836-4833
biblio126@reseaubibliocqlm.qc.ca
Pierre-Yvon Laporte, Responsable
Julie Rémillard, Adjointe
Cécile Rémillard, Bénévole
450-836-2146
Monique Lepage, Bénévole

***Saint-Cyprien:* Bibliothèque de Saint-Cyprien (Alphonse-Desjardins)**
187, rue Principale, Saint-Cyprien QC G0L 2P0
Tél: 418-963-1887
biblio.cyprien@crsbp.net
www.reseaubiblioduquebec.qc.ca
Ginette Gagné, Responsable

***Saint-Cyprien-des-Etchemins:* Bibliothèque municipale de Saint-Cyprien**
399, rue Principale, Saint-Cyprien-des-Etchemins QC G0R 1B0
Tél: 418-383-3476; *Téléc:* 418-383-5269
Sandy DeBlois, Responsable

***Saint-Damase:* Bibliothèque municipale de Saint-Damase**
113, rue St-Étienne, Saint-Damase QC J0H 1J0
Tél: 418-797-3341
damase@reseaubibliomonteregie.qc.ca
Hélène Simard, Responsable

***Saint-Damase-de-l'Islet:* Bibliothèque municipale de Saint-Damase-de-l'Islet**
28, rue de Village est, Saint-Damase-de-l'Islet QC G0R 2X0
Tél: 418-598-9370; *Téléc:* 418-598-9396
stdamase3@hotmail.com
Sylvie Cloutier, Responsable

***Saint-Damase-de-Matapédia:* Bibliothèque de Saint-Damase-de-Matapédia**
18, av du Centenaire, Saint-Damase-de-Matapédia QC G0J 2J0
Tél: 418-776-2103
biblio.damase@crsbp.net
www.reseaubiblioduquebec.qc.ca
Edith Deschênes, Responsable

***Saint-Damien:* Bibliothèque de Saint-Damien**
6960, rue Principale, Saint-Damien QC J0K 2E0
Tél: 450-835-7519
biblio041@reseaubibliocqlm.qc.ca
www.reseaubiblioduquebec.qc.ca
Josée St-Martin, Responsable

***Saint-Damien-de-Buckland:* Bibliothèque Le Bouquin d'Or/Saint-Damien-de-Buckland**
75, rue Saint-Gérard, Saint-Damien-de-Buckland QC G0R 2Y0
Tél: 418-789-2127; *Téléc:* 418-789-2125
www.reseaubiblioduquebec.qc.ca/saint-damien
Marielle Dion-Jobin, Responsable de la bibliothèque
418-789-2125

***Saint-Denis:* Bibliothèque de Saint-Denis**
2, A rte de l'Église, Saint-Denis QC G0L 2R0
Tél: 418-867-8883
biblio.denis@crsbp.net
www.reseaubiblioduquebec.qc.ca
Doris Rivard, Responsable

***Saint-Didace:* Bibliothèque de Saint-Didace**
530A, rue Principale, Saint-Didace QC J0K 2G0
Tél: 450-835-3933; *Téléc:* 450-835-0602
biblio128@reseaubibliocqlm.qc.ca
www.reseaubiblioduquebec.qc.ca
Isabel Lamoureux, Responsable

***Saint-Dominique:* Bibliothèque municipale de Saint-Dominique**
488, Saint-Dominique, Saint-Dominique QC J0H 1L0
Tél: 450-771-0256
dominique@reseaubibliomonteregie.qc.ca
Manon Denault, Responsable

***Saint-Donat:* Bibliothèque de Saint-Donat**
510, rue Desrochers, Saint-Donat QC J0T 2C0
Tél: 819-424-3044; *Téléc:* 819-424-5020
biblio@saintdonat.ca
www.reseaubiblioduquebec.qc.ca/saint-donat
Anita Desmeules, Responsable
Joanne Riopel, Adjointe

***Saint-Donat:* Bibliothèque de Saint-Donat**
101, rue Bérubé, Saint-Donat QC G0K 1L0
Tél: 418-739-3368
biblio.donat@crsbp.net
www.reseaubiblioduquebec.qc.ca
Madeleine Leclerc, Responsable
Micheline Hallé, Bénévole

***Sainte-Adèle:* Bibliothèque Claude-Henri-Grignon**
170, rue Morin, Sainte-Adèle QC J8B 2P7
Tél: 450-229-2921; *Téléc:* 450-229-2283
Stéphanie Lachaine, Responsable
slachaine@ville.sainte-adele.qc.ca

***Sainte-Adèle:* Bibliothèque Jean-Baptiste-Rolland**
1200, rue Claude-Grégoire, Sainte-Adèle QC J8B 1E9
Tél: 450-229-2921; *Téléc:* 450-229-2283
Stéphanie Lachaine, Responsable
slachaine@ville.sainte-adele.qc.ca
Suzanne Legault, Adjointe

***Sainte-Agathe-de-Lotbinière:* Bibliothèque municipale Rayons d'Art**
402A, rue Gosford ouest, Sainte-Agathe-de-Lotbinière QC G0S 2A0
Tél: 418-599-2830; *Téléc:* 418-599-2905
rayons@coopsteagathe.com
www.reseaubiblioduquebec.qc.ca/sainte-agathe
Denise Allard-Martineau, Responsable

***Sainte-Agathe-des-Monts:* Bibliothèque municipale de Sainte-Agathe-des-Monts**
10, rue St-Donat, Sainte-Agathe-des-Monts QC J8C 1P5
Tél: 819-326-2848
biblio49@crsbpl.qc.ca
France Bélanger, Responsable

***Sainte-Angèle-de-Mérici:* Bibliothèque de Sainte-Angèle-de-Mérici**
23, rue de la Fabrique, Sainte-Angèle-de-Mérici QC G0J 2H0
Tél: 418-775-6436
biblio.merici@crsbp.net
www.reseaubiblioduquebec.qc.ca
Guylaine Hudon, Responsable

***Sainte-Angèle-de-Monnoir:* Bibliothèque Sainte-Angèle-de-Monnoir**
1, rue des Loisirs, Sainte-Angèle-de-Monnoir QC J0L 1P0
Tél: 450-460-3644

***Sainte-Angèle-de-Prémont:* Bibliothèque de Sainte-Angèle-de-Prémont**
2451, rue Camirand, Sainte-Angèle-de-Prémont QC J0K 1R0
Tél: 819-268-5079; *Téléc:* 819-268-5536
biblio124@reseaubibliocqlm.qc.ca
www.reseaubiblioduquebec.qc.ca
Denis Beauregard, Responsable

***Sainte-Anne-de-la-Pérade:* Bibliothèque de Sainte-Anne-de-la-Pérade (Armand-Goulet)**
100, rue de la Fabrique, Sainte-Anne-de-la-Pérade QC G0X 2J0
Tél: 418-325-2216; *Téléc:* 418-325-3070
biblio014@reseaubibliocqlm.qc.ca
www.reseaubiblioduquebec.qc.ca
Cécile Fortier, Responsable

***Sainte-Anne-des-Lacs:* Bibliothèque de Sainte-Anne-des-Lacs**
723 chemin Ste-Anne-des-Lacs, Sainte-Anne-des-Lacs QC J0R 1B0
Tél: 450-224-8332; *Téléc:* 450-224-8672
biblio26@crsbpl.qc.ca
www.reseaubiblioduquebec.qc.ca
Hélène Limoges, Responsable

***Sainte-Anne-des-Monts:* Bibliothèque municipale Blanche-Lamontagne**
120, 7e rue ouest, Sainte-Anne-des-Monts QC G4V 2L2
Tél: 418-763-3810; *Téléc:* 418-763-3400
bbosadm@globetrotter.qc.ca
www.villesainte-anne-des-monts.qc.ca/html/biblio.php
Monique Campion
418-763-3810

***Sainte-Anne-des-Plaines:* Bibliothèque publique de Sainte-Anne-des-Plaines**
155, rue des Cèdres, Sainte-Anne-des-Plaines QC J0N 1H0
Tél: 450-478-4337; *Téléc:* 450-478-6733
biblio.sadp@videotron.ca
www.ville.ste-anne-des-plaines.qc.ca/biblio/
Sylviane Dubé, Directrice

***Sainte-Anne-du-Lac:* Bibliothèque de Sainte-Anne-du-Lac**
1B, rue St-François-Xavier, Sainte-Anne-du-Lac QC J0W 1V0
Tél: 819-586-2161; *Téléc:* 819-586-2203
bibsadl@tlb.sympatico.ca
www.reseaubiblioduquebec.qc.ca
Sylvie Giard, Responsable
819-586-2856
Johanne Mélançon, Bénévole
819-586-2198
Claudette Bigras, Bénévole
819-586-2094
Nicole Bélisle, Bénévole
819-586-2408

***Sainte-Aurélie:* Bibliothèque Le Maillon**
151B, ch des Bois-Francs, Sainte-Aurélie QC G0M 1M0
Tél: 418-593-3021; *Téléc:* 418-593-3961
maillon@sogetel.net
www.reseaubiblioduquebec.qc.ca/sainte-aurelie/
JoAnne Leclerc, Responsable
Christiane Giguère, Adjointe

***Sainte-Barbe:* Bibliothèque municipale Lucie Benoît**
468, ch de l'Église, Sainte-Barbe QC J0S 1P0
Tél: 450-371-2424
barbe@reseaubibliomonteregie.qc.ca
Lucie Benoît, Responsable

***Sainte-Béatrix:* Bibliothèque de Sainte-Béatrix**
Pavillon du Village, Sainte-Béatrix QC J0K 1Y0
Tél: 450-883-2245; *Téléc:* 450-883-1772
administration@stebeatrix.com
www.sainte-beatrix.com
Micheline Thibault, Responsable

***Sainte-Brigide-d'Iberville:* Bibliothèque de Sainte-Brigide-d'Iberville**
#100, 509, 9e rang, Sainte-Brigide-d'Iberville QC J0J 1X0
Tél: 450-293-4363; *Téléc:* 450-293-1243
administration@sainte-brigide.qc.ca
www.sainte-brigide.qc.ca
Francine Belzile, Responsable
450-293-7358

***Sainte-Brigitte-de-Laval:* Bibliothèque Le Trivent**
3, rue du Couvent, Sainte-Brigitte-de-Laval QC G0A 3K0
Tél: 418-666-4666; *Téléc:* 418-825-3114
trivent.bibli@csdps.qc.ca
www.reseaubiblioduquebec.qc.ca/sainte-brigitte/
Marie-Ôve Joubert, Responsable
Carole Gagnon, Adjointe

***Sainte-Brigitte-des-Saults:* Bibliothèque de Sainte-Brigitte-des-Saults**
400, rue Principale, Sainte-Brigitte-des-Saults QC J0C 1E0
Tél: 819-336-4460; *Téléc:* 819-336-4410
biblio043@reseaubibliocqlm.qc.ca
www.reseaubiblioduquebec.qc.ca
Jocelyne Guérin, Responsable
Jocelyne Guilbault, Bénévole

***Sainte-Catherine:* Bibliothèque publique de Sainte-Catherine**
5365, boul St-Laurent, Sainte-Catherine QC J5C 1A6
Tél: 450-632-0590; *Téléc:* 450-632-9908
bibliotheque@ville.sainte-catherine.qc.ca
www.ville.sainte-catherine.qc.ca/francais/biblio_accueil.html
Lise Forcier, Directrice
Véronique Desautels, Technicienne en documentation

***Sainte-Cécile-de-Lévrard:* Bibliothèque de Sainte-Cécile-de-Lévrard**
234, rue Principale, Sainte-Cécile-de-Lévrard QC G0X 2M0
Tél: 819-263-0368; *Téléc:* 819-263-2104
biblio113@reseaubibliocqlm.qc.ca
www.reseaubiblioduquebec.qc.ca
Yvette Demers, Responsable

***Sainte-Cécile-de-Masham:* Bibliothèque de Sainte-Cécile-de-Masham (La Pêche)**
5, rue Principale ouest, Sainte-Cécile-de-Masham QC J0X 2W0
Tél: 819-456-2627; *Téléc:* 819-456-4228
admmasham@crsbpo.qc.ca
www.reseaubiblioduquebec.qc.ca/Masham
Gisèle Duguay, Responsable

Sainte-Christine: **Bibliothèque municipale de Sainte-Christine**
629, rue des Loisirs, Sainte-Christine QC J0H 1H0
Tél: 819-858-2828
christine@reseaubibliomonteregie.qc.ca
www.reseaubiblioduquebec.qc.ca
Rosalie Proulx, Responsable

Sainte-Claire: **Bibliothèque municipale de Sainte-Claire**
135, rue Principale, Sainte-Claire QC G0R 2V0
Tél: 418-883-3314; *Téléc:* 418-883-3845
msclaire@globetrotter.qc.ca
Serge Gagnon, Directeur général et secrétaire-trésorier
sgagn@globetrotter.net
418-883-3314

Sainte-Clotilde-de-Beauce: **Bibliothèque municipale de Sainte-Clotilde-de-Beauce**
307, rue du Couvent, Sainte-Clotilde-de-Beauce QC G0N 1C0
Tél: 418-427-2018; *Téléc:* 418-427-2637
pp307@hotmail.com
Paulette Pomerleau, Responsable
418-427-2181
Angèle Grenier, Responsable au prêt (adm.)
418-427-2392
Jocelyne G. Prévost, Responsable des statistiques (adm.)
418-427-5151
Suzanne Therrien, Responsable des PIB (sec. adm.)
418-427-2558

Saint-Edmond-les-Plaines: **Bibliothèque publique de Saint-Edmond**
561, rue Principale, Saint-Edmond-les-Plaines QC G0W 2M0
Tél: 418-274-2591; *Téléc:* 418-274-5629
stedmond@reseaubiblioslsj.qc.ca
Lucie Coté, Responsable

Saint-Édouard: **Bibliothèque municipale de Saint-Édouard**
405B, Montée Lussier, Saint-Édouard QC J0L 1Y0
Tél: 450-454-2056
edouard@reseaubibliomonteregie.qc.ca
www.reseaubiblioduquebec.qc.ca
Fleurette Michaud, Responsable

Saint-Edouard-de-Lotbinière: **Bibliothèque municipale de Saint-Édouard-de-Lotbinière**
105, rue de L'École, Saint-Edouard-de-Lotbinière QC G0S 1Y0
Tél: 418-796-2433; *Téléc:* 418-796-2228
biblsted@globetrotter.qc.ca
Patricia McDonald, Responsable
Diane Chabot, Secretaire-trésorière
Pierre Luc Daigle, Responsable des activités

Saint-Édouard-de-Maskinongé: **Bibliothèque de Saint-Édouard-de-Maskinongé**
3851, rue Notre-Dame, Saint-Édouard-de-Maskinongé QC J0K 2H0
Tél: 819-268-2883
biblio123@reseaubibliocqlm.qc.ca
www.reseaubiblioduquebec.qc.ca
Hélène Robert, Responsable

Sainte-Elisabeth-de-Proulx: **Bibliothèque publique de Sainte-Elisabeth-de-Proulx**
1254, rue Principale, Sainte-Elisabeth-de-Proulx QC G8M 4V2
Tél: 418-276-9494
elisabeth@reseaubiblioslsj.qc.ca
www.reseaubiblioduquebec.qc.ca/portail/index.aspx?page=3&BID=5
Rosanne Carrier-Simard, Responsable

Sainte-Elizabeth: **Bibliothèque de Sainte-Elisabeth (Françoise-Allard-Bérard)**
2270, rue Principale, Sainte-Elizabeth QC J0K 2J0
Tél: 450-759-2875
biblio068@reseaubibliocqlm.qc.ca
www.reseaubiblioduquebec.qc.ca
Josette Lamontagne, Responsable

Sainte-Élizabeth-de-Warwick: **Bibliothèque de Sainte-Élizabeth-de-Warwick**
228, rue Principale, Sainte-Élizabeth-de-Warwick QC J0A 1M0
Tél: 819-358-2429; *Téléc:* 819-358-9192
biblio141@reseaubibliocqlm.qc.ca
www.reseaubiblioduquebec.qc.ca
Christiane Luscher, Responsable
819-358-6980

Céline Parenteau, Adjointe
Denise Gagnon, Bénévole
Pierrette Martel Leblanc, Bénévole
Cécile Morin, Bénévole

Sainte-Émélie-de-l'Énergie: **Bibliothèque de Sainte-Émélie-de-l'Énergie**
241, rue Coutu, Sainte-Émélie-de-l'Énergie QC J0K 2K0
Tél: 450-886-3823; *Téléc:* 450-886-9175
biblio053@reseaubibliocqlm.qc.ca
www.reseaubiblioduquebec.qc.ca
Diane Durand, Responsable

Sainte-Eulalie: **Bibliothèque de Sainte-Eulalie**
757A, rue des Bouleaux, Sainte-Eulalie QC G0Z 1E0
Tél: 819-225-8069; *Téléc:* 819-225-4078
biblio074@reseaubibliocqlm.qc.ca
www.reseaubiblioduquebec.qc.ca
Marjolaine Rheault, Responsable
819-225-4434

Sainte-Famille: **Bibliothèque municipale de Sainte-Famille**
3912-1, ch Royal, Sainte-Famille QC G0A 3P0
Tél: 418-666-4666; *Téléc:* 418-829-2513
biblisfa@csdps.qc.ca
www.reseaubiblioduquebec.qc.ca/sainte-famille
Ernest Labranche, Responsable

Sainte-Flavie: **Bibliothèque Olivar-Asselin**
505, rte de la Mer, Sainte-Flavie QC G0J 2L0
Tél: 418-775-7050
biblio.flavie@crsbp.net
www.reseaubiblioduquebec.qc.ca
Liz Fortin, Responsable

Sainte-Florence: **Bibliothèque de Sainte-Florence**
29, rue des Loisirs, Sainte-Florence QC G0J 2M0
Tél: 418-756-5079
biblio.florence@crsbp.net
www.reseaubiblioduquebec.qc.ca
Gaétane Morin, Responsable

Sainte-Françoise: **Bibliothèque de Sainte-Françoise (Bas-Saint-Laurent)**
31, rue Principale, Sainte-Françoise QC G0L 3B0
Tél: 418-851-3878
biblio.francoise@crsbp.net
www.reseaubiblioduquebec.qc.ca
Édith Rioux, Responsable

Sainte-Françoise: **Bibliothèque de Sainte-Françoise (Centre-du-Québec)**
563, rue Principale, Sainte-Françoise QC G0S 2N0
Tél: 819-287-5838
biblio104@reseaubibliocqlm.qc.ca
www.reseaubiblioduquebec.qc.ca
Diane Bélanger, Responsable

Sainte-Germaine-Boulé: **Bibliothèque de Sainte-Germaine-Boulé**
240, rue Roy, Sainte-Germaine-Boulé QC J0Z 1M0
Tél: 819-787-6477; *Téléc:* 819-787-6477
boule@reseaubiblioatnq.qc.ca
www.reseaubiblioduquebec.qc.ca
Odette Rancourt Audet, Responsable

Sainte-Hedwidge-de-Roberval: **Bibliothèque publique de Sainte-Hedwidge**
1090, rue Principale, Sainte-Hedwidge-de-Roberval QC G0W 2R0
Tél: 418-275-4318
hedwidge@reseaubiblioslsj.qc.ca
www.reseaubiblioduquebec.qc.ca
Michelle Morin, Responsable
418-275-4963
Marie Gagnon, Représentante municipale
Josée-Anne Rodrigue, Bénévole
Hélène Langlais, Bénévole
Denise Bonneau, Bénévole
Dominique Harvey, Bénévole
Caroline Privé, Bénévole
Guy Privé, Bénévole
Carole-Anne Morin, Bénévole

Sainte-Hélène: **Bibliothèque de Sainte-Hélène**
707, rue du Couvent, Sainte-Hélène QC G0L 3J0
Tél: 418-492-3819
biblio.helene@crsbp.net
www.reseaubiblioduquebec.qc.ca
Lucie Bérubé, Responsable
lucieberube42@hotmail.com
418-492-3324

Sainte-Hélène-de-Bagot: **Bibliothèque municipale de Sainte-Hélène-de-Bagot**
384, 6e av, Sainte-Hélène-de-Bagot QC J0H 1M0
Tél: 450-791-2618
helene@reseaubibliomonteregie.qc.ca
www.reseaubiblioduquebec.qc.ca
France Vachon, Responsable

Sainte-Hénédine: **Bibliothèque La Détente/Sainte-Hénédine**
111, rue Principale, Sainte-Hénédine QC G0S 2R0
Tél: 418-935-3993; *Téléc:* 418-935-3113
biblsthe@globetrotter.qc.ca
www.reseaubiblioduquebec.qc.ca/sainte-henedine/
Doris Drouin-Dubreuil, Responsable
Jocelyne Cyr, Adjointe
Louise Bédard, Responsable, PIB
Lise Dion, Responsable, Collection locale

Sainte-Irène: **Bibliothèque de Sainte-Irène**
362, rue de la Fabrique, Sainte-Irène QC G0J 1P0
Tél: 418-629-5705
biblio.irene@crsbp.net
www.reseaubiblioduquebec.qc.ca
Sylvie Chenel, Responsable

Sainte-Julie: **Bibliothèque municipale de Sainte-Julie**
1600, ch du Fer-à-Cheval, Sainte-Julie QC J3E 2M1
Tél: 450-922-7070; *Téléc:* 450-922-7077
biblio@ville.sainte-julie.qc.ca
Marie-Hélène Parent, Bibliothécaire en chef
mhparent@ville.sainte-julie.qc.ca
450-922-7115 ext. 7071

Sainte-Julienne: **Bibliothèque Gisèle-Paré**
2550, rue Marcel-Masse, Sainte-Julienne QC J0K 2T0
Tél: 450-831-3811; *Téléc:* 450-831-4433
biblio43@crsbpl.qc.ca
www.reseaubiblioduquebec.qc.ca/sainte-julienne
Marielle Rompré, Responsable
Carmen Vézina, Adjointe

Saint-Élie-de-Caxton: **Bibliothèque de Saint-Élie-de-Caxton**
50, ch des Loisirs, Saint-Élie-de-Caxton QC G0X 2N0
Tél: 819-221-4095
biblio115@reseaubibliocqlm.qc.ca
www.reseaubiblioduquebec.qc.ca
Charline Plante, Responsable

Saint-Éloi: **Bibliothèque de Saint-Éloi**
456, rue Principale, Saint-Éloi QC G0L 2V0
biblio.eloi@crsbp.net
www.reseaubiblioduquebec.qc.ca
Rachel Tardif, Responsable

Sainte-Louise: **Bibliothèque Idée-Lire**
506, rue Principale, Sainte-Louise QC G0R 3K0
Tél: 418-354-7730
www.reseaubiblioduquebec.qc.ca/sainte-louise
Jacqueline Lizotte, Responsable

Saint-Elphège: **Bibliothèque de Saint-Elphège (La Bouquinerie)**
227A, rue de l'Église, Saint-Elphège QC J0G 1J0
Tél: 450-568-7339; *Téléc:* 450-568-0288
biblio007@reseaubibliocqlm.qc.ca
www.reseaubiblioduquebec.qc.ca
Monique Champagne Lemire, Responsable

Sainte-Luce: **Bibliothèque de Luceville**
67, rue Saint-Pierre est, Sainte-Luce QC G0K 1P0
Tél: 418-739-3534
biblio.luceville@crsbp.net
www.reseaubiblioduquebec.qc.ca
Sylvanne Saint-Laurent, Responsable

Sainte-Luce: **Bibliothèque de Sainte-Luce**
1, rue Langlois, Sainte-Luce QC G0K 1P0
Tél: 418-739-3393
biblio.luce@crsbp.net
www.reseaubiblioduquebec.qc.ca
Luc Bourassa, Responsable

Sainte-Lucie-de-Beauregard: **Bibliothèque A la Bouquinerie**
21, rte des Chutes, Sainte-Lucie-de-Beauregard QC G0R 3L0
Tél: 418-223-3122; *Téléc:* 418-223-3121
www.reseaubiblioduquebec.qc.ca/sainte-lucie
Huguette Rouillard, Responsable
418-223-3613

***Saint-Elzéar:* Bibliothèque de Saint-Elzéar**
144, ch Principal, Saint-Elzéar QC G0C 2W0
Tél: 418-534-4314; *Téléc:* 418-534-2626
www.reseaubiblioduquebec.qc.ca
Lucille Ferlatte, Responsable

***Saint-Elzéar-de-Témiscouata:* Bibliothèque de Saint-Elzéar (Saint-Elzéar-de-Témiscouata)**
320, rue Principale, Saint-Elzéar-de-Témiscouata QC G0L 2W0
Tél: 418-534-3513
biblio.elzear@crsbp.net
www.reseaubiblioduquebec.qc.ca
Thérèse Sirois, Responsable

***Sainte-Madeleine:* Bibliothèque municipale de Sainte-Madeleine**
1040A, rue Saint-Simon, Sainte-Madeleine QC J0H 1S0
Tél: 450-795-3959; *Téléc:* 450-795-3736
madeleine@reseaubibliomonteregie.qc.ca
www.reseaubiblioduquebec.qc.ca
Cathy Collins, Responsable

***Sainte-Marguerite:* Biblio La Bouquine**
235, rue Saint-Jacques, Sainte-Marguerite QC G0S 2X0
Tél: 418-935-7089; *Téléc:* 418-935-3709
www.reseaubiblioduquebec.qc.ca/sainte-marguerite/
Adrienne Gagné, Responsable

***Sainte-Marguerite:* Bibliothèque de Sainte-Marguerite**
15, rue de la Vérendrye, Sainte-Marguerite QC G0J 2Y0
Tél: 418-756-3364
biblio.margot@crsbp.net
www.reseaubiblioduquebec.qc.ca
Colette Marquis, Responsable

***Sainte-Marie:* Bibliothèque Honorius-Provost**
80, rue St-Antoine, Sainte-Marie QC G6E 4B8
Tél: 418-387-2240; *Téléc:* 418-387-2454
jacques.filiatrault@sainte-marie.ca
www.ville.sainte-marie.qc.ca
Jacques Filiatrault, Responsable

***Sainte-Marie-de-Blandford:* Bibliothèque de Sainte-Marie-de-Blandford**
492, rue des Bosquets, Sainte-Marie-de-Blandford QC G0X 2W0
Tél: 819-283-2127; *Téléc:* 819-283-2169
biblio108@reseaubibliocqlm.qc.ca
www.reseaubiblioduquebec.qc.ca
Carmen Bilodeau, Responsable

***Sainte-Marie-Salomé:* Bibliothèque de Sainte-Marie-Salomé**
121, rue Viger, Sainte-Marie-Salomé QC J0K 2Z0
Tél: 450-839-6212; *Téléc:* 450-753-5236
biblio050@reseaubibliocqlm.qc.ca
www.reseaubiblioduquebec.qc.ca
Diane Éthier, Responsable

***Sainte-Marthe-sur-le-Lac:* Bibliothèque municipale de Sainte-Marthe-sur-le-Lac**
3003, ch Oka, Sainte-Marthe-sur-le-Lac QC J0N 1P0
Tél: 450-974-7111; *Téléc:* 450-974-7110
www.saintemarthesurlelac.qc.ca/contenu.aspx?page=154
Micheline Aloi, Commis senior
450-947-7111

***Sainte-Mélanie:* Bibliothèque de Sainte-Mélanie (Louise-Amélie-Panet)**
940, rue Principale, Sainte-Mélanie QC J0K 3A0
Tél: 450-889-5871
biblio111@reseaubibliocqlm.qc.ca
www.reseaubiblioduquebec.qc.ca
Martin Alarie, Responsable

***Saint-Émile-de-Suffolk:* Bibliothèque de Saint-Émile-de-Suffolk**
299, route des Cantons, Saint-Émile-de-Suffolk QC J0V 1Y0
Tél: 819-426-2987; *Téléc:* 819-426-3447
biblio.stemile@mrcpapineau.com
www.reseaubiblioduquebec.qc.ca
Georgette Haineault, Responsable

***Sainte-Monique:* Bibliothèque de Sainte-Monique**
247, rue Principale, Sainte-Monique QC J0G 1N0
Tél: 819-289-2051; *Téléc:* 819-289-2344
biblio052@reseaubibliocqlm.qc.ca
www.reseaubiblioduquebec.qc.ca
Pierrette Beauchemin, Responsable

***Sainte-Monique-Lac-St-Jean:* Bibliothèque publique de Sainte-Monique**
138, rue Honfleur, Sainte-Monique-Lac-St-Jean QC G0W 2T0
Tél: 418-347-4391
monique@reseaubiblioslsj.qc.ca
www.reseaubiblioduquebec.qc.ca/portail/index.aspx?page=3&BI D=5
Normande Gauthier, Directrice

***Sainte-Paule:* Bibliothèque de Sainte-Paule**
102, rue Banville, Sainte-Paule QC G0J 3C0
Tél: 418-737-1378
biblio.paule@crsbp.net
www.reseaubiblioduquebec.qc.ca
Carmen Côté-D'Amour, Responsable

***Sainte-Perpétue:* Bibliothèque de Sainte-Perpétue**
2504, rang St-Joseph, Sainte-Perpétue QC J0C 1R0
Tél: 819-336-6275
biblio094@reseaubibliocqlm.qc.ca
www.reseaubiblioduquebec.qc.ca
Colette Laplante, Responsable

***Sainte-Pétronille:* Bibliothèque municipale de Sainte-Pétronille**
3, ch de l'Église, Sainte-Pétronille QC G0A 4C0
Tél: 418-828-2270; *Téléc:* 418-828-1364
bibliospetro@qc.aira.com
www.reseaubiblioduquebec.qc.ca/sainte-petronille
Lise Paquet, Responsable

***Saint-Épiphane:* Bibliothèque de Saint-Épiphane**
216, rue du Couvent, Saint-Épiphane QC G0L 2X0
Tél: 418-867-3225
biblio.epiphane@crsbp.net
www.reseaubiblioduquebec.qc.ca
Jacqueline Jalbert, Responsable

***Sainte-Rita:* Bibliothèque Sainte-Rita**
23, rue de L'Église est, Sainte-Rita QC G0L 4G0
Tél: 418-963-2967
biblio.rita@crsbp.net
www.reseaubiblioduquebec.qc.ca
Lucille Turcotte, Responsable

***Sainte-Rose-de-Watford:* Bibliothèque municipale de Sainte-Rose-de-Watford**
693, rue Carrier, Sainte-Rose-de-Watford QC G0R 4G0
Tél: 418-267-5264; *Téléc:* 418-267-5812
biblioste-rose@sogetel.net
www.reseaubiblioduquebec.qc.ca/sainte-rose
Lisette Gagnon, Responsable
jlcya@sogetel.net
418-267-5721
Nicole Bisier, Vice-responsable
418-267-5491
Lorraine Roy, Secrétaire
418-267-4512

***Sainte-Rose-du-Nord:* Bibliothèque publique de Ste-Rose-du-Nord**
126, rue Descente-des-Femmes, Sainte-Rose-du-Nord QC G0V 1T0
Tél: 418-675-2250
ste-rose@reseaubiblioslsj.qc.ca
www.reseaubiblioduquebec.qc.ca/portail/index.aspx?page=3&BI D=5
Lise Clermont, Responsable

***Sainte-Sabine:* Bibliothèque Sabithèque**
#203, 4, rue St-Charles, Sainte-Sabine QC G0R 4H0
Tél: 418-383-5788; *Téléc:* 418-383-5488
www.reseaubiblioduquebec.qc.ca/sainte-sabine/
Micheline Cyr, Responsable
Solange Mercier, Adjointe

***Sainte-Sophie-de-Lévrard:* Bibliothèque de Sainte-Sophie-de-Lévrard**
184A, rue St-Antoine, Sainte-Sophie-de-Lévrard QC G0X 3C0
Tél: 819-288-0334; *Téléc:* 819-288-5804
biblio102@reseaubibliocqlm.qc.ca
www.reseaubiblioduquebec.qc.ca
Daniel Désilets, Responsable

***Saint-Esprit:* Bibliothèque de Saint-Esprit (Alice-Parizeau)**
45, rue des Écoles, Saint-Esprit QC J0K 2L0
Tél: 450-831-2274; *Téléc:* 450-839-6070
biblio125@reseaubibliocqlm.qc.ca
Diane Lamarre, Responsable

***Sainte-Thècle:* Bibliothèque de Sainte-Thècle**
301, rue St-Jacques, Sainte-Thècle QC G0X 3G0
Tél: 418-289-3717; *Téléc:* 418-289-3014
biblio016@reseaubibliocqlm.qc.ca
www.reseaubiblioduquebec.qc.ca
Thérèse Lemelin, Responsable

***Sainte-Thérèse:* Bibliothèque municipale de Sainte-Thérèse**
150, boul du Séminaire, Sainte-Thérèse QC J7E 1Z2
Tél: 450-434-1442; *Téléc:* 450-434-6070
ltheriault@ville.sainte-therese.qc.ca
ville.sainte-therese.qc.ca
Lise Thériault, Directrice
Nicole Bouchard, Technicienne, réference, animation, PEB

***Saint-Étienne-de-Beauharnoi:* Bibliothèque municipale de Saint-Étienne-de-Beauharnois**
430, rue de l'Église, Saint-Étienne-de-Beauharnois QC J0S 1S0
Tél: 450-429-6384; *Téléc:* 450-429-6384
etienne@reseaubibliomonteregie.qc.ca
Carole Lalande, Responsable
Francine Boyer, Gestion du PIB et Administration des systèmes informatiques

***Saint-Étienne-des-Grès:* Bibliothèque de Saint-Étienne-des-Grès**
#300, 190, rue Saint-Honoré, Saint-Étienne-des-Grès QC G0X 2P0
Tél: 819-535-5192
biblio019@reseaubibliocqlm.qc.ca
www.reseaubiblioduquebec.qc.ca
Denis Boisvert, Responsable

***Saint-Étienne-des-Grès:* Bibliothèque de Saint-Thomas-de-Caxton**
332, rue des Loisirs, Saint-Étienne-des-Grès QC G0X 2P0
Tél: 819-296-3004
biblio105@reseaubibliocqlm.qc.ca
www.reseaubiblioduquebec.qc.ca
France Bournival, Responsable

***Saint-Eugène:* Bibliothèque publique de Saint-Eugène**
469, rue Principale, Saint-Eugène QC G0W 1B0
Tél: 418-276-7790
steugene@reseaubiblioslsj.qc.ca
www.reseaubiblioduquebec.qc.ca
Lise Lavoie, Responsable
Pauline Dumont, Adjointe

***Saint-Eugène-de-Guigues:* Bibliothèque de Saint-Eugène-de-Guigues**
4, 1ère av ouest, Saint-Eugène-de-Guigues QC J0Z 3L0
Tél: 819-785-4441; *Téléc:* 819-785-2301
eugene@reseaubiblioatnq.qc.ca
www.reseaubiblioduquebec.qc.ca
Lorraine Falardeau, Responsable

***Sainte-Ursule:* Bibliothèque de Sainte-Ursule (C.-J. Magnan)**
215, rue Lessard, Sainte-Ursule QC J0K 3M0
Tél: 819-228-0735; *Téléc:* 819-228-8326
biblio031@reseaubibliocqlm.qc.ca
Suzanne Pilon, Responsable
Lisette Bergeron, Bénévole
Dominique Côté, Bénévole

***Saint-Eusèbe:* Bibliothèque de Saint-Eusèbe**
222B, rue Principale, Saint-Eusèbe QC G0L 2Y0
Tél: 418-899-0150
biblio.eusebe@crsbp.net
www.reseaubiblioduquebec.qc.ca
Gisèle Lebrun Bolduc, Responsable
Sébastien Meunier, Adjoint

***Saint-Eustache:* Bibliothèque municipale Guy-Bélisle**
80, boul Arthur-Sauvé, Saint-Eustache QC J7R 2H7
Tél: 450-974-5035; *Téléc:* 450-974-5054
ngrimard@ville.saint-eustache.qc.ca
biblio.ville.saint-eustache.qc.ca
Nicole Grimard, Responsable
ngrimard@ville.saint-eustache.qc.ca
Danielle Touchette, Technicienne, Animation/Référence
France Genest, Bibliothécaire adjointe
Rina Dupuis, Préposée acquisitions

Sainte-Victoire-de-Sorel: **Bibliothèque municipale de Sainte-Victoire-de-Sorel**
519, ch Ste-Victoire, Sainte-Victoire-de-Sorel QC J0G 1T0
Tél: 450-782-3111
victoire@reseaubibliomonteregie.qc.ca
Micheline Lamoureux, Responsable
Josée Paquette, Responsable, Échanges
Lucille Ayotte, Responsable, Collection locale

Saint-Fabien: **Bibliothèque de Saint-Fabien**
10, 7e Avenue, Saint-Fabien QC G0L 2Z0
Tél: 418-869-2602
biblio.fabien@crsbp.net
www.reseaubiblioduquebec.qc.ca
Raynald Beaulieu, Responsable

Saint-Fabien-de-Panet: **Bibliothèque Fabiothèque/Saint-Fabien-de-Panet**
199, rue Bilodeau, Saint-Fabien-de-Panet QC G0R 2J0
Tél: 418-249-4417; *Téléc:* 418-249-2507
fabiot@globetrotter.qc.ca
www.reseaubiblioduquebec.qc.ca/saint-fabien-de-panet
Michèle Thibodeau, Responsable
418-249-2732

Saint-Faustin-Lac-Carré: **Bibliothèque du Lac**
64, rue de la Culture, Saint-Faustin-Lac-Carré QC J0T 1J1
Tél: 819-688-5434; *Téléc:* 819-688-5644
bibliodulac@municipalite.stfaustin.qc.ca
www.crsbpl.qc.ca/bibliotheques/Saint-Faustin-Lac-Carre.html
Marielle Jacques, Responsable
Nicole Morel, Commis aux prêts
819-688-2645

Saint-Félicien: **Bibliothèque municipale de Saint-Félicien**
#200, 1209, boul Sacré Coeur, Saint-Félicien QC G8K 2R5
Tél: 418-679-2100; *Téléc:* 418-679-1449
biblio@ville.stfelicien.qc.ca
www.stfelicien.biblio.qc.ca
Johanne Laprise, Responsable
Francine Ménard, Technicienne en documentation

Saint-Félicien: **Bibliothèque publique de Saint-Méthode**
3159, rue Saint-Méthode, Saint-Félicien QC G8K 3C2
Tél: 418-679-0757
stmethode@reseaubibliosIsj.qc.ca
Thérèse Fortin, Responsable

Saint-Félix-d'Otis: **Bibliothèque publique de Saint-Félix-d'Otis**
455, rue Principale, Saint-Félix-d'Otis QC G0V 1M0
Tél: 418-544-1144
stfelix@reseaubibliosIsj.qc.ca
www.reseaubiblioduquebec.qc.ca/portail/index.aspx?page=3&BI D=5
Nathalie Simard, Responsable

Saint-Félix-de-Kingsey: **Bibliothèque de Saint-Félix-de-Kingsey**
6105-B, rue Principale, Saint-Félix-de-Kingsey QC J0B 2T0
Tél: 819-848-1400
biblio152@reseaubibliocqlm.qc.ca
www.reseaubiblioduquebec.qc.ca
Pauline Roy, Responsable

Saint-Félix-de-Valois: **Bibliothèque de Saint-Félix-de-Valois**
4863, rue Principale, Saint-Félix-de-Valois QC J0K 2M0
Tél: 450-889-5589; *Téléc:* 450-889-7911
biblio010@reseaubibliocqlm.qc.ca
Suzie Thériault, Responsable

Saint-Ferdinand: **Bibliothèque de Saint-Ferdinand (Onil-Garneau)**
620, rue Notre-Dame, Saint-Ferdinand QC G0N 1N0
Tél: 418-428-9607
biblio049@reseaubibliocqlm.qc.ca
Lucie Lamontagne, Responsable

Saint-Ferréol-les-Neiges: **Bibliothèque Aux Sources/Saint-Ferréol-les-Neiges**
33, rue de l'Église, Saint-Ferréol-les-Neiges QC G0A 3R0
Tél: 418-826-3540; *Téléc:* 418-826-0489
www.reseaubiblioduquebec.qc.ca/saint-ferreol
Lucie Bédard, Responsable
Louisette Bédard, Responsable, l'Animation

Saint-Flavien: **Bibliothèque La Flaviethèque/Saint-Flavien**
6, rue Caux, Saint-Flavien QC G0S 2M0
Tél: 418-728-0025; *Téléc:* 418-728-4190
biblifla@globetrotter.qc.ca
www.reseaubiblioduquebec.qc.ca/saint-flavien
Carole Turgeon, Responsable

Saint-Fortunat: **Bibliothèque municipale de Saint-Fortunat**
173, rue Principale, Saint-Fortunat QC G0P 1G0
Tél: 418-344-5399
www.reseaubiblioduquebec.qc.ca/saint-fortunat
Huguette Garneau, Responsable

Saint-François-d'Assise: **Bibliothèque de Saint-François-d'Assise**
457, ch Central, Saint-François-d'Assise QC G0J 2N0
Tél: 418-299-2099; *Téléc:* 418-299-3037
munstfrs@globetrotter.net
Monelle Gallant, Responsable

Saint-François-de-Sales: **Bibliothèque publique de Saint-François-de-Sales**
255, rue de l'Église, Saint-François-de-Sales QC G0W 1M0
Tél: 418-348-9444
franco@reseaubibliosIsj.qc.ca
www.reseaubiblioduquebec.qc.ca/portail/index.aspx?page=3&BI D=5
Myriam Simard, Responsable
418-348-6736

Saint-François-du-Lac: **Bibliothèque de Saint-François-du-Lac**
480, rue Notre-Dame, Saint-François-du-Lac QC J0G 1M0
Tél: 450-568-1130; *Téléc:* 450-568-7465
biblio158@reseaubibliocqlm.qc.ca
www.reseaubiblioduquebec.qc.ca
Ghislaine Lachapelle, Responsable

Saint-Fulgence: **Bibliothèque publique de Saint-Fulgence**
12, Saint-Basile, Saint-Fulgence QC G0V 1S0
Tél: 418-615-0059
stfulgence@reseaubibliosIsj.qc.ca
www.reseaubiblioduquebec.qc.ca/portail/index.aspx?page=3&BI D=5
Lina Tremblay, Responsable
418-674-2440

Saint-Gabriel-de-Brandon: **Bibliothèque de Saint-Gabriel (Au fil des pages)**
53, rue Beausoleil, Saint-Gabriel-de-Brandon QC J0K 2N0
Tél: 450-835-2212; *Téléc:* 450-835-1493
biblio013@reseaubibliocqlm.qc.ca
Noëlla Ganley, Responsable

Saint-Gabriel-de-Rimouski: **Bibliothèque Le Bouquinier**
103, rue Leblanc, Saint-Gabriel-de-Rimouski QC G0K 1M0
Tél: 418-798-8310; *Téléc:* 418-798-4108
biblio.gabriel@crsbp.net
www.reseaubiblioduquebec.qc.ca
Hélène Thibeault, Responsable
Julie Lepage, Bénévole
Julie Lavoie, Bénévole

Saint-Gédéon: **Bibliothèque publique de Saint-Gédéon**
208, Dequen, Saint-Gédéon QC G0W 2P0
Tél: 418-345-8798
stgedeon@reseaubibliosIsj.qc.ca
www.crsbpsIsj.biblio.qc.ca
Carole Gagnon, Responsable

Saint-Germain: **Bibliothèque de Saint-Germain**
506, rue de la Fabrique, Saint-Germain QC G0L 3G0
Tél: 418-492-5767
biblio.germain@crsbp.net
www.reseaubiblioduquebec.qc.ca
Simone Lévesque, Responsable

Saint-Germain-de-Grantham: **Bibliothèque de Saint-Germain-de-Grantham (Le Signet)**
299, rue Notre-Dame, Saint-Germain-de-Grantham QC J0C 1K0
Tél: 819-395-2644
biblio100@reseaubibliocqlm.qc.ca
www.reseaubiblioduquebec.qc.ca
Louise Gaillard-Simoneau, Responsable
819-395-4463
Pauline Leclerc, Bibliotechnicienne

Saint-Gervais: **Bibliothèque Faubourg de la Cadie**
36A, rue de la Fabrique est, Saint-Gervais QC G0R 3C0
Tél: 418-887-3628; *Téléc:* 418-887-3628
www.reseaubiblioduquebec.qc.ca/saint-gervais
Micheline Trudel, Responsable
Louisette Toussaint, Adjointe
Mariette Labrecque, Responsable, Animation

Saint-Gilles: **Bibliothèque Le Signet**
1540, rue du Couvent, Saint-Gilles QC G0S 2P0
Tél: 418-888-5178; *Téléc:* 418-888-5486
www.reseaubiblioduquebec.qc.ca/saint-gilles
Pascale Bélanger, Responsable
Nicole Aubert, Adjointe

Saint-Guillaume: **Bibliothèque de Saint-Guillaume**
106, rue Saint-Jean-Baptiste, Saint-Guillaume QC J0C 1L0
Tél: 819-396-3754; *Téléc:* 819-396-0184
biblio087@reseaubibliocqlm.qc.ca
www.reseaubiblioduquebec.qc.ca
Jocelyne Taillon, Responsable

Saint-Guy: **Bibliothèque de Saint-Guy**
54, ch Principal, Saint-Guy QC G0K 1W0
Tél: 418-963-1490
biblio.guy@crsbp.net
Nathalie Belisle, Responsable

Saint-Henri-de-Lévis: **Bibliothèque La Reliure/Saint-Henri**
123, rue Belleau, Saint-Henri-de-Lévis QC G0R 3E0
Tél: 418-882-0694; *Téléc:* 418-882-0302
bibhenri@globetrotter.qc.ca
www.reseaubiblioduquebec.qc.ca/saint-henri
Céline Labrecque, Responsable

Saint-Henri-de-Taillon: **Bibliothèque publique de Saint-Henri-de-Taillon**
504, rue Principale, Saint-Henri-de-Taillon QC G0W 2X0
Tél: 418-347-3243; *Téléc:* 418-347-1138
sthenri@reseaubibliosIsj.qc.ca
www.crsbpsIsj.biblio.qc.ca/st-henri-de-taillon
Chantale Fortin, Responsable
418-347-1513

Saint-Hippolyte: **Bibliothèque de Saint-Hippolyte**
871, ch des Hauteurs, Saint-Hippolyte QC J8A 1J2
Tél: 450-224-4137; *Téléc:* 450-224-9927
biblisthip@bellnet.ca
Élise Chaumont, Responsable
Joanne Bonneau, Adjointe

Saint-Honoré-de-Chicoutimi: **Bibliothèque publique de Saint-Honoré**
100, rue Paul-Aimé Hudon, Saint-Honoré-de-Chicoutimi QC G0V 1L0
Tél: 418-673-3790
biblio@ville.sthonore.qc.ca
www.reseaubiblioduquebec.qc.ca/portail/index.aspx?page=3&BI D=5
Hélène Chaput, Coordonnatrice

Saint-Honoré-de-Témiscouata: **Bibliothèque Les Moussaillons**
6B, rue de l'Église, Saint-Honoré-de-Témiscouata QC G0L 3K0
Tél: 418-497-3996
biblio.honore@crsbp.net
www.reseaubiblioduquebec.qc.ca
Hélène Paradis, Responsable
418-497-2316
Dominique Viel, Responsable, Promotion
418-497-2696

Saint-Hugues: **Bibliothèque municipale de Saint-Hugues**
207, rue Saint-Germain, Saint-Hugues QC J0H 1N0
Tél: 450-794-2630; *Téléc:* 450-794-2630
hugues@reseaubibliomonteregie.qc.ca
www.reseaubiblioduquebec.qc.ca
Marie Bernier Lavigne, Responsable

Saint-Hyacinthe: **Médiathèque maskoutaine**
2720, rue Dessaulles, Saint-Hyacinthe QC J2S 2V7
Tél: 450-773-1830; *Téléc:* 450-773-3398
www.mediatheque.qc.ca
Yves Tanguay, Directeur
tanguayy@mediatheque.qc.ca
450-773-1830 ext. 23
Marie-Hélène Charest, Responsable, Services publics
Bibliothèque T.-A.-St-Germain
450-773-1830 ext. 25

Marie-France Pineault, Secrétaire administrative
450-773-1830 ext. 21

Saint-Ignace-de-Loyola: **Bibliothèque de Saint-Ignace-de-Loyola**
621, rue de l'Église, Saint-Ignace-de-Loyola QC J0K 2P0
Tél: 450-836-1831; *Téléc:* 450-836-1400
biblio156@reseaubibliocqlm.qc.ca
www.reseaubiblioduquebec.qc.ca
Andrée Bergeron, Responsable

Saint-Irénée: **Bibliothèque Adolphe-Basile-Routhier**
136, rue Principale, Saint-Irénée QC G0T 1V0
Téléc: 418-452-8221
www.reseaubiblioduquebec.qc.ca/saint-irenee
Micheline Mongrain, Responsable
Denise Gauthier, Adjointe
Claudia Boudreault, Responsable des concours

Saint-Isidore: **Bibliothèque municipale de Saint-Isidore**
5, rue Boyer, Saint-Isidore QC J0L 2A0
Tél: 450-454-9871
isidore@reseaubibliomonteregie.qc.ca
Ginette Goyette, Responsable
Louisette Paré, Responsable, PIB
Nicole Dubuc, Responsable, Échanges

Saint-Isidore: **Bibliothèque municipale La Livrerie**
126, rte Coulombe, Saint-Isidore QC G0S 2S0
Tél: 418-882-5670; *Téléc:* 418-882-5902
www.reseaubiblioduquebec.qc.ca/saint-isidore
Catherine-Émilie Martel, Responsable

Saint-Jacques: **Bibliothèque municipale Marcel-Dugas**
16, rue Maréchal, Saint-Jacques QC J0K 2R0
Tél: 450-839-3926; *Téléc:* 450-839-2387
biblio@st-jacques.org
www.st-jacques.org/bibli/index.html
Francine Roy-Gaudet, Responsable

Saint-Jacques-de-Leeds: **Bibliothèque La Ressource**
425, rue Principale, Saint-Jacques-de-Leeds QC G0N 1J0
Tél: 418-424-3181; *Téléc:* 418-424-0126
www.reseaubiblioduquebec.qc.ca/leeds/
Louise Dionne, Responsable
Martine Bolduc, Responsable, PIB
Sylvie Tanguay, Responsable, Échanges

Saint-Jacques-le-Mineur: **Bibliothèque municipale de Saint-Jacques-le-Mineur**
89, rue Principale, Saint-Jacques-le-Mineur QC J0J 1Z0
Tél: 450-347-1888; *Téléc:* 450-347-5754
jacques@reseaubibliomonteregie.qc.ca
Benoît D'Avignon, Responsable

Saint-Janvier-de-Joly: **Bibliothèque Adrien-Lambert/Saint-Janvier-de-Joly**
729, rue des Loisirs, Saint-Janvier-de-Joly QC G0S 1M0
Tél: 418-728-2984; *Téléc:* 418-728-2984
adrienlambert1936@hotmail.com
www.reseaubiblioduquebec.qc.ca/joly
Marielle Sylvain, Responsable
mariebouffonsylvain@hotmail.com
Monique Turmel, Adjointe

Saint-Jean-Baptiste: **Bibliothèque municipale de Saint-Jean-Baptiste**
3090, rue Principale, Saint-Jean-Baptiste QC J0L 2B0
Tél: 450-467-1786
jean.baptiste@reseaubibliomonteregie.qc.ca
Sylvie Sweeney, Responsable

Saint-Jean-Chrysostome: **Bibliothèques Lévis**
959, rue de l'Hôtel-de-Ville, Saint-Jean-Chrysostome QC G6Z 2N8
Tél: 418-835-4982; *Téléc:* 418-839-2640
bibliolevis@ville.levis.qc.ca
bibliotheques.ville.levis.qc.ca
Suzanne Rochefort, Chef du service des bibliothèques
srochefort@ville.levis.qc.ca

Saint-Jean-de-Brébeuf: **Bibliothèque Bibliomagie/Saint-Jean-de-Brébeuf**
844, rue de l'Église, Saint-Jean-de-Brébeuf QC G6G 0A1
Tél: 418-453-2571; *Téléc:* 418-453-2339
www.reseaubiblioduquebec.qc.ca/saint-jean-de-brebeuf
Solange Bolduc, Responsable

Saint-Jean-de-Dieu: **Bibliothèque de Saint-Jean-de-Dieu**
32, rue Principale sud, Saint-Jean-de-Dieu QC G0L 3M0
Tél: 418-963-3529
biblio.jeandieu@crsbp.net
www.reseaubiblioduquebec.qc.ca
Francine Rioux, Responsable

Saint-Jean-de-Matha: **Bibliothèque de Saint-Jean-de-Matha**
81, rue Sainte-Louise, Saint-Jean-de-Matha QC J0K 2S0
Tél: 450-886-5855
biblio047@reseaubibliocqlm.qc.ca
www.reseaubiblioduquebec.qc.ca
Nicole Léonard, Responsable
450-886-5855

Saint-Jean-Port-Joli: **Bibliothèque Marie-Bonenfant/Saint-Jean-Port-Joli**
7B, place de l'Église, Saint-Jean-Port-Joli QC G0R 3G0
Tél: 418-598-3187; *Téléc:* 418-598-3085
biblio.stjean@globetrotter.net
www.reseaubiblioduquebec.qc.ca/joli
Gilberte Picard, Responsable
Évangéline Dionne, Adjointe
Azeline Leblanc, Responsable, l'Animation
Thérèse Morneau, Responsable, PIB

Saint-Jean-sur-Richelieu: **Bibliothèques municipales de Saint-Jean-sur-Richelieu**
180, rue Laurier, Saint-Jean-sur-Richelieu QC J3B 7B2
Tél: 450-357-2111; *Téléc:* 450-357-2055
www.ville.saint-jean-sur-richelieu.qc.ca
Camille Bricault, Chef, Division bibliothèques
Lise Gosselin, Bibliothécaire responsable
France Gagnon, Bibliotechnicienne
f.gagnon@ville.saint-jean-sur-richelieu.qc.c
Yvan Tourigny, Bibliotechnicien
Sylvette Toutant, Bibliothécaire responsable
Julie Roy, Bibliotechnicienne
Lucie Gauthier, Bibliotechnicienne

Saint-Jérôme: **Bibliothèque Marie-Antoinette-Foucher**
101, place du Curé-Labelle, Saint-Jérôme QC J7Z 1X6
Tél: 450-432-0569; *Téléc:* 450-436-1211
www.ville.saint-jerome.qc.ca/pages/
Chantal Paquin, Bibliothécaire
cpaquin@villesaint-jerome.qc.ca
450-436-1512 ext. 3350

Saint-Joseph-de-Beauce: **Bibliothèque de Saint-Joseph-de-Beauce**
139-100, rue Sainte-Christine, Saint-Joseph-de-Beauce QC G0S 2V0
Tél: 418-397-6160; *Téléc:* 418-397-5715
www.reseaubiblioduquebec.qc.ca/saint-joseph-de-beauce
Gilberte Doyon, Responsable
Gina Poulin, Adjointe
Marie-Reine Vézina, Responsable, Échanges/PIB
Lise Bourque, Responsable, Animation

Saint-Joseph-de-Kamouraska: **Bibliothèque de Saint-Joseph-de-Kamouraska**
298-B, rue Principale, Saint-Joseph-de-Kamouraska QC G0L 3P0
Tél: 418-493-2658
biblio.joseph@crsbp.net
www.reseaubiblioduquebec.qc.ca
Anita Toner, Responsable
418-493-2658

Saint-Joseph-de-Lepage: **Bibliothèque de Saint-Joseph-de-Lepage**
70, rue de la Rivière, Saint-Joseph-de-Lepage QC G5H 3N8
Tél: 418-775-4607; *Téléc:* 418-775-3004
biblio.lepage@crsbp.net
www.reseaubiblioduquebec.qc.ca
Noëlla Dupont, Responsable
Jacqueline Roy, Bénévole
Nathalie Roy, Bénévole

Saint-Joseph-du-Lac: **Bibliothèque de Saint-Joseph-du-Lac**
70, Montée du Village, Saint-Joseph-du-Lac QC J0N 1M0
Tél: 450-623-7833; *Téléc:* 450-623-2889
biblio64@crsbpl.qc.ca
www.reseaubiblioduquebec.qc.ca
Hélène Caron, Responsable
hcaron@ssdl.qc.ca
450-623-1072 ext. 4
Francine Carbonneau, Adjointe
450-623-7633

Saint-Jude: **Bibliothèque St-Jude**
940, rue de Centre, Saint-Jude QC J0H 1P0
Tél: 450-792-2164
Daniele Boulanger, Responsable

Saint-Julien: **Bibliothèque municipale de Saint-Julien**
794, ch Saint-Julien, Saint-Julien QC G0N 1B0
Tél: 418-423-3410; *Téléc:* 418-423-3410
bibliotheque@st-julien.ca
www.reseaubiblioduquebec.qc.ca/saint-julien
Yolande Poirier, Responsable
Yannick Gouin, Responsable, PIB

Saint-Juste-du-Lac: **Bibliothèque de Saint-Juste-du-Lac**
37, ch Principal, Saint-Juste-du-Lac QC G0L 3R0
Tél: 418-899-0374
biblio.juste@crsbp.net
Jeanne Benoist, Responsable

Saint-Juste-du-Lac: **Bibliothèque Lots-Renversés**
Route 295, Saint-Juste-du-Lac QC G0L 1V0
Tél: 418-899-0375
biblio.lotsren@crsbp.net
Leslie Bingham, Responsable

Saint-Justin: **Bibliothèque de Saint-Justin**
1281, rue Gérin, Saint-Justin QC J0K 2V0
Tél: 819-227-2775; *Téléc:* 819-227-4876
biblio056@reseaubibliocqlm.qc.ca
www.reseaubiblioduquebec.qc.ca
Josianne Messier, Responsable

Saint-Lambert: **Bibliothèque municipale de Saint-Lambert**
490, av Mercille, Saint-Lambert QC J4P 2L5
Tél: 450-466-3910; *Téléc:* 450-923-6512
bibliotheque@saint-lambert.ca
Guylaine Pellerin, Directrice
guylaine.pellerin@ville.saint-lambert.qc.ca
405-466-3889 ext. poste
Caroline Régis, Bibliothécaire

Saint-Lazare: **Bibliothèque Biblio-Culture**
116B, rue de la Fabrique, Saint-Lazare QC G0R 3J0
Tél: 418-883-2551; *Téléc:* 418-883-2551
biblio-st-lazare@globetrotter.net
www.reseaubiblioduquebec.qc.ca/saint-lazare
Raoul Laflamme, Responsable
laflammer@globetrotter.net
418-883-3005
Anna-Marie Chabot-Laverdière, Adjointe
Johanne Allard, Responsable, Animation

Saint-Léonard-d'Aston: **Bibliothèque de Saint-Léonard-d'Aston (Lucille-M.-Desmarais)**
146, rue des Écoles, Saint-Léonard-d'Aston QC J0C 1M0
Tél: 819-399-3368
biblio089@reseaubibliocqlm.qc.ca
Sylvie Turmel, Responsable

Saint-Léonard-de-Portneuf: **Bibliothèque Biblio 'Fleur de lin'**
260, rue Pettigrew, Saint-Léonard-de-Portneuf QC G0A 4A0
Tél: 418-337-3961; *Téléc:* 418-337-6742
www.reseaubiblioduquebec.qc.ca/saint-leonard
Ginette Paquet, Responsable
Hélène Cantin, Adjointe
Marie-Paule Langlois, Responsable, PIB
Carole Perron, Responsable, Statistiques

Saint-Léon-le-Grand: **Bibliothèque de Saint-Léon-le-Grand (Bas-Saint-Laurent)**
241, rue Gendron, Saint-Léon-le-Grand QC G0J 2W0
Tél: 418-743-2914
biblio.granleon@crsbp.net
www.reseaubiblioduquebec.qc.ca
Lise Fournier, Responsable

Saint-Léon-le-Grand: **Bibliothèque de Saint-Léon-le-Grand (Mauricie)**
44, rue de la Fabrique, Saint-Léon-le-Grand QC J0K 2W0
Tél: 819-228-3236; *Téléc:* 819-228-8088
biblio029@reseaubibliocqlm.qc.ca
www.reseaubiblioduquebec.qc.ca
Diane Lavergne, Responsable

Saint-Liboire: **Bibliothèque municipale de Saint-Liboire**
21, Place Mauriac, Saint-Liboire QC J0H 1R0
Tél: 450-793-4751
liboire@reseaubibliomonteregie.qc.ca
Julie Girouard, Responsable

***Saint-Liguori:* Bibliothèque de Saint-Liguori**
741, rue Principale, Saint-Liguori QC J0K 2X0
Tél: 450-753-4446; *Téléc:* 450-753-4638
biblio006@reseaubibliocqlm.qc.ca
www.reseaubiblioduquebec.qc.ca
Jeanne Gagné-Richard, Responsable
450-753-4446

***Saint-Lin-Laurentides:* Bibliothèque de Saint-Lin-Laurentides**
920, 12e av, Saint-Lin-Laurentides QC J5M 2W2
Tél: 450-439-2486; *Téléc:* 450-439-1525
biblio@saint-lin-laurentides.com
www.reseaubiblioduquebec.qc.ca/saint-lin-laurentides
Jocelyne Dufort, Responsable
Danielle Gravel, Adjointe

***Saint-Louis-de-Blandford:* Bibliothèque de Saint-Louis-de-Blandford**
80, rue Principale, Saint-Louis-de-Blandford QC G0Z 1B0
Tél: 819-364-7007; *Téléc:* 819-364-2781
biblio116@reseaubibliocqlm.qc.ca
www.reseaubiblioduquebec.qc.ca
Françoise Lafond, Responsable

***Saint-Louis-de-Gonzague:* Bibliothèque municipale de Saint-Louis-de-Gonzague**
140, rue Principale, Saint-Louis-de-Gonzague QC J0S 1T0
Tél: 450-371-9411; *Téléc:* 450-371-7428
louis.gonzague@reseaubibliomonteregie.qc.ca
www.reseaubiblioduquebec.qc.ca
Marie-Andrée Demers, Responsable

***Saint-Louis-du-Ha!Ha!:* Bibliothèque de Saint-Louis-du-Ha!Ha!**
234, rue Commerciale, Saint-Louis-du-Ha!Ha! QC G0L 3S0
Tél: 418-854-4031
biblio.louis@crsbp.net
www.reseaubiblioduquebec.qc.ca
Laurette Lavoie, Responsable

***Saint-Luc-de-Bellechasse:* Bibliothèque L'Éveil/Saint-Luc-de-Bellechasse**
115, rue de la Fabrique, Saint-Luc-de-Bellechasse QC G0R 1L0
Tél: 418-636-2776; *Téléc:* 418-636-2776
bibliotheque@sogetel.net
www.reseaubiblioduquebec.qc.ca/saint-luc
Lisette Bilodeau, Responsable

***Saint-Luc-de-Vincennes:* Bibliothèque de Saint-Luc-de-Vincennes**
660, rue Principale, Saint-Luc-de-Vincennes QC G0X 3K0
Tél: 819-295-3608; *Téléc:* 819-295-3782
biblio097@reseaubibliocqlm.qc.ca
www.reseaubiblioduquebec.qc.ca
Louise Lemire, Responsable
819-295-3603

***Saint-Ludger-de-Milot:* Bibliothèque publique de Saint-Ludger-de-Milot**
739, rue Gaudreault, Saint-Ludger-de-Milot QC G0W 2B0
Tél: 418-373-2568; *Téléc:* 418-373-2554
stludger@reseaubiblioslsj.qc.ca
www.reseaubiblioduquebec.qc.ca/portail/index.aspx?page=3&BID=5
Karine Boutot, Responsable

***Saint-Malachie:* Bibliothèque J.-A.-Kirouac**
1184, rue Principale, Saint-Malachie QC G0R 3N0
Tél: 418-642-5127; *Téléc:* 418-642-2231
jakir@globetrotter.qc.ca
www.reseaubibliodequebec.qc.ca/saint-malachie/
Louise Guénette, Responsable
Francine Moore, Responsable, PIB
Mariette Labrecque, Responsable, Animation

***Saint-Marc-du-Lac-Long:* Bibliothèque Saint-Marc-du-Lac-Long**
14A, rue de l'Église, Saint-Marc-du-Lac-Long QC G0L 1T0
Tél: 418-893-1075; *Téléc:* 418-893-1339
biblio.laclong@crsbp.net
Jeanne-D'Arc Poliquin, Responsable

***Saint-Marcel-de-Richelieu:* Bibliothèque Saint-Marcel-de-Richelieu**
#2, 1060, rue des Ormes, Saint-Marcel-de-Richelieu QC J0L 1R0
Tél: 450-794-2832; *Téléc:* 450-794-1140
marcel@monteregie.crsbp.qc.ca
Nicole Beauchamp, Responsable
450-794-2706

***Saint-Marcellin:* Fautoulire**
336, rte 234, Saint-Marcellin QC G0K 1R0
Tél: 418-798-8164
biblio.marcellin@crsbp.net
www.reseaubiblioduquebec.qc.ca
Mélanie Labbé, Responsable

***Saint-Marc-sur-Richelieu:* Bibliothèque municipale Archambault-Trépanier/Saint-Marc-sur-Richelieu**
102, rue de la Fabrique, Saint-Marc-sur-Richelieu QC J0L 2E0
Tél: 450-584-2258
marc@reseaubibliomonteregie.qc.ca
www.reseaubiblioduquebec.qc.ca
Nancy Bélanger, Responsable

***Saint-Mathias-sur-Richelieu:* Bibliothèque municipale de Saint-Mathias-sur-Richelieu**
50, rue Lussier, Saint-Mathias-sur-Richelieu QC J3L 6A4
Tél: 450-447-0679
mathias@reseaubibliomonteregie.qc.ca
www.reseaubiblioduquebec.qc.ca
France Desautels, Responsable

***Saint-Mathieu:* Bibliothèque municipale de Saint-Mathieu**
299, ch Saint-Édouard, Saint-Mathieu QC J0L 2H0
Tél: 450-659-9528
mathieu@reseaubibliomonteregie.qc.ca
Danielle Routhier, Responsable

***Saint-Mathieu-de-Beloeil:* Bibliothèque municipale Ryane-Provost**
5000, rue des Loisirs, Saint-Mathieu-de-Beloeil QC J3G 2C9
Tél: 450-467-7490
mathieu.beloeil@reseaubibliomonteregie.qc.ca
www.reseaubiblioduquebec.qc.ca
Claude Monast, Responsable

***Saint-Mathieu-de-Rioux:* Bibliothèque de Saint-Mathieu-de-Rioux**
41, rue de l'Église, Saint-Mathieu-de-Rioux QC G0L 3T0
Tél: 418-738-3057
biblio.mathieu@crsbp.net
www.reseaubiblioduquebec.qc.ca
Peggy Dufaut, Responsable

***Saint-Mathieu-du-Parc:* Bibliothèque de Saint-Mathieu-du-Parc (Micheline H.- Gélinas)**
600, ch Saint-Marc, Saint-Mathieu-du-Parc QC G0X 1N0
Tél: 819-532-2345
biblio093@reseaubibliocqlm.qc.ca
www.reseaubiblioduquebec.qc.ca
Suzie Parent, Responsable

***Saint-Maurice:* Bibliothèque de Saint-Maurice**
1380, rue Notre-Dame, Saint-Maurice QC G0X 2X0
Tél: 819-378-7315
biblio026@reseaubibliocqlm.qc.ca
www.reseaubiblioduquebec.qc.ca
Aline Harnois, Responsable

***Saint-Médard:* Bibliothèque de Saint-Médard**
1, rue Principale est, Saint-Médard QC G0L 3V0
Tél: 418-963-1588
biblio.medard@crsbp.net
www.reseaubiblioduquebec.qc.ca
Andrée Beaulieu, Responsable
andreeobeaulieu@hotmail.com

***Saint-Michel:* Bibliothèque municipale Claire-Lazure**
440, place Saint-Michel, Saint-Michel QC J0L 2J0
Tél: 450-454-7995
michel@reseaubibliomonteregie.qc.ca
www.reseaubiblioduquebec.qc.ca
Lucie Longtin, Responsable

***Saint-Michel-de-Bellechasse:* Bibliothèque Benoît-Lacroix**
8, av Saint-Charles, Saint-Michel-de-Bellechasse QC G0R 3S0
Tél: 418-884-2766; *Téléc:* 418-884-2866
biblistmic@globetrotter.net
www.reseaubiblioduquebec.qc.ca/saint-michel
Gilbert Théberge, Responsable

***Saint-Michel-des-Saints:* Bibliothèque de Saint-Michel-des-Saints (Antonio-Saint-Georges)**
390B, rue Matawin, Saint-Michel-des-Saints QC J0K 3B0
Tél: 450-833-5471
biblio044@reseaubibliocqlm.qc.ca
www.reseaubiblioduquebec.qc.ca
Cécile Baudouard, Responsable

***Saint-Michel-du-Squatec:* Bibliothèque Alma-Durand**
149, rue St-Joseph, CP 104, Saint-Michel-du-Squatec QC G0L 4H0
Tél: 418-855-2708; *Téléc:* 418-855-5228
biblio.squatec@crsbp.net
Céline Morin, Responsable
Linda Cyr, Bénévole

***Saint-Modeste:* Bibliothèque de Saint-Modeste**
312, rue Principale, Saint-Modeste QC G0L 3W0
Tél: 418-867-2352
biblio.modeste@crsbp.net
www.reseaubiblioduquebec.qc.ca
Solange Chouinard, Responsable

***Saint-Narcisse:* Bibliothèque de Saint-Narcisse (Gérard-Desrosiers)**
509, rue Massicotte, Saint-Narcisse QC G0X 2Y0
Tél: 418-328-4430; *Téléc:* 418-328-4348
biblio001@reseaubibliocqlm.qc.ca
www.reseaubiblioduquebec.qc.ca
Rose-Alice Lafontaine, Responsable
Louise Lafontaine, Adjointe

***Saint-Narcisse-de-Beaurivag:* Bibliothèque municipale de Saint-Narcisse-de-Beaurivage**
510, rue de l'École, Saint-Narcisse-de-Beaurivag QC G0S 1W0
Tél: 418-475-6464; *Téléc:* 418-475-6880
biblio.st-narcisse@globetrotter.net
www.reseaubiblioduquebec.qc.ca/saint-narcisse
Monique Arlen, Responsable
418-475-6750

***Saint-Nazaire:* Bibliothèque publique de St-Nazaire**
220, rue Principale, Saint-Nazaire QC G0W 2V0
Tél: 418-662-1422; *Téléc:* 418-662-5467
nazaire@reseaubiblioslsj.qc.ca
www.reseaubiblioduquebec.qc.ca/portail/index.aspx?page=3&BID=5
Manon Tremblay, Responsable

***Saint-Nazaire-d'Acton:* Bibliothèque municipale de Saint-Nazaire-d'Acton**
715, rue des Loisirs, Saint-Nazaire-d'Acton QC J0H 1V0
Tél: 819-392-2090
nazaire@reseaubibliomonteregie.qc.ca
Maryse Pelland, Responsable

***Saint-Nérée:* Bibliothèque Biblio Du Centenaire**
2139, route Principale, Saint-Nérée QC G0R 3V0
Tél: 418-243-3649; *Téléc:* 418-243-2136
www.reseaubiblioduquebec.qc.ca/saint-neree
Francine Nadeau, Responsable
Suzanne Corlay, Adjointe

***Saint-Noël:* Bibliothèque de Saint-Noël**
12, rue Saint-Joseph est, Saint-Noël QC G0J 3A0
Tél: 418-776-2549
biblio.noel@crsbp.net
www.reseaubiblioduquebec.qc.ca
Diane Leclerc, Responsable

***Saint-Odilon:* Bibliothèque L'Intello/Saint-Odilon-de-Cranbourne**
111, rue de l'Hôtel-de-Ville, Saint-Odilon QC G0S 3A0
Tél: 418-464-4803; *Téléc:* 418-464-4800
www.reseaubiblioduquebec.qc.ca/saint-odilon
Mariette Vachon, Responsable
418-464-2463
Sylvie Drouin, Responsable, PIB/Extranet
418-464-4134
Odile Ruel, Responsable, Échanges
Lucille Carbonneau, Responsable, Collection locale
418-464-2972
Dany Lessard, Responsable, Statistiques
418-464-4260

***Saint-Omer:* Bibliothèque de Saint-Omer**
106B, rte 132 est, Saint-Omer QC G0C 2Z0
Tél: 418-364-6485
bibliostomer@globetrotter.net
www.reseaubiblioduquebec.qc.ca
Line Arsenault, Responsable

***Saint-Ours:* Bibliothèque municipale de Saint-Ours**
2636, rue de l'Immaculée-Conception, Saint-Ours QC J0G 1P0
Tél: 450-785-2779
ours@reseaubibliomonteregie.qc.ca
www.reseaubiblioduquebec.qc.ca
Lucie Grenier, Responsable

Saint-Pacôme: **Bibliothèque de Saint-Pacôme**
27, rue Saint-Louis, Saint-Pacôme QC G0L 3X0
Tél: 418-852-2356
biblio.pacome@crsbp.net
www.reseaubiblioduquebec.qc.ca
Marc Bélanger, Responsable

Saint-Pamphile: **Bibliothèque Marie-Louise-Gagnon/Saint-Pamphile**
3, rue Elgin sud, Saint-Pamphile QC G0R 3X0
Tél: 418-356-5403; *Téléc:* 418-356-5502
pamphile@globetrotter.net
www.saintpamphile.ca
Micheline Leclerc, Responsable

Saint-Pascal: **Bibliothèque de Saint-Pascal**
470, rue Notre-Dame, Saint-Pascal QC G0L 3Y0
Tél: 418-492-2312
biblio.pascal@crsbp.net
www.reseaubiblioduquebec.qc.ca
Jeannine Desjardins, Responsable

Saint-Patrice-de-Beaurivage: **Bibliothèque Florence-Guay/Saint-Patrice-de-Beaurivage**
470, du Manoir, Saint-Patrice-de-Beaurivage QC G0S 1B0
Tél: 418-596-2439; *Téléc:* 418-596-2430
borivage@globetrotter.qc.ca
www.reseaubiblioduquebe.qc.ca/saint-patrice
Claire Béland, Responsable
450-596-3074

Saint-Paul de l'île-aux-Noi: **Bibliothèque municipale Lucile-Langlois-Éthier**
959C, rue Principale, Saint-Paul de l'île-aux-Noi QC J0J 1G0
Tél: 450-291-5585
paul.ile.noix@reseaubibliomonteregie.qc.ca
www.reseaubiblioduquebec.qc.ca
Roger Langlois, Responsable

Saint-Paul-d'Industrie: **Bibliothèque de Saint-Paul**
18, boul Brassard, Saint-Paul-d'Industrie QC J0K 3E0
Tél: 450-759-3333; *Téléc:* 450-759-6396
biblio071@reseaubibliocqlm.qc.ca
www.reseaubiblioduquebec.qc.ca
Isabelle Plouffe, Responsable

Saint-Paul-de-la-Croix: **Bibliothèque de Saint-Paul-de-la-Croix**
1-B, rue du Parc, Saint-Paul-de-la-Croix QC G0L 3Z0
Tél: 418-898-3095; *Téléc:* 418-898-2322
biblio.croix@crsbp.net
www.reseaubiblioduquebec.qc.ca
Johanne Lagacé, Responsable
418-898-2568
Diane Dubé, Bénévole
418-898-2006
Marjolaine April, Bénévole
Isabelle Lagacé, Bénévole
Jacinthe Dionne, Bénévole
418-898-2179

Saint-Paulin: **Bibliothèque de Saint-Paulin (Jeannine-Julien)**
3051, rue Bergeron, C.P. 39, Saint-Paulin QC J0K 3G0
Tél: 819-268-2425; *Téléc:* 819-268-2890
biblio118@reseaubibliocqlm.qc.ca
www.reseaubiblioduquebec.qc.ca
Lucie Marcouiller, Responsable

Saint-Philippe: **Bibliothèque Saint-Philippe/Le Vaisseau d'Or**
2223, rte Édouard VII, Saint-Philippe QC J0L 2K0
Tél: 450-659-7701; *Téléc:* 450-659-5354
bibliotheque@municipalite.saint-philippe.qc.ca
www.municipalite.saint-philippe.qc.ca
Line Thibodeau, Responsable

Saint-Philippe-de-Néri: **Bibliothèque de Saint-Philippe-de-Néri**
11, rue de l'Église, Saint-Philippe-de-Néri QC G0L 4A0
Tél: 418-498-3843
biblio.philip@crsbp.net
www.reseaubiblioduquebec.qc.ca
Mariette Dumais, Responsable

Saint-Pie: **Bibliothèque municipale de Saint-Pie**
309, rue Notre-Dame, Saint-Pie QC J0H 1W0
Tél: 450-772-2332; *Téléc:* 450-772-2332
pie@reseaubibliomonteregie.qc.ca
Danielle Massé, Responsable

Saint-Pie-de-Guire: **Bibliothèque de Saint-Pie-de-Guire**
445C, rue Principal, Saint-Pie-de-Guire QC J0G 1R0
Tél: 450-784-0232
biblio132@reseaubibliocqlm.qc.ca
www.reseaubiblioduquebec.qc.ca
Sylvie Courchesne, Responsable

Saint-Pierre-de-Broughton: **Bibliothèque Maurice-Couture/Saint-Pierre-de-Broughton**
6, du Couvent, Saint-Pierre-de-Broughton QC G0N 1T0
Tél: 418-424-3450; *Téléc:* 418-424-0389
biblio.m.couture@cgocable.ca
www.reseaubiblioduquebec.qc.ca/broughton
Brigitte Routhier, Responsable

Saint-Pierre-de-l'Ile-d'Orl: **Bibliothèque Oscar-Ferland**
515, rte des Prêtres, Saint-Pierre-de-l'Ile-d'Orl QC G0A 4E0
Tél: 418-828-2962; *Téléc:* 418-828-2855
www.reseaubiblioduquebec.qc.ca/saint-pierre/
Lisette Grégoire, Responsable
Guylaine Pichette, Adjointe
Claudine Rouleau, Responsable, Échanges

Saint-Pierre-les-Becquets: **Bibliothèque de Saint-Pierre-les-Becquets**
108, rue des Loisirs, Saint-Pierre-les-Becquets QC G0X 2Z0
Tél: 819-263-0797; *Téléc:* 819-263-2622
biblio086@reseaubibliocqlm.qc.ca
Francine Bergeron, Responsable

Saint-Placide: **Bibliothèque de Saint-Placide**
73, rue de l'Église, Saint-Placide QC J0V 2B0
Tél: 450-258-1780; *Téléc:* 450-258-0364
biblio@municipalite.saint-placide.qc.ca
www.reseaubiblioduquebec.qc.ca
Danielle Le Moëligou, Responsable
450-258-42

Saint-Polycarpe: **Bibliothèque municipale de Saint-Polycarpe**
7, rue Ste-Catherine, Saint-Polycarpe QC J0P 1X0
Tél: 450-265-3444; *Téléc:* 450-265-3010
polycarpe@reseaubibliomonteregie.qc.ca
www.reseaubiblioduquebec.qc.ca
Suzanne Poirier, Responsable
450-265-3043

Saint-Prime: **Bibliothèque publique de Saint-Prime**
616, rue Principale, Saint-Prime QC G8J 1T4
Tél: 418-251-4976
stprime@reseaubiblioslsj.qc.ca
www.reseaubiblioduquebec.qc.ca/portail/index.aspx?page=3&BID=5
Claudette Tremblay, Responsable
Suzanne Aubin, Secrétaire-trésorière

Saint-Prosper: **Bibliothèque de Saint-Prosper (Livresque)**
371, rue de l'Église, Saint-Prosper QC G0X 3A0
Tél: 418-328-4219; *Téléc:* 418-328-4219
biblio012@reseaubibliocqlm.qc.ca
www.reseaubiblioduquebec.qc.ca
Christiane Couture, Responsable

Saint-Raphaël: **Bibliothèque Jeannine-Marquis-Garant**
88, rue du Foyer, Saint-Raphaël QC G0R 4C0
Tél: 418-243-3437; *Téléc:* 418-243-2605
www.reseaubiblioduquebec.qc.ca/saint-raphael/
René Bouchard, Responsable

Saint-Rémi: **Bibliothèque municipale de Saint-Rémi**
25, Saint-Sauveur, Saint-Rémi QC J0L 2L0
Tél: 450-454-2418; *Téléc:* 450-454-4083
bibliotheque@ville.saint-remi.qc.ca
Patrick Thibert, Responsable
450-454-9227
Monique Black, Technicienne
Françoise Chatelin-Lussier, Préposée au comptoir

Saint-René-de-Matane: **Bibliothèque de Saint-René-de-Matane**
178, av Saint-René, Saint-René-de-Matane QC G0J 3E0
Tél: 418-224-1339
www.municipalite.st-rene-matane.qc.ca
Paulette Dugas, Responsable
418-224-1339
Sandra Blier, Bénévole
418-224-3293

Saint-Robert: **Bibliothèque municipale de Saint-Robert**
1, Aggée-Pelletier, Saint-Robert QC J0G 1S0
Tél: 450-782-2562
robert@reseaubibliomonteregie.qc.ca
Mariette Latour, Responsable

Saint-Roch-de-l'Achigan: **Bibliothèque de Saint-Roch-de-l'Achigan**
30, rue Dr Wilfrid-Locat nord, Saint-Roch-de-l'Achigan QC J0K 3H0
Tél: 450-588-5838; *Téléc:* 450-588-4478
biblio109@reseaubibliocqlm.qc.ca
www.reseaubiblioduquebec.qc.ca
Jocelyne Allard, Responsable

Saint-Roch-de-Mékinac: **Bibliothèque de Saint-Roch-de-Mékinac**
1216, rue Principale, Saint-Roch-de-Mékinac QC G0X 2E0
Tél: 819-646-5635
biblio033@reseaubibliocqlm.qc.ca
www.reseaubiblioduquebec.qc.ca
Claudia Klaus, Responsable

Saint-Roch-de-Richelieu: **Bibliothèque municipale de Saint-Roch-de-Richelieu**
1111, rue du Parc, Saint-Roch-de-Richelieu QC J0L 2M0
Tél: 450-785-2755
roch@reseaubibliomonteregie.qc.ca
Hélène Jackson, Responsable

Saint-Roch-des-Aulnaies: **Bibliothèque Bibli-Aulnaies/Saint-Roch-des-Aulnaies**
1028, de la Seigneurie, Saint-Roch-des-Aulnaies QC G0R 4E0
Tél: 418-856-7045; *Téléc:* 418-354-2059
www.reseaubiblioduquebec.qc.ca/aulnaies
Louise Filion, Responsable
louloufilion@hotmail.com
418-354-2233
Marcelle Dubé, Adjointe
Monique Belzile, Responsable, Échanges

Saint-Rosaire: **Bibliothèque de Saint-Rosaire**
9, rue St-Pierre, Saint-Rosaire QC G0Z 1K0
Tél: 819-795-4861; *Téléc:* 819-795-4861
biblio088@reseaubibliocqlm.qc.ca
www.reseaubiblioduquebec.qc.ca
Jacques Dubois, Responsable

Saint-Samuel: **Bibliothèque de Saint-Samuel**
143, rue de l'Église, Saint-Samuel QC G0Z 1G0
Tél: 819-353-1242; *Téléc:* 819-353-1499
biblio137@reseaubibliocqlm.qc.ca
www.reseaubiblioduquebec.qc.ca
Noëlla Grondin, Responsable
Pierrette Doucet, Adjointe
biblio137@telwarwick.net

Saint-Sauveur: **Bibliothèque de Saint-Sauveur**
33, av de l'Église, Saint-Sauveur QC J0R 1R0
Tél: 450-227-2669; *Téléc:* 450-227-3362
biblio.st-sauveur@cgocable.ca
www.reseaubiblioduquebec.qc.ca
Claudette St-Jacques, Responsable

Saint-Sébastien: **Bibliothèque municipale de Saint-Sébastien**
595, rue de La Fabrique, Saint-Sébastien QC G0Y 1M0
Tél: 819-652-2727
biblio092@reseaubiblioestrie.qc.ca
www.st-sebastien.com
Eric Bernier, Responsable

Saint-Sévère: **Bibliothèque de Saint-Sévère (Denise L. Noël)**
47, rue Principale, Saint-Sévère QC G0X 3B0
Tél: 819-264-5656
biblio119@reseaubibliocqlm.qc.ca
www.reseaubiblioduquebec.qc.ca
Jocelyne Lavigne, Responsable

Saint-Séverin-de-Beauce: **Bibliothèque municipale de Saint-Séverin**
900, rue des Lacs, Saint-Séverin-de-Beauce QC G0N 1V0
Tél: 418-426-2423; *Téléc:* 418-426-1274
biblicle@oricom.ca
www.reseaubiblioduquebec.qc.ca/saint-severin
Cécile Couture, Responsable
Maryse Trépanier, Personnes-ressources du Résseau Biblio
René Leduc, Représentant désigné

Saint-Siméon: **Bibliothèque municipale de Saint-Siméon**
505A, rue Saint-Laurent, Saint-Siméon QC G0T 1X0
Tél: 418-638-2691; *Téléc:* 418-638-5145
www.reseaubiblioduquebec.qc.ca/saint-simeon
Lyse Leblond, Responsable

Saint-Siméon-de-Bonaventure: **Bibliothèque de Saint-Siméon**
116, rue Bélanger, Saint-Siméon-de-Bonaventure QC G0C 3A0
Tél: 418-534-2606; *Téléc:* 418-534-3830
bbostsim@globetrotter.net
www.reseaubiblioduquebec.qc.ca
Huguette Lepage, Responsable
hlepage@globetrotter.net
418-534-3928

Saint-Simon: **Bibliothèque de Saint-Simon**
39, rue de l'Église, Saint-Simon QC G0L 4C0
biblio.simon@crsbp.net
www.reseaubiblioduquebec.qc.ca
France Beauchesne, Responsable
418-738-2517
Gisèle Desharnais, Bénévole
Jocelyn Rioux, Bénévole
418-738-2344

Saint-Simon: **Bibliothèque municipale Lise-Bourque-St-Pierre**
46, rue des Loisirs, Saint-Simon QC J0H 1Y0
Tél: 450-798-2276
simon@reseaubibliomonteregie.qc.ca
Claire Bousquet, Responsable
450-798-2624

Saint-Stanislas: **Bibliothèque publique de Saint-Stanislas**
953, rue Principale, Saint-Stanislas QC G8L 7B4
Tél: 418-276-4476; *Téléc:* 418-276-4476
stanisla@reseaubiblioslsj.qc.ca
www.reseaubiblioduquebec.qc.ca/portail/index.aspx?page=3&BID=5
Line Laprise, Responsable

Saint-Stanislas-de-Kostka: **Bibliothèque Saint-Stanislas-de-Kostka**
117, rue Centrale, Saint-Stanislas-de-Kostka QC J0S 1W0
Tél: 450-370-4650
Christiane Blanchard, Responsable
Manon Demeule, Responsable, achats

Saint-Sulpice: **Bibliothèque de Saint-Sulpice**
215, rue des Loisirs, Saint-Sulpice QC J5W 6C9
Tél: 450-589-7816
biblio133@reseaubibliocqlm.qc.ca
www.reseaubiblioduquebec.qc.ca
Julie Parent, Responsable

Saint-Sylvère: **Bibliothèque de Saint-Sylvère**
260, rte de l'École, Saint-Sylvère QC G0Z 1H0
Tél: 819-285-2699; *Téléc:* 819-285-2075
biblio037@reseaubibliocqlm.qc.ca
www.reseaubiblioduquebec.qc.ca
Linda Searles, Responsable

Saint-Sylvestre: **Bibliothèque municipale de Saint-Sylvestre**
824, rue Principale, Saint-Sylvestre QC G0S 3C0
Tél: 418-596-2427; *Téléc:* 418-596-2384
sylve@globetrotter.qc.ca
Isabelle Gagnon, Responsable
munisylvestre@globetrotter.net
418-596-3400

Saint-Télesphore: **Bibliothèque municipale de Saint-Télesphore**
1421, rte 340, Saint-Télesphore QC J0P 1Y0
Tél: 450-269-2364
telesphore@reseaubibliomonteregie.qc.ca
Lisa Longtin, Responsable

Saint-Tharcisius: **Bibliothèque de Saint-Tharcisius**
55, rue Principale, Saint-Tharcisius QC G0J 3G0
Tél: 418-629-4727
biblio.tharci@crsbp.net
www.reseaubiblioduquebec.qc.ca
Maryse Rioux, Responsable

Saint-Théodore-d-Acton: **Bibliothèque autonome de Saint-Théodore-d'Acton**
1803, rue Principale, Saint-Théodore-d-Acton QC J0H 1Z0
Tél: 450-546-5643
www.st-theodore.com

Saint-Thomas-de-Joliette: **Bibliothèque de Saint-Thomas (Jacqueline-Plante)**
#941, 10, rue Principale, Saint-Thomas-de-Joliette QC J0K 3L0
Tél: 450-759-8173; *Téléc:* 450-759-2530
biblio117@reseaubibliocqlm.qc.ca
www.reseaubiblioduquebec.qc.ca
Média social: www.facebook.com/group.php?gid=159259607457177
Brigitte Brunet, Responsable

Saint-Thomas-Didyme: **Bibliothèque publique de Saint-Thomas-de-Didyme**
31-1, av du Moulin, Saint-Thomas-Didyme QC G0W 1P0
Tél: 418-274-4034
thomas@reseaubiblioslsj.qc.ca
Denise Bergeron, Responsable

Saint-Tite: **Bibliothèque de Saint-Tite (Marielle-Brouillette)**
330, rue du Moulin, Saint-Tite QC G0X 3H0
Tél: 418-365-6203
biblio017@reseaubibliocqlm.qc.ca
www.reseaubiblioduquebec.qc.ca
Noëlla Gauthier, Responsable

Saint-Ubalde: **Bibliothèque Guy-Laviolette**
400, rue de l'Aréna, Saint-Ubalde QC G0A 4L0
Tél: 418-277-2124; *Téléc:* 418-277-2055
www.reseaubiblioduquebec.qc.ca/saint-ubalde/
Odile Tessier, Responsable
Claire Morissette, Responsable, Échanges

Saint-Valentin: **Bibliothèque municipale de Saint-Valentin**
790, 4e Ligne, Saint-Valentin QC J0J 2E0
Tél: 450-291-3948
valentin@reseaubibliomonteregie.qc.ca
www.reseaubiblioduquebec.qc.ca/valentin/
Réjane Hébert Olivier, Responsable

Saint-Valère: **Bibliothèque de Saint-Valère**
2A, rue du Parc, Saint-Valère QC G0P 1M0
Tél: 819-353-3464; *Téléc:* 819-353-3465
biblio127@reseaubibliocqlm.qc.ca
www.reseaubiblioduquebec.qc.ca
Hélène Provencher-Hébert, Responsable

Saint-Valérien: **Bibliothèque de Saint-Valérien**
159, rue Principale, Saint-Valérien QC G0L 4E0
Tél: 418-736-8170
biblio.valerien@crsbp.net
www.reseaubiblioduquebec.qc.ca
Chantal Paquet, Responsable

Saint-Vallier: **Bibliothèque Marie-Josephte-Corrivaux**
365, av de l'Église, Saint-Vallier QC G0R 4J0
Tél: 418-884-3190; *Téléc:* 418-884-2454
www.reseaubiblioduquebec.qc.ca/saint-vallier
Monique Rochefort, Responsable
Suzanne Alain, Adjointe

Saint-Vianney: **Bibliothèque de Saint-Vianney**
170-B, av Centrale, Saint-Vianney QC G0J 3J0
Tél: 418-629-4082
biblio.vianney@crsbp.net
Estelle Allaire, Responsable

Saint-Victor: **Bibliothèque Biblio Luc-Lacourcière**
287, rue Marchand, Saint-Victor QC G0M 2B0
Tél: 418-588-6689; *Téléc:* 418-588-6855
www.reseaubiblioduquebec.qc.ca/saint-victor/
Marc Bélanger, Responsable
Noelline Jacques, Adjointe

Saint-Wenceslas: **Bibliothèque de Saint-Wenceslas**
1240, rue Principale, Saint-Wenceslas QC G0Z 1J0
Tél: 819-224-4055
biblio073@reseaubibliocqlm.qc.ca
www.reseaubiblioduquebec.qc.ca
Jeanne Champagne, Responsable

Saint-Zénon: **Bibliothèque de Saint-Zénon (Danièle-Bruneau)**
6191, rue Principale, Saint-Zénon QC J0K 3N0
Tél: 450-884-0328; *Téléc:* 450-884-5285
biblio048@reseaubibliocqlm.qc.ca
www.reseaubiblioduquebec.qc.ca
Simone L. Boisvert, Responsable

Saint-Zéphirin-de-Courval: **Bibliothèque de Saint-Zéphirin-de-Courval**
950, rue des Loisirs, Saint-Zéphirin-de-Courval QC J0G 1V0
Tél: 450-564-2401; *Téléc:* 450-564-2339
biblio092@reseaubibliocqlm.qc.ca
www.reseaubiblioduquebec.qc.ca
Angèle Lefebvre, Responsable

Saint-Zotique: **Bibliothèque municipale de Saint-Zotique**
1250, rue Principale, Saint-Zotique QC J0P 1Z0
Tél: 450-267-3689
dg@st-zotique.com
www.st-zotique.com
Ginette Léger, Responsable

La Sarre: **Bibliothèque municipale Richelieu de La Sarre**
Maison de la culture, 195, rue Principale, La Sarre QC J9Z 1Y3
Tél: 819-333-2294; *Téléc:* 819-333-2296
www.biblrn.qc.ca/biblls
Lise Gaignard, Directrice
Noëlline Marcoux, Technicienne

Sayabec: **Bibliothèque Quilit**
8B, rue Keable, Sayabec QC G0J 3K0
Tél: 418-536-5431
biblio.sayabec@crsbp.net
www.reseaubiblioduquebec.qc.ca
Thérèse Arsenault, Responsable

Scott: **Bibliothèque municipale de Scott**
1070, rte Kennedy, Scott QC G0S 3G0
Tél: 418-387-1837
munscott@globetrotter.net
www.reseaubiblioduquebec.qc.ca/scott
Roger Pigeon, Responsable
Bédard Jacinthe, Adjointe

Senneterre: **Bibliothèque de Senneterre**
121, 1e rue Est, Senneterre QC J0Y 2M0
Tél: 819-737-8829; *Téléc:* 819-737-4215
senneterre@reseaubiblioatnq.qc.ca
www.reseaubiblioduquebec.qc.ca
Denise Dufour, Responsable
819-737-8322
Réjeanne Laprise, Bénévole
819-737-2429
Jeanne-Mance Matte, Bénévole
819-737-2942

Sept-Iles: **Bibliothèque Louis-Ange-Santerre**
500, av Jolliet, Sept-Iles QC G4R 2B4
Tél: 418-964-3355; *Téléc:* 418-964-3353
www.ville.sept-iles.qc.ca
Sylvie Pelletier, Superviseure
sylvie.pelletier@ville.sept-iles.qc.ca
Claude Charest, Bibliothécaire
claude.charest@ville.sept-iles.qc.ca

Shannon: **Bibliothèque municipale de Shannon**
50, rue St-Patrick, Shannon QC G0A 4N0
Tél: 418-844-1622; *Téléc:* 418-844-2111
biblio@cableshannon.com
www.reseaubiblioduquebec.qc.ca/shannon/
Brigitte Olivier, Responsable
Marie-Josée Monderie, Adjointe
Germaine Pelletier, Responsable, Collection locale

Shawinigan: **Bibliothèque Fabien-LaRochelle**
550, av de l'Hôtel-de-Ville, Shawinigan QC G9N 6V3
Tél: 819-536-7218; *Téléc:* 819-536-0808
bibliotheque@ville.shawinigan.qc.ca
www.shawinigan.ca
Charlotte Lecours, Responsable des bibliothèques

Shawville: **Bibliothèque Shawville/Clarendon/Thorne/ Shawville/Clarendon/Thorne Library**
356, rue Main, Shawville QC J0X 2Y0
Tél: 819-647-3732; *Téléc:* 819-647-3732
admshawville@crsbpo.qc.ca
www.reseaubiblioduquebec.qc.ca/ShawvilleClarendon
Jennifer Davies, Responsable

Sherbrooke: **Bibliothèque municipale Éva-Senécal**
450, rue Marquette, Sherbrooke QC J1H 1M4
Tél: 819-821-5860; *Téléc:* 819-822-6110
bibliotheque@ville.sherbrooke.qc.ca
www.ville.sherbrooke.qc.ca
Linda Travis, Chef, Section bibliothèque
819-821-5862

Luce Mathieu, Responsable, Référence
819-821-5598
André Bruneau, Bibliothécaire, Acquisitions
819-821-5595
Luce Marquis, Bibliothécaire, Catalogage
819-821-5464
Jeanne Desautels, Bibliothécaire, Acquisitions
819-821-5594

***Shipshaw:* Bibliothèque de Shipshaw (Rivage)**
3760, rte Saint-Léonard, Shipshaw QC G7P 1H5
Tél: 418-695-7135; *Téléc:* 418-542-6173
webbiblio@ville.saguenay.qc.ca
www.ville.saguenay.qc.ca
Lyne Racine, Responsable

***Shipshaw:* Bibliothèque de Shipshaw (Rivière)**
4281-A, rue des Pins, Shipshaw QC G7P 1L8
Tél: 418-542-3982; *Téléc:* 418-542-6231
webbiblio@ville.saguenay.qc.ca
www.ville.saguenay.qc.ca
Ginette Tremblay, Responsable

***Sorel-Tracy:* Bibliothèque municipale de Sorel-Tracy**
3015, Place des loisirs, Sorel-Tracy QC J3R 5S5
Tél: 450-780-5600
www.ville.sorel-tracy.qc.ca
Guy Desjardins, Régisseur, Culture & Bibliothèque

***Sorel-Tracy:* Bibliothèque municipale de Sorel-Tracy**
145, rue George, Sorel-Tracy QC J3P 1C7
Tél: 450-780-5600
www.ville.sorel-tracy.qc.ca
Guy Desjardins, Régisseur, Culture & Bibliothèque

***St-Alexandre-de-Kamouraska:* Bibliothèque Saint-Alexandre**
480, av de l'École, St-Alexandre-de-Kamouraska QC G0L 2G0
Tél: 418-495-3123
biblio.alexi@crsbp.net
Hélène Therrien, Responsable

***Stanbridge East:* Bibliothèque Denise-Larocque-Duhamel/ Denise Larocque Duhamel Library**
12A, rue Maple, Stanbridge East QC J0J 2H0
Tél: 450-248-4662
stanbridge@reseaubibliomonteregie.qc.ca
Nicole L'Heureux, Responsable

***Standon:* Bibliothèque l'Étincelle**
514B, rue Principale, Standon QC G0R 4L0
Tél: 418-642-2708; *Téléc:* 418-642-2570
etincel@globetrotter.qc.ca
www.reseaubiblioduquebec.qc.ca/saint-leon
Mario Grenier, Responsable
Odette Genest, Adjointe
Michel Lacasse, Responsable, PIB
Céline Lafontaine, Responsable, Échanges
Monique Moore, Responsable, Collection locale

***Stanstead:* Haskell Free Library Inc.**
1 Church St., Stanstead QC J0B 3E2
Tel: 819-876-2471; *Fax:* 802-873-3634
Other Numbers: Derby Line Phone: 802/873-3022
www.haskellopera.org
Nancy Rumery, Director of Library, Head Librarian
802-873-3022 ext. 201

***St-Barnabé-Nord:* Bibliothèque de Saint-Barnabé**
70, rue Duguay, St-Barnabé-Nord QC G0X 2K0
Tél: 819-264-2085; *Téléc:* 819-264-2079
biblio027@reseaubibliocqlm.qc.ca
www.reseaubiblioduquebec.qc.ca
Luc Gélinas, Responsable

***St-Boniface-de-Shawinigan:* Bibliothèque de Saint-Boniface**
155, rue Langevin, St-Boniface-de-Shawinigan QC G0X 2L0
Tél: 819-535-3330; *Téléc:* 819-535-1242
biblio021@reseaubibliocqlm.qc.ca
www.reseaubiblioduquebec.qc.ca
Chantal Gélinas, Responsable

***St-Charles-de-Bellechasse:* Bibliothèque Jacques-Labrie/Saint-Charles-de-Bellechasse**
2829A, av Royale, St-Charles-de-Bellechasse QC G0R 2T0
Tél: 418-887-6561; *Téléc:* 418-887-6779
biblstch@globetrotter.qc.ca
www.reseaubiblioduquebec.qc.ca/saint-charles
Manon Larochelle, Responsable
Louise Cantin, Adjointe

***St-David-de-Falardeau:* Bibliothèque publique Saint-David-de-Falardeau**
124, boul St-David, St-David-de-Falardeau QC G0V 1C0
Tél: 418-673-6395
stdavid@reseaubiblioslsj.qc.ca
www.reseaubiblioduquebec.qc.ca
Francine Allard, Responsable

***St-Dominique-du-Rosaire:* Bibliothèque de St-Dominique-du-Rosaire**
235, rue Principale, St-Dominique-du-Rosaire QC J0Y 2K0
Tél: 819-727-4144; *Téléc:* 819-727-4344
dominique@reseaubiblioatnq.qc.ca
www.reseaubiblioduquebec.qc.ca
Marcelle Gravelle, Responsable

***Ste-Catherine-de-la-J-Carti:* Bibliothèque Anne-Hébert**
22, rue Louis-Jolliet, Ste-Catherine-de-la-J-Carti QC G3N 2V3
Tél: 418-875-2171; *Téléc:* 418-875-2699
bibliotheque@villescjc.com
www.reseaubiblioduquebec.qc.ca/cartier
Geneviève Roger, Responsable

***Ste-Geneviève-de-Batiscan:* Bibliothèque de Sainte-Geneviève-de-Batiscan (Clément-Marchand)**
2, rue du Centre, Ste-Geneviève-de-Batiscan QC G0X 2R0
Tél: 418-363-2261
biblio036@reseaubibliocqlm.qc.ca
www.reseaubiblioduquebec.qc.ca
Nicole Lahaie, Responsable

***Ste-Geneviève-de-Berthier:* Bibliothèque de Sainte-Geneviève-de-Berthier (Léo-Paul-Desrosiers)**
391, rang de la Rivière-Bayonne sud, Ste-Geneviève-de-Berthier QC J0K 1A0
Tél: 450-836-4333; *Téléc:* 450-836-7260
biblio066@reseaubibliocqlm.qc.ca
www.reseaubiblioduquebec.qc.ca
Gabrielle Desjardins, Responsable

***Ste-Gertrude-Mannville:* Bibliothèque de Sainte-Gertrude**
391, rte 395, Ste-Gertrude-Mannville QC J0Y 2L0
Tél: 819-727-2244; *Téléc:* 819-727-2244
gertrude@crsbpat.qc.ca
Geneviève Michaud, Responsable
Colette Dumais, Responsable, Demandes spéciales

***Ste-Hélène-de-Mancebourg:* Bibliothèque de Sainte-Hélène-de-Mancebourg**
459, ch Rangs 2 et 3, Ste-Hélène-de-Mancebourg QC J0Z 2T0
Tél: 819-333-4609; *Téléc:* 819-333-9591
mancebourg@reseaubiblioatnq.qc.ca
www.reseaubiblioduquebec.qc.ca
Émilienne Jérôme, Responsable
819-333-5766

***Ste-Jeanne-d'Arc-de-Matane:* Bibliothèque de Sainte-Jeanne-d'Arc-de-Matane**
205, rue Principale, Ste-Jeanne-d'Arc-de-Matane QC G0J 2T0
Tél: 418-776-5814
biblio.jeanne@crsbp.net
www.reseaubiblioduquebec.qc.ca
Pauline Proulx, Responsable

***Ste-Lucie-des-Laurentides:* Bibliothèque de Sainte-Lucie-des-Laurentides**
2057, ch des Hauteurs, Ste-Lucie-des-Laurentides QC J0T 2J0
Tél: 819-326-3228; *Téléc:* 819-326-0592
biblio041@crsbpl.qc.ca
www.municipalite.sainte-lucie-des-laurentides.qc.ca
Lorraine Beauchamp, Responsable

***Ste-Marcelline-de-Kildare:* Bibliothèque de Sainte-Marcelline-de-Kildare**
435, 1ère av Pied-de-la-Montagne, Ste-Marcelline-de-Kildare QC J0K 2Y0
Tél: 450-883-2241; *Téléc:* 450-883-2242
biblio135@reseaubibliocqlm.qc.ca
www.reseaubiblioduquebec.qc.ca
Gisèle Labine, Responsable
Nicole Perreault, Adjointe

***Ste-Marguerite-du-Lac-Masso:* Bibliothèque de Sainte-Marguerite-Estérel**
4, rue des Lilas, Ste-Marguerite-du-Lac-Masso QC J0T 1L0
Tél: 450-228-4442; *Téléc:* 450-228-4442
biblio031@crsbpl.qc.ca
www.reseaubiblioduquebec.qc.ca/sainte-marguerite-esterel
Joane Grandmaison, Responsable

***Ste-Séraphine:* Bibliothèque de Sainte-Séraphine**
2660, rue Centre communautaire, Ste-Séraphine QC J0A 1E0
Tél: 819-336-3222; *Téléc:* 819-336-3800
biblio085@reseaubibliocqlm.qc.ca
www.reseaubiblioduquebec.qc.ca
Monique Raîche, Responsable

***Ste-Thérèse-de-la-Gatineau:* Bibliothèque municipale de Sainte-Thérèse-de-la-Gatineau**
29, rue Principale, Ste-Thérèse-de-la-Gatineau QC J0X 2X0
Tél: 819-449-7964; *Téléc:* 819-449-2194
admtherese@crsbpo.qc.ca
www.reseaubiblioduquebec.qc.ca/Ste-Therese-de-la-Gatineau
Josée Riel, Coordonnatrice

***St-François-Xavier-de-Viger:* Bibliothèque de Saint-François-Xavier-de-Viger**
125, rue Principale, St-François-Xavier-de-Viger QC G0L 3C0
Tél: 418-497-2430; *Téléc:* 418-497-2302
biblio.xavier@crsbp.net
www.reseaubiblioduquebec.qc.ca
Diana Morin, Responsable

***St-Jean-de-l'Ile-d'Orléans:* Bibliothèque municipale de Saint-Jean-de-l'Ile-d'Orléans**
10, ch des Côtes, St-Jean-de-l'Ile-d'Orléans QC G0A 3W0
Tél: 418-829-3336; *Téléc:* 418-829-0997
biblio.vm@sympatico.ca
Françoise Laberge, Responsable
Nicole Pelchat, Responsable, Acquisitions

***St-Lambert-Desmeloizes:* Bibliothèque de St-Lambert**
509B, rte du 5e & 8e rang, St-Lambert-Desmeloizes QC J0Z 1V0
Tél: 819-788-2491; *Téléc:* 819-788-2491
lambert@reseaubiblioatnq.qc.ca
www.reseaubiblioduquebec.qc.ca
Jeanne D'Arc Fluet, Responsable

***St-Laurent-de-l'Ile-d'Orléa:* Bibliothèque David-Gosselin/Saint-Laurent-de-l'Ile-d'Orléans**
#1, 1330, ch Royal, St-Laurent-de-l'Ile-d'Orléa QC G0A 3Z0
Tél: 418-828-2529; *Téléc:* 418-828-2170
bibliosaintlaurentiledorleans@gmail.com
www.reseaubiblioduquebec.qc.ca/saint-laurent
Guy Delisle, Responsable
guy.delisle2@gmail.com

***St-Marcel-de-L'Islet:* Bibliothèque municipale de Saint-Marcel**
46, rue Taché est, St-Marcel-de-L'Islet QC G0R 3R0
Tél: 418-356-2691; *Téléc:* 418-356-2820
Rita Avoine, Responsable
Solange Boucher, Adjointe

***St-Nazaire-de-Buckland:* Bibliothèque municipale de St-Nazaire**
PR, St-Nazaire-de-Buckland QC G0R 3T0
Tél: 418-642-2945
René Blais, Responsable
Jacinthe Bruneau, Adjointe

***St-Norbert-d'Arthabaska:* Bibliothèque de Norbertville**
42, rue Landry, St-Norbert-d'Arthabaska QC G0P 1B0
Tél: 819-260-0560
biblio147@reseaubibliocqlm.qc.ca
www.reseaubiblioduquebec.qc.ca
Suzie Leblanc, Responsable

***Stoneham:* Bibliothèque Jean-Luc-Grondin**
325, ch du Hibou, Stoneham QC G0A 4P0
Tél: 418-848-3399; *Téléc:* 418-848-1748
jlgrondin@sympatico.ca
www.reseaubiblioduquebec.qc.ca/stoneham/
Gaétane St-Laurent, Responsable
Mireille Bélanger, Responsable, PIB

***St-Pierre-de-la-Riv.-du-Sud:* Bibliothèque municipale de Saint-Pierre-de-la-Rivière-du-Sud**
620, rue Principale, St-Pierre-de-la-Riv.-du-Sud QC G0R 4B0
Tél: 418-248-8031; *Téléc:* 418-241-1477
biblstpi@globetrotter.qc.ca
www.reseaubiblioduquebec.qc.ca/saint-pierre-r-s
Georgette Roy, Responsable
groy45@globetrotter.net
418-248-2319

***St-Stanislas-de-Champlain:* Bibliothèque Émile-Bordeleau/Saint-Stanislas**
33A, rue du Pont, St-Stanislas-de-Champlain QC G0X 3E0
Tél: 418-328-4556; *Téléc:* 418-328-4121
biblio002@reseaubibliocqlm.qc.ca
www.reseaubiblioduquebec.qc.ca
Ghislaine B. Asselin, Responsable

***Sutton:* Bibliothèque municipale de Sutton**
19, rue Highland, Sutton QC J0E 2K0
Tél: 450-538-5843; *Téléc:* 450-538-4286
sutton@reseaubibliomonteregie.qc.ca
Lisa Charbonneau, Responsable

***Tadoussac:* Bibliothèque municipale de Tadoussac**
162, des Jésuites, Tadoussac QC G0T 2A0
Tél: 418-235-4446; *Téléc:* 418-235-4433
ville@tadoussac.com
www.tadoussac.com
Johanne Hovington, Responsable
418-235-4512

***Taschereau:* Bibliothèque de Taschereau**
50, rue Morin, Taschereau QC J0Z 3N0
Tél: 819-796-2219
taschereau@reseaubiblioatnq.qc.ca
www.reseaubiblioduquebec.qc.ca
Hélène Pelletier, Responsable

***Témiscamingue:* Bibliothèque de Témiscamingue**
40, rue Boucher, Témiscamingue QC J0Z 3R0
Tél: 819-627-9778; *Téléc:* 819-627-3019
biblioTEM@hotmail.com
Suzelle Plante, Responsable
Claudie Gaudet, Responsable écolière

***Terrasse-Vaudreuil:* Bibliothèque Terrasse-Vaudreuil**
74, 7e av, Terrasse-Vaudreuil QC J7V 3M9
Tél: 514-425-0430
Huguette Noël, Responsable

***Terrebonne:* Bibliothèque publique de Terrebonne**
3424, rue Camus, Terrebonne QC J6W 4N7
Tél: 450-470-0933
www.ville.terrebonne.qc.ca/loisirs_bibliotheques-publiques.php
Céline Paquette, Coordonnatrice aux bibliothèques
celine.paquette@ville.terrebonne.qc.ca

***Tête-à-la-Baleine:* Bibliothèque municipale de Tête-à-la-Baleine**
Centre Communautaire, Municipalité de la Côte-Nord-du-Golfe-du-Saint-Laurent, Tête-à-la-Baleine QC G0G 2W0
Tél: 418-787-2244; *Téléc:* 418-787-2241
www.reseaubiblioduquebec.qc.ca
Olive Marcoux, Responsable

***Thetford Mines:* Bibliothèque publique de Black Lake**
Polyvalente de Black Lake, 499, St-Désiré, Thetford Mines QC G6H 1L7
Tél: 418-423-4291; *Téléc:* 418-423-4909
Carmen Poulin, Agente de bureau

***Thurso:* Bibliothèque de Thurso/Lochaber-Partie-Ouest/Lochaber**
341A, rue Victoria, Thurso QC J0X 3B0
Tél: 819-985-3479; *Téléc:* 819-386-0134
admthurso@crsbpo.qc.ca
www.reseaubiblioduquebec.qc.ca/Thurso
Lysette Boyer, Responsable

***Tingwick:* Bibliothèque de Tingwick**
1266, rue St-Joseph, Tingwick QC J0A 1L0
Tél: 819-359-3225; *Téléc:* 819-359-2233
biblio083@reseaubibliocqlm.qc.ca
www.reseaubiblioduquebec.qc.ca
Lyse Brochu, Responsable

***Tourville:* Bibliothèque municipale de Tourville**
946, Principale, Tourville QC G0R 4M0
Tél: 418-359-2106; *Téléc:* 418-359-3671
municipal.tourville@globetrotter.net
Ghislaine Legros, Responsable
418-359-2192

***Très-Saint-Rédempteur:* Bibliothèque municipale de Très-Saint-Rédempteur**
769, rte Principale, Très-Saint-Rédempteur QC J0P 1P0
Tél: 450-451-5203
redempteur@reseaubibliomonteregie.qc.ca
Carolle Lalonde, Responsable

***La Trinité-des-Monts:* Bibliothèque de La Trinité-des-Monts**
12, rue Principale ouest, La Trinité-des-Monts QC G0K 1B0
Tél: 418-779-2272
biblio.trinite@crsbp.net
www.reseaubiblioduquebec.qc.ca
Léonie Morin, Responsable

***Trois-Pistoles:* Bibliothèque Anne-Marie-D'Amours**
145, rue de l'Aréna, Trois-Pistoles QC G0L 4K0
Tél: 418-851-2374; *Téléc:* 418-851-3567
biblio.pistoles@crsbp.net
www.reseaubiblioduquebec.qc.ca
Karen Dionne, Directrice
k.dionne@ville-trois-pistoles.ca

***Trois-Rives:* Bibliothèque de Saint-Joseph-de-Mékinac**
258, rue St-Joseph, Trois-Rives QC G0X 2C0
Tél: 819-646-5686; *Téléc:* 819-646-5686
biblio034@reseaubibliocqlm.qc.ca
www.reseaubiblioduquebec.qc.ca
Georgette Doucet, Responsable

***Trois-Rivières:* Bibliothèques de Trois-Rivières**
1425, place de l'Hôtel-de-Ville, Trois-Rivières QC G9A 5L9
Tél: 819-372-4615
bibliotheque@v3r.net
www.biblio.v3r.net
Michel Lacoursière, Chef de service, Bibliothèques de Trois-Rivières
mlacoursiere@v3r.net
819-372-4645
Lisette Beauchemin, Chef d'équipe
lbeauchemin@v3r.net
Odette Pelletier, Coordination, Services techniques
opelletier@v3r.net
819-372-4641 ext. 4251

***La Tuque:* Bibliothèque municipale de la Tuque**
575, rue St-Eugène, La Tuque QC G9X 2T5
Tél: 819-523-3100; *Téléc:* 819-523-4487
bibliotheque@ville.latuque.qc.ca
Alain Michaud, Bibliothécaire
Julie Gravel, Technicienne en documentation
jgravel@ville.latuque.qc.ca

***Upton:* Bibliothèque municipale d'Upton**
784, rue Saint-Éphrem, Upton QC J0H 2E0
Tél: 450-549-4537
Francine Savoie, Responsable
450-549-4564

***Val-Alain:* Bibliothèque L'Hiboucou**
1198, rue de l'Église, Val-Alain QC G0S 3H0
Tél: 418-744-3313; *Téléc:* 418-744-3222
hiboucou@globetrotter.qc.ca
www.reseaubiblioduquebec.qc.ca/val-alain/
Karine Fleury, Responsable

***Val-Barrette:* Bibliothèque de Val-Barrette**
135, rue St-Joseph, Val-Barrette QC J0W 1Y0
Tél: 819-585-3131; *Téléc:* 819-585-4915
val-barrette@sympatico.ca
www.crsbpl.qc.ca/bibliotheques/Val-Barrette.html
Nicole Thériault, Responsable
ntheriault001@hotmail.com
819-585-2490
Sylvie Giguère, Bénévole
819-585-3803

***Val-Brillant:* Bibliothèque Val-Brillant**
11, rue Saint-Pierre ouest, Val-Brillant QC G0J 3L0
Tél: 418-742-3711
biblio.brillant@crsbp.net
Adrienne Aubut, Responsable

***Valcourt:* Bibliothèque publique Yvonne L. Bombardier**
1002, rue J.A. Bombardier, Valcourt QC J0E 2L0
Tél: 450-532-2250; *Téléc:* 450-532-5807
bylb@fjab.qc.ca
Karine Corbeil, Responsable
k.corbeil@fjab.qc.ca

***Val-d'Espoir:* Bibliothèque de Val-d'Espoir**
1240, 5e Rang est, Val-d'Espoir QC G0C 3G0
www.reseaubiblioduquebec.qc.ca
Lorraine Dallaire, Responsable

***Val-d'Or:* Bibliothèque municipale de Val-d'Or**
600, 7e rue, Val-d'Or QC J9P 3P3
Tél: 819-824-2666; *Téléc:* 819-825-3062
www.ville.valdor.qc.ca
Olivier Barrette, Responsable
barretto@ville.valdor.qc.ca
Colette Gobeil, Bibliotechnicienne
gobeilc@ville.valdor.qc.ca
819-824-2666
Diane Naud, Bibliotechnicienne
naudd@ville.valdor.qc.ca
819-824-2666

***Val-David:* Bibliothèque de Val-David**
1355, rue de l'Académie, Val-David QC J0T 2N0
Tél: 819-322-2900; *Téléc:* 819-322-1307
bibliotheque@valdavid.com
www.reseaubiblioduquebec.qc.ca
Michel Usal, Responsable

***Val-des-Bois:* Bibliothèque de Val-des-Bois/Bowman**
593, rte 309, Val-des-Bois QC J0X 3C0
Tél: 819-454-2280; *Téléc:* 819-454-2211
admvaldesbois@crsbpo.qc.ca
www.reseaubiblioduquebec.qc.ca/Val-des-Bois
Denise Dubois, Responsable

***Val-des-Monts:* Bibliothèque de Perkins (Val-des-Monts)**
17, ch du Manoir, Val-des-Monts QC J8N 7E8
Tél: 819-671-1476; *Téléc:* 819-457-4141
admperkins@crsbpo.qc.ca
www.reseaubiblioduquebec.qc.ca/Perkins
Denise Cécyre, Responsable

***Val-des-Monts:* Bibliothèque de Poltimore/Denholm (Val-des-Monts)**
2720, rte Principale, Val-des-Monts QC J8N 3B6
Tél: 819-457-4467; *Téléc:* 819-457-4141
bibliopoltimore@crsbpo.qc.ca
www.reseaubiblioduquebec.qc.ca/Poltimore
Gabriel Ewen, Responsable

***Val-des-Monts:* Bibliothèque de Saint-Pierre-de-Wakefield (Val-des-Monts)**
24, ch du Parc, Val-des-Monts QC J8N 4H8
Tél: 819-457-1911; *Téléc:* 819-457-9113
admstpierre@crsbpo.qc.ca
www.reseaubiblioduquebec.qc.ca
Colette Prud'Homme, Responsable

***Val-Morin:* Bibliothèque Francine Paquette**
6160, rue Morin, Val-Morin QC J0T 2R0
Tél: 819-324-5672
valmorin@crsbpl.qc.ca
www.reseaubiblioduquebec.qc.ca
Jacqueline Leonard, Responsable

***Val-Paradis:* Bibliothèque de Val-Paradis**
1865-A, ch des Rangs 1 et 10, Val-Paradis QC J0Z 3S0
Tél: 819-941-2046; *Téléc:* 819-941-2485
paradis@reseaubiblioatnq.qc.ca
www.reseaubiblioduquebec.qc.ca
Renée Bégin, Responsable

***Val-Saint-Gilles:* Bibliothèque de Val-Saint-Gilles**
801, rue Principale, Val-Saint-Gilles QC J0Z 3T0
Tél: 819-333-5676; *Téléc:* 819-333-3116
gilles@reseaubiblioatnq.qc.ca
www.reseaubiblioduquebec.qc.ca
Nicole Richer, Responsable

***Varennes:* Bibliothèque Jacques-Lemoyne-de-Sainte-Marie**
2221, boul René-Gaultier, Varennes QC J3X 1E3
Tél: 450-652-3949
m.lamoureux@ville.varennes.qc.ca
www.ville.varennes.qc.ca/biblio/
Michèle Lamoureux, Bibliothécaire

***Vaudreuil-Dorion:* Bibliothèque municipale de Vaudreuil-Dorion**
51, rue Jeannotte, Vaudreuil-Dorion QC J7V 6E6
Tél: 450-455-5588; *Téléc:* 450-455-5653
biblio@ville.vaudreuil-dorion.qc.ca
www.ville.vaudreuil-dorion.qc.ca
Michelle Dupuy, Directrice, Arts et Culture
Hélène Diamond, Chef de division - Bibliothèque
Dominique D'Amour, Technicienne en documentation

Jean Gagnon, Technicien en documentation

***Vendée:* Bibliothèque de Vendée**
1816, ch du Village, Vendée QC J0T 2T0
Tél: 819-681-3372
vendee@crsbpl.qc.ca
www.reseaubiblioduquebec.qc.ca
Jeannine Dallaire, Responsable

***Verchères:* Bibliothèque municipale-scolaire Dansereau-Larose**
36, rue Dalpé, Verchères QC J0L 2R0
Tél: 450-583-3309; *Téléc:* 450-583-3637
vercheres@reseaubibliomonteregie.qc.ca
Sylvie Bissonnette, Responsable

***Victoriaville:* Bibliothèque Charles-Édouard-Mailhot**
2, rue de l'Ermitage, Victoriaville QC G6P 6T2
Tél: 819-758-8441; *Téléc:* 819-758-9432
www.bibliomcq.qc.ca/victoriaville
Louise Grondines, Directrice
louise.grondines@ville.victoriaville.qc.ca

***Villebois:* Bibliothèque de Villebois**
3889, rue de l'Église, Villebois QC J0Z 3V0
Tél: 819-941-2684; *Téléc:* 819-941-2685
villebois@reseaubiblioatnq.qc.ca
www.reseaubiblioduquebec.qc.ca
Marie Vézina, Responsable

***Ville-Marie:* Bibliothèque Ville-Marie 'La Bouquine'**
50, rue Notre-Dame de Lourdes, Ville-Marie QC J9V 1X9
Tél: 819-629-2881
villemarie@reseaubiblioatnq.qc.ca
www.reseaubiblioatnq.qc.ca/villemarie/
Cécile Boily, Responsable

***Wakefield:* Wakefield Library/ Bibliothèque de Wakefield (La Pêche)**
20 Valley Dr., Wakefield QC J0X 3G0
Tel: 819-459-3266; *Fax:* 819-459-8832
contact@wakefieldlibrary.ca
Sue Graham, Coordinator

***Warwick:* Bibliothèque de Warwick (P.-Rodolphe-Baril)**
181, rue St-Louis, Warwick QC J0A 1M0
Tél: 819-358-4325; *Téléc:* 819-358-4326
bibliowarwick@cablevision.com
www.reseaubiblioduquebec.qc.ca
France Gendron, Responsable
819-358-4325
Diane Provencher, Animatrice et préposée aux prêts
Collette Lavasseur-Desroche

***Waterloo:* Bibliothèque publique de Waterloo/ Waterloo Public Library**
650, rue de la Cour, Waterloo QC J0E 2N0
Tél: 450-539-2268
biblio@cacwaterloo.qc.ca
Gisèle Dupuis, Responsable

***Wemotaci:* Bibliothèque de Wemotaci**
CP 222, Wemotaci QC G0X 3R0
Tél: 819-666-2232; *Téléc:* 819-666-2233
biblio064@reseaubibliocqlm.qc.ca
www.reseaubiblioduquebec.qc.ca
Yvette Niquay, Responsable

***Wickham:* Bibliothèque de Wickham**
893, rue Moreau, Wickham QC J0C 1S0
Tél: 819-398-6878; *Téléc:* 819-398-7166
biblio154@reseaubibliocqlm.qc.ca
www.reseaubiblioduquebec.qc.ca
Pierrette Courchesne, Responsable

***Windsor:* Bibliothèque municipale Patrick-Dignan de Windsor**
52, rue St-Georges, Windsor QC J1S 1J5
Tél: 819-845-7115; *Téléc:* 819-845-5516
bibliwin@abacom.com
www.bibliotheque.windsor.qc.ca
Jacynthe Dubois, Technicienne en documentation
duboisj2@abacom.com

***Yamachiche:* Bibliothèque de Yamachiche (J.-Alide-Pellerin)**
440, rue Sainte-Anne, Yamachiche QC G0X 3L0
Tél: 819-296-3580; *Téléc:* 819-296-3542
biblio020@reseaubibliocqlm.qc.ca
www.reseaubiblioduquebec.qc.ca
Hélène Larose, Responsable

Archives

***Alma:* Société d'histoire du Lac-Saint-Jean**
1671, Du Pont, Alma QC G8B 5G2
Tél: 418-668-2606; *Téléc:* 418-668-5851
info@shlsj.org
www.sagamie.org/shlsj/
Gaston Martel, Archiviste

***Amos:* Société d'histoire d'Amos**
222, 1e av est, Amos QC J9T 1H3
Tél: 819-732-6070; *Téléc:* 819-732-3242
societe.histoire@cableamos.com
www.societehistoireamos.com
Pierrette Blais, Archiviste

***Baie-Comeau:* Société historique de la Côte-Nord**
9, av Marquette, Baie-Comeau QC G4Z 1K4
Tél: 418-296-8228; *Téléc:* 418-294-4187
shcn@globetrotter.net
www.shcote-nord.org
Média social:
www.facebook.com/group.php?gid=215657145115493
Pierre Frenette, Président
Marc Champagne, Secrétaire
marcus_spartacus@hotmail.com
Catherine Pellerin, Directrice-archiviste
catherine.pellerin@shcote-nord.org

***Baie-Comeau:* Ville de Baie-Comeau**
19, av Marquette, Baie-Comeau QC G4Z 1K5
Tél: 418-296-8108; *Téléc:* 418-296-3759
souellet@ville.baie-comeau.qc.ca
Sylvain Ouellet, Greffier
souellet@ville.baie-comeau.qc.ca

***Cap-de-la-Madeleine:* Sanctuaire Notre-Dame du Cap**
626, rue Notre-Dame, Cap-de-la-Madeleine QC G8T 4G9
Tél: 819-374-2441; *Téléc:* 819-374-2441
André Boucher, Responsable

***Chambly:* Société d'histoire de la Seigneurie de Chambly**
2445, rue Bourgogne, Chambly QC J3L 2A5
Tél: 450-658-2666
shsc@societehistoirechambly.org
www.societehistoirechambly.org
Paul-Henri Hudon, Président

***Chicoutimi:* Evêché de Chicoutimi**
602, rue Racine est, Chicoutimi QC G7H 1V1
Tél: 418-543-0783; *Téléc:* 418-543-2141
diocese.chicoutimi@videotron.net
www.evechedechicoutimi.qc.ca
Raynald Côté, Chancelier
raynald.cote@evechedechicoutimi.qc.ca

***Chicoutimi:* Séminaire de Chicoutimi**
679, rue Chabanel, Chicoutimi QC G7H 1Z7
Tél: 418-549-0190; *Téléc:* 418-549-1524
lycee.seminaire@lycee-sdec.qc.ca
www.sdec.qc.ca
Clément-Jacques Simard, Archiviste

***Chicoutimi:* Société historique du Saguenay**
930, rue Jacques Cartier est, Chicoutimi QC G7H 7K9
Tél: 418-549-2805; *Téléc:* 418-698-3758
shs@shistoriquesaguenay.com
www.shistoriquesaguenay.com
Louise Bouchard, Directrice générale

***Gaspé:* Centre d'archives de la Gaspésie/Musée de la Gaspésie**
80, boul Gaspé, Gaspé QC G4X 1A9
Tel: 418-368-1534; *Fax:* 418-368-1535
archives@museedelagaspesie.ca
www.museedelagaspesie.ca/cag/french/index.htm
Carlos Suich, Directeur général
direction.musee@globetrotter.net
418-368-1534
Janis Lucas, Archiviste
archive@globetrotter.net
418-368-1534

***Gatineau:* Archives municipales de la Ville de Gatineau**
855, boul de la Gappe, Gatineau QC J8T 8H9
Tél: 819-243-2329; *Téléc:* 819-243-2341
archives@ville.gatineau.qc.ca
www.ville.gatineau.qc.ca/archives/
Bernard Savoie, Responsable, Chef, Section gestion des documents et des archives
Michelyne Mongeon, Archiviste
Louise Bisson, Analyste

***Gatineau:* Western Québec School Board**
170, rue Principale, Gatineau QC J9H 6K1
Tel: 819-864-2336; *Fax:* 819-684-1328
Toll-Free: 800-363-9111
wqsb@wqsb.qc.ca
www.wqsb.qc.ca
Ann Bilodeau, Contact

***Granby:* Société d'histoire de la Haute-Yamaska**
135, rue Principale, Granby QC J2G 2V1
Tél: 450-372-4500
info@shhy.org
www.shhy.org
Richard Racine, Directeur général, archiviste
richard.racine@shhy.info
Johanne Rochon, Responsable de la diffusion, archiviste
johanne.rochon@shhy.info

***Jonquière:* La Commission scolaire de la Jonquière**
3644, rue Saint-Jules, Jonquière QC G7X 7X4
Tél: 418-542-7551; *Téléc:* 418-542-1505
sgeneral@csjonquiere.qc.ca
www.csjonquiere.qc.ca
Christian St-Gelais, Secrétaire général
Serge LeBlanc, Agent d'administration
serge.leblanc@csjonquiere.qc.ca
418-695-1801

***Knowlton:* Brome County Historical Society/ Société historie du comté de Brome**
130 Lakeside, Knowlton QC J0E 1V0
Tel: 450-243-6782
bchs@endirect.qc.ca
Marion L. Phelps, Archivist

***Lac-aux-Sables:* Société d'histoire de Lac-aux-Sables et d'Hervey-Jonction**
40, rue Bourassa, Lac-aux-Sables QC G0X 1M0
Tél: 418-336-2918
shlashj@hotmail.com
www.rabaska.com/histoire/lacauxsables.htm
Annie Gauthier, Responsable
anik3@globetrotter.net

***Lac-Etchemin:* Société du patrimoine de Sainte-Justine-de-Langevin**
212E, 2e av, Lac-Etchemin QC G0R 1S0
Tél: 418-625-1231; *Téléc:* 418-625-5980
etchemin@eccetera.com
Ghislain Royer, Archiviste

***Lachine:* Musée de Lachine**
1, ch du Musée, Lachine QC H8S 4L9
Tél: 514-634-3478; *Téléc:* 514-637-6784
museedelachine@lachine.ca
lachine.ville.montreal.qc.ca/musee

***Lac-Mégantic:* Société d'histoire et du patrimoine de la région de Mégantic**
5086, rue Frontenac, Lac-Mégantic QC G6B 1H3
Tél: 819-583-0876; *Téléc:* 819-583-0878
direction@bibliomegantic.qc.ca
www.bibliomegantic.qc.ca
Daniel Lavoie, Bibliothécaire

***Laval:* Frères des écoles chrétiennes, Montréal**
300, ch du Bord-de-l'Eau, Laval QC H7X 1S9
Tél: 450-689-4151; *Téléc:* 450-689-6260
archives@delasalle.qc.ca
Louis-Marie Côté, Archiviste
archives@delasalle.qc.ca
Claude Gadoury, Personnel

***Laval:* Société d'histoire et de généalogie de l'Ile Jésus**
4290, boul Samson, Laval QC H7W 2G9
Tél: 450-681-9096; *Téléc:* 450-686-8270
shgij@bellnet.ca
www.genealogie.org/club/shgij
Nicole Boyer, Directrice générale

***Lennoxville:* Lennoxville-Ascot Historical & Museum Society**
9 Speid St., Lennoxville QC J1M 1Z3
Tel: 819-564-0409; *Fax:* 819-564-8951
lrider@uplands.ca
www.uplands.ca/eng/lenn-ascot.html
Lillian Rider, Head of Archives

***Longueuil:* Soeurs des Saints Noms de Jésus et de Marie, Longueuil**
80, rue Saint-Charles est, Longueuil QC J4H 1A9
Tél: 450-651-8104; *Téléc:* 450-651-8636
archivessnjm@videotron.ca
Yvonne Painchaud, Archiviste

***Magog:* Société d'histoire du Lac Memphrémagog**
525, Verchères, Magog QC J1X 3K9
memphre@cgocable.ca
www.memphre.com
Jacques Boisvert, Président

***Montréal:* Archevêché de Montréal**
2000, rue Sherbrooke ouest, Montréal QC H3H 1G4
Tél: 514-931-7311; *Téléc:* 514-931-3432
chancellerie@diocesemontreal.org
www.diocesemontreal.org
Mgr. Michel Parent, Archiviste
awalhin@diocesemontreal.org

***Montréal:* Archives de Montréal**
#108R, 275, rue Notre-Dame est, Montréal QC H2Y 1C6
Tél: 514-872-1173; *Téléc:* 514-872-3475
consultation_archives@ville.montreal.qc.ca
www.ville.montreal.qc.ca/archives
Denys Chouinard, Chef de section des archives
dchouinard@ville.montreal.qc.ca
514-872-3496
Mario Robert, Analyste
mrobert@ville.montreal.qc.ca
514-872-2579

***Montréal:* Archives provinciales des Capucins et Bibliothèque franciscaine provinciale des Capucins**
3650, boul de la Rousselière, Montréal QC H1A 2X9
Tél: 514-642-5391; *Téléc:* 514-642-5033
sacre-coeur@videotron.ca
Godefroy-C. Dévost, Bibliothécaire-Archiviste
514-642-5391 ext. 345
France Guilbert, Technicienne en documentation
514-642-5391 ext. 347

***Montréal:* Bank of Montreal**
129, rue Saint-Jacques, étage D, Montréal QC H2Y 1L6
Tel: 514-877-6810; *Fax:* 514-877-7341
yolaine.toussaint@bmo.com
Yolaine Toussaint, Archivist
yolaine.toussaint@bmo.com

***Montréal:* Canadian Jewish Congress/ Congrès Juif Canadien**
1590, av Docteur Penfield, Montréal QC H3G 1C5
Tel: 514-931-7531; *Fax:* 514-931-0548
archives@cjccc.ca
www.cjccc.ca/national_archives
Janice Rosen, Archives Director
archives@cjccc.ca

***Montréal:* Concordia University Archives**
#1015, Hall Bldg., 1455, boul de Maisonneuve ouest, Montréal QC H3G 1M8
Tel: 514-848-2424; *Fax:* 514-848-2857
nancy.marrelli@concordia.ca
archives3.concordia.ca
Nancy Marrelli, Director of Archives
nancy.marrelli@concordia.ca
514-848-2424 ext. 7776

***Montréal:* Congrégation de Notre-Dame de Montréal**
2330, rue Sherbrooke ouest, Montréal QC H3H 1G8
Tél: 514-931-5891; *Téléc:* 514-931-2915
cndarchives@cnd-m.com

***Montréal:* Congrégation de Ste-Croix, Montréal**
4994, ch Côte-des-Neiges, Montréal QC H3V 1A4
Tél: 514-735-1526; *Téléc:* 514-735-7813
administrationprov@religieuxcsc.qc.ca
www.ste-croix.qc.ca/index.php
Marie-Josée Vadnais, Archiviste
514-735-1526 ext. 420

***Montréal:* Frères de St Gabriel, Province de Montréal**
1601, boul Gouin est, Montréal QC H2C 1C2
Tél: 514-387-7337; *Téléc:* 514-387-0735
fsgarchives@bellnet.ca
www.saintgabriel.ca
Philippe Geoffrion, Archiviste

***Montréal:* The Gazette**
200, 1010, rue Ste-Catherine ouest, Montréal QC H3B 5L1
Tel: 514-987-2412; *Fax:* 514-987-2433
library@thegazette.canwest.com
www.canada.com/montreal/montrealgazette
Michael Porritt, Library Administrator
mporritt@thegazette.canwest.com

***Montréal:* McCord Museum**
690, rue Sherbrooke ouest, Montréal QC H3A 1E9
Tel: 514-398-7100; *Fax:* 514-398-5045
francois.cartier@mccord.mcgill.ca
www.musee-mccord.qc.ca
Nicole Vallières, Director, Collection Management
514-398-7100 ext. 282
François Cartier, Archivist
francois.cartier@mccord.mcgill.ca
514-398-7100 ext. 267
François Cartier, Archivist
francois.cartier@mccord.mcgill.ca
514-398-7100 ext. 267

***Montréal:* Montréal Holocaust Memorial Centre/ Centre commémoratif de l'holocauste à Montréal**
5151, ch Côte Sainte-Catherine, Montréal QC H3W 1M6
Tel: 514-345-2605; *Fax:* 514-344-2651
info@mhmc.ca
www.mhmc.ca
Bill Surkis, Executive Director

***Montréal:* Oratoire St-Joseph**
3800, ch Queen-Mary, Montréal QC H3V 1H6
Tél: 514-733-8211; *Téléc:* 514-733-5269
recherche@saint-joseph.org
Daniel Picot, Directeur du centre de recherche et documentation OSJ
514-733-8211 ext. 2331

***Montréal:* Pères Dominicains, Montréal**
2715, ch. de la Côte-Sainte-Catherine, Montréal QC H3T 1B6
Tél: 514-341-2244; *Téléc:* 514-341-3233
archives@dominicains.ca
www.dominicains.ca
Luc Aubin, Archiviste provincial

***Montréal:* Port de Montréal**
Édifice du port de Montréal, 2100, av Pierre-Dupuy, Aile 1, Montréal QC H3C 3R5
Tél: 514-283-3098; *Téléc:* 514-283-6981
www.port-montreal.com
Denise Duguay, Archiviste/Superviseur, Gestion des documents
duguayd@port-montreal.com
514-283-7009

***Montréal:* Séminaire de Saint-Sulpice de Montréal**
116, rue Notre-Dame ouest, Montréal QC H2Y 1T2
Tél: 514-849-6561; *Téléc:* 514-286-9021
ucss.archives@sulpc.org
www.sulpc.org/sulpc_univers_culturel_archives_en.php
Marc Lacasse, Coordinateur
Marc Lacasse, Archiviste, Coordinateur du service
lacasse@cam.org

***Montréal:* Soeurs Grises de Montréal**
138, rue Saint-Pierre, Montréal QC H2Y 2L7
Tél: 514-842-9411; *Téléc:* 514-842-0142
www.sgm.qc.ca
Suzanne Morin, Responsable des archives

***Montréal:* Vidéographe inc**
#504, 460, rue Sainte-Catherine ouest, Montréal QC H3B 1A7
Tél: 514-866-4727; *Téléc:* 514-866-4725
info@videographe.qc.ca
www.videographe.qc.ca

***Nicolet:* Séminaire de Nicolet**
#110, 900, boul Louis-Fréchette, Nicolet QC J3T 1V5
Tél: 819-293-4838; *Téléc:* 819-293-4543
seminairedenicolet@archives-seminaire-nicolet.
archives-seminaire-nicolet.qc.ca
Marie Pelletier, Archiviste
m.pelletier@archives-seminaire-nicolet.qc.ca

***Nicolet:* Les Soeurs de l'Assomption de la Sainte-Vierge**
251, rue Saint-Jean Baptiste, Nicolet QC J3T 1X9
Tél: 819-293-2011; *Téléc:* 819-293-8315
archives@sasv.ca
www.sasv.ca/english/archives.php
Rose-Aimee Richard, Principal Archivist
archives@sasv.ca
Isabelle Périgny, Archiviste

***Oka:* Société d'histoire d'Oka**
2017, ch d'Oka, Oka QC J0N 1E0
Tél: 450-479-8556; *Téléc:* 450-479-8556
www.histoiredoka.ca
Réjeanne Cyr, Présidente

***Oka:* Tsi Ronterihwanonhnha ne Kanienkeha/ Kanehsatake Resource Centre**
407 St Michel, Oka QC J0N 1E0
Tel: 450-479-1651; *Fax:* 450-479-8587
Other Numbers: 450-479-1783
kononkwe@inbox.com
Hilda Nicholas, Director

***Outremont:* Fondation Lionel-Groulx**
261, av Bloomfield, Outremont QC H2V 3R6
Tél: 514-271-4759; *Téléc:* 514-271-6369
info@fondationlionelgroulx.org
www.fondationlionelgroulx.org
Robert Boily, Directeur général
Yves Devin, Bibliothécaire
514-271-4759 ext. 226
Marie Léveillé, Archiviste principale
514-271-4759 ext. 225
François Dumas, Archiviste de référence
514-271-4759 ext. 224

***Pierrefonds:* Montréal Arrondissement Pierrefonds/Roxboro**
13665, boul Pierrefonds, Pierrefonds QC H9A 2Z4
Tel: 514-624-1124; *Fax:* 514-624-1300
amallaire@villemontreal.qc.ca
Anne-Marie Allaire, Archiviste
amallaire@villemontreal.qc.ca
514-624-1011

***La Pocatière:* Evêché de Sainte-Anne-de-la-Pocatière**
#1200, 4, av Painchaud, La Pocatière QC G0R 1Z0
Tél: 418-856-1811; *Téléc:* 418-856-5863
librairie@diocese-ste-anne.net
www.diocese-ste-anne.net/
Céline Hudon, Archiviste
819-856-1811 ext. 131
Doris Laplante, Chancelier
418-856-1811 ext. 122

***La Pocatière:* Société historique de la Côte-du-Sud**
100, 4e av Painchaud, La Pocatière QC G0R 1Z0
Tél: 418-856-2104; *Téléc:* 418-856-2104
archsud@bellnet.ca
www.shcds.org
François Taillon, Directeur, centre des archives

***La Prairie:* Archives des Frères de l'Instruction chrétienne**
870, ch de Saint-Jean, La Prairie QC J5R 2L5
Tél: 450-659-1922; *Téléc:* 450-659-3717
François Boutin, Archiviste
boutinf@jdlm.qc.ca
François Boutin, Archiviste
Albert Pruneau, Collaborateur
André Lemire, Collaborateur
Gaston Roy, Collaborateur

***La Prairie:* Société d'histoire de La Prairie de la Magdeleine**
249, rue Sainte-Marie, La Prairie QC J5R 1G1
Tél: 450-659-1393
histoire@laprairie-shlm.com
www.laprairie-shlm.com/
Edith Gagnon, secrétaire-coordonnatrice

***Québec:* Les Archives de la Ville de Québec**
350, rue St-Joseph est, 4e étage, Québec QC G1K 3B2
Tél: 418-641-6214
greffearchives@ville.quebec.qc.ca
ville.quebec.qc.ca/en/apropos/portrait/archives_historiques.as
Sylvain Ouellet, Director of the Registry and Archives

***Québec:* Archives des Augustines du Monastère de l'Hôpital Général de Québec**
260, boul Langelier, Québec QC G1K 5N1
Tél: 418-692-0461; *Téléc:* 418-692-2668
denisrobitaille@augustines.ca
www.augustines.ca
Colette Huit, Responsable
Juliette Cloutier, Archiviste
418-529-0931 ext. 217

***Québec:* Centrale des syndicats du Québec**
#100, 320, rue St-Joseph est, Québec QC G1K 9E7
Tél: 418-649-8888; *Téléc:* 418-649-8800
documentation@csq.qc.net
www.csq.qc.net
François Gagnon, Conseiller
gagnon.francois@csq.qc.net

Québec: Église catholique de Québec
#114, 1073, boul René-Lévesque ouest, Québec QC G1S 4R5
Tél: 418-688-1211; *Téléc:* 418-688-1399
fabriques@ecdq.org
fabriques.ecdq.org
Rémy Gagnon, Responsable
remy.gagnon@ecdq.org

Québec: Monastère des Augustines de l'Hôtel-Dieu de Québec
75, rue des Remparts, Québec QC G1R 3R9
Tél: 418-692-0461; *Téléc:* 418-692-2668
denisrobitaille@augustines.ca
www.augustines.ca
Claire Gagnon, Archiviste
François Rousseau, Archiviste

Québec: Musée de la Civilisation
16, rue de la Barricade, Québec QC G1K 8W9
Tél: 418-643-2158; *Téléc:* 418-646-8779
Ligne sans frais: 866-710-8031
documentation@mcq.org
www.mcq.org
Danielle Aubin, Responsable
Pierrette Lafond, Technicienne
418-643-2158 ext. 400
Martine Malenfant, Technicienne
mmalenfant@mcq.org
Martine Malenfant, Technicienne
mmalenfant@mcq.org

Québec: Musée du Royal 22e Régiment/ Museum of the Royal 22e Régiment
La Citadelle, Québec QC G1R 4V7
Tel: 418-694-2800; *Fax:* 418-694-2853
information@lacitadelle.qc.ca
www.lacitadelle.qc.ca
Jocelyne Milot, Directrice du musée
information@lacitadell.qc.ca
418-694-2800 ext. 2840
Marcelle Cinq-Mars, Archiviste
418-694-2800 ext. 2885

Québec: Pères Eudistes
6125, av 1 est, Québec QC G1H 2V9
Tél: 418-626-6494; *Téléc:* 418-628-8774
cjmeudes@sympatico.ca
www.eudistes.org/archives.htm
André Samson, Responsable
cjmeudes@sympatico.ca
418-626-6494

Québec: Religieux de St-Vincent-de-Paul (Canada)
2555, ch Ste-Foy, Québec QC G1V 1T8
Tél: 418-650-3441; *Téléc:* 418-650-5459
relsv.qc.ca/relsv
Pierre Grenier, Responsable
pierre.grenier@relsv.qc.ca

Québec: Société d'histoire de Sainte-Foy
CP 8586, Québec QC G1V 4N5
Tél: 418-654-4275
Michel Germain, Vice-Président
418-653-3215

Québec: Soeurs de Saint-Joseph-de-Saint-Vallier, Québec
560, ch Sainte-Foy, Québec QC G1S 2J6
Tél: 418-681-7361; *Téléc:* 418-683-4440
archives.st-joseph@sympatico.ca
www.saint-joseph-fed.org
Louise Talbot, Responsable
Marie-Claude Lavoie

Québec: Soeurs Servantes du Saint-Coeur-de-Marie, Beauport
37, rue des Cascades, Québec QC G1E 2K1
Tél: 418-661-3766; *Téléc:* 418-661-7269
archivesscm@qc.aira.com

Québec: Soeurs Servantes du Saint-Coeur-de-Marie, Québec
598, 8e av, Québec QC G1J 3L7
Tél: 418-529-0672; *Téléc:* 418-529-0332
Madeleine Lamothe, Archiviste

Québec: Soeurs Ursulines de Québec
2, rue du Parloir, Québec QC G1R 4M5
Tél: 418-683-0671
archivesmg@ursulines-uc.com
www.ursulines-uc.com/
Marie Marchand, Responsable, Archives
archurs.qc@bellnet.com
418-695-2523 ext. 254

Repentigny: Commission scolaire des Affluents, Affaires corporatives et gestion de l'information
80, rue Jean-Baptiste-Meilleur, Repentigny QC J6A 6C5
Tél: 450-492-9400; *Téléc:* 450-492-3720
archives@csaffluents.qc.ca
www.csaffluents.qc.ca
Jacques Dufour, Secrétaire général et directeur des communications
jacques.dufour@sg.csaffluents.qc.ca
450-492-9400 ext. 1310
Viviane Rondeau, Régisseuse
viviane.rondeau@rm.csaffluents.qc.ca
450-492-9400 ext. 1370

Rimouski: Archevêché de Rimouski
34, rue de l'Évêché ouest, Rimouski QC G5L 4H5
Tél: 418-723-3320; *Téléc:* 418-722-8978
Sylvain Gosselin, Archiviste
418-723-3320

Rivière-du-Loup: Commission scolaire de Kamouraska - Rivière du Loup
464, rue Lafontaine, Rivière-du-Loup QC G5R 3Z5
www.cskamloup.qc.ca
Mèdia social: twitter.com/#!/cskamloup;
www.facebook.com/cskamloup.qc.ca

Sainte-Agathe-des-Monts: Commission scolaire des Laurentides
13, rue Sainte-Antoine, Sainte-Agathe-des-Monts QC J8C 2C3
Tél: 819-326-0333; *Téléc:* 819-326-2121
archives@cslaurentides.qc.ca
www.cslaurentides.qc.ca
André Bouchard, Directeur Général
boucharda@cslaurentides.qc.ca
819-326-0333 ext. 2004
Michel Goyer, Technicien en documentation

Sainte-Anne-de-Beaupré: Pères rédemptoristes, Sainte-Anne-de Beaupré
10018, av Royale, Sainte-Anne-de-Beaupré QC G0A 3C0
Tél: 418-827-3781; *Téléc:* 418-827-8227
Samuel Baillargeon, Archiviste

Saint-Hyacinthe: Centre d'histoire de Saint-Hyacinthe
650, rue Girouard est, Saint-Hyacinthe QC J2S 2W2
Tél: 450-774-0203; *Téléc:* 450-774-7101
infos@chsth.com
Jean-Noël Dion, Archiviste

Saint-Jean-sur-Richelieu: Société d'histoire du Haut-Richelieu
203, rue Jacques Cartier nord, CP 212, Saint-Jean-sur-Richelieu QC J3B 6Z4
Tél: 450-358-5220
shhr@qc.aira.com
www.genealogie.org
Nicole Poulin, Responsable

Saint-Jérome: Commission scolaire de la Rivière-du-Nord
995, rue Labelle, Saint-Jérome QC J7Z 5N7
Tél: 450-436-5040
tremblayr@csrdn.qc.ca
Rémi Tremblay, Responsable

Saint-Jérome: La Compagnie de Jésus
175, boul des Hauteurs, Saint-Jérome QC J7Z 5E7
Tél: 450-438-3593; *Téléc:* 450-438-6617
Andre Gendron, Bibliothécaire
Martine Proulx, Responsable, services techniques

Saint-Joseph-de-Beauce: Société du patrimoine des Beaucerons/ Beauce Historical Society
#400, 139, rue Sainte-Christine, Saint-Joseph-de-Beauce QC G0S 2V0
Tel: 418-397-6379; *Fax:* 418-397-6379
spb@axion.ca
www.culture-quebec.qc.ca/patrimoine-beauce
Rolland Bouffard, Président
Daniel Carrier, Archiviste

Saint-Laurent: Arrondissement de Saint-Laurent
777, boul Marcel Laurin, Saint-Laurent QC H4M 2M7
Tél: 514-855-6000; *Téléc:* 514-855-4121
chevrier.josee@ville.saint-laurent.qc.ca
Josée Chevrier, Coordonnatrice, Gestion de documents
chevrier.josee@ville.saint-laurent.qc.ca
Yves Drolet, Commis, gestion de documents
drolet.yves@ville.saint-laurent.gc.ca
514-855-6000 ext. 4073

Saint-Laurent: Soeurs de Sainte-Croix, Saint-Laurent
Pavillon Saint-Joseph, 900, ch. Côté Vertu, Saint-Laurent QC H4L 4T9
Tél: 514-747-6132
Suzanne Gratton, Archiviste

Shawinigan: Commission scolaire de l'Énergie
2072, rue Gignac, Shawinigan QC G9N 6V7
Tél: 819-539-6971; *Téléc:* 819-539-7797
Ligne sans frais: 888-711-0013
www.csenergie.qc.ca
Luce Marion, Bibliothécaire
lmarion@csenergie.qc.ca
Minique Champagne, Technicienne

Sherbrooke: Archevêché de Sherbrooke
130, rue de la Cathédrale, Sherbrooke QC J1H 4M1
Tél: 819-563-9934; *Téléc:* 819-562-0125
bibliotheque@diocesedesherbrooke.org
Roger Roy, Vicaire général
vicgeneral@diocesedessherbrooke.org

Sherbrooke: Commission scolaire de la Région-de-Sherbrooke
2955, boul de l'Université, Sherbrooke QC J1K 2Y3
Tél: 819-822-5540; *Téléc:* 819-822-5530
www.csrs.qc.ca
Diane Boivin, Analyste en gestion documentaire
819-843-9266

Sherbrooke: Société d'histoire de Sherbrooke
275, rue Dufferin, Sherbrooke QC J1H 4M5
Tél: 819-821-5406; *Téléc:* 819-821-5417
info@histoiresherbrooke.com
www.histoiresherbrooke.com/
Hélène Liard, Archiviste
helene.liard@histoiresherbrooke.com

Sorel-Tracy: Société historique Pierre-de-Saurel inc
6A, rue St-Pierre, Sorel-Tracy QC J3P 3S2
Tél: 450-780-5739; *Téléc:* 450-746-1655
histoire.archives@shps.qc.ca
Luc Poirier, Président

Stanbridge East: Missisquoi Historical Society
2, rue River, Stanbridge East QC J0J 2H0
Tel: 450-248-3153; *Fax:* 450-248-0420
jantle@museemissisquoi.ca
www.museemissisquoi.ca
Judy Antle, Archivist
jantle@museemissisquoi.ca
450-248-3153
Pamela Realffe, Executive Secretary
prealffe@museemissisquoi.ca
450-248-3153
Heather Darch, Curator
hdarch@museemissisquoi.ca
450-248-3153

Stanstead: Stanstead Historical Society/ Société historique de Stanstead
535, rue Dufferin, Stanstead QC J0B 3E0
Tel: 819-876-7322; *Fax:* 819-876-7936
archives@colbycurtis.ca
www.colbycurtis.ca/eng/archives.html
Aileen Desbarats, Archivist
info@colbycurtis.ca
Kathy Curtis, Assistant Archivist
archives@colbycurtis.ca
Sophie Cormier, Staff
info@colbycurtis.ca

Thetford Mines: Société des archives historiques de la région de l'Amiante
671, boul Frontenac ouest, Thetford Mines QC G6G 1N1
Tél: 418-338-8591; *Téléc:* 418-338-3498
archives@cegepth.qc.ca
www.sahra.qc.ca
Stéphane Hamann, Directeur - Archiviste
Marie-Josée Poirier, Technicienne en documentation

Trois-Rivières: Evêché de Trois-Rivières
362, Bonaventure, Trois-Rivières QC G9A 2B3
Tél: 819-374-1432; *Téléc:* 819-379-2496
archives@evechetr.org
http://diocese-trois-rivieres.org/
Denise Maltais, Archiviste diocésaine
819-379-1432 ext. 2308

Trois-Rivières: **Soeurs Ursulines, Trois-Rivières**
784, rue des Ursulines, Trois-Rivières QC G9A 5B5
Tel: 819-375-6039; *Fax:* 819-691-0490
urstr.archives@cgocable.ca
www.ursulines-uc.com/musees.php#a_tr
Claude Jutras, Directeur du service des archives

Trois-Rivières: **Ville de Trois-Rivières**
370, rue des Forges, Trois-Rivières QC G9A 2H1
Tél: 819-372-4647; *Téléc:* 819-374-9872
archives@v3r.net
Céline Lamy, Archiviste
Brigitte Tremblay, Technicienne

Val-d'Or: **Société d'histoire et de généalogie de Val-d'Or**
600, 7e rue, Val-d'Or QC J9P 3P3
Tél: 819-825-6352; *Téléc:* 819-825-3062
Louiselle Alain, Présidente

Victoriaville: **Commission scolaire des Bois-Francs**
40, boul Bois-Francs, Victoriaville QC G6P 6S5
Tél: 819-758-6453; *Téléc:* 819-758-5827
mprovencher@csbf.qc.ca
www.csbf.qc.ca
Michael Provencher, Secrétariat général
lgingras@csbf.qc.ca
819-758-6453 ext. 22010

Westmount: **Avataq Cultural Institute**
#400, 215 Redfern Ave., Westmount QC H3Z 3L5
Tel: 514-989-9031; *Fax:* 514-989-8789
Toll-Free: 800-361-5029
avataq@avataq.qc.ca
www.avataq.qc.ca
Christelle Cuillert, Archivist
christelle@avataq.qc.ca
514-989-9031 ext. 241
Elisapi Novelinga, Information Agent
elisapi@avataq.qc.ca
514-989-9031 ext. 225

Saskatchewan

Regional Systems

Chinook Regional Library
1240 Chaplin St. West, Swift Current SK S9H 0G8
Tel: 306-773-3186; *Fax:* 306-773-0434
chinook@chinook.lib.sk.ca
www.chinooklibrary.ca/chinook.htm
Michael J. Keaschuk, Director
Myra Leyshon, Assistant Director

Lakeland Library Region (Saskatchewan)
1302 - 100th St., North Battleford SK S9A 0V8
Tel: 306-445-6108; *Fax:* 306-445-5717
info@lakeland.lib.sk.ca
www.lakeland.lib.sk.ca
Annmarie Hillson, Regional Librarian

Palliser Regional Library
366 Coteau St. West, Moose Jaw SK S6H 5C9
Tel: 306-693-3669; *Fax:* 306-692-5657
webmaster@palliser.lib.sk.ca
www.palliserlibrary.ca
Janet Smith, Director
jsmith@palliser.lib.sk.ca
Carolyn Graham, Rural Branch Supervisor
cgraham@palliser.lib.sk.ca
Wanda Burton, Accountant
wburton@palliser.lib.sk.ca

Parkland Regional Library
PO Box 5049, Yorkton SK S3N 3Z4
Tel: 306-783-7022; *Fax:* 306-782-2844
office@parkland.lib.sk.ca
www.parkland.lib.sk.ca
Deirdre Crichton, Regional Library Director
dcrichton@parkland.lib.sk.ca
S. Temoin, Assistant Regional Librarian
stemoin@parkland.lib.sk.ca
L. Corbett, Business Manager
office@parkland.lib.sk.ca
M. Patrick, Systems/ Database Administrator
mpatrick@parkland.lib.sk.ca
P. Anderson, Technician, Acquisitions & Bibliographic Control
panderso@parkland.lib.sk.ca
B. Eckhart, Technician, Interlibrary Loan
beckhart@parkland.lib.sk.ca
P. Stroud, Contact, Information Services
pstroud@parkland.lib.sk.ca

Southeast Regional Library
49 Bison Ave., Weyburn SK S4H 0H9
Tel: 306-848-3100; *Fax:* 306-842-2665
library.srl@southeast.lib.sk.ca
www.southeast.lib.sk.ca
Allan Johnson, CEO & Library Director
allan@southeast.lib.sk.ca

Wapiti Regional Library
145 - 12th St. East, Prince Albert SK S6V 1B7
Tel: 306-764-0712; *Fax:* 306-922-1516
wapiti@panet.pa.sk.ca
www.panet.pa.sk.ca
Kevin Phillip, Acting Regional Director

Wheatland Regional Library
806 Duchess St., Saskatoon SK S7K 0R3
Tel: 306-652-5077; *Fax:* 306-931-7611
admin@wheatland.sk.ca
www.wheatland.sk.ca
Rena Bartsch, Director
rbartsch@wheatland.sk.ca
306-652-4182
Joanne Hardy, Administrative Services Manager
jhardy@wheatland.sk.ca
306-652-5077
Kim Hebig, Assistant Director & Manager, Central Branch
khebig@wheatland.sk.ca
306-652-4183
Saache Heinrich, Youth Services Manager
sheinrich@wheatland.sk.ca
306-652-4184

Public Libraries

Abbey: **Abbey Branch Library**
133 Main St., PO Box 185, Abbey SK S0N 0A0
Tel: 306-689-2202
abbey@chinook.lib.sk.ca
www.chinooklibrary.ca/abbey.htm
Marilyn Turgeon, Librarian

Aberdeen: **Aberdeen Library**
Aberdeen Recreational Complex, 2nd Fl., Aberdeen SK S0K 0A0
Tel: 306-253-4349
aberdeen.library@wheatland.sk.ca
www.wheatland.sk.ca/branches_aberdeen.html

Admiral: **Admiral Branch Library**
PO Box 152, Admiral SK S0N 0B0
Tel: 306-297-4040
www.chinooklibrary.ca/admiral.htm
Shannon Wallis, Librarian

Air Ronge: **Senator Myles Venne School Public Library**
Box 268, Air Ronge SK S0J 3G0
Tel: 306-425-2478; *Fax:* 306-425-2815
Edna Mirasty, Librarian
smvs09@sk.sympatico.ca
306-425-2478
Betsy Dorion, Library Assistant

Alameda: **Alameda Branch Library**
200 - 5th St., Alameda SK S0C 0A0
Tel: 306-489-2066
alameda@southeast.lib.sk.ca
hip.southeast.lib.sk.ca/Southeast/Docs/alameda.html
Dee Anne Schiestel, Chair
Diane Miller, Librarian

Allan: **Allan Library**
216 Main St., Allan SK S0K 0C0
Tel: 306-257-4222
allan.library@sasktel.net
www.wheatland.sk.ca
Sandra Wilson, Library Contact

Alvena: **Alvena Public Library**
Business / Commerce Complex, 101 Main St., Alvena SK S0K 0E0
Tel: 306-943-2003
alvcirc@panet.pa.sk.ca
www.panet.pa.sk.ca
Donna Leschinski, Chair
Joan Gareau, Branch Librarian

Arborfield: **Arborfield Public Library**
Town Office, 201 Main St., PO Box 223, Arborfield SK S0E 0A0
Tel: 306-276-9330
arbcirc@panet.pa.sk.ca

Irene Lindsay, Chair
Ruth Laforge, Branch Librarian
306-769-8533

Archerwill: **Archerwill Public Library**
1st Ave., Archerwill SK S0E 0B0
Tel: 306-323-2128
arccirc@panet.pa.sk.ca
Genene Kimber-Zinger, Chair
Sandi Bender, Branch Librarian

Arcola: **Arcola Branch Library**
127 Main St., Arcola SK S0C 0G0
Tel: 306-455-2321
arcola@southeast.lib.sk.ca
hip.southeast.lib.sk.ca/Southeast/Docs/arcola.html
Shauna Forester, Librarian

Assiniboia: **Assiniboia & District Public Library**
201 - 3rd Ave. West, Assiniboia SK S0H 0B0
Tel: 306-642-3631; *Fax:* 306-642-5622
assiniboia@palliser.lib.sk.ca
www.palliserlibrary.ca
Carol Munro, Branch Librarian

Avonlea: **Avonlea Branch Library**
201 Main St. West, Avonlea SK S0H 0C0
Tel: 306-868-2076; *Fax:* 306-868-2221
avonlea@palliser.lib.sk.ca
www.palliserlibrary.ca
Sheryl Ursu, Librarian
Erica Miller, Branch Librarian

Balgonie: **Balgonie Branch Library**
129 Railway St., Balgonie SK S0G 0E0
Tel: 306-771-2332
balgonie@southeast.lib.sk.ca
Dawn Grad, Librarian

Battleford: **Battleford Branch Library**
201 - 22nd St., Battleford SK S0M 0E0
Tel: 306-937-2646; *Fax:* 306-937-6631
battleford.lib@lakeland.lib.sk.ca
www.lakeland.lib.sk.ca
Rita Kuntz, Branch Librarian

Beauval: **Beauval Public Library**
PO Bag 9000, Beauval SK S0M 0G0
Tel: 306-288-2022; *Fax:* 306-288-2202
sb@pnls.lib.sk.ca
Carol Edguist, Librarian

Beechy: **Beechy Library**
PO Box 154, Beechy SK S0L 0C0
Tel: 306-859-2032
beechy.library@sasktel.net
Lois Meaden, Branch Library Staff Contact

Bengough: **Bengough Branch Library**
301 Main St., Bengough SK S0C 0K0
Tel: 306-268-2022
bengough@southeast.lib.sk.ca
www.southeast.lib.sk.ca/branches.html
Fay Adam, Branch Librarian

Bethune: **Bethune Branch Library**
Community Hall, 524 East St., Bethune SK S0G 0H0
Tel: 306-638-3046; *Fax:* 306-638-3102
bethune@palliser.lib.sk.ca
www.palliserlibrary.ca
Robbie Curtis, Librarian

Bienfait: **Bienfait Branch Library**
414 Main St., Bienfait SK S0C 0M0
Tel: 306-388-2995; *Fax:* 306-388-2223
bienfait@southeast.lib.sk.ca
www.southeast.lib.sk.ca
Bonnie Gibson, Librarian

Big River: **Big River Branch Library**
PO Box 154, Big River SK S0J 0E0
Tel: 306-469-2152
bigcirc@panet.pa.sk.ca
www.panet.pa.sk.ca
Joan Holbrook, Librarian
Susan Maitland, Librarian

Biggar: **Biggar Lionel A. Jones Library**
202 - 3rd Ave. West, Biggar SK S0K 0M0
Tel: 306-948-3911
biggar.library@wheatland.sk.ca
Darlene Stainbrook, Community Librarian
Ruth Hall, Assistant Community Librarian

Birch Hills: **Birch Hills Branch Library**
PO Box 396, Birch Hills SK S0J 0G0
Tel: 306-749-3281
bircirc@panet.pa.sk.ca
Joanne Bzdel, Branch Librarian
Nadia Stevenson, Substitute Librarian

Bjorkdale: **Bjorkdale Public Library**
PO Box 210, Bjorkdale SK S0E 0E0
Tel: 306-886-2119
bjocirc@panet.pa.sk.ca
Janice Willerton, Chair
Lorraine Bishop, Branch Librarian

Blaine Lake: **Blaine Lake Branch Library**
General Delivery, Blaine Lake SK S0J 0J0
Tel: 306-497-3130
blacirc@panet.pa.sk.ca
Lorraine Kouznitsoff, Chair
David Bannister, Branch Librarian

Borden: **Borden Library**
303 - 1st Ave., Borden SK S0K 0N0
Tel: 306-997-2220
borden.lib@lakeland.lib.sk.ca
Diane Sylvester, Branch Librarian
Cyndy Fairbrother, Branch Substitute Librarian
Brock Joncas, Branch Substitute Librarian

Briercrest: **Briercrest Branch Library**
Community Center, Main St. PO Box 97, Briercrest SK S0H 0K0
Tel: 306-799-2137
briercrest@palliser.lib.sk.ca
www.palliserlibrary.ca
Eleanor Anderson, Chair
Lisa Nestman, Branch Librarian

Broadview: **Broadview Branch Library**
515 Main St., PO Box 590, Broadview SK S0G 0K0
Tel: 306-696-2414
broadview@southeast.lib.sk.ca
www.southeast.lib.sk.ca
Sandra Charbonneau, Chair
Winona Hovind, Branch Librarian

Broadview: **Kahkewistahaw First Nation**
PO Box 609, Broadview SK S0G 0K0
Tel: 306-696-3291; *Fax:* 306-696-3201
Toll-Free: 888-691-0188
education@kahkewistahaw.com
www.kahkewistahaw.com
Iris Taypotat, Resource Coordinator

Bruno: **Bruno Branch Library**
522 Main St., Bruno SK S0K 0S0
Tel: 306-369-2353
bruno.library@wheatland.sk.ca
Donna Olchowski, Branch Head
Danielle Demong, Branch Assistant

Buffalo Narrows: **Wisewood Public Library**
PO Box 309, Buffalo Narrows SK S0M 0J0
Tel: 306-235-4240; *Fax:* 306-235-4452
wisewoodlibrary@NLSD113.net
Darlene Petit, Librarian

Burstall: **Burstall Branch Library**
PO Box 309, Burstall SK S0N 0H0
Tel: 306-679-2177
burstall@chinook.lib.sk.ca
www.chinooklibrary.ca/burstall.htm
Janet Albrecht, Chair
Cindy Ressler, Library Assistant

Cabri: **Cabri Branch Library**
Town Hall Complex, Centre St., PO Box 18, Cabri SK S0N 0J0
Tel: 306-587-2911
cabri.chinook@sasktel.net
www.chinooklibrary.ca/cabri.htm
Liz Gossard, Chair
Joy Handwork, Librarian

Candle Lake: **Candle Lake Public Library- Paperback Deposit**
PO Box 136, Candle Lake SK S0J 3E0
Tel: 306-929-3121
Donna Hawrylak, Librarian

Canwood: **Canwood Branch Library**
PO Box 23, Canwood SK S0J 0K0
Tel: 306-468-2501
cancirc@panet.pa.sk.ca
Doris Wideen, Chair
Hildegarde Butz, Branch Librarian

Carlyle: **Carlyle Branch Library**
119 Souris Ave. West, Carlyle SK S0C 0R0
Tel: 306-453-6120
carlyle@southeast.lib.sk.ca
hip.southeast.lib.sk.ca/Southeast/Docs/carlyle.html
Kathy Homer, Chair
306-453-6256
Rita Kyle, Librarian

Carnduff: **Carnduff Branch Library**
Carnduff Education Complex, 506 Anderson Rd., Carnduff SK S0C 0S0
Tel: 306-482-3255
carnduff@southeast.lib.sk.ca
Elizabeth Henger, Chair
306-482-3270
Marjorie Johnson, Librarian
Darlene Davis, School Librarian
Agnes Kimler, School Librarian

Carrot River: **Carrot River Branch Library**
Town Office / Library Complex, Main St., PO Box 1001, Carrot River SK S0E 0L0
Tel: 306-768-2501
carcirc@panet.pa.sk.ca
Carol Stewart, Chair
JoAnne Rempel, Branch Librarian

Central Butte: **Central Butte Branch Library**
271 Butte St., PO Box 276, Central Butte SK S0H 0T0
Tel: 306-796-2222
cent_chinook@hotmail.com
www.chinooklibrary.ca/central
Sylvia Lindquist, Chair
Sandra Yonge, Librarian
Sara Bryan, Library Assistant
Anne Lloyd, Library Assistant

Chaplin: **Chaplin Branch Library**
Hall Complex, 2nd Ave., PO Box 225, Chaplin SK S0H 0V0
Tel: 306-395-2524
chaplin@chinook.lib.sk.ca
www.chinooklibrary.ca/chaplin
Duane Farnel, Chair
Gayla Gane, Librarian
Geria Ball, Library Assistant
Lynn Doell, Library Assistant

Choiceland: **Choiceland Branch Library**
Town Office, 116 - 1st St. East, Choiceland SK S0J 0M0
Tel: 306-428-2216; *Fax:* 306-428-2071
chocirc@panet.pa.sk.ca
Elaine McLean, Chair
Janice Bakker, Branch Librarian

Christopher Lake: **Christopher Lake Branch Library**
Village Office, Hwy. 263, PO Box 27, Christopher Lake SK S0J 0N0
Tel: 306-982-4763
chrcirc@panet.pa.sk.ca
Social Media:
www.facebook.com/pages/Christopher-Lake-Library/165970773430201
Gwen Collee, Chair
Laverne Jones, Branch Librarian

Climax: **Climax Branch Library**
Village Complex, 120 Main St., PO Box 323, Climax SK S0N 0N0
Tel: 306-293-2229
climax@chinook.lib.sk.ca
www.chinooklibrary.ca/climax
Michelle Smith, Chair
Nancy Glenn, Librarian
Lorna Smith, Assistant

Cochin: **Cochin Book Depository**
Hwy. 4, PO Box 190, Cochin SK S0M 0L0
Tel: 306-386-1148; *Fax:* 306-386-2305
cochin.lib@lakeland.lib.sk.ca
Judy Smith, Contact

Coleville: **Coleville Library**
R.M. Bldg., PO Box 45, Coleville SK S0L 0K0
Tel: 306-965-2551
coleville.library@wheatland.sk.ca
www.wheatland.sk.ca/branches_coleville.html
Wendy Bahm, Branch Library Staff Contact

Colonsay: **Colonsay Library**
RM Bldg., PO Box 172, Colonsay SK S0K 0Z0
Tel: 306-255-2232
colonsay.library@wheatland.sk.ca
Val Pidlisney, Branch Library Staff Contact

Conquest: **Conquest Branch Library**
Conquest Community Centre, PO Box 130, Conquest SK S0L 0L0
Tel: 306-856-4555
conquestlibrary@wheatland.sk.ca
www.wheatland.sk.ca/branches_conquest.html

Consul: **Consul Branch Library**
Prescod St., PO Box 121, Consul SK S0N 0P0
Tel: 306-299-2118
consul@chinook.lib.sk.ca
www.chinooklibrary.ca/consul.htm
Jolene Gershon, Chair
Linda Brown, Librarian

Coronach: **Coronach Branch Library**
111A Center St., Coronach SK S0H 0Z0
Tel: 306-267-3260
coronach@palliser.lib.sk.ca
www.palliserlibrary.ca
Colleen Christopherson-Coe, Chair
Marlene McBurney, Branch Librarian
Giselle Wilson, Assistant Librarian

Craik: **Craik Branch Library**
611 - 1st Ave., PO Box 339, Craik SK S0G 0V0
Tel: 306-734-2388; *Fax:* 306-734-2688
craik@palliser.lib.sk.ca
www.palliserlibrary.ca
Wanda Paradis, Chair
Jo McAlpine, Branch Librarian

Crystal Springs: **Crystal Springs Paperback Deposit**
PO Box 28, Crystal Springs SK S0K 1A0
Tel: 306-749-2632
Brenda Fisher, Branch Librarian

Cudworth: **Cudworth Branch Library**
Cudworth Town Complex, 426 - 2nd Ave., PO Box 321, Cudworth SK S0K 1B0
Tel: 306-256-3530; *Fax:* 306-256-3515
cudcirc@panet.pa.sk.ca
Regina Bantle, Chair
Shirley Osmond, Branch Librarian

Cut Knife: **Cut Knife Community Branch Library**
115 Broad St., PO Box 595, Cut Knife SK S0M 0N0
Tel: 306-398-2342
cutknife.lib@lakeland.lib.sk.ca
www.lakeland.lib.sk.ca

Cut Knife: **Poundmaker School Library**
PO Box 640, Cut Knife SK S0M 0N0
Tel: 306-398-4966; *Fax:* 306-398-4058
Corinne Weenie, Librarian

Dalmeny: **Dalmeny Branch Library**
301 Railway Ave., PO Box 850, Dalmeny SK S0K 1E0
Tel: 306-254-2119
dalmeny.library@wheatland.sk.ca
www.wheatland.sk.ca
Dana Perkins, Librarian

Davidson: **Davidson Branch Library**
314 Washington Ave., PO Box 754, Davidson SK S0G 1A0
Tel: 306-567-2022; *Fax:* 306-567-2081
davidson@palliser.lib.sk.ca
www.palliserlibrary.ca
Angela Shaw, Chair
September Brooke, Librarian
Debbie Shearwood, Assistant

Debden: **Debden Public Library**
Village Office, #3, 204 - 2nd Ave. East, Debden SK S0J 0S0
Tel: 306-724-2240
debcirc@panet.pa.sk.ca
Linda Berscheid, Chair
Aline Hannon, Branch Librarian

Delisle: **Delisle Library**
201 - 1st St. West, Delisle SK S0L 0P0
Tel: 306-493-8288
delisle.library@wheatland.sk.ca

Denzil: **Denzil Branch Library**
Brooks Ave., PO Box 188, Denzil SK S0L 0S0
Tel: 306-358-2118; *Fax:* 306-358-4828
denzil.lib@lakeland.lib.sk.ca
www.lakeland.lib.sk.ca

Dinsmore: **Dinsmore Branch Library**
Town Office, 100 Main St., PO Box 369, Dinsmore SK S0L 0T0
Tel: 306-846-2011
dinsmore.library@wheatland.sk.ca
www.wheatland.sk.ca
Mary McBain, Community Librarian
Carol Greuel, Assistant Librarian
Mary Jones, Assistant Librarian

Dodsland: **Dodsland Branch Library**
135 Second Ave., PO Box 100, Dodsland SK S0L 0V0
Tel: 306-356-2180
dodsland.library@sasktel.net
www.wheatland.sk.ca

Drake: **Drake Library**
Francis St., Drake SK S0K 1H0
Tel: 306-363-2101
drake.library@wheatland.sk.ca
www.wheatland.sk.ca/branches_drake.html

Duck Lake: **Duck Lake Public Library**
410 Victoria Ave., Duck Lake SK S0K 1J0
Tel: 306-467-2016
duccirc@panet.pa.sk.ca
Diane Perrin, Branch Librarian
Roberta Tournier, Chair

Dundurn: **Dundurn Branch Library**
300 - 3rd Ave., PO Box 626, Dundurn SK S0K 1K0
Tel: 306-492-2366
dundurn.library@wheatland.sk.ca
www.wheatland.sk.ca
Candace Myers, Branch Head

Eastend: **Eastend Branch Library**
Pottery St., PO Box 91, Eastend SK S0N 0T0
Tel: 306-295-3788
eastend@chinook.lib.sk.ca
www.chinooklibrary.ca/eastend.htm
Gail Bock, Librarian

Eatonia: **Eatonia Branch Library**
PO Box 100, Eatonia SK S0L 0Y0
Tel: 306-967-2224
eatonia.library@wheatland.sk.ca
www.townofeatonia.com/services/library.html
Sandy Guidinger, Chair
Debbie Tweten, Branch Library Staff Member
Garnet Nunweiler, Library Assistant
Melanie Rudy, Library Assistant

Edam: **Edam Library**
1000 Main St., Edam SK S0M 0V0
Tel: 306-397-2223; *Fax:* 306-397-2626
edam.lib@lakeland.lib.sk.ca
Trudy McMurphy, Librarian
Anne Latendresse, Substitute Librarian

Elbow: **Elbow Branch Library**
402 Minto St., Elbow SK S0H 1J0
Tel: 306-854-2220
elbow@palliser.lib.sk.ca
www.palliserlibrary.ca
Janice Scrimbitt, Branch Librarian

Elrose: **Elrose Branch Library**
Town Office, PO Box 185, Elrose SK S0L 0Z0
Tel: 306-378-2808
elrose.library@wheatland.sk.ca
www.wheatland.sk.ca

Estevan: **Estevan Public Library**
701 Souris Ave. North, Estevan SK S4A 2T1
Tel: 306-636-1620; *Fax:* 306-634-5830
estevan@southeast.lib.sk.ca
www.cap.estevan.sk.ca/library
Gregory Salmers, Head Librarian
greg@southeast.lib.sk.ca

Eston: **Eston Branch Library**
218 Main St., Eston SK S0L 1A0
Tel: 306-962-3513
eston.library@wheatland.sk.ca
www.wheatland.sk.ca

Fillmore: **Fillmore Branch Library**
51 Main St., Fillmore SK S0G 1N0
Tel: 306-722-3369
fillmore@southeast.lib.sk.ca
Joy Pollock, Librarian

Fort Qu'appelle: **Fort Qu'Appelle Branch Library**
140 Company Ave. South, Fort Qu'appelle SK S0G 1S0
Tel: 306-332-6411
fort.quappelle@southeast.lib.sk.ca
www.fortquappelle.com/library
Holly Smith, Librarian
306-332-6411

Fort Qu'appelle: **Standing Buffalo Branch Library**
PO Box 248, Fort Qu'appelle SK S0G 1S0
Tel: 306-332-4414
Eleice Bear, Librarian

Fox Valley: **Fox Valley Branch Library**
PO Box 145, Fox Valley SK S0N 0V0
Tel: 306-666-2045
foxvalley@chinook.lib.sk.ca
www.chinooklibrary.ca/fox.htm
Valerie Reinboldt, Librarian

Frontier: **Frontier Branch Library**
211 - 1st St. West, Frontier SK S0N 0W0
Tel: 306-296-4667
frontier@chinook.lib.sk.ca
www.chinooklibrary.ca/frontier.htm
Holly Johnson, Librarian

Gainsborough: **Gainsborough Branch Library**
401 Railway, Gainsborough SK S0C 0Z0
Tel: 306-685-2229
gainsborough@southeast.lib.sk.ca
Marjorie Johnson, Librarian

Glaslyn: **Glaslyn Library**
182 Main St., Glaslyn SK S0M 0Y0
Tel: 306-342-4748; *Fax:* 306-342-4748
glaslyn.lib@lakeland.lib.sk.ca
www.lakeland.lib.sk.ca
Jody Seifert, Librarian

Glenavon: **Glenavon Branch Library**
311 Railway Ave., Glenavon SK S0G 1Y0
Tel: 306-429-2180
glenavon@southeast.lib.sk.ca
hip.southeast.lib.sk.ca/Southeast/Docs/glenavon.html
Heather Wozniak, Librarian

Glentworth: **Glentworth Branch Library**
PO Box 200, Glentworth SK S0H 1V0
Tel: 306-266-4804
glentworth@chinook.lib.sk.ca
www.chinooklibrary.ca/glent.htm
Meryle Iwanicki, Librarian

Goodsoil: **Goodsoil Library**
301 Main St. North, Goodsoil SK S0M 1A0
Tel: 306-238-2155; *Fax:* 306-238-2155
goodsoil.lib@lakeland.lib.sk.ca
www.lakeland.lib.sk.ca
Jolynn Berlinger, Librarian
306-238-2155

Gravelbourg: **Gravelbourg Branch Library**
PO Box 568, Gravelbourg SK S0H 1X0
Tel: 306-648-3177
gravelbourg@chinook.lib.sk.ca
www.chinooklibrary.ca/gravel.htm
Valerie Alix, Librarian

Green Lake: **Dore Lake Book Deposit**
c/o Hamlet of Dore Lake, General Delivery, Green Lake SK S0M 1B0
Tel: 306-832-4528

Grenfell: **Grenfell Branch Library**
1109 Wolseley Ave., Grenfell SK S0G 2B0
Tel: 306-697-2455
grenfell@southeast.lib.sk.ca
hip.southeast.lib.sk.ca/Southeast/Docs/grenfell.html
Ann Neuls, Librarian

Gronlid: **Gronlid Branch Library**
PO Box 192, Gronlid SK S0E 0W0
Tel: 306-277-4633
grocirc@panet.pa.sk.ca
www.panet.pa.sk.ca/branchweb/gronlid/public.htm
Norma Lovell, Librarian

Gull Lake: **Gull Lake Branch Library**
1377 Conrad Ave., Gull Lake SK S0N 1A0
Tel: 306-672-3277
gull@chinook.lib.sk.ca
www.city.swift-current.sk.ca/chinook/gull.htm
Sandra Kettner, Librarian

Hafford: **Hafford Library**
17 Main St., Hafford SK S0J 1A0
Tel: 306-549-2373; *Fax:* 306-549-2333
haffordlibrary@hotmail.com
Carol Herman, Librarian

Hague: **Hague Library**
210 Railway St., Hague SK S0K 1X0
Tel: 306-225-4326
hague.library@wheatland.sk.ca
www.wheatland.sk.ca/branches_hague.html
Lynn Williamson, Branch Librarian
hague.library@sasktel.net

Hanley: **Hanley Branch Library**
112A Lincoln St., Hanley SK S0G 2E0
Tel: 306-544-2546
hanley.library@wheatland.sk.ca
www.wheatland.sk.ca/branches_hanley.html
Ann Rogers, Branch Librarian

Hazlet: **Hazlet Branch Library**
PO Box 73, Hazlet SK S0N 1E0
Tel: 306-678-2155
hazlet@chinook.lib.sk.ca
www.chinooklibrary.ca/hazlet.htm
Elaine Little, Librarian

Herbert: **Herbert Branch Library**
517 Herbert Ave., Herbert SK S0H 2A0
Tel: 306-784-2484
herbert@chinook.lib.sk.ca
www.chinooklibrary.ca/herbert.htm
Jane Epp, Librarian

Hodgeville: **Hodgeville Branch Library**
PO Box 68, Hodgeville SK S0H 2B0
Tel: 306-677-2223
hodgeville@chinook.lib.sk.ca
www.chinooklibrary.ca/hodge.htm
Elizabeth Haubrich, Librarian

Holdfast: **Holdfast Branch Library**
PO Box 205, Holdfast SK S0G 2H0
Tel: 306-488-2000
holdfast@palliser.lib.sk.ca
www.palliserlibrary.ca
Janet Couture, Branch Librarian

Hudson Bay: **Hudson Bay Public Library**
130 Main St., Hudson Bay SK S0E 0Y0
Tel: 306-865-3110; *Fax:* 306-865-2800
hudcirc@panet.pa.sk.ca
Glennys Shewchuk, Librarian

Humboldt: **Humboldt Reid-Thompson Public Library**
705 Main St., Humboldt SK S0K 2A0
Tel: 306-682-2034; *Fax:* 306-682-2035
humcirc@panet.pa.sk.ca
www.panet.pa.sk.ca/BranchDir_list.asp
Rose Ward, Branch Librarian

Ile-a-la-Crosse: **Ile a la Crosse Elementary School**
PO Box 70, Ile-a-la-Crosse SK S0M 1C0
Tel: 306-833-2010; *Fax:* 306-833-2322
Valerie Gardiner, School Librarian
vgardiner@icsd.ca
306-833-2010

Imperial: **Imperial Branch Library**
PO Box 238, 310 Royal St., Imperial SK S0G 2J0
Tel: 306-963-2272; *Fax:* 306-963-2445
imperial@palliser.lib.sk.ca
www.palliserlibrary.ca
Donalda MacLellan, Branch Librarian

Indian Head: **Indian Head Branch Library**
419 Grand Ave., Indian Head SK S0G 2K0
Tel: 306-695-3922
indian.head@southeast.lib.sk.ca
Colleen Reynard, Librarian

Island Lake: **Island Lake Library**
Island Lake First Nations School, Island Lake SK S0M 3G0
Tel: 306-837-4868; *Fax:* 306-837-4558
sli.ill@lakeland.lib.sk.ca
Helen Kowal, Librarian

Kenaston: **Kenaston Library**
PO Box 309, Kenaston SK S0G 2N0
Tel: 306-252-2130
kenaston.library@wheatland.sk.ca
www.wheatland.sk.ca/branches_kenaston.html
Faye McVeigh, Branch Librarian
Vicki Gowler, Library Assistant

***Kennedy:* Kennedy Branch Library**
235 Scott St., Kennedy SK S0G 2R0
Tel: 306-538-2020
kennedy@southeast.lib.sk.ca
Amy Hewson, Librarian

***Kerrobert:* Kerrobert Library**
PO Box 618, Kerrobert SK S0L 1R0
Tel: 306-834-5211; *Fax:* 306-834-2633
kerrobert.library@wheatland.sk.ca
Heather Wack, Branch Library Staff Contact
Marilyn Hering, Chair

***Kincaid:* Kincaid Branch Library**
PO Box 146, Kincaid SK S0H 2J0
Tel: 306-264-3910
kinc.chinook@sasktel.net
www.chinooklibrary.ca/kincaid.htm
Trudy Turgeon, Librarian

***Kindersley:* Kindersley Library**
104 Princess St., Kindersley SK S0L 1S2
Tel: 306-463-4141; *Fax:* 306-463-6834
kindersley.library@wheatland.sk.ca
Marilyn Shea, Librarian

***Kinistino:* Kinistino Branch Library**
PO Box 774, Kinistino SK S0J 1H0
Tel: 306-864-2537
kincirc@panet.pa.sk.ca
Joanne Jansen, Librarian
circ1@sk.sympatico.ca

***Kipling:* Kipling Branch Library**
207 - 6th Ave., Kipling SK S0G 2S0
Tel: 306-736-2911
kipling@southeast.lib.sk.ca
Jody Levey, Head Librarian
Florence Poirier, Assistant Librarian

***Kyle:* Kyle Public Library**
116 Centre St., Kyle SK S0L 1T0
Tel: 306-375-2566
kyle.library@wheatland.sk.ca
Elva Akister, Community Librarian
Jan Rein, Assistant

***Lafleche:* Lafleche Branch Library**
157 Main St., PO Box 132, Lafleche SK S0H 2K0
Tel: 306-472-5466
lafleche@chinook.lib.sk.ca
www.chinooklibrary.ca/lafleche.htm
Gloria McIvor, Librarian

***Lake Alma:* Lake Alma Branch Library**
Hwy. 18, PO Box 216, Lake Alma SK S0C 1M0
Tel: 306-447-2061
lake.alma@southeast.lib.sk.ca
Bernice Bloor, Librarian

***Lampman:* Lampman Branch Library**
302 Main St., Lampman SK S0C 1N0
Tel: 306-487-2202
lampman@southeast.lib.sk.ca
Martha Engel, Librarian

***Landis:* Landis Library**
PO Box 124, Landis SK S0K 2K0
Tel: 306-658-2177
landis.library@wheatland.sk.ca
www.wheatland.sk.ca/branches_landis.html
Vera Halter, Branch Librarian

***Langham:* Langham Library**
PO Box 697, Langham SK S0K 2L0
Tel: 306-283-4362
langham.library@wheatland.sk.ca
www.wheatland.sk.ca/branches_langham.html
Dean Buhr, Community Librarian
Pat C. Wood, Chair

***Lanigan:* Lanigan Library**
PO Box 70, Lanigan SK S0K 2M0
Tel: 306-365-2472
lanigan.library@wheatland.sk.ca
www.wheatland.sk.ca/branches_lanigan.html
Fran Nugent, Branch Library Staff Contact
Harvey Nugent, Branch Assistant

***Lashburn:* Lashburn Branch Library**
95 Main St., Box 160, Lashburn SK S0M 1H0
Tel: 306-285-4144
lashburn.lib@lakeland.lib.sk.ca
Bernadette Evans, Librarian

***Leader:* Leader Branch Library**
151 - 1st St. West, Leader SK S0N 1H0
Tel: 306-628-3830
leader@chinook.lib.sk.ca
www.chinooklibrary.ca/leader.htm
Lois Smith, Librarian
Stephanie Hilger, Staff

***Leask:* Leask Branch Library**
PO Box 117, Leask SK S0J 1M0
Tel: 306-466-4577; *Fax:* 306-466-2000
leacirc@panet.pa.sk.ca
Connie Peake, Librarian

***Leoville:* Leoville Branch Library**
22 Main St., Leoville SK S0J 1N0
Tel: 306-984-2057; *Fax:* 306-984-2337
leocirc@panet.pa.sk.ca
Judy Wandler, Branch Librarian
306-984-2057
Sharon Miners, Substitute Librarian

***Livelong:* Livelong Branch Library**
PO Box 161, Livelong SK S0M 1J0
Tel: 306-845-3395
livelong.lib@lakeland.lib.sk.ca
Inga Sample, Librarian

***Loon Lake:* Loon Lake Branch Library**
PO Box 216, Loon Lake SK S0M 1L0
Tel: 306-837-2186
loonlake.lib@lakeland.lib.sk.ca
www.lakeland.lib.sk.ca
Gwen Lindstrom, Librarian
loonlake.lib@lakeland.lib.sk.ca

***Loreburn:* Loreburn Branch Library**
Village Office, Loreburn SK S0H 2S0
Tel: 306-644-2026
loreburn@palliser.lib.sk.ca
www.palliserlibrary.ca
Janice Scrimbitt, Branch Librarian

***Lucky Lake:* Lucky Lake Library**
101 - 1st Ave. South, Lucky Lake SK S0L 1Z0
Tel: 306-858-2246
luckylake.library@wheatland.sk.ca
www.wheatlandlibrary.sk.ca
Elaine Ylioja, Community Librarian
Caroline Duhaime, Assistant Community Librarian

***Lumsden:* Lumsden Branch Library**
Centennial Hall, 40 - 3rd Ave., Lumsden SK S0G 3C0
Tel: 306-731-2433
lumsden@southeast.lib.sk.ca
Sheila Felix, Librarian

***Luseland:* Luseland Library**
510 Grand Ave., Luseland SK S0L 2A0
Tel: 306-372-4808
luseland.library@wheatland.sk.ca
www.wheatland.sk.ca
Diane Hurford, Branch Library Staff Contact
Ellen-May Anthony, Chair

***Macklin:* Macklin Branch Library**
5001 Press Ave., Macklin SK S0L 2C0
Tel: 306-753-2933; *Fax:* 306-753-3234
macklin.lib@lakeland.lib.sk.ca
Linda Engele, Librarian

***Maidstone:* Maidstone Branch Library**
#102B, 108 - 1st Ave. West, Maidstone SK S0M 1M0
Tel: 306-893-4153; *Fax:* 306-893-4153
maidstone.lib@lakeland.lib.sk.ca
Lorna Foster, Librarian

***Makwa:* Makwa Branch Library**
Box 10, General Delivery, Makwa SK S0M 1N0
Tel: 306-236-3995
makwa.lib@lakeland.lib.sk.ca
Michelle Boehler, Branch Librarian
306-236-3995

***Mankota:* Mankota Branch Library**
PO Box 373, Mankota SK S0H 2W0
Tel: 306-478-2331
mank.chinook@sasktel.net
www.chinooklibrary.ca/mankota.htm
Maggie Brown, Librarian

***Manor:* Manor Branch Library**
45 Main St., Manor SK S0C 1R0
Tel: 306-448-2266; *Fax:* 306-448-2266
manor@southeast.lib.sk.ca
www.southeast.lib.sk.ca
Rita Kyle, Librarian
Decia Knockeart, Assistant

***Maple Creek:* Maple Creek Branch Library**
205 Jasper St., Maple Creek SK S0N 1N0
Tel: 306-662-3522
maplecreek@chinook.lib.sk.ca
www.chinooklibrary.ca/maple.htm
Evelyn Southwood, Librarian

***Marcelin:* Marcelin Branch Library**
Town Office, 1st Ave. South, Marcelin SK S0J 1R0
Tel: 306-226-2110
marcirc@panet.pa.sk.ca
Peggy Brad, Librarian

***Marsden:* Marsden Branch Library**
#104 Centre St., Marsden SK S0M 1P0
Tel: 306-826-5666; *Fax:* 306-826-5666
marsden.lib@lakeland.lib.sk.ca
Denise Polkinghorne, Librarian

***Marshall:* Marshall Branch Library**
13 Main St., Marshall SK S0M 1R0
Tel: 306-387-6155; *Fax:* 306-387-6555
marshall.lib@lakeland.lib.sk.ca
Donna Ferguson, Librarian

***Martensville:* Martensville Library**
PO Box 1180, Martensville SK S0K 2T0
Tel: 306-956-7311
martensville.library@wheatland.sk.ca
Marla Skomar, Head Librarian
Heather Braun, Contact
Stacey Brooman, Contact

***Maryfield:* Maryfield Branch Library**
PO Box 160, Maryfield SK S0G 3K0
Tel: 306-646-2148
maryfield@southeast.lib.sk.ca
Doreen Jurkovich, Librarian

***Mayfair:* Mayfair Branch Library**
Mayfair Central School, PO Box 70, Mayfair SK S0M 1S0
Tel: 306-246-4465
mayfair.lib@lakeland.lib.sk.ca
Janet Cherwinski, Librarian

***Maymont:* Maymont Library**
PO Box 102, Maymont SK S0M 1T0
Tel: 306-389-2006
maymont.lib@lakeland.lib.sk.ca
Cassandra Mireau, Regional Librarian
cmireau@lakeland.lib.sk.ca
306-445-6108 ext. 226

***Meadow Lake:* Meadow Lake Library**
320 Centre St., PO Box 9000, SPMC Mailroom, Meadow Lake SK S9X 1V8
Tel: 306-236-5396; *Fax:* 306-236-6282
meadowlake.lib@lakeland.lib.sk.ca
Tara Million, Librarian

***Meath Park:* Meath Park Branch Library**
PO Box 122, Meath Park SK S0J 1T0
Tel: 306-929-2133; *Fax:* 306-929-2401
Kathryn Hughes, Branch Librarian

***Medstead:* Medstead Branch Library**
209 - 2nd Ave., Medstead SK S0M 1W0
Tel: 306-342-4609
medstead.lib@lakeland.lib.sk.ca
Nissa Shields, Librarian

***Melfort:* Melfort Public Library**
106 Crawford Ave. West, Melfort SK S0E 1A0
Tel: 306-752-2022; *Fax:* 306-752-2022
melcirc@panet.pa.sk.ca
Penny Markland, Librarian

***Meota:* Meota Library**
PO Box 214, Meota SK S0M 1X0
Tel: 306-892-2004
meota.lib@lakeland.lib.sk.ca
Deborah Pearce, Librarian
Juliette Tebay, Substitute Librarian

***Mervin:* Mervin Branch Library**
11 Main St., Mervin SK S0M 1Y0
Tel: 306-845-2784; *Fax:* 306-845-3563

Dawn Simkins, Librarian
306-845-2784

***Meskanaw:* Meskanaw Paperback Deposit**
General Delivery, Meskanaw SK S0K 2W0
Tel: 306-864-3730

***Midale:* Midale Branch Library**
PO Box 185, Midale SK S0C 1S0
Tel: 306-458-2263
midale@southeast.lib.sk.ca
Lydia Duncan, Librarian

***Milden:* Milden Library**
PO Box 7, Milden SK S0L 2L0
Tel: 306-935-4600
milden.library@wheatland.sk.ca
www.wheatland.sk.ca/branches_milden.html
Sandra Frey, Library Assistant

***Milestone:* Milestone Library**
112 Main St., Milestone SK S0G 3L0
Tel: 306-436-2112
milestone@southeast.lib.sk.ca
Diana Cook, Librarian

***Mistatim:* Mistatim Branch Library**
Railway Ave., Mistatim SK S0E 1B0
Tel: 306-889-2008
miscirc@panet.pa.sk.ca
Theresa McHugh, Librarian

***Montmartre:* Montmartre Regional Library**
136 Central, Montmartre SK S0G 3M0
Tel: 306-424-2029
montmartre@southeast.lib.sk.ca
Lillian Ripplinger, Librarian

***Montreal Lake:* Montreal Lake Community Library**
PO Box 150, Montreal Lake SK S0J 1Y0
Tel: 306-663-5602; *Fax:* 306-663-5652
sml@pnls.lib.sk.ca
Blanche Bird, Librarian

***Moose Jaw:* Moose Jaw Public Library**
461 Langdon Cres., Moose Jaw SK S6H 0X6
Tel: 306-692-2787; *Fax:* 306-692-3368
reference.smj@sasktel.net
www.moosejawlibrary.ca
Karon Selzer, Head Librarian
Greg Salmer, Asst. Head Librarian
gsalmer@moosejawlibrary.ca
Laura Shtern, Children's Librarian
childrens.smj@sasktel.net

***Moosomin:* Moosomin Branch Library**
701 Main St., Moosomin SK S0G 3N0
Tel: 306-435-2107
moosomin@southeast.lib.sk.ca
Christie McGonigal, Librarian

***Morse:* Morse Branch Library**
PO Box 64, Morse SK S0H 3C0
Tel: 306-629-3335
morse@chinook.lib.sk.ca
www.chinooklibrary.ca/morse.htm
Donna Fafard, Librarian

***Mortlach:* Mortlach Branch Library**
Main St., Mortlach SK S0H 3E0
Tel: 306-355-2202
mortlach@palliser.lib.sk.ca
www.palliserlibrary.ca
Linda Locke, Branch Librarian

***Mossbank:* Mossbank Branch Library**
310 Main St., Mossbank SK S0H 3G0
Tel: 306-354-2474
mossbank@palliser.lib.sk.ca
www.palliserlibrary.ca
Debbie Sullivan, Branch Librarian

***Naicam:* Naicam Branch Library**
109 Center St., Naicam SK S0K 2Z0
Tel: 306-874-2156
naicirc@panet.pa.sk.ca
Darla Christianson, Librarian
naicirc@panet.pa.sk.ca

***Neilburg:* Neilburg Branch Library**
108 Centre St., Neilburg SK S0M 2C0
Tel: 306-823-4234
neilburg.lib@lakeland.lib.sk.ca
Sharon Schempp, Librarian

***Nipawin:* Nipawin Branch Library**
214 - 2nd Ave. East, Nipawin SK S0E 1E0
Tel: 306-862-4867
nipcirc@panet.pa.sk.ca
www.nipawinlibrary.ca
Nancy Budd, Branch Librarian

***Nokomis:* Nokomis Library**
PO Box 38, Nokomis SK S0G 3R0
Tel: 306-528-2251
nokomis.library@wheatland.sk.ca
Teresda Strachan, Librarian

***North Battleford:* North Battleford Library**
1392 - 101st St., North Battleford SK S9A 1A2
Tel: 306-445-3206; *Fax:* 306-445-6454
www.northbattlefordlibrary.com

***North Battleford:* Saskatchewan Hospital Branch Library**
PO Box 39, North Battleford SK S9A 2X8
Tel: 306-446-6863; *Fax:* 306-446-6810
saskhospital.lib@lakeland.lib.sk.ca
Rita Kuntz, Branch Librarian

***Odessa:* Odessa Branch Library**
PO Box 91, Odessa SK S0G 3S0
Tel: 306-957-2020
odessa@southeast.lib.sk.ca
Sheila Leurer, Librarian

***Ogema:* Ogema Branch Library**
117 Main St., Ogema SK S0C 1Y0
Tel: 306-459-2985
ogema@southeast.lib.sk.ca
hip.southeast.lib.sk.ca/Southeast/Docs/ogema.html
Valerie Dunn, Librarian

***Osler:* Osler Library**
228 Willow Dr., Osler SK S0K 3A0
Tel: 306-239-4774; *Fax:* 306-239-2194
oslerlibrary@yourlink.ca
www.wheatland.sk.ca/branches_osler.html
Tina Remple, Branch Head

***Oungre:* Oungre Branch Library**
PO Box 88, Oungre SK S0C 1Z0
Tel: 306-456-2662
oungre@southeast.lib.sk.ca
Rozann Graefer, Librarian

***Outlook:* Outlook Library**
505 Franklin St. South, Outlook SK S0L 2N0
Tel: 306-867-8823; *Fax:* 306-867-1831
outlook.library@wheatland.sk.ca
Elaine Nadeau, Librarian

***Oxbow:* Oxbow Branch Library/Ada Staples Library**
516 Prospect Ave., Oxbow SK S0C 2B0
Tel: 306-483-5175; *Fax:* 306-483-2276
oxbow@southeast.lib.sk.ca
Marty James, Librarian
Shirley Berntson, Assistant Librarian

***Paddockwood:* Paddockwood Library**
PO Box 178, Paddockwood SK S0J 1Z0
Tel: 306-989-2124; *Fax:* 306-989-2123
padcirc@panet.pa.sk.ca
Joan Carriere, Librarian

***Pangman:* Pangman Library**
PO Box 113, Pangman SK S0C 2C0
Tel: 306-442-2119
pangman@southeast.lib.sk.ca
Carolyn Colbow, Librarian

***Paradise Hill:* Paradise Hill Branch Library**
2nd Ave., Paradise Hill SK S0M 2G0
Tel: 306-344-4741
paradisehill.lib@lakeland.lib.sk.ca
Dianne Palsich, Branch Librarian

***Paynton:* Paynton Branch Library**
General Delivery, Paynton SK S0M 2J0
Tel: 306-895-2175
paynton.lib@lakeland.lib.sk.ca
Linda Peterson, Librarian
Marion McDougall, Head of Reference
204-895-2173

***Pelican Narrows:* Tawowikamik Public Library**
PO Box 100, Pelican Narrows SK S0P 0E0
Tel: 306-632-2022; *Fax:* 306-632-2022
spn@pnls.lib.sk.ca
Margaret Brass, Head Librarian
306-632-2161
Merle Michel, School Library Clerk
Angie McLeod, Public Library Clerk
Josephine Custer, Public Library Clerk

***Pennant Station:* Pennant Branch Library**
General Delivery, Pennant Station SK S0N 1X0
Tel: 306-626-3316
pennant@chinook.lib.sk.ca
www.chinooklibrary.ca/pennant.htm
Sharon Windsor, Librarian

***Perdue:* Perdue Library**
PO Box 253, Perdue SK S0K 3C0
Tel: 306-237-4227
perdue.library@sasktel.net
Mary Lee Sapsford, Librarian

***Pierceland:* Pierceland Library**
Main St., Pierceland SK S0M 2K0
Tel: 306-839-2166
pierceland.lib@lakeland.lib.sk.ca
Ann Hill, Librarian

***Pilger:* Pilger Library**
PO Box 116, Pilger SK S0K 3G0
Tel: 306-367-4809
pilcirc@panet.pa.sk.ca
Delores Pomedli, Head Librarian

***Pilot Butte:* Pilot Butte Branch Library**
PO Box 668, Pilot Butte SK S0G 3Z0
Tel: 306-781-3403
pilot.butte@southeast.lib.sk.ca
Sharon Millie, Librarian

***Plenty:* Plenty Library**
PO Box 70, Plenty SK S0L 2R0
Tel: 306-932-4455
plenty.library@wheatland.sk.ca
www.wheatland.sk.ca/branches_plenty.html
Lynn Halter, Branch Library Staff Contact

***Ponteix:* Ponteix Branch Library**
130 - 1st Ave. East, PO Box 700, Ponteix SK S0N 1Z0
Tel: 306-625-3353
ponteix@chinook.lib.sk.ca
www.chinooklibrary.ca/ponteix.htm
Marie Kouri, Librarian

***Porcupine Plain:* Porcupine Plain Library**
PO Box 162, Porcupine Plain SK S0E 1H0
Tel: 306-278-2488
porcirc@panet.pa.sk.ca
Joanne Yacyshyn, Librarian

***Prairie River:* Prairie River Branch Library**
General Delivery, Prairie River SK S0E 1J0
Tel: 306-889-4521
pracirc@panet.pa.sk.ca
Pat Danku, Librarian
Mary Rovensky, Substitute Librarian
306-899-4501
Jeanette Schweitzer, Substitute Librarian
306-889-4311

***Prelate:* Prelate Branch Library**
Drawer 40, Prelate SK S0N 2B0
Tel: 306-673-2340
prelate@chinook.lib.sk.ca
www.chinooklibrary.ca/prelate.htm
Darlene Wagner, Librarian

***Prince Albert:* John M. Cuelenaere Public Library**
125 - 12th St. East, Prince Albert SK S6V 1B7
Tel: 306-763-8496; *Fax:* 306-763-3816
Toll-Free: 888-975-8165
library@jmcpl.ca
www.jmcpl.ca
Sharon Karr, Acting Director
skarr@jmcpl.ca
306-763-8528
Jaclyn McLean, Assistant Director, Circulation Services
jmclean@jmcpl.ca
306-763-8496 ext. 132
Sharon Karr, Assistant Director
skarr@jmcpl.ca

***Prud'Homme:* Prud'Homme Public Library**
45 Government Rd., Prud'Homme SK S0K 3K0
Tel: 306-654-2221
prucirc@panet.pa.sk.ca
Jennifer Wesdyk, Librarian

***Qu'Appelle:* Qu'Appelle Branch Library**
PO Box 450, Qu'Appelle SK S0G 4A0
Tel: 306-699-2902
quappelle@southeast.lib.sk.ca
Elizabeth Fries, Librarian

***Rabbit Lake:* Rabbit Lake Branch Library**
PO Box 146, Rabbit Lake SK S0M 2L0
Tel: 306-824-2089
rabbitlake.lib@lakeland.lib.sk.ca
Marlene Martens, Librarian
Melita Hildebrand, Assistant Librarian

***Radisson:* Radisson Branch Library**
PO Box 161, Radisson SK S0K 3L0
Tel: 306-827-4521
radisson.lib@lakeland.lib.sk.ca
Shirley Hosegood, Branch Librarian
Kaylla Maxwell, Substitute Librarian

***Radville:* Radville Branch Library**
420 Floren St., Radville SK S0C 2G0
Tel: 306-869-2742
radville@southeast.lib.sk.ca
Shannon Bourassa, Librarian

***Redvers:* Redvers Library**
53B Railway Ave., Redvers SK S0C 2H0
Tel: 306-452-3255
redvers@southeast.lib.sk.ca
Janet Dauvin, Librarian

***Regina:* Forum**
#15, 2010 - 7th Ave., Regina SK S4R 1C2
Tel: 306-780-9413; *Fax:* 306-780-9447
slaforum@sasktel.net
www.lib.sk.ca/sla/newsletter.html

***Regina:* The Medium**
3142 Athol St., Regina SK S4S 1Y7
Tel: 306-373-1660; *Fax:* 306-374-1122
bmcneil@rbe.sk.ca
www.stf.sk.ca/prof_growth/ssc/ssla/medium.html
Barb McNeil, Editor

***Regina:* Regina Public Library**
2311 - 12th Ave., Regina SK S4P 0N3
Tel: 306-777-6000; *Fax:* 306-949-7260
Other Numbers: 306-777-6120 (Info Svs); 306-777-6024 (ILL)
www.reginalibrary.ca
Jeff Barber, Library Director
jbarber@reginalibrary.ca
306-777-6099
Julie McKenna, Deputy Director
jmckenna@reginalibrary.ca
306-777-6074
André Gagnon, Head, Central Public Services
andre@reginalibrary.ca
306-777-6071
Colleen Schommer, Head, Finance & Administration
schommer@reginalibrary.ca
306-777-6060
Amanda Cachia, Director & Curator, Dunlop Art Gallery
acachia@reginalibrary.ca
306-777-6045
Sharon Christie, Manager, Marketing & Communications
schristie@reginalibrary.ca
306-777-6114
Alan Dedman, Manager, Information Technology
adedman@reginalibrary.ca
306-777-6056
John Edgar, Manager, Strategic Initiatives
jedgar@reginalibrary.ca
306-777-6125
Jeff Grant, Manager, Human Resources & Administrator
jgrant@reginalibrary.ca
306-777-6136
Chrystal Hampson, Manager, Collections & Technical Services
champson@reginalibrary.ca
306-777-6001

***Regina Beach:* Regina Beach Branch Library**
133 Donovel Cres., Regina Beach SK S0G 4C0
Tel: 306-729-2062
regina.beach@southeast.lib.sk.ca
www.southeast.lib.sk.ca
Lorie Gejdos, Acting Librarian
Debbie Arsenault

***Riverhurst:* Riverhurst Branch Library**
The Village Square, Box 37, Riverhurst SK S0H 3P0
Tel: 306-353-2130
riverhurst@palliser.lib.sk.ca
www.palliserlibrary.ca
Donna Miner, Librarian

***Rocanville:* Rocanville Branch Library**
218 Ellice St., Rocanville SK S0A 3L0
Tel: 306-645-2088
rocanville@southeast.lib.sk.ca
www.southeast.lib.sk.ca
Catherine Stanhope, Librarian

***Rockglen:* Rockglen Branch Library**
Main St., Rockglen SK S0H 3R0
Tel: 306-476-2350; *Fax:* 306-476-2339
rockglen@palliser.lib.sk.ca
www.palliserlibrary.ca
Claudette Schnell, Branch Librarian

***La Ronge:* Pahkisimon Nuye?áh Library System**
118 Avro Pl., La Ronge SK S0J 1L0
Tel: 306-425-4525; *Fax:* 306-425-4572
Toll-Free: 866-396-8818
pnlsoffice@pnls.lib.sk.ca
www.pnls.lib.sk.ca
Audrey Mark, Director
ae.mark@ pnls.lib.sk.ca
Jocelyn Provost, Library Coordinator
jprovost@ pnls.lib.sk.ca
Harriet Roy, Assistant Director
hroy@pnls.lib.sk.ca

***La Ronge:* La Ronge Public Library**
1222 Hildebrand Dr., La Ronge SK S0J 1L0
Tel: 306-425-2160; *Fax:* 306-425-3883
sla@pnls.lib.sk.ca
www.pnls.lib.sk.ca/laronge/
Rosemary Loeffler, Library Administrator
r.loeffler.sla@pnls.lib.sk.ca
Jocelyn Mark, Contact, Interlibrary Loans
jmark@pnls.lib.sk.ca

***Rosetown:* Rosetown Library**
#201, 5 Ave. East, Rosetown SK S0L 2V0
Tel: 306-882-3566
rosetown.library@wheatland.sk.ca
Lydia Hare, Manager

***Rosthern:* Rosthern Library**
PO Box 27, Rosthern SK S0K 3R0
Tel: 306-232-5377
rosthern.library@wheatland.sk.ca
Agnes Epp, Librarian
Andy Lehmann, Library Staff
Elsie Lehmann, Library Staff
Lillian Gervais, Library Staff

***Rouleau:* Rouleau Branch Library**
204 Main St., Rouleau SK S0G 4H0
Tel: 306-776-2322
rouleau@palliser.lib.sk.ca
www.palliserlibrary.ca
Dee Colibaba, Branch Librarian

***St Benedict:* St Benedict Library**
Centre St., PO Box Box 10, St Benedict SK S0K 3T0
Tel: 306-289-2072
sbencirc@panet.pa.sk.ca
Lee Ann Hannotte, Librarian

***St Brieux:* St Brieux Branch Library**
PO Box 70, St Brieux SK S0K 3V0
Tel: 306-275-2133; *Fax:* 306-275-4907
sbricirc@panet.pa.sk.ca
Kim Ells, Librarian

***St Louis:* St Louis Branch Library**
PO Box 70, St Louis SK S0J 2C0
Tel: 306-422-8511
sloucirc@panet.pa.sk.ca
Birgit Raduenz, Librarian

***St Walburg:* St Walburg Library**
124 Main St., St Walburg SK S0M 2T0
Tel: 306-248-3250; *Fax:* 306-248-3278
stwalburg.lib@lakeland.lib.sk.ca
www.stwalburglibrary.ca
Valerie L'Heureux, Librarian

***Saskatoon:* Saskatoon Public Library**
311 - 23rd St. East, Saskatoon SK S7K 0J6
Tel: 306-975-7558; *Fax:* 306-975-7542
illreps@saskatoonlibrary.ca
www.saskatoonlibrary.ca
Zenon Zuzak, Director of Libraries
z.zuzak@saskatoonlibrary.ca
Bryan Foran, Manager, Branch & Technical Sevices
b.foran@saskatoonlibrary.ca
Anne Craggs, Manager, Public Services, Planning & Development
a.craggs@saskatoonlibrary.ca
Cinda Romuldietz, Manager, Information Technology Services
c.romuldietz@.saskatoonlibrary.ca

***Sceptre:* Sceptre Branch Library**
PO Box 128, Sceptre SK S0N 2H0
Tel: 306-623-4244
sceptre@chinook.lib.sk.ca
www.chinooklibrary.ca/sceptre.htm
Sherry Egeland, Librarian

***Sedley:* Sedley Branch Library**
224 Broadway, Sedley SK S0G 4K0
Tel: 306-885-4506
sedley@southeast.lib.sk.ca
Jocelyn Weinberger, Librarian

***Shaunavon:* Shaunavon Branch Library**
440 Center St., Shaunavon SK S0N 2M0
Tel: 306-297-3844
shaunavon@chinook.lib.sk.ca
www.chinooklibrary.ca/shaunavn.htm
Lorie Gronhovd, Librarian
Carol Simpson, Library Staff

***Shell Lake:* Shell Lake Branch Library**
PO Box 310, Shell Lake SK S0J 2G0
Tel: 306-427-2272; *Fax:* 306-427-2272
shllcirc@panet.pa.sk.ca
Pat Pelchat, Librarian

***Shellbrook:* Shellbrook Branch Library**
105 Railway Ave. West, Shellbrook SK S0J 2E0
Tel: 306-747-3419
Deborah Mervold, Chairperson
d.mervold@sasktel.net
Alanna Carswell, Branch Librarian

***Shellbrook:* Sturgeon Lake Branch Library**
Sturgeon Lake Central School, PO Box 24, Shellbrook SK S0J 2E0
Tel: 306-764-5506
Sharon Daniels, Librarian

***Simmie:* Simmie Branch Library**
PO Box 66, Simmie SK S0N 2N0
Tel: 306-297-6217
www.chinooklibrary.ca/simmie.htm
Grace Olson, Librarian

***Smeaton:* Smeaton Branch Library**
PO Box 149, Smeaton SK S0J 2J0
Tel: 306-426-2049; *Fax:* 306-426-2291
smecirc@panet.pa.sk.ca
Gayle Olson, Librarian

***Sonningdale:* Sonningdale Library**
PO Box 40, Sonningdale SK S0K 4B0
Tel: 306-237-7603
sonningdale.library@wheatland.sk.ca
www.wheatland.sk.ca/branches_sonningdale.html
Connie Guiness, Branch Library Staff Contact
Lynn Ross, Chair

***Speers:* Speers Branch Library**
Main St., Speers SK S0M 2V0
Tel: 306-246-4866
speers.lib@lakeland.lib.sk.ca
Maureen Kachmarski, Branch Librarian

***Spiritwood:* Spiritwood Branch Library**
Box 177, Spiritwood SK S0J 2M0
Tel: 306-883-2337
spicirc@panet.pa.sk.ca
Joyce Carriere, Librarian

***Spruce Home:* Spruce Home Branch Library**
General Delivery, Spruce Home SK S0J 2N0
Tel: 306-764-8377
sprucehomewapiti@yahoo.com
Julie Czychowski, Branch Librarian

***Stanley Mission:* Keethanow Public Library**
PO Box 70, Stanley Mission SK S0J 2P0
Tel: 306-635-2104; *Fax:* 306-635-2050
l.ratt.ssk@pnls.lib.sk.ca
Lucy Ratt, Branch Librarian

Star City: **Star City Branch Library**
PO Box 371, Star City SK S0E 1P0
Tel: 306-863-4364
stacirc@panet.pa.sk.ca
Dena MacKenzie, Librarian

Stewart Valley: **Stewart Valley Branch Library**
Box 1, Stewart Valley SK S0N 2P0
svlibrary@t2.net
www.chinooklibrary.ca/stewart.htm
Kathy King, Librarian

Stoughton: **Stoughton Branch Library**
232 Main St., Stoughton SK S0G 4T0
Tel: 306-457-2484
stoughton@southeast.lib.sk.ca
Laura Lee Knibbs, Librarian

Stranraer: **Stranraer Book Deposit**
PO Box 130, Stranraer SK S0L 3B0
Tel: 306-237-7603
stranraer.library@wheatland.sk.ca
Charlene Bradley, Branch Library Staff

Swift Current: **Swift Current Branch Library**
411 Herbert St. East, Swift Current SK S9H 1M5
Tel: 306-778-2752; *Fax:* 306-773-8769
sc.librarian@sasktel.net
www.city.swift-current.sk.ca/library
Manisha Khetarpal, Librarian

Tisdale: **Tisdale Public Library**
800 - 101st ST., Tisdale SK S0E 1T0
Tel: 306-873-4767
tiscirc@panet.pa.sk.ca
Isabel Hankins-Wilk, Librarian
tisdale_lib@yahoo.com

Tompkins: **Tompkins Library**
PO Box 203, Tompkins SK S0N 2S0
Tel: 306-622-2255
tompkins@chinook.lib.sk.ca
www.chinooklibrary.ca/tompkins.htm
Lynne Baumann, Librarian

Tugaske: **Tugaske Branch Library**
Main St., PO Box 10, Tugaske SK S0H 4B0
Tel: 306-759-2215; *Fax:* 306-759-2253
tugaske@palliser.lib.sk.ca
www.palliserlibrary.ca/tugaske/tugaske.htm
Kathy Russell, Branch Librarian
Manon Bueckert, Assistant Branch Librarian

Turtleford: **Thunderchild Branch Library**
PO Box 600, Turtleford SK S0M 2Y0
Tel: 306-845-4325; *Fax:* 306-845-3339
Susan Wapass, Librarian

Turtleford: **Turtleford Branch Library**
PO Box 146, Turtleford SK S0M 2Y0
Tel: 306-845-2074
turtleford.lib@lakeland.lib.sk.ca
Hilma Copeland, Branch Librarian
Dianne Brett, Branch Librarian

Unity: **Unity Library**
General Delivery, Unity SK S0K 4L0
Tel: 306-228-2802
unity.library@wheatland.sk.ca
Michelle Schumack, Branch Library Staff Contact
Rhelda Winterhalt, Chair
JoAnn Coid, Assistant

Val Marie: **Val Marie Branch Library**
Box 93, Val Marie SK S0N 2T0
Tel: 306-298-2133
valmarie@chinook.lib.sk.ca
www.chinooklibrary.ca/valmarie.htm
Judy Gunter, Librarian

Vanguard: **Vanguard Branch Library**
PO Box 85, Vanguard SK S0N 2V0
Tel: 306-582-2244
vanguard@chinook.lib.sk.ca
www.chinooklibrary.ca/vanguard.htm
Melanie Clark, Librarian

Vibank: **Vibank Branch Library**
101 - 2nd Ave., Vibank SK S0G 4Y0
Tel: 306-762-2270
vibank@southeast.lib.sk.ca
www.southeast.lib.sk.ca
Betty Kuntz, Librarian
vibank@southeast.lib.sk.ca
306-762-2270

Viscount: **Viscount Library**
PO Box 117, Viscount SK S0K 4M0
Tel: 306-944-2155
viscount.library@wheatland.sk.ca
www.wheatland.sk.ca/branches_viscount.html
Carol Brown, Librarian

Vonda: **Vonda Public Library**
316 Main St., Vonda SK S0K 4N0
Tel: 306-258-2035
voncirc@panet.pa.sk.ca
Jennifer Wesdyk, Librarian

Wakaw: **Wakaw Branch Library**
PO Box 464, Wakaw SK S0K 4P0
Tel: 306-233-5552
wakcirc@panet.pa.sk.ca
Lee Ann Hannotte, Librarian

Waldheim: **Waldheim Branch Library**
PO Box 446, Waldheim SK S0K 4R0
Tel: 306-945-2221
waldheim.ca/category/library
Lynn McDonald, Librarian

Wapella: **Wapella Branch Library**
519 South Railway St., Wapella SK S0G 4Z0
Tel: 306-532-4419
wapella@southeast.lib.sk.ca
Sharon Matheson, Librarian

Warman: **Warman Library**
101 Klassen St., Warman SK S0K 4S0
Tel: 306-933-4387
warman.library@wheatland.sk.ca
Margaret-Ann Janzen, Community Librarian

Waskesiu Lake: **Waskesiu Lake Library**
PO Box 202, Waskesiu Lake SK S0J 2Y0
Tel: 306-663-5999
Marilyn Hegel, Librarian

Watrous: **Watrous Library**
306 Main St., Watrous SK S0K 4T0
Tel: 306-946-2244
watrous.library@wheatland.sk.ca
Kathleen Kimmig, Community Librarian
Toni Ambrose, Assistant
Karen Kostenuk, Assistant

Wawota: **Wawota Branch Library**
308 Railway, Wawota SK S0G 5A0
Tel: 306-739-2375
wawota@southeast.lib.sk.ca
Maureen Jensen, Librarian

Weldon: **Weldon Branch Library**
PO Box 55, Weldon SK S0J 3A0
Tel: 306-887-4466
welcirc@panet.pa.sk.ca
Terry Coldevin, Librarian

Weyburn: **Weyburn Public Library**
45 Bison Ave. NE, Weyburn SK S4H 0H9
Tel: 306-842-4352; *Fax:* 306-842-1255
weyburn@southeast.lib.sk.ca
wcapqlx.sasktelwebhosting.com/wpl
Kam Teo, City Librarian
Ilene Lequyere, Library Assistant

White City: **White City Branch Library**
12 Ramm Ave., White City Community Centre, PO Box 308, White City SK S0G 5B0
Tel: 306-781-2118
white.city@southeast.lib.sk.ca
Lori Lee Harris, Branch Librarian
Shayna Hordos, Assistant Librarian

White Fox: **White Fox Branch Library**
301 Elinor St., White Fox SK S0J 3B0
Tel: 306-276-5800
whicirc@panet.pa.sk.ca
Debbie Woods, Librarian

Whitewood: **Whitewood Library**
731 Lalonde St., Whitewood SK S0G 5C0
Tel: 306-735-4233
whitewood@southeast.lib.sk.ca
Irene Blyth, Librarian

Wilkie: **Wilkie Library**
202 - 2nd Ave. East, Wilkie SK S0K 4W0
Tel: 306-843-2616
wilkie.library@wheatland.sk.ca
Terri Dueck, Branch Library Staff Contact

Frances Love, Chair

Willow Bunch: **Willow Bunch Branch Library**
Main St., PO Box 280, Willow Bunch SK S0H 4K0
Tel: 306-473-2405
willowbunch@palliser.lib.sk.ca
www.palliserlibrary.ca
Cindy Philippon, Branch Librarian

Windthorst: **Windthorst Branch Library**
202 Angus St., Windthorst SK S0G 5G0
Tel: 306-224-2159
windthorst@southeast.lib.sk.ca
Jill Taylor, Librarian

Wolseley: **Wolseley Branch Library**
#5, 101 Sherbrooke St., Wolseley SK S0G 5H0
Tel: 306-698-2221
wolseley@southeast.lib.sk.ca
www.southeast.lib.sk.ca
Sharon Jeeves, Librarian
wolseley@southeast.lib.sk.ca
306-698-2221

Wood Mountain: **Wood Mountain Branch Library**
2nd Ave. West, Wood Mountain SK S0H 4L0
Tel: 306-266-2110
woodmountain@palliser.lib.sk.ca
www.palliserlibrary.ca
Edie Klein, Branch Librarian

Yellow Creek: **Yellow Creek Branch Library**
General Delivery, Yellow Creek SK S0K 4X0
Tel: 306-279-2191
yelcirc@panet.pa.sk.ca
Eileen Orenchuk, Librarian

Yellow Grass: **Yellow Grass Branch Library**
213 Souris St., Yellow Grass SK S0G 5J0
Tel: 306-465-2574
yellow.grass@southeast.lib.sk.ca
Betty Guest, Librarian

Young: **Young Library**
114 Main St., Young SK S0K 4Y0
Tel: 306-259-2227
young.library@wheatland.sk.ca
www.wheatland.sk.ca/branches_young.html
Gisele Camber, Branch Library Staff Contact
Elaine Raskell, Chair

Zenon Park: **Zenon Park Paperback Deposit**
920 Park Rd., Zenon Park SK S0E 1W0
Tel: 306-767-2451; *Fax:* 306-767-2548
wapiti@panet.pa.sk.ca
www.panet.pa.sk.ca
Michelle LeBlanc, Librarian

Archives

Duck Lake: **Duck Lake Historical Museum**
5 Anderson Ave., Duck Lake SK S0K 1J0
Tel: 306-467-2057; *Toll-Free:* 866-467-2057
duckmuf@sasktel.net
www.dlric.org/museum.html
Céline Perillat, Curator

Prince Albert: **Prince Albert Historical Society/Museum**
10 River St. East, Prince Albert SK S6V 8A9
Tel: 306-764-2992
historypa@citypa.com
historypa.com
William D. Smiley, Archivist
historypa@citypa.com
James Benson, Assistant
historypa@citypa.com
Harris May, Researcher
historypa@citypa.com

Regina: **RCMP Heritage Centre/ Centre du Patrimoine de la GRC**
5907 Dewdney Ave., Regina SK S4T 0P4
Tel: 306-522-7333; *Toll-Free:* 866-567-7267
info@rcmphc.com
www.rcmpheritagecentre.com
Rhonda Lamb, Manager
306-522-7333 ext. 3017
Jodi Ann Eskritt, Curator
306-522-7333 ext. 3004

Regina: **Regina Firefighters' Museum**
1205 Ross Ave., Regina SK S4P 3C8
Tel: 306-777-7830; *Fax:* 306-777-6807

Jim Kerr, Contact

***Regina:* Saskatchewan Archives Board**
3303 Hillsdale St., Regina SK S4S 6W9
Tel: 306-787-4068; *Fax:* 306-787-1197
info.regina@archives.gov.sk.ca
www.saskarchives.com

Trevor J.D. Powell, Provincial Archivist
306-787-4066

***Regina:* Saskatchewan Genealogical Society**
#110, 1514 - 11th Ave., Regina SK S4P 0H2
Tel: 306-780-9207; *Fax:* 306-780-3615
sgslibrary@sasktel.net
www.saskgenealogy.ca

Megen Ashcroft, Librarian
sgslibrary@sasktel.net
Linda Dunsmore-Porter, Executive Director
ed.sgs@sasktel.net

***Saskatoon:* City of Saskatoon Archives**
88 - 24th St. East, Saskatoon SK S7K 0K4
Tel: 306-975-7811; *Fax:* 306-975-2612
www.saskatoon.ca/org/clerks_office/archives/index.asp

J. Jeffrey O'Brien, City Archivist
jeff.obrien@sasktoon.ca

***Saskatoon:* Mohyla Institute**
1240 Temperance St., Saskatoon SK S7N 0P1
Tel: 306-653-1944; *Fax:* 306-653-1902
mohyla@sasktel.net
www.mohyla.ca
Social Media: www.facebook.com/StPetroMohylaInstitute

***Verigin:* National Doukhobour Heritage Village Inc.**
PO Box 99, Verigin SK S0A 4H0
Tel: 306-542-4441
ndhv@yourlink.ca

Philip Perepelkin, Archivist

***Weyburn:* Soo Line Historical Society**
411 Industrial Lane, Weyburn SK S4H 1W3
Tel: 306-842-2922; *Fax:* 306-842-2922
slhm@sasktel.net

Yukon Territory

Public Libraries

***Destruction Bay:* Destruction Bay Volunteer Branch Library**
General Delivery, Destruction Bay YT Y0B 1H0
Tel: 867-841-5161

***Mayo:* Keno City Volunteer Branch Library**
Site 1, Box 17, Mayo YT Y0B 1M0
Tel: 867-995-2394

***Whitehorse:* Yukon Public Libraries**
2071 - 2nd Ave., Whitehorse YT Y1A 2C6
Tel: 867-667-5239; *Fax:* 867-393-6333
Toll-Free: 800-661-0408
Other Numbers: 867-667-3668 (Reference); 867-667-5228 (Programs)
whitehorse.library@gov.yk.ca
www.ypl.gov.yk.ca

Hans Ott, Chair
wplboard@yahoo.ca
Julie Ourom, Director
867-667-5447

Archives

***Dawson:* Dawson City Museum**
595 Fifth Ave., Dawson YT Y0B 1G0
Tel: 867-993-5291; *Fax:* 867-993-5839
dcmuseum@northwestel.net

Cheryl Thompson, Museum Director/Administration
867-993-5291

***Whitehorse:* Yukon Tourism & Culture**
400 College Dr., Whitehorse YT Y1A 2C6
Tel: 867-667-5321; *Fax:* 867-393-6253
yukon.archives@gov.yk.ca
www.yukonarchives.ca

Ian Burnett, Territorial Archivist
Ian.Burnett@gov.yk.ca
867-667-5321
Heather Jones, Reference Desk Attendant
yukon.archives@gov.yk.ca
867-667-8064
Peggy D'Orsay, Archives Librarian
Peggy.Dorsay@gov.yk.ca
867-667-5625
Clara Rutherford, Accessions Archivist
Clara.Rutherford@gov.yk.ca
867-667-5333
Heather LeDuc, Government Records Archivist
Heather.Leduc@gov.yk.ca
867-667-5926
Leslie Buchan, Government Records Archivist
Lesley.Buchan@gov.yk.ca
867-667-5926

SECTION 13
PUBLISHING

Publishers

Book Publishers

Aardvark Enterprises (Div. of Speers Investments Ltd.)
204 Millbank Dr. SW, Calgary, AB T2Y 2H9
Tel: 403-256-4639
ISBNs: ISBN: 0-921057; ISSN: 0831-1919
Publishers of poems, short stories & how-to books
J. Alvin Speers, President

AB collector publishing
5835 Grant St., Halifax, NS B3H 1C9
Tel: 902-425-6935; *Fax:* 506-385-1981
Toll-Free: 888-748-5514
darklady@nbnet.nb.ca
www.abcollectorpublishing.ca
Publisher of poetry, short stories, biography, drama, works relating to photography, ceramics, art & history, in English, French, German
Astrid Brunner, Publisher

Abbeyfield Publishers
 # 304, 160 Balmoral Ave., Toronto, ON M4V 1J7
Tel: 416-925-6458; *Fax:* 416-925-4165
Toll-Free: 866-370-9407
info@whiteknightbooks.ca
www.whiteknightbooks.ca
Bill Belfontaine, Publisher

ABC Publishing
80 Hayden St., Toronto, ON M4Y 3G2
Tel: 416-924-1332; *Fax:* 416-924-2760
Toll-Free: 800-265-6397
customerservice@afcanada.com
www.afcanada.com
ISBNs: 0-919030, 0-919891, 0-921846
The premier source for Anglican prayer & hymn books, Path books, & parish programming materials & other resources for Church leaders, the Anglican Book Centre & its publishing unit, ABC Publishing, merged with Augsburg Fortress Canada in 2007. Customers may take advantage of shared ordering & distribution channels

Academic Printing & Publishing
#403, 9-3151 Lakeshore Rd., Kelowna, BC V1W 3S9
Tel: 250-764-6427; *Fax:* 250-764-6428
academicpublishing@shaw.ca
www.academicprintingandpublishing.com
ISBNs: ISSNs: 0003-6390; 1206-5269; 1206-3696
Publishers of scholarly books & journals, with emphasis on Philosophy
Roger A. Shiner, Director

Acadiensis Press
Campus House, University of New Brunswick, PO Box 4400, Fredericton, NB E3B 5A3
Tel: 506-453-4978; *Fax:* 506-453-5068
acadnsis@unb.ca
www.lib.unb.ca/Texts/Acadiensis
ISBNs: ISSN: 0044-5871
Publisher of ACADIENSIS: The Journal of the History of the Atlantic Region, & books on the culture & history of Atlantic Canada
Dr. David Frank, Managing Editor

Acorn Press
PO Box 22024, Charlottetown, PE C1A 9J2
Tel: 902-892-8151; *Fax:* 902-566-0756
info@acornpresscanada.com
www.acornpresscanada.com
ISBNs: 1-894838014-9; 1-894838-16-5-64
Publishing books about Prince Edward Island, with emphasis on Prince Edward Island authors, Acorn Press lists works of fiction, poetry, folklore, history & literature for children
Laurie Brinklow, Publisher

Addison-Wesley Publishers Ltd.
PO Box 580, 26 Prince Andrew Pl., Toronto, ON M3C 2T8
Tel: 416-447-5101; *Fax:* 416-443-0948
Toll-Free: 800-387-8028
www.pearsoncanada.ca
ISBNs: 9780321531193; 9780321510105
Addison-Wesley, a Pearson imprint, is a key publisher of technical resources of particular interest to computer programmers, engineers & system administrators. Academic titles include astronomy, mathematics & statistics, economics & finance
MR Allan T. Reynolds, President & CEO, Pearson Canada

Aero Training Products Inc.
#105, 6080 Russ Baker Way, Richmond, BC V7B 1B4
Tel: 604-278-0432; *Fax:* 604-278-4255
Toll-Free: 800-567-3221
www.aerotraining.com
Training materials for pilots & technicians

Aggie Blinkhorn Organization Inc.
PO Box 88549, #101, 13753 - 72nd Ave., Surrey, BC V3W 0X1
Tel: 604-594-7607; *Fax:* 604-594-7289
blinkhorn@estacom.com
ISBNs: ISBN: 0-9696248; SAN: 118-5039

Agogic Publishing
#406, 109 - 10 St., New Westminster, BC V3M 3X7
Tel: 604-290-2692; *Fax:* 604-540-4419
agogic@iglide.net
www.agogic.biz
ISBNs: ISBN: 1-896595
Publishers of learner's guides for guitar

Alexander Press
2875, av Douglas, Montréal, QC H3R 2C7
Tel: 514-738-5517; *Fax:* 514-738-4718
Toll-Free: 866-303-5517
alexanderpress@gmail.com
www.alexanderpress.com
ISBNs: ISBN: 1-896800
Publishes Christian Orthodox books & media in Greek, English & French

Alpel Publishing
CP 203, Chambly, QC J3L 4B3
Tél: 450-658-6205; *Téléc:* 450-658-3514
alpel@videotron.ca
ISBNs: ISBN: 0-9691932, 0-921993
Elie Albala, President

Alpine Book Peddlers
#140, 405 Bow Meadows Cres., Canmore, AB T1W 2W8
Tel: 403-678-2280; *Fax:* 403-678-2840
alpinebk@aeontech.ca
ISBNs: ISBN: 0-9699368, 0-9692631, 0-919934, 0-9692457; SAN: 1187546
John Blum

Alter Ego Editions
5922, rue Jeanne-Mance, Montréal, QC H2V 458
Tel: 514-276-7429; *Fax:* 514-276-7429
books@alterego.montreal.qc.ca
www.alterego.montreal.qc.ca
ISBNs: ISBN: 1-896743
Small independent French-Language publisher

The Alternate Press
#508, 264 Queens Quay West, Toronto, ON M5J 1B5
Tel: 416-260-0303; *Toll-Free:* 800-215-9574
altpress@lifemedia.ca
www.lifemedia.ca/altpress
ISBNs: 0-920118-04-6; 978-0-920118-15-3;0-920118-00-3
An imprint of Life Media, The Alternate Press publishes materials promoting home schooling & natural learning, natural parenting, natural business (home-based & green), & poetry
MS Wendy Priesnitz, Publisher

The Althouse Press
Faculty of Education, University of Western Ontario, 1137 Western Rd., London, ON N6G 1G7
Tel: 519-661-2096; *Fax:* 519-661-3833
press@uwo.ca
www.edu.uwo.ca/althousepress
ISBNs: ISBN: 0-920354; SAN: 115-1142
Dr. Greg Dickinson, Director

Annick Press Ltd.
15 Patricia Ave., Toronto, ON M2M 1H9
Tel: 416-221-4802; *Fax:* 416-221-8400
annickpress@annickpress.com
www.annickpress.com
ISBNs: ISBN: 0-920236, 920303, 1-55037; SAN: 115-0065
Publishers of books for children & young adults; Publishers of Robert Munsch & Loris Lesynski; Publishes approximately 30 books a year
Rick Wilks

Anvil Press
PO Box 3008 MPO, Vancouver, BC V6B 3X5
Tel: 604-876-8710; *Fax:* 604-879-2667
info@anvilpress.com
www.anvilpress.com
ISBNs: ISBN: 1-895636
Brian Kaufman, Publisher

Apple Press Publishing
810 Landresse Ct., Newmarket, ON L3X 1M6
Tel: 905-853-7979; *Fax:* 905-853-1175
Toll-Free: 866-222-8883
info@applepressbooks.com
ISBNs: ISBN: 0-919972
Publishes educational books & resources
George Quinn, President

Aquila Communications Ltd.
2642, rue Diab, Saint-Laurent, QC H4S 1E8
Tel: 514-338-1065; *Fax:* 514-338-1948
Toll-Free: 800-667-7071
aquila@aquilacommunications.com
www.aquilacommunications.com
ISBNs: ISBN: 0-88510, 2-89054; SAN: 115-2483, 115-8295
Publishes French as a Second Language reading materials from grades 4 through college
Mike Kelada, Vice-President & General Manager
Sami Kelada, President/CEO

Arbeiter Ring Publishing
#201E, 121 Osborne St., Winnipeg, MB R3L 1Y4
Tel: 204-942-7058; *Fax:* 204-944-9198
info@arbeiterring.com
www.arbeiterring.com
ISBNs: ISBN: 1-894037
Publishers of books on contemporary politics, culture, and social issues.

Argenta Friends Press
Press Rd., Naksup, BC V0G 1R0
Tel: 250-366-4314; *Fax:* 250-366-4314
afp@look.ca
ISBNs: ISBN: 0-920367
Pat Cattermole

Ariane Editions Inc.
#110, 1209, rue Bernard ouest, Outremont, QC H2V 1V7
Tél: 514-276-2949; *Téléc:* 514-279-4121
info@ariane.qc.ca
www.ariane.qc.ca
ISBNs: ISBN: 2-920987
Martine Vallée
Marc Vallée

Armdale Publications
#203, 10544 - 106 St. NW, Edmonton, AB T5J 2M4
Tel: 780-429-1073; *Fax:* 780-425-5844
armadale@global-serve.net
Winston Mohabir
Haloshini Naideo, Manager

Arsenal Pulp Press Ltd.
#200, 341 Water St., Vancouver, BC V6B 1B8
Tel: 604-687-4233; *Fax:* 604-687-4283
info@arsenalpulp.com
www.arsenalpulp.com
ISBNs: ISBN: 0-88978, 1-55152; SAN: 115-0847
Publisher with over 200 titles in print, including literary fiction & non-fiction; cultural & gender studies; gay, lesbian & multicultural literature; cookbooks & guidebooks.
Robert Ballantyne, Associate Publisher
Brian Lam, Publisher
Janice Beley, Marketing Director

Art Global
384, av Laurier ouest, Montréal, QC H2V 2K7
Tél: 514-272-6111; *Téléc:* 514-272-8609
kermoyan@edirom.com
ISBNs: ISBN: 2-920718
Ara Kermoyan

Art Metropole
788 King St. West, Toronto, ON M5V 1N6
Tel: 416-703-4400; *Fax:* 416-703-4404
info@artmetropole.com
www.artmetropole.com
ISBNs: ISBN: 0-920956; SAN: 156-9902
Publishers of art books & publications
A.A. Bronson, Director

Artel Educational Resources Ltd.
5528 Kingsway, Burnaby, BC V5H 2G2
Tel: 604-435-4949; *Fax:* 604-435-1955
Toll-Free: 800-665-9255
info@arteleducational.ca
www.arteleducational.ca
ISBNs: SAN: 116-029X
Publishes educational resources for schools, institutions, home schoolers & the general public; Includes material for all levels of education, ESL & Special Education
Vern Milani, President

Artery Enterprises Ltd.
PO Box 3302, Langley, BC V3A 4R6
Tel: 604-534-8122; *Fax:* 604-534-8124
Toll-Free: 888-333-1006
info@artery.ca
www.artery.ca
ISBNs: ISBN: 0-920431; SAN: 117-0198

Artextes Éditions / Centre d'information Artexte
#508, 460, rue Sainte-Catherine ouest, Montréal, QC H3B 1A7
Tel: 514-874-0049; *Fax:* 514-874-0316
info@artexte.ca
www.artexte.ca
ISBNs: ISBN:
Publishes critical anthologies, monographs & references dealing with visual, media & interdisciplinary art
François Dion, Director

Asquith House Limited/Michael Preston Associates
94 Asquith Ave., Toronto, ON M4W 1J8
Tel: 416-925-3577; *Fax:* 416-925-8823
Toll-Free: 800-646-6858
m.preston@sympatico.ca
ISBNs: SAN: 115-4915
Publishes educational books, reading programs, maps & globes
M. Preston
P. Preston

Athabasca University
Copyright Office, 1 University Dr., Athabasca, AB T9S 3A3
Tel: 780-675-6204; *Fax:* 780-675-6338
Toll-Free: 800-788-9041
copyright@athabascau.ca
www.athabascau.ca
ISBNs: ISBN: 0-919737
Lori-Ann Claerhout, Copyright Officer

Athena Books
47 Sarrazin Way, Ottawa, ON K2J 4A5
Tel: 613-825-6986;
athena@magma.ca
www.magma.ca/~athena
ISBNs: ISBN: 1-895520
Robert Allan Stewart, President

Atlantic Book Ltd.
PO Box 1910, 35 Cobequid Dr., Truro, NS B2N 5R1
Tel: 902-893-1057; *Fax:* 902-893-1464
Toll-Free: 888-773-7727
atlantic.book@ns.sympatico.ca
ISBNs: SAN: 111-0608

Augsburg Fortress Publishers
500 Trillium Dr., Kitchener, ON N2G 4Y4
Tel: 519-748-2200; *Fax:* 519-748-9835
Toll-Free: 800-265-6397
info@afcanada.com
www.afcanada.com
The publishing wing of the Evangelical Lutheran Church in America, Augsburg Fortress also services the Evangelical Lutheran Church in Canada & publishes Bibles, Bible study resources, multicultural materials, music, & seasonal & special occasion books.
Larry N. Willard, Canadian Operations Director

Aviation Publishers Co. Ltd.
PO Box 1361 B, Ottawa, ON K1P 5R4
Tel: 613-244-8280; *Fax:* 613-244-8281
info@aviationpublishers.com
www.aviationpublishers.com
ISBNs: ISBN: 0-9690054
Publishers of the ground school flight training manual "From the Ground Up" as well as other books on flight training & aeronautical theory.
William N. Peppler, President
Graeme Peppler, General Manager

Backroad Mapbooks
#106, 1500 Hartley Ave., Coquitlam, BC V3K 7A1
Tel: 604-521-6277; *Fax:* 604-521-6260
Toll-Free: 877-520-5670
info@backroadmapbooks.com; hr@backroadmapbooks.com
www.backroadmapbooks.com
Other information: GPS Maps, E-mail: gps@backroadmapbooks.com
Backroad Mapbooks produces up-to-date outdoor recreation Canadian maps & guidebooks.
Russell Mussio, President, rmussio@backroadmapbooks.com
Chris Taylor, Vice-President & Manager, National Sales, ctaylor@backroadmapbooks.com
Andrew Allen, Contact, Mapping Department, aallen@backroadmapbooks.com

Bacon & Hughes Limited
#30, 81 Auriga Dr., Ottawa, ON K2E 7Y5
Tel: 613-226-8136; *Fax:* 613-226-8121
Toll-Free: 800-563-2468
sales@baconandhughes.ca
www.baconandhughes.ca
Bacon & Hughes Limited provides learning resources from early childhood to the secondary level. Teacher resources & French literature are also available.

Bahá'¡ Distribution Service
#9, 945 Middlefield Rd., Toronto, ON M1V 5E1
Tel: 416-609-9900; *Fax:* 416-609-9600
Toll-Free: 800-465-3287
orders@bahaibooksonline.com
www.bahaibooksonline.com

Banff Centre Press
The Banff Centre, PO Box 1020, 107 Tunnel Mountain Dr., Banff, AB T1L 1H5
Tel: 403-762-6410; *Fax:* 403-762-6277
Toll-Free: 800-565-9989
press@banffcentre.ca
www.banffcentre.ca/press
The Banff Centre Press publishes books of contemporary art, culture, & literature.
Mary E. Hofstetter, President & Chief Executive Officer
J.A. (Art) Nutt, Vice-President & Chief Finanacial Officer

The Battered Silicon Dispatch Box
PO Box 204, Shelburne, ON L0N 1S0
Tel: 519-925-3027; *Fax:* 519-925-3482
gav@bmts.com
www.batteredbox.com
ISBNs: ISBN: 1-55246
Publishers of Sherlock Holmes and other out-of-print works by Canadian & international authors
George A. Vanderhurgh

Battle Street Books
175 Battle St., Kamloops, BC V2C 2L1
Tel: 250-372-1119; *Fax:* 250-372-1830
info@battlestreetbooks.com
www.battlestreetbooks.com
Battle Street Books publishes the novels, plays, & short stories of British Columbia writer, Ernest Langford.

BC Decker Inc.
PO Box 620 LCD 1, #310, 69 John St. South, Hamilton, ON L8N 3K7
Tel: 905-522-7017; *Toll-Free:* 800-568-7281
customercare@bcdecker.com
www.bcdecker.com
BC Decker publishes the ACP Medicine & ACS Surgery book products in both print & digital editions, as well as ten specialty medical journals, to serve the informational needs of health care professionals & students.

Béliveau Éditeur
5090, rue de Bellechasse, Montréal, QC H1T 2A2
Tél: 514-253-0403; *Téléc:* 514-256-5078
admin@beliveauediteur.com
www.beliveauediteur.com
ISBNs: ISBN: 2-89092
Spécialités: Affaires, finances, biographies, psychologie et sciences humaines, religion, mathématiques, physique, chimie
Mathieu Béliveau, Président-directeur général

Bendall Books Educational Publishers
PO Box 115, Mill Bay, BC V0R 2P0
Tel: 250-743-2946; *Fax:* 250-743-2910
admin@bendallbooks.com
www.bendallbooks.com
Bendall Books is a publisher & distributor of educational materials for the college & university sector.
Raymond Bendall, Publisher

The Best of Bridge Publishing Ltd.
#800, 120 Eglington Ave. E, Toronto, ON M4P 1E2
Tel: 416-322-6552; *Fax:* 416-322-6936
bestofbridge@robertrose.ca
www.bestofbridge.com
ISBNs: ISBN: 0-9690425
Publishers of cookbooks
Joan Wilson, President

Betelgeuse Books
#516, 3044 Bloor St. West, Toronto, ON M8X 2Y8
Betelgeuse@sympatico.ca
www.maxpages.com/betelgeuse
Betelgeuse Books publishes books about northern Canada.

Between the Lines (BTL)
#404, 720 Bathurst St., Toronto, ON M5S 2R4
Tel: 416-535-9914; *Fax:* 416-535-1484
Toll-Free: 800-718-7201
info@btlbooks.com; editor@btlbooks.com
www.btlbooks.com
Between the Lines provides books with critical perspectives on culture, economics, & society.
Amanda Crocker, Editorial Coordinator
Paula Brill, Marketing & Promotion Coordinator, Marketing & Promotion
Voula Kraniou, Financial Coordinator
Jennifer Tiberio, Design & Production Coordinator

Bibliothèque nationale du Québec
2275, rue Holt, Montréal, QC H2G 3H1
Tel: 514-873-1100; *Fax:* 514-873-9312
Toll-Free: 800-363-9028
info@bnquebec.ca
www.bnquebec.ca
ISBNs: ISBN: 2-550, 2-551
Lise Bissonnette, Présidente et directrice générale

Black Moss Press
2450 Byng Rd., Windsor, ON N8W 3E8
Tel: 519-252-2551; *Fax:* 519-253-7809
www.blackmosspress.com/pages/2OurBooks.html
The literary press publishes Canadian literature, including poetry & short story anthologies.
Marty Gervais, President

Black Rose Books
CP 1258 Place du Parc, Montréal, QC H2W 2R3
Ligne sans frais: 800-565-9523
info@blackrosebooks.net
www.blackrosebooks.net
Black Rose Books publishes critical writing on topics such as philosophy, politics, history, sociology, & hte environment.
Robert Dollins, Editorial Administrator

Blue Heron Press
160 Greenlees Dr., Kingston, ON K7K 6P4
Tel: 613-549-4334;
info@blueheronpress.ca
www.blueheronpress.ca
The literary press specializes in Canadian literature.

Bodhi Publishing
PO Box 144, Kinmount, ON K0M 2A0
Tel: 705-488-3248; *Fax:* 705-488-2455
dana@bodhipublishing.org
www.bodhipublishing.netfirms.com
The charitable organization publishes books by Venerable Namgyal Rinpoche.

The Books Collective
#214-21, 10405 Jasper Ave., Edmonton, AB T5J 3S2
Tel: 780-448-0590; *Fax:* 780-448-0640
admin@bookscollective.com
www.bookscollective.com
ISBNs: ISBN: 1-895836, 0-88878
Candas Jane Dorsey, Contact

Boomerang Éditeur Jeunesse inc.
33, rue de Chenonceau, Blainville, QC J7B 1P6
Tél: 450-430-3259; *Téléc:* 450-430-4607
info@boomerangjeunesse.com
www.boomerangjeunesse.com
Resources for children

Borealis Book Publishers
8 Mohawk Cres., Nepean, ON K2H 7G6
Tel: 613-829-0150; *Fax:* 613-829-7783
Toll-Free: 877-696-2585
drt@borealispress.com
www.borealispress.com
Borealis Book Publishers consists of Borealis Books, Tecumseh Books, Publishing Advisors Inc., Journal of Canadian Poetry, Canadian Critical Editions, & the Parliamentary Handbook / Répertoire Parlementaire Canadien.

Boston Mills Press
c/o Firefly Books, 66 Leek Cres., Richmond Hill, ON L4B 1H1
Tel: 416-499-8412; *Fax:* 416-499-8313
Toll-Free: 800-387-6192
service@fireflybooks.com
ISBNs: 0-919783; 0-919822
Boston Mills Press publishes nonfiction books for adults, including nature, history, travel, & transportation titles. It is a client publisher of Firefly Books.

Bradley Publications
2352 Smith St., Regina, SK S4P 2P6
Tel: 306-525-3305; *Fax:* 306-757-1810

Breakwater Books Ltd.
PO Box 2188, 100 Water St., St. John's, NL A1C 6E6
Tel: 709-722-6680; *Fax:* 709-753-0708
Toll-Free: 800-563-3333
info@breakwater.nf.net
www.breakwaterbooks.com
ISBNs: ISBN: 0-919519, 0-920911, 1-55081; SAN 115-0154
Newfoundland's first publishing house; specializing in educational & curriculum materials, and resources with an emphasis on the history & unique culture of Newfoundland & Labrador
Clyde Rose, President

Brendan Kelly Publishing Inc.
2122 Highview Dr., Burlington, ON L7R 3X4
Tel: 905-335-3359; *Fax:* 905-335-5104
mail@brendankellypublishing.com
www.brendankellypublishing.com
ISBNs: ISBN: 1-895997, 0-9695244
Specialists in the subject areas of mathematics, business, sports & psychology
Brendan Kelly, President

Breton Books & Music
RR#1, Wreck Cove, NS B0C 1H0
Tel: 902-539-5140; *Fax:* 902-539-9117
Toll-Free: 800-565-5140
bretonbooks@ns.sympatico.ca
www.capebretonbooks.com
ISBNs: ISBN: 1-895415
Showcasing Cape Breton authors
Ronald Caplan, President

Brick Books
PO Box 20081, 431 Boler Rd., London, ON N6K 4G6
Tel: 519-657-8579;
brick.books@sympatico.ca
www.brickbooks.ca
ISBNs: ISBN: 0-919626, 1-894078; SAN: 115-0162
Small literary press devoted to the work of Canadian poets
Kitty Lewis, General Manager

Brindle & Glass Publishing Ltd.
6 - 356 Simcoe St., Victoria, BC V8V 1L1
Tel: 250-360-0829;
info@brindleandglass.com
www.brindleandglass.com
Ruth Linka, Publisher

Broadview Press
PO Box 1243, #5, 280 Perry St., Peterborough, ON K9J 7H5
Tel: 705-743-8990; *Fax:* 705-743-8353
customerservice@broadviewpress.com
www.broadviewpress.com
ISBNs: ISBN: 0-921149, 1-55111; SAN: 115-6772
With additional offices in Guelph, Halifax & Calgary; specializing in English Studies & Philosophy
Don LePan, President

Broken Jaw Press Inc. (MAPP)
PO Box 596 A, Fredericton, NB E3B 5A6
Tel: 506-454-5127; *Fax:* 506-454-5127
editors@brokenjaw.com
www.brokenjaw.com
ISBNs: ISBN: 0-921411, 1-896647, 1-55391; SAN: 117-1437
Joe Blades, Publisher

Broquet inc. / Broquet Publishing Company Inc.
97-B, Montee des Bouleaux, Saint-Constant, QC J5A 1A9
Tel: 450-638-3338; *Fax:* 450-638-4338
info@broquet.qc.ca
www.broquet.qc.ca
ISBNs: ISBN: 2-89000
Antoine Broquet, Éditeur

The Brucedale Press
PO Box 2259, Port Elgin, ON N0H 2C0
Tel: 519-832-6025;
brucedale@bmts.com
www.bmts.com/~brucedale
ISBNs: ISBN: 0-9698716, 1-896922
Specializing in Bruce Peninsula & Queen's Bush writers, artists & photographers
Anne Duke Judd, Contact

Bungalo Books
#100, 17 Elk Ct., Kingston, ON K7M 7A4
Tel: 613-374-2494; *Fax:* 613-389-2351
bungalo@pokeweed.com; bungalo@cgocable.net
www.bungalobooks.com
ISBNs: ISBN: 0-921285
Books for children
John Bianchi, President, john@johnbianchi.com
Frank B. Edwards, Publisher

Bunker to Bunker Books
PO Box 914 T, Calgary, AB T2H 2H4
Tel: 403-512-2123;
bunkertobunkerbooks@yahoo.com
www.bunkertobunkerbooks.com
ISBNs: ISBN: 0-9699039
Military firearms books, British & Canadian military collectible books, WW II history
Geoff Todd, Contact

Burgher Books
#504, 555 Richmond St. West, Toronto, ON M5V 3B1
Tel: 416-504-3471; *Fax:* 416-504-6604
info@burgher.com

BuschekBooks
PO Box 74053, 5 Beechwood Ave., Ottawa, ON K1M 2H9
Tel: 613-744-2589; *Fax:* 613-744-2967
contact@buschekbooks.com
www.buschekbooks.com
ISBNs: ISBN: 0-9699904, 1-894543
John Buschek, Publisher

Butterfly Books Ltd.
PO Box 294, Maple Creek, SK S0N 1N0
W.P. Stewart, President

Butterworths Canada Ltd.
#700, 123 Commerce Valley Dr. East, Markham, ON L3T 7W8
Tel: 905-479-2665; *Toll-Free:* 800-668-6481
media@lexisnexis.ca; customerservice@lexisnexis.ca
www.butterworths.ca
ISBNs: ISBN: 0-409
Now a part of LexisNexis Canada, Butterworths' catalogue focuses on Canadian law. Vancouver Office: #920, 355 Burrard St., Vancouver, BC, V6C 2G8, Tel.: 604-684-1462. Ottawa Office: #700, 112 Kent St., Ottawa, ON, K1P 5P2, Tel.: 613-238-3499. Toronto Office: #400, 905 King St. West, Toronto, ON, M6K 3G9, Tel.: 416-862-7656. Montréal Office: #111, 215 rue St. Jacques, Montréal, QC, H2Y 1M6.

Caitlin Press Inc.
8100 Alderwood Rd., Halfmoon Bay, BC V0N 1Y1
Tel: 604-885-9194; *Toll-Free:* 877-964-4953
www.caitlin-press.com
ISBNs: ISBN: 1-894759, 0-920576; SAN: 115-2793
Specializing in BC authors, poetry, stories of the Central Interior and in works by and about BC women.
Vici Johnstone, Publisher & Owner, vici@caitlin-press.com

Callawind Publications Inc. / Publications Callawind inc.
#179, 3551, boul St. Charles, Kirkland, QC H9H 3C4
Tel: 514-685-9109; *Fax:* 514-685-7952
info@callawind.com
www.callawind.com
ISBNs: ISBN: 1-896511
Specializing in cookbooks & children's books; also available in the U.S. from #200, 4501 Forbes Blvd., Lanham, MD, 20706, Tel: 800-462-6420, www.bibliodistribution.com.
Marcy Claman, President

Cambridge University Press
66 Pine St. South, Port Hope, ON L1A 3G1
Tel: 905-885-9315; *Fax:* 905-885-9332
Toll-Free: 877-406-5248
toronto@cambridge.org
www.cambridge.org
ISBNs: ISBN: 0-521; SAN: 281-3769
Cambridge U. Press publishes academic & educational writing from arounds the world, currently over 2500 titles and 200 journals per year. Vancouver office: c/o Curriculum Plus, 40407 Ayr Dr., Box 2319, Vancouver, BC, V0N 3G0, Tel: 800-660-1244, Email: ian.sutherland@shaw.ca
Pamela Robinson, Sales Representative, probinson@cambridge.org

Canada Law Book Inc.
240 Edward St., Aurora, ON L4G 3S9
Tel: 905-841-6472; *Fax:* 905-841-5085
Toll-Free: 800-263-2037
www.canadalawbook.ca
ISBNs: ISBN: 0-88804
Specializing in legal resources (print & online), & current awareness services
Stuart Morrison, President, The Cartwright Group Ltd.
Ruth Epstein, VP, Canada Law Book LL.B.

Canadian Bible Society
10 Carnforth Rd., Toronto, ON M4A 2S4
Tel: 416-757-4171; *Fax:* 416-757-3376
Toll-Free: 800-465-2425
info@biblesociety.ca
www.biblesociety.ca
ISBNs: ISBN: 0-88834; SAN: 112-5559
The Society translates, publishes & distributes the Bible throughout Canada
Rev. Ted Seres, National Director, tseres@biblesociety.ca
Dennis Hillia, Director, Operations, dhillis@biblesociety.ca

Canadian Centre for Community Renewal (CCCR)
PO Box 1161 A, Port Alberni, BC V9Y 7M1
Tel: 250-752-4710; *Fax:* 250-752-4718
Toll-Free: 888-255-6779
www.cedworks.com
ISBNs: 1-895818
CCCR publishes information on the principles of community economic development. The on-line catalogue carries nearly 600 articles, papers, and books available in portable document format (PDF).
Mike Lewis, Executive Director, 250-723-1139, mlewis@cedworks.com
Don McNair, Editor & Publisher, mcnair@cedworks.com

Canadian Circumpolar Institute
1 - 42 Pembina Hall, University of Alberta, Edmonton, AB T6G 2H8
Tel: 403-492-4512; *Fax:* 403-492-1153
ccinst@gpu.srv.ualberta.ca
www.uofaweb.ualberta.ca/polar/
ISBNs: ISBN: 1-896445, 0-919058
Elaine Maloney, Managing Editor, elaine.maloney@ualberta.ca
Cindy S. Mason, Business Manager, 780-492-4512, cindy.mason@ualberta.ca

Canadian Council on Social Development
#100, 190 O'Connor St., Ottawa, ON K2P 2R3
Tel: 613-236-8977; *Fax:* 613-236-2750
council@ccsd.ca.
www.ccsd.ca
ISBNs: ISBN: 0-88810; SAN: 115-284X
CCSD is a non-governmental, not-for-profit publisher in the social development field, with titles covering economic security & poverty, employment & labour market issues, social policies & programs.
Peggy Taillon, President & CEO, ext. 253, taillon@ccsd.ca
Katherine Scott, VP, Research, ext. 245, scott@ccsd.ca

Canadian Educators' Press
1230 White Clover Way, Mississauga, ON L5V 1K7
Tel: 905-826-0578;
cepress@sympatico.ca
ISBNs: ISBN: 1-896191
CEP publishes titles related to Canadian law and law enformcement.
Silma Deonarine, Manager

Canadian Government Publishing
350 Albert St., 4th Floor, Ottawa, ON K1A 0S5
Tel: 613-941-5995; *Fax:* 613-998-1450
Toll-Free: 800-635-7943
publications@pwgsc.gc.ca
publications.gc.ca
ISBNs: ISBN: 0-660, 0-662; SAN: 115-2882
The official publisher for the Government of Canada, CGP publishes priced documents in print, Braille, and large-print formats and on a variety of subjects, such as health, finance, science and education, among others. These publications include books, serials, monographs, maps, pamphlets, and information kits. Formats also include online publishing and electronic publications.

The Canadian Institute for Law, Theology & Public Policy
89 Douglasview Rise SE, Calgary, AB T2Z 2P5
Tel: 403-720-8714; *Fax:* 403-720-8746
ciltpp@cs.com
www.ciltpp.com
ISBNs: ISBN: 1-896363
Publishes books and taps which seek to integrate in depth the Christian faith with public policy issues
Will Moore, President

Canadian Institute of Chartered Accountants (CICA)
277 Wellington St. West, Toronto, ON M5V 3H2
Tel: 416-977-3222; *Fax:* 416-977-8585
www.cica.ca
ISBNs: 1-55385, 0-88800
Published material includes resources for accountants & accounting students.
Doug Baker, Chair FCA

Kevin Dancey, President & CEO FCA, 416-204-3333, Fax: 416-204-3405, kevin.dancey@cica.ca
Peter Hoult, Director, Information & Productivity, 416-204-3330, peter.hoult@cica.ca

Canadian Institute of Resources Law
#3353 MFH, University of Calgary, 2500 University Dr. NW, Calgary, AB T2N 1N4
Tel: 403-220-3200; *Fax:* 403-282-6182
cirl@ucalgary.ca
www.cirl.ca
ISBNs: ISBN: 0-919269; SAN: 115-2904
The Institute publishes the results of its research & proceedings of conferences that it sponsors, on the topic of Natural Resources Law. Titles include, "Canada Energy Law Service."
Richard Neufeld, Chair
J. Owens Saunders, Executive Director, 403-220-3975, josaunde@ucalgary.ca

Canadian Institute of Strategic Studies
#702, 165 University Ave., Toronto, ON M5H 3B8
Tel: 416-322-8128; *Fax:* 416-322-8129
info@ciss.ca
www.ciss.ca
ISBNs: 1-894736, 0-919769; SAN: 115-2912
The Institute publishes books, papers & journals devoted to the research & analysis of Canadian Military Affairs, security affairs & international relations in general.
Sen. Hugh Segal, Chair
Alex Morrison, President

Canadian Institute of Ukrainian Studies Press (CIUS Press)
University of Toronto, Rm. 308, 256 McCaul St., Toronto, ON M5T 1W5
Tel: 416-978-6934; *Fax:* 416-978-2672
cius@chass.utoronto.ca
www.ciuspress.com
ISBNs: 0-920862, 1-895571, 1-894301, 1-894865; SAN: 115-2920
The Institute is the publishing arm of the Canadian Institute of Ukranian Studies. It focuses on original research in English on Ukrainian history, language, literature, contemporary Ukraine, and Ukrainians in Canada. It also publishes English translations of Ukrainian monographs and memoirs.
Dr. Zenon Kohut, Director, CIUS

Canadian International Council (CIC)
#210, 45 Willcocks St., Toronto, ON M5S 1C7
Tel: 416-946-7209; *Fax:* 416-946-7319
Toll-Free: 800-668-2442
info@onlinecic.org
www.onlinecic.org
ISBNs: 0-9866175; SAN: 115-2890
CIC is a non-partisan, nationwide research council which publishes content on Canada's foreign policy.
Jim Balsillie, Chair
Jennifer Jeffs, President
Laura Sunderland, Communications Officer, lsunderland@onlinecic.org

Canadian Museum of Civilization
100 Laurier St., Gatineau, QC K1A 0M8
Tel: 819-776-8387; *Fax:* 819-776-8535
Toll-Free: 800-555-5621
publications@civilization.ca
www.civilization.ca
ISBNs: ISBN: 0-660; SAN: 115-4532
Together with the Canadian War Museum, the CMC publishes a range of books, papers, essays, journals and reports with a focus on Canadian history, prehistory & civilization for both adults and children.
Victor Rabinovitch, President & CEO, 819-776-7116, victor.rabinovitch@civilization.ca
Chantal Schryer, VP, Public Affairs & Publishing, 819-776-8499, chantal.schryer@civilization.ca
Stéphanie Verner, Media Relations Officer, 819-776-7169, stephanie.verner@civilization.ca

Canadian Paperbacks Publishing Ltd.
17 Gwynne Ave., Ottawa, ON K1Y 1X1
Tel: 613-722-1171
ISBNs: ISBN: 0-919554
This is the publisher of "A Dictionary of Canadian Artists," a resource of biographies. The copyright of this 8-volume series however was sold to the National Gallery of Canada (www.gallery.ca) in 2007, where the project continues online.
Colin S. MacDonald, President

Canadian Plains Research Center Press (CPRCP Press)
University of Regina, 3737 Wascana Parkway, Regina, SK S4S 0A2
Tel: 306-585-4758; *Fax:* 306-585-4699
Toll-Free: 866-874-2257
canadian.plains@uregina.ca
www.cprcpress.ca
ISBNs: ISBN: 0-88977; SAN: 115-0278
The CPRCP Press is publishing arm of the University of Regina. It publishes scholarly manuscripts on aspects of life in the Prairie region, as well as non-fiction trade titles concerning the Prairies.
Harry Diaz, Executive Director, harry.diaz@uregina.ca
Brian Mlazgar, Publications Manager, 306-585-4795, brian.mlazgar@uregina.ca

Canadian Scholars' Press Inc. (CSPI)
#801, 180 Bloor St. West, Toronto, ON M5S 2V6
Tel: 416-929-2774; *Fax:* 416-929-1926
info@cspi.org
www.cspi.org
ISBNs: 1-55130, 0-921627, 1-894184
CSPI is an independent publisher of texts, scholarly works, and titles that present themes and issues of interest to the general Canadian market. It also imprints Women's Press and Sumach Press, both with a focus on feminist work which contributes to the social identity of Canada, and also Kellom Books which carries poetry, fiction and non-fiction by men.
Andrew Wayne, President, awayne@cspi.org
Rick Walker, VP, Book Publishing, rick.walker@cspi.org
Drew Hawkins, VP, Custom Publishing, dhawkins@cspi.org

Canadian Urban Institute / Institut urbain du Canada
PO Box 612, #402, 555 Richmond St. W, Toronto, ON M5V 3B1
Tel: 416-365-0816; *Fax:* 416-365-0650
cui@canurb.com
www.canurb.com
ISBNs: 1-895446
Terry Cooke, Chair
Michael Fenn, Interim President & CEO, 416-365-0816, X-233, mfenn@canurb.com

Canadian Water Resources Association (CWRA) / Association canadienne des ressources hydriques
1401 - 14th St., Lethbridge, AB T1H 2W6
Tel: 403-317-0017;
www.cwra.org
ISBNs: 1-896513, 0-9694535
CWRA publishes journals, books & reports on water resources in Canada. Titles include the quarterly publication, Canadian Water Resources Journal, the newsletter, Water News.
Rick Ross, Executive Director, fjross@telusplanet.net

CANAV Books
51 Balsam Ave., Toronto, ON M4E 3B6
Tel: 416-698-7559; *Fax:* 416-693-4344
www.canavbooks.com
ISBNs: ISBN: 0-9690703, 0-91022; SAN: 115-3021
Publishers of books on aviation history
Larry Milberry, Publisher, larry@canavbooks.com

Can-Ed Media Ltd.
43 Moccasin Trail, Toronto, ON M3C 1Y5
Tel: 416-445-3900; *Fax:* 416-445-9976
canedmedia@sympatico.ca
ISBNs: ISBN: 0-920102; SAN: 170-0073
Specializes in dance & fitness recordings & instruction books

Cape Breton University Press
PO Box 5300, 1250 Grand Lake Rd., Sydney, NS B1P 6L2
Tel: 902-563-1955; *Fax:* 902-563-1177
cbu_press@cbu.ca
www.cbu.ca/press
ISBNs: 0-920336, 1-897009; SAN: 115-5458
Publishing arm of Cape Breton University.
Mike R. Hunter, Editor-in-Chief, 902-563-1955, mike_hunter@cbu.ca

Capemara Communications Inc.
4623 William Head Rd., Victoria, BC V9C 3Y7
Tel: 250-474-3935; *Fax:* 250-478-3979
Toll-Free: 800-661-0368
info@capamara.com
capamara.com
This publisher offers specialty magazines and trade newspapers for various industries in Canada and around the world. Titles include: Aquaculture, Hatchery International, Small Farm Canada, Crane & Hoist Canada.

Captus Press
 # 14-15, 1600 Steeles Ave. West, Concord, ON L4K 4M2
Tel: 416-736-5537; *Fax:* 416-736-5793
info@captus.com
www.captus.com
ISBNs: 0-921801, 1-895712, 1-896691, 1-55322
Captus is a publisher of textbooks which provide a Canadian context for university and college courses in the subjects of business, law, disability studies, and Aboriginal economic development.
Randy Hoffman, President

Carraig Books / Livres Carraig
CP 8733, Sainte-Foy, QC G1V 4N6
Tél: 418-651-5918;
carraigbooks@sympatico.ca
ISBNs: 0-9690805, 0-9698581
The company specializes in books on Quebec-Irish history with titles including, "Eyewitness - Grosse Ile - 1847," "The Shamrock Trail, Tracing the Irish in Quebec City."
Marianna O'Gallagher, m.ogallagher@sympatico.ca

Carswell
One Corporate Plaza, 2075 Kennedy Rd., Toronto, ON M1T 3V4
Tel: 416-609-8000; *Fax:* 416-298-5094
Toll-Free: 800-387-5351
carswell.comments@thomson.com
www.carswell.com
ISBNs: 0-459, 0-7798, 0-88820; SAN: 115-0316
Carswell publishes directories, including the Lexpert Legal Directory, Tax & Accounting, Business, Compliance & International.
Don Van Meer, President/CEO

CBC Learning
PO Box 500 A, 205 Wellington St. West, Toronto, ON M5W 1E6
Tel: 416-205-6384; *Fax:* 416-205-2376
Toll-Free: 866-999-3072
cbclearning@cbc.ca
www.cbceds.ca
ISBNs: ISBN: 0-660; SAN: 115-2777
Publishes resources related to CBC programs & programming

CCH Canadian Limited
#300, 90 Sheppard Ave. East, Toronto, ON M2N 3A1
Tel: 416-224-2224; *Fax:* 416-224-2243
Toll-Free: 800-268-4522
cservice@cch.ca; support@cch.ca
www.cch.ca
ISBNs: ISBN: 1-55367, 1-55141, 0-88796, 1-55496; SAN: 115-2785
Publishers of professional information products involving tax, accounting, law, financial planning & human resources
Ian Rhind, President/CEO
Allan Orr, VP, Finance & Administration, aorr@cch.ca

Cedar Cave Books
PO Box 180, Newmarket, ON L3Y 4X1
Fax: 905-895-7613
Toll-Free: 866-895-9296
info@cedarcave.com
www.cedarcave.com/
Cedar Cave Books are self-publishers of a number of non-fiction books, with titles including "Yoga for Cats," and "Florida, Eh?"

Centax Books & Distribution
1150 - 8th Ave., Regina, SK S4R 1C9
Tel: 306-359-7580; *Fax:* 800-823-6829
Toll-Free: 800-667-5595
centax@printwest.com
www.centaxbooks.com
ISBNs: 0-919845, 1-895292, 1-894022, 1-897010
Together with its sister company, Publishing Solutions, Centax produces and markets cookbooks, RCMP history books, business and family management books, family lifestyle, gardening, self-help and sports books.
Dan Marce, General Manager, d.marce@printwest.com
Tracy Wilson, Office Manager, t.wilson@printwest.com
Margo Embury, Director, Operations, m.embury@printwest.com

Centre for Addiction & Mental Health (CAMH)
33 Russell St., Toronto, ON M5S 2S1
Tel: 416-595-6059; *Fax:* 416-593-4694
Toll-Free: 800-661-1111
publications@camh.net
www.camh.net
Other information: 1-800-463-627
ISBNs: 0-88868, 1-77052; SAN 115-0081
CAMH publishes resources for therapists, doctors, nurses, front-line workers, and other professionals in the fields of

addictions & mental health. Materials include research papers, pamphlets, newsletters and journals.

Centre for the Grief Journey Inc.
PO Box 201, 2 - 3415 Dixie Rd., Mississauga, ON L4Y 4J6
Tel: 905-624-8080; *Fax:* 905-624-6742
info@griefjourney.com
www.griefjourney.com
ISBNs: 0-9697841
The company publishes books & other resources to support the grieving process.
Dr. Bill Webster, bwebster@griefjourney.com

Le Centre FORA
432, av Westmount, unité H, Sudbury, ON P3A 5Z8
Tél: 705-524-3672; *Téléc:* 705-524-8535
Ligne sans frais: 888-814-4422
info@centrefora.on.ca
www.centrefora.on.ca
ISBNs: ISBN: 2-921706
Centre francophone d'édition en éducation de base des adultes, et de diffusion de matériel éducatif pour tout âge. Service d'édition: coordination de projects, production, impression, rédaction, etc. Service de diffusion. Bureaux: Sudbury, North Bay.
Yolande Clément, Directrice générale, yclement@centrefora.on.ca

Centre franco-ontarien de ressources pédagogiques
435, rue Donald, Ottawa, ON K1K 4X5
Tél: 613-747-8000; *Téléc:* 613-747-2808
Ligne sans frais: 877-742-3677
cforp@cforp.on.ca
www.cforp.on.ca
Centre multiservices en éducation; développement, édition; production multimedia; programmation; formation professionnelle; imprimerie
Gilles Leroux, Directeur général, x253, robert.arseneault@cforp.on.ca

Céthial Books for Children (Canada) Inc.
PO Box 252 Mount Royal, Montréal, QC H3P 3C5
Tel: 514-278-3333; *Toll-Free:* 800-238-4425
cethial@cethial.com; info@cethial.com
www.cethial.com
ISBNs: ISBN: 1-55274, 1-896933

CGS Communications, Inc.
2521 Nicklaus Ct., Burlington, ON L7M 4V1
Tel: 905-332-0083; *Fax:* 905-319-1641
info@cgscommunications.com
www.cgscommunications.com
ISBNs: ISBN: 0-929079
Published materials include books on career/educational planning and scholarship informaton.

CHA Press
17 York St., Ottawa, ON K1N 9L6
Tel: 613-241-8005; *Fax:* 613-241-5055
custserv@cha.ca
www.cha.ca/cart/catalog/cha-publications.html
ISBNs: ISBN: 0-919100, 1-896151
Pamela C. Fralick, President & CEO

The Charlton Press
PO Box 820 Willowdale B, Toronto, ON M2K 2R1
Tel: 416-488-1418; *Fax:* 416-488-4656
Toll-Free: 800-442-6042
chpress@charltonpress.com
www.charltonpress.com
ISBNs: ISBN: 0-88968: SAN: 115-0235
Publishers of catalogues on 20th century collectables including coins, bank notes & others
W.K. Cross, Publisher

Chenelière Éducation
7001, boul St-Laurent, Montréal, QC H2S 3E3
Tél: 514-273-1066; *Téléc:* 514-276-0324
Ligne sans frais: 800-565-5531
info@cheneliere-education.ca
www.cheneliere.ca
ISBNs: ISBN: 2-89310, 2-89461
Y compris Groupe Beauchemin, Gaëtan Morin Éditeur, et les Publications Graficor
Jacques Rochefort, Président-directeur général, jrochefort@cheneliere.ca
Michel Carl Perron, Vice-président, Production, mcperron@cheneliere.ca

Chestnut Publishing Group
#610, 4005 Bayview Ave, Toronto, ON M2M 3Z9
Tel: 416-224-5824; *Fax:* 416-224-0595
sharkstark@sympatico.ca
www.chestnutpublishing.com
ISBNs: ISBN: 1-894601, 0-9731237, 0-9689552, 0-9688946
CPG publishes educational material for both adult & children, ESL materials, as well as novels & teacher's guides targeted at reluctant readers. It has 4 imprints: Chestnut Publishing, High Interest Publishing (HIP), Lynx Publishing and Patnor Books with its New Start Suspense Series.
Stanley Starkman

Clifford Ford Publications
#15, 120 Walnut Ct., Ottawa, ON K1R 7W2
Tel: 613-237-0550;
crford@cliffordfordpublications.ca
www.cliffordfordpublications.ca
ISBNs: ISBN: 0-919883
This is a publisher of a wide range of sheet music, including Canadian historical anthologies, choral collections and pedagogical music, as well as those works composed by Clifford Ford.

CNIB
1929 Bayview Ave., Toronto, ON M4G 3E8
Tel: 416-486-2500; *Fax:* 416-480-7700
Toll-Free: 800-563-2642
info@cnib.ca
www.cnib.ca
ISBNs: 0-616, 0-921122
CNIB reproduces materials in alternative formats, including DAISY audio, Braille

Coach House Books
401 Huron St., Toronto, ON M5S 2G5
Tel: 416-979-2217; *Fax:* 416-977-1158
Toll-Free: 800-367-6360
mail@chbooks.com
www.chbooks.com
ISBNs: 1-55245, 1-897439, 1-77056
Coach House Books publishes Canadian content across a variety of fields: fiction, poetry, art & architecture, drama & performing arts, children's, social science & travel, including a series of books about Toronto. It has been nominated for a slew of literary awards, such as Griffin Poetry Prizes, Governor General's Awards, Trillium Book Awards, and the Ontario Premier's Award for Excellence in the Arts.
Stan Bevington, Publisher, stan@chbooks.com
Alana Wilcox, Editorial Director, alana@chbooks.com

Codasat Canada Ltd.
3122 Blenheim St., Vancouver, BC V6K 4J7
Tel: 604-228-9952; *Fax:* 604-228-4733
www.codasat.com
In addition to inventory management services, Codasat offers sales & distribution services to small & medium-sized publishers wishing to sell books in the Canadian market.
Sandra Hargreaves, Co-owner

Colombo & Company
42 Dell Park Ave., Toronto, ON M6B 2T6
Tel: 416-782-6853; *Fax:* 416-782-0285
jrc@ca.inter.net
www.colombo.ca
ISBNs: 1-894540, 0-9695092, 1-896308
This is the publishing imprint for books by John Robert Colombo & colleagues, including poetry & poetry anthologies, Canadiana, reference works & quotation collections, mysteries, humour, & translations.
John Robert Colombo, Publisher

Commoners' Publishing Society Inc.
631 Tubman Cres., Ottawa, ON K1V 8L5
Tel: 613-523-2444; *Fax:* 613-260-0401
Toll-Free: 866-890-9489
cheriton@on.aibn.com
www.commonerspublishing.com
ISBNs: 0-88970; SAN: 115-0243
Although by no means limited to men's issues, Commoners' publishes books on parenting, marriage and divorce policy from a male perspecitive.
Glenn Cheriton, President

The Communication Project
9 Lobraico Lane, Whitchurch-Stouffville, ON L4A 7X5
Tel: 905-640-8914; *Fax:* 905-640-2922
Toll-Free: 800-772-7765
tcp@tcpnow.com
www.tcppress.com
ISBNs: ISBN: 1-896232
A research & education group, with an independent press, dedicated to quality books for children & adults in the areas of literacy, science education, life course, & intergenerational relationships

Community Legal Education Ontario (CLEO) / Éducation juridique communautaire Ontario
#600, 119 Spadina Ave., Toronto, ON M5V 2L1
Tel: 416-408-4420; *Fax:* 416-408-4424
cleo@cleo.on.ca
www.cleo.on.ca
ISBNs: 0-88903; SAN: 115-3110
CLEO is a community legal clinic specializing in public legal education and publishing booklets, pamphlets, fact sheets & manuals, all written in clear language for people with low incomes, immigrants & refugees, seniors, injured workers, & women. Topics include workers' rights, landlord & tenant law, immigration law, family law, consumer rights, & women's rights. Most publications are available in French, and some are available in other languages. MOst are free of charge.
Julie Mathews, Chief Privacy Officer, privacyofficer@cleonet.ca

Company's Coming Publishing Limited
2311 - 96 St., Edmonton, AB T6N 1G3
Tel: 780-450-6223; *Fax:* 780-450-1857
info@companyscoming.com
www.companyscoming.com
ISBNs: 1-896891, 1-897069, 1-895455, 0-9690695, 0-9693322, 1-897477
This is the publisher of an extensive array of cookbooks, including a selection of series, with Kids Cooking, Pint Size, and Focus as examples. In addition, Company's Coming publishes a series of craft books.
Grant Lovig, President & Publisher
Gail Lovig, Vice-President, Marketing & Distribution
Kim Hamilton, Marketing Coordinator, 780-450-6223, X-264, kimh@companyscoming.com

Continental Records Company Ltd.
PO Box 7, Streetsville, ON L5M 2B7
Tel: 905-813-9544; *Fax:* 905-812-4993
Toll-Free: 800-494-6129
conrecs@gocontinental.com
www.gocontinental.com
ISBNs: 0-920325
In addition to selling 45 RPM records & unique oldies on CD, Continental Records publishes chart books and music books. Titles include The Record & CD Collector's Directory. The company also offers The Directory of Canadian Recruiters, a compilation of employment firms & organizations.
Neil Patte, President

Continuing Legal Education Society of British Columbia (CLEBC)
#300, 845 Cambie St., Vancouver, BC V6B 5T2
Tel: 604-669-3544; *Fax:* 604-669-9260
Toll-Free: 800-663-0437
custserv@cle.bc.ca
www.cle.bc.ca
ISBNs: 1-55258, 0-86504; SAN: 115-3153
CLEBC specializes in books, papers, case digests & manuals for the legal profession, covering a variety of practice areas including aboriginal law, administrative law, criminal law, family law, labour, real estate, tax and more. An online subscription service is also available.
Susan Munro, Director of Publications, 604-893-2106, smunro@cle.bc

Copp Clark Professional
#1, 1675 Sismet Rd., Mississauga, ON L4W 4K8
Tel: 905-238-2882; *Fax:* 905-238-3413
Toll-Free: 877-389-3378
info@coppclark.com
www.coppclark.com
ISBNs: 0-7730, 0-273
The oldest, continuously active publisher in Canada, Copp Clark publishes resources for the financial trading community, authoritative reference data on holiday observances.
Ronald S. Marr, President & Publisher
Grace D'Alfonso, Editorial Director

Cordillera Books
PO Box 46, 8415 Granville St., Vancouver, BC V6P 4Z9
Tel: 604-261-1695; *Fax:* 604-266-4469
richbook@shaw.ca
ISBNs: 1-895590
Publishers of naval, maritime history and shipping books
S.C. Heal

Cormorant Books Inc.
#230, 215 Spadina Ave., Toronto, ON M5T 2C7
Tel: 416-929-4957; *Fax:* 416-929-3596
Toll-Free: 800-565-9523
www.cormorantbooks.com
ISBNs: 0-920953, 1-896951, 1-897151; SAN: 115-4176
Cormorant Books specializes in fiction emerging Canadian writers, reissues of Canadian literary classics, and English translations of works by Quebec writers. There is a selection of

gay & lesbian literature, as well as non-fiction titles, including historical biographies and memoirs.
J. Marc Coté, President & Publisher

Coteau Books
2517 Victoria Ave., Regina, SK S4P 0T2
Tel: 306-777-0170; *Fax:* 306-522-5152
Toll-Free: 800-440-4471
coteau@coteaubooks.com
www.coteaubooks.com
ISBNs: 0-919926, 1-55050
Coteau Books is a not-for-profit, cooperatively run press specializing in fiction, poetry, drama & fiction for young readers, with some emphasis on Saskatchewan writers.
Nik L. Burton, Managing Editor

Crabtree Publishing Company
616 Welland Ave., St. Catharines, ON L2M 5V6
Tel: 905-682-5221; *Fax:* 800-355-7166
Toll-Free: 800-387-7650
custserv@crabtreebooks.com
www.crabtreebooks.com
ISBNs: 0-7787, 0-86505, 1-4271; SAN: 115-1436
With offices in the U.S., Canada, the U.K. and Australia, Crabtreespecializes in children's non-fiction work & educational products on many curriculum subjects. Material is published in an audio format and in several languages, including Spanish and French. Imprints include: A Bobbie Kalman Book; Leaps and Bounds Books; and Look, Listen, & Learn.
Lisa Antonsen, National Account Manager
Peter Crabtree, President

Cranberry Tree Press
#173, 5060 Tecumseh Rd. East, Windsor, ON N8T 1C1
Fax: 519-945-6207
mail@cranberrytreepress.com
www.cranberrytreepress.com
ISBNs: 0-9681325, 0-9684218, 1-894668
Cranberry Tree Press is a contract, co-operative publishing service with editors & designers on staff.
Lenore Langs, Publisher & Editor

Creative Book Publishing Ltd.
PO Box 8660 A, St. John's, NL A1B 3T7
Tel: 709-748-0813; *Fax:* 709-579-6511
nlbooks@transcontinental.ca
www.creativebookpublishing.ca
ISBNs: 0-920021, 1-895387, 1-894294, 1-897174, 0-920884
Creative Book Publishing specializes in works by Newfoundland & Labrador authors, promoting them to national & international markets. Genres include fiction, poetry, memoirs, history, women's studies and more. Books are published under 3 imprints: Creative Publishers, Killick Press, & Tuckamore Books.
Russell Wangersky, General Manager, rwanger@thetelegram.com
Donna Francis, Editor & Marketing Manager, donna.francis@transcontinental.ca

Crisp Learning Canada
60 Briarwood Ave., Mississauga, ON L5G 3N6
Tel: 905-274-5678; *Fax:* 905-278-2801
Toll-Free: 800-446-4797
info@crisplearning.ca
www.crisplearning.ca
ISBNs: 0-921601; SAN: 116-0478
Crisp Learning publishes a library of books & training manuals specializing in: communication, conflict resolution, presentation skills, telephone skills, sales & marketing, customer service, managing, organizational development, and personal improvement.
Stephen Connolly, President, steveconnolly@homeroom.ca

Cross Canada Books
354 Wellesley St. East, Toronto, ON M4X 1H3
Tel: 416-925-7807; *Fax:* 416-925-9946
Toll-Free: 800-473-4078
doug.fisher@sympatico.ca
ISBNs: 0-920400
Book distributor

Crown Publications Inc.
PO Box 9452 Prov Govt, 563 Superior St., Victoria, BC V8W 9V7
Tel: 250-387-6409; *Fax:* 250-387-1120
Toll-Free: 800-663-6105
crownpub@gov.bc.ca
www.crownpub.bc.ca
ISBNs: ISBN: 0-9696417
Crown Publications is the authorized distributor of British Columbia acts, regulations & related legislative publications, and an authorized agent for Canadian Federal Government publications.
Sherry Brown, Director, 250-356-6876, sherry.brown@gov.bc.ca
Wendy Pope, Manager, 250-356-5392, wendy.pope@gov.bc.ca

Culture Concepts Books
69 Ashmount Cres., Toronto, ON M9R 1C9
Tel: 416-245-8119; *Fax:* 416-245-3383
cultureconcepts@rogers.com
www.cultureconceptsbooks.ca
ISBNs: 0-921472
Culture Concepts Books publishes fiction titles and academic titles in adult education, food, nutrition and culture. Also offered are professional editing services & manuscript evaluation, selected literary agency & book production.
Thelma Barer-Stein, President

Cyclops Press
#1, 164 Browning Ave., Toronto, ON M4K 1W5
mail@cyclopspress.com
www.cyclopspress.com
ISBNs: 1-894177
An independent, artist-run, multimedia, literary micro- publisher specializing in poetry, novels, feature films & videos, CDs, interdisciplinary art projects. Material is distributed through Signature Editions, www.signature-editions.com.
Clive Holden
Alissa York

Dance Collection Danse Publishing
145 George St., Toronto, ON M5A 2M6
Tel: 416-365-3233; *Fax:* 416-365-3169
Toll-Free: 800-665-5320
talk@dcd.ca
www.dcd.ca
ISBNs: ISBN: 0-929003
Publisher of DANCE COLLECTION DANSE MAGAZINE, and books on dance
Miriam Adams, Co-director

Database Directories
588 Dufferin St., London, ON N6B 2A4
Tel: 519-433-1666; *Fax:* 519-430-1131
mail@databasedirectory.com
www.databasedirectory.com
ISBNs: ISBN: 1-896537
Publisher of current contact information on Canadian schools, libraries, book retailers & municipalities
Lesley Classic, CEO

David C. Cook Distribution Canada
PO Box 98, 55 Woodslee Ave., Paris, ON N3L 3E5
Tel: 800-263-2664; *Fax:* 800-461-8575
Toll-Free: 000-000-0000
custserv@davidccook.ca
www.davidccook.ca
ISBNs: SAN: 170-0197
Distribution wing of David C. Cook Publishing, Colorado Springs, CO. Specializing in Christian literature & communication resources

Davus Publishing
150 Norfolk St. South, Simcoe, ON N3Y 2W2
Tel: 519-426-2027; *Fax:* 519-426-0105
davuspub@sympatico.ca
www.kwic.com/davus/
ISBNs: ISBN: 0-915317
Featuring the works of David Beasley, and Major John Richardson, Canada's first novelist
Dr. David Beasley, Publisher

DC Books
PO Box 666 St. Laurent, 950, rue Décarie, Montréal, QC H4L 4V9
Tel: 514-843-8130; *Fax:* 514-939-0569
Toll-Free: 800-591-6250
dcbooks@videotron.ca
www.dcbooks.ca
ISBNs: 0-919688, 1-897190; SAN: 115-8988
DC Books publishes poetry & prose with innovative Canadian emphasis, histories, memoirs, & drama. Also offered are Railfare DC Books about railways & Moosehead Anthology. The house is a Member of the Association of English Editors of Quebec, & the Literary Press Group.
Keith Henderson, Managing Editor
Steve Luxton, Editor-in-chief

Detselig Enterprises Ltd.
c/o Temeron Books Inc., #210, 1220 Kensington Rd. NW, Calgary, AB T2N 3P5
Tel: 403-283-0900; *Fax:* 403-283-6947
temeron@telusplanet.net
www.temerondetselig.com
ISBNs: ISBN: 0-920490, 1-55059; SAN: 115-0324
Specializing in general trade & academic books written by authors from Canada, the U.S., Austria and The Netherlands
T.E. Giles, President

Diffusion Dimedia inc.
539, boul Lebeau, Saint-Laurent, QC H4N 1S2
Tel: 514-336-3941; *Fax:* 514-331-3916
general@dimedia.qc.ca
www.dimedia.qc.ca
Diffuse & distribue des livres de langue française au Canada
Johanne Paquette, Contact

Diffusion du Livre Mirabel
5757, rue Cypihot, Saint-Laurent, QC H4S 1R3
Tél: 514-334-2690; *Téléc:* 514-334-4720
Ligne sans frais: 800-263-3678
erpidlm@erpi.com
www.erpi.com
ISBNs: ISBN: 0-88527
Division d'Éditions du Renouveau Pédagogique Inc.; livres jeunesse & imagerie, informatique, littérature, livres de cuisine, bandes dessinées
Normand Cleroux, Président

Diffusion Inter-Livres
1703, rue Belleville, Lemoyne, QC J4P 3M2
Tél: 450-465-0037; *Téléc:* 450-923-8966
ligueqc@cam.org
www.inter-livres.ca
Joël Coppieter

Doubleday Canada Ltd.
c/o Random House of Canada Limited, One Toronto St., Unit 300, Toronto, ON M5C 2V6
Tel: 416-364-4449; *Fax:* 416-364-6863
Toll-Free: 000-000-0000
www.randomhouse.ca
ISBNs: ISBN: 0-385; SAN: 115-0340
Doubleday Canada is an imprint of Random House of Canada, publishing high quality Canadian literary & commercial fiction from new & established writers, memoirs, history, business, & social & political journalism
John Neale, President
Evaughn Moffat, Vice-President, Sales & Marketing

Douglas & McIntyre Publishing Group
#201, 2323 Quebec St., Vancouver, BC V5T 4S7
Tel: 604-254-7191; *Fax:* 604-254-9099
Toll-Free: 800-387-0117
dm@douglas-mcintyre.com
www.douglas-mcintyre.com
ISBNs: ISBN: 0-88894, 1-55054, 1-55365; SAN: 115-1886, 115-026X
Specializing in high quality Canadian fiction & non-fiction. Imprints: Douglas & McIntyre, Greystone Books
Mark Scott, President
Scott McIntyre, Publisher, Douglas & McIntyre
Rob Sanders, Publisher, Greystone Books

Dovehouse Editions Inc.
1890 Fairmeadow Cres., Ottawa, ON K1H 7B9
Tel: 613-731-7601; *Fax:* 613-731-7601
www.dovehouse.ca
ISBNs: ISBN: 0-919473, 1-895537
Publishers of The Carleton Renaissance Plays in Translation Series, as well as other works in Renaissance Studies; Publications of the Barnabe Riche Society; University of Toronto Italian Studies; and Ottawa Hispanic Studies
Dr. Donald Beecher, Editor

Dragon Hill Publishing Ltd.
5474 Thibault Wynd NW, Edmonton, AB T6R 3P9
Tel: 780-239-4996;
info@dragonhillpublishing.com
www.dragonhillpublishing.com
ISBNs: ISBN: 1-896124
Publishing for the popular adult and youth markets, in the subject areas of self-help, biography, success guides, and traditional cultures
Gary Whyte, Publisher

Drawn & Quarterly
PO Box 48056, Montréal, QC H2V 4S8
Tel: 514-279-2221; *Fax:* 514-279-2221
info@drawnandquarterly.com
www.drawnandquarterly.com
ISBNs: ISBN: 1-896597
Publisher of comic books & graphic novels
Chris Oliveros, Publisher

DreamCatcher Publishing Inc.
55 Canterbury St., Saint John, NB E2L 2C6
Tel: 506-632-4008; *Fax:* 506-632-4009
Toll-Free: 877-631-7323
elizabeth.margaris@dreamcatcherpublishing.ca
www.dreamcatcherpublishing. ca

ISBNs: ISBN: 1-894372
Specializing in Maritime writers, fiction & non-fiction for children & adults
Elizabeth Margaris, Publisher

The Dundurn Group
#500, 3 Church St., Toronto, ON M5E 1M2
Tel: 416-214-5544; *Fax:* 416-214-5556
info@dundurn.com
www.dundurn.com
ISBNs: ISBN: 0-919670, 1-55002, 0-88924, 1-895681, 0-88882, 0-88866,
Specializing in Canadian content in a number of subject areas, including adult & juvenile fiction & non-fiction, history, literature & literary criticism, health, music, travel & business
Kirk Howard, President

Duval Education / Duval Éducation
#100, 233 Dunbar Ave., Montreal, QC H3P 2H4
Tél: 514-932-8229; *Téléc:* 514-932-9175
Ligne sans frais: 888-932-8229
duvalhouse@duvalhouse.com
www.duvalhouse.com
ISBNs: ISBN: 1-55220, 1-895850
Educational resources in English & French, ESL materials, Aboriginal resources
Simon de Jocas, Vice President, simon.dejocas@nelson.com

eastendbooks
45 Fernwood Park Ave., Toronto, ON M4E 3E9
Tel: 416-691-6816; *Fax:* 416-691-2414
info@eastendbooks.com
www.eastendbooks.com
ISBNs: ISBN: 1-896973
A small-press with an Ontario focus, publishing material in a range of subjects, including fiction, travel, current events, modern jazz
Jeanne MacDonald

Écrits des Forges
992-A, rue Royale, Trois-Rivières, QC G9A 4H9
Tél: 819-840-8492;
ecritsdesforges.com
ISBNs: ISBN: 2-89046
Poésie, et essais en poésie
Stéphane Despatie, Director général

ECW Press
#200, 2120 Queen St. East, Toronto, ON M4E IE2
Tel: 416-694-3348; *Fax:* 416-698-9906
info@ecwpress.com
www.ecwpress.com
ISBNs: ISBN: 1-55022, 0-920802, 1-920763; SAN: 115-1274
Publishers of Essays on Canadian Writing, & a diverse selection of contemporary poetry, fiction, writings on culture & politics, biography
Jack David, Co-publisher
Crissy Boylan, Managing Editor

EDIMAG inc.
CP 325 Rosemont, Montréal, QC H1X 3B8
Tél: 514-522-2244; *Téléc:* 514-522-6301
info@edimag.com
www.edimag.com
ISBNs: ISBN: 2-921735, 2-89542
Santé, alimentation & recettes, environnement, connaissances pratiques, jeux & sport, loisirs
Pierre Nadeau, Éditeur

Éditions Actualisation
Place du Parc, #2200, 300, rue Léo-Pariseau, Montréal, QC H2X 4B3
Tél: 514-284-2622; *Téléc:* 514-284-2625
Ligne sans frais: 877-688-0101
admin@actualisation.com
www.actualisation.com
Matériel pour animer des formations, destiné aux formateurs, éducateurs et conseillers en ressources humaines: guides, manuels, questionnaires. Québec: Centre de la technologie, 1995, rue Frank Carrel, bureau 102, 418-688-0100.
Louis Fortin, Président MBA, louis.fortin@actualisation.com

Éditions Anne Sigier inc.
a/s Éditions Médiaspaul, 3965, boul Henri-Bourassa est, Montréal, QC H1H 1L1
Tél: 514-322-7341; *Téléc:* 514-322-4281
mediaspaul@mediaspaul.qc.ca
www.annesigier.qc.ca
ISBNs: ISBN: 2-89129
Bibles, livres de spiritualité chrétienne, beaux-livres
Anne Sigier
Jacques Sigier

Éditions Arts, Lettres et Techniques inc.
12, rue Northcote, Hampstead, QC H3X 1P5
Tél: 514-747-4784
ISBNs: ISBN: 0-921137
Droit, médecine, techniques, sciences, arts
Jacqueline Irali, Présidente

Les Éditions Behaviora inc.
CP 91, 151, ch Bellevue, Eastman, QC J0E 1P0
Tél: 450-297-0515; *Téléc:* 450-297-0516
behaviora@sympatico.ca
www.behaviora.qc.ca
ISBNs: ISBN: 2-7629
Ouvrages de psychologie, de pédagogie, & de sciences sociales
Dr. Rodrigue Otis

Éditions Bellarmin
a/s Éditions Fides, 306, rue Saint-Zotique est, Montréal, QC H2S 1L6
Tél: 514-745-4290; *Téléc:* 514-745-4299
editions@fides.qc.ca
www.fides.qc.ca
ISBNs: ISBN: 0-88502, 2-89007
Michel Maillé, Directeur général

Les Éditions Brault et Bouthillier / Brault & Bouthillier Publishing
4823, rue Sherbrooke ouest, Montréal, QC H3Z 1G7
Tél: 514-932-9466; *Téléc:* 514-932-5929
Ligne sans frais: 866-750-9466
editions@ebbp.ca
www.ebbp.ca
ISBNs: ISBN: 0-88537, 2-7615
Manuels scolaires, ouvrages pédagogiques/parascolaires; français et anglais
Jean Brault, Président
Yves Brault, Vice-président
Paul Beullac, Éditeur

Les Éditions CEC inc.
9001, boul Louis-H.-La Fontaine, Anjou, QC H1J 2C5
Tél: 514-351-6010; *Téléc:* 514-351-3534
Ligne sans frais: 800-363-0494
infoped@ceceditions.com
www.editionscec.com
ISBNs: ISBN: 0-7751, 2-7617
Ouvrages pour tous les ordres d'enseignement - manuels scolaires, ouvrages de référence, grammaires, anthologies littéraires

Éditions CERES
CP 1089 B, Montréal, QC H5B 3K9
Tél: 514-937-7138; *Téléc:* 514-937-9875
editionsceres@gmail.ca
www.editionsceres.ca
ISBNs: ISBN: 0-919089
Les éditions CERES publient exclusivement des livres érudits
C. Stéfane

Les Éditions Chouette
#B-238, 1001, rue Lenoir, Montréal, QC H4C 2Z6
Tél: 514-925-3325; *Téléc:* 514-925-3323
info@editions-chouette.com
www.chouettepublishing.com
Livres Caillou
Christine L'Heureux, Présidente-fondatrice

Les Éditions Cornac
5, rue Sainte-Ursule, Québec, QC G1R 4C7
Tél: 418-692-0377; *Téléc:* 418-692-0605
editionscornac.com
ISBNs: ISBN: 2-921310, 2-89529
Livres jeunesse; poésie; essais; albums illustrés; a pour mission d'encourager l'expression des Premières Nations
Michel Brûlé, Éditeur, michel@editionscornac.com

Les Éditions de l'Hexagone
1010, rue de la Gauchetière est, Montréal, QC H2L 2N5
Tél: 514-523-7993; *Téléc:* 514-282-7530
adpcommandes@messageries-adp.com
www.edhexagone.com
ISBNs: ISBN: 2-89006, 2-89295
Littérature québécoise
Danielle Fournier, Directrice

Les Éditions de l'Homme
955, rue Amherst, Montréal, QC H2L 3K4
Tél: 514-523-1182; *Téléc:* 514-597-0370
adpcommandes@messageries-adp.com
www.editions-homme.com
ISBNs: ISBN: 2-7619, 2-89005, 2-89006
Livres de sciences humaines
Pierre Lespérance, Président
Pierre Bourdon, Vice-président à l'édition

Éditions de l'Instant même
865, av Moncton, Québec, QC G1S 2Y4
Tél: 418-527-8690; *Téléc:* 418-681-6780
info@instantmeme.com
www.instantmeme.com
ISBNs: ISBN: 2-921197, 2-9800635, 2-89502
Romans, essais, nouvelles
Marie Taillon, Directrice générale

Les Éditions de L'IQRC/Les Presses de l'Université Laval
Pavillon Maurice-Pollack, #3103, 2305, rue de l'Université, Québec, QC G1V 0A6
Tél: 418-656-2803; *Téléc:* 418-656-3305
Ligne sans frais: 800-859-7474
presses@pul.ulaval.ca
www.pulaval.com
ISBNs: ISBN: 2-89224
Américana, bioéthique critique, cinéma et société, culture québécoise, éducation, géographie, histoire sociale, lectures, politique
Denis Dion, Directeur général

Les Éditions de la courte échelle
5243, boul Saint-Laurent, Montréal, QC H2T 1S4
Tél: 514-274-2004; *Téléc:* 514-270-4160
info@courteechelle.com
www.courteechelle.com
ISBNs: ISBN: 2-89021; SAN: 116-0249
Un leader de la littérature jeunesse francophone - livres pour les trois à six ans; collection adulte
Hélène Derome, Présidente/Éditrice

Éditions de la Paix
127, rue Lussier, Saint-Alphonse-de-Granby, QC J0E 2A0
Tél: 450-375-4765; *Téléc:* 450-375-4765
info@editpaix.qc.ca
www.editpaix.qc.ca
Jeunesse, patrimoine, romans, poésie, spiritualité
Jean-Paul Tessier, Président-directeur général

Les Éditions de la Pleine Lune
223, 34e av, Lachine, QC H8T 1Z4
Tél: 514-637-6366; *Téléc:* 514-637-6366
editpllune@videotron.ca
www.pleinelune.qc.ca
ISBNs: ISBN: 2-89024
Ouvrages québécois et canadiens
Marie-Madeleine Raoult, Directrice

Éditions de Mortagne
CP 116, Boucherville, QC J4B 5E6
Tél: 450-641-2387; *Téléc:* 450-655-6092
info@editionsdemortagne.com
www.editionsdemortagne.com
ISBNs: ISBN: 2-89074
Biographies, romans, collection 'Lime et citron', guides pratiques, santé, psychologie, astrologie, motivation
Max Permingeat, Président

Les Éditions des Plaines
CP 123, Saint-Boniface, MB R2H 3B4
Tél: 204-235-0078; *Téléc:* 204-233-7741
admin@plaines.mb.ca
www.plaines.mb.ca
ISBNs: ISBN: 0-920944, 2-921353, 2-89611
La maison s'applique à donner la parole aux écrivains de l'Ouest canadien
Doris Touchette, Adjointe administrative

Les Éditions du Blé
340, boul Provencher, Saint-Boniface, MB R3H 0G7
Tél: 204-237-8200; *Téléc:* 204-233-8182
direction@editionsduble.ca
www.livres-disques.ca/editions_ble/home/index .cfm
ISBNs: ISBN: 0-920640, 2-921347
La première maison d'édition francophone de l'Ouest canadien; ouvrages des auteurs de la région - poésie, romans, essais, théâtre, livres pour enfants & adolescents
Lucien Chaput

Éditions du Bois-de-Coulonge
1140, av De Montigny, Sillery, QC G1S 3T7
Tél: 418-683-6332; *Téléc:* 418-683-6332
www.ebc.qc.ca
ISBNs: ISBN: 2-9801397
Services aux collectivités & vente directe au grand public
Richard Leclerc, Propriétaire Ph.D.

Éditions du Boréal
4447, rue Saint-Denis, Montréal, QC H2J 2L2
Tél: 514-287-7401; *Téléc:* 514-287-7664
boreal@editionsboreal.qc.ca
www.editionsboreal.qc.ca

ISBNs: ISBN: 2-89052, 0-7646
Fiction, poésie, essais, histoire, biographies, livres pratiques, collections jeunesse
Pascal Assathiany, Directeur général

Éditions du Nordir
Dép des lettres française, Université d'Ottawa, 60, rue Université, Ottawa, ON K1N 6N5
Tél: 819-243-1253; *Téléc:* 819-243-6201
lenordir@sympatico.ca
www.livres-disques.ca/editions_nordir

ISBNs: ISBN: 0-921272
Biographies, études littéraires, poésie, réflexions sociales

Les Éditions du Noroît
#202, 4609, rue d'Iberville, Montréal, QC H2H 2L9
Tél: 450-727-0005; *Téléc:* 450-723-6660
lenoroit@lenoroit.com
www.lenoroit.com

ISBNs: ISBN: 2-89018
Livres de poésie
Karine Hubert

Les Éditions du Remue-Ménage inc.
#501, 110, rue Ste-Thérèse, Montréal, QC H2Y 1E6
Tél: 514-876-0097; *Téléc:* 514-876-7951
info@editions-remuemenage.qc.ca
www.editions-remuemenage.qc.ca

ISBNs: ISBN: 2-89091
Livres sur les femmes: biographie, culture, développement international, éducation, études féministes, poésie, politique, santé
Rachel Bédard, Éditrice

Éditions du Renouveau Pédagogique inc.
5757, rue Cypihot, Saint-Laurent, QC H4S 1R3
Tél: 514-334-2690; *Téléc:* 514-334-4720
Ligne sans frais: 800-263-3678
info@erpi.com
www.erpi.com

ISBNs: ISBN: 2-7613
Maison d'édition scolaire; matériel didactique pour tous les niveaux d'enseignement
Normand Cléroux, Président

Les Éditions du Septentrion
1300, av Maguire, Québec, QC G1T 1Z3
Tél: 418-688-3556; *Téléc:* 418-527-4978
sept@septentrion.qc.ca
www.septentrion.qc.ca

Spécialisée en histoire, archéologie, science politique, ethnographie, et aux sciences humaines
Denis Vaugeois, Président

Les Éditions du Trécarré
La Tourelle, #800, 1055, boul René-Lévesque est, Montréal, QC H2L 4S5
Tél: 514-849-5259; *Téléc:* 514-849-1388
adpcommandes@messageries-adp.com
www.edtrecarre.com

ISBNs: ISBN: 2-89249, 2-89568
Livres pratiques (cuisine, santé); cahiers d'exercices; littérature jeunesse
Marc Laberge, Président
Colette Laberge, Redactrice en chef

Éditions du Vermillon
305, rue Saint-Patrick, Ottawa, ON K1N 5K4
Tél: 613-241-4032; *Téléc:* 613-241-3109
leseditionsduvermillon@rogers.com
www.leseditionsduvermillion.ca

ISBNs: ISBN: 0-919925, 1-895873, 1-894547, 1-897058
Romans, poésie, bandes dessinées, guides pédagogiques, essais
Monique Bertoli, Directrice générale

Éditions Fides
306, rue Saint-Zotique est, Montréal, QC H2S 1L6
Tél: 514-745-4290; *Téléc:* 514-745-4299
editions@fides.qc.ca
www.fides.qc.ca

ISBNs: ISBN: 2-7621
Littérature (collection de poche 'Bibliothèque québécoise'), essais, livres religieux, ouvrages de référence, beaux livres; collection Éditions Bellarmin
Michel Maillé, Directeur général

Les Éditions Flammarion Ltée
375, av Laurier ouest, Montréal, QC H2V 2K3
Tél: 514-277-8807; *Téléc:* 514-278-2085
info@flammarion.qc.ca
www.flammarion.qc.ca

ISBNs: ISBN: 2-89077
Une maison d'édition généraliste

Jean-Michel Sivry, Président

Éditions Ganesha
CP 484 Youville, Montréal, QC H2P 2W1
Tél: 450-641-2395; *Téléc:* 450-641-2989
courriel@editions-ganesha.qc.ca
www.editions-ganesha.qc.ca

Ouvrages diverses: philosophie, religion/cultes, psychologie
André Beaudoin
Lucie Cournoyer

Les Éditions Héritage
300, rue Arran, Saint-Lambert, QC J4R 1K5
Tél: 514-875-0327; *Téléc:* 514-672-1481
Ligne sans frais: 888-228-1498

ISBNs: ISBN: 2-7625, 0-7773
Luc Payette, Président

Éditions Hurtubise inc
1815, av De Lorimier, Montréal, QC H2K 3W6
Tél: 514-523-1523; *Téléc:* 514-523-9969
Ligne sans frais: 800-361-1664
www.editionshurtubise.com

ISBNs: ISBN: 2-89045, 2-89428
Littérature, beaux livres, jeunesse, éducation
Hervé Foulon, Président-directeur général

Les Éditions JCL inc.
930, rue Jacques-Cartier est, Chicoutimi, QC G7H 7K9
Tél: 418-696-0536; *Téléc:* 418-696-3132
jcl@jcl.qc.ca
www.jcl.qc.ca

ISBNs: ISBN: 2-89431, 2-920176
Éditeur généraliste: romans, histoire, culture, jeunesse
Jean-Claude Larouche, Président

Les Éditions JML inc.
1150, ch des Patriotes nord, Mont-St-Hilaire, QC J3G 4S6
Tél: 450-536-1565; *Téléc:* 450-536-2565
infos@editionsjml.com
www.editionsjml.com

ISBNs: ISBN: 2-89234
Cahiers de préparation de cours, cahiers de titulariat, relevés de notes, relevés d'absences

Éditions l'Artichaut inc.
355, rue Dubé, Rimouski, QC G5L 4W6
Tél: 418-723-1554; *Téléc:* 418-725-4828
artichaut@editionslartichaut.com
www.editionslartichaut.com

ISBNs: ISBN: 2-921288; 2-922998
Matériel didactique axé sur le développement des compétences en langue française (niveaux primaire, secondaire)
Ginette Tremblay, Propriétaire

Les Éditions La Pensée Inc.
4370, rue de l'Hôtel de Ville, Montréal, QC H2W 2H5
Tél: 514-848-9042; *Téléc:* 514-848-9836
Ligne sans frais: 800-667-5442
administration@editions-lapensee.qc.ca
www.editions-lapensee.qc.ca

Marc-Aimé Guérin, President

Les Éditions le Griffon d'argile
7649, boul Wilfrid-Hamel, Sainte-Foy, QC G2G 1C3
Tél: 418-871-6898; *Téléc:* 418-871-6818
Ligne sans frais: 800-268-6898
admin@griffondargile.com
www.griffondargile.com

ISBNs: ISBN: 2-920210, 2-920922, 2-89443
André Gosselin

Les Éditions le Renouveau Charlesbourg inc.
CP 87605 Charlesbourg, 870, carré de Tracy est, Québec, QC G1G 5W6
Tél: 418-628-3445; *Téléc:* 418-624-2277
Ligne sans frais: 877-628-3445
info@editionslerenouveau.com
www.editionslerenouveau.com

Guide de lecture de la Bible, ouvrages du domaine religieux, musique, objets religieux
Jacques Roy, Responsable

Éditions Les 400 Coups
#B550, 1001, rue Lenoir, Montréal, QC H4C 2Z6
Tél: 514-381-1422; *Téléc:* 514-487-8811
info@editions400coups.com
www.editions400coups.com

ISBNs: ISBN: 2-920993, 2-89540
Albums jeunesse, livres d'art, bandes dessinées. Publient également sous les noms de Mille-Iles, de Zone convective, et de Mécanique générale
Myriam Comtois, Responsable, Communications, m.comtois@editions400coups.com

Éditions Liber
2318, rue Bélanger, Montréal, QC H2G 1C8
Tél: 514-522-3227; *Téléc:* 514-522-2007
info@editionsliber.org
www.editionsliber.org

ISBNs: ISBN: 2-921569, 2-89578
Études & essais en philosophie, sciences humaines, littérature
Giovanni Calabrese, Directeur

Éditions Libre Expression
La Tourelle, #800, 1055, boul. René-Lévesque E, Montréal, QC H2L 4S5
Tél: 514-849-5259; *Téléc:* 514-849-1388
www.edlibreexpression.com

ISBNs: ISBN: 2-89111, 2-7648
Fiction, biographie, essais, histoire, culture, guides, beaux livres, livres de poche

Les Éditions Logiques
La Tourelle, #800, 1055, boul René-Lévesque est, Montréal, QC H2L 4S5
Tél: 514-849-5259; *Téléc:* 514-849-1388
adpcommandes@messageries-adp.com
www.edlogiques.com

ISBNs: ISBN: 2-89381
Gestion des affaires, économie, pédagogie, psychologie populaire, philosophie, sociologie

Éditions Marie-France ltée
9900, av des Laurentides, Montréal, QC H1H 4V1
Tél: 514-329-3700; *Téléc:* 514-329-0630
Ligne sans frais: 800-563-6644
editions@marie-france.qc.ca
www.marie-france.qc.ca

ISBNs: ISBN: 2-89168
Informatique, littérature, mathématique, français, français immersion
Jean H. Lachapelle, Président

Éditions MultiMondes
930, rue Pouliot, Québec, QC G1V 3N9
Tél: 418-651-3885; *Téléc:* 418-651-6822
Ligne sans frais: 800-840-3029
multimondes@multim.com
www.multim.com

ISBNs: ISBN: 2-921146, 2-89544
Environnement, santé, jeunesse, muséologie, pédagogie, science et technologie
Jean-Marc Gagnon, Président, jmgagnon@multim.com
Lise Morin, Vice-présidente, lmorin@multim.com

Éditions Paulines
5610, rue Beaubien est, Montréal, QC H1T 1X5
Tél: 514-253-5610; *Téléc:* 514-253-1907
editions@paulines.qc.ca
www.paulines.qc.ca

ISBNs: ISBN: 0-920912
Ouvrages de spiritualité

Les Éditions Perce-Neige ltée
#22, 140 Botsford St., Moncton, NB E1C 4X4
Tél: 506-383-4446; *Téléc:* 506-857-2064
perceneige@nb.aibn.com
perceneige.recf.ca

ISBNs: ISBN: 2-920221
Essaies historiques, études littéraires, contes traditionnels et récits, poésie, romans
Paul Bourque, Directeur général

Éditions Phidal inc./Phidal Publishing Inc.
5740, rue Ferrier, Montréal, QC H4P 1M7
Tel: 514-738-0202; *Fax:* 514-738-5102
Toll-Free: 800-738-7349
customer@phidal.com
www.phidal.com

ISBNs: ISBN: 2-89393, 2-7643
Ouvrages pour enfants
Albert Soussan, Président

Éditions Prise de Parole
#205, 109, rue Elm, Sudbury, ON P3C 1T4
Tél: 705-675-6491; *Téléc:* 705-673-1817
prisedeparole@bellnet.ca
www.livres-disques.ca/prise_parole/

ISBNs: ISBN: 0-920814, 0-921573, 2-89423
Bandes dessinées, beaux livres, contes traditionnels, enfants, ados, études littéraires, poésie, revues, romans
Denise Truax, Directrice générale, prisedeparole@bellnet.ca
Sylvie Lessard, Agente de commercialisation, pdpcommercialisation@bellnet.ca
Alain Mayotte, Directeur administratif, pdpadministration@bellnet.ca

Les Éditions Québec Amérique
329, rue de la Commune ouest, 3e étage, Montréal, QC H2Y 2E1
Tél: 514-499-3000; *Téléc:* 514-499-3010
courrier@quebec-amerique.com
www.quebec-amerique.com
ISBNs: ISBN: 0-88552, 2-89037, 2-7644
Ouvrages de référence, littérature, jeunesse
Jacques Fortin, CEO

Les Éditions Quebecor
7, ch Bates, Montréal, QC H2V 4V7
Tél: 514-270-1746; *Téléc:* 514-270-5313
simard.jacques@quebecoreditions.com
www.quebecoreditions.com
ISBNs: ISBN: 0-88617, 2-89089, 2-9801107
Affaires, alimentation, astrologie, biographie, guides pratiques, littérature, santé, sports, nouvel âge
Jacques Simard, Éditeur

Les Éditions Reynald Goulet inc.
40, rue Mireault, Repentigny, QC J6A 1M1
Tél: 450-654-2626; *Téléc:* 450-654-5433
Ligne sans frais: 800-663-3021
info@goulet.ca
www.goulet.ca
ISBNs: ISBN: 2-89377
Ouvrages de bureautique, d'informatique, de dessin assisté par ordinateur, et l'autoformation au niveau post-secondaire
Reyald Goulet, Président & Dir. général

Éditions Saint-Martin
#501, 7333, place des Roseraies, Anjou, QC H1M 2X6
Tél: 514-529-0920; *Téléc:* 514-352-1764
info@stmartin-decarie.com
www.stmartin-decarie.com
ISBNs: ISBN: 2-89035
Ouvrages grand public; manuels collégials et universitaires. Éditions Saint-Martin a fait l'acquisition de deux autres maisons d'éditions: Décarie éditeur, et Éditions Carcajou.
Stéphane Lavoie, Directeur général

Les Éditions SMG inc.
#203, 5365, boul Jean XXIII, Trois-Rivières, QC G8Z 4A6
Tél: 819-376-5650; *Téléc:* 819-373-2904
ISBNs: ISBN: 2-89094

Les Éditions Stanké
La Tourelle, #800, 1055, boul René-Lévesque Est, Montréal, QC H2L 4S5
Tél: 514-849-5259; *Téléc:* 514-849-1388
info@groupelibrex.com
www.edstanke.com
ISBNs: ISBN: 2-7604, 0-88566
Ouvrages grand public: romans, essais, récits
Alain Stanké, Président & Dir.-gén.
Patrick Leimgruber, Directeur commercial

Les Éditions Thémis
Faculté de droit, Université de Montréal, CP 6128 Centre-Ville, Montréal, QC H3C 3J7
Tél: 514-343-6627; *Téléc:* 514-343-6779
info@editionsthemis.com
www.themis.umontreal.ca
ISBNs: ISBN: 2-920376, 2-89400; SAN: 115-8252
Livres juridiques; Revue juridique Thémis
Stéphane Rousseau, Président et Dir. général

Les Éditions Un Monde différent ltée
#101, 3905, rue Isabelle, Brossard, QC J4Y 2R2
Tél: 450-656-2660; *Téléc:* 450-659-9328
Ligne sans frais: 800-443-2582
info@umd.ca
www.umd.ca
ISBNs: ISBN: 2-89225, 2-92000
Traductions et adaptations de best-sellers américains, ouvrages d'auteurs canadiens et internationaux
Michel Ferron, Éditeur

Les Éditions Vents d'Ouest
185, rue Eddy, Gatineau, QC J8X 2X2
Tél: 819-770-6377; *Téléc:* 819-770-0559
info@ventsdouest.ca
www.ventsdouest.ca
Ado, histoire, romans, essais, nouvelles
Melvin Jomphe, Président

Les Éditions XYZ inc. / XYZ Publishing
1815, av De Lorimier, Montréal, QC H2K 3W6
Tél: 514-525-2170; *Téléc:* 514-525-7537
info@editionsxyz.com
www.editionsxyz.com
ISBNs: ISBN: 2-89261 French; 0-9683601 Eng.
Dominique Lemay, Directrice générale, dominique.lemay@editionsxyz.com
André Vanasse, Conseiller littéraire, andre.vanasse@editionsxyz.com

Éditions Yvon Blais
CP 180, Cowansville, QC J2K 3H6
Tél: 450-266-1086; *Téléc:* 450-263-9256
Ligne sans frais: 800-363-3047
editionsyvonblais.professeurs@thomsonreuters.com
www.editionsyvonblais.c om
ISBNs: ISBN: 2-89451
Éditeur juridique; textes des conférences des formations continues du Barreau du Québec; fiscalité; ressources humaines
Yvon Blais, Président

EDU Reference Publishers Direct Inc.
#3, 109 Woodbine Downs Blvd., Toronto, ON M9W 1Y6
Tel: 416-674-8622; *Fax:* 416-674-6215
eduref@edureference.com
www.edureference.com
ISBNs: ISBN: 0-86596, 0-04150
A distributor - bringing publishers & buyers in the Canadian education community together
Orland Kirkness, President

Educa Books
PO Box 2694 D, Ottawa, ON K1P 5W6
Tel: 613-738-2163; *Fax:* 613-247-0256
educa2@yahoo.com
educa0.tripod.com/edu/
ISBNs: ISBN: 1-895959, 1-55394
Specialists in dictionaries, reference books, language learning resources
L. Martin

EGS Press
#118, 283 Danforth Ave., Toronto, ON M4K 1N2
Tel: 416-829-8014;
info@egspress.com
www.egspress.com
ISBNs: ISBN: 0-9685330
Publisher of research material in the fields of media, the arts & therapy from the European Graduate School, Switzerland, and the annual journal POIESIS: A JOURNAL OF THE ARTS & COMMUNICATION
Stephen K. Levine, Editor-in-Chief

Ekstasis Editions
PO Box 8474 Main, Victoria, BC V8W 3S1
Tel: 250-361-9941; *Fax:* 250-385-3378
Toll-Free: 866-961-9951
ekstasis@islandnet.com
www.ekstasiseditions.com
ISBNs: ISBN: 0-921215, 1-896860, 0-9691289, 1-894800
Literary publisher, with focus on poetry, fiction & criticism; Cherubim Books imprint for Children's & Young Adult books
Richard Olafson

Elsevier Canada
1 Goldthorne Ave., Toronto, ON M8Z 5S7
Tel: 416-253-3640; *Fax:* 416-255-5456
Toll-Free: 800-665-1148
cs.canada@elsevier.com
www.elsevier.ca; www.lb.ca
ISBNs: ISBN: 0-3230, 0-3974, 0-3998, 0-4430, 0-4160, 1-5566, 1-5605
Robert Dingee

Emond Montgomery Publications Limited
60 Shaftesbury Ave., Toronto, ON M4T 1A3
Tel: 416-975-3925; *Fax:* 416-975-3924
Toll-Free: 888-837-0815
info@emp.ca; orders@emp.ca
www.emp.ca
ISBNs: ISBN: 0-920722, 1-55239
Specialists in legal publishing & textbooks
D. Paul Emond, President/CEO

Empyreal Press
PO Box 1708, Champlain, NY
skarwood@videotron.ca
www.skarwood.com
ISBNs: ISBN: 0-921852
An independent literary press, specializing in new & established Canadian writers of poetry, prose & non-fiction
Geoffrey Isherwood, CEO

Environmental Law Centre
#800, 10025 - 106 St., Edmonton, AB T5J 1G4
Tel: 780-424-5099; *Fax:* 780-424-5133
Toll-Free: 800-661-4238
elc@elc.ab.ca
www.elc.ab.ca
ISBNs: ISBN: 0-921503
Publishing objective information about environmental & natural resources law & policy
Cindy Chiasson, Executive Director

Ergo Books
PO Box 1439 B, London, ON N6A 5M2
Tel: 519-432-4357;
ergopro@ergobooks.com
www.ergobooks.com
ISBNs: ISBN: 0-920516; SAN: 115-3374
Specializing in fiction, poetry, humour, local history & memoirs by Southwestern Ontario writers
Winston G. Schell, Publisher

Essence Publishing
20 Hanna Ct., Belleville, ON K8P 5J2
Tel: 613-962-0234; *Fax:* 613-962-3055
Toll-Free: 800-238-6376
info@essence-publishing.com
www.essencegroup.com
ISBNs: ISBN: 1-896400, 1-894169, 1-55306
Specializing in short-run publishing, with emphasis on Christian themes & perspectives

Everyday Publications Inc.
310 Killaly St. West, Port Colborne, ON L3K 6A6
Tel: 905-834-5552; *Fax:* 905-834-8045
books@everydaypubications.org
www.everydaypublications.org
ISBNs: ISBN: 0-88873, 0-919586; SAN: 115-3398
Specializing in books about the Bible, in English, French, Spanish, Portuguese, Swahili & Chinese
R.E. Harlow, Publisher

Exile Editions Ltd.
134 Eastbourne Ave., Toronto, ON M5P 2G6
Fax: 416-969-9556
info@exileeditions.com
www.exileeditions.com
ISBNs: ISBN: 1-550960, 0-920428; SAN: 115-3404
Specializing in fiction, poetry, drama, non-fiction & translations, from established and new writers
Michael Callaghan, Publisher

Exportlivre
289, boul Desaulniers, Saint-Lambert, QC J4P 1M8
Tel: 450-671-3888; *Fax:* 450-671-2121
order@exportlivre.com
www.exportlivre.com
Book export agency, handling orders for books in English & French in the areas of trade & non-trade publications, children's fiction & non-fiction, scientific & technical books, textbooks, scholarly publications & government publications
Thomas Déri, Directeur

Fairmount Books Inc.
120 Duffield Dr., Markham, ON L6G 1B5
Tel: 905-475-0988; *Fax:* 905-475-1072
sales@fairmountbooks.ca
www.fairmountbooks.ca
ISBNs: ISBN: 0-921372; SAN: 106-7886
Wholesaler of remaindered books
Marty Cutler, President

Federation of Ontario Naturalists (FON)
#201, 366 Adelaide St. W., Toronto, ON M5V 1R9
Tel: 416-444-8419; *Fax:* 416-444-9866
Toll-Free: 800-440-2366
info@ontarionature.org
www.ontarionature.org
Publisher of ON Nature; other resources available through the online Shop
Caroline Schultz, Executive Director

Fernwood Publishing Co. Ltd.
PO Box 5, 32 Oceanvista Lane, Site 2A, Black Point, NS B0J 1B0
Tel: 902-857-1388; *Fax:* 902-857-1328
info@fernpub.ca
www.fernwoodpublishing.ca
ISBNs: ISBN: 1-895686, 1-55266
Errol Sharpe, Publisher
Cynthia Martin, Promotions

Fifth House Publishers
#1511, 1800 - 4 St. SW, Calgary, AB T2S 2S5
Tel: 403-571-5230; *Fax:* 403-571-5235
Toll-Free: 800-387-9776
charlene@fitzhenry.ca
www.fitzhenry.ca
ISBNs: ISBN: 0-920079, 1-894004, 1-894856, 1-895618; SAN: 115-1134
Specializing in non-fiction with a Western Canadian emphasis

Charlene Dobmeier, Publisher

Firefly Books Ltd.
66 Leek Cres., Richmond Hill, ON L4B 1H1
Tel: 416-499-8412; *Fax:* 416-499-8313
Toll-Free: 800-387-6192
service@fireflybooks.com
www.fireflybooks.com
Other information: Toll-Free Fax: 800-450-0391
Firefly Books publishes non-fiction books & distributes non-fiction & children's books.
Rob Lidstone, Contact, Sales Operations, Data Export, & Website, rlidstone@fireflybooks.com
Parisa Michailidis, Contact, Special & Corporate Sales, parisa@fireflybooks.com
Ann Quinn, Contact, Schools & Libraries, annq@fireflybooks.com
Diane Vanderkooy, Contact, Rights, dianevan@fireflybooks.com

Fisher House Publishers
10907 - 34A Ave., Edmonton, AB T5J 2T9
Tel: 780-435-2320; *Fax:* 780-468-2058
fisherhousejohn@hotmail.com
www.fisherhouse.com
ISBNs: ISBN: 1-896255
John R. Fisher Ph.D

Fitzhenry & Whiteside Limited
195 Allstate Pkwy., Markham, ON L3R 4T8
Tel: 905-477-9700; *Fax:* 800-260-9777
Toll-Free: 800-387-9776
godwit@fitzhenry.ca
www.fitzhenry.ca
ISBNs: ISBN: 0-55041, 0-88902, 1-55005, 1-894004, 1-895618, 0-7737, 0
Specializing in history, biography, poety, sports, photography, reference resources, and children's and young adult material.
Owner of Red Deer Press Inc., and Fifth House Publishers
Sharon Fitzhenry, President

Flanker Press Ltd.
PO Box 2522 C, St. John's, NL A1C 6K1
Tel: 709-739-4477; *Fax:* 709-739-4420
Toll-Free: 866-739-4420
info@flankerpress.com
www.flankerpress.com
ISBNs: ISBN: 0-9698767, 1-894463
Specializing in regional Newfoundland & Labrador historical fiction & non-fiction titles; imprints include Pennywell Books, & Brazen Books

Fleurbec
198, ch de la Grande-Grillade, Saint-Henri-de-Lévis, QC G0R 3E0
Tél: 418-882-0843; *Téléc:* 418-882-6133
melilot@sympatico.ca
www.fleurbec.com
ISBNs: ISBN: 2-920174
Guides d'identification, ouvrages scientifiques, guide culinaire - plantes sauvages, flore
Gisèle Lamoureux, Dirigeante

Formac Publishing Company Limited
5502 Atlantic St., Halifax, NS B3H 1G4
Tel: 902-421-7022; *Fax:* 902-425-0166
Toll-Free: 800-565-1975
orderdesk@formac.ca
www.formac.ca
ISBNs: ISBN: 0-88780, 0-921921; SAN: 115-1371
Publishers & distributors
James Lorimer, Publisher

49th Avenue Press
100 West 49th Ave., Vancouver, BC V5Y 2Z6
Tel: 604-323-5374; *Fax:* 604-323-5597
lholmes@langara.bc.ca
www.bendallbooks.com
ISBNs: ISBN: 1-896661
Linda Holmes, President

The Fraser Institute
1770 Burrard St., 4th Fl., Vancouver, BC V6J 3G7
Tel: 604-688-0221; *Fax:* 604-688-8539
Toll-Free: 800-665-3558
info@fraserinstitute.ca
www.fraserinstitute.ca
ISBNs: ISBN: 0-88975; SAN: 115-3498
Offices in Vancouver, Calgary, Toronto, Montreal; engaged in research & publication with emphasis on economics, public policy and other issues that affect Canadians
Mark Mullins, Executive Director

Frederick Harris Music Co. Ltd.
#1, 5865 McLaughlin Rd., Mississauga, ON L5R 1B8
Tel: 905-501-1595; *Fax:* 905-501-0929
Toll-Free: 800-387-4013
fhmc@frederickharris.com
www.frederickharris.com
Darlene Dunn, Customer Service Representative

Friday 501
PO Box 31599, Whitehorse, YT Y1A 6L2
Tel: 867-668-3501; *Fax:* 867-668-4472
info@friday501.com
www.friday501.com

Friday Circle
Dept. of English, University of Ottawa, Ottawa, ON K1N 6N5
Tel: 613-562-5800; *Fax:* 613-562-5990
fridaycircle@uottawa.ca
www.fridaycircle.uottawa.ca
ISBNs: ISBN: 1-896362, 1-9697391
Publishing works by faculty, students & alumni of the Creative Writing Program, University of Ottawa
Seymour Mayne, Co-editor

Full Blast Productions
70 Allan Dr., St. Catherines, ON L2N 1E9
Fax: 905-937-2657
Toll-Free: 877-355-2578
fbp@cogeco.ca
www.fullblastproductions.mybisi.com
ISBNs: ISBN: 1-895451
Publisher of English & Spanish language teaching resources

Fundy Guild Inc.
Fundy National Park, #2, 8642, RR#114, Fundy National Park, NB E4H 4V2
Tel: 506-887-6094; *Fax:* 506-887-6008
info@fundyguild.ca
www.fundyguild.ca
ISBNs: ISBN: 0-920383
Publishes books related to the bay of Fundy & Fundy National Park
Beulah Michelin

Gaspereau Press
47 Church Ave., Kentville, NS B4N 2M7
Tel: 902-678-6002; *Fax:* 902-678-7845
Toll-Free: 877-230-8232
info@gaspereau.com
www.gaspereau.com
ISBNs: ISBN: 1-894031
Specializing in contemporary literature by emerging & established Canadian authors, with publishing & printing under one roof
Gary Dunfield, Co-publisher
Andrew Steeves, Co-publisher

General Store Publishing House
PO Box 415, 499 O'Brien Rd., Renfrew, ON K7A 4A6
Tel: 613-432-7697; *Fax:* 613-432-7184
Toll-Free: 800-465-6072
submissions@gsph.com
www.gsph.com
ISBNs: ISBN: 0-919431, 1-896182, 1-894263, 1-897113 SAN: 115-6853
Tim Gordon, President

Georgetown Publications Inc.
34 Armstrong Ave., Georgetown, ON L7G 4R9
Tel: 905-873-8498; *Fax:* 888-595-3009
Toll-Free: 888-595-3008
info@gtwcanada.com
www.georgetownpublications.com
ISBNs: ISBN: 0-9731994, 0-9733149
Distributor for Allison & Busby, American Girl Pubishing, Hampton Roads Publishing, & Large Print Press, among others

Gilpin Publishing
PO Box 597, Alliston, ON L9R 1V7
Tel: 705-424-6507; *Fax:* 705-424-6507
mail@gilpin.ca
www.gilpin.ca
ISBNs: ISBN: 0-921046; SAN: 119-6162
Music publishing - MP3s, CDs, piano methods, instrumental & choral arrangements, sheet music
Wayne Gilpin, Publisher

The Ginger Press
848 - 2 Ave. East, Owen Sound, ON N4K 2H3
Tel: 519-376-4233; *Fax:* 519-376-9871
Toll-Free: 800-463-9937
maryann@gingerpress.com
www.gingerpress.com
ISBNs: ISBN: 0-921773
A bookshop, café, & publishing house, specializing in Owen Sound & area writers & subjects
Maryann Thomas, Publisher

Godwin Books
1212 Hampshire Rd., Victoria, BC V8S 4T1
Tel: 250-414-0215; *Fax:* 250-414-0216
rthomson@islandnet.com
www.godwinbooks.com
ISBNs: ISBN: 0-9696774
Featuring books by Robert Thomson & George Godwin
Robert Stuart Thomson, Editor

Good Medicine Books
PO Box 844, Skookumchuck, BC V0B 2E0
canadiancaboose@yahoo.com
goodmedicinefoundation.com
ISBNs: ISBN: 0-920698
Good Medicine Cutural Foundation publishes a collection of material on a theme of trains, as well documentation & accounts on First Nations People, in particular, the Pikunni.
Adolf Hungry Wolf, Publisher

Goose Lane Editions
#330, 500 Beaverbrook Ct., Fredericton, NB E3B 5X4
Tel: 506-450-4251; *Fax:* 506-459-4991
Toll-Free: 888-926-8377
info@gooselane.com
www.gooselane.com
ISBNs: ISBN: 0-919197, 0-86492, 0-920110; SAN: 115-3420
Small independent publisher of high-quality, award-winning books.
Susanne Alexander, Publisher

Gordon Soules Book Publishers Ltd.
1354-B Marine Dr., West Vancouver, BC V7T 1B5
Tel: 604-922-6588; *Fax:* 604-688-5442
books@gordonsoules.com
www.gordonsoules.com
ISBNs: ISBN: 0-919574, 1-894661, 0-920045; SAN: 115-0987
Publisher of self-help, health, fitness & natural medicine books; cookbooks; tarot decks & tarot books; travel books & maps
Gordon Soules, President

Granville Island Publishing
#212, 1656 Duranleau St., Vancouver, BC V6H 3S4
Tel: 604-688-0320; *Fax:* 604-668-0132
Toll-Free: 877-688-0320
info@granvilleislandpublishing.com
www.granvilleislandpublishing.com
ISBNs: ISBN: 1-894694; SAN: 118-7953
Services for self-published authors
Jo Blackmore, Publisher

Grass Roots Press
6520 - 82 Avenue, Main Floor, Edmonton, AB T6B 0E7
Tel: 780-413-6491; *Fax:* 780-413-6582
Toll-Free: 888-303-3213
info@grassrootsbooks.net
www.literacyservices.com
Specializing in adult literacy resources
DR Pat Campbell, President

Great Plains Publications Ltd.
#420, 70 Arthur St., Winnipeg, MB R3B 1G7
Tel: 204-475-6799; *Fax:* 204-475-0138
info@greatplains.mb.ca
www.greatplains.mb.ca
ISBNs: ISBN: 0-9697804, 1-894283
Specializing in the best books from the Prairies & authors from across Canada
Gregg Shilliday, Publisher

Green Dragon Press
#1009, 2267 Lakeshore Blvd. West, Toronto, ON M8V 3X2
Tel: 416-251-6366; *Fax:* 416-251-6365
www3.sympatico.ca/equity.greendragonpress
ISBNs: ISBN: 1-896781
Publishes books & materials on women's equity

Grey House Publishing Canada
#301 - 555 Richmond St. West, Toronto, ON M5V 3B1
Tel: 416-644-6479; *Fax:* 416-644-1904
Toll-Free: 866-433-4739
info@greyhouse.ca
www.greyhouse.ca
ISBNs: ISBN: 978-1-59237
Publishers of a number of comprehensive Canadian directories including the Canadian Almanac & Directory, Associations Canada, Libraries Canada & the Canadian Parliamentary Guide.
Bryon Moore, General Manager
Robert Lang, Editorial Manager

Grolier
#570, 1700, boul Laval, Laval, QC H7S 2N6
Tel: 450-667-5497; *Fax:* 450-667-7694
Toll-Free: 800-563-3231
customerservice@grolier.qc.ca
www.grolier.ca
ISBNs: ISBN: 0-7172; SAN 115-3668
Publisher of children's books

Groundwood Books
#801, 110 Spadina Ave., Toronto, ON M5V 2K4
Tel: 416-363-4343; *Fax:* 416-363-1017
www.groundwoodbooks.com
ISBNs: ISBN: 0-88899; SAN 115-0391
Publisher of children's books in English & Spanish
Patricia Aldana, Publisher

Groupe Éducalivres inc. - Éditions Études Vivantes
955, rue Bergar, Laval, QC H7L 4Z6
Tél: 514-334-8466; *Téléc:* 514-334-8387
Ligne sans frais: 800-567-3671
commentaires@educalivres.com
www.educalivres.com
ISBNs: ISBN: 2-7607, 0-88586, 0-289022, 0-03-92

Groupe Modulo
#300, 233, av Dunbar, Montréal, QC H3P 2H4
Tel: 514-738-9818; *Fax:* 514-738-5838
Toll-Free: 888-738-9818
www.moduloediteur.com
ISBNs: ISBN: 2-89113, 2-920210, 2-920922, 2-89443, 2-920190, 2-921363
Éditeur au préscolaire et au primaire
Jean Bouchard, Directeur général

GTK Press
#109, 18 Wynford Dr., Toronto, ON M3C 3S2
Tel: 416-385-1313; *Fax:* 416-385-1919
Toll-Free: 866-485-7737
info@gtkpress.com
www.gtkpress.com
ISBNs: ISBN: 1-894318, 1-55137
Publisher of curriculum resources, notably science, technology, mathematics
K.L. Kwong, President & CEO

Guérin éditeur ltée
4501, rue Drolet, Montréal, QC H2T 2G2
Tél: 514-842-3481; *Téléc:* 514-842-4923
Ligne sans frais: 800-398-8337
france.larochelle@guerin-editeur.qc.ca
www.guerin-editeur.qc.ca
ISBNs: ISBN: 2-7601
L'éditeur des écoles. Groupe Guérin: Guérin, éditeur limitée, Les Éditions La Pensée Inc., et LIDEC Inc.
Marc-Aimé Guérin, President

Guernica Editions Inc.
PO Box 117 P, Toronto, ON M5S 2S6
Tel: 416-658-9888; *Fax:* 416-657-8885
Toll-Free: 800-565-9523
guernicaeditions@cs.com
www.guernicaeditions.com
ISBNs: ISBN: 0-919349, 2-89135, 0-920717, 1-55071; SAN: 115-0421
Antonio D'Alfonso, Editor in Chief

Guy Saint-Jean Éditeur
3154, boul Industriel, Laval, QC H7X 4P7
Tél: 450-663-1777; *Téléc:* 450-663-6666
info@saint-jeanediteur.com
www.saint-jeanediteur.com
ISBNs: ISBN: 2-920340, 2-89455
Guides pratiques sur la santé, la psychologie populaire, le sport, le jardinage; beaux-livres; littérature; Green Frog Publishing (www.greenfrogpublishing.com) et MarieGray (www.mariegray.com)
Nicole Saint-Jean

GWEV Publishing Inc.
PO Box 565, Stittsville, ON K2S 1A6
Tel: 613-831-9154; *Fax:* 613-831-4291
Toll-Free: 866-747-3797
Sylvia@gwevpublishing.com
www.gwevpublishing.com
ISBNs: ISBN: 0-9681414, 0-9731300
Publisher of children's books
Sylvia Vincent, Publisher

H.B. Fenn & Company Ltd.
34 Nixon Rd., Bolton, ON L7E 1W2
Tel: 905-951-6600; *Fax:* 905-951-6601
Toll-Free: 800-267-3366
sales@hbfenn.com
www.hbfenn.com
ISBNs: ISBN: 0-919768, 1-55168; SAN: 115-1746
Book distributor
Harold B. Fenn, President

Hades Publications, Inc.
PO Box 1414 M, Calgary, AB T2P 2L6
Tel: 403-254-0160; *Fax:* 403-254-0456
admin@hadespublications.com
www.trickster.com
ISBNs: ISBN: 0-919230, 0-921298
Publishes books and other materials on Magic, Illusion, Conjuring & Variety Arts
Brian Hades, Publisher

Hancock House Publishers Ltd.
19313 Zero Ave., Surrey, BC V3S 9R9
Tel: 604-538-1114; *Fax:* 604-538-2262
Toll-Free: 800-938-1114
sales@hancockhouse.com
www.hancockhouse.com
ISBNs: ISBN: 0-88839, 0-91954; SAN: 115-3730
Publishers of wildlife & nature books
David Hancock, President

Hans Schafler & Co. Ltd.
#2, 1184 Speers Rd., Oakville, ON L6L 2X4
Tel: 905-827-2949; *Fax:* 905-827-2524
Toll-Free: 877-646-9323
info@schafler.com
www.schafler.com
Publishes curriculum books for schools
Lisbeth Schafler

Happy Landings
851 Heritage Dr., RR#4, Merrickville, ON K0G 1N0
Tel: 613-269-2552; *Fax:* 613-269-3962
books@happylandings.com
www.happylandings.com
ISBNs: ISBN: 0-9697322
Publisher of aviation books by Garth Wallace
Liz Wallace, Publisher

Harbour Publishing Co. Ltd.
PO Box 219, Madeira Park, BC V0N 2H0
Tel: 604-883-2730; *Fax:* 604-883-9451
Toll-Free: 800-667-2988
info@harbourpublishing.com
www.harbourpublishing.com
ISBNs: ISBN: 0-920080, 1-55017
Specializing in BC authors & books of the Pacific Northwest
Howard White, President

Harlequin Enterprises Limited
225 Duncan Mill Rd., Toronto, ON M3B 3K9
Tel: 416-445-5860; *Fax:* 416-445-8655
Toll-Free: 800-387-0112
customer_ecare@harlequin.ca
www.eharlequin.com
ISBNs: ISBN: 0-373, 1-55166, 0-778; SAN: 115-3749
Specializing in series romance & fiction for women
Katherine Orr, Vice President, Public Relations

HarperCollins Canada Ltd.
2 Bloor St. East, Toronto, ON M4W 1A8
Tel: 416-975-9334; *Fax:* 416-975-5223
Toll-Free: 800-387-0117
hcorder@harpercollins.com
www.harpercollins.ca
ISBNs: SAN: 150-026X
Canadian imprints include Avon, Greenwillow Books, HarperAudio, HarperBusiness, HarperLargePrint, William Morrow, among many others; specializing in Canadian fiction & non-fiction, for adults & children

Hartley & Marks Publishers
3661 Broadway West, Vancouver, BC V6R 2B8
Tel: 800-277-5887; *Fax:* 800-707-5887
info@hartleyandmarks.com
www.hartleyandmarks.com
ISBNs: ISBN: 0-88179; SAN: 115-3757

Herald Press
#C8, 490 Dutton Dr., Waterloo, ON N2L 6H7
Tel: 519-747-5722; *Fax:* 519-747-5721
Toll-Free: 800-245-7894
hpcan@mph.org
www.heraldpress.com
ISBNs: ISBN: 0-8361; SAN: 116-0931
The trade publishing division of Mennonite Publishing Network; specializing in resources with emphasis on the Anabaptist perspective, biblical studies, mission, family & church life
Ron Rempel, Publisher, Canadian Branch

Heritage House Publishing Co. Ltd.
#108, 17665 - 66A Ave., Surrey, BC V3S 2A7
Tel: 604-574-7067; *Fax:* 604-574-9942
Toll-Free: 800-665-3302
distribution@heritagehouse.ca
www.heritagehouse.ca
ISBNs: ISBN: 0-919214, 1-895811, 1-894384; SAN: 115-8287
Specializing in Western Canadian non-fiction subjects & authors
Rodger Touchie, President

HikingCamping.com
PO Box 8563, Canmore, AB T1W 2V3
Fax: 403-678-3343
nomads@hikingcamping.com
www.hikingcamping.com
Specializing in guidebooks for hikers & campers, works of inspiration, insight & philosophy, & photography

Historical Trails West/Historical Research Centre
1115 - 8th Ave. South, Lethbridge, AB T1J 1P7
Tel: 403-328-3824;
hrc@ourheritage.net
www.ourheritage.net
Specializing in books & resources of Western Canadian interest
Bruce A. Haig, Director

Hogrefe & Huber Publishers
1543 Bayview Ave., Toronto, ON M4G 3B5
Tel: 416-482-6339; *Fax:* 416-617-354
Toll-Free: 800-228-3749
hhpub@hogrefe.com
www.hogrefe.com
ISBNs: ISBN: 0-88937, 0-920887; SAN: 115-379X
Specializing in resources in the areas of applied & experimental psychology, health, pharmacology, psychiatry & neurosciences
DR G.-J. Hogrefe, Publisher

House of Anansi Press
#801, 110 Spadina Ave., Toronto, ON M5V 2K4
Tel: 416-363-4343; *Fax:* 416-363-1017
Toll-Free: 800-663-5714
info@anansi.ca
www.anansi.ca
ISBNs: ISBN: 0-88784; SAN: 115-0391
Specializing in new & established Canadian writers of fiction, non-fiction & poetry, & French-Canadian works in translation
Sarah MacLachlan, President
Lynn Henry, Publisher

Human Kinetics Canada
#100, 475 Devonshire Rd., Windsor, ON N8Y 2L5
Tel: 519-971-9500; *Fax:* 519-971-9797
Toll-Free: 800-465-7301
info@khcanada.com
www.humankinetics.com

Humanitas
228, de la Lande, Rosemère, QC J4A 4J1
Tél: 450-965-6624; *Téléc:* 450-965-8839
humanitas@cyberglobe.net
www.editionshumanitas.com
ISBNs: ISBN: 2-89396, 2-9800950
Art, poésie, romans, essais, théâtre
Constantin Stoiciv

Hyperion Press Limited
300 Wales Ave., Winnipeg, MB R2M 2S9
Tel: 204-256-9204; *Fax:* 204-255-7845
tamos@mts.net
ISBNs: ISBN: 0-920534, 1-895340, 1-895569; SAN: 115-124X
Dr. Marvis Tutiah, President
Arlene Osen, Vice President

Imago Press
30 Laws St., Toronto, ON M6P 2Y7
Tel: 416-604-9741;
imagorediron@rogers.com
http://pages.interlog.com/~imago/
ISBNs: ISBN: 0-920489, 0-9697555
Marshall Hryciuk

Inclusion Press International
47 Indian Trail, Toronto, ON M6R 1Z8
Tel: 416-658-5363; *Fax:* 416-658-5067
inclusionpress@inclusion.com
www.inclusion.com
ISBNs: ISBN: 1-895418
Resource materials with emphasis on diversity, inclusion &

community, for educational institutions, government agencies, human service agencies, First Nations organizations
Jack Pearpoint, Co-publisher
Marsha Forest, Co-publisher

Inner City Books
PO Box 1271 Q, Toronto, ON M4T 2P4
Tel: 416-927-0355; *Fax:* 416-924-1814
info@innercitybooks.net
www.innercitybooks.net
ISBNs: ISBN: 0-919123, 1-894574; SAN: 115-3870
Publishers of studies in Jungian Psychology by Jungian Analysts
Daryl Sharp, President

Insomniac Press
#403, 192 Spadina Ave., Toronto, ON M5T 2C2
Tel: 416-504-6270; *Fax:* 416-504-9313
mike@insomniacpress.com
www.insomniacpress.com
ISBNs: ISBN: 1-895837, 1-894663
Independent press that publishes non-fiction, poetry & fiction
Mike O'Connor, Publisher, mike@insomniacpress.com
Dan Varrette, Managing Editor, dan@insomniacpress.com

Institut de recherches psychologiques, inc. / Institute of Psychological Research Inc.
34, rue Fleury ouest, Montréal, QC H3L 1S9
Tél: 514-382-3000; *Téléc:* 514-382-3007
Ligne sans frais: 800-363-7800
info@i-r-p.ca
www.i-r-p.ca
ISBNs: ISBN: 0-88509, 2-89109
Robert Chevrier

The Institute for Research on Public Policy / L'Institut de recherche en politiques publiques
#200, 1470, rue Peel, Montréal, QC H3A 1T1
Tel: 514-985-2461; *Fax:* 514-985-2559
irpp@irpp.org
www.irpp.org
ISBNs: ISBN: 0-920380, 0-88645; SAN: 115-3889, 115-0537
Specializing in research & publication with emphasis on Canadian public policy, Canadian federalism, economic policy, international relations; publisher of POLICY OPTIONS journal
Suzanne Ostiguy McIntyre, Vice President, Operations
Mel Cappe, President

Institute for Risk Research
University of Waterloo, 200 University Ave. West, Waterloo, ON N2L 3G1
Tel: 519-888-4567; *Fax:* 519-725-4834
irr-neram@uwaterloo.ca
www.irr-neram.ca
ISBNs: ISBN: 0-88898, 0-9696747, 0-9684982
Along with The Network for Environmental Risk Assessment and Management (NERAM), the Institute for Risk Research specializes in research & publications in the areas of risk, risk management for the environment, human health, industrial safety & transportation
Dr. John Shortreed, Executive Committee

Institute of Intergovernmental Relations
Room 301, School of Policy Studies, Queen's University, Kingston, ON K7L 3N6
Tel: 613-533-2080; *Fax:* 613-533-6868
iigr@iigr.ca
www.iigr.ca
ISBNs: ISBN: 0-88911, 1-55339
Specializing in research & publication, with emphasis on Canadian federalism, intergovernmental relations, constitutional reform & social union
Thomas J. Courchene, Director

International Development Research Centre (IDRC) / Le Centre de recherches pour le développement international
PO Box 8500, 150 Kent St., Ottawa, ON K1G 3H9
Tel: 613-236-6163; *Fax:* 613-563-2476
pub@idrc.ca
www.idrc.ca
ISBNs: ISBN: 0-88936, 1-55250
Publishers of IDRC Bulletin, & resources with emphasis on international development, sustainable development, food, health, social issues
Bill Carman, Senior Communications Advisor, Publishing

International Institute for Sustainable Development
161 Portage Ave. East, 6th Floor, Winnipeg, MB R3B 0Y4
Tel: 204-958-7700; *Fax:* 204-958-7710
info@iisd.org
www.iisd.org
ISBNs: ISBN: 1-895536
Specializing in books & other materials with emphasis on the IISD's institutional & research history. Offices in Ottawa, New York & Geneva
David Runnalls, President & CEO
Stuart Slayen, Manager, Publishing & Communications

International Press Publications Inc.
#21, 90 Nolan Ct., Markham, ON L3R 4L9
Tel: 905-946-9588; *Fax:* 905-946-9590
sales@ippbooks.com
www.ippbooks.com
ISBNs: SAN: 170-0049
"Specialists in directories on all subjects from all over the world; largest distributors of books on career guidance, general reference, research, text books, dictionaries; free search for rare & out-of-print books from any country"
Bali Sethi, President

Irwin Law Inc.
#206, 14 Duncan St., Toronto, ON M5H 3G8
Tel: 416-862-7690; *Fax:* 416-862-9236
Toll-Free: 888-314-9014
www.irwinlaw.com
ISBNs: ISBN: 1-55221
Jeffrey Miller, Publisher

Is Five Press
#200, 161 Eglinton Ave. East, Toronto, ON M4P 1J5
Tel: 416-480-2408; *Fax:* 416-480-2546
tom@isfive.com
www.isfive.com
ISBNs: ISBN: 0-920934; SAN: 115-3943
Specializing in books, manuals & curriculum resources in social & environmental subject areas; other services include writing, design, translation & editing

ISER Books
Facilities Management Building, Room FM-2005A, Memorial University, St. John's, NL A1C 5S7
Tel: 709-737-3453; *Fax:* 709-737-4342
iser-books@mun.ca
www.mun.ca/iser
ISBNs: ISBN: 1-894725, 0-919666; SAN: 115-3897
Al Potter, Manager

Island Studies Press
University of Prince Edward Island, 550 University Ave., Charlottetown, PE C1A 4P3
Tel: 902-566-0386; *Fax:* 902-566-0756
iis@upei.ca
www.upei.ca
ISBNs: ISBN: 0-919013
Publisher of books on the history, literature, culture and environment of Prince Edward Island

ITMB Publishing Ltd.
530 West Broadway, Vancouver, BC V5Z 1E9
Tel: 604-879-3621; *Fax:* 604-879-4521
itmb@itmb.com
www.itmb.com
ISBNs: ISBN: 0-921463, 1-895907, 1-55341; SAN: 112-6997
Publisher of travel maps
Jack Joyce, President

J & L Macpherson Educational Services Ltd.
3030 Collens Hill Rd., Kelowna, BC V1Z 1P5
Tel: 250-769-4321; *Fax:* 250-769-3045
jlmltd@fichtner.com
W. John Macpherson
Lydia Macpherson

J. Gordon Shillingford Publishing Inc.
PO Box 86 Corydon Ave., Winnipeg, MB R3M 3S3
Tel: 204-779-6967; *Fax:* 204-779-6970
jgshill@allstream.net
jgshillingford.com
ISBNs: ISBN: 1-896239, 0-919754, 0-969761, 0-920486, 0-968942
Primarily a literary publisher; publishes on average 14 titles/year.
J. Gordon Shillingford, President
Karen Green, Marketing Director
Glenda MacFarlane, Drama Editor
Catherine Hunter, Poetry Editor

J.C. George Enterprises
577 Mount Pleasant Rd., Toronto, ON M4S 2M5
Tel: 416-483-4353; *Fax:* 416-791-8586
mgfa@interlog.com
ISBNs: ISBN: 0-921369
Publishes educational materials & books

J.E.S.L. Educational Products
58 Glen Park Ave., Toronto, ON M6B 2C2
Tel: 416-785-7941; *Fax:* 416-785-7941
jesl@rogers.com
www.interlog.com/~jesl
ISBNs: ISBN: 0-9691264, 0-9684362
Publishes Jewish educational materials
Edmond Y. Lipsitz

J.P. Delf Companies
13020 Delf Pl., Richmond, BC V6V 2A2
Tel: 604-278-4600; *Fax:* 604-276-0118
delf@helix.net
ISBNs: ISBN: 1-55056, 0-969-6208

Jack The Bookman Ltd.
#4, 1150 Kerrisdale Blvd., Newmarket, ON L3Y 8Z9
Tel: 905-836-5999; *Fax:* 905-836-1152
Toll-Free: 800-563-5168
jackthebookman@sympatico.ca
www.jackthebookman.com
Library wholesalers
Scott Davey, Vice-President

James Lorimer & Co. Ltd., Publishers
#1002, 317 Adelaide St. W, Toronto, ON M5V 1P9
Tel: 416-362-4762; *Fax:* 416-362-3939
info@lorimer.ca
www.lorimer.ca
ISBNs: ISBN: 0-88862, 1-55028; SAN: 115-1134
Lynn Schellenberg, Acquisitions Editor, acquisitions@lorimer.ca
Faye Smailes, Children's Book Editor, childrenseditor@lorimer.ca
James Lorimer, Publisher, publisher@lorimer.ca
Allison McDonald, Editorial & Marketing Coordinator, promotion@lorimer.ca

Jesperson Publishing
See Breakwater Books
ISBNs: ISBN: 1-894377, 0-921692, 0-920502
Clyde Rose, Publisher

John Markham & Associates
11210 Elderberry Way, Sidney, BC V8L 5J6
Tel: 250-655-1823; *Fax:* 250-655-1826
Toll-Free: 800-865-1826
jma@jamtags.com

John Wiley & Sons Canada Ltd.
#400, 5353 Dundas St. W, Toronto, ON M9B 6H8
Tel: 416-236-4433; *Fax:* 416-236-4447
Toll-Free: 800-567-4797
canada@wiley.com
www.wiley.com
ISBNs: ISBN: 0-471; SAN: 115-1185
William J. Pesce, President & CEO
Timothy B. King, Sr. Vice-President, Planning & Development
Bill Zerter, Chief Operating Officer, John Wiley & Sons Canada, Ltd.

John Wiley & Sons Inc.
111 River St., Hoboken, NJ
Tel: 201-748-6000; *Fax:* 201-748-6088
info@wiley.com
www.wiley.com
Ellis E. Cousens, Executive Vice President, Chief Financial & Operations Officer
William J. Arlington, Sr. Vice President, Human Resources
Gary M. Rinck, Sr. Vice President, Human Resources

Johnson Gorman Publishers
2003 - 35 Ave. SW, Calgary, AB T2T 2E2
Tel: 403-246-7956; *Fax:* 403-246-8926
ISBNs: ISBN: 0-921835; SAN: 115-0871
Dennis Johnson

Johnstone Training & Consultation (JTC) Inc.
PO Box 1927, Kemptville, ON K0G 1J0
Tel: 613-258-3092; *Fax:* 613-258-9971
Toll-Free: 888-408-6647
jtcinc@jtcinc.ca
www.jtcinc.ca
ISBNs: ISBN: 1-895271
Resource materials for not-for-profits & charities
Laura Kelly

Jordan Music Productions
PO Box 160 M, Toronto, ON M6S 4T3
Tel: 905-938-5050; *Fax:* 905-938-9970
Toll-Free: 800-567-7733
sjordan@sara-jordan.com
www.sara-jordan.com

ISBNs: ISBN: 1-895523, 1-894262, 1-533860; SAN: 118-959X
Publisher & producer of educational songs & music

Juris Analytica Publishing Inc.
604 - 10080 Jasper Ave., Edmonton, AB T5J 1V9
Tel: 780-420-9010; *Fax:* 780-420-9030
ISBNs: ISBN: 0-9698958

The Kashtan Press
22 Gretna Green, Kingston, ON K7M 3J2
Tel: 613-546-8364;
luciuk@luciuk.ca
luciuk.ca/kashtanpress.html
ISBNs: ISBN: 1-896354
Primarily Ukranian & Ukranian/Canadian History
Dr. Lubomyr Luciuk

Ken Haycock & Associates Inc
#343, 101-1001 West Broadway, Vancouver, BC V6H 4E4
Tel: 604-925-0266; *Fax:* 604-925-0566
admin@kenhaycock.com
www.kenhaycock.com
ISBNs: ISBN: 0-920175
Ken Haycock, Publisher
Michelle Rudert, Director, Client Services

Keng Seng Enterprises Inc.
#103, 4000, rue St-Ambroise, Montréal, QC H4C 2C7
Tel: 514-939-3971; *Fax:* 514-989-1922
canada@kengseng.com
www.kengseng.com
ISBNs: ISBN: 1-895494
David Chen, President

Kerrwil Publications Ltd.
#800, 2 St. Clair Ave. E, Toronto, ON M4T 2T5
Tel: 416-622-6736; *Fax:* 416-695-0453
www.kerrwil.com

Key Porter Books Limited
6 Adelaide St. E, 10th Fl., Toronto, ON M5C 1H6
Tel: 416-862-7777; *Fax:* 416-862-2304
info@keyporter.com
www.keyporter.com
ISBNs: ISBN: 0-88619, 1-55013, 1-89555, 1-55228, 1-5263, 1-5536
Publishes about 100 titles per year; covering politics, fiction, history, environment, children's, health, sports, cookbooks & photography
Jordan Fenn, Vice President & Publisher, jordan.fenn@keyporter.com
Paula Sloss, Special & Corporate Sales, 416-862-7777 x222, paula.sloss@keyporter.com
Sandra Homer, Manager, International Rights & Co-editions, 416-862-7777 x260, sandra.homer@keyporter.com
Louise Ward, Production Manager, 416-862-7777 x247, lward@keyporter.com
Rob Howard, Sales & Marketing, 416-862-7777 x235, rob.howard@keyporter.com

Kids Can Press Ltd.
29 Birch Ave., Toronto, ON M4V 1E2
Tel: 416-925-5437; *Fax:* 416-960-5437
Toll-Free: 800-265-0884
info@kidscan.com
www.kidscanpress.com
ISBNs: ISBN: 0-919964, 0-55337, 1-55074; SAN: 115-4001
Specializes in children's literature & children's books
Lisa Lyons, President

Kinbridge Publications
PO Box 89065, RPO Westdale, Hamilton, ON L8S 4R5
Fax: 905-627-0431
ISBNs: ISBN 0-9693233
M.A. Major, Manager

Kindred Productions
1310 Taylor Ave., Winnipeg, MB R3M 3Z6
Tel: 204-669-6575; *Fax:* 204-654-1865
Toll-Free: 800-545-7322
kindred@mbconf.ca
www.kindredproductions.com
ISBNs: ISBN: 0-919797, 0-921788, 1-894791
Publishing & distribution arm of the Mennonite Bretheren Churches in North America.
Marilyn Hudson, Director

Kirkton Press Ltd.
396 Grills Rd., RR#1, Baltimore, ON K0K 1C0
Tel: 905-349-3443; *Fax:* 905-349-3420
Toll-Free: 800-332-3663
kirkton@eagle.ca
www.breakingtheviciouscycle.info
ISBNs: ISBN: 0-9692768
Publishers of *The Vicious Cyclei series of diet/health books.*
Elaine Gottschall, President
Herbert Gottschall, Vice-President

Kitchener News Company Ltd.
PO Box 274 Waterloo, 455 Dutton Dr., Waterloo, ON N2J 4A4
Tel: 519-884-3710; *Fax:* 519-885-4640
Toll-Free: 800-265-8839
www.kitnews.com
ISBNs: ISBN 0-394
Educational books & mass market paperbacks

Knopf Canada
#210, 33 Yonge St., Toronto, ON M5E 1G4
Tel: 416-777-9477; *Fax:* 416-777-9470
ISBNs: ISBN: 0-394, 0-676
Louise Dennys, Publisher

Koala Books of Canada Ltd.
14327 - 95A Ave., Edmonton, AB T5N 0B6
Tel: 780-452-5149; *Fax:* 780-452-5149
jcarolan@nucleus.com
ISBNs: SAN: 169-9385
John Carolan, General Manager

Kosoy Travel Guides
112 Fairholme Ave., Toronto, ON M6B 2W9
Tel: 416-256-0974; *Fax:* 416-256-0974
torcan22@yahoo.com
ISBNs: ISBN: 0-919632; SAN: 115-8724
Ted Kosoy

Kugh Enterprises
PO Box 31821, Whitehorse, YT Y1A 6L3
Tel: 867-633-2118; *Fax:* 867-633-3307
gkarpes@northwestel.net
www.yukonweb.com/tourism/kugh
ISBNs: ISBN: 1-896
Publisher of Wilderness books about the Yukon.
Gus Karpes

Lambrecht Publications
1763 Maple Bay Rd., Duncan, BC V9L 5N6
Tel: 250-748-8722; *Fax:* 250-748-8722
Toll-Free: 877-774-4372
ISBNs: ISBN: 0-919383; SAN: 115-057X
H. Lambrecht, Publisher

Lancaster House
#200, 17 Dundonald St., Toronto, ON M4Y 1K3
Tel: 416-977-6618; *Fax:* 416-977-5873
Toll-Free: 888-298-8841
lan@lancasterhouse.com
www.lancasterhouse.com
ISBNs: ISBN: 0-920450
Publishes information & hosts conferences in the areas of labour & employment law.
Paul Wollaston, General Manager
Vanessa Scott, Editorial Coordinator
Cristina Santos, Production Coordinator/Database Administrator
Norma Nixon, Manager, Customer Service & Database

LandOwner Resource Centre
PO Box 599, 5524 Dickinson St., Manotick, ON K4M 1A5
Tel: 613-692-3571; *Fax:* 613-692-0831
info@lrconline.com
www.lrconline.com
ISBNs: 0-9680992
Publishes information on forestry, agriculture, wildlife, water, soil and other land management issues.

Largy Books
PO Box 6023, Fort McMurray, AB T9H 4W1
Tel: 403-791-1750; *Fax:* 403-791-1750
madame_faucon@hotmail.com
ISBNs: ISBN: 0-9698203

Laurier Books Ltd.
PO Box 2694 D, Ottawa, ON K1P 5W6
Tel: 613-738-2163; *Fax:* 613-247-0256
educa2@yahoo.com
educa0.tripod.com/edu
ISBNs: ISBN: 1-895959, 1-55394; SAN: 168-2806
Publishers of Educational Books, Foreign Language Dictionaries; French Language Dictionaries; Native American Books & Native Languages; Asian Studies books
Marthe Lalwani

Lazara Press
PO Box 2269 Main, Vancouver, BC V6B 3W2
Tel: 604-872-1134; *Fax:* 604-874-6661
www.lazarapress.ca
ISBNs: ISBN: 0-920999
Small, progressive publishing house located in Vancouver. Publishers of poetry, literature, broadsides & chapbooks. Committed to publishing & distributing works that might not otherwise be available.
Penny Goldsmith, Owner/Founder

Learnxs Press
5050 Yonge St., Toronto, ON M2N 5N8
Tel: 416-397-3911;
learnxs.foundation@tbsb.on.ca
ISBNs: ISBN: 0-920020; SAN: 115-4060
Publishing house for the production & sale of innovative learning materials in conjunction with the Toronto District School Board.
Ross Richardson, Production Manager

Leméac Éditeur
4609, rue d'Iberville, 1er étage, Montréal, QC H2H 2L9
Tél: 514-524-5558; *Téléc:* 514-524-3145
lemeac@lemeac.com
www.lemeac.com
ISBNs: ISBN: 2-7609, 0-7761
Notre politique éditoriale essentiellement à caractère littéraire s'inscrit surtout dans les domaines du roman, du théâtre contemporain, de l'essai, de la biographie de personalités ayant marqué le secteur culturel.
Lise P. Bergevin, Directrice générale

LexisNexis Canada Inc.
#700, 123 Commerce Valley Drive E, Markham, ON L3T 7W8
Tel: 905-479-2665; *Fax:* 905-479-2826
Toll-Free: 800-668-6481
info@lexisnexis.ca
www.lexisnexis.ca
ISBNs: ISBN: 0-409, 0-433; SAN: 115-2750
Provider of invormation & services to law professionals, corporations, government & academic institutions through online products.
Michael Pilmer, President & CEO

Libra Information Services
PO Box 353 A, 18 Eastern Ave. Lower Level, Toronto, ON M5W 1C2
Tel: 416-364-0050; *Fax:* 416-364-0606
libra@web.ca
www.web.ca/~libra
Publishers of material on Innovative Health Care methods, and for Social Investors & Conscious Consumers

Librairie Gallimard de Montréal
3700, boul Saint-Laurent, Montréal, QC H2X 2V4
Tél: 514-499-2012; *Téléc:* 514-499-1535
info@gallimardmontreal.com
www.gallimardmontreal.com

Librairie Wilson & Lafleur Ltée
40, rue Notre-Dame est, Montréal, QC H2Y 1B9
Tél: 514-875-6326; *Téléc:* 514-875-8356
Ligne sans frais: 800-363-2327
libraire@wilsonlafleur.com
www.wilsonlafleur.com
ISBNs: ISBN: 2-89127
Éditeur en droit et législation
Claude Wilson

Library Bound
#6-7, 75 Rankin Ave., Waterloo, ON N2V 1W2
Tel: 519-885-3233; *Fax:* 519-885-2662
Toll-Free: 800-363-4728
lbi@librarybound.com
www.librarybound.com
ISBNs: SAN: 116-9203
Also provide services for shelf-ready materials
Heather Bindseil, President, 5198853233 ext.28, heatherb@librarybound.com
Lisa Bendig, Accounting Department, lisab@librarybound.com
Ron Stadnik, Print Collections Development, 5198853233 ext.26, ron@librarybound.com

Lidec Inc.
4350, av de l'Hôtel-de-Ville, Montréal, QC H2W 2H5
Tel: 514-843-5991; *Fax:* 514-843-5252
Toll-Free: 800-350-5991
lidec@lidec.qc.ca
www.lidec.qc.ca
ISBNs: ISBN: 2-7608, 0-7762
La maison Lidec fut fondée par les Frères des écoles chrétiennes pour répondre aux besoins de l'éducation, puis achetée en 1985 par le Groupe Guérin. Lidec se spécialise dans le matériel scolaire de tous les niveaux et de toutes les disciplines. La maison publie des manuels de base et du matériel complémentaire pour l'enseignement primaire, secondaire, collégial et universitaire adaptés aux différents

programmes du Ministère de l'Éducation du Québec et des autres provinces canadiennes.
Marc-Aimé Guérin, President

Life Cycle Books Ltd.
#20, 1149 Bellamy Rd. N, Toronto, ON M1H 1H7
Fax: 866-690-8532
Toll-Free: 800-880-5860
canorders@lifecyclebooks.com
www.lifecyclebooks.com
ISBNs: ISBN: 0-919225; SAN: 115-8417
Publisher of pro-life & abstinence books and other educational materials.

Lifestyle Books
PO Box 42, Grand Falls, NL A2A 2J3
Tel: 709-489-6796; *Fax:* 709-489-6796
c.coish@nf.sympatico.ca
ISBNs: ISBN: 0-9691126, 0-9699031
Cal Coish, President

Lingo Media Inc.
#703, 151 Bloor St. West, Toronto, ON M5S 1S4
Tel: 416-927-7000; *Fax:* 416-927-1222
Toll-Free: 866-927-7011
mkraft@lingomedia.com
www.lingomedia.com
Develops and publishes English Language Learning materials for use in China.
Michael Kraft, mkraft@lingomedia.com
Khurram Qureshi, kqureshi@lingomedia.com

Linguatech éditeur inc.
CP 26026 Salaberry, Montréal, QC H3M 1L0
Tél: 514-336-5207; *Téléc:* 514-336-4736
linguatechediteur@bellnet.ca
home.ican.net/~lingua
ISBNs: ISBN: 2-920342
Publications: dictionnaires et vocabulaires; Actes de congrès; Ouvrages didactiques; Langues de spécialité
André Dubuc, Président
Robert Dubuc, Vice-Président
Odette Dubuc, Secrétaire

Little Brick Schoolhouse Inc.
PO Box 84001, 1235 Trafalgar Rd., Oakville, ON L6H 3J0
Tel: 905-844-4669; *Fax:* 905-690-3400
schoolhouse@cogeco.ca
www.littlebrick.com
ISBNs: ISBN: 0-919788
Publisher of Educational entertainment products dealing with Canadian & American History.
Robert Livesey, President

Lobster Press Limited
1620, rue Sherbrooke ouest, #C & D, Montréal, QC H3H 1C9
Tel: 514-904-1100; *Fax:* 514-904-1101
marketing@lobsterpress.com
www.lobsterpress.com
ISBNs: ISBN: 1-894222, 1-897073, 2-922435
Publisher of children's books
Alison Fripp, President & Publisher
Meghan Nolan, Editor
Stephanie Hindley, Director, Marketing
Ruth Joseph, Office Manager

Lone Pine Publishing
10145 - 81 Ave., Edmonton, AB T6E 1W9
Tel: 780-433-9333; *Fax:* 780-433-9646
Toll-Free: 800-661-9017
info@lonepinepublishing.com
www.lonepinepublishing.com
ISBNs: ISBN: 0-919433, 1-55105; SAN: 115-4125
Focus as a regional publisher in the Rocky Mountains, West Coast & Great Lakes. Focus on nature, outdoor recreation & popular history.
Shane Kennedy, President
Nancy Foulds, Senior Editor
David Cleary, Director of Sales & Marketing

Lorraine Greey Publications Limited
#303, 56 The Esplanade, Toronto, ON M5E 1A7
Tel: 416-366-9729; *Fax:* 416-367-3998
Lorraine Durham Greey, President

Louise Courteau, éditrice inc.
481, Lac St-Louis est, Saint-Zénon, QC J0K 3N0
Tél: 450-884-5958; *Téléc:* 450-884-5913
presse@louisdecourteau.com
www.louisdecorteau.com
Louise Courteau, Éditrice

Loyal Colonies Press
304 Olympus Ave., Kingston, ON K7M 4T9
Tel: 613-389-0866;
tvincent@can.rogers.com
www.bibliofiles.ca/lc_index.cfm
ISBNs: ISBN: 0-929832
Publishers of history books, largely biographies of Canadians; Publishes roughly 2 books per year.
Thomas B. Vincent, Proprietor

Lugus Publications Ltd.
48 Falcon St., Toronto, ON M4S 2P5
Tel: 416-322-5113; *Fax:* 416-484-9512
gethin@la-rampa.com
ISBNs: ISBN: 0-921633, 1-896266
Publishes Children's books and other books & pamphlets.
Annual sales of $200,000 - $350,000
Gethin James, Manager

Lyalta Publishing
4903 Benson Rd. West, Calgary, AB T2L 1R9
Tel: 403-233-2558; *Fax:* 403-266-7078
Toll-Free: 888-322-2558
lyle@lyaltapublishing.com
www.lyaltapublishing.com
ISBNs: ISBN: 0-9699101, 0-9681761
Assists individuals and small organizations in self-publishing
Lyle Manery, Founder

Lynx Images Inc.
PO Box 5961 A, Toronto, ON M5W 1P4
Tel: 416-925-8422; *Fax:* 416-925-8352
website@lynximages.com
www.lynximages.com
ISBNs: ISBN: 0-9698427, 1-894073
Documentary Film production company & publisher. Publishes books dealing with Canadian History & companion books to documentaries.
Russell Floren, President
Barbara Chisolm, Vice-President, Publishing

MacKenzie Art Gallery
3475 Albert St., Regina, SK S4S 6X6
Tel: 306-584-4285; *Fax:* 306-569-8191
sandra.nixon@uregina.ca
www.mackenzieartgallery.ca
ISBNs: ISBN: 1-896470
Publishes books about visual arts and Canadian & local artists

Madison Press Books
#200, 1000 Yonge St., Toronto, ON M4Y 2K2
Tel: 416-923-5027; *Fax:* 416-923-9708
info@madisonpressbooks.com
www.madisonpressbooks.com
Independent publishers of illustrated non-fiction titles; Catalog includes a number of international best-sellers including Robert D. Ballard's 'Discovery of the Titanic'; Also publish children's books & custom publishing programs for corporate clients
Oliver Salzmann, Publisher, 4169235027 ext. 223, osalzmann@madisonpressbooks.com
Alison Maclean, Associate Publisher, amaclean@madisonpressbooks.com

Madonna House Publications
Madonna House, 2888 Dafoe Rd., Combermere, ON K0J 1L0
Tel: 613-756-3728; *Fax:* 613-756-0103
Toll-Free: 888-703-7110
publications@madonnahouse.org
www.madonnahouse.org/publications
ISBNs: ISBN: 0-921440
Non-profic Catholic Christian publisher of religious books, audiobooks, videos, music & cards.
Linda Lambeth

Malcolm Lester & Associates
22 St. Clair Ave. E, 14th Fl., Toronto, ON M4T 2S3
Tel: 416-928-2637; *Fax:* 416-944-3122
malcolm@malcolmlester.com
www.malcolmlester.com
ISBNs: ISBN: 1-9659415
Publisher & publishing consultant; Develop books for other publishers; Develops custom books for corporate clients, individuals & organizations.
Malcolm Lester, malcolm@malcolmlester.com
Andrea Knight, andrea@malcolmlester.com

Map Art
70 Bloor St. East, Oshawa, ON L1H 3M2
Tel: 905-436-2525; *Toll-Free:* 877-231-6277
info@mapart.com
www.mapart.com
Leading publishers of Maps, Atlases, Wall Maps & Street Guides.

Maple Tree Press Inc.
#200, 51 Front St. East, Toronto, ON M5E 1B3
Tel: 416-304-0702; *Fax:* 416-304-0525
info@mapletreepress.com
www.mapletreepress.com
ISBNs: ISBN: 0-919872, 0-920775, 1-895688, 1-897066, 1-894379; SAN: 1
Publishers of non-fiction books for children covering a wide variety of topics including Sports, Humor, Science, Crafts, Canada, History & Culture.
Sheba Meland

Marcus Books
301 Petheram Pl., Newmarket, ON L3X 1J8
Tel: 905-478-2201;
thomas.rieder@sympatico.ca
ISBNs: ISBN: 0-919951; SAN: 115-4249
Thomas Rieder, President

Marshall Cavendish
#3, 109 Woodbine Downs Rd., Toronto, ON M9W 6Y1
Tel: 416-674-8622; *Fax:* 416-674-6215
info@edureference.com
www.marshallcavendish.com
ISBNs: ISBN: 0-7614
Publishes educational, home & library reference & non-fiction titles.
Orland Kirkness

Marvin Melnyk Associates Ltd
PO Box 220, Queenston, ON L0S 1L0
Tel: 905-262-4964; *Fax:* 905-262-4974
Toll-Free: 800-682-0029
meljack@niagara.com
ISBNs: ISBN: 0-919803; SAN: 115-4281
John O. Fritz, Vice-President
Marvin Melnyk, President

Master Point Press
331 Douglas Ave., Toronto, ON M5M 1H2
Tel: 416-781-0351; *Fax:* 416-781-1831
info@masterpointpress.com
www.masterpointpress.com
ISBNs: ISBN: 0-9698461, 1-894154, 1-897106
Publisher of a variety of books on the topic of the card game Bridge; also publishes books on other games, as well as software
Ray Lee, President
Linda Lee, Co-owner

MasterAthlete Book Publishing Group Ltd.
75 Main St., Mount Albert, ON L0G 1M0
Tel: 905-473-9714; *Fax:* 905-473-9715
ISBNs: ISBN: 0-921016; SAN: 118-3613
Liz Roach, President

McArthur & Company
#402, 322 King St. West, Toronto, ON M5V 1J2
Tel: 416-408-4007; *Fax:* 416-408-4081
info@mcarthur-co.com
www.mcarthur-co.com
ISBNs: ISBN: 1-55278; SAN: 117-9713
Publisher & distributor of Canadian & international fiction & non-fiction; Publisher of 63 best-sellers & 21 #1 bestsellers.
Kim McArthur, President, Publisher
Jim Palmeieri, Director, Finance
Jessica Scott, Production & Rights

McClelland & Stewart Ltd. (M&S)
5th Fl., 75 Sherbourne St., Toronto, ON M5A 2P9
Tel: 416-598-1114; *Fax:* 416-598-7764
Toll-Free: 800-788-1074
mail@mcclelland.com
www.mcclelland.com
ISBNs: ISBN: 0-7710; SAN: 115-4192
Publisher of over 100 titles annually, both fiction & non-fiction. Publishers of authors such as Margaret Atwood, Alistair MacLeod, Rohinton Mistry & Jane Urquhart. Publishers of political memoirs, including Pierre Elliott Trudeau's.
Douglas J. Pepper

McGilligan Books
PO Box 16024, 1260 Dundas St. West, Toronto, ON M6J 3W2
Tel: 416-538-0945;
info@mcgilliganbooks.com
www.mcgilliganbooks.com
ISBNs: ISBN: 0-9698064, 1-894692
Publishers of fiction & non-fiction, emphasizing multiracial & multicultural books.
Ann Decter, Publisher

McGill-Queen's University Press
Marketing Dept., McGill-Queen's University Press, 3430 McTavish St., Montréal, QC H3A 1X9
Tel: 514-398-3750; *Fax:* 514-398-4333
Toll-Free: 877-864-8477
mqup@mqup.ca
www.mqup.mcgill.ca
ISBNs: ISBN: 0-88629, 0-7735, 0-88911, 1-55339; SAN: 106-4206
Publisher of non-fiction books, with over 1800 books in print and numerous awards & bestsellers.
Philip Cercone, Executive Director & Senior Editor, 514-398-3750, philip.cercone@mcgill.ca
John Zucchi, Deputy Senior Editor, 514-398-2056, john.zucchi@mcgill.ca
Joan McGilvray, Coordinating Editor, 514-398-3922, joan.mcgilvray@mcgill.ca
Joanne Pisano, Permissions & Rights Coordinator, 514-398-2068, joanne.pisano@mcgill.ca

McGill-Queen's University Press
Queen's University, 144 Barrie St., Kingston, ON K7L 3N6
Tel: 613-533-2155; *Fax:* 613-533-6822
mqup@post.queensu.ca
www.mqup.mcgill.ca
ISBNs: ISBN: 0-7735
Donald H. Akenson, Senior Editor
Kyla Madden, Deputy Senior Editor, 6kmm3@queensu.ca

McGraw-Hill Ryerson Limited
300 Water St., Whitby, ON L1N 9B6
Tel: 905-430-5000; *Fax:* 905-430-5020
Toll-Free: 800-565-5758
cs_queries@mcgrawhill.ca
www.mcgrawhill.ca
ISBNs: ISBN: 0-07; SAN: 115-060X
Publishers of a large quantity of education materials, including textbooks
John Dill, President/CEO

MDAG Publishing
8035 Redtail Ct., Surrey, BC V3W 0N4
Tel: 604-502-0796;
contact@mdag.com
www.mdag.com/publishing
ISBNs: 0-9682039
Released tools & publications produced by the Minesite Drainage Assessment Group

Mediacorp Canada Inc.
21 New St., Toronto, ON M5R 1P7
Tel: 416-964-6069; *Fax:* 416-964-3202
info@mediacorp.ca
www.mediacorp.ca
ISBNs: ISBN: 0-9681447, 1-894450
Publishers of data & publications regarding employment, employers & labour

Megamy Publishing Ltd.
PO Box 3507, Spruce Grove, AB T7X 3A7
Tel: 780-960-3539; *Fax:* 780-960-3539
megamy@compusmart.ab.ca
ISBNs: ISBN: 0-9681916

The Mercury Press
PO Box 672 P, Toronto, ON M5S 2Y4
Tel: 416-531-4338; *Fax:* 416-531-0765
Toll-Free: 800-591-6250
contact@themercurypress.ca
www.themercurypress.ca
ISBNs: ISBN: 0-920544, 1-55128; SAN: 115-009X
Publishers of poetry, fiction, murder mysteries & non-fiction by Canadian authors

Messageries ADP inc.
955, rue Amherst, Montréal, QC H2L 3K4
Tél: 514-523-1182; *Téléc:* 514-521-4434
Ligne sans frais: 800-361-4806
www.messageries-adp.com
Diffuseur et distributeur de livres francophones au Canada; partenaire de 139 maisons d'édition québécoises, françaises, belges et suisses

Michelin North America (Canada) Inc.
Travel Publications, #510, 2540, boul Daniel Johnson, Laval, QC H7T 2T9
Toll-Free: 800-361-8236
ISBNs: ISBN: 2-06; SAN: 115-0618
Publishes maps & travel guides
Jack Haugh

Michi-Mook Enterprises
817 Queen St. East, Sault Ste Marie, ON P6A 2A4
Tel: 705-946-5746; *Fax:* 705-946-3577
ISBNs: ISBN: 1-896579, 0-9698326
Publishes personalized childrens books
Lou Mangone

Mile Oak Publishing Inc.
#81, 20 Mineola Rd. East, Mississauga, ON L5G 4N9
Tel: 905-274-4356;
mile_oak@compuserve.com
www.i75online.com
ISBNs: ISBN: 1-896819
Publishers of the "Along Interstate-75" travel guide.
Dave Hunter, Publisher

Mini Mocho Press
PO Box 57424 Jackson, Hamilton, ON L8P 4X2
Tel: 905-523-1518;
jamesstrecker@sympatico.ca
ISBNs: ISBN: 0-921980
Publishes a catalog of 26 titles featuring primarily authors from Southern Ontario
James Strecker

Misthorn Press
Comp. 11, Site 660, RR#6, Courtenay, BC V9N 8H9
Tel: 250-335-2237; *Fax:* 250-338-8469
ISBNs: ISBN: 0-9680159

MLR Editions Canada
Dept. of English & Film Studies, Wilfrid Laurier Univ, Waterloo, ON N2L 3C5
Tel: 519-884-0710; *Fax:* 519-886-9351
ptiessen@wlu.ca
ISBNs: ISBN: 0-9692539
Paul Tiessen, Publisher

MOD Publishing
4 Fairview Blvd., Toronto, ON M4K 1L9
Tel: 416-466-9275; *Fax:* 416-466-7493
jean.weihs@rogers.com
www.modpublishing.com
ISBNs: ISBN: 0-9684559, 0-9683974, 1-894461
Publishes supplemental educational aids that covers material not covered within current cirriculum

Modus Vivendi
55 rue Jean-Talon Ouest, Montréal, QC H2R 2W8
Tél: 514-272-0433; *Téléc:* 514-272-7234
info@modusaventure.com
www.modusaventure.com
ISBNs: ISBN: 2-921556, 2-92155, 2-89523, 2-922148 (Presses Aventure)
Publishers of non-fiction books covering topics such as arts & crafts, cooking, food & wine, diet & health, games & activities, home renovations and others.
Jean Poitras, Editeur

Monarch Books of Canada
5000 Dufferin St., Toronto, ON M3H 5T5
Tel: 416-663-8231; *Fax:* 416-736-1702
Toll-Free: 800-404-7404
customer_service@monarchbooks.ca
www.monarchbooks.ca
Specializes in distributing Children's books, Teacher Resources, Special Needs, Sports, Reference and more, from a wide range of publishers, as well as bestselling audiobook titles.

Mondia éditeurs inc.
105, rue de Martigny ouest, Saint-Jérome, QC J7Y 2G2
Tél: 514-438-8479; *Téléc:* 514-884-8307
ISBNs: ISBN: 0-88556, 2-89114, 0-9861676

Money Jar Publishing
#2021, 642 Sheppard Ave. East, Toronto, ON M2K 1B9
Tel: 416-223-7312;
millyard@rogers.com
ISBNs: ISBN: 0-9695889
John Millyard, Owner

Montréal Museum of Fine Arts / Musée des beaux-arts de Montréal
PO Box 3000 H, Montréal, QC H3G 2T9
Tel: 514-285-2000;
flavoie@mbamtl.org
www.mbamtl.org; www.mmfa.qc.ca
ISBNs: ISBN: 2-89192
Francine Lavoie, Head, Publishing, flavoie@mbamtl.org

Moonprint Press
PO Box 293, Winnipeg, MB R3C 2G9
Tel: 204-237-5504
Diane Driedger, Co-Publisher
Cecile Guillemot, Co-Publisher

Moose Enterprise Book & Theatre Play Publishing
684 Walls Side Rd., Sault Ste Marie, ON P6A 5K6
Tel: 705-779-3331; *Fax:* 705-779-3331
Toll-Free: 888-826-6698
mooseenterprises@on.aibn.com
www.moosehidebooks.com
ISBNs: ISBN: 0-9698319, 0-9681852, 0-9684909, 0-9686086, 1-894650
Local publishers of plays, children's short stories, non-fiction & fiction works.
Richard Mousseau, Publisher, rmousseau@moosehidebooks.com

Mosaic Press
#1, 1252 Speers Rd., Oakville, ON L6L 5N9
Tel: 905-825-2130; *Fax:* 905-825-2130
info@mosaic-press.com
www.mosaic-press.com
ISBNs: ISBN: 0-88962; SAN: 115-4362, 115-4370
Publishes over 20 original titles each year, with a back catalog of over 500 books covering all genres. Literature; The Arts; Social Studies & INternational Studies
Howard Aster, Publisher

Mother Tongue Publishing Ltd.
290 Fulford-Ganges Rd., Salt Spring Island, BC V8K 2K6
Tel: 250-537-4155; *Fax:* 250-537-4725
info@mothertonguepress.com
www.mothertonguepress.com
ISBNs: ISBN: 1-896949, 0-9698904
Publishers of local authors as well as books on British Columbia art history, art & literature.

Moving to Magazines Ltd.
178 Main St., Unionville, ON L3R 2G9
Tel: 905-479-0641; *Fax:* 905-479-1286
info@movingto.com
www.movingto.com
ISBNs: ISBN: 1-895020
Publishers of the "Moving to" series of publications geared towards people moving to new cities in Canada.
Anita Wood, President/Publisher

Multicultural Books
Richmond Gardens, #307, 6311 Gilbert Rd., Richmond, BC V7C 3V7
Tel: 604-277-3894;
jrmbooks@hotmail.com
ISBNs: ISBN: 0-9694933
Joe M. Ruggier

Multicultural History Society of Ontario
43 Queen's Park Cres. East, Toronto, ON M5S 2C3
Tel: 416-979-2973; *Fax:* 416-979-7947
ISBNs: ISBN: 0-919045
Publishers of a number of journals and non-fiction books dealing with Multicultural History in Ontario

Munsey Music
PO Box 511, Richmond Hill, ON L4C 4Y8
Tel: 905-737-0208; *Fax:* 905-737-0208
info@MunseyMusic.com
www.MunseyMusic.com
ISBNs: ISBN: 0-9697066, 0-9685152; SAN: 116-967X
Terence Munsey, President

Napoleon Publishing/Rendezvous Press
#201, 178 Willowdale Ave., Toronto, ON M2N 4Y8
Tel: 416-730-9052; *Fax:* 416-730-8096
Toll-Free: 877-730-9052
napoleon@napoleonandcompany.com
www.napoleonandcompany.com
ISBNs: ISBN: 0-929141, 1-894917; SAN: 115-0022
Publishers of Children's picture books, novels, biographies & educational resources under the Napoleon Imprint. Rendezvous Press imprint covers general fiction & general interest books.
Sylvia McConnell, President

Native Law Centre
University of Saskatchewan, Rm. 160, Law Bldg. 15 Campus Drive., Saskatoon, SK S7N 5A6
Tel: 306-966-6189; *Fax:* 306-966-6207
native.law@usask.ca
www.usask.ca/nativelaw/
ISBNs: ISBN: 0-88880; SAN: 115-4540
Publishers of materials relating to First Nations & Aboriginal Law in Canada.
Zandra Wilson, Publications Editor, 3069666192, zandra.wilson@usask.ca

NDE Publishing
#15, 30 Wertheim Ct., Richmond Hill, ON L4B 1B9
Tel: 905-727-8580; *Fax:* 905-229-0448
info@ndepublishing.com
www.ndepublishing.com
ISBNs: ISBN: 1-55321, 1-55375

Nelson Education Ltd.
1120 Birchmount Rd., Toronto, ON M1K 5G4
Tel: 416-752-9100; *Fax:* 416-752-8101
Toll-Free: 800-668-0671
inquire@nelson.com
www.nelson.com
ISBNs: ISBN: 0-176; SAN: 115-0669
Canada's leading Educational Publisher. Publishes K-12 textbooks and educational products, as well as higher education, professional learning & business education publications
William D. Rieders, Acting President
Michael Andrews, CFO
Beverly Buxton, Vice-President, School Division
James Reeve, Vice-President, Higher Education Division

New Orphic Publishers
706 Mill St., Nelson, BC V1L 4S5
Tel: 250-354-0494; *Fax:* 250-352-0743
ISBNs: ISBN: 0-9699162, 0-9682800, 1-9687317; 1-894842-04-9
Ernest Hekkanen, President

New Society Publishers
PO Box 189, Gabriola, BC V0R 1X0
Tel: 250-247-9737; *Fax:* 250-247-7471
Toll-Free: 800-567-6772
info@newsociety.com
www.newsociety.com
ISBNs: ISBN: 1-55092, 0-86571
Progressive publishing company that specializes in books about activism & ecological sustainability
Judith Plant

New Star Books Ltd.
#107, 3477 Commercial St., Vancouver, BC V5N 4E8
Tel: 604-738-9429; *Fax:* 604-738-9332
info@newstarbooks.com
www.newstarbooks.com
ISBNs: ISBN: 0-919573, 0-921586, 1-55420; SAN: 115-1908
Publishes 6-10 titles annually covering politically- and socially-based non-fiction as well as fiction, poetry and books on local history & culture.
Rolf Maurer, President/Publisher

New World Publishing
PO Box 36075, Halifax, NS B3J 3S9
Tel: 902-576-2055; *Fax:* 902-576-2095
Toll-Free: 877-211-3334
nwp1@eastlink.ca
www.newworldpublishing.com
ISBNs: ISBN: 1-895814
Francis Mitchell, Managing Editor

NeWest Publishers Ltd.
#201, 8540 - 109 St., Edmonton, AB T6G 1E6
Tel: 780-432-9427; *Fax:* 780-433-3179
Toll-Free: 866-796-5473
info@newestpress.com
www.newestpress.com
ISBNs: ISBN: 0-920316, 0-920897, 1-896300
Western regional press publishing 10-12 books annually
Ruth Linka, General Manager

Newport Bay Publishing Limited
356 Cyril Owen Pl., Victoria, BC V9E 2B6
Tel: 250-479-4616; *Fax:* 250-479-3836
info@newportbay.ca
www.newportbay.ca/publishing
ISBNs: ISBN: 0-921513
Publishers of a small number of books covering the following subjects: biography, world governance, alternative economics, alternative health and medicine, home and garden, media/journalism, Native peoples, nature/environment, philosophy, social sciences, and women/feminism.
Donna Lindenberg

Nightwood Editions
3692 Beach Ave., RR#2, Roberts Creek, BC V0N 2W2
Tel: 604-885-0212; *Fax:* 604-885-0212
info@nightwoodeditions.com
www.nightwoodeditions.com
ISBNs: ISBN: 0-88971; SAN: 115-2661
Publishers of new poetry & fiction by Canadian writers; Also publishes non-fiction works

Nimbus Publishing Ltd.
PO Box 9166, 3731 MacKintosh St., Halifax, NS B3K 5M8
Tel: 902-454-7404; *Fax:* 902-455-5440
Toll-Free: 800-646-2879
info@nimbus.ns.ca
www.nimbus.ns.ca
ISBNs: ISBN: 0-920852, 0-921054, 1-55109; SAN: 115-0685
Terrilee Bulger, Sales & Marketing Manager, tbulger@nimbus.ns.ca
John S. Marshall, President

North Shore Publishing Inc.
2351 Sinclair Circle, Burlington, ON L7P 3C1
Tel: 905-336-2364; *Fax:* 905-336-5110
info@canadianheritagebooks.com
www.canadianheritagebooks.com
ISBNs: ISBN: 1-896899
Publishers of local heritage books in Southern Ontario

Northern Canada Mission Distributors
PO Box 3030, Prince Albert, SK S6V 7V4
Tel: 306-764-3388; *Fax:* 306-764-3390
ncmd@ncem.ca
www.ncem.ca
ISBNs: ISBN: 0-920731, 1-896968
William Dyck

The North-South Institute / L'Institut Nord-Sud
#200, 55 Murray St., Ottawa, ON K1N 5M3
Tel: 613-241-3535; *Fax:* 613-241-7435
nsi@nsi-ins.ca
www.nsi-ins.ca
ISBNs: ISBN: 1-896770; SAN: 115-4605
Publishers of findings made by the North-South Institute
Roy Culpepper, President, rculpepper@nsi-ins.ca
Ann Weston, Vice-President & Coordinator of Research, aweston@nsi-ins.ca

Novalis Publishing
Saint Paul University, 223 Main St., Ottawa, ON K1S 1C4
Tel: 613-236-1393; *Fax:* 613-782-3004
Toll-Free: 800-313-3020
tradebooks@novalis.ca
www.novalis.ca
ISBNs: ISBN: 2-89088, 2-89507; SAN: 115-4621
Religious publishing house in the Catholic Tradition; Publishes in the areas of liturgy, prayer, spirituality, sacramental practice, catechetics, religious education and personal growth.
Michael O'Hearn, Director, mohearn@ustpaul.ca
Kevin Burns, Editorial Director, kburns@ustpaul.ca

NRC Research Press
National Research Council of Canada, 1200 Montreal Rd., Bldg. M-55, Ottawa, ON K1A 0R6
Tel: 613-993-9084; *Fax:* 613-952-7656
pubs@nrc-cnrc.gc.ca.
pubs.nrc-cnrc.gc.ca
Publishes research findings conducted by the National Research Council of Canada
Cameron Macdonald, Director, Publishing

Oasis Press
38 Nina St., Toronto, ON M5R 1Z4
Tel: 416-534-5124; *Fax:* 416-537-8421
allenmorgan@sympatico.ca
oasispress.allenmorgan.com
ISBNs: ISBN: 1-895092
Publishers of story collections for children
Allen Morgan

Oberon Press
#205, 145 Spruce St., Ottawa, ON K1R 6P1
Tel: 613-238-3275; *Fax:* 613-238-3275
oberon@sympatico.ca
www3.sympatico.ca/oberon
ISBNs: ISBN: 0-88750, 0-7780; SAN: 115-0723
Publishers of fiction by Canadian Authors. Publishes 10 new titles annually, and has 650 titles in print.
Nicholas Macklem, President

OCAPT Business Books
27 Donna Marie Dr., Welland, ON L3C 2X7
Tel: 905-735-2967; *Fax:* 905-788-0839
Toll-Free: 888-579-3013
ocapt@iaw.on.ca
www.ocapt.com
ISBNs: ISBN: 0-915299, 1-56327, 0-527, 0-9667843
Publishes books & visual learning products for the manufacturing & service industries
Gail Grimaldi

Ontario Outdoor Publications
PO Box 1414 C, 1431 Stavebank Rd., Mississauga, ON L5G 2V5
Tel: 905-891-1714; *Fax:* 905-891-2352
ISBNs: ISBN: 0-9690474; SAN: 115-4672
K. Duncliffe, President

Oolichan Books
PO Box 10, Lantzville, BC V0R 2H0
Tel: 250-390-4839; *Fax:* 866-299-0026
Toll-Free: 877-390-4839
oolichan@island.net
www.oolichan.com
ISBNs: ISBN: 0-88982; SAN: 115-4680
Publishes poetry, fiction & non-fiction titles including literary criticism, memoirs & books on regional history
Ron Smith, Publisher
Hiro Boga, Managing Editor
Pat Smith, Consulting Editor

Optimum Publishing International Inc.
PO Box 524, Maxville, ON K0C 1T0
Tel: 613-527-2222; *Fax:* 613-527-3333
info@optimumbooks.com
optimumbooks.com
ISBNs: ISBN: 0-88890
Publishers of non-fiction books covering true crime, politics & history

Orca Book Publishers Ltd.
PO Box 5626 B, Victoria, BC V8R 6S4
Tel: 250-380-1229; *Fax:* 250-380-1892
Toll-Free: 800-210-5277
orca@orcabook.com
www.orcabook.com
ISBNs: ISBN: 0-920501, 1-55143; SAN: 115-7485
Publishers of children's books; with ovr 350 titles in print & 60 new titles per year. Picturebooks, Early chapter books, teen novels
Bob Tyrrell, Publisher
Andrew Wooldridge, Associate Publisher
Dayle Sutherland, Marketing Director
Melanie Jeffs, Office Manager

Organisation for Economic Cooperation and Development (OECD)
#650, 2001 L St. NW, Washington, DC
Tel: 202-785-6323; *Fax:* 202-785-0350
Toll-Free: 800-456-6323
washington.contact@oecd.org
www.oecdwash.org
ISBNs: ISBN: 92-64
Sandra Wilson, Head, Center for Public Affairs

Our Schools/Our Selves
107 Earl Grey Rd., Toronto, ON M4J 3L6
Tel: 416-463-6978; *Fax:* 416-463-6978
Toll-Free: 800-565-1975
satu.repo@utoronto.ca
ISBNs: ISBN: 0-921908
Satu Repo

Owl's Head Press
8500 Main St., Alma, NB E4H 1M7
Tel: 506-887-2073
ISBNs: ISBN: 0-920635

Oxford University Press - Canada
70 Wynford Dr., Toronto, ON M3C 1J9
Tel: 416-441-2941; *Fax:* 416-444-0427
Toll-Free: 800-387-8020
customer.service@oup.com
www.oupcanada.com
ISBNs: ISBN: 0-19; SAN: 115-731
One of the oldest publishing companies in the world; Publishers of non-fiction & educational material
David Stover, President
Wendy Moran, Associate Vice-President/Director, Creative Services
David Steele, Vice-President/Director, School Division

P.D. Meany Publishers
145 Westminster Ave., Toronto, ON M6R 1N8
Tel: 416-516-2903; *Fax:* 416-516-7632
info@pdmeany.com
www.pdmeany.com
ISBNs: ISBN: 0-88835; SAN: 115-4273
Publishers of a variety of fiction & non-fiction titles
Pierrek L'Abbé

Pacific Edge Publishing Ltd.
1773 El Verano Dr., Gabriola, BC V0R 1X6
Tel: 250-247-9093; *Fax:* 250-247-9083
Toll-Free: 800-668-8806
info@pacificedgepublishing.com
www.pacificedgepublishing.com
ISBNs: ISBN: 1-895110
Publisher & distributor of educational resources for K-12 teachers.
Chris Sherwood

Pacific Educational Press
Faculty of Education, University of British Columbia, 6365 Biological Sciences Rd., Vancouver, BC V6T 1Z4
Tel: 604-822-5385; *Fax:* 604-822-6603
pep@interchange.ubc.ca
www.pep.educ.ubc.ca
ISBNs: ISBN: 0-88865, 1-895766; SAN: 115-1266
Publishing house of the Faculty of Education at the University of British Columbia; Publishes educational resources
Catherine Edwards, Director

Paideia Press Ltd.
2318 Regional Rd. 81, Jordan Station, ON L0R 1S0
Tel: 905-562-5719; *Fax:* 905-562-7828
ISBNs: ISBN: 0-88815; SAN: 115-4761
John Hultink

Pandora Press
33 Kent Ave., Kitchener, ON N2G 3R2
Tel: 519-578-2381; *Fax:* 519-578-1826
Toll-Free: 866-696-1678
judith@pandorapress.com
www.pandorapress.com
ISBNs: ISBN: 0-9698762, 0-9685543, 1-894710
Judith Jutzi, Manager, judith@pandorapress.com

Paperplates Books
19 Kenwood Ave., Toronto, ON M6C 2RB
Tel: 416-651-2551; *Fax:* 416-651-2910
paper@perkolator.com
www.paperplates.org
Small Publishing House; Publishes short fiction & personal essays
Bernard Kelly
Cary Fagan

Parkland Publishing
501 Mount Allison Pl., Saskatoon, SK S7H 4A9
Tel: 306-242-7731;
info@parklandpublishing.com
www.parklandpublishing.com
Publishes non-fiction books about Saskatchewan, hiking in Saskatchewan & trivia about Saskatchewan
Robin Kaplan, Co-founder
Arlene Kaplan, Co-founder

Pathway Publishers
RR#4, Aylmer, ON N5H 2R3
ISBNs: ISBN: 0-919374
Amish & Anabaptist Publishing House

Pearson Education Canada Inc.
26 Prince Andrew Pl., Toronto, ON M3C 2T8
Tel: 416-447-5101; *Fax:* 416-443-0948
Toll-Free: 800-263-9965
www.pearsoncanada.ca
ISBNs: 9780131113497; 9780131228436; 9780131280397
A Pearson Canada imprint, Pearson Education Canada Inc. is the largest publisher of print & electronic curriculum materials in Canada
MR Allan T. Reynolds, President & CEO, Pearson Canada

Pedlar Press
PO Box 26 P, 191 Madison Ave., Toronto, ON M5S 2S6
Tel: 416-534-2011; *Fax:* 416-535-9677
ISBNs: ISBN: 0-9681884, 0-9686522, 0-9732140

Pegasus Publishing
PO Box 26, Causeway Rd., Site 19, Seaforth, NS B0J 1N0
Tel: 902-827-3204;
jenniblackmore@eastlink.ca
ISBNs: ISBN: 0-9692552
Jenni Blackmore

Pembroke Publishers Limited
538 Hood Rd., Markham, ON L3R 3K9
Tel: 905-477-0650; *Fax:* 905-477-3691
mary@pembrokepublishers.com
www.pembrokepublishers.com
ISBNs: ISBN: 0-921217, 1-55138
Publisher of educational resources for parents & teachers covering: Reading & Writing; Grammar & Speaking; Thinking & drama; Classroom management & major issues in education
Claudia Connolly, General Manager
Mary Macchiusi, President

Pemmican Publications Inc.
150 Henry Ave., Winnipeg, MB R3B 0J7
Tel: 204-589-6346; *Fax:* 204-589-2063
pemmican@pemmican.mb.ca
www.pemmican.mb.ca
ISBNs: ISBN: 0-91943, 0-921827; SAN: 115-1657
Publishers of children's books, fiction & non-fiction related to Metis culture & heritage.
Andreen Hourie, Managing Editor

Pendas Productions
525 Canterbury Rd., London, ON N6G 2N5
Tel: 519-434-8555;
pendas@pennkemp.ca
www.pennkemp.ca
ISBNs: ISBN: 0-920820
Gavin Stairs

Penguin Books Canada Ltd.
#700, 90 Eglinton Ave. East, Toronto, ON M4P 2Y3
Tel: 416-925-2249; *Fax:* 416-925-0068
info@penguin.ca
www.penguin.ca
ISBNs: 9781592403691; 9780140260670; 9780142004272
Penguin Books Canada is a division of Pearson Canada, & publishes paperback & hardcover books in a range of subjects, for adults & children. Winner of the 2008 Canadian Booksellers Association Publisher of the Year Award
MR David Davidar, President
MS Yvonne Hunter, Director, Publicity & Marketing

Penumbra Press
PO Box 940, Manotick, ON K4M 1A8
Tel: 613-692-5590; *Fax:* 613-692-5589
john@penumbrapress.ca
www.penumbrapress.com
ISBNs: ISBN: 0-921254, 0-929806, 1-894131; SAN: 115-0774
Small fine-art & literary publishing house; Publishes Northern and Native literatures; children's literature; poetry; translations of Scandinavian literature; history; mythology; art books
John Flood, President

Phaidon Press Inc.
14 Glenwood Ave., Toronto, ON M6P 3C6
Tel: 416-761-1755; *Fax:* 416-761-9316
enquiries@phaidon.com
www.phaidon.com
Publisher of books on the visual arts

Picasso Publications Inc.
#3904, 10080 Jasper Ave., Edmonton, AB T5J 1V9
Tel: 780-420-1070; *Fax:* 780-420-0475
sales@picassopublications.com
ISBNs: ISBN: 1-55279

Pippin Publishing Corp.
PO Box 242 Don Mills, Toronto, ON M3C 2S2
Tel: 416-510-2918; *Fax:* 416-510-3359
jld@pippinpub.com
www.pippinpub.com
ISBNs: ISBN: 0-88751; SAN: 115-3293
Jonathan Lovat Dickson

Playwrights Canada Press
#230, 215 Spadina Ave., Toronto, ON M5T 2C7
Tel: 416-703-0013; *Fax:* 416-408-3402
publisher@playwrightscanada.com
www.playwrightscanada.com
ISBNs: ISBN: 0-88754, 0-919834
Publishes roughly 32 books of plays, theatre history & criticism annually
Angela Rebeiro, Project Coordinator, editor@playwrightscanada.com
Annie Gibson, Publisher

Pokeweed Press
#337, 829 Norwest Rd., Kingston, ON K7P 2N3
Tel: 613-374-2494;
publisher@pokeweed.com
www.pokeweed.com
ISBNs: ISBN: 1-894323
Frank B. Edwards, Publisher

Polar Bear Press
35 Price Andrew Pl., Toronto, ON M3C 2H2
Tel: 416-449-4000; *Fax:* 416-449-9924
Toll-Free: 800-490-4049
north49@idirect.com
ISBNs: ISBN: 1-896757

Polestar Book Publishers
An Imprint of Raincoast Books, 9050 Shaughnessy St., Vancouver, BC V6P 6E5
Tel: 604-323-7100; *Fax:* 604-323-2600
Toll-Free: 800-663-5714
info@raincoast.com
www.raincoast.com
ISBNs: ISBN: 0-919591, 1-896095
Michelle Benjamin, Publisher

Pontifical Institute of Mediaeval Studies, Dept. of Publications
59 Queen's Park Cres. East, Toronto, ON M5S 2C4
Tel: 416-926-7142; *Fax:* 416-926-7258
pontifex@chass.utoronto.ca
www.pims.ca
ISBNs: ISBN: 0-88844; SAN: 115-0804
Small University Press publishing the results of research carried out by all medievalists
Rev. James K. McConica, President CSB, OC

Porcupine's Quill Inc.
68 Main St., Erin, ON N0B 1T0
Tel: 519-833-9158; *Fax:* 519-833-9845
pql@sentex.net
www.sentex.net/~pql
ISBNs: ISBN: 0-88984; SAN: 115-0820
Small publishing house, Publishers of Canadian poetry & literature
Tim Inkster, Publisher
Elke Inkster, Publisher

Portage & Main Press
#100, 318 McDermot Ave., Winnipeg, MB R3A 0A2
Tel: 204-987-3500; *Fax:* 866-734-8477
Toll-Free: 800-667-9673
books@pandmpress.com
www.portageandmainpress.com
ISBNs: ISBN: 0-919566, 1-89110, 1-895411, 1-55379
Publishers of educational books & resources for teachers
Catherine Gerbosi, President

Potlatch Publications Limited
30 Berryhill Ave., Waterdown, ON L0R 2H4
Tel: 905-689-2104; *Fax:* 905-689-1632
robtnielsen@aol.com
www.angelfire.com/on3/potlatch
ISBNs: ISBN: 0-919676; SAN: 115-1355
Robert Nielsen, President

Pottersfield Press
83 Leslie Rd., East Lawrencetown, NS B2Z 1P8
Tel: 902-827-4517; *Fax:* 902-455-3652
Toll-Free: 800-646-2879
www.pottersfieldpress.com
ISBNs: ISBN: 0-919001, 1-895900; SAN: 115-0790
Publishers of a number of non-fiction books, including local history & geography; memoirs; & biographies
Lesley Choyce

Power Engineering Books Ltd.
7 Perron St., St Albert, AB T8N 1E3
Tel: 780-458-3155; *Fax:* 780-460-2530
Toll-Free: 800-667-3155
sales@powerengbooks.com
www.powerengbooks.com
ISBNs: SAN: 115-4850
Andrew Benko

Prairie House Books
PO Box 84007 Market Mall, Calgary, AB T3A 5C4
Tel: 403-202-5438; *Fax:* 403-202-5437
phbooks@telusplanet.net
ISBNs: ISBN: 1-895012
Wayne Magnuson, Editor/Publisher

Prentice-Hall Canada Inc.
26 Prince Andrew Place, Don Mills, ON M3C 2T8
Tel: 416-447-5101; *Fax:* 416-443-0948
cdn_ordr@prenhall.com
www.pearsoncanada.ca
ISBNs: 9780137149445; 9780205608171
A Pearson Canada (Pearson Education) imprint.
MR Allan T. Reynolds, President & CEO, Pearson Canada

The Press of the Nova Scotia College of Art & Design
5163 Duke St., Halifax, NS B3J 3J6
Tel: 902-444-9600; *Fax:* 902-425-2420
thepress@nscad.ns.ca
www.nscad.ns.ca/press/press_relaunched.php
ISBNs: ISBN: 0-919616
Publishers of scholarly works in the fields of contemporary art, craft & design

Susan McEachern, Editorial Director

Les Presses de l'Université de Montréal
306, rue Saint-Zotique est, Montréal, QC H2S 1L6
Tél: 514-343-6933; *Téléc:* 514-343-2232
pum@umontreal.ca
www.pum.umontreal.ca
ISBNs: ISBN: 2-7606
A pour mandat le diffusion des résultats de la recherche universitaire (livres, revues, édition électronique); la transférence des connaissances scientifiques à un large public; participation à la vie de la Cité; et contribution au rayonnement national et international de l'Université de Montréal
Antoine Del Busso, Directeur général, delbussa@pum.umontreal.ca

Presses de l'Université du Québec
Édifice Le Delta 1, #450, 2875, boul Laurier, Sainte-Foy, QC G1V 2M2
Tél: 418-657-4399; *Téléc:* 418-657-2096
Ligne sans frais: 800-859-7474
puq@puq.ca
www.puq.ca
ISBNs: ISBN: 0-7770, 2-7605, 2-920073
Céline Fournier, Directrice générale, 4186574399
Micheline Auger, Secrétaire de direction, 4186574399
Bianca Drapeau, Directrice du marketing, 4186574075 x.224, bianca.drapeau@puq.ca

Les Presses de l'Université Laval
#3103, Pavillon Maurice-Pollack, 2305, rue de l'Université, Québec, QC G1V 0A6
Tél: 418-656-2803; *Téléc:* 418-656-3305
Ligne sans frais: 800-859-7474
presses@pul.ulaval.ca
www.pulaval.com
ISBNs: ISBN: 2-7637, 2-89224
Ouvrages didactiques, manuels, travaux savants; diffuseur et distributeur
Denis Dion, Directeur général, denis.dion@pul.ulaval.ca
Louise Saint-Michel, Secrétaire, louise.saint-michel@pul.ulaval.ca

Presses Inter Universitaires
PO Box 36, Cap-Rouge, QC G1Y 3C6
Tel: 418-657-6050; *Fax:* 418-657-7630
ISBNs: ISBN: 2-89441

The Prince Edward Island Museum & Heritage Foundation
2 Kent St., Charlottetown, PE C1A 1M6
Tel: 902-368-6600; *Fax:* 902-368-6608
mhpei@gov.pe.ca
www.peimuseum.com
ISBNs: ISBN: 0-920434

Probe International
225 Brunswick Ave., Toronto, ON M5S 2M6
Tel: 416-964-9223; *Fax:* 416-964-8239
www.probeinternational.org
ISBNs: ISBN: 0-919849, 1-85383, 0-7656

Productive Publications
#1210, 1930 Yonge St., Toronto, ON M4S 1Z4
Tel: 416-483-0634; *Fax:* 416-322-7434
productivepublications@rogers.com
www.productivepublications.ca
ISBNs: ISBN: 0-920847, 1-896210, 1-55270; SAN: 117-1712
Iain Williamson, Owner

Prosveta Inc.
3950 Albert Mines, North Hatley, QC J0B 2C0
Tel: 819-564-8212; *Fax:* 819-564-1823
Toll-Free: 800-854-8212
prosveta@prosveta-canada.com
www.prosveta-canada.com
ISBNs: ISBN: 1-895978
Publishers of books related to philosophy & meditation authored by Omraam Mikhael Aivanhov
Huguette Paquin, Vice-Presidente

Psycan Corporation
#12, 120 West Beaver Creek Rd., Richmond Hill, ON L4B 1L2
Tel: 905-731-8795; *Fax:* 905-731-5029
Toll-Free: 800-263-3558
mail@psycan.com
www.psycan.com
Family-owned & operated publisher of eductional & clinical resources

Ptarmigan Press
1372 - 16th Ave., Campbell River, BC V9W 2E1
Tel: 250-286-0878; *Fax:* 250-286-9749
info@kaskgraphics.com
www.kaskgraphics.com/ptarmigan/
ISBNs: ISBN: 0-919537; SAN: 116-0281
Small publishing house; Publisher of non-fiction covering Fishing; Hiking; Local history; Autobiography; Cooking; How To; Health; Sexual Abuse
Ann Kask

Public Works & Government Services Canada - Depository Services Program / Travaux public et services gouvernement aux Canada - Progra
350 Albert St., 4th Fl., Ottawa, ON K1A 0S5
Tel: 613-993-1695; *Fax:* 613-941-2410
dsp-psd@pwgsc.gc.ca
dsp-psd.pwgsc.gc.ca
ISBNs: ISBN: 0-662, 0-660; SAN: 115-2882
Publishes federal government publications and distribute them to oublic & academic libraries.
Christine Leduc, Director, 6139965959

Publications Ontario
50 Grosvenor St., Toronto, ON M7A 1N8
Tel: 416-326-5300; *Fax:* 416-613-566
Toll-Free: 800-668-9938
www.publications.serviceontario.ca
ISBNs: ISBN: 0-7743, 0-7729, 0-7778
Publishers of government publications, including driver's handbook, fire codes, building codes, agricultural publications, employment standards & occupational health & safety
Marg Munro, Manager
Eric Steeves, Director

Publishers Group Canada
#402, 559 College St., Toronto, ON M6G 1A9
Tel: 416-934-9900; *Fax:* 416-934-1410
Toll-Free: 800-747-8147
graham@pgcbooks.ca
www.pgcbooks.ca
ISBNs: SAN: 117-0171
Distributors of a large number of non-fiction, fiction & children's books for a large number of publishers.
Graham Fidler, Exec. Vice-President, ext. 203, graham@pgcbooks.ca
Suzanne Wice, Director, Sales & Marketing, ext. 207, suzanne@pgcbooks.ca

Purich Publishing Ltd.
PO Box 23032 Market Mall, Saskatoon, SK S7J 5H3
Tel: 306-373-5311; *Fax:* 306-373-5315
purich@sasktel.net
www.purichpublishing.com
ISBNs: ISBN: 1-895830
Publishers of books dealing with Aboriginal & Social Justice Issues; Law & Western Canadian History; Focus on the university, college & reference market
K. Bolstad
D. Purich

Quarry Press
20 Hatter St., Kingston, ON K7M 2L5
Tel: 613-548-8429; *Fax:* 613-548-1556
ISBNs: ISBN: 0-919627, 1-55082; SAN: 115-4958
Bob Hilderley, Publisher

Québec dans le Monde
CP 8503 Sainte-Foy, #404, 1001, route de l'Eglise, Québec, QC G1V 4N5
Tél: 418-659-5540; *Téléc:* 418-659-4143
info@quebecmonde.com
www.quebecmonde.com
ISBNs: ISBN: 2-921309, 2-89525, 2-9801130; SAN: 116-8657
Denis Turcotte, Directeur général

Québec Science Éditeur
#300, 4388, rue St-Denis, Montréal, QC H2J 2L1
Tél: 514-843-6888; *Téléc:* 514-843-4897
courrier@quebecscience.qc.ca
www.cybersciences.com
ISBNs: ISBN: 2-920073
Jean-Yves Poirier, jypoirier@velo.qc.ca
Raymond Lemieux, Rédacteur en chef

Quill & Quire
111 Queen St. East, Toronto, ON M5C 1S2
Tel: 416-364-3333; *Fax:* 416-595-5415
www.quillandquire.com
Publishers of directories of publishers

Quintin Publishers / Éditions Michel Quintin
PO Box 340, 4770, rue Foster, Waterloo, QC J0E 2N0
Tel: 450-539-3774; *Fax:* 450-539-4905
info@editionsmichelquintin.ca
www.editionsmichelquintin.ca
ISBNs: ISBN: 2-920438, 2-89435; SAN: 116-5356
Michel Quintin, Président-directeur général
Johanne Ménard, Édition scientifique, jmenard@editionsmichelquintin.ca
Mélanie Roy, Coordonnatrice, production, info@editionsmichelquintin.ca

R.G. Mitchell Family Books Inc.
565 Gordon Baker Rd., Toronto, ON M2H 2W2
Tel: 416-499-4615; *Fax:* 416-499-6340
Toll-Free: 800-268-3445
info@rgm.ca
www.rgm.ca
ISBNs: SAN: 168-4604
David Freeland, President
Keith Chesire, Chair

Rainbird Press
4890 Mackenzie St., Vancouver, BC V6L 2R6
Tel: 604-224-4756; *Fax:* 604-224-4740
michaelbullock@hotmail.com
m_bullock.tripod.com
ISBNs: ISBN: 0-9690504, 0-9684894
Publishers of the poetry of Michael Bullock.
Lori-Ann Latremouille

Raincoast Books Distribution Ltd.
9050 Shaughnessy St., Vancouver, BC V6P 6E5
Tel: 604-323-7100; *Fax:* 604-323-2600
Toll-Free: 800-663-5714
info@raincoast.com
www.raincoast.com
ISBNs: ISBN: 0-920417, 1-895714, 1-55192, 1-896095, 0-919591; SAN 115
Full-service book distributor and former publisher (Publishing operations closed in January of 2008).
Allan MacDougall, President/CEO

Rand McNally Canada Inc.
90A Royal Crest Ct., Markham, ON L3R 9X6
Tel: 905-477-8480; *Fax:* 905-477-7408
Toll-Free: 800-205-6277
customerservicecanada@randmcnally.com
www.randmcnally.ca
ISBNs: ISBN: 0-88640
Publishers of maps and atlases

Random House of Canada Ltd.
#300, 1 Toronto St., Toronto, ON M5C 2V6
Tel: 416-364-4449; *Fax:* 416-364-6863
ISBNs: ISBN: 0-394, 0-679; SAN: 115-088X
Louise Dennys, Vice-President

Random House of Canada Ltd.
2775 Matheson Blvd. East, Mississauga, ON L4W 4P7
Tel: 905-624-0672; *Fax:* 905-624-6217
Toll-Free: 800-668-4247
www.randomhouse.com
ISBNs: ISBN: 0-394, 0-679 0-449, 0-553 0-385 0-7704, 0-676; SAN: 201-
Large publisher of best-selling & award-winning books; distributor of many international authors
Brad Martin, President & COO
David Kent, Publisher
Katheleen Bain, Vice-President, Sales & Marketing

Reach for Unbleached!
Attn. D. Broten, PO Box 39, Whaletown, BC V0P 1Z0
Tel: 250-935-6992;
dbroten@rfu.org
www.rfu.org
ISBNs: 0-9680431
Publishers of environmental education material about paper & pulp mill monitoring

Reader's Digest Association (Canada) Ltd.
1100, boul René Levesque ouest, Montréal, QC H3B 5H5
Tel: 514-940-0751; *Fax:* 514-940-3637
Toll-Free: 866-736-3382
trade@readersdigest.ca
www.readersdigest.ca
ISBNs: ISBN: 0-88850; SAN 115-0898, 115-4974
Andrea C. Martin, President/CEO

Red Deer Press
#1512, 1800 - 4th St. SW, Calgary, AB T2S 2S5
Tel: 403-509-0800; *Fax:* 403-228-6503
rdp@reddeerpress.com
www.reddeerpress.com

ISBNs: ISBN: 0-88995; SAN: 115-0871
Publishes picture books, junior, juvenile, Young Adult fiction and non-fiction and adult non-fiction titles
Richard Dionne, Publisher, 4035090804, dionne@reddeerpress.com
Peter Carver, Children's Editor

Reference Press
PO Box 70, Teeswater, ON N0G 2S0
Tel: 519-392-6634; *Fax:* 519-392-6634
refpress@wcl.on.ca
www.libris.ca/refpress
ISBNs: ISBN: 0-919981; SAN: 115-687X
Publisher of Canadian reference materials & software for use in school & public libraries
Gordon Ripley

Reflections
PO Box 178, Gabriola, BC V0R 1X0
Tel: 250-247-8685
ISBNs: ISBN: 0-9692570

Renouf Publishing Co. Ltd. / Éditions Renouf limitées
#1, 5369 Canotek Rd., Ottawa, ON K1J 9J3
Tel: 613-745-2665; *Fax:* 613-745-7660
Toll-Free: 866-767-6766
orders@renoufbooks.com
www.renoufbooks.com
ISBNs: ISBN: 0-88852; SAN: 170-8066
Publishers of over 35 international organizations' publiations & documents
Gordon Grahame, President
Avrum Kerzner, Comptroller
Brigid Grahame, General Manager

Repository Press
Comp. 8, Site 29, RR#7, Prince George, BC V2N 2J5
Tel: 250-562-7074; *Fax:* 250-561-7094
harris@cnc.bc.ca
ISBNs: ISBN: 0-920104; SAN: 115-5016
John Harris, Publisher/Editor
Joanne Armstrong, Marketing

The Resource Centre Inc.
PO Box 190, Waterloo, ON N2J 3Z9
Tel: 519-885-0826; *Fax:* 519-747-5629
Toll-Free: 800-923-0330
sales@theresourcecentre.com
www.theresourcecentre.com
ISBNs: ISBN: 0-920701; SAN: 115-5032
Publishers of educational resources, including books on ESL, Language & Writing among other subjects
N. Gridgeman, President

Revue Cap-aux-Diamants
CP 26 Haute-Ville, #2113, 1, côte de la Fabrique, Québec, QC G1R 4M8
Tél: 418-656-5040; *Téléc:* 418-656-7282
revue.cap-aux-diamants@hst.ulaval.ca
www.capauxdiamants.org
ISBNs: ISBN: 2-920069
Yves Beauregard

River City Press
PO Box 752, Sarnia, ON N7T 7J7
Tel: 519-344-5284; *Fax:* 519-344-5284
ISBNs: ISBN: 0-920940
Mel Cameron

Riverwood Publishers Ltd.
471 Eagle St., Newmarket, ON L3Y 1K7
Tel: 905-853-8887; *Fax:* 905-853-3330
Toll-Free: 800-561-2674
info@riverwoodpub.com
www.riverwoodpub.com
ISBNs: ISBN: 1-895121; SAN: 116-1288
Publishers of children's books & Canadian distributors of Usborne Books, a respected children's book publisher.
Ron Charlesworth, President

Robert Davies Multimedia Publishing / Éditions multimedia Robert Davies inc.
9 Parkside Pl., Montréal, QC H3Z 1T3
Tel: 514-934-5433; *Fax:* 514-937-8765
Toll-Free: 800-481-2440
rdppub@rdppub.com
www.rdppub.com
ISBNs: ISBN: 1-895854, 1-55207, 2-89019, 2-89462
Robert Davies, Publisher

Robert Rose Inc.
120 Eglington Ave. E, Toronto, ON M4P 1E2
Tel: 416-322-6552; *Fax:* 416-322-6936
www.fireflybooks.com/RR.html
ISBNs: ISBN: 1-896503, 0-7788
Publishers of cookbooks; Distributed by Firefly Books
Robert J. Dees

Robin Brass Studio Inc.
PO Box 335 R, Montréal, QC H2S 2R0
Tel: 514-272-7463; *Fax:* 514-272-7971
rbrass@sympatico.ca
www.rbstudiobooks.com
ISBNs: ISBN: 1-896941; SAN: 115-5040
Small publishing house producing primarily non-fiction, especially within the area of military history & other Canadian history; Also designs and produces books under contract for other publishers & organizations

Rocky Mountain Books
#108, 17665 - 66A Ave., Surrey, BC V3S 2A7
Tel: 604-574-7067; *Toll-Free:* 800-665-3302
distribution@heritagehouse.ca
www.rmbooks.com
ISBNs: ISBN: 0-921102; SAN: 115-5040
Publisher of outdoor activity guidebooks, historical accounts of Canadian mountaineering and other adventures, biographies & related non-fiction
Tony Daffern, Publisher

Ronsdale Press
3350 West 21st Ave., Vancouver, BC V6S 1G7
Tel: 604-738-4688; *Fax:* 604-731-4548
ronsdale@shaw.ca
www.ronsdalepress.com
ISBNs: ISBN: 0-921870, 1-55380; SAN: 116-2454
Publishers of fiction, poetry, regional history, biography and autobiography, books of ideas about Canada, as well as children's books; Presently has roughly 140 books in print.
Ronald B. Hatch, Director

Roseway Publishing Co. Ltd.
32 Oceanvista Lane, Site 2A, Box 5, Black Point, NS B0T 1B0
Tel: 902-857-1388; *Fax:* 902-857-1328
info@rosewaypublishing.ca
www.rosewaypublishing.com, www.selfpublishingspecialists.com
ISBNs: ISBN: 0-9694180, 1-896496
Small publishing house; Publishes plays & fiction & non-fiction books of local interest
Kathleen K. Tudor, Owner/Manager

Routledge/Taylor & Francis Books
#2102, 110 Erskine Ave., Toronto, ON M4P 1Y4
Tel: 416-482-4562; *Fax:* 416-482-3043
probinson@taylorandfrancis.com
www.routledge-ny.com
ISBNs: ISBN: 0-415, 0-87830
Publishers of educational & academic resources for the college/university market
Colin Jones, President

Rowland & Jacob Inc.
52 Hazelton Ave., Toronto, ON M5R 2E2
Tel: 416-921-9557; *Fax:* 416-921-0408
ISBNs: ISBN: 0-921430
Publishers of travel guides for major Canadian cities

The Rowman & Littlefield Publishing Group
Canadian Sales Office, 10 Cushendun Rd., Toronto, ON M1E 2B3
Tel: 416-282-3592;
donmacivor@rogers.com
www.rowmanlittlefield.com
Canadian sales office for large international publisher focusing on non-fiction books for the academic market

The Royal Astronomical Society of Canada
136 Dupont St., Toronto, ON M5R 1V2
Tel: 416-924-7973; *Fax:* 416-924-2911
Toll-Free: 844-626-2665
mempub10001@rasc.ca
www.rasc.ca
Publishes journals and guides to astronomy
Jo Taylor, Membership & Publications Clerk

Rubicon Publishing Inc.
PO Box 69596, Oakville, ON L6J 7R4
Tel: 905-849-8777; *Fax:* 905-849-7579
contact@rubiconpublishing.com
www.rubiconpublishing.com
ISBNs: ISBN: 0-921156; SAN: 115-432X
Publisher of educational resources for students and educators for grades K-12.
Kimberley Wulf
Maggie Goh

Safety Sense Enterprises
PO Box 9512 T, Ottawa, ON K1G 3V2
Tel: 613-830-9342; *Fax:* 613-830-4284
ISBNs: ISBN: 0-9695568
Hon. Heward Graffley, President/CEO

Salal Press
PO Box 36060, Victoria, BC V9A 7J5
Tel: 250-384-0305; *Fax:* 250-384-0351
salal@horizon.bc.ca
ISBNs: ISBN: 1-894012
Small publisher of novels and non-fiction books
Clare Thorbes

Sandhill Publishing
#4, 3308 Appaloosa Rd., Kelowna, BC V1V 2G9
Tel: 250-491-1446; *Fax:* 250-491-4066
Toll-Free: 800-667-3848
info@sandhillbooks.com
www.sandhillbooks.com
ISBNs: ISBN: 0-920923; SAN: 115-2181
Distributor for Small Press & Independent Publishers
Nancy Wise

Saunders Book Company
PO Box 308, 199 Campbell St., Collingwood, ON L9Y 3Z7
Tel: 705-445-4777; *Fax:* 705-445-9569
Toll-Free: 800-461-9120
info@saundersbook.ca
www.saundersbook.ca
ISBNs: SAN: 169-9768
Publishers of books for educational books & fiction for K-12 schools & libraries
John Saunders, President
James Saunders, Sales, james.saunders@saundersbook.ca

Saxon House Canada
PO Box 6947 A, Toronto, ON M5W 1X6
Tel: 416-488-7171; *Fax:* 416-488-2989
ISBNs: ISBN: 0-9693934
Publishers of history books
W.H. Wallace, General Manager

Scholar's Choice
PO Box 7214, 2323 Trafalgar St., London, ON N5Y 5S7
Tel: 519-453-7470; *Fax:* 519-455-2853
Toll-Free: 800-265-1095
sales@scholarschoice.ca
www.scholarschoice.ca
ISBNs: ISBN: 0-88809; SAN: 170-0014
Publisher & retailer of educational materials
Scott Webster, President
Cindy Webster, Executive Vice-President

Scholastic Canada Ltd. / Éditions Scholastic
175 Hillmount Rd., Markham, ON L6C 1Z7
Tel: 905-887-7323; *Fax:* 905-887-1131
custsev@scholastic.ca
www.scholastic.ca
ISBNs: ISBN: 0-590; SAN: 115-5164
Leading publishers & distributors of children's books & educational materials in French & English
Iole Lucchese, Co-President
Linda Goswell, Co-President

School Book Fairs Limited
2201 Dunwin Dr., Mississauga, ON L5L 1X2
Tel: 905-828-6620; *Fax:* 905-828-2761
Toll-Free: 800-268-4557
sbf@sbfmedia.com
www.sbfmedia.com
ISBNs: ISBN: 0-921932; SAN 115-5083
Publisher & distributor of mass market & trade paperbacks for schools; Also publish educational resource books

Script Publishing Inc.
#200, 839 - 5th Ave. SW, Calgary, AB T2P 3C8
Tel: 403-547-3400; *Fax:* 403-241-8575
ISBNs: ISBN: 0-9694287, 1-896015
Publishers of scripts & plays
P. Douglas McArthur, President

Second Story Press
#401, 20 Maud St., Toronto, ON M5S 2R4
Tel: 416-537-7850; *Fax:* 416-537-0588
info@secondstorypress.ca
www.secondstorypress.on.ca
ISBNs: ISBN: 0-929005, 1-896764; SAN: 115-1134
Publishers of roughly 8 titles per sesaon, spanning adult fiction & non-fiction; children's fiction, non-fiction & picture books; Young

Adult fiction & non-fiction. Special interest areas include Judaica, Ability Issues, Coping with Cancer & Queer rights
Margie Wolf, President

Self-Counsel Press Ltd.
1481 Charlotte Rd., North Vancouver, BC V7J 1H1
Tel: 604-986-3366; *Fax:* 604-986-3947
Toll-Free: 800-663-3007
www.self-counsel.com
ISBNs: ISBN: 0-88908, 1-55180; SAN: 115-0545
Publisher of self-help law books & books for small business
Diana R. Douglas, President

September Dreams Publishing
PO Box 44085 Southcentre PO, 9419 Fairmount Dr. SE, Calgary, AB T2J 7C5
Tel: 403-519-7418;
viktor@septemberdreams.com
www.septemberdreams.com
ISBNs: ISBN: 0-9695763
Publishers of four books covering business, computer, humour & lifestyle
Viktor E. Oey
Rudy W. Oey

Septembre éditeur inc.
CP 9425 Sainte-Foy, 2825, ch des Quatre-Bourgeois, Québec, QC G1V 4B8
Tél: 418-658-7272; *Téléc:* 418-652-0986
Ligne sans frais: 800-361-7755
serviceclientele@septembre.com
www.septembre.com
ISBNs: ISBN: 2-930433, 2-89471
Matériel didactique; éducation; emplois; formation; littérature jeunesse; management; ressources humaines; métiers; orientation; outils pédagogiques
Martin Rochette, Président-directeur général

Services documentaires multimedia inc.
#620, 5650, rue d'Iberville, Montréal, QC H2GH3L 3T1
Tél: 514-382-0895; *Téléc:* 514-384-9139
informations@sdm.qc.ca
www.sdm.qc.ca
ISBNs: ISBN: 2-89059, 0-88523
Denis Lévesque, Directeur Général
Claude Jourdain, Direction de l'info. et du dév. tech.
Diane Dallaire-Talbot, Directrice, l'Exploration

Servidec
50 Main St., Ottawa, ON K1S 1B2
Tel: 613-237-5577; *Fax:* 613-230-1762
Toll-Free: 800-265-0375

Shard Press
102 Garnet Ave., Toronto, ON M6G 1V7
Tel: 416-538-2679; *Fax:* 416-538-2679
kyril@shard.com
www.shard.com
ISBNs: ISBN: 0-9696455
Cyril Chen

Sheltus & Picard Inc.
CP 1321, Bedford, QC J0J 1A0
Tél: 450-248-7319; *Téléc:* 450-248-2057
cp.jas.rm@acbm.net
ISBNs: ISBN: 0-9696296
Small publisher specializing in local history
J.A. Sheltus, President/CEO
C. Picard, Vice-President & Editor

Shoreline Press
23, rue Sainte-Anne, Sainte-Anne-de-Bellevue, QC H9X 1L1
Tel: 514-457-5733; *Fax:* 514-457-5733
shoreline@sympatico.ca
www.shorelinepress.ca
ISBNs: ISBN: 0-9695180, 0-9698752, 1-896754; SAN 116-9564
Independent press publishing specializing in memoirs & titles of local interest
Judy Isherwood, Owner & Publisher

Sierra Club Books
85 Second St., 2nd Fl., San Francisco, CA
Tel: 415-977-5500; *Fax:* 415-977-5799
booksinfo@sierraclub.org
www.sc.org/books/

Signature Editions
PO Box 206 Corydon, Winnipeg, MB R3M 3S7
Tel: 204-779-7803; *Fax:* 204-779-6970
signature@allstream.net
www.signature-editions.com
ISBNs: ISBN: 0-921833, 1-897109; SAN: 115-0723
Karen Haughian, Publisher

Simon & Schuster Canada
#600, 625 Cochrane Dr., Markham, ON L3R 9R9
Tel: 905-943-9942; *Fax:* 905-943-9026
Toll-Free: 800-268-3216
info@simonandschuster.ca
www.simonsayscanada.com
ISBNs: ISBN: 1-55525, 0-38224, 0-945299; SAN: 115-4788
Publishers of a large catalog of books covering all aspects of fiction & non-fiction
Deborah Woods, President
Susan Stoddart, Chair

Simply Read Books Inc.
#501, 5525 West Blvd., Vancouver, BC V6M 3W6
Tel: 604-727-2960; *Fax:* 604-263-5707
info@simplyreadbooks.com
www.simplyreadbooks.com
Publishers of fiction for children & young adults

Sinai Multi-lingual Books
7356 Ontario St., Vancouver, BC V5X 3B8
Tel: 604-327-6694; *Fax:* 604-327-6694
info@booksm.com
www.booksm.com
ISBNs: ISBN: 1-896277
Publishes books in English, French, Arabic, Chinese, German, Russian & Spanish
Cynthia Wong

Singing Shield Productions
104 Ray Blvd., Thunder Bay, ON P7B 4C4
Tel: 807-344-8355; *Fax:* 807-344-8355
pebarr@tbaytel.net
ISBNs: ISBN: 0-9691717; SAN: 115-5784
Elinor Barr

Sister Vision Press
101 Dewson St., Toronto, ON M6H 1H4
Tel: 416-533-9353
ISBNs: ISBN: 0-920813, 1-896705
Stephanie Martin
Makeda Silvera

Snowapple Press
PO Box 66024 Heritage, Edmonton, AB T6J 6T4
Tel: 403-437-0191; *Fax:* 403-437-0191
ISBNs: ISBN: 1-895592
Guy Tessier, Publisher

Socadis Inc.
420, rue Stinson, Ville Saint-Laurent, QC H4N 3L7
Tel: 514-331-3300; *Fax:* 514-745-3282
Toll-Free: 800-361-2847
socinfo@socadis.com
www.socadis.com

Society to Overcome Pollution
716 St. Ferdinand, Montréal, QC H4C 2T2
Tel: 514-932-7267

Sound & Vision Publishing Ltd.
#103, 109 Beech Ave., Toronto, ON M4E 3H5
www.soundandvision.com
ISBNs: ISBN: 0-920151; SAN: 115-0979
Publishers of books about contemporary music & music history
Geoff Savage, Publisher

Southwest Québec Publishing
PO Box 539, 27, rue Prince, 2e étage, Huntingdon, QC J0S 1H0
Tel: 450-264-6200; *Fax:* 450-264-5387
ISBNs: ISBN: 1-895656
Maurice J. King, President
Janet Hicks, Editor

Spindrift Publishing
PO Box 50, Barrington, NS B0W 1E0
Tel: 902-637-2569; *Fax:* 902-637-2324
ISBNs: ISBN: 0-9691458
Hattie Perry, Publisher

Statistics Canada
c/o Circulation Management, 120 Parkdale Ave., Ottawa, ON K1A 0T6
Tel: 613-951-7277; *Fax:* 613-951-1584
Toll-Free: 800-700-1033
order@statcan.ca
www.statcan.ca
ISBNs: ISBN: 0-660, 0-662
Publishes research and information conducted by Statistics Canada

Steller Press Ltd.
#13, 4335 West 10 Ave., Vancouver, BC V6R 2H6
Tel: 604-222-2955; *Fax:* 604-222-2965
info@stellerpress.com
www.stellerpress.com
ISBNs: ISBN: 1-894143
Regional publisher; focusing on books for the Pacific Northwest & Lower Mainland
Steve Paton

Stoneycroft Publishing
PO Box 1710, RR#1, Yarmouth, NS B5A 4A5
Tel: 902-742-2667;
stuarttrask@eastlink.ca
ISBNs: ISBN: 1-896269
Gwen G. Trask

Studio Word
228 Park Ridge Cl., Camrose, AB T4V 4P1
Tel: 780-672-2551; *Fax:* 780-672-5887
studioword@studioword.com
www.studioword.com
ISBNs: ISBN: 0-969, 0-968, 1-894361
Publishes training manuals for popular software applications
Lois Larson, Owner

Subway Books Ltd.
#203, 1819 Pendrell St., Vancouver, BC V6G 1T3
Tel: 604-488-1388
ISBNs: ISBN: 0-9681660
Publishes books on social issues, non-fiction topics, biographies & poetry

Sumach Press
#202, 1415 Bathurst St., Toronto, ON M5R 3H8
Tel: 416-531-6250; *Fax:* 416-531-3892
info@sumachpress.com
www.sumachpress.com
ISBNs: ISBN: 1-894549, 1-896764, 0-929005; SAN: 115-1134
Publishers of feminist writing
Lois Pike

Summerthought Publishing
PO Box 2309, Banff, AB T1L 1C1
Tel: 403-762-0531; *Fax:* 403-762-3095
info@summerthought.com
www.summerthought.com
ISBNs: ISBN: 0-919934; SAN: 115-2149
Publisher of the Canadian Rockies Trail Guide
Andrew Hempstead, Publisher

Summit Educational Services
PO Box 149, Richmond Hill, ON L4C 4X9
Tel: 905-883-9427; *Fax:* 905-770-8576
Toll-Free: 800-741-5956
admin@summit-ed.com
www.summit-ed.com
ISBNs: ISBN: 1-895187
Arlene Marks, President

Sun-Scape Enterprises Ltd.
290 Healey Rd., Bolton, ON L7E 1C9
Tel: 905-951-3155; *Fax:* 905-951-9712
ISBNs: ISBN: 0-919842
Kenneth George Mills

Talon Books Ltd.
PO Box 2076, 278 East 1st Ave., Vancouver, BC V6B 3S3
Tel: 604-444-4889; *Fax:* 604-444-4119
info@talonbooks.com
www.talonbooks.com
ISBNs: ISBN: 0-88922; SAN: 115-5334; Telebook: S1150391
Publishers specializing in poetry, drama & literary criticism. Also publishes fiction & non-fiction
Karl Siegler, President
Christy Siegler, Marketing & Promotion
Kevin Williams, Sales & Marketing Coordinator, kevin@talonbooks.com
Gregory Gibson, Production Coordinator, production@talonbooks.com

Tanager Press
145 Troy St., Mississauga, ON L5G 1S8
contact@tanagerpress.com
www.tanagerpress.com
ISBNs: ISBN: 1-895410
Publishes resources for those learning guitar & musical theory
N. Ledwidge
J. Neveleff

Tangled Web Audio
#133, 1063 King St. West, Hamilton, ON L8S 1L8
Tel: 905-522-5349; *Fax:* 905-522-0711
ISBNs: ISBN: 1-896552

Tantalas Books
PO Box 255, 10 Towers Ave., Gander, NL A1V 1W6
Tel: 709-656-8833; *Fax:* 709-651-3849
ISBNs: ISBN: 0-9695519

Taylor & Francis
325 Chestnut St., 8th Fl., Philadelphia, PA
Tel: 215-625-8900; *Fax:* 215-625-2940

TechnoKids Inc.
1282A Cornwall Rd., Oakville, ON L6J 7W5
Tel: 905-631-9112; *Fax:* 905-631-9113
Toll-Free: 800-221-7921
information@technokids.com
www.technokids.com
ISBNs: ISBN: 1-894995
Publisher of technology cirriculum for schools

Temeron Books Inc.
#210, 1220 Kensington Rd. NW, Calgary, AB T2N 3P5
Tel: 403-283-0900; *Fax:* 403-283-6947
temeron@telusplanet.net
www.temerondetselig.com
ISBNs: ISBN: 1-895510, 1-55059, 0-920490; SAN: 115-0324
Publishers of educational resources in the fields of psychology, social & political science; history, biography & memoirs; Health; K9 Training & Information; Living & Social Interaction
T.E. Giles, President

Ten Speed Press
c/o Hornblower Books, #1202, 200 Woolner Ave., Toronto, ON M6N 1Y4
Tel: 416-461-7973; *Fax:* 416-461-0365
Toll-Free: 800-404-4446
alan@tenspeed.ca
www.tenspeed.com/canada.htm
ISBNs: ISBN: 0-89815, 1-58008, 0-89087, 1-883672, 1-58246, 1-58761

Terrific Titles for Young Readers
52 Hazelton Ave, Toronto, ON M5R 2E2
Tel: 416-921-9557

Theytus Books
Green Mountain Rd., Lot 45, RR#2, Comp. 8, Site 50, Penticton, BC V2A 6J7
Tel: 250-493-7181; *Fax:* 250-493-5302
info@thaytusbooks.ca
www.theytusbooks.ca
ISBNs: ISBN: 0-919441, 1-894778; SAN: 115-1517
Aboriginal-owned & operated publishing house; Focus is on publishing books of Aboriginal literature, children's books, history, culture, politics & educational materials
Anita Large, Publishing Manager

Thistledown Press Ltd.
633 Main St., Saskatoon, SK S7H 0J8
Tel: 306-244-1722; *Fax:* 306-244-1762
tdpress@thistledownpress.com
www.thistledownpress.com/
ISBNs: ISBN: 0-920066, 1-894345, 0-920633, 1-895449
Publishes poetry & fiction for adults & young adults by Canadian writers; Also publishes resources for teachers
Allan Forrie, Publisher, editorial@thistledownpress.com
Jackie Forrie, Publishing & Production Manager, tdpress@thistledownpress.com
Taylor Leedahl, Promotions Manager, taylor.leedahl@thistledownpress.com
Kathy Painchaud, Marketing, marketing@thistledownpress.com

Thomas Allen & Son Ltd.
390 Steelcase Rd. East, Markham, ON L3R 1G2
Tel: 905-475-9126; *Fax:* 905-475-4255
Toll-Free: 800-458-5504
info@t-allen.com
www.thomas-allen.com
ISBNs: ISBN: 0-919028, 088762; SAN: 115-1762
Publishers of award-winning bestsellers; Publish a small, highly-focused list of no more than 10-12 books a year, both fiction & non-fiction
T.J. Allen

Thompson Educational Publishing, Inc.
20 Ripley Ave., Toronto, ON M6S 3N9
Tel: 416-766-2763; *Fax:* 416-766-0398
Toll-Free: 877-366-2763
publisher@thompsonbooks.com
www.thompsonbooks.com
ISBNs: ISBN: 1-55077; SAN: 115-0391
Publishes educational texts in the social sciences & humanities
Keith Thompson, President

Tikka Books
PO Box 203, Chambly, QC J3L 4B3
Tel: 450-658-6205;
leila@tikkabooks.com
www.tikkabooks.com
ISBNs: ISBN: 1-896106; 0-921993
Independent publishing house
Leila Pelposaari, Publisher

Timeless Books
#423, 215 Spadina Ave., Toronto, ON M5T 2C7
Tel: 416-644-1030; *Fax:* 416-644-0116
contact@timeless.org
www.timeless.org
ISBNs: ISBN: 0-931454, 2-9044616
Publishers of teachings on yoga, including poetry & spiritual biography; Also publishes classic books & audio
Andrew Wedman, Publisher, andrew@timeless.org
Clea McDougall, Editor, clea@timeless.org
Kendra Ward, Managing Editor, kendra@timeless.org

Times Mirror Professional Publishing
130 Flaska Dr., Markham, ON L6G 1B8
Tel: 905-470-6739; *Fax:* 905-470-0050
ISBNs: ISBN: 0-8016; SAN: 115-4389

TouchWood Editions Ltd.
Editorial & Marketing, #6, 356 Simcoe St., Victoria, BC V8V 1L1
Tel: 250-360-0829; *Fax:* 250-385-0829
info@touchwoodeditions.com
www.touchwoodeditions.com
ISBNs: ISBN: 0-920663, 1-894898
Publishes books with a focus on history, historical fiction, biography, food, nautical subjects, mysteries & art/architecture
Pat Touchie, President

Tradewind Books
#202, 1807 Maritime Mews, Vancouver, BC V6H 3W7
Tel: 604-662-4405; *Fax:* 604-730-0454
tradewindbooks@eudoramail.com
www.tradewindbooks.com
ISBNs: ISBN: 1-896580
Publishers of children's literature recognized internationally
Michael Katz

Tralco Educational Services Inc.
#101, 1030 Upper James St., Hamilton, ON L9C 6X6
Tel: 905-575-5717; *Fax:* 905-575-1783
Toll-Free: 888-487-2526
sales@tralco.com
www.tralco.com
ISBNs: ISBN: 0-921376, 1-894738, 1-55409
Publishes supplementary materials for second-language education; Publishes in French, German, Spanish, ESL & Italian. Also produces activity books, videos, audio cassettes, games & software
Karen Traynor, President

Tree Frog Press Ltd.
10144 - 89 St., Edmonton, AB T5H 1P7
Tel: 780-429-1947;
www.bookpublishers.ab.ca/members/treefrog.html
ISBNs: ISBN: 0-88967; SAN: 115-1053
Involved in custom book production for self-publishers & organizations & families
Allan Shute, Editor & Publisher

Tree House Press Inc.
#2, 110 Lansing Dr., Hamilton, ON L8W 3A1
Fax: 905-574-0228
Toll-Free: 800-776-8733
contact@treehousepress.com
www.treehousepress.com
ISBNs: ISBN: 1-895165
Publishes educational resources specifically made for each province's educational standards

Trent University. Academic Skills Centre
Trent University, PO Box 4800, 1600 West Bank Dr., Peterborough, ON K9J 7B8
Tel: 705-748-1720; *Fax:* 705-748-1830
acdskills@trentu.ca
www.trentu.ca/academicskills
ISBNs: ISBN: 0-9693668, 1-894674

Tri-Fold Books (Distributor)
141 King St., Guelph, ON N1E 4P7
Tel: 519-821-9901; *Fax:* 519-821-5333
Toll-Free: 800-572-2300
info@trifoldbooks.com
ISBNs: SAN: 106-4320
Douglas N. Cass, Owner

Trifolium Books Inc.
A Fitzhenry & Whiteside Company, 195 Allstate Pkwy., Markham, ON L3R 4T8
Tel: 905-477-9700; *Fax:* 905-477-9179
Toll-Free: 800-387-9776
bookinfo@fitzhenry.ca
www.fitzhenrty.ca
ISBNs: ISBN: 1-895579, 1-55244
Publishes practical resources in science, technology, information technology, mathematics, careers, general business and life skills, for schools (elementary and secondary), trade professional and reference and library markets.
Sharon Fitzhenry

Trout Lily Press
940 Holly Ave., Winnipeg, MB R3T 1W5
www.sju.ca/troutlily/
Very small independent publisher of poetry & prose

TSAR Publications
PO Box 6996 A, Toronto, ON M5W 1X7
Tel: 416-483-7191; *Fax:* 416-486-0706
inquiries@tsarbooks.com
www.tsarbooks.com
ISBNs: ISBN: 0-929661, 1-894770
Publishes 6-8 titles of fiction, poetry & non-fictoin (literary criticism, history) annually.

Tumbleweed Press
#4, 1853A Avenue Rd., Toronto, ON M5M 2G3
Tel: 416-781-4010; *Fax:* 416-781-2764
info@tumblebooks.com
www.tumbleweed-press.com
ISBNs: ISBN: 0-9683303, 0-9680678
Custom publishers of children's books to be used for marketing purposes

TUNS Press
Faculty of Architecture & Planning, Dalhousie University, PO Box 1000, Halifax, NS B3J 2X4
Tel: 902-494-3925; *Fax:* 902-423-6672
tuns.press@dal.ca
tunspress.dal.ca
ISBNs: ISBN: 0-929112
Publishing arm of the Faculty of Architecture & Planning at Dalhousie University

Turnstone Press
#018, 100 Arthur St., Winnipeg, MB R3B 1H3
Tel: 204-947-1555; *Fax:* 204-942-1555
editor@turnstonepress.com
www.turnstonepress.com
ISBNs: ISBN: 0-88801; SAN: 115-1096
Publishers of fiction, literary criticism, poetry & non-fiction; Imprints include Turnstone Press which publishes mysteries, thrillers & noir fiction
Manuela David, Managing Editor
Patrick Gunter, Marketing Director

Ulverscroft Large Print (Canada) Ltd.
PO Box 80038, Burlington, ON L7L 6B1
Tel: 905-637-8734; *Fax:* 905-333-6788
Toll-Free: 888-860-3365
ulpbcan@worldchat.com
www.ulverscroft.com
ISBNs: ISBN: 0-7089
Publishers of large print books, producing 84 large print books monthly.
Diane van Veen

Ulysses Travel Guides / Éditions Ulysse
4176, rue Saint-Denis, Montréal, QC H2W 2M5
Tel: 514-843-9447; *Fax:* 514-843-9448
info@ulysses.ca
www.ulyssesguides.com
ISBNs: ISBN: 2-921444, 2-89464; SAN: 115-7167
Publishers of Canadian travel guides covering all areas of the country with a focus on Québec
Daniel Desjardins

Umberto Press
PO Box 42086, 2300 Oak Bay Ave., Victoria, BC V8R 6T4
Tel: 250-721-7239; *Fax:* 250-592-6463

United Church Publishing House
#300, 3250 Bloor St. West, Toronto, ON M8X 2Y4
Tel: 416-231-5931; *Fax:* 416-231-3103
Toll-Free: 800-288-7365
bookpub@united-church.ca
www.united-church.ca/ucph
ISBNs: ISBN: 0-919000, 1-55134; SAN: 111-6002
Rebekah Chevalier, Director, Publishing P, 4162317680 ext 4034, rchevali@united-church.ca

University Extension Press
#237 Williams Bldg., University of Saskatchewan, 221 Cumberland Ave. N, Saskatoon, SK S7N 1M3
Tel: 306-966-5558; *Fax:* 306-966-5567
extension.press@usask.ca
www.extension.usask.ca
Perry Millar, Managing Editor
Bertram Wolfe, Director

University of Alberta Press
Ring House 2, University of Alberta, Edmonton, AB T6G 2E1
Tel: 780-492-3662; *Fax:* 780-492-0719
www.uap.ualberta.ca
ISBNs: ISBN: 0-88864; SAN: 118-9794
Linda D. Cameron, Director, 7804920717, linda.cameron@ualberta.ca

University of British Columbia Press
2029 West Mall, Vancouver, BC V6T 1Z2
Tel: 604-822-5959; *Fax:* 604-822-6083
Toll-Free: 877-377-9378
frontdesk@ubcpress.ca
www.ubcpress.ca
ISBNs: ISBN: 0-7748; SAN: 115-1118
Publishing branch of the University of British Columbia; Largest scholarly press in Western Canada; Publishes 50-60 books annually with over 800 published since establishment; Specialties include political science, native studies, forestry, Asian studies, Canadian history, environmental studies, planning & urban studies.
R. Peter Milroy, Director

University of Calgary Press
2500 University Dr. NW, Calgary, AB T2N 1N4
Tel: 403-220-7578; *Fax:* 403-282-0085
Toll-Free: 800-663-5714
ucpress@ucalgary.ca
www.uofcpress.com
ISBNs: ISBN: 0-919813, 1-895176, 1-55238; SAN: 115-0871
Publishing arm of the University of Calgary
Donna Livingstone, Director, 4032203511, livingsd@ucalgary.ca
Karen Buttner, Editorial Secretary, 4032203979, kbuttner@ucalgary.ca
John King, Senior Editor, 4032204208, jking@ucalgary.ca
Peter Enman, Editor, 4032202606, enman@ucalgary.ca

University of Manitoba Press
301 St. John's College, University of Manitoba, Winnipeg, MB R3T 2M5
Tel: 204-474-6465; *Fax:* 204-474-7566
uofm_press@umanitoba.ca
www.umanitoba.ca/publications/uofmpress
ISBNs: ISBN: 0-88755; SAN: 115-5474
Publishing arm of the University of Manitoba; Publishes 6-8 scholarly works annually; Best known for Native History, Canadian History, Native Studies & Canadian literary studies.
David Carr, Director, 2044749242, carr@cc.umanitoba.ca
Cheryl Miki, Marketing Coordinator, 2044749495, miki@cc.umanitoba.ca
Pat Sanders, Managing Editor, 2044747338, sandersp@cc.umanitoba.ca

University of Ottawa Press (UOP/PUO) / Presses de l'Université d'Ottawa
542 King Edward St., Ottawa, ON K1N 6N5
Tel: 613-562-5246; *Fax:* 613-562-5247
Toll-Free: 800-565-9523
press@uottawa.ca
www.uopress.uottawa.ca
ISBNs: ISBN: 0-7766, 2-7603
Canada's oldest French Language university press & the only Bilingual University press in North America
Marie Clausén, Managing Editor, 6135625800 ext 3064, msec@uottawa.ca
Eric Nelson, Editor, Acquisitions, 6135625800 ext 3065, enelson@uottawa.ca
Heidi Laing, Editor, Livres Français, 6135625800 ext 1562, hlaing@uottawa.ca

University of Toronto Centre of Criminology
14 Queen's Park Cres. W., Toronto, ON M5S 3K9
Tel: 416-978-7124; *Fax:* 416-978-4195
criminology.publications@utoronto.ca
www.criminology.utoronto.ca
ISBNs: ISBN: 0-919584
In-house publishing facility to showcase research of Centre faculty & graduate students
Rita Donelan, Assistant to the Director

University of Toronto Press
#700, 10 St. Mary St., Toronto, ON M4Y 2W8
Tel: 416-978-2239; *Fax:* 416-978-4738
Toll-Free: 800-565-9523
publishing@utpress.utoronto.ca
www.utpress.utoronto.ca
ISBNs: ISBN: 0-8020; SAN: 115-1134, 115-3234
Publishing arm of the University of Toronto
Anne Laughlin, Managing Editor, 4169782239 ext236, alaughlin@utpress.utoronto.ca
Charley LaRose, Publications Co-ordinator, 4169782239 ext237, clarose@utpress.utoronto.ca

Up Here Publishing
#800, 4920 - 52th St., Yellowknife, NT X1A 3T1
Tel: 867-766-6710; *Fax:* 867-873-9876
Toll-Free: 800-661-0861
www.uphere.ca
Ronne Heming, Vice-President, ronne@outcrop.com

Véhicule Press
PO Box 125 Place du Parc, Montréal, QC H2W 4A3
Tel: 514-844-6073; *Fax:* 514-844-7543
vp@vehiculepress.com
www.vehiculepress.com
ISBNs: ISBN: 0-919890, 1-55065; SAN: 115-1150
Simon Dardick, Co-Publisher
Nancy Marrelli, Co-Publisher

Vesta Publications Ltd.
PO Box 1641, Cornwall, ON K6H 5R9
Tel: 613-932-7735;
vesta@primus.ca
ISBNs: ISBN: 0-919806, 1-55065; SAN: 115-5520
Stephen Gill, Editor

Visual Arts Ontario
#225, 215 Spadina Ave., Toronto, ON M5T 2C7
Tel: 416-591-8883; *Fax:* 416-591-2432
info@vao.org
www.vao.org
ISBNs: ISBN: 0-920708; SAN: 115-5539
Publishes materials that address the interests of visual artists in Ontario
Hennie L. Wolff

VLB Éditeur
1010, rue de la Gauchetière est, Montréal, QC H2L 2N5
Tél: 514-523-7993; *Téléc:* 514-282-7530
adpcommandes@messageries-adp.com
www.edvlb.com
ISBNs: ISBN: 2-89005
Martin Balthazar, Éditeur

Voyageur Publishing
1474 Clayton Rd., RR1, Almonte, ON K0A 1A0
Tel: 613-256-9435; *Fax:* 613-256-9435
info@voyageurpublishing.ca
www.voyageurpublishing.ca/
ISBNs: ISBN: 0-921842
Publishers of Canadian History books with a Christian Perspective
Liz Jefferson, Promotions Contact

Wall & Emerson, Inc.
205 Bethune College, 4700 Keele St., Toronto, ON M3J 1P3
Tel: 416-467-8685; *Fax:* 416-352-5368
Toll-Free: 877-409-4601
wall@wallbooks.com
www.wallbooks.com
ISBNs: ISBN: 1-895131, 0-921332; SAN: 116-0486
Client publisher of the University of Toronto Press; Publishes textbooks for universities & colleges, primarily in adult education, science, history of science, mathematics, English as a second language, and industrial engineering
Byron E. Wall, President

Warwick Publishing
#200, 161 Frederick St., Toronto, ON M5A 4P3
Tel: 416-596-1555; *Fax:* 416-596-1520
nick@warrickgp.com
www.warwickgp.com
ISBNs: ISBN: 1-895629, 1-894020, 1-894622
Publishes daily interest, non-fiction trade books with a focus on sports, food & drink, and personal finance.
Nick Pitt

Waterloo Music Co. Ltd.
3 Regina St. North, Waterloo, ON N2J 4A5
Tel: 519-886-4990; *Fax:* 519-886-4999
ISBNs: ISBN: 0-88909, 0-88797; SAN: 157-9363
William Brubacher, President

Weigl Educational Publishers Ltd.
6325 - 10 St. SE, Calgary, AB T2H 2Z9
Tel: 403-233-7747; *Fax:* 403-233-7769
info@weigl.com
www.weigl.com
ISBNs: ISBN: 0-9690637, 0-919879, 1-896990; SAN: 115-1312, 115-5536
Publishers of educational resources & books
Linda Weigl, President & Publisher

West Coast Paradise Publishing
PO Box 2093 Main, Sardis, BC V2R 1A5
Tel: 604-824-9528; *Fax:* 604-824-9541
rya@shaw.ca
rg.anstey.ca
ISBNs: ISBN: 0-9697494, 1-896779, 1-897031
Self-publishers of over 50 books by Robert G. Anstey
Yvonne Anstey

White Knight Books
#304, 160 Balmoral Ave., Toronto, ON M4V 1J7
Tel: 416-925-6548; *Fax:* 416-925-4165
info@whiteknightbooks.ca
www.whiteknightbooks.ca
ISBNs: 978-1-89745-603-3
Publisher of books in a range of subject areas, including Biography; Business; Canadian History; Education; Health & Medicine; Humour; Personal Finance; Poetry; Self-Help; Travel. For White Knight Book Distribution Services Ltd., consult www.whiteknightbookdistribution.com
Bill Belfontaine, Publisher
Karen Thomas, Creative Director, White Knight Books, design@whiteknightbooks.ca
Bill Husion, Sales Consultant, White Knight Distribution Services Lt
Jody Hronek, Special Sales, White Knight Book Distribution Services

Whitecap Books Ltd.
351 Lynn Ave., North Vancouver, BC V7J 2C4
Tel: 604-980-9852; *Fax:* 604-980-8197
whitecap@whitecap.ca
www.whitecap.ca
ISBNs: ISBN: 1-895099, 1-55110, 1-55285; SAN: 115-1290
Currently publishes more than 300 Canadian & foreign titles; Primary emphasis is in the areas of food & wine, but also publish children's fiction & non-fiction; travel sports & transportation.
Michael Burch, President
Nick Rundall, Vice-President
Robert McCullogh, Publisher
Meghan Spong, Production Manager

Whitecap Books Ltd.
#306, 20 Maud St., Toronto, ON M5V 2M5
Tel: 416-469-1555; *Fax:* 416-504-3376
customerservice@whitecap.ca
www.whitecap.ca/
Michael E. Burch, President

Whitlands Publishing Ltd.
4444 Tremblay Dr., Victoria, BC V8N 4W5
Tel: 250-477-0192;
info@whitlands.com
www.whitlands.com
ISBNs: ISBN: 0-9685061, 0-9734383
Publishers of novels by J. Robert Whittle

Wildlife Conservation
2300 Southam Blvd., Bronx, NY
Tel: 718-220-6876; *Fax:* 718-584-2625
subscribe@wcs.org
www.wildlifeconservation.org

Wilfrid Laurier University Press
75 University Ave. West, Waterloo, ON N2L 3C5
Tel: 519-884-0710; *Fax:* 519-725-1399
press@wlu.ca
www.wlupress.wlu.ca
ISBNs: ISBN: 0-88920; SAN: 115-1525
Publishing arm of Wilfrid Laurier University; Publishes 28-30 titles annually in the fields of history, literature, sociology, social work, life writing, film and media studies, aboriginal studies, women's studies, philosophy, & religious studies
Brian Henderson, Director, x6123, brian@press.wlu.ca
Lisa Quinn, Acquisitions Editor, x2843, quinn@press.wlu.ca
Rob Kohlmeier, Managing Editor, x6119, rob@press.wlu.ca

Wilson et Lafleur
40, rue Notre-Dame, Montréal, QC H2Y 1B9
Tél: 514-875-6326; *Téléc:* 514-875-8356
librarie@wilsonlafleur.com
www.wilsonlafleur.com
ISBNs: ISBN: 2-89127

Claude Wilson, Président

Windflower Communications
67 Flett Ave., Winnipeg, MB R2K 3N3
Tel: 204-668-7475; *Fax:* 204-661-8530
Toll-Free: 800-465-6564
windflower@brandtfamily.com
ISBNs: ISBN: 1-895308
Publishes 2-4 books annually
Gilbert G. Brandt, President
Susan Brandt, Vice-President
SuAnn Brandt Goertzen, Manager, Wholesale Division

Winslow Publishing
PO Box 38012, 550 Eglinton Ave. West, Toronto, ON M5N 3A8
Tel: 416-789-4733;
winslow@interlog.com
www.winslowpublishing.com
ISBNs: ISBN: 0-921199
Michelle West

Wolsak & Wynn Publishers Ltd.
#102, 69 Hughson St. N, Hamilton, ON L8R 1G5
Tel: 905-972-9885; *Fax:* 905-972-8589
info@wolsakandwynn.ca
www.wolsakandwynn.ca
ISBNs: ISBN: 0-919897
Publishers of award-winning poetry; 122 titles in all

Women's Press
#801, 180 Bloor St. West, Toronto, ON M5S 2V6
Tel: 416-929-2774; *Fax:* 416-929-1926
info@womenspress.ca
www.womenspress.ca
ISBNs: ISBN: 0-88961, 0-921881, 0-7737, 0-921556; SAN: 115-5628
Publishes high-quality feminist writing
Jack Wayne, President, jwayne@cspi.org
Megan Mueller, Editorial Director, meganmueller@cspi.org

Wood Lake Publishing
9025 Jim Bailey Rd., Kelowna, BC V4V 1R2
Tel: 250-766-2778; *Fax:* 250-766-2736
Toll-Free: 800-299-2926
info@woodlake.com
www.woodlakebooks.com
ISBNs: ISBN: 1-55145, 1-896836; SAN: 117-7436
Publishers of religious books and religious education tools
Lois Huey Heck, Marketing Manager
Bonnie Schlosser, Publisher

Word of Mouth Production
299 Booth Ave., Toronto, ON M4M 2M7
Tel: 416-462-0670; *Fax:* 416-462-0682
mail@torontofunplaces.com
www.torontofunplaces.com
ISBNs: ISBN: 0-9684432
Publishes a directory of recreation activities to do in the GTA and southern Ontario
Nathalie Prézeau

Wordwrights Canada
PO Box 456 O, Toronto, ON M4A 2P1
Tel: 416-752-0689; *Fax:* 416-752-0689
wordwrights@sympatico.ca
www.wordwrights.ca
ISBNs: ISBN: 0-920835
Self-publishers of poetry
Susan Ioannou

Work 4 Projects Ltd.
CP 400, Succ Victoria, Westmount, QC H3Z 2V8
Tel: 514-489-4941; *Fax:* 514-489-5505

Wuerz Publishing Ltd.
895 McMillan Ave., Winnipeg, MB R3M 0T2
Tel: 204-956-0308; *Fax:* 204-956-5053
ISBNs: ISBN: 0-929963
Steve Wuerz

YYZ Books
#140, 401 Richmond St. West, Toronto, ON M5V 3A8
Tel: 416-598-4546; *Fax:* 416-598-2282
yyz@yyzartistsoutlet.org
www.yyzartistsoutlet.org
ISBNs: ISBN: 0-920397
Publishes a variety of current writing focusing on art & culture

Magazine & Newspaper Publishers

AgMedia Inc.
58 Teal Dr., Guelph, ON N1C 1G4
Tel: 519-763-4044; *Fax:* 519-763-4482
publisher@betterfarming.com

Agricultural Publishing Co Ltd.
#1504, One Yonge St., Toronto, ON M5E 1E5
Tel: 416-364-5324; *Fax:* 416-364-5857

Alberta Business Research Ltd
200-10621 100 Ave. NW, Edmonton, AB T5J 0B3
Tel: 780-429-1610; *Fax:* 780-421-7677

Andrew John Publishing
#220, 115 King St. West, Dundas, ON L9H 1V1
Tel: 905-628-4309; *Fax:* 905-628-6847
info@andrewjohnpublishing.com
www.andrewjohnpublishing.com
Andrew John Publishing Inc. is a trade oriented publishing house with a focus on health sciences and specializing in association and society publishing. They publish, for example, "Wavelength", "Caslpo", "Canadian Hearing Report", "College Contact" and "Listen Ecoute".

Annex Publishing & Printing Inc.
#220, 6200 Dixie Rd., Mississauga, ON L5T 2E1
Tel: 905-795-0110; *Fax:* 905-795-2967
bookstore@annexweb.com
A variety of publications including Bakers Journgal, Canadian Pizza Magazine, Canadian Florist, and Canadian Poultry.

Annex Publishing & Printing Inc.
PO Box 530, 105 Donly Dr. South, Simcoe, ON N3Y 4N5
Tel: 519-429-3966; *Fax:* 519-429-3112
Toll-Free: 800-265-2827
mfredericks@annexweb.com
www.annexweb.com
Michael Fredericks, President, Magazine division, mfredericks@annexweb.com

Annex Publishing & Printing Inc.
PO Box 530, 105 Donly Dr. South, Simcoe, ON N3Y 4N5
Tel: 519-429-3966; *Fax:* 519-429-3112
Toll-Free: 888-404-1129
amatthews@annexweb.com (A.Matthews: Pro. Manager)
www.annexweb.com
AnnexWeb publishes publications such as "Bakers Journal", "Canadian Chiropractor", "Canadian Florist", "Canadian Firefighter", "Canadian Pizza", "Wings", and "Helicopter". They also publish books on a variety of topics such as baking, horticulture, pizza, and horses.
Fredericks Michael, President and CEO, mfredericks@annexweb.com
Diane Kleer, VP/Group Publisher (Annex Publishing Divison), dkleer@annexweb.com

Armadale Publications Inc.
PO Box 1193 Main PO, 203 10544 106SE, Edmonton, AB T5H 2X6
Tel: 780-429-1073; *Fax:* 780-425-5844
armadale@global-serve.net
ww.albertaoilandgas.com
Cal Kelly, Editor

August Communications Ltd.
2151 Portage Ave., #A, Winnipeg, MB R3J 0L4
Tel: 204-957-0265; *Fax:* 204-957-0217
Toll-Free: 888-573-1136
Gladwyn D. Nickel, Publisher

Bale Communications Inc.
#1463, 1011 Upper Middle Rd. East, Oakville, ON L6H 5Z9
Tel: 416-252-9400; *Fax:* 416-252-8002
info@adnews.com
www.adnews.com
Bale Communications publishes Adnews, A Canadian publication that offers daily advertising & marketing news.
Rob Bale, Publisher
Derek Winkler, Editor

Battlefords Publishing Ltd.
892 - 104th St., North Battleford, SK S9A 1M9
Tel: 306-445-7261; *Fax:* 306-445-3223
Toll-Free: 866-549-9979
battlefords.publishing@sasktel.net
Battlefords Publishing Ltd. is a newspaper & web printing company.
Alana Schweitzer, Publisher

Baum Publications Ltd.
#201, 2323 Boundary Rd., Vancouver, BC V5M 4V8
Tel: 604-291-9900; *Fax:* 604-291-1906
circulation@baumpub.com
www.baumpub.com
Baum Publications Ltd. publishes specialty trade publications, such as Contractors Magazine, Heavy Equipment Guide, Oil & Gas Product News, & Recycling Product News.
Engelbert J. Baum, President, ebaum@baumpub.com
Ken Singer, Publisher & Vice-President, ksinger@baumpub.com
Melvin Date Chong, Controller & Vice-President, mdatechong@baumpub.com
Tina Anderson, Manager, Production, tanderson@baumpub.com

Baxter Publications Inc.
310 Dupont St., Toronto, ON M5R 1V9
Tel: 416-968-7252; *Fax:* 416-968-2377
baxgroup@baxter.net; humanres@baxter.net
www.baxter.net
Baxter Publications is the publisher of education products & travel industry products. Services include web design & development, web hosting, & digital publishing.

Bayard Presse Canada Inc.
4475, rue Frontenac, Montréal, QC H2H 2S2
Tel: 514-522-3936; *Fax:* 514-522-1761

Becker Associates
#202, 10 Morrow Ave., Toronto, ON M6R 2J1
Tel: 416-538-1650; *Fax:* 416-489-1713
info@beckerassociates.ca
www.beckerassociates.ca
Other information: Montréal Phone: 514-274-0742
Becker Associates offers services such as editorial management, production management, & web-based publishing for publications & scholarly journals.
Adam Becker, President, Publications & Web, abecker@beckerassociates.ca

Bowes Publishers Ltd.
PO Box 1620, Kenora, ON P9N 3X7
Tel: 807-468-5555; *Fax:* 807-468-1060
mail@kenoraenterprise.com
www.lotwenterprise.com
ISBN: 0-9782505

Bowes Publishers Ltd.
1540 North Routledge Pk, London, ON N6H 5L6
Tel: 780-986-2271; *Fax:* 780-986-6397
bowes@bowesnet.com
www.bowesnet.com
Newspaper network, online resources, company directory.
Margaret Choja, Office Manager, 519-657-5510, mchoja@bowes.com

Breton Communications Inc.
#202, 495 boul. St-Martin ouest, Laval, QC H7M 1Y9
Tel: 450-629-6005; *Fax:* 450-629-6044
breton.com@bretoncom.com
www.bretoncom.com
Martine Breton, President, martine@bretoncom.com

Brunico Communications Ltd.
#100, 366 Adelaide St. West, Toronto, ON M5V 1R9
Tel: 416-408-2300; *Fax:* 416-408-0870
brunico@magic.ca
www.brunico.com
Through print, electronic publications and industry events, Brunico connects indicviduals and organizations, building communities specializing in the entertainment and marketing sectors. Brunico Marketing Inc., the California subsidiary of Brunico Communications Ltd., produces Brunico's entertainment and marketing conferences in New York, Washington, Los Angeles and other U.S. cities.

Bryarhouse Publishing Ltd.
10893 Old River Rd., Komoka, ON N0L 1R0
Tel: 519-657-2088; *Fax:* 519-657-2796

Business Information Group
#800, 12 Concorde Pl., Toronto, ON M3C 4J2
Tel: 416-442-5600; *Fax:* 416-442-2191
Toll-Free: 800-668-2374
www.businessinformationgroup.ca
ISBNs: 1-55257, 0-919217, 0-919378, 0-9693221, 0-911448
Trade & technical magazines
Bruce Creighton, President

Business Information Group
#705, East Tower, 1, rue Holiday est, Pointe-Claire, QC H9R 5N3

Byrne Publishing Group Inc
#10 - 1753 Dolphin Ave., Kelowna, BC V1Y 8A6
Tel: 250-861-5399; *Fax:* 250-868-3040
Toll-Free: 888-311-1119
info@okanaganlife.com
www.okanaganlife.com

Cameron Publications Ltd.
42 Borden Ave., Dartmouth, NS B3B 1C8
Tel: 902-468-1635; *Fax:* 902-468-1623

Campbell Communications Inc.
PO Box 5310, 1218 Langley St., 3rd Fl., Victoria, BC V8R 6S4
Tel: 250-388-7231; *Fax:* 250-385-3563
focusadmin@shaw.ca
www.focusonline.ca

ISBNs: ISBN: 1-895297
Publisher of FOCUS Magazine
Leslie Campbell, Publisher & Editor

Canada Wide Media Limited
4180 Lougheed Hwy., 4th Fl., Burnaby, BC V5C 6A7
Tel: 604-299-7311; *Fax:* 604-299-9188
cwm@canadawide.com
www.canadawide.com
Canada Wide Media provides a range of media services and products, in printed publications and digital media.
Peter Legge, President & Publisher LL.D, plegge@canadawide.com
Heather Parker, Senior Vice-President CGA, hparker@canadawide.com
Samantha Legge, Vice-President, Marketing, slegge@canadawide.com
Corinne Smith, Vice-President, Production, csmith@canadawide.com

Canadian Arctic Resources Committee
488 Gladstone Ave, Ottawa, ON K1N 8V4
Tel: 613-759-4284; *Fax:* 613-237-3845
Toll-Free: 866-949-9006
www.carc.org

ISBNs: ISSN: 0380-5522
Publisher of Northern Perspectives journal, & other publications dealing with the long-term environmental and social wellbeing of northern Canada and its peoples. Yellowknife office: 5003 - 48 St., P.O. Box 1705, Yellowknife, NT, X1A 2P3, Email: davidg@carc.org.
Charles Birchall, Chair
Jan Glyde, Contact, janglyde@carc.org

Canadian Committee on Labour History
Peace Hills Trust Tower, Athabasca University, 1200, 10011 - 109 St., Edmonton, AB T5J 3S8
cclh@athabascau.ca
www.cclh.ca
ISBNs: ISBN: 0-9692060, 0-9695835, 1-894000; SAN: 115-4168
Publisher of Labour/Le Travail: Journal of Canadian Labour Studies, as well as books & bulletins around the subject of labour history.
Alvin Finkel, President, alvinf@athabascau.ca
Rhonda Hinther, Vice-President, rhonda.hinther@civilization.ca
Gregory S. Kealey, Treasurer, gkealey@unb.ca

Canadian Controlled Media Communications
#101, 5397 Eglinton Ave. West, Toronto, ON M9C 5K6
Tel: 416-928-2909; *Fax:* 416-966-1181
Toll-Free: 800-320-6420
www.ccmc.ca
CCMC is a sports and entertainment marketing company with ventures in publishing, radio and television, internet, event production and media creation. Published products include SCOREGolf and CFL Illustrated.

Canadian Energy Research Institute
#150, 3512 - 33rd St. NW, Calgary, AB T2L 2A6
Tel: 403-282-1231; *Fax:* 403-284-4181
ceri@ceri.ca
www.ceri.ca
ISBNs: 0-920522, 1-896091; SAN: 115-2866
CERI is an independent, not-for-profit research establishment created through a partnership of industry, academia, and government. It aims to provide relevant, objective economic research in energy and related environmental issues. CERI's publications are categorized into Studies and Periodicals. Studies are reports published by the Institute on completion of study projects.
Peter Howard, Interim President & CEO, 403-220-2379, phoward@ceri.ca

Canadian Government Publishing
350 Albert St., 4th Floor, Ottawa, ON K1A 0S5
Tel: 613-941-5995; *Fax:* 613-954-5779
Toll-Free: 800-635-7943
publications@pwgsc.gc.ca
publications.gc.ca
The Government of Canada's official publisher, CGP publishes priced documents in print, Braille, and large-print formats and on a variety of subjects, such as health, finance, science and education, among others. These publications include books, serials, monographs, maps, pamphlets, and information kits.Formats also include online publishing and electronic publications. Hours M-F 8am-5pm.

Canadian Home Publishers
#120, 511 King St. West, Toronto, ON M5V 2Z4
Tel: 416-593-0204; *Fax:* 416-591-1630
chheditorial@canhomepub.com
www.houseandhome.com

Lynn Reeves, President & Publisher
Kirby Miller, VP & General Manager

Canadian Institute of Mining, Metallurgy & Petroleum (CIM) / Institut canadien des mines, de la métallurgie et du pétrol
#1250, 3500 boul de Maisonneuve ouest, Westmount, QC H3Z 3C1
Tel: 514-939-2710; *Fax:* 514-939-2714
cim@cim.org
www.cim.org
ISBNs: 1-894475, 0-919086, 1-926872
Chris Twigge-Molecey, President, 905-403-3926, Fax: 905-855-7629, ctwigge-molecey@hatch.ca
Jean Vavrek, Executive Director, ext. 1301, Fax: 514-939-2714, jvavrek@cim.org
Angela Hamlyn, Dir., Media & Communications, ext. 1303, ahamlyn@cim.org

Canadian Medical Association
1867 Alta Vista Dr., Ottawa, ON K1G 5W8
Tel: 613-731-9331; *Fax:* 613-565-5471
Toll-Free: 866-971-9171
pubs@cmaj.ca
www.cmaj.ca; www.cma.ca
ISBNs: 1-894391, 0-920169, 1-897490
The Association publishes the Canadian Medical Association Journal (CMAJ) in print and online. CMAJ showcases innovative research and ideas aimed at improving health. It publishes original clinical research, analyses and reviews, news and editorials.

Canstar Community News Ltd.
1355 Mountain Ave., Winnipeg, MB R2X 3B6
Tel: 204-697-7000
Published titles include such community newspapers as The Herald, The Lance, The Metro and The Times.

Carswell
One Corporate Plaza, 2075 Kennedy Rd., Toronto, ON M1T 3V4
Tel: 416-609-8000; *Fax:* 416-298-5094
carswell.customerrelations@thomson.com
www.carswell.com
ISBNs: 0-459, 0-7798, 0-88820
Carswell publishes information and electronic research solutions to the legal, tax, finance, accounting and human resources markets. Its material is integrated information available in a range of formats, including books, looseleaf services, journals, newsletters, CD-ROMS and online.
Don Van Meer, President & CEO

CHMM Inc.
#4, 951 Denison St., Markham, ON L3R 3W9
Tel: 905-305-6155; *Fax:* 905-305-6255
comments@solidwastemag.com
http://www.solidwastemag.com
The company publishes Solid Waste & Recycling Magazine, providing environmental information to industry and government. Topics include: Recycling, Diversion, Composting, The Haulers Page, Landfill Technology, Equipment, Regulation Roundup, and Final Analysis. The publication is available to qualified Canadians for free.

Chronicle Information Resources Ltd.
#306, 555 Burnhamthorpe Rd., Toronto, ON M9C 2Y3
Tel: 416-916-2476; *Fax:* 800-865-1632
Toll-Free: 866-632-4766
health@chronicle.org
www.chronicle.ca

ISBNs: 0-9685848
This is a privately-held independent producer of periodicals, newsletters, websites and information for medical practitioners, and for the pharmaceutical and biotech industries. Publications include, "The Chronicle of Cancer Therapy," "The Chronicle Neurology Network," and "The Skin Book."
R.Allan Ryan, Editorial Director, allan.ryan@chronicle.ca

CLB Media Inc.
240 Edward St., Aurora, ON L4G 3S9
Tel: 905-727-0077; *Fax:* 905-727-0017
www.clbmedia.ca
CLB Media properties include more than 26 business-to-business publications and web sites in such fields as industrial/manufacturing, logging/milling, workplace management, security and automotive.

CMP Publications
PO Box 34097, Halifax, NS B3J 3S1
Tel: 902-425-1320; *Fax:* 902-425-1325
cmp@cmppublications.com
www.cmppublications.com
ISBNs: 0-9693595, 0-9739494
The company is dedicated to researching, publishing and / or distributing information and books related to the natural and social sciences. Titles include themes on fisheries, agriculture, construction, environment, recycling and more.

Cottage Life Books
54 St. Patrick St., Toronto, ON M5T 1V1
Tel: 416-599-2000; *Fax:* 416-599-0500
Toll-Free: 877-874-5253
clmag@cottagelife.com
www.cottagelife.com

ISBNs: 0-9696922
In addition to keeping a website with a plethora of information about cottage lifestyle, the company publishes Cottage Life magazine and distributes a small selection of cottage-related books.
Al Zikovitz, Publisher, zikovitz@cottagelife.com
Stacie Smith, Media Contact, 416-910-8112, smithcommunications@sympatico.ca

Craig Kelman & Associates Ltd.
2020 Portage Ave., 3rd Fl., Winnipeg, MB R3J 0K4
Tel: 204-985-9780; *Fax:* 204-985-9799
info@kelman.ca
www.kelman.ca
ISBNs: 0-9694013
CK&A is a full-service contract publisher of magazines, newsletters & directories. Staff includes writers, editors & designers.
Chris Kelman, 866-985-9791, chris@kelman.ca

CTC Communications Corp.
#102, 155A Matheson Blvd. West, Mississauga, ON L5R 3L5
Tel: 905-712-3636; *Fax:* 905-712-2935
info@ctccomm.com
www.ctccomm.com

Dakota Design & Advertising Ltd.
Bay 114, 3907 - 3A St. NE, Calgary, AB T2E 6S7
Tel: 403-250-1128; *Fax:* 403-250-1194

Directories International Limited
PO Box 84021, 1235 Trafalgar Rd., Oakville, ON L6H 1A1
Tel: 905-337-3030; *Fax:* 905-452-8133
mansoor@emanon.com
Newspaper manufacturers

Les Éditions Apex inc. / Apex Publications Inc.
185, rue Saint-Paul, Québec, QC G1K 3W2
Tél: 418-692-2110; *Téléc:* 800-664-2739
Ligne sans frais: 800-905-7468
info@photolife.com
www.photolife.com
Éditeur de périodiques: "Photo Life", et "Photo Solution"
Valérie Racine, Rédactrice en chef, editor@photolife.com

Les Editions du Journal de l'Assurance
#100, 321, rue de la Commune ouest, Montréal, QC H2Y 2E1
Tél: 514-289-9595; *Téléc:* 514-289-9527
reception@journal-assurance.ca
www.journal-assurance.ca
Publications: "FlashFinance.ca", "Le Journal de l'assurance", "CarrièresAssurance.ca", "Le Congrès de l'assurance et de l'investissement", "QuébecInc.", et "The Insurance & Investment Journal".
Serge Therrien, Président et éditeur, serge.therrien@journal-assurance.ca

Les Éditions du Monde alimentaire inc.
#102, 200, rue MacDonald, Saint-Jean-sur-Richelieu, QC J3B 8J6
Tel: 450-349-0107; *Fax:* 450-349-6923

Les Éditions forestières
#203, 1175, rue Lavigerie, Québec, QC G1V 4P1
Tél: 418-877-4583; *Téléc:* 418-877-6449
www.lemondeforestier.ca
Publication: Le journal "Le Monde forestier"
Guy Lavoie, Directeur général, direction@lemondeforestier.ca

Les Éditions Héritage
300, rue Arran, Saint-Lambert, QC J4R 1K5
Tél: 514-875-9012; *Téléc:* 514-672-5448
Luc Payette, Président

Éditions Infopresse inc.
4310, boul St-Laurent, Montréal, QC H2W 1Z3
Tél: 514-842-5873; *Téléc:* 514-842-2422
redaction@infopresse.com
www.infopresse.com
"Le Portail du marketing, de la publicité et des communications."
Bruno Gautier, Président et éditeur
Sandrine Archambault, Directrice générale,
frederic.bruniquel@infopresse.com

Les Éditions Rogers limitée
#800, 1200, av McGill College, Montréal, QC H3B 4G7
Tél: 514-845-5141; *Téléc:* 514-845-7503
www.leseditionsrogers.ca
Brian Segal, Président/Chef de la direction

Editions Versicolores inc.
1320 Saint-Joseph Blvd., Québec, QC G2K 1G2
Tel: 418-628-8690; *Fax:* 418-628-0524

Egress Enterprises Inc
PO Box 1094 A, 1476 Latta Rd., Kelowna, BC V1P 1B4
Tel: 250-765-6065; *Fax:* 250-765-7346

English Literary Studies (ELS)
Dept. of English, University of Victoria, PO Box 3070, Victoria, BC V8W 3W1
Tel: 250-721-7237; *Fax:* 250-721-6498
hedyt@uvic.ca
www.engl.uvic.ca
ISBNs: ISBN: 0-920604; SAN: 115-3366
Hedy Miller

L'Escale Nautique
175, rue Saint-Paul, Québec, QC G1K 3W2
Tél: 418-692-3779; *Téléc:* 418-694-6904
production@escalenautique.qc.ca
www.escalenautique.qc.ca
Le leader de la presse nautique au Québec; publications y compris le journal "L'Escale nautique", et "Guide du tourisme nautique"
Michel Veilleux, Directeur général

Family Communications Inc.
65 The East Mall, Toronto, ON M8Z 5W3
Tel: 416-537-2604; *Fax:* 416-538-1794
sales@canadianbride.com
www.canadianbride.com
Family Communications is Canada's largest privately-held, independent publisher of women's magazines, holding a leading position in Canada's bridal, new parent and home buying markets through its flagship titles: "Today's Bride", "Best Wishes", "Mon Bébé", "Expecting", "C'est Pour Quand", etc..

Family Communications Inc./Communications Famille inc.
#1, 37 Hanna Ave., Toronto, ON M6K 1X1
Tel: 450-622-0091; *Fax:* 450-622-0099
Manon Le Moyne, Editeur

Farm Business Communications
PO Box 9800, Winnipeg, MB R3C 3K7
Tel: 204-944-5760; *Fax:* 204-942-8463
Bob Willcox, 204-944-5751, bob.willcox@fbcpublishing.com
John Morriss, 204-944-5754, john.morriss@fbcpublishing.com

Farm Papers Ltd.
#105B, 9547 - 152 St., Surrey, BC V3R 5Y5
Tel: 604-585-3131; *Fax:* 604-585-1504

Formula Publications Ltd.
4-447 Speers Rd., Oakville, ON L6K 3S7
Tel: 905-842-6591; *Fax:* 905-842-6843
www.carguidemagazine.com
Manufactor / Distributor

Giroux Publishing
102 Ellis St., Penticton, BC V2A 4L5
Tel: 250-493-0942; *Fax:* 250-493-7526
Toll-Free: 800-361-7526
cgiroux@awinc.com

Globe Interactive
444 Front St. West, Toronto, ON M5V 2S9
Tel: 416-585-5250; *Fax:* 416-585-5249
Toll-Free: 800-268-9128
www.theglobeandmail.com
ISBNs: ISBN: 0-921925
Publisher of The Globe & Mail daily newspaper, in print & online
Jim Sheppard, Executive Editor, Online News

Groupe Bomart
#204, 905 Michèle-Bohec, Blainville, QC J7C 5J6
Tél: 450-435-3131; *Téléc:* 450-435-3884
www.bomartgroup.com
Spécialisée dans l'édition de magazines dans le domaine du camionnage, de transport, de la logistique et des affaires

Groupe Constructo
#200, 1500, boul Jules-Poitras, Saint-Laurent, QC H4N 1X7
Tél: 514-745-5720; *Téléc:* 514-339-2267
Ligne sans frais: 800-363-0910
www.constructo.ca
Constructo is a divison of Transcontinental and a partner of CGI for SEAO.
Manon Bouchard, Marketing contact, 514-856-6609,
manon.bouchard@trancontinental.ca

Groupe Magazines S.A. Inc.
#300, 275, boul des Braves, Terrebonne, QC J6W 3H6
Tel: 450-964-7590; *Fax:* 450-964-2327

Groupe Ro-na Dismat
#100, 1570, ch Ampere, Boucherville, QC J4B 7L4
Tel: 405-641-7526; *Fax:* 405-641-6688

GSA Publishing Group
#200, 1104 Hornby St., Vancouver, BC V6Z 1V8
Tel: 604-689-2909; *Fax:* 604-689-2989
sales@gsapublishing.com
www.gsapublishing.com
Travel magazine for travel agents.

Helpard Publishing Inc.
#401, rte 7575 Trans Canada, Saint-Laurent, QC H4T 1V6
Tel: 514-956-1361; *Fax:* 514-956-1461

Herald Publishing Co.
PO Box 280, Dundalk, ON N0C 1B0
Tel: 519-923-2203; *Fax:* 519-923-2747
www.herald-publishing.com

Homes for Sale Magazine Ltd.
178 Main St., Unionville, ON L3R 2G9
Tel: 905-479-4663; *Fax:* 905-479-4482
Toll-Free: 800-363-4663
info@homesmag.com
www.homesmag.com/
Various publications including Homes Magazine, Active Adult Magazine, Condo Life Magazine, Moving To Magazines, Ontario Design Trade Sourcebook, and Renovation and Decor Magazine.
Michael Rosset, Publisher
Risë Levy, Editor
Natalie Armstrong, Circulation Manager

Homes Publishing Group
178 Main St., Unionville, ON L3R 2G9
Tel: 905-479-4663; *Fax:* 905-479-1286
Toll-Free: 800-363-4663
info@homesmag.com
www.homesmag.com/
HOMES Publishing Group publishes titles such as "Homes Magazines", "Active Adult Magazine", "Condo Life Magazine", and "Moving To Magazines".
Liz Bonser, Director of Sales

Horse Publications Group
PO Box 670, 225 Industrial Pkwy. South, Aurora, ON L4G 4J9
Tel: 905-727-0107; *Fax:* 905-841-1530
Toll-Free: 800-505-7428
editor@horse-canada.com
www.horse-canada.com
Publications includes Horse Sport, Horse-Canada & Canadian Thoroughbred, and Horsepower.
Jennifer Anstey, Publisher, Staff, janstey@horse-canada.com
Susan Stafford, Mangaging Editor (Horse Sport), Staff, editor@horse-canada.com
Lee Benson, Mangaging Editor (Horse-Canada), Staff, info@horse-canada.com
Jennifer Morrison, Mangaging Editor (Canadian Thoroughbred), Staff, teditor@horse-canada.com

IG Publications Ltd.
PO Box 3090, 101 Owl St., Banff, AB T1L 1C7
Tel: 403-760-3484; *Fax:* 403-760-2341
igpub@telusplanet.net
www.igpublications.com
Publishes travel information for B.C.

Insurancewest Media Ltd.
PO Box 3311 Terminal, Vancouver, BC V6B 3Y3
Tel: 604-874-1001; *Fax:* 604-874-3922
manager@insurancewest.ca
www.insurancewest.ca
Publishes a variety of publications such as "The BC Broker", "Insurancewest", "Alberta Insurance Directory", and "British Columbia Insurance Directory".

Investment Executive Inc.
100 - 25 Sheppard Ave. W., Toronto, ON M2N 6S7
Tel: 416-227-8266; *Fax:* 416-218-3544
Toll-Free: 888-366-4200
support@investmentexecutive.com
www.investmentexecutive.com

Ishcom Publications Ltd.
#201, 2065 Dundas St. East, Mississauga, ON L4X 2W1
Tel: 905-206-0150; *Fax:* 905-206-9972
Toll-Free: 800-201-8596

JCFT Forest Communications Inc.
#14, rue 90 Morgan, Baie-d'Urfé, QC H9X 3A8
Tel: 514-457-2211; *Fax:* 514-457-2558
jcft@qc.aira.com; info@forestcommunications.com
www.forestcommunications.com
Publishes "Canadian Wood Products", Canadian Forest Industries", and "Opérations Forestieres".

Journal la Nouvelle Édition
2030 boul Pie-IX, Montréal, QC H1V 2C8
Tél: 514-257-1000; *Téléc:* 514-257-7505
www.journaledition.com
"Journal des gens d'affaires de Montréal"; actualités économiques
Alain Dulong, Président/Éditeur, a.dulong@journaledition.com

JuneWarren Publishing Ltd.
#300, 5735 - 7 St. NE, Calgary, AB T2E 8V3
Tel: 780-944-9333; *Fax:* 780-944-9500
Toll-Free: 800-563-2946
marketing@junewarren.com
www.junewarren.com
Bill Whitelaw, Publisher

Kenilworth Publishing
#710, 15 Wertheim Ct., Richmond Hill, ON L4B 3H7
Tel: 905-771-7333; *Fax:* 905-771-7336

Kerrwil Publications Ltd.
2 St.Clair Ave.E, Suite 800, Toronto, ON M4T 2T5
Tel: 416-703-7167; *Fax:* 416-531-0348
peter@kerrwil.com

Key Publishers
59 Front St. East, 2nd Fl., Toronto, ON M5E 1B3
Tel: 416-364-3333; *Fax:* 416-594-3374

Kingston Publications
PO Box 1352, 11 Princess St., Kingston, ON K7L 1A1
Tel: 613-549-8442; *Fax:* 613-549-4333

Koocanusa Publications Inc.
100-100 7th Ave. South, Cranbrook, BC V1C 2J4
Tel: 250-426-7253; *Fax:* 250-426-4125
Toll-Free: 800-665-2382
koocanusa@cintek.com
www.koocanusapublications.com
Magazine and directory publishing.

Kostuch Publications Ltd.
101-23 Lesmill Rd., Toronto, ON M3B 3P6
Tel: 416-447-0888; *Fax:* 416-447-5333
mlima@foodservice.ca
www.foodserviceworld.com
Publisher serving the foodservice and hospitality markets in Canada such as "Foodservice and Hospitality" and "Hotelier".
Kostuch Mitch, President and Group Publisher,
mkostuch@foodservice.ca
Rosanna Caira, Editor and Publisher, rcaira@foodservice.ca

Kylix Media Inc
5165 Sherbrooke St., Montréal, QC H4A 1T6
Tel: 514-481-5892; *Fax:* 514-481-9699

Landscape Ontario Horticultural Trades Association
7856 - 5th Line South, RR#4, Milton, ON L9T 2X8
Tel: 905-875-1805; *Fax:* 905-875-0183
Toll-Free: 800-265-5656
LANDSCAPEONTARIO@SPECTRANET.CA
www.HORT-TRADES.COM
Crispin Co, Circulation Manager
Rita Weedenburg, Publisher
Linda Erskine, Editor

Laurentian Technomedia Inc. (LTI)
501 Oakdale Rd., Toronto, ON M3N 1W7
Tel: 416-746-7360; *Fax:* 416-746-1421
www.lti.on.ca

LexisNexis Canada Ltd.
#700, 123 Commerce Valley Dr. East, Markham, ON L3T 7W8
Tel: 905-479-2665; *Fax:* 905-479-3758
Toll-Free: 800-668-6481
sales@lexisnexis.ca
www.lexisnexis.ca

Lighthouse Publishing Ltd
353 York St., Bridgewater, NS B4V 3K2
Tel: 902-543-2457; *Fax:* 902-543-2228
lighthse@fox.nstn.ca
fox.nstn.ca/~lighthse/

Malcolm Média
3650, boul Pitfield, Pierrefonds, QC H8Y 3L4
Tel: 514-327-4464; *Fax:* 514-327-0514

Malcolm Publishing Inc.
3100 de la Concorde East Blvd. Suite 213, Laval, QC H7E 2B8
Tel: 450-665-0271; *Fax:* 450-665-2974
hclmag.media@videotron.ca
www.harrowsmithcountrylife.ca
Publishes Harrowsmith Country Life.

Martin Charlton Communications
#300, 1914 Hamilton St., Regina, SK S4N 3N6
Tel: 306-584-1000; *Fax:* 306-352-4110
www.martincharlton.ca
This is a public relations consultant with services including writing, graphic design, media training, communications planning, among others.

McLeish Communications Inc.
1, rue Pacifique, Sainte-Anne-de-Bellevue, QC H9X 1C5
Tel: 514-457-2423; *Fax:* 514-457-2577

MediaEdge Communications Inc.
#1000, 5255 Yonge St., Toronto, ON M2N 6P4
Tel: 416-512-8186; *Fax:* 416-512-8344
Toll-Free: 866-216-0860
www.mediaedge.ca
Publications including Building Strategies, Canadian Apartment Magazine, CondoBusiness, Construction Business, and Design Quarterly.
Kevin Brown, President

Mediconcept Inc.
#300, 3333, boul Cote-Vertu, Saint-Laurent, QC H4R 2N1
Tel: 514-331-4561; *Fax:* 514-336-1129
medicopea@netaxis.qc.ca

Mercury Publications Ltd.
1740 Wellington Ave., Winnipeg, MB R3H 0E8
Tel: 204-954-2085; *Fax:* 204-954-2057

Metro Guide Publishing
1300 Hollis St., Halifax, NS B3J 1T6
Tel: 902-420-9943; *Fax:* 902-429-9058
publishers@metroguide.ca
Sheila Blair, Publisher

Moorshead Magazines Ltd.
#500, 505 Consumers Rd., Toronto, ON M2J 4V8
Tel: 416-491-3699; *Fax:* 416-491-3996
www.moorshead.com
Publications include Family Chronicle; Internet-genealogy; History Magazine.

Multi-Vision Publishing Inc.
#1100, 655 Bay St., Toronto, ON M5G 2K4
Tel: 416-595-9944; *Fax:* 416-595-7217

National Research Council of Canada - NRC Research Press
Bldg. M-55, Montréal Rd., Ottawa, ON K1A 0R6
Tel: 613-993-0362; *Fax:* 613-952-7656
pubs@nrc-cnrc.gc.ca
www.nrc.ca/cisti/journals/rj.html
Publisher of scholarly journals since 1929. They are part of the Canada Institute for Scientific and Technical Information and publish 16 journals, monographs, conference proceedings, and allied publications.
Bruce P. Dancik, Editor-in-Chief, pubs@nrc-cnrc.gc.ca

Naylor Communications Ltd.
100 Sutherland Ave., Winnipeg, MB R2W 3C7
Tel: 204-947-0222; *Fax:* 204-947-2047
Toll-Free: 800-665-5456
cpopper@naylor.com
www.naylor.com
Provides customized association marketing communications, including magazines, member directories, online buyers' guides, e-newsletters, digital magazines, show guides, and event marketing and promotion materials. Their products are to "build IMAGE" and generate significant non-dues revenue for our association partners. Publications includes "Icon", "The Clarifier", "Who's Who", "Connections", "Pace", and "Association Leadership".
Robert Thompson, Publisher

NCC Specialty Publications
11 Thornhill Dr., Dartmouth, NS B3B 1R9
Tel: 902-468-8027; *Fax:* 902-468-2425

New Age Times Ink.
356 Dupont St., Toronto, ON M5R 1V9
Tel: 416-964-0528

News Canada Inc.
#810, 111 Peter St., Toronto, ON M5V 2H1
Tel: 416-599-9900; *Fax:* 416-599-9700
Toll-Free: 888-855-6397
www.newscanada.com
*Provides print editors with feature news stories of interest to their readers.

Norris-Whitney Communications Inc.
#7, 23 Hannover Dr., St Catharines, ON L2W 1A3
Tel: 905-641-3471; *Fax:* 905-641-1648
Toll-Free: 877-746-4692
info@nor.com
www.nor.com
Norris-Whitney Communications Inc. is an international communications company specializing in the music, audio, and lighting fields.

North Huron Publishing Inc.
PO Box 429, 404 Queen St., Blyth, ON N0M 1H0
Tel: 519-523-4311; *Fax:* 519-523-9140
Publications include; The Citizen, The Rural Voice, and Stops Along the Way.

North Island Publishing Ltd.
#8, 1606 Sedlescomb Dr., Mississauga, ON L4X 1M6
Tel: 905-625-7070; *Fax:* 905-625-4856
www.mastheadonline.ca
Bill Shields, Editor (The Magazine About Magazines), 905-625-7070

North Superior Publishing Inc.
1145 Barton St., Thunder Bay, ON P7B 5N3
Tel: 807-623-2348; *Fax:* 807-623-7515
nspinc@tbaytel.net
www.northsuperiorpublishing.com
Publishes "Golfing News", "Business", and "Snowmobile News".
Sylvia Gomez, Sales Rep, 807-623-2348, sylvia@northsuperiorpublishing.com

Northern Star Communications Ltd.
900 - 6 Ave. SW, 5th Fl., Calgary, AB T2P 3K2
Tel: 403-263-6881; *Fax:* 403-263-6886
Toll-Free: 800-052-6417
editor@northernstar.ab.ca
www.northernstar.ab.ca
Four oilpatch magazines- "The Roughneck", "Energy Processing Canada", "Propane Canada" and "The Roughneck Buy and Sell", as well as the annual "Alberta Gas Plant Directory" and volume one of the "Roughneck Joke Book".
Scott, Publisher, scott@northernstar.ab.ca

Nytek Publishing Inc., Division of New Communications Group Ltd.
451 Attwell Dr., Toronto, ON M9W 5C4
Tel: 416-242-8088; *Fax:* 416-242-8085
rshuker@nytek.ca
Simon Blake, Editor
Jim Gillen, National Sales Manager
Bill Begin, Publisher
Ron Shuker, Executive Editor
Pat Glionna, Circulation Manager

Omnicom Publications Inc.
#300, 512 King St. East, Toronto, ON M5A 1M1
Tel: 416-955-1550; *Fax:* 416-955-1391

Ontario Association of Certified Engineering Technicians & Technologists
#404, 10 Four Seasons Pl., Toronto, ON M6B 6H7
Tel: 416-621-9621; *Fax:* 416-621-8694
info@oacett.org
www.oacett.org
OACETT will be the foremost organization for advancing the engineering and applied science technology profession. They are dedicated to excellence in the engineering and applied science technology profession in a manner that serves and protects the public interest.

The Ontario Historical Society
34 Parkview Ave., Toronto, ON M2N 3Y2
Tel: 416-226-9011; *Fax:* 416-226-2740
ohs@historicalsociety.ca
www.ontariohistoricalsociety.ca

OP Publishing Ltd.
#900, 1080 Howe St., Vancouver, BC V6Z 2T1
Tel: 604-606-4644; *Fax:* 604-687-1925
Toll-Free: 800-816-0747
info@oppublishing.com
www.oppublishing.com
Publishes magazines such as "Fishing", "Cottage", "Pacific Yachting", "Western Sportsman", "Outdoor Edge", "Canadian Aviator", "BC Marine Parks Guide", and "BC Fishing".
Mark Yelic, Publisher

OT Communications
1025-101 Sixth Ave. SW, Calgary, AB T2P 3P4
Tel: 403-264-3270; *Fax:* 403-264-3276
Toll-Free: 800-465-0322
info@otcommunications.com
www.otcommunications.com

Ottawa News Publishing
#3B, 15 Antares Dr., Nepean, ON K2E 7Y9
Tel: 613-723-5970; *Fax:* 613-723-1862
Newspapers

Our Kids Publications Ltd.
4242 Rockwood Rd., Mississauga, ON L4W 1L8
Tel: 905-272-1843; *Fax:* 905-272-0474
agatha@ourkids.net
www.ourkids.net
Magazine "Our Kids Go to Camp" is devoted to helping parents find the right camp for their children and "Our Kids Go To School" is devoted to helping parents find the "best education for their kids".
Agatha Stawicki, Director, Marketing & Advertising

Pacific Island Publishers Co. Ltd.
818 Broughton St., Victoria, BC V8W 1E4
Tel: 250-383-3633; *Fax:* 250-480-3233
info@wheremagazine.com

Parkhurst Publishing
400 McGill St., 3rd Fl., Montréal, QC H2Y 2G1
Tel: 514-397-8833; *Fax:* 514-397-0228
www.parkpub.com
ISBNs: 0-9688648, 0-9698972, 0-9732870
Parkhurst is a medical publishing house providing a wide range of medical media journals and educational communications to physicians and patients. Toronto office: 416-489-8045.

Perks Publications Inc.
3 Kennett Dr., Whitby, ON L1P 1L5
Tel: 905-430-7267; *Fax:* 905-430-6418
Toll-Free: 877-880-4877
admin@perkspub.com
www.perkspub.com
Publishes Trade Magazines, Journals, Periodicals, and News Letter for Associations across the county.
Tanja Nowotny, Editor/Art Director, 905-697-8905, Fax: 905-697-2596, tanja@perkspub.com

Pilot Press Ltd.
#213, 3347 Oak St., Victoria, BC V8X 1R2
Tel: 250-658-6575; *Fax:* 250-658-6576
Toll-Free: 800-656-7598
pilotpress@shaw.ca

Plesman Communications Inc.
400-2005 Sheppard Ave. East, Toronto, ON M2N 6S7
Tel: 416-467-9562; *Fax:* 416-497-6022

Plesman Communications Inc.
Tour B, #305, 1470, rue Peel, Montréal, QC H3A 1T1

Polyscience Publications Inc.
PO Box 148, 44 Seize Arpents, Morin-Heights, QC J0R 1H0
Tel: 450-226-5870; *Fax:* 450-226-5866
polysc@ietc.com

Post Newspapers Inc.
340 Sheppard Ave. East, Toronto, ON M2N 3B4
Tel: 416-250-7979; *Fax:* 416-250-1737
postnews@idirect.com

Postmedia Network Inc.
1450 Don Mills Rd., Toronto, ON M3B 3R5
Tel: 416-383-2300;
www.postmedia.com
The company is a publisher by circulation of paid English-language daily newspapers. Titles include: National Post, Vancouver Sun, Edmonton Journal, Calgary Herald, Star Phoenix, Ottawa Citizen, (Montréal) Gazette. Online titles include Canada.com and Dose.ca.
Ron Osborne, Chair
Paul Godfrey, President & CEO
Doug Lamb, Executive VP & CFO
Gillian Akai, VP, Legal Affairs, 416-383-2550, gakai@postmedia.com

Progress Publishing Co Ltd.
#510, 1489 Marine Dr., West Vancouver, BC V7T 1B8
Tel: 604-922-6717; *Fax:* 604-922-1739

Publicom inc.
CP 365, #400, 1055, côte du Beaver Hall, Montréal, QC H2Y 3H1
Tél: 514-274-0004; *Téléc:* 514-274-5884

Publicor
7, ch Bates, Outremont, QC H2V 4V7
Tel: 514-270-1100; *Fax:* 514-270-6900
Andre Vilder, Editor

Publiédition inc.
620, boul Industriel, Saint-Jean-sur-Richelieu, QC J3B 7X4
Tel: 514-856-7821; *Fax:* 514-359-0836

Pulsus Group Inc.
2902 South Sheridan Way, Oakville, ON L6J 7L6
Tel: 905-829-4770; *Fax:* 905-829-4799
pulsus@pulsus.com
www.pulsus.com
Privately owned Canadian company which publishes "The Canadian Journal of Cardiology", "The Canadian Journal of Gastroenterology", "The Canadian Journal of Infectious Diseases & Medical Microbiology", "The Canadian Journal of Plastic Surgery", "Canadian Respiratory Journal", "Pain Research & Management", "Paediatrics & Child Health", and "Experimental & Clinical Cardiology".
LeBlanc Ann, Vice-President, 905-829-4770 ext 124
Lisa Robb, Director of Advertising Sales, 905-829-4770 ext 143

Reed Construction Data
4285 Canada Way, Burnaby, BC V5G 1H2
Tel: 604-433-8164; *Fax:* 604-433-9549
Toll-Free: 800-465-6475

Rive-nord medias inc.
896, rue de Puyjalon, Baie-Comeau, QC G5C 1N1
Tel: 418-589-5900; *Fax:* 418-589-5263

Robins Southern Printing (1990) Ltd.
1320 - 36 St. North, Lethbridge, AB T1H 5H8
Tel: 403-328-5114; *Fax:* 403-328-5443

Rodar International Inc.
84 Hymus Blvd., Pointe-Claire, QC H9R 1E4
Tel: 514-697-7738; *Fax:* 514-697-4114
cjo.cancer.ctrl@sympatico.ca

Rogers Media Inc.
1 Mount Pleasant Rd., Toronto, ON M4Y 2Y5
Tel: 416-764-2000

Rogers Publishing Ltd.
1 Mount Pleasant Rd., Toronto, ON M4Y 2Y5
Tel: 416-764-2000
Publications include "Canadian Business", "Chatelaine", "Flare", "Todays' Parents", "Macleans", "Money Sense", "Profit", "Marketing", "Lou Lou" and "Ontario Out of Doors" as well as Quebec magazines "L'actualité", "Le Bulletin", "Châtelaine", et "Lou Lou".
John H. Tory, President & CEO

Salon Communications Inc.
#1902, 365 Bloor St. East, Toronto, ON M4W 3L4
Tel: 416-869-3131; *Fax:* 416-869-3008

Sawmill Creek Communications
PO Box 1800, #11, 4040 Creditview Rd., Mississauga, ON L5C 3Y8
Tel: 905-569-1800; *Fax:* 905-569-1818

Solstice Publishing Inc.
47 Soho Sq., Toronto, ON M5T 2Z2
Tel: 416-595-1252; *Fax:* 416-595-7255
Toll-Free: 800-263-5295

Southam Information & Technology Group Inc.
280 Yorkland Blvd., Willowdale, ON M2J 4Z6
www.southam.com

STA Communications Inc.
#306, 955, boul St-Jean, Pointe-Claire, QC H9R 5K3
Tel: 514-695-7623; *Fax:* 514-695-8554
cme@sta.ca
www.stacommunications.com
Journals include "Diagnosis", "CME", "Clinicien", Cardiology", and"Pharmaceutical".
Paul Brand, Contact (Montreal office), 541-695-8393 ext.220, paulb@sta.ca

Stitches: the Journal of Medical Humour
CLB Media Inc., 240 Edward St., Aurora, ON L4G 3S9
Tel: 905-727-0077; *Fax:* 905-727-0017
stiches@stichesmagaine.com; knuenhuis@cllbmedia.ca
www.stitchesmagazine.com
Medical humor magazine.
Simon Hally, Associate Publisher & Editor

Stone & Cox Ltd.
500-111 Peter St., Toronto, ON M5V 2H1
Tel: 416-599-0772; *Fax:* 416-599-0867
cathysp@cdnins.com
Cathy St Pierre, Contact, 416-599-0772 ext 103, Fax: 416-599-0867, cathysp@cdnins.com

Suggitt Publishing Ltd.
950 Bell Tower, 10104 103 Ave., Edmonton, AB T5J 0H8
Tel: 780-413-6163; *Fax:* 780-413-6185
Toll-Free: 877-784-4488
Consumer magazines.

Sundance Publications Ltd.
PO Box 939, 423 Mountain Ave., Neepawa, MB ROJ 1HO
Tel: 204-476-2309; *Fax:* 204-476-5802
neepress@mts.net
www.neepawapress.com
Publications such as the Neepawa Press.
Jack Gibson, Publisher, gibson@neepawapress.com

Sunrise Publishing
2213B Hanselman Ct., Saskatoon, SK S7L 6A8
Tel: 306-244-5668; *Fax:* 306-244-5679
Toll-Free: 800-247-5743
http://sunrisepublish.com

Swan Erickson Publishing Inc.
#1235, 1011 Upper Middle Rd. East, Oakville, ON L6H 5Z9
Tel: 905-475-4231; *Fax:* 905-475-3512

Synergistic Publications
132 Adrian Cres., Markham, ON L3P 7B3
Tel: 905-472-2801; *Fax:* 905-472-3091
www.canadiandefencereview.ca

Thomson Healthcare Communications
#200, 1120 Birchmount Rd., Scarborough, ON M1K 5G4
Tel: 416-750-8900; *Fax:* 416-751-8126

Thornhill Publications Ltd.
#16, 7780 Woodbine Ave., Markham, ON L3R 2N7
Tel: 905-475-1743

Today's Parent Group
269 Richmond St. West, Toronto, ON M5V 1X1
Tel: 416-596-8680; *Fax:* 416-596-1991

Toro Communications
#224, 2560 Matheson Blvd. East, Mississauga, ON L4W 4Y9
Tel: 905-238-5625; *Fax:* 905-000-0000
Periodical publishers

Town Media Inc., a division of Osprey Media Group
1074 Cooke Blvd., Burlington, ON L7T 4A8
Tel: 905-634-8003; *Fax:* 905-634-7661
info@townmedia.ca
www.townmedia.ca

Trajan Publishing Corp.
PO Box 28103 Lakeport, #10, 600 Ontario St., St Catharines, ON L2N 7P8
Tel: 905-646-7744; *Fax:* 905-646-0995
Toll-Free: 800-408-0352
office@tranjan.ca
www.trajan.com
Produces "Antique & Collectibles Showcase" and "Canadian Coin News& Canadian Stamp News".
Judy Sheluk, Editor (Antique and Collectibles Showcase), acseditor@rogers.com

Transcontinental ITBusiness Group
#100, 25 Sheppard Ave. West, Toronto, ON M2N 6S7
Tel: 416-733-7600

Transcontinental Media Inc.
1100, boul René-Lévesque ouest, 24e étage, Montréal, QC H3B 4X9
Tél: 514-392-9000; *Téléc:* 514-392-1489
Ligne sans frais: 800-361-5479
www.transcontinental-media.com
Publishes a variety of magazines, newspapers, and books. Magazines include Canadian Living, Coup de pouce, Elle Canada and Sytle at home. They also publish a variety of books and educational materials.

Transcontinental Publications G.T. Inc.
#500, 2608 Granville St., Vancouver, BC V6H 3V3

Transcontinental Specialty Publications/Holiday Media
Suite 609, 1888 Brunswick Ave., Halifax, NS B3J 3J8
Tel: 902-425-8255; *Fax:* 902-425-8118
Toll-Free: 800-537-5507
jnearing@holidaymedia.ca, dhillier@holidaymedia.ca
www.holidaymedia.ca
Dan Hillier, Account Exec (Toronto & Area; Lake Country and Northlan, dhillier@holidaymedia.ca
Studley Serena, Account Executive (Kitchener; Hamilton; W & E Ontario), sstudley@holidaymedia.ca

Tribute Publishing Inc.
71 Barber Greene Rd., Toronto, ON M3C 2A2
Tel: 416-445-0544; *Fax:* 416-445-2894
generalinfo@tribute.ca
www.tribute.ca
Entertainment magazine

Turbopress Inc.
4105, boul Matte, Brossard, QC J4Y 2P4
Tel: 450-444-1103; *Fax:* 514-738-4929
Toll-Free: 800-561-0318
www.turbopress.net

TVA Publications
7, ch Bates, Outremont, QC H2V 4V7
Tel: 514-270-1100; *Fax:* 514-270-6900
Toll-Free: 800-663-4984
Periodicals, publishing.

University of Calgary Press
2500 University Dr. NW, Calgary, AB T2N 1N4
Tel: 403-220-7578; *Fax:* 403-282-0085
ucomail@ucalgary.ca
www.ucalgary.ca/UofC/departments/UP
Dr. Geoffrey Simmins, 403-220-3511, simmins@ucalgary.ca

University of Toronto Press Inc.
5201 Dufferin St., Toronto, ON M3H 5T8
Tel: 416-667-7838; *Fax:* 416-667-7881
journals@utpress.utoronto.ca
www.utpjournals.com
Publishes a variety of journals including "Bookbird: a journal of international children's literature", "The Canadian Journal on Aging", "The Canadian Journal of Information and Library Sciences", "Eighteenth Century Fiction","SIMILE: Studies in Media and Information Literacy Education", and "Ulimate Reality and Meaning".
Anne Marie Corrigan, Vice-President (Journals), 416-667-7777 ext7838, acorrigan@utpress.utoronto.ca

Velo Québec Éditions
1251, rue Rachel est, Montréal, QC H2J 2J9
Tel: 514-521-8356; *Fax:* 514-521-5711

Westcoast Publishing Ltd
1496 West 72nd Ave., Vancouver, BC V6P 3C8
Tel: 604-266-7433; *Fax:* 604-263-8620
fish@west_coast.com

Wood Mountain Post Provincial Park
#530, 3211 Albert St., Regina, SK S4S 5W6
Tel: 306-787-9572; *Fax:* 306-787-7000
Toll-Free: 800-205-7070
Sioux First Nations & NWMP arifacts; open June-Sept

Youngblood Publishing
Suite 404, 4580 Dufferin St., North York, ON M3H 5Y2
Tel: 416-665-7333; *Fax:* 416-665-7226

Youth Culture Inc.
#245, 401 Richmond St. West, Toronto, ON M5V 1X3
Tel: 416-595-1313; *Fax:* 416-595-1312
info@youthculture.com
www.youthculture.com
Magazines are directed and marketed towards teens and "tweens".
Kaaren Whitney-Vernon, President, CEO, and Group Publisher, karen@youthculture.com
Sarah Graham, Associate Editor (Vervegirl, Fuel, Desperado & Bangzone, sara@youthculture.com

Zanny Ltd.
11966 Woodbine Ave., Gormley, ON L0H 1G0
Tel: 905-887-5048; *Fax:* 905-887-0764

Newspapers

Alberta

Daily Newspapers in Alberta

***Calgary:* Calgary Herald**
PO Box 2400 M, 215 - 16 St. SE, Calgary, AB T2P 0W8
Tel: 403-235-7100; *Fax:* 403-235-7379
Toll-Free: 800-327-9219
www.calgaryherald.com
Circulation: 140,000 *Frequency:* Morning
Peter Menzies, General Manager
Brendan T. Hughes, Vice-President, Advertising
Malcolm Kirk, Editor-in-chief

***Calgary:* The Calgary Sun**
2615 - 12 St. NE, Calgary, AB T2E 7W9
Tel: 403-410-1010; *Fax:* 403-250-4258
www.calgarysun.com
Circulation: 66,394, Mon.-Sat.; 97,050, Sun. *Frequency:* Morning
Guy Huntingford, Publisher
Chris Nelson, Editor-in-chief

***Edmonton:* The Edmonton Journal**
PO Box 2421, 10006 - 101 St., Edmonton, AB T5J 2S6
Tel: 780-429-5100; *Fax:* 780-429-5604
www.edmontonjournal.com
Circulation: Mon.-Thu./Sat. 131,306, Fri. 148,701, Sun., 128,306 *Frequency:* Morning
Linda Hughes, President & Publisher
Heather Boyd, City Editor

***Edmonton:* The Edmonton Sun**
#250, 4990 - 92 Ave., Edmonton, AB T6B 3A1
Tel: 780-468-0100; *Fax:* 780-468-0139
mailbag@edmontonsun.com
www.edmontonsun.com
Circulation: 74,173 M-Sa; 113,092 Su *Frequency:* Morning
Gordon Norrie, Publisher & CEO
Graham Dalziel, Editor-in-chief

***Fort McMurray:* Fort McMurray Today**
c/o Sun Media Inc., PO Box 4008, 8550 Franklin Ave., Fort McMurray, AB T9H 3G1
Tel: 780-743-8186; *Fax:* 780-715-3820
today@fortmcmurraytoday.com
www.fortmcmurraytoday.com
Circulation: 6,043, Mon.-Thu.; 7,248, Fri. *Frequency:* Afternoon/evening, Mon.-Fri.
Tim O'Rouke, Publisher
Michael Hall, Managing Editor

***Grande Prairie:* Daily Herald-Tribune**
PO Box 3000, 10604 - 100 St., Grande Prairie, AB T8V 6V4
Tel: 780-532-1110; *Fax:* 780-532-2120
dht@bowesnet.com
www.dailyheraldtribune.com
Circulation: 8,384 M-Th; 12,830 F *Frequency:* Monday-Friday; Afternoon
Doug Hare, Asst. Publisher
Fred Rinne, Managing Editor
Kent Keebaugh, Publisher

***Lethbridge:* The Lethbridge Herald**
Southern Alberta Newspapers, PO Box 670, 504 - 7th St. South, Lethbridge, AB T1J 3Z7
Tel: 403-328-4411; *Fax:* 403-328-4536
www.lethbridgeherald.com
Circulation: 18,950, Sun.-Thu.; 23,213, Fri., 20,386, Sat. *Frequency:* Morning
Bob Carey, General Manager & Vice-President
Doyle MacKinnon, Managing Editor

***Medicine Hat:* Medicine Hat News**
Southern Alberta Newspapers, PO Box 10, 3257 Dunmore Rd. SE, Medicine Hat, AB T1A 7E6
Tel: 403-527-1101; *Fax:* 403-527-1244
Toll-Free: 800-682-2476
www.medicinehatnews.com
Mike Hertz, Publisher

***Red Deer:* Red Deer Advocate**
PO Box 5200, 2950 Bremner Ave., Red Deer, AB T4N 5G3
Tel: 403-343-2400; *Fax:* 403-341-6560
editorial@reddeeradvocate.com
www.reddeeradvocate.com
Circulation: 17,440 *Frequency:* Afternoon
Joe McLaughlin, Editor
Fred Gorman, Publisher

Other Newspapers in Alberta

***Airdrie:* Airdrie City View**
PO Box 5368, Bay 5, 213 Main St. North, Airdrie, AB T4B 2T9
Tel: 403-948-1885; *Fax:* 403-948-2554
production@airdriecityview.com
www.airdriecityview.com
Circulation: 11,997 *Frequency:* Fri.
Cam Christianson, Publisher
Nathan Anderson, Editor

***Airdrie:* Airdrie Echo**
PO Box 3820, 112 First Ave. NE, Airdrie, AB T4B 2B9
Tel: 403-948-7280; *Fax:* 403-912-2341
airdrieprod@bowesnet.com
www.airdrieecho.com
Other information: Editorial Email: airdrie.echo@shaw.ca
Circulation: 13,725 *Frequency:* Wednesday
Don Scotten, Publisher

***Athabasca:* Athabasca Advocate**
4917B - 49th St., Athabasca, AB T9S 1C5
Tel: 780-675-9222; *Fax:* 780-675-3143
Circulation: 3,612 *Frequency:* Tuesday
Ross Hunter, Publisher

***Banff:* The Banff Crag & Canyon**
PO Box 129, 201 Bear St., 2nd Fl., Banff, AB T1L 1H2
Tel: 403-762-2453; *Fax:* 403-762-5274
www.banffcragandcanyon.com
Circulation: 6,970 *Frequency:* Tuesday
Kim Oliver, Publisher
Dave Husdal, Editor

***Banff:* Summit UP**
PO Box 129, 201 Bear St., 2nd Fl., Banff, AB T0L 0C0
Tel: 403-762-2453; *Fax:* 403-762-5274
editor@banffcragandcanyon.com
Circulation: 16,280 *Frequency:* Weekly
Candis Zell, Circulation/Subscription
Al Guthrow, Publisher
Dave Husdal, Editor

***Barrhead:* Barrhead Leader**
PO Box 4520, Barrhead, AB T7N 1A4
Tel: 780-674-3823; *Fax:* 780-674-6337
leader@barrhead.greatwest.ca
www.greatwest.ca
Circulation: 3,841 *Frequency:* Tuesday
Carol Farnalls, Publisher
Ray Wangen, Editor

***Bashaw:* Bashaw Star**
PO Box 188, 4909 - 50th St., Bashaw, AB T0B 0H0
Tel: 780-372-3608; *Fax:* 780-372-4445
stetnews@telusplanet.net
Circulation: 564 *Frequency:* Tuesday
Audrey Brown, Publisher

***Bassano:* Bassano Times**
PO Box 780, 216 - 3rd St., Bassano, AB T0J 0B0
Tel: 403-641-3636; *Fax:* 403-641-3952
btimes@telusplanet.net
Circulation: 568 *Frequency:* Tuesday
Mary Lou Brooks, Publisher & Editor-in-chief

***Beaumont:* La Nouvelle Beaumont News**
5021B - 52nd Ave., Beaumont, AB T4X 1E5
Tel: 780-929-6632; *Fax:* 780-929-6634
beaunews@telusplanet.net
dispatchnews.ca
Circulation: 4,999 *Frequency:* Friday
Mary Ann Johnston, Publisher
George Brown, Editor

***Beaverlodge:* Beaverlodge Advertiser**
PO Box 300, 920 First Ave., Beaverlodge, AB T0H 0C0
Tel: 780-354-2460; *Fax:* 780-354-2460
Circulation: 1,180 *Frequency:* Wednesday
Trevor Harris, Publisher

***Blairmore:* The Crowsnest Pass Promoter**
PO Box 1019, 13343 - 20 Ave., Blairmore, AB T0K 0E0
Tel: 403-562-8884; *Fax:* 403-562-2242
publisher@crowsnestpasspromoter.com
www.crowsnestpasspromoter.com
Circulation: 1,576 *Frequency:* Friday
Kathy Taylor, Editor & Publisher

***Blairmore:* The Pass Herald**
Crowsnest Mall, PO Box 960, Blairmore, AB T0K 0E0
Tel: 403-562-2248; *Fax:* 403-562-8379
passherald@shaw.ca
www.passherald.net
Circulation: 2,220 *Frequency:* Tuesday
Gail Sygutek, Publisher

***Bonnyville:* Bonnyville Nouvelle**
5304 - 50 Ave., Bonnyville, AB T9N 1Y4
Tel: 780-826-3876; *Fax:* 780-826-7062
nouvelle@greatwest.com
www.greatwest.ca
Circulation: 3,626 *Frequency:* Monday; English & French
Dave Hutton, Publisher

***Bow Island:* County Commentator & Cypress Courier**
PO Box 580, 147 - 5th Ave., Bow Island, AB T0K 0G0
Tel: 403-545-2258; *Fax:* 403-545-6886
dpilon@my403.com
www.bowislandcommentator.com
Circulation: 5,842
Coleen Campbell, Publisher

***Brooks:* Brooks & County Chronicle**
PO Box 1568 Main, Brooks, AB T1R 1C4
Tel: 403-793-2252;
www.brooksinthenews.com
Circulation: 11,712 *Frequency:* Monday
M. Joan Brees, Publisher

***Brooks:* Brooks Bulletin**
PO Box 1450, 124 - 3rd St. West, Brooks, AB T1R 1C3
Tel: 403-362-5571; *Fax:* 403-362-5080
editor@brooksbulletin.com
www.brooksbulletin.com
Circulation: 4,569 *Frequency:* Tuesday
James Nesbitt, Sr., Publisher

***Calgary:* Calgary Community Digest**
#453, 3545 - 32nd Ave. NE, Calgary, AB T1Y 6M6
Tel: 403-271-8275; *Fax:* 604-875-0336
digestnews@yahoo.ca
Circulation: 25,000 *Frequency:* Tuesday
N. Ebrahim, Manager, Advertisements

***Calgary:* Calgary Herald Your City**
PO Box 2400 M, 215 - 16th St. SE, Calgary, AB T2P 0W8
Tel: 403-235-7538; *Fax:* 403-235-7379
Circulation: 115,000 *Frequency:* Thursday; 2 city area editions
Dan Gaynor, Publisher

***Calgary:* Le Chinook**
6415 Larkspur Way, Calgary, AB T3E 5P9
Tél: 403-232-5488; *Téléc:* 403-232-5489
lechinook@shaw.ca
Circulation: 10 000 *Frequency:* Mensuel; français
Agathe Fillion

***Camrose:* Camrose Booster**
4925 - 48 St., Camrose, AB T4V 1L7
Tel: 780-672-3142; *Fax:* 780-672-2518
ads@camrosebooster.com
camrosebooster.com
Circulation: 12,941 *Frequency:* Tuesday
Blain Fowler, Publisher
Berdie Fowler, Editor

***Camrose:* Camrose Canadian**
4903 - 49 Ave., Camrose, AB T4V 0M9
Tel: 780-672-4421; *Fax:* 780-672-5323
production@camrosecanadian.com
www.camrosecanadian.com
Circulation: 12,948 *Frequency:* Sunday
Lynne Chernin, Publisher
Elaine Pennington, Editor

***Canmore:* Canmore Leader**
#100, 50 Lincoln Park, Canmore, AB T1W 1N8
Tel: 403-678-2365; *Fax:* 403-678-2996
info@canmoreleader.com
www.canmoreleader.com
Circulation: 6,856 *Frequency:* Wednesday
Kim Oliver, Publisher

***Canmore:* Rocky Mountain Outlook**
PO Box 8610, Canmore, AB T1W 2V3
Tel: 403-609-0220;
www.rockymountainoutlook.ca
Circulation: 12,404 *Frequency:* Thu.
Carol Picard, Editor

***Cardston:* Temple City Star**
PO Box 2060, 80 - 2nd Ave. West, Cardston, AB T0K 0K0
Tel: 403-653-4664; *Fax:* 403-653-4006
tempcity@telusplanet.net
www.templecitystar.com
Circulation: 3,000 *Frequency:* Thursday
Robert Smith, Publisher

***Castor:* Castor Advance**
PO Box 120, Castor, AB T0C 0X0
Tel: 403-882-4044; *Fax:* 403-882-2010
Circulation: 873 *Frequency:* Thursday
Aubrey Brown, Publisher
Stewart Brown, Editor

***Claresholm:* Claresholm Local Press**
PO Box 520, 4913 - 2nd St. West, Claresholm, AB T0L 0T0
Tel: 403-625-4474; *Fax:* 403-625-2828
www.claresholmlocalpress.ca
Circulation: 1,839 *Frequency:* Wednesday
Rob Vogt, Editor
Roxanne Thompson, General Manager

***Coaldale:* Sunny South News**
PO Box 30, Coaldale, AB T1M 1M2
Tel: 403-345-3081;
www.sunnysouthnews.com
Circulation: 3,576 *Frequency:* Tuesday
Coleen Campbell, Publisher

***Cochrane:* Calgary Country**
Bay 8, 206 - 5th Ave. West, Cochrane, AB T4C 1X3
Tel: 403-932-3500; *Fax:* 403-932-3935
www.calgarycountry.com
Darryl Mills, Editor
Bob Doornenbal, Publisher

***Cochrane:* Cochrane Eagle**
126A River Ave., Cochrane, AB T4C 2C2
Tel: 403-932-6588; *Fax:* 403-851-6520
www.cochraneeagle.com
Circulation: 12,200 *Frequency:* Weekly
Jack Tennant, Publisher
Ian Tennant, Editor

***Cochrane:* Rocky View Times/Cochrane Times**
206 - 5th Ave. West, Bay 8, Cochrane, AB T4C 1X3
Tel: 403-932-3500; *Fax:* 403-932-3935
www.cochranetimes.com
Circulation: 10,000 *Frequency:* Wednesday
Bob Doornenbal, Publisher

***Cold Lake:* Cold Lake Sun**
PO Box 268, 5517 - 55 St., Cold Lake, AB T9M 1P1
Tel: 780-594-5881; *Fax:* 780-594-2120
gcclsun@telusplanet.net
www.coldlakesun.com
Circulation: 5,849 *Frequency:* Tuesday
Raymon Picco, Publisher

***Cold Lake:* The Courier**
Centennial Bldg. #67, PO Box 6190 Forces, Cold Lake, AB T9M 2C5
Tel: 780-594-5206; *Fax:* 780-594-2139
thecourier@telus.net
www.thecouriernewspaper.ca
Circulation: 3,000 *Frequency:* Tuesday
Joy Smith, Editor
Diana Warbeck, Manager

***Consort:* Consort Enterprise**
PO Box 129, 5008 - 52nd St., Consort, AB T0C 1B0
Tel: 403-577-3337; *Fax:* 403-577-3611
consort_enterprise@awnet.net
consortenterprise.awna.com
Circulation: 1,285 *Frequency:* Wednesday
Carol Bruha, Publisher

***Coronation:* Coronation Review**
PO Box 70, 4923 Victoria Ave., Coronation, AB T0C 1C0
Tel: 403-578-4111; *Fax:* 403-578-2088
coronews@wildroseinternet.ca
www.coronationreview.com
Circulation: 1,140 *Frequency:* Monday
Joyce Webster, Publisher
Joyce Webster, Editor

***Didsbury:* Didsbury Review**
PO Box 760, 2017 - 19th Ave., Didsbury, AB T0M 0W0
Tel: 403-335-3301; *Fax:* 403-335-8143
mereview@airenet.com
www.didsburyreview.ca/
Circulation: 3,001 *Frequency:* Tuesday
Murray Elliott, Publisher

***Drayton Valley:* Drayton Valley Western Review**
PO Box 6960, 4905 - 52nd Ave., Drayton Valley, AB T7A 1S3
Tel: 780-542-5380; *Fax:* 780-542-9200
dvwr@incentre.net
www.draytonvalleywesternreview.com
Circulation: 4,301 *Frequency:* Tuesday
Kelly Stone, Publisher
Graham Long, Editor

***Drumheller:* Drumheller Mail**
PO Box 1629, Drumheller, AB T0J 0Y0
Tel: 403-823-2580; *Fax:* 403-823-3864
information@drumhellermail.com
www.drumhellermail.com
Circulation: 4,826 *Frequency:* Wednesday
Ossie Sheddy

***Drumheller:* The Drumheller Valley Times**
PO Box 1627, 110 - 3 Ave. West, Drumheller, AB T0Y 0Y0
Tel: 403-823-6397; *Fax:* 403-823-6813
info@valleytimes.ca
www.valleytimes.ca
Circulation: 5,549 *Frequency:* Tuesday
Isabell Fooks, Publisher

***Edmonton:* Beverly Page**
PO Box 51034, Highland Post Office, Edmonton, AB T5W 5G5
Tel: 780-479-3959
Circulation: 15,000
Marcel Dalton, Publisher

***Edmonton:* Edmonton Examiner**
#250, 4990 - 92 Ave., Edmonton, AB T6B 3A1
Tel: 780-444-5450; *Fax:* 780-451-1421
www.edmontonexaminer.com
Circulation: 136,477 *Frequency:* Wednesday
Barry Hanson, Editor
John Caputo, Publisher

***Edmonton:* Journal Le Franco**
#201, 8627 - 91 St., Edmonton, AB T6C 3N1
Tel: 780-465-6581; *Fax:* 780-469-1129
journal@lefranco.ab.ca
www.lefranco.ab.ca
Circulation: 3,500 *Frequency:* Vendredi; français
Éric Batalla, Directeur

***Edson:* Edson Leader**
PO Box 6330, 4820 - 3rd Ave., Edson, AB T7E 1T8
Tel: 780-723-3301; *Fax:* 780-723-5171
leadernews@telusplanet.net
www.edsonleader.com
Circulation: 2,824 *Frequency:* Monday
Derek Pyne, Publisher
Chandra Lye, Editor

***Edson:* The Weekly Anchor**
PO Box 6870, 420 - 50 St., Edson, AB T7E 1V2
Tel: 780-723-5787; *Fax:* 780-723-5725
anchor@yellowhead.com
www.weeklyanchor.com
Circulation: 6,100 *Frequency:* Every other Mon.
Craig McArthur, Publisher

***Elk Point:* Elk Point Review**
PO Box 309, 4809 - 50 Ave., Elk Point, AB T0A 1A0
Tel: 780-724-4087
Circulation: 602 *Frequency:* Tuesday
Clare Gauvreau, Publisher

***Fairview:* Fairview Post**
PO Box 1900, 10118 - 110 St., Fairview, AB T0H 1L0
Tel: 780-835-4925; *Fax:* 780-835-4227
info@fairviewpost.com
www.fairviewpost.com
Circulation: 2,256 *Frequency:* Tuesday
Scott Fitzpatrick, Publisher
Natasha Botha, Editor

***Falher:* Smoky River Express**
PO Box 644, 217 Main St. SW, Falher, AB T0H 1M0
Tel: 780-837-2585; *Fax:* 780-837-2102
srexpress@telus.net
www.smokyriverexpress.com
Circulation: 2,166 *Frequency:* Wednesday
Kevin Laliberte, Editor
Jeff Burgar, Publisher

***Fort MacLeod:* Macleod Gazette**
PO Box 720, 310 - 24th St., Fort MacLeod, AB T0L 0Z0
Tel: 403-553-3391; *Fax:* 403-553-2961
ftmgazet@telusplanet.net
www.fortmacleodgazette.com
Circulation: 1,309 *Frequency:* Wednesday
Frank McTighe, Publisher

***Fort Saskatchewan:* Fort Saskatchewan Record**
#155, 10420 - 98 Ave., Fort Saskatchewan, AB T8L 2N6
Tel: 780-998-7070; *Fax:* 780-998-5515
fortsaskrecord@telusplanet.net
www.fortsaskatchewanrecord.com
Circulation: 16,780 *Frequency:* Tuesday, Friday
Wayne Jobb, Publisher

***Grande Cache:* Grande Cache Mountaineer**
2702 Pine Plaza, PO Box 660, Grande Cache, AB T0E 0Y0
Tel: 780-827-3539; *Fax:* 780-827-3530
gcnews@telus.net
grandecachenews.awna.com
Circulation: 1,296 *Frequency:* Tuesday
Noel Edey, Publisher
Arthur Veitch, Editor

***Grande Prairie:* Peace Country Sun**
PO Box 3000, 10604 - 100 St., Grande Prairie, AB T8V 6V4
Tel: 780-532-1110; *Fax:* 780-532-2120
www.peacecountrysun.com
Circulation: 19,721 *Frequency:* bi-weekly; also Peace Country Farmer (circ. 29,190)
Kent Keebaugh, Publisher

***Grimshaw:* The Mile Zero News**
PO Box 1010, Grimshaw, AB T0H 1W0
Tel: 780-332-2215; *Fax:* 780-332-4380
milezeronews@mackreport.ab.ca
Circulation: 1,292 *Frequency:* Wednesday

***Hanna:* Hanna Herald**
PO Box 790, Hanna, AB T0J 1P0
Tel: 403-854-3366; *Fax:* 403-854-3256
haherald@telusplanet.net
www.hannaherald.com
Circulation: 2,455 *Frequency:* Tuesday
Mario Prusina, Publisher

***Hardisty:* The Hardisty World**
PO Box 419, 5135 - 50 St., Hardisty, AB T0B 1V0
Tel: 780-888-3836; *Fax:* 780-888-3850
hworld@telusplanet.net
www.hardistyworld.awna.com/
Rob Rondeau, Publisher

***High Level:* High Level Echo**
PO Box 1018, 10006 - 97 St., High Level, AB T0H 1Z0
Tel: 780-926-2000; *Fax:* 780-926-2001
Circulation: 1,599 *Frequency:* Wednesday
Tom Mihaly, Publisher

***High Prairie:* South Peace News**
c/o South Peace News, PO Box 1000, 4901 - 51 Ave., High Prairie, AB T0G 1E0
Tel: 780-523-4484; *Fax:* 780-523-3039
spn@inetnorth.net
www.southpeacenews.com
Circulation: 1,813 *Frequency:* Wednesday
May Burgar, Publisher

***High River:* High River Times**
618 Centre St. South, High River, AB T1V 1E9
Tel: 403-652-2034; *Fax:* 403-652-3962
info@highrivertimes.com
www.highrivertimes.com
Circulation: 12,930 *Frequency:* Wednesday, Friday

Nancy Middleton, Publisher

***Hinton:* Hinton Parklander**
104 McLeod Ave., Hinton, AB T7V 2A9
Tel: 780-865-3115; *Fax:* 780-865-1252
bbentt@telusplanet.net
www.hintonparklander.com
Circulation: 2,569 *Frequency:* Monday
Tyler Waugh, Publisher
Bradley Fehr, Editor

***Hythe:* Hythe Headliner**
Hythe Family & Community Support Services, PO Box 622, 10011A - 100 St., Hythe, AB T0H 2C0
Tel: 780-356-2004; *Fax:* 780-356-2009
headliner@telus.net
www.hythe.ca
Circulation: 1,000 *Frequency:* Bi-weekly
Monica Shaw, Director
Gisela Everton, Manager, Advertisements

***Innisfail:* Innisfail Province**
4932 - 49th St., Innisfail, AB T4G 1N2
Tel: 403-227-3477; *Fax:* 403-227-3330
rbrinson@innisfail.greatwest.ca
www.innisfailprovince.com
Circulation: 8,425 *Frequency:* Tuesday
Ray Brinson, Publisher

***Irricana:* Carstairs Courier**
PO Box 40, Irricana, AB T0M 1B0
Tel: 403-337-2806; *Fax:* 403-337-3160
www.carstairscourier.awna.com
Circulation: 2,951 *Frequency:* Tuesday
Jackie Taylor, Publisher

***Irricana:* Crossfield Five Village Weekly**
c/o Tall Taylor Publishing Ltd., PO Box 40, 2nd Ave. & 2nd St., Irricana, AB T0M 1B0
Tel: 403-935-4221; *Fax:* 403-935-4981
deal@wheel-deal.com
www.wheel-deal.com
Circulation: 14,555

***Jasper:* Jasper Booster**
PO Box 940, 622 Connaught, Jasper, AB T0E 1E0
Tel: 780-852-3620; *Fax:* 780-852-3384
jbooster@incentre.net
www.jasperbooster.com
Circulation: 797 *Frequency:* Wednesday
Mary-Ann Kostiuk, Publisher

***La Crete:* Northern Pioneer**
PO Box 571, La Crete, AB T0H 2H0
Tel: 780-928-4000
Circulation: 999

***Lac La Biche:* Lac La Biche Post**
PO Box 508, 10211 - 101 St., Lac La Biche, AB T0A 2C0
Tel: 780-623-4221; *Fax:* 780-623-4230
Circulation: 2,832 *Frequency:* Tuesday
Rob McKinley, Publisher

***Lacombe:* Lacombe Globe**
5022 - 50th St., Lacombe, AB T4L 1W8
Tel: 403-782-3498; *Fax:* 403-782-5850
publisher@lacombglobe.com
www.lacombeglobe.com
Circulation: 2,911 *Frequency:* Tuesday
Mary-Ann Kostiuk, Publisher
Lisa Joy, Editor

***Lamont:* Lamont Farm 'N' Friends**
PO Box 800, Lamont, AB T0B 2R0
Tel: 780-421-9715; *Fax:* 780-942-2515
redwater@shaw.ca
Circulation: 21,922 *Frequency:* Tuesday
Ed Cowley, Publisher/Editor

***Leduc:* Leduc Representative**
4504 - 61 Ave., Leduc, AB T9E 3Z1
Tel: 780-986-2271; *Fax:* 780-986-6397
editor-rep@webcoleduc.com
www.leducrep.com
Circulation: 12,881 *Frequency:* Friday
Neil Sutcliffe, Publisher

***Lethbridge:* Lethbridge Shopper**
234 - 12th St. B North, Lethbridge, AB T1H 2K7
Tel: 403-329-8225; *Fax:* 403-329-8211
www.theshoppergroup.com
Circulation: 35,500 *Frequency:* Saturday
Brian Legoff, Manager

***Lloydminster:* Lloydminster Meridian Booster**
5714 - 44th St., Lloydminster, AB T9V 0B6
Tel: 780-875-3362; *Fax:* 780-875-3423
booster@telusplanet.net
www.meridianbooster.com
Circulation: 43,041 *Frequency:* Monday, Wednesday, Friday
Shaun Jessome, Publisher
Dana Smith, Managing Editor

***Manning:* Manning Banner Post**
PO Box 686, Manning, AB T0H 2M0
Tel: 780-836-3588; *Fax:* 780-836-2820
bannerpost@mackreport.ab.ca
Circulation: 1,200 *Frequency:* Wednesday
Tim Mihlay, Publisher

***Mayerthorpe:* The Freelancer**
PO Box 599, Mayerthorpe, AB T0E 1N0
Tel: 780-786-2602; *Fax:* 780-786-2663
may-free@telusplanet.net
www.mayerthorpefreelancer.com
Circulation: 1,254 *Frequency:* Wednesday
Jim Gray, Publisher

***Medicine Hat:* Medicine Hat Shopper**
922 Allowance Ave. SE, Medicine Hat, AB T1A 3G7
Tel: 403-527-5777; *Fax:* 403-526-7352
rheizelman@ac403.com
www.shoppergroup.com
Circulation: 23,688 *Frequency:* Saturday
Ron Heizelman, General Manager

***Medicine Hat:* Prairie Post**
3257 Dunmore Rd. SE, Medicine Hat, AB T1B 3R2
Tel: 403-527-1101; *Fax:* 403-528-2276
Toll-Free: 800-682-2476
jtennant@prairie-post.com
www.prairie-post.com
Circulation: 24,500 *Frequency:* Fri.
Jim Tennant, General Manager
Mike Hertz, Group Publisher

***Morinville:* The Free Press**
PO Box 3005, Morinville, AB T8R 1P7
Tel: 780-939-3309; *Fax:* 780-939-3093
redwater@shaw.ca
Circulation: 9,452 *Frequency:* Tuesday
Ed Cowley, Publisher

***Morinville:* The Morinville Free Press**
PO Box 3005, Morinville, AB T8R 2P7
Tel: 780-939-3309; *Fax:* 780-939-3093
redwater@shaw.ca
Circulation: 9,452 *Frequency:* Tuesday
Ed Cowley, Editor

***Morinville:* Morinville Mirror**
10205 - 100 Ave., Morinville, AB T8R 1P9
Tel: 780-939-2133; *Fax:* 780-939-2425
mirror1@telusplanet.net
www.morinvillemirror.com
Circulation: 10,048 *Frequency:* Wednesday
Sonia Fedorus, Publisher
Lawrence Gleason, Editor

***Morinville:* Redwater Tribune**
10205 - 100 Ave., Morinville, AB T8R 1P9
Tel: 780-460-8868; *Fax:* 780-939-2425
tribnews@bowesnet.com
www.redwatertribune.com
Circulation: 3,701 *Frequency:* Wednesday
Sonia Fedorus, Publisher

***Nanton:* Nanton News**
PO Box 429, 2129 - 20 St., Nanton, AB T0L 1R0
Tel: 403-646-2023; *Fax:* 403-646-2848
natnnews@telusplanet.net
www.nantonnews.com
Circulation: 1,012 *Frequency:* Wednesday
Nancy Middleton, Publisher

***Okotoks:* The Western Wheel**
PO Box 150, 9 McRae St., Okotoks, AB T1S 2A2
Tel: 403-938-6397; *Fax:* 403-938-2518
info@westernwheel.com
www.westernwheel.com
Circulation: 14,370 *Frequency:* Wednesday
Paul Rockley, Publisher

***Olds:* Mountain View County News**
6102 - 46 St., Olds, AB T4H 1M5
Tel: 403-556-3351; *Fax:* 403-556-3464
oldsgaz@telusplanet.net
Circulation: 14,465 *Frequency:* Every other Fri.

***Olds:* The Olds Albertan**
PO Box 3910, 5021 - 51 St., Olds, AB T4H 1P6
Tel: 403-556-7510; *Fax:* 403-556-7515
albertan@olds.greatwest.ca
www.oldsalbertan.awna.com
Circulation: 6,675 *Frequency:* Tuesday
Murray Elliott, Publisher

***Olds:* Olds Albertan**
PO Box 3910, 6102 - 46 St., Olds, AB T4H 1P6
Tel: 403-556-7510; *Fax:* 403-556-3464
oldsgaz@telusplanet.net
oldsalbertan.awna.com
Circulation: 6,675 *Frequency:* Tuesday
Murray Elliott, Publisher

***Onoway:* The Lac Ste. Anne Bulletin**
PO Box 822, Onoway, AB T0E 1V0
Tel: 780-967-4754; *Fax:* 780-967-4756
tbulletin@icrossroads.com
Frequency: Fri.

***Oyen:* Oyen Echo**
109 - 6th Ave. East, Oyen, AB T0J 2J0
Tel: 403-664-3622; *Fax:* 403-664-3622
oyenecho@telusplanet.net
oyenecho.awna.com
Circulation: 1,446 *Frequency:* Tuesday
Ronald Holmes, Publisher

***Peace River:* Peace River Record-Gazette**
PO Box 6870, 10009 - 100 Ave., Peace River, AB T8S 1S6
Tel: 780-624-2591; *Fax:* 780-624-8600
news@prrecordgazette.com
www.prrecordgazette.com
Circulation: 2,834 *Frequency:* Tuesday
Scott Fitzpatrick, Publisher

***Pincher Creek:* Pincher Creek Echo**
PO Box 1000, 714 Main St., Pincher Creek, AB T0K 1W0
Tel: 403-627-3252; *Fax:* 403-627-3949
www.pinchercreekecho.com
Circulation: 2,432 *Frequency:* Friday
Kathy Taylor, Publisher

***Ponoka:* Ponoka News & Advertiser**
PO Box 4217, 5010 - 50th Ave., Ponoka, AB T4J 1R6
Tel: 403-783-3311; *Fax:* 403-783-6300
publisher@ponokanews.com
www.ponokanews.com/
Circulation: 6,257 *Frequency:* Wednesday
Tiffany Williams, Editor

***Provost:* Provost News**
PO Box 180, 5111 - 50th St., Provost, AB T0B 3S0
Tel: 780-753-2564; *Fax:* 780-753-6117
www.provostnews.ca
Circulation: 1,981 *Frequency:* Wednesday
Richard Holmes, Publisher

***Red Deer:* Red Deer Express**
#121, 5301 - 43 St., Red Deer, AB T4N 1C8
Tel: 403-346-3356; *Fax:* 403-347-6620
adviser@reddeer.greatwest.ca
www.reddeerexpress.com
Circulation: 39,104 *Frequency:* Wed.
Graham Schofield, Publisher
Sean McCann, Editor

***Red Deer:* Red Deer Life**
2950 Bremner Ave., PO Bag 5200, Red Deer, AB T4N 5G3
Frequency: Sunday

***Redwater:* The Review**
PO Box 850, Redwater, AB T0A 2W0
Tel: 780-942-2023; *Fax:* 780-942-2515
redwater@shaw.ca
Circulation: 7,742 *Frequency:* Tuesday
Wanda Cowley, Publisher
Edwin Cowley, Editor

***Rimbey:* Rimbey Review**
PO Box 244, 5001 - 50 Ave., Rimbey, AB T0C 2J0
Tel: 403-843-4909; *Fax:* 403-843-4907
publisher@rimbeyreview.com
www.rimbeyreview.com
Circulation: 5,419 *Frequency:* Tuesday
Doug Wyrostok, Publisher

Rocky Mountain House: The Mountaineer
4814 - 49 St., Rocky Mountain House, AB T4T 1S8
Tel: 403-845-3334; *Fax:* 403-845-5570
editor@rmh-mountaineer.com
rmh-mountaineer.awna.com
Circulation: 4,301 *Frequency:* Tuesday
Glen Mazza, Publisher
Brian Mazza, Editor

Rycroft: The Central Peace Signal
PO Box 250, Rycroft, AB T0H 3A0
Tel: 780-765-3604; *Fax:* 780-765-2188
admin@cpsignal.com
www.centralpeacesignal.com
Circulation: 2,389 *Frequency:* Tuesday
Dan Zahara, Publisher

Sedgewick: The Community Press
PO Box 99, Sedgewick, AB T0B 4C0
Tel: 780-384-3641; *Fax:* 780-384-2244
info@thecommunitypress.com
www.thecommunitypress.com
Circulation: 2,722 *Frequency:* Tuesday
Kerry Anderson, Publisher

Sherwood Park: The News
168 Kaska Rd., Sherwood Park, AB T8A 4G7
Tel: 780-464-0033; *Fax:* 780-464-8512
parknews@telusplanet.net
www.sherwoodparknews.com
Circulation: 21,386 *Frequency:* Wednesday
David Clarke, Editor
B. Wayne Jobb, Publisher

Sherwood Park: Strathcona County This Week
#154A, 150 Chippewa Rd., Sherwood Park, AB T8A 6A2
Tel: 780-464-5176; *Fax:* 780-467-4125
thisweek@telusplanet.net
www.strathconathisweek.com
Circulation: 24,435 *Frequency:* Friday
Andreas Morse, Senior Reporter
Mike Ivanik, Sales Coordinator

Slave Lake: Lakeside Leader
PO Box 849, 103 - 3rd St. NE, Slave Lake, AB T0G 2A0
Tel: 780-849-4380; *Fax:* 780-849-3903
www.lakesideleader.com
Circulation: 3,544 *Frequency:* Wednesday
Mary Burgar, Publisher

Slave Lake: Slave Lake Scope
PO Box 1130, Slave Lake, AB T0G 2A0
Tel: 780-849-4350; *Fax:* 780-849-2433
Circulation: 1,018 *Frequency:* Saturday
Bruce Thomas, Publisher

Smoky Lake: Smoky Lake Signal
PO Box 328, Smoky Lake, AB T0A 3C0
Tel: 780-656-4114; *Fax:* 780-656-4361
www.smokylake.com/index.php
Circulation: 1,639 *Frequency:* Wednesday
Lorne Taylor, Publisher

Spruce Grove: Calmar Community Voice
PO Box 3595, Spruce Grove, AB T7X 3A8
Tel: 780-962-9228; *Fax:* 780-962-1021
comvoice@telusplanet.net
www.com-voice.com
Circulation: 3,000 *Frequency:* Every other Tue.
Elaine Lewchuck, Publisher

Spruce Grove: The Examiner
PO Box 4206, 322 McLeod Ave., Spruce Grove, AB T7X 2K5
Tel: 780-962-4257; *Fax:* 780-962-0658
ritas@bowesnet.com
www.sprucegroveexaminer.com
Circulation: 9,342 *Frequency:* Friday
Rita Sharek, Publisher

Spruce Grove: Onoway Community Voice
PO Box 3595, 15A Alberta Ave., Spruce Grove, AB T7X 3A8
Tel: 780-962-9228; *Fax:* 780-962-1021
comvoice@telusplanet.net
www.com-voice.com
Circulation: 5,000 *Frequency:* Every other Tue.
Elaine Lewchuck, Publisher

Spruce Grove: Wabamun Community Voice
PO Box 3595, 15A Alberta Ave., Spruce Grove, AB T7X 3A8
Tel: 780-962-9228; *Fax:* 780-962-1021
sales@com-voice.com
com-voice.com
Circulation: Zone 1 6,000; Zone 2 5,000; Zone 3 3,500; Total 14,500 *Frequency:* Every other Tue.
Elaine Lewchuck, Publisher

St Albert: Saint City News
#145, 44 Riel Dr., St Albert, AB T8N 5C4
Tel: 780-460-8000; *Fax:* 780-460-2437
www.saintcitynews.com
Circulation: 24,397 *Frequency:* Fri.
John Roberts, Publisher

St Albert: St. Albert Gazette
PO Box 263 Main, St Albert, AB T8N 1N3
Tel: 780-460-5500; *Fax:* 780-460-8220
www.stalbertgazette.com
Circulation: 44,142 *Frequency:* Wednesday, Saturday
Duff Jamison, Publisher
Sue Gawlak, Managing Editor

St Michael: Elk Island Triangle
PO Box 170, St Michael, AB T0B 4B0
Tel: 780-896-2223; *Fax:* 780-896-2281
Toll-Free: 866-896-2333
trinews@telusplanet.net
Circulation: 1,600 *Frequency:* 1st & 3rd Fri./mth.
Joanne Paltzat, Publisher

St Paul: St. Paul Journal
PO Box 159, 4813 - 50th Ave., St Paul, AB T0A 3A0
Tel: 780-645-3342; *Fax:* 780-645-2346
www.spjournal.com
Circulation: 4,171 *Frequency:* Tuesday
Claire Gauvreau, Publisher

Stettler: Stettler Independent
PO Box 310, 4810 - 50th Ave., Stettler, AB T0C 2L0
Tel: 403-742-2395; *Fax:* 403-742-8050
stetnews@telusplanet.net
stetnews.awna.com
Circulation: 3,323 *Frequency:* Wednesday
Marlene Conibear, Publisher

Stony Plain: Stony Plain Reporter
5006 - 50 St., Stony Plain, AB T7Z 1T3
Tel: 780-963-2291; *Fax:* 780-963-9716
stony_plain_reporter@awnet.net
www.stonyplainreporter.com
Circulation: 9,636 *Frequency:* Friday
Inez Scheideman, Publisher

Strathmore: Strathmore Standard
PO Box 2250, 136 - 2nd Ave., Strathmore, AB T1P 1K2
Tel: 403-934-3021; *Fax:* 403-934-5011
editorial@strathmorestandard.com
www.strathmorestandard.com
Circulation: 5,512 *Frequency:* Thursday
Gary Hickling, Editor

Sundre: Sundre Round-Up
PO Box 599, Sundre, AB T0M 1X0
Tel: 403-638-3577; *Fax:* 403-638-3077
roundup@sundre.greatwest.ca
sundreroundup.com
Circulation: 2,308 *Frequency:* Tuesday
Ray Lachambre, Publisher

Swan Hills: Swan Hills Grizzly Gazette
PO Box 1000, 4924 Plaza Ave., Swan Hills, AB T0G 2C0
Tel: 780-333-2100; *Fax:* 780-333-2111
sgazette@telusplanet.net
shgazette.awna.com
Circulation: 500 *Frequency:* Tuesday
Carol Webster, Publisher

Sylvan Lake: Eckville Echo
#103, 5020 - 50A St., Sylvan Lake, AB T4S 1R2
Tel: 403-887-2331; *Fax:* 403-887-2081
echo@sylvanlakenews.com
www.eckvilleecho.com
Circulation: 2,293 *Frequency:* Fri.
Barry Hibbert, Publisher

Sylvan Lake: Sylvan Lake News
#103, 5020 - 50A St., Sylvan Lake, AB T4S 1R2
Tel: 403-887-2331; *Fax:* 403-887-2081
production@sylvanlakenews.com
www.sylvanlakenews.com
Circulation: 7,500 *Frequency:* Friday
Barry Hibbert, Publisher

Taber: Taber Times
4822 - 53 St., Taber, AB T1G 1W4
Tel: 403-223-2266; *Fax:* 403-223-1408
tabads@my403.com
www.tabertimes.com
Circulation: 2,870 *Frequency:* Wednesday
Garrett Simmons, Editor
Coleen Campbell, Publisher

Three Hills: The Capital
PO Box 158, 411 Main St., Three Hills, AB T0M 2A0
Tel: 403-443-5331; *Fax:* 403-443-7331
three_hills_capital@awna.com
threehillscapital.awna.com
Circulation: 4,133 *Frequency:* Wednesday
Timothy J. Shearlaw, Publisher

Tofield: Tofield Mercury
PO Box 150, 5312 - 50 St., Tofield, AB T0B 4J0
Tel: 780-662-4046; *Fax:* 780-662-3735
tofmerc@telusplanet.net
Circulation: 1,457 *Frequency:* Tuesday
Kerry Anderson, Publisher

Two Hills: Two Hills & County Chronicle
PO Box 668, 4708-50 Street, Two Hills, AB T0B 4K0
Tel: 780-657-2524; *Fax:* 780-657-2534
chroni2h@telus.net
Circulation: 1,604 *Frequency:* Tuesday
Ruven Rajoo, Publisher

Valleyview: Valley Views
PO Box 787, 4713 - 50th St., Valleyview, AB T0H 3N0
Tel: 780-524-3490; *Fax:* 780-524-4545
valley_views@awna.com
valleyviewspub.awna.com
Circulation: 1,270 *Frequency:* Wednesday
Joan Plaxton, Publisher

Vauxhall: Vauxhall Advance
PO Box 302, 516 - 2nd Ave. North, Vauxhall, AB T0K 2K0
Tel: 403-654-2122;
www.vauxhalladvance.com
Circulation: 673 *Frequency:* Thursday
Coleen Campbell, Publisher

Vegreville: Vegreville News Advertiser
PO Box 810, Vegreville, AB T9C 1R9
Tel: 780-632-2861; *Fax:* 780-632-7981
Toll-Free: 800-522-4127
editor@newsadvertiser.com
www.newsadvertiser.com
Circulation: 10,700 *Frequency:* Monday
Arthur Beaudrette, General Manager
Dan Beaudrette, Publisher

Vegreville: Vegreville Observer
PO Box 489, Vegreville, AB T9C 1R6
Tel: 780-632-2353; *Fax:* 780-632-3235
news@vegobserver.ca
Circulation: 7,426 *Frequency:* Wednesday
Daniel Beaudette, Publisher, Editor, and Advertising Manager
Arthur Beaudette, General Manager

Vermilion: Vermilion Standard
4917 - 50 Ave., Vermilion, AB T9X 1A6
Tel: 780-853-5344; *Fax:* 780-853-5203
news@vermilionstandard.com
www.vermilionstandard.com
Circulation: 2,722 *Frequency:* Tuesday
Dan Macpherson, Publisher and General Manager

Veteran: Veteran Eagle
PO Box 462, Veteran, AB T0C 2S0
Tel: 403-575-3892; *Fax:* 403-575-3938
veagle@agt.net
www.geocities.com/veteraneagle
Circulation: 525 *Frequency:* Thursday
Les Hainer, Publisher

Viking: The Weekly Review
PO Box 240, 5311 - 50th St., Viking, AB T0B 4N0
Tel: 780-336-3422; *Fax:* 780-336-3223
wrnews@telusplanet.net
www.vikingweeklyreview.com
Circulation: 1,252 *Frequency:* Tuesday
Patricia Harcourt, Editor

Vulcan: Vulcan Advocate
PO Box 389, 211 Centre St., Vulcan, AB T0L 2B0
Tel: 403-485-2036; *Fax:* 403-485-6938
publisher@vulcanadvocate.com
www.vulcanadvocate.com
Circulation: 2,095 *Frequency:* Wednesday
Nancy Middleton, Publisher
Catherine Pooley, Editor, Pooley

Wainwright: Wainwright Review
414 - 10th St., Wainwright, AB T9W 1P5
Tel: 780-842-4465; *Fax:* 780-842-2760
kelly@starnews.ca
www.starnews.ca

Circulation: 2,014 *Frequency:* Wed.
Roger Holmes, Publisher
; roger@starpress.ca
Derek Kilbourn, Associate Editor
; derek@starnews.ca

Wainwright: Wainwright Star Regional
414 - 10 St., Wainwright, AB T9W 1P5
Tel: 780-842-4465; *Fax:* 780-842-2760
starnews@telusplanet.net
starnews.ca
Circulation: 8,800 *Frequency:* Wednesday; also Wainwright Star Chronicle (circ: 1,937)
Rogers Holmes, Publisher

Westlock: Westlock News
9871 - 107th St., Westlock, AB T7P 1R9
Tel: 780-349-3033; *Fax:* 780-349-3677
news@westlock.greatwest.ca
Circulation: 3,889 *Frequency:* Monday
George Blais, Publisher
Brian Bachynski, General Manager

Wetaskiwin: Wetaskiwin Times Advertiser
PO Box 6900, 5104 - 53rd Ave., Wetaskiwin, AB T9A 2G5
Tel: 780-352-2231; *Fax:* 780-352-4333
editor@wetaskiwintimes.com
www.wetaskiwintimes.com
Circulation: 10,316 *Frequency:* Monday
Brian Bentt, Publisher

Whitecourt: Whitecourt Star
PO Box 630, 4732 - 50th Ave., Whitecourt, AB T7S 1N7
Tel: 780-778-3977; *Fax:* 780-778-6459
general@whitecourtstar.com
www.whitecourtstar.com
Circulation: 2,844 *Frequency:* Wednesday
Pam Allain, Publisher

British Columbia

Daily Newspapers in British Columbia

Dawson Creek: Peace River Block News
Hollinger Canadian Newspapers L.P., 901 - 100th Ave., Dawson Creek, BC V1G 1W2
Tel: 250-782-4888; *Fax:* 250-782-6770
prbsales@pris.bc.ca
Circulation: 2,177 *Frequency:* Monday-Friday; also Peace River Block News Sunday Regional (Sunday, circ. 10,000)
Jamie Durham, Managing Editor
Susan Rand, Publisher

Fort St John: Alaska Highway News
Hollinger Canadian Newspapers L.P., 9916 - 98th St., Fort St John, BC V1J 3T8
Tel: 250-785-5631; *Fax:* 250-785-3522
ahnews@awink.com
www.canada.com/cityguides/fortstjohn/index.html
Circulation: 3,844 *Frequency:* Monday-Friday
Ginette Graves, Associate Publisher
Dustin Walker, Managing Editor
William Julian, Publisher

Kamloops: The Daily News, Kamloops
Hollinger Canadian Newspapers L.P., 393 Seymour St., Kamloops, BC V2C 6P6
Tel: 250-372-2331; *Fax:* 250-372-0823
www.kamloopsnews.ca
Circulation: 13,643 *Frequency:* Morning
Don Herron, Publisher

Kelowna: Capital News
2495 Enterprise Way, Kelowna, BC V1X 7K2
Tel: 250-763-3212; *Fax:* 250-862-5275
nlark@kelownacapnews.com
www.kelownacapnews.com
Circulation: 157,854 *Frequency:* Wednesday, Friday, Sunday
Nigel Lark, Publisher

Kelowna: Daily Courier
550 Doyle Ave., Kelowna, BC V1Y 7V1
Tel: 250-762-4445; *Fax:* 250-762-3866
www.kelownadailycourier.ca
Circulation: 17,000 *Frequency:* Morning
Alison Yesilcimen, Publisher

Kimberley: The Daily Bulletin
335 Spokane St., Kimberley, BC V1A 1Y9
Tel: 250-427-5333; *Fax:* 250-427-5336
bulletin@cyberlink.bc.ca
www.dailytownsman.com
Circulation: 1,800 *Frequency:* Afternoon

Nanaimo: Nanaimo Harbour City Star
B1-2575 McCullough Rd., Nanaimo, BC V9S 5W5
Tel: 250-729-4200; *Fax:* 250-729-4256
cduddy@nanaimodailynews.com
www.nanaimodailynews.com
Circulation: 91,931 *Frequency:* Wed., Sat.
Cale Cowan, Managing Editor
Curt Duddy, Publisher

Nelson: Daily News
266 Baker St., Nelson, BC V1L 4H3
Tel: 250-352-3552; *Fax:* 250-352-2418
ndnews@netidea.com
www.nelsondailynews.com
Circulation: 4,347 *Frequency:* Afternoon

Penticton: Herald
186 Nanaimo Ave. West, Penticton, BC V2A 1N4
Tel: 250-492-4002; *Fax:* 250-492-2403
www.pentictonherald.ca
Circulation: 8,235 *Frequency:* Morning, Mon.-Sat.
André Martin, General Manager

Port Alberni: Alberni Valley Times
4918 Napier St., Port Alberni, BC V9Y 3H5
Tel: 250-723-8171; *Fax:* 250-723-0586
www.avtimes.net
Circulation: 6,100 *Frequency:* Monday-Friday
Rick Methot, Publisher
Karen Boden, Managing Editor

Prince George: Prince George Citizen
PO Box 5700, 150 Brunswick St., Prince George, BC V2L 5K9
Tel: 250-562-2441; *Fax:* 250-562-7453
news@princegeorgecitizen.com
www.princegeorgecitizen.com
Circulation: 16,011 *Frequency:* Monday
Del Laverdure, Publisher

Prince Rupert: Daily News
801 - 2nd Ave. West, Prince Rupert, BC V8J 1H6
Tel: 250-624-6781; *Fax:* 250-624-2851
Toll-Free: 800-343-0022
prdnews@citytel.net
www.canada.com/cityguides/princerupert/index.html
Frequency: Evening, Mon.-Fri.
Rodney Venis, Managing Editor
Lynda Lafleur, Publisher

Trail: Trail Daily Times
Hollinger Canadian Newspapers L.P., 1163 Cedar Ave., Trail, BC V1R 4B8
Tel: 250-368-8551; *Fax:* 250-368-8550
sales@trailtimes.ca
Circulation: 5,490 *Frequency:* Afternoon; also West Kootenay Weekender (23,000), Fri.
Tracy Gilchrist, Editor
Barbara Blatchford, Publisher

Vancouver: Metro Vancouver
#250, 1190 Homer St., Vancouver, BC V6B 2X6
Tel: 604-602-1002; *Fax:* 866-254-6504
www.metronews.ca
Frequency: 145,000
Mary Kemmis, Publisher/Managing Director

Vancouver: The Province
#1, 200 Granville St., Vancouver, BC V6C 3N3
Tel: 604-605-2000; *Fax:* 604-605-2720
www.canada.com/vancouver/theprovince/index.html
Circulation: 216,074 *Frequency:* Morning, Sun.-Fri.
Wayne Moriarty, Editor-in-chief

Vancouver: The Vancouver Sun
Pacific Newspaper Group Inc., #1, 200 Granville St., Vancouver, BC V6C 3N3
Tel: 604-605-2000; *Fax:* 604-605-2308
info@png.canwest.com
www.canada.com/vancouversun/info/index.html
Circulation: 196,903 Mon.-Thu., 252,000 Fri., 253,900 Sat.
Frequency: Morning
Dennis Skulsky, Publisher
Patricia Graham, Editor-in-chief

Victoria: Times Colonist
PO Box 300, 2621 Douglas St., Victoria, BC V8T 4M2
Tel: 250-380-5211; *Fax:* 250-380-5353
www.canada.com/victoriatimescolonist/index.html
Circulation: 77,000 *Frequency:* Morning

Other Newspapers in British Columbia

100 Mile House: The 100 Mile House Advisor
PO Box 490, 351A South Birch Ave., 100 Mile House, BC V0K 2E0
Tel: 250-395-1053; *Fax:* 250-395-1057
editor@100milehouseadvisor.com
Circulation: 6,084 *Frequency:* Wed.
Tari Meade, Publisher

100 Mile House: 100 Mile House Free Press
PO Box 459, #3, 536 Horse Lake Rd., 100 Mile House, BC V0K 2E0
Tel: 250-395-2219; *Fax:* 250-395-3939
100milefreepress@bcnewsgroup.com
www.100milefreepress.net
Circulation: 3,631 *Frequency:* Wednesday
Iris Phillips, Editor

Abbotsford: Abbotsford News
34375 Gladys Ave., Abbotsford, BC V2S 2H5
Tel: 604-853-1144; *Fax:* 604-850-5426
editor@abbynews.com
www.abbynews.com
Circulation: 124,288 *Frequency:* Tuesday, Thursday, Saturday
Josh O'Connor, Publisher
Rick Rake, Editor

Abbotsford: Abbotsford Times
#1, 30887 Peardonville Rd., Abbotsford, BC V2T 6K2
Tel: 604-854-5244; *Fax:* 604-854-1140
editorial@abbotsfordtimes.com
www.abbotsfordtimes.com
Circulation: 88,281 *Frequency:* Tuesday, Friday
Rod Thomson, Publisher

Agassiz: Agassiz-Harrison Observer
PO Box 129, Agassiz, BC V0M 1A0
Tel: 604-796-4300; *Fax:* 604-796-2081
observer@uniserve.com
www.agassizharrisonobserver.com
Circulation: 4,349 *Frequency:* Wednesday
Andrew Franklin, Publisher
Darla Dickinson, Editor

Aldergrove: Aldergrove Star
27106 Fraser Hwy., Aldergrove, BC V4W 3P6
Tel: 604-856-8303; *Fax:* 604-856-5212
www.aldergrovestar.com
Circulation: 10,700 *Frequency:* Thursday
Dwayne Weldendorf, Publisher
Kurt Langmann, Editor

Armstrong: Armstrong Advertiser
PO Box 610, 3400 Okanagan St., Armstrong, BC V0E 1B0
Tel: 250-546-3121; *Fax:* 250-546-3636
armadver@telus.net
www.northokanagan.net
Circulation: 2,500 *Frequency:* Wednesday
J.H. Jamieson

Ashcroft: Ashcroft-Cache Creek Journal
PO Box 190, 128 - 4th St., Ashcroft, BC V0K 1A0
Tel: 250-453-2261; *Fax:* 250-453-9625
journal@uniserve.com
www.ash-cache-journal.com
Circulation: 1,179 *Frequency:* Tuesday
Tuula Opheim, Publisher

Barriere: North Thompson Star/Journal
PO Box 1020, Barriere, BC V0E 1E0
Tel: 250-672-5611;
advertising@starjournal.net
www.starjournal.net
Circulation: 836 *Frequency:* Monday
Al Kirkwood, Publisher
Jill Hayward, Editor

Bowen Island: Bowen Island Undercurrent
PO Box 130, Government Rd., Bowen Island, BC V0N 1G0
publisher@northshoreoutlook.com
www.bowenislandundercurrent.com
Frequency: Fri.
Linda Stewart, Publisher

Bowen Island: Undercurrent
PO Box 130, Bowen Island, BC V0N 1G0
Tel: 604-947-2442; *Fax:* 604-947-0148
undercurrent@bcnewsgroup.com
www.bowenislandundercurrent.com
Circulation: 1,400 *Frequency:* Fri.
Edythe Hanen, Editor
Dave McCullough, Publisher

***Burnaby:* Burnaby Now**
#201A, 3430 Brighton Ave., Burnaby, BC V5A 3H4
Tel: 604-444-3451; *Fax:* 604-444-3460
www.burnabynow.com
Circulation: 98,155 *Frequency:* Saturday, Wednesday
Brad Alden, Publisher
Pat Tracy, Editor

***Burnaby:* Burnaby/New Westminster News Leader**
6569 Kingsway, Burnaby, BC V5E 1E1
Tel: 604-438-6397;
publisher@burnabynewsleader.com
www.burnabynewsleader.com
Circulation: 61,463 *Frequency:* Thursday, Saturday
Tracy Keenan, Publisher

***Burnaby:* New Westminster Record**
#201A, 3430 Brighton Ave., Burnaby, BC V5A 3H4
Tel: 604-444-3451; *Fax:* 604-444-3460
editorial@royalcityrecord.com
www.royalcityrecord.com
Circulation: 32,821 *Frequency:* Saturday, Wednesday
Pat Tracy, Editor
Brad Alden, Publisher

***Burns Lake:* Lakes District News**
PO Box 309, 23 - 3rd Ave., Burns Lake, BC V0J 1E0
Tel: 250-692-7526; *Fax:* 250-692-3685
newsroom@ldnews.net
www.ldnews.net
Circulation: 1,864 *Frequency:* Wednesday
Laura Blackwell, Publisher

***Campbell River:* Campbell River Courier-Islander**
PO Box 310, 1040 Cedar St., Campbell River, BC V9W 5B5
Tel: 250-287-7464; *Fax:* 250-287-8891
editor@island.net
Circulation: 15,470 *Frequency:* Wednesday
Neil Cameron, Publisher

***Campbell River:* Campbell River Mirror**
#104, 250 Dogwood St., Campbell River, BC V9W 2X9
Tel: 250-287-9227; *Fax:* 250-287-3238
mirror@island.net
www.campbellrivermirror.com
Circulation: 31,765 *Frequency:* Wednesday, Friday
Zena Williams, Publisher
Alistair Taylor, Editor

***Campbell River:* Campbell River North Islander**
PO Box 310, 1040 Cedar St., Campbell River, BC V9W 5B5
Tel: 250-287-7464; *Fax:* 250-287-8891
editor@island.net
Circulation: 21,142 *Frequency:* Fri.
Neil Cameron, Publisher

***Campbell River:* North Islander**
1040 Cedar St., Campbell River, BC V9W 5B5
Tel: 250-287-7464;
www.northislandmidweek.com
Circulation: 21,142 *Frequency:* Fri.
Neil Cameron, Publisher
Paul Rudan, Editor

***Castlegar:* Castlegar News**
#1, 425 Columbia Ave., Castlegar, BC V1N 1G8
Tel: 250-365-6397; *Fax:* 250-365-6390
publisher@castlegarnews.com
www.castlegarnews.com
Circulation: 6,600 *Frequency:* Wed.
Ken Alexander, Editor
Mike Johnstone, Publisher

***Chetwynd:* Chetwynd Echo**
5208 North Access Rd., Chetwynd, BC V0C 1J0
Tel: 250-788-2246;
echo@chetwyndecho.com
chetwyndecho.com
Circulation: 1,300 *Frequency:* Tuesday

***Chilliwack:* Chilliwack Progress**
45860 Spadina Ave., Chilliwack, BC V2P 6H9
Tel: 604-702-5550;
editor@theprogress.com
www.theprogress.com
Circulation: 65,614 *Frequency:* Tuesday, Friday, Saturday
Andrew Franklin, Publisher
Gregg Knill, Editor

***Chilliwack:* Chilliwack Times**
45951 Tretheway Ave., Chilliwack, BC V2P 1K4
Tel: 604-792-9117; *Fax:* 604-792-9300
editorial@chilliwacktimes.com
www.chilliwacktimes.com
Circulation: 27,000 *Frequency:* Tuesday, Friday
Ken Goudswaard, Editor

***Clearwater:* North Thompson Times**
Brookfield Mall, PO Box 2592, RR#2, Clearwater, BC V0E 1N0
Tel: 250-674-3343;
newsroom@clearwatertimes.com
www.clearwatertimes.com
Circulation: 1,334 *Frequency:* Monday
Al Kirkwood, Publisher

***Coquitlam:* The Now**
#1, 2700 Barnet Hwy., Coquitlam, BC V3B 1B8
Tel: 604-942-4192;
publisher@theonnews.com
www.thenownews.com
Circulation: 54,525 *Frequency:* Wed., Fri.
Bob Moody, Publisher

***Courtenay:* Comox Valley Echo**
407D - 5th St., Courtenay, BC V9N 1J7
Tel: 250-334-4722; *Fax:* 250-334-3172
echo@mars.ark.com
www.canada.com/vancouverisland/comoxvalleyecho/index.h tml
Circulation: 22,776 *Frequency:* Tuesday
Sean Doran, Contact

***Courtenay:* Comox Valley Record**
PO Box 3729, 765 McPhee Ave., Courtenay, BC V9N 7P1
Tel: 250-338-5811; *Fax:* 250-338-5568
editor@comoxvalleyrecord.com
www.comoxvalleyrecord.com
Circulation: 44,124 *Frequency:* Wednesday, Friday
Mark Allen, Editor
Grant Lawrence, Publisher

***Cranbrook:* Cranbrook Daily Townsman**
822 Cranbrook St. North, Cranbrook, BC V1C 3R9
Tel: 250-426-5201; *Fax:* 250-426-5003
accounting@dailytownsman.com
www.dailytownsman.com
Circulation: 3,800 *Frequency:* Monday-Friday
Steen Jorgensen, Publisher

***Cranbrook:* The Kootenay Advertiser**
1510 - 2nd St. North, Cranbrook, BC V1C 3L2
Tel: 250-489-3455; *Fax:* 250-489-3743
Toll-Free: 800-665-2382
advertising@kootenayadvertiser.com
www.kootenayadvertiser.com
Circulation: 28,090 *Frequency:* Monday, Friday; TV listing supplement, 7 Days Magazine (Mon.)
Darcy Wiebe, Publisher
Kerstin Renner, Editor

***Creston:* Creston Valley Advance**
PO Box 1279, 1018 Canyon St., Creston, BC V0B 1G0
Tel: 250-428-2266; *Fax:* 250-428-3320
advance@kootenay.com
www.crestonvalley.com/advance
Circulation: 3,141 *Frequency:* Thursday
Steen Jorgenson, General Manager
Brian Lawrence, Editor

***Dawson Creek:* Dawson Creek Mirror**
1316 Alaska Ave., Dawson Creek, BC V1G 1Z3
Tel: 250-782-9424; *Fax:* 250-782-9454
Circulation: 8,200 *Frequency:* Friday

***Dawson Creek:* Tumbler Ridge Observer**
PO Box 620, 901 - 100 Ave., Dawson Creek, BC V0C 2W0
Tel: 250-242-5343; *Fax:* 250-782-6770
prbsales@pris.bc.ca
www.tumblerridgenews.com
Circulation: 1,500 *Frequency:* Wednesday
Loraine Funk, Publisher
Susan Rand, Publisher

***Delta:* Delta Optimist**
207-4840 Delta St., Delta, BC V4K 2T6
Tel: 604-946-4451; *Fax:* 604-946-5680
editor@delta-optimist.com
www.delta-optimist.com
Circulation: 33,754 *Frequency:* Wednesday, Saturday
Ted Murphy, Editor

***Delta:* South Delta Leader**
#7, 1363 - 56 St., Delta, BC V4L 2P7
Tel: 604-948-3640; *Fax:* 604-943-8619
newsroom@southdeltaleader.com
www.southdeltaleader.com
Circulation: 15,827 *Frequency:* Fri.
Lisa Farquharson, Publisher
Chris Bryan, Editor

***Duncan:* Cowichan News Leader**
#2, 5380 Trans Canada Hwy., Duncan, BC V9L 6W4
Tel: 250-746-4471;
publisher@cowichannewsleader.com
www.cowichannewsleader.com
Circulation: 20,595 *Frequency:* Wednesday
Jim Parker, Publisher
John McKinley, Editor

***Duncan:* The Pictorial**
#2, 5380 Trans Canada Hwy., Duncan, BC V9L 6W4
Tel: 250-746-4471; *Fax:* 250-746-8529
www.cowichannewsleader.com/
Circulation: 23,153 *Frequency:* Sunday
John McKinley, Editor
Bill Macadam, Editor

***Fernie:* Fernie Free Press**
342 - 2nd Ave., PO Bag 5000, Fernie, BC V0B 1M0
Tel: 250-423-4666; *Fax:* 250-423-3110
Toll-Free: 866-337-6437
freepres@shawcable.com
www.thefreepress.ca
Circulation: 1,851 *Frequency:* Wednesday
Cina Wales-Green, Publisher

***Fort Nelson:* Fort Nelson News**
PO Box 600, #3, 4448 - 50th Ave. North, Fort Nelson, BC V0C 1R0
Tel: 250-774-2357; *Fax:* 250-774-3612
editorial@fortnelsonnews.ca
www.fortnelsonnews.ca
Circulation: 2,238 *Frequency:* Wednesday
Judith Kenyon, Editor

***Fort St James:* Fort St. James Caledonia Courier**
PO Box 1298, 366 Stuart Dr., Fort St James, BC V0J 1P0
Tel: 250-996-8482; *Fax:* 250-996-7973
www.caledoniacourier.com
Circulation: 825 *Frequency:* Wednesday
Scott Farmer, Publisher

***Fort St John:* North Peace Express**
9909 100 Ave., Fort St John, BC V1J 1Y4
Tel: 250-787-7030;
abnews@awink.com
www.nenews.ca
Circulation: 25,000 *Frequency:* Wed.
Bruce Lantz, Publisher

***Fort St John:* The Northerner**
9916 - 98A Ave., Fort St John, BC V1J 1S2
Tel: 250-785-5631; *Fax:* 250-785-3522
graphicsnorth@awink.com
www.thenortherner.ca
Circulation: 7,500 *Frequency:* Wednesday
Dustin Walker, Editor
William Julian, Publisher

***Gabriola:* Gabriola Sounder**
1001 Pat Burns Ave., Gabriola, BC V0R 1X2
Tel: 250-247-9337; *Fax:* 250-247-8147
sounder@island.net
www.soundernews.com
Circulation: 3,580 *Frequency:* Monday
Sue de Carteret, Editor
Bill de Carteret, Publisher

***Gold River:* The Record**
PO Box 279, Gold River, BC V0P 1G0
Tel: 250-283-2324;
record@island.net
www.island.net/~record
Circulation: 1,300 *Frequency:* Twice monthly
Lynne West, Associate Publisher
Jerry West, Editor

***Grand Forks:* Boundary Weekender**
7255 Riverside Drive, Grand Forks, BC V0H 1H0
Tel: 250-442-2191; *Fax:* 250-442-3336
gfgazedt@sunshinecable.com
www.canwestmediaworks.com
Circulation: 4,208 *Frequency:* Friday
Sandra Watts, Publisher
Richard Finnigan, Editor

***Grand Forks:* Grand Forks Gazette**
PO Box 700, 7330 - 2nd St., Grand Forks, BC V0H 1H0
Tel: 250-442-2191; *Fax:* 250-442-3336
gfgazedt@sunshinecable.com
Circulation: 2,807 *Frequency:* Wednesday
Sandra Barron, Publisher

Jason Harshenin, Editor

Greenwood: Big White Mountaineer
PO Box 99, Greenwood, BC V0H 1J0
Tel: 250-445-2233; Fax: 250-445-2243
Circulation: 5,000

Greenwood: Boundary Creek Times Mountaineer
PO Box 99, Greenwood, BC V0H 1J0
Tel: 250-445-2233; Fax: 250-445-2243
bctimes@direct.ca
Circulation: 1,894 Frequency: Friday
Reed Turcotte, Publisher

Hagensborg: Coast Mountain News
PO Box 250, 1290 Hwy. 20, Hagensborg, BC V0T 1H0
Tel: 250-982-2696; Fax: 250-982-2512
cmnews@belco.bc.ca
Circulation: 1,150 Frequency: Every other Thu.

Hope: Hope Standard
PO Box 1090, 540 Wallace St., Hope, BC V0X 1L0
Tel: 604-869-2421; Fax: 604-869-7351
www.hopestandard.com
Circulation: 2,062 Frequency: Thursday
Simone Rolph, Editor
Andrew Franklin, Publisher

Houston: Houston Today Newspaper
PO Box 899, 3232 Hwy. 6, Houston, BC V0J 1Z0
Tel: 250-845-2890; Fax: 250-845-7893
www.houston-today.com
Circulation: 1,076 Frequency: Wednesday
Mary Ann Ruiter, Publisher

Invermere: The Valley Echo
PO Box 70, 530 - 13th St., Invermere, BC V0A 1K0
Tel: 250-342-9216; Fax: 250-342-3930
www.invermerevalleyecho.com
Circulation: 2,971 Frequency: Wednesday
Sheila Tutty, Publisher
Ian Cobb, Editor

Kamloops: Kamloops This Week
1365B Dalhousie Dr., Kamloops, BC V2C 5P6
Tel: 250-374-7467;
ktw@bcnewsgroup.com
www.kamloopsthisweek.com
Circulation: 88,680 Frequency: Wednesday, Friday, Sunday
Kelly Hall, Publisher
Christopher Foulds, Managing Editor

Keremeos: Keremeos Review
PO Box 130, 613 - 7 Ave., Keremeos, BC V0X 1N0
Tel: 250-499-2653; Fax: 250-499-2645
review@nethop.net
www.keremeosreview.com
Circulation: 1,344 Frequency: Thu.
Chuck Bennett, Publisher

Keremeos: The Review
PO Box 220, 613 7th Ave., Keremeos, BC V0X 1N0
Tel: 250-499-2653; Fax: 250-499-2645
reviewads@nethop.net
www.keremosreview.com
Frequency: Thu.
Chuck Bennett, Publisher

Kitimat: Northern Sentinel
626 Enterprise Ave., Kitimat, BC V8C 2E4
Tel: 250-632-6144; Fax: 250-639-9373
advertising@northernsentinel.com
www.northernsentinel.com
Circulation: 1,655 Frequency: Wednesday; also Weekend Advertiser (Sat., circ. 15,650)
Sandra Dugdale, Publisher

Kitimat: Weekend Advertiser
626 Enterprise Ave., Kitimat, BC V8C 2G4
Tel: 250-632-6144; Fax: 250-639-9373
advertising@northernsentinel.com
www.northernsentinel.com
Circulation: 15,800
Sandra Dugdale, Publisher
; publisher@northernsentinel.com

Ladysmith: Ladysmith-Chemainus Chronicle
PO Box 400, 341 - 1st Ave., Ladysmith, BC V9G 1A3
Tel: 250-245-2277; Fax: 250-245-2260
lccedit@vinewsgroup.com
www.ladysmithchronicle.com
Circulation: 2,640 Frequency: Tuesday
Richard Dutka, Publisher
Jason Youmans, Editor

Lake Country: Lake Country Calendar
#3 3370 Beaver Lake Rd., Lake Country, BC V4V 1S7
Tel: 250-766-4688; Fax: 250-766-4645
calendar@cablelan.net
www.lakecountrynews.net
Circulation: 6,758 Frequency: Wednesday, Saturday
Jack McCarthy, Publisher

Lake Cowichan: Lake Cowichan Gazette
PO Box 10, 170E Cowichan Lake Rd., Lake Cowichan, BC V0R 2G0
Tel: 250-749-4383; Fax: 250-749-4385
www.lakecowichangazette.com
Circulation: 936 Frequency: Wed.
Dennis Skalicky, Publisher

Lake Errock: Valley Express
PO Box 84, Lake Errock, BC V0M 1N0
Tel: 604-820-1930
Circulation: 4,000
Joanne Taylor, Publisher

Langley: Langley Advance News
#112, 6375 - 202nd St., Langley, BC V2Y 1N1
Tel: 604-534-8641; Fax: 604-534-3383
editorial@langleyadvance.com
www.langleyadvance.com
Circulation: 81,580 Frequency: Tuesday, Friday
Bob Groeneveld, Editor
Liz Lynch, General Manager

Langley: Langley Times
PO Box 3097, 20258 Fraser Hwy., Langley, BC V3A 4R3
Tel: 604-533-4157; Fax: 604-533-0219
www.langleytimes.com
Circulation: 117,264 Frequency: Wednesday, Friday, Sunday
Dwane Weidendorf, Publisher
Frank Bucholtz, Editor

Lantzville: The Lantzville Log
Lantzville Log Society, PO Box 268, 6958 Jacks Rd., Lantzville, BC V0R 2H0
Tel: 250-390-2847; Fax: 250-390-2847
info@thelog.ca
www.thelog.ca
Circulation: 3,626 Frequency: Ist Mon. of month
Wanda Cullen, Contact

Lazo: Comox Totem Times
PO Box 1000 Main, 19 Wing, CFB Comox, Lazo, BC V0R 2K0
Tel: 250-339-2541; Fax: 250-339-5209
Circulation: 2,000 Frequency: Monthly

Lillooet: Bridge River-Lillooet News
PO Box 709, Lillooet, BC V0K 1V0
Tel: 250-256-4219; Fax: 250-256-4210
Toll-Free: 877-300-8569
lillooetnews@cablelan.net
www.lillooetnews.net
Circulation: 1,581 Frequency: Wednesday
Bain Gair, Publisher

Lumby: Lumby Valley Times
PO Box 408, 2062 Park Ave., Lumby, BC V0E 2G0
Tel: 250-547-6990; Fax: 250-547-6992
lvt@telus.net
Circulation: 2,600 Frequency: Wed.
Rod Neufeld, Publisher

Mackenzie: The Times
PO Box 609, 540 Mackenzie Blvd., Mackenzie, BC V0J 2C0
Tel: 250-997-6675; Fax: 250-997-4747
thetimes@mackbc.com
Circulation: 1,500 Frequency: Tuesday
Jackie Benton, Editor

Maple Ridge: The Maple Ridge- Pitt Meadows News
22328 - 119th Ave., Maple Ridge, BC V2X 2Z3
Tel: 604-467-1122; Fax: 604-463-4731
editor@mapleridgenews.com
www.mapleridgenews.com
Circulation: 59,724 Frequency: Wed., Sat.
Michael Hall, Editor
Jim Coulter, Publisher

Maple Ridge: Maple Ridge-Pitt Meadows Times
Unit 2, 22345 North Ave., Maple Ridge, BC V2X 8T2
Tel: 604-463-2281; Fax: 604-463-9943
www.mrtimes.com
Circulation: 27,400 Frequency: Tuesday, Friday
Fred Armstrong, Publisher

Merritt: Merritt Herald
PO Box 9, 2090 Granite Ave., Merritt, BC V1K 1B8
Tel: 250-378-4241; Fax: 250-378-6818
newsroom@merrittherald.com
www.merrittherald.com
Circulation: 1,404 Frequency: Wednesday
Rick Proznick, Publisher

Merritt: The Merritt News
PO Box 939, Merritt, BC V1K 1B8
Tel: 250-378-8876
Circulation: 5,094 Frequency: Friday
Tracy McCall, Publisher

Merritt: Valley Express
PO Box 9, 2090 Granite Ave., Merritt, BC V1K 1B8
Tel: 250-378-4241; Fax: 250-378-6818
mvherald@uniserve.com
Circulation: 5,442 Frequency: Saturday
Rick Proznick, Publisher

Mission: Mission City Record
33047 - 1st Ave., Mission, BC V2V 1G2
Tel: 604-826-6221; Fax: 604-826-8266
mcrecord@uniserve.com
www.missioncityrecord.com
Circulation: 10,780 Frequency: Thu.
Josh O'Connor, Publisher
Jason Roessle, Editor

Nakusp: Arrow Lakes News
PO Box 189, 203 Broadway Ave., Nakusp, BC V0G 1R0
Tel: 250-265-3823;
newsroom@arrowlakesnews.com
www.arrowlakesnews.com
Circulation: 1,040 Frequency: Wednesday
Lynda Lafleur, Publisher

Nanaimo: Harbour City Star
B1-2575 McCullough Rd., #B1, Nanaimo, BC V9S 5W5
Tel: 250-729-4200;
www.nanaimodailynews.com
Circulation: 91,931 Frequency: Wed., Sat.
Curt Duddy, Publisher
; wking@island.net

Nanaimo: Nanaimo News Bulletin
777 Poplar St., Nanaimo, BC V9S 2H7
Tel: 250-753-3707;
publisher@nanaimobulletin.com
www.nanaimobulletin.com
Circulation: 98,079 Frequency: Tuesday, Thursday, Saturday
Roy Linder, Publisher

Nelson: Kootenay Weekly Express
554 Ward St., Nelson, BC V1L 1S9
Tel: 250-354-3910; Fax: 250-352-5075
Toll-Free: 800-665-3288
express@expressnews.bc.ca
www.expressnews.ca
Circulation: 11,801 Frequency: Wednesday
Nelson Becker, Publisher

Nelson: West Kootenay Weekender
266 Baker St., Nelson, BC V1L 4H3
Tel: 250-352-3552; Fax: 250-352-2418
weekender@nelsondailynews.com
Circulation: 26,646 Frequency: Friday; supplement to Nelson Daily News, Trail Daily Times
John A. Smith, Publisher

North Vancouver: North Shore News
100 - 126 East 15th St., North Vancouver, BC V7L 2P9
Tel: 604-985-2131; Fax: 604-985-2104
editor@nsnews.com
www.nsnews.com
Circulation: 192,584 Frequency: Wednesday, Friday, Sunday
Doug Foot, General Manager
Terry Peters, Managing Editor

North Vancouver: North Shore Outlook
#104, 980 West 1st St., North Vancouver, BC V7P 3N4
Tel: 604-903-1000; Fax: 604-903-1001
www.northshoreoutlook.com
Circulation: 58,183 Frequency: Thu.
Linda Stewart, Publisher
Andrew McCredie, Editor

Oliver: Oliver Chronicle
PO Box 880, 36083 - 97th St., Oliver, BC V0H 1T0
Tel: 250-498-3711; Fax: 250-498-3966
olivernews@img.net
www.oliverchronicle.com
Other information: Advertising Email: ads@oliverchronicle.com

Circulation: 2,393 *Frequency:* Wednesday
Michael Newman, Publisher

***Osoyoos:* Osoyoos Times**
PO Box 359, 8712 Main St., Osoyoos, BC V0H 1V0
Tel: 250-495-7225; *Fax:* 250-495-6616
news@osoyoostimes.com
www.osoyoostimes.com
Circulation: 2,340 *Frequency:* Wednesday
Chuck Bennett, Editor-in-chief
Chris Stodola, Publisher & General Manager

***Parksville:* Parksville Qualicum News**
PO Box 1180, #4, 154 Middleton Ave., Parksville, BC V9P 2H2
Tel: 250-248-4341; *Fax:* 250-248-4655
www.pqbnews.com
Circulation: 33,562 *Frequency:* Tuesday, Friday
Julie Chambers, Publisher

***Peachland:* The Peachland Signal**
PO Box 1300, 4478 - 3rd St., RR# 7, Peachland, BC V0H 1X7
Tel: 250-767-2004; *Fax:* 250-767-3306
Toll-Free: 877-867-7977
signal@shawcable.com
Circulation: 1,491 *Frequency:* Thu.
Darren Bayrack, Publisher

***Peachland:* Peachland View**
#102A, 4200 Beach Ave., Peachland, BC V0H 1X6
Tel: 250-767-7771; *Fax:* 250-767-3337
peachlandview@shaw.ca
Circulation: 3,500
Kathie McClinton

***Pender Island:* Gulf Islands, Island Tides**
PO Box 55, Pender Island, BC V0N 2M0
Tel: 250-629-3660; *Fax:* 250-629-3838
news@islandtides.com
www.islandtides.com
Circulation: 17,500
Christa Grace-Warrick, Publisher

***Penticton:* Penticton Western News**
2250 Camrose St., Penticton, BC V2A 8R1
Tel: 250-492-3636; *Fax:* 250-492-9843
western@img.net
www.pentictonwesternnews.com
Circulation: 61,316 *Frequency:* Wednesday, Friday, Sunday
Dan Ebanal, Editor
Mark Walker, Publisher

***Port Alberni:* Pennyworth**
4656 Margaret St., Port Alberni, BC V9Y 6H2
Tel: 250-723-3709;
pennywth@uniserve.com
Circulation: 10,885 *Frequency:* Wednesday
Linda Patterson

***Port Coquitlam:* The Tri-City News**
1405 Broadway St., Port Coquitlam, BC V3C 6L6
Tel: 604-525-6397;
brian@tricitynews.com
www.tricitynews.com
Circulation: 161,637 *Frequency:* Wednesday, Friday, Sunday
Brian McCristall, Publisher

***Port Hardy:* North Island Gazette**
PO Box 458, 7305 Market St., Port Hardy, BC V0N 2P0
Tel: 250-949-6225; *Fax:* 250-949-7655
publisher@northislandgazette.com
northislandgazette.com
Circulation: 2,228 *Frequency:* Wednesday
Teresa Bird, Publisher

***Powell River:* Powell River Peak**
4400 Marine Ave., Powell River, BC V8A 2K1
Tel: 604-485-5313; *Fax:* 604-485-5007
publisher@prpeak.com
www.prpeak.com
Circulation: 11,680 *Frequency:* Wed., Fri.
Joyce Carlson, Publisher
Laura Walz, Editor

***Prince George:* Prince George Free Press**
1773 South Lyon St., Prince George, BC V2N 1T3
Tel: 250-564-0005; *Fax:* 250-562-0025
editor@pgfreepress.com
pgfreepress.com
Circulation: 59,590 *Frequency:* Wed., Fri.
Dennis Chapman, Publisher
Darlene Osborne, General Manager
Bill Phillips, Editor

***Prince George:* Prince George This Week**
145 Brunswick St., Prince George, BC V2L 2B2
Tel: 250-563-9988; *Fax:* 250-562-5012
Circulation: 32,500 *Frequency:* Sunday; also Central Interior Buy & Sell (Wed. 8,000)
Christine Skorepa, Editor

***Princeton:* Similkameen News Leader**
PO Box 956, 226A Bridge St., Princeton, BC V0X 1W0
Tel: 250-295-4149; *Fax:* 250-295-4103
Toll-Free: 888-350-9969
george@thenewsleader.ca
www.thenewsleader.ca
Circulation: 1,400
W. George Elliott, Publisher/Owner

***Princeton:* Similkameen Spotlight**
PO Box 340, Princeton, BC V0X 1W0
Tel: 250-295-3535; *Fax:* 250-295-7322
editor@similkameenspotlight.com
www.similkameenspotlight.com
Circulation: 1,372 *Frequency:* Wednesday
Geri Swanson, Publisher
Richard MacKenzie, Editor

***Queen Charlotte:* Queen Charlotte Islands Observer**
PO Box 205, 623 - 7th St., Queen Charlotte, BC V0T 1S0
Tel: 250-559-4680; *Fax:* 250-559-8433
observer@qcislands.net
www.qciobserver.com
Circulation: 1,444 *Frequency:* Thursday

***Quesnel:* Cariboo Observer**
188 Carson Ave., Quesnel, BC V2J 2A8
Tel: 250-992-2121;
advertising@quesnelobserver.com
www.quesnelobserver.com
Circulation: 14,162 *Frequency:* Wednesday, Sunday
Darcy Wiebe, Publisher
Andrea Johnston, Editor

***Quesnel:* The Quesnel Advisor**
369C Anderson Dr., Quesnel, BC V2J 2G1
Tel: 250-992-5572; *Fax:* 250-992-6044
editorial@quesneladvisor.com
www.quesneladvisor.com
Circulation: 7,546 *Frequency:* Wed.
Kim Saunders, Publishers

***Revelstoke:* Revelstoke Times Review**
PO Box 20, Revelstoke, BC V0E 2S0
Tel: 250-837-4667;
www.revelstoketimesreview.com
Circulation: 2,040 *Frequency:* Wednesday
Mavis Cann, Publisher
David F. Rooney, Editor

***Richmond:* Richmond Review**
#140, 5671 No. 3 Rd., Richmond, BC V6X 2C7
Tel: 604-247-3700;
www.richmondreview.com
Circulation: 94,215 *Frequency:* Thu., Sat.
Josh O'Connor, Publisher

***Salmon Arm:* Salmon Arm Observer**
PO Box 550, 51 Hudson Ave., Salmon Arm, BC V1E 4N7
Tel: 250-832-2131; *Fax:* 250-832-5140
newsroom@saobserver.net
www.saobserver.net
Other information: Ad Email: advertising@saobserver.net
Circulation: 3,687 *Frequency:* Wednesday
Tracy Hughes, Editor
Ron Lovestone, Publisher

***Salmon Arm:* The Shuswap Market News**
PO Box 550, Salmon Arm, BC V1E 4N7
Tel: 250-832-2131; *Fax:* 250-832-5140
newsroom@saobserver.net
www.saobserver.net
Other information: Ad Email: advertising@saobserver.net
Circulation: 14,786 *Frequency:* Friday
Ron Lovestone, Publisher
Tracy Hughes, Editor

***Salt Spring Island:* Gulf Islands Driftwood**
Driftwood Publishing Ltd., 328 Lower Ganges Rd., Salt Spring Island, BC V8K 2V3
Tel: 250-537-9933; *Fax:* 250-537-2613
Toll-Free: 877-537-9933
driftwood@gulfislands.net
www.gulfislands.net
Circulation: 4,311 *Frequency:* Wednesday
Penny Sakamoto, Publisher

***Sechelt:* Coast Reporter**
PO Box 1388, 5485 Warf Rd., Sechelt, BC V0N 3A0
Tel: 604-885-4811; *Fax:* 604-885-4818
classified@coastreporter.net
www.coastreporter.net
Circulation: 13,123 *Frequency:* Fri.
Peter Kvarnstrom, Publisher

***Sicamous:* Eagle Valley News**
PO Box 113, 1133 Parksville St., Sicamous, BC V0E 2V0
Tel: 250-836-2570; *Fax:* 250-836-2661
evnews@bcnewsgroup.com
Circulation: 942 *Frequency:* Wednesday
Ron Lovestone, Publisher
Tracy Hughes, Editor

***Sidney:* Peninsula News Review**
9726 First St., Sidney, BC V8L 3C9
Tel: 250-656-1151; *Fax:* 250-656-5526
penreview@vinewsgroup.com
www.peninsulanewsreview.com
Circulation: 13,796 *Frequency:* Wednesday
Susan Hodgson, Publisher
Judy Reimche, Editor

***Smithers:* Interior News**
PO Box 2560, Smithers, BC V0J 2N0
Tel: 250-847-3266; *Fax:* 250-847-2995
advertising@interior-news.com
www.interior-news.com
Circulation: 3,838 *Frequency:* Wednesday
Vic Swan, Publisher

***Sooke:* Sooke News Mirror**
PO Box 339, 6711 Eustace Rd., Sooke, BC V0S 1N0
Tel: 250-642-5752; *Fax:* 250-642-4767
rod@vinewsgroup.com
www.sookenewsmirror.com
Circulation: 5,394 *Frequency:* Wednesday
Rod Sluggett, Publisher

***Squamish:* Squamish Chief**
PO Box 3500, 38117 - 2nd Ave., Squamish, BC V8B 0B9
Tel: 604-892-9161; *Fax:* 604-892-8483
www.squamishchief.com
Circulation: 3,866 *Frequency:* Friday
Cathryn Atkinson, Editor
Tim Shoults, Publisher

***Summerland:* Summerland Review**
PO Box 309, 13224 Victoria Rd., Summerland, BC V0H 1Z0
Tel: 250-494-5406;
www.summerlandreview.com/
Circulation: 2,327 *Frequency:* Thursday
Mark Walker, Publisher
John Arendt, Editor

***Surrey:* Apna Roots**
#103, 12414 - 82nd Ave., Surrey, BC V3W 3E9
Tel: 604-599-5021; *Fax:* 604-599-5415
staff@apnaroots.com
www.apnaroots.com
Circulation: 15,000 *Frequency:* Weekly
Rue Hayer Bains, Publisher

***Surrey:* Cloverdale Reporter News & Traveling Times**
17586 - 56A Ave., Surrey, BC V3S 1G3
Tel: 604-575-2405; *Fax:* 604-575-2406
crnews@shaw.ca
www.cloverdalereporter.com
Circulation: 20,000
Ursula Maxwell, Publisher/Managing Editor

***Surrey:* Indo-Canadian Times**
#103, 12414 - 82nd Ave., Surrey, BC V3W 3E9
Tel: 604-599-5408; *Fax:* 604-599-5415
indo@direct.ca, indo@telus.net
www.indo-canadiantimes.com
Circulation: 32,000 *Frequency:* Weekly; Punjabi
Rupinder Hayer, Publisher

***Surrey:* The Indo-Canadian Voice**
#200, 12732 - 80th Ave., Surrey, BC V3W 3A7
Tel: 604-502-6100; *Fax:* 604-502-6111
ads@voiceonline.com
www.voiceonline.com/voice/thisweek/
Circulation: 15,000 *Frequency:* Weekly
Vinnie Combow, Editor

***Surrey:* The Leader**
#205, 5450 - 152nd St., Surrey, BC V3S 5J9
Tel: 604-575-2744;
newsroom@surreyleader.com
www.surreyleader.com
Circulation: 259,235 *Frequency:* Wednesday, Friday, Sunday
Bruce McAuliffe, Publisher
; publisher@surreyleader.com
Andrew Holota, Editor

***Surrey:* The Link**
#101, 13463 - 78th Ave., Surrey, BC V3W 0A8
Tel: 604-591-5160; *Fax:* 604-591-2113
linknews@smartt.com
www.thelinkpaper.ca
Circulation: 17,000 *Frequency:* Saturday
Rakesh Puri, General Manager

***Surrey:* Surrey Now**
#201, 7889 - 132nd St., Surrey, BC V3W 4N2
Tel: 604-572-0064; *Fax:* 604-572-6438
ghollick@thenownewspaper.com
www.thenownewspaper.com
Circulation: 115,000 *Frequency:* Tuesday, Friday
Gary Hollick, Publisher

***Terrace:* The Terrace Standard**
3210 Clinton Ave., Terrace, BC V8G 5R2
Tel: 250-638-7283; *Fax:* 250-638-8432
newsroom@terracestandard.com
www.terracestandard.com
Circulation: 7,963 *Frequency:* Wednesday; also The Skeena Marketplace (Sat., circ. 10,200)
Rod Link, Publisher

***Ucluelet:* The Westerly News**
PO Box 317, 1701 Peninsula Rd., Ucluelet, BC V0R 3A0
Tel: 250-726-7029; *Fax:* 250-726-4282
westnews@ukeecable.net
home.ukeecable.net/%7Ewestnews
Circulation: 1,108 *Frequency:* Wednesday
Susan McIntyre, Publisher

***Valemount:* The Valley Sentinel**
PO Box 688, 1012 Commercial Dr., Valemount, BC V0E 2Z0
Tel: 250-566-4425; *Fax:* 250-566-4528
sentinel@valemount.com
www.thevalleysentinel.com
Circulation: 1,013 *Frequency:* Wednesday
William J. Mahoney, Publisher

***Vancouver:* East Side Revue**
1574 West 6th Ave., Vancouver, BC V6J 1R2
Tel: 604-738-1411;
www.vancourier.com
Circulation: 118,802 *Frequency:* Wednesday, Friday
Rod Raglin, Publisher

***Vancouver:* L'Express du Pacifique**
#227A, 1555, 7e av ouest, Vancouver, BC V6J 1S1
Tél: 604-736-3734; *Téléc:* 604-736-3740
administration@lexpress.org
www.lexpress.org
Circulation: 1 800 *Frequency:* Lundi; aux deux semaines
Stéphanie Descôteaux
Raphael Perdrau, directeur de la publication
Cécil Lepage, journaliste

***Vancouver:* The False Creek News**
661A Market Hill, Vancouver, BC V5Z 4B5
Tel: 604-875-9626; *Fax:* 604-875-0336
fcnews@hotmail.com
Circulation: 25,000 *Frequency:* Fri.
A. Juma, Publisher

***Vancouver:* Jewish Independent**
#200, 291 East 2nd Ave., Vancouver, BC V5T 1B8
Tel: 604-689-1520;
editor@jewishindependent.ca
www.jewishbulletin.ca
Circulation: 5,000 *Frequency:* Weekly

***Vancouver:* The Vancouver Courier**
1574 - West 6th Ave., Vancouver, BC V6J 1R2
Tel: 604-738-1411;
www.vancourier.com
Circulation: 24,358 *Frequency:* Friday
Peter Ballard, Publisher

***Vancouver:* West Side Revue**
1736A - 33rd Ave. East, Vancouver, BC V5N 3E2
Tel: 604-327-1665
Circulation: 7,700 *Frequency:* Sunday
Rod Raglin, Publisher

***Vancouver:* WestEnder**
200-1490 W. Broadway, Vancouver, BC V6H 4E8
Tel: 604-606-8686;
www.westender.com
Circulation: 56,064 *Frequency:* Thursday
James Craig, Publisher
Michael White, Editor

***Vanderhoof:* Omineca Express**
PO Box 1007, 150 West Columbia, Vanderhoof, BC V0J 3A0
Tel: 250-567-9258; *Fax:* 250-567-2070
www.ominecaexpress.com
Circulation: 1,460 *Frequency:* Wednesday
Scot Farmer, Publisher
Allan Wishart, Editor

***Vernon:* The Morning Star**
4407 - 25th Ave., Vernon, BC V1T 1P5
Tel: 250-545-3322; *Fax:* 250-542-1510
morningstarads@bcnewsgroup.com
www.vernonmorningstar.com
Circulation: 101,536 *Frequency:* Wednesday, Friday, Sunday
Karen Hill, Publisher
Glenn Mitchell, Editor

***Victoria:* Country Life in B.C.**
3917 Mildred St., Victoria, BC V8Z 7A2
Tel: 250-708-0085; *Fax:* 250-708-0095
countrylifeinbc@shaw.ca
www.countrylifeinbc.com
Circulation: 8,900 *Frequency:* Monthly
Peter Wilding, Publisher & Editor

***Victoria:* Esquimalt News**
818 Broughton St., Victoria, BC V8W 1E4
Tel: 250-381-5664; *Fax:* 250-386-2624
wporter@vinewsgroup.com
www.esquimaltnews.com
Circulation: 14,071 *Frequency:* Wednesday, Friday
Vern Faulkner, Editor
Kirk Freeman, Publisher

***Victoria:* Goldstream News Gazette**
PO Box 7310 D, #117, 777 Goldstream Ave., Victoria, BC V9B 2X4
Tel: 250-478-9552; *Fax:* 250-478-6545
www.goldstreamgazette.com
Circulation: 33,123 *Frequency:* Wednesday, Friday
Andrew Topf, Editor
Penny Sakamoto, Publisher

***Victoria:* Lookout**
c/o CFB Esquimalt, PO Box 17000 Forces, 1522 Esquimalt Rd., Victoria, BC V9A 7N2
Tel: 250-363-3014; *Fax:* 250-363-3015
frontoffice@lookoutnewspaper.com
www.lookoutnewspaper.com
Circulation: 4,021 *Frequency:* Monday; English & French
Melissa Atkinson, Publisher

***Victoria:* Oak Bay News**
818 Broughton St., Victoria, BC V8W 1E4
Tel: 250-598-4123; *Fax:* 250-386-2624
www.oakbaynews.com
Circulation: 14,114 *Frequency:* Wednesday, Friday
Kirk Freeman, Publisher
Jim Zeeben, Editor

***Victoria:* Saanich News**
818 Broughton St., Victoria, BC V8W 1E4
Tel: 250-920-2090;
saanichnews@pinc.com
www.saanichnews.com
Circulation: 65,904 *Frequency:* Wednesday, Friday
Penny Sakamoto, Publisher
Jim Zeeben, Editor

***Victoria:* Victoria News**
818 Broughton St., Victoria, BC V8W 1E4
Tel: 250-386-3484; *Fax:* 250-386-2624
www.vicnews.com
Circulation: 23,165 W; 23,500 F; Total 46,665 *Frequency:* Wednesday, Friday
Kirk Freeman, Publisher
Keith Norbury, Editor

***Westbank:* Westside Weekly**
550 Doyle Ave., Westbank, BC V1Y 7V1
Tel: 250-470-0748;
www.kelownadailycourier.ca
Circulation: 18,316 *Frequency:* Wed.
Alison Yesilcimen, Publisher

***Whistler:* The Whistler Question**
#238, 4370 Lorimer Rd., Whistler, BC V0N 1B4
Tel: 604-932-5131; *Fax:* 604-932-2862
general@whistlerquestiom.com
www.whistlerquestion.com
Circulation: 10,000 *Frequency:* Thursday
Stephanie Matches, Publisher
David Burke, Editor

***White Rock:* The Peace Arch News**
1545 Johnston Rd., White Rock, BC V4B 3Z6
Tel: 604-531-1711; *Fax:* 604-531-7977
publisher@peacearchnews.com
www.peacearchnews.com
Circulation: 63,067
Rob Demone, Editor
Linda Hooton, Publisher

***Williams Lake:* The Cariboo Advisor**
68 North Broadway, Williams Lake, BC V2G 1C1
Tel: 250-398-5516; *Fax:* 250-398-5855
writeus@caribooadvisor.com
www.caribooadvisor.com
Circulation: 12,004 *Frequency:* Wed.

***Williams Lake:* Tribune Weekend**
188 - 1st Ave. North, Williams Lake, BC V2G 1Y8
Tel: 250-392-2331;
www.wltribune.com
Circulation: 6,196 *Frequency:* Tuesday, Thursday; also the Weekender (circ. 10,300)
Lorne Doerkson, Publisher
Bill Phillips, Editor

Manitoba

Daily Newspapers in Manitoba

***Brandon:* Brandon Sun**
501 Rosser Ave., Brandon, MB R7A 0K4
Tel: 204-727-2451;
www.brandonsun.com
Circulation: 16,470; Sat. 22,358 *Frequency:* Evening
Ewan Pow, Publisher
William E. Chester, General Manager

***Flin Flon:* The Reminder**
10 North Ave., Flin Flon, MB R8A 0T2
Tel: 204-687-3454; *Fax:* 204-687-4473
online@ffdailyreminder.com
www.r-online.ca
Circulation: 3,800 *Frequency:* Afternoon

***Portage la Prairie:* Portage Daily Graphic**
PO Box 130, 1941 Saskatchewan Ave. West, Portage la Prairie, MB R1N 3B4
Tel: 204-857-3427; *Fax:* 204-239-1270
ads.dailygraphic@shawcable.com
www.portagedailygraphic.com
Circulation: 4,300
Barry Clayton, Publisher

***Winnipeg:* Winnipeg Free Press**
1355 Mountain Ave., Winnipeg, MB R2X 3B6
Tel: 204-697-7122; *Fax:* 204-697-7370
letters@freepress.mb.ca
www.winnipegfreepress.com
Circulation: 119,738 Mon.-Fri., 166,422 Sat., 115,652 Sun.
Frequency: Morning
Murdoch Davis, Publisher
Bob Cox, Editor
John Sullivan, Associate Editor
204-697-7293

***Winnipeg:* The Winnipeg Sun**
1700 Church Ave., Winnipeg, MB R2X 3A2
Tel: 204-694-2022; *Fax:* 204-697-0759
wpgsun@wpgsun.com
www.winnipegsun.com
Circulation: 45,407 Mon.-Sat., 58,712 Sun. *Frequency:* Morning
Ed Huculak, Publisher

Other Newspapers in Manitoba

***Altona:* Altona Red River Valley Echo**
PO Box 700, Altona, MB R0G 0B0
Tel: 204-324-5001; *Fax:* 204-324-1402
altona.echo@rnts.net
www.altonaecho.com
Circulation: 6,400 *Frequency:* Friday
Rick Reimer, General Manager

Baldur: **Baldur-Glenboro Gazette**
PO Box 280, Baldur, MB R0K 0B0
Tel: 204-535-2127; *Fax:* 204-827-2207
gazette@mts.net
www.baldur-glenborogazette.ca
Circulation: 1,866 *Frequency:* Tuesday
Travis Johnson, Publisher
Mike Johnson, Publisher

Beausejour: **The Clipper Weekly**
PO Box 2033, 27A - 3rd St. South, Beausejour, MB R0E 0C0
Tel: 204-268-4700; *Fax:* 204-268-3858
mail@clipper.mb.ca
www.clipper.mb.ca
Circulation: 11,407 *Frequency:* Monday
Kimberley MacAulay, Publisher

Beausejour: **The Review**
726 Park Ave., Beausejour, MB R0E 0C0
Tel: 204-467-2421; *Fax:* 204-268-4570
info@valleytimes.ca
www.beausejourreview.com
Circulation: 6,904 *Frequency:* Fri.
Lana Meier, Publisher

Bladur: **Glenboro Gazette**
PO Box 280, Bladur, MB R0K 0B0
Tel: 204-535-2127; *Fax:* 204-827-2207
www.baldur-glenborogazette.ca
Circulation: 1,866 *Frequency:* Tuesday
Michael Johnson, Co-Publisher
Travis Johnson, Co-Publisher

Boissevain: **Boissevain Recorder**
PO Box 220, 561 Stephen St., Boissevain, MB R0K 0E0
Tel: 204-534-6479; *Fax:* 204-534-2977
brecorder@mts.net
www.boissevainrecorder.mb.ca
Circulation: 1,351 *Frequency:* Saturday
Lorraine Houston, Publisher & Editor

Brandon: **Westman Review**
501 Rosser Ave., Brandon, MB R7A 0K4
Tel: 204-727-2451; *Fax:* 204-727-0385
Circulation: 20,000 *Frequency:* Sunday

Brandon: **Wheat City Journal**
800 Rosser Ave., Brandon, MB R7A 6N5
Tel: 204-725-0209; *Fax:* 204-725-3021
info@wheatcityjournal.ca
www.wheatcityjournal.ca
Circulation: 20,962 *Frequency:* Thursday (Weekly).
Kyla Henderson, Editor

Carberry: **Carberry News-Express**
PO Box 220, Carberry, MB R0K 0H0
Tel: 204-834-2153; *Fax:* 204-834-2714
letters@carberrynews.ca
www.carberrynews.ca
Circulation: 1,146 *Frequency:* Monday
Angie Reynolds, Advertising Manager
John Lupton, Editor & Publisher

Carman: **The Valley Leader**
70 Main St. South, Carman, MB R0G 0J0
Tel: 204-745-2051; *Fax:* 204-745-3976
www.carmanvalleyleader.com
Circulation: 5,852 *Frequency:* Friday
Rick Reimer, Publisher

Cartwright: **Southern Manitoba Review**
PO Box 249, Cartwright, MB R0K 0L0
Tel: 204-529-2342; *Fax:* 204-529-2029
www.southernmanitobareview.com
Circulation: 867 *Frequency:* Thursday
Vicky M. Wallace, Publisher

Darlingford: **The Southern Shopper & Review**
RR#2, Darlingford, MB R0G 0L0
Frequency: Fri.

Dauphin: **Dauphin Herald**
PO Box 548, 120 - 1st Ave., NE, Dauphin, MB R7N 2V4
Tel: 204-638-4420; *Fax:* 204-638-8760
dherald@mts.net
www.dauphinherald.com
Circulation: 5,426 *Frequency:* Tuesday
Robert Gilroy, Publisher

Emerson: **The Southeast Journal**
PO Box 68, Emerson, MB R0A 0L0
Tel: 204-373-2493; *Fax:* 204-373-2084
www.connecta.com
Circulation: 2,984 *Frequency:* Saturday
Brenda Piett, Publisher

Grandview: **Grandview Exponent**
PO Box 39, Grandview, MB R0L 0Y0
Tel: 204-546-2555; *Fax:* 204-546-3081
expos@mts.net
www.grandviewexponent.com
Circulation: 1,178 *Frequency:* Tuesday
Clayton Chaloner, Publisher & Editor

Killarney: **Killarney Guide**
PO Box 670, 417 William Ave., Killarney, MB R0K 1G0
Tel: 204-523-4611; *Fax:* 204-523-4445
Circulation: 2,396 *Frequency:* Friday
Garry Struth, Publisher

Lac du Bonnet: **Lac du Bonnet Leader**
83 - 3 St., Lac du Bonnet, MB R0E 1A0
Tel: 204-467-2421; *Fax:* 204-345-6344
leader@mts.net
www.lacdubonnetleader.com
Circulation: 5,013 *Frequency:* Friday
Lana Meier, Publisher

Manitou: **Manitou Western Canadian**
PO Box 190, 424 Ellis Ave. East, Manitou, MB R0G 1G0
Tel: 204-242-2555; *Fax:* 204-242-3137
Circulation: 1,516 *Frequency:* Tuesday
Grant Howatt, Co-Publisher

Melita: **Deloraine Times & Star**
PO Box 820, Melita, MB R0M 1L0
Tel: 204-747-2249; *Fax:* 204-747-3999
deltimes@mb.sympatico.ca
Circulation: 1,278 *Frequency:* Saturday
Bruce Schwanke, Publisher

Melita: **Melita New Era**
PO Box 820, 128 Main St., Melita, MB R0M 1L0
Tel: 204-522-3491; *Fax:* 204-522-3648
newera@mts.net
Circulation: 1,713 *Frequency:* Saturday
Bruce Schwanke, Publisher

Minnedosa: **Minnedosa Tribune**
PO Box 930, 14 - 3rd Ave., SW, Minnedosa, MB R0J 1E0
Tel: 204-867-3816; *Fax:* 204-867-5171
trib@minnedosatribune.com
www.minnedosatribune.com
Circulation: 2,894 *Frequency:* Monday
Jennifer Muth, Publisher

Morden: **The Morden Times**
104 - 8th St., Morden, MB R6M 1Y7
Tel: 204-822-4421; *Fax:* 204-822-4079
news@mordentimes.com
www.mordentimes.com
Circulation: 6,798 *Frequency:* Friday
Rick Reimer, Publisher

Neepawa: **Neepawa Banner**
PO Box 699, 423 Mountain Ave., Neepawa, MB R0J 1H0
Tel: 204-476-2309; *Fax:* 204-476-5802
gibson@neepawapress.com
www.neepawabanner.com
Circulation: 11,171 *Frequency:* Monday
Ken Waddell, Publisher & Editor

Neepawa: **Neepawa Press**
PO Box 939, 423 Mountain Ave., Neepawa, MB R0J 1H0
Tel: 204-476-2309; *Fax:* 204-476-5802
neepress@mts.net
www.neepawapress.com
Circulation: 8,676 *Frequency:* Monday
Jack Gibson, Publisher

Pilot Mound: **The Sentinel Courier**
PO Box 179, 13 Railway Ave., Pilot Mound, MB R0G 1P0
Tel: 204-825-2772; *Fax:* 204-825-2439
sentinel@mts.net
Circulation: 1,010 *Frequency:* Tuesday
Sheila Howell, Publisher

Portage la Prairie: **Central Manitoba Shopper & News**
1943 Saskatchewan Ave. West, Portage la Prairie, MB R1N 3B4
Frequency: Tuesday

Portage la Prairie: **Central Plains Herald-Leader**
PO Box 130, 1941 Saskatchewan Ave. West, Portage la Prairie, MB R1N 3B4
Tel: 204-857-3427; *Fax:* 204-239-1270
www.cpheraldleader.com
Circulation: 10,577 *Frequency:* Saturday
Berry Clayton, Publisher

Reston: **Reston Recorder**
PO Box 10, Reston, MB R0M 1X0
Tel: 204-877-3321; *Fax:* 204-877-3115
recorder@mb.sympatico.ca
www.rmofpipestone.com/recorder/advertise.htm
Circulation: 893 *Frequency:* Saturday
Bruce Schwanke, Publisher

Rivers: **Rivers Banner**
PO Box 70, Rivers, MB R0K 1X0
Tel: 204-328-7494; *Fax:* 204-328-5212
riversbanner@inetlink.ca
www.riversbanner.com
Circulation: 1,862 *Frequency:* Saturday
Ken Waddell, Publisher
Sheila Runions, General Manager

Roblin: **Roblin Review**
PO Box 938, 119 - 1st Ave. NW, Roblin, MB R0L 1P0
Tel: 204-937-8377; *Fax:* 204-937-8212
roblinreview@mts.net
Circulation: 1,731 *Frequency:* Tuesday
Brent Wright, Publisher

Russell: **Russell Banner**
PO Box 100, Russell, MB R0J 1W0
Tel: 204-773-2069; *Fax:* 204-773-2645
rbanner@mts.net
www.russellbanner.com
Circulation: 1,534 *Frequency:* Tuesday
R.I. Gilroy, Publisher

Saint-Boniface: **La Liberté**
CP 190, 383 Provencher Blvd., Saint-Boniface, MB R2H 3B4
Tél: 204-237-4823; *Téléc:* 204-231-1998
la-liberte@la-liberte.mb.ca
www.journaux.apf.ca/laliberte
Circulation: 6 000 *Frequency:* Vendredi; français
Sylviane Lanthier, Directrice générale

Selkirk: **Selkirk Journal**
PO Box 190, 217 Clandeboye Ave., Selkirk, MB R1A 0X2
Tel: 204-482-7402; *Fax:* 204-482-3336
sjournal@mts.net
www.selkirkjournal.com
Circulation: 18,363 *Frequency:* Friday
Lana Meier, Publisher

Shilo: **Shilo Stag**
T-114 Community Centre, CFB Shilo, Shilo, MB R0K 2A0
Tel: 204-765-3000; *Fax:* 204-765-3014
stag@escape.ca
Circulation: 3,000 *Frequency:* Thursday; Bi-weekly
Janine Avery, Editor

Shoal Lake: **Crossroads This Week**
PO Box 160, 353 Station Rd., Shoal Lake, MB R0J 1Z0
Tel: 204-759-2644; *Fax:* 204-759-2521
gnesbitt@mts.net
www.crossroadsthisweek.com
Circulation: 2,943 *Frequency:* Saturday
Greg Nesbitt, Publisher

Souris: **Souris Plaindealer**
PO Box 488, 2 Crescent Ave. East, Souris, MB R0K 2C0
Tel: 204-483-2070; *Fax:* 204-483-3866
Circulation: 1,425 *Frequency:* Saturday
Bruce Schwanke, Publisher

Steinbach: **The Carillon**
PO Box 1290, 377 Main St., Steinbach, MB R5G 1A5
Tel: 204-326-3421; *Fax:* 204-326-4860
Toll-Free: 800-442-0463
info@thecarillon.com
www.thecarillon.com
Circulation: 10,651 *Frequency:* Thursday
Rick Derksen, Publisher

Stonewall: **The Interlake Spectator**
PO Box 190, Stonewall, MB R0C 2Z0
Tel: 204-642-2421; *Fax:* 204-642-8275
ispec@mts.net
www.interlakespectator.com
Circulation: 14,341 *Frequency:* Friday
Lana Meier, Publisher

***Stonewall:* Stonewall Argus & Teulon Times**
PO Box 190, 410 Main St., Stonewall, MB R0C 2Z0
Tel: 204-467-2421; *Fax:* 204-467-5967
interlakepublishing@shaw.ca
stonewallargusteulontimes.com
Circulation: 3,731 *Frequency:* Friday
Lana Meier, Publisher

***Swan River:* Swan Valley Star & Times**
PO Box 670, 704 Main St., Swan River, MB R0L 1Z0
Tel: 204-734-3858; *Fax:* 204-734-4935
info@starandtimes.ca
www.starandtimes.ca
Circulation: 3,746 *Frequency:* Tuesday
Brian Gilroy, General Manager

***The Pas:* Opasquia Times**
PO Box 750, 148 Fischer Ave., The Pas, MB R9A 1K8
Tel: 204-623-3435; *Fax:* 204-623-5601
Circulation: 4,111
Brian Gilroy, Publisher

***Thompson:* Nickel Belt News**
PO Box 887, 141 Commercial Pl., Thompson, MB R8N 1N8
Tel: 204-677-4534; *Fax:* 204-677-3681
Circulation: 5,125 *Frequency:* Monday

***Thompson:* Thompson Citizen**
PO Box 887, 141 Commercial Pl., Thompson, MB R8N 1N8
Tel: 204-677-4534; *Fax:* 204-677-3681
precambrian@mts.net
www.thompsoncitizen.net
Circulation: 2,770 *Frequency:* Monday, Wednesday, Friday
John Barker, Editor
Diana Hiscock, General Manager

***Treherne:* The Times**
PO Box 50, Treherne, MB R0G 2V0
Tel: 204-723-2542; *Fax:* 204-723-2754
trehernetimes@mts.net
Circulation: 2,788 *Frequency:* Monday
Gary Lodwick, Publisher

***Virden:* Virden Empire Advance**
PO Box 250, 300 Nelson St. West, Virden, MB R0M 2C0
Tel: 204-748-3931; *Fax:* 204-748-1816
empire12@mts.net
Circulation: 2,585 *Frequency:* Saturday
Grant/Marlain Shoemaker, Publisher
Brent Fitzpatrick, Editor

***Winkler:* The Winkler Times**
PO Box 1356, Winkler, MB R6W 4B3
Tel: 204-325-4771; *Fax:* 204-325-5059
www.winklertimes.com
Circulation: 6,531 *Frequency:* Friday
Rick Reimer, Publisher

***Winnipeg:* Farmers' Independent Weekly**
PO Box 1846 Main, Winnipeg, MB R3C 3R1
Tel: 204-254-7253; *Fax:* 204-257-4263
info@fiwonline.com
www.fiwonline.com
John Morriss, Publisher & Editor

***Winnipeg:* Headingley Headliner**
1465 St. James St., Winnipeg, MB R3H 0W9
Tel: 204-798-0800; *Fax:* 204-953-4300
headliner@man.net
www.canstarnews.com
Circulation: 5,320 *Frequency:* Fri.
Bob Verge, Publisher

***Winnipeg:* The Herald**
1465 St. James St., Winnipeg, MB R3H 0W9
Tel: 204-789-0800; *Fax:* 204-953-4300
www.canstarnews.com
Circulation: 36,692 *Frequency:* Thu.
Bryan Metcalfe, Publisher

***Winnipeg:* The Jewish Post & News**
113 Hutchings St., Winnipeg, MB R2X 2V4
Tel: 204-694-3332; *Fax:* 204-694-3916
jewishp@mts.net
www.jewishpostandnews.com
Circulation: 2,600 *Frequency:* Wednesday; supplement, Lifestyles (3 times a year; circ. 30,000)
Matt Bellan, Editor
Bernie Bellan, Business Manager

***Winnipeg:* The Lance**
1465 St. James St., Winnipeg, MB R3H 0W9
Tel: 204-789-0800; *Fax:* 204-953-4300
www.canstarnews.com
Circulation: 55,665 *Frequency:* Thu.
Bryan Metcalfe, Publisher

***Winnipeg:* The Metro**
1465 St. James St., Winnipeg, MB R3H 0W9
Tel: 204-789-0800; *Fax:* 204-953-4300
www.canstarnews.com
Circulation: 52,944 *Frequency:* Thu.
Bryan Metcalfe, Publisher

***Winnipeg:* the Times**
1465 St. James St., Winnipeg, MB R3H 0W9
Tel: 204-789-0800; *Fax:* 204-953-4300
tcweeklies@transcontinental.ca
www.canstarnews.com
Circulation: 34,736 *Frequency:* Wed.
Dale Penner, Publisher & General Manager

***Winnipeg:* Voxair**
PO Box 17000 Forces, 17 Wing Winnipeg, Winnipeg, MB R3J 3Y5
Tel: 204-833-2500; *Fax:* 204-833-2809
voxair@mts.net
www.voxair.ca
Circulation: 4,000 *Frequency:* Every other Wed.; English & French
Lt.Col. P. Conway, Editor-in-chief

New Brunswick

Daily Newspapers in New Brunswick

***Caraquet:* L'Acadie Nouvelle**
CP 5536, 476, boul St-Pierre ouest, Caraquet, NB E1W 1B7
Tél: 506-727-4444; *Téléc:* 506-727-7620
infos@acadienouvelle.com
www.acadienouvelle.com/acadienouvelle/index.cfm
Circulation: 16 800 *Frequency:* Matin; français

***Fredericton:* Daily Gleaner**
984 Prospect St. West, Fredericton, NB E3B 5A2
Tel: 506-452-6670;
info@canadaeast.com
www.canadaeast.com/dg/
Circulation: 30,200 *Frequency:* Monday-Saturday

***Moncton:* The Times-Transcript**
PO Box 1001, 939 Main St., Moncton, NB E1C 8P3
Tel: 506-859-4900; *Fax:* 506-859-4904
news@timestranscript.com
www.canadaeast.com/tt/
Circulation: 38,394 *Frequency:* Monday-Friday

***Saint John:* The New Brunswick Telegraph Journal**
PO Box 2350, 210 Crown St., Saint John, NB E2L 3V8
Tel: 506-632-8888; *Fax:* 506-633-6758
Toll-Free: 877-389-6397
newsroom@nbpub.com
www.canadaeast.com/tp/
Circulation: 41,362 *Frequency:* Monday-Saturday

Other Newspapers in New Brunswick

***Bathurst:* Northern Light**
PO Box 416, Bathurst, NB E2A 1P4
Tel: 506-546-4491; *Fax:* 506-546-1491
Circulation: 5,516 *Frequency:* Tuesday
Maurice Aube, Publisher

***Campbellton:* L'Aviron**
#406, 113, rue Robeberry, Campbellton, NB E3N 2G6
Tél: 506-753-7637; *Téléc:* 506-753-3628
atelier.campbellton@hebdosquebecor.com
hebdosquebecor.com
Circulation: 6,100 *Frequency:* Vendredi
Louise Decary, Rédactrice-en-chef

***Campbellton:* The Tribune**
PO Box 486, 6 Shannon St., Campbellton, NB E3N 3G9
Tel: 506-753-4413; *Fax:* 506-759-9595
tribune@tribpub.nb.ca
www.tribpub.nb.ca
Circulation: 4,066 *Frequency:* Wednesday; English & French
Nancy Cook, Publisher

***Campbellton:* La Voix du Restigouche**
6 Shannon St., Campbellton, NB E3N 2Y2
Tél: 506-753-4413; *Téléc:* 506-759-9595
nouvelles@tribunenb.ca
www.tribpub.nb.ca
Circulation: 15,073 *Frequency:* Saturday
Nancy Cook, Publisher

***Dieppe:* Journal Dieppe Journal**
988, rue Champlain, Dieppe, NB E1A 1P8
Tél: 506-388-8200; *Téléc:* 506-388-8201
journaldieppejournal@nb.aibn.com
www.dieppejournal.ca
Circulation: 6,178 *Frequency:* Fri.

***Edmundston:* Le Madawaska**
20, rue St. François, Edmundston, NB E3V 1E3
Tél: 506-735-5575; *Téléc:* 506-735-8086
grondin.paul@brunswicknews.com
apf.ca/lemadawaska
Circulation: 9 000 *Frequency:* Mercredi; bilingue
Paul Grondin

***Edmundston:* La République**
20, rue St. François, Edmundston, NB
Tél: 506-735-5575

***Grand Falls:* Victoria County Star**
PO Box 7363, 229 Broadway Blvd., Grand Falls, NB E3Z 2K1
Tel: 506-473-3083; *Fax:* 506-473-3105
rickard.mark@victoriastar.ca
Circulation: 2,549 *Frequency:* Wednesday
Hermel Volpe, Publisher

***Grand Sault:* La Cataracte**
CP 7363, 229, boul Broadway, Grand Sault, NB E3Z 2K1
Tél: 506-473-3083
Circulation: 5 300 *Frequency:* Wed.
Don Calhoun, Publisher

***Hampton:* The Hampton Herald**
242 Main St., Hampton, NB E5N 6B8
Tel: 506-832-5613; *Fax:* 506-832-3353
tnherald@nbnet.nb.ca
www.ossekeag.ca/hampton-herald

***Hampton:* The Sussex Herald**
242 Main St., Hampton, NB E5N 6B8
Tel: 506-832-5613; *Fax:* 506-832-3353
www.ossekeag.ca/sussex.htm

***Miramichi:* Miramichi Leader**
PO Box 500, Miramichi, NB E1V 3M6
Tel: 506-773-5853; *Fax:* 506-622-7422
news@miramichileader.com
www.miramichileader.com
Circulation: 10,506 *Frequency:* Monday, Wednesday
Bill MacIntosh, Publisher
Nick Stephens, Editor

***Miramichi:* Miramichi Weekend**
PO Box 500, 175 General Manson Way, Miramichi, NB E1V 3M6
Tel: 506-773-5853;
news@miramichileader.com
www.miramichileader.com
Circulation: 7,105 *Frequency:* Friday
Bill MacIntosh, Publisher
Cathy Carnahan, Editor

***Oromocto:* Oromocto Post-Gazette**
281 Restigouche Rd., Oromocto, NB E2V 2H5
Tel: 506-357-9813
Circulation: 15,533 *Frequency:* Saturday
Eric Lawson, Publisher

***Richibucto:* L'Étoile de Kent**
#2, 9406, rue Principale, Richibucto, NB E4W 4E1
Tél: 506-523-6231; *Téléc:* 506-523-6520
redaction@journaletoile.com
Frequency: Samedi
Mario Tardiff

***Riverview:* The County Chronicle**
75 Canusa Dr., Riverview, NB E1B 2W6
Tel: 506-387-4085; *Fax:* 506-387-9096
ctychron@nbnet.nb.ca
Circulation: 8,500
David Singer, Publisher

***Sackville:* Sackville Tribune-Post**
80 Main St., Sackville, NB E4L 4A7
Tel: 506-536-2500; *Fax:* 506-536-4024
tribune@nbnet.nb.ca
Circulation: 2,603 *Frequency:* Wednesday
Paul Ramsay, Publisher
Scott Doherty, Editor

***Shediac:* Le Moniteur Acadien**
CP 5191, 817, Boudreau Ouest, Shediac, NB E4P 8T9
Tél: 506-532-6680; *Téléc:* 506-532-6681
moniteur@rogers.com
www.capacadie.com/moniteuracadien

Circulation: 5 132 *Frequency:* Mercredi, français
Carole Landry, Rédactrice en chef

St Stephen: International Money Saver
179A King St., St Stephen, NB E3L 2E4
Tel: 506-466-5072; *Fax:* 506-466-5717
moneysav@nbnet.nb.ca
Circulation: 15,000 *Frequency:* Saturday

St Stephen: St. Croix Courier
PO Box 250, St Stephen, NB E3L 2X2
Tel: 506-466-3220; *Fax:* 506-466-9950
jim@stcroixcourier.ca
www.stcroixcourier.com
Circulation: 4,019 *Frequency:* Tuesday; also: Courier Weekend, Atlantic Coast Guide
Leith Orr, Publisher

Sussex: Kings County Record
593 Main St., Sussex, NB E4E 7H5
Tel: 506-433-1070; *Fax:* 506-432-3532
news@kingscorecord.com
Circulation: 4,795 *Frequency:* Tuesday
Beverly Gauvreau, Publisher
Gisele McKnight, Editor

Woodstock: The Bugle
110 Carleton St., Woodstock, NB E7M 1E4
Tel: 506-328-8863; *Fax:* 506-328-3208
Circulation: 4,341 *Frequency:* Tuesday
Ken Langdon, Publisher
Jim Dumville, Editor

Woodstock: Bugle Observer
110 Carleton St., Woodstock, NB E7M 1E4
Tel: 506-328-8863; *Fax:* 506-328-3208
Circulation: 5,341 *Frequency:* Tuesday
Ken Langdon, Publisher

Newfoundland & Labrador

Daily Newspapers in Newfoundland & Labrador

Corner Brook: The Western Star
PO Box 460, 160 West St., Corner Brook, NL A2H 6E7
Tel: 709-634-4348; *Fax:* 709-637-4675
Toll-Free: 800-454-4348
newsroom@thewesternstar.com
www.thewesternstar.com
Circulation: 52,500 *Frequency:* Daily; Morning, Mon.- Sat.
Robert Verge, Publisher
Richard Williams, Editor

St. John's: The Telegram
PO Box 5970, Columbus Dr., St. John's, NL A1C 5X7
Tel: 709-364-6300; *Fax:* 709-364-9333
telegram@thetelegram.com
www.thetelegram.com
Circulation: 33,065 Mon.-Fri., 58,887 Sat., 33,693 Sun.
Frequency: Monday-Friday pm; Saturday-Sunday am
Miller H. Ayre, Publisher
Russell Wangersky, Managing Editor

Other Newspapers in Newfoundland & Labrador

Carbonear: The Compass
PO Box 760, 176 Water St., Carbonear, NL A1Y 1C3
Tel: 709-596-6458;
www.cbncompass.ca
Circulation: 4,776 *Frequency:* Tuesday
Scott Courage, Publisher

Clarenville: The Packet
8B Thompson St., Clarenville, NL A5A 1Y9
Tel: 709-466-2243;
www.thepacket.ca
Circulation: 4,979 *Frequency:* Monday
Scott Courage, Publisher

Gander: Beacon
PO Box 420, Gander, NL A1V 1W8
Tel: 709-256-4371; *Fax:* 709-256-3826
info@beaconnl.ca
www.ganderbeacon.ca
Circulation: 4,585 *Frequency:* Monday
Paul Banks, Manager/Editor

Grand Falls-Windsor: Advertiser
PO Box 129, Grand Falls-Windsor, NL A2A 2J4
Tel: 709-489-2162;
www.gfwadvertiser.ca
Circulation: 5,819 *Frequency:* Monday, Thursday
Scott Courage, Publisher

Happy Valley-Goose Bay: The Labradorian
PO Box 39 B, Happy Valley-Goose Bay, NL A0P 1E0
Tel: 709-896-3341;
www.thelabradorian.ca
Circulation: 2,019 *Frequency:* Monday
Shawn Woodford, Publisher

Harbour Breton: The Coaster
PO Box 188, Harbour Breton, NL A0G 1P0
Tel: 709-489-2162;
www.thecoaster.ca
Circulation: 1,702 *Frequency:* Tuesday
Scott Courage, Publisher

Labrador City: The Aurora
PO Box 423, Labrador City, NL A2V 2K7
Tel: 709-944-2957;
www.theaurora.ca
Circulation: 1,869 *Frequency:* Monday
Shawn Woodford, Publisher

Lewisporte: The Pilot
PO Box 1210, Lewisporte, NL A0G 3A0
Tel: 709-535-6910; *Fax:* 709-535-8640
www.lportepilot.ca
Circulation: 3,686 *Frequency:* Wed.
Scott Courage, Publisher

Lumsden: Kittiwake Commentary
PO Box 130, Lumsden, NL A0G 3E0
Tel: 709-530-2111; *Fax:* 709-530-2221
Circulation: 4,500 *Frequency:* Monthly
James Combden, Editor
Audrey Manning, Publisher

Marystown: The Southern Gazette
PO Box 1116, Marystown, NL A0E 2M0
Tel: 709-279-3188; *Fax:* 709-279-2628
www.southerngazette.ca
Circulation: 3,816 *Frequency:* Tuesday
Scott Courage, Publisher

Paradise: The Shoreline News
PO Box 3065, Paradise, NL A1L 3W2
Tel: 709-834-2169; *Fax:* 709-834-4364
tsnews@avint.net
Circulation: 14,800 *Frequency:* Sunday
Franklin Petten, Publisher

Placentia: The Charter
PO Box 450, Placentia, NL A0B 2Y0
Tel: 709-227-5240;
www.thecharter.ca
Circulation: 1,011 *Frequency:* Monday
Scott Courage, Publisher

Port Aux Basques: The Gulf News
PO Box 1090, Port Aux Basques, NL A0M 1C0
Tel: 709-695-3671;
www.gulfnews.ca
Circulation: 2,720 *Frequency:* Monday
Shawn Woodford, Publisher

Springdale: The Nor-Wester
PO Box 28, Springdale, NL A0J 1T0
Tel: 709-673-3721; *Fax:* 709-673-4171
www.thenorwester.ca
Circulation: 3,239 *Frequency:* Wed.
Scott Courage, Publisher

St Anthony: The Northern Pen
PO Box 520, St Anthony, NL A0K 4S0
Tel: 709-454-2191; *Fax:* 709-454-3718
northernpen@nf.sympatico.ca
www.northernpen.ca
Circulation: 5,186 *Frequency:* Monday
Shawn Woodford, Publisher
Allan Bock, Editor

St. John's: The Express
PO Box 8660 A, St. John's, NL A1B 3T7
Tel: 709-722-8500; *Fax:* 709-579-7745
express@optipress.ca
www.theexpress.ca
Circulation: 41,386 *Frequency:* Wednesday
Scott Courage, Publisher

St. John's: Le Gaboteur
65 chemin Ridge, St. John's, NL A1B 4P5
Tél: 709-753-9585; *Téléc:* 709-753-9586
gaboteur@nf.sympatico.ca
www.gaboteur.ca
Circulation: 1 000 *Frequency:* Bi-mensuel; français

Stephenville: The Georgian
PO Box 283, Stephenville, NL A2N 2Z4
Tel: 709-643-4531; *Fax:* 709-643-5041
georgian@optipress.ca
www.thegeorgian.ca
Circulation: 2,029 *Frequency:* Tuesday
Shawn Woodford, Publisher

Northwest Territories

Other Newspapers in Northwest Territories

Fort Smith: Slave River Journal
PO Box 990, 207 McDougall Rd., Fort Smith, NT X0E 0P0
Tel: 867-872-2784; *Fax:* 867-872-2754
Toll-Free: 888-355-6729
editor.srj@auroranet.nt.ca
www.srji.com
Circulation: 1,346 *Frequency:* Wednesday
Don Jaque, Publisher
Sandra Jaque, Managing Editor

Hay River: The Hub
8-4 Courtoreille St., Hay River, NT X0E 1G2
Tel: 867-874-6577; *Fax:* 867-874-2679
editor@hayriverhub.com
www.hayriverhub.com
Circulation: 2,322 *Frequency:* Wednesday
Chris Brodeur, Publisher

Yellowknife: L'Aquilon
CP 1325, Yellowknife, NT X1A 2N9
Tél: 867-873-6603; *Téléc:* 867-873-2158
aquilon@internorth.com
www.aquilon.nt.ca
Circulation: 1,000 *Frequency:* Vendredi; français
Alain Bessette, Publisher

Yellowknife: Deh Cho Drum
PO Box 2820, Yellowknife, NT X1A 2R1
Tel: 867-873-4031;
advertising@nnsl.com
www.nnsl.com
Circulation: 1,458 *Frequency:* Thu.
Petra Ehrke, Manager, National/Territorial Advertising

Yellowknife: Den Cho Drum
PO Box 2820, Yellowknife, NT X1A 2R1
Tel: 867-873-4031;
nnsl@nnsl.com
www.nnsl.com
Circulation: 1,458 *Frequency:* Thursday
J.W. Sigvaldson, Publisher
Michael Scott, General Manager

Yellowknife: Nunavut News North
PO Box 2820, 5108 - 50th St., Yellowknife, NT X1A 2R1
Tel: 867-873-4031; *Fax:* 867-873-8507
advertising@nnsl.com
www.nnsl.com
Circulation: 6,592 *Frequency:* Monday
Jack Sigvaldason, Publisher

Yellowknife: NWT News North
PO Box 2820, 5108 - 50th St., Yellowknife, NT X1A 2R1
Tel: 867-873-4031; *Fax:* 867-873-8507
nnsl@nnsl.com
www.nnsl.com
Circulation: 9,158 *Frequency:* Monday
Sig Sigvaldason, Publisher
Bruce Valpy, Managing Editor

Yellowknife: Yellowknifer
PO Box 2820, 5108 - 50th St., Yellowknife, NT X1A 2R1
Tel: 867-873-4031; *Fax:* 867-873-8507
nnsl@nnsl.com
www.nnsl.com
Circulation: 5,220 W; 5,875 F; 11,095 Total *Frequency:* Wednesday, Friday
J.W. Sigvaldason, Publisher

Nova Scotia

Daily Newspapers in Nova Scotia

Amherst: Daily News
PO Box 280, 147 South Albion St., Town Square, Amherst, NS B4H 3Z2
Tel: 902-667-5102; *Fax:* 902-667-0419
dcole@amherstdaily.com
www.amherstdaily.com
Circulation: 3,700 *Frequency:* Monday-Saturday
Darrell Cole, Managing Editor

Halifax: The Chronicle Herald, The Sunday Herald
PO Box 610, Halifax, NS B3J 2T2
Tel: 902-426-2811; *Fax:* 902-426-1158
newsroom@herald.ca
www.herald.ns.ca
Circulation: 114,000

Halifax: The Daily News
1601 Lower Water St., Halifax, NS B3P 3J6
Tel: 902-444-4444;
info@hfxnews.ca
www.hfxnews.ca
Circulation: 55,000 *Frequency:* Monday-Sunday
Jamie Thomson, Publisher

New Glasgow: The News
PO Box 159, 352 East River Rd., New Glasgow, NS B2H 5E2
Tel: 902-928-3500; *Fax:* 902-752-1945
news@ngnews.ca
www.newglasgownews.com
Circulation: 8,086 *Frequency:* Evening
Richard Russell, Publisher
Dave Glenen, Managing Editor

Sydney: Cape Breton Post
PO Box 1500, 255 George St., Sydney, NS B1P 6K6
Tel: 902-564-5451; *Fax:* 902-562-7077
news@cbpost.com
www.cbpost.com
Circulation: 27,300 *Frequency:* Morning
Fred Jackson, Managing Editor

Truro: Truro Daily News
PO Box 220, 6 Louise St., Truro, NS B2N 5C3
Tel: 902-893-9405; *Fax:* 902-893-0518
news@trurodaily.com
www.trurodaily.com
Circulation: 7,200 *Frequency:* Monday-Saturday

Other Newspapers in Nova Scotia

Amherst: The Citizen
PO Box 280, 10 Lawrence St., Amherst, NS B4H 3Z2
Tel: 902-667-5102; *Fax:* 902-667-0419
www.amherstdaily.com
Circulation: 3,262 *Frequency:* Saturday
Richard Russell, Publisher

Antigonish: The Casket
PO Box 1300, 88 College St., Antigonish, NS B2G 2L7
Tel: 902-863-4370; *Fax:* 902-863-1943
editor@thecasket.ca
www.thecasket.ca
Circulation: 5,097 *Frequency:* Wednesday
Brian Lazzuri, Editor
Ken Sims, Publisher

Bass River: The Shoreline Journal
RR#1, Bass River, NS B0M 1B0
Tel: 902-647-2968; *Fax:* 902-647-2194
Toll-Free: 800-406-1426
shoreline@ns.sympatico.ca
Frequency: last Thu. of every month
Donna Benoit, Contact

Berwick: Berwick Register
227 Commercial St., Berwick, NS B0P1E0
Tel: 902-538-3180; *Fax:* 902-538-8583
www.berwickregister.ca
Circulation: 2,186 *Frequency:* Wed.

Bridgewater: Bridgewater Bulletin
353 York St., Bridgewater, NS B4V 3K2
Tel: 902-543-2457; *Fax:* 902-543-2228
mail@lighthouse.ns.ca
www.lighthouse.ns.ca
Circulation: 7,108 *Frequency:* Wednesday
Lynn Hennigar, President

Bridgewater: Progress Enterprise
353 York St., Bridgewater, NS B4V 3K2
Tel: 902-634-8863; *Fax:* 902-634-3572
www.lighthouse.ns.ca
Circulation: 3,038 *Frequency:* Wednesday
Lynn Hennigar, Publisher

Enfield: The Laker
287 Hwy. 2, Enfield, NS B2T 1C9
Tel: 902-883-3181; *Fax:* 902-883-3180
leith@advocatemediainc.com
Circulation: 5,151 *Frequency:* Monthly
Leith Orr

Enfield: The Weekly Press
287 Hwy. 2, Enfield, NS B2T 1C9
Tel: 902-883-3181; *Fax:* 902-420-0524
leith@advocatemediainc.com
www.enfieldweeklypress.com
Circulation: 1,877 *Frequency:* Wednesday
Leith Orr, Publisher

Greenwood: The Aurora
PO Box 99, CFB Greenwood, Greenwood, NS B0P 1N0
Tel: 902-765-1494; *Fax:* 902-765-1717
aurora@auroranewspaper.com
www.auroranewspaper.com
Circulation: 5,900 *Frequency:* Monday; English & French
Stephen Boates, Manager, Publisher

Guysborough: Guysborough Journal
PO Box 210, 48 Main St., Guysborough, NS B0H 1N0
Tel: 902-533-2851; *Fax:* 902-533-2750
advertising@guysboroughjournal.ca
www.guysboroughjournal.com
Circulation: 2,018 *Frequency:* Wed.
Allan Murphy, Owner
Helen Murphy, Owner

Halifax: The Coast, Halifax's Weekly
5435 Portland Pl., Halifax, NS B3K 6R7
Tel: 902-422-6278; *Fax:* 902-425-0013
coast@thecoast.ns.ca
www.thecoast.ca
Circulation: 20,000 *Frequency:* Weekly
Christine Oreskovich, Publisher
Kyle Shaw, Editor
Catherine Salisbury, President

Inverness: The Oran
PO Box 100, 15767 Central Ave., Inverness, NS B0E 1N0
Tel: 902-258-3400; *Fax:* 902-258-2632
oran@ns.aliantzinc.ca
www.oran.ca
Circulation: 4,509 *Frequency:* Wednesday
Rankin MacDonald, Editor
Frank MacDonald, Publisher

Kentville: The Advertiser
PO Box 430, Kentville, NS B4N 3X4
Tel: 902-681-2121; *Fax:* 902-681-0830
nsclassified@kentvilleadvertiser.ca
www.novanewsnow.com
Circulation: 5,508 *Frequency:* Tuesday
Caroline Andrews, Publisher

Kentville: Digby Courier
PO Box 430, 9185 Commercial St., Kentville, NS B4N 3X4
Tel: 902-245-4715; *Fax:* 902-245-6136
editor@digbycourier.ca
www.digbycourier.ca
Circulation: 1,801 *Frequency:* Thursday
John DeMings, Editor

Kentville: Hants Journal
PO Box 430, 9185 Commercial St., Kentville, NS B4N 3X4
Tel: 902-681-2121; *Fax:* 902-798-5451
journal.optipresspublishing.com
Circulation: 3,154 *Frequency:* Thursday
Caroline Andrews, Publisher

La Butte: Le Courrier de la Nouvelle-Écosse
9250, Route 1, La Butte, NS B0W 2L0
Tel: 902-769-3078; *Fax:* 902-769-3869
abonnements@lecourrier.com
www.lecourrier.com
Circulation: 1,546 *Frequency:* Vendredi; français
Marie-Claude Dion, Editor-in-chief

Liverpool: Liverpool Advance
PO Box 10, 271 Main St., Liverpool, NS B0T 1K0
Tel: 902-354-3441; *Fax:* 902-354-2455
info@theadvance.ca
www.atlanticnewsnet.ca
Circulation: 2,620 *Frequency:* Tuesday
Caroline Andrews, Publisher

Middleton: The Annapolis County Spectator
PO Box 880, 87 Commercial St., Middleton, NS B0S 1P0
Tel: 902-825-3457;
www.annapolisspectator.ca
Circulation: 3,090 *Frequency:* Thursday
Caroline Andrews, Publisher

Middleton: Bridgetown Monitor
PO Box 880, 87 Commercial St., Middleton, NS B0S 1P0
Tel: 902-665-4441; *Fax:* 902-665-4014
Circulation: 1,445 *Frequency:* Tuesday; also Mirror-Examiner (Wed.)
Kirk Cross, Publisher

Middleton: The Mirror-Examiner
PO Box 880, Middleton, NS B0S 1P0
Tel: 902-825-3457; *Fax:* 902-825-6707
Circulation: 2,411 *Frequency:* Wed.
Garnet Austen, Publisher
Lawrence Powell, Editor

Oxford: Oxford Journal
PO Box 10, Oxford, NS B0M 1P0
Tel: 902-447-2051; *Fax:* 902-447-2055
thejournal@ns.sympatico.ca
Circulation: 2,460 *Frequency:* Wednesday
Charlie Weeks, Editor
Paul Marchant, Publisher

Pictou: Pictou Advocate
PO Box 1000, 21 George St., Pictou, NS B0K 1H0
Tel: 902-485-8014; *Fax:* 902-752-4816
leith@advocatemediainc.com
www.pictouadvocate.com
Circulation: 3,173 *Frequency:* Wednesday
Leith Orr, Publisher
Jason Warren, Editor

Pictou: The Tatamagouche Light
PO Box 1000, Pictou, NS B0K 1H0
Tel: 902-485-8014
Circulation: 4,015 *Frequency:* Monday
Leith Orr, Publisher

Port Hawkesbury: The Reporter
2 MacLean Ct., Port Hawkesbury, NS B9A 3K2
Tel: 902-625-3300; *Fax:* 902-625-1701
Circulation: 4,390 *Frequency:* Tuesday, Friday
Rick Cluett, Publisher

Shelburne: The Coast Guard
PO Box 100, 164 Water St., Shelburne, NS B0T 1W0
Tel: 902-875-3244; *Fax:* 902-875-3454
www.novanewsnow.com
Circulation: 4,058 *Frequency:* Tuesday
Caroline Andrews, Publisher

Springhill: Springhill & Parrsboro Record
PO Box 670, 72 Main St., Springhill, NS B0M 1X0
Tel: 902-597-3731; *Fax:* 902-667-1402
www.springhillrecord.com
Circulation: 1,673 *Frequency:* Wednesday
Kevin Cummings, General Manager

Yarmouth: The Vanguard
PO Box 128, 2 Second St., Yarmouth, NS B5A 4B1
Tel: 902-742-7111; *Fax:* 902-742-2311
www.novanews.com
Circulation: 5,242 *Frequency:* Tuesday
Caroline Andrews, Publisher

Nunavut

Other Newspapers in Nunavut

Iqaluit: Nunatsiaq News
PO Box 8, Iqaluit, NU X0A 0H0
Tel: 867-979-5357; *Fax:* 867-979-4763
editor@nunatsiaq.com
www.nunatsiaq.com
Circulation: 5,916 *Frequency:* Friday; English & Inuktitut
Steven Roberts, Publisher

Yellowknife: Kivalliq News
PO Box 2820, Yellowknife, NU X1A 2R1
Tel: 867-873-4031; *Fax:* 867-873-8507
advertising@nnsl.com
www.nnsl.com
Circulation: 1,746 *Frequency:* Wed.
Petra Ehrke, Advertising Manager

Ontario

Daily Newspapers in Ontario

Barrie: Barrie Examiner
Osprey Media Group, 571 Bayfield St. North, Barrie, ON L4M 4Z9
Tel: 705-726-6537; *Fax:* 705-728-7717
news@thebarrieexaminer.com
www.thebarrieexaminer.com
Circulation: 10,558 *Frequency:* Evening, Mon.-Sat.
Mike Beaudin, Managing Editor
Mike Power, Publisher

Belleville: **The Intelligencer**
45 Bridge St. East, Belleville, ON K8N 5C7
Tel: 613-962-9171; *Fax:* 613-962-9652
newsroom@intelligencer.ca
www.intelligencer.ca/webapp/sitepages/
Circulation: Mon.-Fri., Sun. 16,998; Sat. 18,000 *Frequency:* Afternoon
Roger Cazabon, Managing Editor

Brantford: **The Expositor**
Southam Publications, PO Box 965, 53 Dalhousie St., Brantford, ON N3T 5S8
Tel: 519-756-2020; *Fax:* 519-756-4911
www.brantfordexpositor.ca
Circulation: 22,082 *Frequency:* Morning
Michael Pearce, Publisher

Brockville: **Recorder & Times**
PO Box 10, 1600 California Ave., Brockville, ON K6V 5T8
Tel: 613-342-4441; *Fax:* 613-342-4456
Toll-Free: 800-267-4434
editor@recorder.ca
www.recorder.ca
Circulation: 13,500 *Frequency:* Evening, Mon.-Sat.
Jeff Lawson, Manager, Advertising
Bob Pearce, Publisher

Chatham: **Chatham Daily News**
Osprey Media Group, PO Box 2007, 45 - 4th St., Chatham, ON N7M 5M6
Tel: 519-354-2000; *Fax:* 519-354-9489
news@chathamdailynews.ca
www.chathamdailynews.ca/webapp/sitepages
Circulation: 13,373 *Frequency:* Evening
Bruce Corcoran, Managing Editor

Cobourg: **Cobourg Daily Star**
Northumberland Publishers, PO Box 400, 99 King St. West, Cobourg, ON K9A 4L1
Tel: 905-372-0131; *Fax:* 905-372-4966
cdsletters@northumberlandtoday.com
www.northumberlandtoday.com
Circulation: 4,503 *Frequency:* Evening
Darren J. Murphy, Publisher
Mandy Martin, Managing Editor

Cornwall: **Standard-Freeholder**
44 Pitt St., Cornwall, ON K6J 3P3
Tel: 613-933-3160; *Fax:* 613-933-7521
www.standard-freeholder.com
Circulation: 14,800 *Frequency:* Morning, Mon.-Sat.
Milton Ellis, Publisher

Fort Frances: **Daily Bulletin**
PO Box 339, 116 - 1st St. East, Fort Frances, ON P9A 3M7
Tel: 807-274-5373; *Fax:* 807-274-7286
Toll-Free: 800-465-8508
news@fortfrances.com
www.fftimes.com
Circulation: 2,500 *Frequency:* Afternoon
J.R. Cumming, Publisher
Mike Behan, Editor

Guelph: **The Guelph Mercury**
#8, 14 Macdonell St., Guelph, ON N1H 6P7
Tel: 519-822-4310; *Toll-Free:* 866-871-9868
editor@guelphmercury.com
www.guelphmercury.com/
Circulation: 40,578 *Frequency:* Evening
Phil Andrews, Managing Editor

Hamilton: **The Hamilton Spectator**
PO Box 300, 44 Frid St., Hamilton, ON L8N 3G3
Tel: 905-526-3333; *Fax:* 905-526-1395
Toll-Free: 800-263-6902
www.thespec.com
Circulation: 103,664 Mon.-Fri., 118,606 Sat. *Frequency:* Evening
Pat Collins, Publisher
; pcollins@thespec.com
MarkGary Goodale, Director, Circulation & Marketing
; mgoodale@thespec.com

Kenora: **Daily Miner & News**
PO Box 1620, 33 Main St. South, Kenora, ON P9N 3X7
Tel: 807-468-5555; *Fax:* 807-468-4318
minerandnews@norcomcable.com
www.kenoradailyminerandnews.com
Circulation: 4,000 *Frequency:* Evening
Mitch Wolfe, Publisher

Kingston: **The Kingston Whig-Standard**
PO Box 2300, 6 Cataraqui St., Kingston, ON K7L 4Z7
Tel: 613-544-5000; *Fax:* 613-530-4122
kinwhig@thewhig.com
www.thewhig.com
Circulation: 27,695 Mon.-Fri., 38,822 Sat. *Frequency:* Morning & evening
Fred Laflamme, Publisher
Christina Spencer, Editor

Kirkland Lake: **Northern Daily News**
Osprey Media Group, PO Box 1030, 8 Duncan Ave., Kirkland Lake, ON P2N 3L4
Tel: 705-567-5321; *Fax:* 705-567-6162
news@northernnews.ca
www.northernnews.ca/webapp/sitepages/
Circulation: 5,800 *Frequency:* Evening
Joe O'Grady, Managing Editor

Kitchener: **The Record**
160 King St. East, Kitchener, ON N2G 4E5
Tel: 519-894-2231; *Fax:* 519-894-3829
recordlibrary@therecord.com
www.therecord.com
Circulation: 81,702 *Frequency:* Morning, 6 days a week
Lynn Haddrall, Editor

Lindsay: **The Lindsay Daily Post**
17 William St. North, Lindsay, ON K9V 3A3
Tel: 705-324-2113; *Fax:* 705-324-0174
linretail@thepost.ca
www.thepost.ca
Circulation: 5,500 *Frequency:* Morning
Andy Wheeler, Publisher
Andrew Carroll, Editor

London: **The London Free Press**
PO Box 2280, 369 York St., London, ON N6A 4G1
Tel: 519-679-6666; *Fax:* 519-667-4523
Toll-Free: 800-265-4105
letters@lfpress.com
www.lfpress.com
Circulation: 91,716 Sun.-Fri., 110,223 Sat. *Frequency:* Morning
Paul Berton, Editor-in-chief
Susan Muszak, Publisher & CEO

Niagara Falls: **Review**
Niagara Newspaper Group, PO Box 270, 4801 Valley Way, Niagara Falls, ON L2E 6T6
Tel: 905-358-5711; *Fax:* 905-356-0785
citydesk@nfreview.com
www.niagarafallsreview.ca
Circulation: 17,000 *Frequency:* Morning
David A. Beattie, Publisher
Joe Wallace, Editor

North Bay: **North Bay Nugget**
Osprey Media Group, 259 Worthington St. West, North Bay, ON P1B 8J6
Tel: 705-472-3200; *Fax:* 705-472-1438
nugget@nugget.ca
www.nugget.ca
Circulation: 29,000 *Frequency:* Evening, Mon.-Fri.; morning, Sat.
Paul McCuaig, Publisher
John Size, Managing Editor

Orillia: **Packet & Times**
Osprey Media Group, 31 Colborne St. East, Orillia, ON L3V 1T4
Tel: 705-325-1355; *Fax:* 705-325-7691
www.orilliapacket.com
Circulation: 13,092
Andrea Demeer, Publisher
Casandra Bellefeuille, Editor

Ottawa: **Le Droit**
CP 8860 T, #222, 47 Clarence St., Ottawa, ON K1N 3J9
Tél: 613-562-0111; *Téléc:* 613-562-7572
ledroit@ledroit.com
www.cyberpresse.ca/droit
Circulation: 33 281 lun.-ven., 40 638 sam. *Frequency:* Matin; français
Jacques Pronovost, Editeur/Président
Andre Larocque, Rédacteur

Ottawa: **Metro Ottawa**
#402, 116 Albert St., Ottawa, ON K1P 5G3
Tel: 613-236-5058; *Fax:* 866-253-2024
ottawalistings@metronews.ca
www.metronews.ca
Other information: Toll Free Fax: 1-866-253-2024
Circulation: 60,000
Dara Mottahed, Publisher

Ottawa: **The Ottawa Citizen**
PO Box 5020, 1101 Baxter Rd., Ottawa, ON K2C 3M4
Tel: 613-829-9100; *Fax:* 613-726-1198
Toll-Free: 800-267-6100
www.ottawacitizen.com
Circulation: 129,852 Mon.-Fri., 161,901 Sat., 129,749 Sun.
Jim Orban, Publisher & General Manager
Scott Anderson, Editor

Ottawa: **The Ottawa Sun**
6 Antares Dr., Ottawa, ON K1G 5H7
Tel: 613-739-7000; *Fax:* 613-739-8041
oped@sunpub.com
www.ottawasun.com
Circulation: 25,176 Mon.-Fri., 55,197 Sun., 47,710 Sat.
Frequency: Morning
Mike Therien, Editor-in-chief
Rick Gibbons, Publisher

Owen Sound: **Sun Times**
Osprey Media Group, PO Box 200, 290 - 9th St. East, Owen Sound, ON N4K 3P2
Tel: 519-376-2250; *Fax:* 519-376-7190
cmcmenemy@thesuntimes.ca
www.owensoundsuntimes.com
Circulation: 24,198 *Frequency:* Evening

Pembroke: **The Daily Observer**
Osprey Media Group, 186 Alexander St., Pembroke, ON K8A 4L9
Tel: 613-732-3691; *Fax:* 613-732-2226
editor@thedailyobserver.ca
www.thedailyobserver.ca
Circulation: 5,950 *Frequency:* Evening
Peter Lapinskie, Managing Editor

Peterborough: **Examiner**
Osprey Media Group, PO Box 3890, 730 Kingsway, Peterborough, ON K9J 8L4
Tel: 705-745-4641; *Fax:* 705-741-3217
news1@ptbo.igs.net
www.thepeterboroughexaminer.com
Circulation: 25,453 Mon.-Sat., 23,367 Sun. *Frequency:* Morning
Jim Ambrose, Publisher
Ed Arnold, Managing Editor

Port Hope: **Port Hope Evening Guide**
Osprey Media Group, 97 Walton St., Port Hope, ON L1A 1N4
Tel: 905-885-2471; *Fax:* 905-885-7442
www.northumberlandtoday.com
Francis Baker, Managing Editor
Rob Forbes, Publisher & General Manager

Sarnia: **Observer**
Osprey Media Group, 140 South Front St., Sarnia, ON N7T 7M8
Tel: 519-344-3641; *Fax:* 519-332-2951
Toll-Free: 800-668-0564
editorial@theobserver.ca
www.theobserver.ca
Circulation: 22,415 *Frequency:* Monday-Friday evening; Saturday morning
Daryl Smith, Publisher
Rod Hilts, Managing Editor

Sault Ste Marie: **Sault Star**
145 Old Garden River Rd., Sault Ste Marie, ON P6A 5M5
Tel: 705-759-3030; *Fax:* 705-759-0102
ssmstar@saultstar.com
www.saultstar.com
Circulation: 20,003, Mon. - Sat. *Frequency:* Evening (morning Sat.)

Simcoe: **Tuesday Times Reformer**
PO Box 370, 50 Gilberston Dr., Simcoe, ON N3Y 4L2
Tel: 519-426-5710; *Fax:* 519-426-9255
refedit@bowesnet.com
www.simcoereformer.ca
Circulation: 19,630 *Frequency:* Tuesday
Kim Novak, Managing Editor

St Catharines: **The St Catharines Standard**
17 Queen St., St Catharines, ON L2R 5G5
Tel: 905-684-7251; *Fax:* 905-684-6032
standard@stcatharinesstandard.ca
www.scstandard.com
Circulation: 33,000 Mon.-Fri., 47,000 Sat. *Frequency:* Afternoon
Andrea Krilluck, Managing Editor
Paul McCuaig, Publisher

***St Thomas:* The St. Thomas Times-Journal**
16 Hincks St., St Thomas, ON N5R 5Z2
Tel: 519-631-2790; *Fax:* 519-631-5653
Toll-Free: 800-663-3410
www.stthomastimesjournal.com
Circulation: 7,971 *Frequency:* Evening
Bev Ponton, Publisher
Ross Porter, Managing Editor

***Stratford:* The Beacon-Herald**
PO Box 430, 16 Packham Rd., Stratford, ON N5A 6T6
Tel: 519-271-2220; *Fax:* 519-271-1031
Toll-Free: 800-265-8577
bhadvertising@bowesnet.com
www.stratfordbeaconherald.com
Circulation: 11,457 *Frequency:* Daily
Amber Olgilvie, Publisher
Larke Turnbull, City Editor

***Sudbury:* The Sudbury Star**
33 MacKenzie St., Sudbury, ON P3C 4Y1
Tel: 705-674-5271; *Fax:* 705-674-6834
thesudburystar@thesudburystar.com
www.thesudburystar.com/webapp/sitepage s/
Circulation: 26,333 Mon.-Sat., 23,960 Sun. *Frequency:* Morning
Roger Cazebon, Managing Editor
Dan Johnson, Publisher

***Thunder Bay:* The Chronicle-Journal**
Horizon Operations (Canada) Ltd., 75 South Cumberland St., Thunder Bay, ON P7B 1A3
Tel: 807-343-6200; *Fax:* 807-345-3582
editor@chroniclejournal.com
www.chroniclejournal.com
Frequency: 29,110 Mon.-Fri.; 31,764 Sat.; 26,513 Sun.
Brian Dryden, Managing Editor
Colin Bruce, Publisher

***Timmins:* Daily Press**
c/o Osprey Media Group Inc., 187 Cedar St. South, Timmins, ON P4N 7G1
Tel: 705-268-5050; *Fax:* 705-268-7373
news@thedailypress.ca
www.timminspress.com
Circulation: 13,541 *Frequency:* Morning
Bruce Cowan, Publisher & General Manager
David McGee, Managing Editor

***Toronto:* Daily Racing Form**
47 Voyageur Ct. North, Toronto, ON M9W 4Y2
Tel: 416-798-1911; *Fax:* 416-798-1919
Circulation: 3,570 Mon., 5,529 Tue.-Fri. 9,558 Sat., 8,465 Sun.
Frequency: Morning
Bill Tallon, Editor

***Toronto:* The Globe and Mail**
444 Front St. West, Toronto, ON M5V 2S9
Tel: 416-585-5600; *Fax:* 416-585-5102
www.globeandmail.com
Circulation: 316,428 *Frequency:* Morning, Mon. to Sat.; also Report on Business Magazine, Globe Television
Isabella Cattelan, CFO
Phillip Crawley, Publisher & CEO
John Stackhouse, Editor-in-chief
; jstackhouse@globeandmail.com

***Toronto:* Metro Toronto**
703, 1 Concorde Gate, Toronto, ON M3C 3N6
Tel: 416-486-4900; *Fax:* 416-482-8097
www.metronews.ca
Circulation: 220,000
Greg Lutes, Publisher

***Toronto:* National Post**
300-1450 Don Mills Rd., Toronto, ON M3B 3R5
Tel: 416-383-2300; *Fax:* 416-383-2305
www.nationalpost.com
Frequency: Monday-Friday (175,238); Saturday (217,115)
Gordon Fisher, President
Douglas Kelly, Publisher
Mark Spencer, Vice-President, Advertising Sales
Jonathan Harris, Vice-President, Digital Media
Santina Zito, Vice-President, Operations
Stephen Meurice, Editor-in-chief

***Toronto:* Toronto 24 hours**
333 King St. East, Toronto, ON M5A 3X5
Tel: 416-350-6400; *Fax:* 416-350-6523
Circulation: 238,612
Bob Harris, Publisher

***Toronto:* The Toronto Star**
One Yonge St., Toronto, ON M5E 1E6
Tel: 416-367-4500; *Fax:* 416-869-4328
city@thestar.ca
www.thestar.com
Circulation: 390,163 Mon.-Fri., 566,706 Sat., 347,790 Sun.
Frequency: Morning, 2 editions
John D. Cruickshank, Publisher
Michael Cooke, Editor
; lettertoed@thestar.ca

***Toronto:* The Toronto Sun**
Sun Media Corp., 333 King St. East, Toronto, ON M5A 3X5
Tel: 416-947-2222; *Fax:* 416-368-0374
www.torontosun.com
Circulation: 179,004, Mon.-Fri., 151,101, Sat., 311,689, Sun.
Frequency: Morning
Mike Power, Publisher
James Wallace, Editor-in-chief
; james.wallace@sunmedia.ca

***Welland:* The Tribune**
PO Box 278, 228 East Main St., Welland, ON L3B 5P5
Tel: 905-732-2411; *Fax:* 905-732-3660
tribune@wellandtribune.ca
www.wellandtribune.ca
Circulation: 14,260
Mike Walsh, Publisher & General Manager
George Duma, Managing Editor

***Windsor:* The Windsor Star**
167 Ferry St., Windsor, ON N9A 4M5
Tel: 519-255-5768; *Fax:* 519-255-5520
letters@win.southam.ca
www.canada.com/windsorstar
Circulation: 72,514 Mon.-Fri., 82,127 Sat. *Frequency:* Morning
Marty Beneteau, Editor
Jim McCormack, Publisher

***Woodstock:* Sentinel-Review**
16 Brock St., Woodstock, ON N4S 8A5
Tel: 519-537-2341; *Fax:* 519-537-3049
osn@annexweb.com
www.woodstocksentinelreview.com
Circulation: 9,600 *Frequency:* Evening; supplement - CoverStory (weekly, circ. 15,200)
Pat Logan, Group Publisher

Other Newspapers in Ontario

***Ailsa Craig:* Middlesex Banner**
PO Box 433, 175 Main St., Ailsa Craig, ON N0M 1A0
Tel: 519-293-1095;
www.banner.on.ca
Circulation: 1,170 *Frequency:* Wed.
Brad Harness, Publisher

***Ajax:* Ajax/Pickering News Advertiser**
130 Commercial Ave., Ajax, ON L1S 2H5
Tel: 905-683-5110; *Fax:* 905-683-7363
www.durhamregion.com
Circulation: 142,337 *Frequency:* Wednesday, Friday, Sunday
Tim Whittaker, Publisher
Tony Doyle, Editor

***Alexandria:* Glengarry News**
PO Box 10, 3 Main St., Alexandria, ON K0C 1A0
Tel: 613-525-2020; *Fax:* 613-525-3824
gnews@glengarrynews.ca
www.glengarrynews.ca
Circulation: 6,242 *Frequency:* Wednesday
J. T. Grossmith, Publisher

***Alliston:* Alliston Herald**
PO Box 280, #22, 169 Dufferin St. South, Alliston, ON L9R 1E6
Tel: 705-435-6228; *Fax:* 705-435-3342
www.simcoe.com
Circulation: 23,475 *Frequency:* Wednesday, Friday
Joe Anderson, Publisher

***Amherstburg:* The Amherstburg Echo**
238 Dalhousie St., Amherstburg, ON N9V 1W4
Tel: 519-736-2147; *Fax:* 519-736-8384
echooffice@bowesnet.com
www.amherstburgecho.com
Circulation: 8,283 *Frequency:* Tuesday

***Arnprior:* Arnprior Chronicle-Guide**
116 John St. North, Arnprior, ON K7S 2N6
Tel: 613-623-6571; *Fax:* 613-623-7518
dwalter@runge.net
www.runge.net
Circulation: 2,400 *Frequency:* Tuesday

Bryan Wiltsie, Publisher

***Arthur:* Arthur Enterprise-News**
PO Box 310, 106 Charles St. East, Arthur, ON N0G 1A0
Tel: 519-848-2410; *Fax:* 519-848-3665
enterprise@wellingtonnorth.com
www.wellingtonnorth.com
Circulation: 748 *Frequency:* Friday
Lynne Pinnegar, Publisher

***Atikokan:* Atikokan Progress**
PO Box 220, 109 Main St. East, Atikokan, ON P0T 1C0
Tel: 807-597-2731; *Fax:* 807-597-6103
progress@nwon.com
Circulation: 1,513 *Frequency:* Monday
Eve Shine, Publisher
Michael P. McKinnon, Editor

***Aurora:* The Auroran**
#3, 75 Mary St., Aurora, ON L4G 1G3
www.auroran.com
Rosemary Schumaker, Publisher
Ron W. Wallace, Editor

***Aylmer:* Aylmer Express**
PO Box 160, Aylmer, ON N5H 2R9
Tel: 519-773-3126; *Fax:* 519-773-3147
Circulation: 3,886 *Frequency:* Wednesday
John Hueston, Publisher

***Ayr:* Ayr News**
PO Box 1173, Ayr, ON N0B 1E0
Tel: 519-632-7432; *Fax:* 519-632-7743
Circulation: 3,588 *Frequency:* Wednesday
James W. Schmidt, Publisher
John P. Schmidt, Editor

***Bancroft:* Bancroft Times**
PO Box 1894, 93 Hastings St. North, Bancroft, ON K0L 1C0
Tel: 613-332-2300; *Fax:* 613-332-4887
bancroft-times@sympatico.ca
Circulation: 4,971 *Frequency:* Thursday
David Walker, Publisher

***Barrie:* Barrie Advance**
21 Patterson Rd., Barrie, ON L4N 7W6
Tel: 705-726-0573; *Fax:* 705-726-9350
www.simcoe.com
Circulation: 112,078 *Frequency:* Wednesday, Friday
Joe Anderson, Publisher

***Barrie:* Super Shopper, Buy, Trade & Sell**
124 Brock St., Barrie, ON L4N 2M2
Tel: 705-726-6015; *Fax:* 705-726-6015
Toll-Free: 800-461-7585
ads@supershopper.com
www.supershopper.com
Circulation: 13,271 *Frequency:* Thursday
Laurie Crosson

***Barrys Bay:* Barry's Bay This Week**
PO Box 220, 41 Bay St., Barrys Bay, ON K0J 1B0
Tel: 613-756-2944; *Fax:* 613-756-2994
bsummers@barrysbaythisweek.com
www.barrysbaythisweek.com
Circulation: 2,642 *Frequency:* Wednesday
David Zilstra, General Manager
Douglas Gloin, Editor

***Beamsville:* Grimsby/West Lincoln Independent**
PO Box 400, 4309 Central Ave., Beamsville, ON L0R 1B0
Tel: 905-563-5393; *Fax:* 905-563-7977
twilkins@rannie.com
west.niagaracommunitynewspapers.com
Circulation: 45,526 *Frequency:* Wednesday, Friday
Tom Wilkinson, Editor

***Beamsville:* Lincoln Post Express**
PO Box 400, 4991 King St., Beamsville, ON L0R 1B0
Tel: 905-563-5393; *Fax:* 905-563-7977
Circulation: 2,260

***Beeton:* Beeton/New Tecumseth Times**
PO Box 310, Beeton, ON L0G 1A0
Tel: 905-729-2287; *Fax:* 905-729-2541
admin.syp@rogers.com
Circulation: 2,490 *Frequency:* Wed.
John Archibald, Publisher
Bruce Haire, Publisher

***Beeton:* Caledon Citizen**
PO Box 310, 34 Main St. West, Beeton, ON L0G 1A0
Tel: 905-857-6626; *Fax:* 905-857-6363
editor@caledoncitizen.com
www.caledoncitizen.com

Circulation: 9,814 *Frequency:* Wednesday
Bruce Haire, Publisher
Mark Pavilons, Editor

Beeton: Innisfil Scope
PO Box 310, 34 Main St. West, Beeton, ON L0G 1A0
Tel: 905-729-2287; *Fax:* 905-729-2541
admin.syp@rogers.com
www.innisfilscope.com
Circulation: 11,755 *Frequency:* Wednesday
John Archibald, General Manager
Bruce Haire, Publisher

Beeton: King Township Sentinel
PO Box 310, Beeton, ON L0G 1A0
Tel: 905-729-2287; *Fax:* 905-729-2541
admin.syp@rogers.com
www.kingsentinel.com
Circulation: 6,499 *Frequency:* Wed.
John Archibald, Publisher
Bruce Haire, Publisher

Beeton: Woodbridge Advertiser
PO Box 379, 2 Main St. West, Beeton, ON L0G 1A0
Tel: 905-729-4501; *Fax:* 905-729-3961
Toll-Free: 888-285-4501
info@ontariosauctionpaper.com
Circulation: 5,500 *Frequency:* Thu.
Karl Mallette, Publisher

Belle Ewart: The Innisfil Enterprise
PO Box 222, Belle Ewart, ON L0L 1C0
Tel: 705-456-2424; *Fax:* 705-456-8249
innisfilenterprise.ca
Carol McPherson, Publisher

Belle River: Lakeshore News
PO Box 429, Belle River, ON N0R 1A0
Tel: 519-728-1082; *Fax:* 519-728-4551
www.windsoressexnews.com
Circulation: 1,759 *Frequency:* Wednesday
William Harris, Editor
Gary Baxter, Publisher

Belleville: Belleville Shopper's Market
PO Box 446, 365 North Front St., Belleville, ON K8N 5A5
Tel: 613-962-3422; *Fax:* 613-962-1353
www.shoppersmarket.on.ca
Circulation: 42,800 *Frequency:* Saturday
Charles Parker, General Manager

Belleville: Campbellford Shield
20 Hanna Court, Belleville, ON K8P 5J2
Tel: 613-962-0234;
www.shieldmedia.ca
Circulation: 4,920 *Frequency:* Friday
Earl Jones, Publisher

Belleville: Hastings Shield
20 Hanna Court, Belleville, ON K8P 5J2
Tel: 613-962-0234; *Fax:* 613-472-5026
www.shieldmedia.ca
Circulation: 2,534 *Frequency:* Friday
Earl Jones, Publisher

Belleville: Madoc Shield
20 Hanna Court, Belleville, ON K8P 5J2
Tel: 613-962-0234;
www.shieldmedia.ca
Circulation: 2,885 *Frequency:* Friday
Earl Jones, Publisher

Belleville: Marmora Shield
20 Hanna Court, Belleville, ON K8P 5J2
Tel: 613-962-0234;
www.shieldmedia.ca
Circulation: 2,117 *Frequency:* Friday
Nancy Derrer, Editor

Belleville: Norwood Shield
20 Hanna Court, Belleville, ON K8P 5J2
Tel: 613-962-0234;
www.shieldmedia.ca
Circulation: 2,469 *Frequency:* Friday
Earl Jones, Piblisher

Belleville: Prince Edward Free Press
PO Box 7500, RR#7, Belleville, ON K8N 4Z7
Frequency: Tuesday

Belleville: Stirling Shield
20 Hanna Court, Belleville, ON K8P 5J2
Tel: 613-962-0234;
www.shieldmedia.ca

Circulation: 2,872 *Frequency:* Fri.
Earl Jones, Publisher

Blenheim: Blenheim News-Tribune
PO Box 160, 62 Talbot St. West, Blenheim, ON N0P 1A0
Tel: 519-676-3321; *Fax:* 519-676-3454
Circulation: 2,548 *Frequency:* Wednesday
Peter Laurie, Publisher

Blyth: The Citizen
PO Box 429, 404 Queen St., Blyth, ON N0M 1H0
Tel: 519-523-4792; *Fax:* 519-523-9140
norhuron@scsinternet.com
www.northhuron.on.ca
Circulation: 1,976 *Frequency:* Thursday
Keith Roulston, Publisher
Bonnie Gropp, Editor

Bolton: Caledon Enterprise
PO Box 99, #4A, 12612 Hwy. 50, Bolton, ON L7E 5T1
Tel: 905-857-3433; *Fax:* 905-857-5002
www.metroland.com
Circulation: 28, 054 *Frequency:* Wednesday 13,193; Saturday 14,861
Bill Anderson, General Manager

Borden: The Borden Citizen
S-138, PO Box 1000 Main, Rafah Cres., Borden, ON L0M 1C0
Tel: 705-423-2496; *Fax:* 705-423-3452
Circulation: 6,000 *Frequency:* Wednesday; English & French
Col. W. Reid, Publisher

Bothwell: The Spirit of Bothwell
261 Main St., Bothwell, ON N0P 1C0
Tel: 519-695-2508; *Fax:* 519-695-5078
spirit@ciaccess.com
www.spiritofbothwell.com
Circulation: 725 *Frequency:* Wed.
Dean Muharrem, Publisher

Bracebridge: Bracebridge Examiner
PO Box 1049, 16 Manitoba St., Bracebridge, ON P1L 1V2
Tel: 705-645-8771; *Fax:* 705-645-1718
exanews@muskoka.com
www.bracebridgeexaminer.com
Circulation: 5,463 *Frequency:* Wednesday
Joe Anderson, Publisher

Bracebridge: Muskoka Sun
PO Box 1600, #203, 175 Manitoba St., Bracebridge, ON P1L 1V6
Tel: 705-645-4463; *Fax:* 705-645-3928
sun@muskoka.com
Circulation: 24,500 *Frequency:* Thu.; also Muskoka Life (annually)

Bracebridge: The Muskokan
PO Box 1049, 16 Manitoba St., Bracebridge, ON P1L 1V2
Tel: 705-645-8771; *Fax:* 705-645-1718
muskokan@muskoka.com
www.muskokan.com
Circulation: 25,000 *Frequency:* Thursday
Andrew Wagner-Chazalon, Editor
Ted Britton, Publisher

Bradford: Bradford West Gwillimbury Times
PO Box 1570, 74 John St. West, Bradford, ON L3Z 2B8
Tel: 905-775-4471; *Fax:* 905-775-4489
info@times.net
www.times.net
Circulation: 11,000 *Frequency:* Saturday
Miriam King, Editor
Richard Fonger, Publisher

Brampton: Brampton Pennysaver
#1, 56 Bramsteele Rd., Brampton, ON L6W 3M7
Tel: 905-454-0854; *Fax:* 905-450-5792
pennysaver_production@wwwdc.com
www.torontowestpennysaver.com
Circulation: 177,367 *Frequency:* Sunday; also publish: Caledon Pennysaver, Malton Pennysaver, Mississauga Pennysaver & Rexdale Pennysaver
Dale Davis, General Manager

Brampton: Le Régional
99 Professors Lake Pkwy., Brampton, ON L6S 4P8
Tél: 905-790-3229; *Téléc:* 905-790-9127
Ligne sans frais: 800-525-6752
info@leregional.com
www.leregional.com
Circulation: 10,000 *Frequency:* Mercredi
Christiane Beaupré, Rédactrice en chef

Brighton: The Independent
PO Box 1030, 1 Young St., Brighton, ON K0K 1H0
Tel: 613-475-0255; *Fax:* 613-475-4546
newsroom@eastnorthumberland.com
www.indynews.ca
Circulation: 18,505 *Frequency:* Wednesday
Stasha Conolly, Publisher

Brockville: St. Lawrence EMC
7712 Kent Blvd., Brockville, ON K6V 7H6
Tel: 613-342-0305; *Fax:* 613-498-0307
stlemc@storm.com
www.perfprint.ca
Frequency: Fri.
Duncan Weir, Publisher

Burford: Burford Times
PO Box 100, 115 King St., Burford, ON N0E 1A0
Tel: 519-449-5478; *Fax:* 519-449-5478
burfordtimes@brant.net
www.burfordtimes.com
Circulation: 2,000 *Frequency:* Wednesday
Bill Johnston, Publisher & Editor

Burks Falls: Almaguin News
PO Box 518, 185 Ontario St., Burks Falls, ON P0A 1C0
Tel: 705-382-9996; *Fax:* 705-382-3440
Toll-Free: 800-731-6397
news@almaguinnews.com
www.almaguinnews.com
Circulation: 3,783 *Frequency:* Wednesday
Joe Anderson, Publisher
Bruce Hickey, Editor

Burks Falls: Burks Falls Marketplace
PO Box 518, 183 Ontario St., Burks Falls, ON P0A 1C0
Tel: 705-382-3843; *Fax:* 705-382-3440
Toll-Free: 800-731-6397
news@almaguinnews.com
www.almaguinnews.com
Circulation: 12,600; Almaguin News 6,200 *Frequency:* Friday
Peter Barr, Publisher
Allan Dennis, Editor

Burlington: Burlington Post
#1, 5040 Mainway, Burlington, ON L7L 7G5
Tel: 905-632-4444;
www.haltonsearch.com
Circulation: 46,777 W, 57,619 F, 46,781 Su *Frequency:* Wednesday, Friday, Sunday
Niel Oliver, Publisher

Burlington: Cityscope
1343 Headen Rd., Burlington, ON L7M 1X4
Tel: 905-637-2900; *Fax:* 905- -
Circulation: 53,000
Dave de Jong, Publisher

Caledonia: Grand River Sachem
3 Sutherland St. West, Caledonia, ON N3W 1C1
Tel: 905-765-4441; *Fax:* 905-765-3651
sachem@sachem.on.ca
www.sachem.on.ca
Circulation: 18,110 *Frequency:* Friday
Neil Dring, Publisher
Neil Dring, Editor

Caledonia: The Regional News This Week
345 Argyle St. South, Caledonia, ON N3W 1L8
Tel: 905-765-4210; *Fax:* 905-765-3563
Circulation: 21,200 *Frequency:* Wed.
Christine Pickup, Publisher

Caleton Place: Almonte Gazette
PO Box 430, 53 Bridge St., Caleton Place, ON K7C 3P5
Tel: 613-257-1303; *Fax:* 613-257-7373
cpcedit@runge.net
www.runge.net
Circulation: 1,988 *Frequency:* Wednesday
Diane Pinder-Moss, Editor
Derek Walter, Publisher

Cambridge: Cambridge Times
1460 Bishop St., Cambridge, ON N1R 7N6
Tel: 519-623-7395;
www.cambridgetimes.ca
Circulation: 127,025 *Frequency:* Tuesday, Thursday, Friday
Peter Winkler, Publisher

Cannington: Brock Citizen
30 Cameron St. East, Cannington, ON L0E 1E0
Tel: 705-432-8842; *Fax:* 705-324-5694
showard@mykawartha.com
www.mykawartha.com

Circulation: 7,110 *Frequency:* Friday
Bruce Danford, Publisher
Scott Howard, Editor

***Carleton Place:* The Canadian**
PO Box 430, 53 Bridge St., Carleton Place, ON K7C 3P5
Tel: 613-257-1303; *Fax:* 613-257-7373
dpindermoss@runge.net
www.runge.net
Circulation: 2,561 *Frequency:* Tuesday
Diane Pinder-Moss, Editor
Derek Walter, Publisher, Sales

***Cayuga:* The Haldimand Press**
PO Box 100, Cayuga, ON N0A 1E0
Tel: 905-768-3111; *Fax:* 905-772-5465
press.c@news-net.ca
Circulation: 4,307 *Frequency:* Wednesday
Robert Hall, Publisher

***Chatham:* Chatham This Week**
#7, 930 Richmond St., Chatham, ON N7M 5J5
Tel: 519-351-7331; *Fax:* 519-351-7774
www.chathamthisweek.com
Circulation: 18,550 *Frequency:* Wednesday
Peter Epp, Editor

***Chatham:* Chatham-Kent Pennysaver**
#7, 930 Richmond St., Chatham, ON N7M 5L1
Tel: 519-351-4362; *Fax:* 519-351-2452
Toll-Free: 877-351-7331
chathampennysaver@bowesnet.com
www.chathampennysaver.com
Circulation: 30,000 *Frequency:* Friday
Ken Oliver, Publisher

***Chesterville:* Chesterville Record**
PO Box 368, Chesterville, ON K0C 1H0
Tel: 613-448-2321; *Fax:* 613-448-3260
www.agrinews.ca
Circulation: 1,941 *Frequency:* Wednesday
Robin Morris, Publisher

***Clinton:* Clinton News-Record**
PO Box 39, 53 Albert St., Clinton, ON N0M 1L0
Tel: 519-482-3443; *Fax:* 519-482-7341
clinton.news@bowesnet.com
www.clintonnewsrecord.com
Circulation: 2,438 *Frequency:* Wednesday
Tom Williscraft, Publisher

***Cobden:* Cobden Sun**
PO Box 100, 36 Crawford St., Cobden, ON K0J 1K0
Tel: 613-646-2380; *Fax:* 613-628-3291
cobdensun@nrtco.net
Circulation: 1,374 *Frequency:* Wednesday
Ron Tracey, Publisher

***Cobourg:* Northumberland News**
#212, 884 Division St., Cobourg, ON K9A 5V6
Tel: 905-373-7355; *Fax:* 905-373-4719
www.northumberlandnews.com
Circulation: 44,954 *Frequency:* Wed., Fri.
Tim Whittaker, Publisher

***Cochrane:* Cochrane Times-Post**
PO Box 10, 171 - 6th Ave., Cochrane, ON P0L 1C0
Tel: 705-272-3344; *Fax:* 705-272-3434
www.cochranetimespost.com
Circulation: 2,200 *Frequency:* Fri.
Wayne Major, Publisher

***Colborne:* Colborne Chronicle**
PO Box 208, 11 King St. East, Colborne, ON K0K 1S0
Tel: 905-355-2843; *Fax:* 905-355-1639
cchronicle@rol.ca
www.northumberlandtoday.com
Circulation: 913 *Frequency:* Thursday
Mike Walsh, Publisher

***Collingwood:* Collingwood Enterprise-Bulletin**
PO Box 98, 77 St. Marie St., Collingwood, ON L9Y 3Z4
Tel: 705-445-4611; *Fax:* 705-444-6477
editorial@theenterprisebulletin.com
www.theenterprisebulletin.com
Circulation: 18,591 *Frequency:* Wednesday, Friday; also Enterprise-Bulletin This Week (Fri., circ. 13,652)
Doreen Sykes, Publisher
Morgan Ian Adams, Editor

***Collingwood:* Collingwood/Wasaga Beach Connection**
4-155 First St., Collingwood, ON L9Y 1A4
Tel: 705-444-1875; *Fax:* 705-444-1876
connection@simcoe.com
www.collingwoodconnection.com
Circulation: 19,640 *Frequency:* Friday
Joe Anderson, Publisher
Larry Culham, Editor

***Cornwall:* Le Journal**
113 Montréal Rd., Cornwall, ON K6H 1B2
Tél: 613-938-1433; *Téléc:* 613-938-2798
rlduplan@glen-net.ca
Circulation: 2,300 *Frequency:* Jeudi; français
Roger Duplantie, President

***Cornwall:* Seaway News**
29 - 2nd St. East, Cornwall, ON K6H 1Y2
Tel: 613-933-0014; *Fax:* 613-933-0024
info@cornwallseawaynews.com
www.cornwallseawaynews.com
Circulation: 34,964 *Frequency:* Friday
Rick Shaver, Editor & General Manager
R.N. Aubry, Publisher

***Deep River:* North Renfrew Times**
PO Box 310, 11 Champlain St., Deep River, ON K0J 1P0
Tel: 613-584-4161; *Fax:* 613-584-1062
drcanrt@magma.ca
www.northrenfrewtimes.com
Circulation: 2,226 *Frequency:* Wednesday
Terry Myers, Editor
Terry Myers, Editor-in-chief

***Delhi:* Delhi News-Record**
237 Main St., Delhi, ON N4B 2M4
Tel: 519-582-2510; *Fax:* 519-582-4040
www.delhinewsrecord.com
Circulation: 1,447 *Frequency:* Wednesday
Cam McKnight, Publisher
Greg MacLachlin, Editor

***Dorchester:* Dorchester Signpost**
15 Bridge St., Dorchester, ON N0L 1G2
Tel: 519-268-7337; *Fax:* 519-268-3260
Circulation: 2,370 *Frequency:* Wednesday
Fred Huxley, Publisher

***Drayton:* The Community News**
PO Box 189, 41 Wellington St. North, Drayton, ON N0G 1P0
Tel: 519-638-3066; *Fax:* 519-638-3066
Toll-Free: 800-708-9555
www.wellingtonadviser.com
Circulation: 4,689 *Frequency:* Friday
W.H. Adsett, Publisher

***Dresden:* North Kent Leader**
PO Box 490, 254 Main St., Dresden, ON N0P 1M0
Tel: 519-683-4485; *Fax:* 519-683-4355
www.northkentleader.com
Circulation: 929 *Frequency:* Wednesday
Jim Blake, Publisher

***Dryden:* Dryden Observer**
PO Box 3009, Dryden, ON P8N 2Y9
Tel: 807-223-2390; *Fax:* 807-223-2907
Toll-Free: 800-465-7230
lauriep@drydenobserver.ca
www.drydenobserver.ca
Circulation: 3,945 *Frequency:* Wednesday
Warner Bloomfield, Editor
Roy Wilson, President & Publisher

***Dundalk:* Dundalk Herald**
PO Box 280, Dundalk, ON N0C 1B0
Tel: 519-923-2203; *Fax:* 519-923-2747
Circulation: 2,053 *Frequency:* Wednesday
Matthew Walls, Publisher
Mary Fowler, Editor

***Dundalk:* Flesherton Advance**
PO Box 280, Dundalk, ON N0C 1B0
Tel: 519-923-2203; *Fax:* 519-923-2747
Circulation: 1,634 *Frequency:* Wed.
Matt Walls, Publisher
Cathy Walls, General Manager

***Dundas:* Ancaster News**
47 Cootes Dr., Dundas, ON L9H 1B5
Tel: 905-628-6313; *Fax:* 905-628-6313
www.ancasternews.com
Circulation: 12,591 *Frequency:* Friday
Neil Oliver, Publisher

***Dundas:* Dundas Star News**
47 Cootes Dr., Dundas, ON L9H 1B5
Tel: 905-628-6313; *Fax:* 905-628-5485
www.dundasstarnews.com
Circulation: 18,047 *Frequency:* Friday
Neil Oliver, Publisher

***Dundas:* Hamilton Mountain News**
47 Cootes Dr., Dundas, ON L9H 1B5
Tel: 905-628-6313;
www.hamiltonmountainnews.com
Circulation: 48,883 *Frequency:* Friday
John Rousseau, Associate Publisher

***Dundas:* Stoney Creek News**
47 Cootes Dr., Dundas, ON L9H 1B5
Tel: 905-628-6313;
www.stoneycreeknews.com
Circulation: 29,791 *Frequency:* Fri.
Neil Oliver, Publisher

***Dunnville:* Dunnville Chronicle**
131 Lock St. East, Dunnville, ON N1A 1J6
Tel: 905-774-7632; *Fax:* 905-774-5744
www.dunnvillechronicle.ca
Circulation: 2,642 *Frequency:* Wednesday; also CoverStory (Sat.)
Mike Walsh, Publisher

***Eganville:* Eganville Leader**
PO Box 310, 154 John St., Eganville, ON K0J 1T0
Tel: 613-628-2332; *Fax:* 613-628-3291
leader@nrtco.net
www.eganvilleleader.com
Circulation: 4,931 *Frequency:* Wednesday
Ron Tracey, Co-Publisher
Gerald Tracey, Editor & Co-Publisher

***Elliot Lake:* Elliot Lake Standard**
14 Hillside Dr. South, Elliot Lake, ON P5A 1M6
Tel: 705-848-7195; *Fax:* 705-848-0249
Toll-Free: 800-463-6408
standard@elliottlakestandard.ca
www.elliotlakestandard.ca
Circulation: 4,564 *Frequency:* Wednesday
Ray Ethelston, Publisher

***Elmira:* Elmira Independent**
PO Box 128, 24 Church St. West, Elmira, ON N3B 2Z5
Tel: 519-669-5155; *Fax:* 519-669-5928
editor@elmiraindependent.com
www.elmiraindependent.com
Circulation: 3,320 *Frequency:* Friday
Gail Martin, Editor

***Elmira:* Woolwich Observer**
20B Arthur St., North, Elmira, ON N3B 1Z9
Tel: 519-669-5790; *Fax:* 519-669-5753
info@woolwichobserver.com
www.woolwichobserver.com
Circulation: 12,689 *Frequency:* Saturday
Joe Merlihan, Publisher

***Erin:* Erin Advocate**
#5, 8 Thompson Cres., Erin, ON N0B 1T0
Tel: 519-833-9603; *Fax:* 519-833-9605
editorial@erinadvocate.com
www.metroland.com
Circulation: 2,200 *Frequency:* Wednesday
Ken Nugent, Publisher

***Espanola:* Mid-North Monitor**
#15, 417 - 2nd Ave., Espanola, ON P5E 1L1
Tel: 705-869-0588; *Fax:* 705-869-0587
ads@midnorthmonitor.com
www.midnorthmonitor.com
Circulation: 3,492 *Frequency:* Wednesday
Ray Ethleston, Publisher

***Essex:* Essex Free Press**
16 Centre St., Essex, ON N8M 1N9
Tel: 519-776-4268; *Fax:* 519-776-4014
essexfreepress@on.aibn.com
essexfreepress.reinvented.net
Circulation: 3,460 *Frequency:* Wednesday
Laurie Brett, Publisher

***Etobicoke:* Bloor West Villager**
307 Humberline Dr., Etobicoke, ON M9W 5V1
Tel: 416-767-3644; *Fax:* 416-767-4880
www.insidetoronto.ca
Circulation: 38,571 *Frequency:* Fri.
Betty Carr, Publisher
Deborah Bodine, Editor-in-chief

Exeter: **Exeter Times-Advocate**
PO Box 850, 424 Main St., Exeter, ON N0M 1S0
Tel: 519-235-1331; *Fax:* 519-235-0766
www.southhuron.com
Circulation: 3,775 *Frequency:* Wednesday
Jim Beckett, Publisher

Fergus: **Fergus-Elora News-Express**
PO Box 130, 390 Tower St. South, Fergus, ON N1M 2W7
Tel: 519-843-1310; *Fax:* 519-843-1334
editor@centrewellington.com
www.centrewellington.com
Circulation: 3,587 *Frequency:* Wednesday
John Roberts, General Manager

Fergus: **The Wellington Advertiser**
PO Box 252, 180 St. Andrew St. East, Fergus, ON N1M 2W8
Tel: 519-843-5410; *Fax:* 519-843-7607
info@wellingtonadvertiser.com
www.wellingtonadvertiser.com
Circulation: 39,071 *Frequency:* Friday
W.H. Adsett, Publisher

Fonthill: **The Voice of Pelham**
PO Box 40, 111 Regional Rd. 20, Fonthill, ON L0S 1E0
Tel: 905-892-8690; *Fax:* 905-892-0823
thevoice@vaxxine.com
www.thevoiceofpelham.ca
Circulation: 8,528 *Frequency:* Wed.
Shawn Taylor, Editor

Fort Erie: **The Times**
PO Box 1219, #1, 450 Garrison Rd., Fort Erie, ON L2A 1N2
Tel: 905-871-3100; *Fax:* 905-871-5243
feeditor@cogeco.net
times.niagaracommunitynewspapers.com
Circulation: 12,043 *Frequency:* Saturday
Tim Dundas, Publisher

Fort Frances: **Fort Frances Times**
PO Box 339, 116 - 1st St. East, Fort Frances, ON P9A 3M7
Tel: 807-274-5373; *Fax:* 807-274-7286
Toll-Free: 800-465-8508
www.fortfrances.com
Circulation: 5,240 *Frequency:* Wednesday
Jim Cumming, Publisher
Mike Behan, Editor

Gananoque: **Gananoque Reporter**
79 King St. East, Gananoque, ON K7G 1E8
Tel: 613-382-2156; *Fax:* 613-382-3010
reporter@tipgananoque.com
www.gananoquereporter.com
Circulation: 3,616 *Frequency:* Wednesday
Ken Koyama, Publisher

Georgetown: **Georgetown Independent/Free Press**
#29, 280 Guelph St., Georgetown, ON L7G 4B1
Tel: 905-873-0301; *Fax:* 905-873-0398
www.independentfreepress.com
Circulation: 42,299 *Frequency:* Wednesday, Friday
John McGhie, Editor
Ken Nugent, Publisher

Geraldton: **Times Star**
PO Box 490, 414 Main St., Geraldton, ON P0T 1M0
Tel: 807-854-1919; *Fax:* 807-854-1682
tstar@astrocom-on.com
www.timestar.ca
Circulation: 1,293 *Frequency:* Wednesday
Stephane Parent, Publisher

Glencoe: **Transcript & Free Press**
PO Box 400, 243 Main St., Glencoe, ON N0L 1M0
Tel: 519-287-2615; *Fax:* 519-287-2408
tranfree@excelco.on.ca
Circulation: 2,069 *Frequency:* Wednesday
Dale Hayter, Publisher
Marie Williams-Gagnon, Editor

Gloucester: **L'Express d'Orléans / Orleans Express**
#30, 5300 Canotek Rd., Gloucester, ON K1J 8R7
Tél: 613-744-4800; *Téléc:* 613-744-8232
production_orleans@transcontinental.ca
journaux.apf.ca/expressorleans
Circulation: 36,500 *Frequency:* Mardi; français
Madeleine Joanisse, Éditeur
Florence Bolduc, Rédacteur en chef

Goderich: **Goderich Signal-Star**
PO Box 220, 120 Huckins St., Goderich, ON N7A 4B6
Tel: 519-524-2614; *Fax:* 519-524-5145
gssads@bowesnet.com
www.goderichsignalstar.com
Circulation: 5,530 *Frequency:* Wed; also Focus (every other Fri.)
Dave Sykes, Publisher
Ron Bunoy, Editor

Gore Bay: **The Manitoulin West Recorder**
PO Box 235, Meredith St., Gore Bay, ON P0P 1H0
Tel: 705-282-2003; *Fax:* 705-282-2432
therecorder@bellnet.ca
www.manitoulin.ca/recorder_etc/recorder.html
Circulation: 1,961 *Frequency:* Friday
Rick McCutcheon, Publisher

Grand Bend: **The Lakeshore Advance**
PO Box 1195, 58 Ontario St. North, Grand Bend, ON N0M 1T0
Tel: 519-238-5383; *Fax:* 519-238-5131
ladvance@bowesnet.com
www.lakeshoreadvance.com
Circulation: 1,587 *Frequency:* Wed.
Neil Clifford, General Manager
Linda Hillman-Rapley, Editor

Gravenhurst: **Gravenhurst Banner**
PO Box 849, 140 Muskoka Rd. South, Gravenhurst, ON P1P 1X2
Tel: 705-687-6674; *Fax:* 705-687-7213
Circulation: 3,043 *Frequency:* Wednesday
Joe Anderson, Publisher

Gravenhurst: **Muskoka Today**
140 - 1st St. South, Gravenhurst, ON P1P 1H5
Tel: 705-687-5777; *Fax:* 705-687-1009
Toll-Free: 800-240-2329
news@muskokatoday.com
www.muskokatoday.com
Circulation: 10,000
Lois Cooper, Editor
Mark Clairmont, Publisher

Grimsby: **Grimsby Lincoln News**
32 Main St. West, Grimsby, ON L3M 1R4
Tel: 905-945-8392; *Fax:* 905-945-3916
info@thegrimsbylincolnnews.com
www.thegrimsbylincolnnews.com
Circulation: 22,093 *Frequency:* Wed.
Ian Oliver, Publisher

Guelph: **Guelph Pennysaver**
86 Dawson Rd., Guelph, ON N1H 1A8
Tel: 519-823-5070; *Fax:* 519-823-2161
classifieds@guelphpennysaver.com
www.guelphpennysaver.com
Circulation: 47,300 *Frequency:* Friday
Rocky Nash, General Manager

Guelph: **The Guelph Tribune**
#1, 27 Woodlawn Rd. West, Guelph, ON N1H 1G8
Tel: 519-763-3333; *Fax:* 519-763-4814
gtribune@sentex.net
www.guelphtribune.ca
Circulation: 84,356 *Frequency:* Tuesday 39,808, Friday 44,548
Dwayne Weidendorf, Publisher

Haliburton: **Haliburton County Echo**
PO Box 360, 146 Highland St., Haliburton, ON K0M 1S0
Tel: 705-457-1037; *Fax:* 705-457-3275
info@haliburtonecho.on.ca
www.haliburtonecho.ca
Circulation: 4,302 *Frequency:* Tuesday
Don Smith, Publisher
Martha Perkins, Editor

Hamilton: **Dundas-Ancaster Recorder**
PO Box 68041 Blakely, Hamilton, ON L8M 3M7
Tel: 905-385-7192; *Fax:* 905- -
Circulation: 13,000 *Frequency:* Tuesday
Margaret Casey, Publisher

Hamilton: **Hamilton Recorder**
PO Box 68041 Blakely, Hamilton, ON L8M 3M7
Tel: 905-385-7192; *Fax:* 905- -
Circulation: 20,000 *Frequency:* Wednesday
Margaret Casey, Publisher

Hanover: **The Post**
413 - 18th Ave., Hanover, ON N4N 3S5
Tel: 519-364-2001; *Fax:* 519-364-6950
postads@thepost.on.ca
www.thepost.on.ca
Lori Gillespie, Managing Editor
Marie David, Publisher

Harcourt: **The Highlands Courier**
PO Box 88, Harcourt, ON K0L 1X0
Tel: 705-448-1388; *Fax:* 705-448-1394
hillo@sympatico.ca
Circulation: 1,000 *Frequency:* Monthly
Andrea Hillo, Publisher/Owner

Harrow: **Harrow News**
PO Box 310, 563 Queen St., Harrow, ON N0R 1G0
Tel: 519-738-2542; *Fax:* 519-738-3874
harnews@mnsi.net
Circulation: 1,360 *Frequency:* Tuesday
Cecil MacKenzie, Publisher

Hawkesbury: **Le Carillon**
CP 1000, Hawkesbury, ON K6A 3H1
Tél: 613-632-4155; *Téléc:* 613-632-6122
nouvelles@eap.on.ca
www.lecarillon.ca
Circulation: 19,587 *Frequency:* Mercredi; français
Bertrand Castonguay, Publisher

Hawkesbury: **Hawkesbury Tribune/Express**
PO Box 1000, 299, rue Principale est, Hawkesbury, ON K6A 3H1
Tel: 613-632-4155; *Fax:* 613-632-8601
pub@eap.on.ca
Circulation: 23,750 *Frequency:* Friday; English & French
Roger Duplantie

Hawkesbury: **Le/The Regional**
124, rue Principale est, Hawkesbury, ON K6A 1A3
Tel: 613-632-0112; *Fax:* 613-632-0277
Toll-Free: 888-477-3566
regional@hawk.igs.net
Circulation: 32,800 *Frequency:* Fri.; English & French
André Cayer
Sylvain Roy

Hearst: **Le Nord**
CP 2320, 813, rue Georges, Hearst, ON P0L 1N0
Tél: 705-372-1233; *Téléc:* 705-362-5954
lenord@lenord.on.ca
www.lenord.on.ca
Circulation: 3 500 *Frequency:* Mercredi; français et anglais
André Bolduc, Rédacteur-en-chef
Omer Cantin, Éditeur/Publisher

Huntsville: **Huntsville Forester**
11 Main St. West, Huntsville, ON P1H 2C6
Tel: 705-789-5541; *Fax:* 705-789-9381
news@huntsvilleforester.com
www.huntsvilleforester.com
Circulation: 6,305 *Frequency:* Wednesday
Joe Anderson, Publisher

Huntsville: **Muskoka Advance**
11 Main St. West, Huntsville, ON P1H 2C5
Tel: 705-645-8771; *Fax:* 705-645-1718
Circulation: 23,509 *Frequency:* Sunday

Ignace: **Ignace Driftwood**
PO Box 989, 153 Balsam St., Ignace, ON P0T 1T0
Tel: 807-934-6482; *Fax:* 807-934-6667
driftwood@bellnet.ca
Circulation: 445 *Frequency:* Wednesday
Dennis Smyk, Publisher

Ingersoll: **Ingersoll Times**
19 King St. West, Ingersoll, ON N5C 2J2
Tel: 519-485-3631; *Fax:* 519-485-6652
ingersoll@bowesnet.com
www.ingersolltimes.com
Circulation: 2,235 *Frequency:* Wednesday
Pat Logan, Publisher

Iroquois Falls: **The Enterprise**
PO Box 834, 727 Synagogue St., Iroquois Falls, ON P0K 1G0
Tel: 705-232-4081; *Fax:* 705-232-4235
Circulation: 2,345 *Frequency:* Thursday
W.C. Cavell, Publisher

Kanata: **Kanata Kourier-Standard**
#202, 240 Terrence Matthews Cres., Kanata, ON K2M 2C4
Tel: 613-591-3060; *Fax:* 613-591-8503
www.runge.net
Circulation: 24,430 *Frequency:* Friday
Brian Wiltsie, Publisher

Kanata: **Stittsville News**
#202, 240 Terrence Matthews Cres., Kanata, ON K2M 2C4
Tel: 613-836-1357; *Fax:* 613-836-5621
www.runge.net
Circulation: 1,935 *Frequency:* Tuesday

Bryan Wiltsie, Publisher

Kapuskasing: L'Horizon
2 Queen St., Kapuskasing, ON P5N 1G6
Tél: 705-335-5850; *Téléc:* 705-335-5958
horizon@nt.net
Frequency: Vendredi; aussi Le/The Weekender (Vendredi)

Kapuskasing: Kapuskasing Northern Times
51 Riverside Dr., Kapuskasing, ON P5N 1A7
Tel: 705-335-2283; *Fax:* 705-337-1222
kaptimes@bowesnet.com
www.kapuskasingtimes.com
Circulation: 2,912 *Frequency:* Wednesday; English & French
Wayne Major, Publisher

Kemptville: The Chieftain
PO Box 529, 29 Plaza Dr., Kemptville, ON K0E 1K0
Tel: 613-652-4395; *Fax:* 613-652-2508
comnew@magmacom.com
www.runge.net
Circulation: 648 *Frequency:* Wednesday
Fred Runge, Publisher

Kemptville: Kemptville Advance
PO Box 1420, Kemptville, ON K0G 1J0
Tel: 613-258-3451; *Fax:* 613-258-7734
news@comnews.ca
www.runge.net
Circulation: 2,031 *Frequency:* Wednesday
Chris Webb, Publisher
Ashley Kulp, Editor

Kenora: Kenora Lake of the Woods Enterprise
PO Box 1620, 33 Main St., Kenora, ON P9N 3X7
Tel: 807-468-6397; *Fax:* 807-468-1060
info@kenoraenterprise.com
www.lotwenterprise.com
Circulation: 9,400 *Frequency:* Saturday
Jim Blight

Keswick: Georgina Advocate
461 The Queensway South, Keswick, ON L4P 2C9
Tel: 905-476-7753; *Fax:* 905-476-5785
www.yorkregion.com
Circulation: 16,757 *Frequency:* Thursday
Ian Proudfoot, Publisher

Kincardine: The Independent
PO Box 1240, 840 Queen St., Kincardine, ON N2Z 2Z4
Tel: 519-396-3111; *Fax:* 519-396-3899
indepen@bmts.com
www.independent.on.ca
Circulation: 2,203 *Frequency:* Wednesday
Eric Howald, Publisher

Kincardine: Kincardine News
719 Queen St., Kincardine, ON N2Z 1Z9
Tel: 519-396-2963; *Fax:* 519-396-3790
kincardine@bowesnet.com
www.kincardinenews.com
Circulation: 3,736 *Frequency:* Wednesday
Carol McKnight, Publisher
Troy Patterson, Editor

Kingston: Frontenac Gazette
1748 Bath Rd., Kingston, ON K7M 4Y2
Tel: 613-389-8884; *Fax:* 613-389-1870
heritagenewspaper@bellnet.ca
Circulation: 10,045 *Frequency:* Tuesday
Darryl Cembal, President

Kingston: The Heritage Newspaper
1784 Bath Rd., Kingston, ON K7M 4Y2
Tel: 613-389-8884; *Fax:* 613-389-1870
heritagenewspaper@bellnet.ca
www.whatsonkingston.com/heritage/
Circulation: 26,596 *Frequency:* Friday
Darryl Cembal, President

Kingston: Kingston This Week
607 Gardiners Rd., Kingston, ON K7M 3Y4
Tel: 613-389-7400;
news@kingstonthisweek.com
www.kingstonthisweek.com
Circulation: 97,444 *Frequency:* Tuesday, Friday
Ken Koyama, Publisher

Kingsville: Kingsville Reporter
17 Chestnut St., Kingsville, ON N9Y 1J9
Tel: 519-733-2211; *Fax:* 519-733-6464
www.kingsreporter.emporium.on.ca
Circulation: 2,350 *Frequency:* Tuesday
Greg Sims, Publisher

Kitchener: Pennysaver
685 Wabanaki Dr., Kitchener, ON N2C 2G3
Tel: 519-894-1400; *Fax:* 519-894-5401
www.kitchenerpennysaver.com
Frequency: Saturday

Lakefield: Lakefield Herald
PO Box 1000, 74 Bridge St., Lakefield, ON K0L 2H0
Tel: 705-652-5114; *Fax:* 705-652-6912
Toll-Free: 877-652-6594
info@lakefieldherald.com
www.lakefieldherald.com
Circulation: 1,036 *Frequency:* Friday
Simon Conolly, Publisher

Lasalle: LaSalle Post
1775 Sprucewood Ave., Lasalle, ON N9J 1X7
Tel: 519-250-2880; *Fax:* 519-250-2881
lapost@windsoressexnews.com
www.windsoressexnews.com
Circulation: 9,768 *Frequency:* Wed.
Gary Baxter, Publisher

Leamington: Leamington Post & Shopper
27 Princess St., Leamington, ON N8H 2X8
Tel: 519-326-4434; *Fax:* 519-326-2171
leampost@wincom.net
www.leamingtonpostandshopper.com
Circulation: 5,000 *Frequency:* Wednesday; also Leamington Shopper (Sat., circ. 17,000)
Linda Gage, Manager, Sales
Don Gage, Publisher
Mike Thibodeau, Editor

Lindsay: Bobcaygeon Independent
96 Albert St. South, Lindsay, ON K9V 3H7
Tel: 705-324-8600; *Fax:* 705-324-5694
Circulation: 1,700 *Frequency:* Wednesday
Lois Tuffin, Editor-in-chief

Lindsay: Fenelon Falls Gazette
c/o Lindsay This Week, 96 Albert St. South, Lindsay, ON K9V 3H7
Frequency: Tuesday
Bruce Danford, Publisher

Listowel: Listowel Banner
PO Box 97, 185 Wallace Ave. North, Listowel, ON N4W 3H2
Tel: 519-291-1660; *Fax:* 519-291-3771
gbisch@northperth.com
www.northperth.com
Circulation: 3,480 *Frequency:* Wednesday; also Independent & Independent Plus (Fri.)
Bill Huether, General Manager
Patrick Raftis, Editor

Little Current: The Manitoulin Expositor
PO Box 369, One Manitowaning Rd., Little Current, ON P0P 1K0
Tel: 705-368-2744; *Fax:* 705-368-3822
theexpositor@etown.net
www.manitoulin.ca
Circulation: 5,703 *Frequency:* Wednesday
R.L. McCutcheon, Publisher
Jim Moodie, Editor

London: London Pennysaver
369 York St., London, ON N6A 4G1
Tel: 519-667-5486; *Fax:* 519-667-4573
pennyreaderads@londonpennysaver.com
www.londonpennysaver.com
Circulation: 144,000 *Frequency:* Friday
Marj Bastow, General Manager

London: The Londoner
PO Box 7400, London, ON N5Y 4X3
Tel: 519-673-5005; *Fax:* 519-673-4624
www.thelondoner.ca
Circulation: 107,623 *Frequency:* Wed.
Alan Glaser, Publisher
Philip McLeod, Editor

Lucknow: Lucknow Sentinel
PO Box 400, 619 Campbell St., Lucknow, ON N0G 2H0
Tel: 519-528-2822; *Fax:* 519-528-3529
lucksent@bowesnet.com
www.lucknowsentinel.com
Circulation: 1,639 *Frequency:* Wednesday
Pat Livingston, Publisher
Sara Bender, Editor

Manitouwadge: Echo
PO Box 550, #8, Hallmark Sq., Manitouwadge, ON P0T 2C0
Tel: 807-826-3788; *Fax:* 807-826-3910
echo_manitouwadge@hotmail.com
Circulation: 610 *Frequency:* Wednesday
B.J. Schermann, Publisher

Manotick: Manotick Messenger
PO Box 567, 1165 Beaverwood Rd., Manotick, ON K4M 1A5
Tel: 613-692-6000; *Fax:* 613-692-3758
newsfile@bellnet.ca
www.storm.ca/~newsfile/
Circulation: 955 *Frequency:* Wed.
Jeff Morris, Publisher

Manotick: The Manotick Review
PO Box 102, 1142 Tighe St., Manotick, ON K4M 1A2
Tel: 613-432-3655; *Fax:* 613-692-2456
comnews@magmacom.com
www.runge.net/mercury
Circulation: 342 *Frequency:* Wed.
Bryan Wiltsie, Publishing

Manotick: Ottawa-South This Month
PO Box 102, 1142 Tighe St., Manotick, ON K4M 1A2
Tel: 613-692-3211; *Fax:* 613-692-2456
comnews@magma.ca
Circulation: 17,063
Peter Peers, Manager, Sales
Brian Crawford, Publisher
Joe Morin, Editor

Marathon: Marathon Mercury
PO Box 369, 14 Peninsula Rd., Marathon, ON P0T 2E0
Tel: 807-229-1520; *Fax:* 807-229-1595
marathonmercury@shaw.ca
Circulation: 1,341 *Frequency:* Tuesday
Garry R. McInnes, Publisher

Markham: Markham Economist & Sun
9 Heritage Rd., Markham, ON L3P 1M3
Tel: 905-294-2200; *Fax:* 905-294-1538
www.yorkregion.com
Circulation: 179,476 *Frequency:* Tuesday, Thursday, Saturday
Ian Proudfoot, Publisher
Dave Teetzel, Editor

Marmora: Land O'Lakes Sun
PO Box 250, Marmora, ON K0K 2M0
Tel: 613-472-2431; *Fax:* 613-472-5026
zoo@kos.net
Circulation: 5,565 *Frequency:* Saturday
Brian Dunning, Editor

Mattawa: Mattawa Recorder
PO Box 67, 341 McConnell St., Mattawa, ON P0H 1V0
Tel: 705-744-5361; *Fax:* 705-744-5361
Circulation: 1,050 *Frequency:* Sunday
Heather Edwards, Contact

Meaford: Express
68 Sykes St. North, Meaford, ON N4L 1R2
Tel: 519-538-1421; *Fax:* 519-538-5028
Toll-Free: 866-771-6235
themeafordexpress@rogers.com
Circulation: 2,544 *Frequency:* Wed.
Doug Rowe, Publisher

Midland: Free Press
PO Box 37, Midland, ON L4R 4K6
Tel: 705-526-5431; *Fax:* 705-526-1771
freepress@midlandfreepress.com
www.midlandfreepress.com
Circulation: 5,429 *Frequency:* Wed., Fri.
Sandy Coghlan, Publisher

Midland: Midland/Penetanguishene Mirror
PO Box 77, 488 Dominion Ave., Midland, ON L4R 1P6
Tel: 705-527-5500; *Fax:* 705-527-5467
themirror@simcoe.com
www.midlandmirror.com
Circulation: 14,026 W; 19,404 F *Frequency:* Wednesday, Friday
Joe Anderson, Publisher

Midland: Penetanguishene Free Press
PO Box 37, 845 King St., Unit 4, Midland, ON L4R 4K3
Tel: 705-526-5431; *Fax:* 705-526-1771
freepress@midlandfreepress.com
www.midlandfreepress.com
Circulation: 6,657 *Frequency:* Tuesday, Friday
Sandy Coghlan, General Manager

Mildmay: **Mildmay Town Crier Weekly**
PO Box 190, 100 Elora St., Mildmay, ON N0G 2J0
Tel: 519-367-2681; *Fax:* 519-367-5417
thecrier@wightman.ca
Circulation: 1,800 *Frequency:* Wednesday
John H. Hafermehl, Publisher

Millbrook: **The Green Hills Gazette**
69 King St. East, Millbrook, ON L0A 1G0
Frequency: Thursday

Millbrook: **Millbrook Times**
PO Box 285, 5 Lisa Court, Millbrook, ON L0A 1G0
Tel: 705-932-3001
Circulation: 1,816 *Frequency:* Thu.
Beverley Martin, Publisher

Milton: **Milton Canadian Champion**
PO Box 248, 191 Main St, Milton, ON L9T 4N9
Tel: 905-878-2341; *Fax:* 905-878-4943
www.haltonsearch.com
Circulation: 38,934 *Frequency:* Tuesday, Friday
Karen Smith, Editor

Minden: **The Times**
PO Box 97, 134 Bobcaygeon Rd., Minden, ON K0M 2K0
Tel: 705-286-1288; *Fax:* 705-286-4768
editor@mindentimes.ca.ca
www.mindentimes.ca
Circulation: 2,891 *Frequency:* Wednesday
Martha Perkins, Editor
David Zilstra, Publisher
Don Smith, Publisher

Mississauga: **Mississauga Booster**
5650 Keaton Cres., Unit A, Mississauga, ON L5R 3G3
Tel: 905-890-4606; *Fax:* 905-890-3999
http://webhome.idirect.com/~booster/start.html
Circulation: 120,000 *Frequency:* Every other Fri.
Paul McCallion, Publisher
Ron Lenyk, Publisher

Mississauga: **Mississauga News**
3145 Wolfedale Rd., Mississauga, ON L5C 3A9
Tel: 905-273-8111; *Fax:* 905-273-9119
www.mississauganews.com
Circulation: 367,941 *Frequency:* Wed., Fri., Sun; supplement, Community News (Wed.)
Ron Lenyk, Publisher

Mississauga: **The Weekly Voice**
#212, 6705 Tomken Rd., Mississauga, ON L5T 2J6
Tel: 905-795-8282; *Fax:* 905-795-9801
info@weeklyvoice.com
www.weeklyvoice.com
Circulation: 30,000 (English); 20,000 (Punjabi) *Frequency:* Fri.
Jazz Samra, Publisher

Mitchell: **Mitchell Advocate**
PO Box 669, 42 Montreal St., Mitchell, ON N0K 1N0
Tel: 519-348-8431; *Fax:* 519-348-8836
abader@bowesnet.com
www.mitchelladvocate.com
Circulation: 2,479 *Frequency:* Wednesday
Andy Bader, Publisher

Morrisburg: **Morrisburg Leader**
PO Box 891, 41 Main St., Morrisburg, ON K0C 1X0
Tel: 613-543-2987; *Fax:* 613-543-3643
Circulation: 2,111 *Frequency:* Wednesday
Sam Laurin, Publisher & Editor
Bonnie McNairn, Managing Editor

Mount Forest: **Mount Forest Confederate**
PO Box 130, 277 Main St. South, Mount Forest, ON N0G 2L0
Tel: 519-323-1550; *Fax:* 519-323-4548
editor@mountforest.com
www.mountforest.com
Circulation: 2,649 *Frequency:* Wednesday
Lynne Pinnegar, Publisher

Napanee: **Napanee Beaver**
72 Dundas St. East, Napanee, ON K7R 1H9
Tel: 613-354-6641; *Fax:* 613-354-2622
beaver@bellnet.ca
www.napaneebeaver.com
Circulation: 2,385 *Frequency:* Wednesday
Seth DuChene, Editor
Jean Morrison, Publisher

Napanee: **The Napanee Guide**
#11, 2 Dairy Ave., Napanee, ON K7R 3T1
Tel: 613-354-6648; *Fax:* 613-354-6708
www.napaneeguide.com
Circulation: 14,101 *Frequency:* Friday
Ken Koyama, Publisher

Nepean: **Alta Vista Canterbury News**
#3B, 15 Antares Dr., Nepean, ON K2E 7Y9
Tel: 613-723-5970; *Fax:* 613-723-1862
ottnews@ottnews.ca
Circulation: 36,000 *Frequency:* Every other Thu.; also Britannia/Lincoln Heights News, Carlingwood/Baseline News, Glebe & Ottawa South News, Westboro/Hampton Park News
Michael Wollock, Publisher
Tom Collins, Editor

Nepean: **Barrhaven Independent**
PO Box 29011, Nepean, ON K2J 4A9
Tel: 613-825-9858; *Fax:* 613-692-3758
newsfile@bellnet.ca
www.barrhavenindependent.on.ca
Circulation: 17,445 *Frequency:* Fri.
Derek Dunn, Editor

Nepean: **Nepean This Week**
#200, 9 Camelot Dr., Nepean, ON K2G 5W6
Tel: 613-723-7951; *Fax:* 613-723-9589
publisher@nepeanthisweek.com
www.nepeanthisweek.com
Circulation: 44,757 *Frequency:* Fri.
Chris Webb, Publisher

New Hamburg: **New Hamburg Independent**
PO Box 670, 77 Peel St., New Hamburg, ON N3A 1E7
Tel: 519-662-1240; *Fax:* 519-662-3521
Toll-Free: 800-563-3578
editor@newhamburgindependent.ca
www.newhamburgindependent.ca
Circulation: 3,060 *Frequency:* Wed.
Neil Oliver, Publisher
Cal Bosveld, Publisher

New Liskeard: **Journal O'Courant**
CP 1358, New Liskeard, ON P0J 1P0
Tél: 705-647-9898
Frequency: Wed.

New Liskeard: **The Temiskaming Speaker**
PO Box 580, 18 Wellington St., New Liskeard, ON P0J 1P0
Tel: 705-647-6791;
www.northernontario.ca
Circulation: 4,840 *Frequency:* Wed.
Dave Armstrong, Publisher

Newmarket: **Newmarket Era Banner**
PO Box 236, 580 Steven Ct., Newmarket, ON L3Y 4X1
Tel: 905-773-7627; *Fax:* 905-773-7626
www.yorkregion.com
Circulation: 174,637 *Frequency:* Tuesday, Thursday, Sunday
Ian Proudfoot, Publisher

Niagara Falls: **Niagara Falls News**
4949 Victoria Ave., Niagara Falls, ON L2E 4C7
Tel: 905-357-2440; *Fax:* 905-357-1620
twilkinson@niagaracommunitynewspapers.com
falls.niagaracommunitynewspape rs.com

Niagara Falls: **Niagara Shopping News**
4949 Victoria Ave., Niagara Falls, ON L2E 4C7
Tel: 905-357-2440; *Fax:* 905- -
Circulation: 29,650 *Frequency:* Friday

Nipigon: **Nipigon-Red Rock Gazette**
PO Box 1057, 145 Railway St., Nipigon, ON P0T 2J0
Tel: 807-887-3583; *Fax:* 807- -
Circulation: 1,008 *Frequency:* Tuesday
Linda Harbison, Publisher

North York: **Canadian Jewish News**
 # 205, 1500 Don Mills Rd., North York, ON M3B 3K4
Tel: 416-391-1836;
www.cjnews.com
Circulation: 41,302 *Frequency:* Thur.
Vera Gillman, Advertising Manager
Mordechai Ben-Dat, Editor

Norwich: **Norwich Gazette**
PO Box 459, 4 Washington St., Norwich, ON N0J 1P0
Tel: 519-863-2262; *Fax:* 519-863-3229
norwich@bowesnet.com
www.norwichgazette.ca
Circulation: 1,433 *Frequency:* Wed.
Pat Logan, Publisher

Jennifer Vandermeer, Editor

Oakville: **Milton Shopping News**
1158 South Service Rd. West, Oakville, ON L6L 5T7
Tel: 905-827-2244; *Fax:* 905-827-2308
Circulation: 18,700 *Frequency:* Tuesday, Friday
Bill Whitaker Sr.

Oakville: **Oakville Beaver**
467 Speers Rd., Oakville, ON L6K 3S4
Tel: 905-845-3824;
www.insidehalton.com; www.metroland.com
Circulation: 139,631 *Frequency:* Wed., Fri., Sun.; also North News (Fri.), & Oakville Marketplace (Tue.)
Oakville's community newspaper; print and online editions
Neil Oliver, Publisher
Jill David, Editor-in-Chief

Oakville: **Oakville Shopping News**
1158 South Service Rd. West, Oakville, ON L6L 5T7
Tel: 905-827-2244; *Fax:* 905-827-2308
Circulation: 46,500 *Frequency:* Wed., Fri.
Bill Whitaker Sr.

Oakville: **Oakville Today**
#10, 2526 Speers Rd., Oakville, ON L6L 5M2
Tel: 905-825-2229; *Fax:* 905-825-8315
newsroom@oakvilletoday.ca
www.oakvilletoday.ca
Circulation: 26,800 *Frequency:* Thu.
Lars Melander, Publisher

Ohsweken: **Tekawennake - Six Nations & New Credit**
PO Box 130, Ohsweken, ON N0A 1M0
Tel: 519-753-0077; *Fax:* 519-753-0011
teka@tekanews.com
www.tekanews.com
Circulation: 2,500 *Frequency:* Wednesday
Scott Smith

Orangeville: **Orangeville Banner**
37 Mill St., Orangeville, ON L9W 2M4
Tel: 519-941-1350; *Fax:* 519-941-9600
banner@orangevillebanner.com
www.orangeville.com
Circulation: 19,115 Tue.; 23,055 Fri. *Frequency:* Tuesday, Friday
Keith Poole, Publisher

Orangeville: **Orangeville Citizen**
10 - 1st St., Orangeville, ON L9W 2C4
Tel: 519-941-2230; *Fax:* 519-941-9361
mail@citizen.on.ca
www.citizen.on.ca
Circulation: 11,983 *Frequency:* Thursday
Tom Claridge, Editor
Alan Claridge, Publisher

Orillia: **Orillia Today**
25 Ontario St., Unit 1, Orillia, ON L3V 6H1
Tel: 705-329-2058; *Fax:* 705-329-2059
www.orilliatoday.com
Circulation: 41,430 *Frequency:* Wed., Fri.
Joe Anderson, Publisher

Orono: **Orono Weekly Times**
PO Box 209, 5310 Main St., Orono, ON L0B 1M0
Tel: 905-983-5301;
oronotimes@speedline.ca
Circulation: 1,067 *Frequency:* Wed.
Margaret Zwart, Publisher

Oshawa: **Oshawa/Whitby This Week, Clarington This Week, Canadian Statesman**
PO Box 481, 865 Farewell Ave., Oshawa, ON L1H 7L5
Tel: 905-579-4400; *Fax:* 905-579-2238
www.durhamregion.com
Circulation: 147,467 *Frequency:* Wed., Fri., Sun.
Tim Whittaker, Publisher
Chris Bovie, Editor-in-chief

Ottawa: **Centretown News**
c/o St. Patrick's Bldg., Carleton University School of Journ, #531, 1125 Colonel By Dr., Ottawa, ON K1S 5B6
Tel: 613-520-7410; *Fax:* 613-520-4068
ctown@carleton.ca
www.carleton.ca/ctown/home/homeNew.htm
Circulation: 16,000 *Frequency:* Every other Fri.
Klaus Pohle, Publisher

Ottawa: **Greenboro Hunt Club Park News**
#3B, 15 Antares Dr., Ottawa, ON K2E 7Y9
Tel: 613-723-5970; *Fax:* 613-723-1862
ottnews@ottnews.ca

Circulation: 36,000 *Frequency:* Every other Thu.
Mike Wollock, Publisher

***Ottawa:* The Hill Times**
69 Sparks St., Ottawa, ON K1P 5A5
Tel: 613-232-5952; *Fax:* 613-232-9055
www.thehilltimes.ca
Circulation: 12,947 *Frequency:* Monday
Jim Creskey, Publisher
Kate Malloy, Editor

***Ottawa:* Hunt Club Riverside News**
#3B, 15 Antares Dr., Ottawa, ON K2E 7Y9
Tel: 613-723-5970; *Fax:* 613-723-1862
ottnews@ottnews.ca
Circulation: 36,000 *Frequency:* Thu.
Mike Wollock, Publisher

***Ottawa:* Ottawa Pennysaver**
PO Box 9729 T, 6 Antares Dr., Phase III, Ottawa, ON K1G 5H7
Tel: 613-733-4099; *Fax:* 613-733-7107
www.ottawapennysaver.com
Frequency: Saturday

***Ottawa:* The Spectrum**
Boyd McRubie Communications Inc., PO Box 16130 F, Ottawa, ON K2C 3S9
Tel: 613-226-2738;
thespectrum@hotmail.com
Circulation: 6,000 *Frequency:* Monthly, except July & August
Ewart Walters

***Ottawa:* The Star**
#30, 5300 Canotek Rd., Ottawa, ON K1J 8R7
Tel: 613-744-4800; *Fax:* 613-744-1976
thestar@transcontinental.ca
www.neighbourhoodnews.ca
Circulation: 35,000 *Frequency:* Tuesday
Terry Tyo, Publisher

***Owen Sound:* Markdale Standard**
209 9th St. East, Owen Sound, ON N4K 5P2
Tel: 519-376-2250;
themarkdalestandard@bmts.com
www.markdalestandard.com
Circulation: 648 *Frequency:* Wednesday
Cheryl McMenemy, Publisher & General Manager

***Palmerston:* Minto Express**
PO Box 757, 171 William St., Palmerston, ON N0G 2P0
Tel: 519-343-2440; *Fax:* 519-343-2267
www.mintoexpress.com
Circulation: 1,260 *Frequency:* Tuesday
Paul Teahen, General Manager
Patrick Raftis, Editor

***Paris:* Paris Star**
59 Grand River St. North, Paris, ON N3L 2N9
Tel: 519-442-7866; *Fax:* 519-442-3100
parisstar@bowesnet.com
www.parisstaronline.com
Circulation: 1,638 *Frequency:* Wed.
Andrea DeMeer, Publisher

***Parkhill:* Forest Standard**
PO Box 400, Parkhill, ON N0M 2K0
Tel: 519-786-5242; *Fax:* 519-786-4884
standard@xcelco.on.ca
www.foreststandard.com
Circulation: 2,481 *Frequency:* Thursday
Dale Hayter, Publisher

***Parkhill:* Parkhill Gazette**
PO Box 400, 165 King St., Parkhill, ON N0M 2K0
Tel: 519-294-6264; *Fax:* 519-294-6391
Circulation: 1,177 *Frequency:* Thursday
Dale Hayter, Publisher

***Parry Sound:* Parry Sound Beacon Star**
PO Box 370, 67 James St., Parry Sound, ON P2A 1T6
Tel: 705-746-2104; *Fax:* 705-746-8369
www.parrysoundbeaconstar.com
Circulation: 3,688 *Frequency:* Saturday
Fred Heidman, General Manager

***Parry Sound:* Parry Sound North Star**
PO Box 370, 67 James St., Parry Sound, ON P2A 2X4
Tel: 705-746-2105; *Fax:* 705-746-8369
www.parrysoundnorthstar.com
Circulation: 4,101 *Frequency:* Wed.
Fred Heidman, General Manager

***Penetanguishene:* Le Goût de Vivre**
343, av Lafontaine, RR#3, Penetanguishene, ON L9M 1R3
Tél: 705-533-3349; *Téléc:* 705-533-3422
legout-de-vivre@sympatico.ca
www.journaux.apf.ca/legoutdevivre
Circulation: 1 000 *Frequency:* 1er et 3e jeudi du mois; français

***Perth:* Perth Courier**
PO Box 156, 39 Gore St. East, Perth, ON K7H 3E3
Tel: 613-267-1100; *Fax:* 613-267-3986
courier@perth.igs.net
www.perthcourier.com
Circulation: 4,836 *Frequency:* Wed.
John W. Clement, Publisher
Ian Gray, Editor

***Petawawa:* Petawawa Post**
Bldg. P-106, Petawawa, ON K8H 2X3
Tel: 613-687-5511;
petawawapost@bellnet.ca
www.psppetawawa.com/petawawapost.cfm
Circulation: 7,700 *Frequency:* Tuesday
Carol Bullied, Editor

***Peterborough:* Peterborough This Week**
884 Ford St., Peterborough, ON K9J 5V3
Tel: 705-749-3383; *Fax:* 705-749-0074
www.mykawartha.com
Circulation: 96,277 *Frequency:* Wed., Fri.
Bruce Danford, Publisher

***Petrolia:* The Petrolia Topic**
PO Box 40, 4182 Petrolia Line, Petrolia, ON N0N 1R0
Tel: 519-882-1770; *Fax:* 519-882-3212
www.petroliatopic.com
Circulation: 2,422 *Frequency:* Wed.
Daryl Smith, Publisher

***Picton:* Picton Gazette**
PO Box 80, Picton, ON K0K 2T0
Tel: 613-476-3201; *Fax:* 613-476-3464
gazette@connect.reach.net
www.pictongazette.com
Circulation: 2,170 *Frequency:* Wed.; The Picton Gazette Regional (Sat., circ. 10,602)
Jean M. Morrison, Publisher

***Port Colborne:* In Port**
149 King St., Port Colborne, ON L3K 4G3
Tel: 905-834-4521; *Fax:* 905-834-5422
itait@wellandtribune.ca
www.wellandtribune.ca
Circulation: 5,300 *Frequency:* Wed.
Mike Walsh, Publisher

***Port Dover:* Port Dover Maple Leaf**
PO Box 70, 351 Main St., Port Dover, ON N0A 1N0
Tel: 519-583-0112; *Fax:* 519-583-3200
info@inportdover.com
www.inportdover.com
Circulation: 3,163 *Frequency:* Wed.
Stan Morris, Publisher

***Port Elgin:* Shoreline Beacon**
PO Box 539, 694 Goderich St., Port Elgin, ON N0H 2C0
Tel: 519-832-9001; *Fax:* 519-389-4793
shoreline@bmts.com
www.shorelinebeacon.com
Circulation: 4,510 *Frequency:* Wed.
Carol McKnight, Publisher

***Port Perry:* Port Perry Star**
180 Mary St, #11, Port Perry, ON L9L 1C4
Tel: 905-985-7383; *Fax:* 905-985-3708
advertising@portperrystar.com
www.ducharmregion.com
Circulation: 23,400 *Frequency:* Wed., Fri.
Tim Whittaker, Publisher

***Prescott:* Prescott Journal**
PO Box 549, 231 King St. West, Prescott, ON K0E 1T0
Tel: 613-925-4265; *Fax:* 613-925-3472
slp@ripnet.com
www.prescottjournal.com
Circulation: 2,441 *Frequency:* Wed.
Lisa D. Taylor, Publisher

***Rainy River:* Rainy River Record**
PO Box 280, 312 - 3rd St., Rainy River, ON P0W 1L0
Tel: 807-852-3366; *Fax:* 807-852-4434
info@rainyriverrecord.com
www.rainyriverrecord.com
Circulation: 788 *Frequency:* Tuesday
J.R. Cumming, Publisher

Ken Johnston, Editor

***Rainy River:* The Westend Weekly**
PO Box 66, Rainy River, ON P0W 1L0
Tel: 807-852-3815; *Fax:* 807-852-4011
Circulation: 8,600 *Frequency:* Wed.
Ron McAllister, Publisher
Jacquie Dufresne, Editor-in-chief

***Renfrew:* Renfrew Mercury**
PO Box 400, 35 Opeongo Rd., Renfrew, ON K7V 1A8
Tel: 613-432-3655; *Fax:* 613-432-6689
rmedit@runge.net
www.runge.net
Circulation: 4,006 *Frequency:* Tuesday
Fred Runge, Publisher
Lucy Hass, Editor

***Renfrew:* Renfrew Weekender**
PO Box 400, 35 Opeongo Rd., Renfrew, ON K7V 4A8
Tel: 613-432-3655; *Fax:* 613-432-6689
rmedit@runge.net
www.runge.net
Circulation: 14,795 *Frequency:* Friday
Lucy Hass, Editor
Fred Runge, Publisher
Derek Walter, General Manager

***Richmond Hill:* The Liberal**
PO Box 390, 1550 16th Ave., Richmond Hill, ON L4B 3K9
Tel: 905-881-3373; *Fax:* 905-881-9924
www.yorkregion.com
Circulation: 197,459 *Frequency:* Tuesday 45,443; Thursday 76,048; Sunday 75,968
Ian Proudfoot, Publisher
Debora Kelly, Editor-in-chief

***Richmond Hill:* Vaughan Citizen**
Suite 100, 1550 16th Avenue Bld.F, Richmond Hill, ON L4B 3K9
Tel: 905-881-3373; *Fax:* 905-660-3118
www.yorkregion.com
Other information: Toronto Line: 416/661-0047
Circulation: 42,924 Th; 42,000 Su; 84,924 total *Frequency:* Thursday, Sunday
Ian Proudfoot, Publisher

***Ridgetown:* The Ridgetown Independent News**
PO Box 609, 1 Main St., Ridgetown, ON N0P 2C0
Tel: 519-674-5205; *Fax:* 519-674-2573
Circulation: 2,200 *Frequency:* Wed.
Jim Brown, Publisher

***Rockland:* Journal Vision Prescott/Russell**
PO Box 897, 1579 Laurier, Rockland, ON K4K 1L5
Tel: 613-446-6456; *Fax:* 613-446-1381
vision@eap.on.ca
Circulation: 18,100

***Russell:* Russell Villager**
PO Box 550, 191 Castor St., Russell, ON K4R 1E1
Tel: 613-445-3804; *Fax:* 613-445-3843
villager@magma.ca
Circulation: 989 *Frequency:* Wed.
Robin Morris, Managing Publisher

***Sarnia:* Lambton-Sarnia Pennysaver**
1383 Confederation St., Sarnia, ON N7S 5P1
Tel: 519-336-1100; *Fax:* 519-336-1833
info@sarniamedia.com
www.sarniamedia.com
Circulation: 45,700 *Frequency:* Saturday

***Sarnia:* Sarnia This Week**
1383 Confederation St., Sarnia, ON N7S 5P1
Tel: 519-336-1100; *Fax:* 519-336-1833
www.sarniamedia.com
Circulation: 24,026 *Frequency:* Wed.
Linda Leblanc, Publisher

***Sault Ste Marie:* Sault Ste Marie This Week**
PO Box 188, 2 Towers St., Sault Ste Marie, ON P6A 5L6
Tel: 705-949-6111; *Fax:* 705-942-8596
stwnews@saultthisweek.com
www.saultthisweek.com/webapp/sitepages/
Circulation: 34,047 *Frequency:* Wed.
Fred Bright, Publisher

***Schreiber:* Terrace Bay Schreiber News**
PO Box 720, 303 Scotia St., Schreiber, ON P0T 2S0
Tel: 807-824-2021
Circulation: 481 *Frequency:* Tuesday
Linda Harbison, Publisher

Seaforth: **Seaforth Huron Expositor**
PO Box 69, 11 Main St., Seaforth, ON N0K 1W0
Tel: 519-527-0240; *Fax:* 519-527-2858
seaforth@bowesnet.com
www.seaforthhuronexpositor.com
Circulation: 2,020 *Frequency:* Wed.
Tom Williscraft, Publisher
Susan Hundertmark, Editor

Shelburne: **Shelburne Free Press & Economist**
PO Box 100, Shelburne, ON L0N 1S0
Tel: 519-925-2832; *Fax:* 519-925-5500
www.citizen.on.ca
Circulation: 2,108 *Frequency:* Thursday
Thomas Claridge, Publisher

Simcoe: **Tuesday Times-Reformer**
PO Box 370, 50 Gilbertson Dr., Simcoe, ON N3Y 4L2
Tel: 519-426-5710; *Fax:* 519-426-9255
www.simcoereformer.ca
Circulation: 19,630 *Frequency:* Tuesday
Cam McKnight, Publisher

Sioux Lookout: **Sioux Lookout Bulletin**
PO Box 1389, 40 Front St., Sioux Lookout, ON P8T 1B9
Tel: 807-737-3209; *Fax:* 807-737-3084
office@siouxbulletin.com
www.siouxbulletin.com
Circulation: 4,444 *Frequency:* Wed.
Dick MacKenzie, Publisher

Sioux Lookout: **Wawatay News**
Wawatay Native Communications Society, PO Box 1180, Sioux Lookout, ON P8T 1B7
Tel: 807-737-2951; *Fax:* 807-737-3224
bryanp@wawatay.on.ca
www.wawatay.on.ca
Circulation: 9,050 *Frequency:* Every other Thu.; English, Ojibwe & Cree
Bryan Phelan, Publisher and General Manager

Smiths Falls: **Perth Record News EMC**
PO Box 158, 65 Lorne St. South, Smiths Falls, ON K7A 4T1

Smiths Falls: **Smiths Falls Record News**
PO Box 158, 65 Lorne St., Smiths Falls, ON K7A 4T1
Tel: 613-283-3182; *Fax:* 613-283-7480
Circulation: 11,000 *Frequency:* Tuesday
Duncan Weir, Publisher

St Catharines: **Thorold News**
PO Box 86, 140 Welland Ave. North, St Catharines, ON L2R 2N6
Tel: 905-688-4332; *Fax:* 905-688-6313
stcatharinesnews@bellnet.ca
www.thorold.niagaracommunitynewspapers.com
Circulation: 6,827 *Frequency:* Wed.
Tim Dundas, Publisher

St George: **The Paris Chronicle**
PO Box 354, St George, ON N0E 1N0
Tel: 519-837-4187;
cmparafenko@hotmail.com
Circulation: 3,800 *Frequency:* Monthly, last Friday
Carol Parafenko

St Marys: **St Marys Journal-Argus**
PO Box 1030, 115 Queen St. East, St Marys, ON N4X 1B7
Tel: 519-284-2440; *Fax:* 519-284-3650
editor@stmarys.com
www.stmarys.com
Circulation: 2,621 *Frequency:* Wed.
Laura Payton, Editor

St Thomas: **Elgin County Market**
16 Hincks St., St Thomas, ON N5R 5Z2
Tel: 519-631-3782; *Fax:* 519-631-3759
www.elgincountymarket.com
Circulation: 30,600
Linda Axelson, Publisher

Stayner: **Angus-Borden Sun**
PO Box 80, 250 Main St. East, Stayner, ON L0M 1S0
Tel: 705-428-2638; *Fax:* 705-428-6909
schalsun@bmts.com
www.simcoe.com
Circulation: 5,000 *Frequency:* Wed.
Joe Anderson, Publisher
John Devine, Editor-in-chief

Stirling: **The Belleville-Quinte Community Press**
PO Box 88, 14 Demerest Rd., Stirling, ON K0K 3E0
Tel: 613-967-8467; *Fax:* 613-395-2992
general@communitypress-online.com
www.communitypress-online.com
Circulation: 38,211 *Frequency:* Fri.
Dan Kennedy, Publisher

Stirling: **The Community Press**
PO Box 88, Stirling, ON K0K 3E0
Tel: 613-395-3015; *Fax:* 613-395-2992
general@communitypress-online.com
www.communitypress-online.com
Circulation: 10,494 *Frequency:* Friday
Alan Coxwell, Publisher

Stirling: **The Community Press (East Ed.)**
PO Box 88, Stirling, ON K0K 3E0
Tel: 613-395-3015; *Fax:* 613-395-2992
general@communitypress-online.com
www.communitypress-online.com
Circulation: 10,000 *Frequency:* Fri.

Stouffville: **Stouffville Sun-Tribune**
34 Civic Ave., Stouffville, ON L4A 1H2
Tel: 905-640-2612; *Fax:* 905-640-8778
www.yorkregion.com
Circulation: 18,374 *Frequency:* Thu., Sat.
Ian Proudfoot, Publisher
Debora Kelly, Editor-in-chief

Stratford: **Inside Stratford/Perth**
PO Box 23016, #4, 285 Lorne Ave., Stratford, ON N5A 7V8
Tel: 519-272-0051; *Fax:* 519-272-0067
inside@primus.ca
www.insidestratfordperth.com
Circulation: 24,086 *Frequency:* Fri.
Nancy Johnson, Publisher
Richard Johnson, Editor

Stratford: **Marketplace**
PO Box 430, 16 Packham Rd., Stratford, ON N5A 6T6
Tel: 519-271-2220; *Fax:* 519-271-1026
Toll-Free: 800-265-8577
beaconherald@bowesnet.com
www.stratfordbeaconherald.com
Circulation: 16,000 *Frequency:* weekly
Dave Carter, Publisher

Stratford: **Stratford City Gazette**
413 Hibernia St., Stratford, ON N5A 5W2
Tel: 519-271-8002;
www.southwesternontario.ca/sw/news/stratford/
Circulation: 13,490 *Frequency:* Fri.
Kevin McCann, General Manager
Jim Hagarty, Editor

Strathroy: **Strathroy Age-Dispatch**
8 Front St. East, Strathroy, ON N7G 1Y4
Tel: 519-245-2370; *Fax:* 519-245-1647
agedispatch@strathroyonline.com
www.strathroyagedispatch.com
Circulation: 4,070 *Frequency:* Wed.
Denise Armstrong, Manager, Advertising
Steve Down, Publisher
Dave Cameron, Editor

Sturgeon Falls: **Sturgeon Falls Tribune**
206 King St., Sturgeon Falls, ON P2B 1R7
Tel: 705-753-2930; *Fax:* 705-753-5231
tribune@westnipissing.com
Circulation: 2,661 *Frequency:* Tuesday; English & French
Suzanne Gammon, Publisher

Sudbury: **Journal Le Voyageur**
525, av Notre-Dame, Sudbury, ON P3C 5L1
Tél: 705-673-3377; *Téléc:* 705-673-5854
Ligne sans frais: 866-688-7027
levoyageur@levoyageur.ca
www.levoyageur.ca
Circulation: 8 700 *Frequency:* Mercredi; français
Gouled Hassan, Administration
Réjean Grenier, Éditeur
Yves Nadeau, Directeur, Marketing
William Levasseur, Rédacteur

Sudbury: **Northern Life**
158 Elgin St., Sudbury, ON P3E 3N5
Tel: 705-673-5667; *Fax:* 705-673-4652
resource@northernlife.ca
www.northernlife.ca
Circulation: 90,727 *Frequency:* Wed., Fri.
Abbas Homayed, Publisher

Sudbury: **South Side Story**
#204, 469 Bouchard St., Sudbury, ON P3E 2K8
Tel: 705-523-2339; *Fax:* 705-523-8499
Circulation: 47,100
Colin Firth, Contact

Tavistock: **Tavistock Gazette**
PO Box 70, 119 Woodstock South, Tavistock, ON N0B 2R0
Tel: 519-655-2341; *Fax:* 519-655-3070
gazette@tavistock.on.ca
www.tavistock.on.ca
Circulation: 1,323 *Frequency:* Wed.
William Gladding, Publisher

Tecumseh: **Shoreline Week**
1614 Lesperance Rd., Tecumseh, ON N8N 1Y2
Tel: 519-735-2080; *Fax:* 519-735-2082
shoreline@windsoressexnews.com
www.windsoressexnews.com
Circulation: 15,024 *Frequency:* Wed.
Gary Baxter, Publisher

Thamesville: **Thamesville Herald**
PO Box 580, 65 London Rd., Thamesville, ON N0P 2K0
Tel: 519-692-3825; *Fax:* 519- -
Circulation: 772 *Frequency:* Wed.
Allison Humphrey, Publisher

Thessalon: **The North Shore Sentinel**
PO Box 640, 155 Main St., Thessalon, ON P0R 1L0
Tel: 705-842-2504; *Fax:* 705-842-2679
Circulation: 2,315 *Frequency:* Wed.
Randy Rankin, Publisher

Thornbury: **The Courier Herald**
PO Box 190, 51 Bruce St. S, Thornbury, ON N0H 2P0
Tel: 519-599-3760; *Fax:* 519-599-3214
www.bluemountainschamber.ca/courier
Circulation: 1,100 *Frequency:* Wed.; also Meaford Express (Wed., circ. 2,521)
Kathy Taylor, Publisher

Thorold: **Niagara This Week**
#1, 3550 Schmon Pkwy., Thorold, ON L2V 4Y6
Tel: 905-688-2444;
www.niagarathisweek.com
Circulation: 342,000 *Frequency:* Wed., Fri.
Mike Williscraft, Director of Editorial

Thunder Bay: **Thunder Bay's Source**
87 North Hill St., Thunder Bay, ON P7A 5V6
Tel: 807-346-2600; *Fax:* 807-345-9923
ldunick@dougallmedia.com
www.tbsource.com
Circulation: 48,000 *Frequency:* Fri.
Leith Dunick, Publisher

Tilbury: **Tilbury Times**
PO Box 490, Tilbury, ON N0P 2L0
Tel: 519-682-0411; *Fax:* 519-682-3633
tiltimes@ciaccess.com
www.windsoressexnews.com
Circulation: 1,962 *Frequency:* Wed.
Gary Baxter, Publisher
Bob Odette, Associate Editor

Tillsonburg: **Tillsonburg Independent**
PO Box 190, 25 Townline Rd., Tillsonburg, ON N4G 4H6
Tel: 519-688-6397; *Fax:* 519- -
www.tillsonburgnews.ca
Circulation: 10,201 *Frequency:* Wed.
Cam McKnight, Publisher

Tillsonburg: **Tillsonburg News**
PO Box 190, 25 Townline Rd., Tillsonburg, ON N4G 4H6
Tel: 519-688-4400; *Fax:* 519-842-3511
www.tillsonburgnews.ca
Circulation: 8,019 *Frequency:* Monday, Friday
Cam McKnight, Publisher

Timmins: **Les Nouvelles**
187, rue Cedar, Timmins, ON P4N 7G1
Tél: 705-268-2955; *Téléc:* 705-268-3614
lesnouv@vianet.ca
www.apf.ca/lesnouvelles
Frequency: Mercredi; français
Doris Bouchard, Editor
Bruce Cowan, Publisher

Timmins: **Timmins Times**
815 Pine St. South, Timmins, ON P4N 8S3
Tel: 705-268-6252; *Fax:* 705-268-2255
times@timminstimes.com
www.timminstimes.com

Circulation: 37,416 *Frequency:* Wed., Fri.
Heather Duhns, Managing Editor
Linda Leblanc, Publisher

***Tobermory:* The Bruce Peninsula Press**
PO Box 89, 39 Legion St., Tobermory, ON N0H 2R0
Tel: 519-596-2658; *Fax:* 519-596-8030
Toll-Free: 800-794-4480
info@tobermorypress.com
Circulation: 3,000 *Frequency:* 16 times a year
John Francis, Publisher
Holly Dunham, Editor

***Toronto:* The Annex Gleaner**
154 Harbord St., Toronto, ON M5S 1H2
Tel: 416-504-6987; *Fax:* 416-504-8792
editor@gleaner.on.ca
Circulation: 33,500 *Frequency:* also The Liberty Gleaner, Village Gleaner
Brian Burchell, Publisher
Anne Marie Brissenden, Editor-in-chief

***Toronto:* The Bay Street Times**
#514, 5334 Yonge St., Toronto, ON M2N 6V1
Tel: 416-949-6332; *Fax:* 416-997-6697
editor@baystreetimes.com
www.baystreettimes.com
Frequency: Monthly

***Toronto:* Bayview Post**
30 Lesmill Rd., Toronto, ON M3B 2T6
Tel: 416-250-7979; *Fax:* 416-250-1737
info@postcitymagazines.com
www.postcitymagazines.com
Circulation: 30,000 *Frequency:* also North Toronto Post, North York Post, Richmond Hill Post
Lorne London, Publisher

***Toronto:* Beach Metro Community News**
2196 Gerrard St. East, Toronto, ON M4E 2C7
Tel: 416-698-1164; *Fax:* 416-698-1253
admin@beachmetro.com
www.beachmetro.com
Circulation: 30,000 *Frequency:* Tuesday
Sheila Blinoff, General Manager
Carole Stimmell, Editor

***Toronto:* Beach Riverdale Mirror**
100 Tempo Ave., Toronto, ON M2H 2N8
Tel: 416-493-4400; *Fax:* 416-493-6190
www.insidetoronto.ca
Circulation: 21,228 *Frequency:* Fri.
Betty Carr, Publisher

***Toronto:* Downtown Bulletin**
#121, 260 Adelaide St. East, Toronto, ON M5A 1N1
Tel: 416-929-0011;
info@communitybulletin.ca
www.thebulletin.ca
Circulation: 60,000 *Frequency:* Monday, Monthly
Frank Touby, Editor
Paulette Touby, Publisher

***Toronto:* East York Mirror**
100 Tempo Ave., Toronto, ON M2H 3S5
Tel: 416-493-4400; *Fax:* 416-493-6190
www.insidetoronto.ca/to/eastyork/
Circulation: 35,302 *Frequency:* Fri.
Betty Carr, Publisher
Deborah Bodine, Editor-in-chief

***Toronto:* Etc...News**
201 Leslie St., Toronto, ON M4M 3C6
Tel: 416-465-7554; *Fax:* 416-778-7540
etcnews@sympatico.ca
www.etcnews.ca
Circulation: 25,000 *Frequency:* 16 times a year; every 3rd Thurs.
Bruce Brackett, Publisher
; brackett@sympatico.ca
Terry Brackett, Editor

***Toronto:* Etobicoke Guardian**
307 Humberline Dr., Toronto, ON M9W 5V1
Tel: 416-675-4390; *Fax:* 416-675-9296
etg@mirror-guardian.com
www.insidetoronto.ca
Circulation: 138,838 *Frequency:* Wed., Fri.
Tony Poland, Editor-in-chief
Betty Carr, Publisher

***Toronto:* European Reporter**
PO Box 6039, Toronto, ON L5P 1B2
Tel: 647-274-8689; *Fax:* 905-281-9436
mail@europeanreporter.com
www.europeanreporter.com
Frequency: Bi-weekly

***Toronto:* L'Express**
17 Carlaw Ave., Toronto, ON M4M 2R6
Tel: 416-465-2107; *Fax:* 416-465-3778
express@lexpress.to
www.lexpress.to
Circulation: 20,000 *Frequency:* Mardi; français; et: L'Observateur, London; L'Information, Hamilton/Burlington & Le Courrier d'Oshawa, Métro Courrier
D.P. Mazare

***Toronto:* Hi-Rise**
#121, 95 Leeward Glenway, Toronto, ON M3C 2Z6
Tel: 416-424-1393; *Fax:* 416-467-8262
sec.valdunn@vif.com
www.hi-risenews.com
Circulation: 60,000 *Frequency:* Monthly
Valerie Dunn

***Toronto:* New Canada**
#500, 120 Eglinton Ave. East, Toronto, ON M4P 1E2
Tel: 416-481-7793; *Fax:* 416- -
Toll-Free: 888-667-5877
humanrights@sympatico.ca
www.hrrrc.ca
Circulation: 10,000 *Frequency:* Fri.; English, Urdu & Panjabi
Hasanat Ahmad Syed, Editor-in-chief

***Toronto:* The New Canadian**
524 Front St. West, Toronto, ON M5V 1B8
Tel: 416-593-1583; *Fax:* 416-593-1871
newcdn@japancominc.com
Circulation: 10,000 *Frequency:* Thu.; English & Japanese
Shin Kawai, Publisher

***Toronto:* North York Mirror**
100 Tempo Ave., Toronto, ON M2H 3S5
Tel: 416-493-4400; *Fax:* 416-493-6190
www.insidetoronto.ca/to/northyork/
Circulation: 193,559 *Frequency:* Wed., Fri.
Betty Carr, Publisher
David Harvey, Editor-in-chief

***Toronto:* Our Toronto Free Press**
#200, 49 Elm St., Toronto, ON M5G 1H1
Tel: 416-977-0183; *Fax:* 416-977-1322
www.canadafreepress.com
Frequency: Tuesday
Judi McLeod, Editor & Owner

***Toronto:* Scarborough Mirror**
100 Tempo Ave., Toronto, ON M2H 3S5
Tel: 416-493-4400; *Fax:* 416-493-6190
scm@torontocommunitynews.com
www.insidetoronto.ca/to/scarborough/
Circulation: 227,965 *Frequency:* Wed., Fri.
Betty Carr, Publisher
Alan Shackleton, Editor-in-chief

***Toronto:* Share**
658 Vaughan Rd., Toronto, ON M6E 2Y5
Tel: 416-656-3400; *Fax:* 416-656-0691
share@interlog.com
www.sharenews.com
Circulation: 50,000
Arnold A. Auguste, Publisher

***Toronto:* Thornhill Post**
30 Lesmill Rd., Toronto, ON M2N 3B4
Tel: 416-250-7979; *Fax:* 416-250-1737
admin@postcitymagazines.com
www.postcitymagazines.com
Circulation: 30,000 *Frequency:* Fri.
Lorne London, Publisher

***Toronto:* Toronto Street News**
c/0 LoveCry, 1024 Queen St. East, Toronto, ON M4M 1K4
Tel: 416-406-0099;
debramoon-ivil.tripod.com/thetorontostreetnews/id1.html
Circulation: 3,000 *Frequency:* Weekly
Victor Fletcher, Publisher

***Toronto:* Town Crier**
101 Wingold Ave., Toronto, ON M6B 1P8
Tel: 416-785-4300; *Fax:* 416-488-4918
info@towncrieronline.ca
www.towncrieronline.ca

Frequency: Monthly; nine separate newspapers: Bayview Mills TC, Bloor-Annex TC (circ. 30,000); Beach Riverdale TC (circ. 30,000); Leaside-Rosedale TC (circ. 25,000); North Toronto TC (circ. 30,000) Forest Hill T
Eric McMillan, Managing Editor
Lori Abittan, President & Publisher

***Toronto:* The Village Post**
30 Lesmill Rd., Toronto, ON M3B 2T6
Tel: 416-250-7979; *Fax:* 416-250-1737
postnews@idirect.com
Circulation: 27,000
Lorne London, Publisher

***Toronto:* The Villager**
#206, 2323 Bloor St. West, Toronto, ON M8X 1B6
Tel: 416-239-3029; *Fax:* 416-767-4880
www.thevillager.ca
Circulation: 42,351 *Frequency:* Fri.
Dave Harvey, Contact

***Toronto:* The Women's Post**
#804, 2 Carlton St., Toronto, ON M5B 1J3
Tel: 416-964-5850; *Fax:* 416-964-6142
www.womenspost.ca
Circulation: 71,818 *Frequency:* Bi-monthly
Sarah Whatmough-Thomson, Editor

***Toronto:* York Guardian**
100 Tempo Ave., Toronto, ON M2H 3S5
Tel: 416-493-4400; *Fax:* 416-493-6190
www.insidetoronto.com/news/york?thePub=york
Circulation: 30,000 *Frequency:* Fri.
Betty Carr, Publisher
Deborah Bodine, Editor-in-chief

***Trenton:* Trentonian**
41 Quinte St., Trenton, ON K8V 5R3
Tel: 613-392-6501; *Fax:* 613-392-0505
newsroom@trentonian.ca
www.trentonian.ca
Circulation: 6,642 *Frequency:* Monday, Wednesday, Friday

***Tweed:* Tweed News**
PO Box 550, Tweed, ON K0K 3J0
Tel: 613-478-2017; *Fax:* 613-478-2749
thenews@magma.ca
Circulation: 1,111 *Frequency:* Wed.
Rodger Hanna, Publisher & Editor
Roseann Trudeau, Circulation Manager

***Uxbridge:* Times-Journal**
PO Box 459, 16 Bascom St., Uxbridge, ON L9P 1M9
Tel: 905-852-9141; *Fax:* 905-852-9341
jpirone@durhamregion.com
www.durhamregion.com
Circulation: 16,941 *Frequency:* Wed, Fri.
Tim Whittaker, Publisher
; jpirone@durhamregion.com

***Vankleek Hill:* Vankleek Hill Review**
PO Box 160, 76 Main St. East, Vankleek Hill, ON K0B 1R0
Tel: 613-678-3327; *Fax:* 613-678-2700
Toll-Free: 877-678-3327
review@thereview.on.ca
www.thereview.on.ca
Circulation: 3,662 *Frequency:* Wed.; English & French
Louise Sproule, Publisher
Richard Mahoney, Editor

***Virgil:* Niagara Advance**
PO Box 430, Virgil, ON L0S 1T0
Tel: 905-468-3283; *Fax:* 905-468-3137
notleditorial@cogeco.net
Circulation: 7,331 *Frequency:* Saturday
Tim Dundas, Publisher
Penny Coles, Editor

***Walkerton:* Walkerton Herald-Times**
PO Box 190, 10 Victoria St., Walkerton, ON N0G 2V0
Tel: 519-881-1600; *Fax:* 519-881-0276
www.walkerton.com
Circulation: 2,200 *Frequency:* Wed.
John McPhee, General Manager

***Wallaceburg:* Wallaceburg Courier Press**
1542 Dufferin Ave., Wallaceburg, ON N8A 2W9
Tel: 519-627-1488; *Fax:* 519-627-0640
couriernews@kent.net
www.wallaceburgcourierpress.com
Circulation: 11,168 *Frequency:* Wed.
Dean Muharrem, Publisher

Wallaceburg: **Wallaceburg News**
538 James St., Wallaceburg, ON N8A 2N9
Tel: 519-627-2557; *Fax:* 519-627-1261
www.thewallaceburgnews.ca
Frequency: Wed.
Wayne Snider, Managing Editor
Daryl Smith, Publisher

Wasaga Beach: **Stayner Sun**
1456B Mosley St., Wasaga Beach, ON L9Z 2B9
Tel: 705-428-2638; *Fax:* 705-422-2446
www.staynersun.ca
Circulation: 1,128 *Frequency:* Wed.
Joe Anderson, Publisher

Wasaga Beach: **The Wasaga Sun**
1456B Mosley St., Wasaga Beach, ON L9Z 2B9
Tel: 705-428-2638; *Fax:* 705-422-2446
www.wasagasun.ca
Circulation: 7,457 *Frequency:* Wed.
Joe Anderson, Publisher

Waterdown: **Flamborough Review**
PO Box 20, 30 Main St. North, Waterdown, ON L0R 2H0
Tel: 905-689-4841; *Fax:* 905-689-3110
www.haltonsearch.com
Circulation: 13,662 *Frequency:* Fri.

Waterloo: **Waterloo Chronicle**
#20, 279 Weber St. North, Waterloo, ON N2J 3H8
Tel: 519-886-2830; *Fax:* 519-886-9383
www.waterloochronicle.ca
Circulation: 31,564 *Frequency:* Wednesday (weekly)
Neil Oliver, Publisher

Watford: **Watford Guide-Advocate**
PO Box 99, 5292 Nauvoo Rd., Watford, ON N0M 2S0
Tel: 519-876-2809; *Fax:* 519-876-2322
guideadvocate@execulink.com
Circulation: 1,160 *Frequency:* Thursday (weekly).
Dale Hayter, Publisher

Wawa: **Wawa/Algoma News Review**
PO Box 528, 37 Ste-Marie St., Wawa, ON P0S 1K0
Tel: 705-856-2267; *Fax:* 705-856-4952
Toll-Free: 800-461-9209
waprint2@ontera.net
Circulation: 1,060 *Frequency:* Wed.
W. Robert Avis, Publisher & Editor
Krystal Gignac, Advertising Manager

West Lorne: **The Chronicle**
PO Box 100, 167 Main St., West Lorne, ON N0L 2P0
Tel: 519-768-2220; *Fax:* 519-768-2221
chronicle@bowesnet.com
www.thechronicle-online.com
Frequency: Thu.

Westport: **The Review-Mirror**
PO Box 130, 15 Church St., Westport, ON K0G 1X0
Tel: 613-273-8000; *Fax:* 613-273-8001
revmir@rideau.net
www.review-mirror.com
Circulation: 1,929 *Frequency:* Thur.
Howard Crichton, Publisher

Wheatley: **Wheatley Journal**
PO Box 10, 14 Talbot West, Wheatley, ON N0P 2P0
Tel: 519-825-4541; *Fax:* 519-825-4546
Circulation: 946 *Frequency:* Wed.
Rick Epplett, Publisher

Wiarton: **Wiarton Echo**
PO Box 220, 573 Berford St., Wiarton, ON N0H 2T0
Tel: 519-534-1560; *Fax:* 519-534-4616
wiartonecho@bmts.com
www.wiartonecho.com
Circulation: 2,593 *Frequency:* Wed.
Keith Gilbert, Publisher

Winchester: **Winchester Press**
c/o 2woMor Publications Inc., PO Box 399, Winchester, ON K0C 2K0
Tel: 613-774-2524; *Fax:* 613-774-3967
news@winchesterpress.on.ca
www.winchesterpress.on.ca
Circulation: 9,964 *Frequency:* Wed.
Donna Rushford, Publisher/Advertising Manager
Allen VanBridger, Co-Publisher/Managing Editor

Windsor: **Journal Le Rempart**
7515, chemin Forest Glade, Windsor, ON N8T 3P5
Tel: 519-948-4139; *Fax:* 519-948-0628
info@lerempart.ca
www.lerempart.ca
Circulation: 1 000 *Frequency:* Mercredi; français
Denis Poirier, Publisher

Windsor: **Windsor Pennysaver**
#400, 4525 Rhodes Dr., Windsor, ON N8W 5R8
Tel: 519-966-4500; *Fax:* 519-966-3660
classified@windsorpennysaver.com
www.windsorpennysaver.com
Circulation: 119,000 *Frequency:* Fri.

Wingham: **Wingham Advance-Times**
PO Box 390, 5 Diagonal Rd., Wingham, ON N0G 2W0
Tel: 519-357-2320; *Fax:* 519-357-2900
editor@wingham.com
www.wingham.com
Circulation: 1,988 *Frequency:* Wed.
Kathy Steele, Publisher and General Manager

Woodstock: **Oxford Shopping News**
16 Brock St., Woodstock, ON N4S 3B4
Tel: 519-537-6657; *Fax:* 519-537-8542
www.oxfordshoppingnews.com
Circulation: 28,284 *Frequency:* Tuesday
Pat Logan, Publisher

Prince Edward Island

Daily Newspapers in Prince Edward Island

Charlottetown: **The Guardian**
PO Box 760, 165 Prince St., Charlottetown, PE C1A 7L8
Tel: 902-629-6000; *Toll-Free:* 800-267-6397
comments@theguardian.pe.ca
www.theguardian.pe.ca
Circulation: 21,023 *Frequency:* Morning
Don Brander, Publisher
Gary MacDougall, Managing Editor

Summerside: **Journal Pioneer**
PO Box 2480, 4 Queen St., Summerside, PE C1N 4K5
Tel: 902-436-2125; *Fax:* 902-436-3027
info@journalpioneer.com
www.journalpioneer.com
Circulation: 10,257 *Frequency:* Evening
Darlene Shea, Managing Editor
Sandy Rundle, Publisher

Other Newspapers in Prince Edward Island

Alberton: **West Prince Graphic**
PO Box 339, 4 Railway St., Alberton, PE C0B 1B0
Tel: 902-853-3320; *Fax:* 902-853-3071
jean.kenny@westprince.com
www.peicanada.com
Circulation: 6,016 *Frequency:* Wed.
Paul MacNeill, Publisher and General Manager

Montague: **The Eastern Graphic**
PO Box 790, 567 Main St. South, Montague, PE C0A 1R0
Tel: 902-838-2515; *Fax:* 902-838-4392
Toll-Free: 800-806-5443
www.peicanada.com
Circulation: 5,396 *Frequency:* Wed.
Paul MacNeill, Publisher

Summerside: **La Voix Acadienne**
5, av Maris Stella, Summerside, PE C1N 6M9
Tél: 902-436-6005; *Téléc:* 902-888-3976
pub@lavoixacadienne.com
www.lavoixacadienne.com
Circulation: 1 100 *Frequency:* Mercredi; français
Marcia Enman, Directrice général

Québec

Daily Newspapers in Québec

Chicoutimi: **Le Quotidien du Saguenay-Lac-St-Jean**
1051, boul Talbot, Chicoutimi, QC G7H 5C1
Tél: 418-545-4474; *Téléc:* 418-690-8824
www.cyberpresse.ca/quotidien
Circulation: 29 131 *Frequency:* Matin; français
Guy Granger, Président & Éditeur
Michel Simard, Rédacteur-en-chef

Granby: **La Voix de L'Est**
76, rue Dufferin, Granby, QC J2G 9L4
Tél: 450-375-4555; *Téléc:* 450-777-7221
www.cyberpresse.ca/vde/
Circulation: 14 955 lun.-ven., 18,563 sam. *Frequency:* Matin; français
Jacques Pronovost, Président & Éditeur

Montréal: **Le Devoir**
2050, rue de Bleury, 9e étage, Montréal, QC H3A 3M9
Tél: 514-985-3333; *Téléc:* 514-985-3390
redaction@ledevoir.com
www.ledevoir.com
Circulation: 24 582 lun.-ven., 39 084 sam. *Frequency:* Matin; français
Josée Boileau, Rédactrice-en-chef

Montréal: **Le Journal de Montréal**
4545, rue Frontenac, Montréal, QC H2H 2R7
Tél: 514-521-4545; *Téléc:* 514-525-5442
http://lejournaldemontreal.canoe.ca
Circulation: 265 573 lun.-ven., 316 457 sam., 265 610 dim.
Frequency: Matin; français
Lyne Robitaille, Présidente et Éditrice

Montréal: **Metro**
#700, 625, av du President Kennedy, Montréal, QC H3A 1K2
Tel: 514-286-1066; *Fax:* 514-286-9310

Montréal: **The Montréal Gazette**
#200, 1010 St. Catherine St. West, Montréal, QC H3B 5L1
Tel: 514-987-2222; *Fax:* 514-987-2399
www.montrealgazette.com
Circulation: 148,000 Mon.-Fri.; 217,000 Sat.; 138,000 Sun.
Raymond Brassard, Managing Editor
514-987-2508

Montréal: **La Presse**
7, rue St-Jacques, Montréal, QC H2Y 1K9
Tél: 514-285-7000; *Téléc:* 514-285-6808
www.cyberpresse.ca
Circulation: 185 609 lun.-ven., 268 236 sam., 194 012 dim.
Frequency: Matin; français
Guy Crevier, Président et éditeur
Éric Trottier, Vice-président et éditeur adjoint

Montréal: **Quotidien 24 heures Montréal**
465 McGill St., 3rd Fl., Montréal, QC H2Y 4B4
Tel: 514-373-2424; *Fax:* 514-373-2400
information@24-heures.ca
toronto.24hrs.ca
Circulation: 134,691
Serge Gosselin, Editor

Québec: **Le Soleil**
CP 1547 Terminus, 410, boul Charest est, Québec, QC G1K 7J6
Tél: 418-686-3394; *Téléc:* 418-686-3374
redaction@lesoleil.com
www.cyberpresse.ca/le-soleil
Circulation: 181 380 *Frequency:* Matin; français
Claude Gagnon, Président & éditeur
Raymond Tardif, Éditeur adjoint

Sherbrooke: **The Record**
PO Box 1200, 1195 Galt East, Sherbrooke, QC J1K 1A1
Tel: 819-569-9525; *Fax:* 819-569-3945
Toll-Free: 800-463-9525
www.sherbrookerecord.com
Circulation: 25,135 *Frequency:* Monday-Friday
Randy Kinnear, Publisher
Sharon McCully, Editor-in-chief

Sherbrooke: **La Tribune**
1950, rue Roy, Sherbrooke, QC J1K 2X8
Tél: 819-564-5450; *Téléc:* 819-564-8098
Ligne sans frais: 800-567-6955
redaction@latribune.qc.ca
www.cyberpresse.ca
Circulation: 32 000 lun.-ven., 42 000 sam. *Frequency:* Matin; français
Louise Boisvert, President and editor
Louise Boisvert, Présidente et éditrice

Trois-Rivières: **Le Nouvelliste**
CP 668, 1920, rue Bellefeuille, Trois-Rivières, QC G9A 3Y2
Tél: 819-376-2501; *Téléc:* 819-691-4356
noured@lenouvelliste.qc.ca
www.cyberpresse.ca/nouvelliste
Circulation: 45 000 lun.-ven., 48 000 sam. *Frequency:* Matin; français
Alain Turcotte, Rédactrice-en-chef
Raymond Tardif, Éditeur

Vanier: **Le Journal de Québec**
450, rue Bechard, Vanier, QC G1M 2E9
Tél: 418-683-1573; *Téléc:* 418-683-8886
commentaires@journaldequebec.com
www.journaldequebec.com
Circulation: 98 490 lun.-ven., 121 943 sam., 100 575304 dim.
Frequency: Matin; français
Jean-Claude L'Abbée, Éditeur et Chef de la direction
Serge Côté, Rédacteur en chef

Other Newspapers in Québec

Acton Vale: **La Pensée de Bagot**
962, rue St-André, Acton Vale, QC J0H 1A0
Tél: 450-546-3271; *Téléc:* 450-546-3491
publicite@lapensee.qc.ca
www.lapensee.qc.ca
Circulation: 13 660 *Frequency:* Dimanche
Michel Dorais, Directeur

Alma: **Le Lac Saint-Jean**
100 rue St-Joseph sud local #01, Alma, QC G8B 7A4
Tél: 418-668-4545; *Téléc:* 418-668-8522
redaction_alma@transcontinental.ca
www.lelacstjean.com
Circulation: 19 716 *Frequency:* Samedi
Gaston Martin

Amqui: **L'Avant-poste**
59, St-Benoît ouest, Amqui, QC G5J 2E4
Tél: 418-629-3443; *Téléc:* 418-629-2919
avantposte@globetrotter.net
www.hebdosquebecor.com/avp/index_avp.asp
Circulation: 8 815 *Frequency:* Saturday
Michèle Bérubé, Rédactrice-en-chef

Asbestos: **Les Actualités**
78, rue St-Jean, Asbestos, QC J1T 3R3
Tél: 819-879-6681; *Téléc:* 819-879-2355
fernand.lallier@hebdesquebecor.com
www.hebdosquebecor.com/aca/index_aca. asp
Circulation: 14 800 *Frequency:* Samedi
Fernand Lallier, Éditeur
Louise Jutras, Rédactrice-en-chef

Baie-Comeau: **Baie-Comeau-Objectif Plein Jour**
#309, 625, boul Laflèche, Baie-Comeau, QC G5C 1C5
Tél: 418-589-5900; *Téléc:* 418-589-5263
Circulation: 16 366 *Frequency:* Vendredi; aussi Plein jour sur la Manicouagan (mercredi, tirage 15 866)

Baie-Comeau: **Journal Haute Côte Nord Est**
965, Parfondeval, Baie-Comeau, QC G5C 2W8
Tel: 418-589-2090; *Fax:* 418-589-9989
journalhcn.baiecomeau@globetrotter.net
Circulation: 15 378

Baie-Comeau: **Le Plein-Jour en Haute Côte-Nord**
#309, 625, boul Laflèche, Baie-Comeau, QC G5C 1C5
Tél: 418-589-5900; *Téléc:* 418-589-5263
objectif@globetrotter.net
www.hebdosquebecor.com/pjh/index_pjh.asp
Circulation: 6 468 *Frequency:* Vendredi
Claude Mercier, Directeur général

Baie-Saint-Paul: **L'Hebdo Charlevoisien**
45, Raymond Mailloux, Baie-Saint-Paul, QC G3Z 1W2
Tél: 418-665-1299; *Téléc:* 418-665-2051
lhebdo.charlevoisien@sympatico.ca
www.journalhebdocharlevoisien.com
Circulation: 13 033 *Frequency:* Saturday
Guy Charlebois, Directeur de production
Charles Warren, Directeur

Beaulac-Garthby: **Le Contact de Beaulac-Garthby**
CP 58, 9, rue de la Chapelle, Beaulac-Garthby, QC G0Y 1BO
Tél: 418-458-2737; *Téléc:* 418-458-2737
contactbg2002@yahoo.ca
Circulation: 355
Andree Sautier, Redactrice-en-chef
Serge Frederick, President

Beloeil: **L'Oeil Régional**
393, boul Laurier, Beloeil, QC J3G 4H6
Tél: 450-467-1821; *Téléc:* 450-467-3087
journal@oeilregional.com
www.oeilregional.com
Circulation: 30 000 *Frequency:* Samedi
Guy Gilbert, Éditeur
Bernard Blanchard, Rédacteur-en-chef

Boucherville: **Journal La Relève Inc.**
528, rue St-Charles, Boucherville, QC J4B 3M5
Tél: 450-641-4844; *Téléc:* 450-641-4849
lareleve@lareleve.qc.ca
www.lareleve.qc.ca
Circulation: 54 650 *Frequency:* Jeudi et Vendredi
Charles Desmarteau, Directeur général

Boucherville: **La Seigneurie**
391, boul de Montagne, Boucherville, QC J4B 1B7
Tél: 450-641-3360; *Téléc:* 450-655-9752
info@la-seigneurie.qc.ca
www.hebdos.net/lsb
Circulation: 29 421 *Frequency:* Samedi
Serge Landry, Éditeur

Brossard: **Brossard-Eclair**
#A105, 7900, boul Taschereau, Brossard, QC J4X 1C2
Tel: 450-466-3344; *Fax:* 450-466-9019
infos@brossardeclair.qc.ca
www.hebdosquebecor.com/bre/index_bre.asp
Circulation: 23 880 *Frequency:* Mardi; French & English
Léo Gagnon, Rédacteur-en-chef

Brossard: **Le Journal de St-Hubert**
#A105, 7900, boul Taschereau, Brossard, QC J4X 1C2
Tél: 450-466-0036; *Téléc:* 450-466-9019
info@journaldesainthubert.qc.ca
www.journaldesainthubert.qc.ca
Circulation: 28 000 *Frequency:* Mercredi
Léo Gagnon, Rédacteur

Buckingham: **Le Bulleín de la Lièvre**
435, rue Principale, Buckingham, QC J8L 2G8
Tél: 819-986-5089; *Téléc:* 819-986-2073
Circulation: 11 351 *Frequency:* Dimanche
Michel Blais, Éditeur

Cantley: **L'Écho de Cantley**
188, montée de la Source, Boite 1, Comp. 9, Cantley, QC J8V 3J2
Tél: 819-827-3496; *Téléc:* 819- -
echo.cantley@sympatico.ca
Circulation: 2 400
Steve Harris

Cap-aux-Meules: **Le Radar**
CP 8183, Cap-aux-Meules, QC G4T 1R3
Tél: 418-986-2345; *Téléc:* 418-986-6358
Ligne sans frais: 866-986-2345
leradar@lino.com
www.leradar.qc.ca
Circulation: 3 000 *Frequency:* Vendredi; français
Achille Hubert, Éditeur
Marielle Ouellet, Rédactrice-en-chef

Chambly: **Le Journal de Chambly**
CP 175, 1685, rue Bourgogne, Chambly, QC J3L 4B3
Tél: 450-658-6516; *Téléc:* 450-658-3785
info@journaldechambly.com
www.hebdos.net/jdc/
Circulation: 21 237 *Frequency:* Mardi
Carole Pronovost, Rédactrice-en-chef

Châteauguay: **Le Soleil du Samedi**
82, rue Salaberry sud, Châteauguay, QC J6J 4J6
Tél: 450-692-8552; *Téléc:* 450-692-3460
info@ cybersoleil.com
www.cybersoleil.com
Circulation: 28 197 *Frequency:* Samedi

Chibougamau: **Le Jamesien**
CP 250, 317, 3e rue, Chibougamau, QC G8P 2K7
Tél: 418-748-6406; *Téléc:* 418-748-2421
www.hebdosquebecor.com
Circulation: 10,000 *Frequency:* Samedi

Chicoutimi: **Le Progrès Dimanche**
1051, boul Talbot, Chicoutimi, QC G7H 5C1
Tél: 418-690-8800; *Téléc:* 418-690-8805
Circulation: 44 500 *Frequency:* Dimanche
Claude Gagnon, Éditeur

Coaticook: **Le Progrès de Coaticook**
72, rue Child, Coaticook, QC J1A 2B1
Tél: 819-849-9846; *Téléc:* 819-849-1041
progres@leprogres.net
www.leprogres.net
Circulation: 8 600 *Frequency:* Samedi
Henri Gérin, Éditrice

Cookshire: **Le Haut Saint-François**
CP 976, 212, rue Principale est, Cookshire, QC J0B 1M0
Tél: 819-875-5501; *Téléc:* 819-875-5327
jourhsf@globetrotter.net
www.microtec.net/~jourhsf
Circulation: 17 500 *Frequency:* 20 fois par an
Maxime Doyon, Président

Courcelette: **Journal Adsum**
CP 1000 Forces, Garnison Valcartier, bâtisse 200, local 102, Courcelette, QC G0A 4Z0
Tél: 418-844-5000; *Téléc:* 418-844-6934
tadsum@forces.gc.ca
Circulation: 5 500
Col. erry Champagne, Éditeur

Cowansville: **Le Guide/The Guide**
121, rue Principale, Cowansville, QC J2K 1J3
Tél: 450-263-5288; *Téléc:* 450-263-9435
leguide@canadafrancais.com
www.journal-leguide.com
Circulation: 17 884 *Frequency:* Samedi
Martine Chagnon, Directrice general

Daveluyville: **Le Causeur**
539, rte Principale, Daveluyville, QC G0Z 1C0
Tél: 819-367-2210; *Téléc:* 819-367-4011
lecauseur@yahoo.ca
Circulation: 1 100
Lucie Boulanger, Coordonnatrice

Delson: **Le Reflet**
11, rte 132, Delson, QC J0L 1G0
Tél: 450-635-9146; *Téléc:* 450-635-4619
info@lereflet.qc.ca
www.lereflet.qc.ca
Circulation: 31 700 *Frequency:* Samedi
Robert Fichaud, Éditeur
Hélène Gingras, Rédactrice-en-chef

Disraéli: **Le Cantonnier**
888, St-Antoine, Disraéli, QC G0N 1E0
Tél: 418-449-1888; *Téléc:* 418-449-1889
lecantonnier@lino.com
www.lecantonnier.com
Jean-Denis Grimard, Rédacteur en chef

Dolbeau-Mistassini: **Nouvelles Hebdo**
1741, des Pins, Dolbeau-Mistassini, QC G8L 1M9
Tél: 418-276-6211; *Téléc:* 418-276-6166
nh@destination.ca
www.nouvelles-hebdo.qc.ca
Circulation: 13 369
Michel Aubé, Éditeur

Dolbeau-Mistassini: **Le Point**
1570, boul Wallberg, Dolbeau-Mistassini, QC G8L 1H4
Tél: 418-276-5110; *Téléc:* 418-276-5354
atelierlepoint@qc.aira.com
www.lepoint.ca
Circulation: 12 375 *Frequency:* Dimanche
Diane Audet, Directrice générale

Dollard-Des Ormeaux: **Le Messager Lachine Dorval**
3677, boul. des Sources, Dollard-Des Ormeaux, QC H9B 2K4
Tél: 514-685-4690; *Téléc:* 514-685-3923
www.messagerlachine.com
Circulation: 23 100 *Frequency:* Sunday; English & French
Michel Bessette, Éditeur

Dollard-des-Ormeaux: **The Chronicle**
3677, boul des Sources, Dollard-des-Ormeaux, QC H9B 2T6
Tél: 514-685-4690; *Téléc:* 514-685-3452
www.westislandchronicle.com
Circulation: 14 800 *Frequency:* Wed.
Albert Kramberger, Éditeur

Dollard-des-Ormeaux: **Cités Nouvelles / City News**
3677, boul des Sources, Dollard-des-Ormeaux, QC H9B 2T6
Tel: 514-685-4690; *Fax:* 514-685-3923
www.citesnouvelles.com
Circulation: 55 000 *Frequency:* Sunday; English & French

Donnacona: **Le Courrier de Portneuf**
CP 1030, 276, rue Notre-Dame, Donnacona, QC G3M 1G7
Tél: 418-285-0211; *Téléc:* 418-285-2441
www.courrierdeportneuf.com
Circulation: 31 953 *Frequency:* Samedi
Josee-Anne Fiset, Directrice general

***Drummondville:* L'Express**
1050, rue Cormier, Drummondville, QC J2C 2N6
Tél: 819-478-8171; *Téléc:* 819-478-4306
lorraine.paquet@transcontinental.ca
www.expressparole.com
Circulation: 46 089 *Frequency:* Dimanche
Jean-Claude Bonneau, Rédacteur-en-chef
Johanne Marceau, Éditeur

***Drummondville:* La Parole**
1050, rue Cormier, Drummondville, QC J2C 2N6
Tél: 819-478-8171; *Téléc:* 819-478-4306
lorraine.paquet@transcontinental.ca
www.expressparole.com
Circulation: 43 070 *Frequency:* Mercredi
Jean-Claude Bonneau, Rédacteur-en-chef
Johanne Marceau, Éditeur

***Farnham:* L'Avenir & des Rivières**
322A, rue Principale est, Farnham, QC J2N 1L7
Tél: 450-293-3138; *Téléc:* 450-293-2093
lavence@canadafrancais.com
avenir-rivieres.com
Circulation: 14 390 *Frequency:* Samedi

***Fermont:* Le Trait d'Union du Nord**
1 Centre L.J. Patterson, CP 561, Fermont, QC G0G 1J0
Tél: 418-287-3655; *Téléc:* 418-287-3874
journalisteTDN@.diffusionfermont.ca
Circulation: 1 700
Eric Cyr, Rédacteur-en-chef

***Forestville:* Journal Haute Côte-Nord Ouest**
#100, 31 rte 138 ouest, Forestville, QC G0T 1E0
Tél: 418-587-2090; *Téléc:* 418-587-6407
journhcn@globetrotter.net
www.journalhautecotenord.com
Circulation: 6 285 *Frequency:* Vendredi
Luc Brisson

***Fort-Coulonge:* Fort Coulonge/Pontiac Journal / Le Journal de Pontiac**
PO Box 279, 289, Hwy. 148, Fort-Coulonge, QC J0X 1V0
Tel: 819-683-3583; *Fax:* 819-683-2977
journalpontiac@bellnet.ca
Circulation: 9,855 *Frequency:* Every other Wed.; English & French
Dana Bertrand, Circulation Manager
Fred Ryan, Publisher & Editor

***Gatineau:* Aylmer Bulletin**
#C-10, 181, rue Principale, Gatineau, QC J9H 6A6
Tel: 819-684-4755; *Fax:* 819-684-6428
Toll-Free: 800-486-7678
abawqp@videotron.ca
www.bulletinaylmer.com
Circulation: 17,645 *Frequency:* Wed.
Lynne Lavery, General Manager
Fred Ryan, Publisher

***Gatineau:* Le Régional Aylmer/Hull**
#30, 160, boul de l'Hopital, Gatineau, QC J8T 8J1
Tél: 819-568-7736; *Téléc:* 819-568-8728
www.info07.com/
Circulation: 10 650 *Frequency:* Mercredi

***Gatineau:* Le Régional d'Aylmer**
#30, boul de l'Hopital, Gatineau, QC J8T 8J1
Tél: 819-684-0097; *Téléc:* 819-776-1668
regional@magma.ca
Circulation: 11,905
Jacques Blais, Éditeur
Bryan Kirk, Rédacteur-en-chef

***Gatineau:* La Revue de Gatineau**
#106, 430, boul de l'Hôpital, Gatineau, QC J8V 1T7
Tél: 819-568-7736; *Téléc:* 819-568-7038
www.info07.com
Circulation: 41 174 *Frequency:* Mercredi
Yves Blondin, Éditeur

***Gatineau:* Week-end Outaouais**
#106, 430, boul de L'Hôpital, Gatineau, QC J8V 1T7
Tel: 819-568-7736; *Fax:* 819-568-7038
Circulation: 50 903 *Frequency:* Samedi
Sylvain Dupras, Editeur-en-chef

***Gatineau:* West Québec Post**
#C-10, 181, rue Principale, Gatineau, QC J9H 6A6
Tel: 819-684-4755; *Fax:* 819-684-6428
Toll-Free: 800-486-7678
abawqp@videotron.ca
Circulation: 5,238 *Frequency:* Fri.
Lynne Lavery, General Manager
Fred Ryan, Publisher

***Granby:* Le Citoyen**
#2, 189, rue Dufferin, Granby, QC J2G 4X2
Tél: 450-777-1636; *Téléc:* 450-378-4980
Circulation: 17 500 *Frequency:* Samedi
Charles Gagnon, Éditeur

***Granby:* Journal l'Express**
#5, 398, rue Principale, Granby, QC J2G 2W6
Tél: 450-777-4515; *Téléc:* 450-777-4516
monjournalexpress.com
Circulation: 39 500 *Frequency:* Hebdomadaire
Claude Hébert, Redactrice-en-chef

***Granby:* La voix de l'est plus**
76, rue Dufferin, Granby, QC J2G 9L4
Tél: 450-375-6850; *Téléc:* 450-777-4865
Circulation: 47 222 *Frequency:* Saturday
Pierre Gobeil, Éditeur

***Grande-Vallée:* Le Phare, l'autre vision**
3, Saint-François-Xavier est, Grande-Vallée, QC G0E 1K0
Tél: 418-393-2161; *Téléc:* 418-393-2274
journallephare@chez.com
www.chez.com/journallephare
Circulation: 1 325
Noël-Denis Samson, Président

***Grosse Isle:* First Informer**
2-246 Ch. Principale, Grosse Isle, QC G4T 6A8
Tel: 418-985-2100; *Fax:* 418-985-2274
first@duclos.net
www.firstinformer.com
Circulation: 619 *Frequency:* Fri.
Joy Davies, Publisher

***Hudson:* Hudson/St. Lazare Gazette**
PO Box 70, Hudson, QC J0P 1H0
Tel: 450-458-5482; *Fax:* 450-458-3337
hudsongazette@videotron.ca
www.hudsongazette.com
Circulation: 16,000 *Frequency:* Wed.
Was Lake of Two Mountains Gazette. First English Quebec weekly on the web.
G. Jones, Publisher & Editor

***Huntingdon:* The Gleaner**
66 Chateauguay, Huntingdon, QC J0S 1H0
Tel: 450-264-5364; *Fax:* 450-264-9521
info@gleaner-source.com
www.gleaner-source.com
Circulation: 3,328 *Frequency:* Wed.; English & French
Patrice Laflamme, French Editor
; plaflamme@gleaner-source.com
Andre Castagnier, Publisher
; acastagnier@gleaner-source.com
Susanne J. Brown, Editor
; editorial@gleaner-source.com

***Joliette:* L'Action**
342, Beaudry nord, Joliette, QC J6E 6A6
Tél: 450-759-3664;
infolanaudiere@transcontinental.ca
www.laction.com
Circulation: 46 700 *Frequency:* Dimanche

***Joliette:* L'Action Montcalm**
262, boul l'Industrie, Joliette, QC J6E 3Z1
Tél: 450-759-3664; *Téléc:* 450-759-9828
André Nadeau, Éditeur
Francine Rainville, Rédactrice-en-chef

***Joliette:* L'Expression de Lanaudière**
342, Beaudry nord, Joliette, QC J6E 6A6
Tél: 450-752-0447; *Téléc:* 450-759-0945
Circulation: 45 195 *Frequency:* Dimanche
Jean-Pierre Malo, Éditeur
André Lafrenière, Rédacteur-en-chef

***Jonquière:* Le Réveil**
CP 520, 3388, boul St-François, Jonquière, QC G7X 7W4
Tél: 418-695-2601; *Téléc:* 418-695-0530
Ligne sans frais: 800-387-2601
atelier.reveil@hebdosquebecor.com
www.lereveil.com
Circulation: 70 529 *Frequency:* Dimanche
Diane Audet, Directrice générale

***Jonquière:* Le Réveil**
CP 520, 3388, boul St-François, Jonquière, QC G7X 7W4
Tél: 418-695-2601; *Téléc:* 418-695-1391
Ligne sans frais: 800-387-2601
atelier.reveil@hebdosquebecor.com
www.lereveil.com
Circulation: 71 416 *Frequency:* Dimanche; aussi Le Point (samedi, 13 067)
Diane Audet, Contact

***Knowlton:* Brome County News**
88-A Lakeside St., Knowlton, QC J0E 1V0
Tel: 450-242-1188; *Fax:* 450-243-5155
Toll-Free: 800-463-9525
newsroom@sherbrookerecord.com
www.sherbrookerecord.com
Circulation: 12,307 *Frequency:* Wed.
Elanor Brown, Editor
Randy Kinnear, Publisher

***L'Islet:* Le Hublot**
CP 347, 62, ave 5, L'Islet, QC G0R 2C0
Tél: 418-247-7345; *Téléc:* 418-247-5085
lehublot@caramail.com
Circulation: 1 735 *Frequency:* Last Thurs. of the month
Jean-François Pelletier, Président

***La Malbaie:* Le Plein Jour Charlevoix**
#110, 249, rue Nairn, La Malbaie, QC G5A 1M4
Tél: 418-665-6121; *Téléc:* 418-665-3105
redaction@pleinjour.com
www.hebdosquebecor.com
Circulation: 12 725 *Frequency:* Vendredi
Benoit Paré

***La Salle:* Magazine Ile des Soeurs / Nuns Island Magazine**
420 rue Lafleur, La Salle, QC H8R 3H6
Tél: 514-363-5656; *Téléc:* 514-363-3895
pierre.vigneault@transcontinental.ca
www.lemagazineids.com
Circulation: 8 091 *Frequency:* Wed.; English & French
Pierre Vigneault, Éditeur

***La Salle:* Le Messager Verdun**
420, rue Lafleur, La Salle, QC H8R 3H6
Tél: 514-363-5656; *Téléc:* 514-363-3895
lussierp@transcontinental.ca
www.messagerverdun.com
Circulation: 24 500 *Frequency:* Sunday; English & French

***La Salle:* La Voix Populaire**
420, rue Lafleur, La Salle, QC H8R 3H6
Tél: 514-363-5656; *Téléc:* 514-363-3895
,arilyse.hamelin@transcontinental.ca
www.lavoixpopulaire.com
Circulation: 23 500 *Frequency:* Dimanche
Mathieu Robert-Perron, Directeur de l'information
; mathieu.robert-perron@transcontinental.c

***La Tuque:* L'Echo de La Tuque**
324, rue St-Joseph, La Tuque, QC G9X 1L2
Tél: 819-523-6141;
www.lechodelatuque.com/
Circulation: 6 802

***Lac-Etchemin:* La Voix du Sud**
1516A, rte 277, Lac-Etchemin, QC G0R 1S0
Tél: 418-625-7471; *Téléc:* 418-625-5200
Ligne sans frais: 866-325-8649
production_lacetchemin@transcontinental.ca
www.lavoixd usud.com
Circulation: 22 434 *Frequency:* Samedi
Caroline Gilbert, Éditeur
André Poulin, Rédacteur-en-chef

***Lac-Mégantic:* L'Echo de Frontenac**
5040, boul des Vétérans, Lac-Mégantic, QC G6B 2G5
Tél: 819-583-1630; *Téléc:* 819-583-1124
Ligne sans frais: 866-583-1630
hebdo@echodefrontenac.com
www.echodefrontenac.com
Circulation: 9 134 *Frequency:* Dimanche; français
Gaétan Poulin, Éditeur
Rémi Tremblay, Rédacteur-en-chef

***Lachenaie:* Le Trait d'Union**
#210, 1300, Grande Allée, Lachenaie, QC J6W 4M4
Tél: 450-964-4400;
www.letraitdunion.com

***Lachute:* L'Argenteuil**
52, rue Principale, Lachute, QC J8H 3A8
Tél: 450-562-2494; *Téléc:* 450-562-1434
roger@eap.on.ca
www.largenteuil.ca
Circulation: 15 000 *Frequency:* Mercredi; français
Evelyne Bergeron, Rédacteur-en-chef

***Lachute:* Progrès Watchman**
52, rue Principale, Lachute, QC J8H 3A8
Tel: 450-562-8593; *Fax:* 450-562-1434
Toll-Free: 800-561-5738
www.progres-watchman.ca
Circulation: 13 000 *Frequency:* Samedi
Evelyne Bergeron, Editor

***Lasalle:* Le Messager de LaSalle**
420, Lafleur, Lasalle, QC H8R 3H6
Tel: 514-363-5656; *Fax:* 514-363-3895
boulangerp@transcontinental.ca
www.messagerlasalle.com
Circulation: 32 200 *Frequency:* Sunday; English & French
Jean-Guy Marceau, Éditeur

***Lasalle:* Weekly Post/L'Hebdo de Ville Mount-Royal**
#70, 410, rue Lafleur, Lasalle, QC H8R 3H6
Tel: 514-739-3302; *Fax:* 514-739-3304
Frequency: Thur.; English & French

***Laurier-Station:* Le Peuple Lotbinière**
CP 130, 1000, ch St-Joseph, Laurier-Station, QC G0S 1N0
Tél: 418-728-2131; *Téléc:* 418-728-4819
redaction.lotbiniere@hebdosquebecor.com
www.peuplelotbiniere.com
Circulation: 12 390 *Frequency:* Dimanche; français
Denys Simoneau, Éditeur

***Laval:* The Chomedey News**
250, 657, boul Curé-Labelle, Laval, QC H7V 2T8
Tel: 450-978-9999; *Fax:* 450-687-6330
www.chomedeynews.ca
Circulation: 28,965 *Frequency:* Thu.
George Bakoyannis, Publisher

***Laval:* Courrier Laval**
189, av Laval, Laval, QC H7N 3V8
Tél: 450-667-4360; *Téléc:* 450-667-9498
www.courrierlaval.com
Circulation: 108 375 *Frequency:* Dimanche; aussi Courrier du Jeudi
François Charbonneau, Éditeur

***Laval:* Vivre**
828 - 79 av, Laval, QC H7V 3J1
Tél: 450-973-8787; *Téléc:* 450-973-8414
ccvm@videotron.ca
www.ccvm.org
Circulation: 5 000
Johane Papineau, Directrice

***Lennoxville:* The Townships Sun**
PO Box 28, 7 Conley St., Lennoxville, QC J1M 1Z3
Tel: 819-566-7424; *Fax:* 819-566-7424
townsun@abacom.com
Circulation: 696 *Frequency:* Monthly
David Wright, Editor

***Lévis:* Le Peuple**
CP 1200, 421, rue Dorimene Des Jardins, Lévis, QC G6V 6R8
Tél: 418-833-9398; *Téléc:* 418-833-8177
bertrand.picard@hebdosquebecor.com
www.peuplelevis.com
Circulation: 57 087 *Frequency:* Samedi

***Lingwick:* Le Reflet du Canton de Lingwick**
#306, 72, rte 108, Lingwick, QC J0B 2Z0
Tél: 819-877-3560;
refletgt@axion.ca
www.axion.ca/~reflet
Frequency: 9/an
Daniel Pezat, Président

***Longueuil:* Point Sud**
#200, 24, rue De Gentilly, Longueuil, QC J4H 1Y8
Tél: 450-677-2626; *Téléc:* 450-442-2663
info@pointsud.ca
www.pointsud.ca

***Louiseville:* L'Echo d'Autray et de Maskinongé**
43, St-Louis, Louiseville, QC J5V 2C7
Tél: 819-228-5532; *Téléc:* 819-228-9379
Ligne sans frais: 877-228-5532
lyne.baribeau@transcontinental.ca
www.lechoam.com
Circulation: 27 200 *Frequency:* Dimanche
Lyne Baribeau, Éditrice

***Magog:* Le Reflet du Lac**
#104, 101, rue Du Moulin, Magog, QC J1X 4A1
Tél: 819-843-3500; *Téléc:* 819-843-3085
www.lerefletdulac.com
Circulation: 23 359 *Frequency:* Samedi

***Malartic:* Le Courrier de Malartic**
CP 4020, Malartic, QC J0Y 1Z0
Tél: 819-757-4712; *Téléc:* 819-757-4712
Circulation: 1 200 *Frequency:* Mardi; français
Denyse Roberge, Éditrice

***Maniwaki:* La Gatineau**
114, rue de la Ferme, Maniwaki, QC J9E 3J9
Tél: 819-449-1725; *Téléc:* 819-449-5108
Circulation: 11 100 *Frequency:* Vendredi; français
Marguette Ceré, Directrice

***Matane:* La Voix Gaspesienne**
#107, 305, rue de la Gare, Matane, QC G4W 3J2
Tél: 418-562-4040; *Téléc:* 418-562-4607
www.hebdosquebecor.com/vxg/index_vxg.asp
Circulation: 5 013 *Frequency:* Mercredi; aussi La Voix du dimanche
Romain Pelletier, Rédacteur-en-chef

***Mont-Joli:* L'Information**
135, rue Doucet, Mont-Joli, QC G5H 1R6
Tél: 418-775-4381; *Téléc:* 418-775-7768
www.hebdosquebecor.com/ifm/index_ifm.asp
Circulation: 10 500 *Frequency:* Dimanche

***Mont-Laurier:* Le Choix d'Antoine-Labelle**
369, boul Paquette, Mont-Laurier, QC J9L 1K5
Tél: 819-623-3112; *Téléc:* 819-623-6224
Ligne sans frais: 888-484-8181
www.journallechoix.qc.ca
Circulation: 16 890 *Frequency:* Vendredi
Luc Bélanger, Éditeur

***Mont-Laurier:* L'Echo de la Lievre**
534, de la Madonne, Mont-Laurier, QC J9L 1S5
Tél: 819-623-5250; *Téléc:* 819-623-7148
www.hebdosquebecor.com/edl/index_edl.asp
Circulation: 16 000 *Frequency:* Samedi

***Mont-Royal:* Greek Canadian Reportage**
PO Box 54025, Mont-Royal, QC H3P 3H4
Tel: 514-279-7772
Circulation: 15,000 *Frequency:* Weekly; Greek
Anthony Bartzakos, Publisher & Editor

***Mont-Tremblant:* L'Information du Nord**
1107, rue de Saint-Jovite, Mont-Tremblant, QC J8E 3J9
Tél: 819-425-8658; *Téléc:* 819-425-7713
info.nord@hebdoqquebecor.com
www.hebdosquebecor.com/ifj/index_ifj.asp
Circulation: 14 300 *Frequency:* Vendredi
Daniel Deslauriers, Rédacteur-en-chef

***Montmagny:* L'Oie Blanche**
70, rue de l'Anse, Montmagny, QC G5V 3S7
Tél: 418-248-8227; *Téléc:* 418-248-4033
oieblanc@globetrotter.net
www.oieblanc.com/oie3/index.asp
Circulation: 19 672 *Frequency:* Samedi
France Fortin

***Montmagny:* Le Peuple de la Côte-du-Sud**
80, boul Taché est, Montmagny, QC G5V 3S7
Tél: 418-248-0415; *Téléc:* 418- -
www.hebdosquebecor.com/pcs/index_pcs.asp
Circulation: 21 073 *Frequency:* Samedi

***Montréal:* Le Couac**
CP 222, Montréal, QC H3K 3G5
info@lecouac.org
www.lecouac.org

***Montréal:* Courrier Ahuntsic**
1569, rue Fleury est, Montréal, QC H2C 1S7
Tél: 514-381-4414; *Téléc:* 514-381-1278
www.courrierahuntsic.com
Frequency: Dimanche

***Montréal:* Échos du Vieux-Montréal**
234, rue St-Paul ouest, Montréal, QC H2Y 1Z9
Tél: 514-844-2133; *Téléc:* 514-844-5858
echos@pubrde.com
Circulation: 15 000
Denise Di Candido, Chief Editor
Vincent Di Candido, Président

***Montréal:* Le Journal de Mont-Royal**
6965 6e ave., Montréal, QC H2A 3E3
Tél: 514-270-8088;
www.expressoutrement.com
Frequency: also Le Point d'Outremont, L'Etoile du Plateau & Mile End

***Montréal:* Journal de Rosemont**
6965, 6e Avenue, Montréal, QC H2A 3E3
Tél: 514-270-8088; *Téléc:* 514-270-8368
cerasis@transcontinental.ca
www.journalderosemont.com
Circulation: 59 588
Sylvia Cerasi, Rédactrice-en-chef
Sylviane Lussier, Éditrice

***Montréal:* Journal L'Itinéraire**
2103, rue Sainte-Catherine est, 3e étage, Montréal, QC H2K 2H9
Tél: 514-597-0238; *Téléc:* 514-597-1544
itineraire@itineraire.ca
www.itineraire.ca
Circulation: 13 000 *Frequency:* bimensuel
Jocelyne Sénécal, Directrice des ressources humines
Serge Lareault, Directeur général

***Montréal:* Le Monde**
CP 201 St-Michel, Montréal, QC H2A 3L8
Tél: 514-722-7708; *Téléc:* 514-722-3667
lemonde@arobas.net
Circulation: 22 000 *Frequency:* Monthly
Raymond Gagnon, President

***Montréal:* National Review of Medicine**
400 McGill St., 3rd Fl., Montréal, QC H2Y 2G1
Tel: 514-397-8833; *Fax:* 514-397-0228
Toll-Free: 800-663-7403
editor@nationalreviewofmedicine.com
www.nationalreviewofmedicine.com
Circulation: 41,761 *Frequency:* 21 times a year
David Elkins, Executive Editor

***Montréal:* Nouvelles de l'Est**
6965, 6e Ave., Montréal, QC H2A 3E3
Tél: 514-270-8088; *Téléc:* 514-270-8368
pinely@transcontinental.ca
www.nouvellesdelest.com
Circulation: 24 629
Yannick Pinel, Rédacteur-en-chef
Sylviane Lussier, Éditrice & Directrice

***Montréal:* Nouvelles Parc-Extension News**
#250, 657, boul Curé-Labelle, Montréal, QC H7V 2T8
Tel: 450-978-9999; *Fax:* 450-687-6330
http://px-news.com/
Frequency: Saturday; English & French
George Bakoyannis, Co-Publisher, General Director

***Montréal:* Place Publique**
3516, Place du Parc, Montréal, QC H2X 2H7
Tél: 514-844-6917;
placepub@cam.org
Circulation: 25 000
Alex Frettier, Rédacteur en chef

***Montréal:* Le Plateau**
6965, 6e av, Montréal, QC H2A 3E3
Tél: 514-270-8088; *Téléc:* 514-270-8368
lussiers@transcontinental.ca
www.leplateau.com
Circulation: 34 132
Sylviane Lussier, Éditeur
Alain Perron, Rédacteur-en-chef

***Montréal:* Progrès Saint-Léonard**
#212, 8770, boul Langelier, Montréal, QC H1P 3C6
Tél: 514-899-5888; *Téléc:* 514-899-5984
www.progresstleonard.com
Circulation: 30 592 *Frequency:* Mercredi
Jean Touchette, Éditeur
Jacques Boulanger, Éditeur

***Montréal:* Progrès Villeray**
6965, 6e Ave., Montréal, QC H2A 3E3
Tél: 514-270-8088; *Téléc:* 514-270-8368
www.leprogresvilleray.com
Circulation: 22 576
Alain Perron, Rédacteur-en-chef
Sylviane Lussier, Éditrice

***Montréal:* Reflet de Société/Le Journal de la rue**
4237, rue Ste-Catherine est, Montréal, QC H1V 1X4
Tél: 514-256-9000; *Téléc:* 514-256-9444
journal@journaldelarue.ca
www.cafegraffiti.net
Circulation: 60 000 *Frequency:* 6 fois par an
Raymond Viger, Redacteur en chef

***Montréal:* Le Soi-disant**
4240, rue Ontario est, Montréal, QC H1V 1K1
Tél: 514-257-9028; *Téléc:* 514-252-7425

Circulation: 5 000
Richard Aubry, Président

Montréal: **Le Ville-Marie**
6965, 6e av, Montréal, QC H2A 3E3
Tél: 514-270-8088; *Téléc:* 514-270-8368
www.leville-marie.com

Montréal: **Visions Voisins / Neighbour Visions**
770 Rachel east (3rd Fl), Montréal, QC H2W 2M5
Tél: 514-277-7801; *Téléc:* 514-277-8919
afarrell@cdn-news.com
Circulation: 4 000
Ann Farrell, Rédactrice

Montréal: **Vue sur la Bourgogne**
755, rue des Seigneurs, Montréal, QC H3J 1K2
Tél: 514-596-4978; *Téléc:* 514-596-4981
Circulation: 5 500
Miriam Rouleau-Perez, Responsable

Napierville: **Coup D'Oeil**
350, rue St-Jacques, Napierville, QC J0J 1L0
Tél: 450-245-3344; *Téléc:* 450-245-7419
Ligne sans frais: 800-363-4542
coupdoeil@canadafrancois.com
www.journal-coupdoeil.com
Circulation: 12 072 *Frequency:* Samedi
Claude Trahan, Directeur de la publication
Charles Couture, Directeur édition et distribution

Natashquan: **Le Portageur**
CP 40, 50, ch d'en haut, Natashquan, QC G0G 2E0
Tél: 418-726-3736; *Téléc:* 418-726-3714
secom@globetrotter.net
Circulation: 548 *Frequency:* Mercredi
Nicole Lessard

New Carlisle: **The Gaspé Spec**
CP 99, 128, boul Gerard D. Levesque, New Carlisle, QC G0C 1Z0
Tél: 418-752-5400; *Téléc:* 418-752-6932
specs@globetrotter.net
www.gaspespec.com/
Circulation: 3,022 *Frequency:* Sunday
Sharon Farrell, Publisher

New Richmond: **L'Echo de la Baie**
140, boul Perron ouest, New Richmond, QC G0C 1B0
Tél: 418-392-5083; *Téléc:* 418-392-6605
www.hebdosquebecor.com/eba/index_eba.asp
Frequency: Dimanche
Alain St-Amand, Directeur général régional

Nicolet: **Le Courrier du Sud**
3255 Marie-Victorin, Nicolet, QC J3T 1X5
Tél: 450-646-3333; *Téléc:* 450-674-0205
Ligne sans frais: 866-646-3332
journal@courrierdusud.com
www.lecourrierdusud.com
Circulation: 127 350 *Frequency:* Samedi aussi Longueuil Extra (mercredi, tirage 50 000)
Lucie Masse

Nicolet: **Le Courrier-Sud**
Medias Trancontinental, 3255, rue Marie Victorin, Nicolet, QC J3T 1X5
Tél: 819-293-4551; *Téléc:* 819-293-8758
nancy.allaire@transcontinental.ca
www.lecourriersud.com
Circulation: 21 105 *Frequency:* Dimanche
Emilie Vallée, Rédactrice
Nancy Allaire, Editrice
Suzanne Blanchette, Secrétaire de direction

Outremont: **L'Express d'Outremont/de Mont-Royal**
6965 6e ave., Outremont, QC H2V 2K8
Tél: 514-270-8088;
redactionexpress@transcontinental.ca
www.expressoutremont.com
Circulation: 28 748 *Frequency:* Jeudi, hebdo
Mario Marois, Éditeur
Marilaine Bolduc-Jacob, Rédactrice en chef

Port-Cartier: **Le Port-Cartois**
10, des Pins, Port-Cartier, QC G5B 2A5
Tél: 418-766-5322; *Téléc:* 418-766-5329
redaction.portcartois@hebdosquebecor.com
www.hebdosquebecor.com
Circulation: 3 600 *Frequency:* Dimanche
Jean-Guy Gougeon

Préissac: **L'Alliance**
180, av du Lac, Préissac, QC J0Y 2E0
Tél: 819-759-4141; *Téléc:* 819-759-4142
journalalliance@cablevision.qc.ca
Circulation: 1 000 *Frequency:* Mensuel
Estelle Gelot, Présidente

Québec: **L'Actuel**
#900, 1265, boul Charest ouest, Québec, QC G1N 4V4
Tél: 418-686-6400; *Téléc:* 418-686-4841
www.quebechebdo.com
Circulation: 38 000 *Frequency:* Samedi
François Cattapan, Rédacteur en chef

Québec: **L'Appel**
#900, 1265, boul Charest ouest, Québec, QC G1N 4V4
Tél: 418-686-6400; *Téléc:* 418-686-4841
www.quebechebdo.com
Circulation: 52 000 *Frequency:* Samedi
François Cattapan, Rédacteur en chef

Québec: **Beauport Express**
Hebdos Transcontinental à Québec, #900, 1265, boul Charest ouest, Québec, QC G1N 4V4
Tél: 418-686-6400; *Téléc:* 418-686-1086
yvan.rancourt@transcontinental.ca
www.beauportexpress.com
Circulation: 38 700 *Frequency:* Hebdomadaire
Alain Lepage, Éditeur
Yvan Rancourt, Directeur des ventes

Québec: **Charlesbourg Express**
Médias-Transcontinental, #900, 1265, boul Charest ouest, Québec, QC G1N 4V4
Tél: 418-686-6400; *Téléc:* 418-686-4841
www.quebechebdo.com
Circulation: 30 100 *Frequency:* Samedi
François Cattapan, Rédacteur en chef

Québec: **Journal Droit de Parole**
412, 3e av, Québec, QC G1L 2W1
Tél: 418-648-8043;
cbv@oricom.ca
droitdeparole.org
Circulation: 15 000 *Frequency:* bi-hebdomadaire
Gilles Simard, Rédacteur-en-chef
Claude Giguère, Journaliste

Québec: **Journal Jacques-Cartier**
Médias-Transcontinental, #900, 1265, boul Charest ouest, Québec, QC G1N 4V4
Tel: 418-686-3036;
www.lejacquescartier.com
Circulation: 9,500 *Frequency:* au 2 mois
François Cattapan, Rédacteur en chef

Québec: **Journal le Carrefour**
#20, 580, Grande Allée est, Québec, QC G1R 2K2
Tél: 418-649-0775; *Téléc:* 418-649-7531
carrefour@webnet.qc.ca
Circulation: 72 500 *Frequency:* Dimanche
Martin Claveau, Éditeur
Nicolas Godbout, Rédacteur-en-chef

Québec: **Journal Québec Express**
#900, 1265, boul Charest ouest, Québec, QC G1N 4V4
Tél: 418-686-6400;
www.quebechebdo.com
Frequency: Dimanche

Québec: **Quebec Chronicle-Telegraph**
#101, 1248, che. Ste-Foy, Québec, QC G1X 2M5
Tel: 418-650-1764; *Fax:* 418-650-5172
qct@videotron.ca
www.qctonline.com
Circulation: 1,854 *Frequency:* Wed.
Karen Macdonald, Publisher

Québec: **Québec Express**
Médias-Transcontinental, #900, 1265, boul Charest ouest, Québec, QC G1N 4V4
Tel: 418-686-6400;
www.quebechebdo.com
Circulation: 38 000
François Cattapan, Rédacteur en chef

Québec: **La Quête**
729, Côte d'Araham, Québec, QC G1R 1A1
Tél: 418-649-2388; *Téléc:* 418-649-7770
laquete@archipelentraide.com
www.archipelentraide.com
Circulation: 3 000
Bernard Hélie, Coordonnateur

Repentigny: **L'Artisan**
1004, rue Notre-Dame, Repentigny, QC J5Y 1S9
Tél: 450-581-5120; *Téléc:* 450-581-4515
www.journallartisan.com
Circulation: 46 432 *Frequency:* Mardi; aussi Hebdo Rive-Nord (dimanche, tirage 39 900)
Jacques Boulanger, Éditeur

Repentigny: **Hebdo Rive-Nord**
1004, rue Notre-Dame, Repentigny, QC J5Y 1S9
Tél: 450-581-5120; *Téléc:* 450-581-6509
boulangery@transcontinental.ca
www.hebdorivenord.com
Circulation: 46 457 *Frequency:* Dimanche
Yannick Boulanger, Éditeur

Richelain: **Journal Servir**
Garnison St-Jean, CP 100 Bureau Chef, Richelain, QC J0J 1R0
Tél: 450-358-7099; *Téléc:* 450-358-7423
journalservin@videotron.net
Circulation: 3 300 *Frequency:* English & French
Gaëtane Dion, Rédactrice-en-chef

Rimouski: **L'Avantage Votre Journal**
183, St-Germain ouest, Rimouski, QC G5L 4B8
Tél: 418-722-0205; *Téléc:* 418-723-4237
bgleeson@lavantage.qc.ca
www.lavantage.qc.ca
Circulation: 40 586 *Frequency:* Vendredi
Bill Gleeson

Rimouski: **L'Avant-Poste Gaspesien**
CP 410, 73, rue Saint-Germain est, Rimouski, QC G5L 7C4
Tél: 418-723-4800; *Téléc:* 418-722-4078
Frequency: Dimanche

Rimouski: **Le Hâvre**
CP 3217 A, 217, av Léonidas, Rimouski, QC G5L 9G6
Tél: 418-689-4518; *Téléc:* 418- -
Circulation: 8 430 *Frequency:* Dimanche
Karine Boudreau, Rédactrice-en-chef

Rimouski: **Le Pharillon**
CP 3217 A, 217, av Léonidas, Rimouski, QC G5L 9G6
Tél: 418-368-3242; *Téléc:* 418-368-1705
www.hebdosquebecor.com/pha/index_pha.asp
Circulation: 8 618 *Frequency:* Dimanche
Michèle Lemieux, Rédactrice-en-chef

Rimouski: **Le Progrès Echo**
CP 3217, 217, av Léonidas, Rimouski, QC G5L 9G6
Tél: 418-721-1212; *Téléc:* 418-723-1855
www.progresecho.com
Circulation: 30 492 *Frequency:* Dimanche
Ernie Wells, Rédacteur-en-chef

Rimouski: **Le Rimouskois**
CP 3217, 271, av Leœnidas, Rimouski, QC G5L 9G6
Tél: 418-721-1212; *Téléc:* 418-723-1855
www.hebdosquebecor.com/rim/index_rim.asp
Circulation: 24 059 *Frequency:* Mercredi
Ernie Wells, Rédacteur-en-chef

Rimouski: **Vision Terre et Forêt**
CP 3217 A, 217, av Léonidas, Rimouski, QC G5L 9G6
Tél: 418-721-1222; *Téléc:* 418-721-1222
atelier.rimouski@editionsbelcor.com
www.hebdosquebecor.com/vis/index_vis .asp
Circulation: 6 500
Alice Roussell, Rédacteur-en-chef

Rivière-Portneuf: **Nouvelles d'icitte**
CP 310, Rivière-Portneuf, QC G0T 1P0
Tél: 418-238-5566; *Téléc:* 418-238-2793
Circulation: 800
Denise Fournier, Rédactrice-en-chef

Rivière-du-Loup: **Info Dimanche**
72, rue Fraser, Rivière-du-Loup, QC G5R 1C6
Tél: 418-862-1911; *Téléc:* 418-862-6165
journal@infodimanche.com
www.infodimanche.com
Circulation: 29 118 *Frequency:* Dimanche
Mario Pelletier, Rédacteur-en-chef
Michel Chalifour, Éditeur

Rivière-du-Loup: **Info Dimanche**
72, rue Fraser, Rivière-du-Loup, QC G5R 1C6
Tél: 418-862-1911; *Téléc:* 418-862-6165
journal@infodimanche.com
www.infodimanche.com
Circulation: 30 000 *Frequency:* Dimanche
Mario Pelletier, Rédacteur en chef

***Rivière-du-Loup:* Saint-Laurent Portage**
16, rue du Domaine, Rivière-du-Loup, QC G5R 2P5
Tél: 418-862-1774; *Fax:* 418-862-4387
grapho.ede_st@sympatico.ca
www.hebdosquebecor.com/slp/
Circulation: 39 000 *Frequency:* Dimanche
Richard Gauthier

***Roberval:* L'Etoile du Lac**
#101, 797 boul. Saint-Joseph, Roberval, QC G8H 2L4
Tél: 418-275-2911; *Téléc:* 418-275-2834
production_roberval@transcontinental.ca
www.letoiledulac.com
Circulation: 14 158 *Frequency:* Samedi

***Roberval:* L'Horizon**
#101, 797, boul St-Joseph, Roberval, QC G8H 2L4
Tél: 418-236-4432; *Téléc:* 418-236-9144
Circulation: 450

***Rouyn-Noranda:* Le Citoyen Rouyn-Noranda**
CP 490, 25 rue Gamble est, Rouyn-Noranda, QC J9X 5C4
Tél: 819-797-2450; *Téléc:* 819-762-4361
Circulation: 18 760 *Frequency:* Dimanche; supplement, Journal du Nord-Ouest
Andre Renaud, Directeur
819/762-4361

***Rouyn-Noranda:* La Frontière**
CP 490, 25, rue Gamble est, Rouyn-Noranda, QC J9X 5C4
Tél: 819-762-4361; *Téléc:* 819-797-2450
www.hebdosquebecor.com/fro/index_fro.asp
Circulation: 5 626 *Frequency:* Mercredi

***Saint-André-Avellin:* La Petite Nation**
CP 240, 70, rue Principale, Saint-André-Avellin, QC J0V 1W0
Tél: 819-983-2725; *Téléc:* 819-983-6844
Ligne sans frais: 800-567-6898
Circulation: 9 600 *Frequency:* Dimanche
Michel Blais, Rédacteur

***Saint-Anselme:* Le Tour des ponts**
#102, 134, rue Principale, Saint-Anselme, QC G0R 2N0
Tél: 418-885-9867; *Téléc:* 418-885-9834
Circulation: 1 425
Jacquelin Guillemette, Président

***Saint-Basile-le-Grand:* Journal L'Impact**
#101, 155, Sir Wilfrid Laurier, Saint-Basile-le-Grand, QC J3N 1A9
Tél: 450-441-7252; *Téléc:* 450-441-4497
journallimpact@videotron.ca
www.journallimpact.com

***Saint-Bruno:* L'Écho de Saint-Bruno**
1688, Place Seigneuriale, Saint-Bruno, QC J3V 4E4
Tél: 450-653-5295; *Téléc:* 450- -
Circulation: 10 000 *Frequency:* Mensuel

***Saint-Bruno:* Le Journal de Saint-Bruno**
1507, rue Roberval, Saint-Bruno, QC J3V 3P8
Tél: 450-653-3685; *Téléc:* 450-653-6967
www.journaldest-bruno.qc.ca
Circulation: 14 900 *Frequency:* Samedi

***Saint-Bruno:* Les Versants du Mont-Bruno**
1488, rue Montarville, Saint-Bruno, QC J3V 3T5
Tél: 450-441-5300; *Téléc:* 450-441-5450
www.versants.com
Circulation: 18 000

***Saint-Bruno-Lac-Saint-Jea:* Le Brunois**
197, rue Jauvin, Saint-Bruno-Lac-Saint-Jea, QC G0W 2L0
Tél: 418-343-3437; *Téléc:* 418-343-2662
Circulation: 1 000
Jacques Demers, Rédacteur en chef

***Saint-Bruno-de-Kamouraska:* Le Trait d'Union de St-Bruno**
CP 3, 4, rue du Couvent, Saint-Bruno-de-Kamouraska, QC G0L 2M0
Tél: 418-492-7849; *Téléc:* 418-492-2612
trdunion@globetrotter.net
Constance Gagné, Présidente

***Saint-Denis-de-Brompton:* Le Saint-Denisien**
CP 244, 1495, route 222, Saint-Denis-de-Brompton, QC J0B 2P0
Tél: 819-572-4445; *Téléc:* 819-562-2888
stdenisi@abacom.com
Circulation: 1 175
Johanne Carrier, Président

***Saint-Donat:* Journal Altitude**
CP 1350, 365, rue Principale, Saint-Donat, QC J0T 2C0
Tél: 819-424-2610; *Téléc:* 819-424-3615
journalaltitude@bellnet.ca
www.st-donat.com/journal.html
Circulation: 3,700 *Frequency:* Vendredi; français
Jean Lafortune, Rédacteur-en-chef

***Saint-Eustache:* La Concorde**
53, rue St-Eustache, Saint-Eustache, QC J7R 2L2
Tél: 450-472-3440; *Téléc:* 450-472-1629
laconcorde@groupejcl.com
www.linfonet.com/concframe.cfm
Circulation: 45 300 *Frequency:* Mercredi; aussi L'Eveil (dimanche; tirage 37 400)
Jean-Claude Langlois, Éditeur
Rémi Binette, Rédacteur en chef

***Saint-Eustache:* L'Éveil**
53, rue St-Eustache, Saint-Eustache, QC J7R 2L2
Tél: 450-472-3440; *Téléc:* 450-472-1638
Circulation: 45 720 *Frequency:* Samedi
Jean-Claude Langlois, Éditeur
Rémi Binette, Rédacteur-en-chef

***Saint-Eustache:* Le Nord Info**
53, rue St-Eustache, Saint-Eustache, QC J4R 2L2
Tél: 450-435-6537; *Téléc:* 450-435-7968
pub@groupejcl.com
www.groupejcl.com
Circulation: 57 000 *Frequency:* Samedi
Jean-Claude Langlois, Éditeur

***Saint-Hippolyte:* Le Sentier**
CP 135, Saint-Hippolyte, QC J8A 3P5
Tél: 450-563-1975; *Téléc:* 450-563-1059
journal.lesentier@videotron.ca
www.inter-actif.qc.ca/le-sentier/
Circulation: 4 000
Manon Dagenais, Présidente

***Saint-Hyacinthe:* Le Clairon Regional de St-Hyacinthe**
655, av Ste-Anne, Saint-Hyacinthe, QC J2S 5G4
Tél: 450-773-6028; *Téléc:* 450-773-3115
publicite@courrierclairon.qc.ca
www.leclairon.qc.ca
Circulation: 33 985 *Frequency:* Samedi
Benoit Chartier, Editor, Ventes

***Saint-Hyacinthe:* Le Courrier de Saint-Hyacinthe**
655, rue Ste-Anne, Saint-Hyacinthe, QC J2S 5G4
Tél: 450-773-6028; *Téléc:* 450-773-3115
info@lecourrier.qc.ca
www.lecourrier.qc.ca
Circulation: 13 605 *Frequency:* Mercredi; français
Martin Bourassa, Rédacteur-en-chef

***Saint-Jean-sur-Richelieu:* Le Canada Français**
84, rue Richelieu, Saint-Jean-sur-Richelieu, QC J3B 6X3
Tél: 450-347-0323; *Téléc:* 450-347-4539
canadaf@canadafrancais.com
www.canadafrancais.com
Circulation: 18 955 *Frequency:* Mercredi; aussi Le Richelieu Dimanche (dimanche)
Robert Paradis, Éditeur

***Saint-Jean-sur-Richelieu:* Le Richelieu Dimanche**
84, rue Richelieu, Saint-Jean-sur-Richelieu, QC J3B 6X3
Tél: 450-347-0323; *Téléc:* 450-347-4539
Circulation: 35 795
Robert Paradis, Éditeur

***Saint-Jérome:* L'Echo du Nord**
179, rue St-Georges, Saint-Jérome, QC J7Z 4Z8
Tél: 450-436-5887; *Téléc:* 450-436-5904
www.hebdosquebecor.com/edl/index_edl.asp
Circulation: 7 500 *Frequency:* Mercredi
Andre Juteau, Éditeur
Claude Lamarche, Rédacteur-en-chef

***Saint-Jérome:* Journal Le Mirabel**
179, rue St-Georges, Saint-Jérome, QC J7Z 4Z8
Tél: 450-436-8200; *Téléc:* 450-436-8912
Circulation: 39 430 *Frequency:* Samedi

***Saint-Jérome:* Journal Le Nord**
393, boul des Laurentides, Saint-Jérome, QC J7Z 4L9
Tél: 450-438-8383; *Téléc:* 450-438-4174
editeur@journallenord.qc.ca
www.journallenord.com
Circulation: 40 012 *Frequency:* Mercredi
François Laferrière, Éditeur

***Saint-Lambert:* Saint-Lambert Journal**
574, rue Victoria, Saint-Lambert, QC J4P 2J5
Tél: 450-671-0014; *Fax:* 450- -
Circulation: 10,800 *Frequency:* Wed.; English & French

***Saint-Laurent:* Les Nouvelles Saint-Laurent / Saint-Laurent News**
#304, 685, boul Décarie, Saint-Laurent, QC H4L 5G4
Tél: 514-855-1292; *Téléc:* 514-855-1855
gauthiera@transcontinental.ca
www.nouvellessaint-laurent.com
Circulation: 27 499 *Frequency:* Sunday; English & French
Alexandre Gauthier, Rédacteur-en-chef

***Saint-Laurent:* The Suburban**
#105, 7575 Trans-Canada Hwy., Saint-Laurent, QC H4T 1V6
Tel: 514-484-1107; *Fax:* 514-484-9616
suburban@thesuburban.com
www.thesuburban.com
Circulation: West End: 64,000; West Island: 41,000; East End: 25,000 *Frequency:* Wed.: West End, West Island; Thu.: East End
Michael Sochaczevski, Publisher
Sari Medicoff, Operations Manager

***Saint-Malo:* L'Informalo**
50, ch Aukland, Saint-Malo, QC J0B 2Y0
Tél: 819-658-3587; *Téléc:* 819-658-1019
clevesque29@hotmail.com
Circulation: 450 *Frequency:* Bimestrielle, 1er mardi à chaque 2 mois

***Saint-Pamphile:* L'Écho d'en Haut**
#209, 25, rue Principale, Saint-Pamphile, QC G0R 3X0
Tél: 418-356-5491; *Téléc:* 418-356-5491
Circulation: 2 915
Claudel Pelletier, Président

***Saint-Pascal:* Le Placoteux**
491, av d'Anjou, Saint-Pascal, QC G0L 3Y0
Tél: 418-492-2706; *Téléc:* 418-492-9706
association@leplacoteux.qc.ca
www.leplacoteux.qc.ca
Circulation: 17 469 *Frequency:* Dimanche
Bruno Lacroix, Editeur

***Saint-Pierre-Ile-d'Orléan:* Autour de l'île**
CP 124, Saint-Pierre-Ile-d'Orléan, QC G0A 4E0
Tél: 418-828-0330; *Téléc:* 418-828-0741
autourdelile@videotron.ca
Circulation: 3 400 *Frequency:* 6/an
Léo- Desaulniers, Président

***Saint-Siméon:* Le Goéland**
CP 250, 127, boul Perron ouest, Saint-Siméon, QC G0C 3A0
Tél: 418-534-2026; *Téléc:* 418-534-4353
Circulation: 610
Antoinette Arsenault, Éditrice

***Saint-Tite:* L'Hebdo Mekinac/des Chenaux**
CP 4057, Saint-Tite, QC G0X 3H0
Tél: 819-537-5111; *Téléc:* 819-537-5471
gilles.guay@transcontinental.ca
www.lhebdomekinacdeschenaux.com
Circulation: 13 081 *Frequency:* Samedi; français
Gilles Guay, Éditeur

***Sainte-Adèle:* Le Journal des Pays D'en Haut**
102, rue Morin, Sainte-Adèle, QC J8B 2P7
Tél: 450-229-6664; *Téléc:* 450-229-6063
www.hebdosquebecor.com/pdh/index_pdh.asp
Circulation: 23 000 *Frequency:* Mercredi
Kim Nymark, Directrice générale

***Sainte-Anne:* Le Point d'Impact**
194B, boul Sainte-Anne, Sainte-Anne, QC J0N 1H0
Circulation: 6 000 *Frequency:* Samedi

***Sainte-Anne-de-Beaupré:* L'Autre Voix**
#230, 9749, boul Ste-Anne, Sainte-Anne-de-Beaupré, QC G0A 3C0
Tél: 418-827-1511; *Téléc:* 418-827-1513
info@lautrevoix.com
www.lautrevoix.com
Mathieu Tremblay, Éditeur

***Sainte-Anne-des-Monts:* Le Riverain**
21-A, boul. Ste-Anne Est, Sainte-Anne-des-Monts, QC G4V 1M4
Tél: 418-763-7777; *Téléc:* 418-763-7778
atelier.matane@hebdoquebecor.com
www.hebdosquebecor.com/riv/index_riv.as p
Circulation: 5,749 *Frequency:* Dimanche

Allen Cormier, Rédacteur-en-chef

***Sainte-Brigitte-de-Laval:* Le Lavalois**
CP 1020, Sainte-Brigitte-de-Laval, QC G0A 3K0
Tél: 418-907-7172; *Téléc:* 418-907-7172
lelavalois@ccapcable.com
pages.ccapcable.com/lavalois/?page=100
Circulation: 1 300 *Frequency:* 10/an
Lucille Thomassin, Présidente

***Sainte-Geneviève-de-Batis:* Le Bulletin des Chenaux**
#220, 44, Rivière-à-Vaeillette, Sainte-Geneviève-de-Batis, QC G0X 2R0
Tél: 418-362-2134; *Téléc:* 418-362-2861
redaction@lebulletindeschenaux.com
www.lebulletindescheneaux.com
Circulation: 9 000
Fanny Prince, Directrice générale

***Sainte-Julie:* L'Information Ste-Julie**
#2, 566, rue Jules-Choquet, Sainte-Julie, QC J3E 1W6
Tél: 450-649-0719; *Téléc:* 450-649-7748
info@infodeste-julie.qc.ca
www.hebdos.net/isj/
Circulation: 19 363 *Frequency:* Samedi
Serge Landry, Éditeur
Yves Bélanger, Rédacteur-en-chef

***Sainte-Marie:* Beauce Media**
CP 400, 1147, boul Vachon, Sainte-Marie, QC G0S 2Y0
Tél: 418-387-8000; *Téléc:* 418-387-4495
www.hebdosquebecor.com/bem/index_bem.asp
Circulation: 16 807 *Frequency:* Lundi

***Sainte-Marie:* Beauce Week-End**
450, 2e av, Sainte-Marie, QC G6E 1B6
Tél: 418-387-6969; *Téléc:* 418-387-5223
Ligne sans frais: 877-387-6969
bweekend@dynamiques.com
www.dynamiques.com/dynamiques/bwe.html
Circulation: 19 400 *Frequency:* Vendredi
Nicolas Lapointe, Directeur

***Sainte-Thérèse:* Le Courrier de Groulx**
#204, 190, rue Curé Labelle, Sainte-Thérèse, QC J7E 2X5
Tél: 450-434-4144; *Téléc:* 450-434-3142
Circulation: 54 072 *Frequency:* Samedi
Donald Brouillette, Rédacteur-en-chef

***Sainte-Thérèse:* Journal Le Courrier**
#204, 190, boul Labelle, Sainte-Thérèse, QC J7E 2X5
Tél: 450-434-4144; *Téléc:* 450-434-3142
Ligne sans frais: 866-434-4144
louis.sauvageau@transcontinental.ca
www.journallecourrier.com
Circulation: 55 472 *Frequency:* Samedi
Louis Sauvageau, Editor
Linda Veilleux, Directrice de tirage

***Sainte-Thérèse:* La Voix des Milles-Iles**
50B, rue Turgeon, Sainte-Thérèse, QC J7E 3H4
Tél: 450-435-6537; *Téléc:* 450-435-0588
pubnordinfo@groupejcl.com
www.linfonet.com; www.groupejcl.com
Circulation: 57 000 *Frequency:* Mercredi
Jean-Claude Langlois, Éditeur

***Saint-Élie-d'Orford:* L'Info**
CP 157, Saint-Élie-d'Orford, QC J0B 2S0
Tél: 819-829-9639; *Téléc:* 819-566-5218
Circulation: 3 000
Jean Charron, Directeur

***Saint-Étienne-des-Grès:* Le Stéphanois**
CP 282, 1260, rue St-Alphonse, Saint-Étienne-des-Grès, QC G0X 2P0
Tél: 819-535-2089; *Téléc:* 819-535-5118
lestephanois@cgocable.ca
www.lestephanois.ca/
Circulation: 1 700
Gilbert Bournival, Président

***Sept-Iles:* Le Nord-Est**
365, boul Laure, Sept-Iles, QC G4R 2X1
Tél: 418-962-4100; *Téléc:* 418-962-0439
www.hebdosquebecor.com/nes/index_nes.asp
Circulation: 13 510 *Frequency:* Dimanche; aussi Le Nord-Est Plus (mercredi)

***Shawinigan:* L'Hebdo du St-Maurice**
CP 10, 2102, av Champlain, Shawinigan, QC G9N 6T8
Tél: 819-537-5111; *Téléc:* 819-537-5471
michel.matteau@transcontinental.ca
www.lhebdodustmaurice.com
Circulation: 30 511 *Frequency:* Samedi; français
Michel Matteau, Éditeur

***Shawville:* The Equity**
PO Box 4300, 133 Centre St., Shawville, QC J0X 2Y0
Tel: 819-647-2204; *Fax:* 819-647-2206
news@theequity.ca
www.theequity.ca
Circulation: 3,362 *Frequency:* Upd from CCNA
Heather Dickson, Publisher

***Sherbrooke:* Entrée Libre**
#317, 187, rue Laurier, Sherbrooke, QC J1H 4Z4
Tél: 819-821-2270; *Téléc:* 819-566-2664
Circulation: 9 000
Normand Gilbert, Président

***Sherbrooke:* La Nouvelle de Sherbrooke**
1950, rue Roy, Sherbrooke, QC J1K 2E8
Tél: 819-566-8022; *Téléc:* 819-563-1977
Circulation: 47 000 *Frequency:* Mercredi
Céline Maheu, Éditrice
Denis Duchaine, Rédacteur-en-chef

***Shipshaw:* La Vie d'Ici**
4681, rue Saint-Léonard, Shipshaw, QC G7P 1J4
Tél: 418-542-6252; *Téléc:* 418-542-0850
Circulation: 1 200 *Frequency:* Mensuel
Claire Duchesne, Présidente

***Sorel:* Les 2 Rives**
77, rue George, Sorel, QC J3P 1C2
Tél: 450-742-9408; *Téléc:* 450-742-2493
les2rives@les2rives.com
www.hebdos.net/drs
Circulation: 28 000 *Frequency:* Mardi
Pierre Plante, Éditeur
Louise Grégoire-Racicot, Rédactrice-en-chef

***Sorel-Tracy:* Journal La Voix**
58, rue Charlotte, Sorel-Tracy, QC J3P 1G3
Tél: 450-743-8466; *Téléc:* 450-742-8567
info@journallavoix.net
www.journallavoix.net
Circulation: 29 125 *Frequency:* Hebdomadaire, samedi
Johanne Berthiaume, Éditrice/Dir. gén.
; j.berthiaume@journallavoix.net
Hélène Goulet, Rédactrice
; h.goulet@journallavoix.net

***St-Charles-de-Bellechasse:* Au fil de la Boyer**
CP 316, 8B ave Commerciale, St-Charles-de-Bellechasse, QC G0R 2TO
Tél: 418-882-4242; *Téléc:* 418-887-5050
laboyer@laboyer.com
www.laboyer.com
Circulation: 1 000
Jean-Pierre Paré, Éditeur

***St-Fabien-de-Panet:* Le Réveil**
199B, rue Bilodeau, St-Fabien-de-Panet, QC G0R 2J0
Tél: 418-249-2128; *Téléc:* 418-249-2138
lereveil@sogetel.net
Frequency: Mensuel
Thérèse Bilodeau, Présidente

***St-François:* L'Echo de St-François**
534, ch St-François ouest, St-François, QC G0R 3A0
Tél: 418-259-2177; *Téléc:* 418-259-2177
echosf@globetrotter.net
Circulation: 675 *Frequency:* Mensuel
Lorraine Lamonde, Présidente

***St-Georges:* Éclaireur Progrès/Beauce Nouvelle**
12625, 1e av, St-Georges, QC G5Y 2E4
Tél: 418-228-8858; *Téléc:* 418-227-0268
eclaprog@globetrotter.net
www.hebdosquebecor.com/ecl/index_ecl.asp
Circulation: 28 700 *Frequency:* Mercredi, Vendredi
Michel Roy, Directeur de l'information

***St-Jean:* L'Attisée**
CP 847, 318, rue Verreault, 2e étage, St-Jean, QC G0R 3G0
Tél: 418-598-9590; *Téléc:* 418-598-7588
journalattisee@videotron.ca
Circulation: 2 250
Benoit Lévesque, Éditeur

***St-Laurent:* Courrier Bordeaux/Cartierville**
#304, 685, boul, Décarie, St-Laurent, QC H4L 5G4
Tél: 514-855-1292; *Téléc:* 514-381-1278
www.courrierbc.com
Circulation: 17 237 *Frequency:* Dimanche
Jacques Dion, Éditeur

***St-Léonard:* L'Avenir de l'Est**
 # 210, 8770 boulevard Langelier, St-Léonard, QC H1P 3C6
Tél: 514-899-5888; *Téléc:* 514-899-5001
www.avenirdelest.com
Circulation: 42 314

***St-Léonard:* Le Flambeau de l'Est**
#210, 8770, boul Langelier, St-Léonard, QC H1P 3C6
Tél: 514-899-5888; *Téléc:* 514-899-5001
www.flambeaudelest.com

***St-Léonard:* Guide de Montréal-Nord**
#210, 8770, boul Lanaelier, St-Léonard, QC H1P 3C6
Tél: 514-899-5888; *Téléc:* 514-899-5001
www.guidemtlnord.com
Circulation: 32 841
Sylviane Lussier, Éditrice
Marie-Josée Chouinard, Rédactrice-en-chef

***St-Léonard:* Le Guide Montréal-Nord**
#210, 8770, boul Langelier, St-Léonard, QC H1P 3C6
Tél: 514-899-5888; *Téléc:* 514-899-5001
www.guidemtlnord.com

***St-Léonard:* L'Informateur de Rivières-Des-Prairies**
#210, 8770 boul. Langelier, St-Léonard, QC H1P 3C6
Tél: 514-899-5888; *Téléc:* 514-899-5001
www.linformateurrdp.com

***St-Pierre-du-Sud:* Le Pierr'Eau**
645, 2e av, St-Pierre-du-Sud, QC G0R 4B0

***St-Sauveur:* Journal La Vallée**
#104, 94, de la Gare, St-Sauveur, QC J0R 1R6
Tél: 450-227-4646; *Téléc:* 450-227-8144
www.hebdosquebecor.com/jlv/index_jlv.asp
Circulation: 28,000
André Guillemette, Éditeur

***St-Sauveur-des-Monts:* Le Journal de la Vallée**
#104, 94, de la Gare, St-Sauveur-des-Monts, QC J0R 1R0
Circulation: 31 300 *Frequency:* Vendredi

***Stanstead:* Stanstead Journal**
269 Dufferin St., Stanstead, QC J0B 3E2
Tel: 819-876-7514; *Téléc:* 819-876-7515
Ligne sans frais: 800-567-1259
journal@stansted.journal.com
www.stanstead-journal.com
Circulation: 2 700 *Frequency:* Wed.
Jean-Yves Durocher, Publisher & Editor

***Témiscaming:* Contact**
CP 566, 32, rue Simon, Témiscaming, QC J0Z 3R0
Tél: 819-627-9050; *Téléc:* 819-627-1794
contact@cablevision.qc.ca
Circulation: 1 000 *Frequency:* Bilingual
Elaine Ouellet, Rédactrice-en-chef

***Terrebonne:* La Revue de Terrebonne**
231, rue Ste-Marie, Terrebonne, QC J6W 3E4
Tél: 450-964-4444; *Téléc:* 450-471-1023
ventes@larevue.qc.ca
www.larevue.qc.ca
Other information: Montréal: 514/990-7314
Circulation: 50 800 *Frequency:* Mercredi
Gilles Bordonado, Propriétaire

***Thetford Mines:* Le Courrier Frontenac**
CP 789, 541, boul Smith nord, Thetford Mines, QC G6G 5V3
Tél: 418-338-5181; *Téléc:* 418-338-5482
publicite@courrierfrontenac.com
www.courrierfrontenac.com
Circulation: 20 750 *Frequency:* Vendredi; aussi Courrier Affaires & Économie (bimensuel)
Danie Blais, Rédacteur-en-chef

***Trois-Rivières:* La Gazette Populaire**
942, rue Ste-Geneviève, Trois-Rivières, QC G9A 3X6
Tél: 819-375-4012; *Téléc:* 819-375-9670
info@lagazettepopulaire.com
www.lagazettepopulaire.com
Circulation: 75 000 *Frequency:* Mensuel
Jean-Marc Lord, Rédacteur

***Trois-Riviéres:* L'Hebdo-Journal**
#205, 525, rue Barkoff, Trois-Riviéres, QC G8T 2A5
Tél: 819-379-1490; *Téléc:* 819-379-0705
redaction.hj@transcontinental.ca
www.lhebdojournal.com
Circulation: 48 900 *Frequency:* Samedi

Trois-Rivières: **Le Tour d'y voir**
991, rue Champflour, Trois-Rivières, QC G9A 1Z8
Tél: 819-375-0484; *Téléc:* 819-371-3827
tdv@tr.cgocable.ca
www.tdv.qc.ca
Circulation: 1 000
Sonia Lavergne, Directrice

Val-David: **Ski-se-dit**
2600, rue Monty, Val-David, QC J0T 2N0
Tél: 819-322-7969; *Téléc:* 819-322-7904
ski-se-dit@bellnet.ca
Circulation: 3 000 *Frequency:* Mensuel
Françoise Gilbert, Présidente

Val-d'Or: **Le Citoyen de la Vallée de l'Or**
1462, rue de la Québécoise, Val-d'Or, QC J9P 5H4
Tél: 819-874-4545; *Téléc:* 819-874-4547
citoyens@cablevision.qc.ca
www.hebdosquebecor.com/cvo/index_cvo.asp
Frequency: Dimanche
André Renaud, Directeur général régional

Val-d'Or: **Les Echos Abitibiens**
1462, rue de la Québécoise, Val-d'Or, QC J9P 5H4
Tél: 819-825-3755; *Téléc:* 819-825-0361
Circulation: 17 700 *Frequency:* Mercredi; (Amos, Lasarre, Malartic, Matagami)

Val-des-Monts: **Journal l'Envol**
12, Potvin, Val-des-Monts, QC J8N 7B2
Tél: 819-671-1502; *Téléc:* 819-671-7463
envol.desmonts@sympatico.ca
Circulation: 11 500 *Frequency:* Mensuel
Nicole A. Thibodeau, Contact

Valleyfield: **Journal Le Suroît**
#201, 52, rue Nicholson, Valleyfield, QC J6T 4M8

Valleyfield: **Le Journal St-François**
55, rue Jacques Cartier, Valleyfield, QC J6T 4R4
Tél: 450-371-6222; *Téléc:* 450-371-7254
info@st-francois.com
www.st-francois.com
Circulation: 31 000
Diane Dumont, Directrice générale

Valleyfield: **Le Soleil de Salaberry-de-Valleyfield**
20, rue Académie, Valleyfield, QC J6T 6M9
Tél: 450-373-8555; *Téléc:* 450-373-8666
redacval@lesoleil.qc.ca
www.hebdos.net/lsv/default.asp
Circulation: 30 200
Andre Mooney
; a.mooney@lesoleil.qc.ca

Vaudreuil-Dorion: **L'Etoile de l'Outaouais**
469, av St-Charles, Vaudreuil-Dorion, QC J7V 2N4
Tél: 450-455-6111; *Téléc:* 450-455-0596
Circulation: 34 324 *Frequency:* Mercredi
Angèle Marcoux Prévost, Éditrice

Vaudreuil-Dorion: **1ère Édition du Sud-Ouest**
469, av St-Charles, Vaudreuil-Dorion, QC J7V 2N4
Tel: 514-597-2231; *Fax:* 514-597-1932
peinfo@hebdosdusuroit.com
Circulation: 48 770 *Frequency:* Saturday; English & French
Isabelle Boutin

Victoriaville: **L'Avenir de l'Erable**
43, rue Notre-Dam, Victoriaville, QC G6P 3Z4
Tél: 819-758-6211; *Téléc:* 819-362-2216
www.lanouvelle.net
Circulation: 11 049 *Frequency:* Dimanche
Normand Poulin, Rédacteur-en-chef

Victoriaville: **La Nouvelle de Victoriaville**
CP 130, 43, rue Notre-Dame est, Victoriaville, QC G6P 3Z4
Tél: 819-758-6211; *Téléc:* 819-758-0417
www.lanouvelle.net
Circulation: 42 074 *Frequency:* Dimanche
Sylvie Côté, Éditrice
Manon Samson, Rédactrice-en-chef

Victoriaville: **L'Union**
43, rue Notre-Dame est, Victoriaville, QC G6P 3Z4
Tél: 819-759-6211; *Téléc:* 819-758-2759
www.lanouvelle.net
Circulation: 25 968 *Frequency:* Mercredi
Sylvie Côté, Éditrice
Manon Samson, Rédactrice-en-chef

Ville LaSalle: **Westmount Examiner**
420, LaFleur, Ville LaSalle, QC H8R 3H6
Tel: 514-363-5656; *Fax:* 514-937-6365
larsenw@transcontinental.ca
www.westmountexaminer.com
Circulation: 9,800 *Frequency:* Thur.

Ville-Marie: **Le Reflet**
Le Reflet Témiscamien inc., 22, rue Ste-Anne, Ville-Marie, QC J9V 2B7
Tél: 819-622-1313; *Téléc:* 819-622-1333
le.reflet@cablevision.qc.ca
www.journallereflet.com
Circulation: 9 700 *Frequency:* Vendredi
Karen LaChapelle, Directrice

Ville-Marie: **Le Témiscamien**
22, rue Sainte-Anne, Ville-Marie, QC J9V 2B7
Tél: 819-622-1313; *Téléc:* 819-622-1333
www.journallereflet.com
Circulation: 8 500 *Frequency:* Mercredi

Wakefield: **The Low Down to Hull & Back News**
PO Box 99, Wakefield, QC J0X 3G0
Tel: 819-459-2222; *Fax:* 819-459-3831
thelowdown@earthlink.net
www.lowdownonline.com
Circulation: 2,990 *Frequency:* Wed.
Nikki Mantell, Publisher

Windsor: **L'Etincelle**
193, rue St-Georges, Windsor, QC J1S 1J7
Tél: 819-845-2705; *Téléc:* 819-845-5520
journal@letincelle.qc.ca
www.letincelle.qc.ca
Circulation: 10 093 *Frequency:* Samedi
Claude Frenette, Éditeur

Évain: **Ensemble pour bâtir**
CP 424, 200, rue Côté ouest, Évain, QC J0Z 1Y0
Tél: 819-768-2495
Circulation: 1 400
Jocelyne Maynard, Présidente

Saskatchewan

Daily Newspapers in Saskatchewan

Moose Jaw: **Times-Herald**
44 Fairford St. West, Moose Jaw, SK S6H 1V1
Tel: 306-692-6441; *Fax:* 306-692-2101
moose.jaw.times@sasknet.sk.ca
www.mjtimes.sk.ca
Circulation: 10,500 *Frequency:* Evening
Rob Clark, Publisher
Rob Clark, Publisher/General Manager

North Battleford: **Battlefords News-Optimist**
Battlefords Publishing Ltd., PO Box 1029, 892 - 104th St., North Battleford, SK S9A 3E6
Tel: 306-445-7261; *Fax:* 306-445-3223
Toll-Free: 866-549-9979
battlefords.publishing@sasktel.net
Circulation: 2,997 *Frequency:* Wed.; also Regional Optimist/Advertiser-Post, Fri.
Alana Schweitzer, Contact

Prince Albert: **Daily Herald**
30 - 10th St. East, Prince Albert, SK S6V 0Y5
Tel: 306-764-4276; *Fax:* 306-763-3119
editorial@paherald.sk.ca
www.paherald.sk.ca
Circulation: 8,784 *Frequency:* Evening
Ian Jensen, Publisher & General Manager

Regina: **The Leader-Post**
PO Box 2020, 1964 Park St., Regina, SK S4P 3G4
Tel: 306-565-8211; *Fax:* 306-565-8812
www.leader-post.sk.ca/
Circulation: 70,203 *Frequency:* Afternoon
Greg MacLean, Publisher
Bob Hughes, Editor

Saskatoon: **The StarPhoenix**
204 - 5th Ave. North, Saskatoon, SK S7K 2P1
Tel: 306-657-6231; *Fax:* 306-657-6437
Toll-Free: 800-667-2002
spnews@sp.canwest.com
www.thestarphoenix.com
Circulation: 54,093 Mon.-Thu., 62,117 Fri., 51,199 Sat.
Frequency: Morning
Steve Gibb, Editor
Dale Brin, Publisher

Other Newspapers in Saskatchewan

Assiniboia: **Assiniboia Times**
PO Box 910, 410 - 1st Ave. East, Assiniboia, SK S0H 0B0
Tel: 306-642-5901; *Fax:* 306-642-4519
Circulation: 2,413 *Frequency:* Fri.
Glen Hall, Publisher

Biggar: **Biggar Independent**
PO Box 40, 102 - 3rd Ave. West, Biggar, SK S0K 0M0
Tel: 306-948-3344; *Fax:* 306-948-2133
Circulation: 1,891 *Frequency:* Monday
Daryl Hasein, Publisher

Canora: **Canora Courier**
PO Box 746, Canora, SK S0A 0L0
Tel: 306-563-5131; *Fax:* 306-563-6144
Circulation: 1,639 *Frequency:* Wed.
Brant Kersey, Publisher

Canora: **Kamsack Times**
PO Box 746, Canora, SK S0A 0L0
Tel: 306-563-5131; *Fax:* 306-563-6144
Circulation: 1,260 *Frequency:* Thu.
Brant Kersey, Publisher

Canora: **Norquay North Star**
PO Box 746, Canora, SK S0A 0L0
Tel: 306-563-5131; *Fax:* 306-563-6144
Circulation: 599 *Frequency:* Wed.
Brant Kersey, Publisher

Canora: **Preeceville Progress**
PO Box 746, Canora, SK S0A 0L0
Tel: 306-563-5131; *Fax:* 306-563-6144
Circulation: 1,169 *Frequency:* Thur.
Brant Kersey, Publisher

Carlyle: **Carlyle Observer**
PO Box 160, 132 Main St., Carlyle, SK S0C 0R0
Tel: 306-453-2525; *Fax:* 306-453-2938
observer@saskte.net
www.carlyleobserver.com
Circulation: 3,076 *Frequency:* Fri.
Cindy Moffatt, General Manager

Carnduff: **Carnduff Gazette-Post News**
PO Box 220, 106 Broadway St., Carnduff, SK S0C 0S0
Tel: 306-482-3252; *Fax:* 306-482-3373
www.sasknews.com/info/carnduff.shtml
Circulation: 1,246 *Frequency:* Monday
Bill Grass, Publisher

Coronach: **Triangle News**
PO Box 689, Coronach, SK S0H 0Z0
Tel: 306-267-3381; *Fax:* 306-267-3381
Circulation: 1,000 *Frequency:* Monday
Randall Burns, Publisher

Craik: **Craik Weekly News**
PO Box 360, 221 - 3rd St., Craik, SK S0G 0V0
Tel: 306-734-2313; *Fax:* 306- -
Circulation: 880 *Frequency:* Tuesday
Harve Friedel, Publisher

Cut Knife: **Highway 40 Courier**
PO Box 639, 200 Steel St., Cut Knife, SK S0M 0N0
Tel: 306-398-4901; *Fax:* 306-398-4909
ckcouriernews@sasktel.net
Circulation: 579 *Frequency:* Wed.
Lorie Gibson, Publisher

Davidson: **Davidson Leader**
PO Box 786, 205 Washington Ave., Davidson, SK S0G 1A0
Tel: 306-567-2047; *Fax:* 306-567-2900
lmt@sasktel.net
Circulation: 1,319 *Frequency:* Monday
Tara de Ryk, Publisher & Editor

Esterhazy: **Esterhazy Miner-Journal**
PO Box 1000, 606 - 2nd Ave., Esterhazy, SK S0A 0X0
Tel: 306-745-6669; *Fax:* 306-745-2699
miner.journal@sasktel.net
www.minerjournal.com
Circulation: 1,627 *Frequency:* Monday
Brenda Matchett, Publisher

Estevan: **Estevan Lifestyles**
PO Box 783, Estevan, SK S4A 2A6
Tel: 306-634-5112; *Fax:* 306-634-2588
lifestyles@sasktel.net
www.sasklifestyles.com
Circulation: 7,918 *Frequency:* Fri.
Teresa Howie, Publisher
Teresa Howie, Editor

***Estevan:* Estevan Mercury**
PO Box 730, 68 Souris Ave. North, Estevan, SK S4A 2A6
Tel: 306-634-2654; *Fax:* 306-634-3934
www.estevanmercury.ca
Circulation: 3,308 *Frequency:* Wed.
Peter Ng, Publisher

***Estevan:* Estevan Southeast Trader Express**
PO Box 730, Estevan, SK S4A 2A6
Tel: 306-634-2654;
www.estevanmercury.ca
Circulation: 8,661 *Frequency:* Fri.
Andrea Heath, Publisher
Robert Heath, Publisher

***Estevan:* The Southeast Trader Express**
PO Box 730, 68 Souris Ave. North, Estevan, SK S4A 2A6
Tel: 306-634-2654; *Fax:* 306-634-3934
mercury_merc1@sasktel.net
www.estevanmercury.ca
Circulation: 8,661 *Frequency:* Fri.
Peter Ng, Publisher

***Eston:* Eston Press Review**
PO Box 787, 112 Main St. West, Eston, SK S0L 1A0
Tel: 306-962-3221; *Fax:* 306-962-4445
Circulation: 1,042 *Frequency:* Tuesday
Stuart Crump, Publisher
Tim Crump, Editor

***Foam Lake:* Foam Lake Review**
PO Box 550, 325 Main St., Foam Lake, SK S0A 1A0
Tel: 306-272-3262; *Fax:* 306-272-4521
Circulation: 1,582 *Frequency:* Monday
Bob Johnson, Publisher

***Fort Qu'appelle:* Fort Qu'Appelle Times**
PO Box 940, 141 Broadway St. West, Fort Qu'appelle, SK S0G 1S0
Tel: 306-332-5526; *Fax:* 306-332-5414
forttimes@sasktel.net
Circulation: 1,462 *Frequency:* Tuesday
Sandra Huber, Publisher

***Gravelbourg:* Gravelbourg Tribune**
PO Box 1017, 611 Main St., Gravelbourg, SK S0H 1X0
Tel: 306-648-3479; *Fax:* 306-648-2520
gravelbourgtribune@sasktel.net
Circulation: 1,221 *Frequency:* Monday
Paul Boisvert, Publisher

***Grenfell:* Broadview Express**
PO Box 189, 813 Desmond St., Grenfell, SK S0G 2B0
Tel: 306-697-2722; *Fax:* 306-697-2689
stoneprint@sasktel.net
Circulation: 526 *Frequency:* Tuesday
Dwayne Stone, Publisher

***Grenfell:* Grenfell Sun**
PO Box 189, 813 Desmond St., Grenfell, SK S0G 2B0
Tel: 306-697-2722; *Fax:* 306-697-2689
stoneprint@sasktel.net
Circulation: 1,114 *Frequency:* Tuesday
Dwayne Stone, Publisher

***Gull Lake:* Gull Lake Advance**
PO Box 628, 1462 Conrad, Gull Lake, SK S0N 1A0
Tel: 306-672-3373; *Fax:* 306-672-3573
gladvance@sasktel.net
glcn.com/town/business/peters/peters.htm
Circulation: 1,245 *Frequency:* Tuesday
John Peters, Publisher

***Herbert:* Herbert Herald**
PO Box 399, 716 Herbert Ave., Herbert, SK S0H 2A0
Tel: 306-784-2422; *Fax:* 306-784-3246
Circulation: 1,663 *Frequency:* Tuesday
Rhonda Ens, Publisher & Editor

***Hudson Bay:* Hudson Bay Post Review**
PO Box 10, 20 Railway Ave., Hudson Bay, SK S0E 0Y0
Tel: 306-865-2771; *Fax:* 306-865-2340
post.review@sasktel.net
Circulation: 1,243 *Frequency:* Wed.
Larry Mitchell, Publisher

***Humboldt:* Humboldt Journal**
PO Box 970, Humboldt, SK S0K 2A0
Tel: 306-682-2561; *Fax:* 306-682-3322
journal.ads@sasktel.net
Circulation: 10,650 *Frequency:* Sunday, Wednesday; also, Humboldt Trader Regional (Sun.)
Kent Peters, Publisher

***Indian Head:* Indian Head-Wolseley News**
PO Box 70, 311 Grand Ave., Indian Head, SK S0G 2K0
Tel: 306-695-3565
Circulation: 1,735 *Frequency:* Tuesday
Ken McCabe, Publisher

***Ituna:* The Ituna News**
PO Box 413, Ituna, SK S0A 1N0
Tel: 306-795-2412; *Fax:* 306-795-3621
Circulation: 822 *Frequency:* Monday
Bob Johnson, Publisher

***Kindersley:* Kerrobert Citizen Dispatch**
PO Box 1150, 919 Main St., Kindersley, SK S0L 1S0
Tel: 306-463-4611; *Fax:* 306-463-6505
Circulation: 611 *Frequency:* Wed.
Tim Crump, Editor
Barry Malindine, Manager, Sales
Stewart Crump, General Manager

***Kindersley:* Kindersley Clarion**
PO Box 1150, 919 Main St., Kindersley, SK S0L 1S0
Tel: 306-463-4611; *Fax:* 306-463-6505
Circulation: 2,308 *Frequency:* Wed.
Stewart Crump, Publisher

***Kindersley:* The Leader News**
PO Box 1150, 919 Main St., Kindersley, SK S0L 1S0
Tel: 306-463-4611; *Fax:* 306-463-6505
Circulation: 1,025 *Frequency:* Wed.

***Kindersley:* The Luseland Dispatch**
PO Box 1150, 919 Main St., Kindersley, SK S0L 1S0
Tel: 306-463-4611; *Fax:* 306-463-6505
Circulation: 846

***Kindersley:* West Central Crossroads**
PO Box 1150, 919 Main St., Kindersley, SK S0L 1S0
Tel: 306-463-4611; *Fax:* 306-463-6505
Circulation: 14,886 *Frequency:* Monday
Stewart Crump, Publisher

***Kipling:* Kipling Citizen**
PO Box 329, Kipling, SK S0J 2S0
Tel: 306-736-2535; *Fax:* 306-736-8445
www.kiplingcitizen.com
Circulation: 1,547 *Frequency:* Fri.
Michael Kearns, Publisher

***La Ronge:* La Ronge Northerner**
PO Box 1350, 715 La Ronge Ave., La Ronge, SK S0J 1L0
Tel: 306-425-3344; *Fax:* 306-425-2827
Circulation: 1,485 *Frequency:* Thursday
Brenda Fitch, Publisher

***Langenburg:* Langenburg Four-Town Journal**
PO Box 68, Langenburg, SK S0A 2A0
Tel: 306-743-2617; *Fax:* 306-743-2299
Circulation: 1,463 *Frequency:* Wed.
Bill Johnston, Publisher

***Lanigan:* Lanigan Advisor**
PO Box 1029, 80 Downing Dr., Lanigan, SK S0K 2M0
Tel: 306-365-2010; *Fax:* 306-365-3388
Circulation: 1,072 *Frequency:* Monday
Linda Mallett, Publisher

***Lumsden:* New Waterfront Press**
PO Box 507, 635 James St. North, Lumsden, SK S0G 3C0
Tel: 306-731-3143; *Fax:* 306-731-2277
watpress@sasktel.net
Circulation: 3,795 *Frequency:* Thursday; 4 supplements (Agriculture, Farm Progress Show, Remembrance Day, Christmas)
Lucien Chouinard, Publisher
Jacqueline Chouinard, Publisher

***Macklin:* Macklin Mirror**
PO Box 100, Macklin, SK S0L 2C0
Tel: 306-753-2424; *Fax:* 306-753-2424
macklinmirror@sasktel.net
Circulation: 990 *Frequency:* Wed.
Robert Brost, Editor

***Maidstone:* Maidstone Mirror**
PO Box 1029, 892-104 St., Maidstone, SK S9A 3T6
Tel: 306-445-7261; *Fax:* 306-445-3223
Toll-Free: 866-549-9979
battlefords.publishing@sasktel.net
Circulation: 533 *Frequency:* Wed.
Alana Schweitzer, Manager, Sales
Becky Doig, Editor

***Maple Creek:* Maple Creek & Southwest Advance Times**
PO Box 1328, Maple Creek, SK S0N 1N0
Tel: 306-662-2100; *Fax:* 306-662-5005
www.maplecreektimes.ca
Circulation: 2,278 *Frequency:* Tuesday
Mike Hertz, Publisher

***Maple Creek:* Maple Creek News**
PO Box 1328, 116 Harder St., Maple Creek, SK S0N 1N0
Tel: 306-662-2133; *Fax:* 306-662-3092
www.maplecreeknews.com
Circulation: 2,500 *Frequency:* Thursday
Mike Hertz, Publisher

***Meadow Lake:* Meadow Lake Progress**
PO Box 879, 311 Centre St., Meadow Lake, SK S9X 1Y6
Tel: 306-236-5265; *Fax:* 306-236-3130
editor@meadowlakeprogress.com
www.meadowlakeprogress.com
Circulation: 2,703 *Frequency:* Sunday
Donna Ritco, Publisher

***Meadow Lake:* Northern Pride**
205A - 3rd Ave. East, Meadow Lake, SK S9X 1Z4
Tel: 306-236-5353; *Fax:* 306-236-5962
Circulation: 4,281 *Frequency:* Tuesday
Terry Villeneuve, Publisher

***Melfort:* Kinistino/Birch Hills Post Gazette**
PO Box 1300, Melfort, SK S0E 1A0
Tel: 306-752-5737; *Fax:* 306-752-5358
Circulation: 1,257 *Frequency:* Wed.
Ken Sorenson, Publisher

***Melfort:* Melfort Journal**
PO Box 1300, 901 Main St., Melfort, SK S0E 1A0
Tel: 306-752-5737; *Fax:* 306-752-5358
Toll-Free: 800-752-9559
journal@melfortjournal.com
www.melfortjournal.com
Circulation: 2,774 *Frequency:* Tuesday
Ken Sorenson, Publisher, Advertising
Ken Sorenson, General Manager
Greg Wiseman, Editor

***Melville:* Melville Advance**
PO Box 1420, Melville, SK S0A 2P0
Tel: 306-728-5448; *Fax:* 306-728-4004
editor@melvilleadvance.com
www.melvilleadvance.com
Circulation: 2,818 *Frequency:* Wed.
Mark Orosz, Publisher
Lin Orosz, Publisher

***Moose Jaw:* Moose Jaw This Week**
44 Fairford St. West, Moose Jaw, SK S6H 6E4
Tel: 306-692-6441; *Fax:* 306-692-2101
Circulation: 19,478 *Frequency:* Sunday
Rob Clark, Publisher

***Moosomin:* Moosomin World-Spectator**
PO Box 250, 624 Main St., Moosomin, SK S0G 3N0
Tel: 306-435-2445; *Fax:* 306-435-3969
world_spectator@sasktel.net
www.world-spectator.com
Circulation: 3,128 *Frequency:* Monday
Kevin Weedmark, Publisher & Editor

***Nipawin:* Nipawin Journal**
PO Box 2014, 220 Centre St., Nipawin, SK S0E 1E0
Tel: 306-862-4618; *Fax:* 306-862-4566
njournal@sk.sympatico.ca
www.nipawinjournal.com
Circulation: 3,115 *Frequency:* Wed.
Ryan Kiedowski, Editor
Kathy McAuley, Publisher

***Nokomis:* Southey, The Market Connection**
PO Box 340, 103 First Ave. West, Nokomis, SK S0G 3R0
Tel: 306-528-2020; *Fax:* 306-528-2090
lmt@sasktel.net
Circulation: 10,700
Lyle Emmons, Publisher

***Nokomis:* Strasbourg, Last Mountain Times**
PO Box 340, Nokomis, SK S0G 3R0
Tel: 306-528-2020; *Fax:* 306-528-2090
lmt@sasktel.net
Circulation: 1,323 *Frequency:* Tuesday; also The Market Connection (10,700)
Lyle Emmons, Publisher

***North Battleford:* News-Optimist Sunday Edition**
PO Box 1029, North Battleford, SK S9A 3E6
Tel: 306-445-7261; *Fax:* 306-445-3223
Toll-Free: 866-549-9979
battlefords.publishing@sasktel.net
Circulation: 2,997 *Frequency:* Wed.
Alana Schweitzer, Manager, Sales
Becky Doig, Editor

***North Battleford:* Regional Optimist**
PO Box 1029, 892 - 104 St., North Battleford, SK S9A 3E6
Tel: 306-445-7261; *Fax:* 306-445-3223
Toll-Free: 866-549-9979
battlefords.publishing@sasktel.net
Circulation: 14,056 *Frequency:* Fri.
Alana Schweitzer, Publisher

***North Battleford:* Turtleford Northwest Neighbours**
PO Box 1029, North Battleford, SK S9A 3E6
Tel: 306-445-7261; *Fax:* 306-445-3223
Toll-Free: 866-549-9979
battlefords.publishing@sasktel.net
Circulation: 819 *Frequency:* Wed.
Alana Schweitzer, Manager, Sales
Becky Doig, Editor

***Outlook:* The Outlook**
PO Box 1717, 108 Saskatchewan Ave. East, Outlook, SK S0L 2N0
Tel: 306-867-8262; *Fax:* 306-867-9556
www.theoutlook.ca
Circulation: 2,170 *Frequency:* Monday
Terry Jenson, Publisher

***Oxbow:* Oxbow Herald**
PO Box 420, Oxbow, SK S0C 2B0
Tel: 306-483-2323; *Fax:* 306-483-5258
oxbow.herald@sasktel.net
www.oxbowherald.com
Circulation: 1,329 *Frequency:* Monday
Ken Pedlar, Publisher

***Pierceland:* The Beaver River Banner**
PO Box 700, Pierceland, SK S0M 2K0
Tel: 306-839-4496; *Fax:* 306-839-2306
br.banner@sasktel.net
Circulation: 1,715 *Frequency:* Tuesday
Robin Harrison, Publisher
Brad Harrison, Publisher

***Radville:* Radville Star**
PO Box 370, Radville, SK S0C 2G0
Tel: 306-869-2202; *Fax:* 306-869-2533
radstar@hotmail.com
Circulation: 1,128 *Frequency:* Wed.
George Hay, Publisher

***Redvers:* The Optimist**
PO Box 490, Redvers, SK S0C 2H0
Tel: 306-452-3363; *Fax:* 306-452-6408
Circulation: 1,577 *Frequency:* Saturday
Bruce Schwanke, Publisher

***Regina:* Journal L'eau vive**
410, av Victoria, Regina, SK S4N 0P6
Tél: 306-347-0481; *Téléc:* 306-565-3450
direction@accesscomm.ca
www.leauvive.net
Circulation: 1,400 *Frequency:* Thursday
Réjeanne Geoffrion-Flichel, Directrice générale

***Regina:* Regina Sun**
PO Box 2020, 1964 Park St., Regina, SK S4P 3G4
Tel: 306-565-8250; *Fax:* 306-565-8350
Circulation: 67,318 Wed.; 68,212 Sun. city, 20,528 Sun. rural
Frequency: Wed., Sun.

***Rosetown:* Rosetown Eagle**
PO Box 130, Rosetown, SK S0L 2V0
Tel: 306-882-4202; *Fax:* 306-882-4204
rosetown.eagle@sasktel.net
Circulation: 2,190 *Frequency:* Monday
Danny Pagé, Publisher

***Rosthern:* Saskatchewan Valley News**
PO Box 10, Rosthern, SK S0K 3R0
Tel: 306-232-4865; *Fax:* 306-232-4694
valleynews@sasktel.net
Circulation: 2,785 *Frequency:* Wed.
Renay Kowalczyk, Editor

***Saskatoon:* Saskatoon Sun**
204 - 5th Ave. North, Saskatoon, SK S7K 2P1
Tel: 306-657-6231; *Fax:* 306-657-6437
Toll-Free: 800-667-2002
spnews@sp.canwest.com
Circulation: 96,200 *Frequency:* Sunday
Wayne Roberts, Editor
Dale Brin, Publisher

***Shaunavon:* Shaunavon Standard**
PO Box 729, Shaunavon, SK S0N 2M0
Tel: 306-297-4144; *Fax:* 306-297-3357
standard@sk.sympatico.ca
Circulation: 1,700 *Frequency:* Tuesday
Leslie Corrins, Publisher

***Shellbrook:* Shellbrook Chronicle**
PO Box 10, Shellbrook, SK S0J 2E0
Tel: 306-747-2442; *Fax:* 306-747-3000
www.shellbrookchronicle.com
Circulation: 4,478 *Frequency:* Fri.
Clark Pepper, Publisher

***Shellbrook:* Spiritwood Herald**
PO Box 10, Shellbrook, SK S0J 2E0
Tel: 306-747-2442; *Fax:* 306-747-3000
www.spiritwoodherald.com
Circulation: 2,770 *Frequency:* Fri.
Clark Pepper, Publisher

***Swift Current:* The Southwest Booster**
PO Box 1330, 30 - 4th Ave. NW, Swift Current, SK S9H 3X4
Tel: 306-773-9321; *Fax:* 306-773-9136
boosternews@swbooster.com
www.swbooster.com
Circulation: 19,100 *Frequency:* Saturday
Bob Watson, Publisher
Scott Anderson, Editor

***Tisdale:* Tisdale Recorder**
PO Box 1660, Tisdale, SK S0E 1T0
Tel: 306-873-4515; *Fax:* 306-873-4712
Circulation: 1,554 *Frequency:* Wed.
Larry Mitchell, Publisher

***Unity:* The Northwest Herald**
PO Box 309, Unity, SK S0K 4L0
Tel: 306-228-2267; *Fax:* 306-228-2767
northwest.herald@sasktel.net
Circulation: 1,793 *Frequency:* Monday
Dan Feser, Co-Publisher
Lisa Feser, Co-Publisher

***Unity:* Press**
PO Box 309, 304 Main St., Unity, SK S0K 4L0
Tel: 306-228-2267; *Fax:* 306-228-2767
northwest.herald@sasktel.net
Circulation: 672 *Frequency:* Monday
Joanne Urlacher, Publisher

***Wadena:* Kelvington Radio**
PO Box 100, Wadena, SK S0A 4J0
Tel: 306-338-2231; *Fax:* 306-338-3421
wadena.news@sasktel.net
Circulation: 988 *Frequency:* Wed.
Bruce Squires, Co-Publishers
Alison Squires, Co-Publishers

***Wadena:* Wadena News**
PO Box 100, 101 1st St. N.E., Wadena, SK S0A 4J0
Tel: 306-338-2231; *Fax:* 306-338-3421
wadena.news@sasktel.net
Circulation: 3,114 *Frequency:* Wed.
Bruce Squires, Co-Publisher
Alison Squires, Co-Publisher

***Wakaw:* Wakaw Recorder**
PO Box 9, Wakaw, SK S0K 4P0
Tel: 306-233-4325; *Fax:* 306-233-4386
Circulation: 2,159 *Frequency:* Wed.
Dwayne Biccum, Publisher

***Warman:* The Country Press**
PO Box 880, Warman, SK S0K 4S0
Tel: 306-934-6191; *Fax:* 306-668-8250
countrypress@sasktel.net
Circulation: 11,351 *Frequency:* Wed.
C. Lynn Handford, General Manager

***Watrous:* Watrous Manitou**
PO Box 100, 309 Main St., Watrous, SK S0K 4T0
Tel: 306-946-3343; *Fax:* 306-946-2026
watrous.manitou@sasktel.net
Circulation: 1,827 *Frequency:* Monday
Nicole Lay, Publisher
Robin Lay, Publisher

***Watson:* East Central Connection**
#100-102 Main St., Watson, SK S0E 1T0
Tel: 306-287-4388; *Fax:* 306-287-3308
eastcentral@sk.sympatico.ca
Circulation: 9,139 *Frequency:* Fri.
Karen Mitchell, Publisher

***Watson:* The Naicam News**
PO Box 576, #100, 102 Main St., Watson, SK S0K 4V0
Tel: 306-287-4388; *Fax:* 306-287-3308
Circulation: 330 *Frequency:* Fri.
Karen Mitchell, Publisher

***Watson:* Watson Witness**
PO Box 129, 313 Railway Ave. West, Watson, SK S0K 4V0
Tel: 306-287-3245; *Fax:* 306-287-4333
Circulation: 1,562 *Frequency:* Wed.
Ken Sopkow, Publisher

***Weyburn:* Weyburn Review**
PO Box 400, Weyburn, SK S4H 2K4
Tel: 306-842-7487; *Fax:* 306-842-0282
production@weyburnreview.com
www.weyburnreview.com
Circulation: 4,139 *Frequency:* Wed.; also Weyburn Booster (Mon.; Circ. 12,990; Sat.; Circ.7,698)
Darryl Ward, Publisher
Patricia Ward, Editor-in-chief

***Weyburn:* Weyburn This Week**
19 - 11th St. NE, Weyburn, SK S4H 1J1
Tel: 306-842-3900; *Fax:* 306-842-2515
weyburnthisweek@sasktel.net
www.weyburnthisweek.com
Circulation: 6,048 *Frequency:* Fri.
Penny Tochor, General Manager
Troy Kramm, Editor

***Whitewood:* Whitewood Herald**
PO Box 160, Whitewood, SK S0G 5C0
Tel: 306-735-2230; *Fax:* 306-735-2899
www.whitewoodherald.sk.ca
Circulation: 812 *Frequency:* Monday
Elaine Ashfield, Publisher

***Wolseley:* The RTown News**
PO Box 89, 219 Poplar St., Wolseley, SK S0G 5H0
Tel: 306-698-2271; *Fax:* 306-698-2808
unos@sasktel.net
www.saskfarmnews.com
Circulation: 2,200 *Frequency:* Fri. (50 times a year)
Rick Dahlman, Editor/Publisher

***Wolseley:* The Wolseley Bulletin**
PO Box 89, 284 Oak St., Wolseley, SK S0G 5H0
Tel: 306-698-2271; *Fax:* 306-698-2808
www.saskfarmnews.com
Circulation: 273 *Frequency:* Fri.
Eleanor Dahlman, Publisher

***Wynyard:* Wynyard Advance/Gazette**
Bowes Publishers Limited, PO Box 10, 117 Ave. B East, Wynyard, SK S0A 4T0
Tel: 306-554-2224; *Fax:* 306-554-3226
w.advance@sasktel.net
www.wynyardadvance.com
Circulation: 1,757 *Frequency:* Monday
Bob Johnson, Publisher

***Yorkton:* The News Review Extra**
18 - 1st Ave. North, Yorkton, SK S3N 1J4
Tel: 306-783-7355; *Fax:* 306-783-9138
info@yorktonnews.com
www.yorktonnews.com
Circulation: 6,575 *Frequency:* Thursday
Ken Chyz, Publisher

***Yorkton:* Yorkton This Week**
PO Box 1300, 20 Third Ave., Yorkton, SK S3N 2X3
Tel: 306-782-2465; *Fax:* 306-786-1898
www.yorktonthisweek.com
Circulation: 4,680 *Frequency:* Wed.
Neil Thom, Publisher

Yukon Territory

Daily Newspapers in Yukon Territory

Whitehorse: **The Whitehorse Star**
2149 - 2nd Ave., Whitehorse, YT Y1A 1C5
Tel: 867-668-2060; *Fax:* 867-668-7130
star@whitehorsestar.com
www.whitehorsestar.com
Circulation: Mon.-Thu. 2,900; Fri. 4,200 *Frequency:* Weekdays
Jackie Pierce, Publisher
Jim Butler, Editor
403/667-4481

Other Newspapers in Yukon Territory

Whitehorse: **L'Aurore boréale**
302, rue Strickland, Whitehorse, YT Y1A 2K1
Tél: 867-667-2931; *Téléc:* 867-667-2932
auroredir@afy.yk.ca
www.afy.ca/aurore
Circulation: 945 *Frequency:* Bi-mensuel; français
Marie-Hélène Comeau, Journaliste
Odette Poirier, Coordonatrice, Publicité
Cécile Girard, Directrice

Whitehorse: **Yukon News**
211 Wood St., Whitehorse, YT Y1A 2E4
Tel: 867-667-6285; *Fax:* 867-668-3755
stever@yukon-news.com
www.yukon-news.com
Circulation: Mon 5,248 Wed. 5,613, Fri 7,243; Total 18,104.
D.S. Robertson, Publisher
Richard Mostyn, Editor

Magazine Name Index

D

E

Magazines

Business

Advertising, Marketing, Sales

Adnews Insight Magazine
#1463, 1011 Upper Middle Rd., Oakville, ON L6H 5Z9
Tel: 416-252-9400; *Fax:* 416-252-8002
info@adnews.com
www.adnews.com
Frequency: 4 times a year
Robert A. Bale, Publisher
Derek Winkler, Editor

Adnews Online Daily
#1463, 1011 Upper Middle Rd. East, Oakville, ON L6H 5Z9
Tel: 416-252-9400; *Fax:* 416-252-8002
info@adnews.com
www.adnews.com
Circulation: 33,000 *Frequency:* Daily
Robert Bale, Publisher

Blitz Magazine Inc
#544, 1489 Marine Dr., West Vancouver, BC V7T 1B8
Tel: 604-921-8735; *Fax:* 604-921-8738
Toll-Free: 866-632-5489
editor@blitzmagazine.com
www.blitzmagazine.com
Circulation: 10,000 *Frequency:* 6 times a year
Louise Aird, Publisher & Editor-in-chief

Boards
#500, 366 Adelaide St. West, Toronto, ON M5V 1R9
Tel: 416-408-2300; *Fax:* 416-408-0870
Toll-Free: 866-262-7371
drankin@brunico.com
www.boardsmag.com
Circulation: 11,250
Russell Goldstein, Publisher, rgoldstein@brunico.com
Rae Ann Fera, Editor, raeann@boardsmag.com

Canadian Advertising Rates & Data
1 Mount Pleasant Rd., 7th Fl., Toronto, ON M4Y 2Y5
Tel: 416-764-2000; *Fax:* 416-764-1709
Toll-Free: 800-265-3561
www.cardonline.ca
Circulation: 2,100 *Frequency:* Monthly
Bruce Richards, Publisher, bruce.richards@cardonline.rogers.com
Bruce Richards, Publisher

Canadian Direct Marketing News
#302, 137 Main St. North, Markham, ON L3P 1Y2
Tel: 905-201-6600; *Fax:* 905-201-6601
Toll-Free: 800-688-1838
home@dmn.ca
www.dmn.ca
Circulation: 8,058 *Frequency:* Monthly, plus annual directory of suppliers & annual directories The List of Lists...The DM Industry Sourcebook & the Canadian Call Centre Industry Directory
Ron Glen, Editor
Mark Henry, Ad Sales
Steve Lloyd, Publisher & President

The Chronicle of Healthcare Marketing
Tel: 905-273-9116; *Fax:* 905-273-4322
Toll-Free: 866-633-4766
health@chronicle.org
www.chronicle.ca
Circulation: 2,159 *Frequency:* 9 times a year
Mitchell Shannon, Publisher
R. Allan Ryan, Editorial Director

Contact
Canadian Professional Sales Assn., #800, 310 Front St., Toronto, ON M5V 3B5
Tel: 416-408-2685; *Fax:* 416-408-2684
www.cpsa.com
Circulation: 37,125 *Frequency:* 6 times a year
Bernadette Johnson, Editor
Harvey Copeman, Vice-President, Sales & Marketing

Direct Marketing News
#302, 137 Main St. North, Markham, ON L3P 1Y2
Tel: 905-201-6600; *Fax:* 905-201-6601
www.dmn.ca
Ron Glen, Editor

Ethnic Media & Markets
1 Mount Pleasant Rd., 7th Fl., Toronto, ON M4Y 2Y5
Tel: 416-764-1606; *Fax:* 416-764-1709
bruce.richards@cardonline.rogers.com
www.cardonline.ca
Circulation: 1,500 *Frequency:* 2 times a year
Bruce Richards, Publisher

Imprint Canada
#16, 190 Marycroft Ave., Woodbridge, ON L4L 5Y2
Tel: 905-856-2600; *Fax:* 905-856-2667
Toll-Free: 877-895-7022
feedback@imprintcanada.com
www.imprintcanada.com
Circulation: 6,700
Tony Muccilli, Publisher

Infopresse
Tél: 514-842-5873; *Téléc:* 514-842-2422
redaction@infopresse.com
www.infopresse.com
Circulation: 7 500 *Frequency:* 10 fois par an
Charles Grandmont, Rédacteur-en-chef
Bruno Gautier, Éditeur

Kidscreen
#500, 366 Adelaide St. West, Toronto, ON M5V 1R9
Tel: 416-408-2300; *Fax:* 416-408-0870
Toll-Free: 800-543-4512
dmacneil@brunico.com
www.kidscreen.com
Circulation: 11,500 *Frequency:* Monthly
Donna MacNeil, Vice-President & Group Publisher, dmacneil@brunico.com
Jocelyn Christie, Editor

Marketing Magazine
Tel: 416-596-5853; *Fax:* 416-596-3482
www.marketingmag.ca
Circulation: 10,187 *Frequency:* Weekly
Richard Elliott, Executive Publisher

Marketwire
48 Yonge St., 8 Fl., Toronto, ON M5E 1G6
Tel: 416-362-0885; *Fax:* 416-955-0705
Toll-Free: 888-299-0338
www.marketwirecanada.com
Other information: Toll Free Fax: 1-800-363-9296
Michael J. Nowlan, President & CEO

The National List of Advertisers
1 Mount Pleasant Rd., 7th Fl., Toronto, ON M4Y 2Y5
Tel: 416-764-2000; *Fax:* 416-764-1709
bruce.richards@cardonline.rogers.com
www.cardonline.ca
Circulation: 1,467 *Frequency:* Annually, December
Bruce Richards, Publisher

Publication Profiles
1 Mount Pleasant Rd., 7th Fl., Toronto, ON M4Y 2Y5
Tel: 416-764-2000; *Fax:* 416-764-1709
Toll-Free: 800-265-3561
bruce.richards@cardonline.rogers.com
www.cardonline.ca
Circulation: 1,432 *Frequency:* Annually, April
Bruce Richards, Publisher

Sales Promotion
Tel: 905-634-2100; *Fax:* 905-634-2238
www.sp-mag.com
Circulation: 14,000 *Frequency:* 6 times a year
Jackie Roth, Publisher
Nathan Mallet, Editor

Sign Media
Tel: 905-771-7333; *Fax:* 905-771-7336
Toll-Free: 800-409-8688
editor@kenilworth.com
www.signmedia.ca
Circulation: 13,200 *Frequency:* 6 times a year
Ellen Kral, Publisher
Blair Adams, Editorial Director
Erik Tolles, Sales Manager

Silver Screen
383 Lawrence Ave. West, Toronto, ON M5M 1B9
Tel: 416-488-3393; *Fax:* 416-488-5217
malcolm@msilver.com
www.msilver.com
Circulation: 1,800
Malcolm Silver, Publisher

Strategy
Tel: 416-408-2300; *Fax:* 416-408-0870
cmacdonald@brunico.com
www.strategymag.com
Circulation: 13,152 *Frequency:* 12 times a year
Claire MacDonald, Associate Publisher

Architecture

Award Magazine
4180 Lougheed Hwy., Burnaby, BC V5C 6A7
Tel: 604-299-7311; *Fax:* 604-299-9188
cwm@canadawide.com
www.canadawide.com
Circulation: 8,500 *Frequency:* 6 times a year
Les Wiseman, Editor
Peter Legge, Publisher

Canadian Architect
#800, 12 Concord Place, Toronto, ON M3C 4J2
Tel: 416-510-6845; *Fax:* 416-510-5140
Toll-Free: 800-268-7742
editors@canadianarchitect.com
www.canadianarchitect.com
Circulation: 10,323 *Frequency:* Monthly
Tom Arkell, Publisher

Construction Canada
Tel: 905-771-7333; *Fax:* 905-771-7336
Toll-Free: 800-409-8688
sales@constructioncanada.net
www.constructioncanada.net
Circulation: 12,109 *Frequency:* 6 times a year
Ellen Kral, Publisher
Blair Adams, Editorial Director
Cora Golden, Sales Director

Info-Link
#270, 3044 Bloor St. West, Toronto, ON M8X 2Y8
Tel: 416-604-7552;
info@infolinkcanada.com
www.infolinkcanada.com
Frequency: 4 times a year

Perspectives
c/o Canadian Association Publishers, PO Box 90510, 230 Markham Rd., Toronto, ON M1J 3N7
Tel: 416-955-1550; *Fax:* 416-955-1391
jeaton@capmagazines.ca
www.capmagazines.ca
Circulation: 6,200 *Frequency:* 4 times a year
Kelly Chase, Production
Jim Eaton, Publisher
Gordon Grice, Editor

Automobile, Cycle, & Automotive Accessories

L'Automobile
Tél: 514-630-5955; *Téléc:* 514-630-5980
Ligne sans frais: 800-363-1327
garbour@lautomobile.ca
Circulation: 12 829 *Frequency:* 6 fois par an; français
Guy Arbour, Éditeur et Rédacteur-en-chef

Automotive Parts & Technology
c/o Newcom Business Media Inc., 451 Attwell Dr., Toronto, ON M9W 5C4
Tel: 416-614-0955; *Fax:* 416-614-2781
info@aptmag.ca
www.aptmag.ca
Jim Glionna, Publisher

Automotive Service Data Book
Tel: 416-445-6641; *Fax:* 416-442-2261
Frequency: Annually, December
David Booth, Editor

Bike Trade Canada
#200, 260 Spadina Ave., Toronto, ON M5T 2E4
Tel: 416-977-2100; *Fax:* 416-977-9200
Toll-Free: 866-977-3325
info@pedalmag.com
www.pedalmag.com
Circulation: 5,000 *Frequency:* 3 times a year
Benjamin A. Sadavoy, Publisher & Editor
Sarah Carlin, Circulation

Bodyshop
Tel: 416-510-6763; *Fax:* 416-442-2213
www.bodyshopbiz.com
Circulation: 11,917 *Frequency:* 6 times a year
Andrew Ross, Publisher, aross@bodyshopbiz.com
JD Ney, Editor, jdney@bodyshopbiz.com

Canadian Auto World
c/o Formula Media Group, #4, 447 Speers Rd., Oakville, ON L6K 3S7
Tel: 905-842-6591; *Fax:* 905-842-4432
www.wheels.ca
Circulation: 4,529 *Frequency:* 6 times a year
Joseph Knycha, Editor-in-chief
J. Scott Robinson, Publisher

Canadian Technician
451 Attwell Dr., Toronto, ON M9W 5C4
Tel: 416-614-0955; *Fax:* 416-614-2781
www.canadiantechnician.com
Mark Vreugdenhill, Publisher
Allan Janssen, Editor

Collision Quarterly
Automotive Retailer Publishing Company Ltd., #1, 8980 Fraserwood Ct., Burnaby, BC V5J 5H7
Tel: 604-432-7987; *Fax:* 604-432-1756
publish@ara.bc.ca
www.ara.bc.ca
Circulation: 6,179 *Frequency:* 4 times a year
Kara Cunningham, Publisher & Editor
Kelly Johnston, Circulation Manager

Collision Repair Magazine
86 John St., Thornhill, ON L3T 1Y2
Tel: 905-889-3544; *Fax:* 905-889-4680
collisionrepair@rogers.com
www.collisionrepairmag.com
Darryl Simmons, Publisher
Mike Davey, Editor

Jobber News
Tel: 416-445-5600; *Fax:* 416-442-2213
www.autoserviceworld.com
Circulation: 11,136 *Frequency:* Monthly
Andrew Ross, Publisher

Octane
Fulcrum Publications, #201, 508 Lawrence Ave. West, Toronto, ON M5A 1A1
Tel: 416-504-0504; *Fax:* 416-256-3002
info@fulcrum.ca
www.fulcrum.ca
Circulation: 9,000 *Frequency:* 6 times a year

Revue Le Garagiste
Publications Rousseau et associés, 2938, Terrasse Abenaquis, Longueuil, QC J4M 2B3
Tél: 450-448-2220; *Téléc:* 450-448-1041
Ligne sans frais: 888-748-2220
admin@p-rousseau.com
www.legaragiste.com
Circulation: 18 200 *Frequency:* 8 fois par an
Rémy L. Rousseau, Éditeur

Service Station & Garage Management
Tel: 416-442-2275; *Fax:* 416-442-2213
Toll-Free: 800-268-7742
rtelford@ssgm.com
www.autoserviceworld.com
Other information: 1-800-387-0273 (U.S.)
Circulation: 31,200 *Frequency:* Monthly
Robert Telford, Publisher

Taxi News
38 Fairmount Cres., Toronto, ON M4L 2H4
Tel: 416-466-2328; *Fax:* 416-466-4220
taxinews@the-wire.com
www.taxinews.com
Circulation: 9,800 *Frequency:* Monthly
John Duffy, Publisher
William McOuat, Editor

Aviation & Aerospace

Airforce
c/o Airforce Productions Ltd., PO Box 2460 D, #400, 222 Somerset St. West, Ottawa, ON K1P 5W6
Tel: 613-232-2303; *Fax:* 613-232-2156
Toll-Free: 866-351-2322
vjohnson@airforce.ca
www.airforce.ca
Circulation: 16,526 *Frequency:* 4 times a year
Vic Johnson, Editor

Aviation Business Directory - Eastern Directory
#900, 1080 Howe St., Vancouver, BC V6Z 2T1
Tel: 604-606-4644; *Fax:* 604-687-1925
Toll-Free: 800-656-7598
markyelic@oppublishing.com
www.aviatormag.com
Frequency: annual
Jack Scholfield, Publisher
Katherine Kjaer, Manager, Sales

Aviation Business Directory - Western Directory
#900, 1080 Howe St., Vancouver, BC V6Z 2T1
Tel: 780-643-3962; *Fax:* 604-687-1925
Toll-Free: 800-656-7598
markyelic@oppublishing.com
www.aviationbusinessdirectories.com
Frequency: annual
Mark Yelic, Publisher, myelic@outdoorgroupmedia.com
Russ Niles, Editor, canadianaviator@xplornet.com

Canadian Aviator Magazine
#213, 3347 Oak St., Victoria, BC V8X 1R2
Tel: 250-658-6575; *Fax:* 250-658-6576
Toll-Free: 800-656-7598
sales@canadianaviatormagazine.com
www.canadianaviatormagazine.com
Circulation: 16,000 *Frequency:* 6 times a year
Mark Yelic, Publisher
Katherine Kjaer, Advertising Sales, pilotpresssale@shaw.ca
Garth Eichel, Editor, 250/386-6575, pilotpressedit@shaw.ca

Canadian Flight
#207, 75 Albert St., Ottawa, ON K1P 5E7
Tel: 613-236-4901; *Fax:* 613-236-8646
editorial@copanational.org
www.copanational.org
Circulation: 18,000 *Frequency:* Monthly; includes: Canadian Homebuilt Aircraft News, Canadian Ultralight News, Executive Flight News, Seaplane News, Aircraft Maintenance Engineers News, Canadian Plane Trade, Aviation Museum News
Michel Hell, Publisher

Helicopters
PO Box 530, 105 Donly Dr. South, Simcoe, ON N3Y 4N5
Tel: 519-428-3471; *Fax:* 519-429-3094
www.helicoptersmagazine.com
Frequency: 4 times a year

ICAO Journal
International Civil Aviation Organization, 999, rue University, Montréal, QC H3C 5H7
Tel: 514-954-8222; *Fax:* 514-954-6376
icaohq@icao.int
www.icao.int
Circulation: 15,000 *Frequency:* 6 issues a year; English, French & Spanish editions
Eric MacBurnie, Editor

Western & Eastern Canada - Aviation Business Directory
#900, 1080 Howe St., Vancouver, BC V6Z 2T1
Tel: 604-606-4644; *Fax:* 604-687-1925
markyelic@oppublishing.com
www.canadianaviatormagazine.com
Frequency: annual
Katherine Kjaer, Manager, Sales
Mark Yelic, Publisher

Wings
Toll-Free: 888-599-2228
www.wingsmagazine.com
Frequency: 6 times a year
Drew McCarthy, Editor

Baking & Bakers' Supplies

Bakers Journal
105 Donly Drive S., Simcoe, ON N3Y 4N5
Toll-Free: 888-599-2228
editor@bakersjournal.com
www.bakersjournal.com
Circulation: 6,800 *Frequency:* 10 times a year
Martin McAnulty, Publisher, mmcanulty@annexweb.com
Brian Hartz, Editor, bhartz@annexweb.com

La Fournée
Les Éditions Comestibles inc., 615, av Notre-Dame, Saint-Lambert, QC J4P 2K8
Tél: 514-990-6967; *Téléc:* 514-990-6967
Circulation: 4 718 *Frequency:* 4 fois par an; français
Lyne Gosselin, Editor

Barbers & Beauticians

Canadian Hairdresser Magazine
11 Spadina Rd., Toronto, ON M5R 2S9
Tel: 416-923-1111; *Fax:* 416-968-1031
Toll-Free: 800-588-5221
info@canhair.com
www.canhair.com
Circulation: 30,112 *Frequency:* 10 times a year
Joan Harrison, Managing Editor

Salon Magazine
Tel: 416-869-3131; *Fax:* 416-869-3008
Toll-Free: 800-720-6665
frontdesk@beautynet.com
www.beautynet.com
Circulation: 35,000 *Frequency:* 8 times a year; English (circ. 25,000) & French (circ. 10,000) editions
Brian Light, President
Gregory Robins, Website Producer

Boating & Yachting

Boating Business
Tel: 905-842-6591; *Fax:* 905-842-6843
Circulation: 5,375 *Frequency:* 6 times a year
J. Scott Robinson, Publisher
Valerie Tryer, Circulation Coordinator

Books

Access
c/o Ontario Library Association, #201, 50 Wellington St., Toronto, ON M5E 1C8
Tel: 416-363-3388; *Fax:* 416-941-9581
Toll-Free: 866-873-9867
info@accessola.com
www.accessola.com
Circulation: 4,500 *Frequency:* 4 times a year
Lori Knowles, Editor

Canadian Bookseller
Canadian Booksellers Association, #700, 789 Don Mills Rd., Toronto, ON M3C 1T5
Tel: 416-467-7883; *Fax:* 416-467-7886
Toll-Free: 866-788-0790
enquiries@cbabook.org
www.cbabook.org
Circulation: 2,500 *Frequency:* 6 times a year
Susan Dayus, Publisher & Executive Director

Feliciter
c/o Canadian Library Association, 328 Frank St., Ottawa, ON K2P 0X8
Tel: 613-232-9625; *Fax:* 613-563-9895
publishing@cla.ca
www.cla.ca
Circulation: 3,000 *Frequency:* 6 times a year
Don Butcher, Executive Director

Quill & Quire
111 Queen St. East, 3rd Fl., Toronto, ON M5C 1S2
Tel: 416-364-3333; *Fax:* 416-595-5415
info@quillandquire.com
www.quillandquire.com
Circulation: 5,265 *Frequency:* Monthly; supplement, Canadian Publishers' Directory (June & Dec.); ISSN: 0033-6491
Alison Jones, Publisher, 416/364-3333, ext.31

Teacher Librarian
The Scarecrow Press, Inc., 15200 NBN Way, Blue Ridge Summit, PA 17214
Tel: 717-794-3800; *Fax:* 717-794-3833
admin@teacherlibrarian.com
www.teacherlibrarian.com
Circulation: 7,500-10,000 *Frequency:* 5 times a year; ISSN: 1481-1782
Kim Tabor, Managing Editor
David V. Loertscher, Co-Editor
Esther Rosenfeld, Co-Editor
Edward Kurdyla, Publisher

Brides, Bridal

Weddings & Honeymoons
65 Helena Ave., Toronto, ON M6G 2H3
Tel: 416-653-4986; *Fax:* 416-653-2291
barwed@interlog.com
www.weddingshoneymoons.com
Circulation: 30,000 *Frequency:* 3 pa; ISSN: 1192-764X
Joyce Barshow, Publisher & Editor-in-chief

Broadcasting

Broadcast Dialogue
18 Turtle Path, Site 1, Box 150, Brechin, ON L0K 1B0
Tel: 705-484-0752;
broadcastdialogue@rogers.com
www.broadcastdialogue.com
Circulation: 7,200
Howard Christensen, Publisher, howard@broadcastdialogue.com
Barry Hamelin, Executive Director, barry@broadcastdialogue.comm

Broadcaster
Tel: 416-510-6871; *Fax:* 416-510-5134
Toll-Free: 800-268-7742
jcook@broadcastermagazine.com
www.broadcastermagazine.com
Circulation: 7,670 *Frequency:* monthly
James A. Cook, Publisher

Mediacaster
Tel: 416-510-6878; *Fax:* 416-510-5140
www.mediacastermagazine.com
Circulation: 6,800 *Frequency:* 12 times a year
Grenville Pinto, Publisher

Playback
#500, 366 Adelaide St. West, Toronto, ON M5V 1R9
Tel: 416-408-2300; *Fax:* 416-408-0870
Toll-Free: 888-278-6426
www.playbackmag.com
Circulation: 9,052 *Frequency:* 25 times a year
Peter Vamos, Publisher

Building & Construction

Alberta Construction Magazine
#300, 5735 - 7 St. NE, Calgary, AB T2E 8V3
Tel: 403-265-3700; *Fax:* 403-265-3706
Toll-Free: 888-563-2946
marketing@junewarren.com
www.junewarren.com
Circulation: 8,500 *Frequency:* 6 times a year; also Alberta Constuction Association Membership Roster & Buyers' Guide (annual, May)
Chaz Osburn, Editor

Alberta Construction Service & Supply Directory
6111 - 91 St. NW, Edmonton, AB T6E 6V6
Tel: 780-944-9333; *Fax:* 780-944-9500
Toll-Free: 800-563-2946
theath@junewarren.com
www.junewarren.com
Circulation: 10,000 *Frequency:* Annually
Agnes Zalewski, Publisher

Atlantic Construction Journal
Transcontinental Specialty Publications, #609, 1888 Brunswick St., Dartmouth, NS B3J 3J9
Tel: 902-468-8027; *Fax:* 902-468-2425
Toll-Free: 800-537-5507
acj@hfnews.ca
Circulation: 15,000 *Frequency:* 4 times a year
Naster Tracz, Senior Account Executive
Ken Partridge, Editor

BSDA Newsmagazine
Building Supply Dealers Assn. of BC, #2, 19299 - 94th Ave., Surrey, BC V4N 4E6
Tel: 604-513-2205; *Fax:* 604-513-2206
bsdabc@telus.net
www.bsdabc.com
Circulation: 1,000 *Frequency:* 4 times a year
George Tracy

Building & Construction Trades Today
PO Box 186, 27 St. Clair Ave. East, Toronto, ON M4T 2M1
Tel: 416-944-1217; *Fax:* 416-944-0133
hize@earthlink.net
Circulation: 2,000-2,500 *Frequency:* 8 times a year
Alan Heisey, Publisher
Jason Kieffer, Editor

Building Magazine
#800, 12 Concorde Place, Toronto, ON M3C 2J4
Tel: 416-442-5600; *Fax:* 416-442-2191
Toll-Free: 800-668-2374
www.building.ca
Circulation: 10,737 *Frequency:* 6 times a year
Tom Arkell, Senior Publisher, 416-510-6806, tomarkell@canadianarchitect.com

Canadian Apartment Magazine

Circulation: 7,000 *Frequency:* 6 times a year
Ellie Chesnutt, Editor

Canadian Contractor

Tel: 416-764-1656; *Fax:* 416-764-1484
dchestnut@rmpublishing.com
canadiancontractormagazine.com
Circulation: 45,000 *Frequency:* 4 times a year
David Chestnut, Associate Publisher

Canadian Property Management

Tel: 416-512-8186; *Fax:* 416-512-8344
Circulation: 12,504 *Frequency:* 8 times a year
Tony Robinson, Publisher

Canadian Renovator Magazine
PO Box 7400, London, ON N5Y 4X3
Tel: 519-471-8412; *Fax:* 519-473-7859
Toll-Free: 877-707-3639
drawlings@bowesnet.com
renopub.com
Circulation: 13,200 *Frequency:* 5 times a year
Don Rawlings, Publisher & Editor

Canadian Roofing Contractor & Design
3 Kennett Dr., Whitby, ON L1P 1L5
Tel: 905-430-7267; *Fax:* 905-430-6418
Toll-Free: 877-880-4877
mike@perkspub.com
www.perkspub.com
Circulation: 6,000 *Frequency:* 4 times a year
Michael Nosko, Publisher

Canadian Window & Door Manufacturer

Tel: 519-657-2088; *Fax:* 519-657-2796
Frequency: 2 times a year
Bruce Munro, Editor

CondoBusiness

Tel: 416-512-8186; *Fax:* 416-512-8344
info@mediaedge.ca
www.mediaedge.ca
Circulation: 2,500 *Frequency:* 8 times a year
Angela Altass, Editor
Tracy Ryan, Publisher

Construire
L'Association de la Construction du Québec, #205, 7400, boul des Galeries-d'Anjou, Anjou, QC H1M 3M2
Tél: 450-963-4339; *Téléc:* 450-625-6065
Ligne sans frais: 888-868-3424
communication@acq.org
www.rep-comm.ca
Circulation: 27 400 *Frequency:* 6 fois par an; français
Monique Thomas, Rédactrice
Pierre Leduc, Directeur, ventes

Daily Commercial News
Reed Construction Data, 500 Hood Rd., 4th Fl., Markham, ON L3R 9Z3
Tel: 905-752-5547; *Fax:* 905-752-5448
sonia.kalraali@reedbusiness.com
www.dailycommercialnews.com
Circulation: 4,000 *Frequency:* Daily
Mark Casaletto, Publisher

Equipment Journal
Pace Publishing Limited, #6, 5160 Explorer Dr., Mississauga, ON L4W 4T7
Tel: 905-629-7500; *Fax:* 905-629-7988
Toll-Free: 800-667-8541
ej@equipmentjournal.com
www.equipmentjournal.com
Circulation: 23,500 *Frequency:* 17 issues a year, every 3 weeks
John Baker, Publisher

Formes
6718, rue Chambord, Montréal, QC H2G 3C3
Tél: 514-736-7637; *Téléc:* 514-272-3477
info@formes.ca
www.formes.ca
Frequency: 6 fois par an

Heavy Construction News On-Site

Tel: 416-764-2000; *Fax:* 416-764-1733
www.on-sitemag.com
Circulation: 22,984 *Frequency:* 7 times a year
Jim Barnes, Editor
Peter Leonard, Publisher

Heavy Equipment Guide

Tel: 604-291-9900; *Fax:* 604-291-1906
www.baumpub.com
Circulation: 26,575 *Frequency:* 10 times a year
Engelbert J. Baum, Publisher
Lawrence Buser, Editor

Home Builder Magazine
4819 St. Charles Blvd., Pierrefonds, QC H9H 3C7
Tel: 514-620-2200; *Fax:* 514-620-6300
homebuilder@work4.ca
www.homebuildercanada.com
Circulation: 26,418 *Frequency:* 6 times a year
Nachmi Artzy, Publisher

HPAC Magazine/Buyer's Guide
1 Mount Pleasant Rd., Toronto, ON M4Y 2Y5
Tel: 416-764-2000; *Fax:* 416-764-1746
bruce.meacock@hpacmag.rogers.com
www.hpacmag.com
Circulation: 16,379 *Frequency:* annually (August)
Bruce Meacock, Publisher

Journal Constructo
#200, 1500, boul Jules-Poitras, Saint-Laurent, QC H4N 1X7
Tél: 514-745-5720; *Téléc:* 514-339-2267
Ligne sans frais: 800-363-0910
groupeconstructo@transcontinental.ca
www.constructo.ca
Circulation: 2 611 *Frequency:* 80 fois par an; français
Anik Girard, Éditeur
Marie Vaillancourt, Chef de L'Information

Le Journal de L'Habitation
Médias-Transcontinental, #900, 1265, boul Charest ouest, Québec, QC G1N 4V4
Tél: 418-686-6400; *Téléc:* 418-686-4841
www.journalhabitation.com
Circulation: 28 000 *Frequency:* 2 times a month
François Cattapan, Rédacteur en chef

Journal of Commerce
#101, 4299 Canada Way, Burnaby, BC V5G 1H3
Tel: 604-433-8164; *Fax:* 604-433-9549
Toll-Free: 888-878-2121
jocinfor@reelbusiness.com
www.joconl.com
Circulation: 1,800 *Frequency:* 2 times a week

LBMAO Reporter
#27, 5155 Spectrum Way, Mississauga, ON L42 5A1
Tel: 905-625-1084; *Fax:* 905-625-3006
reporter@lbmao.on.ca
www.lbmao.on.ca
Circulation: 1,750 *Frequency:* 6 times a year
David Campbell, President

Ontario Home Builder
1074 Cooke Blvd., Burlington, ON L7T 4A8
Tel: 905-634-8003; *Fax:* 905-634-7661
Toll-Free: 800-387-0109
info@ohba.ca
www.homesontario.com
Circulation: 8,084 *Frequency:* 5 times a year
Wayne Nanciso, Publisher

Ottawa Construction News
#202, 1 Cleopatra Dr., Ottawa, ON K2G 3W9
Tel: 613-224-3460; *Fax:* 613-224-1076
Toll-Free: 888-432-3555
editor@constructionnrgroup.com
www.ottawaconstructionnews.com
Circulation: 12,000 *Frequency:* 12 times a year
Mark Buckshon, Publisher
Terry Tinkess, Editor

Québec Habitation
5930, boul Louis-H.-Lafontaine, Anjou, QC H1M 1S7
Tél: 514-353-9960; *Téléc:* 514-353-0835
Ligne sans frais: 800-468-8160
quebec-hab@apchq.com
www.quebec-habitation.com
Circulation: 30 000 *Frequency:* 6 fois par an; français
Lise Plante, Éditeur
Jean Garon, Rédactrice-en-chef

Sanitation Canada
3 Kennett Dr., Whitby, ON L1P 1L5
Tel: 905-430-7267; *Fax:* 905-430-6418
Toll-Free: 877-880-4877
mike@perkspub.com
www.perkspub.com
Circulation: 5,134 *Frequency:* 6 times a year
Michael Nosko, Publisher

Toronto Construction News
Reed Construction Data, 500 Hood Rd., 4th Fl., Markham, ON L3R 9Z3
Tel: 905-752-5539; *Fax:* 905-750-5450
Toll-Free: 800-465-6475
www.dailycommercialnews.com
Circulation: 4,000 *Frequency:* 7 times a year
Patrick McConnell, Publisher

Business & Finance

Advisor's Edge
One Mount Pleasant Rd., Toronto, ON M4Y 2Y5
Tel: 416-764-3859; *Fax:* 416-764-3943
service@advisor.ca
www.advisor.ca
Circulation: 40,000 *Frequency:* 12 times a year
Advisor's Edge magazine is an independent Canadian publication focused solely on the information needs of Canadian retail financial advisors (brokers, financial planners, insurance specialists, mutual fund salespeople and bank-based consultants). With a strong emphasis on practice management, the magazine helps advisors stay on top of industry trends, investment insurance products and strategies, as well as marketing and client relationship best practices
Donna Kerry, Publisher, donna.kerry@rci.rogers.com
Philip Porado, Executive Editor, philip.porado@rci.rogers.com

Les Affaires
1100, boul René-Lévesque ouest 24e étage, Montréal, QC H3B 4X9
Tél: 514-392-9000; *Téléc:* 514-392-1586
Ligne sans frais: 800-361-5479
lesaffaires.redaction@transcontinental.ca
www.lesaffai res.com
Circulation: 90 000 *Frequency:* 52 fois par an; français; aussi Affaires 500, PME, Affaires plus (10 fois par an, 93 288)
Principal journal d'affaires de langue française au Canada, fondé en 1928. Ce tabloïd tout en couleur paraît le samedi et a un tirage de 88 000 exemplaires, surtout vendus au Québec. Il est publié par les Publications Transcontinental Inc. Il est reconnu pour sa couverture des grandes sociétés canadiennes, des petites et moyennes entreprises québécoises, de l'économie canadienne et des affaires publiques. La moitié de son contenu est consacrée aux finances personnelles et aux placements avec diverses pages spécialisées, des tableaux et des graphiques
Michel Lord, Éditeur
Jean-Paul Gagné, Rédacteur-en-chef, pierre.marcoux@transcontinental.ca

Affaires Plus Magazine
1100, boul René-Lévesque 24e étage, Montréal, QC H3B 4X9
Tél: 514-392-9000; *Téléc:* 514-392-4726
aplus@transcontienal.ca
www.lesaffaires.com
Circulation: 88 806 *Frequency:* 12 fois par an; français
Créé en 1978, le magazine Affaires PLUS est le magazine d'affaires au plus fort tirage et au plus fort lectorat au Québec. C'est aussi la plus personnelle des publications d'affaires de Médias Transcontinental. Le magazine est bâti autour de trois axes: mon argent, ma carrière, ma vie, qui déterminent à la fois le positionnement et le contenu d'Affaires PLUS
Stéphane Labrèche, Rédacteur en chef, stephane.labreche@transcontinental.ca

Alberta Venture
10259 - 105 St., Edmonton, AB T5J 1E3
Tel: 780-990-0839; *Fax:* 780-425-4921
Toll-Free: 866-227-4276
admin@albertaventure.com
www.albertaventure.com
Circulation: 40,800 *Frequency:* 10 times a year
Alberta Venture is the only province-wide magazine that keeps you informed about Alberta's business community. Covers trends, issues, people and events that set the pace for Canada's fastest growing economy
Ruth Kelly, Editor

Atlantic Business Magazine
PO Box 2356 C, 197 Water St., St. John's, NL A1C 6E7
Tel: 709-726-9300; *Fax:* 709-726-3013
www.atlanticbusinessmagazine.com

Circulation: 33,000 *Frequency:* 6 times a year
Founded in 1989, Atlantic Business Magazine is an independently owned, bi-monthly glossy publication that covers all areas of business within the four Atlantic provinces.
Hubert Hutton, Publisher, hhutton@atlanticbusinessmagazine.com
Dawn Chafe, Editor, dchafe@atlanticbusinessmagazine.com

Avantages
#800, 1200, ave McGill College, Montréal, QC H3B 4G7
Tél: 514-843-2510; *Téléc:* 514-843-2182
www.revueavantages.ca
Circulation: 5 159 *Frequency:* 8 fois par an; français
Avantages is a French-language pension and benefits publication produced to meet the needs of the Quebec marketplace. Avantages provides information and analysis on pensions, benefits, healthcare and investments to key decision-makers who manage employer-sponsored pension and benefits plans in Quebec
Alexandre Daudelin, Rédacteur-en-chef, alexandre.daudelin@avantages.rogers.com
Jean Goulet, Éditeur, jean.goulet@rci.rogers.com

Backbone Magazine
c/o Publimedia Communications Inc., 187 Rondoval Cres., North Vancouver, BC V7N 2W6
Tel: 905-918-0567; *Fax:* 604-986-5309
info@backbonemag.com
www.backbonemag.com
Circulation: 115,000 *Frequency:* 6 times per year
Backbone magazine's aim is to provide business people with a tangible tool to enhance the way they do business in Canada's New Economy
Steve Dietrich, Publisher, sdietrich@backbonemag.com
Peter Wolchak, Editor, pwolchak@backbonemag.com

Le Banquier/Canadian Banker
Canadian Bankers Association, CP 348, Commerce Ct. West, 30th Fl., Toronto, ON M5L 1G2
Tél: 416-362-6092; *Téléc:* 416-362-7705
Ligne sans frais: 800-263-0231
cbacallcentre@cba.ca
www.cba.ca
Circulation: 8 400 *Frequency:* 4 fois par an; français/anglais
Canadian Banker and Le Banquier are published four times annually by the Canadian Bankers Association. The magazines aim to keep their readers informed about the broad trends and changes in banking and the financial-services industry

BCBusiness Magazine
4180 Lougheed Hwy. 4th Fl., Burnaby, BC V5C 6A7
Tel: 604-299-7311; *Fax:* 604-299-9188
Toll-Free: 800-663-0518
ttjaden@canadawide.com
www.bcbusinessmagazine.com
Circulation: 26,000 *Frequency:* Monthly; ISSN: 0849-481X
An authoritative voice on the province's business scene, BCBusiness goes beyond the headlines to give readers valuable, relevant insights into today's trends and issues
Peter Legge, Publisher, ttjaden@canadawide.com
Matt O'Grady, Editor, mogrady@canadawide.com
John Bucher, Editor, jbucher@canadawide.com

Benefits & Pensions Monitor
#501, 245 Fairview Mall Dr., Toronto, ON M2J 4T1
Tel: 416-494-1066; *Fax:* 416-494-2536
info@powershift.ca
www.bpmmagazine.com
Circulation: 22,850 *Frequency:* 12 times a year
Benefits and Pensions Monitor is published eight times a year. Benefits and Pensions Monitor had to be different from the other industry magazine to succeed. It had to provide a unique editorial focus on issues that affect the industry. Monitor delivers. Today, Monitor has the industry's highest audited circulation.
John McLaine, Publisher & Editorial Director, jmclaine@powershift.ca
Joe Hornyak, Executive Editor, jhornyak@powershift.ca

Benefits Canada
One Mount Pleasant Rd. 12th Floor, Toronto, ON M4Y 2Y5
Tel: 416-764-3915; *Fax:* 416-764-3938
paulb.williams@rci.rogers.com
www.benefitscanada.com
Circulation: 17,000 *Frequency:* 12 times a year; English & French
Provides information and analysis on pensions, benefits, healthcare and investments to key decision-makers who manage employer-sponsored pension and benefits plans. The publication targets the plan sponsor community, particularly those employers with more than 500 employees
Paul Williams, Publisher & Vice President, 416-764-3848, PaulO.williams@rci.rogers.com
Alyssa Hodder, Editor, 416-764-3823, alyssa.hodder@rci.rogers.com

BIZ Magazine
1074 Cooke Blvd, Hamilton, ON L7T 4A8
Tel: 905-522-6117; *Fax:* 905-529-2242
info@townmedia.ca
Circulation: 24,000 *Frequency:* 4 times a year
Business publication in the Hamilton/Burlington region, with award-winning features, profiles, real-life photography and controversial opinions
Arend Kirsten, Editor

The Bottom Line
#700, 123 Commerce Valley Dr. East, Markham, ON L3T 7W8
Tel: 905-415-5804; *Fax:* 905-479-3758
tbl@butterworths.ca
www.thebottomlinenews.com
Circulation: 30,428 *Frequency:* 16 times a year
The Bottom Line is an independent and specialized business periodical that keeps accredited professional accountants, financial managers, and consultants abreast of news, trends, and technology within the industry
Robert Kelly, Managing Editor
Gary P. Rodrigues, Publisher

Business Bulletin
Mississauga Board of Trade, #701, 77 City Centre Dr., Mississauga, ON L5B 1M5
Tel: 905-273-6151; *Fax:* 905-273-4937
info@mbot.com
www.mbot.com
Circulation: 22,000 *Frequency:* 11 times a year
Business Bulletin has been replaced by the mbot magazine. mbot magazine is our dynamic business resource and reference tool. It provides an array of practical articles and advice that address the issues, news and trends important to businesses of all sizes and scopes in Mississauga as well as companies located outside the City. mbot magazine replaces our tabloid-style newspaper Business Bulletin.
Naveen Atwal, External Communications, 905-273-3523, naveena@mbot.com

Business Central Magazine
#304, 4820 Gaetz Ave., Red Deer, AB T4N 4A4
Tel: 403-309-5587; *Fax:* 403-346-3044
Circulation: 5,000 *Frequency:* 6 times a year
Donald C. Sylvester, Publisher & Editor

Business Examiner - North
777B Poplar St., Nanaimo, BC V9S 2H7
Tel: 250-754-8344; *Fax:* 250-754-8304
Toll-Free: 800-332-7355
merv@businessexaminer.net
www.businessexaminer.net
Circulation: 14,000 *Frequency:* Monthly
Steve Weatherbee, Editor

Business Examiner - South Island Edition
818 Broughton St., Victoria, BC V8W 1E4
Tel: 250-381-3926; *Fax:* 250-381-5606
www.businessexaminer.net
Circulation: 14,400 *Frequency:* 24 times a year
Bill MacAdam, Publisher
Simon Lindley, Publisher/Sales Manager, simon@businessexaminer.net
Steve Weatherbee, Editor, editor@businessexaminer.net

The Business Executive
#220, 466 Speers Rd., Oakville, ON L6K 3W9
Tel: 905-845-8300; *Fax:* 905-845-9086
wpeters@busexec.com
www.busexec.com
Circulation: 30,000 *Frequency:* 12 times a year
The Business Executive is Southern Ontario's only business-to-business newspaper published on a monthly basis. The Business Executive is divided into sections to allow the readers to pick and choose subjects of most interest to them. Some of the sections include: Real Estate & Construction, Finance, Business News, People and Lifestyles, Computers and Technology, International Trade & Travel.
Thomas Peters, Publisher, t.peters@busexec.com
Wendy Peters, Editor, wpeters@busexec.com

Business in Calgary
#1025, 101 - 6th Ave. SW, Calgary, AB T2P 3P4
Tel: 403-264-3270; *Fax:* 403-264-3276
Toll-Free: 800-465-0322
info@businessincalgary.com
www.businessincalgary.com
Circulation: 30,735 *Frequency:* Monthly
A monthly publication dedicated to producing intelligent, colorful articles about the people, trends and events that make Calgary a prominent business centre in the west.
Camie Leard, Editor, editor@businessincalgary.com
Pat Ottmann, Publisher, pat@businessincalgary.comcom
Tim Ottmann, Publisher, tim@businessincalgary.comcom

Business London
PO Box 7400, London, ON, ON N5Y 4X3
Tel: 519-472-7601; *Fax:* 519-473-7859
editorial@businesslondon.ca
www.businesslondon.ca
Circulation: 12,000 *Frequency:* Monthly
The Magazine provides unparalleled behind-the-scenes coverage, chronicling companies on the move and putting faces to faceless events.
Gord Delamont, Publisher, editorial@businesslondon.ca

Business Trends
1383 Confederation St., Sarnia, ON N7S 5P1
Tel: 519-336-1100; *Fax:* 519-336-1833
businesstrends@cogeco.net
www.sarniabusinesstrends.com
Circulation: 6,300 *Frequency:* 12 times a year
Covers business trends in the Sarnia area
Gord Bowes, Editor
Kirsten Anderson, Account Manager

Business Voice
1300 Hollis St., Halifax, NS B3J 1T6
Tel: 902-420-9943; *Fax:* 902-429-9058
publishers@metroguide.ca
www.metroguidepublishing.ca/bv.php
Circulation: 7,500 *Frequency:* 10 times a year
Business Voice is Halifax's leading business magazine, offering unrivalled access to Metro's decision-makers. Business Voice is the official voice of the Halifax Chamber of Commerce: 95% of members read most or every issue. It keeps readers updated on Chamber policies and activities, plus develop-ments in the business community
Sheila Blair, Publisher

BusinessWoman Canada Magazine
PO Box 31010, Barrie, ON L4N 0B3
Tel: 705-722-9692; *Fax:* 705-722-7268
Toll-Free: 877-251-7226
Circulation: 20,000 *Frequency:* 4 times a year
Donna Messer, Editor

Businest
#800, 625 boul René-Lévesque Ouest, Montréal, QC H3B 1R2
Tél: 514-866-3131; *Téléc:* 514-866-3030
Ligne sans frais: 800-361-7262
infos@reseauselect.com
www.reseauselect.com
Circulation: 20 100 *Frequency:* Mensuel; français
Publication qui couvre de domaine des affaires, et dessert les professionnels, les entreprises et les gens d'affaires le territoire de La Pocatière aux les-de-la-Madeleine, et la Côte-Nord
Ernie Wells, Rédacteur-en-chef

CA Magazine
277 Wellington St. West, Toronto, ON M5V 3H2
Tel: 416-977-3222; *Fax:* 416-204-3409
CAmagazine@cica.ca
www.camagazine.com
Circulation: 72,500 *Frequency:* 10 times a year; English & French
CAmagazine is published by the Canadian Institute of Chartered Accountants (CICA) ten times a year. Articles about careers in chartered accounting are featured while current issues are discussed and explained. The magazine also deals with a wide variety of business topics from the Chartered Accountant's perspective
Christian Bellavance, Editor-in-chief

Canada Japan Journal
Japan Advertising Ltd., #410, 1199 West Pender St., Vancouver, BC V6E 2R1
Tel: 604-688-2486; *Fax:* 604-688-1487
Toll-Free: 888-245-2549
japanad@telus.net
www.canadajournal.com
Circulation: 15,750 *Frequency:* Monthly; Japanese
Taka Aoki, Editor

Canadian Association Publishers
PO Box 90510, 230 Markham Rd., Scarborough, ON M1J 3N7
Tel: 416-955-1550; *Fax:* 416-955-1391
info@capmagazines.ca
www.capmagazines.ca
Circulation: 30,650 *Frequency:* Semi-annual
Business Resources Canada is Canada's premier Small Business Resource Directory for Owners and Entrepreneurs. Published quarterly, Business Resources Canada, with its combined directory and magazine format, guides and inspires

Canadians who are starting or growing a business as their career.
Kelly Chase, Production, production@capmagazines.ca
Jim Eaton, Publishing Enquiries, jeaton@capmagazines.ca
Adrienne Ramsay, Advertising

Canadian Business
One Mount Pleasant Rd. 11th Floor, Toronto, ON M4Y 2Y5
Tel: 416-764-1200; *Fax:* 416-764-1404
adsales@canadianbusiness.com
www.canadianbusiness.com/canadian_business_ magazine
Circulation: 84,000 *Frequency:* 24 times a year; ISSN: 0008-3100
Canadian Business, Canada's best-selling business magazine, captures the attention of Canada's business leaders with topical, timely stories that matter to corporate managers and executives. Written for an audience with an orientation to the future, its compelling insight inspires readers to capitalize on change
Joe Chidley, Editor
Deborah Rosser, Publisher

Canadian Business Franchise/L'entreprise
c/o Kenilworth Media Inc., #710, 15 Wertheim Ct., Richmond Hill, BC L4B 3H7
Tel: 905-771-7333; *Fax:* 905-771-7336
Toll-Free: 800-409-8688
info@kenilworth.com
www.cgb.ca
Frequency: Bi-monthly
Canadian Business Franchise Magazine is a bi-monthly publication that features articles on franchise advice from bankers, lawyers and franchise specialists. The magazine is in its eleventh year of production and is the best selling Franchise magazine in Canada
Colin Bradbury, Publisher & Editor
Tuesday Royko, Editorial Assistant

Canadian German Trade
#1500, 480 University Ave., Toronto, ON M5G 1V2
Tel: 416-598-3355; *Fax:* 416-598-1840
info@germanchamber.ca
www.germanchamber.ca
Circulation: 2,500 *Frequency:* 6 times a year
Covers news concerning the Canadian and German economy, special articles which are of interest to the Canadian and German business community, as well as updated economic datanews concerning the Canadian and German economy, special articles which are of interest to the Canadian and German business community, as well as updated economic data
Sonya Deevy, Contact

Canadian Investment Review
One Mount Pleasant Ave., 12th Fl., Toronto, ON M4Y 2Y5
Tel: 416-764-3867; *Fax:* 416-764-3934
www.investmentreview.com
Frequency: 4 times a year
Canada's leading forum for academics, institutional investors and industry practitioners to exchange ideas on the capital markets, investment and economic theory, and the related sociology and demographics.
Caroline Cakebread, Editor, caroline.cakebread@rogers.com
Paul Williams, Publisher, VP, Healthcare and Financial, don.bisch@rogers.comogers.com

The Canadian Manager
Canadian Institute of Management, 15 Collier St., Lower Level, Barrie, ON L4M 1G5
Tel: 705-725-8926; *Fax:* 705-725-8196
Toll-Free: 800-387-5774
office@cim.ca
www.cim.ca
Circulation: 4,500 *Frequency:* 4 times a year
The Canadian Manager is published 4 times per year by the Canadian Institute of Management, with a readership over 12,000 (approx.)
Anna Victoria Wong, Editor/Manager, awong@baseconsulting.ca

Canadian Not-For-Profit News
One Corporate Plaza, 2075 Kennedy Rd., Toronto, ON M1T 3V4
Tel: 416-609-8000; *Fax:* 416-298-5094
www.carswell.com
Frequency: Monthly
Source of current information on the tax implications and practical considerations relating to the most relevant and timely issues surrounding registered charities and other non-profit organizations

The Canadian Taxpayer
Tel: 416-609-8000; *Fax:* 416-298-5082
Toll-Free: 800-387-5164
carswell.orders@thomson.com
www.carswell.com
Circulation: 1,000 *Frequency:* 24 times per year
The Taxpayer is the flagship publication of the Canadian Taxpayers Federation (CTF). It is published six times a year and contains comprehensive updates on CTF happenings and accomplishments around the country. It features articles written by CTF researchers and spokespersons. Guest editorial writers also contribute to this publication.
Robert Freeman, Vice-President

Canadian Treasurer
c/o Treasury Management Association of Canada, #1010, 8 King St. East, Toronto, ON M5C 1B5
Tel: 416-367-8500; *Fax:* 416-367-3240
Toll-Free: 800-449-8622
info@tmac.ca
www.tmac.ca
Circulation: 5,313 *Frequency:* 6 times a year
TMAC's bimonthly magazine, Canadian Treasurer, brings directly to you the latest trends in treasury management. Canadian Treasurer reaches treasury professionals of major corporate and government organizations throughout Canada. It is also distributed to other organizations within the Canadian financial community, the U.S. and around the world. Circulation includes the top 1,000 companies in Canada.
Bruce McDougall, Managing Editor
Mike Whiston, Executive Director

Central Nova Business News
Advocate Print & Publishing Ltd., PO Box 1000, 181 Brown's Point Rd., Pictou, NS B0K 1H0
Tel: 902-893-0375; *Fax:* 902-893-1353
Circulation: 1,500 *Frequency:* Monthly
The official Publication of the Truro and District Chamber of Commerce
Jason Warren, Editor

CGA Magazine
#800, 1188 Georgia St. West, Vancouver, BC V6E 4A2
Tel: 604-669-3555; *Fax:* 604-689-5845
Toll-Free: 800-663-1529
jward@cga-canada.org
www.cga-online.org/canada
Circulation: 60,000 *Frequency:* 6 times a year; English & French
CGA Magazine profiles current issues relevant to professional accountancy and discusses news and trends in the business and regulatory environment. Printed 6 times a year, this glossy publication is distributed to 68,000 CGA students, members, and leaders in the business, government, education and regulatory communities.
Barbara Cameron, Publisher
Peggy Homan, Associate Publisher/Editor

China's Wired!
#400, 1235 Bay St., Toronto, ON M5R 3K4
Tel: 416-966-9391; *Fax:* 416-699-1165
www.flyingarmchair.com
Frequency: 12 times a year (internet)
China's Wired! Your Guide to the Internet in China, is the first book written on the Internet and its use and potential in the People's Republic of China. China's Wired! is designed to be the Internet guide on the PRC for investors and entrepreneurs

CMA Management Magazine
c/o Society of Management Accountants of Canada, Miss. Exec., #1400, One Robert Speck Pkwy., Mississauga, ON L4Z 3M3
Tel: 905-949-4200; *Fax:* 905-949-0888
Toll-Free: 800-263-7622
info@cma-canada.org
www.managementmag.com
Circulation: 48,000 *Frequency:* 9 times a year; English & French
Management is an outstanding business magazine specifically tailored to help you make informed business decisions and give you a strategic advantage. It provides effective, practical solutions to your most pressing business challenges. It features the latest trends in management strategies with sharp, fresh editorial and attention-grabbing design.
David Fletcher, Publisher
Robert Colman, Editor-in-chief

Commerce & Industry
1740 Wellington Ave., Winnipeg, MB R3H 0E8
Tel: 204-954-2085; *Fax:* 204-954-2057
mp@mercury.mb.ca
www.mercury.mb.ca
Circulation: 18,154 *Frequency:* 6 times a year
A national publication focused on the industrial, manufacturing, resource, transportation and construction sectors. Each issue offers a large variety of sector analysis, in-depth company profiles and reports on key areas of interest to the magazine's target audience.
Al Kaglik, National Account Manager, al@mercury.mb.ca
Frank Yeo, Publisher
Edna Saito, Production Manager

Commerce News
Edmonton Chamber of Commerce, #700, 9990 Jasper Ave., Edmonton, AB T5J 1P7
Tel: 780-426-4620; *Fax:* 780-424-7946
info@edmontonchamber.com
www.edmontonchamber.com
Circulation: 36,000 *Frequency:* 11 times a year
Published by the Edmonton Chamber of Commerce, reaches an estimated audience of over 150,000 business readers per issue. It is direct mailed eleven times per year to every Chamber member and subscriber (4,500 copies), to all Edmonton area businesses, government and association leaders around the region, and to all Alberta Chambers of Commerce (25,500 copies).
Martin Salloum, Publisher
Chris O'Brien, Editor
Rita Boyce, Ad Sales
Kimberly Nishikaze, Managing Editor

Corporate Ethics Monitor
Lawrence Plaza, PO Box 54034, Toronto, ON M6A 3B7
Tel: 416-783-6776; *Fax:* 416-783-7386
info@ethicscan.ca
www.ethicscan.ca
Circulation: 400 *Frequency:* Bi-monthly
Each sixteen page issue of the bi-monthly Corporate Ethics Monitor ($297 Canadian for one year, $456 CDN for foreign subscriptions) is laden with articles and stories that deal with recognizing and enhancing ethics in the workplace. Expect to find original research, timely articles, provocative perspectives, and practical ideas. The reporting on comparative business practices reflects dozens of hours of interviews, data base retrieval, fact checking and preparation of tables, charts and profiles. All this, plus insightful articles from regular columnists, an OPEN FORUM for executives, a Face to Face debate section, and lively book reviews.

Defined Benefit Monitor
#501, 245 Fairview Mall Dr., Toronto, ON M2J 4T1
Frequency: 2 times a year
John McLaine, Publisher

Defined Contribution Monitor
#501, 245 Fairview Maill Dr., Toronto, ON M2J 4T1
Frequency: 2 times a year
John McLaine, Publisher

EDGE
#302, 55 World Town Centre Ct., Scarborough, ON M1P 4X4
Tel: 416-290-0240; *Toll-Free:* 800-387-5312
info@itbusiness.ca
www.itbusiness.ca
Circulation: 16,640 *Frequency:* 12 times a year
EDGE (Executives in a Digital Global Economy) is a non-technical, monthly magazine for CEOs, CFOs, CIOs and other senior executives who want to know how information technology can be used to transform their business. Through a combination of case studies, executive profiles and a look at best practices, EDGE not only demystifies IT, it shows how organizations can achieve competitive advantage.
Martin Slofstra, Editorial Director
Joe Tersigni, Publisher
Dave Web, Writer and Editor

L'Edition Le Journal des Gens d'Affaires
Tél: 514-257-1000; *Téléc:* 514-257-7505
Circulation: 29 700
Carole Le Hirez, Rédacteur-en-chef
Lise Thériault, Éditeur

Entreprendre
Editions Qualité Performante inc., #660, 1600, boul St-Martin est, Laval, QC H7G 4R8
Tél: 450-669-8373; *Téléc:* 450-669-9078
Ligne sans frais: 800-479-1777
message@entreprendre.ca
www.entreprendre.ca
Circulation: 45 000 *Frequency:* 10 fois par an; français
Le magazine Entreprendre rejoint un auditoire exceptionnel de décideurs du monde des affaires. Outil d'information qui développe des références et éclaire la nature profonde de l'entrepreneurship au Québec

Edmond Bourque, Publisher

Exchange Magazine for Business
#10, 160 Frobisher Dr., Waterloo, ON N2V 2B1
Tel: 519-886-0298; *Fax:* 519-886-6409
editor@exchangemagazine.com
www.exchangemagazine.com
Circulation: 17,500 *Frequency:* 8 times a year
Covers business news in the Kitchener-Waterloo area
Jon Rohr, Editor-in-chief

Finance et Investissement
Tel: 514-392-9000; *Fax:* 514-392-4726
Toll-Free: 800-361-5479
www.finance-investissement.com
Circulation: 18,000 *Frequency:* 14 times a year
Depuis son lancement en novembre 1999, le journal Finance et Investissement est devenu la source d'information privilégiée des représentants en épargne collective, des conseillers en valeurs mobilières, des conseillers en sécurité financière et des planificateurs financiers
Sylvain Bedard, Publisher, sylvain.bedard@transcontinental.ca

Financial Post Business
#300, 1450 Don Mills Rd., Toronto, ON M3B 3R5
Tel: 416-383-2300; *Fax:* 416-386-2836
editorial@nationalpostbusiness.com
www.nationalpostbusiness.com
Circulation: 289,000 *Frequency:* 12 times a year
Brian Banks, Editor

FlashFinance
#100, 321, rue de la Commune, Montréal, QC H2Y 2E1
Tel: 514-289-9595; *Fax:* 514-289-9527
flash@flashfinance.ca
www.flashfinance.ca
Circulation: 2 000 *Frequency:* Weekly
Outil privilégié d'information du monde de l'assurance et de la finance, FlashFinance.ca joint des milliers de dirigeants de compagnies d'assurance, de propriétaires de cabinets, de directeurs de courtage, et de conseillers financiers
Serge Therrien, Publisher

The FP Survey of Industrials
Financial Post Data Group, 1450 Don Mills Rd., 2nd Fl., Toronto, ON M3B 2X7
Tel: 416-442-2121; *Fax:* 416-442-2968
fpdg@canwest.com
Circulation: 3,870 *Frequency:* Annually, August
Financial and operational information on publicly traded Canadian companies

Franchise Canada Directory
Canadian Franchise Association, #300, 2585 Skymark Ave., Mississauga, ON L4W 4L5
Tel: 905-625-2896; *Fax:* 905-625-9076
Toll-Free: 800-665-4232
jschofield@cfa.ca
www.cfa.ca
Frequency: Annually
John Schofield, Editor

Franchise Canada Magazine
Canadian Franchise Association, #116, 5399 Eglinton Ave. West, Toronto, ON M9C 5K6
Tel: 416-695-2896; *Fax:* 416-695-1950
Toll-Free: 800-665-4232
info@cfa.ca
www.cfa.ca
Circulation: 6,000 *Frequency:* 6 times a year
A bi-monthly magazine geared at entrepreneurs interested in acquiring a franchise. Franchise Canada Magazine will contain top-notch editorial from leading authorities in the industry as well as countless tips on how to establish a successful franchise.
John Scofield, Editor

Gestion
3000, ch de la Côte-Sainte-Catherine, Montréal, QC H3T 2A7
Tél: 514-340-6677; *Téléc:* 514-340-6975
revue.gestion@hec.ca
revue.hec.ca/gestion
Circulation: 3 500 *Frequency:* 4 fois par an; français
La Revue Gestion a pour but de favoriser la diffusion des connaissances dans tous les domaines de la gestion en français. Particulièrement populaire au Québec, la revue est également lue dans d'autres régions francophones. Offre à ses lecteurs des articles inédits présentant les dernières recherches, des analyses critiques, des synthèses et des réflexions originales dans le domaine de la gestion en Amérique du nord
Michel Vézina, Rédacteur-en-chef

GST & Commodity Tax
One Corporate Plaza, 2075 Kennedy Rd., Toronto, ON M1T 3V4
Tel: 416-609-8000; *Fax:* 416-298-5094
www.carswell.com
The exclusive source for what leading experts are saying about the latest developments in GST, federal and provincial sales and commodity taxes, and customs and excise duties

Halton Business Times
#1, 5040 Mainway, Burlington, ON L7L 7G5
Tel: 905-632-4444; *Fax:* 905-632-9162
thepost@worldchat.com
Circulation: 12,000 *Frequency:* 12 times a year
Ian Oliver, Publisher
Karen Smith, Editor

Huronia Business Times
Kozlov Centre, #243, 400 Bayfield St., Barrie, ON L4M 5A1
Tel: 705-728-3090; *Fax:* 705-734-9600
businesstimes@simcoe.com
www.huroniabusinesstimes.com
Circulation: 12,000 *Frequency:* 12 times a year
Purchased by Metroland Business Publications in September of 1998, Huronia Business Times, and its sister publication the Mississauga Business Times, was formerly owned by North Island Publishing from 1992-1998. Metroland also publishes five other Business Times newspapers in southern Ontario
Martin Melbourne, Editor
Shaun Sauve, General Manager

In Business Windsor
1775 Sprucewood, La Salle, ON N9J 1X7
Tel: 519-250-2880; *Fax:* 519-250-2881
gbaxter@inbusinesswindsor.com
www.inbusinesswindsor.com
Circulation: 10,500 *Frequency:* 12 times a year
Monthly publication which highlights business news in the Windsor area
Jenine Fry, Associate Editor
Gary Baxter, Publisher

Info-ACAIQ
Association des courtiers et agents immobilier du Québec, #300, 6300, rue Auteuil, Brossard, QC J4Z 3P2
Tél: 450-676-4800; *Téléc:* 450-676-7801
Ligne sans frais: 800-440-5110
info@acaiq.com
www.acaiq.com
Circulation: 16 000
L'Info ACAIQ est le journal des professionnels du courtage immobilier du Québec. Il couvre divers sujets relatifs à l'application de la Loi sur le courtage immobilier, aux règlements de la profession, au marché immobilier en plus de questions d'ordre juridique et déontologique reliées à la pratique du courtage immobilier

Investment Executive
#100, 25 Sheppard Ave. West, Toronto, ON M2N 6S7
Tel: 416-733-7600; *Fax:* 416-218-3544
twilmott@investmentexecutive.com
www.investmentexecutive.com
Circulation: 50,200 *Frequency:* 16 times a year
Investment Executive is Canada's national newspaper for financial service industry professionals. Investment Executive is published 16 times a year and reaches more than 120,000 financial advisors. Investment Executive has gained the respect of its readers by offering intelligent, informed coverage of the financial services industry and providing insightful information for advisors on topics as diverse as mutual funds, investment research, technology, estate planning, tax, building relationships with clients and developing products and services for the client of the future.
Tessa Wilmott, Editor-in-chief, twilmott@investmentexecutive.com

Investor's Digest of Canada
#700, 133 Richmond St. West, Toronto, ON M5H 3M8
Tel: 416-869-1177; *Fax:* 416-869-0616
Toll-Free: 800-504-8846
customers@mplcomm.com
www.adviceforinvestors.com
Circulation: 42,912 *Frequency:* 24 times a year
Devoted to uncovering profitable opportunities in every area of investing, using the insights of Canada's leading investment professionals
Michael Popovich, Editor
Barrie Martland, Publisher

Italcommerce
Italian Chamber of Commerce in Canada, #1150, 550, rue Sherbrooke ouest, Montréal, QC H3A 1B9
Tel: 514-844-4249; *Fax:* 514-844-4875
Toll-Free: 800-263-4372
info.montreal@italchambers.net
www.italchamber.qc.ca
Frequency: 3 times a year; French, English & Italian
A pour mission de promouvoir et soutenir les échanges commerciaux entre le Québec, le Canada et l'Italie. Le magazine est diffusé au Canada, en Italie ainsi que dans 60 autres pays où on retrouve des chambres de commerce italiennes
Pasquale Iacobacci, Managing Editor

ITBusiness Report
#302, 55 Town Ct., Scarborough, ON M1P 4X4
Tel: 416-290-0240;
info@itbusiness.ca
www.itbusiness.ca
Circulation: 20,000 *Frequency:* 12 times a year
Covers Canada's IT industry: the key players, the important issues, the decision-making processes. Provides informative, incisive and unbiased coverage examining Canadian case studies, news stories and applications. It provides an overview of trends and technologies, and looks at Canadian product availability and costs
Joe Tersigni, Publisher, jtersigni@itworldcanada.com
Neil Sutton, Editor

Ivey Business Journal
c/o Richard Ivey School of Business, University of Western O, London, ON N6A 3K7
Tel: 519-661-3208; *Fax:* 519-661-3882
www.iveybusinessjournal.com
Circulation: 12,013 *Frequency:* 6 times a year; ISSN: 1481-8248
For more than 70 years, the Ivey Business Journal has delivered incisive, practical articles about managing. Covers articles about e-business, managing uncertainty, knowledge management, marketing, strategy and other topics that managers need to know more about to steer their firms to success
Ed Pearce, Publisher
Stephen Bernhut, Editor

Journal Économique de Québec
#900, 1265, boul Charest ouest, Québec, QC G1N 4V4
Tél: 418-686-6400; *Téléc:* 418-868-1086
Ligne sans frais: 888-293-0999
redacjeq@transcontinental.ca
Circulation: 19 000 *Frequency:* Hebdomadaire
Yvon Giroux, Rédacteur-en-chef

Kootenay Business Magazine
Tel: 250-426-7253; *Fax:* 250-426-4125
Toll-Free: 800-663-8555
info@kpimedia.com
www.kootenaybiz.com
Circulation: 9,400 *Frequency:* 6 times a year
Kootenay Business magazine is free to businesses within the Kootenay/ Columbia/ Boundary/ Revelstoke area
Keith Powell, Publisher, keith@kpimedia.com

Le lien économique
#2, 500, rue Somerset ouest, Ottawa, ON K1R 5J8
Tél: 613-858-1336; *Téléc:* 613-234-1148
sara.grenier@lelieneconomique.com
Circulation: 13 500 *Frequency:* 6 fois par an
Le Lien économique est lu par des décideurs de tous les secteurs de l'économie: Propriétaires et gestionnaires d'entreprises dans tous les secteurs d'activité commerciale : manufactures, institutions financières, services de santé, vente au détail, services et haute technologie
Réjean Grenier, Éditeur et rédacteur en chef

Magazine PME
1100, boul René-Lévesque 24e étage, Montréal, QC H3B 4X9
Tél: 514-392-9000; *Téléc:* 514-392-2026
Circulation: 35 922 *Frequency:* 10 fois par an; français
Couvre les petites et moyennes entreprises au Québec
Marie Quinty, Rédactrice en chef
Pierre Duhamel, Editeur

The Manitoba Broker
#3C, 2020 Portage Ave., Winnipeg, MB R3J 0K4
Tel: 204-985-9785; *Fax:* 204-985-9795
info@kelman.mb.ca
Circulation: 1,300 *Frequency:* 4 times a year
Has timely industry releated articles by feature writers and advertisements of interest to Manitoba brokers
Terry Ross, Editor-in-chief

Manitoba Business Magazine
#508, 294 Portage Ave., Winnipeg, MB R3C 0B9
Tel: 204-943-2931; *Fax:* 204-943-2942
Toll-Free: 888-477-4620
mbm@mts.net
www.manitobabusinessmagazine.com
Circulation: 8,000 *Frequency:* 10 times a year
Ritchie Gage, Editor

Marketplace Magazine
PO Box 523, 910 Queen St., Kincardine, ON N2Z 2Y9
Tel: 519-396-9142; *Fax:* 519-396-3555
Toll-Free: 877-396-9142
marketplace@bmts.com
Circulation: 13,000 *Frequency:* 12 times a year
James Pannell, Publisher
Linda Pannell, General Manager

mbot Magazine
Mississauga Board of Trade, 701-77 City Dr., Mississauga, ON L5B 1M5
Tel: 905-273-6151; *Fax:* 905-273-4937
info@mbot.com
www.mbot.com
Circulation: 5,000 *Frequency:* 11 times a year
Sheryl McKean, President & CEO

Mississauga Business Times
3145 Wolfedale Rd., Mississauga, ON L5C 3A9
Tel: 905-273-8111; *Fax:* 905-273-8219
www.mississauganews.com
Circulation: 40,000 *Frequency:* Monthly
The News is a perennial newspaper award winner, including best newspaper in Ontario and Canada, on several occasions. The Mississauga News is delivered three times a week to houses.
Rick Drennan, Editor, rdrennan@mississauga.net
Ron Lenyk, Publisher

Monday Report on Retailers
One Mount Pleasant Rd., 7th Fl., Toronto, ON M4Y 2Y5
Tel: 416-764-1463; *Fax:* 416-764-1711
www.mondayreport.ca
Frequency: Weekly
Canada's premier information resource for people seeking in-depth, up to-date data on the retail, food service and shopping centre industries in Canada
Don Douloff, Managing Editor

MoneySense
One Mount Pleasant Rd., 11th Fl., Toronto, ON M4Y 2Y5
Tel: 416-764-1400; *Fax:* 416-764-1404
adsales@moneysense.com
www.canadianbusiness.com/moneysense_magazine
Circulation: 106,600 *Frequency:* 6 times a year
MoneySense is Canada's leading personal finance magazine. Each issue contains insightful and informative columns and articles to help you make the most of your money. MoneySense magazine is published seven times a year by Rogers Media.
Ian McGugan, Editor
Deborah Rosser, Publisher

National Post Business, FP 500
#300, 1450 Don Mills Rd., Toronto, ON M3B 3R5
Tel: 416-383-2300; *Fax:* 416-386-2836
Toll-Free: 800-668-7678
feedback@canada.com
www.nationalpostbusiness.com
Circulation: 289,000 *Frequency:* Annually, June
Ranking of Canada's largest corporations
Brian Banks, Editor

North Country Business
PO Box 180, Bracebridge, ON P1L 1T6
Tel: 705-646-1314; *Fax:* 705-645-6424
info@muskokamagazine.com
http://ospreymediagroup.com
Circulation: 5,259 *Frequency:* 12 times a year
Donald Smith, Publisher

Northern Ontario Business
Laurentian Publishing Co., 158 Elgin St., Sudbury, ON P3E 3N5
Tel: 705-673-5705; *Fax:* 705-673-9542
Toll-Free: 800-757-2766
info@nob.on.ca
www.northernontariobusiness.com
Circulation: 10,000 *Frequency:* Monthly
Northern Ontario Business is printed every month and is the only publication devoted to the region's business community
Patricia Mills, Publisher, pmills@nob.on.ca
Kelly Louiseize, Managing Editor, kellyl@nob.on.ca

Northwest Business Magazine
Dakota Design & Advertising Ltd., 3907 - 3A St. NE, Bay 114, Calgary, AB T2E 6S7
Tel: 403-250-1128; *Fax:* 403-250-1194
dakotade@telusplanet.net
Circulation: 15,000 *Frequency:* 10 times a year
Regional business magazine that focuses on developments affecting the resource sectors in Northern BC, Alberta, Northwest Territories
Kathryn Engel, Editor

Nova Scotia Business Journal
Transontinental Specialty Publications, #609, 1888 Brunswick St., Halifax, NS B3J 3J8
Tel: 902-468-8027; *Fax:* 902-468-1775
info@transcontinental.ca
www.novascotiabusinessjournal.com
Circulation: 15,000 *Frequency:* Monthly
This established business-to-business journal, published 12 times a year, features coverage of premier events, local success stories, issues affecting Nova Scotia's many business sectors, and sought-after special features.
Barbt McCay Cashin, Editor

Office@Home
PO Box D-79, Bowen Island, BC V0N 1G0
Tel: 604-947-2275; *Fax:* 604-947-0633
officeathome@dowco.com
Frequency: 4 times a year
Dave Sharrock, Publisher
Dale Gagne, Editor

Okanagan Business Magazine
Byrne Publishing Group Inc., #10, 1753 Dolphin Ave., Kelowna, BC V1Y 8A6
Tel: 250-861-5399; *Fax:* 250-868-3040
Toll-Free: 888-311-1119
info@okanaganlife.com
www.okanaganlife.com
Circulation: 25,000 *Frequency:* 10 times a year
Okanagan Life captures the essence of life and lifestyles in the Okanagan with informative and entertaining stories on Okanagan food and wine, Okanagan travel, Valley music and entertainment, Okanagan real estate, fashion trends, Okanagan personalities, Okanagan business profiles, community activism, and much more. Okanagan Life Magazine is distributed to 24,460 Okanagan Valley homes, businesses, newsstands and subscribers making it the only city or regional magazine in North America to match or exceed the circulation of the region's largest daily newspaper.
Paul Byrne, Publisher

Ontario Industrial Magazine
#1159, 1011 Upper Middle Rd. East, Oakville, ON L6H 5Z9
Tel: 416-446-1404; *Fax:* 416-446-0502
Toll-Free: 800-624-2776
sales@oim-online.com
www.oim-online.com
Circulation: 20,000 *Frequency:* Monthly
OIM provides the very latest information about manufacturing technology, material handling products, industrial equipment & services, financial management and general business news
Keith Laverty, Publisher
Bill Bryson, Editorial Advisor

L'Opportuniste
450, 2e av, Sainte-Marie, QC G6E 1B6
Tél: 418-387-6969; *Téléc:* 418-387-5223
Ligne sans frais: 877-387-6969
redactionopp@dynamiques.com
www.dynamiques.com
Frequency: Mensuel

Ottawa Business Journal
Transcontinental Media, #30, 5300 Canotek Rd., Ottawa, ON K1J 8R7
Tel: 613-744-4800; *Fax:* 613-744-8232
obj@transcontinental.ca
www.ottawabusinessjournal.com
Circulation: 16,300 *Frequency:* 51 times a year
Ottawa Business Journal is the leading source of local business news and information for Canada's national capital region. Every Monday, the newspaper provides authoritative and in-depth news coverage on the sectors that comprise Ottawa's vibrant business scene, ranging from technology to commercial real estate and corporate finance to hospitality.
Michael Curran, Publisher

Partners, Italy & Canada
Italian Chamber of Commerce of Toronto, #1502, 80 Richmond St. West, Toronto, ON M5H 2A4
Tel: 416-789-7169; *Fax:* 416-789-7160
info.toronto@italchambers.net
www.italchambers.ca
Circulation: 12,000 *Frequency:* 4 times a year
partners is the official publication of the Italian Chamber of Commerce of Toronto. Published quarterly, the magazine features editorials and special reports written by international experts and tackles themes such as business ethics, design, multiculturalism, foreign trade, arts and entertainment. Through interviews and company profiles, partners is the voice of the Canadian, Italian and international business community.
Corrado Paina, Editorial Director, paina@italchambers.ca
Emily Saso, Managing Editor, saso@italchambers.ca

Port of Halifax
1300 Hollis St., Halifax, NS B3J 1T6
Tel: 902-420-9943; *Fax:* 902-429-9058
swhite@metroguide.ca
www.metroguidepublishing.ca/port.php
Circulation: 20,000
Port of Halifax Magazine features information about the Port of Halifax along with stories of interest to the international shipping community
Sheila Blair, Publisher

Profit: The Magazine for Canadian Entrepreneurs
One Mount Pleasant Rd., 11th Fl., Toronto, ON M4Y 2Y5
Tel: 416-764-1402; *Fax:* 416-764-1404
www.canadianbusiness.com
Circulation: 102,600 *Frequency:* 6 times a year; ISSN: 1183-1324
Published six times per year and boasting circulation of 101,000 and readership of 373,000, PROFIT delivers the highest composition of business decision-makers and managers / owner / professionals amongst all PMB measured English-language magazines in Canada
Deborah Rosser, Publisher

Progress
Penthouse, #1201, 1660 Hollis St., Halifax, NS B3J 1V7
Tel: 902-494-0999; *Fax:* 902-494-0997
progress@progresscorp.com
www.progresscorp.com
Circulation: 26,513 *Frequency:* 10 times a year; ISSN: 0046-6735
Pamela Scott Crace, Editor

Québec Enterprise
#200, 5, Place du Commerce, Ile des Soeurs, Montréal, QC H3E 1M8
Tél: 514-842-5492; *Téléc:* 514-842-5375
Ligne sans frais: 866-303-5492
magazine@quebecenterprise.com
www.quebecentreprise.com
Circulation: 25,000 *Frequency:* 5 fois par an; français
Magazine d'affaires couvrant les activités industrielles de toutes les régions du Québec
Daniel Boisvert, Président-éditeur

Québec Franchise & Occasions d'Affaires
CP 57, Youville, QC H2P 2V2
Tél: 514-383-0034; *Téléc:* 514-383-0057
info@quebec-franchise.qc.ca
www.quebec-franchise.qc.ca
Circulation: 10 000 copies *Frequency:* 6 times a year, French, 25% English
Spécialisé dans la franchise et les opportunités d'affaires au Québec et au Canada
Jacques Desforges, Editor

Québec inc
#100, 321, rue de la Commune ouest, Montréal, QC H2Y 2E1
Tél: 514-289-9595; *Téléc:* 514-289-9527
quebecinc@quebecinc.ca
www.quebecinc.ca/
Circulation: 33 231 *Frequency:* 8 fois par an
Magazine pour gens d'affaires du Québec
Claude Breton, Rédacteur en chef
Serge Therrien, Éditeur

Report on Business Magazine (ROB)
c/o The Globe and Mail, 444 Front St. West, Toronto, ON M5V 2S9
Tel: 416-585-5000; *Fax:* 416-585-3327
newsroom@globeandmail.com
www.theglobeandmail.com
Frequency: 11 times a year
Canada's premier business magazine is distributed nationwide with The Globe and Mail to targeted circulation. The thought-provoking and important business stories reach an

influential and educated audience. As a pro-business, pro-Canada and pro-reader magazine, it charts the path of business like no other publication in this country
Philip Crawley, Publisher and CEO

Revue Commerce
1100, boul René-Lévesque ouest, 24e étage, Montréal, QC H3B 4X9
Tél: 514-392-9000; *Téléc:* 514-392-2026
www.lesaffaires.com/publications/commerce.fr.html
Circulation: 37,766 *Frequency:* Mensuel; français; ISSN: 0380-9811
Magazine d'actualité qui couvre le monde des affaires
Diane Bérar, Rédactrice en chef

Senior Executive
Beacon Publishing Inc., 2150 Fillmore Cres., Ottawa, ON K1J 6A4
Tel: 613-747-1138; *Fax:* 613-747-7319
!publisher@seniorexec.ca!
www.seniorexec.ca
Circulation: 20,000 *Frequency:* 6 times a year
Senior Executive magazine features informative articles on topics such as: management techniques; service improvement;business developments; success stories; best practices; IM and IT; innovative use of technology; financial management; personal finance; innovative organizational approaches; modern comptrollership; risk management; policy issues; personnel and retention issues; stress management; transformations; horizontal management;and partnering innovations/successes/challenges between business and government.
John Kiska, Associate Editor
Jonathan Calof, Associate Editor
Chris MacLean, Managing Editor, !cmaclean@seniorexec.ca!
John Kiska, Associate Editor

SOHO Business Report
439A Marmont St., Coquitlam, BC V3K 4S4
Tel: 604-936-5815; *Fax:* 604-936-5805
Toll-Free: 888-963-5815
info@SOHObusinessreport.com
www.sohobusinessreport.com
Circulation: 40,000 *Frequency:* 4 times a year
SOHO Business Report is a quarterly magazine begun in 1989, when the SOHO-based business phenomenon was just a "blip" on the screen of public consciousness. It originated in Abbotsford, British Columbia, Canada from the home of founding publisher Barbara Mowat. Starting as a small newsletter, it first started as The B.C. Home Business Report, and was designed to help link home-based businesses across the province, providing the lone entrepreneur with practical tips and sensible advice on running their business. The newsletter was in demand, and soon other regional editions followed in Alberta and Ontario. Then in 1994, Home Business Report went national. After all these years, it was time for the magazine to enter its teenage growth spurt and the SOHO Business Report emerged as a celebration of over a decade and a half of helping entrepreneurs
Chad Thiessen, Publisher

Sounding Board
World Trade Center, #400, 999 Canada Pl., Vancouver, BC V6C 3E1
Tel: 604-681-2111; *Fax:* 604-681-0437
contactus@boardoftrade.com
www.boardoftrade.com
Circulation: 12,000 *Frequency:* 10 times a year
As the official monthly publication of The Vancouver Board of Trade, the Sounding Board newspaper provides analysis and discussion of regional and national issues facing the business community. The paper has a primary circulation of 12,000 and a conservatively estimated total readership of 30,000. Sounding Board is published 10 times per year by The Board, Vancouver's chamber of commerce.
Darcy Rezac, Managing Director, 604-641-1255
Tracy Campbell, Editor

Thompson's World Insurance News
PO Box 1027, Waterloo, ON N2J 4S1
Tel: 519-579-2500; *Fax:* 519-745-7321
mpub@sympatico.ca
www.thompsonsnews.com
Frequency: Weekly
Canada's only independent weekly for p&c insurance professionals, has been the industry's most trusted news source for more than a decade
Mark Publicover, Managing Editor

Thunder Bay Business
1145 Barton Street, Thunder Bay, ON P7B 5N3
Tel: 807-623-2348; *Fax:* 807-623-7515
nspinc@tbaytel.net
www.thunderbaybusiness.ca
Circulation: 5,000 *Frequency:* Monthly
Northwestern Ontario business publication
Scott Sumner, Publisher & Editor

Toronto Business Magazine
11966 Woodbine Ave., Gormley, ON L0H 1G0
Tel: 905-887-5048; *Fax:* 905-887-0764
Circulation: 48,085 *Frequency:* 6 times a year
Janet Gardiner, Publisher

The Toronto Stock Exchange Daily Record
130 King St. West, 3rd Fl., Toronto, ON M5X 1J2
Tel: 416-947-4655; *Fax:* 416-814-8811
Circulation: 1,000 *Frequency:* Daily
Toronto Stock Exchange publishes the names of conditionally approved companies in the Daily Record, a daily TSX publication
Catherine McGravey, Publisher & Editor

The Toronto Stock Exchange Monthly Review
130 King St., 3rd Fl., Toronto, ON M5X 1J2
Tel: 416-947-4655; *Fax:* 416-814-8811
Circulation: 2,000 *Frequency:* 12 times a year
Monthly bulletin containing market information for companies traded on the Toronto Stock Exchange
Catherine McGravey, Publisher & Editor

Trade & Commerce
1700 Church Ave., Winnipeg, MB R2X 3A2
Tel: 204-632-2606; *Fax:* 204-694-3040
tcommerce@wpgsun.com
www.tradeandcom.com
Circulation: 10,000 *Frequency:* 4 times a year
Trade & Commerce magazine produces annual "Market Surveys" on all Canadian provinces and territories, that review overall economic performance and highlight investment and growth opportunities in specific communities. Each of the year's five issues also profiles leading companies operating within the surveyed regions. The Access Americas section features attractive U.S. and international locations for Canadian business and industrial expansion. Distributed nationally to top managers in Canada fastest growing companies
George Mitchell, Publisher

YorkU
York University, West Office Bldg., 4700 Keele St., Toronto, ON M3J 1P3
Tel: 416-736-5058; *Fax:* 416-736-5681
editor@yorku.ca
www.yorku.ca/yorku
Circulation: 180,000 alumni editions *Frequency:* 5 times a year; includes 3 for alumni
YorkU is the magazine of York University
Berton Woodward, Publications Director

Camping & Outdoor Recreation

Camping Canada's Dealer News
Camping Canada Ltd., #5, 1020 Brevik Pl., Mississauga, ON L4W 4N7
Tel: 905-624-8218; *Fax:* 905-624-6764
Circulation: 56,000
William E. Taylor, Publisher
Peter Tasler, Editor-in-chief

Chemicals & Chemical Process Industries

Canadian Chemical News / L'Actualité chimique canadienne
c/o The Chemical Institute of Canada, #550, 130 Slater St., Ottawa, ON K1P 6E2
Tel: 613-232-6252; *Fax:* 613-232-5862
editorial@accn.ca
www.accn.ca
Circulation: 5,500 *Frequency:* 10 times a year
Michelle Piquettee, Editor-in-chief
Heather Dana Munroe, Managing Editor

Canadian Process Equipment & Control News
#29, 588 Edward Ave., Richmond Hill, ON L4C 9Y6
Tel: 905-770-8077; *Fax:* 905-770-8075
cpe@cpecn.com
www.cpecn.com
Circulation: 24,127 *Frequency:* 6 times a year
Mike Overment, Editor

Industrial Process Products & Technology
#1235, 1011 Upper Middle Rd. East, Oakville, ON L6H 5Z9
Tel: 905-475-4231; *Fax:* 905-475-3512
Toll-Free: 800-572-4231
mswan@ippt.ca
www.ippt.ca
Circulation: 24,190 *Frequency:* 6 times a year
Michael Swan, Publisher

Clothing & Accessories

Canadian Apparel Magazine
Canadian Apparel Federation, #504, 124 O'Connor St., Ottawa, ON K1P 5M9
Tel: 613-231-3220; *Fax:* 613-231-2305
Toll-Free: 800-661-1187
info@apparel.ca
www.apparel.ca
Circulation: 25,466 *Frequency:* 6 times a year
Bob Kirke, Publisher
Marsha Ross, Managing Editor

Kids Creations
c/o Children's Apparel Manufacturers' Association, #3110, 6900, boul Decarie, Montréal, QC H3X 2T8
Tel: 514-731-7774; *Fax:* 514-731-7459
cama@apparel.org
www.cama-apparel.org
Circulation: 12,000 *Frequency:* 4 times a year; English & French
Patrick Thomas, Business Manager & Executive Director
Andrea Taylor, Editor

Style
#701, 555 Richmond St. West, Toronto, ON M5V 3B1
Tel: 416-203-6737; *Fax:* 416-203-1057
rod@style.ca; leslie@style.ca
www.style.ca
Circulation: 12,000 *Frequency:* 5 times a year
Rod Morris, Publisher
Leslie Wu, Editor

Computing & Technology

CIO Canada
#302, 55 Town Centre Ct., Toronto, ON M1P 4X4
Tel: 416-290-0240; *Fax:* 416-290-0238
www.itworldcanada.com
Circulation: 8,000 *Frequency:* 12 times a year
David Carrey, Editor

Communications & Networking
Tel: 416-733-7600;
info@itbusiness.ca
www.itbusiness.ca
Circulation: 18,053 *Frequency:* 12 times a year
Joe Tersigni, Publisher

Computer Dealer News
Tel: 416-733-7600;
cdnsales@itbusiness.ca
www.itbusiness.ca
Circulation: 18,859 *Frequency:* 18 times a year
Paolo Del Nibletto, Editor

Computer World Canada
#302, 55 Town Centre Ct., Toronto, ON M1P 4X4
Tel: 416-290-0240; *Fax:* 416-290-0238
computerworld_canada@itworldcanada.com
www.itworldcanada.com
Circulation: 40,000 *Frequency:* 25 times a year
Dan McLean, Publisher
Greg Enright, Editor

Computing Canada
Tel: 416-733-7600; *Fax:* 416-227-8300
info@itbusiness.ca
www.itbusiness.ca
Circulation: 40,000 *Frequency:* 26 times a year
Joe Tersigni, Publisher

ConnectIT
17 Moodie Dr., Richmond Hill, ON L4C 8C9
Tel: 905-763-1200; *Fax:* 905-886-6216
swexler@integratedmar.com
www.integratedmar.com

Direction Informatique
Tél: 416-733-7600; *Téléc:* 416-227-8324
Ligne sans frais: 800-387-5012
directioninformatique@transcontinental.ca
www.directio ninformatique.com
Circulation: 17 939 *Frequency:* 10 fois par an; français
Stephanie Manseau, Coordonatrice de Production
Patrice-Guy Martin, Rédacteur
Marc Meloche, Directeur des Ventes

eChannelLine
17 Moodie Dr., Richmond Hill, ON L4C 8C9
Tel: 905-763-1200; *Fax:* 905-886-6216
Toll-Free: 800-465-2059
swexler@integratedmar.com
www.integratedmar.com
Circulation: 36,000 *Frequency:* daily
Steve Wexler, Editor-in-chief, Special Projects

HUB: Digital Living Magazine
c/o Piccolo Publishing Inc., 775 B The Queensway, Toronto, ON M8Z 1N1
Tel: 416-348-9666; *Fax:* 416-348-9553
Toll-Free: 800-465-3517
www.hubcanada.com

IT for Industry
1 Mount Pleasant Rd., 7th Fl., Toronto, ON M4Y 2Y5
Tel: 416-764-1546; *Fax:* 416-764-1742
Toll-Free: 800-268-9119
Joe.Terrett@plant.rogers.com
www.itforindustry.com
Circulation: 20,100 *Frequency:* 6 times a year
Dan Bordun, Publisher
Joe Terrett, Editor

Network Cabling
Tel: 905-727-0077; *Fax:* 905-727-0017
www.networkcabling.ca
Circulation: 9,200 *Frequency:* 6 times a year
Peter Young

Network World Canada
#302, 55 Town Centre Ct., Toronto, ON M1P 4X4
Tel: 416-290-0240; *Fax:* 416-290-0238
www.itworldcanada.com
Circulation: 16,000 *Frequency:* 24 times a year
Michael Martin, Editor

Technologies for Worship Magazine
3891 Holborn Rd., Queensville, ON L0G 1R0
Tel: 905-473-9822; *Fax:* 905-473-9928
info@tfwm.com
www.tfwm.com
Circulation: 30,000 *Frequency:* bi-monthly
Shelagh Rogers, Founder
Kevin Rogers Cobus, Editor

Technology in Government
Tel: 416-733-7600; *Fax:* 416-227-8300
info@itbusiness.ca
www.itbusiness.ca
Circulation: 19,437 *Frequency:* Monthly
Joe Tersigni, Publisher

Conventions & Meetings

Conventions Meetings Canada
1 Mount Pleasant Rd., 7th Fl., Toronto, ON M4Y 2Y5
Tel: 416-764-1635; *Fax:* 416-764-1419
steve.dempsey@mtg.rogers.com
www.meetingscanada.com
Circulation: 10,586 *Frequency:* Annually
Stephen Dempsey, Publisher

Meeting Places
BIV Media Group, #500, 1155 West Pender St., Vancouver, BC V6E 2P4
Tel: 604-688-2398; *Fax:* 604-688-6058
Circulation: 13,000
Paul Harris, Editor
Gail Clark, Publisher

Meetings & Incentive Travel (M&IT)
Tel: 416-764-1635; *Fax:* 416-764-1419
Circulation: 10,764 *Frequency:* 6 times a year
Steven Dempsey, Publisher

Cosmetics

Cosmetics Magazine
Tel: 416-764-1664; *Fax:* 416-764-1704
Circulation: 12,000 *Frequency:* 6 times a year; also Cosmetiques (3 fois par an; français)
James R. Hicks, Publisher

Credit

The Atlantic Co-operator
Atlantic Co-operative Publishers, 123 Halifax St., Moncton, NB E1C 8N5
Tel: 506-858-6617; *Fax:* 506-858-6615
editor@theatlanticco-opoperator.coop
www.theatlanticco-operator.coop
Circulation: 17,500 English; 3,500 French *Frequency:* 9 times a year; English & French
The Atlantic Co-operator is a monthly newspaper covering all aspects of co-operation values and principles in Atlantic Canada and around the world. We are published 9 times a year in both French and English by the Atlantic Co-operative Publishers and distributed throughout Atlantic Canada and les Iles-de-la-Madeleine, in Québec.
Jennifer MacLeod, Publisher
Mark Higgins, Editor, 506-858-6614
Jennifer MacLeod, Publisher

Dentistry

Canadian Journal of Dental Hygiene
c/o Canadian Dental Hygienists Assn., 96 Centrepointe Dr., Ottawa, ON K2G 6B1
Tel: 613-224-5515; *Fax:* 613-224-7283
Toll-Free: 800-267-5235
info@cdha.ca
www.cdha.ca
Circulation: 11,400 *Frequency:* 6 times a year
Susan A. Ziebarth, Executive Director
Susanne Sunell, Scientific Editor

Denturism Canada - The Journal of Canadian Denturism / Denturologie Canada
Tel: 204-985-9780; *Fax:* 204-985-9795
Toll-Free: 866-985-9780
info@kelman.ca
www.kelman.ca
Other information: Toll Free Fax: 1-866-985-9799
Circulation: 1,909 *Frequency:* 4 times a year
Kevin Hill, Editor

Journal de l'Ordre des dentistes du Québec
Ordre des dentistes du Québec, 625, boul René-Lévesque ouest, 15e étage, Montréal, QC H3B 1R2
Tél: 514-875-8511; *Téléc:* 514-875-9049
journal@odq.qc.ca
www.odq.qc.ca
Circulation: 5 300 *Frequency:* 10 fois par an; French
Dr. Denis Forest, Rédacteur

Journal of the Canadian Dental Association / Journal de l'Association Dentaire Canadienne
1815 Alta Vista Dr., Ottawa, ON K1G 3Y6
Tel: 613-523-1770; *Fax:* 613-523-7736
Toll-Free: 800-267-6354
reception@cda-adc.ca
www.cda-adc.ca
Circulation: 19,600 *Frequency:* 11 times a year; English & French
Dr. John O'Keefe, Editor

Manitoba Dentist
Cutting Edge Communications, #2, 1248 Pembina Hwy., Winnipeg, MB
Tel: 204-669-2377; *Fax:* 204-669-2336
Circulation: 1,700 *Frequency:* Annually
Jamie Parcells, Publisher

Ontario Dentist
4 New St., Toronto, ON M5R 1P6
Tel: 416-922-3900; *Fax:* 416-922-9005
www.oda.on.ca
Circulation: 7,000 *Frequency:* 10 times a year
Julia Kuipers, Managing Editor

Oral Health
Tel: 416-510-6785; *Fax:* 416-510-5140
Toll-Free: 800-268-7742
msummerfield@oralhealthjournal.com
www.oralhealthjournal.com
Other information: Toll Free: U.S. 1-800-387-0273
Circulation: 17,200 *Frequency:* Monthly
Melissa Summerfield, Publisher

Directories & Almanacs

Almanach du Peuple
#213, 3100, boul de la Concorde Est, Laval, QC H7E 2B8
Tél: 450-665-0271;
adv-pub.media@videotron.ca
Circulation: 125 000 *Frequency:* Annuellement; français
Luc Lemay, Éditeur
Robert Ferland, Directeur, Marketing

Buildcore
Reed Construction Data, 500 Hood Rd., 4th Fl., Markham, ON L3R 9Z3
Tel: 905-752-5450; *Fax:* 866-309-5774
Toll-Free: 800-465-6475
buildcore@reedbusiness.com
www.buildcore.com
Other information: Toll Free Fax: 1-800-570-5399
Circulation: 8,500 *Frequency:* Quarterly
Denise Holtby, Editor
David Dehaas, Publisher

Canadian Forces Base Kingston Official Directory
PO Box 1352, #205, 11 Princess St., Kingston, ON K7L 5C6
Tel: 613-549-8442; *Fax:* 613-549-4333
editorial@kingstonpublications.com
Circulation: 3,000 *Frequency:* Annually, March; English & French
Liza Nelson, Publisher

Frasers
Tel: 416-764-1467; *Fax:* 416-764-1710
suzanne.mccauley@frasers.rogers.com
www.frasers.com
Circulation: 6,000; 15,000 CD-Rom *Frequency:* Annually, March
Gloria Gallagher, Publisher

Sources
#305, 489 College St., Toronto, ON M6G 1A5
Tel: 416-964-7799; *Fax:* 416- -
www.sources.com
Circulation: 14,000 *Frequency:* 2 times a year
Ulli Diemer, Publisher

Drugs

L'actualité pharmaceutique
Tél: 514-843-2105; *Téléc:* 514-843-2183
caroline.belisle@rci.rogers.com
www.pharmacyconnects.com
Circulation: 6 000 *Frequency:* 12 fois par an; français
Caroline Bélisle, Éditeur
Caroline Baril, Rédacteur

The Canadian Journal of Hospital Pharmacy / Le Journal canadien de la pharmacie hospitalière
The Cdn. Society of Hospital Pharmacists, #3, 30 Concourse Gate., Ottawa, ON K2E 7V7
Tel: 613-736-9733; *Fax:* 613-736-5660
cjhpedit@cshp.ca
www.cshp.ca
Circulation: 3,200 *Frequency:* 7 times a year; English & French
Mary Ensom, Editor

Canadian Pharmaceutical Journal
1785 Alta Vista Dr., Ottawa, ON K1G 3Y6
Tel: 613-523-7877; *Fax:* 613-523-2332
Toll-Free: 800-917-9489
cpj@pharmacists.ca
www.pharmacists.ca
Circulation: 18,076 *Frequency:* 6 times a year
Leesa D. Bruce, Publisher
Renée Dykeman, Managing Editor
Rosemary R. Killeenn, Editor

Le Pharmactuel
L'Association des pharmaciens des établissements de santé, #320, 4050, rue Molson, Montréal, QC H1VH3A 1T1
Tél: 514-286-0776; *Téléc:* 514-286-1081
apes@globetrotter.net
www.pharmactuel.com
Circulation: 1 800 *Frequency:* 5 fois par an
Louise Mallet, ADES Editor

Pharmacy Post
Tel: 416-764-2000; *Fax:* 416-764-3931
www.pharmacyconnects.com
Circulation: 18,800 *Frequency:* 12 times a year; OTC Report (Apr.)
Janet Smith, Executive Publisher
Vicki Wood, Editor

Pharmacy Practice
Tel: 416-764-3926; *Fax:* 416-764-3931
rosalind.stefanac@pharmacygroup.rogers.com
www.pharmacyconnects.com
Circulation: 20,387 *Frequency:* 12 times a year

Rosalind Stefanac, Editor

Québec Pharmacie
#800, 1200, av McGill College, Montréal, QC H3B 4G7
Tél: 514-843-2569; *Téléc:* 514-843-2183
www.quebecpharmacie.org
Circulation: 7 350 *Frequency:* 10 fois par an; français
Hélène Blanchette, Editor

Education

Agenda
c/o Ontario English Catholic Teachers' Association, #400, 65 St. Clair Ave. East, Toronto, ON M4T 2Y8
Tel: 416-925-2493; *Fax:* 416-925-7764
Toll-Free: 800-268-7230
a.oconnor@oecta.on.ca
www.oecta.on.ca
Circulation: 46,000 *Frequency:* Sept.-June monthly (7 times during school year)
Aleda O'Connor, Director, Communications

The ATA Magazine
The Alberta Teachers' Association, 11010 - 142 St., Edmonton, AB T5N 2R1
Tel: 780-447-9400; *Fax:* 780-455-6481
www.teachers.ab.ca
Circulation: 42,000 *Frequency:* 4 times a year
Timothy Johnston, Editor
Raymond Gariépy, Managing Editor

Canadian Vocational Journal
Canadian Vocational Association, 645, rue Labonté, Longueuil, QC J4H 2R5
Tel: 450-442-2353; *Fax:* 450-442-2353
cva_acfp@ca.inter.net
cva-acfp.ca/journal/vol37no1_cover.htm
Frequency: 4 times a year electronically; English & French

CAUT Bulletin ACPPU
2675 Queensview Dr., Ottawa, ON K2B 8K2
Tel: 613-820-2270; *Fax:* 613-820-2417
duhaime@caut.ca
www.caut.ca
Circulation: 41,000 *Frequency:* 10 times a year
Greg Allain, President
James Turk, Executive Director
Liza Duhaime, Managing Editor

Education Forum
c/o Ontario Secondary School Teachers' Federation, 60 Mobile Dr., Toronto, ON M4A 2P3
Tel: 416-751-8300; *Fax:* 416-751-3875
Toll-Free: 800-267-7867
claytom@osstf.on.ca
www.osstf.on.ca
Circulation: 49,323 *Frequency:* 3 times a year
Renate Brandon, Advertising Director
Marianne Clayton, Assistant Editor
Janice Grant, Traffic Coordinator
Pierre Côté, Editor

Education Today
Ontario Public School Boards Assn., 439 University Ave. 18th Fl., Toronto, ON M5G 1Y8
Tel: 416-340-2540; *Fax:* 416-340-7571
webmaster@opsba.org
www.opsba.org
Circulation: 3,500 *Frequency:* 3 times a year; ISSN: 0843-5081
Catherine Watson, Editor

Educational Digest
11966 Woodbine Ave., Gormley, ON L0H 1G0
Tel: 905-887-5048; *Fax:* 905-887-0764
Circulation: 76,216 *Frequency:* 4 times a year
Janet Gardiner, Publisher

ESL in Canada Directory
PO Box 75117, 20 Bloor St. East, Toronto, ON M4W 3T3
Tel: 416-608-4194; *Fax:* 416-513-0026
info@eslincanada.com
www.eslincanada.com
Frequency: 2 times a year
Ross McBride, Production Manager

Green Teacher: Education for Planet Earth
95 Robert St., Toronto, ON M5S 2K5
Tel: 416-960-1244; *Fax:* 416-925-3474
info@greenteacher.com
www.greenteacher.com
Circulation: 7,200 *Frequency:* 4 times a year; ISSN: 1192-1285
Tim Grant, Co-Editor
Gail Littlejohn, Co-Editor

The Manitoba Teacher
The Manitoba Teachers' Society, 191 Harcourt St., Winnipeg, MB R3J 3H2
Tel: 204-888-7961; *Fax:* 204-831-0877
Toll-Free: 800-262-8803
gstephenson@mbteach.org
www.mbteach.org/mbteacher.htm
Circulation: 17,000 *Frequency:* 7 times a year
George Stephenson, Editor

OPC Register
180 Dundas St. West, Toronto, ON M5G 1Z8
Tel: 416-322-6600; *Fax:* 416-322-6618
Frequency: 4 times a year

Professionally Speaking / Pour parler profession
Ontario College of Teachers, 121 Bloor St. East, Toronto, ON M4W 3M5
Tel: 416-961-8800; *Fax:* 416-961-8822
Toll-Free: 888-534-2222
ps@oct.ca
www.oct.ca
Circulation: 218,570 *Frequency:* 4 times a year
Richard Lewko, Publisher
Philip Carter, Editor

Quebec Home & School News
Québec Federation of Home & School Associations, #560, 3285, boul Cavendish, Montréal, QC H4B 2L9
Tel: 514-481-5619; *Fax:* 514-481-5610
Toll-Free: 888-808-5619
info@qfhsa.org
www.qfhsa.org
Circulation: 7,600 distribution; 5,900 paid distribution *Frequency:* 4 times a year
Notorized publications data as of Sept. 2005
Donna Norris, President
Helen Koeppe, Editor

Teach Magazine
#206, 258 Wallace Ave., Toronto, ON M6P 3M9
Tel: 416-537-2103; *Fax:* 416-537-3491
info@teachmag.com
www.teachmag.com
Circulation: 22,000 *Frequency:* 5 times a year
Wili Liberman, Publisher & Editor

The Teacher
c/o Nova Scotia Teachers Union, 3106 Joseph Howe Dr., Halifax, NS B3L 4L7
Tel: 902-477-5621; *Fax:* 902-477-3517
Toll-Free: 800-565-6788
theteacher@nstu.ca
www.nstu.ca
Circulation: 13,000 *Frequency:* 10 times a year; Sept. to June
Angela Murray, Editor
Wayne Noseworthy, Executive Director
Mary-Lou Donnelly, President

University Affairs / Affaires universitaires
c/o Assn. of Universities & Colleges of Canada, #600, 350 Albert St., Ottawa, ON K1R 1B1
Tel: 613-563-1236; *Fax:* 613-563-9745
ua@aucc.ca
www.aucc.ca; www.universityaffairs.ca; www.affairesuniversitaires.ca
Circulation: 18,153 *Frequency:* 10 times a year; English & French; ISSN: 0041-9257
Christine Tausig Ford, Publisher
Peggy Berkowitz, Editor

Electrical Equipment & Electronics

CNS Cabling Networking Systems
#800, 12 Concorde Place, Toronto, ON M3C 4J2
Tel: 416-510-5111; *Fax:* 416-510-5134
Toll-Free: 800-268-7742
mlevy@cnsmagazine.com
www.cablingsystems.com
Circulation: 10,313 *Frequency:* 6 times a year
Maureen Levy, Publisher
Paul Barker, Editor

Electrical Business
www.ebmag.com
Circulation: 18,500 *Frequency:* Monthly
Bill Begin, Publisher

Electrical Line
3105 Benbow Rd., West Vancouver, BC V7V 3E1
Tel: 604-922-5516; *Fax:* 604-922-5312
info@electricalline.com
www.electricalline.com

Circulation: 20,789 *Frequency:* 6 times a year
Ken Buhr, Editor
Kevin Buhr, Publisher

Électricité Québec
5925, boul Decarie, Montréal, QC H3W 3C9
Tél: 514-738-2184; *Téléc:* 514-738-2192
info@cmeq.org
www.cmeq.org
Circulation: 9 834 *Frequency:* 6 fois par an; français
Hélène Rioux, Éditrice et rédactrice-en-chef

Electricity Today
Hurst Communications, #215, 1885 Clements Rd., Pickering, ON L1W 3V4
Tel: 905-686-1040; *Fax:* 905-509-4451
hq@electricityforum.com
www.electricityforum.com
Circulation: 12,255 *Frequency:* 8 times a year
Randolph Hurst, Publisher

EP&T
LVP Media Inc., #27, 1200 Aerowood Dr., Mississauga, ON L4W 2S7
Tel: 905-624-8100; *Fax:* 905-624-1760
info@ept.ca
www.ept.ca
Circulation: 24,000 *Frequency:* 8 times a year; also EP&T's Electrosource Product Reference Guide & Telephone Directory (annually, Jan.)
Robert Luton, Publisher

Report on Wireless
#1800, 160 Elgin St., Ottawa, ON K2P 2P7
Tel: 613-230-1984; *Fax:* 613-230-3793
phoffman@decima.ca
www.decima.ca
Frequency: Weekly
Perry Hoffman, Editor

Emergency Services

Canadian Emergency News
1121 Newscastle Rd., Drumheller, AB T0J 0Y2
Tel: 403-823-2290; *Toll-Free:* 800-567-0911
cen@emsnews.com
www.emsnews.com
Circulation: 4,000 *Frequency:* 6 times a year
Lyle Blumhagen, Publisher/Editor

Engineering

Aggregates & Roadbuilding Magazine
105 Donly Drive South, Simcoe, ON N3Y 4N5
Tel: 514-487-9868; *Fax:* 514-487-9276
www.rocktoroad.com
Circulation: 11,400 *Frequency:* 6 times a year
Andy Bateman, Editor, abateman1@cogeco.ca
Scott Jamieson, Group Publisher, sjamieson@annexweb.com

Annuaire Téléphonique de la Construction du Québec
CP 590, 22, rue St-Charles, Sainte-Thérèse, QC J7E 2A4
Tél: 450-437-1600; *Téléc:* 450-437-0723
optilog@optilog.com
www.optilog.com
Circulation: 7 200 *Frequency:* Annuellement; français
Michel Vaudrin, Éditeur & Rédacteur

Canadian Consulting Engineer
#800, 12 Concorde Place, Toronto, ON M4C 4J2
Tel: 416-510-5111; *Fax:* 416-510-5134
Toll-Free: 800-268-7742
bparsons@ccemag.com
www.canadianconsultingengineer.com
Circulation: 8,476 *Frequency:* 7 times a year
Maureen Levy, Publisher
Bronwen Parsons, Editor, 416/510-5119

Construction Alberta News
#50, 22 Rowland Cres., St Albert, AB T8N 5B3
Tel: 780-460-8004
Frequency: 2 times a year

Engineering Dimensions
#1000, 25 Sheppard Ave. West, Toronto, ON M2N 6S9
Tel: 416-224-1100; *Fax:* 416-224-8168
Toll-Free: 800-339-3716
webmaster@peo.on.ca
www.peo.on.ca
Other information: Toll Free Fax: 1-800-268-0496
Circulation: 68,000 *Frequency:* 6 times a year
Connie Mucklestone, Publisher

Geomatica
#400, 1390 Prince of Wales Dr., Ottawa, ON K2C 3N6
Tel: 613-224-9851; *Fax:* 613-224-9577
editgeo@magma.ca
www.cig-acsg.ca
Circulation: 1,059 *Frequency:* 4 times a year; English & French
Kelly Dean, Editor

Innovation
c/o Assn. of Professional Engineers & Geoscientists of BC, #200, 4010 Regent St., Burnaby, BC V5C 6N2
Tel: 604-430-8035; *Fax:* 604-430-8085
Toll-Free: 888-430-8035
apeginfo@apeg.bc.ca
www.apeg.bc.ca
Circulation: 22,000 *Frequency:* 6 times a year
Melinda Lau, Publications Specialist & Managing Editor
Derek Doyle, Executive Director & Registrar

Ontario Professional Surveyor
1043 McNicoll Ave., Toronto, ON M1W 3W6
Tel: 416-491-9020; *Fax:* 416-491-2576
Toll-Free: 800-268-0718
admin@aols.org
www.aols.org
Circulation: 1,400 *Frequency:* 4 times a year
Maureen Mountjoy, Editor

The Ontario Technologist
CLB Media Inc., 240 Edward St., Aurora, ON L4G 3S9
Tel: 905-727-0077; *Fax:* 905-727-0017
arush@clbmedia.ca
www.oacett.org
Circulation: 21,240 *Frequency:* 6 times a year
Angela Rush, Sales Representative

The PEGG
APEGGA, Scotia One, #1500, 10060 Jasper Ave. NW, Edmonton, AB T5J 4A2
Tel: 780-426-3990; *Fax:* 780-425-1722
Toll-Free: 800-661-7020
email@apegga.org
www.apegga.org
Circulation: 47,000 *Frequency:* 10 times a year
George Lee, Managing Editor

PLAN
Ordre des ingenieurs du Québec, Gare Windsor, #350, 1100, rue de la Gauchetière ouest, Montréal, QC H3B 2S2
Tél: 514-845-6141; *Téléc:* 514-845-1833
Ligne sans frais: 800-461-6141
plan@oiq.qc.ca
www.oiq.qc.ca
Circulation: 49 000 *Frequency:* 9 fois par an; français
Daniel Boismenu, Editeur
Geneviève Terreault, Coordonatrice
France Cadieux, Publicité

Plan Canada
Canadian Institute of Planners, #801, 116 Albert St., Ottawa, ON K1P 5G3
Tel: 613-237-7526; *Fax:* 613-237-7045
Toll-Free: 800-207-2138
general@cip-icu.ca
www.cip-icu.ca
Circulation: 4,715 *Frequency:* 4 times a year
Michele Garneau, Publisher
Mark Seasons, Chair, Editorial Board

Publiquip Inc.
490, Gilles Villeneuve, Berthierville, QC J0C 1A0
Tél: 450-836-3666; *Téléc:* 450-836-7401
ftrepanier@publiquip.com
www.publiquip.com
Circulation: 43 506 *Frequency:* Mensuel; français
Gilles Chevigny, Éditeur

Supply Post
#105, 26730 - 56th Ave., Langley, BC V4W 3X5
Tel: 604-607-5577; *Fax:* 604-607-0533
Toll-Free: 800-663-4802
robert.watson@supplypost.com
www.supplyline.com
Circulation: 14,436 *Frequency:* 11 times a year
Robert Watson, General Manager

Environment & Nature

Eco Week.ca
#800, 12 Concorde Pl., Toronto, ON M3C 4J2
Tel: 416-442-5600; *Fax:* 416-510-5148
dorchard@ecolog.com
www.ecoweek.ca
Frequency: weekly
Formally EcoLog Week, this publication aims to show its readers how to live a green lifestyle, as well keeping the public up-to-date on environmental issues of the day, including the environmental regulatory programs, new developments in waste-treatment, and how to get involved with local environmentalist organizations.
Deborah Orchard, Editor

EcoCompliance.ca
#800, 12 Concorde Place, Toronto, ON M3C 4J2
Tel: 416-422-5600; *Fax:* 416-510-5148
Toll-Free: 888-702-1111
llubka@ecolog.com
www.ecocompliance.ca
Frequency: Monthly
A monthly national newsletter that examines the developments and amendments in Canadian environmental law. It gives its readers commentary on new legislation, proposed environmental bills, changing environmental legislation, and all other issues affecting enviromental law policies in Canada.
Lidia Lubka, Associate Publisher

Ecoforestry
Ecoforestry Institute Society, PO Box 5070 B, Victoria, BC V8R 6N3
Tel: 250-595-0655; *Fax:* 250- -
journal@ecoforestry.ca
ecoforestry.ca
Frequency: quarterly
Journal looks at issues relating to the forestry industry using a low-impact approach to forest management. Its goal is to increase public awareness of ecoforestry by working with community organizations, offering workshops to the public and providing information.

EnviroLine
PO Box 77042 Chinatown, 4905 - 23 Ave. NW, Calgary, AB T2G 5J8
Tel: 403-263-3272; *Fax:* 403-263-3280
enviroline@shaw.ca; enviroca@cadvision.com
Circulation: 500 *Frequency:* 20 times a year
Provides Western Canadian resource industries with reviews of important and up-to-date environmental issues.
Mark Lowey, Publisher & Editor

Environmental Reviews
M-55, 1200 Montreal Rd., Ottawa, ON K1A 0R6
Tel: 613-993-9101; *Fax:* 613-952-9907
Toll-Free: 877-672-2672
pubs@nrc-cnrc.gc.ca; info@nrc-cnrc.gc.ca
pubs.nrc-cnrc.gc.ca
Circulation: 300 *Frequency:* Annually; ISSN: 1208-6053
Publication presents reviews on a range of environmental issues and topics, emphasizing the effects humans have on natural and manmade ecosystems. Topics investigated in this publication include climate change, air and marine pollution, erosion and agroforestry.
Bruce P. Dancik, Editor
Bushra Waheed, Managing Editor
Cameron Macdonald, Director

Recycling Canada
PO Box 378, Campbellford, ON K0L 1L0
Tel: 705-653-1112; *Fax:* 705-653-1113
dbp@personainternet.com
Mark Sabourin, Publisher & Editor

Recycling Product News
#201, 2323 Boundary Rd., Vancouver, BC V5M 4V8
Tel: 604-291-9900; *Fax:* 604-291-1906
ebaum@baumpub.com
www.baumpub.com
Circulation: 18,000 *Frequency:* 8 times a year
Publication focuses on products, technologies services and industry news in recycling and waste management, ranging from composting to scrap metal.
Engelbert J. Baum, Publisher
Keith Barker, Editor

Vecteur Environnement
#220, 911, rue Jean-Talon est, Montréal, QC H2R 1V5
Tél: 514-270-7110; *Téléc:* 514-270-7154
info@reseau-environnement.com
www.reseau-environnement.com
Circulation: 4 000 *Frequency:* 5 fois par an; français
Revue de l'industrie, des sciences et techniques de l'environnement du Québec; publiée par RÉSEAU environnement
Martine Boivin, Rédactrice-en-chef

European

Gateway to Czech Trade
#1006, 909 Bay St., Toronto, ON M5S 3G2
Tel: 416-929-3432; *Fax:* 416-929-3432
trade@ccrcc.net
www.ccrcc.net
Circulation: 4,500
L.J. Novotny, Publisher & Editor

Fire Protection

Atlantic Firefighter
Hilden Publishing Ltd., #456, 6 - 295 Queen St. East, Brampton, NS L6W 4S6
Toll-Free: 800-555-2514
info@atlanticfirefighter.ca
www.atlanticfirefighter.ca
Circulation: 6,200 *Frequency:* 11 times a year
Jennifer Brown, Publisher & Editor

Canadian Firefighter & EMS Quarterly
105 Donly Dr. South, Simcoe, ON N3Y 4N5
Toll-Free: 800-265-2827
firefightcan@annexweb.com
www.firefightingincanada.com
Circulation: 7,500 *Frequency:* 4 times a year
Martin McAnulty, Publisher
Jim Haley, Editor

Fire Fighting in Canada
Toll-Free: 800-265-2827
fire@annexweb.com
www.firefightingincanada.com
Circulation: 5,200 *Frequency:* 8 times a year
James Haley, Editor
Martin J. McAaulty, Publisher

The Fire Services Journal
6 Hillman Dr., Ajax, ON L1S 6X9
Tel: 905-428-8465; *Fax:* 905-683-9572
fire@interlog.com
www.fsj.on.ca
Circulation: 14,185 *Frequency:* 6 times a year
David Ross, Editor-in-chief
Sue Wells, Editor
Dan Haden, Publisher

Fisheries

Atlantic Fisherman
130 Wright Ave., Dartmouth, NS B3B 1R6
Tel: 902-422-4990; *Fax:* 902-422-4278
Circulation: 3,818 *Frequency:* Monthly
Ian Ross, Editor

The Fisherman
326 - 12th St., 1st Fl., New Westminster, BC V3M 4H6
Tel: 604-519-3638; *Fax:* 604-524-6944
fisherman@ufawu.org
Circulation: 7,700 *Frequency:* 4 times a year
Sean Griffin, Editor

Northern Aquaculture
4623 William Head Rd., Victoria, BC V9J 1R3
Tel: 250-478-3973; *Fax:* 250-478-3979
editor@naqua.com
www.naqua.com
Circulation: 3,600 *Frequency:* 12 times a year
Peter Chettleburgh, Publisher

The Sou'Wester
Transcontinental Media, #609, 1888 Brunswick St., Halifax, NS B3J 3J8
Tel: 902-425-8255; *Fax:* 902-468-1775
Circulation: 10,500 *Frequency:* 12 times a year
Jeff Nearing, Publisher

Floor Coverings

Coverings
Mayville Publishing (Canada) Ltd., 990 County Rd. 18, Cherry Valley, ON K0K 1P0
Tel: 613-476-4244; *Fax:* 613-476-5233
coverings@floorpage.com
www.floorpage.com
Circulation: 7,100 *Frequency:* 8 times a year
Peter Spragg, Publisher
Gillian Spragg, Administration

Surface
2105, rue de Salaberry, St-Bruno-de-Montarville, QC J3V 4N7
Tél: 450-441-4243; *Téléc:* 450-441-6997
soury@biz.videotron.ca
soury.ca/surface
Circulation: 5 500 *Frequency:* 5 fois par an; français
Marcel Soury, Rédacteur-en-chef

Florists

Canadian Florist
PO Box 530, 105 Donly Dr. South, Simcoe, ON N3Y 4N5
Fax: 519-429-3094
Toll-Free: 888-599-2228
dmccarthy@annexweb.com
florist.hortport.com
Circulation: 5,394 *Frequency:* 6 times per year
Drew McCarthy, Editorial Director
Sue Fredericks, Publisher

Food & Beverage

L'Actualité Alimentaire
615, Notre-Dame, Saint-Lambert, QC J4P 2K8
Tél: 514-990-6967; *Téléc:* 514-990-6967
mlemire@editionscomestibles.com
www.actualitealimentaire.com
Circulation: 5 000
Martin Lemire, Rédacteur

Canadian Pizza Magazine
PO Box 530, 105 Donly Dr. South, Simcoe, ON N3Y 4N5
Tel: 519-429-5177; *Fax:* 519-429-3094
Toll-Free: 888-599-2228
dgeerlinks@annexweb.com
www.canadianpizzamag.com
Circulation: 9,500 *Frequency:* 8 times a year
Diane Kleer, Publisher
Cam Wood, Editor

Food in Canada
Tel: 416-764-1503; *Fax:* 416-764-1755
www.foodincanada.com
Circulation: 9,200 *Frequency:* 9 times a year
Ingrid Eilbracht, Publisher

Footwear

Canadian Footwear Journal
241, rue Senneville, Senneville, ON H9X 3X5
Tel: 514-457-8787; *Fax:* 514-457-5832
cfj@shoetrades.com
www.shoetrades.com
Circulation: 7,000 *Frequency:* 8 times a year; plus Retail Buyers' Guide (annual), Shoemaking Buyers' Guide (annual)
Shirley Boake, Associate Publisher
Barbara McLeish, Editor

Forest & Lumber Industries

Canadian Forest Industries
#14, rue 90 Morgan, Baie-d'Urfé, QC H9X 3A8
Tel: 514-457-2211; *Fax:* 514-457-2558
jcft@qc.aira.com
www.forestcommunications.com
Circulation: 14,600 *Frequency:* 8 times a year
Tim Tolton, Publisher
Guy Fortin, Publisher
Scott Jamieson, Editor

Canadian Wood Products
Tel: 514-457-2211; *Fax:* 514-457-2558
info@forestecommunications.com
www.forestcommunications.com/cwp/
Circulation: 7,340 *Frequency:* 6 times a year
Tim Tolton, Publisher
Scott Jamieson, Editor

Directory of Ontario Lumber & Building Materials Retailers, Buyers' Guide & Product Directory
Lumber & Building Materials Association of Ontario, #27, 5155 Spectrum Way, Mississauga, ON L4W 5A1
Tel: 905-625-1084; *Fax:* 905-625-3006
www.lbmao.on.ca
Frequency: Annually, October

The Forestry Chronicle
Canadian Institute of Forestry, #504, 151 Slater St., Ottawa, ON K1P 5H3
Tel: 613-234-2242; *Fax:* 613-234-6181
cif@cif-ifc.org
www.cif-ifc.org
Circulation: 2,800 *Frequency:* 6 times a year
Roxanne M. Comeau, Publisher

Logging & Sawmilling Journal
PO Box 86670, 211 East 1st St., North Vancouver, BC V7L 1B4
Tel: 604-990-9970; *Fax:* 604-990-9971
Toll-Free: 866-405-6462
stanhope@forestnet.com
www.forestnet.com
Circulation: 16,200 *Frequency:* 10 times a year
Robert Stanhope, Publisher

Logging Management
Tel: 604-298-3005; *Fax:* 604-298-3966
Circulation: 20,000 *Frequency:* 4 times a year
Heri R. Baum, Publisher

Madison's Canadian Lumber Directory
PO Box 2486, #209, 980 West 1st St., Vancouver, BC V6B 3W7
Tel: 604-984-6838; *Fax:* 604-984-6572
madrep@direct.ca
www.madisonsreport.com
Circulation: 1,200 *Frequency:* Annually, Spring
Laurence Cater, Publisher

Mid-Canada Forestry & Mining
Tel: 204-985-9780; *Fax:* 204-985-9795
info@kelman.mb.ca
Circulation: 3,400 *Frequency:* 4 times a year
Terry Ross, Editor

Le Monde forestier
Tél: 418-877-4583; *Téléc:* 418-877-6449
journal@lemondeforestier.ca
www.lemondeforestier.ca
Circulation: 18 500 *Frequency:* 10 fois par an; français
Alain Castonguay, Rédacteur-en-chef

Opérations forestières et de scierie
#14, 90, rue Morgan, Baie d'Urfe, QC H9X 3A8
Tél: 514-457-2211; *Téléc:* 514-457-2558
info@forestcommunications.com
www.forestcommunications.com/of/
Circulation: 5 436 *Frequency:* 4 fois par an; français
Guy Fortin, Éditeur/Rédacteur

Yardstick
100 Southerland Ave., Winnipeg, MB R2W 3C7
Tel: 204-947-0222; *Fax:* 204-947-2047
Toll-Free: 800-665-2456
www.naylor.com
Circulation: 1,669 *Frequency:* 6 times a year; also WRLA Directory & Buyers' Guide (annually, Jan.)
Jonah O'Neill, Editor

Funeral Service

The Canadian Funeral Director Magazine
HPL Publishers, 1 Hanlan Ct., Whitby, ON L1N 9X4
Tel: 905-686-7161; *Fax:* 905-686-2159
info@thefuneralmagazine.com
www.thefuneralmagazine.com
Frequency: Monthly
Scott Hillier, Publisher & Editor

Canadian Funeral News
#1025, 101 - 6th Ave. SW, Calgary, AB T2P 3P4
Tel: 403-264-3270; *Fax:* 403-264-3276
Toll-Free: 800-465-0322
info@otcommunications.com
www.otcommunications.com/cfnindex.html
Frequency: Monthly
Patrick Ottmann, Publisher
Cammie Leard, Editor

Network
#1025, 101 - 6th Ave. SW, Calgary, AB T2P 3P4
Tel: 403-264-3270; *Fax:* 403-264-3276
Toll-Free: 800-465-0322
info@otcommunications.com
www.otcommunications.com/networkcontact.html
Frequency: 6 times a year
Patrick Ottman, Publisher
Cammie Leard, Editor

Fur Trade

The Canadian Trapper
Coyote Communications Inc., 32 Willoughby Dr., St Albert, AB T8N 3R3
Tel: 780-459-4734; *Fax:* 780-459-4731
Circulation: 5,778 *Frequency:* 6 times a year; also Alberta Trapper, 4 times a year (circ. 1,800); BC Trapper Magazine, 4 times a year (circ. 1,500)
Becky McIntosh, Publisher

Gardening & Garden Equipment

Canadian Garden Centre & Nursery
Tel: 519-429-3966; *Fax:* 519-429-3094
Circulation: 4,000 *Frequency:* 6 times a year
Anja Sonnenberg, Editor
Diane Geerlinks, Publisher

Greenhouse Canada
PO Box 530, 105 Donly Dr. South, Simcoe, ON N3Y 4N5
Tel: 519-235-2400; *Fax:* 519-235-0798
Toll-Free: 888-599-2228
pdarbishire@annexweb.com
www.greenhousecanada.com
Circulation: 5,500 *Frequency:* Monthly
Peter Darbishire, Publisher

Gifts

CGTA Retail News
Canadian Gift & Tableware Association, 42 Voyager Ct. South, Toronto, ON M9W 5M7
Tel: 416-679-0170; *Fax:* 416-679-1868
Toll-Free: 800-611-6100
retailnews@cgta.org
www.cgta.org
Circulation: 16,529 *Frequency:* 6 times a year
Tom Foran, Publisher
Erica Kirkland, Editor

Gifts & Tablewares
#800, 12 Concord Place, Toronto, ON M3C 4J2
Tel: 416-510-6826; *Fax:* 416-510-5134
Toll-Free: 800-268-7742
bbishop@gifts-and-tablewares.com
www.gifts-and-tablewares.com
Circulation: 15,010 *Frequency:* 7 times a year
Brenda Bishop, Publisher
Lori Smith, Editor

Glass

Glass Canada
Tel: 519-235-2400; *Fax:* 519-235-0798
ais@aiscommunications.net
Circulation: 5,800 *Frequency:* 6 times a year
Chris Skalkos, Editor
Peter Phillips, Publisher

Government

Forum
Federation of Canadian Municipalities, 24 Clarence St., Ottawa, ON K1N 5P3
Tel: 613-241-5221; *Fax:* 613-241-7440
www.fcm.ca
Frequency: 6 times a year; English & French
Robert Ross, Managing Editor

Government Purchasing Guide
Kenilworth Media Inc., #710, 15 Wertheim Ct., Richmond Hill, ON L4B 3H7
Tel: 905-771-7333; *Fax:* 905-771-7336
Toll-Free: 800-409-8688
sales@gpgmag.ca
www.gpgmag.ca
Circulation: 10,220 *Frequency:* 6 times a year
Ellen Kral, Publisher
Cora Golden, Director, Sales
Blair Adams, Editorial Director

MERX
#1000, 38 Antares Dr., Nepean, ON K2E 7V2
Tel: 800-964-6379; *Fax:* 888-235-5800
Toll-Free: 800-964-6379
merx@merx.com
www.merx.com

Municipal Redbook

Tel: 604-433-8164; *Fax:* 604-433-9549
Toll-Free: 888-878-2121
jocinfo@reedbusiness.com
www.journalofcommerce.com
Circulation: 2,000 *Frequency:* Annually

Municipal World
PO Box 399 Main, St Thomas, ON N5P 3V3
Tel: 519-633-0031; *Fax:* 519-633-1001
mwadmin@municipalworld.com
www.municipalworld.com
Circulation: 7,500 *Frequency:* Monthly
Susan Gardner, Executive Editor

Optimum Online: The Journal of Public Sector Management
The Summit Group, #100, 263 Holmwood Ave., Ottawa, ON K1S 2P8
Tel: 613-688-0763; *Fax:* 613-688-0767
Toll-Free: 800-575-1146
info@optimumonline.ca
www.optimumonline.ca
Circulation: 10,000
Gilles Paquet, Editor

Parliamentary Names & Numbers
Sources, #305, 489 College St., Toronto, ON M6G 1A6
Tel: 416-964-7799; *Fax:* 416- -
www.sources.com
Circulation: 500 *Frequency:* 2 times a year
Ulli Diemer, Publisher

Scott's Government Index
#800, 12 Concorde Place, Toronto, ON M3C 4J2
Tel: 416-442-2010; *Fax:* 416-510-6870
Toll-Free: 800-408-9431
pstuckey@scottsdirectories.com
www.scottsgi.ca
Paul Stuckey, Group Publisher
Barb Peard, Editor

Urba
Union des municipalitiés de Québec, #680, 680, rue Sherbrooke ouest, Montréal, QC H3A 2M7
Tél: 514-282-7700; *Téléc:* 514-282-8893
lpmenard@umq.qc.ca
www.umq.qc.ca
Circulation: 6 600 *Frequency:* 6 fois par an; français
Laurent Paul Ménard, Rédacteur

Graphic Arts

Applied Arts
#411, 18 Wynford Dr., Toronto, ON M3C 3S2
Tel: 416-510-0909; *Fax:* 416-510-0913
art@appliedartsmag.com
www.appliedartsmag.com
Circulation: 12,000 *Frequency:* 6 times a year; ISSN: 1196-1775
Roberta Heckhausen, Publisher, rosetta@appliedartsmag.com
Peter Giffen, Editor, editor@appliedartsmag.com

The Graphic Exchange
Brill Communications Inc., 25 Elm Ave., Toronto, ON M4W 1M9
Tel: 416-961-1325; *Fax:* 416-961-0941
Circulation: 13,394 *Frequency:* 6 times a year
Dan Brill, Publisher & Editor

Grocery Trade

L'Alimentation
Les Editions du marchand québécois, 1298, rue St-Zotique est, Montréal, QC H2S 1N7
Tél: 514-271-6922; *Téléc:* 514-271-1308
dbeaudin@l-alimentation.com
www.l-alimentation.com
Circulation: 15 700 *Frequency:* 10 fois par an; français
Diane Beaudin, Éditrice

Canadian Grocer

Tel: 416-764-2000; *Fax:* 416-764-1523
www.bizlink.com/cangrocer.htm
Circulation: 20,000 *Frequency:* 10 times a year
Karen James, Publisher

Grocer Today
4189 Lougheed Hwy., 4th Fl., Burnaby, BC V5C 6A7
Tel: 604-299-7311; *Fax:* 604-299-9188
cwm@canadawide.com
www.canadawide.com
Circulation: 14,812 *Frequency:* 10 times a year
Les Wiseman, Editor
Peter Legge, Publisher

Western Grocer

Tel: 204-954-2085; *Fax:* 204-954-2057
mp@mercury.mb.ca
www.mercury.mb.ca
Circulation: 16,005 *Frequency:* 6 times a year
Frank Yeo, Publisher
Kelly Gray, Editor

Hardware Trade

Hardware & Home Centre Magazine
#800, 12 Concorde Place, Toronto, ON M3C 4J2
Tel: 416-510-5106; *Fax:* 416-510-5140
eopasini@centremagazine.com
www.centremagazine.com
Circulation: 15,167 *Frequency:* 8 times a year
Greg Paliouras, Publisher
Elena Opasini, Editor

Hardware Merchandising

Tel: 416-764-1672; *Fax:* 416-764-1484
stephen.payne@rci.rogers.com
www.bizlink.com/hardwaremerchandising.htm
Circulation: 14,881 *Frequency:* 6 times a year
Stephen Payne, Publisher

Home Improvement Retailing
Powershift Communications Inc., #501, 245 Fairview Mall Dr., Toronto, ON M2J 4T1
Tel: 416-494-1066; *Fax:* 416-494-2536
info@powershift.ca
www.hirmagazine.com
Circulation: 15,500 *Frequency:* 6 times a year
Dante Piccinin, Publisher

Quart de Rond
Assn. des détaillants de matériaux de construction du Québec, 474, rue Trans-Canada, Longueuil, QC J4G 1N8
Tél: 450-646-5842; *Téléc:* 450-646-6171
Ligne sans frais: 877-723-6220
information@admacq.qc.ca
www.admacq.qc.ca
Circulation: 3 200 *Frequency:* 8 fois par an; français
Donald O'Hara, Éditeur

Health & Medical

L'Actualité Médicale

Tél: 514-843-5141; *Téléc:* 514-843-2183
Circulation: 18 258 *Frequency:* 40 fois par an; français
Catherine Choquette, Rédactrice

The Alberta Doctors' Digest
Alberta Medical Association, 12230 - 106 Ave. NW, Edmonton, AB T5N 3Z1
Tel: 780-482-2626; *Fax:* 780-482-5445
Toll-Free: 800-270-9680
amamail@albertadoctors.org
www.albertadoctors.org
Circulation: 8,300 *Frequency:* 6 times a year
Dr. Dennis W. Jirsch, Editor

British Columbia Medical Journal
c/o BC Medical Association, #115, 1665 West Broadway, Vancouver, BC V6J 5A4
Tel: 604-638-2815; *Fax:* 604-638-2917
Toll-Free: 800-972-2262
journal@bcma.bc.ca
www.bcma.org/public/bc_medical_journal/overview.htm;
www.bcmj.org
Circulation: 10,500 *Frequency:* 10 times a year
Jay Draper, Managing Editor M.D., JDraper@bcma.bc.ca

Canadian Association of Radiologists Journal (CARJ/JACR) / Journal l'assn canadienne des radiologistes
Department of Radiology, HHSC - MUMC Site, 1200 Main St. West, Hamilton, ON L8N 3Z5
Fax: 905-521-1390
carj@mcmaster.ca
www.carj.ca
Circulation: 1,800 *Frequency:* 5 times a year; English & French
Emphasizes medical education and continuing professional development fo r radiologists
Dr. Craig Coblentz, Editor-in-chief

Canadian Chiropractor

Tel: 519-429-5174; *Fax:* 519-429-3094
www.canadianchiropractor.ca
Circulation: 5,800 *Frequency:* 7 times a year
David Stubbs, Editor
Diane Geerlinks, Publisher

Canadian Family Physician
College of Family Physicians of Canada, 2630 Skymark Ave., Mississauga, ON L4W 5A4
Tel: 905-629-0900; *Fax:* 905-629-0893
Toll-Free: 800-387-6197
www.cfpc.ca/cfp
Circulation: 35,000 *Frequency:* Monthly
Dr. Diane Kelsall, Scientific Editor

Canadian Healthcare Manager

Tel: 416-764-2000; *Fax:* 416-764-3930
www.chmonline.ca
Circulation: 19,000 *Frequency:* 8 times a year
Kim Laudrum, Editor
Alison Webb, Publisher

Canadian Healthcare Technology
#207, 1118 Centre St., Thornhill, ON L4J 7R9
Tel: 905-709-2330; *Fax:* 905-709-2258
info2@canhealth.com
www.canhealth.com
Circulation: 12,715 *Frequency:* 8 times a year
Jerry Zeidenberg, Publisher

Canadian Journal of Anesthesia / Journal Canadien d'Anesthésie
c/o Canadian Anesthesiologists' Society, #208, 1 Eglinton Ave. East, Toronto, ON M4P 3A1
Tel: 416-480-0602; *Fax:* 416-480-0320
cja@cas.ca
www.cas.ca
Circulation: 5,000 *Frequency:* Monthly
Dr. Donald R. Miller, Editor
Phillipe Ménard, Managing Editor

Canadian Journal of Cardiology
2902 South Sheridan Way, Oakville, ON L6J 7L6
Tel: 905-829-4770; *Fax:* 905-829-4799
pulsus@pulsus.com
www.pulsus.com
Circulation: 15,500 *Frequency:* 14 times a year
Robert B. Kalina, Publisher
Dr. E.R. Smith, Editor-in-chief

Canadian Journal of Cardiology

Circulation: 15,500 *Frequency:* 14 times a year
Dr. E. Smith, Editor

Canadian Journal of Continuing Medical Education (CME)

Tel: 514-695-7623; *Fax:* 514-695-8554
cme@sta.ca
www.stacommunications.com
Circulation: 35,544 *Frequency:* 12 times a year
Robert E. Passaretti, Publisher

The Canadian Journal of Diagnosis

Tel: 514-695-7623; *Fax:* 514-695-8554
diagnosis@sta.ca
www.stacommunications.com
Circulation: 35,266 *Frequency:* Monthly
Robert Passaretti, Publisher

Canadian Journal of Dietetic Practice & Research / Revue canadienne de la pratique et de la recherche en diété
#5, 500 Cochrane Dr., Markham, ON L3R 8E2
Tel: 905-940-0200; *Fax:* 905-940-0204
www.dietitians.ca
Circulation: 5,305 *Frequency:* 4 times a year; French & English
Marsha Sharp, CEO

Canadian Journal of Emergency Medicine (CJEM/JCMU) / Journal canadien de la médecine d'urgence
Canadian Association of Emergency Physicians, #104, 1785 Alta Vista Dr., Ottawa, ON K1G 3Y6
Tel: 613-523-3343; *Fax:* 613-523-0190
Toll-Free: 800-463-1158
cjem@caep.ca
www.caep.ca

Circulation: 4,000 *Frequency:* 6 times a year
Grant Innes, Editor-in-chief

Canadian Journal of Gastroenterology

Tel: 905-829-4770; *Fax:* 905-829-4799
pulsus@pulsus.com
www.pulsus.com
Circulation: 13,700 *Frequency:* Monthly
Robert B. Kalina, Publisher
Dr. P. Adams, Editor-in-chief

Canadian Journal of Geriatrics
#220, 115 King St. West, Dundas, ON L9H 1V1
Tel: 905-628-4309; *Fax:* 905-628-6847
brobinson@andrewjohnpublishing.com
www.andrewjohnpublishing.com
Circulation: 15,500 *Frequency:* 4 times a year
John D. Birkby, Publisher

Canadian Journal of Infectious Diseases & Medical Microbiology

Tel: 905-829-4770; *Fax:* 905-829-4799
pulsus@pulsus.com
www.pulsus.com
Circulation: 8,800 *Frequency:* 6 times a year
Robert B. Kalina, Publisher
Dr. L.E. Nicolle, Editor-in-chief

Canadian Journal of Infectious Diseases & Medical Microbiology

Circulation: 9,600 *Frequency:* 6 times a year
Dr. L. Nicolle, Editor

Canadian Journal of Medical Laboratory Science (CJMLS)
Cdn. Society for Medical Laboratory Science, PO Box 2830 LCD 1, Hamilton, ON L8N 3N8
Tel: 905-528-8642; *Fax:* 905-528-4968
Toll-Free: 800-263-8277
Alison@csmls.org
www.csmls.org
Circulation: 16,000 *Frequency:* 6 times a year; English & French editions
Alison McLennan, Publisher

Canadian Journal of Medical Radiation Technology / Le Journal Canadien des Techniques en Radiation Médicale
Canadian Assn. of Medical Radiation Technologists, 85 Albert St., 10th Fl., Ottawa, ON K1P 6A4
Tel: 613-234-0012; *Fax:* 613-234-1097
Toll-Free: 800-463-9729
www.camrt.ca/english/publications/journal.asp
Circulation: 10,468 *Frequency:* 4 times a year; English & French
Christiane Ménard, Director of Communications

Canadian Journal of Neurological Sciences
#709, 7015 MacLeod Trail SW, Calgary, AB T2H 2K6
Tel: 403-229-9575; *Fax:* 403-229-1661
journal@cjns.org
www.cjns.org
Circulation: 1,600 *Frequency:* 4 times a year; English & French
G. Bryan Young, Editor
Dan Morin, CEO

The Canadian Journal of Occupational Therapy / Revue canadienne d'ergothérapie
Carleton Technology & Training Centre, #3400, 1125 Colonel By Dr., Ottawa, ON K1S 5R1
Tel: 613-523-2268; *Fax:* 613-523-2552
Toll-Free: 800-434-2268
publications@caot.ca
www.caot.ca
Circulation: 7,000 *Frequency:* 5 times a year; English & French
Marcia Finlayson, Editor

Canadian Journal of Ophthalmology
Canadian Ophthalmological Society, #610, 1525 Carling Ave., Ottawa, ON K1Z 8R9
Tel: 613-729-6779; *Fax:* 613-729-7209
Toll-Free: 800-267-5763
cos@eyesite.ca
www.eyesite.ca
Circulation: 1,300 *Frequency:* 7 times a year
Dr. Graham E. Trope, Editor in Chief

The Canadian Journal of Plastic Surgery / Journal canadien de chirurgie plastique
2902 South Sheridan Way, Oakville, ON L6J 7L6
Tel: 905-829-4770; *Fax:* 905-829-4799
pulsus@pulsus.com
www.pulsus.com
Circulation: 5,200 *Frequency:* 4 times a year; English with French abstracts
Dr. P.E. Wyshynski, Editor-in-chief
Robert B. Kalina, Publisher

Canadian Journal of Plastic Surgery

Circulation: 13,000 *Frequency:* 4 times a year
Dr. P. Wyshynski, Editor

Canadian Journal of Public Health (CJPH) / Revue canadienne de santé publique
Canadian Public Health Association, #400, 1565 Carling Ave., Ottawa, ON K1Z 8R1
Tel: 613-725-3769; *Fax:* 613-725-9826
cjph@cpha.ca
www.cpha.ca
Circulation: 2,300 *Frequency:* Bi-monthly; English & French
Patricia Huston, Hon. Scientific Editor
Elinor Wilson, Executive Managing Editor

Canadian Journal of Rural Medicine (CJRM) / Journal canadien de la médecine rurale

Tel: 613-731-9331; *Fax:* 613-523-0937
pubs@cma.ca
www.cma.ca/cjrm
Circulation: 7,000 *Frequency:* 4 times a year
John Wootton, Editor-in-chief M.D.
Suzanne Kingsmill

Canadian Journal of Surgery (CJS/JCC) / Journal canadien de chirurgie

Tel: 613-731-9331; *Fax:* 613-523-0937
Toll-Free: 800-267-9703
pubs@cma.ca
www.cma.ca/cjs
Circulation: 2,900 *Frequency:* 6 times a year; English & French
A peer reviewed journal meeting the medical education needs of Canada's surgical specialists
Garth L. Warnick, Co-Editor M.D.
J.P. Waddell, Co-Editor M.D.

Canadian Medical Association Journal (CMAJ/JAMC) / Journal de l'Association médicale canadienne

Tel: 613-731-9331; *Fax:* 613-565-5471
Toll-Free: 800-663-7336
pubs@cma.ca
www.cmaj.ca
Circulation: 62,000 *Frequency:* 25 times a year; English; some French
For canadian physicians; reflects the complexities of modern medical practice through concise reports on original research, peer commentaries and review articles

Canadian Nursing Home
c/o Health Media, 14453 - 29A Ave., White Rock, BC V4P 1P7
Tel: 604-535-7933; *Fax:* 604-535-9000
www.nursinghomemagazine.ca
Circulation: 3,000 *Frequency:* 4 times a year
Agnes Forster, Managing Editor
Frank Fagan, Editor

Canadian Respiratory Journal

Tel: 905-829-4770; *Fax:* 905-829-4799
Toll-Free: 866-879-4770
pulsus@pulsus.com
www.pulsus.com
Circulation: 15,600 *Frequency:* 8 times a year
Robert B. Kalina, Publisher
Dr. N. Anthonisen, Editor-in-chief

The Chronicle of Cardiovascular & Internal Medicine

Tel: 905-273-9116; *Fax:* 905-273-4322
health@chronicle.org
www.chronicle.ca
Circulation: 5,843 *Frequency:* 6 times a year
Mitchell Shannon, Publisher
R. Allan Ryan, Editorial Director

The Chronicle of Neurology & Psychiatry

Tel: 905-273-9116; *Fax:* 905-273-4322
Toll-Free: 866-633-4766
health@chronicle.org
www.chronicle.ca/neuro.htm
Circulation: 6,189 *Frequency:* 9 times a year
Mitchell Shannon, Publisher
R. Allan Ryan, Senior Editor

The Chronicle of Skin & Allergy

Tel: 905-273-9116; *Fax:* 905-273-4322
Toll-Free: 866-633-4766
health@chronicle.org
www.chronicle.ca
Circulation: 7,045 *Frequency:* 9 times a year
R. Allan Ryan, Senior Editor
Mitchell Shannon, Publisher

The Chronicle of Urology & Sexual Medicine

Tel: 905-273-9116; *Fax:* 905-273-4322
Toll-Free: 866-633-4766
health@chronicle.org
www.chronicle.ca
Circulation: 5,020 *Frequency:* 6 times a year
Mitchell Shannon, Publisher
R. Allan Ryan, Senior Editor

Clinical & Investigative Medicine (CIM) / Médecine clinique et expérimentale
Canadian Society for Clinical Investigation, 774 Echo Dr., Ottawa, ON K1S 5N8
Tel: 613-730-6240; *Fax:* 613-730-1116
csci@rcpsc.edu
www.csci-scrc.medical.org
Circulation: 1,000 *Frequency:* 6 times a year
David Bevan, Editor

Clinical & Refractive Optometry

Tel: 514-331-4561; *Fax:* 514-336-1129
info@mediconcept.ca
www.mediconcept.ca
Circulation: 3,065 *Frequency:* 12 times a year
Lawrence Goldstein, Publisher
Dr. Barbara Caffery, Editor-in-chief

Clinical & Surgical Ophthalmology

Tel: 514-331-4561; *Fax:* 514-336-1129
info@mediconcept.ca
www.mediconcept.ca
Circulation: 1,500 *Frequency:* 12 times a year
Dr. Steve Arshinoff, Editor
Lawrence Goldstein, Publisher

Le Clinicien
#306, 955 Boul. St. John, Pointe-Claire, QC H9R 5K3
Tél: 514-695-7623; *Téléc:* 514-695-8554
clinicien@sta.ca
www.stacommunications.com
Circulation: 12 149 *Frequency:* Mensuel; français
Robert Passaretti, Éditeur

Coup d'oeil
Breton Communications Inc., #202, 495, boul St-Martin ouest, Laval, QC H7M 1Y9
Tél: 450-629-6005; *Téléc:* 450-629-6044
Ligne sans frais: 888-462-2112
breton.com@bretoncom.com
www.bretoncom.com
Circulation: 4,055 *Frequency:* 6 fois par an
Martine Breton, President

CrossCurrents: The Journal of Addiction & Mental Health
Centre for Addiction & Mental Health, 33 Russell St., Toronto, ON M5S 2S1
Tel: 416-595-6714; *Fax:* 416-593-4694
hema_zbogar@camh.net
www.camh.net/publications
Circulation: 3,000 *Frequency:* 4 times a year
Hema Zbogar, Editor

Dental Practice Management

Tel: 416-510-6785; *Fax:* 416-510-5140
Toll-Free: 800-268-7742
cwilson@oralhealthjournal.com
www.oralhealthjournal.com
Other information: Toll Free: U.S. 1-800-387-0273
Circulation: 18,700 *Frequency:* 4 times a year

Catherine Wilson, Editor

Dermatology Times of Canada
#102, 155A Matheson Blvd. West, Mississauga, ON L5R 3L5
Tel: 905-286-9800; *Fax:* 905-286-9811
Toll-Free: 800-561-7516
info@ctccomm.com
www.ctccomm.com
Circulation: 6,800 *Frequency:* 6 times a year
M.E. Farley, Publisher
K. Pearsall, Managing Editor
Karen Tousignant, Advertising

Doctor's Review
400 McGill, 3rd Fl., Montréal, QC H2Y 2G1
Tel: 514-397-8833; *Fax:* 514-397-0228
Toll-Free: 800-663-7403
drletters@parkpub.com
www.doctorsreview.com
Circulation: 40,000 *Frequency:* Monthly
David Elkins, Publisher
Annarosa Sabbadini, Editor

doctorNS
Doctors Nova Scotia, 5 Spectacle Lake Dr., Dartmouth, NS B3B 1X7
Tel: 902-468-1866; *Fax:* 902-468-6578
kelly.stoddard@doctorsns.com
www.doctorsns.com
Circulation: 3,000 *Frequency:* 10 times a year
Kelly Stoddard, Editor

Fitness Business Canada
30 Mill Pond Dr., Georgetown, ON L7G 4S6
Tel: 905-873-0850; *Fax:* 905-873-8611
www.fitnet.ca
Graham Longwell, Publisher
Barb Gormley, Managing Editor

FMWC Newsletter
Federation of Medical Women of Canada, 780 Echo Dr., Ottawa, ON K1S 5R7
Tel: 613-569-5881; *Fax:* 616-569-4432
Toll-Free: 877-771-3777
fmwcmain@fmwc.ca
www.fmwc.ca
Other information: Toll Free Fax: 1-877-772-5777
Circulation: 1,000 *Frequency:* 3 times a year
Gail Beck, President

Gastroenterology Canada
Circulation: 10,041 *Frequency:* 4 times a year
Michael E. Farley, Publisher

Geriatrics & Aging
#300, 162 Cumberland St., Toronto, ON M5R 3N5
Tel: 416-480-9478; *Fax:* 416-480-2740
www.geriatricsandaging.ca
Circulation: 25,270 *Frequency:* 10 times a year
Michael Yasny, Publisher
Kristin Casady, Editorial Director

Guide to Canadian Healthcare Facilities
c/o Canadian Healthcare Association, 17 York St., Ottawa, ON K1N 9J6
Tel: 613-241-8005; *Fax:* 613-241-9481
custserv@cha.ca
www.cha.ca
Circulation: 1,300 *Frequency:* annual
Eleanor Sawyer, Director, Publishing
Nola Haddadian, Managing Editor

HEALTHbeat
#319, 9768 - 170 St., Edmonton, AB T5T 5L4
Tel: 780-413-9342; *Fax:* 780-413-9328
Toll-Free: 800-727-0782
info@mccronehealthbeat.com
www.mccronehealthbeat.com
Circulation: 40,000 *Frequency:* 12 times a year
Jan Henry, Publisher

Healthcare Management FORUM / Forum gestion des soins de santé
Canadian College of Health Service Executives, 292 Somerset St. West, Ottawa, ON K2P 0J6
Tel: 613-235-7218; *Fax:* 613-235-5451
Toll-Free: 800-363-9056
cchse@cchse.org
www.cchse.org
Circulation: 3,500 *Frequency:* 4 times a year
Patricia Brown, Managing Editor

Hospital News, Canada
Trader Media Corp, 15 Apex Rd., Toronto, ON M6A 2V6
Tel: 416-781-5516; *Fax:* 416-781-5499
editor@hospitalnews.com
www.hospitalnews.com
Circulation: 32,650 *Frequency:* Monthly
Julie Abelsohn, Publisher

Journal of Otolaryngology
Tel: 905-522-7017; *Fax:* 905-522-7839
info@bcdecker.com
www.bcdecker.com
Circulation: 1,113 *Frequency:* 6 times a year

Journal of Psychiatry & Neuroscience (JPN) / Revue de psychiatrie & de neuroscience
Tel: 613-731-9331; *Fax:* 613-523-0937
Toll-Free: 800-267-9703
pubs@cma.ca
www.cma.ca/jpn
Circulation: 7,200 *Frequency:* 6 times a year, English & French
R.T. Joffe, Co-Editor M.D.
S.N. Young, Co-Editor M.D.

The Journal of Rheumatology
Journal of Rheumatology Publishing Co. Ltd., #901, 365 Bloor St. East, Toronto, ON M4W 3L4
Tel: 416-967-5155; *Fax:* 416-967-7556
jrheum@jrheum.com
www.jrheum.com
Circulation: 3,500 *Frequency:* Monthly
Duncan A. Gordon, Editor-in-chief

Journal of the Canadian Chiropractic Association
1396 Eglinton Ave. West, Toronto, ON M6C 2E4
Tel: 416-781-5656; *Fax:* 416-781-7344
Circulation: 5,384 *Frequency:* 4 times a year
Dr. Allan Gotlib, Editor

Journal SOGC
Society of Obstetrician & Gynaecology of Canada, 780 Echo Dr., Ottawa, ON K1P 5J3
Tel: 613-730-4192; *Fax:* 613-730-4314
Toll-Free: 800-561-2416
helpdesk@sogc.com
www.sogc.org/jogc
Circulation: 9,970 *Frequency:* 13 times a year; English with French abstracts
Timothy Rowe, Editor in Chief

Long Term Care
Ontario Long Term Care Association, #202, 345 Renfrew Dr., Markham, ON L3R 9S9
Tel: 905-470-8995; *Fax:* 905-470-9595
info@oltca.com
www.oltca.com
Circulation: 6,000 *Frequency:* 4 times a year

Medactuel-FMC
c/o Éditions Santé Rogers media, 1001, boul de Maisonneuve ouest, 10e étage, Montréal, QC H3A 3E1
Tél: 514-843-2539
Circulation: 11 158 *Frequency:* 15 fois par an
Catherine Choquette, Rédactrice-en-chef

Le Médecin du Québec
Quebec Federation of General Practitioners, #1000, 1440, rue St-Catherine ouest, Montréal, QC H3G 1R8
Tél: 514-878-1911; *Téléc:* 514-878-4455
Ligne sans frais: 800-361-8499
info@fmoq.org
www.fmoq.org
Circulation: 17 900 *Frequency:* Mensuel; français
Louise Roy, Rédacteur M.D.

Médecine/sciences
#800, 500, Sherbrooke ouest, Montréal, QC H3A 3C6
Tél: 514-288-2247; *Téléc:* 514-288-0520
medecine.sciences@bellnet.caa
Circulation: 2 007 *Frequency:* 10 fois par an
Michel Bergeron, Directeur général

The Medical Post
Tel: 416-764-3887; *Fax:* 416-764-1207
info@medicalpost.rogers.com
www.mdpassport.com
Circulation: 47,755 *Frequency:* 48 times a year
Nancy Kent, Associate Publisher

Nutrition - Science en Evolution
#1220, 2155, rue Guy, Montréal, QC H3H 2R9
Tel: 514-393-3733; *Fax:* 514-393-3582
Toll-Free: 888-393-8528
opdq@opdq.org
www.opdq.org
Circulation: 2,500 *Frequency:* 3 times a year; French
Paul-Guy Duhamel, President

Obesity Surgery
PO Box 1002, 5863 Leslie St., Toronto, ON M2H 1J8
Tel: 416-224-5055; *Fax:* 416-224-5455
journal@obesitysurgery.com
www.obesitysurgery.com
Circulation: 2,300 *Frequency:* 12 times a year
Frances Deitel, Publisher

Obstetrics & Gynaecology Canada
Circulation: 10,000 *Frequency:* 4 times a year
Michael E. Farley, Publisher
Kathy Pearsall, Managing Editor

Occupational Therapy Now / Actualités ergothérapiques
CTTC Bldg., #3400, 1125 Coloney By Dr., Ottawa, ON K1S 5R1
Tel: 613-523-2268; *Fax:* 613-523-2552
Toll-Free: 800-434-2268
subscriptions@caot.ca
www.caot.ca
Circulation: 6,500 *Frequency:* 6 times a year
Fern Swedlove, Editor

Oncology Exchange
400 McGill St., 3rd Fl., Montréal, QC H2Y 2G1
Tel: 514-397-8833; *Fax:* 514-397-0228
Toll-Free: 800-663-7403
www.oncologyex.com
Circulation: 6,000 *Frequency:* 6 times a year

Ontario Medical Review
Ontario Medical Assn., #300, 525 University Ave., Toronto, ON M5G 2K7
Tel: 416-599-2580; *Fax:* 416-340-2232
Toll-Free: 800-268-7215
kim_secord@oma.org
www.oma.org
Circulation: 27,000 *Frequency:* 11 times a year
Jeff Henry, Editor
Elizabeth Petruccelli, Managing Editor
Kim Secord, Circulation Manager

Optical Prism
Nusand Publishing Inc., #1113, 250 the East Mall, Toronto, ON M9B 6L3
Tel: 416-233-2487; *Fax:* 416-233-1746
info@opticalprism.ca
www.opticalprism.ca
Circulation: 10,609 *Frequency:* 10 times a year
Robert May, Publisher
Kim Edwards, Editor

Opti-Guide
Breton Communications Inc., #202, 495, boul St-Martin ouest, Laval, QC H7M 1Y9
Tel: 450-629-6005; *Fax:* 450-629-6044
Toll-Free: 888-462-2112
breton.com@bretoncom.com
www.opti-guide.com
Circulation: 5,481 *Frequency:* Annually
Martine Breton, President

L'Optométriste
#740, 1265, rue Berri, Montréal, QC H2L 4X4
Tél: 514-288-6272; *Téléc:* 514-288-7071
Ligne sans frais: 888-505-6786
aoq@aoqnet.qc.ca
Circulation: 4 400 *Frequency:* 6 fois par an; français

Paediatrics & Child Health
Tel: 905-829-4770; *Fax:* 905-829-4799
Toll-Free: 866-879-9770
pulsus@pulsus.com
www.pulsus.com
Circulation: 14,500 *Frequency:* 10 times a year
Robert Kalina, Publisher
Dr. E. Ford-Jones, Editor
Dr. N. MacDonald, Editor

Pain Research & Management

Tel: 905-829-4770; *Fax:* 905-829-4799
Toll-Free: 866-879-4770
pulsus@pulsus.com
www.pulsus.com
Circulation: 15,300 *Frequency:* 4 times a year
Robert Kalina, Publisher
Dr. K. Craig, Editor

Parkhurst Exchange
400, rue McGill, 3e étage, Montréal, QC H2Y 2G1
Tel: 514-397-8833; *Fax:* 514-397-0228
Toll-Free: 800-663-7403
parkex@parkpub.com
www.parkpub.com
Circulation: 39,453 *Frequency:* 12 times a year
Madeleine Pantais, Publisher

Patient Care

Tel: 416-764-2000; *Fax:* 416-764-1207
Toll-Free: 888-766-7043
Circulation: 27,256 *Frequency:* 12 times a year
Golda Goldman, Editor

Perspectives in Cardiology
#306, 955 Boul. St. Jean, Pointe-Claire, QC H9R 5K3
Tel: 514-695-7623; *Fax:* 514-695-8554
cardio@sta.ca
www.stacommunications.com
Circulation: 15,270 *Frequency:* 10 times a year
Robert Passaretti, Publisher

Physicians' Computing Chronicle

Tel: 905-273-9116; *Fax:* 905-273-4322
Toll-Free: 866-633-4766
health@chronicle.org
www.chronicle.ca
Circulation: 33,682 *Frequency:* 6 times a year
Mitchell Shannon, Publisher
R. Allan Ryan, Senior Editor

Physiotherapy Canada

Tel: 905-522-7017; *Fax:* 905-522-7839
Toll-Free: 800-387-8679
www.physiotherapy.ca
Circulation: 9,500 *Frequency:* 4 times a year
Dr. Susan R. Harris, Scientific Editor
Kathy Hay, Journal Coordinator

Psychology Ontario
Ontario Psychological Association, #221, 730 Yonge St., Toronto, ON M4Y 2B7
Tel: 416-961-5552; *Fax:* 416-961-5516
info@psych.on.ca
www.psych.on.ca
Circulation: 1,450 *Frequency:* 4 times a year
Dr. Mario Cappelli, Editor
Sandra Traub, Publication Manager

Rehab & Community Care Medicine
BCS Communications Ltd., 101 Thorncliffe Park Dr., Toronto, ON M4H 1M2
Tel: 416-421-7944; *Fax:* 416-421-0966
Toll-Free: 800-798-6282
reception@bcsgroup.com
www.bscgroup.com
Circulation: 20,500 *Frequency:* 4 times a year
Caroline Tapp-McDougall, Publisher

Stitches: The Journal of Medical Humour
240 Edward St., Aurora, ON L4G 3S9
Tel: 905-727-0077; *Fax:* 905-727-0017
Toll-Free: - - 0
stitches@stitchesmagazine.com
www.stitchesmagazine.com
Circulation: 38,652 *Frequency:* Bi-monthly
Michael Moriarty, Publisher
Randall Willis, Editor

Strategy: The Financial Digest for Physicians
Canadian Medical Association, 1867 Alta Vista Dr., Ottawa, ON K1G 3Y6
Tel: 613-731-4552; *Fax:* 613-736-5367
Circulation: 41,500
Stephen Prudhomme, Publisher

Synergie
#400, 505, boul de Maisonneuve ouest, Montréal, QC H3A 3C2
Tél: 514-282-4251; *Téléc:* 514-282-4289
michel.lauzier@ssss.gouv.qc.ca
www.aqesss.qc.ca
Circulation: 6 212 *Frequency:* 10 fois par an; français
Marie-Hélène Juneau, Rédactrice
Michel Lauzier, Directeur commercial, Publicité

Urology Times of Canada
#102, 155A Matheson Blvd. West, Mississauga, ON L5R 3L5
Tel: 905-712-3636; *Fax:* 905-712-2935
Toll-Free: 800-561-7516
info@ctccomm.com
www.ctccomm.com
Circulation: 4,800 *Frequency:* 6 times a year
Mike Farley, Publisher
K. Pearsall, Managing Editor
Karen Tousignant, Advertising

Heating, Plumbing, Air Conditioning

Contracting Canada Magazine
1697 Kelsey Ct., Mississauga, ON L5L 3J8
Tel: 905-569-2777; *Fax:* 905-569-2444
don.beaulieu@rogers.com
www.contractingcanada.com
Circulation: 30,000 *Frequency:* 4 times a year
Don B. Beaulieu, Publisher

Heating Plumbing Air Conditioning

Tel: 416-764-2000; *Fax:* 416-764-1746
www.hpacmag.com
Circulation: 16,312 *Frequency:* 7 times a year; also Buyers Guide (annually, Aug.)
W. Bruce Meacock, Publisher
Kerry Turner, Editor

Inter-mécanique du bâtiment (CMMTQ)
8175, boul St-Laurent, Montréal, QC H2P 2M1
Tél: 514-382-2668; *Téléc:* 514-382-1566
Ligne sans frais: 800-465-2668
cmmtq@cmmtq.org
www.cmmtq.org
Circulation: 6 000 *Frequency:* 10 fois par an; français
André Dupuis, Rédacteur-en-chef

Plumbing & HVAC Product News

Tel: 416-242-8088; *Fax:* 416-242-8085
rshuker@nytek.ca
www.plumbingandhvac.ca
Circulation: 17,982 *Frequency:* 6 times a year
Simon Blake, Editor, sblake@nytek.ca
Ronald H. Shuker, Executive Editor, rshuker@nytek.ca

Hotels & Restaurants

Atlantic Restaurant News
#301, 2065 Dundas St. West, Mississauga, ON L4X 2W1
Tel: 905-206-0150; *Fax:* 905-206-9972
Toll-Free: 800-201-8596
www.can-restaurantnews.com
Circulation: 5,500 *Frequency:* 6 times a year
Steve Isherwood, Publisher, sisherwood@can-restaurantnews.com

Bar & Beverage Business

Tel: 204-954-2085; *Fax:* 204-954-2057
mp@mercury.mb.ca
www.barandbeverage.com
Circulation: 17,063 *Frequency:* 6 times a year
Frank Yeo, Publisher
Kelly Gray, Editor

BC Restaurant News
British Columbia Restaurant & Foodservices Association, 439 Helmcken St., Vancouver, BC V6B 2E6
Tel: 604-669-2239; *Fax:* 604-669-6175
Toll-Free: 877-669-2239
info@bcrfa.com
www.bcrfa.com
Frequency: 8 times a year
Jason McRobbie, Editor

Canadian Lodging News

Tel: 905-206-0150; *Fax:* 905-206-9972
Toll-Free: 800-201-8596
mandrews@can-lodgingnews.com
Circulation: 9,000 *Frequency:* 4 times a year
Steven Isherwood, Publisher

Le Chef du service alimentaire
252, St-André, Saint-Étienne-de-Lauzon, QC G6J 1E8
Tél: 418-831-5317; *Téléc:* 418-831-5172
Ligne sans frais: 800-363-1727
lechef@magazinelechef.com
www.magazinelechef.com
Circulation: 20 286 *Frequency:* 6 fois par an; français
Maurice LeBlanc, Publisher
Christiane Rioux, Editor-in-chief

Foodservice & Hospitality

Tel: 416-447-0888; *Fax:* 416-447-5333
mkostuch@foodservice.ca
www.foodserviceworld.com
Circulation: 25,120 *Frequency:* 12 times a year
Mitch Kostuch, President/Publisher
Rosanna Caira, Associate Publisher/Editor

Foodservice News
#1000, 5255 Yonge St., Toronto, ON M2N 6P4
Tel: 416-512-8186; *Fax:* 416-512-8344
Toll-Free: 866-216-0860
Circulation: 21,347 *Frequency:* 9 times a year
Arthur Mensher, Publisher

Hotelier
#101, 23 Lesmill Rd., Toronto, ON M3B 3P6
Tel: 416-447-0888; *Fax:* 416-447-5333
rcaira@foodservice.ca
www.foodserviceworld.com
Circulation: 9,000 *Frequency:* 8 times a year
Mitch Kostuch, President
Rosanna Caira, Editor & Publisher

Ontario Restaurant News
#201, 2065 Dundas St. East, Mississauga, ON L4X 2W1
Tel: 905-206-0150; *Fax:* 905-206-9972
Toll-Free: 800-201-8596
info@can-restaurantnews.com
www.can-restaurantnews.com
Circulation: 16,500 *Frequency:* 12 times a year
Steven Isherwood, Publisher

Pacific/Prairie Restaurants

Tel: 905-206-0150; *Fax:* 905-206-9972
Toll-Free: 800-201-8596
cisherwood@can-restaurantnews.com
www.can-restaurantnews.com
Circulation: 14,500 *Frequency:* 6 times a year
Steven Isherwood, Publisher
Colleen Isherwood, Editor

Western Hotelier

Tel: 204-954-2085; *Fax:* 204-954-2057
mp@mercury.mb.ca
www.mercury.mb.ca
Circulation: 5,200 *Frequency:* 5 times a year
Frank Yeo, Publisher
Kelly Gray, Editor, editorial@mercury.mb.ca
Kristi Balon, Editorial Coordinator, editorial@mercury.mb.ca

Western Restaurant News

Tel: 204-954-2085; *Fax:* 204-954-2057
mp@mercury.mb.ca
www.mercury.mb.ca
Circulation: 14,523 *Frequency:* 6 times a year
Frank Yeo, Publisher
Kelly Gray, Editor, editorial@mercury.mb.ca

Housewares

Canadian Home Style Magazine
Lorell Communication Inc., 146 Cavendish Ct., Oakville, ON L6J 5S2
Tel: 905-338-0799; *Fax:* 905-338-5657
homestylemag@home.com
Frequency: 6 times a year
Laurie O'Halloran, Publisher & Editor

Human Resources

Canadian HR Reporter
1 Corporate Plaza, 2075 Kennedy Rd., Toronto, ON M1T 3V4
Tel: 416-609-8000; *Fax:* 416-298-5031
john.hobel@thomson.com
www.hrreporter.com
Circulation: 10,800 *Frequency:* 22 times a year
John Hobel, Publisher & Editor

Human Resources Professional

Tel: 204-947-0222; *Fax:* 204-947-2047
Toll-Free: 800-665-2456
wayne@naylor.com

Circulation: 12,000 *Frequency:* 6 times a year
Martin Rissin, Publisher

Workplace News

Tel: 905-841-6472; *Fax:* 905-841-5078
shughes@clbmedia.ca
www.wpnonline.com

Circulation: 10,000 *Frequency:* Monthly
Jackie Roth, Publisher
Nathan Mallett, Editor

Industrial & Industrial Automation

Advanced Manufacturing
240 Edward St., Aurora, ON L4G 3S9

Tel: 905-727-0077; *Fax:* 905-727-0017
www.advancedmanufacturing.com

Circulation: 17,363 *Frequency:* 6 times a year
Klaus B. Pirker, Publisher
Andre Voshart, Acting Editor, avoshart@clbmedia.ca

Canadian Electronics

Tel: 905-727-0077; *Fax:* 905-727-0017
ce@clbmedia.ca
www.canadianelectronics.ca

Circulation: 23,393 *Frequency:* 6 times a year; also annual web & product directory
Roger Heritage, Publisher, rheritage@clbmedia.ca

Canadian Industrial Equipment News

Tel: 416-442-5600; *Fax:* 416-442-2214
mking@cienmagazine.com
CIENMagazine.com

Circulation: 21,293 *Frequency:* Monthly
Michael King, Publisher
Olga Markovich, Editor
Dianne Rakoff, Circulation Manager

Industrial Sourcebook

Tel: 905-727-0077; *Fax:* 905-727-0017
www.industrialsourcebook.com

Circulation: 18,000 *Frequency:* Annually
Frank Shoniker, Publisher

Le Journal Industriel du Québec
2370, rue Henri-Bourassa Est, Montréal, QC H2B 1T6

Tél: 514-388-8801; *Téléc:* 514-388-7871
ygauthier@industriel.qc.ca
www.industriel.qc.ca

Circulation: 20 000 *Frequency:* 10 fois par an; français
Yvan Gauthier, Publisher

Manufacturing Automation

Tel: 905-727-0077; *Fax:* 905-727-0017
www.automationmag.com

Circulation: 20,300 *Frequency:* 7 times a year
Klaus Pirker, Senior Publisher

MCI
P.A.P. Communications Inc., 1627, boul Bastien, Québec, QC G2K 1H1

Tél: 418-623-3383; *Téléc:* 418-623-5033
Ligne sans frais: 800-387-3383
info@magazinemci.com
www.magazinemci.com

Circulation: 23 000 *Frequency:* 6 fois par an; français
Andre Pageau, Editor

PEM: Plant Engineering & Maintenance (PEM)

Tel: 905-727-0077; *Fax:* 905-727-0017
www.pem-mag.com

Circulation: 18,494 *Frequency:* 7 times a year
Frank Schoniker, Publisher

Plant

Tel: 416-764-2000; *Fax:* 416-764-1742
www.plant.ca

Circulation: 30,000 *Frequency:* 12 times a year
Joe Terrett, Editor

Produits pour l'industrie québécoise

Tél: 905-727-0077; *Téléc:* 905-727-0017
tgouldson@clbmedia.ca
www.pig-mag.ca

Frequency: 6 fois par an; français
Linda Nadon, Éditeur
Tim Goulsdon, Rédacteur

Industrial Safety

Accident Prevention
Industrial Accident Prevention Assn (IAPA)., #300, 5110 Creekbank Rd., Mississauga, ON L4W 0A1

Tel: 905-614-4272; *Fax:* 905-614-1414
Toll-Free: 800-316-4272
apmag@iapa.ca
www.iapa.ca

Circulation: 12,500 *Frequency:* 5 times a year
Scott Williams, Editor

Canadian Occupational Safety

Tel: 905-727-0077; *Fax:* 905-727-0017
www.cos-mag.com

Circulation: 14,000 *Frequency:* 6 times a year
Cocoe Horsley, Publisher
Jennifer Brown, Editor

OHS Canada Magazine (OH&S Canada)

Tel: 416-442-2122; *Fax:* 416-442-2191
Toll-Free: 800-668-2374
astelmakowich@ohscanada.com
www.ohscanada.com

Circulation: 10,587 *Frequency:* 8 times a year
Peter Boxer, Publisher
Angela Stelmakowich, Editor

Travail et santé
CP 1089, Napierville, QC J0J 1L0

Tél: 450-245-7285; *Téléc:* 450-245-0593
travail.sante@sympatico.ca
www.travailetsante.net

Frequency: 4 fois par an; français
Robert Richards, Rédacteur

Insurance

Alberta Insurance Directory
PO Box 3311 Terminal, 661 Market Hill, Vancouver, BC V5Z 4B5

Tel: 604-874-1001; *Fax:* 604-874-3922
manager@insurancewest.ca
www.insurancewest.ca

Circulation: 1,555 *Frequency:* Annually
The directory, started in 1982, is considered the recognized reference authority. It contains full, accurate and up-to-date listings in Alberta of 600 general insurance broker offices, 100 independent adjusting offices, 280 general and life insurer offices, and 50 insurance association and government-related offices. In addition, 2700 senior insurance personnel are listed and cross-referenced; 100 trades and suppliers also included. The 230-page coil-bound book is used primarily by general insurance brokers, adjusters and insurers in Alberta.
Linda Helme, Publisher & Editor & Advertising Sales
Bill Earle, Publisher & Editor & Advertising Sales

The BC Broker
PO Box 3311 Terminal, 661 Market Hill, Vancouver, BC V5Z 4B5

Tel: 604-874-1001; *Fax:* 604-874-3922
manager@insurancewest.ca
www.insurancewest.ca

Circulation: 3,500 *Frequency:* 6 times a year
The official publication of the Insurance Brokers Association of British Columbia (IBABC), the magazine is published six times a year - February, April, June, August, October and December. Circulation is 3500 of which 2600 is to member insurance brokers, the balance going to insurance companies, adjusters and suppliers to the industry. The BC Broker is an ideal medium for advertisers who wish to reach a target audience of all or part of the B.C. general insurance industry market. Not only does its circulation cover virtually all the key decision makers, it is also widely recognized as the best provincial insurance publication in Canada.
Bill Earle, Publisher & Managing Editor & Advertising Sales
Jim Bensley, Publisher & Managing Editor & Advertising Sales

British Columbia Insurance Directory
PO Box 3311 Terminal, 661 Market Hill, Vancouver, BC V5Z 4B5

Tel: 604-874-1001; *Fax:* 604-874-3922
manager@insurancewest.ca
www.insurancewest.ca

Circulation: 2,563 *Frequency:* Annually, April
The directory, started in 1964, is considered the recognized reference authority. It contains full, accurate and up-to-date listings in B.C. of 950 general insurance broker offices, 160 independent adjusting offices, 250 general and life insurer offices, and 60 insurance association and government-related offices. In addition, 5000 senior insurance personnel are listed and cross-referenced; 200 trades and suppliers also included. The 340-page coil-bound book is used primarily by general insurance brokers, adjusters and insurers in B.C.
Bill Earle, Editor & Publisher & Advertising Sales
Jim Bensley, Editor & Publisher & Advertising Sales

Canadian Insurance
#500, 111 Peter St., Toronto, ON M5V 2H1

Tel: 416-599-0772; *Fax:* 416-599-0867
info@cdnins.com
www.cdnins.com

Circulation: 11,600 *Frequency:* Monthly
Canadian Insurance magazine provides leading coverage of the news, events and trends that shape the p&c insurance industry. Focus is on the issues of claims management, information technology; global & commercial risks, reinsurance, loss prevention, adjusters, risk management, brokers & underwriters, environment, and financial services
Barbara Aarsteinsen, Editor, baarsteinsen@cdnins.com
John D. Wyndham, Publisher, jwyndham@cdnins.com

Canadian Insurance Claims Directory
#700, 10 St Mary St., Toronto, ON M4Y 2W8

Tel: 416-978-2239; *Fax:* 416-978-4738
Toll-Free: 800-565-9523
publishing@utpress.utoronto.ca
www.utppublishing.com

Circulation: 1,500 *Frequency:* Annually, May
This directory is published yearly to facilitate the forwarding of insurance claims throughout Canada and the United States. Its subscribers are adjusters, firms specializing in counsel to the insurance industry, insurance companies, and industrial and government offices. Listed are a total of 1600 independent adjusting offices, which offer dependable service to claims forwarders, as well as some 100 insurance counsel, who are experienced in insurance defense litigation.
Gwen Peroni, Editor

Canadian Underwriter
#800, 12 Concorde Pl., Toronto, ON M3C 4J2

Fax: 416-510-6809
Toll-Free: 800-268-7742
www.cdnunderwriter.com

Circulation: 10,061 *Frequency:* Monthly; also Rehabilitation & Medical Services Guide, Litigation Services Guide, Insurance Marketer, Annual Statistical Issue, Ontario Insurance Directory
Canadian Underwriter is a professional Insurance and Risk Management magazine covering all aspects of Canada's property and casualty Insurance Market. Covers all the insurance news and insight into the issues, events and people affecting this $30 billion market. Reporting on all sectors of the market, including: brokers; insurers; reinsurance; claims; risk management; associations; legislation; legal; technology; insurer statistical review and all other related Insurance topics
David Gambrill, Editor, 416-510-6796, david@canadianunderwriter.ca
Steve Wilson, Senior Publisher, 416-510-6800, steve@canadianunderwriter.ca

Forum
c/o Advocis, 350 Bloor St. East, 2nd Fl., Toronto, ON M4W 3W8

Tel: 416-444-5251; *Fax:* 416-444-8031
info@advocis.ca
www.advocis.ca

Circulation: 18,100 *Frequency:* 12 times a year
Peter Wilmshurst, Publisher
Kristin Doucet, Editor

General Insurance Register

Tel: 416-599-0772; *Fax:* 416-599-0867
info@cdnins.com
www.cdnins.com

Circulation: 5,500 *Frequency:* Annually, January
Lists insurance Adjusters, Appraisers, Legal firms in Canada; Consultants, Engineering, Investigation, Rehabilitation, Replacement, Restoration and other services companies; also lists Brokers, Intermediaries and Managing Agents
J. Wyndham, Publisher & Editor

The Insurance Journal
#100, 321 Rue de la Commune West, Montreal, QC H2Y 2E1
Tel: 514-289-9595; *Fax:* 514-289-9527
idesk@insurance-journal.ca
www.insurance-journal.ca
Circulation: 15 500 *Frequency:* 10 times a year
The Insurance Journal targets financial advisors, life insurance producers, financial planners, and general insurance brokers in Canada. The magazine publishes news and examines trends in the development of insurance and financial products, such as group and individual insurance, disability insurance, mutual funds, segregated funds, health care management, and information technology. Published 10 times per year.
Serge Therrien, Publisher, serge.therrien@insurance-journal.ca
Donna Glasgow, Editor in Chief, donna.glasgow@insurance-journal.ca

Insurancewest
PO Box 3311 Terminal, 661 Market Hill, Vancouver, BC V5Z 4B5
Tel: 604-874-1001; *Fax:* 604-874-3922
manager@insurancewest.ca
www.insurancewest.ca
Circulation: 6,000 *Frequency:* 6 times a year
Launched in 1996, this bi-monthly magazine (formerly a quarterly) circulates to 6000 in Canada's four western provinces - virtually every insurance industry decision-maker in the west. Insurancewest is about insurance people and companies
Bill Earle, Publisher & Editor & Advertising Sales
Jim Bensley, Publisher & Editor & Advertising Sales

Le Journal de l'Assurance
#100, 321, Rue de la Commune West, Montreal, QC H2Y 2E1
Tél: 514-289-9595; *Téléc:* 514-289-9527
Circulation: 26 000 *Frequency:* 10 times a year; français; ISSN: 1198-4678
Journal de l'assurance is a French-language news magazine that targets life insurance producers, general insurance brokers, financial planners, and financial advisors in Quebec
Serge Therrien, Publisher, serge.therrien@insurance-journal.ca
Donna Glasgow, Editor-in-Chief, donna.glasgow@insurance-journal.ca

Ontario Insurance Directory
#800, 12 Concorde Place, Toronto, ON M3C 4J2
Tel: 416-442-2122; *Fax:* 416-442-2191
Toll-Free: 800-668-2374
Circulation: 3,500 *Frequency:* Annually, December
Personal address and telephone book dedicated solely to the Ontario insurance industry
Steve Wilson, Senior Publisher
Cathy Donaghy, Associate Editor

Interior Design & Decor

Azure
#601, 460 Richmond St. West, Toronto, ON M5V 1Y1
Tel: 416-203-9674; *Fax:* 416-203-9842
azure@azureonline.com
www.azuremagazine.com
Circulation: 30,000 *Frequency:* 8 times a year; ISSN: 0829-982X
Sergio Sgaramella, Publisher
Catherine Osborne, Senior Editor
Nelda Rodger, Editor

Canadian Facility Management & Design
#338, 4195 Dundas St. West, Toronto, ON M8X 1Y4
Tel: 416-236-5856; *Fax:* 416-236-5219
Circulation: 6,538 *Frequency:* 6 times a year
Arvid Stonkus, Publisher & Production Manager

Canadian Interiors
800, 12 Concorde Place, Toronto, ON M3C 4J2
Tel: 416-442-5600; *Fax:* 416-442-2191
Toll-Free: 800-668-2374
www.canadianinteriors.com
Circulation: 11,847 *Frequency:* 6 times a year
Martin Spreer, Publisher, 416-510-6766, mspreer@canadianinteriors.com

Ontario Design
Tel: 905-479-4663; *Fax:* 905-479-4482
Toll-Free: 800-363-4663
info@ontariodesigntrade.com
www.ontariodesigntrade.com
Circulation: 12,000 *Frequency:* Annually
Michael Rosset, Publisher

Jewellery & Giftware

Canadian Jeweller
Style Communications, #701, 555 Richmond St. West, Toronto, ON M5V 3B1
Tel: 416-203-6737; *Fax:* 416-203-1057
Toll-Free: 877-789-5315
canjewel@style.ca
www.canadianjeweller.com
Circulation: 5,400 *Frequency:* 7 times a year
John Peters, Publisher
Carol Besler, Editor

Journalism

L'edition Nouvelles
8030, rue Marie Lefranc, Laval, QC H7Y 2C2
Tel: 450-962-7610; *Fax:* 450-962-7092
Toll-Free: 866-639-7226
dcoggins@newscanada.com
www.newscanada.com
Circulation: 1 451 *Frequency:* mensuel
Ruth Douglas, President & Publisher

Media
Canadian Association of Journalists, #B224, 1385 Woodroffe Ave., Ottawa, ON K2G 1V8
Tel: 613-526-8061; *Fax:* 613-521-3904
caj@igs.net
www.eagle.ca/caj
Circulation: 4,000 *Frequency:* 4 times a year
David McKie, Publisher

News Canada / L'Édition Nouvelles
Tel: 416-599-9900; *Fax:* 416-599-9700
www.newscanada.com
Frequency: Monthly
Ruth Douglas, President/Publisher

Press Review
PO Box 368 A, Toronto, ON M5W 1C2
Tel: 416-368-0512; *Fax:* 416-366-0104
info@pressreview.ca
www.pressreview.ca
Circulation: 8,500 *Frequency:* 4 times a year
Jana Cassidy, Publisher

Ryerson Review of Journalism
School of Journalism, Ryerson University, 350 Victoria St., Toronto, ON M5B 2K3
Tel: 416-979-5000; *Fax:* 416-979-5216
reynolds@ryerson.ca
www.rrj.ca
Circulation: 4,500 *Frequency:* 2 times a year; ISSN: 0838-0651
Paul Knox, Publisher
Bill Reynolds, Editorial Instructor

Landscaping

GreenMaster
Tel: 905-771-7333; *Fax:* 905-771-7336
Toll-Free: 800-409-8688
editor@kenilworth.com
www.kenilworth.com
Circulation: 4,948 *Frequency:* 6 times a year
Ellen Kral, Publisher
Blair Adams, Editorial Director
Cora Golden, Director, Advertising Sales

Horticulture Review: The Voice of Landscape Ontario
Tel: 905-875-1805; *Fax:* 905-875-0183
Circulation: 2,837 *Frequency:* Monthly
Lee Ann Knudson, Publisher
Sarah Wills, Editorial Director

Hortwest
c/o BC Landscape & Nursery Association, #102, 5783 - 176A St., Surrey, BC V3S 6S6
Tel: 604-574-7772; *Fax:* 604-574-7773
Toll-Free: 800-421-7963
bnelson@bclna.com
www.canadanursery.com; www.gardenwise.bc.ca
Circulation: 1,250 *Frequency:* 10 times a year
Karen DeJong, Managing Editor
Barb Nelson, Manager, Advertising, b-nelson@telus.net

Landscape Trades
7856 5th Line South, RR #4, Milton, ON L9T 2X8
Tel: 905-875-1805; *Fax:* 905-875-0183
Toll-Free: 800-265-5656
sarahw@landscapeontario.com
www.hort-trades.com
Circulation: 8,226 *Frequency:* 9 times a year
Sarah Willis, Editorial Director

Landscaping & Groundskeeping
Tel: 604-291-9900; *Fax:* 604-291-1906
www.baumpub.com
Circulation: 14,229 *Frequency:* 6 times a year
Engelbert Baum, Publisher
Lawrence Buser, Editor

Prairie Landscape Magazine
Aurora Design, PO Box 85127 APPO, Calgary, AB T2A 7R7
Tel: 403-273-6917; *Fax:* 403-313-6917
prairielandscape@shaw.ca
Circulation: 1,050 *Frequency:* 6 times a year
Jennett Jackson, Publisher

Québec Vert
1320, boul. Saint-Joseph, Québec, QC G2K 1G2
Tél: 418-628-8690; *Téléc:* 418-628-0524
Ligne sans frais: 800-463-1576
editions@versicolores.ca
www.quebecvert.com
Circulation: 3 167 *Frequency:* 8 fois par an; français
Claire Bélisle, Éditeur

Turf & Recreation
275 James St., Delhi, ON N4B 2B2
Tel: 519-582-8873; *Fax:* 519-582-8877
Toll-Free: 800-525-6825
turf@on.aibn.com
www.turfandrec.com
Circulation: 15,000 *Frequency:* 7 times a year
Bart Crandon, Publisher

Laundry & Dry Cleaning

Fabricare Canada
Todd's Your Answer Ltd., PO Box 968, Oakville, ON L6J 5E8
Tel: 905-337-0516; *Fax:* 905-337-0525
martodd@cogeco.ca
www.fabricarecanada.com
Circulation: 6,300 *Frequency:* 6 times a year
Marcia Todd, Publisher & Editor

Legal

The Advocate
Editorial Office, #1600, 925 West Georgia St., Vancouver, BC V6C 3C2
Tel: 604-685-3456; *Fax:* 604-631-9190
tswoods@lawsonlundell.com
Circulation: 11,000 *Frequency:* 6 times a year
The periodical's observation of its theme "Of interest to the lawyer and in the lawyer's interest" has made it a welcome and invaluable resource for lawyers throughout British Columbia
Thomas S. Wood, Editor

Canadian Bar Review / La Revue du Barreau canadien
c/o Canadian Bar Foundation, #500, 865 Carling Ave., Ottawa, ON K1S 5S8
Tel: 613-237-2925; *Fax:* 613-237-0185
Toll-Free: 800-267-8860
info@cba.org
www.cba.org
Circulation: 36,200 on-line *Frequency:* 3 times a year; English & French
The official, bilingual learned legal journal of the CBA, the Canadian Bar Review is published online three times a year. Fully searchable archives of the Bar Review, dating back to 1923, are available in PDF format. The Review directly meets the educational objective of the CBA. It is frequently cited in the Supreme Court of Canada and boasts an international reputation for quality and excellence.
Prof. Beth Bilson, Editor-in-chief

Canadian Lawyer
240 Edward St., Aurora, ON L4G 3S9
Tel: 905-841-6480; *Fax:* 905-841-5078
cleditor@clbmedia.ca
www.canadianlawyermag.com
Circulation: 28,000 *Frequency:* 11 times a year; ISSN: 0703-2129
Canadian Lawyer is the first national consumer-style magazine devoted exclusively to lawyers. It's the magazine that Canada's

legal professionals turn to the most for coverage of the news, events and issues that are continually shaping the profession
Karen Lorimer, Publisher, klorimer@clbmedia.ca
Jim Middlemiss, Editor, cleditor@clbmedia.ca

Le Journal du Barreau
445, boul St-Laurent, Montréal, QC H2Y 3T8
Tél: 514-954-3440; *Téléc:* 514-954-3477
Ligne sans frais: 800-361-8495
journaldubarreau@barreau.qc.ca
www.barreau.qc.ca
Circulation: 26 000 *Frequency:* 12 fois par an; français
Le Journal du Barreau, édité par le Service des communications, est la publication phare du monde juridique québécois. Il traite de l'évolution de l'exercice de la profession d'avocat, de différents domaines du droit, du système judiciaire et des aspects du droit liés aux enjeux de société
Virginie Savard, Assistante en communications

Law Times
240 Edward St., Aurora, ON L4G 3S9
Tel: 905-841-6481; *Fax:* 905-727-0017
gcohen@clbmedia.ca
www.lawtimesnews.com
Circulation: 12,700 *Frequency:* 40 times a year
Ontario's source of legal affairs news and commentary. News Flash: Our weekly coverage offers analysis and insight into the legal profession's key players, news events and court rulings. Focus Sections: Each issue explores in detail a topic of compelling interest to Ontario's legal profession. Our focus sections cover topics as diverse as computer software, private investigators and forensic services
Kimberlee Pascoe
Gail Cohen, Editor, gcohen@clbmedia.ca
Karen Lormier, Publisher, klorimer@clbmedia.ca

LawNow
c/o University of Alberta, 174 University Campus NW, #4-36, 8303 - 112 St., Edmonton, AB T6G 2T4
Tel: 780-492-1751; *Fax:* 780-492-6180
lawnow@ualberta.ca
www.lawnow.org
Circulation: 2,500 *Frequency:* 6 times a year; ISSN: 0841-2626
Each issue of LawNow magazine includes articles on a featured THEME, as well as a SPECIAL REPORT section. Upcoming Themes include Family Law, and Landmark Cases. Upcoming Special Reports include Administrative Law, and Law and the Disadvantaged.
Lois Gander, Publisher

The Lawyers Weekly
#700, 123 Commerce Valley Dr., Markham, ON L3T 7W8
Tel: 905-479-2665; *Fax:* 905-479-6460
Toll-Free: 800-668-6481
tlw@lexisnexis.ca
www.thelawyersweekly.ca
Circulation: 21,400 *Frequency:* 48 times a year
Published since 1983, The Lawyers Weekly was the first newspaper for the Canadian legal profession. It serves the national market with bureaus in Ottawa and Toronto and correspondents across the country. Published 48 times a year, The Lawyers Weekly provides lawyers with information essential to maintaining and building a successful practice in today's competitive business environment.
Tim Wilbur, Managing Editor
Gary Rodrigues, Publisher

McGill Law Journal / Revue de droit de McGill
3644 Peel St., Montréal, QC H3A 1W9
Tel: 514-398-7397; *Fax:* 514-398-7360
journal.law@mcgill.ca
lawjournal.mcgill.ca
Circulation: 1,330 *Frequency:* 4 times a year; English & French
The McGill Law Journal is an academic legal journal established in 1952 by the students of the McGill University Faculty of Law. More than fifty years later, and still entirely student-run, we remain committed to the advancement of legal scholarship in both the common and civil law. Amongst university law journals, McGill's is especially unique as a result of its bilingual, bijuridical character, and its success as the most frequently quoted university law journal by the Supreme Court of Canada.
Christine Stecura, Managing Editor

Le Monde Juridique
6050, av de L'Authion, Montréal, QC H1M 2S4
Tél: 514-353-3549; *Téléc:* 514-353-4159
agmonde@videotron.ca
Circulation: 10 000 *Frequency:* 10 fois par an; français
Magazine des juristes du Québec
André Gagnon, Éditeur & Rédacteur

National
Tel: 416-764-3910; *Fax:* 416-764-3933
Circulation: 38,400 *Frequency:* 8 times a year; English & French
National is the official magazine of the Canadian Bar Association. It tracks and analyzes the latest trends and developments in the law, provides practice and career information to lawyers, informs members of CBA activities and explores issues of importance to Canadian law practitioners
Jim Farley, Publisher

Ontario Legal Directory
University of Toronto Press, #700, 10 St. Mary St., Toronto, ON M4Y 2W8
Tel: 416-978-2239; *Fax:* 416-978-4738
Toll-Free: 800-565-9523
publishing@utpress.utoronto.ca
www.utppublishing.com
Circulation: 5,500 *Frequency:* Annually, February
Accuracy and completeness of detail have characterized the Ontario Legal Directory since 1925, when the first annual edition of the Toronto Legal Directory was published. With over 30,000 listings of lawyers, law firms, federal and provincial courts and government offices, each complete with names, addresses, telephone and fax numbers, and e-mail and web addresses, the Ontario Legal Directory places all the information you need right at your fingertips. The Blue Pages put governments and courts information right up front, organized in easy-to-find categories with thumb-tab indexing.
Lynn N. Browne, Editor

The Ontario Reports
#700, 123 Commerce Valley Dr. East, Markham, ON L3T 7WB
Tel: 905-479-2665; *Fax:* 905-479-3758
Toll-Free: 800-668-6481
Frequency: Weekly
Published by the Law Society of Upper Canada through LexisNexis Canada, the Ontario Reports, Third Series provides in full text, leading cases decided at all levels of Ontario courts. Published 52 times per year, the soft cover parts also contain official Law Society notices (i.e., Practice Directions), government notices of interest to the legal profession, fee schedules, lawyers announcements and advertising. A personally addressed copy is sent to each of the Law Society's members each Friday.
Sarojini Pillay, Editor

Osgoode Hall Law Journal
Osgoode Hall Law School of York University, 4700 Keele St., Toronto, ON M3J 1P3
Tel: 416-736-5354; *Fax:* 416-736-5869
journal@osgoode.yorku.ca
www.ohlj.ca
Circulation: 1,500 *Frequency:* 4 times a year, plus index; English or French
The Journal has acquired a reputation for excellence in publishing scholarly articles that represent a wide range of perspectives about law and legal institutions
Jamie Cameron, Editor-in-chief
John Boadway, Managing Editor
Yvonne Massop, Journal Coordinator
Val Culp, Managing Editor

The Scrivener Magazine
PO Box 44, #1220, 625 Howe St., Vancouver, BC V6C 2T6
Tel: 604-681-4516; *Fax:* 604-681-7258
Toll-Free: 800-663-0343
scrivener@notaries.bc.ca
www.notaries.bc.ca
Circulation: 6,000 *Frequency:* 4 times a year
The Scrivener is published quarterly by The Society of Notaries Public of British Columbia. Celebrates the Notary's role in drafting, communicating, authenticating, and getting the facts straight. Strives to publish articles about points of law and the Notary profession for the education and enjoyment of its members, their Allied Professionals, and the public
Val Wilson, Editor-in-chief

Lighting

Professional Lighting & Production
Tel: 905-641-1512; *Fax:* 905-641-1648
Toll-Free: 877-746-4692
info@nor.com
www.professional-lighting.com
Circulation: 10,200 *Frequency:* 4 times a year
Jim Norris, Publisher

Machinery Maintenance

Machinery & Equipment MRO
Tel: 416-510-5600; *Fax:* 416-510-5134
Toll-Free: 800-387-0273
broebuck@mromagazine.com
www.mro-esource.com
Circulation: 19,000 *Frequency:* 6 times a year
Nick Naunheimer, Publisher
William Roebuck, Editor

Materials Handling & Distribution

Gestion & Logistique
Tél: 450-435-3131; *Téléc:* 450-435-3884
gestionlogistique@bomartgroup.com
www.bomartgroup.com
Circulation: 10 104 *Frequency:* 10 fois par an
Ginette Marsolais, Directrice générale
Pierre Gravel, Éditeur
Elanka A. Todorov, Rédacteur-en-chef
André Perreault, Gestion, Circulation

Materials Management & Distribution
Tel: 416-764-1537; *Fax:* 416-764-1739
emily.atkins@mmd.rogers.com
www.mmdonline.com
Circulation: 19,000 *Frequency:* Monthly; also Data Capture Communication & Commerce (4 times a year)
Supply chain magazine covering information management & transportation
Emily Atkins, Editor
Warren Patterson, Publisher

Metalworking

Canadian Machinery & Metalworking
1 Mount Pleasant Rd., 7th Fl., Toronto, ON M4Y 2Y5
Tel: 416-764-1540; *Fax:* 416-764-1735
larry.bonikowsky@rci.rogers.com
www.canadianmetalworking.com
Circulation: 20,500 *Frequency:* 10 times a year
Larry Bonikowsky, Publisher
Mary Scianna, Editor

Metalworking Production & Purchasing
Tel: 905-727-0077; *Fax:* 905-727-0017
mpp@clbmedia.ca
www.metalworkingcanada.com
Circulation: 20,129 *Frequency:* 6 times a year; also The Canadian Machine Tool Dealer
Nigel Bishop, Publisher

Military

Canadian Defence Review
PO Box 305, 21 Main St., Markham, ON L3P 3J8
Tel: 905-472-2801; *Fax:* 905-472-3091
info@canadiandefencereview.com
www.canadiandefencereview.com
Circulation: 10,470 *Frequency:* 6 times a year
Peter A. Kitchen, Publisher
Nick Stephens, Managing Editor
Dianne Osadchuk, Circulation Manager

Mining

Canadian & American Mines Handbook
Tel: 416-442-5600; *Fax:* 416-510-5187
Toll-Free: 800-668-2374
mineshandbook@northernminer.com
www.northernminer.com
Frequency: Annually, November
Doug Donnelly, Publisher
Diane Giancola, Editor

Canadian Miner
285 Lynn Ave., North Vancouver, BC V7J 2C3
Tel: 604-980-0794; *Fax:* 604-980-7123
Toll-Free: 800-570-3366
subscriptions@canadianminer.com
Circulation: 3,250 *Frequency:* 4 times a year
Michael J. McGrath, Editor

Canadian Mining Journal
Tel: 416-510-6891; *Fax:* 416-510-5138
Toll-Free: 800-268-7742
www.canadianminingjournal.com

Circulation: 10,045 *Frequency:* 9 times a year
Jane Werniuk, Editor
Ray Perks, Publisher

CIM Bulletin

Tel: 514-939-2710; *Fax:* 514-939-2714
cim@cim.org
www.cim.org
Circulation: 10,213 *Frequency:* 10 times a year
H. Ednie, Editor

CIM Directory
#855, 3400 de Maisonneuve Blvd. West, Montréal, QC H3Z 3B8
Tel: 514-939-2710; *Fax:* 514-939-2714
cim@cim.org
www.cim.org
Circulation: 10,531 *Frequency:* Annually
Perla Gantz, Editor
Yvan Jacques, Publisher

CIM Reporter
#855, 3400 de Maisonneuve Blvd. West, Montréal, QC H3Z 3B8
Tel: 514-939-2710; *Fax:* 514-939-2714
cim@cim.org
www.cim.org
Circulation: 6,582
H. Ednie, Editor
Yvan Jacques, Publisher

FP Survey-Mines & Energy

Tel: 416-442-2121; *Fax:* 416-442-2968
helpdesk@canwest.com
www.fpinfomart.ca
Circulation: 4,300 *Frequency:* Annually, August

Mineral Exploration
4180 Lougheed Hwy., 4th Fl., Burnaby, BC V5C 6A7
Tel: 604-299-7311; *Fax:* 604-299-9188
cwm@canadawide.com
www.canadawide.com; www.amebc.ca/mineralexploration.htm
Circulation: 3,000 *Frequency:* 4 times a year
Peter Legge, Publisher/President

Mining Sourcebook

Tel: 416-510-6891; *Fax:* 416-510-5138
www.canadianminingjournal.com
Circulation: 5,861 *Frequency:* Annually, November
Ray Perks, Publisher, rperks@canadianminingjournal.com

The Northern Miner

Tel: 416-510-6768; *Fax:* 416-510-5137
tnm@northernminer.com
www.northernminer.com
Circulation: 16,874 *Frequency:* Weekly
Doug Donnelly, Publisher

The Prospector Investment and Exploration News
#360, 7360 - 137th St., Surrey, BC V3R 1A3
Tel: 604-580-1844; *Fax:* 604-580-1019
info@miningandinvestment.com
www.miningandinvestment.com
Circulation: 25,000 *Frequency:* 6 times a year
Kasey Gordon, Publisher
Samantha D. Amara, Editor

Motor Trucks & Buses

L'Echo du Transport

Tél: 450-435-3131; *Téléc:* 450-435-3884
editions@bomartgroup.com
www.lechodutransport.com
Circulation: 19 063 *Frequency:* 10 fois par an; français
Pierre Gravel, Éditeur
Eric Bérard, Rédacteur-en-chef
Manon Laviolette, Directrice, Ventes

highwaySTAR
451 Attwell Dr., Toronto, ON M9W 5C4
Tel: 416-614-2200; *Fax:* 416-614-8861
rolf@highwaystar.ca
highwaystarmagazine.com
Circulation: 40,470 *Frequency:* 12 times a year
Rolf Lockwood, Publisher/Editorial Director
Jim Park, Editor

Manitoba Ship-by-Truck Directory

Tel: 204-985-9780; *Fax:* 204-985-9795
info@kelman.mb.ca
Circulation: 1,000 *Frequency:* Annually

Motor Truck

Tel: 416-510-5123; *Fax:* 416-510-5143
www.trucknews.com
Circulation: 20,477 *Frequency:* 6 times a year
Lou Smyrlis, Editorial Director
Julie Kuzeljevich, Managing Editor

Over the Road
18 Parkglen Dr., Ottawa, ON K2G 3G9
Tel: 613-224-9947; *Fax:* 613-224-8825
otr@otr.on.ca
www.overtheroad.ca
Frequency: 12 times a year
Steve Jenkins, Editor

Today's Trucking
New Communications Group Inc., 451 Attwell Dr., Toronto, ON M9W 5C4
Tel: 416-614-2200; *Fax:* 416-614-8861
rolf@todaystrucking.com
www.todaystrucking.com
Circulation: 30,000 *Frequency:* 10 times a year
Rolf Lockwood, Publisher
Peter Carter, Editor

Truck News

Tel: 416-510-5123; *Fax:* 416-510-5143
www.trucknews.com
Circulation: 71,824 *Frequency:* Monthly
Rob Wilkins, Publisher
Lou Smyrlis, Editorial Director

Truck West

Tel: 416-510-5123; *Fax:* 416-510-5143
www.trucknews.com
Circulation: 20,782 *Frequency:* 12 times a year
Rob Wilkins, Publisher
Lou Smyrlis, Editorial Director

La Voix du vrac
#235, 670, rue Bouvier, Québec, QC G2J 1A7
Tél: 418-623-7923; *Téléc:* 418-623-0448
revue@ancai.com
www.ancai.com
Circulation: 9 491 *Frequency:* 6 fois par an; français
Alain Simard, Éditeur

Western Canada Highway News

Tel: 204-985-9785; *Fax:* 204-985-9795
Toll-Free: 866-985-9780
info@kelman.ca
Circulation: 4,000 *Frequency:* 4 times a year
Craig Kelman, Publisher
T. Ross, Editor

Music

Canadian Music Trade

Tel: 905-641-1512; *Fax:* 905-641-1648
Toll-Free: 877-746-4692
mail@nor.com
www.canadianmusictrade.com
Circulation: 3,500 *Frequency:* 6 times a year
Jim Norris, Publisher

Music Directory Canada

Tel: 905-641-1512; *Fax:* 905-641-1648
Toll-Free: 800-265-8481
info@nor.com
www.musicdirectorycanada.com
Circulation: 6,000
Jim Norris, Publisher

Professional Sound

Tel: 905-641-1512; *Fax:* 905-641-1648
Toll-Free: 877-746-4692
info@nor.com
www.professional-sound.com
Circulation: 10,400 *Frequency:* 6 times a year
Jim Norris, Publisher

Nursing

Alberta RN
College & Association of Registered Nurses of Alberta, 11620 - 168 St., Edmonton, AB T5M 4A6
Tel: 780-451-0043; *Fax:* 780-452-3276
Toll-Free: 800-252-9392
carna@nurses.ab.ca
www.nurses.ab.ca
Circulation: 28,000 *Frequency:* 9 times a year
Margaret Ward-Jack, Managing Editor
Rachel Champagne, Editor

Canadian Journal of Cardiovascular Nursing
c/o Canadian Council of Cardiovascular Nurses, 84 Isabella St., Pembroke, ON K8A 5S5
Tel: 613-735-0952; *Fax:* 613-735-7983
heather@pappin.com
www.CardiovascularNurse.com
Circulation: 700 *Frequency:* 4 times a year
Bruce Pappin, Managing Editor

Canadian Nurse
Canadian Nurses Assn., 50 Driveway, Ottawa, ON K2P 1E2
Tel: 613-237-2133; *Fax:* 613-237-3520
Toll-Free: 800-361-8404
info@canadian-nurse.com
www.canadian-nurse.com
Circulation: 120,815 *Frequency:* 9 times a year
Muriel Hurst, Editor-in-chief

Canadian Oncology Nursing Journal
The Victoria Centre, 84 Isabella St., Pembroke, ON K8A 5S5
Tel: 613-735-0952; *Fax:* 613-735-7983
www.pappin.com
Circulation: 1,000 *Frequency:* 4 times a year; English & French
Bruce M. Pappin, Managing Editor
Dr. Heather Porter, Editor-in-chief

Infirmière canadienne
Canadian Nurses Assn., 50 Driveway, Ottawa, ON K2P 1E2
Tél: 613-237-2159; *Téléc:* 613-237-3520
Ligne sans frais: 800-361-8404
redaction@infirmiere-canadienne.com
www.infirmiere-canadienne.com
Circulation: 3 000 *Frequency:* 9 fois par an
Lucille Auffrey, Editor-in-chief

Newsbulletin
Saskatchewan Registered Nurses' Association, 2066 Retallack St., Regina, SK S4S 7X5
Tel: 306-359-4200; *Fax:* 306-525-0849
Toll-Free: 800-667-9945
info@srna.org
www.srna.org
Circulation: 10,000 *Frequency:* 5 times a year
Shirley McKay, Director Registrar

Nursing B.C.
2855 Arbutus St., Vancouver, BC V6J 3Y8
Tel: 604-736-7331; *Fax:* 604-738-2272
nursingbc@crnbc.ca
www.crnbc.ca
Circulation: 34,454 *Frequency:* 5 times a year
Bruce Wells, Editor, wells@crnbc.ca

Perspective Infirmière
4200, boul Dorchester ouest, Montréal, QC H3Z 1V4
Tél: 514-935-2501; *Téléc:* 514-935-2055
Ligne sans frais: 800-363-6048
revue@oiiq.org
www.oiiq.org
Circulation: 66 913 *Frequency:* 6 fois par an; français
Marlène Lavoie, Secrétaire de rédaction
Colette Pilon-Bergman, Rédactrice

Registered Nurse Journal
#1600, 438 University Ave., Toronto, ON M5G 2K8
Tel: 416-599-1925; *Fax:* 416-599-1926
Toll-Free: 800-268-7199
smackinnon@rnao.org
www.rnao.org
Circulation: 24,000 *Frequency:* 6 times a year
Sine MacKinnon, Publisher

The Registered Practical Nursing Journal
Bldg. 4, #200, 5025 Orbitor Dr., Mississauga, ON L4W 4Y5
Tel: 905-602-4664; *Fax:* 905-602-4666
Toll-Free: 877-602-4664
info@rpnao.org
www.rpnao.org
Circulation: 5,500 *Frequency:* 4 times a year
Joanne Young Evans, Executive Director

Santé Québec
Ordre des infirmières & infirmiers auxiliaires du Québec, 531, rue Sherbrooke est, Montréal, QC H2L 1K2
Tél: 514-282-9511; *Téléc:* 514-282-0631
Ligne sans frais: 800-283-9511
oiiaq@oiiaq.org
www.oiiaq.org
Circulation: 23 000 *Frequency:* 3 fois par an; français et anglais
Catherine-Dominique Nantel, Rédactrice-en-chef & Éditrice

Packaging

Canadian Packaging
1 Mount Pleasant Rd., 7th Fl., Toronto, ON M4Y 2Y5
Tel: 416-764-1497; *Fax:* 416-764-1755
stephen.dean.@packaging.rogers.com
www.canadianpackaging.com
Circulation: 13,626 *Frequency:* 9 times a year
Stephen Dean, Publisher
George Guidoni, Editor

Paint, Finishes, Coatings

Coatings Magazine
Tel: 416-764-1554; *Fax:* 416-764-1740
Toll-Free: 800-382-4957
pete.wilkinson@coatings.rogers.com
www.coatingsmagazine.com
Circulation: 8,400 *Frequency:* 7 times a year
Pete Wilkinson, Publisher

Petroleum, Oil & Gas

Alberta Oil & Gas Directory
Tel: 780-429-1073; *Fax:* 780-425-5844
armadale@nucleus.com
www.global-serve.net
Circulation: 10,000 *Frequency:* Annually
Haloshini Naidoo, Manager
Winston Mohabir, Publisher

Canada-Z Oil Gas Mining Directory
Tel: 780-429-1073; *Fax:* 780-425-5844
armadale@nucleus.com
www.global-serve.net
Circulation: 10,000 *Frequency:* Annually
Haloshini Naidoo, Manager
Winston Mohabir, Publisher

Canadian Oil Register
#300, 999 - 8 St. SW, Calgary, AB T2R 1N7
Tel: 403-209-3500; *Fax:* 403-245-8666
www2.canadianoilregister.com
Frequency: Annually, September
Doreen McArthur, Manager

Canadian Oilfield Gas Plant Atlas
6111 - 91 St. NW, Edmonton, AB T6E 6V6
Tel: 780-944-9333; *Fax:* 780-944-9500
Toll-Free: 800-563-2946
www.junewarren.com
Circulation: 4,000 *Frequency:* Bi-annual
Agnes Zalewski, Publisher

Canadian Oilfield Service & Supply Directory
Tel: 780-944-9333; *Fax:* 780-944-9500
Frequency: Annually
Bill Whitelaw, Publisher

Energy Processing/Canada
Tel: 403-263-6881; *Fax:* 403-263-6886
Toll-Free: 800-526-4177
energy@northernstar.ab.ca
www.northernstar.ab.ca
Circulation: 9,866 *Frequency:* 6 times a year
Scott Jeffrey, Publisher
Heather DeSimone, Sales Manager

The Journal of Canadian Petroleum Technology
The Petroleum Society, #425, 500 - 5 Ave. SW, Calgary, AB T2P 3L5
Tel: 403-237-5112; *Fax:* 403-262-4792
info@petsoc.org
www.petsoc.org
Circulation: 3,800 *Frequency:* 12 times a year
Nancy Hawthorne, Editor

Nickle's New Technology Magazine
#300, 999 - 8 St. SW, Calgary, AB T2R 1N7
Tel: 403-209-3500; *Fax:* 403-245-8666
www.nickles.com
Frequency: 8 times a year
Maurice Smith, Editor

Ocean Resources
162 Trider Cres., Dartmouth, NS B3B 1R6
Tel: 902-422-4990; *Fax:* 902-422-4728
www.ocean-resources.com
Frequency: 8 times a year
Joanne Elliott, Editor

Oil & Gas Inquirer
6111 - 91 St. NW, Edmonton, AB T6E 6V6
Tel: 780-944-9333; *Fax:* 780-944-9500
Toll-Free: 800-563-2946
marketing@junewarren.com
www.junewarren.com
Circulation: 10,000 *Frequency:* Monthly
Janet Howes, Editor

The Oil & Gas Magazine
#201, 1062 Topsail Rd., Mount Pearl, NF A1N 5E6
Tel: 709-722-5444; *Fax:* 709-722-4555
Info@oilandgasmagazine.ca
www.oilworks.com
Frequency: Bi-monthly
Bill Abbott, Editor

Oil & Gas Network
#300, 840 - 6th Ave. SW, Calgary, AB T2P 3E5
Tel: 403-539-1165; *Fax:* 403-206-7753
www.oilgas.net
Frequency: 6 times a year
Shelly Brimble, Editor

Oil & Gas Product News
Tel: 604-291-9900; *Fax:* 604-291-1906
www.baumpub.com
Circulation: 10,708 *Frequency:* 6 times a year
Engelbert J. Baum, Publisher
Morena Zanotto, Editor

Oilsands Review
#300, 5735 - 7 St. NE, Calgary, AB T2E 8V3
Tel: 403-265-3700; *Fax:* 403-265-3706
Circulation: 12,000 *Frequency:* Monthly
Deborah Jaremko, Editor

Oilweek
9915 - 56 Ave. NW, Edmonton, AB T6E 5L7
Tel: 780-944-9333; *Fax:* 780-944-9500
marketing@junewarren.com
Circulation: 10,000 *Frequency:* 12 times a year Oil Week Magazine; 52 times a year Oilweek Newsletter
Darrell Stonehouse, Managing Editor
Bill Whitelaw, Publisher

Propane-Canada
Tel: 403-263-6881; *Fax:* 403-263-6886
Toll-Free: 800-526-4177
propane@northernstar.ab.ca
www.northernstar.ab.ca
Circulation: 8,800 *Frequency:* 6 times a year
Scott Jeffrey, Publisher
Lisa McGuire, Advertising Sales
Alister Thomas, Editor

The Roughneck
#500, 900 - 6th Ave. SW, Calgary, AB T2P 3K2
Tel: 780-263-6881; *Fax:* 780-423-6886
Circulation: 6,527 *Frequency:* 12 times a year
Scott Jeffrey, Publisher

Photography

Master Guide
185 St-Paul St., Québec, QC G1K 3W2
Tel: 418-692-2110; *Fax:* 418-692-3392
Toll-Free: 800-905-7468
www.photolife.com
Other information: Toll Free Fax: 1-800-644-2739
Circulation: 6,500 *Frequency:* Annually
Guy J. Poirier, Publisher
Xavier Bonaccasi, Editor

Photo Life Buyers' Guide
185, rue St-Paul, Québec, QC G1K 3W2
Toll-Free: 800-905-7468
sales@photolife.com
www.photolife.com
Other information: Toll Free Fax: 1-800-664-2739
Circulation: 65,000 *Frequency:* Annually
Xavier Bonaconsi, Editor
Guy Poirier, Publisher

Photo Sélection
185, rue St-Paul, Québec, QC G1K 3W2
Tél: 418-692-2110; *Téléc:* 418-692-3392
Ligne sans frais: 800-905-7468
info@photoselection.com
www.photoselection.com
Circulation: 10 000 *Frequency:* 6 fois par an; français
Xaviar Bonacorsi, Rédacteur en Chef
Xavier Bonacorsi, Rédacteur

Plastics

Canadian Plastics
Tel: 416-442-5600; *Fax:* 416-510-5143
www.canplastics.com
Circulation: 10,402 *Frequency:* 12 times a year
Judith Nancekivell, Senior Publisher, 416/442-2067

Canadian Plastics Directory & Buyer's Guide
#800, 12 Concorde Place, Toronto, ON M3C 4J2
Tel: 416-442-5600; *Fax:* 416-510-5134
Toll-Free: 800-268-7742
cmacdonald@canplastics.com
www.canplastics.com
Circulation: 10,959 *Frequency:* Annually
Judith Nancekivell, Publisher
Bill Young, Associate Publisher

Plastics in Canada Magazine
Tel: 416-764-1514; *Fax:* 416-764-1740
www.bizlink.com/plasticsincanada.htm
Circulation: 10,500 *Frequency:* 6 times a year
Nick Passingham, Publisher
Edward Mason, Editor

Police

Blue Line Magazine
#254, 12A - 4981 Hwy. 7 East, Markham, ON L3R 1N1
Tel: 905-640-3048; *Fax:* 905-640-7547
blueline@blueline.ca
www.blueline.ca
Circulation: 12,000 *Frequency:* 10 times a year
Morley S. Lymburner, Publisher/Editor
Mark Reesor, Senior Editor

Tour of Duty
Toronto Police Assn., 180 Yorkland Blvd., Toronto, ON M2J 1R5
Tel: 416-491-4301; *Fax:* 416-494-4948
editor@tpassn.com
Circulation: 9,245 *Frequency:* Monthly

Power & Power Plants

Nuclear Canada Yearbook
Canadian Nuclear Association, #1610, 130 Albert St., Ottawa, ON K1P 5G4
Tel: 613-237-4262; *Fax:* 613-237-0989
huntc@cna.ca
www.cna.ca
Circulation: 3,500 *Frequency:* Annually
Colin Hunt, Publisher & Editor

Printing & Publishing

Canadian Printer
Tel: 416-764-1509; *Fax:* 416-764-1738
www.canadianprinter.com
Circulation: 11,500 *Frequency:* 8 times a year
Susan Ritcey, Publisher
Doug Picklyk, Editor

Estimators' & Buyers' Guide
Tel: 905-625-7070; *Fax:* 905-625-4856
Frequency: Annually
Alexander Donald, Publisher

Grafika
Tél: 514-842-5873; *Téléc:* 514-842-2422
redaction@infopresse.com
www.infopresse.com
Circulation: 6 000 *Frequency:* 10 fois par an
Bruno Gautier, Éditeur
Mélanie Rudel-Tessier, Rédactrice en chef

Graphic Arts Magazine
#202, 1180 Kingdale Rd., Newmarket, ON L3Y 4W1
Tel: 905-830-4394; *Fax:* 905-830-9345
joe@graphicartsmagazine.com
www.graphicartsmagazine.com
Circulation: 11,200 *Frequency:* 10 times a year
Joe Mulcahy, Publisher
Scott Bury, Editor

Graphic Monthly
Tel: 905-625-7070; *Fax:* 905-625-4856
Toll-Free: 800-331-7408
www.graphicmonthly.ca
Circulation: 10,372 *Frequency:* 6 times a year
Alexander Donald, Publisher

Livre d'ici
#55, 222, Cours Dominion, Montréal, QC H3J 2X1
Tel: 514-933-8033; *Fax:* 514-933-7958
livredici.com
Circulation: 1,600
Jacques Therriault, Publisher

Le Maître Imprimeur
5400, rue Chemin, Saint-Laurent, QC H4S 1P6
Tél: 514-388-9311; *Téléc:* 514-388-0188
Circulation: 5 000 *Frequency:* 10 fois par an; français
Christine Veznia, Éditeur

Masthead
Tel: 905-625-7070; *Fax:* 905-625-4856
wshields@masthead.ca
www.mastheadonline.com
Circulation: 2,800 *Frequency:* 6 times a year; ISSN 0832-512X
Doug Bennet, Publisher

The Publisher
#300, 8 Market St., Toronto, ON M5E 1M6
Tel: 416-482-1090; *Fax:* 416-482-1908
Toll-Free: 877-305-2262
publisher@ccna.ca
www.communitynews.ca; www.ccna.ca
Circulation: 750 *Frequency:* 10 times a year
Lyne Hennigar, Publisher
John Hinds, Editor

Second Impressions
35 Mill Dr., St Albert, AB T8N 1J5
Tel: 780-458-9889; *Fax:* 780-458-9839
secondimpressions@second-impressions.com
www.second-impressions.com
Circulation: 9,000 *Frequency:* 6 times a year
Loretta Puckrin, Publisher

Product Engineering & Design

Design Engineering
1 Mount Pleasant Rd., 7th Fl., Toronto, ON M4Y 2Y5
Tel: 416-764-1534; *Fax:* 416-764-1735
alan.macpherson@de.rogers.com
www.design-engineering.com
Circulation: 19,000 *Frequency:* 8 times a year
Alan Macpherson, Associate Publisher
Mike Mcleod, Editor

Design Product News
Tel: 905-727-0077; *Fax:* 905-727-0017
dpn@clbmedia.ca
www.clbmedia.ca
Circulation: 20,407 *Frequency:* 6 times a year
Nigel Bishop, Publisher
Mike Edwards, Editor
James Zammit, Circulation Manager

Pulp & Paper

Mill Product News
Tel: 604-298-3005; *Fax:* 604-298-3966
www.baumpub.com
Circulation: 20,137 *Frequency:* 6 times a year
Heri R. Baum, Publisher
Gunnar Mardon, Editor

Les Papetières du Québec
Business Information Group, #705, Tour Est, 1, rue Holiday, Pointe-Claire, QC H9R 5N3
Tél: 514-630-5955; *Téléc:* 514-630-5980
Ligne sans frais: 800-363-1327
jbussiere@pulpandpapercanada.com
www.pulpandpapercanada.com
Circulation: 4 348 *Frequency:* 5 fois par an; français
Jim Bussiere, Éditeur-en-chef
Jaclin Ouellet, Rédacteur-en-chef

Pulp & Paper Canada
Business Information Group, #705, Tour Est, 1, rue Holiday, Pointe-Claire, QC H9R 5N3
Tel: 514-630-5955; *Fax:* 514-630-5980
Toll-Free: 800-363-1327
jbussiere@pulpandpapercanada.com
www.pulpandpapercanada.com
Circulation: 9,698 *Frequency:* Monthly; also Annual Directory (Dec.)
Jim Bussiere, Publisher
Anya Orzechowska, Editor

Purchasing

Canadian Trade Index
#208, 2085 Hurontario St., Mississauga, ON L5A 4G1
Tel: 905-290-1818; *Fax:* 905-290-1760
Toll-Free: 877-463-6284
owenmediainfocti@owen-media.com
www.ctidirectory.com
Frequency: Annually, May
Hugh Owen, President

Purchasing B2B
Tel: 416-764-1499; *Fax:* 416-764-1740
www.purchasingb2b.ca
Circulation: 19,292 *Frequency:* 10 times a year
Tim Dimopoulos, Publisher

Real Estate

Canadian Appraiser / L'Évaluateur Canadien
#3C, 2020 Portage Ave., Winnipeg, MB R3J 0K4
Tel: 204-985-9780; *Fax:* 204-985-9795
info@kelman.ca
www.kelman.ca
Circulation: 5,961 *Frequency:* 4 times a year
Craig Kelman, Editor

Canadian Office Guide
2014 Stavebank Rd., Mississauga, ON L5C 1T2
Tel: 905-273-7950; *Fax:* 905-273-3816
www.factorygroup.com/magaz.htm
Frequency: Annually

Canadian Property Guide
#1000, 33 Yonge St., Toronto, ON M5E 1S9
Tel: 416-359-2550; *Fax:* 416-359-2538
cmildon@royallepage.com
www.canadianpropertyguide.com
Circulation: 70,000 *Frequency:* Bi-annual
Caroline Mildon

Espace Montréal
#9235, 800, rue de la Gauchetière ouest, Montréal, QC H5A 1K6
Tél: 514-879-1559; *Téléc:* 514-879-1556
Ligne sans frais: 800-232-9846
espace@espacequebec.com
www.espacepublications.com
Circulation: 10 000 *Frequency:* 4 fois par an
Andrew Cross, Publisher & Editor

Espace Québec
#9235, 800, de la Gauchetière ouest, Montréal, QC H5A 1K6
Tél: 514-879-1559; *Téléc:* 514-879-1556
Ligne sans frais: 800-232-9846
andrew@espacequebec.com
www.espacepublications.com
Circulation: 5 000 *Frequency:* 2 fois par an
Andrew Cross, Éditeur/Rédacteur

REM: Canada's Magazine for Real Estate Professionals
House Magazine Inc., 808 Coxwell Ave., Toronto, ON M4C 3E4
Tel: 416-425-3504; *Fax:* 416-406-0882
www.remonline.com
Circulation: 50,000 *Frequency:* 12 times a year
Heino Molls, Publisher
Jim Adair, Editor, jim@remonline.com

The Western Investor
Business in Vancouver Media Group, #501, 1155 West Pender St., Vancouver, BC V6E 2P4
Tel: 604-669-8500; *Fax:* 604-669-2154
www.westerninvestor.com
Circulation: 16,000 *Frequency:* Monthly
Cheryl Carter, Publisher
Frank O'Brien, Editor

Rental & Leasing Equipment

Canadian Rental Service
Tel: 519-235-2400; *Fax:* 519-235-0798
Circulation: 3,543 *Frequency:* 9 times a year
Chris Skalkos, Editor

Contractors Magazine
Tel: 604-291-9900; *Fax:* 604-291-1906
www.baumpub.com
Circulation: 14,021 *Frequency:* 6 times a year
Engelbert Baum, Publisher
Keith Barker, Editor

Retailing

Canadian Retailer
#800, 1255 Bay St., Toronto, ON M5R 2A9
Tel: 416-922-6678; *Fax:* 416-922-8011
Toll-Free: 888-373-8245
www.retailcouncil.org/cdnretailer
Circulation: 15,000 *Frequency:* 6 times a year
Theresa Rogers, Editor-in-chief
Diane Brisebois, Publisher

Science, Research & Development

Bio Business
#202, 30 Beaver Creek Rd. East, Richmond Hill, ON L4B 1J2
Tel: 905-886-5040; *Fax:* 905-886-6615
Toll-Free: 800-613-6353
cforbes@jesmar.com
www.biobusinessmag.com
Circulation: 15,000 *Frequency:* 4 times a year
Christopher Forbes, Publisher

Biochemistry & Cell Biology / Biochimie & biologie cellulaire
National Research Council of Canada, Ottawa, ON K1A 0R6
Tel: 613-993-0362; *Fax:* 613-952-7656
pubs@nrc-cnrc.gc.ca
pubs.nrc-cnrc.gc.ca
Circulation: 1,150 *Frequency:* Bi-monthly; English & French
Cameron Macdonald, Director
Bruce P. Dancik, Editor
Judy Busnarda, Managing Editor

Camford Chemical Report
38 Groomsport Cres., Toronto, ON M1T 2K9
Tel: 416-740-5604; *Fax:* 416-291-3406
ccr@camfordinfo.com
www.camfordinfo.com
Frequency: 50 times a year
Bob Douglas, Publisher

Canadian Biotech News
Canadian Biotech News Service, 110 Ebb Tide Dr., Winnipeg, MB R3X 2H9
Tel: 415-591-5474; *Fax:* 415-591-5401
canadianbiotech@yahoo.com
www.canadianbiotechnews.com
Circulation: 3,500 *Frequency:* 12 times a year; ISSN: 1188-455X
Peter Winter, Editor-in-chief
Jeff Miller, Publisher

Canadian Geotechnical Journal / Revue canadienne de géotechnique
National Research Council of Canada, Ottawa, ON K1A 0R6
Tel: 613-993-0362; *Fax:* 613-952-7656
pubs@nrc-cnrc.gc.ca
pubs.nrc-cnrc.gc.ca
Circulation: 2,600 *Frequency:* 6 times a year; English & French
Cameron Macdonald, Director
Bruce P. Dancik, Editor
Bushra Waheed, Managing Editor

Canadian Journal of Botany / Revue canadienne de botanique
National Research Council of Canada, Ottawa, ON K1A 0R6
Tel: 613-993-0362; *Fax:* 613-952-7656
pubs@nrc-cnrc.gc.ca
pubs.nrc-cnrc.gc.ca
Circulation: 1,550 *Frequency:* Monthly; English & French
Cameron Macdonald, Director
Bruce P. Dancik, Editor
Cecily Pearson, Managing Editor

Canadian Journal of Chemistry / Revue canadienne de chimie
National Research Council of Canada, Ottawa, ON K1A 0R6
Tel: 613-993-0362; *Fax:* 613-952-7656
pubs@nrc-cnrc.gc.ca
pubs.nrc-cnrc.gc.ca
Circulation: 1,700 *Frequency:* Monthly; English & French
Cameron Macdonald, Director
Dr. R.H. Lipson, Editor
Judy Buscarda, Managing Editor

Canadian Journal of Civil Engineering / Revue canadienne de génie civil
National Research Council of Canada, Ottawa, ON K1A 0R6
Tel: 613-993-0362; *Fax:* 613-952-7656
pubs@nrc-cnrc.gc.ca
pubs.nrc-cnrc.gc.ca
Circulation: 3,200 *Frequency:* 6 times a year; English & French
Cameron Macdonald, Director
Bruce P. Dancik, Editor
Bushra Waheed, Managing Editor

Canadian Journal of Earth Sciences / Revue canadienne des sciences de la Terre
National Research Council of Canada, Ottawa, ON K1A 0R6
Tel: 613-993-0362; *Fax:* 613-952-7656
pubs@nrc-cnrc.gc.ca
pubs.nrc-cnrc.gc.ca
Circulation: 2,400 *Frequency:* Monthly; English & French
Cameron Macdonald, Director
Bruce P. Dancik, Editor
Bushra Waheed, Managing Editor

Canadian Journal of Fisheries & Aquatic Science / Journal canadien des sciences halieutiques et aquatiques
National Research Council of Canada, Ottawa, ON K1A 0R6
Tel: 613-993-0362; *Fax:* 613-952-7656
pubs@nrc-cnrc.gc.ca
pubs.nrc-cnrc.gc.ca
Circulation: 2,400 *Frequency:* Monthly
Bruce P. Dancik, Editor
Cecily Pearson, Managing Editor
Cameron Macdonald, Director

Canadian Journal of Forest Research / Revue canadienne de recherche forestière
National Research Countil of Canada, Ottawa, ON K1A 0R6
Tel: 613-993-0362; *Fax:* 613-952-7656
pubs@nrc-cnrc.gc.ca
pubs.nrc-cnrc.gc.ca
Circulation: 900 *Frequency:* Monthly; English & French
Cameron Macdonald, Director
Bruce P. Dancik, Editor
Donald S. Mavinic, Assistant Editor
Cecily Pearson, Managing Editor

Canadian Journal of Microbiology / Revue canadienne de microbiologie
National Research Council of Canada, Ottawa, ON K1A 0R6
Tel: 613-993-0362; *Fax:* 613-952-7656
pubs@nrc-cnrc.gc.ca
pubs.nrc-cnrc.gc.ca
Circulation: 1,675 *Frequency:* Monthly; English & French
Bruce P. Dancik, Editor
Cameron Macdonald, Director
Donald S. Mavinic, Assistant Editor
Judy Busnarda, Managing Editor

Canadian Journal of Physics / Revue canadienne de physique
National Research Council of Canada, Ottawa, ON K1A 0R6
Tel: 613-993-0362; *Fax:* 613-952-7656
pubs@nrc-cnrc.gc.ca
pubs.nrc-cnrc.gc.ca
Circulation: 850 *Frequency:* Monthly; English & French
Cameron MacDonald, Director
Bushra Waheed, Managing Editor
Bruce P. Dancik, Editor

Canadian Journal of Physiology & Pharmacology / Revue canadienne de physiologie & pharmacologie
Natioanl Research Council of Canada, Ottawa, ON K1A 0R6
Tel: 613-993-0362; *Fax:* 613-952-7656
pubs@nrc-cnrc.gc.ca
pubs.nrc-cnrc.gc.ca
Circulation: 975 *Frequency:* Monthly; English & French
Cameron Macdonald, Director
Bruce P. Dancik, Editor
Donald S. Mavinic, Assistant Editor
Judy Busnarda, Managing Editor

Canadian Journal of Zoology / Revue canadienne de zoologie
National Research Council of Canada, Ottawa, ON K1A 0R6
Tel: 613-993-0362; *Fax:* 613-952-7656
pubs@nrc-cnrc.gc.ca
pubs.nrc-cnrc.gc.ca
Circulation: 1,250 *Frequency:* Monthly; English & French
Cameron Macdonald, Director
Bruce P. Dancik, Editor
Cecily Pearson, Managing Editor

Genome / Génome
National Research Council of Canada, Ottawa, ON K1A 0R6
Tel: 613-993-0362; *Fax:* 613-952-7656
pubs@nrc-cnrc.gc.ca
pubs.nrc-cnrc.gc.ca
Circulation: 1,350 *Frequency:* 6 times a year; English & French
Cameron MacDonald, Director
Cecily Pearson, Managing Editor
Bruce P. Dancik, Editor

LAB Business
#202, 30 East Beaver Creek Rd., Richmond Hill, ON L4B 1J2
Tel: 905-886-5040; *Fax:* 905-886-6615
cforbes@jesmar.com
www.labbusinessmag.com
Circulation: 30,250 *Frequency:* 5 times a year
Christopher Forbes, Publisher

Laboratory Buyers Guide
Tel: 416-510-6835; *Fax:* 416-510-5140
lburt@labcanada.com
www.labcanada.com
Circulation: 20,000 *Frequency:* Annually
Leslie Burt, Publisher/Editor

Laboratory Product News
Tel: 416-510-6835; *Fax:* 416-510-5140
Toll-Free: 800-268-7742
lburt@labcanada.com
www.labcanada.com
Circulation: 20,000 *Frequency:* 6 times a year
Leslie Burt, Publisher/Editor

The Microscopical Society of Canada Bulletin
c/o Dept. of Physics, Acadia University, Wolfville, NS B4P 2R6
Tel: 902-585-1318;
michael.robertson@acadiau.ca
msc.rsvs.ulaval.ca/english/pages/bulletin.html
Circulation: 650 *Frequency:* 4 times a year; ISSN 0383-1825
Dr. Michael Robertson, Editor

OSMT Advocate
#402, 234 Eglinton Ave. East, Toronto, ON M4P 1K5
Tel: 416-485-6768; *Fax:* 416-485-7660
Toll-Free: 800-461-6768
osmt@osmt.org
www.osmt.org
Circulation: 3,000 *Frequency:* 4 times a year
Blanca McArthur, Executive Director

Physics in Canada / La Physique au Canada
#112, McDonald Bldg., 150 Louis Pasteur Ave., Ottawa, ON K1N 6N5
Tel: 613-562-5614; *Fax:* 613-562-5615
cap@physics.uottawa.ca
www.cap.ca
Circulation: 1,623 *Frequency:* 6 times a year; French & English
Béla Joȼs, Editor

Security

Canadian Security
Tel: 905-727-0077; *Fax:* 905-727-0017
sfenninger@clbmedia.ca
www.canadiansecuritymag.com
Circulation: 16,000 *Frequency:* 9 times a year
Jennifer Brown, Editor

Security Products & Technology News
Tel: 905-727-0077; *Fax:* 905-727-0017
www.sptnews.ca
Circulation: 12,000 *Frequency:* 10 times a year
Frank Shoniker, Publisher
Jennifer Brown, Editor

Shipping & Marine

Canadian Sailings
#200, 5165, rue Sherbrooke ouest, Montréal, QC H4A 1T6
Tel: 514-934-0373; *Fax:* 514-934-4708
www.canadiansailings.com
Circulation: 9,000 *Frequency:* Weekly
Joyce Hammock, Publisher & Editor

Harbour & Shipping
#200, 1865 Marine Dr., West Vancouver, BC V7V 1J7
Tel: 604-922-6717; *Fax:* 604-922-1739
harbour_shipping@bc.sympatico.ca
Circulation: 2,200 *Frequency:* Monthly
Murray D. McLellan, President/Publisher
Allison Smith, Editor

Sporting Goods & Recreational Equipment

Golf Business Canada
#105, 955 Green Valley Cres., Ottawa, ON K1C 3V4
Tel: 613-226-3616; *Fax:* 613-226-4148
ngcoa@ngcoa.ca
www.ngcoa.ca
Circulation: 4,000 *Frequency:* 4 times a year
Pamela Stewart, Editor

Jim Rennie's Sports Letter
PO Box 1000, 101 Pretty River Pkwy. South, Collingwood, ON L9Y 4L4
Tel: 705-445-7161; *Fax:* 705-445-8650
rennies@rennies.net
Circulation: 2,000 *Frequency:* Weekly
Jim Rennie, Publisher & Editor

Motorsport Dealer & Trade
Point One Media Inc., #3, 2232 Wilgress Rd., Nanaimo, BC V9S 4N4
Fax: 250-758-8665
Toll-Free: 877-755-8665
info@pointonemedia.com
www.mdtcanada.net
Circulation: 3,500 *Frequency:* 6 times a year
Jim Aikins, Editor
Lara Perraton, Group Publisher

Pool & Spa Marketing
Hubbard Marketing & Publishing Ltd., #12, 270 Esna Park Dr., Markham, ON L3R 1H3
Tel: 905-513-0090; *Fax:* 905-513-1377
Toll-Free: 800-268-5503
richard@poolspamarketing.com
www.poolspamarketing.com
Circulation: 8,000 *Frequency:* 7 times a year
Richard Hubbard, Publisher

Telecommunications

Canadian New Media
#1800, 160 Elgin St., Ottawa, ON K2P 2P7
Tel: 613-230-1984; *Fax:* 613-230-3793
jlewis@decima.com
www.decima.com
James Lewis, Editor

Wireless Telecom
#1110, 130 Albert St., Ottawa, ON K1P 5G4
Tel: 613-233-4888; *Fax:* 613-233-2032
info@cwta.ca
www.cwta.ca
Circulation: 7,273 *Frequency:* 3 times a year

Television, Radio, Video & Home Appliances

Marketnews
Bomar Publishing Inc., #102, 701 Evans Ave., Toronto, ON M9C 1A3
Tel: 416-667-9945; *Fax:* 416-667-0609
jtomson@marketnews.ca
www.marketnews.ca
Circulation: 11,200 *Frequency:* Monthly
John Thomson, Associate Publisher, jtomson@marketnews.ca
Bob Grierson, Publisher, bgrierson@marketnews.ca
Robert Franner, Editor, rfranner@marketnews.ca
Erik Devantier, Creative Director

Media Names & Numbers
Sources, #305, 489 College St., Toronto, ON M6G 1A5
Tel: 416-964-7799; *Fax:* 416- -
www.sources.com
Circulation: 500 *Frequency:* annually
Ulli Diemer, Publisher

Première Video Magazine
#100, 102 Atlantic Ave., Toronto, ON M6K 1X9
Tel: 416-539-8800; *Fax:* 416-539-8511
Circulation: 7,900 *Frequency:* 12 times a year
Salah Bachir, President

Textiles

Canadian Textile Journal
#3000, rue Boullé, Saint-Hyacinthe, QC J2S 1H9
Tel: 450-778-1870; *Fax:* 450-778-9016
Toll-Free: 877-288-8878
rleclerc@gcttg.com
www.textilejournal.ca
Circulation: 2,500 *Frequency:* 7 times a year
Daniel Bertrand, Editor-in-chief

The Textile Journal
3000, rue Boulle, Saint-Hyacinthe, QC J2S 1H9
Tel: 450-778-1870; *Fax:* 450-778-9016
rleclerc@ctt.ca
www.textilejournal.ca
Roger Leclerc

Toys

Toys & Games
Chelsie Communications Inc., #216, 61 Alness St., Toronto, ON M3J 2H2
Tel: 416-663-9229; *Fax:* 416-663-2353
cantoymag@look.ca
www.toysandgamesmag.com
Circulation: 5,000 *Frequency:* 6 times a year
Graham Kennedy, Publisher

Transportation, Shipping & Distribution

Atlantic Construction & Transportation Journal
#609, 1888 Brunswick St., Halifax, NS B3J 3J8
Tel: 902-468-8027; *Fax:* 902-425-8118
ken.partridge@transcontinental.ca
Circulation: 12,500 *Frequency:* 4 times a year
Jeff Nearing, General Manager

Canadian Automotive Fleet
#110, 295 The West Mall, Toronto, ON M9C 4Z4
Tel: 416-383-0302; *Fax:* 416-383-0313
caf@fleetbusiness.com
www.fleetbusiness.com
Circulation: 12,474 *Frequency:* 7 times a year
Jake McLaughlin, Publisher & Editor

Canadian Transit Forum
#710, 15 Wertheim Ct., Richmond Hill, ON L4B 3H7
Tel: 905-771-7333; *Fax:* 905-771-7336
ellenkrai@kenilworth.com
www.kenilworth.com
Circulation: 1,800 *Frequency:* 6 times a year
Ellen Krai, Publisher

Canadian Transportation Logistics
#800, 12 Concorde Place, Toronto, ON M3C 4J2
Tel: 416-510-5108; *Fax:* 416-510-5134
nick@ctl.ca
www.ctl.ca
Circulation: 17,665 *Frequency:* 11 times a year
Nick Krukowski, Publisher
Lou Smyrlis, Editorial Director

Guide du Transport par Camion
Tél: 450-435-3131; *Téléc:* 450-435-3884
guidedutransport@bomartgroup.com
www.bomartgroup.com
Circulation: 3 000 *Frequency:* annuel; français
Pierre Gravel, Président et éditeur
Ginette Marsolais, Conception

Logistics Magazine
#115, 916, boul Ste-Adèle, Sainte-Adèle, QC J8B 2N2
Tel: 450-229-7777; *Fax:* 450-229-3233
www.logistics-mag.com
Frequency: Bi-monthly
Michel Trudeau, Editor

Maritime Magazine
Tel: 418-692-3779; *Fax:* 418-692-5198
Toll-Free: 877-595-3779
pterrien@maritimemag.com
Circulation: 11,000 *Frequency:* 4 times a year; French & English
Covers Marine Transport Industry
Léo YRyanen, Rédacteur en chef

Routes et Transports
A.Q.T.R., #200, 1255, rue University, Montréal, QC H3B 3B2
Tél: 514-523-6444; *Téléc:* 514-523-2666
info@aqtr.qc.ca
www.aqtr.qc.ca
Circulation: 3 500 *Frequency:* 4 fois par an; français
Jean Auden, Editor

Travel

Bulletin Voyages
78 boul Saint-Joseph Ouest, Montréal, QC H2T 2P4
Tél: 514-287-9773; *Téléc:* 514-842-6180
Circulation: 9 062 *Frequency:* Hebdomadaire; français
Jean-Pierre Kerten, Éditeur

Canada Journal
KLR Communications, 44 Cameron Cres., Toronto, ON M4G 1Z8
Tel: 416-487-0166; *Fax:* 416-487-2452
mail@canadajournal.ca
www.canadajournal.ca
Circulation: 27,000 *Frequency:* bi-weekly; German
Klaus Ruland, Publisher/Editor

Canadian Travel Press
310 Dupont St., Toronto, ON M5R 1V9
Tel: 416-968-7252; *Fax:* 416-968-2377
dmcclung@baxter.net
www.travelpress.com
Circulation: 13,000 *Frequency:* Thu.- weekly; summer - bi-weekly
David McClung, President
Edith Baxter, Editor

Canadian Traveller
ACT Communications Inc., #203, 1104 Hornby St., Vancouver, BC V6Z 1V8
Tel: 604-699-9990; *Fax:* 604-699-9993
info@canadiantraveller.net
www.canadiantraveller.net
Circulation: 14,782 *Frequency:* Monthly
Rex Armstead, Publisher
Stephen Fountaine, Associate Publisher
Janice Strong, Associate Editor

GSA: The Travel Magazine for Western Canada
Tel: 604-689-2909; *Fax:* 604-689-2989
Toll-Free: 888-286-6148
sales@gsa.publishing.com
www.gsapublishing.com
Circulation: 5,100 *Frequency:* 26 times a year
Frank Cumming, Publisher
Lynda Cumming, Editor

Le Magazine l'agent de voyages inc.
CP 38, Anjou, QC H1K 4G5
Tél: 514-881-9637; *Téléc:* 514-881-8292
info@planisphere.qc.ca
Circulation: 8 500 *Frequency:* 7 fois par an; français
Michel Villeneuve, Éditeur

Personnel Guide to Canada's Travel Industry
Tel: 416-968-7252; *Fax:* 416-968-2377
sales@baxter.net
www.personnelguide.ca
Circulation: 4,500 *Frequency:* 2 times a year
David McClung, President

Tourisme Plus
#301, 11800, 5e av, Montréal, QC H1E 7C1
Tél: 514-881-8583; *Téléc:* 514-881-8292
production@planisphere.qc.ca
Circulation: 9 200 *Frequency:* 46 fois par an; français
Michel Villeneuve, Rédacteur-en-chef

Travel Courier
310 Dupont St., Toronto, ON M5R 1V9e
Tel: 416-968-7252; *Fax:* 416-968-2377
www.travelpress.com
Circulation: 11,191 *Frequency:* Weekly, Thu.
Edith Baxter, Editor-in-chief

Travelweek
Concepts Travel Media Ltd., #100, 282 Richmond St. East, Toronto, ON M5A 1P4
Tel: 416-365-1500; *Fax:* 416-365-1504
Toll-Free: 800-727-1429
travelweek@travelweek.ca
www.travelweek.ca
Circulation: 12,420 *Frequency:* Weekly
Patrick Dineen, Editor

Voyage en Groupe / Group Travel
590, ch St-Jean, La Prairie, QC J5R 2L1
Tél: 450-444-5870; *Téléc:* 450-444-4720
voyageengroupe@bellnet.ca
www.revue-voyage-groupe.com
Circulation: 13 000 *Frequency:* 6 fois par an; français
Monique Papineau, Éditrice

Vending & Vending Equipment

Canadian Vending & Coin Box Amusement News
PO Box 530, 105 Donly Dr. Aouth, Simcoe, ON N3Y 4N5
Tel: 519-429-5177; *Fax:* 519-429-3094
Toll-Free: 888-599-2228
dkleer@annexweb.com
www.canadianvending.com
Circulation: 3,900 *Frequency:* 10 times a year
Diane Geerlinks, Publisher

Veterinary

The Canadian Veterinary Journal / La Revue Vétérinaire Canadienne
c/o Canadian Veterinary Medical Association, 339 Booth St., Ottawa, ON K1R 7K1
Tel: 613-236-1162; *Fax:* 613-236-9681
Toll-Free: 800-567-2862
admin@cvma-acmv.org
canadianveterinarians.net/publications-journal-issue.aspx
Circulation: 5,500 *Frequency:* Monthly; English & French
Dr. W.C.D. Hare, Editor-in-chief

Le Vétérinarius
#200, 800, av Sainte-Anne, Saint-Hyacinthe, QC J2S 5G7
Tél: 450-774-1427; *Téléc:* 450-774-7635
Ligne sans frais: 800-267-1427
omvq@omvq.qc.ca
www.omvq.qc.ca
Circulation: 2 500 *Frequency:* 6 fois par an; français
Mathieu Bilodeau, Rédacteur-en-chef

Water & Wastes Treatment

Canadian Environmental Protection
Tel: 604-291-9900; *Fax:* 604-291-1906
ebaum@baumpub.com
www.baumpub.com
Circulation: 20,127 *Frequency:* 8 times a year
Morena Zanotto, Editor
Engelbert J. Baum, Publisher

Environmental Science & Engineering Magazine
Environmental Science & Engineering Publications Inc., #30, 220 Industrial Pkwy. South, Aurora, ON L4G 3V6
Tel: 905-727-4666; *Fax:* 905-841-7271
Toll-Free: 888-254-8769
steve@esemag.com
www.esemag.com
Circulation: 19,000 *Frequency:* 6 times a year; ISSN 0835-605X
Steve Davey, Publisher & Editor

Ground Water Canada
Tel: 519-235-2400; *Fax:* 519-235-0798
cskalkos@annexweb.com
Circulation: 3,842 *Frequency:* 4 times a year
Chris Skalkos, Editor

Hazardous Materials Management Magazine
#800, 12 Concorde Pl., Toronto, ON M3C 4J2
Tel: 416-442-5600; *Fax:* 416-510-5133
Toll-Free: 888-702-1111
gcrittenden@solidwastemag.com
www.hazmatmag.com
Circulation: 14,048 *Frequency:* Bi-monthly; ISSN 0843-9303
Guy Crittenden, Editor
Brad O'Brien, Publisher

Maritime Provinces Water & Wastewater Report
Transcontinental Media, #609, 1888 Brunswick St., Halifax, NS B3J 3J8
Tel: 902-468-8027; *Fax:* 902-468-2425
barb.cashin@transcontinental.ca
www.mpwwa.ca/newsletter.asp
Circulation: 2,567 *Frequency:* 4 times a year
Barb McCay Cashin, Editor

Solid Waste & Recycling Magazine
Tel: 416-510-6798; *Fax:* 416-510-5133
cvitello@solidwastemag.com
www.solidwastemag.com
Circulation: 10,000 *Frequency:* 6 times a year; ISSN: 1206-0879
Brad O'Brien, Publisher & Sales Manager
Guy Crittenden, Editor

Woodworking

2 x 4
Editions C.R. Inc., PO Box 1010, Victoriaville, QC G6P 8Y1
Tel: 819-752-4243; *Fax:* 819-382-2970
c-roy@ivic.qc.ca
www.2x4.net
Circulation: 8,000 *Frequency:* 4 times a year; English & French
Claude Roy, Publisher
Bernard Gauthier, Editor, info@bernardgauthier.com

Woodworking
240 Edward St., Aurora, ON L4G 3S9
Tel: 905-272-0077; *Fax:* 905-272-0017
woodworking@clbmedia.ca
www.woodworkingcanada.com
Circulation: 11,190 *Frequency:* 6 times a year; also Woodworking Sourcer (annually)
Bert Kleiser, Publisher
Adam Freill, Editor

Consumer

Advertising, Marketing, Sales

Adbusters
1234 - West 7th Ave., Vancouver, BC V6H 1B7
Tel: 604-736-9401; *Fax:* 604-737-6021
Toll-Free: 800-663-1243
info@adbusters.org
www.adbusters.org
Circulation: 120,000 *Frequency:* 6 times a year; ISSN: 0847-9097
Kalle Lasn, Publisher

Airline Inflight

enRoute
#707, 4200 boul. St-Laurent, Montréal, QC H2W 2R2
Tel: 514-844-2001; *Fax:* 514-844-6001
info@enroutemag.net
www.enroutemag.com
Circulation: 149,478 *Frequency:* Monthly; English & French

Animals

Animals' Voice
Ontario SPCA, 16586 Woodbine Ave., RR#3, Newmarket, ON L3Y 4V8
Tel: 905-898-7122; *Fax:* 905-853-8643
info@ospca.on.ca
www.ospca.on.ca
Circulation: 100,000 *Frequency:* 2 times a year
Vicki Quigley, Editor, vquigley@ospca.on.ca

Canine Review
PO Box 40215 Highfield, Calgary, AB T2G 5G6
Tel: 403-236-0557; *Fax:* 403-236-3271
Toll-Free: 866-236-0557
editor@canine-review.com
www.canine-review.com
Circulation: 2,000 *Frequency:* 10 pa
Karen Milne, Editor
Merla Thomson, Publisher

Dog Sport
131 McElderry Rd., Guelph, ON N1G 4J8
Tel: 519-837-9257; *Fax:* 519-837-4976
www.dogsportmagazine.com
Anne B. Douglas, Editor

Dogs in Canada
Apex Publishing Ltd., #200, 89 Skyway Ave., Toronto, ON M9W 6R4
Tel: 416-798-9778; *Fax:* 416-798-9671
info@dogsincanada.com
www.dogsincanada.com
Circulation: 40,000 *Frequency:* Monthly (13 pa, including Dogs in Canada Annual)
Ann McDonagh, Publisher

Dogs in Canada Annual
Apex Publishing Ltd., #200, 89 Skyway Ave., Toronto, ON M9W 6R4
Tel: 416-798-9778; *Fax:* 416-798-9671
info@dogsincanada.com
www.dogsincanada.com
Circulation: 120,000 *Frequency:* Annually
Ann McDonagh, Publisher

Dogs, Dogs, Dogs!
PO Box 157 Brooklin, Toronto, ON L1M 1B5
Tel: 416-203-8186; *Fax:* 905-620-0805
info@dogsx3.com
www.dogsx3.com
Frequency: 6 times a year
Jackie Lindsay, Publisher & Editor

Magazine Animal
141, rue des Perce Neige, Otterburn Park, QC J3H 5V1
Tél: 450-467-0064; *Téléc:* 450-467-0060
www.magazineanimal.com
Frequency: 10 fois par an
France Philippon, Éditrice

Modern Dog
#202, 343 Railway St., Vancouver, BC V6A 1A4
Tel: 604-734-3131; *Fax:* 604-734-3031
info@moderndogmagazine.com
www.moderndogmagazine.com
Frequency: 4 times a year
Connie Wilson, Editor-in-chief

Pets Magazine
Tel: 905-771-7333; *Fax:* 905-771-7336
Toll-Free: 877-738-7624
editor@petsmagazine.ca
www.petsmagazine.ca
Circulation: 36,565 *Frequency:* 6 pa
Cora Golden, Director, Advertising Sales
Blair Adams, Editor-in-chief
Ellen Kral, Publisher

Pets Quarterly Magazine
PO Box 90510, 230 Markham Rd., Scarborough, ON M1J 3N7
Tel: 416-955-1550; *Fax:* 416-955-1391
jeaton@capmagazines.ca
www.capmagazines.ca/petsquarterly/index.html
Circulation: 53,800 *Frequency:* 4 pa
Kelly Chase, Editor
Adrienne Ramsay, Manager, Advertising
Jim Eaton, Publisher

Arts, Art & Antiques

Border Crossings
#500, 70 Arthur St., Winnipeg, MB R3B 1G7
Tel: 204-942-5778; *Fax:* 204-949-0793
Toll-Free: 866-825-7165
bordercrossings@mts.net
bordercrossingsmag.com
Circulation: 5,500 *Frequency:* 4 pa; ISSN: 0831-2559
Meeka Walsh, Editor
Robert Enright, Editor-at-large

C international contemporary art magazine
C The Visual Arts Foundation, PO Box 5 B, Toronto, ON M5T 2T2
Tel: 416-539-9495; *Fax:* 416-539-9903
Toll-Free: 800-745-6312
general@cmagazine.com
www.cmagazine.com
Circulation: 3,000 *Frequency:* 4 pa; ISSN: 1480-5472

Canadian Art
#210, 51 Front St. East, Toronto, ON M5E 1B3
Tel: 416-368-8854; *Fax:* 416-368-6135
Toll-Free: 800-222-4762
info@canadianart.ca
www.canadianart.ca
Circulation: 23,500 *Frequency:* 4 pa; ISSN: 0825-3854
Melony Ward, Publisher, mward@canadianart.ca
Richard Rhodes, Editor, rhodes@canadianart.ca

Capers Aweigh Annual Anthology
142 Lornest, Sydney, NS B1P 4H4
Tel: 902-849-0822; *Fax:* 902-564-4144
capersaweigh@hotmail.com
Circulation: 500 *Frequency:* Annually
John MacNeil, Publisher

Cityart Magazine
PO Box 1063 F, Toronto, ON M4Y 2T7
Tel: 416-925-5564; *Fax:* 416-925-2972
info@artfocus.com
www.artfocus.com/cityart.html
Circulation: 8,000 *Frequency:* 3 pa
Pat Fleisher, Publisher/Editor

Dance International
The Vancouver Ballet Society, Level 6, 677 Davie St., Vancouver, BC V6B 2G6
Tel: 604-681-1525; *Fax:* 604-681-7732
danceint@direct.ca
www.danceinternational.org
Circulation: 4,000 *Frequency:* 4 pa; ISSN: 1189-9816
Maureen Riches, Editor

Downhomer Magazine
43 James Lane, St. John's, NL A1E 3H3
Tel: 709-726-5113; *Fax:* 709-726-2135
mail@downhomer.com
www.downhomer.com
Circulation: 35,180 *Frequency:* Monthly
Ron Young, Publisher

ETC Montréal
#250, 1435, rue St-Alexandre, Montréal, QC H3A 2G4
Tél: 514-848-1125; *Téléc:* 514-848-0071
etcmtl@dsuper.net
www.etcmontreal.com
Circulation: 2 500 *Frequency:* 4 fois par an
Isabelle Lelarge, Rédacteur-en-chef

Galleries West
#301, 690 Princeton Way SW, Calgary, AB T2P 5J9
Tel: 403-234-7097; *Fax:* 403-243-4649
www.gallerieswest.ca
Frequency: 3 times a year
Jennifer MacLeod, Editor

Inter
Les Éditions intervention, 345, rue du Pont, Québec, QC G1K 6M4
Tél: 418-529-9680; *Téléc:* 418-529-6933
infos@inter-lelieu.org
www.inter-lelieu.org
Circulation: 1 200 *Frequency:* 3 fois par an

Inter, art actuel
345, rue du Pont, Québec, QC G1K 6M4
Tel: 418-529-9680; *Fax:* 418-529-6933
edinter@total.net
Circulation: 1 200 *Frequency:* 3 times a year; ISSN: 0825-8708
Nathalie Perreault, Coordinator

Inuit Art Quarterly
Inuit Art Foundation, 2081 Merivale Rd., Ottawa, ON K2G 1G9
Tel: 613-224-8189; *Fax:* 613-224-2907
iaq@inuitart.org
www.inuitart.org
Circulation: 3,500 *Frequency:* 4 pa; ISSN: 0831-6708
Marybelle Mitchell, Editor

Jump Magazine
#306, 6021 Yonge St., Toronto, ON M2M 3W2
Tel: 416-657-8884; *Fax:* 416-658-5385
info@blackpages.ca
www.blackpages.ca
Circulation: 50,000 *Frequency:* quarterly
Lynrod Douglas, Publisher

Muse
Canadian Museums Assn., #400, 280 Metcalfe St., Ottawa, ON K2P 1R7
Tel: 613-567-0099; *Fax:* 613-233-5438
info@museums.ca
www.museums.ca
Circulation: 2,500 *Frequency:* 6 pa; English & French; ISSN: 0820-0165

Muzik Etc./Drums Etc.
753, rue Ste-Hélène, Longueuil, QC J4K 3R5
Tel: 450-651-4257; *Fax:* 450-670-8683
montrealdrumfest.com
Circulation: 30,000 *Frequency:* 6 times a year
Serge Gamache, Publisher

Ralph Anelillo, Editor

The National Ballet of Canada Souvenir Magazine
#101, 5397 Eglinton Ave. West, Toronto, ON M9C 5K6
Tel: 416-928-2909; *Fax:* 416-966-1181
Toll-Free: 800-320-6420
debby@scoregolf.com
Circulation: 6,000 *Frequency:* Annually
Kim Locke, Publisher

Ontario Craft
Designers Walk, #300, 170 Bedford Rd., Toronto, ON M5R 2K9
Tel: 416-925-4222; *Fax:* 416-925-4223
ontariocraftscouncil@craft.on.ca
www.craft.on.ca
Circulation: 2,500 *Frequency:* 2 pa; ISSN: 0229-1320
Deborah Kirkegaard, Program & Development Officer

Parachute
#501, 4060, boul St-Laurent, Montréal, QC H2W 1Y9
Tel: 514-842-9805; *Fax:* 514-842-9319
info@parachute.ca
www.parachute.ca
Circulation: 4,000 *Frequency:* 4 pa; ISSN: 0318-7020
C. Pontbriand, Rédacteur

Qui Fait Quoi
#200, 3430, rue Saint-Denis, Montréal, QC H2X 3L3
Tel: 514-842-5333; *Fax:* 514-842-6717
info@qfq.com
www.qfq.com
Other information: n7
Circulation: 7,000 *Frequency:* 9 times a year
Claude Desjardins, Publisher

Rotunda
c/o Royal Ontario Museum, 100 Queen's Park, Toronto, ON M5S 2C6
Tel: 416-586-5758; *Fax:* 416-586-5649
sandrap@rom.on.ca
www.rom.on.ca
Circulation: 27,000 *Frequency:* 3 pa; ISSN: 0035-8495
Sandra Piller, Executive Editor

Sequences
CP 26 Haute-Ville, Québec, QC G1R 4M8
Tél: 418-656-5040; *Téléc:* 418-656-7282
revue.cap-aux-diamants@hst.ulaval.ca
www.revuesequences.com
Circulation: 1 400 *Frequency:* 6 fois par an
Elie Castiel, Rédacteur-en-chef
Yves Beauregard, Directeur

Slate
155 King St. East, Kingston, ON K7L 2Z9
Tel: 613-542-3717; *Fax:* 613-542-1447
Toll-Free: 800-871-8093
info@slateartguide.com
www.slateartguide.com
Circulation: 12,000 *Frequency:* 8 pa
Allan Lochhead, Publisher

Spirale
6742, rue Saint-Denis, Montréal, QC H3K 1G6
Tél: 514-934-5651; *Téléc:* 514-934-6390
spiralemagazine@yahoo.com
www.spiralemagazine.com
Circulation: 1 500
Pierre L'Hérault, Direction

Storyteller Magazine
TYO Communications, 3687 Twin Falls Pl., Ottawa, ON K1V 1W6
Tel: 613-521-9734; *Fax:* 613-521-1753
info@storytellermagazine.com
www.storytellermagazine.com
Circulation: 2,000 *Frequency:* 4 times a year
Terry Tyo, Publisher

Take One
#482, 283 Danforth Ave., Toronto, ON M4K 1N2
Tel: 416-944-1096; *Fax:* 416-465-4356
takeone@interlog.com
www.takeonemagazine.ca
Circulation: 5,000 *Frequency:* 4 times a year; ISSN: 1192-5507
Wyndham Wise, Publisher

Vie des Arts
#400, 486, rue Sainte-Catherine ouest, Montréal, QC H3B 1A6
Tél: 514-282-0205; *Téléc:* 514-282-0235
arts@qc.aira.com
www.viedesarts.com
Circulation: 3 386 *Frequency:* 4 fois par an; français avec section en anglais; ISSN: 0042-5435
Bernard Lévy, Rédacteur

Westbridge Art Market Report
1737 Fir St., Vancouver, BC V6J 5J9
Tel: 604-736-1014; *Fax:* 604-734-4944
info@westbridge-fineart.com
www.westbridge-fineart.com
Published free online only
Anthony R. Westbridge, Publisher & Editor

Automobile, Cycle, & Automotive Accessories

Canadian Biker
735 Market St., Victoria, BC V8T 2E2
Tel: 250-384-0333; *Fax:* 250-384-1832
Toll-Free: 800-667-5667
canbike@canadianbiker.com
www.canadianbiker.com
Circulation: 20,000 *Frequency:* 10 pa; ISSN: 1196-7218
Len Creed, Editor & Publisher
Marilyn Piercey, Circulation Manager

Canadian Classics & Performance
PO Box 342, O'Leary, PE C0B 1V0
Tel: 902-859-3869; *Fax:* 902-859-1539
Toll-Free: 877-859-1539
dale@lidstonepub.pe.ca
www.canadianclassicsmag.com
Circulation: 11,000 *Frequency:* 12 times a year
Dale Lidstone, Publisher, dale@lidstonepub.pe.ca

Canadian International Auto Show Program
#4, 447 Speers Rd., Oakville, ON L6K 3S7
Tel: 905-842-6591; *Fax:* 905-842-6843
Circulation: 50,000 *Frequency:* Annually
J. Scott Robinson, Publisher

Carguide/Le Magazine Carguide
Tel: 905-842-6591; *Fax:* 905-842-6843
mailbox@FormulaPublications.com
www.CarguideMagazine.com
Circulation: 333,043 *Frequency:* 6 pa; English & French editions
Joe Knycha, Editor-in-chief
J. Scott Robinson, Publisher

Cycle Canada
Tel: 450-444-5773; *Fax:* 514-444-6773
Toll-Free: 866-522-5656
www.cyclecanadamagazine.net
Circulation: 38,000 *Frequency:* 10 pa; ISSN: 0319-2822
Costa Mouzouris, Editor
Jean Lemieux, Publisher

Lemon-Aid Magazine / Roulez sans vous faire rouler
c/o Automobile Protection Association, 292, boul St-Joseph ouest, Montréal, QC H2V 2N7
Tel: 514-272-5555; *Fax:* 514-273-0797
apamontreal@apa.ca
www.apa.ca

Luxury Vehicles Magazine
3 Ainsley Gardens, Toronto, ON M9A 1M5
Tel: 416-233-2171
Circulation: 177,405 *Frequency:* Quarterly
John D. Duncan, Publisher
Bob English, Editor, 519/833-2089

Le Monde de l'Auto
LC Media inc., 4105, boul Matte, Brossard, QC J4Y 2P4
Tél: 450-444-5773; *Téléc:* 450-444-6773
Ligne sans frais: 866-522-5656

Le Monde du VTT
215, rue Principale, Saint-Amable, QC J0L 1N0
Tél: 450-922-9010; *Téléc:* 450-922-8211
info@motomag.qc.ca
Circulation: 9 560 *Frequency:* 6 times a year
Richard Jetté, Éditeur

Moto Journal
Tél: 514-738-9439; *Téléc:* 514-738-4929
Ligne sans frais: 800-561-0318
turbocirculation@qc.aibn.com
www.motojournalmagazine.net
Circulation: 12 644 *Frequency:* 10 fois par an; ISSN: 0319-2865
Didier Constant, Éditeur
Claude Leonard, Rédacteur

Motocycliste
Fédération Motocycliste du Québec, #208, 4875, boul Métropolitan est, Montréal, QC H1R 3J2
Tél: 514-252-8121; *Téléc:* 514-252-7857
fmq@fmq.qc.ca
www.fmq.qc.ca
Circulation: 15 500 *Frequency:* 5 fois par an

MOTOMAG
1730 - 55e av, Lachine, QC H8T 3J5
Tél: 514-631-6550; *Téléc:* 514-631-0591
Circulation: 11 234 *Frequency:* 6 fois par an
Genevieve Pepin, Chief Editor
Michel Crepault, Publisher

Old Autos
PO Box 250, 348 Main St., Bothwell, ON N0P 1C0
Tel: 519-695-2303; *Fax:* 519-695-3716
Toll-Free: 800-461-3457
www.oldautos.ca
Circulation: 19,263 *Frequency:* 24 pa
Murray McEwan, Publisher/Editor

Ottawa-Gatineau International Auto Show Program
#4, 447 Speers Rd., Oakville, ON L6K 3S7
Tel: 905-842-6591; *Fax:* 905-842-6843
jknycha@formulapublications.com
www.formulamediagroup.com
Circulation: 10,000 *Frequency:* Annually
J. Scott Robinson, Publisher

Performance Racing News
1009678 Ontario Inc., 593 Yonge St., Toronto, ON M4Y 1Z4
Tel: 416-922-7223; *Fax:* 416-922-8001
Toll-Free: 800-667-7223
editor@prn.com
www.prnmag.com
Circulation: 11,691 *Frequency:* 12 pa
Frank Spezzano, Group Publisher
Neal Jones, Editor-in-chief

Pole Position
553, rue Calixa-Lavallée, Beloeil, QC J3G 4B6
Tel: 450-464-4076; *Fax:* 450-464-7742
info@poleposition.ca
www.poleposition.ca
Circulation: 16,625 *Frequency:* 8 times a year
Philippe Brasseur, Editor

Vancouver International Auto Show Program
Carling Media, #70, 10551 Shellbridge Way, Richmond, BC V6X 2W9
Tel: 604-214-9964; *Fax:* 604-214-9965
autoshowinfo@newcardealers.ca
www.bcautoshow.com
Circulation: 50,000
Glen Ringdal, Publisher

Vélo Mag
Tél: 514-521-8356; *Téléc:* 514-521-5711
Ligne sans frais: 800-567-8356
velomag@velo.qc.ca
www.velomag.com
Circulation: 15 000 *Frequency:* 6 fois par an; français
Jacques Sennechael, Rédacteur-en-chef

World of Wheels
1 Yonge St., Toronto, ON M5E 1P9
Tel: 416-869-4010; *Fax:* 416-869-4183
editor@wheels.ca, torstar@torstar.ca
www.wheels.ca
Circulation: 26,099 *Frequency:* 6 pa; ISSN: 0824-5487
Michael Bettencourt, Managing Editor
J. Scott Robinson, Publisher

Aviation & Aerospace

Canadian Aviation Historical Society Journal
PO Box 705 P, Toronto, ON M5S 2Y4
Tel: 416-410-9774; *Fax:* 416-923-3425
cahsnatmem@sympatico.ca
www.cahs.com
Circulation: 1,100 *Frequency:* 4 pa
W. Wheeler, Editor

Babies & Mothers

The Baby & Child Care Encyclopaedia
Tel: 416-537-2604; *Fax:* 416-538-1794
admin@parentscanada.com
Circulation: 100,000 *Frequency:* 2 pa (May & Nov.)
Donald G. Swinburne, Publisher

Best Wishes
Tel: 416-537-2604; *Fax:* 416-538-1794
Toll-Free: 866-457-3320
admin@parentscanada.com
www.parentscanada.com
Circulation: 142,260 *Frequency:* 2 pa (May & Nov.)
Donald G. Swinburne, Publisher
Susan Pennell-Sebekos, Editor, susanp@parentscanada.com

C'est Pour Quand? Revue prénatale
2260, des Patriotes, Laval, QC H7L 3K8
Tél: 450-622-0091; *Téléc:* 450-622-0099
mlemoyne@qc.aira.com
Circulation: 43 000 *Frequency:* 2 fois par an; français
Manon Le Moyne, Éditrice & Rédactrice-en-chef

The Compleat Mother - The Magazine of Pregnancy, Birth & Breastfeeding
PO Box 38033, Calgary, AB T3K 5G9
Tel: 403-255-0246; *Fax:* 403- -
thecompleatmother@shaw.ca
www.thecompleatmother.com
Circulation: 8,000 *Frequency:* 4 pa
Angela van Son, Publisher & Editor

Expecting Magazine
Tel: 416-537-2604; *Fax:* 416-538-1794
admin@parentscanada.com
www.parentscanada.com
Circulation: 146,649 *Frequency:* 3 times a year
Donald G. Swinburne, President

Grossesse
468, boul Roland-Thierrien, Longueuil, QC J4H 4E3
Tél: 450-677-2556; *Téléc:* 450-677-4097
Circulation: 20 000 *Frequency:* 2 fois par an
Richard Desmarais, Rédacteur

Mère Nouvelle
1 Mount Pleasant Rd., 8th Fl., Toronto, ON M4Y 2Y5
Tél: 416-764-2850; *Téléc:* 416-764-2894
maria.paguirigan@tpg.rogers.com
toronto.todaysparent.com
Circulation: 35 700 *Frequency:* 2 fois par an
Holly Bennett, Rédactrice

Mon Bébé Revue Postnatale
2260, des Patriotes, Laval, QC H7L 3K8
Tél: 450-622-0091; *Téléc:* 450-622-0099
mlemoyne@qc.aira.com
Circulation: 43 000 *Frequency:* 2 fois par an; français
Manon Le Moyne, Éditrice & Rédactrice-en-chef

Newborn
1 Mount Pleasant Rd., 8th Fl., Toronto, ON M4Y 2Y5
Tel: 416-764-2844; *Fax:* 416-764-2894
Tiziana.Roberts@tpg.rogers.com
toronto.todaysparent.com
Circulation: 132,875 *Frequency:* 2 pa; English & French editions
Holly Bennett, Editor
Tiziana Roberts, Publisher

Spécial Bébé
186, rue Val Chenaie, Rosemère, QC J7A 4B6
Tél: 514-331-0661; *Téléc:* 514-331-8821
Circulation: 38 000 *Frequency:* 2 fois par an
Ronald Lapierre, Rédacteur

Today's Parent Pregnancy & Birth
1 Mount Pleasant Rd., 8th Fl., Toronto, ON M4Y 2Y5
Tel: 416-764-2883; *Fax:* 416-764-2801
askus@todaysparent.com
www.todaysparent.com
Circulation: 132,875 *Frequency:* 2 pa
Holly Bennett, Editor
Tiziana Roberts, Publisher

Boating & Yachting

Boat Guide
Tel: 905-842-6591; *Fax:* 905-842-6843
boatbiz@idirect.ca
www.carguideca.com
Circulation: 60,000 *Frequency:* 2 pa
Scott Robinson, Publisher
Lizanne Madigan, Editor

Boating East Ports & Cruising Guide
Marble Rock Rd., RR#2, Gananoque, ON K7G 2V4
Tel: 613-382-5735; *Fax:* 613-382-8326
boateast@kos.net
Circulation: 20,000 *Frequency:* Annually, May
K. Christensen, Contact

Boats & Places
#13, 130 Saunders Rd., Barrie, ON L4N 9A8
Tel: 705-725-4669; *Fax:* 705-725-4669
info@boatsandplaces.com
www.boatsandplaces.com
Circulation: 24,692 *Frequency:* 6 times per year
Brian Minton, Publisher
Amanda Dyer Comission, Editor

Canadian Yachting
Kerrwil Publications Limited, #201, 49 Bathurst St., Toronto, ON MV5 2P2
Tel: 416-703-7167; *Fax:* 416-703-1330
www.cymagazine.ca
Circulation: 24,500 *Frequency:* 6 pa; ISSN: 0384-0999
Elizabeth Kerr, Publisher

DIY Boat Owner
PO Box 118, Lindsay, ON K9V 4R8
Tel: 705-359-2094; *Fax:* 705-359-2097
Toll-Free: 888-658-2628
info@diy-boat.com
www.diy-boat.com
Circulation: 20,000 *Frequency:* 4 times a year
Jan Mundy, Publisher & Editor

L'Escale Nautique
Tél: 418-863-5055; *Téléc:* 418-692-5198
redaction@escalenautique.qc.ca
www.escalenautique.qc.ca
Circulation: 12 000 *Frequency:* 4 fois par an, plus guide nautique; français
Michel Sacco, Rédacteur-en-chef

Gam on Yachting
#202, 250 The Esplanade, Toronto, ON M5A 1J2
Tel: 416-368-1559; *Fax:* 416-368-2831
gam@passport.ca
www.gamonyachting.com
Circulation: 13,500 *Frequency:* 8 pa
Craig M. Green, Manager, Sales
Karin Larson, Publisher & Editor

Ontario Sailor Magazine
91 Hemmingway Dr., Courtice, ON L1E 2C2
Tel: 905-434-7409; *Fax:* 905-434-1654
sails@istar.ca
www.ontariosailormagazine.ca
Circulation: 8,000/issue *Frequency:* 7 times a year
Sandra McDowell, Publisher
Greg McDowell, Managing Editor

Pacific Yachting
#900, 1080 Howe St., Vancouver, BC V6Z 2T1
Tel: 604-606-4644; *Fax:* 604-687-1925
Toll-Free: 800-816-0747
info@oppublishing.com
www.oppublishing.com
Circulation: 16,975 *Frequency:* Monthly
Mark Yelic, Publisher
Peter Robson, Editor

Les Plaisanciers
#310, 970, Montée de Liesse, Saint-Laurent, QC H4T 1W7
Tél: 514-856-0788; *Téléc:* 514-856-0790
roy@magazinelesplaisanciers.com
Circulation: 20 000 *Frequency:* 5 fois par an; français
Roy Baird, Sr., Publisher
Claude Leonard, Editor

Port Hole / Le Hublot
c/o Canadian Power & Sail Squadrons, 26 Golden Gate Ct., Toronto, ON M1P 3A5
Tel: 416-293-2438; *Fax:* 416-293-2445
Toll-Free: 888-277-2628
hqg@cps-ecp.ca
www.cps-ecp.ca
Circulation: 28,000 *Frequency:* 4 pa; English & French
Joan Eyolfson Cadham, Editor-in-chief

Power Boating Canada
#5, 1020 Brevik Pl., Mississauga, ON L4W 4N7
Tel: 905-624-8218; *Fax:* 905-624-6764
www.powerboating.com
Frequency: 7 pa
William Taylor, Publisher
Steve Fennel, Editor

Québec Yachting
912, rue Bellerive, Longueuil, QC J4J 1A7
Tél: 450-670-0377; *Téléc:* 450-670-5262
quebecyachting@videotron.ca
Circulation: 10 500 *Frequency:* 6 fois par an; français
Pierre Hudon, Co-Editor
Henri R. de Cotret, Co-Editor

Windsport Magazine
SBC Media Inc., #3266, 2255B Queen St. East, Toronto, ON M4E 1G3
Tel: 416-406-2400; *Fax:* 416-406-0656
info@windsport.com
www.windsport.com
Circulation: 26,000 *Frequency:* 4 pa
John Bryja, Editor

Books

Amphora
c/o Alcuin Society, PO Box 3216, Vancouver, BC V6B 3X8
Tel: 604-937-3293;
info@alcuinsociety.com
www.alcuinsociety.com
Circulation: 340 *Frequency:* Quarterly; ISSN: 0003-200x
Rollin Milroy, amphora@alcuinsociety.com

BC BookWorld
A.R.T. BookWorld Productions, 3516 West 13th Ave., Vancouver, BC V6R 2S3
Tel: 604-736-4011; *Fax:* 604-736-4011
bookworld@telus.net
www.bcbookworld.com
Circulation: 100,000 *Frequency:* 4 times a year; ISSN 0847-7728
Alan Twigg, Publisher
David Lester, Editor

Brides, Bridal

Mariage Québec
#1301, 1155, rue Université, Montréal, QC H3B 3A7
Tél: 514-284-2552; *Téléc:* 514-284-4492
info@mariagequebec.com
www.mariagequebec.com
Circulation: 22 915 *Frequency:* 2 fois par an; français
Denyse Clermont, Éditrice
Claude LaFramboise, Directeur de la direction

Sposa Magazine
c/o Jasmin Publishing, #202, 55 York St., Toronto, ON M5J 1R7
Tel: 416-364-5899; *Fax:* 416-364-5996
editor@sposa.com
www.sposa.com
Circulation: 50,000 *Frequency:* 2 pa
Gulshan Sippy, Editor

Today's Bride
Tel: 416-537-2604; *Fax:* 416-538-1794
Circulation: 99, 361 *Frequency:* 2 pa
Donald G. Swinburne, Publisher

WeddingBells
#320, 111 Queen St. East, Toronto, ON M5C 1S2
Tel: 416-364-3333; *Fax:* 416-594-3374
feedback@weddingbells.ca
www.weddingbells.ca
Circulation: 103,500 *Frequency:* 2 pa; ISSN: 1203-0392
Alethea Wakefield, Associate Publisher

Business & Finance

The Bay Street Bull
#208, 80 Park Lawn Rd., Toronto, ON M8Y 3H8
Tel: 416-252-4356; *Fax:* 416-252-0838
info@thebaystreetbull.com
www.thebaystreetbull.com
Magazine for men and women who make up Canada's leading business community
Stephen Petherbridge, Publisher

Business in Vancouver
102 East 4th St., Vancouver, BC V5T 1G2
Tel: 604-688-2398; *Fax:* 604-688-1963
www.biv.com
Circulation: 16,000 *Frequency:* Weekly, Tue.
Business in Vancouver is an award-winning weekly newspaper serving Greater Vancouver since 1989. Targeted at business decision-makers, it provides local business news and information every Tuesday and reaches more than 62,000+ readers a week.
Tom Siba, Publisher

Business Niagara Magazine
159 York St., St Catharines, ON L2R 6E9
Tel: 905-682-4509; *Fax:* 905-682-8219
www.bizniagara.com

Circulation: 20,000
Released bi-monthly by Osprey Media Group Inc., Business Niagara Magazine reaches over 20,000 registered businesses and is geared to everyone from a one-person operation to a large publicly traded organization.
Mishka Balsom, Publisher

Canadian MoneySaver
PO Box 370, 5540 Loyalist Pkwy., Bath, ON K0H 1G0
Tel: 613-352-7448; *Fax:* 613-352-7700
moneyinfo@canadianmoneysaver.ca
www.canadianmoneysaver.ca

Circulation: 69,700 *Frequency:* 9 pa
Canadian MoneySaver is an acclaimed investment advisory with a recognized reputation for providing a trustworthy and down-to-earth service since 1981. Canadian MoneySaver publishes monthly with three double issues (July/August, November/December and March/April).
Dale Ennis, Publisher/Editor-in-Chief

Canadian Shareowner Magazine
#806, 4 King St. West, Toronto, ON M5H 1B6
Tel: 416-595-9600; *Fax:* 416-595-0400
Toll-Free: 800-268-6881
magazine@ShareOwner.com
www.shareowner.com

Circulation: 20,876 *Frequency:* 6 pa; ISSN: 0836-0960
Periodical offering a proprietary Stock Selection Guide to find stocks in which subscribers ought to consider investing
John T. Bart, Publisher & Editor

Pensez-y bien!
Les Éditions EJS, 13, ch du Pied-de-Roi, Lac Beaufort, QC G0A 2C0
Tél: 418-686-1940; *Téléc:* 418-871-0972
info@ejs.qc.ca
www.ejs.qc.ca

Circulation: 150 000 *Frequency:* 4 fois par an; français
Les articles présentent et expliquent les services et les produits financiers
France Bégin, Éditeur

Votre Avoir: La revue de vos Finances Personnelles
#2001, 1500, rue Notre Dame, Montréal, QC H8S 2E3
Tél: 514-639-5355; *Téléc:* 514-639-8880
info@votreavoir.com
www.votreavoir.com

Circulation: 34,000 *Frequency:* 6 times a year
Revue de finances personnelles
Roger Déry, Éditeur

Camping & Outdoor Recreation

Camping Caravaning
Communication Camping Caravaning, CP 1000 M, 4545, av Pierre de Coubertin, Montréal, QC H1V 3R2
Tél: 514-252-3003; *Téléc:* 514-254-0694
Ligne sans frais: 866-237-3722
communication@fqcc.qc.ca
www.campingquebec.com

Circulation: 46 000 *Frequency:* 8 fois par an
Paul Laquerre, Rédacteur-en-chef

Camping in Ontario
Ontario Private Campground Assn., #8, 220 Royal Crest Ct., Markham, ON L43 9Y2
Fax: 905-947-9501
Toll-Free: 877-672-2226
opca@campinginontario.ca
www.campinginontario.ca

Circulation: 200,000 *Frequency:* Annually, January
Beth Potter, Executive Director

explore
Quarto Communications, 54 St. Patrick St., Toronto, ON M5T 1V1
Tel: 416-599-2000; *Fax:* 416-599-0800
Toll-Free: 877-874-5253
explore@explore-mag.com
www.explore-mag.com

Circulation: 30,000 *Frequency:* 6 pa; 0714-816X
Al Zikovitz, Publisher
James Little, Editor

Kanawa: Canada's Paddling Magazine
Paddle Canada, PO Box 20069 Taylor-Kidd, Kingston, ON K7P 2T6
Tel: 613-521-7267; *Fax:* 613-547-6292
Toll-Free: 888-252-6292
info@paddlingcanada.com
www.paddlingcanada.com

Circulation: 21,000 *Frequency:* 4 times a year; ISSN: 1198-9580
Anne Baxter, Managing Director
Richard Alexander, President, Canadian Recreational Canoeing Association

RV Gazette
Explorer RV Club, #6, 328 Mill St., Beaverton, ON L0K 1A0
Tel: 705-426-1419; *Fax:* 705-426-1403
Toll-Free: 800-999-0819
info@rvgazette.com
www.rvgazette.com

Circulation: 13,304 *Frequency:* 6 times a year
Marcia Anderson, General Manager

Vie en Plein Air
#310, 970, Montée de Liesse, Saint-Laurent, QC H4T 1W7
Tél: 514-856-0787; *Téléc:* 514-856-0790

Circulation: 20 000 *Frequency:* 4 fois par an; français
Claude Leonard, Éditeur

Children's

ChickaDEE
#400, 10 Lower Spadina Ave., Toronto, ON M5V 2Z2
Tel: 416-340-2700; *Fax:* 416-340-9769
Toll-Free: 800-551-6957
chickadee@owlkids.com
www.owlkids.com

Circulation: 95,000 *Frequency:* 10 pa; ISSN: 0707-4611
Mary Vincent, Publisher

Chirp
#400, 10 Lower Spadina Ave., Toronto, ON M5V 2Z2
Tel: 416-340-2700; *Fax:* 416-340-9769
Toll-Free: 800-551-6957
chirp@owlkids.com
www.owlkids.com

Circulation: 75,000 *Frequency:* 10 times a year; ISSN: 1206-4580
Sarah Trusty, Assistant Editor

Les Débrouillards
4475, rue Frontenac, Montréal, QC H2H 2S2
Tél: 514-844-2111; *Téléc:* 514-278-3030
scientifix@lesdebrouillards.qc.ca
www.lesdebrouillards.qc.ca

Circulation: 37 000 *Frequency:* 10 fois par an; français
Félix Maltais, Éditeur
Isabelle Vaillancourt, Rédactrice-en-chef

Les Explorateurs
Les Publications BLD, 4475, rue Frontenac, Montréal, QC H2H 2S2
Tél: 514-844-2111; *Téléc:* 514-278-3030
lesexplorateurs@lesdebrouillards.qc.ca
www.lesexplos.qc.ca

Félix Maltais, Éditeur
Sarah Perreault, Rédactrice en chef

Famous Kids
#100, 102 Atlantic Ave., Toronto, ON M6K 1X9
Tel: 416-539-8800; *Fax:* 416-539-8511

Frequency: 4 times a year
Salah Bachir, Publisher

J'Aime Lire
4475, rue Frontenac, Montréal, QC H2H 2S2
Tél: 514-844-2111; *Téléc:* 514-278-3030
Ligne sans frais: 800-313-3020
redaction@bayardpresse.qc.ca
www.bayardjeunesse.ca

Circulation: 23 000
Suzanne Spino, Directrice générale

Kids Tribute
71 Barber Greene Rd., Toronto, ON M3C 2A2
Tel: 416-445-0544; *Fax:* 416-445-2894
generalinfo@tribute.ca
www.tribute.ca

Circulation: 300,000 *Frequency:* 4 pa
Sandra Stewart, Publisher & Editor

kidsworld Magazine
#301, 177 Danforth Ave., Toronto, ON M4K 1N2
Tel: 416-466-4956; *Fax:* 416-466-5002
kidsworld@kidsworld-online.com
www.kidsworld-online.com

Circulation: 300,000 *Frequency:* 5 pa
Michael Sheasgreen, Publisher

The Magazine not for Adults / Le Magazine Interdit aux Adultes
643 Queen St. East, Toronto, ON M4M 1G4
Tel: 416-778-8727; *Fax:* 416-778-8726
letters@themagazine.ca
www.themagazine.ca

Circulation: 3,800,000 *Frequency:* 12 times a year
Eric Conroy, Publisher

OWL Magazine
#400, 10 Lower Spadina Ave., Toronto, ON M5V 2Z2
Tel: 416-340-2700; *Fax:* 416-340-9769
Toll-Free: 800-551-6957
owl@owlkids.com
www.owlkids.com

Circulation: 75,000 *Frequency:* 10 pa; ISSN: 0382-6627
Craig Battle, Associate Editor

Planète 912
#301, 177 Danforth Ave., Toronto, ON M4K 1N2
Tel: 416-466-4956; *Fax:* 416-466-5002

Circulation: 75,000 *Frequency:* 5 times a year
Michael Sheasgreen, Publisher
Martine Becquet, Editor

YES Mag: Canada's Science Magazine For Kids
#501, 3960 Quadra St., Victoria, BC V8X 4A3
Tel: 250-477-5543; *Fax:* 250-477-5390
info@yesmag.ca
www.yesmag.ca

Circulation: 18,000 *Frequency:* bi-monthly
David Garrison, Publisher

City Magazine

Avenue
RedPoint Media Group Inc., #105, 1210 - 20th Ave. SE, Calgary, AB T2G 1M8
Tel: 403-240-9055; *Fax:* 403-240-9059
info@redpointmedia.ca
www.avenuemagazine.ca

Circulation: 27,000 *Frequency:* 10 times a year
Gary Davies, Publisher, gdavies@redpointmedia.ca
Jennifer Hamilton, Managing Editor, jhamilton@redpointmedia.ca
Kathe Lemon, Editor, klemon@redpointmedia.ca

eye
625 Church St., 6th Fl., Toronto, ON M4Y 2G1
Tel: 416-596-4393; *Fax:* 416-504-4341
www.eye.net

Circulation: 95,893 *Frequency:* Weekly
Peter Burke, Publisher

Fast Forward Weekly
Great West Publishing, #206, 1210 - 20th Ave. SE, Calgary, AB T2G 3G2
Tel: 403-244-2235; *Fax:* 403-244-1431
info@ffwd.greatwest.ca
www.ffwdweekly.com

Circulation: 24,000 *Frequency:* Weekly

The Georgia Straight
1701 West Broadway St., Vancouver, BC V6J 1Y3
Tel: 604-730-7000; *Fax:* 604-730-7010
info@straight.com
www.straight.com

Circulation: 115,238 *Frequency:* Weekly
Dan McLeod, Publisher/Editor, 604/730-7088

Le Guide Prestige Montréal
#700, 2160, de la Montagne, Montréal, QC H3G 2T3
Tel: 514-982-9823; *Fax:* 514-289-9160
tamara@prestipresse.com

Circulation: 150,000 *Frequency:* 4 times a year; English & French
Peter Weiss, Publisher
André Ducharme, Editor-in-chief

Hamilton Magazine

Tel: 905-634-8003; *Fax:* 905-634-7661
info@townmedia.ca
www.hamiltonmagazine.com

Circulation: 39,901 *Frequency:* 5 pa
Wayne Narciso, Publisher
David Young, Editor

HighGrader
PO Box 624, Timmins, ON P4N 1E9
Tel: 705-266-4950; : highgrader@nt.net
www.highgradermagazine.com
Circulation: 2,500
Brit Griffin, Publisher

Hour
Communications Voir Inc., 355, rue Ste-Catherine ouest, 7e étage, Montréal, QC H3B 1A5
Tel: 514-848-0777; *Fax:* 514-848-9004
info@hour.ca
www.hour.ca
Circulation: 49,000 *Frequency:* 52 pa
Jamie O'Meara, Editor-in-chief

In Montréal
1, Carré Cummings Sq., Montréal, QC H3W 1M6
Tel: 514-345-2645; *Fax:* 514-345-2655
info@inmontreal.com
Frequency: 6 pa

International Guide, Banff
Tel: 403-760-3484;
igpub@telusplanet.net
www.igpublications.com
Circulation: 18,000
Wayne Kehoe, Publisher
Cherie Rautio, Editor

Kingston Life Magazine
PO Box 1352, Kingston, ON K7L 5C6
Tel: 613-549-8442; *Fax:* 613-549-4333
Frequency: 4 times a year
Mary Laflamme, Publisher

Legacy
9667 - 87th Ave., Edmonton, AB T6C 1K5
Tel: 780-439-0705; *Fax:* 780-439-0549
legacy@legacymagazine.ab.ca
www.legacymagazine.ab.ca
Circulation: 8,700 *Frequency:* 4 times a year; ISSN: 1203-5769
Barbara Dacks, Publisher

Lethbridge Living
PO Box 22005 Henderson Lake, 1518 - 3rd Ave. S, Lethbridge, AB T1K 6X5
Tel: 403-381-1454; *Fax:* 403-329-0264
editor@lethbridgeliving.com
lethbridgeliving.com
Circulation: 15,000 *Frequency:* 4 times a year
Martin Oordt, Editor
Mary Oordt, Managing Editor

London City Life Magazine
1147 Gainsborough Rd., London, ON N6H 5L5
Tel: 519-471-2907; *Fax:* 519-473-7859
Circulation: 31,000 *Frequency:* 6 pa
Gord Delamont, Publisher & Editor

Monday Magazine
Island Publisher Ltd., 818 Broughton St., Victoria, BC V8W 1E4
Tel: 250-382-6188; *Fax:* 250-382-6014
publisher@mondaymag.com
www.mondaymag.com
Circulation: 40,000 *Frequency:* Weekly
Jim Parker, Publisher

Montreal Mirror
Communications Gratte-Ciel ltée, 465 McGill St., 3rd Fl., Montréal, QC H2Y 4B4
Tel: 514-393-1010; *Fax:* 514-393-3173
letters@mtl-mirror.com
www.montrealmirror.com
Circulation: 70,000 *Frequency:* Weekly; Thursday
Alastair Sutherland, Editor-in-charge

Montréal Scope
#202, 4416, boul St-Laurent, Montréal, QC H2W 1Z5
Tel: 514-933-3333; *Fax:* 514-933-4286
info@montrealscope.com
Circulation: 40,000 *Frequency:* 15 pa
Priscilla Baritte, Head Editor & Coordinator

Moving to Magazines.. / Emménager-à
Tel: 905-479-0641; *Fax:* 905-479-1286
info@movingto.com
www.movingto.com
Circulation: 240,000 *Frequency:* Annually, or bi-annual issues cover all major Canadian cities & areas; 2 bilingual issues, Montréal, Ottawa/Hull
Michael Rosset

Niagara Life Magazine (a division of Downtowner Publications Inc.)
#1, 3550 Schmon Pkwy., Thorold, ON L2V 4Y5
Tel: 905-641-1984; *Fax:* 905-641-0682
niagaralife@on.aibn.com
www.niagaralifemag.com
Circulation: 45,000 *Frequency:* 8 times a year
Ian Oliver, Publisher
Gail Todd, Managing Editor

Northword Magazine
PO Box 817, Smithers, BC V0J 2N0
Tel: 250-847-4600; *Fax:* 250-847-4668
www.northword.ca
Frequency: 4 times a year

Now
189 Church St., Toronto, ON M5B 1Y7
Tel: 416-364-1300; *Fax:* 416-364-1168
alice@nowtoronto.com
www.nowtoronto.com
Circulation: 108,779 *Frequency:* Weekly; Thursday
Alice Klein, Editor/CEO
Michael Hollett, Editor/Publisher

Off-Centre Magazine
PO Box 1384, Vernon, BC V1T 7H4
Tel: 250-558-3979; *Fax:* 250-558-3912
info@off-centre.ca
www.off-centre.ca
Circulation: 17,000 *Frequency:* Monthly
Leanne Allen, Publisher

Okanagan Life Magazine
Byrne Publishing Group Inc., #10, 1753 Dolphin Ave., Kelowna, BC V1Y 8A6
Tel: 250-861-5399; *Fax:* 250-868-3040
Toll-Free: 888-311-1119
info@okanaganlife.com
www.okanaganlife.com
Circulation: 25,000 *Frequency:* 10 pa
J. Paul Byrne, Publisher

Ottawa City Magazine
MacKenzie Publishing, #300, 111 Sparks St., Ottawa, ON K1P 5B5
Tel: 613-688-5433; *Fax:* 613-688-1994
olife@magma.ca
Circulation: 35,500 *Frequency:* 6 times a year
Dan Donovan, Publisher
Harvey Chartrand, Editor

Ottawa Life Magazine
1A Springfield Rd., Ottawa, ON K1M 1C8
Tel: 613-688-5433; *Fax:* 613-688-1994
info@ottawalife.com
www.ottawalife.com
Circulation: 40,000 *Frequency:* 6 times a year
Harvey Chartrand, Editor

The Ottawa X Press
Communications Voir Inc., #204, 396 Cooper St., Ottawa, ON K2P 2H7
Tel: 613-237-8226; *Fax:* 613-237-8220
Toll-Free: 877-632-8647
info@ottawaexpress.ca
www.ottawaxpress.ca
Circulation: 29,344 *Frequency:* Weekly, Thu.
Matthew Harrison, Editor-in-chief

Pique Newsmagazine
#202, 1390 Alpha Lake Rd., Whistler, BC V0N 1B1
Tel: 604-938-0202; *Fax:* 604-938-0201
mail@piquenewsmagazine.com
www.piquenewsmagazine.com
Circulation: 16,500 *Frequency:* Weekly, Fri.
Kathy Barnett, Publisher
Darren ROberts, Director, Advertising
Bob Barnett, Editor

the prairie dog
#201, 1836 Scarth St., Regina, SK S4P 2G3
Tel: 306-757-8522; *Fax:* 306-352-9686
reception@prairiedogmag.com
prairiedog.inregina.com
Circulation: 16,000 *Frequency:* Bi-weekly
April Bourgeois, Publisher
Stephen Whitworth, Editor

Profile Kingston
PO Box 91, Kingston, ON K7L 4V6
Tel: 613-546-6723; *Fax:* 613-546-0707
editor@profilekingston.com
www.profilekingston.com
Circulation: 16,000 *Frequency:* 6 times a year
Bonnie Golomb, Publisher

Pulse Niagara
Dynasty Communications Inc., #208, 243 Church St., St Catharines, ON L2R 3E8
Tel: 905-682-5999; *Fax:* 905-682-1414
www.pulseniagara.com
Circulation: 18,000 *Frequency:* Weekly
Ron Kilpatrick, Publisher/Editor

Thunder Bay Guest Magazine
87 North Hill St., Thunder Bay, ON P7A 5V6
Tel: 807-345-2625; *Fax:* 807-345-9923
info@thunderbaypost.com
Circulation: 12,469 *Frequency:* 9 pa
Richard Sadick, Publisher

Toronto Events Calendar
#460, 20 Eglinton Ave. East, Toronto, ON M4P 1A9
Tel: 416-782-3322; *Fax:* 416-787-9299
info@torontoeventscalendar.com
www.torcalendar.com
Frequency: 2 pa; January, June
R.S. Diamond, Editor
Sybil Levine, Publisher

Toronto Life
#320, 111 Queen St. East, Toronto, ON M5C 1S2
Tel: 416-364-3333; *Fax:* 416-861-1169
editorial@torontolife.com
www.torontolife.com
Circulation: 91,692 *Frequency:* Monthly; ISSN: 0049-4194
John Macfarlane, Editor

UPtown Magazine
Rosebud Publications Ltd., 1465 St. James St., Winnipeg, MB R3H 0W9
Tel: 204-949-4370; *Fax:* 204-949-4376
source@uptownmag.com
www.uptownmag.com
Circulation: 17,000 *Frequency:* Weekly
John Kendle, Editor

Vancouver Magazine
Transcontinental Publishing, #500, 2608 Granville St., Vancouver, BC V6H 3V3
Tel: 604-877-7732; *Fax:* 604-877-4823
mail@vancouvermagazine.com
www.vancouvermagazine.com
Circulation: 48,000 *Frequency:* 11 pa
Kim Peacock, Publisher
Gary Stephen Ross, Editor-in-chief

Victoria Boulevard
PO Box 5417 LCD 9, Victoria, BC V8R 6S4
Tel: 250-598-8111; *Fax:* 250-598-3183
baypub@telus.net
www.victoriaboulevard.com
Circulation: 45,000 *Frequency:* Bi-monthly
Evelyn Butler, Publisher

Visitor's Choice, Vancouver
#500, 1155 West Pender St., Vancouver, BC V6E 2P4
Tel: 604-608-5180; *Fax:* 604-608-5181
Toll-Free: 800-867-5141
info@visitorschoice.com
www.visitorschoice.com
Circulation: 795,000
Pierre Pelletier, Publisher

Voilà Québec
1255, rue Maguire, Sillery, QC G1T 1Z2
Tel: 418-694-1272; *Fax:* 418-694-1119
info@voilaquebec.com
Circulation: 70,000 *Frequency:* 4 pa; English & French
Curtis J. Sommerville, Publisher
Lynn Magee, Editor

Voir Gatineau-Ottawa
#200, 396, rue Cooper, Ottawa, ON K2P 2H7
Tél: 613-237-8226; *Téléc:* 613-237-8220
www.voir.ca
Frequency: Hebdomadaire, français
Jean-François Landré, Directeur général
Mélissa Proulx, Rédactrice-en-chef

Voir Montréal
375, rue Ste-Catherine ouest, 7e étage, Montréal, QC H3B 1A5
Tél: 514-848-0805; *Téléc:* 514-848-9004
www.voir.ca
Circulation: 102 000
Christophe Bergeron, Rédacteur-en-chef

Voir Québec
470, rue de la Couronne, Québec, QC G1K 6G2
Tél: 418-522-7777; *Téléc:* 418-522-7779
info@qc.voit.ca
www.voir.ca
Circulation: 41 725 *Frequency:* Hebdomadaire; français, aussi Voir Québec City; 52 par an
Benoit Paré, Directeur général
David Desjardins, Rédacteur-en-chef

Vue Weekly
10303 - 108th St., Edmonton, AB T5J 1L7
Tel: 780-426-1996; *Fax:* 780-426-2889
chris@vueweekly.com
www.vueweekly.com
Circulation: 24,274 *Frequency:* Weekly
Ross Moroz, Managing Editor
Ron Garth, Publisher & Editor

What's Happening Magazine
553 Morrison Point Rd., RR#2, Milford, ON KOK 2P0
Tel: 613-476-6175; *Fax:* 613-476-1050
whatshappening@primus.ca
Circulation: 6,000 *Frequency:* 4 pa
Gudrun Gallo, Editor

Where Calgary
St. Joseph Media Inc., #250, 125 - 9 Ave. SE, Calgary, AB T2G 0P6
Tel: 403-299-1888; *Fax:* 403-299-1899
info_calgary@where.ca
www.where.ca/calgary
Circulation: 46,500 *Frequency:* Bi-monthly
Brian French, Publisher

Where Edmonton
Tanner Publishing Ltd., #4, 9343 - 50 St., Edmonton, AB T6B 2L5
Tel: 780-465-3362; *Fax:* 780-448-0424
info@whereedmonton.com
www.whereedmonton.com
Circulation: 33,240 *Frequency:* 6 times a year
Rob Tanner, Publisher

Where Halifax
Tel: 902-420-9943; *Fax:* 902-429-9058
publishers@metroguide.ca
www.where.ca/halifax
Circulation: 220,000 *Frequency:* 10 pa
Sheila Blair-Reid, Publisher

Where Ottawa
St. Joseph Media, 226 Argyle Ave., Ottawa, ON K2P 1B9
Tel: 613-230-0333; *Fax:* 613-230-4441
dianne@capitalpublishers.com
www.where.ca/ottawa
Circulation: 19,081 *Frequency:* Monthly
Melanie Scott, Editor
Dianne Wing, Publisher

Where Toronto
111 Queen St. East, Toronto, ON M5C 1S2
Tel: 416-364-3333; *Fax:* 416-594-3375
editorial@wheretoronto.com
www.wheretoronto.com
Circulation: 74,988 *Frequency:* Monthly
Anne Gibson, Editor-in-chief

Where Victoria
818 Broughton St., Victoria, BC V8W 1E4
Tel: 250-383-3633; *Fax:* 250-480-3233
info@wherevictoria.com
www.where.ca/victoria
Circulation: 64,320 *Frequency:* 6 pa
Anna Scolnick, Publisher

Where Winnipeg
Fanfare Magazine Group, #400, 112 Market Ave., Winnipeg, MB R3B 0P4
Tel: 204-943-4439; *Fax:* 204-947-5463
www.wherewinnipeg.com
Circulation: 33,708 *Frequency:* 6 pa
Brad Hughes, Editor-in-chief
Laurie Hughes, Publisher

Windsor Life Magazine
#318, 5060 Tecumseh Rd. East, Windsor, ON N8T 1C1
Tel: 519-979-5433; *Fax:* 519-979-9237
publisher@windsorlife.com
www.windsorlife.com
Circulation: 79,373 Windsor & Essex County *Frequency:* 8 times a year
Robert E. Robinson, Publisher
Hal Sullivan, Editor

YVR Skytalk
#306, 5400 Airport Rd. South, Richmond, BC V7B 1B4
Tel: 604-736-6754; *Fax:* 604-736-6750
jstewart@westerndriver.com
www.yvr.ca/authority/news/skytalk.asp
Circulation: 68,000 *Frequency:* Monthly
Patrick Stewart, Publisher

Computing & Technology

Atout Micro
CP 240, Saint-Isidore, QC G0S 2S0
Tél: 418-882-5214; *Ligne sans frais:* 866-826-1089
atout@atoutmicro.ca
www.atoutmicro.ca
Other information: Sans frais: 1-866-826-1089
Circulation: 8 000
François Picard, Éditeur & Rédacteur en chef

INFORMATION Highways: The Magazine about Online Information
e-Content Institute, 60 Waterloo Ave., Toronto, ON M3H 3Y2
Tel: 416-488-7372; *Fax:* 416-488-7078
info@econtentinstitute.org
www.econtentinstitute.org
Circulation: 5,000 *Frequency:* 6 pa
David Shinwell, Publisher

We Compute
483 Kennedy Rd., Toronto, ON M1K 2B1
Tel: 416-264-6938; *Fax:* 416-266-3614
editors@we-compute.com
Circulation: 150,000 *Frequency:* 12 times a year
Eric Macmillan, Editor
George Bachir, Publisher

Culture, Current Events

Edges: New Planetary Patterns
655 Queen St. East, Toronto, ON M4M 1G4
Tel: 416-691-2316; *Fax:* 416-691-2491
Toll-Free: 877-691-1422
ica@icacan.ca
www.icacan.ca
Circulation: 12,000 *Frequency:* 3 pa
Fred Simons, Executive Director
Leah Taylor, Editor

Fuse
#454, 401 Richmond St. West, Toronto, ON M5V 3A8
Tel: 416-340-8026; *Fax:* 416-340-0494
info@fusemagazine.org
www.fusemagazine.org
Circulation: 3,300 *Frequency:* 4 pa; ISSN: 0838-603X
Michael Maranda, Associate Publisher
Izida Zorde, Associate Editor

MIX: Independent Art & Culture Magazine
Parallélogramme Artist-Run Culture & Publishing Inc., #446, 401 Richmond St. West, Toronto, ON M5V 3A8
Tel: 416-506-1012; *Fax:* 416-506-0141
editor@mixmagazine.com
www.mixmagazine.com
Circulation: 120,000 *Frequency:* 4 pa; English & French; ISSN: 1204-5349
Claudia McKoy, Editor-in-Chief

The Newfoundland Herald
PO Box 2015, St. John's, NL A1C 5R7
Tel: 709-726-7060; *Fax:* 709-726-6971
www.nfldherald.com
Circulation: 23,913 *Frequency:* Weekly
Mark Dwyer, Managing Editor

Saltscapes Publishing Inc.
#501, 40 Alderney Dr., Dartmouth, NS B2Y 2N5
Tel: 902-464-7258; *Fax:* 902-464-3755
Toll-Free: 877-311-5877
subscriptions@saltscapes.com
www.saltscapes.com
Circulation: 40,000 *Frequency:* 6 times a year
Jim Gourlay, Publisher
Heather White, Editor

This Magazine
Red Maple Foundation, #396, 401 Richmond St. West, Toronto, ON M5V 3A8
Tel: 416-979-9429; *Fax:* 416-979-1143
info@thismagazine.ca
www.thismagazine.ca
Circulation: 8,000 *Frequency:* 6 times a year; ISSN: 1491-2678
Jessica Johnston, Editor
Lisa Whittington-Hill, Publisher

Education

Life Learning Magazine
Life Media, #508, 264 Queen's Quay West, Toronto, ON M5J 1B5
Tel: 416-260-0303; *Toll-Free:* 800-215-9574
publisher@lifelearningmagazine.com
www.lifelearningmagazine.com
Circulation: 35,000
Wendy Priesnitz, Editor
Rolf Priesnitz, Publisher

Entertainment

CineAction: Radical Film Criticism & Theory
#705, 40 Alexander St., Toronto, ON M4Y 1B5
Tel: 416-964-3534; *Fax:* 416- -
smorr@the-wire.com
Circulation: 4,000 *Frequency:* 3 pa; ISSN: 0826-9866
Robin Wood
Susan Morrison

Cinema Scope
465 Lytton Blvd., Toronto, ON M5N 1S5
www.cinema-scope.com
Mark Peranson, Publisher & Editor
Andrew Tracy, Managing Editor

En Primeur
71 Barber Greene Rd., Toronto, ON M3C 2A2
Tel: 416-445-0544; *Fax:* 416-445-2894
www.enprimeur.ca
Circulation: 105,000
Sandra I. Stewart, Publisher

En Primeur Jeunesse
Tél: 416-445-0544; *Téléc:* 416-445-2894
www.enprimeur.ca
Circulation: 50 000 *Frequency:* 4 fois par an; français

Famous Magazine
1303 Yonge St., Toronto, ON M4T 2Y9
Tel: 416-539-6600; *Fax:* 416-539-6616
customerservice@cineplex.com
Circulation: 500,000 *Frequency:* 12 times a year

Festival Cinemas
2236 Queen St. East, Toronto, ON M4E 1G2
Tel: 416-691-7330
Circulation: 85,000

Inside Entertainment
134 Peter St., 3rd Fl., Toronto, ON M5V 2H2
Tel: 416-367-7658;
www.insideeonline.com
Frequency: 9 times a year
Kendon Polak, Editor-in-chief

Magazine Le Clap
#370, 2360, ch Ste-Foy, Sainte-Foy, QC G1V 4H2
Tél: 418-653-2470; *Téléc:* 418-653-6018
leclap@clap.qc.ca
www.clap.qc.ca
Circulation: 100 000 *Frequency:* 7 fois par an; français

Marquee
Marquee Media Inc., 1325 Burnhamthorpe Rd. East, Mississauga, ON L4Y 3V8
Tel: 905-274-7174; *Fax:* 905-274-9799
marquee@marquee.ca
Circulation: 150,000 *Frequency:* 7 pa
David Haslam, Publisher
Michael Bukovac, President

The Mosaic
PO Box 130, 105 Garafraxa St. North, Durham, ON N0G 1R9
Tel: 519-369-2716; *Fax:* 519-369-2311
Circulation: 3,000
Vi Bland, Publisher

Playboard
Arch-Way Publishers, #3, 11720 Voyageur Way, Richmond, BC V6X 3G9
Tel: 604-278-5881; *Fax:* 604-278-5813
theatre@shawbiz.ca
Circulation: 15,000 *Frequency:* 10 pa
Alan Slater, Publisher & Editor

Preview
1700 Church Ave., Winnipeg, MB R2X 3A2
Tel: 204-694-2022; *Fax:* 204-694-2347
www.canoe.ca/winnipegsun
Circulation: 70,700
Ed Huculak, Publisher

Satellite Direct
1420 Parsons Rd. SW, Edmonton, AB T6X 1M5
Tel: 780-424-6222; *Fax:* 780-426-0279
Toll-Free: 800-661-3203
info@captivemultimedia.com
www.satguide.com
Circulation: 19,397 *Frequency:* 12 times a year
Steven R. Vogel, Publisher
Gene Kosowan, Editor

Scene Magazine
PO Box 2302, London, ON N6A 4E3
Tel: 519-642-4780; *Fax:* 519-642-0737
bret@scenemagazine.com
www.scenemagazine.com
Circulation: 18,500 *Frequency:* 25 pa
Bret Downe, Editor-in-chief

SEE Magazine
#200, 10275 Jasper Ave., Edmonton, AB T5J 1X8
Tel: 780-430-9003; *Fax:* 780-432-1102
info@see.greatwest.ca
www.seemagazine.com
Circulation: 24,000 *Frequency:* Weekly, Thu.
Gord Nielsen, Publisher
Zoltan Varadi, Music Editor
Kevin Wilson, News Editor

Teen Tribute
Tel: 416-445-0544; *Fax:* 416-445-2894
advertising@tribute.ca
www.tribute.ca
Circulation: 300,000 *Frequency:* 4 times a year
Robin Stevenson, Editor
Sandra Stewart, Publisher

Teleguide
9185 Commercial St., New Minas, NS B4N 3G1
Tel: 902-681-2121; *Fax:* 902-681-0830
Circulation: 28,000
Caroline Andrews, Publisher

Tribute Magazine
Tel: 416-445-0544; *Fax:* 416-445-2894
generalinfo@tribute.ca
www.tribute.ca
Circulation: 500,450 *Frequency:* 9 pa
Sandra Stewart, Editorial Director

TV Channels
44 Fairford St. West, Moose Jaw, SK S6H 6E4
Tel: 306-692-6441; *Fax:* 306-692-2101
timesads@sk.sympatico.ca
www.mjtimes.sk.ca
Circulation: 10,500
Rob Clark, Publisher

View Weekly
370 Main St. West, Hamilton, ON L8P 1K3
Tel: 905-527-3343; *Fax:* 905-527-3721
info@viewmag.com
www.viewmag.com
Circulation: 30,000 *Frequency:* Weekly
Sarah Cairns, Editor-in-chief
Marcus Rosen, Publisher

Visitor Magazine
PO Box 41030, Waterloo, ON N0K 3K0
Tel: 519-886-2831; *Fax:* 519-886-6409
jonr@visitor.on.ca
www.visitor.on.ca
Circulation: 100,000
John Rohr, Publisher

Environment & Nature

Alternatives Journal: Canadian Environmental Ideas & Action
c/o Faculty of Environmental Studies, University of Waterloo, 200 University Ave. West, Waterloo, ON N2L 3G1
Tel: 519-888-4442; *Fax:* 519-746-0292
Toll-Free: 866-437-2587
infoalternativesjournal.ca
www.alternativesjournal.ca
Circulation: 4,500 *Frequency:* 6 pa; ISSN: 1205-7398
A theme-based publication dedicated to illustrating the relationships between the environment and social justice, politics and the economy. It looks at the challenges and issues related to the interaction of humanity and the environment, and the responses to those issues.
Nicola Ross, Executive Editor

The Atlantic Salmon Journal
Atlantic Salmon Federation, PO Box 5200, St Andrews, NB E5B 3S8
Tel: 506-529-1033; *Fax:* 506-529-4438
tiffinic@nb.aibn.com
www.asf.ca
Circulation: 11,000 *Frequency:* 4 times a year
This magazine is the world's oldest publication regarding conservation-minded salmon angling, covering issues related to fly-fishing for Atlantic salmon and the over-all protection of the species.
Martin Silverstone, Editor

British Columbia Environmental Report
c/o British Columbia Environmental Network, #122, 718-333 Brooksbank Ave., North Vancouver, BC V7J 3V6
Tel: 604-515-1969;
editor@ecobc.org; network@bcen.bc.ca
www.ecobc.org
The British Columbia Environmental Report is a journal which features news, analysis, events, & reviews about British Columbia environmental topics.
Dave Stevens, Chair, Board of Directors
Chris Blake, Executive Coordinator

Canadian Environmental Protection
#201, 2323 Boundary Rd., Vancouver, BC V5M 4V8
Tel: 604-291-9900; *Fax:* 604-291-1906
ebaum@baumpub.com
www.baumpub.com
Circulation: 20,000 *Frequency:* 8 times a year
This publication is one of Canada's most popular environmental trade publications, with four marketplace issues, an internet version and industry supplements. Some issues this magazine covers are bio-fuels, specialty gasses and air pollution.

Canadian Geographic
c/o Royal Canadian Geographical Society, 39 McArthur Ave., Ottawa, ON K1L 8L7
Tel: 613-745-4629; *Fax:* 613-744-0947
editorial@canadiangeographic.ca
www.canadiangeographic.ca
Circulation: 222,000 *Frequency:* 6 times a year; ISSN: 0706-2168
Publication aims to promote Canada both to Canadians and around the world. It looks at issues relating to the nature and wildlife within Canada, and what can be done to preserve the natural Canadian landscape.
John L. Thomson, CEO & Publisher
Rick Boychuk, Editor

Canadian Wildlife
350 Michael Cowpland Dr., Kanata, ON K2M 2W1
Tel: 613-599-9594; *Fax:* 613-599-4428
Toll-Free: 800-563-9453
info@cwf-fcf.org
www.cwf-fcf.org
Frequency: 6 times a year
Aimed at both teenagers and adults, this magazine covers issues relating to Canadian and international wildlife, and reports on the work of the Canadian Wildlife Federation.

Environmental Science & Engineering Magazine
#30, 220 Industrial Parkway South, Aurora, ON L4G 3V6
Tel: 905-727-4666; *Fax:* 905-841-7271
sandra@esemag.com
www.esemag.com
Circulation: 19,000 *Frequency:* 6 times a year
This publicationis the largest documentary magazine in Canada and has articles on various environmental issues, including air pollution, water filtration, hazerdous waste, alternative energy, greenhouse gasses, among others.

EnviroZine
70 Crémazie St., 7th Fl., Gatineau, QC K1A 0H3
Tel: 819-997-2800; *Fax:* 819-994-1412
Toll-Free: 800-668-6767
enviroinfo@ec.gc.ca
www.ec.gc.ca/envirozine
Circulation: available online only *Frequency:* monthly ISSN: English ed. ISSN 1499-1411; French ed. 1499-142X
This webzine covers a wide range of environmental issues that are of importance to Canadians. It provides information in several categories, such as Air, Climate Change, Environmental Action, Nature and Wildlife, Pollution, Science & Technology, Water, and Weather, and attracts readers from 58 countries.

Green Living Magazine
Key Publishers Company Ltd., #400, 70 the Esplanade, Toronto, ON M5E 1R2
Tel: 416-360-0044; *Fax:* 416-362-2387
info@green-living.ca
www.greenlivingmagazine.ca
Circulation: 150,000 *Frequency:* quarterly
Green Living Magazine attempts to promote living a green lifestyle to its readers by providing information about organics, health, the environment and eco-consumer products. They support sustainable and healthy living and publicizing the green message.
Laurie Simmonds, Publisher

Journal of Environmental Engineering & Science
M-55, 1200 Montreal Rd., Ottawa, ON K1A 0R6
Tel: 613-993-9084; *Fax:* 613-952-7656
Toll-Free: 800-668-1222
pubs@nrc-cnrc.gc.ca
pubs.nrc-cnrc.gc.ca
Frequency: 6 times a year ISSN: 1496-256X
This publication provides a forum for the discussion of environmental engineering & science research. Topics this journal explores include environmental engineering, physical & analytical sciences, life sciences related to environmental issues, health sciences, & oceanography.

La Maison du 21e siècle
2955, lac Lucerne, Sainte-Adèle, QC J8B 3K9
Tél: 450-228-1555; *Téléc:* 450-228-1555
info@21esiecle.qc.ca
www.21esiecle.qc.ca
Frequency: 4 fois par an
André Fauteux, Éditeur

Natural Life
Life Media, #508, 264 Queens Quay West, Toronto, ON M5J 1B5
Tel: 416-260-0303; *Toll-Free:* 800-215-9574
natural@life.ca
www.life.ca
Circulation: 35,000 *Frequency:* 6 pa; ISSN 0701-8002
This independently owned magazine has an international focus on providing intelligent and in-depth practical information on issues such as healthy cooking, organic gardening, sustainable homes, natural parenting, wellness and natural healing, eco-leisure and eco-travel and sustainable business.
Wendy Priesnitz, Editor
Rolf Priesnitz, Publisher

Nature Canada
c/o Nature Canada, #900, 84 Albert St., Ottawa, ON K1P 6A4
Tel: 613-562-3447; *Fax:* 613-562-3371
Toll-Free: 800-267-4088
info@naturecanada.ca
naturecanada.ca
Circulation: 26,400 *Frequency:* 4 pa; ISSN: 0374-9894
The mission of this magazine is to protect nature, its diversity and the processes that sustain it, and does this by providing information regarding several environmental topics including bird conservation, wilderness protection, endangered species and national parks. The publication supports community-based efforts to protect wildlife; encourages the development of an effective network of parks and protected areas across Canada; and promoting biodiversity in Canada and abroad.

ON Nature
Federation of Ontario Naturalists, #201, 366 Adelaide St. West, Toronto, ON M5V 1R9
Tel: 416-444-8419; *Fax:* 416-444-9866
Toll-Free: 800-440-2366
onnature@ontarionature.org
www.ontarionature.org
Circulation: 14,500 *Frequency:* 4 pa; ISSN: 0227-793X
ON Nature attempts to bring its readers closer to nature by providing information about Ontario's natural areas and wildlife, and by providing insight into current environmental issues. Magazine features articles by nature specialists, colour

photography, information regarding wilderness travel and up-to-date news on conservation battles.
Caroline Schultz, Executive Director
Victoria Foote, Editor

Québec Oiseaux
1251, rue Rachel est, Montréal, QC H2S 2J9
Tél: 514-521-8356; *Téléc:* 514-521-5711
quebecoiseaux@aqgo.qc.ca
www.quebecoiseaux.qc.ca
Circulation: 7 928 *Frequency:* 4 fois par an
Michel Préville, Rédacteur-en-chef

Shared Vision
#301, 873 Beatty St., Vancouver, BC V6B 2M6
Tel: 604-733-5062; *Fax:* 604-731-1050
publisher@shared-vision.com
www.shared-vision.com
Circulation: 42,000 *Frequency:* 12 times a year
This publication attempts to help its readers live healthy, happy lives while creating and maintaining a sustainable society. The magazine features information on topics including green living, natural wellness, and organic food.
Rebecca Edhraim, Publisher

Solid Waste & Recycling
#800, 12 Concorde Place, Toronto, ON M3C 4J2
Tel: 416-510-6798; *Fax:* 416-510-5133
Toll-Free: 888-702-1111
bobrien@solidwastemag.com
www.solidwastemag.com
Circulation: 9,426 *Frequency:* 6 times a year
This publication dicusses all issues and topics pertaining to recyling and waste management.

The Sustainable Times
1225 Prospect Bay Rd., Prospect Village, NS B3T 2A6
Tel: 902-850-2510;
times@chebucto.ns.ca
www.sustainabletimes.ca
Circulation: online only
A webzine that discusses and publicizes global issues including environmetalism, the Third World, and Fair Trade. The webzine is published by CUSO, which works for sustainable developtment in places such as Africa, Asia, Latin America and the Caribbean.
Sean Kelly, Editor

Watershed Sentinel
c/o Watershed Sentinel Educational Society, PO Box 39, Whaletown, BC V0P 1Z0
Tel: 250-935-6992; *Fax:* 250-935-6992
editor@watershedsentinel.ca
www.watershedsentinel.ca
Circulation: 5,000 *Frequency:* 6 pa
This West Coast based publication focuses on how humanity affect the environment around them, by looking at issues such as logging and fishing practices and air and water pollution. It covers both bioregional and global perspectives on topics such as the environment, health and sustainability.
Delores Broten, Publisher & Editor

Women & Environments International Magazine
HNES Building, room 234, York University, 4700 Keele St., Toronto, ON M3J 1P3
Tel: 416-736-2100; *Fax:* 416-736-5679
weimag@yorku.ca
www.weimag.com
Circulation: 2,000 *Frequency:* 2 pa
Publication examines the relationships between women and the environment from a feminist perspective. It provides a forum for academic research and theory, professional practice and community experience and covers topics such as ecology and environmental activism, community development, childcare, and urban and rural agriculture.
Prabha Khosla
Reggie Modlich

Families

BC Parent Magazine
PO Box 72086, Sasamat RPO, Vancouver, BC V6R 4P2
Tel: 604-221-0366;
bcparent@shaw.ca
www.bcparent.ca
Circulation: 50,000 *Frequency:* 9 times a year
Elizabeth Shaffer, Editor, eshaffer@telus.net

Calgary's Child Magazine
#723, 105-150 Crowfoot Cres. NW, Calgary, AB T3G 3T2
Tel: 403-241-6066; *Fax:* 403-286-9731
calgaryschild@shaw.ca
www.calgaryschild.com
Circulation: 70,000 *Frequency:* 6 times a year
Ellen Percival, Publisher

City Parent
Torstar Direct Services, #600, 625 Church St., Toronto, ON M4Y 2G1
Tel: 416-596-4347; *Fax:* 416-596-4360
Toll-Free: 800-265-3673
cityparent@torstardirect.com
www.cityparent.com
Circulation: 77,785 *Frequency:* 12 times a year
Neil Oliver, Publisher
Jane Muller, Editor-in-chief

Divorce Magazine
#1179, 2255B Queen St. East, Toronto, ON M4E 1G3
Tel: 416-368-8853; *Fax:* 416-368-4978
danc@divorcemag.com
www.divorcemagazine.com
Circulation: 170,000 *Frequency:* 4 times a year
Dan Couvrette, Publisher

Edmonton's Child Magazine
#208, 14218 Stony Plain Rd., Edmonton, AB T5N 3R3
Tel: 780-484-3360; *Fax:* 780-486-1844
Toll-Free: 866-484-3360
edmchild@telus.net
www.edmontonschild.com
Circulation: 30,000 *Frequency:* 6 times a year
Jane Martin, CEO/Publisher

Island Parent Magazine
#A-10, 830 Pembroke St., Victoria, BC V8T 1H9
Tel: 250-388-6905; *Fax:* 250-388-6920
Toll-Free: 888-372-0862
mail@islandparent.ca
www.islandparent.ca
Circulation: 20,000 *Frequency:* Monthly
Paul Abra, Publisher
Mada Johnson, Editor

Junior
Versant Média Inc., 468, boul Rolland-Therrien, Longueuil, QC J4H 4E3
Tél: 450-677-2556; *Téléc:* 450-677-4099
Circulation: 23 579 *Frequency:* 4 fois par an; français
Richard Desmarais, Rédacteur

Le Magazine Enfants Québec
300, rue Arran, Staint-Lambert, QC J4R 1K5
Tél: 450-875-9612; *Téléc:* 450-672-5448
magazineenfants@editionsheritage.com
www.enfantsquebec.com
Circulation: 60 600 *Frequency:* 12 fois par an; français
Eve Christian, Rédactrice
Sylvie Payette, Éditrice

Our Kids Go to Camp
4242 Rockwood Rd., Mississauga, ON L4W 1L8
Tel: 905-272-1843; *Fax:* 905-272-0474
fun@ourkids.net
www.ourkids.net
Circulation: 200,000 *Frequency:* Annually
Agatha Stawicki, Managing Editor

Our Kids Go to School
4242 Rockwood Rd., Mississauga, ON L4W 1L8
Tel: 905-272-1843; *Fax:* 905-272-0474
fun@ourkids.net
www.ourkids.net
Circulation: 250,000 *Frequency:* Annually
Agatha Stawicki, Managing Editor

Owl Canadian Family
#400, 10 Lower Spadina Ave., Toronto, ON M5V 2Z2
Tel: 416-340-2700; *Fax:* 416-340-9769
owlfamily@m-v-p.com
www.owlkids.com/owl/
Circulation: 66,768 *Frequency:* 6 times a year
Mary Beth Leatherdale, Editor

Pomme d'Api Québec
4475, rue Frontenac, Montréal, QC H2H 2S2
Tél: 514-844-2111; *Téléc:* 514-278-3030
Ligne sans frais: 800-313-3020
redaction@bayardpresse.qc.ca
www.bayardjeunesse.ca
Circulation: 16 000
Suzanne Spino, Directrice générale

7 Jours
7, ch Bates, Montréal, QC H2V 4V7
Tél: 514-848-7000; *Téléc:* 514-848-7070
Ligne sans frais: 800-367-0667
7jours@tva-publications.com
Circulation: 121 540 *Frequency:* Hebdomadaire
Jocelyn Poirier, Président

Today's Parent
1 Mount Pleasant Rd., 8th Fl., Toronto, ON M4Y 2Y5
Tel: 416-764-2883; *Fax:* 416-764-2801
www.todaysparent.com
Circulation: 175,000 *Frequency:* 11 times a year; also Prenatal Class Guide (annual); ISSN: 0823-9258
Linda Lewis, Editor

Fashion

Clin d'oeil
Tél: 514-848-7164; *Téléc:* 514-270-7079
clindoeil@publicor.ca
Circulation: 60 372 *Frequency:* Mensuel; français
Claire Syril, Éditeur
Mitsou Gélinas, Directeur de la publication

Dolce Magazine
#1, 60 Winges Rd., Woodbridge, ON L4L 6B1
Tel: 905-264-6789; *Fax:* 905-264-3787
dolce.ca
Michelle Zerillo-Sosa, Publisher & Editor-in-chief

Fashion Magazine
St. Joseph Media, #320, 111 Queen St. East, Toronto, ON M5C 1S2
Tel: 416-364-3333; *Fax:* 416-594-3374
www.fashionmagazine.com
Circulation: 124,927 *Frequency:* 10 times a year; ISSN: 0049-4194
Ceri Marsh, Editor-in-chief
Michelle Bilodeau, Assoc. Editor
Giorgina Bigioni, Publisher

Flare
Tel: 416-764-2871; *Fax:* 416-764-2864
Toll-Free: 800-268-6823
david.hamilton@rci.rogers.com
www.flare.com
Circulation: 158,904 *Frequency:* Monthly; ISSN: 0708-4927
David Hamilton, Publisher

Glow
Tel: 416-764-2886; *Fax:* 416-764-2488
mail@glow.rogers.com
www.glow.ca
Frequency: 6 times a year; English & French

Good Life Connoisseur
#317, 1489 Marine Dr., West Vancouver, BC V7T 1B8
Tel: 604-925-0313;
www.goodlifecanada.com
Frequency: 4 times a year
Terry Tremaine, Publisher & Editor

LOULOU
#1700, 1200 McGill College Ave., Montréal, QC H3B 4G7
Tel: 514-843-2189; *Fax:* 514-843-2189
loulou.infoweb@rci.rogers.com
www.louloumagazine.com
Circulation: 8 times a year; English & French
Marie-Joseé Desmarais, Publisher/Editor
Claude LaFramboise, Executive Editor

Nuvo Magazine
#200, 460 Nanaimo St., Vancouver, BC V5L 4W3
Tel: 604-899-9380; *Fax:* 604-899-1450
www.nuvomagazine.com
Frequency: 4 times a year
Jim Tobler, Editor

VMM
303, av Saint-Denis, Saint-Lambert, QC J4P 2G5
Tél: 450-465-0009; *Téléc:* 450-465-2110
info@imagellan.com
www.imagellan.com
Circulation: 50 000 *Frequency:* 4 fois par an; français
Marie-Claude Guérin, Rédactrice

Fifty-Plus Adults

Active Adult
178 Main St., Unionville, ON L3R 2G9
Tel: 905-479-4663; *Fax:* 905-479-4482
Toll-Free: 800-363-4663
nsicilia@homesmag.com
www.activeadultmag.com
Circulation: 100,000 *Frequency:* 3 times a year
Michael Rosset, Publisher

Patrick Tivy, Editor

Bel Age

Tél: 514-499-0561; *Téléc:* 514-499-9112
belage@transcontinental.ca
Circulation: 145 872 *Frequency:* 11 fois par an; français
Lucie Desaulniers, Éditrice

CARP Magazine

Kemur Publishing, #702, 27 Queen St. East, Toronto, ON M5C 2M6
Tel: 416-363-5562; *Fax:* 416-363-7394
magazine@kemur.ca
www.50Plus.com
Circulation: 219,506 *Frequency:* 9 times a year
Gord Poland, Publisher
Bonnie Baker-Cowan, Editor

Choices After 50

EMC Marketing Associates Ltd., PO Box 1291, Saint John, NB E2L 4H8
Tel: 506-658-0754; *Fax:* 506-633-0868
emc@nb.aibn.com
Circulation: 20,000 *Frequency:* Bi-monthly
Carol Maber, Editor

Comfort Life

Tel: 905-272-1843; *Fax:* 905-272-0474
info@comfortlife.ca
www.comfortlife.ca
Circulation: 250,000 *Frequency:* Annually
Hugh Wesley, Executive Director

Community Resource Directory

Tel: 250-765-3886; *Fax:* 250-765-7346
Frequency: Annual
Joel A. Rickard, Publisher

The Edmonton Senior

Tel: 780-429-1610; *Fax:* 780-421-7677
abrnews@shaw.ca
seniorsgotravel.com
Circulation: 60,000 *Frequency:* 12 times a year
Lorne Silverstein, Publisher
Colin Smith, Editor

Fifty-Five Plus

c/o Coyle Publishing Inc., #220, 362 Terry Fox Dr., Kanata, ON K2K 2P5
Tel: 613-271-8903; *Fax:* 613-271-8905
publisher@fifty-five-plus.com
www.fifty-five-plus.com
Circulation: 45,000 *Frequency:* 8 times a year
George Coyle, Publisher
Pat den Boer, Editor

Focus 50+

#13-215, 4 Alliance Blvd., Barrie, ON L4M 5J1
Tel: 705-735-2144; *Fax:* 705-735-6002
focusplus@csolve.net
Circulation: 11,500 *Frequency:* 12 times a year
Taylor Ledden, Editor
Jeanneke Van Hattem, Publisher

Gold Mine Manitoba

#202, 63 Albert St., Winnipeg, MB R3B 1G4
Tel: 204-949-4371; *Fax:* 204-949-4818
prime.editorial@uptownmag.com
Circulation: 15,000 *Frequency:* Quarterly
Dianne Biggs, Publisher
John Ross, General Manager

Good Times

Transcontinental Media, #100, 25 Sheppard Ave., Toronto, ON M2N 6S7
Tel: 416-733-7600; *Fax:* 416-218-3630
Toll-Free: 888-290-1466
goodtimes.pub@mail.transcontinental.ca
www.goodtimes.ca
Circulation: 157,086 *Frequency:* 11 times a year
Francine Tremblay, Publisher

The Independent Times

K.W. Publishing Ltd., #360, 7360 - 137 St., Surrey, BC V3W 1A3
Tel: 604-580-1844; *Fax:* 604-580-1019
kweditor@telus.net
Circulation: 50,000 *Frequency:* 10 times a year
K. Gordon, Publisher
Wanda Boyd, Editor

Le Journal du Bel Age

Senior Publications, #900, 2001, rue University, Montréal, QC H3A 2A6
Tél: 514-499-0561; *Téléc:* 514-499-9112
Circulation: 70,000 *Frequency:* 10 fois par an; français
Francine Tremblay, Éditrice

Kerby News

1133 - 7th Ave. SW, Calgary, AB T2P 1B2
Tel: 403-265-0661; *Fax:* 403-264-7047
kerbynews@kerbycentre.com
www.kerbynews.com
Circulation: 25,000 *Frequency:* Monthly
Barry Whitehead, Editor

Mainly for Seniors Lambton-Kent

140 South Front St., Sarnia, ON N7T 7M8
Tel: 519-882-1770; *Fax:* 519-882-3212
Circulation: 4,400 *Frequency:* Monthly

The Montrealer

342 Ballantyne North, Montreal Lake, QC H4X 2C5
Tel: 514-369-7000; *Fax:* 514-369-1362
foryoung@mlink.net
www.themontrealeronline.com
Circulation: 30,000 *Frequency:* Monthly
Peter Kerr, Publisher

Our World 50+

PO Box 68034 Crowfoot NW, Calgary, AB T3G 3N8
Tel: 403-208-1235; *Fax:* 403-208-0004
ow@ow50.com
www.ow50.com
Circulation: 20,000 *Frequency:* 6 times a year
Karen Cottingham, Publisher

Prime Time

Metroland Printing, Publishing & Distributing Ltd., 884 Ford St., Peterborough, ON K9J 5V3
Tel: 705-749-3383; *Fax:* 705-749-0074
bdanford@mykawartha.com
Circulation: 7,100 *Frequency:* Monthly
Bruce Danford, Publisher & General Manager
Paul Relinger, Editor

Prime Times News

Rosebud Publications Ltd., 1465 St. James St., Winnipeg, MB R3H 0W9
Tel: 204-789-0800; *Fax:* 204-953-4300
Circulation: 10,000 *Frequency:* 24 times a year
John Proven, Publisher
John Kendle, Editor

The Saskatchewan Senior

PO Box 1010, Regina, SK S4P 3B2
Tel: 306-525-8988; *Fax:* 306-525-8031
clay@sasksenior.com
www.sasksenior.com
Circulation: 18,529 *Frequency:* 11 times a year
Clay Stacey, Publisher & Editor

The Seniors Choice

PO Box 41075, South RPO, Lake Country, BC V4V 1Z7
Tel: 250-765-6065; *Fax:* 250-765-7346
Toll-Free: 800-866-2755
ads@seniorschoice.com
www.seniorschoice.com
Circulation: 15,000 *Frequency:* Monthly
James E. Archibald, Publisher
Patricia Archibald, Editor

The Seniors Review

#B2, 11 Bond St., St Catharines, ON L2R 4Z4
Tel: 905-687-9861; *Fax:* 905-687-6911
Toll-Free: 800-627-3111
seniorsreview@seniorsreview.com
Circulation: 40,000
David Irwin, Publisher
Carol Anderson, Editor

The Silver Pages

24 Cherryhill Dr., Grimsby, ON L3M 3B5
Tel: 905-309-1525; *Fax:* 905-309-1524
info@thesilverpages.ca
www.thesilverpages.ca
Circulation: 50,000 *Frequency:* 6 times a year
John Bauslaugh, Publisher
Tim Miller, Editorial Director

Virage

CP 1000 M, 4545, av Pierre-de-Coubertin, Montréal, QC H1V 3R2
Tél: 514-252-3017; *Téléc:* 514-252-3154
fadoq@fadoq.ca
www.fadoq.ca
Circulation: 215 027 *Frequency:* 4 fois par an
Martine Langlois, Éditrice
Lyne Rémillard, Rédacteur-en-chef

Fishing & Hunting

Alberta Fishing Guide

#6C, 5571 - 45 St., Red Deer, AB T4N 1L2
Tel: 403-347-5079; *Fax:* 403-341-5454
Circulation: 27,825 *Frequency:* Annually, March
Barry Mitchell, Publisher

Aventure chasse et pêche

332, rue Veilleux, Saint-Simon-les-Mines, QC G0M 1K0
Tel: 418-774-4443; *Fax:* 418-774-4444
cregimbald@qacp.com
www.qacp.com
Circulation: 50,600 *Frequency:* 4 times a year
Claude Regimbald, Marketing Manager
Denis Lapointe, Production Manager

Bateaux de pêche

#310, 970, Montée de Liesse, Saint-Laurent, QC H4T 1W7
Tel: 514-856-0787; *Fax:* 514-856-0790
Circulation: 18,000
Roy Baird, Publisher

BC Fishing Recreation Guide & Atlas

#900, 1080 Howe St., Vancouver, BC V6Z 2T1
Tel: 604-606-4644; *Fax:* 604-687-1925
Toll-Free: 800-816-0747
info@oppublishing.com
www.oppublishing.com
Circulation: 15,000 *Frequency:* Annually, Saltwater (Jan.); Freshwater (Jan.)
Mark Yelic, Publisher
Mike Mitchell, Editor

BC Outdoors Hunting & Shooting

#900, 1080 Howe St., Vancouver, BC V6Z 2T1
Tel: 604-606-4644; *Fax:* 604-687-1925
Toll-Free: 800-816-0747
info@oppublishing.com
www.oppublishing.com
Circulation: 25,000 *Frequency:* 2 times a year
Mark Yelic, Publisher
Mike Mitchell, Editor

BC Sport Fishing Magazine

#900, 1080 Howe St., Vancouver, BC V6Z 2T1
Tel: 604-606-4644; *Fax:* 604-687-1925
Toll-Free: 800-816-0747
info@oppublishing.com
www.oppublishing.com
Circulation: 23,195 *Frequency:* 6 times a year
Mark Yelic, Publisher
Mike Mitchell, Editor

The Canadian Fly Fisher

256 1/2 Front St., 2nd Fl., Belleville, ON K8N 2Z2
Tel: 613-966-8017; *Fax:* 613-966-4192
Toll-Free: 888-805-5608
info@canflyfish.com
www.canflyfish.com
Chris Marshall, Editor

Eastern Woods & Waters

#501, 40 Alderney Dr., Dartmouth, NS B2Y 2N5
Tel: 902-464-3757; *Fax:* 902-464-3755
Circulation: 13,681 *Frequency:* 6 times a year
Jim Gourlay, Publisher & Editor

Island Angler

30 Acacia Ave., Nanaimo, BC V9R 3L4
Tel: 250-753-2227; *Fax:* 250-753-2295
editor@islandangler.net
www.islandangler.net
Circulation: 15,000
Andrew Kolasinski, Publisher

Newfoundland Sportsman

PO Box 13754 A, 36 Pippy Pl., St. John's, NL A1B 4G5
Tel: 709-754-3515; *Fax:* 709-454-2490
www.newfoundlandsportsman.com
Circulation: 17,692 *Frequency:* 6 times a year
Dwight J. Blackwood, Publisher
Gordon Follet, Editor

Ontario Out of Doors
Tel: 416-764-1652; *Fax:* 416-764-1751
mail@ontariooutofdoors.com
www.fishontario.com
Circulation: 92,026 *Frequency:* 10 times a year
Matt Nicholls, Editor/Associate Publisher
Alison de Groot, Publisher

Outdoor Canada
#100, 25 Sheppard Ave. West, Toronto, ON M2N 6S7
Tel: 416-733-7600; *Fax:* 416-227-8296
walsh@outdoorcanada.ca
www.outdoorcanada.ca
Circulation: 82,574 *Frequency:* 8 times a year; ISSN: 0315-0542
Patrick Walsh, Editor
Jaqueline Howe, Publisher

The Outdoor Edge
c/o Keywest Marketing Ltd., PO Box 173, Debden, SK
Tel: 306-724-2233; *Fax:* 306-724-4448
odedge@sasktel.net
Circulation: 54,517 *Frequency:* 6 times a year
Mark Yelic, Publisher

Saskatchewan Fishing & Hunting
Tourism Saskatchewan, 1922 Park St., Regina, SK S4P 3V7
Tel: 306-787-9685; *Fax:* 306-787-0715
Toll-Free: 877-237-2273
belva.schlosser@sasktourism.com
www.sasktourism.com
Circulation: 85,000 *Frequency:* Annually

Sentier Chasse-Pêche
Tél: 450-665-0271; *Téléc:* 450-665-2974
Ligne sans frais: 800-563-6738
redaction@sentierchassepeche.com
www.sentierchassepeche.com
Circulation: 80 000 *Frequency:* 11 fois par an; français
Luc Lemay, Éditeur
Jeannot Ruel, Rédacteur

Western Sportsman
#900, 1080 Howe St., Vancouver, BC V6Z 2T1
Tel: 604-606-4644; *Fax:* 604-687-1925
Toll-Free: 800-816-0747
info@oppublishing.com
www.oppublishing.com
Circulation: 25,933 *Frequency:* 6 times a year; ISSN: 0709-1532
Dave Webb, Editor
Mark Yelic, Publisher

Food & Beverage

Appeal
Tel: 604-299-7311; *Fax:* 604-299-9188
cwm@canadawide.com
www.canadawide.com
Circulation: 230,000 *Frequency:* 2 times a year
Kim Mah, Editor
Peter Legge, Publisher

La Barrique
#414, 5165, rue Sherbrooke Ouest, Montréal, QC H4A 1T6
Tél: 514-481-5892; *Téléc:* 514-481-9699
labarrique@majesticlaser.com
Circulation: 12 000 *Frequency:* 6 fois par an; français
Aldo Parise, Rédacteur-en-chef adjoint
Nick Hamilton, Rédacteur-en-chef
Marylin Barker, Directrice de tirage

BC Wine Trails
2250 Camrose St., Penticton, BC V2A 8R1
Tel: 250-492-3636
Circulation: 15,000 *Frequency:* 4 times a year
Dani Greene, Manager

Coffee & Beverage Magazine
2C Fairfield Rd., Toronto, ON M4P 1T1
Tel: 416-932-2743; *Fax:* 596-979-3
coffee@primus.ca
www.coffeeandbeverage.ca
Circulation: 10,000 *Frequency:* 5 times a year
Vida Radovanovic, Publisher

Coup de Pouce Cuisine
Transcontinental Publications, #900, 2001, rue University, Montréal, QC H3A 2A6
Tél: 514-499-0561; *Téléc:* 514-499-1844
Frequency: 5 fois par an; français
Francine Tremblay, Éditrice
France Lefebvre, Rédacteur

Elite Wine, Food & Travel Magazine
PO Box 37, #5, 23 McCleary Ct., Concord, ON L4K 1B2
Tel: 905-760-1724; *Fax:* 905-760-1718
editor@elitewinefoodtravel.com
www.elitewinefoodtravel.com
Circulation: 10,000 *Frequency:* 4 times a year; ISSN: 72906-86110
Anna Cavaliere, Editor

Flavours
www.flavoursmagazine.ca
Frequency: 4 times a year
Brandon Boone, Editor-in-chief

Food & Drink
Liquor Control Board of Ontario, 55 Lakeshore Blvd. East, Toronto, ON M5E 1A4
Tel: 416-365-5900; *Fax:* 416-365-5935
Toll-Free: 800-668-5226
foodanddrink@lcbo.com
www.lcbo.com/fooddrink
Circulation: 500,000 *Frequency:* 6 times a year; English & French
Judy Dunn, Editor
Wayne Leek, Publisher

Le Guide Cuisine
Communication Duocom Inc., #203, 90, rue Sainte-Anne, Sainte-Anne-de-Bellevue, QC H9X 1L8
Tél: 514-457-0144; *Téléc:* 514-457-0226
info@leguidecuisine.com
www.leguidecuisine.com
Circulation: 47 000 *Frequency:* 5 times a year
Nicolas Vallée, Éditeur

Tidings
Tel: 514-481-5892; *Fax:* 514-481-9699
editor@tidingsmag.com
www.tidingsmag.com
Circulation: 29,200 *Frequency:* 8 times a year; ISSN: 0228-6157
Aldo Parise, Editor-in-chief

Toronto Wine & Cheese Show Guide
467 Speers Rd., Oakville, ON L6K 3S4
Tel: 905-815-0017; *Fax:* 905-887-0764
Toll-Free: 800-265-3673
marti.milks@sympatico.ca
www.towineandcheese.com
Circulation: 33,500 *Frequency:* 1 times a year
Janet Gardiner, Publisher

Fraternal, Service Clubs, Associations

KIN Magazine
c/o Kin Canada (Kinsmen & Kinette Clubs of Canada), Cambridge, ON N3H 5C6
Tel: 519-653-1920; *Fax:* 519-650-1091
Toll-Free: 800-742-5546
mrickard@kinclubs.ca
www.kinclubs.ca
Circulation: 10,000 *Frequency:* 3 print (Feb., June, Oct.); 3 online (April, Aug. & Dec.)
Michelle Rickard, Editor

Mensa Canada Communications
Mensa Canada Society, PO Box 1570, Kingston, ON K7L 5C8
Tel: 613-547-0824; *Fax:* 613-531-0626
mensa@eventsmgt.com
www.canada.mensa.org
Circulation: 2,100 *Frequency:* 6 times a year
Phyrne Parker, President

Papyrus
c/o Rameses Temple, A.A.O.N.M.S., 3100 Keele St., Toronto, ON M3M 2H4
Tel: 416-633-6317; *Fax:* 416-633-6345
Circulation: 7,200 *Frequency:* 6 times a year
Otto Yoworski, Editor

The Sentinel
c/o Loyal Orange Association, 94 Sheppard Ave. West, Toronto, ON M2N 1M5
Tel: 416-223-1690; *Fax:* 416-223-1324
sentinel@orange.ca
www.orange.ca
Circulation: 4,000 *Frequency:* 4 times a year
Jeremy Dowdell, Editor

Gardening & Garden Equipment

Canadian Gardening
#100, 25 Sheppard Ave. West, Toronto, ON M2N 6S7
Tel: 416-218-3570; *Fax:* 416-227-8298
satterthwaite@canadiangardening.com
www.canadiangardening.com
Circulation: 153,000 *Frequency:* 8 times a year; ISSN: 0847-3463
Aldona Satterthwaite, Editor-in-chief
Jacqueline Howe, Publisher

Canadian Organic Grower
323 Chapel St., Ottawa, ON K1N 7Z2
Tel: 613-216-0741; *Fax:* 613-236-0743
Toll-Free: 888-375-7383
office@cog.ca
www.cog.ca/magazine.htm
Circulation: 2,600 *Frequency:* 4 times a year
Janet Wallace, Editor, janet@cog.ca

Fleurs, plantes et jardins
Tél: 418-686-3036; *Téléc:* 418-628-0524
Ligne sans frais: 800-463-1576
Circulation: 55 506 *Frequency:* 9 fois par an; français
Francine Tremblay, Éditeur
Sophie Banford, Rédacteur

Gardening Life
#120, 511 King St. West, Toronto, ON M5V 2Z4
Tel: 416-593-0204; *Fax:* 416-591-1630
Toll-Free: 800-559-8868
mail@canhomepub.com
www.gardeninglife.ca
Circulation: 95,797 *Frequency:* 6 times a year; ISSN: 1203-858X
Giorgina Bigioni, Publisher
Caren Watkins, Editor-in-chief

Gardens West
Cornwall Publishing Co. Ltd., PO Box 2680, Vancouver, BC V6B 3W8
Tel: 604-879-4991; *Fax:* 604-879-5110
Toll-Free: 800-263-1088
grow@gardenswest.com
www.gardenswest.com
Circulation: 40,000 *Frequency:* 9 times a year
Dorothy Horton, Publisher/Editor

GardenWise Magazine
4180 Lougheed Hwy., 4th Fl., Burnaby, BC V5C 6A7
Tel: 604-299-7311; *Fax:* 604-299-9188
Toll-Free: 800-663-0518
cwm@canadawide.com
www.canadawide.com
Circulation: 35,000 *Frequency:* 6 times a year
Peter Legge, Publisher
Karen Foss, Associate Publisher
Carol Pope, Editor

Manitoba Gardener
130A Cree Cres., Winnipeg, MB R3J 3W1
Tel: 204-940-2700; *Fax:* 204-940-2727
Toll-Free: 888-680-2008
ddobbie@pegasuspublications.net
www.localgardener.net
Circulation: 6,628 *Frequency:* 6 times a year
Dorothy Dobbie, Publisher
Joan Cohen, Editor

Ontario Gardener
#107A, 219 Dufferin St., Toronto, ON M6K 3J1
Tel: 416-963-3434; *Fax:* 416-963-5929
www.localgardener.net/ontario/
Frequency: 6 times a year
Shauna Dobbie, Publisher & Editor

Gay/Lesbian

Capital Xtra
#503, 251 Bank St., Ottawa, ON K2P 1X3
Tel: 613-237-7133; *Fax:* 613-237-6651
capxtra@capital.xtra.ca
Circulation: 20,000 *Frequency:* monthly
Brandon Matheson, Publisher & Editor-in-chief

Gaiety.ca
#1, 438 Parliament St., Toronto, ON M5A 3A5
Tel: 416-944-2963; *Fax:* 416-944-9013
gaiety.ca
Frequency: 3 times a year
Joanna M. Valius, Editor

Perceptions
PO Box 8581, Saskatoon, SK S7K 6K7
Tel: 306-244-1930; *Fax:* 306-665-1280
perceptions@shaw.ca
Circulation: 1,500
Gens Hellquist, Publisher

XTRA West!
#501, 1033 Davie St., Vancouver, BC V6E 1M7
Tel: 604-684-9696; *Fax:* 604-684-9697
xtrawest@xtra.ca
www.xtra.ca
Circulation: 30,000 *Frequency:* Bi-weekly
Ken Hickling, Publisher, ken.hickling@xtra.ca

Xtra!
#200, 491 Church St., Toronto, ON M4Y 2C6
Tel: 416-925-6665; *Fax:* 416-925-6674
info@xtra.ca
www.xtra.ca
Circulation: 42,000
Brandon Matheson, Publisher & Editor-in-chief

General Interest

Access Magazine
Trafalgar Publications, 79 Portsmouth Dr., Toronto, ON M1C 5C8
Tel: 416-335-0747; *Fax:* 416-335-0748
crossfire@accessmag.com
www.accessmag.com
Circulation: 150,000 *Frequency:* 10 times a year
Sean Plummer, Editor

Active Living
2276 Rosedene Rd., St Ann's, ON L0R 1Y0
Tel: 905-957-6016; *Fax:* 905-957-6017
activeliv@aol.com
www.activelivingmagazine.com
Circulation: 50,000 *Frequency:* 4 times a year, plus Active Living's Buyers' Guide Product & Service Directory (annual)
Kimberley Barrada, Editor
Jeffrey Tiessen, Publisher

L'Agora
CP 96, Ayer's Cliff, QC J0B 1C0
Tél: 819-849-6360;
agora.qc.ca
Circulation: 10 000
Hélène Laberge, Rédactrice-en-chef
Jacques Dufresne, Éditeur

Alberta Views
#208, 320 - 23 Ave. SW, Calgary, AB T2S 0J2
Tel: 403-243-5334; *Fax:* 403-243-8599
Toll-Free: 877-212-5334
avadmin@albertaviews.ab.ca
www.albertaviews.ab.ca
Circulation: 20,000 *Frequency:* 8 times a year
Jackie Flanagan, Publisher & Editor

Angus Magazine
PO Box 306, 298 Main St., Mattawa, ON P0H 1V0
Tel: 705-744-4954; *Fax:* 705-744-4955
www.angusmagazine.com
Kevin J. Pecore, Editor-in-chief

CAA Magazine
Redwood Custom Communications, 37 Front St. East, Toronto, ON M5E 1B3
Tel: 416-360-7339; *Fax:* 416-640-6164
caamagazine@redwoodcc.com
redwoodcc.com
Frequency: 4 times a year
Tracy Howard, Editor

The Canadian Forum
5502 Atlantic St., Halifax, NS B3H 1G4
Tel: 902-421-7022; *Fax:* 902-425-0166
Frequency: 10 times a year; ISSN: 0008-3631
Robert Chodos, Editor

Canadian Immigrant Magazine
#228, 4401 Still Creek Dr., Burnaby, BC V5C 6G9
Tel: 604-872-0102; *Fax:* 604-709-0102
www.thecanadianimmigrant.com

Canadian Newcomer
222 Parkview Hill Cres., Toronto, ON M4B 1R8
Tel: 416-406-4719; *Fax:* 416-757-7086
cnmag@rogers.com
www.cnmag.ca
Dale Sproule, Publisher

Contact
Cité Universitaire, Université Laval, 3577, Pavillon Alphonse-Desjardins, Québec, QC G1K 7P4
Tél: 418-656-7266; *Téléc:* 418-656-2809
magazine.contact@dap.ulaval.ca
Circulation: 37 125 *Frequency:* 3 fois par an; français
Louise Desautels, Manager/Editor

Continuité
82, Grande-Allée ouest, Québec, QC G1R 2G6
Tél: 418-647-4525; *Téléc:* 418-647-6483
continuite@cmsq.qc.ca
www.cmsq.qc.ca/continuite
Circulation: 5 000 *Frequency:* 4 fois par an; français
Sophie Marcotte, Rédactrice en chef

The Country Connection
PO Box 100, Boulter, ON K0L 1G0
Tel: 613-332-3651; *Toll-Free:* 866-332-3651
magazine@pinecone.on.ca
www.pinecone.on.ca
Circulation: 5,000 *Frequency:* 4 times a year; ISSN: 1486-0643
Gus Zylstra, Publisher & Managing Editor

Dernière heure
7, chemin Bates, Outremont, QC H2V 4V7
Tel: 514-848-7000; *Fax:* 514-270-9079
Circulation: 26 798 *Frequency:* Hebdomadaire; français
Isabelle Clément, Éditrice

Digital Journal Magazine
PO Box 1046, Toronto, ON M5C 2K4
Tel: 416-410-9675;
www.digitaljournal.com
Christopher A. Hogg, Editor-in-chief

Eye for the Future
493 Markham St., Toronto, ON M6G 2L1
Tel: 416-654-5858; *Fax:* 416-654-5898
Circulation: 50,000 *Frequency:* 10 times a year
Elizabeth Rizzuto, Publisher

fab Magazine
511 Church St., 2nd Fl., Toronto, ON M4Y 2C9
Tel: 416-925-5221; *Fax:* 416-925-4817
Circulation: 31,000 *Frequency:* 26 times a year
Michael Schwarz, Publisher

The Family Herald Magazine
PO Box 1042, Chatham, ON N7M 5L6
Tel: 519-352-4359
Circulation: 10,000 *Frequency:* quarterly
Lorn LeDrew, Publisher

The Flag & Banner
International Flag & Banner Inc., 1755 - 4th Ave. West, Vancouver, BC V6J 1M2
Tel: 604-736-8161; *Fax:* 604-736-6439
Toll-Free: 800-663-8681
editor@flagshop.com
www.flagshop.com
Circulation: 14,000 *Frequency:* 2 times a year
Doreen Braveman, Editor
Dan Bogdon, Production Assistant

Focus Magazine
Campbell Communicatons Inc., PO Box 5310, Victoria, BC V8R 6S4
Tel: 250-388-7231; *Fax:* 250-383-1140
focusadmin@shaw.ca
www.focusonline.ca
Circulation: 35,000 *Frequency:* Monthly
Leslie Campbell, Publisher

Fugues
1212, St-Hubert, Montréal, QC H2L 3Y7
Tel: 514-848-1854; *Fax:* 514-845-7645
www.fugues.com
Circulation: 50,000 *Frequency:* 14 times a year
Maurice Nadeau, Publisher

Georgian Bay Today
PO Box 186, 27 St. Clair Ave. East, Toronto, ON M4T 2M1
Tel: 416-944-1217; *Fax:* 416-944-0133
hize@earthlink.net
Circulation: 2,000 *Frequency:* 4 times a year
Michael Ufford, Editor
Alan Heisey, Publisher

Going Natural
Federation of Canadian Naturists, PO Box 186 D, Toronto, ON M9A 4X2
Tel: 905-304-4836;
editor@fcn.ca
www.fcn.ca/GN.html
Circulation: 2,500 *Frequency:* 4 times a year
Dr. Paul Rapoport, Editor

Harrowsmith Country Life
#213, 3100 de la Concorde East Blvd., Laval, QC H7E 2B8
Tel: 450-665-0271; *Fax:* 450-665-2974
Toll-Free: 800-563-6738
hclmag.media@videotron.ca
www.harrowsmithcountrylife.ca
Circulation: 129,000 *Frequency:* 6 times a year; ISSN: 1190-8416
Tom Cruickshank, Editor
Michel Paradis, Vice-President & Group Publisher

Humanist in Canada
PO Box 943, Duncan, BC V9L 3Y2
Tel: 250-748-0962; *Fax:* 250-746-6672
editor@humanistincanada.com
www.humanistincanada.com
Circulation: 1,500 *Frequency:* 4 times a year; ISSN: 0018-7402
Gary Bauslaugh, Editor

ICI Montreal
Communications Gratte-Ciel ltée, 465, rue McGill, 3e étage, Montréal, QC H2Y 4B4
Tel: 514-393-1010; *Fax:* 514-393-3756
ici@ici-mirror.com
Circulation: 80,154 *Frequency:* Weekly, Thu.
Pierre Thibeault, Editor-in-charge

Kindred Spirits of PEI
#3, 5 Gerald McCarville Dr., Kensington, PE C0B 1M0
Tel: 902-836-5502;
kws@annesociety.org
www.annesociety.org
Circulation: 5,000 *Frequency:* 4 times a year; English
George Campbell, Publisher & Editor

Legion Magazine
Canvet Publications Ltd., 86 Aird Pl., Ottawa, ON K2L 0A1
Tel: 613-235-8741; *Fax:* 613-233-7159
magazine@legion.ca
www.legionmagazine.com
Circulation: 313,217 *Frequency:* 6 times a year
Mac Johnston, Editor & General Manager

Lifestyles
A.T.E. Publishing Co. Ltd., PO Box 1000, #24, 155 East Beaver Creek Rd., Richmond Hill, ON L4B 2N1
Tel: 905-881-3070; *Fax:* 905-731-6000
atopmag@aol.com
Frequency: 6 times a year
Gabriel Erem, Publisher
P.S. Henley, Managing Editor

Living Safety / Famille Avertie
c/o Canada Safety Council, 1020 Thomas Spratt Place, Ottawa, ON K1G 5L5
Tel: 613-739-1535; *Fax:* 613-739-1566
csc@safety-council.org
www.safety-council.org
Circulation: 25,000 *Frequency:* 4 times a year
Jack A. Smith, General Manager

Le Lundi
Tél: 514-848-7164; *Téléc:* 514-270-7079
Circulation: 27 589 *Frequency:* Hebdomadaire; français
Sylvie Bourgeault, Publisher

Magazine Prestige
305, boul René-Lévesque ouest, Québec, QC G1S 1S1
Tél: 418-683-5333; *Téléc:* 418-683-2899
info@magazineprestige.com
www.magazineprestige.com
Frequency: 11 fois par an
Jean Frenette, Rédacteur-en-chef

Muskoka Magazine
PO Box 180, Bracebridge, ON P1L 1T6
Tel: 705-646-1314; *Fax:* 705-645-6424
info@muskokamagazine.com
www.muskokamagazine.com
Circulation: 14,550 *Frequency:* 7 times a year
Jenny Cressman, Editor
Richard Everett, Manager, Sales
Donald Smith, Publisher & Editor

Nouvelles CSQ
Centrale des syndicats du Québec, 9405, rue Sherbrooke est, Montréal, QC H1L 6P3
Tél: 514-356-8888; *Téléc:* 514-356-9999
allaire.luc@csq.qc.net
www.csq.qc.net
Circulation: 103 000 *Frequency:* 5 fois par an; français
Louise Rochefort, Directrice

On the Bay Magazine
#201, 186 Hurontario St., Collingwood, ON L9Y 4T4
Tel: 705-444-9192; *Fax:* 705-444-5658
www.onthebaymagazine.com
Frequency: 6 times a year
Janet Lees, Editor

Our Canada
1100, boul René Levesque ouest, Montréal, QC H3B 5H5
Tel: 514-940-0751; *Fax:* 514-940-0751
Frequency: 6 times a year

Pacific Rim Magazine
100 West 49th Ave., Vancouver, BC V5Y 2Z6
Tel: 604-323-5648; *Fax:* 604-323-5393
erains@langara.bc.ca
www.langara.bc.ca/publishing/prm
Circulation: 18,000
Elizabeth Rains, Publisher, erains@langara.bc.ca
Keith Murray, Manager, Advertising Sales, kmurray@langara.bc.ca

Profile Markting & Publishing
#201, 212 East Miles St., Thunder Bay, ON P7C 1J6
Tel: 807-621-0400; *Fax:* 807-767-7352
santacom@tbaytel.net
Circulation: 40,000 *Frequency:* Monthly
Gillian Hamilton, Editor-in-chief
Orville Santa, Publisher

Protégez-Vous
#305, 2120, rue Sherbrooke est, Montréal, QC H1T 1C2
Tél: 514-873-3000; *Téléc:* 514-223-7160
courrier@pv.qc.ca
www.pv.qc.ca
Circulation: 151 145 *Frequency:* 12 fois par an; français
David Clerk, Contact

R.G.
CP 915 C, Montréal, QC H2L 4V2
Tél: 514-523-9463; *Téléc:* 514-523-2214
info@rgmag.com
www.rgmag.com
Circulation: 11 500
Alain Bouchard, Éditeur

Reader's Digest / Sélection du Reader's Digest
1100, boul René Lévesque ouest, Montréal, QC H3B 5H5
Tel: 514-940-0751; *Fax:* 514-940-3637
Toll-Free: 800-465-0780
customerservice@readersdigest.ca
www.rd.ca; www.selection.ca
Circulation: 1,200,000 *Frequency:* Monthly; English & French editions
Andrea C. Martin, President & CEO
Antoni Cioffi, Vice-President & CFO
Mathieu Péloquin, Vice-President, Marketing
Linda Melrose, Production Manager

Safarir
#501, 407, St-Laurent, Montréal, QC H2Y 2Y5
Tél: 514-396-5179;
www.safarir.com
Frequency: 12 fois par an; français
Sylvain Bolduc, Éditeur

Sélection du Reader's Digest
1100, boul René-Lévesque ouest, Montréal, QC H3B 5H5
Tel: 514-940-0751; *Fax:* 514-940-3637
Toll-Free: 888-459-3333
www.selectionrd.ca
Circulation: 242,970 *Frequency:* Monthly
Robert Goyette, Rédacteur-en-chef

Shunpiking, Nova Scotia's Discovery Magazine
6211 North St., Halifax, NS B3L 1P4
Tel: 902-444-4922; *Fax:* 902-444-7599
shunpike@shunpiking.com
www.shunpiking.com
Circulation: 25,000
Tony Seed, Publisher
Richard LeBlanc, Marketing Director

Times 10
#402, 10175 - 114 St., Edmonton, AB T5K 2L4
Tel: 780-415-5616; *Fax:* 780-455-6540
www.times10.org
Frequency: 10 times a year
Dennis Cambly, On Line Editor

Touring: Travel, Automobile, Lifestyle Magazine
c/o Medias Transcontinental S.E.N.C., 1100 René Lévesque Blvd., 24th Fl., Montréal, QC H3B 4X9
Tel: 514-392-9000; *Fax:* 514-392-1489
ghislaine.mercille@transcontinental.ca
Circulation: 625,000 *Frequency:* 4 times a year; English & French
Jean-Louis Gauthier, Editor-in-chief
Ghislaine Mercille, Sales Manager

University of Toronto Magazine
University of Toronto, Div. of University Advancement, 21 King's College Circle, Toronto, ON M5S 3J3
Tel: 416-946-7575; *Fax:* 416-978-3958
uoft.magazine@utoronto.ca
www.magazine.utoronto.ca
Circulation: 252,000 *Frequency:* 4 times a year
Scott Anderson, Editor & Manager

Up Here: Explore Canada's Far North
PO Box 1350, Yellowknife, NT X1A 2N9
Tel: 867-766-6711; *Fax:* 867-873-9876
Toll-Free: 800-661-0861
kathy@uphere.ca
www.uphere.ca
Circulation: 24,827 *Frequency:* 8 times a year; ISSN: 0828-4253
Jake Kennedy, Editor
Marion LaVigne, Publisher

Western Living
Transcontinental Media, #560, 2608 Granville St., Vancouver, BC V6H 3V3
Tel: 604-877-7732; *Fax:* 604-877-4849
wlmail@westernlivingmagazine.com
www.westernlivingmagazine.com
Circulation: 195,500 *Frequency:* 10 times a year; ISSN: 0824-0604
Lance Neale, Publisher
Jim Sutherland, Editor

Westworld Alberta
4180 Lougheed Hwy., 4th Fl., Burnaby, BC V5C 6A7
Tel: 604-299-7311; *Fax:* 604-299-9188
cwm@canadawide.com
www.canadawide.com
Circulation: 413,479 *Frequency:* 5 times a year
Peter Legge, Publisher
Anne Rose, Editor

Westworld British Columbia
4180 Lougheed Hwy., 4th Fl., Burnaby, BC V5C 6A7
Tel: 604-299-7311; *Fax:* 604-299-9188
cwm@canadawide.com
www.canadawide.com
Circulation: 502,239 *Frequency:* 4 times a year; also Westworld Saskatchewan (circ. 106,607, 4 times a year), Westworld Alberta (circ. 413,479, 5 times a year)
Peter Legge, Publisher
Anne Rose, Editor

Westworld Saskatchewan
1480 Lougheed Hwy., 4th Fl., Burnaby, BC V5C 6A7
Tel: 604-299-7311; *Fax:* 604-299-9188
cwm@canadawide.com
www.canadawide.com
Circulation: 110,000 *Frequency:* 4 times a year
Peter Legge, Publisher
Sheila Hansen, Editor

Yours for Fun
PO Box 518, 185 Ontario St., Burks Falls, ON P0A 1C0
Tel: 705-382-3943; *Fax:* 705-382-3440
news@almaguinnews.com
www.almaguinnews.com
Circulation: 60,000
Peter Barr, Publisher

Health & Medical

Abilities Magazine
c/o Canadian Abilities Foundation, #401, 340 College St., Toronto, ON M5T 3A9
Tel: 416-923-1885; *Fax:* 416-923-9829
info@abilities.ca
www.abilities.ca
Circulation: 45,000 *Frequency:* 4 times a year; ISSN: 0845-4469
Jaclyn Law, Managing Editor
Raymond D. Cohen, Editor-in-chief

Alive Magazine
Alive Publishing Group Inc., #100 - 12751 Vulcan Way, Richmond, BC V6V 3C8
Toll-Free: 800-663-6580
editorial@alive.com
www.alive.com
Circulation: 250,000 *Frequency:* 12 times a year

beyond fitness
#502, 3535 St. Charles Blvd., Kirkland, QC H9H 5B9
Tel: 514-697-5888; *Fax:* 514-693-0833
beyondfit@bellnet.ca
Circulation: 150,000 *Frequency:* 11 times a year
Pierre Martineau, President & Publisher
Laura Warf, Fitness Editor
Amanda Vogel, Fashion Editor
André Thibault, Administration & Circulation Manager

Canada's Family Guide to Home Health Care & Wellness Solutions
BCS Communications Ltd., 101 Thorncliffe Park Dr., Toronto, ON M4H 1M2
Tel: 416-421-7997; *Fax:* 416-421-0966
www.bcsgroup.com
Circulation: 30,000 *Frequency:* 4 times a year
Caroline Tapp-McDougall, Publisher

Capital Santé
Tél: 514-499-0317; *Téléc:* 514-849-9779
capitalsantepub@mail.transcontinental.ca
Circulation: 49 594 *Frequency:* 10 fois par an; français
Francine Tremblay, Éditrice
Jean-Louis Gauthier, Rédacteur

Common Ground Magazine
#204, 4381 Fraser St., Vancouver, BC V5V 4G4
Tel: 604-733-2215; *Fax:* 604-733-4415
Toll-Free: 800-365-8897
admin@commonground.ca
www.commonground.ca
Circulation: 70,000 *Frequency:* 12 times a year
Joseph Roberts, Publisher

Diabetes Dialogue
#1400, 522 University Ave., Toronto, ON M5G 2R5
Tel: 416-363-3373; *Fax:* 416-363-7067
Toll-Free: 800-226-8464
Membership@diabetes.ca.
www.diabetes.ca
Circulation: 45,510 *Frequency:* 4 times a year
Amir Hanna, Editor-in-chief

Family Health
PO Box 2421, Edmonton, AB T5J 2S6
Tel: 780-429-5189; *Fax:* 780-498-5661
Circulation: 120,000 *Frequency:* 4 times a year; ISSN 0830-0305
Robert Clarke, Publisher

Future Health
c/o Canadians for Health Research, PO Box 126, Westmount, QC H3Z 2T1
Tel: 514-398-7478; *Fax:* 514-398-8361
info@chrcrm.org
www.chrcrm.org
Circulation: 2,000 *Frequency:* 4 times a year; English, some French
Heather Pengelley, Editor

The Health Journal: Canada's Authorative Health Forum
Gemini Communications Inc., #2200, 4950 Yonge St., Toronto, ON M2N 6K1
Tel: 416-218-5568; *Fax:* 416-221-4668
thehealthjournal@sympatico.ca
Circulation: 214,572 *Frequency:* 5 times a year
Chantal Goudreau, Publisher

Health'N Vitality
#502, 3535, St-Charles, Kirkland, QC H9H 5B9
Tel: 514-697-5888; *Fax:* 514-693-0833
vitalitemag@qc.aira.com
Circulation: 200,000 *Frequency:* 6 times a year
Pierre Martineau, President
Kate Tompkins, Editor-in-chief
André Thibault, Circulation Manager

Healthcare Information Management & Communications Canada
5782 - 172 St., Edmonton, AB T6M 1B4
Tel: 780-489-4521; *Fax:* 780-489-3290
healthcare@shaw.ca
www.hcccinc.com
Circulation: 6,000 *Frequency:* 5 times a year
Steven A. Huesing, Publisher & Editor

HeartBeat
PO Box 1, Site 100, RR#1, Carvel, AB T0E 0H0
Tel: 780-380-2; *Fax:* 780-892-3401
pnewman@xplornet.com
www.heartbeatangels.com
Circulation: 4,600 *Frequency:* 4 times a year
Pauline Newman, Publisher

Impact Magazine
2007 - 2nd St. SW, Calgary, AB T2S 1S4
Tel: 403-228-0605; *Fax:* 403-228-0627
info@impactmagazine.ca
www.impactmagazine.ca
Frequency: Bi-monthly
Elaine Kupser, Publisher
Louise Hodgson-Jones, Editor

Lifestyle & Wellness
2813 Victoria Park Ave., Toronto, ON M1W 1A1
Tel: 416-492-6598; *Fax:* 416-492-6725
landwmag@rogers.com
Circulation: 30,000 *Frequency:* 4 times a year
Sheila McKenzie-Barnswell

Magazine Vie et santé
#200, 5 Place du Commerce, Verdun, QC H3E 1M8
Tél: 514-842-5492; *Téléc:* 514-842-5375
info@vie-sante.com
vieetsante.branchez-vous.com
Frequency: 8 fois par an
Veronique Tremblay, Rédactrice-en-chef

Synchronicity
PO Box 63118, 2604 Kensington Rd., NW, Calgary, AB T2N 4S5
Tel: 403-270-9544; *Fax:* 403-270-7407
info@synchronicitymagazine.ca
www.synchronicitymagazine.ca
Circulation: 37,000 *Frequency:* 6 times a year; ISSN: 1198-760X
Doreen Nystrom, Editor/President
Joy Nystrom, Publisher/Secretary

Vision Magazine
Breton Communications Inc., #202, 495, boul St-Martin ouest, Laval, QC H7M 1Y9
Tel: 450-629-6005; *Fax:* 450-629-6044
Toll-Free: 888-462-2112
breton.com@bretoncom.com
www.bretoncom.com
Circulation: 11,435 *Frequency:* 6 times a year
Martine Breton, Présidente

Vitalité Québec Mag
#502, 3535, boul St-Charles, Kirkland, QC H9H 5B9
Tél: 514-697-5888; *Téléc:* 514-693-0833
vitalitemag@qc.aira.com
Circulation: 40 000 *Frequency:* 10 fois par an; français
André Thibault, Directeur, Administration et diffusion
Monick Juliette Élie, Rédacteur-en-chef
Pierre Martineau, Président

Vitality Magazine: Toronto's Monthly Wellness Journal
356 Dupont St., Toronto, ON M5R 1V9
Tel: 416-964-0528; *Fax:* 416- -
advertising@vitalitymagazine.com
www.vitalitymagazine.com; www.wholelifecanada.com
Circulation: 52,000 *Frequency:* 10 times a year
Julia Woodford, Editor

WHOLifE JOURNAL
#15, 2301 St. Henry Ave., Saskatoon, SK S7M 0P6
Tel: 306-653-1283; *Fax:* 306-653-3291
Toll-Free: 800-780-3564
editor@wholife.com
www.wholife.com
Circulation: 17,000 *Frequency:* 6 times a year
Covers natural health & wellness for body, mind & sprirt, plus environmental issues
Melva Armstrong, Publisher

History & Genealogy

Canada's History Magazine
Canada's National History Society, #478, 167 Lombard Ave., Winnipeg, MB R3B 0T6
Tel: 204-988-9300; *Fax:* 204-988-9309
Toll-Free: 800-816-6777
thebeaver@historysociety.ca
www.canadashistory.ca
Circulation: 45,000 *Frequency:* 6 times a year; ISSN: 0005-7517
Deborah Morrison, President/CEO

Family Chronicle
Tel: 416-491-3699; *Fax:* 416-491-3996
Toll-Free: 888-326-2476
publisher@familychronicle.com
www.familychronicle.com
Frequency: 6 times a year
Halvor Moorshead, Publisher

Heritage/Patrimoine
5 Blackburn Ave., Ottawa, ON K1N 8A2
Tel: 613-237-1066; *Fax:* 613-237-5987
heritagecanada@heritagecanada.org
www.heritagecanada.org
Frequency: 4 times a year; ISSN: 1480-6924
Carolyn Quinn, Editor

Kayak: Canada's History Magazine for Kids
Canada's National History Society, #478, 167 Lombard Ave., Winnipeg, MB R3B 0T6
Tel: 204-988-9300; *Fax:* 204-988-9309
Toll-Free: 800-816-6777
info@kayakmag.ca
www.kayakmag.ca
Circulation: 16,000 *Frequency:* 6 times a year; ISSN: 1712-3984
Deborah Morrison, President/CEO

The Loyalist Gazette
#202, 50 Baldwin St., Toronto, ON M5T 1L4
Tel: 416-591-1783; *Fax:* 416-591-7506
uela@becon.org
www.uelac.org
Circulation: 2,500 *Frequency:* 2 times a year
Robert McBride, Editor

Newfoundland and Labrador Studies
Memorial University of Newfoundland, St. John's, NL A1C 5S7
Tel: 709-737-7474; *Fax:* 709-737-7560
nlstudies@mun.ca
www.mun.ca/nls/
Bi-annual, interdisciplinary journal about the society & culture of Newfoundland & Labrador
Al Potter

OHS Bulletin
34 Parkview Ave., Toronto, ON M2N 3Y2
Tel: 416-226-9011; *Fax:* 416-226-2740
bulletin@ontariohistoricalsociety.ca
www.ontariohistoricalsociety.ca
Circulation: 2,500 *Frequency:* 5 times a year
Sheila Creighton, Editor
Patricia K. Neal, Executive Director

Hobbies

The Canadian Amateur
CARF Publications, #217, 720 Belfast Rd., Ottawa, ON K1G 0Z5
Tel: 613-244-4367; *Fax:* 613-244-4369
Toll-Free: 877-273-8304
rachq@rac.ca
www.rac.ca
Circulation: 7,200 *Frequency:* 6 times a year
Alan Griffin

Canadian Coin News
PO Box 28103 Lakeport, St. Catherines, ON L2N 7P8
Tel: 905-646-7744; *Fax:* 905-646-0995
Toll-Free: 800-408-0352
bret@trajan.ca
www.canadiancoinnews.com
Circulation: 8,500 *Frequency:* 26 times a year; ISSN: 0702-3162
Bret Evans, Managing Editor & Associate Publisher
Hans Niedermair, News Editor

Canadian Railway Modeller
c/o North Kildonan Publications, PO Box 99 F, 355 Henderson Hwy., Winnipeg, MB R2L 2A5
Tel: 204-668-0168; *Fax:* 204-669-9821
morgant@cdnrwymod.com
www.cdnrwymod.com
Circulation: 25,000 *Frequency:* 6 times a year
Morgan B. Turney, Editor
John Longhurst, Editor

Canadian Sports Collector
PO Box 28103 Lakeport, 600 Ontario St., St. Catherines, ON L2N 7P8
Tel: 905-646-7744; *Fax:* 905-646-0995
Toll-Free: 800-408-0352
pwinkler@trajan.ca
www.sportscollector.ca
Circulation: 7,500 *Frequency:* Monthly; ISSN: 1492-3513
Paul Winkler, Publisher

Canadian Stamp News
PO Box 28103 Lakeport, St. Catherines, ON L2N 7P8
Tel: 905-646-7744; *Fax:* 905-646-0995
Toll-Free: 800-408-0352
bret@trajan.ca
www.canadianstampnews.ca
Circulation: 5,000 *Frequency:* 26 times a year; ISSN: 0702-3145
Paul Winkler, Publisher
Bret Evans, Editor

ÉCHEC+
c/o La Fédération Québécoise des Échecs, CP 640 C, Montréal, QC H2L 4L5
Tél: 514-252-3034; *Téléc:* 514-251-8038
info@fqechecs.qc.ca
www.fqechecs.qc.ca
Circulation: 2 000 *Frequency:* 6 fois par an; français
Louis Morin, Rédacteur

Metalcraft
345 Munster Ave., Toronto, ON M8Z 3C6
Tel: 416-232-0330; *Fax:* 416-234-1516
info@metalcraftmag.com
www.metalcraftmag.com
Frequency: 4 times a year
Nestor Gula, Editor

Model Aviation Canada
#9, 5100 South Service Rd., Burlington, ON L7L 6A5
Tel: 905-632-9808; *Fax:* 905-632-3304
maachq@on.aibn.com
www.maac.ca
Circulation: 12,600 *Frequency:* 6 times a year
Keith Morison, Editor, 403/282-0837

Philatélie Québec
275, rue Bryant, Sherbrooke, QC J1J 3E6
Tél: 819-252-3035; *Téléc:* 819-563-6482
sdu@videotron.ca
Circulation: 1 500 *Frequency:* 6 fois par an; français
Guy Desrosiers, Editeur

Homes

ARIDO Journal
#220, 6 Adelaide St. East, Toronto, ON M5C 1H6
Tel: 416-921-2127; *Fax:* 416-921-3660
Toll-Free: 800-334-1180
ltheoret@arido.on.ca
www.arido.on.ca
Circulation: 4,000
Lori Theoret, Publisher

Canadian Home & Country
#100, 25 Sheppard Ave. West, Toronto, ON M2N 6S7
Tel: 416-733-7600; *Fax:* 416-227-8298
editorial@canadianhomeandcountry.com
www.canadianhomeandcountry.com
Circulation: 140,000 *Frequency:* 7 times a year; ISSN: 0838-9330
Erin McLaughlin, Editor

Canadian Home Workshop
c/o Quarto Communications, 54 St. Patrick St., Toronto, ON M5T 1V1
Tel: 416-599-2000; *Toll-Free:* 800-465-6183
www.canadianhomeworkshop.com
Frequency: 6 times a year; ISSN: 1485-8509
Canadian Home Workshop magazine provides information about woodworking & home improvement. Features include do-it-yourself projects & reviews of tools & products.
Douglas Thomson, Editor
Randy Craig, Director, Advertising & Marketing
Amy McCleverty, Director, Art
Jodi Brooks, Manager, Production
Heather Maxwell-Tufford, Manager, Circulation

Canadian Homes & Cottages
The In-Home Show, #4, 2650 Meadowvale Blvd., Mississauga, ON L5N 6M5
Tel: 905-567-1440; *Fax:* 905-567-1442
Toll-Free: 888-830-6696
sgriffin@homesandcottages.com
www.homesandcottages.com
Circulation: 79,099 *Frequency:* 6 times a year
Steven Griffin, Publisher
Janice Naisby, Editor-in-chief

Canadian House & Home
Canadian Home Publishers, #120, 511 King St. West, Toronto, ON M5V 2Z4
Tel: 416-593-0204; *Fax:* 416-591-1630
Toll-Free: 800-559-8868
advertising@hhmedia.com
www.canadianhouseandhome.com
Circulation: 249,124 *Frequency:* 10 times a year; ISSN: 0826-7642
Lynda Reeves, Publisher
Cobi Ladner, Editor

Canadian Living
#100, 25 Sheppard Ave. West, Toronto, ON M2N 6S7
Tel: 905-733-7600; *Fax:* 905- -
letters@canadianliving.com
www.canadianliving.com
Circulation: 533,370 *Frequency:* 12 times a year; ISSN: 0382-4624
Debbie Gibson, Publisher

Classic Homestyles Home Plans
102 Ellis St., Penticton, BC V2A 4L5
Tel: 250-493-0942; *Fax:* 250-493-7526
plan@westhomeplanners.com
Circulation: 10,000 *Frequency:* Annually
G.T. Giroux, Publisher
Michael A. Giroux, Editor

Condo Life Magazine
178 Main St., Unionville, ON L3R 2G9
Tel: 905-479-4663; *Fax:* 905-479-4482
Toll-Free: 800-363-4663
info@homesmag.com
www.condolifemag.com
Circulation: 140,000
Michael Rosset, Publisher
Patrick Tivy, Editor

Cottage Life
54 Patrick St., Toronto, ON M5T 1V1
Tel: 416-599-2000; *Fax:* 416-599-0800
Toll-Free: 877-874-5253
clmag@cottagelife.com
www.cottagelife.com
Circulation: 70,000 *Frequency:* 6 times a year
Al Zikovitz, Publisher
Penny Caldwell, Editor

Cottage Magazine
#900, 1080 Howe St., Vancouver, BC V6Z 2T1
Tel: 604-606-4644; *Fax:* 604-687-1925
Toll-Free: 800-816-0747
info@oppublishing.com
www.oppublishing.com
Circulation: 13,195 *Frequency:* 6 times a year
Mark Yelic, Publisher
Desiree Daniel, Editor

The Cottager
PO Box 40, Victoria Beach, MB R0E 2C0
Tel: 204-756-8381; *Fax:* 204-756-2662
magazine@thecottager.mb.ca
www.thecottager.com
Circulation: 10,000
Glenn Halgren
Cathy Halgren, Circulation

Décoration Chez-Soi
Tél: 514-848-7164; *Téléc:* 514-270-7079
Circulation: 74 174 *Frequency:* 10 fois par an; français
Pierre Deschênes, Directeur

Décormag
Trancontinental Media, 1100, boul. René-Lévesque Ouest, 24e étage, Montréal, QC H3A 4X9
Tél: 514-392-9000; *Téléc:* 514-848-9779
redaction@decormag.com
www.decormag.com
Circulation: 84 542 *Frequency:* 11 fois par an; français
Marie-Christine Tremblay, Édimestre
Michèle Dubreuil, Directrice

Del Condominium Life
4800 Dufferin St., Toronto, ON M3H 5S9
Tel: 416-739-5143; *Fax:* 416-661-4538
pmackellar@delcondo.com
delpropertymanagement.com
Circulation: 32,500 *Frequency:* 3 times a year
Patricia MacKellar, Editor/Production Manager

Designer Showcase
1300 Hollis St., Halifax, NS B3J 1T6
Tel: 902-420-9943; *Fax:* 902-429-9058
publishers@metroguide.ca
www.metroguide.ca
Circulation: 8,000
Trevor Adams, Editor
Sheila Blair, Publisher

Designers' Best Home Plans
Tel: 250-493-0942; *Fax:* 250-493-7526
plan@westhomeplanners.com
www.westhomeplanners.com
Circulation: 10,000 *Frequency:* Annually
G.T. Giroux, Publisher
Michael A. Giroux, Editor-in-chief

East Coast Living
1300 Hollis St., Halifax, NS 3J 1T6
Tel: 902-420-9943; *Fax:* 902-429-9058
publishers@metroguide.ca
www.metroguidepublishing.ca
Circulation: 34,100 *Frequency:* 2 times a year
Sheila Blair, Publisher

Home Digest
1416 Stonehampton Ct., Pickering, ON L1V 7C9
Tel: 905-509-9900; *Fax:* 905-509-9990
homedigest@sympatico.ca
www.homedigest.ca
Circulation: 700,000 *Frequency:* 4 times a year
Barry Holmes, Publisher
William Roebuck, Editor

Homes Magazine
Tel: 905-479-4663; *Fax:* 905-479-4482
Toll-Free: 800-363-4663
info@homesmag.com
www.homesmag.com
Circulation: 100,000 *Frequency:* 9 times a year
Michael Rosset, Publisher
Patrick Tivy, Editor

Les Idées de ma maison
7, Chemin Bates, Outremont, QC H2V 4V7
Tél: 514-848-7000; *Téléc:* 514-270-7079
Circulation: 65 493 *Frequency:* 10 fois par an; français
Béatrix Marik, Rédactrice

Les idées Réno-Dépôt
Tél: 514-848-7164; *Téléc:* 514-270-7079
Circulation: 120 000 *Frequency:* 2 fois par an
Michel Blain, Rédacteur

Maison d'Aujourd'hui
3390, boul Métropolitain est, Montréal, QC H2A 1A4
Tel: 514-729-0000; *Fax:* 514-729-2552
courriel@maisonmax.com
www.maisondirect.com
Circulation: 50 000 *Frequency:* semi-annuel
Phillippe Massé, Président

Planimage Magazines
#105, 1501, rue Ampere, Boucherville, QC J4B 5Z5
Tel: 450-641-7526; *Fax:* 450-641-6688
Toll-Free: 800-752-6744
info@planimage.com
www.planimage.com
Circulation: 30 000 *Frequency:* 6 times a year
Daniel Therrien, Publisher & Editor

Plans de Maisons du Québec
Tél: 514-848-7164; *Téléc:* 514-848-7079
Frequency: 4 fois par an; français
Claude Leclerc, Rédacteur

Practical Homes Home Plans
Tel: 250-493-0942; *Fax:* 250-493-7526
plan@westhomeplanners.com
www.westhomeplanners.com
Circulation: 10,000 *Frequency:* Annually
G.T. Giroux, Publisher
Michael A. Giroux, Editor-in-chief

Proven & Popular Home Plans
Tel: 250-493-0942; *Fax:* 250-493-7526
plan@westhomeplanners.com
www.westhomeplanners.com
Circulation: 10,000 *Frequency:* Annually
G.T. Giroux, Publisher
Michael A. Giroux, Editor-in-chief

Real Estate News
1400 Don Mills Rd., Toronto, ON M3B 3N1
Tel: 416-443-8113; *Fax:* 416-443-9185
ren@thestar.ca
www.toronto.com/realestatenews
Circulation: 99,442 *Frequency:* Weekly
Mirella Torchia, General Manager

Real Estate Victoria
Monday Publications, 818 Broughton St., Victoria, BC V8W 1E4
Tel: 250-381-9171; *Fax:* 250-381-9172
rev@revweekly.com
www.revweekly.com
Circulation: 20,000 *Frequency:* Weekly
Glenda Turner, Publisher, gturner@monday.com

Renovation & Decor Magazine
178 Main St., Unionville, ON L3R 2G9
Tel: 905-479-4663; *Fax:* 905-479-4482
Toll-Free: 800-363-4663
nsicilia@homesmag.com
www.homespublishinggroup.com
Circulation: 75,000
Michael Rosset, Publisher

Rénovation Bricolage
7, ch Bates, Outremont, QC H2V 4V7
Tél: 514-848-7164; *Téléc:* 514-270-6918
renobrico@tva-publications.com
Circulation: 33 270 *Frequency:* 9 fois par an; français
Claude Leclerc, Éditeur/Rédacteur

Select Home Designs
#102, 9440 - 202 St., Langley, BC V1M 4A6
Tel: 604-881-1124; *Fax:* 604-881-2114
sales@selecthomedesigns.com
www.selectaplan.com
Circulation: 82,500 *Frequency:* 3 times a year
Steve Riley, Publisher

Sounder Profiles Newsmagazine
#6A, 17675 - 66 Ave., Surrey, BC V3S 7X1
Tel: 604-574-6530; *Fax:* 604-574-6529
Circulation: 40,000 *Frequency:* monthly
Arlie McClurg, Publisher

Style at Home: Canada's Decorating Magazine
#100, 25 Sheppard Ave. West, Toronto, ON M2N 6S7
Tel: 416-733-7600; *Fax:* 416-218-3632
letters@styleathome.com
styleathome.com
Circulation: 235,000 *Frequency:* 12 times a year; ISSN: 1206-5870
Jacqueline Howe, Publisher
Gail Johnston Habs, Editor

Horses, Riding & Breeding

Atlantic Horse & Pony
PO Box 1509, Liverpool, NS B0T 1K0
Tel: 902-354-5411; *Fax:* 902- -
Circulation: 4,000 *Frequency:* 6 times a year
Dirk van Loon, Editor

Canadian Arabian Registry/News
#113, 37 Athabascan Ave., Sherwood Park, AB T8A 4H3
Tel: 780-416-4990; *Fax:* 780-416-4860
editor@cahr.ca
www.cahr.ca
Circulation: 2,200 *Frequency:* 4 times a year
Nicole Toren, Editor
Shari Christie, Administrator/Registrar

The Canadian Sportsman
PO Box 129, 25 Old Plank Rd., Straffordville, ON N0J 1Y0
Tel: 519-866-5558; *Fax:* 519-866-5596
gfoerster@canadiansportsman.ca
www.canadiansportsman.ca
Frequency: Bi-weekly
Gary Foerster, Publisher
Dave Briggs, Editor

Canadian Thoroughbred

Tel: 905-727-0107; *Fax:* 905-841-1530
Toll-Free: 800-505-7428
info@horse-canada.com
www.horse-canada.com
Circulation: 4,500 *Frequency:* 6 times a year
Jennifer Anstey, Publisher
Lee Benson, Editor

The Corinthian/Horse Sport

Tel: 905-727-0107; *Fax:* 905-841-1530
Toll-Free: 800-505-7428
info@horse-canada.com
www.horse-canada.com
Circulation: 10,000 *Frequency:* 12 times a year
Jennifer Anstey, Publisher

Courrier Hippique
CP 1000 M, 4545, av Pierre-de-Coubertin, Montréal, QC H1V 3R2
Tél: 514-252-3030; *Téléc:* 514-252-3165
courrier@hippique.qc.ca
www.hippique.qc.ca
Circulation: 7 000 *Frequency:* 6 times a year
Laure Chazerand, Rédactrice-en-chef

Horse & Country Canada
PO Box 203, #23, 845 Dakota St., Winnipeg, MB R2M 5M3
Tel: 204-256-7467; *Fax:* 204-257-2467
horsecountry@mts.net
www.horsecountry.ca
Circulation: 12,000 *Frequency:* 6 times a year
Linda Hazelwood, Publisher & Editor

Horse-Canada.com
PO Box 670, 225 Industrial Pkwy. South, Aurora, ON L4G 4J9
Tel: 905-727-0107; *Fax:* 905-841-1530
Toll-Free: 800-505-7428
info@horse-canada.com
www.horse-canada.com
Circulation: 17,000 *Frequency:* 6 times a year
Jennifer Anstey, Publisher
Lee Benson, Editor

Horsepower: Magazine for Young Horse Lovers
PO Box 670, Aurora, ON L4G 4J9
Tel: 905-727-0107; *Fax:* 905-841-1530
Toll-Free: 800-505-7428
janstey@horse-canada.com
www.horse-canada.com
Circulation: 16,000 *Frequency:* 6 times a year
Jennifer Anstey, Publisher
Susan Stafford, Editor

Horses All
629 Evermeadow Rd. SW, Calgary, AB T2Y 4W8
Tel: 403-249-8770; *Fax:* 403-249-8769
www.horsesall.com
Circulation: 7,000 *Frequency:* Monthly
Steve Mark, Publisher
Cindy Mark, Editor

Pacific & Prairie Horse Journal
PO Box 2190, Sidney, BC V8L 3S8
Tel: 250-655-8883; *Fax:* 250-655-8913
Toll-Free: 800-299-3799
editor@horsejournals.com
www.horsejournals.com
Circulation: 20,000 *Frequency:* 12 times a year
Kathy Smith, Publisher/Editor

The Rider
PO Box 10072, 487 Book Rd. West, Ancaster, ON L9K 1P2
Tel: 905-648-2035; *Fax:* 905-648-6977
Toll-Free: 877-743-3715
therider@worldchat.com
www.therider.com
Circulation: 7,000 *Frequency:* Monthly
Aidan Finn, Editor

Trot
c/o Standardbred Canada, 2150 Meadowvale Blvd., Mississauga, ON L5N 6R6
Tel: 905-858-3060; *Fax:* 905-858-3089
trotmagazine@standardbredcanada.ca
Frequency: Monthly
Chris Roberts, Manager & Editor

Interior Design & Decor

Homefront
BCS Communications Ltd., 101 Thorncliffe Park Dr., Toronto, ON M4H 1M2
Tel: 416-421-7944; *Fax:* 416-421-0966
Toll-Free: 800-298-6282
dostal@bcsgroup.com
www.homefrontmagazine.ca
Circulation: 35,000 *Frequency:* 4 times a year
Helmut Dostal, Publisher

Plaisirs de Vivre/Living in Style
#1703, 1115 Sherbrooke St. West, Montréal, QC H3A 1H3
Tel: 514-982-9823; *Fax:* 514-289-9160
pdv@prestipresse.com
Circulation: 70,198 *Frequency:* 6 times a year; English & French
Peter Weiss, Publisher
Céline Tremblay, Editor-in-chief
Steve Robins, Associate Publisher

Labour, Trade Unions

Our Times
#407, 15 Gervais Dr., Toronto, ON M3C 1Y8
Tel: 416-703-7661; *Fax:* 416-703-9094
Toll-Free: 800-648-6131
office@ourtimes.ca
www.ourtimes.ca
Circulation: 8,000 *Frequency:* 4 times a year

Socialist Worker
PO Box 339 E, Toronto, ON M6H 4E3
Tel: 416-972-6391; *Fax:* 416-972-6319
sworker@sympatico.ca
www.socialist.ca
Circulation: 2,000 *Frequency:* 24 times a year; ISSN 0836-7094
Paul Kellogg, Editor

Literary

The Antigonish Review
PO Box 5000, St. Francis Xavier University, Antigonish, NS B2G 2W5
Tel: 902-867-3962; *Fax:* 902-867-5563
tar@stfx.ca
www.antigonishreview.com
Circulation: 900 *Frequency:* 4 times a year; ISSN: 0003-5661
Bonnie McIsaac, Office Manager
Gerald Trites, Editor

ARC: Canada's National Poetry Magazine
PO Box 81060, Ottawa, ON K1P 1B1
Tel: 613-729-3550;
arc@arcpoetry.ca
www.arcpoetry.ca
Circulation: 1,200 *Frequency:* 2 times a year; ISSN: 0705-6397
Anita Lahey, Editor
Pauline Conley, Managing Editor

Brick: A Literary Journal
PO Box 537 Q, Toronto, ON M4T 2M5
Tel: 416-593-9684; *Fax:* 416- -
info@brickmag.com
www.brickmag.com
Circulation: 2,200 *Frequency:* 2 times a year; ISSN: 0382-8565
M. Redhill

Canadian Notes & Queries
The Porcupine's Quill, 68 Main St., Erin, ON N0B 1T0
Tel: 519-833-9158; *Fax:* 519-833-9845
pql@sentex.net
www.sentex.net/~pql
Circulation: 500 *Frequency:* 2 times a year; ISSN: 0576-5803
Tim Inkster, Publisher
John Metcalf, Editor

The Capilano Review
2055 Purcell Way, North Vancouver, BC V7J 3H5
Tel: 604-984-1712; *Fax:* 604-990-7837
tcr@capcollege.bc.ca
www.capcollege.bc.ca/thecapilanoreview/
Circulation: 900 *Frequency:* 3 times a year; ISSN: 0315-3754
Jenny Pennberthy, Editor

The Claremont Review
Claremont Review Publishers, 4980 Wesley Rd., Victoria, BC V8Y 1Y9
Tel: 250-658-5221; *Fax:* 250-658-5387
editor@theclaremontreview.ca
www.theclaremontreview.ca
Circulation: 1,000 *Frequency:* 2 times a year; ISSN: 1188-5068
Susan Stenson, Editor
Lucy Bashford, Managing Editor

Contemporary Verse 2
 # 207, 100 Arthur St., Winnipeg, MB R3B 1H3
Tel: 204-949-1365; *Fax:* 204-942-5754
cv2@mts.net
www.contemporaryverse2.ca
Circulation: 650 *Frequency:* 4 times a year; ISSN: 0831-9502
Clarise Foster, Managing Editor

The Dalhousie Review
Dalhousie University, 6209 University Ave., Halifax, NS B3H 4R2
Tel: 902-494-2541; *Fax:* 902-494-3561
dalhousie.review@dal.ca
dalhousiereview.dal.ca
Circulation: 700 *Frequency:* 3 times a year
Jennifer Lambert, Production Manager
Anthony Stewart, Editor

Descant
Descant Arts & Letters Foundation, PO Box 314 P, Toronto, ON M5S 2S8
Tel: 416-593-2557; *Fax:* 416-593-9362
info@descant.on.ca
www.descant.on.ca
Circulation: 1,200 *Frequency:* 4 times a year; ISSN: 0382-909X
Karen Mulhallen, Editor

Exile
134 Eastbourne Ave., Toronto, ON M5P 2G6
Tel: 416-485-4885;
exq@exilequarterly.com
www.exilequarterly.com
Circulation: 1,200 *Frequency:* 4 times a year
Michael Callaghan, Publisher

The Fiddlehead
Campus House, PO Box 4400 A, 11 Garland Ct., Fredericton, NB E3B 5A3
Tel: 506-453-3501; *Fax:* 506-453-5069
fiddlehd@unb.ca
www.Lib.unb.ca/Texts/Fiddlehead
Circulation: 1,000 *Frequency:* 4 times a year; ISSN: 015-0630
Ross Leckie, Editor

Geist
#200, 341 Water St., Vancouver, BC V6B 1B8
Tel: 604-681-9161; *Fax:* 604-669-8250
Toll-Free: 800-434-7834
geist@geist.com
www.geist.com
Circulation: 8,000 *Frequency:* 4 times a year; ISSN: 1181-6554
Stephen Osborne, Editor

Grain
PO Box 67, Saskatoon, SK S7K 3K1
Tel: 306-244-2828; *Fax:* 306-244-0255
grainmag@sasktel.net
www.grainmagazine.ca
Circulation: 1,700 *Frequency:* 4 times a year; ISSN: 1491-0497
Kent Bruyneel, Editor

The Malahat Review
University of Victoria, PO Box 1700 CSC, Victoria, BC V8W 2Y2
Tel: 250-721-8524; *Fax:* 250-472-5051
malahat@uvic.ca
www.malahatreview.ca
Circulation: 1,000 *Frequency:* 4 times a year; ISSN: 0025-1216
John Barton, Editor

Matrix
#502, 1400, boul de Maisonneuve ouest, Montréal, QC H3G 1M8
Tel: 514-848-2357; *Fax:* 514-848-4501
matrix@alcor.concordia.ca
alcor.concordia.ca/~matrix
Circulation: 1,500 *Frequency:* 4 times a year; ISSN 0318-3610
R.E.N. Allen, Editor

The New Quarterly
c/o St. Jerome's University, 290 Westmount Rd. North, Waterloo, ON N2L 3G3
Tel: 519-884-8111; *Fax:* 519-884-5759
editor@newquarterly.net
newquarterly.net
Circulation: 1,000 *Frequency:* 4 times a year; ISSN: 0227-0455
Covers Canadian writers & writing
Kim Jernigan, Editor

Nuit blanche
#403, 1026, rue St-Jean, Québec, QC G1R 1R7
Tél: 418-692-1354; *Téléc:* 418-692-1355
nuitblanche@nuitblanche.com
www.nuitblanche.com

Circulation: 2 800 *Frequency:* 4 fois par an; français
Anne-Marie Guérineau, Directrice

On Spec Magazine
The Copper Pig Writers' Society, PO Box 4727, Edmonton, AB T6E 5G6
Tel: 780-413-0215; *Fax:* 780-413-1538
onspec@onspec.ca
www.onspec.ca
Circulation: 2,000 *Frequency:* 4 times a year; ISSN: 0843-476X
Diane Walton, Managing Editor

paperplates
19 Kenwood Ave., Toronto, ON M6C 2R8
Tel: 416-651-2551; *Fax:* 416-651-2910
magazine@paperplates.org
www.paperplates.org
Frequency: 4 issues a year; ISSN: 1183-3742, online
Bernard Kelly, Publisher & Editor

Prairie Fire
Prairie Fire Press Inc., #423, 100 Arthur St., Winnipeg, MB R3B 1H3
Tel: 204-943-9066; *Fax:* 204-942-1555
prfire@mts.net
www.prairiefire.ca
Circulation: 1,500 *Frequency:* 4 times a year; ISSN: 0821-1124
Janine Tschuncky, Operations Manager
Andris Taskans, Editor
Heidi Harms, Associate Editor

Prairie Journal
Prairie Journal Press, PO Box 61203 Brentwood, Calgary, AB T2L 2K6
prairiejournal@yahoo.com
www.geocities.com/prairiejournal
Circulation: 600 *Frequency:* 2 times a year; ISSN: 0827-2921
A. Burke

Prism International
Buch., #E462, Dept. of Creative Writing, UBC, 1866 Main Mall, Vancouver, BC V6T 1Z1
Tel: 604-822-2514; *Fax:* 604-822-3616
prism@interchange.ubc.ca
www.prism.arts.ubc.ca
Circulation: 1,200 *Frequency:* 4 times a year; ISSN: 0032-8790
Jamella Hagen, Executive Editor
Kellee Ngan, Executive Editor

Rampike Magazine
c/o Dept. of English, University of Windsor, 401 Sunset Ave., Windsor, ON N9B 3P4
Tel: 519-253-3000; *Fax:* 519-971-3676
jirgins@uwindsor.ca
Circulation: 4,000 *Frequency:* 2 times a year; ISSN: 0711-7647
Karl E. Jirgins, Editor/Publisher

The Readers Showcase
Tel: 780-413-6163; *Fax:* 780-413-6185
Toll-Free: 877-784-4488
www.suggitt.com
Circulation: 380,895 *Frequency:* 6 pa

sub-TERRAIN Magazine
PO Box 3008 MPO, Vancouver, BC V6B 3X5
Tel: 604-876-8710; *Fax:* 604-879-2667
subter@portal.ca
www.subterrain.ca
Circulation: 3,500 *Frequency:* 3 issues a year; ISSN: 0840-7533
Brian Kaufman, Editor

TickleAce
PO Box 5353, St. John's, NL A1C 5W2
Tel: 709-754-6610; *Fax:* 709-754-5579
tickleace@nfld.com
Circulation: 1,000 *Frequency:* 2 times a year; ISSN: 0823-6399
Bruce Porter, Editor

West Coast Line
2027 East Annex, Simon Fraser University, 8888 Universi, Burnaby, BC V5A 1S6
Tel: 604-291-4287; *Fax:* 604-291-4622
wcl@sfu.ca
Circulation: 800 *Frequency:* 3 times a year; ISSN: 1182-4271
Michael Barnholden, Managing Editor

White Wall Review
63 Gould St., Toronto, ON M5B 1E9
Tel: 416-977-9924; *Fax:* 416-977-7709
Frequency: Annually; ISSN: 0712-8991

Men's

Highrise Magazine
83 Clansman Blvd., Toronto, ON M2H 1X7
info@highrisemag.com
www.highrisemag.com
Frequency: 4 times a year
Cynthia Cully, Editor-in-chief

Military

Esprit de Corps
#204, 1066 Somerset St. West, Ottawa, ON K1Y 4T3
Tel: 613-725-5060; *Fax:* 613-725-1019
Toll-Free: 800-361-2791
espritdecorp@idirect.com
www.espritdecorps.ca
Circulation: 15,000
Scott Taylor, Publisher

Music

Beatlology Magazine
#90, 260 Adelaide St. East, Toronto, ON M5A 1N1
www.beatlology.com
Andrew Croft, Publisher, publisher@beatlology.com
Charles Iscove, Editor, editor@beatlology.com

Canadian Musician
Tel: 905-641-3471; *Fax:* 905-641-1648
Toll-Free: 877-746-4692
mail@nor.com
www.canadianmusician.com
Circulation: 27,000 *Frequency:* 6 times a year
Jim Norris, Publisher

Chart
Chart Communications Inc., #200, 41 Britain St., Toronto, ON M5A 1R7
Tel: 416-363-3101; *Fax:* 416-363-3109
chart@chartattack.com
www.chartattack.com
Circulation: 40,000 *Frequency:* Monthly; ISSN: 1198-7235
Edward Skira, Co-Publisher
Nada Laskovski, Co-Publisher

Country Music News
PO Box 7323 Vanier Terminal, Ottawa, ON K1L 8E4
Tel: 613-745-6006; *Fax:* 613-745-0576
Larry@CountryMusicNews.ca
www.countrymusicnews.ca
Circulation: 6,500 *Frequency:* Monthly
Larry Delaney, Publisher & Editor, Larry@CountryMusicNews.ca

Crescendo
Toronto Musicians' Assn., #500, 15 Gervais Dr., Toronto, ON M3C 1Y8
Tel: 416-421-1020; *Fax:* 416-421-7011
Toll-Free: 800-463-6333
info@torontomusicians.org
www.torontomusicians.org
Circulation: 4,000 *Frequency:* 3 times a year
Allan MacMillan, Publisher
Brian Blain, Managing Editor

Exclaim!
#966, 7-B Pleasant Blvd., Toronto, ON M4T 1K2
Tel: 416-535-9735; *Fax:* 416-535-0566
exclaim@exclaim.ca
www.exclaim.ca
Circulation: 102,000 *Frequency:* Monthly
Ian Danzig, Publisher

Musicworks: The Journal of Sound Explorations
#358, 401 Richmond St. West, Toronto, ON M5V 3A8
Tel: 416-977-3546;
sound@musicworks.ca
www.musicworks.ca
Circulation: 3,000 *Frequency:* 3 times a year; English & French; ISSN: 0225-686X
Gayle Young, Editor

Opera Canada
#244, 366 Adelaide St. East, Toronto, ON M5A 3X9
Tel: 416-363-0395; *Fax:* 416-363-0396
Circulation: 5,575 *Frequency:* 5 times a year; ISSN: 0030-3577
Wayne Gooding, Editor

Opus
161 Frederick St., Toronto, ON M5A 4P3
Tel: 416-596-1480; *Fax:* 416-596-9793
www.warwickgp.com/opus/main/main.htm
Frequency: 4 times a year
Rick MacMillan, Editor-in-chief

La Scena Musicale
5409, rue Waverly, Montréal, QC H2T 2X8
Tel: 514-274-1128; *Fax:* 514-274-9456
Toll-Free: 877-948-2520
info@scena.org
www.scena.org
Circulation: 42,000 *Frequency:* monthly
Wah Keung Chan, Publisher/Editor

TRIBE Magazine
PO Box 65053, 358 Danforth Ave., Toronto, ON M4K 3Z2
Tel: 416-778-4115; *Fax:* 416-405-9473
editor@tribe.ca
www.tribemagazine.com
Circulation: 35,000 *Frequency:* 10 times a year
Alex Dordevic, Publisher/Editor

WHOLENOTE: Toronto's Music, Classical & New
#503, 720 Bathurst St., Toronto, ON M5S 2R4
Tel: 416-603-3786; *Fax:* 416-603-4791
info@thewholenote.com
www.thewholenote.com
Circulation: 36,000
Allan Pulker, Publisher

News

L'Actualité
#800, 1200 av. McGill College, Montréal, QC H3B 4G7
Tél: 514-843-2564; *Téléc:* 514-843-2186
redaction@lactualite.rogers.com
www.lactualite.com
Circulation: 187 700 *Frequency:* 20 fois par an; français; ISSN: 03830-8714
Carole Beaulieu, Rédactrice

Behind the Headlines
Canadian Institute of International Affairs, #302, 205 Richmond St. West, Toronto, ON M5V 1V3
Tel: 416-977-9000; *Fax:* 416-977-7521
Toll-Free: 800-668-2442
mailbox@ciia.org
www.ciia.org
Frequency: 4 times a year
The Hon. Barbara McDougall
Robert Johnstone, Editor

Broken Pencil
PO Box 203 P, Toronto, ON M5S 2S7
Tel: 416-204-1700;
editor@brokenpencil.com
www.brokenpencil.com
Circulation: 3,000 *Frequency:* 3 times a year; ISSN: 1201-8996
Anna Bowness, Editor

Columbia Journal
PO Box 2633 Main, Vancouver, BC V6B 3W8
Tel: 604-266-6552; *Fax:* 604-267-3342
cjournal@telus.net
www.columbiajournal.ca
Circulation: 20,000 *Frequency:* 12 times a year
Jim Lipkovits, Publisher
Marco Procaccini, Editor

Le Courrier Parlementaire
30 Grande-Allée ouest, Québec, QC G1R 2G6
Tel: 418-640-4211; *Fax:* 418- -
editeur@courrierparlementaire.com
www.courrierparlementaire.com
Denis Massicotte, Publisher

Inroads
3777 Kent Ave., #A, Montréal, QC H3S 1N4
Tel: 514-731-8383; *Fax:* 514- -
inroads@canada.com
www.inroadsjournal.ca
Frequency: 2 times a year; ISSN: 0315-7911
Robert Chodos, Managing Editor

Maclean's
1 Mount Pleasant Rd., 11th Fl., Toronto, ON M4Y 2Y5
Tel: 416-764-1300; *Fax:* 416-764-1332
Toll-Free: 800-268-9119
service@macleans.ca
www.macleans.ca
Circulation: 401,080 *Frequency:* Weekly
Ken Whyte, Publisher/Editor-in-Chief

Northwest Compass
PO Box 21034, Prince Rupert, BC V8J 2P4
Tel: 250-627-7777; *Fax:* 250-627-7756
www.northwestcompass.com

Rob Ritchie, Publisher
Bob Colebrook, Editor

TIME
Time Canada Ltd., North Tower, #602, 175 Bloor St. East, Toronto, ON M4W 3R8
Tel: 416-929-1115; *Fax:* 416-929-0019
Toll-Free: 800-668-9934
joan_brehl@timeinc.com
www.timecanada.com
Circulation: 225,000 *Frequency:* Weekly
Joan Brehl, Managing Director
George Russell, President

Photography

Blackflash
Buffalo Berry Press, PO Box 7381 Main, 12 - 23rd St. East, 2nd Fl., Saskatoon, SK S7K 4J3
Tel: 306-374-5115; *Fax:* 306-665-6568
editor@blackflash.ca
www.blackflash.ca
Circulation: 1,300 *Frequency:* 3 times a year; ISSN: 0826-3922
John Shelling, Managing Editor

Photo Life
Apex Publications, 185, rue St-Paul, Québec, QC G1K 3W2
Toll-Free: 800-905-7468
editor@photolife.com
www.photolife.com
Other information: Toll Free Fax: 1-800-664-2739
Circulation: 55,000 *Frequency:* 6 times a year; ISSN: 0700-3021
Guy Poirier, Publisher
Anita Dammer, Editor-in-chief

Productions Ciel Variable
#204, 661, rue Rose-de-Lima, Montréal, QC H4C 2L7
Tel: 514-390-1193; *Fax:* 514-390-8802
info@cielvariable.ca
www.ceilvariable.ca
Circulation: 1,850 *Frequency:* 4 times a year; English & French; ISSN: 0831-3091
Jacques Doyen, Directeur

Political

bout de papier
#412, 47 Clarence St., Ottawa, ON K1N 9K1
Tel: 613-241-1391; *Fax:* 613-241-5911
boutdepapier@pafso.com
Circulation: 2,800 *Frequency:* 4 times a year; English & French; ISSN: 305-500
Debra Hulley, Managing Editor

Briarpatch
2138 McIntyre St., Regina, SK S4P 2R7
Tel: 306-525-2949; *Fax:* 306-565-3430
info@briarpatchmagazine.com
www.briarpatchmagazine.com
Circulation: 2,000 *Frequency:* 8 times a year; ISSN 0703-8968
Shayna Stock, Publisher, publisher@briarpatchmagazine.com
Dave Oswald Mitchell, Managing Editor, editor@briarpatchmagazine.com

Canadian Dimension
#2B, 91 Albert St., Winnipeg, MB R3B 1G5
Tel: 204-957-1519; *Fax:* 204-943-4617
Toll-Free: 800-737-7051
www.canadiandimension.mb.ca
Circulation: 3,500 *Frequency:* 6 times a year; ISSN: 0008-3402
Cy Gonick, Publisher & Coordinating Editor

Dialogue Magazine
Gabriel Communications, 6227 Groveland Dr., Nanaimo, BC V9V 1B1
Tel: 250-758-9877; *Fax:* 250-758-9855
dialogue@dialogue.ca
www.dialogue.ca
Circulation: 1,000 *Frequency:* 6 times a year
Maurice J. King, Publisher
Janet Hicks, Editor

Peace Magazine
PO Box 248 P, Toronto, ON M5S 2S7
Tel: 416-588-8748; *Fax:* 416-789-4508
office@peacemagazine.org
www.peacemagazine.org
Circulation: 2,500 *Frequency:* 4 times a year; ISSN: 0826-9521
Metta Spencer, Chair
Verda McDonald, Treasurer

Printing & Publishing

Devil's Artisan: A Journal of the Printing Arts
c/o The Porcupine's Quill, 68 Main St., Erin, ON N0B 1T0
Tel: 519-833-9158; *Fax:* 519-833-9845
pql@sentex.net
www.sentex.net/~pql
Circulation: 800 *Frequency:* 2 times a year; ISSN: 0225-7874
Tim Inkster, Publisher
Don McLeod, Editor

Religious & Denominational

The Anglican
135 Adelaide St. East, Toronto, ON M5C 1L8
Tel: 416-363-6021; *Fax:* 416- -
Frequency: Monthly
Stuart Mann, Editor

Anglican Journal
c/o Anglican Church of Canada, 80 Hayden St., Toronto, ON M4Y 3G2
Tel: 416-924-9192; *Fax:* 416-921-4452
editor@national.anglican.ca
www.anglicanjournal.com
Circulation: 215,000 *Frequency:* 10 times a year
Steven Brickenden, Editorial Assistant
Leanne Larmontoin, Editor

BC Christian News
#200, 20316 - 56th Ave., Langley, BC V3A 3Y7
Tel: 604-534-1444; *Fax:* 604-534-2970
admin@canadianchristianity.com
www.canadianchristianity.com
Circulation: 37,000 *Frequency:* Monthly
Flyn Ritchie, Publisher & Editor, editor@canadianchristianity.com
David Dawes, Managing Editor, ddawes@canadianchristianity.com

Canada Lutheran
#302, 393 Portage Ave., Winnipeg, MB R3B 3H6
Tel: 204-984-9172; *Fax:* 204-984-9185
Toll-Free: 888-786-6707
canaluth@elcic.ca
www.elcic.ca
Circulation: 14,000 *Frequency:* 8 times a year
Trina Gallop, Managing Editor

Canadian Jewish News
#205, 1500 Don Mills Rd., Toronto, ON M4B 3K8
Tel: 416-391-1836; *Fax:* 416-391-0949
www.cjnews.com
Circulation: 50,000 *Frequency:* Weekly
Mordechai Ben-Dat, Editor
Gary Laforet, General Manager

Canadian Mennonite
#C5, 490 Dutton Dr., Waterloo, ON N2L 6H7
Tel: 519-884-3810; *Fax:* 519-884-3331
Toll-Free: 800-378-2524
editor@canadianmennonite.org
canadianmennonite.org
Circulation: 17,000 *Frequency:* 24 times a year
Timothy Miller Dyck, Editor

The Canadian Messenger
c/o Jesuit Fathers, 661 Greenwood Ave., Toronto, ON M4J 4B3
Tel: 416-466-1195; *Fax:* 416- -
Circulation: 14,000 *Frequency:* 11 times a year
Rev. F.J. Power, Editor

Catholic Insight
PO Box 625 Adelaide, 31 Adelaide St. East, Toronto, ON M5C 2J8
Tel: 416-204-9601; *Fax:* 416-204-1027
reach@catholicinsight.com
www.catholicinsight.com
Circulation: 3,700 *Frequency:* 11 times a year; ISSN: 1192-5671
Fr. Alphonse de Valk, Publisher

Catholic New Times
80 Sackville St., Toronto, ON M5A 3E5
Tel: 416-361-0761; *Fax:* 416-361-0796
editor@catholicnewtimes.org
www.catholicnewtimes.org
Frequency: 20 times a year
Diane Bisson, Publisher/Editor

The Catholic Register
#401, 1155 Yonge St., Toronto, ON M4T 1W2
Tel: 416-934-3410; *Fax:* 416-934-3409
news@catholicregister.org
www.catholicregister.org
Circulation: 33,000 *Frequency:* 47 times a year
Joseph Sinasac, Editor

Christian Courier
c/o Reformed Faith Witness, 1 Hiscott St., St Catharines, ON L2R 1C7
Tel: 905-682-8311; *Fax:* 905-682-8313
Toll-Free: 800-969-4838
editor@christiancourier.ca
www.christiancourier.ca
Circulation: 3,500 *Frequency:* Bi-weekly
Harry DerNederlanden, Editor-in-chief

ChristianCurrent
PO Box 725, Winnipeg, MB R3C 2K3
Tel: 204-982-2060; *Fax:* 204-947-5632
www.christiancurrent.com
Brian Koldyk, Publisher
Robert White, Managing Editor

ChristianWeek
#204, 424 Logan Ave., Winnipeg, MB R3A 0R4
Tel: 204-982-2060; *Fax:* 204-947-5632
Toll-Free: 800-263-6695
admin@christianweek.org
www.christianweek.org
Circulation: 5,000 *Frequency:* Every other Tue., except every 3 weeks in Dec.
Doug Koop, Editorial Director

Clarion
1 Beghin Ave., Winnipeg, MB R2J 3X5
Tel: 204-663-9000; *Fax:* 204-633-9202
premier@premierprinting.ca
www.premierprinting.ca
Circulation: 3,000 *Frequency:* Bi-weekly
W. Gortemaker, Publisher

Edmonton Jewish Life
7200 - 156 St. NW, Edmonton, AB T5R 1X3
Tel: 780-488-7276; *Fax:* 780-484-4978
ejlife@shaw.ca
Circulation: 1,500 *Frequency:* Monthly
John Bresler, Publisher
Neil Loomer, Editor

Edmonton Jewish News
#300, 10036 Jasper Ave., Edmonton, AB T5J 2W2
Tel: 780-421-7966; *Fax:* 780-424-3951
Circulation: 2,000
David Moser, Publisher

Faith Today
c/o The Evangelical Fellowship of Canada, PO Box 3745, Markham, ON L3R 0Y4
Tel: 905-479-5885; *Fax:* 905-479-4742
ft@efc-canada.com
www.faithtoday.ca
Circulation: 20,000 *Frequency:* 6 times a year
Gail Reid, Managing Editor
Bruce Clemenger, Publisher

Gospel Herald
c/o Gospel Herald Foundation, 4904 King St., Beamsville, ON L0R 1B6
Tel: 905-563-7503; *Fax:* 905-563-7503
Toll-Free: 866-722-2264
maxc@strathmorecofc.ca
www.gospelherald.org
Circulation: 1,320 *Frequency:* Monthly
Wayne Turner, Editor
Max E. Craddock, Managing Editor

Huron Church News
190 Queens Ave., London, ON N6A 6H7
Tel: 519-434-6893; *Fax:* 519-673-4151
Bishop Bruce Howe, Publisher
David Parson, Editor

Island Catholic News
PO Box 5424 LCD 9, Victoria, BC V8R 6S4
Tel: 250-727-9420; *Fax:* 250-727-3647
icn@islandnet.com
Circulation: 2,000 *Frequency:* Monthly
Marnie Butler, Senior Editor
Patrick Jamieson, Managing Editor

Jewish Free Press
8411 Elbow Dr. SW, Calgary, AB T2V 1K8
Tel: 403-252-9423; *Fax:* 403-255-5640
jewishfp@telus.net
Circulation: 2,000 *Frequency:* Semi-monthly
Richard Bronstein, Publisher

The Jewish Tribune
15 Hove St., Toronto, ON M3H 4Y8
Tel: 416-633-6224; *Fax:* 416-630-2159
editor@jewishtribune.ca
www.jewishtribune.ca/TribuneV2/
Circulation: 60,000 *Frequency:* weekly
Norm Gordner, Editor

Living Light News
#200, 5306 - 89th St., Edmonton, AB T6E 5P9
Tel: 780-468-6397; *Fax:* 780-468-6872
shine@livinglightnews.org
www.livingnews.org
Circulation: 50,000 *Frequency:* Bi-Monthly
Jeff Caporale, Editor-in-chief

London Jewish Community News
536 Huron St., London, ON N5Y 4J5
Tel: 519-673-3310; *Fax:* 519-673-1161
Frequency: quarterly

Mennonite Brethren Herald
Canadian Mennonite Brethren Conference, 1310 Taylor Ave., Winnipeg, MB R2M 3Z6
Tel: 204-654-5760; *Fax:* 204-654-1865
Toll-Free: 888-669-6575
mbherald@mbconf.ca
www.mbherald.com
Circulation: 17,500 *Frequency:* Monthly
Dora Dueck, Assistant Editor
Laura Kalmar, Editor
Helga Kasdorf, Manager, Circulation & Advertising

The New Brunswick Anglican
773 Glengarry Place, Fredericton, NB E3B 5Z8
Tel: 506-459-5358; *Fax:* 506- -
awatts@nbnet.nb.ca
fredericton.anglican.org
Circulation: 10,000 *Frequency:* 10 times a year
Rt. Rev. Claude Miller, Publisher

The New Freeman
1 Bayard Dr., Saint John, NB E2L 3L5
Tel: 506-653-6806; *Fax:* 506-653-6818
tnf@nbnet.nb.ca
Circulation: 7,480 *Frequency:* Weekly
Margie Trafton, Editor

Niagara Anglican
c/o Anglican Diocese of Niagara, Cathedral Place, 252 James St. North, Hamilton, ON L8R 2L3
Tel: 905-573-0962; *Fax:* 905- -
dihutton@mountaincable.com
Circulation: 16,175 *Frequency:* Monthly exc. July & Aug.
Christopher Grabiec, Editor

L'Oratoire / The Oratory
3800, ch Queen Mary, Montréal, QC H3V 1H6
Tel: 514-733-8211; *Fax:* 514-733-9735
revue@osj.qc.ca
www.saint-joseph.org
Circulation: 7,500 English; 42,000 French *Frequency:* 6 fois par an; français
Nathalie Dumas, Rédactrice-en-chef

Ottawa Jewish Bulletin
21 Nadolny Sachs, Ottawa, ON K2A 1R9
Tel: 613-798-4696; *Fax:* 613-798-4730
bulletin@jccottawa.com
www.ottawajewishbulletin.com
Circulation: 2,500 *Frequency:* 19 times a year

Outlook
#3, 6184 Ash St., Vancouver, BC V5Z 3G9
Tel: 604-324-5101; *Fax:* 604-325-2470
outlook@vcn.bc.ca
www.vcn.bc.ca/outlook/
Frequency: 6 times a year; ISSN: 0834-0242
Carl Rosenberg, Editor-in-chief

Prairie Messenger
Benedictine Monks of St. Peter's Abbey, PO Box 190, Muenster, SK S0K 2Y0
Tel: 306-682-1772; *Fax:* 306-682-5285
pm.ads@stpeterspress.ca
www.stpeters.sk.ca/prairie_messenger
Circulation: 7,000 *Frequency:* 46 times a year
Rev. Peter Novecosky, Editor OSB

Presbyterian Record
50 Wynford Dr., Toronto, ON M3C 1J7
Tel: 416-441-1111; *Fax:* 416-441-2825
Toll-Free: 800-619-7301
record@presbyterianrecord.ca
www.presbyterianrecord.ca
Circulation: 42,000 *Frequency:* Monthly exc. Aug.
David Harris, Editor

Présence Magazine
2715, ch Côte Ste-Catherine, Montréal, QC H3T 1B6
Tel: 514-739-9797; *Fax:* 514-739-1664
presence@presencemag.qc.ca
www.presencemag.qc.ca
Circulation: 2,000 *Frequency:* 8 times a year
Marie-Thérèse Guilbault, Editor-in-chief
Gilles Leblanc, Director

Shalom
#508, 5670 Spring Garden Rd., Halifax, NS B3J 1H6
Tel: 902-422-7491; *Fax:* 902-425-3722
atlanticjewishcouncil@theajc.ns.ca
www.theajc.ns.ca
Circulation: 1,400 *Frequency:* 3 times a year
Jon Goldberg, Editor

Studies in Religion / Sciences Religieuses
#347 Arts, University of Alberta, Edmonton, AB T6G 2E6
Tel: 780-492-2879; *Fax:* 780-492-2715
willi.braun@ualberta.ca
www.ccsr.ca
Circulation: 1,400 *Frequency:* 4 times a year
Marc Dumas, Editor-in-chief
Willi Braun, Managing Editor

Sunday Magazine
PO Box 53529, PO Box 53529, Broadmead RPO, Victoria, BC V8X 5K2
Tel: 250-592-6026; *Fax:* 250-592-8217
Toll-Free: 877-992-6071
info@sundaymagazine.org
www.sundaymagazine.org
Circulation: 11,000
Tony Reynolds, Publisher & Editor

Testimony
The Penetecostal Assemblies of Canada, 2450 Milltower Ct., Mississauga, ON L5N 5Z6
Tel: 905-542-7400; *Fax:* 905-542-7313
testimony@paoc.org
www.paoc.org/testimony
Circulation: 14,000 *Frequency:* Monthly
Stacey McKenzie, Editor

The United Church Observer
478 Huron St., Toronto, ON M5R 2R3
Tel: 416-960-8500; *Fax:* 416-960-8477
general@ucobserver.org
www.ucobserver.org
Circulation: 80,000 *Frequency:* 11 times a year; ISSN: 0041-7238
Muriel Duncan, Editor

La Voix Sépharade
#216, 1, carré Cummings, Montréal, QC H3W 1M6
Tél: 514-733-4998; *Téléc:* 514-733-3158
info@csq.qc.ca
Frequency: 5 fois par an
Élie Benchetrit, Directeur
Daniel N. Sebban, Rédacteur-en-chef

The War Cry
2 Overlea Blvd., Toronto, ON M4H 1P4
Tel: 416-422-6117; *Fax:* 416-422-6120
warcry@can.salvationarmy.org
warcry.salvationarmy.ca
Circulation: 20,000 *Frequency:* Monthly
Maj. Ken Smith, Editor

Western Catholic Reporter
8421 - 101 Ave., Edmonton, AB T6A 0L1
Tel: 780-465-8030; *Fax:* 780-465-8031
wcr@wcr.ab.ca
www.wcr.ab.ca
Circulation: 37,015 *Frequency:* 44 times a year
Glen Argan, Managing Editor

Science, Research & Development

Découvrir: La revue de la recherche
425, rue de la Gauchetière est, Montréal, QC H2L 2M7
Tél: 514-849-0045; *Téléc:* 514-849-5558
decouvrir@acfas.ca
www.acfas.ca/decouvrir
Circulation: 10 000 *Frequency:* 6 fois par an; français
Danielle Ouellet, Éditrice & Rédactrice

Québec Science
#300, 4388, rue St-Denis, Montréal, QC H2J 2L1
Tél: 514-843-6888; *Téléc:* 514-843-4897
courrier@quebecscience.qc.ca
www.cybersciences.com
Circulation: 32 000 *Frequency:* 10 fois par an; français
Raymond Lemieux, Rédacteur-en-chef

Spectre Magazine
#259, 7400, boul St-Laurent, Montréal, QC H2R 2Y1
Tel: 514-948-6422; *Fax:* 514-948-6423
diane.apsq@videotron.ca
www.apsq.org
Circulation: 3,000
Diane Poulin, Editor-in-chief

Social Welfare

Canadian Social Work & CASW Bulletin / Travail social canadien et Bulletin de l'ACTS
Myropen Publications Ltd., #402, 383 Parkdale Ave., Ottawa, ON K1Y 4R4
Tel: 613-729-6668; *Fax:* 613-729-9608
casw@casw-acts.ca
www.casw-acts.ca
Circulation: 16,000 *Frequency:* English/French; 3 times a year
Eugenia Repetur Moreno, Executive Director

Community Action: Canada's Community Service Newspaper
41 Marbury Cres., Toronto, ON M3A 2G3
Tel: 416-449-6766; *Fax:* 416-444-5850
Circulation: 12,010 *Frequency:* 11 times a year
Leon Kumove, Publisher

Human Rights TRIBUNE
#301, One Nicholas St., Ottawa, ON K1N 7B7
Tel: 613-789-7407; *Fax:* 613-789-7414
tribune@hri.ca
www.hri.ca/tribune
Circulation: 2,000 *Frequency:* 3 times a year; ISSN: 1192-3822
Gemma Richardson, Editor

Perception
Canadian Council on Social Development, #100, 190 O'Connor St., Ottawa, ON K2P 2R3
Tel: 613-236-8977; *Fax:* 613-236-2750
council@ccsd.ca
www.ccsd.ca
Frequency: 2 times a year; English & French
Nancy Perkins, Communications Coordinator

WhyNot Magazine
Canadian Foundation for Physically Disabled Persons, 731 Runnymede Ave., Toronto, ON M6N 3V7
Tel: 416-760-7351; *Fax:* 416-760-9405
whynot@sympatico.ca
www.cfpdp.com
Frequency: 3 times a year
Bill McQuat, Editor
Vim Kochhar, Publisher
Larry Allen, Editor

Sports & Recreation

Athletics: Canada's National Track & Field/Running Magazine
#211, 3 Concorde Gate, Toronto, ON M3C 3N7
Tel: 416-426-7215; *Fax:* 416-426-7358
ontrack@eol.ca
www.otfa.ca
Circulation: 4,000 *Frequency:* 8 times a year; ISSN 0229-4966
John Craig, Editor
Cecil Smith, Managing Director

Atlantic Snowmobiler
#510, 527 Beaverbrook Ct., Fredericton, NB E3B 1X6
Tel: 506-444-6489; *Fax:* 506-444-6453
Circulation: 20,000 *Frequency:* 4 times a year
Terrence D. Kehoe, Publisher

BC Hockey Now
#300, 92 Lonsdale Ave., North Vancouver, BC V7M 2E6
Tel: 604-990-1432; *Fax:* 604-990-1433
www.bchockey.com
Frequency: 18 times a year; also Alberta Hockey Now & Ontario Hockey Now
Don McIntosh, Publisher, dmcintosh@hockeynow.ca
Andrew Chong, Editor, andrewchong@hockeynow.ca

Below the Belt Boxing Magazine
#1712, 1478 Pilgrims Way, Oakville, ON L6M 3G7
Tel: 416-336-1947;
dameon@belowthebelt.tv
www.belowthebelt.tv

Canadian Cyclist
7 Barker St., Paris, ON N3L 2H4
Tel: 519-442-7905; *Fax:* 519-442-5259
news@canadiancyclist.com
www.canadiancyclist.com
Circulation: 8,000
Tracy Harkness, Publisher
Robert Jones, Editor

Canadian Rodeo News
#223, 2116 - 27 Ave. NE, Calgary, AB T2E 7A6
Tel: 403-250-7292; *Fax:* 403-250-6926
editor@rodeocanada.com
www.rodeocanada.com
Circulation: 4,000 *Frequency:* Monthly
Darell Hartlen, Editor

Diver Magazine
241 East 1st St., North Vancouver, BC V7K 1B4
Tel: 604-988-0711; *Fax:* 604-988-0747
mail@divermag.com
www.divermag.com
Circulation: 7,000 *Frequency:* 8 times a year
Phil Nuytten, Publisher
Virginia Cowell, Editor

Flagstick Golf Magazine
8197 Parkway Rd., Metcalfe, ON K0A 2P0
Tel: 613-821-0888; *Fax:* 613-821-4888
info@flagstick.com
www.flagstick.com
Circulation: 20,000 *Frequency:* 6 times a year
Jeff Bauder, Publisher

Golf Guide
16410 - 137 Ave., Edmonton, AB T5L 4H8
Tel: 780-447-2128; *Fax:* 780-447-1933
Frequency: Annually, April
Paul McCracken, Publisher

Golf International
c/o Media Transcontinental, 1100, boul René Lévesque ouest, 24e étage, Montréal, QC H3B 4X9
Tél: 514-392-9000; *Téléc:* 514-392-1489
Ligne sans frais: 800-361-5479
www.transcontinental-gtc.com
Circulation: 40 000 *Frequency:* 6 fois par an; français
Luc Desjardins, President & CEO

Golf West
Tel: 250-426-7253; *Fax:* 250-426-4125
Toll-Free: 800-663-8555
info@kpimedia.com
www.mygolfwest.com
Circulation: 30,000 *Frequency:* Annually, Spring
Jooy Jacob, Writer
Keith G. Powell, Publisher
Amber Cowie, Writer

Hockey News
Transcontinental Media Inc., #100, 25 Sheppard Ave. West, Toronto, ON M2N 6S7
Tel: 416-227-8237; *Fax:* 416-340-2786
Circulation: 103,350 *Frequency:* 42 times a year
Gerald McGroarty, Publisher & Editor-in-chief

Hot Sled
#5, 1020 Brevik Pl., Mississauga, ON L4W 4N7
Tel: 905-624-8218; *Fax:* 905-624-6764
info@hotsled.com
www.hotsled.com
Circulation: 75,000
William E. Taylor, Publisher

Le Journal Québec Quilles / Bowling Québec
CP 126 Anjou, Montréal, QC H1L 4N7
Tél: 514-351-5224; *Téléc:* 514-351-6818
qcquilles@videotron.ca
Frequency: 5 fois par an; français
Yves Larocque, Éditeur

The Leader
#100, 1345 Baseline Rd., Ottawa, ON K2C 0A7
Tel: 613-224-5131; *Fax:* 613-224-5982
smuehlherr@scouts.ca
www.scouts.ca
Circulation: 38,000 *Frequency:* 10 times a year; ISSN: 0711-5377
Susan Muehlherr, Executive Editor

MARCHE-Randonnée
CP 1000 M, 4545, ave. Pierre-De Coubertin, Montréal, QC H1V 3R2
Tél: 514-252-3157; *Téléc:* 514-252-5137
Ligne sans frais: 866-252-2065
revuemarche@fqmarche.qc.ca
www.fqmarche.qc.ca/revue.asp
Circulation: 8 225 *Frequency:* 4 fois par an
Raymond Dulude, Advertising
Daniel Pouplot, Production Manager
Louise Giroux, Co-ordinatrice

Motoneige Québec
4545, av Pierre-de-Coubertin, Montréal, QC H1V 3R2
Tél: 514-252-3163; *Téléc:* 514-254-2066
michel.garneau@fcmq.qc.ca
Circulation: 60 000 *Frequency:* 4 fois par an; français
Michel Garneau, Directeur de la rédaction

MX Performance
593 Yonge St., Toronto, ON M4Y 1Z4
Tel: 416-922-7223; *Fax:* 416-922-8001
Frequency: Bi-monthly
Noel Simpson, Managing Editor

National Rugby Post
13228 - 76 St., Edmonton, AB T5C 1B6
Tel: 780-476-0268; *Fax:* 780-473-1066
hector@oanet.com
www.rugbypost.com
Circulation: 6,000 *Frequency:* 6 times a year
David C. Graham, Publisher

Northwestern Ontario Golfing News
Tel: 807-623-2348; *Fax:* 807-623-7515
nspinc@tbaytel.net
Circulation: 2,000 *Frequency:* 5 times a year
Scott Sumner, Publisher & Editor

Northwestern Ontario Snowmobile News
Tel: 807-623-2348; *Fax:* 807-623-7515
nspinc@tbaytel.net
Circulation: 2,000 *Frequency:* 7 times a year
Scott A. Summer, Publisher & Editor

Ontario Golf
Town Media, 1074 Cooke Blvd., Burlington, ON L7T 4A8
Tel: 905-634-8003; *Fax:* 905-634-7661
info@townmedia.ca
www.golfontario.ca
Circulation: 55,000 *Frequency:* 4 times a year
Wayne Narcisco, Publisher

Ontario Snowmobiler
78 Main St. South, Newmarket, ON L3Y 3Y6
Tel: 905-898-8585; *Fax:* 905-898-8071
Toll-Free: 888-661-7469
ontariosnowmobile@bellnet.ca
www.ontariosnowmobiler.com
Circulation: 70,000 *Frequency:* 5 times a year
Raymond D. Kehoe, Publisher
Terrence D. Kehoe, CEO

Ontario Tennis
Ontario Tennis Association, #200, 1 Shoreham Dr., Toronto, ON M3N 3A7
Tel: 416-514-1100; *Fax:* 416-514-1112
Toll-Free: 800-387-5066
ota@tennisontario.com
www.tennisontario.com
Circulation: 20,000 *Frequency:* 3 times a year

Outdoor Sportsman
PO Box 13754 A, 36 Pippy Pl., St. John's, NL A1B 4G5
Tel: 709-754-3515; *Fax:* 709-754-7490
customerservice@newfoundlandsportsman.com
newfoundlandsportsman.com
Circulation: 14,621 *Frequency:* 6 times a year
Dwight J. Blackwood, Publisher
Gordon Follett, Editor

Pacific Golf Magazine
Tel: 604-299-7311; *Fax:* 604-299-9188
cwm@canadawide.com
www.canadawide.com
Circulation: 25,000 *Frequency:* 4 times a year
Peter Legge, Publisher
Stephen Thomas, General Sales Manager

Pedal Magazine
#703, 317 Adelaide St. West, Toronto, ON M5V 1P9
Tel: 416-977-2100; *Fax:* 416-977-9200
info@pedalmag.com
www.pedalmag.com
Circulation: 18,000 *Frequency:* 6 pa; ISSN: 1191-2685
Benjamin Sadavoy, Publisher & Editor

Physical Education Digest
11 Cerilli Cres., Sudbury, ON P3E 5R3
Fax: 705-523-3331
Toll-Free: 800-544-8782
pedigest@cyberbeach.net
www.pedigest.com
Circulation: online only *Frequency:* website database
Dick Moss, Publisher

Québec Soccer
6900, rue St-Denis, 3e étage, Montréal, QC H2S 2S2
Tél: 514-278-6399; *Téléc:* 514-278-9737
journal@quebecsoccer.com
www.quebecsoccer.com
Circulation: 40 000 *Frequency:* 12 fois par an; français
Pascal Cifarelli, Publisher
Matthias Van Halst, Editor-in-chief

SBC Skateboard Magazine
#3266, 2255B Queen St. East, Toronto, ON M4E 1G3
Tel: 416-406-2400; *Fax:* 416-406-0656
info@sbcskateboard.com
www.sbcskateboard.com
Circulation: 25,000 *Frequency:* 5 times a year
Steve Jarrett, Publisher
Ryan Stutt, Managing Editor

SCORE - Canada's Golf Magazine
Tel: 416-928-2909; *Fax:* 416-928-1181
Toll-Free: 800-320-6420
info@scoregolf.com
www.scoregolf.com
Circulation: 142,438 *Frequency:* 6 times a year
Bob Weeks, Managing Editor
Kim Locke, Publisher

SCORE Golf for Women
Tel: 416-928-2909; *Fax:* 416-966-1181
Frequency: Annually

SCORE Golf Québec
#101, 5397 Eglinton Ave. West, Toronto, ON M9C 5K6
Tél: 416-928-2909; *Téléc:* 416-966-1181
scoresls@idirect.com
Circulation: 35,000 *Frequency:* 4 fois par an
Peter Robinson, Editor, robinson@scoregolf.com
Kim Locke, Publisher

Ski Canada
47 Soho Sq., Toronto, ON M5T 2Z2
Tel: 416-595-1252; *Fax:* 416-595-7255
Toll-Free: 888-666-9754
info@skicanadamag.com
www.skicanadamag.com
Circulation: 40,733 *Frequency:* 6 times a year
Iain MacMillan, Editor
Paul Green, Publisher

Ski Press/Ski Presse
1395, rue Marie-Victorin, Saint-Bruno, QC J3V 6B7
Tél: 450-653-1033; *Téléc:* 450-653-1038
Ligne sans frais: 888-854-3121
info@skipressmag.com
www.skipressworld.com
Circulation: 182,000 *Frequency:* 4 times a year
Jean Marc Blais, Publisher
Jules Older, Editor-in-chief, English version

Ski& Ride West
Tel: 250-426-7253; *Fax:* 250-426-4125
Toll-Free: 800-663-8555
info@kpimedia.com
www.koocanusapublications.com
Circulation: 30,000 *Frequency:* Annually, Fall

Jeff Cummings, Editor
Keith G. Powell, Publisher

SkiTrax
#703, 317 Adelaide St. West, Toronto, ON M5V 1P9
Tel: 416-977-2100; *Fax:* 416-977-9200
info@skitrax.com
www.skitrax.com
Circulation: 30,000 *Frequency:* 4 times a year; ISSN: 1191-2677
Benjamin Sadavoy, Publisher

Sno Riders West
Tel: 250-426-7253; *Fax:* 250-426-4125
Toll-Free: 800-663-8555
info@kpimedia.com
www.snoriderswest.com; www.riderswestmag.com
Frequency: 5 times a year; fall (41,000), winter (30,000), mid-winter (32,000), spring (32,000), summer (32,000)
Jeff Cummings, Editor
Keith G. Powell, Publisher

Snowboard Canada Magazine
SBC Media, #3266, 2255B Queen St. East, Toronto, ON M4E 1G3
Tel: 416-406-2400; *Fax:* 416-406-0656
info@snowboardcanada.com
Circulation: 73,000 *Frequency:* 4 times a year
Steve Jarrett, Publisher

Sporting Scene
22 Maberley Cres., West Hill, ON M1C 3K8
Tel: 416-284-0304;
sportingscene@yahoo.com
Circulation: 24,000 *Frequency:* 11 times a year
Peter Martens, Publisher & Editor-in-chief

Squash Life
c/o Squash Ontario, 1185 Eglinton Ave. East, Toronto, ON M3C 3C6
Tel: 416-426-7201; *Fax:* 416-426-7393
www.squashontario.com
Circulation: 5,000 *Frequency:* 3 times a year
Sherry Funston, Executive Director & Managing Editor

Supertrax International
#187, 762 Upper James St., Hamilton, ON L9C 3A2
Tel: 905-286-2135; *Fax:* 905-286-6308
info@supertraxmag.com
www.supertraxmag.com
Circulation: 76,520 *Frequency:* 4 times a year; English & French
Mark Lester, Publisher
Kent Lester, Executive Editor

Sweep! Curling's Magazine
#12, 6655 Kitimat Rd., Mississauga, ON L5N 6J4
Tel: 905-542-0539; *Fax:* 905-567-8920
sweep@sweepmag.com
www.sweepmag.com
Circulation: 8,000 *Frequency:* 6 times a year
Bob Garvin, Editor

Swim News
356 Sumach St., Toronto, ON M4X 1V4
Tel: 416-963-5599; *Fax:* 416- -
swimnews@swimnews.com
www.swimnews.com
Circulation: 4,300 *Frequency:* 10 times a year
N.J. Thierry, Publisher

Volleyball Canada Magazine
#202, 5510 Canotek Rd., Gloucester, ON K1J 9J5
Tel: 613-748-5681; *Fax:* 613-748-5727
info@volleyball.ca
www.volleyball.ca
Circulation: 35,000 *Frequency:* 4 times a year
Greg Smith, Publisher

Wakeboard SBC Magazine
#3266, 2255B Queen St. East, Toronto, ON M4E 1G3
Tel: 416-406-2400; *Fax:* 416-406-0656
info@sbcmedia.com
www.sbcmedia.com
Circulation: 36,000 *Frequency:* 2 times a year
Steve Jarrett, Publisher

WaveLength Magazine
1773 El Verano Dr., Gabriola Island, BC V0R 1X6
Tel: 250-247-9093; *Fax:* 250-247-9083
Toll-Free: 800-668-8806
RMumford@WavelengthMagazine.com
www.wavelengthmagazine.com
Circulation: 22,000 *Frequency:* 6 times a year
Ron Mumford, Publisher

Diana Mumford, Editor

Television, Radio, Video & Home Appliances

Audio Ideas Guide
#12, 860 Dufferin St., King City, ON L7B 1K5
Tel: 905-833-7177; *Fax:* 905-833-7178
mail@audio-ideas.on.ca
www.audio-ideas.com
Frequency: Quarterly
Andrew Marshall, Editor/Publisher, andrew@audio-ideas.com

The Brandon Sun TV Book
501 Rosser Ave., Brandon, MB R7A 5Z6
Tel: 204-727-2451; *Fax:* 204-725-0976
Circulation: 14,843 *Frequency:* Weekly
Bill Chester, General Manager

Feature (Your Premium Entertainment Magazine)
Tel: 514-939-5024; *Fax:* 514-939-8027
editor@feature.ca
www.featuremagazine.com
Circulation: 930,000 *Frequency:* Monthly
Marvin Boisvert, Publisher
David Sherman, Editor

Globe Television
Globe & Mail, 444 Front St. West, Toronto, ON M5V 2S9
Tel: 416-585-5567; *Fax:* 416-585-5599
Frequency: Weekly
Andrew Ryan, Editor

The Inner Ear Report
Disticor Magazines, #14, 695 Westney Rd. South, Ajax, ON L1S 6M9
Tel: 905-619-6565; *Fax:* 905-619-2903
Circulation: 16,000 *Frequency:* 4 times a year

Post TV
The National Post Company, 1450 Don Mills Rd., Toronto, ON M3B 3R5
Tel: 416-383-2300; *Fax:* 416-442-2212
Circulation: 104,000 *Frequency:* 52 times a year

Primeurs
Tél: 514-939-5024; *Téléc:* 514-939-8027
editor@feature.ca
www.featuremagazine.com
Circulation: 409 000 *Frequency:* Mensuel; français
Marvin Boisvert, Éditeur
Mireille Duhamel, Rédactrice
Nathalie Abitbol, Directrice de tirage

StarWeek Magazine
c/o Toronto Star, One Yonge St., Toronto, ON M5E 1E6
Tel: 416-869-4244; *Fax:* 416-869-4103
Circulation: 645,181 *Frequency:* Weekly
Gord Stimmell, Editor

Sunday Sun Television Magazine
Calgary Sun, 2615 - 12 St. NE, Calgary, AB T2E 7W9
Tel: 403-250-4220; *Fax:* 403-250-4258
Circulation: 63,794 *Frequency:* Weekly
Guy Huntingford, Publisher
Chris Nelson, Editor-in-chief

Sunday Sun Television Magazine
c/o Edmonton Sun, #250, 4990 - 92 Ave., Edmonton, AB T6B 3A1
Tel: 780-468-0100; *Fax:* 780-468-0233
Circulation: 95,860 *Frequency:* Weekly
Graham Delziel, Editor

Sunday Sun Television Magazine
c/o Ottawa Sun, 6 Antares Dr., Ottawa, ON K1G 5H7
Tel: 613-739-7000; *Fax:* 613- -
Circulation: 54,267 *Frequency:* Weekly
Rick Gibbons, Publisher

Sunday Sun Television Magazine
c/o Toronto Sun, 333 King St. East, Toronto, ON M5A 3X5
Tel: 416-947-2000; *Fax:* 416-947-2441
Circulation: 400,652 *Frequency:* Weekly

Télé Horaire
c/o Le Journal de Montréal, 4545, rue Frontenac, Montréal, QC H2H 2R7
Tél: 514-521-4545; *Téléc:* 514-525-5442
www.journalmtl.com
Circulation: 326 440 *Frequency:* Hebdomadaire; français
Raymond Fortin, Director, Special Projects & Sections

Télé Horaire (Québec)
c/o Le Journal de Québec, 450, rue Bechard, Vanier, QC G1M 2E9
Tél: 418-683-1573; *Téléc:* 418-683-1027
www.journaldequebec.com
Circulation: 126 689 *Frequency:* Hebdomadaire; français
Jean-Claude L'Abbée, Éditeur

Téléromans
Trustmedia, 7, ch Bates, Outremont, QC H2V 4V7
Tél: 514-848-7000; *Téléc:* 514-843-7079
Circulation: 46 000 *Frequency:* 2 fois par an; français
Clair Syril, Vice-President & General Manager

TV 7 Jours
Tél: 514-848-7164; *Téléc:* 514-270-7079
Circulation: 92 361 *Frequency:* Hebdomadaire; français

TV Guide
Transcontineal Media Inc., #100, 25 Sheppard Ave. West, Toronto, ON M2N 6S7
Tel: 416-733-7600; *Fax:* 416-733-3568
Toll-Free: 800-387-1163
www.tvguide.ca
Circulation: 281,955 *Frequency:* Weekly; ISSN: 1191-5315
Jamie Hubbard, Editor

TV Hebdo
Tél: 514-848-7000; *Téléc:* 514-270-7079
Circulation: 123 670 *Frequency:* Hebdomadaire
Claire Syril, Président

TV Scene, Fort McMurray
8550 Franklin Ave., Bag 4008, Fort McMurray, AB T9H 3G1
Tel: 780-743-8186; *Fax:* 780-790-1006
today@bowesnet.com
www.fortmcmurraytoday.com
Circulation: 8,205 *Frequency:* Weekly
Tim O'Rourke, Publisher

TV This Week
6 Louise St., Truro, NS B2N 5C3
Tel: 902-893-9405; *Fax:* 902-893-0518
Circulation: 11,000
Peter Padbury, Publisher

TV Times, Calgary
PO Box 2400 M, 215 - 16th St. SE, Calgary, AB T2P 0W8
Tel: 403-235-7100; *Fax:* 403-235-7379
www.calgaryherald.com
Circulation: 150,000

TV Times, Edmonton
10006 - 101 St., Edmonton, AB T5J 0S1
Tel: 780-429-5100; *Fax:* 780-429-5500
www.edmontonjournal.com
Circulation: 150,000
Linda Hughes, Publisher
Allan Mayer, Editor-in-chief

TV Times, St. Catharines
17 Queen St., St Catharines, ON L2R 5G5
Tel: 905-684-7251; *Fax:* 905-684-8011
Circulation: 44,600
Paul McCraig, Publisher

TV Times, Windsor
167 Ferry St., Windsor, ON N9A 4M5
Tel: 519-255-5711; *Fax:* 519-255-5515
Circulation: 87,275
Jim McCormack, Publisher

TV Week Magazine
4180 Lougheed Hwy., 4th Fl., Burnaby, BC V5C 6A7
Tel: 604-299-7311; *Fax:* 604-299-9188
Toll-Free: 800-663-0518
cwm@canadawide.com
www.canadawide.com
Circulation: 80,000 *Frequency:* Weekly
Peter Legge, Publisher
Brent Furdyk, Editor

TV Week Stratford
PO Box 430, 16 Packham Rd., Stratford, ON N5A 6T6
Tel: 519-271-2220; *Fax:* 519-271-1026
Toll-Free: 800-265-8577
jkastner@bowesnet.com
stratfordbeaconherald.com
Circulation: 11,475 *Frequency:* Weekly
John Kastner, Editor
Dave Carter, Publisher

TVOntario Magazine
TV Ontario, PO Box 200 Q, 2180 Yonge St., 5th Fl., Toronto, ON M4T 2T4
Tel: 416-484-2600; *Fax:* 416-484-6285
Frequency: 10 times a year
Angela Garde, Editor

Voila
c/o GESCA, 7, rue St-Jacques, Montréal, QC H2Y 1K9
Tél: 514-285-7306; *Téléc:* 514-845-8129
Frequency: Hebdomadaire; français

The Winnipeg Sun TV Magazine
1700 Church Ave., Winnipeg, MB R2X 3A2
Tel: 204-694-2022; *Fax:* 204-632-8709
wpgsun@wpgsun.com
Circulation: 44,337 *Frequency:* Weekly
Ed Huculak, Publisher

Travel

Above & Beyond Magazine
PO Box 13142, Kanata, ON K2K 1X3
Tel: 613-599-4190; *Fax:* 613-599-4191
Toll-Free: 877-227-2842
info@arcticjournal.ca
Circulation: 20,000 *Frequency:* 6 pa
Tom Koelbel, Publisher & Editor

Bear Country
1475 West Walsh St., Thunder Bay, ON P7E 4X6
Tel: 807-474-2636; *Fax:* 807-474-2658
pgresham@bearskinairlines.com
bearskinairlines.com
Circulation: 10,000 *Frequency:* 4 times a year
Patti Gresham, Production Manager & Editor

British Columbia Magazine
1803 Douglas St., 3rd Fl., Victoria, BC V8T 5C3
Tel: 250-356-5860; *Fax:* 250-356-5896
Toll-Free: 800-663-7611
orders@bcmag.ca
www.bcmag.ca
Other information: Toll Free Fax: 1-800-308-4533
Circulation: 125,000 *Frequency:* 4 times a year
Don Foxford, Publisher
Anita Willis, Editor, editor@bcmag.ca

Dreamscapes Travel & Lifestyle Magazine
3 Bluffwood Dr., Toronto, ON M2H 3L4
Tel: 416-497-5353; *Fax:* 416-497-0871
Toll-Free: 888-700-4464
gtm@ca.inter.net
www.dreamscapes.ca
Circulation: 110,000 *Frequency:* 8 times a year
Sandra Kitchen, Publisher
Donna Vieira, Editor
Joe Turkel, President & Group Publisher

Espaces
#205, 911, rue Jean-Talon est, Montréal, QC H2R 1V5
Tél: 514-277-3477; *Téléc:* 514-277-3822
info@espaces.qc.ca
www.espaces.qc.ca
Circulation: 50 000 *Frequency:* 6 times a year
Marie Eisenmann, Rédactrice en chef

Family Getaways
4242 Rockwood Rd., Mississauga, ON L4W 1L8
Tel: 905-272-1843; *Fax:* 905-272-0474
fun@ourkids.net
www.ourkids.net
Circulation: 100,000 *Frequency:* annual
Agatha Stawicki, Managing Editor

Geo Plein Air
Tél: 514-521-8356; *Téléc:* 514-521-5711
Ligne sans frais: 800-567-8356
geopleinair@velo.qc.ca
www.geopleinair.com
Circulation: 25 358 *Frequency:* 7 fois par an; français
Magazine québécois de la nature et de l'aventure
Pierre Hamel, Éditeur
Nathalie Schneider, Rédactrice en chef

Great Getaways Guide
Vancouver, Coast & Mountains Tourism, #250, 1508 West 2nd Ave., Vancouver, BC V6J 1H2
Tel: 604-739-9011; *Fax:* 604-739-0153
Toll-Free: 800-667-3306
info@vcmbc.com
www.vcmbc.com/greatgetaways/
Jennifer Huitema, Director, Communications

Greater Halifax Visitor Guide
1300 Hollis St., Halifax, NS B3J 1T6
Tel: 902-420-9943; *Fax:* 902-429-9058
publishers@metroguide.ca
www.metroguidepublishing.ca
Circulation: 240,000 *Frequency:* Annually
Sheila Blair, Publisher

HolidayMaker
Wild Boar Publications, PO Box 10, 23260 - 88 Ave., Fort Langley, BC V1M 2R4
Tel: 604-888-4037; *Fax:* 604-888-6663
holidaymaker@telus.net
www.cwtleisure.ca/holidaymaker/
Circulation: 86,500 *Frequency:* 2 times a year
Chris Potter, Publisher & Editor

Horizon Travel Magazine
#303, 65 Front St. East, Toronto, ON M5E 1B5
Tel: 416-603-8900; *Fax:* 416-603-8901
horizon@horizontravelmag.com
www.horizontravelmag.com
Frequency: 6 times a year
Amir Shirazi, Publisher
Denise Shirazi, Editor-in-chief

Key to Kingston
Osprey Media, PO Box 1352, 11 Princess St., Kingston, ON K7L 5C6
Tel: 613-549-8442; *Fax:* 613-549-4333
Circulation: 22,500 *Frequency:* 8 pa
Mary Laflamme, Publisher

The Laurentians Tourist Guide / Les Laurentides Guide Touristique
#14, 142, rue de la Chapelle, Mirabel, QC J7J 2C8
Tel: 450-436-8532; *Fax:* 450-436-5309
info-tourisme@laurentides.com
www.laurentides.com
Circulation: 73,000, English edition; 202,000, French edition
Frequency: Annually; English & French editions
Diane Leblond, General Manager

müv
#202, 3863, boul Saint-Laurent, Montréal, QC H2W 1Y1
Tél: 514-286-9696; *Téléc:* 514-284-9152
info@muvmag.com
www.muvmag.com
Frequency: 4 fois par an
Julie Boisvert, Rédactrice-en-chef

99 North Magazine
4180 Lougheed Hwy., Burnaby, BC V5C 6A7
Tel: 604-299-7311; *Fax:* 604-299-9188
cwm@canadawide.com
www.canadawide.com
Circulation: 100,000 *Frequency:* 2 times a year
Samantha Legge, General Manager

Outpost: Canada's Travel Magazine
#201, 425 Queen St. West, Toronto, ON M5V 2A5
Tel: 416-972-6527; *Fax:* 416-972-6645
www.outpostmagazine.com
Circulation: 28,000 *Frequency:* Bi-monthly
Matthew Robinson, Publisher
Larry Frolick, Editor

Presse Voyages
19, rue La Gallois, Gatineau, QC J8V 2H3
Tel: 819-246-9855;
tvcanada@videotron.ca
Circulation: 5,000 *Frequency:* Bi-monthly
Ynes De Lara, Publisher

La Revue Voil à Québec
#201, 735, boul. Wilfrid-Hamel, Québec, QC G1M 2R1
Tél: 418-694-1272; *Téléc:* 418-694-1119
Ligne sans frais: 888-694-1272
Circulation: 265 000
Curtis J. Sommerville, Éditeur
Lynn Magee, Rédactrice-en-chef

Rocky Mountain Visitor's Magazine
Tel: 250-426-7253; *Fax:* 250-426-4125
Toll-Free: 800-663-8555
info@kpimedia.com
koocanusapublications.com
Circulation: 40,000 May; 30,000 Nov. *Frequency:* Semi-annually
Jeff Cummings, Editor
Keith G. Powell, Publisher

Saskatchewan Vacation Guide
Tourism Saskatchewan, 1922 Park St., Regina, SK S4P 3V7
Tel: 306-787-9685; *Fax:* 306-787-0715
Toll-Free: 877-237-2273
www.sasktourism.com
Circulation: 195,000 *Frequency:* annually

The Travel Society Magazine
#218, 1033 Bay St., Toronto, ON M5S 3A5
Tel: 416-926-0111; *Fax:* 416-926-0222
brit@thetravelsociety.com
www.thetravelsociety.com
Circulation: 7,000
Nigel D. Raincock, Publisher
Ann Wallace, Editor

Where Canadian Rockies
#250, 125 - 9 Ave. SE, Calgary, AB T2G 0P6
Tel: 403-299-1897; *Fax:* 403-299-1899
info@whererockies.com
www.wherecanadianrockies.com
Circulation: 240,000 summer; 145,000 winter *Frequency:* 2 pa; English with some Japanese
Jack Newton, Publisher

Where Vancouver
2208 Spruce St., Vancouver, BC V6H 2P3
Tel: 604-736-5586; *Fax:* 604-736-3465
infovancouver@where.ca
www.where.ca
Circulation: 53,000 *Frequency:* Monthly
Peggie Terry, Publisher

Women's & Feminist

L'Actuelle
1043, rue Tiffin, Longueuil, QC J4P 3G7
Tél: 450-442-3983; *Téléc:* 450-442-4363
cerfer@videotron.ca
www.cfq.qc.ca
Circulation: 50 000 *Frequency:* 5 fois par an; français
Publication officielle des Cercles de Fermières du Québec

Canadian Guider
c/o Girl Guides of Canada, 50 Merton St., Toronto, ON M4S 1A3
Tel: 416-487-5281; *Fax:* 416-487-5570
bryantc@girlguides.ca
www.girlguides.ca
Circulation: 30,891 *Frequency:* 3 times a year
Deborah Del Duca

Canadian Woman Studies / Les Cahiers de la Femme
210 Founders College, York University, 4700 Keele St., Toronto, ON M3J 1P3
Tel: 416-736-5356; *Fax:* 416-736-5765
cwscf@yorku.ca
www.yorku.ca/cwscf
Circulation: 5,000 *Frequency:* 4 times a year; ISSN: 0713-3235
Luciana Ricciutelli, Editor

Chatelaine
1 Mount Pleasant Rd., 8th Fl., Toronto, ON M4Y 2Y5
Tel: 416-764-1888; *Fax:* 416-764-2891
Toll-Free: 800-268-6812
lise.ravary@chatelaine.com
www.chatelaine.com
Circulation: 675,016 *Frequency:* Monthly; ISSN 0009-1995
Sara Angel, Editor-in-Chief
Lise Ravary, Editorial Director

Châtelaine
Tél: 514-845-5141; *Téléc:* 514-843-2183
www.chatelaine.qc.ca
Circulation: 203 014 *Frequency:* Mensuel; français; ISSN: 0317-2635
Lise Ravary, Éditeur

City Woman Magazine
Capital Publishers, 226 Argyle St., Ottawa, ON K2E 6Z5
Tel: 613-230-0333; *Fax:* 613-230-4441
www.capitalpublishers.com
Circulation: 30,000 *Frequency:* 4 times a year
Dianne Wing
Steve Ball

Coup de Pouce
#900, 2001, rue University, Montréal, QC H3A 2A6
Tél: 514-499-0317; *Téléc:* 514-848-9779
www.transcontinental.com
Circulation: 228 071 *Frequency:* 12 fois par an; ISSN: 0822-3033

Francine Tremblay, Éditeur
France Lefebvre, Rédacteur-en-chef

Edmonton Woman
Tel: 780-424-1221; *Fax:* 780-421-7677
abrnews@shaw.ca
www.edmontonwoman.com
Circulation: 25,000 *Frequency:* 6 times a year
Lorne Silverstein, Publisher
Colin Smith, Editor-in-chief

elevate magazine
#1902, 365 Bloor St. East, Toronto, ON M4W 3L4
Tel: 416-869-3131; *Fax:* 416-869-3008
www.elevatemagazine.com
Brian Light, Publisher
Chantel Simmons, Editor-in-chief

Elle Canada
Transcontinental Media, #100, 25 Sheppard Ave. West, Toronto, ON M2N 6S7
Tel: 416-218-3604;
www.ellecanada.com
Jacqueline Howe, Publisher
Noreen Flanagan, Sr. Editor

Elle Québec
Publications Transcontinental-Hachette, #900, 2001, rue University, Montréal, QC H3A 2A6
Tél: 514-499-0491; *Téléc:* 514-848-9779
Circulation: 88 398 *Frequency:* Mensuel; français
Francine Tremblay, Éditrice
Sylvie Poirier, Rédactrice-en-chef

Femme d'Aujourd'hui
Tél: 514-848-7164; *Téléc:* 514-270-7079
Circulation: 47 000 *Frequency:* Mensuel; français
Sandra Cliche, Editorial Director

Femme Plus
Tél: 514-270-1100; *Téléc:* 514-270-7079
femmeplus@publicor.ca
Circulation: 52 204 *Frequency:* Mensuel; français
Claire Syril, Éditrice
Hélène Matteau, Directrice

FQ Magazine
134 Peter St., 3rd Fl., Toronto, ON M5V 2H2
Tel: 416-367-7664; *Fax:* 416-367-7659
Frequency: 5 times a year
Jeanne Beker, Editor-in-chief

Homemaker's Magazine / Madame
Transcontinental Media, #100, 25 Sheppard Ave. West, Toronto, ON M2N 6S7
Tel: 416-733-7600; *Fax:* 416-733-8683
Circulation: 512,000 *Frequency:* 8 times a year
Kathy Ullyott, Editor-in-chief

The Look
St. Joseph Media, #320, 111 Queen St. East, Toronto, ON M5C 1S2
Tel: 416-364-3333; *Fax:* 416-595-7217
thelook@thelookmagazine.ca
www.thelookmagazine.ca
Circulation: 199,718 *Frequency:* 4 times a year
David Livingstone, Editor-in-chief

Madame
Transcontinental Media, #900, 2001, rue Université, Montréal, QC H3A 2A6
Tél: 514-499-0317; *Téléc:* 514-848-9779
Circulation: 109 634 *Frequency:* 9 fois par année
Jean-Louis Gauthier, Rédacteur

Magazine les Ailes de la mode
Les Editions San Francisco inc., 50, rue de Lauzon, Boucherville, QC J4B 1E6
Tél: 450-449-1313; *Téléc:* 450-449-1317
Circulation: 29 751 *Frequency:* 6 fois par an
Claude Fortin, Éditeur
Julie Brisson, Rédactrice-en-chef
Camille Roberge, Rédactrice

Orah Magazine
Canadian Hadassah-WIZO, #900, 1310, av Greene, Westmount, QC H3Z 2B8
Tel: 514-937-9431; *Fax:* 514-933-6483
natoff@canadian-hadassah-wizo.org
www.canadian-hadassah-wizo.org
Circulation: 14,000 *Frequency:* 2 times a year
Rochelle Levinson, Editor-in-chief
Lily Frank, National Exec. Vice-President

Room of One's Own
PO Box 46160 D, Vancouver, BC V6J 5G5
contactus@roommagazine.com
www.roommagazine.com
Circulation: 1,100 *Frequency:* 4 times a year; ISSN: 0316-1609

Youth

The Canadian Leader
Canyouth Publications, #100, 1345 Baseline Rd., Ottawa, ON K2C 0A7
Tel: 613-224-5131; *Fax:* 613-224-3571
leader@scouts.ca
www.scouts.ca/leader
Circulation: 37,000 *Frequency:* 10 times a year
Ross Francis, Executive Editor

Cool! Le magazine qui bouge
Tél: 514-848-7164; *Téléc:* 514-270-7079
cool@tva-publications.com
Circulation: 62 000 *Frequency:* 12 fois par an
Marie-Claude Bonneau, Director

Fashion 18
St. Joseph Media, 111 Queen St. East, Toronto, ON M5C 1S2
Tel: 416-364-3333;
www.fashion18.com
Frequency: 4 times a year
Giorgina Bigioni, Publisher

Faze Magazine
#2400, 4936 Yonge St., Toronto, ON M2N 6S3
Tel: 416-222-3060; *Fax:* 416-222-2097
letters@fazeteen.com
www.fazeteen.com
Frequency: 5 times a year
Paul Zander, Publisher

Filles Clin d'oeil
Tél: 514-848-7000; *Téléc:* 514-270-7079
fillescool.canoe.com
Frequency: Mensuel; français

Filles d'aujourd'hui
7, Chemin Bates, Outremont, QC H2V 4V7
Tél: 514-270-1100; *Téléc:* 514-270-7079
fillesdaujourdhui@publicor.ca
tva.canoe.com
Circulation: 56 030 *Frequency:* Mensuel; français
Claire Sgril, Éditrice
Isabelle Jomphe, Rédactrice-en-chef
Francine Trudeau, Directrice

Fuel
#245, 401 Richmond St. West, Toronto, ON M5V 1X3
Tel: 416-595-1313; *Fax:* 416-595-1312
kay@youthculture.com
www.fuelpowered.com
Circulation: 119,268 *Frequency:* 7 times a year
Sara Graham, Editor

Magazine Adorable
#102, 50, rue Queen, Montréal, QC H3C 2N5
Tél: 514-761-0556; *Téléc:* 514-761-0085
www.adorable.qc.ca
Circulation: 13 173 *Frequency:* 10 fois par année; français
Patrice Demers, Éditeur
Violaine Trudeau, Rédactrice-en-chef

Vervegirl
#245, 401 Richmond St. West, Toronto, ON M5V 1X3
Tel: 416-595-1313; *Fax:* 416-595-1312
Toll-Free: 888-292-5559
nigel@youthculture.com
www.vervegirl.com
Circulation: 178,851 *Frequency:* 8 times a year
Sara Graham, Associate Editor
Jaishree Drepaul, Editor-in-chief

What's Hers Magazine
#108, 93 Lombard Ave., Winnipeg, MB R3B 3B1
Tel: 204-985-8160; *Fax:* 204-943-8991
Toll-Free: 800-665-9428
www.whatshers.com
Circulation: 180,000 *Frequency:* 5 times a year
Nancy Moore, Publisher
Barbara Chabai, Editor-in-chief

What's His Magazine
#106, 93 Lombard Ave., Winnipeg, MB R3B 3B1
Tel: 204-985-8160; *Fax:* 204-943-8991
letters@whatshis.com
www.whatshis.com
Circulation: 100,000 *Frequency:* 5 times a year
Barbara Chabai, Editor-in-chief
Nancy Moore, Publisher

Youthink
1275 West 6th Ave, 2nd Fl., Vancouver, BC V6H 1A6
Tel: 604-732-6397; *Fax:* 604-732-6390
Toll-Free: 866-370-6462
andrew@youthink.ca
www.youthink.ca
Circulation: 69,987 *Frequency:* 10 times a year
Andrew Sloan, Publisher

Ethnic

Aboriginal

Alberta Native News
#207, 11460 Jasper Ave., Edmonton, AB T5K 0M1
Tel: 780-421-7966; *Fax:* 780-424-3951
editor@albertanativenews.com
www.albertanativenews.com
Circulation: 14,000 *Frequency:* 12 times a year
David Moser, Publisher

Alberta Sweetgrass
13245 - 146 St., Edmonton, AB T5L 4S8
Tel: 780-455-2700; *Fax:* 780-455-7639
market@ammsa.com
www.ammsa.com/sweetgrass/
Circulation: 7,000 *Frequency:* Monthly
Bert Crowfoot, Publisher
Laura Suthers, Editor

The Drum
Taiga Communications, #554, 70 Arthur St., Winnipeg, MB R3B 1G7
Tel: 204-943-1500; *Fax:* 204-943-1160
staff@taiga-communications.com
www.firstperspective.ca
Circulation: 15,000 *Frequency:* monthly
James Wastasecoot, Publisher
Joseph Quesnel, Editor

First Nations Free Press
363 Sioux Rd., Sherwood Park, AB T8A 4W7
Tel: 780-449-1803; *Fax:* 780-449-1807
Toll-Free: 800-830-1803
fnfp@telus.net
Frequency: Monthly
Flo Baker, Publisher

The First Perspective & The Drum
Taiga Communications Inc., #554, 70 Arthur St., Winnipeg, MB R3B 1G7
Tel: 204-943-1500; *Fax:* 204-943-1160
staff@taiga-communications.com
www.taiga-communications.com
Circulation: 10,000 *Frequency:* Monthly
James Wastasecoot, Publisher
Len Kruzenga, Editor

Ha-Shilth-Sa
PO Box 1383, Port Alberni, BC V9Y 7M2
Tel: 250-724-5757; *Fax:* 250-723-0463
Toll-Free: 877-677-1131
hashilthsa@nuuchahnulth.org
www.nuuchahnulth.org
Circulation: 3,100
Denise Ambrose, Regional Reporter
Annie Watts, Office Manager

Inuvik Drum
PO Box 2820, 5108 - 50 St., Yellowknife, NT X1A 2R1
Tel: 867-777-4545; *Fax:* 867-777-4412
inuvikdrum@nnsl.com
www.nnsl.com
Circulation: 1,634
Jack Sigvaldson, Publisher
Bruce Valpy, Managing Editor
Petra Ehrke, National/Territorial Manager

Journal of Aboriginal Tourism
PO Box 1240 M, Calgary, AB T2P 2L2
Tel: 403-228-9984; *Fax:* 403-229-3598
eao@telusplanet.net

Circulation: 7,800 *Frequency:* Annual Directory of Canadian Aboriginal Tourism (Jan.-Feb.); annual directory of Cultural Heritage Tourism (Sept.-Oct.)
Edmund A. Oliverio, Editorial Director

Kahtou News: The Voice of B.C.'s First Nations
PO Box 192, 5526 Sinku Dr., Sechelt, BC V0N 3A0
Tel: 604-885-7391; *Fax:* 604-885-7397
Toll-Free: 800-561-4311
kahtou@dcc.net
www.kahtou.com
Circulation: 12,431 *Frequency:* Monthly
Stan Dixon, Publisher & Editor

Ktuqcqakyam Newsletter
7468 Mission Rd., Cranbrook, BC V1C 7E5
Tel: 250-417-4022; *Fax:* 250-489-2438
dlalande@ktunaxa.org
www.ktunaxa.com
Circulation: 700 *Frequency:* Bi-monthly
Donna Kraus-Hagerman, Contact

Mi'kmaq-Maliseet Nation News
PO Box 1590, 57 Martin Cres., Truro, NS B2N 5V3
Tel: 902-895-2038; *Fax:* 902-893-3030
marketing@cmmns.com
Frequency: Monthly
Don Julien, Publisher
Art Stevens, Managing Editor

The Nation: The News & Cultural Magazine of the James Bay Cree
#3018, 5505, boul St. Laurent, Montréal, QC H2T 1S6
Tel: 514-272-3077; *Fax:* 514-278-9914
beesum@beesum-communications.com
www.beesum-communications.com
Circulation: 6,730 *Frequency:* 26 times a year; English & James Bay Cree
Aaron MacDevitt, Sales Representative

Native Journal
#57096, 2020 Sherwood Dr., Sherwood Park, AB T8A 5L7
Tel: 780-448-9693; *Fax:* 780-448-9694
Toll-Free: 866-526-8688
elaine@nativejournal.ca
www.nativejournal.ca
Frequency: Monthly
Elaine Shuflita, Publisher
Lisa Doucet, Publisher

Native Youth News
363 Sioux Rd., Sherwood Park, AB T8A 4W7
Tel: 780-449-1803; *Fax:* 780-449-1807
Toll-Free: 800-830-1803
fnfpltd@telusplanet.net
Frequency: Monthly
Flo Baker, Publisher

Natotawin
PO Box 10880, Opaskwayak, MB R0B 2J0
Tel: 204-627-7066;
gabriel.constant@opaskwayak.ca
www.opaskwayak.mb.ca/natotawin
Circulation: 1,000 *Frequency:* Weekly
Gabriel Constant, Editor

New Breed Magazine
c/o Gabriel Dumont Institute, #2, 604 - 22nd St. West, Saskatoon, SK S7M 5W1
Tel: 306-657-5716; *Fax:* 306-244-0252
darren.prefontaine@gdi.gdins.org
www.metismuseum.ca
Circulation: 1,000 *Frequency:* 3 times a year
Darren Préfontaine
David Morin
Karon Shmon

Nunavut News/North
c/o Northern News Services Ltd., PO Box 2820, Yellowknife, NT X1A 2R1
Tel: 867-979-5990; *Fax:* 867-979-6010
editor@nunavutnews.com
www.nnsl.com
Frequency: Weekly
J.W. (Sig) Sigvaldason, Publisher
Mike Scott, General Manager

Raven's Eye
13245 - 146 St., Edmonton, AB T5L 4S8
Tel: 780-455-2700; *Fax:* 780-455-7639
market@ammsa.com
www.ammsa.com/raven
Circulation: 6,500 *Frequency:* Monthly
Bert Crowfoot, Publisher

Saskatchewan Sage
13245 - 146 St., Edmonton, AB T5L 4S8
Tel: 780-455-2700; *Fax:* 780-455-7639
Toll-Free: 800-661-5469
market@ammsa.com
www.ammsa.com/sage/
Circulation: 6,000 *Frequency:* Monthly
Bert Crowfoot, Publisher
Cheryl Petten, Editor

Secwepemc News, The Voice of the Shuswap Nation
Secwepemc Cultural Education Society, #311, 355 Yellowhead Hwy., Kamloops, BC V2H 1H1
Tel: 250-828-9783; *Fax:* 250-372-1127
communic@secwemc.org
www.secwepemc.org
Circulation: 5,000 *Frequency:* Monthly
Kathy Manuel, Managing Editor

Turtle Island News
PO Box 329, Ohsweken, ON N0A 1M0
Tel: 519-445-0868; *Fax:* 519-445-0865
news@theturtleislandnews.com
www.theturtleislandnews.com
Circulation: 10,000 *Frequency:* Weekly
Lynda Powless, Publisher & Editor

Western Native News Ltd.
#330, 10115 - 100A St., Edmonton, AB T5J 2W2
Tel: 780-421-7966; *Fax:* 780-424-3941
nativenews@telus.net
David Moser, Publisher
Deborah Shatz, Editor

Windspeaker
13245 - 146 St., Edmonton, AB T5L 4S8
Tel: 780-455-2700; *Fax:* 780-455-7639
market@ammsa.com
www.ammsa.com/windspeaker
Circulation: 25,500 *Frequency:* Monthly
Bert Crowfoot, Publisher
Debora Steel, Managing Editor

African-Canadian & Caribbean Canadian Communi

Caribbean Camera
#212, 55 Nugget Ave., Toronto, ON M1S 3L1
Tel: 416-412-2905; *Fax:* 416-412-2134
caribbeancamera@aol.com
www.thecaribbeancamera.com
Circulation: 35,000 *Frequency:* Weekly; 2 editions: Montreal & Toronto
Raynier Maharaj, Editor

Equality News
1646 Victoria Park Ave., Toronto, ON M1R 1P7
Tel: 416-759-6397
Circulation: 37,000 *Frequency:* Weekly
Bhaskar Sharma, Publisher & Managing Editor

The Jamaican Weekly Gleaner
1390 Eglinton Ave. West, Toronto, ON M6C 2E4
Tel: 416-784-3002; *Fax:* 416-784-5719
Toll-Free: 800-565-3961
gleanercan@gleanerna.com
www.jamaica-gleaner.com
Circulation: 110,000 *Frequency:* Weekly; also The Jamaican Weekly Star, The Black Pages Directory
Maxwell Wynter, General Manager
Yulanda Gordon, Editor

Pride News Magazine
#304, 5200 Finch Ave., Toronto, ON M1S 4Z5
Tel: 416-335-1719; *Fax:* 416-335-1723
pridenews@bellnet.ca
www.pridenewsmagazine.com
Circulation: 25,000
Michael Van Cooten, Publisher & Editor

Somali Press
PO Box 30097, 2141 Kipling Ave., Toronto, ON M9W 6T1
Tel: 416-242-7777; *Fax:* 416-242-3603
Axmed M.I. Barkhadle, Editor-in-chief

Word: Toronto's Urban Culture Magazine
Working Word Cooperative Ltd., #123, 4-2880 Queen St. East, Brampton, ON L6S 6H4
Tel: 905-799-1630; *Fax:* 905-799-2788
editor@wordmag.com
www.wordmag.com
Circulation: 50,000 *Frequency:* 9 times a year
Angela Baldassarre, Editor
Phillip Vassell, Publisher

Arabic

Al-Mughtarib Weekly Newspaper
PO Box 48113, 60 Dundas St. East, Mississauga, ON L5A 4G8
Fax: 905-949-0117
Toll-Free: 866-771-9358
Frequency: Weekly
Saleh Rafai, Editor-in-chief

Al-Mustakbal
#6, 1305, Mazurette, Montréal, QC H4N 1G8
Tel: 514-334-0909; *Fax:* 514-332-5419
info@almustakbal.com
www.almustakbal.com
Circulation: 12,000
Joseph Nakhlé, Editeur
Ibrahim Ghorqyebo, Rédacteur-en-chef

Arab Guide
368 Queen St. East, 2nd Fl., Toronto, ON M5A 1T1
Tel: 416-362-0304; *Fax:* 416-861-0238
Circulation: 5,000
E. Elgamal, Editor
F. Ahmed, Publisher

Arab News International
602 Millwood Rd., Toronto, ON M5A 1K8
Tel: 416-362-0307; *Fax:* 416-861-0238
info@arabnews.ca
Frequency: Bi-weekly
Salah Allam, Publisher
Eynass El Masri, Managing Editor

Arabbusiness International
368 Queen St. East, 2nd Fl., Toronto, ON M5A 1T1
Tel: 416-362-0304; *Fax:* 416-861-0238
allam@octoline.com
Circulation: 6,000
S. Allam, Publisher
N. Soliman, Editor & Manager, Advertising

ARC Arabic Journal
368 Queen St. East, Toronto, ON M5A 1T1
Tel: 416-362-0304; *Fax:* 416-861-0238
Circulation: 5,000
Emad Nafeh, Editor

Canada & the Arab World
602 Millwood Rd., Toronto, ON M5A 1K8
Tel: 416-362-0307; *Fax:* 416-861-0238
info@arabnews.ca
Circulation: 5,000
Salah Allam, Publisher
Ibrahim Salama, Editor

Egypt & the Arab World in Canada
#521, 1117, rue Ste-Catherine, Montréal, QC H3B 1H9
Tel: 514-288-0188; *Fax:* 514-288-1944
georgesaad@videotron.ca
Frequency: 4 times a year
George Saad, Editor-in-chief

El-Mahroussa Magazine
Egyptian Canadian Friendship Association Inc., 879, av St-Charles, Chomedey, QC H7V 3T5
Tel: 450-687-0273; *Fax:* 450-505-1880
masri1993@hotmail.com
www.el-mahrousaonline.com
Circulation: 12,000 *Frequency:* 12 issues a year; Arabic & French
Nancy Youssef, Chief of Staff

El-Masri Newspaper
879, av St-Charles, Laval, QC H7V 3T5
Tel: 450-687-0273; *Fax:* 450-505-1880
ads@el-masrionline.com
www.el-masrionline.com
Circulation: 12,000 *Frequency:* Bi-weekly; Arabic & French
Adel Iskander, General Director

The Iran Star
#205, 72 Steeles Ave. West, Thornhill, ON L4J 1A1
Tel: 905-763-9770; *Fax:* 905-763-9771
iranstar@iranstar.com
www.iranstar.com
Circulation: 12,500
Bijan Binesh, Editor-in-chief
Shahram Binesh, Editor & Coordinator

Middle East Report
368 Queen St. East, 2nd Fl., Toronto, ON M5A 1T1
Tel: 416-362-0304; *Fax:* 416-861-0238
allam@idirect.com

Circulation: 5,000
N. Soliman, Editor & Manager, Advertising

Armenian

Abaka
Tekeyan Armenian Cultural Association of Montréal, 825, rue Manoogian, Saint-Laurent, QC H4N 1Z5
Tel: 514-747-6680; *Fax:* 514-747-6162
abaka@bellnet.ca
Circulation: 1,000 *Frequency:* Weekly; Tabloid; Armenian, French & English
Arsène Mamourian, Editor

Horizon
3401, rue Olivar-Asselin, Montréal, QC H4J 1L5
Tel: 514-332-3757; *Fax:* 514-332-4870
manager.horizonweekly@bellnet.ca
Circulation: 2,000
Vahakn Karakashian, Editor

Lradou Newsletter
3401, rue Olivar-Asselin, Montréal, QC H4J 1L5
Tel: 514-333-1616; *Fax:* 514-333-1612
ars-canada@bellnet.ca
www.ars-canada.ca
Frequency: Annually

Pourastan
Parish Council of St. Gregory, 615, av Stuart, Outremont, QC H2V 3H2
Tel: 514-279-3066; *Fax:* 514-279-8008
sounpkr.kor@qc.aira.com
www.armeniancathedral.ca
Circulation: 700
Father Boyajan

Bulgarian

Bulgarian Horizons
#7, 648A Yonge St., Toronto, ON M4Y 2A6
Tel: 416-962-7100; *Fax:* 416-962-7101
maksim1@mail.com
www.bulgarianhorizons.com
Circulation: 2,000
Maxim Bozhilov, Editor

Celtic

Celtic Heritage
PO Box 8805 A, #204, 1454 Dresden Row, Halifax, NS B3K 5M4
Tel: 902-835-6244; *Fax:* 902-835-0080
editorial@celticheritage.ns.ca
www.celticheritage.ns.ca
Circulation: 5,800 *Frequency:* 6 times a year; ISSN: 1202-7553
Angus M. MacQuarrie, Publisher
Alexa Thompson, Editor

Chinese

The Capital Chinese News
#203, 1390 Prince of Wales Dr., Ottawa, ON K2C 3N6
Tel: 613-837-3564; *Fax:* 613-834-1193
Frequency: Monthly
Ping J. Chiu, Publisher & Editor-in-chief

Chinese Canadian Community News
80 Florence St., Ottawa, ON K1R 7W6
Tel: 613-232-8403; *Fax:* 613-232-4953
cccny.g@cyberus.ca
Yu Qin Guo, Publisher
King Wan Wu, Editor

The Chinese Journal
10553A - 97 St., Edmonton, AB T5H 2L4
Tel: 780-424-0213; *Fax:* 780-428-7117
chinesejournal@telusplanet.net
Circulation: 7,000 *Frequency:* Weekly
Vicki Lim, Publisher
Grace Chi, Editor

Chinese News
#11, 50 Weybright Ct., Toronto, ON M1S 5A8
Tel: 416-504-0761; *Fax:* 416-504-4928
Frequency: Weekly
Jack Jia, Publisher

The Chinese Press
1123, rue Clark, 2e étage, Montréal, QC H2Z 1K3
Tel: 514-397-9969; *Fax:* 514-397-9929
cpreader@chinesepress.com
www.chinesepress.com
Circulation: 25,000 *Frequency:* Weekly
Crescent Chau, Publisher/Editor

Herald Monthly
#205, 3325 Victoria Park Ave., Toronto, ON M1W 2R8
Tel: 416-492-4578; *Fax:* 416-492-6570
toronto@cchc.org
www.cchc.org
Circulation: 75,000 *Frequency:* Monthly
Helena Lee, Chief Editor

Jasmine
218 Viewmount Ave., Toronto, ON M6B 1T8
Tel: 416-901-5201; *Fax:* 416-901-5202
info@jasminemagazine.com
www.jasminemagazine.com
Circulation: 4 times a year
English print - 18-34 years old Asian female
Amy Lan, Publisher

Ming Pao Daily News
1355 Huntingwood Dr., Toronto, ON M1S 3J1
Tel: 416-321-0088; *Fax:* 416-321-5377
Circulation: 73,000 M; 62,000 Tu; 71,000 W-Th; 66,000 F; 97,000 Sa *Frequency:* Daily; Chinese
Jeannie Lee, Regional General Manager
Frankie Chow, Manager, Advertising

Ming Pao Daily News, Western Edition
5368 Parkwood Pl., Richmond, BC V6V 2N1
Tel: 604-231-8992; *Fax:* 604-231-9882
Frequency: Daily
Agnes Wong, Manager, Advertising
Lydia Yu, Manager, Sales Service

Modesty Magazine
#115, 18 Crown Steel Dr., Markham, ON L3R 9X8
Tel: 905-513-1232; *Fax:* 905-513-0483
modestygroup@rogers.com
www.modestymagazine.com
Circulation: 10,000-20,000 annually
Ivy Lee, Publisher & Editor

Popular Lifestyle & Entertainment Magazine
3248 Cambie St., Vancouver, BC V5Z 2W4
Tel: 604-872-1285; *Fax:* 604-872-0677
info@plem.com
www.plem.com
Circulation: 75,953 *Frequency:* Monthly
Patrick Wong, President & Editor-in-chief
Amanda Pi, Managing Editor
Lorna Chan, Account Executive

Les Presses Chinoises
1123, rue Clark, 2e étage, Montréal, QC H2Z 1K3
Tél: 514-397-9969; *Téléc:* 514-397-9929
cpmarket@chinesepress.com
www.chinesepress.com
Circulation: 25 000 *Frequency:* Weekly
Amy Tsang

Rice Paper
PO Box 74174 Hillcrest, Vancouver, BC V5V 5C8
Tel: 604-879-5962;
info@ricepaperonline.com
www.ricepaperonline.com
Circulation: 3,000 *Frequency:* 4 times a year
Jessica Gin-Jade, Editor-in-chief

Shing Wah News
#203, 1252 Lawrence Ave. East, Toronto, ON M3A 1C3
Tel: 416-778-1854; *Fax:* 416-778-6340
willywecheng@hotmail.com
Frequency: Monthly
W. Cheng, President

Sing Pao Vancouver Chinese News
1296 Kingsway, Vancouver, BC V5V 3E1
Tel: 604-872-6968; *Fax:* 604-872-1608
Circulation: 50,000 *Frequency:* Daily
Shing Pao, Publisher

Sing Tao Daily
417 Dundas St. West, Toronto, ON M5T 1G6
Tel: 416-596-8140; *Fax:* 416-599-6688
Frequency: Daily
Robert Lang, Chief Editor

World Journal (Toronto)
415 Eastern Ave., Toronto, ON M4M 1B7
Tel: 416-778-0889; *Fax:* 416-778-1037
editorial@worldjournal.net
www.worldjournal.com
Circulation: 30,000 *Frequency:* Daily
Paul Chang, Editor-in-chief
David Ting, President

World Journal (Vancouver)
2288 Clark Dr., Vancouver, BC V5N 3G8
Tel: 604-876-1338; *Fax:* 604-876-3728
Frequency: Daily; Chinese
Kuo-Liang Swei, Editor
Richard Lin, President

Croatian

Glasnik Hrvatske Seljacke Stranke
PO Box 82187, Burnaby, BC V5C 5P2
Tel: 604-524-2813; *Fax:* 604-521-0030
georged@smart.com
Circulation: 800 *Frequency:* Monthly
George Durkovich, Editor

Dutch

De Nederlandse Courant
1945 Four Seasons Dr., Burlington, ON L7P 2Y3
Tel: 905-333-3615;
courant@sympatico.cadsecourant.com
www.denederlandsecourant.com
Circulation: 5,800 *Frequency:* 25 pa; Dutch & English
Theo Luykenaar, Publisher

The Windmill Herald
PO Box 3006 LCD1, Langley, BC V3A 4R3
Tel: 604-532-1733; *Fax:* 604-532-1734
windmill@godutch.com
www.godutch.com
Circulation: 12,500

Estonian

Eesti Elu/Estonian Life
3 Madison Ave., Toronto, ON M5R 2S2
Tel: 416-733-4550; *Fax:* 416-733-0944
eetoimetus@eestielu.ca
www.eesti.ca
Circulation: 2,300 *Frequency:* Weekly; Estonian
Elle Puusaag, Editor
Juri Laansoo, General Manager

Filipino

Filipiniana News
1531 Queen St. West, Toronto, ON M6R 1A5
Tel: 416-534-7836; *Fax:* 416-535-9491
filipiniananews@rogers.com
Circulation: 10,000 *Frequency:* Monthly

Filipino Journal
46 Pincarrow Rd., Winnipeg, MB R3Y 1E3
Tel: 204-489-8894; *Fax:* 204-489-1575
info@filipinojournal.com
filipinojournal.com
Circulation: 4,500 *Frequency:* 24 pa
Linda Natividad-Cantiveros, Publisher/Editor-in-chief

The North American Filipino Star
4950, rue Queen Mary, Penthouse, Montréal, QC H3W 1X3
Tel: 514-485-7861; *Fax:* 514-485-3076
filipinostar@yahoo.com
Circulation: 5,000 *Frequency:* Monthly
Zenaida Ferry-Kharroubi, Publisher & Chief Editor

The Philippine Reporter
807 Queen St. East, Toronto, ON M4M 1H8
Tel: 416-461-8694; *Fax:* 416-461-7399
thephilreporter@on.aibn.com
www.philreporter.com
Circulation: 10,000 *Frequency:* 24 pa
Hermie Garcia, Publisher & Editor

Finnish

Vapaa Sana
#308, 191 Eglinton Ave. East, Toronto, ON M4P 1K1
Tel: 416-321-0808; *Fax:* 416-321-0811
markus@vapaasana.com
www.vapaasana.com
Circulation: 2,500 *Frequency:* Weekly
Matti Termiseva, Editor
Markus Ratty, General Manager

German

Albertaner
3635 - 28th St., Edmonton, AB T6T 1N4
Tel: 780-465-7526; *Fax:* 780-465-3140
ajoop@planet.eon.net
Circulation: 3,500
Arnim Joop, Publisher & Editor

Der Bote
Mennonite Church Canada, 600 Shaftesbury Blvd., Winnipeg, MB R3P 0M4
Tel: 204-888-6781; *Fax:* 204-831-5675
Toll-Free: 866-888-6785
ijamzenlamp@mennonitechurch.ca
Circulation: 3,300 *Frequency:* Bi-weekly
Ingrid Jamzen, Editor

Deutsche Presse
#303, 455 Spadina Ave., Toronto, ON M5S 2G8
Tel: 416-595-9714; *Fax:* 416-595-9716
Frequency: Weekly
Rolf Meyer, Publisher

Deutsche Zeitung
85 Inglis St., Ayr, ON N0B 1E0
Tel: 519-632-7700; *Fax:* 519-632-8700
Toll-Free: 888-749-0606
deutschezt@golden.net
Circulation: 7,500 *Frequency:* Weekly; German
Erhard Matthaes, Editor

Die Mennonitische Post
383 Main St., Steinbach, MB R5G 1Z4
Tel: 204-326-6790
Circulation: 5,000 *Frequency:* 23 pa

Echo Germanica
383 Vaughan Rd., Toronto, ON M6C 2N8
Tel: 416-652-1332; *Fax:* 416-658-6909
editor@echoworld.com
www.echoworld.com
Circulation: 16,000
Sybille Forster-Rentmeister, Publisher/Editor-in-chief

Freundschaft/Friendship
Central-Organization of German-Sudeten-Clubs in Canada, 20 Banff Rd., Toronto, ON M4S 2V5
Tel: 416-483-8240; *Fax:* 416- -
Circulation: 200
Rolf Lorenz

German Canadian Business & Trade Directory
2255B Queen St. East, Box 106, Toronto, ON M4E 1G3
Tel: 416-465-9957; *Fax:* 416-465-8169
directory@germancanadian.com
www.germancanadian.com
Circulation: 5,000
Eva Wazda, Publisher

Mennonitische Rundschau
1310 Taylor Ave., Winnipeg, MB R3M 3Z6
Tel: 204-669-6575; *Fax:* 204-654-1865
mr@mbconf.ca
www.rundschau.ca
Circulation: 2,200 *Frequency:* Monthly; German
Marianne Dulder, Editor

Greek

Courier Grec
765, rue Jean-Talon ouest, Montréal, QC H3N 1S3
Tel: 514-278-9299; *Fax:* 514-278-4572
Frequency: Weekly
Iraklis Theodorakopoulos, Editor

drassis/Greek Canadian Action
#250, 657, boul Curé Labelle, Laval, QC H7V 2T8
Tel: 450-978-0070; *Fax:* 514-687-6330
Circulation: 44,300 *Frequency:* Weekly
George Guzmas, Publisher

Greek Canadian Tribune / Ellinokanadiko Vima
7835, av Wiseman, Montréal, QC H3N 2N8
Tel: 514-272-6873; *Fax:* 514-272-3157
info@bhma.net
www.bhma.net
Circulation: 13,000 *Frequency:* Weekly; Greek & English
Christos Manikis, Publisher & Editor

Greek Press
6 Chester Ave., Toronto, ON M4K 2Z9
Tel: 416-465-3243; *Fax:* 416-604-2480
info@greekpress.ca
www.greekpress.ca
Circulation: 6,000 *Frequency:* Bi-weekly
Constantine Kranias, Publisher/Editor

H Poh
2975, Brighton, Montréal, QC H3S 1T7
Tel: 514-342-0808;
hpoh@videotron.ca
Circulation: 20,000 *Frequency:* Weekly
Kostas Georgoulis, Publisher

Hellenic Hamilton News
#2, 8 Morris Ave., Hamilton, ON L8L 1X7
Tel: 905-549-9208; *Fax:* 905-549-7935
Circulation: 5,300 *Frequency:* Monthly; Greek
Panos Andronidis, Publisher & Editor

The Hellenic News
Alpha Omega Communications, 37 Hillsmount Rd., London, ON N6K 1W1
Tel: 519-472-4807; *Fax:* 519-471-6116
alpha_omega_com@hotmail.com
Frequency: Monthly
George N. Drossos, Managing Editor

Hellenic-Canadian Chronicles
Ledra Publishing Co. Ltd., 437 Danforth Ave., Toronto, ON M4K 1P1
Tel: 416-465-4628; *Fax:* 416-465-6592
Circulation: 6,000 *Frequency:* Weekly; English & Greek
Peter Maniatakos, Editor

Patrides, A North American Review
PO Box 266 O, Toronto, ON M4A 2N3
Tel: 416-921-4229; *Fax:* 416-921-0723
saras@patrides.com
www.patrides.com
Circulation: 160,000 *Frequency:* Bi-weekly
Kathy Saras, Publisher
Thomas Saras, Editor-in-chief

Hungarian

Kanadai Magyarsag
74 Advance Rd., Toronto, ON M8Z 2T7
Tel: 416-233-3131; *Fax:* 416-233-5984
Frequency: Weekly
Csaba Gaal, Editor & Manager

Menorah-Egyenloseg
PO Box 54017 Lawrence Plaza, #312, 1089 Bathurst St., Toronto, ON M6A 3B7
Tel: 416-780-9168; *Fax:* 416-780-9167
Circulation: 4,500 *Frequency:* Bi-weekly, Friday
William Koseras, Publisher & Editor

Icelandic

Logberg-Heimskringla
The Sterling Bldg., #100, 283 Portage Ave., Winnipeg, MB R3B 2B5
Tel: 204-284-5686; *Fax:* 204-284-7099
Toll-Free: 866-564-2374
lh@lh-inc.ca
www.lh-inc.ca
Circulation: 2,000 *Frequency:* 24 pa Friday; English & Icelandic

Italian

Corriere Canadese
101 Wingold Ave., Toronto, ON M6B 1P8
Tel: 416-785-4300; *Fax:* 416-781-4329
Toll-Free: 877-503-5077
corriere@corriere.com
www.corriere.com
Circulation: 29,500 *Frequency:* Monday-Saturday
Paola Bernardini, Managing Editor
Lori Abittan, General Manager/COO
Elena Caprile, Editor-in-chief

Corriere Italiano
6900, rue St-Denis, Montréal, QC H2S 2S2
Tel: 514-279-4536; *Fax:* 514-279-3900
pubital@biz.videotron.ca
Circulation: 20 500 *Frequency:* Weekly
Carole Gagliardi, President & Editor

Donna
#100, 166 Woodbridge Ave., Woodbridge, ON L4L 2S7
Tel: 905-856-2823; *Fax:* 905-856-2825
lospecchio@msn.com
Circulation: 18,500 *Frequency:* 4 times a year
Giovanna Tozzi, Managing Editor

L'Eco D'Italia
Marco Polo World News, #302, 3680 East Hastings St., Vancouver, BC V5K 2A9
Tel: 604-294-8707; *Fax:* 604-291-1707
marcopolonews@shaw.ca
Circulation: 5,900 *Frequency:* Weekly
Rino Vultaggio, Editor/Publisher

La Gazzetta
909 Howard Ave., Windsor, ON N9A 1S3
Tel: 519-253-8883; *Fax:* 519-253-3280
Frequency: Weekly; Italian & English
Rita Bison, Managing Editor

Il Cittadino Canadese
#209, 5960, rue Jean Talon est, Saint-Léonard, QC H1S 1M2
Tel: 514-253-2332; *Fax:* 514-253-6574
Circulation: 38,000 *Frequency:* Weekly
Basilio Giordano, Publisher

Il Congresso
Cura Enterprises Ltd., 9227 - 169 Ave., Edmonton, AB T5Z 1X3
Tel: 780-424-3010; *Fax:* 780-424-3037
ilcongresso@shaw.ca
Circulation: 7,500 *Frequency:* 12 pa; Italian
Alessandro Urso, Publisher & Editor

Il Rincontro / La Recontre
6675, av Wilderton, Montréal, QC H3S 2L8
Tel: 514-739-4213; *Fax:* 514-344-8238
tony.vellone@videotron.ca
Circulation: 11,500 *Frequency:* Monthly; Italian
Tony Vellone, Editor

Insieme
4358, rue Charleroi, Montréal, QC H1H 1T3
Tel: 514-328-2062; *Fax:* 514-328-6562
insieme@multimedianova.com
Circulation: 38,000 *Frequency:* Weekly; Italian
Lori Abittan, Publisher
Mimmo Forte, Editor

Lo Specchio/Vaughan
#100, 166 Woodbridge Ave., Woodbridge, ON L4L 2S7
Tel: 905-856-2823; *Fax:* 905-856-2825
editorial@lospecchio.com
www.lospecchio.com
Circulation: 28,000 *Frequency:* Weekly
Sergio Tagliavini, Editor

L'Ora Di Ottawa
203 Louisa St., Ottawa, ON K1R 6Y9
Tel: 613-232-5689; *Fax:* 613-563-2573
info@loradiottawa.ca
Circulation: 2,115 *Frequency:* Weekly
Donatella Votano
Luciano Gonella, Editor

Tandem
101 Wingold Ave., Toronto, ON M6B 1P8
Tel: 416-785-4300; *Fax:* 416-781-4329
Toll-Free: 877-503-5077
corriere@corriere.com
www.tandemnews.com
Circulation: 55,000 *Frequency:* Weekly
Angela Baldassarre, Managing Editor
Lori Abittan, General Manager/COO
Elena Caprile, Editor-in-chief

Vita Italiana
PO Box 1098, Toronto, ON M9L 2R8
Tel: 416-656-2050; *Fax:* 416-780-0208
mcvarano@hotmail.com
Frequency: 24 times per year
Dr. Mario Caligure Varano, Editor

Japanese

Japanese Canadian National Museum (JCNM)
#120, 6688 Southoaks Cres., Vancouver, BC V5S 4M7
Tel: 807-777-8000; *Fax:* 807-777-7001
jcnmas@telus.net
www.jcnm.ca
Grace Eiko Thomson, Executive Director

The Montreal Bulletin
8155, rue Rousselot, Montréal, QC H2E 1Z7
Tel: 514-723-5551;
bulletin@dsuper.net
Circulation: 500
Mary Burke, Managing Editor

Nikkei Voice
6 Garamond Ct., Toronto, ON M3C 1Z5
Tel: 416-386-0287; *Fax:* 416-386-0136
nikkeivoice@bellnet.com
Frequency: Monthly
Frank Moritsugu, Publisher

Korean

Korea Central Daily
655 Bloor St. West, Toronto, ON M6G 1L1
Tel: 416-533-5533; *Fax:* 416-533-5500
toronto.koreadaily.com
Hyo Kim, Publisher

James Lim, Editor-in-Chief

The Korea Times Daily
287 Bridgeland Ave., Toronto, ON M6A 1Z6
Tel: 416-787-1111; *Fax:* 416-781-7777
www.koreatimes.net
Circulation: 17,000 *Frequency:* 6 pa; Korean
Woon Y. Kim, Editor-in-chief
Lawrence M. Kim, Publisher

Latin American

El Mundo Latino News
3050 Kirwin Ave., Mississauga, ON L5A 2K6
Tel: 905-306-7929; *Fax:* 905-279-2702
info@elmundolatinonews.ca
www.elmundolatinonews.ca
Circulation: 10,000 *Frequency:* Weekly
Ana Griselda Romero, Publisher

El Popular
2413 Dundas St. West, Toronto, ON M6P 1X3
Tel: 416-531-2495; *Fax:* 416-531-7187
editor@diarioelpopular.com
Frequency: Weekly
Eduardo Uruena, Publisher

Reporte Latino
PO Box 1098, Toronto, ON M9L 2R8
Tel: 416-656-2050; *Fax:* 416-780-0208
Frequency: Monthly
Dr. Mario Caligiure Varano, Editor

Lithuanian

Teviskes Ziburiai/Lights of Homeland
2185 Stavebank Rd., Mississauga, ON L5C 1T3
Tel: 905-275-4672; *Fax:* 905-290-9802
tevzib@pathcom.com
Circulation: 2,800 *Frequency:* Weekly
P. Gaida, Editor-in-chief
J. Kuras, Chair

Macedonian

Macedonia
PO Box 97589, 364 Old Kingston Rd., Toronto, ON M1C 4Z1
Tel: 416-288-7673; *Fax:* 416-286-0712
Tanas Jovanovska, Editor

Roots
2145 Danforth Ave., Toronto, ON M4C 1K2
Tel: 416-691-7184; *Fax:* 416-691-3439

Multicultural

Community Digest
#216, 1755 Robson St., Vancouver, BC V6G 3B7
Tel: 604-875-8313; *Fax:* 604-875-0336
digestnews@yahoo.com
Circulation: 25,000 *Frequency:* Weekly
N. Ebrahim, Publisher

Ethno-Cultural Networker
c/o 129 Browning Blvd., Winnipeg, MB R3K 0L1
Tel: 204-774-3569
Frequency: Monthly

FACES: Canada's Multicultural Magazine
Multicultural Council of Saskachewan, 369 Park St., Regina, SK S4N 5B2
Tel: 306-721-2769; *Fax:* 306-721-3342
mcos@accesscomm.ca
mcos.sask.com
Circulation: 1,500 *Frequency:* 4 times a year
Wade Luzny, CEO

New Canada Weekly
#500, 120 Eglinton Ave. East, Toronto, ON M4P 1E2
Tel: 416-481-7793; *Fax:* 416- -
humanrights@sympatico.ca
hrrrc.ca
Circulation: 10,000 *Frequency:* Weekly; English & Urdu
Hasanat Ahmad Syed, Publisher & Editor

Peel Multicultural Scene
Peel Multicultural Council, 6630 Turner Valley Rd., Mississauga, ON L5N 2P1
Tel: 905-819-1144; *Fax:* 905-542-3950
pmcgeneral@peelmc.com
www.peelmc.com
Circulation: 400
Naveed Chaudhey

Persian

Sarmayeh/Investment
Sarmayeh Publications, #415, 5795 Yonge St., Toronto, ON M2M 4J3
Tel: 416-221-1400; *Fax:* 416-221-1451
sarmayeh@idirect.com
Circulation: 7,000
Arman Parsi, Editor/Sales Manager

Shahrvand
#208, 4610 Dufferin St., Toronto, ON M3H 5S4
Tel: 905-739-1086; *Fax:* 905-739-6418
www.shahrvand.com
Circulation: 30,000 *Frequency:* Tuesday, Friday
Hassan Zerehi, Editor-in-chief

Polish

Czas Polish Times
207 Cathedral Ave., Winnipeg, MB R2W 0X2
Tel: 204-582-4392;
czaspol@mts.net
Circulation: 651 *Frequency:* Weekly
Krystyna Gajda, President

Glos Polski/Polish Voice
71 Judson St., Toronto, ON M8Z 1A4
Tel: 416-201-9601; *Fax:* 416-201-9602
info@glospolski.com
Circulation: 6,000
Czeslaw Zacharski, Editor-in-chief

Polish Business Directory
777C The Queensway, Toronto, ON M8Z 1N4
Tel: 416-255-9182; *Fax:* 416-255-9893
Toll-Free: 877-742-9455
mail@master.on.ca
www.przewodnikhandlowy.com
Circulation: 40,000 *Frequency:* annually
Martin Chlapowski
Robert Wagner

The Polish Canadian Courier/Nowy Kurier
12 Foch Ave., Toronto, ON M8W 3X1
Tel: 416-259-4353; *Fax:* 416-259-4353
zkopc549@rogers.com
www.nowykurier.com
Circulation: 20,000 *Frequency:* Weekly; Polish & English
Jolanta Kowalewska-Cabaj, Publisher & Editor-in-chief

Zwiazkowiec
c/o Polonia Media Ltd., 22 Roncesvalles Ave., Toronto, ON M6R 2K3
Tel: 416-531-2491; *Fax:* 416-531-5153
Frequency: Weekly

Portuguese

Alem-Fronteiras
585 Queen St. South, Kitchener, ON N2G 1W9
Tel: 519-745-3233; *Fax:* 519-745-3395
legacytr@golden.net
Circulation: 1,000

Correio Português/Portuguese Mail
793 Ossington Ave., Toronto, ON M6G 3T8
Tel: 416-532-9894; *Fax:* 416-532-1475
correioportugues@tht.net
Circulation: 122,000 *Frequency:* 24 pa
Antonio Ribeiro, Publisher

Gente Modesta
256B Lansdowne Ave., Toronto, ON L6T 3Z8
Tel: 416-531-0833; *Fax:* 416-531-0770
sino@interlog.com
Circulation: 4,950 *Frequency:* Monthly
Severiano Da Silva, Editor & Publisher

Golo/Goal
977 College St., Toronto, ON M6H 1A6
Tel: 416-538-1788; *Fax:* 416-538-7953
golo@solnet.com
www.solnet.com
Circulation: 12,000 *Frequency:* Weekly
Antonio Perinu, Publisher
Alice Perinu, Editor-in-chief

O Mundial
1148 Ellice Ave., Winnipeg, MB R3G 0E6
Tel: 204-786-7689; *Fax:* 204-775-6549
omundial@shaw.ca
Circulation: 2,000 *Frequency:* Monthly
Manuel Guerra, Editor-in-chief

Sol Portugues/Portuguese Sun
977 College St., Toronto, ON M6H 1A6
Tel: 416-538-1788; *Fax:* 416-538-7953
sol@solnet.com
www.solnet.com
Circulation: 12,000 *Frequency:* Weekly
Antonio Perinu, Publisher
Alice Perinu, Editor-in-chief

Voice Luso-Canadian Newspaper
428 Ossington Ave., Toronto, ON M6J 3A7
Tel: 416-534-3177; *Fax:* 416-534-6441
voice@ftn.net
Frequency: Weekly
Joaquim R. Baptista, Publisher & Editor

A Voz de Portugal
4231, boul St-Laurent, Montréal, QC H2W 1Z4
Tel: 514-284-1813; *Fax:* 514-284-6150
Toll-Free: 866-684-1813
jornal@avozdeportugal.com
www.avozdeportugal.com
Circulation: 10,000 *Frequency:* Weekly
Sylvio Martins, Editor, sylviomartins@avozdeportugal.com

Romanian

Romanian Voice
PO Box 78010 Westcliffe, Hamilton, ON L9C 7N5
Tel: 905-387-1832; *Fax:* 905-388-4651
Frequency: Monthly
George Balasu, Director
Eugene Barasan, Chief Editor
Mihaela Moisin, Manager

Russian

Gazeta Plus
#108, 5987 Bathurst St., Toronto, ON M2R 1Z3
Tel: 416-226-4777; *Fax:* 416-226-0374
Toll-Free: 877-877-5240
info@infogazeta.com
Circulation: 12,000 *Frequency:* Weekly
Boris Nusenbaum
Eugene Koutcher

ISKRA: Voice of the Doukhobors
PO Box 3024, Castlegar, BC V1N 3H4
Tel: 250-365-3613; *Fax:* 250-365-5477
info@iskra.ca
iskra.ca
Circulation: 1,100
Lisa Poznikoff, Editor

Nasha Gazeta
592 Champagne Dr., Toronto, ON M3J 2T9
Tel: 416-725-8337; *Fax:* 416-757-9713
info@exo.ca
Circulation: 10,000 *Frequency:* Weekly
G. Kukuy, President
T. Sergeeva, Managing Editor
I. Toutchinski, Editor-in-chief

Russian Canadian INFO
#108, 5987 Bathurst St., Toronto, ON M2R 1Z3
Tel: 416-226-4777; *Fax:* 416-226-0374
Toll-Free: 877-877-5240
info@infogazeta.com
www.ruscanada.com
Circulation: 15,000 *Frequency:* Weekly
Boris Nusenbaum
Eugene Koutcher

The Voice of Community
308 Blue Haven, Dollard-des-Ormeaux, QC H9G 2K3
Tel: 514-696-8955; *Fax:* 514-696-9493
Circulation: 9,000
Mark Groysberg, Publisher & Editor

Serbian

Kanadski Srbobran
Serbian League of Canada, 335 Britannia Ave., Hamilton, ON L8H 1Y4
Tel: 905-549-4079; *Fax:* 905-549-8552
Circulation: 755 *Frequency:* Bi-monthly
Dragan Ciric, Manager

Kisobran
#368, 3495 Cambie St., Vancouver, BC V5Z 4R3
Tel: 604-731-9446;
kisobran@telus.net; redakcija@kisobran.com
www.kisobran.com
Circulation: 4,000 *Frequency:* monthly

Dragan Andrejevic, Publisher

Serbia
269 Glover Rd., Stoney Creek, ON L8E 5H6
Tel: 905-643-3341; *Fax:* 905-643-3341
serbrad@sympatico.ca
Frequency: Monthly
David Damjanovic, Publisher & Editor

Srpsko Bratsvo
1 Secroft Cres., Toronto, ON M3N 1R5
Tel: 416-663-3409; *Fax:* 416-665-3564
Frequency: Monthly
William Durovic, Editor-in-chief
Drag D. Georgevic, Editor

Voice of Canadian Serbs
c/o Serbian National Shield Society of Canada, #303, 1900 Sheppard Ave. East, Toronto, ON M2J 4T4
Tel: 416-496-7881; *Fax:* 416-493-0335
Circulation: 1,500 *Frequency:* Monthly; Serbian & English
Bora Dragasevich, Editor

Slovak, Czech

Kanadske Listy / Canadian Pages
388 Atwater Ave., Mississauga, ON L5G 2A3
Tel: 905-278-4116; *Fax:* 905- -
mirko388@allstream.net
Circulation: 2,200 *Frequency:* Bi-monthly; Czech
Mike Janecek, Publisher & Editor
Jana Janeckova-Bayerova, Secretary

Novy Domov
Masaryk Memorial Institute Inc., 450 Scarborough Golf Club Rd., Toronto, ON M1G 1H1
Tel: 416-439-9557;
novydom@sympatico.ca
Frequency: Bi-weekly
Jan Rotbauer, Editor

Satellite 1-416
PO Box 176 E, Toronto, ON M6H 4E2
Tel: 416-530-4222; *Fax:* 416-530-0069
satellite1-416@rogers.com
www.satellite1-416.com
Circulation: 1,600
Ales Brezina, Publisher & Editor

South Asian

Ahmadiyya Gazette Canada
10610 Jane St., Maple, ON L6A 3A2
Tel: 905-303-4000; *Fax:* 905-832-3220
gazette@ahmadiyya.ca
www.ahmadiyya.ca
Frequency: English, French & Urdu
Hasan Muhammad Khan, Editor-in-chief, editor@ahmadiyyagazette.ca
S.H. Hadi, Urdu Editor
M. Nadeem A. Siddiq, Editor

Al-Hilal/Crescent
338 Hollyberry Trail, Toronto, ON M2H 2P6
Tel: 416-493-4374; *Fax:* 416-493-4374
lowaisi@rogers.com
Circulation: 4,200 *Frequency:* Bi-monthly
M.L. Owaisi, Publisher
Farida Abdullah, Editor

Bazm
4248, rue Hugo, Pierrefonds, QC H9H 2V7
Tel: 514-620-2041; *Fax:* 419-828-7613
bazm1989@yahoo.ca
Frequency: Monthly
Saira Watsy, Publisher & Chief Editor
Itaat Wasty, Sr. Editor

Canadian Times of India
7 Axsmith Cres., Main Fl., Toronto, ON M2J 3K2
Tel: 416-490-0091; *Fax:* 416-490-9592
umeshvijaya@msn.com
Circulation: 22,500
Umesh Vijaya, Publisher & Editor

Charhdi Kala
#6, 7743 - 128th St., Surrey, BC V3W 4E6
Tel: 604-590-6397; *Fax:* 604-591-6397
cknewsgroup@telus.net
Circulation: 15,000 *Frequency:* Weekly; Punjabi & English
Gurpreet Singh Sahota, Editor

Desi News
37 Firestone Rd., Toronto, ON M9C 4N1
Tel: 416-695-4357; *Fax:* 416-621-2691
desinews@rogers.com
www.e-desinews.com
Circulation: 30,000 *Frequency:* Monthly
G.A. Easwar, Publisher
Shagorika Easwar, Editor

Eastern News
5790 Riverside Pl., Mississauga, ON L5M 4W9
Tel: 905-858-7525; *Fax:* 905-858-7951
mkhan@theeasternnews.com
Circulation: 7,500 *Frequency:* 24 pa
Alia Sultana, Publisher
Masood Khan, Editor

Gujarat Express
20 Eldwood Pl., Brampton, ON L6V 3N3
Tel: 905-890-6919; *Fax:* 905-457-7096
Circulation: 7,500 *Frequency:* Weekly
Amit Bhatt, Publisher

Gujarat Vartman
250 Norfinch Dr., Toronto, ON M3N 1Y4
Tel: 416-736-1640; *Fax:* 416-736-0848
Frequency: Monthly; Gujarti
J.D. Shah, Editor

India Calling
#1908, 41 Mabelle Ave., Toronto, ON M9A 5A9
Tel: 416-233-9577
Sanyogta Singh, Publisher
Sonia Singh, Publisher & Editor-in-chief

India Journal
#11, 2355 Derry Rd. East, Mississauga, ON L5S 1V6
Tel: 905-405-0420; *Fax:* 905-405-0428
indiajournal@indiajournal.ca
www.indiajournal.ca
Circulation: 22,000
Harjinder Singh, Publisher

Indo Caribbean World
312 Brownridge Dr., Thornhill, ON L4J 5X1
Tel: 905-738-5005; *Fax:* 905-738-3927
Circulation: 30,000 *Frequency:* 2 times per month
Harry Ramkhelawan, Publisher & Editor

Indo-Canadian Awaaz
#200, 12732 - 80 Ave., Surrey, BC V3W 3A3
Tel: 604-502-6100; *Fax:* 604-501-6111
new@voiceonline.com
Circulation: 10,000 *Frequency:* weekly
Vinnie Combow, Editor
Rajesh Gupta, Publisher

Journal Apna Watan
4021, boul Notre Dame, Laval, QC H7W 1S8
Tel: 450-681-3108;
apnawatan2002@yahoo.com
Circulation: 5,000 *Frequency:* Monthly
Arshad Randhawa, Editor

Kerala Express
18 Greenbrook Dr., Toronto, ON M6M 2J9
Tel: 416-654-0431; *Fax:* 416- -
Circulation: 2,000 *Frequency:* Bi-weekly; Malayalam
J.P. George, Publisher

Pakeeza International
Tel: 905-337-3030; *Fax:* 905-338-1364
pakeeza@mansoor.com
Circulation: 8,000 *Frequency:* Wednesday; Urdu
Sabih Mansoor, Publisher & Editor

Sangam
7 Axsmith Cres., Toronto, ON M3J 3K2
Tel: 416-490-0091; *Fax:* 416-490-9592
umeshvijaya@msn.com
Circulation: 22,500
Umesh Vijaya, Publisher/Editor

Sanjh Savera/Dust and Dawn
#2, 2575 Steeles Ave. East, Brampton, ON L6T 5T1
Tel: 905-789-7787; *Fax:* 905-789-7717
info@sanjhsavera.com
www.sanjhsavera.com
Circulation: 15,000
Nirmal Hansa, Publisher

Shama/Flame
5790 Riverside Pl., Mississauga, ON L5M 4W9
Tel: 905-826-6397; *Fax:* 905-858-7951
nkhan@theeasternnews.com
Circulation: 5,000 *Frequency:* Semi-monthly; Urdu
Alia Sultana, Publisher & Editor

The South Asian Voice
Tel: 905-337-3030; *Fax:* 905-338-1364
southasianvoice@mansoor.com
Circulation: 8,000 *Frequency:* Wednesday; English & Urdu
Sabih Mansoor, Publisher

Thamilar Thakaval
PO Box 3 F, Toronto, ON M4Y 2L4
Tel: 416-920-9250; *Fax:* 416-921-6576
tamilsinfo@sympatico.ca
Circulation: 5,000 *Frequency:* Monthly
Thiru S. Thiuchelvam, Editor-in-chief

The Times of Sri Lanka
58 Sundial Cres., Toronto, ON M4A 2J8
Tel: 416-445-5390; *Fax:* 416-285-8494
timeslanka@rogers.com
Circulation: 5,000
Upali Obeyesekere, Managing Editor

The Weekly Voice
#212, 6705 Tomken Rd., Mississauga, ON L5T 2J6
Tel: 905-795-8282; *Fax:* 905-795-9801
info@weeklyvoice.com
www.weeklyvoice.com
Circulation: 50,000
Binoy Thomas, Editor

Spanish

Noticero De Norte a Sur
295 Vaughan Rd., Toronto, ON M6C 2N3
Tel: 416-653-8942; *Fax:* 416-653-6441
denorteasur@on.aibn.com
www.denorteasur.com
Circulation: 60,000 *Frequency:* Monthly
Emilia Modolo, Editor

La Voz de Montreal
#112, 6225, Place North Crest, Montréal, QC H3S 2T5
Tel: 514-253-2739; *Fax:* 514-343-9697
lavoz@sympatico.ca
Circulation: 15,000 *Frequency:* 12 times a year
Gilberto Miranda, Director

Swedish

Scandinavian Press
1294 - 7th Ave. West, Vancouver, BC V6H 1B6
Tel: 604-731-6381; *Fax:* 604-731-2292
office@nordicway.com
www.nordicway.com
Frequency: 4 times a year; ISSN: 1201-3447
Anders Neumuller, Publisher & Editor

Swedish Press
1294 - 7th Ave. West, Vancouver, BC V6H 1B6
Tel: 604-731-6381; *Fax:* 604-731-2292
office@nordicway.com
www.nordicway.com
Circulation: 6,000 *Frequency:* Monthly; English & Swedish; ISSN: 0839-2323
Anders Neumuller, Publisher & Editor

Ukrainian

Homin Ukrainy
83 Christie St., Toronto, ON M6G 3B1
Tel: 416-516-2443; *Fax:* 416-516-4033
homin@on.aibn.com
Circulation: 1,000 *Frequency:* Weekly; Ukrainian & English
M. Shepetyk, Publisher
O. Romanyshyn, Editor

Moloda Ukraina
12 Minstrel Dr., Toronto, ON M8Y 3G4
Tel: 416-255-8604; *Fax:* 416-961-9609
Walentina Rodak, Contact

Novy Shliakh/New Pathway
New Pathway Publishers Ltd., 145 Evans Ave., Toronto, ON M5Z 5X8
Tel: 416-960-3424; *Fax:* 416-960-1442
npweekly@look.ca
www.infoukes.com/newpathway
Circulation: 4,500 *Frequency:* Weekly; also New Pathway Almanac (annual)

Leslie Salnick, President

Progress Ukrainian Catholic News
233 Scotia St., Winnipeg, MB R2V 1V7
Tel: 204-338-7801; *Fax:* 204-339-4006
progress@archeparchy.ca
www.archeparchy.ca/progress/
Circulation: 4,900
Rev. Mikhail Kouts, Associate Editor
Lydia Firman, Business Manager
Most Rev. Richard Soo, Managing Editor SJ

Promin
PO Box 57268 Jackson, Hamilton, ON L8P 4X1
Tel: 905-572-9626; *Fax:* 905-524-5362
promin@networx.on.ca
Circulation: 1,600
Orysia Sushko, Editor-in-chief

Ukrainian News
c/o Edmonton Lasergraphics, #1, 12227 - 107 Ave., Edmonton, AB T5M 1Y9
Tel: 780-488-3860; *Fax:* 780-488-3859
ukrnews@interbaun.com
Circulation: 3,274 *Frequency:* Bi-weekly; English & Ukrainian
Marco Levytsky, Publisher & Editor
Vitaly Shevchenko, Chief, KYIV Bureau
Irene Hladki, Manager, Advertising & Production

Ukrainsky Holos
842 Main St., Winnipeg, MB R2W 3N8
Tel: 204-589-5871; *Fax:* 204-586-3618
presstr@mbsympatico.ca
Circulation: 2,100 *Frequency:* Bi-Weekly; Ukrainian & English
Maria Bosak

Visnyk/The Herald
9 St. John's Ave., Winnipeg, MB R2W 1G8
Tel: 204-582-0996; *Fax:* 204-582-5241
Toll-Free: 877-586-3093
visnyk@uocc.ca
www.uocc.ca
Circulation: 10,000 *Frequency:* Monthly; English & Ukrainian
Rev. Andrew Jarmus, Editor-in-chief

Zhinochy Svit / Woman's World
Ukrainian Women's Organization of Canada, 145 Evans Ave., Toronto, ON M8Z 5X8
Tel: 416-960-5297; *Fax:* 416-960-1442
Circulation: 2,000 *Frequency:* 4 pa; English & Ukrainian
Lesia Panko, Editor

Vietnamese

Lang Van
PO Box 218 U, Toronto, ON M8Z 5P1
Tel: 905-607-8010; *Fax:* 905-607-8011
langvan@ilap.com
Circulation: 5,000
Nguyen Huu Nghia, Publisher/Editor-in-chief

Thôi Bâo/Time News
1114 College St., Toronto, ON M6H 1B6
Tel: 416-925-8607; *Fax:* 416-925-0695
mails@thoibao.com
www.thoibao.com
Circulation: 14,500 *Frequency:* Weekly
Lee Nguyen, Manager
Dave Nguyen, Publisher

Vietnam Time Magazine Edmonton
PO Box 284 Main, Edmonton, AB T5J 2J1
Tel: 780-429-4781; *Fax:* 780-429-4781
thoibao@telus.net
Circulation: 1,500
Thanh Nguyen, Publisher

Farm

Farm Publication

The Ad-Viser
Farm Press Ltd., 1320 - 36th St. North, Lethbridge, AB T1H 5H8
Tel: 403-328-5114; *Fax:* 403-328-5443
Toll-Free: 877-328-0048
adsales@farmpressltd.com
www.farmpressgroup.com
Circulation: 20,159 *Frequency:* Every other Thu.
Jeff Sarich, Publisher

Agri Digest
Site 26, Comp. 32, RR#2, Chase, BC V0E 1M0
Tel: 250-679-5362; *Fax:* 250-675-6851
Toll-Free: 800-555-7102
meaghen@elltel.net
www.agridigest.com
Circulation: 10,546 *Frequency:* 12 times a year; Aug. issue - Agri Digest Directory (annual)
Fran Kay, Publisher
Jodi Houghton, Editor

Agricom
2474 Champlain St., Clarence Creek, ON K0A 1N0
Tél: 613-488-2651; *Téléc:* 613-488-2541
info.agricom@lavoieagricole.ca
www.lavoieagricole.ca/agri_com.cfm
Circulation: 5 000 *Frequency:* 22 times a year
Pierre Glaude, Publisher

Alberta Beef
#202, 2915 - 19 St. NE, Calgary, AB T2E 7A2
Tel: 403-250-1090; *Fax:* 403-291-9546
info@beefnews.com
www.albertabeef.ca
Circulation: 8,700 *Frequency:* 12 times a year
Garth McClintock, Publisher

Alberta Farmer Express
1666 Dublin Ave., Winnipeg, MB R3H OH1
Tel: 204-954-1400; *Fax:* 204-954-1422
www.albertafarmexpress.ca
Circulation: 29,500 *Frequency:* 12 times per year
Will Verboven, Editor, will.verboven@fbcpublishing.com
Dave Bedard, Daily News Editor, daveb@fbcpublishing.com

Barley Country
c/o Alberta Barley Commission, #200, 3601A - 21 St. NE, Calgary, AB T2E 6T5
Tel: 403-291-9111; *Fax:* 403-291-0190
Toll-Free: 800-265-9111
abbarley@albertabarley.com
www.albertabarley.com
Circulation: 35,000 *Frequency:* 4 times a year
Terry Bullick, Editor, tbullick@telusplanet.net
Nikki Barnes, Advertising, Project Coordinator

BC Dairy Directory
PO Box 724, Summerland, BC V0H 1Z0
Tel: 250-496-5707; *Fax:* 250-496-5132
Toll-Free: 888-324-7347
info@bcdairydirectory.com
www.bcdairydirectory.com
Circulation: 1,450 *Frequency:* Annually, June
Karin McCarty, Editor

Beef in B.C. Inc.
c/o B.C. Cattlemen's Association, #4, 10145 Dallas Dr., Kamloops, BC V2C 6T4
Tel: 250-573-3611; *Fax:* 250-573-5155
beefinbc@kamloops.net
www.cattlemen.bc.ca
Circulation: 2,200 *Frequency:* 7 times a year
Bob France, Editor

Better Farming
ON
Tel: 519-763-4044; *Fax:* 519-763-4482
publisher@betterfarming.com
www.betterfarming.com
Circulation: 43,000
Paul Nolan, Publisher & Advertising Director
Don Stoneman, Senior Staff Editor, 519-654-9106, Fax: 519-654-9357, dstoneman@betterfarming.com
Robert Irwin, Managing Editor, 613-678-2232, Fax: 613-678-5993, rirwin@betterfarming.com

Better Pork
Tel: 519-763-4044; *Fax:* 519-763-4482
Circulation: 6,403 *Frequency:* 6 times a year

Le Bulletin des Agriculteurs
#800, 1200, av McGill College, Montréal, QC H3B 4G7
Tél: 514-845-5141; *Téléc:* 514-843-2180
info@lebulletin.rogers.com
www.lebulletin.com
Circulation: 24 000 *Frequency:* Mensuel; français
Simon M. Guertin, Éditeur
Yvon Thérien, Rédacteur-en-chef

CAAR Communicator
#107, 1090 Waverley St., Winnipeg, MB R3T 3P4
Tel: 204-989-9300; *Fax:* 204-989-9306
Toll-Free: 800-463-9323
www.caar.org
Circulation: 4,700 *Frequency:* 5 times a year
J. Ryrie

Canada's Who's Who Of The Poultry Industry
Tel: 519-429-3966; *Fax:* 516-429-3094
Toll-Free: 888-599-2228
jbauslaugh@annexweb.com
www.canadianpoultrymag.com
Circulation: 5,300 *Frequency:* Annually, July
John Bauslaugh, Publisher
Kristy Nudds, Editor

Canadian Ayrshire Review
4865, boul Laurier ouest, Saint-Hyacinthe, QC J2S 3V4
Tel: 450-778-3535; *Fax:* 451-778-3531
info@ayrshire-canada.com
www.ayrshire-canada.com
Circulation: 1,500 *Frequency:* Bi-monthly; English & French
Linda Ness, Business Manager

Canadian Cattlemen: The Beef Magazine
PO Box 9800, Winnipeg, MB R3C 3K7
Tel: 204-944-5753; *Fax:* 204-942-8463
gren@fbcpublishing.com
www.agcanada.com
Circulation: 26,825 *Frequency:* Monthly
Gren Winslow, Editor

Canadian Guernsey Journal
Canadian Guernsey Assn., RR#5, Guelph, ON N1H 6J2
Tel: 519-836-2141; *Fax:* 519-763-6582
guernsey@gencor.ca
www.guernseycanada.ca
Circulation: 250 *Frequency:* annual
Vivianne M. Macdonald, Managing Editor

Canadian Hereford Digest
5160 Skyline Way NE, Calgary, AB T2E 6V1
Tel: 403-274-1734; *Fax:* 403-275-4999
info@herefordddigest.com
www.herefordddigest.com
Circulation: 2,500; 8,000 (commercial issue) *Frequency:* 7 times a year; English & French
Kurt Gilmore, Publisher & Editor

The Canadian Horsetrader
PO Box 219, Dutton, ON N0L 1J0
Tel: 519-762-3993; *Fax:* 519-762-0572
pams@wwdc.com
www.horsetradermagazine.com
Circulation: 10,000

Canadian Jersey Breeder
#9, 350 Speedvale Ave. West, Guelph, ON N1H 7M7
Tel: 519-821-1020; *Fax:* 519-821-2723
info@jerseycanada.com
www.jerseycanada.com
Circulation: 1,400 *Frequency:* 5 times a year
Ryan Barrett, Editor

Canadian Poultry Magazine
Tel: 519-429-3966; *Fax:* 519-429-3094
Toll-Free: 888-599-2228
jbauslaugh@annexweb.com
www.canadianpoultrymag.com
Circulation: 5,300 *Frequency:* 12 times a year
Kristy Nudds, Editor
John Bauslaugh, Advertising Manager

Canola Country
Saskatchewan Canola Growers Association, #210, 111 Research Dr., Saskatoon, SK S7N 3R2
Tel: 306-668-2380; *Fax:* 306-975-1126
lkuchenski@innovationplace.com
Circulation: 1,100 *Frequency:* 4 times a year
Lanette Kuchenski, Editor

Canola Digest
315 Pacific Ave., Winnipeg, MB R3A 0M2
Tel: 204-947-6912; *Fax:* 204-947-9136
www.canola-council.org
Circulation: 50,405 *Frequency:* 4 times a year
Kelly Funke, Editor

Canola Guide
Tel: 204-944-5569; *Fax:* 204-944-5562
www.agcanada.com
Circulation: 26,012 *Frequency:* 4 times a year
Cory Bourdeau'hui, Editor

Central Alberta Farmer
Tel: 780-986-2271; *Fax:* 780-986-6397
cafarmer@ccinet.ab.ca
www.albertafarmer.com
Circulation: 32,800 *Frequency:* 12 times a year
Neil Sutcliffe, Publisher

Central Alberta Life
PO Box 5200, 2950 Bremner Ave., Red Deer, AB T4N 5G3
Tel: 403-343-2400; *Fax:* 403-342-4051
Circulation: 38,460 *Frequency:* Twice weekly
Fred Gorman, Publisher

Charolais Banner
#1, 2241 Alberts St., Regina, SK S4P 2V5
Tel: 306-546-3940; *Fax:* 306-546-3942
charolaisbanner@sasktel.net
www.charolaisbanner.com
Circulation: 1,900 *Frequency:* 5 times a year
Candace By, Managing Editor

Le Coopérateur Agricole
#200, 9001, boul de l'Acadie, Montréal, QC H4N 3H7
Tél: 514-384-6450; *Téléc:* 514-858-2025
cooperateur@lacoop.coop
www.lacoop.coop/cooperateur
Circulation: 20 718 *Frequency:* 10 fois par an; français
André Léger, Advertising Manager
Patrick Dupuis, Rédacteur-en-chef

Country Guide
Tel: 204-944-5754; *Fax:* 204-942-8463
jay@fbcpublishing.com
www.agcanada.com
Circulation: 42,000 (West & East editions) *Frequency:* 11 times a year; also Corn-Soy Guide
Jay Whetter, Editor

Dairy Contact
PO Box 549, 4914 - 50th St., Onoway, AB T0E 1V0
Tel: 780-967-2929; *Fax:* 780-967-2930
dccontact@icrossroads.com
Frequency: Monthly
Allen Parr, Editor

Dairy Update
Tel: 204-944-5569; *Fax:* 204-944-5562
www.agcanada.com
Circulation: 44,405 *Frequency:* 9 times a year
G. Winslow, Editor

Drainage Contractor
Tel: 519-235-2400; *Fax:* 519-235-0798
pdarbishire@annexweb.com
drainagecontractor.com
Circulation: 8,000 *Frequency:* Annually
Peter Darbishire, Editor

Eastern Ontario Agrinews
PO Box 368, 7 King St., Chesterville, ON K0C 1H0
Tel: 613-448-2321; *Fax:* 613-448-3260
rm@agrinewsinteractive.com
agrinewsinteractive.com
Circulation: 14,000 *Frequency:* Monthly
Robin R. Morris, Publisher

Farm Focus
Optipress Publishing, PO Box 128, 2 Second St., Yarmouth, NS B5A 4B1
Tel: 902-742-7111; *Fax:* 902-742-2311
www.atlanticfarmfocus.ca
Circulation: 5,990 *Frequency:* 24 times a year
Mark Richardson, Publisher

Farm Market
930 Richmond St., Chatham, ON N7M 5J5
Tel: 519-351-7331; *Fax:* 519-351-2452
farmmarketnew@bowesnet.com
Circulation: 12,518 *Frequency:* 25 times a year
Peter Epp, Editor
Dean Muharren, Publisher

Farming for Tomorrow
#204, 2114 Robinson St., Regina, SK S4T 2P7
Toll-Free: 888-213-9999
info@farmingfortomorrow.ca
www.farmingfortomorrow.ca
Other information: Toll Free Fax: 1-888-213-9999
Circulation: 67,400 *Frequency:* 2 times a year
Tom Bradley, Editor/Publisher

Feather Fancier Newspaper
5739 Telfer Rd., Sarnia, ON N7T 7H2
Tel: 519-542-6859; *Fax:* 519-542-4168
featherfancier@ebtech.net
www.featherfancier.on.ca
Circulation: 1,800 *Frequency:* 11 times a year
Paul Monteith, Editor/Publisher

Fruit & Vegetable Magazine
Tel: 519-429-3966; *Fax:* 519-429-3094
Toll-Free: 800-265-2827
fruitedit@annexweb.com
www.fruitandveggie.com
Circulation: 7,000 *Frequency:* 8 times a year
Peter Darbishire, Publisher
Marg Land, Editor

Germination
Issues Ink, #203, 897 Corydon Ave., Winnipeg, MB R3M 0W7
Tel: 204-453-1965; *Fax:* 204-475-5247
issues@issuesink.com
www.germination.ca
Circulation: 5,000 *Frequency:* 5 times a year
Robynne Anderson, Editor

Gestion et Technologie Agricoles
655, av Sainte-Anne, Saint-Hyacinthe, QC J2S 5G4
Tél: 450-773-6028; *Téléc:* 450-773-3115
publicite@courrierclarion.qc.ca
www.lecourrier.qc.ca
Circulation: 20 000 *Frequency:* 11 fois par an; français
Guy Roy, Directeur

Grainews
Tel: 204-944-5567; *Fax:* 204-944-5562
Toll-Free: 800-665-1362
cory@fbcpublishing.com
www.agcanada.com
Circulation: 28,771 *Frequency:* 18 times a year
Cory Bourdeaud'hui, Editor

Holstein Journal
#210, 30 East Beaver Creek Rd., Richmond Hill, ON L4B 1J2
Tel: 905-886-4222; *Fax:* 905-866-0037
peter@holsteinjournal.com
www.holsteinjournal.com
Circulation: 4,900 *Frequency:* Monthly; English & French
G. Peter English, Publisher
Bonnie Cooper, Editor

Island Farmer
PO Box 790, 567 Main St., Montague, PE C0A 1R0
Tel: 902-838-2515; *Fax:* 902-838-4392
Toll-Free: 800-806-5443
pmacneill@islandpress.ca
www.peicanada.com
Circulation: 2,244 *Frequency:* 26 times a year
Paul MacNeill, Publisher
Andy Walker, Editor

The Limousin Leader
Bollum Marketing, PO Box 10, Site 11, RR#1, Airdrie, AB T4B 2A3
Tel: 403-948-4768; *Fax:* 403-948-7531
rhonda@limousinleader.com
www.limousinleader.com
Frequency: 4 times a year
Randy Bollum, Editor

Ma Revue de machinerie agricole
Section Rouge Média Inc., 468, boul Roland-Therrien, Longueuil, QC J4H 4E3
Tél: 450-677-2556; *Téléc:* 450-677-4099
info@marevueagricole.com
www.marevueagricole.com
Circulation: 35 000 *Frequency:* 11 fois par an; français
Louise Gionet, Directeure des ventes publicitaires

The Manitoba Co-Operator
PO Box 9800 Main, 220 Portage Ave., Winnipeg, MB R3C 3K7
Tel: 204-944-5569; *Fax:* 204-944-5562
www.agcanada.com
Circulation: 11,939 *Frequency:* Weekly; supplements Seed Manitoba (annual); Yield Manitoba (annual); ISSN: 0025-2239
Andy Sirski, Editorial Director

Manitoba Farmers' Voice
Frequency: 4 times a year
Kevin Hill, Editor

Manitoba FarmLIFE
#300, 2050 Cume Blvd., Brandon, MB R7A 5Y1
Tel: 204-727-5459; *Fax:* 204-729-8965
Toll-Free: 888-756-7770
farmlife@mts.net
www.farmpressgroup.com
Circulation: 28,000 *Frequency:* 26 times a year
Dale Coulter, Manager

Niagara Farmers' Monthly
PO Box 52, 131 College St., Smithville, ON L0R 2A0
Tel: 905-957-3751; *Fax:* 905-957-0088
editor@niagarafarmers.com
Circulation: 21,078 *Frequency:* 11 times a year
Maribeth Fitts, Editor

The Northern Horizon
901 - 100th Ave., Dawson Creek, BC V1G 1W2
Tel: 250-782-4888; *Fax:* 250-782-6300
Circulation: 29,000 *Frequency:* Bi-weekly

Northern Horse Review
Tel: 403-250-1128; *Fax:* 403-250-1194
ingrids@telusplanet.net
www.northernhorsereview.com
Circulation: 15,000 *Frequency:* Monthly
Ingrid Schulz, Co-Publisher & Editor, ingrid@telusplanet.net
Ruth Dunbar, Co-Publisher

Northwest Farmer/Rancher
PO Box 1029, 892 - 104th St., North Battleford, SK S9A 3E6
Tel: 306-445-7621; *Fax:* 306-445-3223
Toll-Free: 866-549-9979
battlefords.publishing@sasktel.net
Circulation: 16,800 *Frequency:* 6 times a year
Alana Schweitzer, General Manager
Doug Collie, Editor

Ontario Beef
Ontario Cattlemen's Assn., 130 Malcolm Rd., Guelph, ON N1K 1B1
Tel: 519-824-0334; *Fax:* 519-824-9101
ontbeef@cattle.guelph.on.ca
www.cattle.guelph.on.ca
Circulation: 20,000 *Frequency:* 5 times a year
Lianne Appleby, Editor
Donna Corbet, Circulation Manager

Ontario Beef Farmer
Tel: 519-473-0010; *Fax:* 519-473-2256
Circulation: 10,310 *Frequency:* 5 times a year
Mervyn J. Hawkins, Publisher
Paul Mahon, Editor

Ontario Corn Producer
c/o Ontario Corn Producers Assn., 90 Woodlawn Rd. West, Guelph, ON N1H 1B2
Tel: 519-837-1660; *Fax:* 519-837-1674
ontcorn@ontariocorn.org
www.ontariocorn.org/magazine.html
Circulation: 22,000 *Frequency:* 9 times a year
Brenda Miller-Sanford, Editor

Ontario Dairy Farmer
Tel: 519-473-0010; *Fax:* 519-473-2256
Toll-Free: 800-567-3276
www.ontariofarmer.com
Circulation: 7,445 *Frequency:* 8 times a year
Mervyn J. Hawkins, Publisher

Ontario Farmer
Tel: 519-473-0010; *Fax:* 519-473-2256
www.ontariofarmer.com
Circulation: 32,127 *Frequency:* Weekly, Tue.
Mervyn J. Hawkins, Publisher
Paul Mahon, Editor

Ontario Hog Farmer
Tel: 519-473-0010; *Fax:* 519-473-2256
www.ontariofarmer.com

Circulation: 4,830 *Frequency:* 8 times a year
Mervyn J. Hawkins, Publisher

Ontario Milk Producer
Dairy Farmers of Ontario, 6780 Campobello Rd., Mississauga, ON L5N 2L8
Tel: 905-821-8970; *Fax:* 905-821-3160
Circulation: 10,791 *Frequency:* Monthly
Bill Dimmick, Editor

Porc Québec - Québec Hog Industry Magazine
555, boul Roland Therrien, Longueuil, QC J4H 4E9
Tél: 450-679-0530; *Téléc:* 450-679-0102
rloiseau@upa.qc.ca
Circulation: 3 000 *Frequency:* 5 times a year
Dominique Blanchard, Production Manager

Prairie Farmer
PO Box 1356, 500 Main St., Winkler, MB R6W 4B3
Tel: 204-325-4771; *Fax:* 204-325-5059
Toll-Free: 888-565-8357
Circulation: 26,000 *Frequency:* 25 times a year
Rick Reimer, Publisher

Prairie Hog Country
PO Box 5536, Leduc, AB T9E 2A1
Tel: 780-986-0962; *Fax:* 780-980-9640
hogcountry@shaw.ca
www.prairiehogcountry.ca
Circulation: 4,800 *Frequency:* 6 times a year
Calvin Daniels, Copy Editor
Laurie Brandly, Publisher

Le Producteur de lait québécois
Fédération des producteurs de lait du Québec, 555, boul Roland Thérrien, Longueuil, QC J4H 3Y9
Tél: 450-679-0530; *Téléc:* 450-670-4788
rloiseau@laterre.ca
www.lait.org
Circulation: 9 338 *Frequency:* 10 fois par an; français
Jean Vigneault, Éditeur-en-chef

Producteur Plus
CP 147, Farnham, QC J2N 2R4
Tél: 450-293-8282; *Téléc:* 450-293-8554
leonard.pigeon@producteurplus.com
Circulation: 18 644 *Frequency:* 8 fois par an; français
Léonard Pigeon, Éditeur et Rédacteur-en-chef

Pro-farm
#300, 2216 Lorne St., Regina, SK S4P 2M7
Tel: 306-586-5866; *Toll-Free:* 888-776-3276
wcwga@wcwga.ca
Circulation: 9,000 *Frequency:* 4 times a year
Shannon McArton, Editor
Shelley Collins, Circulation Manager

Québec Farmers' Advocate
Maison l'UPA, 555, boul Roland-Therrien, Longueuil, QC J4H 3Y9
Tel: 450-679-0530; *Fax:* 450-463-5291
qfa@upa.qc.ca
www.quebecfarmers.org
Circulation: 3,722 *Frequency:* 11 times a year

Regional Country News
115 Queen St. East, St Marys, ON N4X 1B7
Tel: 519-284-2440; *Toll-Free:* 888-270-1604
editor@regionalcountrynews.com
www.regionalcountrynews.com
Circulation: 18,000 *Frequency:* Monthly
Stew Slater, Editor
Bill Huether, Publisher

Richelieu Agricole
#800, 625 boul Rene-Levesque, Montréal, QC H3B 1R2
Tél: 514-866-3131; *Téléc:* 514-866-3030
Ligne sans frais: 800-361-7262
infos@reseauselect.com
www.reseauselect.com
Circulation: 15 700 *Frequency:* 12 fois par an
Gilles Lévesque, Rédacteur-en-chef
Lucie Leduc, General Manager

Rural Roots
30 - 10th Ave. East, Prince Albert, SK S6V 0Y5
Fax: 306-922-4237
rural.roots@paherald.sk.ca
www.paherald.sk.ca
Circulation: 31,992 *Frequency:* 52 times a year
Ian Jensen, Publisher
Ruth Griffiths, Editor

The Rural Voice
Tel: 519-523-4311; *Fax:* 519-523-9140
Circulation: 13,293 *Frequency:* Monthly; ISSN: 0703-7724
Keith Roulston, Publisher

Saskatchewan Farm Life
2206A Ave. C North, Saskatoon, SK S7L 6C3
Tel: 306-242-5723; *Fax:* 306-668-6164
Toll-Free: 888-924-6367
Circulation: 56,200 *Frequency:* 26 times a year
Dan Moores, Publisher

Sheep Canada
1489 Rte. 560, Deerville, NB E7K 1W7
Tel: 506-328-3599; *Fax:* 506-328-8165
Toll-Free: 888-241-5124
gallivan@sheepcanada.com
www.sheepcanada.com
Frequency: 4 times a year
Dr. Cathy Gallivan, Editor

Simmental Country
#13, 4101 - 19 St. NE, Calgary, AB T2E 7C4
Tel: 403-250-5255; *Fax:* 403-250-5121
country@simmental.com
www.simmental.com
Circulation: 1,800 *Frequency:* Monthly

Specialty Farms
PO Box 530, 105 Donly Dr. South, Simcoe, ON N3Y 4N5
Tel: 519-429-5190; *Fax:* 519-429-3094
Toll-Free: 888-599-2228
mland@annexweb.com
www.specialtyfarms.ca
Other information: Toll-Free Fax: 1-888-404-1129
Circulation: 3,500 *Frequency:* 6 times a year
Peter Darbishire, Publisher
Sharon Kauk, Advertising Manager
Marg Land, Editor

La Terre de chez nous
555, boul Roland Therrien, Longueuil, QC J4H 3Y9
Tél: 450-679-8483; *Téléc:* 450-670-4788
lhamon@laterre.ca
laterre.ca
Circulation: 38 620 *Frequency:* Hebdomadaire; français
Loïc Hamon, Rédacteur-en-chef

Union Farmer Quarterly
National Farmers Union, 2717 Wentz Ave., Saskatoon, SK S7K 4B6
Tel: 306-652-9465; *Fax:* 306-664-6226
nfu@nfu.ca
www.nfu.ca
Circulation: 5,000 *Frequency:* 4 times a year
Terry Pugh, Editor

Voice of the Farmer
PO Box 490, 254 Main St., Dresden, ON N0P 1M0
Tel: 519-683-4485; *Fax:* 519-683-4355
Frequency: Biweekly; also - Voice of the: Huron Farmer, Kent Farmer, Lambton Farmer, Middlesex Farmer, Elgin Farmer, Perth Farmer, Oxford Farmer, Waterloo Farmer; monthly Voice of: York Farmer, Durham Farmer, Vi
Mary Baxter, Editor

Western Dairy Farmer Magazine
Tel: 780-986-2271; *Fax:* 780-986-6397
editor-wdf-caf@webcoleduc.com
www.westerndairyfarmer.com
Circulation: 6,962 *Frequency:* 6 times a year
Diana MacLeod, Editor
Neil Sutcliffe, Publisher

Western Hog Journal
Alberta Pork Producers Development Corp., 4828 - 89 St., Edmonton, AB T6E 5K1
Tel: 780-474-8288; *Fax:* 780-479-5128
Circulation: 4,315 *Frequency:* 4 times a year, 1 special Banff pork seminar edition
Jody Wacowich, Editor

The Western Producer
PO Box 2500, 2310 Millae Ave., Saskatoon, SK S7K 2C4
Tel: 306-665-3544; *Fax:* 306-934-2401
Toll-Free: 800-667-6978
newsroom@producer.com
www.producer.com
Circulation: 70,000 *Frequency:* Weekly
Ken Zacharias, Publisher
Barb Glen, Editor

Scholarly

Literary

Event
c/o Douglas College, PO Box 2503, New Westminster, BC V3L 5B2
Tel: 604-527-5293; *Fax:* 604-527-5095
event@douglas.bc.ca
event.douglas.bc.ca
Circulation: 1,250 *Frequency:* 3 times a year; ISSN: 0315-3770
Billeh Nickerson, Editor
Ian Cockfield, Managing Editor
Rick Maddocks, Editor

Scholarly Publication

Acadiensis: Journal of the History of the Atlantic Region / Revue d'Histoire de la Région Atlantique
Campus House, University of New Brunswick, PO Box 4400 A, Fredericton, NB E3B 5A3
Tel: 506-453-4978; *Fax:* 506-453-5068
acadiensis@unb.ca
www.lib.unb.ca/Texts/Acadiensis
Circulation: 900 *Frequency:* 2 times a year; English & French; ISSN: 0044-5851
Bill Parenteau, Editor
Nicole Lang, Editor, nlang@umce.ca
Stephen Dutcher, Managing Editor, nlang@umce.ca

Annals of Air & Space Law / Annales de droit aérian et spatial
Institute & Centre of Air & Space Law, McGill University, 3661, rue Peel, Montréal, QC H3A 1X1
Tel: 514-398-5095; *Fax:* 514-398-8197
edannals.law@mcgill.ca
www.mcgill.ca/iasl/annals
Circulation: 1,000 *Frequency:* annually
Prof.Dr. Paul S. Dempsey, Editor

Anthropologica
Wilfrid Laurier University Press, 2-139 DAWB, 75 University Ave. West, Waterloo, ON N2L 3C5
Tel: 519-884-0710; *Fax:* 519-725-1399
press@wlu.ca
www.anthropologica.ca
Circulation: 625 *Frequency:* 2 times a year
Dr. Leslie Jermyn, Managing Editor, ljermyn@chass.utoronto.ca
Andrew Lyons, Editor-in-chief, andrewpaullyons@gmail.com

Arctic
c/o Arctic Institute of North America, University of Calgary, 2500 University Dr. NW, Calgary, AB T2N 1N4
Tel: 403-220-7515; *Fax:* 403-282-4609
kmccullo@ucalgary.ca
www.artic.ucalgary.ca
Circulation: 1,500 *Frequency:* 4 times a year; ISSN: 0004-0843
Dr. Karen McCullough, Editor, 403/220-4049
Dr. Benoît Beauchamp, Executive Director, 403/220-7516

ARIEL - A Review of International English Literature
Department of English, University of Calgary, 2500 University Dr. NW, Calgary, AB T2N 1N4
Tel: 403-220-4657; *Fax:* 403-289-1123
ariel@ucalgary.ca
Circulation: 850 *Frequency:* 4 times a year
Pamela McCallum, Editor

Atlantis: A Women's Studies Journal
Institute for the Study of Women, Mount Saint Vincent Univer, Halifax, NS B3M 2J6
Tel: 902-457-6319; *Fax:* 902-443-1352
atlantis@msvu.ca
www.msvu.ca/atlantis
Circulation: 500 *Frequency:* 2 times a year
Linda Kealey, General Editor
Annalee Lepp, General Editor
Katherine Side, General Editor

BC Studies: The British Columbian Quarterly
Buchanan E, #162, 1866 Main Mall, Vancouver, BC V6T 1Z1
Tel: 604-822-3727; *Fax:* 604-822-0606
info@bcstudies.com
www.bcstudies.com
Circulation: 700 *Frequency:* 4 times a year
Leanne Coughlin, Editor

Canadian Children's Literature (CCL) / Littérature Canadienne pour la Jeunesse
Centre for Research in Young People's Texts and Cultures, University of Winnipeg, 515 Portage Ave., Winnipeg, MB R3B 2E9
Tel: 204-786-9351; *Fax:* 204-774-4134
ccl@uwinnipeg.ca
ccl.uwinnipeg.ca
Circulation: 900 *Frequency:* 4 times a year; English & French; ISSN 0319-0080
Perry Nodelman, Editor
Marie Davis, Associate Editor
Anne Rusnak, Associate Editor

Canadian Ethnic Studies / Études Ethniques au Canada
University of Calgary, 2500 University Dr. NW, Calgary, AB T2N 1N4
Tel: 403-220-7257; *Fax:* 403-210-8764
ces@ucalgary.ca
www.ss.ucalgary.ca/ces
Circulation: 1,800 *Frequency:* 3 times a year; ISSN: 0008-3496
Dr. James Frideres, Editor

Canadian Foreign Policy / La Politique étrangère du Canada
2116 Dunton Tower, Carleton University, 1125 Colonel By Dr., Ottawa, ON K1S 5B6
Tel: 613-520-6696; *Fax:* 613-520-3981
cfp@carleton.ca
www.carleton.ca/cfpj
Frequency: 3 times a year
Maureen Molot, Editor
Sarah Geddes, Managing Editor

The Canadian Historical Review
5201 Dufferin St., Toronto, ON M3H 5T8
Tel: 416-667-7810; *Fax:* 416-667-7881
journals@utpress.utoronto.ca
www.utpjournals.com/chr/chr.html
Circulation: 1,700 *Frequency:* 4 times a year; English & French; ISSN: 0008-3755
Ken Cruikshank, Co-Editor
Sylvie Dépatie, Co-Editor

Canadian Journal of Development Studies / Revue canadienne d'études du développement
c/o University of Ottawa, 542 King Edward Ave., Ottawa, ON K1N 6N5
Tel: 613-562-5800; *Fax:* 613-562-5361
cjds@uottawa.ca
www.cjds.ca
Circulation: 500 *Frequency:* 4 times a year, plus 1 special issue; English & French
Henry Veltmeyer, Co-Editor
Scott Simon, Co-Editor

Canadian Journal of Economics / Revue canadienne d'economique
CIREQ, Université de Montréal, PO Box 6128 Centre Ville, #C-6086, 3150, Jean-Brillant, Montréal, QC H3C 3J7
Tel: 514-343-2104; *Fax:* 514-343-5831
cje@umontreal.ca
economics.ca/cje
Circulation: 3,200 *Frequency:* 4 times a year
Dwayne Benjamin, Managing Editor

Canadian Journal of Higher Education / La Revue canadienne d'enseignement supérieur
c/o The Canadian Society for the Study of Higher Education, 220 Sinnot Building, 70 Dysart St., Winnipeg, MB R3T 2N2
Tel: 204-474-8309; *Fax:* 204-474-7607
csshe@cc.umanitoba.ca
www.umanitoba.ca/csshe
Circulation: 550 *Frequency:* 3 times a year
Keith Archer, Editor

Canadian Journal of History (CJH) / Annales canadiennes d'histoire
Dept. of History, University of Saskatchewan, 9 Campus Dr., Saskatoon, SK S7N 5A5
Tel: 306-966-5794; *Fax:* 306-966-5852
cjh@duke.usask.ca
www.usask.ca/history/cjh
Circulation: 725 *Frequency:* 3 times a year; ISSN: 0008-4107
John McCannon, Editor
Linda Dietz, Managing Editor

The Canadian Journal of Information & Library Science
5201 Dufferin St., Toronto, ON M3H 5T8
Tel: 416-667-7810; *Fax:* 416-667-7881
journals@utpress.utoronto.ca
www.utpjournals.com/cjils/cjils.html
Circulation: 400 *Frequency:* 4 times a year
Lynne McKechnie, Editor

Canadian Journal of Law & Society (CJLS/RCDS) / Revue Canadienne Droit et Société
Dept des sciences juridiques, UQAM, CP 8888 Centre-Ville, Montréal, QC H3C 3P8
Tél: 514-987-3000; *Téléc:* 514-987-4784
www.acds-clsa.org/en/rcds
Circulation: 700 *Frequency:* Biennially; English & French
Ruth Murbach, Editor

Canadian Journal of Linguistics / Revue Canadienne de Linguistique
5201 Dufferin St., Toronto, ON M3H 5T8
Tel: 416-667-7810; *Fax:* 416-667-7881
journals@utpress.utoronto.ca
www.utpjournals.com/cjl/cjl.html
Circulation: 900 *Frequency:* 4 times a year
Rose-Marie Dechaine, Editor

Canadian Journal of Mathematics
CMS, 5201 Dufferin St., Toronto, ON M3H 5T8
Tel: 416-667-7810; *Fax:* 416-667-7881
journals@utpress.utoronto.ca
www.utpjournals.com/cjm/cjm.html
Circulation: 1,225 *Frequency:* 6 times a year
James B. Carrell, Editor
Nassif Ghoussoub, Editor

Canadian Journal of Philosophy
Tel: 403-220-3514; *Fax:* 403-282-0085
ucpmail@ucalgary.ca
www.uofcpress.com/UCP/CJP.html
Circulation: 875 *Frequency:* 4 times a year plus supplementary volume
Dr. M. Stingl, Editorial Board Coordinator

Canadian Journal of Program Evaluation / La Revue canadienne d'évaluation de programme
PO Box 450 A, 145 Jean-Jacques-Lussier, Ottawa, ON K1N 6N5
Tel: 613-562-5800; *Fax:* 613-562-5146
cjpe@uottawa.ca
www.evaluationcanada.ca
Circulation: 1,900 *Frequency:* Bi-annually; English & French
Prof. J. Bradley Cousins, Editor

Canadian Journal of Psychiatry
#701, 141 Laurier Ave. West, Ottawa, ON K1P 5J3
Tel: 613-234-2815; *Fax:* 613-234-9857
subscriptions@cpa-apc.org
www.cpa-apc.org/Publications/cjpHome.asp
Circulation: 6,100 *Frequency:* 12 times a year
Dr. Joel Paris, Editor-in-chief

Canadian Journal of Psychoanalysis / Revue canadienne de psychanalyse
7000, Côte-des-Neiges, Montréal, QC H3S 2C1
Tel: 514-738-9847; *Fax:* 514-738-6393
cjp-rcp@qc.aira.com
Circulation: 650 *Frequency:* Bi-annually; ISSN 1195-3330
Brian M. Robertson, Editor

The Canadian Journal of Sociology / Cahiers canadiens de sociologie
5201 Dufferin St., Toronto, ON M3H 5T8
Tel: 416-667-7810; *Fax:* 416-667-7881
journals@utpress.utoronto.ca
www.utpjournals.com/cjs/cjs.html
Circulation: 1,100 *Frequency:* 4 times a year; English with French abstracts; ISSN: 0318-6431
Kevin D. Haggerty, Editor

Canadian Journal of Women & The Law (CJWL/RFD) / Revue Femmes et Droit
University of Toronto Press - Journals Division, 5210 Dufferin St., Toronto, ON M3H 5T8
Tel: 416-667-7810; *Fax:* 416-667-7881
www.utpjournals.com/cjwl
Frequency: 2 times a year; English & French

Canadian Journal on Aging / La Revue Canadienne du Vieillissement
5201 Dufferin St., Toronto, ON M3H 5T8
Tel: 416-667-7810; *Fax:* 416-667-7881
journals@utpress.utoronto.ca
www.utpjournals.com/cja/cja.html
Circulation: 1,600 *Frequency:* 4 times a year; English & French; ISSN: 0714-9808
Mark W. Rosenberg, Editor

Canadian Literature
c/o University of British Columbia, Buchanan E158, 1866 Main Mall, Vancouver, BC V6T 1Z1
Tel: 604-822-2780; *Fax:* 604-822-5504
can.lit@ubc.ca
www.canlit.ca
Circulation: 1,200 *Frequency:* 4 times a year
Donna Chin, Managing Editor
Laurie Ricou, Editor

Canadian Mathematical Bulletin
5201 Dufferin St., Toronto, ON M3H 5T8
Tel: 416-667-7810; *Fax:* 416-667-7881
journals@utpress.utoronto.ca
www.utpjournals.com/cmb/cmb.html
Circulation: 775 *Frequency:* 4 times a year
Maung Min-Oo, Editor-in-chief
Andrew J. Nicas, Editor-in-chief

Canadian Modern Language Review (CMLR/RCLV) / Le Revue canadienne des langues vivantes
5201 Dufferin St., Toronto, ON M3H 5T8
Tel: 416-667-7810; *Fax:* 416-667-7881
journals@utpress.utoronto.ca
www.utpjournals.com/cmlr/cmlr.html
Circulation: 1,000 *Frequency:* 4 times a year; English & French; ISSN: 0008-4506
Larry Vandergrift, Co-Editor
Tracey Derwing, Co-Editor

Canadian Poetry: Studies, Documents, Reviews
Dept. of English, University of Western Ontario, Richmond St. North, London, ON N6A 3K7
Tel: 519-673-1164; *Fax:* 519-661-3776
dbentley@uwo.ca
www.canadianpoetry.ca
Circulation: 400 *Frequency:* 2 times a year
D.M.R. Bentley, Editor

Canadian Public Administration (CPA/APC) / Administration publique du Canada
#401, 1075 Bay St., Toronto, ON M5S 2B1
Tel: 416-924-8787; *Fax:* 416-924-4992
ntl@ipac.ca; ntl@iapc.ca
www.ipac.ca; www.iapc.ca
Circulation: 3,600 *Frequency:* 4 times a year; ISSN: 008-4840
Barbara Wake Carroll, Editor

Canadian Public Policy / Analyse de Politique
CIREQ - Université de Montréal, PO Box 6128 Centre-Ville, Montréal, QC H3C 3J7
Tel: 514-343-2104; *Fax:* 514-343-5831
cpp@umontreal.ca
economics.ca/cpp
Circulation: 1,500 *Frequency:* 4 times a year; English & French; ISSN: 0317-0861
James B. Davis, Managing Editor

Canadian Review of American Studies
5201 Dufferin St., Toronto, ON M3H 5T8
Tel: 416-667-7810; *Fax:* 416-667-7881
journals@utpress.utoronto.ca
www.utpjournals.com/cras/cras.html
Circulation: 400 *Frequency:* 3 times a year; English & French
Priscilla Walton, Editor

Canadian Review of Sociology & Anthropology / Revue canadienne de sociologie et d'anthropologie
SB-323, 1455, boul de Maisonneuve West, Montréal, QC H3G 1M8
Tel: 514-848-8780; *Fax:* 514-848-8780
info@csaa.ca
www.csaa.ca
Circulation: 1,428 *Frequency:* 4 times a year; French & English
Harley Dickinson, Managing Editor

Canadian Theatre Review
5201 Dufferin St., Toronto, ON M3H 5T8
Tel: 416-667-7810; *Fax:* 416-667-7881
journals@utpress.utoronto.ca
www.utpjournals.com/ctr
Circulation: 650 *Frequency:* 4 pa; ISSN: 0315-0836
Ann Wilson, Co-Editor

Rick Knowles, Co-Editor
Harry Lane, Co-Editor
Reid Gilbert, Co-Editor
Catherine Graham, Co-Editor
Andrew Houston, Co-Editor

Cartographica
5201 Dufferin St., Toronto, ON M3H 5T8
Tel: 416-667-7810; *Fax:* 416-667-7881
journals@utpress.utoronto.ca
www.utpjournals.com/carto/carto.html
Circulation: 900 *Frequency:* 4 times a year
Jeremy Crampton, Co-Editor
Roger Wheate, Co-Editor
Clifford Wood, Co-Editor

Economics Working Papers
Dept. of Economics, McMaster University, #426, Kenneth Taylor Hall, Hamilton, ON L8S 4M4
Tel: 905-525-9140; *Fax:* 905-521-8232
econ@mcmaster.ca
socserv2.socsci.mcmaster.ca/~econ/rsrch/index.html
Frequency: 4 times a year

Eighteenth-Century Fiction
Tel: 416-667-7810; *Fax:* 416-667-7881
journals@utpress.utoronto.ca
www.utpjournals.com
Circulation: 750 *Frequency:* 4 times a year
Jacqueline Langille, Managing Editor
Peter Walmsley, Co-Editor
Julie Park, Co-Editor

Energy Studies Review
c/o MIES, KTH 330, McMaster University, Hamilton, ON L8S 4M4
Tel: 905-525-9140; *Fax:* 905-777-8344
mies@mcmaster.ca
www.socsci.mcmaster.ca/mies/
Frequency: 2 times a year; ISSN: 0843-4379
Prof. Joseph A. Doucet, Editor

Environments: A Journal of Interdisciplinary Studies
Geography & Environmental Studies, Wilfred Laurier University, Waterloo, ON N2L 3C5
Tel: 519-884-0710; *Fax:* 519-725-1342
www.fes.uwaterloo.ca/research/environments/
Circulation: 400 *Frequency:* 3 times a year; ISSN: 0711-6780
D. Scott Slocombe, Editor, sslocomb@wlu.ca

Essays on Canadian Writing (ECW)
#200, 2120 Queen St. East, Toronto, ON M4E 1E2
Tel: 416-694-3348; *Fax:* 416-698-9906
info@ecwpress.com
www.ecw.ca
Circulation: 1,200 *Frequency:* 3 times a year; ISSN: 0313-0300
Jack David, Publisher & Editor

Exceptionality Education Canada
c/o Lindsey Leenaars, Uni. of Alberta, #6, 102 Education North, Edmonton, AB T6G 2G5
Tel: 780-492-0800; *Fax:* 780-492-1318
eecj@ualberta.ca
www.uofaweb.ualberta.ca/eec
Circulation: 250 *Frequency:* 3 times a year
Judy Lupart, Editor
Christina M. Rinaldi, Editor
Jessica Whitley, Associate Editor
Lindsey Leenaars, Editorial Assistant

Infor
5201 Dufferin St., Toronto, ON M3H 5T8
Tel: 416-667-7810; *Fax:* 416-667-7881
journals@utpress.utoronto.ca
www.utpjournals.com/infor/infor.html
Circulation: 400 *Frequency:* 4 times a year
Bernard Gendron, Editor

Interculture
4917, rue Saint-Urbain, Montréal, QC H2T 2W1
Tel: 514-288-7229; *Fax:* 514-844-6800
info@iim.qc.ca
www.iim.qc.ca
Circulation: 900 *Frequency:* 2 times a year; English & French editions; ISSN: 0828-797X (English), 0712-1571 (French)
Robert Vachon, Publisher

International Journal
c/o Canadian Institute of International Affairs, #302, 205 Richmond St. West, Toronto, ON M5V 1V3
Tel: 416-997-9000; *Fax:* 416-977-7521
mailbox@ciia.org
www.ciia.org
Circulation: 1,300 *Frequency:* 4 times a year; ISSN: 0020-7020
David Haglund, Co-Editor
Joseph Jodcel, Co-Editor

Intersections : Canadian Journal of Music/Revue canadienne de musique
PO Box 507 Q, Toronto, ON M4T 2M5
Tel: 416-483-7282; *Fax:* 416-489-1713
journals@interlog.com
www.cums-smuc.ca
Circulation: 400 *Frequency:* 2 times a year; ISSN 1911-0146; French
Prof. Mary Woodside, Editor
François de Médicis, Rédacteur

Journal of Baha'i Studies / La Revue des Études Bahá'¡es/La Revista des Estudios Bahá'¡
34 Copernicus St., Ottawa, ON K1N 7K4
Tel: 613-233-1903; *Fax:* 613-233-3644
editor@bahai-studies.ca
www.bahai-studies.ca
Circulation: 2,000 *Frequency:* biannual; English, French & Spanish; ISSN: 0838-0430
Anne Furlong, Editor

Journal of Canadian Art History / Annales d'histoire de l'art canadien
c/o EV-3.819, Concordia University, 1455, boul de Maisonneuve ouest, Montréal, QC H3G 1M8
Tel: 514-848-2424; *Fax:* 514-848-4584
jcah@vax2.concordia.ca
art-history.concordia.ca/JCAH/index.html
Circulation: 550 *Frequency:* 2 times a year; English & French
Sandra Paikowsky, Publisher

Journal of Canadian Poetry
Dept. of English, University of Ottawa, Ottawa, ON K1N 6N5
Tel: 613-562-5800; *Fax:* 613-562-5975
dstaines@uottawa.ca
Circulation: 350 *Frequency:* Annually
David Staines, Editor

Journal of Canadian Studies / Revue d'Études Canadiennes
c/o Trent University, 1600 West Bank Dr., Peterborough, ON K9J 7B8
Tel: 705-748-1279; *Fax:* 705-748-1110
jcs_rec@trentu.ca
Circulation: 1,300 *Frequency:* 4 times a year; English & French
Robert M. Campbell
Kerry Cannon, Managing Editor

Journal of Law & Social Policy / Revue des lois et des politiques sociales
Clinic Resource Office, Legal Aid Ontario, #41, 425 Adelaide St. West, Toronto, ON M5V 3C1
Tel: 416-204-5408; *Fax:* 416-204-5422
Toll-Free: 800-668-8258
jlsp@lao.on.ca
www.legalaid.on.ca
Circulation: 230 *Frequency:* Annually; ISSN 0829-3929
Margaret Capes, Editor
Andrew Bolter, Editor

Journal of Scholarly Publishing
5201 Dufferin St., Toronto, ON M3H 5T8
Tel: 416-667-7810; *Fax:* 416-667-7881
journals@utpress.utoronto.ca
www.utpjournals.com/jsp/jsp.html
Circulation: 800 *Frequency:* 4 times a year; ISSN: 1198-9742
Tom Radko, Editor

Journal of Ukrainian Studies
CIUS Press, #125, 10 Orde St.res., Toronto, ON M5T 1N7
Tel: 416-978-6934; *Fax:* 416-978-2672
zakydalsky@sympatico.ca
www.utoronto.ca/cius/
Circulation: 250
Taras Zakydalsky, Managing Editor, zakydalsky@sympatico.ca

Labour, Capital & Society: A Journal on the Third World / Travail, capital et société
c/o Dr. Suzanne Dansereau, Intl. Development Studies Program, Saint Mary's University, Halifax, NS B3H 3C3
Tel: 902-420-5793;
journallcs-tcs@smu.ca
www.marua.com/journallcs/index.html
Circulation: 700 *Frequency:* 2 times a year; English & French
Dr. Suzanne Dansereau, Editor

Labour/Le Travail
FM 2005, Faculty of Arts Publications, Memorial University of Newfoundland, St. John's, NL A1C 5S7
Tel: 709-737-2144; *Fax:* 709-737-4342
cclh@mun.ca
www.mun.ca/cclh
Circulation: 1,000 *Frequency:* 2 times a year; English & French; ISSN: 0700-3862
Bryan D. Palmer, Editor-in-chief
Irene Whitfield, Managing Editor, 709/737-3453

Material Culture Review
c/o University of Cape Breton, PO Box 5300, Sydney, NS B1P 6L2
Tel: 902-563-1604; *Fax:* 902-563-1177
www.uccbpress.ca/MCReview.htm
Circulation: 400 *Frequency:* 2 times a year; ISSN: 1183-1073
Richard McKinnon, Managing Editor

McGill Journal of Education / Revue des sciences de l'éducation McGill
c/o Faculty of Education, McGill University, 3700, rue McTavish, Montréal, QC H3A 1Y2
Tel: 514-398-4246; *Fax:* 514-398-4529
ann.keenan@mcgill.ca
Circulation: 500 *Frequency:* 3 times a year; English & French
Anthony Paré, Editor
Ann Keenan, Managing Editor

McMaster Journal of Theology & Ministry
c/o McMaster Divinity College, McMaster University, 1280 Main St. West, Hamilton, ON L8S 4K1
Tel: 905-525-9140; *Fax:* 905-577-4782
mjtm@mcmaster.ca
www.mcmaster.ca/mjtm
Frequency: annual
Wendy J. Porter, Editor

Le Médecin Vétérinaire du Québec
Ordre des médecins vétérinaires du Québec, #200, 800, av Ste-Anne, Saint-Hyacinthe, QC J2S 5G7
Tél: 450-774-1427; *Téléc:* 450-774-7635
Ligne sans frais: 800-267-1427
omvq@omvq.qc.ca
www.omvq.qc.ca
Circulation: 2 500 *Frequency:* 4 fois par an; français
Jean Piérard, Rédacteur-en-chef d.m.v.

Modern Drama
5201 Dufferin St., Toronto, ON M3H 5T8
Tel: 416-667-7810; *Fax:* 416-667-7881
journals@utoronto.ca
www.utpjournals.com/md/md.html
Circulation: 1,700 *Frequency:* 4 times a year; ISSN: 0026-7694
Alan Ackerman, Editor

The Monograph - Journal of the Ont. Assn. for Geographic & Environmental Education
Ontario Association for Geographic & Environmental Education, PO Box 507 Q, Toronto, ON M4T 2M5
Tel: 416-483-7282; *Fax:* 416-489-1713
journals@interlog.com
www.oagee.org
Circulation: 800 *Frequency:* 4 times a year; ISSN 0048-1973
Gary Birchall, Editor

Mosaic: A Journal for the Interdisciplinary Study of Literature
#208, Tier Bldg., University of Manitoba, Winnipeg, MB R3T 2N2
Tel: 204-474-9763; *Fax:* 204-474-7584
mosaic_journal@umanitoba.ca
www.umanitoba.ca/mosaic
Circulation: 900 *Frequency:* 4 times a year; ISSN: 0027-1276
Lisa Muirhead, Production Manager
Donna Danyluk, Manager, Subscriptions
Jackie Pantel, Business, Submissions & Systems Manager
Dawne McCance, Editor

Mouseion, Journal of the Classical Association of Canada/ Revue de la Societé canadienne des ét
Department of Classics, Memorial University of Newfoundland, St. John's, NF A1C 5S7
Tel: 709-737-7914
Frequency: 3 times a year; English & French
Dr. Mark Joyal, Editor
Dr. J. Butrica, Editor, jbutrica@mun.ca
Dr. L. Stirling, Editor

Newfoundland and Labrador Studies
Faculty of Arts Publications, Memorial University of Newfoun, FM 2005, St. John's, NL A1C 5S7
Tel: 709-737-2144; *Fax:* 709-737-4342
nlstudies@mun.ca
www.mun.ca/nls
Circulation: 350 *Frequency:* 2 times a year; English & French; ISSN: 0823-1737
Ron Rompkey, Chair
Irene Whitfield, Managing Editor

Ontario History
Tel: 416-226-9011; *Fax:* 416-226-2740
ohs@ontariohistoricalsociety.ca
www.ontariohistoricalsociety.ca
Circulation: 1,200 *Frequency:* 2 times a year
Thorald J. Tronrud, Editor
Patricia K. Neal, Executive Director

Pacific Affairs
c/o University of British Columbia, #164, 1855 West Mall, Vancouver, BC V6T 1Z2
Tel: 604-822-4534; *Fax:* 604-822-9452
enquiry@pacificaffairs.ubc.ca
pacificaffairs.ubc.ca
Circulation: 1,600 *Frequency:* 4 times a year; ISSN: 0030-851X
Jacquelilne Garnett, Managing Editor
Pittman Potter, Chair, Editorial Board
Timothy Cheek, Editor

The Philantropist / Le Philanthrope
The AGORA Foundation, PO Box 507 Q, Toronto, ON M4T 2M5
Tel: 416-483-7282; *Fax:* 416-489-1713
journals@interlog.com
www.thephilanthropist.ca
Circulation: 450 *Frequency:* 4 times a year
Donald Bourgeois, Editor

Policy Options / Options politiques
Inst. for Research on Public Policy, #200, 1470, rue Peel, Montréal, QC H3A 1T1
Tel: 514-985-2461; *Fax:* 514-985-2559
irpp@irpp.org
www.irpp.org
Circulation: 2,000 *Frequency:* 10 times a year; ISSN: 0226-5893
L. Ian MacDonald, Editor

Prairie Forum: Journal of the Canadian Plains Research Center
Canadian Plains Research Center, University of Regina, Regina, SK S4S 0A2
Tel: 306-585-4795; *Fax:* 306-585-4699
brian.mlazgar@uregina.ca
www.cprc.ca
Circulation: 300 *Frequency:* 2 times a year; ISSN: 0317-6282
Dr. Patrick Douaud, Editor

Public Sector Management et Secteur Publique
#401, 1075 Bay St., Toronto, ON M5S 2B1
Tel: 416-924-8787; *Fax:* 416-924-4992
ntl@ipac.ca; ntl@iapc.ca
www.ipac.ca; www.iapc.ca
Circulation: 4,000 *Frequency:* 3 times a year; ISSN: 1183-1081
Patrice Dutil, Editor

Queen's Quarterly
Queen's University, Kingston, ON K7L 3N6
Tel: 613-533-2667; *Fax:* 613-533-6822
qquarter@post.queensu.ca
www.queensu.ca/quarterly
Circulation: 3,000 *Frequency:* 4 times a year; ISSN: 0033-6041
Dr. Boris Castel, Editor
Penny Roantree, Business Manager

Relational Child & Youth Care Practice
School of Child & Youth Care, Ryerson University, SHE Bldg., 350 Victoria St., Toronto, ON M5B 2K3
Tel: 416-598-5923; *Fax:* 416-979-5209
rcycp@ryerson.ca
Circulation: 450 *Frequency:* 4 times a year
Gerry Fewster, Founding Editor
Carol Stuart, Managing Editor
Dr. T. Garfat, Co-Editor

Renaissance & Reformation / Renaissance et réforme
CRRS Publications, Victoria University, 71 Queen's Park Cres. East, Toronto, ON M5S 1K7
Tel: 416-585-4465; *Fax:* 416-585-4430
crrs.publications@utoronto.ca
www.RenRef.ca
Circulation: 700 *Frequency:* 4 times a year; ISSN 0034-429X

Michael O'Connor, Managing Editor

Resources for Feminist Research
Ontario Institute for Studies in Education/University of Tor, 252 Bloor St. West, Toronto, ON M5S 1V6
Tel: 416-923-6641; *Fax:* 416-926-4725
rfrdrf@oise.utoronto.ca
www.oise.utoronto.ca/rfr
Circulation: 2,000 *Frequency:* 2 times a year; ISSN: 0707-8412
Philinda Masters, Editor

Revue canadienne de linguistique appliquée / Canadian Journal of Applied Linguistics
Institut des langues secondes, Université d'Ottawa, 600 King Edward, Ottawa, ON K1N 6N5
Tél: 613-562-5743; *Téléc:* 613-562-5126
hknoerr@uottawa.ca
www.aclacaal.org
Frequency: 2 fois par an
Hélène Knoerr, Editor

Russell: The Journal of Bertrand Russell Studies
The Bertrand Russell Research Centre, TSH #619, McMaster Uni, Main St. West, Hamilton, ON L8S 4M2
Tel: 905-525-9140; *Fax:* 905-577-6930
blackwk@mcmaster.ca
www.humanities.mcmaster.ca/~russell/journal.htm
Circulation: 400 *Frequency:* 2 times a year
Kenneth Blackwell, Editor

Science Fiction Studies
c/o Veronica Hollinger, Cultural Studies Program, Trent University, Peterborough, ON K9J 7B8
Tel: 705-748-1011; *Fax:* 705-748-1826
vhollinger@trentu.ca
www.depauw.edu/sfs
Circulation: 800 *Frequency:* 3 times a year
Arthur B. Evans, Managing Editor

Scientia Canadensis - Journal of the History of Cdn. Science, Technology & Medicine
Canadian Science & Technology Historical Association, PO Box 8509 T, Ottawa, ON K1G 3H9
Circulation: 200 *Frequency:* Annually; ISSN 0829-2507
Stéphane Castonguay, Editor-in-chief

Scrivener Creative Review
c/o McGill University, 853, rue Sherbrooke ouest, Montréal, QC H3A 2T6
Tel: 514-398-6588; *Fax:* 514-398-8146
scrivener.review@gmail.com
arts.mcgill.ca/english/scrivener/
Circulation: 500 *Frequency:* Annually; ISSN: 0227-5090
Lisa Guimond, Editor
Andrew Cleland, Editor

Seminar
5201 Dufferin St., Toronto, ON M3H 5T8
Tel: 416-667-7810; *Fax:* 416-667-7881
journals@utpress.utoronto.ca
www.utpjournals.com/seminar/seminar.html
Circulation: 770 *Frequency:* 4 times a year
Raleigh Whitinger, Editor

Social History / Histoire Sociale
5201 Dufferin St., Toronto, ON M3H 5T8
Tel: 416-667-7810; *Fax:* 416-667-7881
journals@utpress.utoronto.ca
www.utpjournals.com/hssh/hssh.html
Circulation: 500 *Frequency:* 2 times a year
Chad Gaffield, Editor
Gordon Darroch, Editor

Studies in Canadian Literature / Études en littérature canadienne
Campus House, PO Box 4400, 11 Garland Ct., Fredericton, NB E3B 5A3
Tel: 506-453-3501; *Fax:* 506-453-5069
scl@unb.ca
www.Lib.unb.ca/Texts/SCL
Circulation: 500 *Frequency:* 2 times a year
J.C. Ball, Editor
S.R. Campbell, Managing Editor
J. Andrews, Editor

Studies in Political Economy
Carleton University, Colonel By Dr., Ottawa, ON K1S 5B6
Tel: 613-520-2600; *Fax:* 613-520-3713
spe@carleton.ca
www.carleton.ca/spe
Circulation: 600 *Frequency:* 2 times a year
Hélène Pellerin

Tessera
Études littéraires, UQAM, CP 8888 Centre-Ville, Montréal, QC H3C 3P8
Tél: 514-987-3000; *Téléc:* 514-987-8218
delvaux.martine@uqam.ca
Circulation: 500 *Frequency:* 2 times a year; ISSN: 0840-4631
Martine Delvaux, Co-Editor

Theatre Research in Canada / Recherches théâtrales au Canada
Graduate Centre for Study of Drama, University of Toronto, 214 College St., 3rd Fl., Toronto, ON M5T 2Z9
Tel: 416-978-7984; *Fax:* 416-971-1378
tric.rtac@utoronto.ca
www.lib.unb.ca/Texts/TRIC/
Circulation: 350 *Frequency:* 2 times a year; English & French
Bruce Barton, Editor

The Tocqueville Review / La Revue Tocqueville
5201 Dufferin St., Toronto, ON M3H 5T8
Tel: 416-667-7781; *Fax:* 416-667-7881
journals@utpress.utoronto.ca
www.utpjournals.com/ttr/ttr.html
Circulation: 400 *Frequency:* 2 times a year; English & French
Michel Forsé, Co-Editor
Françoise Mélonio, Co-Editor
Laurence Gullec, Co-Editor
Cheryl Welch, Co-Editor

Topia: A Canadian Journal of Cultural Studies
c/o 3013 Tel Centre, York University, 4700 North Keele St., Toronto, ON M3J 1P3
Tel: 416-736-2100; *Fax:* 416-736-5392
topia@yorku.ca
www.yorku.ca/topia
Circulation: 300 *Frequency:* 2 times a year; ISSN: 1206-0143
Jody Berland, Editor

Transcultural Psychiatry
Psychiatry Dept., McGill University, 1033, av des Pins ouest, Montréal, QC H3A 1A1
Tel: 514-398-7302; *Fax:* 514-398-4370
Laurence.Kirmayer@mcgill.ca
www.mcgill.ca/tcpsych/publications
Circulation: 500 *Frequency:* 4 times a year
Laurence J. Kirmayer, Editor M.D.
Sing Lee, Associate Editor M.D.
Roland Littlewood, Associate Editor M.D., PhD
Leslie Swartz, Associate Editor PhD

Ultimate Reality & Meaning
5201 Dufferin St., Toronto, ON M3H 5T8
Tel: 416-667-7810; *Fax:* 416-667-7881
journals@utpress.utoronto.ca
www.utpjournals.com/uram/uram.html
Circulation: 380 *Frequency:* 4 times a year
John F. Perry, Editor
J. Patrick Mohr, Executive Editor

University of Toronto Law Journal
5201 Dufferin St., Toronto, ON M3H 5T8
Tel: 416-667-7810; *Fax:* 416-667-7881
journals@utpress.utoronto.ca
www.utpjournals.com/utlj/utlj.html
Circulation: 700 *Frequency:* 4 times a year
Karen Knop, Editor

University of Toronto Quarterly
5201 Dufferin St., Toronto, ON M3H 5T8
Tel: 416-667-7810; *Fax:* 416-667-7881
journals@utpress.utoronto.ca
www.utpjournals.com/utq/utq.html
Circulation: 1,100 *Frequency:* 4 times a year
Brian Corman, Editor

Urban History Review / Revue d'Histoire Urbaine
Tel: 416-483-7282; *Fax:* 416-489-1713
subscribe@urbanhistoryreview.ca
www.urbanhistoryreview.ca
Circulation: 400 *Frequency:* 2 times a year; ISSN 0703-0428
Michèle Dagenais, Co-Editor
Robert Lewis, Co-Editor

Windsor Review
c/o Dept. of English, University of Windsor, #2, 104 Chrysler Hall North, Windsor, ON N9B 3P4
Tel: 519-253-3000; *Fax:* 519-971-3676
uwrevu@uwindsor.ca
athena.uwindsor.ca/units/english/English.nsf
Circulation: 500 *Frequency:* 2 times a year; ISSN: 0042-0352

University

Student Guides

Acces Media
#31, 1124, ch Marie-Anne est, Montréal, QC H2J 2B7
Tel: 514-524-1182; *Fax:* 514-524-7771
Toll-Free: 800-391-1182
info@accesmedia.com
www.accesmedia.com
Circulation: 300,000
Edgar Donelle

The Student Traveller
The Canadian Federation of Students - Services, #100, 45 Charles St. East, Toronto, ON M4Y 1S2
Tel: 416-966-2887; *Fax:* 416-966-4043
suben@travelcuts.com
www.travelcuts.com
Circulation: 130,000 *Frequency:* 2 times a year
Lisa Trainor, Editor

Welcome Back Student Magazine
Osprey Media Group, PO Box 1352, #205, 111 Princess St., Kingston, ON K7L 5C6
Tel: 613-549-8442; *Fax:* 613-549-4333
kingmags@kos.net
Circulation: 18,500 *Frequency:* Annually
Mary Laflamme, Publisher & Editor

University & Student Publications

Algonquin Times
1385 Woodroffe Ave., Ottawa, ON K2G 1V8
Tel: 613-727-4723; *Fax:* 613-727-7743
times@algonquincollege.com
www.algonquincollege.com
Kris Lapenskie, Online Editor

L'Alinéa
781, rue Notre Dame, Repentigny, QC J5Y 1B4
Tel: 450-470-0911; *Fax:* 450-581-1567
infocom@collanaud.qc.ca
www.collanaud.qc.ca

antiThesis
99 University Ave., Kingston, ON K7L 3N6
Tel: 613-533-2000; *Fax:* 613-533-6300
antithesis@sgps.ca
www.queensu.ca

Aquinian
PO Box 4400 A, Fredericton, NB E3B 5G3
Tel: 506-452-0532; *Fax:* 506-452-0617
www.stu.ca

Argosy Weekly
62A York St., Sackville, NB E4L 1H3
Tel: 506-364-2300;
argosy@mta.ca
www.mta.ca
Dan Wortman, Managing Editor
Julie Stephenson, Editor

The Argus
955 Oliver Rd., Thunder Bay, ON P7B 5E1
Tel: 807-343-8110; *Fax:* 807-343-8023
www.lakeheadu.ca

Arthur
#104, 751 George St., Peterborough, ON K9H 7P5
Tel: 705-745-3535; *Fax:* 705-745-3534
editors@trentarthur.ca
www.trentu.ca
James Burrows, Editor
Ariel Sharratt, Editor

At Guelph
50 Stone Rd. East, Guelph, ON N1G 2W1
Tel: 519-824-4120; *Fax:* 519-767-1693
www.uoguelph.ca
Barbara Chance, Editor

The Athenaeum
C/O Acadia University, 50 Acadia St., Wolfville, NS B4P 2R6
Tel: 902-542-2201; *Fax:* 902-585-1072
www.acadiau.ca

L'Attribut
9155, rue St-Hubert, Montréal, QC H2M 1Y8
Tel: 514-389-5921; *Fax:* 514-389-5762
www.collegeahuntsic.qc.ca

Bandersnatch
CP 2000, 21275, rue Lakeshore, Sainte-Anne-de-Bellevue, QC H9X 3L9
Tél: 514-457-6610; *Téléc:* 514-457-1655
bandersnatch@johnabbott.qc.ca
www.johnabbott.qc.ca

Bricklayer
PO Box 5005, 100 College Blvd., Red Deer, AB T4N 5H5
Tel: 403-342-3300; *Fax:* 403-340-8940
www.rdc.ab.ca

Brock Press
500 Glenridge Ave., St Catharines, ON L2S 3A1
Tel: 905-688-5550; *Fax:* 905-688-2789
www.brocku.ca

Brunswickan
PO Box 4400 A, Fredericton, NB E3B 5A3
Tel: 506-453-4666; *Fax:* 506-453-5158
trudya@unb.ca
www.unb.ca

The Buzz
c/o Newnham Campus, 1750 Finch Ave. East, Toronto, ON M2J 2X5
Tel: 416-491-5050;
www.senecac.on.ca/

The Cadre
550 University Ave., Charlottetown, PE C1A 4P3
Tel: 902-566-0439; *Fax:* 902-566-0420
www.upei.ca

Le Calvaire
60, rue de l'Évêché ouest, Rimouski, QC G5L 4H6
Tel: 418-723-1880; *Fax:* 418-724-4961
infoscol@cegep-rimouski.qc.ca
www.cegep-rimouski.qc.ca

The Campus
PO Box 5000, Lennoxville, QC J1M 1Z7
Tel: 819-822-9600; *Fax:* 819-822-9661
Toll-Free: 1 8-0 5-7 27
liaison@ubishops.ca
www.ubishops.ca

Campus Times
C/O University of British Columbia #164, 1855 West Mall, Vancouver, BC V6T 1Z2
Tel: 604-822-2211;
www.ubc.ca

Capilano Courier
2055 Purcell Way, North Vancouver, BC V7J 3H5
Tel: 604-986-1911; *Fax:* 604-984-4985
switchboard@capcollege.bc.ca
www.capcollege.bc.ca

CAS
1455, boul de Maisonneuve ouest, Montréal, QC H3G 1M8
Tel: 514-848-2424; *Fax:* 514-848-2621
communications@concordia.ca
www.concordia.ca

Cascade
33844 King Rd., Abbotsford, BC V2S 7M8
Tel: 604-504-7441; *Fax:* 604-855-7614
www.ucfv.ca

The Charlatan
1125 Colonel By Dr., Ottawa, ON K1S 5B6
Tel: 613-520-7400;
www.carleton.ca

The Chronicle
PO Box 385, 2000 Simcoe St. North, Oshawa, ON L1H 7L7
Tel: 905-721-2000; *Fax:* 905-721-3113
www.durhamcollege.ca

Cityside
3737 Wascana Pkwy., Regina, SK S4S 0A2
Tel: 306-585-4402; *Fax:* 306-585-4997
www.uregina.ca

The Cord Weekly
75 University Ave. West, Waterloo, ON N2L 3C5
Tel: 519-884-0710;
www.wlu.ca

La Criée
616, av St-Rédempteur, Matane, QC G4W 1L1
Tel: 418-562-1240; *Fax:* 418-566-2115
comcegep@cgmatane.qc.ca
www.cegep-matane.qc.ca

La Crise
1660, boul de l'Entente, Québec, QC G1S 4S3
Tel: 418-688-8310; *Fax:* 418-688-1539
communications@cegep-fxg.qc.ca
www.cegep-fxg.qc.ca

The Crown
777 Garner Rd. East, Ancaster, ON L9K 1J4
Tel: 905-648-2131; *Fax:* 905-648-2134
mvanbev@redeemer.ca
www.redeemer.ca

D'Épiderme
175, rue De La Vérendrye, Sept-Iles, QC G4R 5B7
Tel: 418-962-9848; *Fax:* 418-962-3852
info@cegep-sept-iles.qc.ca
www.cegep-sept-iles.qc.ca

D.E.C. express
537, boul Blanche, Baie-Comeau, QC G5C 2B2
Tel: 418-589-5707; *Fax:* 418-589-9842
Toll-Free: 1 8-0 4-3 20
www.cegep-baie-comeau.qc.ca

de Fouille-moi
235, rue Saint-Jacques, Granby, QC J2G 3N1
Tel: 450-372-6614; *Fax:* 450-372-6565
www.cegepgranby.qc.ca

Dialog Newspaper
PO Box 1015 B, Toronto, ON M5T 2T9
Tel: 416-415-2000; *Fax:* 416-415-4493
Toll-Free: 1 8-0 2-5 20
info@gbrownc.on.ca
www.gbrownc.on.ca

The Echo
821, av Ste-Croix, Saint-Laurent, QC H4L 3X9
Tel: 514-744-7500; *Fax:* 514-744-7023
info@vaniercollege.qc.ca
www.vaniercollege.qc.ca

Eclosion
2410, ch Ste-Foy, Sainte-Foy, QC G1V 1T3
Tel: 418-659-6630; *Fax:* 418-659-7576
www.cegep-ste-foy.qc.ca

L'Ecorché
100, rue Duquet, Sainte-Thérèse, QC J7E 3G6
Tel: 450-430-3120; *Fax:* 450-971-7872
info@clg.qc.ca
www.clg.qc.ca

L'Électic
3000, av Boullé, Saint-Hyacinthe, QC J2S 1H9
Tel: 450-773-6800; *Fax:* 450-773-9971
info@cegepsth.qc.ca
www.cegepsth.qc.ca

The Emery Weal
1301 - 16 Ave. NW, Calgary, AB T2M 0L4
Tel: 403-284-8110; *Fax:* 403-284-7112
www.sait.ca
Canada's premier technical institute by 2010

The Endeavour
3000 College Dr. South, Lethbridge, AB T1K 1L6
Tel: 403-320-3200; *Fax:* 403-320-1461
Toll-Free: 1 8-0 5-2 01
info@lethbridgecollege.ab.ca
www.lethbridgecollege.ab.ca

L'Entremetteur
333, boul Cité-des-Jeunes, Hull, QC J8Y 6M5
Tél: 819-770-4012; *Téléc:* 819-770-8167
www.coll-outao.qc.ca

Etcetera
North Campus, 205 Humber College Blvd., Toronto, ON M9W 5L7
Tel: 416-675-5005; *Fax:* 416-675-2427
enquiry@humber.ca
www.humber.ca

L'Exemplaire
3000, boul Tracy, Sorel-Tracy, QC J3R 5B9
Tel: 450-742-6651; *Fax:* 450-742-1878
info@cegep-sorel-tracy.qc.ca
www.cegep-sorel-tracy.qc.ca

Express This
299 College Dr. SE, Medicine Hat, AB T1A 3Y6
Tel: 403-529-3811; *Fax:* 403-504-3517
info@mhc.ab.ca
www.mhc.ab.ca

Folio
114 St. - 89 Ave., Edmonton, AB T6G 2E1
Tel: 780-492-3111;
www.ualberta.ca

Le Forcep
205, rue Mgr Bourget, Lévis, QC G6V 6Z9
Tel: 418-833-5110; *Fax:* 418-833-7323
www.clevislauzon.qc.ca

Free Forum
3330 - 22nd Ave., Prince George, BC V2N 1P8
Tel: 250-562-2131; *Fax:* 250-561-5816
Toll-Free: 1 8-0 3-1 81
askcnc@cnc.bc.ca
www.cnc.bc.ca

Le Front
Universite de Moncton, Centre Etudiant, 2e Etage, Moncton, NB E1A 3E9
Tel: 506-858-4000; *Fax:* 506-858-4379
www.umoncton.ca

Gargoyle
15 King's College Circle, Toronto, ON M5S 3H7
Tel: 416-978-3170; *Fax:* 416-978-6019

The Gauntlet
2500 University Dr. NW, Calgary, AB T2N 1N4
Tel: 403-220-5110; *Fax:* 403-282-8413
www.ucalgary.ca

Gazette
1459 Oxford St., Halifax, NS B3H 4R2
Tel: 902-494-2211; *Fax:* 902-494-2319
www.dal.ca

The Georgian Eye
One Georgian Dr., Barrie, ON L4M 3X9
Tel: 705-728-1968; *Fax:* 705-722-5123
inquire@georgianc.on.ca
www.georgianc.on.ca

La Gifle
CP 97, 3500, rue De Courval, Trois-Rivières, QC G9A 5E6
Tél: 819-376-1721; *Téléc:* 819-693-4663
dir.generale@cegeptr.qc.ca
www.cegeptr.qc.ca

Golden Ram
PO Box 550, Truro, NS B2N 5E3
Tel: 902-893-6722; *Fax:* 902-895-5529
www.nsac.ns.ca/

The Gradzette
134 Services Building, 97 Dafoe Rd., Winnipeg, MB R3T 2N2
Tel: 204-474-8880;
www.umanitoba.ca

Le Grafitti
3200, ch Côte Ste-Catherine, Montréal, QC H3T 1C1
Tel: 514-342-9342; *Fax:* 514-342-6607
mapril@brebeuf.qc.ca
www.brebeuf.qc.ca

Great Northern Way Campus
3700 Willingdon Ave., Burnaby, BC V5G 3H2
Tel: 604-434-5734; *Fax:* 604-431-6917
www.bcit.ca

L'Hermes
CP 1018, 30, boul du Séminaire nord, Saint-Jean-sur-Richelieu, QC J3B 7B1
Tél: 450-347-5301; *Téléc:* 450-358-9350
communications@cstjean.qc.ca
www.cstjean.qc.ca

Impact Campus
Cité universitaire, Québec, QC G1K 7P4
Tel: 418-656-3333; *Fax:* 418-656-2809
sg@sg.ulaval.ca
www.ulaval.ca

in Extremis
475, rue du Parc, Sherbrooke, QC J1E 4K1
Tél: 819-564-6350; *Téléc:* 819-564-1579
communications@cegepsherbrooke.qc.ca
www.cegepsherbrooke.qc.ca

L'Infomane
10555, av de Bois-de-Boulogne, Montréal, QC H4N 1L4
Tel: 514-332-3000; *Fax:* 514-332-5857
www.bdeb.qc.ca

The Intercamp
City Centre Campus, 10700 - 104 Ave., Edmonton, AB T5J 4S2
Tel: 780-497-5401; *Fax:* 780-497-5405
www.macewan.ca

L'Interdit
1300, 8e av, Québec, QC G1J 5L5
Tél: 418-647-6600; *Téléc:* 418-647-6798
info@climoilou.qc.ca
www.climoilou.qc.ca

L'Interêt
3000, ch de la Côte-Sainte-Catherine, Montréal, QC H3T 2A7
Tél: 514-340-6000; *Téléc:* 514-340-6411
www.hec.ca

The Interrobang
PO Box 7005, 1460 Oxford St. East, London, ON N5Y 5R6
Tel: 519-452-4430; *Fax:* 519-452-4420
www.fanshawec.ca

Jargon
166 Bedford Hwy., Halifax, NS B3M 2J6
Tel: 902-457-6117; *Fax:* 902-457-6498
www.msvu.ca

Le Jets
1100, rue Notre-Dame ouest, Montréal, QC H3C 1K3
Tél: 514-396-8800; *Téléc:* 514-396-8950
www.etsmtl.ca

The Journal
923 Robie St., Halifax, NS B3H 3C3
Tel: 902-420-5400; *Fax:* 902-420-5566
www.smu.ca

Journal l'actif
CP 610, Shawinigan, QC G9N 6V8
Tél: 819-539-6401; *Téléc:* 819-539-2435
information@collegeshawinigan.qc.ca
www.collegeshawinigan.qc.ca

Kwantlen Chronicle
12666 - 72 Ave., Surrey, BC V3W 2M8
Tel: 604-599-2100; *Fax:* 604-599-2068
www.kwantlen.bc.ca

Lion's Tale
1457 London Rd., Sarnia, ON N7S 6K4
Tel: 519-542-7751; *Fax:* 519-541-2418
www.lambton.on.ca

MacMedia (McLaughlin College)
4700 Keele St., Toronto, ON M3J 1P3
Tel: 416-736-2100; *Fax:* 416-736-5700
www.yorku.ca

Magnetic North
PO Box 60, 443 Northern Ave., Sault Ste Marie, ON P6A 5L3
Tel: 705-759-6774; *Fax:* 705-759-3273
Toll-Free: 1 8-0 4-1 22
www.saultc.on.ca/

Le Majeur
675, boul Auger ouest, Alma, QC G8B 2B7
Tel: 418-668-2387; *Fax:* 418-668-7336
college@calma.qc.ca
www.calma.qc.ca

Mars' Hill
7600 Glover Rd., Langley, BC V2Y 1Y1
Tel: 604-888-6158; *Fax:* 604-888-5729

Le Matulu
10748, boul Saint-Vital, Montréal-Nord, QC H1H 4T3
Tel: 514-322-8111; *Fax:* 512- -
dg@marievictorin.qc.ca
www.marievictorin.qc.ca

The Medium
3359 Mississauga Rd., Mississauga, ON L5L 1C6
Tel: 905-828-5399; *Fax:* 905-569-4301
www.erin.utoronto.ca/

The Meliorist
4401 University Dr., Lethbridge, AB T1K 3M4
Tel: 403-329-2201; *Fax:* 403-329-2097
www.uleth.ca

The Mike
81 St. Mary St., Toronto, ON M4S 1J4
Tel: 416-926-1300; *Fax:* 416-926-7266

La Minerve
625, av Ste-Croix, Saint-Laurent, QC H4L 3X7
Tel: 514-747-6521; *Fax:* 514-748-1249
www.cegep-st-laurent.qc.ca

Le Motdit
945, ch de Chambly, Longueuil, QC J4H 3M6
Tel: 450-679-2631; *Fax:* 450-679-5570
www.collegeem.qc.ca

Mouton Noir
960, rue St-Georges, Drummondville, QC J2C 6A2
Tel: 819-478-4671; *Fax:* 819-478-8823
dg@cdrummond.qc.ca
www.cdrummond.qc.ca/cegep/index.htm

The Muse
PO Box 4200, 230 Elizabeth Ave., St. John's, NL A1C 5S7
Tel: 709-737-8000; *Fax:* 709-737-4569
www.mun.ca

Navigator
900 Fifth St., Nanaimo, BC V9R 5S5
Tel: 250-753-3245; *Fax:* 250-740-6473
www.mala.bc.ca

Le Nénu phare
534, rue Jacques-Cartier est, Chicoutimi, QC G7H 1Z6
Tel: 418-549-9520; *Fax:* 418-549-1315
dirgene@cegep-chicoutimi.qc.ca
www.cegep-chicoutimi.qc.ca

news@niagara
Welland Campus, 300 Woodlawn Rd., Welland, ON L3C 7L3
Tel: 905-735-2211; *Fax:* 905-736-6000
webmaster@niagarac.on.ca
www.niagarac.on.ca

Nexus
Lansdowne Campus, 3100 Foul Bay Rd., Victoria, BC V8P 5J2
Tel: 250-370-3550; *Fax:* 250-370-3551
www.camosun.bc.ca

NightViews
350 Victoria St., Toronto, ON M5B 2K3
Tel: 416-979-5000;
inquire@ryerson.ca
www.ryerson.ca

Nomad
King & Portsmouth, 100 Portsmouth Ave., Kingston, ON K7L 5A6
Tel: 613-544-5400; *Fax:* 613-545-3923
www.sl.on.ca

Le Nordet
140, 4e av, La Pocatière, QC G0R 1Z0
Tel: 418-856-1525; *Fax:* 418-856-4589
information@cglapocatiere.qc.ca
www.cglapocatiere.qc.ca/cg

The Nugget
11762 - 106 St., Edmonton, AB T5G 2R1
Tel: 780-471-7400; *Fax:* 780-471-8583
registrar@nait.ca
www.nait.ca

Opus
PO Box 398, 1450 Nakina Dr., Thunder Bay, ON P7C 4W1
Tel: 807-475-6110; *Fax:* 807-623-4512
Toll-Free: 1 8-0 4-5 54
www.confederationc.on.ca/

L'Original déchainé
Ramsey Lake Rd., Sudbury, ON P3E 2C6
Tel: 705-675-1151; *Fax:* 705-675-4891
admissions@laurentian.ca
www.laurentian.ca
Teaching is in French & English. Certain faculties offer parallel programs in both languages.

Other Press
PO Box 2503, New Westminster, BC V3L 5B2
Tel: 604-527-5400; *Fax:* 604-527-5095
registrar@douglas.bc.ca
www.douglas.bc.ca/

Over the Edge
3333 University Way, Prince George, BC V2N 4Z9
Tel: 250-960-5555; *Fax:* 250-960-5794
www.unbc.ca

The Papercut
3880, Côte-des-Neiges, Montréal, QC H3H 1W1
Tel: 514-931-8792; *Fax:* 514-931-8790
www.marianopolis.edu

Pars ailleurs
169, rue Champlain, Salaberry-de-Valleyfield, QC J6T 1X6
Tel: 450-373-9441; *Fax:* 450-377-6035
courrier@colval.qc.ca
www.colval.qc.ca

The Peak
8888 University Dr., Burnaby, BC V5A 1S6
Tel: 604-291-3111;
www.sfu.ca

La Petite Caisse
555, boul de l'Université, Chicoutimi, QC G7H 2B1
Tél: 418-545-5011; *Téléc:* 418-545-5012
www.uqac.uquebec.ca

The Phoenix
1000 KLO Rd., Kelowna, BC V1Y 4X8
www.okanagan.bc.ca

La Pige
2505, rue St-Hubert, Jonquière, QC G7X 7W2
Tel: 418-547-2191; *Fax:* 418-547-6965
cegep@cjonquiere.qc.ca
www.cjonquiere.qc.ca

The Pioneer
PO Box 4200, Belleville, ON K8N 5B9
Tel: 613-969-1913; *Fax:* 613-962-1376
liaison@loyalistc.on.ca
www.loyalistcollege.com

Plant
3040, rue Sherbrooke ouest, Montréal, QC H3Z 1A4
Tel: 514-931-8731; *Fax:* 514-931-5181
www.dawsoncollege.qc.ca

Le Polyscope
CP 6079 Centre-ville, Montréal, QC H3C 3A7
Tél: 514-340-4711;
www.polymtl.ca

Le Profane
425, boul du Collège, Rouyn-Noranda, QC J9X 5E5
Tél: 819-762-0931; *Téléc:* 819-762-2071
cegepat.qc.ca

Quartier Libre
CP 6128 Centre-Ville, Montréal, QC H3C 3J7
Tél: 514-343-6111; *Téléc:* 514-343-2098
www.umontreal.ca

Quill
270 - 18th St., Brandon, MB R7A 6A9
Tel: 204-728-9520; *Fax:* 204-726-4573
www.brandonu.ca

Reflector
4825 Richard Rd. SW, Calgary, AB T3E 6K6
Tel: 403-440-6111; *Fax:* 403-440-5938
slscalia@mtroyal.ca
www.mtroyal.ca

La Réplique
475, rue Notre-Dame est, Victoriaville, QC G6P 4B3
Tel: 819-758-6401; *Fax:* 819-758-8126
www.cgpvicto.qc.ca

Le Republique
255, rue Ontario est, Montréal, QC H2X 1X6
Tél: 514-982-3437; *Téléc:* 514-982-3400
www.cvm.qc.ca

République étudiante
6400, 16e av, Montréal, QC H1X 2S9
Tel: 514-376-1620; *Fax:* 514-376-1440
mdionne@crosemont.qc.ca
www.crosemont.qc.ca

Réseau/U.Q. Network
475, rue de l'Église, Québec, QC G1K 9H7
Tél: 418-657-3551; *Téléc:* 418-657-2132
cscuq@uqss.uquebec.ca
www.uquebec.ca

Le Réveil
200, av de la Cathédrale, Winnipeg, MB R2H 0H7
Tel: 204-233-0210

The Ring
PO Box 1700 CSC, Victoria, BC V8W 2Y2
Tel: 250-721-7211; *Fax:* 250-721-7212
www.uvic.ca

La Rotonde
550 Cumberland St., Ottawa, ON K1N 6N5
Tel: 613-562-5700; *Fax:* 613-562-5103
Toll-Free: 1 8-7 8-8 82
www.uottawa.ca

The Satellite
PO Box 2034, Hamilton, ON L8N 3T2
Tel: 905-575-1212; *Fax:* 905-575-2378
www.mohawkcollege.ca

Le Script
9, rue Monseigneur Gosselin, Lévis, QC G6V 5K1
Tel: 418-833-1249; *Fax:* 418-833-1974
lvezina@collegedelevis.qc.ca

Le Sentier
CP 7300, Saint-Félicien, QC G8K 2R8
Tél: 418-679-5412; *Téléc:* 418-679-0238
www.cstfelicien.qc.ca

The Sheaf
105 Admin. Place, Saskatoon, SK S7N 5A2
Tel: 306-966-4343; *Fax:* 306-966-4530
www.usask.ca

The Sheridan Sun
Trafalgar Road Campus, 1430 Trafalgar Rd., Oakville, ON L6H 2L1
Tel: 905-845-9430; *Fax:* 905-815-4148
infosheridan@sheridaninstitute.ca
www.sheridaninstitute.ca

The Shield
1400 Barrydowne Rd., Sudbury, ON P3A 3V8
Tel: 705-566-8101;
info@cambrianc.on.ca
www.cambrianc.on.ca

The Silhouette
1280 Main St. West, Hamilton, ON L8S 4K1
Tel: 905-525-9140; *Fax:* 905-521-1504
www.mcmaster.ca

Siren
PO Box 631 A, Scarborough, ON M1K 5E9
Tel: 416-289-5000; *Fax:* 416-439-7358
www.centennialcollege.ca

The 60th Meridian
PO Box 5300, 1250 Grand Lake Rd., Sydney, NS B1P 6L2
Tel: 902-539-5300; *Fax:* 902-562-0119
Toll-Free: 1 8-0 4-4 72
www.capebretonu.ca

Sommets
2500, boul de l'Université, Sherbrooke, QC J1K 2R1
Tel: 819-821-7686;
information@usherbrooke.ca
www.usherbrooke.ca

Spoke
299 Doon Valley Dr., Kitchener, ON N2G 4M4
Tel: 519-748-5220; *Fax:* 519-748-3505
www.conestogac.on.ca/

Strand
73 Queen's Park Cres. East, Toronto, ON M5S 1K9
Tel: 416-585-4524; *Fax:* 416-585-4584
www.vicu.utoronto.ca

Student Connection
8115 Franklin Ave., Fort McMurray, AB T9H 2H7
Tel: 780-791-4800; *Fax:* 780-791-1555
Toll-Free: 1 8-0 2-1 14
registrar@keyano.ca
www.keyano.ca

Suites
CP 8888 Centre-Ville, Montréal, QC H3C 3P8
Tél: 514-987-3000;
www.uqam.ca

The Surveyor
Administrative Services, 140 Weymouth St., Charlottetown, PE C1A 4Z1
Tel: 902-629-4217; *Fax:* 902-629-4239
info@hollandc.pe.ca
www.hollandc.pe.ca/

The Tablet
845, rue Sherbrooke ouest, Montréal, QC H3A 2T5
Tel: 514-398-4455; *Fax:* 514-398-4455
www.mcgill.ca

The Three Penny Beaver
Sutherland Campus, 599 Brealey Dr., Peterborough, ON K9J 7B1
Tel: 705-749-5530; *Fax:* 705-749-5540
copeland@flemingc.on.ca
www.flemingc.on.ca/

The Toike Oike
21 King's College Circle, Toronto, ON M5S 1A1
Tel: 416-978-2011;
www.utoronto.ca

Le Trait d'Union
3800, rue Sherbrooke est, Montréal, QC H1X 2A2
Tel: 514-254-7131; *Fax:* 514-253-7637
communic@cmaisonneuve.qc.ca
www.cmaisonneuve.qc.ca

L'Ulcère
80, rue Frontenac, Rivière-du-Loup, QC G5R 1R1
Tél: 418-862-6903; *Téléc:* 418-862-4959
sercom@cegep-rdl.qc.ca
www.cegep-rdl.qc.ca

Underground
1265 Military Trail, Toronto, ON M1C 1A4
Tel: 905-287-8872; *Fax:* 905-287-7525
www.scar.utoronto.ca/

The Uniter
401 Sunset Ave., Windsor, ON N9B 3P4
Tel: 519-253-3000; *Fax:* 519-973-7050
www.uwindsor.ca

The Uniter
515 Portage Ave., Winnipeg, MB R3B 2E9
Tel: 204-786-7811; *Fax:* 204-786-8983
adm@uwinnipeg.ca
www.uwinnipeg.ca

Uquarium
300, allée des Ursulines, Rimouski, QC G5L 3A1
Tél: 418-723-1986;
uqar@uqar.qc.ca
www.uqar.qc.ca

UW Gazette
200 University Ave. West, Waterloo, ON N2L 3G1
Tel: 519-885-1211; *Fax:* 519-884-8009
www.uwaterloo.ca/

V.C.C. Voice
1155 East Broadway, Vancouver, BC V5T 4V5
Tel: 604-871-7000; *Fax:* 604-871-7100
www.vcc.ca

Le Virus
Pavillion Alexandre-Taché, CP 1250 Hull, 283, boul Alexandre-Taché, Gatineau, QC J8X 3X7
Tél: 819-595-3900; *Téléc:* 819-595-3924
www.uqo.ca

The Voice
1 University Dr., Athabasca, AB T9S 3A3
Tel: 780- -; *Fax:* 780-675-6437
Toll-Free: 1 8-0 7-8 90
www.athabascau.ca

The Voice
100 West 49th Ave., Vancouver, BC V5Y 2Z6
Tel: 604-323-5511; *Fax:* 604-323-5555
geninfo@langara.bc.ca
www.langara.bc.ca

Vox-Populi
1111, rue Lapierre, Lasalle, QC H8N 2J4
Tel: 514-364-3320; *Fax:* 514-364-7130
courrier@claurendeau.qc.ca
www.claurendeau.qc.ca

Le Voyeur
445, boul de l'Université, Rouyn-Noranda, QC J9X 5E4
Tél: 819-762-0971; *Téléc:* 819-797-4727
www.uqat.ca

Le Voyeur
CP 500 Bureau-chef, 3351, boul des Forges, Trois-Rivières, QC G9A 5H7
Tél: 819-376-5011; *Téléc:* 819-376-5012
www.uqtr.ca

Wallaceburg Campus
2000 Talbot Rd. West, Windsor, ON N9A 6S4
Tel: 519-966-1656; *Fax:* 519-972-3811
info@stclaircollege.ca
www.stclaircollege.ca

Watch
6350 Coburg Rd., Halifax, NS B3H 2A1
Tel: 902-422-1271; *Fax:* 902-423-3357
www.ukings.ns.ca

Western News
#2, 1151 Richmond St., London, ON N6A 5B8
Tel: 519-661-2111;
www.uwo.ca

Window
300 Huron, Toronto, ON M5S 3J6
Tel: 416-978-2460; *Fax:* 416-978-0554

Xaverian Weekly
PO Box 5000, Antigonish, NS B2G 2W5
Tel: 902-863-3300; *Fax:* 902-867-5153
www.stfx.ca

Le Zèle
475, boul de l'Avenir, Laval, QC H7N 5H9
Tel: 450-975-6100; *Fax:* 450-975-6116
cmontmorency.qc.ca

SECTION 14
RELIGION

Broad Faith Based Associations

Action des Chrétiens pour l'abolition de la torture (ACAT) / Action by Christians for the Abolition of Torture
15, rue de Castelnau ouest, Montréal QC H2R 2W3 Canada
Tél: 514-890-6169; *Téléc:* 514-890-6484
info@acatcanada.org
www.acatcanada.org

Également appelé: ACAT Canada
Aperçu: *Dimension:* moyenne; *Envergure:* nationale; *Organisme sans but lucratif; fondée en 1984*
Finances: *Budget de fonctionnement annuel:* $50,000-$100,000
Personnel: 2 membre(s) du personnel; 30 bénévole(s)
Membre: 600; *Montant de la cotisation:* 30 $-80 $; *Critères d'admissibilite:* ouvert; *Comités:* Commission des interventions; Financement; Relations publiques; Ressourcement
Activités: Campagne annuelle; *Listes de destinataires:* Oui *Bibliothèque:* Oui rendez-vous
Description: Dans un but d'engagement évangélique, encourager les différentes communautés Chrétiennes du Canada à porter ensemble, par la prière, les souffrances des victimes de la torture; dans un but éducatif, sensibiliser particulièrement les Chrétiens au scandale de la torture (par l'information et la formation aux droits de la personne); dans un but de soulager la misère des victimes de la torture, apporter une aide concrète par l'envoi de lettres et pétitions aux responsables de torture et des lettres d'encouragement aux victimes
Affiliation(s): Fédération internationale de l'action des Chrétiens pour l'abolition de la torture (FIACAT)

Adventive Cross Cultural Initiatives (ACCI)
89 Auriga Dr., Nepean ON K2E 7Z2 Canada
Tel: 613-298-1546; *Fax:* 613-225-7455
lauren@adventive.ca
www.adventive.ca

Previous Name: New Life League
Overview: A small national charitable organization founded in 1986
Finances: *Annual Operating Budget:* Less than $50,000; *Funding Sources:* Donations
Staff: 4 staff member(s); 1 volunteer(s)
Activities: *Internships:* Yes
Description: To operate as an international, interdenominational Christian missionary organization; To minister through printing & literature, children's homes, national workers, evangelism, & church planting; *Member of:* Canadian Council of Christian Charities

Alcoholics for Christ Canada
1277 Fennell Ave. East, Hamilton ON L8T 1T3 Canada
Tel: 905-383-4160
afc@execulink.com
www.alcoholicsforchrist.ca

Overview: A small national organization
Description: To direct & restore the alcoholic or substance abuser, the family member, & the adult child to a sincere & dedicated relationship with Jesus Christ

American Academy of Religion (AAR)
#300, 825 Houston Mill Rd., Atlanta GA 30329-4205 USA
Tel: 404-727-3049; *Fax:* 404-727-7959
aaw@aarweb.org; membership@aarweb.org
www.aarweb.org

Overview: A medium-sized national charitable organization founded in 1909
Chief Officer(s):
John R. Fitzmier, Executive Director & Treasurer
jfitzmier@aarweb.org
Emilie M. Townes, President
Michel Desjardins, Secretary
Membership: 10,000+; *Fees:* Schedule; *Member Profile:* Teachers; Research scholars; *Committees:* Academic Relations; Executive; Finance; Graduate Student; International Connections; Nominations; Program; Publications; Public Understanding of Religion; Regions; Status of Racial & Ethnic Minorities in the Profession; Status of Women in the Profession; Teaching & Learning; Theological Education Steering Committee
Activities: Governance Task Force; Job Placement Task Force; Religion in the Schools Task Force; Sustainability Task Force; Status of Lesbian, Gay, Bisexual, & Transgendered Persons in the Profession; Awards for Excellence in the Study of Religion Book Award Juries; History of Religions Jury; Research Grants Jury; *Speaker Service:* Yes
Awards: Book Awards
For scholarly publications that contribute to the study of religion
Journalism Awards
For best in-depth reporting on topics related to religion
Ray L. Hart Service Award
Martin E. Marty Public Understanding of Religion Award
AAR Award for Excellence in Teaching
Religion and the Arts Award
Annual Meeting Travel Grants
Wabash Center For Teaching & Learning In Theology & Religion
Regional Development Grants
Publications: Journal of the American Academy of Religion
Type: Journal *Frequency:* q.
Profile: Scholarly articles of world religious traditions & methodologies
Openings: Employment Opportunities for Scholars of Religion
Accepts Advertising
In the Field
Type: Newsletter
Profile: Calls for papers, grant news, conference announcements, & other opportunities for scholars of religion
Description: The American Academy of Religion promotes research, teaching & scholarship in the field of religion.
Member of: American Council of Learned Societies

The Apostolic Church in Canada
c/o New Life Centre, 220 Adelaide St. North, London ON N6B 3H4 Canada
Tel: 519-852-7755
nlt@apostolic.ca
www.apostolic.ca

Overview: A small national organization founded in 1934
Finances: *Annual Operating Budget:* $500,000-$1.5 Million
Staff: 15 staff member(s)
Membership: 500-999
Activities: *Internships:* Yes

Associated Gospel Churches (AGC) / Association des églises évangéliques (AEE)
1500 Kerns Rd., Burlington ON L7P 3A7 Canada
Tel: 905-634-8184; *Fax:* 905-634-6283
admin@agcofcanada.com
www.agcofcanada.com

Overview: A medium-sized national charitable organization founded in 1925
Finances: *Annual Operating Budget:* $250,000-$500,000
Staff: 5 staff member(s)
Membership: 21,400 members; 140+ churches; *Fees:* 4% of revenue minus missions support; *Committees:* Doctrine & Credentials; Finance & Administration; Communication; Church Growth; Church Renting
Description: To glorify God by partnering together in obedience to the Great Commandment & the Great Commission; to become a movement of healthy, reproducing churches
Affiliation(s): World Relief; World Team; UFM International; Evangelical Fellowship of Canada

Association of Unity Churches Canada
2631 Kingsway Dr., Kitchener ON N2C 1A7 Canada
Tel: 519-894-0810
info@unitycanada.org
www.unitycanada.org

Also Known As: Unity
Overview: A small national charitable organization founded in 1978
Chief Officer(s):
Doris Lewis, President
info@unityvictoria.ca
Pat Ball, Exec. Assistant
revpatball@gmail.com
Finances: *Annual Operating Budget:* $50,000-$100,000
Membership: 20 churches
Activities: *Internships:* Yes; *Speaker Service:* Yes
Description: Unity is a Christian association asserting that reunion with God in mind brings certain fulfillment in life. It is a registered charity, BN: 118794544RR0001.
Affiliation(s): Association of Unity Churches USA

Atlantic Episcopal Assembly (AEA) / Assemblée des évêques de l'Atlantique
Diocesan Centre, 60 Bouchard St., Edmundston NB E3V 3K1 Canada
Tel: 506-735-5578; *Fax:* 506-735-4271

Overview: A small local organization founded in 1967
Chief Officer(s):
Léo Grégoire, I.V.Dei, Secretary-Treasurer
François Thibodeau, C.F.M., President
Terrence Prendergast, S.J.
Finances: *Annual Operating Budget:* Less than $50,000
Membership: 12; *Committees:* Exécutif; Affaires sociales
Description: Proposer l'évangile de Jésus Christ dans les diverses situations de la vie ainsi que ses implications pratiques de notre temps; echange d'information pour les évêques

The Bible League of Canada / Société canadienne pour la distribution de la Bible
PO Box 5037, Burlington ON L7R 3Y8 Canada
Tel: 905-319-9500; *Fax:* 905-319-0484
Toll-Free: 800-363-9673
admin@thebibleleague.ca
www.thebibleleague.ca

Previous Name: World Home Bible League
Overview: A large international charitable organization founded in 1949
Chief Officer(s):
Dick Kranendonk, Executive Director
J. Ellens, President
Finances: *Annual Operating Budget:* $3 Million-$5 Million; *Funding Sources:* Donations
Staff: 15 staff member(s)
Activities: *Speaker Service:* Yes *Library:* Library
Description: To introduce people to Jesus Christ; to spread God's Word worldwide
Member of: Canadian Council of Christian Charities; International Association of Bible Leagues
Affiliation(s): The Bible League

Brethren in Christ
2700 Bristol Circle, Oakville ON L6H 6EH Canada
Tel: 905-339-2335; *Fax:* 905-337-2120
biccanada@bellnet.ca
www.bic-church.org

Overview: A medium-sized international charitable organization founded in 1788
Finances: *Annual Operating Budget:* $500,000-$1.5 Million; *Funding Sources:* Congregational giving
Staff: 8 staff member(s)
Membership: 3,450 + 43 congregations in Canada; *Member Profile:* North American membership is about 20,000 with significant churches in other countries including India, Japan, Zambia, Zimbabwe, Nicaragua, Cuba, Venezuela, Columbia, South Africa
Activities: *Speaker Service:* Yes; *Rents Mailing List:* Yes
Member of: Evangelical Fellowship of Canada
Affiliation(s): Mennonite Central Committee; Canadian Holiness Federation

British Israel World Federation (Canada) Inc. (BIWF)
313 Sherbourne St., Toronto ON M5A 2S3 Canada
Tel: 416-921-5996; *Fax:* 416-921-9511
info@british-israel-world-fed.ca
www.british-israel-world-fed.ca

Overview: A small international charitable organization founded in 1929
Chief Officer(s):
Douglas C. Nesbit, President
Membership: 1,200; *Fees:* $10
Activities: Meetings; *Speaker Service:* Yes
Publications: The Kingdom Herald
Profile: Magazine, 10 issues published annually
Description: To proclaim the Gospel of the Kingdom of God as contained in the Holy Bible

Canada's National Bible Hour (CNBH)
PO Box 1210, St Catharines ON L2R 7A7 Canada
Tel: 905-684-1401
gonow@missiongo.org
www.missiongo.org/biblehour.html

Overview: A small national organization founded in 1925
Chief Officer(s):
Brian Albrecht, President, GOM
Len Lane, Contact
len@missiongo.org
Description: The Hour is a bible-teaching ministry, & Canada's oldest religious broadcast, heard from coast to coast. It is sponsored by Global Outreach Mission (GOM), an organization dedicated to evangelism & missions.
Member of: Global Outreach Mission

Canadian Association for Pastoral Practice & Education (CAPPE) / Association canadienne pour la pratique et l'éducation pastorales (ACPEP)
660 Francklyn St., Halifax NS B3H 3B5
Tel: 902-820-3085; *Fax:* 902-820-3087
Toll-Free: 866-442-2773
office@cappe.org
www.cappe.org

Overview: A medium-sized national organization founded in 1965
Finances: *Funding Sources:* Membership dues
Fees: $200 associate members, with any amount of CPE or PCE training, & corporate members; $400 certified specialists or teaching supervisors; *Member Profile:* Persons involved in a variety of ministries, in settings such as parishes, prisons & correctional facilities, pastoral counselling centres, health care facilities, & industrial facilities

Activities: Offering educational programs for both clergy & lay persons; Providing certification for supervisors & specialists; Creating networking opportunities
Publications: Canadian Association for Pastoral Practice & Education Handbook
Type: Handbook
Profile: Information about accreditation, certification, & practice
CAPPE [Canadian Association for Pastoral Practice & Education] / ACPEP National E-Newsletter
Type: Newsletter *Price:* Free with membership in the Canadian Association for Pastoral Practice & Education
CAPPE [Canadian Association for Pastoral Practice & Education] / ACPEP Annual Report
Type: Yearbook *Frequency:* a. *Price:* Free with membership in the Canadian Association for Pastoral Practice & Education
Description: To support persons involved in pastoral care & pastoral counselling in Canada; To set standards & monitor professional practice; To accredit educational centres in a range of settings

Canadian Bible Society (CBS) / Société biblique canadienne
10 Carnforth Rd., Toronto ON M4A 2S4
Toll-Free: 800-465-2425
info@biblesociety.ca; communications@biblesociety.ca (Media)
www.biblesociety.ca
Social Media: www.facebook.com/CanadianBibleSociety; www.twitter.com/CanadianBible
Overview: A large national charitable organization founded in 1904
Finances: *Funding Sources:* Donations; Sale of gifts; Fundraising
Activities: Offering various programs to share God's Word, such as Operation Bible for the Canadian military, & welcoming newcomers to Canada with God's message
Publications: Canadian Bible Society Annual Report
Type: Yearbook *Frequency:* a.
Description: To translate, publish, & distribute Bibles, New Testaments, & other Scriptures throughout Canada & Bermuda
Member of: United Bibles Societies

Canadian Foodgrains Bank Association Inc. (CFGB) / Association de la banque canadienne de grains inc.
PO Box 767, #400, 393 Portage Ave., Winnipeg MB R3B 3H6 Canada
Tel: 204-944-1993; *Fax:* 204-943-2597
Toll-Free: 800-665-0377
cfgb@foodgrainsbank.ca
www.foodgrainsbank.ca
Also Known As: Foodgrains Bank
Overview: A large international charitable organization founded in 1983
Finances: *Funding Sources:* Donations; Fundraising
Membership: 15; *Member Profile:* Canadian church agencies
Activities: Improving community development; Protecting & building sustainable economic livelihoods; Encouraging peace-building; Strengthening Canadian & international policy & action towards hunger issues; Increasing public awareness & engagement; Collecting grain & cash donations from donors
Publications: Breaking Bread
Type: Newsletter
Food Justice Update
Type: Newsletter *Frequency:* 3 pa
Canadian Foodgrains Bank Annual Report
Type: Yearbook *Frequency:* a.
Description: To provide a Christian response to hunger; to share resources with & support hungry populations outside Canada to achieve food security; to reduce hunger in developing countries

The Canadian Orthodox Church (COC) / L'Église Orthodoxe canadienne (EOC)
37323 Hawkins Pickle Rd., Dewdney BC V0M 1H0 Canada
Tel: 604-826-9336; *Fax:* 604-820-5247
synaxis@new-ostrog.org
www.orthodoxcanada.org
Overview: A medium-sized national organization founded in 1970
Finances: *Funding Sources:* Publications; candle factory sales
Membership: 2,000
Activities: *Speaker Service:* Yes *Library:* Library (Open to Public) by appointment
Member of: Ukrainian Orthodox Church, Kiev, Ukraine
Affiliation(s): The Nemanjic Institute for Serbo-Byzantine Studies; Centre for Canadian Orthodox Studies

Canadian Society for the Study of Religion (CSSR) / Société canadienne pour l'étude de la religion (SCER)
c/o Dr. Mark D. Chapman, #100, 30 Carrier Dr., Toronto ON M9W 5T7 Canada
mchapman@alumni.uwaterloo.ca
www.ccsr.ca/cssr
Overview: A small national organization founded in 1966
Chief Officer(s):
Michel Desjardins, President
mdesjardins@wlu.ca
Mark Chapman, Membership Secretary
mchapman@alumni.uwaterloo.ca
Richard Mann, Treasurer
Richard_mann@carleton.ca
Fees: $50 students; $60 part-time & retired persons; $90 regular; *Member Profile:* Scholars engaged in various academic approaches to the study of religion
Publications: Studies in Religion / Sciences Religieuses
Type: Journal *Price:* Free with CSSR membership
Canadian Society for the Study of Religion Bulletin
Type: Newsletter *Frequency:* s-a. *Editor:* Mark Chapman *ISSN:* 0708-952X *Price:* Free with CSSR membership
Profile: CSSR activies, member news, departmental news, & conference information
Description: To promote research in the study of religion, with particular reference to Canada; to encourage a critical examination of the teaching of the discipline
Member of: International Association for the History of Religions (IAHR)
Affiliation(s): Canadian Federation for the Humanities & Social Sciences (CFHSS)

Canadian Society of Biblical Studies (CSBS) / Société canadienne des études bibliques (SCEB)
c/o Prof. Robert A. Derrenbacker, Jr., Regent College, 5800 University Blvd., Vancouver BC V6T 2E4 Canada
rderrenbacker@regent-college.edu
www.ccsr.ca/csbs
Overview: A small national organization founded in 1933
Fees: $35 students & retired & unemployed persons; $72 full membership; *Member Profile:* Individuals interested in all aspects of the academic study of the Bible
Publications: Studies in Religion / Sciences Religieuses
Type: Journal *Price:* Free with CSBS membership
Profile: Refereed articles
The CSBS [Canadian Society of Biblical Studies] / SCÉB [Société canadienne des études bibliques] Bulletin
Type: Yearbook *Frequency:* a. *Editor:* Richard S. Ascough *Price:* Free with CSBS membership
Profile: CSBS membership news, events, annual general meeting minutes, & financial statements
Canadian Society of Biblical Studies Membership Directory
Type: Directory
Description: To stimulate the critical investigation of the classical biblical literature & related literature

Canadian Society of Patristic Studies (CSPS) / Association canadienne des études patristiques
c/o Dr. S. Muir, Religious Studies, Concordia University College of AB, 7128 Ada Blvd., Edmonton AB T5B 4E4
www.ccsr.ca/csps
Overview: A small national organization founded in 1975
Chief Officer(s):
Tim Hegedus, President
Lorraine Buck, Vice-President
George Bevan, Secretary
Steven Muir, Treasurer
Fees: $48 studemts & retired members (with subscription); $65 regular members (including subscription); *Committees:* Program; Nominating
Publications: Canadian Society of Patristic Studies Bulletin
Type: Newsletter *Frequency:* s-a. *Editor:* Adriana Bara
Profile: Society activities, including information about recent & upcoming conferences, membership updates, research, & other scholarly activities in patristics
Description: To encourage the academic study of the Church Fathers
Member of: Canadian Federation for the Humanities & Social Sciences / Fèdèration canadienne des sciences humaines

Canadian Theological Society (CTS) / Société théologique canadienne
c/o N. Jesson, St. Thomas More College, University of Saskatchewan, 1437 College Dr., Saskatoon SK S7N 0W6 Canada
www.ccsr.ca/cts/
Overview: A small national organization founded in 1955
Chief Officer(s):
Michael Bourgeois, President, 416-585-4534, Fax: 416-585-4516
michael.bourgeois@utoronto.ca
Bob McKeon, Treasurer
rmckeon@shaw.ca
Nicholas Jesson, Officer, Communications, 306-652-1595
jesson@ecumenism.net
Fees: $86 full members; $61 associate members; $45 student, retired, & unwaged members; *Member Profile:* Theologians, clergy, scholars, & students from universities, seminaries, & churches; Lay people
Activities: *Awareness Events:* Annual Student Essay Contest
Description: To promote theological reflection & writing in Canada
Member of: Canadian Corporation for the Study of Religion (CCSR)
Affiliation(s): Congress of the Humanities & Social Sciences

Canadian Theosophical Society Inc. / Association théosophique canadienne inc.
27 Northmount Cr. NW, Calgary AB T2K 2V6 Canada
Tel: 403-275-7817
office@theosophical.ca
www.theosophical.ca
Overview: A medium-sized national charitable organization founded in 1924
Finances: *Annual Operating Budget:* Less than $50,000; *Funding Sources:* Memberships; Donations
Membership: 100-499; *Fees:* $25; *Member Profile:* From all across Canada & all backgrounds
Activities: Promotion of Theosophy or wisdom, whatever the source
Publications: The Light Bearer
Type: Magazine *Frequency:* q. *Price:* Free with Canadian Theosophical Association membership; $20 Canada non-members
Description: To form a nucleus of the Universal Brotherhood of Humanity, without distinction of race, creed, sex, caste, or colour; to encourage the study of comparative religion, philosophy, & science; to investigate unexplained laws of nature & the powers latent in man
Member of: Theosophical Society, India
Affiliation(s): 70 other countries

Carrefour Humanisation Santé
CP 12, 1431, Fullum, Montréal QC H2K 3M3 Canada
Tél: 514-544-4154; *Téléc:* 514-259-0857
carrefour.humanisation@videotron.ca
www.carrefourhumanisationsante.org
Nom précédent: Carrefour des Chrétiens du Québec pour la Santé
Aperçu: *Dimension:* petite; *Envergure:* provinciale
Membre(s) du bureau directeur:
Andrée Chapleau-Lorrain, Co-présidente
Pierre Côté, Co-président
Description: Carrefour Humanisation-Santé est une association sans but lucratif qui vise l'humanisation des milieux de soins et de services de santé, en s'inspirant des valeurs judéo-chrétiennes. Elle met l'accent sur l'harmonisation entre la dimension humaine et spirituelle.

Centre for Faith & the Media
PO Box 5694, Stn. A, Calgary AB T2H 1Y1 Canada
Toll-Free: 877-210-0077
info@faithandmedia.org
www.faithandmedia.org
Overview: A small national organization
Chief Officer(s):
Richelle Wiseman, Executive Director
Description: To inform, advise & help media & the general public achieve a stronger understanding of spiritual history, practices & values in Canadian society

Chosen People Ministries (Canada)
PO Box 897, Stn. B, 291 Sheppard Ave. West, Toronto ON M2K 2R1 Canada
Tel: 416-250-0177; *Fax:* 416-250-9235
Toll-Free: 888-442-5535
info@cpmcanada.ca
www.cpmcanada.ca
Also Known As: Beth Sar Shalom Mission
Overview: A medium-sized national charitable organization founded in 1967
Chief Officer(s):
Joseph Gray, Director
Finances: *Annual Operating Budget:* $500,000-$1.5 Million; *Funding Sources:* Donations
Staff: 11 staff member(s)
Activities: *Speaker Service:* Yes
Description: To bring the Gospel of Jesus to Jewish people

Christ for the Nations (Canada) Inc. (CFNI)
19533 - 64 Ave., Surrey BC V4N 3G6 Canada
Tel: 604-514-2364; *Fax:* 604-514-2604
Toll-Free: 888-999-2364
info@cfnc.ca
www.cfni.bc.ca

Also Known As: Christ for the Nations Bible College
Overview: A small national charitable organization founded in 1978
Membership: 1-99
Description: To prepare spiritually mature servant leaders who are competent in Ministry & who influence their world by living as Jesus did
Member of: The Christ for the Nations Association of Bible Schools
Affiliation(s): Association for Biblical Higher Education

Christian Medical & Dental Society of Canada (CMDS)
246 Main St., #B, Steinbach MB R5G 1Y8 Canada
Tel: 204-326-2523; *Fax:* 204-326-3098
Toll-Free: 888-256-8653
office@cmdscanada.org
www.cmdscanada.org

Overview: A medium-sized provincial organization founded in 1971
Chief Officer(s):
Roger Gingerich, Executive Director
Abraham Ninan, President
Rudy W. Hamm, Treasurer
Sue McLoughlin, Secretary
Finances: *Funding Sources:* Dues; Donations
Fees: $325 Full-time Medical & Dental Practitioners; $165 Part-time Practitioners; $50 Residents; $25 Medical or Dental Students or Missionaries; *Member Profile:* Christian physicians, dentists, & students who wish to integrate faith with professional practice
Activities: Offers workshops & conferences; supports a toll-free helpline for medical & dental trainees; publishes a Members Directory & other literature; offers mission opportunities; provides investment services
Description: CMDS has the following mission: to uphold a Christian view of medicine & dentistry; to understand & minister to the spiritual needs of patients & colleagues; to create educational materials about public policy & health; to develop programs that promote a Christian view of medical ethics; & to support local group activities, plan conferences, & locate mentorship & other opportunities.
Member of: Practitioners Christian Medical & Dental Association

Christos Metropolitan Community Church
427 Bloor St. West, Toronto ON M5S 1X7 Canada
Tel: 416-435-1211; *Fax:* 416-922-8587
christosmcc@hotmail.com
www.christosmcc.com

Also Known As: Christos MCC
Overview: A small local charitable organization founded in 1984
Chief Officer(s):
Deana Dudley, Pastor
Judi Bonner, Secretary
Finances: *Annual Operating Budget:* Less than $50,000
Staff: 1 staff member(s); 8 volunteer(s)
Membership: 30
Activities: Weekly worship services; spirituality-based study groups; social events
Member of: Universal Fellowship of Metropolitan Community Churches

Church Council on Justice & Corrections (CCJC) / Conseil des églises pour la justice et la criminologie
#303, 200 Isabella St., Ottawa ON K1S 1V7 Canada
Tel: 613-563-1688; *Fax:* 613-237-6129
info@ccjc.ca
www.ccjc.ca

Overview: A medium-sized national charitable organization founded in 1972
Finances: *Annual Operating Budget:* $250,000-$500,000
Staff: 3 staff member(s)
Membership: 46 directors + 292 supporting; *Fees:* $40 individuals; $200 organizations; *Committees:* Steering
Activities: *Internships:* Yes; *Speaker Service:* Yes *Library:* Library
Awards: Ron Wiebe Restorative Justice Award
Description: To strengthen churches' ministry in fields of crime prevention, justice & corrections; to initiate, encourage & support programs which sensitize congregations & educate volunteer groups to participate in development of community responses to crime, justice & corrections; to promote a healing justice; to examine & respond to policy concerns with assistance of churches; to call on churches to address issues; to provide resources to churches & other related organizations.
Member of: National Associations Active in Criminal Justice
Affiliation(s): The Network - Interaction for Conflict Resolution

The Church Lads' Brigade (CLB)
PO Box 28126, St. John's NL A1B 4J8 Canada
Tel: 709-722-1737
clb@nf.aibn.com
www.theclb.ca

Overview: A medium-sized national organization founded in 1892
Chief Officer(s):
Keith Arns, Chair
Sterling Pritchett, Secretary
Finances: *Annual Operating Budget:* $50,000-$100,000; *Funding Sources:* Donations; building rentals; fundraising
Staff: 1 staff member(s); 200 volunteer(s)
Membership: 800; *Fees:* $20; *Member Profile:* Boys & girls of all religious affiliations
Activities: Youth activities; recreational, educational & social; *Internships:* Yes *Library:* CLB Archives (Open to Public) by appointment
Description: The advancement of Christ's kingdom among youth, the promotion of Christian charity, reverence, discipline, self-respect, respect for others & all that lends towards true Christian character
Affiliation(s): The Church Lads' & Church Girls' Brigade (UK)

Church of the Good Shepherd
116 Queen St. North, Kitchener ON N2H 2H7 Canada
Tel: 519-743-3845; *Fax:* 519-743-3375
secretary@churchofthegoodshepherd.ca
www.churchofthegoodshepherd.ca

Also Known As: Swedenborgian Church
Overview: A small local organization
Chief Officer(s):
John Maine, Minister
Membership: 140 individual

Community of Christ - Canada East Mission
390 Speedvale Ave. East, Guelph ON N1E 1N5 Canada
Tel: 519-822-4150; *Fax:* 519-822-1236
Toll-Free: 888-411-7537
info@communityofchrist.ca
www.communityofchrist.ca/east/east.htm

Also Known As: Saints' Church
Previous Name: Reorganized Church of Jesus Christ of Latter Day Saints (Canada)
Overview: A medium-sized local charitable organization founded in 1830
Description: To promote communities of joy, hope, love, & peace

Community of Christ - Canada West Mission
6415 Ranchview Dr. NW, Calgary AB T3G 1B5 Canada
Tel: 403-239-8070; *Fax:* 403-239-3542
Toll-Free: 877-411-2632
darrell@communityofchrist.ca
www.communityofchrist.ca/west/west.htm

Overview: A medium-sized local organization
Chief Officer(s):
Darrell Belrose, Mission President
Publications: The Mission Messenger
Type: Newsletter
Profile: Articles & events to inform members & friends of the church
Family Camps, Youth Camps, Retreats
Type: Directory
Profile: Dates, directors & registrars of upcoming camps & retreats
Description: To promote communities of joy, hope, love, & peace

The Coptic Orthodox Church (Canada)
St. Mark's Coptic Orthodox Church, 41 Glendinning Ave., Toronto ON M1W 3E2 Canada
Tel: 416-494-4449; *Fax:* 416-494-4196
mail@coptorthodox.ca
www.stmark.toronto.on.coptorthodox.ca

Overview: A small national organization
Chief Officer(s):
M.A. Marcos, Protopriest
Membership: 45,000
Member of: The Canadian Council of Churches; Coptic Orthodox Patriarchate

Council on Homosexuality & Religion (CHR) / Conseil de l'homosexualité et la religion
PO Box 1912, Winnipeg MB R3C 3R2 Canada
Tel: 204-772-8215; *Fax:* 204-478-1160
Toll-Free: 888-399-0005
cvogel@mts.net

Overview: A small national charitable organization founded in 1976
Finances: *Annual Operating Budget:* Less than $50,000; *Funding Sources:* Donations
Staff: 5 volunteer(s)
Membership: 40 individuals + 21 organizations; *Fees:* Schedule
Activities: Administers the Manitoba Gay & Lesbian Legal Defense Fund & the Victims of Homophobic Violence Memorial; distributes publications; provides referrals for union ceremonies & the like; *Internships:* Yes; *Speaker Service:* Yes *Library:* Library
Description: To foster the welfare of homosexually-oriented persons & promote the understanding & acceptance of homosexuality within religious institutions; to provide counselling & referral services; to conduct workshops, seminars & lectures; to provide a library & a range of publications on homosexuality & religion; to assist others in the same activities
Member of: Association for Manitoba Archives; Manitoba Library Association; Social Planning Council

Creation Science Association of British Columbia
PO Box 39577, White Rock BC V4B 5L6 Canada
Tel: 604-535-0019
info@creationbc.org
www.creationbc.org

Overview: A small provincial charitable organization founded in 1968
Chief Officer(s):
George Pearce, President
Finances: *Annual Operating Budget:* Less than $50,000
Staff: 25 volunteer(s)
Membership: 125 individual; *Fees:* $15 individual
Activities: *Speaker Service:* Yes *Library:* Yes by appointment
Description: To compile scientific as well as Biblical evidence which supports creation & contradicts evolution & to communicate this information to schools, churches & the general public

Creation Science of Saskatchewan Inc. (CSSI)
PO Box 26, Kenaston SK S0G 2N0 Canada
Tel: 306-252-2842; *Fax:* 306-252-2842
gbmiller@sasktel.net
www.creation-science.sk.ca

Overview: A small provincial charitable organization founded in 1978
Chief Officer(s):
Rudi Fast, President
Finances: *Annual Operating Budget:* Less than $50,000; *Funding Sources:* Donations
Staff: 13 volunteer(s)
Membership: 15 institutional + 140 individual; *Fees:* $10 institutional; $10 individual
Activities: Meetings; speakers; book tables; tours; summer camp; *Speaker Service:* Yes *Library:* Yes by appointment
Description: To share scientific & scriptural evidence for special creation & the Creator

CrossTrainers Canada
PO Box 1426, Bradford ON L3Z 2B7 Canada
Tel: 416-697-0147; *Fax:* 905-775-0444
ct@ctministries.ca
www.ctministries.ca

Overview: A small local organization
Chief Officer(s):
Jodi Greenstreet, Co-founder
Patti LaRose, Co-founder
Joshua Schrader, Director, The Hub Youth Centre
Finances: *Funding Sources:* Corporate sponsors
Staff: 5 staff member(s)
Activities: Connections Centre with True Vibe program, Playzone, cafe & special events; The Hub Youth Centre with A Hand Up Clothing Room; Mercy House, a women's shelter
Description: The association is a Christian ministry organization with members from several local churches serving the Bradford community. It is a registered charity, BN: 889735023RR0001.

Diocèse militaire du Canada
USFC (O), Site Uplands, Édifice 469, Ottawa ON K1A 0K2 Canada
Tél: 613-990-7824; *Téléc:* 613-991-1056
rc.milord@on.aibn.com
www.missa.org

Aperçu: *Dimension:* petite; *Envergure:* nationale; *Organisme sans but lucratif; fondée en 1987*
Activités: *Bibliothèque:* Centre d'entraînement des aumôniers de Borden
Description: Fournir une dimension spirituelle et morale à toutes les activités affectant le moral et le bien-être des membres catholiques des Forces canadiennes, leurs familles et les employés civils du Ministère de la Défense nationale; *Membre de:* La Conférence des évêques catholiques du Canada

Direction Chrétienne Inc.
#520, 1450, rue City Councillors, Montréal QC H3A 2E6 Canada
Tél: 514-878-3035; *Téléc:* 514-878-8048
info@direction.ca
www.direction.ca
Également appelé: Christian Direction
Aperçu: *Dimension:* petite; *Envergure:* provinciale; *Organisme sans but lucratif; fondée en 1964*
Finances: *Budget de fonctionnement annuel:* $500,000-$1.5 Million
Personnel: 13 membre(s) du personnel; 3 bénévole(s)
Membre: 1-99
Description: Rendre visite aux communautés chrétiennes locales et particulièrement celles des grands centres urbains afin de se faire connaître et partager son mandat

Edmonton & District Council of Churches (EDCC)
c/o Garneau United Church, #123, 11148 - 84 Ave., Edmonton AB T6G 0V8 Canada
Tel: 780-439-2501; *Fax:* 780-439-3067
garneau@uccedm.org
Overview: A small local organization founded in 1942
Finances: *Annual Operating Budget:* Less than $50,000
Staff: 1 staff member(s); 7 volunteer(s)
Membership: 22; *Fees:* $60 denominational member; $30 individual member; *Member Profile:* Christian denominations; *Committees:* Ecumenical Coordinators; Week of Prayer for Christian Unity Service Planning Committee; Way of the Cross Planning Committee; No Room in the Inn Planning Committee
Activities: Organization of events; distribution of information; participation in interdenominational projects; *Awareness Events:* Week of Prayer for Christian Unity, Jan.; Good Friday Way of the Cross; No Room in the Inn Fundraising for Low Income Housing, Dec.
Awards: Rev. Marilyn McClung Memorial Award for Ecumenism
Description: To express through fellowship, consultation, cooperation, & service, the essential unity of the Christian church; to maintain open relationships & foster dialogue with other faith groups & inter-faith organizations; to provide support & monitoring for chaplaincy programs
Affiliation(s): Canadian Council of Churches

Église Réformée St-Jean
3407A, av du Musee, Montréal QC H4E 4L7 Canada
Tél: 514-767-3165
info@erq.qc.ca
www.stjean.erq.qc.ca
Aperçu: *Dimension:* moyenne; *Envergure:* provinciale
Membre(s) du bureau directeur:
Jean Zoellner, Pastor
Description: The majority of our members are French-speaking Québecers practising various occupations in society, blue and white collared workers. People coming from a wide range of cultural, regional and national backgrounds also contribute to a rich diversity. People of all ages can be found amongst us: young children, adolescents, students, the middle-aged and the retired. The dynamic nature of our church can be seen in the presence of many young families. We recognise that the Lord Jesus Christ, head of the Church, has assembled us, with our children in a community which holds one vision, one love, one faith and one hope: to live for His Glory and to serve Him where He has placed us.
Affiliation(s): Christian Reformed Church; Presbyterian Church of North America

Fédération nationale du MFC - Mouvement des Femmes Chrétiennes (MFC)
CP 174, 49, boul Lanaudière, Sainte-Anne-de-la-Pérade QC G0X 2J0 Canada
Tél: 418-325-2338; *Téléc:* 418-325-2255
mfcnational@sympatico.ca
www.mfcnational.com
Aperçu: *Dimension:* grande; *Envergure:* nationale; *Organisme sans but lucratif; fondée en 1962*
Membre(s) du bureau directeur:
Claire Duchesneau, Secrétaire
Finances: *Budget de fonctionnement annuel:* Moins de $50,000
Personnel: 1 membre(s) du personnel; 700 bénévole(s)
Membre: 8000; *Montant de la cotisation:* 15$; *Critères d'admissibilite:* Femmes de tout âge, condition et culture
Activités: Rencontre mensuelle sur le programme d'action; formation
Description: Un mouvement d'action catholique générale, il forme des femmes efficaces et dynamiques sur le plan familial, paroissial, social, et chrétien afin de transformer le milieu de vie par des projects concrets et en utilisant la méthode de l'action catholique; *Membre de:* Regroupement des Organismes Volontaires d'Éducation Populaire

Focus on the Family Canada
#200, 20486 - 64 Ave., Langley BC V2Y 2V5 Canada
Tel: 604-539-7900; *Fax:* 604-539-7999
Toll-Free: 800-661-9800
letters@fotf.ca
www.fotf.ca
Overview: A large national charitable organization founded in 1982
Finances: *Annual Operating Budget:* Greater than $5 Million; *Funding Sources:* Donations
Staff: 72 staff member(s); 250 volunteer(s)
Activities: Community Impact Seminars; *Library:* Library
Description: To strengthen & encourage the Canadian family through education & resources
Member of: Canadian Council of Christian Charities

Fondation Père-Eusèbe-Ménard
1195, rue Sauvé est, Montréal QC H2C 1Z8 Canada
Tél: 514-274-7645; *Téléc:* 514-274-7647
Ligne sans frais: 800-665-7645
info@fondationperemenard.org
www.fondationperemenard.org
Aperçu: *Dimension:* petite; *Envergure:* internationale; *Organisme sans but lucratif; fondée en 1970*
Membre(s) du bureau directeur:
Nicole Bernard, Directrice générale
Finances: *Budget de fonctionnement annuel:* $1.5 Million-$3 Million
Personnel: 3 membre(s) du personnel; 10 bénévole(s)
Membre: 15 000+
Activités: La Fondation travaille en partenariat avec les Missionnaires de Saints-Apôtres présents dans les pays d'intervention pour assurer la croissance des Églises locales en contribuant particulièrement à la formation de futurs prêtres et agents de pastorale, et pour améliorer les conditions de vie inhumaines de nos frères et soeurs dans ces pays
Description: Encourager les personnes qui le désirent à appuyer les efforts de développement et d'évangélisation des populations défavorisées dans le Tiers-Monde

Foursquare Gospel Church of Canada
#307, 2099 Lougheed Hwy., Port Coquitlam BC V3B 1A8 Canada
Tel: 604-941-8414; *Fax:* 604-941-8415
info@foursquare.ca
www.foursquare.ca
Overview: A medium-sized national charitable organization founded in 1981
Finances: *Annual Operating Budget:* $250,000-$500,000
Staff: 3 staff member(s)
Membership: 67 churches
Member of: Evangelical Fellowship of Canada

Full Gospel Business Men's Fellowship in Canada (FGBMFI)
#403, 50 Gervais Dr., Toronto ON M3C 1Z3 Canada
Tel: 416-449-7272; *Fax:* 416-449-9743
fgbmfi@allstream.net
www.fgbmfi.ca
Overview: A medium-sized national charitable organization founded in 1964
Finances: *Annual Operating Budget:* $100,000-$250,000
Staff: 2 staff member(s); 2 volunteer(s)
Membership: 1,000-4,999; *Fees:* $60 individual
Activities: National convention; *Internships:* Yes; *Speaker Service:* Yes
Description: To reach men at all levels of our modern society, calling them to God, & releasing them into their respective gifts & talents through the Holy Spirit
Member of: Full Gospel Business Men's Fellowship International

General Church of the New Jerusalem in Canada
c/o Olivet Church of the New Jerusalem, 279 Burnhamthorpe Rd., Toronto ON M9B 1Z6 Canada
Tel: 416-239-3054; *Fax:* 416-239-4935
assistant@olivetnewchurch.org
www.newchurch.org/societies/toronto
Overview: A small national organization
Chief Officer(s):
James Cooper, Pastor
Nathan Cole, Assistant Pastor
Member of: General Church of the New Jerusalem

General Conference of the Canadian Assemblies of God / Conférence générale des assemblées de dieu canadiennes
6724, rue Fabre, Montréal QC H2G 2Z6 Canada
Tel: 514-279-1100; *Fax:* 514-279-1131
info@caogonline.org
www.caogonline.org
Previous Name: Italian Pentecostal Church of Canada
Overview: A small national charitable organization founded in 1912
Chief Officer(s):
David Quackenbush, General Treasurer
Alberico DeVito, Overseer Emeritus
David Mortelliti, General Superintendent
David DiStaulo, General Secretary
Mario Catalano, Overseer
Finances: *Annual Operating Budget:* $100,000-$250,000
Staff: 2 staff member(s); 3 volunteer(s)
Membership: 6,000 + 21 affiliated churches
Activities: Hosting an annual conference; *Internships:* Yes
Description: To provide distinctive ministry to the Italian community, extending to all Canadians, regardless of language, nationality, or race; To proclaim the gospel of Jesus Christ in the power of the Holy Spirit throughout Canada & the world, based on the biblical standard of ministry in the New Testament
Member of: The Evangelical Fellowship of Canada; Canadian Council of Christian Charities

Global Outreach Mission Inc.
PO Box 1210, St Catharines ON L2R 7A7 Canada
Tel: 905-684-1401; *Fax:* 905-684-3069
Toll-Free: 866-483-5787
glmiss@on.aibn.com
www.missiongo.org/contact.html
Previous Name: European Evangelistic Crusade, Inc.
Overview: A small international organization founded in 1943
Affiliation(s): Interdenominational Foreign Mission Association

Good News Broadcasting Association of Canada
#3 Lower, 40 Centre Street, Chatham ON N7M 5W3 Canada
Toll-Free: 800-663-2425
bttb@backtothebible.ca
www.backtothebible.ca
Also Known As: Back to the Bible Canada
Overview: A small local charitable organization
Chief Officer(s):
Byron Reaume, CFO & Director of Stewardship
Bob Beasley, CEO
Member of: Canadian Council of Christian Charities; Evangelican Fellowship of Canada

Greek Orthodox Metropolis of Toronto (Canada)
86 Overlea Blvd., Toronto ON M4H 1C6 Canada
Tel: 416-429-5757; *Fax:* 416-429-4588
metropolis@gocanada.org
www.gocanada.org
Previous Name: Greek Orthodox Church (Canada)
Overview: A large national organization
Membership: Over 50,000
Description: There are 76 Greek Orthodox Communities in Canada under the jurisdiction of the Greek Orthodox Metropolis of Toronto (Canada)
Member of: The Canadian Council of Churches

Habitat for Humanity Canada (HFHC) / Habitat pour l'Humanité Canada
40 Albert St., Waterloo ON N2L 3S2 Canada
Tel: 519-885-4565; *Fax:* 519-885-5225
Toll-Free: 800-667-5137
habitat@habitat.ca
www.habitat.ca
Overview: A medium-sized national charitable organization founded in 1985
Chief Officer(s):
Stewart Hardacre, President & CEO
Finances: *Annual Operating Budget:* $3 Million-$5 Million; *Funding Sources:* Corporate & individual donations of cash & building materials
Staff: 20 staff member(s); 15 volunteer(s)
Membership: 72 local affiliates
Activities: Ed Schreyer Work Project; All Women Build Project; *Speaker Service:* Yes *Library:* Yes (Open to Public)
Description: To provide affordable & adequate housing for God's people in need by mobilizing local communities, volunteers & material & financial resources in wide-ranging, inclusive partnerships; to support, encourage, facilitate & empower those affiliates to build affordable homes in partnership with needy families.
Member of: Habitat for Humanity International

Holy Face Association
CP 1000, Succ A, Montréal QC H3C 2W9 Canada
Tel: 514-747-0357; *Fax:* 514-747-9147
holyface@holyface.com
Overview: A small national charitable organization founded in 1975
Chief Officer(s):
Gordon Deery, Contact
Finances: *Annual Operating Budget:* $250,000-$500,000; *Funding Sources:* Donations

Staff: 20 volunteer(s)
Membership: 15,000-49,999
Activities: *Speaker Service:* Yes *Library:* Yes by appointment
Description: The goal of this apostolate is reparation to God (Father, Son and Holy Spirit) through contemplative devotion to the Holy Face of Jesus

Independent Assemblies of God International - Canada
PO Box 653, Chatham ON N7M 5K8 Canada
Tel: 519-352-1743; *Fax:* 519-351-6070
pmcphail@ciaccess.com
www.iaogcan.com

Also Known As: IAOGI Canada
Overview: A small national charitable organization founded in 1918
Chief Officer(s):
Paul McPhail, General Secretary
Finances: *Annual Operating Budget:* $100,000-$250,000; *Funding Sources:* Membership fees; offerings
Staff: 2 staff member(s); 12 volunteer(s)
Membership: 500 churches/ministries; *Fees:* $100; *Member Profile:* Must be called by God to preach His Word
Activities: *Awareness Events:* National Convention, May; *Speaker Service:* Yes
Publications: The Canadian Mantle
Type: Newsletter *Frequency:* 3x/yr
Member of: Independent Assemblies of God International

Institut Séculier Pie X (ISPX) / Pius X Secular Institute
CP 7731, Succ. Succ. Charlesbourg, 1645, 80e rue Est, Québec QC G1G 5W6 Canada
Tél: 418-626-5882; *Téléc:* 418-624-2277
info@ispx.org
www.ispx.org

Aperçu: *Dimension:* petite; *Envergure: internationale; Organisme sans but lucratif; fondée en 1939*
Finances: *Budget de fonctionnement annuel:* $100,000-$250,000
Membre: 17 consacrés + 250 associés
Activités: Apostolat catholique; évangélisation; présence au monde; *Service de conférenciers:* Oui
Description: Évangéliser les milieux populaires par la présence et par des activités apostoliques; *Membre de:* Conférence canadienne des instituts séculiers; Conférence mondiale des instituts séculiers

Institut Voluntas Dei / Voluntas Dei Institute
7385, boul Parent, Trois-Rivières QC G9A 5E1 Canada
Tel: 819-375-7933; *Fax:* 819-691-1841
ivd.cent@cgocable.ca
www.voluntasdei.org

Also Known As: I.V. Dei
Overview: A small international charitable organization founded in 1958
Finances: *Annual Operating Budget:* $100,000-$250,000
Staff: 3 staff member(s)
Membership: 752; *Member Profile:* Clerics & laymen who commit their lives to the service of Jesus Christ; married people as associate members who live out the same ideal & same apostolic project as the celibate members
Activities: *Internships:* Yes
Description: To make known & communicate God's love for all to all people; to be present in every milieu; apostolic objective is "to create peace & brotherhood in Jesus Christ"
Member of: Roman Catholic Church

Integrity/Calgary
1121 - 14th Ave. SW, Calgary AB T2R 0P3 Canada
Tel: 403-276-9266
calgary@integritycanada.org
members.aol.com/DWFrancis/integrity.html

Overview: A small local organization
Member Profile: Gay & lesbian Anglicans & their friends

Integrity/Toronto
PO Box 873, Stn. F, Toronto ON M4Y 2N9 Canada
Tel: 416-925-9872
toronto@integritycanada.org
www.toronto.integritycanada.org

Overview: A small local organization founded in 1975
Finances: *Annual Operating Budget:* Less than $50,000; *Funding Sources:* Donations
Staff: 6 volunteer(s)
Membership: 100 individual; *Fees:* $15
Description: International organization of gay & lesbian Anglicans & their friends; to help its members discover & affirm that we can be both Christian & gay/lesbian/bisexual/transgender
Affiliation(s): Integrity Inc. - USA

Integrity/Vancouver
PO Box 2797, Stn. Main, Vancouver BC V6B 3X2 Canada
Tel: 604-432-1230
vancouver@integritycanada.org
www.vancouver.integritycanada.org

Overview: A small local charitable organization
Finances: *Annual Operating Budget:* Less than $50,000
Staff: 14 volunteer(s)
Membership: 50-100; *Fees:* $20; *Member Profile:* Gay, lesbian, bisexual, transgendered Anglicans
Activities: Monthly services on first Sunday, St. Paul's Anglican Church; monthly potluck dinners at members' homes; *Speaker Service:* Yes
Affiliation(s): Integrity Inc. - USA

International Institute of Integral Human Sciences (IIIHS) / Institut international des sciences humaines intégrales
PO Box 1445, Stn. H, Montréal QC H3G 2N3 Canada
Tel: 514-937-8359; *Fax:* 514-937-5380
iiihs@iiihs.org
www.iiihs.org

Overview: A medium-sized international organization
Membership: 10,000; *Fees:* $15
Activities: Corporate Divisions: SSF-IIIHS National & Regional Chapters; International College of Human Sciences; International Academy for Research & Advanced Studies; International Council of World Religions & Cultures; The Order of the Transfiguration
Description: An interdisciplinary, professional association for scientists, scholars, and spiritual leaders worldwide, who are involved in the sciences of human consciousness & healing, paradigms for the convergence of science, spirituality & humane values in the world, & new insights into the potential of the human spirit.

International Society for Krishna Consciousness (Toronto Branch) (ISKCON) / Subuddhi Deri Dasi
243 Avenue Rd., Toronto ON M5R 2J6 Canada
Tel: 416-922-5415; *Fax:* 416-922-1021
toronto@pamho.net
www.iskcon.com

Also Known As: ISKCON Toronto - Hare Krishna Movement
Overview: A medium-sized local charitable organization founded in 1966
Chief Officer(s):
Subuddhi Dasi, President
Finances: *Annual Operating Budget:* $3 Million-$5 Million; *Funding Sources:* Donations from congregations & festivals
Staff: 10 staff member(s); 20 volunteer(s)
Membership: 700 institutional; 2,000 individual; *Fees:* $1,100
Activities: Distribution of free food; taking care of seniors & youth; *Internships:* Yes *Library:* Library (Open to Public)
Description: To preach Krishna Consciousness around the world, following in the footsteps of the founder & spiritual master, His Divine Grace A.C. Bhaktivedanta Swami Prabhupada.

International Society of Toronto for Hungarian Church History
Regis College, 15 St. Mary St., Toronto ON M4Y 2R5 Canada
Tel: 416-922-2476; *Fax:* 416-922-2773
t.horvath@utoronto.ca

Also Known As: METEM
Overview: A small international charitable organization founded in 1990
Finances: *Annual Operating Budget:* Less than $50,000; *Funding Sources:* Charitable organizations & funds; fundraising
Staff: 3 staff member(s); 50 volunteer(s)
Membership: 400; *Fees:* $36; *Member Profile:* Scholarship & interest in Hungarian church history; *Committees:* Canadian; Hungarian; International
Activities: Congress banquets; *Library:* Library by appointment
Description: To promote research in Hungarian church history by preparing & publishing an encyclopedia, collecting documents & sources; to support publications related to the purpose of the Society; to promote public interest in the history of places related to church history in Canada & Hungary; to establish & maintain suitable quarters & facilities to hold meetings & exhibitions for discussing problems related to church history in general; to establish funds & scholarships for university students studying church history; to promote historical & archaeological research
Affiliation(s): METEM - Hungary

Jeunes canadiens pour une civilisation chrétienne
880, av Louis Frechette, Québec QC G1S 3N3 Canada
Tél: 418-683-5222

Aperçu: *Dimension:* petite; *Envergure: locale; fondée en 1977*
Membre(s) du bureau directeur:
Sébastien Bolduc
Description: Travailler avec la jeunesse pour préserver les principes catholiques et éducatifs

Jews for Jesus
#402, 1315 Lawrence Ave. East, Toronto ON M3A 3R3 Canada
Tel: 416-444-7020; *Fax:* 416-444-1028
toronto@jewsforjesus.ca
www.jewsforjesus.ca

Overview: A small local charitable organization
Chief Officer(s):
Andrew Barron, Canadian Director
Member of: Canadian Council of Christian Charities; Evangelical Fellowship of Canada; Interdenominational Foreign Mission Association

Latin American Mission Program (LAMP)
81 Prince St., Charlottetown PE C1A 4R3 Canada
Tel: 902-368-7337; *Fax:* 902-368-7180

Overview: A small international organization
Finances: *Annual Operating Budget:* $50,000-$100,000; *Funding Sources:* Share Lent collections taken up annually in all parishes
Membership: 20
Activities: Educational events; orientation & support for missionaries
Description: To send out & receive back missionaries; to learn from the dispossessed & oppressed & to stand with them in building a society of justice; to develop & encourage a Faith response based on the life & struggle of dispossessed peoples; to participate in "return mission" by working with groups committed to social justice in Canada & developing education programs in PEI which analyze the causes of exploitation of the poor & which exposes the reality of their lives
Affiliation(s): Les missionnaires du Sacre-Coeur; Scarboro Foreign Mission Society

Missionaires de la Royauté du Christ / Missionaries of the Kingship of Christ
5750, boul Rosemont, Montréal QC H1T 2H2 Canada
Tél: 514-259-2542

Aperçu: *Dimension:* petite; *Envergure: locale*

Les Missions des Soeurs Missionnaires du Christ-Roi
4730, boul Lévesque ouest, Chomedey QC H7W 2R4 Canada
Tél: 450-687-2100
missionsmcr@hotmail.com

Également appelé: Missions MCR
Aperçu: *Dimension:* moyenne; *Envergure: internationale; Organisme sans but lucratif; fondée en 1979*
Membre(s) du bureau directeur:
S. Evva Melanson, Contact
Finances: *Budget de fonctionnement annuel:* Moins de $50,000
Personnel: 1 membre(s) du personnel
Membre: 213 institutionnel
Activités: *Bibliothèque:* Oui (Bibliothèque publique)
Description: Organiser, administrer, maintenir une oeuvre dont les fins sont la religion, la charitépromouvoir l'éducation et le bien-être, particulièrement en ce qui a trait aux différents buts qu'il s'est fixéaide internationale

Multifaith Action Society (MAS)
#5, 305 - 41 Ave. West, Vancouver BC V5Y 2S5 Canada
Tel: 604-321-1302; *Fax:* 604-321-1370
admin@multifaithaction.org
www.multifaithaction.org

Previous Name: Canadian Ecumenical Action
Overview: A small national charitable organization founded in 1972
Finances: *Annual Operating Budget:* Less than $50,000
Staff: 3 staff member(s)
Membership: 200; *Fees:* $25 individual; $40 couple; *Member Profile:* Members come from many religious faiths: Aboriginal, Baha'i, Buddhist, Christian, Hindu, Muslim, Jain, Jewish, Sikh, Unitarian, Zoroastrian; *Committees:* Program; Calendar; Development; Personnel; Advocacy
Activities: Lectures & conferences promoting interreligious dialogue; forums on faith; environmental awareness programs within religious communities; faith centre visits; *Speaker Service:* Yes
Description: MAS is a non-profit organization promote interfaith & multifaith dialogue & understanding. It provides information & resources on world religions to the community & develops community service programs. It is a registered charity, BN: 122214505RR0001.
Member of: Affiliation of Multicultural Societies & Service Agencies of BC; Vancouver Multicultural Society

Les Oblates missionnaires de Marie Immaculée (OMMI) / Oblate Missionaries of Mary Immaculate
#100, 7535, boul Parent, Trois-Rivières QC G9A 5E1 Canada
Tél: 819-375-7317; *Téléc:* 819-691-1769
ommi@ommi-is.org
www.ommi-is.org
Aperçu: *Dimension:* petite; *Envergure: internationale; fondée en 1952*
Membre(s) du bureau directeur:
Claire Nantel, Presidente-directrice générale

OMF International - Canada (OMF)
5155 Spectrum Way, Bldg. 21, Mississauga ON L4W 5A1 Canada
Tel: 905-568-9971; *Fax:* 905-568-9974
Toll-Free: 888-657-8010
omfcanada@omf.ca
www.ca.omf.org
Also Known As: Overseas Missionary Fellowship
Previous Name: China Inland Mission
Overview: A medium-sized international organization founded in 1865
Membership: 1,300 missionaries worldwide; *Member Profile:* Four years post-secondary education
Member of: Interdenomination Foreign Mission Association
Affiliation(s): Evangelical Fellowship of Canada

Ontario Consultants on Religious Tolerance (OCRT)
PO Box 27026, Stn. Frontenac, Kingston ON K7M 8W5 Canada
Fax: 613-547-9015
ocrt4@religioustolerance.org
www.religioustolerance.org
Overview: A small provincial organization founded in 1995
Chief Officer(s):
B.A. Robinson, Coordinator
Finances: *Annual Operating Budget:* Less than $50,000; *Funding Sources:* Lecture fees; donations; banner ads
Staff: 1 staff member(s); 5 volunteer(s)
Membership: 1-99
Activities: *Speaker Service:* Yes
Description: To promote religious tolerance & expose religious hatred & misinformation

Pioneer Clubs Canada Inc.
#100, 3350 South Service Rd., Burlington ON L7N 3M6 Canada
Tel: 905-681-2883; *Fax:* 905-681-3256
Toll-Free: 800-465-5437
info@pioneerclubs.ca
www.pioneerclubs.ca
Also Known As: Pioneer Girls/Pioneer Boys
Overview: A large national licensing charitable organization founded in 1974
Chief Officer(s):
Jessica Breski, Executive Director
jbreski@pioneerclubs.ca
Finances: *Annual Operating Budget:* $250,000-$500,000
Staff: 9 staff member(s)
Membership: 216 institutional; 16,000 individual; *Fees:* $12 child
Activities: *Speaker Service:* Yes
Description: To serve God by assisting churches & other ministries in helping children & youth make Christ Lord in every aspect of life
Affiliation(s): Canadian Council of Christian Charities

Presbyterian Church in Canada (PCC) / Église presbytérienne au Canada
50 Wynford Dr., Toronto ON M3C 1J7 Canada
Tel: 416-441-1111; *Fax:* 416-441-2825
Toll-Free: 800-619-7301
hamilton@presbyterian.ca
www.presbyterian.ca
Overview: A large national organization founded in 1875
Finances: *Funding Sources:* Congregations
Membership: 125,509; *Member Profile:* Presbyteries; congregations; communicants on roll; ministers
Activities: *Library:* Knox College & Presbyterian College Libraries (Open to Public)
Member of: The Canadian Council of Churches; World Alliance of Reformed Churches; World Council of Churches; Action By Churches Together; Ecumenical Advocacy Alliance

Prison Fellowship Canada / Fraternite des prisons du Canada
PO Box 19510 RPO Manulife, Toronto ON M4W 3T9 Canada
Tel: 416-848-4793; *Fax:* 416-961-7190
Toll-Free: 888-470-2748
info@prisonfellowship.ca
www.prisonfellowship.ca
Overview: A small national organization
Chief Officer(s):
Eleanor Clitheroe, President/CEO
Jim Cavanagh, Contact, Kingston Office, 613-530-1205
Description: To challenge, equip, & serve the body of Christ in its ministry to prisoners, ex-prisoners, their families, & victims; to promote the advancement of restorative justice
Member of: Prison Fellowship International

The Reformed Episcopal Church of Canada - Diocese of Central & Eastern Canada (REC)
PO Box 2532, 320 Armstrong St., New Liskeard ON P0J 1P0 Canada
Tel: 705-647-4565; *Fax:* 705-647-1340
trinityfed@hotmail.com
recus.org; www.reccec.homestead.com
Overview: A medium-sized provincial charitable organization founded in 1886
Chief Officer(s):
Alison Buffet, Secretary
Michael Fedechko, Bishop Ordinary
Finances: *Annual Operating Budget:* Less than $50,000; *Funding Sources:* Donations
Staff: 4 volunteer(s)
Membership: 210 + 6 churches; *Committees:* Standing; Constitution & Canons; Church Extension
Activities: Synodical Council, 3rd week of Sept.; *Library:* Library (Open to Public) by appointment
Description: We believe the Bible to be the inspired, the only infallible, inerrant, authoritative Word of God

The Reformed Episcopal Church of Canada - Diocese of Western Canada & Alaska (RECWCAN)
2604 Quadra St., Victoria BC V8T 4E4 Canada
Tel: 250-727-3722; *Fax:* 250-727-3722
recwcan@islandnet.com
www.recwcan.ca
Overview: A small national licensing charitable organization founded in 1874
Chief Officer(s):
John Boudewyn, Treasurer, 250-544-0098
Jack Cryderman, Secretary, 250-339-4014
Charles W. Dorrington, Diocesan Bishop, 250-652-8850
Finances: *Annual Operating Budget:* Less than $50,000; *Funding Sources:* Offerings; bequests; church assessments
Staff: 2 staff member(s)
Membership: 300; *Fees:* Church offerings; *Committees:* Council; Vestry; Executive; Standing; Synod
Activities: Douglas House Retirement Home Ministry; Victoria Prayer Counselling; Healing Rooms; *Internships:* Yes; *Speaker Service:* Yes *Library:* Diocesan Office Library by appointment
Description: To reach out to those outside the existing congregation; establish new churches; assist congregations within the Diocese; receive congregations wishing to affiliate with the Reformed Episcopal Church; ordain candidates into the ministry
Affiliation(s): Common Cause Network

Religious Freedom Council of Christian Minorities
PO Box 223, Stn. A, Vancouver BC V6C 2M3 Canada
Tel: 250-492-3376
Also Known As: Bible Holiness Movement
Overview: A small local organization founded in 1979
Chief Officer(s):
Wesley H. Wakefield, Chair
Finances: *Annual Operating Budget:* Less than $50,000
Staff: 4 volunteer(s)
Activities: *Speaker Service:* Yes *Library:* Bible Holiness Movement by appointment
Awards: Religious Freedom Essay Contest Award
Description: To act as a sponsored organization of the Bible Holiness Movement

Romanian Orthodox Deanery of Canada
PO Box 4023, Regina SK S4P 3R9 Canada
romanianorthodoxdeanery.org
Overview: A small national organization
Chief Officer(s):
Nathaniel Popp, Archbishop, 517-522-4800
nathaniel@roea.org
Ionel Cudritescu, Dean, Eastern Canada, 416-614-1942
icudritescu5303@rogers.com
Michael Lupu, Dean, Western Canada, 403-203-7033
fatherlupu@shaw.ca
Description: The Romanian Orthodox Episcopate of America is grouped geographically into 7 deaneries & the Deanery of Canada is one of them, with 30 parishes across the country. It is non-profit, registered charity, BN: 888289642RR0001.
Member of: Romanian Orthodox Episcopate of America; Orthodox Church in America

Saint Swithun's Society
427 Lynett Cres., Richmond Hill ON L4C 2V6 Canada
Tel: 905-883-0984
norman@stswithunssociety.ca
www.stswithunssociety.ca
Overview: A small local organization founded in 1974
Chief Officer(s):
Norman McMullen, KStG, President
Kevin Dark, KStG, Vice-President
Elisabeth Stenson, Sec.-Treas.
Finances: *Annual Operating Budget:* Less than $50,000
Staff: 3 staff member(s)
Membership: 300; *Member Profile:* Non-denominational, non-political/sectarian & inclusive
Activities: Annual Celebration; *Library:* Yes (Open to Public)
Awards: Honourary Memberships
Awarded annually to those individuals who best represent the aims of the Society
Gonzo Award
Awarded to member who has given special service to the Society
Raging Bull
Awarded to member who has given special service to the Society
Umbrage Award
For annoying behaviour by an individual or group found to have offended the greatest number of people
Description: To promote feelings of goodwill; to encourage the celebration of Saint Swithun's Day (July 15) & to pattern members' lives after the example of our Patron
Affiliation(s): Friends of Winchester Cathedral (England)

The Salvation Army in Canada
Territorial Headquarters, Canada & Bermuda, 2 Overlea Blvd., Toronto ON M4H 1P4 Canada
Tel: 416-425-2111; *Toll-Free:* 800-725-2769
www.salvationarmy.ca
Social Media: www.facebook.com/salvationarmy?ref=ts
Overview: A large international charitable organization founded in 1882
Finances: *Annual Operating Budget:* $3 Million-$5 Million
Staff: 152 staff member(s)
Membership: 343 Corps (congregations); 165 social institutes across Canada
Activities: *Speaker Service:* Yes
Description: To preach the Gospel of Jesus Christ; to supply basic human needs; to provide personal counselling & undertake the spiritual & moral regeneration & physical rehabilitation of all persons in need who come within its sphere of influence regardless of race, colour, creed, sex or age
Member of: Evangelical Fellowship of Canada

Samaritan House Ministries Inc.
630 Rosser Ave., Brandon MB R7A 0K7 Canada
Tel: 204-726-0758; *Fax:* 204-729-9951
exec@samaritanhouse.net
samaritanhouse.net
Overview: A small local charitable organization founded in 1987
Activities: *Internships:* Yes; *Speaker Service:* Yes
Description: To provide support & services to at-risk populations - the homeless, those living in poverty, people with literacy challenges or persons leaving abusive relationships

Seicho-No-Ie Toronto Centre
662 Victoria Park Ave., Toronto ON M4C 5H4 Canada
Tel: 416-690-8686; *Fax:* 416-690-3917
www.snitoronto.ca
Also Known As: Home of Infinite Growth
Previous Name: Seicho-No-Ie Canada Truth of Life Centre
Overview: A small national organization founded in 1963
Chief Officer(s):
Nana Ishii, Contact
Fees: $60
Description: Provides a place of worship for those who believe in the Seicho-No-Ie Humanity Enlightenment Movement, which says that all religions emanate from one universal god.
Member of: Seicho-No-Ie (Canada)

Serbian Orthodox Church in the United States of America & Canada - Diocese of Canada
7470 McNiven Rd., RR#3, Campbellville ON L0B 1B0 Canada
Tel: 905-878-0043; *Fax:* 905-878-1909
vladika@istocnik.com
www.istocnik.com
Overview: A medium-sized national charitable organization founded in 1983
Chief Officer(s):
Davor Milicevic, Episcopal Secretary, 905-878-3438
Finances: *Annual Operating Budget:* $500,000-$1.5 Million; *Funding Sources:* Donations; parish taxes; dispensations
Staff: 23 staff member(s)

Membership: 150,000; *Committees:* Diocesan Executive Board; Diocesan Assembly
Activities: *Library:* Holy Transfiguration (Open to Public) by appointment
Description: To serve the Serbian Orthodox community & teach the Orthodox faith & culture

Seventh-day Adventist Church in Canada (SDACC) / Église adventiste du septième jour au Canada
1148 King St. East, Oshawa ON L1H 1H8 Canada
Tel: 905-433-0011; *Fax:* 905-433-0982
communications@sdacc.org
www.sdacc.org
Overview: A large national charitable organization founded in 1901
Finances: *Annual Operating Budget:* $3 Million-$5 Million; *Funding Sources:* Donations
Staff: 23 staff member(s)
Membership: 55,000
Activities: Adventist Development & Relief Agency (ADRA); It Is Written Canada; Christian Record Services
Description: To be a significant Christian movement that recognizes the unique role to which Christ has called it & the urgency of the message of salvation & judgment; to lead people to salvation in Jesus; to teach them the biblical faith & discipline of the Christian life; to equip them to serve with their God-given abilities through the leadership of our various administrative & ministry teams; to proclaim Christ; to nurture believers; to serve humanity

Société internationale de sociologie des religions (SISR) / International Society for the Sociology of Religion (ISSR)
Bremveldstraat 16, Herent B-3020 Belgium
sisr@soc.kuleuven.be
www.sisr.org
Aperçu: *Dimension:* petite; *Envergure: internationale; fondée en 1948*
Finances: *Budget de fonctionnement annuel:* Moins de $50,000; *Fonds:* Cotisations des membres
Personnel: 2 bénévole(s)
Membre: 300; *Montant de la cotisation:* 106 E; *Critères d'admissibilite:* En sciences sociales des religions

Société québécoise pour l'étude de la religion
Bureau R303, Université Concordia, 1455, rue de Maisonneuve ouest, Montréal QC H3G 1M8 Canada
Tél: 514-848-2076; *Téléc:* 514-848-4541
www.er.uqam.ca/nobel/sqer/
Aperçu: *Dimension:* petite; *Envergure: provinciale; fondée en 1989*
Membre(s) du bureau directeur:
Alain Bouchard, Président
alain.bouchard@ftsr.ulaval.ca
Description: Promouvoir la recherche, l'enseignement et la diffusion des connaissances dans les disciplines ayant pour objet l'étude de la religion

Spiritual Science Fellowship/International Institute of Integral Human Sciences (SSF-IIIHS)
PO Box 1445, Stn. H, 1974, rue de Maisonneuve ouest, Montréal QC H3G 2N3 Canada
Tel: 514-937-8359; *Fax:* 514-937-5380
info@iiihs.org
www.iiihs.org
Overview: A small local charitable organization
Chief Officer(s):
Marilyn Z. Rossner
Membership: 10,000; *Fees:* $15; gifts
Activities: *Internships:* Yes; *Speaker Service:* Yes
Description: To provide spiritual services, educational programs, & pastoral ministrations for persons, regardless of religious background, who desire to understand experiences of psyche & spirit, & to dedicate themselves to personal spiritual growth & psychic development, in an atmosphere of informed free-thought & enquiry

Taoist Tai Chi Society of Canada
134 Darcy St., Toronto ON M5T 1K3 Canada
Tel: 416-656-2110; *Fax:* 416-654-3937
headoffice@taoist.org
www.taoist.org
Overview: A medium-sized national organization founded in 1970
Finances: *Funding Sources:* Membership fees
Staff: 20 staff member(s)
Membership: 15,000; *Fees:* $20; *Member Profile:* Open to everyone
Activities: *Awareness Events:* National Taoist Tai Chi Awareness Day, first Sat. after Labour Day
Description: To make Taoist Tai Chi available to all &, through its teaching & practice, promote health improvement, cultural exchange & helping others

TEAM of Canada Inc. (TEAM)
2635 - 32 St. SW, Calgary AB T3E 2R8 Canada
Tel: 403-248-2344; *Fax:* 403-207-6025
Toll-Free: 800-295-4160
team@teamcanada.org
www.teamcanada.org
Also Known As: The Evangelical Alliance Mission of Canada Inc.
Overview: A medium-sized international charitable organization founded in 1969
Finances: *Annual Operating Budget:* $1.5 Million-$3 Million
Staff: 6 staff member(s)
Membership: 1-99
Activities: *Internships:* Yes; *Speaker Service:* Yes *Library:* Resource Centre
Description: To help churches send missionaries to establish reproducing churches among the nations, to the Glory of God
Member of: Canadian Council of Christian Charities

Teamwork Children's Services International
5983 Ladyburn Cres., Mississauga ON L5M 4V9
Tel: 905-542-1047
jchacha@teamworkchildrenservices.com
www.teamworkchildrenservices.com
Overview: A small international charitable organization
Chief Officer(s):
Joel Chacha, Program Director
Finances: *Funding Sources:* Donations
Description: To provide orphaned & disadvantaged children in rural areas of Africa a safe & secure faith-based home environment; To provide the children with good health, education, & vocational training, enabling them to become self-supporting & productive citizens

Ukrainian Orthodox Church of Canada
Ecumenical Patriarchate, 9 St. Johns Ave., Winnipeg MB R2W 1G8 Canada
Tel: 204-586-3093; *Fax:* 204-582-5241
Toll-Free: 877-586-3093
consistory@uocc.ca
www.uocc.ca
Overview: A large national organization founded in 1918
Membership: 120,000
Activities: *Speaker Service:* Yes *Library:* Library (Open to Public) by appointment

Union mondiale des organisations féminines catholiques (UMOFC) / World Union of Catholic Women's Organizations (WUCWO)
37, rue Notre-Dame des Champs, Paris F-75006 France
wucwoparis@wanadoo.fr
www.wucwo.org
Aperçu: *Dimension:* grande; *Envergure: internationale; fondée en 1910*
Membre: Over 50,000; *Critères d'admissibilite:* Organisation féminine catholique ayant 3 ans d'existance; *Comités:* Commissions Permanentes - Droits Humains; Développement et Coopération; Femmes et Église; Famille; Oecuménisme; Comités permanents - International; Finances; Procédures; Liturgie
Activités: Groupe de travail sur la violence contre les femmes, santé et prises de décisions; éducation; droits humains
Description: Promouvoir l'apport des femmes catholiques à la communauté ecclésiale et humaine; étudier et encourager la participation des femmes dans la mission d'évangélisation de l'Église; promouvoir une action qui rend les femmes capables de mieux remplir leur rôle dans l'Église et dans la société*Membre de:* Conférence des Organisations Internationales Catholiques (OIC)
Affiliation(s): Catholic Women's League of Canada; Ukrainian Catholic Women's League of Canada; Association féminine d'éducation d'action sociale; Mouvement des femmes chrétiennes - Inter-Montréal

Union of Spiritual Communities of Christ
PO Box 3024, Castlegar BC V1N 3H4 Canada
Tel: 250-365-5477
info@iskra.ca
iskra.ca
Overview: A small national organization
Chief Officer(s):
Lisa Poznikoff, Contact
Description: The Union of Spiritual Communities of Christ (USCC) is a registered Canadian charitable society dedicated to the sustainability and enrichment of the Doukhobor Life-Concept based on the Law of God and the Teachings of Jesus Christ

The United Brethren Church in Canada
501 Whitelaw Rd., Guelph ON N1K 1E7 Canada
Tel: 519-836-0180; *Fax:* 519-821-8385
brian.magnus@ubcanada.org
www.ubcanada.org
Previous Name: Ontario Conference, Church of the United Brethren in Christ
Overview: A small national charitable organization founded in 1856
Finances: *Annual Operating Budget:* $50,000-$100,000; *Funding Sources:* Donations
Staff: 1 staff member(s)
Membership: 12 churches; *Fees:* Schedule; *Member Profile:* Personal knowledge of God through faith in Christ; desire to live a life conforming to biblical principles
Activities: *Library:* At Emmanuel Bible College Library
Description: To organize groups of people into congregations to worship God; to make effective application of principles of righteousness in the Society
Member of: Church of the United Brethren in Christ, International
Affiliation(s): Evangelical Fellowship of Canada

VISION TV
#230, 171 East Liberty St., Toronto ON M6K 3P6 Canada
Tel: 416-368-3194; *Fax:* 416-368-9774
Toll-Free: 888-321-2567
visiontv@visiontv.ca
www.visiontv.ca
Overview: A medium-sized national charitable organization founded in 1988
Chief Officer(s):
William D. Roberts, President & CEO
Peter Miller, Chief Operating Officer, Programming
Gail Thomson, Dir., Audience, Brand & Marketing, Communications & Marketing
Mark Prasuhn, Chief Content Officer
Finances: *Annual Operating Budget:* Greater than $5 Million; *Funding Sources:* Sale of airtime; advertising; cable fees
Staff: 70 staff member(s); 3 volunteer(s)
Description: To reflect & illuminate the full spectrum of faith & religious belief which make up Canada's diverse society; to build bridges of knowledge & understanding between faiths & cultures; licenced to provide paid access to all eligible religious & faith communities & broadcast ministries; also mandated to broadcast non-sectarian programs based on values, ethics & spirituality on a wide variety of issues & themes
Member of: Canadian Association of Broadcasters; North American Interfaith Network
Affiliation(s): North American Broadcasters Association

Watch Tower Bible & Tract Society of Canada
PO Box 4100, Halton Hills ON L7G 4Y4 Canada
Tel: 905-873-4100; *Fax:* 905-873-4554
www.watchtower.org
Also Known As: Jehovah's Witnesses
Overview: A medium-sized national organization
Description: Serving Jehovah's Witnesses in Canada

The Wesleyan Church of Canada - Atlantic District
229 Beulah Rd., Browns Flat NB E5M 2R5 Canada
Tel: 506-468-2286; *Fax:* 506-468-2004
office@atlanticdistrict.com
www.atlanticdistrict.com
Overview: A medium-sized local organization

The Wesleyan Church of Canada - Central Canada District
17 St. Paul St., Belleville ON K8N 1A4 Canada
Tel: 613-966-7527; *Fax:* 613-968-6190
ccd@on.aibn.com
www.ccdwesleyan.com
Also Known As: The Wesleyan Methodist Church of Canada
Overview: A medium-sized national charitable organization founded in 1897
Finances: *Annual Operating Budget:* $500,000-$1.5 Million; *Funding Sources:* District churches
Staff: 3 staff member(s)
Membership: 1,736; *Member Profile:* Covenant members & community members
Activities: *Internships:* Yes
Awards: Five Star Award
Description: To create a context that produces healthy churches
Affiliation(s): Tyndale Seminary; World Hope International; World Relief Canada; Bethany Bible College; Outreach Canada; Evangelical Fellowship of Canada

Women's Inter-Church Council of Canada (WICC) / Conseil oecuménique des chrétiennes du Canada
47 Queen's Park Cres. East, Toronto ON M5S 2C3
Tel: 416-929-5184; *Fax:* 416-929-4064
wicc@wicc.org
www.wicc.org
Overview: A medium-sized national organization founded in 1918
Finances: *Funding Sources:* World Day of Prayer offerings
Member Profile: Representatives from the Anglican Church of Canada, the Canadian Baptist Ministries, the Christian Church (Disciples of Christ), the Evangelical Lutheran Church in Canada, the Mennonite Central Committee, the Presbyterian Church in Canada, the Religious Society of Friends, the Roman Catholic Church, the Salvation Army, & the United Church of Canada; Membership is by appointment & election; *Committees:* Program; Communications; Membership & Nominating; Finance
Activities: Establishing the Ecumenical Network for Women's Justice; Preparing policy statements on issues such as racial justice & health care; Granting funds for a variety of projects that benefit women & children in Canada & around the world; Coordinating the Fellowship of the Least Coin program in Canada; Providing education, such as theology workshops
Publications: WICC News
Type: Newsletter *Frequency:* s-a.
Profile: Updates on the work of the Women's Inter-Church Council of Canada, including results of project grants & forthcoming events
Description: To focus on national & international issues affecting women, growth in ecumenism, action for social justice, & the sharing of spirituality & prayer

World Conference on Religion & Peace (Canada) (WCRP)
#490-1, 333 Queen Mary Rd., Montréal QC H3Z 1A2 Canada
Tel: 514-343-7869
patrice.brodeur@umontreal.ca
www.wcrp.org
Also Known As: Religions for Peace (Canada)
Overview: A medium-sized national organization founded in 1975
Chief Officer(s):
Patrice Claude Brodeur, President
Membership: 100-499; *Fees:* $100 institutional; $10 student; $25 individual; $15 senior
Activities: Meetings; occasional conferences; newsletter
Description: To establish peace & justice at the local, national & international levels; to encourage members to work together with like-minded organizations on issues of social & economic justice, human rights, ecological harmony, arms limitation & nuclear disarmament; to aim for world peace through interfaith dialogue & applied ethics
Affiliation(s): World Conference on Religion & Peace (International)

World Council of Churches
PO Box 2100, 150, rte de Ferney, Geneva CH-1211 Switzerland
oikoumene.org
Overview: A medium-sized international organization
Chief Officer(s):
Luzia Wehrle, Administrative Assistant, General Secretariat
Affiliation(s): International Council of World Religions & Cultures

World-Wide Bible Study Association
PO Box 98590, 873 Jane St., Toronto ON M6N 4C0 Canada
Tel: 416-766-1855
richard.kruse@sympatico.ca
www.ibcschool.ca
Also Known As: International Bible Correspondence School
Overview: A small local organization founded in 1968
Chief Officer(s):
Richard Kruse, Director

Worldwide Church of God Canada
#101, 5660 - 192 St., Surrey BC V3S 2V7 Canada
Tel: 604-575-2705; *Fax:* 604-575-2758
info@wcg.ca
www.wcg.ca
Overview: A small national organization
Description: To proclaim the gospel of Jesus Christ around the world & to help members grow spiritually

Wycliffe Bible Translators of Canada, Inc. (WBT)
4316 - 10th St. NE, Calgary AB T2E 6K3 Canada
Tel: 403-250-5411; *Fax:* 403-250-2623
Toll-Free: 800-463-1143
info@wycliffe.ca
www.wycliffe.ca
Also Known As: Wycliffe Canada
Overview: A large national charitable organization founded in 1968
Chief Officer(s):
David Ohlson, Executive Director
Finances: *Annual Operating Budget:* Greater than $5 Million; *Funding Sources:* Charitable donations; CIDA funding for literacy projects
Staff: 146 staff member(s); 50 volunteer(s)
Membership: 501 individual
Activities: Monthly newsletter on website; *Internships:* Yes; *Speaker Service:* Yes *Library:* Resource Centre (Open to Public)
Description: To empower indigenous peoples worldwide for spiritual, personal & social growth through Bible translations & other language-related ministries
Member of: Evangelical Fellowship of Canada; Canadian Council of Christian Charities
Affiliation(s): Wycliffe Bible Translators International; Summer Institute of Linguistics; Canada Institute of Linguistics; Wycliffe Associates Canada

Yasodhara Ashram Society
PO Box 9, Kootenay Bay BC V0B 1X0 Canada
Tel: 250-227-9224; *Fax:* 250-227-9494
Toll-Free: 800-661-8711
yashram@netidea.com
www.yasodhara.org
Overview: A small international charitable organization founded in 1963
Finances: *Annual Operating Budget:* $500,000-$1.5 Million
Staff: 15 volunteer(s)
Membership: 125; *Fees:* $25
Activities: *Internships:* Yes; *Speaker Service:* Yes *Library:* Library by appointment
Description: To maintain a centre for adults engaged in a life of spiritual intent; to provide instruction in & opportunities for religious & spiritual practice

Yonge Street Mission (YSM)
270 Gerrard St. East, Toronto ON M5A 2G4 Canada
Tel: 416-929-9614; *Fax:* 416-929-7204
Toll-Free: 800-416-5111
ysm@ysm.on.ca
www.ysm.on.ca
Overview: A medium-sized local charitable organization founded in 1896
Chief Officer(s):
Rick Tobias, Executive Director
Finances: *Annual Operating Budget:* Greater than $5 Million; *Funding Sources:* Donations; churches; individuals; businesses; foundations; grants
Staff: 80 staff member(s); 500 volunteer(s)
Activities: Recreation; education; social & family events; relief; housing; *Internships:* Yes; *Speaker Service:* Yes
Description: To bring God's peace, dignity & justice to the poor & needy in downtown Toronto

Youth for Christ - Canada
PO Box 93008, #135, 19705 Fraser Highway, Langley BC V3A 8H2 Canada
Tel: 604-595-2498; *Fax:* 604-595-2473
Toll-Free: 800-899-9322
info@yfccanada.com
www.yfccanada.com
Overview: A medium-sized national organization
Chief Officer(s):
Dave Brereton, National Director
Shirley Loewen, Office Manager
Activities: Responsible, effective & culturally sensitive evangelism of youth, communicating & caring in ways that are relevant to this generation
Description: To impact every young person in Canada with the person, work & teachings of Jesus Christ & discipling them into the Church

Yukon Church Heritage Society (YCHS)
PO Box 31461, Whitehorse YT Y1A 6K8 Canada
Tel: 867-668-2555; *Fax:* 867-667-6258
logchurch@yknet.yk.ca
Also Known As: Old Log Church Museum
Overview: A small provincial charitable organization founded in 1982
Chief Officer(s):
Susan Twist, Director/Curator
L. Thistle, President
Finances: *Annual Operating Budget:* $50,000-$100,000
Staff: 1 staff member(s); 8 volunteer(s)
Membership: 25; *Fees:* $10
Activities: Operates Old Log Church Museum; *Library:* Yes (Open to Public) by appointment
Description: To promote & preserve church history in the Yukon
Member of: Yukon Historical & Museums Association
Affiliation(s): Canadian Museums Association

Zoroastrian Society of Ontario (ZSO)
3590 Bayview Ave., Toronto ON M2M 3S6 Canada
Tel: 416-733-4586
info@zso.org
www.zso.org
Overview: A small provincial charitable organization founded in 1971
Finances: *Annual Operating Budget:* $100,000-$250,000; *Funding Sources:* Membership fees; donations; investment income
Staff: 1 staff member(s); 200 volunteer(s)
Membership: 1,000; *Fees:* $70 family; $40 individual; $20 seniors & students; *Member Profile:* Zoroastrians living in Ontario; *Committees:* 15 sub-committees reporting to elected executive committee
Activities: Religious, cultural, youth, religious classes, seniors activities; sponsors 100th Scout Group; *Library:* ZSO Library by appointment
Awards: Volunteer of the Year
4 volunteer awards given per year
Description: Meeting the religious & cultural needs of the Zoroastrian community of Ontario
Affiliation(s): Federation of North American Zoroastrian Associations

Specific Faith Based Associations

Anglican

The Anglican Church of Canada (ACC) / L'Église anglicane du Canada
80 Hayden St., Toronto ON M4Y 3G2 Canada
Tel: 416-924-9192; *Fax:* 416-968-7983
information@national.anglican.ca
www.anglican.ca
Social Media: www.facebook.com/canadiananglican; twitter.com/generalsynod
Previous Name: Church of England in Canada
Overview: A large national charitable organization founded in 1893
Membership: 800,000 members; 2,346 churches
Activities: *Library:* Library by appointment
Description: To proclaim & celebrate the gospel of Jesus Christ in worship & action, as a partner in the world-wide Anglican Communion & the universal church; to value our heritage of faith, reason, liturgy, tradition, bishops & synods, & the rich variety of life in community; to acknowledge that God calls us to greater diversity of membership, wider participation in ministry & leadership, better stewardship in God's creation & a strong resolve in challenging attitudes & structures which cause injustice
Member of: Canadian Council of Churches

Anglican Foundation of Canada
Anglican Church House, 80 Hayden St., Toronto ON M4V 3G2 Canada
Tel: 416-924-9199; *Fax:* 416-924-8672
foundation@anglicanfoundation.org
www.anglicanfoundation.org
Overview: A small national charitable organization founded in 1957
Chief Officer(s):
John Wright, Executive Director
jwright@anglicanfoundation.org
Kavitha Gunaseelan, Executive Assistant
kgunaseelan@anglicanfoundation.org
Activities: *Speaker Service:* Yes
Description: To assist parishes, dioceses & programs of Anglican Church of Canada with low interest loans &/or grants
Affiliation(s): World Council of Churches

The Church Army in Canada
105 Mountain View Dr., Saint John NB E2J 5B5 Canada
Tel: 506-642-2210; *Fax:* 506-657-8217
Toll-Free: 888-316-8169
hello@churcharmy.com
www.churcharmy.com
Overview: A medium-sized national charitable organization founded in 1929
Finances: *Annual Operating Budget:* $500,000-$1.5 Million; *Funding Sources:* Individuals; churches; foundations
Staff: 50 staff member(s)
Membership: 1-99
Activities: *Speaker Service:* Yes *Library:* Cowan Memorial Library
Description: To bring people from all walks of life into a living relationship with Jesus Christ
Affiliation(s): Anglican Church of Canada

Baha'i Faith

Association for Baha'i Studies (ABS) / Association d'études Baha'is
34 Copernicus St., Ottawa ON K1N 7K4 Canada
Tel: 613-233-1903; *Fax:* 613-233-3644
abs-na@bahai-studies.ca
www.bahai-studies.ca
Previous Name: Canadian Association for Studies in the Baha'i Faith
Overview: A medium-sized international charitable organization founded in 1975
Finances: *Annual Operating Budget:* $100,000-$250,000; *Funding Sources:* Grants; Conference & Literature revenue; Membership fees
Staff: 2 staff member(s)
Membership: 2,000; *Fees:* $50 adult; $60 couple; $25 student/senior; $60 institution; $999 life
Activities: *Library:* Library (Open to Public) by appointment
Description: To foster Baha'i scholarship & to demonstrate the value of this scholarly approach; to promote courses of study on the Baha'i faith; to foster relationships with various leaders of thought & persons of capacity; to publish scholarly materials examining the Baha'i faith, especially on its application to the concerns & needs of humanity; to organize annual meetings & develop chapters of the Association around the world

Baha'i Community of Ottawa
211 McArthur Ave., Ottawa ON K1L 6P6 Canada
Tel: 613-297-9406; *Toll-Free:* 800-433-3284
www.bahai-ottawa.org
Overview: A small local organization
Membership: 9 sectors
Description: To support the development of the Baha'i Faith Community in Ottawa, Ontario.

The Bahá'í Community of Canada / La communauté bahá'íe du Canada
Baha'i National Centre, 7200 Leslie St., Thornhill ON L3T 6L8 Canada
Tel: 905-889-8168; *Fax:* 905-889-8184
secretariat@cdnbnc.org
www.ca.bahai.org
Overview: A large national charitable organization founded in 1844
Finances: *Annual Operating Budget:* Greater than $5 Million; *Funding Sources:* Contributions from members
Staff: 30 staff member(s)
Membership: 30,000
Activities: *Awareness Events:* Unity in Diversity Week, Nov.; *Speaker Service:* Yes *Library:* Library (Open to Public) by appointment
Description: An independent religion based on the writings of Baha'u'llah, 1817-1892, teaching the oneness of humanity, the common divine source of all the great religions, equality of the sexes & eventual world government; headquarters in Haifa, Israel; 5-6 million adherents in 214 countries & territories; Canada's 30,000 Baha'is are located in some 1,500 centres, 261 of which elect local governing councils called Spiritual Assemblies; National Spiritual Assembly of Baha'is of Canada incorporated by Act of Parliament in 1949
Affiliation(s): Baha'i International Community

Baptists

Association d'églises baptistes évangéliques au québec
7415, boul Gouin ouest, Montréal QC H4K 1B8 Canada
Tél: 514-337-2555; *Téléc:* 514-337-8892
association@aebeq.qc.ca
www.aebeq.qc.ca
Aperçu: *Dimension:* moyenne; *Envergure:* nationale
Membre: 65 000
Activités: Camps de jeunes; retraites; congrès; cohortes; *Stagiaires:* Oui; *Service de conférenciers:* Oui
Description: Aider les églises à: communiquer l'évangile de Jésus-Christ à tous les Québécois; former des disciples et des leaders; devenir plus solides et se reproduire; *Membre de:* Fellowship of Evangelical Baptist Churches in Canada

Baptist Convention of Ontario & Québec (BCOQ)
#100, 304 The East Mall, Toronto ON M9B 6E2 Canada
Tel: 416-622-8600; *Fax:* 416-622-2308
bcoq@baptist.ca
www.baptist.ca
Overview: A large local organization founded in 1887
Finances: *Annual Operating Budget:* $3 Million-$5 Million; *Funding Sources:* Member churches
Staff: 15 staff member(s)
Membership: 375
Activities: *Internships:* Yes *Library:* Library (Open to Public)
Description: A family of churches building Christ's kingdom; supports & enables member churches to be healthy, mission congregations as we serve God together
Affiliation(s): Baptist Women of Ontario and Quebec; McMaster Divinity College; Canadian Council of Churches; Evangelical Fellowship of Canada; Canadian Council of Christian Charities

Canadian Baptist Ministries
Canadian Baptist Place, 7185 Millcreek Dr., Mississauga ON L5N 5R4 Canada
Tel: 905-821-3533; *Fax:* 905-826-3441
info@cbmin.org
www.cbmin.org
Merged from: Canadian Baptist International Ministries; Canadian Baptist Federation
Overview: A medium-sized national organization founded in 1912
Finances: *Annual Operating Budget:* Greater than $5 Million; *Funding Sources:* Member churches; individuals; CIDA
Staff: 112 staff member(s); 540 volunteer(s)
Membership: 250,000 + 1,000 churches; *Member Profile:* Members of churches affiliated with the four conventions/unions; *Committees:* Public Affairs
Activities: Partners in Mission - 75 missionaries serving in Asia, Africa, Latin America, Europe & Canada; The Sharing Way - relief & development ministries in 13 countries, working in areas of agricultural & community development, community health, etc.; Canadian Baptist Volunteers - short-term ministry opportunities; Canada Caucus - consensus building among the churches in Canada; *Library:* Daniel Global Mission Resource Room
Description: To unite, encourage & enable Canadian Baptist Churches in their national & international endeavor to fulfill the commission of our Lord Jesus Christ, in the power of the Holy Spirit, proclaiming the gospel & sharing the love of God to all people.
Member of: Canadian Council of Christian Charities
Affiliation(s): Baptist World Alliance

Canadian Baptists of Western Canada (CBWC)
#1100, 550 - 11 Ave. SW, Calgary AB T2R 1M7 Canada
Tel: 403-228-9559; *Fax:* 403-228-9048
Toll-Free: 800-820-2479
info@cbwc.ca
www.cbwc.ca
Previous Name: The Baptist Union of Western Canada
Overview: A medium-sized local charitable organization founded in 1908
Finances: *Funding Sources:* Church congregations
Staff: 12 staff member(s)
Membership: 178 congregations representing 100,000 worshippers; *Committees:* Western Canada Missions; Evangelism; Finance; Youth
Activities: *Internships:* Yes
Affiliation(s): Baptist World Alliance

Canadian Convention of Southern Baptists (CCSB) / Convention canadienne des baptistes du Sud
100 Convention Way, Cochrane AB T4C 2G2 Canada
Tel: 403-932-5688; *Fax:* 403-932-4937
Toll-Free: 888-442-2272
office@ccsb.ca
www.ccsb.ca
Overview: A medium-sized national charitable organization founded in 1985
Chief Officer(s):
Gérald J. Taillon, Executive Director
Alan Braun, President
Finances: *Funding Sources:* Member churches
Staff: 8 staff member(s); 4 volunteer(s)
Membership: 10,189
Activities: *Library:* Resource Centre (Open to Public)
Publications: The Baptist Horizon
Type: Journal *Frequency:* bi-m. *Editor:* Debbie Shelton *ISSN:* 1195-4744
Profile: CCSB news
Description: To help churches build the Kingdom of God; a church for every person across Canada & around the world
Affiliation(s): Southern Baptist Convention

Convention of Atlantic Baptist Churches (CABC) / Convention des Églises Baptistes de l'Atlantique
1655 Manawagonish Rd., Saint John NB E2M 3Y2 Canada
Tel: 506-635-1922; *Fax:* 506-635-0366
www.baptist-atlantic.ca
Also Known As: Atlantic Baptist Convention
Previous Name: United Baptist Convention of the Maritime Provinces
Overview: A medium-sized local charitable organization founded in 1905
Activities: Providing seminars, conferences, stewardship education, & retreats; *Speaker Service:* Yes
Publications: Convention Update
Type: Newsletter *Frequency:* m.
Youth & Family Update
Type: Newsletter *Frequency:* m.
Description: To resource pastors, churches, & people; to facilitate a shared mission on behalf of churches; to establish & maintain professional standards & ethics for clergy

Buddhism

Buddhist Association of Canada - Cham Shan Temple
7254 Bayview Ave., Toronto ON L3T 2R6 Canada
Tel: 905-886-1522
www.chamshantemple.org/en
Overview: A small national organization founded in 1973
Chief Officer(s):
Dayi Shi, President & Abbot
Activities: Seminars, sutra reading groups, meditation retreats; *Library:* Yes
Description: In addition to the main worship hall & 2 congregation halls, the Buddhist temple also includes a Dharma seminary for the Chinese community to learn Buddhism.

Jodo Shinshu Buddhist Temples of Canada
11786 Fentiman Pl., Richmond BC V7E 6M6 Canada
Tel: 604-272-3330; *Fax:* 604-272-6865
jsbtcheadquarters@shaw.ca
www.bcc.ca
Previous Name: Buddhist Churches of Canada
Overview: A medium-sized national charitable organization founded in 1933
Chief Officer(s):
Leslie Kawamura, Director, Living Dharma Centre
Finances: *Annual Operating Budget:* $100,000-$250,000
Staff: 9 staff member(s)
Membership: 2,500; *Fees:* $45
Activities: *Speaker Service:* Yes *Library:* Library by appointment
Description: Propagation of Buddhism
Affiliation(s): Jodo Shinshu Hongwanji, Kyoto

The Palyul Foundation of Canada
c/o Orgyan Osal Cho Dzong, Buddhist Monastery & Retreat Centre, 1755 Lingham Lake Rd., RR#3, Box 68, Madoc ON K0K 2K0 Canada
Tel: 613-967-7432; *Fax:* 416-604-8101
palyul@ca.inter.net
www.palyulcanada.org
Overview: A small local charitable organization founded in 1981
Activities: Classes on Buddhism, meditation, ritual practices; retreats; empowerments; celebration of Buddhist holy days & festivals
Description: Dedicated to the preservation & advancement of the teachings of the Nyingma lineage of Vajrayana Buddhism

Union of Vietnamese Buddhist Churches in Canada
229 Ave. Y South, Saskatoon SK S7M 3J4 Canada
Tel: 306-978-0085
www.buddhismcanada.com/sask.html
Previous Name: The General Committee Vietnamese Buddhism in Canada
Overview: A medium-sized national organization founded in 1983
Finances: *Funding Sources:* Membership dues
Staff: 9 staff member(s); 7 volunteer(s)
Activities: *Speaker Service:* Yes *Library:* Bibliothèque Tam Bao Som (Open to Public) by appointment
Description: To preach Buddhism; to preserve traditional culture of the Vietnamese

Catholicism

Alberta Catholic School Trustees Association
#325, 9940 - 106 St., Edmonton AB T5K 2N2 Canada
Tel: 780-484-6209; *Fax:* 780-484-6248
admin@acsta.ab.ca
www.acsta.ab.ca
Overview: A medium-sized provincial organization
Affiliation(s): Canadian Catholic School Trustees Association

Assemblée des évêques catholiques du Québec (AEQ) / Assembly of Québec Catholic Bishops
3331, rue Sherbrooke est, Montréal QC H1W 1C5 Canada
Tél: 514-274-4323; *Téléc:* 514-274-4383
aeq@eveques.qc.ca
www.eveques.qc.ca
Nom précédent: Assemblée des Évêques du Québec
Aperçu: *Dimension:* moyenne; *Envergure:* provinciale; *Organisme sans but lucratif; fondée en 1871*
Finances: *Budget de fonctionnement annuel:* $500,000-$1.5 Million

Personnel: 8 membre(s) du personnel
Membre: 37; *Critères d'admissibilite:* Évêque diocésain; évêque auxiliaire; *Comités:* Éducation; Laicat; Ministères; Missions; Affaires sociales; Théologie; Communications; Prospective; Législation; Administration; Relations interculturelles; Pastorale des Autochtones
Description: Ôtre un lieu d'échange et de concertation où ses membres s'entraident dans la recherche d'actions à entreprendre pour rendre l'Église au Québec toujours plus vivante et engagée dans la société et la culture contemporaines
Affiliation(s): Conférence des évêques catholiques du Canada

Association des parents catholiques du Québec (APCQ)
#406, 7400, boul Saint-Laurent, Montréal QC H2R 2Y1 Canada
Tél: 514-276-8068; *Téléc:* 514-948-2595
Ligne sans frais: 866-376-8068
apcq406@bellnet.ca
www.apcqc.net
Aperçu: *Dimension:* grande; *Envergure: provinciale; Organisme sans but lucratif; fondée en 1966*
Finances: *Budget de fonctionnement annuel:* $50,000-$100,000
Personnel: 2 membre(s) du personnel; 25 bénévole(s)
Membre: 4 000; *Montant de la cotisation:* 12$; *Critères d'admissibilite:* Familles; *Comités:* Éducation de la foi; comité provincial d'enseignement privécarrefour famille-Québec
Activités: Secrétariat permanent; périodique; colloques; conférences; cours; congrès parents-jeunes; pétitions; rédactions de mémoires; *Service de conférenciers:* Oui
Description: Regroupe des parents catholiques pour promouvoir et défendre leurs droits et leurs intérêts selon les valeurs catholiques en matière d'éducation, de famille et de culture par l'information et la représentation de ses membres auprès de la population et des autorités civiles et religieuses; *Membre de:* Regroupement Inter-Organismes pour une politique familiale au Québec
Affiliation(s): Organisation internationale de l'enseignement catholique (OIEC)

Augustines de la Miséricorde de Jésus
2655, rue Guillaume - Le Pelletier, Québec QC G1C 3X7 Canada
Tél: 418-628-8860
secretaire@augustines.org
www.augustines.org
Aperçu: *Dimension:* petite; *Envergure:* locale
Membre(s) du bureau directeur:
Claire Gagnon, Supérieure générale
Description: Les trois dimensions de la vie spirituelle des Augustines d'hier et de demain sont: communion fraternelle; louange et intercession; et miséricorde

Auxiliaires du clergé catholique
12350, rue Fort Lorette, Montréal QC H2C 3C8 Canada
Tél: 514-384-0880
Aperçu: *Dimension:* moyenne; *Envergure: provinciale; fondée en 1939*
Membre(s) du bureau directeur:
Odette Desmarteau, Présidente
Finances: *Budget de fonctionnement annuel:* Moins de $50,000
Membre: 150

Benedictine Sisters of Manitoba (OSB)
225 Masters Ave., Winnipeg MB R4A 2A1 Canada
Tel: 204-338-4601; *Fax:* 204-339-8775
stbens@mts.net
www.mts.net/~stbens/
Also Known As: Sisters of the Order of St. Benedict
Overview: A small provincial charitable organization founded in 1912
Chief Officer(s):
Virginia Evard, Director, Communications
Irene Burzynski, OSB, Prioress
Finances: *Funding Sources:* Donations
Staff: 35 staff member(s); 30 volunteer(s)
Membership: 33
Activities: Programs in spirituality, personal growth & a variety of retreats; *Library:* St. Benedict's Monastery Library by appointment
Description: To witness Jesus Christ, through community life & prayer, contemplative living, hospitality, service to the people of God & stewardship of all God's gifts
Member of: Federation of St. Gertrude

Calgary Catholic Immigration Society (CCIS)
120 - 17th Ave., 3rd Fl., Calgary AB T2S 2T2 Canada
Tel: 403-262-2006; *Fax:* 403-262-2033
contact@ccis-calgary.ab.ca
www.ccis-calgary.ab.ca
Overview: A small international organization
Activities: Pre-employment training & counseling; community outreach for families & seniors; temporary accommodation facility; Integrated Resettlement Program
Description: CCIS is a non-profit organization which provides settlement & integration services to immigrants & refugees in Southern Alberta.

Canadian Catholic Historical Association - English Section (CCHA) / Société canadienne d'histoire de l'église catholique - Section anglaise
c/o St. Michael's College, 81 St. Mary St., Toronto ON M5S 1J4 Canada
Tel: 905-893-9754; *Fax:* 416-934-3444
www.umanitoba.ca/colleges/st_pauls/ccha/ccha.html
Overview: A medium-sized national organization founded in 1933
Finances: *Annual Operating Budget:* Less than $50,000; *Funding Sources:* Membership fees; donations
Staff: 11 volunteer(s)
Membership: 100-499; *Fees:* $50 Canadian; US$50 American; $30 student; $60 French-English
Activities: Annual scholarly conference at the Canadian Congress
Description: The Association promotes interest & research in the history of the Canadian Catholic Church, its dioceses, religious communities, institutions, parishes, buildings, sites, & personalities. It is divided into English & French sections.

Canadian Catholic School Trustees' Association (CCSTA) / Association canadienne des commissaires d'écoles catholique
Catholic Education Centre, 570 West Hunt Club Rd., Nepean ON K2G 3R4 Canada
Tel: 613-224-4455; *Fax:* 613-224-3187
ccsta@ottawacatholicschools.ca
www.ccsta.ca
Overview: A medium-sized national organization founded in 1960
Finances: *Funding Sources:* Sponsoships
Membership: 7 associations; *Member Profile:* Provincial & territorial Catholic school trustees' associations in Canada
Activities: Promoting Catholic education; Providing professional development opportunities for trustees; Collaborating with the Canadian Conference of Catholic Bishops; Liaising with Canadian government agencies & other Catholic education organizations; *Awareness Events:* Catholic Education Week
Publications: CCSTA [Canadian Catholic School Trustees' Association] Newsletter
Type: Newsletter
Profile: Includes CCSTA activities, conferences, & provincial reports
Build Bethlehem Everywhere - A Statement on Catholic Education
Type: Book
Description: To protect the right to Catholic education in Canada; to promote excellence in Catholic education across Canada

Canadian Catholic Students Association (CCSA)
Canada
cccmadmin@cccm.ca
www.cccm.ca
Social Media: www.facebook.com/group.php?gid=2230853889
Overview: A small national charitable organization
Chief Officer(s):
Lori Neale, National Coordinator, 416-506-0183
Victoria Tuason, President & Central Representative
central.rep@cccm.ca
Maureen Callaghan, Atlantic Representative & Contact, Communications
ccsa.communications@cccm.ca
Sharayhah Ulrich, Western Representative & Contact, Social Justice
ccsa.socialjustice@cccm.ca
Finances: *Funding Sources:* Donations
Member Profile: Persons who support the purpose of the association
Activities: Supporting prayerful, pastoral action; *Awareness Events:* Catholic Students' Week, March
Description: To unite Catholic students on Canadian post-secondary campuses; To nurture Christian student leadership
Affiliation(s): Canadian Catholic Campus Ministry; the International Movement of Catholic Students - Canada

Canadian Conference of Catholic Bishops (CCCB) / Conférence des évêques catholiques du Canada (CECC)
2500 Don Reid Dr., Ottawa ON K1H 2J2 Canada
Tel: 613-241-9461; *Fax:* 613-241-9048
cecc@cccb.ca
www.cccb.ca
Previous Name: Canadian Catholic Conference
Overview: A small national charitable organization founded in 1943
Member Profile: Diocesan bishops in Canada; Coadjutor Bishops; Auxiliary Bishops; Titular Bishops of any rite within the Catholic Church
Activities: Providing aid to developing countries & Christian education; Offering a forum for bishops to share experiences & insights
Publications: A Simple Guide to the Daily Mass Readings
Type: Yearbook *Frequency:* a. *Price:* $3
Workbook for Lectors and Gospel Readers
Type: Yearbook *Frequency:* a. *ISBN:* 978-0-88997-572-9 *Price:* $15
Sourcebook for Sundays and Seasons
Type: Yearbook *Frequency:* a. *ISBN:* 978-1-56854-674-2 *Price:* $18
Children's Daily Prayer
Type: Yearbook *Frequency:* a. *ISBN:* 978-1-56854-662-9 *Price:* $18
Daily Prayer
Type: Yearbook *Frequency:* a. *Price:* $15
At Home with the Word
Type: Yearbook *Frequency:* a. *Price:* $9
Description: To exercise pastoral functions for Catholics in Canada

Canadian Jesuits International (CJI)
#100, 1325 Bay St., Toronto ON M5R 2C4 Canada
Tel: 416-962-4500; *Fax:* 416-962-4501
Toll-Free: 800-448-2148
www.canadianjesuitsinternational.ca
Also Known As: Canadian Jesuit Missions
Overview: A medium-sized national charitable organization founded in 1955
Membership: 100-499
Activities: Support projects in Africa, India, Nepal, Jamaica, & Ukraine
Publications: Mission News
Type: Newsletter *Frequency:* 3 pa
Profile: News & stories about people in developing countries
Description: Committed to the service of faith & the promotion of justice for the poor of the world; especially dedicated to the educational needs of women, children, elderly & indigenous people at home & abroad

Canadian Latvian Catholic Association
34 Edenvale Cres., Toronto ON M9A 4A4 Canada
Tel: 416-244-4576; *Fax:* 416-244-1513
Overview: A medium-sized national organization founded in 1949
Finances: *Annual Operating Budget:* Less than $50,000
Staff: 10 volunteer(s)
Membership: 3,000 individual; *Fees:* $10 individual

Carrefour des mouvements d'action catholique
435, rue du Roi, Québec QC G1K 2X1 Canada
Tél: 418-525-6187; *Téléc:* 418-525-6081
Nom précédent: Comité diosésain d'action catholique
Aperçu: *Dimension:* petite; *Envergure:* locale
Description: Groupe de coordination des associations d'action catholique dans le diocèse de Québec

Catholic Biblical Association of Canada (CBAC)
#1407, 2300 Confederation Pkwy., Mississauga ON L5B 1R5 Canada
Tel: 416-406-4398; *Fax:* 416-406-5139
www.cbac.org
Previous Name: Canadian Catholic Biblical Association
Overview: A medium-sized national charitable organization founded in 1974
Finances: *Annual Operating Budget:* $100,000-$250,000
Fees: $30; *Committees:* Media & Communications; Resource; Program; Finance
Activities: *Rents Mailing List:* Yes *Library:* Resource Centre (Open to Public)
Description: To foster knowledge & love of the Word of God as found in the Scriptures, through provision of a variety of sources, primarily to the Catholic community.
Affiliation(s): World Catholic Biblical Federation

Catholic Biblical Federation (CBF) / Fédération biblique catholique (FBC)
St. Ottilien 86941 Germany
gensec@c-b-f.org
www.c-b-f.org
Overview: A small international charitable organization founded in 1969
Membership: 300+ in 130 countries
Activities: Workshops; Plenary Assembly
Affiliation(s): Catholic Biblical Association of Canada

Catholic Charities of The Archdiocese of Toronto
#400, 1155 Yonge St., Toronto ON M4T 1W2 Canada
Tel: 416-934-3401; *Fax:* 416-934-3402
info@catholiccharitiestor.org
www.catholiccharitiestor.org
Previous Name: Council of Catholic Charities
Overview: A medium-sized local licensing charitable organization founded in 1913
Finances: *Annual Operating Budget:* $250,000-$500,000
Staff: 1 staff member(s); 10 volunteer(s)
Activities: *Speaker Service:* Yes
Description: Catholic Charities of the Archdiocese of Toronto is dedicated to ensuring the provision of health and social sciences and to provide leadership and advocacy on behalf of the member agencies and those in need. The people served live and work throughout the Greater Toronto Area, as well as, in Simcoe, Durham, Peel, and York.
Affiliation(s): Catholic Family Services of Toronto & 26 member agencies

Catholic Children's Aid Society of Hamilton (CCAS)
735 King St. East, Hamilton ON L8M 1A1 Canada
Tel: 905-525-2012; *Fax:* 905-525-5606
karen.dolyniuk@hamiltonccas.on.ca
www.hamiltonccas.on.ca
Overview: A small local charitable organization founded in 1954
Finances: *Annual Operating Budget:* Greater than $5 Million; *Funding Sources:* Ontario Ministry of Community & Social Services
Staff: 180 staff member(s); 191 volunteer(s)
Membership: 100-499; *Fees:* $10
Activities: Annual general meeting; *Awareness Events:* Serendipity Auction, Nov.; *Internships:* Yes; *Speaker Service:* Yes
Description: To provide child welfare services to the Roman Catholic population of the City of Hamilton
Member of: Ontario Association of Children's Aid Societies
Affiliation(s): Council of Catholic Service Organziations

Catholic Children's Aid Society of Toronto (CCAS)
26 Maitland St., Toronto ON M4Y 1C6 Canada
Tel: 416-395-1500; *Fax:* 416-395-1581
pr@ccas.toronto.on.ca
www.ccas.toronto.on.ca
Previous Name: Catholic Children's Aid Society of Metropolitan Toronto
Overview: A medium-sized local organization founded in 1894
Finances: *Funding Sources:* Provincial government; private donations
Activities: Parental healthcare & child management training; foster care; Central Adoption Centre; *Awareness Events:* Child Abuse Prevention Campaign
Description: CCAS investigates concerns that a child may be abused or neglected, then assesses the risk to the child & develops a plan to keep the child safe. It is mandated to provide protective services to Catholic children at any time. It is a registered charity, BN: 129863577RR0001.
Member of: Catholic Charities of the Archdiocese of Toronto

Catholic Community Services Inc. (CCS) / Services communautaires catholiques inc.
1857, boul de Maisonneuve ouest, Montréal QC H3H 1J9 Canada
Tel: 514-937-5351; *Fax:* 514-937-5548
info@ccs-montreal.org
www.ccs-montreal.org
Overview: A medium-sized local organization founded in 1974
Chief Officer(s):
Bruno J. Mital, Managing Director
brunom@ccs-montreal.org
Finances: *Annual Operating Budget:* $1.5 Million-$3 Million
Staff: 33 staff member(s); 1104 volunteer(s)
Membership: 65; *Fees:* $10
Activities: Youth groups; home sharing; administrative & support services; community organization & development; family support programs; personal development & support groups; camping services; Almage Senior Centre; Teapot Senior Centre; Good Shepherd Community Centre; Home Support Program; volunteer coordination; Home Day Care Program; *Speaker Service:* Yes
Description: To provide a broad spectrum of social services on behalf of the English-speaking Catholic community of the Diocese of Montréal

Catholic Education Foundation of Ontario (CEFO)
80 Sheppard Ave. East, Toronto ON M2N 6E8 Canada
Tel: 416-229-5326; *Fax:* 416-229-5345
Overview: A small provincial charitable organization founded in 1976
Chief Officer(s):
John J. Flynn, Executive Secretary
Description: To foster & promote the principles of Catholic education; to support parents in their role as primary educators; to assist the Church in its pastoral responsibilities to the schools; to encourage the establishment of Catholic schools; to promote equity of educational funding in Ontario

Catholic Family Service of Ottawa (CFS Ottawa) / Service familial catholique d'Ottawa
310 Olmstead St., Ottawa ON K1L 7K3 Canada
Tel: 613-233-8478; *Fax:* 613-233-9881
info@cfsottawa.ca
www.cfsottawa.ca
Previous Name: Catholic Family Service of Ottawa-Carleton
Overview: A small local charitable organization founded in 1940
Finances: *Annual Operating Budget:* $1.5 Million-$3 Million; *Funding Sources:* Provincial/municipal government; United Way; private donations
Staff: 34 staff member(s); 15 volunteer(s)
Membership: 50
Activities: *Internships:* Yes *Library:* Library (Open to Public)
Description: CFS Ottawa offers a range of social services in English & French to all residents of the Ottawa-Carleton area. Services include counselling, support to the victims or witnesses of family violence or sexual abuse, advocacy, community development. It is a registered charity, BN: 118841105RR0001.
Member of: Family Service Canada

Catholic Family Services of Hamilton (CFS)
#201, 447 Main St. East, Hamilton ON L8N 1K1
Tel: 905-527-3823; *Fax:* 905-546-5779
Toll-Free: 877-527-3823
intake@cfshw.com
www.cfshw.com
Previous Name: Catholic Family Services of Hamilton-Wentworth
Overview: A small local organization founded in 1944
Finances: *Funding Sources:* Government of Canada; Province of Ontario; City of Hamilton; United Way of Burlington & Greater Hamilton; Foundations such as ON Trillium Foundation
Activities: Offering programs, such as the Employee Assistance Program, Debt Management Program, K.I.D.S. (Kids in Divorced / Separated Situations), Men's Anti-Violence & Abuse Program, & the Senior's Intervention & Support Program; Providing mediation services, in areas such as the workplace, credit, estates, & commerce; Offering consumer credit education to the general public; Offering money management coaching
Description: To provide individual, marriage, family, & credit counselling services in the Hamilton & Burlington communities
Member of: Ontario Association of Credit Counselling Service
Affiliation(s): Ontario Community Support Association; ONTCHILD; Family Services Ontario; Canadian Association for Community Care; Continuing Gerontological Education Cooperative; Older Persons' Mental Health & Addictions Network; Ontario Association on Developmental Diabilities; Ontario Case Managers Association; Ontario Gerontology Association; Ontario Partnership on Aging Development Disabilities

Catholic Family Services of Peel Dufferin (CFSPD)
Emerald Centre, #400, 10 Kingsbridge Garden Circle, Mississauga ON L5R 3K6 Canada
Tel: 905-897-1644; *Fax:* 905-897-2467
Toll-Free: 888-940-0584
info@cfspd.com
www.cfspd.com
Previous Name: Peel Dufferin Catholic Services
Overview: A small local charitable organization founded in 1981
Finances: *Annual Operating Budget:* $500,000-$1.5 Million
Staff: 30 staff member(s); 85 volunteer(s)
Activities: Individual, couple & family therapy; support groups; workshops; *Internships:* Yes; *Speaker Service:* Yes
Description: CFSPD is a multi-service counselling agency that supports families coping with difficulties, notably violence, trauma & abuse. Services are available in many languages to help people deal with such problems as depression, anxiety, grief, marital difficulties, parent-child conflict, developmental transitions & cutural adjustments. Offices in Mississauga & Brampton have walk-in clinics. The Society is a registered charity, BN: 119087823RR0001.
Member of: Catholic Charities; Archdiocese of Toronto; United Way of Peel Region

Catholic Family Services of Simcoe County (CFSSC)
#5, 20 Bell Farm Rd., Barrie ON L4M 6E4 Canada
Tel: 705-726-2503; *Fax:* 705-726-2570
info@cfssc.ca
www.cfssc.ca
Previous Name: Catholic Family Life Centre-Simcoe South; North Simcoe Catholic Family Life Centre
Overview: A small local charitable organization founded in 1979
Finances: *Annual Operating Budget:* $250,000-$500,000; *Funding Sources:* Charities; United Way
Staff: 20 staff member(s)
Membership: 1-99
Activities: Family, individual & group counselling; family life education
Description: To offer professional social services to all residents of Simcoe South; services will be directed to the treatment of troubled families & individuals, as well as to strengthening & enriching family life & individual functioning in all their dimensions & contexts

Catholic Family Services of Toronto (CFS Toronto) / Services familiaux catholiques de Toronto
Catholic Pastoral Centre, #200, 1155 Yonge St., Toronto ON M4T 1W2 Canada
Tel: 416-921-1163; *Fax:* 416-921-1579
info@cfsofto.org
www.cfsofto.org
Previous Name: Catholic Welfare Bureau
Overview: A medium-sized local charitable organization founded in 1922
Finances: *Annual Operating Budget:* $1.5 Million-$3 Million
Staff: 35 staff member(s); 18 volunteer(s)
Activities: *Library:* Library
Description: CFS Toronto is a non-profit, counselling agency for individuals, couples, & families. Within the context of Catholic beliefs, it offers a range of specialised programs, as well as a safe environment for women & families who are victims of abuse. It is a registered charity, BN: 100844919RR0001.
Member of: Catholic Charities of the Archdiocese of Toronto
Affiliation(s): Family Service Canada; Family Service Ontario

Catholic Family Services of Windsor-Essex County
6038 Empress St., Windsor ON N8T 1B5 Canada
Tel: 519-254-5164; *Fax:* 519-254-0611
intake@cfswindsor-essex.com
Previous Name: Windsor Catholic Family Service Bureau
Overview: A small local charitable organization founded in 1947
Finances: *Annual Operating Budget:* $250,000-$500,000; *Funding Sources:* United Way; government; fees
Staff: 8 staff member(s); 2 volunteer(s)
Activities: *Speaker Service:* Yes
Description: To strengthen the ability of individuals, families & communities to reach their potential within the context of Catholic beliefs, values & teachings, while affirming the cultural, racial & specific differences of people
Member of: Family Service Canada; Family Service Ontario

The Catholic Foundation of Manitoba / Fondation catholique du Manitoba
#5, 434 Archibald St., Winnipeg MB R2J 0X5 Canada
Tel: 204-233-4268; *Fax:* 204-233-1800
cfmb@mts.net
catholicfoundation.mb.ca
Overview: A medium-sized provincial organization founded in 1964
Chief Officer(s):
Tom Lussier, President
Description: The vision of the Catholic Foundation is to provide for the needy, better the situation of the underprivileged, promote cultural advancement and scientific research, and promote the cultural life of the Catholic community of Manitoba by encouraging the funding of endowments and by providing prudent management of funds and responsible distribution of the derived revenue

Catholic Health Association of British Columbia (CHABC)
9387 Holmes St., Burnaby BC V3N 4C3 Canada
Tel: 604-524-3427; *Fax:* 604-524-3428
smhouse@shawlink.ca
chabc.bc.ca
Overview: A medium-sized provincial organization founded in 1940
Membership: 114; *Committees:* Mission Intergration; Pastral Care; Ethics
Description: To witness to the healing ministry and abiding presence of Jesus. Inspired by the Gospel, this Association strives to have a universal concern for health as a condition for full human development.
Member of: Catholic Health Association of Canada; Health Employers Association of British Columbia

Affiliation(s): Euthanasia Prevention Coalition; Canadian Association of Parish Nurse Ministries

Catholic Health Association of Canada (CHAC) / Association catholique canadienne de la santé (ACCS)
1247 Kilborn Pl., Ottawa ON K1H 6K9 Canada
Tel: 613-731-7148; *Fax:* 613-731-7797
info@chac.ca
www.chac.ca
Previous Name: Catholic Hospital Association of Canada
Overview: A large national charitable organization founded in 1939
Finances: *Funding Sources:* Membership dues
Membership: 7 provincial associations + 23 sponsors & owners of health care organizations + 96 hospitals, long-term care organizations & health care professionals; *Fees:* $750 corporate member; $250 associate member; $50 individual member; *Member Profile:* Membership includes provincial associations, sponsors & owners of health care organizations, hospitals, long-term care organizations, health care professionals, affiliate organizations, & individuals.
Awards: CHAC Performance Citation Award
Established 1981; awarded annually to an individual who makes an outstanding contribution to health care in a Christian context, who exhibits exemplary leadership of a national effort at building the Christian community & unselfish dedication to others
Publications: Health Ethics Guide
Number of Pages: 132 *Price:* $12.50 members; $18 non-members
Lift Up Your Hearts to the Lord
Number of Pages: 104 *Price:* $4 members; $8 non-members
A Compendium of the Catholic Health Association of Canada
Number of Pages: 392 *Price:* $15
World Day of the Sick Kit
Price: $15
Living With Hope
Price: $2/copy
Description: The Association strengthens & supports the ministry of Catholic health care organizations & providers through advocacy & governance.

Catholic Health Association of Manitoba (CHAM) / Association catholique manitobaine de la santé (ACMS)
SBGH Education Bldg., #N5067, 409 Taché Ave., Winnipeg MB R2H 2A6 Canada
Tel: 204-235-3136; *Fax:* 204-235-3811
executivedirector@cham.mb.ca
www.cham.mb.ca
Overview: A medium-sized provincial charitable organization founded in 1943
Fees: $20 personal members; $100 associate members; *Member Profile:* Organizations; Health care facilities; Individuals
Activities: Promoting collaboration in health care services; Providing education to health care professionals, parish workers, & volunteers; Engaging in advocacy activities for the needs of the vulnerable & disadvantaged; Promoting the dignity & sacredness of each person; *Awareness Events:* CHAC World Day of the Sick
Publications: CHAM [Catholic Health Association of Manitoba] Newsletter
Type: Newsletter
Profile: Educational information for members & CHAM activities
Description: To carry out the healing ministry of the Catholic Church in the delivery of both health & social services in Manitoba; to treat the people of Manitoba with compassion & respect for all; to recognize the spiritual dimension integral to health & healing
Affiliation(s): Bishops of Manitoba; Diocese of Churchill-Hudson Bay, Northwest Territories

Catholic Health Association of Saskatchewan (CHAS)
1702 - 20 St. West, Saskatoon SK S7M 0Z9 Canada
Tel: 306-655-5330; *Fax:* 306-655-5333
cath.health@sasktel.net
www.chassk.ca
Overview: A medium-sized provincial charitable organization founded in 1943
Fees: $25 person members; $75 associations; *Member Profile:* Institutions, groups, & individuals who are interested in Catholic health care & support the work of the association
Activities: Providing education & resources to members; Offering programs, such as the Parish Home Ministry of Care Program & the Catholic Health Leadership Program; Engaging in advocacy activities with government; Providing both provincial & national networking opportunities; *Awareness Events:* Mission Week; World Day of the Sick *Library:* Catholic Health Association of Saskatchewan Resource Library
Description: To provide leadership in mission, ethics, spiritual care, & social justice in Saskatchewan; to promote the sanctity of life & the dignity of all

Catholic Health Corporation of Ontario (CHCO)
PO Box 1879, 712 College Ave. West, Guelph ON N1H 7A1 Canada
Tel: 519-767-5600; *Fax:* 519-767-5602
chco@chco.ca
www.chco.ca
Overview: A medium-sized provincial organization
Description: Sponsors member institutions and thereby continues and strengthens Catholic health care in Ontario

Catholic Health of Alberta (ACHC)
9810 - 165 St., Edmonton AB T5P 3S7 Canada
Tel: 780-481-9900; *Fax:* 780-455-4150
Previous Name: Alberta Catholic Health Corporation
Overview: A small provincial organization
Chief Officer(s):
Patrick Dumelie,, Interim CEO

Catholic Missions in Canada (CMIC) / Missions catholiques au Canada
#201, 1155 Yonge St., Toronto ON M4T 1W2 Canada
Tel: 416-934-3424; *Fax:* 416-934-3425
Toll-Free: 866-937-2642
info@cmic.info
www.cmic.info
Previous Name: Catholic Church Extension Society of Canada
Overview: A large national charitable organization founded in 1908
Finances: *Funding Sources:* Donations; Fundraising
Activities: Supporting over 600 missionaries who serve in home mission communities throughout Canada
Publications: Catholic Missions in Canada
Type: Magazine
Profile: Information about missionaries who serve in home mission communities across Canada
Catholic Missions in Canada Annual Report
Type: Yearbook *Frequency:* a.
Profile: Featuring information on CMIC's expenses & distributions
Description: To keep the Catholic faith in remote & poor communities throughout Canada

Catholic Organization for Life & Family (COLF) / Organisme catholique pour la vie et la famille (OCVF)
2500 Don Reid Dr., Ottawa ON K1H 2J2 Canada
Tel: 613-241-9461; *Fax:* 613-241-9048
colf@colf.ca
www.colf.ca
Overview: A small national organization founded in 1996
Chief Officer(s):
Jean Gagnon, Chair
Michèle Boulva, Director
Lea Singh, Assistant Director
Jocelyne Pagé, Administrative Assistant
Finances: *Funding Sources:* Donations
Activities: Promoting the teaching of the Catholic Church in circumstances from conception to natural death; Preparing & providing educational resources; Strengthening the role of the family; Participating in public debate about the family & respect for life; Collaborating with the Canadian Conference of Catholic Bishops & the Knights of Columbus
Publications: Catholic Organization for Life & Family Activity Report
Type: Yearbook *Frequency:* a.
Profile: Details about the organization's activities, projects, & initiatives
Stem Cells: Astonishing Promises . . . But at What Cost?
Euthanasia & Assisted Suicide — Urgent Questions
Life in the Balance: Workshop on Euthanasia & Assisted Suicide
Type: Guide
Description: To build a civilization of love; to promote respect for human life & the important role of the family

The Catholic Principals' Council of Ontario (CPCO)
#400, 161 Eglinton Ave. East, Toronto ON M4P 1J5 Canada
Tel: 416-483-1556; *Fax:* 416-483-2554
Toll-Free: 888-621-9190
info@cpco.on.ca
www.cpco.on.ca
Overview: A small provincial organization
Chief Officer(s):
Clara Pitoscia, Executive Director
director@cpco.on.ca
Paul Lacalamita, President
president@cpco.on.ca
Finances: *Annual Operating Budget:* $1.5 Million-$3 Million
Staff: 6 staff member(s); 6 volunteer(s)
Membership: 2,000 members who are principals & vice-principals in more than 1,300 elementary & secondary separate schools across Ontario; *Committees:* Communications; Member Security; Professional Development; Finance; Issues in Catholic Education
Activities: Advocacy, professional development; legal services; *Speaker Service:* Yes
Description: CPCO is a voluntary, professional association that serves more than 2,100 principals and vice-principals in twenty-nine Catholic school boards across Ontario

Congrégation de Sainte-Croix - Les Frères de Sainte-Croix / Congregation of Holy Cross
3745, ch Queen Mary, Montréal QC H3V 1A7 Canada
Tél: 514-737-6660; *Téléc:* 514-341-0739
saintecroixcsc@yahoo.ca
Aperçu: *Dimension:* petite; *Envergure:* locale
Membre(s) du bureau directeur:
Réjean Charette, Supérieur provincial
Description: Congrégation religieuse catholique qui oeuvre en éducation, en milieu paroissial et dans divers autres secteurs de la société

Congregation of St-Basil (Basilian Fathers) (CSB)
95 St. Joseph St., Toronto ON M5S 3C2 Canada
Tel: 416-921-6674; *Fax:* 416-920-3413
basilian@basilian.org
www.basilian.org
Also Known As: Basilian Fathers
Overview: A small international organization founded in 1822
Finances: *Annual Operating Budget:* Less than $50,000
Staff: 3 volunteer(s)
Membership: 325; *Member Profile:* Priests; students for the priesthood
Activities: *Library:* Library by appointment
Description: Roman Catholic congregation of priests whose primary apostolate is education, parishes & Hispanic ministry in Canada, USA, Mexico, Colombia, & France
Member of: RC Church

Council of Catholic School Superintendents of Alberta
AB Canada
superintendents@ccssa.ab.ca
www.ccssa.ab.ca
Overview: A small provincial organization
Membership: 35
Description: Provides a forum for discussion regarding the direction & development of Catholic Education in Alberta

Development & Peace / Développement et paix
1425, boul René-Lévesque ouest, 3e étage, Montréal QC H3G 1T7 Canada
Tel: 514-257-8711; *Fax:* 514-257-8497
Toll-Free: 888-234-8533
info@devp.org
www.devp.org
Social Media: facebook.com/devpeace
Also Known As: Canadian Catholic Organization for Development & Peace
Overview: A large international charitable organization founded in 1967
Finances: *Annual Operating Budget:* Greater than $5 Million; *Funding Sources:* Donations; CIDA (Canadian International Development Agency) provides grants for projects & programs
Staff: 70 staff member(s); 5000 volunteer(s)
Membership: 13,000; *Fees:* 5$
Activities: Financial support of projects in the developing world; emergency relief; advocacy on crises/issues in developing countries
Publications: Development & Peace Annual Report
Frequency: a.
Global Village Voice [a publication of Development & Peace]
Type: Newsletter *Frequency:* 3 pa *ISSN:* 0383-6703
Description: An official, volunteer-driven arm of the Canadian Catholic Church for international development, the organization aims to educate the Canadian population about the causes of poverty. It fosters solidarity, forming alliances with groups in developing countries, & promotes alternatives to unfair social, political & economic structures. Head offices are in Toronto & Montreal. It is a registered charity, BN: 118829902RR0001.
Member of: Caritas Internationalis; Conseil canadien pour la coopération internationale/Canadian Council for International Cooperation
Affiliation(s): Asia Partnership for Human Development; Coopération internationale pour le développement et la solidarité

Dignity Canada Dignité
PO Box 2102, Stn. D, Ottawa ON K1P 5W3 Canada
Tel: 613-746-7279
info@dignitycanada.org
www.dignitycanada.org

Overview: A medium-sized national organization
Chief Officer(s):
Dennis Benoit, President, 604-669-3677
pilgrim8220@hotmail.com
Frank Testin, Sec.-Treas., 780-990-1696
trainlvr@compusmart.ab.ca
Finances: *Funding Sources:* Donations
Activities: Encouraging spiritual development, education, & social involvement
Description: To voice the concerns of Roman Catholic sexual minorities; To promote the development of sexual theology, justice, & acceptance of the lesbian & gay community; To reinforce a sense of dignity & to encourage gay men & lesbian women to become more active members in the Church & society

Dignity Toronto Dignité
175 Windermere Ave., Toronto ON M6S 3J8 Canada
Tel: 416-925-9872
dignity-toronto@canada.com
www.dignitycanada.org/dtd.html
Overview: A small local organization founded in 1974
Finances: *Annual Operating Budget:* Less than $50,000
Membership: 20; *Fees:* $30
Activities: Monthly liturgical meeting to support gay & lesbian Roman Catholics; social gatherings
Description: To support & affirm gay & lesbian Roman Catholics through spiritual development, education, social involvement, equity issues, social events
Member of: Dignity Canada Dignité

Dignity Vancouver Dignité
PO Box 3016, Stn. Terminal, Vancouver BC V6B 3X5 Canada
vancouver@dignitycanada.org
Overview: A small local organization founded in 1977
Chief Officer(s):
Dennis Benoit, President, 604-669-3677
president@dignitycanada.org
Finances: *Annual Operating Budget:* Less than $50,000
Membership: 12; *Fees:* $35 individual; *Member Profile:* Roman Catholic gays, lesbians, friends
Description: The organization works within the Catholic Church & with other Catholic groups to reform the church's theological stance pertaining to sexual minorities. It supports gay & lesbian Catholics & their friends, encouraging participation in educational, spiritual, & social activities.
Member of: Dignity Canada Dignité

Dignity Winnipeg Dignité
PO Box 1912, Winnipeg MB R3C 3R2 Canada
Tel: 204-779-6446; *Fax:* 204-284-0132
dignitywinnipeg@yahoo.ca
www.dignitycanada.org/chapters.html#winnipeg
Overview: A small provincial organization founded in 1970
Finances: *Annual Operating Budget:* Less than $50,000
Staff: 3 volunteer(s)
Membership: 20; *Fees:* $25 (optional); *Member Profile:* Gay & lesbian people; non-gay men & women, encompassing a broad spectrum of professions, political beliefs, ethnic & linguistic backgrounds & economic levels
Activities: Regular liturgies/discussion groups; annual retreat; social events; brochures; *Speaker Service:* Yes
Description: To bring together gay & lesbian Catholics & their friends; To encourage a process of self-understanding & personal integration with respect to issues, including spirituality & sexuality
Member of: Dignity Canada Dignité

Foundation of Catholic Community Services Inc (FCCS)
#310, 1857, boul de Maisonneuve ouest, Montréal QC H3H 1J9 Canada
Tel: 514-934-1326; *Fax:* 514-934-0453
foundationcathcom@yahoo.ca
Overview: A small local organization founded in 1932
Chief Officer(s):
Mary Ellen Bayard, Adminstrator
Membership: 100 individual

Frères de Notre-Dame de la Miséricorde / Brothers of Our Lady of Mercy
1149, ch Tour du Lac nord, Lac-Sergent QC G0A 2J0 Canada
Tél: 418-875-2792; *Téléc:* 418-875-4829
fndm@cite.net
Aperçu: *Dimension:* petite; *Envergure: internationale; Organisme sans but lucratif; fondée en 1839*
Membre(s) du bureau directeur:
Omer Beaulieu, Délégué du Supérieur général
Finances: *Budget de fonctionnement annuel:* Moins de $50,000
Personnel: 1 membre(s) du personnel; 6 bénévole(s)
Membre: 9
Description: Rassembler des personnes en vue d'un travail apostolique auprès des jeunes et particulièrement auprès des personnes éprouvant des difficultés

Holy Childhood Association (HCA)
3329 Danforth Ave., #D, Toronto ON M1L 4T3 Canada
Tel: 416-699-7077; *Fax:* 416-699-9019
Toll-Free: 800-897-8865
hca@missionsocieties.ca
www.missionsocieties.ca
Also Known As: Children Helping Children
Overview: A medium-sized international charitable organization founded in 1843
Description: To develop mission awareness through a school program for elementary Catholic school children; to provide aid to children in developing countries.
Member of: Pontificial Mission Societies

Jesuit Development Office (JDO)
c/o Jesuit in English Canada, Provincial Office, 43 Queen's Park Cres. East, Toronto ON M5S 2C3 Canada
Tel: 416-481-9154; *Fax:* 416-920-5799
www.jesuits.ca
Overview: A medium-sized international charitable organization founded in 1940
Membership: under 200
Description: To raise & provide the funds necessary for the support of Jesuit brothers & priests in formation, in ministry & in their senior years
Member of: Jesuit Fathers & Brothers of Upper Canada

LAUDEM, L'Association des musiciens liturgiques du Canada
1085, rue de la Cathédrale, Montréal QC H3B 2V3 Canada
Tél: 514-866-1661; *Téléc:* 514-767-1168
info@laudem.org
www.laudem.org
Nom précédent: L'Association des organistes liturgiques du Canada
Aperçu: *Dimension:* petite; *Envergure: nationale; fondée en 1992*
Membre(s) du bureau directeur:
Hélène Dugal, Présidente
Membre: 117; *Critères d'admissibilite:* Laudem accueille parmi ses membres actifs les organistes professionnels, amateurs et étudiants, titulaires, assistants, ou remplaçants dans les paroisses, sanctuaires, dessertes et communautés religieuses d'expression française de l'Église canadienne; Laudem accueille en outre parmi ses membres donateurs toutes les personnes intéressées à promouvoir les buts pour lesquels l'association a été créé
Description: De réunir les organistes liturgiques pour la promotion et le développement de leur ministère dans l'Église catholique romaine; *Membre de:* Fédération francophone des amis de l'orgue

Little Brothers of the Good Shepherd / Petits Frères du Bon-Pasteur
Good Shepherd Centre, PO Box 1003, 135 Mary St., Hamilton ON L8N 3R1 Canada
Tel: 905-528-9109; *Fax:* 905-528-6967
info@goodshepherdcentres.ca
www.goodshepherdcentres.ca
Overview: A small local organization founded in 1964
Chief Officer(s):
Richard MacPhee, Executive Director
Finances: *Annual Operating Budget:* $500,000-$1.5 Million
Activities: Housing for battered women & children; residence for homeless youth; men's hostel; food bank & food line; speakers on topics dealing with violence & abuse; *Speaker Service:* Yes

Messagères de Notre-Dame de l'Assomption (MNDA)
1671, ch de Château-Bigot, Charlesbourg QC G2L 1H4 Canada
Tél: 418-626-7492
Aperçu: *Dimension:* petite; *Envergure: locale; Organisme sans but lucratif; fondée en 1964*
Membre(s) du bureau directeur:
Lucie Dorval, Présidente
Finances: *Budget de fonctionnement annuel:* Moins de $50,000
Membre: 200 membres auxiliaires; 10 membres engagés, célibataires et veuves; *Montant de la cotisation:* 100$

Missionary Sisters of The Precious Blood
685 Finch Ave. West, Toronto ON M2R 1P2 Canada
Tel: 416-630-3298
srkatericps@hotmail.com
www.cpsmissionarysisters.com
Overview: A small international organization founded in 1885
Finances: *Funding Sources:* donations
Staff: 60 staff member(s)
Description: Involved in early childhood education and teaching at the elementary, secondary, and college levels. Also work in health care services as nurses, doctors, administrators, physical and occupational therapists, hospital chaplains, caregivers for the elderly, with AIDs patients and in nutrition education. Serves in social work, parish ministry, domestic work, gardening, religious education, work with the mentally and physically handicapped, retreat work, art, and in ministry to the Hispanic and First Nations people.

Mosaic Counselling & Family Services
400 Queen St. South, Kitchener ON N2G 1W7
Tel: 519-743-6333
info@mosaiconline.ca
www.mosaiconline.ca
Previous Name: Catholic Family Counselling Centre; Catholic Social Services; Catholic Welfare Bureau
Overview: A small local charitable organization founded in 1952
Finances: *Annual Operating Budget:* $3 Million-$5 Million; *Funding Sources:* United Way; Government of Canada; Province of Ontario; Regional Municipality of Waterloo; Foundations, such as Pathways to Education Canada
Activities: Offering individual, group, & credit counselling; Providing workplace & employee assistance programs; Offering community outreach services; *Library:* Mosaic Counselling & Family Services Library
Awards: Leadership Award
For exceptional contribution to the well being of families in Canada
Description: To provide full-service professional counselling services in Kitchener & the surrounding region; *Member of:* Canadian Association of Credit Counselling Services; Ontario Association of Credit Counselling Services; United Way of Kitchener-Waterloo & Area; Family Service Ontario

New Brunswick Catholic Health Association (NBCHA)
1773 Water St., Miramichi NB E1N 1B2 Canada
Tel: 506-778-5302; *Fax:* 506-778-5303
nbcha@nb.aibn.com
www.chanb.com/chanb/
Also Known As: Catholic Health Association of New Brunswick
Overview: A small provincial organization founded in 1986
Membership: 300
Description: The New Brunswick Catholic Health Association is a provincial Christian organization promoting health care in the tradition of the Catholic Church. The Association fosters healing in all its aspects: Physical, psychological, social and spiritual

Newman Foundation of Toronto
89 St. George St., Toronto ON M5S 2E8 Canada
Tel: 416-979-2468; *Fax:* 416-596-6920
secretary@newmantoronto.com
www.newmantoronto.com
Overview: A small local charitable organization
Chief Officer(s):
W.F. Morneau, President
Patrick O'Dea, Director
Description: To maintain & support Roman Catholic chaplaincy on University of Toronto campus

Ontario Conference of Catholic Bishops / Conférence des évêques catholiques de l'Ontario
#800, 10 St. Mary St., Toronto ON M4Y 1P9 Canada
Tel: 416-923-1423; *Fax:* 416-923-1509
occb@occb.on.ca
www.occb.on.ca
Overview: A small provincial organization
Description: The Ontario Conference of Catholic Bishops is the association of the Catholic bishops of the Province of Ontario in the service of Catholics of Ontario. Involved in providing information and instruction about the principles and moral positions of the Church on all aspects of life

Ontario English Catholic Teachers' Association (CLC) (OECTA)
#400, 65 St. Clair Ave. East, Toronto ON M4T 2Y8 Canada
Tel: 416-925-2493; *Fax:* 416-925-7764
Toll-Free: 800-268-7230
m.despault@oecta.on.ca
www.oecta.on.ca
Overview: A large provincial organization founded in 1944
Chief Officer(s):
James Ryan, President
j.ryan@oecta.on.ca
Marshall Jarvis, General Secretary
m.jarvis@oecta.on.ca
Membership: 36,000; *Fees:* $950
Description: Committed to the advancement of Catholic education; to provide professional services, support, protection & leadership

Member of: Canadian Teachers' Federation; Canadian Labour Congress; Ontario Federation of Labour
Affiliation(s): Ontario Teachers' Federation

Orthodox Church in America Archdiocese of Canada (OCA ADOC)
Office of the Bishop, PO Box 179, Spencerville ON K0E 1X0 Canada
Tel: 613-925-5226; *Fax:* 613-925-1521
vladyka@archdiocese.ca
www.archdiocese.ca/home.htm
Also Known As: Orthodox Church in Canada
Previous Name: Russian Orthodox Greek Catholic Church (Metropolia)
Overview: A medium-sized international organization founded in 1902
Membership: 10,000+
Description: A component of the Orthodox Church in America, an autocephalous (self-governing) church with territorial jurisdiction in Canada, the USA & Mexico; its doctrine & worship are those of the world-wide One Holy Catholic & Apostolic Church
Member of: Canadian Council of Churches; Churches of Manitoba; Orthodox Clergy Association of Québec

Pax Romana
CP 374, 15, rue du Grand-Bureau, Geneva 24 CH-1211 Switzerland
international_secretariat@paxromana.org
www.paxromana.org
Également appelé: International Catholic Organization
Nom précédent: International Movement of Catholic Students; International Catholic Movement for Intellectual & Cultural Affairs
Aperçu: *Dimension:* grande; *Envergure: internationale; fondée en 1921*
Membre(s) du bureau directeur:
Bernard Hyon, Secretary General
Activités: Pax Romana has consultative status with the United Nations Economic & Social Council, UNESCO & the European Council, & has accredited representatives to those organisations in New York, Vienna, Paris, Geneve & Strasbourg
Description: Aims, through its various professional & intellectual commitments in society & the Church, to engage in pro-active dialogue between Christian faith & cultures in order to promote the evangelization of cultures & the inculturation of the Gospel for the realization of the Kingdom of God
Affiliation(s): Mouvement d'étudiants chrétiens du Québec; Association of Canadian Catholic Students

Religious of The Sacred Heart / Religieuses du Sacré-Coeur
#811, 325 Dalhousie St., Ottawa ON K1N 7G2 Canada
Tel: 613-241-4050; *Fax:* 613-241-3142
sshcph@on.aibn.com
www.sshc.ca
Also Known As: Society of the Sacred Heart
Overview: A small local charitable organization founded in 1800
Chief Officer(s):
Mary Finlayson, Provincial Superior
Membership: 1-99
Activities: *Library:* Provincial Archives (Open to Public) by appointment
Description: To make known the love of Jesus in the world, through educaton & social justice activities

St. John's Cathedral Polish Catholic Church
186 Cowan Ave., Toronto ON M6K 2N6 Canada
Tel: 416-532-8249; *Fax:* 416-532-4653
stjohnscathedralcc@sympatico.com
Previous Name: Polish National Catholic Church of Canada
Overview: A small national organization
Chief Officer(s):
Joris Vercammen, Bishop Administrator
Finances: *Annual Operating Budget:* $100,000-$250,000
Membership: 300
Member of: The Canadian Council of Churches

ShareLife
1155 Yonge St., Toronto ON M4T 1W2 Canada
Tel: 416-934-3400; *Fax:* 416-934-3412
Toll-Free: 800-263-2595
slife@archtoronto.org
www.sharelife.org
Overview: A large international charitable organization founded in 1976
Finances: *Annual Operating Budget:* $500,000-$1.5 Million
Membership: 34 organizations
Activities: *Awareness Events:* Kickoffs; *Speaker Service:* Yes
Description: ShareLife is the Catholic Community's response to helping the whole community through Catholic agencies by effectively raising & allocating funds
Member of: International Catholic Stewardship Council
Affiliation(s): Canadian Centre for Philanthropy

Sisters Adorers of the Precious Blood / Soeurs Adoratrices du Précieux Sang
301 Ramsay Rd., London ON N6G 1N7 Canada
Tel: 519-473-2499; *Fax:* 519-473-6590
sremwalsh@pbsisters.on.ca
www.vocations.ca
Overview: A small local charitable organization founded in 1861
Chief Officer(s):
Eileen Mary Walsh, General Superior

Sisters of Charity of Halifax (SC)
215 Seton Rd., Halifax NS B3M 0C9 Canada
Tel: 902-406-8077; *Fax:* 902-457-3506
communications@schalifax.ca
www.schalifax.ca
Overview: A small local organization founded in 1849
Chief Officer(s):
Carrie Flemming, Advancement Associate
advancement@schalifax.ca
Ruth Jeppesen, Director, Communications
Membership: 500
Description: To develop a sensitivity to the oppressed through presence, prayer & ministry to others

Sisters of Mary of The Miraculous Medal
81 Lunness Rd., Toronto ON M8W 4M7 Canada
Tel: 416-259-2808; *Fax:* 416-259-2808
Overview: A small local charitable organization
Chief Officer(s):
Mirta Rezar, Sr. Superior
Finances: *Annual Operating Budget:* Less than $50,000
Staff: 3 staff member(s)
Membership: 100-499
Activities: Nursing order

Sisters of Saint Joseph of Pembroke (CSJ)
1127 Pembroke St. West, Pembroke ON K8A 5R3 Canada
Tel: 613-735-5650; *Fax:* 613-732-1788
csjadmin@csjpembroke.ca
www.csjpembroke.ca
Overview: A small local organization founded in 1921
Chief Officer(s):
Mary McGuire, General Superior
Membership: 1-99
Description: The Sisters of St. Joseph of Pembroke are a group of fifty Roman Catholic women religious based in eastern Ontario

Sisters of Saint Joseph of Peterborough (CSJ)
PO Box 566, Mount Saint Joseph, Peterborough ON K9J 6Z6 Canada
Tel: 705-750-1688; *Fax:* 705-745-1377
csjteamtwo@nexicom.net
Overview: A small local charitable organization founded in 1890
Chief Officer(s):
Helen Russell, Vocation Director
Membership: 90
Description: To respond to the poor & most needy, particularly where the need is not already met

Sisters of Saint Joseph of Sault Ste Marie
2025 Main St. West, North Bay ON P1B 2X6 Canada
Tel: 705-474-3800; *Fax:* 705-495-3028
csjnbay@ontera.net
www.csjssm.ca
Overview: A small local organization
Description: Lives and works that all people may be united with God and with one another

Sisters of the Child Jesus (SEJ) / Soeurs de l'Enfant-Jésus
318 Laval St., Coquitlam BC V3K 4W4 Canada
Tel: 604-939-7545; *Fax:* 604-939-7549
gpainchaud@shaw.ca
members.shaw.ca/gmlamy
Also Known As: Sisters of Instruction of the Child Jesus
Overview: A small local charitable organization founded in 1667
Chief Officer(s):
Gilberte Painchaud, Provincial Superior
Description: To be a presence of love to the Father & to others for the definite purpose of awakening & deepening the faith; to enable people to grow in the uniqueness of their person as created by God & to liberate themselves from all that prevents their being truly human; to bring hope & direction to contemporaries; to be at the service of the least favoured, the marginalized & those who have no voice in society

Sisters of the Sacred Heart / Suore del Sacro Cuore di Ragusa
1 Edward St., Welland ON L3C 5H2 Canada
Tel: 905-732-4542
Overview: A small local charitable organization founded in 1889
Membership: 600 worldwide
Activities: Day care, schools, orphanages, retirement homes for the elderly, parish work, home visits, missions, nursing
Description: To live an apostolic life in the church & society through the works of beneficence among the poor & needy; to instruct & educate youth; to collaborate in parish pastoral work, especially through the teaching of catechism

Société canadienne d'histoire de l'Église Catholique - Section française (SCHEC) / Canadian Catholic Historical Association - French Section
SCHEC, Université du Québec à Trois-Rivières, 3351, boul des Forges, Trois-Rivières QC G9A 5H7 Canada
Tél: 819-376-5011; *Téléc:* 819-376-5179
www.cieq.ca/schec
Aperçu: *Dimension:* moyenne; *Envergure: nationale; fondée en 1933*
Membre(s) du bureau directeur:
René Hardy, Président
Finances: *Budget de fonctionnement annuel:* Moins de $50,000
Personnel: 4 bénévole(s)
Membre: 150 individu; 100 institutionnel; *Montant de la cotisation:* 30$ individu; 40$ institutionnel; *Critères d'admissibilite:* La Société compte des membres dans toutes les parties du Canada de même qu'en Europe et aux États-Unis; les membres peuvent être des individus, ou des institutions publiques ou privées, tels des dépôts d'archives, bibliothèques, diocèses, communautés religieuses
Description: Grouper les personnes intéressées à l'histoire de l'Église catholique au Canada; stimuler l'intérêt pour cette histoire dans le grand public; tenir des congrès annuels dans diverses régions du Canada afin de susciter un dialogue entre chercheurs participants et de promouvoir les travaux d'histoire régionale

Société catholique de la Bible (SOCABI) / Catholic Bible Society
#608, 7400, boul St-Laurent, Montréal QC H2R 2Y1 Canada
Tél: 514-274-4381; *Téléc:* 514-274-5184
socabi@bellnet.ca
www.interbible.org/socabi
Aperçu: *Dimension:* moyenne; *Envergure: nationale; Organisme sans but lucratif; fondée en 1940*
Finances: *Budget de fonctionnement annuel:* $100,000-$250,000
Personnel: 6 membre(s) du personnel; 3 bénévole(s)
Membre: 130; *Montant de la cotisation:* 45$ tous les trois ans; *Critères d'admissibilite:* Implication dans le pastorale biblique; *Comités:* Administration; Financement
Activités: Service de librairie; conférences sur cassettes; cours par correspondance; cours d'initiation et formation; voyage en Israël; retraites; publication d'articles; *Bibliothèque:* Oui (Bibliothèque publique) rendez-vous
Description: Rendre la bible accessible au plus grand nombre de personnes possible, en facilitant la lecture et la compréhension; *Membre de:* Association canadienne des périodiques catholiques
Affiliation(s): World Catholic Federation for the Biblical Apostolate

The Society of St. Peter the Apostle
3329 Danforth Ave., Toronto ON M1L 4T3 Canada
Tel: 416-699-7077; *Fax:* 416-699-9019
Toll-Free: 800-897-8865
missions@missionsocieties.ca
www.missionsocieties.ca
Overview: A small national charitable organization founded in 1889
Finances: *Annual Operating Budget:* $500,000-$1.5 Million
Activities: Funds the training of local clergy & religious missions; *Speaker Service:* Yes
Description: To educate local clergy & religious men & women in developing countries

Soeurs Auxiliatrices
1637, rue St-Christophe, Montréal QC H2L 3W7 Canada
Tél: 514-522-4452; *Téléc:* 514-524-1448
auxiqc@point-net.com
Aperçu: *Dimension:* petite; *Envergure: provinciale; fondée en 1856*
Membre(s) du bureau directeur:
Maria-Paule Lebél
Suzanne Loiselle
Andrée Brosseau

Les Soeurs de Sainte-Anne
#22, 1950, rue Provost, Lachine QC H8S 1P7 Canada
Tél: 514-637-3783; *Téléc:* 514-637-5400
accueil@ssacong.org
www.ssacong.org/

Aperçu: *Dimension:* petite; *Envergure: internationale; Organisme sans but lucratif; fondée en 1850*
Finances: *Budget de fonctionnement annuel:* $100,000-$250,000
Description: Impliquée dans l'éducation, les soins de santé, l'animation pastorale et sociale en divers milieux

Soeurs de Sainte-Marie de Namur / Sisters of Saint Mary of Namur
156, voul. Lorrain, Gatineau QC J8P 2G2 Canada
Tél: 819-663-5736
cdjeunes@comnet.ca
Aperçu: *Dimension:* petite; *Envergure: internationale; Organisme sans but lucratif; fondée en 1819*
Membre(s) du bureau directeur:
Réjeanne Roussel, Secrétaire-trésorière
Françoise Sabourin, Supérieure provinciale
Suzanne Martineau, Secrétaire-trésorière, 613-725-3427
ssmnproc@sympatico.ca
Finances: *Budget de fonctionnement annuel:* $250,000-$500,000
Membre: 1-99

Soeurs de Saint-Joseph de Saint-Vallier (SSJ)
860, av Louis-Fréchette, Québec QC G1S 3N3 Canada
Tél: 418-683-9653; *Téléc:* 418-681-8781
ssjvallier1903@videotron.ca
Aperçu: *Dimension:* petite; *Envergure: locale; fondée en 1683*
Membre(s) du bureau directeur:
Berthe Fortin, Supérieure générale, 418-681-2989
Membre: 165

Soeurs missionnaires Notre-Dame des Anges / Missionary Sisters of Our Lady of the Angels
323, rue Queen, Lennoxville QC J1M 1K8 Canada
Tél: 819-569-9248; *Téléc:* 819-569-9180
mindalen@videotron.ca
Aperçu: *Dimension:* petite; *Envergure: internationale; Organisme sans but lucratif; fondée en 1919*
Membre: 142
Description: The congregation is exclusively at the service of the missionary Church. Its specific mission is the formation of religious sisters, catechists and committed lay people. In addition, they respond to the needs of the local churches by working in the medical, social and educational fields when it is possible

Sovereign Military Hospitaller Order of St-John of Jerusalem of Rhodes & of Malta - Canadian Association / Ordre souverain militaire hospitalier de St-Jean de Jérusalem, de Rhodes et de Malte - Association canadienne
#302, 1247 Kilborn Pl., Ottawa ON K1H 6K9 Canada
Tel: 613-731-8897; *Fax:* 613-731-1312
wgs@bellnet.ca
www.orderofmaltacanada.org
Previous Name: Association of Canadian Knights of the Sovereign Military Order of Malta
Overview: A medium-sized national charitable organization founded in 1953
Chief Officer(s):
Peter Quail, Q.C., President
Finances: *Annual Operating Budget:* $100,000-$250,000; *Funding Sources:* Donations
Staff: 1 staff member(s); 259 volunteer(s)
Membership: 100-499
Description: To act as a Roman Catholic religious, chivalric & charitable organization; To provide assistance for: Good Shepherd Refuge, St. Francis, Second Mile Club, Providence Centre in Toronto, Czech Republic, Safe Motherhood Project, Nigeria, & ambulance brigades, Montréal, Cap-de-la-Madeleine, Ste. Anne de BeaupréAffiliation(s): Sovereign Military Order of Malta

Spiritans, the Congregation of the Holy Ghost
Laval House, 121 Victoria Park Ave., Toronto ON M4E 3S2 Canada
Tel: 416-691-9319; *Fax:* 416-698-1884
communications@spiritans.com
www.spiritans.com
Overview: A medium-sized national organization
Chief Officer(s):
Pat Fitzpatrick, Contact
Description: Roman Catholic religious congregation specializing in education & mission

Christian

The Antiochan Orthodox Christian Archdiocese of North America
Antiochian Orthodox Christian Archdiocese, PO Box 5238, Englewood NJ 07631-5238 USA
Tel: 201-871-1355; *Fax:* 201-871-7954
archdiocese@antiochian.org
www.antiochian.org
Overview: A small national organization founded in 1875
Membership: 275 parishes, 19 in Canada
Description: The Antiochan Orthodox Community in Canada is under the jurisdiction of the Patriarch of Antioch & all the East, with headquarters in Damascus, Syria. There are five churches in Canada & eight missions. The headquarters for all churches in North America is the Antiochan Orthodox Christian archdiocese, in Englewood, New Jersey, under Archbishop Philip Salica
Affiliation(s): Canadian (Can-Am) Region

Armenian Holy Apostolic Church - Canadian Diocese (AHAC)
615, av Stuart, Outremont QC H2V 3H2 Canada
Tel: 514-276-9479; *Fax:* 514-276-9960
adiocese@armenianchurch.ca
www.armenianchurch.ca
Overview: A medium-sized national charitable organization founded in 1984
Chief Officer(s):
Bagrat V. Galstanian, Bishop
Silva Mangassarian, Executive Secretary
Finances: *Annual Operating Budget:* $250,000-$500,000; *Funding Sources:* Donations; parish dues
Staff: 6 staff member(s)
Membership: Over 50,000; *Member Profile:* Baptized in the Armenian faith; *Committees:* Endowment Fund
Activities: Humanitarian Aid to Armenia; *Library:* Library (Open to Public) by appointment
Description: To preserve & promote Christian & national heritage; humanitarian aid to Armenia
Affiliation(s): Canadian Council of Churches

Association of Christian Churches in Manitoba (ACCM) / Association des églises chrétiennes du Manitoba
151 de la Cathedrale Ave., Winnipeg MB R2H 0H6 Canada
Tel: 204-237-9851
Previous Name: Ecumenical Committee of Manitoba
Overview: A medium-sized provincial organization founded in 1990
Finances: *Annual Operating Budget:* Less than $50,000
Description: To bring Christian churches into living encounter with one another; to provide a network of news & events which can help member churches act together in all matters except those in which deep differences compel us to act separately; to act as common Christian voice & media contact on issues of spiritual & social concern in the Province

Association of Christian Schools International (ACSI)
PO Box 65130, 731 Chapel Hills Dr., Colorado Springs CO 80962-5130 USA
Tel: 719-528-6906; *Fax:* 719-531-0631
info@acsi.org
www.acsi.org
Overview: A medium-sized international organization founded in 1978
Finances: *Funding Sources:* Membership fees
Membership: 5300 schools/colleges in 100 countries; *Fees:* Schedule; *Member Profile:* Christian school; affirmation of ACSI statement of faith
Activities: Teacher conferences; student leadership conferences; board/administrator conferences; district principals meetings; music events; professional development days; *Speaker Service:* Yes
Description: ACSI is an association of Protestant schools. It strives for school improvement, professional development & a provision of resources to enable Christian educators & schools worldwide to effectively prepare students for life.

Canadian Church Press (CCP)
8 MacDonald Ave., Hamilton ON L8P 4N5 Canada
Tel: 905-521-2240
info@canadianchurchpress.com
www.canadianchurchpress.com
Overview: A small national organization founded in 1957
Chief Officer(s):
Glen Argan, President
wcr@wcr.ab.ca
Trina Gallop, Vice-President
tgallop@elcic.ca
Pamela Richardson, Treasurer
pamela_richardson@can.salvationarmy.org
Finances: *Funding Sources:* Sponsorships
Activities: Offering fellowship for members; Supporting members; Conducting professional development workshops
Awards: General Canadian Church Press Awards
A.C. Forrest Award
Publications: Canadian Church Press Membership Directory
Type: Directory
Profile: Listings of publication members, associate members, & honorary life members
Description: To promote high standards of religious journalism; to encourage a positive Christian influence on contemporary society

Canadian Council of Christian Charities (CCCC)
#1, 43 Howard Ave., Elmira ON N3B 2C9 Canada
Tel: 519-669-5137; *Fax:* 519-669-3291
mail@cccc.org
www.cccc.org
Overview: A medium-sized national licensing charitable organization founded in 1972
Chief Officer(s):
John Pellowe, CEO
Finances: *Annual Operating Budget:* $500,000-$1.5 Million
Staff: 14 staff member(s); 56 volunteer(s)
Membership: 3,000; *Fees:* $185-$500
Activities: Education; training on legal, financial & leadership issues
Publications: Charities Handbook
Price: Free with CCCC membership; $95 non-members
CCCC [Canadian Council of Christian Charities] Bulletin
Type: Newsletter *Frequency:* 5-7 pa *Accepts Advertising Editor:* Heather Hanson *ISSN:* 0838-6803 *Price:* Free with CCCC membership; $45 non-members
Profile: CCCC news & information & legislative developments for executives, administrators, & stewardship representatives of Christian charities operating under Canadian law
Description: To encourage the Canadian Christian community to a biblical stewardship of all He has entrusted to us by integrating practical concepts of administration, development & accountability with the spiritual concerns of ministry

The Canadian Council of Christians & Jews (CCCJ) / Conseil canadien des chrétiens et des juifs
PO Box 17, 4211 Yonge St., Toronto ON M2P 2A9 Canada
Tel: 416-597-9693; *Fax:* 416-597-9775
Toll-Free: 800-663-1848
info@cccj.ca
www.cccj.ca
Overview: A medium-sized national charitable organization founded in 1947
Finances: *Annual Operating Budget:* $250,000-$500,000; *Funding Sources:* Private; corporate; government for special projects
Staff: 4 staff member(s)
Membership: 100-499
Activities: Educational workshops/forums; research; public service announcements; *Awareness Events:* Brotherhood/Sisterhood Week, 3rd week of Feb. *Library:* Library by appointment
Awards: Human Relations Award
Made to outstanding Canadians who have made a significant contribution towards bringing people together regardless of race, religion, or social status, in an atmosphere of understanding & respect; the award is made annually & is approved by a National Nominating Committee from the Board of Directors of CCCJ
Good Servant Medal
Created to commemorate the retirement of Richard D. Jones, O.C., LL.D., after 30 years of continuous service to CCCJ, as founder & principal officer, 1947-1977; recognizes individuals who have rendered extraordinary service to their community beyond the call of duty without seeking public recognition
Publications: The Canadian Council of Christians & Jews Annual Report
Frequency: a.
The Word [a publication of The Canadian Council of Christians & Jews]
Type: Newsletter
Description: Non-sectarian organization that builds on our common heritage in pursuit of our goal to eradicate discrimination, prejudice & bigotry in Canadian society through education, research, communication & community building. The CCCJ promotes religious, racial & cultural equality through programming for young people
Affiliation(s): International Council of Christians & Jews

Canadian Society of Church History (CSCH) / Société canadienne d'histoire de l'Église
c/o Robynne R. Healey, Dept. of History, Trinity Western University, 7600 Glover Rd., Langley BC V2Y 1Y1 Canada
robynne.healey@twu.ca
www.augustana.ab.ca/csch/

Overview: A small national organization founded in 1960
Fees: $36 students; $53 retired academics; $60 individuals;
Member Profile: Historians of Christianity in Canada & the United States
Publications: Historical Papers: Canadian Society of Church History
Type: Journal *Frequency:* a. *Editor:* Robynne Rogers Healey
Price: Free with CSCH membership
Profile: A selection of papers delivered at the CSCH annual meeting
Description: To encourage research in the history of Christianity, especially the history of Christianity in Canada
Member of: Canadian Corporation for Studies in Religion; Congress of Social Sciences & Humanities

Christian Blind Mission International (CBMI)
PO Box 800, 3844 Stoufville Rd., Stouffville ON L4A 7Z9 Canada
Tel: 905-640-6464; *Fax:* 905-640-4332
Toll-Free: 800-567-2264
cbm@cbmcanada.org
www.cbmcanada.org
Overview: A medium-sized international charitable organization founded in 1978
Finances: *Annual Operating Budget:* Greater than $5 Million
Staff: 28 staff member(s); 45 volunteer(s)
Activities: Talking Book Library; Craft Store; works with nearly 600 mission agencies, local churches, Christian relief organizations & self-help groups overseas; *Rents Mailing List:* Yes *Library:* Talking Book Library (Open to Public)
Description: With core values based on Christian faith, CBMI serves the blind & disabled in the developing world, irrespective of nationality, race, sex, or religion; prevents & treats blindness & other disabilities through medical care, rehabilitation training & integration programs; helps people to help themselves.
Member of: Canadian Council of Christian Charities

Christian Brethren Churches of Québec (CBCQ) / Églises de frères chrétiens du Québec (EFCQ)
#101, 1520, rue King ouest, Sherbrooke QC J1J 2G2 Canada
Tel: 819-820-1693; *Fax:* 819-821-9287
Also Known As: Plymouth Brethren
Overview: A medium-sized provincial charitable organization founded in 1942
Chief Officer(s):
Richard Strout, Secretary
Finances: *Annual Operating Budget:* Less than $50,000;
Funding Sources: Dues from local churches
Staff: 2 volunteer(s)
Description: To handle affairs for local affiliated churches regarding government & affairs of civil status

Christian Catholic Church Canada (CCRCC) / Église catholique-chrétien Canada
PO Box 2043, Stn. Hull, Gatineau QC J8X 3Z2 Canada
Tel: 613-738-2942; *Fax:* 613-738-7835
info@ccrcc.ca
www.ccrcc.ca
Previous Name: Canadian Chapter of the International Council of Community Churches
Overview: A large international charitable organization founded in 1858
S.A. Thériault, Ph.D, Th.D, Bishop Ordinary
Finances: *Annual Operating Budget:* Less than $50,000;
Funding Sources: Clergy; churches; benefactors
Staff: 15 staff member(s); 25 volunteer(s)
Membership: 1,000-4,999; *Fees:* $200 church; $50 clergy;
Committees: Order of the Crown of Thorns
Activities: Church Ministry; Seminary Program; counselling & mediation services; *Library:* Archives (Open to Public) by appointment
Description: Advancing the kingdom of God through worship, pastoral work & fellowship. Parishes in Ottawa-Gatineau, North Bay, Montreal
Affiliation(s): International Council of Community Churches (ICCC), ICCC Canada, World Council of Churches

Christian Children's Fund of Canada (CCFC)
1200 Denison St., Markham ON L3R 8G6 Canada
Tel: 905-754-1001; *Toll-Free:* 800-263-5437
supporter-services@ccfcanada.ca
www.ccfcanada.ca
Overview: A large international organization founded in 1960
Finances: *Annual Operating Budget:* Greater than $5 Million
Staff: 100 staff member(s); 200 volunteer(s)
Membership: 30,000+; *Fees:* $35/month suggested donation
Activities: International development; working to help those affected by HIV/AIDS; water & sanitation; health & nutrition; gender issues; poverty; micro-enterprise development; education; environmental sustainability; *Internships:* Yes; *Speaker Service:* Yes
Description: A child-centred international development organization, the CCFC focusses on community development ministry, starting with basic assistance & leading to programs stressing self-help & eventual independence. Working with colleagues & partners in developing countries, CCFC reaches out to children & families of all faiths
Member of: Canadian Council for International Cooperation
Affiliation(s): Canadian Direct Marketing Association; National Society of Fundraising Executives

Christian Church (Disciples of Christ) in Canada (DISCAN) / Église chrétienne (Disciples du Christ) au Canada
PO Box 1, Springfield ON N0L 2J0 Canada
Tel: 519-269-9800
ccinca@eastlink.ca
www.disciplesofchrist.ca
Previous Name: All-Canada Committee of the Christian Church (Disciples of Christ)
Overview: A small national charitable organization founded in 1922
Finances: *Annual Operating Budget:* $100,000-$250,000;
Funding Sources: Donations
Staff: 2 staff member(s)
Membership: 4,000 + 30 churches; *Committees:* Archives; Biennial Convention; Christian Nurture, Service, Witness; Church Development; College; Ministry
Activities: *Internships:* Yes; *Speaker Service:* Yes *Library:* Resource Centre
Member of: The Canadian Council of Churches
Affiliation(s): The Christian Church (Disciples of Christ) in USA

Christian Episcopal Church of Canada (CECC)
St. Saviour's Anglican Church, 9280 #2 Rd., Richmond BC V6E 3C8 Canada
Tel: 604-275-7422
Also Known As: Traditional Anglican Church in Canada
Overview: A small national charitable organization founded in 1991
Chief Officer(s):
Robert D. Redmile
Finances: *Annual Operating Budget:* $100,000-$250,000;
Funding Sources: Donations
Staff: 12 staff member(s); 40 volunteer(s)
Membership: 450; *Fees:* Free-will offerings; *Member Profile:* Baptised & confirmed Anglican Christians; *Committees:* Parochial Church Council, Assembly & Consistory; Diocesan Synod & Diocesan Council
Activities: Traditional Anglican faith & worship according to the Book of Common Prayer
Member of: Anglican Communion
Affiliation(s): Christian Episcopal Church in the USA

Christian Health Association of Alberta (CHAA)
132 Warwick Rd., Edmonton AB T5X 4P8 Canada
Tel: 780-488-8074; *Fax:* 780-475-7968
chaaa@compusmart.ab.ca
www.chaaa.ab.ca
Previous Name: Catholic Health Care Conference of Alberta
Overview: A medium-sized provincial charitable organization founded in 1943
Finances: *Annual Operating Budget:* $50,000-$100,000
Staff: 1 staff member(s); 13 volunteer(s)
Membership: 22 health facilities + 29 associate + 48 personal + 10 life; *Fees:* $25 individual; $75 associate
Description: Represents the shared vision & values of those seeking to make visible Jesus the Healer; provides support & leadership to members & the community through education, advocacy & collaboration

Christian Record Services Inc.
PO Box 31119, #119, 1300 King St. East, Oshawa ON L1H 8N9 Canada
Tel: 905-436-6938; *Fax:* 905-436-7102
Toll-Free: 888-899-0006
crs-ncb@hotmail.com
www.crsblindservices.ca
Also Known As: National Camps for the Blind
Previous Name: Christian Record Braille Foundation Inc.
Overview: A medium-sized national charitable organization founded in 1899
Finances: *Annual Operating Budget:* $500,000-$1.5 Million;
Funding Sources: Public contribution
Staff: 14 staff member(s)
Activities: Magazines in braille, large print & on audio cassette; full-vision books (a combination of print & braille for blind parents with sighted children); Bible Correspondence School (Bible study guides available in braille, in large print, on audio cassettes & in easy English for the deaf); National Camps for the Blind; personal visitation; glaucoma screenings; deaf services.; *Library:* Lending Library for the Blind (Open to Public)
Description: To enrich the lives of blind, deaf, visually, physically & hearing impaired persons regardless of race, creed, economic status or sex.
Member of: Christian Camping International; Canadian Camping Association

Christian Reformed Church in North America (CRCNA)
PO Box 5070, Stn. LCD 1, 3475 Mainway, Burlington ON L7R 3Y8 Canada
Tel: 905-336-2920; *Fax:* 905-336-8344
Toll-Free: 800-730-3490
crcna@crcna.org
www.crcna.org
Overview: A large international organization founded in 1857
Chief Officer(s):
Bruce Adema, Director, Canadian Ministries
Finances: *Annual Operating Budget:* Greater than $5 Million;
Funding Sources: Gifts & donations
Staff: 225 staff member(s)
Membership: In US & Canada: 275,000 members in more than 1,000 congregations; *Committees:* Abuse Prevention; Back to God Hour; Calvin College; Calvin Theological Seminary; CRC Publications; Home Missions; World Missions; World Relief; Chaplaincy Ministries; CRC Loan Fund; Disability Concerns; Fund for Smaller Churches; Pastor-Church Relations; Pensions & Insurance; Race Relations; Historical; Interchurch Relations; Sermons for Reading Services
Activities: *Awareness Events:* Sea to Sea Celebration Rally; *Speaker Service:* Yes
Description: The Denominational Office in Canada coordinates the work of the Church in Canada, overseeing the Committee for Contact with the Government (social justice issues), urban Aboriginal Ministry Centres (Edmonton, Regina, Winnipeg), & ecumenical involvement in KAIROS task forces (KAIROS: Canadian Ecumenical Justice Initiatives)
Affiliation(s): National Association of Evangelicals; Reformed Ecumenical Council; World Alliance of Reformed Churches; Canadian Council of Churches; Evangelical Fellowship of Canada

Christian Reformed World Relief Committee of Canada (CRWRC)
PO Box 5070, 3475 Mainway, Burlington ON L7R 3Y8 Canada
Tel: 905-336-2920; *Fax:* 905-336-8344
Toll-Free: 800-730-3490
crwrc@crcna.org
www.crwrc.org
Overview: A large international charitable organization founded in 1962
Finances: *Annual Operating Budget:* Greater than $5 Million;
Funding Sources: Christian Reformed Churches; CIDA; other denominations
Staff: 40 staff member(s)
Membership: 15,000-49,999
Activities: *Awareness Events:* World Hunger Week, 1st week of Nov.; *Internships:* Yes; *Speaker Service:* Yes *Library:* CRWRC Development Education Library (Open to Public)
Description: To engage God's people in redeeming resources & developing gifts in collaborative activities of love, mercy, justice & compassion.
Member of: Canadian Foodgrains Bank; Canadian Council of Christian Charities; Canadian Council for International Cooperation.
Affiliation(s): Christian Reformed Church in North America

Christian Science / La Première Église du Christ, Scientiste
The First Church of Christ, Scientist, 210 Massachusetts Ave., Boston MA 02115 USA
Tel: 617-450-2000; *Fax:* 617-450-3790
Toll-Free: 800-775-2775
info@churchofchristscientist.org
www.tfccs.com; www.marybakereddy.org
Social Media: twitter.com/CSmediaNews
Also Known As: The Mother Church
Overview: A large international organization founded in 1879
Chief Officer(s):
Mary M. Trammell, Chair
Phil Davis, Manager, Committee on Publication
Victor Westberg, Manager, The Christian Science Publishing Society
sales@cspc.com
Finances: *Annual Operating Budget:* Greater than $5 Million;
Funding Sources: Donations
Staff: 850 staff member(s)
Membership: 2,200 churches in over 70 countries; *Fees:* Per capita tax of not less than 1$; *Member Profile:* The Church is open those who are "believer(s) the doctrines of Christian

Science textbook: Science & Health with Key to the Scriptures, by Rev. Mary Baker Eddy."
Activities: Sunday worship services, Wednesday testimonial meetings; Sunday School for children; worldwide speakers bureau; retail book stores; Christian Science Reading Rooms; Christian Science programs & Weekly Bible Lessons are broadcast on public media; *Internships:* Yes; *Speaker Service:* Yes *Library:* Mary Baker Eddy Library for the Betterment of Humanity (Open to Public) by appointment
Publications: The Christian Science Monitor
Type: newspaper *Frequency:* daily
Profile: www.csmonitor.com
The Christian Science Journal
Type: magazine *Frequency:* monthly
Profile: www.spirituality.com/journal
Description: Christian Scientists believe in one God, the Bible & in Christ Jesus as the Messiah. They believe that the application of the laws of God are practical & provable, hence scientific.

Christian Stewardship Services (CSS)
#214A, 500 Alden Rd., Markham ON L3R 5H5
Tel: 905-947-9262; *Fax:* 905-947-9263
Toll-Free: 800-267-8890
admin@csservices.ca
www.csservices.ca
Overview: A medium-sized national charitable organization founded in 1976
Finances: *Funding Sources:* Christian charities, including churches & schools; Social service organizations
Activities: Providing advice about will & estate planning; Offering the Growing & Giving program, featuring presentations & workshops
Publications: Advancing Stewardship
Type: Newsletter *Frequency:* s-a.
Profile: Information about the organization & its work
Christian Stewardship Services Annual Report
Type: Yearbook *Frequency:* a.
Description: To connect families, faith, & finances for efficient estate & gift planning; To promote Biblical stewardship
Member of: Canadian Council of Christian Charities
Affiliation(s): Diaconal Ministries of the Christian Reformed Church

Christians Concerned for Racial Equality
PO Box 223, Stn. A, Vancouver BC V6C 2M3 Canada
Tel: 250-492-3376
Overview: A small national organization founded in 1979
Chief Officer(s):
Wesley H. Wakefield, Chair
Finances: *Annual Operating Budget:* Less than $50,000
Staff: 4 volunteer(s)
Membership: 1-99
Activities: Against slavery & racism; *Speaker Service:* Yes *Library:* Bible Holiness Movement by appointment
Description: To act as a sponsored organization of The Bible Holiness Movement
Member of: The Bible Holiness Movement

Citizens for Public Justice (CPJ)
#501, 309 Cooper St., Ottawa ON K2P 0G5 Canada
Fax: 613-232-1275
Toll-Free: 800-667-8046
cpj@cpj.ca
www.cpj.ca
Overview: A medium-sized national organization
Chief Officer(s):
Joe Gunn, Executive Director
Membership: 1500; *Fees:* $50 individual; $25 low income; $10 student
Activities: *Internships:* Yes
Description: To promote public justice in Canada by shaping key public policy debates through research and analysis, publishing and public dialogue. CPJ encourages citizens, leaders in society and governments to support policies and practices which reflect God's call for love, justice and stewardship.

Congregational Christian Churches in Canada (CCCC)
Dunsdon Plaza, #405, 241 Dunsdon St., Brantford ON N3R 7C3 Canada
Tel: 519-751-0606; *Fax:* 519-751-0852
Toll-Free: 866-868-8702
admincccc@bellnet.ca
www.cccc.ca
Overview: A small national charitable organization founded in 1821
Finances: *Annual Operating Budget:* $100,000-$250,000
Staff: 2 staff member(s)
Membership: 8,000 + 100 churches across Canada
Activities: *Internships:* Yes
Description: To celebrate & serve Jesus Christ in the 21st century through shared concern for others.

Gospel Tract & Bible Society
PO Box 180, Ste. Anne MB R5H 1R1 Canada
Tel: 204-355-4975
info@gospeltract.ca
Overview: A small national organization
Description: Publishes Christian religious tracts; affiliated with Church of God in Christ, Mennonite.

Hamilton & District Christian Churches Association
147 Chedoke Ave., Hamilton ON L8P 4P2 Canada
Overview: A small local organization founded in 1890
Membership: 13+; *Fees:* Proportional; *Member Profile:* Mainline denominations in Hamilton
Activities: Pre-ordinating ecumenical work of denominations in Hamilton
Description: To strengthen the work & witness of Jesus Christ by fostering cooperation among Christians of different traditions
Member of: The Canadian Council of Churches

Indian Métis Christian Fellowship (IMCF)
3131 Dewdney Ave., Regina SK S4T 0Y5 Canada
Tel: 306-359-1096; *Fax:* 306-359-0103
imcfr@sasktel.net
metfel.sasktelwebsite.net
Overview: A small local organization founded in 1978
Chief Officer(s):
Bert Adema, Director
Finances: *Annual Operating Budget:* $100,000-$250,000
Membership: 30 individual
Activities: Drop-in ministry; daily prayer circle; soup & bannock lunch; computer club
Description: IMCF is an urban aboriginal ministry supported by the Christian Reformed Church in North America - Canada. Its mission is to develop a worshipping, working community through serving the spiritual & social needs of aboriginal people in Regina.
Affiliation(s): Canadian Ministry Board; Indian Family Center, Winnipeg; Native Healing Centre, Edmonton

Intercede International
201 Stanton St., Fort Erie ON L2A 3N8 Canada
Tel: 905-871-1773; *Fax:* 905-871-5165
Toll-Free: 800-871-0882
friends@intercedenow.ca
www.intercedenow.ca
Previous Name: Christian Aid Mission
Overview: A medium-sized international charitable organization founded in 1953
Finances: *Annual Operating Budget:* $500,000-$1.5 Million; *Funding Sources:* Private donations
Staff: 10 staff member(s); 50 volunteer(s)
Membership: 10; *Committees:* Audit Review
Activities: Sponsorship programs; relief aid; equipment & materials provisions; Missions cafe held in major cities; *Speaker Service:* Yes *Library:* Library (Open to Public) by appointment
Description: To aid, encourage & strengthen indigenous new testament Christianity, particularly where Christians are impoverished, few, or persecuted; to encourage Christian witness & ministry to the international community in North America
Member of: Canadian Council of Christian Churches
Affiliation(s): Evangelical Fellowship of Canada

Inter-Varsity Christian Fellowship of Canada (IVCF)
64 Prince Andrew Pl., Toronto ON M3C 2H4 Canada
Tel: 416-443-1170; *Toll-Free:* 800-668-9766
inquiries@ivcf.ca; donorservices@ivcf.ca
www.ivcf.ca
Overview: A medium-sized national charitable organization founded in 1929
Finances: *Funding Sources:* Donations
Activities: Offering Pioneer Camps across Canada; Providing ministry at university & college campuses; Offering travel opportunities through Inter-Varsity's World Services' Global Partnerships; Participating in the Urbana Student Mission Convention
Description: To help young people live a transformed life in Jesus Christ

Lifewater Canada
#194, 307 Euclid Ave., Thunder Bay ON P7E 6G6 Canada
Tel: 807-622-4848; *Fax:* 807-577-9798
Toll-Free: 888-543-3426
gehrelji@yahoo.com
www.lifewater.ca
Overview: A small international organization
Chief Officer(s):
Jim Gehrels, President
Member Profile: Hydrogeologists, well drillers, educators, engineers, environmental scientists, businessmen & many other people with diverse skills & training
Description: Christian organization dedicated to ensuring that people everywhere have access to adequate supplies of safe water; to train & equip Nationals with drill rigs & hand pumps so they can solve their own water problems; to place as many technical documents on-line as possible so they can benefit people everywhere, regardless of affiliation

M2/W2 Association - Restorative Christian Ministries (M2/W2)
#208, 2825 Clearbrook Rd., Abbotsford BC V2T 6S3 Canada
Tel: 604-859-3215; *Fax:* 604-859-1216
Toll-Free: 800-298-1777
info@m2w2.com
www.m2w2.com
Also Known As: Man-to-Man/Woman-to-Woman
Overview: A small provincial charitable organization founded in 1966
Chief Officer(s):
Wayne Northey, Co-Director
Bernie Martens, Co-Director
Finances: *Annual Operating Budget:* $250,000-$500,000; *Funding Sources:* 65% community fundraising; 35% federal & provincial government contracts
Staff: 11 staff member(s); 400 volunteer(s)
Membership: 190; *Fees:* $10; *Member Profile:* Wide range of people whose common interest is the focus of M2/W2; *Committees:* Finance/Promotion; Program/New Initiatives; Personnel
Activities: Organizing annual promotion dinners; *Speaker Service:* Yes
Description: To mutually transform lives - one relationship at a time; To see individuals & communities in British Columbia safer, transformed, reconciled, & restored through justice, accountability, partnerships, mutual support, mediation, education & prevention; To provide one-to-one volunteers for men & women in British Columbia prisons, combined with pre- & post-release support & resources; To counsel prisoners, ex-prisoners, & their families; To prevent crime through one-to-one support for parents of young children at risk
Member of: Canadian Council of Christian Charities

Micah House
c/o 333 King St. East, Hamilton ON L8N 1C1 Canada
Tel: 905-296-4387
info@micahhouse.ca
www.micahhouse.ca
Social Media: www.twitter.com/micah_house
Overview: A small local organization founded in 2005
Chief Officer(s):
Ian Innis, Chair
Scott Jones, Executive Director
Finances: *Funding Sources:* Donations
Staff: 6 staff member(s)
Member Profile: Christians from a variety of churches & organizations in Hamilton, Ontario
Activities: *Awareness Events:* Walkathon
Description: To demonstrate God's love to newly arrived refugees in Hamilton, Ontario

National Christian School Association
PO Box 26005, Saskatoon SK S7K 8C1 Canada
Tel: 306-280-9991
lbrunelle@aceministries.com
www.aisca.ab.ca/associations.htm
Also Known As: School of Tomorrow Canada
Previous Name: Canadian National Accelerated Christian Education Association
Overview: A small national organization founded in 1991
Chief Officer(s):
Lou Brunelle, President
Finances: *Annual Operating Budget:* Less than $50,000; *Funding Sources:* Provincial dues
Staff: 24 volunteer(s)
Membership: 100-499
Description: To continue to assure Canadians of the freedom to choose alternative Christian education
Affiliation(s): Federation of Independent Schools in Canada

New Apostolic Church Canada
319 Bridgeport Rd. East, Waterloo ON N2J 2K9 Canada
Tel: 519-884-2862; *Toll-Free:* 866-622-7828
info@naccanada.org
www.newapostolicchurch.com
Overview: A medium-sized international organization
Membership: 4,283,287 internationally
Description: The New Apostolic Church comprises a world-wide community of Christian worshippers that are growing into the future together. We take a balanced approach to our bible-based

faith and enjoy life and the many benefits that come from faith, family and friendship.
Member of: New Apostolic Church (International)

Ontario Alliance of Christian Schools (OACS)
790 Shaver Rd., Ancaster ON L9G 3K9 Canada
Tel: 905-648-2100; *Fax:* 905-648-2110
oacs@oacs.org
www.oacs.org
Overview: A medium-sized provincial organization founded in 1952
Finances: *Annual Operating Budget:* $500,000-$1.5 Million; *Funding Sources:* Membership dues
Staff: 15 staff member(s); 200 volunteer(s)
Membership: 1-99; *Fees:* Schedule; *Committees:* Finance; Education; PR; Planning; Government Relations; Personnel
Activities: *Speaker Service:* Yes; *Rents Mailing List:* Yes
Description: To promote independent schools in Ontario; to promote Christian education in Canada; to provide educational services for member schools; to lobby government for educational choice. Canada's largest & oldest independent school organization, representing 79 schools with approximately 14,000 students.
Affiliation(s): Christian Schools International; Christian Schools Canada

Ontario Christian Music Assembly
90 Topcliff Ave., Toronto ON M3N 1L8 Canada
Tel: 416-636-9779; *Fax:* 905-775-2230
Overview: A small provincial organization founded in 1961
Chief Officer(s):
Érick De Bellefeuille, Président
Membership: 130 individual
Activities: Spring & Christmas concerts series; annual christian festival concert

Prairie Association of Christian Librarians (PACL)
Briercrest College & Seminary, 510 College Dr., Caronport SK S0H 0S0 Canada
Tel: 306-756-3262; *Fax:* 306-756-5588
library@briercrest.ca
www.pacl.ca
Overview: A small local organization
Chief Officer(s):
Brad Doerksen, Sec.-Treas.
bdoerksen@briercrest.ca
Finances: *Annual Operating Budget:* Less than $50,000
Membership: 1-99

Project Peacemakers
745 Westminster Ave., Winnipeg MB R3G 1A5 Canada
Tel: 204-775-8178; *Fax:* 204-784-1339
info@projectpeacemakers.org
www.projectpeacemakers.org
Social Media:
facebook.com/pages/project-peacemakers/108617822532248
Overview: A small international charitable organization founded in 1983
Finances: *Annual Operating Budget:* Less than $50,000; *Funding Sources:* Member donations; church grants
Staff: 2 staff member(s); 30 volunteer(s)
Membership: 200; *Fees:* $25 one year; $40 two years; $8 low income
Activities: Concerts; film festivals; protests; witness-for-peace delegations; forums; *Speaker Service:* Yes *Library:* Library (Open to Public)
Publications: Peace Projections
Type: newsletter *Frequency:* quarterly
Description: Project Peacemakers is a group of people working for peace from a faith perspective. Its activities are varied, from peace delegations in war zones to educational forums on such issues as child soldiers & violent video games.
Member of: Project Ploughshares
Affiliation(s): Canadian Centre for Arms Control & Disarmament; Manitoba Environmental Network; Mennonite Central Committee; Peace Alliance Winnipeg; Manitoba Japanese-Canadian Citizens Association

REHOBOTH Christian Ministries
3920 - 49th Ave., Stony Plain AB T7Z 2J7 Canada
Tel: 780-963-4044; *Fax:* 780-963-3075
stonyplain@ rehoboth.ab.ca
rehoboth.ab.ca
Also Known As: Christian Association for the Mentally Handicapped of Alberta
Overview: A medium-sized provincial charitable organization founded in 1976
Chief Officer(s):
Wally Mulder, Executive Director
Finances: *Annual Operating Budget:* Greater than $5 Million; *Funding Sources:* Provincial government; membership fees; donations; church offerings
Staff: 411 staff member(s); 950 volunteer(s)
Membership: 4,600; *Fees:* $10; *Member Profile:* Everybody accepting our mission statement; *Committees:* Regional Advisory
Activities: Residential, vocational & recreational support for individuals who live with disabilities; summer camp program; fundraising golf tournament
Description: To convey God's love to persons with disabilities through support, advocacy & public education, & by providing opportunities for personal growth & meaningful participation in society
Member of: Alberta Association of Rehabilitation Centres; Canadian Council of Christian Charities; Canadian Centre for Philanthropy
Affiliation(s): Christian Stewardship Services

Samaritan's Purse Canada
20 Hopewell Way NE, Calgary AB T3J 5H5 Canada
Tel: 403-250-6565; *Fax:* 403-250-6567
Toll-Free: 800-663-6500
canada@samaritan.org
www.samaritanspurse.ca
Also Known As: Operation Christmas Child
Overview: A large international charitable organization founded in 1973
Finances: *Annual Operating Budget:* Greater than $5 Million; *Funding Sources:* Donations
Staff: 60 staff member(s); 1300 volunteer(s)
Activities: Operation Christmas Child packages; Turn on the Tap access to safe water program; *Internships:* Yes; *Speaker Service:* Yes
Description: A nondenominational evangelical Christian international relief organization with projects around the globe, meeting both physical & spiritual needs of people who are victims of war, poverty, natural disasters, disease & famine. Focus is on emergency relief & development programs, medical projects. International offices in Canada, Australia, Germany, Ireland, the Netherlands, the U.S. & the U.K.
Member of: Canadian Council of Christian Charities
Affiliation(s): Samaritan's Purse USA

Society of Christian Schools in British Columbia (SCSBC)
Fosmark Centre, Trinity Western University, 7600 Glover Rd., Langley BC V2Y 1Y1
Tel: 604-888-6366; *Fax:* 604-888-2791
contact@scsbc.ca; scsbc@twu.ca (Library & membership information)
www.scsbc.ca
Previous Name: Southwest British Columbia League of Christian Schools
Overview: A small provincial organization founded in 1976
Membership: 1-99; *Member Profile:* Christian school campuses & societies in British Columbia
Activities: Monitoring government policies & regulations regarding Christian schoools, & advising schools about government relations; Promoting Christian education throughout British Columbia; Offering workshops; Publishing resource handbooks; Assisting new Christian schools & expanding schools; Supporting digital learning; *Library:* Society of Christian Schools in British Columbia Resource Library
Publications: The Link
Type: Newsletter *Frequency:* q.
Profile: Information for Christian school, staff, & committee members, including new resources & school news & events
eBulletin
Type: Newsletter
Profile: Information, such as Ministry of Education updates, society policies, & forthcoming workshops & courses, sent regularly to member school board members, principals, curriculum coordinators, & preschool directors
For the Love of Your Child
Type: Booklet *Number of Pages:* 20
Profile: Christian education information
SCSBC Administrative Handbook
Type: Handbook
Profile: General guidelines to shape school policy & practice
Educating for Life Today & Tomorrow: Resource Manual for High School Guidance
Type: Manual
Educating toward Wisdom
Type: Booklet
Profile: A resource for curriculum leaders & administrators in Christian schools
Educating with Heart & Mind: Principles for Curriculum in Christian Schools
Type: Booklet
Profile: A collection of biblical perspective statements
Good Teaching Comes from the Inside
Type: Booklet
Profile: Information for school leaders & teachers
SCSBC Internal Control Checklist
Type: Booklet
Profile: Internal controls which may be suitable for SCSBC schools & other independent schools
International Education Program: Student Coordinator Handbook
Type: Handbook
Profile: Information for schools initiating or restructuring an international student program
La Joie de la langue française
Type: Booklet
Profile: A resource for both elementary & secondary French teachers
The SCSBC Language Arts Handbook
Type: Handbook
Profile: Fundamental principles for language arts education
Learning Together in the Middle
Type: Booklet
Profile: Renewing middle level education in Christian schools
Living, Loving, & Learning: A Kindergarten Handbook
Type: Handbook
Profile: A resource for kindergarten teachers in Christian schools
Responding to a School Emergency
Type: Booklet
Profile: School emergency preparedness
Serving All Children Well
Type: Booklet
Profile: Information for Christian educators
The SCSBC Visual Arts Activity Handbook
Type: Booklet
Profile: Direction for visual arts programs in Christian schools
Description: To serve Christian schools in British Columbia; To seek support in the provision of Christian education; To develop policies & curriculum outlines & units
Affiliation(s): Christian Schools International (CSI); Christian Schools Canada (CSC); Christian Teachers Association of British Columbia; Christian Principals Association of British Columbia

Strathcona Christian Academy Society
1011 Cloverbar Rd., Sherwood Park AB T8A 4V7 Canada
Tel: 780-449-2787; *Fax:* 780-449-3954
sca@ei.educ.ab.ca
www.ei.educ.ab.ca/sch/sca/
Overview: A small local organization
Chief Officer(s):
Robert McCoy, Director, Advancement
Finances: *Annual Operating Budget:* $3 Million-$5 Million; *Funding Sources:* Regional Government
Staff: 47 staff member(s); 120 volunteer(s)
Description: To challenge students, through Christ-centred education, to know Jesus Christ as Savior & Lord in order to pursue a life of Godly character, personal & academic excellence & service to others

World Fellowship of Orthodox Youth - Syndesmos
Syndesmos General Secretariat, PO Box 66051, Holargos 15510 Greece
syndesmos@syndesmos.org
www.syndesmos.org
Also Known As: Syndesmos
Overview: A small international organization founded in 1953
Finances: *Annual Operating Budget:* $50,000-$100,000; *Funding Sources:* Orthodox churches; Orthodox church organisations; council of Eurpoe; European Christina Diakonia age
Staff: 2 staff member(s); 4 volunteer(s)
Membership: 121 organizations in 42 countries; *Fees:* $500 affiliated; *Member Profile:* Christian Orthodox youth organizations & theological schools; *Committees:* Publications
Activities: Orthodox youth camps, festivals, encounters, seminars, consultations, conferences, training courses, workshops; *Internships:* Yes *Library:* Yes (Open to Public)
Description: To serve as a bond of unity among Orthodox youth movements, organisations & theological schools around the world, promoting a consciousness of the catholicity of the Orthodox faith; to foster relations, coordination & mutal aid among them; to promote among young people a full understanding of the Orthodox faith & the mission of the Church in the contemporary world & an active participation of youth in ecclesial life; to promote a way of life founded in eucharistic communion, in the Gospel & in patristic teaching, for witness & service to the world; to assist & promote Orthodox effocrts for visible Christian unity & for positive relations with people of other faiths; to encourage reflection & action on issues affecting the lives of Orthodox Christians & the local churches; to be an instrument for furthering cooperation & deeper communion between the Orthodox Church & the Oriental Orthodox Churches

Ecumenism

The Canadian Churches' Forum for Global Ministries / Le forum des églises canadiennes pour les ministères globaux
47 Queens Park Cres. East, Toronto ON M5S 2C3 Canada
Tel: 416-924-9351; *Fax:* 416-978-7821
director@ccforum.ca
www.ccforum.ca
Previous Name: Ecumenical Forum of Canada
Overview: A medium-sized international charitable organization founded in 1921
Chief Officer(s):
Jonathan Schmidt, Co-director
Alice Schuda, Co-director
Finances: *Annual Operating Budget:* $100,000-$250,000; *Funding Sources:* Churches; religious orders; individuals
Staff: 2 staff member(s); 30 volunteer(s)
Membership: 1-99
Activities: Mission Personnel Programs, Jan., July & Sept.; Annual Katherine Hockin Award & Dinner; International Visitor; *Library:* Library by appointment
Awards: Katharine Hockin Award for Global Mission & Ministry
Publications: Forum Focus [a publication of the The Canadian Churches' Forum for Global Ministries]
Type: Newsletter *Frequency:* a. *Editor:* Alice Schuda & Jonathan Schmidt
Profile: Letters from overseas, information about mission personnel programs, book reviews, articles by international visitors, articles related to global mission, & updates on Forum staff & board members
Description: To provide ecumenical orientation & re-entry programs for mission personnel; to stimulate ecumenical dialogue on issues of mission, global concerns & social justice; to prepare individuals to serve faithfully in mission in an ever-changing world
Member of: International Association for Mission Studies; Forum on International Personnel; Forum on Mutuality in Mission
Affiliation(s): Canadian Council of Churches

The Canadian Council of Churches (CCC) / Le Conseil canadien des églises
47 Queen's Park Crescent East, Toronto ON M5S 2C3 Canada
Tel: 416-972-9494; *Fax:* 416-927-0405
Toll-Free: 866-822-7645
admin@ccc-cce.ca
www.ccc-cce.ca
Overview: A large national charitable organization founded in 1944
Finances: *Annual Operating Budget:* $250,000-$500,000; *Funding Sources:* Member churches
Staff: 4 staff member(s); 2 volunteer(s)
Membership: 10 original member churches, 4 affiliates
Activities: Sponsor of Project Ploughshares; maintains dialogue with all faith groups
Description: To engage in ecumenical education & training; to address issues of justice, liberty, peace, human rights in keeping with principals inherent in the Christian Gospel; to promote understanding among member churches & with other Christian churches & religious organizations in Canada; to provide coordinating services for preparation of statements, programs, activities & resources; to aid in development of ecumenism in Canada; to provide a forum in which members & interested parties can discuss, study & act on issues of faith & worship
Affiliation(s): Anglican Church of Canada; Baptist Convention of Ontario & Québec; Canadian Conference of Catholic Bishops; British Methodist Episcopal Church; Canadian Diocese of the Armenian Orthodox Church; Christian Church (Disciples of Christ); Christian Reformed Church in North America; Coptic Orthodox Church; Ethiopian Orthodox Church; Greek Orthodox Church; Evangelical Lutheran Church in Canada; Mennonite Church Canada; Orthodox Church in America; Polish National Catholic Church of Canada; Presbyterian Church in Canada; Reformed Church in America; Religious Society of Friends; Salvation Army

The Churches' Council on Theological Education in Canada: an Ecumenical Foundation (CCTE) / Le Conseil des Églises pour l'éducation théologique au Canada: une fondation oecuménique
47 Queen's Park Cres., Toronto ON M5S 2C3 Canada
Tel: 416-928-3223; *Fax:* 416-928-3563
director@ccte.ca
www.ccte.ca
Overview: A small national organization founded in 1962
Chief Officer(s):
Robert Faris, Executive Director
Robert Smith, President
Finances: *Annual Operating Budget:* $100,000-$250,000
Staff: 2 staff member(s); 24 volunteer(s)
Membership: 24 individual
Description: To provide for the coordination of consultation, research, & administration of grants awarded by the Council, in order to promote the development of theological education for ministry
Affiliation(s): Association of Theological Schools

Student Christian Movement of Canada (SCM) / Mouvement d'étudiant(e)s chrétien(ne)s
310 Danforth Ave., Toronto ON M4K 1N6 Canada
Tel: 416-463-4312; *Fax:* 416-463-9410
info@scmcanada.org
www.scmcanada.org
Overview: A medium-sized national charitable organization founded in 1921
Finances: *Annual Operating Budget:* $50,000-$100,000
Staff: 2 staff member(s)
Membership: 500; *Member Profile:* Groups at Canadian universities
Description: National, ecumenical student organization; to encourage members in theological/social reflection & in actions for social change. Offices in Toronto & Winnipeg
Member of: World Student Christian Federation

World Association for Christian Communication (WACC) / Association mondiale pour la communication
308 Main St., Toronto ON M4C 4X7 Canada
Tel: 416-691-1999; *Fax:* 416-691-1997
wacc@waccglobal.org
www.waccglobal.org
Overview: A small international charitable organization founded in 1975
Membership: 1,000-4,999; *Fees:* US$120 corporate; US$40 personal; US$10 student; *Member Profile:* Individuals, churches, church-related agencies, media producers, educational institutions, secular communication organizations, & persons who share WACC's mission
Activities: *Speaker Service:* Yes *Library:* Library by appointment
Publications: Media Development
Type: Journal *Frequency:* q. *Price:* US$40 individual; US$50-US$75 libraries & institutions
Profile: Theory & practice of communication worldwide
No-Nonsense Guides
Number of Pages: 6
Profile: Different aspects of communication for practitioners & activists
Description: Communication for social change is promoted by WACC through advocacy, education, training, & the creation & sharing of knowledge. Areas of chief concern include media diversity, equal & affordable access to communication & knowledge, media & gender justice, & the relationship between communication & power.
Member of: UNESCO; ECOSOC

Evangelism

Africa Inland Mission International (Canada) (AIM) / Mission à l'intérieur de l'Afrique (Canada)
1641 Victoria Park Ave., Toronto ON M1R 1P8 Canada
Tel: 416-751-6077; *Fax:* 416-751-3467
Toll-Free: 877-407-6077
general.can@aimint.net
www.aimcanada.org
Also Known As: AIM Canada
Overview: A medium-sized international charitable organization founded in 1895
Finances: *Annual Operating Budget:* $1.5 Million-$3 Million; *Funding Sources:* Donations from churches & individuals
Staff: 8 staff member(s); 3 volunteer(s)
Membership: 135; *Committees:* Finance; Personnel; Projects
Description: Evangelization of people within Eastern & Central Africa & Islands around India Ocean; to plant & establish churches; to train leadership for those churches; to provide medical, educational & agricultural services
Member of: Africa Inland Mission International, Bristol, England; Interdenominational Foreign Mission Association

Baptist Foundation, Alberta, Saskatchewan & the Territories, Inc. (B-FAST)
14323 - 107A Ave. NW, Edmonton AB T5N 1G2 Canada
Tel: 780-451-4878; *Fax:* 780-758-4453
info@febcast.com
Overview: A small local organization founded in 1982
Chief Officer(s):
Nanja Reynolds, Office Manager
Membership: 15 individual
Description: Funding capital projects for Fellowship of Evangelical Baptist Churches in Alberta, Saskatchewan & the Territories

Baptist General Conference of Canada (BGCC)
#205, 15824 - 131 Ave., Edmonton AB T5V 1J4 Canada
Tel: 780-438-9127; *Fax:* 780-435-2478
info@bgc.ca
www.bgc.ca
Overview: A large national charitable organization founded in 1981
Finances: *Funding Sources:* Churches; individuals; BGC Stewardship Foundation
Staff: 5 staff member(s); 12 volunteer(s)
Membership: 7,000+ individuals + 106 churches; *Member Profile:* Agreement with our Affirmation of Faith, Distinctives & ministry goals; *Committees:* Global Ministries; Equipping Ministries; Women; Youth; Regents - Canadian Baptist Seminary; Finance
Activities: Global Ministries; new church development; leadership training; youth programs; women's ministries; international development consulting; *Library:* BGC Canada Archives by appointment
Description: To unite churches in a fellowship that is scriptual in doctrine, evangelical in character & irenic (peaceful) in spirit, & seeking to fulfil the Great Commission of Christ (Mt.28: 19-20) in Canada & abroad
Member of: Evangelical Fellowship of Canada

Billy Graham Evangelistic Association of Canada (BGEAC)
20 Hopewell Ave. NE, Calgary AB T3J 5H5 Canada
Tel: 403-219-2300; *Fax:* 403-250-6567
Toll-Free: 800-293-3717
www.billygraham.ca
Overview: A small national charitable organization founded in 1968
Chief Officer(s):
Fred Weiss, Executive Director
Steve Wile, Director, Ministry
Finances: *Funding Sources:* Donations
Staff: 21 staff member(s)
Activities: Television & radio broadcasts; schools of evangelism; evangelistic crusades; teaching seminars
Description: The goal is to expose those who are searching to the message of Christ; to help edify the Christian body in Canada
Affiliation(s): Bill Graham Evangelistic Association USA

Child Evangelism Fellowship of Canada
PO Box 165, Stn. Main, 189 Henderson Highway, Winnipeg MB R3C 2G9 Canada
Tel: 204-943-2774; *Fax:* 204-943-9967
Toll-Free: 866-943-2774
info@cefcanada.org
www.cefcanada.org
Also Known As: CEF Canada
Overview: A medium-sized national charitable organization founded in 1937
Finances: *Annual Operating Budget:* $500,000-$1.5 Million; *Funding Sources:* Individual, corporate & church donations
Staff: 45 staff member(s); 200 volunteer(s)
Membership: 8
Activities: Children's Ministries Institute; offers courses/programs, materials & training for Christian education among children
Description: CEF Canada is a bible-centred organization of born-again believers whose purpose is to evangelize & disciple children with the gospel of Jesus Christ.
Member of: Canadian Council of Christian Charities; Evangelical Fellowship of Canada
Affiliation(s): Child Evangelism Fellowship Inc.; CEF of Nations

The Christian & Missionary Alliance in Canada (C&MA) / L'Alliance chrétienne et missionnaire au Canada
#100, 30 Carrier Dr., Toronto ON M9W 5T7 Canada
Tel: 416-674-7878; *Fax:* 416-674-0808
info@cmacan.org
www.cmacan.org
Also Known As: The Alliance Church
Overview: A large national charitable organization founded in 1972
Finances: *Annual Operating Budget:* Greater than $5 Million; *Funding Sources:* Donations
Staff: 1200 staff member(s)
Membership: 430 churches + 300 missionaries + 43,700 baptized + 127,000 inclusive members
Description: To proclaim the truth of God's Word & to disciple people of all nations, particularly where Christ has not been named, emphasizing the Lordship of Jesus Christ & the person & work of the Holy Spirit, & looking for the coming of the Lord; to establish & nurture churches related in fellowship with C&MA around the world, dedicated to evangelism & missions; to establish local churches throughout Canada; to teach & train believers for the work of the ministry of Christ; to provide

fellowship for individual believers of kindred spirit with one another without affecting their denominational relations; to encourage the cooperation of such evangelical groups of churches or Christians as may be disposed to send their missionaries through C&MA & contribute their missionary offerings through the general treasury
Member of: Alliance World Fellowship
Affiliation(s): Evangelical Fellowship of Canada

Emmanuel International (Canada) (EIC)
PO Box 4050, 3967 Stouffville Rd., Stouffville ON L4A 8B6 Canada
Tel: 905-640-2111; *Fax:* 905-640-2186
info@e-i.org
www.e-i.org
Overview: A large national charitable organization founded in 1975
Finances: *Annual Operating Budget:* $1.5 Million-$3 Million; *Funding Sources:* Government; donations
Staff: 14 staff member(s); 3 volunteer(s)
Membership: 1-99
Activities: *Internships:* Yes
Description: To encourage, strengthen & assist churches worldwide to meet the spiritual & physical needs of the poor in accordance with the Holy Scriptures through programs of relief, rehabilitation, community development, evangelism & church planting
Member of: Canadian Council of Christian Charities

Evangelical Covenant Church of Canada (ECCC)
PO Box 34025, RPO Fort Richmond, Winnipeg MB R3T 5T5 Canada
Tel: 204-269-3437; *Fax:* 204-269-3584
Toll-Free: - - 020
messengr@escape.ca
www.canadacovenantchurch.org
Overview: A medium-sized national charitable organization founded in 1904
Chief Officer(s):
Jeff Anderson, ECCC Conference Superintendent
Finances: *Funding Sources:* Donations
Member Profile: Evangelical Covenant Churches in Canada
Member of: World Relief Canada; The Evangelical Fellowship of Canada; The Canadian Council of Christian Charities

Evangelical Fellowship of Canada (EFC) / Alliance évangélique du Canada
+, PO Box 3745, Stn. MIP, #300, 600 Alden Rd., Markham ON L3R 0Y4 Canada
Tel: 905-479-5885; *Fax:* 905-479-4742
Toll-Free: 866-302-3362
efc@evangelicalfellowship.ca
www.evangelicalfellowship.ca
Social Media: facebook.com/theefc
Overview: A medium-sized national charitable organization founded in 1964
Finances: *Annual Operating Budget:* $1.5 Million-$3 Million; *Funding Sources:* General & corporate donations; member & subscriber fees
Staff: 20 staff member(s); 90 volunteer(s)
Membership: 32 evangelical denominations + 110 organizations + 1,200 churches
Activities: Task forces: Evangelism; Women in Ministry; Aboriginal; Global Mission; Commissions: Education; Religious Liberty; Social Action; *Speaker Service:* Yes
Awards: Brian Stiller Leadership Award
Description: EFC is the national association of evangelical Christians in Canada. Its aims are to be a public advocate of the gospel of Jesus Christ; to provide an evangelical identity which unites Canadian Christians of diverse backgrounds; to express biblical views on current issues; to assist individuals & groups in proclaiming the gospel & advancing Christian values.
Member of: World Evangelical Fellowship

Evangelical Medical Aid Society (EMAS)
PO Box 820, Stn. Main, 3967 Stouffville Road, Stouffville ON L4A 7Z9 Canada
Tel: 905-642-4661; *Fax:* 905-640-2186
Toll-Free: 866-648-0664
info@emascanada.org
www.emascanada.org
Overview: A small international charitable organization founded in 1948
Chief Officer(s):
Hendrik Visser, M.D., Chair
Finances: *Annual Operating Budget:* $500,000-$1.5 Million
Staff: 1 staff member(s); 175 volunteer(s)
Membership: 25 individual
Description: To operate as a global medical ministry, revealing Christ's love; To work with national groups to provide assistance in healing & teaching

The Evangelical Order of Certified Pastoral Counsellors of America (EOCPCA)
#210, 3017 St. Clair Ave., Burlington ON L7N 3P5 Canada
Tel: 905-639-0137; *Fax:* 905-333-8901
admin@eocpc.com
www.eocpc.com
Previous Name: Order of Certified Pastoral Counsellors of America
Overview: A medium-sized national organization founded in 1982
Chief Officer(s):
Stephen Hambly, Contact
shambly@eocpc.com
Finances: *Annual Operating Budget:* $500,000-$1.5 Million
Staff: 3 staff member(s)
Membership: 1,200 individual; *Fees:* $75-250
Description: To promote a Christian-oriented order; to certify & accredit pastoral counsellors by federal charter
Member of: Canadian Christian Counsellors Association; Canadian Christian Clinical Counsellors College
Affiliation(s): California State Christian University

Evangelical Tract Distributors (EDT)
PO Box 146, Stn. Main, 12151 - 67 St. NW, Edmonton AB T5J 2G9 Canada
Tel: 780-477-1538; *Fax:* 780-477-3795
etdsupport@evangelicaltract.com
www.evangelicaltract.com
Overview: A small national organization founded in 1935
Chief Officer(s):
John Harder, President/Managing Director
Publications: The Evangelist
Type: newsletter *Frequency:* monthly
Description: EDT is a non-profit organization that prints & distributes Christian gospel tracts free of charge. It is a registered charity, BN: 130522659RR0001.

Fellowship of Evangelical Baptist Churches in Canada
PO Box 457, 351 Elizabeth St., Guelph ON N1H 6K9 Canada
Tel: 519-821-4830; *Fax:* 519-821-9829
president@fellowship.ca
www.fellowship.ca
Overview: A large national organization
Finances: *Annual Operating Budget:* Greater than $5 Million
Staff: 16 staff member(s)
Membership: 501 churches
Activities: *Library:* Archives
Description: To glorify God & to proclaim the good news of Jesus Christ, evangelizing our generation & producing healthy, growing churches in Canada & around the world

Gideons International in Canada
501 Imperial Rd. North, Guelph ON N1H 7A2 Canada
Tel: 519-823-1140; *Fax:* 519-767-1913
Toll-Free: 888-482-4253
info@gideons.ca; tcg@gideons.ca
www.gideons.ca
Overview: A medium-sized international charitable organization founded in 1911
Chief Officer(s):
Paul Mercer, Executive Director
Finances: *Funding Sources:* Membership fees; voluntary donations
Membership: 1,000-4,999; *Member Profile:* Christian business & professional people
Activities: Sharing faith; Placing Bibles & New Testaments in institutions; Distributing New Testaments to selected groups
Publications: Gideon News
Type: Newsletter
The Canadian Gideon: The Official Publication of The Gideons International in Canada
Type: Magazine *Editor:* Neil Bramble *Price:* $15
Profile: Information & resources for Gideon & Auxiliary members
Description: The interdenominational lay association communicates God's Word in Canada & around the world.

Jack West Evangelistic Association
#401, 76 Rochampton Ave., St Catharines ON L2M 7W5 Canada
Overview: A small local charitable organization founded in 1966
Chief Officer(s):
Jack West, Contact
Membership: 100 individual
Activities: *Speaker Service:* Yes

Lighthouse Mission
669 Main St., Winnipeg MB R3B 1E3 Canada
Tel: 204-943-9669
Overview: A small local organization founded in 1911
Chief Officer(s):
Scott Miller, Contact
Activities: Operates a soup kitchen; distributes clothing to the needy
Description: Provides food and services to the needy in Winnipeg.

Living Bible Explorers (LBE)
600 Burnell St., Winnipeg MB R3G 2B7 Canada
Tel: 204-786-8667; *Fax:* 204-775-7525
Toll-Free: 866-786-8667
lbe1@mts.net
livingbibleexplorers.com
Overview: A small local charitable organization founded in 1969
Chief Officer(s):
Lainie Loiselle, Chair
George Hill, General Manager
Finances: *Annual Operating Budget:* $250,000-$500,000; *Funding Sources:* Provincial government; individual churches; foundations
Staff: 7 staff member(s); 100 volunteer(s)
Membership: 700 individual; *Member Profile:* Manitobans who have a tangible interest by working, volunteering or giving to the work
Activities: Boys & Girls Clubs; summer camps; weekend camps; weekly kids church; teens church; food distribution; weekly home visitation; annual banquet, Mar.; *Internships:* Yes; *Speaker Service:* Yes *Library:* Resource Library (Open to Public)
Description: To develop relationships with children & teens from inner city homes in an effort to evangelize them & to promote discipleship with a view to integrating them into the life & care of Bible-believing churches
Member of: Canadian Council of Christian Charities

Society for International Ministries (SIM Canada)
10 Huntingdale Blvd., Toronto ON M1W 2S5 Canada
Tel: 416-497-2424; *Fax:* 416-497-2444
Toll-Free: 800-294-6918
info@sim.ca
www.sim.ca
Overview: A small international organization founded in 1893
Finances: *Annual Operating Budget:* $3 Million-$5 Million
Staff: 30 staff member(s)
Membership: 300
Description: To evangelize the unreached & minister to human need

Solbrekken Evangelistic Association of Canada
PO Box 44220, Stn. Garside, Edmonton AB T5V 1N6 Canada
Tel: 780-460-8444
mswm@telusplanet.net
www.mswm.org
Also Known As: Max Solbrekken World Mission
Overview: A small national charitable organization founded in 1961
Chief Officer(s):
Max Solbrekken, President
Donna Solbrekken, Secretary
Description: To promote the gospel
Affiliation(s): Europa for Kristus, Oslo, Norwey

Friends

Canadian Friends Service Committee (CFSC) / Secours Quaker Canadien
60 Lowther Ave., Toronto ON M5R 1C7 Canada
Tel: 416-920-5213; *Fax:* 416-920-5214
cfsc-office@quaker.ca
www.cfsc.quaker.ca
Also Known As: Religious Society of Friends (Quakers)
Overview: A medium-sized national charitable organization founded in 1931
Finances: *Annual Operating Budget:* $500,000-$1.5 Million; *Funding Sources:* Individuals; meetings
Staff: 7 staff member(s); 40 volunteer(s)
Activities: Peace & social justice work; *Internships:* Yes; *Speaker Service:* Yes *Library:* Friends House Library (Open to Public)
Publications: Quaker Concern
Type: Newsletter *Frequency:* 3 pa *Editor:* M. Egan, J. Preston, G. Broughtone
Profile: CFSC information & feature articles on CFSC concerns
Description: To unify & expand the concerns of Friends (Quakers)
Member of: The Canadian Council of Churches; Kairos: Canadian Ecumenical Justice Initiatives; Project Ploughshares; Canadian Council for Refugees; War Resistors Support Campaign

Friends Historical Association (FHA)
Quaker Collection, Haverford College, 370 Lancaster Ave., Haverford PA 19041-1392 USA
Tel: 610-896-1161; *Fax:* 610-896-1102
fha@haverford.edu
www.haverford.edu/library/fha/fha.html
Overview: A medium-sized international charitable organization founded in 1873
Chief Officer(s):
Kenneth Carroll, President
Joelle Bertolet, Office Manager
Finances: *Annual Operating Budget:* Less than $50,000; *Funding Sources:* Membership dues; subscriptions; donations
Staff: 1 staff member(s); 21 volunteer(s)
Membership: 800; *Fees:* $15; *Member Profile:* Friends & interested historians; *Committees:* Membership; Publication; Historical Research; Finance; Curatorial; Development
Activities: Pilgrimages to historic Friends Meetings; lectures; *Rents Mailing List:* Yes
Publications: Quaker History
Type: Journal *Frequency:* s-a *Editor:* Charles L. Cherry
Description: To promote the study, preservation & publication of material relating to the history of the Religious Society of Friends
Affiliation(s): Conference of Quaker Historians & Archivists

Friends Historical Society - London (FHS)
c/o Friends House, 173 Euston Rd., London NW1 2BJ United Kingdom
Overview: A small international organization founded in 1903
Finances: *Funding Sources:* Membership fees
Membership: 400
Description: To encourage the study of Quaker history
Member of: Association of Denominational Historical Societies & Cognate Libraries

Hinduism

Hindu Society of Alberta
14225 - 133 Ave., Edmonton AB T5L 4W3 Canada
Tel: 780-451-5130; *Fax:* 780-451-5130
webmaster@hindusociety.ab.ca
www.hindusociety.ab.ca
Overview: A small provincial charitable organization founded in 1967
Chief Officer(s):
Jivan Kayande, President, 780-459-3852
Membership: 500
Activities: Classes in yoga & meditation; language classes; lectures & seminars on history & religion; religious celebrations; music & dance performances; hall rentals; *Library:* library
Description: The Society is a cultural, social & religious institute catering to the needs of those influenced by Hinduism. It is a registered charity, BN: 118958370RR0001.

Islam/Muslim

Ahmadiyya Movement in Islam (Canada) (AMI) / Mouvement Ahmadiyya en Islam (Canada)
Baitul Islam Mosque, 10610 Jane St., Maple ON L6A 3A2 Canada
Tel: 905-303-4000; *Fax:* 905-832-3220
info@ahmadiyya.ca
www.ahmadiyya.ca
Social Media: www.facebook.com/group.php?gid=2259487439
Overview: A large international charitable organization founded in 1966
Finances: *Annual Operating Budget:* $500,000-$1.5 Million; *Funding Sources:* Contributions from members
Staff: 5 staff member(s); 30 volunteer(s)
Membership: 200 million+ followers in 170 countries
Activities: *Speaker Service:* Yes *Library:* Reference Library (Open to Public) by appointment
Description: Seeks to establish, maintain & conduct mosques & to carry on the teachings of the Holy Koran; to establish, maintain, organize & unify Muslims & particularly the members of Ahmadiyya Movement in Islam; to conduct public or private meetings of a religious nature & to establish, maintain & conduct classes for Islamic education & to employ instructors; to employ, send out & direct Muslim missionaries to preach the Holy Koran & its principles highlighting peaceful co-existence of adherents of different religions
Member of: Horizon Interfaith Council

Ahmadiyya Muslim Centre
525 Kylemore Ave., Winnipeg MB R3L 1B5 Canada
Tel: 204-475-2642; *Fax:* 204-452-2455
www.ahmadiyya.ca
Overview: A small local organization founded in 1979
Membership: 1-99
Activities: *Library:* Library

Association des Projets charitables Islamiques / Association of Islamic Charitable Projects
6691, av du Parc, Montréal QC H2V 4J1 Canada
Tél: 514-274-6194; *Téléc:* 514-274-0011
Aperçu: *Dimension:* petite; *Envergure:* locale
Membre(s) du bureau directeur:
Bassam Derbas, 514-945-1549
Maher Bissany, 514-892-2295
Description: Dénonce tout acte de terrorisme et promouvoit le support envers la communauté musulmane

Canadian Council of Muslim Women (CCMW) / Conseil canadien des femmes musulmanes
PO Box 154, Gananoque ON K7G 2T7 Canada
Tel: 613-383-2847
info@ccmw.com
www.ccmw.com
Overview: A medium-sized national organization founded in 1982
Finances: *Annual Operating Budget:* Less than $50,000; *Funding Sources:* Fundraising; public funds
Staff: 20 volunteer(s)
Membership: 100-499; *Fees:* Schedule; *Member Profile:* Practising Muslim women
Activities: Affirmative Action/Women's Issues; Community Associations; Cultural Diversity; Education/Islamic; Gender Equality; Gender Issues; Immigrant Women; Inter-Faith Relations; International Islamic Affairs; Islam; Islamic Activities; Islamic Information; Islamic Religious Matters; Minority Women's Issues; Mosques/Islamic Centres; Muslim Community; Muslims; Religion; Religious Activities; Religious Publications; Religious Tolerance; Status of Women; Women's Associations/Advocacy Groups; Women's Image Development; Women's Issues; *Speaker Service:* Yes
Publications: CCMW [Canadian Council of Muslim Women] National Newsletter
Type: Newsletter
Description: To assist Muslim women in participating effectively in Canadian society & to promote mutual understanding with women of other faiths; our goals: Equity, Equality, Empowerment

Council on American-Islamic Relations Canada (CAIR-CAN)
PO Box 13219, Ottawa ON K2K 1X4 Canada
Tel: 613-254-9704; *Fax:* 613-254-9810
Toll-Free: 866-524-0004
info@caircan.ca
www.caircan.ca
Overview: A small international organization
Chief Officer(s):
Selma Djukic, Acting Chair
Ihsaan Gardee, Executive Director, 613-853-4111
Activities: Seminars & workshops; publication of guides, handbooks & media resource kits
Description: CAIR-CAN is a nonprofit organization promoting the civic engagement of Canadian Muslims, the protection of their human rights, & the education of non-Muslims so they may hold an accurate understanding of Islam. It is active in the areas of media relations, anti-discrimination & political advocacy.

International Development & Relief Foundation (IDRF)
#210, 2 Berkeley St., Toronto ON M5A 4J5 Canada
Tel: 416-497-0818; *Fax:* 416-497-0686
Toll-Free: 866-497-4373
office@idrf.ca
www.idrf.ca
Overview: A small international organization founded in 1985
Finances: *Annual Operating Budget:* $500,000-$1.5 Million
Staff: 5 staff member(s)
Activities: Providing aid worth more than $8 million to people in 15 countries
Description: To empower the disadvantaged peoples of the world, through emergency relief & participatory development programs based on the Islamic principles of human dignity, self-reliance, & social justice
Affiliation(s): Canadian Council for International Cooperation

Islamic Affairs Council of Québec (IACQ)
1830, Thierry, Brossard QC J4W 2M8 Canada
Tel: 450-672-8027
naseer@library.mcgill.ca
Overview: A small local organization founded in 1991
Chief Officer(s):
Syed Naseer, President
Finances: *Annual Operating Budget:* Less than $50,000
Staff: 5 volunteer(s)
Description: Seeks effective cooperation among Islamic organizations & Muslims of all nationalities or schools of thought; seeks better understanding of Islam; assists media by open discussion; takes part in multicultural activities

Islamic Association of Nova Scotia (IANS)
42 Leaman Dr., Dartmouth NS B3A 2K9 Canada
Tel: 902-469-9490
info@islamnovascotia.ca
www.islamnovascotia.ca
Previous Name: Islamic Association of the Maritimes
Overview: A small local organization
Fees: $50 single; $100 family; $25 student

Islamic Association of Saskatchewan (Saskatoon)
222 Copland Cres., Saskatoon SK S7H 2Z5 Canada
Tel: 306-665-6424
info@islamiccenter.sk.ca
www.islamiccenter.sk.ca
Overview: A small provincial organization founded in 1968
Chief Officer(s):
Khalil-Ur Rehman, President
Shakeel Akhtar, Secretary
Activities: Operates Islamic Centre; represents Muslims; provides activities; responsible for Muslim Cemetery
Affiliation(s): Multi-Faith Group; Saskatchewan Organization for Heritage Language; Saskatchewan Intercultural Association; Saskatchewan Forum for "Racialized" Canadians; Saskatchewan Council for International Cooperation

Islamic Foundation of Toronto
441 Nugget Ave., Toronto ON M1S 5E1 Canada
Tel: 416-321-0909; *Fax:* 416-321-1995
info@islamicfoundation.ca
www.islamicfoundation.ca
Also Known As: Nugget Mosque
Overview: A small local charitable organization founded in 1969
Finances: *Annual Operating Budget:* $3 Million-$5 Million
Staff: 72 staff member(s)
Membership: 1,000-4,999; *Committees:* DAwah; Library; School Board; Social Services
Activities: Full time Islamic school, JK to Grade 10; part-time evening Islamic school; Arabic language centre for adults; Friday & Sunday schools; *Library:* Yes (Open to Public)

Islamic Information Centre (IIC)
312 Lisgar St., Ottawa ON K2P 0E8 Canada
Tel: 613-232-0210; *Fax:* 613-232-0210
mail@islamottawa.com
www.islamottawa.com
Also Known As: Daw'ah Centre
Overview: A small national organization founded in 1993
Chief Officer(s):
Sulaiman Khan, Director
Finances: *Annual Operating Budget:* $50,000-$100,000
Staff: 2 staff member(s); 10 volunteer(s)
Membership: 35; *Fees:* $50; *Committees:* Business; Conference; Daw'ah; Membership; Newsletter
Activities: *Speaker Service:* Yes *Library:* Islamic Information (Open to Public)
Member of: Muslim Community Council of Ottawa
Affiliation(s): Islam Care Centre

Islamic Information Foundation (IIF)
8 Laurel Lane, Halifax NS B3M 2P6 Canada
Tel: 902-445-2494; *Fax:* 902-445-2494
Overview: A small national charitable organization founded in 1981
Finances: *Annual Operating Budget:* $100,000-$250,000; *Funding Sources:* Sale of religious material; donations
Staff: 4 volunteer(s)
Membership: 40 individuals
Activities: *Speaker Service:* Yes
Description: To promote better understanding of Islam among Muslims & Christians through information provided in print, audio & video forms & through lecture, seminars & interfaith dialogues

Islamic Propagation Centre International (Canada) (IPCI (Canada))
5761 Coopers Ave., Mississauga ON L4Z 1R9 Canada
Tel: 905-507-3323; *Fax:* 905-507-3323
zsyed@ipci-canada.com
www.ipci-canada.com
Also Known As: Jama Masjid Mississauga
Overview: A small local charitable organization founded in 1984
Finances: *Annual Operating Budget:* $50,000-$100,000
Staff: 2 staff member(s); 100 volunteer(s)
Membership: 100 student; 1,000 individual; *Fees:* $200 individual; *Committees:* Fundraising; Eid & Ramadhan; Executive
Activities: Congregation; marriages; family counselling; summer & evening school for kids; *Speaker Service:* Yes *Library:* IPC Office Library (Open to Public) by appointment

Description: The Centre offers a selection of resource material for those interested in learning about Islam. Topics covered include comparative religion, history, culture, lifestyle, politics, law & women in Islam. It is a registered charity, BN: 886810191RR0001.

Manitoba Islamic Association (MIA)
247 Hazelwood Ave., Winnipeg MB R2M 4W1 Canada
Tel: 204-256-1347
editorialboard@miaonline.org
www.miaonline.org
Overview: A small provincial organization founded in 1976
Fees: $30; *Member Profile:* Muslim persons in Manitoba who abide by the association's rules & regulations; Associate members are non-Muslim persons in Manitoba; *Committees:* Takaful Fund
Activities: Accepting applications for financial assistance, through the Takaful Fund; Providing funeral services to the Muslim community, through partnership with Cropo Funeral Services; Offering services for marriage; Conducting Sunday Qur'an classes for children & the MIA Al Nur Weekend Islamic School; Sponsoring the Al-Hamd Learning Center, which offers an Arabic & Islamic educational program for preschoolers
Awards: MIA / MSA University Scholarships
Publications: Manitoba Muslim
Type: Newsletter *Accepts Advertising*
Profile: Editorials, reports, articles, announcements, community news, & local events

Muslim Association of Canada (MAC)
#332, 1568 Merivale Rd., Ottawa ON K2G 5Y7 Canada
Tel: 613-321-5000; *Fax:* 613-321-5001
mac@macnet.ca
www.macnet.ca
Overview: A medium-sized national organization
Activities: Schools & community centres; educational & other projects; youth projects; outreach
Description: Seeks to promote a balanced, constructive & integrated Islamic presence in Canada; operates in 11 Canadian cities

Muslim Association of New Brunswick (MANB)
1100 Rothesay Rd., Saint John NB E2H 2H8 Canada
Tel: 506-633-1675
info@manb.ca
www.manb.ca
Overview: A medium-sized provincial organization
Chief Officer(s):
Tareq Shah, President
Description: The Muslim Association of New Brunswick (MANB) is a Saint John-based, nonprofit organization found to present, serve and educate the Muslim community in the Saint John Area. MANB aims to; strengthen access to Islamic education, facilitate community outreach and interaction with other religious organizations and community groups, consolidate the social fabric of the community, and sustain Islamic work by encouraging and building endowments.

Muslim Community of Québec (MCQ) / Communauté musulmane du Québec
7445, av Chester, Montréal QC H4V 1M4 Canada
Tel: 514-484-2967; *Fax:* 514-484-3802
Also Known As: Mosque of Montréal
Overview: A small local organization founded in 1979
Chief Officer(s):
Mohammed M. Amin, Founder
Finances: *Annual Operating Budget:* $500,000-$1.5 Million
Membership: 500
Activities: *Speaker Service:* Yes
Description: To facilitate Muslim religious life

Muslim Education & Welfare Foundation of Canada (MEWFC)
2580 McGill St., Vancouver BC V5K 1H1 Canada
Tel: 604-255-9941; *Fax:* 604-255-9941
Also Known As: Almuassasatul Islamiyah Lit-Tarbiyah War-Riaayah (Canada)
Overview: A medium-sized national charitable organization founded in 1987
Activities: *Library:* Jannat Bibi Library
Awards: Jannat Bibi Award of Educational Excellence
Description: To provide for the educational, religious & welfare needs of the Muslim community

Muslim World League - Canada
#3, 6680 Campobello Rd., Mississauga ON L5N 2L8 Canada
Tel: 905-542-1050; *Fax:* 905-542-1054
mwl@mwlcanada.org
www.mwlcanada.org
Overview: A small national organization founded in 1985
Member Profile: Muslims
Activities: *Rents Mailing List:* Yes *Library:* Library (Open to Public)
Description: The League is a non-profit, non-governmental organization that serves the religious needs of Muslims in Canada. It promotes Islam & Islamic teachings among Canadian Muslims & helps non-Muslims grasp an accurate understanding of the religion. It also serves as a resource centre, publishing booklets & flyers on current issues.
Affiliation(s): Muslim World League, Makkah, Saudia Arabia

Ottawa Muslim Community Circle (OMCC)
PO Box 29105, Stn. Barrhaven, Nepean ON K2J 4A9 Canada
Tel: 613-825-7059; *Fax:* 613-825-4667
omcc@magma.ca
www.magma.ca/~omcc
Overview: A small local organization founded in 1984
Chief Officer(s):
Mahmood Rasheed, President
Finances: *Annual Operating Budget:* Less than $50,000
Staff: 15 volunteer(s)
Membership: 400
Activities: Social services; seminars & conferences
Description: To foster unity among various Muslims; to promote better understanding of Muslims & Islam among Canadians of other faiths; to maintain cultural identity

Scarborough Muslim Association (SMA)
2665 Lawrence Ave. East, Toronto ON M1P 2S2 Canada
Tel: 416-750-2253; *Fax:* 416-750-1616
info@smacanada.ca
www.smacanada.ca
Overview: A small local organization
Chief Officer(s):
Yakub Hatia, President

Windsor Islamic Association (WIA)
c/o Windsor Mosque, 1320 Northwood Dr., Windsor ON N9W 1A4 Canada
Tel: 519-966-2355
presidentwia@yahoo.com
www.wiao.org
Overview: A small local organization founded in 1964
Chief Officer(s):
Ismail Peer, President
Hussein Khalaf, Vice-President
Abdelkader Tayebi, Secretary
Description: Serves a population of over 25,000 Muslims in the Windsor locality
Affiliation(s): World Muslim League

Judaism

Canadian Council for Reform Judaism
#301, 3845 Bathurst St., Toronto ON M3H 3N2 Canada
Tel: 416-630-0375; *Fax:* 416-630-5089
Toll-Free: 800-560-8242
ccrj@urj.org
urj.org/ccrj/
Previous Name: Canadian Council of Reform Rabbis
Overview: A medium-sized national organization
Description: The CCRJ is the Canadian region of the Union for Reform Judaism Congregations, and serves as the umbrella organization for Reform Judaism in Canada, representing about 10,000 households in 26 affiliated congregations.
Member of: Union for Reform Judaism

Congregation Beth Israel - British Columbia
4350 Oak St., Vancouver BC V6H 2N4 Canada
Tel: 604-731-4161; *Fax:* 604-731-4989
info@bethisrael.ca
www.bethisrael.ca
Overview: A small local organization founded in 1932
Chief Officer(s):
Catherine Epstein, President
Jonathan Infeld, Klei Kodesh
rabbiinfeld@bethisrael.ca
Shannon Etkin, Executive Director
shannon@bethisrael.ca
Activities: Youth programs; Hebrew school; facility rental; Rabbi Wilfred & Phyllis Solomon Museum; *Library:* Moe Cohen Library (Open to Public)
Description: The congregation is dedicated to the strengthening of all aspects of Jewish life, including worship & Torah study, religious, educational & social activities for all ages, & the observance of life cycle events.
Member of: United Synagogue of Conservative Judaism

National Council of Jewish Women of Canada
#118, 1588 Main St., Winnipeg MB R2V 1Y3 Canada
Tel: 204-339-9700; *Fax:* 204-334-3779
info@ncjwc.org
www.ncjwc.org
Overview: A medium-sized national charitable organization founded in 1897
Description: To further human welfare in the Jewish & general communities; to help fulfill unmet needs & to serve the individual & the community.
Member of: UNESCO Canadian Subcommission of the Status of Women; Jewish Women Against Domestic Violence; Coalition for Agunot Rights
Affiliation(s): International Council of Jewish Women

Orthodox Rabbinical Council of British Columbia
#401, 1037 West Broadway, Vancouver BC V6H 1E3 Canada
Tel: 604-731-1803; *Fax:* 604-731-1804
info@bckosher.org
www.bckosher.org
Also Known As: BC Kosher
Overview: A small provincial charitable organization founded in 1983
Finances: *Annual Operating Budget:* $100,000-$250,000
Staff: 4 staff member(s); 6 volunteer(s)
Membership: 1-99
Activities: Providing information about Kashruth (kosher food - kashruth symbol BCK); *Speaker Service:* Yes

Shaare Zion Congregation
5575 Côte St. Luc Rd., Montréal QC H3X 2C9 Canada
Tel: 514-481-7727; *Fax:* 514-481-1219
Webmaster@shaarezion.org
www.shaarezion.org
Overview: A small local charitable organization
Chief Officer(s):
David Moscovitch, Executive Director
Gerry Silverman, President
Affiliation(s): United Synagogue of Conservative Judaism

Toronto Association of Synagogue & Temple Administrators
1445 Eglinton Ave. West, Toronto ON M6C 2E6 Canada
Tel: 416-783-6103; *Fax:* 416-783-9923
Overview: A small local organization
Chief Officer(s):
Barbara Berke, President
Finances: *Annual Operating Budget:* Less than $50,000
Membership: 12; *Fees:* $50; *Member Profile:* Executive directors of synagogues & temples

Vaad Harabonim (Orthodox Rabbinical Council)
3600 Bathurst St., Toronto ON M6A 2C9 Canada
Tel: 416-787-1631; *Fax:* 416-785-5378
Also Known As: Rabbinical Council of Ontario
Overview: A small provincial organization founded in 1982
Finances: *Annual Operating Budget:* Less than $50,000
Membership: 40
Description: To serve & guide the Jewish community

Lutheran

Canadian Lutheran World Relief (CLWR)
1080 Kingsbury Ave., Winnipeg MB R2P 1W5 Canada
Tel: 204-694-5602; *Fax:* 204-694-5460
Toll-Free: 800-661-2597
clwr@clwr.mb.ca
www.clwr.org
Overview: A large national charitable organization founded in 1946
Finances: *Annual Operating Budget:* Greater than $5 Million; *Funding Sources:* Lutheran churches; Canadian International Development Agency; Province of Saskatchewan
Staff: 20 staff member(s)
Activities: We Care kits & quilts; study tours; *Speaker Service:* Yes
Publications: Partnership Newsletter [a publication of the Canadian Lutheran World Relief]
Type: Newsletter *Frequency:* q. *Editor:* Lorne Kletke *ISSN:* 1916-2308
Profile: Inspirational stories about people in the developing world
Four Corners [a publication of the Canadian Lutheran World Relief]
Type: Newsletter *Frequency:* s-a.
Profile: News about alternative trade to create opportunities for artists in the developing world
Canadian Lutheran World Relief Annual Report
Type: Yearbook *Frequency:* a.
Profile: Distributed to CLWR donors
Canadian Lutheran World Relief Bulletin of Reports
Type: Yearbook *Frequency:* a.
Profile: CLWR activities & financial information
CLWR [Canadian Lutheran World Relief] News Briefs
Type: Newsletter *Frequency:* w.
Profile: Summary of significant CLWR-related news events in Canada or around the world

CLWR [Canadian Lutheran World Relief] Monthly Briefs
Frequency: m.
Profile: Information for constituents about events in the developing world & the response of Canadians
Description: To provide development programming in Africa, Asia, Latin America & the Middle East, to provide emergency relief in case of disaster, to enable sponsorships for refugee resettlement in Canada. Focus is on development, peace building, alternative approaches to trade, education & community building. Offices in Winnipeg, Toronto, Burnaby, Bolivia & Zambia
Member of: Canadian Council for International Cooperation; Manitoba Council for International Cooperation
Affiliation(s): Canadian Foodgrains Bank; Inter-Church Action

Estonian Evangelical Lutheran Church Consistory (EELC Consistory)
383 Jarvis St., Toronto ON M5B 2C7 Canada
Tel: 416-925-5465; *Fax:* 416-925-5688
e.e.l.k@eelk.ee
www.eelk.ee/eelcabroad.html
Overview: A small national organization founded in 1950
Membership: 7,200 + 13 churches
Description: EELC is an independent, self-governing church which functions on democratic grounds, calls together congregations, ordains pastors, holds services & carries out religious ceremonies according to the Service Book, the Statutes & the established order. The Consistory is the government of the EELC.
Affiliation(s): Lutheran World Federation; World Council of Churches

Evangelical Lutheran Church in Canada (ELCIC)
#302, 393 Portage Ave., Winnipeg MB R3B 3H6 Canada
Tel: 204-984-9150; *Fax:* 204-984-9185
Toll-Free: 888-786-6707
www.elcic.ca
Overview: A medium-sized national charitable organization founded in 1986
Finances: *Annual Operating Budget:* $1.5 Million-$3 Million; *Funding Sources:* Donations
Staff: 20 staff member(s)
Membership: 153,000 individuals; 607 congregations; *Member Profile:* Current members in a congregation
Description: The Church shares the gospel of Jesus Christ with people in Canada & around the world through the proclamation of the Word, celebration of the sacraments, & through service in Christ's name. It functions through three major entities: nationally as the ELCIC, regionally as synods, & locally as congregations.
Member of: Canadian Council of Churches; Lutheran Council in Canada; Lutheran World Federation; World Council of Churches

Lutheran Association of Missionaries & Pilots (LAMP)
4966 - 92 Ave. NW, Edmonton AB T6B 2V4 Canada
Tel: 780-466-8507; *Fax:* 780-466-6733
Toll-Free: 800-307-4036
office@lampministry.org
www.lampministry.org
Overview: A small international organization founded in 1970
Chief Officer(s):
Ron Ludke, Executive Director
Finances: *Annual Operating Budget:* $500,000-$1.5 Million
Staff: 300+ volunteer(s)
Activities: *Speaker Service:* Yes *Library:* Yes (Open to Public)
Description: A cross-cultural ministry sharing Jesus Christ with God's people in remote areas of Canada
Affiliation(s): Lutheran Church Canada; Evangelical Lutheran Church in Canada

Lutheran Bible Translators of Canada Inc. (LBTC)
PO Box 934, Kitchener ON N2G 4E3 Canada
Tel: 519-742-3361; *Fax:* 519-742-5989
Toll-Free: 866-518-7071
info@lbtc.ca
www.lbtc.ca
Overview: A small international charitable organization founded in 1974
Finances: *Annual Operating Budget:* $250,000-$500,000
Staff: 5 staff member(s)
Membership: 1-99
Activities: *Speaker Service:* Yes
Description: To bring people to faith in Jesus Christ through Bible translations & literacy work
Affiliation(s): Canadian Council of Christian Charities

Mennonites

Calgary Mennonite Centre for Newcomers Society
#125, 920 - 36th St. NE, Calgary AB T2A 6L8 Canada
Tel: 403-569-3325; *Fax:* 403-248-5041
newcomer@cmcn.ab.ca
www.centrefornewcomers.ca
Overview: A small local organization founded in 1988
Chief Officer(s):
Dale Taylor, Executive Director, Centre for Newcomers, 403-537-8800
Member Profile: Members beyond the Mennonite constituency is enoucraged.
Activities: Calgary Career Show for immigrant youth; preschool activities for immigrant children; employment preparation courses; anti-bullying workshop; EthniCity Catering Program; ESL classes
Description: The Society is a not-for-profit, registered charity that operates the Centre for Newcomers, assisting refugees & immigrants arriving in Calgary to meet their settlement needs.
Affiliation(s): Canadian Red Cross

Canadian Conference of Mennonite Brethren Churches
1310 Taylor Ave., Winnipeg MB R3M 3Z6 Canada
Tel: 204-669-6575; *Fax:* 204-654-1865
Toll-Free: 888-669-6575
www.mbconf.ca
Overview: A medium-sized national organization founded in 1945
Chief Officer(s):
David Wiebe, Executive Director
Finances: *Funding Sources:* Donations
Staff: 19 staff member(s)
Membership: 31,264; *Committees:* Mennonite Central Committee; Mennonite Disaster Service; Manitoba Missions/Service
Activities: *Library:* Centre for M.B. Studies (Open to Public)
Publications: Mennonite Brethren Herald
Frequency: m.
Profile: Feature articles, columns, letters, news, people, & events for the Mennonite Brethren community
Chinese Manitoba Brethren Herald
Frequency: m.
Profile: Written in Chinese, the Herald serves the conference's Chinese community
Le Lien
Frequency: bi-m.
Profile: Written in French, the publication serves the conference's francophone churches in Québec
Description: To glorify God, to nurture & equip members to live the Christian life, & to mobilize them for ministry

Evangelical Mennonite Conference (EMC)
440 Main St., Steinbach MB R5G 1Z5 Canada
Tel: 204-326-6401; *Fax:* 204-326-1613
messenger@emconf.ca
www.emconf.ca
Overview: A medium-sized national charitable organization founded in 1812
Chief Officer(s):
Tim Dyck, General Secretary
Finances: *Annual Operating Budget:* $1.5 Million-$3 Million; *Funding Sources:* Donations
Membership: 7,300
Activities: *Library:* EMC Archives
Description: To encourage local churches to work together on missions in Canada & around the world

Evangelical Mennonite Mission Conference (EMMC)
PO Box 52059, Stn. Niakwa, Winnipeg MB R2M 5P9 Canada
Tel: 204-253-7929; *Fax:* 204-256-7384
info@emmc.ca
www.emmc.ca
Previous Name: Rudnerweider Mennonite Church
Overview: A medium-sized national charitable organization founded in 1959
Chief Officer(s):
Jake Friesen, Executive Director & Moderator
Al Kehler, Conference Pastor
al@emmc.ca
Gin Thiessen, Secretary
Henry Derksen, Treasurer
Activities: *Library:* EMMC Resource Centre; EMMC Media Library
Affiliation(s): Mennonite Central Committee of Canada; Mennonite World Conference; Mennonite Foundation of Canada; Mennonite Foundation of Canada

MBMS International (MBMSI) / Mennonite Brethren Mission & Service International
International & Western Canada (BC), #302, 32025 George Ferguson Way, Abbotsford BC V2T 2K7 Canada
Tel: 604-859-6267; *Fax:* 604-589-6422
Toll-Free: 866-964-7627
mbmsi@mbmsi.org
www.mbmsi.org
Also Known As: Board of Missions & Services of the Mennonite Brethren Churches of North America
Overview: A medium-sized local charitable organization founded in 1900
Finances: *Annual Operating Budget:* Greater than $5 Million; *Funding Sources:* Voluntary contributions; grants
Staff: 2 staff member(s)
Activities: Cross-cultural mission agency of Mennonite Brethren churches in Canada & the US; *Internships:* Yes; *Speaker Service:* Yes
Description: To make disciples & plant churches globally through church planting & envangelism, discipleship & leadership training & social ministry
Member of: Evangelical Fellowship of Mission Agencies

Mennonite Central Committee Canada (MCCC)
134 Plaza Dr., Winnipeg MB Canada
Tel: 204-261-6381; *Fax:* 204-269-9875
Toll-Free: 888-622-6337
canada@mennonitecc.ca
www.mcc.org/canada
Overview: A large international charitable organization founded in 1920
Description: To operate as a relief & development service agency; To promote relief, development, & peace
Member of: Mennonite Central Committee

Mennonite Church Canada (MC Canada)
600 Shaftesbury Blvd., Winnipeg MB R3P 0M4 Canada
Tel: 204-888-6781; *Fax:* 204-831-5675
Toll-Free: 866-888-6785
office@mennonitechurch.ca; resources@mennonitechurch.ca
www.mennonitechurch.ca
Also Known As: Conference of Mennonites in Canada
Overview: A medium-sized national charitable organization founded in 1903
Chief Officer(s):
Robert J. Suderman, General Secretary
rjsuderman@mennonitechurch.ca
Finances: *Funding Sources:* Donations
Staff: 40 staff member(s)
Membership: 33,000 baptized believers in 225 congregations & 5 area conferences
Activities: *Library:* Resource Centre
Description: To form a people of God; To become a global church; To grow leaders

Mennonite Economic Development Associates Canada
#I-106, 155 Frobisher Dr., Waterloo ON N2V 2E4 Canada
Tel: 519-725-1633; *Fax:* 519-725-9083
Toll-Free: 800-665-7026
meda@meda.org
www.meda.org
Also Known As: MEDA Canada
Overview: A medium-sized international charitable organization founded in 1953
Finances: *Annual Operating Budget:* $1.5 Million-$3 Million
Membership: 3,000 Canada & US
Activities: *Library:* Library by appointment
Description: To be committed to the nurture & expression of Christian faith in a business setting; To enable members to integrate biblical values & business principles in their daily lives; To address the needs of the disadvantaged through programs of economic development

Mennonite Foundation of Canada (MFC)
#12, 1325 Markham Rd., Winnipeg MB R3T 4J6 Canada
Tel: 204-488-1985; *Fax:* 204-488-1986
Toll-Free: 800-772-3257
contact@mennofoundation.ca
www.mennofoundation.ca
Overview: A medium-sized national charitable organization founded in 1974
Finances: *Annual Operating Budget:* $500,000-$1.5 Million
Staff: 12 staff member(s)
Membership: 24; *Member Profile:* Representatives of 7 conferences
Activities: *Speaker Service:* Yes *Library:* Yes (Open to Public)
Description: The Foundation was established to accumulate, manage & distribute financial resources exclusively for charitable purposes, as a means, for example, of supporting the Mennonite Community by providing loans to churches & related organizations. Resources provide stewardship education &

service from an Anabaptist perspective. It is a registered charity, BN: 129253308RR0001.
Affiliation(s): Mennonite Church Canada; Evangelical Mennonite Mission Conference; Mennonite Church Eastern Canada; Northwest Mennonite Conference; Evangelical Mennonite Conference; Chortitzer Mennonite Conference; Evangelical Missionary Church of Canada

Northwest Mennonite Conference
PO Box 1316, 2025 - 20 Ave., Didsbury AB T0M 0W0 Canada
Tel: 403-335-9805; *Fax:* 403-335-9548
www.nwmc.ca
Overview: A medium-sized local organization
Chief Officer(s):
Carol Gelleny, Contact
Membership: 14 congregations; *Committees:* Congregational Ministries; Congregational Leadership; Missions & Service; Stewardship
Member of: Mennonite Church North America

Methodists

The Bible Holiness Movement / Mouvement de sainteté biblique
PO Box 223, Stn. A, Vancouver BC V6C 2M3 Canada
Tel: 250-492-3376
www.bible-holiness-movement.com
Previous Name: The Bible Holiness Mission
Overview: A medium-sized international charitable organization founded in 1949
Finances: *Annual Operating Budget:* $100,000-$250,000; *Funding Sources:* Unsolicited gifts from Christian believers
Staff: 16 staff member(s); 6 volunteer(s)
Membership: 93,658 worldwide in 89 countries; 954 Canadian; *Fees:* None
Activities: *Internships:* Yes; *Speaker Service:* Yes *Library:* Library by appointment
Description: To emphasize the original Methodist faith of salvation & scriptural holiness, with principles of discipline, non-conformity, & non-resistance, & to administer overseas indigenous missionary centres in West Africa, the Philippines, East Africa & the West Indies; South Korea, India
Member of: Christian Holiness Partnership; National Black Evangelical Association; Anti-Slavery International
Affiliation(s): Religious Freedom of Council of Christian Minorities; Christians Concerned for Racial Equality

Free Methodist Church in Canada (FMCIC) / Église méthodiste libre du Canada
4315 Village Centre Ct., Mississauga ON L4Z 1S2 Canada
Tel: 905-848-2600; *Fax:* 905-848-2603
ministrycentre@fmc-canada.org
www.fmc-canada.org
Overview: A medium-sized national organization founded in 1880
Finances: *Annual Operating Budget:* $1.5 Million-$3 Million
Staff: 11 staff member(s)
Membership: 12,000+ attendees at 144 churches
Activities: *Internships:* Yes; *Speaker Service:* Yes
Description: To make known to people everywhere God's call to wholeness through forgiveness & holiness in Jesus Christ & to invite into membership & to equip for ministry all who respond in faith; to see healthy churches within the reach of all people in Canada & beyond.
Member of: Free Methodist World Conference
Affiliation(s): Evangelical Fellowship of Canada; Canadian Council of Christian Charities; World Relief Canada

Mormonism

Church of Jesus Christ of Latter-day Saints (Mormons)
c/o Toronto Ontario Temple, 10060 Bramalea Rd., Brampton ON L6R 1A1 Canada
Tel: 905-799-1122
www.lds.org
Overview: A medium-sized national organization founded in 1830
Membership: 178,000 members + 324 congregations in Canada
Activities: *Speaker Service:* Yes *Library:* Family History Library by appointment

Pentecostal

Apostolic Church of Pentecost of Canada Inc. (ACOP) / Église apostolique de Pentecôte du Canada inc.
International Office, #119, 2340 Pegasus Way NE, Calgary AB T2E 8M5 Canada
Tel: 403-273-5777; *Fax:* 403-273-8102
acop@acop.ca
www.acop.ca
Overview: A small national licensing charitable organization founded in 1921
Finances: *Annual Operating Budget:* $1.5 Million-$3 Million; *Funding Sources:* Donations
Staff: 30 staff member(s)
Membership: 155 affiliated churches + 436 members; *Fees:* Varies
Activities: *Internships:* Yes; *Speaker Service:* Yes *Library:* Library by appointment
Description: To provide fellowship, encouragement & accountability in the proclamation of the Gospel of Jesus Christ by the Power of the Holy Spirit
Affiliation(s): Evangelical Fellowship of Canada

Church of God of Prophecy in Canada
Eastern Canada Head Office, 5145 Tomken Rd., Mississauga ON L4W 1P1 Canada
Tel: 905-625-1278; *Fax:* 905-625-1316
info@cogop.ca
www.cogop.ca
Overview: A medium-sized national charitable organization
Finances: *Annual Operating Budget:* $100,000-$250,000
Staff: 3 staff member(s)
Membership: 31 churches
Activities: *Internships:* Yes; *Speaker Service:* Yes
Description: The Church of God of Prophecy has its roots in the Holiness/Pentecostal tradition and has felt a special burden to call attention to the principle of unity in the body of Christ, while faithfully proclaiming the gospel of Jesus Christ before a watching world.

Pentecostal Assemblies of Canada (PAOC) / Assemblées de la Pentecôte du Canada
2450 Milltower Ct., Mississauga ON L5N 5Z6 Canada
Tel: 905-542-7400; *Fax:* 905-542-7313
info@paoc.org
www.paoc.org
Overview: A large national charitable organization founded in 1919
Finances: *Annual Operating Budget:* Greater than $5 Million; *Funding Sources:* Local churches; individuals
Staff: 50 staff member(s)
Membership: 1,100 churches, 3,500 pastors representing 235,000 parishoners; *Committees:* General Executive; Administrative; Overseas Missions
Activities: Task Force; Work Force; Volunteers in Mission; Short-Term Missions; Volunteers in Special Assignment; ERDO (Emergency Relief & Development Overseas); Child Care Plus; *Library:* The PAOC Archives (Open to Public) by appointment
Description: PAOC makes disciples everywhere by the proclamation & practice of the gospel of Christ in the power of the Holy Spirit with the goal to establish local congregations & to train spiritual leaders.
Affiliation(s): World Pentecost; Pentecostal/Charismatic Churches of North America; Pentecostal World Fellowship; World Assemblies of God Fellowship; Focus on the Family; Canadian Foodgrains Bank; Pentecostal European Mission; Seeds International; VisionLEDD; Canadian Council of Christian Charities; Every Home for Christ; Evangelical Missiological Society; Evangelical Fellowship of Canada; Canadian Children's Ministries Network; Canadian Bible Society; Family Life Ministries; Society of Pentecostal Studies

The Pentecostal Assemblies of Newfoundland & Labrador (PAON)
PO Box 8895, Stn. A, 57 Thorburn Rd., St. John's NL A1B 3T2 Canada
Tel: 709-753-6314; *Fax:* 709-753-4945
info@paonl.ca
www.paonl.ca
Overview: A medium-sized provincial charitable organization founded in 1911
Finances: *Annual Operating Budget:* $1.5 Million-$3 Million
Membership: 40,000
Activities: *Internships:* Yes; *Speaker Service:* Yes *Library:* Library/Resource Centre by appointment
Description: To promote evangelism, world missions, famine relief, & education
Affiliation(s): Pentecostal Fellowship of North America

Protestants

Grand Orange Lodge of Canada
94 Sheppard Ave. West, Toronto ON M2N 1M5 Canada
Tel: 416-223-1690; *Fax:* 416-223-1324
Toll-Free: 800-565-6248
secretary@grandorangelodge.ca
www.grandorangelodge.ca
Also Known As: Loyal Orange Association
Previous Name: The Grand Orange Lodge of British America
Overview: A large national organization founded in 1830
Finances: *Annual Operating Budget:* Less than $50,000; *Funding Sources:* Membership dues
Staff: 8 staff member(s)
Membership: 100,000; *Fees:* Schedule; *Member Profile:* Protestant faith
Activities: *Awareness Events:* Annual Golf Tournament
Description: To encourage its members to actively participate in the Protestant church of their choice; to actively support the Canadian system of government; to anticipate legislation & its impact on the civil & religious liberties of all Canadians; to provide social activities which will enrich the lives of its members; to participate in benevolent activities which will enrich our communities & our country
Member of: Imperial Orange Council of the World

Operation Mobilization Canada (OM)
84 West St., Port Colborne ON L3K 4C8 Canada
Tel: 905-835-2546; *Fax:* 905-835-2533
Toll-Free: 877-487-7777
info@cdn.om.org
www.omcanada.org
Overview: A small international charitable organization founded in 1966
Finances: *Annual Operating Budget:* $1.5 Million-$3 Million
Staff: 25 staff member(s)
Activities: *Speaker Service:* Yes *Library:* Library
Description: Missionary training movement operating in 80 countries with 6,000 people in program every year; mobilizes & trains young Protestant believers for mission fields.
Member of: Evangelical Fellowship of Canada; Canadian Council of Christian Charities

Taoism

Fung Loy Kok Institute of Taoism
1376 Bathurst St., 2nd Fl., Toronto ON M5R 3J1 Canada
Tel: 416-656-2110; *Fax:* 416-654-3937
fungloykok@ttcs.org
Overview: A small international organization

Unitarian

Canadian Unitarian Council (CUC) / Conseil unitarien du Canada
#018, 1179A King St. West, Toronto ON M6K 3C5 Canada
Tel: 416-489-4121; *Fax:* 416-489-9010
info@cuc.ca
www.cuc.ca
Also Known As: Unitarian Church
Overview: A medium-sized national charitable organization founded in 1961
Finances: *Annual Operating Budget:* $250,000-$500,000; *Funding Sources:* Donations; membership dues
Staff: 6 staff member(s); 20 volunteer(s)
Membership: 50 institutional + 25 individual; *Fees:* $80 individual; congregations - assessment per member; *Committees:* Lay & Chaplaincy; Social Responsibility
Activities: *Library:* CUC Library by appointment
Publications: The Canadian Unitarian
Frequency: 3 pa *Accepts Advertising ISSN:* 0527-9860 *Price:* Free for members of CUC congregations; $15 non-members
Canadian Unitarian Council National Directory
Type: Directory *Price:* Free for members of CUC congregations
Description: To enhance, nurture & promote Unitarian & Universalist religion in Canada; to provide support for religious exploration, spiritual growth & social responsibility
Affiliation(s): International Association for Religious Freedom; International Council of Unitarians & Universalists

First Unitarian Congregation of Toronto
175 St.Clair Ave. West, Toronto ON M4V 1P7 Canada
Tel: 416-924-9654; *Fax:* 416-924-9655
administrator@firstunitariantoronto.org
www.firstunitariantoronto.org
Overview: A small national charitable organization founded in 1845
Finances: *Annual Operating Budget:* $250,000-$500,000
Staff: 9 staff member(s); 25 volunteer(s)
Membership: 306 individual
Activities: *Internships:* Yes *Library:* Library by appointment

Description: To serve the religious needs of those who embrace Unitarian Universalist principles, who respect the free exercise of private judgment in all matters of belief & who live in the Metropolitan Toronto area
Member of: Canadian Unitarian Council

USC Canada
#705, 56 Sparks St., Ottawa ON K1P 5B1 Canada
Tel: 613-234-6827; *Fax:* 613-234-6842
Toll-Free: 800-565-6872
info@usc-canada.org
www.usc-canada.org
Also Known As: Unitarian Service Committee of Canada
Overview: A medium-sized international charitable organization founded in 1945
Chief Officer(s):
Jackie Boisvenue, Media Relations Officer
Lise Latrémouille, Director, International Programs
Ron Cross, Communications Officer
Francine Longtin, Director, Finance and Administration
Susan Walsh, Executive Director
Finances: *Annual Operating Budget:* Greater than $5 Million; *Funding Sources:* Support from the general public; bequests; foundations & corporations; investment income; government
Staff: 22 staff member(s)
Membership: 1,000; *Member Profile:* Membership is offered to individuals supporting USC through volunteer or financial means; *Committees:* Finance; Executive; Programs
Activities: Communications/Media Program; Development Education Program to raise awareness about development issues & their impact on our lives in Canada; Fundraising & Volunteer Program; Overseas Program to work in partnership with people in the developing world to build self-reliant communities; *Speaker Service:* Yes; *Rents Mailing List:* Yes *Library:* Library by appointment
Description: Committed to enhancing human development through an international partnership of people linked in the challenge to reduce poverty
Member of: Canadian Council for International Cooperation

United Church of Christ

Affirm United / S'affirmer Ensemble
PO Box 57057, Stn. Somerset, Ottawa ON K1R 1A1 Canada
affirmunited@affirmunited.ca
www.affirmunited.ca
Overview: A medium-sized national organization founded in 1982
Chief Officer(s):
Read Sherman, Communications Coordinator
Finances: *Annual Operating Budget:* Less than $50,000
Staff: 20 volunteer(s)
Membership: 500 individual; *Fees:* $40 individual/household; $100 institutional
Activities: *Speaker Service:* Yes
Description: To affirm gay, lesbian, bisexual & transgender people & their friends, within The United Church of Canada; to provide a network of supports among affirming ministries & regional groups; to act as a point of contact for individuals; to speak to the church in a united fashion encouraging it to act prophetically & pastorally both within & beyond the church structure.
Affiliation(s): United Church of Canada

Boys & Girls Clubs of Alberta
J. Percy Page Centre, 11759 Groat Rd., Edmonton AB T5M 3K6 Canada
Tel: 780-415-1734; *Fax:* 780-415-1737
www.bgccan.com/clubresults.asp?l=e&location=ab
Social Media: www.facebook.com/group.php?gid=24403790656
Overview: A medium-sized provincial organization
Finances: *Annual Operating Budget:* $100,000-$250,000
Staff: 2 staff member(s)
Membership: 15,000-49,999
Activities: Counselling; conflict resolution training; street safety
Description: The Clubs offer educational, recreational & skills development programs & services to children from pre-school to young adulthood. Activities are scheduled after school, evenings & weekends, providinge a safe, supportive place where children & youth can build positive relationships, & develop confidence & skills.
Member of: Boys & Girls Clubs of Canada

Boys & Girls Clubs of Manitoba
Central Region, #204, 7100 Woodbine Ave., Markham ON L3R 5J2 Canada
Tel: 416-535-9675; *Fax:* 905-477-2056
www.bgccan.com/clubresults.asp?l=e&location=mb
Overview: A medium-sized provincial organization
Chief Officer(s):
Sandra Morris, Central Region Director
smorris@bgccan.com
Brittany Tough, Central Region Coordinator
btough@bgccan.comm
Activities: Counselling; conflict resolution training; street safety
Description: The Clubs offer educational, recreational & skills development programs & services to children from pre-school to young adulthood. Activities are scheduled after school, evenings & weekends, providinge a safe, supportive place where children & youth can build positive relationships, & develop confidence & skills.
Member of: Boys & Girls Clubs of Canada

Boys & Girls Clubs of New Brunswick
Maritime Region, c/o #204, 7100 Woodbine Ave., Markham ON L3R 5J2 Canada
Tel: 902-469-1550
www.bgccan.com/clubresults.asp?l=e&location=nb
Overview: A medium-sized provincial organization
Activities: Counselling; conflict resolution training; street safety
Description: The Clubs offer educational, recreational & skills development programs & services to children from pre-school to young adulthood. Activities are scheduled after school, evenings & weekends, providinge a safe, supportive place where children & youth can build positive relationships, & develop confidence & skills.
Member of: Boys & Girls Clubs of Canada

Boys & Girls Clubs of Québec / Clubs garçons et filles du Québec
Region de Québec, c/o #204, 7100 Woodbine Ave., Markham ON L3R 5J2 Canada
Tél: 905-477-7272; *Téléc:* 905-477-2056
www.bgccan.com/clubresults.asp?l=e&location=qc
Aperçu: *Dimension:* moyenne; *Envergure: provinciale*
Membre de: Boys & Girls Clubs of Canada

Boys & Girls Clubs of Saskatchewan
J. Percy Page Centre, 11759 Groat Rd., Edmonton AB T5M 3K6 Canada
Tel: 780-415-1734; *Fax:* 780-415-1737
Toll-Free: 877-615-1734
www.bgccan.com/clubresults.asp?l=e&location=sk
Overview: A medium-sized provincial organization
Finances: *Annual Operating Budget:* $100,000-$250,000
Staff: 2 staff member(s)
Activities: Counselling; conflict resolution training; street safety
Description: The Clubs offer educational, recreational & skills development programs & services to children from pre-school to young adulthood. Activities are scheduled after school, evenings & weekends, providinge a safe, supportive place where children & youth can build positive relationships, & develop confidence & skills.
Member of: Boys & Girls Clubs of Canada

Boys & Girls Clubs of Yukon
Pacific Region, PO Box 20222, 1434 Graham St., Kelowna BC V1Y 9H2 Canada
Tel: 250-762-3914; *Fax:* 250-762-6562
www.bgccan.com/clubresults.asp?l=e&location=yt
Overview: A medium-sized provincial organization
Activities: Counselling; conflict resolution training; street safety
Description: The Clubs offer educational, recreational & skills development programs & services to children from pre-school to young adulthood. Activities are scheduled after school, evenings & weekends, providinge a safe, supportive place where children & youth can build positive relationships, & develop confidence & skills.
Member of: Boys & Girls Clubs of Canada

KAIROS: Canadian Ecumenical Justice Initiatives / Initiatives canadiennes oecuméniques pour la justice
#200, 310 Dupont St., Toronto ON M5R 1V9 Canada
Tel: 416-463-5312; *Fax:* 416-463-5569
Toll-Free: 877-403-8933
info@kairoscanada.org
www.kairoscanada.org
Social Media: www.twitter.com/kairoscanada
Previous Name: Ecumenical Coalition for Economic Justice; GATT-Fly
Overview: A small national organization founded in 1973
Finances: *Annual Operating Budget:* $100,000-$250,000
Staff: 4 staff member(s)
Fees: $100
Activities: *Speaker Service:* Yes
Description: To undertake a program of research & action with churches & popular groups emphasizing coalition-building & social transformation; five churches have participated in the Coalition since its inception: the Anglican Church of Canada, the Canadian Conference of Catholic Bishops, the Evangelical Lutheran Church in Canada, the Presbyterian Church in Canada, the United Church of Canada
Member of: Action Canada Network
Affiliation(s): Canadian Council of Churches

Manitoba CGIT Association
PO Box 52073, Winnipeg MB R2M 5P9 Canada
Tel: 204-254-2378
cgit@cgitmanitoba.ca
Also Known As: Canadian Girls in Training - Manitoba
Previous Name: National CGIT Association - Manitoba & Northwestern Ontario
Overview: A small local organization

Maritime Regional CGIT Committee
PO Box 383, Pictou NS B0K 1H0 Canada
Tel: 902-485-4011
g.cmacdonald@ns.sympatico.ca
Also Known As: Canadian Girls in Training - Maritimes
Previous Name: National CGIT Association - Maritime Regional Committee
Overview: A small local organization
Chief Officer(s):
Chris MacDonald, Contact

National Alliance of Covenanting Congregations (NACC)
489 East Osborne Rd., North Vancouver BC V7N 1M4 Canada
Tel: 604-987-9876; *Fax:* 604-987-9835
geoff@unitedrenewal.org
www.unitedrenewal.org
Overview: A large national charitable organization founded in 1991
Chief Officer(s):
Geoff Wilkins, Chair
Finances: *Annual Operating Budget:* $50,000-$100,000; *Funding Sources:* Donations
Staff: 1 volunteer(s)
Membership: 100 congregations; 15,000 members; *Member Profile:* All congregational members; spectrum of congregations rural to urban, coast to coast
Activities: *Speaker Service:* Yes *Library:* NACC Resources/Yoke Study Centre (Open to Public)
Publications: NACC [National Alliance of Covenanting Congregations] News Briefs
Type: Newsletter *Frequency:* q. *Editor:* Geoff Wilkins
Description: To offer support & fellowship to United Churches wishing to uphold traditional theology & to work for reform & renewal in the United Church of Canada
Affiliation(s): United Church of Canada

Ontario CGIT Association
PO Box 371, Norwich ON N0J 1P0 Canada
Tel: 519-863-6760; *Fax:* 519-863-6760
ontario@cgit.ca
www.cgit.ca
Also Known As: Canadian Girls in Training - Ontario
Previous Name: National CGIT Association - Ontario
Overview: A small provincial charitable organization founded in 1915
Finances: *Annual Operating Budget:* Less than $50,000
Staff: 1 staff member(s); 150 volunteer(s)
Membership: 350; *Member Profile:* Teen girls & adult women; *Committees:* Leadership Training; Camps; Publicity & Promotion
Activities: Leadership training weekend; camp council leadership training for senior girls; Red Maple Leaf Program
Affiliation(s): The United Church of Canada; The Presbyterian Church in Canada

Provincial CGIT Board of BC
c/o J. Grinnell, 13780 Hill Rd., Ladysmith BC V9G 1G7 Canada
Tel: 250-245-4016
grinncon@nanaimo.ark.com
Also Known As: Canadian Girls in Training - BC
Previous Name: National CGIT Association - BC Provincial Board
Overview: A small provincial organization

Saskatchewan CGIT Committee
3624 - 28th Ave., Regina SK S4S 2N6 Canada
saskcgit@accesscomm.ca
www.cgit.ca/saskatchewan
Also Known As: Canadian Girls in Training - Saskatchewan
Previous Name: National CGIT Association - Saskatchewan Committee
Overview: A small provincial organization
Chief Officer(s):
Alice Monks, Chair

SECTION 15
SPORTS

Associations & Organizations

Aquatic Sports

American & Canadian Underwater Certification Inc.
379 West St., Brantford, ON N3R 3V9, Canada
Tel: 519-750-5767; *Fax:* 519-750-5769
acuchq@acuc.ca
www.acuc.es
Affiliation(s): World Diving Federation; Undersea Hyperbaric Medical Society
Nancy Hilton, Office Manager
R.W. Cronkwright, President
Marg Cronkwright, Vice-President

Aquatic Federation of Canada / Fédération canadienne des sports aquatiques
4 Calgary St., St. John's, NL A1A 3W2, Canada
Tel: 709-753-2398; *Fax:* 709-753-2398
whogan@nl.rogers.com
www.swimming.ca/AFC.aspx
Affiliation(s): Synchro Canada; Canadian Amateur Diving Association Inc.; Water Polo Canada; Swimming Canada
Bill Hogan, President

Athabasca Landing Pool Association (ALPA)
4705 - 48th Ave., Athabasca, AB T9S 1R3, Canada
Tel: 780-675-5656; *Fax:* 780-675-4700
athpool@telusplanet.net
Jaymie Mullin, Manager
Alan Fisher, President

Canadian Aquafitness Leaders Alliance Inc. (CALA)
125 Lilian Dr., Toronto, ON M1R 3W6, Canada
Tel: 416-751-9823; *Fax:* 416-755-1832
Toll-Free: 888-751-9823
cala_aqua@mac.com
www.calainc.org
Affiliation(s): CanFitPro; BCRPA; Ontario Fitness Council; Go50 (UK); AGEconcern (UK); LEAD (Ger.); Univ. of Stellenbosch (SA); H2Oz (Aus.)
Charlene Kopansky, President

Water Polo Canada (WPC)
#12, 1010 Polytek St., Gloucester, ON K1G 9H9, Canada
Tel: 613-748-5682; *Fax:* 613-748-5777
dvilleneuve@waterpolo.ca
www.waterpolo.ca
Affiliation(s): Aquatic Federation of Canada
Debbie Villeneuve, Manager of Administration

Archery

Alberta Bowhunters Association (ABA)
c/o Mark Walliser, #8, 7957 - 49 Ave., Red Deer, AB T4P 2V5, Canada
www.bowhunters.ca
Brent Watson, President
Gun Lemke, Secretary

Archers Association of Nova Scotia (AANS)
NS, Canada
president@aans.ca
www.aans.ca
Lindsey Poehl, President

Archery Association of New Brunswick (AANB)
1003 Duckcove Lane, Saint John, NB E2M 3G3, Canada
Tel: 506-647-5766
contact@archerynb.ca
www.archerynb.ca
Robert McIntyre, Provincial President

Fédération de tir à l'arc du Québec (FTAQ)
CP 1000, Succ. M, 4545, av Pierre-de Coubertin, Montréal, QC H1V 3R2, Canada
Tél: 514-252-3054; *Téléc:* 514-252-3165
ftaq@ftaq.qc.ca
www.ftaq.qc.ca
Gabriela Cosovan, Directrice technique

Federation of Canadian Archers Inc. (FCA) / Fédération canadienne des archers inc.
#108, 2255 St. Laurent Blvd., Ottawa, ON K1G 4K3, Canada
Tel: 613-260-2113; *Fax:* 613-260-2114
information@fca.ca
www.fca.ca
Kathleen Millar, Executive Director
Roger Murray, President

International Archery Federation (IAF) / Fédération internationale de tir à l'arc (FITA)
Maison du Sport International, Avenue de Rhodanie 54, Lausanne, 1007, Switzerland
Tel: 41-21-614-3050; *Fax:* 41-21-614-3055
info@archery.org
www.archery.org
Affiliation(s): Federation of Canadian Archers Inc.
Ugur Erdener, President
Tom Dielen, Secretary General

Moncton Archers & Bowhunters Association
99 West Lane, Coal Branch, NB E4T 4K1, Canada
Tel: 506-785-9806
spencers@nb.sympatico.ca
Affiliation(s): New Brunswick Archery Association; Canadian Archery Association
Charles Spencer, President

Ontario Association of Archers Inc. (OAA)
PO Box 45, Stn. Caledon Village, Caledon, ON L7K 3L3, Canada
Tel: 519-927-3256; *Fax:* 519-927-9137
info@oaa-archery.on.ca
www.oaa-archery.on.ca
Adam Thomas, President
Cathy Fischer, Secretary

Saskatchewan Archery Association (SAA)
PO Box 5, RR#2, Site 6, Craven, SK S0G 0W0, Canada
Tel: 306-775-0385
rlakeman.coram@sasktel.net
www.saskarchery.com
Robert Lakeman, President

Arm Wrestling

World Arm Wrestling Federation
135 - 29th St. East, Prince Albert, SK S6V 1Y5, Canada
Tel: 306-763-0899
fred.roy@sasktel.net
waf.homestead.com

Athletics

Association régionale du sport collégial de l'Ile de Montréal (ARSCIM)
a/s FQSE, CP 1000, Succ. M, 4545, av Pierre-de-Coubertin, Montréal, QC H1V 3R2, Canada
Tél: 514-252-3300; *Téléc:* 514-254-3292
infos@arscim.qc.ca
www.arscim.qc.ca
Robert Dussault, Directeur général

Association régionale du sport étudiant de l'Abitibi-Témiscamingue (ARSEAT)
375, ave. Centrale, Val-d'Or, QC J9P 1P4, Canada
Tél: 819-825-2047; *Téléc:* 819-825-0125
Ligne sans frais: 866-626-2047
mlangelier@ulsat.qc.ca
www.ulsat.qc.ca/lsat/pages/sportetudiant.php
Affiliation(s): Fédération québécoise du sport étudiant
Pierre Boulerice, Président
Serge Hurtubise, Vice-président

Association régionale du sport étudiant de la Côte-Nord (ARSECN)
110, rue Comeau, Sept-Iles, QC G4R 1J4, Canada
Tél: 418-968-3731; *Téléc:* 418-968-4033
sport.etudiant.cn@globetrotter.net
sportetudiantcotenord.qc.ca
Gilles Briand, Président

Association régionale du sport étudiant de la Mauricie (ARSEM)
260, rue Dessureault, Trois-Rivières, QC G8T 9T9, Canada
Tél: 819-693-5805; *Téléc:* 819-693-1189
www.arsem.qc.ca
Micheline Guillemette, Directrice générale

Association régionale du sport étudiant de Laval
#221, 3235, St-Martin Est, Laval, QC H7E 5G8, Canada
Tél: 450-664-1917; *Téléc:* 450-664-7832
info@sportslaval.qc.ca
www.sportslaval.qc.ca
Richard Courteau, Directeur général

Association régionale du sport étudiant de Québec et Chaudière-Appalaches (ARSEQCA)
2450, ch Ste-Foy, Québec, QC G1V 1T2, Canada
Tél: 418-657-7678; *Téléc:* 418-657-1367
mleclerc@sportetudiant.qc.ca
www.sportetudiant.qc.ca
Daniel Veilleux, Directeur général

Association régionale du sport étudiant du Richelieu (ARSER)
École secondaire Gérard-Filion, 1330, boul. Curé-Poirier Ouest, Longueuil, QC J4K 2G8, Canada
Tél: 450-463-4055; *Téléc:* 450-463-4229
sport_etudiant@csmv.qc.ca
www.arser.qc.ca/site/index.html
Sylvie Cornellier, Directrice générale

Association régionale du sport étudiant Lac Saint-Louis
2900, rue Lake, Dollard-des-Ormeaux, QC H9B 2P1, Canada
Tél: 514-855-4230; *Téléc:* 514-685-4643
administration@arselsl.qc.ca
www.arselsl.qc.ca
Serge Bélanger, Directeur général

Association régionale du sport étudiant Laurentides-Lanaudière
430, boul. Arthur-Sauvé, Saint-Eustache, QC J7R 6V6, Canada
Tél: 450-419-8786; *Téléc:* 450-419-8892
ginette.laforest@cssmi.qc.ca
www7.cssmi.qc.ca/sportell
Jacinthe Lussier, Directrice générale

Athletics Alberta
Percy Page Centre, 11759 Groat Rd., Edmonton, AB T5M 3K6, Canada
Tel: 780-427-8792; *Fax:* 780-427-8899
info@athleticsalberta.com
www.athleticsalberta.com
Peter Ogilvie, Executive Director
Sheryl Mack, Office Manager

Athletics Manitoba
#214, 200 Main St., Winnipeg, MB R3C 4M2, Canada
Tel: 204-925-5743; *Fax:* 204-925-5792
office@athleticsmanitoba.com
www.athleticsmanitoba.com
Rob Guy, Managing Director

Athletics New Brunswick (ANB) / Athlétisme du Nouveau-Brunswick
Tel: 506-457-4122; *Fax:* 506-325-9420
ncactm@nb.aibn.com
www.anb.ca
Annette Wetmore, Secretary
Harold Nicholson, President

Athletics Nova Scotia
5516 Spring Garden Rd, 4th Fl., Halifax, NS B3J 1G6, Canada
Tel: 902-425-5450; *Fax:* 902-425-5606
athletics@sportnovascotia.ca
www.athleticsnovascotia.ca
Jonathan Brill, Executive-Chair
Dan Bainard, CEO

Athletics PEI
55 Villa Ave., Charlottetown, PE C1A 2B2, Canada
Tel: 902-566-6861; *Fax:* 902-368-4548
Barrie Stanfield, Treasurer

Athletics Yukon
4061 - 4th Ave., Whitehorse, YT Y1A 1H1, Canada
Tel: 867-668-2545
info@athleticsyukon.ca
www.athleticsyukon.ca
Chris Locke, President

British Columbia Athletics
#120, 3820 Cessna Dr., Richmond, BC V7B 0A2, Canada
Tel: 604-333-3550; *Fax:* 604-333-3551
bcathletics@bcathletics.org
www.bcathletics.org
Brian McCalder, President & CEO

Canadian Wheelchair Basketball Association (CWBA) / Association canadienne de basketball en fauteuil roulant (ACBFR)
#B2, 2211 Riverside Dr., Ottawa, ON K1H 7X5, Canada
Tel: 613-260-1296; *Fax:* 613-260-1456
Toll-Free: 877-843-2922
info@wheelchairbasketball.ca
www.wheelchairbasketball.ca

Affiliation(s): Canada Basketball
Wendy Gittens, Executive Director
Steven Bach, President

Fédération québécoise d'athlétisme (FQA)
CP 1000, Succ. M, 4545, av Pierre-de Coubertin, Montréal, QC H1V 3R2, Canada
Tél: 514-252-3041; *Téléc:* 514-252-3042
fqa@athletisme.qc.ca
www.athletisme.qc.ca
Jean-Paul Baert, Directeur général

Greater Montreal Athletic Association (GMAA) / Association régionale du sport scolaire
#101, 5925, av Monkland, Montréal, QC H4A 1G7, Canada
Tel: 514-482-8555; *Fax:* 514-487-0121
gmaa@gmaa.ca
www.gmaa.ca
Don McEwen, Executive Director

National Association of Collegiate Directors of Athletics (NACDA)
PO Box 16428, 24651 Detroit Rd., Westlake, Cleveland, OH 44116, USA
Tel: 440-892-4000; *Fax:* 440-892-4007
www.nacda.com
Mike Cleary, Executive Director

Newfoundland & Labrador Athletics Association (NLAA)
PO Box 21406, RPO MacDonald Dr., St. John's, NL A1A 5G6, Canada
Tel: 709-576-1303; *Fax:* 709-576-7493
athletics@nlaa.ca
www.nlaa.ca
Affiliation(s): Athletics North-East; Mariners Athletics Club; Nautilus Running Club; New World Running Club; Pearlgate T&F Club; Trappers Running Club; Trinity-Conception Athletics Club; Westerland Track Club
Bob Walsh, President
Alison Walsh, Treasurer
George Stanoev, Technical Director

Ontario Track & Field Association (OTFA)
#211, 3 Concorde Gate, Toronto, ON M3C 3N7, Canada
Tel: 416-426-7215; *Fax:* 416-426-7358
ontrack@eol.ca
www.otfa.ca
Bill Stephens, Chair

Saskatchewan Athletics
2020 College Dr., Saskatoon, SK S7N 2W4, Canada
Tel: 306-664-6744; *Fax:* 306-664-6761
athletics@sasktel.net
www.saskathletics.ca
Bob Reindl, Executive Director
Janine Platana, Admin Assistant

World Masters Athletics
Via Padre Leopoldo da Castel-Nuovo 1, Assenza di Brenzon, I-370 10, Italy
info@world-masters-athletics.org
www.world-masters-athletics.org

Automobile Racing

Motorsport Club of Ottawa (MCO) / Club des sports moteur d'Ottawa
PO Box 65006, RPO Merivale Mall, Nepean, ON K2G 5Y3, Canada
Tel: 613-788-0525
registrar@mco.org
www.mco.org
Affiliation(s): ASN Canada FIA; CASC-OR; Rallysport Ontario
Pat McDermott, President

Toronto Autosport Club (TAC)
#1214, 2267 Lakeshore Dr. West, Toronto, ON M8V 3X2, Canada
president@torontoautosportclub.ca
www.torontoautosportclub.ca
Dietmar Seelemnayer, President

Aviation

Canada's Aviation Hall of Fame (CAHF)
c/o Reynolds-Alberta Museum, PO Box 6360, Wetaskiwin, AB T9A 2G1, Canada
Tel: 780-361-1351; *Fax:* 780-361-1239
cahf@telusplanet.net
www.cahf.ca
John Holding, Chair
David R. Crone, Curator
Julie Stalker, Administrator

Badminton

Badminton Alberta
c/o Alberta Badminton Centre, 60 Patterson Blvd. SW, Calgary, AB T3H 2E1, Canada
Tel: 403-297-2722; *Fax:* 403-297-2706
Toll-Free: 888-397-2722
info@badmintonalberta.ca
www.badmintonalberta.ca
Jeff Bell, Executive Director

Badminton BC
#252, 3820 Cessna Dr., Richmond, BC V7B 0A2, Canada
Tel: 604-333-3595; *Fax:* 604-333-3594
Toll-Free: 800-483-2473
info@badmintonbc.com
www.badmintonbc.com
Brock Turner, Executive Director
Ken Thiesen, Operations & Programs Manager

Badminton Canada
#99, 2201 Riverside Dr., Ottawa, ON K1H 8K9, Canada
Tel: 613-569-2424; *Fax:* 613-569-3232
badminton@badminton.ca
www.badminton.ca
Affiliation(s): International Badminton Federation
Sonia Blanchard, Office Administrator
Kyle Hunter, Executive Director

Badminton New Nouveau Brunswick
PO Box 355, Stn. Main, Bathurst, NB E2A 3Z3, Canada
Tel: 506-783-4654
badminton@bnnb.ca
www.bnnb.ca
Maurice Boudreau, President
Daryl Beers, Executive Director

Badminton Newfoundland & Labrador Inc.
PO Box 21248, #213, 810 East White Hills Rd., St. John's, NL A1A 5B2, Canada
Tel: 709-576-7606; *Fax:* 709-576-7493
badminton@sportnl.ca
www.sportnl.ca/badminton/index.html
Janice Reid Boland, Executive Director

Badminton Québec
4940, rue Hochelaga est, Montréal, QC H1V 1E7, Canada
Tél: 514-252-3066; *Téléc:* 514-252-3175
badmintonquebec@videotron.ca
www.badmintonquebec.com
Maryse Bellavance, Directrice générale

International Badminton Federation (IBF)
Stadium Badminton Kuala Lumpur, Batu 3 «, Jalan Cheras, Kuala Lumpur, 56000, Malaysia
Tel: 603-9283 7155; *Fax:* 603-9284 71553
bwf@internationalbadminton.org
www.internationalbadminton.org
Kang Young Joong, President

Manitoba Badminton Association
200 Main St., Winnipeg, MB R3C 4M2, Canada
Tel: 204-925-5679; *Fax:* 204-925-5703
Toll-Free: 888-243-0890
badminton@shawbiz.ca
www.badminton.mb.ca
Ron Waterman, President
Connie Blamie, Executive Director

Nova Scotia Badminton Association
5516 Spring Garden Rd., Halifax, NS B3J 1G6, Canada
Tel: 902-425-5450; *Fax:* 902-425-5606
nsbadminton@sportnovascotia.ca
www.nsba.ca
Jennifer Petrie, Executive Director
Linda Pride, President

NWT Badminton Association
4407 School Draw Ave., Yellowknife, NT X1A 2K2, Canada
Tel: 867-669-2606
jimu@ssimicro.com
www.nwtbadminton.yk.com
Jim Umpherson, President

Ontario Badminton Association (OBA)
#209, 3 Concorde Gate, Toronto, ON M3C 3N7, Canada
Tel: 416-426-7192; *Fax:* 416-426-7346
info@ontariobadminton.on.ca
www.ontariobadminton.on.ca
Affiliation(s): Badminton Canada; Badminton World Federation
Val Butler, Executive Director

Prince Edward Island Badminton Association
c/o Sport PEI, PO Box 302, Charlottetown, PE C1A 7K7, Canada
Tel: 902-368-4262; *Fax:* 902-368-4548
Dawna Woodside, President

Saskatchewan Badminton Association (SBA)
3615 Pasqua St., Regina, SK S4S 6W8, Canada
Tel: 306-780-9368; *Fax:* 306-780-9369
saskbadminton@sasktel.net
www.saskbadminton.ca
Frank Gaudet, Executive Director

Yukon Badminton Association
4061 - 4th Ave., Whitehorse, YT Y1A 1H1, Canada
Tel: 867-668-4821
bluestone@northwestel.net
Michael Muller, President
Randy Carlson, Vice-President

Ball Hockey

British Columbia Ball Hockey Association (BCBHA)
1302 Cliveden Ave., Delta, BC V3M 6G4, Canada
Tel: 604-812-6720; *Fax:* 604-588-7760
www.bcbha.com
Affiliation(s): Canadian Ball Hockey Association
Wade Traversy, President
Kris Little, Vice-President
Rob Moxness, Secretary
Roger Sidhu, Treasurer

Canadian Ball Hockey Association / Association canadienne de hockey-balle
#5, 56 Pennsylvania Ave., Concord, ON L4K 3V9, Canada
Tel: 905-832-6200; *Fax:* 905-856-1331
info@cbha.com
www.cbha.com
Domenic de Gironimo, President

Manitoba Ball Hockey Association
200 Main St., Winnipeg, MB R3C 4M2, Canada
Tel: 204-925-5602
mbha1@hotmail.com
www.manitobaballhockey.com
Jeff Dzikowcz, President

New Brunswick Ball Hockey Association (NBBHA)
16 Reflection Lane, Quispamsis, NB E2E 6E7, Canada
Tel: 506-333-7772; *Fax:* 506-847-8585
sheila@committedtoyourgoals.com
Sheila Elliott, Contact

Newfoundland & Labrador Ball Hockey Association (NLBHA)
PO Box 2579, Stn. C, St. John's, NL A1C 6K1, Canada
Tel: 709-729-0689
paulbarron@gov.nl.ca
Paul Barron, President

Nova Scotia Ball Hockey Association
100 Auburn Drive, Dartmouth, NS B2W 3S6, Canada
Tel: 902-462-5433; *Fax:* 902-477-0243
Affiliation(s): Canadian Ball Hockey Association; Sport Nova Scotia
Bill Davidson, Contact

Ontario Ball Hockey Association (OBHA)
#5, 56 Pennsylvania Ave., Concord, ON L4K 3V9, Canada
Tel: 905-738-3320; *Fax:* 905-738-3321
www.ontarioballhockey.ca
Affiliation(s): Canadian Ball Hockey Association; International Street & Ball Hockey Association; Sport Canada; Canadian Hockey Association
Mauro Cugini, Executive Director

Québec Ball Hockey Association
#203, 5960 Jean-Talon E, St. Leonard, QC H1S 1M2, Canada
Tel: 514-251-9346; *Fax:* 514-251-8285
info@ballhockeynews.ca
www.ballhockeynews.ca
Tony Iannitto

Wild Rose Ball Hockey Association
7604 - 182 St., Edmonton, AB T5T 1Y9, Canada
Tel: 780-970-0637; *Fax:* 780-484-9957
info@wrbha.com
www.wrbha.com
Craig Thiessen, Contact

Baseball

Baseball Alberta (BA)
Percy Page Centre, 11759 Groat Rd., Edmonton, AB T5M 3K6, Canada
Tel: 780-427-8943; *Fax:* 780-427-9032
bradwolansky@baseballalberta.com
www.baseballalberta.com
Affiliation(s): Alberta Amateur Baseball Council

Baseball BC
#310, 15225 - 104th Ave., Surrey, BC V3R 6Y8, Canada
Tel: 604-586-3310; *Fax:* 604-586-3311
info@baseball.bc.ca
www.baseball.bc.ca

Baseball Canada / Fédération canadienne de baseball amateur
2212 Gladwin Cres., #A7, Ottawa, ON K1B 5N1, Canada
Tel: 613-748-5606; *Fax:* 613-748-5767
info@baseball.ca
www.baseball.ca
Affiliation(s): Canadian Olympic Association
Jim Baba, Director General
Ray Carter, President

Baseball New Brunswick (BNB) / Baseball Nouveau-Brunswick
#13, 900 Hanwell Rd., Fredericton, NB E3B 6A2, Canada
Tel: 506-451-1329; *Fax:* 506-451-1325
baseballnb2003@nb.aibn.com
www.baseballnb.ca
Affiliation(s): Sport New Brunswick; Baseball Atlantic

Baseball Nova Scotia (BNS)
5516 Spring Garden Rd., 4th Fl., Halifax, NS B3J 1J, Canada
Tel: 902-425-5450; *Fax:* 902-425-5606
www.baseballnovascotia.com
Brad Lawlor, Executive Director

Baseball Ontario
#3, 131 Sheldon Dr., Cambridge, ON N1R 6S2, Canada
Tel: 519-740-3900; *Fax:* 519-740-6311
baseball@baseballontario.com
www.baseballontario.com
Affiliation(s): Little League Ontario
Mary-Ann Smith, Administrative Director

Fédération du baseball amateur du Québec
CP 1000, Succ. M, 4545, av Pierre-de Coubertin, Montréal, QC H1V 3R2, Canada
Tél: 514-252-3075; *Téléc:* 514-252-3134
info@baseballquebec.qc.ca
www.baseballquebec.qc.ca

Little League Canada / Petite ligue Canada
235 Dale Ave., Ottawa, ON K1G 0H6, Canada
Tel: 613-731-3301; *Fax:* 613-731-2829
canada@littleleague.org
www.littleleague.ca
Roy Bergerman, President & Chair
Marthe Dubroy, Secretary
Bruce Campbell, Treasurer

Manitoba Baseball Association
200 Main St., Winnipeg, MB R3C 4M2, Canada
Tel: 204-925-5763; *Fax:* 204-925-5928
info.baseball@sport.mb.ca
www.baseballmanitoba.ca
Morgan de Peña, Executive Director

Newfoundland Baseball
83 Ashford Dr., Mount Pearl, NL A1N 3N7, Canada
Tel: 709-368-2819; *Fax:* 709-368-6080
nlbaseball@nl.rogers.com
www.sport.ca/nlbaseball
John Janes, President

Prince Edward Island Amateur Baseball Association
PO Box 302, Charlottetown, PE C1A 7K7, Canada
Tel: 902-368-4208; *Fax:* 902-368-4548
Toll-Free: 800-235-5687
kmcintosh@sportpei.pe.ca
www.baseballpei.ca
Kelsey McIntosh, Executive Director

Saskatchewan Baseball Association (SBA)
1870 Lorne St., Regina, SK S4P 2L7, Canada
Tel: 306-780-9237; *Fax:* 306-352-3669
mramage@sasktel.net
www.saskbaseball.ca
Mike Ramage, Executive Director

Basketball

Basketball Alberta
Percy Page Centre, 11759 Groat Rd., Edmonton, AB T5M 3K6, Canada
Tel: 780-427-9044; *Fax:* 780-427-9124
bballab@basketballalbert.ab.ca
www.basketballalberta.ca
Bob Mitchell, President
Brian Anstice, Vice President

Basketball BC
#310, 7155 Kingsway, Burnaby, BC V5E 2V1, Canada
Tel: 604-718-7852; *Fax:* 604-525-7762
hoopsbc@basketball.bc.ca
www.basketball.bc.ca
Michael Hind, Executive Director

Basketball Manitoba
200 Main St., Winnipeg, MB R3C 4M2, Canada
Tel: 204-925-5775; *Fax:* 204-925-5929
Toll-Free: 800-282-8069
info@basketball.mb.ca
www.basketball.mb.ca
Adam Wedlake, Executive Director

Basketball New Brunswick (BNB) / Basketball Nouveau-Brunswick
#13, 900 Hanwell Rd., Fredericton, NB E2E 6A2, Canada
Tel: 506-849-4667; *Fax:* 506-451-1325
info@basketball.nb.ca
www.basketball.nb.ca
Affiliation(s): New Brunswick Association of Approved Basketball Officials; New Brunswick Interscholastic Athletic Association
Carolyn Peppin, Executive Director
Norval McConnell, President

Basketball Nova Scotia
5516 Spring Garden Rd., 4th Fl., Halifax, NS B3J 1G6, Canada
Tel: 902-425-5450; *Fax:* 902-425-5606
bnsadmin@basketball.ns.ca
www.basketball.ns.ca
Affiliation(s): Sport Nova Scotia
Peter Halpin, President
Liam Blanchard, Executive Director

Basketball PEI
PO Box 302, 40 Enman Cres., Charlottetown, PE C1A 7K7, Canada
Tel: 902-368-4208; *Fax:* 902-368-4208
Toll-Free: 800-247-6712
info@basketballpei.ca
www.basketballpei.ca
Stephen Marchbank, Executive Director

Basketball Saskatchewan Inc. (BSI)
2205 Victoria Ave., Regina, SK S4P 0S4, Canada
Tel: 306-780-9264; *Fax:* 306-525-4009
mbarr@basketballsask.com
www.basketballsask.com
Affiliation(s): Sask Sport
Marg Barr, Executive Director

Canada Basketball
#11, 1 Westside Dr., Toronto, ON M9C 1B2, Canada
Tel: 416-614-8037; *Fax:* 416-614-9570
info@basketball.ca
www.basketball.ca
Affiliation(s): 10 provincial + 2 territorial associations; Canadian Interuniversity Athletic Union; Canadian Colleges Athletic Association; Canadian School Sports Federation; Toronto Raptors; Canadian Wheelchair Basketball Association; Canadian Association of Basketball Officials; National Association of Basketball Coaches of Canada; Women's Basketball Coaches Association
Wayne Parrish, Executive Director & CEO

Fédération de basketball du Québec (FBBQ) / Québec Basketball Federation
CP 1000, Succ. M, 4545, av Pierre-De Coubertin, Montréal, QC H1V 3R2, Canada
Tél: 514-252-3057; *Téléc:* 514-252-3357
Ligne sans frais: 866-557-3057
basket@basketball.qc.ca
www.basketball.qc.ca
Daniel Méthot, Directeur général

Newfoundland & Labrador Basketball Association
PO Box 21029, St. John's, NL A1A 5B2, Canada
Tel: 709-576-0247; *Fax:* 709-576-8787
nlba@sportnf.com
www.nlba.nf.ca
Bill Murphy, Executive Director
Roger Head, Secretary-Treasurer
Bas Kavanagh, President

Ontario Basketball
#311, 3 Concorde Gate, Toronto, ON M3C 3N7, Canada
Tel: 416-426-7200; *Fax:* 416-426-7360
info@basketball.on.ca
www.basketball.on.ca
Affiliation(s): Provincial Sports Organizations Council; Canada Basketball; Toronto Raptors Basketball Club; NBA Canada; Coaches Association of Ontario; Canadian Sports Centre; and other provincial basketball organizations
Michele O'Keefe, Executive Director
Ken Urbach, President
Greg Verner, Vice President

STARS Sports Association
PO Box 15, Okotoks, AB T1S 1A4, Canada
Tel: 403-938-3475; *Fax:* 403-938-3625
info@starsvolleyball.ca; info@starsbasketball.com

Biathlon

Biathlon Alberta
Bob Niven Training Centre, #100, 88 Canada Olympic Rd., Calgary, AB T3B 5R5
Tel: 403-202-6548; *Fax:* 403-297-2702
info@biathlon.ca
www.biathlon.ca
Ken Davies, President
Andy Holmwood, Executive Director

Biathlon Canada
#111, 2197 Riverside Dr., Ottawa, ON K1H 7X3, Canada
Tel: 613-748-5608; *Fax:* 613-748-5762
jthomson@biathloncanada.ca
www.biathloncanada.ca
Affiliation(s): International Biathlon Union; Canadian Olympic Committee
Joanne Thomson, Executive Director
Chris Lindsay, Coordinator, Technical Programs

Bicycling

Alberta Bicycle Association (ABA)
Percy Page Centre, 11759 Groat Rd., Edmonton, AB T5M 3K6, Canada
Tel: 780-427-6352; *Fax:* 780-427-6438
Toll-Free: 877-646-2453
info@albertabicycle.ab.ca
www.albertabicycle.ab.ca
Heather Lothian, Executive Director

Bicycle Newfoundland & Labrador
PO Box 2127, Stn. C, St. John's, NL A1C 5R6, Canada
Tel: 709-738-2597
admin@bnl.nf.ca
www.bnl.nf.ca
Leon Organ, President

Bicycle Nova Scotia (BNS)
5516 Spring Garden Rd., 4th Fl., Halifax, NS B3J 1G6, Canada
Tel: 902-425-5454; *Fax:* 902-425-5606
staff@bicycle.ns.ca
www.bicycle.ns.ca
Tamara Stephen, Office Administrator

Bicycle Trade Association of Canada (BTAC) / Association canadienne de l'industrie du vélo (ACIV)
17 Main St. North, Newmarket, ON L3Y 3Z6, Canada
Tel: 905-853-5031; *Fax:* 905-853-7632
Toll-Free: 866-528-2822
info@btac.org
www.btac.org
Janet O'Connell, Executive Director

Canadian Cycling Association (CCA) / Association cycliste canadienne
#203, 2197 Riverside Dr., Ottawa, ON K1H 7X3, Canada
Tel: 613-248-1353; *Fax:* 613-248-9311
general@canadian-cycling.com
www.canadian-cycling.com/
Lorraine Lafrenière, CEO

Cycling Association of the Yukon
4061, 4th Avenue, Whitehorse, YT Y1A 1H1, Canada
Tel: 867-668-4990; *Fax:* 867-668-8212
sue.richards@gov.yk.ca
Sue Richards, President

Cycling British Columbia (CBC)
#201, 210 West Broadway, Vancouver, BC V5Y 3W2, Canada
Tel: 604-737-3034; *Fax:* 604-737-3141
assist@cycling.bc.ca
www.cycling.bc.ca
Ryan Keith, Chief Executive Officer

Cycling PEI (CPEI)
Sport PEI, PO Box 302, 40 Enman Cresent, Charlottetown, PE C1A 7K7, Canada
Tel: 902-368-4985; *Fax:* 902-368-4548
mconnolly@sportpei.pe.ca
www.cpei.ca
Mike Connolly, Executive Director

Edmonton Bicycle & Touring Club (EBTC)
PO Box 52017, Stn. Garneau, Edmonton, AB T6G 2T5, Canada
Tel: 780-424-2453
info@bikeclub.ca
www.bikeclub.ca
Affiliation(s): Alberta Bicycle Association
Sid Bennett, President

Fédération québécoise des sports cyclistes (FQSC) / Québec Cycling Sports Federation
4545, av Pierre-de-Coubertin, Montréal, QC H1V 3R2, Canada
Tél: 514-252-3071; *Téléc:* 514-252-3165
reception@fqsc.net
www.fqsc.net
Affiliation(s): Association cycliste canadienne; Union cycliste internationale; Sports-Québec; Regroupement loisir Québec
Simon Thériault, Directeur technique
Louis Barbeau, Directeur général
André Michaud, Président

Ontario Cycling Association (OCA) / Association cycliste ontarienne
#307, 3 Concorde Gate, Toronto, ON M3C 3N7
Tel: 416-426-7416; *Fax:* 416-426-7349
info@ontariocycling.org; ocamagazine@ontariocycling.org
www.ontariocycling.org
Affiliation(s): Canadian Cycling Association
Duncan Vipond, President
Malcolm Eade, Vice-President, Administration & Finance
Glenn Meeuwisse, Vice-President, High Performance
Matthias Schmidt, Vice-President, Development
Jim Crosscombe, Executive Director
Denise Kelly, Director, Provincial Coaching
Chris Baskys, Coordinator, Membership
Nicky Pearson, Coordinator, BMX Growth & Development

Saskatchewan Cycling Association
2205 Victoria Ave., Regina, SK S4P 0S4, Canada
Tel: 306-780-9299; *Fax:* 306-525-4009
cycling@accesscomm.ca
www.saskcycling.ca
Wayne Walker, President

Toronto Bicycling Network
PO Box 279, #200, 131 Bloor St. West, Toronto, ON M5S 1R8, Canada
Tel: 416-760-4191
info@tbn.ca
www.tbn.ca
Brian Mclean, President

Vélo New Brunswick
536 McAllister Rd., Riverview, NB E1B 4G1, Canada
Tel: 506-474-0214
Christine.Martin@velo.nb.ca
www.velo.nb.ca
Affiliation(s): Sport New Brunswick
Kelly Murray, President
Michelle Chase, Vice-President
Sheila Colbourne, Executive Director

Vélo Québec
1251, rue Rachel est, Montréal, QC H2J 2J9, Canada
Tél: 514-521-8356; *Téléc:* 514-521-5711
Ligne sans frais: 800-567-8356
velo_quebec@velo.qc.ca
www.velo.qc.ca
Jean-François Pronovost, Directeur général

Blindness

Blind Sports Nova Scotia
c/o CNIB, 6136 Almon St., Halifax, NS B3K 1T8, Canada
Tel: 902-453-1480; *Fax:* 902-454-6570
info@blindsportsnovascotia.ca
www.blindsportsnovascotia.ca
Yvon Clement, President

Boating

Canadian International Dragon Boat Festival Society
110 Keefer St., Vancouver, BC V6A 1X4, Canada
Tel: 604-688-2382; *Fax:* 604-677-2147
www.adbf.com
Ann Phelps, General Manager

Canadian Power & Sail Squadrons (Canadian Headquarters) (CPS) / Escadrilles canadiennes de plaisance (ECP)
26 Golden Gate Ct., Toronto, ON M1P 3A5, Canada
Tel: 416-293-2438; *Fax:* 416-293-2445
Toll-Free: 888-277-2628
hgg@cps-ecp.ca
www.cps-ecp.ca
Alain Brière, Executive Director
John Gullick, Manager, Government & Special Programs

Bobsledding & Luge

Alberta Bobsleigh Association
Bob Niven Training Centre, #205, 88 Canada Olympic Rd. SW, Calgary, AB T3B 5R5, Canada
Tel: 403-297-2721; *Fax:* 403-286-7213
slide@albertabobsleigh.com
www.albertabobsleigh.com
Tim Dyrgas, President

Alberta Luge Association (ALA)
Rm 201, BNTC, 88 Canada Olympic Rd. SW, Calgary, AB T3B 5R5, Canada
Tel: 403-202-6570; *Fax:* 403-247-5497
admin@albertaluge.com
www.albertaluge.com
Affiliation(s): Canadian Luge Association
Darryl Gunn, President

Bobsleigh Canada Skeleton
140 Canada Olympic Rd. SW, Calgary, AB T3B 5R5, Canada
Tel: 403-247-5950; *Fax:* 403-247-5951
ddreher@bobsleigh.ca
www.bobsleigh.ca/
Affiliation(s): Fédération internationale de bobsleigh et de tobogganing
Shane Pearsall, Managing Director

Canadian Luge Association / Association canadienne de luge
88 Canada Olympic Rd. SW, Calgary, AB T3B 5R5, Canada
Tel: 403-202-6581; *Fax:* 403-247-8820
tfarstad@coda.ca
www.luge.ca
Tim Farstad, Executive Director

Fédération internationale de bobsleigh et de tobogganing
Via Piranesi, 44/B, Milan, 120137, Italy
Tél: 39-02-7395-1819; *Téléc:* 39-02-7000-8071
egarde@tin.it
www.fibt.com
Affiliation(s): Canadian Amateur Bobsleigh & Tobogganing Association
Ivo Ferriani, Président
Ermanno Gardella, Secrétaire général

Fédération Internationale de Luge de Course (FIL) / International Luge Federation
Rathausplatz 9, Berchtesgaden, 83471, Germany
Tél: 49-86-526-6960; *Téléc:* 49-86-526-6969
office@fil-luge.org
www.fil-luge.org
Affiliation(s): Canadian Luge Association
Josef Fendt, Président
Svein Romstad, Secrétaire général

Bowling

Alberta 5 Pin Bowlers' Association (A5-PBA)
432 - 14 St. South, Lethbridge, AB T1J 2X7, Canada
Tel: 403-320-2695; *Fax:* 403-320-2676
Toll-Free: 800-762-3075
a5pba@telusplanet.net
www.alberta5pin.com
Annette Bruneau, President

Bowling Federation of Canada / Fédération des quilles du Canada
c/o Administrator, #206, 720 Belfast Rd., Ottawa, ON K1G 0Z5, Canada
Tel: 613-744-5090; *Fax:* 613-744-2217
info@canadabowls.ca
www.canadabowls.ca
Affiliation(s): Bowling Proprietors Association of Canada; Canadian 5-pin Bowlers Association; Canadian Tenpin Federation.
Sheila Carr, Interim Administrator

Bowling Federation of Saskatchewan
#101, 1805 - 8th Ave., Regina, SK S4R 1E8, Canada
Tel: 306-780-9412; *Fax:* 306-780-9455
bowling@sasktel.net
saskbowl.com
Rhonda Sereda, Executive Director

Bowling Proprietors' Association of BC
#209, 332 Columbia St., New Westminster, BC V3L 1A6, Canada
Tel: 604-522-2990; *Fax:* 604-522-2055
bowl4fun@bowlbc.com
www.bowlbc.com
Ken Clarke, President

Bowling Proprietors' Association of Canada (BPAC)
#10A, 250 Shields Ct., Markham, ON L3R 9W7, Canada
Tel: 905-479-1560; *Fax:* 905-479-8613
info@bowlcanada.ca
www.bowlcanada.ca
Mariano Meconi, President
Paul Oliveira, Executive Director

Bowling Proprietors' Association of Ontario (BPAO)
#202, 500 Alden Rd., Markham, ON L3R 5H5, Canada
Tel: 905-940-8200
bpao@bpao.ca
www.bpao.ca
Affiliation(s): Bowling Proprietors' Association of Canada
Walter J. Valentan, Secretary
Don Gorman, President/Chair
Margaret Gorman, Administrative Assistant

Canadian 5 Pin Bowlers' Association (C5PBA) / Association canadienne des cinq quilles (AC5Q)
#206, 720 Belfast Rd., Ottawa, ON K1G 0Z5, Canada
Tel: 613-744-5090; *Fax:* 613-744-2217
c5pba@c5pba.ca
www.c5pba.ca
Affiliation(s): Bowling Federation of Canada
Sheila Carr, Executive Director
Mel Osmond, President
Don MacIver, Corporate Sec.-Treas.

Canadian Tenpin Federation, Inc. (CTF) / Fédération canadienne des dix-quilles, inc.
916 3 Ave. N., Lethbridge, AB T1H 0H3, Canada
Tel: 403-381-2830; *Fax:* 403-381-6247
www.gotenpinbowling.ca
Affiliation(s): Fédération internationale des quilleurs
Stan May, Executive Director

Fédération de pétanque du Québec
CP 1000, Succ. M, 4545, av Pierre-de Coubertin, Montréal, QC H1V 3R2, Canada
Tél: 514-252-3077
petanque@loisirquebec.qc.ca
www.petanque.qc.ca
Denise Coutu, Secrétaire administrative

Manitoba Five Pin Bowling Federation, Inc.
#219, 200 Main St., Winnipeg, MB R3C 4M2, Canada
Tel: 204-925-5766; *Fax:* 204-925-5767
Toll-Free: 800-282-8069
www.mfpbf.org
Deanne Zilinsky, Executive Director

New Brunswick Candlepin Bowlers Association
PO Box 4315, 11 Sawyer Rd., Woodstock, NB E7M 6B7, Canada
Tel: 506-328-8418
Bill Hamilton, Contact

Northwest Territories 5 Pin Bowlers' Association (NWT5PBA)
PO Box 2643, Yellowknife, NT X1A 2P9, Canada
Tel: 867-873-8189; *Fax:* 867-873-8237
gary@nwt5pba.ca
www.nwt5pba.ca
Gary Black, President

Ontario 5 Pin Bowlers' Association (O5PBA)
#302, 3 Concorde Gate, Toronto, ON M3C 3N7, Canada
Tel: 416-426-7167; *Fax:* 416-426-7364
o5pba@o5pba.ca
www.o5pba.ca
Rhonda Gifford, Program Coordinator
Harold Stoddart, Technical Director
Al Hong, Executive Director

Prince Edward Island Five Pin Bowlers Association Inc.
c/o Sport PEI, PO Box 302, Charlottetown, PE C1A 7K7, Canada
Tel: 902-368-4110; *Fax:* 902-368-4548
Toll-Free: 800-247-6712
sports@sportpei.pe.ca
www.pei5pba.com
Sue MacPherson, President

Saskatchewan 5 Pin Bowlers' Association
#100, 1805 - 8th Ave., Regina, SK S4R 1E8, Canada
Tel: 306-780-9412; *Fax:* 306-780-9455
bowling@sasktel.net
saskbowl.com
Affiliation(s): Bowling Federation of Saskatchewan
Rhonda Sereda, Executive Director

Youth Bowling Canada (YBC)
c/o Bowl Canada, #10A, 250 Shields Ct., Markham, ON L3R 9W7, Canada
Tel: 905-479-1560; *Fax:* 905-479-8613
info@bowlcanada.ca
www.youthbowling.ca; www.bowlcanada.ca
Mariano Meconi, President, Bowl Canada
Paul Oliveira, Executive Director, Bowl Canada

Boxing

Boxing Alberta
Percy Page Centre, 11759 Groat Rd., Edmonton, AB T5M 3K6, Canada
Tel: 780-427-6515; *Fax:* 780-427-1205
www.boxingalberta.com
Jim Titley, President
Dennis Belair, Executive Director

Boxing BC Association
250 Willingdon Ave., Burnaby, BC V5C 5E9, Canada
Tel: 604-291-7921; *Fax:* 604-291-7927
boxingbc@telus.net
www.boxing.bc.ca
Affiliation(s): Canadian Amateur Boxing Association
Scotty Jackson, President

Boxing Ontario
#202, 3 Concorde Gate, Toronto, ON M3C 3N7, Canada
Tel: 416-426-7250; *Fax:* 416-426-7367
info@boxingontario.com
www.boxingontario.com
Affiliation(s): Canadian Amateur Boxing Association (CABA); Association International de Boxe Amateur (AIBA); Ontario Ministry of Health Promotion
Tom Hennessey, President
Matt Kennedy, Executive Director

Boxing Saskatchewan
PO Box 4711, Regina, SK S4P 3Y3, Canada
Tel: 306-525-6678; *Fax:* 306-569-3454
skboxing@accesscomm.ca
www.boxingsask.com
Affiliation(s): Canadian Amateur Boxing Association
Frank Fiacco, President
Graham Craig, Executive Director

Calgary Boxing & Wrestling Commission (CBWC)
PO Box 2100, Stn. M #63, Calgary, AB T2P 2M5, Canada
Tel: 403-268-5367
Candy S. Schacter, Chair

Canadian Amateur Boxing Association (CABA) / Association canadienne de boxe amateur (ACBA)
888 Belfast Rd., Ottawa, ON K1G 0Z6
Tel: 613-238-7700; *Fax:* 613-238-1600
caba@boxing.ca
www.boxing.ca
Affiliation(s): International Amateur Boxing Association
Robert G. Crête, Executive Director
Daniel Trépanier, Coordinator, Technical
Michelle Ethier, Registrar & Accountant

Edmonton Combative Sports Commission (ECSC)
10250 - 101 St. NW, 13th Fl., Edmonton, AB T6J 3P4, Canada
Tel: 780-495-0382; *Fax:* 780-429-6976
ecsc.ca
Affiliation(s): Association of Boxing Commissions
Pat Reid, Executive Director

Fédération québécoise de boxe olympique (FQBO)
CP 1000, Succ. M, 4545, av Pierre-de Coubertin, Montréal, QC H1V 3R2, Canada
Tél: 514-252-3047; *Téléc:* 514-254-2144
Ligne sans frais: 866-241-3779
info@fqbo.qc.ca
www.fqbo.qc.ca
Kenneth Piché, Directeur général
Victoria Sullivan-Smith, Adjointe administrative

Manitoba Amateur Boxing Association
#302, 200 Main St., Winnipeg, MB R3C 4M2, Canada
Tel: 204-925-5658
Rosemary Broadbent

Manitoba Boxing Commission
#420, 213 Notre Dame Ave., Winnipeg, MB R3B 1N3, Canada
Tel: 204-945-8954; *Fax:* 204-945-1675
mansport@sport.mb.ca
Henry Janzen, Chair
Dan Vandal, Contact

Broomball

Alberta Broomball Association
Percy Page Centre, 11759 Groat Rd., Edmonton, AB T5M 3K6, Canada
Tel: 780-459-7668; *Fax:* 780-460-0527
neigel@telus.net
Greg Mastervick, President

British Columbia Broomball Society
c/o 5356 Lochside Dr., Victoria, BC V8Y 2G7, Canada
www.bcbroomball.ca
Rick Przybysz, President
Bruce MacRae, Sec.-Treas.

Broomball Newfoundland & Labrador
734 Birch St., Labrador City, NL A2V 1C8, Canada
Tel: 709-944-5780; *Fax:* 709-944-5780
clarkep@nf.sympatico.ca
Harold Clarke, President

Canadian Broomball Federation / Fédération canadienne de ballon sur glace
#302, 200 Main St., Winnipeg, MB R3C 4M2, Canada
Tel: 204-925-5656; *Fax:* 204-925-5703
cbfbroomball@shaw.ca
www.broomball.ca

Federation of Broomball Associations of Ontario
515 Gascon St., Russell, ON K4R 1C6, Canada
Tel: 613-445-0904; *Fax:* 613-445-9844
gerry.wever@ontariobroomball.ca
www.ontariobroomball.ca
Gerry Wever, President

Fédération québécoise de ballon sur glace
CP 1000, Succ. M, 4545, av Pierre-de Coubertin, Montréal, QC H1V 3R2, Canada
Tél: 514-252-3078; *Téléc:* 514-252-3051
info@fqbg.net
www.fqbg.net
Richard Mimeau, Président

Manitoba Amateur Broomball Association (MABA)
#305, 200 Main St., Winnipeg, MB R3C 4M2, Canada
Tel: 204-925-5668; *Fax:* 204-925-5703
Toll-Free: 866-792-7666
info@mbbroomball.com
www.mbbroomball.com
Alan Park, President
Scott Marohn, Vice President

Northwest Territories Broomball Association
Stn. 529 Range Lake Road, Yellowknife, NT X1A 3Y1, Canada
nwtbroomball@yahoo.ca
www.nwtbroomball.com
Jan Vallillee, President

Saskatchewan Broomball Association (SBA)
2205 Victoria Ave., Regina, SK S4P 0S4, Canada
Tel: 306-780-9215; *Fax:* 306-525-4009
saskbroomball@sasktel.net
www.saskbroomball.ca
Greg Perreaux, Executive Director

Canoeing & Rafting

Alberta Sprint Racing Canoe Association
11759 Groat Rd., Edmonton, AB T5M 3K6, Canada
Tel: 780-203-3987
arsca@shaw.ca
www.albertasprintcanoe.com
Rick Hill, President

Association québécoise de canoë-kayak de vitesse (AQCKV)
CP 1000, Succ. M, 4545, av Pierre-de Coubertin, Montréal, QC H1V 3R2, Canada
Tél: 514-252-3086; *Téléc:* 514-252-3094
directeur.technique@aqckv.qc.ca
www.aqckv.qc.ca
Luc Therrien, Président

Canoe Kayak New Brunswick
c/o Doug Forbes, 42 Third St., Rothesay, NB E2H 1M9, Canada
Tel: 506-849-0793
communications@canoekayaknb.org
www.canoekayaknb.org
Tim Humes, President

Canoe Kayak Nova Scotia (CKNS)
5516 Spring Garden Rd., 4th Fl., Halifax, NS B3J 1G6, Canada
Tel: 902-425-5454; *Fax:* 902-425-5606
canoens@sportnovascotia.ca
www.ckns.ca
Ike Whitehead, Administrator

Canoe Newfoundland & Labrador
PO Box 23072, Stn. Churchill Sq., St. John's, NL A1B 4J9, Canada
Tel: 709-364-1601; *Fax:* 709-368-8357
tumblehome.nfld@gmail.com
www.canoenfld.ca
Corey Locke, President

Canoe Ontario
c/o OCSRA, 570 Blenheim Cres., Oakville, ON L6J 6P6, Canada
Tel: 905-337-8314
jorlando1@cogeco.ca
www.canoeontario.ca
Affiliation(s): Ontario Canoe Sprint Racing Affiliation; Ontario Marathon Canoe Racing Association; Whitewater Ontario
John Orlando, Treasurer

CanoeKayak BC
20585 - 124A Ave., Maple Ridge, BC V2X 0M6, Canada
Tel: 604-465-5268; *Fax:* 604-460-0587
info@canoekayakbc.ca
www.canoekayakbc.ca
Mary Jane Abbot, Executive Director

CanoeKayak Canada (CKC)
#705, 2197 Riverside Dr., Ottawa, ON K1H 7X3, Canada
Tel: 613-260-1818; *Fax:* 613-260-5137
christine@canoekayak.ca
www.canoekayak.ca
Anne Merklinger, Director General
Christine Lafontaine, Administrative Coordinator

CanoeKayak Canada - Atlantic Division
c/o Sport NS, 5516 Spring Garden Rd., 4th Fl., Halifax, NS B3J 3G6, Canada
Tel: 902-425-5450; *Fax:* 902-425-5606
ccaatlantic@sportnovascotia.ca
www.ccaatlantic.ca
Liz Orton, Program Coordinator

Fédération québécoise du canot et du kayak (FQCK)
CP 1000, Succ. M, 4545, av Pierre-de Coubertin, Montréal, QC H1V 3R2, Canada
Tél: 514-252-3001; *Téléc:* 514-252-3091
info@canot-kayak.qc.ca
www.canot-kayak.qc.ca
Pierre Trudel, Directeur général

Ikaluktutiak Paddling Association
PO Box 125, Cambridge Bay, NU X0B 0C0, Canada
Tel: 867-983-2068
ipanorth69@gmail.com
Rob Harmer, President

Manitoba Paddling Association Inc. (MPA)
200 Main St., Winnipeg, MB R3C 4M2, Canada
Tel: 204-925-5678; *Fax:* 204-925-5703
mpa@sport.mb.ca; dragonboat@sport.mb.ca
www.mpa.mb.ca
Jeff Dzikowicz, Executive Director
Robin McClure, President
Marcia Hrechkosy, Secretary
Bob Hunter, Treasurer

New Brunswick Competitive Canoe Association
c/o Sport New Brunswick, 181 Kennebecasis River Rd., Hampton, NB E5N 6L1, Canada
nbcca_m@hotmail.com
J. Timothy Flood, President

Newfoundland & Labrador Paddling Association (NLPA)
103« Forest Rd., St. John's, NL A1A 1E4, Canada
Affiliation(s): Kayak Newfoundland & Labrador; Tumblehome Recreational Canoe Club
Allan Goodridge, President
Brian Hemeon, Vice-President, Canoeing
Darren MacDonald, Vice-President, Kayaking
Neil Burgess, Secretary
Alex Mcgruer, Treasurer

Paddle Manitoba
PO Box 2663, Winnipeg, MB R3C 4B3, Canada
Tel: 204-338-6722
info@paddle.mb.ca
www.paddle.mb.ca
Affiliation(s): Manitoba Paddling Association
Catherine Holmen, President

Prince Edward Island Canoe Kayak Association
RR#4, Alliston, Montague, PE C0A 1R0, Canada
Tel: 902-962-3883; *Fax:* 902-962-3883
justin.heidi@windsinc.com
www.windsinc.com/canoekayak/canoekayak.htm
Justin Richard Batten, President

Prince Edward Island Recreational Canoeing Association
PO Box 5604, RR#5, Charlottetown, PE C1A 7J8, Canada
Tel: 902-368-6355; *Fax:* 902-368-6186
Shawn Shea, Chair

Recreational Canoeing Association BC (RCABC)
1755 East 7th Ave., Vancouver, BC V5N 1S1, Canada
Tel: 604-253-5410; *Fax:* 604-253-5490
sec@bccanoe.com
www.bccanoe.com
Alan Thomson, President
Jean Chandler, Secretary

Whitewater Kayaking Association of British Columbia (WKABC)
PO Box 91549, Stn. West Vancouver, Vancouver, BC V7V 3P2, Canada
Tel: 604-515-6376
admin@whitewater.org
www.whitewater.org

Affiliation(s): Outdoor Recreation Council of BC
Don Butler, President

Whitewater Ontario
411 Carnegie Beach Rd., Port Perry, ON L9L 1B6, Canada
Tel: 905-985-4585; *Fax:* 905-985-5256
Toll-Free: 888-322-2849
info@whitewaterontario.ca
www.whitewaterontario.ca
Claudia Kerkoff, Vice-President

Yukon Canoe & Kayak Club
PO Box 40080, 3 Sitka Cres., Whitehorse, YT Y1A 6M6, Canada
Tel: 867-456-4827
current@yckc.ca
www.yckc.ca
Eyvi Smith, President

Cerebral Palsy

Canadian Cerebral Palsy Sports Association (CCPSA) / Association canadienne de sport pour paralytiques cérébraux (ACPSA)
PO Box 41009, 1910 St. Laurent Blvd., Ottawa, ON K1G 5K9, Canada
Tel: 613-748-1430; *Fax:* 613-748-1355
Toll-Free: 866-247-9934
ccpsa@bellnet.ca
www.ccpsa.ca
Affiliation(s): Canadian Paralympic Committee; Cerebral Palsy International Sport & Recreation Association
Sandy Hermiston, President

Cerebral Palsy Sports Association of British Columbia (CPSABC)
6235A - 136th St., Surrey, BC V3X 1H3, Canada
Tel: 604-599-5240; *Fax:* 604-599-5241
Toll-Free: 877-711-3111
sportinfo@telus.net
www.cpsports.com
Affiliation(s): Sport BC
Terri Moore, Executive Director

Manitoba Cerebral Palsy Sports Association (MCPSA)
200 Main St., Winnipeg, MB R3C 1A8, Canada
Tel: 204-925-5682; *Fax:* 204-925-5703

Sport Ability Alberta
Percy Page Centre, 11759 Groat Rd., Edmonton, AB T5M 3K6, Canada
Tel: 780-422-2904; *Fax:* 780-422-2663
Toll-Free: 866-282-4356
acpsa@telusplanet.net
Sandy Hermiston, President
Norma Lorincz, Executive Director

Coaching

Coaches Association of British Columbia (CABC)
#200, 3820 Cessna Drive, Richmond, BC V7B 0A2, Canada
Tel: 604-333-3600; *Fax:* 604-333-3450
info@coaches.bc.ca
www.coaches.bc.ca
Gordon May, Executive Director

Coaches Association of PEI (CAPEI)
PO Box 302, Charlottetown, PE C1A 7K7, Canada
Tel: 902-569-0583; *Fax:* 902-368-4548
Toll-Free: 800-247-6712
cgcrozier@sportpei.pe.ca
www.coachespei.ca
Cheryl G. Crozier, Executive Director

Coaching Association of Canada (CAC) / Association canadienne des entraîneurs
#300, 141 Laurier Ave. West, Ottawa, ON K1P 5J3, Canada
Tel: 613-235-5000; *Fax:* 613-235-9500
coach@coach.ca
www.coach.ca
Affiliation(s): Professional Arm: Canadian Professional Coaches Association
John Bales, CEO
Gaëtan Robitaille, COO

Commonwealth Games

The Commonwealth Games Association of Canada Inc. (CGAC) / Association canadienne des jeux du Commonwealth inc.
#120, 2255 St. Laurent Blvd., Ottawa, ON K1G 4K3, Canada
Tel: 613-244-6868; *Fax:* 613-244-6826
info@commonwealthgames.ca
www.commonwealthgames.ca
Affiliation(s): Commonwealth Games Federation - London, England
Kelly Laframboise, Administrative Coordinator
Thomas Jones, CEO

Croquet

Fédération des clubs de croquet du Québec (FCCQ)
CP 1000, Succ. M, 4545, av Pierre-de Coubertin, Montréal, QC H1V 3R2, Canada
Tél: 514-252-3032
croquet@fqjr.qc.ca
www.fqjr.qc.ca/croquet.html
Yves Bédard, Président

Curling

Alberta Curling Federation (ACF)
11759 Groat Rd., Edmonton, AB T5M 3K6, Canada
Tel: 780-643-0809; *Fax:* 780-427-8103
jim@albertacurling.ab.ca
www.albertacurling.ab.ca
J.W. (Jim) Pringle, Executive Director
Kathy Odegard, Office Manager

Canadian Curling Association (CCA) / Association canadienne de curling
1660 Vimont Ct., Cumberland, ON K4A 4J4, Canada
Tel: 613-834-2076; *Fax:* 613-834-0716
Toll-Free: 800-550-2875
cca@curling.ca
www.curling.ca
Affiliation(s): World Curling Federation
Greg Stremlaw, CEO

Curl BC
#320, 1367 West Broadway, Vancouver, BC V6H 4A9, Canada
Tel: 604-737-3040; *Fax:* 604-737-1476
Toll-Free: 800-667-2875
curling@curlbc.ca
www.curlbc.ca
Scott Braley, Executive Director & CEO
Terry Vandale, President

Curling Québec
CP 1000, Succ. M, 4545, av Pierre-de Coubertin, Montréal, QC H1V 3R2, Canada
Tél: 514-252-3088; *Téléc:* 514-252-3342
Ligne sans frais: 888-292-2875
info@curling-quebec.qc.ca
www.curling-quebec.qc.ca
Marco Berthelot, Directeur général

Manitoba Curling Association (MCA)
#309, 145 Pacific Ave., Winnipeg, MB R3B 2Z6, Canada
Tel: 204-925-5723; *Fax:* 204-925-5720
mca@curlmanitoba.org
www.curlmanitoba.org
Affiliation(s): Canadian Curling Association
Shane Ray, Executive Director
Cole Skinner, Event/Media Coordinator
Cindy Maddock, President

New Brunswick Curling Association (NBCA) / Association de Curling du Nouveau-Brunswick (ACNB)
PO Box 812, Moncton, NB E1C 8N6, Canada
Tel: 506-854-9143; *Fax:* 506-388-5708
Toll-Free: 800-592-2875
nbca@nb.sympatico.ca
www.nbcurling.nb.ca
Affiliation(s): Curl Atlantic
Tradina Meadows-Forgeron, Executive Director
Jerry McCann, President
Catherine MacLean, Treasurer

Newfoundland & Labrador Curling Association
c/o Bob Osborne, 54 Hoyles Ave., St. John's, NL A1B 1E3
Tel: 709-738-3640
www.curlingnl.ca
Bob Osborne, President
Roy Hodder, Vice-President
Baxter House, Secretary
Carl C. Loughlin, Treasurer
Jean Blackie, Coordinator, Technical
Len Kostaszek, Coordinator, Tournament

Northern Alberta Curling Association (NACA)
#110, 9440 - 49 St., Edmonton, AB T6B 2M9, Canada
Tel: 780-440-4270; *Fax:* 780-463-4519
naca@planet.eon.net
northernalbertacurling.com
Marylynn Morris, Executive Director

Northern Ontario Curling Association
PO Box 940, Unit #4, 214 Main St. West, Atikokan, ON P0T 1C0, Canada
Tel: 807-597-8730; *Fax:* 807-597-4241
Toll-Free: 888-597-8730
info@curlnoca.ca
www.curlnoca.ca
Leslie Kerr, Executive Director
Al Gemmell, President

Northwest Territories Curling Association
c/o PO Box 11089, Yellowknife, NT X1A 3X7, Canada
nwtca@auroranet.nt.ca
www.curlingnwt.ssimicro.com
Jennifer Keith, Secretary

Northwestern Ontario Curling Association (NWOCA)
433 Catherine St., Thunder Bay, ON P7E 1K9, Canada
Tel: 807-622-8254; *Fax:* 807-626-9622
www.norontcurl.tripod.com
Colleen Syrja, Sec.-Treas.
Don R. MacLeod, President

Northwestern Québec Curling Association (NWQCA) / Association de curling du Nord-Ouest québécois
281, 3e rue est, Amos, QC J9T 2A7, Canada
Tel: 819-732-2089; *Fax:* 819-732-1617
Claude Noel, Secretary

Ontario Curling Association (OCA)
Office Mall 2, #2B, 1400 Bayly St., Pickering, ON L1W 3R2, Canada
Tel: 905-831-1757; *Fax:* 905-831-1083
Toll-Free: 877-668-2875
doug@ontcurl.com
www.ontcurl.com
Affiliation(s): Curl Ontario
Doug Bakes, Executive Director

Ottawa Valley Curling Association (OVCA)
PO Box 40129, Ottawa, ON K1V 0W8, Canada
Tel: 613-521-5822; *Fax:* 613-521-5344
Toll-Free: 800-385-6621
events@ovca.com
www.ovca.com
Affiliation(s): Curling Quebec
Perry Anderson, President
Lily Ooi, Coordinator, Events

Peace Curling Association (PCA)
PO Box 265, Grande Prairie, AB T8V 3A4, Canada
Tel: 780-532-4782; *Fax:* 780-538-2485
peaccurl@telusplanet.net
www.peacecurl.org
Bob Cooper, President

Prince Edward Island Curling Association (PEICA)
PO Box 302, 40 Enman Cres., Charlottetown, PE C1A 7K7, Canada
Tel: 902-368-4986; *Fax:* 902-368-4548
glucas@sportpei.pe.ca
www.peicurling.com
Affiliation(s): Sports PEI, Curl Atlantic
Ray McCourt, President

Saskatchewan Curling Association (SCA)
613 Park St., Regina, SK S4N 5N1, Canada
Tel: 306-780-9202; *Fax:* 306-780-9404
Toll-Free: 877-722-2875
saskcurling@sasktel.net
www.saskcurl.com/sca/scahome.htm
Del Jones, President

Southern Alberta Curling Association (SACA)
#720, 3 St. NW, Calgary, AB T2N 1N9, Canada
Tel: 403-246-9300; *Fax:* 403-246-9349
curling@saca.ca
www.saca.ca
Brent Syme, General Manager

Temiskaming & Northern Ontario Curling Association
c/o Stephen Chenier, PO Box 735, Englehart, ON P0J 1H0, Canada
Tel: 705-647-2589; *Fax:* 705-544-8525
jcdhh@ntl.sympatico.ca
www.tnoca.curlingclub.ca
Stephen Chenier, Secretary/Treasurer

World Curling Federation (WCF)
74 Tay St., Perth, PH2 8N, Scotland
Tel: 44-173-845-1630; *Fax:* 44-173-845-1641
wcf@dial.pipex.com
www.worldcurling.net
Lester Harrison, President
Kate Caithness, Vice-President
Mike Thomson, Secretary General

Yukon Curling Association (YCA)
4061 - 4th Ave., Whitehorse, YT Y1A 1H1, Canada
Tel: 867-668-7121; *Fax:* 867-667-4237
yca@sportyukon.com
yukoncurling.inthehack.com
Affiliation(s): Watson Lake Curling Club; Mayo Curling Club
Gord Zealand, President

Deafness

Alberta Deaf Sports Association (ADSA)
11404 - 142 St., Edmonton, AB T5M 1V1, Canada
adsa@shaw.ca
adsa.deafalberta.org
Arista Haas, President
Ryan Bercier, Vice-President
Brenda Hillcox, Secretary

Diabetes

Diabetes Exercise & Sports Association (DESA)
#604, 310 West Liberty, Louisville, KY 40202, USA
Fax: 502-581-0207
Toll-Free: 800-898-4322
desa@diabetes-exercise.org
www.diabetes-exercise.org
Guy Hornsby, Chair
Doug Dressman, Executive Director

Diving

Alberta Diving
426 Reeves Cres., Edmonton, AB T6R 2A4, Canada
Tel: 780-988-5571; *Fax:* 780-988-7753
www.albertadiving.ca
Cindy Casper, President
Susan Zwaenepoel, Vice-President
Barbara Dauphinais, Executive Director
Jim MacDonald, Secretary
Curtis Yano, Treasurer

British Columbia Diving
2630 Dogwood Dr., Surrey, BC V4A 3K5, Canada
Tel: 604-541-9332; *Fax:* 604-541-9303
info@bcdiving.ca
www.bcdiving.ca
Bev Boys, Executive Director
Joyne MacDonald, Manager, Operations

Dive Ontario
216 Gilwood Park Dr., Penetanguishene, ON L9M 1Z6, Canada
Tel: 705-355-3483; *Fax:* 705-355-4663
info@diveontario.com
www.diveontario.com
Affiliation(s): Community & recreation centres around the province
Janice Moore, President

Diving Plongeon Canada (DPC) / Association canadienne du plongeon amateur Inc.
#703, 2197 Riverside Dr., Ottawa, ON K1H 7X3, Canada
Tel: 613-736-5238; *Fax:* 613-736-0409
cada@diving.ca
www.diving.ca
Affiliation(s): Aquatics Federation of Canada; Swimming Natation Canada; Synchronized Swimming; Water Polo Canada
Penny Joyce, Chief Operating Officer
Mitch Geller, Chief Technical Officer
Nancy Brawley, Director, National Team
Kathy Seaman, President

Fédération du plongeon amateur du Québec (FPAQ)
CP 1000, Succ. M, 4545, av Pierre-de-Coubertin, Montréal, QC H1V 3R2, Canada
Tél: 514-252-3096; *Téléc:* 514-252-3094
fpaq@plongeon.qc.ca
www.plongeon.qc.ca
Isabelle Cloutier, Directrice exécutive

Fédération québécoise des activités subaquatiques (FQAS)
CP 1000, Succ. M, 4545, av Pierre-de Coubertin, Montréal, QC H1V 3R2, Canada
Tél: 514-252-3009; *Téléc:* 514-254-1363
Ligne sans frais: 866-391-8835
info@fqas.qc.ca
www.fqas.qc.ca
Affiliation(s): Confédération mondiale des activités subaquatiques
Jean-Sébastien Naud, Directeur général

Manitoba Diving Association
Sport Manitoba Building, 200 Main St., Winnipeg, MB R3C 1A8, Canada
Tel: 204-925-5654; *Fax:* 204-925-5703
headcoach@panamdiving.com
www.manitobadiving.com
Jim Lambie, Head Coach

Manitoba Underwater Council (MUC)
PO Box 711, Winnipeg, MB R3C 2K3, Canada
Tel: 204-632-8508
info@manunderwater.com
www.manunderwater.com

Ontario Underwater Council (OUC)
#104, 1185 Eglinton Ave. East, Toronto, ON M3C 3C6, Canada
Tel: 416-426-7033; *Fax:* 416-426-7280
ouc@underwatercouncil.com
www.underwatercouncil.com
Raimund Krob, President

Saskatchewan Diving
1870 Lorne St., Regina, SK S4P 2L7, Canada
Tel: 306-780-9405; *Fax:* 306-781-6021
skdiving@accesscomm.ca
www.saskdiving.ca
Karen Swanson, Provincial Administrator
Carol Lunn, President

Equestrian Sports & Activities

Alberta Equestrian Federation (AEF)
#100, 251 Midpark Blvd. SE, Calgary, AB T2X 1S3, Canada
Tel: 403-253-4411; *Fax:* 403-252-5260
Toll-Free: 877-463-6233
www.albertaequestrian.com
Dixie Crowson, President
Sonia Dantu, Executive Director

Atlantic Canada Trail Riding Association
Sylvia Gillies, #344 Route 875, Belleisle Creek, NB E5P 1C8, Canada
Roy Drinnan, Chair

British Columbia Competitive Trail Riders Association (BCCTRA)
c/o 2980 Giovando Road, Nanaimo, BC V9X 1K5, Canada
Tel: 250-245-4405
nicole.vaugeois@viu.ca
www.bcctra.ca
Nicole Vagueois, Sec.-Treas.

Canadian Sport Horse Association (CSHA)
PO Box 970, 7904 Franktown Rd., Richmond, ON K0A 2Z0, Canada
Tel: 613-686-6161; *Fax:* 613-686-6170
csha@canadian-sport-horse.org
www.c-s-h-a.org
Paul Morgan, President
David Lancaster, Treasurer

Distance Riders of Manitoba Association (DRMA)
PO Box 47, Gr 36, RR#2, Dugald, MB R0E 0K0, Canada
Tel: 204-444-2314
www.kucera.mb.ca/drma

Affiliation(s): American Endurance Ride Conference
Myna Cryderman, President
Linda Cruden, Membership Director

Drive Canada
PO Box 2062, Vancouver, BC V6B 3S3, Canada
Tel: 604-875-1905; *Fax:* 604-857-9582
drivecanada@shaw.ca
www.drivecanada.org
Affiliation(s): American Driving Society
Simon Rosenman, President

Endurance Riders Association of British Columbia (ERABC)
c/o 1624 Duncan Dr., Delta, BC V4L 1S2, Canada
info@erabc.com
www.erabc.com
Affiliation(s): Endurance Canada
Terre O'Brennan, Ride Manager

Endurance Riders of Alberta (ERA)
c/o President, PO Box 418, Seba Beach, AB T0E 2B0, Canada
Tel: 780-797-5404
www.enduranceridersofalberta.com
Affiliation(s): Canadian Long Distance Riding Association
Carol Wadey, Treasurer
Owen Fulcher, President

Equestrian Association for the Disabled
8360 Leeming Rd., RR#3, Mount Hope, ON L0R 1W0
Tel: 905-679-8323; *Fax:* 905-679-1705
www.tead.on.ca
Jim Sykes, Chair & President
Patrick Warner, Vice-President
Hilary Webb, Executive Director
Gord Hyland, Treasurer
Trish Brakewell, Coordinator
Pat Bullock, Instructor, Riding

Equine Canada (EC) / Canada Hippique
#100, 2685 Queensview Dr., Ottawa, ON K2B 8K2, Canada
Tel: 613-248-3433; *Fax:* 613-248-3484
Toll-Free: 866-282-8395
inquiries@equinecanada.ca
www.equestrian.ca
Affiliation(s): Provincial Partners: Horse Council of B.C., Alberta Equestrian Federation, Saskatchewan Horse Federation, Manitoba Horse Council, Ontario Equestrian Federation, Fédération Équestre du Quebec, New Brunswick Equestrian Association, PEI Horse Council, Nova Scotia Equestrian Federation, Newfoundland Equestrian Association, Canadian Pony Club
Akaash Maharaj, CEO

Fédération équestre du Québec inc. (FEQ)
CP 1000, Succ. M, 4545, av Pierre-de-Coubertin, Montréal, QC H1V 3R2, Canada
Tél: 514-252-3053; *Téléc:* 514-252-3165
infocheval@feq.qc.ca
www.feq.qc.ca
Richard Mongeau, Directeur général

Horse Council British Columbia (HCBC)
27336 Fraser Hwy., Aldergrove, BC V4W 3N5, Canada
Tel: 604-856-4304; *Fax:* 604-856-4302
Toll-Free: 800-345-8055
reception@hcbc.ca; membership@hcbc.ca; education@hcbc.ca
www.hcbc.ca
Lisa Laycock, Executive Director
Sarah Bradley, President
Susan Harrison, Secretary
Gary Patterson, Treasurer

Horse Trials New Brunswick
c/o Donna Lee Cole, 7515 Rte.102, Browns Flat, NB E5M 2N8, Canada
Tel: 506-468-2098
www.htnb.org
Affiliation(s): Horse Trials Canada
Donna Lee Cole, President
Louise McSheffrey, Secretary

Horse Trials Nova Scotia (HTNS)
60 Rockwell Drive, Mount Uniacke, NS B0N 1Z0, Canada
Tel: 902-866-3889
www.htns.org
Affiliation(s): Horse Trials Canada; Nova Scotia Equestrian Federation
Kim Elliott-Foster, President

Island Horse Council (IHC)
PO Box 1887, Charlottetown, PE C1A 7N5, Canada
islandhorsecouncil@yahoo.ca
www.islandhorsecouncil.ca
Affiliation(s): Equine Canada
Ken Smith, Chair
Bobbi Jo Duffy, Treasurer

Manitoba Horse Council Inc.
#207, 200 Main St., Winnipeg, MB R3C 4M2, Canada
Tel: 204-925-5718; *Fax:* 204-925-5792
admin@manitobahorsecouncil.ca
www.manitobahorsecouncil.ca
Dave Myers, President
Sheilagh Antoniuk, Executive Director

Manitoba Trail Riding Club Inc.
838 Alfred Ave., Winnipeg, MB R2X 0T6, Canada
Kelli.Hayhurst@pwgsc.gc.ca
www.mbtrailridingclub.ca
Affiliation(s): Canadian Long Distance Riding Association
Kelli Hayhurst, President
Mary Anne Kirk, Treasurer

New Brunswick Equestrian Association (NBEA)
c/o Sport NB, #13, 900 Hanwell Rd., Fredericton, NB E3B 6A3, Canada
Tel: 506-454-2353; *Fax:* 506-454-2363
generalinfo@equestrian.nb.ca
www.equestrian.nb.ca
Jeremy Hoyt, President
Jennifer Everett, Secretary

Newfoundland Equestrian Association (NEA)
PO Box 372, Stn. C, St. John's, NL A1C 5J9, Canada
www.horsenewfoundland.com
Katrina Butler, President
Sheila Anstey, Vice-President & Director, Competitions
Katie Murray, Secretary
Cathy Favre, Treasurer

North American Riding for the Handicapped Association (NARHA)
PO Box 33150, Denver, CO 80233, USA
Tel: 303-452-1212; *Fax:* 303-252-4610
Toll-Free: 800-369-7433
narha@narha.org
www.narha.org
Carol Nickell, CEO

Nova Scotia Distance Riding Association (NSDRA)
RR#3, Site 802, Newport, NS B0N 2A0, Canada
Affiliation(s): Canadian Long Distance Riding Association

Nova Scotia Equestrian Federation
5516 Spring Garden Rd., 4th Fl., Halifax, NS B3J 1G6, Canada
Tel: 902-425-5450; *Fax:* 902-425-5606
nsef@sportnovascotia.ca
www.horsenovascotia.ca
Heather Myrer, Executive Director

Ontario Competitive Trail Riding Association Inc. (OCTRA)
R.R.#4, Tottenham, ON L0G 1W0, Canada
Tel: 905-936-3362
webmaster@octra.on.ca
www.octra.on.ca
Affiliation(s): Horse Ontario; Ontario Equestrian Federation
Mark Ford, President
Joe Mezenberg, Vice-President
Marg Murray, Secretary
Kelly Corbyn, Treasurer

Ontario Equestrian Federation (OEF)
#203, 9120 Leslie St., Richmond Hill, ON L4B 3J9, Canada
Tel: 905-709-6545; *Fax:* 905-709-1867
Toll-Free: 877-441-7112
horse@horse.on.ca
www.horse.on.ca
Affiliation(s): Equine Guelph; Ontario Trails Council; Ontario Federation of Agriculture
Deborah Thompson, Executive Director
Gary Yaghdjian, President
Kathy Fremes, Secretary

Ontario Horse Trials Association (OHTA)
#186, 3-304 Stone Rd. West, Guelph, ON N1G 4W4, Canada
ohta@hotmail.ca
www.horsetrials.on.ca
Glenn McMechan, President
Robin Campbell, Secretary

Ontario Trail Riders Association (OTRA)
PO Box 3038, Elmvale, ON L0L 1P0, Canada
www.otra.ca
Affiliation(s): Ontario Trails Council; Ontario Equestrian Federation
Janice Clegg, President

Saskatchewan Horse Federation (SHF)
2205 Victoria Ave., Regina, SK S4P 0S4, Canada
Tel: 306-780-9244; *Fax:* 306-525-4009
sk.horse@sasktel.net
www.saskhorse.ca
Affiliation(s): Sask Sport; Western College Veterinary Medicine; SK Agriculture & Food (SAF)
Mae Smith, Executive Director

Saskatchewan Long Riders
C/O Diane Trundle, Stn. 429, Balgonie, SK S0G 0E0, Canada
Tel: 306-978-1225; *Fax:* 306-230-1224
bsutherland@shaw.ca
www.sasklongriders.com
Affiliation(s): Canadian Long Distance Riding Association
Rachel Croskery, President

Trail Riding Alberta Conference (TRAC)
738 Wheeler Road, Edmonton, AB T6M 2E8, Canada
Tel: 403-486-0957
shanharms@shaw.ca
www.trailriding.ab.ca
Affiliation(s): Canadian Long Distance Riding Association
Brent Seufert, President

Fencing

Alberta Fencing Association (AFA)
Percy Page Centre, 11759 Groat Rd., Edmonton, AB T5M 3K6, Canada
Tel: 780-427-9474; *Fax:* 780-447-5959
info@fencing.ab.ca
www.fencing.ab.ca
Nicolas Allen, Executive Director

British Columbia Fencing Association (BCFA)
c/o #15, 12900 Jack Bell Dr., Richmond, BC V6V 2V8, Canada
www.fencing.bc.ca
John French, President

Canadian Fencing Federation (CFF) / Fédération canadienne d'escrime
10 Masterson Dr., St Catharines, ON L2T 3P1, Canada
Tel: 647-476-2401; *Fax:* 647-476-2402
cff@fencing.ca
www.fencing.ca
Affiliation(s): Fédération internationale d'escrime
Stephen Symons, President
Ron Dewar, Vice-President

Fédération d'escrime du Québec
CP 1000, Succ. M, 4545, av Pierre-de-Coubertin, Montréal, QC H1V 3R2, Canada
Tél: 514-252-3045; *Téléc:* 514-254-3451
info@escrimequebec.qc.ca
www.escrimequebec.qc.ca
Maître Dominique Teisseire, Directeur, technique et administratif

Fencing Association of Nova Scotia (FANS) / Association d'escrime de la Nouvelle-Écosse
c/o Sport Nova Scotia, 5516 Spring Garden Rd., 4th Fl., Halifax, NS B3J 3G6
Fax: 902-425-5606
www.chebucto.ns.ca/SportFit/Fencing
Diane Buote, President
Michael Barton, Treasurer
Bob Gillis, Registrar
Florian Friedrich, Technical Director
Janessa Green, Administrative Coordinator

Manitoba Fencing Association (MFA)
200 Main St., Winnipeg, MB R3C 4M2, Canada
Tel: 204-925-5696; *Fax:* 204-925-5703
fencingmb@shawbiz.ca
www.fencing.mb.ca
Marian McLennan, Executive Director
Paul Smith, President
Chris Whitmore, Vice-President, Technical
Kathy Borgfjord, Vice-President, Finance
Michel Allard, Vice-President, Athlete Programs
Dave Dessens, Vice-President, Sport Development

New Brunswick Fencing Association (NBFA)
c/o 20 Glenburn Ct., Saint John, NB E2K 3Y9, Canada
Tel: 506-633-7047
execdir@fencingnb.ca
www.fencingnb.ca

Jane Corey, President
Tammy Crowley, Secretary

Newfoundland & Labrador Fencing Association (N&LFA)
#168, Unit 50 Hamlyn Road Plaza, St. John's, NL A1E 5X7, Canada
Fax: 709-368-8830
nlfencing@gmail.com
sites.google.com/site/nlfencing/

Justin So, President

Ontario Fencing Association (OFA) / Association d'escrime de l'Ontario
984 Main St. West, Hamilton, ON L8S 1B2, Canada
Tel: 905-525-6693
info@fencingontario.ca
fencingontario.ca/cms

Ranil Sonnadara, President
June McGuire, Executive Director

Prince Edward Island Fencing Association (PEIFA)
c/o Sport PEI, PO Box 302, 40 Enman Cres., Charlottetown, PE C1A 7K7, Canada
Tel: 905-368-4110; *Fax:* 905-386-4548
Toll-Free: 800-247-6712
sports@sportpei.pe.ca
www.upei.ca/~fencing

Saskatchewan Fencing Association (SFA)
510 Cynthia St., Saskatoon, SK S7L 7K7, Canada
Tel: 306-975-0823; *Fax:* 306-242-8007
saskfencing@shaw.ca
saskfencing.com

Affiliation(s): Saskatchewan Sport
Lynn Seguin, Executive Assistant

Field Hockey

Fédération de hockey sur gazon Québec / Québec Field Hockey Federation
CP 1000, Succ. M, 4545, av Pierre-de Coubertin, Montréal, QC H1V 3R2, Canada
Tél: 514-426-8405; *Téléc:* 514-426-9418
hockeysurgazon@yahoo.com
Affiliation(s): Field Hockey Canada; Sports Canada
Harbir Bhamrah, Président

Field Hockey Alberta (FHA)
#1, 2135 Westmount Rd. NW, Calgary, AB T2N 3N3, Canada
Tel: 403-670-0014; *Fax:* 403-670-0018
Toll-Free: 888-670-0018
info@fieldhockey.ab.ca
fieldhockey.ab.ca

Liz Allan, Executive Director

Field Hockey Canada (FHC) / Hockey sur gazon Canada
#240, 1101 Prince of Wales Dr., Ottawa, ON K2C 3W7, Canada
Tel: 613-521-8774; *Fax:* 613-521-0261
fhc@fieldhockey.ca
www.fieldhockey.ca

Mary Cicinelli, President
Suzzanne Nicholson, Executive Director
Ian Clark, Administrative Coordinator

Field Hockey Manitoba (FHM)
200 Main St., Winnipeg, MB R3C 4M2, Canada
Tel: 204-925-5794; *Fax:* 204-925-5703
fieldhockeymb@shawbiz.ca
www.fieldhockeymb.org

Arnold D'Souza, President
Geoffrey Govia, Executive Director

Field Hockey Nova Scotia
NS, Canada
www.fieldhockey.ns.ca

Mike Fearon, President

Field Hockey Ontario (FHO)
PO Box 1037, Erin, ON N0B 1T0, Canada
Tel: 905-492-1680
fhoboard@gmail.com
www.fieldhockeyontario.netfirms.com

Ann Doggett, President

New Brunswick Field Hockey Association (NBFHA)
c/o 2341 Golden Grove Rd., Saint John, NB E2N 1Z8, Canada
Tel: 506-634-1241
sara.hayward@nbed.nb.ca

Sara Hayward, President

Saskatchewan Field Hockey Association
1860 Lorne St., Regina, SK S4P 2L7, Canada
Tel: 306-780-9256; *Fax:* 306-781-6021
sfha@sasktel.net
www.saskfieldhockey.ca

Stefanie Sloboda, Technical Director

Firearms

Buckskinners Muzzleloading Association, Limited
PO Box 4127, Stn. Champlain Place, Dieppe, NB E1A 6E8, Canada
Tel: 506-576-1959; *Fax:* 506-859-1249
buckskinnersweb@yahoo.com
buckskinnersweb.weebly.com
Affiliation(s): New Brunswick Wildlife Federation
Shirley Stuart, Contact

Football

Alberta Amateur Football Association (AAFA)
Percy Page Centre, 11759 Groat Rd., Edmonton, AB T5M 3K6, Canada
Tel: 780-427-8108; *Fax:* 780-427-0524
bfryer@telus.net
www.footballalberta.ab.ca

Neil Gerritsen, President
Brian Fryer, Executive Director

Canadian Football Hall of Fame & Museum
58 Jackson St. West, Hamilton, ON L8P 1L4, Canada
Tel: 905-528-7566; *Fax:* 905-528-9781
info@cfhof.ca
www.cfhof.ca

Steve Howse, Chair
Mark DeNobile, Executive Director
Meghan Sturgeon, Curator

Canadian Football League (CFL) / Ligue canadienne de football (LCF)
50 Wellington St. East, 3rd Fl., Toronto, ON M5E 1C8, Canada
Tel: 416-322-9650; *Fax:* 416-322-9651
info@cfl.ca
www.cfl.ca

Mark Cohon, Commissioner
Michael Copeland, COO
Jamie Dykstra, Director, Communications

Canadian Football Officials Association
c/o Ontario Region, 73 Alpaca Dr., Toronto, ON M1J 2Z9, Canada
Tel: 416-431-7887
webcommittee@cfoa-acof.ca
www.cfoa-acof.ca

Mike Groleau, President

Canadian Junior Football League (CJFL)
9611 RR#1, Richmond, BC V7E 1R8, Canada
Tel: 604-277-8133; *Fax:* 604-277-8136
ronald_white@telus.net
www.cjfl.net

Antonio Iadeluca, Commissioner

Canadian University Football Coaches Association (CUFCA)
c/o Huskies Football, St. Mary's University, Halifax, NS B3H 3C3, Canada
Tel: 902-420-5550
Affiliation(s): Canadian Interuniversity Athletic Union
Blake Nill, President

Football BC
10605 - 135 St., Surrey, BC V3T 4C8, Canada
Tel: 604-583-9363; *Fax:* 604-583-9939
footballbc@footballbc.org
www.playfootball.bc.ca

Football Canada
#100, 2255 St. Laurent Blvd., Ottawa, ON K1G 4K3, Canada
Tel: 613-564-0003; *Fax:* 613-564-6309
info@footballcanada.com
footballcanada.com

Richard Munro, CEO
Bob Swan, Technical Consultant
Cara Lynch, Manager, Non-Contact Programs
Josh Sacobie, Technical Coordinator
Christine Piché, Administrative Coordinator

Football Nova Scotia Association
#536, 1657 Barrington St., Halifax, NS B3J 2A1, Canada
Tel: 902-454-5105; *Fax:* 902-425-5606
footballns@ns.aliantzinc.ca
www.footballnovascotia.ca
Affiliation(s): Canadian Amateur Football Association
Richard MacLean, President
Rob Manson, Vice-President

Football Québec (FFAQ) / Fédération de football amateur de Québec
CP 1000, Succ. M, 4545, av Pierre-de-Coubertin, Montréal, QC H1V 3R2, Canada
Tél: 514-252-3059; *Téléc:* 514-252-5216
jeancharles@football.qc.ca
www.football-quebec.com
Affiliation(s): National Football Federation of Canada
René Robillard, Président

Ontario Football Alliance
#B11, 100 Crimea St., Guelph, ON N1H 2Y6, Canada
Tel: 519-780-0200; *Fax:* 519-780-0705
otf@on.aibn.com
www.ontariotacklefootball.com

Peter Repac, President

Foundations

Dr. James Naismith Basketball Foundation / La fondation de basketball Dr James Naismith
PO Box 1030, 14 Bridge St., Almonte, ON K0A 1A0, Canada
Tel: 613-256-0492; *Fax:* 613-256-7883
naismith@trytel.com
Affiliation(s): Basketball Canada
John Gosset, Executive Director
Allen G. Rae, President

Royal Canadian Golf Association Foundation
#1, 1333 Dorval Dr., Oakville, ON L6M 4X7, Canada
Tel: 905-849-9700; *Fax:* 905-845-7040
Toll-Free: 800-263-0009
khewson@rcga.org
www.rcga.org

Karen Hewson, Executive Director

Fundraising

WinSport Canada
88 Canada Olympic Rd. SW, Calgary, AB T3B 5R5, Canada
Tel: 403-247-5452; *Fax:* 403-286-7213
info@coda.ca
www.winsportcanada.ca
Affiliation(s): Canadian Olympic Committee; Canadian Paralympic Committee
Trevor Nakka, Chair

Golf

Alberta Golf Association (AGA)
#22, 11410 - 27 St. SE, Calgary, AB T2Z 3R6, Canada
Tel: 403-236-4616; *Fax:* 403-236-2915
Toll-Free: 888-414-4849
info@albertagolf.org
www.albertagolf.org

Brent Ellenton, Executive Director

Association des golfeurs professionnels du Québec (AGP)
435, boul. Saint-Luc, Saint-Jean-sur-Richelieu, QC J2W 1E7, Canada
Tél: 450-349-5525; *Téléc:* 450-349-6640
agpinfo@agp.qc.ca
www.agp.qc.ca

Jean Trudeau, Directeur général

Association des surintendants de golf du Québec (ASGQ) / Québec Golf Superintendents Association (QSGA)
CP 642, Succ. B, Montréal, QC H3B 3K3, Canada
Tél: 514-285-4874; *Téléc:* 514-282-4292
info@asgq.org
www.asgq.org
Christian Pilon, Président

British Columbia Golf Association (BCGA)
#2105, 21000 Westminster Hwy., Richmond, BC V6V 2S9, Canada
Tel: 604-279-2580; *Fax:* 604-207-9535
Toll-Free: 888-833-2242
info@bcga.org
www.bcga.org
Affiliation(s): Canadian Golf Foundation; Professional Golf Association of BC; Canadian Ladies Golf Association of BC; Golf Course Superintendents Association of BC; International Association of Golf Administrators; National Golf Foundation; Pacific Coast Golf Association; Pacific Northwest Golf Association
George Faithfull, President
Kris Jonasson, Executive Director

British Columbia Golf Superintendents Association (BCGSA)
PO Box 807, 231 Nootka Cres., Lake Cowichan, BC V0R 2G0, Canada
Tel: 250-749-6703; *Fax:* 250-749-6702
admin@bcgsa.com
www.bcgsa.com
Ginny Tromp, Executive Administrator
Rob Wilke, BCGSA President
Jerry Rousseau, Treasurer

British Columbia Professional Golfers Association
3540 Morgan Creek Way, Surrey, BC V3C 0J7, Canada
Tel: 604-536-7878; *Fax:* 604-536-7879
Toll-Free: 800-667-4653
brian@pgabc.org
www.bcpga.org
Brian Butters, Executive Director
Troy Peverley, President

Canadian Caribbean Amateur Golfers Association (CCAGA)
#718, 7305 Woodbine Ave, Markham, ON L3R 3V7, Canada
Fax: 905-420-8421
info@ccaga.ca
www.ccaga.ca

Canadian Golf Industry Association / Association canadienne de l'industrie du golf
7 Aspendale Dr., Toronto, ON M1P 4J5, Canada
Tel: 416-289-1305; *Fax:* 416-289-1412
cgiacgi@bellnet.ca
Chuck Fitzpatrick, Executive Director

Canadian Golf Superintendents Association (CGSA) / Association canadienne des surintendants de golf
#205, 5520 Explorer Dr., Mississauga, ON L4W 5L1
Tel: 905-602-8873; *Fax:* 905-602-1958
Toll-Free: 800-387-1056
cgsa@golfsupers.com
www.golfsupers.com
Kenneth S. Cousineau, Executive Director
Greg Holden, President
Debbie Amirault, Vice-President
Tim Kubash, Secretary-Treasurer

Canadian Professional Golfers' Association (CPGA) / Association canadienne des golfeurs professionnels
13450 Dublin Line, RR#1, Acton, ON L7J 2W7, Canada
Tel: 519-853-5450; *Fax:* 519-853-5449
Toll-Free: 800-782-5764
cpga@cpga.com
www.cpga.com
Gary Bernard, Interim Executive Director

Canadian Society of Club Managers (CSCM) / La Société canadienne des directeurs de club
2943B Bloor St. West, Toronto, ON M8X 1B3, Canada
Tel: 416-979-0640; *Fax:* 416-979-1144
Toll-Free: 877-376-2726
national@cscm.org
www.cscm.org
Elizabeth Di Chiara, Executive Director

Golf Association of Ontario (GAO)
PO Box 970, Uxbridge, ON L9P 1N3, Canada
Tel: 905-852-1101; *Fax:* 905-852-8893
Toll-Free: 800-668-2949
administration@gao.ca
www.gao.ca
Stephen James, President
David Mills, Executive Director

Golf Manitoba Inc.
420 - 145 Pacific Ave., Winnipeg, MB R3B 2Z6, Canada
Tel: 204-925-5730; *Fax:* 204-925-5731
golfmb@golfmanitoba.mb.ca
golfmanitoba.mb.ca
Rob MacDonald, President
Dave Comaskey, Executive Director

Golf Newfoundland & Labrador (GNL)
77 Morgan Dr., Gander, NL A1V 2K3, Canada
Tel: 709-722-2470; *Fax:* 709-722-8104
golf@hnl.ca
www.golfnewfoundland.ca
Greg Hillier, President

Golf Québec
#110, 415, rue Bourke, Dorval, QC H9S 3W9, Canada
Tél: 514-633-1088; *Téléc:* 514-633-1074
golfquebec@golfquebec.org
www.golfquebec.org
Diane Dunlop-Hébert, President
Jean-Pierre Beaulieu, Directeur général

National Golf Course Owners Association Canada (NGCOA)
#105, 955 Green Valley Cres., Ottawa, ON K2C 3V4, Canada
Tel: 613-226-3616; *Fax:* 613-226-4148
Toll-Free: 866-626-4262
ngcoa@ngcoa.ca
www.ngcoa.ca
Jeff Calderwood, CEO
Nathalie Lavallée, Director, Communications & Member Services

New Brunswick Golf Association (NBGA) / Association de golf du nouveau brunswick
PO Box 1555, Stn. A, Fredericton, NB E3B 1G2, Canada
Tel: 506-451-1324; *Fax:* 506-451-1348
nbgolf@nbnet.nb.ca
www.nbga.nb.ca
Pierre Arsenault, Executive Director

Nova Scotia Golf Association (NSGA)
#4, 24 Simmonds Dr., Dartmouth, NS B3B 1R3, Canada
Tel: 902-468-8844; *Fax:* 902-484-5327
adminexec@ns.aliantzinc.ca
www.nsga.ns.ca
David Campbell, Executive Director
Shelley Pineault, Executive Assistant

Prince Edward Island Golf Association
PO Box 51, Charlottetown, PE C1A 7K2, Canada
Tel: 902-393-3293; *Fax:* 902-628-2260
peiga@peiga.ca
www.peiga.ca
Don Chandler, Executive Director
Jean Kelly, President

Royal Canadian Golf Association (RCGA) / Association royale de golf du Canada
Golf House, #1, 1333 Dorval Dr., Oakville, ON L6M 4X7, Canada
Tel: 905-849-9700; *Fax:* 905-845-7040
cboag@rcga.org
www.rcga.org
Affiliation(s): World Amateur Golf Council
Scott Simmons, Executive Director
Peter Beresford, COO
Rick Desrochers, Senior Director, Corporate Planning

Saskatchewan Golf Association
510 Cynthia St., Saskatoon, SK S7L 7K7, Canada
Tel: 306-975-0850; *Fax:* 306-975-0840
info@saskgolf.ca
www.saskgolf.ca
Daniel Rauckman, Executive Director

Gymnastics

Alberta Gymnastics Federation (AGF)
#207, 5800 - 2 St. SW, Calgary, AB T2H 0H2, Canada
Tel: 403-259-5500; *Fax:* 403-259-5588
Toll-Free: 800-665-1010
info@abgym.ab.ca
www.abgym.ab.ca
Scott Hayes, President & CEO

Fédération de gymnastique du Québec (FGQ) / Québec Gymnastics Federation
CP 1000, Succ. M, 4545, av Pierre-de-Coubertin, Montréal, QC H1V 3R2, Canada
Tél: 514-252-3043; *Téléc:* 514-252-3169
info@gymnastique.qc.ca
www.gymnastique.qc.ca
Robert Paquin, Directeur général
Claude Aubertin, Président
Raymond Paquin, Vice-président

Gymnastics B.C. (GBC)
#230, 3820 Cessna Dr., Richmond, BC V3B 0A2, Canada
Tel: 604-333-3496; *Fax:* 604-333-3499
Toll-Free: 800-556-2242
info@gymnastics.bc.ca
www.gymnastics.bc.ca
Moira Gooksetter, CEO
Twyla Ryan, President

Gymnastics Canada Gymnastique (GCG)
#120, 1900 City Park Dr., Ottawa, ON K1J 1A3, Canada
Tel: 613-748-5637; *Fax:* 613-748-5691
info@gymcan.org
www.gymcan.org
Affiliation(s): Fédération internationale de gymnastique
Jean-Paul Caron, President & CEO

Gymnastics Newfoundland & Labrador Inc.
PO Box 21248, Stn. MacDonald Dr., St. John's, NL A1A 5B2, Canada
Tel: 709-576-0146; *Fax:* 709-576-7493
gymnastics@sportnl.ca
www.gymnastics.nl.ca
Bob Godden, President
Carol White, Executive Director

Gymnastics Nova Scotia (GNS)
5516 Spring Garden Rd., 4th Fl., Halifax, NS B3J 1G6
Tel: 902-425-5450; *Fax:* 902-425-5606
gns@sportnovascotia.ca
www.gymns.ca
Byron Topp, President
Angela Gallant, Executive Director
Vaughn Arthur, Chair, Fair Play & Equity
Nick Lenehan, Chair, Competition
Eleanor Melrose, Chair, Education & Recreation
Cathy Huntington, Secretary
Steve Lowe, Treasurer

Gymnastics PEI
Sport PEI, PO Box 302, Charlottetown, PE C1A 7K7, Canada
Tel: 902-368-4262; *Fax:* 902-368-4548
gflood@sportpei.pe.ca
www.sportpei.pe.ca
Glen Flood, Executive Director

Gymnastics Saskatchewan
1870 Lorne St., Regina, SK S4P 2L7, Canada
Tel: 306-780-9229; *Fax:* 306-780-9475
info@gymsask.com
www.gymsask.com
Klara Miller, Executive Director

Manitoba Gymnastics Association
200 Main St., Winnipeg, MB R3C 4M2, Canada
Tel: 204-925-5781; *Fax:* 204-925-5932
mangym@sport.mb.ca
www.gymnastics.mb.ca
Kathy Stoesz, Executive Director

New Brunswick Gymnastics Association (NBGA) / Association gymnastique du Nouveau-Brunswick
110 Rivercrest Ave., Riverview, NB E1B 1M7, Canada
Tel: 506-384-6242; *Fax:* 506-384-6244
nbga@gym.nb.ca
user.fundy.net/nbga/
Reid Middleton, President
Nathalie Colpitts, Executive Director

Ontario Gymnastic Federation (OGF)
#214, 3 Concorde Gate, Toronto, ON M3C 3N7
Tel: 416-426-7100; *Fax:* 416-426-7377
Toll-Free: 866-565-0650
info@ogf.com
www.ogf.com

Affiliation(s): Gymnastics Canada
Ruth Simpson, Chief Executive Officer
Linda Clifford, President
Angel Crossman, Secretary & Director, Policies & Procedures
Sean Holmes, Technical Director, Gymnastics Program Development
Yuliana Korolyova, Coordinator, Education
Colleen O'Hare, Coordinator, Membership Services
Terri Parsons, Coordinator, Administrative Services

Rhythmic Gymnastics Alberta (RGA)
c/o Percy Page Centre, 11759 Groat Rd., 3rd Fl., Edmonton, AB T5M 3K6, Canada
Tel: 780-427-8152; *Fax:* 780-427-8153
Toll-Free: 800-881-2504
rga@rgalberta.com
www.rgalberta.com

Joan Jack, President
Odette Lindstrom, Treasurer
Helen Marchak, Vice-President

Yukon Gymnastics Association
4061 - 4th Ave., Whitehorse, YT Y1A 1H1, Canada
Tel: 867-668-4794; *Fax:* 867-667-4237
polarett@internorth.com
www.polarettes.org

Kelly Mock, Technical Director

Halls of Fame

Alberta Sports Hall of Fame & Museum (ASHFM)
#30, Riverview Park, Red Deer, AB T4N 1E3, Canada
Tel: 403-341-8614; *Fax:* 403-341-8619
postmaster@albertasportshalloffame.com
www.albertasportshalloffame.com

Donna Hateley, Managing Director

British Columbia Sports Hall of Fame & Museum
Gate A, BC Place Stadium, 777 Pacific Blvd. South, Vancouver, BC V6B 4Y8, Canada
Tel: 604-687-5520; *Fax:* 604-687-5510
sportsinfo@bcsportshalloffame.com
www.bcsportshalloffame.com

Affiliation(s): International Association of Sports Museums & Halls of Fame
Colin Brown, Chair

Canada's Sports Hall of Fame / Temple de la renommée des sports du Canada
Exhibition Place, 115 Princes' Blvd., Toronto, ON M6K 3C3, Canada
Tel: 416-260-6789; *Fax:* 416-260-9347
info@cshof.ca
www.cshof.ca

Sheryn Posen, COO
J. Trevor Eyton, Chair

Canadian Golf Hall of Fame & Museum (CGHF) / Musée et Temple canadien de la renommée du golf
Glen Abbey Golf Club, 1333 Dorval Dr., Oakville, ON L6M 4X7, Canada
Tel: 905-849-9700; *Fax:* 905-845-7040
rdands@golfcanada.ca
www.rcga.org

Scott Simmons, Executive Director, Golf Canada
Meggan Gardner, Curator, Canadian Golf Hall of Fame & Museum
Jason Cheong, Assistant, Canadian Golf Hall of Fame & Museum

Canadian Lacrosse Hall of Fame
302 Royal Ave., New Westminster, BC V3L 1H7, Canada
Tel: 604-527-4640; *Fax:* 604-527-4641
allan@lacrosse.ca

Allan Blair, Curator

Canadian Olympic Hall of Fame / Temple de la renommée olympique du Canada
c/o COC, #1400, 85 Albert St., Ottawa, ON K1P 6A4, Canada
Tel: 613-244-2020; *Fax:* 613-244-0169
www.olympic.ca/en/programs/canadian-olympic-hall-fame

Manitoba Sports Hall of Fame & Museum (MSHF&M)
200 Main St., 2nd Fl., Winnipeg, MB R3C 4M2, Canada
Tel: 204-925-5735; *Fax:* 204-925-5792
www.halloffame.mb.ca

Affiliation(s): Sport Manitoba
Rick Brownlee, Executive Director

New Brunswick Sports Hall of Fame / Temple de la renommée sportive du N.-B.
Clark Bldg., PO Box 6000, 503 Queen St., Fredericton, NB E3B 5H1, Canada
Tel: 506-453-3747; *Fax:* 506-459-0481
deborah.williams@gnb.ca
www.nbsportshalloffame.nb.ca

Affiliation(s): International Sports Heritage Association
Jamie Wolverton, Executive Director

Northwestern Ontario Sports Hall of Fame & Museum
219 May St. South, Thunder Bay, ON P7E 1B5, Canada
Tel: 807-622-2852; *Fax:* 807-622-2736
nwosport@tbaytel.net
www.nwosportshalloffame.com

Kathryn Dwyer, Curator
Diane Imrie, Executive Director

Nova Scotia Sport Heritage Centre
#446, 1800 Argyle Street, Halifax, NS B3J 3N8, Canada
Tel: 902-421-1266; *Fax:* 902-425-1148

Bill Robinson, Executive Director

Ottawa Sports Hall of Fame Inc. (OSHOF) / Temple de la renommée des sports d'Ottawa
Ottawa, ON, Canada
Tel: 613-562-6515
frank.lambros@NBPCD.com
www.ottawasportshalloffame.com

Tom Deacon, Chair

Prince Edward Island Sports Hall of Fame & Museum Inc.
PO Box 1523, Summerside, PE C1N 4K4, Canada
Tel: 902-436-0423; *Fax:* 902-436-0960
publicrelations@sportpei.pe.ca
www.peisportshalloffame.ca

Clair Sudsbury, Chair

Saskatchewan Sports Hall of Fame & Museum (SSFHM)
2205 Victoria Ave., Regina, SK S4P 0S4, Canada
Tel: 306-780-9232; *Fax:* 306-780-9427
sshfm@sasktel.net
www.sshfm.com

Sheila Kelly, Executive Director

Handball

Alberta Team Handball Federation (ATHF)
Percy Page Centre, 11759 Groat Rd., Edmonton, AB T5M 3K6, Canada
Tel: 780-415-2666; *Fax:* 780-422-2663
Handballalberta@gmail.com
www.teamhandball.ab.ca

Rick Ryll, President/CEO
Amber Smart, Chief Information Officer

Balle au mur Québec (BAMQ) / Québec Handball Association
CP 1000, Succ. M, 4545, av Pierre-de-Coubertin, Montréal, QC H1V 3R2, Canada
Tél: 514-252-3062
info@sports-4murs.qc.ca
www.balleaumur.qc.ca

Affiliation(s): Association canadienned de Balle au mur
Michel Foster, Directeur général
Danny Bell, Président

Canadian Handball Association (CHA) / Fédération de balle au mur du Canada
30 Melwood Ave., Halifax, NS B3N 1E3, Canada
Tel: 902-477-2902; *Fax:* 902-431-3145
handball@cdnhandball.ca
www.cdnhandball.ca

Brian Goto, President
Mike Wilson, Treasurer

Canadian Team Handball Federation (CTHF) / Fédération canadienne de handball olympique (FCHO)
453, rue Jacob-Nicol, Sherbrooke, QC J1J 4E5, Canada
Tel: 819-563-7937; *Fax:* 819-563-5352
f.lebeau@videotron.ca
www.handballcanada.ca

Affiliation(s): International Handball Federation; Pan American Team Handball Federation; Commonwealth Handball Federation
François LeBeau, COO
Ward Hrabi, President

Fédération québécoise de handball olympique
CP 1000, Succ. M, 4545, av Pierre-de-Coubertin, Montréal, QC H1V 3R2, Canada
Tél: 514-252-3067; *Téléc:* 514-251-8882
handball@handball.qc.ca
www.handball-elite.com

Michelle Lortie, Directrice

Manitoba Team Handball Federation
#311, 200 Main St., Winnipeg, MB R3C 4M2, Canada
Tel: 204-925-5652; *Fax:* 204-925-5703
NancyKarpinsky@hotmail.com
www.handballmanitoba.com

Nancy Karpinsky, President

New Brunswick Team Handball Association
585, Pointe des Ferguson, Tracadie-Sheila, NB E1X 1C6, Canada
Tél: 506-395-7722; *Téléc:* 506-395-3809

Adair Losier, President

Newfoundland & Labrador Handball Federation
c/o School of Human Kinetics, Memorial Univ., St. John's, NL A1C 5S7, Canada
Tel: 709-737-8684
rwheeler@mun.ca

Ralph Wheeler, Contact

Team Handball Federation of British Columbia
Vancouver, BC, Canada
info@vancouverhandball.ca
www.vancouverhandball.ca

Deborah Magdee, President

Hang Gliding

British Columbia Hang Gliding & Paragliding Association (BCHPA)
www.bchpa.ca

Nance Margit, President

Hang Gliding & Paragliding Association of Atlantic Canada (HPAAC)
General Delivery, Diligent River, NS B0M 1H0, Canada
Tel: 902-254-2972
jnewman@eastlink.ca
www.hpaac.ca

Affiliation(s): Hang Gliding & Paragliding Association of Canada
Judith Newman, Contact

Hang Gliding & Paragliding Association of Canada (HPAC) / Association canadienne de vol libre (ACVL)
5 Millennium Dr., Stratford, PE C1B 2H2, Canada
Fax: 902-367-3358
Toll-Free: 877-370-2078
admin@hpac.ca
www.hpac.ca

Domagoj Juretic, President
Sam Jeyes, Business Manager

Health

Island Fitness Council
#2, 1216 Sand Cove Rd., Saint John, NB E2M 5V8, Canada
Tel: 506-672-1993; *Fax:* 506-672-8762
Toll-Free: 888-790-1411
membershipservices@fitnessnb.ca
www.fitnessnb.ca

Affiliation(s): National Fitness Leadership Alliance

Physical & Health Education Canada / Éducation physique et santé Canada
#301, 2197 Riverside Dr., Ottawa, ON K1H 7X3
Tel: 613-523-1348; *Fax:* 613-523-1206
Toll-Free: 800-663-8708
info@phecanada.ca
www.phecanada.ca

Mark Jones, President
Andrea Grantham, Executive Director
Sharon May, Director, Programs

Hearing

Canadian Deaf Ice Hockey Federation (CDIHF)
c/o C. Cooper, #137, 201 Queen Victoria Dr., Hamilton, ON L8W 1W7
cdihf@rogers.com
www.cdihf.deafhockey.com
Affiliation(s): Canadian Hockey Association; Ontario Deaf Sports Association, Inc.; Canadian Deaf Sports Association
Danny Daniels, President
Eugene Franciosi, Vice-President
Brenda Stanley, Secretary
Raymond Patterson, Treasurer

Hiking

Federation of Mountain Clubs of British Columbia
PO Box 19673, 130 West Broadway, Vancouver, BC V5T 4E7, Canada
Tel: 604-873-6096; *Fax:* 604-873-6086
fmcbc@mountainclubs.bc.ca
www.mountainclubs.bc.ca
Patrick R. Harrison, President
Ron Ford, Registrar
Brian Jones, Manager
Peter Rothermel, Vice-President

Hockey

British Columbia Amateur Hockey Association (BCAHA) / Association de hockey amateur de la Colombie-Britannique
6671 Oldfield Rd., Saanichton, BC V8M 2A1, Canada
Tel: 250-652-2978; *Fax:* 250-652-4536
info@bchockey.net
www.bchockey.net
Barry Petrachenko, Executive Director
Ed Mayert, President

Canadian Adult Recreational Hockey Association (CARHA)
#610, 1420 Blair Pl., Ottawa, ON K1J 9L8, Canada
Tel: 613-244-1989; *Fax:* 613-244-0451
Toll-Free: 800-267-1854
hockey@carhahockey.ca
www.carhahockey.ca
Mike Peski, President

Canadian Hockey League
#201, 305 Milner Ave., Toronto, ON M1B 3V4, Canada
Tel: 416-332-9711; *Fax:* 416-332-1477
www.chl.ca
Tim Van Overbeek, Contact

Fédération internationale de hockey (FIH) / International Hockey Federation
Résidence du Parc, Rue du Valentin 61, Lausanne, 1004, Switzerland
Tél: 41-21-641-0606; *Téléc:* 41-21-641-0607
nicole.delaloye@worldhockey.org
www.worldhockey.org
Affiliation(s): Field Hockey Canada
Leandro Negre, President

Hockey Canada
#N204, 801 King Edward Ave., Ottawa, ON K1N 6N5, Canada
Tel: 613-562-5677; *Fax:* 613-562-5676
Toll-Free: 800-667-2242
nsouliere@hockeycanada.ca
www.hockeycanada.ca
Affiliation(s): International Ice Hockey Federation
Bob Nicholson, President
Al Morris, Chairman

Hockey Development Centre for Ontario (HDCO)
#312, 3 Concorde Gate, Toronto, ON M3C 3N7, Canada
Tel: 416-426-7252; *Fax:* 416-426-7348
Toll-Free: 888-843-4326
hockey@hdco.on.ca
www.hdco.on.ca
Wayne Dillon, Executive Director
Wayne Salatino, Chair

Hockey Manitoba
508 - 145 Pacific Ave., Winnipeg, MB R3B 2Z6, Canada
Tel: 204-925-5755; *Fax:* 204-925-5761
info@hockeymanitoba.mb.ca
www.hockeymanitoba.mb.ca
Affiliation(s): Hockey Canada
Brian Franklin, President
Peter Woods, Executive Director
Bernie Reichardt, Director, Hockey Development

Hockey New Brunswick (HNB) / Hockey Nouveau-Brunswick
PO Box 456, 861 Woodstock Rd., Fredericton, NB E3B 4Z9, Canada
Tel: 506-453-0089; *Fax:* 506-453-0868
www.hnb.ca
Brian Whitehead, Executive Director
Tom Donovan, President
Pat MacFadzen, Director, Administration

Hockey Newfoundland & Labrador (NLHA) / Association de hockey de Terre-Neuve et Labrador
PO Box 176, 13B High St., Grand Falls-Windsor, NL A2A 2J4, Canada
Tel: 709-489-5512; *Fax:* 709-489-2273
office@hockeynl.ca
www.hockeynl.ca
Craig Tulk, Executive Director
Tamar Hobbs, Administrative Assistant

Hockey North
3506 McDonald Dr., Yellowknife, NT X1A 2H1, Canada
Tel: 867-874-6903; *Fax:* 867-874-4603
ccarriere@northwestel.net
www.hockeynorth.ca
Cheryl Carriere, Executive Director

Hockey Northwestern Ontario (HNO)
#100, 216 Red River Rd., Thunder Bay, ON P7B 1A6, Canada
Tel: 807-623-1542; *Fax:* 807-623-0037
info@hockeyhno.com
www.hockeyhno.com
John Pucci, General Manager
Ron MacKinnon, Development Coorindator

Hockey Nova Scotia
#200, 6300 Lady Hammond Rd., Halifax, NS B3K 2R6, Canada
Tel: 902-454-9400; *Fax:* 902-454-3883
www.hockeynovascotia.ca
Darren Cossar, Executive Director

Hockey PEI
PO Box 302, 40 Enman Cres., Charlottetown, PE C1A 7K7, Canada
Tel: 902-368-4334; *Fax:* 902-368-4337
info@hockeypei.com
www.hockeypei.com
Rob Newson, Executive Director

Hockey Québec (FQHG)
#210, 7450, boul. les Galeries d'Anjou, Montréal, QC H1M 3M3, Canada
Tél: 514-252-3079; *Téléc:* 514-252-3158
info@hockey.qc.ca
www.hockey.qc.ca
Gérard Bélanger, Président
Sylvain B. Lalonde, Directeur général

International Hockey Hall of Fame & Museum (IHHOF)
PO Box 82, 277 York St., Kingston, ON K7L 4V6, Canada
Tel: 613-544-2355; *Fax:* 613-544-2844
info@ihhof.com
www.ihhof.com
Mark Potter, President

International Hockey Heritage Centre
c/o MacDonnell Group Consulting Ltd., #1100, 1505 Barrington St., Halifax, NS B3J 3K5, Canada
Tel: 902-425-3980; *Fax:* 902-423-7593
info@hockeyland.ca
www.hockeyland.ca
Ralston MacDonnell, Project Manager
Wayne Russell, Chair

International Ice Hockey Federation (IIHF)
Brandschenkestrasse 50, Zurich, CH-8027, Switzerland
Tel: 41-1-562-2200; *Fax:* 41-1-562-2229
office@iihf.com
www.iihf.com
Affiliation(s): Hockey Canada
Horst Lichtner, General Secretary
René Fasel, President

Minor Hockey Alliance of Ontario
71 Albert St., Stratford, ON N5A 3K2, Canada
Tel: 519-273-7209; *Fax:* 519-273-2114
alliance@alliancehockey.com
www.alliancehockey.com
Tony Martindale, Executive Director

Northern Ontario Hockey Association (NOHA)
108 Lakeshore Dr., North Bay, ON P1A 2A8, Canada
Tel: 705-474-8851; *Fax:* 705-474-6019
noha@noha.on.ca
www.noha.on.ca
Affiliation(s): Ontario Hockey Federation
Bryce Kulik, President
Chris May, Executive Director

Nova Scotia Minor Hockey Council
#910, 6080 Young St., Halifax, NS B3K 5L2, Canada
Tel: 902-455-8320; *Fax:* 902-454-3883
Toll-Free: 800-313-8320
Affiliation(s): Nova Scotia Hockey Association
Cliff Pottie, Executive Director
Tom O'Keefe, Chairman

Ontario Hockey Federation (OHF)
Sport Alliance of Ontario Bldg., #212, 3 Concorde Gate, Toronto, ON M3C 3N7
Tel: 416-426-7249; *Fax:* 416-426-7347
info@ohf.on.ca
www.ohf.on.ca
Affiliation(s): Minor Hockey Alliance of Ontario; Greater Toronto Hockey League; Northern Ontario Hockey Association; Ontario Minor Hockey Association; Ontario Hockey Association; Ontario Hockey League; Ontario Women's Hockey Association
Joe Drago, Executive Director
Bill Bowman, 1st Vice-President
Frank Pindar, 2nd Vice-President
Phil McKee, Executive Director
Wayne Tod, Secretary-Treasurer
Ryan Berg, Coordinator, Hockey Development
Cheryl Boston, Coordinator, Communications, Marketing, & Events

Ontario Minor Hockey Association (OMHA)
#3, 25 Brodie Dr., Richmond Hill, ON L4B 3K7
Tel: 905-780-6642; *Fax:* 905-780-0344
omha@omha.net
www.omha.net
Affiliation(s): Ontario Hockey Federation
Marg Ensoll, President
Richard Ropchan, Executive Director
Kevin Boston, Director, Marketing & Events
Ian Taylor, Director, Development
Bill Rowney, Treasurer
Mark Dickie, Manager, Communications & IT

Ontario Women's Hockey Association (OWHA) / Association de hockey féminin de l'Ontario
#3, 5155 Spectrum Way, Mississauga, ON L4W 5A1, Canada
Tel: 905-282-9980; *Fax:* 905-282-9982
info@owha.on.ca
owha.on.ca
Fran Rider, President

Ottawa & District Hockey Association (ODHA) / Association de hockey du district d'Ottawa
#D 300, 1247 Kilborn Pl., Ottawa, ON K1H 6K9, Canada
Tel: 613-224-7686; *Fax:* 613-224-6079
rts-ed@odha.com
www.odha.com
Richard T. Sennott, Executive Director

Pan American Hockey Federation (PAHF)
46 Barton St., Ottawa, ON K1S 4R7, Canada
Tel: 819-956-8023; *Fax:* 819-956-8019
info@panamhockey.org
www.panamhockey.org

Saskatchewan Hockey Association (SHA) / Association de hockey de la Saskatchewan
#2, 575 Park St., Regina, SK S4N 5B2, Canada
Tel: 306-789-5101; *Fax:* 306-789-6112
carissal@sha.sk.ca
www.sha.sk.ca
Al Hubbs, President
Kelly McClintock, General Manager

Sledge Hockey of Canada (SHOC)
c/o Hockey Canada, #N204, 801 King Edward Ave., Ottawa, ON K1N 6N5, Canada
Tel: 613-562-5677; *Fax:* 613-562-5676
cchampagne@hockeycanada.ca
www.hockeycanada.ca
Adam Crockatt, Manager

Western Hockey League (WHL)
#1, 3030 Sunridge Way NE, Calgary, AB T1Y 7K4, Canada
Tel: 403-693-3030; *Fax:* 403-693-3031
info@whl.ca
www.whl.ca
Ron Robison, Commissioner

Horse Racing

Alberta Horse Trials Association
c/o Joanne Cameron, 21 Greenbrier Cres., St Albert, AB T8N 1A2, Canada
Tel: 780-922-3170
mgaglione@xplornet.com
www.albertahorsetrials.com
Affiliation(s): Canadian Equestrian Federation
George Balogh, President

Association Trot & Amble du Québec (ATAQ)
#230, 5375, rue Paré, Montréal, QC H4P 1P7, Canada
Tél: 514-731-9484; *Téléc:* 514-731-7687
Ligne sans frais: 800-731-9484
courses@qc.aira.com
www.trotetamble.ca/fr/index.html
Michel St-Louis, Président

Jockey Club of Canada / Jockey Club du Canada
PO Box 66, Stn. B, Toronto, ON M9W 5K9, Canada
Tel: 416-675-7756; *Fax:* 416-675-6378
jockeyclub@bellnet.ca
www.jockeyclubcanada.com
Richard Bonnycastle, Steward
Bridget Bimm, Executive Director

Jockeys Benefit Association of Canada (JBAC)
c/o Thoroughbred Race Office, 555 Rexdale Blvd., Toronto, ON M9W 5L2, Canada
Tel: 416-798-8715
jbacmanager@mac.com
jbac.ca/trainers/jbac
Chad Hoverson, President
Robert King, Secretary-Manager

Ontario Horse Racing Industry Association (OHRIA)
PO Box 456, 555 Rexdale Blvd., Toronto, ON M9W 5L4, Canada
Tel: 416-679-0741; *Fax:* 416-679-9114
ohria@ohria.com
www.ohria.com
Hector Clouthier, Executive Director

Horses

Saskatchewan Standardbred Horsemen's Association
PO Box 4122, Regina, SK S4P 3W5, Canada
Tel: 306-757-4755
Ron McLeod, President

Kayaking

Canoe Kayak Saskatchewan (CKS)
1870 Lorne St., Regina, SK S4P 2L7, Canada
Tel: 306-729-4220; *Fax:* 306-729-4216
cks@accesscomm.ca
www.saskcanoe.ca
Jan Hanson, Executive Director
Fiona Vincent, President
Jeanette Hamilton, Treasurer

Fédération québécoise de canoë-kayak d'eau vive
CP 1000, Succ. M, 4545, av Pierre-de Coubertin, Montréal, QC H1V 3R2, Canada
Tél: 514-252-3099; *Téléc:* 514-252-3094
fqckev@kayak.qc.ca
www.kayak.qc.ca
Patrick Lévesque, Coordonnateur

Ontario Recreational Canoeing and Kayaking Association (ORCKA)
#411, 1185 Eglinton Ave. East, Toronto, ON M3C 3C6, Canada
Tel: 416-426-7016; *Fax:* 416-426-7363
info@orca.on.ca
www.orca.on.ca
Gordon Haggert, President

Paddle Canada (PC) / Pagaie Canada
PO Box 20069, Stn. RPO Taylor-Kidd, Kingston, ON K7P 2T6, Canada
Tel: 613-547-3196; *Fax:* 613-547-4880
Toll-Free: 888-252-6292
info@paddlingcanada.com
www.paddlingcanada.com
Affiliation(s): Active Living Alliance for Canadians with a Disability; Canadian Heritage Rivers System; Girl Guides of Canada
Sue J. Hopson, Business Manager

Wilderness Canoe Association (WCA)
PO Box 91068, 2901 Bayview Ave., Toronto, ON M2K 2Y6, Canada
Tel: 416-223-4646
info@wildernesscanoe.ca
www.wildernesscanoe.ca
Aleks Gusev, Chair

Labour Unions

Canadian Football League Players' Association (CFLPA) / Association des joueurs de la ligue de football canadienne
#207, 603 Argus Rd., Oakville, ON L6J 6G6, Canada
Tel: 905-844-7852; *Fax:* 905-844-5127
Toll-Free: 800-616-6865
admin@cflpa.com
www.cflpa.com
Stu Laird, President
Mike O'Shea, 1st Vice-President
Jay McNeil, 2nd Vice-President
Sean Fleming, Member-at-Large
Edward Molstad, Legal Counsel
Fred James, Benefits Chairman
Deanne Mitchell, Executive Assistant

Major League Baseball Players' Association (Ind.) / Association des joueurs de la Ligue majeure de baseball (ind.)
12 East 49th St., 24th Fl., New York, NY 10017, USA
Tel: 212-826-0808; *Fax:* 212-752-4378
feedback@mlbpa.org
www.majorleaguebaseball.com/
Donald M. Fehr, Executive Director
Gene Orza, Chief Operating Officer

Professional Hockey Players' Association (PHPA)
#701, 1 St Paul St., St Catharines, ON L2R 7L2, Canada
Tel: 905-682-4800; *Fax:* 905-682-4822
phpa@phpa.com
www.phpa.com
Larry Landon, Executive Director

Lacrosse

British Columbia Lacrosse Association (BCLA)
4041B Remi Pl., Burnaby, BC V5A 4J8, Canada
Tel: 604-421-9755; *Fax:* 604-421-9775
info@bclacrosse.com
www.bclacrosse.com
Rochelle Winterton, Executive Director

Canadian Lacrosse Association (CLA) / Association canadienne de crosse (ACC)
#B4, 2211 Riverside Dr., Ottawa, ON K1H 7X5, Canada
Tel: 613-260-2028; *Fax:* 613-260-2029
info@lacrosse.ca
www.lacrosse.ca
Affiliation(s): International Lacrosse Federation; International Federation of Women's Lacrosse Associations; Fédération internationale d'Inter-crosse; Canadian Lacrosse Foundation; Sport Canada; Coaching Association of Canada
David Miriguay, CLA General Manager

Fédération de crosse du Québec (FCQ)
CP 1000, Succ. M, 4545, av Pierre-de Coubertin, Montréal, QC H1V 3R2, Canada
Tél: 514-252-3058; *Téléc:* 514-251-8038
crosse@crosse.qc.ca
www.crosse.qc.ca
Affiliation(s): Sports Québec; Regroupement Loisir Québec
Joe Cambria, Président

Lacrosse Nova Scotia
PO Box 3010 South, Halifax, NS B3J 3G6, Canada
Tel: 902-233-1783; *Fax:* 902-425-5606
bill.brydon@rcmp-grc.gc.ca
www3.ns.sympatico.ca/hami/
Affiliation(s): Canadian Lacrosse Association; Sport Nova Scotia
Stephen Brown, Vice-President, Administration
Wayne Finck, Vice-President, Technical Development
Brian Thompson, Vice-President, Finance

Ontario Lacrosse Association
#607, 1185 Eglinton Ave. East, Toronto, ON M3C 3C6, Canada
Tel: 416-426-7068; *Fax:* 416-426-7382
info@ontariolacrosse.com
www.ontariolacrosse.com
Stan Cockerton, Executive Director

Saskatchewan Lacrosse Association
2205 Victoria Ave., Regina, SK S4P 0S4, Canada
Tel: 306-780-9216; *Fax:* 306-525-4009
lacrosse@sasktel.net
www.sasklacrosse.net
Dale Measner, Executive Director

Lawn Bowling

Bowls BC (BBC)
#148, 5525 West Blvd., Vancouver, BC V6M 3W6, Canada
www.bowlsbc.ca
Affiliation(s): World Bowls Board; World Indoor Bowls Board
Keith Terlson, President
Pat Cutt, Vice-President
Marjorie Mitchell, Treasurer
Juanita Tucker, Secretary

Bowls Canada Boulingrin (BCB)
#207, 720 Belfast Rd., Ottawa, ON K1G 0Z5, Canada
Tel: 613-244-0021; *Fax:* 613-244-0041
Toll-Free: 800-567-2695
office@bowlscanada.com
www.bowlscanada.com
Affiliation(s): Commonwealth Games Association of Canada
Kevin Penny, Executive Director

Bowls Manitoba
200 Main St., Winnipeg, MB R3C 4M2, Canada
Tel: 204-925-5694; *Fax:* 204-925-5703
bowls@shawbiz.ca
www.bowls.mb.ca
Cathy Derewianchuk, Executive Director

Bowls Saskatchewan Inc.
#102, 1860 Lorne St., Regina, SK S4P 2L7, Canada
Tel: 306-780-9426; *Fax:* 306-781-6021
bowlsask@sasktel.net
www.bowls.sk.ca
Karen Swanson, Executive Director
Jean Roney, President

Lawn Bowls Association of Alberta
Percy Page Centre, 11759 Groat Rd., 3rd Fl., Edmonton, AB T5M 3K6, Canada
Tel: 780-427-8119; *Fax:* 780-452-5932
lawnbowl@telusplanet.net
www.bowls.ab.ca
David Simpson, President
Mary Ward, Secretary
Margaret Bruce, Treasurer

New Brunswick Lawn Bowling Association
929A Cloverdale Rd., Riverview, NB E1B 5E6, Canada
rkhm118@aol.com
Dugald Richford, Executive Secretary

Ontario Lawn Bowls Association
c/o Elaine Stevenson, 23018 Lakeridge Rd., RR#2, Sunderland, ON L0C 1H0
Tel: 705-228-8058
olba@olba.ca
www.olba.ca
Arja Nesbitt, President
Elaine Houtby, Vice-President
Alan Dean, 2nd Vice-President
Bob O'Neil, Executive Director
Edith Pedden, Secretary
Richard Peart, Treasurer

Prince Edward Island Lawn Bowling Association
Sport PEI, PO Box 302, Charlottetown, PE C1A 7K7, Canada
Tel: 902-368-4110
sharonrenner@eastlink.ca
Sharon Renner, President

Québec Lawn Bowling Federation / Fédération de Boulingrin du Québec
#662 Oak Ave., Saint-Lambert, QC J4P 2R6, Canada
www.qlbf.org
Debbie Smits, Contact

Libraries

North American Sport Library Network (NASLIN)
c/o University of Calgary Law Library, 2500 University Dr. NW, Calgary, AB T2N 1N4, Canada
Tel: 403-220-6097; *Fax:* 403-282-6837
gghent@ucalgary.ca
www.naslin.org
Affiliation(s): International Association for Sports Information
Gretchen Ghent, Chair

Martial Arts

Association de taekwondo du Québec
CP 1000, Succ. M, 4545, av Pierre-de Coubertin, Montréal, QC H1V 3R2, Canada
Tél: 514-252-3198; *Téléc:* 514-254-7075
Ligne sans frais: 800-762-9565
info@taekwondo-quebec.ca
www.taekwondo-quebec.ca
Jean Faucher, Président
Richard Gagné, Vice-président

Canadian Chito-Ryu Karate-Do Association
89 Curlew Ave., Toronto, ON M3A 2P8, Canada
Tel: 416-444-5310
www.canadianchitoryu.ca
David Smith, President
Derek J. Ryan, Vice-President

Canadian Jiu-jitsu Association Inc. / Association canadienne du jiu-jitsu inc.
c/o Pro Spar Martial Arts Centre, #10, 4 Alliance Blvd., Barrie, ON L4M 5J1, Canada
Tel: 705-725-9186
Toll-Free: 800-352-1338
info@canadianjiujitsu.com
www.canadianjiujitsu.com
Affiliation(s): World Council of Jiu-Jitsu Organizations
Gary Pilon, Vice-President/Treas.
Terry Yanke, President

Canadian Kendo Federation (CKF) / Fédération canadienne de kendo
8013 Hunter St., Burnaby, BC V5A 2B8
Tel: 604-420-0438; *Fax:* 604-420-1971
hokusa@kendo-canada.com
www.kendo-canada.com
Hiro Okusa, President
Yoshiaki Taguchi, Vice-President
Christian d'Orangeville, 2nd Vice-President
Kim Taylor, Secretary
John Maisonneuve, Treasurer

Confederation of Canadian Wushu Organizations
#22-25B, 2370 Midland Ave., Toronto, ON M1S 5C6, Canada
Tel: 416-321-5913; *Fax:* 416-321-5068
cdnwushu@rogers.com
www.canadawushu.com
Sunny Tang, National President

Judo Alberta
11759 Groat Rd., Edmonton, AB T5M 3K6, Canada
Tel: 780-427-8379; *Fax:* 780-447-1915
Toll-Free: 866-919-5836
judo@judoalberta.com
www.judoalberta.com
Affiliation(s): International Judo Federation
Garry Yamashita, President

Judo British Columbia
4421 Prince Albert St., Vancouver, BC V5V 4K1, Canada
Tel: 604-734-3197; *Fax:* 604-251-3197
info@judobc.ca
www.judobc.ca
Renée Hock, Executive Director

Judo Manitoba
c/o Sport Manitoba, #310, 200 Main St., Winnipeg, MB R3C 4M2, Canada
Tel: 204-925-5691; *Fax:* 204-925-5703
judomb@sport.mb.ca
www.judomanitoba.mb.ca
John Wenham, Executive Director
David Minuk, President

Judo New Brunswick / Judo Nouveau Brunswick
#13, 900 Hanwell Rd., Fredericton, NB E3B 6A2, Canada
Tel: 506-451-1322; *Fax:* 506-451-1325
judonb@nb.aibn.com
www.sport.nb.ca/judonb/
Jean Pierre Cantin, Executive Director

Judo Newfoundland
#112, Hamlyn Rd. Plaza, Unit 50, St. John's, NL A1E 5X7, Canada
Fax: 709-722-2573
Toll-Free: 877-879-5836
judo@nfld.com
www.judonl.ca
Blair Bradbury, President

Judo Nova Scotia
224 Victoria Rd., Bridgewater, NS B4V 2P1, Canada
Tel: 902-543-2836; *Fax:* 902-527-4847
tim.lohnes@abitibibowater.com
www.judons.ca
Tim Lohnes, President

Judo Ontario
1185 Eglinton Ave. East, Toronto, ON M3C 3C6, Canada
Tel: 416-426-7006; *Fax:* 416-426-7390
Toll-Free: 866-553-5836
info@judoontario.ca
www.judoontario.ca
Ron Wilson, Executive Director
Charles Formosa, President
Mohamad Hassani, Secretary General

Judo Prince Edward Island
40 Enman Cres., Charlottetown, PE C1E 1E6, Canada
Tel: 902-368-4262; *Fax:* 902-368-4548
gflood@sportpei.pe.ca
sites.townsquare.ca/JudoPEI/index.cfm
John Wilbert, President

Judo Saskatchewan
c/o Registrar, 3130 Parkland Dr., Regina, SK S4V 1W5, Canada
Tel: 306-789-7395
abyuen@sasktel.net
www.judosask.ca
Affiliation(s): International Judo Federation
T.V. Taylor, President
Bev Yuen, Registrar

Judo-Québec inc
CP 1000, Succ. M, 4545, av Pierre-de-Coubertin, Montréal, QC H1V 3R2, Canada
Tél: 514-252-3040; *Téléc:* 514-254-5184
info@judo-quebec.qc.ca
www.judo-quebec.qc.ca
Affiliation(s): Fédération internationale de Judo; Union panaméricaine du Judo
Daniel De Angelis, Président
Patrick Esparbès, Directeur général
Patrick Vesin, Coordonnateur technique

Karate BC (KBC)
#225, 3820 Cessna Dr., Richmond, BC V7B 0A2, Canada
Tel: 604-333-3610; *Fax:* 604-333-3612
info@karatebc.org
www.karatebc.org
Affiliation(s): National Karate Association; Sport BC; Sport Canada; Canadian Olympic Association
Dan Wallis, President
Robert G. Tuss, Executive Director
Ken Corrigan, Treasurer

Karate Manitoba
200 Main St., Winnipeg, MB R3C 4M2, Canada
Tel: 204-925-5682; *Fax:* 204-925-5703
colettem@highspeedcrow.ca
www.karatemanitoba.ca
Meron Solonynka, President
Cindy Glacken, Treasurer
Bill Murray, Secretary

Karate New Brunswick
294 Water St., St Andrews, NB E5B 1B7, Canada
david.langley@gnb.ca
karatenb.com
Rick MacMichael, Treasurer
Joe Hatfield, Secretary
Paul Oliver, President

Karate Ontario
#160, 2 County Ct. Blvd., Brampton, ON L6W 4V1, Canada
Tel: 905-455-2170
info@karateontario.org
www.karateontario.org
Affiliation(s): World Karate Federation; Sport Alliance of Ontario; Coaches Assocation of Ontario
Joshua Drury, Secretary

Karaté Québec
CP 1000, Succ. M, 4545, rue Pierre de Coubertin, Montréal, QC H1V 3R2, Canada
Tél: 514-252-3161; *Téléc:* 514-252-3036
info@karatequebec.com
www.karatequebec.com
Mohamed Jelassi, Coordonnateur général

Manitoba Tae Kwon-Do Association
200 Main St., Winnipeg, MB R3C 4M2, Canada
Tel: 204-925-5682; *Fax:* 204-925-5703
tkd-exec@rainyday.mb.ca
K.S. Cho, President

National Tae Kwon-Do Federation
c/o Whitecroft Hall, #314, 52313 Range Rd. 232, Sherwood Park, AB T8B 1B5, Canada
Tel: 780-468-3418
www.ntf.ca
Wilfred Ho, President & Founder

Newfoundland & Labrador WTF (World Taekwondo Federation) Tae Kwon Do Association
PO Box 28083, 48 Kenmount Rd., St. John's, NL A1B 4J8, Canada
www.nltkd.ca
Affiliation(s): WTF Canada; Sport Canada; Sport NL; Kukkiwon
Neil Tucker, President
Paul Gosse, Vice-President
Sheila McGrath, Secretary
Lisa Collette, Treasurer

Ontario Taekwondo Association
#201, 2355 Keele Street, Toronto, ON M6M 4A2, Canada
Tel: 416-245-8582
otasecretarygeneral@yahoo.com
www.taekwondo.on.ca
Hwa Sun Myung, President
Yoneh Chae, Secretary General

Police Martial Arts Association
PO Box 7303, Sub. #12, Riverview, NB E1B 4T9, Canada
Tel: 506-387-5126
pmaa@nbnet.nb.ca
www.policemartialarts.org
Rannie MacDonald
Foster MacLeod

Prince Edward Island Karate Association (PEIKA)
PO Box 640, Montague, PE C0A 1R0, Canada
Tel: 902-892-3640
www.karatepei.ca
Affiliation(s): Sport PEI; National Karate Association
Erick A. Silva, Treasurer
Ken Roper, President
Lori Beck, Secretary

Yukon Judo
4061 - 4th Ave., Whitehorse, YT Y1A 1H1, Canada
Tel: 867-668-4236; *Fax:* 867-667-4237
jessup@klondiker.com
Penny Prysnuk, President

Massage Therapy

Canadian Sport Massage Therapists Association (CSMTA) / Association canadienne des massothérapeutes du sport
#306, 50 Eccleston Dr., Toronto, ON M4A 1K8, Canada
Tel: 416-285-1745; *Fax:* 416-285-1914
natoffice@csmta.ca
www.csmta.ca

Affiliation(s): Canadian Olympic Committee; Expert Provider Group
Trish Scheidel, President
Joanne Baker, National Office Coordinator
Aurel Hamran, President, Alberta Chapter
Kim Mark-Goldsworthy, President, BC Chapter
Johanna Thackwray, President, Ontario Chapter
Al Bodnarchuk, President, Saskatchewan Chapter

Mediation

Sport Dispute Resolution Centre of Canada
#950, 1080 Beaver Hall Hill, Montréal, QC H2Z 1S8, Canada
Tel: 450-686-1245; *Fax:* 450-686-1246
Toll-Free: 866-733-7767
info@adrsportred.ca
www.adrsportred.ca
Allan J. Stitt, President
Benoit Girardin, Executive Director

Motorcycles

Association des motocyclistes gais du Québec (AMGQ)
CP 36, Succ. C, Montréal, QC H2L 4J7, Canada
Tél: 514-247-9564
info@amgq.org
www.amgq.org
Adam Roy, Président

Canadian Motorcycle Association (CMA) / Association motocycliste canadienne
PO Box 448, Hamilton, ON L8L 8C4, Canada
Tel: 905-522-5705; *Fax:* 905-522-5716
registration@canmocycle.ca
www.canmocycle.ca
Affiliation(s): Fédération internationale motocycliste; Canadian Olympic Association; North American Motorcycle Union
Marilyn Bastedo, General Manager
Joseph Godsall, President

Fédération motocycliste du Québec (FMQ) / Quebec Motorcyclist Federation
#208, 4875, boul Métropolitain est, Montréal, QC H1R 3J2, Canada
Tél: 514-252-8121; *Téléc:* 514-252-7857
fmq@fmq.qc.ca
www.fmq.qc.ca
Jacques Lafontaine, Président

Mountaineering

The Alpine Club of Canada (ACC) / Club alpin du Canada
PO Box 8040, Indian Flats Rd., Canmore, AB T1W 2T8, Canada
Tel: 403-678-3200; *Fax:* 403-678-3224
info@alpineclubofcanada.ca
www.alpineclubofcanada.ca
Affiliation(s): International Union of Alpinist Associations
Lawrence White, Executive Director
Peter Muir, President

Association of Canadian Mountain Guides (ACMG) / Association des guides de montagne canadiens
PO Box 8341, Canmore, AB T1W 2V1, Canada
Tel: 403-678-2885; *Fax:* 403-609-0070
acmg@acmg.ca
www.acmg.ca
Keith Reid, President
Peter Tucker, Executive Director

British Columbia Mountaineering Club
PO Box 2674, Vancouver, BC V6B 3W8, Canada
Tel: 604-268-9502
info@bcmc.ca
www.bcmc.ca
Affiliation(s): Federation of Mountain Clubs of BC
David Scanlon, President

Native Peoples

Aboriginal Sport & Recreation Association of British Columbia (ASRA)
#4, 2475 Mt. Newton X Rd., Saanichton, BC V8M 2B7, Canada
Tel: 250-544-8172; *Fax:* 250-544-8173
asra@asra.ca
www.asra.ca
Alex Nelson, President & CEO
Patrick Chénier, General Manager
Gordon Celesta, Operations Manager
Karen Henry, Program Manager
Linda Bristol, Office Manager

Aboriginal Sport Circle
Roundpoint Memorial Bldg., #7, 34 McCumber Rd., Akwesasne Mohawk Territory, Cornwall Island, ON K6H 5R7, Canada
Tel: 613-938-1176; *Fax:* 613-938-9181
rbrant@aboriginalsportcircle.ca
www.aboriginalsportcircle.ca
Viginia Doucett, Executive Director

Netball

British Columbia Netball Association
3468 Triumph St., Vancouver, BC V5K 1T8, Canada
Tel: 604-293-1820; *Fax:* 604-293-1851
netball_info@bcnetball.net
www.bcnetball.net

Fédération de Netball du Québec / Québec Amateur Netball Federation
5617, av Jellicoe, Montréal, QC H4W 1Z5, Canada
Tél: 514-486-2769
quebecnetball@yahoo.ca
www.netballquebec.com
Avice Roberts-Joseph, Présidente

Netball Alberta
PO Box 270, 7620 Elbow Dr. SW, Calgary, AB T2V 1K2, Canada
Tel: 403-238-8041
info@albertanetball.com
www.netballalberta.com
Affiliation(s): International Federation of Netball Associations
Paula MacWilliam, President

Obesity

Active Healthy Kids Canada / Jeunes en forme Canada
#1804 - 2 Bloor St. E, Toronto, ON M4W 1A8, Canada
Tel: 416-913-0238; *Fax:* 416-913-1541
info@activehealthykids.ca
www.activehealthykids.ca
Michelle Brownrigg, Chief Executive Officer

Olympic Games

Canadian Olympic Committee (COC) / Comité olympique canadien
#900, 21 St Clair Ave. East, Toronto, ON M4T 1L9, Canada
Tel: 416-962-0262; *Fax:* 416-967-4902
www.olympic.ca
Chris Rudge, CEO

Vancouver Organizing Committee for the 2010 Olympic & Paralympic Winter Games
#400, 1095 West Pender St., Vancouver, BC V6E 2M6, Canada
Tel: 778-328-2010; *Fax:* 778-328-2011
Toll-Free: 877-408-2010
www.vancouver2010.com
John Furlong, CEO

Orienteering

Alberta Orienteering Association (AOA)
#128, 4307 - 130 Ave. SE, Calgary, AB T2Z 3V8, Canada
Tel: 403-697-5750
pascale@orienteeringalberta.ca
www.orienteeringalberta.ca
Don Riddle, President
J.P. Buysschaert, Treasurer
Pascale Levesque, Executive Director

Canadian Orienteering Federation (COF) / Fédération canadienne de course d'orientation
1239 Colgrove Ave. NE, Calgary, AB T2C 5C3, Canada
Tel: 403-283-0807; *Fax:* 403-451-1681
info@orienteering.ca
www.orienteering.ca
Affiliation(s): International Orienteering Federation
Charlotte MacNaughton, President

Manitoba Orienteering Association Inc. (MOA)
200 Main St., Winnipeg, MB R3C 4M2, Canada
Tel: 204-925-5706; *Fax:* 204-925-5792
info@orienteering.mb.ca
www.orienteering.mb.ca
Affiliation(s): Sports Manitoba
Jennifer Hamilton, President
Dave Graupner, Treasurer

Orienteering Association of British Columbia (OABC)
4337 San Cristo Pl., Victoria, BC V8N 5G5, Canada
www.orienteeringbc.ca
Affiliation(s): Canadian Orienteering Federation (COF); Coaching Association of Canada
John Rance, President
Alex Kerr, Secretary

Orienteering Association of Nova Scotia (OANS)
c/o Andrew Harding, 5516 Spring Garden Rd., 4th Fl., Halifax, NS B3J 1G6, Canada
Tel: 902-446-2295; *Fax:* 902-425-5606
info@orienteeringns.ca
www.orienteeringns.ca
Andrew Harding, Executive Director
Michael Price, President
Dale Ellis, Vice-President
Ian Folkins, Treasurer

Orienteering Ontario Inc.
2163 Third Side Rd., Campbellville, ON L0P 1B0, Canada
Tel: 416-284-5580
Toll-Free: 888-810-9990
admin@orienteering.on.ca
www.orienteering.on.ca

Orienteering Québec (OQ) / Fédération québécoise de course d'orientation
, Canada
Tel: 450-433-3624
orientering_quebec@orienteeringquebec.ca
www.orienteeringquebec.ca
Michael MacConaill, President
Randall Kemp, Vice-President
Colin Kirk, Treasurer

Yukon Orienteering Association (YOA)
4061 - 4th Ave., Whitehorse, YT Y1A 1H1, Canada
info@yukonorienteering.ca
www.yukonorienteering.ca
Barbara Scheck, President
Jean-François Roldan, Vice-President

Parachuting

Alberta Sport Parachuting Association (ASPA)
#63, 2505 - 42 St., Edmonton, AB T6L 7G8, Canada
admin@aspa.ca
www.aspa.ca
Affiliation(s): Canadian Sport Parachuting Association
Henry Komant, Acting President
Tina Connolly, Program Coordinator

Canadian Sport Parachuting Association (CSPA) / Association canadienne du parachutisme sportif (ACPS)
300 Forced Rd., Russell, ON K4R 1A1, Canada
Tel: 613-445-1881; *Fax:* 613-445-2698
office@cspa.ca
www.cspa.ca
Judy Donnelly, Executive Secretary
Tim Grech, President

Manitoba Sport Parachute Association (MSPA)
#309, 200 Main St., Winnipeg, MB R3C 4M2, Canada
Tel: 204-925-5682; *Fax:* 204-925-5703
president@mspa.mb.ca
www.mspa.mb.ca
Jill Forbes, President

Sport Parachute Association of Saskatchewan
PO Box 37056, Regina, SK S4S 7K3, Canada
Tel: 306-934-8528
www.skydive.sk.ca
Craig Skihar, President
Burk Reiman, Vice-President

Pentathlon

Alberta Modern Pentathlon Association
info@albertapentathlon.com
albertapentathlon.com
Joanne Willis, President

Canadian Modern Pentathlon Association (CAMPA) / Association canadienne du pentathlon moderne
70 Como Gardens, Hudson, QC J0P 1H0, Canada
Tel: 450-458-7974; *Fax:* 450-458-1746
president@pentathloncanada.ca
www.pentathloncanada.ca
Affiliation(s): Union internationale de pentathlon moderne et biathlon
Angela Ives, President

Physical Education & Training

Association régionale du sport étudiant de l'Est du Québec (ARSEEQ)
60, rue de L'Evêché ouest, Rimouski, QC G5L 4H6, Canada
Tél: 418-723-1880; *Téléc:* 418-722-0457
marcboud@cegep-rimouski.qc.ca
www.arseeq.net
Affiliation(s): Fédération québécoise du sport étudiant
Marc Boudreau, Directeur

Association régionale du sport étudiant de Montréal (ARSEM)
#200, 7800, boul. Métropolitain Est, Montréal, QC H1K 1A1, Canada
Tél: 514-645-6923; *Téléc:* 514-354-8632
secretariat@arsemontreal.com
www.arsemontreal.com
Jacques Desrochers, Directeur général
Dominique Blanc, Secrétaire

Fédération des éducateurs et éducatrices physiques enseignants du Québec (FEEPEQ)
2500, boul de l'Université, Sherbrooke, QC J1K 2R1, Canada
Tél: 819-821-8000; *Téléc:* 819-821-7970
feepeq.information@usherbrooke.ca
www.feepeq.com
Affiliation(s): Sports Québec; Fédération québécoise du sport étudiant
Dav Bergeron, Président
Nathalie Morneau, Directrice, Opérations

Ontario Physical & Health Education Association (OPHEA)
#608, 1 Concorde Gate, Toronto, ON M3C 3N6
Tel: 416-426-7120; *Fax:* 416-426-7373
Toll-Free: 888-446-7432
info@ophea.org
www.ophea.org
Mark Seaton, President
Chris Markham, Executive Director & CEO
Jennifer Cowie Bonne, Director, Marketing & Development
Gwen Slauenwhite, Director, Finance & Administration
Brenda Whitteker, Director, Programs

Saskatchewan Physical Education Association (SPEA)
#306, 104 - 5th St. NE, Weyburn, SK S4H 0Z1, Canada
Tel: 306-842-0978; *Fax:* 306-842-2465
spea@xplornet.com
www.speaonline.ca
Affiliation(s): Canadian Association for Health, Physical Education, Recreation, & Dance; Saskatchewan Teachers' Federation
Holly Stevens, Executive Director
Vic Stynsky, President

Physical Fitness

Alberta Fitness Leadership Certification Association (AFLCA)
Percy Page Bldg., 11759 Groat Rd., 3rd Fl., Edmonton, AB T5M 3K6, Canada
Tel: 780-492-4435; *Fax:* 780-455-2264
Toll-Free: 866-348-8648
general@provincialfitnessunit.ca
www.provincialfitnessunit.ca
Katherine MacKeigan, Executive Director

The Canadian Association of Fitness Professionals / Association canadienne des professionnels en conditionnement physique
#110, 255 Consumers Rd., Toronto, ON M2J 1R4, Canada
Tel: 416-493-3515; *Fax:* 416-493-1756
Toll-Free: 800-667-5622
info@canfitpro.com
www.canfitpro.com
Maureen Hagan, Executive Director
Kathy Ash, Contact, Administration

Canadian Fitness & Lifestyle Research Institute (CFLRI) / Institut canadien de la recherche sur la condition physique et le mode de vie
#201, 185 Somerset St. West, Ottawa, ON K2P 0J2, Canada
Tel: 613-233-5528; *Fax:* 613-233-5536
info@cflri.ca
www.cflri.ca
Lawrence Brawley, Chair
Cora Lynn Craig, President & Chief Scientist

Canadian Society for Exercise Physiology (CSEP) / Société canadienne de physiologie de l'exercice (SCPE)
#370, 18 Louisa St., Ottawa, ON K1R 6Y6
Tel: 613-234-3755; *Fax:* 613-234-3565
Toll-Free: 877-651-3755
info@csep.cap; support@csep.ca (member directory inquiries)
www.csep.ca
Affiliation(s): Public Health Agency of Canada - Physical Activity Unit
Brian MacIntosh, Executive Director
Audrey Hicks, President
Mike Plyley, Vice-President, Research
Panagiota Klentrou, Treasurer
Mary Duggan, Manager, Administration
Charles Akben-Marchand, Director, Health & Fitness Program

Certified Professional Trainers Network (CPTN)
122 D'Arcy St., Toronto, ON M5T 1K3, Canada
Tel: 416-979-1654; *Fax:* 416-979-1466
info@cptn.com
www.cptn.com
Susan Lee, President

National Association of Physical Activity & Health (NAPAH)
Tel: 416-879-2348; *Fax:* 416-879-1905
Toll-Free: 866-228-3492
info@napah.ca
www.napah.ca

Physical Culture Association of Alberta
Percy Page Centre, 11759 Groat Rd., Edmonton, AB T5M 3K6, Canada
Tel: 780-415-1744
physicalculture@hotmail.com
www.physicalculture.ca
Lesley McEwan, Executive Director

The Recreation Association / L'Association récréative
2451 Riverside Dr., Ottawa, ON K1H 7X7, Canada
Tel: 613-733-5100; *Fax:* 613-736-6234
racentre@racentre.com
www.racentre.com
Rick Baker, General Manager
John Ossowski, President

Polo

Canadian Polo Association (CPA)
#301, 250 Consumers Rd., Toronto, ON M2J 4V6
Tel: 416-494-0724; *Fax:* 416-495-8723
Toll-Free: 888-494-0724
info@polocanada.ca
www.polocanada.ca
Affiliation(s): Canadian Amateur Athletic Association (RCAAA); Federation of International Polo (FIP); Equine Canada; Ontario Equestrian Federation (OEF); International Olympic Committee (IOC)
Justin R. Fogarty, President
Don. B. Pennycook, Vice-President
Wayne Venhuizen, Secretary
Dave Offen, Treasurer

Powerlifting

Canadian Powerlifting Organization (CPO)
PO Box 51180 RPO Beddington, Calgary, AB T3K EV9, Canada
Fax: 403-698-2434
powerlifting@gmail.com; info@wpc-canada.com
www.worldpowerlifting.com/cpo

Canadian Powerlifting Union (CPU)
#17, 1063 Coteau St. West, Moose Jaw, SK S6H 5G3, Canada
Tel: 306-694-6116; *Fax:* 306-693-3301
jbutt@sasktel.net
www.powerlifting.ca
Affiliation(s): International Powerlifting Federation
Jeff Butt, President

Nova Scotia Powerlifting Association
Sydney, NS B1P 3W7, Canada
Tel: 902-567-0893
president@nspowerlifting.org
www.nspowerlifting.org
Cliff Samms, Vice-President
John Fraser, President

Ontario Powerlifting Association
412 Big Creek Rd., Caledonia, ON N3W 2G9, Canada
Tel: 905-765-5345
info@ontariopowerlifting.org
www.ontariopowerlifting.org
Bill Jamison, President

Racquetball

Association québécoise de racquetball (AQR)
CP 1000, Succ. M, 4545, av Pierre-de-Coubertin, Montréal, QC H1V 3R2, Canada
Tél: 514-252-3062
info@sports-4murs.qc.ca
www.sports-4murs.qc.ca/racquetball/accueil-AQR.html
Michel Gagnon, Président

British Columbia Racquetball Association (BCRA)
1282 - 7th Ave. West, Vancouver, BC V6H 1B6, Canada
Tel: 604-737-1786; *Fax:* 604-737-1786
bcracquetball@hotmail.com
www.racquetballbc.ca
Cheryl McKeeman, President, Memberships
Cal Smith, Vice-President, Officiating & Communication
David Serra, Secretary, Junior Development
Diana Hambley, Treasurer, Ranking

Canadian Racquetball Association (CRA) / Association canadienne de racquetball
25 Golflinks Dr., Ottawa, ON K2J 4Y1, Canada
Tel: 613-692-5394
emlane@rogers.com
www.racquetball.ca
Affiliation(s): Canadian Sport Council; Canadian Olympic Association; Coaching Association of Canada
Usher Barnoff, President

New Brunswick Racquetball Association (NBRA)
24 Baxter St., Lower Coverdale, NB E1J 1B4, Canada
Tel: 506-387-4196
moorbar@rogers.com
Barry Moore, NB Provincial Representative, Racquetball Canada

Newfoundland Racquetball Association
16 Fairhaven Pl., St. John's, NL A1W 4S2, Canada
Tel: 709-364-9151; *Fax:* 709-364-9151
measton@roadrunner.nf.net
Eric Easton, Vice-President
Dino Sauntuccione, Secretary

Racquetball Manitoba
#304, 200 Main St., Winnipeg, MB R3C 4M2, Canada
Tel: 204-925-5666; *Fax:* 204-925-5703
rball@shawbiz.ca
members.shaw.ca/racquetball
Jennifer Saunders, Executive Director

Racquetball Ontario (RO)
5591 McAdam Rd., Mississauga, ON L4Z 1N4, Canada
Tel: 519-584-0235
info@racquetballontario.ca
www.racquetballontario.ca
John Ursino, President

Racquetball PEI
c/o Sport PEI, PO Box 302, Charlottetown, PE C1A 7K7, Canada
Tel: 902-368-4110; *Fax:* 902-368-4548
postie@vapordragon.ca
Allan Postie, President

Recreation

Canadian Volkssport Federation (CVF) / Fédération canadienne volkssport (FCV)
PO Box 2668, Stn. D, Ottawa, ON K1P 5W7, Canada
Tel: 613-234-7333
cvffcv@bellnet.ca
www.walks.ca
Benoît Pinsonneault, President

Coalition for Active Living
#301, 2197 Riverside Dr., Ottawa, ON K1H 7X3, Canada
Tel: 613-277-9979
info@activeliving.ca
www.activeliving.ca
Christa Costas-Bradstreet, Co-Chair
Nancy Dubois, Co-Chair

Fitness New Brunswick (NBCFAL) / Conditionnement physique Noueau-Brunswick (CCPVANB)
#2, 1216 Sand Cove Rd., Saint John, NB E3M 5V8, Canada
Tel: 506-672-1993; *Fax:* 506-672-8762
Toll-Free: 888-790-1411
membershipservices@fitnessnb.ca
www.fitnessnb.ca
Affiliation(s): Atlantic Canadian Society for Exercise Physiology (CSEP) Health & Fitness Program (H&FP); National Fitness Leadership Alliance (NFLA)
Gina Simpson, Executive Director
Lauren Rogers, President

International Masterathlete Federation (IMAF)
PO Box 185, Richmond Hill, ON L4B 4R5, Canada
Tel: 905-473-9714; *Fax:* 905-473-9715
Toll-Free: 888-883-3315
Liz Roach, President
Iain Douglas, Vice-President

International Orienteering Federation (IOF)
Radiokatu 20, Slu, FI-00093, Finland
Tel: 358-9-3481-3112; *Fax:* 358-9-3481-3113
iof@orienteering.org
www.orienteering.org
Affiliation(s): Canadian Orienteering Federation
Barbro Rönnberg, Secretary General
Anna Zeelig, Assistant to the Secretary General

Paralympics PEI
c/o Royalty Center House Of Sport, PO Box 841, 40 Enman Cres., Charlottetown, PE C1A 7L9, Canada
Tel: 902-368-4540; *Fax:* 902-368-4548
info@website.paralympicspei.pe.ca
www.paralympicspei.pe.ca
Tracy Stevenson, Executive Director

Sport Alliance of Ontario
3 Concorde Gate, Toronto, ON M3C 3N7, Canada
Tel: 416-426-7000; *Fax:* 416-426-7381
jjoseph@sportalliance.com
www.sportalliance.com
Jim Bradley, CEO
Larry Rudner, Interim CFO

Rhythmic Sportive Gymnastics

Canadian Rhythmic Sportive Gymnastic Federation (CRSGF) / Fédération canadienne de gymnastique rythmique sportive
c/o 2288 Covington Pl., Victoria, BC V8N 5N6, Canada
Tel: 250-472-3322; *Fax:* 250-472-2659
dfrattaroli@shaw.ca
Danielle Frattaroli, GCG-RG Program Coordinator

Rhythmic Gymnastics Manitoba Inc. (RGM)
Sport Manitoba Bldg., 200 Main St., Winnipeg, MB R3C 4M2, Canada
rhythmic@sport.mb.ca
www.rgmanitoba.com
Affiliation(s): Sport Manitoba; Rhythmic Gymnastics Canada; Gymnastics Canada; International Gymnastics Federation; Canadian Sport Centre - Manitoba; Coaching Manitoba; Gymnastics Manitoba
Zlatica Stauder, Executive Director
Raymond Chu, President
Susan Yurkiw, Vice-President

Rifles

British Columbia Rifle Association (BCRA)
43583 Bracken Dr., Chilliwack, BC V2R 4A3, Canada
Tel: 604-793-0300; *Fax:* 604-793-4385
contact@bcrifle.org
www.bcrifle.org
Affiliation(s): Responsible Firearms Owners Coalition of British Columbia
Robert Pitcairn, Secretary

British Columbia Target Sports Association
PO Box 496, Kamloops, BC V2C 5L2, Canada
Tel: 250-374-6705
targetsports@bctsa.bc.ca
www.bctsa.bc.ca

Manitoba Provincial Rifle Association Inc. (MPRA)
795 Valour Rd., Winnipeg, MB R3G 3B3, Canada
Tel: 204-783-0768
www.manitobarifle.ca
Affiliation(s): Sports Manitoba
John C. Chapman, President

Nova Scotia Rifle Association (NSRA)
PO Box 482, Dartmouth, NS B2Y 3Y8, Canada
Tel: 902-456-7468
nsrifle@ns.sympatico.ca
www.nsrifle.org
Affiliation(s): Shooting Federation of Canada
A.S. Webber, President
D.G. Beaulieu, Secretary

Province of Québec Rifle Association (PQRA) / Association de tir de la province de Québec (ATPQ)
PO Box 141, St Augustin de Desmaures, QC G2N 1W5, Canada
Tel: 418-878-4195
jacques.denis@globetrotter.net
www.pqra.org
Jacques Denis, President

Shooting Federation of Canada (SFC) / Fédération de tir du Canada (FTC)
45 Shirley Blvd., Nepean, ON K2K 2W6, Canada
Tel: 613-727-7483; *Fax:* 613-727-7487
info@sfc-ftc.ca
www.sfc-ftc.ca
Affiliation(s): Canadian Shooting Sports Association
Reg Potter, President

Ringette

British Columbia Ringette Association (BCRA) / Association de ringuette de Colombie-Britannique
#319, 789 West Pender St., Vancouver, BC V6C 1H2, Canada
Fax: 604-629-0876
www.bcringette.org
Glen Ritchie, President
Donna Mihalcheon, Vice President

Fédération sportive de ringuette du Québec
CP 1000, Succ. M, 4545, av Pierre-de-Coubertin, Montréal, QC H1V 3R2, Canada
Tél: 514-252-3085; *Téléc:* 514-254-1069
ringuette@ringuette-quebec.qc.ca
www.ringuette-quebec.qc.ca
Florent Gravel, Président

International Ringette Federation
#201, 5510 Chemin Canotek Rd., Gloucester, ON K1J 9J4, Canada
Tel: 613-748-5655; *Fax:* 613-748-5860
ringette@ringette.ca
www.ringette.ca
David Patterson, Executive Director

Manitoba Ringette Association (MRA) / Association de ringuette du Manitoba
Sport Manitoba, #309, 200 Main St., Winnipeg, MB R3C 4M2, Canada
Tel: 204-925-5710; *Fax:* 204-925-5925
ringette@sport.mb.ca
www.manitobaringette.ca
Affiliation(s): Sport Manitoba
Cheryl Adlard, Executive Director
Melanie Perkins, Technical Director

Northwest Territories Ringette / Association de ringuette des Territoires Nord-Ouest
#2, 496 Range Lake Rd., Yellowknife, NT X1A 3R5, Canada
Tel: 867-920-7419; *Fax:* 867-920-2843
nwt_ringette@yahoo.com
Affiliation(s): Ringette Alberta
Miles Harris, President

Ontario Ringette Association (ORA) / Association de ringuette de l'Ontario
#207, 3 Concorde Gate, Toronto, ON M3C 3N7, Canada
Tel: 416-426-7204; *Fax:* 416-426-7359
info@ontario-ringette.com
www.ontario-ringette.com
Ellorie Hanson, President
Mike Beaton, Executive Director

Ringette Association of Saskatchewan (RAS) / Association de ringuette de Saskatchewan
#204, 1860 Lorne St., Regina, SK S4P 2L7, Canada
Tel: 306-780-9432; *Fax:* 306-780-9460
executivedirector@ringettesask.com
www.ringettesask.com
Darrell Liebrecht, President
Crystal Gellner, Executive Director

Ringette Canada (RC) / Ringuette Canada
#201, 5510 Canotek Rd., Ottawa, ON K1J 9J4, Canada
Tel: 613-748-5655; *Fax:* 613-748-5860
ringette@ringette.ca
www.ringette.ca
Jim Dawson, President
David Patterson, Executive Director

Ringette New Brunswick (RNB) / Ringuette Nouveau-Brunswick
c/o Marise Aufrey, Administrative Assistant, 940 Centrale St., Memramcook, NB E4K 3T4, Canada
Tel: 506-758-2546
MariseA@rrsb.nb.ca
www.sport.nb.ca/ringette/
Ron Richard, President
Hélène L. Beaulieu, Vice-President

Ringette Nova Scotia
5516 Spring Garden Rd., 4th Fl., Halifax, NS B3J 1G6, Canada
Tel: 902-425-5450; *Fax:* 902-425-5606
ringette@sportnovascotia.ca
www.ringette.ns.ca
Lindsay Bennett, Executive Director
Dennis Barnhart, President

Ringette PEI
PO Box 302, Charlottetown, PE C1A 7K7, Canada
Tel: 902-368-4208; *Fax:* 902-362-4548
www.ringettepei.ca
Kelsey McIntosh, Executive Director
Ian MacIsaac, President
Dan Delaney, Vice-President
Susan McInnis, Treasurer

Rowing

Alberta Rowing Association (ARA)
Percy Page Centre, 11759 Groat Rd., Edmonton, AB T5M 3K6, Canada
Tel: 780-427-8154; *Fax:* 780-422-2663
albertarows@can.rogers.com
www.albertarowing.ca
Carol Hermansen, President

Association québécoise d'aviron (AQA)
CP 1000, Succ. M, 4545, av Pierre-de Coubertin, Montréal, QC H1V 3R2, Canada
Tél: 514-252-3191; *Téléc:* 514-252-3094
info@avironquebec.ca
www.avironquebec.ca
Matteo Cendamo, Président

Ontario Rowing Association (ORA)
#210, 3 Concorde Gate, Toronto, ON M3C 3N7, Canada
Tel: 416-426-7002; *Fax:* 416-426-7309
admin@rowontario.ca
www.rowontario.ca
Affiliation(s): Ontario Sport Council
Derek Ventor, Executive Director

Rowing Canada Aviron (RCA) / Association canadienne d'aviron amateur
100 - 4636 Elk Lake Dr., Victoria, BC V8Z 5M1, Canada
Fax: 250-361-4211
Toll-Free: 877-722-4769
rca@rowingcanada.org
www.rowingcanada.org
Affiliation(s): Fédération Internationale des Sociétés d'Aviron; Canadian Olympic Association
Donna Atkinson, Executive Director

Rowing Newfoundland
PO Box 50536, SS#3, St. John's, NL A1B 4M2, Canada
Tel: 709-753-8515
Adrian Miller, President

Saskatchewan Rowing Association
510 Cynthia St., Saskatoon, SK S7L 7K7, Canada
Tel: 306-975-0876; *Fax:* 306-242-8007
saskrowing@sasktel.net
www.saskrowing.ca
Affiliation(s): Rowing Aviron Canada, Saskatchewan Sports Hall of Fame & Museum, Saskatchewan Coaches Association
Siobhan McLaughlin, Head Coach/Executive Director
Bruce Acton, President

Rugby

Alberta Rugby Football Union
Percy Page Centre, 11759 Groat Rd., Edmonton, AB T5M 3K6, Canada
Tel: 780-415-1773; *Fax:* 780-422-5558
Toll-Free: 866-784-2922
rugbyab@telus.net
www.rugbyalberta.com
Bert Radford, President

British Columbia Rugby Union
#203, 210 West Broadway, Vancouver, BC V5Y 3W2, Canada
Tel: 604-737-3065; *Fax:* 604-737-3916
bcrugby@telus.net
www.bcrugby.com
Louise Wheeler, Manager, Member Services
Jeff Sauvé, CEO

Fédération de rugby du Québec (FRQ) / Quebec Rugby Union
CP 1000, Succ. M, 4545, av Pierre-de Coubertin, Montréal, QC H1V 3R2, Canada
Tél: 514-252-3189; *Téléc:* 514-252-3159
rugbyquebec@rugbyquebec.qc.ca
www.rugbyquebec.qc.ca
Nicholas Clapinson, Directeur

Newfoundland & Labrador Rugby Union
349 Old Broad Cove Rd., St. Phillips, NL A1M 3N2, Canada
Tel: 709-895-2608; *Fax:* 709-895-0214
tjacobs@nl.rogers.com
www.rockrugby.ca
Tom Jacobs, President

Nova Scotia Rugby Football Union
5516 Spring Garden Rd., Halifax, NS B3J 1G6, Canada
Tel: 902-425-5450; *Fax:* 902-425-5606
rugby@sportnovascotia.ca
www.rugbyns.ns.ca
Affiliation(s): International Rugby Board
Marty Williams, CEO

Ontario Rugby Union (ORU)
#702A, 1185 Eglinton Ave. East, Toronto, ON M3C 3C6, Canada
Tel: 416-426-7050; *Fax:* 416-426-7369
rugbyregistration@osrc.com
www.rugbyontario.com
Affiliation(s): Canadian Rugby Union
Allen Piggott, Executive Director

Saskatchewan Rugby Union (SRU)
510 Cynthia St., Saskatoon, SK S7L 7K7, Canada
Tel: 306-975-0895; *Fax:* 306-242-8007
sru@sasktel.net
www.saskrugby.com

Sailing

Alberta Sailing Association (ASA)
4915 Graham Dr. SW, Calgary, AB T3E 4L3, Canada
Tel: 403-617-9092
info@albertasailing.com
www.albertasailing.com
Peter MacDougal, Executive Director & Head Coach
Ron Hewitt, President

Association maritime du Québec (AMQ)
#500, 621, rue Stravinski, Brossard, QC J4X 1Y7, Canada
Tél: 450-466-1777; *Téléc:* 450-466-6056
Ligne sans frais: 877-560-1777
info@nautismequebec.com
www.nautismequebec.com
Walter Timmerman, Président
Yves Paquette, Directeur général
Walter Timmerman, Vice-président

British Columbia Sailing Association
#223, 3820 Cessna Dr., Richmond, BC V7B 0A2, Canada
Tel: 604-333-3628; *Fax:* 604-333-3626
crew@bcsailing.bc.ca
www.bcsailing.bc.ca
Affiliation(s): Canadian Yachting Association; International Sailing Federation; Sport BC
Tine Moberg-Parker, Executive Director

Canadian Albacore Association (CAA)
PO Box 98093, 970 Queen St. East, Toronto, ON M4M 1J8, Canada
info@albacore.ca
www.albacore.ca
Jeff Beitz, Commodore
Mary Free, Treasurer

Canadian Yachting Association (CYA) / Association canadienne de yachting
Portsmith Olympic Harbour, 53 Yonge St., Kingston, ON K7M 6G4, Canada
Tel: 613-545-3044; *Fax:* 613-545-3045
Toll-Free: 877-416-4720
sailcanada@sailing.ca
www.sailing.ca
Affiliation(s): International Sailing Federation; International Sailing Schools Association
Gerry Giffin, President

Manitoba Sailing Association Inc. (MSA)
#406, 200 Main St., Winnipeg, MB R3C 4M2, Canada
Tel: 204-925-5650; *Fax:* 204-925-5624
sailing@sport.mb.ca
www.sailmanitoba.com
Ivan McMorris, President
Brigitte Smutny, Executive Director

Ontario Sailing / Association de voile de l'Ontario
65 Guise St. East, Hamilton, ON L8L 8B4, Canada
Tel: 905-572-7245; *Fax:* 905-572-6056
Toll-Free: 888-672-7245
info@ontariosailing.ca
www.ontariosailing.ca
Glenn Lethbridge, Executive Director

S.A.L.T.S. Sail & Life Training Society (SALTS)
PO Box 5014, Stn. B, Victoria, BC V8R 6N3, Canada
Tel: 250-383-6811; *Fax:* 250-383-7781
Toll-Free: 888-383-6811
info@salts.ca
www.salts.ca
Loren Hagerty, Executive Director

Tanzer 22 Class Association
PO Box 11122, Stn. H, Nepean, ON K2H 7T9, Canada
president@tanzer22.com
www.tanzer22.com
Affiliation(s): Canadian Yachting Association; United States Sailing Association

Schools

Prince Edward Island School Athletic Association (PEISAA)
109 Water St., Summerside, PE C1N 1A8, Canada
Tel: 902-888-8037; *Fax:* 902-432-2659
grturtle@gov.pe.ca
www.edu.pe.ca/peisaa
Garth Turtle, Executive Director
Lona Ryan, Game Reporting
Gerald MacCormack, Secretary-Treasurer

Senior Citizens

Alberta Senior Citizens Sport & Recreation Association (ASCSRA)
#101, 525 - 11 Ave. SW, Calgary, AB T2R 0C9, Canada
Tel: 403-297-2703; *Fax:* 403-297-6669
ascsra@telus.net
www.alberta55plus.ca
Affiliation(s): Alberta Sport, Recreation, Parks & Wildlife Foundation

Shooting Sports

Alberta Federation of Shooting Sports (AFSS)
Percy Page Centre, 11759 Groat Rd., Edmonton, AB T5M 3K6, Canada
Tel: 780-415-1775; *Fax:* 780-422-2663
afss@abshooters.org
www.abshooters.org
Bernie Harrison, President
Trudie Snider, Office Manager

Alberta Metallic Silhouette Association
2306 - 22nd St. South, Lethbridge, AB T1K 2K2, Canada
Tel: 403-327-7552
amsa@albertasilhouetteshooting.ca
www.silhouette-alberta.org
Affiliation(s): Shooting Federation of Canada; Alberta Federation of Shooting Sports
Ralph Oler, President
Kathy Oler, Sec.-Treas.

Atlantic Marksmen Association
PO Box 181, Stn. Dartmouth Main, Dartmouth, NS B2Y 3Y3, Canada
Tel: 902-469-2062
boudreau@chebucto.ns.ca
www.atlanticmarksmen.ca
Edward Doane, President

Calgary & District Target Shooters Association
612 - 500 Country Hills Blvd. NE, #142, Calgary, AB T3K 5K3, Canada
Tel: 403-275-3257; *Fax:* 403-291-5579
cowboy@cdtsa.org
www.cdtsa.org
Affiliation(s): Alberta Federation of Shooting Sports; Alberta Fish & Game Association; Alberta Black Powder Association; Alberta Metallic Silhouette Association

Canadian Shooting Sports Association
#106, 3 Director Ct., Vaughan, ON L4L 4S5, Canada
Tel: 905-265-0692; *Fax:* 905-265-9794
Toll-Free: 888-873-4339
info@cdnshootingsports.org
www.cdnshootingsports.org
Affiliation(s): Ontario Council of Shooters; Shooting Federation of Canada

Canadian Trapshooting Association (CTA)
RR#1, Penhold, AB T0M 1R0, Canada
Tel: 403-886-2600; *Fax:* 403-886-2600
Bob Brown, President

Dominion of Canada Rifle Association (DCRA) / L'Association de tir dominion du canada
45 Shirley Blvd., Ottawa, ON K2K 2W6, Canada
Tel: 613-829-8281; *Fax:* 613-829-0099
office@dcra.ca
www.dcra.ca
Jim Thompson, Executive Director
Stan E. Frost, Executive Vice-President
T.F. deFaye, President

Fédération québécoise de tir (FQT) / Québec Shooting Federation
CP 1000, Succ. M, 4545, av Pierre-De Coubertin, Montréal, QC H1V 3R2, Canada
Tél: 514-252-3056; *Téléc:* 514-252-3060
fqt@fqtir.qc.ca
www.fqtir.qc.ca
Affiliation(s): Regroupment Loisir Québec; Sports Québec
Yvon Morissette, Directeur exécutif
Gérald Tousignant, Président

Manitoba Provincial Handgun Association
200 Main St., Winnipeg, MB R3C 4M2, Canada
Tel: 204-925-5682; *Fax:* 204-925-5703
mpha@handgun.mb.ca
www.handgun.mb.ca
Randy Myrdal, President

Ontario Muzzle Loading Association (OMLA)
c/o Irene Wardell, 372 Beattie St., Strathroy, ON N7G 2X6, Canada
www.omla.ca
Irene Wardell, President
Russ Moore, Vice-President
Vivian Moore, Secretary
George Wortner, Treasurer

Ontario Provincial Trapshooting Association
c/o 273 Bousfield Cres., Milton, ON L9T 3N5, Canada
Tel: 905-878-5669
info@trapshooting.on.ca
www.trapshooting.on.ca
Smokey Smith, President
Gord Kerr, Secretary-Treasurer

Ontario Rifle Association
PO Box 60, Locust Hill, ON L0H 1J0, Canada
Tel: 905-294-8266; *Fax:* 905-294-1213
jimc.thompson@sympatico.ca
www.ontariorifleassociation.org
Affiliation(s): Dominion of Canada Rifle Association

Ontario Skeet Shooting Association (OSSA)
PO Box 96, Hampton, ON L0B 1J0, Canada
Tel: 905-263-8174; *Fax:* 905-263-4870
info@ontarioskeet.com
www.ontarioskeet.com
Bill Marsh, Secretary
Brad McRae, President

Saskatchewan Black Powder Association (SBPA)
PO Box 643, Saskatoon, SK S7K 3L7, Canada
www.sbpa.ca

Saskatchewan Provincial Rifle Association Inc. (SPRA)
20 Acadia Bay, Regina, SK S4S 4T6, Canada
Tel: 306-586-0617; *Fax:* 306-586-7547
fullbore.rifle@saskrifle.ca
www.saskrifle.ca

Shooting Federation of Nova Scotia (SFNS)
PO Box 28023, Dartmouth, NS B2W 6E2, Canada
Tel: 902-462-7048; *Fax:* 902-462-7048
marcom79@ns.sympatico.ca
Ray Fisher, President

Yellowknife Shooting Club (YKSC)
PO Box 2931, Yellowknife, NT X1A 2R2, Canada
Tel: 867-873-3212; *Fax:* 867-873-9008
mail@yellowknifeshootingclub.ca
yellowknifeshootingclub.ca
Affiliation(s): NWT Federation of Shooting Sports; Shooting Federation of Canada; NRA
Barry Taylor, President
Jim Robinson, Vice-President

Skating

Alberta Amateur Speed Skating Association (AASSA)
2500 University Dr. NW, Calgary, AB T2N 1N4, Canada
Tel: 403-220-7911; *Fax:* 403-220-9226
aassa@ucalgary.ca
www.albertaspeedskating.ca
Wendy Walker, Office Administrator

British Columbia Speed Skating Association
PO Box 2023, Stn. A, Abbotsford, BC V2T 3T8, Canada
Tel: 604-746-4349; *Fax:* 604-746-4549
lorna@speed-skating.bc.ca
www.speed-skating.bc.ca
Ted Houghton, Executive Director

Fédération de patinage artistique du Québec (FPAQ)
CP 1000, Succ. M, 4545, av Pierre-de-Coubertin, Montréal, QC H1V 3R2, Canada
Tél: 514-252-3073; *Téléc:* 514-252-3170
patinage@patinage.qc.ca
www.patinage.qc.ca
Josée Beauséjour, Directeur exécutif

Fédération de Patinage de Vitesse du Québec
930, av Roland Beaudin, Sainte-Foy, QC G1V 4H8, Canada
Tél: 418-651-1973; *Téléc:* 418-651-1977
fpvq@fpvq.org
www.fpvq.org
Robert Dubreuil, Directeur général

International Skating Union (ISU) / Union Internationale de Patinage
Chemin de Primerose 2, Lausanne, 1007, Switzerland
Tel: 41-21-612-6666; *Fax:* 41-21-612-6677
info@isu.ch
www.isu.org
Fredi Schmid, General Secretary

Manitoba Speed Skating Association
145 Pacific Ave., Winnipeg, MB R3B 2Z6, Canada
Tel: 204-925-5657; *Fax:* 204-925-5792
Toll-Free: 888-628-9921
mssa@shawbiz.ca
www.mbspeedskating.org
Paul Daeninck, President

Newfoundland & Labrador Speed Skating Association (NLSSA)
81 Birchy Cove Dr., Corner Brook, NL A2H 6W8, Canada
Tel: 709-785-1403
rzrenos@gmail.com

Nunavut Speed Skating Association
PO Box 761, Iqaluit, NU X0A 0H0, Canada
Tel: 867-979-1226; *Fax:* 867-975-3384
jtmaurice@northwestel.net
www.nunavutspeedskating.ca
John Maurice, President

NWT Speed Skating Association
PO Box 2664, Yellowknife, NT X1A 2P9, Canada
pamela@ssimicro.com
www.nwtspeedskating.ca
Pam Dunbar, President

Saskatchewan Amateur Speed Skating Association (SASSA)
2205 Victoria Ave., Regina, SK S4P 0S4, Canada
Tel: 306-780-9400; *Fax:* 306-525-4009
sassa@sasktel.net
www.saskspeedskating.ca
Affiliation(s): Sask Sport Inc.
Shawn MacLennan, Executive Director

Skate Canada / Patinage Canada
865 Shefford Rd., Ottawa, ON K1J 1H9, Canada
Tel: 613-747-1007; *Fax:* 613-748-5718
Toll-Free: 888-747-2372
skatecanada@skatecanada.ca
www.skatecanada.ca
William Thompson, CEO
Benoît Lavoie, President

Skate Ontario
99 Cabot Cr., Sault Ste Marie, ON P6C 5X8, Canada
Tel: 705-949-9219
skateontario@sympatico.ca
www.skateontario.org
John Greenwood, President

Speed Skate New Brunswick
246 St. Pierre East Blvd., Caraquet, NB E1E 1B1, Canada
Tel: 506-727-6334; *Fax:* 506-727-6334
speedskatenb@gmail.com
ssnb.homestead.com
Ray Harris, President
Peter Steele, Provincial Coach

Speed Skate Nova Scotia
10 Thistle Dr., North Sydney, NS B2A 3R1, Canada
Tel: 902-794-8954
laurolea@ns.sympatico.ca
Terri Dixon, President

Speed Skate PEI
PO Box 383, Charlottetown, PE C1A 7K7, Canada
Tel: 902-628-6606
info@speedskatepei.ca
www.speedskatepei.com
Wendy A. Francis, President
Alban Moran, Secretary

Speed Skating Canada (SSC) / Patinage de vitesse Canada
#402, 2781 Lancaster Rd., Ottawa, ON K1B 1A7, Canada
Tel: 613-260-3669; *Fax:* 613-260-3660
ssc@speedskating.ca
www.speedskating.ca
Affiliation(s): International Skating Union
Jean R. Dupré, Director General
Brian Rahill, Director of Sport
Mylène Croteau, Manager of Communications

Yukon Speed Skating Association
11 Buttercup Pl., Whitehorse, YT Y1A 5V1, Canada
Tel: 867-668-4591; *Fax:* 867-393-8101
Bruce Henry, Branch President

Skiing

Alberta Freestyle Ski Association (AFSA)
88 Canada Olympic Rd. SW, Calgary, AB T3B 5R5, Canada
Tel: 403-297-2718; *Fax:* 403-202-2522
info@abfreestyle.com
www.abfreestyle.com
Affiliation(s): Canadian Feestyle Ski Association
Gord Campbell, Executive Director
Larry Bilton, Chair
Al Ulsifer, Vice-Chair
Neil Orr, Treasurer

Alpine Canada ALPIN
#153, 401 - 9th Ave. SW, Calgary, AB T2P 3C5, Canada
Tel: 403-777-3200; *Fax:* 403-777-3213
info@canski.org
www.canski.org
Gary Allan, President
Jennifer Duggan, Manager, National Services

Association des stations de ski du Québec (ASSQ)
#100, 7665, rue Larrey, Anjou, QC H1J 2T7, Canada
Tél: 514-493-1810; *Téléc:* 514-493-3975
lbissonnette@assq.qc.ca
www.quebecskisurf.com
Claude Péloquin, Président-directeur général

British Columbia Alpine Ski Association
#403, 1788 West Broadway, Vancouver, BC V6J 1Y1, Canada
Tel: 604-678-3070; *Fax:* 604-678-8073
info@bcalpine.com
www.bcalpine.com
Bruce Goldsmid, CEO

Canadian Association of Nordic Ski Instructors (CANSI)
c/o Secrétariat, 8 Douglas Rd., Chelsea, QC J9B 1K4
Tel: 819-360-6700; *Fax:* 819-827-0017
office@cansi.ca; membership@cansi.ca
www.cansi.ca
Jeff Hampshire, President
Françoise Chatenoud, Office Coordinator

Canadian Freestyle Ski Association / Association canadienne de ski acrobatique
808 Pacific St., Vancouver, BC V6Z 1C2, Canada
Tel: 604-714-2233; *Fax:* 604-714-2232
info@freestyleski.com
www.freestyleski.ca
Affiliation(s): Canadian Ski & Snowboard Association
Peter Judge, CEO

Canadian Masters Cross-Country Ski Association (CMCSA) / Association canadienne des maîtres en ski de fond
c/o 2 MacNeil Cres., Stephenville, NL A2N 3E3, Canada
www.canadian-masters-xc-ski.ca/en_index.htm
Affiliation(s): World Masters Cross-Country Ski Association; Cross-Country Canada
Bruce Legrow, National Director

Canadian Ski Coaches Federation (CSCF) / Fédération des entraîneurs de ski du Canada
#220, 4900 Jean Talon ouest, Montréal, QC H4P 1W9, Canada
Tel: 514-748-2648; *Fax:* 514-748-2476
Toll-Free: 800-811-6428
national@snowpro.com
www.snowpro.com/csia/e
Michel Lamothe, Chief Executive Officer

Canadian Ski Council (CSC) / Conseil canadien du ski
21 Fourth St. East, Collingwood, ON L9Y 1T2, Canada
Tel: 705-445-9140; *Fax:* 705-445-0525
info@skicanada.org
www.skicanada.org
Affiliation(s): Canadian Association for Disabled Skiing; Canadian Association of Nordic Ski Instructors; Canadian Ski Area Operators' Association; Canadian Ski Association; Canadian Ski Instructors' Alliance; Canadian Ski Coaches Federation; Canadian Ski Patrol System; Canadian Association of Snowboard Instructors; National Snow Industries Association
Colin S. Chedore, President

Canadian Ski Instructors' Alliance (CSIA) / Alliance des moniteurs de ski du Canada
#220, 4900, Jean Talon ouest, Montréal, QC H4P 1W9, Canada
Tel: 514-748-2648; *Fax:* 514-748-2476
Toll-Free: 800-811-6428
national@snowpro.com
www.snowpro.com/csia/e
Affiliation(s): International Ski Instructors Association
Martin Jean, National Program Director
Michel Lamothe, CEO

Canadian Ski Marathon (CSM) / Marathon canadien de ski
#200, 81 Jean-Prolux, Gatineau, QC J8Z 1W2, Canada
Tel: 819-770-6556; *Fax:* 819-770-7428
Toll-Free: 877-770-6556
ski@csm-mcs.com
www.csm-mcs.com
Affiliation(s): Tourisme Outaouais; Tourisme Laurentides
Gregory Koegl, President

Canadian Ski Patrol System (CSPS) / Patrouille canadienne de ski (OPCS)
4531 Southclark Pl., Ottawa, ON K1T 3V2, Canada
Tel: 613-822-2245; *Fax:* 613-822-1088
Toll-Free: 900-565-2777
info@skipatrol.ca
www.csps.ca
John Leu, Executive Director
Brian Low, Chair
Bill Powell, Corporate Secretary

Canadian Snowsports Association (CSA) / L'Association canadienne des sports d'hiver (ACSH)
#202, 1451 West Broadway, Vancouver, BC V6H 1H6, Canada
Tel: 604-734-6800; *Fax:* 604-669-7954
lillianalderton@hotmail.com
www.canadaskiandsnowboard.net
Chris Robinson, President
David Pym, Managing Director

Cross Country Alberta (CCA)
Percy Page Centre, 11759 Groat Rd., Edmonton, AB T5M 3K6, Canada
Tel: 780-415-1738; *Fax:* 780-427-0524
manager@xcountryab.net
www.xcountryab.net
Ken Hewitt, Chair
Michael Neary, Manager, Sport

Cross Country British Columbia
#106, 3003 - 30th St., Vernon, BC V1T 9J5, Canada
Tel: 250-545-9600; *Fax:* 250-545-9614
office@crosscountrybc.ca
www.crosscountrybc.ca

Cross Country Canada (CCC) / Ski de fond Canada (SFC)
c/o Bill Warren Training Centre, #100, 1995 Olympic Way, Canmore, AB T1W 2T6, Canada
Tel: 403-678-6791; *Fax:* 403-678-3644
Toll-Free: 877-609-3215
info@cccski.com
www.cccski.com
Affiliation(s): Canadian Ski & Snowboard Association
Jim McCarthy, President
Davin MacIntosh, Executive Director
Cathy Sturgeon, Director, Administration & Communication

Cross Country New Brunswick / Ski de fond Nouveau-Brunswick
1450 Maria Street, Bathurst, NB E2A 3G2, Canada
Tel: 506-548-5707; *Fax:* 506-542-2638
skis@nbnet.nb.ca
www.xcski-nb.ca
Marie-Eve Cyr, Contact

Cross Country Ontario
738 River Street, Thunder Bay, ON P7A 3S8, Canada
Tel: 807-768-4617; *Fax:* 807-768-8368
admin@xco.org
www.xco.org
Liz Inkila, Administrator

Cross Country Saskatchewan (CCS)
1860 Lorne St., Regina, SK S4P 2L7, Canada
Tel: 306-780-9240; *Fax:* 306-780-9462
ccs@sasktel.net
www.crosscountrysask.ca
Dave Martinuk, President
Alana Ottenbreit, Executive Director

Cross Country Ski Association of Manitoba
Sport for Life Centre, 145 Pacific Ave., Winnipeg, MB R3B 2Z6, Canada
Tel: 204-925-5639; *Fax:* 204-231-0297
info@ccski.mb.ca
www.ccski.mb.ca
Affiliation(s): Sport Manitoba
Richard Huybers, Chair
Karin McSherry, Executive Director

Cross Country Ski Nova Scotia (CCSNS)
5516 Spring Garden Rd., 4th Fl., Halifax, NS B3J 1G6, Canada
Tel: 902-425-5450; *Fax:* 902-425-5606
ccsns@sportnovascotia.ca
www.crosscountryskins.com
Kenzie MacDonald, Treasurer

Cross Country Yukon (CCY)
4061 - 4th Ave., Whitehorse, YT Y1A 1H1, Canada
Tel: 867-334-9220; *Fax:* 867-667-4237
xcyukon@northwestel.net
www.crosscountryyukon.com
Alain Masson, Coordinator

Fédération québécoise de la montagne et de l'escalade (FQME)
CP 1000, Succ. M, 4545, av Pierre-de-Coubertin, Montréal, QC H1V 3R2, Canada
Tél: 514-252-3004; *Téléc:* 514-252-3201
Ligne sans frais: 866-204-3763
fqme@fqme.qc.ca
www.fqme.qc.ca
Affiliation(s): Union internationale des associations d'alpinisme
André St-Jacques, Directeur des opérations

National Snow Industries Association (NSIA) / Association nationale des industries de la neige
#810, 245, av Victoria, Montréal, QC H3Z 2M6, Canada
Tel: 514-939-7370; *Fax:* 514-939-7371
Toll-Free: 800-263-6742
central.station@nsia.ca
www.nsia.ca
Anna Di Meglio, President
Nicole Garand, Administration & Customer Service

Northwest Territories Ski Division
c/o PO Box 682, Yellowknife, NT X1A 2N5, Canada
Tel: 867-873-4782
cygnus@theedge.ca
Brenda Hans

Ontario Track 3 Ski Association
PO Box 67, Stn. D, #4, 61 Advance Rd., Toronto, ON M9A 4X1, Canada
Tel: 416-233-3872; *Fax:* 416-233-7862
Toll-Free: 877-308-7225
track3@track3.org
www.track3.org
Henk Engels, Executive Director

Ski Hawks Ottawa
522 Hillcrest Ave., Ottawa, ON K2A 2M9, Canada
Tel: 613-725-2472
Affiliation(s): Canadian Association for Disabled Skiing; Canadian Association for Disabled Skiers-National Capital Division
Bruce Meredith, Treasurer

Ski-Québec
CP 1000, Succ. M, 4545, av Pierre de Coubertin, Montréal, QC H1V 3R2, Canada
Tél: 514-252-3089; *Téléc:* 514-252-5282
johanne@skiquebec.qc.ca
www.skiquebec.qc.ca
Sylvie Halou, Directrice générale

Snowbound
#1, 733 Ross Ave. East, Timmins, ON P4N 8S8, Canada
Tel: 705-264-4700; *Fax:* 705-268-3585
Toll-Free: 800-575-3210
Chantal Pépin, Contact

Union internationale des associations d'alpinisme (UIAA) / International Union of Alpine Associations
c/o International Mountaineering & Climbing Federation, Monbijoustrasse 61/Postfach, 23, Bern, CH-3000, Switzerland
Tel: 41-(0)31-370-18-28; *Fax:* 41-(0)31-370-18-38
office@uiaa.ch
www.uiaa.ch
Affiliation(s): Alpine Club of Canada; Fédération québécoise de la montagne
Judith Safford, Executive Director

Snowboarding

Canadian Association for Disabled Skiing (CADS) / Association canadienne pour les skieurs handicapés (ACSH)
91 Nelson St., Barrie, ON L4M 4K4
Tel: 705-725-4845; *Fax:* 705-725-4804
michelle.bavington@sympatico.ca
www.disabledskiing.ca
David O'Brien, Executive Director
Al Matile, President
Helen Grimm, Secretary
Jeff Laidlaw, Treasurer

Canadian Association of Snowboard Instructors (CASI) / Association canadienne des moniteurs de surf des neiges (ACMS)
#220, 4900, Jean-Talon ouest, Montréal, QC H4P 1W9, Canada
Tel: 514-748-2648; *Fax:* 514-748-2476
Toll-Free: 800-811-6428
national@casi-acms.com
www.casi-acms.com
Affiliation(s): Canadian Ski Instructors Alliance; Canadian Snowboard Federation
Dan Genge, Executive Director

HeliCat Canada
#102, 810 Waddington Dr., Vernon, BC V1T 8T3, Canada
Tel: 250-542-9020; *Fax:* 250-542-5070
info@helicatcanada.com
www.helicatcanada.com
John Forrest, President

Snowmobiles

Alberta Snowmobile Association (ASA)
11759 Groat Rd., Edmonton, AB T5M 3K6, Canada
Tel: 780-427-2695; *Fax:* 780-415-1779
info@altasnowmobile.ab.ca
www.altasnowmobile.ab.ca
Affiliation(s): Canadian Council of Snowmobile Organizations
Louise A. Sherren, Executive Director

British Columbia Snowmobile Federation (BCSF)
Stn. 400, 2439 Poulton Ave., Houston, BC V0Y 1Z0, Canada
Tel: 250-845-7705; *Fax:* 250-845-7715
Toll-Free: 877-537-8716
office@bcsf.org
www.bcsf.org
Affiliation(s): International Snowmobile Council; Canadian Council of Snowmobile Organizations
Les Auston, Executive Director

Canadian Council of Snowmobile Organizations (CCSO) / Conseil canadien des organismes de motoneige (CCOM)
PO Box 21059, Thunder Bay, ON P7A 8A7
Tel: 807-345-5299
ccso.ccom@tbaytel.net
www.ccso-ccom.ca
Kevin Sweetland, President
Patrick McGrath, 1st Vice-President, Communications
Brenda R. Welsh, Secretary-Treasurer
Craig Giles, National Coordinator, Safety

Fédération des clubs de motoneigistes du Québec (FCMQ)
CP 1000, Succ. M, 4545, av Pierre-de Coubertin, Montréal, QC H1V 3R2, Canada
Tél: 514-252-3076; *Téléc:* 514-254-2066
info@fcmq.qc.ca
www.fcmq.qc.ca
Mario Côté, Président

Great Slave Snowmobile Association
4209 - 49A Ave., Yellowknife, NT X1A 1B3, Canada
Tel: 867-766-4353
bruceh@sub-arctic.ca
www.yktrailriders.com
Affiliation(s): Canadian Council of Snowmobile Organizations; International Snowmobile Council
Bill Braden, President

Klondike Snowmobile Association
PO Box 9034, 29 Wann Rd., Whitehorse, YT Y1A 4A2, Canada
Tel: 867-667-7680
klonsnow@yknet.ca
www.ksa.yk.ca
Affiliation(s): Trans Canada Trail - Yukon

Ontario Federation of Snowmobile Clubs (OFSC)
#9, 501 Welham Rd., Barrie, ON L4N 8Z6
Tel: 705-739-7669; *Fax:* 705-739-5005
www.ofsc.on.ca

Saskatchewan Snowmobile Association Inc. (SSA)
PO Box 533, 221 Centre St., Regina Beach, SK S0G 4C0, Canada
Tel: 306-729-3500; *Fax:* 306-729-3505
Toll-Free: 800-499-7533
sasksnow@sasktel.net
www.sasksnowmobiling.sk.ca
Barry Bradshaw, Chair
George Belchamber, Co-Chair

Snowmobilers Association of Nova Scotia (SANS)
5516 Spring Garden Rd., 4th Fl., Halifax, NS B3J 3G6, Canada
Tel: 902-425-5450; *Fax:* 902-425-5606
info@snowmobilersNS.com
www.snowmobilersns.com
John Cameron, General Manager

Snowmobilers of Manitoba Inc.
2121 Henderson Hwy., Winnipeg, MB R2G 1P8, Canada
Tel: 204-940-7533; *Fax:* 204-940-7531
info@snoman.mb.ca
www.snoman.mb.ca
Affiliation(s): Canadian Council of Snowmobile Organizations
Duncan Stokes, Executive Director

Thunder Bay Adventure Trails
PO Box 29190, Thunder Bay, ON P7B 6P9, Canada
Tel: 807-939-7533
tbat_den@hotmail.com
www.tbat.ca

Soaring

Aéro-Club des Outardes
1455, de Biencourt, Montréal, QC H4E 1T1, Canada
Tél: 514-465-7806
francisco45@gmail.com
aeroclubdesoutardes.iquebec.com
Jacques Fairpault, Président

Air Sailing Club
144 Maple St., Guelph, ON N1G 2G7, Canada
Tel: 519-836-7049
stephen.szikora@sympatico.ca
Stephen Szikora

Alberta Soaring Council
PO Box 13, Black Diamond, AB T0L 0H0, Canada
Tel: 403-933-4968
asc@platinum.ca
www.soaring.ab.ca
Phil Stade, Executive Director

Association de vol à voile Champlain
10, 745 de Martigny, Montréal, QC H2B 2N1, Canada
Tél: 450-771-0500
champlain@videotron.ca
www.avvc.qc.ca

Base Borden Soaring
PO Box 286, Borden, ON L0M 1C0, Canada
Tel: 705-424-1200
users.csolve.net/~ourplace/
Ray Leiska

Bonnechere Soaring Club
PO Box 1081, Deep River, ON K0J 1P0, Canada
Tel: 613-584-4636; *Fax:* 613-584-4636
Iver Theilmann

Central Alberta Gliding Club
4309 Grandview Blvd., Red Deer, AB T4N 3E7, Canada
Tel: 403-340-3506
hammondv@telus.net
www.cagcsoaring.ca
Affiliation(s): Alberta Soaring Council
Drew Hammond, President

Club de vol à voile de Québec
CP 9276, Sainte-Foy, QC G1V 4B1, Canada
Tél: 418-337-4905
www.cvvq.net
Richard Noël, Président

Cu Nim Gliding Club
113 Midridge Pl. SW, Calgary, AB T2X 1E4, Canada
Tel: 403-630-4332
www.soaring.ab.ca/exec.html
Affiliation(s): Alberta Soaring Council
Danny Russell

Edmonton Soaring Club (ESC)
PO Box 472, Edmonton, AB T5J 2K1, Canada
Tel: 780-363-3860
www.edmontonsoaringclub.com
Affiliation(s): Alberta Soaring Council; other soaring clubs
Gary Hill, President
Bob Hagen, Facilities Manager

Gatineau Gliding Club
PO Box 8145, Stn. T, Ottawa, ON K1G 3H6, Canada
Tel: 613-673-5386
ggc@gatineauglidingclub.ca
www.gatineauglidingclub.ca

Grande Prairie Soaring Society
PO Box 64, Hythe, AB T0H 2C0, Canada
soaring.ab.ca/gpss
Lloyd Sherk, President
Terry Hatfield, Sec.-Treas.

London Soaring Club
130 Holcroft St. West, Ingersoll, ON N5C 2B8, Canada
Tel: 519-661-7844
info@londonsoaringclub.ca
www.londonsoaringclub.ca
Cal Gillett, Treasurer

Manitoba Soaring Council
200 Main St., Winnipeg, MB R3C 4M2, Canada
Tel: 204-925-5682; *Fax:* 204-925-5703
www.wgc.mb.ca/msc/Manitoba_Soaring_Council_Home_Page.htm

Montréal Soaring Council (MSC) / Club de Vol à Voile MSC
PO Box 1804, Hawkesbury Airfield, Saint-Laurent, QC H4L 4W6, Canada
Tel: 613-632-5438
alainlaprade@hotmail.com
www.flymsc.org
Arvind K. Jain, Administration

Ontario Soaring Association
10 Courtwood Pl., Toronto, ON M2K 1Z9, Canada
Tel: 416-223-6487
Walter Chmela, Contact

Pemberton Soaring Centre
Pemberton, BC V0N 2L1, Canada
Tel: 604-894-5727; *Fax:* 604-894-5776
Toll-Free: 800-831-2611
info@pembertonsoaring.com
www.pembertonsoaring.com
Rudy Rozsypalek

Prince Albert Gliding & Soaring Club (PAG&SC)
219 Scissons Ct., Saskatoon, SK S7S 1B7, Canada
Tel: 306-249-1859
www.soar.sk.ca/pagsc
Affiliation(s): Soaring Association of Saskatchewan; Soaring Association of Canada
Keith Andrews, President
Don Klassen, Treasurer

Regina Gliding & Soaring Club
PO Box 4093, Regina, SK S4P 3W5, Canada
Tel: 306-536-4119
fly@soar.regina.sk.ca
www.soar.regina.sk.ca

Saskatoon Soaring Club
510 Cynthia St., Saskatoon, SK S7L 7K7, Canada
Tel: 306-975-0844
j.toles@sasktel.net
www.ssc.soar.sk.ca
John Toles, Secretary

Soaring Association of Canada (SAC) / Association canadienne de vol à voile (ACVV)
#107, 1025 Richmond Rd., Ottawa, ON K2B 8G8, Canada
Tel: 613-829-0536; *Fax:* 613-829-9497
sac@sac.ca
www.sac.ca
Affiliation(s): Aero Club of Canada; International Gliding Commission of the Fédération Aéronautique Internationale
John Toles, President
James F. McCollum, Executive Director

Soaring Nova Scotia
c/o Charles Yeates, #110, 105 Dunbrack St., Halifax, NS B3M 3G7, Canada
Tel: 902-443-0094
www.soarns.ca
Larry Bogan, Chair
Charles Yeates, Sec-Treas.

SOSA Gliding Club
PO Box 81, Rockton, ON L0R 1X0, Canada
Tel: 519-740-9328
sosa@sosaglidingclub.com
www.sosaglidingclub.com
Dave Springford, President/Treasurer

Toronto Soaring Club
c/o President, 58 River Ridge Rd., Barrie, ON L4N 7E8, Canada
Tel: 705-735-4422
dellis@rogers.com
www.toronto-soaring.ca
Dave Ellis, President

Winnipeg Gliding Club (WGC)
PO Box 1255, Winnipeg, MB R3C 2Y4, Canada
Tel: 204-735-2868
info@wgc.mb.ca
www.wgc.mb.ca

York Soaring Association
10 Courtwood Pl., Toronto, ON M2K 1Z9, Canada
Tel: 416-223-6487; *Fax:* 416-223-6487
robertocentazzo@yorksoaring.com
www.yorksoaring.com
Walter Chmela, President

Soccer

Alberta Soccer Association
Commonwealth Stadium, 1100 Stadium Rd., Edmonton, AB T5H 4E2, Canada
Tel: 780-474-2200; *Fax:* 780-474-6300
Toll-Free: 866-250-2200
www.albertasoccer.com
Ron Axelson, Executive Director

British Columbia Soccer Association
#510, 375 Water St., Vancouver, BC V6B 5C6, Canada
Tel: 604-299-6401; *Fax:* 604-299-9610
bcsoccer@gmail.com
www.bcsoccer.net
Bjorn Osieck, Executive Director

Canadian Soccer Association (CSA) / Association canadienne de soccer
237 Metcalfe St., Ottawa, ON K2P 1R2, Canada
Tel: 613-237-7678; *Fax:* 613-237-1516
info@soccercan.ca
www.canadasoccer.com
Affiliation(s): Féderation Internationale de Football Association, FIFA; Football Confederation; Canadian Olympic Association
Dominic Maestracci, President
Richard Scott, Director, Communications

Fédération de soccer du Québec
955, av Bois-de-Boulogne, Laval, QC H7N 4G1, Canada
Tél: 450-975-3355; *Téléc:* 450-975-1001
courriel@federation-soccer.qc.ca
www.federation-soccer.qc.ca
Brigitte Frot, Directrice générale

Newfoundland & Labrador Soccer Association
PO Box 21029, St. John's, NL A1A 5B2, Canada
Tel: 709-576-0601; *Fax:* 709-576-0588
nlsa@sportnl.ca
www.nlsa.ca
Doug Redmond, President
Dragan Mirkovic, Technical Director

Northwest Territories Soccer Association (NWTSA)
PO Box 11089, Yellowknife, NT X1A 3X7, Canada
Tel: 867-669-8326; *Fax:* 867-669-8327
Toll-Free: 800-661-0797
www.nwtkicks.ca
Affiliation(s): Sport North Federation
Melanie Kornacki, Sport Consultant
Ryan Fequet, President

Ontario Soccer Association (OSA)
7601 Martin Grove Rd., Vaughan, ON L4L 9E4, Canada
Tel: 905-264-9390; *Fax:* 905-264-9445
TheOSA@soccer.on.ca
www.soccer.on.ca
Colin Linford, President
Dan Tomlinson, Secretary
Brian Avey, Executive Director

Prince Edward Island Soccer Association (PEISA)
PO Box 1863, 40 Enman Cres., Charlottetown, PE C1A 7N5, Canada
Tel: 902-368-6251; *Fax:* 902-569-7693
admin@peisoccer.com
www.peisoccer.com
Gerald MacDonald, President
Daphne Andrews, Secretary/Registrat
Colleen Arsenault, Treasurer

Saskatchewan Soccer Association Inc. (SSA)
1870 Lorne St., Regina, SK S4P 2L7, Canada
Tel: 306-780-9225; *Fax:* 306-780-9480
k.sumner@sasksoccer.com
www.sasksoccer.com
Bonnie Lee Copeman, Business Administrator

Soccer New Brunswick
#2, 125 Russ Howard Dr., Moncton, NB E1C 0L7, Canada
Tel: 506-382-7529; *Fax:* 506-382-5621
office@soccernb.org
www.soccernb.org
Jeff Salvis, Executive Director

Soccer Nova Scotia
210 Thomas Raddall Dr., Halifax, NS B3S 1K3, Canada
Tel: 902-445-0265; *Fax:* 902-445-0258
soccerns@ns.sympatico.ca
www.soccerns.ns.ca
George Athanasiou, Executive Director

Yukon Soccer Association
4061 - 4th Ave., Whitehorse, YT Y1A 1H1, Canada
Tel: 867-633-4625; *Fax:* 867-667-4237
yukonsoccer@sportyukon.com
www.yukonsoccer.yk.ca
Kim King, Administrator

Softball

Alberta Amateur Softball Association (AASA)
9860 - 33 Ave., Edmonton, AB T6N 1C6, Canada
Tel: 780-461-7735; *Fax:* 780-461-7757
calie@softballalberta.ca
www.softballalberta.ca
Affiliation(s): Western Canada Softball Association
Michele Patry, Executive Director

British Columbia Amateur Softball Association (BCASA)
PO Box 45570, Stn. Sunnyside Mall, 2201 - 148th St., Surrey, BC V4A 9N3, Canada
Tel: 604-531-0044; *Fax:* 604-531-8831
info@softball.bc.ca
www.softball.bc.ca
Dennis Bidin, President

Ontario Rural Softball Association
RR#1, Innerkip, ON N0J 1M0, Canada
Tel: 519-469-3593
www.ontarioruralsoftball.ca/index.php
Carl Littlejohns, Secretary
Dennis Wilson, President

Softball Canada
#212, 223 Colonnade Rd., Ottawa, ON K1H 7X3, Canada
Tel: 613-523-3386; *Fax:* 613-523-5761
info@softball.ca
www.softball.ca
Hugh Mitchener, CEO
Kevin Quinn, President

Softball Manitoba
200 Main St., Winnipeg, MB R3C 4M2, Canada
Tel: 204-925-5673; *Fax:* 204-925-5703
softball@softball.mb.ca
www.softball.mb.ca
Bill Finch, President

Softball NB Inc. (SNB) / Softball Nouveau-Brunswick Inc.
4242 Water St., Miramichi, NB E1N 4L2, Canada
Tel: 506-773-3507; *Fax:* 506-773-5630
softball@softballnb.ca
www.softballnb.ca
Bev Adams, President
Réjean Léger, Sec.-Treas.
Peter McLean, Executive & Technical Director

Softball Newfoundland & Labrador
PO Box 21165, St. John's, NL A1A 5B2, Canada
Tel: 709-576-7231; *Fax:* 709-576-7081
softball@sportnl.ca
www.softball.nf.ca
Lloyd Power, President

Softball Ontario
#305, 1185 Eglinton Ave. East, Toronto, ON M3C 3C6, Canada
Tel: 416-426-7150; *Fax:* 416-426-7368
info@softballontario.ca
www.softballontario.ca
Wendy Cathcart, Executive Director

Softball Québec
CP 1000, Succ. M, 4545, av Pierre-de Coubertin, Montréal, QC H1V 3R2, Canada
Tél: 514-252-3061; *Téléc:* 514-252-3134
cgagnon@softballquebec.com
www.softballquebec.com
Sophie Bédard, Présidente

Softball Saskatchewan
2205 Victoria Ave., Regina, SK S4P 0S4, Canada
Tel: 306-780-9235; *Fax:* 306-780-9483
info@softball.sk.ca
www.softball.sk.ca
Guy Jacobson, Executive Director

Softball Yukon
18 Stewart Rd., Whitehorse, YT Y1A 3S3, Canada
sbyukon@whtvcable.com
www.softballyukon.com
Rob Andison, President

Sport Medicine

Alberta Athletic Therapists Association
PO Box 61115, Kensingston RPO, Calgary, AB T2N 4S6
Tel: 403-220-8957
info@aata.ca
www.aata.ca
Breda Lau, President
Sarah Klassen, Secretary

Athletic Therapy Association of British Columbia (ATABC)
c/o Camosun College Interurban Campus, #PISE 306E, 4371 Interurban Rd., Victoria, BC V9E 2C5, Canada
mail@athletictherapybc.ca
www.athletictherapybc.ca
Noreen Ortilla, President
Kelly Uniewski, Registrar

Atlantic Provinces Athletic Therapists Association
c/o Memorial University, PO Box 4200, 2300 Elizabeth Ave., St. John's, NL A1C 5S7, Canada
Tel: 709-737-3442
contact@apata.ca
www.apata.ca
Shauna Stone, President

Canadian Academy of Sport Medicine (CASM) / Académie canadienne de médecine du sport (ACMS)
#4, 5330 Canotek Rd., Ottawa, ON K1J 9C1
Tel: 613-748-5851; *Fax:* 613-748-5792
Toll-Free: 877-585-2394
bfalardeau@casm-acms.org
www.casm-acms.org
Affiliation(s): World Federation of Sport Medicine
Dawn Haworth, Executive Director

Canadian Athletic Therapists Association (CATA) / Association canadienne des thérapeutes du sport
#402, 1040 - 7th Ave. SW, Calgary, AB T2P 3G9, Canada
Tel: 403-509-2282; *Fax:* 403-509-2280
info@athletictherapy.org
www.athletictherapy.org
Grant Slessor, Executive Director

Corporation des thérapeutes du sport du Québec (CTSQ)
Concordia University, #SP165.04, 7141, rue Sherbrooke ouest, Montréal, QC H4B 1R6, Canada
Tél: 514-848-2424
admin@ctsq.qc.ca
www.ctsq.qc.ca
Christina Grace, President
Diana Berardi, General Manager

Manitoba Athletic Therapists Association Inc. (MATA)
University of Manitoba, 233 Investors Group Athletic Centre, 75 Sidney Smith St., Winnipeg, MB R3T 2N2, Canada
Tel: 204-474-6004; *Fax:* 204-474-7680
mail@mata.mb.ca
www.mata.mb.ca
Mike Hutton, President

Ontario Athletic Therapists Association
283 Danforth Avenue, Toronto, ON M4K 1N2, Canada
Tel: 416-845-4993
president@athletictherapist.on.ca
www.athletictherapist.on.ca
Drew Laskoski, President

Saskatchewan Athletic Therapists Association (SATA)
Tel: 306-291-6069
karihiebert@yahoo.ca
www.smscs.ca/sata.htm
Kari Hiebert, President

Sport Medicine Council of Alberta (SMCA)
Percy Page Centre, 11759 Groat Rd., Edmonton, AB T5M 3K6, Canada
Tel: 780-415-0812; *Fax:* 780-422-3093
smca@sportmedab.ca
www.sportmedab.ca
Dwayne Laing, President

Sport Medicine Council of British Columbia
1325 Keith Road, North Vancouver, BC V7J 1J3, Canada
Tel: 604-903-3880; *Fax:* 604-929-3877
Toll-Free: 888-755-3375
info@sportmedbc.com
www.sportmedbc.com
Lynda Cannell, President/CEO

Sport Medicine Council of Manitoba Inc.
#403, 200 Main St., Winnipeg, MB R3C 4M2, Canada
Tel: 204-925-5750; *Fax:* 204-925-5624
cbaker@sport.mb.ca
sportmed.mb.ca
Scott Leckie, Presidnet

Sports Medicine Council of Nova Scotia (SMCNS)
50 West Porters Lake Rd., Porters Lake, NS B3E 1K2, Canada
Fax: 902-435-4491
kelliott@smcns.ca
www.smcns.ca
Affiliation(s): Sport Medicine & Science Council of Canada
Kate Elliott, President

Sport Sciences

Canadian Society for Psychomotor Learning & Sport Psychology (CSPLSP) / Société canadienne d'apprentissage psychomoteur et de psychologie du sport (SCAPPS)
c/o Dr. N. Holt, Faculty of Physical Ed. & Rec., University of Alberta, Van Vliet Centre, Edmonton, AB T6G 2H9
nick.holt@ualberta.ca
www.scapps.org
Nick Holt, President
Sean Horton, Secretary-Treasurer

Ontario Association of Sport & Exercise Sciences (OASES)
295 Broadway, Orangeville, ON L9W 1L2, Canada
Tel: 519-925-2265; *Fax:* 519-925-9853
Affiliation(s): Canadian Society for Exercise Physiology
Patricia Clark, Executive Director

Sports

Alberta Schools' Athletic Association (ASAA)
Percy Page Centre, 11759 Groat Rd., Edmonton, AB T5M 3K6, Canada
Tel: 780-427-8182; *Fax:* 780-415-1833
info@asaa.ca
www.asaa.ca
Affiliation(s): National Federation of State High School Associations
John F. Paton, Executive Director
Dave M. Jones, President

Amateur Athletic Union (AAU)
PO Box 22049, 1910 Hotel Plaza Blvd., Lake Buena Vista, FL 32830, USA
Tel: 407-934-7200; *Fax:* 407-934-7242
Toll-Free: 800-228-4872
anita@aausports.org
www.aausports.org
Bobby Dodd, President/CEO
Mike Killpack, Director, Sports

Arctic Winter Games International Committee (AWGIC)
#400, 5201 - 50 Ave., Yellowknife, NT X1A 3S9, Canada
Tel: 867-873-7245; *Fax:* 867-920-6467
www.awg.ca
Lloyd Bentz, Secretary
Gerry Thick, President
Wendell Shiffler, Vice-President
Ian D. Legaree, Technical Director

Association régionale du sport étudiant du Saguenay-Lac St-Jean (ARSESLSJ)
CEGEP de Chicoutimi, 534, rue Jacques Cartier Est, Chicoutimi, QC G7H 1Z6, Canada
Tél: 418-543-3532; *Téléc:* 418-693-0503
arse@arseslsj.qc.ca
www.arseslsj.qc.ca
Éric Benoit, Directeur général

Athletes CAN
#301, 1376 Bank St., Ottawa, ON K1H 7Y3, Canada
Tel: 613-526-4025; *Fax:* 613-526-9735
Toll-Free: 888-832-4222
info@athletescan.com
www.athletescan.com
Guy Tanguay, CEO
Claire Carver-Dias, President

Athletes International
#2702, 3550 Jeanne Mauce, Montréal, QC H2X 3P7
Tel: 514-982-9989; *Fax:* 514-982-0111
Toll-Free: 800-344-1810
info@athletes-int.com
www.athletes-int.com
Peter Schleicher, President

Atlantic University Sport Association (AUSA)
#403, 5657 Spring Garden Rd., Halifax, NS B3J 3R4, Canada
Tel: 902-425-4235; *Fax:* 902-425-7825
feedback@atlanticuniversitysport.com
www.atlanticuniversitysport.com

The Boomerang Association of Canada (BAC)
www.canboom.org
Andy Cross, Contact

British Columbia Games Society
#200, 990 Fort St., Victoria, BC V8V 3K2, Canada
Tel: 250-387-1375; *Fax:* 250-387-4489
info@bcgames.org
www.bcgames.org
Kelly Mann, President & CEO

British Columbia School Sports (BCSS)
#100, 4585 Canada Way, Burnaby, BC V5G 4L6, Canada
Tel: 604-737-3066; *Fax:* 604-737-9844
info@bcschoolsports.ca
www.bcschoolsports.ca
Affiliation(s): USA National Federation of State High Schools
Sue Keenan, Executive Director
Raj Puri, President

Canada Games Council (CGC) / Conseil des jeux du Canada
#701, 2197 Riverside Dr., Ottawa, ON K1H 7X3, Canada
Tel: 613-526-2320; *Fax:* 613-526-4068
canada.games@canadagames.ca
www.canadagames.ca
Sue Hylland, President/CEO
Kelly-Ann Paul, Director of Sport

Canadian Centre for Ethics in Sport (CCES) / Centre canadien pour l'éthique dans le sport
#350, 955 Green Valley Cr., Ottawa, ON K2C 3V4, Canada
Tel: 613-521-3340; *Fax:* 613-521-3134
info@cces.ca
www.cces.ca
Affiliation(s): True Sport Foundation
Roger Jackson, Chair
Paul Melia, CEO

Canadian Colleges Athletic Association / Association canadienne du sport collégial
c/o St. Lawrence College, 2 Belmont St., Cornwall, ON K6H 4Z1, Canada
Tel: 613-937-1508; *Fax:* 613-937-1530
sandra@ccaa.ca
www.ccaa.ca
Affiliation(s): Atlantic Colleges Athletic Association; Fédération québécoise du sport étudiant; Ontario Colleges Athletic Association; Alberta Colleges Athletic Conference; British Columbia Colleges Athletic Association
Sandra Murray-MacDonell, Executive Director

Canadian Paintball Association
92 Arlington Ave., Oshawa, ON L1G 2N6, Canada
admin@canadianpaintball.ca
www.canadianpaintball.ca
Jody L.E. McLeod, Contact

Canadian Sport Tourism Alliance (CSTA)
#600, Lisgar St., Ottawa, ON K2P 0C2, Canada
Tel: 613-688-5843; *Fax:* 613-238-3878
info@canadiansporttourism.com
www.canadiansporttourism.com
Janet Gates, Chair
Rick Traer, CEO

Canadian Ultimate Players Association (CUPA)
200 Main St., Winnipeg, MB R3C 4M2, Canada
Toll-Free: 888-691-1080
info@canadianultimate.com
www.canadianultimate.com
Danny Saunders, Executive Director

Fédération québécoise du sport étudiant (FQSE)
CP 1000, Succ. M, 4545, av Pierre-De Coubertin, Montréal, QC H1V 3R2, Canada
Tél: 514-252-3300; *Téléc:* 514-254-3292
www.fqse.qc.ca; www.sportetudiant.com
Yves Paquette, Président

Fraser Valley Soccer Referees' Association (FVSRA)
10945B River Rd, Delta, BC V4C 2R8, Canada
Tel: 604-588-3959
www.fraservalleysoccerreferees.com
David Miller, President

International Curling Information Network Group (ICING)
73 Appleford Rd., Hamilton, ON L9C 6B5, Canada
Tel: 905-389-7781
psmith@icing.org
www.icing.org
Peter M. Smith, Contact

Judo Canada
#212, 1725 St. Laurent, Ottawa, ON K1G 3V4, Canada
Tel: 613-738-1200; *Fax:* 613-738-1299
info@judocanada.org
www.judocanada.org
Affiliation(s): International Judo Federation
Andrzej Sadej, Director General
Phil Moreau, Administrative Coordinator

Manitoba High Schools Athletic Association (MHSAA)
#405, 200 Main St., Winnipeg, MB R3C 4M2, Canada
Tel: 204-925-5640; *Fax:* 204-925-5624
info@mhsaa.ca
www.mhsaa.mb.ca
Morris Glimcher, Executive Director
Don Hurton, President

Nova Scotia School Athletic Federation
5516 Spring Garden Rd., Halifax, NS B3J 3G6, Canada
Tel: 902-425-8662; *Fax:* 902-425-5606
dweston@sportnovascotia.ca
nssaf.ednet.ns.ca
Darrell Dempster, Executive Director
Dianne Weston, Secretary

Ontario Federation of School Athletic Associations (OFSAA) / Fédération des associations du sport scolaire de l'Ontario
#204, 3 Concorde Gate, Toronto, ON M3C 3N7
Tel: 416-426-7391; *Fax:* 416-426-7317
lindsey@ofsaa.on.ca (Newsletter)
www.ofsaa.on.ca
Martin Ritsma, President
Lynn Kelman, Vice-President
Doug Gellatly, Executive Director
Lindsey Evanoff, Coordinator, Marketing & Communications

Orienteering New Brunswick (ONB)
34 Fairview Dr., Moncton, NB E1E 3C7, Canada
Tel: 506-389-8091
www.orienteering.nb.ca
Affiliation(s): International Orienteering Federation
David Ross, President
Paul Looker, Secretary

Ottawa Carleton Ultimate Association (OCUA)
PO Box 142, 99 Fifth Ave., Ottawa, ON K1S 5P5, Canada
Tel: 613-860-6282
board@ocua.ca
www.ocua.ca
Marci Morris, Executive Director
Neil Saravanamuttoo, President
Shawn Roussy, Treasurer

Sask Sport Inc.
1870 Lorne St., Regina, SK S4P 2L7, Canada
Tel: 306-780-9300; *Fax:* 306-781-6021
sasksport@sasksport.sk.ca
www.sasksport.sk.ca
Jim Burnett, General Manager

School Sports Newfoundland & Labrador (SSNL)
PO Box 8700, Bldg. 810, Pleasantville, NL A1B 4J6, Canada
Tel: 709-729-2795; *Fax:* 709-729-2705
ssnl@sportnl.ca
www.schoolsportsnl.ca
Karen Richard, Executive Director

Société des Jeux de l'Acadie inc. (SJA)
#210, 702, rue Principale, Petit-Rocher, NB E8J 1V1, Canada
Tél: 506-783-4207; *Téléc:* 506-783-4209
sja1@nbnet.nb.ca
www.jeuxdelacadie.org
Stéphane Hachey, Président
Mario Doucet, Directeur général

Sport BC
#260, 3820 Cessna Dr., Richmond, BC V7B 0A2, Canada
Tel: 604-333-3400; *Fax:* 604-333-3401
info@sport.bc.ca
www.sport.bc.ca
Paul Varian, President/CEO

Sport Manitoba
200 Main St., Winnipeg, MB R3C 4M2, Canada
Tel: 204-925-5600; *Fax:* 204-925-5916
Toll-Free: 866-774-2220
info@sport.mb.ca
www.sportmanitoba.ca
Jeff Hnatiuk, President/CEO
Tara Skibo, Communications/Public Relations

Sport New Brunswick / Sport Nouveau-Brunswick
#13, 900 Hanwell Rd., Fredericton, NB E3B 6A2, Canada
Tel: 506-451-1320; *Fax:* 506-451-1325
director@sportnb.com
www.sportnb.com
Jason Dickson, Executive Director

Sport North Federation
Don Cooper Building, PO Box 11089, 4908 - 49 St., Yellowknife, NT X1A 3X7, Canada
Tel: 867-669-8326; *Fax:* 867-669-8327
Toll-Free: 800-661-0797
www.sportnorth.com
Doug Rentmeister, Executive Director

Sport Nova Scotia (SNS)
PO Box 3010, Stn. South, 5516 Spring Garden Rd., Halifax, NS B3J 1G6, Canada
Tel: 902-425-5450; *Fax:* 902-425-5606
sportns@sportnovascotia.ca
www.sportnovascotia.ca
Jamie Ferguson, CEO

Sport PEI Inc.
PO Box 302, Charlottetown, PE C1A 7K7, Canada
Tel: 902-368-4110; *Fax:* 902-368-4548
Toll-Free: 800-247-6712
sports@sportpei.pe.ca
www.sportpei.pe.ca
Lyall Huggan, Special Projects
Gemma Koughan, Executive Director
Wendy Reid, President
Nick Murray, Communications
Lisa MacKay, Finance & Administration

Sport Yukon
4061 - 4 Ave., Whitehorse, YT Y1A 1H1, Canada
Tel: 867-668-4236; *Fax:* 867-667-4237
news@sportyukon.com
www.sportyukon.com
George Arcand, President

Sports-Québec
CP 1000, Succ. M, 4545, av Pierre-De Coubertin, Montréal, QC H1V 3R2, Canada
Tél: 514-252-3114; *Téléc:* 514-254-9621
sports@sportsquebec.com
www.sportsquebec.com
André-François Lafond, Directeur général

True Sport Foundation / Fondation sport pur
#350, 955 Green Valley Crescent, Ottawa, ON K2C 3V4, Canada
Tel: 613-526-6043; *Fax:* 613-521-3134
Toll-Free: 888-995-8899
info@truesport.ca
www.truesportfoundation.ca
Victor Lachance, Executive Director

Sports for the Disabled

Active Living Alliance for Canadians with a Disability (ALACD) / Alliance de vie active pour les canadiens/canadiennes ayant un handicap
#104, 720 Belfast Rd., Ottawa, ON K1G 0Z5, Canada
Tel: 613-244-0052; *Fax:* 613-244-4857
Toll-Free: 800-771-0663; *TTY:* 888-771-0663
info@ala.ca
www.ala.ca
Affiliation(s): Canadian Amputee Sports Association; Canadian Association for Disabled Skiing; Canadian Association for Health, Physical Education, Recreation & Dance; Canadian Blind Sports Association; Canadian Cerebral Palsy Sports Association; Canadian Deaf Sports Association; Canadian Intramural Recreation Association; Canadian National Institute for the Blind; Canadian Paralympic Committee; Canadian Paraplegic Association; Canadian Parks/Recreation Association; Canadian Red Cross Society; Canadian Special Olympics; Learning Disabilities Association of Canada; National Network for Mental Health
Jane Arkell, Director

Alberta Amputee Sports & Recreation Association (AASRA)
PO Box 708, Stn. M, Calgary, AB T2P 2J3, Canada
Tel: 403-201-0507; *Fax:* 403-256-7611
Toll-Free: 800-501-0507
info@aasra.ab.ca
www.aasra.ab.ca
Gwen Davies, Executive Director

Alberta Northern Lights Wheelchair Basketball Society
6788 - 99th St., Edmonton, AB T6E 5B8, Canada
Tel: 780-433-4310; *Fax:* 780-431-1764
Toll-Free: 800-465-2992
info@albertanorthernlights.com
www.albertanorthernlights.com

Alberta Sports & Recreation Association for the Blind (ASRAB)
#007, 15 Colonel Baker Pl. NE, Calgary, AB T2E 4Z3, Canada
Tel: 403-262-5332; *Fax:* 403-265-7221
Toll-Free: 888-882-7722
marilyn@asrab.ab.ca
www.asrab.ab.ca
Marilyn McIntosh, Executive Director
Peter Wettlaufer, President

Association des sports pour aveugles de Montréal (ASAM)
CP 95, Succ. M, Montréal, QC H1V 3L6, Canada
Tél: 514-252-3178; *Téléc:* 514-254-1303
infoasam@sportsaveugles.qc.ca
www.sportsaveugles.qc.ca/asam
Affiliation(s): Association sportive des aveugles du Québec
Gérald Cousineau, Président
Guillaume Thibault, Vice-président

Association québécoise des sports en fauteuil roulants (AQSFR)
CP 1000, Succ. M, 4545, rue Pierre-de-Coubertin, Montréal, QC H1V 3R2, Canada
Tél: 514-252-3108; *Téléc:* 514-254-9793
aqsfr@aqsfr.qc.ca
www.aqsfr.qc.ca
José Malo, Directrice générale

Association sportive des aveugles du Québec inc. (ASAQ)
CP 1000, Succ. M, 4545, av Pierre-de Coubertin, Montréal, QC H1V 3R2, Canada
Tél: 514-252-3178; *Téléc:* 514-254-1303
infoasaq@sportsaveugles.qc.ca
www.sportsaveugles.qc.ca
Nathalie Chartrand, Directrice générale

Blind Sailing Association of Canada (BSAC)
45 Brahms Ave., Toronto, ON M2H 1H3, Canada
Tel: 416-489-2433; *Fax:* 416-489-2433
info@blindsailing.ca
www.blindsailing.ca
David Brown, President
Grant Robinson, Vice-President
Randy Nelson, Treasurer

British Columbia Blind Sports & Recreation Association (BCBSRA)
#330, 5055 Joyce St., Vancouver, BC V5R 6B2, Canada
Tel: 604-325-8638; *Fax:* 604-325-1638
info@bcblindsports.bc.ca
www.bcblindsports.bc.ca
Affiliation(s): International Blind Sports Association; BC Sport & Fitness Council for the Disabled
Brian Cowie, President
Tami Grenon, Vice President

British Columbia Deaf Sports Federation (BCDSF)
#254, 3820 Cessna Dr., Richmond, BC V7B 0A2, Canada
Fax: 604-738-7175; *TTY:* 604-333-3606
bcdeafsports@telus.net
www.bcdeafsports.bc.ca
Affiliation(s): BC Sport & Fitness Council for the Disabled
Roger Chan, President
Mandy Harker, Media/Programming

British Columbia Disability Sports (BCDS)
#217, 12837 - 76th Ave., Surrey, BC V3W 2V3, Canada
Tel: 604-598-7890; *Fax:* 604-598-7892; *TTY:* 604-598-7890
info@disabilitysport.org
www.disabilitysport.org
Affiliation(s): Sportability BC; Deaf Sports Federation of BC; Disabled Skiers Association of BC; Canadian Amputee Sports Association BC Division; BC Blind Sports & Recreation Association; BC Therapeutic Riding Association; Disabled Sailing Association of BC; BC Sledge Hockey & Ice Picking; Wheeling Eights Square Dance Club; BC Wheelchair Basketball Society
Jane Samletzki, Executive Director

British Columbia Wheelchair Sports Association (BCWSA)
#210 - 3820 Cessna Dr., Richmond, BC V7B 0A2, Canada
Tel: 604-333-3520; *Fax:* 604-333-3450
Toll-Free: 877-737-3090
info@bcwheelchairsports.com
www.bcwheelchairsports.com
Kathy Newman, Executive Director

Canadian Amputee Golf Association (CAGA)
PO Box 6091, Stn. A, Calgary, AB T2H 2L4, Canada
canamps@caga.ca
www.caga.ca
Gwen Davies, President

Canadian Amputee Sports Association (CASA) / Association canadienne des sports pour amputés
1399 Weslemkoon Lake Rd., Gilmour, ON K0L 1W0, Canada
Tel: 613-474-1397
bobfox1@hotmail.com
www.canadianamputeesports.ca
Affiliation(s): Canadian Paralympic Committee; Hockey Canada
Robert Fox, President

Canadian Association for Disabled Skiing - Alberta (CADS Alberta)
11759 Groat Rd., Edmonton, AB T5M 3K6, Canada
Tel: 780-427-8104; *Fax:* 780-427-0524
info@cadsalberta.ca
www.cadsalberta.ca
Affiliation(s): Canadian Ski Instructors' Alliance (CSIA), Canadian Association of Snowboard Instructors (CASI)
Mike Low, President
Allyson Szafranski, Executive Coordinator

Canadian Association for Disabled Skiing - Newfoundland & Labrador Division
6 Albany Pl., St. John's, NL A1E 1Y2, Canada
Tel: 709-753-3625; *Fax:* 709-777-4884
margaret.tibbo@easternhealth.ca
Marg Tibbo, Secretary

Canadian Association for Disabled Skiing Nova Scotia
c/o Alpine Ski Nova Scotia, 5516 Spring Garden Rd., Halifax, NS B3J 1G6, Canada
Tel: 902-425-5450; *Fax:* 902-425-5606
alpinens@sportnovascotia.ca
Lorraine Burch

Canadian Blind Sports Association Inc. / Association canadienne des sports pour aveugles inc.
#325, 5055 Joyce St., Vancouver, BC V5R 6B2, Canada
Tel: 604-419-0480; *Fax:* 604-419-0481
Toll-Free: 866-604-0480
jane@canadianblindsports.ca
www.canadianblindsports.ca
Affiliation(s): International Blind Sports Association; Canadian Paralympic Committee; Active Living Alliance
Jane D. Blaine, Executive Director

Canadian Deaf Sports Association (CDSA) / Association des sports des sourds du Canada (ASSC)
#202A, 10217, boul Pie IX, Montréal, QC H1H 3Z5, Canada
Tel: 514-321-4520; *Fax:* 514-321-2937
Toll-Free: 800-855-0511
office@assc-cdsa.com
www.assc-cdsa.com
Affiliation(s): International Committee of Sports for the Deaf
Kimberley D. Rizzi, Executive Director
Bradford Bentley, External Relations Director
Greg Desrosiers, President

Canadian Electric Wheelchair Hockey Association (CEWHA)
#920, 200 Yorkland Blvd., Toronto, ON M2J 5C1, Canada
Tel: 416-757-8544; *Fax:* 416-490-9334
info@cewha.ca
www.cewha.ca

Canadian Paralympic Committee (CPC) / Comité paralympique canadien
#1401, 85 Albert St., Ottawa, ON K1P 6A4, Canada
Tel: 613-569-4333; *Fax:* 613-569-2777
reachus@paralympic.ca
www.paralympic.ca
Affiliation(s): International Paralympic Committee
Brian MacPherson, Director General
Manali Haridas, Coordinator, Office and Leadership

Canadian Wheelchair Sports Association (CWSA) / Association canadienne des sports en fauteuil roulant (ACSFR)
#108, 2255 St. Laurent Blvd., Ottawa, ON K1G 4K3, Canada
Tel: 613-523-0004; *Fax:* 613-523-0149
info@cwsa.ca
www.cwsa.ca
Affiliation(s): International Stoke Mandeville Wheelchair Sports Federation
Cathy Cadieux, Executive Director
Donald Royer, President

Commission de Ski pour Personnes Handicapées du Québec (CSPHQ)
165 Place Lilas, Pincourt, QC J7V 5B6, Canada
Tél: 514-425-8894; *Téléc:* 514-425-8894
hwohler@yahoo.com
Henry Wohler, President

Disabled Sailing Association of BC
#207, 3077 Granville Street, Vancouver, BC V6H 3J9, Canada
Tel: 604-668-6464; *Fax:* 604-688-6463
dsa@disabilityfoundation.org
www.disabilityfoundation.org/dsa

Affiliation(s): BC Sport & Fitness Council for the Disabled
Kirk Duncan, Program Coordinator

Disabled Skiers Association of BC (DSABC)
#220, 3820 Cessna Dr., Richmond, BC V7B 0A2, Canada
Tel: 604-333-3630; *Fax:* 604-333-3450
disabledskiers@telus.net
www.disabledskiingbc.com
Brian Forrester, Executive Director
Kevin ter Kuile, President

International Committee of Sports for the Deaf (ICSD) / Comité international des Sports des Sourds (CISS)
528 Trail Ave., Frederick, MD 21701, USA
Fax: 301-620-2990
info@ciss.org
www.ciss.org; www.deaflympics.com
Affiliation(s): Canadian Deaf Sports Association
Craig A. Crowley, President

Manitoba Amputee Sport & Recreation Association
286 Harvard Ave., Winnipeg, MB R3M 0K8, Canada
Tel: 204-489-9278; *Fax:* 204-488-1094
rootel@shaw.ca
Raquel Godin, Contact

Manitoba Blind Sport Association
#311, 200 Main St., Winnipeg, MB R3C 4M2, Canada
Tel: 204-925-5694; *Fax:* 204-925-5703
blindsport@shawbiz.ca
www.blindsport.mb.ca
Cathy Drewianchuk, Executive Director

Manitoba Wheelchair Sports Association
200 Main St., Winnipeg, MB R3C 4M2, Canada
Tel: 204-925-5790; *Fax:* 204-925-5792
mwsa@sport.mb.ca
www.mwsa.ca
Tricia Klassen, Executive Director

National Capital Sports Council of the Disabled Inc. (NCSCD) / Le Conseil des sports des handicapées de la capitale nationale inc. (CSHCN)
#104, 720 Belfast Rd., Ottawa, ON K1G 0Z5, Canada
Tel: 613-569-7632; *Fax:* 613-244-4857
ncscd@ncscd.ca
www.ncscd.ca

New Brunswick Deaf Sports Association
#902, 656 Brunswick Dr., Saint John, NB E2L 3S5, Canada
Tel: 506-642-3903
Eugene Frost, President

Ontario Amputee & Les Autres Sports Association (OALASA)
#102, 1185 Eglinton Ave. East, Toronto, ON M3C 3C6, Canada
Tel: 519-659-7452
www.oalasa.org
Rodney Reimer, President
Douglas Walker, Treasurer
Archie Watts, Secretary

Ontario Blind Sport Association (OBSA)
#104, 3 Concorde Gate, Toronto, ON M3C 3N6, Canada
Tel: 416-426-7191; *Fax:* 416-426-7361
Toll-Free: 888-711-1112
matt@osrc.com
www.blindsports.on.ca
Shirley Shelby, President

Ontario Deaf Sports Association
#303, 3 Concorde Gate, Toronto, ON M3C 3N7, Canada
Tel: 416-413-0299
office@ontariodeafsports.on.ca
www.ontariodeafsports.on.ca
Rohan Smith, President

Ontario Wheelchair Sports Association (OWSA)
#102, 1185 Eglinton Ave. East, Toronto, ON M3C 3C6, Canada
Tel: 416-426-7189; *Fax:* 416-426-7361
info@ontwheelchairsports.org
www.ontwheelchairsports.org
Affiliation(s): Canadian Wheelchair Sports Association
Barb Montemurro, President
Michael Suraci, Executive Director

Paralympic Sports Association (Alberta) (PSA)
10024 - 79 Ave., Edmonton, AB T6E 1R5, Canada
Tel: 780-439-8687; *Fax:* 780-432-0486
info@parasports.net
www.parasports.net
Affiliation(s): Wheelchair Sports Alberta
Kim McDonald, Executive Director

ParaSport Ontario
#104, 3 Concorde Gate, Toronto, ON M3C 3N7, Canada
Tel: 416-426-7187; *Fax:* 416-426-7361
Toll-Free: 800-265-1539
info@parasportontario.ca
www.parasportontario.ca
Affiliation(s): Ontario Amputee & Les Autres Sports Association; Ontario Blind Sports Association; Ontario Cerebral Palsy Sports Association; Ontario Wheelchair Sports Association
Cathy Vincelli, Executive Director

Saskatchewan Blind Sports Association Inc.
510 Cynthia St., Saskatoon, SK S7L 7K7, Canada
Tel: 306-975-0888
Toll-Free: 877-772-7798
sbsa.sk@shaw.ca
www.saskblindsports.ca
Tony Badger, Executive Director
Jerry Johnson, President

Saskatchewan Deaf Sports Association
1860 Lorne St., Regina, SK S4P 2L7, Canada
Toll-Free: 800-855-0511
www.saskdeafsports.ca
Affiliation(s): Regina Deaf Athletic Club; Saskatoon Deaf Athletic Club; Saskatchewan Sport Inc.; Canadian Deaf Sports Assn.
Kenneth Hoffman, President
Dale Birley, Administrator

Saskatchewan Ski Association - Skiing for Disabled (SASKI)
17 Clark Cres., Saskatoon, SK S7H 3L8, Canada
Tel: 306-374-7745; *Fax:* 306-955-5979
sask.ski@sasktel.net
www.saski.ca
Alana Ottenbreit, Executive Director
Pat Prokopchuk, Contact, Skiing for Disabled
Doug Sylvester, Contact, Biathlon

Saskatchewan Wheelchair Sports Association (SWSA)
510 Cynthia St., Saskatoon, SK S7L 7K7, Canada
Tel: 306-975-0824; *Fax:* 306-975-0825
info@swsa.ca
www.swsa.ca
Judy Peddle, Executive Director

Special Olympics Alberta (SOA)
Percy Page Centre, 11759 Groat Rd., Edmonton, AB T5M 3K6, Canada
Tel: 780-415-0719; *Fax:* 780-422-2663
Toll-Free: 800-444-2883
info@specialolympics.ab.ca
www.specialolympics.ab.ca
Carmen Wyton, President & CEO

Wheelchair Sports Alberta
Percy Page Center, 11759 Groat Rd., Edmonton, AB T5M 3K6, Canada
Tel: 780-427-8699; *Fax:* 780-427-8723
Toll-Free: 888-453-6770
wsa1@telus.net
www.abwheelchairsport.ca
Mike Sandomirsky, Executive Director

Wheelchair Sports Association of Newfoundland & Labrador (WSANL)
40 Imogene Cr., Paradise, NL A1L 1H5, Canada
Tel: 709-782-0487
gpower@cwsa.ca
Gary Power, President

Sports, Amateur

Alberta Amateur Wrestling Association (AAWA)
Percy Page Centre, 11759 Groat Rd., Edmonton, AB T5M 3K6, Canada
Tel: 780-415-0140; *Fax:* 780-427-0524
aawa@ocii.com
www.albertawrestling.ab.ca
Jerry Derewonko, President
Tammie Bradley, Executive Director
Michael Drought, Technical Director

Hockey Alberta / Hockey l'Alberta
#1, 7875 - 48 Ave., Red Deer, AB T4P 2K1, Canada
Tel: 403-342-6777; *Fax:* 403-346-4277
operations@hockeyalberta.ca
www.hockey-alberta.ca
Rob Litwinski, General Manager
Brad Robbins, Senior Manager, Operations & Member Services
Tim Leer, Senior Manager, Hockey Development

Ontario Speed Skating Association (OSSA)
Memorial Hall, PO Box 1179, 2 Queen St., 2nd Fl., Lakefield, ON K0L 2H0, Canada
Tel: 705-652-0653; *Fax:* 705-652-1227
jdeschenes@speedskatingontario.org
www.speedskatingontario.org
Jackie Deschenes, Executive Director
Bill Allen, Director of Sport

Sport Newfoundland & Labrador
PO Box 8700, St. John's, NL A1B 4J6, Canada
Tel: 709-576-4932; *Fax:* 709-576-7493
sportnl@sportnl.ca
www.sportnl.ca
Troy Croft, Executive Director

Squash

Squash Alberta
3415 - 3rd Ave. NW, Calgary, AB T2N 0M4, Canada
Tel: 403-270-7344; *Fax:* 403-270-8445
Toll-Free: 877-646-6566
lynn@squashalberta.com
www.squashalberta.com
Lynn Nixon, Executive Director

Squash British Columbia
4867 Ontario St., Vancouver, BC V5H 3H4, Canada
Tel: 604-737-3084; *Fax:* 604-736-3527
info@squashbc.com
www.squashbc.com
John Roche, President

Squash Canada
#401, 2197 Riverside Dr., Ottawa, ON K1H 7X3, Canada
Tel: 613-731-7385; *Fax:* 613-731-6291
squash.canada@squash.ca
www.squash.ca
Linda MacPhail, Executive Director
Robert Wyma, President

Squash Manitoba
145 Pacific Ave., Winnipeg, MB R3B 2Z6, Canada
Tel: 204-925-5661; *Fax:* 204-925-5792
squash@sportmanitoba.ca
www.squashmb.org
Lynn Colliou, Executive Director

Squash New Brunswick
276 Parkhurst Dr., Fredericton, NB E3B 2J9, Canada
Tel: 506-457-0877; *Fax:* 506-443-0830
russky@unb.ca
www.squashnb.ca

Squash Nova Scotia
PO Box 3010, Stn. Park Lane Centre, #401, 5516 Spring Garden Rd., Halifax, NS B3J 3G6, Canada
Tel: 902-425-5450; *Fax:* 902-425-5606
gcouture@ns.sympatico.ca
www.squashns.ca

Squash Ontario
#308, 3 Concorde Gate, Toronto, ON M3C 3N7
Tel: 416-426-7201; *Fax:* 416-426-7393
Toll-Free: 888-741-5111
info@squashontario.com
www.squashontario.com
Tom Craig, President
Sherry Funston, Executive Director
Geoffrey Johnson, Program Coordinator
Laura Mauer, Administrative Coordinator

Squash P.E.I.
C/O Sport PEI, PO Box 302, Stn. Enman Cres., Charlottetown, PE C1A 7K7, Canada
Tel: 902-566-0338
meleclair@edu.pe.ca
www.squashpei.org
Steven Banks, President
Nicole Blanchard, Secretary
Des Lecky, Treasurer

Squash Québec
CP 1000, Succ. M, 4545, av Pierre-de Coubertin, Montréal, QC H1V 3R2, Canada
Tél: 514-252-3062; Téléc: 514-252-3103
info@sports-4murs.qc.ca
www.squash.qc.ca
Barry Faguy, Président

Squash Yukon
PO Box 31226, Whitehorse, YT Y1A 5P7, Canada
Tel: 867-667-7071; Fax: 867-668-6442
squashyukon@yknet.yk.ca
www.squashyukon.yk.ca
Jim Gilpin, President

Swimming

Fédération de natation du Québec
CP 1000, Succ. M, 4545, av Pierre-de-Coubertin, Montréal, QC H1V 3R2, Canada
Tél: 514-252-3200; Téléc: 514-252-3232
fnq@fnq.qc.ca
www.fnq.qc.ca
Bernard Charron, directeur général

International Amateur Swimming Federation (IASF) / Fédération internationale de natation amateur (FINA)
Av. de l'Avant-Poste 4, Lausanne, 1005, Switzerland
Tel: 41-21-310-4710; Fax: 41-21-312-6610
www.fina.org
Bartolo Consolo, Hon. Secretary
Julio C. Maglione, President
Cornel Marculescu, Executive Director

Solo Swims of Ontario Inc. (SSO)
32 Coxwell Cres., Brantford, ON N3P 1Z1, Canada
www.soloswims.com
Greg Taylor, President & Secretary

Swim Alberta
Percy Page Centre, 11759 Groat Rd., Edmonton, AB T5M 3K6, Canada
Tel: 780-415-1780; Fax: 780-415-1788
office@swimalberta.ca
www.swimalberta.ca
Doug Bird, President
James Hood, General Manager

Swim BC
#204, 4475 Viewmont Ave., Victoria, BC V8Z 6L8, Canada
Tel: 250-479-2069; Fax: 250-479-3021
markschuett@swim.bc.ca
www.swim.bc.ca
Mark Hahto, Executive Director

Swim Manitoba / Natation Manitoba
#224, 200 Main St., Winnipeg, MB R2C 4M2, Canada
Tel: 204-925-5778; Fax: 204-925-5792
office@swimmanitoba.mb.ca
www.swimmanitoba.mb.ca
Cathie Pickerl, President
Michael McMullen, Vice-President
Sharra Hinton, Treasurer

Swim Nova Scotia (SNS)
5516 Spring Garden Rd., Halifax, NS B3J 1G6, Canada
Tel: 902-425-5450; Fax: 902-425-5606
swimming@sportnovascotia.ca
www.swimnovascotia.com
Lynn Sitland, President
Bette El-Hawary, Executive Director

Swim Ontario
#206, 3 Concorde Gate, Toronto, ON M3C 3N7, Canada
Tel: 416-426-7220; Fax: 416-426-7356
info@swimontario.com
www.swimontario.com
John Vadeika, Executive Director

Swim Saskatchewan
2205 Victoria Ave., Regina, SK S4P 0S4, Canada
Tel: 306-780-9291; Fax: 306-525-4009
marjwalton@swimsask.ca
www.swimsask.ca
Marj Walton, Executive Director

Swimming New Brunswick
#13, 900 Hanwell Rd., Fredericton, NB E3B 6A3, Canada
Tel: 506-451-1323; Fax: 506-451-1325
swimnb@nbnet.nb.ca
www.swimnb.ca
Maurice Leger, President

Swimming Newfoundland & Labrador
PO Box 21248, Stn. Macdonald Dr., St. John's, NL A1A 5B2, Canada
Tel: 709-576-7946; Fax: 709-576-7493
swimnl@sportnl.ca
www.swimnl.nfld.net
Corina Hartley, Executive Director

Swimming Prince Edward Island
PO Box 302, Charlottetown, PE C1A 7K7, Canada
Tel: 902-569-0583; Fax: 902-368-4548
cgcrozier@sportpei.pe.ca
www.swimpei.com
Cheryl Crozier, Executive Director

Swimming/Natation Canada
#700, 2197 Riverside Dr., Ottawa, ON K1H 7X3, Canada
Tel: 613-260-1348; Fax: 613-260-0804
natloffice@swimming.ca
www.swimming.ca
Affiliation(s): Aquatic Federation of Canada
Pierre Lafontaine, CEO/National Coach
Mark Hahto, COO
Larry Clough, CFO
Martin Richard, Communications Director

Synchro Alberta
The Percy Page Centre, 11759 Groat Rd., Edmonton, AB T5M 3K6, Canada
Tel: 780-415-1789; Fax: 780-415-0056
syncro@synchroalberta.com
www.synchroalberta.com
Chris Hampshire, President

Synchro BC
#301, 1367 West Broadway, Vancouver, BC V6H 4A9, Canada
Tel: 604-737-3169; Fax: 604-738-7175
synchrobc@telus.net
www.synchro.bc.ca
Twyla Ryan, Executive Director
Cathy Chapell, Office Coordinator

Synchro Canada / Association canadienne de nage synchronisée amateur
#200, 1010 Polytek St., Unit 14, Gloucester, ON K1J 9H9, Canada
Tel: 613-748-5674; Fax: 613-748-5724
catherine@synchro.ca
www.synchro.ca
Catherine Gosselin-Després, Chief Operations Officer
Diane Oligny, Chief Technical Officer

Synchro Manitoba
200 Main St., Winnipeg, MB R3C 4M2, Canada
Tel: 204-925-5693; Fax: 204-925-5703
info@synchromb.ca
www.synchromb.ca
Affiliation(s): Manitoba Sports Federation
Allison Gervais, Executive Director

Synchro Newfoundland & Labrador
1 Pine Bud Pl., St. John's, NL A1B 1N1, Canada
Tel: 709-722-0439
Lorna Proudfoot, Contact

Synchro Ontario
#303, 1185 Eglinton Ave. East, Toronto, ON M3C 3C6, Canada
Tel: 416-426-7110; Fax: 416-426-7376
lmakins@osrc.com
www.synchroontario.com
Leslie Makins, Executive Director

Synchro PEI
PO Box 302, Charlottetown, PE C1A 7K7, Canada
Tel: 902-892-1873
lucillecarter@aol.com
www.sportpei.pe.ca
Lucille Carter, President

Synchro Saskatchewan
#209, 1860 Lorne St., Regina, SK S4P 2L7, Canada
Tel: 306-780-9227; Fax: 306-780-9445
synchro.sk@sasktel.net
www.synchrosask.com
Kathleen Reynolds, Executive Director

Synchro-Québec
CP 1000, Succ. M, 4545, av Pierre-de Coubertin, Montréal, QC H1V 3R2, Canada
Tél: 514-252-3087; Téléc: 514-252-5658
Ligne sans frais: 866-537-3164
fnsq@synchroquebec.qc.ca
www.synchroquebec.qc.ca

Table Soccer

Canadian Table Soccer Federation
8311, rue Ouimet, Brossard, QC J4Y 3B3, Canada
Tel: 514-668-2326
secretary@canadafoos.com
Eric Dunn, President
Adam Imanpoor, Secretary

Ontario Table Soccer Association & Tour
Tel: 905-812-9994
Toll-Free: 866-247-7702
info@ontariotablesoccer.com
www.ontariotablesoccer.com
Mario Recupero, Executive Director

Table Tennis

Alberta Table Tennis Association (ATTA)
Percy Page Centre, 11759 Groat Rd., Edmonton, AB T5M 3K6, Canada
Tel: 780-427-8588; Fax: 866-273-6708
atta@abtabletennis.com
www.abtabletennis.com
Affiliation(s): International Table Tennis Federation
Joseph Chan, President
Judy Ellefson, Program Coordinator

British Columbia Table Tennis Association
#227 - 3820 Cessna Drive, Richmond, BC V7B 0A2, Canada
Tel: 604-333-3655; Fax: 604-333-3450
bctta@hotmail.com
www.bctta.ca
Amelia Ho, President

Canadian Table Tennis Association (CTTA) / Association canadienne de tennis de table
#400, 2211 Riverside Dr., Ottawa, ON K1H 7X5, Canada
Tel: 613-733-6272; Fax: 613-733-7279
ctta@ctta.ca
www.ctta.ca
Affiliation(s): Sports Council of Canada
Manali Haridas, Office Administrator
Tony Kiesenhofer, Director General

Fédération de tennis de table du Québec (FTTQ)
CP 1000, Succ. M, 4545, av Pierre-de Coubertin, Montréal, QC H1V 3R2, Canada
Tél: 514-252-3064; Téléc: 514-251-8038
www.tennisdetable.ca/
Jacques Plamandon, Directeur général

Manitoba Table Tennis Association (MTTA)
145 Pacific Ave., Winnipeg, MB R3B 2Z6, Canada
Tel: 204-925-5690; Fax: 204-925-5916
table.tennis@sportmanitoba.ca
www.mtta.ca
Affiliation(s): International Table Tennis Federation
Ron Edwards, Executive Director
Dan Racicot, President
Ryan Szajkowski, Vice-President, Administration
Greg Chan, Vice-President, Technical

Ontario Table Tennis Association (OTTA)
PO Box 42040, Stn. Conestoga, 550 King St. North, Waterloo, ON N2L 6K5, Canada
Toll-Free: 877-396-6601
larry.laughlen@ottacanada.com
www.ottacanada.com
Larry Laughlen, President

Prince Edward Island Table Tennis Association (PEITTA)
3 Hurry Rd., RR#10, Charlottetown, PE C1E 1Z4, Canada
Tel: 902-368-2360
nchishti@biovectra.com
Todd Gaudin, Vice-President
Lorne Clow, Secretary
Wade Gregory, Treasurer
Najam Chishti, President

Saskatchewan Table Tennis Association Inc. (STTA)
John V. Remai Centre, 510 Cynthia St., Saskatoon, SK S7N 7K7, Canada
Tel: 306-975-0835
info@sasktabletennis.ca
www.sasktabletennis.ca
Dwayne Yachiw, Program Coordinator
Joseph Chan, President
Edward Hung, Vice-President

Teaching

British Columbia Physical Education Provincial Specialist Association
c/o B.C. Teachers' Federation, #100, 550 West 6th Ave., Vancouver, BC V5Z 4P2, Canada
Tel: 604-871-2283; *Fax:* 604-871-2286
www.bctf.bc.ca/pebc
Debbie Keel, President

Tennis

Alberta Tennis Association (ATA)
11759 Groat Rd., Edmonton, AB T5M 3K6, Canada
Tel: 780-415-1661; *Fax:* 780-415-1693
info@tennisalberta.com
www.tennisalberta.com
Darryl Szafranski, Chief Executive Officer
Eva Wolicki, Technical Director

International Tennis Federation (ITF)
Bank Lane, Roehampton, London, SW15 5XZ, United Kingdom
Tel: 44-20-8878-6464; *Fax:* 44-20-8392-4744
www.itftennis.com
Affiliation(s): Tennis Canada
Francesco Ricci Bitti, President
Juan Margets, Executive Vice-President

Nova Scotia Tennis Association
5516 Spring Garden Rd., Halifax, NS B3J 1G6, Canada
Tel: 902-425-5450; *Fax:* 902-425-5606
tennisns@sportnovascotia.ca
www.tennisnovascotia.ca
Roger Keating, Executive Director

Ontario Tennis Association (OTA)
#200, 1 Shoreham Dr., Toronto, ON M3N 3A7
Tel: 416-514-1100; *Fax:* 416-514-1112
Toll-Free: 800-387-5066
ota@tennisontario.com
www.tennisontario.com
Michel Lecavalier, President
Jim Boyce, Executive Director
Simon Bartram, Vice-President
Scott Fraser, Vice-President, Finance & Administration
Glenna Poick, Vice-President, Marketing & Communications
Liz Wood, Vice-President, Membership & Regional Development

Prince Edward Island Tennis Association
PO Box 302, 40 Enman Cres., Charlottetown, PE C1A 7K7, Canada
Tel: 902-368-4985; *Fax:* 902-368-4548
mconnolly@sportpei.pe.ca
www.tennispei.ca
Mike Connolly, Executive Director
Brian Hall, Technical Director

Tennis BC
#204, 210 West Broadway, Vancouver, BC V5Y 3W2, Canada
Tel: 604-737-3086; *Fax:* 604-737-3124
tbc@tennisbc.org
tennisbc.org
Ryan Clark, Chief Executive Officer

Tennis Canada
Rexall Centre, #100, 1 Shoreham Dr., Toronto, ON M3N 3A6, Canada
Tel: 416-665-9777; *Fax:* 416-665-9017
Toll-Free: 877-283-6647
info@tenniscanada.com
www.tenniscanada.com
Michael S. Downey, President & CEO
Tony Eames, Chair

Tennis Manitoba
#303, 200 Main St., Winnipeg, MB R3C 4M2, Canada
Tel: 204-925-5660; *Fax:* 204-925-5703
tennismb@shawbiz.ca
www.tennismanitoba.com
Rick Bochinski, Executive Director
Brigitte Epp, Administrative Assistant

Tennis New Brunswick
PO Box 604, Fredericton, NB E3B 5A6, Canada
Tel: 506-444-0885
tnb@tennisnb.net
www.tennisnb.net

Tennis Newfoundland & Labrador
Bldg. 810, PO Box 8700, Stn. Pleasantville, St. John's, NL A1B 4J6, Canada
Tel: 709-765-0426; *Fax:* 709-722-1670
tennis@sportnl.ca
www.tennisnl.ca
Ryan Maarschalk, Technical Director

Tennis Northwest Territories
PO Box 671, Yellowknife, NT X1A 2N5, Canada
Tel: 867-873-2018
eastarm@ssimicro.com
www.tennisnwt.ca
Fran Hurcomb, President

Tennis Québec (TQ)
285, rue Faillon ouest, Montréal, QC H2R 2W1, Canada
Tél: 514-270-6060; *Téléc:* 514-270-2700
courrier@tennis.qc.ca
www.tennis.qc.ca
Jean François Manibal, Directeur général
Réjean Genois, Président

Tennis Saskatchewan
2205 Victoria Ave., Regina, SK S4P 0S4, Canada
Tel: 306-780-9410; *Fax:* 306-525-4009
tennissask@sasktel.net
www.tennissask.com
Affiliation(s): Sask Sport Incorporated
Rory Park, Executive Director

Therapeutic Riding

Antigonish Therapeutic Riding Association
50 The Heights, Antigonish, NS B2G 1K5, Canada
Tel: 902-863-1479
www.nsnet.org/riding/

British Columbia Therapeutic Riding Association (BCTRA)
25768 - 128th Ave., Maple Ridge, BC V4R 1C4, Canada
Tel: 604-462-9884; *Fax:* 604-462-9597
supremehm@shaw.ca
vcn.bc.ca/bctra
Affiliation(s): Horse Council BC; Sports & Fitness Council for the Disabled
Jane James, President

Canadian Therapeutic Riding Association / Association canadienne d'équitation thérapeutique
#11, 5420 Hwy. 6 North, RR#5, Guelph, ON N1H 6J2, Canada
Tel: 519-767-0700; *Fax:* 519-767-0435
ctra@golden.net
www.cantra.ca
Lisa Burd, President
Donna Naylor, Executive Director

Cavalier Riding Club Ltd. (CRC)
c/o Ashton Ridge Equestrian Centre, 711 Pine Glen Rd., Pine Glen, NB E1J 1S1, Canada
Tel: 506-386-2596
mgs500@gmail.com
ashton-ridge.com/cavalier.htm
Mark G. Stevens, President

Central Ontario Developmental Riding Program (CODRP)
Pride Stables, 584 Pioneer Tower Rd., Kitchener, ON N2P 2H9, Canada
Tel: 519-653-4686; *Fax:* 519-653-5565
info@pridestables.com
www.codrp.com; www.pridestables.com
Affiliation(s): Ontario Therapeutic Riding Association (ONTRA)
Heather Mackneson, Executive Director

Community Association for Riding for the Disabled (CARD)
4777 Dufferin St., Toronto, ON M3H 5T3, Canada
Tel: 416-667-8600; *Fax:* 416-739-7520
card.info@sympatico.ca
www.card.ca
Affiliation(s): Ontario Therapeutic Riding Association
Abbey Simbrow, Executive Director

Comox Valley Therapeutic Riding Society (CVTRS)
PO Box 3666, Courtenay, BC V9N 7P1, Canada
Tel: 250-338-1968; *Fax:* 250-338-4137
cvtrs@telus.net
www.cvtrs.com
Affiliation(s): North American Handicapped Riding Association
Margaret Hind, Coordinator

Errington Therapeutic Riding Association (ETRA)
Pyramid Stables, PO Box 462, 7581 Harby Rd., Lantzville, Parksville, BC V9P 2G6, Canada
etrainfo@shaw.ca
islandpages.com/etra/
Affiliation(s): BC Therapeutic Riding Association; Canadian Therapeutic Riding Association
Tom Roy, President

Halifax Area Leisure & Therapeutic Riding Association
The Stables, 1690 Bell Rd., Halifax, NS B3H 2Z3, Canada
Tel: 902-860-0697
haltr@bengallancers.com
www.bengallancers.com/haltr.html
Affiliation(s): Sport Canada; Equine Canada
Sally Murphy, Contact

Lanark County Therapeutic Riding Programme (LCTRP)
103 Judson St., Carleton Place, ON K7C 2S5, Canada
Tel: 613-257-7121; *Fax:* 613-257-2675
Toll-Free: 800-667-2617
info@therapeuticriding.ca
www.therapeuticriding.ca
Susan Cressy, Contact

Lethbridge Handicapped Riding Association
RR#8-24-6, Lethbridge, AB T1J 4P4, Canada
Tel: 403-328-2165
lhra@telusplanet.net
Nancy Conan, Contact
Cory Conan, Contact

Little Bits Therapeutic Riding Association
PO Box 29016, Stn. Lendrum, Edmonton, AB T6H 5Z6, Canada
Tel: 780-476-1233
info@littlebits.ca
www.littlebits.ca

Manitoba Riding for the Disabled Association Inc. (MRDA)
200 Main St., 2nd Fl., Winnipeg, MB R3C 4M2, Canada
Tel: 204-925-5905; *Fax:* 204-925-5792
mrda@shawcable.com
www.mrda.cc
Peter Manastyrsky, Executive Director

Mirabel Morgan Special Riding Centre
1201 - 2nd Line South, RR#1, Bailieboro, ON K0L 1B0, Canada
Tel: 705-939-6485
mirabel.ms@sympatico.ca
Colleen Baptist, Contact

Mount View Special Riding Association (MVSRA)
5629 - 49 Ave., Olds, AB T4H 1G5, Canada
Tel: 403-556-7247

New Brunswick Therapeutic Riding
860 Mitchell St., Fredericton, NB E3B 6C5, Canada
Tel: 506-455-1621
Carol Morrison

Nova Scotia Riding for the Disabled Association (NSRDA)
608 West Lawrencetown Rd., Lawrencetown, NS B2Z 1S5, Canada
Tel: 902-435-9344; *Fax:* 902-434-0545
salliemurphy@hotmail.com
Affiliation(s): Nova Scotia Equestrian Federation; Recreation Council on Disability in Nova Scotia
Sallie Murphy, Sec.-Treas.

Ontario Therapeutic Riding Association (OnTRA) / Association ontarienne d'équitation thérapeutique
RR#1, 54117 Heritage Line, Straffordville, ON N0J 1Y0, Canada
www.ontra.ca
Viki Davidson LaCombe, President

Pacific Riding for Developing Abilities (PRDA)
1088 - 208 St., Langley, BC V2Z 1T4, Canada
Tel: 604-530-8717; *Fax:* 604-530-8617
admin@prda.ca
www.prda.ca
Affiliation(s): Ishtar Transition Housing Society; Burnaby Association for Community Inclusion
Donna Morris, Administration Manager
Michelle Meacher, Program Manager

PARD Therapeutic Riding (PARD)
PO Box 1654, Peterborough, ON K9J 5S4, Canada
Tel: 705-742-6441
info@pard.ca
www.pard.ca
Joanna Primavesi, President

Peace Area Riding for the Disabled (PARDS)
PO Box 2, Site 24, RR#1, Grande Prairie, AB T8V 2Z8, Canada
Tel: 780-538-3211; *Fax:* 780-538-3683
pards@telusplanet.net
www.pards.ca
Jennifer Douglas, Executive Director

Quinte Therapeutic Riding Association (QUINTRA)
PO Box 22129, Belleville, ON K8N 5V7, Canada
Tel: 613-395-4472
barbara.davis@sympatico.ca
www.quintra.org
Affiliation(s): United Way of Quinte
Barb Davis, Contact

SARI Therapeutic Riding
12659 Medway Rd., RR#1, Arva, ON N0M 1C0, Canada
Tel: 519-666-1123; *Fax:* 519-666-1971
office@sari.ca
www.sari.ca
Affiliation(s): Ontario Therapeutic Riding Association
Heather Zak, Executive Director

Saskatchewan Therapeutic Riding Association
PO Box 1072, North Battleford, SK S9A 3E6, Canada
Tel: 306-398-2889
Ed Gendall, Contact

Sunrise Therapeutic Riding & Learning Centre
6920 Concession 1, RR#2, Puslinch, ON n0B 2J0, Canada
Tel: 519-837-0558; *Fax:* 519-837-1233
info@sunrise-therapeutic.ca
www.sunrise-therapeutic.ca
Affiliation(s): Ontario's Promise
Ann Caine, Executive Director
Suzy Bender, Head Instructor

Therapeutic Ride Algoma
188 Upton Rd., Sault Ste Marie, ON P6A 3W4, Canada
Tel: 705-759-2935; *Fax:* 705-541-5700
Toll-Free: 877-526-4438
slavik@sympatico.ca
www.ridealgoma.com

Victoria Riding for Disabled Association (VRDA)
PO Box 43032, Stn. Victoria North, Victoria, BC V8X 3G2, Canada
Tel: 250-658-6272
vrda@shaw.ca
www.members.shaw.ca/vrda
Affiliation(s): B.C. Therapeutic Riding Association; Horse Council of British Columbia

Windsor Essex Therapeutic Riding Association (WETRA) / Association d'équitation thérapeutique Windsor-Essex
4465 Huron Church Line Rd., Windsor, ON N9H 1H3, Canada
Tel: 519-969-1261; *Fax:* 519-969-4016
wetra@on.aibn.com
www.wetra.ca
Affiliation(s): Ontario Therapeutic Riding Association
Sue Klotzer, Program Director

Track & Field Sports

Achilles Canada
119 Snowden Ave., Toronto, ON M4N 2A8, Canada
Tel: 416-485-6451; *Fax:* 416-485-0823
bmclean@idirect.com
www.achillestrackclub.ca
Brian McLean, Contact

Athletics Canada / Athlétisme Canada
#B1-110, 2445 St-Laurent Blvd, Ottawa, ON K1G 6C3, Canada
Tel: 613-260-5580; *Fax:* 613-260-0341
athcan@athletics.ca
www.athletics.ca
Affiliation(s): International Amateur Athletic Federation
Joanne Mortimore, CEO

Canadian Masters Athletic Association (CMAA)
426 Valermo Dr., Toronto, ON M8W 2L9, Canada
Tel: 416-252-7047
masters@sympatico.ca
www.canadianmastersathletics.com
Brian Keaveney, President
Joan Christiensen, Membership

Northwest Territories Track & Field Association
PO Box 11089, Yellowknife, NT X1A 3X7, Canada
Fax: 867-669-8327
Toll-Free: 800-661-0797
Joe LeBlanc, President

Ontario Masters Track & Field Association (OMTFA)
1185 Eglinton Ave. East, Toronto, ON M3C 3C6, Canada
Tel: 416-426-4427; *Fax:* 416-426-7358
douglasj.smith@sympatico.ca
www.ontariomasters.ca
Doug Smith, President
Paul Osland, Vice-President

Ontario Roadrunners Association
#158, 2255B Queen St. East, Toronto, ON M4E 1G3, Canada
Tel: 416-691-9556
info@ontarioroadrunners.com
www.ontarioroadrunners.com

Transportation

Toronto Cycling Committee (TCC)
850 Coxwell Ave., 2nd Fl., Toronto, ON M4C 5R1, Canada
Tel: 416-392-7592
btww@toronto.ca
www.toronto.ca/cycling
Adrian A. Heaps, Chair

Triathlon

Alberta Triathlon Association (ATA)
11759 Groat Rd., Edmonton, AB T5M 3K6
Tel: 780-427-8616; *Fax:* 780-427-8628
Toll-Free: 866-888-7448
psm@triathlon.ab.ca
www.triathlon.ab.ca
Kenneth Sackley, President
Stephen Paiano, Executive Director

Ontario Association of Triathletes (OAT)
#205, 3 Concorde Gate, Toronto, ON M3C 3N7, Canada
Tel: 416-426-7025; *Fax:* 416-426-7303
info@triathlonontario.com
www.triathlonontario.com
Linda Kirk, Executive Director
Steve Harrigan, President

Triathlon Canada
#106, 3 Concorde Gate, Toronto, ON M3C 3N7, Canada
Tel: 416-426-7180; *Fax:* 416-426-7294
info@triathloncanada.com
www.triathloncanada.com
Alan Trivett, Executive Director

Triathlon Newfoundland & Labrador
PO Box 113, 1 Union St., Corner Brook, NL A2H 6C3, Canada
Tel: 709-634-9570; *Fax:* 709-634-9417
triathlon@nf.sympatico.ca
Affiliation(s): International Triathlon Union
Allen Vansen, President

Triathlon Québec
CP 1000, Succ. M, 4545, av Pierre-de-Coubertin, Montréal, QC H1V 3R2, Canada
Tél: 514-252-3121; *Téléc:* 514-252-5328
info@triathlonquebec.org
www.triathlonquebec.org
Affiliation(s): Triathlon Canada
Benoît-Hugo St-Pierre, Directeur

Universities & Colleges

Alberta Colleges Athletic Conference (ACAC)
Percy Page Centre, 11759 Groat Rd., Edmonton, AB T5M 3K6, Canada
Tel: 780-427-8068; *Fax:* 780-427-9289
office@acac.ab.ca
www.acac.ab.ca
Robert D. Day, Executive Director
Wade Kolmel, President
Alan Rogan, Vice-President, Operations
Leigh Goldie, Vice-President, Finance
Laurie de Grace, Coordinator, Marketing & Communications

British Columbia Colleges' Athletic Association (BCCAA)
100 West 49th Ave., Vancouver, BC V5X 2X6, Canada
Tel: 604-439-9325; *Fax:* 604-439-9245
www.bccaa.ca
Affiliation(s): Canadian Colleges Athletics Association (CCAA)
Clayton Munro, President
Bruce Hunter, Chair, Discipline
Elise Le Brun, Chair, Eligibility

Canadian Council of University Physical Education & Kinesiology Administrators (CCUPEKA) / Conseil canadien des administrateurs universitaires en éducation physique et kinésiologie (CCAUEPK)
c/o Dr. J. Starkes, Department of Kinesiology, McMaster University, Hamilton, ON L8S 4K1, Canada
www.ccupeka.ca
Janet Starkes, Coordinator, Accreditation Council

Canadian Interuniversity Sport (CIS) / Sport interuniversitaire canadien (SIC)
#N205, 801 King Edward, Ottawa, ON K1N 6N5, Canada
Tel: 613-562-5670; *Fax:* 613-562-5669
cisoffice@universitysport.ca
www.cis-sic.ca
Affiliation(s): Atlantic University Sport; Québec Student Sport Federation; Ontario University Athletics; Canada West Universities Athletic Association
Marg McGregor, CEO

Ontario Colleges Athletic Association (OCAA)
#201m 3 Concorde Gate, Toronto, ON M3C 3N7, Canada
Tel: 416-426-7043; *Fax:* 416-426-7308
admin@ocaa.com
www.ocaa.com
Mark Couch, Sport Services Coordinator
Lindsay Bax, Marketing/Communications
Blair Webster, Executive Director
Ron Fearon, President

Ontario University Athletics (OUA) / Sports universitaires de l'Ontario
#230, 1119 Fennell Ave. East, Hamilton, ON L8T 1S2, Canada
Tel: 905-540-5148; *Fax:* 905-574-2840
info@oua.ca
www.oua.ca
Ward Disle, Executive Director

Volleyball

Alberta Volleyball Association (AVA)
Percy Page Centre, 11759 Groat Rd., Edmonton, AB T5M 3K6, Canada
Tel: 780-415-1703; *Fax:* 780-415-1700
info@albertavolleyball.com
www.albertavolleyball.com
Affiliation(s): Federation of Outdoor Volleyball Associations
Terry Gagnon, Executive Director
Gail Senkiw, Office Manager

Fédération de volleyball du Québec (FVBQ)
CP 1000, Succ. M, 4545, av Pierre-de Coubertin, Montréal, QC H1V 3R2, Canada
Tél: 514-252-3065; *Téléc:* 514-252-3176
info-fvbq@volleyball.qc.ca
www.volleyball.qc.ca
Affiliation(s): Sports Québec; Regroupement loisirs Québec
Alain D'Amboise, Directeur général
Charles H. Cardinal, Président

International Volleyball Association / Fédération Internationale de Volleyball (FIVB)
Edouard-Sandoz 2-4, Lausanne, 1006, Switzerland
Tel: 41-21-345-3535; *Fax:* 41-21-345-3545
info@fivb.org
www.fivb.ch

Affiliation(s): Canadian Volleyball Association
Jizhong Wei, President

Manitoba Volleyball Association (MVA)
200 Main St., Winnipeg, MB R3C 4M2, Canada
Tel: 204-925-5783; *Fax:* 204-925-5786
mbvolley@sport.mb.ca
www.manitobavolleyball.com
Affiliation(s): Volleyball Canada
Greg Jarvis, Executive Director
Leanne Leskiw, President
Pat Alexander, Vice-President & Treasurer
Colin Glass, Secretary

Newfoundland & Labrador Volleyball Association (NLVA)
PO Box 21248, St. John's, NL A1A 5B2, Canada
Tel: 709-576-0817; *Fax:* 709-576-7493
nlvaruss@sportnl.ca
www.nlva.net
Russell Jackson, Executive Director
Eric Hiscock, President
Mike Murrran, Elite Development Chair

Northwest Territories Volleyball Association (NWTVA)
Tel: 867-920-2712
terrel_hobbs@nwtvolleyball.ca
www.nwtvolleyball.ca
Terrell Hobbs, President & Regl Official Chair
Micher Haener, Vice-President
Ryan Nichols, Secretary
Kim Weir, Treasurer

Ontario Volleyball Association (OVA)
#304, 3 Concorde Gate, Toronto, ON M3C 3N7, Canada
Tel: 416-426-7316; *Fax:* 416-426-7109
Toll-Free: 800-563-5938
ova@ontariovolleyball.org
www.ontariovolleyball.org
Kristine Drakich, President
Orest Stanko, Executive Director
Jason Trepanier, Technical Director

Saskatchewan Volleyball Association
1750 McAra St., Regina, SK S4N 6L4, Canada
Tel: 306-780-9250; *Fax:* 306-780-9288
officemanager@saskvolleyball.ca
www.saskvolleyball.ca
Dalene Phillips, President
Dan Medford, Executive Director
Tammy Schneider, Office Manager

Volleyball BC
Harry Jerome Sports Centre, 7564 Barnet Hwy., Burnaby, BC V5A 1E7, Canada
Tel: 604-291-2007; *Fax:* 604-291-2602
contact@volleyballbc.ca
www.volleyballbc.ca
Tom Caverly, Executive Director

Volleyball Canada (VC)
#202, 5510 Canotek Rd., Gloucester, ON K1J 9J5, Canada
Tel: 613-748-5681; *Fax:* 613-748-5727
info@volleyball.ca
www.volleyball.ca
Affiliation(s): International Volleyball Federation; Canadian Olympic Association; Coaching Association of Canada
John-Paul Cody-Cox, Executive General
Hugh Wong, President

Volleyball New Brunswick
#13, 900 Hanwell Rd., Fredericton, NB E3B 6A3, Canada
Tel: 506-451-1346; *Fax:* 506-451-1325
vnb@nb.aibn.com
www.vnb.nb.ca
James Cress, Executive Director
John Richard, President

Volleyball Nova Scotia
5516 Spring Garden Rd., 4th Floor, Halifax, NS B3J 1G6, Canada
Tel: 902-425-5450; *Fax:* 902-425-5606
vns@sportnovascotia.ca
www.volleyballnovascotia.ca
Liam Blanchard, Executive Director
Steve Stuart, Treasurer
Eugene Tan, President

Volleyball Prince Edward Island
PO Box 302, Charlottetown, PE C1N 7K7, Canada
Tel: 902-569-0583; *Fax:* 902-368-4548
Toll-Free: 800-247-6712
cgcrozier@sportpei.pe.ca
www.volleyballpei.com
Affiliation(s): Sport PEI
Cheryl Crozier, Executive Director
Krista Walsh, President
Harvey Mazerolle, Vice-President

Volleyball Yukon
4061 - 4th Ave., Whitehorse, YT Y1A 1H1, Canada
Tel: 867-334-4592; *Fax:* 867-667-4237
bunpalamar@whtvcable.com
www.volleyballyukon.com
Tara Wardle, President
Bunne Palamar, Executive Director

Water Polo

Alberta Water Polo Association (AWPA)
PO Box 54, 2225 Macleod Trail South, Edmonton, AB T2G 5B6, Canada
Tel: 403-475-6747; *Fax:* 403-475-6748
office@albertawaterpolo.ca
www.albertawaterpolo.ca
Mike Erickson, President

British Columbia Water Polo Association (BCWPA)
#227, 3820 Cessna Dr., Richmond, BC V7B 0A2, Canada
Tel: 604-333-3480; *Fax:* 604-333-3450
bcwaterpolo@telus.net
www.bcwaterpolo.com
Dave Soul, Executive Director

Fédération de Water-Polo du Québec (FWPQ) / Water Polo Québec
CP 1000, Succ. M, 4545, Pierre de Coubertin, Montréal, QC H1V 3R2, Canada
Tél: 514-252-3098; *Téléc:* 514-252-5658
waterpolo@waterpolo-quebec.qc.ca
www.waterpolo-quebec.qc.ca
Jean Thomas, Directeur général
Guy Lapointe, Président

Manitoba Water Polo Association Inc.
#304, 200 Main St., Winnipeg, MB R3C 4M2, Canada
Tel: 204-925-5777; *Fax:* 204-925-5730
mwpa@shaw.ca
www.mbwaterpolo.com
Marilyn Thorington, President
Joy Halliday, Secretary

Ontario Water Polo Association (OWPA) / L'Association de water polo d'Ontario
#206, 3 Concorde Gate, Toronto, ON M3C 3N7, Canada
Tel: 416-426-7028; *Fax:* 416-426-7356
info@ontariowaterpolo.ca
www.ontariowaterpolo.ca
Ross McDonald, Technical Director

Water Polo Saskatchewan Inc.
1860 Lorne St., Regina, SK S4P 2L7, Canada
Tel: 306-780-9260; *Fax:* 306-780-9467
admin@wpsask.ca
www.wpsask.ca
Jymmi Kaye-Demchuk, Executive Director

Water Skiing

Fédération québécoise de ski nautique (FQSN)
CP 1000, Succ. M, 4545, av Pierre-de Coubertin, Montréal, QC H1V 3R2, Canada
Tél: 514-252-3092; *Téléc:* 514-252-3186
louissimard@skinautiquequebec.qc.ca
www.skinautiquequebec.qc.ca
Louis Simard, Président

Nova Scotia Water Ski Association (NSWSA)
PO Box 783, Dartmouth, NS B2Y 3Z3, Canada
nswsa@aol.com
www.nswsa.com
Gary Allen, President

Ontario Water Ski Association (OWSA)
#307, 1185 Eglinton Ave. East, Toronto, ON M3C 3C6, Canada
Tel: 416-426-7092; *Fax:* 416-426-7378
info@wswo.ca
www.wswo.ca
Paul Roberts, President

Water Ski - Wakeboard Manitoba
200 Main St., Winnipeg, MB R3C 4M2, Canada
Tel: 204-925-5700; *Fax:* 204-925-5703
waterski@waterski.mb.ca
www.waterski.mb.ca
Katja Smutny, Executive Director
Kevin Polley, President

Water Ski & Wakeboard Alberta (WSWA)
Percy Page Centre, 11759 Groat Rd., Edmonton, AB T5M 3K6, Canada
Tel: 780-415-0088; *Fax:* 780-422-2663
Toll-Free: 866-258-2754
info@wswa.ca
www.wswa.ca
Affiliation(s): Water Ski Canada; International Water Ski Federation
Rose Dufty, President
Dallas Harrop, Executive Director

Water Ski & Wakeboard British Columbia (WSWBC)
PO Box 42049, Stn. RPO North, Lake Country, BC V4V 1Z8, Canada
Toll-Free: 888-696-6677
info@wswbc.org
www.wswbc.org
Kim McKnight, Executive Director
Dale Erb, President
Ian Kellow, Vice-President

Water Ski & Wakeboard Canada / Ski nautique et planche Canada
#210, 223 Colonnade Rd. South, Ottawa, ON K2E 7K3, Canada
Tel: 613-526-0685; *Fax:* 613-526-4380
wswc@waterski-wakeboard.ca
www.waterski-wakeboard.ca
Glenn Bowie, President
Dan Wolfenden, Executive Director

Water Ski & Wakeboard Saskatchewan
PO Box 202, Warman, SK S0K 4S0, Canada
Tel: 306-931-2901; *Fax:* 306-249-3062
sheri@wswsask.com
www.wswsask.com
Sheri Seiferling, Executive Director
Berk Summach, President

Women in Sports

Canadian Association for the Advancement of Women & Sport & Physical Activity (CAAWS) / Association canadienne pour l'avancement des femmes du sport et de l'activité physique (ACAFS)
#202N, 801 King Edward Ave., Ottawa, ON K1N 6N5
Tel: 613-562-5667; *Fax:* 613-562-5668
caaws@caaws.ca
www.caaws.ca
Karin Lofstrom, Executive Director
Sydney Millar, Manager, National Program
Stéphanie Legault, Manager, Marketing & Projects
Jessica Lowe, Administrator & Office Coordinator

Field Hockey BC (FHBC) / Hockey sur gazon C-B
#202, 210 Broadway West, Vancouver, BC V5Y 3W2, Canada
Tel: 604-737-3046; *Fax:* 604-737-6488
info@fieldhockeybc.com
www.fieldhockeybc.com
Mark Saunders, Executive Director

Ladies' Golf Union (LGU)
The Scores, St. Andrews, Fife, KY16 9AT, United Kingdom
Tel: 44-13-34-475811; *Fax:* 44-13-34-472818
info@lgu.org
www.lgu.org
Affiliation(s): Canadian Ladies' Golf Association
Maureen Lockett, President
Shona Malcolm, CEO

Nova Scotia Curling Association (NSCA)
5516 Spring Garden Rd., 4th Fl., Halifax, NS B3J 1G6, Canada
Tel: 902-421-2875; *Fax:* 902-425-5606
nsca@sportnovascotia.ca
www.nscurl.com
Affiliation(s): Canadian Curling Association
Jeremiah Anderson, Executive Director
Shirley Osborne, President

Wrestling

British Columbia Wrestling Association (BCWA)
#335, 2416 Main St., Vancouver, BC V5T 3E2, Canada
Tel: 604-737-3092; *Fax:* 604-737-6043
info@bcwrestling.com
www.bcwrestling.com

Affiliation(s): BC School Sports
MaryAnn DeCorby, Executive Director

Canadian Amateur Wrestling Association (CAWA) / Association canadienne de lutte amateur
#7, 5370 Canotek Rd., Gloucester, ON K1J 9E6
Tel: 613-748-5686; *Fax:* 613-748-5756
info@wrestling.ca
www.wrestling.ca

Tamara Medwidsky, Executive Director
Doug Cox, President
Clint Kingsbury, Manager, Domestic Development
Dave Mair, Manager, High Performance
Dave McKay, National Coach, Senior Men
Leigh Vierling, National Coach, Senior Women

Lutte NB Wrestling
gdouc5110@rogers.com
www.luttenbwrestling.ca
Greg Doucette, Vice-President, Administration
Don Ryan, President

Manitoba Freestyle Wrestling Association
200 Main St., Winnipeg, MB R3C 4M2, Canada
Tel: 204-925-5670; *Fax:* 204-925-5703
mbfreewr@mb.sympatico.ca
Nat Brigante, Executive Director/Coach

Newfoundland & Labrador Amateur Wrestling Association (NLAWA)
1 Wade's Ln., Flatrock, NL A1K 1C3, Canada
Fax: 709-643-5103
contact@nlawa.com
www.nlawa.com

Randy Ralph, President

Ontario Amateur Wrestling Association (OAWA)
#213, 3 Concorde Gate, Toronto, ON M3C 3N7, Canada
Tel: 416-426-7274; *Fax:* 416-426-7343
admin@oawa.ca
www.oawa.ca
Affiliation(s): International Amateur Wrestling Association; Canadian Amateur Wrestling Association
Tim MaGarrey, Provincial Director

Saskatchewan Amateur Wrestling Association (SAWA)
510 Cynthia St., Saskatoon, SK S7L 7K7, Canada
Tel: 306-975-0822; *Fax:* 306-242-8007
sk.wrestling@shaw.ca
www.saskwrestling.com
Anna-Beth Zulkoskey, Executive Director

Wrestling Nova Scotia
General Delivery, Bear River, NS B0S 1B0, Canada
Tel: 902-857-1761
wrestlingns@canada.com
www.wrestlingnovascotia.ca

Peter Coulthard, President
Scott Aldridge, Vice-President
Debbie MacDonald, Sec.-Treas.

Wrestling PEI
Sport PEI, PO Box 302, Charlottetown, PE C1A 7K7, Canada
Tel: 902-368-4110; *Fax:* 902-368-4548
Toll-Free: 800-247-6712
gflood@sportpei.pe.ca
www.sportpei.pe.ca

Glen Flood, Executive Director

Professional Leagues & Teams

Baseball, Professional: Major League

Major League Baseball/MLB
245 Park Ave.
31st Fl.
New York, NY 10167
212-931-7800
866-800-1275
Fax: 212-945-5654
www.mlb.com

Allan (Bud) H. Selig, Baseball Commissioner
Bob DuPuy, President/Chief Operating Officer
Jimmie Lee Solomon, Executive VP, Baseball Development
Tim Brosnan, Executive Vice President, Business
Rob Manfred, Executive VP, Labor Relations & HR
John McHale, Jr., Executive VP, Administration, & Chief Information Officer
Jonathan Mariner, Executive VP, Finance
Joe Torre, Executive VP, Baseball Operations
Nature of Service:
Administrates professional baseball. Established and enforces rules regarding franchise operation. Supervises national radio and television contracts. Handles publicity and marketing of baseball and legal matters pertaining to baseball as an industry. Operates the World Series and All-Star games.
Membership Requirements:
Teams operating in the American or National Leagues.
Year Founded:
1920
Sponsors:
Ameriquest Mortgage; Anheuser Busch; Baby Ruth; Bank of America; DHL; FIA Card Services, NA; Gatorade; General Motors/Chevrolet; Gillette; Intercontinental Hotels Group/Holiday Inn; MasterCard International; Nestle; Nike; Pepsi-Cola; Sharp; Taco Bell; Wheaties; XM Satellite Radio.

Teams:

Toronto Blue Jays
Rogers Centre
One Blue Jays Way, #3200
Toronto, ON M5V 1J1
416-341-1000
888-654-6529
Fax: 416-341-1250
http://toronto.bluejays.mlb.com
Alex Anthopoulos, SVP, Baseball Operations/General Manager
Keith Pelley, President/Chief Executive Officer
Howard Starkman, Vice President of Special Projects
Jay Stenhouse, Vice President Communications
George Poulis, Head Trainer
Matthew Shuber, Director of Business Affairs & Legal Counsel
Jay Sartori, Assistant Manager
Perry Minasian, Director, Scouting
Stephen Brooks, Senior VP & Business Operations
Jason Diplock, VP of Ticket Sales & Service
Mario Coutinho, Vice President Stadium Operations/Security
Honsing Leung, Senior Manager, Business Development
Cito Gaston, Team Manager
John Farrell, Team Manager
Heather Connolly, Admin, Baseball Operations
Stadium:
Rogers Centre.
Stadium Seating Capacity:
50,516
Publications:
Inside Pitch newsletter.

Baseball, Professional: Minor League

Canadian American Association of Professional Baseball
1415 Highway 54 West, #210
Durham, NC 27707
919-401-8150
Fax: 919-401-8152
www.canamleague.com

Teams:

Quebec Capitals
Le Stade De Québec
100 Rue Du Cardinal Maurice-Roy
Quebec, QC G1K 8Z1
418-521-2255
Fax: 418-521-2266
baseball@capitalesdequebec.com
www.capitalesdequebec.com
Miles Wolff, Director of Baseball Operations
Alexandre Harvey, General Manager
Michel Laplante, President
Pier-Luc Nappert, Director Of Marketing & Communications
Ballpark:
La Stade de Québec.
Ballpark Description:
Opened in 1939. Seating Capacity: 4,800
Team History:
Eastern Canada League - 1923; Quebec-Ontario-Vermont League - 1924; Quebec Provincial League - 1940; Canadian-American League - 1941-42, 1946-50, 2005-present; Provincial League - 1951-55; Eastern League - 1971-77; Northern League - 1999-2002; Northeast League - 2003-04.
Publications:
Le Journal de Québec; Le Soleil; Media Matin Québec
Media Broadcast:
CHRC 800 AM

Northwest League
P.O. Box 1645
Boise, Idaho 83701
208-429-1511
Fax: 208-429-1525
mail@northwestleague.com
http://www.northwestleague.com

Bob Richmond, President
Todd Rahr, Vice President

Teams:

Vancouver Canadians
4601 Ontario St
Vancouver, BC V5V 3H4
604-872-5232
Fax: 604-872-1714
staff@canadianbaseball.com
www.canadianbaseball.com
Jake Kerr, Owner
Jeff Mooney, Owner
Andy Dunn, President
Jason Takefman, General Manager
jtakefman@canadiansbaseball.com
Graham Wall, Vice President
gwall@canadiansbaseball.com
Rob Fai, Director Media/Broadcast
JC Fraser, Assistant General Manager/Ballpark Operations
jcfraser@canadiansbaseball.com
Years in League:
1967-71, 1979-present.
Ballpark:
Nat Bailey Stadium.
Ballpark Description:
Opened in 1951. Seating Capacity: 6,500
Media Broadcast:
The TEAM Sports Radio 1040-AM.

Basketball, Professional

National Basketball Association/NBA
645 Fifth Ave.
New York, NY 10121
212-407-8000
Fax: 212-832-3861
info@nba.com
www.nba.com

David Stern, Commissioner
Adam Silver, Deputy Commissioner, & Chief Operating Officer
Carol Sawdye, Executive Vice President

Description:
The premier professional basketball league in North America. Many of the world's best players play in the NBA, and the overall standard of the competition is considerably higher than any other professional competition. The NBA was founded in New York City on June 6, 1946 as the Basketball Association of America (BAA). It adopted the name National Basketball Association in the fall of 1949 after adding several teams from the rival National Basketball League.
Business Ventures:
NBA City (Restaurants) - A partnership with Ralph Burnet/RWB Financial.
Publications:
Official NBA Guide, annual; NBA Register, annual; NBA Basketball Encyclopedia.
Membership Requirements:
Approval of the franchise by Board of Governors.

Teams:

Toronto Raptors
Air Canada Center
40 Bay St., #400
Toronto,ON M5J 2X2
416-815-5600
Fax: 416-359-9332
www.raptors.com
Richard Peddie, President/Chief Executive Officer
Tom Anselmi, Executive VP/Chief Operating Officer
Ian Clarke, Executive VP/Chief Financial Officer
Dwayne Casey, Head Coach
Larry Tanenbaum, Chairman of the Board

History:
Founded in 1995 in Toronto.
Arena:
Air Canada Center. Seating Capacity: 19,800

Football, Professional

Canadian Football League/CFL
50 Wellington St. E
3rd Fl.
Toronto, ON M5E 1C8
416-322-9650
Fax: 416-322-9651
www.cfl.ca

Mark Cohon, Commissioner
Michael Copeland, Chief Operating Officer
Kevin McDonald, Vice President, Football Operations
Matt Maychak, VP, Communications
Douglas Allison, Director, Finance and Administration
Adrian Sciarra, Director, Partnerships

Teams:

B.C. Lions
10605- 135th St.
Surrey, BC V6B 4Y9
604-930-5466
Fax: 604-583-7882
www.bclions.com
David Braley, Owner
Wally Buono, General Manager/Head Coach
Roy Shivers, Director of Player Personnel
George Chayka, Vice President, Business
Dennis Skulsky, President/CEO
Jamie Taras, Director, Community Relations
Jamie Cartmell, Director, Communications
Carol Longmuir, Finance Administrator
Phil Adams, Director, Corporate Partnerships

Calgary Stampeders
Calgary Stampeder Football Club
McMahon Stadium
1817 Crowchild Trail NW
Calgary, AB T2M 4R6
403-289-0205
Fax: 403-289-7850
stampeder@stampeders.com
www.stampeders.com
John Forzani, Chairman
Lyle Bauer, President
Doug Mitchell, Governor
Bob Viccars, Executive Member
Stan Schwartz, Executive Vice-President
Valerie Pak, Director Marketing
Jamie Seguin, Director of Game Operations
John Hufnagel, Head Coach/General Manager
Tanya Mettimano, Director Ticketing & Customer Relations

Edmonton Eskimos
Edmonton Eskimo Football Club
11000 Stadium Road
Edmonton, AB T5B 2R7
780-448-1525
Fax: 780-429-3452
comments@esks.com
www.esks.com
Rick LeLacheur, President/Chief Executive Officer
Eric Tillman, General Manager & Director of Football Operations
Kavis Reed, Head Coach
Greg Treble, Director of Business Operations
Cathy Presniak, Vice President of Finance
Dan McKinnon, Assistant General Manager
Paul Jones, Director Player Personnel
Dave Jamieson, Vice President of Communication & Broadcast

Hamilton Tiger-Cats
1 Jarvis St.
Hamilton, ON L8R 3J2
905-547-2287
Fax: 905-547-8423
www.ticats.com
Robert F. Young, Owner
Bob, O'Billovich, General Manager
Adam Provost, Executive Vice President
Scott Mitchell, President
Jim Edmands, VP, Sales & Marketing
Mark Bowden, VP, Business Affairs
Dan Deighton, VP, Finance
Scott McNaughton, Manager, Media Relations
Marcel Bellefeuille, Head Coach
Bob Young, Caretaker

Montreal Alouettes
4545 Pierre-De-Coubertin
Montreal, PQ H1V 3L6
514-253-0008
Fax: 514-253-8821
info@montrealalouettes.com
www.montrealalouettes.com
Robert Wetenall, Owner
Paul Harris, Director
Laurie Bennett, VP Business Operations
Olivier Poulin, Director Communications
Larry Smith, President/Chief Executive Officer
Jim Popp, VP/GM/Director Football Operations
Richard Blais, VP, Corporate Partnerships
Claude Rochon, VP, Marketing/Communications
crochon@montrealalouettes.com
Marcel Desjardins, Assistant General Manager
Olivier Poulin, Director of Communications
Marc Trestman, Head Coach

Saskatchewan Roughriders
Mosaic Stadium
1910 Piffles Taylor Way, Box 1966
Regina, SK S4P 3E1
306-569-2323
888-474-3377
Fax: 306-566-4280
www.saskriders.com
Rob Pletch, Chairman
Jim Hopson, President/CEO
Steve Mazurak, VP, Marketing/Sales
Shannon Chinn, Manager Corporate Partnerships/Game Day Operations
Eric Tillman, GM/Director of Football Operations
Craig Reynolds, Chief Financial Officer
Hugh McKay, Manager Facilities and Stadium Operations
Gail Mund, Manager, Ticket Operations
gailm@saskriders.com
Ryan Whippler, Director, Communications
Mark Habicht, Director, Retail Sales
Ken Miller, Head Coach

Toronto Argonauts
212 King St. West, #501
Toronto, ON M5V 1J6
416-341-2700
Fax: 416-341-2714
www.argonauts.ca
David Braley, Owner
Bob Nicholson, President/CEO
Jason Colero, Manager Community Relations
David Bedford, VP, Marketing & Communications
Carlos Ferreira, VP, Marketing & Events
Mike Hagen, Director Player Personnel
Eric Holmes, Director, Communications
Jim Barker, Head Coach & General Manager

Winnipeg Blue Bombers
1465 Maroons Road
Winnipeg, MB R3G 0L6
204-784-2583
Fax: 204-783-5222
bbombers@bluebombers.com
www.bluebombers.com
Jim Bell, President
Bill Watchorn, Board Chairperson
Jerry Maslowsky, VP, Marketing
Ross Hodgkinson, Director, Football Operations
Ken Moll, Director of Player Personnel
Darren Cameron, Director of Media Operations
Joe Mack, Vice President & GM of Football Operations
Paul LaPolice, Head Coach

Hockey, Professional (NHL)

National Hockey League/NHL
1185 Ave. of the Americas
15th Fl.
New York, NY 10020
212-789-2000
Fax: 212-789-2020
www.nhl.com

Gary Bettman, Commissioner
Steve Solomon, Chief Operating Officer
Brian Jennings, Executive Vice President of Marketing
Keith Ritter, SVP New Business Development
Doug Perlman, SVP Television/Media Ventures
(212)789-2000
William Daly, EVP/Chief Legal Officer
Jim Haskins, VP Consumer Products/Marketing
Adam Acone, VP Broadcasting/Programming
Scott Carmichael, Vice President Club Marketing
Andrew Judelson, Group VP Corporate Marketing
Ken Yaffe, Group VP/Managing Director
Ed Home, President NHL Enterprises
Lisa Schoeck, Director Human Resources
Susan Cohig, SVP Club Consulting & Services
John Collins, Senior Executive Vice President
Year Founded:
1917
Description:
League of professional hockey teams
Membership Requirements:
Approval by NHL Board of Governors
Publications:
NHL Rule Book, annual; NHL Schedule, annual; NHL MEDIA DIRECTORY, annual; NHL Official Guide and Record Book, annual
Additional Offices:
75 International Blvd, Ste 300, Rexdale, Ont, Canada M9W 6L9. 416 798-0809; FAX: 416 798-0819. Montreal Office: 1800 McGill College Ave, Ste 2600, Montreal, P.Q., Canada H3A 3J6. 514 288-9220; FAX: 514 284-0300

Teams:

Calgary Flames
PO Box 1540
Station M
Calgary, AB T2P 3B9
403-777-2177
888-5-FLAMES
Fax: 403-777-2171
www.calgaryflames.com
Murray Edwards, Owner
Alvin Libin, Owner
Allan Markin, Owner
Jeffrey McCaig, Owner
Clayton Riddell, Owner
Byron Seaman, Owner
Ken King, President/Chief Executive Officer
Lyle Edwards, Chairman
Brent Sutter, Head Coach
Troy Ward, Assistant Coach
Dave Lowry, Assistant Coach
Rob Cookson, Assistant Coach
John Bean, Senior Vice President
Year Founded:
1972
Description:
The Calgary Flames are a National Hockey League team based in Calgary, Alberta
Home Arena:
Pengrowth Saddledome

Edmonton Oilers
11230 110th St.
2nd Fl.
Edmonton, AB T5G 3H7
780-414-4000
Fax: 780-409-5848
www.edmontonoilers.com
Patrick LaForge, President/Chief Executive Officer
Kevin Lowe, President, Hockey Operations
Darryl Boessenkool, VP Finance/Chief Financial Officer
Allan Watt, VP Communications/Broadcast
Steve Tambellini, General manager
Steve Katzman, Chief Marketing Officer
Mike Sillinger, Director of Player Development
Tom Renney, Head Coach
Ralph Krueger, Assistant Coach
Kelly Buchberger, Assistant Coach
Steve Smith, Assistant Coach
Year Founded:
1972
Description:
The Edmonton Oilers are a National Hockey League team based in Edmonton, Alberta
Home Arena:
Rexall Place

Montreal Canadiens
1275 Saint Antoine St. W
Montreal, QC H3C 5L2
514-932-2582
Fax: 514-932-8285
www.canadiens.com
Geoff Molson, President/Owner
Pierre Gauthier, Executive Vice President

Jacques Aube, Vice President/General Manager
Fred Steer, Chief Financial Officer
Jacques Martin, Head Coach
Perry Pearn, Assistant Coach
Pierre Groulx, Assistant Coach
Year Founded:
1909
Description:
The Montreal Canadiens are the oldest established National Hockey League team
Home Arena:
Centre Bell

Ottawa Senators
1000 Palladium Drive
Kanata, ON K2V 1A5
613-599-0250
Fax: 613-599-0358
info@ottawasenators.com
www.ottawasenators.com
Eugene Melnyk, Owner/Chairman/Governor
Cyril Leeder, President/Alternate Governor
Bryan Murray, Executive Vice President/General Manager
Erin Crowe, Chief Financial Officer
Anders Hedberg, Director Player Personnel
Steve Keogh, Director Communications
Paul MacLean, Head Coach
Dave Cameron, Assistant Coach
Tim Murray, Assistant General Manager
Year Founded:
1992
Description:
The Ottawa Senators are a National Hockey League team based in Ottawa, Ontario Canada
Home Arena:
Scotiabank Place

Toronto Maple Leafs
50 Bay St., #500
Toronto, ON M5J 2L2
416-815-5400
Fax: 416-359-9331
www.torontomapleleafs.com
Brian Burke, President/General Manager
Tom Anselmi, Executive Vice President/COO
Ian Clarke, Executive Vice President/CFO, Business Development
Pat Park, Director Media Relations
Ron Wilson, Head Coach
Rob Zettler, Assistant Coach
Jim Hughes, Director of Player Development
Scott Gordon, Assistant Coach
Year Founded:
1917
Description:
The Toronto Maple Leafs are a National Hockey League team based in Toronto, Ontario
Home Arena:
Air Canada Centre

Vancouver Canucks
800 Griffiths Way
Vancouver, BC V6B 6G1
604-899-7400
855-899-7401
Fax: 604-899-7401
info@canucks.com
www.canucks.com
Francesco Aquilini, Chairman & Governor
Mike Gillis, President/General Manager
Lorne Henning, VP Player Personnel
Laurence Gilman, VP Hockey Operations
Dave Gagner, Director, Player Development
Alain Vigneault, Head Coach
Rick Bowness, Associate Coach
Newell Brown, Assistant Coach
Darryl Williams, Assistant Coach
Roland Melanson, Goaltending Coach
Year Founded:
1970
Description:
The Vancouver Canucks are a National Hockey League team based in Vancouver, British Columbia
Home Arena:
Rogers Arena

Winnipeg Jets
260 Hargrave street
Winnipeg, MB R3C 5S5
204-987-7825
Fax: 204-926-5555
www.jets.nhl.com
Jim Ludlow, President/ CEO
Mark Chipman, Chairman
Kevin Cheveldayoff, EVP/ General Manager
Norva Riddell, Senior Vice President Sales & Marketing
Craig Heisinger, Director of Hockey Operations
Claude Noel, Head Coach
Year Founded:
2011
Description:
The Winnipeg Jets are a National Hockey League team based in Winnipeg, Manitoba. The franchise was formerly known as the Atlanta Thrashers until their purchase in 2011.
Home Arena:
MTS Centre

Hockey, Professional: Minor League

American Hockey League/AHL
1 Monarch Place, #2400
Springfield, MA 01144
413-781-2030
Fax: 413-733-4767
info@theahl.com
www.theahl.com

David Andrews, President/CEO
Jim Mill, Executive VP, Hockey Operations
Drew Griffin, Director, Finance & Administration
Year Founded:
1936
Description:
Promotes and operates the sport of professional ice hockey
Membership Requirements:
Purchase of a franchise
Publications:
Official guide and record book; Rule book; Schedule; Year End Statistical Package

Teams:

Hamilton Bulldogs
101 York Blvd
Hamilton, ON L8R 3L4
905-529-8500
Fax: 905-777-2360
info@hamiltonbulldogs.com
www.hamiltonbulldogs.com
Michael Andlauer, Majority Owner/Chairman
Glenn Stanford, President/Governor
Derek Wills, Director, Broadcasting & Communications
Robert Jefferies, Director, Finance
Paul Giordano, Director, Brand Marketing
Julien BriseBois, General Manager
Guy Boucher, Head Coach
Daniel Lacroix, Assistant Coach
Martin Raymond, Assistant Coach
Home Ice:
Copps Coliseum

Manitoba Moose
260 Hargrave
Winnipeg, MB R3C 5S5
204-987-7825
Fax: 204-926-5555
www.moosehockey.com
Mark Chipman, Chairman/Governor
Jim Ludlow, President/CEO
John Offert, Chief Operating Officer
Audrey Ma, Controller
Craig Heisinger, SVP/General Manager
Norva Riddell, SVP, Sales & Marketing
Scott Brown, Director, Corporate Communications & Hockey Operations
Robert Thorsten, VP, People & Patron Services
Scott Arniel, Head Coach
Keith McCambridge, Assistant Coach
Rick St.Croix, Assistant Coach
Bruce Southern, Director, Player Personnel
Home Ice:
MTS Centre

Toronto Marlies
100 Princess Blvd
Toronto, ON M6K 3C3
416-263-3900
Fax: 416-263-3901
www.torontomarlies.com
Peter Church, General Manager
Michael Cosentino, Director, Business Operations
Brad Lynn, Manager, Hockey Operations & Communications
Dallas Eakins, Head Coach
Gord Dineen, Assistant Coach
Derek King, Assistant Coach
Home Ice:
Ricoh Coliseum

Ontario Hockey League
305 Milner Ave., #208
Scarborough, ON M1B 3V4
416-299-8700
Fax: 416-299-8787
ohl@chl.ca
www.ontariohockeyleague.com

David Branch, Commissioner
Sherwood Bassin, Chairman
Year Founded:
1896

Teams:

Barrie Colts
555 Bayview Drive
Barrie, ON L4N 8Y2
705-722-6587
Fax: 705-721-9709
operations@barriecolts.com
www.barriecolts.com
Howie Campbell, President
Jim Payetta, VP of Business Development and Marketing
Dale Hawerchuk, Head Coach
Jay Wells, Assistant Coach
Todd Miller, Assistant Coach
Home Ice:
Barrie Molson Centre

Belleville Bulls
265 Cannifton Road
Belleville, ON K8N 4V8
613-966-8338
Fax: 705-966-8761
hockey@bellevillebulls.com
www.bellevillebulls.com
Gord Simmonds, Owner/Governor
George Burnett, General Manager/Head Coach
Robert Vaughan, Founder
Barclay Branch, Assistant General Manager
David Steenburgh, Director of Business Operations
Home Ice:
Yardmen

Brampton Battalion
7575 Kennedy Road S
Brampton, ON L6W 4T2
905-874-2393
Fax: 905-874-2394
info@battalionhockey.com
www.battalionhockey.com
C. Scott Abbott, Owner/Governor
Michael Griffin, President
Stan Butler, Director Hockey Operations & Head Coach
Phil Ercolani, Marketing, Sales & Media Relations
Gord Smith, Player Development
Jamie Allison, Assistant Coach
Kelly Harper, Assistant Coach
Mike Tamburro, Goaltending Coach
Binne Brouwer, Head Trainer
Greg Phillips, Assistant Trainer
Home Ice:
Brampton Centre

Guelph Storm
55 Wyndham St. N
Guelph, ON N1H 7T8
519-837-9690
Fax: 519-837-9692
info@guelphstorm.com
www.guelphstorm.com
Rick Hoyle, President
Lindsay Pink, Media Relations Manager
Mike Kelly, Vice President/General Manager
Scott Walker, Head Coach
Chris Hajt, Assistant Coach
Home Ice:
Guelph Sports Entertainment Centre

Kingston Frontenacs
PO Box 665
Kingston, ON K7I 4X1
613-542-4042
Fax: 613-542-2834
kgnfront@kos.net
www.kingstonfrontenacs.com
Doug Springer, President/Governor
Jeff Stilwell, Director Sales/Marketing
Doug Gilmour, General Manager
Todd Gill,Head Coach
Darren Keily, Assistant Coach
Craig Belfer, Head Trainer
Home Ice:
Kingston Memorial Centre

Kitchener Rangers
400 East Ave.
Kitchener, ON N2H 1Z6
519-576-3700
Fax: 519-576-7571
info@kitchenerrangers.com
www.kitchenerrangers.com
Steve Bienkowski, Chief Operating Officer
Craig Campbell, President
Steve Spott, General Manager/Head Coach
Paul Fixter, Associate Coach
Troy Smith, Assistant Coach
Brandon Merli, Strength Trainer
Dan Lebold, Head Trainer
Home Ice:
Kitchener Memorial Auditorium

London Knights
99 Dundas St.
London, ON N6A 6K1
519-681-0800
Fax: 519-668-7291
info@londonknights.com
www.londonknights.com
Dale Hunter, President/Head Coach
Mark Hunter, Vice President/General Manager
Trevor Whiffen, Governor
Jim McKellar, Assistant General Manager
Geoffrey Hare, Director Marketing
Misha Donskov, Assistant Coach
Home Ice:
John Labatt Centre

Mississauga St. Michael's Majors
5500 Rose Cherry Place
Mississauga, ON L4Z 4B6
905-502-7788
Fax: 905-502-0169
administration@majors.ca
www.stmichaelsmajors.com
Roger Lajoje, Executive Vice President
Rick Radovski, Vice President Marketing/Sales
James Boyd, General Manager/Head Coach
Kelly Harper, Assistant General Manager
Brad May, Assistant General Manager
Home Ice:
Hershey Centre

Oshawa Generals
99 Athol St. E
Oshawa, ON L1H 1J8
905-433-0900
Fax: 905-433-0868
admin@oshawagenerals.com
www.oshawagenerals.com
Rocco Tullio, President/Governor
John McMahon, Vice President/Governor
Chris DePiero, General Manager/Head Coach
Joe Cirella, Assistant General Manager/Associate Coach
Mark Fitzgerald, Sports Conditioning coach
Bryan Boyes, Head TrainerHome Ice:
Civic Auditorium

Ottawa 67's
Lansdowne Park
1015 Bank St.
Ottawa, ON K1S 3W7
613-232-6767
Fax: 613-232-5582
ottawa67s@chl.ca
www.ottawa67s.com
Jeff Hunt, Owner/Governor
Patrick Whalen, President/CEO
Randy Burgess, Vice-President
Chris Byrne, Head Coach/General Manager
Larry Skinner, Assistant Coach
Bobby Brooks, Assistant coach
Neil Hoch, Head Trainer
Home Ice:
Ottawa Civic Centre

Owen Sound Attack
1900 - 3rd Ave. E
Owen Sound, ON N4K 2M6
519-371-7452
Fax: 519-371-7990
attack@bmts.com
www.attackhockey.com
Bob Severs, Owner/President
Dale DeGray, General Manager
Ray McKelvie, Business Manager
Brent Fisher, Director of Marketing and Public Relations
Greg Ireland, Head Coach
Terry Virtue, Assistant Coach
Home Ice:
Harry Lumley Bayshore Community Centre

Peterborough Petes
151 Landsdowne St. W
Peterborough, ON K9J 1Y4
705-743-3681
Fax: 705-743-5497
petes@gopetesgo.com
www.gopetesgo.com
Jim Devlin, President
Jeff Twohey, General Manager
Aaron Garfat, Director Marketing/Public Relations
Pete Dalliday, Director of Ticket Sales
Mike Pelino, Head Coach
Jody Hull, Assistant Coach
Brian Miller, Head Trainer
Home Ice:
Peterborough Memorial Centre

Sarnia Sting
1455 London Road
Sarnia, ON N7S 6K7
519-542-4494
Fax: 519-542-2388
buzz@sarniasting.com
www.sarniasting.com
Larry Ciccarelli, President
Bill Abercrombie, VP Operations
Bill Abercrombie, VP of Operations
Dean Collver, Director of Business Operations
Jacques Beaulie, Head Coach/General Manager
Trevor Letowski, Associate Coach
Chad Oliver, Head Trainer
Home Ice:
Sarnia Sports Entertainment Centre

Sault Ste. Marie Greyhounds
269 Queen St. E
Sault Ste. Marie, ON P6A 1Y9
705-253-5976
Fax: 705-945-9458
info@soogreyhounds.com
www.soogreyhounds.com
Lou Lukenda, President
Gerry Liscumb, Public Relations Director
Kyle Dubas, General Manager
Mike Stapleton, Head Coach
Nick Warriner, Assistant Coach
Lorne Robinson, Equipment Manager
Home Ice:
Sault Memorial Gardens

Sudbury Wolves
240 Elgin St. S
Sudbury, ON P3E 3N6
705-675-3941
Fax: 705-675-3944
info@sudburywolves.com
www.sudburywolves.com
Mark Burgess, CEO/Chairman of the Board
Blaine Smith, President/General Manager
Trent Cull, Head Coach
Jeff Beukeboom, Assistant Coach
Ken MacKenzie, Assistant General Manager
Home Ice:
Sudbury Community Arena

Windsor Spitfires
334 Wyandotte St. E
Windsor, ON N9A 3H6
519-254-9256
Fax: 519-254-9257
frontoffice@windsorspitfires.com
www.windsorspitfires.com
Bob Boughner, President/Head Coach
Warren Rychel, Vice President/General Manager
Peter Dobrich, Governor/Treasurer
Steve Horne, Director of Business Development
Bob Jones, Assistant Coach
D.J. Smith, Assistant Coach
Mark Turner, Video Coach
Home Ice:
Windsor Arena

Quebec Major Junior Hockey League
1205 Ampère, #101
Boucherville, QC J4B 7M6
450-650-0500
Fax: 450-650-0510
hockey@lhjmq.qc.ca
www.lhjmq.qc.ca
Gilles Courteau, Commissioner
Marcel Patenaude, Executive Vice-President
Richard Trottier, Director Officiating
Photi Sotiropoulos
Pierre Leduc, Director Hockey Operations
Description:
Member of Canadian Hockey League

Teams:

Acadie-Bathurst Titan
850 St. Anne St.
Bathurst, NB E2A 6X2
506-549-3300
Fax: 506-549-3355
letitan@nbnet.nb.ca
www.letitan.com
Earl Dimitroff, Director Marketing
Sylvain Courturier, General Manager
Eric Dubois, Head Coach
Gianni Cantini, Assistant Coach
Nathan Belliveau, Head Trainer
Home Ice:
K.C. Irving Regional Centre

Baie-Comeau Drakkar
70 Ave. Michel-Hémon
Baie-Comeau, QC G4Z 2A5
418-296-2522
Fax: 418-296-0011
drakkar@globetrotter.net
www.le-drakkar.com
Paul Joncas, President
Steve Ahern, General Manager
Pierre Lebreux, Governor
Stéphane Hains, Head Coach
Jean Cormier, Assistant Coach
Dominic Boucher, Goalie Coach
Michel Larocque, Head Trainer
Home Ice:
Henry Leonard Center

Cape Breton Screaming Eagles
479 George St.
Sydney, NS B1P 6G9
902-567-6378
Fax: 902-567-6303
admin@capebretoneagles.com
www.capebretoneagles.com
Richard Morency, Governor
Paul MacDonald, President & Director of Business Operations
Peter MacDonald, Director of Marketing
Bill Sidney, Director of Sales
Mario Durocher, General Manager/Head Coach
John Hanna, Assistant Coach
Blair Joseph, Assistant Coach
John Kibyuk, Assistant Coach
Alain Chabbert, Head Trainer
Home Ice:
Centre Georges Vezina

Chicoutimi Saguenéens
643 Bégin
C.P. 323
Chicoutimi, QC G7H 5C2
418-549-9489
Fax: 418-549-1645
sagueneens@videotron.ca
www.sagueneens.com
Richard Martel, General Manager
Marc-Etienne Hubert, Head Coach
Mario Durocher, Assistant Coach
Carl Bouchard, Assistant General Manager
Home Ice:
Centre Georges Vezina

Drummondville Voltigeurs
300 Cockburn St.
Drummondville, QC J2C 4L6
819-477-9400
Fax: 819-477-0561
info@voltigeurs.ca
www.voltigeurs.ca
Louis Brousseau, Governor
Dominic Ricard, General Manager
Mario Duhamel, Head Coach
Dennis Gauthier, Assistant Coach
Alain Couturier, Head Trainer

Gatineau Olympiques
Station Hull
125 Carillon St.
PO Box 1251
Gatineau, QC J8X 3X7
819-777-0661
Fax: 819-777-6933
hockey@lesolympiques.net
www.lesolympiques.net
Alain Sear, President
Daniel Brunet, Marketing Manager
Benoit Grouix, Manager/Head Coach
Guy Lalonde, Assistant Coach
Jonathan Carrier, Assistant Coach
Michel Vallière, Goalie Coach
Serge Haché, Head Trainer
Home Ice:
Robert Gatineau Arena

Halifax Mooseheads
5284 Duke St.
Halifax, NS B3J 3L2
902-496-5993
Fax: 902-423-6413
mooseheads@halifaxmooseheads.ca
www.halifaxmooseheads.ca
Cam Russell, General Manager/Head Coach
Tipper Leblanc, Assistant General Manager
Brian Urquhart, Vice President, Business Operations
Chris Donnelly, Associate Coach
Jeff MacLeod, Assistant Coach
Jason Troini, Assistant Coach
Ian Cox, Head Trainer
Home Ice:
Halifax Metro Center

Moncton Wildcats
100 Midland Drive
Dieppe, NB E1A 6X4
506-382-5555
Fax: 506-858-2222
info@moncton-wildcats.com
www.moncton-wildcats.com
Jean Brousseau, Governor
Andrew Benson, Marketing Manager
Jeff Rose, General Manager
Danny Flynn, Director of Hockey Operations/Head Coach
Fabian Joseph, Associate Coach
Darryl Seward, Assistant Coach
Home Ice:
Moncton Coliseum

Montreal Juniors
4110, boul LaSalle
Montréal, QC H4G 2A5
514-670-2100
Fax: 514-670-2258
info@juniordemontreal.com
www.juniordemontreal.com
Farrel Miller, Governor
Martin Routhier, President
Éric Tessier, Tickets Director
Jérôme Burke, Controller
Valérie Clément, Director of Communications
Sonya Lamoureux, Director of Corporate Relations
Pascal Vincent, General Manager/Head Coach
Dominique Ducharme, Assistant Coach
Joel Bouchard, Assistant Coach
Alain Grenier, Goaltending Coach
Dominic Boudriau, Head Trainer
Home Ice:
Auditorium de Verdun

P.E.I. Rocket
46 Kensington Road
Charlottetown, PE C1A 5H7
902-892-7349
Fax: 902-892-7350
administration@peirocket.com
www.peirocket.com
Serge Savard, Jr., President/Governor
Kent Hudson, General Manager
Nathan Baker, Director of Sales & Marketing
Tom Tessier, Media Relations Manager
Guy Chouinard, Head Coach & Director of Hockey Operations
Corrado Micalef, Assistant Coach
Jamie Blanchard, Goalie Coach
Andrew MacNeill, Trainer
Home Ice:
Charlottetown Civic Centre

Quebec Remparts
250 Wilfrid Hamel
Quebec, QC G1L 5A7
418-525-1212
Fax: 418-525-2242
info@remparts.qc.ca
www.remparts.qc.ca
Julien Gagnon, Governor
Claude Rousseau, President
Lucie Cloutier,Director Communications/Marketing
Myriam Raby, Controller
Louis Painchaud, Vice President Operations
Roy Patrick, Head Coach
Martin Laperriere, Assistant Coach
Gabriel Hardy, Head Trainer
Benoit Fortier, Goalie Coach
Home Ice:
Colisee Pepsi

Rimouski Oceanic
111 2nd St. W
PO Box 816
Rimouski, QC G5L 7C9
418-723-4444
Fax: 418-725-0944
hockey@oceanic.qc.ca
www.oceanic.qc.ca
Camille Leblanc, Governor
Henri Martin, President
Phillipoe Boucher, General Manager
Yannick Dumais, Assistant General Manager
Andre Jolicoeur, Hockey Operations Manager
Serge Beausoleil, Head Coach
Daniel Renaud, Assistant Coach
Donald Dufresne, Assistant Coach
Francis St-Pierce, Head Trainer
Home Ice:
Rimouski Coliseum

Rouyn-Noranda Huskies
218 Murdoch Ave.
Rouyn-Noranda, QC J9X 1E6
819-797-3022
Fax: 819-797-4311
admin@huskies.qc.ca
www.huskies.qc.ca
Pierre Cloutier, Governor
Jacques Blais, President
Ian Clermont, Director of Administration
Andre Tourigny, General Manager/Head Coach
Garry Parke, Assistant Coach
Mario Pouliot, Assistant Coach
Matt Doyle, Head Trainer
Home Ice:
Dave Keon Arena

Saint John Sea Dogs
99 Station St., #200
Saint John, NB E2L 4X4
506-657-3647
Fax: 506-696-0611
info@saintjohnseadogs.com
www.saintjohnseadogs.com
Wayne Long, President
Mike McGraw, Vice President
Scott McCain, Chief Executive Officer
Mike Kelly, Director of Hockey Operations
Gérard Gallant, Head Coach
Yvon Vautour, Assistant Coach
David Kelly, Head Trainer
Home Ice:
Harbour Station

Shawinigan Cataractes
1200, rue des Cèdres
Shawinigan, QC G9N 1P6
819-537-6327
Fax: 819-537-3538
cats@cataractes.qc.ca
www.cataractes.qc.ca
Mario Clermont, Governor
Martin Mondou, General Manager
Louis Caron, President
Eric Veilleux, Head Coach
Alain Petit, Assistant Coach
Patrick Leonard, Head Trainer
Home Ice:
Arena Jacques-Plante

Val D'Or Foreurs
810 6th Ave.
Val-D'or, QC J9P 1B4
819-824-0093
Fax: 819-824-7602
admin@foreurs.qc.ca
www.foreurs.qc.ca
Glenn Mullan, Governor
Louis Blanchette, President
Mario Carrière, Director Hockey Operations
Marc-André Dumont, Head Coach
Joey Bucci, Assistant Coach
Mario Carriere, General Manager
Maxime Paquin, Head Trainer
Home Ice:
Palais des Sports

Victoriaville Tigers
400 boul. Jutras Est
PO Box 857
Victoriaville, QC G6P 7W7
819-752-6353
Fax: 819-758-2846
info@tigresvictoriaville.com
www.tigersvictoriaville.com
Jean Marcotte, Governor
Eric Bernier, President
Patrick Villeneuve, Director Finance
Alain Danault, Director Marketing/Media Relations
Jérôme Mésonéro, General Manager
Yanick Jean, Head Coach
Simon Olivier, Assistant Coach
Patrick Villeneuve, Head Trainer
Home Ice:
Colisee des Bois-Francs

Western Hockey League
1 - 3030 Sunridge Way NE
Calgary, AB T1Y 7K4
403-693-3030
Fax: 403-693-3031
info@whl.ca
www.whl.ca
Ron Robison, Commissioner
Richard Doerksen, VP Hockey
Yvonne Bergmann, VP Operations
Corey Flett, Director Communications
Kevin Muench, Director Officiating
Jim Donlevy, Director, Education Services
Ed Chynoweth, Chairman

Teams:

Brandon Wheat Kings
#2 1175 - 18th St.
Brandon, MB R7A 7C5
204-726-3535
Fax: 204-726-3540
office@wheatkings.com
www.wheatkings.com
Kelly McCrimmon, General Manager/Governor
Rick Dillabough, Director of Sales and Marketing
Al MacPherson, Director of Player Personnel
Dwayne Glywoychuck, Assistant Coach
Darren Ritchie, Assistant Coach
Grant Ammann, Athletic Trainer
Home Ice:
Keystone Arena

Calgary Hitmen
PO Box 1540
Station M
Calgary, AB T2P 3B9
403-571-2200
Fax: 403-571-2211
info@hitmenhockey.com
www.hitmenhockey.com
Ken King, Governor/President/CEO
Kelly Kisio, Director Marketing
Rick Dillabough, Director Of Sales
Mike Moore, Director of Business Operations
Mike Williamson, Head Coach
Joel Otto, Assistant Coach
Will McMillan, Head Trainer
Home Ice:
Pengrowth Saddledome

Chilliwack Bruins
45323 Hodgins Ave.
Chilliwack, BC V2P 8G1
604-792-4625
Fax: 604-795-4656
info@chilliwackbruins.com
www.chilliwackbruins.com
Brian Burke, Owner
Jim Bond, Owner
Moray Keith, Owner
Darryl Porter, Owner
Glen Sather, Owner
Marc Habscheid, General Manager/Head Coach
Bob Rouse, Assistant Coach/Assistant General Manager
Peter Hay, Assistant Coach
Brady Robinson, Goaltender Coach
Matt Auerbach, Head Trainer
Home Ice:
Prospera Centre

Edmonton Oil Kings
11913 Wayne Gretzky Drive S
Edmonton, AB T5B 1Z7
780-409-3700
Fax: 780-409-3701
www.oilkings.ca
Patrick LaForge, Governor
Nick Wilson, Alternate Governor & VicPresident of Business Operations
Bob Green, General Manager
Kelly Row, Manager, Communications
Steve Pleau, Head Coach
Rocky Thompson, Assistant Coach
Darryl Weinberger, Assistant Coach
Terrill Lobo, Head Trainer
Home Ice:
Prospera Centre

Kamloops Blazers
300 Lorne St.
Kamloops, BC V2C 1W1
250-828-1144
Fax: 250-828-7822
info@blazerhockey.com
www.blazerhockey.com
Murray Owen, President/Governor
Craig Bonner, General Manager
Matt Recchi, Director Player Personnel
Guy Charron, Head Coach
Dave Hunachak, Assistant Coach
Home Ice:
Interior Savings Centre

Kelowna Rockets
#101-1223 Water St.
Kelowna, BC V1Y 9V1
250-860-7825
Fax: 250-860-7880
info@kelownarockets.com
www.kelownarockets.com
Bruce Hamilton, President/General Manager
Lorne Frey, Assistant GM/Director Player Personnel
Ryan Huska, Head Coach
Ryan Cuthbert, Assistant Coach
Dan Lambert, Assistant Coach
Jeff Thorburn, Athletic Therapist
Home Ice:
Prospera Place

Kootenay Ice
#2 - 1777 2nd St. N
Cranbrook, BC V1C 7G9
250-417-0322
Fax: 250-417-0323
info@kootenayice.net
www.kootenayice.net
Jeff Chynoweth, President/General Manager
Tiffany Harris-Johnson, Director of Marketing
Kris Knoblauch, Head Coach
Todd Johnson, Assistant Coach
Jerry Bancks, Assistant Coach
Home Ice:
Cranbrook Rec Plex

Lethbridge Hurricanes
Enmax Centre
2510 Scenic Drive S
Lethbridge, AB T1J 7J1
403-328-1986
Fax: 403-329-1622
info@lethbridgehurricanes.com
www.lethbridgehurricanes.com
Herman Elfring, Governor
Don Clark, President
Rich Preston, General Manager/Head Coach
Matt Kabayama, Assistant Coach
Brad Robson, Assistant General Manager
Home Ice:
Enmax Center

Medicine Hat Tigers
155 Ash Ave. SE
Medicine Hat, AB T1A 7G2
403-526-2666
Fax: 403-526-3072
admin@tigershockey.com
www.tigershockey.com
Darrell Maser, Governor/President
Brent Maser, Vice President
Dave Andjelic, Director of Marketing/Public Relations
Brad McEwan, General Manager
Shaun Clouston, Head Coach
Darren Kruger, Assistant Coach
Mikki Lanuk, Head Trainer
Home Ice:
The Arena

Moose Jaw Warriors
PO Box 74
Moose Jaw, SK S6H 4N7
306-694-5711
Fax: 306-692-7833
warriors1@mjwarriors.com
www.mjwarriors.ca
Darin Chow, Governor
Chad Taylor, President
Corey Nyhagen, Director, Corporate Sales and Marketing
Marnel Rasmussen, Director, Community Relations
Jeff Truitt, Director of Hockey Operations
Dave Hunchak, Head Coach
Kevin Higo, Assistant Coach
Curtis Amiot, Head Trainer
Home Ice:
Moose Jaw Civic Center

Prince Albert Raiders
690 - 32nd St. E
Prince Albert, SK S6V 2W8
306-764-4263
Fax: 306-764-5454
info@raiderhockey.com
www.raiderhockey.com
Dale McFee, President
Bruno Campese, General Manager/Head Coach
Steve Young, Assistant General Manager/Assistant Coach
Craig Bedard, Assistant Coach
Home Ice:
Art Hauser Centre

Prince George Cougars
#102, 2187 Ospika Blvd S
Prince George, BC V2N 6Z1
250-561-0783
Fax: 250-561-0743
cougars@mag-net.com
www.pgcougars.com
Rick Brodsky, President
Dallas Thompson, General Manager
Brandi Brodsky, Vice President
Wade Klippenstein, Director of Player Personnel
Dean Clark, Head Coach
Brent Arsenault, Assistant Coach
Ramandeep Singh Dhanjal, Head Trainer
Home Ice:
CN Center

Red Deer Rebels
4847-19th St., Unit C
Red Deer, AB T4R 2N7
403-341-6000
Fax: 403-341-6009
rebels@telusplanet.net
www.reddeerrebels.com
Brent Sutter, Owner/President/Governor
Jerry Van Someren, VP of Business Operations
Greg McConkey, VP of Business Development
Randy Peterson, Director of Scouting & Player Development
Jesse Wallin, VP of Hockey Operations/Head Coach
Bryce Thoma, Assistant Coach
Dave Horning, Head Trainer
Home Ice:
Enmax Centrium

Regina Pats
PO Box 104
Regina, SK S4P 2Z5
306-522-5604
Fax: 306-569-1021
pats@reginapats.com
www.reginapats.com
Russ Parker, Owner/President/Governor
Diane Parker, Owner/President/Governor
Brent Parker, General Manager
Cliff Mapes, Vice President of Business Operations
Dan Plaster, Director of Communications and Media Relations
Chris Hutchinson, Corporate Sales
Curtis Hunt, Head Coach
Shaun Sutter, Assistant Coach
Greg Mayer, Head Trainer/Equipment Manager
Home Ice:
Brandt Centre

Saskatoon Blades
201-3515 Thatcher Ave.
Saskatoon, SK S7R 1C4
306-975-8844
Fax: 306-934-1097
info@saskatoonblades.com
www.saskatoonblades.com
Jack Brodsky, Owner/Governor
Mike Jenkins, Director of Business Operations
Lorne Molleken, General Manager/Head Coach
Dave Struch, Associate Coach
Steve Hildebrand, Head Trainer
Home Ice:
Credit Union Centre

Swift Current Broncos
PO Box 2345
Swift Current, SK S9H 4X6
306-773-1509
Fax: 306-773-5406
s.c.broncos@sasktel.net
www.scbroncos.com
Ben Wiebe, Governor
Al Stewart, Alternate Governor/Chairman
Jordan Wall Director of Business Operations
Keegan Goodrich, Public/Media Relations Director
Mark Lamb, General Manager/Head Coach
Tim Kehler, Assistant Coach
Jamie LeBlanc, Head Trainer
Sheldon Ferguson, Assistant General Manager/Director of Hockey Operations
Home Ice:
Centennial Civic Centre

Vancouver Giants
100 North Renfrew St.
Vancouver, BC V5K 3N7
604-444-2687
Fax: 604-254-2687
info@vancouvergiants.com
www.vancouvergiants.com
Ron Toigo, Owner
Gordie Howe, Owner
Pat Quinn, Owner
Sultan Thiara, Owner
Colleen Howie, Owner
Paul Lucrezi, Director of Ticket Sales & Marketing
Scott Bonner, General Manager
Jason Ripplinger, Director of Player Personnel
Don Hay, Head Coach
Ian Gallagher, Strength & Conditioning Coach

Glen Hanlon, Assistant Coach
Nick Murray, Athletic Trainer
Home Ice:
Pacific Coliseum

Lacrosse

National Lacrosse League
9 East 45th St.
5th Fl.
New York, NY 10017
212-764-1390
Fax: 917-510-9890
www.nll.com
George Daniel, Interim Commissioner
Tatia Mays-Russell, Chief Financial Ocer
Brian Lemon, VP Operations
Doug Fritts, VP Communications
Scott Neiss, Director of Operations
Jason Lai, Director of Team Business Development
Description:
Founded 1997. Professional Indoor Lacrosse League.

Teams:

Calgary Roughnecks
555 Saddledome Rise SE
Calgary, AB T2G 2W1
403-777-4646
Fax: 403-777-3695
info@calgaryroughnecks.com
www.calgaryroughnecks.com
Ken King, President/CEO
John Bean, Governor/CFO
Dave Pym, Head Coach
Mike Board, General Manager
Description:
Arena: Pengrowth Saddledome

Edmonton Rush
137 Turbo Drive
Sherwood Park, AB T8H 2J6
780-732-7874
Fax: 780-467-7854
info@edmontonrush.com
www.edmontonrush.com
Bruce Urban, Owner/Governor
Gord Sawyer, President
Derek Keenan, General Manager/Head Coach
Todd Lorenz, Offensive Coach
Jeremy Tallevi, Defensive Coach
Description:
Arena: Rexall Place

Toronto Rock
416 North Service Road East, #100
Oakville, ON L6H 5R2
416-596-3075
Fax: 905-339-3473
info@torontorock.com
www.torontorock.com
Jamie Dawick, President
Troy Cordingley, Head Coach
Matt Sawyer, Assistant Coach
Terri Giberson, Business Manager
Description:
Air Canada Centre

Soccer

Canadian Soccer League
5160 Explorer Drive
Mississauga, ON L5T 1C8
905-564-2297
Fax: 905-671-6450
info@canadiansoccerleague.com
www.canadiansoccerleague.com
Vincent Ursini, Chairman
Pino Jazbec, League Administrator
Tony Camacho, Director of Officials
Stan Adamson, Director of Media

Teams:

Brampton Lions
8820 Jane St.
Vaughan, ON L4K 2M9
647-999-8484
Fax: 905-760-2820
pionadi@bramptonlionsfc.ca
www.bramptonlionsfc.ca
Antonio Carvalho, President
Armando Costa, Director of Soccer Operations/Head Coach
Victor Cameira, Manager

London City
PO Box 125
Station B
London, ON N6A 4V6
519-672-5425
Fax: 519-438-4625
Markus Gauss, President
Ryan Gauss, CEO/Vice President/General Manager
Luka Shaqiri, Head Coach

North York Astros
1589 Weston Road
Toronto, ON M9N 1T4
416-240-1718
Fax: 416-240-1648
astros@northyorkastros.ca
www.northyorkastros.ca
Bruno Ierullo, General Manager
Jorge Collazo, Director Of Football

Portugal FC
964 The Queensway
Toronto, ON M6H 1A2
416-417-2349
Fax: 416-731-9501
info@portugalfc.ca
www.portugalfc.ca
Isac Cambas, President
Juan Carlos Ramirez Gaston, Director of Soccer
Daniel Amaral, Head Coach

Serbian White Eagles
30 Titan Road, Unit 15
Toronto, ON M8Z 5Y2
416-252-4762
dragan@serbianwhiteeagles.ca
www.serbianwhiteeagles.ca
Dragan Bakoc, President
Dusko Prijic, Head Coach
Mario Ostojic, Sports Director

St Catharines Wolves
125 Vansickle Road
St. Catharines, ON L2S 3X5
905-682-7621
Fax: 905-682-8811
armanddifruscio@hotmail.com
Armand Di Fruscio, General Manager
James McGilivary, Head Coach

TFC Academy
BMO Field
170 Princes' Blvd.
Toronto, ON M6K 3C3
416-815-5400
Fax: 416-815-5452
http://torontofc.ca/academy
Anthony Capotosto, Assistant Coach
Stuart Neely, General Manager/Head Coach

Toronto Croatia
89 Queen St. S
Mississauga, ON L5M 2K7
905-812-7868
Fax: 905-828-7753
jzaradic@sympatico.ca
www.torontocroatia.com
Joe Pavicic, President
Ivan Kulis, General Manager
Arapovic Pero, Head Coach
Alen Vukobrad, Assistant Coach

Major League Soccer
110 E 42nd St, Tenth Fl.
New York, NY 10017
212-450-1200
Fax: 212-450-1300
feedback@mlssoccer.com
www.mlssoccer.com
Don Garber, Commissioner
Mark Abbott, President
Kathy Carter, President, Soccer United Marketing

Teams:

Toronto FC
BMO Field
170 Princes' Blvd.
Toronto, ON M6K 3C3
416-360-4625
www.torontofc.ca
Paul Beirne, Business Operations Director
Earl Cochrane, Team Operations Director
Aron Winter, Head Coach
Cesar Velasco, Director, Marketing & Communications

United Soccer Leagues
1715 N. Westshore Blvd
Ste 825
Tampa, FL 33607
813-963-3909
Fax: 813-963-3807
www.uslsoccer.com
Francisco Marcos, Senior Director
Tim Holt, President
Jay Preble, Director Public Relations

Teams:

Ottawa Fury
458 Maclaren St.
Fl. 2
Ottawa, ON K1R 5K6
613-235-3879
Fax: 613-567-3879
www.ottawafury.com
John Pugh, Owner/CEO
Melanie Rutherford, Director of Operations
Klaus Linnenbruegger, Head Coach

Thunder Bay Chill
191 Hazelwood Drive
Thunder Bay, ON P7G 1Y5
807-623-5911
Fax: 807-344-7177
tbchill@tbaytel.net
www.thunderbaychill.com
John Marrello, General Manager
Tony Colistro, Head Coach

Toronto Lynx Soccer Club
100 Westmore Drive, #8
Toronto, ON M9V 5C3
416-251-4625
Fax: 416-251-7054
lynx@lynxsoccer.com
www.lynxsoccer.com
Danny Stewart, Head Coach

Facilities

Arenas & Stadiums

Air Canada Centre
50 Bay St, #500
Toronto, ON M5J 2X2
416-815-5500
Fax: 416-359-9332
www.theaircanadacentre.com
Beth Robertson, Marketing Vice President/COO
Seating Capacity:
Basketball-19,800; Hockey-18,800; Concerts-19,800; Theatre-5,200; also 1020 Club Seats, 40 Platinum Lounges, 65 Executive Suites, and 32 Theatre Suites.
Tenant(s):
NBA - Toronto Raptors basketball, NHL - Toronto Maple Leafs hockey, NLL - Toronto Rock lacrosse.

BC Place Stadium
777 Pacific Blvd
Vancouver, BC V6B 4Y8
604-669-2300
Fax: 604-661-3412
stadium@bcpavco.com
www.bcplacestadium.com
Crosley Howard, General Manager
Brian Griffin, Director Of Construction
Graham Ramsay, Director, Business Development Division
Harvey Repp, Director Of Operations
Seating Capacity:
60,000
Description:
Future host of the 2010 Winter Olympic Games Opening/Closing Ceremonies.

Bell Centre
1909 Ave. Des
Montreal, QC H3B 5E8
514-932-2582
Fax: 514-9892871
services@bellcentre.ca
www.bellcentre.ca
Eric Molson, Chairman
Daniel O'Neill, Chief Executive Officer
Pierre Boivin, Team President
Aldo Giampaolo, EVP
Tenant(s):
NHL - Montreal Canadiens Hockey, NLL - Montreal Express Lacrosse.
Permanent Seating Capacity:
21,500

BMO Field
170 Princes' Blvd
Toronto, ON M6K 363
Seating Capacity:
20,000
Description:
Home of the Toronto FC. Held the FIFA U-20 World Championships in July of 2007.

Calgary Exhibition & Stampede
1410 Olympic Way SE
Calgary, AB T2P 2K8
403-261-0101
800-661-1260
Fax: 403-265-7197
reception3@calgarystampede.com
www.calgarystampede.com
Warren Connell, Chief Operating Officer
Laurie Schild, Vice President Marketing
Gordon Fache, Vice President

Canad Inns Stadium
1430 Maroons Road
Winnipeg, MB R3G 0L5
204-784-2583
Seating Capacity:
29,503
Playing Surface:
Artificial
Teams:
Winnipeg Blue Bombers

Canwest Global Park
One Portage Ave. E
Winnipeg, MB R3B 3N3
204-982-2273
Fax: 204-982-2274
goldeyes@goldeyes.com
www.goldeyes.com
Scott Horn, Facility Manager
Tom Thiessen, Box Office Manager
Sport:
Baseball
Team:
Winnipeg Goldeyes
Capacity:
6,266

Colisee Pepsi De Quebec
250 Blvd Wilfrid-Hamel
Quebec, QC G1L 5A7
418-691-7110
Fax: 418-691-7249
info@expocite.com
www.expocite.com
Bruno St-Onge, Manager, Operations
Mark Sparrow, General Manager
Arena Seating Capacity:
15,399.00
Year Founded:
1950

Commonwealth Stadium
11000 Stadium Road
PO Box 2359
Edmonton, AB T5J 2R7
780-944-7561
Seating Capacity:
60,217
Playing Field:
Grass
Teams:
Edmonton Eskimos

Copps Coliseum
101 York Blvd
Hamilton, ON L8R 3L4
905-546-4040
Fax: 905-527-6856
www.hecfi.on.ca/copps
Description:
Seats 19,000

Enmax Centre
2510 Scenic Drive S
Lethbridge, AB T1K 1N2
403-320-4040
Fax: 403-327-3620
enmaxcentre@lethbridge.ca
www.lethbridge.ca
Kim Gallucci, General Manager
Jill Henderson, Events Manager

Frank Clair Stadium
1015 Bank St.
Ottawa, ON K1S 3W7
Seating Capacity:
30,927
Playing Surface:
Artificial
Teams:
Ottawa Renegades

General Motors Place
800 Griffith Way
Vancouver, BC V6B 6G1
604-899-7400
Fax: 604-899-7401
www.canucks.com
Steven H Bellringer, President
Leila Bell-Irving, Business Development VP
Valerie Lewis, Suites
Owned by:
Orca Bay Sports & Entertainment
Tenant(s):
NHL - Vancouver Canucks Hockey, NLL - Vancouver Ravens Lacrosse.
Permanent Seating Capacity:
20,000

Halifax Metro Centre
1800 Argyle St, #416, PO Box 955
Halifax, NS B3J 2V9
902-421-8000
Fax: 902-422-2922
judith@wtcchmc.com
www.halifaxmetrocentre.com
Scott D Ferguson, Operations VP
(902)421-1302
scott@wtechmc.com
Deanna A Sperry, Marketing Manager
(902)421-1302
deanna@halifaxmetrocentre.com
Ralph J Williams, Events Booking Manager
(902)421-1302
ralph@halifaxmetrocentre.com
Robert Logan, Corporate Sales Manager
(902)421-1302
robertl@halifaxmetrocentre.com
Arena Seating Capacity:
10,000

Hamilton Entertainment & Convention Facilities, Inc.
10 MacNab St, S.
Hamilton, ON L8P 4Y3
905-546-3100
Fax: 905-521-0924
hectemp@hamilton.ca
www.hecfi.on.ca
Brad Calder, Acting Manager Director/Chief Executive
Debra Vivian, Marketing/Public Relations Manager
Rick Difilippo, Business Services Director
John Elder, Programming Manager
Permanent Seating Capacity:
17,500

Harbour Station
99 Station St
Saint John, NB E2L 4X4
506-632-6103
Fax: 506-632-6121
mail@harbourstation.nb.ca
www.harbourstation.nb.ca
Michael Caddell, General Manager
Ewan Cameron, Operations Director
Brenda Lee, Box Office Manager

Ivor Wynne Stadium
75 Balsam Ave. N
Hamilton, ON L8L 8C1
905-546-4246
Seating Capacity:
35,000
Playing Surface:
Artificial
Teams:
Hamilton Tigercats

John Labatt Centre
99 Dundas St.
London, ON N6A 6K1
519-667-5700
Fax: 519-432-3386
info@johnlabattcentre.com
www.johnlabattcentre.com
Brian Ohl, General Manager
Chris Campbell, Marketing Director
Gary Turrell, Operations Director
Arena Seating Capacity:
10,000
Clients:
Harlem Globetrotters, Stars on Ice, US Hot Rod Monster Jam, Sesame St., Disney on Ice, various concerts.
Nature of Service:
Multi-purpose Sports, Entertainment Facility.

Landsdowne Park
1015 Bank St
Ottawa, ON K1S 3W7
613-580-2429
Fax: 613-564-1619
lansdowne@ottawa.ca
www.lansdownepark.ca
Richard Haycock, General Manager
Arena Seating Capacity:
10,000
Stadium Seating Capacity:
35,000

Le Stade De Quebec
100 Rue Du Cardinal Maurice-Roy
Quebec City, QC,CANADA G1K 8Z1
418-521-2255
Fax: 418-521-2266
baseball@capitalesdequebec.com
www.capitalesdequebec.com
Sport:
Baseball
Team:
Capitales de Quebec
Capacity:
4,800
Sport:
Baseball
Team:
Capitales de Quebec

Lynx Stadium
300 Coventry Rd
Ottawa, ON K1K 4P5
613-747-5969
Fax: 613-747-0003
lynx@ottawalynx.com
www.ottawalynx.com
Melissa Rumble, Director Ticket Operations
(613)747-5969
rumble@ottawalynx.com
Steve Benhott, Head Groundskeeper
(613)747-5969
lynxcrew@hotmail.com
Matt Horan, Head Groundskeeper
(613)747-5969
lynxcrew@hotmail.com
Seating Capacity
10,332.00
Track Type
Natural grass
Track Size
325 feet LF and RF, 404 feet CF

McMahon Stadium
1817 Crowchild Trail NW
Calgary, AB T2M 4R6
403-282-2044
Fax: 403-282-2018
mcmahonstadium@shaw.ca
John Haverstock, Manager
Year Opened:
1960

Seating Capacity:
36,000 permanent with 10,000 additional seats available.
Description:
Home to the Calgary Stampeders and the University of Calgary Dinos.
Events:
Held the opening and closing ceremonies of the 1988 Olympic Winter Games. Opening ceremonies of the 1997 World Police/Fire Games. CFL Grey Cup Championship games in 1975, 1993, 2000 and 2009.

Molson Stadium
475 Pine Ave. W
Montreal, QC H2W 1S4
514-398-7000
www.athletics.mcgill.ca/facilities
Phil Quintal, Facilities Manager
Eyal Baruch, Assistant Manager, Events
Playing Surface:
FieldTurf

MTS Centre
300 Portage Ave.
Winnipeg, MB R3C 5S4
(204) 987-7825
www.mtscentre.ca
Jim Ludlow, President & CEO
Kevin Cheveldayoff, Executive VP & General Manager
Dorian Morphy, Senior Director of Marketing
Permanent Seating Capacity:
Hockey - 15,015
Tenant(s):
NHL - Winnipeg Jets

Northlands Park
Box 1480
Edmonton, AB T5J 2N5
780-471-7210
888-800-7275
Fax: 780-471-8195
info@northlands.com
www.northlands.com
Dale Leschuitta, President
Ken Knowles, Designate General Manager
Gerry Stoll, Entertainment/Booking Manager
Duane Vienneau, Sales Business Unit Manager
Permanent Seating Capacity:
17,099
Facility:
Edmonton Coliseum

Olympic Stadium
4141 Pierre De Coubertin Ave
Montreal, QB H1V 3N7
514-252-4441
Fax: 514-252-4440
rio@rio.gouv.qc.ca
www.rio.gouv.qc.ca
David Heurtel, Chief Executive Officer
Suzanne Audet, President
Stadium Seating Capacity:
55,389

Pacific Coliseum
2901 East Hasting St.
Vancouver, BC V5K 5J1
604-253-2311
Fax: 604-251-7768
sales@pne.bc.ca
www.pne.bc.ca
Mike McDaniel, President/Chief Executive Officer
Peter Male, Sales VP
(604)251-7787
peterm@pne.bc.ca
Shelley Frost, Marketing VP
Arena Seating Capacity:
17,300
Clients:
Boys Basketball, Old Timers Hockey, Slam City Jam.
Nature of Service:
Ice Hockey Services, Catering, Event Concessions, Arena Configurations, Video, Scoreboard.
Tenant(s):
Vancouver Giants, Weston Hockey League.

Ricoh Coliseum
100 Princes' Blvd
Exhibition Place
Toronto, ON M6K 3C3
416-263-3000
Fax: 416-263-3901
www.ricohcoliseum.com
Vince Bozzo, General Manager
Nathalie Burri, Event Service Manager
Food & Beverage:
Centerplate Inc.
Management Firm:
O&Y/SMG Canada
Permanent Seating Capacity:
10,000
Tenant(s):
AHL - Toronto Roadrunners hockey

Rogers Centre
One Blue Jays Way
Toronto, ON M5V 1J1
416-341-3000
Fax: 416-341-3101
guestservices@rogerscentre.com
www.rogerscentre.com
Silvio D'Addario, Chief Operating Officer
Mario Coutinho, Director Operations
Owned by:
Sportsco International, L.P.
Tenants:
MLB - Toronto Blue Jays baseball, CFL - Toronto Argonauts football.
Permanent Seating Capacity:
53,506 - Football; 51,517 - Baseball.

Sarnia Sports and Entertainment Centre
1455 London Road
Sarnia, ON N7S 1P6
519-541-1000
Fax: 519-541-0303
info@ssec.on.ca
www.ssec.on.ca
Ryan Chamney, Events Manager
Edgar Hunt, Finance Manager
Trevor Sanderson, Operations Manager
Tenant(s):
OHL - Sarnia Sting hockey.
Permanent Seating Capacity:
5,500

Saskatchewan Place
101-3515 Thatcher Ave
Saskatoon,SK S7R 1C4
306-975-3155
Fax: 306-975-2907
Info@creditunioncentre.com
www.saskatchewanplace.com
Kenneth H Wood, General Manager
Will Antonishyn, Finance Manager
Brian Swidrovich, Business Development Manager
Scott Ford, Marketing/Events Manager
Description:
Saskatchewan Place is the province's premier, multi-purpose trade, sports and entertainment facility. 110,000 sq.ft. of trade show space; free parking for over 3000 vehicles, 13,000 seating space.
Permanent Seating Capacity:
11,301

Saskatoon Kinsmen/Henk Ruys Soccer Centre
219 Primrose Drive
Saskatoon, SK S7K 2J9
306-975-3400
Fax: 306-975-3407
www.saskatoonsoccer.com
John Tomchuk, General Manager
Grace Kachur, Administrative Assistant
DeAnn Eckdahl, Financial Administrator
deann.eckdahl@sk.sympatico.ca
Murray Waters, Food/Beverage Manager
Nature of Sports Service:
A multi-purpose facility dedicated to soccer, including four indoor pitches, internal restaurant, concession and lounge. 84,000 sq. feet.

Scotiabank Place
1000 Palladium Dr
Kanata, ON K2V 1A5
613-599-0100
Fax: 613-599-0359
feedback@scotiabankplace.com
www.scotiabankplace.com
Tom Conroy, VP/Executive Director
Krista Pogue, Director Media/Marketing
Owned by:
capital Sports Properties
Tenant(s):
NHL - Ottawa Senators hockey.
Permanent Seating Capacity:
18,500

Scotiabank Saddledome
555 Saddledome Rise SE
Calgary, AB T2G 2W1
403-777-4636
Fax: 403-777-3695
customerservice@calgaryflames.com
www.pengrowthsaddledome.com
Libby Raines, Vice President, Building Operations
Garry McKenzie, Marketing VP
George Greenwood, Operations Manager
John Vidalin, Advertising/Promotions Director
Owned by:
Calgary Flames Ltd. Partnership (20 year lease from Saddledome Foundation, City of Calgary).
Tenant(s):
NHL - Calgary Flames hockey; NLL - Calgary Roughnecks lacrosse; WHL - Calgary Hitmen hockey.
Permanent Seating Capacity:
18,800

Taylor Field
2940-10th Ave.
Regina, SK S4P 3B8
306-569-2323
Seating Capacity:
27,637
Playing Surface:
Artificial
Teams:
Saskatchewan Roughriders and Regina Rams High School Football

Telus Field
10233 96 Ave. N.W.
Edmonton, AB T5K OA5
780-414-4450
Fax: 780-414-4475
www.eks.com
Heather Sayers, Ticket Manager
Don Benson, Stadium Operations Manager
Sport:
Baseball.
Team:
Edmonton Trappers.
Capacity:
9,200

Winnipeg Arena
1430 Maroons Rd
Winnipeg, MB R3G 0L5
204-784-2583
888-780-7328
Fax: 204-783-5222
Colinne Dowbyhuz, Event Service Manager
Seating Capacity:
29,503

Race Tracks

Clinton Raceway
147 Beech St.
Clinton, ON N0M 1LO
519-482-5270
Fax: 519-482-1489
info@clintonraceway.com
www.clintonraceway.com
Jessica Carnochan, Marketing Director
Murray Watt, President
Description:
Horse race track.

Flamboro Downs
967 Highway #5 W
PO Box 8220
Hamilton, ON L9H 6Y6
905-627-3561
Fax: 905-627-0480
info@flamborodowns.com
www.flamborodowns.com
Neil McCoag, Racing Secretary
Ron Barr, Marketing Manager

Mosport International Raceway
3233 Concession Road #10, RR #5
Bowmanville, ON L1C 3K6
905-983-9141
Fax: 905-983-5195
info@mosports.com
www.mosport.com
Myles Brandt, President/General Manager
Andrew Foxman, Sales Director
Glenn Butt, Marketing Director
Janet Brandt, Food Service Manager
Notes:
Purchased by Panoz Motorsports.
Description:
Motor Speedway.

Sanair International Raceway
669 Petit Rang St.-Francois
PO Box 222
St.-Pie,QB J0H 1W0
450-772-6400
Fax: 450-772-2236
www.sanairracing.com
Description:
Auto race track.

Shannonville Motorsport Park
7047 Old Hwy #2
PO Box 259
Shannonville, ON K0K 3A0
613-969-1906
Fax: 613-966-6890
info@shannonville.com
www.shannonville.com
Jean Gauthier, Owner

Description:
Auto Race Track.
Long Track:
4.03km.
Pro Track:
2.47km
Fabi Circuit:
2.23km.

Stampede Park
1410 Olympic Way SE
2300 Stampede Trail SE
Calgary, AB T2G 2W1
403-261-0214
Fax: 403-265-7009
www.stampede-park.com
Patti Hunt, Promotions & Advertising Manager

Sudbury Downs
2070 Old Burwash Rd
Sudbury, ON P3E 4Z4
705-855-9001
Fax: 705-855-5434
sudburydowns@gmail.com
www.sudburydowns.com
Patrick Macisaac, President
Ken Le Drew, General Manager
Year Founded:
1974
Nature of Sports Service:
Harness horse race track.

Western Fair Entertainment Centre
316 Rectory St
PO Box 7550
London, ON N5Y 5P8
519-438-7203
800-619-4629
Fax: 519-679-3124
info@westernfair.com
www.westernfair.com
Hugh Mitchell, CEO
Dave Taylor, Senior Marketing Manager
dtaylor@westernfair.com
Ian Fleaming, Raceway Manager
ifleaming@westernfair.com
Pam Kelly, Assistant Raceway Manager
pkelly@westernfair.com
Description:
Founded 1960. Harness horse race track.
Seating capacity:
4,500

Windsor Raceway
5555 Ojibway Parkway
PO Box 998
Windsor, ON N9A 6P6
519-969-8311
Fax: 519-969-0780
youbet@windsorraceway
www.windsorraceway.com
Patrick Soulliere, President
Richard Jacob, VP Operations
Description:
Horse race track.

Woodbine Racetrack
555 Rexdale Blvd
Rexdale, ON M9W 5L2
416-675-7223
888-675-7223
Fax: 416-213-2129
www.woodbine-racetrack.com
David Willmot, Chairman/Chief Executive Officer
Nickolas Eaves, President/Chief Operating Officer

Woodstock Raceway
875 Nellis St
PO Box 234
Woodstock, ON N4S 7W8
519-537-5717
Fax: 519-421-7374
wdstock@windsorraceway.com
www.windsorraceway.com
Paul Masters, General Manager

SECTION 16
TRANSPORTATION

Associations

Aerospace Industries Association of Canada (AIAC) / Association des industries aérospatiales du Canada
#1200, 60 Queen St., Ottawa ON K1P 5Y7 Canada
Tel: 613-232-4297; *Fax:* 613-232-1142
info@aiac.ca
www.aiac.ca
Previous Name: Air Industries Association of Canada
Overview: A large national organization founded in 1962
Membership: 400; *Committees:* Airworthiness; International Exhibition; Technology Council; Defence Procurement Council; Suppliers Council; Space Council
Activities: *Library:* Library
Description: To promote & facilitate the continued success & growth of this strategic industry; to establish & maintain a public policy environment that enables sustained aerospace industry growth; to strengthen the international competitiveness of all aerospace firms in Canada; to strengthen Canadian aerospace SME capabilities & position them as "suppliers of choice"; to represent & involve the full range of aerospace companies that operate in Canada

Air Canada Pilots Association (ACPA) / L'Association des pilotes d'Air Canada
#205, 6299 Airport Rd., Mississauga ON L4V 1N3 Canada
Tel: 905-678-9008; *Fax:* 905-678-9016
Toll-Free: 800-634-0944
info@acpa.ca
acpa.ca
Overview: A medium-sized national organization founded in 1995
Finances: *Annual Operating Budget:* $3 Million-$5 Million
Staff: 20 staff member(s); 50 volunteer(s)
Membership: 3,100
Affiliation(s): Association of Star Alliance Pilots

Air Line Pilots Association, International - Canada (ALPA)
#1301, 155 Queen St., Ottawa ON K1P 6L1 Canada
Tel: 613-569-5668; *Fax:* 613-569-5681
www.alpa.org
Social Media:
www.facebook.com/pages/We-Are-ALPA/200676905671
Previous Name: Canadian Air Line Pilots Association
Overview: A large national organization founded in 1931
Finances: *Funding Sources:* Membership dues
Staff: 10 staff member(s); 360 volunteer(s)
Membership: 2,200 + 19 locals in Canada; *Member Profile:* Active airline pilots employed by airlines in Canada; *Committees:* Air Safety; Aeromedical; Insurance
Activities: In Québec call 1-888-337-2033
Description: To promote & represent the interests of the airline pilot profession & to safeguard the rights of individual members; to promote & maintain the highest standards of flight safety; to function as trade union & professional association
Affiliation(s): International Federation of Air Line Pilots' Associations; Canadian Labour Congress

Air Transport Association of Canada (ATAC) / Association du transport aérien du Canada
#700, 255 Albert St., Ottawa ON K1P 6A9
Tel: 613-233-7727; *Fax:* 613-230-8648
atac@atac.ca
www.atac.ca
Overview: A medium-sized national organization founded in 1934
Membership: 200; *Member Profile:* Operators; Associates; Affiliates
Activities: Engaging in lobbying activities; *Speaker Service:* Yes
Description: To advance the issues that affect members from the commercial aviation & flight training industries as well as avaiation industry suppliers

Airport Management Council of Ontario
10 Geddes Cres., Barrie ON L4N 7B3 Canada
Tel: 705-726-2626; *Fax:* 705-739-8520
Toll-Free: 877-636-2626
amco@amco.on.ca
www.amco.on.ca
Overview: A small provincial organization founded in 1985
Membership: 51 airports + 44 businesses
Activities: Workshops, presentations, conventions; *Speaker Service:* Yes *Library:* Resource
Description: AMCO is committed to the sustainability of airports nationally. It monitors the airport industry, lobbies, provides networking opportunities and training to airports & businesses that work to enhance airport operations.

Alberta Construction Trucking Association (ACTA)
PO Box 4520, Stn. C, Calgary AB T2T 5N3 Canada
Tel: 403-244-4487; *Fax:* 403-244-2340
Previous Name: Alberta Gravel Truckers Association
Overview: A medium-sized provincial organization
Description: To develop & promote the business of transporting construction & construction-related material

Alberta Motor Transport Association (AMTA)
3660 Blackfoot Trail SE, Calgary AB T2G 4E6 Canada
Tel: 403-243-4161; *Fax:* 403-243-4610
Toll-Free: 800-267-1003
amtamsc@amta.ca
www.amta.ca
Merged from: Alberta Trucking Industry Safety Association; Alberta Trucking Association
Overview: A medium-sized provincial organization
Membership: 12,000; *Member Profile:* All sectors of the highway transportation industry; *Committees:* Injury Reduction & Training; Compliance & Regulatory Affairs; Member Services
Activities: Six regional meetings
Description: To take a leadership role in fostering a healthy, vibrant industry. PUBLICATIONS: Quaterly Newsletter; Annual Source Book; Western Canada Highway News Magazine.
Member of: Canadian Council of Motor Transport Administrators

Alberta Pioneer Railway Association
PO Box 70014, Stn. Londonderry, Edmonton AB T5C 3R6 Canada
Tel: 780-472-6229; *Fax:* 780-968-0167
hdixon@incentre.net
www.railwaymuseum.ab.ca
Also Known As: Alberta Railway Museum
Overview: A small provincial charitable organization founded in 1968
Finances: *Annual Operating Budget:* $50,000-$100,000; *Funding Sources:* Grants; donations
Membership: 50; *Fees:* $30 regular; $35 family; $20 senior; $10 associate; *Member Profile:* Railway enthusiasts; retired railway workers
Activities: Operates Alberta Railway Museum; *Library:* John Rechner Memorial Library (Open to Public) by appointment
Description: To collect, preserve, restore, exhibit & interpret artifacts which represent the history & social impact of the railways in Western Canada, with emphasis on Canadian National Railways & Northern Alberta Railways & their predecessors in northern & central Alberta
Member of: Alberta Museums Association; Museums Canada
Affiliation(s): Heritage Canada

Amalgamated Transit Union (AFL-CIO/CLC) / Syndicat uni du transport (FAT-COI/CTC)
5025 Wisconsin Ave. NW, Washington DC 20016 USA
Tel: 202-537-1645; *Fax:* 202-244-7824
www.atu.org
Overview: A medium-sized international organization

Association des propriétaires d'autobus du Québec (APAQ)
#107, 225, boul Charest est, Québec QC G1K 3G9 Canada
Tél: 418-522-7131; *Téléc:* 418-522-6455
apaq@apaq.qc.ca
www.apaq.qc.ca
Aperçu: *Dimension:* moyenne; *Envergure: provinciale; Organisme sans but lucratif; fondée en 1926*
Finances: *Budget de fonctionnement annuel:* $500,000-$1.5 Million
Personnel: 11 membre(s) du personnel
Membre: 250 sociétés; *Montant de la cotisation:* Barème (entre 240$ et 8 000$); *Critères d'admissibilite:* Transportateurs par autocars; vendeurs de produits touristiques pour les groupes; *Comités:* Scolaire; Interurbain; Nolise
Activités: Congrès annuel, Bienvenue Québec, Golf
Description: Défendre les intérêts des enterprises offrant des services de transport collectif de personnes par autobus et autocars; *Membre de:* Association de l'industrie touristique du Canada

Association du camionnage du Québec inc. (ACQ) / Québec Trucking Association Inc.
#200, 6450, rue Notre Dame ouest, Montréal QC H4C 1C4 Canada
Tél: 514-932-0377; *Téléc:* 514-932-1358
Ligne sans frais: 800-361-5813
info@carrefour-acq.org
www.carrefour-acq.org
Aperçu: *Dimension:* moyenne; *Envergure: provinciale; Organisme sans but lucratif; fondée en 1951*
Finances: *Budget de fonctionnement annuel:* $500,000-$1.5 Million
Personnel: 13 membre(s) du personnel
Membre: 600 sociétés + 251 associés; *Critères d'admissibilite:* transporteurs et locateurs publics & privés
Activités: *Stagiaires:* Oui
Description: Favoriser l'amélioration des normes de sécurité, d'efficacité et d'éthique dans l'industrie du camionnage; maintenir un contact avec l'autorité gouvernementale, les usagers des services de camionnage et le public en général; soutenir le perfectionnement professionnel; soutenir les entreprises dans la défense de leurs intérêts.
Affiliation(s): Union Internationale des Transports Routiers - Genève; American Trucking Association - Washington, DC

Association du transport écolier du Québec (ATEQ)
#300, 5300, boul des Galeries, Québec QC G2K 2A2 Canada
Tél: 418-622-6544; *Téléc:* 418-622-6595
Ligne sans frais: 877-622-6544
courrier@ateq.qc.ca
www.ateq.qc.ca
Aperçu: *Dimension:* moyenne; *Envergure: provinciale; fondée en 1962*
Membre: 700 transporteurs scolaires; *Montant de la cotisation:* Barème

Association du transport urbain du Québec (ATUQ)
#8090, 800, rue de la Gauchetière, Montréal QC H5A 1J6 Canada
Tél: 514-280-4640; *Téléc:* 514-280-7053
info@atuq.com
www.atuq.com
Aperçu: *Dimension:* moyenne; *Envergure: provinciale; fondée en 1983*
Description: Organisme de concertation et de représentation politique qui a pour mandat d'assurer la promotion du transport en commun et la défense des intérêts de ses membres auprès des partenaires de l'industrie et des différentes instances gouvernementales

Association nationale des camionneurs artisans inc. (ANCAI)
#235, 670, rue Bouvier, Québec QC G2J 1A7 Canada
Tél: 418-623-7923; *Téléc:* 418-623-0448
infos@ancai.com
www.ancai.com
Aperçu: *Dimension:* moyenne; *Envergure: provinciale; fondée en 1966*
Finances: *Budget de fonctionnement annuel:* $500,000-$1.5 Million
Personnel: 10 membre(s) du personnel
Membre: 5 000; *Montant de la cotisation:* 185$; *Critères d'admissibilite:* Camionneur propriétaire de son véhicule
Activités: Congrès annuel; Tirage camion
Description: Défendre les intérêts des transporteurs en vrac (gravier et forêts) auprès des gouvernements, organismes patronaux et entreprises privées

Association of Canadian Port Authorities (ACPA)
#1502, 85 Albert St., Ottawa ON K1P 6A4 Canada
Tel: 613-232-2036; *Fax:* 613-232-9554
leroux@acpa-ports.net
www.acpa-ports.net
Previous Name: Canadian Port & Harbour Association
Overview: A medium-sized national organization founded in 1958
Finances: *Annual Operating Budget:* $50,000-$100,000; *Funding Sources:* Membership fees; seminars
Staff: 1 staff member(s)
Membership: 18 corporate + 17 associate; *Fees:* $750 associate & affiliate; $100 individual; *Committees:* Constitution; Finance & Administration; Marketing; Public Relations; Operations & Environment; Past Presidents; Real Property Management
Activities: Annual conferences where papers are given by experts in the field of port operations & where members inspect the host port's dock & industrial facilities; port-related research; special seminars; *Speaker Service:* Yes
Description: To encourage, mentor & stimulate the development of excellence within Canadian ports
Affiliation(s): American Association of Port Authorities

Association québécoise du transport aérien (AQTA)
Aéroport international Jean-Lesage, 600, 6e av de l'Aéroport, Québec QC G2G 2T5 Canada
Tél: 418-871-4635; *Téléc:* 418-871-8189
aqta@aqta.ca
www.aqta.ca
Aperçu: *Dimension:* moyenne; *Envergure: provinciale; Organisme sans but lucratif; fondée en 1975*
Membre: 130; *Montant de la cotisation:* Barème; *Critères d'admissibilite:* Transporteurs aériens et fournisseurs de produits et services liés à l'aviation
Description: Voué à la défense et la promotion des intérêts de tous les secteurs du transport aérien

Association québécoise du transport et des routes inc. (AQTR)
#200, 1255, rue University, Montréal QC H3B 3B2 Canada
Tél: 514-523-6444; *Téléc:* 514-523-2666
info@aqtr.qc.ca
www.aqtr.qc.ca
Aperçu: *Dimension:* grande; *Envergure: provinciale; fondée en 1965*
Finances: *Budget de fonctionnement annuel:* $500,000-$1.5 Million
Personnel: 7 membre(s) du personnel; 100+ bénévole(s)
Membre: 950; *Montant de la cotisation:* 270 $; *Critères d'admissibilité:* Secteur privé - Ingénieur conseils; Entrepreneurs; Fournisseurs et manufacturiers; Laboratoires; Transporteurs; Architectes et urbanistes; Étudiants; Spécialistes en environnement; Secteur public et parapublic - Ministères; Municipalités; Maisons d'enseignement; Sociétés de transport; Autres sociétés, départements et services publics; *Comités:* Directions techniques - Infrastructures de transport; Transport des personnes; Circulation; Sécurité dans les transports; Transport aérien; Recherche et développement; Comités - Transport des marchandises; Environnement; Revue; Congrès; Activités municipales
Activités: Regrouper les personnes impliquées dans les techniques du transport; encourager les échanges multidisciplinaires et favoriser la collaboration entre différents secteurs; recommander toute mesure permettant de développer des techniques du transport; *Listes de destinataires:* Oui
Description: Assumer un leadership technique; définir des règles en matière de sécurité et d'environnement; favoriser l'échange international des expertises; promouvoir la recherche et le développement des expertises et des produits en transport; promouvoir la formation dans le domaine des transports; assumer la représentativité de l'AQTR par la participation aux principaux forums sur les transports; contribuer à servir la société par l'éducation et l'information du grand public.

Association Sectorielle Transport Entreposage (ASTE)
#301, 6455, boul Jean-Talon est, Montréal QC H1S 3E8 Canada
Tél: 514-955-0454; *Téléc:* 514-955-0449
Ligne sans frais: 800-361-8906
info@aste.qc.ca
www.aste.qc.ca
Aperçu: *Dimension:* moyenne; *Envergure: provinciale; fondée en 1983*
Membre: 1-99
Description: L'Association Sectorielle Transport Entreposage est une organisme en prèvention, autonome et paritaire, sans but lucratif, fondé et administré par des reprétants des employeurs et des syndicats.

Atlantic Provinces Trucking Association (APTA)
#400, 725 Champlain St., Dieppe NB E1A 1P6 Canada
Tel: 506-855-2782; *Fax:* 506-853-7424
Toll-Free: 866-866-1679
apta@apta.ca
www.apta.ca
Overview: A medium-sized local organization founded in 1950
Membership: 400 corporate & individual; *Member Profile:* Open to anyone having an interest in the trucking industry in Atlantic Canada, including common carriers, owner-operators & private fleets; *Committees:* Accident Review; Associated Trades Council; Broker; Common Carrier; Group Insurance; Marine; Membership; New Brunswick Legislative; Newfoundland Legislative; Nova Scotia Legislative; Prince Edward Island Legislative; Safety Council; Workers Compensation
Activities: Infrastructure improvements; complete twinning of the highway between Halifax & Saint John; elimination of motor carrier plates & fees; simplification of multiple registration & other tax collection systems in North America to allow for "one-stop shipping"; establishment of training programs; Annual Meeting & Convention; Atlantic Truck Show; Spring Maintenance Seminar; *Rents Mailing List:* Yes
Description: To promote an efficient, safe & environmentally sound trucking industry in Atlantic Canada. PUBLICATIONS: Atlantic Trucking Magazine (quaterly); Atlantic Report Newsletter (monthly) (only to members).

British Columbia Aviation Council (BCAC)
PO Box 32366, Stn. YVR Domestic Terminal, Richmond BC V7B 1W2 Canada
Tel: 604-278-9330; *Fax:* 604-278-8210
info@bcaviationcouncil.org
www.bcaviationcouncil.org
Overview: A small provincial organization founded in 1936
Finances: *Funding Sources:* Membership fees
Description: A self-sustaining organization with the mission to "promote the safe and orderly development of aviation and aviation services to the province of British Columiba."

British Columbia Ferry & Marine Workers' Union (CLC) (BCFMWU) / Syndicat des travailleurs marins et de bacs de la Colombie-Britannique (CTC)
1511 Stewart Ave., Nanaimo BC V9S 4E3 Canada
Tel: 250-716-3454; *Fax:* 250-716-3455
Toll-Free: 800-663-7009
mailroom@bcfmwu.com
www.bcfmwu.com
Also Known As: Ferry Workers' Union
Overview: A medium-sized provincial organization founded in 1977
Finances: *Annual Operating Budget:* $1.5 Million-$3 Million; *Funding Sources:* Union dues
Staff: 9 staff member(s)
Membership: 4,400; *Fees:* $60 initiation fee; 1.5% of gross monthly income
Description: To unite in the Union all workers eligible for membership; to seek the best possible wage standards & improvements in the conditions of employment for these workers & to represent members in protecting & maintaining their rights; to act as the representative of the membership; to establish free child day care for all individuals; to engage in educational, legislative, political, civic, social, welfare, community & other activities to safeguard & promote economic & social benefits & justice for all workers, unionized & non-unionized.
Affiliation(s): BC Federation of Labour; National Union of Public & General Employees (NUPGE)

British Columbia Railway Historical Association (BCRHA)
1148 Balmoral Rd., Victoria BC V8T 1B1 Canada
Tel: 250-383-7063
bcrha@shaw.ca
www.trainweb.org/bcrha
Overview: A small provincial charitable organization founded in 1961
Finances: *Annual Operating Budget:* Less than $50,000; *Funding Sources:* Donations; book sales; membership dues
Staff: 30 volunteer(s)
Membership: 5 associate + 1 senior/lifetime + 30 individual; *Fees:* $15 full; $4 associate; *Member Profile:* Interest in BC railway history; *Committees:* Acquisitions; Book Sales; New Book Review; Financial
Activities: Research & publication of books on BC railway history; *Library:* Library (Open to Public)
Description: To preserve railway exhibits, manuscripts & film of BC railways
Member of: Heritage Society of BC

British Columbia Supercargoes' Association
#206, 3711 Delbrook Ave., North Vancouver BC V7N 3Z4 Canada
Tel: 604-878-1258; *Fax:* 604-904-6545
admin@supercargoes.bc.ca; president@supercargoes.bc.ca
www.supercargoes.bc.ca
Overview: A medium-sized provincial organization founded in 1952
Finances: *Annual Operating Budget:* $50,000-$100,000; *Funding Sources:* Membership dues
Staff: 8 volunteer(s)
Membership: 12; *Member Profile:* Marine professionals in the shipping industry
Description: To provide expert marine cargo planning & onsite management & supervision of shiploading & discharge of all types of cargoes & vessels on the west coast of North America

British Columbia Trucking Association (BCTA)
#100, 20111 - 93A Ave., Langley BC V1M 4A9 Canada
Tel: 604-888-5319; *Fax:* 604-888-2941
Toll-Free: 800-565-2282
bcta@bctrucking.com
www.bctrucking.com
Previous Name: BC Motor Transport Association
Overview: A large provincial organization founded in 1913
Finances: *Annual Operating Budget:* $500,000-$1.5 Million; *Funding Sources:* Membership dues
Staff: 8 staff member(s)
Membership: 1,000 corporate; *Fees:* $325-$400; *Member Profile:* Trucking company operating in BC or supplier to trucking industry; *Committees:* Convention; Insurance; International; Labour; Freight Claims & Hazardous Goods; Safety; Truxpo; Vehicle Standards
Activities: *Speaker Service:* Yes; *Rents Mailing List:* Yes *Library:* Yes by appointment
Description: To act as the recognised voice of the commercial road transportation industry in British Columbia, by consulting & communicating with the industry, government & the public; to promote a prosperous, safe, efficient & responsible road transportation industry; to provide programs & services to members

Bytown Railway Society (BRS)
PO Box 47076, Ottawa ON K1B 5P9 Canada
Tel: 613-745-1201; *Fax:* 613-745-1201
info@bytownrailwaysociety.ca
www.bytownrailwaysociety.ca
Overview: A medium-sized national charitable organization founded in 1969
Finances: *Annual Operating Budget:* $100,000-$250,000; *Funding Sources:* Publications sale; memberships
Staff: 60 volunteer(s)
Membership: 20 corporate + 3 senior/lifetime + 1,225 individual; *Fees:* $40/year plus $2.00 GST or $5.20 HST; *Committees:* Publications
Activities: Restoration/preservation of owned railway equipment; *Library:* Library (Open to Public) by appointment
Description: To promote an interest in railways & railway history, with particular emphasis on Canadian railways. PUBLICATIONS: Canadian Trackside Guide, The Quebec Railway Light and Power Company, Montreal Streetcars- Vol.2. People and Places, Montreal and Southern Counties Railway Co., The Ottawa Streetcar Company, Hamilton's Other Railway.

Canadian Aeronautics & Space Institute (CASI) / Institut aéronautique et spatial du Canada
#104, 350 Terry Fox Dr., Ottawa ON K2K 2W5 Canada
Tel: 613-591-8787; *Fax:* 613-591-7291
casi@casi.ca; membership@casi.ca
www.casi.ca
Previous Name: Canadian Aeronautical Institute (CAI)
Merged from: Institute of Aircraft Technicians; Ottawa Aeronautical Society; US Institute of Aeronautical Science
Overview: A medium-sized national licensing organization founded in 1954
Membership: 1,600; *Fees:* $36.75 juniors; $63 seniors; $94.50 associates & individuals
Activities: Facilitating communications among the Canadian aeronautics & space community; Developing members' skills
Description: To advance the art, science, engineering, & applications of aeronautics & associated technologies in Canada; to promote Canadian competence & international competitiveness
Affiliation(s): Canadian Air Cushion Technology Society; Canadian Navigation Society; Canadian Remote Sensing Society

Canadian Airports Council (CAC) / Conseil des aéroports du Canada
#706, 350 Sparks St., Ottawa ON K1R 7S8
Tel: 613-560-9302; *Fax:* 613-560-6599
sharon.redden@cacairports.ca
www.cacairports.ca
Overview: A medium-sized national organization founded in 1991
Finances: *Funding Sources:* Sponsorships
Membership: 48; *Member Profile:* Canadian airports (CAC members are also members of Airports Council International - North America)
Activities: Preparing submissions to governmental bodies & agencies
Description: To act as the voice for Canadian airports on a great range of important issues
Member of: Airports Council International - North America (ACI-NA)
Affiliation(s): Air Transport Association of Canada (ATAC); Canadian International Freight Forwarders Association (CIFFA); Canadian Chamber of Commerce; Canadian Tourism Commission; Tourism Industry Association of Canada (TIAC)

Canadian Association of Movers (CAM) / Association canadienne des déménageurs (ACD)
#404, 2200 Sherobee Rd., Mississauga ON L5A 3Y3 Canada
Tel: 905-848-6579; *Fax:* 905-848-8499
Toll-Free: 866-860-0065
admin@mover.net
www.mover.net
Overview: A small national organization
Membership: 100-499
Activities: Government & political affairs; membership development; volunteer participation & recognition; van lines; public affairs & publications; research & development; education & training; professional ethics & standards; organizational competency
Description: To further the interests of the owner-managed moving & storage companies by providing for its members leadership, motivation, research, education, programs of mutual benefit, consultation & technical advice
Affiliation(s): American Moving & Storage Association

Canadian Association of Railway Suppliers / Association canadienne des fournisseurs de chemins de fer
#901, 99 Bank St., Ottawa ON K1P 6B9 Canada
Tel: 613-237-3888; *Fax:* 613-237-4888
info@railwaysuppliers.ca
www.railwaysuppliers.ca
Previous Name: Canadian Railway & Transit Manufacturers Association
Overview: A medium-sized national organization
Membership: 18 organizations; *Fees:* Schedule

Canadian Automobile Association (CAA) / Association canadienne des automobilistes
National Office, #200, 1145 Hunt Club Rd., Ottawa ON K1V 0Y3 Canada
Tel: 613-247-0117; *Fax:* 613-247-0118
info@national.caa.ca
www.caa.ca
Overview: A large national organization founded in 1913
Finances: *Funding Sources:* Membership dues
Staff: 25 staff member(s)
Membership: 5+million; *Member Profile:* CAA British Columbia; Alberta Motor Association; CAA Saskatchewan; CAA Manitoba; CAA Mid-Western Ontario; CAA South Central Ontario; CAA Niagara; CAA Central Ontario; CAA North & East Ontario; CAA Québec; CAA Maritimes
Activities: *Speaker Service:* Yes *Library:* Yes
Description: To promote, develop & implement programs & information relating to the rights, responsibilities & needs of the motorist as a consumer
Affiliation(s): Alliance internationale de tourisme; Fédération internationale de l'automobile; Federacion interamericana de touring y automovil-clubes; Commonwealth Motoring Conference; American Automobile Association

Canadian Aviation Historical Society (CAHS)
PO Box 2700, Stn. D, 156 St. Pierre Rd., Ottawa ON K1P 5W7 Canada
www.cahs.com
Overview: A small national charitable organization founded in 1962
Finances: *Funding Sources:* Donations
Fees: CAD$40 Canadian members; $50 USA; $60 overseas; *Member Profile:* Individuals with an interest in the history of aviation
Activities: Supporting research in Canadian aeronautical history
Description: The Society collects & disseminates information about Canada's aviation heritage. It aims to foster public interest in the field. It is a registered charity, BN: 118829589RR0001.

Canadian Aviation Maintenance Council (CAMC) / Conseil canadien de l'entretien des aéronefs (CCEA)
#155, 955 Green Valley Cres., Ottawa ON K2C 3V4 Canada
Tel: 613-727-8272; *Fax:* 613-727-7018
Toll-Free: 800-448-9715
secretariat@camc.ca
www.camc.ca
Overview: A medium-sized national organization founded in 1992
Finances: *Annual Operating Budget:* $250,000-$500,000; *Funding Sources:* Aviation maintenance industry; Human Resources Development Canada; federal government
Staff: 5 staff member(s)
Membership: 1,000-4,999; *Fees:* Initial: $84/2 yrs; Renewal $59.50/2 yrs; Certified $89.49/2 yrs
Activities: *Internships:* Yes
Description: To develop occupational training standards & facilitate the implementation of a human resources strategy for the Canadian Aviation Maintenance Industry.

Canadian Bus Association (CBA) / Association canadienne de l'autobus
c/o #2001, 45 O'Connor St., Ottawa ON K1P 1A4 Canada
Tel: 613-238-1800; *Fax:* 613-241-4936
mresnick@rothwellgroup.ca
Previous Name: Canadian Motor Coach Association
Overview: A medium-sized national organization founded in 1936
Membership: 100 companies
Description: To act as the national voice of the Canadian bus industry; to act as a national forum for the discussion of bus-related issues & the establishment of positions in relation to industry-wide areas of concern; to function as a technical & operational information gathering & exchange mechanism; to further the objectives of safety, convenience & quality of the motor coach industry.

Canadian Business Aviation Association (CBAA) / Association canadienne de l'aviation d'affaires (ACAA)
#430, 55 Metcalfe St., Ottawa ON K1P 6L5 Canada
Tel: 613-236-5611; *Fax:* 613-236-2361
info@cbaa.ca
www.cbaa.ca
Previous Name: Canadian Business Aircraft Association Inc.
Overview: A medium-sized national organization founded in 1962
Finances: *Annual Operating Budget:* $500,000-$1.5 Million; *Funding Sources:* Membership dues; convention/tradeshow
Staff: 9 staff member(s)
Membership: 150 business + 5 commercial + 108 associate + 12 affiliate + 9 affiliated organizations; *Member Profile:* Business: owns or operates a Canadian privately or state registered aircraft as an aid to conduct its business; Commercial: owns or operates Canadian commercially registered aircraft; Associate: businesses primarily concerned with aviation activities, including the manufacture of aircraft; Affiliate: owns or operates aircraft exclusively registered in a nation other than Canada
Activities: Leadership; excellence; collaboration; ethics
Description: CBAA acts as a collective voice for the business aviation community in Canada, assisting its members in all aviation related matters, & promoting the Canadian business community globally.
Affiliation(s): National Business Aviation Association; International Business Aviation Council; European Business Aircraft Association

Canadian Council of Motor Transport Administrators (CCMTA) / Conseil canadien des administrateurs en transport motorisé (CCATM)
2323 St. Laurent Blvd., Ottawa ON K1G 4J8 Canada
Tel: 613-736-1003; *Fax:* 613-736-1395
ccmta-secretariat@ccmta.ca
www.ccmta.ca
Overview: A medium-sized national charitable organization founded in 1940
Finances: *Funding Sources:* Member assessments; special projects; membership fees
Membership: 100-499; *Member Profile:* Members include representatives of provincial, territorial, & federal governments, & associate members from transportation related organizations.; *Committees:* Drivers & Vehicles; Compliance & Regulatory Affairs; Road Safety Research & Policies
Activities: Developing strategies & programs; Managing a communications network, called the Interprovincial Record Exchange system; *Rents Mailing List:* Yes
Description: CCMTA coordinates operational matters dealing with the administration, regulation, & control of motor vehicle transportation & highway safety.

Canadian Federation of AME Associations (CFAMEA)
837 Charlotte St., Fredericton NB E3B 1M7 Canada
Tel: 506-452-1809; *Fax:* 506-452-8251
www.cfamea.com
Also Known As: Aircraft Maintenance Engineers Association
Overview: A medium-sized national organization
Finances: *Annual Operating Budget:* Less than $50,000; *Funding Sources:* Membership dues
Staff: 6 volunteer(s)
Membership: 1,000-4,999
Activities: Liaison with government concerning aircraft maintenance & AME licensing

Canadian Ferry Operators Association (CFOA) / Association canadienne des opérateurs de traversiers
c/o Anthonie A. de Hoog, CFOA Executive Director, 21 Meredith Dr., Sussex Corner NB E4E 2T8 Canada
Tel: 506-433-4810; *Fax:* 506-432-9505
adehoog@cfoa.ca
www.cfoa.ca
Overview: A small national organization founded in 1987
Finances: *Funding Sources:* Sponsorships
Membership: 37; *Member Profile:* Major ferry owners & operators in Canada
Activities: Providing opportunities for discussion of matters of interest to members; Promoting the safety, reliability, & efficiency of Canadian ferry operators; Providing representation at regulatory forums such as CMAC
Description: To establish & maintain a standard of professional & technical excellence in the operation of Canadian ferries; to promote & protect the interests of members of the association

Canadian Flight Instructors Association
579 Kingston Rd., Ajax ON L1S 6M1 Canada
Tel: 905-683-8986; *Fax:* 905-683-6977
bill@jsdavidson.ca
Overview: A small national organization

Canadian Heartland Training Railway
PO Box 1174, Camrose AB T4V 1X2 Canada
Tel: 780-679-4008; *Fax:* 780-672-4032
www.chtr.ca
Overview: A small national organization
Description: To support the practical training needs of the railway industry in Canada & around the world
Member of: Railway Association of Canada; Railway Suppliers Association of Canada

Canadian Industrial Transportation Association (CITA) / Association canadienne de transport industriel (ACTI)
#405, 580 Terry Fox Dr., Ottawa ON K2L 4C2 Canada
Tel: 613-599-3283; *Fax:* 613-599-1295
info@cita-acti.ca
www.cita-acti.ca
Overview: A medium-sized national organization
Finances: *Annual Operating Budget:* $250,000-$500,000; *Funding Sources:* Membership dues
Staff: 3 staff member(s)
Membership: 400 major shippers
Activities: Advocacy; education; *Speaker Service:* Yes *Library:* Library (Open to Public)
Description: CITA-ACTI actively promotes a competitive and cost effective North American transportation system serving Canada and its NAFTA allies. Their vision is to be recognized as the "National Voice" of industrial transportation in Canada through increased membership and member representation in all regions of the county.

Canadian Institute of Traffic & Transportation (CITT) / Institut canadien du trafic et du transport
#400, 10 King St. East, Toronto ON M5C 1C3 Canada
Tel: 416-363-5696; *Fax:* 416-363-5698
info@citt.ca
www.citt.ca
Social Media:
www.facebook.com/group.php?gid=148552441716
Overview: A medium-sized national organization founded in 1958
Membership: 2,000; *Fees:* $275; *Member Profile:* Members must complete course of study to hold the designation, CITT
Activities: Offers the CITT Diploma Program
Description: Designation granting body in logistics management.

Canadian International Freight Forwarders Association, Inc. (CIFFA) / Association des transitaires internationaux canadiens, inc. (ATIC)
#480, 170 Attwell Dr., Toronto ON M9W 5Z5 Canada
Tel: 416-234-5100; *Fax:* 416-234-5152
Toll-Free: 866-282-4332
ciffa@ciffa.com
www.ciffa.com
Overview: A large international organization founded in 1948
Finances: *Annual Operating Budget:* $500,000-$1.5 Million; *Funding Sources:* Membership dues; education fees
Staff: 5 staff member(s); 20 volunteer(s)
Membership: 188 regular + 94 associate; *Fees:* Schedule; *Committees:* AGM; Bylaws; Counsel; Education; Electronic Data Interchange; Ethics/Standards; FIATA; Judicial; Logistics Institute; Membership; Public Relations; Road & Rail; Sea Freight; Ways & Means
Activities: CIFFA Professional Training Program; education courses; dangerous goods courses, topical workshops
Description: To represent & support members of the Canadian international freight forwarding industry in providing the highest level of quality & professional services to their clients.
Member of: Federation internationale des associations de transitaires et assimiles
Affiliation(s): International Federation of Freight Forwarders Associations

Canadian Marine Pilots' Association (CMPA) / Association des pilotes de la marine canadienne
#1302, 155 Queen St., Ottawa ON K1P 6L1
Tel: 613-232-7777; *Fax:* 613-232-7667
cmpa@tnpa.ca
www.marinepilots.ca
Overview: A small national organization founded in 1966
Membership: 400; *Member Profile:* Marine pilots in Canada
Activities: Upholding a Code of Conduct for Canadian pilots; Contributing to matters of safety & regulatory issues; Collaborating with marine stakeholders to maintain a vibrant marine sector
Description: To represent Canadian marine pilots; To raise awareness of marine pilots' role to protect public safety; To ensure a healthy Canadian marine sector

Member of: International Maritime Pilots' Association; Canadian Merchant Service Guild
Affiliation(s): International Maritime Organization

Canadian National Railways Police Association (Ind.) (CNRPA) / Association des policiers des chemins de fer nationaux du Canada (ind.)
6479 Miller's Grove, Mississauga ON L5N 3E5 Canada
Tel: 905-824-0856; *Fax:* 905-824-4584
fjmorgan@ica.net
www.cnrpa.ca
Also Known As: CNR Police Association
Overview: A small national organization founded in 1923
Membership: 159 + 7 locals

Canadian Northern Society (CNoS)
PO Box 1174, Camrose AB T4V 1X2 Canada
Tel: 780-672-3099
canadiannorthern@telus.net
www.canadiannorthern.ca
Overview: A small local charitable organization founded in 1987
Finances: *Funding Sources:* Donations
Fees: $20 full members; $10 associate; *Committees:* Camrose Railway Station Park & Morgan Railway Garden; Meeting Creek Grain Elevator & Railway Station Heritage Site; Big Valley Railway Station & Roundhouse Interpretive Park; Fundraising; Canora Chronicle; Finance & Audit
Description: To preserve prairie heritage

Canadian Owners & Pilots Association (COPA)
#207, 75 Albert St., Ottawa ON K1P 5E7 Canada
Tel: 613-236-4901; *Fax:* 613-236-8646
copa@copanational.org
www.copanational.org
Overview: A medium-sized national charitable organization founded in 1954
Finances: *Annual Operating Budget:* $500,000-$1.5 Million; *Funding Sources:* Membership dues; advertising
Staff: 9 staff member(s); 20 volunteer(s)
Membership: 17,000; *Fees:* $50 individual; $250 corporate; *Member Profile:* Pilots & aircraft owners; corporate members; *Committees:* Air Navigation Services National Advisory Group; Canadian Aviation Regulation Advisory Committee
Activities: COPA Flight Chapters located across Canada; *Library:* Library (Open to Public)
Description: The recognized voice of general aviation in Canada

Canadian Parking Association (CPA)
#350, 2255 St. Laurent Blvd., Ottawa ON K1G 4K3 Canada
Tel: 613-727-0700; *Fax:* 613-727-3183
info@canadianparking.ca
www.canadianparking.ca
Also Known As: Association canadienne du stationnement
Overview: A medium-sized national organization founded in 1983
Membership: 320; *Fees:* $475 full
Description: The Association is the national organization that represents the parking industry & provides a dynamic forum for learning & sharing to enhance member's ability to serve the public & improve the economic vitality of communities.

Canadian Ports Clearance Association
#500, 101 Syndicate Ave. North, Thunder Bay ON P7C 3V4 Canada
Tel: 807-623-8491; *Fax:* 807-623-2676
Previous Name: British Columbia Grain Shippers Clearance Association; Lake Shippers Clearance Association
Overview: A small national organization
Description: Shipping agent

Canadian Professional Logistics Institute / Institut canadien des professionnels de la logistique
#200, 160 John St., Toronto ON M5V 2E5 Canada
Tel: 416-363-3005; *Fax:* 416-363-5598
Toll-Free: 877-363-3005
loginfo@loginstitute.ca
www.loginstitute.ca
Also Known As: The Logistics Institute
Previous Name: Professional Logistics Institute of Canada
Overview: A medium-sized national organization founded in 1990
Finances: *Annual Operating Budget:* $500,000-$1.5 Million; *Funding Sources:* Membership dues; training tuition
Staff: 4 staff member(s); 5 volunteer(s)
Membership: 1,400 professional + 60 institutional + 50 associate; *Fees:* $395 professional; $99 associate; $875 corporate; *Member Profile:* Members must meet a professional standard developed & maintained by the Institute; *Committees:* Administration; Admissions; Legal; Marketing; Policy Development; Professional Development; R & D; Rules
Activities: *Internships:* Yes; *Speaker Service:* Yes
Description: To establish professional standards, certification & a program of professional development for the Logistics community.
Affiliation(s): Canadian Institute of Traffic & Transportation; Canadian International Freight Forwarders Association

Canadian Railroad Historical Association (CRHA) / Association canadienne d'histoire ferroviaire
110, rue St-Pierre, Saint-Constant QC J5A 1G7 Canada
Tel: 450-632-2410; *Fax:* 450-638-1563
info@exporail.org
www.exporail.org
Overview: A medium-sized national charitable organization founded in 1932
Membership: 1,100; *Fees:* $36
Activities: *Library:* Library/Archives (Open to Public) by appointment
Description: To collect, preserve & disseminate information/items relating to the history of railways in Canada

Canadian Seaplane Pilots Association (CSPA)
#1001, 75 Albert St., Ottawa ON K1P 5E7 Canada
Tel: 613-236-4901; *Fax:* 613-236-8646
Overview: A medium-sized national organization
Finances: *Annual Operating Budget:* $50,000-$100,000
Staff: 2 staff member(s); 10 volunteer(s)
Membership: 400; *Fees:* US$28
Activities: Fly-ins; safety seminars
Description: To maintain communications among seaplane pilots; to represent them at all levels of government; to help develop regulations conducive to safe & pleasurable flying; to prepare & disseminate educational material; to advance among its members information & knowledge of seaplane flying.
Affiliation(s): Seaplane Pilots Association International

Canadian Shipowners Association (CSA) / Association des armateurs canadiens (AAC)
#705, 350 Sparks St., Ottawa ON K1R 7S8 Canada
Tel: 613-232-3539; *Fax:* 613-232-6211
csa@shipowners.ca
www.shipowners.ca
Previous Name: Dominion Marine Association
Overview: A medium-sized national organization founded in 1903
Membership: 8 corporate
Activities: Monitors Canadian & US government legislative/regulatory actions, initiatives by various international marine organizations, political trends, public policy relating to navigation, safety & the Canadian shipping environment; executes strategic communications & public relations campaigns to effectively represent the interests of member companies
Description: To promote an economic & competitive Canadian marine transportation industry; to support a national policy conducive to the development & maintenance of the Canadian flag merchant fleet in the inland, coastal & Arctic waters of Canada & foster the growth of a Canadian flag deep sea merchant fleet.
Member of: International Chamber of Shipping; International Shipping Federation; Chamber of Maritime Commerce; Canada Maritime Law Association

Canadian Transport Lawyers Association
c/o S.S.T. Thibault, Heenan Blaikie LLP, #600, 900, rue René-Lévesque ouest, Québec QC G1R 2B5 Canada
www.ctla.ca
Overview: A small national organization
Fees: $100 - $195; *Member Profile:* Lawyers engaged in transportation law, regulatory policy, procedure, & related legal interests

Canadian Transport Workers Union (Ind.) (CTWU) / Syndicat canadien des travailleurs du transport (ind.)
c/o Local #213, 73 Misty St., Kitchener ON N2B 3V6 Canada
Tel: 519-896-2671
Overview: A small national organization
Membership: 90 + 2 locals

Canadian Transportation Equipment Association (CTEA) / Association d'équipement de transport du canada (AETC)
#3B, 16 Barrie Blvd., St Thomas ON N5P 4B9 Canada
Tel: 519-631-0414; *Fax:* 519-631-1333
transportation@ctea.on.ca
www.ctea.ca
Overview: A medium-sized national organization founded in 1963
Membership: 544; *Member Profile:* Commercial vehicle & component manufacturers; Dealers & distributors; Service providers
Activities: Lobbying; Providing access to technical & regulatory information; Offering networking opportunities; Encouraging research
Description: To promote excellence in commercial vehicle manufacturing; to develop standard practices

Canadian Transportation Research Forum (CTRF) / Groupe de recherches sur les transports au Canada
PO Box 23033, Woodstock ON N4T 1R0 Canada
Tel: 519-421-9701; *Fax:* 519-421-9319
feedback@ctrf.ca, cawoudsma@ctrf.ca
www.ctrf.ca
Overview: A medium-sized national charitable organization founded in 1967
Finances: *Annual Operating Budget:* Less than $50,000
Staff: 21 volunteer(s)
Membership: 320; *Fees:* $129; *Member Profile:* Open to anyone interested in any aspect of transportation; membership is individual rather than corporate; present membership is drawn from carriers, shippers, consultants & suppliers in the commercial sector, the policy, regulatory, planning & research environments at all levels of government, students & professors at universitites & community colleges
Description: To promote the development of research in transportation & related fields; to publish research papers through media & through national & regional forum meetings.

Canadian Trucking Alliance (CTA) / L'Alliance canadienne du camionnage (ACC)
324 Somerset St. West, Ottawa ON K2P 0J9 Canada
Tel: 613-236-9426; *Fax:* 866-823-4076
info@cantruck.ca
www.cantruck.com
Overview: A medium-sized national organization founded in 1937
Member Profile: Motor carriers & associated trades
Activities: *Speaker Service:* Yes
Description: To promote business excellence in trucking; to participate in the development of public policy which supports the economic growth, safety & prosperity of the industry; to provide services, including research, development, products & information to meet the needs of the industry. PUBLICATIONS: Dangerous Goods: A Trucker's Guide; Crossing International Borders:A Trucker's Guide; National Safety Code: A Trucker's Guide.

Canadian Trucking Human Resources Council (CTHRC) / Conseil canadien des ressources humaines en camionnage
#203, 720 Belfast Rd., Ottawa ON K1G 0Z5 Canada
Tel: 613-244-4800; *Fax:* 613-244-4535
info@cthrc.com
www.cthrc.com
Overview: A medium-sized national organization
Activities: Conducting research; Training; Offering advice; Liaising with industry members
Description: To respond to the human resource needs of the trucking industry
Affiliation(s): CCA Truck Driver Training Ltd.; Capilano Truck Driver Training Institute; JVI Provincial Transportation & Safety Academy; Mountain Transport Institute Ltd.; Red Deer College; SK Driver Training Ltd.; Wheels On Ltd. / Training & Driver Training

Canadian Urban Transit Association (CUTA) / Association canadienne du transport urbain (ACTU)
#1401, 55 York St., Toronto ON M5J 1R7
Tel: 416-365-9800; *Fax:* 416-365-1295
transit@cutaactu.ca
www.cutaactu.ca
Overview: A large national organization founded in 1904
Membership: 503; *Member Profile:* Transit systems; Manufacturers & suppliers of transit equipment; Federal, provincial, & municipal government agencies; Consultants; Affiliated individuals & companies; *Committees:* Business Members; Communications & Public Affairs; Human Resources; Technical Services; Transit Board Members
Activities: Conducting research & preparing statistics; Providing technical & operational information; Liaising with government; Partnering with other transportation associations & community development stakeholders; Engaging in advocacy activities; Raising public awareness of transit's contributions to communities; *Library:* Canadian Urban Transit Association Library (Open to Public)
Description: To represent the public transit community throughout Canada; To strengthen the industry

Canadians for Responsible & Safe Highways (CRASH)
PO Box 1042, Stn. B, Ottawa ON K1P 5R1 Canada
Tel: 613-860-0529; *Fax:* 613-567-6204
Toll-Free: 800-530-9945

Overview: A small national organization
Description: CRASH strives to ensure that safety, environmental & economic concerns are fully considered by governments when the latter establish & administer regulations pertaining to trucking operations on public highways.

Carefree Society Transportation Service
2832 Queensway St., Prince George BC V2L 4M5 Canada
Tel: 250-562-1394; *Fax:* 250-562-1393
carefree_society@telus.net
Also Known As: Carefree Society
Overview: A small local charitable organization founded in 1971
Finances: *Annual Operating Budget:* $250,000-$500,000; *Funding Sources:* Provincial government; regional government
Staff: 12 staff member(s); 10 volunteer(s)
Membership: 15; *Fees:* $6; *Committees:* Accessible Transportation Awareness
Description: To provide transportation services for the disabled in our community
Affiliation(s): BC Transit

Central British Columbia Railway & Forest Industry Museum Society
850 River Rd., Prince George BC V2L 5S8 Canada
Tel: 250-563-7351; *Fax:* 250-563-3697
trains@pgrfm.bc.ca
www.pgrfm.bc.ca
Also Known As: Railway & Forestry Museum
Overview: A small local charitable organization founded in 1983
Finances: *Annual Operating Budget:* $50,000-$100,000
Staff: 6 staff member(s); 15 volunteer(s)
Membership: 75; *Fees:* $15-$40
Activities: *Awareness Events:* Steam Day; Forester Day; Family Carnival *Library:* Canfor Library by appointment
Description: Administers Prince George Railway & Forest Industry Museum
Member of: Canadian Railway Historical Association; Canadian Museum Association; British Columbia Museum Association; American Railway Museum Association

Chamber of Maritime Commerce (CMC) / Chambre du commerce maritime (CCM)
#700, 350 Sparks St., Ottawa ON K1R 7S8 Canada
Tel: 613-233-8779; *Fax:* 613-233-3743
email@cmc-ccm.com
www.cmc-ccm.com
Previous Name: Great Lakes Waterways Development Association
Overview: A large national organization founded in 1959
Finances: *Annual Operating Budget:* $250,000-$500,000; *Funding Sources:* Membership dues
Staff: 4 staff member(s)
Membership: 180+ institutional; *Member Profile:* Major Canadian & American shippers, ports & marine service providers, domestic & international shipowners
Activities: *Speaker Service:* Yes
Description: To bring together all sectors of the economy that rely on a cost efficient & safe marine transportation system

Chartered Institute of Logistics & Transport (CILT)
Earlstrees Court, Earlstrees Rd., Corbyn NN17 4Ax United Kingdom
enquiry@ciltuk.org.uk
www.cilt-international.com
Previous Name: Chartered Institute of Transport
Overview: A medium-sized international charitable organization founded in 1919
Finances: *Annual Operating Budget:* Greater than $5 Million; *Funding Sources:* Membership dues
Staff: 21 staff member(s)
Membership: 23,000 in UK; 33,000 worldwide; *Fees:* Schedule; *Member Profile:* Professionals in transport & logistics; *Committees:* Membership; Education
Activities: Providing education programs, lecture meetings, & training; Presenting transport reports; *Speaker Service:* Yes *Library:* Chartered Institute of Logistics & Transport Library (Open to Public)
Description: To promote, encourage & coordinate the study & advancement of the science & art of transportation in all its branches
Affiliation(s): Integrated in UK with Institute of Logistics UK section now titled Institute of Logistics & Transport

Chartered Institute of Logistics and Transport in North America (CILT) / Institut agréé de la logistique et des transports Amérique du Nord
#900, 275 Slater St., Ottawa ON K1P 5H9 Canada
Tel: 613-688-1438; *Fax:* 613-688-0966
ghonima@ciltna.com
www.ciltna.com
Also Known As: CILT in North America
Previous Name: Chartered Institute of Transport in Canada
Overview: A medium-sized international organization founded in 1919
Finances: *Funding Sources:* Membership fees
Staff: 1 staff member(s); 15 volunteer(s)
Membership: 460; *Member Profile:* Individuals with experience, interest & education in the transportation field.; *Committees:* Regional
Description: To promote, encourage, coordinate study & advancement of science & art of transportation.
Member of: Chartered Institute of Transport

Chatham Railroad Museum Society
PO Box 434, 2 McLean St., Chatham ON N7M 5K5 Canada
Tel: 519-352-3097
Overview: A small local charitable organization founded in 1989
Membership: 1-99
Description: To present history from a retired CN baggage car

Club de trafic de Québec
CP 72, Saint-Jean-Chrysostome QC G6Z 2L3 Canada
Tél: 418-654-5446; *Téléc:* 418-619-1044
jcoulombe@videotron.ca
www.clubtraficqc.org
Aperçu: *Dimension:* moyenne; *Envergure:* provinciale; *Organisme sans but lucratif; fondée en 1960*
Finances: *Budget de fonctionnement annuel:* $100,000-$250,000
Membre: 235; *Montant de la cotisation:* 75$
Description: Regrouper les représentants oeuvrant dans le domaine du transport de la grande région de Québec

Company of Master Mariners of Canada
c/o R. Wallace, 305 Michigan St., Victoria BC V8V 1R6 Canada
www.mastermariners.ca
Overview: A medium-sized national organization founded in 1967
Finances: *Funding Sources:* Membership dues
Membership: 455; *Fees:* $70-$140; *Member Profile:* Master Mariners
Activities: *Speaker Service:* Yes
Description: The Company is a central body of command-level mariners that represents senior officers of the Canadian Merchant Service. It maintains the standard of ability & professional conduct of the officers, & also develops education, training & qualifications for young cadets. It helps liaison between Canada's commercial, governmental & military fleets.
Affiliation(s): Master Mariner organizations in the UK, USA, South Africa, Australia & NZ

Dewdney-Alouette Railway Society (DARS)
22520 - 116 Ave., Maple Ridge BC V2X 0S4 Canada
Tel: 604-463-5311; *Fax:* 604-463-5317
mrmuseum@telus.net
Overview: A small local organization founded in 1979
Finances: *Annual Operating Budget:* Less than $50,000
Staff: 25 volunteer(s)
Membership: 2 senior/lifetime + 27 individual; *Fees:* $30; *Member Profile:* 20 hour apprenticeship
Activities: Port Haney diorama; *Library:* Library
Description: The Society preserves the railway history of Maple Ridge, promotes the craft of model railroading, & offers advice to the public who are engaged in the building & operating of model railroads.
Affiliation(s): National Model Railway Association; Pacific Northwest Region 7th Division Society; BC Heritage Society; Maple Ridge Historical Society; Maple Ridge Museum

Edmonton Radial Railway Society (ERRS)
PO Box 76057, Stn. Southgate, Edmonton AB T6H 5Y7 Canada
Tel: 780-437-7721; *Fax:* 780-437-3095
info@edmonton-radial-railway.ab.ca
www.edmonton-radial-railway.ab.ca
Overview: A small national charitable organization founded in 1980
Finances: *Annual Operating Budget:* $50,000-$100,000; *Funding Sources:* Municipal, provincial & federal governments; donations
Staff: 100 volunteer(s)
Membership: 100; *Fees:* $20
Activities: Operating 2 historic street railway lines within Edmonton from May to Oct.; streetcar museum; streetcar chartering service; *Library:* Library
Description: The Society collects, preserves & restores vintage streetcars, primarily those from 1908-1951.
Member of: Canadian Museum Association
Affiliation(s): Association of Railway Museums; Alberta Museums Association

Electric Vehicle Council of Ottawa Inc. (EVCO)
PO Box 4044, Stn. E, Ottawa ON K1S 5B1 Canada
info@evco.ca
www.evco.ca
Overview: A small local organization founded in 1980
Finances: *Annual Operating Budget:* Less than $50,000; *Funding Sources:* Memberships
Membership: 80; *Fees:* $5 student; $25 electronic; $30 paper
Description: To provide information about electric road vehicles, in Canada & worldwide

Electric Vehicle Society of Canada (EVS)
21 Burritt Rd., Toronto ON M1R 3S5
Tel: 416-755-4324; *Fax:* 416-755-4324
info@evsociety.ca
www.evsociety.ca
Overview: A medium-sized national organization founded in 1991
Fees: $20 students, spouses, & seniors; $30 adults; $50 families; $100 corporations; *Member Profile:* Engineers; Environmentalists; Enthusiasts for electric energy for propulsion
Activities: Providing a forum for member discussions; Examining modes of electric transportation
Description: To investigate & promote clean transportation technologies

Freight Carriers Association of Canada (FCA)
#3-4, 427 Garrison Rd., Fort Erie ON L2A 6E6 Canada
Tel: 905-994-0560; *Fax:* 905-994-0117
Toll-Free: 800-559-7421
info@fca-natc.org
www.fca-natc.org
Previous Name: Canadian Transport Tariff Bureau Association
Overview: A medium-sized national organization founded in 1939
Finances: *Annual Operating Budget:* $1.5 Million-$3 Million; *Funding Sources:* Membership fees; sales of publications & software
Staff: 17 staff member(s)
Membership: 100; *Fees:* Based on revenues; *Member Profile:* For-hire motor carriers; *Committees:* Tariff Advisory; Québec Comité Consultatif
Activities: Carrier meetings; seminars; research; info gathering & dissemination; *Speaker Service:* Yes
Description: To provide quality information, products & services to users, providers & third parties involved in motor carrier transportation. PUBLICATIONS: Fuel Price and Surcharge Information Bulletin (weekly); Currency Exchange Bulletin (2X/month -14th and last day of the month).
Affiliation(s): North American Transportation Council

Hope Air / Vols d'espoir
Procter & Gamble Bldg., #703, 4711 Yonge St., Toronto ON M2N 6K8 Canada
Tel: 416-222-6335; *Fax:* 416-222-6930
Toll-Free: 877-346-4673
mail@hopeair.org
www.hopeair.org
Previous Name: Mission Air Transportation Network
Overview: A small national charitable organization founded in 1985
Finances: *Annual Operating Budget:* $250,000-$500,000; *Funding Sources:* Corporate; private donations; government
Staff: 4 staff member(s); 30 volunteer(s)
Membership: 1-99; *Committees:* Air Coordination; Funding; Finance; Office Administrations; Planning; Public Relations
Description: To provide free air transportation to Canadians in financial need who must travel between their own communities & recognized facilities for medical care

Huntsville & Lake of Bays Railway Society
26 Centre St. North, Huntsville ON P1H 1X4 Canada
Tel: 705-635-2227; *Fax:* 705-635-2227
nicholls@vianet.ca
www.portageflyer.org
Also Known As: The Portage Railway
Overview: A small local charitable organization founded in 1984
Finances: *Annual Operating Budget:* Less than $50,000; *Funding Sources:* Fundraising; Rotary Club; local industry; donations
Staff: 15 volunteer(s)
Membership: 145; *Fees:* $35
Activities: A fully functional operating railway
Description: Maintains & displays original artifacts of the old Huntsville & Lake of Bays Railway, plus vintage railway equipment of the turn of the century
Affiliation(s): Muskoka Heritage Place

Industrial Truck Association (ITA)
#460, 1750 K St. NW, Washington DC 20006 USA
Tel: 202-296-9880; *Fax:* 202-296-9884
www.indtrk.org

Overview: A medium-sized international organization
Finances: *Annual Operating Budget:* $1.5 Million-$3 Million
Staff: 5 staff member(s)
Membership: 100; *Fees:* Varies; *Member Profile:* Manufacturers of forklifts & suppliers
Description: Represents the manufacturers of lift trucks & their suppliers who do business in Canada, the United States or Mexico

INFORM Inc.
5 Hanover Sq., 19th Fl., New York NY 10004 USA
Tel: 212-361-2400; *Fax:* 212-361-2412
inform@informinc.org
www.informinc.org
Overview: A medium-sized international charitable organization founded in 1974
Finances: *Annual Operating Budget:* $1.5 Million-$3 Million; *Funding Sources:* Individual donors; Foundations; Government; Corporate contributions; Book sales
Staff: 25 staff member(s); 5-10 volunteer(s)
Membership: 1,000; *Fees:* $35
Activities: Researching strategies to prevent chemical hazards & to develop sustainable products & practices; *Internships:* Yes; *Speaker Service:* Yes
Description: To examine the effects of business practices on the environment & human health
Member of: Earthshare

Intermodal Association of North America (IANA)
#1100, 11785 Beltsville Dr., Calverton MD 20705 USA
Tel: 301-982-3400; *Fax:* 301-982-4815
iana@intermodal.org
www.intermodal.org
Overview: A medium-sized international organization founded in 1991
Finances: *Annual Operating Budget:* $3 Million-$5 Million
Staff: 21 staff member(s)
Membership: 700; *Committees:* Conference Planning; Education & Training; Electronic Business Solutions; Maintenance & Repair, Operations & P.R.
Description: IANA is the leading industry trade association representing the combined interests of intermodal freight transportation companies & their suppliers

International Air Transport Association / Association du transport aérien international
PO Box 113, 800, Place Victoria, Montréal QC H4Z 1M1 Canada
Tel: 514-874-0202; *Fax:* 514-874-9632
www.iata.org
Overview: A small international organization founded in 1945
Description: To promote safe, regular & economical air transport for the benefit of the peoples of the world; to foster air commerce; to study the problems connected with air transport; to provide a means for collaboration among the air transport enterprises engaged directly or indirectly in international air transport service; to cooperate with the International Civil Aviation Organization & other international organizations; to furnish for governments a forum for developing industry working standards &, as appropriate, coordinating international fares & rates; to simplify the travelling process for the general public
Affiliation(s): International Civil Aviation Organization

International Association of Ports & Harbours (IAPH)
7F South Tower, New Pier Takeshiba, 1-16-1 Kaigan, Minato-Ku, Tokyo 105-0022 Japan
info@iaphworldports.org
www.iaphworldports.org
Overview: A large international organization founded in 1955
Finances: *Annual Operating Budget:* $1.5 Million-$3 Million; *Funding Sources:* Membership fees
Staff: 7 staff member(s)
Membership: 360; *Fees:* Schedule; *Member Profile:* 90 maritime countries are represented; *Committees:* Finance, Constitution & By-Laws; Long Range Planning/Review; Port Safety, Environment & Marine Operations; Dredging Task Force; Legal Protection; Trade Facilitation; Cargo Operations; Ship Trends; Combined Transport & Distribution; Port Planning & Construction; Trade Policy; Membership; Communication & Networking; Human Resources Development
Activities: *Library:* Library (Open to Public)
Description: To promote the development of the international port & maritime industry by fostering cooperation among members in order to build a more cohesive partnership among the world's ports & harbors, thereby promoting peace in the world & the welfare of mankind; to ensure that the industry's interests & views are represented before international organizations involved n the regulation of international trade & transportation & incorporated in the regulatory initiatives of these organizations; & to collect, analyse, exchange & distribute information on developing trends in international trade, transportation, ports & the regulations of these industries
Affiliation(s): International Maritime Organization; United Nations Conference on Trade & Development; United Nations Economic & Social Council; Permanent International Association of Navigation Congresses; International Cargo Handling Coordination Association; International Maritime Pilots Association; International Association of Independent Tanker Owners; Baltic & International Martime Council

International Industry Working Group (IIWG)
International Air Transport Association, PO Box 113, 800, Place Victoria, Montréal QC H4Z 1M1 Canada
Tel: 514-874-0202; *Fax:* 514-874-9632
obrienm@iata.org
www.iata.org
Overview: A small international organization founded in 1970
Membership: 50; *Member Profile:* Aircraft & aeroengine manufacturers; airlines & airport authorities
Description: To promote & develop an open exchange of information to minimize interface problems through well-informed design, development & operation of both aircraft & airports; to study jointly solutions to major problems which impede the development of the air transport system

International Maritime Organization (IMO) / Organisation maritime internationale
4 Albert Embankment, London SE1 7SR United Kingdom
info@imo.org
www.imo.org
Overview: A large international organization founded in 1948
Finances: *Annual Operating Budget:* Greater than $5 Million; *Funding Sources:* Government
Staff: 300 staff member(s)
Membership: 166 governments; *Fees:* Based on shipping fleet tonnage; *Committees:* Maritime Safety; Marine Environment Protection; Legal; Technical Cooperation; Facilitation
Activities: *Library:* Library by appointment
Description: To encourage the adoption of high standards in matters concerning maritime safety, security, efficiency of navigation & control of marine pollution from ships

Locomotive & Railway Historical Society of Western Canada
#4104, 2120 Southland Dr. SW, Calgary AB T2V 4W3 Canada
Tel: 403-265-9229; *Fax:* 403-261-1057
laniganj@telus.net
Overview: A small local charitable organization founded in 1985
Finances: *Annual Operating Budget:* Less than $50,000
Staff: 9 volunteer(s)
Membership: 9
Activities: Preservation & restoration of important historic Canadian railway equipment; *Speaker Service:* Yes
Description: To promote the preservation of railway equipment integral to the history of Western Canada; to act in a consultative capacity on heritage rail projects
Member of: Canadian Council for Railway Heritage

Manitoba Trucking Association
25 Bunting St., Winnipeg MB R2X 2P5 Canada
Tel: 204-632-6600; *Fax:* 204-694-7134
info@trucking.mb.ca
www.trucking.mb.ca
Overview: A medium-sized provincial organization founded in 1932
Finances: *Funding Sources:* Membership dues & fundraising through services
Staff: 5 staff member(s)
Membership: 350 organizations; *Member Profile:* PSV Carriers; City Transportation; Private Fleet; Household Goods Carriers; Associated Trades; Vehicle Maintenance; *Committees:* Associated Trades (Members, Executive); Vehicle Maintenance Council; Maintenace Council Executive
Activities: *Library:* Library by appointment
Description: Serves the needs of the trucking industry & its interested parties by promoting a healthy business environment & advocating safety, education, & responsibility.
Affiliation(s): Canadian Trucking Alliance; Canadian Council of Motor Transport Administrators; Canadian Trucking Human Resource Council; Winnipeg Chamber of Commerce; Manitoba Chamber of Commerce; Infrastructure Council of Manitoba; Employers' Task Force on Workers' Compensation; Manitoba Employers' Council

Motorcycle & Moped Industry Council (MMIC) / Le Conseil de l'industrie de la motocyclette et du cyclomoteur (CIMC)
#201, 3000 Steeles Ave. East, Markham ON L3R 4T9 Canada
Tel: 416-491-4449; *Fax:* 416-493-1985
Toll-Free: 877-470-6642
info@mmic.ca
www.mmic.ca
Overview: A small national organization founded in 1971
Finances: *Annual Operating Budget:* $500,000-$1.5 Million
Staff: 7 staff member(s); 15 volunteer(s)
Membership: 150 corporate; 500 individual; *Fees:* Schedule
Description: The Motorcycle and Moped Industry Council (MMIC) is a national, non-profit trade association that represents the manufacturers and distributors of street legal motorcycles and related products and services in Canada.

National Association of Railroad Passengers (NARP)
#308, 900 - 2 St. NE, Washington DC 20002-3557 USA
Tel: 202-408-8362; *Fax:* 202-408-8287
narp@narprail.org
www.narprail.org
Overview: A medium-sized international charitable organization founded in 1967
Finances: *Annual Operating Budget:* $250,000-$500,000; *Funding Sources:* Membership dues
Staff: 4 staff member(s)
Membership: 23,000; *Fees:* $35 individual; $45 family; $25 senior
Activities: *Rents Mailing List:* Yes *Library:* Library (Open to Public)
Description: To encourage & promote a more balanced US transporation system including promotion of federal & state policies beneficial to all forms of rail service, urban rail transit, rural public transportation & intermodal terminals
Affiliation(s): Transport 2000 Ltd.

National Transportation Brokers Association
PO Box 238, Markham ON L3P 3J7 Canada
Tel: 416-798-7211
info@ntba-brokers.com
www.ntba-brokers.com
Overview: A medium-sized national organization
Fees: $200; *Member Profile:* Freight brokerage services providers
Description: Promotes and continually improves business relationships among shippers, carriers, government and freight brokers

New Brunswick Potato Shippers Association
8824 Route 2, Grand Falls NB E3Z 1P8 Canada
Tel: 506-473-5520; *Fax:* 506-473-6701
tatered@nbnet.nb.ca
Overview: A small provincial organization
Description: The shippers association monitors industry growth

The Ninety-Nines Inc./International Organization of Women Pilots
4300 Amelia Earhart Rd., Oklahoma City OK 73159 USA
Tel: 405-685-7969; *Fax:* 405-685-7985
Toll-Free: 800-994-1929
99s@ninety-nines.org
www.ninety-nines.org
Also Known As: 99's
Overview: A small international charitable organization founded in 1929
Finances: *Annual Operating Budget:* $250,000-$500,000
Staff: 4 staff member(s); 4 volunteer(s)
Membership: 5,400 worldwide; *Fees:* US$65 for US; US$57 Canadian; US$44 other countries; *Member Profile:* Women pilots
Activities: *Speaker Service:* Yes *Library:* 99s Museum of Women Pilots
Description: To promote world fellowship through flight; to provide networking & scholarship opportunities for women & aviation education in the community; to preserve the unique history of women in aviation

North America Railway Hall of Fame
RPO Centre, PO Box 20040, St Thomas ON N5P 4H4 Canada
Tel: 519-633-2535; *Fax:* 519-633-3087
info@narhf.org
www.narhf.org
Overview: A small national charitable organization founded in 1996
Description: To establish a tribute to those who have made significant contributions relating to the railway industry in North America; honour railway organizations, related innovations & technical accomplishments; preserve & display a collection of library materials & railway heritage artifacts related to the Hall of Fame inductees; to educate the public about the impact of railway transportation on history & the development of communities, nations & international relations

Northern Air Transport Association (NATA)
PO Box 2457, Yellowknife NT X1A 2P8 Canada
Tel: 867-920-2985; *Fax:* 867-920-2983
nata-yzf@theedge.ca
www.nata-yzf.ca
Overview: A small local organization founded in 1977
Member Profile: Northern air carriers

Activities: Advocating for Northern air transport; Establishing partnerships with governments & within the transportation industry; *Speaker Service:* Yes
Description: To promote safe & effective Northern air transportation

Northwestern Ontario Air Carriers Association (NOACA)
PO Box 4075, 143 Cedar Point Dr., Sioux Lookout ON P8T 1J9 Canada
Tel: 807-737-7470; *Fax:* 807-583-2812
Overview: A small local organization

Ontario Community Transit Association (OCTA)
#306, 4141 Yonge St., Toronto ON M2P 2A8
Tel: 416-229-6222; *Fax:* 416-229-6281
www.octa.on.ca
Previous Name: Ontario Urban Transit Association
Overview: A medium-sized provincial organization founded in 1997
Fees: Annual fees for transportation service providers & suppliers based on transportation operating budget or net sales; $160 non-profit organizations; *Member Profile:* Representatives of public transit systems; Health & social service agency transportation providers; Government representatives; Suppliers to the industry; Consultants
Activities: Engaging in advocacy activities; Sharing information
Description: To strengthen & improve public transit services in Ontario; To ensure excellence & sustainability in public transit

Ontario Good Roads Association (OGRA)
#2, 6355 Kennedy Rd., Mississauga ON L5T 2L5
Tel: 905-795-2555; *Fax:* 905-795-2660
info@ogra.org
www.ogra.org
Social Media: www.twitter.com/Ont_Good_Roads
Overview: A medium-sized provincial organization founded in 1894
Finances: *Funding Sources:* Membership fees; Sponsorships
Membership: 400+ municipalities; *Member Profile:* Ontario municipalities; First Nations communities; Corporations; Life & honourary members; *Committees:* Executive; Policy; Member Services; Nominating; Combined Conference; Companions Program
Activities: Advocating for the collective interests of municipal transportation & works departments; Analyzing policies; Reviewing legislation; Consulting with stakeholders & partners; Offering education & training opportunities
Description: To represent the transportation & public works-related interests of Ontario's municipalities & First Nation communities; To deliver programs & services that meet the needs of members; To support municipalities in the provision of effective & efficient transportation systems throughout Ontario

Ontario Milk Transport Association (OMTA)
#301, 660 Speedvale Ave. West, Guelph ON N1K 1E5 Canada
Overview: A medium-sized provincial organization founded in 1967
Membership: 60 companies; *Member Profile:* Transporters of milk, such as producer-owned co-operatives, which collect raw milk from Ontario farms & take it to processing plants in Ontario, Quebec, & Manitoba

Ontario Traffic Conference (OTC)
#2, 6355 Kennedy Rd., Mississauga ON L5T 2L5 Canada
Tel: 647-346-4050; *Fax:* 647-346-4060
info@otc.org
www.otc.org
Social Media: twitter.com/ontariotraffic
Overview: A medium-sized provincial organization
Description: To improve traffic conditions & traffic safety in municipalities of Ontario

Ontario Trucking Association (OTA)
555 Dixon Rd., Toronto ON M9W 1H8 Canada
Tel: 416-249-7401; *Fax:* 416-245-6152
info@ontruck.org
www.ontruck.org
Overview: A large provincial organization founded in 1926
Finances: *Funding Sources:* Membership fees
Membership: 1,700 member companies; *Committees:* Axle Weight; Credit; Education; Executive; Social/Labour; Tech./Ops; Convention; Dues; Membership; Insurance; Finance; Environmental Issues
Activities: Drug Testing Consortium; training courses & seminars; Trucking Industry Compensation & Benefits Report; *Speaker Service:* Yes *Library:* Library
Description: Canada's largest trade association representing companies & industry suppliers; provides political advocacy, education & information services to North American freight transport companies with operations in Ontario.

Ontario Trucking Association Education Foundation Inc.
555 Dixon Rd., Toronto ON M9W 1H8 Canada
Tel: 416-249-7401; *Fax:* 416-245-6152
education.foundation@ontruck.org
Overview: A small provincial charitable organization
Finances: *Annual Operating Budget:* Less than $50,000
Staff: 1 staff member(s); 5 volunteer(s)
Membership: 18

Operation Lifesaver (OL) / Opération Gareautrain
#1401, 99 Bank St., Ottawa ON K1P 6B9 Canada
Tel: 613-564-8100; *Fax:* 613-567-6726
admin@operationlifesaver.ca
www.operationlifesaver.ca
Overview: A small national organization founded in 1981
Finances: *Annual Operating Budget:* $250,000-$500,000; *Funding Sources:* Transport Canada; Railway Association of Canada
Staff: 2 staff member(s); 150 volunteer(s)
Activities: *Awareness Events:* OL Rail Safety Week, April
Description: To create an awareness by the general public of the potential hazards of rail/highway crossings; to improve drivers' & pedestrians' behaviour at these intersections; to inform the public of the dangers associated with trespassing on railway property; & to reduce the number of accidents resulting in fatalities, injuries & monetary losses

Pharmaceutical & Personal Care Logistics Association (PPCLA) / Association de logistique des soins personnels et pharmaceutiques
PO Box 40598, Stn. Six Points Plaza, Toronto ON M9B 6K8 Canada
Tel: 416-232-6817; *Fax:* 416-232-6818
Toll-Free: 866-293-1238
ppcla@ppcla.org
www.ppcla.org
Previous Name: Pharmaceutical & Toilet Preparations Traffic Association
Overview: A medium-sized national organization founded in 1958
Finances: *Annual Operating Budget:* Less than $50,000
Staff: 1 volunteer(s)
Membership: 47 institutional; *Fees:* $350; *Member Profile:* Logistics managers in the pharmaceutical & personal care industries
Description: To develop & promote the interchange of ideas & information concerning traffic & transportation matters of the pharmaceutical & toilet preparations industry; to foster fair dealings & cordial relationships among members & between representatives of the various modes of transportation employed by members

Private Motor Truck Council of Canada (PMTC) / Association canadienne du camionnage d'entreprise (ACCE)
#115, 1660 North Service Rd. East, Oakville ON L6H 7G3 Canada
Tel: 905-827-0587; *Fax:* 905-827-8212
Toll-Free: 877-501-7682
info@pmtc.ca
www.pmtc.ca
Overview: A medium-sized national organization founded in 1977
Finances: *Annual Operating Budget:* $250,000-$500,000; *Funding Sources:* Seminars; social events; membership fees
Staff: 4 staff member(s)
Membership: 400; *Member Profile:* Private truck fleets or suppliers to same; private truck fleets operated by companies whose principal business is other than transportation, but use their own truck fleets to further their business
Activities: Seminars; annual conference; benchmarking and best practices survey; National Vehicle Graphics Design Competition
Description: Recognized as the leader of the private trucking community in Canada; represents the varied interests of private fleet operators with integrity & sound business practices.
Member of: North American Private Truck Council
Affiliation(s): National Private Truck Council

The Railway Association of Canada (RAC) / L'Association des chemins de fer du Canada (ACFC)
#901, 99 Bank St., Ottawa ON K1P 6B9 Canada
Tel: 613-567-8591; *Fax:* 613-567-6726
rac@railcan.ca
www.railcan.ca
Overview: A large national organization founded in 1917
Finances: *Annual Operating Budget:* Greater than $5 Million; *Funding Sources:* Members fees
Staff: 23 staff member(s)
Membership: 55 railways & 40 associates; *Fees:* $2,000 minimum; *Member Profile:* Railway companies operating in Canada; *Committees:* Policy; Accounting; Finance; Human Resources; Safety & Operations Management; Taxation
Activities: Operation Lifesaver
Description: To promote the commercial viability & the safe & efficient operation of the Canadian railway industry; to act on behalf of, or work jointly with, member companies to promote public policy & regulation that provides equitable treatment between shipping modes; to provide factual information on the railway industry for the public, government & industry, & to provide the views of the industry on public policy issues.
PUBLICATIONS: Interchange; Canadian Railway Medical Rules Handbook; Locomotive Emissions Monitoring Program 2009; Canada's Railway Lead North America.
Affiliation(s): Association of American Railroads

Recreational Aircraft Association (RAA) / Réseau aéronefs amateur
22 - 4881 Fountain St. North, Breslau ON N0B 1M0 Canada
Tel: 519-648-3030; *Toll-Free:* 800-387-1028
raa@raa.ca
www.raa.ca
Previous Name: Experimental Aircraft Association of Canada
Overview: A medium-sized national organization founded in 1983
Finances: *Annual Operating Budget:* $100,000-$250,000; *Funding Sources:* Membership dues
Staff: 1 staff member(s); 150 volunteer(s)
Membership: 2,000; *Fees:* $40; *Committees:* 12 regional
Activities: Fly-ins across Canada; *Speaker Service:* Yes
Description: To be a national leader in the development & advancement of recreational aviation; to promote recreational flying & building of amateur built aircraft, restorations of classic & antique aircraft
Affiliation(s): Recreational Aviation Foundation

Saskatchewan Trucking Association (STA)
1335 Wallace St., Regina SK S4N 3Z5 Canada
Tel: 306-569-9696; *Fax:* 306-569-1008
Toll-Free: 800-563-7623
ttoope@sasktrucking.com
www.sasktrucking.com
Overview: A medium-sized provincial licensing organization founded in 1937
Finances: *Annual Operating Budget:* $250,000-$500,000; *Funding Sources:* Membership fees; sponsorship of programs
Staff: 5 staff member(s)
Membership: 300; *Fees:* Schedule
Activities: Truck Driver Roadeos
Description: Helps the industry fight its battles in everything from deregulation to weights and measures. Represents the industry in discussions with government

The Shipping Federation of Canada / La Fédération maritime du Canada
#326, 300, rue St-Sacrement, Montréal QC H2Y 1X4 Canada
Tel: 514-849-2325; *Fax:* 514-849-8774
Toll-Free: 877-534-7367
info@shipfed.ca
www.shipfed.ca
Overview: A medium-sized national organization founded in 1903
Finances: *Funding Sources:* International shipping
Staff: 8 staff member(s)
Membership: 83; *Member Profile:* Direct involvement in steamship business; *Committees:* Customs; Dangerous Goods; EDI; Immigration; Pilotage; Railways; Tanker Safety
Activities: To protect members in all matters affecting the operation of shipping from & to Eastern Canada, the St. Lawrence River, the Great Lakes & Arctic ports; areas of concern include pilotage, pollution, navigation aids, port operations, port charges, & federal government legislation & regulation

Shipyard General Workers' Federation of British Columbia (CLC) / Fédération des ouvriers des chantiers navals de la Colombie-Britannique (CTC)
#130, 111 Victoria Dr., Vancouver BC V5L 4C4 Canada
Tel: 604-254-8204; *Fax:* 604-254-7447
office@bcshipyardworkers.com
www.bcshipyardworkers.com
Overview: A medium-sized provincial organization
Membership: 1,100 + 3 locals
Affiliation(s): Machinists, Fitters & Helpers Industrial Union #3, Marine Workers & Boilerworkers' Industrial Union #1, Shipwrights, Joiners & Caulkers' Industrial Union #9

Société des traversiers du Québec (STQ)
250, rue Saint-Paul, Québec QC G1K 9K9 Canada
Tél: 418-643-2019; *Téléc:* 418-643-7308
Ligne sans frais: 877-787-7483
stq@traversiers.gouv.qc.ca
www.traversiers.gouv.qc.ca
Aperçu: *Dimension:* petite; *Envergure: provinciale; fondée en 1971*
Finances: *Budget de fonctionnement annuel:* Plus de $5 Million
Membre: 100-499
Description: Contribuer à la mobilité des personnes et des marchandises en assurant des services de transport maritime de qualité, sécuritaires et fiables, favorisant ainsi l'essor social, économique et touristique du Québec

Sydney & Louisburg Railway Historical Society / Le Musée de chemin de fer de Sydney à Louisburg
7330 Main St., Louisbourg NS B1C 1P5 Canada
Also Known As: S&L Museum
Overview: A small local organization founded in 1973
Finances: *Annual Operating Budget:* Less than $50,000
Staff: 6 volunteer(s)
Membership: 210; *Fees:* $10
Activities: Annual reunion, Sept.; *Awareness Events:* Samuel B. Morse - Museum Day, July 1 *Library:* Resource Centre (Open to Public) by appointment
Description: To commemorate the history of the S&L Railway by preserving & displaying the artifacts & documents which survive; to commemorate the people who worked for the S&L Railway; to explain the local & commercial history of the area which relates to the S&L Railway; to explain & commemorate the general themes of railway & transportation history & technology
Member of: Federation of the Nova Scotian Heritage; Heritage Canada

Teamsters Canada Rail Conference (TCRC) / Conference ferroviaire de Teamsters Canada (CFTC)
#1710, 130 Albert St., Ottawa ON K1P 5G4 Canada
Tel: 613-235-1828; *Fax:* 613-235-1069
info@teamstersrail.ca
www.teamstersrail.ca
Previous Name: Brotherhood of Locomotive Engineers
Overview: A medium-sized national organization
Membership: 16,000 in 21 divisions; *Fees:* $15
Activities: *Library:* Library (Open to Public)

Toronto Transportation Society (TTS)
PO Box 5187, Stn. A, Toronto ON M5W 1N5 Canada
ttswebmaster@torontotransportationsociety.org
www.torontotransportationsociety.org
Overview: A small local organization founded in 1973
Finances: *Funding Sources:* Membership dues
Staff: 7 volunteer(s)
Membership: 131; *Fees:* $20; *Committees:* Executive; Trips & Excursions
Activities: *Library:* Yes
Description: To afford persons interested in transportation by land, facilities for discussion & exchange of information

Transport Action Canada
Bronson Centre, PO Box 858, Stn. B, #303, 211 Bronson Ave., Ottawa ON K1P 5P9 Canada
Tel: 613-594-3290; *Fax:* 613-594-3271
info@transport-action.ca
www.transport-action.ca
Previous Name: Transport 2000 Canada
Overview: A medium-sized national charitable organization founded in 1976
Finances: *Annual Operating Budget:* $50,000-$100,000; *Funding Sources:* Donations
Staff: 15 volunteer(s)
Membership: 1,500; *Fees:* $35 regular; $30 senior; $50 family; $75 affiliate non-profit; $170corporate
Activities: Research, public education & advocacy, representation of the consumer interests before federal, provincial, municipal public hearings & regulatory bodies, direction of consumer complaints to public carriers; *Speaker Service:* Yes *Library:* Library (Open to Public)
Description: National federation of environmental & consumer groups concerned about the importance of transportation on our environment & quality of life; to inform Canadians of the need for a coherent national transport policy which recognizes that conservation of resources must be a priority & that access to good public transportation is a right of all Canadians; to work for the improvement & greater use of bus & rail transportation in the interests of public safety, social equity & the protection of the environment; to press for the coordination of all transport services for the benefit of users; to demand more attention to the needs of pedestrians, cyclists & public transport users; to maximize the use of the energy-efficient rail & marine modes for the shipment of freight. PUBLICATIONS: National Transport Newsletter.
Affiliation(s): Transport 2000 International

Transportation Association of Canada (TAC) / Association des transports du Canada (ATC)
2323 St. Laurent Blvd., Ottawa ON K1G 4J8 Canada
Tel: 613-736-1350; *Fax:* 613-736-1395
secretariat@tac-atc.ca
www.tac-atc.ca
Previous Name: Roads & Transportation Association of Canada
Overview: A large national organization founded in 1970
Finances: *Annual Operating Budget:* Greater than $5 Million
Staff: 30 staff member(s); 500 volunteer(s)
Membership: 550 corporate; *Fees:* Schedule; *Committees:* Technical & Research; Editing & Publications; Rules of the Road; Project; Technical Steering; Asphalts Advisory; Operations; Pavements; Structures; Aviation; Conference Technical Program; Geometric Design; Goods Movement; Soils & Materials; Traffic; Transit Planning; Technology
Activities: *Library:* Technical Information Centre by appointment
Description: To promote the provision of safe, efficient, effective & environmentally sustainable transportation services in support of Canada's social & economic goals; to act as a neutral forum for the discussion of transportation issues & matters; to act as a technical focus in the highway transportation area. PUBLICATIONS: TAC News.

Truck Training Schools Association of Ontario Inc. (TTSAO)
Fax: 519-858-0920
Toll-Free: 866-475-9436
training@ttsao.com
www.ttsao.com
Overview: A small national licensing organization founded in 1992
Finances: *Annual Operating Budget:* $100,000-$250,000
Staff: 7 staff member(s)
Membership: 75; *Fees:* Schedule
Activities: *Internships:* Yes
Description: To provide the trucking industry with the highest quality driver training programs for entry level individuals that earn & maintain public confidence, adhering to sound & ethical business practices
Affiliation(s): Ontario Trucking Association; Ministry of Education, Ministry of Transportation

Truckers Association of Nova Scotia
PO Box 1527, 184 Arthur St., Truro NS B2N 5V2 Canada
Tel: 902-895-7447; *Fax:* 902-897-0487
Toll-Free: 800-232-6631
contact@tans.ca
www.tans.ca
Overview: A medium-sized provincial organization founded in 1968
Description: Promotes all matters aiding the development and improvement of the trucking industry and the allied trades in Nova Scotia, including social, recreational, benevolent, educational and charitable activities. In addition, the Truckers Association of Nova Scotia makes presentations to government and other regulatory bodies in relation to the economic welfare of the trucking industry and is the main proponent in gaining access to the provincial haul rates and beneficial changes to the contract specifications used by the contractors

Ultralight Pilots Association of Canada (UPAC) / Association canadienne des pilotes d'avions ultra-légers
907289 Township Rd. 12, RR#4, Bright ON N0J 1B0 Canada
Tel: 519-684-7628
www.upac.ca
Overview: A small national organization
Finances: *Annual Operating Budget:* Less than $50,000; *Funding Sources:* Membership fees
Staff: 10 volunteer(s)
Membership: 500+; *Fees:* $40; *Member Profile:* Interest in ultralight aviaton
Activities: Video library for members; *Library:* Video Library (Open to Public)
Description: To promote ultralight aviation in Canada

Union of Canadian Transportation Employees (UCTE) / Union canadienne des employés des transports (UCET)
#702, 233 Gilmour St., Ottawa ON K2P 0P2 Canada
Tel: 613-238-4003; *Fax:* 613-236-0379
ucte_webmaster@psac.com
www.ucte.com
Overview: A medium-sized national organization
Membership: 7,500 + 90 locals
Description: The Union represents members working in the public & private sectors of the Canadian transportation industry (ports, airports, NAV Canada, pilotage authorities, transportation companies, canals, the Dept. of Transport, lighthouses, ships and Canadian Coast Guard bases)

United Transportation Union (AFL-CIO/CLC) - Canada
71 Bank St., 7th Fl., Ottawa ON K1P 5N2 Canada
Tel: 613-747-7979; *Fax:* 613-747-2815
Overview: A medium-sized national organization
Membership: 8,500 + 79 locals
Member of: United Transportation Union (AFL-CIO/CLC), Cleveland USA

University of Toronto Institute for Aerospace Studies
Faculty of Applied Science & Engineering, 4925 Dufferin St., Toronto ON M3H 5T6 Canada
Tel: 416-667-7700; *Fax:* 416-667-7799
info@utias.utoronto.ca
www.utias.utoronto.ca
Overview: A medium-sized national organization founded in 1949
Membership: 68
Activities: *Library:* Library
Description: UTIAS is a graduate studies and research institute, forming part of the faculty of Applied Science and Engineering at the University of Toronto.
Affiliation(s): Canadian Aeronautics & Space Institute; Institute for Space & Terrestrial Science; Canadian Space Agency; Intelligent Sensing for Innovative Structures Canada

Upper Canada Railway Society
PO Box 122, Stn. A, Toronto ON M5W 1A2 Canada
Tel: 416-921-4023
ucrs@btinternet.com
Overview: A small national organization founded in 1941
Membership: 600; *Fees:* $29
Description: To work to preserve history & railways of Canada
Member of: Community Heritage Project

The Van Horne Institute for International Transportation & Regulatory Affairs
#620 Earth Sciences Bldg., 2500 University Dr. NW, Calgary AB T2N 1N4 Canada
Tel: 403-220-8455; *Fax:* 403-282-4663
vanhorne@ucalgary.ca
www.vanhorne.info/
Overview: A small international organization founded in 1991
Finances: *Annual Operating Budget:* Less than $50,000; *Funding Sources:* Private sector
Staff: 4 staff member(s)
Membership: 60; *Member Profile:* Government; industry; education; *Committees:* Centre for Transportation; Centre for Regulatory Affairs; Centre for Innovation & Communication
Activities: Transporation research & education; programs to assist in improving the efficiency & equity of transportation & regulated industries; *Speaker Service:* Yes; *Rents Mailing List:* Yes *Library:* Library (Open to Public)
Description: To contribute to public policy development & education in the areas of transportation & regulated industries. PUBLICATIONS: On-Trac.
Affiliation(s): University of Calgary; University of Alberta; Southern Alberta Institute of Technology

Vintage Locomotive Society Inc.
PO Box 33021, RPO Polo Park, Winnipeg MB R3G 3N4 Canada
Tel: 204-832-5259; *Fax:* 866-751-2348
info@pdcrailway.com
www.pdcrailway.com
Also Known As: Prairie Dog Central Steam Train
Overview: A small local charitable organization founded in 1968
Finances: *Annual Operating Budget:* $250,000-$500,000
Staff: 170 volunteer(s)
Membership: 170 individuals; *Fees:* $25 full; $15 junior; $40 family; *Committees:* Restoration-Locomotive; Restoration-Coaches; Painting; Sign Work; Public Relations; Advertising; Photography; Operations & Maintenance
Activities: *Speaker Service:* Yes
Description: To collect, restore for operation & maintain steam locomotives & rolling stock of early part of twentieth-century; to provide source of historical information relating to origin & past operation of acquired equipment & buildings

West Coast Railway Association (WCRA)
PO Box 2790, Vancouver BC V6B 3X2 Canada
Tel: 604-524-1011; *Fax:* 604-876-4104
Toll-Free: 800-722-1233
info@wcra.org
www.wcra.org
Overview: A small local charitable organization founded in 1961

Finances: *Annual Operating Budget:* $500,000-$1.5 Million; *Funding Sources:* Tours; government grants; donations; fundraising; foundation
Staff: 12 staff member(s); 150 volunteer(s)
Membership: 600 individual; *Fees:* Schedule; *Member Profile:* Interest in railways past & present; *Committees:* Museum; Tours; Collections; Motive Power; Children; Education
Activities: Develops & operates West Coast Railway Heritage Park in Squamish B.C. - collection of over 60 locomotives, freight & passenger cars; operates tour progrm; other community event; Day out with Thoma, June; *Speaker Service:* Yes *Library:* Archives (Open to Public) by appointment
Description: Collects, preserves, restores, operates & exhibits artifacts relating to the history of railways, especially those of BC; the West Coast Railway Heritage Park in Squamish BC develops educational exhibits on railway heritage for all age groups; the tour program encourages the public to travel today's railways to see Canada
Member of: Association of Rail Museums; Tourist Railroad Association

Western Transportation Advisory Council (WESTAC)
#1140, 800 Pender St. West, Vancouver BC V6C 2V6 Canada
Tel: 604-687-8691; *Fax:* 604-687-8751
infoservices@westac.com
www.westac.com
Overview: A small local organization founded in 1973
Finances: *Annual Operating Budget:* $500,000-$1.5 Million; *Funding Sources:* Membership fees; project fees; professional services fees
Staff: 4 staff member(s)
Membership: 52 corporate; *Fees:* Revenue-related scale; *Member Profile:* Carriers; shippers; ports & terminals; labour unions; government
Activities: *Library:* Library by appointment
Description: To advance Western Canadian economy through the improvement of the region's transportation system.

Companies

Airline Companies

ACE Aviation Holdings Inc.
5100, boul de Maisonneuve ouest, Montréal, QC H4A 3T2
www. aceaviation.com; www.aircanada.ca
Profile: Air Canada, Aeroplan, Jazz, and ACTS are subsidiaries of ACE Aviation.
Monte R. Brewer, President & CEO, Air Canada
Duncan Dunne, EVP/CFO
Sydney Isaacs, SVP Corporate Affairs/Cheif Administrative Officier
Greg Cote, SVP Corporate Development/Chief Legal Officer
Jack McLean, Controller

Aer Lingus
Suite 130, 300 Jericho Quadrangle, Jericho, NY 11753
Tel: 516-622-4022; *Fax:* 516-752-2045
Toll-Free: 866-886-8844
groupsusa@aerlingus.com
www.flyaerlingus.com

Aeroflot - Russian Airlines
PO Box 61, #1908, 1 Queen St. East, Toronto, ON M5C 2C5
Tel: 416-642-1653; *Fax:* 416-642-1658
info@aeroflotcanada.com
www.aeroflotcanada.com
Gelena Bakholdina, Marketing and advertising events
omosheva@aeroflot.ru

Aerolineas Argentinas
Rm. 1600, 51 East 42nd St., New York, NY
Tel: 212-542-8880; *Fax:* 212-542-8881
Toll-Free: 800-333-0276
salesnyc@usaerolinesas.aero
www.aerolineas.com.ar
Vilma Castellino, Manager, Rep World

Air Canada
7373, boul de la Côte-Vertu ouest, Montréal, QC H4S 1Z3
Tel: 514-422-5000; *Fax:* 514-422-5789
www.aircanada.ca
Ticker Symbol: AC
Profile: Scheduled air transportation; Travel agencies; Arrangement of transportation of freight & cargo
Lise Fournel, Sr. Vice-President, E-Commerce
Joseph D. Randell, President, Air Canada Jazz
Joshua Koshy, CFO & Exec. Vice-President
Duncan Dee, Sr. Vice-President, Corporate Affairs

Air Canada Jazz
c/o Halifax International Airport, 310 Goudey Dr., Enfield, NS B2T 1E4
Tel: 902-873-5000; *Fax:* 902-873-2098
websupport@flyjazz.ca
Profile: At Jazz, their priorities include safe, efficient, and on-time operations and have over 4,300 employees. They have a fleet of 36 planes.

Air Creebec
PO Box 430, 101, 7th St., Val-d'Or, QC J9P 4P4
Tél: 819-825-8355; *Téléc:* 418-748-6030
www.aircreebec.ca
Profile: Air Creebec aims to provide safe, reliable, and efficient air transportation within Eeyou Istchee and beyond.
Albert Diamond, President

Air France
 # 1510, 2000 rue Mansfield, Montreal, QC H3A 3A3
Tel: 514-847-1106; *Fax:* 514-847-5013
Toll-Free: 800-667-2747
www.airfrance.ca
Jean-Cyril Spinette, Chairman and CEO
Pierre-Henri Gourgeon, President and Chief Operating Officier
Philippe Calavia, CEO
Alain Bassil, EVP- Air France Industries
Francois Brousse, SVP Corporate Communications
Pascal de Izaguirre, EVP Ground Operations
Bruno Matheu, EVP Marketing/Network Management
Bruno Matheu, EVP Marketing/Network Management
Edouard Odier, EVP Information Technology
Gilbert Rovetto, EVP Flight Operations

Air India Ltd.
#218, 5955 Airport Rd., Mississauga, ON L4V 1R9
Tel: 905-405-2160; *Fax:* 905-405-2169
Toll-Free: 800-625-6424
yyz@airindiacanada.ca
www.airindia.com
V. Thulasidas, Chairman and Managing Director, Air India
M. Kacker, Chief Vigiliance Officer/Offg. Executive Director-Secur
Amod Sharma, Director Finance
K.M. Unni, Director Engineering
V.K. Verma, Director Commercial
Jitender Bhargava, Executive Director-Coordination
S. Ranganathan, Executive Director Ground Services
Deepak Anand, Executive Director Operations
Paul Lakra, Executive Director-Mumbai Airport
I.S. Vhatkar, General Manager Properties/Facilities

Air Nootka
PO Box 19, Gold River, BC V0P 1G0
Tel: 250-283-2255; *Fax:* 250-283-2256
info@airnootka.com
http://www.airnootka.com/
Profile: Air Nootka takes pride in providing the best service to new and longtime customers. A floatplane operation based out of Gold River, British Columbia. They service all of Vancouver Island, including Victoria, Nanaimo, Comox, Campbell River, and Kyuquot, as well as Vancouver.

Air North Airlines
Fax: 867-393-4601
office@flyairnorth.com
www.flyairnorth.com
Profile: Frequent departures from all supported aiports; Great Value Cargo service at the price of general freight (ground service); Cargo Friendly Cargo can be taken directly to the Airport and quickly processed while you wait.

Air St-Pierre
c/o Air Saint-Pierre, PO Box 1660, 1 Bell Blvd., Enfield, NS B2T 1K2
Tel: 902-873-3566; *Fax:* 902-873-3567
halifax@airsaintpierre.com
www.airsaintpierre.com

Air Transat
5959 Côte-Vertu Blvd., Montréal, QC H4S 2E6
Tel: 514-636-3630; *Toll-Free:* 866-435-0011
information@airtransat.com
www.airtransat.com
Profile: Air Transat is a wholly owned subsidiary of Transat A.T. Inc. They specialize in both scheduled and charter flights from Canada to vacation destinations. In the winter months, the majority of flights are between Canada to vacation desintations. In the winter months, the majority of flights are between Canada and the Caribbean/USA and in the summer between Canada and many European countries. Year-round schedule services operate between Europe and Canada. The Air Transat fleet of 15 aircraft serves over 90 destinations in 25 countries.

Pierre Ménard, Vice-President, Operations

Alitalia
#202, 5915 Airport Rd., Mississauga, ON L4V 1T1
Tel: 905-673-2442; *Fax:* 905-673-6089
Toll-Free: 800-268-9277
atitaliasupport@alicos.net
www.alitalia.ca
Berardino Libonati, Chairman

American Airlines Inc.
Lester B. Pearson Airport, PO Box 6005, Stn Toronto AMF, Mississauga, ON L5P 1B6
Tel: 905-612-7266; *Fax:* 905-612-0144
Toll-Free: 800-433-7300
www.aa.com
A.W. Pliszka, General Manager, Toronto

Austrian Airlines
2085, Union St., Montréal, QC H3A 2C3
Tel: 514-842-2500; *Fax:* 514-842-3300
Toll-Free: 888-817-4444
www.aua.com
Pierre Doueihi, Manager

Avianca
#1102, 1 St. Clair Ave. West, Toronto, ON M4V 1K6
Tel: 416-969-8817; *Fax:* 416-969-9926
Toll-Free: 800-387-8667
www.avianca.com

British Airways
c/o British Airways Customer Relations, USA, East Elmhurst, NY 11369-0098
www.british-airways.com
Bernie Herenberg

BWIA West Indies Airways
#401, 40 Holly St., Toronto, ON M4S 3C3
Toll-Free: 800-920-4225
mail@caribbean-airlines.com
www.caribbean-airlines.com
Peter Davies, CEO
Ian Brunton, EVP Operations
Anne Cole, VP Human Resource Services
Roy Harrypersad, VP Finance
Derek De Gannes, VP Information Services
Rachel Laquis, VP Legal/Corporate Services
Robert Bodish, Regional Director North America
Mark Garcia, Director Quality Assurance
Francois Pariseau, Director Marketing
Arthur Lok Jack, Chairman

CanJet Airlines
PO Box 980, Enfield, NS B2T 1R6
Tel: 902-873-7800; *Fax:* 902-873-6580
Toll-Free: 800-809-7777
www.canjet.com

Central Mountain International
PO Box 998, 6431 Airport Rd., Smithers, BC V0J 2N0
Tel: 250-877-5000; *Fax:* 250-874-3744
info@flycma.com
Profile: 300+ employees. Centreal Mountain Air is pleased to offer selected cargo services to a majority of our route network destinations. we endeavor to provide our cusomters with a convenient and economical cargo product. Established in 1987 Central Mountain Air (CMA) is a Western Canadian privately owned and operated company offering scheduled and charter flights to over 17 British Columbia and Alberta communities.

CHC Helicopter Corporation
4740 Agar Dr., Richmond, BC V7B 1A3
Tel: 604-276-7500;
communications@chc.ca
www.chc.ca
Ticker Symbol: FLY
Profile: Nonscheduled & scheduled air transportation; Airports, flying fields & airport terminal services; Vocational schools
Sylvain A. Allard, CEO
Jo Mark Zurel, CFO & Sr. Vice-President

Continental Airlines
PO Box 4607, Houston, TX 77210-4607
Fax: 832-235-1806
Toll-Free: 800-346-3133
www.continental.com
Profile: Subsidary company: Continental Mirconesia, Inc.
Larry Kellner, Chairman/CEO
Jeffery Smisek, President Continental Airlines
Jim Compton, EVP Marketing
Jeff Misner, EVP/CFO
Mark Moran, EVP Operations

Ron Anderson-Lehman, SVP/CIO
Rebecca Cox, SVP Government Affairs
Dave Hilfman, SVP Sales

Cubana
620, rue St-Jacques, Montréal, QC H3C 1C7
Tel: 514-871-1222; *Fax:* 514-871-1227
Toll-Free: 888-667-1222
ventas@qc.aira.com
www.cubana.cu
Ramon Valdivia

Czech Airlines
#1510, 401 Bay St., Toronto, ON M5H 2Y4
Tel: 416-363-3174; *Fax:* 416-363-0239
Toll-Free: 800-641-0641
www.czechairlines.com
Ladislav Slipka, Regional Director

El Al Israel Airlines
#701, 151 Bloor St. West, Toronto, ON M5S 1S4
Tel: 416-967-4222; *Fax:* 416-967-1643
Toll-Free: 800-361-6174
www.elal.co.il

Finnair G.S.A Canada
Vista Centre, Core C, #235, 6500 Silver Dart Dr., Mississauga, ON L5P 1B2
Tel: 416-222-0740; *Fax:* 416-678-8949
Toll-Free: 800-461-8651
feedback@ca.finnair.com
www.finnair.com
Tommi Mormonen, Managing Director

First Air
20 Cope Dr., Kanata, ON K2M 2V8
Tel: 613-254-6200; *Fax:* 613-254-6398
Toll-Free: 800-267-1247
reservat@firstair.ca
www.firstair.ca
Profile: Specializes in travel to Northern Canada. First Air operates a versatile fleet of 17 aircraft for regularly scheduled passenger and air cargo services. The fellt of well-maintained, modern aircraft also provides First Air with the size and flexibility to meet your air charter services requirements. First Air offers scheduled service to 28 destinations in Nunavut, Northwest Territories, Manitoba, Alberta, Yukon, Quebec, and Ontario operating a fleet of 20 aircraft. The Inuit owned airline has over 1,000 employees, of which more than 450 work and live in the north.
Rick Lefebvre, Director Sales, Eastern Region
Mike Olsen, Director Sales, Western Region
Scott Bateman, VP Commercial Operations
Don Orr, VP Flight Operations/Maintenance
Jim Ballingall, VP Marketing/Sales
Jan Traversy, VPVP Finance

Harbour Air Seaplanes
1095 West Waterfront Rd., Vancouver, BC
Tel: 604-274-1277; *Fax:* 604-274-1200
Toll-Free: 800-665-0212
rreid@harbourair.com
www.harbour-air.com

Harmony Airways, Inc.
Corporate Office, 3600 Lysander Lane, Richmond, BC V7B 1C2
Tel: 604-248-7800; *Fax:* 604-248-7800
Toll-Free: 866-868-6789

Helijet International
c/o Vancouver International Airport, 5911 Airport Rd. South, Richmond, BC V7B 1B5
Tel: 604-273-4688; *Fax:* 604-273-5301
passengerServices@helijet.com
www.helijet.com
Profile: Helijet are the first scheduled helicopter service in Canada and since their inception in 1986, they now have a fleet of 10 helicopters and airplanes with a staff of over 100 employees. They also have cargo services which ship time sensitive envelops and packages with speed and reliability.

Icelandair
#410, 5950 Symphony Woods Rd., Columbia, MD
Tel: 410-715-1600; *Fax:* 410-715-3547
Toll-Free: 800-223-5500
america@icelandair.is
www.icelandair.com
J¢n Karl ¢lafsson, CEO/President, The Americas
Andri Ass Grétarsson, SVP Finance/Resource Management
Guòjòn Arngr¡msson, VP Corporate Communications
Guòmundur Pálsson, SVP Operations
Gunnar Már Sigurfinnsson, SVP Marketing/Sales

Hjörtur Porgilsson, VP Information Technology
Jens Bjarnason, SVP Technical Services
Una Eyp¢rsd¢ttir, VP Human Resources

Japan Airlines
#2515, 1075 West Georgia St., Vancouver, BC V6E 3C9
Toll-Free: 800-525-3663
www.japanair.com
Haruka Nishimatsu, President/CEO

Korean Air
1813 Wilshire Blvd., Los Angeles, CA 90057
Tel: 905-676-8440; *Fax:* 213-484-5790
Toll-Free: 800-438-5000
www.koreanair.com

LanChile
#902, 18 King St. East, Toronto, ON M5C 1C4
Tel: 416-862-0807; *Fax:* 416-862-5453
www.lanchile.cl

LOT Polish Airlines
Clarica Centre Tower, 10th Fl., #3080, 3300 Bloor St. West., Toronto, ON M8X 2X3
Tel: 416-236-4242; *Fax:* 416-776-3152
Toll-Free: 800-668-5928
lotyto@lot.com
www.lot.com
Wojciech Maciszewski, General Manager

Lufthansa German Airlines
PO Box 939, 31 Adelaide St. E, Toronto, ON M5K 2K3
Tel: 905-612-5000; *Fax:* 416-360-3605
Toll-Free: 800-563-5954
www.lufthansa.com
Justin Gosling, General Manager, Passenger Sales, Canada

Malev Hungarian Airlines
#909, 175 Bloor St. East, Toronto, ON M4W 3R8
Tel: 416-944-0093; *Fax:* 416-944-0095
Toll-Free: 866-379-7313
toronto@malev.hu
www.malev.hu
Attila Gogh

Martinair Holland
#1503, 111 Richmond St. West, Toronto, ON M5H 2G4
Tel: 416-364-3672; *Fax:* 800-561-8083
www.martinair.ca

Mexicana
1315 Skyway Dr., Bakersfield, CA 93308
Tel: 661-387-9755;
www.mexicana.com
Erika Flores, "Person in Charge"
Manuel Borja Chico, CEO

Northern Thunderbird Air Inc.
#101, 4245 Hangar Rd., Prince George, BC V2N 4M6
Tel: 250-963-9611; *Fax:* 250-963-8422
Toll-Free: 800-963-9611
infoWntair.ca
www.ntair.ca
Bill Hesse, General Manager
Bernice Hesse, Operations Manager
Ed Goodkey, Controller
Shawna Finch, Maintenance Manager

Northwest/KLM Royal Dutch Airlines
Passgenger Refund Department MS C6455, 7500 Airline Dr., Minneapolis, MN 55450-1101
Tel: 612-726-2422;
www.nwa.com

Olympic Airways
#503, 80 Bloor St. West, Toronto, ON M5S 2V1
Tel: 416-964-2720; *Fax:* 416-920-3686
sales.yyz@olympicairlines.ca
www.olympic-airways.gr

Pacific Coastal Airlines
c/o Vancouver International Airport, Unit 2, 4440 Cowely Crest., Richmond, BC V7B 1B8
Tel: 604-214-2358; *Fax:* 604-273-4485
www.pacific-coastal.com
Daryl Smith, CEO/Director

PIA Pakistan International Airlines
#500, 131 Bloor St. West, Toronto, ON M5S 1P7
Tel: 416-926-8747; *Fax:* 416-926-0507
Toll-Free: 800-387-1375
www.piac.com.pk
Zaffar A. Khan, Chairman

Purolator Courier Ltd.
#100, 5995 Avebury Rd., Mississauga, ON L5R 3T8
Tel: 905-712-1251; *Fax:* 905-712-6696
suggestions@purolator.com
www.purolator.com
Profile: Air courier services
Robert C. Johnson, President/CEO
Sheldon Bell, Sr. Vice-President & CFO

Royal Jordanian
#940, 1801, av McGill College, Montréal, QC H3A 2N4
Tel: 514-288-1655; *Fax:* 514-288-7572
Toll-Free: 800-363-0711
yultbrj@rja.com.jo
www.rja.com.jo/
Omar Kamal, Area Manager, Canada

Skyservice Airlines Inc.
c/o Corporate Office, 31 Fasken Dr., Etobicoke, ON M9W 1K6
Tel: 416-679-5700; *Fax:* 416-678-5654
Toll-Free: 888-571-0094
customer_service@skyservice.com
www.skyservice.com

Swiss International Air Lines
#800, 1555, rue Peel, Montréal, QC H3A 3L8
Tel: 514-954-5600; *Fax:* 514-954-5619
Toll-Free: 877-359-7947
www.swiss.com
Olivier Schlegel, General Manager

Tango
Air Canada Centre, 7373, boul Côte-Vertu ouest, Montréal, QC H4Y 1H4
Tel: 514-422-5000;
www.flytango.com

Trans North Helicopters
PO Box 8, 115 Range Rd., Whitehorse, YK Y1A 5X9
Tel: 867-668-2177; *Fax:* 867-668-3420
email@tntaheli.com
http://www.tntaheli.com
Arden Meyer, General Manager
Rob Fletcher, Operations Manager
Charlie Hoeller, Director of Maintenance
Doug Kerley, Chief Pilot
Diane Barnhart, Accountant

Transat A.T. Inc.
Place du Parc, #600, 300, rue Léo-Pariseau, Montréal, QC H2X 4C2
Tel: 514-987-1660; *Fax:* 514-987-8035
info@transat.com
www.transat.com
Ticker Symbol: TRZ
Profile: Offices of holding companies; Air transportation, scheduled; Travel agencies; Airports, flying fields, & airport terminal services; Tour operators
Jean-Marc Eustache, President/CEO
Nelson Gentiletti, CFO & Vice-President, Finance & Administration
Jean-Marc Bélisle, Vice-President/Chief Information Officer

United Airlines
77 W. Wacker Dr., Chicago, IL 60601
Tel: 847-700-4000; *Fax:* 847-700-4081
Toll-Free: 800-241-6522
www.ual.com

Varig
#1108, 77 Bloor St. West, Toronto, ON M5S 1M2
Tel: 416-926-7500; *Fax:* 416-926-1536
Toll-Free: 800-898-2744
www.varig.com.br

WestJet
5055 - 11 St. NE, Calgary, AB T2E 8N4
Tel: 403-444-2600; *Fax:* 403-444-2301
Toll-Free: 888-2 W-STJE
customercare@westjet.com
www.westjet.com
Profile: Their fleet is the most modern of any large commercial airline which is comprised of 62 Boeing Next-Generation 737 aircrafts equipped with more legroom, leather seats and live seatback televisions on more than 85% of its fleet.
Sean Durfy, President
Donald Bell, Executive VP of Culture

WestJet Airlines Ltd.
5055 - 11 St. NE, Calgary, AB T2E 8N4
Tel: 403-444-2600; *Fax:* 403-444-2301
investor_relations@westjet.com
www.westjet.com
Ticker Symbol: WJA
Profile: Scheduled air transportation throughout North America
Clive J. Beddoe, President & Chair
Alexander (Sandy) Campbell, CFO/Sr. Vice President, Finance
Russ Hall, Exec. Vice-President, Guest Service & Information Technology

Zip Air Inc.
8050 - 22 St. NE, Calgary, AB T2E 7H6
Tel: 604-270-5676; *Fax:* 604-276-3433

Zoom Airlines Inc.
#200, 380 Hunt Club Rd., Ottawa, ON K1V 1C1
Tel: 613-235-9666; *Fax:* 613-231-7340
custrel@flyzoom.com
www.flyzoom.com
Kris Dolinky, President & CEO

Maritime Shipping

Admiral Marine Inc.
#207-7035 Maxwell Rd., Mississauga, ON L5S 1R5
Tel: 905-564-8788; *Fax:* 905-564-1440
admiral@admiralmarine.ca
www.admiralmarine.ca
Profile: Canstar Ocean Line through Admiral Marine operate a regular break-bulk/conventional service from North America to Europe with transshipment via Antwerp to Eastern Europe, the Middle East and Africa. Canstar is a full service transportation consulting company that specializes in the shipment of over-dimensional, ro.ro, break-bulk, heavy lift, and project cargoes.

Algoma Central Corporation
#1000, 103 Church St., St Catharines, ON L2R 3C4
Tel: 905-687-7888; *Fax:* 905-687-7882
gdwight@algonet.com
www.algonet.com
Ticker Symbol: ALC
Profile: Algoma Central Corporation operates vessels throughout the Great Lakes-St. Lawrence Waterway from the Gulf of St. Lawrence, through all 5 Great Lakes. The corporation owns 19 Canadian-flagged dry-bulk vessels. The operational and commercial activities of the Canadian-flag dry-bulk team are managed by Seaway Marine Transport, a partnership with Upper Great Lakes Shipping Inc., an unrelated company. The Corporation also has an interest in one tug and one barge.
Tim S. Dool, President/CEO
G.D. Wight, Vice-President, Finance
Robert Cook, Director, Information Services
Kevin Reid, Director, Safety

American President Lines Ltd.
#728, 185 The West Mall, Etobicoke, ON M9C 5L5
Tel: 416-620-7790; *Fax:* 416-620-7723
www.apl.com
Profile: APL provides customers around the world with container transportation services through a network combining high-quality intermodal operations with state-of-the-art information technology.
David Goodwin, Vice President, Corporate Affairs
Mike Zampa, Director, Corporate Communications

Anglo-Eastern Ship Management Ltd.
www.angloeasterngroup.com
Profile: Currently the Anglo-Eastern Group looks after a varied fleet and crew base trading and operates worldwide.
Peter Cremers, President

Canada Steamship Lines Inc.
759 Victoria Square, Montreal, QC H2Y 2K3
Tel: 514-982-3800; *Fax:* 514-982-3802
ships@cslmtl.com
csl.ca/new/
Profile: Since 1945 Canada Steamship Lines and its affiliates have been part of the lifeblood of the Canadian economy. Throughout the years, Canada Steamship lines has consistently fulfilled the needs of its clients by providing the supply lines necessary to ensure the survival and prosperity of many industry sectors. Today, Canada Steamship Lines is considered a visionary pioneer in its field and a commendable success story for Canada.
Gerald Carter, President
Claude Dumais, Vice President, Technical Operations
Kirk Jones, Director, Transportation Services

Celtic Maritime
1066 Thierry, La Salle, QC H8N 2Y6
Tel: 514-932-6464; *Fax:* 514-932-6565
info@celticmaritime.com
www.celticmaritime.com
Anthony Morahan, Administrative Contact

CSL Group Inc.
759, carré Victoria, Montréal, QC H2Y 2K3
Tel: 514-982-3800; *Fax:* 514-982-3802
ships@cslmtl.com
www.thecslgroup.ca
Profile: Specializes in bulk transportation & self-loading technology
Meredith (Sam) Hayes, President/CEO
Pierre Richard, Vice-President, Finance & Administration

F.K. Warren Ltd.
Cogswell Tower, #209, 2000 Barrington St., Halifax, NS B3J 2X1
Tel: 902-423-8136; *Fax:* 902-429-1326
www.fkwarren.ca
Profile: F.K. Warren brings together technological, human, and material resources to ensure we meet our of supplying efficient and quality service to those in the Marine and Offshore industries. Provides a comprehensive range of Marine Agency Services at all porst throughout Atlantic Canada.
Gordon Smith, President
gsmith@fkwarren.ca
Richard Danells, Vice President
rdanells@fkwarren.ca

Fednav Limited
#3500, 1000, rue de la Gauchetière ouest, Montréal, QC H3B 4W5
Tel: 514-878-6500; *Fax:* 514-878-6642
info@fednav.com
www.fednav.com
Profile: Deep sea foreign transportation of freight; Freight transportation on the Great Lakes-St.Lawrence Seaway; Marine cargo handling
Laurence F. Pathy, President/CEO

Groupe Desgagnés Inc.
21 Marché-Champlain St., Québec, QC G1K 8Z8
Tel: 418-692-1000; *Fax:* 418-692-6044
info@degagnes.com
www.groupedesgagnes.com
Profile: Groupe Desgagnés' entire history has been marked by sustained, carefully orchestrated efforts that have helped ensure its growth and maintain its position as a shipping industry leader. Purchasing vessels, creating subsidiaries, forming partnerships - this strategy of diversification and combining strengths has helped keep us growing. The fleet includes 14 vessels and 1 barge; 6 vessels for the transportation of general and dry bulk cargo; 7 tankers and 1 barge for the transportation of liquid bulks; 1 passenger and cargo vessels serving the Middle and Lower North shore.
Louis-Marie Beaulieu, CEO

Holmes Maritime Inc.
1345 Hollis St., Halifax, NS B3J 1T8
Tel: 902-422-0400; *Fax:* 902-422-9439
info@holmesmaritime.com
www.holmesmaritime.com
Profile: Holmes Maritime Inc. is a privately owned Canadian headquartered in Halifax, Nova Scotia, providing port agency and logistics services to international ship owners and operators throughout eastern Canada and along the Great Lakes.
Louis Homes, President

Logistec Corporation
#1500, 360, rue Saint-Jacques, Montréal, QC H2Y 1P5
Tel: 514-844-9381; *Fax:* 514-843-5217
corp@logistec.com
www.logistec.com
Ticker Symbol: LGT
Profile: Deep sea foreign transportation of freight; Freight transportation on the Great Lakes & the St. Lawrence Seaway; Marine cargo handling; Various water transportation services; Refuse systems
Madeleine Paquin, President/CEO
Jean-Claude Dugas, Assistant Sec./Treasurer & Vice-President, Finance
Nicole Paquin, Vice-President, Information Systems

Marine Atlantic Inc.
Baine Johnston Centre, #802, 10 Fort William Pl., St. John's, NL A1C 1K4
Tel: 709-772-8957; *Fax:* 709-772-8956
Toll-Free: 800-341-7981
info@marine-atlantic.ca
www.marine-atlantic.ca
Profile: Deep sea domestic transportation of freight; Ferries; Various water transportation of passengers
Sidney J. Hynes, Chair/CEO
Murray Hupman, Chief Information Officer
Anthony deHoog, Sr. Technical Manager

Montship Inc.
Purdy's Wharf Tower 1, #1502, 1959 Upper Water St., Halifax, NS B3J 3N2
Tel: 902-420-9184; *Fax:* 902-422-6010
ops@montshipmaritime.com
www.montship.ca
Profile: Montship Maritime Inc.'s objective is to ensure the outgoing competitiveness of our Maritime operation, and to continue to provide top quality service for our valued Principals.
Kirk Tyler, General Manager
902-420-9184, ktyler@montship.ca
Dennis Merner, Port Superintendent
902-420-9184, dmerner@montship.ca

N.M. Paterson & Sons Limited
PO Box 24, GRP 210, RR2 ., Winnipeg, MB R3C 2E6
Tel: 204-694-4445; *Fax:* 204-694-4446
winnipeg_terminal@patersongrain.com
www.patersongrain.com
Profile: Freight transportation on the great lakes-st.lawrence seaway; Wholesales-grain and field beans
Andrew B. Paterson, CEO
J.B. Gresham, Treasurer/CFO

Oceanex Inc.
#2550, 630 René-Lévesque Blvd. West, Montreal, QC H3B 1S6
Tel: 514-875-9244; *Fax:* 514-877-0226
www.oceanex.com
Profile: With our modern fleet, state-of-the-art technology and hands-on experience, Oceanex ensures you of prompt, relieable and cost-effective pick-up, handling and delivery of any of the industry's cargo needs. From full-load or LTL, the Oceanex track record for outstanding intermodal freight service and customer satisfaction remains second to none. To Newfoundland from anywhere in North America and just in time...every time. That's what you can count on from Oceanex, your Newfoundland connection.
Peter Henrico, President & CEO
Daniel Bélisle, Vice President, Finance & Administration
Glenn Etchegary, Vice President, Operations
Peter Grayton, Sales Manager

Rigel Shipping Canada
PO Box 5151, 3521 Route 134, Shediac, NB E4P 8T9
Tel: 506-533-9000; *Fax:* 506-533-9010
www.rigelcanada.com
Profile: Dedicated to being a quality, technology driven company that provides safe, efficient, environmentally friendly, corteous, and cost-effective marine transportation to our partners and clients.
Brian Ritchie, President
Scott Lewis, General Manager
Shirley Cripps, Human Resources Manager

Robert Redford
2 Place Alexis Nihon, #1777, 3500 de Maisonneuve West, Montreal, QC H3Z 3C1
Tel: 514-845-5201; *Fax:* 514-845-6490
info@redford.ca
www.robertredford.com
Profile: Since 1945, the company has acted exclusively as General Steamship Agents. The company is the oldest Canadian steamship agency organization. It is a wholly owned Canadian company.
Ross Kennedy, President
514-887-5201
Donny Coelho, Operations Manager
514-924-5209
Andrew Digby, Vice President, Operations
514-928-5203

Seaway Marine Transport
#300, 20 Corporate Park, St. Catharines, ON L2S 3W2
Tel: 905-988-2600; *Fax:* 905-988-1803
www.seawaymarinetransport.com
Profile: Seaway Marine Transport Manages the largest and most versatile fleet of self-unloading vessels and the largest fleet of gearless bulk carriers operating on the Great Lakes, St. Lawrence River and the waters of eastern Canada. This is comprised of 22 self-unloading vessels and 12 gearless bulk cargo vessels.
Allister Paterson, President & CEO
Dennis McPhee, Director, Marketing

Senator Lines
#1000, 465 rue St. Jean, Montreal, QC H2Y 2R6
Tel: 514-845-9800; *Fax:* 514-845-8182
www.senatorlines.com
Profile: Our company is motivated by a multi-national team spirit. With our fast and reliable scheduled container services, we can provide your goods with excellent connections to people in the strong-growth markets - Europe-the Middle and Far East, Asia, Canada, South America and the whole Mediterranean region.
Hans-Hermann Mohr, CEO
Jong-Seong Hahm, Vice President

Upper Lakes Group Inc.
49 Jackes Ave., Toronto, ON M4T 1E2
Tel: 416-920-7610; *Fax:* 416-922-6159
inquiries@upperlakes.com
www.upperlakes.com
Profile: Upper Lakes Group Inc. is a client focused full service provider, moving, handling, and storing wet and dry bulk commodoties and dry bulk commodities and containerized cargoes in the Great Lakes, across Canada, and around the world. We manage an integrated group of companies offering innovative solutions to our customers, and growth, sustainability, and profitability to our shareholders.
Pat Loduca, President & CEO
ploduca@upperlakes.com
Sam Amendola, Vice President & CFO, Finance
samendola@upperlakes.com
Ewa Chudecki, Vice President, Human Resources
eshudecki@upperlakes.com

Wallenius Wilhelmsen Logistics
#1700, 1959 Upper Water St., Halifax, NS B3J 3N2
Tel: 902-425-2873; *Fax:* 902-425-9820
www.wwlamericas.com
Profile: We shall create business success for our customers by providing logistics solutions for the distribution of rolling and selected static cargo in a changing global market - with maximum reliability, quality, and cost-effectiveness.
Andrea Farrison, Manager, Public Relations
Elana Brennan, Manager, Marketing Communications

Railroad Companies

Agence métropolitaine de transport
500, Place d'Armes, 25e étage, Montréal, QC H2Y 2W2
Tel: 514-287-2464; *Fax:* 514-287-2460
tram@amt.qc.ca
www.amt.qc.ca
Joël Gauthier, Président/CEO

Alberta Prairie Railway
PO Box 1600, Stettler, AB T0C 2L0
Tel: 403-742-2811; *Fax:* 403-742-2844
info@absteamtrain.com
www.absteamtrain.com
Don Gillespie

Alberta RailNet Inc.
9410 - 92 Ave., Grande Prairie, AB T8V 7A6
Tel: 780-831-0407;
railnet1@telusplanet.net
www.albertarailnet.com

Algoma Central Railway Inc.
PO Box 130, 129 Bay St., Sault Ste Marie, ON P6A 6Y2
Tel: 705-946-7300; *Fax:* 705-541-2989
Toll-Free: 800-242-9287
www.agawacanyontourtrain.com
Profile: "Rail service, Sault Ste Marie to Hearst, Ont."

BC Rail Ltd.
#660-221 West Esplanade, North Vancouver, BC V7M 3J3
Tel: 604-678-4735; *Fax:* 604-678-4736
www.bcrproperties.com/bcrco/
Profile: "Full & intermodal service with CP & CN connections; 1,388 miles of track; 125 locomotives; 10,050 freight cars"
Kevin Mahoney, President/CEO

British Columbia Railway Company
#400, 221 West Esplanade Ave, North Vancouver, BC V7M 3J3
Tel: 604-678-4735; *Fax:* 604-678-4736
www.bcrco.com
Profile: Offices of holding companies; Real estate operators of nonresidential buildings; Real estate agents & managers; Railroads, line-haul operating; Marine cargo handling
Kevin Mahoney, President/CEO
Michael Kaye, CFO & Vice-President, Finance

Burlington Northern Santa Fe (Manitoba) Inc.
963 Lindsay St., Winnipeg, MB R3N 1X6
Tel: 204-453-4415; *Fax:* 204-477-0046

Burlington Northern Sante Fe Railway
PO Box 961056, 2650 Lou Menk Dr., Fort Worth, TX 76161-0056
Toll-Free: 800-795-2673
www.bnsf.com
Profile: "31,000 miles (70 miles in Canada); 200,000 railcars; 4,000 locomotives"
Matthew K. Rose, Chair/President/CEO

Canadian National Railway Company
935, rue de la Gauchetière ouest, Montréal, QC H3B 2M9
Tel: 514-399-0052; *Fax:* 514-399-5985
Toll-Free: 888-888-5909
contact@cn.ca
www.cn.ca
Ticker Symbol: CNR
Profile: Railroads & line-haul operating; Railroad switching & terminal establishments. Founded in 1919; 21,685 employees.
E. Hunter Harrison, President/CEO
Claude Mongeau, CFO & Exec. Vice-President
Fred Grigsby, Sr. Vice-President & Chief Information Officer
J.V. Raymond Cyr, Chair, Environment, Safety & Security Committee

Canadian National Railway Company
935 de La Gauchetiere St. West, Montreal, QC H3B 2M9
Toll-Free: 888-888-5909
contact@cn.ca
www.cn.ca
Hunter Harrison, President & CEO

Canadian Pacific Railway
401 - 9th Ave. SW, Calgary, AB T2P 4Z4
Tél: 403-319-7000; *Téléc:* 403-319-7567
Ligne sans frais: 800-716-9132
www.cpr.ca
Fred J. Green, President & CEO

Canadian Pacific Railway Limited
#500, 401 - 9th Ave. SW, Calgary, AB T2P 4Z4
Tel: 403-319-7000; *Toll-Free:* 888-333-6370
investor@cpr.ca
www.cpr.ca
Ticker Symbol: CP
Profile: Transcontinental carrier; Rail network operates in Canada & the USA. Founded in 1881; over 15,000 employees
Fred J. Green, CEO
Michael R. Lambert, Exec. Vice-President/CFO
Allen H. Borak, Vice-President, Information Services

Cando Contracting Ltd.
740 Rosser Ave., 4th Fl., Brandon, MB R7A 0K9
Tel: 204-725-2627; *Fax:* 204-725-4100
info@candoltd.com
www.candoltd.com
Profile: "Operates 4 shortlines: Barrie/Collingwood Railway, Central Manitoba Railway Inc., Athabasca Northern, Orangeville-Brampton"
Gord Peters, President

Cape Breton & Central Nova Scotia Railway
PO Box 2240, 121 King St., Stellarton, NS B0K 1S0
Tel: 902-752-3357; *Fax:* 902-752-2713
Toll-Free: 800-565-5715
Jim Ryan, General Manager

Cartier Railway Company
Rte. 138, Port Cartier, QC G5B 2H3
Tel: 514-285-2064; *Fax:* 514-285-1978
Profile: "416 km; 21 locomotives; 1,365 cars"
Guy Dufresne, President/CEO

Central Western Railway
Associated Centre, #306, 13220 St-Albert Trail, Stettler, AB T5L 5W1
Tel: 780-448-5877; *Fax:* 780-742-1477
www.railamerica.com
Shawn Smith, General Manager
shawn.smith@railamerica.com

CN
935, rue de la Gauchetière ouest, Montréal, QC H3B 2M9
Fax: 204-987-9310
Toll-Free: 888-888-5909
cn@wpg.fanfuil.com
www.cn.ca
Profile: "17,544 route miles of track in Canada & the US.; 1,450 diesel locomotives; 61,500 freight cars"
E. Hunter Harrison

Consolidated Rail Corporation
PO Box 41416, 2001 Market St., 29th Fl., Philadelphia, PA 19103
Tel: 215-209-2000; *Fax:* 215-209-4819
info@conrail.com
www.conrail.com
Profile: "66 route miles in Québec, from New York-Québec border to Montréal. Includes owned lines, leased lines & trackage rights. Total route miles US & Canada, 13,068"
T.T. O'Toole, President

CSX Transportation Inc.
500 Water St., Jacksonville, FL 33202
Tel: 904-359-3200;
www.csxt.com
Profile: 166 miles in Canada
Michael J. Ward, Chair/President/CEO

E&N Railway
PO Box 581, 23 Esplanade, Nanaimo, BC V9R 5L3
Tel: 250-754-9222

Essex Terminal Railway Co.
PO Box 24025, 1601 Lincoln Rd., Windsor, ON N8Y 4Y9
Tel: 519-973-8222; *Fax:* 519-973-7234
www.essexterminalrailway.com
Profile: Freight only; 24 miles of main track (CN CP CSX NS connect); 5 locomotives; 5 cars
B.G. McKeown, President

GO Transit
#600, 20 Bay St., Toronto, ON M5J 2W3
Tel: 416-869-3200; *Fax:* 416-869-3525
Toll-Free: 888-438-6646
publicrelations@gotransit.com
www.gotransit.com
Gary W. McNeil, Managing Director

Goderich-Exeter Railway Company Ltd.
#2, 126 Weber St. West, Kitchener, ON N2H 3Z9
Tel: 519-749-8000; *Fax:* 519-749-8088
www.railamerica.com
Cheryl Ford, General Manager

Greater Winnipeg Water District Railway
598 Plinguet St., Winnipeg, MB R2J 2W7
Tel: 204-986-4118; *Fax:* 204-986-3562
Profile: Express Co.-None~92 miles; 3 locomotives; 150 cars
T. Hutchinson, Railway Supervisor

Huron Central Railway Inc.
30 Oakland Ave., Sault Ste Marie, ON P6A 2T3
Tel: 705-254-4511; *Fax:* 705-254-5056
Garth E. Rushton, General Manager

Kelowna Pacific Railway Ltd.
2806 - 27 Ave., Vernon, BC V1T 9K4
Tel: 250-549-1473; *Fax:* 250-549-1589
kenf@smartt.com
Kenneth Fitzgerald, Chairman & CEO

Mackenzie Northern Railway
#306, Associated Centre, 13220 St. Albert Trail, Edmonton, AB T5L 4W1
Tel: 780-448-5855; *Fax:* 780-448-5658

New Brunswick Southern Railway Company Limited
11 Gifford Rd., Saint John, NB E2M 4X7
Tel: 506-632-4654; *Fax:* 506-632-5818
www.nbsouthern.com
Ian Simpson, General Manager

Norfolk Southern Corporation
Three Commercial Place, Norfolk, VA 23510-9241
Tel: 757-629-2600; *Fax:* 757-629-2607
www.nscorp.com
Profile: "Operating Subsidiary: Norfolk Southern Railway Co.~Track miles 21,500 (245 miles in Canada); 3,000 locomotives; 19,000 road haul equipment"
Charles Moorman, Chairman/President/CEO

OC Transpo
1500 St. Laurent Blvd., Ottawa, ON K1G 0Z8
Tel: 613-741-6440; *Fax:* 613-230-6543
ocinfo@octranspo.com
www.octranspo.com
Alex Cullen, Chairman

Ontario Northland Transportation Commission
555 Oak St. East, North Bay, ON P1B 8L3
Tel: 705-472-4500; *Fax:* 705-476-5598
Toll-Free: 800-363-7512
info@ontc.on.ca
www.ontc.on.ca

Profile: (Owned by Province of Ontario)~700 miles; 26 locomotives; 700 cars
Steve Carmichael, President & CEO

Ontario Southland Railway Inc.
383 Everglade Cres., London, ON N6H 4M8
Tel: 519-471-9606; *Fax:* 519-471-7334
info@osrinc.ca
www.osrinc.ca

Québec North Shore & Labrador Railway Company
PO Box 1000, Sept-Iles, QC G4R 4L5
Tél: 418-968-7497; *Téléc:* 418-968-7926
robitaim@ironore.ca
www.ironore.ca
M. Robitaille, General Manager

Québec Railway Corporation
#525, 1010, rue Sherbrooke ouest, Montréal, QC H3A 2R7
Tél: 514-982-0917; *Téléc:* 514-849-2319
cnplus.cn.ca
Profile: "Operates the following shortlines: Ottawa Central Railway (OCRR), New Brunswick East Coast Railway (NBEC), Chemin de fer Charlevoix (CFC), Chemin de fer de la Matapédia et du Golfe inc. (CFMG)"
Marc Laliberté, President

Roberval & Saguenay Railway Company
PO Box 1277, Jonquière, QC G7S 4K8
Tél: 418-699-3685; *Téléc:* 418-699-2069
Profile: Express Co.-None (Canadian National Railway connects)~54 miles; 11 locomotives; 189 cars
Claude Chamberland, Vice President

Rocky Mountaineer Rail
#100, 1150 Station St., Vancouver, BC V6A 2X7
Tel: 604-606-7245; *Fax:* 604-606-7250
Toll-Free: 877-460-3200
reservations@rockymountaineer.com
www.rockymountaineer.com
Peter Armstrong, President & CEO

South Simcoe Railway
PO Box 186, Tottenham, ON L0G 1W0
Tel: 905-936-5815;
info@steamtrain.com
www.steamtrain.com
Eric Smith, President

Southern Manitoba Railway
PO Box 253, #2, 156 Boyne, Morris, MB R0G 1K0
Tel: 204-746-2722; *Fax:* 204-746-2749
cnplus.cn.ca
Steve Van Wagenen, General Manager

Southern Ontario Railway
PO Box 953, 241 Stuart St. West, Hamilton, ON L8N 3P9
Tel: 905-777-1234;
www.railamreica.com
Stuart Thomas, General Manager

Southern Railway of British Columbia Limited
2102 River Dr., New Westminster, BC V3M 6S3
Tel: 604-521-1966; *Fax:* 604-526-0914
www.sryraillink.com
Profile: (freight only)~75 miles; 19 locomotives; 475 cars
John van der Burch, President

Toronto Terminals Railway Company Ltd.
#402, Union Station, 65 Front St. West, Toronto, ON M4J 1E6
Tel: 416-864-3440;
www.ttrly.com
S.L. Spares, Director of Operations

Trillium Railway
PO Box 218, 265 King St., Port Colborne, ON L3K 5V8
Tel: 905-835-2772; *Fax:* 905-835-8943
wayne.ettinger@trilliumrailway.com
www.trilliumrailway.com
Wayne Ettinger, President & CEO

VIA Rail Canada Inc.
PO Box 8116 A, #500, 3, Place Ville Marie, Montréal, QC H3C 3N3
Tel: 514-871-6000; *Fax:* 514-871-6619
www.viarail.ca
Profile: Railroads, line-haul operating; Local & suburban transit
Paul Côté, President/CEO
J. Roger Paquette, CFO
Paul Raynor, Director, Corporate Communications
Michael Greenberg, Vice-President, Procurement, Real Estate & Environment

Via Rail Canada Inc.
#500, 3, Place Ville-Marie, Montréal, QC H3B 2C9
Tél: 514-871-6000; *Téléc:* 514-871-6117
www.viarail.ca
Profile: (passenger services only)
Paul Côté, President & CEO

Wabush Mines
PO Box 878, Sept-Iles, QC G4R 4L4
Tél: 418-964-3000; *Téléc:* 418-962-9876
Profile: Wabush Mines represents both the Arnaud Railway Company & the Wabush Lake Railway
D. Lebel, General Manager

West Coast Express Ltd.
#295, 601 West Cordova, Vancouver, BC V6B 1G1
Tel: 604-488-8906; *Fax:* 604-689-3896
www.westcoastexpress.com
Doug Kelsey, President & CEO

White Pass & Yukon Route
PO Box 435, 231 Second Ave., Skagway, AK 99840-0435
Tel: 907-983-2214; *Fax:* 907-983-2734
Toll-Free: 800-343-7373
info@whitepass.net
www.whitepassrailroad.com
Profile: Express Co.-None 40 miles; 20 locomotives; 59 cars
Gary C. Danielson, President

Windsor & Hantsport Railway Co.
PO Box 578, 2 Water St., Windsor, NS B0N 2T0
Tel: 902-798-0798;
cnplus.cn.ca
James Taylor, General Manager

Public Transit Systems

100 Mile House Transit System (Paratransit)
c/o LDN Transportation, 6119 Reita Cres., 100 Mile House, BC V0K 2E0
Tel: 250-395-2834;
lnieson@telus.net
www.bctransit.com/regions/one
Profile: The 100 Mile House Transit System has many routes which offer service to major residenial areas of 100 Mile House, 103 Mile and 108 Ranch. It also has several accessible services, including rural transit service, HandyDART and priority seating.

Agence métropolitaine de transport
500, Place d'Armes, 25e étage, Montréal, QC H2Y 2W2
Tél: 514-287-8726; *Téléc:* 514-276-2460
Ligne sans frais: 888-702-8726
www.amt.qc.ca
Profile: AMT's mission is to improve the efficiency of personal travel in the metropolitan area by promoting the use of public transit. AMT is therefore responsible for the planning, coordination, integration and promotion of public transit services (bus, metro, taxi-bus, commuter trains and adapted transit), as well as for improving the efficiency of roads of metropolitan significance.
Joel Gauthier, Président/CEO

Barrie Transit
24 Maple Ave., Barrie, ON L4N 7W4
Tel: 705-739-4209
Profile: The City of Barrie offers both conventional bus service with Barrie Transit and specialized transit services for people with mobility restrictions with Barrie Accessible Community Transportation Service (BACTS)

BC Transit
520 Gorge Rd. East, Victoria, BC V8W 2P3
Tel: 250-385-2551; *Fax:* 250-995-5639
nancy_longphee@bctransit.com
www.bctransit.com
Profile: BC Transit provides planning, marketing, fleet and funding support for all transit services in BC, except for the Greater Vancouver region. BC Transit's fleet of 20 fuel cell buses will be the world's first to be placed in regular transit operation.

Belleville Transit
City Hall, 169 Front St., Belleville, ON K8N 2Y8
Tel: 613-962-1925
Profile: Belleville Transit operates 6 days a week, Monday to Saturday, inclusive with 9 routes servicing the urban area of the city. The fleet consists of 14 coaches travelling approximately 2,300 kilometers per day and carries 3,000 riders daily

Boundary Transit System
c/o Interior Health Authority, Hardy View Lodge, PO Box 2647, 2320 - 78 Ave., Grand Forks, BC V0H 1H0
Tel: 250-443-2080; *Fax:* 250-442-8331
trish.hallstrom@interiorhealth.ca
www.bctransit.com/regions/bdy
Profile: The Boundary Transit System has many routes within Grand Forks, with trips to and from Greenwood on Fridays. It also has several accessible services, including HandyDART and priority seating.

Brampton Transit
185 Clark Blvd., Brampton, ON L6T 4G6
Tel: 905-874-2750;
www.brampton.ca/transit/home.taf
Profile: Brampton Transit provides approximately 583,000 transit service hours per year

Brandon Transportation Services
900 Richmond Ave. East, Brandon, MB R7A 6A2
Tel: 204-729-2300; *Fax:* 204-729-2485
Profile: Brandon City Transit offers many services to the community, including Handi-Transit, an environmentally friendly way of traveling, and specialized schedules.
Bob MacDonald, City Transportation Manager

Brantford Transit
64 Darling St., Brantford, ON N3T 6G6
Tel: 519-753-3847; *Fax:* 519-750-0491
mspicer@brantford.ca
www.city.brantford.on.ca/transit
Profile: Operated by the Engineering Department of the Corporation of the City of Brantford. The fleet consists of 25 buses

British Columbia Ferry Services Inc.
1112 Fort St., Victoria, BC V8V 4V2
Tel: 250-386-3431; *Fax:* 250-388-7754
www.bcferries.com
Profile: Ferries
David Hahn, President/CEO

British Columbia Rapid Transit Company Ltd. (SkyTrain
6800 - 14 Ave., Burnaby, BC V3N 4S7
Tel: 604-520-3641; *Fax:* 604-521-2818
www.skytrain.info/index.html
Profile: The SkyTrain in Vancouver, British Columbia, Canada is an advanced light rapid transit system operating fully automated trains on two lines. Built for the Expo 86 World's Fair, it has since become the world's longest automated light rapid transit system. The system uses the same family of linear induction motor-driven trains as the Scarborough RT line in Toronto, the Putra LRT in Kuala Lumpur, Malaysia, and the JFK AirTrain in New York.

Burlington Transit
3332 Harvester Rd., Burlington, ON L7N 3M8
Tel: 905-639-0550; *Fax:* 905-335-7878
transit&traffic@burlington.ca

Calgary Transit
c/o City of Calgary, PO Box 2100 M, Calgary, AB T2P 2M5
TPCT043@calgary.ca
www.calgarytransit.com
Profile: Calgary Transit serves a population of 991,759 with the help of 960 vehicles on more than 161 routes
John Hubbell, Director

Campbell River Transit System
1050 - 9 Ave., Campbell River, BC V9W 4C2
Tel: 250-287-7433; *Fax:* 250-287-7488
transit@oberon.ark.com
www.bctransit.com/regions/cam
Profile: The Campbell River Transit System has several services available to the community, including three types of Accessible Service, including Low Floor Busses, handyDART and the Taxi Saver Program. It has routes to most major destinations in Campbell River, and to Willow Point and Oyster Bay.

Cape Breton Transit
320 Esplanade, Sydney, NS B1P 7B9
Tel: 902-539-8124; *Fax:* 902-564-0481
epw@cbrm.ns.ca
www.cbrm.ns.ca
Profile: Transit Cape Breton offers the community travel within Industrial Cape Breton, including Loonie Days every Saturday, and discounted tickets.

Castlegar Regional Transit System
c/o Trail Transit Services Inc., 8170 Old Waneta Rd., Trail, BC V1R 4W9
Tel: 250-365-3100; *Fax:* 250-364-2418
dennis.trailtransit@shawlink.ca
www.bctransit.com/regions/cas
Profile: The Castlegar Regional Transit system has routes to Downtown and the College. It also has several accessible services, including rural transit services, HandyDART and priority seating.

Central Fraser Valley Transit System
c/o Township Transit Services Inc., 1225 Riverside Rd., Abbotsford, BC V2S 7P1
Tel: 604-854-3232; *Fax:* 604-854-3598
inquiries@townshiptransit.com
www.busonline.ca/regions/cfv
Profile: The Central Fraser Valley Transit System has several services available to the community, including routes to most major destinations in the City of Abbotsford and the District of Mission, as well as accessible services such as low floor busses, HandyDART and a taxi saver program.

Chatham Transit
c/o Municipality of Chatham-Kent, PO Box 640, 315 King St. West, Chatham, ON N7M 5K8
Tel: 519-360-1998

Chilliwack Transit
44580 Yale Rd. West, Chilliwack, BC V2R 4H1
Tel: 604-795-3838; *Fax:* 604-795-5110
inquiries@townshiptransit.com
www.bctransit.com/regions/chw
Profile: The Chilliwack Transit System has several routes available to the community, which go to most major destinations in the City of Chilliwack, and to Rosedale, Popkum, Agassiz and Harrison Hot Springs, including service to Minter Gardens, Bridal Falls and Dusty's Dino Town. It also has accessible services including low floor busses, HandyDART, a specializex HandyDART flex route and a taxi saver program.

Clearwater & Area Transit System (Paratransit)
c/o Yellowhead Community Services, 612 Park Dr., Clearwater, BC V0E 1N0
Tel: 250-674-3935;
jack.k@yellowheadcs.ca
www.bctransit.com/regions/clr
Profile: The Clearwater & Area transit system services an area that covers Vavenby, Birch Island, Clearwater and Blackpool. On the last Thursday of every month the bus goes to Kamloops and back to Clearwater. It has several accessible services including door-to-door services and priority seating.

Coast Mountain Bus Company
13401 - 108 Ave., Surrey, BC V3T 5T4
Tel: 604-953-3000;
info@coastmountainbus.com
www.coastmountainbus.com
Profile: Coast Mountain Bus Company (CMBC) is a vital link in the Greater Vancouver multi-modal public transportation network. You experience our service when you ride a CMBC bus, or cross Vancouver harbour on SeaBus ferry service. Coast Mountain Bus Company (CMBC) operates conventional buses, smaller community shuttles, SeaBus and, soon, a fleet of state-of-the-art trolley buses in Greater Vancouver, in the largest single transit service area in Canada.

Cobourg Transit
c/o Town of Cobourg, 55 King St. West, Cobourg, ON K9A 2M2
Tel: 905-373-0582
Profile: Cobourg Transit is a fully accessible community transit system that combines a fixed route service with the flexibility of door-to-door service for eligible riders

Codiac Transit Commission
140 Millennium Blvd., Moncton, NB E1E 2G8
Tel: 506-857-2008; *Fax:* 506-859-2680
www.codiactransit-moncton.com
Profile: Transit system for Moncton with express routes, charters and airport routes.

Comox Valley Transit System
1635 Knight Rd., Comox, BC V9N 5N1
Tel: 250-339-5426; *Fax:* 250-339-2797
karen_sankey@hotmail.com
www.bctransit.com/regions/com
Profile: Comox Valley Transit has several routes available to the community, which go to Cumberland, Royston/Buckley Bay, Courtenay, Comox, and BC Ferries and the airport. It has accessible services including low floor busses, HandyDART and a taxi saver program.

Cornwall Transit
PO Box 877, 863 Second St. West, Cornwall, ON K6J 1H5
Tel: 613-930-2636; *Fax:* 613-932-9906
cityhall@city.cornwall.on.ca
Profile: The City operated transit system transports approximately 525,000 passengers annually
Gerry Godard, Senior Supervisor

Cowichan Valley Regional Transit System
#8, 180 Central Rd., Duncan, BC V9L 4X3
Tel: 250-746-4841;
rick.salewski@greyhound.ca
www.transitbc.com/regions/cow/
Profile: The Cowichan Valley Regional Transit System has several routes to the Duncan/North Cowichan area, including Quamichan, Mt Prevost and Maple Bay; the Cowichan Lake area, including Youbou and Honeymoon Bay; and the South End communities including Mill Bay, Shawnigan Lake, Cobble Hill and Cowichan Bay. It also has accessible services including low floor busses and priority seating.

Cranbrook Transit System
C/O Gray Line of Victoria, 1229 Crambrook St. North, Cranbrook, BC V1C 3S6
Tel: 250-426-3331; *Fax:* 250-426-5101
john.darula@suncity.bc.ca
www.bctransit.com/regions/cra
Profile: Cranbrook Transit System has several routes available to the community, and many services, such as low-floor busses, HandyDART, etc. for those who are in need of them.

Creston Valley Transit System
c/o Grouse Mountain Transportation, 1607 Canyon St., Creston, BC V0B 1G5
Tel: 250-428-5533; *Fax:* 250-428-2658
crestonchamber@kootnay.com
www.bctransit.com/regions/cre
Profile: The Creston Valley Transit System has routes that go to most of the major destinations in the area. It also has several accessible services including door to door service and priority seating.

Dawson Creek Transit System
10105 - 13A St., Dawson Creek, BC V1G 3V7
Tel: 250-784-3600; *Fax:* 250-782-3203
jchute@dawsoncreek.ca
www.bctransit.com/regions/daw
Profile: Dawson Creek Transit system has several routes available to the community, which go to most of the major destinations in Dawson Creek. It has several low floor busses and priority seating.

Durham Region Transit
605 Rossland Rd. East, Whitby, ON L1N 6A3
Tel: 905-668-7711; *Fax:* 905-668-1567
www.durhamregiontransit.com
Profile: Durham Region Transit (DRT) is an integrated transit system serving all communities in Durham Region. The service area is divided into West, East, Centre and North service sectors. Door to door transit for disabled passengers is provided by Specialized Services

Edmonton Transit System
PO Box 2610 Main, Edmonton, AB T5J 3R5
Tel: 780-496-1611; *Fax:* 780-496-1670
etransit@edmonton.ca
Profile: Today, Edmonton Transit's fleet encompasses over 847 diesel and trolley buses, and 29 community buses. The system covers more than 150 routes, including a Light Rail Transit (LRT) system with 37 vehicles and 11 stations. ETS also offers transportation to persons with disabilities, called the Disabled Adult Transit Service (DATS)

Fort St. John Transit System
c/o Nordbo Services Ltd., 10404 - 87 Ave., Fort St John, BC V1J 5K7
Tel: 250-787-9373;
nordbo@awink.com
www.bctransit.com/regions/fsj/
Profile: The Fort St. John Transit system has many routes available to the community, reaching most of the major destinations in the city. It has low floor busses for easy accessibility, and priority seating.

Fredericton Transit
PO Box 130, Fredericton, NB E3B 4Y7
Tel: 506-460-2200; *Fax:* 506-460-2211
transit@fredericton.ca
www.fredericton.ca
Profile: The City of Fredericton Transit Division operates 27 buses on eight routes, Monday to Saturday, 6:30 am until 11:00 pm, providing safe, affordable mobility to those in the community who do not have access to or choose not to use a private vehicle. In addition we operate chartered busing to various school, tour, and conference groups in and around Fredericton, and a parallel service, Dial-A-Bus, for persons with a disability.
Alex MacNeill, Contact

GO Transit
#600, 20 Bay St., Toronto, ON M5J 2W3
Tel: 416-869-3600; *Fax:* 416-869-3525
www.gotransit.com
Profile: GO Transit is Canada's first, and Ontario's only, interregional public transit system, linking Toronto with the surrounding regions of the Greater Toronto Area (GTA). The system began operating in May 1967 and carries 49 million passengers a year by train & bus

GP Transit
City Hall, PO Bag 4000, Grande Prairie, AB T8V 6V3
Tel: 780-538-0337; *Fax:* 780-538-667
gptransit@cityofgp.com
Profile: For over 24 years, GP transit has served the citizens of Grand Prairie, Alberta. Fares range from $1.50 to $2.00 per ride, and children under 12 ride free when accompanied by a paying passenger.

Grand River Transit
250 Strasburg Rd., Kitchener, ON N2E 3M6
Tel: 519-585-7555;
www.grt.ca/web/transit.nsf/fmFrontPage?openform

Greater Sudbury Transit
c/o City of Sudbury, PO Box 5000 A, Sudbury, ON P3A 593
Tel: 705-675-3333; *Fax:* 705-560-4571
Profile: Operates a fleet of 42 buses
Roger Sauvé, Director
roger.sauve@city.greatersudbury.on.c

Greater Vancouver Transportation Authority (TransLink
#1600, 4720 Kingsway, Burnaby, BC V5H 4N2
Tel: 604-453-4500;
www.translink.bc.ca
Profile: TransLink, the Greater Vancouver Transportation Authority, is a small organization involved with transportation planning, administration of service contracts with subsidiary companies and contractors, the management of capital projects, financial management and planning, public affairs and supporting business functions.

Guelph Transit
City Hall, 59 Carden St., Guelph, ON N1H 3A1
Tel: 519-822-1811; *Fax:* 519-822-1322
transit@guelph.on.ca
Profile: Guelph Transit has 20 low-floor conventional buses in its fleet and guarantees accessible service on ten of its transit routes

The Hamilton Street Railway Company
2200 Upper James St., Hamilton, ON L0R 1W0
Tel: 905-528-4200; *Fax:* 905-679-7305
hsrserve@hamilton.ca
www.myhamilton.ca/myhamilton/CityandGovernment/City
Profile: Operates over 30 bus routes serving Hamilton, Stoney Creek, Dundas, Ancaster and Burlington. Buses run seven days a week on most routes, from around 5:30 a.m. to 1:00 a.m. the next morning
Don Hull, Director

Hazeltons' Regional Transit System
c/o Farwest Bus Lines Ltd., 5251 First Ave., New Hazelton, BC V0J 1Y0
Tel: 250-847-2134; *Toll-Free:* 877-842-2131
phil.malnis@farwestgroup.com
www.bctransit.com/regions/haz
Profile: The Hazeltons' Regional Transit System has routes to most communities within the Hazeltons', as well as major destinations like Wrinch Memorial Hospital, Northwest Community College, First Nations Education Centre and the historic Village of 'Ksan. It also has routes to Moricetown and Smithers on Tuesday and Thursdays. It has accessible services which include door to door service and priority seating.

Kamloops Transit System
1550 Ord Rd., Kamloops, BC V2B 7V4
Tel: 250-376-6373; *Fax:* 250-376-7398
coordinators@farwestgroup.com
www.bctransit.com/regions/kam
Profile: The Kamloops Transit System has several routes available to the public which go to all regions of Greater Kamloops. It also has several services available, including low floor busses, HandyDART, a Taxi Saver Program and priority seating.

Kaslo Transit System (Paratransit)
c/o Arrow & Slocan Lakes Community Services, PO Box 100, 205 - 6 Ave. North, Nakusp, BC V0G 1R0
Tel: 250-265-3674; *Fax:* 250-265-3378
jbrown@aslcs.com

Kelowna Regional Transit System
c/o Farwest Transit Services Inc., 1494 Hardy St., Kelowna, BC V1Y 8H2
Tel: 250-860-8140;
m.docherty@kelownatransit.com
www.busonline.ca/regions/kel
Profile: The Kelowna Transit System has several routes available to the public, which go to all regions of Greater Kelowna. It also has many accessible services, including low floor busses, HandyDART, a Taxi Saver program and priority seating.

Kimberley Transit System
260 - 4 Ave., Kimberley, BC V1A 2R6
Tel: 250-423-2015;
carole.rausch@interiorhealth.ca
www.bctransit.com/regions/kim
Profile: The Kimberley Transit System has routes within the City of Kimberley, and makes a round-trip to Cranbrook every 1st and 3rd Monday of the month. It also has several accessible services, including door to door service and priority seating.

Kings Transit Authority
PO Box 100, Kentville, NS B4N 3W3
Tel: 902-678-7310; *Fax:* 902-678-2545
Toll-Free: 888-546-4442
info@kingstransit.ns.ca
www.kingstransit.ns.ca
Profile: King Transit Authority is a public tranist system that operates in teh Annapolis Country between the towns of Bridgetown, Annapolis Royal and Greenwood. Their service also extends to Cornwallis Park and Upper Clements Park, as well as Digby County to Weymouth.
Andrew A. Paterson, General Manager

Kitimat Transit System
c/o Coastal Bus Lines Ltd., 780 Lahakas Blvd. South, Kitimat, BC V8C 1T9
Tel: 250-632-4444;
phil.malnis@farwestgroup.com
www.bctransit.com/regions/kit
Profile: The Kitimat Transit System has many routes that go to most of the major destinations in Kitimat. It also has several accessible services, including low floor busses, HandyDART, and priority seating.

Kootenay Boundary Transit System
8170 Old Waneta Rd., Trail, BC V1R 4W9
Tel: 250-364-3262; *Fax:* 250-364-2418
dennis.trailtransit@shawlink.ca
www.bctransit.com/regions/kob
Profile: The Kootenay Transit System has several routes available to the community that go to most of the major destinations in Trail. It also has many accessible services, including low floor busses, HandyDART, and priority seating.

Lethbridge Transit
619 - 4 Ave. North, Lethbridge, AB T1H 0K4
Tel: 403-320-3885; *Fax:* 403-380-3876
wbest@lethbridge.ca
Profile: Lethbridge Transit's mission is to provide a safe and efficient public transportation system that allows community access to economic, social, educational or leisure opportunities.

London Transit Commission
450 Highbury Ave. North, London, ON N5W 5L2
Tel: 519-451-1347;
www.londontransit.ca
Profile: L.T.C. services 32 routes (19 accessible). Annual ridership reaches 18.3 million
Larry E. Ducharme, General Manager

Medicine Hat Transit
333 - 6 Ave. SE, Medicine Hat, AB T1A 2S6
Tel: 403-529-8214; *Fax:* 403-527-5844
transit_dept@medicinehat.ca
Profile: The City of Medicine Hat operates a public transportation system, which is available and accessible to all residents of the community. Medicine Hat Transit makes every attempt to be responsive to the needs of residents and other community partners. Efficient use of human and physical resources, customer service and satisfaction, and a leadership role in providing a integrated transit system which meets the needs of our community, are just some of the objectives of our Transit Operations Plan.

Metro Transit
c/o Transit Services, Halifax Regional Municipalit, 200 Ilsley Ave., Dartmouth, NS B3B 1V1
Tel: 709-490-4000;
contactHRM@halifax.ca
www.region.halifax.ns.ca/metrotransit
Profile: Metro Transit has many services available to the community, including Accessible Low-Floor Buses, Charter Services, FRED (Free Rides Everwhere in Dowtown Halifax) as well as using more environmentally friendly biodiesal fuel.

Metrobus
245 Freshwater Rd., St. John's, NL A1B 1B3
Tel: 709-570-2020; *Fax:* 866-843-5287
infoservices@metrobus.com
www.metrobus.com
Profile: St. John's Metrobus System has recently been revitalized and is now offering more frequent services, more direct routes, reduced travel times and more express routes.

Mississauga Transit
975 Central Parkway West, Mississauga, ON L5C 3B1
Tel: 905-615-4636;
transit.info@mississauga.ca
www.mississauga.ca/portal/residents/publictransit
Profile: City operated since 1974 with a fleet of over 300 buses

Moose Jaw Transit System
City Hall, 228 Main St. North, Moose Jaw, SK S6H 3J8
Tel: 306-694-4488; *Fax:* 306-694-4022
transit@city.moose-jaw.sk.ca
Profile: The City of Moose Jaw Transit System offers bus service to all areas of the community. Routes are designed to provide the most efficient service possible to the citizens of Moose Jaw. Charter Service is also available, as is a Special Needs Service.

Nakusp Transit System (Paratransit)
c/o Arrow & Slocan Lakes Community Services, PO Box 100, 205 - 6 Ave. North, Nakusp, BC V0G 1R0
Tel: 250-265-3674; *Fax:* 250-265-3378
jbrown@aslcs.com

Nanaimo Regional Transit System
6300 Hammond Bay Rd., Nanaimo, BC V9T 6N2
Tel: 250-390-4531; *Fax:* 250-390-2757
Toll-Free: 877-604-4111
transprt@rdn.bc.ca
www.rdn.bc.ca
Profile: Nanaimo Regional Transit System provides both regular transit and HandyDART custom transit service. Regional Transit is operated by the Regional District of Nanaimo in partnership with BC Transit. We serve the area from Cedar in the south of the Regional District to Qualicum Beach in the north.
Anita Wajouda

Nelson/Slocan Valley Transit
c/o City of Nelson Public Works, #101, 310 Ward St., Nelson, BC V1L 5S4
Tel: 250-352-8228;
rod@city.nelson.bc.ca
www.bctransit.com/regions/nel
Profile: The Nelson/Slocan Valley Transit System has several routes which go to most of the major destinations in the area, as well as many rural stops in Taghum, Blewett, Beasley, Bonnington, South Slocan, Playmor, Shore Acres, Crescent Valley, Slocan Park, Passmore, Winlaw and Appledale. It also has accessible services including low floor busses, HandyDART and priority seating.

Niagara Transit Commission
4320 Bridge St., Niagara Falls, ON L2E 2R7
Tel: 905-356-1179; *Fax:* 905-356-5576
Toll-Free: 866-336-1119
info@niagaratransit.com
www.niagaratransit.com
Profile: Niagara Transit has supplied public transportation for the City of Niagara Falls since 1960. Presently supplies the city with 10 bus routes
Terry Librock, General Manager

North Bay Transit
PO Box 360, 200 McIntyre St. East, North Bay, ON P1B 8H8
Tel: 705-474-0419; *Fax:* 705-476-5308
Profile: Operates a fleet of 25 buses
Peter Reid, Transit Manager
705-474-0626, peter.reid@cityofnorthbay.ca

Oakville Transit
c/o Town of Oakville, PO Box 310, Oakville, ON L6J 5A6
Tel: 905-815-2020; *Fax:* 905-338-4166
transit-info@oakville.ca
www.oakvilletransit.com
Profile: Oakville Transit has been providing bus service to Oakville since 1972

Osoyoos Transit System
c/o South Okanagan Transit Society - Osoyoos Bapti, 8606 - 92nd Ave., Osoyoos, BC V0H 1V2
Tel: 250-495-8054; *Toll-Free:* 888-706-9752
obc@cablerocket.com
www.busonline.ca/regions/oso
Profile: Osoyoos Transit System operates Monday through Thursday, with Monday catering to destinations between Osoyoos and Kelowna Airport, including Oliver, Okanagan Falls, Penticton, Summerland, Peachland, Westbank and Kelowna, and Tuesday through Thursday servicing all destinations between Osoyoos and Summerland, including Oliver, Okanagan Falls and Penticton. It also has accessible services including handyDART and priority seating.

Ottawa Carleton Regional Transit Commission
1500 St. Laurent Blvd., Ottawa, ON K1G 0Z8
Tel: 613-741-6440;
ocinfo@ottawa.ca
www.octranspo.com
Profile: Has 911 buses in fleet; covers 225 routes and has over 2,200 employees
Janet Stavinga, Chair

Penticton Transit System
301 Warren Ave. East, Penticton, BC V2A 3M1
Tel: 250-492-4042;
mattb@berryandsmith.com
www.bctransit.com/regions/pen
Profile: The Penticton Transit System has many routes available both in the community and in rual areas. It also has several accessible services, including low floor busses, HandyDART, a taxi saver program and priority seating.

Peterborough Transit
c/o City of Peterborough, 190 Simcoe St., Peterborough, ON K9H 2H7
Tel: 705-745-0525;
jkimble@city.peterborough.on.ca
www.peterborough.ca/Living/City_Services/Transporta
Profile: Services the City of Peterborough, Ontario with regular and Handi-Van transit services. All regular Peterborough Transit routes now have fully accessible buses
Jim Kimble, Manager

Port Alberni/Clayoquot Transit
c/o Western Bus Lines, 4521 - 10 Ave., Port Alberni, BC V9Y 4X9
Tel: 250-723-3341; *Fax:* 250-723-8115
wbl@telus.net
www.bctransit.com/regions/pta
Profile: The Port Alberni/Clayoquot Transit System has several routes that go to most of the major destinations in the area, as well as many accessible services, including low floor busses, handyDART and priority seating.

Powell River Regional Transit System
c/o Powell River Municipal Transportation, 6910 Duncan St., Powell River, BC V8A 1W2
Tel: 604-485-4287; *Fax:* 604-485-4219
bprice@cdpr.bc.ca
www.bctransit.com/regions/pow
Profile: The Powell River Transit System has many routes available to the community, which go to most of the major destinations in the area. It also has several accessible services, including a rural transit service, low floor busses, HandyDART and priority seating.

Prince George Transit System
1041 Great St., Prince George, BC V2N 2K8
Tel: 250-563-0011; *Fax:* 250-564-4901
rick@bc.pwt.ca
www.bctransit.com/regions/prg
Profile: The Prince George Transit System has many routes that go to most of the major regions in the area. It also has several accessible services available to the community, including community travel training, low floor busses, HandyDART, a taxi saver program and priority seating.

Prince Rupert/Port Edward Transit
c/o Coastal Bus Lines Ltd., 225 - 2 Ave. West, Prince Rupert, BC V8J 1G4
Tel: 250-624-6400; *Fax:* 250-624-6432
bart.carrigan@farwestgroup.com
www.bctransit.com/regions/prr
Profile: The Prince Rupert/Port Edward Transit system has several routes available to the community that go to most of the major destinations in the area, as well as many accessible services, including low floor busses, HandyDART, a taxi saver program and door to door service.

Princeton & Area Transit System (Paratransit)
c/o Princeton & District Community Services, PO Box 1960, 47 Harold Ave., Princeton, BC V0X 1W0
Tel: 250-295-6666; *Fax:* 250-295-6214
Toll-Free: 800-291-0911
pcomserv@cablerocket.com
Profile: The Princeton and Area Transit System runs Monday through Friday, with door-to-door trips within Princeto and to and from Penticton, Hedley, Keremeos and Coalmont.
Lynn Pelly, Contact

Quesnel Transit System
c/o Five Five Transport, 355C Vaughan St., Quesnel, BC V2J 2T1
Tel: 250-992-1109;
fivefive@quesnelbc.ca
www.busonline.ca/regions/que
Profile: Quesnel Transit has several routes that go to most of the major destinations in the area, as well as many accessible services, including HandyDART and priority seating.

Red Deer Transit
PO Box 5008, Red Deer, AB T4N 3T4
Tel: 403-342-8225; *Fax:* 403-342-8222
transit@reddeer.ca
Profile: Red Deer Transit has several services available to the community, including Low Floor Buses, Overload Busses, Charter Bus Services, and a Citizen's Action Bus.

Regina Transit
PO Box 1790, 333 Winnipeg St., Regina, SK S4P 3C8
Tel: 306-777-7726; *Fax:* 306-949-7211
www.reginatransit.com
Profile: The City of Regina Transit System has several services available to the community, including a charter service, a safebus, night stops, and paratransit.

Réseau de transport de la capitale (RTC-Québec)
720, rue des Rocailles, Québec, QC G2J 1A5
Tél: 418-627-2351; *Téléc:* 418-641-6716
www.stcuq.qc.ca

Le Réseau de transport de Longueuil
Centre administratif, 1150, boul Marie-Victorin, Longueuil, QC J4G 2M4
Tél: 450-463-0131;
www.rtl-longueuil.qc.ca
Profile: Le Réseau de transport de Longueuil's (RTL) mission is to improve the quality of life of citizens in the territory served by the RTL by meeting their evolving transportation needs through the promotion and cost-effective operation of various quality and environmentally friendly public transportation means."
Pierre Del Fante, Dir.-gén.

Saint John Transit Commission
PO Box 3860 B, 951 Fairville Blvd., Saint John, NB E2M 5C2
Tel: 506-658-4700; *Fax:* 506-658-4704
Profile: The Saint John Transit Commission was established in 1979 to provide scheduled transit service to the city. It is the largest public transit system in New Brunswick in terms of both mileage and passengers. Saint John Transit's ridership is approximately 50 percent higher than the average for Canadian cities with a population of between 50,000 and 150,000.

St. Albert Transit
235 Carnegie Dr., St Albert, AB T8N 5A7
Tel: 780-418-6060; *Fax:* 780-459-4050
transit@st-albert.net
Profile: St-Albert Transit (StAT) local routes serve all neighbourhoods within the City of St. Albert, connecting with StAT commuter services to Edmonton destinations at either (or both) the Village Transit Station or St. Albert Centre Exchange. Edmonton destinations include downtown, the University of Alberta, MacEwan, NAIT, Government Centre and West Edmonton Mall.

St Catherines Transit Commission
2012 First St. Louth, RR#3, St Catharines, ON L2S 3V9
Tel: 905-687-5555;
phil@yourbus.com
www.yourbus.com

Sarnia Transit
1169 Michener Rd., Sarnia, ON N7S 4W3
Tel: 519-336-3271; *Fax:* 519-336-3361
transit@city.sarnia.on.ca
www.sarnia.ca/visit.asp?sectionid=53
Profile: Operates and maintains a fleet of 25 buses on the conventional transit system and 6 specialized vehicles on their Care-a-Van service (provided to people with disabilities)
Jim Stevens, Director

Saskatchewan Transportation Company
2041 Hamilton St., Regina, SK S4P 2E2
Tel: 306-787-3340;
info@stcbus.com
www.stcbus.com
Profile: Saskatchewan Transit has been providing passenger and freight transportation services for over 60 years, and provides passenger transportation and parcel express services throughout Saskatchewan operating main terminals in Regina, Saskatoon and Prince Albert with an additional 206 rural agencies in the Province.

Saskatoon Transit Services
c/o City of Saskatoon, 222 - 3rd Ave. North, Saskatoon, SK S7K 0J5
Tel: 306-975-3100; *Fax:* 306-975-7532
transit.services@saskatoon.ca
Profile: Saskatoon Transit's mission is to provide cost-effective, safe and affordable public transit services using clean and enviornmentally friendly public equipment that enables all residents to access work, education, health care, shopping, social and recreational opportunities.

Sault Ste. Marie Transit
111 Huron St., Sault Ste Marie, ON P6A 5P9
Tel: 705-759-5848; *Fax:* 705-759-5834
d.scott@cityssm.on.ca
Profile: The Sault Ste. Marie Transit has a fleet of 28 regular Transit vehicles, 7 Para Transit buses, and 1 Community Bus
Don Scott, Transit Manager
d.scott@cityssm.on.ca

Société de transport de l'Outaouais
111, rue Jean-Proulx, Gatineau, QC J8Z 1T4
Tél: 819-770-7900; *Téléc:* 819-770-5987
www.sto.ca
Profile: The mission of the Société de transport de l'Outaouais is to provide residents of the municipalities in its area, which includes the Gatineau urban area as well as Cantley and Chelsea, with a reliable public transit system that meets their needs at a reasonable cost for users, taxpayers and these municipalities. They have 246 busses, 259 shelters, 11 million kilometers travelled each ear, 56 bus routes, comprised of 41 regular, 13 express and 2 interzone routes).

Société de transport de Laval
2250, av Francis-Hughes, Laval, QC H7S 2C3
Tél: 450-662-5400; *Téléc:* 450-662-5459
pgiard@stl.laval.qc.ca
www.stl.laval.qc.ca
Profile: The Société de transport de Laval ha 34 bus routes, covering a total distance of 627 km, has approx. 22 hours of daily service on weekdays, and 21 hours on weekends, and covers 13.4 million km in a year. It has 463 drivers, 225 busses, 281 bus shelters and 2300 bus stops.
Pierre Giard, Directeur général

Société de transport de Montréal
800, rue de la Gauchetière ouest, Montréal, QC H5A 1J6
Tél: 514-786-4636;
www.stm.info
Profile: Transport Montreal, or STM, has both a bus, para-transit and metro system. It provides 1.3 million trips on its system every day, with 1503 busses, 89 mini paratransit busses and 759 metro cars.

Société de transport de Sherbrooke
895, rue Cabana, Sherbrooke, QC J1K 2M3
Tél: 819-564-2687; *Téléc:* 819-564-1069
service.clientele@sts.qc.ca
www.sts.qc.ca

Squamish Transit System
c/o Whistler Transit Ltd., #101, 1055 Millar Creek Rd., Whistler, BC V0N 1B0
Tel: 604-938-0388;
scott@whistlertransit.pwt.ca
www.bctransit.com/regions/squ
Profile: The Squamish Transit System has many routes that go to Valleycliffe, Brackendale, Highlands, Downtown, Woodfibre Ferry, Garibaldi Highlands and most major destinations in Squamish. It also has accessible services including low floor busses, HandyDART and priority seating.

Stratford Transit
60 Corcoran St., Stratford, ON N5A 1V7
Tel: 519-271-0250

Strathcona Transit
2001 Sherwood Dr., Sherwood Park, AB T8A 3W7
Tel: 780-417-7187; *Fax:* 780-417-7176
transit@strathcona.ab.ca
Profile: Strathcona's Transit's mission is to provide an effective, efficient and customer-focused transit service that aligns with the County's three pillars of sustainability: environmental, economic and social.

Sunshine Coast Transit System
5920 Mason Rd., Sechelt, BC V0N 3A0
Tel: 604-885-6899;
transit@scrd.bc.ca
www.bctransit.com/regions/sun
Profile: The Sunshine Coast Transit System has many routes that go to the most built-up residential neighbourhoods between the Langdale, Gibsons and Sechelt. In addition, there is service to Halfmoon Bay and limited service on Saturday, Sunday and holidays to Secret Cove in the summertime.

Terrace Regional Transit System
c/o Coastal Bus Lines Ltd., 4904 Hwy. 16 West, Terrace, BC V8G 1L8
Tel: 250-635-4991; *Fax:* 250-635-6417
phil.malnis@farwestgroup.com
www.bctransit.com/regions/ter
Profile: The Terrace Regional Transit System has many routes through the City of Terrace and the Regional District of Kitimat-Stikine. It also has several accessible services including low floor busses, Handy-DART and priority seating.

Thunder Bay Transit
570 Fort William Rd., Thunder Bay, ON P7B 2Z8
Tel: 807-684-3744; *Fax:* 807-345-5744
www.thunderbay.ca/index.cfm?fuse=html&pg=728
Profile: Operates with a fleet of 49 buses on 17 routes
Alex Grant, Manager

Timmins Transit
220 Algonquin Blvd. East, Timmins, ON P4N 1B3
Tel: 705-360-2654; *Fax:* 705-360-2698
transit@timmins.ca
www.timminstransit.ca/new
Profile: Timmins Transit is a service operated by the City of Timmins. They operate a fleet of over 25 buses, low floor buses, and accessible mini-buses
David Onodera, Transit Superintendent
david.onodera@city.timmins.on.ca

Toronto Transit Commission
1900 Yonge St., Toronto, ON M4S 1Z2
Tel: 416-393-4000; *Fax:* 416-338-0210
www.city.toronto.on.ca/ttc
Profile: Operates a subway system which is linked with buses, streetcars, and light rail transit. The TTC dates to 1892

Transit Windsor
3700 North Service Rd. East, Windsor, ON N8W 5X2
Tel: 519-944-4141; *Fax:* 519-944-5121
tw@city.windsor.on.ca
www.citywindsor.ca/transitwindsor
Profile: Fleet consists of 99 transit coaches, including 49 low floor vehicles

Trius Tours Ltd.
PO Box 2288, 22 Garfield St., Charlottetown, PE C1A 8C1
Tel: 902-566-5664; *Fax:* 902-566-3497
trius.tours@pei.aibn.com
Profile: Trius Tours has 2-54 passenger motor coaches, 12-47 passenger motor coaches and 5-15 passenger vans which provide scenic tours of Prince Edward Island.
George M. Brookins, Contact

Vernon Regional Transit System
4210 - 24 Ave., Vernon, BC V1T 1M2
Tel: 250-545-7286;
vernontransit@shawcable.ca
www.bctransit.com/regions/ver
Profile: The Vernon Regional Transit System has many routes available to the community which go to to most major destinations in the City of Vernon, to the District of Coldstream, and Spallumcheen, Armstrong, Endergy, Lavington, Whitevale and Lumby. It has accessible services including community travel training, a taxi saver program, low floor busses and HandyDART.

Victoria Regional Transit Commission
c/o BC Transit, 520 Gorge Rd. East, Victoria, BC V8W 2P3
Tel: 250-385-2551; *Fax:* 250-995-5639
nancy_longphee@bctransit.com
www.bctransit.com/regions/vic
Profile: The Victoria Regional Transit System began operation on 22 February 1890 with a fleet of four street cars. The system now serves approximately 312,000 persons and operates in a 400-square-kilometre area. The peak fleet in operation is 178 buses operating on 36 conventional routes, and 40 vans

providing custom door-to-door service for people who cannot ride the conventional buses.
Barbara Harris, Contact

WAVE Whistler & Valley Express
#101, 1055 Millar Creek Rd., Whistler, BC V0N 1B0
Tel: 604-932-4020;
scott@whistlertransit.pwt.ca
www.bctransit.com/regions/whi
Profile: The Whistler and Valley Express, or WAVE, runs through Emerald Estates, Alpine Meadows, Spruce Grove, White Gold, Nesters, Tapleys Farm, Blueberry Hill, Whistler Village, the Upper Village, Alta Vista, Nordic Whistler Creek, Tamarisk, Function Junction and Pemberton. It has racks on which you can attach your bicycles or skis, and runs from 5:30 am to 3:00 am, 365 days a year.

Welland Transit
c/o City Hall, 60 East Main St., Welland, ON L3B 3X4
Tel: 905-735-1700;
transit@welland.ca
www.city.welland.on.ca/Transit/wTransit.html
Margaret Fortin, Office Coordinator

West Coast Express Ltd.
#295, 601 West Cordova, Vancouver, BC V6B 1G1
Tel: 604-488-8906; *Fax:* 604-689-3896
wcecustomerservice@translink.bc.ca
www.westcoastexpress.com
Profile: West Coast Express (WCE) is an efficient commuter rail service linking Mission, Port Haney, Maple Ridge, Pitt Meadows, Port Coquitlam, Coquitlam and Port Moody with downtown Vancouver. They operate ten trains and two TrainBuses per day, Monday to Friday. There are five trains westbound from Mission to Vancouver in the morning peak commuter period and five trains eastbound from Vancouver to Mission in the afternoon. There is a morning TrainBus from Mission to Vancouver and an evening bus from Vancouver to Mission. West Coast Express does not run on weekends or statutory holidays.
Doug Kelsey, President & CEO

Whitehorse Transit
139 Tlingit St., Whitehorse, YT Y1A 2Y6
Tel: 867-668-8394;
transit@city.whitehorse.yk.ca
Profile: Whitehorse Transit runs six days a week, with no service on Sundays or holidays. There is also a Handy Bus which provides door-to-door service for those who are unable to use regular transit.
Dave Muir, Transit Manager

Winnipeg Transit
421 Osborne St., Winnipeg, MB R3L 2A2
Tel: 204-986-5717;
transit@winnipeg.com
winnipegtransit.com
Profile: Winnipeg Transit has 68 fixed routes throughout the city, including main line routes, express routes and suburban feeders, as well as a 'Handi-Transit' system.

Wood Buffalo Transit
9909 Franklin Ave., Fort McMurray, AB T9H 2K4
Tel: 780-743-4157; *Fax:* 780-799-5899
transit@woodbuffalo.ab.ca
Profile: The Fort McMurray Public Transit System provides efficient bus service on a fixed route, fixed schedule basis. Offering eight regular routes and service five days a week, it carries 900,000 riders annually and links all of Fort McMurray's subdivisions through direct or feeder connections. The service is reduced on weekends and not available on some statutory holidays. It is free for seniors and children under five years of age.

York Region Transit
50 High Tech Rd., 5th Fl., Richmond Hill, ON L4B 4N7
Tel: 905-762-2100;
transitinfo@york.ca
www.yorkregiontransit.com
Profile: YRT offers more than 100 routes including conventional services, GO Shuttles, Express services, community buses and high school, college and university services

Trucking Companies

American Cartage Ltd.
#101-9366 200A St., Langley, BC V1M 4B3
Tel: 604-513-3681; *Fax:* 604-513-3677
www.americancartage.com
Profile: To ensure prompt, safe delivery of marine containers to and from Vancouver's busy waterfront terminals.
Gloria Vander Schaaf, President

AMJ Campbell Inc.
1445 Courtneypark Dr., Mississauga, ON L5T 2E3
Tel: 905-795-3785; *Fax:* 905-670-3787
www.amjcampbell.com
Ticker Symbol: AMJ
Profile: Local trucking with storage; Trucking, except local
Bruce Bowser, President/CEO
Richard Smith, CFO

Bulk Carriers (PEI) Ltd.
PO Box 153, 779 Bannockburn Rd., Cornwall, PE C0A 1H0
Tel: 902-675-2600; *Fax:* 902-675-3100
info@bulkcarrierspei.com
www.bulkcarrierspei.com
Profile: With a fleet made up of reefer trailers, we haul primarily food products throughout 48 States and all the Canadian Provinces.
Jack Kelly, President

Canadian American Transportation Inc.
4 rue du Transport, Coteau-du-Lac, QC J0P 1B0
Tel: 450-763-6363; *Fax:* 450-763-2400
Toll-Free: 800-363-5313
cat@cat.ca
www.cat.ca
Profile: For over 25 years, we have listened to our customers and responded to their needs with services that met their requirements. As a result, our efforts have awarded us the reputation of being a leader in the transportation industry. C.A.T. also offers logistics services and a partnership program with other transportation companies enabling opportunities to serve you better.
Daniel Goyette, President

Canadian Freightways
Lake City Industrial Park, 7867 Express St., Burnaby, BC V5A 1S8
Tel: 604-420-4044; *Fax:* 604-420-4312
http://cf.cfmvmt.com
Profile: North American Coverage: Canadian Freightways provides services to 25,000 points across Canada and the U.S. through an integrated network of regional carriers including sister companies Epic Express and Click Express and strategic partners Averitt Express, New England Motor Freight, Midwest Motor Express and the Connection Company. Regional Expertise: Each partner in their North American network is a regional specialist providing overnight and second day service within their region. Partners operate local Service Centers and are represented by professional drivers and sales teams in key economic communities.
Ralph Wettstein, Vice-President

Can-Truck Inc.
655 Bloor St. West, Oshawa, ON L1J 5Y6
Tel: 905-404-6622; *Fax:* 905-404-6620
donf@can-truck.com
www.can-truck.com
Profile: Concentrates mainly on truckload freight including consolation and distribution throughout North America
Don Flesch, President
Frank Cassano, General Manager

Challenger Motor Freight Inc.
300 Maple Grove Rd., Cambridge, ON N3E 1B7
Tel: 519-653-6226; *Fax:* 519-653-9810
Toll-Free: 800-265-6358
info1@challenger.com
www.challenger.com
Profile: Challenger transports goods between Canada and anywhere in North America. Has a full range of transportation, warehousing and logistics services
Dan Einwechter, Chairman & CEO

Challenger Motor Freight Inc.
300 Maple Grove Rd., Cambridge, ON N3E 1B7
Tel: 519-653-6226; *Fax:* 519-653-9810
Toll-Free: 800-265-6358
info1@challenger.com
www.challenger.com
Profile: Constantly challenging ourselves to set new standards of quality and performance through leadership, respect and commitment.
Dan Einwechter, Chairman & CEO

Contrans Income Fund
PO Box 1210, 1179 Ridgeway Rd., Woodstock, ON N4S 8P6
Tel: 519-421-4600; *Fax:* 519-539-9220
info@contrans.ca
www.contrans.ca
Ticker Symbol: CSS
Profile: Offices of holding companies; Long-distance trucking
Stan G. Dunford, Chair/CEO
Gregory W. Rumble, President/COO
James S. Clark, CFO & Vice-President, Finance
Kim Barnes, Manager, Management Information Systems

CRS-Express Inc.
2100, 95e rue, Saint-Georges, QC G5Y 8J3
Tel: 418-227-7379; *Fax:* 418-227-7381
Toll-Free: 800-807-7379
www.crs-express.com
Profile: CRS Express is dedicated to excellence in the transportation industry. Pur customers will receive high quality services by a professional and complete transport.

Essen Transport Ltd.
PO Box 2229, Winkler, MB R6W 4B9
Tel: 204-325-5200; *Fax:* 204-325-5252
Toll-Free: 800-760-3776
www.essentransport.com
Profile: Their focus on teamwork continues to satisfy new customers with effective supply chain management that consistently delivers on time. Essen Transport's team uses cutting edge logistics to track inbound and outbound shipments for over 100 reputable companies in Canada and the US .

Ghost Transportation Services
715E-46th St. West, Saskatoon, SK S7L 6A1
Tel: 306-249-3515; *Fax:* 306-249-3335
customerservice@ghosttrans.com
www.ghosttrans.com
Profile: Ghost Transportation Services' diversity and flexibility are the keys. Whether it be warehousing, the shipment of raw materials, transportation or distribution of finished products, our dedication to satisfy our customer's needs and wants provides mutual success.
Clay Dowling, President

GN Transport
163 Bowes Rd., Concord, ON L4K 1H3
Tel: 905-760-2888; *Fax:* 905-760-2040
info@gntransport.com
www.gntransport.com
Profile: With deregulation firmly in place, GN Transport Ltd. has expanded to serve our customers more effectively and to generate business opportunities within Ontario, and cross border into the United States.

Go Transport Ltd.
88 Golden Dr., Coquitlam, BC V3K 6T1
Tel: 604-945-8300; *Fax:* 604-945-8305
Toll-Free: 888-363-6699
dispatch@gotransport.ca
www.gotransport.ca
Mark Maarsman, President

Grimshaw Trucking LP
11510-151 St., Edmonton, AB T5M 3N6
Tel: 780-414-2880; *Fax:* 780-455-7818
Toll-Free: 888-414-2850
www.grimshaw-trucking.com
Profile: A highly respected transportation company in Western Canada.
Graham McDonald, Vice President

Group Express Inc.
170 Main St. N., Alexandria, ON K0C 1A0
Tel: 613-525-1275; *Fax:* 613-525-1278
traffic@groupexpress.ca
www.groupexpress.ca
Profile: Groupex will provide our customers with quality transportation services of the highest value while emphasizing sustainable growth and public safety as measures of corporate strength and security for our employees.
Reynald Blais, President
Jeff ManKinnon, Traffic Manager

Harold Newell & Son Trucking Ltd.
R.R. #1, Barrington, NS B0W 1E0
Tel: 902-637-2243; *Fax:* 902-637-1563
trucking@ns.sympatico.ca
www.tcfb.com/trucking

International Truck and Engine Corporation Canada
5500 North Service Rd., 4th Fl., Burlington, ON L7L 5H7
Tel: 905-332-3323; *Fax:* 905-332-2965
www.internationaldelivers.com
Profile: Dealers of trucks, buses, vans: engines, parts, services & financing
James J. Schumacher, President

Kindersley Transport Inc.
660 Aldford Ave., Delta, BC V3M 6X1
Tel: 604-522-4002; *Fax:* 604-525-2955
customerservice@kindersleytransport.com
www.kindersleytransport.com

Profile: One of the largest, most modern fleets based in Western Canada providing truckload and less-than-truckload services through a network of strategically located service centers in Canada and the U.S.
Erwen Siemens, President

KO Transport Inc.
651 Burlington St. E., Hamilton, ON L8L 4J5
Tel: 905-544-9000;
info@kotransport.com
www.kotransport.com
Profile: KO Transport is a family-owned and operated business. Established in 1933, KO Transport has been in business since 1933, servicing the Southern Ontario region and points well beyond.

Kooi Trucking Inc.
PO Box 70, Scotland, ON N0E 1R0
Tel: 519-446-3333; *Fax:* 519-446-3999
info@kooitruckinginc.com
www.kooitruckinginc.com
Profile: Kooi Trucking Inc. is an experienced freight company, specializing in the transportatoin needs of North American importers and exporters since 1993.
Sue Kooi, President

Lark Transport Inc.
2880 Saskatchewan Ave. W., Portage la Prairie, MB R1N 3B9
Tel: 888-444-5257; *Fax:* 888-246-9365
www.larktransport.com
Profile: Lark Transport Inc. is proud to be a Canadian based freight transportation company.
Reynold Plett, Contact, Sales
reynold@larktransport.com
Rene Painchaud, Contact, Dispatch
rene@larktransport.com

Lighthouse Transport Services Ltd.
PO Box 38010, #2-150 Wright Ave., Dartmouth, NS B3B 1X2
Tel: 902-468-3696; *Fax:* 902-468-5267
Toll-Free: 800-770-5457
colleen@lighthousetransport.com
www.lighthousetransport.com
Profile: Offers FTL and LTL transport, container transport, warehousing and crating, oversized cargo moves, pilot car services, flatbed moves, deconsolidations, in bond warehousing, exclusive deliveries, in bond transport.
Ernest O'Toole, President

Motrux Inc.
731 Belgrave Way, Delta, BC V3M 5R8
Tel: 604-527-1000; *Fax:* 604-527-1002
Toll-Free: 800-663-3436
info@motrux.com
www.motrux.com
Profile: Over the years Motrux has evolved from a designated carrier, serving only a few specific customers in Western Canada, to one that now serves many customers across a variety of industries - throughout North America.

Mullen Transportation Inc.
PO Box 87, 1 Maple Leaf Rd., Aldersyde, AB T0L 0A0
Tel: 403-652-8888; *Fax:* 403-601-8301
ir@mullentransportation.com
www.mullen-trans.com
Ticker Symbol: MTL
Profile: Offices of holding companies; Long-distance trucking; Local trucking with storage; Various oil & gas fields services
Murray K. Mullen, CEO/Chair
Stephen H. Lockwood, President & Co-CEO
David E. Olsen, CFO & Vice-President, Finance

Overland Freight Courrier
#300-10362 King George Hwy., Surrey, BC V3T 2W5
Tel: 604-580-4600; *Fax:* 604-580-4601
Toll-Free: 800-698-2111
admin@overland.ca
www.welightentheload.com
Profile: We are a diverse group of Canadian individuals who try to provide our customers with no surprises LTL-freight-courier service in British Columbia Canada, Alberta Canada, and the Western United States of America.

Pacific Coast Express Ltd.
#220-185 Golden Dr., Coquitlam, BC V3K 6T1
Toll-Free: 800-667-6061
www.pcx.ca/pacificcoast.htm
Profile: Pacific Coast Express Ltd. is a wholly owned operating unit of Landtran Systems Inc., Western Canada's largest integrated regional distribution company. The primary service offered by the company is expedited LTL/TL, dry van motor freight service between all points in Western Canada and core markets in Arizona, California, Oregon Washington and Mexico. We also provide selected service to points in the Idaho and Utah markets from British Columbia and Alberta, as well as domestic transportation to and from Vancouver Island.
Al Turner, President

Phantom Freightlines
5300 86 Ave. SE, Calgary, AB T2C 47L
Tel: 403-219-1008; *Fax:* 403-219-1016
www.phantomfreightlines.com
Profile: Phantom Freightlines is a family-owned, Alberta based business that specializes in the transportation of time sensitive and delicate materials for over 25 years. From meat and produce, to flowers and plants, we understand the unique needs of temperature controlled cargo and pride ourselves on providing safe, hassle-free delivery 365 days a year across Canada and the United States.
Scott Decker, Director, Corporate Development
Lindsey Kydd, Vice President, Sales and Marketing

Polar Express Transportation Ltd.
#4, 10097-201 St., Langley, BC V1M 3G4
Tel: 604-888-3729; *Fax:* 604-888-3759
jplowman@polarexpresstrans.com
www.polarexpresstrans.com
Profile: Starting January 2000 with one 10 ton and one tractor/trailer we began hauling refrigerated goods to/from Seattle/Tacoma, WA and Vancouver, BC. Using this foundation we have grown to become the West's best choice for handling refrigerated goods moving between the US and Canada.

Premium Trucknig Ltd.
PO Box 39, 449 Lower Rd., Arichat, NS B0E 1A0
Tel: 902-226-3474; *Fax:* 902-226-0026
www.premiumseafoods.ns.ca/ptrucking.php
Profile: Premium Trucking Ltd. provides world-class transportation services at a fair price. The company owns and operates a fleet of high-quality vehicles, which includes five delivery trucks and two tractor-trailers.
Edgar Sampson, President

Redline Transport
PO Box 22, R.R. #4, Brandon, MB R7A 5Y4
Tel: 204-727-1673; *Fax:* 204-725-3548
Toll-Free: 800-367-0375
redline@escape.ca
www.redlinetransport.com
Profile: Redline Transport has remained an important part of the rural economy. Redline Transport changed ownership in September 2005, when it was bought be Robert & Lynda Moffatt in Strathclair. Redline continues to grow with more than 20 trucks on the road and offices in both Rivers and Brandon.
Ron Bouchardd, General Manager

Rockman Transport
10765 Cote de Lisse #56, Dorval, QC H9P 1A7
Tel: 514-422-1085; *Fax:* 514-422-1083
www.rockmantransport.com
Profile: A bonded transport company with facilities at Montreal and Ottawa, serving the CL and LCL container deliveries for the major Maritime Companies for over 20 years, Rockman Trucking is equipped with recent and well kept equipment to ensure prompt and timely deliveries. We can deliver any size container; from 20' to 53'. Whether regular, High Cube, Open top or Reefer containers for Imports as well as Exports purposes.

Rolls Right Industry
2961 Norland Ave., Burnaby, BC V5B 3A9
Tel: 604-298-0080; *Fax:* 604-298-1366
info@rollsright.ca
www.rollsright.ca
Profile: At Rolls Right Industries, we understand that our customers depend on timely deliveries to maintain proper inventory levels, fully-stocked shelves and secure sales. Whether your are a local supplier to the retail sector or a custom broker moving containers, with a wide range of time sensitive freight transportation services, Rolls Right will get you there.

Shadow Lines Transportation Group
9818 198B St., Langley, BC V1M 2X5
Tel: 604-888-2976; *Fax:* 604-888-2459
www.shadowlines.com
Profile: Shadow Lines has over 35 years experience as a service based transportation company. We operate in Canada from British Columbia to Ontario and throughout the 48 states of the continental USA.

Swift Dispatch Service Ltd.
32 West 5th Ave., Vancouver, BC V5Y 1H5
Tel: 604-873-5422; *Fax:* 604-879-2311
info@swiftdispatch.com

TLI FlatDecks Inc.
1260 Cliveden Ave., Delta, BC V3M 6Y1
Tel: 877-517-1177; *Fax:* 604-527-1175
www.tliflatdecks.net
Profile: We are an international flat deck specialized carrier, based in Delta BC, servicing all of North America. As a bonded carrier with terminals across Canada, we offer cross dock and reload services at all our locations. We have 24-hour dispatch and all types of trailers, including heavy haul units. Continuous improvement is the cornerstone of a growing, innovative company.
John Stokes, Contact

TMT Freight System
14 Cadetta Rd., Brampton, ON L6T 3Z8
Tel: 905-794-9845; *Fax:* 905-794-9846
Toll-Free: 888-817-4410
info@tmtfreight.com
www.tmtfreight.com
Profile: TMT Freight System was emerged as an innovative company in the year 1993 and over our nearly 13 year history; we have dedicated our efforts to being a container carrier with a strong motto of on time delivery with care and safety.
Bobby Mahal, President
Jasbir Sanghera, Vice Prestident

Trailmobile Canada Limited
455 Gibraltar Dr., Mississauga, ON L5T 2S9
Tel: 905-565-9500; *Fax:* 905-565-9525
hq@trailmobile.com
www.trailmobile.com
Profile: Manufacturers of truck trailers
Tom Wiseman, President
Bert Clay, Vice-President, Sales & Marketing

TransForce Income Fund
6600, ch St-François, Montréal, QC H4S 1B7
Tel: 514-856-7500; *Fax:* 514-332-9527
administration@transforce.ca
www.transforce.ca
Ticker Symbol: TFI
Profile: Long-distance trucking; Local trucking without storage
Alain Bedard, President/CEO & Chair
Salvatore Vitale, CFO

TransForce Income Fund
#300, 8585 Trans-Canada Highway, Saint-Laurent, QC H4S 1Z6
Tel: 514-331-4000; *Fax:* 514-337-4200
administration@transforce.ca
www.transforce.ca
Profile: TransForce Income Fund creates value for unitholders by managing and investing in a growing network of independent operating companies. The Fund, through these subsidiaries, is the leader in Canada's transportation and logistics industry.
Alain Bedard, President & CEO

Trappers Transport Ltd.
2475 Day St., Winnipeg, MB R2C 2Z2
Tel: 204-697-7647; *Fax:* 204-633-5569
www.trapperstransport.com
Profile: We specialize in the transportation of refrigerated LTL or Full Loads throughout North America. Our maintenance shop services or repairs all makes and models of trucks, trailers, heavy equipment and reefer units.
Dan Omeniuk, President & CEO
Pankaj Sharma, Vice President & CFO, Finance

Trimac Corporation
PO Box 3500 M, #1700, 800 - 5th Ave. SW, Calgary, AB T2P 2P9
Tel: 403-298-5100; *Fax:* 403-298-5146
info@trimac.com
www.trimac.com
Ticker Symbol: TMA.UN
Profile: The company provides services in highway transportation of bulk commodities.
Terry Owen, President/CEO
416-298-5101, Fax: 416-298-5355, tjowen@trimac.com
Ed Malysa, Vice-President/CFO
416-298-5176, Fax: 416-298-5146, emalysa@trimac.com

Vitran Corporation Inc.
#701, 185 The West Mall, Toronto, ON M9C 5L5
Tel: 416-596-7664; *Fax:* 416-596-8039
webmaster@vitran.com
www.vitran.com
Ticker Symbol: VTN
Profile: Long-distance trucking; Arrangement of transportation of freight & cargo; General warehousing & storage; Refuse systems
Rick E. Gaetz, President/CEO
Sean P. Washchuk, CFO & Vice-President, Finance

West Arm Truck Lines
1077 Columbia Rd., Castlegar, BC V1N 4K5
Tel: 250-365-2127; *Fax:* 250-365-5658
Toll-Free: 800-363-9247
info@westarm.com
www.westarm.com
Profile: West Arm Truck Lines is the premier freight service provider in Southern British Columbia and Alberta. We provide overnight LTL service to all major centres in these areas. Well maintained, late model equipment and the most up to date computer technology allow the people of West Arm Truck Lines to deliver on commitments to our customers.
Michael Revane, Contact
michael_revane@westarm.com

Yanke Group of Companies
2815 Lorne Ave., Saskatoon, SK S7J 0S5
Tel: 306-955-4221; *Fax:* 306-955-5663
Toll-Free: 800-667-7988
yanke_sales@yanke.ca
www.yanke.ca
Profile: During the last 30 years, our founder has seen Yanke expand from a mere two trucks to a fleet of more than 400, and flourish from 33 employees to over 700. Cancom satellite systems. Instant shipment tracking. National weather monitoring system. Why does Yanke do all of this? We strive to stay ahead of our time to make sure that we are always on time.

Zeena Transport
PO Box 759, Morden, MB R6M 1A7
Tel: 204-822-4915; *Fax:* 204-822-4687
www.zeenatransport.com
Profile: We are proud to offer our customers the best refrigerated and dry van service possible. We accomplish this by utilizing dependable, up-to-date equipment and well trained, dependable employees.
Henry Giesbrecht, President
Reynold Hildebrand, Operations Manager

Transportation Manufacturers & Services

Atlas Cold Storage Income Trust
5255 Yonge St., Toronto, ON M2N 5P8
Tel: 416-512-2352; *Fax:* 416-512-2353
Toll-Free: 888-642-3333
inquiries@atlascold.com
www.atlascold.com
Ticker Symbol: FZR
Profile: Refrigerated warehousing & storage
J. David Williamson, President/CEO
Kevin Glass, Sr. Vice-President & CFO
Robert Lockie, Vice-President, Information Technology Operations

Bombardier Inc.
800, boul René-Lévesque ouest, Montréal, QC H3B 1Y8
Tel: 514-861-9481; *Fax:* 514-861-7053
www.bombardier.com
Ticker Symbol: BBD
Profile: Manufacturers of railroad equipment, aircraft, aircraft engines & engine parts, aircraft parts & auxiliary equipment, various transportation equipment; Personal credit institutions; Real estate land subdividers & developers
Laurent Beaudoin, Chair/CEO
Pierre Beaudoin, President/COO, Bombardier Aerospace
Pierre Alary, Sr. Vice-President/CFO

Dynetek Industries Ltd.
4410 - 46 Ave. SE, Calgary, AB T2B 3N7
Tel: 403-720-0262; *Fax:* 403-720-0263
invest@dynetek.com
www.dynetek.com
Ticker Symbol: DNK
Profile: Manufacturers of cylinders, fuel cell storage systems
Robb D. Thompson, President/CEO
Karen Y. Minton, Vice-President, Finance & Administration

Glendale International Corp.
353 Iroquois Shore Rd., Oakville, ON L6H 1M3
Tel: 905-844-2870; *Fax:* 905-844-2907
info@glendaleint.com
www.glendaleint.com
Ticker Symbol: GIN
Profile: Manufacturers of motor homes, travel trailers & campers, radio & television broadcasting & communications equipment, printed circuit boards, & various electronic components
Edward C. Hanna, President/CEO & Chair
Philip L. Szabo, Vice-President/CFO & Secretary

Greyhound Canada Transportation Corp.
877 Greyhound Way SW, Calgary, AB T3C 3V8
Tel: 403-260-0877; *Fax:* 403-260-0779
canada.info@greyhound.ca
www.greyhound.ca
Profile: Intercity & rural bus transportation; travel agencies; courier services
Dave Leach, Sr. Vice President, Canada

Héroux-Devtek inc
Tour est, #658, 1111, rue St-Charles, Longueuil, QC J4K 5G4
Tel: 450-679-3330; *Fax:* 450-679-3666
ir@herouxdevtek.com
www.herouxdevtek.com
Ticker Symbol: HRX
Profile: Manufacturers of aircraft parts & auxiliary equipment; Wholesalers of transportation equipment & supplies; Airports, flying fields & airport terminal services
Gilles Labbé, President/CEO
Réal Bélanger, CFO & Exec. Vice-President

Intier Automotive Inc.
521 Newpark Blvd., Newmarket, ON L3Y 4X7
Tel: 905-898-5200; *Fax:* 905-898-4178
info@intier.com
www.intier.com
Ticker Symbol: IAI.A
Profile: Develops & manufactures vehicle interiors; Consumer research
Donald J. Walker, President/CEO
Michael E. McCarthy, CFO & Exec. Vice-President
Georg Kirchbaumer, Chief Technology Officer

Lear Canada Ltd.
PO Box 9758, 530 Manitou Dr., Kitchener, ON N2G 4C2
Tel: 519-895-1600; *Fax:* 519-895-3248
www.lear.com
Profile: Designs, tests & produces automotive interiors
Donald J. Stebbins, President/COO, Americas
David C. Wajsgras, CFO & Sr. Vice-President, Lear Corporation

Linamar Corporation
287 Speedvale Ave. West, Guelph, ON N1H 1C5
Tel: 519-836-7550; *Fax:* 519-836-9175
investorrelations@linamar.com
www.linamar.com
Ticker Symbol: LNR
Profile: Manufacturers of motor vehicle parts & accessories, fabricated plate work, carburetors, pistons, piston rings, valves, farm machinery equipment, aircraft parts & auxiliary equipment, pumps & pumping equipment; Wholesalers of farm & garden machinery & equipment
Linda Hasenfratz, President/CEO
Csaba Havasi, Group President, Europe
Peggy Mulligan, CFO/ Exec. Vice-President & Treasurer
Mark Stoddart, Chief Technology Development Officer & Vice-President, Marketing

Magellan Aerospace Corporation
3160 Derry Rd. East, Mississauga, ON L4T 1A9
Tel: 905-677-1889; *Fax:* 905-677-5658
info@aerospace.com
www.magellanaerospace.com
Ticker Symbol: MAL
Profile: Manufacturers of aircraft parts & auxiliary equipment, aircraft engines & engine parts
Richard A. Neill, President/CEO
John B. Dekker, Secretary/Vice-President, Finance
Donald C. Lowe, Chair, Risk Management & Environmental Committee

Magna International Inc.
337 Magna Dr., Aurora, ON L4G 7K1
Tel: 905-726-2462; *Fax:* 905-726-7164
www.magnaint.com
Ticker Symbol: MG
Profile: Manufacturers of motor vehicle parts & accessories, automotive stampings, various fabricated metal products, motor vehicles & passenger car bodies, vehicular lighting equipment, various fabricated textile products, public building & related furniture; Wholesalers of motor vehicle supplies & new parts; Racing, including track operation; Various amusement & recreation services
Siegfried Wolf, Co-CEO
Vincent J. Galifi, CFO & Exec. Vice-President, Finance

NAV Canada
PO Box 3411 D, 77 Metcalfe St., Ottawa, ON K1P 5L6
Tel: 613-563-5588; *Fax:* 613-563-3426
Toll-Free: 800-876-4693
service@navcanada.ca
www.navcanada.ca
Profile: Provides, maintains & enhances an air navigation service
John W. Crichton, President/CEO
R.A. (Sandy) Morrison, Chair
William G. Fenton, Treasurer/CFO & Vice-President, Finance
John Morris, Director, Communications
Sidney Koslow, Vice-President/Chief Technology Officer

Northstar Aerospace
105 Bedford Rd., Toronto, ON M5R 2K4
Tel: 416-364-5852; *Fax:* 416-362-5334
www.northstar-aerospace.com
Ticker Symbol: NAS
Profile: Manufacturers of motor vehicle parts & accessories, aircraft parts & auxiliary equipment, speed changers, industrial high-speed drives, gears, aircraft engines & engine parts; Airports, flying fields & airport terminal services
Mark Emery, President/CEO
Thomas E. Connerty, CFO

Pratt & Whitney Canada Corp.
1000, boul Marie-Victorin, Longueuil, QC J4G 1A1
Tel: 450-677-9411; *Fax:* 450-647-3620
communications@pwc.ca
www.pwc.ca
Profile: Manufacturers of aircraft engines & engine parts; Wholesalers of transportation equipment & supplies
Alain M. Bellemare, President
Miguel C. Doyon, Vice-President, Finance
Amal M. Girgis, Chief Information Officer
John Saabas, Exec. Vice-President

Prevost Car Inc.
35, boul Gagnon, Sainte-Claire, QC G0R 2V0
Tel: 418-883-3391; *Fax:* 418-883-4157
www.prevostcar.com
Profile: Manufacturers of intercity coaches & coach shells for motorhomes & specialty conversion
Gaetan Bolduc, President/CEO

Public Storage Canadian Properties
First Canadian Place, #6600, 100 King St. West, Toronto, ON M5X 1B8
Toll-Free: 866-772-2623
investor@publicstorage.ca
www.publicstoragecanada.com
Ticker Symbol: PUB
Profile: General warehousing & storage
David P. Singelyn, President
Vincent R. Chan, Vice-President/Controller

Rolls-Royce Canada ltée
9500, ch de la Côte-de-Liesse, Montréal, QC H8T 1A2
Tel: 514-636-0964; *Fax:* 514-636-9969
www.rolls-royce.com
Profile: Airports, flying fields & airport terminal services; Manufacturers of steam, gas, hydraulic turbines & turbine generator units
Pierre Racine, President/CEO
Stephane Guerin, CFO

Spar Aerospace Limited
Edmonton International Airport, PO Box 9864, Edmonton, AB T5J 2T2
Tel: 780-890-6300; *Fax:* 780-890-6652
www.spar.ca
Profile: Aviation services: aircraft programs; Component maintenance, repair & operation; Support services
Patrice M. Pelletier, President

ThyssenKrupp Budd Canada Inc.
PO Box 1204, Kitchener, ON N2G 4G8
Tel: 519-895-1000; *Fax:* 519-895-0099
Ticker Symbol: BUD
Profile: Manufacturers of motor vehicle parts & accessories; Wholesalers of motor vehicle supplies & new parts
Micheal Balavich, President
David A. Robinson, CFO & Controller

The Toronto Transit Commission
1900 Yonge St., Toronto, ON M4S 1Z2
Tel: 416-393-4000; *Fax:* 416-482-0478
www.ttc.ca
Profile: Operates & maintains urban transit system: buses, subways, streetcars & trolleys
R. Ducharme, CEO
Mike Roche, CFO
John Cannon, Chief Information Officer

Tri-White Corporation
#1400, 1 University Ave., Toronto, ON M5J 2P1
Tel: 416-367-6877; *Fax:* 416-367-6890
www.tri-white.com
Ticker Symbol: TWH
Profile: Local & suburban transit; Local passenger transportation
K. (Rai) Sahi, Chair/CEO
Donald W. Turple, CFO
Beverley Flynn, Corporate Counsel & Secretary

Uniglobe Travel International L.P.
#900, 1199 West Pender St., Vancouver, BC V6E 2R1
Tel: 604-718-2600; *Fax:* 604-718-2678
info@uniglobetravel.com
www.uniglobetravel.com
Profile: Travel franchise specializing in corporate travel services for small to medium accounts as well as individual travelers.
U. Gary Charlwood, Chair/CEO
Tracy Bartram, CFO & Exec. Vice-President

Vector Aerospace Corporation
#300, 105 Bedford Rd., Toronto, ON M5R 2K4
Tel: 416-925-1143; *Fax:* 416-925-7214
investorinfo@vectoraerospace.ca
www.vectoraerospace.ca
Ticker Symbol: RNO
Profile: Manufacturers of aircraft parts & auxiliary equipment; Electrical & electronic repair shops; Various repair shops & related services
Donald Jackson, President/CEO
Randal L. Levine, Sr. Vice-President/CFO & Corporate Secretary

Versacold Income Fund
2115 Commissioner St., Vancouver, BC V5L 1A6
Tel: 604-255-4656; *Fax:* 604-255-4330
info@versacold.com
www.versacold.com
Ticker Symbol: ICE
Profile: Refrigerated logistics services: storage & transportation
H. Brent Sugden, Chair/President & CEO
Joel M. Smith, CFO & Exec. Vice-President

Wescast Industries Inc.
150 Savannah Oaks Dr., Brantford, ON N3T 5L8
Tel: 519-750-0000; *Fax:* 519-720-1629
investor.relations@wescast.com
www.wescast.com
Ticker Symbol: WCS
Profile: Manufacturers of motor vehicle parts & accessories; Wholesalers of motor vehicle supplies & new parts
Edward G. Frackwiak, Chair/CEO
Dave Dean, Vice-President, Finance

World Point Terminals Inc.
#303, 407 - 8th Ave. SW, Calgary, AB T2P 1E5
Tel: 403-261-3700; *Fax:* 403-282-3323
Ticker Symbol: WPO
Profile: Various transportation services; Special warehousing & storage; Manufacturers of petroleum refining
Bruce N. Calvin, President
Steven G. Twele, CFO

Government Agency Guide

AIRPORTS & AVIATION
See Also: Transportation
Canadian Air Transport Security Authority, 99 Bank St., 13th Fl., Ottawa, ON K1P 6B9
Fax: 613-991-6726, 888-294-2202
Institute for Aerospace Research, 1200 Montreal Rd., Ottawa, K1A 0R6 ON
613-991-5738, Fax: 613-952-7214
Transport Canada, Place de Ville, 330 Sparks St., Tower C, Ottawa, K1A 0N5 ON
613-990-2309, Fax: 613-954-4731, minTC@tc.gc.ca
Transportation Appeal Tribunal of Canada, 333 Laurier Ave. West, 12th Fl., Ottawa, ON K1A 0N5
613-990-6906, Fax: 613-990-9153, info@tatc.gc.ca

Newfoundland & Labrador
Department of Transportation & Works, Confederation Bldg., West Block, 6th Fl., PO Box 8700, St. John's, A1B 4J6 NL
709-729-3679, Fax: 709-729-4285, twminister@gov.nl.ca

Northwest Territories
Airports, YK Centre, 4922 - 28th St., 4th fl., PO Box 1320, Yellowknife, X1A 2L9 NT
867-873-7725, Fax: 867-873-0297
Department of Transportation, Lahm Ridge Bldg., 4501 50 Ave., PO Box 1320, Yellowknife, X1A 2L9 NT
867-920-3460, Fax: 867-873-0363

Nunavut
Department of Community & Government Services, J.G. Brown Bldg., PO Box 1000 700,Iqaluit, X0A 0H0 NU
867-975-5400, Fax: 867-975-5305

Ontario
Ministry of Transportation, Ferguson Block, 77 Wellesley St. West, 3rd Fl., Toronto, M7A 1Z8 ON
416-235-4686, Fax: 416-327-9185, 800-268-4686

Saskatchewan
Saskatchewan Highways & Infrastructure, 1855 Victoria Ave., Regina, S4P 3T2 SK
306-787-4800,

Yukon Territory
Yukon Highways & Public Works, PO Box 2703, Whitehorse, Y1A 2C6 YT
867-393-7193, Fax: 867-393-6218, 800-661-0408, hpw-info@gov.yk.ca

RAIL TRANSPORTATION
See Also: Transportation
Transportation Safety Board of Canada, 200 Promenade du Portage, 4th Fl., Ottawa, K1A 1K8 ON
819-994-3741, Fax: 819-997-2239, 800-387-3557
Via Rail Canada Inc., #500, 3, Place Ville-Marie, Montréal, H3B 2C9 QC
514-871-6000, Fax: 514-871-6768

Manitoba
Manitoba Infrastructure & Transportation, Legislative Building, #203, 450 Broadway Ave., Winnipeg, R3C 0V8 MB
204-945-3723, Fax: 204-945-7610

New Brunswick
Department of Transportation, Kings Pl., 440 KingSt., PO Box 6000, Fredericton, E3B 5H8 NB
506-453-3939, Fax: 506-453-2900, Transportation.Web@gnb.ca

Newfoundland & Labrador
Department of Transportation & Works, Confederation Bldg., West Block, 6th Fl., PO Box 8700, St. John's, A1B 4J6 NL
709-729-3679, Fax: 709-729-4285, twminister@gov.nl.ca

Nova Scotia
Department of Transportation & Infrastructure Renewal, Johnston Bldg., 1672 Granville St., 2nd Fl., PO Box 186, Halifax, B3J 2N2 NS
902-424-2297, Fax: 902-424-0171, 888-432-3233, tpwpaff@gov.ns.ca

Ontario
GO Transit, #600, 20 Bay St., Toronto, ON M5J 2W3
416-869-3600, Fax: 416-869-1755, 888-438-6646

Quebec
Société du port ferroviaire Baie-Comeau-Hauterive, 18, rte Maritime, Baie-Comeau, QC G4Z 2L6
418-296-6785, Fax: 418-296-2377, soport@globetrotter.qc.ca
Ministère des Transports, 700, boul René-Lévesque est, 27e étage, Québec, G1R 5H1 QC
Fax: 514-643-1269, 888-355-0511, communications@mtq.gouv.qc.ca

Saskatchewan
Saskatchewan Highways & Infrastructure, 1855 Victoria Ave., Regina, S4P 3T2 SK
306-787-4800

TRANSPORTATION
Atlantic Pilotage Authority Canada, #910, 2000 Barrington St., Halifax, B3J 3K1 NS
902-426-2550, Fax: 902-426-4004
Canadian Air Transport Security Authority, 99 Bank St., 13th Fl., Ottawa, ON K1P 6B9
Fax: 613-991-6726, 888-294-2202
Canadian Coast Guard, Centennial Towers, #6S018, 200 Kent St., Ottawa, K1A 0E6 ON
613-998-1573, Fax: 613-990-2780
Canadian Transportation Agency, Les Terrasses de la Chaudière, 15, rue Eddy, Gatineau, K1A 0N9 QC
819-997-0344, Fax: 819-997-6727, 888-222-2592, info@otc-cta.gc.ca
Centre for Surface Transportation Technology, 2320 Lester Rd., Ottawa, K1V 1S2 ON
613-998-9639, Fax: 613-957-0831, inquiries.cstt@nrc-cnrc.gc.ca
Federal Bridge Corporation Limited, #1210, 55 Metcalfe St., Ottawa, ON K1P 6L5
613-993-6880, Fax: 613-993-6945, info@federalbridge.ca
Great Lakes Pilotage Authority, 202 Pitt St., 2nd fl., PO Box 95, Cornwall, K6H 5R9 ON
613-933-2991, Fax: 613-932-3793, administration@glpa-apgl.com
Institute for Aerospace Research, 1200 Montreal Rd., Ottawa, K1A 0R6 ON
613-991-5738, Fax: 613-952-7214
Laurentian Pilotage Authority Canada, #1501, 555, boul René-Lévesque ouest, Montréal, H2Z 1B1 QC
514-283-6320, Fax: 514-496-2409, administration@apl.gc.ca
Marine Atlantic Inc., Baine Johnston Centre, #802, 10 Fort William Place, St. John's, A1C 1K4 NL
709-772-8957, Fax: 709-772-8956, 800-341-7981, info@marine-atlantic.ca
Old Port of Montréal Corporation Inc., 333, rue de la Commune ouest, Montréal, H2Y 2E2 QC
514-283-5256, Fax: 514-283-8423
Pacific Pilotage Authority Canada, #1000, 1130 Pender St. West, Vancouver, V6E 4A4 BC
604-666-6771, Fax: 604-666-1647, info@ppa.gc.ca
Parc Downsview Park Inc., #1, 35 Carl Hall Rd., Toronto, M3K 2B6 ON
613-952-2222, Fax: 613-952-2225, info@pdp.ca
St. Lawrence Seaway Management Corporation, 202 Pitt St., Cornwall, K6J 3P7 ON
613-932-5170, Fax: 613-932-7286, marketing@seaway.ca
Transport Canada, Place de Ville, 330 Sparks St., Tower C, Ottawa, K1A 0N5 ON
613-990-2309, Fax: 613-954-4731, minTC@tc.gc.ca
Transportation Appeal Tribunal of Canada, 333 Laurier Ave. West, 12th Fl., Ottawa, ON K1A 0N5
613-990-6906, Fax: 613-990-9153, info@tatc.gc.ca
Transportation Safety Board of Canada, 200 Promenade du Portage, 4th Fl., Ottawa, K1A 1K8 ON
819-994-3741, Fax: 819-997-2239, 800-387-3557
Via Rail Canada Inc., #500, 3, Place Ville-Marie, Montréal, H3B 2C9 QC
514-871-6000, Fax: 514-871-6768

Alberta
Automobile Insurance Rate Board, Terrace Bldg., #200, 9515 - 107 St. NW, Edmonton, AB T5K 2C3
780-427-5428, Fax: 780-644-7771, airb@gov.ab.ca
Alberta Infrastructure & Transportation, Twin Atria Bldg., 4999 - 98 Ave., Edmonton, T6B 2X3 AB
780-427-2731, Fax: 780-466-3166,-310-0000
Transportation Safety Board, Twin Atria Bldg., 4999 - 98 Ave., Edmonton, AB T6B 2X3
780-427-7178, Fax: 780-422-9739

British Columbia
British Columbia Ferry Commission, PO Box 1497, Comox, BC V9M 8A2
250-339-2714, info@bcferrycommission.com
British Columbia Transit, 520 Gorge Rd. East, PO Box 610, Victoria, BC V8W 2P3
250-385-2551, Fax: 250-995-5639
British Columbia Ferry Services Inc., 1112 Fort St., Victoria, V8V 4V2 BC
250-381-1401, 888-223-3779
Passenger Transportation Board, #202, 940 Blanshard St., PO Box 9850 Prov Govt, Victoria, BC V8W 9T5
250-953-3777, Fax: 250-953-3788, ptboard@gov.bc.ca
Ministry of Transportation & Infrastructure, 940 Blanshard St., PO Box 9850 Prov Govt,Victoria, V8W 9T5 BC
250-387-3198, Fax: 250-356-7706, tran.webmaster@gov.bc.ca
Transportation Planning & Policy Department, #5C, 940 Blanshard St., PO Box 9850 Prov Govt,Victoria, V8W 9T5 BC
250-387-5062, Fax: 250-387-6431

Manitoba
Highway Traffic Board/Motor Transport Board, #200, 301 Weston St., Winnipeg, MB R3E 3H4
204-945-8912, Fax: 204-783-6529
Manitoba Infrastructure & Transportation, Legislative Building, #203, 450 Broadway Ave., Winnipeg, R3C 0V8 MB
204-945-3723, Fax: 204-945-7610
License Suspension Appeal Board/Medical Review Committee, #200, 301 Weston St., Winnipeg, MB R3E 3H4
204-945-7350, Fax: 204-948-2682
Taxicab Board, #200, 301 Weston St., Winnipeg, MB R3E 3H4
Fax: 204-948-2315

New Brunswick
New Brunswick Transportation Authority, Kings Place, 440 King St., PO Box 6000, Fredericton, NB E3B 5H1
506-453-3939, Fax: 506-453-2900
Department of Transportation, Kings Pl., 440 KingSt., PO Box 6000, Fredericton, E3B 5H8 NB
506-453-3939, Fax: 506-453-2900, Transportation.Web@gnb.ca

Newfoundland & Labrador
Department of Transportation & Works, Confederation Bldg., West Block, 6th Fl., PO Box 8700, St. John's, A1B 4J6 NL
709-729-3679, Fax: 709-729-4285, twminister@gov.nl.ca

Northwest Territories
Highways, 4510 - 50 Ave., 2nd fl., PO Box 1320, Yellowknife, X1A 2L9 NT
867-920-8771, Fax: 867-873-0288
Department of Transportation, Lahm Ridge Bldg., 4501 50 Ave., PO Box 1320, Yellowknife, X1A 2L9 NT
867-920-3460, Fax: 867-873-0363

Nova Scotia
Department of Transportation & Infrastructure Renewal, Johnston Bldg., 1672 Granville St., 2nd Fl., PO Box 186, Halifax, B3J 2N2 NS
902-424-2297, Fax: 902-424-0171, 888-432-3233, tpwpaff@gov.ns.ca

Nunavut
Department of Community & Government Services, J.G. Brown Bldg., PO Box 1000 700,Iqaluit, X0A 0H0 NU
867-975-5400, Fax: 867-975-5305
Department of Economic Development & Transportation, #1104 Inuksugait Plaza, PO Box 1000 1500,Iqaluit, X0A 0H0 NU
867-975-7800, Fax: 867-975-7870, 888-975-5999, edt@gov.nu.ca

Ontario
GO Transit, #600, 20 Bay St., Toronto, ON M5J 2W3
416-869-3600, Fax: 416-869-1755, 888-438-6646
Licence Appeal Tribunal (LAT), 1 St. Clair Ave. West, 12th Fl., Toronto, ON M4V 1K6
416-314-4260, Fax: 416-314-4270, 800-255-2214
Niagara Falls Bridge Commission, PO Box 395, Niagara Falls, L2E 6T8 ON
905-354-5641, Fax: 905-353-6644
Ontario Highway Transport Board, 151 Bloor St. West, 10th Fl., Toronto, ON M5S 2T5
416-326-6732, Fax: 416-326-6738, ohtb@mto.gov.on.ca
Owen Sound Transportation Company Ltd., RR#5, Hwy 6 & 21, Owen Sound, ON N4K 5N7
519-376-8740
Road User Safety Division, #191, Bldg A, 1201 Wilson Ave., Toronto, M3M 1J8 ON
416-235-2999, Fax: 416-235-4153
Ministry of Transportation, Ferguson Block, 77 Wellesley St. West, 3rd Fl., Toronto, M7A 1Z8 ON
416-235-4686, Fax: 416-327-9185, 800-268-4686

Prince Edward Island
Department of Transportation & Public Works, Jones Bldg., 11 Kent St., PO Box 2000, Charlottetown, C1A 7N8 PE
902-368-5100, Fax: 902-368-5395

Quebec
Abitibi-Témiscamingue-Nord-du-Québec, 80, av Québec, Rouyn-Noranda, J9X 6R1 QC
819-763-3271, Fax: 819-763-3493, datnq@mtq.gouv.qc.ca
Bas-Saint-Laurent-Gaspésie-Iles-de-la-Madeleine, #101, 92, 2e rue ouest, Rimouski, G5L 8E6 QC
418-727-3674, Fax: 418-727-3673, dtbgi@mtq.gouv.qc.ca
Capitale-Nationale, 475, boul de l'Atrium, 2e étage, Québec, G1H 7H9 QC
418-643-1911, Fax: 418-646-0003, dcnat@mtq.gouv.qc.ca
Chaudière-Appalaches, 1156, boul de la Rive-Sud, Saint-Romuald, G6W 5M6 QC
418-839-5581, Fax: 418-834-7338, dtca@mtq.gouv.qc.ca
Commission des transports du Québec, 200, ch Sainte-Foy, 7e étage, Québec, QC G1R 5V5
Fax: 418-644-8034, 888-461-2433, courrier@ctq.gouv.qc.ca
Côte-Nord, #110, 625, boul Laflèche, Baie-Comeau, G5C 1C5 QC
418-295-4765, Fax: 418-295-4766, dtcn@mtq.gouv.qc.ca
Est-de-la-Montérégie, 201, place Charles-Lemoyne, 5e étage, Longueuil, J4K 2T5 QC
450-677-3413, Fax: 450-442-1317, dtem@mtq.gouv.qc.ca
Estrie, #2.02, 200, rue Belvédère nord, Sherbrooke, J1H 4A9 QC
819-820-3280, Fax: 819-820-3118, dte@mtq.gouv.qc.ca
Ile-de-Montréal, 440, boul René-Lévesque ouest, 10e étage, Montréal, H2Z 2A6 QC
514-873-7781, Fax: 514-864-3867, dtim@mtq.gouv.qc.ca
Laurentides-Lanaudière, 222, rue Saint-Georges, 2e étage, Saint-Jérôme, J7Z 4Z9 QC
450-569-3057, Fax: 450-569-3072, dll@mtq.gouv.qc.ca
Laval-Mille-Iles, 1725, boul Le Corbusier, Laval, H7S 2K7 QC
450-680-6330, Fax: 450-973-4959, dtlmi@mtq.gouv.qc.ca
Mauricie-Centre-du-Québec, 100, rue Laviolette, 4e étage, Trois-Rivières, G9A 5S9 QC
819-371-6896, Fax: 819-371-6136, dmcq@mtq.gouv.qc.ca
Ouest-de-la-Montérégie, #200, 180, boulevard d'Anjou, Châteauguay, J6K 1C4 QC
450-698-3400, Fax: 450-698-3452, dtom@mtq.gouv.qc.ca
Outaouais, #5.110, 170, rue de l'Hôtel-de-Ville, Gatineau, J8X 4C2 QC
819-772-3849, Fax: 819-772-3338, dto@mtq.gouv.qc.ca
Saguenay-Lac-Saint-Jean-Chibougamau, 3950, boul Harvey, Jonquière, G7X 8L6 QC
418-695-7916, Fax: 418-695-7926, dt.slsjc@mtq.gouv.qc.ca
Société de l'assurance automobile du Québec, 333, boul Jean-Lesage, CP 19600 Terminus, Québec, QC G1K 8J6
418-643-7620, Fax: 418-644-0339, 800-361-7620, courrier@saaq.gouv.qc.ca
Société des traversiers du Québec, 250, rue Saint-Paul, Québec, QC G1K 9K9
418-643-2019, Fax: 418-643-7308, stq@traversiers.gouv.qc.ca
Société du port ferroviaire Baie-Comeau-Hauterive, 18, rte Maritime, Baie-Comeau, QC G4Z 2L6
418-296-6785, Fax: 418-296-2377, soport@globetrotter.qc.ca
Ministère des Transports, 700, boul René-Lévesque est, 27e étage, Québec, G1R 5H1 QC
Fax: 514-643-1269, 888-355-0511, communications@mtq.gouv.qc.ca

Saskatchewan
Saskatchewan Highways & Infrastructure, 1855 Victoria Ave., Regina, S4P 3T2 SK
306-787-4800
Saskatchewan Highway Traffic Board, 1550 Saskatchewan Dr., Regina, SK S4P 0E4
306-775-6674

Yukon Territory
Yukon Community Services, PO Box 2703, Whitehorse, Y1A 2C6 YT
867-667-5811, Fax: 867-393-6295, 800-661-0408, inquiry@gov.yk.ca
Driver Control Board, 308 Steele St., PO Box 2703, Whitehorse, YT Y1A 2C6
867-667-3774, Fax: 867-393-6483, dcb@gov.yk.ca
Yukon Highways & Public Works, PO Box 2703, Whitehorse, Y1A 2C6 YT
867-393-7193, Fax: 867-393-6218, 800-661-0408, hpw-info@gov.yk.ca
Yukon Motor Transport Board, PO Box 2703, Whitehorse, YT Y1A 2C6
867-667-5782, Fax: 867-393-6408, Laurie.Hrynuik@gov.yk.ca

Port Authorities

Fraser River Port Authority
400 - 625 Agnes St., New Westminster, BC V3M 5Y4
Tel: 604-524-6655; *Fax:* 604-524-1127
info@frpa.com
www.fraserportauthority.com
Profile: The Fraser River Port Authority is a federally mandated port authority operating under the Canada Marine Act. It administers Fraser River Port, a major deep-sea port located on the main arm of the Fraser River, south of Vancouver, British Columbia

Halifax Port Authority
1215 Marginal Rd., Halifax, NS B3H 4P8
Tel: 902-426-8222; *Fax:* 902-426-7335
www.portofhalifax.ca
Profile: Cargo: Bulk Cargo (Oil, Fuel, Gypsum) - 8.8 million metric tones Breakbulk Cargo (Iron/Steel, Machinery, Rubber) - 136,000 metric tones Roll-on, Roll-off Cargo (Cars and Trucks) - 216,000 metric tones Containerized Cargo - 4.6 million metric tones

Hamilton Port Authority
605 James St. North, 6th Floor, Hamilton, ON L8L 1K1
Tel: 905-525-4330; *Fax:* 905-528-6554
Toll-Free: 800-263-2131
cargo@hamiltonport.ca
www.hamiltonport.ca

Montreal Port Authority
Édifice du port de Montréal, Aile N§ 1, Cité du Havre, Montréal, QC H3C 3R5
Tel: 514-283-7011; *Fax:* 514-283-0829
info@port-montreal.com
www.port-montreal.com
Profile: The Montreal Port Authority's mandate is to facilitate domestic and international trade and thereby contribute to the attainment of local, regional and national socioeconomic objectives

Nanaimo Port Authority
104 Front St., Nanaimo, BC V9R 5H7
Tel: 250-753-4146; *Fax:* 250-753-4899
info@npa.ca
www.npa.ca/en/index.htm
Profile: The NPA administers the federal harbour from the Nanaimo Assembly Wharf to the Petro-Canada dock on Newcastle Channel and extending to Newcastle and Protection Islands

North Fraser Port Authority
7911 Grauer Rd., Richmond, BC V7B 1N4
Tel: 604-273-1866; *Fax:* 604-273-3772
www.nfpa.ca/engindex.html
Profile: Our mission is to provide innovative and responsible leadership in the administration of the North Arm's river highway and to ensure that all development enhances the economic opportunity, recreational potential and environmental integrity of the area

Port Alberni Port Authority
2750 Harbour Rd., Port Alberni, BC V9Y 7X2
Tel: 250-723-5312; *Fax:* 250-723-1114
www.portalberniportauthority.ca/english/index.html
Profile: Committed to the continued waterfront development of the Alberni Inlet and the economic sustainability of the Alberni Valley

Port of Belledune
112, Shannon Dr., Belledune, NB E8G 2W2
Tel: 506-522-1200; *Fax:* 506-522-0803
info@portofbelledune.ca
www.portofbelledune.ca
Profile: To develop to the fullest, the services and facilities of the port, to enable it to become the anchor of economic development in Northern New Brunswick. Existing infrastructures can handle any product & merchandise, We can handle Bulk, break bulk, containers, trailer, liquid, RoRo, Space and storage available for available for lease, Low storage and rental cost, Customize rate available, Custom Bonded available, Space available for break cargo, Industrial location

Prince Rupert Port Authority
200 - 215 Cow Bay Rd., Prince Rupert, BC V8J 1A2
Tel: 250-627-8899; *Fax:* 250-627-8980
pcorp@rupertport.com
www.rupertport.com
Profile: Significant changes in world trade patterns have shifted the focus of the Prince Rupert Port Authority (PRPA) and have already resulted in new initiatives, including a cruise and container port. Significant opportunities for industrial development mark the next phase in development potential at the port

Quebec Port Authority
PO Box 2268, 150 rue Dalhousie, Québec, QC G1K 7P7
Tel: 418-648-3640;
www.portquebec.ca
Profile: The mission of the Québec Port Authority is to promote and develop maritime trade, to serve the economic interests of the Quebec area and of Canada and to ensure that it is profitable while respecting both its community and the environment

Saguenay Port Authority
6600, rue Quai-Marcel-Dionne, La Baie, QC G7B 3N9
Tel: 418-697-0250; *Fax:* 418-697-0243
info@portsaguenay.ca
www.portsaguenay.ca
Profile: The Port of Saguenay is the only public port in the Saguenay-Lac-St-Jean area. It is a port recognized for its strategic importance to the country's trade and economy. This international seaport is also part of the essential infrastructures of the municipality and the region and generates several hundred jobs. The port is the cornerstone of the community of Saguenay-Lac-St-Jean. It is an element of Canada's transportation infrastructure and offers a marine gateway to global markets

Saint John Port Authority
133 Prince William St., 5th Floor, Saint John, NB E2L 2B5
Tel: 506-636-4869; *Fax:* 506-636-4443
port@sjport.com
www.sjport.com

Sept-Iles Port Authority
1 Quai Mgr-Blanche, Sept-Iles, QC G4R 5P3
Tel: 418-968-1231; *Fax:* 418-962-4445
www.portsi.com/eg/default.htm

Toronto Port Authority
60 Harbour St., Toronto, ON M5J 1B7
Tel: 416-863-2000; *Fax:* 416-863-4830
www.torontoport.com
Profile: Maintains a paved facility of over 50 acres centrally located, adjacent to downtown Toronto. The yard provides convenience, with excellent access to the railroads, as well as all major highways. This facility is fully bonded and has 24-hour security

Vancouver Port Authority
100 The Pointe, 999 Canada Pl., Vancouver, BC V6C 3T4
Tel: 604-665-9000; *Fax:* 604-665-9007
Toll-Free: 888-767-8826
public_affairs@portvancouver.com
www.portvancouver.com
Profile: Marine cargo handling; Regulation & administration of transportation programs. The Port of Vancouver handled 79.4 million tonnes in 2006, up 4% from 2005's 76.5 million tonnes

Windsor Port Authority
#502, 251 Goyeau St., Windsor, ON N9A 6V2
Tel: 519-258-5741; *Fax:* 519-258-5905
wpa@portwindsor.com
www.portwindsor.com
Profile: The mission of the Windsor Port Authority is to manage, develop, and promote the Port of Windsor for the benefit of its stakeholders and ensure the general security of the port while remaining sensitive to the need for a high degree of safety and environmental responsibility

SECTION 17
UTILITIES

Associations

American Public Works Association (APWA)
#700, 2345 Grand Blvd., Kansas City MO 64108-2625 USA
Tel: 816-472-6100; *Fax:* 816-472-1610
Toll-Free: 800-848-2792
apwa@apwa.net
www.apwa.net
Overview: A medium-sized international organization founded in 1938
Chief Officer(s):
Peter King, Executive Director, 202-218-6700
pking@apwa.net
Kaye Sullivan, Deputy Executive Director/COO, 816-595-5233
ksullivan@apwa.net
Finances: *Annual Operating Budget:* Greater than $5 Million; *Funding Sources:* Membership dues; Federal grants; Products
Staff: 50 staff member(s); 250+ volunteer(s)
Membership: 26,000; *Fees:* Schedule; *Member Profile:* Public agencies, private sector companies, & individuals engaged in public works services; *Committees:* Transportation; Solid Waste; Water Resources; Engineering & Technology; Management & Leadership; Emergency Management; Fleet Services; Facilities & Grounds; Utility & Public Right of Way
Description: To provide high quality public works goods & services

Association de l'industrie électrique du Québec (AIEQ)
#320, 2000, rue Mansfield, Montréal QC H3A 2Y9 Canada
Tél: 514-281-0615; *Téléc:* 514-281-7965
aieq@aieq.net
www.aieq.net
Nom précédent: Club d'électricité du Québec inc.
Aperçu: *Dimension:* moyenne; *Envergure:* provinciale; *Organisme sans but lucratif; fondée en 1916*
Membre(s) du bureau directeur:
Jean-François Samray, Président et directeur général
Finances: *Budget de fonctionnement annuel:* $500,000-$1.5 Million
Personnel: 7 membre(s) du personnel
Membre: 152; *Montant de la cotisation:* Selon le nombre d'employés au Québec; *Critères d'admissibilite:* Membres industriels; *Comités:* Consultatif; Finances; Services aux membres; Promotion; Débats projects
Activités: Déjeuners; conférences; activités sociales; *Service de conférenciers:* Oui
Description: Etre porte parole de l'industrie 'électrique au Québec; favoriser la circulation de toute information et intérêt pour les membres et l'industrie électrique en général; contribuer au développement de nos membres et à la promotion de leurs intérêts par des initiatives de concertation et de représentation; encourager l'utilisation rationnelle des ressources dans une perspective de développement

Association of Major Power Consumers in Ontario (AMPCO)
Sterling Tower, 372 Bay St., Toronto ON M5H 2W9 Canada
Tel: 416-260-0280; *Fax:* 416-260-0442
info@ampco.org
www.ampco.org
Overview: A large provincial organization founded in 1975
Finances: *Funding Sources:* Membership fees
Staff: 1 staff member(s)
Membership: 42; *Fees:* Based on electrical energy usage; *Member Profile:* Companies that are major manufacturers, employers, & power consumers (represents key industries - mining, pulp & paper, automobile manufacturing, petro-chemicals, metals, consumer products, steel, etc.); *Committees:* Transition Issues; Executive
Description: To represent Ontario's electricity-intensive companies; to ensure reliability of power supply to support the economy of Ontario & to advocate a fair & equitable pricing system for electricity; to present views on energy matters to such groups as the Ontario Energy Board, the Ontario Government, Ontario Hydro, the news media, & the general public; to provide decision makers with recommendations on resolving issues

Association québécoise du gaz naturel (AQGN)
#207, 560, boul. Henri-Bourassa Ouest, Montréal QC H3L 1P4 Canada
Tél: 514-339-9399; *Téléc:* 514-339-9353
aqgn@aqgn.com
www.aqgn.com
Aperçu: *Dimension:* petite; *Envergure:* provinciale
Membre(s) du bureau directeur:
Ginette Gamache, Directrice générale
Montant de la cotisation: 450$ régulier; 2 500$ aviseur
Description: L'Association Québécoise du Gaz Naturel regroupe les gens d'affaires intéressés par le développement de l'industrie du gaz naturel au Québec

Canadian Association of Members of Public Utility Tribunals (CAMPUT) / Association canadienne des membres des tribunaux d'utilité publique
#646, 200 North Service Rd. West, Oakville ON L6M 2Y1 Canada
Tel: 905-827-5139; *Fax:* 905-827-3260
info@camput.org
www.camput.org
Previous Name: Canadian Association of Utility Commissioners
Overview: A small national organization founded in 1976
Member Profile: Federal, provincial, & territorial boards & commissions which regulate electric, water, gas, & pipeline utilities in Canada; *Committees:* Regulatory Affairs; Education
Activities: Educating & training commissioners & staff of public utility tribunals; Communicating with members; Liaising with parallel regulatory organizations
Description: To improve public utility regulation in Canada

Canadian Association of Petroleum Producers (CAPP) / Association canadienne des producteurs pétroliers
#2100, 350 - 7 Ave. SW, Calgary AB T2P 3N9 Canada
Tel: 403-267-1100; *Fax:* 403-261-4622
communication@capp.ca; membership@capp.ca;
publications@capp.ca
www.capp.ca
Merged from: Canadian Petroleum Association; Independent Petroleum Association of Canada
Overview: A large national organization founded in 1992
Membership: 100+ producer members + 150 associate members; *Member Profile:* Producer members range from two person operations to internationally recognized corporations employing thousands; Associate members provide services, such as drilling, baniking, & computing, for Canada's oil & gas industry
Activities: Reviewing, analyzing, & recommending industry policy positions; Participating in regulatory change dialogues; Representing the industry on multi-sector international, federal, & provincial consultation bodies; Communicating with governments, regulators, stakeholders, & the public; Offering seminars & workshops; Providing industry trends, statistics, & research information; Informing members of industry standards & guidelines; Monitoring pipeline expansions; Improving coordinated land use planning processes
Description: To represent companies that produce Canada's natural gas & crude oil; To enhance the economic sustainability of the Canadian upstream petroleum industry; To ensure work is conducted in a safe & environmentally & socially responsible manner; To work with government to develop regulatory requirements

Canadian Clean Power Coalition (CCPC)
c/o Bob Stobbs, Executive Director, 2901 Powerhouse Dr., Regina SK S4N 0A1 Canada
www.canadiancleanpowercoalition.com
Overview: A medium-sized national organization
Chief Officer(s):
Bob Stobbs, Executive Director, 306-566-3326
bstobbs@saskpower.com
David Lewin, Chair, 780-412-3196
dlewin@epcor.ca
Member Profile: Canadian coal & coal-fired electricity producers
Activities: Addressing environmental issues with governments & stakeholders
Description: To secure a future for coal-fired electricity generation, along with a mix of fuels such as solar, wind, hydro, & nuclear; to research & develop clean coal technology

Canadian Electricity Association (CEA) / Association canadienne de l'électricité (ACE)
#1100, 350 Sparks St., Ottawa ON K1R 7S8 Canada
Tel: 613-230-9263; *Fax:* 613-230-9326
info@electricity.ca
www.electricity.ca
Overview: A medium-sized national organization founded in 1891
Chief Officer(s):
Pierre Guimond, President & Chief Executive Officer, 613-230-4762
Francis Bradley, Vice-President, Policy Development, 613-230-5027
Sandra Schwartz, Vice-President, Policy Advocacy, 613-230-9876
Louisa Hood, Director, Communications, 613-688-2954
Angela Macleod, Corporate Secretary, 613-230-7384
Richard Lussier, Controller, 613-688-2065
Member Profile: Members generate, transmit, & distribute electrical energy to residential, commercial, institutional, & industrial customers throughout Canada
Activities: Analyzing national & international business issues; Providing a national forum for the electricity business; Advocating industry views; Helping companies in evolving markets; Communicating findings about concerns such as mercury emissions & electric & magnetic fields
Publications: Forced Outage Performance of Transmission Equipment [a publication of the Canadian Electricity Association]
Type: Yearbook *Frequency:* a.
Profile: Produced by the Performance Excellence & Benchmarking program of the Canadian Electricity Association, the report addresses the performance of transmission equipment in Canada
Generation Equipment Status [a publication of the Canadian Electricity Association]
Type: Yearbook *Frequency:* a.
Profile: Produced by the Performance Excellence & Benchmarking program of the Canadian Electricity Association, the report features information on the performance of electrical generating units in Canada
Annual Service Continuity Report on Distribution System Performance in Electrical Utilities
Type: Yearbook *Frequency:* a.
Profile: Produced by the Performance Excellence & Benchmarking program of the Canadian Electricity Association, the report contains information about industry standard metrics for electricity distribution, including system average interruption frequency index & the system average interruption duration index
Electricity Annual
Type: Yearbook *Frequency:* a.
Profile: The Canadian Electricity Association's yearly industry review
The CEA [Canadian Electricity Association] Member Directory
Type: Directory *Frequency:* a. *Price:* $15 members; $65 non-members
Profile: Contact information for the Canadian electricity industry's major players, in addition to information about the operations of the Canadian Electricity Association's member companies
Description: To act as the voice of the Canadian electricity business

Canadian Energy Workers Association (CEWA)
#202, 10707 - 100 Ave., Edmonton AB T5J 3M1 Canada
Tel: 780-420-7887
cewa@cewa.ca
www.cewa.ca
Previous Name: Canadian Utilities & Northland Utilities Employees' Association; Alberta Power Employees' Association
Overview: A small national organization founded in 1969
Activities: Engaging in problem solving between members & management; Creating programs for members in the areas of safety, security, & skills development; Offering an annual bursary program
Description: To represent the interests of members, by serving as a bargaining agent for matters related to working relations with employers

Canadian Gas Association (CGA) / Association canadienne du gaz
#809, 350 Sparks St., Ottawa ON K1R 7S8
Tel: 613-748-0057; *Fax:* 613-748-9078
info@cga.ca
www.cga.ca
Overview: A large national organization founded in 1907
Chief Officer(s):
Timothy M. Egan, President & Chief Executive Officer
tegan@cga.ca
Paula Dunlop, Director, Public Affairs & Strategy
pdunlop@cga.ca
Bryan Gormely, Director, Policy, Economics, & Information
bgormley@cga.ca
Jim Tweedie, Director, Operations, Safety, & Integrity Management
jtweedie@cga.ca
Valerie Prokop, Manager, Finance & Corporate Services
vprokop@cga.ca
Member Profile: Equipment manufacturers; Distribution companies; Transmission companies; Service providers
Activities: Advancing policy positions with federal & provincial decision makers; Developing educational information
Publications: Canadian Natural Gas Magazine
Type: Magazine *Frequency:* s-a. *Accepts Advertising Editor:* Suzy Richardson
Profile: CGA news, feature articles, & a buyers' guide for the natural gas distribution industry in Canada
Canadian Gas Association Membership Directory
Type: Directory
Profile: Available for current CGA members
Canadian Gas Association Market Updates
Profile: Topics include natural gas markets pre-heating season, post-heating season, supply, & demographics

Description: To act as the voice of the natural gas distribution industry in Canada

Canadian Hydropower Association (CHA) / Association canadienne de l'hydroélectricité

#1300, 340 Albert St., Ottawa ON K1R 7Y9 Canada
Tel: 613-751-6655; *Fax:* 613-751-4465
info@canhydropower.org
www.canhydropower.org

Overview: A small national organization founded in 1998
Membership: 16 generators; 21 industry; 8 associate; *Member Profile:* Hydroelectic generation; hydroelectric industry; Associated associations and organizations
Description: To provide leadership for the responsible growth & prosperity of the Canadian hydropower industry

Canadian Petroleum Law Foundation

PO Box 4143, Stn. C, Calgary AB T2T 5M9 Canada
Tel: 403-237-2423
lara.h.pella@esso.ca
www.cplf.org

Overview: A small national organization founded in 1963
Chief Officer(s):
Ben Rogers, President
ben.rogers@blakes.com
Miles Pittman, Treasurer
miles.pittman@fmc-law.com
Description: To study oil & gas laws

Canadian Public Works Association (CPWA) / Association Canadienne des Travaux Publics

#191, 253 College St., Toronto ON M5T 1R5 Canada
Tel: 202-408-9541; *Fax:* 202-408-9542
cpwa@cpwa.net
www.cpwa.net

Overview: A medium-sized national organization founded in 1938
Membership: 1,800
Description: Their mission statement is to be recognized as the "voice of public works" in Canada; to create a forum for public works professionals in Canada to exchange inforamation, develop ideas, and share skills, knowledge, and technologies on issues unique to Canada; to increase membership and participation.

Compressed Gas Association, Inc. (CGA)

4221 Walney Rd., 5th Fl., Chantilly VA 20151-2923 USA
Tel: 703-788-2700; *Fax:* 703-961-1831
cga@cganet.com
www.cganet.com

Overview: A small international organization founded in 1913
Finances: *Funding Sources:* Membership dues
Staff: 14 staff member(s)
Membership: 150; *Fees:* Schedule
Awards: Compressed Gas Association Safety Awards
Description: To promote, develop & coordinate technical & standardization activities in compressed gas industries in interest of public safety

Electricity Distributors Association (EDA)

#1100, 3700 Steeles Ave. West, Vaughan ON L4L 8K8 Canada
Tel: 905-265-5300; *Fax:* 905-265-5301
Toll-Free: 800-668-9979
email@eda-on.ca
www.eda-on.ca

Previous Name: Municipal Electric Association
Overview: A large provincial organization founded in 1986
Finances: *Annual Operating Budget:* Greater than $5 Million; *Funding Sources:* Membership dues
Staff: 18 staff member(s); 100 volunteer(s)
Membership: 256; *Fees:* $750 commercial member; *Member Profile:* Public & privately owned electricity distributors
Description: To be the voice of Ontario's electricity distributors, the publicly & privately owned companies that deliver electricity to Ontario homes, businesses & public institutions. Focus is on advocacy & representation to government, analysis of legislation & market regulations, communication & networking among members & industry colleagues

Electro-Federation Canada Inc. (EFC)

#200, 5800 Explorer Dr., Mississauga ON L4W 5K9 Canada
Tel: 905-602-8877; *Fax:* 905-602-5686
Toll-Free: 866-602-8877
info@electrofed.com
www.electrofed.com

Overview: A medium-sized national organization founded in 1995
Chief Officer(s):
Milos Jancik, President/CEO
mjancik@electrofed.com
Ken Frankum, Chair
Harald Henze, Treasurer
Larry Moore, Vice-President, Consumer Councils
lmoore@electrofed.com
Joseph Neu, Vice-President, Engineering, Codes & Standards
jneu@electrofed.com
Membership: 300 companies; *Member Profile:* Companies that manufacture, distribute, & service electrical, electronics, & telecommunications products; *Committees:* Canadian Appliance Manufacturers Association; Consumer Electronics Marketers of Canada; Electrical Equipment Manufacturers Association of Canada; Supply & Manufacturers' Reps Councils; Installation Maintenance & Repair Sector Council & Trade Association; Electro-Federation Canada Alumni Association
Activities: Collecting & disseminating market data; Providing networking opportunities; Hosting annual conferences; Researching; Offering educational programs; Communicating with members; Promoting the industry; Conducting surveys
Description: To represent members provincially, federally, & internationally on issues affecting the electro-technical business

Gas Processing Association Canada (GPAC)

#505, 900 - 6th Ave. SW, Calgary AB T2P 3K2 Canada
Tel: 403-705-0223; *Fax:* 403-263-6886
info@gpacanada.com
www.gpacanada.com

Previous Name: Canadian Gas Processors Association
Overview: A medium-sized national organization founded in 1960
Finances: *Annual Operating Budget:* Less than $50,000; *Funding Sources:* Membership dues
Staff: 17 volunteer(s)
Membership: 450 individual; *Fees:* $75 Regular, $9 Retired; *Member Profile:* Open to those employed in companies processing gaseous & liquid hydrocarbons; *Committees:* Safety; Research; Environment; Membership; Publications
Activities: *Library:* Library
Description: To promote interaction & exchange of ideas & technology that will add value to those who are involved with or affected by the hydrocarbon processing industry
Affiliation(s): Gas Processors Association (USA)

Independent Power Producers Association of British Columbia

#26, 181 Ravine Dr., Port Moody BC V3H 4T3 Canada
Tel: 604-461-4778; *Fax:* 604-469-3717
steve.davis@ippbc.com
www.ippbc.com

Overview: A small provincial organization
Chief Officer(s):
Steve Davis, President
Description: To develop a viable independent power industry in British Columbia that serves the public interest by providing cost-effective electricity through the efficient & environmentally responsible development of the Province's energy resources

Independent Power Producers Society of Alberta (IPPSA)

#400, 505 - 8th Ave. SW, Calgary AB T2P 1G2 Canada
Tel: 403-282-8811; *Fax:* 403-256-8342
Evan.Bahry@ippsa.com
www.ippsa.com

Overview: A small provincial organization
Chief Officer(s):
Evan Bahry, Executive Director
Membership: 185; *Fees:* $250-$10,000; *Member Profile:* Power suppliers, retailers & supporting industries

Industrial Gas Users Association Inc. (IGUA) / Association des consommateurs industriels de gaz (ACIG)

#1201, 99 Metcalfe St., Ottawa ON K1P 6L7 Canada
Tel: 613-236-8021; *Fax:* 613-230-9531
www.igua.ca

Overview: A medium-sized national organization founded in 1973
Finances: *Annual Operating Budget:* $500,000-$1.5 Million; *Funding Sources:* Membership dues
Staff: 3 staff member(s)
Membership: 39 corporate; *Fees:* Based on gas consumption, $1,200-$36,099; *Member Profile:* Open to end users of natural gas
Description: To provide a coordinated & effective voice for industrial firms depending on natural gas as fuel or feedstock; to represent industrial users of natural gas before regulatory boards & governments

Municipal Equipment & Operations Association (Ontario) Inc.

38 Summit Ave., Kitchener ON N2M 4W5 Canada
Tel: 519-741-2780; *Fax:* 519-741-2750
admin@meoa.org
www.meoa.org

Overview: A medium-sized provincial organization
Membership: 270
Description: A network of individuals working directly with equipment & operations, to exchange information, promote high standards in the field & cost effective public service in Ontario.

Natural Gas Employees' Association

#100, 10612 - 124th St. NW, Edmonton AB T5N 1S4 Canada
Tel: 780-483-9330; *Fax:* 780-469-2504

Overview: A small national organization
Chief Officer(s):
Brad Crocker, President

NOIA

Atlantic Place, #602, 215 Water St., St. John's NL A1C 6C9 Canada
Tel: 709-758-6610; *Fax:* 709-758-6611
www.noianet.com

Also Known As: Newfoundland & Labrador Oil & Gas Industries Association
Overview: A medium-sized provincial organization founded in 1977
Chief Officer(s):
Robert Cadigan, President & CEO
Finances: *Annual Operating Budget:* $500,000-$1.5 Million; *Funding Sources:* Membership fees; conferences, seminars & special events
Staff: 10 staff member(s); 100 volunteer(s)
Membership: 450; *Fees:* Schedule; *Member Profile:* Those who develop, manufacture & market products & services in the oil & gas industry, both offshore & onshore; *Committees:* Board of Directors; Petroleum Research & Information; Membership Services & Internal Communications; External Relations; Finance & Human Resources; Policy & Positions
Activities: Promotes development of East Coast Canada's hydrocarbon resources & facilitates its membership's participation in oil & gas industries; *Library:* Library by appointment
Awards: NOIA Hibernia Commemorative Scholarship
Eligibility: Newfoundland post-secondary students planning to pursue a career in a petroleum-related field
Description: To assist, promote & facilitate the participation of members in ocean industries, with particular emphasis on oil & gas, to enhance their growth & development; to promote the growth of ocean industry; to act as a focal point for representations to government bodies & agencies; to act as a source of information & education for members

Offshore/Onshore Technologies Association of Nova Scotia (OTANS)

#400, 1718 Argyle St., Halifax NS B3J 3N6 Canada
Tel: 902-425-4774; *Fax:* 902-422-2332
otans@otans.com
www.otans.com

Overview: A small provincial organization founded in 1982
Finances: *Funding Sources:* Membership dues
Staff: 5 staff member(s); 19 volunteer(s)
Membership: 346; *Fees:* $475-$950
Description: To identify, promote & support the development of opportunities both offshore & onshore in the oil & gas industry

Ontario Municipal Water Association (OMWA)

c/o Doug Parker, 43 Chelsea Cres., Belleville ON K8N 4Z5
Tel: 613-966-1100; *Fax:* 613-966-3024
Toll-Free: 888-231-1115
dparker@omwa.org
www.omwa.org

Overview: A medium-sized provincial organization
Membership: 180+ public drinking water authorities in Ontario; *Fees:* Schedule, based upon population; *Member Profile:* Ontario's public water supply authorities
Activities: Reviewing policy, & legislative, & regulatory issues; Liaising with government, agencies, & associations to maintain safe & sustainable water sources; Lobbying to improve conditions; Promoting high standards of treatment, infrastructure, & operations; Offering technical training for operating authorities, operators, & owners of drinking water systems; Encouraging dissemination of information for public education
Publications: Ontario Municipal Water Association Members' Handbook
Type: Handbook
Councillors Handbook: Stewardship Responsibilities Under the Safe Drinking Water Act
Type: Handbook
Description: To act as the voice of municipal water supply in Ontario; To ensure the safety, quality, reliability, & sustainability of drinking water in Ontario
Affiliation(s): Ontario Water Works Association (a section of the American Water Works Association)

Ontario Petroleum Institute Inc. (OPI)

#104, 555 Southdale Rd. East, London ON N6E 1A2 Canada
Tel: 519-680-1620; *Fax:* 519-680-1621
opi@ontpet.com
www.ontpet.com

Overview: A medium-sized provincial organization founded in 1963
Finances: *Funding Sources:* Sponsorships
Member Profile: Geologists in Ontario; Geophysicists; Explorationists; Producers; Contractors; Petroleum engineers; Companies involved in the oil & gas, hydrocarbon storage, & solution mining industries
Activities: Liaising with government agencies; Disseminating information to members; Increasing public awareness of the importance of the industry in Ontario
Publications: OPI [Ontario Petroleum Institute Inc.] Newsletter
Type: Newsletter *Accepts Advertising ISSN:* 14802201
Profile: Membership updates, reports, conferences, & legislation information
Ontario Petroleum Institute Annual Conference & Trade Show Proceedings
Type: Yearbook *Frequency:* a.
Description: To promote responsible exploration & development by Ontario's oil, gas, hydrocarbon storage, & solution-mining industries

Ontario Propane Association

#11, 1155 North Service Rd. West, Oakville ON L6M 3E3 Canada
Tel: 905-469-1941; *Fax:* 905-469-1942
opa@propane.ca
www.propane.ca

Overview: A medium-sized provincial licensing organization founded in 1996
Chief Officer(s):
René Chartier, President & Secretary
Finances: *Annual Operating Budget:* $100,000-$250,000
Staff: 55 volunteer(s)
Membership: 100-499; *Member Profile:* Producers; wholesalers; retailers; equipment suppliers & trainers; *Committees:* Responsible Management Plan; Emergency Response Assistance Plan; Member Services; Technical, Standards & Training
Activities: Annual conference; regional meetings
Awards: Gas Technician Scholarship
The Steven Sparling Scholarships
Description: To promote the safe handling & increased use of propane; to work toward a favourable environment for propane; to serve as a resource centre for its members; to act as the principal voice of the propane industry in Ontario

Petrolia Discovery Foundation Inc.

PO Box 1480, Petrolia ON N0N 1R0 Canada
Tel: 519-882-0897; *Fax:* 519-882-4209
petdisc@xcelco.on.ca
www.petroliadiscovery.com

Overview: A small national charitable organization founded in 1980
Finances: *Annual Operating Budget:* $100,000-$250,000
Staff: 2 staff member(s); 35 volunteer(s)
Membership: 35 individual
Activities: *Speaker Service:* Yes
Description: To preserve & conserve oil heritage

Pipe Line Contractors Association of Canada (PLCAC)

#201, 1075 North Service Rd. West, Oakville ON L6M 2G2 Canada
Tel: 905-847-9383; *Fax:* 905-847-7824
plcac@pipeline.ca
www.pipeline.ca

Overview: A small national organization founded in 1954
Finances: *Annual Operating Budget:* $500,000-$1.5 Million; *Funding Sources:* Membership dues
Staff: 3 staff member(s)
Membership: 34 regular + 66 associate + 17 honorary; *Member Profile:* Open to pipe line contractors or suppliers

Propane Gas Association of Canada Inc. (PGAC) / Association canadienne du gaz propane inc.

#800, 717 - 7th Ave. SW, Calgary AB T2P 3C4
Tel: 403-543-6500; *Fax:* 403-543-6508
Toll-Free: 877-784-4636
info@propanegas.ca
www.propanegas.ca

Overview: A medium-sized national licensing organization founded in 1967
Membership: 270+; *Member Profile:* Producers; Wholesalers; Retailers; Transporters; Manufacturers of appliances, cylinders, & equipment; Associates
Activities: Providing industry related training & emergency response; Promoting the interests of the industry; Engaging in regulatory relations
Publications: 1075news bytes [a publication of the Propane Gas Association of Canada Inc.]
Type: Newsletter *Frequency:* m.
Profile: For members
1075news talk [a publication of the Propane Gas Association of Canada Inc.]
Type: Newsletter *Frequency:* bi-m.
Profile: Also published in every edition of Propane Canada magazine
Description: To act as the national voice of the Canadian propane industry; To supports its members in the development of a safe, environmentally responsible Canadian propane industry
Affiliation(s): Propane Training Institute, a division of the PGAC; Liquefied Petroleum Gas Emergency Response Corporation, a wholly owned subsidiary of the PGAC

Small Explorers & Producers Association of Canada (SEPAC)

#1060, 717 - 7th Ave. SW, Calgary AB T2P 0Z3 Canada
Tel: 403-269-3454; *Fax:* 403-269-3636
info@sepac.ca
www.sepac.ca

Overview: A small national organization founded in 1986
Chief Officer(s):
Jim Screaton, Chair
Gary Leach, Executive Director
Membership: 387 corporate; *Fees:* $500-$3,335
Description: To represent & promote the interests of small producers & explorers, not only to government & regulatory bodies, but to other sectors of the conventional oil & gas industry; to educate the public at large about the importance of emerging companies in resource development in Western Canada, & investment opportunities available in the growing segment of the oilpatch; to propose long-term, effective fiscal & operating strategies for the ongoing health & vitality of this important sector of the Canadian economy

The Society of Energy Professionals

#300, 425 Bloor St. East., Toronto ON M4W 3R4 Canada
Tel: 416-979-2709; *Fax:* 416-979-5794
Toll-Free: 866-288-1788
society@society.on.ca
www.thesociety.ca

Previous Name: Society of Ontario Hydro Professional & Administrative Employees
Overview: A medium-sized provincial organization founded in 1944
Chief Officer(s):
Rodney Sheppard, President
Finances: *Annual Operating Budget:* $1.5 Million-$3 Million; *Funding Sources:* Membership dues
Staff: 14 staff member(s); 300 volunteer(s)
Membership: 7,000 + 265 locals; *Fees:* $10 per week; *Member Profile:* Professional, administrative, & associated personnel of Ontario Hydro; *Committees:* Operations; Negotiating; Health & Safety; Training; Member Services; External Relations; Communications
Description: To represent the interests of the professional, administrative, & associated employees in all aspects of their employment with Ontario Hydro
Affiliation(s): Canadian Court of Utility Professionals & Associated Societies (CCUPAS)

Society of Petroleum Engineers (SPE)

PO Box 833836, Richardson TX 75083-3836 USA
Tel: 972-952-9393; *Fax:* 972-952-9435
Toll-Free: 800-456-6863
spedal@spe.org
www.spe.org

Overview: A large international organization founded in 1957
Chief Officer(s):
Mark A. Rubin, Executive Director
Finances: *Annual Operating Budget:* $3 Million-$5 Million
Staff: 87 staff member(s)
Membership: 79,000+ (active operations in some 50 countries); *Member Profile:* Managers, engineers, operating personnel & scientists engaged in the exploration, drilling & production sectors of the global oil & gas industry
Activities: *Internships:* Yes; *Speaker Service:* Yes *Library:* Library (Open to Public)
Description: To collect, disseminate & exchange technical knowledge concerning the exploration, development & production of oil & gas resources & related technologies for the public benefit; provide opportunities for professionals to enhance their technical & professional competence

United Utility Workers' Association of Canada (UUWA)

1207 - 20 Ave. NW, Calgary AB T2M 1G2 Canada
Tel: 403-284-4521; *Fax:* 403-282-1598
www.uuwac.org

Overview: A small provincial organization
Chief Officer(s):
Grace Thostenson, Business Manager
Finances: *Annual Operating Budget:* $500,000-$1.5 Million
Staff: 3 staff member(s); 60 volunteer(s)
Membership: 900; *Member Profile:* Employees of TransAlta Utilities, Fortis, AltaLink, Dataco, SNC-Lavalin ATP Inc, TransAlta Corporation

Utility Contractors' Association of Ontario Inc. (UCA)

#201, 1075 North Service Rd. West, Oakville ON L6M 2G2 Canada
Tel: 905-847-7305; *Fax:* 905-847-7824
info@pipeline.ca
www.uca.on.ca

Overview: A medium-sized provincial organization founded in 1968
Chief Officer(s):
Barry L. Brown, General Manager
Finances: *Annual Operating Budget:* $100,000-$250,000; *Funding Sources:* Membership dues
Membership: 35

World Petroleum Congress (WPC) / Congrès mondiaux du pétrole

#1, 1 Duchess St., 4th Fl., London W1W 6AN United Kingdom
secretariat@world-petroleum.org
www.world-petroleum.org

Overview: A medium-sized international organization founded in 1933
Chief Officer(s):
Pierce Riemer, Director General
pierce@world-petroleum.org
Ulrike von Lonski, Director of Communications
ulrike@world-petroleum.org
Finances: *Funding Sources:* Membership dues; royalties; levy on registration
Staff: 4 staff member(s)
Membership: 57 countries; *Fees:* Schedule; *Member Profile:* Major oil producing & consuming nations of the world; each country has a National Committee made up of representatives of the oil industry, academic & research institutions, & government departments; *Committees:* Permanent Council; Executive Board; Scientific Program; Congress Arrangements; Environmental Affairs; Development
Description: To help the oil industry in the development of petroleum resources & the use of petroleum products for the benefit of mankind; to promote petroleum science & technology; to encourage the application of scientific advances & the transfer of technology
Affiliation(s): IEA; OPEN; United Nations

Companies

Alberta

AltaGas Income Trust

#1700, 355 - 4th Ave. SW, Calgary, AB T2P 0J1
Tel: 403-691-7575; *Fax:* 403-691-7576
Toll-Free: 888-890-2715
feedback@altagas.ca
www.altagas.ca
Ticker Symbol: ALA

Profile: The energy infrastructure organization acquires, grows, & optimizes gas & power infrastructure. AltaGas Income Trust focuses upon renewable energy sources.
David W. Cornhill, B.Sc.(Hons), MBAChair/CEO
Richard M. Alexander, BBM, CFA, CMAPresident/COO
David Wright, B.Sc., M.Sc., LLBExec. Vice-President, Strategy & Corporate Development
Deborah S. Stein, CFO & Vice-President, Finance
James (Jim) Bracken, CASr. Vice-President, Major Projects
Gregory A. Aarssen, B.Sc.(Hons), MBA, LLBVice-President, Corporate Affairs
Denis C. Fonteyne, Chair, Environment Occupational Health & Safety Committee

AltaGas Utility Group Inc.

#540, 355 - 4 Ave. SW, Calgary, AB T2P 0J1
Tel: 403-806-3310; *Fax:* 403-806-3311
information@altagasutility.com
www.altagasutilitygroup.com
Ticker Symbol: AUI

Profile: AltaGas Utility Group Inc. is involved in the natural gas distribution marketplace. The company invests in infrastructure-based utility & related businesses. It holds interest in the following companies: AltaGas Utilities Inc., Inuvik Gas Ltd., Heritage Gas Limited, & Ikhil Joint Venture.
Patricia Newson, CAPresident/CEO
403-806-3330, patricia.newson@altagasutility.com
Jared Green, Vice-President, Controller, & Corporate Secretary
403-806-3320, jared.green@altagasutility.com

ATCO Ltd.
#1400, 909 - 11th Ave. SW, Calgary, AB T2R 1N6
Tel: 403-292-7500; *Fax:* 403-292-7623
info@atco.com
www.atco.com
Ticker Symbol: ACO
Profile: The management holding company consists of the following main divisions: utilities, which includes natural gas & electricity transmission & distribution; power generation, which features the operation of hydroelectric, coal, & natural gas fired power plants; & global enterprises, which comprises ATCO Frontec, ATCO Midstream, ATCO Structures, ATCO Travel, ATCO I-Tek, & ATCO Noise Management.
Nancy C. Southern, President/CEO
Karen M. Watson, Sr. Vice-President/CFO
Michael M. Shaw, Managing Director, ATCO Ltd., Global Enterprises, Corp. Dev., & ATCO Group
Siegfried W. Kiefer, Chief Information Officer & Managing Director, Utilities

BP Canada Energy Company
240-4th Ave., SW, Calgary, AB T2P 2H8
Tel: 403-233-1313;
www.bp.com
Profile: BP is an energy company which provides its customers with fuel for transportation, energy for heat & light, retail services, & petrochemical products.
Tony Hayward, Group Chief Executive

Canadian Hydro Developers, Inc.
#500, 1324 - 17 Ave. SW, Calgary, AB T2T 5S8
Tel: 403-269-9379; *Fax:* 403-244-7388
canhydro@canhydro.com
www.canhydro.com
Ticker Symbol: KHD
Profile: Canadian Hydro Developers, Inc. owns, develops, & operates generating facilities, which are certified, or slated for certification, under Environment Canada's EcoLogo Program. Renewable power generation facilities are situated in Quebec, Ontario, Alberta, & British Columbia. The renewable generation portfolio includes water, wind, & biomass technologies. The company's wholly-owned subsidiary is Canadian Renewable Energy Corporation.
John D. Keating, CAChief Executive Officer
jkeating@canhydro.com
Ross Keating, P.EngPresident, Operations & Development
Kent Brown, CAExec. Vice-Presidnet/CFO
kbrown@canhydro.com
Keith O'Regan, P.Eng, B.B.A.Exec. Vice-President/COO
Steve O'Gorman, Manager, Marketing & Communications
403-298-0262

Canadian Utilities Limited
#1400, 909 - 11th Ave. SW, Calgary, AB T2R 1N6
Tel: 403-292-7500; *Fax:* 403-292-7623
investors@canadian-utilities.com
www.canadian-utilities.com
Ticker Symbol: CU
Profile: Part of the ATCO Group of Companies, Canadian Utilities Limited is engaged in natural gas & electricity transmission & distribution, as well as technology, logistics, & energy services.
Nancy C. Southern, President/CEO
Karen M. Watson, Sr. Vice-President/CFO
Siegfried W. Kiefer, Chief Information Officer & Managing Director, Utilities
Susan R. Werth, Sr. Vice-President & Chief Administration Officer

CU Inc.
#1600, 909 - 11 Ave. SW, Calgary, AB T2R 1N6
Tel: 403-292-7500; *Fax:* 403-292-7532
www.canadian-utilities.com
Ticker Symbol: CIU.PR.A
Profile: A wholly owned subsidiary of Canadian Utilities Limited, CU Inc. is involved in natural gas & electricity transmission & distribution, as well as power generation. CU Inc.'s subsidiaries include CU Water Limited, ATCO Gas & Pipelines Ltd., ATCO Electric Ltd., & Alberta Power (2000) Ltd.
N.C. Southern, President/CEO & Chair
K.M. (Karen) Watson, Sr. Vice-President/CFO
403-292-7502

Enbridge Income Fund
Fifth Avenue Place, #3000, 425 - 1st St. SW, Calgary, AB T2P 3L8
Tel: 403-231-3900; *Fax:* 403-231-3920
webmaster@enbridgeincomefund.com
www.enbridgeincomefund.com
Ticker Symbol: ENF.UN
Profile: The unincorporated, open-ended trust is the owner of the following organizations: Enbridge Pipelines (Saskatchewan) Inc. (Saskatchewan System); NRGreen Power Limited Partnership (50% interest); wind power projects; & Alliance Canada Pipeline (50% interest). Enbridge is also developing electrical generation opportunities with waste heat. Operations are conducted in western Canada.
James A. Schultz, President
John K. Whelen, CFO & Vice-President, Business Development
David K. Wudrick, Treasurer
James E.R. Lord, Corporate Secretary
Jennifer Varey, Manager, Corporate Communications
403-508-6568, jennifer.varey@enbridge.com
Kurtis Griffeth, Sr. Advisor, Investor Relations
403-266-7924, kurtis.griffeth@enbridge.com

ENMAX Corporation
141 - 50 Ave. SE, Calgary, AB T2G 4S7
Tel: 403-514-3000; *Fax:* 403-310-2010
Toll-Free: 877-571-7111
customercare@enmax.com
www.enmax.com
Profile: ENMAX Corporation provides electricity & natural gas energy services in Alberta.
Gary Holden, President/CEO
David Halford, CFO & Exec. Vice-President, Finance

EPCOR Power Equity Ltd.
Investor Relations, EPCOR Centre, 10065 Jasper Ave., Edmonton, AB T5J 3B1
Tel: 780-412-4297; *Fax:* 780-412-3808
Toll-Free: 866-896-4636
InvestorInquiries@epcorpowerlp.ca
www.epcor.ca
Ticker Symbol: EPP.PR.A
Profile: EPCOR's business & power generation assets, plus other assets in the United States, are indirectly held by EPCOR Power Equity Ltd.
Don Lowry, President/CEO
Mark Wiltzen, Sr. Vice-President/CFO
Brian Vaasjo, Exec. Vice-President/COO
Denise Carpenter, Sr. Vice-President, Public & Government Affairs
Peter Arnold, Sr. Vice-President, Human Resources & Corporate Health & Safety

EPCOR Power L.P.
EPCOR Centre, 10065 Jasper Ave., 20th Fl., Edmonton, AB T5J 3B1
Tel: 780-412-4297; *Fax:* 780-412-3808
Toll-Free: 866-896-4636
investorinquiries@epcorpowerlp.ca
www.epcorpowerlp.ca
Ticker Symbol: EP.UN
Profile: EPCOR Power L.P. is a limited partnership, which is involved in the generation of electricity & steam, through it ownership & operation of a portfolio power plants. Earnings & cash flows are derived from this activity. The Partnership's wholly-owned power generation assets are situated in Canada & the United States. The General Partner of the Partnership, EPCOR Power Services Ltd., is responsible for management of the Partnership.
Brian T. Vaasjo, President, EPCOR Power Services Ltd.
Stuart Lee, Chief Financial Officer, EPCOR Power Services Ltd.
Kathryn Chisholm, Sr. Vice-President, General Counsel & Corporate Secretary, EPCOR Power Services Ltd.
Tim LeRiche, Contact, Media Inquiries
780-969-8238
Randy Mah, Contact, Unitholder & Analyst Inquiries

FortisAlberta
320 17th Avenue SW, Calgary, AB T2S 2V1
Tel: 403-514-4000; *Fax:* 403-514-4001
Toll-Free: 866-717-3113
www.fortisalberta.com
Profile: FortisAlberta provides power to various communities in Alberta. It is affliated with the Fortis Family of Companies.
Nipa Chakravarti, Vice-President, Customer Service
Karl W. Smith, President and CEO

Keyera Facilities Income Fund
#600, 144 - 4 Ave. SW, Calgary, AB T2P 3N4
Tel: 403-205-8300; *Fax:* 403-205-8303
ir@keyera.com
www.keyera.com
Ticker Symbol: KEY.UN
Profile: The Keyera Facilities Income Fund is an unincorporated open-ended trust. It owns 100% interest in Keyera Energy Canada Partnership. Keyera is engaged in the following activities: gathering & processing natural gas; storing & transporting natural gas liquids & crude oil; & marketing natural gas liquids.
Jim V. Bertram, President/CEO
Dean Setoguchi, Vice-President/CFO
Graham Balzun, Vice-President, Engineering & Corporate Responsibility
Ron Daniels, Manager, Manager, Information Technology
403-205-7635
Tanis Fiss, Manager, Financial Communications
Murray Selle, Manager, Health & Safety
Rod Sikora, Manager, Environment
403-205-8335
W. John Cobb, Director, Investor Relations
403-205-7673

MAXIM Power Corp.
#1210, 715 - 5th Ave. SW, Calgary, AB T2P 2X6
Tel: 403-263-3021; *Fax:* 403-263-9125
maxim@maximpowercorp.com
www.maximpowercorp.com
Ticker Symbol: MXG
Profile: MAXIM Power Corp. is an independent power producer. The company is involved in the acquisition, development, ownership, & operation of environmentally responsible power projects. Its assets include coal & natural gas powered generators in western Canada, the United States, & France.
John R. Bobenic, President/CEO
Xavier Embroise, President, COMAX France S.A.S.
Michael R. Mayder, CFO & Vice-President, Finance
Ian Sanchez, Vice-President, Corporate Development
Jamie Urquhart, Vice-President, Operations

Medicine Hat Electric
2172 Brier Park Place NW, Medicine Hat, AB T1C 1S6
Tel: 403-529-8262; *Fax:* 403-502-8060
elecdist@medicinehat.ca
Profile: Responsible for providing electrical power, natural gas, water treatment & supply, and waste management services to the city of Medicine Hat

Pristine Power
#1450, 645 - 7th Avenue SW, Calgary, AB T2P 4G8
Tel: 403-444-6401; *Fax:* 403-444-6784
gkrause@pristinepower.ca
www.pristinepower.ca
Ticker Symbol: PPX
Profile: Develops, owns, and operates independent power plants to produce and sell electricity

TransAlta Corporation
PO Box 1900 M, 110 - 12 Ave. SW, Calgary, AB T2P 2M1
Tel: 403-267-7110; *Fax:* 403-267-2590
investor_relations@transalta.com
www.transalta.com
Ticker Symbol: TA
Profile: TansAlta Corporation is engaged in coal & gas-fired generation. The company carries out its activities in Canada, the United States, Mexico, & Australia.
Stephen G. Snyder, President/CEO
Brian Burden, Exec. Vice-President/CFO
William D.A. Bridge, Exec. Vice-President, Generation Technology & Procurement
Dawn Farrell, Exec. Vice-President, Commercial Operations & Development
Mike Williams, Exec. Vice-President, Human Resources, Information Technology & Communication
Ken Stickland, Exec. Vice-President, Legal, SD, & Environmental Health & Safety

TransAlta Power, L.P.
PO Box 1900 M, 110 - 12 Ave. SW, Calgary, AB T2P 2M1
Tel: 403-267-7110; *Fax:* 403-267-2590
investor_relations@transalta.com
www.transalta.com
Ticker Symbol: TA
Profile: Unit investment trusts, certificate/closed-end management offices; Electric services
Stephen G. Snyder, President & CEO
Brian Burden, Chief Financial Officer

TransCanada Corp.
450 - 1 St. SW, Calgary, AB T2P 5H1
Tel: 403-920-2000; *Fax:* 403-920-2200
communications@transcanada.com
www.transcanada.com
Ticker Symbol: TRP
Profile: TransCanada Corporation is engaged in the pipelines & energy business. Pipelines are located in Canada, the United States, & Mexico. Power operations & natural gas storage are part of the energy segment.
Harold N. Kvisle, President/CEO
Alexander J. Pourbaix, President, Energy
Russell K. Girling, President, Pipelines
Gregory A. Lohnes, Exec. Vice-President/CFO
Sarah E. Raiss, Exec. Vice-President, Corporate Services
Sean McMaster, General Counsel & Exec. Vice-President, Corporate
Don Wishart, Exec. Vice-President, Operations & Engineering

British Columbia

Atlantic Power Corp.
#1900, 355 Burrard Street, Vancouver, BC V6L 2G8
Tel: 617-977-2700; *Fax:* 617-977-2410
info@atlanticpowercorporation.com
www.atlanticpowercorporation.com
Ticker Symbol: ATP.UN

Atlantic Power Corporation
#1900, 355 Burrard St., Vancouver, BC V6L 2G8
Tel: 617-977-2700; *Fax:* 617-977-2410
info@atlanticpowercorporation.com
www.atlanticpowercorporation.com

British Columbia Hydro
6911 Southpoint Dr., Burnaby, BC V3N 4X8
Tel: 604-224-9376; *Fax:* 604-528-3137
Toll-Free: 800-224-9376
www.bchydro.com
Profile: Electric services
Bev Van Ruyven, Acting President/CEO
Charles Reid, Exec. Vice President/CFO
Robert J. Steele, Chief Information Officer
Chris O'Riley, Vice-President, Engineering

British Columbia Utilities Commission
PO Box 250, 900 Howe St., Vancouver, BC V6Z 2N3
Tel: 604-660-4700; *Fax:* 604-660-1102
Toll-Free: 800-663-1385
commission.secretary@bcuc.com
www.bcuc.com
Profile: The British Columbia Utilities Commission is an independent regulatory agency of the Provincial Government. The Commission's primary responsibility is the regulation of British Columbia's natural gas & electricity utilities. It also regulates intra-provincial pipelines & universal compulsory automobile insurance.
Len Kelsey, Chair

EarthFirst Canada Inc.
2960 B Jutland Road, Victoria, BC V8T 5K2
Tel: 250-381-1208; *Fax:* 250-381-1298
dnewell@earthfirstcanada.com
www.earthfirstcanada.com
Ticker Symbol: EF
Profile: Developer, builder, owner and operator of windpower projects throughout Canada

Plutonic Power Corp.
#600, 888 Dunsmuir Street, Vancouver, BC V6C 3K4
Tel: 604-669-4999; *Fax:* 604-682-3727
elisha.moreno@plutonic.ca
www.plutonic.ca
Ticker Symbol: PCC
Profile: Clean energy company focused on hydroelectric projects in British Columbia

Powerex Corp.
#1400, 666 Burrard St., Vancouver, BC V6C 2X8
Tel: 604-891-5000; *Fax:* 604-891-6060
Toll-Free: 800-220-4907
Brian.Moghadam@powerex.com (Business Dev)
www.powerex.com
Profile: As a wholly-owned subsidiary of BC Hydro, Powerex markets BC Hydro's surplus electricity. Powerex is a participant in energy markets across North America, where it supplies & buys wholesale power, natural gas, ancillary services, & environmental products.
Amit Budhwar, Director, Risk Management
604-891-5041
Deb Armour, Director, Compliance
604-891-5063
Bernice Crick, Manager, Credit Risk Management
604-895-7093
Andrew Newell, Manager, Market Risk Management
604-891-6093
Jay Ratzlaff, Manager, Contract Management
604-895-7067

Primary Energy Recycling Corp.
#129, 2000 York Road, Oak Brook, IL
Tel: 630-371-0505; *Fax:* 630-371-0673
investorinfo@primaryenergy.com
www.primaryenergyrecycling.com
Ticker Symbol: PRI.UN
Profile: Owns and operates recycled energy projects

Spectra Energy Inc.
#1000, 1055 West Georgia St., Vancouver, BC V6E 3K9
Tel: 604-488-8000; *Fax:* 604-488-8500
www.duke-energy.com
Profile: Natural gas transmission & distribution; Electric services; Crude petroleum, natural gas & natural gas liquids extraction; Natural gas transmission; Special warehousing & storage.
Gregory L. Ebel, President/CEO
John Patrick Reddy, Chief Financial Officer

Terasen Gas
PO Box 6666 Terminal, Vancouver, BC V6B 6M9
Tel: 250-979-4900; *Fax:* 888-224-2720
Toll-Free: 888-224-2710
customerservice@tersengas.com
www.terasengas.com
Profile: Tersan Gas delivers natural gas & piped propane to homes & businesses throughout BC. It has approximately 900,000 customers in 125 communities & provides service to 95% of BC's natural gas customers.

Manitoba

Manitoba Hydro
PO Box 815 Main, 360 Portage Ave., Winnipeg, MB R3C 2P4
Tel: 204-480-5900; *Fax:* 204-475-0069
Toll-Free: 888-624-9376
publicaffairs@hydro.mb.ca
www.hydro.mb.ca
Profile: Manitoba Hydro is a major energy utility. It serves electric & natural gas customers in Manitoba.
Bob Brennan, President & Chief Executive Officer
Vince Warden, Chief Financial Officer & Senior Vice-President, Finance & Administration
Ken Adams, Senior Vice-President, Power Supply
Ed Tymofichuk, Vice-President, Transmission
Gerry Rose, Vice-President, Customer Care & Marketing
Lyn Wray, Vice-President, Corporate Planning & Strategic Analysis
Brad Ireland, Contact, Corporate Health & Safety

New Brunswick

Bell Aliant Regional Communications Income Fund
1 Brunswick Sq., 5th Fl., Saint John, NB E2L 4L4
Tel: 877-248-3113; *Fax:* 877-498-2464
investors@bell.aliant.ca
www.bell.aliant.ca
Ticker Symbol: BA.UN
Profile: The wireline company operates in Atlantic Canada, Quebec, & Ontario.
Karen H. Sheriff, President/CEO
Glen LeBlanc, Exec. Vice-President/CFO
Fred Crooks, Chief Legal Officer & Exec. Vice-President, Corporate Services
David Rathbun, Exec. Vice-President, Bell Aliant, & President, xwave (Bell Alliant's Information Technology Division)
Chuck Hartlen, Sr. Vice-President, Customer Experience, Chief Information Office

Fortis Inc.
Fortis Bldg., PO Box 8837, #1201, 139 Water St., St. John's, NL A1B 3T2
Tel: 709-737-2800; *Fax:* 709-737-5307
investorrelations@fortisinc.com
www.fortisinc.com
Ticker Symbol: FTS
Profile: Fortis Inc. is an international distribution utility holding company, which serves gas & electricity customers. The company also owns hotels & commercial real estate in Canada.
H. Stanley Marshall, President/CEO
Barry V. Perry, CFO & Vice-President, Finance
Ronald W. McCabe, General Counsel & Corporate Secretary

New Brunswick Power Distribution & Customer Svs. Corp
PO Box 2000, 515 King St., Fredericton, NB E3B 4X1
Tel: 506-458-4444; *Fax:* 506-458-4000
Toll-Free: 800-663-6272
customerservices@nbpower.com
www.nbpower.com
Profile: NB Power provides safe & sustainable energy services to homes, businesses, & facilities in New Brunswick. Electricity is generated at sixteen facilities.
David D. Hay, President & Chief Executive Officer
Darrell Bishop, Executive Vice-President, Strategic Planning
Darren Murphy, Vice-President, Transmission, Distribution, & Customer Service
Wayne Snowdon, Vice-President, Generation (Conventional)
Gaëtan Thomas, Vice-President, Nuclear

Newfoundland & Labrador Hydro
Hydro Place, PO Box 12400, 500 Columbus Dr., St.John's, NL A1B 4K7
Tel: 709-737-1400; *Fax:* 709-737-1800
Toll-Free: 888-737-1296
hydro@nlh.nl.ca; tenders@nlh.nl.ca
www.nlh.nl.ca
Profile: Newfoundland & Labrador Hydro is the primary generator of safe & reliable electricity to residents, utilities, & industries across the province. The company's assets include hydroelectric generating stations, high-voltage terminal stations, lower-voltage interconnected distribution stations, diesel plants, gas turbines, transmission & distribution lines, & an oil-fired plant.
Ed Martin, President & Chief Executive Officer
Derrick Sturge, Chief Financial Officer & Vice-President, Finance
Jim Haynes, Vice-President, Regulated Operations
John Mallam, Vice-President, Engineering Services
Gerard McDonald, Vice-President, Human Resources & Organizational Effectiveness

Newfoundland Power Inc.
PO Box 8910, 55 Kenmount Rd., St. John's, NL A1B 3P6
Tel: 709-737-2802; *Fax:* 709-737-2903
Toll-Free: 800-663-2802
contactus@newfoundlandpower.com
www.newfoundlandpower.com
Profile: Newfoundland Power Inc. is engaged in the operation of an integrated generation, transmission, & distribution system. Safe, reliable electricity is supplied to the island portion of Newfoundland & Labrador.
Earl Ludlow, President & Chief Executive Officer
Peter Alteen, Vice-President, Regulation & Planning
Jocelyn Perry, Chief Financial Officer & Vice-President, Finance
Gary Smith, Vice-President, Customer Operations & Engineering
Peter Collins, Manager, Customer Relations & Information Technology

Saint John Energy
PO Box 850, Saint John, NB E2L 4C7
Tel: 506-658-5252; *Fax:* 506-658-0868
Toll-Free: 877-907-5550
www.sjenergy.com
Profile: Responsible for providing electricity to the city of Saint John. Other services include tree trimming, rental of water heaters, street light repair
Eric Marr, President/CEO

Nova Scotia

Emera Incorporated
Barrington Tower, Scotia Square, PO Box 910, 1894 Barrington St., 18th Fl., Halifax, NS B3J 2W5
Tel: 902-450-0507; *Fax:* 902-428-6112
Toll-Free: 888-450-0507
investors@emera.com
www.emera.com
Ticker Symbol: EMA
Profile: The holding company is involved in the energy sector. Emera Inc.'s subsidiaries include Bangor Hydro-Electric Company, Nova Scotia Power Inc., Emera Energy, Maritimes & Northeast Pipeline, Brunswick Pipeline, Emera Utility Services, & Grand Bahama Power Ltd.
Christopher Huskilson, President/CEO
Rob Bennett, President/CEO, Nova Scotia Power Inc.
Robert Hanf, President/COO, Bangor Hydro Electric Company
Robin McAdam, President, Brunswick Pipeline Company Ltd.
Nancy Tower, F.C.A.Chief Financial Officer
902-429-6991, nancy.tower@emera.com
Wayne Crawley,, CAVice-President, Corporate Strategy & Development
James Spurr, General Counsel & Vice-President, Government Relations

Jennifer Nicholson, CADirector, Investor Relations & Strategic Development
902-428-6347, jennifer.nicholson@emera.com

Northwest Territories Power Corporation
4 Capital Dr., Hay River, NT X0E 1G2
Tel: 867-874-5200;
info@ntpc.com
www.ntpc.com
Profile: Northwest Territories Power Corporation generates & delivers power across the Northwest Territories. The corporation operates 28 separate power systems. Northwest Territories Power Corporation attempts to reduce its environmental impact with natural gas engines in Inuvik, rather than shipping in diesel.
Leon Courneya, FCAPresident & Chief Executive Officer
Judith Goucher, MAChief Financial Officer & Director, Finance
John Locke, Chief Information Officer & Director, Information Technology
Brian Willows, Chief Operating Officer
Stephen Kerrows, Director, Engineering
Robert Schmidt, Director, Hydro Region

Nova Scotia Power Inc.
PO Box 910, #1800, 1894 Barrington St., Halifax, NS B3J 2W5
Tel: 902-450-0507; *Fax:* 902-428-6112
Toll-Free: 800-428-6230
investors@emera.com
www.nspower.ca
Ticker Symbol: NSI
Profile: Nova Scotia Power Inc. is engaged in the generation, transmission, & distribution of electric power across Nova Scotia.
Rob Bennett, President/CEO
Sarah MacDonald, President/COO, Emera Utility Services & Vice-President Human Resources
Rick Janega, Exec. Vice-President, Business Infrastructure & Optimization
Greg Blunden, CATreasurer & Vice-President, Finance
Mark Savory, Vice-President, Technical & Construction Services
Gerald Weseen, General Manager, Communications & Public Affairs
James Taylor, General Manager, Environmental Planning & Monitoring

Ontario

Algonquin Power Income Fund
2845 Bristol Circle, Oakville, ON L6H 7H7
Tel: 905-465-4500; *Fax:* 905-465-4514
apif@algonquinpower.com
www.algonquinpower.com
Ticker Symbol: APF
Profile: Algonquin Power Income Fund is an open-ended investment trust. It owns or has interests in a portfolio of renewable power & sustainable infrastructure assets throughout Canada & the United States. The Trust's facilities include the following: hydroelectric generation, wind energy, energy from waste, landfill gas, biomass-fired generation, natural gas cogeneration, water distribution, & wastewater treatment.
Chris K. Jarrat, Managing Director, Development
David Bronicheski, CFO & Managing Director, Administration
David C. Kerr, Managing Director, Power Generation & Corporate Services
Ian E. Robertson, Managing Director, Utilities

Atomic Energy of Canada Limited
2251 Speakman Dr., Mississauga, ON L5K 1B2
Tel: 905-823-9040; *Fax:* 905-823-1290
Toll-Free: 866-886-2325
info@aecl.ca
www.aecl.ca
Profile: Manufacturers of various industrial inorganic chemicals, measuring & controlling devices, special industry machinery; Commercial physical & biological research; Management services; Electric services
Hugh MacDiarmid, President/CEO
Glenna Carr, Chair of the Board
Jonathan Lundy, Sr. Vice-President, General Counsel and Corporate Secretary

Brantford Power Inc.
84 Market St. 3rd Fl., Brantford, ON N3T 5N8
Tel: 519-751-3522; *Fax:* 519-753-6130
brantfordpower@brantford.ca
www.brantfordpower.com
Profile: Brantford Power strives to provide safe, reliable, & competitively priced services to customers, while providing value for municipal shareholder.
George Mychailenko, CEO/General Manager
519-751-3522, gmychailenko@brantford.ca
Ann Elwood, Administrative Coordinator
aelwood@brantford.ca
Brian D'Amboise, Chief Financial Officer
damboise@brantford.ca

Cambridge & North Dumfries Hydro Inc.
PO Box 1060, 1500 Bishop St., Cambridge, ON N1R 5X6
Tel: 519-621-3530; *Fax:* 519-621-0383
Profile: Cambridge & North Dumfries Hydro Inc. is a local distribution company which delivers electricity to the community on a not-for-profit basis. Local distribution rates are approved by the Ontario Energy Board.
Grotheer President/CEO
jgrotheer@camhydro.com
Jeff Brown, Director of Operations
jbrown@camhydro.com
M.Jane Hale-MacDonald, Director, Human Resources
jhalemcdonald@camhydro.com

Countryside Power Income Fund
#920, 495 Richmond St., London, ON N6A 5A9
Tel: 519-435-0298; *Fax:* 519-435-0396
Profile: Indirectly invested in the U.S. Energy Biogas Corporation loans & royalty interest; Has a direct ownership of the District Energy Systems

Creststreet Power & Income Fund LP
#1450, 70 University Ave., Toronto, ON M5J 2M4
Tel: 416-864-6330; *Fax:* 416-862-8950
info@creststreet.com
www.creststreet.com
Ticker Symbol: CRS.DB
Profile: Owns & operates two wind energy projects in Quebec & Nova Scotia

Energy Savings Income Fund
#2630, 100 King St. West, Toronto, ON M5X 1E1
Tel: 416-367-2998; *Fax:* 416-367-4749
fundinfo@energysavingsincomefund.com
www.esif.ca
Ticker Symbol: SIF
Profile: The open-ended, limited purpose trust is involved in the sale of natural gas & electricity to both residential & commercial customers. Operating affiliates inlcude Ontario Energy Savings L.P., Energy Savings (Manitoba) L.P., Energy Savings (Quebec) L.P., ES (B.C.) Limited Partnership, Alberta Energy Savings L.P., Illinois Energy Savings Corp., New York Energy Savings Corp., Indiana Energy Savings Corp., & Energy Savings Texas Corp.
Ken Hartwick, CAPresident/CEO
Peter Bloch, CAChief Financial Officer
905-795-4206, pbloch@energysavings.com
Scott Gahn, Exec. Vice-President, U.S. Energy Savings

Enersource Hydro Mississauga
3240 Mavis Rd., Mississauga, ON L5C 3K1
Tel: 905-273-9050; *Fax:* 905-566-2731
info@enersource.com
www.enersource.com
Profile: Provides electricity to the City of Mississauga
Roland Herman, Exec. Vice-President/COO
Ray Rauber, Vice-Presiednt, Engineering & Operations

FortisOntario
PO Box 1218, 1130 Bertie St., Fort Erie, ON L2A 5Y2
Tel: 905-871-0330;
www.cornwallelectric.com
Profile: FortisOntario is an innovative growth company with core businesses focused on electricity distribution, transmission, & generation. It is 100% Canadian owned & is affliated with the Fortis Family of Companies.
Bill Daley, President and CEO
905-994-3631, Fax: 905-994-2202
Glen King, Vice President, Finance and CFO
905-994-3643, Fax: 905-994-2200

Grimsby Power Incorporated
231 Roberts Rd., Grimsby, ON L3M 5N2
Tel: 905-945-5437; *Fax:* 905-945-9933
info@grimsbypower.com
www.grimsbypower.com
Profile: Grimsby Power Incorporated provides customers in Grimsby with electricity.
Vacant, President

Guelph Hydro Electric Systems Inc.
395 Southgate Dr., Guelph, ON N1G 4Y1
Tel: 519-822-3010; *Fax:* 519-822-0960
bbagley@guelphhydro.com
www.guelphhydro.com
Profile: Guelph Hydro Electric Systems Inc. is Guelph's and Rockwood's electricity distribution company. They deliver electricity, maintain the lines to homes and businesses provide 24-hr emergency service and ensure that the local distribution system meets Guelph's and Rockwood's growing needs.

Hydro One Inc.
483 Bay St., 15th Fl., Toronto, ON M5G 2P5
Tel: 416-345-6867; *Fax:* 416-345-6225
Toll-Free: 877-955-1155
investor.relations@hydroone.com
www.hydroone.com
Profile: HydroOne is the largest electricity delivery company in Ontario. It is a holding company for various subsidiaries. It provides electric services in Toronto.
Larua Forumusa, President/CEO
Sandy Struthers, CFO
Maureen Wareham, Secretary
Myles D'Arcey, Customer Operations
Peter Gregg, Corporate and Regulatory Affairs

Independent Electricity System Operator
PO Box 4474 A, Toronto, ON M5W 4E5
Tel: 905-403-6900; *Fax:* 905-403-6921
customer.relations@ieso.ca
www.ieso.ca
Profile: The IESO balances the supply of & demand for electricity in Ontario & then directs its flow across the province's transmission lines. The IESO works at the heart of Ontario's power system, connecting all participants that produce electricity, transmitters that send it across the province, retailers that buy & sell it, industries & businesses that use it in large quantities, & local distribution companies that deliver it to homes.
Paul Murphy, B.Sc., P.Eng.President and CEO
paul.murphy@ieso.ca

Kenora Hydro Electric Corp. Ltd
City Hall, 1 Main St. South, Kenora, ON P9N 3X2
Tel: 807-467-2000;
service@kenora.ca
Profile: Distributes electricity to the towns of Kenora and Keewatin; has 12 employees dedicated to the delivery of electricity to its customers
Dave Sinclair, President/CEO

London Hydro
111 Horton St., London, ON N6A 4J8
Tel: 519-661-5503; *Fax:* 519-661-5838
admin@londonhydro.com
www.londonhydro.com
Profile: The sole shareholder of London Hydro is the City of London. London Hydro provides London residents & businesses with electricity, through a network of overhead & underground power lines.
Peter Johnson, Chair
Vinay Sharma, Chief Executive Officer

Macquarie Power & Infrastructure Income Fund
Brookfield Place, #3100, 181 Bay St., Toronto, ON M5J 2T3
Tel: 416-848-3500; *Fax:* 416-607-5073
mpt@macquarie.com
www.macquarie.com/mpt
Ticker Symbol: MPT.UN
Profile: Macquarie Power & Infrastructure Income Fund makes investments in essential infrastructure assets. It focuses upon power infrastructure.

Niagara Peninsula Energy Inc.
PO Box 120, 7447 Pin Oak Dr., Niagara Falls, ON L2E 6S9
Tel: 905-356-2681; *Fax:* 905-356-0118
Toll-Free: 877-270-3938
info@npei.ca
www.npei.ca
Profile: Niagara Peninsula Energy Inc. provides local electricity distribution & related services in the Township of West Lincoln, the City of Niagara Falls, the Town of Pelham, & the Town of Lincoln. It serves both business & residential customers.
Brian Wilkie, President & Chief Executive Officer
Margaret Battista, Vice-President, Customer Service & Information Technology
Margaret Battista, Vice-President, Customer Service & Information Technology
Tom Sielicki, Vice-President, Engineering
Suzanne Wilson, Vice-President, Finance

Ontario Power Generation Inc.
700 University Ave., Toronto, ON M5G 1X6
Tel: 416-592-2555; *Toll-Free:* 877-592-2555
investor.relations@opg.com; media@opg.com
www.opg.com; mypowercareer@opg.com
Profile: The electricity generation company operates in a safe & environmentally responsible manner to generate & sell electricity throughout Ontario. Assets include sixty-five hydroelectric generating stations, five fossil generating stations, & three nuclear generating stations.
Tom Mitchell, President & Chief Executive Officer

John Murphy, Executive Vice President, Hydro
Janice Dunlop, Chief Ethics Officer & Senior Vice-President, Human Resources
Donn Hanbidge, Chief Financial Officer & Senior Vice-President
Wayne Robbins, Chief Nuclear Officer
Robert Boguski, Senior Vice-President, Business Services & Information Technology
Charles Pautler, Vice-President, Public Affairs

Oshawa PUC Networks Inc.
100 Simcoe St. South, Oshawa, ON L1H 7M7
Tel: 905-723-4623; *Fax:* 905-743-5222
contactus@opuc.on.ca
www.opuc.on.ca
Profile: Oshawa PUC Networks distributes electricity to homes & businesses in Oshawa.
Atul Mahajanal, President & Chief Executive Officer
Mike Leslie, P. Eng.Vice-President, Engineering & Operations
Phil Martin, Vice-President, Finance & Regulatory Compliance
Nadeige Carter, Coordinator, Conservation Project

Peterborough Utilities Group
PO Box 4125 Main, 1867 Ashburnham Dr., Peterborough, ON K9J 6Z5
Tel: 705-748-9300; *Fax:* 705-748-6761
info@peterboroughutilities.ca
www.peterboroughutilities.ca
Profile: Peterborough Utilities Group delivers & sells utility-related products & services.
Larry Doran, President & Chief Executive Officer
John Stephenson, Chief Financial Officer, Secretary-Treasurer & Vice-President, Corporate Service
Larry Franks, Vice-President, Information Technology Services
Jeff Guilbeault, Vice-President, Electric Utility Services
Wayne Stiver, Vice-President, Water Utility Services
John Wynsma, Vice-President, Generation & Retail Services
Carrissa McCaw, Director, Human Resources & Safety

Toronto Hydro Corporation
14 Carlton St., Toronto, ON M5B 1K5
Tel: 416-542-3100; *Fax:* 416-542-3452
contactus@torontohydro.com
www.torontohydro.com
Profile: Offices of holding companies; Electric services; Natural gas distribution.
David S. O'Brien, President/CEO
David Dobbin, President, Toronto Hydro Telecom
Jean-Sebastien Couillard, CFO
Blair H. Peberdy, Vice-President, Communications & Public Affairs
Anthony M. Haines, President
Ave Lethbridge, Vice-President, Organizational Effectiveness
Lawrence Wilde, Vice-President and General Counsel

Universal Energy Group Ltd.
#1700, 25 Sheppard Avenue West, Toronto, ON M2N 6S6
Tel: 416-673-1162; *Fax:* 416-673-4790
splummer@uegl.ca
www.universalenergygroup.ca
Ticker Symbol: UEG
Profile: Electricity and natural gas company focused in Ontario and Michigan

Utilities Kingston
PO Box 790, Kingston, ON K7L 4X7
Tel: 613-456-0000;
info@utilitieskingston.com
www.utilitieskingston.com
Profile: Utilities Kingston is responsible for supplying, distributing and metering electricity and natural gas in the City Central. Also responsible for supplying, distributing and metering water and for collecting, pumping and treating sewage for the entire city of Kingston

Wellington North Power Inc.
PO Box 359, 290 Queen St. West, Mount Forest, ON N0G 1A0
Tel: 519-323-1710; *Fax:* 519-323-2425
wnp@wellingtonnorthpower.com
www.wellingtonnorthpower.com
Profile: The distribution company delivers electricity & maintains service to residents & businesses. Wellington North Power Inc. serves the areas of Arthur, Mount Forest, & Holstein in Ontario.
Judy Rosebrugh, President & Chief Executive Officer
jrosebrugh@wellingtonnorthpower.com

Westario Power Inc.
24 Eastridge Rd., RR#2, Walkerton, ON N0G 2V0
Tel: 519-507-6937; *Toll-Free:* 866-978-2746
customer.service@westario.com
www.westario.com
Profile: Westario Power Inc. is engaged in the safe & reliable delivery of electricity. It is owned by the municipalities it serves. FortisOntario also has a 10% interest in Westario Power.
Lisa Milne, CGAPresident & Chief Executive Officer
Patrick Protomanni, P. Eng.Manager, System Reliability

Prince Edward Island

Maritime Electric
c/o Island Customer Service Centre, PO Box 1328, 180 Kent St., Charlottetown, PE C1A 7N2
Fax: 902-629-3630
Toll-Free: 800-670-1012
customerservice@maritimeelectric.com
www.maritimeelectric.com
Profile: Maritime Electric operates according to the Electric Power Act & the Renewable Energy Act to deliver electricity on Prince Edward Island.
Fred J. O'Brien, President & Chief Executive Officer
J. William Geldert, CFO, Corporate Secretary, & Vice-President, Finance & Administration
John D. Gaudet, Vice-President, Corporate Planning & Energy Supply
Kim A. Griffin, Manager, Corporate Communications & Public Affairs
Gil A. Jubainville, Manager, Information Technology

Québec

Boralex Inc.
36, rue Lajeunesse, Kingsey Falls, QC J0A 1B0
Tel: 819-363-5860; *Fax:* 819-363-5866
info@boralex.com
www.boralex.com
Ticker Symbol: BLX
Profile: The electricity producer provides the following types of power generation: natural gas cogeneration, hydroelectric, wind power, & wood-residue.
Patrick Lemaire, President/CEO
Jean-François Thibodeau, Vice-President/CFO
Claude Audet, Vice-President/Chief Operating Officer
Patricia Lemaire, Director, Public Affairs & Communications
514-985-1353, Fax: 514-985-1355,
patricia.lemaire@boralex.com
Gabriel Ouellet, Technical Director, Biomass, Quebec & USA
Gilles Shooner, Environmental Consultant & Member, Environmental, Health, & Safety Committee

Boralex Power Income Fund
36 Lajeunesse Street, Kingsey Falls, QC J0A 1B0
Tel: 819-363-5860; *Fax:* 819-363-5866
info@boralex.com
www.boralex.com/trust
Ticker Symbol: BPT.UN
Profile: Open-ended limited purpose trust; owns hydroelectricity, wood residue and natural gas power stations in Quebec and New York

Gaz Métro inc
1717, rue du Havre, Montréal, QC H2K 2X3
Tel: 514-598-3444; *Fax:* 514-598-3144
Toll-Free: 800-361-4005
info@gazmetro.com
www.gazmetro.com
Ticker Symbol: GZM
Profile: Offices of holding companies; Natural gas transmission & distribution; Retail in household appliance stores; Equipment rental & leasing
Sophie Brochu, President/CEO
Pierre Despars, Vice-President, Finance & Corporate Affairs
Stéphanie-Hélène Leclerc, Contact, Public & Governmental Affairs
E. Morin, Director, Engineering, Geomatics & Technology
J.-P. Noël, Director, Regulatory Matters, Rates & Environment

Gaz Métro Limited Partnership
1717, rue du Havre, Montréal, QC H2K 2X3
Tel: 514-598-3444; *Fax:* 514-598-3144
investors@gazmetro.com
www.gazmetro.com
Ticker Symbol: GZM
Profile: Gaz Métro Limited Partnership focuses upon the distribution of natural gas, through its interests in natural gas transmission companies. The company is also engaged in the sale of goods in the energy & fiber optics fields, as well as the diagnosis & rehabilitation of drinking water & wastewater infrastructures. In order to reduce greenhouse gas emissions, Gaz Métro has adopted an environmental policy, an environmental management system, & energy efficiency programs.
Sophie Brochu, President/CEO
Pierre Despars, Exec. Vice-President/CFO
Martin Imbleau, Vice-President, Operations & Major Projects
Marc Lemieux, Corporate Secretary & Vice-President, Legal Affairs

Great Lakes Hydro Income Fund
#200, 480, boul de la Cité, Gatineau, QC J8T 8R3
Tel: 819-561-2722; *Fax:* 819-561-7188
Toll-Free: 888-327-2722
unitholderenquiries@greatlakeshydro.com
www.greatlakeshydro.com
Ticker Symbol: GLH
Profile: Electric services; Open-ended management investment offices.
Richard Legault, President/CEO
Donald Tremblay, CFO & Vice-President
Harry A. Goldgut, Chairman of the Board and Director

Hydro-Québec
75, boul René-Lévesque ouest, Montréal, QC H2Z 1A4
Tel: 514-289-2211; *Fax:* 514-289-5773
Toll-Free: 800-790-2424
www.hydroquebec.com
Profile: Electricity services in Quebec
Thierry Vandal, President/CEO
Joseph Benarrosh, President, JJDS Capital inc.
Daniel Garant, CFO & Exec. Vice-President, Finance
Marie-José Nadeau, Secretary General/Exec. Vice-President, Corporate Affairs

Innergex Renewable Energy Inc.
#1255, 1111, rue Saint-Charles ouest, Longueuil, QC J4K 5G4
Tel: 450-928-2550; *Fax:* 450-928-2544
jtrudel@innergex.com
www.innergex.com
Ticker Symbol: INE
Profile: Innergex Renewable Energy develops & operates renewable power generating facilities. If focuses upon the wind power & hydroelectric sectors.
Michel Letellier, MBAPresident/CEO
Jean Perron, Vice-President/CFO
Michèle Beauchamp, LL.B., LL.M.,Corporate Secretary & Vice-President, Legal Affairs
Guy Dufort, Vice-President, Public Affairs
Peter Grover, Eng.Vice-President, Project Management
Jean Trudel, MBAVice-President, Finance & Investor Relations

Saskatchewan

Saskatoon Light & Power
322 Brand Rd., Saskatoon, SK S7K 0J5
Tel: 306-975-2414; *Fax:* 306-975-3057
www.city.saskatoon.sk.ca/org/electrical
Profile: Founded in 1906, Saskatoon Light & Power distributes electrical services to citizens & businesses of the Saskatoon area that lies roughly within the 1958 boundary. The utility is also responsible for the street light system for the city.

SaskEnergy Incorporated
1777 Victoria Ave., Regina, SK S4P 4K5
Tel: 306-777-9225; *Toll-Free:* 800-567-8899
www.saskenergy.com
Profile: The natural gas distribution company is a provincial Crown corporation. SaskEnergy Incorporated delivers safe & environmentally friendly natural gas to customers throughout Saskatchewan. The company also works with independent natural gas retailers to offer natural gas appliances, maintenance, & financing.
Doug Kelln, President & Chief Executive Officer
Dennis Terry, Chief Financial Officer & Vice-President, Finance
Dean Reeve, Executive Vice-President
Daryl Posehn, Senior Vice-President, Gas Supply & Business Development
Mark Guillet, Vice-President, General Counsel, & Corporate Secretary

Yukon Territory

Yukon Electrical Company Limited
#100, 1100 - 1st Ave., Whitehorse, YT Y1A 3T4
Tel: 867-633-7000; *Fax:* 867-668-6692
Toll-Free: 800-661-0513
www.yukonelectrical.com
Profile: The Yukon Electrical Company Limited is a private, investor-owned utility which provides electrical services to Yukoners. The company works to design & construct its facilities in a way that reduces pollution & the impact of operations upon the environment.
Jerome Babyn, General Manager

Government Agency Guide

CONSERVATION & ECOLOGY

See Also: Heritage Resources; Natural Resources

Canadian Heritage, 15 Eddy St., Gatineau, K1A 0M5 QC
819-997-0055, 866-811-0055

Canadian Polar Commission, Constitution Square, #1710, 360 Albert St., Ottawa, K1R 7X7 ON
613-943-8605, Fax: 613-943-8607, 888-765-2701, mail@polarcom.gc.ca

Environment Canada, 10 Wellington St., Gatineau, K1A 0H3 QC
819-997-2800, Fax: 819-994-1412, 800-668-6767, enviroinfo@ec.gc.ca

Commission for Environmental Cooperation, Secretariat, #200, 393, rue St-Jacques ouest, Montréal, H2Y 1N9 QC
514-350-4300, Fax: 514-350-4314, info@cec.org

Fisheries Resource Conservation Council, PO Box 2001 D, Ottawa, ON K1P 5W3
613-998-0433, Fax: 613-998-1146, info@frcc-ccrh.ca

Natural Resources Canada, 580 Booth St., Ottawa, K1A 0E4 ON
613-995-0947, Fax: 613-992-7211

Parks Canada, 25 Eddy St., Gatineau, K1A 0M5 QC
888-773-8888, information@pc.gc.ca

Alberta

Alberta Environmental Appeal Board, Peace Hills Trust Tower, #306, 10011 - 109 St. NW, Edmonton, AB T5J 3S8
780-427-6207, Fax: 780-427-4693

Alberta Special Areas Board, 212 - 2nd Ave. West, PO Box 820, Hanna, AB T0J 1P0
403-854-5600, Fax: 403-854-5527, specarea@telusplanet.net

Alberta Used Oil Management Association, Scotia One, Scotia Place, #1050, 10060 Jasper Ave., Edmonton, AB T5J 3R8
780-414-1510, Fax: 780-414-1519, reception@usedoilrecycling.ca

Beverage Container Management Board, #1010, 10707 - 100 Ave., Edmonton, AB T5J 3M1
780-424-3193, Fax: 780-428-4620, 888-424-7671, info@bcmb.ab.ca

Clean Air Strategic Alliance, Centre West Bldg, 10035 - 108 St., 10th Fl., Edmonton, AB T5J 3E1
780-427-9793, Fax: 780-422-3127, casa@casahome.org

Alberta Environment, South Tower, Petroleum Plaza, 9915 - 108 St., Main Fl., Edmonton, T5K 2G8 AB
780-427-2700, Fax: 780-422-4086,-310-0000, env.infocent@gov.ab.ca

Natural Resources Conservation Board, Sterling Place, 9940 - 106 St., 4th Fl., Edmonton, AB T5K 2N2
780-422-1977, Fax: 780-427-0607, 866-383-6722

British Columbia

British Columbia Assessment Authority, 1537 Hillside Ave., Victoria, BC V8T 4Y2
250-595-6211, Fax: 250-595-6222, info@bcassessment.ca

Ministry of Environment, PO Box 9339 Prov Govt,Victoria, V8W 9M1 BC
250-387-1161, Fax: 250-387-5669, www.envmail@gov.bc.ca

Environmental Appeal Board, 747 Fort St., 4th Fl., PO Box 9425 Prov Govt, Victoria, BC V8W 9V1
250-387-3464, Fax: 250-356-9923, eabinfo@gov.bc.ca

Environmental Stewardship Division, 2975 Jutland Rd., 5th Fl., PO Box 9339 Prov Govt,Victoria, V8T 5J9 BC
250-356-0121, Fax: 250-953-3414

Forest Practices Board, 1675 Douglas St., 3rd Fl., PO Box 9905 Prov Govt, Victoria, BC V8W 9R1
250-387-7964, Fax: 250-387-7009, 800-994-5899, fpboard@gov.bc.ca

Fraser Basin Council, Central Office, 470 Granville St., 1st Fl., Vancouver, BC V6C 1V5
604-488-5350, Fax: 604-488-5351, info@fraserbasin.bc.ca

Mediation & Arbitration Board, #310, 9900 - 100 Ave., Fort St John, BC V1J 5S7
250-787-3403, Fax: 250-787-3228, mab.office@gov.bc.ca

Northern Interior, 1011 - 4 Ave., 5th Fl., Prince George, V2L 3H9 BC
250-565-6100, Fax: 250-565-6671, www.for.gov.bc.ca/rni

Manitoba

Clean Environment Commission, #305, 155 Carlton St., Winnipeg, MB R3C 3H8
204-945-0594, Fax: 204-945-0090

Manitoba Conservation, 200 Saulteaux Cres., Winnipeg, R3J 3W3 MB
204-945-6784, 800-214-6497, mincon@leg.gov.mb.ca

Ecological Reserves Advisory Committee, c/o Manitoba Conservation, Parks & Natural Areas Branch, 200 Saulteaux Cres., Winnipeg, MB R3J 3W3
204-945-4148, Fax: 204-945-0012, hhernandez@gov.mb.ca

Manitoba Conservation Districts Commission, Secretariat c/o Planning & Coordination Branch, 123 Main St., PO Box 20000, Neepawa, MB R0J 1H0
204-476-7033, Fax: 204-476-7539, whildebran@gov.mb.ca

New Brunswick

Assessment & Planning Appeal Board, #201, 435 King St., PO Box 6000, Fredericton, NB E3B 5H1
506-453-2126, Fax: 506-444-4881,

Department of the Environment, Marysville Place, 20 McGloin St., PO Box 6000, Fredericton, E3B 5H1 NB
506-453-2690, Fax: 506-457-4991

Newfoundland & Labrador

Department of Environment & Conservation, Confederation Bldg., West Block, 4th Fl., PO Box 8700, St. John's, A1B 4J6 NL
709-729-2664, Fax: 709-729-6639, 800-563-6181, info@gov.nl.ca

Northwest Territories

Department of Environment & Natural Resources, PO Box 1320, Yellowknife, X1A 2L9 NT

Nova Scotia

Environmental & Natural Areas Management, PO Box 697, Halifax, B3J 3T8 NS
902-424-3571

Department of Natural Resources, Founder's Square, 1701 Hollis St., 3rd Fl., PO Box 698, Halifax, B3J 2T9 NS
902-424-5935, Fax: 902-424-0594, 800-565-2224

Ontario

Ministry of Environment, 135 St. Clair Ave. West, Toronto, M4V 1P5 ON
416-325-4000, Fax: 416-325-3159, 800-565-4923

Ministry of Natural Resources, Whitney Block, #6630, 99 Wellesley St. West, 6th Fl., Toronto, M7A 1W3 ON
800-667-1940

Niagara Escarpment Commission, 232 Guelph St., Georgetown, L7G 4B1 ON
905-877-5191, Fax: 905-873-7452

Prince Edward Island

Department of Environment, Energy & Forestry, Jones Bldg., 11 Kent St., 4th & 5th Fl., PO Box 2000, Charlottetown, C1A 7N8 PE
902-368-5000, Fax: 902-368-5830

Environmental Advisory Council, 11 Kent St., PO Box 2000, Charlottetown, PE C1A 7N8

Department of Tourism, PO Box 2000, Charlottetown, C1A 7N8 PE
800-463-4734

Quebec

Comité consultatif de l'environnement Kativik, CP 930, Kuujjuaq, QC J0M 1C0
819-964-2961, Fax: 819-964-0694, ndea@krg.ca

Ministère du Développement durable, de l'Environnement et des Parcs, Édifice Marie-Guyart, 675, boul René-Lévesque est, 29e étage, Québec, G1R 5V7 QC
418-521-3830, Fax: 418-646-5974, 800-561-1616, info@mddep.gouv.qc.ca

Fondation de la faune du Québec, Place Iberville II, #420, 1175, av Lavigerie, Québec, QC G1V 4P1
418-644-7926, Fax: 418-643-7655, 877-639-0742, ffq@riq.qc.ca

Société de développement de la Baie James, 110, boul Matagami, CP 970, Matagami, QC J0Y 2A0
819-739-4717, Fax: 819-739-4329

Société québécoise de récupération et de recyclage, Siège social, #200, 420, boul Charest est, Québec, QC G1K 8M4
418-643-0394, Fax: 418-643-6507, 866-523-8290, info@recyc-quebec.gouv.qc.ca

Saskatchewan

Saskatchewan Assessment Management Agency, #200, 2201 - 11 Ave., Regina, S4P 0J8 SK
306-924-8000, Fax: 306-924-8070, 800-667-7262, info.request@sama.sk.ca

Saskatchewan Environment, 3211 Albert St., 2nd Fl., Regina, S4S 5W6 SK
306-953-3750, Fax: 306-787-9544, 800-567-4224, inquiry@serm.gov.sk.ca

Saskatchewan Conservation Data Centre, 3211 Albert St., Regina, SK S4S 5W6
306-787-9038, Fax: 306-787-9544

Saskatchewan Watershed Authority, 111 Fairford St. East, Moose Jaw, SK S6H 7X9
306-694-3900, Fax: 306-694-3465, comm@swa.ca

Yukon Territory

Alsek Renewable Resource Council, PO Box 2077, Haines Junction, YT Y0B 1L0
867-634-2524, Fax: 867-634-2527

Carmacks Renewable Resource Council, PO Box 122, Carmacks, YT Y0B 1C0
867-863-6838, Fax: 867-863-6429, carmacksrrc@lscfn.ca

Dawson District Renewable Resource Council, PO Box 1380, Dawson City, YT Y0B 1G0
867-993-6976, Fax: 867-993-6093, dawsonrrc@yknet.yk.ca

Yukon Environment, PO Box 2703, Whitehorse, Y1A 2C6 YT
867-667-5652, Fax: 867-393-6213, 800-661-0408, environmentyukon@gov.yk.ca

Mayo District Renewable Resources Council, PO Box 249, Mayo, YT Y0B 1M0
867-996-2942, Fax: 867-996-2948, mayorrc@yknet.yk.ca

North Yukon Renewable Resources Council, PO Box 80, Old Crow, YT Y0B 1N0
vgrrc@yknet.yk.ca

Selkirk Renewable Resources Council, PO Box 32, Pelly Crossing, YT Y0B 1P0
867-537-3937, Fax: 867-537-3939, selkirkrre@yknet.yk.ca

Teslin Renewable Resource Council, PO Box 186, Teslin, YT Y0A 1B0
867-390-2323, Fax: 867-390-2919, teslinrrc@yknet.yk.ca

Yukon Land Use Planning Council, #201, 307 Jarvis St., Whitehorse, YT Y1A 2H3
867-667-7397, Fax: 867-667-4624, ylupc@planyukon.ca

ENERGY

See Also: Natural Resources

Atomic Energy of Canada Limited, Head Office, 2251 Speakman Dr., Mississauga, L5K 1B2 ON
905-823-9040, webmaster@aecl.ca

Canadian Nuclear Safety Commission, 280 Slater St., PO Box 1046 B,Ottawa, K1P 5S9 ON
613-995-5894, Fax: 613-995-5086, 800-668-5284, info@cnsc-ccsn.gc.ca

Indian Oil & Gas Canada, #100, 9911 Chula Blvd., Tsuu T'ina (Sarcee), AB T2W 6H6
Fax: 403-292-5618

National Energy Board, 444 - 7 Ave. SW, Calgary, T2P 0X8 AB
403-292-4800, Fax: 403-292-5503, 800-899-1265, info@neb-one.gc.ca

Alberta

Alberta Energy & Utilities Board, 640 - 5 Ave. SW, Calgary, AB T2P 3G4
403-297-8311, Fax: 403-297-7336

Alberta Energy Research Institute, AMEC Place, #2540, 801 - 6 Ave. SW, Calgary, AB T2P 3W2
403-297-8650, Fax: 403-297-3638, aeri@gov.ab.ca

Alberta Energy, North Petroleum Plaza, 9945 - 108 St., 7th Fl., Edmonton, T5K 2G6 AB
780-427-7425, Fax: 780-422-0698, 780-310-0000

British Columbia

Ministry of Energy, Mines & Petroleum Resources, PO Box 9318 Prov Govt,Victoria, V8W 9N3 BC
250-952-0241

British Columbia Hydro, 333 Dunsmuir St., 18th Fl., Vancouver, V6B 5R3 BC
604-224-9376, Fax: 604-623-4467, 800-224-9376

Oil & Gas Commission, #100, 10003 - 110 Ave., Fort St John, BC V1J 6M7
250-261-5700, 800-663-7867

Powerex Corp., #1400, 666 Burrard St., Vancouver, BC V6C 2X8
604-891-5000, Fax: 604-891-6060, 800-220-4907, customer.service@bchydro.com

Powertech Labs Inc., 12388 - 88 Ave., Surrey, BC V8W 7R7
604-590-7500, Fax: 604-590-5347, info@powertechlans.com

British Columbia Utilities Commission, 900 Howe St., 6th Fl., PO Box 250, Vancouver, V6Z 2N3 BC
604-660-4700, Fax: 604-660-1102, 800-663-1385, commission.secretary@bcuc.com

Manitoba

Manitoba Hydro, PO Box 815 Main,Winnipeg, R3C 2P4 MB
204-474-3311, Fax: 204-475-0069, publicaffairs@hydro.mb.ca

Petroleum, #360, 1395 Ellice Ave., Winnipeg, R3G 3P2 MB
204-945-6577, Fax: 204-945-0586

Manitoba Science, Technology, Energy & Mines, #333, 450 Broadway, Winnipeg, R3C 0V8 MB

New Brunswick

Efficiency NB, #101, 33 Charlotte St., Saint John, NB E2L 2H3
506-643-7826, Fax: 506-643-7835, 866-643-8833

Department of Energy, Brunswick Square, #100M, 1 Germain St., PO Box 5001, Saint John, E2L 4Y9 NB
506-658-3180, Fax: 506-658-3191

Department of Natural Resources, PO Box 6000, Fredericton, E3B 5H1 NB
506-453-2510, Fax: 506-444-5839, dnrweb@gnb.ca

New Brunswick Power Group of Companies, 515 King St., PO Box 2000, Fredericton, E3B 4X1 NB
506-458-4444, Fax: 506-458-4000, questions@nbpower.com

Newfoundland & Labrador
Canada-Newfoundland Offshore Petroleum Board, TD Place, 140 Water St., 5th Fl., St. John's, NL A1C 6H6
709-778-1400, Fax: 709-778-1473, postmaster@cnlopb.nl.ca
Churchill Falls (Labrador) Corporation Limited, Hydro Place, 500 Columbus Dr., PO Box 12500, St. John's, A1B 4K7 NL
709-737-1859, Fax: 709-737-1816
Newfoundland & Labrador Hydro, Hydro Place, Columbus Dr., PO Box 12400, St. John's, A1B 4K7 NL
709-737-1400, Fax: 709-737-1800
Newfoundland & Labrador Board of Commissioners of Public Utilities, PO Box 21040, St. John's, A1A 5B2 NL
709-726-8600, Fax: 709-726-9604, 866-782-0006, ito@pub.nf.ca
Twin Falls Power Corporation, PO Box 12500, St. John's, A1B 3T5 NL

Northwest Territories
Department of Environment & Natural Resources, PO Box 1320, Yellowknife, X1A 2L9 NT
Northwest Territories Power Corporation, 4 Capital Dr., Hay River, X0E 1G2 NT
867-874-5200, Fax: 867-874-5229, info@ntpc.com

Nova Scotia
Canada-Nova Scotia Offshore Petroleum Board, TD Centre, 1791 Barrington St., 6th Fl., Halifax, NS B3J 3K9
902-422-5588, Fax: 902-422-1799, postmaster@cnsopb.ns.ca
Department of Energy, Bank of Montreal Bldg., #400, 5151 George St., PO Box 2664, Halifax, B3J 3P7 NS
902-424-4575, Fax: 902-424-0528, energyinfo@gov.ns.ca
Nova Scotia Utility & Review Board, 1601 Lower Water St., 3rd Fl., PO Box 1692 M,Halifax, B3J 3S3 NS
902-424-4448, Fax: 902-424-3919, uarb.board@gov.ns.ca

Ontario
Ministry of Energy and Infrastructure, Hearst Block, 900 Bay St., 4th Fl., Toronto, M7A 2E1 ON
416-327-6758, Fax: 416-327-0033, 888-668-4939
Ministry of Environment, 135 St. Clair Ave. West, Toronto, M4V 1P5 ON
416-325-4000, Fax: 416-325-3159, 800-565-4923
Hydro One Inc., North Tower, 483 Bay St., Toronto, M5G 2P5 ON
416-345-5000, 877-955-1155, webmaster@HydroOne.com
Independent Electricity System Operator, PO Box 4474 A,Toronto, M5W 4E5 ON
905-403-6900, Fax: 905-403-6921, 888-448-7777, customer.relations@ieso.ca
Ontario Energy Board, #2700, 2300 Yonge St., Toronto, ON M4P 1E4
416-481-1967, Fax: 416-440-7656, 888-632-6273
Ontario Power Authority, #1600, 120 Adelaide St. West, Toronto, ON M5H 1T1
416-967-7474, Fax: 416-967-1947, info@powerauthority.on.ca
Ontario Power Generation, 700 University Ave., Toronto, M5G 1X6 ON
416-592-2555, 877-592-2555

Prince Edward Island
Department of Environment, Energy & Forestry, Jones Bldg., 11 Kent St., 4th & 5th Fl., PO Box 2000, Charlottetown, C1A 7N8 PE
902-368-5000, Fax: 902-368-5830
PEI Energy Corporation, Jones Bldg., 11 Kent St., 4th Fl., PO Box 2000, Charlottetown, PE C1A 7N8
902-894-0288, Fax: 902-368-0290

Quebec
Agence de l'efficacité énergétique, #B-405, 5700, 4e av ouest, Québec, QC G1H 6R1
418-627-6379, Fax: 418-643-5828, 877-727-6655, aee@aee.gouv.qc.ca
Hydro-Québec, 75, boul René-Lévesque ouest, 20e étage, Montréal, H2Z 1A4 QC
514-289-2211
Régie de l'énergie, Tour de la Bourse, #255, 800, Place Victoria, CP 1, Montréal, QC H4Z 1A2
514-873-2452, Fax: 514-873-2070, 888-873-2452, secretariat@regie-energie.qc.ca
Société d'énergie de la Baie-James, 888, de Maisonneuve est, 2e étage, Montréal, H2L 5B2 QC
514-286-2020

Saskatchewan
Saskatchewan Energy & Resources, #300, 2103 - 11th Ave., Regina, S4P 3Z8 SK
306-787-2528, Fax: 306-787-8447, 866-727-5427
Saskatchewan Power Corporation (SaskPower), 2025 Victoria Ave., Regina, S4P 0S1 SK
306-566-2121, Fax: 306-566-2330, 800-667-4749
SaskEnergy Incorporated, 1777 Victoria Ave., Regina, S4P 4K5 SK
306-777-9225, Fax: 306-777-9200, 800-567-8899

Yukon Territory
Yukon Energy, Mines & Resources, PO Box 2703, Whitehorse, Y1A 2C6 YT
867-667-5466, Fax: 867-667-8601, 800-661-0408, emr@gov.yk.ca

HYDRO ELECTRIC POWER

National Energy Board, 444 - 7 Ave. SW, Calgary, T2P 0X8 AB
403-292-4800, Fax: 403-292-5503, 800-899-1265, info@neb-one.gc.ca

Alberta
Alberta Energy & Utilities Board, 640 - 5 Ave. SW, Calgary, AB T2P 3G4
403-297-8311, Fax: 403-297-7336
Alberta Utilities Consumer Advocate, TD Tower, 10088 - 102 Ave., Edmonton, T5J 2Z1 AB
780-644-5130, Fax: 780-644-5129, 866-714-4455, UtilitiesConsumerAdvocate@gov.ab.

British Columbia
British Columbia Hydro, 333 Dunsmuir St., 18th Fl., Vancouver, V6B 5R3 BC
604-224-9376, Fax: 604-623-4467, 800-224-9376
Powertech Labs Inc., 12388 - 88 Ave., Surrey, BC V8W 7R7
604-590-7500, Fax: 604-590-5347, info@powertechlans.com

Manitoba
Manitoba Hydro, PO Box 815 Main,Winnipeg, R3C 2P4 MB
204-474-3311, Fax: 204-475-0069, publicaffairs@hydro.mb.ca

New Brunswick
New Brunswick Electric Finance Corporation, #376, 670 King St., PO Box 6000, Fredericton, NB E3B 5H1
506-453-3952, Fax: 506-453-2053
New Brunswick Power Group of Companies, 515 King St., PO Box 2000, Fredericton, E3B 4X1 NB
506-458-4444, Fax: 506-458-4000, questions@nbpower.com

Newfoundland & Labrador
Churchill Falls (Labrador) Corporation Limited, Hydro Place, 500 Columbus Dr., PO Box 12500, St. John's, A1B 4K7 NL
709-737-1859, Fax: 709-737-1816
Newfoundland & Labrador Hydro, Hydro Place, Columbus Dr., PO Box 12400, St. John's, A1B 4K7 NL
709-737-1400, Fax: 709-737-1800
Twin Falls Power Corporation, PO Box 12500, St. John's, A1B 3T5 NL

Northwest Territories
Northwest Territories Power Corporation, 4 Capital Dr., Hay River, X0E 1G2 NT
867-874-5200, Fax: 867-874-5229, info@ntpc.com

Nova Scotia
Nova Scotia Utility & Review Board, 1601 Lower Water St., 3rd Fl., PO Box 1692 M,Halifax, B3J 3S3 NS
902-424-4448, Fax: 902-424-3919, uarb.board@gov.ns.ca

Ontario
Hydro One Inc., North Tower, 483 Bay St., Toronto, M5G 2P5 ON
416-345-5000, 877-955-1155, webmaster@HydroOne.com
Independent Electricity System Operator, PO Box 4474 A,Toronto, M5W 4E5 ON
905-403-6900, Fax: 905-403-6921, 888-448-7777, customer.relations@ieso.ca
Ontario Power Authority, #1600, 120 Adelaide St. West, Toronto, ON M5H 1T1
416-967-7474, Fax: 416-967-1947, info@powerauthority.on.ca
Ontario Power Generation, 700 University Ave., Toronto, M5G 1X6 ON
416-592-2555, 877-592-2555

Quebec
Hydro-Québec, 75, boul René-Lévesque ouest, 20e étage, Montréal, H2Z 1A4 QC
514-289-2211
Société d'énergie de la Baie-James, 888, de Maisonneuve est, 2e étage, Montréal, H2L 5B2 QC
514-286-2020

Saskatchewan
Saskatchewan Power Corporation (SaskPower), 2025 Victoria Ave., Regina, S4P 0S1 SK
306-566-2121, Fax: 306-566-2330, 800-667-4749

OIL & NATURAL GAS RESOURCES

See Also: Energy; Natural Resources

Indian Oil & Gas Canada, #100, 9911 Chula Blvd., Tsuu T'ina (Sarcee), AB T2W 6H6
Fax: 403-292-5618
National Energy Board, 444 - 7 Ave. SW, Calgary, T2P 0X8 AB
403-292-4800, Fax: 403-292-5503, 800-899-1265, info@neb-one.gc.ca

Alberta
Alberta Energy & Utilities Board, 640 - 5 Ave. SW, Calgary, AB T2P 3G4
403-297-8311, Fax: 403-297-7336
Alberta Energy, North Petroleum Plaza, 9945 - 108 St., 7th Fl., Edmonton, T5K 2G6 AB
780-427-7425, Fax: 780-422-0698, 780-310-0000

British Columbia
Ministry of Energy, Mines & Petroleum Resources, PO Box 9318 Prov Govt,Victoria, V8W 9N3 BC
250-952-0241
Oil & Gas Commission, #100, 10003 - 110 Ave., Fort St John, BC V1J 6M7
250-261-5700, 800-663-7867
British Columbia Utilities Commission, 900 Howe St., 6th Fl., PO Box 250, Vancouver, V6Z 2N3 BC
604-660-4700, Fax: 604-660-1102, 800-663-1385, commission.secretary@bcuc.com

Manitoba
Petroleum, #360, 1395 Ellice Ave., Winnipeg, R3G 3P2 MB
204-945-6577, Fax: 204-945-0586
Surface Rights Board, #360, 1395 Ellice Ave., Winnipeg, MB R3G 3P2
204-945-0731, Fax: 204-948-2578, 800-282-8069, bmiskimmin@gov.mb.ca

Newfoundland & Labrador
Canada-Newfoundland Offshore Petroleum Board, TD Place, 140 Water St., 5th Fl., St. John's, NL A1C 6H6
709-778-1400, Fax: 709-778-1473, postmaster@cnlopb.nl.ca

Nova Scotia
Canada-Nova Scotia Offshore Petroleum Board, TD Centre, 1791 Barrington St., 6th Fl., Halifax, NS B3J 3K9
902-422-5588, Fax: 902-422-1799, postmaster@cnsopb.ns.ca
Nova Scotia Utility & Review Board, 1601 Lower Water St., 3rd Fl., PO Box 1692 M,Halifax, B3J 3S3 NS
902-424-4448, Fax: 902-424-3919, uarb.board@gov.ns.ca

Nunavut
Department of Environment, PO Box 1000 1300,Iqaluit, X0A 0H0 NU
867-975-7700, Fax: 867-975-7742, 866-222-9063, environment@gov.nu.ca

Ontario
Ministry of Natural Resources, Whitney Block, #6630, 99 Wellesley St. West, 6th Fl., Toronto, M7A 1W3 ON
800-667-1940

Saskatchewan
SaskEnergy Incorporated, 1777 Victoria Ave., Regina, S4P 4K5 SK
306-777-9225, Fax: 306-777-9200, 800-567-8899,

PUBLIC UTILITIES

Alberta
Alberta Energy & Utilities Board, 640 - 5 Ave. SW, Calgary, AB T2P 3G4
403-297-8311, Fax: 403-297-7336
Alberta Utilities Consumer Advocate, TD Tower, 10088 - 102 Ave., Edmonton, T5J 2Z1 AB
780-644-5130, Fax: 780-644-5129, 866-714-4455, UtilitiesConsumerAdvocate@gov.ab.

British Columbia
British Columbia Hydro, 333 Dunsmuir St., 18th Fl., Vancouver, V6B 5R3 BC
604-224-9376, Fax: 604-623-4467, 800-224-9376
British Columbia Transmission Corporation, Four Bentall Centre, #1100, 1055 Dunsmuir St., PO Box 49260, Vancouver, V7X 1V5 BC
604-699-7300, Fax: 604-699-7333, 866-647-3334, contact.us@bctc.com
British Columbia Utilities Commission, 900 Howe St., 6th Fl., PO Box 250, Vancouver, V6Z 2N3 BC
604-660-4700, Fax: 604-660-1102, 800-663-1385, commission.secretary@bcuc.com

Manitoba
Manitoba Hydro, PO Box 815 Main,Winnipeg, R3C 2P4 MB
204-474-3311, Fax: 204-475-0069, publicaffairs@hydro.mb.ca

Public Utilities Board, #400, 330 Portage Ave., Winnipeg, MB R3C 0C4
204-945-2638, Fax: 204-945-2643, 866-854-3698, publicutilities@gov.mb.ca

New Brunswick

NB Board of Commissioners of Public Utilities, #1400, 15 Market Sq., PO Box 5001, Saint John, NB E2L 4Y9
506-658-2504, Fax: 506-643-7300, 866-766-2782, general@pub.nb.ca

New Brunswick Power Group of Companies, 515 King St., PO Box 2000, Fredericton, E3B 4X1 NB
506-458-4444, Fax: 506-458-4000, questions@nbpower.com

Newfoundland & Labrador

Churchill Falls (Labrador) Corporation Limited, Hydro Place, 500 Columbus Dr., PO Box 12500, St. John's, A1B 4K7 NL
709-737-1859, Fax: 709-737-1816

Newfoundland & Labrador Hydro, Hydro Place, Columbus Dr., PO Box 12400, St. John's, A1B 4K7 NL
709-737-1400, Fax: 709-737-1800

Newfoundland & Labrador Board of Commissioners of Public Utilities, PO Box 21040, St. John's, A1A 5B2 NL
709-726-8600, Fax: 709-726-9604, 866-782-0006, ito@pub.nf.ca

Northwest Territories

Northwest Territories Power Corporation, 4 Capital Dr., Hay River, X0E 1G2 NT
867-874-5200, Fax: 867-874-5229, info@ntpc.com

Northwest Territories Water Board, 5114 - 49th St., PO Box 1326, Yellowknife, X1A 1N9 NT
867-765-0106, Fax: 867-765-0114, info@nwtwb.com

Nova Scotia

Nova Scotia Utility & Review Board, 1601 Lower Water St., 3rd Fl., PO Box 1692 M,Halifax, B3J 3S3 NS
902-424-4448, Fax: 902-424-3919, uarb.board@gov.ns.ca

Ontario

Hydro One Inc., North Tower, 483 Bay St., Toronto, M5G 2P5 ON
416-345-5000, 877-955-1155, webmaster@HydroOne.com

Independent Electricity System Operator, PO Box 4474 A,Toronto, M5W 4E5 ON
905-403-6900, Fax: 905-403-6921, 888-448-7777, customer.relations@ieso.ca

Ontario Power Generation, 700 University Ave., Toronto, M5G 1X6 ON
416-592-2555, 877-592-2555

Prince Edward Island

Island Regulatory & Appeals Commission, National Bank Tower, #501, 134 Kent St., PO Box 577, Charlottetown, C1A 7L1 PE
902-892-3501, Fax: 902-566-4076, 800-501-6268, irac@irac.pe.ca

Quebec

Hydro-Québec, 75, boul René-Lévesque ouest, 20e étage, Montréal, H2Z 1A4 QC
514-289-2211

Régie de l'énergie, Tour de la Bourse, #255, 800, Place Victoria, CP 1, Montréal, QC H4Z 1A2
514-873-2452, Fax: 514-873-2070, 888-873-2452, secretariat@regie-energie.qc.ca

Saskatchewan

Saskatchewan Power Corporation (SaskPower), 2025 Victoria Ave., Regina, S4P 0S1 SK
306-566-2121, Fax: 306-566-2330, 800-667-4749

Saskatchewan Water Corporation (SaskWater), #200, 111 Fairford St. East, Moose Jaw, S6H 1C8 SK
306-694-3098, Fax: 306-694-3207, 888-230-1111, comm@saskwater.com

SaskEnergy Incorporated, 1777 Victoria Ave., Regina, S4P 4K5 SK
306-777-9225, Fax: 306-777-9200, 800-567-8899

Yukon Territory

Yukon Utilities Board, #19, 1114 - 1st Ave., PO Box 31728, Whitehorse, YT Y1A 6L3
867-667-5058

A

B

C

D

F

G

H

I

J

L

M

O

P

Q

R

S

T

U

V

W

X

Y

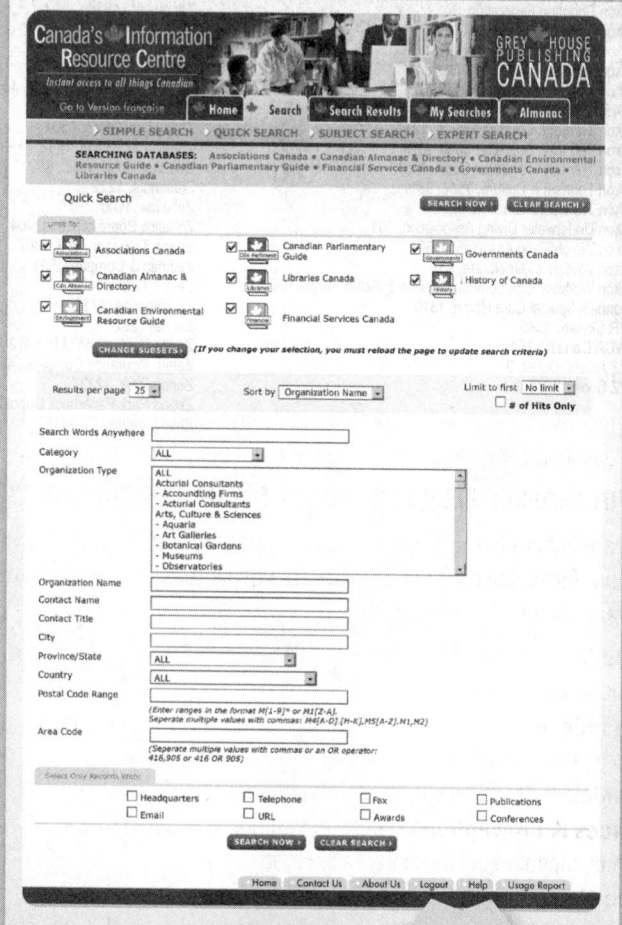

Libraries Canada

Gain Access to Complete and Detailed Information on Canadian Libraries

Libraries Canada brings together the most current information from across the entire Canadian library sector, including libraries and branch libraries, educational libraries, regional systems, resource centres, archives, related periodicals, library schools and programs, provincial and governmental agencies and associations.

As the nation's leading library directory for over 20 years, Libraries Canada gives you access to almost 10,000 names and addresses of contacts in these institutions. Also included are valuable details such as library symbol, number of staff, operating systems, library type and acquisitions budget, hours of operation—all thoroughly indexed and easy to find.

Available in print and online, Libraries Canada delivers easily accessible, quality information that has been verified and organized for easy retrieval. Five easy-to-use indexes assist you in navigating the print edition while the online version utilizes multiple index fields that help you get results.

INSTANT ACCESS TO CANADIAN LIBRARY SECTOR INFORMATION

Developed for publishers, advocacy groups, computer hardware suppliers, Internet service providers and other diverse groups which provide products and services to the library community; associations that need to maintain a current list of library resources in Canada; and research departments, students and government agencies which require information about the types of services and programs available at various research institutions, Libraries Canada will help you find the information you need—quickly and easily.

EXPERT SEARCH OPTIONS AVAILABLE WITH ONLINE VERSION...

Available on Grey House Canada's CIRC interface, you can choose between Expert and Quick search to pinpoint information. Designed for both novice and advanced researchers, you can conduct simple text searches as well as powerful Boolean searches, plus you can narrow your search by using index fields such as name or type of institution, headquarters, location, area code, contact name or title and postal code. Save your searches to build on at a later date or use the mark record function to view, print, e-mail or export your selected records.

Online subscribers have the option to instantly generate their own contact lists and export them into spreadsheets for further use. A great alternative to high cost list broker services.

Libraries Canada gives you all the essentials for each institution:

- name, address, contact information, key personnel, number of staff
- collection information, type of library, acquisitions budget, subject area, special collection
- user services, number of branches, hours of operation, ILL information, photocopy and microform facilities, for-fee research, Internet access
- systems information, details on electronic access, operating and online systems, Internet and e-mail software, Internet connectivity, access to electronic resources
- additional information including associations, publications and regional systems

With almost 60% of the data changing annually it has never been more important to have the latest version of Libraries Canada.

GREY HOUSE PUBLISHING CANADA

For more information please contact Grey House Publishing Canada by Tel.: (866)-433-4739 or (416) 644-6479
Fax: (416) 644-1904 | info@greyhouse.ca | www.greyhouse.ca